DICTIONNAIRE LAROUSSE

FRANÇAIS ANGLAIS

ANGLAIS FRANÇAIS

21, rue du Montparnasse
75283 Paris Cedex 06, France

ISBN 978-2-03-582518-6
Larousse, Paris

ISBN 978-2-03-542132-6
Diffusion/Sales : Houghton Mifflin Company, Boston
Library Of Congress CIP Data has been applied for

LAROUSSE

FRENCH ENGLISH

ENGLISH FRENCH

DICTIONARY

**POUR CETTE ÉDITION/
FOR THIS EDITION**

Coordination générale / Managing Editor
Janice McNeillie

Rédaction / Editors
Marie-Hélène Corréard, Valerie Grundy, Marie Ollivier-Caudray, Donald Watt

Composition / Typesetting
APS - Chromostyle, Sharon McTeir, Cluny Sheeler

Illustration / Illustrations
Jacqueline Bloch, Laurent Blondel, Noël Blotti, Franck Bouttevin, Jacques Cartier, Fabrice Dadoun, David Ducros, Jos Fichet, Christian Godard, Jean-Luc Guérin, Philippe Guinot, Xavier Hüe, Marc Legrand, Guilbert Macé, Emmanuel Mercier, Patrick Morin, Claude Poppé, Bernard Rocamora, Dominique Roussel, Dominique Sablons, Michel Saemann, Tom Sam You, Patrick Taëron, Jacques Toutain, Archives Larousse

Cartographie / Cartography
Krystyna Mazoyer

**POUR L'ÉDITION PRÉCÉDENTE/
FOR THE LAST EDITION**

Coordination générale / Managing Editor
Marc Chabrier

Rédaction / Editors
Harry Campbell, Marie-Hélène Corréard, Marie Ollivier, Garrett White, John Williams

**POUR LA DEUXIÈME ÉDITION /
FOR THE SECOND EDITION**

Coordination générale / Managing Editor
Ralf Brockmeier

Responsables de la rédaction / Senior Editors
Valérie Katzaros, Frances Illingworth

Rédaction / Editors
Laurence Larroche, Michael Mayor, Sophie Marin, Cammy Richelli, Cécile Vanwalleghem

POUR LA PREMIÈRE ÉDITION / FOR THE FIRST EDITION

Direction de la rédaction / General Editor
Faye Carney

Coordination éditoriale / Coordinating Editor
Claude Nimmo

Rédaction / Editors

Valérie Katzaros, Rose Rociola, Claude Le Guyader, Laurence Larroche

Martyn Back, Michael Mayor, Martin Crowley, Ruth Blackmore

avec / with

Cécile Vanwalleghem, Anne Lecroart, Sophie Marin, Bernard Giraud, Anne Landelle, Carole Coen, Catherine Julia, Sabine Citron, Isabelle Rosselin, Marie-Paule Poncelet, Nadine Mongeard

David Hallworth, Karen Lawson, Jane Rogoyska, Margaret Jull Costa, Stephen Curtis, Claire Evans, Jane Goldie, Patrick White, Steve Garner, Peter Cross, Paul Duffy, Simon Fraser, Edwin Carpenter

Comité de lecture / Advisory Panel
Jacques van Roey, Jean-François Allain
Geoffrey Bremner, Trevor Peach

Autres collaborateurs / Other Contributors
David Jones, Hélène Houssemaine-Florent, Marie-Noëlle Lamy, John Scullard

AU LECTEUR

Le Larousse français-anglais / anglais-français est un ouvrage de référence destiné aux étudiants, aux lycéens, aux enseignants de l'université et du secondaire, ainsi qu'à tous ceux qui ont un intérêt particulier pour la langue anglaise et la culture anglo-saxonne.
Conçu de manière à répondre au mieux aux critères de qualité d'un dictionnaire, il allie richesse et actualité de la nomenclature, convivialité de la présentation et fiabilité. Les mots et expressions qui y figurent offrent une image fidèle de la langue contemporaine et un soin tout particulier a été accordé à la sélection des néologismes, notamment dans des domaines essentiels tels que l'informatique et le monde des affaires. Par ailleurs, l'anglais américain a fait l'objet d'un traitement privilégié et l'accueil de canadianismes, d'helvétismes et de belgicismes courants donne à cet ouvrage une dimension véritablement internationale.
La structure des articles ainsi que la typographie ont été étudiées de manière à mettre en relief les mots composés et les locutions. Les différents sens et niveaux de langue sont clairement indiqués afin de faciliter l'accès à la traduction appropriée.
Partant du principe qu'un dictionnaire est aussi un pont entre les cultures et les sociétés, nous avons voulu privilégier cette dimension en offrant à l'utilisateur une meilleure compréhension de la langue et de la culture étrangères. De nombreuses gloses et notes culturelles s'efforcent ainsi d'expliquer lorsque traduire n'est pas possible, lorsqu'il faut aller au-delà du lexique.
Dans l'intention affirmée de répondre aux besoins spécifiques du lecteur, notamment en ce qui concerne l'expression dans l'autre langue, le Larousse français-anglais / anglais-français propose des modules regroupant, autour d'un certain nombre de thèmes tels que l'approbation, l'indignation ou la comparaison, des phrases adaptées à des situations typiques. Celles-ci viennent ainsi enrichir l'information lexicale contenue dans les entrées correspondantes.
Cet outil de communication idéal entre le français et l'anglais doit vivre avec son temps. Dans un souci constant d'innovation et d'amélioration, nous nous adressons à vous, lecteurs, pour vous engager à participer à cette entreprise qui n'est jamais vraiment terminée, en nous faisant part de vos observations, de vos critiques, de vos suggestions.

L'Éditeur

TO OUR READERS

The Larousse French-English/English-French Dictionary is a reference book designed for students and teachers of French at both school and university level, as well as for all those with an active interest in the French language and culture.
Our continuing aim has been to meet the three criteria that make for quality in dictionaries: comprehensive and up-to-date coverage, ease of use and reliability. Entries have been carefully chosen to provide an accurate and idiomatic reflection of French and English as they are written and spoken today. Special attention has been given to new words and phrases, especially in essential fields such as business, information technology and International affairs. The text also reflects the international nature of the two languages: many Swiss, Belgian and Canadian terms are included and American English has been given generous treatment throughout.
The carefully structured layout and clear presentation make it easy to identify set phrases and compounds. The various nuances of meaning and register of a word are clearly indicated to avoid ambiguity and to make access to the appropriate translation as straightforward as possible.
The above features are considered essential components of today's larger bilingual dictionaries. However the Larousse French-English/English-French Dictionary goes one step further in recognizing that sometimes a translation alone is not enough to render the full meaning of certain words and expressions, many of which have a cultural resonance for which there is no equivalent in the other language. Special emphasis is placed on such 'culture-bound' items, using explanatory glosses to explain their full implications and relevance to the non-native speaker. In addition to having a translation or gloss, certain entries have boxed cultural notes attached to them which provide essential background information to the foreign user.
An additional feature of this dictionary is a practical guide to functional language. Boxed usage modules, based on themes such as expressing opinions, certainty, agreement etc, give example sentences showing typical expressions and structures you need to express yourself in everyday situations, and which cannot be shown in a traditional dictionary entry.
Language evolves and any good dictionary has a commitment to keep up to date with the changing needs of its users. The task of innovating and revising is an ongoing one, and we invite you to take part in this venture by sending us your comments and criticisms.

The Publisher

COMMENT UTILISER CE DICTIONNAIRE

mot d'entrée

headword

introduit une catégorie grammaticale

introduces a grammatical category

transcription phonétique dans l'alphabet phonétique international

pronunciation shown in International Phonetic Alphabet

diplomate [diplɔmat] ◇ *adj* diplomatic.
◇ *nmf* POLIT & *fig* diplomat.
◇ *nm* CULIN diplomat pudding.

numéros d'homographes

homograph numbers

forme féminine

feminine form

numéros indiquant les divisions sémantiques à l'intérieur d'une catégorie grammaticale

numbered sense divisions within a grammatical category

indicateurs de domaine

specialist field labels

synonyme du mot d'entrée

synonym of the headword

avocat[1] [avɔka] *nm* BOT avocado (pear).
avocat[2], **e** [avɔka, at] *nm, f* **1.** DR lawyer, barrister *UK*, attorney-at-law *US* ⊙ **~ d'affaires** business lawyer ■ **~ de la défense** counsel for the defence, ≃ defending counsel *UK*, ≃ defense counsel *US* ■ **~ général** ≃ counsel for the prosecution *UK*, ≃ prosecuting attorney *US* ■ **~ plaidant** court lawyer *UK*, trial attorney *US* **2.** [porte-parole] advocate, champion ■ **se faire l'~ d'une mauvaise cause** to advocate *ou* to champion a lost cause ⊙ **~ du diable** devil's advocate ■ **se faire l'~ du diable** to be devil's advocate.

introduit une sous-entrée

introduces a sub-entry

numéro qui renvoie aux tableaux de conjugaison des verbes français

cross-reference number to French verb tables

restaurer [3] [rɛstɔre] *vt* **1.** [édifice, œuvre d'art] to restore **2.** *litt* [rétablir] to restore, to reestablish ■ **~ la paix** to restore peace **3.** *litt* [nourrir] to feed.
◆ **se restaurer** *vp (emploi réfléchi)* to have something to eat.

signalisation précise des sens et du contexte

meaning and context clearly labelled

introduit un glissement de sens à l'intérieur d'une division sémantique

indicates a shift in meaning within a sense division

clôture [klotyr] *nf* **1.** [barrière - en bois] fence ; [- en fil de fer] railings **2.** [fermeture] closing ■ **'~ annuelle'** 'annual closure' ■ **j'ai assisté à la ~** I attended the closing ceremony ▌[fin] end ■ **~ des inscriptions le 20 décembre** UNIV the closing date for enrolment is December 20th **3.** BOURSE close ■ **à la ~** at the close **4.** [dans un monastère] enclosure.

les locutions et les mots composés considérés comme des unités de sens autonomes sont présentés en sous-entrée

fixed phrases and compound nouns with distinct meanings are presented as sub-entries

fuseau, x [fyzo] *nm* **1.** [bobine] spindle ■ **dentelle/ouvrage aux ~x** bobbin lace/needlework **2.** [vêtement] stirrup pants **3.** GÉOM lune.
◆ **en fuseau** ◇ *loc adj* tapered, spindle-shaped.
◇ *loc adv* : **tailler qqch en ~** to taper sthg.
◆ **fuseau horaire** *nm* time zone ■ **changer de ~ horaire** to go into a different time zone.

symbole remplaçant le mot d'entrée

symbol used to replace headword

introduit des expressions figées

introduces fixed phrases and usages

les pluriels ayant leur propre sens sont présentés en sous-entrée

plural nouns with a distinct meaning are presented as sub-entries

reste [rɛst] *nm* **1.** [suite, fin] rest ■ **si vous êtes sages, je vous raconterai le ~ demain** if you're good, I'll tell you the rest of the story tomorrow ■ **et (tout) le ~!** and so on (and so forth)! ■ **tout le ~ n'est que littérature/qu'illusion** everything else is just insignificant/an illusion ⊙ **sans attendre** *ou* **demander son ~** without (any) further ado ■ **être** *ou* **demeurer en ~** to be outdone, to be at a loss **2.** [résidu - de nourriture] food left over, leftovers (of food) ; [- de boisson] drink left over ; [- de tissu, de papier] remnant, scrap ■ CINÉ out-takes ■ **un ~ de jour** *ou* **de lumière** a glimmer of daylight ■ **un ~ de sa gloire passée** a vestige *ou* remnant of his past glory **3.** MATH remainder.
◆ **restes** *nmpl* **1.** [d'un repas] leftovers **2.** [vestiges] remains **3.** [ossements] (last) remains **4.** *fam loc* **elle a de beaux ~s** she's still beautiful despite her age.
◆ **du reste** *loc adv* besides, furthermore, moreover.

transcription phonétique des formes de l'adjectif

pronunciation of declined adjectives indicated

information grammaticale sur les autres formes de l'adjectif

extra grammatical information provided for adjectives

beau [bo] *(devant nm commençant par voyelle ou h muet* **bel** [bɛl]) *(f* **belle** [bɛl], *mpl* **beaux** [bo], *fpl* **belles** [bɛl]) *adj*

HOW TO USE THE DICTIONARY

catégorie grammaticale regroupant les composés formés à partir d'un nom utilisé en apposition

compound category given when a noun is used as a modifier

computer [kəm'pju:tər] <> *n* [electronic] ordinateur *m*. <> *comp* : **~ model** modèle *m* informatique ▪ **~ network** réseau *m* informatique ▪ **~ printout** sortie *f* papier.

computer-aided design *n* conception *f* assistée par ordinateur.

computer dating *n rencontres sélectionnées par ordinateur.*

computer game *n* jeu *m* électronique.

les mots composés s'écrivant avec un trait d'union ou considérés comme des unités de sens autonomes font l'objet d'entrées à part entière

hyphenated compound words, and compound words that have their own distinct meanings treated as headwords

indique qu'il s'agit d'un nom déposé

indicates a registered trademark

MiniDisc® ['mɪnɪdɪsk] *n* Minidisc® *m*.

variantes orthographiques britannique et américaine

British and American spelling variants given

draught *UK*, **draft** *US* [drɑ:ft] *n* **1.** [breeze] courant *m* d'air **2.** [in fireplace] tirage *m* **3.** [drink - swallow] trait *m*, gorgée *f*.

titres d'œuvres littéraires, cinématographiques, etc. connues

titles of well-known books, films etc provided

high noon *n* plein midi *m* ▪ **at ~** à midi pile ▪ **'High Noon'** ***Zinnemann*** 'le Train sifflera trois fois'.

équivalent culturel

cultural equivalent

Punch [pʌntʃ] *pr n* ≃ Polichinelle ▪ **~-and-Judy show** ≃ (spectacle *m* de) guignol *m* ▪ **as pleased as ~** heureux comme un roi.

PUNCH AND JUDY

Le *Punch and Judy show* est un spectacle très apprécié des enfants en Grande-Bretagne. Les représentations ont le plus souvent lieu dans un jardin public ou sur une plage. On y retrouve les personnages de Punch le Bossu, de sa femme Judy, avec qui il se querelle constamment, et de leur chien Toby.

informations supplémentaires de nature culturelle ou encyclopédique

extra information of a cultural or encyclopedic nature

explication donnée sous forme de glose lorsqu'il n'y a pas de traduction directe

explanatory gloss provided where there is no direct translation

pharming ['fɑ:mɪŋ] *n culture ou élevage de plantes ou animaux génétiquement modifiés pour la fabrication de produits pharmaceutiques.*

précisions sur la traduction

extra information that clarifies the translation

cloth cap *n* casquette *f (symbole de la classe ouvrière britannique).*

transcription phonétique des acronymes

pronunciation of acronyms

FAQ [fak, ɛfeɪ'kju:] (*abbrev of* **frequently asked questions**) *n* COMPUT foire *f* aux questions, FAQ *f*.

renvoi à la forme développée lorsqu'il n'y a pas d'équivalent de l'abréviation

cross-reference to the full form of an abbreviation where there is no equivalent

DST *n* (*abbrev of* **daylight saving time**).

renvoi des formes contractées des verbes aux formes complètes

contracted verb forms provided with cross-references to full forms

had *(weak form* [həd], *strong form* [hæd]*) pt & pp* ▷ **have**.

renvoi des formes irrégulières des verbes à l'infinitif

cross-reference from irregular verb forms to main verb

he's [hi:z] = **he is, he has**.

renvoi des pluriels irréguliers aux entrées au singulier

cross-reference from irregular plurals

selves [selvz] *pl* ▷ **self**.

renvoi des variantes orthographiques aux entrées principales

cross-reference from alternative spelling

gypsy ['dʒɪpsɪ] (*pl* **gypsies**) = **gipsy**.

ABBREVIATIONS USED IN THIS DICTIONARY
ABRÉVIATIONS UTILISÉES DANS CE DICTIONNAIRE

abbreviation	*abbr/abrév*	abréviation
absolute	*abs*	absolu
'en usage abs' indicates a transitive verb used without a direct object: **il boit beaucoup**		'en usage abs' signale un verbe transitif employé sans complément d'objet : **il boit beaucoup**
adjective	*adj*	adjectif
phrase functioning as adjective	*adj phr*	locution ayant valeur d'adjectif
adverb	*adv*	adverbe
phrase functioning as adverb	*adv phr*	locution ayant valeur d'adverbe
archaic	*arch*	archaïque
crime slang	*arg crime*	argot du milieu
drugs slang	*arg drogue*	argot de la drogue
military slang	*arg mil*	argot militaire
school slang	*arg scol*	argot scolaire
university slang	*arg univ*	argot universitaire
article	*art*	article
Australian English	*Austr*	anglais australien
auxiliary verb	*aux vb*	auxiliaire
before noun	*avant n*	avant le nom
indicates that an adjective is used attributively, i.e. directly before the noun it modifies		souligne les cas où un adjectif est nécessairement antéposé
Belgian French	*Belgique*	belgicisme
countable noun	*C*	substantif comptable
i.e. a noun which can exist in the plural and be used with 'a'		désigne un substantif anglais qui peut être employé au pluriel et avec 'a'
Canadian English	*Canada*	anglais du Canada
cardinal	*card*	cardinal
compound-forming noun	*comp*	substantif formant des composés
shows noun headword used as a noun modifier, e.g. **computer** in **computer course, law** in **law degree**		s'applique à un substantif employé en apposition : **computer** dans **computer course, law** dans **law degree**
comparative	*compar*	comparatif
conjunction	*conj*	conjonction
phrase functioning as conjunction	*conj phr*	locution ayant valeur de conjonction
continuous	*cont*	progressif
compound	*comp*	composés
crime slang	*crime sl*	argot du milieu
definite	*def/déf*	défini
demonstrative	*dem/dém*	démonstratif
determiner	*det*	déterminant
phrase functioning as determiner	*det phr*	locution ayant valeur de déterminant
diminutive	*dimin*	diminutif
direct	*dir*	direct
drugs slang	*drugs sl*	argot de la drogue
especially	*esp*	particulièrement
euphemism	*euph*	euphémisme
exclamation	*excl*	interjection
feminine	*f*	féminin
informal	*fam*	familier
figurative	*fig*	figuré
formal	*fml*	soutenu
generally, in most cases	*gen/gén*	généralement
Swiss French	*Helv*	helvétisme
humorous	*hum*	humoristique
impersonal	*impers*	impersonnel
indefinite	*indef/indéf*	indéfini
indicative	*indic*	indicatif
indirect	*indir*	indirect
informal	*inf*	familier
infinitive	*infin*	infinitif
offensive	*injur*	injurieux

inseparable shows that the object of a phrasal verb cannot come between the verb and the particle, e.g. **I looked after him** BUT NOT **I looked him after**	*insep*	inséparable indique qu'un verbe anglais à particule ('phrasal verb') ne peut pas être séparé de sa particule, c'est-à-dire qu'un complément d'objet ne peut être inséré entre les deux, par exemple **I looked after him** ET NON **I looked him after**
exclamation	*interj*	interjection
interrogative	*interr*	interrogatif
invariable applied to a noun, indicates that the plural and singular forms are the same, e.g. **garde-boue (des garde-boue); sheep (four sheep).** Applied to an adjective, indicates that feminine, masculine and plural forms are the same, e.g. **vieux jeu (ils sont/elle est vieux jeu)**	*inv*	invariable avec un nom, signifie que la forme du pluriel est identique à la forme du singulier : **garde-boue (des garde-boue) ; sheep (four sheep).** Avec un adjectif, signifie que la forme du féminin et celle du pluriel sont identiques à la forme du masculin : **vieux jeu (ils sont/elle est vieux jeu)**
Irish English	*Ireland*	anglais irlandais
ironic	*iro/iron*	ironique
literary	*lit/litt*	littéraire
phrase(s)	*loc*	locution(s)
phrase functioning as adjective	*loc adj*	locution ayant valeur d'adjectif
phrase functioning as adverb	*loc adv*	locution ayant valeur d'adverbe
phrase functioning as conjunction	*loc conj*	locution ayant valeur de conjonction
phrase functioning as correlative conjunction	*loc corrél*	locution ayant valeur de conjonction corrélative
phrase functioning as determiner	*loc dét*	locution ayant valeur de déterminant
phrase functioning as exclamation	*loc interj*	locution ayant valeur d'interjection
phrase functioning as preposition	*loc prép*	locution ayant valeur de préposition
phrase functioning as pronoun	*loc pron*	locution ayant valeur de pronom
masculine	*m*	masculin
military slang	*mil sl*	argot militaire
noun modifier a noun functioning as an adjective and which can only be used attributively, i.e. before the noun it modifies	*modif*	substantif ayant valeur d'adjectif et devant obligatoirement être antéposé
noun	*n*	nom
negative	*neg/nég*	négatif
feminine noun	*nf*	nom féminin
feminine noun used in the plural	*nfpl*	nom féminin pluriel
masculine noun	*nm*	nom masculin
masculine or feminine noun shows that a noun may be either masculine or feminine: **un architecte/une architecte**	*nmf*	nom masculin ou féminin indique qu'un nom peut être masculin ou féminin : **un architecte/une architecte**
masculine and feminine forms indicates a noun with a different form in the masculine and the feminine, e.g. **inspecteur/inspectrice**	*nm, f*	formes masculine et féminine s'applique à un substantif ayant une forme différente au masculin et au féminin, par exemple **inspecteur/inspectrice**
masculine noun used in the plural	*nmpl*	nom masculin pluriel
proper noun	*npr*	nom propre
plural proper noun	*npr pl*	nom propre pluriel
plural noun	*npl*	nom pluriel
numeral	*num*	numéral
New Zealand English	*New Zealand*	anglais néo-zélandais
object	*obj*	objet
officially recognized term some terms (especially borrowings from English) are considered substandard by the Académie française; terms marked 'offic' are recognized as acceptable alternatives for these, but are unlikely to be as widely used	*offic*	terme officiellement recommandé par l'Académie
onomatopoeia	*onomat*	onomatopée
ordinal	*ord*	ordinal
oneself	*o.s.*	
pejorative	*pej/péj*	péjoratif

personal/person	*pers*	personnel/personne
phrase(s)	*phr*	locution(s)
plural	*pl*	pluriel
plural proper noun	*pl pr n*	nom propre pluriel
possessive	*poss*	possessif
past participle	*pp*	participe passé
literal meaning	*pr*	sens propre
predeterminer	*predet*	mot placé avant un déterminant et exprimant un degré ou une quantité
phrase functioning as predeterminer	*predet phr*	locution ayant valeur de 'predeterminer' (voir ci-dessus)
prefix	*pref/préf*	préfixe
preposition	*prep/prép*	préposition
phrase functioning as preposition	*prep phr*	locution ayant valeur de préposition
present	*pres/prés*	présent
proper noun	*pr n*	nom propre
pronoun	*pron*	pronom
phrase functioning as pronoun	*pron phr*	locution ayant valeur de pronom
proverb	*prov*	proverbe
past tense	*pt*	passé
something	*qqch*	quelque chose
somebody/someone	*qqn*	quelqu'un
relative	*rel*	relatif
French Canadian	*Québec*	québécisme
South African English	*South Africa*	anglais d'Afrique du Sud
somebody, someone	*sb*	quelqu'un
school slang	*school sl*	argot scolaire
Scottish English	*Scotland*	anglais écossais
separable shows that the object of a phrasal verb can come between the verb and the particle, e.g. **I let her in, he helped me out**	*sep*	séparable indique qu'un verbe anglais à particule peut être séparé de sa particule par un complément d'objet : **I let her in, he helped me out**
takes singular verb	*sg*	employé avec un verbe au singulier
singular	*sing*	singulier
slang	*sl*	argot
formal	*sout*	soutenu
specialized term or usage	*spec/spéc*	terme ou sens spécialisé
something	*sthg*	quelque chose
subjunctive	*subj*	subjonctif
subject	*subj/suj*	sujet
superlative	*superl*	superlatif
always	*tjrs*	toujours
uncountable noun i.e. an English noun which is never used in the plural or with 'a'; used when the French equivalent is or can be a plural, e.g. **applause** *n* **(U) applaudissements** *mpl*; **battement** *nm* **beating (U)**	*U*	substantif non comptable substantif anglais qui ne s'utilise qu'au singulier et dont l'équivalent français est ou peut être un pluriel : **applause** *n* **(U) applaudissements** *mpl*; **battement** *nm* **beating** *n* **(U)**
British English	*UK*	anglicisme
American English	*US*	américanisme
usually	*usu*	le plus souvent
link verb followed by a predicative adjective or noun e.g. **tomber malade, être professeur**	*v attr*	verbe suivi d'un attribut par exemple : **tomber malade, être professeur**
verb	*vb/v*	verbe
intransitive verb	*vi*	verbe intransitif
impersonal verb	*v impers*	verbe impersonnel
pronominal verb	*vp*	verbe pronominal
intransitive pronominal verb	*vpi*	verbe pronominal intransitif
transitive pronominal verb	*vpt*	verbe pronominal transitif
transitive verb	*vt*	verbe transitif

SYMBOLS

SYMBOLES

▶	Separates expressions which are not set (given before the symbol) from more fixed expressions.	Sépare les emplois non figés (présentés avant le symbole) des expressions figées.
|	Indicates a shift of meaning within a sense category.	Indique un glissement de sens à l'intérieur d'une division sémantique.
≃	Indicates that the translation given is an approximate cultural equivalent.	Indique que la traduction est une équivalence culturelle approximative.
®	Indicates that the item is a registered trademark.	Indique que le terme est une marque déposée.
△	Warns the user that a lexical item or particular meaning is very colloquial, and thus should be used with caution by non-native speakers.	Avertit l'usager qu'un terme ou un sens est très familier et qu'il devra être employé avec prudence par le locuteur étranger.
▲	Warns the user that a lexical item or particular meaning is either vulgar or racist.	Avertit l'usager qu'un terme ou un sens est vulgaire ou raciste.
	Politics and institutions.	Politique et institutions.
	Historical event.	Fait historique.
	Geographical term.	Terme géographique.
	Cultural box.	Notice culturelle.
	School and education.	Enseignement et scolarité.
	Usage module.	Module d'usage.

TRADEMARKS

Words considered to be trademarks have been designated in this dictionary by the symbol ®. However, neither the presence nor the absence of this symbol should be regarded as affecting the legal status of any trademark.

LES NOMS DE MARQUE

Les noms de marque sont désignés dans ce dictionnaire par le symbole ®. Néanmoins, ni ce symbole ni son absence éventuelle ne peuvent être considérés comme susceptibles d'avoir une incidence quelconque sur le statut légal d'une marque.

A NOTE ON ENGLISH COMPOUNDS

As in most modern dictionaries, we give lexicalized compounds (i.e. nouns consisting of more than one word) the same prominence as simplex headwords. This means that compounds that are considered as independent units of meaning appear as entries in their own right.

LES MOTS COMPOSÉS ANGLAIS

À l'instar de la plupart des dictionnaires actuels, nous accordons aux mots composés lexicalisés (c'est-à-dire aux substantifs composés de plus d'un mot) la même importance qu'aux mots simples. Ainsi, les composés anglais considérés comme des unités de sens autonomes font l'objet d'une entrée à part entière.

FRENCH VERBS

French verbs have a number (from [1] to [116]) which refers to the conjugation tables given in the dictionary. This number is not repeated for reflexive verbs when these appear as sub-entries.

LES VERBES FRANÇAIS

Les verbes français sont suivis d'une numérotation (de [1] à [116]) qui renvoie aux tableaux de conjugaison présentés dans l'ouvrage. Ce chiffre n'est pas répété après les verbes pronominaux lorsque ceux-ci sont présentés en sous-entrées.

FIELD LABELS
DOMAINES

acoustics	ACOUST	acoustique
administration	ADMIN	administration
aeronautics	AERON / AÉRON	aéronautique
agriculture	AGRIC	agriculture
anatomy	ANAT	anatomie
anthropology	ANTHR	anthropologie
antiquity	ANTIQ / ARCHÉOL	antiquité
archeology	ARCHEOL	archéologie
architecture	ARCHIT	architecture
arms	ARM	armement
art	ART	art
astrology	ASTROL	astrologie
astronomy	ASTRON	astronomie
astronautics	ASTRONAUT	astronautique
audio	AUDIO	audio
cars	AUT / AUTO	automobile
banking	BANK / BANQUE	banque
Bible	BIBLE	Bible
biology	BIOL	biologie
botany	BOT	botanique
stock exchange	BOURSE	Bourse
boxing	BOX	boxe
bridge	BRIDGE	bridge
cards	CARDS	cartes
hunting	CHASSE	chasse
chemistry	CHEM / CHIM	chimie
chess	CHESS	échecs
cinema	CIN / CINÉ	cinéma
civil engineering	CIV ENG	travaux publics
climbing	CLIMBING	alpinisme
commerce	COMM	commerce
computing	COMPUT	informatique
construction	CONSTR	construction
sewing	COUT	couture
cricket	CRICKET	cricket
cooking	CULIN	cuisine
cycling	CYCL	cyclisme
dance	DANCE / DANSE	danse
dentistry	DENT	dentisterie
law	DR	droit
ecology	ECOL / ÉCOL	écologie
economics	ECON / ÉCON	économie
school	ÉDUC	éducation
electricity	ELEC / ÉLECTR	électricité
electronics	ELECTRON / ÉLECTRON	électronique
entomology	ENTOM	entomologie
horseriding	EQUIT / ÉQUIT	équitation
fencing	ESCRIME	escrime
ethnology	ETHN	ethnologie
fencing	FENCING	escrime
finance	FIN	finance
fishing	FISHING	pêche
football	FTBL / FOOTBALL	football
games	GAMES	jeux
geography	GEOGR / GÉOG	géographie
geology	GEOL / GÉOL	géologie
geometry	GEOM / GÉOM	géométrie
golf	GOLF	golf
grammar	GRAM / GRAMM	grammaire
gymnastics	GYM	gymnastique
heraldry	HERALD / HÉRALD	héraldique
history	HIST	histoire
horticulture	HORT	horticulture
hunting	HUNT	chasse
ice hockey	ICE HOCKEY	hockey sur glace
printing	IMPR	imprimerie
industry	INDUST	industrie

computing	**INFORM**	informatique
games	**JEUX**	jeux
jewellery	**JOAILL**	joaillerie
judo	**JUDO**	judo
law	**LAW**	droit
linguistics	**LING**	linguistique
literature	**LIT / LITTÉR**	littérature
logic	**LOGIC /**	logique
marketing	**MARKETING**	marketing
mathematics	**MATHS / MATH**	mathématiques
mechanics	**MECH / MÉCAN**	mécanique
medicine	**MED / MÉD**	médecine
carpentry	**MENUIS**	menuiserie
metallurgy	**METALL / MÉTAL**	métallurgie
meteorology	**METEOR / MÉTÉOR**	météorologie
military	**MIL**	militaire
mining	**MIN**	mines
mineralogy	**MINER / MINÉR**	minéralogie
music	**MUS**	musique
mythology	**MYTH / MYTHOL**	mythologie
nautical	**NAUT**	nautique
nuclear physics	**NUCL PHYS / NUCL**	physique nucléaire
oenology	**OENOL / ŒNOL**	œnologie
optics	**OPT**	optique
ornithology	**ORNITH**	ornithologie
fishing	**PÊCHE**	pêche
petroleum industry	**PETR / PÉTR**	industrie du pétrole
pharmaceuticals	**PHARM**	pharmacie
philosophy	**PHILOS**	philosophie
phonetics	**PHON**	phonétique
photography	**PHOT / PHOTO**	photographie
physics	**PHYS**	physique
physiology	**PHYSIOL**	physiologie
poetry	**POET / POÉSIE**	poésie
politics	**POL / POLIT**	politique
press	**PRESS**	presse
printing	**PRINT**	imprimerie
psychology	**PSYCHOL**	psychologie
radio	**RADIO**	radio
rail	**RAIL**	rail
religion	**RELIG**	religion
rowing	**ROWING**	aviron
rugby	**RUGBY**	rugby
sailing	**SAIL**	voile
school	**SCH**	éducation
science	**SCI / SC**	sciences
sewing	**SEW**	couture
skiing	**SKI**	ski
sociology	**SOCIOL**	sociologie
sport	**SPORT**	sport
stock exchange	**ST EX**	Bourse
bull fighting	**TAUROM**	tauromachie
technology	**TECH / TECHNOL**	technologie
telecommunications	**TELEC / TÉLÉCOM**	télécommunications
tennis	**TENNIS**	tennis
textiles	**TEX / TEXT**	textiles
theatre	**THEAT / THÉÂTRE**	théâtre
transport ***UK***, transportation ***US***	**TRANSP**	transport
civil engineering	**TRAV PUB**	travaux publics
television	**TV**	télévision
typography	**TYPO**	typographie
university	**UNIV**	université
veterinary science	**VET / VÉTÉR**	médecine vétérinaire
viniculture	**VINIC**	viniculture
zoology	**ZOOL**	zoologie

TRANSCRIPTION PHONÉTIQUE

Voyelles anglaises

[ɪ]	pit, big, rid
[e]	pet, tend
[æ]	pat, bag, mad
[ʌ]	putt, cut
[ɒ]	pot, log
[ʊ]	put, full
[ə]	mother, suppose
[iː]	bean, weed
[ɑː]	barn, car, laugh
[ɔː]	born, lawn
[uː]	loop, loose
[ɜː]	burn, learn, bird

Diphtongues

[eɪ]	bay, late, great
[aɪ]	buy, light, aisle
[ɔɪ]	boy, foil
[əʊ]	no, road, blow
[aʊ]	now, shout, town
[ɪə]	peer, fierce
[eə]	pair, bear, share
[ʊə]	poor, sure, tour

Semi-voyelles

[j]	you, spaniel
[w]	wet, why, twin

Consonnes

[p]	pop, people
[b]	bottle, bib
[t]	train, tip
[d]	dog, did
[k]	come, kitchen
[g]	gag, great
[tʃ]	chain, wretched
[dʒ]	jig, fridge
[f]	fib, physical
[v]	vine, livid
[θ]	think, fifth
[ð]	this, with
[s]	seal, peace
[z]	zip, his
[ʃ]	sheep, machine
[ʒ]	usual, measure
[h]	how, perhaps
[m]	metal, comb
[n]	night, dinner
[ŋ]	sung, parking
[l]	little, help
[r]	right, carry

Notes sur la transcription phonétique

Anglais-Français

1. Accents primaire et secondaire
Les symboles [ˈ] et [ˌ] indiquent respectivement un accent primaire et un accent secondaire sur la syllabe suivante.

2. Prononciation du 'r' final
Le symbole [ʳ] indique que le 'r' final d'un mot anglais ne se prononce que lorsqu'il forme une liaison avec la voyelle du mot suivant ; le 'r' final est presque toujours prononcé en anglais américain.

3. Anglais britannique et américain
Les différences de prononciation entre l'anglais britannique et l'anglais américain ne sont signalées que lorsqu'elles sortent du cadre de règles générales préétablies. Le 'o' de **dog**, par exemple, est généralement plus allongé en anglais américain, et ne bénéficie pas d'une seconde transcription phonétique. En revanche, des mots comme **schedule, clerk, cliché,** etc, dont la prononciation est moins évidente, font l'objet de deux transcriptions phonétiques.

4. Mots ayant deux prononciations
Nous avons choisi de ne donner que la prononciation la plus courante du mot, sauf dans les cas où une variante est particulièrement fréquente, comme par exemple le mot **kilometre** [ˈkɪləmiːtəʳ, kɪˈlɒmɪtəʳ].

5. Les formes accentuées et atones
La prononciation de certains mots monosyllabiques anglais varie selon le degré d'emphase qu'ils ont dans la phrase ; **the**, par exemple, se prononce [ðiː] en position accentuée, [ðə] en position atone, et [ðɪ] devant une voyelle. Ces informations sont présentées de la manière suivante dans le dictionnaire: **the** [weak form [ðə], before vowel [ðɪ], strong form [ðiː]].

Français-Anglais

1. Le symbole ['] représente le 'h aspiré' français, par exemple **hachis** ['aʃi].

2. Comme le veut la tendance actuelle, nous ne faisons pas de distinction entre le 'a' de **pâte** et celui de **patte,** tous deux transcrits [a].

3. Prononciation du 'e' muet
Lorsque le 'e' peut ne pas être prononcé dans le discours continu, il a été mis entre parenthèses, comme par exemple pour le mot **cheval** [ʃ(ə)val].

PHONETIC TRANSCRIPTION

French vowels

[i] fille, île
[e] pays, année
[ɛ] bec, aime
[a] lac, papillon
[o] drôle, aube
[ɔ] hotte, automne
[u] outil, goût
[y] usage, lune
[θ] aveu, jeu
[œ] peuple, bœuf
[ə] le, je

Nasal vowels

[ɛ̃] limbe, main
[ɑ̃] champ, ennui
[ɔ̃] ongle, mon
[œ̃] parfum, brun

Semi-vowels

[j] yeux, lieu
[w] ouest, oui
[ɥ] lui, nuit

Consonants

[p] prendre, grippe
[b] bateau, rosbif
[t] théâtre, temps
[d] dalle, ronde
[k] coq, quatre
[g] garder, épilogue
[f] physique, fort
[v] voir, rive
[s] cela, savant
[z] fraise, zéro
[ʃ] charrue, schéma
[ʒ] rouge, jabot
[m] mât, drame
[n] nager, trône
[ɲ] agneau, peigner
[l] halle, lit
[r] arracher, sabre

Notes on phonetic transcription

French-English

1. The symbol ['] has been used to represent the French 'h aspiré', e.g. **hachis** ['aʃi].

2. We have followed the modern tendency not to distinguish between the 'a' in **pâte** and the 'a' in **patte**. Both are represented in the text by the phonetic symbol [a].

3. Internal schwa

In cases where the schwa [ə] is likely to be ignored in connected speech but retained in the citation form, the [ə] has been shown in brackets, e.g. **cheval** [ʃ(ə)val].

English-French

1. Primary and secondary stress

The symbol [ˈ] indicates that the following syllable carries primary stress and the symbol [ˌ] that the following syllable carries secondary stress.

2. Pronunciation of final 'r'

The symbol [ʳ] in English phonetics indicates that the final 'r' is pronounced only when followed by a word beginning with a vowel. Note that it is nearly always pronounced in American English.

3. British and American English

Differences between British and American pronunciation have not been shown where the pronunciation can be predicted by a standard set of rules, for example where the 'o' in **dog** is lengthened in American English. However, phonetics have been shown for the more unpredictable cases of **schedule, clerk, cliché** etc.

4. Alternative pronunciations

Our approach being primarily functional rather than descriptive, we have avoided giving variant pronunciations unless both variants are met with equal frequency, e.g. **kilometre** [ˈkɪləmiːtəʳ, kɪləmɪːtəʳ].

5. Strong and weak forms

The pronunciation of certain monosyllabic words varies according to their prominence in a sentence, e.g. **the** when stressed is pronounced [ðiː]; when unstressed, [ðə] and before a vowel [ðɪ]. This information is presented in the text as follows: **the** [weak form [ðə], before vowel [ðɪ], strong form [ðiː]].

NOTES CULTURELLES

Les notes culturelles apportent, sous la forme de développements encyclopédiques, des informations complémentaires sur certains aspects culturels de la langue anglaise dont le sens ne peut être rendu de manière satisfaisante par une traduction ou une glose. Ces notes permettent à l'utilisateur francophone de percevoir, au-delà des mots, toute la signification des grands événements de l'histoire du Royaume-Uni et des États-Unis et de certains traits de leur civilisation, qu'il s'agisse d'institutions politiques, de patrimoine culturel ou de particularités de la vie quotidienne.

La liste ci-dessous donne les titres des notes culturelles figurant dans la partie anglais-français du dictionnaire. Celles-ci apparaissent dans des encadrés à la fin des entrées auxquelles elles sont rattachées.

ALAMO : THE ALAMO
ALBERT : THE ALBERT HALL
A-LEVEL
ALEXANDRA PALACE
APRIL : APRIL FOOLS' DAY
ARAB
ARCHBISHOP
ARMISTICE DAY
ASIAN
BACKBENCHER
BALD EAGLE
BARBICAN
BARNARDOS
BAY OF PIGS : THE BAY OF PIGS
BEST MAN
BIG BEN
BINGO
BLACK COUNTRY : THE BLACK COUNTRY
BLOCK VOTE
BLOOMSBURY GROUP
BOER : THE BOER WAR
BOND STREET
BOOKER PRIZE
BOSTON TEA PARTY
BOW BELLS
BRING-AND-BUY SALE
BRITAIN : THE BATTLE OF BRITAIN
BRITISH COUNCIL
BRITISH LIBRARY
BRITISH TELECOM
BROADSHEET
CAPITOL HILL
CARNABY STREET
CAROL SERVICE
CAUCUS
CHARGE : THE CHARGE OF THE LIGHT BRIGADE
CHECKS AND BALANCES
CHURCH : THE CHURCH OF ENGLAND
CITY : THE CITY
CIVIL WAR
CIVIL WAR : THE ENGLISH CIVIL WAR
CLUB
COLONEL BLIMP
COMING OF AGE
COMMON LAW
CONGRESS
CONSTITUTION
CONTINENTAL BREAKFAST
CORN : THE CORN LAWS
CORONATION STREET
COVENT GARDEN
CRACKER
DAFFODIL
DATE
DECLARATION OF INDEPENDENCE : THE DECLARATION OF INDEPENDENCE
DEPRESSION : THE GREAT DEPRESSION
DIAL : DIAL-A-...
DOWNING STREET
DREAM : "I HAVE A DREAM"
DRURY LANE
DUKE OF EDINBURGH'S AWARD SCHEME
DUST BOWL : THE DUST BOWL
EDINBURGH FESTIVAL
ELECTION : MID-TERM ELECTIONS
EMANCIPATION : THE EMANCIPATION PROCLAMATION
ENGLISH BREAKFAST
ESKIMO
ETON
FABIAN SOCIETY : THE FABIAN SOCIETY
FALKLAND : THE FALKLANDS WAR
FÊTE
FINANCIAL TIMES
FINANCIAL YEAR
FISCAL YEAR
FLAG DAY
FLEET STREET
GCSE
GETTYSBURG ADDRESS : THE GETTYSBURG ADDRESS
GLORIOUS REVOLUTION : THE GLORIOUS REVOLUTION
GOLD RUSH : THE GOLD RUSH
GOTHIC : GOTHIC NOVEL
GRAMMAR SCHOOL
GREENHAM COMMON
GRETNA GREEN
GROUND ZERO
GUNPOWDER PLOT : THE GUNPOWDER PLOT
GUY FAWKES' NIGHT
HABEAS CORPUS : THE HABEAS CORPUS ACT
HENLEY REGATTA
HIGHLAND GAMES
HOME RULE
HONOURABLE
HOUSE
HOUSE OF COMMONS
HOUSE OF LORDS
HOUSE OF REPRESENTATIVES
INDEPENDENCE : THE AMERICAN WAR OF INDEPENDENCE
INDUSTRIAL : THE INDUSTRIAL REVOLUTION
INTERNMENT
IRA
IRISH : THE IRISH FREE STATE
JACOBITE : THE JACOBITES
JP : JUSTICE OF THE PEACE
KENNEDY : THE KENNEDY ASSASSINATION
KOREAN : THE KOREAN WAR
L-DRIVER
LEEK
LICENSING HOURS
LITTLE BIGHORN : THE BATTLE OF LITTLE BIGHORN
LOG CABIN
LOUISIANA PURCHASE : THE LOUISIANA PURCHASE
LOYALIST
LUDDITE : THE LUDDITE RIOTS
MAGNA CARTA
MARSHALL PLAN
MAYFLOWER : THE MAYFLOWER COMPACT
McCARTHYISM
MEXICAN : THE MEXICAN WAR
MIDNIGHT : THE MIDNIGHT RIDE
MINUTEMAN : MINUTEMEN
MONROE DOCTRINE
NORMAN : THE NORMAN CONQUEST
NORTHERN IRELAND
PANTOMIME
PEARL HARBOR
PEASANT : THE PEASANTS' REVOLT
PENTAGON
PILGRIM FATHERS : THE PILGRIM FATHERS
POLITICALLY CORRECT
POOR LAW : THE POOR LAWS
PORTON DOWN
POTATO : THE POTATO FAMINE
PRIMARY : PRIMARIES
PRIVY COUNCIL
PROHIBITION
PROTECTORATE : THE PROTECTORATE
PUB
PUBLIC SCHOOL
PUNCH AND JUDY
PURITAN : THE PURITANS
QUANGO
RADIO
RECONSTRUCTION : THE RECONSTRUCTION
REFORM : THE GREAT REFORM BILLS
RESTORATION : THE RESTORATION
RETIREMENT AGE
RHYMING SLANG
ROYAL SOCIETY : THE ROYAL SOCIETY
SCHOOL : COMPREHENSIVE SCHOOL
SECOND CLASS : SECOND-CLASS MAIL
SENATE
SHADOW : SHADOW CABINET
SHAMROCK
SHOT : THE SHOT HEARD AROUND THE WORLD
SINN FÉIN
SOMERSET HOUSE
SOUTH SEA BUBBLE : THE SOUTH SEA BUBBLE
SPANISH-AMERICAN : THE SPANISH-AMERICAN WAR
SPANISH ARMADA : THE SPANISH ARMADA
SPEAKER : SPEAKER OF THE HOUSE
SPEECH DAY
SPONSORED WALK
STAMP : THE STAMP ACT
STATE OF THE UNION ADDRESS
STRAWBERRY : STRAWBERRIES AND CREAM
STRIKE : THE GENERAL STRIKE
STUDENTS' UNION
SUBURB UNION
SUFFRAGETTES : THE SUFFRAGETTES
SUNDAY PAPERS
SUPREME COURT
TABLOID
TEA
TERRACE
TEXT MESSAGING
THANKSGIVING
THISTLE
TRAFFIC WARDEN
TRAIL : THE TRAIL OF TEARS
TRANSCONTINENTAL : THE TRANSCONTINENTAL RAILROAD
UNIVERSITY
VALENTINE : THE SAINT VALENTINE'S DAY MASSACRE
VIETNAM : THE VIETNAM WAR
VILLAGE GREEN
WALL STREET : THE WALL STREET CRASH
WAR : THE WARS OF THE ROSES
WAR : THE WAR OF THE WORLDS
WATERGATE
WESTMINSTER
WHITEHALL
WINTER : THE WINTER OF DISCONTENT
YE : YE OLDE
YEARBOOK
YELLOW LINE : YELLOW LINES

CULTURAL NOTES

The cultural notes provide extra information, in the form of encyclopedic entries, on certain aspects of culture that cannot be fully rendered by a translation or gloss. They give the foreign user native-speaker access to the full meaning behind certain cultural items including major historical events, public institutions, places of interest and general features of everyday life.

Below is a list of the cultural notes on France in this dictionary. They appear immediately after the entry to which they are attached.

ACADÉMIE : L'ACADÉMIE FRANÇAISE
AGRÉGATION : L'AGRÉGATION
ALGÉRIE : LA GUERRE D'ALGÉRIE
ALSACE
ALSACE-LORRAINE
AMNISTIE
ANCIEN : ANCIEN RÉGIME
ANGLO-SAXON
ANTILLES
APOSTROPHE : APOSTROPHES
AQUITAIN : AQUITAINE
ARABE
ARCHIVES : LES ARCHIVES NATIONALES
ARCHIVES : LES ARCHIVES DÉPARTEMENTALES
ASCENSION : L'ASCENSION
ASIATIQUE
ASSEDIC
ASSEMBLÉE : L'ASSEMBLÉE NATIONALE
ASSOMPTION : L'ASSOMPTION
AUTOROUTE
AUVERGNE
AVIGNON : LE FESTIVAL D'AVIGNON
BACCALAURÉAT
BAIL
BANLIEUE
BASSE-NORMANDIE
BASTILLE : LA BASTILLE
BD
BEAUBOURG
BEUR
BIBLIOTHÈQUE : LA BIBLIOTHÈQUE NATIONALE
BISTROT
BIZUTAGE
BOUQUINISTE : BOUQUINISTES
BOURGOGNE
BRETAGNE
CABINET
CADRE
CAFÉ
CALENDRIER : CALENDRIER RÉPUBLICAIN
CANAL : CANAL +
CANEBIÈRE : LA CANEBIÈRE
CANTON
CAPES
CARTE : CARTE DE SÉJOUR
CAUTION
CENTRE
CHAMBRE : LA CHAMBRE DES DÉPUTÉS
CHAMPAGNE-ARDENNE
CHARCUTERIE
CHARGE : CHARGES
CHARGÉ : CHARGÉ DE COURS
CINÉMATHÈQUE : LA CINÉMATHÈQUE FRANÇAISE
CLASSE : CLASSES PRÉPARATOIRES
CNRS
CODE : CODE POSTAL
COEFFICIENT
COHABITATION : LA COHABITATION
COLLÈGE : LE COLLÈGE DE FRANCE
COLONIE : COLONIE DE VACANCES
COMÉDIE : LA COMÉDIE-FRANÇAISE
COMITÉ : COMITÉ D'ENTREPRISE
COMMUNE
COMMUNE : LA COMMUNE
COMPOSTER
CONCIERGE
CONSEIL : LE CONSEIL CONSTITUTIONNEL
CONSEIL : LE CONSEIL D'ÉTAT
CONSEIL : LE CONSEIL DES MINISTRES
CONSEIL : CONSEIL GÉNÉRAL
CONSEIL : CONSEIL RÉGIONAL
CONSEIL : CONSEIL SUPÉRIEUR DE LA MAGISTRATURE
CONSEIL : CONSEIL MUNICIPAL
CONSEILLER : CONSEILLER MUNICIPAL
CONSTAT
COQ : LE COQ GAULOIS
CORSE : LA CORSE
COUR : COUR D'ASSISES
COUR : COUR DE CASSATION
COUR : COUR DES COMPTES
CRS
CURE : CURE THERMALE
DÉCENTRALISATION
DÉCLARATION : DÉCLARATION D'IMPÔTS
DÉCLARATION : LA DÉCLARATION DES DROITS DE L'HOMME ET DU CITOYEN
DÉCOLONISATION : LA DÉCOLONISATION
DÉPARTEMENT
DEUG : DEUG, DEUST
DOM-TOM
DRAGÉE
DREYFUS : L'AFFAIRE DREYFUS
ÉCOLE : L'ÉCOLE LAÏQUE
EIFFEL : LA TOUR EIFFEL
ÉLECTION : ÉLECTIONS
ÉLYSÉE : L'ÉLYSÉE
ÉTAT : LES ÉTATS GÉNÉRAUX
FÊTE
FONCTIONNAIRE
FRANCHE-COMTÉ
FRANCOPHONIE
FRONT : LE FRONT POPULAIRE
GENDARMERIE
GRAND : GRANDE ÉCOLE
HAGUE : LA HAGUE
HALLE : LES HALLES
HAUSSMANN
HAUTE-NORMANDIE
HÔTEL : L'HÔTEL DE LA MONNAIE
IGN
ÎLE-DE-FRANCE
IMMATRICULATION
IMPÔT : IMPÔTS LOCAUX
IMPRIMERIE : L'IMPRIMERIE NATIONALE
INSTITUT : L'INSTITUT DE FRANCE
JEU : LE JEU DES MILLE FRANCS
JOURNAL : LE JOURNAL OFFICIEL
JUILLET : FÊTE DU 14 JUILLET
LANGUEDOC-ROUSSILLON
LICENCE
LIMOUSIN
LORRAINE
LUMIÈRE : LE SIÈCLE DES LUMIÈRES
MAGHRÉBIN
MAGINOT : LA LIGNE MAGINOT
MAGISTRAT
MAI : MAI 68
MAIRE
MAIRIE
MAISON : MAISON DE LA CULTURE
MAÎTRISE
MARAIS : LE MARAIS
MARIAGE
MARIANNE
MARSEILLAIS : LA MARSEILLAISE
MATIGNON
MIDI-PYRÉNÉES
MINITEL
MJC
MONEO
MONTPARNASSE
MUGUET
MUNICIPAL : MUNICIPALES
MUTUEL : MUTUELLE
NANTES : L'ÉDIT DE NANTES
NORD-PAS-DE-CALAIS
NOUVEAU : LA NOUVELLE VAGUE
OCCUPATION : L'OCCUPATION
ORSEC : LE PLAN ORSEC
PALAIS : PALAIS DES PAPES
PÂQUES : LES CLOCHES DE PÂQUES
PARIS
PAYS : PAYS DE LA LOIRE
PEINE : PEINE DE MORT
PERMIS : PERMIS DE CONDUIRE
PICARDIE
PIÈCE
PIED-NOIR
PION
PLAN : PLAN VIGIPIRATE
PMU
POITOU-CHARENTES
POLICE : POLICE NATIONALE
POLYTECHNIQUE : ÉCOLE POLYTECHNIQUE
POSTE : LA POSTE
PRÉFECTURE
PRÉFET
PRÉSIDENTIEL : LES PRÉSIDENTIELLES
PRESSE
PROVENCE-ALPES-CÔTE-D'AZUR
QUAI
QUÉBEC : LE QUÉBEC
RÉGIME : RÉGIME DE SÉCURITÉ SOCIALE
RÉGION
RELEVÉ : RELEVÉ D'IDENTITÉ BANCAIRE
RENSEIGNEMENT : LES RENSEIGNEMENTS GÉNÉRAUX
RENTRÉE : LA RENTRÉE
RÉSISTANCE : LA RÉSISTANCE
RESTO : LES RESTOS DU CŒUR
RETRAITE
RÉVOLUTION : LA RÉVOLUTION FRANÇAISE
RHÔNE-ALPES
RIVE : RIVE DROITE, RIVE GAUCHE
ROSE
RPR
RTT
RUE
SAINT-GERMAIN-DES-PRÉS
SAMU
SANS-CULOTTE : LES SANS-CULOTTES
SAVON : SAVON DE MARSEILLE
SÉCURITÉ : SÉCURITÉ SOCIALE
SEIZIÈME : SEIZIÈME
SÉNAT : SÉNAT
SERVICE : SERVICE MILITAIRE OU NATIONAL
SYNDIC
TIMBRE : TIMBRE FISCAL
TOUR : TOUR DE FRANCE
TOUSSAINT
VERLAN
VERSAILLES
VICHY : LE GOUVERNEMENT DE VICHY
VIGNETTE
ZONE

USAGE MODULES

The Usage Modules give typical examples of ways in which you can express yourself in French in a particular situation or context.
They appear at the bottom of the page containing the entry to which they are attached (in some cases the module is on the preceding or following page); for example, 'Giving orders' is on the same page as the entry 'order'.
The module shows you different ways of giving orders in French, whereas the entry 'order' shows you how to translate the word itself. Below is a list of the 'Usage Modules' to be found in this dictionary.

Advice
Agreement
Apologies
Certainty
Comparisons
Complaints
Concede :
  Conceding a point
Conditional :
  Conditional clauses
Congratulations
Correct :
  Correcting someone
Disagreement
Disapproval
Dislike
Explanations
Fear
Goodbyes
Meet :
  Arranging to meet somebody
Obligation
Offers
Order :
  Giving orders
Permission
Preferences
Prohibition
Refusals
Regrets
Requests
Subject :
  Changing the subject
Suggestions
Summarizing
Suppositions
Surprise
Sympathy
Thanks :
  Saying thank you
Threats
Wishes

LES MODULES « USAGE »

Les modules « usage » offrent des exemples de tournures à employer lorsque l'on veut s'exprimer en anglais dans une situation donnée. Ils apparaissent au bas de la page comprenant l'entrée à laquelle ils sont rattachés (dans quelques cas, le module se trouve sur la page qui suit ou qui précède celle où figure l'entrée correspondante). Ainsi, « Donner des ordres » figure sur la même page que l'entrée « ordre ». Le module indique les différentes façons de formuler des ordres en anglais, tandis que l'entrée « ordre » permet de traduire le mot lui-même dans ses diverses acceptions. On trouvera ci-dessous la liste des modules « usage » présentés dans ce dictionnaire.

L'accord
La certitude
La comparaison
Compatir
Comprendre : Dire qu'on a compris/
  qu'on n'a pas compris
La condition
Les conseils
Crainte : Exprimer ses craintes
Les demandes
Le désaccord
La désapprobation
Les excuses
L'explication
Les félicitations
Les goûts
L'incertitude
L'indifférence
L'indignation
L'interdiction
Les invitations
Les menaces
L'obligation
L'opinion
Ordre : Donner des ordres
La permission
La persuasion
Les plaintes
La préférence
Les présentations
Les propositions
Raison : Donner raison à quelqu'un
Le refus
Regret : Exprimer des regrets
Les remerciements
Les rendez-vous
Résumer : Résumer ses idées
Revoir : Dire au revoir
Les souhaits
La suggestion
Sujet : Changer de sujet
La supposition
La surprise
Tort : Donner tort à quelqu'un
Les vœux

FRANÇAIS-ANGLAIS
FRENCH-ENGLISH

a, A [a] *nm* a, A ■ **de A à Z** from A to Z, *voir aussi* **g**.

a (*abr écrite de* **are**) a.

a [a] *v* ▻ **avoir**.

A 1. (*abr écrite de* **ampère**) A, Amp **2.** = **autoroute 3.** [sur une voiture] *indicates that the driver has recently obtained his or her licence.*

à [a] (*contraction de à avec le devant consonne ou h aspiré* **au**, *contraction de à avec les* **aux** [o]) *prép*

> **A.** DANS L'ESPACE
> **B.** DANS LE TEMPS
> **C.** MARQUANT LE MOYEN, LA MANIÈRE
> **D.** MARQUANT L'APPARTENANCE
> **E.** INDIQUANT L'ATTRIBUTION, LA DESTINATION
> **F.** INTRODUISANT UNE ÉVALUATION, UN RAPPORT DISTRIBUTIF
> **G.** MARQUANT DES RAPPORTS DE CAUSE OU DE CONSÉQUENCE
> **H.** SUIVI DE L'INFINITIF
> **I.** MARQUANT LA CARACTÉRISATION, LE BUT
> **J.** SERVANT DE LIEN SYNTAXIQUE

A. DANS L'ESPACE

1. [indiquant la position] at ■ [à l'intérieur de] in ■ [sur] on ■ **il habite à la campagne** he lives in the country ■ **elle habite au Canada** she lives in Canada ■ **il est à l'hôpital** he's in hospital *UK OU* in the hospital *US* ■ **elle travaille à l'hôpital** she works at the hospital ■ **il fait 45°C au soleil** it's 45°C in the sun ■ **quand on est à 2 000 m d'altitude** when you're 2,000 m up ■ **elle attendait à la porte** she was waiting at *ou* by the door ■ **au mur/plafond** on the wall/ceiling ■ **c'est au rez-de-chaussée** it's on the ground floor ■ **j'ai une ampoule au pied** I've got a blister on my foot ■ **je l'ai entendu à la radio** I heard it on the radio ■ **à ma droite** on *OU* to my right ■ **vous tournez à gauche après le feu** you turn left after the traffic lights ■ **la gare est à 500 m d'ici** the station is 500 m from here

2. [indiquant la direction] to ■ **aller à Paris/aux États-Unis/à la Jamaïque** to go to Paris/to the United States/to Jamaica ■ **aller au cinéma** to go to the cinema

3. [indiquant la provenance, l'origine] : **puiser de l'eau à la fontaine** to get water from the fountain ■ **retenir l'impôt à la source** to deduct tax at source ■ **remonter à l'origine d'une affaire** to get to the root of a matter

B. DANS LE TEMPS

1. [indiquant un moment précis] at ■ [devant une date, un jour] on ■ [indiquant une époque, une période] in ■ **à 6 h** at 6 o'clock ■ **il ne rentrera qu'à 8 h** he won't be back before 8 ■ **à Noël** at Christmas ■ **à l'aube/l'aurore/midi** at dawn/daybreak/midday ■ **le 12 au soir** on the evening of the 12th ■ **à mon arrivée** on my arrival ■ **à ma naissance** when I was born ■ **à l'automne** in (the) autumn *UK*, in the fall *US* ■ **au XVIIe siècle** in the 17th century ■ **vous allez quelque part à Noël?** are you going somewhere for Christmas?

2. [indiquant un délai] : **nous sommes à deux semaines de Noël** there are only two weeks to go before Christmas, Christmas is only two weeks away ■ **il me tarde d'être à dimanche** *fam* I can't wait till Sunday ■ **à demain/la semaine prochaine/mardi** see you tomorrow/next week/(on) Tuesday

C. MARQUANT LE MOYEN, LA MANIÈRE

1. [indiquant le moyen, l'instrument, l'accompagnement] : **peindre à l'eau/à l'huile** to paint in watercolours/oils ■ **marcher au fuel** to run off *OU* on oil ■ **cousu à la main** hand-sewn ■ **jouer qqch à la guitare** to play sthg on the guitar ■ **cuisiner au beurre** to cook with butter ■ **aller à pied/à bicyclette/à cheval** to go on foot/by bicycle/on horseback

2. [indiquant la manière] : **à voix haute** out loud ■ **je l'aime à la folie** I love her to distraction ■ **nous pourrions multiplier les exemples à l'infini** we could cite an infinite number of examples ■ **à toute vitesse** at full speed ■ **au rythme de deux par semaine** at the rate of two a week ■ **à jeun** on *OU* with an empty stomach ■ **faire qqch à la russe/turque** to do sthg the Russian/Turkish way ■ **un film policier à la Hitchcock** a thriller in the style of *OU* à la Hitchcock

D. MARQUANT L'APPARTENANCE

◗ **encore une idée à Papa!** *fam* another of Dad's ideas! ■ **je veux une chambre à moi** I want my own room *OU* a room of my own ■ **c'est un ami à moi qui m'a parlé de vous** *fam* it was a friend of mine who told me about you

E. INDIQUANT L'ATTRIBUTION, LA DESTINATION

◗ **je suis à vous dans une minute** I'll be with you in a minute ■ **c'est à moi de jouer/parler** it's my turn to play/to speak ■ **ce n'est pas à moi de le faire** it's not up to me to do it ■ **à M. le directeur** [dans la correspondance] to the manager ■ **à notre fille bien-aimée** [sur une tombe] in memory of our beloved daughter ■ **à toi pour toujours** yours for ever

F. INTRODUISANT UNE ÉVALUATION, UN RAPPORT DISTRIBUTIF

1. [introduisant un prix] : **un livre à 20 euros** a book which costs 20 euros, a book worth 20 euros ■ **'tout à 2 euros'** 'everything 2 euros'

2. [indiquant un rapport, une mesure] : **vendus à la douzaine/au poids/au détail** sold by the dozen/by weight/individually ■ **les promotions s'obtiennent au nombre d'années d'ancienneté** promotion is in accordance with length of service

3. [introduisant un nombre de personnes] : **ils ont soulevé le piano à quatre** it took four of them to lift the piano ■ **à deux, on aura vite fait de repeindre la cuisine** between the two of us, it won't take long to repaint the kitchen ■ **nous travaillons à sept dans la même pièce** there are seven of us working in the same room ■ **ils sont venus à plusieurs** several of them came

4. [indiquant une approximation] : **je m'entraîne trois à cinq heures par jour** I practise three to five hours a day ■ **j'en ai vu 15 à 20** I saw 15 or 20 of them

G. MARQUANT DES RAPPORTS DE CAUSE OU DE CONSÉQUENCE

1. [indiquant la cause] : **à ces mots, il s'est tu** on hearing these words, he fell silent ■ **on l'a distribué à sa demande** it was given out at his request
2. [indiquant la conséquence] : **il lui a tout dit, à ma grande surprise** he told her everything, much to my surprise ■ **à la satisfaction générale** to the satisfaction of all concerned
3. [d'après] : **je l'ai reconnu à sa voix/démarche** I recognized (him by) his voice/walk ■ **à sa mine, on voit qu'il est en mauvaise santé** you can tell from the way he looks that he's ill ■ **à ce que je vois/comprends** from what I see/understand ■ **à ce qu'elle dit, le mur se serait écroulé** according to her *ou* to what she says, the wall collapsed

H. SUIVI DE L'INFINITIF

1. [indiquant l'hypothèse, la cause] : **tu vas te fatiguer à rester debout** you'll get tired standing up ■ **à t'entendre, on dirait que tu t'en moques** listening to you, I get the feeling that you don't care ■ **à bien considérer les choses...** all things considered...
2. [exprimant l'obligation] : **la somme est à régler avant le 10** the full amount has to *ou* must be paid by the 10th ■ **c'est une pièce à voir absolument** this play is really worth seeing ■ **les vêtements à laver/repasser** the clothes to be washed/ironed
3. [exprimant la possibilité] : **il n'y a rien à voir/à manger** there's nothing to see/to eat
4. [en train de] : **il était assis là à bâiller** he was sitting there yawning
5. [au point de] : **ils en sont à se demander si ça en vaut la peine** they've got to the stage of wondering whether or not it's worth the effort

I. MARQUANT LA CARACTÉRISATION, LE BUT

➜ **l'homme au pardessus** the man in *ou* with the overcoat ■ **une chemise à manches courtes** a short-sleeved shirt, a shirt with short sleeves ■ **un pyjama à fleurs/rayures** flowery/stripy pyjamas ■ **des sardines à l'huile** sardines in oil ■ **glace à la framboise** raspberry ice cream ■ **tasse à thé** tea cup ■ **machine à coudre** sewing machine ■ **'bureau à louer'** 'office for rent'

J. SERVANT DE LIEN SYNTAXIQUE

1. [introduisant le complément du verbe] : **parler à qqn** to talk to sb ■ **téléphoner à qqn** to phone sb ■ **aimer à faire qqch** *litt* to like to do sthg, to like doing sthg ■ **il consent à ce que nous y allions** he agrees to our going ■ **dire à qqn de faire qqch** to tell sb to do sthg ■ **rendre qqch à qqn** to give sthg back to sb, to give sb sthg back
2. [introduisant le complément d'un nom] : **l'appartenance à un parti** membership of a party ■ **son dévouement à notre cause** her devotion to our cause
3. [introduisant le complément de l'adjectif] : **c'est difficile à dessiner** it's difficult to draw.

AB **1.** *(abr écrite de* **assez bien***) fair grade (as assessment of schoolwork),* ≃ C+, ≃ B- **2.** *(abr écrite de* **agriculture biologique***) food label guaranteeing that a product is made from at least 95% organic ingredients (100% in the case of a single ingredient).*

abaisse [abɛs] *nf* [en pâtisserie] piece of rolled-out pastry.

abaisse-langue [abɛslɑ̃g] *nm inv* tongue-depressor, tongue spatula.

abaissement [abɛsmɑ̃] *nm* **1.** [d'une vitre] lowering ■ [d'une manette - en tirant] pulling down ; [- en poussant] pushing down **2.** *fig* humbling, humiliation, abasement *litt.*

abaisser [4] [abese] *vt* **1.** [faire descendre - vitre] to lower ; [- store] to pull down *(sép)* ; [- voilette] to let down *(sép)* ; [- pont-levis] to lower, to let down *(sép)* ; [- température] to lower ■ **~ la manette** [en tirant] to pull the lever down ; [en poussant] to push the lever down **2.** *litt* [individu, pays] to humble, to abase **3.** MATH [perpendiculaire] to drop ■ [chiffre] to carry **4.** MUS to transpose down *(sép)* **5.** CULIN to roll out *(sép)* **6.** JEUX to lay down *(sép)*.

◆ **s'abaisser** *vpi* **1.** [vitre, pont-levis] to be lowered ■ [voile, rideau] to fall ■ [paupière] to droop **2.** [être en pente - champ] to slope down ■ **le terrain s'abaisse vers le fleuve** the land drop away towards the river.

◆ **s'abaisser à** *vp+prép* : **s'~ à des compromissions** to stoo to compromise ■ **il ne s'abaisserait pas à mentir** he would no demean himself by lying.

abandon [abɑ̃dɔ̃] *nm* **1.** [fait de rejeter] abandonment, rejec tion ■ **faire ~ de qqch à qqn** to donate sthg (freely) to sb ➜ **~ du domicile conjugal** DR desertion of the marital home ■ **~ d'enfant** DR abandonment (of one's child) ■ **~ de famille** DR de sertion ■ **~ de poste** MIL dereliction of duty **2.** [fait d'être rejeté] **éprouver un sentiment d'~** to feel abandoned **3.** [état négligé neglected state ■ **les lieux étaient dans un (état de) grand ~** th place was shamefully neglected **4.** [absence de contrainte abandon, freedom ■ **dans ses bras, elle avait connu un délicieu ~** she'd experienced such sweet surrender in his arm ■ **avec ~** [parler] freely ; [danser, rire] with gay abandon **5.** SPOR withdrawal ■ **il y a eu ~ par Vigor juste avant l'arrivée** Vigo dropped out just before the finish.

◆ **à l'abandon** ◇ *loc adj* : **un potager à l'~** a neglecte kitchen garden.

◇ *loc adv* : **laisser son affaire/ses enfants à l'~** to neglect one' business/one's children.

abandonné, e [abɑ̃dɔne] *adj* **1.** [parc] neglected ■ [mine, exploitation] disused ■ [village] deserted ■ [maison, voiture] abandoned ■ [vêtement, chaussure] discarded **2.** [enfant, animal abandoned.

abandonner [3] [abɑ̃dɔne] *vt* **1.** [quitter - enfant, chien] to abandon ; [- épouse] to leave, to desert ; [- lieu] to abandon to leave ; [- poste] to desert, to abandon ■ **abandonné de tous** forsaken by all **2.** [faire défaut à] to fail, to desert, to forsake ■ **mes forces m'abandonnent** *litt* my strength is failing me **3.** [renoncer à - projet, principe] to discard, to abandon ; [- hypothèse] to abandon ; [- course] to drop out of ; [- études] to give up ; [- carrière] to give up, to leave ; [- droit, privilège] to relinquish, to renounce ■ **~ le pouvoir** to leave *ou* to retire from *ou* to give up office ■ **elle abandonne la géographie** she's dropping geography ➜ **~ la partie** *pr* to give up ; *fig* to throw in the sponge *ou* towel **4.** [livrer] : **~ qqn à** to leave *ou* to abandon sb to ■ **il vous a abandonné à votre triste sort** he's left you to your unhappy fate *pr & hum* **5.** *(en usage absolu)* [dans une lutte, une discussion] to give up ■ **il ne comprendra jamais, j'abandonne** he'll never understand, I give up.

◆ **s'abandonner** *vpi* **1.** [se laisser aller] to let (o.s.) go ■ **elle s'abandonna dans ses bras** she surrendered herself to him **2.** [s'épancher] to open one's heart.

◆ **s'abandonner à** *vp+prép* [désespoir] to give way to ■ [rêverie] to drift off into ■ [plaisirs] to give o.s. up to.

abaque [abak] *nm* **1.** [pour compter] abacus **2.** ARCHIT abacus.

abasourdi, e [abazurdi] *adj* stunned.

abasourdir [32] [abazurdir] *vt* **1.** [stupéfier] to stun ■ **la nouvelle nous avait abasourdis** we were stunned by the news **2.** [suj: bruit, clameur] to stun, to deafen.

abasourdissant, e [abazurdisɑ̃, ɑ̃t] *adj* [bruit] shattering, deafening ■ [nouvelle] stunning.

abasourdissement [abazurdismɑ̃] *nm* stupefaction *sout*, amazement.

abat *etc v* ▷ **abattre.**

abâtardir [32] [abatardir] *vt* [race, individu] to cause to degenerate.

abatis [abati] *nm* *Québec* *land being deforested for cultivation.*

abat-jour [abaʒur] *nm inv* lampshade, shade.

abats [aba] *nmpl* [de porc, de bœuf] offal *(U)* ■ [de volaille] giblets.

abattage [abataʒ] *nm* **1.** [d'arbres] felling **2.** [d'animaux] slaughter, slaughtering **3.** MIN extraction, extracting **4.** *fam loc* **avoir de l'~** to be full of go.

abattant [abatɑ̃] *nm* flap, drop-leaf.

abattement [abatmɑ̃] *nm* **1.** [épuisement - physique] exhaustion ; [- moral] despondency, dejection **2.** [rabais] reduction ▪ **~ (fiscal)** tax allowance.

abattis [abati] ◇ *nm* **1.** MIL abatis, abattis **2.** [dans une forêt] felled trees.
◇ *nmpl* [de volaille] giblets.

abattoir [abatwar] *nm* slaughterhouse, abattoir.

abattre [83] [abatr] *vt* **1.** [faire tomber - arbre] to cut down *(sép)*, to fell ; [- mur] to pull *ou* to knock down *(sép)* ; [- quille] to knock down *(sép)* ▪ **~ de la besogne** *ou* **du travail** *fam fig* to get through a lot of work **2.** [suj: vent, tempête etc] to knock down *(sép)* ▪ **l'arbre fut abattu par le vent** the tree was blown down **3.** [mettre à plat - main, battant] to bring down *(sép)* ▶ **~ ses cartes** *ou* **son jeu** *pr* to lay down one's cards ; *fig* to lay one's cards on the table, to show one's hand **4.** [faire retomber - blé, poussière] to settle ; [- vent] to bring down *(sép)* **5.** [tuer - personne] to shoot (down) ; [- avion] to shoot *ou* to bring down *(sép)* ; [- lièvre] to shoot ; [- perdrix] to shoot, to bring down *(sép)* ; [- animal domestique] to put down *(sép)* ; [- animal de boucherie] to slaughter **6.** [démoraliser] to shatter ▪ [épuiser] to drain, to wear out *(sép)* ▪ **la défaite l'a complètement abattu** [moralement] the defeat completely crushed him ▶ **ne nous laissons pas ~** let's not let things get us down.
◆ **s'abattre** *vpi* [s'écrouler - maison] to fall down ; [- personne] to fall (down), to collapse ▪ **l'arbre s'est abattu** the tree came crashing down.
◆ **s'abattre sur** *vp+prép* **1.** [pluie] to come pouring down on ▪ [grêle] to come pelting *ou* beating down on ▪ [coups] to rain down on ▪ **le malheur/la maladie venait de s'~ sur nous** suddenly we'd been struck by disaster/disease **2.** [se jeter sur] to swoop down on.

abattu, e [abaty] *adj* **1.** [démoralisé] despondent, dejected, downcast ▪ **d'un air ~** dejectedly, dispiritedly **2.** [épuisé] exhausted, worn-out.

abat-vent [abavɑ̃] *nm inv* **1.** [d'une cheminée] (chimney) cowl **2.** HORT windbreak.

abbatial, e, aux [abasjal, o] *adj* abbey *(modif)*.
◆ **abbatiale** *nf* abbey.

abbaye [abei] *nf* abbey ▪ **l'~ de Cîteaux** *the abbey where the Cistercian order was founded in 1098 by Robert de Molesmes* ▪ **l'~ de Clairvaux** *the most famous of the Cistercian monasteries founded by Saint Bernard* ▪ **l'~ de Thélème** *Rabelais' aristocratic utopia in 'Gargantua'*.

abbé [abe] *nm* **1.** [d'une abbaye] abbot **2.** [ecclésiastique] *title formerly used in France for members of the secular clergy.*

abbesse [abɛs] *nf* abbess.

abc [abese] *nm inv* **1.** [base] basics, fundamentals **2.** [livre] primer, alphabet book.

abcès [apsɛ] *nm* abscess ▪ **crever** *ou* **ouvrir** *ou* **vider l'~** *fig* to make a clean breast of things.

abdication [abdikasjɔ̃] *nf* abdication.

abdiquer [3] [abdike] ◇ *vt* [pouvoir] to abdicate, to surrender ▪ [responsabilité, opinion] to abdicate, to renounce.
◇ *vi* to abdicate, to give in ▪ **il abdique facilement devant ses enfants** he gives in easily to his children ▪ **elle n'abdiquera jamais devant les syndicats** she'll never give way to the unions.

abdomen [abdɔmɛn] *nm* abdomen.

abdominal, e, aux [abdɔminal, o] *adj* abdominal.
◆ **abdominaux** *nmpl* **1.** [muscles] stomach *ou* abdominal muscles **2.** [exercices] : **faire des abdominaux** to do exercises for the stomach muscles.

abdos [abdo] *nmpl* **1.** [muscles] abs, stomach muscles **2.** [exercices] stomach exercises, abs (exercises) ▪ **faire des ~** to do abs *ou* stomach exercises.

abducteur [abdyktœr] ◇ *adj m* **1.** ANAT abductor **2.** [tube] delivery *(modif)*.
◇ *nm* ANAT abductor muscle.

abécédaire [abesedɛr] *nm* primer, alphabet book.

abeille [abɛj] *nf* bee.

aberrant, e [abɛrɑ̃, ɑ̃t] *adj* **1.** [comportement] deviant, aberrant ▪ [prix] ridiculous ▪ [idée] preposterous, absurd **2.** BIOL aberrant.

aberration [abɛrasjɔ̃] *nf* **1.** [absurdité] aberration ▪ **par quelle ~ avait-elle dit oui?** whatever had possessed her to say yes? **2.** BIOL & OPT aberration.

abêtir [32] [abetir] *vt* to dull the mind of.
◆ **s'abêtir** *vpi* to become mindless *ou* half-witted.

abêtissant, e [abetisɑ̃, ɑ̃t] *adj* stupefying, dulling, mind-numbing.

abêtissement [abetismɑ̃] *nm* **1.** [action] : **l'~ des enfants par la télévision** the mind-numbing effects of television on children **2.** [résultat] dull-wittedness.

abhorrer [3] [abɔre] *vt litt* to loathe, to abhor.

abîme [abim] *nm* **1.** *litt* [gouffre] abyss, chasm, gulf **2.** *litt* [infini] depths ▪ **plongé dans des ~s de perplexité** utterly nonplussed **3.** [distance mentale] abyss, gulf, chasm ▪ **il y a un ~ entre nous sur le problème de l'euthanasie** there's a gulf between us on the issue of euthanasia.

abîmé, e [abime] *adj* **1.** [vêtement] ruined ▪ [livre, meuble] damaged **2.** *fam* [personne, visage] beaten up ▪ **il est bien ~** he was beaten up pretty badly, he's in a pretty bad state.

abîmer [3] [abime] *vt* **1.** [gâter - aliment, vêtement] to spoil ; [- meuble] to damage ; [- yeux] to ruin ▪ **tu vas ~ ta poupée!** you'll break your dolly! **2.** *fam* [meurtrir] to injure ▪ **ils l'ont bien abîmé** they've made a right mess of him ▶ **~ le portrait à qqn** to smash sb's face in△.
◆ **s'abîmer** ◇ *vpt* : **s'~ la santé** *pr* to ruin one's health ▪ **je ne vais pas m'~ la santé à l'aider** *fam fig* why should I break my neck to help him?
◇ *vpi* **1.** [aliment] to spoil, to go off *UK ou* bad ▪ [meuble] to get damaged **2.** *litt* [navire] to sink, to founder.
◆ **s'abîmer dans** *vp+prép litt* [se plonger dans] : **s'~ dans ses pensées** to be lost *ou* deep in thought ▪ **s'~ dans le désespoir** to be plunged in despair ▪ **abîmé dans ses pensées** deep in thought ▪ **abîmé dans le désespoir** in the depths of despair.

abject, e [abʒɛkt] *adj* despicable, contemptible ▪ **il a été ~ avec elle** he behaved despicably towards her ▪ **d'une manière ~e** abjectly.

abjection [abʒɛksjɔ̃] *nf* **1.** [état] utter humiliation **2.** [caractère vil] abjectness, vileness ▪ **l'~ de son comportement** his vile behaviour.

abjuration [abʒyrasjɔ̃] *nf sout* abjuration.

abjurer [3] [abʒyre] *vt & vi sout* to recant.

ablatif, ive [ablatif, iv] *adj* ablative.
◆ **ablatif** *nm* ablative (case) ▪ **~ absolu** ablative absolute.

ablation [ablasjɔ̃] *nf* **1.** MÉD removal, ablation *spéc* **2.** GÉOL & TECHNOL ablation.

ablette [ablɛt] *nf* bleak.

ablution [ablysjɔ̃] *nf* **1.** RELIG [du corps, du calice] ablution **2.** *hum* [toilette] : **faire ses ~s** to perform one's ablutions.

abnégation [abnegasjɔ̃] *nf* abnegation, self-denial ▪ **avec ~** selflessly.

aboie *etc v* ⊳ **aboyer**.

aboiement [abwamɑ̃] *nm* **1.** [d'un chien] bark ▪ **des ~s** barking **2.** *fig & péj* ranting, raving.

abois [abwa] ◆ **aux abois** *loc adj* **1.** CHASSE at bay **2.** *fig* **être aux ~** to have one's back against *ou* to the wall.

abolir [32] [abɔlir] *vt* to do away *(insép)* with, to abolish.

abolition [abɔlisjɔ̃] *nf* abolition.

abolitionnisme [abɔlisjɔnism] *nm* abolitionism.

abolitionniste [abɔlisjɔnist] *adj & nmf* abolitionist.

abominable [abɔminabl] *adj* **1.** [désagréable - temps, odeur] appalling, abominable **2.** [abject - crime] heinous, abominable, vile ■ **l'~ homme des neiges** the abominable snowman.

abominablement [abɔminabləmɑ̃] *adv* [laid, cher, habillé] horribly, frightfully ■ **~ (mal) organisé** appallingly *ou* abominably badly organized.

abomination [abɔminasjɔ̃] *nf* **1.** [acte, propos] abomination ■ **ce chou-fleur au gratin, c'est une ~** that cauliflower cheese is revolting ■ **il dit des ~s** he says appalling things **2.** [sentiment] loathing, detestation, abomination ■ **avoir qqch en ~** to abhor *ou* to loathe sthg.

abondamment [abɔ̃damɑ̃] *adv* [servir, saler] copiously ■ [rincer] thoroughly ■ **elle a ~ traité la question** she has amply *ou* fully dealt with the question.

abondance [abɔ̃dɑ̃s] *nf* **1.** [prospérité] affluence ■ **vivre dans l'~** to live in affluence **2.** [grande quantité] : **une ~ de citations/détails** a wealth of quotations/details ◆ **~ de biens ne nuit pas** *prov* there's no harm in having too much.
◆ **en abondance** *loc adv* in abundance, in plenty ■ **des fautes en ~** an abundance of mistakes.

abondant, e [abɔ̃dɑ̃, ɑ̃t] *adj* [en quantité - nourriture] abundant, copious ; [- récolte] bountiful ; [- vivres] plentiful ; [- végétation] luxuriant, lush ; [- larmes] copious ; [- chevelure] luxuriant, thick ■ **d'~es illustrations/recommandations** a wealth of illustrations/recommendations.

abondement [abɔ̃dmɑ̃] *nm* employer's contribution *(to savings or share ownership scheme)*.

abonder [3] [abɔ̃de] *vi* **1.** [foisonner] to be plentiful ■ **~ en** to abound in, to be full of ■ **son livre abonde en anecdotes** her book is rich in anecdotes **2.** *fig & sout* **~ dans le sens de** to be in complete agreement with, to go along with.

abonné, e [abɔne] *nm, f* **1.** PRESSE & TÉLÉCOM subscriber **2.** [au théâtre, au concert, au stade] season ticket-holder **3.** *fam hum* [habitué] : **c'est un ~ aux gaffes** he's always putting his foot in it **4.** INFORM : **~ itinérant** roaming subscriber.

abonnement [abɔnmɑ̃] *nm* **1.** PRESSE subscription ■ **prendre un ~ à** to take out a subscription to **2.** [pour un trajet, au théâtre, au stade] season ticket **3.** TÉLÉCOM rental.

abonner [3] [abɔne] *vt* **1.** [inscrire à] : **~ qqn à qqch** [journal] to take out a subscription for sb to sthg ; [théâtre, concert, stade] to buy sb a season ticket for sthg ■ **être abonné à un journal** to subscribe to a paper **2.** [pour un service] : **être abonné au gaz** to have gas ■ **être abonné au téléphone** to have a phone, to be on the phone *UK* ■ **encore une contravention? décidément, tu es abonné!** *hum* another parking ticket? you're making rather a habit of this, aren't you?
◆ **s'abonner** *vp (emploi réfléchi)* : **s'~ à** [un journal] to take out a subscription to ; [au théâtre, au concert, au stade] to buy a season ticket for.

abord [abɔr] *nm* **1.** [contact] manner ■ **elle est d'un ~ déconcertant/chaleureux** she puts you off your stride/makes you feel very welcome when you first meet her ■ **être d'un ~ facile/difficile** to be approachable/unapproachable **2.** [accès - à une côte] approach ; [- à une maison] access ■ **d'un ~ facile** [demeure] easy to get to ; [texte] easy to understand *ou* to get to grips with.
◆ **abords** *nmpl* [alentours] surroundings ■ **les ~s de la tour** the area around the tower.
◆ **aux abords** *loc adv* all around ■ **dans le château et aux ~s** in and around the castle.
◆ **aux abords de** *loc prép* : **aux ~s de la ville** on the outskirts of the town.
◆ **d'abord** *loc adv* **1.** [en premier lieu] first ■ **nous irons d'~ à Rome** we'll go to Rome first **2.** [au début] at first, initially, to begin with ■ **j'ai cru (tout) d'~ qu'il s'agissait d'une blague** at first *ou* to begin with I thought it was a joke **3.** [introduisant une restriction] to start with, for a start ■ **d'~, tu n'es même pas prêt!** to start with *ou* for a start, you're not even ready! **4.** [de toute façon] anyway.
◆ **dès l'abord** *loc adv* at the outset, from the (very) beginning.

abordable [abɔrdabl] *adj* **1.** [peu cher - prix] reasonable ; [- produit] reasonably priced, affordable **2.** [ouvert - patron, célébrité] approachable **3.** [facile - texte] accessible ; [- problème] that can be discussed **4.** NAUT [côte] accessible.

abordage [abɔrdaʒ] *nm* **1.** [manœuvre - d'assaut] boarding ; [- avec un éperon] grappling ■ **à l'~!** away boarders! **2.** [collision] collision ■ **l'~ s'est produit à la sortie du chenal** the two boats collided as they came out of the fairway **3.** [approche - du rivage] coming alongside ; [- d'un quai] berthing.

aborder [3] [abɔrde] ◇ *vt* **1.** [accoster - passant] to accost, to walk up to *(insép)*, to approach ■ **quand le policier l'a abordé** when the detective came *ou* walked up to him **2.** [arriver à l'entrée de] to enter ■ **je suis tombé de vélo au moment où j'abordais la dernière montée/le virage** I fell off my bike as I was coming up to the last climb/the bend **3.** [faire face à - profession] to take up *(sép)* ; [- nouvelle vie] to embark on *(insép)* ; [- tâche] to tackle, to get to grips with ; [- retraite] to approach ■ **à 18 ans, on est prêt à ~ la vie** when you're 18, you're ready to start out in life **4.** [se mettre à examiner - texte, problème] to approach ■ **chez nous, on n'abordait pas ces sujets-là** we never used to mention those topics in our house ■ **il n'a pas eu le temps d'~ le sujet** he didn't have time to get onto *ou* to broach the subject **5.** NAUT [attaquer] to board ■ [percuter] to collide with *(insép)*, to ram into *(insép)*.
◇ *vi* to (touch) *ou* reach land ■ **nous abordons à Gênes demain** we reach Genoa tomorrow.

aborigène [abɔriʒɛn] ◇ *adj* **1.** [autochtone] aboriginal ■ [d'Australie] Aboriginal, native Australian **2.** BOT indigenous.
◇ *nmf* [autochtone] aborigine ■ [autochtone d'Australie] Aborigine, Aboriginal, native Australian.

abortif, ive [abɔrtif, iv] *adj* abortive.

aboucher [3] [abuʃe] *vt* **1.** [tuyaux] to butt, to join up *(sép)*, to join end to end **2.** [gens] to bring together ■ **~ qqn avec** to put sb in touch *ou* contact with.
◆ **s'aboucher** *vpi* : **s'~ avec qqn** [se mettre en rapport avec qqn] to get in touch with sb ; [se lier avec qqn] to team up with sb.

abouler [3] △ [abule] *vt* to hand *ou* to give over *(sép)* ■ **aboule ton fric!** cough up!
◆ **s'abouler**△ *vpi* to come along.

aboulie [abuli] *nf* abulia, aboulia.

about [abu] *nm* butt *(of a beam)*.

abouti, e [abuti] *adj* **1.** [projet, démarche] successful **2.** [œuvre] accomplished.

aboutir [32] [abutir] *vi* **1.** [réussir - projet, personne] to succeed ■ **l'entreprise n'a pas abouti** the venture fell through *ou* never came to anything **2.** [finir] : **~ en prison** to end up in prison **3.** MÉD to come to a head.
◆ **aboutir à** *v+prép* **1.** [voie, rue] to end at *ou* in, to lead to ■ [fleuve] to end in ■ **cette route aboutit à la prison** this road ends at the prison **2.** [avoir pour résultat] to lead to, to result in ■ **de bonnes intentions qui n'aboutissent à rien** good intentions which come to nothing ■ **tu aboutiras au même résultat** you'll arrive at *ou* get the same result.

aboutissants [abutisɑ̃] *nmpl* : **les tenants et les ~** the ins and outs.

aboutissement [abutismɑ̃] *nm* [conclusion] (final) outcome, result ■ [résultat positif] success.

aboyer [13] [abwaje] *vi* **1.** [animal] to bark **2.** *péj* [personne] to bark ■ **~ après** *ou* **contre qqn** to yell at sb.

abracadabra [abrakadabra] *nm* abracadabra.

abracadabrant, e [abrakadabrɑ̃, ɑ̃t] *adj* bewildering.

Abraham [abraam] *npr* Abraham.

abrasif, ive [abrazif, iv] *adj* abrasive.
◆ **abrasif** *nm* abrasive.

abrasion [abrazjɔ̃] *nf* **1.** [action de frotter] abrasion, wearing off ■ [résultat] abrasion **2.** GÉOL abrasion.

abrégé [abreʒe] *nm* **1.** [d'un texte] summary **2.** [livre] abstract, epitome *sout* ▪ **faire un ~ de qqch** to make a précis of sthg.
◆ **en abrégé** ◇ *loc adj* [mot, phrase] in abbreviated form.
◇ *loc adv* [écrire] in brief, in an abridged version ▪ **en ~, voici ce qui s'est passé** here's what happened in a nutshell.

abréger [22] [abreʒe] *vt* **1.** [interrompre - vacances] to curtail, to cut short, to shorten ; [- vie] to cut short, to put an (early) end to ▪ **~ les souffrances de qqn** *euphém* to put an end to sb's suffering **2.** [tronquer - discours] to cut ; [- texte] to cut, to abridge ; [- conversation] to cut short ; [- mot] to abbreviate, to truncate *sout* ▪ *(en usage absolu)* **abrège!** [ton agressif] get to the point!
◆ **pour abréger** *loc adv* : **Catherine, ou Cath pour ~** Catherine, or Cath for short ▪ **pour ~, nous avons échoué** to cut a long story short, we failed.

abreuver [5] [abrœve] *vt* **1.** [faire boire - animaux] to water **2.** *fig* **~ qqn d'insultes** to shower sb with abuse ▪ **elle l'abreuvait d'éloges** she heaped praise upon him ▪ **nous sommes abreuvés d'images de violence** we get swamped with violent images.
◆ **s'abreuver** *vpi* **1.** [animal] to drink **2.** *fam* [personne] to drink.

abreuvoir [abrœvwar] *nm* [bac] (drinking) trough ▪ [plan d'eau] watering place.

abréviation [abrevjasjɔ̃] *nf* abbreviation.

abri [abri] *nm* **1.** [cabane] shelter, refuge ▪ [toit] shelter ▪ [sous terre] shelter ▪ [improvisé] shelter ▪ **~ antiatomique** *ou* **antinucléaire** (nuclear) fallout shelter ▪ **~ à vélos** bicycle stand **2.** *fig* refuge.
◆ **à l'abri** *loc adv* **1.** [des intempéries] : **être à l'~** to be sheltered ▪ **mettre qqn à l'~** to find shelter for sb ▪ **se mettre à l'~** to take cover, to shelter **2.** [en lieu sûr] in a safe place ▪ **mettre sa fortune à l'~ dans le pétrole** to invest one's money safely in oil.
◆ **à l'abri de** *loc prép* **1.** [pluie] sheltered from ▪ [chaleur, obus] shielded from ▪ [regards] hidden from **2.** *fig* **nos économies nous mettront à l'~ de la misère** our savings will shield us against poverty *ou* will protect us from hardship ▪ **à l'~ des contrôles** safe from checks ▪ **personne n'est à l'~ d'une erreur/d'un maître-chanteur** anyone can make a mistake/fall victim to a blackmailer.

Abribus® [abribys] *nm* bus shelter.

abricot [abriko] ◇ *nm* BOT apricot.
◇ *adj inv* apricot, apricot-coloured.

abricotier [abrikɔtje] *nm* apricot tree.

abrité, e [abrite] *adj* sheltered.

abriter [3] [abrite] *vt* **1.** [protéger] : **~ qqn/qqch de la pluie** to shelter sb/sthg from the rain ▪ **~ qqn/qqch du soleil** to shade sb/sthg ▪ **le versant abrité** [du soleil] the shady slopes ; [du vent] the sheltered slopes **2.** [loger - personnes] to house, to accommodate ; [- société, machine] to house.
◆ **s'abriter** *vp (emploi réfléchi)* : **s'~ de la pluie/du vent** to shelter from the rain/from the wind ▪ **s'~ du soleil** to shade o.s. from the sun ▪ **s'~ derrière la loi/ses parents** *fig* to hide behind the law/one's parents.

abrivent [abrivɑ̃] *nm* windbreak.

abrogation [abrɔgasjɔ̃] *nf* repeal, rescinding, abrogation *sout.*

abroger [17] [abrɔʒe] *vt* to repeal, to rescind, to abrogate *sout.*

abrupt, e [abrypt] *adj* **1.** [raide - côte] steep, abrupt ; [- versant] sheer **2.** [brusque - manières] abrupt, brusque ; [- refus] blunt, abrupt, curt ; [- personne] short, sharp, abrupt ; [- changement] abrupt, sudden, sharp.
◆ **abrupt** *nm* steep slope.

abruptement [abryptəmɑ̃] *adv* [répondre] abruptly, brusquely, curtly ▪ [changer] abruptly, suddenly ▪ **ne le lui dis pas trop ~** don't just blurt it out in front of her.

abruti, e [abryti] *nm, f fam* idiot ▪ **quelle ~e, j'ai oublié ton livre** like a fool I've forgotten your book.

abrutir [32] [abrytir] *vt* **1.** [abêtir] to turn into an idiot **2.** [étourdir] to stupefy ▪ **abruti de fatigue** numb *ou* dazed with tiredness ▪ **abruti par l'alcool** stupefied with drink ▪ **après trois heures d'algèbre, je suis complètement abruti!** after three hours of algebra, I feel completely punch-drunk! **3.** [accabler] : **~ qqn de conseils** to pester sb with endless advice.
◆ **s'abrutir** ◇ *vp (emploi réfléchi)* **s'~ de travail** to overwork o.s., to work o.s. into the ground.
◇ *vpi* [s'abêtir] to turn into an idiot.

abrutissant, e [abrytisɑ̃, ɑ̃t] *adj* **1.** [qui rend bête] mind-numbing **2.** [qui étourdit] stupefying **3.** [qui fatigue] wearing, exhausting.

abrutissement [abrytismɑ̃] *nm* mindless state ▪ **l'~ des enfants par la télévision** the mind-numbing effects of television on children.

Abruzzes [abryz] *npr fpl* : **les ~** the Abruzzi.

ABS (*abr de* **Antiblockiersystem**) *nm inv* ABS.

abscisse [apsis] *nf* abscissa.

abscons, e [apskɔ̃, ɔ̃s] *adj litt* abstruse.

absence [apsɑ̃s] *nf* **1.** [fait de n'être pas là] absence ▪ **cette décision a été prise pendant mon ~** this decision was taken in my absence *ou* while I was away ▪ **sa troisième ~** [à l'école] the third time he's been away from *ou* missed school ; [au travail] the third time he's been off work ; [à une réunion] the third time he's stayed away from *ou* not attended the meeting ▪ **comment supporterai-je ton ~?** how shall I cope with you not being there *ou* around? **2.** [de goût, d'imagination] lack, absence ▪ **~ d'idéaux** lack of ideals **3.** [défaillance] : **~ (de mémoire)** mental blank ▪ **elle a des ~s par moments** her mind wanders at times, at times she can be absent-minded **4.** DR absence.
◆ **en l'absence de** *loc prép* in the absence of ▪ **en l'~ de son fils** in her son's absence, while her son is/was away ▪ **en l' ~ de symptômes, il m'est difficile de me prononcer** since there are no symptoms, it is hard for me to say.

absent, e [apsɑ̃, ɑ̃t] ◇ *adj* **1.** [personne - de l'école] absent ; [- du travail] off work, absent ; [- de son domicile] away ▪ **il était ~ de la réunion** he was not present at the meeting **2.** [inattentif] absent ▪ **regard ~** vacant look **3.** [chose] missing ▪ [sentiment] lacking ▪ **un regard d'où toute tendresse est ~e** a look entirely devoid of tenderness.
◇ *nm, f* [du travail, de l'école] absentee ▪ [dans une famille] absent person ▪ **on ne fait pas cours, il y a trop d'~s** we're not having a lesson today, there are too many pupils missing *ou* away ◗ **les ~s ont toujours tort** *prov* the absent are always in the wrong.

absentéisme [apsɑ̃teism] *nm* absenteeism ▪ **~ scolaire** truancy.

absentéiste [apsɑ̃teist] ◇ *adj* absentee.
◇ *nmf* absentee ▪ **les ~s** [au travail] persistent absentees.

absenter [3] [apsɑ̃te] ◆ **s'absenter** *vpi* to be absent ▪ **s'~ de son travail** to be off *ou* to stay away from work ▪ **s'~ du lycée** to be away from *ou* to miss school ▪ **je ne m'étais absentée que quelques minutes** I'd only gone out for a few minutes.

abside [apsid] *nf* apse.

absidiole [apsidjɔl] *nf* apsidiole.

absinthe [apsɛ̃t] *nf* **1.** [boisson] absinthe **2.** BOT wormwood, absinthe.

absolu, e [apsɔly] *adj* **1.** [total - liberté] absolute, complete ; [- repos] complete ; [- silence] total ▪ **un dénuement ~** abject poverty ▪ **en cas d'~e nécessité** when absolutely necessary **2.** POLIT [pouvoir, monarque, majorité] absolute **3.** [sans nuances] absolute ▪ [intransigeant] uncompromising, rigid ▪ **refus ~ d'obtempérer** outright refusal to comply **4.** CHIM, MATH & PHYS absolute **5.** LING [ablatif, construction] absolute.
◆ **absolu** *nm* **1.** PHILOS : **l'~** the Absolute **2.** LING absolute construction ▪ **verbe construit à l'~** transitive verb constructed without an object.
◆ **dans l'absolu** *loc adv* in absolute terms.

absolument [apsɔlymɑ̃] *adv* **1.** [entièrement - croire, avoir raison] absolutely, entirely ; [- ravi, faux] absolutely, completely ; [- défendu] strictly ▪ **personne, ~ personne ne doit sortir** no-one, absolutely no-one must go out ▪ **~ pas** not at all ▪ **~ rien** absolutely nothing, nothing whatsoever **2.** [à tout prix] absolutely ▪ **il faut ~ lui parler** we must speak to him without fail, we simply must speak to him **3.** [oui] absolutely ▪ **vous y croyez? – ~!** do you believe in it? – totally! ▪ **il a raison! – ~!** he's right! – absolutely! **4.** LING absolutely.

absolution [apsɔlysjɔ̃] *nf* **1.** RELIG absolution ▪ **donner l'~ à qqn** to give sb absolution **2.** DR acquittal.

absolutisme [apsɔlytism] *nm* absolutism.

absolutiste [apsɔlytist] *adj* & *nmf* absolutist.

absolvait *etc v* ▻ **absoudre**.

absorbant, e [apsɔrbɑ̃, ɑ̃t] *adj* **1.** [tissu] absorbent **2.** [lecture] absorbing, gripping **3.** PHYS absorbative.

absorber [3] [apsɔrbe] *vt* **1.** [éponger - gén] to absorb, to soak up *(sép)* ; [- avec un buvard] to blot ; [- avec une éponge] to sponge off *(sép)* **2.** ACOUST & PHOTO [lumière] to absorb ▪ [bruit] to absorb, to deaden **3.** [consommer - aliment] to take, to consume ; [- bénéfices, capitaux] to absorb ▪ ÉCON [entreprise] to take over *(sép)*, to absorb ▪ **cette manœuvre vise à faire ~ la Dalco par l'Imalux** this move is designed to allow Imalux to take over Dalco **4.** [préoccuper - suj: travail] to absorb, to engross, to occupy ; [- suj: pensée] to absorb, to grip ▪ **très absorbée par son activité politique** very much engrossed in her political activities **5.** [faire s'intégrer - réfugiés, nouveaux élèves, innovation] to absorb.

◆ **s'absorber dans** *vp+prép* to become absorbed in ▪ **s'~ dans un livre** to be engrossed in a book ▪ **s'~ dans ses pensées** to be lost *ou* deep in thought.

absorption [apsɔrpsjɔ̃] *nf* **1.** [ingestion] swallowing, taking **2.** [pénétration] absorption ▪ **masser jusqu'à ~ complète par la peau** massage well into the skin **3.** [intégration] assimilation ▪ **~ d'une entreprise par une autre** ÉCON takeover of one company by another **4.** PHYSIOL absorption.

absoudre [87] [apsudr] *vt* **1.** RELIG to absolve **2.** *litt* [pardonner] to absolve ▪ **je l'ai absous de ses erreurs de jeunesse** I forgave him his youthful indiscretions **3.** DR to dismiss.

abstenir [40] [apstənir] ◆ **s'abstenir** *vpi* POLIT to abstain.

◆ **s'abstenir de** *vp+prép* [éviter de] to refrain *ou* to abstain from ▪ **abstiens-toi de la critiquer** don't criticize her ▪ *(en usage absolu)* **dans ce cas, mieux vaut s'~** in that case, it's better not to do anything ▪ **'pas sérieux s'~'** 'serious applications only'.

abstention [apstɑ̃sjɔ̃] *nf* **1.** POLIT abstention **2.** [renoncement] abstention.

abstentionnisme [apstɑ̃sjɔnism] *nm* abstention.

abstentionniste [apstɑ̃sjɔnist] *adj* & *nmf* abstentionist.

abstenu, e [apstəny] *pp* ▻ **abstenir**.

abstient *etc v* ▻ **abstenir**.

abstinence [apstinɑ̃s] *nf* **1.** RELIG abstinence ▪ **faire ~** to refrain from eating meat **2.** [chasteté] abstinence.

abstinent, e [apstinɑ̃, ɑ̃t] *adj* & *nm, f* abstinent.

abstint *etc v* ▻ **abstenir**.

abstraction [apstraksjɔ̃] *nf* **1.** [notion] abstraction, abstract idea **2.** [fait d'isoler] abstraction ▪ **faire ~ de** [ignorer] to take no account of, to ignore, to disregard ▪ **~ faite de** apart from, leaving aside ▪ **~ faite de la forme** style apart.

abstraire [112] [apstrɛr] *vt* **1.** [séparer] to abstract **2.** PHILOS to abstract.

◆ **s'abstraire** *vpi* to cut o.s. off.

abstrait, e [apstrɛ, ɛt] **1.** ▻ **abstraire 2.** [conçu par l'esprit] abstract **3.** [non appliqué - science, pensée] theoretical, abstract, pure **4.** [ardu] abstract, obscure *péj* **5.** *péj* [irréel] theoretical, abstract **6.** ART abstract, non-representational **7.** LING & MATH abstract.

◆ **abstrait** *nm* **1.** PHILOS : **l'~** the abstract ; [notions] abstract ideas, the theoretical plane **2.** ART [art] abstract *ou* non-representational art ▪ [artiste] abstract *ou* non-representational artist.

◆ **dans l'abstrait** *loc adv* in the abstract ▪ **dans l'~, il est facile de critiquer** it's easy to be critical if you just look at things in the abstract.

abstraitement [apstrɛtmɑ̃] *adv* in the abstract, abstractly.

abstrayait *v* ▻ **abstraire**.

absurde [apsyrd] <> *adj* **1.** [remarque, idée] absurd, preposterous ▪ [personne] ridiculous, absurd ▪ **ne soyez pas ~!** don't be absurd *ou* talk nonsense! **2.** [oubli, contretemps] absurd **3.** PHILOS absurd.

<> *nm* **1.** [absurdité] absurd **2.** LITTÉR, PHILOS & THÉÂTRE : **l'~** the absurd.

absurdement [apsyrdəmɑ̃] *adv* absurdly, ludicrously.

absurdité [apsyrdite] *nf* **1.** [irrationalité] absurdity **2.** [parole, action] absurdity ▪ **ne dis pas d'~s!** don't be absurd *ou* talk nonsense!

Abu Dhabi [abudabi] *npr* Abou Dhabi.

abus [aby] *nm* **1.** [excès - de stupéfiants, de médicament] abuse ▪ **~ d'alcool** excessive drinking, alcohol abuse ▪ **l'~ de somnifères** taking too many sleeping pills ▪ **faire des ~** to overindulge ◗ **il y a de l'~** *fam* that's a bit much **2.** [injustice] injustice ▪ **les ~** excesses **3.** DR misuse ▪ **~ d'autorité** misuse *ou* abuse of authority ▪ **~ de confiance** breach of trust **4.** LING **~ de langage** misuse of language.

abuser [3] [abyze] *vt litt* to deceive, to mislead.

◆ **abuser de** *v+prép* **1.** [consommer excessivement] to overuse ▪ **~ de la boisson** to drink too much ▪ **~ de ses forces** to overtax o.s. **2.** [mal utiliser - autorité, privilège] to abuse, to misuse **3.** [exploiter - ami, bonté, patience] to take advantage of, to exploit ▪ **~ de la situation** to take unfair advantage of the situation ▪ *(en usage absolu)* **je crains d'~** I wouldn't like to impose ▪ **je veux bien t'aider mais là, tu abuses!** I don't mind helping you but there is a limit! ▪ **dites donc, la queue est faite pour tout le monde, faudrait pas ~!** *fam* hey, queue up like everybody else, can't you? **4.** *euphém* [violer] to sexually abuse.

◆ **s'abuser** *vpi* to be mistaken ▪ **si je ne m'abuse** if I'm not mistaken, correct me if I'm wrong.

abusif, ive [abyzif, iv] *adj* **1.** [immodéré] excessive ▪ **15 euros, c'est ~!** 15 euros, that's a bit much! **2.** [outrepassant ses droits - père, mère] domineering **3.** [incorrect] misused ▪ **l'emploi ~ du mot "réaliser"** misuse of the word "réaliser".

abusivement [abyzivmɑ̃] *adv* **1.** [de façon injuste] wrongly, unfairly **2.** [de façon incorrecte] wrongly, improperly ▪ **le terme "réaliser" est employé ~** the word "réaliser" is used incorrectly **3.** [de façon excessive] excessively.

abyssal, e, aux [abisal, o] *adj* abyssal.

abysse [abis] *nm* : **l'~** the abyssal zone.

AC *nf* = **appellation contrôlée**.

acabit [akabi] *nm péj* **de cet ~** of that type ▪ **son amie est du même ~** she and her friend are two of a kind ▪ **ils sont tous du même ~** they are all (pretty much) the same, they are all much of a muchness *UK*.

acacia [akasja] *nm* acacia.

académicien, enne [akademisjɛ̃, ɛn] *nm, f* [membre - d'une académie] academician ; [- de l'Académie française] member of the French Academy *ou* Académie française.

académie [akademi] *nf* **1.** [société savante] learned society academy ▪ **l'Académie des sciences** the Academy of Science ▪ **l'Académie française** the French Academy, the Académie Française *(learned society of leading men and women of letters)* **2.** [école] academy ▪ **~ de danse/musique** academy of dance/music **3.** [salle] : **~ de billard** billiard hall **4.** ART nude **5.** *fam* [corps] body, figure **6.** ADMIN & ÉDUC ≃ local education authority *UK*, ≃ school district *US*.

L'ACADÉMIE FRANÇAISE

Originally a group of men of letters who were encouraged by Cardinal Richelieu in 1635 to become an official body. *L'académie française* consists of forty distinguished writers known as *les Quarante* or *les Immortels*. Its chief task is to produce a definitive dictionary and to be the ultimate authority in matters concerning the French language.

académique [akademik] *adj* **1.** [d'une société savante] academic ■ [de l'Académie française] of the French Academy *ou* Académie française **2.** *péj* [conventionnel] academic ■ **danse ~** ballet dancing **3.** ÉDUC : **l'année ~** *Suisse* & *Québec* the academic year **4.** PHILOS : **philosophe ~** Platonic philosopher.

académisme [akademism] *nm* academicism.

Acadie [akadi] *npr f* : **(l')~** Acadia.

acadien, enne [akadjɛ̃, ɛn] *adj* Acadian.
◆ **Acadien, enne** *nm, f* Acadian.
◆ **acadien** *nm* LING Acadian.

acajou [akaʒu] ◇ *nm* **1.** BOT mahogany (tree) ■ [anacardier] cashew **2.** MENUIS mahogany.
◇ *adj inv* [couleur] mahogany.

acanthe [akɑ̃t] *nf* acanthus.

a capella [akapela] *loc adv* & *loc adj inv* MUS a capella.

acariâtre [akarjatr] *adj* [caractère] sour ■ [personne] bad-tempered.

acarien [akarjɛ̃] *nm* acarid.

accablant, e [akablɑ̃, ɑ̃t] *adj* [chaleur] oppressive ■ [preuve, témoignage, vérité] damning ■ [travail] exhausting ■ [douleur] excruciating ■ [chagrin] overwhelming ■ **il est d'une stupidité ~e** he's too stupid for words.

accablement [akabləmɑ̃] *nm* **1.** [désespoir] dejection, despondency ■ **saisi d'un grand ~** utterly dejected **2.** [dû à la chaleur] (heat) exhaustion.

accabler [3] [akable] *vt* **1.** [abattre - suj: fatigue, chaleur] to overcome, to overwhelm ; [- suj: soucis] to overcome ; [- suj: chagrin, deuil, travail] to overwhelm ■ **accablé de soucis** careworn **2.** [accuser - suj: témoignage] to condemn ■ **je ne veux pas l'~ mais il faut reconnaître qu'elle a commis des erreurs** I don't want to be too hard on her but it has to be said that she made some mistakes **3.** [couvrir] : **~ qqn de : ~ qqn d'injures** to heap abuse upon *ou* to hurl insults at sb ■ **~ qqn de critiques** to be highly critical of sb ■ **~ la population d'impôts** to overtax the population ■ **~ qqn de conseils** to pester sb with advice.

accalmie [akalmi] *nf* [du bruit, du vent, de la pluie, d'un combat, d'une crise politique] lull ■ [d'une maladie] temporary improvement ■ [de souffrances] temporary relief *ou* respite ■ [du commerce] slack period ■ [dans le travail, l'agitation] break ■ **l'~ qui précède l'orage** the lull *ou* calm before the storm.

accaparant, e [akaparɑ̃, ɑ̃t] *adj* [travail, études, enfant] demanding.

accaparement [akaparmɑ̃] *nm* [d'une conversation, d'une personne] monopolization.

accaparer [3] [akapare] *vt* **1.** [monopoliser - conversation, personne] to monopolize ; [- victoires, récompenses] to carry off *(insép)* ; [- places] to grab ■ **ne laisse pas les enfants t'~** don't let the children monopolize you *ou* take you over **2.** [absorber - suj: travail, soucis] to absorb ■ **il est complètement accaparé par ses études** he's wrapped up *ou* completely absorbed in his studies ■ **son travail l'accapare** her work takes up all her time.

accastiller [3] [akastije] *vt* to provide with a superstructure NAUT.

accédant, e [aksedɑ̃, ɑ̃t] *nm, f* : **un ~ à la propriété** a new home-owner.

accéder [18] [aksede] ◆ **accéder à** *v+prép* **1.** [atteindre - trône] to accede to ; [- poste, rang] to rise to ; [- indépendance, gloire] to gain, to attain ; [- lieu] to reach ■ **on accède à la maison par un petit chemin** you get to the house via a narrow path, access to the house is by a narrow path ■ **~ à la propriété** to become a home-owner **2.** [accepter - demande, requête] to grant ; [- désir] to meet, to give in to **3.** [connaître - culture] to attain a degree of ; [- secrets, documents] to gain access to.

accélérateur, trice [akseleratœr, tris] *adj* accelerating.
◆ **accélérateur** *nm* accelerator ■ **~ de particules** particle accelerator.

accélération [akselerasjɔ̃] *nf* **1.** AUTO, MÉCAN & PHYS acceleration **2.** [accroissement du rythme - du cœur, du pouls] acceleration ; [- d'un processus] speeding up ■ **l'~ de l'histoire** the gathering pace of historical events.

accéléré [akselere] *nm* fast motion.
◆ **en accéléré** ◇ *loc adj* speeded-up, accelerated.
◇ *loc adv* speeded-up.

accélérer [18] [akselere] ◇ *vt* [allure] to accelerate ■ [rythme cardiaque] to raise, to increase ■ [pouls] to quicken ■ [démarches, travaux] to speed up ■ **~ le pas** to quicken one's pace ■ **~ le mouvement** *fam* to get things moving.
◇ *vi* **1.** AUTO to accelerate ■ **allez, accélère!** come on, step on it! **2.** *fam* [se dépêcher] : **accélère un peu!** come on, get going *ou* move!
◆ **s'accélérer** *vpi* [pouls, cœur] to beat faster ■ **son débit s'accélère** he's talking faster and faster.

accent [aksɑ̃] *nm* **1.** [prononciation] accent ■ **avoir un ~** to speak with *ou* to have an accent ■ **il n'a pas d'~** he doesn't have an accent ■ **l'~ du midi** a southern (French) accent **2.** PHON stress ■ **~ tonique** tonic accent ; [signe] stress mark ■ **mettre l'~ sur** *pr* to stress ; *fig* to stress, to emphasize **3.** [signe graphique] accent ■ **~ grave/circonflexe/aigu** grave/circumflex/acute (accent) ■ **e ~ grave/aigu** e grave/acute **4.** [inflexion] note, accent ■ **un ~ de sincérité/d'émotion** a note of sincerity/of emotion ■ **avoir l'~ de la vérité** to ring true.
◆ **accents** *nmpl* [son] : **les ~s d'un accordéon** the strains of an accordion.

accentuation [aksɑ̃tɥasjɔ̃] *nf* **1.** PHON stressing, accentuation ■ **l'~, en anglais, se définit ainsi** the stress pattern of English is defined as follows **2.** [système graphique] use of accents **3.** [exagération - d'une ressemblance, d'une différence, des traits] emphasizing ; [- d'un effort] intensification, increase ; [- du chômage, d'une crise] increase, rise.

accentué, e [aksɑ̃tɥe] *adj* **1.** PHON [son, syllabe] stressed, accented ■ **voyelle non ~e** unstressed vowel **2.** [dans l'écriture] accented **3.** [exagéré - traits, défaut] marked, pronounced ; [- tendance, crise] increased, stronger.

accentuer [7] [aksɑ̃tɥe] *vt* **1.** PHON [son, syllabe] to accent, to accentuate, to bring out *(insép)* **2.** [dans l'écriture] to put an accent on **3.** [rendre plus visible - ressemblance, différence] to accentuate, to bring out *(insép)*, to emphasize ; [- forme, traits] to emphasize, to accentuate, to highlight **4.** [augmenter - effort] to increase, to intensify ; [- chômage, crise] to increase.
◆ **s'accentuer** *vpi* [contraste, ressemblance] to become more marked *ou* apparent *ou* pronounced ■ [tendance] to become more noticeable ■ [chômage] to rise, to increase ■ [crise] to increase in intensity.

acceptabilité [akseptabilite] *nf* acceptability.

acceptable [akseptabl] *adj* [offre, condition] acceptable ■ [attitude] decent, acceptable ■ [travail] fair, acceptable ■ [repas] decent ■ [réponse] satisfactory ■ [prix] fair, reasonable.

acceptation [akseptasjɔ̃] *nf* **1.** [accord] acceptance **2.** FIN & DR acceptance.

accepter [4] [aksepte] *vt* **1.** [recevoir volontiers - cadeau, invitation] to accept ■ *(en usage absolu)* **ne fais pas tant d'histoires, accepte!** don't make such a fuss, say yes! ■ [s'engager volontiers dans - défi, lutte] to take up *(sép)* **2.** [admettre - hypothèse, situation, excuse] to accept ; [- condition] to agree to, to accept ; [- mort, échec, sort] to accept, to come to terms with ; [- requête] to grant ■ **~ que : j'accepte que cela soit difficile** I agree that it is *ou* might be difficult ■ **j'accepte qu'il vienne** I agree to him coming ■ **~ de faire qqch** to agree to do sthg **3.** [tolérer - critique, hypocrisie] to take, to stand for, to put up with *(insép)*

■ **il accepte tout de sa femme** he'd put up with anything from his wife ■ **~ que : elle accepte qu'il lui parle** she puts up with him talking to her ■ **il n'a pas accepté qu'elle le quitte** he just couldn't take *ou* accept her leaving him ■ **~ de** to be prepared to **4.** [accueillir] to accept ■ **elle a tout de suite été acceptée dans la famille** she was readily accepted *ou* made welcome by the family ■ **acceptez-vous les cartes de crédit?** do you take credit cards? **5.** FIN to accept.
◆ **s'accepter** *vp (emploi réfléchi)* to accept o.s. ■ **je me trouvais trop grosse, maintenant je m'accepte telle que je suis** I used to think of myself as too fat, now I've learned to live with the way I am.

acception [aksɛpsjɔ̃] *nf* meaning, sense ■ **dans toutes les ~s du mot** *ou* **du terme** in every sense of the word.
◆ **sans acception de** *loc prép* [gén] without taking into account.

accès [aksɛ] *nm* **1.** [entrée] access ■ **un ~ direct à** *ou* **sur la route** direct access to the road ■ **'~ interdit'** 'no entry', 'no admittance' ■ **'~ réservé aux voyageurs munis de billets'** 'ticket-holders only' ■ **'~ réservé au personnel'** 'staff only' ■ **d'~ facile, facile d'~** [lieu] accessible ; [île] easy to get to ; [personne] approachable ; [œuvre] accessible ■ **d'~ difficile, difficile d'~** [lieu] hard to get to ; [personne] not very approachable, unapproachable ; [œuvre] difficult ■ **avoir ~ à** [lieu, études, profession] to have access to ■ **donner ~ à** [lieu] to lead to ; [musée, exposition] to allow entry to ; [études, profession] to lead to, to open the way to **2.** [chemin, voie] way in, access, entrance ■ **les ~ de la ville** the approaches to the town ■ **'~ aux trains** *ou* **quais'** 'to the trains' **3.** [crise de folie, de jalousie] fit ■ **un ~ de colère** a fit of anger, an angry outburst ■ **un ~ de fièvre** MÉD a bout of fever ; *fig* a sudden burst of activity ■ **un ~ de joie** a surge of happiness ■ **un ~ de tristesse** a wave of sadness **4.** INFORM access ■ **~ aléatoire/direct** random/direct access ■ **port d'~** access port.
◆ **par accès** *loc adv* in fits and starts ■ **ça le prenait par ~** it came over him in waves.

accessibilité [aksesibilite] *nf* accessibility.

accessible [aksesibl] *adj* [livre, œuvre] accessible ■ [personne] approachable ■ [lieu] accessible ■ **~ au public** open to the public ■ **les toilettes doivent être ~s aux handicapés** toilets must have disabled access ■ **un luxe qui n'est pas ~ à tous** a luxury that not everyone can afford ■ **être ~ à la pitié** to be capable of pity.

accession [aksɛsjɔ̃] *nf* **1.** [arrivée] : **~ à : ~ au trône** accession *ou* acceding to the throne ■ **depuis son ~ au poste/rang de...** since he rose to the post/rank of... ■ **le pays fête son ~ à l'indépendance** the country's celebrating becoming independent *ou* achieving independence ■ **faciliter l'~ à la propriété** to make it easier for people to become home-owners **2.** DR accession.

accessit [aksesit] *nm* ≃ certificate of merit *UK*, ≃ Honourable Mention *US*.

accessoire [akseswar] <> *adj* [avantage] incidental ■ **des considérations ~s** considerations of secondary importance ◉ **des frais ~s** incidentals, incidental expense ■ **des avantages ~s** fringe benefits.
<> *nm* **1.** [considérations secondaires] : **laissons l'~ de côté** let's get to the point **2.** [dispositif, objet] accessory ■ **~ automobile/informatique/vestimentaire** car/computer/fashion accessory **3.** CINÉ, THÉÂTRE & TV prop **4.** INFORM : **~s de bureau** desk accessories.

accessoirement [akseswarmɑ̃] *adv* **1.** [secondairement] secondarily **2.** [éventuellement] if necessary, if need be.

accessoiriser [3] [akseswarize] *vt* [voiture] to accessorize, to add accessories to ■ [tenue] to brighten up with accessories.

accessoiriste [akseswarist] *nmf* **1.** CINÉ, THÉÂTRE & TV props person, propman (*f* props girl) **2.** AUTO car accessories dealer.

accident [aksidɑ̃] *nm* **1.** [chute, coup] accident ■ [entre véhicules] crash, accident, collision ■ **un ~ est si vite arrivé** accidents happen so easily ■ **~ d'avion/de voiture** plane/car crash ■ **~ de la circulation** *ou* **route** road accident ■ **la police est sur le lieu de l'~** the police are at the scene of the accident ◉ **~ du travail** industrial accident **2.** [fait imprévu] mishap, accident ■ **~ (de parcours)** hitch ■ **ce n'était pas prévu, c'est un ~** it wasn't planned, it was an accident **3.** MÉD : **~ de santé** (sudden) health problem **4.** *euphém* [incontinence] accident **5.** GÉOL : **un ~ de terrain** an uneven piece of ground **6.** PHILOS accident **7.** MUS accidental.
◆ **par accident** *loc adv* accidentally, by accident *or* chance, as chance would have it.

accidenté, e [aksidɑ̃te] <> *adj* **1.** [endommagé - voiture, avion] damaged **2.** [inégal - terrain] uneven, broken, irregular **3.** *sout* [mouvementé - destin, vie] eventful, chequered.
<> *nm, f* injured person, casualty ■ **~ du travail** victim of an industrial injury ■ **~ de la route** road casualty.

accidentel, elle [aksidɑ̃tɛl] *adj* **1.** [dû à un accident] accidental ■ [dû au hasard] fortuitous *sout*, incidental, accidental **2.** PHILOS accidental.

accidentellement [aksidɑ̃tɛlmɑ̃] *adv* **1.** [dans un accident] in an accident ■ [par hasard] accidentally **2.** PHILOS accidentally.

accidenter [3] [aksidɑ̃te] *vt* [personne] to injure, to wound ■ [véhicule] to damage.

accidentologie [aksidɑ̃tɔlɔʒi] *nf* accident research, accidentology.

accidentologue [aksidɑ̃tɔlɔg] *nmf* accident researcher, accidentologist.

acclamation [aklamasjɔ̃] *nf* acclamation *litt*, applause ■ **être accueilli par les ~s de la foule** to be cheered by the crowd.
◆ **par acclamation** *loc adv* by popular acclaim, by acclamation.

acclamer [3] [aklame] *vt* to acclaim, to applaud, to cheer ■ **se faire ~** to be cheered.

acclimatation [aklimatasjɔ̃] *nf* acclimatization, acclimation *US*.

acclimatement [aklimatmɑ̃] *nm* acclimatization, acclimation *US*.

acclimater [3] [aklimate] *vt* **1.** BOT & ZOOL to acclimatize, to acclimate *US* **2.** [adopter] : **~ un usage étranger** to adopt a foreign practice.
◆ **s'acclimater** *vpi* **1.** BOT & ZOOL to acclimatize, to become acclimatized **2.** [personne] to adapt ■ **il s'est bien acclimaté à la vie parisienne** he's adapted *ou* taken to the Parisian way of life very well.

accointances [akwɛ̃tɑ̃s] *nfpl péj* contacts, links ■ **il a des ~ en haut lieu** he has friends in high places.

accolade [akɔlad] *nf* **1.** [embrassade] embrace ■ **donner l'~ à qqn** to embrace sb ■ **recevoir l'~** to be embraced **2.** HIST accolade **3.** [signe] brace, bracket.

accoler [3] [akɔle] *vt* **1.** [disposer ensemble] to place *ou* to put side by side **2.** [joindre par une accolade] to bracket together.

accommodant, e [akɔmɔdɑ̃, ɑ̃t] *adj* accommodating, obliging.

accommodation [akɔmɔdasjɔ̃] *nf* **1.** [acclimatement] acclimatization, acclimation *US* ■ [adaptation] adaptation **2.** OPT focusing.

accommodement [akɔmɔdmɑ̃] *nm* **1.** [accord] arrangement ■ **trouver des ~s avec sa conscience** to come to terms with one's conscience **2.** POLIT compromise.

accommoder [3] [akɔmɔde] <> *vt* **1.** [adapter] to adapt, to adjust, to fit **2.** CULIN to prepare ■ **~ une viande en ragoût** to make *ou* to prepare a stew.
<> *vi* OPT to focus.
◆ **s'accommoder à** *vp+prép* to adapt to.
◆ **s'accommoder de** *vp+prép* to put up with ■ **il s'accommode d'une modeste retraite** he's content *ou* satisfied with a small pension.

accompagnateur, trice [akɔ̃paɲatœr, tris] *nm, f* **1.** [de touristes] guide, courier ▪ [d'enfants] group leader, accompanying adult ▪ [de malades] nurse **2.** MUS accompanist.

accompagnement [akɔ̃paɲmɑ̃] *nm* **1.** CULIN [d'un rôti] trimmings ▪ [d'un mets] garnish ▪ **servi avec un ~ de petits légumes** served with mixed vegetables **2.** MUS accompaniment.

accompagner [3] [akɔ̃paɲe] *vt* **1.** [escorter - ami] to go with ▪ **~ qqn à l'aéroport** [gén] to go to the airport with sb ; [en voiture] to take sb to the airport ▪ **~ qqn en ville** [à pied] to walk into town with sb ; [en voiture] to drive sb into town ▪ **~ un groupe de touristes** to accompany a group of sightseers, to take some sightseers on a tour ▪ **elle vient toujours accompagnée** she never comes alone, she always brings somebody with her ▪ **je serai accompagné de ma cousine** I'll come with my cousin ▪ **il vaut mieux être seul que mal accompagné** you're better off alone than in bad company ▪ **~ un mourant** *fig* to be with a dying man to the end ▪ **~ qqn du regard** to follow sb with one's eyes ▪ **nos vœux/pensées vous accompagnent** our wishes/thoughts are with you **2.** [compléter] to go with ▪ **un échantillon de parfum accompagne tout achat** a sample of perfume comes with every purchase ▪ **une sauce pour ~ vos poissons** a sauce to complement your fish dishes ▪ **~ qqch de : accompagné de vin blanc, c'est un délice** served with white wine, it's delicious **3.** MUS to accompany, to provide an accompaniment for.

◆ **s'accompagner** *vp (emploi réfléchi)* MUS : **s'~ à un instrument** to accompany o.s. on an instrument.

◆ **s'accompagner de** *vp+prép* to come with ▪ **ses phrases s'accompagnent d'une menace** his remarks contain a threat.

accompli, e [akɔ̃pli] *adj* **1.** [parfait] accomplished **2.** [révolu] : **elle a vingt ans ~s** she's turned *ou* over 20 **3.** LING perfective.

accomplir [32] [akɔ̃plir] *vt* **1.** [achever - mandat, obligation] to fulfil ; [- mission, travail] to accomplish, to carry out ▪ **~ de bonnes actions** to do good (deeds) ▪ **~ de mauvaises actions** to commit evil (deeds) ▪ **il n'a rien accompli à ce jour** up to now he hasn't achieved *ou* accomplished anything **2.** [réaliser - miracle] to perform ▪ **~ un exploit technique** to perform a feat of engineering ▪ **~ les dernières volontés de qqn** to carry out sb's last wishes.

◆ **s'accomplir** *vpi* **1.** [être exécuté - vœu] to come true, to be fulfilled ; [- prophétie] to come true ▪ **la volonté de Dieu s'accomplira** God's will shall be done **2.** [s'épanouir - personnalité] to become rounded out.

accomplissement [akɔ̃plismɑ̃] *nm* **1.** [exécution] : **après l'~ de votre mission** after carrying out your mission **2.** [concrétisation] : **l'~ d'une prophétie** the realization of a prophecy ▪ **l'~ d'un exploit sportif/d'un miracle** the performance of an athletic feat/of a miracle.

accord [akɔr] *nm* **1.** [approbation] consent, agreement ▪ **demander l'~ de qqn** to ask for sb's consent ▪ **donner son ~ à** to consent to ▪ **d'un commun ~** by mutual agreement
2. [entente] agreement ▪ [harmonie] harmony ▪ **il faut un bon ~ entre les participants** the participants must all get on well with each other ▪ **vivre en parfait ~** to live in perfect harmony ▪ **~ de l'expression et de la pensée** harmony between expression and thought
3. [convention] agreement ▪ **conclure un ~ avec** to come to an agreement with ◗ **~ d'entreprise** *ou* **d'établissement** collective agreement ▪ **~ commercial** commercial agreement ▪ **~ de paiement** payment agreement ▪ **~ de principe** agreement in principle ▪ **~ salarial** wage settlement ▪ **les ~s d'Évian** *the agreement signed on 18 March 1962 establishing a cease-fire in Algeria and recognizing the country's independence* ▪ **les ~s de Grenelle** *an agreement between the government and trade unions (27 May, 1968) improving wages and working conditions and aimed at ending workers' support for student disturbances* ▪ **Accord général sur les tarifs douaniers et le commerce** General Agreement on Tariffs and Trade ▪ **Accord de libre-échange nord-américain** North American Free Trade Agreement
4. LING agreement, concord ▪ **~ en genre/nombre** gender/number agreement
5. MUS [son] chord, concord ▪ [réglage] tuning ▪ **~ parfait** triad *ou* common chord.

◆ **d'accord** *loc adv* : **être d'~ (avec qqn)** to agree (with sb) ▪ **ils ne sont pas d'~** they don't agree, they disagree ▪ **je suis d'~ pour qu'on lui dise** I agree that she should be told *ou* to her being told ▪ **(je ne suis) pas d'~!** [je refuse] no (way)! ; [c'est faux] I disagree! ▪ **tu viens? – d'~** are you coming? – OK ▪ **(c'est) d'~ pour ce soir** it's OK for tonight ▪ **j'ai enfin réussi à les mettre d'~** I've finally managed to get them to agree ▪ **se mettre d'~ (sur qqch)** to agree (on sthg) ▪ **ils n'arrivent pas à se mettre d'~** they can't agree to reach an agreement ▪ **mettez-vous d'~, je ne comprends rien à ce que vous dites** get your story straight, I can't understand a word of what you're saying ▪ **mettons-nous bien d'~, c'est vous le responsable** let's get one thing straight, you're in charge ▪ **tomber d'~** to come to an agreement ▪ **tomber d'~ sur qqch** to agree on sthg.

◆ **en accord avec** *loc prép* : **en ~ avec qqn** : **en ~ avec le chef de service, nous avons décidé que...** together with the head of department, we have decided that ▪ **en ~ avec les directives** according to the guidelines ▪ **en ~ avec notre politique commerciale** in line with *ou* in keeping with our business policy ▪ **en ~ avec le style du mobilier** in keeping with the furniture.

Voir module d'usage

accord-cadre [akɔrkadr] (*pl* **accords-cadres**) *nm* framework *ou* outline agreement.

accordéon [akɔrdeɔ̃] *nm* MUS accordion.

◆ **en accordéon** *loc adj* [chaussettes] wrinkled ▪ [voiture] crumpled.

L'ACCORD

I quite *ou* totally agree. Je suis tout à fait d'accord.

I couldn't agree (with you) more. Je suis entièrement de votre avis.

I agree wholeheartedly with what you said. Je suis entièrement d'accord avec ce que tu as dit.

I'm inclined to agree (with you). Je suis assez d'accord (avec toi).

You're quite *ou* absolutely right. Vous avez absolument raison.

I think you were right to tell him to leave. À mon avis, vous avez eu raison de lui dire de partir.

That's just *ou* exactly what I was thinking. C'est exactement ce que je pensais.

Those are my feelings exactly. Je partage votre sentiment là-dessus.

I couldn't have put it better myself. Je n'aurais pas dit mieux moi-même.

I would have done exactly the same in your situation. À ta place, j'aurais fait exactement la même chose.

You've made the right decision there. Tu as pris la bonne décision.

I'll go along with that. Je suis d'accord.

That's fine *ou* OK by me. Pas de problème.

That sounds like a good idea. Ça semble être une bonne idée.

I don't see why not. Pourquoi pas ?

accordéoniste [akɔrdeɔnist] *nmf* accordionist.

accorder [3] [akɔrde] *vt* **1.** [octroyer - congé, permission] to give, to grant ; [- faveur] to grant ; [- subvention] to grant, to award ; [- interview] to give ▪ **~ la grâce d'un** *ou* **sa grâce à un condamné** to grant a condemned man a pardon, to extend a pardon to a condemned man ▪ **~ la main de sa fille à qqn** to give sb one's daughter's hand in marriage ▪ **~ toute sa confiance à qqn** to give sb one's complete trust ▪ **~ de l'importance à qqch** to attach importance to sthg ▪ **~ de la valeur aux objets** to set a value on things ▪ **je vous accorde une heure, pas plus** I'll allow you one hour, no more ▪ **voulez-vous m'~ cette danse?** may I have this dance? **2.** [concéder] : **~ à qqn que** to admit to *ou* to grant sb that ▪ **vous m'accorderez que, là, j'avais raison** you must admit that on this point I was right ▪ **ils sont jeunes, je vous l'accorde** granted, they're young, they're young I grant you **3.** [harmoniser] : **~ les couleurs d'une pièce** to harmonize *ou* to coordinate the colours of a room **4.** GRAMM to make agree ▪ **~ le verbe avec le sujet** to make the verb agree with the subject **5.** MUS [piano, guitare] to tune ▪ **les musiciens accordent leurs instruments** [avant un concert] the players are tuning up ➋ **il faudrait ~ vos violons!** make your minds up!, get your stories straight!

◆ **s'accorder** ◇ *vpi* **1.** [être du même avis] : **s'~ à : tous s'accordent à dire que...** they all agree *ou* concur that... ▪ **s'~ pour : ils se sont accordés pour baisser leurs prix** they agreed among themselves that they would drop their prices **2.** [s'entendre] : **on ne s'est jamais accordé (tous les deux)** we two never saw eye to eye *ou* got along **3.** [être en harmonie - caractères] to blend ; [- opinions] to match, to tally, to converge ▪ **ce qu'il dit ne s'accorde pas avec sa personnalité** he's saying things which are out of character **4.** GRAMM to agree ▪ **s'~ en genre avec** to agree in gender with **5.** MUS to tune up.

◇ *vpt* : **s'~ quelques jours de repos** to take a few days off.

accordeur [akɔrdœr] *nm* (piano) tuner.

accorte [akɔrt] *adj f litt* pleasant, comely ▪ **une femme rondelette et ~** an attractively buxom woman.

accostage [akɔstaʒ] *nm* **1.** NAUT drawing *ou* coming alongside **2.** [d'une personne] accosting.

accoster [3] [akɔste] ◇ *vt* **1.** [personne] to go up to *(insép)*, to accost **2.** NAUT to come *ou* to draw alongside.

◇ *vi* NAUT to berth.

accotement [akɔtmɑ̃] *nm* **1.** [d'une route] shoulder, verge *UK* ▪ **'~s non stabilisés'** 'soft shoulders, soft verges *UK*' ▪ **'~s stabilisés'** 'hard shoulders' **2.** RAIL shoulder.

accoter [3] [akɔte] *vt* to lean ▪ **maisons accotées à la colline** houses hugging the hillside.

◆ **s'accoter à, s'accoter contre** *vp+prép* to lean against.

accotoir [akɔtwar] *nm* armrest.

accouchée [akuʃe] *nf woman who has recently given birth.*

accouchement [akuʃmɑ̃] *nm* [travail] childbirth, labour ▪ [expulsion] delivery ▪ **pendant mon ~** while I was giving birth *ou* in labour ➋ **~ prématuré** *ou* **avant terme** premature delivery ▪ **~ dirigé** induced delivery ▪ **~ sans douleur** painless delivery *ou* childbirth ▪ **~ sous X** *a woman's right to anonymity in childbirth* ▪ **~ à terme** full term delivery.

accoucher [3] [akuʃe] ◇ *vi* **1.** [avoir un bébé] to have a baby, to give birth ▪ **pendant qu'elle accouchait** while she was giving birth *ou* in labour ▪ **j'accouche en juin** my baby's due in June **2.** △ [parler] : **accouche!** spit it out!, let's have it!

◇ *vt* : **c'est lui qui l'a accouchée** he delivered her baby.

◆ **accoucher de** *v+prép* **1.** [enfant] to give birth to, to have ▪ **~ de jumeaux** to have twins **2.** *fam* [produire] to come up with, to produce.

accoucheur, euse [akuʃœr, øz] *nm, f* obstetrician.

accouder [3] [akude] ◆ **s'accouder** *vpi* : **s'~ à** *ou* **sur qqch** to lean (one's elbows) on sthg ▪ **s'~ à la fenêtre** to lean out of the window ▪ **être accoudé à qqch** to lean on sthg.

accoudoir [akudwar] *nm* armrest.

accouplement [akupləmɑ̃] *nm* **1.** [raccordement] linking, joining ▪ MÉCAN coupling, connecting ▪ ÉLECTR connecting **2.** AGRIC yoking, coupling **3.** ZOOL mating.

accoupler [3] [akuple] *vt* **1.** [raccorder - mots] to link *ou* to join (together) ▪ MÉCAN to couple, to connect ▪ ÉLECTR to connect **2.** AGRIC [pour le trait] to yoke *ou* to couple together *(sép)* **3.** ZOOL to mate.

◆ **s'accoupler** *vpi* [animaux] to mate.

accourir [45] [akurir] *vi* to run, to rush ▪ **elle est accourue pour le voir** she hurried *ou* rushed to see him ▪ **elle l'appelle et accourt** all she has to do is whistle and he comes running.

accoutrement [akutrəmɑ̃] *nm* outfit.

accoutrer [3] [akutre] *vt péj* to dress up *(sép)* ▪ **comme te voilà accoutré!** you do look ridiculous in that outfit!

◆ **s'accoutrer** *vp (emploi réfléchi) péj* to get dressed up.

accoutumance [akutymɑ̃s] *nf* **1.** [adaptation] habituation **2.** [d'un toxicomane] addiction, dependency.

accoutumé, e [akutyme] *adj* usual, customary.

◆ **comme à l'accoutumée** *loc adv sout* as usual, as always.

accoutumer [3] [akutyme] *vt* : **~ qqn à (faire) qqch** to accustom sb to (doing) sthg, to get sb used to (doing) sthg.

◆ **s'accoutumer à** *vp+prép* to get used to.

accréditation [akreditasjɔ̃] *nf* FIN accreditation.

accréditer [3] [akredite] *vt* [rumeur, nouvelle] to substantiate, to give credence to ▪ [personne] to accredit ▪ **~ qqn auprès de** to accredit sb to.

◆ **s'accréditer** *vpi* [rumeur] to gain ground.

accréditeur [akreditœr] *nm* surety.

accréditif, ive [akreditif, iv] *adj* : **lettre accréditive** letter of credit.

◆ **accréditif** *nm* [lettre] letter of credit ▪ [crédit] credit.

accro [akro] *fam* ◇ *adj* hooked ▪ **être ~ à qqch** [drogue] to be hooked on sthg ; *fig* to be hooked on *ou* really into sthg.

◇ *nmf* fanatic ▪ **c'est un ~ du football** he's really mad on football.

accroc [akro] *nm* **1.** [déchirure] tear, rip ▪ **faire un ~ à sa chemise** to tear *ou* to rip one's shirt **2.** *fam* [entorse] breach, violation ▪ **faire un ~ au règlement** to bend the rules **3.** [incident] snag, hitch ▪ **un voyage sans ~** *ou* **~s** an uneventful trip.

accrochage [akrɔʃaʒ] *nm* **1.** [suspension - d'un tableau] hanging ▪ ART small exhibition **2.** [fixation - d'un wagon] hitching (up), coupling ; [- d'une remorque] hitching (up) **3.** [collision entre véhicules] collision ▪ **ce n'est qu'un tout petit ~** it's only a scratch **4.** [querelle] quarrel, squabble ▪ **avoir un ~ avec qqn** to clash with sb **5.** MIL skirmish, engagement **6.** SPORT [en boxe] clinch ▪ [entre deux coureurs] tangle.

accroche [akrɔʃ] *nf* attention-getter, attention-catcher *(in advertising)*.

accroche-cœur [akrɔʃkœr] *(pl inv ou pl* **accroche-cœurs**) *nm* kiss-curl *UK*, spit curl *US*.

accroche-plat [akrɔʃpla] *(pl inv ou pl* **accroche-plats**) *nm* plate-hanger.

accrocher [3] [akrɔʃe] ◇ *vt* **1.** [suspendre - tableau] to hang ; [- manteau, rideau] to hang up *(sép)*

2. [saisir] to hook ▪ **chaque enfant essaie d'~ un paquet** each child tries to hook up a parcel

3. [relier] : **~ qqch à** to tie sthg (on) to ▪ **~ un wagon à un train** to couple *ou* to hitch a wagon to a train ▪ **~ un pendentif à une chaîne** to attach a pendant to a chain

4. *fam* [aborder] to corner, to buttonhole, to collar

5. [retenir l'intérêt de] to grab the attention of ▪ [attirer - regard] to catch ▪ **il faut ~ le lecteur dès les premières pages** we must make the reader sit up and take notice from the very beginning of the book ▪ **qui accroche le regard** eye-catching ▪ **ses bijoux accrochaient la lumière** her jewels caught the light ▪ *(en usage absolu)* **un slogan qui accroche** a catchy slogan

6. [déchirer - collant, vêtement] to snag, to catch

7. [heurter - piéton] to hit ■ **il a accroché l'aile de ma voiture** he caught *ou* scraped my wing
8. MIL to engage in a skirmish with.
◇ *vi* **1.** [coincer - fermeture, tiroir] to jam, to stick ■ **des skis qui accrochent** skis that don't run smoothly ■ *fig* [buter] to be stuck ■ **j'accroche sur la traduction de ce mot** I just can't come up with a good translation for this word
2. *fam* [bien fonctionner] : **ça n'a pas accroché entre eux** they didn't hit it off ■ **je n'ai jamais accroché en physique** I never really got into physics ■ **en musique, il a tout de suite accroché** he took to music straight away.
◆ **s'accrocher** ◇ *vp (emploi passif)* to hang, to hook on.
◇ *vp (emploi réciproque)* **1.** [entrer en collision - voitures] to crash (into each other), to collide ; [- boxeurs] to clinch
2. [se disputer] to clash ■ **ils ne peuvent pas se supporter, ils vont s'~ tout de suite** they can't stand each other so they're bound to start arguing straight away.
◇ *vpi fam fam* [persévérer - athlète, concurrent] to apply o.s. ■ **avec lui, il faut s'~!** he's hard work!
◇ *vpt loc* **tu peux te l'~!**△ [tu ne l'auras jamais] you can whistle for it! ; [tu ne l'auras plus] you can kiss it goodbye!
◆ **s'accrocher à** *vp+prép* : **accroche-toi à la poignée!** hang on (tight) to the handle! ■ **s'~ au pouvoir/à la vie/à qqn** *fig* to cling to power/to life/to sb.
◆ **s'accrocher avec** *vp+prép* to clash with.

accrocheur, euse [akrɔʃœr, øz] *fam* ◇ *adj* **1.** [tenace - vendeur] pushy **2.** [attirant - titre, slogan, tube] catchy ; [- sourire] beguiling ■ **une publicité accrocheuse** an eye-catching advertisement.
◇ *nm, f* fighter.

accroire [akrwar] *vt (à l'infinitif seulement) litt* **faire** *ou* **laisser ~ qqch à qqn** to mislead sb into believing sthg ■ **en faire ~ à qqn** to try to deceive sb.

accrois *etc*, **accroissait** *v* ▻ **accroître.**

accroissais ▻ **accroître.**

accroissement [akrwasmɑ̃] *nm* **1.** [augmentation] : **l'~ de la population** population growth ■ **avec l'~ de leur pouvoir d'achat** with their increased purchasing power **2.** MATH increment.

accroître [94] [akrwatr] *vt* [fortune, sentiment] to increase ■ [désordre] to spread ■ [domaine] to add (on) to ■ [popularité] to enhance.
◆ **s'accroître** *vpi* [tension] to rise ■ [sentiment] to grow ■ [population] to rise, to increase, to grow.

accroupir [32] [akrupir] ◆ **s'accroupir** *vpi* to squat *ou* to crouch (down).

accroupissement [akrupismɑ̃] *nm* **1.** [action] squatting, crouching **2.** [position] squatting position.

accru, e [akry] ◇ *pp* ▻ **accroître.**
◇ *adj* [fortune] increased, larger ■ [sentiment] deeper ■ [popularité] enhanced.

accu [aky] *nm fam* battery.

accueil [akœj] *nm* **1.** [réception - d'invités] welcome, greeting ■ **faire bon ~ à qqn** to give sb a warm welcome ■ **faire mauvais ~ à qqn** to give sb a cool reception ■ **faire bon/mauvais ~ à une proposition** *fig* to receive a proposal warmly/coldly **2.** [bureau, comptoir] desk, reception.
◆ **d'accueil** *loc adj* [discours, cérémonie] welcoming ■ [hôtesse, hall] reception *(modif)* ■ [pays] host *(modif)*.

accueillant, e [akœjɑ̃, ɑ̃t] *adj* [peuple, individu] welcoming, friendly ■ [sourire] warm, welcoming ■ [maison] hospitable ■ **peu ~** [endroit] inhospitable ; [personne] unwelcoming, cold.

accueillir [41] [akœjir] *vt* **1.** [aller chercher] to meet **2.** [recevoir] : **~ qqn froidement** to give sb a cool reception ■ **être très bien/mal accueilli** to get a very pleasant/poor welcome ■ **il a été accueilli par des bravos** he was greeted with cheers ■ **~ une idée avec scepticisme/enthousiasme** to greet an idea with scepticism/enthusiasm ■ **le projet a été très mal accueilli par la direction** the project got a cool reception *ou* response from the management **3.** [héberger] to house, to accommodate ■ **l'hôpital peut ~ 1 000 malades** the hospital can accommodate 1,000 patients ■ **j'étais sans abri et ils m'ont accueilli** I was homeless and they took me in *ou* gave me a home.

acculer [3] [akyle] ◇ *vt* **1.** [bloquer] : **~ qqn contre qqch** to drive sb back against sthg **2.** [contraindre] : **~ qqn à** : **~ qqn à la faillite** to push sb into bankruptcy ■ **~ qqn au désespoir** to drive sb to despair.
◇ *vi* NAUT to list by the stern.

acculturation [akyltyrasjɔ̃] *nf* acculturation, cultural adaptation.

acculturer [3] [akyltyre] *vt* : **~ un groupe ethnique** to help an ethnic group adjust to a new cultural environment.

accumulateur [akymylatœr] *nm* **1.** BANQUE, INFORM & MÉCAN accumulator **2.** ÉLECTR (storage) battery, storage cell.

accumulation [akymylasjɔ̃] *nf* **1.** [action] accumulation, amassing, building up ■ [collection] mass ■ **devant cette ~ de preuves/démentis** faced with this mass of proof/with repeated denials **2.** ÉLECTR storage.

accumuler [3] [akymyle] *vt* **1.** [conserver - boîtes, boutons] to keep *ou* to hoard (in large quantities), to accumulate ; [- denrées] to stockpile, to hoard ; [- papiers] to keep **2.** [réunir - preuves] to pile on *(sép)*, to accumulate ; [- fortune, argent] to amass ■ **mais tu les accumules!** *fam* [les bêtises] you never stop, do you?
◆ **s'accumuler** *vpi* to accumulate, to mount (up), to pile up ■ **les toxines s'accumulent dans l'organisme** there is a build-up of toxins in the body.

accusateur, trice [akyzatœr, tris] ◇ *adj* [silence, regard] accusing ■ [bilan] incriminating ■ [preuve] accusatory, incriminating.
◇ *nm, f* [dénonciateur] accuser.
◆ **accusateur** *nm* HIST : **~ public** public prosecutor *(during the French Revolution)*.

accusatif [akyzatif] *nm* accusative.

accusation [akyzasjɔ̃] *nf* **1.** DR charge, indictment ■ **mettre qqn en ~** to indict *ou* to charge sb **2.** [reproche] accusation, charge ■ **lancer une ~ contre qqn/un parti** to make an accusation against sb/a party.

accusatoire [akyzatwar] *adj* accusatory.

accusé, e [akyze] *nm, f* defendant ■ **~, levez-vous!** the accused will stand!
◆ **accusé de réception** *nm* acknowledgment of receipt.

accuser [3] [akyze] *vt* **1.** [désigner comme coupable] to accuse ■ **je ne t'accuse pas!** I'm not saying you did it! ■ **tout l'accuse** everything points to his guilt ■ **~ qqn de qqch** to accuse sb of sthg ■ **il a accusé le jury de favoritisme** he accused the jury of being biased ■ **on m'accuse d'avoir menti** I'm being accused of lying ■ **J'accuse** *title of an open letter to the French President which appeared in 'l'Aurore' in January 1898, in which Emile Zola insisted that Alfred Dreyfus had been unjustly incriminated* ▮ DR : **~ qqn de meurtre/viol** to charge sb with murder/rape ■ **de quoi l'accuse-t-on ?** what's the charge against him?
2. [rejeter la responsabilité sur] to blame, to put the blame on
3. [accentuer] to highlight, to emphasize, to accentuate ■ **la lumière accuse les reliefs** sunlight emphasizes the outlines
4. [indiquer] : **la Bourse accuse une forte baisse** the stock market is registering heavy losses ■ **son visage accuse une grande fatigue** her face shows how tired she is ■ **il accuse ses cinquante ans** he's fifty and looks it ■ **le compteur accuse 130 km/h** the meter's registering *ou* reading 130 km/h
5. *loc* **~ réception de** to acknowledge receipt of ■ **~ le coup** [en boxe] to reel with the punch ; [fatigue] to show the strain ; [moralement] to take it badly ■ **elle a drôlement accusé le coup, dis donc!** *fam* you can tell she's really been through it!
◆ **s'accuser** *vp (emploi réfléchi)* to accuse o.s. ■ **la seule chose dont je peux m'~, c'est de...** the only fault I would admit to is...

ace [ɛs] *nm* ace SPORT.

acéphale [asefal] *adj* acephalous.

acerbe [asɛrb] *adj* **1.** [parole, critique] cutting, acerbic ■ **d'un ton ~** crisply **2.** *litt* [goût] bitter.

acéré, e [asere] *adj* **1.** [lame, pointe] sharp **2.** *fig & sout* [critique, propos] biting, caustic.

acétate [asetat] *nm* CHIM acetate.

acétique [asetik] *adj* acetic.

acétone [asetɔn] *nf* acetone.

acétyle [asetil] *nm* acetyl.

acétylène [asetilɛn] *nm* acetylene.

acétylsalicylique [asetilsalisilik] *adj* acetylsalicylic.

ACF (*abr de* **Automobile Club de France**) *npr m French automobile association*, ≃ AA *UK*, ≃ RAC *UK*, ≃ AAA *US*.

ach. = **achète.**

achalandage [aʃalɑ̃daʒ] *nm* DR clientele.

achalandé, e [aʃalɑ̃de] *adj* : **bien ~** well-stocked ■ **mal ~** short on merchandise.

acharné, e [aʃarne] ◇ *adj* [combat, lutte] fierce ■ [travail] relentless ■ [travailleur] hard ■ [joueur] hardened ■ **il est ~ à votre perte** *ou* **à vous perdre** he is set *ou* bent *ou* intent on ruining you.
◇ *nm, f* : **un ~ du travail** a workaholic.

acharnement [aʃarnəmɑ̃] *nm* [dans un combat] fury ■ [dans le travail] relentlessness, perseverance ■ **son ~ à réussir** his determination to succeed ■ **~ au travail** dedication to work.
◆ **avec acharnement** *loc adv* [combattre] tooth and nail, furiously ■ [travailler] relentlessly ■ [résister] fiercely.

acharner [3] [aʃarne] ◆ **s'acharner** *vpi* **1.** [tourmenter qqn] : **s'~ sur** *ou* **contre** *ou* **après qqn** to persecute *ou* to hound sb ■ **les médias s'acharnent sur** *ou* **contre moi** I'm being hounded by the press ■ **le sort s'acharne sur lui** he's dogged by bad luck **2.** [persévérer] : **s'~ sur qqch** to work (away) at sthg ■ **cesse de t'~ sur ce nœud!** just leave that knot alone! ■ **s'~ à faire qqch** to strive to do sthg ■ **je m'acharne à lui faire mettre son écharpe** I'm always trying to get him to wear his scarf ■ *(en usage absolu)* **inutile de t'~, tu ne la convaincras pas** it's no use struggling, you won't persuade her.

achat [aʃa] *nm* **1.** [fait d'acheter] purchasing, buying ■ **faire un ~** to purchase *ou* to buy something ■ **faire un ~ à crédit** to buy something on credit **2.** [article acheté] purchase, buy ■ **réglez vos ~s à la caisse** pay (for your purchases) at the cash desk ■ **un sac rempli d'~s** a bag full of shopping ■ **c'est un bon/mauvais ~** it's a good/bad buy ➤ **~ groupé** package.
◆ **à l'achat** *loc adv* : **la livre fait 1,6 euros à l'~** the buying rate for sterling is 1.6 euros.

acheminement [aʃminmɑ̃] *nm* [de marchandises] conveying, forwarding, shipment ■ [de troupes] moving ■ [de trains] routing ■ **~ du courrier** mail delivery.

acheminer [3] [aʃmine] *vt* **1.** [marchandises] to convey, to forward ■ **~ des produits par avion** to ship products by plane **2.** MIL to convey, to move ■ **~ des troupes vers** *ou* **sur le front** to move troops up to the front *ou* up the line **3.** RAIL to route ■ **~ un train vers** *ou* **sur** to route a train to *ou* towards.
◆ **s'acheminer vers** *vp+prép* [endroit] to head for ■ [accord, solution] to move towards.

acheter [28] [aʃte] *vt* **1.** [cadeau, objet d'art, denrée] to buy, to purchase *sout* ■ **~ des actions** *ou* **une part d'une entreprise** to buy into a business ■ **~ qqch au kilo** to buy sthg by the kilo ■ **~ qqch comptant/en gros/d'occasion/à crédit** to buy sthg cash/wholesale/second-hand/on credit ■ **~ des boutons/oranges au détail** to buy buttons/oranges singly ■ **~ qqch à qqn** [pour soi] to buy sthg from sb ; [pour le lui offrir] to buy sb sthg, to buy sthg for sb ■ **je lui ai acheté sa vieille voiture** I bought his old car from *ou* off him ■ **si ça te plaît, je te l'achète** I'll buy you it *ou* it for you if you like it ■ *(en usage absolu)* **achetez français!** buy French (products)! **2.** [échanger - liberté, paix] to buy **3.** [soudoyer - témoin, juge] to bribe, to buy (off) ; [- électeurs] to buy ■ **ne crois pas que tu pourras m'~** you must understand I won't be bought ■ **il s'est fait ~ par la Mafia** he was bought by the Mafia.
◆ **s'acheter** ◇ *vp (emploi passif)* to be on sale ■ **où est-ce que ça s'achète?** where can you buy it?
◇ *vpt* : **s'~ qqch** to buy o.s. sthg ➤ **s'~ une conduite** to turn over a new leaf.

acheteur, euse [aʃtœr, øz] *nm, f* **1.** [client] buyer, purchaser ■ **trouver un ~ pour qqch** to find a buyer for *ou* to find somebody to buy sthg **2.** [professionnel] buyer **3.** DR vendee.

achevé, e [aʃve] *adj* [sportif, artiste] accomplished ■ [œuvre] perfect ■ [style] polished ■ **d'un ridicule ~** *sout* utterly ridiculous ■ **d'une bêtise ~e** completely stupid ■ **c'est un imbécile ~** he's a complete idiot *ou* fool.
◆ **achevé d'imprimer** *nm* colophon.

achèvement [aʃɛvmɑ̃] *nm* completion.

achever [19] [aʃve] *vt* **1.** [finir - repas, discours, lettre] to finish, to end, to bring to a close *ou* an end ; [- journal, livre] to reach the end of, to finish ■ **~ sa vie à l'hôpital** to end one's days in hospital ■ **laisse-le ~ sa phrase** let him finish what he's saying ■ **~ de faire qqch** to finish doing sthg ■ **ils avaient juste achevé de rembourser le crédit** they'd just got through paying off the debt ■ **~ de mettre au point une invention** to put the final touches to an invention ■ *(en usage absolu)* [finir de parler] to finish (talking) **2.** [tuer - animal] to destroy ; [- personne] to finish off *(sép)* **3.** *fam* [accabler] to finish off **4.** *fam* [ruiner] to finish off *(sép)*, to clean out *(sép)*.
◆ **s'achever** *vpi* [vie, journée, vacances] to come to an end, to draw to a close *ou* an end ■ [dîner, film] to end, to finish ■ **ainsi s'achève notre journal** RADIO & TV (and) that's the end of the news ■ **le livre s'achève sur une note d'espoir/un chapitre consacré à la peinture** the book ends on a hopeful note/with a chapter on painting.

Achille [aʃil] *npr* Achilles.

achoppement [aʃɔpmɑ̃] *nm* ⊳ **pierre.**

achopper [3] [aʃɔpe] *vi* : **~ sur** *pr & vieilli* to stumble on *ou* over ; *fig* to come up against, to meet with ■ **elle achoppe sur les "r"** she can't pronounce her r's.

achromatique [akrɔmatik] *adj* achromatic.

acide [asid] ◇ *adj* **1.** [goût] acidic, acid, sour ■ [propos] cutting, caustic **2.** CHIM & ÉCOL acid.
◇ *nm* **1.** CHIM acid ■ **~ aminé** amino acid ■ **~ gras saturé/insaturé** saturated/unsaturated fatty acid ■ **~ sulfurique** sulphuric *UK ou* sulfuric *US* acid **2.** △ *arg crime* acid△.

acidification [asidifikasjɔ̃] *nf* acidification.

acidifier [9] [asidifje] *vt* to acidify.
◆ **s'acidifier** *vpi* to acidify.

acidité [asidite] *nf* **1.** [d'un goût, d'un fruit] acidity, sourness ■ [d'un propos] tartness, sharpness **2.** CHIM, GÉOL & MÉD acidity.

acido-basique [asidobazik] (*pl* **acido-basiques**) *adj* acido-basic.

acidulé, e [asidyle] *adj* acidulous.

acier [asje] *nm* steel ■ **~ inoxydable/trempé** stainless/tempered steel.
◆ **d'acier** *loc adj* MÉTALL steel *(modif)* ■ *fig* [regard] steely ■ **muscles/cœur d' ~** muscles/heart of steel.

aciérage [asjeraʒ] *nm* **1.** MÉTALL [fabrication] steeling ■ [durcissement] case-hardening **2.** IMPR steel-engraving.

aciérer [18] [asjere] *vt* **1.** MÉTALL to steel, to case-harden **2.** IMPR to engrave on steel.

aciérie [asjeri] *nf* steelworks, steel plant.

acmé [akme] *nm & nf* **1.** *litt* [apogée] acme *litt*, summit, height **2.** MÉD climax.

acné [akne] *nf* acne ■ **avoir de l'~** to suffer from *ou* to have acne ➤ **~ juvénile** teenage acne.

acnéique [akneik] ◇ *adj* acned.
◇ *nmf* acne sufferer.

acolyte [akɔlit] *nm* **1.** RELIG acolyte **2.** [complice] sidekick.

acompte [akɔ̃t] *nm* **1.** [avance sur - une commande, des travaux] down payment ; [- un salaire] advance ; [- un loyer] deposit ■ **payer par** *ou* **en plusieurs ~s** to pay in instalments ■ **donner**

ou **verser un ~ de 500 euros (sur)** [achat] to make a down payment of 500 euros (on) ▶ **~ provisionnel** [d'un impôt] instalment **2.** [avant-goût] foretaste, preview.

aconit [akɔnit] *nm* aconite BOT.

a contrario [akɔ̃trarjo] ◇ *loc adj inv* converse.
◇ *loc adv* conversely.

acoquiner [3] [akɔkine] ◆ **s'acoquiner** *vpi péj* **s'~ à** *ou* **avec qqn** to take *ou* to team up with sb ■ **il s'est acoquiné avec Pierrot** he and Pierrot have teamed up together.

Açores [asɔr] *npr fpl* : **les ~** the Azores.

à-côté [akote] (*pl* **à-côtés**) *nm* **1.** [aspect - d'une question] side issue ; [- d'une histoire, d'un événement] side *ou* secondary aspect **2.** [gain] bit of extra money ■ **se faire des ~s** *fam* to make some extra money ▮ [frais] incidental expense.

à-coup [aku] (*pl* **à-coups**) *nm* **1.** [secousse - d'un moteur, d'un véhicule] cough, judder ; [- d'une machine] jerk, jolt **2.** [de l'économie] upheaval.
◆ **par à-coups** *loc adv* [travailler] in spurts ■ [avancer] in fits and starts.

acousticien, enne [akustisjɛ̃, ɛn] *nm, f* acoustician.

acoustique [akustik] ◇ *adj* acoustic.
◇ *nf* [science] acoustics *(sing)* ■ [qualité sonore] acoustics *(pl)*.

acquéreur [akerœr] *nm* purchaser, buyer ■ **se rendre** *ou* **devenir ~ : il veut se rendre** *ou* **devenir ~** he wants to buy *ou* to purchase ■ **il s'est rendu** *ou* **il est devenu ~ de...** he's become the owner of...

acquérir [39] [akerir] *vt* **1.** [biens] to buy, to purchase, to acquire ■ [fortune] to acquire ■ **~ qqch par héritage** to come into sthg ▶ **bien mal acquis ne profite jamais** *prov* ill-gotten gains seldom prosper *prov* **2.** *fig* [habitude] to develop ■ [célébrité] to attain, to achieve ■ [droit] to obtain ■ [expérience] to gain ■ [savoir-faire] to acquire ■ [information, preuve] to obtain, to acquire, to get hold of ■ **~ de la valeur** to increase in value ■ **~ la conviction/la certitude que** to become convinced/certain that ■ **~ qqch à qqn : sa réaction lui a acquis l'estime de tous** her reaction won her everybody's esteem ■ **ce stage est destiné à leur faire ~ une expérience pratique** this course is designed to give them practical experience **3.** *sout* [au passif] : **être acquis à qqn : il vous est entièrement acquis** he backs you fully ■ **mon soutien vous est acquis** you can be certain of my support ■ **être acquis à qqch : l'électorat n'est pas encore acquis à cette idée** the electorate hasn't fully accepted *ou* hasn't quite come round to that idea yet.
◆ **s'acquérir** ◇ *vp (emploi passif)* : **la souplesse s'acquiert par des exercices** you become supple by exercising.
◇ *vpt* : **s'~ la confiance de qqn** to gain *ou* to win sb's trust.

acquêt [akɛ] *nm* acquest.

acquiert *etc v* ▷ **acquérir**.

acquiescement [akjɛsmɑ̃] *nm* [accord] agreement ■ [consentement] assent, agreement ■ **donner son ~ à une requête** to assent to a request.
◆ **d'acquiescement** *loc adj* [geste, signe] approving.

acquiescer [21] [akjese] *vi* to agree, to approve ■ **~ d'un signe de tête** to nod (one's) approval ■ **~ à qqch** to assent *ou* to agree to sthg.

acquis, e [aki, iz] ◇ *pp* ▷ **acquérir**.
◇ *adj* [avantage, droit, fait] established ■ [fortune, titre] acquired ■ **tenir qqch pour ~ : je tiens votre soutien pour ~** I take it for granted that you'll support me ■ *(tournure impersonnelle)* **il est ~ que la couche d'ozone est en danger** it is an established fact that the ozone layer is at risk.
◆ **acquis** *nm* **1.** [savoir] knowledge ■ **fonctionner sur des ~ anciens** to get by on what one already knows **2.** [expérience] experience ■ **avoir de l'~** to be experienced **3.** [avantages, droits] established privileges, rights to which one is entitled ■ **les ~ sociaux** social benefits.

acquisition [akizisjɔ̃] *nf* **1.** [apprentissage] acquisition **2.** [achat] purchase ■ **faire l'~ d'une maison** to buy *ou* to purchase a house **3.** INFORM : **~ de données** data acquisition.

acquit [aki] *nm* COMM receipt ■ **'pour ~'** 'paid, received (with thanks)'.
◆ **par acquit de conscience** *loc adv* in order to set my/his *etc* mind at rest.

acquittable [akitabl] *adj* **1.** DR liable to be acquitted **2.** FIN payable.

acquitté, e [akite] *nm, f person who has been acquitted.*

acquittement [akitmɑ̃] *nm* **1.** [règlement - d'une facture, d'un droit] payment ; [- d'une obligation] discharge ; [- d'une promesse] fulfilment ; [- d'une dette] paying off ; [- d'une fonction, d'un travail] performance ; [- d'un engagement] fulfilment **2.** DR acquittal.

acquitter [3] [akite] *vt* **1.** [payer - facture, note] to pay, to settle ; [- droits] to pay ; [- lettre de change] to receipt **2.** [libérer] : **~ qqn de : ~ qqn d'une dette/d'une obligation** to release sb from a debt/from an obligation **3.** DR to acquit.
◆ **s'acquitter de** *vp+prép* [obligation] to discharge ■ [promesse] to carry out ■ [dette] to pay off ■ [fonction, travail] to perform ■ [engagement] to fulfil.

acra [akra] *nm Creole fried fish or vegetable ball.*

acre [akr] *nf* **1.** HIST [en France] ≃ 5 200 m² **2.** [au Canada] acre *UK (= 4 047 m²)*.

âcre [akr] *adj* [saveur, odeur] acrid ■ *litt* [propos, ton] bitter.

âcreté [akrəte] *nf* **1.** [d'une saveur, d'une odeur] acridness, acridity **2.** *litt* [d'un propos, d'un ton] bitterness.

acrimonie [akrimɔni] *nf* acrimony, acrimoniousness.

acrimonieux, euse [akrimɔnjø, øz] *adj* acrimonious.

acrobate [akrɔbat] *nmf* [gén] acrobat ■ [au trapèze] trapeze artist.

acrobatie [akrɔbasi] *nf* **1.** SPORT acrobatics *(pl)* **2.** *fig* **il a réussi à remonter son affaire par quelques ~s** he managed to save his business by doing some skilful manoeuvring **3.** AÉRON : **~s en vol** aerobatics *(pl)*.

acrobatique [akrɔbatik] *adj* acrobatic.

acronyme [akrɔnim] *nm* acronym.

acropole [akrɔpɔl] *nf* acropolis, citadel.

Acropole [akrɔpɔl] *npr f* : **l'~** the Acropolis.

acrostiche [akrɔstiʃ] *nm* acrostic.

acrylique [akrilik] *adj* & *nm* acrylic.

actant [aktɑ̃] *nm* agent.

acte [akt] *nm*

> **A.** SÉQUENCE
> **B.** ACTION
> **C.** ACTION LÉGALE, POLITIQUE
> **D.** DOCUMENT ADMINISTRATIF, LÉGAL

A. SÉQUENCE

1. MUS & THÉÂTRE act ■ **une pièce en un seul ~** a one-act play **2.** *fig* period, episode ■ **sa mort annonçait le dernier ~ de la campagne d'Italie/de la Révolution** his death ushered in the last episode of the Italian campaign/the Revolution

B. ACTION

1. [gén] action, act ■ **juger qqn sur ses ~s** to judge sb by his/her actions ■ **passer aux ~s** to take action, to act ▶ **~ de bravoure** act of bravery, brave deed, courageous act ■ **~ gratuit** PHILOS gratuitous act, acte gratuit *spéc* ■ **~ sexuel** sex act ■ **~ de terrorisme** terrorist action, act of terrorism ■ **~ de vengeance** act of revenge ■ **faire ~ de candidature** [chercheur d'emploi] to submit one's application, to apply ; [maire] to stand *UK*, to run *US* ■ **faire ~ d'autorité** to show one's authority ■ **faire ~ de bonne volonté** to show willing ■ **faire ~ de présence** to put in an appearance
2. MÉD : **~ chirurgical** *ou* **opératoire** operation ■ **~ (médical)** [consultation] (medical) consultation ; [traitement] (medical) treatment

3. PSYCHOL : **passer à l'~** [gén] to act ; [névrosé, psychopathe] to act out ▶ **~ manqué** acte manqué ▪ **c'était peut-être un ~ manqué** maybe subconsciously I/he did it deliberately
4. RELIG ▶ **~ de charité** act of charity ▪ **~ de foi** act of faith ; HIST [pendant l'Inquisition] auto-da-fé

C. ACTION LÉGALE, POLITIQUE
1. DR act, action ▪ **~ administratif** administrative act ▪ **~ juridique** legal transaction ▪ **faire ~ de : faire ~ de citoyen** to act in one's capacity as a citizen ▪ **faire ~ d'héritier** to come forward as a beneficiary ▪ **faire ~ de témoin** to act as a witness, to testify
2. POLIT [en France] : **~ de gouvernement** act of State ▮ [en Grande-Bretagne] : **Acte du Parlement** act of Parliament ▪ **l'Acte unique européen** the Single European Act

D. DOCUMENT ADMINISTRATIF, LÉGAL
1. ADMIN certificate ▪ **~ de décès** death certificate ▪ **~ de l'état civil** *certificate delivered by the registrar of births, deaths and marriages* ▪ **~ de mariage** marriage certificate ▪ **~ de naissance** birth certificate ▪ **demander ~ de qqch** to ask for formal acknowledgment of sthg ▪ **je demande ~ du fait que...** I want it on record that... ▪ **donner ~ de qqch** [constater légalement] to acknowledge sthg formally ▪ **donner ~ à qqn de qqch** *fig* to acknowledge the truth of what sb said ▪ **dont ~** duly noted *ou* acknowledged ▪ **prendre ~ de qqch** [faire constater légalement] to record sthg ; [noter] to take a note of *ou* to note sthg
2. [en droit pénal] : **~ d'accusation** (bill of) indictment ▪ **quel est l'~ d'accusation?** what is the charge?
3. [en droit civil] : **~ authentique** *ou* **notarié** notarial act ▪ **~ de cession** conveyance ▪ **~ de donation** deed of covenant, gift ▪ **~ d'huissier** writ ▪ **~ de succession** attestation of inheritance *ou* will
4. [en droit commercial] : **~ d'association** partnership agreement *ou* deed, articles of partnership ▪ **~ de vente** bill of sale.
◆ **actes** *nmpl* **1.** [procès-verbaux] proceedings ▪ [annales] annals **2.** RELIG : **les Actes des apôtres** the Acts of the Apostles.

acteur, trice [aktœr, tris] *nm, f* CINÉ & THÉÂTRE actor (*f* actress) ▪ **~ de genre** character actor.
◆ **acteur** *nm fig* protagonist ▪ **les ~s du drame** the people involved in the drama.

actif, ive [aktif, iv] *adj* **1.** [qui participe - membre, militaire, supporter] active ▪ **participer de façon** *ou* **prendre une part active à** to take part fully *ou* an active part in **2.** [dynamique - vie] busy, active ; [- personne] active, lively, energetic ▪ **la Bourse a été très active aujourd'hui** trading on the stock market was brisk today **3.** [qui travaille - population] working, active **4.** [efficace - remède, substance] active, potent ; [- shampooing] active **5.** ÉLECTR, LING & OPT active **6.** CHIM active, activated.
◆ **actif** *nm* **1.** LING active voice, *voir aussi* **pluriel 2.** [travailleur] member of the active *ou* working population ▪ **les ~s** the active *ou* working population **3.** FIN & DR [patrimoine] credit, credits, asset, assets ▪ **mettre** *ou* **porter une somme à l'~ de qqn** to add a sum to sb's assets ▪ **mettre qqch à l'~ de qqn** *fig* to credit sb with sthg ▪ **avoir qqch à son ~** to have sthg to one's credit ▶ **~ fictif/réel** fictitious/real assets ▪ **~ net** net assets.
◆ **active** *nf* MIL : **l'active** the regular army.

action [aksjɔ̃] *nf* **1.** [acte] action, act ▪ **responsable de ses ~s** responsible for his actions ▶ **une ~ de grâces** an offering of thanks ▪ **bonne/mauvaise ~** good/evil deed ▪ **faire une bonne ~** to do a good deed ▪ **faire une mauvaise ~** to commit an evil deed ▪ **faire de mauvaises ~s** to commit evil (deeds)
2. [activité] action *(U)* ▪ **l'~ du gouvernement a été de laisser les forces s'équilibrer** the government's course of action was to let the various forces balance each other out ▪ **passer à l'~** [gén] to take action ; MIL to go into action ▪ **assez parlé, il est temps de passer à l'~** enough talking, let's get down to it *ou* take some action ▪ **dans le feu de l'~, en pleine ~** right in the middle *ou* at the heart of the action ▪ **l'~ se passe en Europe/l'an 2000** the action takes place in Europe/the year 2000
3. [intervention] action ▪ **un conflit qui nécessite une ~ immédiate de notre part** a conflict necessitating immediate action on our part ▪ **une ~ syndicale est à prévoir** some industrial action is expected ▶ **~ directe** direct action ▪ **l'Action française** *French nationalist and royalist group founded in the late nineteenth century*
4. [effet] action, effect ▪ **l'~ de l'acide sur le métal** the action of acid on metal ▪ **un médicament à l'~ lente** a slow-acting medicine
5. FIN share ▪ **ses ~s ont baissé/monté** *fig & hum* his stock has fallen/risen *fig* ▶ **~ de capital** ≃ ordinary share ▪ **~ différée/nominative** deferred/registered stock ▪ **~ ordinaire** ordinary share ▪ **~ au porteur** transferable *ou* bearer share ▪ **~s cotées en Bourse** common stock ▪ **~ préférentielle** preference share *UK*, preferred share *US* ▪ **capital en ~s** equity capital ▪ **dividende en ~s** bonus issue *UK*, stock dividend *US* ▪ **société par ~s** joint-stock company
6. DR action, lawsuit ▪ **intenter une ~ contre** *ou* **à qqn** to bring an action against sb, to take legal action against sb, to take sb to court ▶ **~ civile/en diffamation** civil/libel action
7. ADMIN : **~ sanitaire et sociale** health and social services
8. MIL & PHYS action ▪ **à double ~** double-action
9. GRAMM action ▶ **verbe d'~** action verb
10. *Suisse* [vente promotionnelle] sale, special offer.
◆ **d'action** *loc adj* **1.** [mouvementé - roman] action-packed ▪ **film d'~** action film
2. [qui aime agir] : **homme/femme d'~** man/woman of action
3. POLIT & SOCIOL : **journée/semaine d'~** day/week of action.
◆ **en action** *loc adv & loc adj* in action ▪ **être en ~** to be in action ▪ **ils sont déjà en ~ sur les lieux** they're already busy on the scene ▪ **entrer en ~** [pompiers, police] to go into action ; [loi, règlement] to become effective, to take effect ▪ **mettre qqch en ~** to set sthg in motion ▪ **la sirène s'est/a été mise en ~** the alarm went off/was set off.
◆ **sous l'action de** *loc prép* due to, because of.

actionnable [aksjɔnabl] *adj* actionable.

actionnaire [aksjɔnɛr] *nmf* shareholder, stockholder.

actionnariat [aksjɔnarja] *nm* **1.** [système] shareholding **2.** [actionnaires] : **l'~** the shareholders.

actionner [3] [aksjɔne] *vt* **1.** [mettre en mouvement - appareil] to start up *(sép)* ; [- sirène] to set off *(sép)* ; [- sonnette] to ring ▪ **le moteur est actionné par la vapeur** the engine is steam-powered *ou* steam-driven **2.** DR : **~ qqn** to bring an action against *ou* to sue sb.

activateur [aktivatœr] *nm* activator.

activation [aktivasjɔ̃] *nf* **1.** [d'un processus, de travaux] speeding up *ou* along, hastening **2.** CHIM & PHYS activation.

active [aktiv] *f* ▷ **actif**.

activé, e [aktive] *adj* CHIM & PHYS activated.

activement [aktivmɑ̃] *adv* actively ▪ **participer ~ à qqch** to take an active part *ou* to be actively engaged in sthg.

activer [3] [aktive] *vt* **1.** [feu] to stoke (up) ▪ [travaux, processus] to speed up *(sép)* **2.** *fam* [presser] : **active le pas!** get a move on! **3.** CHIM & PHYS to activate.
◆ **s'activer** *vpi* **1.** [s'affairer] to bustle about **2.** *fam* [se dépêcher] : **il est tard, dis-leur de s'~!** it's late, tell them to get a move on.

activisme [aktivism] *nm* activism.

activiste [aktivist] *adj & nmf* activist, militant.

activité [aktivite] *nf* **1.** [animation] activity *(U)* ▪ **le restaurant/l'aéroport débordait d'~** the restaurant/airport was very busy **2.** ADMIN & ÉCON : **avoir une ~ professionnelle** to be actively employed ▪ **être sans ~** to be unemployed ▪ **~ lucrative** gainful employment **3.** [occupation] activity ▪ **mes ~s professionnelles** my professional activities ▶ **~s dirigées** guided activities ▪ **~s d'éveil** discovery classes **4.** ASTRON & PHYSIOL activity ▪ **~ cérébrale** brain activity.
◆ **en activité** *loc adj* [fonctionnaire, militaire] (currently) in post ▪ [médecin] practising ▪ **rester en ~** ADMIN to remain in gainful employment.
◆ **en pleine activité** *loc adj* [industrie, usine] fully operational ▪ [bureau, restaurant] bustling ▪ [marché boursier, secteur] very busy ▪ **être en pleine ~** [très affairé] to be very busy ; [non retraité] to be in the middle of one's working life.

actrice [aktris] *f* ▷ **acteur**.

actuaire [aktɥɛr] *nmf* actuary.

actualisation [aktɥalizasjɔ̃] *nf* **1.** [mise à jour - d'un texte] updating ▪ **faire l'~ d'un ouvrage** to update a work **2.** PHILOS actualization **3.** ÉCON & FIN discounting **4.** LING realization.

actualiser [3] [aktɥalize] *vt* **1.** [manuel] to update, to bring up to date **2.** PHILOS & LING to actualize.

actualité [aktɥalite] *nf* **1.** [caractère actuel] topicality **2.** [événements récents] current developments ▪ **l'~ médicale/scientifique** medical/scientific developments ▪ **se tenir au courant de l'~ politique/théâtrale** to keep abreast of political/theatrical events ▪ **une question d'une ~ brûlante** a question of burning importance.
◆ **actualités** *nfpl* : **les ~s** [les informations] current affairs, the news.
◆ **d'actualité** *loc adj* [film, débat, roman] topical ▪ **c'est un sujet d'~** it's very topical (at the moment).

actuariel, elle [aktɥarjɛl] *adj* actuarial.

actuel, elle [aktɥɛl] *adj* **1.** [présent] present, current ▪ **sous le gouvernement ~** under the present government ▪ **l'~ président** the President in office ▪ **dans les circonstances ~les** under the present circumstances **2.** [d'actualité] topical **3.** PHILOS & RELIG actual.

actuellement [aktɥɛlmɑ̃] *adv* [à présent] at present, at the moment ▪ [de nos jours] nowadays, currently.

acuité [akɥite] *nf* **1.** ACOUST shrillness **2.** [intensité - de l'intelligence] sharpness ; [- d'une crise] severity ; [- du regard] penetration ; [- d'un chagrin] keenness ; [- d'une douleur] intensity, acuteness **3.** MÉD acuity, acuteness ▪ **~ visuelle** acuteness of vision.

acuponcteur, trice, acupuncteur, trice [akypɔ̃ktœr, tris] *nm, f* acupuncturist.

acuponcture, acupuncture [akypɔ̃ktyr] *nf* acupuncture.

acyclique [asiklik] *adj* acyclic.

ADAC [adak] (*abr de* **avion à décollage et atterrissage courts**) *nm* STOL.

adage [adaʒ] *nm* **1.** [maxime] adage, saying **2.** DANSE adagio.

adagio [adadʒjo] *nm & adv* adagio.

Adam [adɑ̃] *npr* Adam.

adamantin, e [adamɑ̃tɛ̃, in] *adj* ANAT & *litt* adamantine.

adaptabilité [adaptabilite] *nf* adaptability.

adaptable [adaptabl] *adj* adaptable.

adaptateur, trice [adaptatœr, tris] *nm, f* [personne] adapter, adaptor.
◆ **adaptateur** *nm* [objet] adapter, adaptor.

adaptatif, ive [adaptatif, iv] *adj* adaptive.

adaptation [adaptasjɔ̃] *nf* **1.** [flexibilité] adaptation ▪ **faculté d'~** adaptability ▪ **ils n'ont fait aucun effort d'~** they didn't try to adapt **2.** CINÉ, THÉÂTRE & TV adaptation, adapted version ▪ **~ scénique/cinématographique** stage/screen adaptation.

adapter [3] [adapte] *vt* **1.** [fixer] : **~ qqch à** *ou* **sur** : **~ un embout à un tuyau/un filtre sur un objectif** to fit a nozzle onto a pipe/a filter onto a lens **2.** [harmoniser qqch avec] : **~ qqch à** : **~ son discours à son public** to fit one's language to one's audience ▪ **adapté aux circonstances** appropriate ▪ **la méthode n'est pas vraiment adaptée à la situation** the method isn't very appropriate for this situation **3.** CINÉ, THÉÂTRE & TV to adapt ▪ **adapté d'une nouvelle de...** adapted from a short story by...
◆ **s'adapter** *vpi* **1.** [s'ajuster] : **s'~ à** to fit ▪ **s'~ sur** to fit on **2.** [s'habituer] to adapt (o.s.) ▪ **savoir s'~** to be adaptable ▪ **elle n'a pas pu s'~ à ce milieu** she couldn't adjust to this social circle ▪ **il s'est bien adapté à sa nouvelle école** he has settled down well in his new school.

ADAV [adav] (*abr de* **avion à décollage et atterrissage verticaux**) *nm* VTOL.

ADD (*abr écrite de* **analogique digital digital**) ADD.

addenda [adɛ̃da] *nm inv* addenda.

addiction [adiksjɔ̃] *nf* (drug) addiction.

additif, ive [aditif, iv] *adj* MATH & PHOTO additive.
◆ **additif** *nm* **1.** [à un texte] additional clause **2.** [ingrédient] additive.

addition [adisjɔ̃] *nf* **1.** [ajout] addition ▪ **faire des ~s à un texte** to add to a text **2.** MATH sum ▪ **faire une ~** to add (figures) up, to do a sum **3.** [facture] bill *UK*, check *US*.

additionnel, elle [adisjɔnɛl] *adj* additional.

additionner [3] [adisjɔne] *vt* **1.** MATH [nombres] to add (up) ▪ **~ 15 et 57** to add 15 and 57, to add 15 to 57, to add together 15 and 57 **2.** [altérer] : **~ qqch de** : **du vin/lait additionné d'eau** watered-down wine/milk.
◆ **s'additionner** *vpi* to build up.

adducteur [adyktœr] <> *adj m* [muscle] adductor ▪ [canal] feeder.
<> *nm* [muscle] adductor ▪ [canal] feeder (canal).

adduction [adyksjɔ̃] *nf* **1.** ANAT adduction **2.** TRAV PUB : **~ d'eau** water conveyance.

Adélie [adeli] *npr* ▷ **terre**.

adénome [adenom] *nm* adenoma.

adepte [adɛpt] *nmf* **1.** RELIG & POLIT follower **2.** *fig* **faire des ~s** to become popular ▪ **les ~s du tennis** tennis fans ▪ **c'est une ~ de romans policiers** she's an avid reader of detective novels.

adéquat, e [adekwa, at] *adj* suitable, appropriate.

adéquatement [adekwatmɑ̃] *adv* suitably, appropriately.

adéquation [adekwasjɔ̃] *nf* appropriateness.

adhérence [aderɑ̃s] *nf* **1.** [par la colle, le ciment] adhesion **2.** [au sol] adhesion, grip ▪ **le manque d'~ d'une voiture** a car's lack of *ou* poor road-holding **3.** ANAT adhesion.

adhérent, e [aderɑ̃, ɑ̃t] <> *adj* **1.** [gén] adherent ▪ **~ à la route** with good road-holding **2.** BOT adherent, adnate.
<> *nm, f* member.

adhérer [18] [adere] ◆ **adhérer à** *v+prép* **1.** [coller sur] to adhere to ▪ **~ à la route** to hold the road ▪ (*en usage absolu*) **une colle qui adhère rapidement** a glue that sticks quickly **2.** [se rallier à - opinion] to adhere to, to support ; [- cause] to support ; [- idéal] to adhere to ; [- association] to join, to become a member of ▪ **ils promettent n'importe quoi pour faire ~ les gens à leur parti** they make all sorts of promises to get people to join their party.

adhésif, ive [adezif, iv] *adj* adhesive, sticky.
◆ **adhésif** *nm* **1.** [substance] adhesive **2.** [ruban] sticky tape, Sellotape® *UK*, Scotch tape® *US*.

adhésion [adezjɔ̃] *nf* **1.** [accord] support, adherence ▪ **donner son ~ à un projet** to give one's support to *ou* to support a project **2.** [inscription] membership ▪ **l'~ au club est gratuite** club membership is free ▪ **de plus en plus d'~s** more and more members.

adhésivité [adezivite] *nf* adhesiveness.

ad hoc [adɔk] *loc adj inv* **1.** [approprié] appropriate, suitable **2.** [destiné à tel usage - règle, raisonnement, commission] ad hoc ▪ **juge ~** specially appointed judge ▪ **réunions ~** meetings (organized) on an ad hoc basis.

adieu, x [adjø] *nm* farewell *litt*, good-bye ▪ **des ~x émouvants** an emotional parting ▪ **faire ses ~x à qqn** to say good-bye *ou* one's farewells to sb ▪ **faire ses ~x à la scène/au music-hall** to make one's final appearance on stage/on a music-hall stage ▪ **dire ~ à qqn** to say good-bye *ou* farewell to sb ▪ **tu peux dire ~ à ta voiture/tes ambitions** you can say good-bye to your car/ambitions.
◆ **adieu** *interj* farewell *litt*, goodbye ▪ **~ Berthe!** *fam* that's the end of it!
◆ **d'adieu** *loc adj inv* [baiser] farewell (*modif*) ▪ [regard, cadeau] parting.

à-Dieu-va(t) [adjøva(t)] *interj* it's in God's hands.

adipeux, euse [adipø, øz] *adj* [tissu, cellule] adipose ▪ [visage] puffed up, puffy.

adiposité [adipozite] *nf* adiposity.

adjacent, e [adʒasɑ̃, ɑ̃t] *adj* adjacent, adjoining ▪ **~ à qqch** adjacent to *ou* adjoining sthg.

adjectif, ive [adʒɛktif, iv], **adjectival, e, aux** [adʒɛktival, o] *adj* adjective *(modif)*, adjectival.
◆ **adjectif** *nm* adjective.

adjectivement [adʒɛktivmɑ̃] *adv* adjectivally, as an adjective.

adjectiver [3] [adʒɛktive], **adjectiviser** [3] [adʒɛktivize] *vt* to use as an adjective.

adjoindre [82] [adjwɛ̃dr] *vt* **1.** [ajouter] : **~ à** to add to ▪ **~ une véranda à une pièce** to add a conservatory *ou* veranda on to a room **2.** [associer] : **~ qqn à : on m'a adjoint un secrétaire/une assistante** I was given a secretary/an assistant.
◆ **s'adjoindre** *vpt* : **s'~ qqn** to take sb on.

adjoint, e [adʒwɛ̃, ɛ̃t] ◇ *adj* assistant *(modif)*.
◇ *nm, f* [assistant] assistant ▪ **~ au maire** deputy mayor ▪ **~ d'enseignement** assistant teacher.
◆ **adjoint** *nm* MIL adjunct.

adjonction [adʒɔ̃ksjɔ̃] *nf* **1.** [fait d'ajouter] adding ▪ **'sans ~ de sucre/sel'** 'with no added sugar/salt' **2.** [chose ajoutée] addition ▪ **biffer les ~s** to cross out the addenda.

adjudant, e [adʒydɑ̃, ɑ̃t] *nm, f* **1.** MIL [dans l'armée de terre] ≃ warrant officer 2nd class *UK*, ≃ warrant officer *US* ▪ [dans l'armée de l'air] ≃ warrant officer *UK*, ≃ chief master sergeant *US* **2.** *fam hum* **bien, mon ~!** yes sir!

adjudant-chef, adjudante-chef [adʒydɑ̃ʃɛf, adʒydɑ̃tʃɛf] *(mpl* **adjudants-chefs**, *fpl* **adjudantes-chefs**) *nm, f* [dans l'armée de terre] ≃ warrant officer 1st class *UK*, ≃ chief warrant officer *US* ▪ [dans l'armée de l'air] ≃ warrant officer *UK*, ≃ chief warrant officer *US*.

adjudicataire [adʒydikatɛr] *nmf* **1.** [aux enchères] successful bidder **2.** [d'un appel d'offres] successful tenderer.

adjudicateur, trice [adʒydikatœr, tris] *nm, f* **1.** [dans des enchères] seller **2.** [dans un appel d'offres] awarder *(of a contract)*.

adjudication [adʒydikasjɔ̃] *nf* **1.** [enchères] auction sale ▪ [attribution] auctioning (off) **2.** COMM [appel d'offres] invitation to tender *UK ou* bid *US* ▪ [attribution] awarding, allocation.
◆ **en adjudication** *loc adv* : **mettre une propriété en ~** to put a property up for (sale by) auction ▪ **mettre un marché en ~** to put a contract out to tender.
◆ **par adjudication, par voie d'adjudication** *loc adv* **1.** [aux enchères] by auction **2.** COMM by tender.

adjuger [17] [adʒyʒe] *vt* **1.** [aux enchères] : **~ qqch à qqn** to knock sthg down to sb ▪ **~ un objet au plus offrant** to sell an item to the highest bidder ▪ **une fois, deux fois, trois fois, adjugé, vendu!** going, going, gone! ▪ **adjugé, vendu!** *fig* gone!, done! **2.** [attribuer] : **~ un contrat/marché à qqn** to award a contract/market to sb ▪ **~ une note à qqn** to give sb a mark *UK ou* grade *US*.
◆ **s'adjuger** *vpt* to take ▪ **elle s'est adjugé la plus jolie chambre** she took *ou* commandeered the prettiest room.

adjuration [adʒyrasjɔ̃] *nf sout* plea, entreaty.

adjurer [3] [adʒyre] *vt sout* to entreat, to implore.

adjuvant, e [adʒyvɑ̃, ɑ̃t] *adj* adjuvant, auxiliary.
◆ **adjuvant** *nm* **1.** MÉD [médicament] adjuvant **2.** [produit] additive.

ad lib(itum) [adlib(itɔm)] *loc adv* ad lib.

admettre [84] [admɛtr] *vt* **1.** [laisser entrer - client, spectateur] to allow *ou* to let in *(sép)* ▪ **'on n'admet pas les animaux'** 'pets are not allowed', 'no pets' ▪ **les enfants de moins de 10 ans ne sont pas admis** children under the age of 10 are not admitted **2.** MÉCAN to let in *(sép)*
3. [recevoir] : **~ qqn dans un groupe** to let *ou* to allow sb into a group ▪ **~ qqn dans un club** to admit sb to (membership of) a club ▪ **faire ~ qqn dans un club** to sponsor sb for membership of a club ▪ **elle a été admise à l'Académie/à l'hôpital** she was elected to the Académie/admitted to hospital
4. ÉDUC to pass ▪ **être admis** to pass ▮ [dans une classe] : **il ne sera pas admis en classe supérieure** he won't be admitted to *ou* allowed into the next year *UK ou* class *US*
5. [reconnaître] to admit to ▪ **j'admets mon erreur/mon incertitude** I admit I was wrong/I am unsure ▪ **j'admets m'être trompé** I admit *ou* accept that I made a mistake ▪ **il faut ~ que c'est un résultat inattendu** you've got to admit the result is unexpected ▮ [accepter] : **il n'a pas reçu ta lettre, admettons** OK, so he didn't get your letter ▪ **~ que : j'admets que les choses se sont/se soient passées ainsi** I accept that things did happen/may have happened that way
6. [permettre - suj: personne] to tolerate, to stand for *(insép)* ; [- suj: chose] to allow, to admit *ou* to be susceptible of *sout* ▪ **tout texte admet de multiples interprétations** any text can lend itself to many different readings ▪ **un ton qui n'admet pas la discussion** *ou* **réplique** a tone brooking no argument ▪ **le règlement n'admet aucune dérogation** there shall be no breach of the regulations ▪ **je n'admets pas d'être accusé sans preuve** I refuse to let myself be accused without proof ▪ **je n'admets pas qu'on me parle sur ce ton!** I won't tolerate *ou* stand for this kind of talk!
7. [supposer] to assume.
◆ **admettons que** *loc conj* let's suppose *ou* assume, supposing, assuming.
◆ **en admettant que** *loc conj* supposing *ou* assuming (that).

administrateur, trice [administratœr, tris] *nm, f* **1.** [dans une société] director ▪ **il est l'~/elle est l'administratrice de l'entreprise** he's/she's the director of the firm ➋ **~ de biens** property manager ▪ **~ judiciaire** receiver **2.** [dans les affaires publiques] administrator **3.** [dans une institution, une fondation] trustee **4.** INFORM : **~ de site (Web)** webmaster.

administratif, ive [administratif, iv] *adj* administrative.

administration [administrasjɔ̃] *nf* **1.** [fait de donner] : **l'~ d'un remède/sédatif** administering a remedy/sedative **2.** [gestion - d'une entreprise] management ; [- d'une institution] administration ; [- de biens] management, administration ; [- d'un pays] government, running ; [- d'une commune] running ▪ **la mauvaise ~ d'une société** mismanagement of a company ➋ **~ légale** guardianship **3.** [fonction publique] : **l'Administration** the Civil Service ▪ **entrer dans l'Administration** to become a civil servant, to enter the Civil Service **4.** [service public] : **~ communale** local government ▪ **l'~ des Douanes** the Customs and Excise *UK*, the Customs Service *US* ▪ **l'~ des Eaux et forêts** the Forestry and Wildlife Commission ▪ **l'~ des Impôts** the Inland Revenue *UK*, the Internal Revenue Service *US* **5.** [équipe présidentielle] : **l'Administration Bush** the Bush administration.

administré, e [administre] *nm, f* citizen.

administrer [3] [administre] *vt* **1.** [diriger - entreprise] to manage ; [- institution, fondation, département, bien] to administer, to run ; [- succession] to be a trustee of ; [- pays] to govern, to run ; [- commune] to run **2.** [donner - remède, sacrement] to administer ; [- gifle, fessée] to give ▪ **se faire ~ les derniers sacrements** to be given the last rites **3.** *sout* [preuve] to produce, to adduce ▪ **~ la justice** to apply the law.

admirable [admirabl] *adj* admirable.

admirablement [admirabləmɑ̃] *adv* wonderfully.

admirateur, trice [admiratœr, tris] *nm, f* admirer.

admiratif, ive [admiratif, iv] *adj* admiring ▪ **son regard était ~** he looked impressed.

admiration [admirasjɔ̃] *nf* admiration, wonder ▪ **avoir** *ou* **éprouver de l'~ pour** to admire ▪ **être en ~ devant qqn/qqch** to be filled with admiration for sb/sthg.

admirativement [admirativmɑ̃] *adv* admiringly.

admirer [3] [admire] *vt* to admire ▪ **je l'admire, ça n'a pas dû être facile** I'm full of admiration for him, it can't have been easy ■ **il m'a fait ~ sa voiture** he showed off his car to me ■ **elle nous a fait ~ la vue de la terrasse** she took us onto the terrace so that we could admire the view.

admis, e [admi, iz] *pp* ▷ **admettre.**

admissibilité [admisibilite] *nf* **1.** [d'une proposition, d'un procédé] acceptability **2.** ÉDUC [après la première partie] *eligibility to take the second part of an exam* ■ [après l'écrit] *eligibility to take the oral exam.*

admissible [admisibl] *adj* **1.** [procédé, excuse] acceptable ■ **il n'est pas ~ que...** it is unacceptable that... **2.** ÉDUC [après la première partie] *eligible to take the second part of an exam* ■ [après l'écrit] *eligible to take the oral exam.*

admission [admisjɔ̃] *nf* **1.** [accueil] admission, admittance, entry ■ **demande d'~** [à l'hôpital] admission form ; [dans un club] membership application **2.** ÉDUC : **~ à un examen** passing an exam ■ **son ~ à la faculté** his admission to *ou* his being admitted to the university **3.** MÉCAN induction **4.** TECHNOL intake **5.** BOURSE : **~ à la cote** admission to quotation.

admonestation [admɔnɛstasjɔ̃] *nf litt* admonition *litt.*

admonester [3] [admɔnɛste] *vt litt* to admonish.

admonition [admɔnisjɔ̃] *nf* **1.** *litt* [reproche] admonition *litt* **2.** RELIG admonition.

ADN (*abr de* **acide désoxyribonucléique**) *nm* DNA.

ado [ado] (*abr de* **adolescent**) *nmf fam* teenager.

adolescence [adɔlesɑ̃s] *nf* adolescence ■ **il a eu une ~ difficile** he was a difficult teenager.

adolescent, e [adɔlesɑ̃, ɑ̃t] *nm, f* adolescent, teenager.

adonis [adɔnis] *nm* Adonis ■ **ce n'est pas un ~!** he's no beauty!

Adonis [adɔnis] *npr* Adonis.

adonner [3] [adɔne] ◆ **s'adonner à** *vp+prép* [lecture, sport, loisirs] to devote o.s. to, to go in for ■ [travail, études] to devote o.s. to, to immerse o.s. in ■ **s'~ à la boisson/au jeu** to take to drink/to gambling.

adoptable [adɔptabl] *adj* adoptable.

adoptant, e [adɔptɑ̃, ɑ̃t] ◇ *adj* adopting.
◇ *nm, f* adopter.

adopté, e [adɔpte] ◇ *adj* adopted.
◇ *nm, f* adoptee.

adopter [3] [adɔpte] *vt* **1.** [enfant] to adopt ■ **ses beaux-parents l'ont tout de suite adoptée** *fig* her in-laws took an instant liking to her **2.** [suivre - cause] to take up *(sép)* ; [- point de vue] to adopt, to approve ; [- politique] to adopt, to take up ; [- loi, projet] to adopt, to pass ; [- mode] to follow, to adopt ■ **ils ont fait ~ le projet de loi par l'Assemblée** they managed to get the bill through Parliament **3.** [se mettre dans - position, posture] to adopt, to assume **4.** [emprunter - nom] to assume ; [- accent] to put on *(sép)* ■ **~ un profil bas** to adopt a low profile.

adoptif, ive [adɔptif, iv] *adj* [enfant] adopted ■ [parent] adoptive ■ [patrie] adopted.

adoption [adɔpsjɔ̃] *nf* **1.** [d'un enfant] adoption **2.** [d'une loi, d'un projet] adoption, passing.
◆ **d'adoption** *loc adj* [pays] adopted ■ **c'est un Parisien d'~** he's Parisian by adoption, he's adopted Paris as his home town.

adorable [adɔrabl] *adj* **1.** [charmant - personne] adorable ; [- endroit] beautiful ; [- vêtement] lovely ; [- sourire] charming **2.** RELIG worthy of adoration, adorable.

adorablement [adɔrabləmɑ̃] *adv* adorably.

adorateur, trice [adɔratœr, tris] *nm, f* **1.** RELIG worshipper **2.** [admirateur] fan, admirer.

adoration [adɔrasjɔ̃] *nf* **1.** RELIG worship, adoration **2.** [admiration] adoration ■ **être en ~ devant qqn** to dote on *ou* to worship sb.

adorer [3] [adɔre] *vt* **1.** [aimer - personne] to adore, to love ; [- maison, robe, livre] to love, to adore ■ **elle adore les roses/lire/qu'on lui écrive** she loves roses/to read/to get letters **2.** RELIG to adore, to worship.
◆ **s'adorer** *vp (emploi réciproque)* to adore each other.

adossé, e [adose] *adj* : **être ~ à** : **elle était ~e au mur** she was leaning against the wall ■ **une maison ~e à la colline** a house built right up against the hillside.

adosser [3] [adose] *vt* : **~ qqch à** *ou* **contre qqch** to put sthg (up) against sthg.
◆ **s'adosser** *vpi* : **s'~ à** *ou* **contre qqch** to lean against sthg.

adouber [3] [adube] *vt* **1.** [chevalier] to dub **2.** JEUX to adjust.

adoucir [32] [adusir] *vt* **1.** [rendre plus doux - peau, regard, voix, eau] to soften ; [- amertume, caractère, acidité] to take the edge off ■ **l'âge l'a beaucoup adouci** he's mellowed a lot with age ■ **du miel pour ~ votre thé** honey to sweeten your tea **2.** [atténuer - couleur, propos, dureté] to tone down *(sép)* ; [- difficulté, antagonisme] to ease **3.** [rendre supportable - peine, punition] to reduce, to lessen the severity of ; [- chagrin] to ease ■ **ils s'efforcent d'~ les conditions de vie des prisonniers** they try to make the prisoners' living conditions less harsh **4.** MÉTALL to temper down *(sép)*, to soften **5.** MÉTÉOR [temps, température] to make warmer *ou* milder.
◆ **s'adoucir** *vpi* **1.** [devenir plus doux - peau, voix, lumière] to soften ; [- regard] to soften ; [- personne, caractère] to mellow **2.** MÉTÉOR [temps, température] to become milder **3.** [s'atténuer - pente] to become less steep ; [- accent] to become less broad **4.** ŒNOL to mellow.

adoucissant, e [adusisɑ̃, ɑ̃t] *adj* emollient.
◆ **adoucissant** *nm* **1.** MÉD emollient **2.** [pour le linge] fabric conditioner.

adoucissement [adusismɑ̃] *nm* **1.** [de la peau, de l'eau] softening ■ [d'un caractère] softening, mellowing ■ **un imperceptible ~ de son regard/sa voix** an imperceptible softening in his look/voice **2.** [estompage - d'une couleur, d'un contraste] softening, toning down **3.** [atténuation - d'une peine] reduction **4.** MÉTÉOR : **~ de la température** rise in temperature **5.** MÉTALL tempering, softening.

adoucisseur [adusisœr] *nm* : **~ (d'eau)** water softener.

ad patres [adpatrɛs] *loc adv fam* **envoyer qqn ~** to send sb to (meet) his maker.

adr. 1. = **adresse 2.** = **adresser.**

adrénaline [adrenalin] *nf* adrenalin.

adressage [adrɛsaʒ] *nm* addressing ■ **~ multiple** multiple selection.

adresse [adrɛs] *nf* **1.** [domicile] address ■ **parti sans laisser d'~** gone without leaving a forwarding address ◐ **une bonne ~** [magasin] a good shop *UK ou* store *US* ; [restaurant] a good restaurant ; [hôtel] a good hotel **2.** [discours] formal speech, address **3.** [dans un dictionnaire] headword **4.** INFORM address ■ **~ de courriel, ~ électronique** email address ■ **~ Web** Web adress, URL **5.** [dextérité] skill ■ **jeu d'~** game of skill **6.** [subtilité] cleverness, adroitness ■ **répondre avec ~** to give a tactful answer.
◆ **à l'adresse de** *loc prép* intended for, aimed at.

adresser [4] [adrese] *vt* **1.** [paquet, enveloppe] to address ■ **~ qqch à qqn** to address sthg to sb ■ **cette lettre vous est adressée** this letter is addressed to you *ou* has your name on the envelope **2.** [envoyer] : **~ qqch à qqn** [gén] to address *ou* to direct sthg to sb ; [par courrier] to send *ou* to forward sthg to sb ■ **~ CV détaillé à Monique Bottin** send detailed CV to Monique Bottin **3.** [destiner] : **~ qqch à qqn** [une remarque] to address sthg to *ou* to direct sthg at sb ■ **~ la parole à qqn** to speak to sb ■ **~ un compliment à qqn** to pay sb a compliment ■ **~ un reproche à qqn** to level a reproach at sb ■ **nous ne vous adressons aucun reproche** we don't blame you in any way ■ **~ des prières à Dieu** to pray to God ■ **il leur adressait des regards furieux** he looked at them with fury in his eyes, he shot furious glances at them ■ **le clin d'œil m'était sans doute adressé** the wink was undoubtedly meant for *ou* intended for *ou* aimed at me ■ **~ un signe à qqn** to wave at sb ■ **~ un sourire à qqn** to smile at sb

4. [diriger - personne] : **~ un malade à un spécialiste** to refer a patient to a specialist ▪ **on m'a adressé à vous** I've been referred to you **5.** INFORM to address.
◆ **s'adresser à** *vp+prép* **1.** [parler à] to speak to, to address ▪ **c'est à vous que je m'adresse** I'm talking to you ▪ **le ministre s'adressera d'abord aux élus locaux** the minister will first address the local councillors ▪ **s'~ à la conscience/générosité de qqn** *fig* to appeal to sb's conscience/generosity **2.** [être destiné à] to be meant for *ou* aimed at ▪ **à qui s'adresse cette remarque?** who's this remark aimed at? **3.** [pour se renseigner] : **adressez-vous à la concierge** you'd better see the porter ▪ **il faut vous ~ au syndicat d'initiative** you should apply to the tourist office ▪ **je ne sais pas à qui m'~** I don't know who to go to.

adret [adrɛ] *nm* sunny side *(of a valley)*.

Adriatique [adrijatik] ◇ *adj* Adriatic ▪ **la mer ~** the Adriatic Sea.
◇ *npr f* : **l'~** the Adriatic (Sea).

adroit, e [adrwa, at] *adj* **1.** [habile - gén] deft, dexterous ; [- apprenti, sportif, artisan] skilful ▪ **être ~ de ses mains** to be clever with one's hands **2.** [astucieux - manœuvre] clever ; [- diplomate] skilful ; [- politique] clever ▪ **la remarque n'était pas bien ~e** it was a rather clumsy thing to say.

adroitement [adrwatmɑ̃] *adv* **1.** [avec des gestes habiles] skilfully **2.** [astucieusement] cleverly.

ADSL (*abr de* **asymmetric digital subscriber line**) *nm* ADSL ▪ **passer à l'~** to switch *ou* upgrade *ou* go over to ADSL ▪ **le confort de l'~** the convenience of ADSL.

adulateur, trice [adylatœr, tris] *litt* ◇ *adj* adulatory.
◇ *nm, f* adulator.

adulation [adylasjɔ̃] *nf litt* adulation.

aduler [3] [adyle] *vt litt* to adulate, to fawn upon *(insép)*.

adulescent, e [adylesɑ̃, ɑ̃t] *nm, f* overgrown teenager, kidult.

adulte [adylt] ◇ *adj* **1.** [individu] adult ▪ [attitude] mature ▪ **devenir ~** to become an adult, to grow up **2.** ZOOL full-grown, adult ▪ BOT full-grown.
◇ *nmf* adult ▪ **livres/films pour ~s** adult books/films.

adultération [adylterasjɔ̃] *nf* adulteration.

adultère [adyltɛr] ◇ *adj* [relation] adulterous ▪ **femme ~** adulteress ▪ **homme ~** adulterer.
◇ *nmf litt* adulterer *(f* adulteress).
◇ *nm* [infidélité] adultery ▪ **commettre l'~ avec qqn** to have an adulterous relationship with sb, to commit adultery with sb.

adultérin, e [adylterɛ̃, in] *adj* adulterine.

ad valorem [advalɔrɛm] *loc adj inv* DR [taxe] ad valorem.

advenir [40] [advənir] *vi* to happen.
◆ **il advient** *v impers* : **qu'est-il advenu de lui?** what *ou* whatever became of him? ▪ **il advient que...** it (so) happens that... ▪ **il advint que je tombai malade** it (so) happened that I fell ill, I happened to fall ill ▪ **quoi qu'il advienne, quoi qu'il puisse advenir** come what may, whatever may happen ➊ **advienne que pourra** come what may.

adventice [advɑ̃tis] *adj* PHILOS adventitious.

adventiste [advɑ̃tist] *adj* & *nmf* Adventist.

advenu, e [advəny] *pp* ▷ **advenir**.

adverbe [advɛrb] *nm* adverb.

adverbial, e, aux [advɛrbjal, o] *adj* adverbial.

adverbialement [advɛrbjalmɑ̃] *adv* [employer] adverbially.

adversaire [advɛrsɛr] *nmf* adversary, opponent ▪ **je n'ai pas peur de l'~** I'm not afraid of the opposition.

adverse [advɛrs] *adj* **1.** [bloc, opinion] opposing ▪ **dans les rangs ~s, on ne croit pas aux privatisations** privatizations aren't popular with the opposition **2.** *litt* [circonstances] adverse **3.** DR opposing.

adversité [advɛrsite] *nf* adversity ▪ **poursuivi par l'~** the victim of many misfortunes.

advient, advint *etc v* ▷ **advenir**.

ad vitam aeternam [advitametɛrnam] *loc adv* for ever.

aède [aɛd] *nm* poet *(in Ancient Greece)*.

AELE (*abr de* **Association européenne de libre-échange**) *npr f* EFTA.

AEN (*abr de* **Agence pour l'énergie nucléaire**) *npr f French atomic energy agency,* ≃ AEA.

aérateur [aeratœr] *nm* **1.** CONSTR ventilator **2.** AGRIC aerator.

aération [aerasjɔ̃] *nf* TECHNOL [d'une pièce] airing, ventilation ▪ **il faudrait un peu d'~ dans cette chambre** this room needs airing.

aéré, e [aere] *adj* **1.** [chambre] well-ventilated, airy **2.** [présentation, texte] well-spaced.

aérer [18] [aere] *vt* **1.** [ventiler - chambre, maison] to air, to ventilate **2.** [alléger] : **aère un peu ton texte avant de le rendre** improve the presentation of your text before handing it in.
◆ **s'aérer** *vp (emploi réfléchi)* to get some fresh air ▪ **s'~ l'esprit/les idées** to clear one's mind/one's thoughts.

aérien, enne [aerjɛ̃, ɛn] *adj* **1.** AÉRON [tarif, base, raid, catastrophe] air *(modif)* ▪ [combat, photographie] aerial ▪ **nos forces ~nes** our air forces **2.** [à l'air libre - câble] overhead **3.** [léger - mouvement] light, floating ▪ **d'une légèreté ~ne** as light as air **4.** TÉLÉCOM overhead.
◆ **aérien** *nm* aerial.

aérobic [aerɔbik] *nm* aerobics *(U)*.

aérobie [aerɔbi] ◇ *adj* aerobic.
◇ *nm* aerobe, aerobium.

aéro-club [aerɔklœb] (*pl* **aéro-clubs**) *nm* flying club.

aérodrome [aerɔdrom] *nm* airfield.

aérodynamique [aerɔdinamik] ◇ *adj* [étude, soufflerie] aerodynamic ▪ [ligne, profil, voiture] streamlined.
◇ *nf* aerodynamics *(U)*.

aérodynamisme [aerɔdinamism] *nm* aerodynamics *(U)*.

aérofrein [aerɔfrɛ̃] *nm* air brake.

aérogare [aerɔgar] *nf* [pour les marchandises] airport building ▪ [pour les voyageurs] air terminal.

aéroglisseur [aerɔglisœr] *nm* hovercraft.

aérogramme [aerɔgram] *nm* aerogramme.

aéromodélisme [aerɔmɔdelism] *nm* model aircraft making.

aéronaute [aerɔnot] *nmf* aeronaut.

aéronautique [aerɔnotik] ◇ *adj* aeronautic, aeronautical.
◇ *nf* aeronautics *(U)*.

aéronaval, e, als [aerɔnaval] *adj* [bataille] air and sea *(modif)*.
◆ **aéronavale** *nf* : **l'~e** ≃ Fleet Air Arm *UK*, ≃ Naval Air Command *US*.

aéronef [aerɔnɛf] *nm* aircraft.

aéronomie [aerɔnɔmi] *nf* aeronomy.

aérophagie [aerɔfaʒi] *nf* wind, aerophagia *spéc* ▪ **avoir** *ou* **faire de l'~** to have wind.

aéroport [aerɔpɔr] *nm* airport.

aéroporté, e [aerɔpɔrte] *adj* MIL airborne.

aéroportuaire [aerɔpɔrtɥɛr] *adj* airport *(modif)*.

aéropostal, e, aux [aerɔpɔstal, o] *adj* airmail *(modif)*.
◆ **Aéropostale** *npr f* : **l'Aéropostale** HIST *first French airmail service between Europe and South America* ; [filiale d'Air France] *subsidiary of Air France.*

aérosol [aerɔsɔl] *nm* COMM aerosol.

◆ **en aérosol** *loc adj* spray *(modif)* ■ **nous l'avons aussi en ~** we also have it in spray form.

aérospatial, e, aux [aerɔspasjal, o] *adj* aerospace *(modif)*.
◆ **aérospatiale** *nf* **1.** SC aerospace science **2.** INDUST aerospace industry.

aérostat [aerɔsta] *nm* aerostat.

aérostation [aerɔstasjɔ̃] *nf* aerostation.

aérostatique [aerɔstatik] ◇ *adj* aerostatic, aerostatical. ◇ *nf* aerostatics *(U)*.

aéroterrestre [aerɔterɛstr] *adj* air and land *(modif)*.

Aérotrain® [aerɔtrɛ̃] *nm* hovertrain.

aérotransporté, e [aerɔtrɑ̃spɔrte] *adj* airborne.

AF *nfpl* = **allocations familiales**.

Afars [afar] *npr mpl* **1.** [peuple] Afars **2.** GÉOGR & *vieilli* **Territoire français des ~ et des Issas** Territory of the Afars and Issas.

affabilité [afabilite] *nf sout* affability, friendliness.

affable [afabl] *adj sout* affable, friendly ■ **sous des dehors ~s** behind a benign façade.

affabulateur, trice [afabylatœr, tris] *nm, f* inveterate liar.

affabulation [afabylasjɔ̃] *nf* **1.** LITTÉR plot construction **2.** PSYCHOL mythomania.

affabuler [3] [afabyle] ◇ *vi* to invent stories. ◇ *vt* LITTÉR [intrigue] to construct.

affadir [32] [afadir] *vt* **1.** [aliments] to make bland *ou* tasteless **2.** [ternir] to make dull, to cause to fade.
◆ **s'affadir** *vpi* **1.** [aliments] to become tasteless **2.** [couleur] to fade ■ **dans sa deuxième période, ses couleurs se sont affadies** in his second period, he paints in duller shades.

affadissement [afadismɑ̃] *nm* **1.** [d'un mets] loss of taste, increased blandness **2.** [d'une couleur - par le soleil] fading ; [- par un pigment] dulling.

affaibli, e [afebli] *adj* weakened ■ **utiliser un mot dans son sens ~** to use a word in its weaker sense.

affaiblir [32] [afeblir] *vt* **1.** [personne] to weaken **2.** [atténuer] to weaken ■ **le brouillard affaiblit tous les sons** the fog muffles all sounds **3.** [armée, institution] to weaken, to undermine **4.** [monnaie] to weaken.
◆ **s'affaiblir** *vpi* **1.** [dépérir] to weaken, to become weaker ■ **s'~ de jour en jour** to get weaker and weaker every day, to get weaker by the day **2.** [s'atténuer - signification, impact] to weaken, to grow weaker ; [- lumière] to fade.

affaiblissement [afeblismɑ̃] *nm* [d'une personne, d'une idée, d'un sentiment] weakening ■ [d'une lumière, d'un bruit] fading.

affaire [afɛr] *nf* **1.** [société] business, firm, company ■ **monter une ~** to set up a business ■ **remonter une ~** to put a business back on its feet ■ **gérer** *ou* **diriger une ~** to run a business ■ **l'~ familiale** the family business
2. [marché] (business) deal *ou* transaction ■ **faire ~ avec qqn** to have dealings with sb ■ **conclure une ~ avec qqn** to clinch a deal with sb ■ **faire beaucoup d'~s** to do a lot of business ■ **une ~ (en or)** *fam* an unbeatable bargain ■ **faire une (bonne) ~** to get a (good) bargain ■ **à mon avis, ce n'est pas une ~ !** I wouldn't exactly call it a bargain! ■ **ils font des ~s en or** they're doing terrific business ■ **(c'est une) ~ conclue !, c'est une ~ faite !** it's a deal! ■ **l'~ ne se fera pas** the deal's off ■ **l'~ n'est pas encore faite !** *pr* the deal isn't clinched yet ; *fig* it's by no means a foregone conclusion ■ **c'est une ~ entendue !** we agree on that! ▶ **lui, c'est vraiment pas une ~ !** *fam* [il est insupportable] he's a real pain! ; [il est bête] he's no bright spark!
3. [problème, situation délicate] business ■ **une mauvaise** *ou* **sale ~** a nasty business ■ **ce n'est pas une mince ~, c'est tout une ~** it's quite a business ■ **quelle** *ou* **la belle ~ !** *iron* so what (does it matter)? ■ **c'est une autre ~** that's another story *ou* a different proposition ▶ **c'est une ~ de gros sous** it's a huge scam ■ **sortir** *ou* **tirer qqn d'~** [par amitié] to get sb out of trouble ; [médicalement] to pull sb through ■ **être sorti** *ou* **tiré d'~** [après une aventure, une faillite] to be out of trouble *ou* in the clear ; [après une maladie] to be off the danger list ■ **on n'est pas encore tirés d'~** we're not out of the woods yet
4. [scandale] : **~ d'État** affair of state ■ **n'en fais pas une ~ d'État !** *fig* don't blow the thing up out of all proportion! ■ **~ (politique)** (political) scandal *ou* affair ■ **l'~ Dreyfus** the Dreyfus affair ‖ [crime] murder ■ [escroquerie] business, job ■ **être sur une ~** to be in on a job
5. [procès] trial, lawsuit, case ■ **l'~ est jugée demain** the trial concludes tomorrow ■ **saisir un tribunal d'une ~** to bring a case before a judge ▶ **~ civile/correctionnelle** civil/criminal action
6. [ce qui convient] : **j'ai votre ~** *fam* I've got just the thing for you ■ **la mécanique c'est pas/c'est son ~** *fam* car engines aren't exactly/are just his cup of tea ■ **faire l'~ (de qqn) : la vieille casserole fera l'~** the old saucepan'll do ▶ **je vais lui faire son ~** *fam* I'll sort *ou* straighten him out!
7. [responsabilité] : **fais ce que tu veux, c'est ton ~** do what you like, it's your business *ou* problem ■ **en faire son ~** to take the matter in hand, to make it one's business ■ **l'architecte ? j'en fais mon ~** I'll deal with *ou* handle the architect
8. [question] : **dis-moi l'~ en deux mots** tell me briefly what the problem is ■ **l'âge/l'argent/le temps ne fait rien à l'~** age/money/time doesn't make any difference ■ **c'est l'~ d'une seconde** it can be done in a trice ■ **c'est l'~ d'un coup de fil** *fam* all it takes is a phone call ■ **c'est une ~ de vie ou de mort** it's a matter of life and death ■ **~ de principe** matter of principle ■ **~ de goût** question of taste ■ **pour une ~ de souveraineté territoriale** over some business to do with territorial sovereignty
9. *loc* **avoir ~ à** to (have to) deal with ■ **avoir ~ à forte partie** to have a strong *ou* tough opponent ■ **avoir ~ à plus fort/plus malin que soi** to be dealing with someone stronger/more cunning than o.s. ■ **il vaut mieux n'avoir pas ~ à lui** it's better to avoid having anything to do with him ■ **tu vas avoir ~ à moi si tu tires la sonnette !** if you ring the bell, you'll have me to deal with! ■ **elle a eu ~ à moi quand elle a voulu vendre la maison !** she had me to contend with when she tried to sell the house! ■ **être à son ~ : à la cuisine, il est à son ~** in the kitchen *ou* when he's cooking he's in his element ■ **tout à son ~, il ne m'a pas vu entrer** he was so absorbed in what he was doing, he didn't see me come in.
◆ **affaires** *nfpl* **1.** COMM & ÉCON business *(U)* ■ **les ~s vont bien/mal** business is good/bad ■ **être dans les ~s** to be a businessman (*f* businesswoman) ■ **les ~s sont les ~s !** business is business! ■ **pour ~s** [voyager, rencontrer] for business purposes, on business ▶ **voyage/repas d'~s** business trip/lunch
2. ADMIN & POLIT affairs ■ **être aux ~s** to run the country, to be the head of state ■ **depuis qu'il est revenu aux ~s** since he's been back in power ▶ **les ~s courantes** everyday matters ■ **les ~s de l'État** the affairs of state ■ **~s intérieures** internal *ou* domestic affairs ■ **~s internationales** international affairs ■ **~s publiques** public affairs ■ **les Affaires sociales** the Social Services (department)
3. [situation matérielle] : **ses ~s** his business affairs, his financial situation ■ **mettre de l'ordre dans ses ~s (avant de mourir)** to put one's affairs in order (before dying) ‖ [situation personnelle] : **s'il revient, elle voudra le revoir et ça n'arrangera pas tes ~s** if he comes back, she'll want to see him and that won't help the situation ■ **mêle-toi de tes ~s !** mind your own business!, keep your nose out of this! ■ **c'est mes ~s, ça te regarde pas !** *fam* that's MY business! ▶ **~s de cœur** love life
4. [objets personnels] things, belongings, (personal) possessions ■ **ses petites ~s** *hum* his little things ; *péj* his precious belongings.
◆ **en affaires** *loc adv* when (you're) doing business, in business ■ **être dur en ~s** [gén] to drive a hard bargain, to be a tough businessman (*f* businesswoman).
◆ **toutes affaires cessantes** *loc adv* forthwith ■ **toutes ~s cessantes, ils sont allés chez le maire** they dropped everything and went to see the mayor.

affairé, e [afere] *adj* busy ■ **prends un air ~** look busy, pretend you've got a lot to do ■ **ils entraient et sortaient d'un air ~** they were bustling in and out.

affairement [afɛrmɑ̃] *nm litt* bustle.

affairer [4] [afere] ◆ **s'affairer** *vpi* to bustle ▪ **il est toujours à s'~ dans la maison** he's always bustling about the house ▪ **s'~ auprès de qqn** to fuss around sb.

affairisme [aferism] *nm péj* money-making.

affairiste [aferist] *nmf péj* speculator.

affaissé, e [afese] *adj* : **le sol était ~** the ground had subsided ▪ **il était ~ sur sa chaise** he was slumped in his chair.

affaissement [afɛsmɑ̃] *nm* **1.** [effondrement] subsidence ▪ **~ de sol, ~ de terrain** subsidence **2.** [relâchement - d'un muscle, des traits] sagging **3.** [dépression] collapse, breakdown.

affaisser [4] [afese] *vt* GÉOL [terrain, sol] to cause to sink *ou* to subside.
◆ **s'affaisser** *vpi* **1.** [se tasser - gén] to subside, to collapse, to sink ; [- bâtiment] to collapse ▪ **à l'image, on voit la tour s'~ après l'explosion** on the screen, you can see the tower collapsing after the blast **2.** [s'affaler] to collapse, to slump ▪ **s'~ sur un canapé** to collapse *ou* to slump onto a couch **3.** ÉCON [monnaie, marché] to collapse, to slump.

affalement [afalmɑ̃] *nm* collapsing, slumping.

affaler [3] [afale] *vt* NAUT [voile] to haul down *(sép)*.
◆ **s'affaler** *vpi* : **s'~ dans un fauteuil** to flop into an armchair ▪ **s'~ sur le sol** to collapse on the ground.

affamé, e [afame] <> *adj* famished, starving ▪ **~ de** *litt* hungry for.
<> *nm, f* starving person.

affamer [3] [afame] *vt* to starve.

affameur, euse [afamœr, øz] *nm, f* starver.

affect [afɛkt] *nm* affect.

affectation [afɛktasjɔ̃] *nf* **1.** [manière] affectation ▪ **il n'y a aucune ~ dans son langage** her language is not at all affected ▪ **avec ~** affectedly **2.** [attribution] allocation ▪ **l'~ de l'aile sud aux services administratifs** allocating the south wing to administration **3.** [assignation] appointment, nomination ▪ MIL posting ▪ **il a reçu son ~ en Allemagne** MIL he was posted to Germany.

affecté, e [afɛkte] *adj* [personne] affected, mannered ▪ **parler d'une manière ~e** to speak affectedly.

affecter [4] [afɛkte] *vt* **1.** [feindre] to affect, to feign ▪ **~ une grande joie** to pretend to be overjoyed ▪ **il a affecté l'indifférence** he feigned indifference, he put on a show of indifference **2.** [présenter - une forme] : **~ la forme d'un cône** to be cone-shaped **3.** [assigner] to allocate, to assign ▪ **~ des crédits à la recherche** to allocate funds to research **4.** [nommer - à une fonction] to appoint, to nominate ; [- à une ville, un pays] to post ▪ **être affecté à un poste** to be appointed to a post ▪ **son père l'a fait ~ à Paris** his father got him a post in Paris **5.** [atteindre] to affect ▪ **le virus a affecté les deux reins** both kidneys were affected by the virus **6.** [émouvoir] to affect, to move ▪ **très affecté par cette lettre/l'accident de ses parents** greatly affected by this letter/his parents' accident **7.** MATH to modify.

affectif, ive [afɛktif, iv] *adj* **1.** [problème, réaction] emotional **2.** PSYCHOL affective.

affection [afɛksjɔ̃] *nf* **1.** [attachement] affection, fondness, liking ▪ **avoir de l'~ pour** to be fond of, to have a fondness for, to have a liking for ▪ **prendre qqn en ~** to become fond of sb ▪ **une marque** *ou* **un signe d'~** a token of love *ou* affection **2.** MÉD disease, disorder **3.** PSYCHOL affection.

affectionné, e [afɛksjɔne] *adj* [dans une lettre] loving.

affectionner [3] [afɛksjɔne] *vt* **1.** [objet, situation] to be fond of **2.** [personne] to like, to feel affection for.

affectivité [afɛktivite] *nf* **1.** [réactions] : **l'~** emotionality *spéc*, emotional life **2.** [caractère] sensitivity.

affectueusement [afɛktɥøzmɑ̃] *adv* **1.** [tendrement] affectionately, fondly **2.** [dans une lettre] : **bien ~** kindest regards.

affectueux, euse [afɛktɥø, øz] *adj* loving, affectionate ▪ **elle le regardait d'un air ~** she was looking at him fondly *ou* affectionately.

afférent, e [aferɑ̃, ɑ̃t] *adj* **1.** DR : **~ à** accruing to, relating to **2.** *sout* **~ à** [qui se rapporte à] relating *ou* relevant to ▪ **voici les renseignements ~s à l'affaire** here is information relating *ou* relevant to the matter **3.** MÉD [nerf, vaisseau] afferent.

affermer [3] [afɛrme] *vt* to lease *ou* to rent (out).

affermir [32] [afɛrmir] *vt* **1.** [consolider - mur] to reinforce, to strengthen **2.** [rendre plus ferme] to strengthen, to tone *ou* to firm up *(sép)* ▪ **lotion tonique pour ~ votre peau** toning lotion for your skin **3.** [assurer] to strengthen ▪ **~ sa position** to strengthen one's position ▪ **~ sa voix** to steady one's voice.
◆ **s'affermir** *vpi* **1.** [puissance, influence] to be strengthened ▪ [investissements, monnaie] to strengthen **2.** [muscle, chair] to firm *ou* to tone up, to get firmer.

affermissement [afɛrmismɑ̃] *nm* [d'un pont] strengthening, consolidating ▪ [de la peau] toning ▪ [d'une monnaie] strengthening.

affichage [afiʃaʒ] *nm* **1.** [sur une surface] posting ▪ **'~ interdit'** 'stick no bills' **2.** INFORM display ▪ **~ numérique** digital display.

affiche [afiʃ] *nf* **1.** [annonce officielle] public notice ▪ [image publicitaire] advertisement, poster ▪ [d'un film, d'une pièce, d'un concert] poster ▪ **~ électorale** election poster **2.** CINÉ & THÉÂTRE : **en tête d'~, en haut de l'~** at the top of the bill ➲ **tenir l'~** to run ▪ **quitter l'~** to close.
◆ **à l'affiche** *loc adv* : **être à l'~** to be on ▪ **mettre une pièce à l'~** to put a play on, to stage a play ▪ **rester à l'~** to run.

afficher [3] [afiʃe] *vt* **1.** [placarder] to post *ou* to stick up *(sép)* **2.** [annoncer] to bill, to have on the bill ▪ **on affiche complet pour ce soir** the house is full tonight **3.** *péj* [exhiber] to show off *(sép)*, to display, to flaunt *péj* ▪ **~ son désespoir** to make one's despair obvious ▪ **~ sa fortune/une liaison** to flaunt one's wealth/an affair **4.** INFORM to display.
◆ **s'afficher** *vpi péj* **elle s'affiche avec lui** she makes a point of being seen with him.

affichette [afiʃɛt] *nf* small poster.

afficheur [afiʃœr] *nm* billposter, billsticker.

affichiste [afiʃist] *nmf* poster designer.

affilage [afilaʒ] *nm* sharpening *(of a blade)*.

affilé, e [afile] *adj* [aiguisé] sharp ▪ **un poignard bien ~** a well-sharpened dagger.
◆ **d'affilée** *loc adv* : **il a pris plusieurs semaines de congé d'~e** he took several weeks' leave in a row ▪ **deux/trois heures d'~e** for two/three hours at a stretch.

affiler [3] [afile] *vt* [couteau, lame] to sharpen.

affiliation [afiljasjɔ̃] *nf* affiliation ▪ **demander son ~ à une organisation** to apply for membership of an organization.

affilié, e [afilje] <> *adj* affiliated ▪ **non ~** nonaffiliated.
<> *nm, f* affiliate.

affilier [9] [afilje] ◆ **s'affilier** *vp (emploi réfléchi)* **s'~ à** to affiliate o.s. *ou* to become affiliated to.

affiloir [afilwar] *nm* whetstone.

affinage [afinaʒ] *nm* [d'un fromage] maturing ▪ [du coton] fining ▪ [d'un métal, de sucre] fining, refining.

affine [afin] *adj* MATH [application, espace, géométrie] affine.

affiner [3] [afine] *vt* **1.** [purifier - verre, métal] to refine **2.** [adoucir - traits] to fine down **3.** [raffiner - goût, sens] to refine **4.** [mûrir] : **~ du fromage** to allow cheese to mature.
◆ **s'affiner** *vpi* **1.** [se raffiner] to become more refined **2.** [mincir] to become thinner.

affinité [afinite] *nf* **1.** [sympathie] affinity ▪ **avoir des ~s avec qqn** to have an affinity with sb **2.** CHIM affinity.

affirmatif, ive [afirmatif, iv] *adj* **1.** [catégorique] affirmative ▪ **il a été très ~ à ce sujet** he was quite positive about it ▪ **parler d'un ton ~** to speak affirmatively **2.** LING affirmative, *voir aussi* **pluriel**.
◆ **affirmatif** *adv* : **~!** affirmative!
◆ **affirmative** *nf* : **répondre par l'affirmative** to answer yes *ou* in the affirmative ▪ **nous aimerions savoir si vous serez libre**

mercredi; dans l'affirmative, nous vous prions de... we'd like to know if you are free on Wednesday; if you are *ou* if so, please...

affirmation [afirmasjɔ̃] *nf* **1.** [gén] affirmation **2.** DR solemn affirmation **3.** LOGIQUE affirmation.

affirmativement [afirmativmɑ̃] *adv* affirmatively.

affirmer [3] [afirme] *vt* **1.** [assurer] to assert, to affirm *sout* ▪ **rien ne permet encore d' ~ qu'il s'agit d'un acte terroriste** there is no firm evidence as yet that terrorists were involved ▪ **elle affirme ne pas l'avoir vu de la soirée** she maintains she didn't see him all evening ▪ **le Premier ministre a affirmé son désir d'en finir avec le terrorisme** the Prime Minister stated his desire to put an end to terrorism ▪ **la semaine dernière, affirma-t-il** last week, he said **2.** [exprimer - volonté, indépendance] to assert.
◆ **s'affirmer** *vpi* [personne] to assert o.s. ▪ [qualité, désir, volonté] to assert *ou* to express itself.

affixe [afiks] *nm* affix.

affleurement [aflœrmɑ̃] *nm* **1.** GÉOL outcrop **2.** MENUIS levelling.

affleurer [5] [aflœre] <> *vt* [étagère, planches] to level.
<> *vi* [écueil] to show on the surface ▪ GÉOL [filon] to outcrop ▪ *fig* to show through.

affliction [afliksjɔ̃] *nf litt* affliction.

affligé, e [afliʒe] *adj* afflicted.

affligeant, e [afliʒɑ̃, ɑ̃t] *adj* **1.** *litt* [attristant] distressing **2.** [lamentable] appalling, pathetic ▪ **d'une ignorance ~e** appallingly ignorant.

affliger [17] [afliʒe] *vt* **1.** [atteindre] to afflict, to affect ▪ **être affligé d'un handicap** to be afflicted with a handicap ▪ **elle est affligée d'un prénom ridicule** *fig* & *hum* she's cursed with a ridiculous first name **2.** *litt* [attrister] to aggrieve *litt*, to affect ▪ **sa mort m'a beaucoup affligé** his death affected me greatly.
◆ **s'affliger** *vpi litt* to be distressed, to feel grief ▪ **s'~ de** to be distressed about, to grieve over.

affluence [aflyɑ̃s] *nf* **1.** [foule] crowd ▪ **il y a ~** it's crowded **2.** *litt* [richesses] affluence.

affluent, e [aflyɑ̃, ɑ̃t] *adj* [fleuve, rivière] tributary.
◆ **affluent** *nm* tributary, affluent.

affluer [3] [aflye] *vi* **1.** [couler] to rush ▪ **le sang afflua à son visage** blood rushed to her face ▪ **les capitaux affluent** *fig* money's flowing *ou* rolling in **2.** [arriver] to surge ▪ **les manifestants affluaient vers la cathédrale** the demonstrators were flocking to the cathedral.

afflux [afly] *nm* **1.** [de sang] rush, afflux *sout* **2.** [de voyageurs] influx, flood **3.** ÉLECTR surge (of current).

affolant, e [afɔlɑ̃, ɑ̃t] *adj* **1.** [inquiétant] frightening, terrifying **2.** *fam* [en intensif] appalling.

affolé, e [afɔle] *adj* **1.** [bouleversé] panic-stricken **2.** [boussole] spinning.

affolement [afɔlmɑ̃] *nm* **1.** [panique] panic ▪ **pas d'~!** don't panic! ▪ **sans ~** in a cool(, calm) and collected way **2.** [d'une boussole] spinning.

affoler [3] [afɔle] *vt* **1.** [terrifier] to throw into a panic ▪ [bouleverser] to throw into turmoil ▪ **les poulains étaient affolés** the foals were running around panick-stricken **2.** *litt* [sexuellement] to drive wild with desire.
◆ **s'affoler** *vpi* **1.** [s'effrayer] to panic ▪ **elle s'affole toujours à l'idée de partir** she always panics *ou* gets frantic at the thought of going away **2.** [boussole] to spin.

affranchi, e [afrɑ̃ʃi] <> *adj* **1.** HIST [esclave] freed **2.** [émancipé] emancipated, liberated.
<> *nm, f* **1.** HIST [esclave libéré] freed slave **2.** △ *arg crime* shady character.

affranchir [32] [afrɑ̃ʃir] *vt* **1.** HIST [esclave] to (set) free **2.** [colis, lettre] to stamp, to put a stamp *ou* stamps on ▪ **paquet insuffisamment affranchi** parcel with insufficient postage on it **3.** △ *arg crime* [renseigner] : **~ qqn** to give sb the lowdown, to tip sb off *(sép)* **4.** JEUX [carte] to clear.
◆ **s'affranchir** *vpi* [colonie] to gain one's freedom ▪ [adolescent] to gain one's independence ▪ [opprimé] to become emancipated *ou* liberated ▪ **s'~ de la domination étrangère** to throw off foreign domination.

affranchissement [afrɑ̃ʃismɑ̃] *nm* **1.** [d'une lettre - avec des timbres] stamping ; [- à l'aide d'une machine] franking ; [- prix] postage ▪ **dispensé d'~** post-free, postage paid ▪ **~ insuffisant** insufficient postage **2.** [libération] freeing ▪ **après leur ~** after they were set free.

affres [afr] *nfpl litt* pangs ▪ **les ~ de la jalousie** the pangs of jealousy ▪ **les ~ de la création** the throes of creativity.

affrètement [afrɛtmɑ̃] *nm* chartering.

affréter [18] [afrete] *vt* [avion, navire] to charter.

affréteur [afretœr] *nm* charterer, charter company.

affreusement [afrøzmɑ̃] *adv* **1.** [en intensif] dreadfully, horribly, terribly ▪ **elle a été ~ mutilée** she was horribly mutilated **2.** [laidement] : **~ habillé/décoré** hideously dressed/decorated.

affreux, euse [afrø, øz] *adj* **1.** [répugnant] horrible, ghastly **2.** [très désagréable] dreadful, awful.
◆ **affreux** *nm fam* [mercenaire] (white) mercenary *(in Africa)*.

affriolant, e [afrijɔlɑ̃, ɑ̃t] *adj* alluring, appealing ▪ **des dessous ~s** sexy underwear.

affrioler [3] [afrijɔle] *vt* to excite, to allure.

affriquée [afrike] LING <> *adj f* [consonne] affricative.
<> *nf* affricate.

affront [afrɔ̃] *nm* affront ▪ **essuyer** *ou* **subir un ~** to be affronted *ou* offended ▪ **faire un ~ à qqn** to affront sb.

affrontement [afrɔ̃tmɑ̃] *nm* confrontation ▪ **l'~ de deux idéologies** the clash *ou* conflict of ideologies.

affronter [3] [afrɔ̃te] *vt* **1.** [ennemi, mort] to face ▪ [problème] to face (up to), to square up to *(insép)* **2.** MENUIS [planche] to butt-joint.
◆ **s'affronter** *vp (emploi réciproque)* to confront one another ▪ **deux thèses s'affrontent dans le débat sur la peine de mort** there are two opposing theories in the debate on the death penalty.

affublement [afybləmɑ̃] *nm* rigout.

affubler [3] [afyble] *vt péj* [habiller] to rig out *(sép)* ▪ **on l'avait affublé d'un surnom idiot** *fig* the poor boy had been given an absurd nickname.
◆ **s'affubler de** *vp+prép péj* to rig o.s. out in.

affût [afy] *nm* **1.** ARM carriage, mount **2.** OPT [d'un télescope] frame.
◆ **à l'affût** *loc adv* : **se mettre à l'~** CHASSE to hide out.
◆ **à l'affût de** *loc prép* **1.** CHASSE : **être à l'~ de** to be lying in wait for **2.** [à la recherche de] : **il est toujours à l'~ des ragots/des articles les plus récents** he's always on the look-out for juicy bits of gossip/the latest articles ▪ **à l'~ d'un sourire** begging for a smile.

affûter [3] [afyte] *vt* to grind, to sharpen.

affûteur [afytœr] *nm* grinder.

afghan, e [afgɑ̃, an] *adj* Afghan.
◆ **Afghan, e** *nm, f* Afghan, Afghani.

Afghanistan [afganistɑ̃] *npr m* : **(l')~** Afghanistan.

aficionado [afisjɔnado] *nm* aficionado ▪ **les ~s du football** football enthusiasts.

afin [afɛ̃] ◆ **afin de** *loc prép* in order to, so as to.
◆ **afin que** *loc conj (suivi du subjonctif)* in order *ou* so that ▪ **préviens-moi si tu viens ~ que je puisse préparer ta chambre** tell me if you are coming so that I can prepare your bedroom.

AFNOR, Afnor [afnɔr] (*abr de* **Association française de normalisation**) *npr f French industrial standards authority*, ≃ BSI *UK*, ≃ ASA *US*.

a fortiori [afɔrsjɔri] *loc adv* a fortiori, even more so, with all the more reason.

AF-P (*abr de* **Agence France-Presse**) *npr f French national news agency*.

AFPA [afpa] (*abr de* **Association pour la formation professionnelle des adultes**) *npr f government body promoting adult vocational training*.

africain, e [afrikɛ̃, ɛn] *adj* African.
◆ **Africain, e** *nm, f* African.

africaniser [3] [afrikanize] *vt* to Africanize.

africanisme [afrikanism] *nm* Africanism.

africaniste [afrikanist] *nmf* Africanist.

afrikaans [afrikɑ̃s] *nm* LING Afrikaans.

afrikaner [afrikanɛr], **afrikaander** [afrikɑ̃dɛr] *adj* Afrikaner.
◆ **Afrikaner, Afrikaander** *nmf* Afrikaner.

Afrique [afrik] *npr f* : **(l')**~ Africa ■ **(l')~ australe** Southern Africa ■ **(l')~ noire** Black Africa ■ **(l')~ du Nord** North Africa ■ **(l')~ du Sud** South Africa.

afro [afro] *adj inv* afro.

afro-américain, e [afroamerikɛ̃, ɛn] (*mpl* **afro-américains**, *fpl* **afro-américaines**) *adj* Afro-American.
◆ **Afro-Américain, e** *nm, f* Afro-American.

afro-antillais, e [afroɑ̃tijɛ, ɛz] (*mpl inv, fpl* **afro-antillaises**) *adj* Afro-Caribbean.
◆ **Afro-Antillais, e** *nm, f* Afro-Caribbean.

afro-asiatique [afroazjatik] (*pl* **afro-asiatiques**) *adj* **1.** GÉOGR Afro-Asian **2.** LING Afro-Asiatic.
◆ **Afro-Asiatique** *nmf* Afro-Asian.

afro-brésilien, enne [afrobreziljɛ̃, ɛn] (*mpl* **afro-brésiliens**, *fpl* **afro-brésiliennes**) *adj* Afro-Brazilian.
◆ **Afro-Brésilien, enne** *nm, f* Afro-Brazilian.

afro-cubain, e [afrokybɛ̃, ɛn] (*mpl* **afro-cubains**, *fpl* **afro-cubaines**) *adj* Afro-Cuban.

after-shave [aftœrʃɛv] (*pl inv*) ◇ *adj* aftershave ■ **une lotion ~** aftershave (lotion).
◇ *nm* aftershave (lotion).

AG (*abr de* **assemblée générale**) *nf* GM.

agaçant, e [agasɑ̃, ɑ̃t] *adj* [irritant] irritating, annoying.

agacement [agasmɑ̃] *nm* irritation, annoyance ■ **montrer de l'~** to show irritation.

agacer [16] [agase] *vt* **1.** [irriter] to irritate, to annoy ■ **ses plaisanteries m'agacent** his jokes get on my nerves ■ **le jus de citron agace les dents** lemon juice sets one's teeth on edge **2.** *litt* [exciter] to excite, to titivate.

agacerie [agasri] *nf* piece of flirtatiousness *ou* of coquettish behaviour ■ **faire de petites ~s à qqn** to tease sb.

agape [agap] *nf* RELIG & *arch* agape.
◆ **agapes** *nfpl hum* feast ■ **faire des ~s** to have a feast.

agate [agat] *nf* agate.

agave [agav], **agavé** [agave] *nm* agave.

AGE (*abr de* **assemblée générale extraordinaire**) *nf* EGM.

âge [aʒ] *nm* **1.** [nombre d'années] age ■ **quel ~ as-tu?** how old are you? ■ **quand j'avais ton ~** when I was your age ■ **être du même ~ que** to be the same age *ou* as old as ■ **à ton ~, on ne pleure plus** you're old enough not to cry now ■ **un garçon/une fille de ton ~ ne doit pas...** a boy/a girl (of) your age shouldn't... ■ **d'un ~ avancé** getting on *ou* advanced in years ■ **d'un ~ canonique** *hum* ancient ■ **d'un certain ~** *euphém* [dame, monsieur] middle-aged ■ **à cause de son jeune/grand ~** because he's so young/old ■ **avancer en ~** to be getting on in years ■ **avoir l'~ (de faire qqch) : il veut se marier, c'est normal, il a l'~** he wants to get married, it's normal at his age ■ **il a l'~ de prendre sa retraite** he's old enough to retire ■ **j'ai passé l'~!** I'm too old (for this kind of thing)! ■ **tu as passé l'~ de jouer aux billes** you're too old to be playing with marbles ■ **c'est de mon/son ~ : les boums, c'est de son ~** they all want to have parties at that age ■ **ce n'est pas de ton ~!** [tu es trop jeune] you're not old enough! ; [tu es trop vieux] you're too old (for it)! ■ **tu es d'~ à** *ou* **en ~ de comprendre** you're old enough to understand ■ **je ne suis plus d'~ à** *ou* **en ~ de faire du camping** I'm too old to go camping ■ **avec l'~, il s'est calmé** he mellowed with age *ou* as he grew older ■ **les effets de l'~** the effects of ageing ■ **prendre de l'~** to age, to get older ■ **j'ai mal aux genoux – c'est l'~!** my knees hurt – you're getting old! ■ **on ne lui donne vraiment pas son ~** he doesn't look his age at all ■ **quel ~ me donnez-vous?** how old do you think I am? ■ **elle ne fait** *ou* **ne paraît pas son ~** she doesn't look her age, she looks younger than she actually is ■ **elle n'a pas d'~** she seems ageless ■ **sans ~** ageless ■ **un whisky vingt ans d'~** a twenty-year-old whisky ▶ **avoir l'~ légal (pour voter)** to be old enough to vote, to be of age ■ **l'~ scolaire** compulsory school age ■ **un enfant d'~ scolaire** a school-age child, a child of school age ■ **on a l'~ de ses artères** you're as old as you feel **2.** [période] age, time (of life) ■ **la quarantaine, c'est l'~ des grandes décisions** forty is the time (of life) for making big decisions ▶ **l'~ adulte** [gén] adulthood ; [d'un homme] manhood ; [d'une femme] womanhood ■ **l'~ bête** *fam ou* **ingrat** the awkward *ou* difficult age ■ **l'~ critique** the change of life ■ **l'~ mûr** maturity ■ **l'~ de raison** the age of reason ■ **l'~ tendre** the tender years ■ **l'~ viril** manhood ■ **ne te plains pas, c'est le bel ~!** don't complain, these are the best years of your life *ou* you're in your prime! ■ **le premier ~** infancy ■ **le troisième ~** [période] old age ; [groupe social] senior citizens ■ **le quatrième ~** [période] advanced old age ; [groupe social] very old people **3.** ARCHÉOL age ■ **l'~ de bronze** the Bronze Age ■ **l'~ de fer** the Iron Age ■ **l'~ d'or** MYTHOL & *fig* the golden age **4.** PSYCHOL : **~ mental** mental age ■ **il a un ~ mental de cinq ans** he has a mental age of five.
◆ **à l'âge de** *loc prép* : **je l'ai connu à l'~ de 17 ans** [j'avais 17 ans] I met him when I was 17 ; [il avait 17 ans] I met him when he was 17 ■ **on est majeur à l'~ de 18 ans** 18 is the age of majority.
◆ **en bas âge** *loc adj* [enfant] very young *ou* small.
◆ **entre deux âges** *loc adj* [personne] middle-aged.

âgé, e [aʒe] *adj* **1.** [vieux] old ■ **elle est plus ~e que moi** she's older than I am **2.** [de tel âge] : **~ de : être ~ de 20 ans** to be 20 years old ■ **une jeune fille ~e de 15 ans** a 15-year-old girl.

agence [aʒɑ̃s] *nf* **1.** [bureau] agency ■ **~ immobilière** estate agent's *UK*, real-estate office *US* ■ **~ matrimoniale** marriage bureau ■ **~ de presse** press *ou* news agency ■ **~ de publicité** advertising agency ■ **~ de renseignements** information bureau ■ **~ de voyages** travel agency ■ **Agence France-Presse** = **AF-P** ■ **Agence nationale pour l'emploi** = **ANPE** ■ **l'~ Tass** Tass, the Tass news agency **2.** [succursale] branch ■ **quand vous passerez à l'~** when you next visit the branch.

agencement [aʒɑ̃smɑ̃] *nm* [d'un lieu] layout, design ■ [d'un texte] layout ■ [d'éléments] order, ordering.

agencer [16] [aʒɑ̃se] *vt* **1.** [aménager] to lay out ■ **un studio bien agencé** a well laid-out studio flat **2.** [organiser] to put together (*sép*), to construct.

agenda [aʒɛ̃da] *nm* diary ■ **~ électronique** personal digital assistant, PDA ; [moint puissant] electronic organizer.

agenouiller [3] [aʒnuje] ◆ **s'agenouiller** *vpi* to kneel (down) ■ **il refuse de s'~ devant le pouvoir** *fig* he refuses to bow to authority.

agent [aʒɑ̃] *nm* **1.** COMM & POLIT agent ■ ADMIN official, officer ■ **~ artistique** agent ■ **~ d'assurances** insurance agent ■ **~ de change** stockbroker ■ **~ commercial** sales representative ■ **~ comptable** accountant ■ **~ de conduite** [d'un train] train driver ■ **~ consulaire** consular agent ■ **~ double** double agent ■ **~ électoral** canvasser ■ **~ immobilier** estate agent *UK*, real estate agent *US*, realtor *US* ■ **~ de liaison** MIL liaison officer ■ **~ littéraire** literary agent ■ **~s de maîtrise** lower management ■ **~ secret** secret agent

2. [policier] : ~ **(de police)** [homme] policeman, constable *UK*, patrolman *US* ; [femme] policewoman, woman police constable *UK*, woman police officer *US* ■ ~ **de la circulation** traffic policeman ■ **s'il vous plaît, monsieur l'~** excuse me, officer
3. [cause - humaine] agent ; [- non humaine] factor ■ **elle a été l'un des principaux ~s de la révolution** she was a prime mover in the revolution ■ ~ **atmosphérique/économique** atmospheric/ economic factor ■ ~ **de conservation** preservative
4. CHIM & SC agent ■ ~ **pathogène** pathogen ■ ~ **chimique** chemical agent
5. GRAMM agent.

agglomérat [aglɔmera] *nm* **1.** GÉOL agglomerate **2.** LING cluster.

agglomération [aglɔmerasjɔ̃] *nf* **1.** [ville et sa banlieue] town ■ **l'~ parisienne** Paris and its suburbs, greater Paris **2.** TRANSP built-up area **3.** [assemblage] conglomeration.

aggloméré, e [aglɔmere] *adj* agglomerate.
◆ **aggloméré** *nm* **1.** MIN briquet, briquette **2.** CONSTR chipboard ■ GÉOL conglomerate ■ [de liège] agglomerated cork.

agglomérer [18] [aglɔmere] *vt* [pierre, sable] to aggregate ■ [charbon] to briquet ■ [métal] to agglomerate.
◆ **s'agglomérer** *vpi* to agglomerate, to aggregate.

agglutinant, e [aglytinɑ̃, ɑ̃t] *adj* LING & MÉD agglutinative.

agglutination [aglytinasjɔ̃] *nf* **1.** LING & MÉD agglutination **2.** *péj* [masse] mass.

agglutiner [3] [aglytine] *vt* to mass *ou* to pack together *(sép)*.
◆ **s'agglutiner** *vpi* to congregate ■ **ils s'agglutinaient à la fenêtre** they were all pressing up against the window.

aggravant, e [agravɑ̃, ɑ̃t] *adj* aggravating ■ **et, fait ~, il avait oublié l'argent** and he'd forgotten the money, which made things worse.

aggravation [agravasjɔ̃] *nf* [d'une maladie, d'un problème] aggravation, worsening ■ [de l'inflation] increase ■ **son état de santé a connu une ~** his health has worsened.

aggraver [3] [agrave] *vt* [mal, problème] to aggravate, to make worse, to exacerbate ■ **n'aggrave pas ton cas** don't make your position worse than it is ■ **ces mesures ne feront qu'~ l'inflation** these measures will only serve to worsen inflation.
◆ **s'aggraver** *vpi* to get worse, to worsen ■ **son état s'est aggravé** his condition has worsened ■ **la situation s'aggrave** the situation is getting worse.

agile [aʒil] *adj* nimble, agile ■ **un esprit ~** an agile mind.

agilement [aʒilmɑ̃] *adv* [grimper, se mouvoir] nimbly, agilely.

agilité [aʒilite] *nf* agility.

agio [aʒjo] *nm* (bank) charge ■ **payer 50 euros d'~s** to pay 50 euros in bank charges.

agir [32] [aʒir] *vi*

A. AVOIR UNE ACTIVITÉ
B. AVOIR UN EFFET
C. DANS LE DOMAINE JURIDIQUE

A. AVOIR UNE ACTIVITÉ
1. [intervenir] to act, to take action ■ **en cas d'incendie, il faut ~ vite** in the event of a fire, it is important to act quickly ■ **sur les ordres de qui avez-vous agi?** on whose orders did you act? ■ **faire ~ : est-ce la jalousie qui l'a fait ~?** was it jealousy that made her do it? ■ ~ **auprès de qqn** [essayer de l'influencer] to try to influence sb
2. [passer à l'action] to do something ■ **assez parlé, maintenant il faut ~!** enough talk, let's have some action!
3. [se comporter] to act, to behave ■ **bien/mal ~ envers qqn** to behave well/badly towards sb ■ **tu n'as pas agi loyalement** you didn't play fair ■ **il a agi en bon citoyen** he did what any honest citizen would have done ■ ~ **selon sa conscience** to act according to one's conscience, to let one's conscience be one's guide

B. AVOIR UN EFFET
1. [fonctionner - poison, remède] to act, to take effect, to work ; [- élément nutritif] to act, to have an effect ; [- détergent] to work ■ **laisser ~ la justice** to let justice take its course ■ **pour faire ~ le médicament plus efficacement** to increase the efficiency of the drug
2. [avoir une influence] : ~ **sur** to work *ou* to have an effect on

C. DANS LE DOMAINE JURIDIQUE
to act in a court of law ■ ~ **contre qqn** [en droit pénal] to prosecute sb ; [en droit civil] to sue sb ■ ~ **au nom de** *ou* **pour qqn** to act on behalf of *ou* for sb.
◆ **s'agir de** *v impers* **1.** [être question de] : **il s'agit de : je voudrais te parler - de quoi s'agit-il?** I'd like to talk to you - what about? ■ **de qui s'agit-il?** who is it? ■ **je voudrais vous parler d'une affaire importante, voici ce dont il s'agit** I'd like to talk to you about an important matter, namely this ■ **le criminel dont il s'agit** the criminal in question ■ **mais enfin, il s'agit de sa santé!** but her health is at stake (here)! ■ **je peux te prêter de l'argent - il ne s'agit pas de ça** *ou* **ce n'est pas de ça qu'il s'agit** I can lend you some money - that's not the point *ou* the question ■ **s'il ne s'agissait que d'argent, la solution serait simple!** if it were only a question of money, the answer would be simple! ■ **une augmentation? il s'agit bien de cela à l'heure où l'on parle de licenciements** *iron* a rise? that's very likely now there's talk of redundancies *iron* ■ **quand il s'agit d'aller à la chasse, il trouve toujours le temps!** when it comes to going hunting, he can always find time! ■ **quand il s'agit de râler, tu es toujours là!** you can always be relied upon to moan! ■ **une voiture a explosé, il s'agirait d'un accident** a car has exploded, apparently by accident ■ **il s'agirait d'une grande première scientifique** it is said to be an important first for science **2.** [falloir] : **il s'agit de : maintenant, il s'agit de lui parler** now we must talk to her ■ **il s'agissait pour moi d'être convaincant** I had to be convincing ■ **il s'agit de savoir si...** the question is whether... ■ **il s'agirait d'obéir!** [menace] you'd better do as you're told! ■ **dis donc, il ne s'agit pas de se perdre!** come on, we mustn't get lost now! ■ **il s'agit bien de pleurer maintenant que tu l'as cassé!** you may well cry, now that you've broken it!
◆ **s'agissant de** *loc prép* **1.** [en ce qui concerne] as regards, with regard to **2.** [puisque cela concerne] : **un service d'ordre ne s'imposait pas, s'agissant d'une manifestation pacifique** there was no need for a police presence, given that this was a peaceful demonstration.

âgisme [aʒism] *nm* age discrimination, agism.

agissant, e [aʒisɑ̃, ɑ̃t] *adj* **1.** [entreprenant] active **2.** [efficace] efficient, effective ■ **un remède ~** an effective remedy.

agissements [aʒismɑ̃] *nmpl* machinations, schemes.

agitateur, trice [aʒitatœr, tris] *nm, f* POLIT agitator.
◆ **agitateur** *nm* CHIM beater, agitator.

agitation [aʒitasjɔ̃] *nf* **1.** [mouvement - de l'air] turbulence ; [- de l'eau] roughness ; [- de la rue] bustle **2.** [fébrilité] agitation, restlessness ■ **être dans un état d'~ violente** to be extremely agitated ■ **l'~ régnait dans la salle** [excitation] the room was buzzing with excitement ; [inquiétude] there was an uneasy atmosphere in the room **3.** MÉD & PSYCHOL agitated depression **4.** POLIT unrest ■ ~ **syndicale** industrial unrest.

agité, e [aʒite] ◇ *adj* **1.** [mer] rough, stormy **2.** [personne - remuante] restless ; [- angoissée] agitated, worried **3.** [troublé - vie] hectic ; [- nuit, sommeil] restless.
◇ *nm, f* **1.** MÉD & PSYCHOL disturbed (mental) patient **2.** [excité] : **c'est un ~** he can't sit still for a minute.

agiter [3] [aʒite] *vt* **1.** [remuer - liquide] to shake ; [- queue] to wag ; [- mouchoir, journal] to wave about *(insép)* ■ ~ **les bras** to flap *ou* to wave one's arms ■ **'~ avant usage** *ou* **de s'en servir'** 'shake well before use' **2.** [brandir] to brandish ■ ~ **le spectre de qqch devant qqn** to threaten sb with the spectre of sthg **3.** [troubler] to trouble, to upset ■ **une violente colère l'agitait** he was in the grip of a terrible rage **4.** [débattre] to debate, to discuss.
◆ **s'agiter** *vpi* **1.** [bouger] to move about ■ **s'~ dans son sommeil** to toss and turn in one's sleep ■ **cesse de t'~ sur ta chaise!** stop fidgeting about on your chair! ■ **tu t'agites trop, ne te fais**

donc pas tant de souci you're too restless, don't worry so much **2.** *fam* [se dépêcher] to get a move on **3.** [se révolter] to be restless *ou* in a state of unrest **4.** [mer] to become rough.

agneau, x [aɲo] *nm* **1.** ZOOL lamb ■ **c'est un ~!** *fig* he's as meek *ou* gentle as a lamb! ➲ **~ de lait** suckling lamb **2.** CULIN lamb *(U)* ■ **côtelettes d'~** lamb chops **3.** [en appellatif] : **viens mon ~ (joli)!** come on lambkin! ■ **mes ~x, vous allez me dire la vérité maintenant!** now, my little friends, you're going to tell me the truth! **4.** [fourrure] lamb, lambskin ■ [peau] lambskin **5.** RELIG : **l'Agneau (de Dieu)** the Lamb (of God) ■ **l'~ mystique** the mystic lamb ■ **l'~ pascal** the Paschal Lamb.

agnelage [aɲəlaʒ] *nm* [naissance] lambing ■ [période] lambing season *ou* time.

agneler [24] [aɲəle] *vi* to lamb.

agnelle [aɲɛl] *nf* young ewe.

Agnès [aɲɛs] *npr* THÉÂTRE *character in Molière's 'l'École des femmes', the archetype of the naive and innocent woman.*

agnosticisme [agnɔstisism] *nm* agnosticism.

agnostique [agnɔstik] *adj & nmf* agnostic.

agonie [agɔni] *nf* death throes, pangs of death, death agony ■ **il a eu une longue ~** he died a slow and painful death ■ **l'~ de l'empire** *fig* the death throes of the empire ■ **être à l'~** *pr* to be at the point of death ; *fig* to suffer agonies.

agonir [32] [agɔnir] *vt sout* **~ qqn d'injures** *ou* **d'insultes** to hurl abuse at sb.

agonisant, e [agɔnizɑ̃, ɑ̃t] ◇ *adj* dying.
◇ *nm, f* dying person.

agoniser [3] [agɔnize] *vi* to be dying.

agora [agɔra] *nf* **1.** [espace piétonnier] concourse **2.** ANTIQ agora.

agoraphobe [agɔrafɔb] *adj & nmf* agoraphobic.

agoraphobie [agɔrafɔbi] *nf* agoraphobia.

agrafe [agraf] *nf* [pour papier] staple ■ [pour vêtement] hook, fastener ■ [pour bois ou métal] clamp ■ MÉD clamp.

agrafer [3] [agrafe] *vt* **1.** [papiers] to staple (together) ■ [bords d'un tissu] to hook *ou* to fasten (up) **2.** △ *arg crime* [arrêter] to nick△ *UK*, to bust△ *US*.

agrafeuse [agraføz] *nf* stapler.

agraire [agrɛr] *adj* agrarian.

agrammatical, e, aux [agramatikal, o] *adj* ungrammatical.

agrandir [32] [agrɑ̃dir] *vt* **1.** [élargir - trou] to enlarge, to make bigger ; [- maison, jardin] to extend ; [- couloir, passage] to widen ■ **la Communauté agrandie** the enlarged Community ■ **~ le cercle de ses activités** to enlarge the scope of one's activities ■ **j'ai besoin de partenaires pour ~ mon affaire** I need partners to expand my business **2.** *litt* [exalter - âme, pensée] to elevate, to uplift **3.** [faire paraître grand] : **on avait agrandi la scène par des décors transparents** the stage had been made to look bigger by the use of see-through sets **4.** IMPR & PHOTO [cliché, copie] to enlarge, to blow up *(sép)* ■ [sur écran] to magnify.
◆ **s'agrandir** *vpi* **1.** [s'élargir] to grow, to get bigger ■ **le cercle de famille s'agrandit** the family circle is widening **2.** ÉCON to expand **3.** [avoir plus de place] : **nous voudrions nous ~** we want more space for ourselves.

agrandissement [agrɑ̃dismɑ̃] *nm* **1.** PHOTO enlargement **2.** [d'un appartement, d'une affaire] extension.

agrandisseur [agrɑ̃disœr] *nm* enlarger PHOTO.

agrarien, enne [agrarjɛ̃, ɛn] *adj & nm, f* agrarian.

agréable [agreabl] *adj* pleasant, nice, agreeable ■ **je la trouve plutôt ~ physiquement** I think she's quite nice-looking ■ **il ne souhaite que vous être ~** he only wants to be nice to you ■ **il me serait bien ~ de le revoir** I would love to see him again ■ **~ à : une couleur ~ à l'œil** *ou* **à voir** a colour pleasing to the eye ■ **voilà quelqu'un qui est ~ à vivre** he's/she's really easy to get on with.

agréablement [agreabləmɑ̃] *adv* pleasantly, agreeably.

agréé, e [agree] *adj* **1.** DR registered **2.** TÉLÉCOM : **'appareil ~'** *France Télécom approved.*

agréer [15] [agree] *vt* [dans la correspondance] : **veuillez ~ mes sentiments distingués** yours faithfully *UK*, sincerely yours *US*.
◆ **agréer à** *v+prép litt* to please, to suit.

agrég [agrɛg] *nf fam* = **agrégation** *(sens 1)*.

agrégat [agrega] *nm* [de roches, de substances] aggregate ■ *fig & péj* conglomeration, mish-mash *péj*.

agrégatif, ive [agregatif, iv] ◇ *adj* UNIV [candidat, étudiant] *who is studying to take the agrégation.*
◇ *nm, f* UNIV agrégation candidate.

agrégation [agregasjɔ̃] *nf* **1.** UNIV *high-level competitive examination for teachers* **2.** [assemblage] agglomeration.

L'AGRÉGATION

This is a prestigious professional qualification for teachers in France. Those who pass the challenging competitive exam for the ***agrég*** become ***professeurs titulaires***, and as such are entitled to higher pay and a less onerous timetable.

agrégé, e [agreʒe] ◇ *adj* **1.** UNIV *who has passed the agrégation* **2.** [assemblé] agglomerated.
◇ *nm, f* UNIV *person who has passed the agrégation (and commands certain salary and timetable privileges within the teaching profession).*

agréger [22] [agreʒe] *vt* **1.** [assembler] to agglomerate (together) **2.** [intégrer] : **~ qqn à** to incorporate sb into.
◆ **s'agréger** *vpi* [s'assembler] to form a mass.
◆ **s'agréger à** *vp+prép* to incorporate o.s. into.

agrément [agremɑ̃] *nm sout* **1.** [attrait] charm, appeal, attractiveness **2.** [accord] approval, consent ■ **agir avec l'~ de ses supérieurs** to act with one's superiors' approval *ou* consent.
◆ **d'agrément** *loc adj* [jardin, voyage] pleasure *(modif)*.

agrémenter [3] [agremɑ̃te] *vt* : **~ qqch avec** *ou* **de** to decorate sthg with ■ **une lettre agrémentée de quelques expressions à l'ancienne** a letter graced *ou* adorned with a few quaint old phrases.

agrès [agrɛ] *nmpl* **1.** SPORT piece of apparatus ■ **elle a eu 20 aux (exercices aux) ~** she got 20 for apparatus work **2.** NAUT lifting gear ■ [sur un ballon] tackle.

agresser [4] [agrese] *vt* **1.** [physiquement] to attack, to assault ■ **se faire ~** to be assaulted **2.** [verbalement] to attack ■ **pourquoi m'agresses-tu ainsi? je n'ai fait que dire la vérité!** why are you being so aggressive towards me? I only told the truth! **3.** [avoir un effet nocif sur] to damage.

agresseur [agrɛsœr] ◇ *adj m* [État, pays] attacking.
◇ *nm* [d'une personne] attacker, assailant, aggressor ■ [d'un pays] aggressor ■ **elle n'a pas pu voir son ~** she couldn't see her assailant *ou* the person who assaulted her.

agressif, ive [agrɛsif, iv] *adj* **1.** [hostile - personne, pays] aggressive, hostile, belligerent *litt* **2.** [oppressant - musique, image] aggressive **3.** [dynamique] dynamic, aggressive **4.** PSYCHOL [acte, pulsion] aggressive.

agression [agrɛsjɔ̃] *nf* **1.** [attaque - contre une personne] attack, assault ; [- contre un pays] aggression ■ **être victime d'une** *ou* **subir une ~** to be assaulted ■ **les ~s de la vie moderne** *fig* the stresses and strains of modern life **2.** PSYCHOL aggression.

agressivement [agrɛsivmɑ̃] *adv* aggressively.

agressivité [agrɛsivite] *nf* aggressivity, aggressiveness.

agreste [agrɛst] *adj litt* rustic.

agricole [agrikɔl] *adj* agricultural, farming *(modif)* ■ **un pays ~** an agricultural country.

agriculteur, trice [agrikyltœr, tris] *nm, f* farmer.

agriculture [agrikyltyr] *nf* agriculture, farming ■ **~ raisonnée** sustainable agriculture, sustainable farming.

agripper [3] [agripe] *vt* **1.** [prendre] to grab, to snatch **2.** [tenir] to clutch, to grip.
◆ **s'agripper** *vpi* to hold on ■ **s'~ à qqch** to cling to *ou* to hold on (tight) to sthg.

Agro [agro] *npr nickname for ENSA.*

agroalimentaire [agroalimɑ̃tɛr] ◇ *adj* food-processing *(modif).*
◇ *nm* : **l'~** the food-processing industry, agribusiness.

agrochimie [agroʃimi] *nf* agrochemistry.

agro-industrie [agroɛ̃dystri] (*pl* **agro-industries**) *nf* : **l'~** [en amont de l'agriculture] the farm machines, implements and fertilizers industry ; [en aval de l'agriculture] the food-processing industry, agribusiness.

agrologie [agrɔlɔʒi] *nf* agrology.

agronome [agrɔnɔm] *nmf* agronomist.

agronomie [agrɔnɔmi] *nf* agronomics *(sing).*

agronomique [agrɔnɔmik] *adj* agronomic, agronomical.

agrotourisme [agroturism] *nm* agrotourism.

agrume [agrym] *nm* citrus fruit.

aguerrir [32] [agerir] *vt* to harden, to toughen (up).
◆ **s'aguerrir** *vpi* to become tougher.

aguets [agɛ] ◆ **aux aguets** *loc adv* : **être aux ~** to be on watch *ou* the lookout.

aguichant, e [agiʃɑ̃, ɑ̃t] *adj* seductive, enticing, alluring.

aguiche [agiʃ] *nf* teaser *(in advertising).*

aguicher [3] [agiʃe] *vt* to seduce, to entice, to allure.

aguicheur, euse [agiʃœr, øz] ◇ *adj* seductive, enticing, alluring.
◇ *nm, f* tease.

ah [a] ◇ *interj* **1.** [renforce l'expression d'un sentiment] ah, oh **2.** [dans une réponse] : **il est venu – ~ bon!** he came – did he (really)? ■ **ils n'en ont plus en magasin – ~ bon!** [ton résigné] they haven't got any more in stock – oh well! ■ **~ non alors!** certainly not! ■ **~ oui?** really?
◇ *nm inv* ah ■ **pousser des oh et des ~** to ooh and ah.

ahaner [3] [aane] *vi litt* to puff and pant.

ahuri, e [ayri] ◇ *adj* **1.** [surpris] dumbfounded, amazed, stunned **2.** [hébété] stupefied, dazed ■ **il avait l'air complètement ~** he looked as if he was in a daze.
◇ *nm, f* idiot.

ahurir [32] [ayrir] *vt* to stun, to daze.

ahurissant, e [ayrisɑ̃, ɑ̃t] *adj* stunning, stupefying ■ **je trouve ça ~** I think it's appalling.

ahurissement [ayrismɑ̃] *nm* daze ■ **son ~ était tel qu'il ne m'entendait pas** he was so stunned that he didn't even hear me.

ai *etc v* ▷ **avoir.**

aï [ai] *nm* ZOOL ai, three-toed sloth.

aiche [ɛʃ] *nf* bait.

aide[1] [ɛd] ◇ *nm* **1.** [assistant - payé] assistant ; [- bénévole] helper ■ **les ~s du président** the presidential aides **2.** *(comme adj; avec ou sans trait d'union)* assistant *(modif)* **3.** MIL : **~ de camp** aide-de-camp.
◇ *nf* : **~ familiale** [travailleuse familiale] home help ; [jeune fille au pair] au pair.

aide[2] [ɛd] *nf* **1.** [appui] help, assistance, aid ■ **avec l'~ de mon frère** with help from my brother *ou* my brother's help ■ **elle y est arrivée sans l'~ de personne** she succeeded with no help at all *ou* unaided *ou* without anyone's help ■ **à l'~!** help! ■ **appeler à l'~** to call for help ■ **offrir son ~ à qqn** to give sb help, to go to sb's assistance ■ **venir en ~ à qqn** to come to sb's aid ■ **que Dieu vous vienne en ~** may God help you **2.** INFORM : **~ contextuelle** *ou* **en ligne** online help **3.** [don d'argent] aid ⊙ **~ au développement économique (des pays du tiers-monde)** economic aid (to third world countries) ■ **~ humanitaire** humanitarian aid ■ **~ judiciaire** ≃ legal aid ■ **~ à la mobilité** relocation allowance *(paid to job seekers)* ■ **~ personnalisée au logement** ≃ housing benefit *(U)* ■ **~ à la reconversion des entreprises** industrial reconversion grants.
◆ **aides** *nfpl* ÉQUIT aids.
◆ **à l'aide de** *loc prép* **1.** [avec] with the help of ■ **marcher à l'~ de béquilles** to walk with crutches **2.** [au secours de] : **aller/venir à l'~ de qqn** to go/to come to sb's aid.

aide-comptable [ɛdkɔ̃tabl] (*pl* **aides-comptables**) *nmf* accountant's assistant.

aide-éducateur, trice [ɛdedykatœr, tris] *nm, f* ÉDUC teaching assistant.

aide-mémoire [ɛdmemwar] *nm inv* notes.

aider [4] [ede] *vt* **1.** [apporter son concours à] to help ■ **je me suis fait ~ par mon frère** I got my brother to help me ■ **~ qqn à faire qqch** to help sb (to) do sthg ■ **il a aidé la vieille dame à monter/descendre** he helped the old lady up/down ■ *(en usage absolu)* to help (out) **2.** [financièrement] to help out, to aid, to assist ■ **il a fallu l'~ pour monter son affaire** she needed help to set up her business ■ **subventions pour ~ l'industrie** subsidies to industry **3.** *(en usage absolu)* [favoriser] : **ça aide** *fam* it's a help ■ **des diplômes, ça aide** qualifications come in handy ■ **la fatigue aidant, je me suis endormi tout de suite** helped by exhaustion, I fell asleep right away ■ **elle l'oubliera, le temps aidant** she'll forget him in time ⊙ **il n'est pas aidé!** *fam* he hasn't got much going for him!
◆ **aider à** *v+prép* to help ■ **~ à la digestion** to help digestion ■ **ça aide à passer le temps** it helps to pass the time.
◆ **s'aider** ◇ *vp (emploi réfléchi)* : **aide-toi, le ciel t'aidera** *prov* God helps those who help themselves *prov.*
◇ *vp (emploi réciproque)* to help each other.
◆ **s'aider de** *vp+prép* to use ■ **marcher en s'aidant d'une canne** to walk with a stick.

Aides [ɛd] *npr French Aids charity.*

aide-soignant, e [ɛdswaɲɑ̃, ɑ̃t] (*mpl* **aides-soignants,** *fpl* **aides-soignantes**) *nm, f* nursing auxiliary *UK*, nurse's aid *US.*

aie *etc v* ▷ **avoir.**

aïe [aj] *interj* [cri - de douleur] ouch ; [- de surprise] : **~, la voilà!** oh dear *ou* oh no, here she comes!

aïeul, e [ajœl] *nm, f* grandparent, grandfather (*f* grandmother).

aïeux [ajø] *nmpl litt* forefathers, ancestors ■ **ah, mes ~, travailler avec lui n'est pas une sinécure!** *hum* heavens, working with him is no easy task!

aigle [ɛgl] ◇ *nm* ORNITH eagle ■ **~ des mers** sea eagle ■ **~ royal** golden eagle ■ **avoir des yeux** *ou* **un regard d'~** to be eagle-eyed ■ **ce n'est pas un ~** *hum* he's no great genius.
◇ *nf* ORNITH (female) eagle.

aiglefin [ɛgləfɛ̃] = **églefin.**

aiglon [ɛglɔ̃] *nm* eaglet ■ **l'Aiglon** *name given to Napoleon II.*

aiglonne [ɛglɔn] *nf* (female) eaglet.

aigre [ɛgr] ◇ *adj* **1.** [acide - vin] acid, sharp ; [- goût, lait] sour ■ **le lait est devenu ~** the milk has turned *ou* gone sour **2.** [perçant - voix, son] shrill, sharp **3.** [vif - bise, froid] bitter **4.** [méchant] cutting, harsh, acid ■ **elle répondit d'un ton ~** she retorted acidly.
◇ *nm* ⊙ **tourner à l'~** [lait] to turn sour ; [discussion] to turn sour *ou* nasty.

aigre-doux, aigre-douce [ɛgrədu, ɛgrədus] (*mpl* **aigres-doux,** *fpl* **aigres-douces**) *adj* CULIN sweet-and-sour ■ **ses lettres étaient aigres-douces** *fig* his letters were tinged with bitterness.

aigrefin [ɛgrəfɛ̃] *nm* swindler.

aigrelet, ette [ɛgrəlɛ, ɛt] *adj* [odeur, saveur] sourish ■ [son, voix] shrillish ■ [propos] tart, sour, acid.

aigrement [ɛgrəmɑ̃] *adv* sourly, tartly, acidly.

aigrette [ɛgrɛt] *nf* **1.** ORNITH egret **2.** [décoration] aigrette.

aigreur [ɛgrœr] *nf* **1.** [acidité] sourness **2.** [animosité] sharpness, bitterness ▪ **ses propos étaient pleins d'~** his remarks were very bitter.
◆ **aigreurs** *nfpl* : **avoir des ~s (d'estomac)** to have heartburn.

aigri, e [egri] ◇ *adj* bitter, embittered.
◇ *nm, f* embittered person.

aigrir [32] [egrir] ◇ *vt* [lait, vin] to make sour ▪ [personne] to embitter, to make bitter.
◇ *vi* [lait] to turn (sour), to go off.
◆ **s'aigrir** *vpi* [lait] to turn (sour), to go off ▪ [caractère] to sour ▪ [personne] to become embittered.

aigu, ë [egy] *adj* **1.** [perçant - voix] high-pitched, shrill *péj*, piercing *péj* ; [- glapissement, hurlement] piercing, shrill ▪ **on entendait la sonnerie ~ë du téléphone** we heard the shrill ringing of the telephone ▪ ACOUST & MUS high-pitched **2.** [effilé] sharp **3.** [pénétrant - esprit, intelligence] sharp, keen ▪ **avoir un sens ~ de l'observation** *ou* **un regard ~** to be an acute observer **4.** [grave - crise, douleur] severe, acute, extreme ▪ MÉD [phase, appendicite] acute ▪ **au stade le plus ~ du conflit** at the height of the conflict.
◆ **aigu** *nm* high pitch ▪ **l'~, les ~s** treble range.

aigue-marine [ɛgmarin] (*pl* **aigues-marines**) *nf* aquamarine.

aiguillage [egɥijaʒ] *nm* **1.** RAIL [manœuvre] shunting, switching ▪ [dispositif] shunt, switch **2.** INFORM switching.

aiguille [egɥij] *nf* **1.** COUT needle ➊ **~ à tricoter/repriser** knitting/darning needle **2.** MÉD needle **3.** [d'une montre, d'une pendule] hand ▪ [d'un électrophone] arm ▪ [d'une balance] pointer ▪ [d'une boussole] needle ▪ **la petite ~, l'~ des heures** the hour hand ▪ **la grande ~, l'~ des minutes** the minute hand **4.** GÉOGR needle, high peak **5.** BOT needle ▪ **~ de pin/de sapin** pine/fir tree needle **6.** RAIL switch, shunt, points **7.** [tour, clocher] spire.

aiguillée [egɥije] *nf* length of thread *(on a needle)*.

aiguiller [3] [egɥije] *vt* **1.** RAIL to shunt, to switch **2.** [orienter - recherche] to steer ▪ **on l'a aiguillé vers une section scientifique** he was steered *ou* guided towards the sciences.

aiguillette [egɥijɛt] *nf* **1.** [vêtement] aglet **2.** CULIN [de canard, d'oie] strip of breast ▪ [de bœuf] : **~ (de rumsteck)** top of the rump (of beef).
◆ **aiguillettes** *nfpl* MIL aglets.

aiguilleur [egɥijœr] *nm* **1.** RAIL pointsman *UK*, switchman *US* **2.** AÉRON : **~ (du ciel)** air traffic controller.

aiguillon [egɥijɔ̃] *nm* **1.** ENTOM sting **2.** BOT thorn **3.** [bâton] goad **4.** *litt* [motivation] incentive, stimulus, motivating force.

aiguillonner [3] [egɥijɔne] *vt* **1.** [piquer - bœuf] to goad **2.** [stimuler - curiosité] to arouse ; [- personne] to spur on, to goad on.

aiguisage [eg(ɥ)izaʒ], **aiguisement** [eg(ɥ)izmɑ̃] *nm* sharpening, grinding.

aiguiser [3] [eg(ɥ)ize] *vt* **1.** [rendre coupant - couteau, lame] to sharpen ▪ **bien aiguisé** sharp **2.** [stimuler - curiosité] to stimulate, to rouse ; [- faculté, sens] to sharpen ; [- appétit] to whet, to stimulate.

aiguiseur, euse [eg(ɥ)izœr, øz] *nm, f* sharpener, grinder.

aïkido [ajkido] *nm* aikido ▪ **faire de l'~** to do aikido.

ail [aj] (*pl* **ails** *ou pl* **aulx** [o]) *nm* garlic.
◆ **à l'ail** *loc adj* garlic *(modif)*.

aile [ɛl] *nf* **1.** ZOOL wing ▪ *fig* **avoir des ~s** to run like the wind ▪ **avoir un petit coup dans l'~** *fam* to be tipsy ▪ **couper** *ou* **rogner les ~s à qqn** to clip sb's wings ▪ **donner des ~s à qqn** to give *ou* to lend sb wings ▪ **prendre qqn sous son ~** to take sb under one's wing **2.** [d'un moulin] sail ▪ [d'un avion] wing ▪ **~ (delta), ~ libre, ~ volante** LOISIRS hang glider **3.** AUTO wing *UK*, fender *US* **4.** ANAT : **les ~s du nez** the nostrils **5.** ARCHIT wing **6.** SPORT wing **7.** MIL wing, flank.

ailé, e [ele] *adj* winged.

aileron [ɛlrɔ̃] *nm* **1.** ZOOL [d'un poisson] fin ▪ [d'un oiseau] pinion **2.** AÉRON aileron.

ailette [ɛlɛt, ɛr] *nf* **1.** [d'un radiateur] fin **2.** [d'une turbine] blade **3.** ARM fin.

ailier, ère [elje, ɛr] *nm, f* SPORT [au football] winger ▪ [au rugby] wing.

aillade [ajad] *nf* CULIN [sauce] garlic sauce ▪ [vinaigrette] garlic vinaigrette ▪ [tranche de pain] *slice of bread rubbed with olive oil and garlic and then toasted.*

aille *etc v* ▷ **aller**.

ailler [3] [aje] *vt* [gigot, rôti] to put garlic in ▪ [croûton] to rub garlic on.

ailleurs [ajœr] *adv* somewhere else, elsewhere ▪ **on ne trouve ça nulle part ~** you won't find that anywhere else ▪ **il est ~!** he's miles away!
◆ **d'ailleurs** *loc adv* **1.** [de toute façon] besides, anyway ▪ **d'~ je sais bien que tu n'en veux pas** besides, I know quite well that you don't want any **2.** [de plus] what's more ▪ **je n'en sais rien et d'~ je ne tiens pas à le savoir** I don't know anything about it and what's more I don't want to know **3.** [du reste] for that matter ▪ **je ne les aime pas, elle non plus d'~** I don't like them, nor does she for that matter **4.** [à propos] incidentally ▪ **nous avons dîné dans un restaurant, très bien d'~** we had dinner in a restaurant which, incidentally, was very good **5.** [bien que] although, while.
◆ **par ailleurs** *loc adv* **1.** [d'un autre côté] otherwise **2.** [de plus] besides, moreover.

ailloli [ajɔli] = aïoli.

aimable [ɛmabl] *adj* **1.** [gentil] kind, pleasant, amiable ▪ **soyez assez ~ de nous prévenir si vous ne venez pas** please be kind enough to let us know if you aren't coming ▪ **peu ~** not very nice ▪ **vous êtes trop ~, merci beaucoup** you're most kind, thank you very much ▪ **c'est très ~ à vous** it's very kind of you ▪ **'nous prions notre aimable clientèle de bien vouloir...'** 'would patrons kindly...' ➊ **il est ~ comme une porte de prison** *fam* [en ce moment] he's like a bear with a sore head ; [toujours] he's a miserable so-and-so **2.** *litt* [digne d'amour] lovable ▪ [séduisant] attractive.

aimablement [ɛmabləmɑ̃] *adv* kindly, pleasantly, amiably.

aimant[1] [ɛmɑ̃] *nm* **1.** [instrument] magnet **2.** [oxyde de fer] magnetite.

aimant[2]**, e** [ɛmɑ̃, ɑ̃t] *adj* loving, caring.

aimanter [3] [ɛmɑ̃te] *vt* to magnetize.

aimer [4] [eme] *vt* **1.** [d'amour] to love ▪ **je l'aime beaucoup** I'm very fond of him ▪ **je l'aime bien** I like him ▪ **qui m'aime me suive** *(allusion à Philippe VI de Valois)* anyone want to join me? **2.** [apprécier - vin, musique, sport] to like, to love, to be fond of ▪ **je n'aime plus tellement le jazz** I'm not so keen on jazz now ▪ **jamais tu ne me feras ~ la voile!** you'll never persuade me to like sailing! ▪ **j'aime à croire** *ou* **à penser que tu m'as dit la vérité cette fois** *sout* I'd like to think that you told me the truth this time ▪ **~ mieux** [préférer] to prefer ▪ **~ autant** *ou* **mieux** to prefer ▪ **pas de dessert, merci, j'aime autant** *ou* **mieux le fromage** no dessert, thanks, I'd much rather have cheese ▪ **j'aime autant** *ou* **mieux ça** it's just as well ▪ **elle aime autant** *ou* **mieux que tu y ailles** she'd rather you *ou* she'd prefer it if you went ▪ **~ que : il aime que ses enfants l'embrassent avant d'aller au lit** he loves his children to kiss him good night ▪ **je n'aime pas qu'on me mente/que tu rentres si tard** I don't like to be told lies/your coming home so late **3.** *(au conditionnel)* [souhaiter] : **j'aimerais un café s'il vous plaît** I'd like a coffee please ▪ **j'aimerais bien te voir** I'd really like to see you ▪ **j'aimerais tant te voir heureux** I'd so love to see you happy.
◆ **s'aimer** ◇ *vp (emploi réfléchi)* to like o.s. ▪ **je ne m'aime pas** I don't like myself ▪ **je m'aime bien en bleu/avec les cheveux courts** I think I look good in blue/with short hair.
◇ *vp (emploi réciproque)* to love each other ▪ **les trois frères ne s'aimaient pas** the three brothers didn't care for *ou* like each other ▪ **un couple qui s'aime** a loving *ou* devoted couple ▪ *litt* [faire l'amour] to make love.

aine [ɛn] *nf* groin.

aîné, e [ene] <> *adj* : **l'enfant ~** [de deux] the elder *ou* older child ; [de plusieurs] the eldest *ou* oldest child.
<> *nm, f* **1.** [entre frères et sœurs] : **l'~** [de deux] the elder *ou* older boy ; [de plusieurs] the eldest *ou* oldest boy ▪ **l'~e** [de deux] the elder *ou* older girl ; [de plusieurs] the eldest *ou* oldest girl **2.** [doyen] : **l'~** [de deux] the older man ; [de plusieurs] the oldest man ▪ **l'~e** [de deux] the older woman ; [de plusieurs] the oldest woman.
◆ **aînés** *nmpl sout* [d'une famille, d'une tribu] : **les ~s** the elders.

aînesse [enɛs] *nf* ▷ **droit**.

AINS [ainɛs] (*abr de* **anti-inflammatoire non stéroïdien**) *nm* NSAID.

ainsi [ɛ̃si] *adv* **1.** [de cette manière] this *ou* that way ▪ **je suis ~ faite** that's the way I am ▪ **puisqu'il en est ~** since that is the case, since that is the way things are ▪ **s'il en était vraiment ~** if this were really so *ou* the case ▪ **c'est toujours ~** it's always like that ▪ **tout s'est passé ~** this is how it happened ▪ **on voit ~ que...** in this way *ou* thus we can see that... ▪ **~ s'achève notre émission** this concludes our programme ▪ **~ va le monde** it's the way of the world *ou* the way things go **2.** [par conséquent] so, thus ▪ **~ tu n'as pas réussi à le voir?** so you didn't manage to see him? ▪ **~ soit-il** RELIG amen ; *hum* so be it **3.** [par exemple] for instance, for example.
◆ **ainsi que** *loc conj* **1.** [comme] as ▪ **~ que je l'ai fait remarquer...** as I pointed out... **2.** [et] as well as ▪ **mes parents ~ que mes frères seront là** my parents will be there as well as my brothers **3.** *litt* [exprimant une comparaison] like.
◆ **et ainsi de suite** *loc adv* and so on, and so forth.
◆ **pour ainsi dire** *loc adv* **1.** [presque] virtually **2.** [si l'on peut dire] so to speak, as it were ▪ **elle est pour ~ dire sa raison de vivre** she's his reason for living, so to speak *ou* as it were.

aïoli [ajɔli] *nm* **1.** [sauce] aïoli, garlic mayonnaise **2.** [plat provençal] *dish of cod and poached vegetables served with aïoli sauce.*

air [ɛr] *nm* **1.** [apparence] air, look ▪ **"bien sûr", dit-il d'un ~ guilleret/inquiet** "of course," he said, jauntily/looking worried ▪ **il avait un ~ angoissé/mauvais** he looked anxious/very nasty ▪ **ne te laisse pas prendre à son faux ~ de gentillesse** don't be taken in by his apparent kindness ▪ **son témoignage a un ~ de vérité qui ne trompe pas** his testimony sounds unmistakably genuine ▪ **avoir l'~ : Maria, tu as l'~ heureux** *ou* **heureuse** Maria, you look happy ▪ **elle n'a pas l'~ satisfait** *ou* **satisfaite** she doesn't look as if she's pleased ▪ **cette poire a l'~ mauvaise, jette-la** this pear looks (as though it's) rotten, throw it away ▪ **tu avais l'~ fin!** *fam* you looked a real fool! ▪ **avoir l'~ de : il a l'~ de t'aimer beaucoup** he seems to be very fond of you ▪ **je ne voudrais pas avoir l'~ de lui donner des ordres** I wouldn't like (it) to look as though I were ordering him about ▪ **ça a l'~ d'un** *ou* **d'être un scarabée** it looks like a beetle ▪ **ça m'a tout l'~ (d'être) traduit de l'anglais** *fam* it looks to me as though it's been translated from English ▪ **il a peut-être la rougeole - il en a tout l'~** he may have measles - it certainly looks like it ▶ **avoir un petit ~ penché** *fam ou* **des petits ~s penchés** *fam* to look pensive ▪ **avec son ~ de ne pas y toucher** *ou* **sans avoir l'~ d'y toucher, il arrive toujours à ses fins** though you wouldn't think it to look at him, he always manages to get his way ▪ **l'~ de rien** *fam ou* **de ne pas en avoir** *fam* **: je me suis approchée, l'~ de rien** *ou* **de ne pas en avoir, et je lui ai flanqué ma main sur la figure** ▪ *fam* I walked up, all innocent, like, and gave him a slap in the face ▪ **ça n'a l'~ de rien comme ça, mais c'est une lourde tâche** it doesn't look much but it's quite a big job ▪ **elle n'a pas l'~ comme ça, mais elle sait ce qu'elle veut!** *fam* you wouldn't think it to look at her, but she knows what she wants! ▪ **sans en avoir l' ~ : sans en avoir l'~, elle a tout rangé en une heure** she tidied up everything in an hour without even looking busy ▪ **je suis arrivée au bout de mon tricot, sans en avoir l'~!** I managed to finish my knitting, though it didn't seem that I was making any progress! ▪ **prendre** *ou* **se donner des ~s** to give o.s. airs ▪ **prendre de grands ~s** to put on airs (and graces *UK*
2. [ressemblance] likeness, resemblance ▪ **un ~ de famille** *ou* **parenté** a family resemblance *ou* likeness ▶ **il a un faux ~ de James Dean** he looks a bit like James Dean
3. MUS [mélodie] tune ▪ [à l'opéra] aria ▪ **avec lui c'est toujours le même ~!** *fig & péj* he should change his tune! ▶ **c'est l'~ qui fait la chanson** it's not what you say, it's the way you say it
4. [qu'on respire] air ▪ **la pollution/température de l'~** air pollution/temperature ▶ **~ conditionné** [système] air-conditioning ▪ **ils ont l'~ conditionné** their building is air-conditioned ▪ **~ comprimé** compressed air ▪ **~ liquide** liquid air ▪ **prendre l'~** to get some fresh air, to take the air *vieilli* ▪ **déplacer** *ou* **remuer beaucoup d'~** *péj* to make a lot of noise *fig* ▪ **(allez,) de l'~!** *fam* come on, beat it!
5. [vent] : **il fait** *fam ou* **il y a de l'~ aujourd'hui** it's breezy today ; [beaucoup] it's windy today
6. [ciel] air ▪ **dans l'~** *ou* **les ~ s** (up) in the air *ou* sky *ou* skies *litt* ▪ **prendre l'~** [avion] to take off, to become airborne, to take to the air ▪ **transport par ~** air transport
7. [ambiance] atmosphere ▪ **de temps en temps, il me faut l'~ du pays natal** I need to go back to my roots from time to time ▶ **vivre de l'~ du temps** to live on (thin) air.
◆ **à air** *loc adj* [pompe] air *(modif)*.
◆ **à l'air** *loc adv* : **j'ai mis tous les vêtements d'hiver à l'~** I put all the winter clothes out for an airing ▪ **mettre son derrière à l'~** to bare one's bottom.
◆ **à l'air libre** *loc adv* out in the open.
◆ **au grand air** *loc adv* [dehors] (out) in the fresh air.
◆ **dans l'air** *loc adv* in the air ▪ **il y a de l'orage dans l'~** *pr & fig* there's a storm brewing ▪ **influencé par les idées qui sont dans l'~** influenced by current ideas ▪ **la révolution est dans l'~** revolution is in the air ▪ **il y a quelque chose dans l'~!** there's something going on!
◆ **de l'air** *loc adj* [hôtesse, mal, musée] air *(modif)*.
◆ **en l'air** <> *loc adj* **1.** [levé] in the air, up ▪ **les pattes en l'~** with its feet in the air ▪ **les mains en l'~!** hands up!
2. [non fondé - promesse] empty ▪ **encore des paroles en l'~!** more empty words! ▪ **je ne fais pas de projets en l'~** when I make a plan, I stick to it.
<> *loc adv* **1.** [vers le haut] (up) in the air ▪ **jeter** *ou* **lancer qqch en l'~** to throw sthg (up) in the air ▪ **tirer en l'~** to fire in the air ▪ **regarde en l'~** look up
2. *fig* rashly ▪ **parler en l'~** to say things without meaning them ▪ **flanquer** *fam ou* **foutre**[△] **qqch en l'~** [jeter] to chuck sthg out, to bin sthg ; [gâcher] to screw sthg up[△].

airain [ɛrɛ̃] *nm litt* bronze.

Airbag® [ɛrbag] *nm* Airbag®.

Airbus® [ɛrbys] *nm* Airbus®.

aire [ɛr] *nf* **1.** [terrain] area ▪ **~ de jeu** playground ▪ **~s de repos** rest areas *(along a road)*, ≃ lay-bys *UK* ▪ **~ de stationnement** parking area **2.** AÉRON & ASTRON : **~ d'atterrissage** landing area ▪ **~ d'embarquement** boarding area ▪ **~ de lancement** launching site **3.** GÉOL : **~ continentale** continental shield **4.** MATH area **5.** AGRIC floor ▪ **~ de battage** threshing floor **6.** [nid d'aigle] eyrie.

airelle [ɛrɛl] *nf* [myrtille] blueberry, bilberry ▪ [rouge] cranberry.

aisance [ɛzɑ̃s] *nf* **1.** [naturel] ease ▪ **danser/jongler avec ~** to dance/to juggle with great ease ▪ **parler une langue avec ~** to speak a language fluently **2.** [prospérité] affluence ▪ **vivre dans l'~** to live a life of ease **3.** COUT : **donner de l'~ à la taille** to let a garment out at the waist.

aise [ɛz] *litt* <> *adj* delighted ▪ **je suis bien ~ de vous revoir** I'm delighted to see you again.
<> *nf* [plaisir] pleasure, joy ▪ **il ne se sentait plus d'~** he was utterly contented ▪ **son accueil nous a comblés d'~** her welcome filled us with joy.
◆ **aises** *nfpl* creature comforts ▪ **il aime ses ~s** he likes his creature comforts ▪ **prends tes ~s, surtout!** *iron* do make yourself comfortable, won't you?
◆ **à l'aise, à son aise** *loc adj & loc adv* : **je suis plus à l'~ avec mes vieilles pantoufles** I feel more at ease with my old slippers on ▪ **on est mal à l'~ dans ce fauteuil** this armchair isn't very comfortable ▪ **être à l'~** [riche] to be well-to-do *ou* well-off ▪ **nous sommes bien plus à l'~ depuis que ma femme travaille** we're better off now my wife's working ▪ **il s'est senti mal à l'~ pendant toute la réunion** *fig* he felt ill-at-ease during the entire meeting ▪ **il nous a mis tout de suite à l'~** *ou* **à notre ~** he put us at (our) ease right away ▪ **mettez-vous donc à l'~** *ou* **à votre ~** make yourself comfortable ▶ **à ton ~!** please yourself! ▪ **à votre ~** as you please ▪ **tu en parles à ton ~** it's easy for you to talk ▪ **en prendre à son ~ : il en prend à son ~!**

he's a cool customer! ▪ **être à l'~ dans ses baskets** *fam* to be together ▪ **on y sera ce soir, à l'~!** *fam* we'll be there tonight, no hassle *ou* sweat! ▪ **tu crois qu'on va y arriver? – à l'~!** *fam* do you think we'll manage? – easily!

aisé, e [eze] *adj* **1.** [facile] easy **2.** [prospère] well-to-do, well-off.

aisément [ezemɑ̃] *adv* easily ▪ **il est ~ reconnaissable à cause de sa cicatrice** he's easy to recognize because of his scar.

aisselle [ɛsɛl] *nf* **1.** ANAT armpit **2.** BOT axile.

Aix-la-Chapelle [ɛkslaʃapɛl] *npr* Aachen.

AJ *nf* = **auberge de jeunesse**.

ajaccien, enne [aʒaksjɛ̃, ɛn] *adj* from Ajaccio.
◆ **Ajaccien, enne** *nm, f inhabitant of or person from Ajaccio* ▪ **les Ajacciens** the people of Ajaccio.

Ajaccio [aʒaksjo] *npr* Ajaccio.

ajonc [aʒɔ̃] *nm* gorse *(U)*, furze *(U)*.

ajouré, e [aʒure] *adj* **1.** COUT [nappe, napperon] openwork *(modif)*, hemstitched **2.** ARCHIT with an openwork design.

ajourer [3] [aʒure] *vt* **1.** COUT [nappe] to hemstitch **2.** ARCHIT to decorate with openwork.

ajourné, e [aʒurne] <> *adj* [date, élection, réunion] postponed ▪ [candidat] referred ▪ [soldat] deferred.
<> *nm, f* [étudiant] referred student ▪ [soldat] deferred soldier.

ajournement [aʒurnəmɑ̃] *nm* **1.** [renvoi] postponement, deferment, adjournment **2.** DR summons **3.** [d'un candidat] referral ▪ [d'un soldat] deferment.

ajourner [3] [aʒurne] *vt* **1.** [différer] to postpone, to defer *sout*, to put off *(sép)* ▪ **l'avocat a fait ~ le procès** the lawyer requested a postponement of the trial *ou* asked for the trial to be postponed **2.** DR to summon, to subpoena **3.** [étudiant] to refer ▪ [soldat] to defer.

ajout [aʒu] *nm* addition ▪ **quelques ~s dans la marge** a few additions *ou* addenda in the margin.

ajouter [3] [aʒute] *vt* **1.** [mettre] to add ▪ **ajoute donc une assiette pour ton frère** lay an extra place *ou* add a plate for your brother **2.** MATH to add ▪ **ils ont ajouté 15 % de service** they added on 15% for the service ▪ **~ 10 à 15** to add 10 and 15 (together), to add 10 to 15 ▪ **pour obtenir le dernier résultat, ~ les deux sommes** to get the final result add both sums together **3.** [dire] to add ▪ **il est parti sans rien ~** he left without saying another word ▪ **je n'ai plus rien à ~** I have nothing further to say *ou* to add ▪ **ajoutez à cela qu'il est têtu** added to this, he's stubborn **4.** *sout* **~ foi à** [croire] to believe, to give credence to *sout*.
◆ **ajouter à** *v+prép* to add to.
◆ **s'ajouter** *vpi* to be added ▪ **vient s'~ là-dessus le loyer** the rent is added *ou* comes on top ▪ **s'~ à : son licenciement s'ajoute à ses autres problèmes** the loss of his job adds to his other problems.

ajustable [aʒystabl] *adj* adjustable.

ajustage [aʒystaʒ] *nm* **1.** INDUST fitting **2.** [des pièces de monnaie] gauging.

ajusté, e [aʒyste] *adj* close-fitting.

ajustement [aʒystəmɑ̃] *nm* **1.** [modification - d'un projet] adjustment, adaptation ; [- des prix, des salaires, des statistiques] adjusting, adjustment **2.** INDUST fitting.

ajuster [3] [aʒyste] *vt* **1.** [adapter] to fit ▪ **~ un vêtement** COUT to alter a garment ▪ **~ qqch à** *ou* **sur** to fit sthg to *ou* on **2.** [mécanisme, réglage] to adjust **3.** ARM : **~ un lapin** CHASSE to aim at a rabbit ⊙ **~ son coup** *ou* **tir** *pr* to aim one's shot ▪ **tu as bien ajusté ton coup** *ou* **tir** *fig* your aim was pretty accurate, you had it figured out pretty well **4.** [arranger - robe, coiffure] to rearrange ; [- cravate] to straighten **5.** ÉQUIT to adjust **6.** INDUST to fit **7.** [en statistique] to adjust.
◆ **s'ajuster** *vpi* to fit.

ajusteur [aʒystœr] *nm* fitter.

Alabama [alabama] *npr m* : **l'~** Alabama.

alacrité [alakrite] *nf litt* alacrity, eagerness.

alaise [alɛz] *nf* drawsheet ▪ **~ en caoutchouc** rubber sheet *ou* undersheet.

alambic [alɑ̃bik] *nm* still (for making alcohol).

alambiqué, e [alɑ̃bike] *adj* convoluted, involved, tortuous.

alanguir [32] [alɑ̃gir] *vt* [suj: chaleur, fatigue] to make listless *ou* languid *ou* languorous ▪ [suj: oisiveté, paresse] to make indolent *ou* languid ▪ [suj: fièvre] to make feeble, to enfeeble.
◆ **s'alanguir** *vpi* to grow languid ▪ **elle s'alanguissait peu à peu** [devenait triste] her spirits gradually fell ; [n'offrait plus de résistance] she was weakening gradually.

alanguissement [alɑ̃gismɑ̃] *nm* languor.

alarmant, e [alarmɑ̃, ɑ̃t] *adj* alarming.

alarme [alarm] *nf* **1.** [dispositif] : **~ antivol** burglar alarm **2.** [alerte] alarm ▪ **donner l'~** *pr* to give *ou* to raise the alarm ; *fig* to raise the alarm **3.** [inquiétude] alarm, anxiety ▪ **à la première ~** at the first sign of danger.
◆ **d'alarme** *loc adj* [dispositif, signal, sonnette] alarm *(modif)*.

alarmer [3] [alarme] *vt* **1.** [inquiéter - suj: personne, remarque] to alarm ; [- suj: bruit] to startle **2.** [alerter - opinion, presse] to alert.
◆ **s'alarmer** *vpi* to become alarmed ▪ **il n'y a pas de quoi s'~** there's no cause for alarm.

alarmiste [alarmist] *adj* & *nmf* alarmist.

Alaska [alaska] *npr m* : **(l')~** Alaska ▪ **la route de l'~** the Alaska Highway.

albanais, e [albanɛ, ɛz] *adj* Albanian.
◆ **Albanais, e** *nm, f* Albanian.

Albanie [albani] *npr f* : **(l')~** Albania.

albâtre [albatr] *nm* **1.** MINÉR alabaster **2.** [objet] alabaster (object).
◆ **d'albâtre** *loc adj litt* [blanc] : **des épaules d'~** alabaster shoulders, shoulders of alabaster.

albatros [albatros] *nm* ORNITH & SPORT albatross.

albinisme [albinism] *nm* albinism.

albinos [albinos] *adj* & *nmf* albino.

Albion [albjɔ̃] *npr f* Albion.

album [albɔm] *nm* **1.** [livre] album ▪ **~ à colorier** colouring *ou* painting book ▪ **~ (de) photos** photograph album **2.** [disque] album, LP.

albumen [albymɛn] *nm* albumen.

albumine [albymin] *nf* albumin.

alcali [alkali] *nm* alkali.

alcalin, e [alkalɛ̃, in] *adj* CHIM alkaline.
◆ **alcalin** *nm* alkali.

alcaliniser [3] [alkalinize] *vt* to alkalinize.

alcaloïde [alkalɔid] *nm* alkaloid.

alcazar [alkazar] *nm* alcazar.

Alceste [alsɛst] *npr main character in Molière's 'le Misanthrope', who shuns society.*

alchimie [alʃimi] *nf* alchemy.

alchimique [alʃimik] *adj* alchemical.

alchimiste [alʃimist] *nmf* alchemist.

alcool [alkɔl] *nm* **1.** [boissons alcoolisées] : **l'~** alcohol ▪ **je ne bois pas d'~** I don't drink (alcohol) ▪ **boisson sans ~** non-alcoholic drink ▪ **bière sans ~** alcohol-free beer ▮ [spiritueux] : **~ de prune** plum brandy ▪ **il ne tient pas l'~** he can't take his drink **2.** CHIM & PHARM alcohol, spirit ▪ **~ à brûler** methylated spirits, meths *UK* ▪ **~ éthylique** ethyl alcohol ▪ **~ de menthe** medicinal mint spirit ▪ **~ méthylique** methyl alcohol, methanol ▪ **~ pur** raw spirits ▪ **~ à 90°** surgical spirit.
◆ **à alcool** *loc adj* [réchaud, lampe] spirit *(modif)*.

alcoolémie [alkɔlemi] *nf* alcohol level *(in the blood)*.

alcoolique [alkɔlik] <> *adj* alcoholic.

<> *nmf* alcoholic ■ **Alcooliques anonymes** Alcoholics Anonymous.

lcoolisation [alkɔlizasjɔ̃] *nf* **1.** CHIM alcoholization **2.** MÉD alcoholism.

lcoolisé, e [alkɔlize] *adj* **1.** [qui contient de l'alcool] : **boissons ~es** alcoholic drinks *ou* beverages *sout*, intoxicating liquors *sout* ■ **non ~** nonalcoholic ■ **bière peu ~e** low-alcohol beer **2.** *fam* [personne] drunk.

lcooliser [3] [alkɔlize] *vt* **1.** [convertir en alcool] to alcoholize, to convert to alcohol **2.** [additionner d'alcool] to add alcohol to.
◆ **s'alcooliser** *vpi fam* [s'enivrer] to get drunk ■ [être alcoolique] to drink.

lcoolisme [alkɔlism] *nm* alcoholism.

lcoolo [alkɔlo] *nmf fam* alkie.

lcoomètre [alkɔmɛtr] *nm* alcoholometer.

lco(o)test® [alkɔtɛst] *nm* **1.** [appareil] breathalyser **2.** [vérification] breath test.

lcôve [alkov] *nf* alcove, recess.
◆ **d'alcôve** *loc adj* [secret, histoire] intimate.

léa [alea] *nm* unforeseen turn of events ■ **tenir compte des ~s** to take the unforeseen *ou* unexpected into account ■ **les ~s de l'existence** the ups and downs of life.

léatoire [aleatwar] *adj* **1.** [entreprise, démarche] risky, hazardous, chancy ■ **c'est ~** it's uncertain, there's nothing definite about it **2.** DR [contrat] aleatory **3.** FIN : **gain ~** chance *ou* contingent gain ■ **profit ~** contingent profit **4.** INFORM random access **5.** MATH random **6.** MUS aleatory.

léatoirement [aleatwarmɑ̃] *adv* **1.** [par hasard] by chance, at random **2.** [de façon risquée] riskily, in a risky *ou* chancy manner.

lémanique [alemanik] *adj* & *nmf* Alemannic.

lena [alena] (*abr de* **Accord de libre-échange nord-américain**) *nm* NAFTA.

lentour [alɑ̃tur] *adv* : **dans la campagne ~** in the surrounding countryside ■ **tout ~** all around.
◆ **alentours** *nmpl* neighbourhood, vicinity, (surrounding) area ■ **les ~s de la ville** the countryside around the city ■ **il doit être dans les ~s** [tout près] he's somewhere around (here) ■ **aux ~s de** [dans l'espace, le temps] around ■ **aux ~s de minuit** round (about) *ou* some time around midnight.

léoutiennes [aleusjɛn] *npr fpl* : **les (îles) ~** the Aleutian Islands, *voir aussi* **île**.

lerte[1] [alɛrt] *adj* [démarche] quick, alert ■ [esprit] lively, alert ■ [style] lively, brisk ■ [personne] spry.

lerte[2] [alɛrt] *nf* **1.** [signal] alert ■ **donner l'~** to give the alert ■ **~!** [aux armes] to arms! ; [attention] watch out! ➲ **fausse ~** false alarm ■ **~ aérienne** air raid *ou* air strike warning ■ **~ à la bombe** bomb scare **2.** [signe avant-coureur] alarm, warning sign ■ **à la première ~** at the first warning ■ **l'~ a été chaude** that was a close call.
◆ **d'alerte** *loc adj* warning, alarm *(modif)*.
◆ **en alerte, en état d'alerte** *loc adv* on the alert ■ **toutes les casernes de pompiers étaient en état d'~** the entire fire service was on standby *ou* the alert.

lertement [alɛrtəmɑ̃] *adv* alertly, briskly, in a lively manner.

lerter [3] [alɛrte] *vt* **1.** [alarmer] to alert **2.** [informer - autorités] to notify, to inform ; [- presse] to alert ■ **nous avons été alertés par les résidents eux-mêmes** the local residents themselves drew our attention to the problem ■ **~ qqn de** to alert sb to.

lèse [alɛz] = **alaise**.

léser [18] [aleze] *vt* to ream, to bore.

levin [alvɛ̃] *nm* alevin, young fish.

leviner [3] [alvine] *vt* to stock (with young fish).

lexandre [alɛksɑ̃dr] *npr* : **~ le Grand** Alexander the Great.

Alexandrie [alɛksɑ̃dri] *npr* Alexandria.

alexandrin, e [alɛksɑ̃drɛ̃, in] *adj* **1.** HIST Alexandrian **2.** LITTÉR Alexandrine.
◆ **Alexandrin, e** *nm, f* Alexandrian.
◆ **alexandrin** *nm* LITTÉR Alexandrine.

alezan, e [alzɑ̃, an] *adj* & *nm, f* chestnut ■ **~ clair** sorrel.

algarade [algarad] *nf* quarrel.

algèbre [alʒɛbr] *nf* algebra ■ **pour moi, c'est de l'~** *fam* it's all Greek to me, I can't make head nor tail of it.

algébrique [alʒebrik] *adj* algebraic, algebraical.

algébriste [alʒebrist] *nmf* algebraist.

Algéco® [alʒeko] *nm* Portakabin®.

Alger [alʒe] *npr* Algiers.

Algérie [alʒeri] *npr f* : **(l')~** Algeria ■ **la guerre d'~** the Algerian War.

LA GUERRE D'ALGÉRIE

The most bitter of France's post-colonial struggles, 1954-62. In a country dominated by a million white settlers, the *pieds noirs*, the government's failure to crush the revolt of the *Front de libération nationale* (FLN), despite massive military intervention, led settlers and army officers to attempt a takeover of the colony. The recall to power of General de Gaulle (1958), and the *Accords d'Évian* (1962), led to Algeria's independence and the resettlement of the *pieds noirs* in France.

algérien, enne [alʒerjɛ̃, ɛn] *adj* Algerian.
◆ **Algérien, enne** *nm, f* Algerian.

algérois, e [alʒerwa, az] *adj* from Algiers.
◆ **Algérois, e** *nm, f inhabitant of or person from Algiers.*

algol [algɔl] *nm* ALGOL.

Algonkin, Algonquin [algɔ̃kɛ̃] *npr m* Algonquin ■ **les ~s** the Algonquin.
◆ **algonkin, algonquin** *nm* Algonquin.

algorithme [algɔritm] *nm* algorithm.

algorithmique [algɔritmik] *adj* algorithmic.

algue [alg] *nf* (piece of) seaweed, alga *spéc.*

alias [aljas] *adv* alias, a.k.a.

alibi [alibi] *nm* **1.** DR alibi ■ **un ~ en or** the perfect alibi **2.** [prétexte] alibi, excuse.

alicament [alikamɑ̃] *nm* [avec additifs] nutraceutical, dietary supplement ■ [biologique] organic food *(consumed for its health benefits)*.

aliénable [aljenabl] *adj* alienable.

aliénant, e [aljenɑ̃, ɑ̃t] *adj* alienating.

aliénation [aljenasjɔ̃] *nf* **1.** PHILOS & POLIT alienation **2.** PSYCHOL : **~ mentale** insanity, mental illness **3.** [perte - d'un droit, d'un bien] loss, removal **4.** DR alienation, transfer of property ■ **~ de biens** disposal of property.

aliéné, e [aljene] <> *adj* **1.** PHILOS & POLIT alienated **2.** PSYCHOL insane, mentally disturbed.
<> *nm, f* PSYCHOL mental patient.

aliéner [18] [aljene] *vt* **1.** [abandonner - indépendance, liberté, droit] to give up *(sép)* ■ DR to alienate **2.** [supprimer - droit, liberté, indépendance] to remove, to confiscate **3.** PHILOS & POLIT to alienate.
◆ **s'aliéner** *vpt* : **s'~ qqn** to alienate sb ■ **je me suis aliéné leur amitié** *sout* I caused them to turn away *ou* to become estranged *sout* from me.

Aliénor [aljenɔr] *npr* : **~ d'Aquitaine** Eleanor of Aquitaine.

alignement [aliɲmɑ̃] *nm* **1.** [rangée] line, row ■ **mettre qqch dans le même ~ que** to bring sthg into line *ou* alignment with ■ **être à** *ou* **dans l'~** to be *ou* to stand in line ■ **se mettre à** *ou* **dans l'~** to fall into line ■ **ne pas être à** *ou* **dans l'~** to be out of line **2.** *fig* aligning, bringing into alignment ■ **leur ~ sur la**

politique des socialistes their coming into line with the socialists' policy ◘ **~ monétaire** monetary alignment *ou* adjustment **3.** DR building line.
◆ **alignements** *nmpl* [de menhirs] standing stones *(arranged in a row)*, alignments.

aligner [3] [aliɲe] *vt* **1.** [mettre en rang] to line up *(sép)*, to align **2.** MIL [soldats, tanks] to line up *(sép)*, to form into lines ■ [divisions] to line up ■ ADMIN & MIL to bring into alignment **3.** [présenter - preuves] to produce one by one ; [- en écrivant] to string together *(sép)* ; [- en récitant] to string together, to reel off *(sép)* **4.** [mettre en conformité] : **~ qqch sur** to line sthg up with, to bring sthg into line with ■ **chaque membre doit ~ sa politique sur celle de la Communauté** each member state must bring its policies into line with those of the Community **5.** △ *loc* **les ~** [payer] to cough up, to fork out.
◆ **s'aligner** *vpi* **1.** [foule, élèves] to line up, to form a line ■ [soldats] to fall into line **2.** △ *loc* **il peut toujours s'~!** he's got no chance (of getting anywhere)!
◆ **s'aligner sur** *vp+prép* [imiter - nation, gouvernement] to fall into line *ou* to align o.s. with.

aligot [aligo] *nm* CULIN *mashed potatoes blended with garlic and soft cheese, a speciality of the Auvergne region.*

aligoté [aligɔte] *nm* aligoté (wine).

aliment [alimɑ̃] *nm* **1.** [nourriture] (type *ou* kind of) food ■ **citez trois ~s** list three types of food *ou* three different foods ■ **l'eau n'est pas un ~** water is not (a) food *ou* has no food value ‖ [portion] (piece of) food ■ **des ~s** food, foodstuffs ■ **la plupart des ~s** most food *ou* foodstuffs ◘ **~s pour bébé/chien** baby/dog food ■ **~s congelés/diététiques** frozen/health food **2.** *fig* & *litt* **l'~ de** *ou* **un ~ pour l'esprit** food for thought **3.** [dans les assurances] interest, risk.
◆ **aliments** *nmpl* DR maintenance.

alimentaire [alimɑ̃tɛr] *adj* **1.** COMM & MÉD food *(modif)* ■ **sac/papier ~** bag/paper for wrapping food **2.** [pour gagner de l'argent] : **œuvre ~** potboiler ■ **je fais des enquêtes mais c'est purement ~** I do surveys, but it's just to make ends meet **3.** [de la digestion] alimentary **4.** TECHNOL feeding, feeder *(modif)* **5.** DR [obligation] maintenance *(modif)*.

alimentation [alimɑ̃tasjɔ̃] *nf* **1.** [fait de manger] (consumption of) food ■ [fait de faire manger] feeding **2.** [régime] diet ■ **une ~ carnée** a meat-based diet **3.** COMM [magasin] grocer's ■ [rayon] groceries ■ [activité] : **l'~** food distribution, the food (distribution) trade **4.** TECHNOL supply ■ **assurer l'~ d'une pompe en électricité** to supply electricity to a pump ■ **ils ont l'~ en eau** they have running water **5.** MIL [d'une armée] arms supply.

alimenter [3] [alimɑ̃te] *vt* **1.** [nourrir - malade, bébé] to feed **2.** TECHNOL [moteur, pompe] to feed ■ [ville] to supply ■ **~ qqn en eau** to supply sb with water **3.** [approvisionner - compte] to put money into ■ **~ les caisses de l'État** to be a source of revenue *ou* cash for the Government **4.** [entretenir - conversation] to sustain ; [- curiosité, intérêt] to feed, to sustain ; [- doute, désaccord] to fuel.
◆ **s'alimenter** *vp (emploi réfléchi)* [gén] to eat ■ **elle ne s'alimente plus depuis une semaine** she hasn't had any solid food for a week ■ **s'~ bien/mal** to have a good/poor diet ‖ [bébé] to feed o.s.
◆ **s'alimenter en** *vp+prép* [se procurer] : **comment le village s'alimente-t-il en eau?** how does the village get its water?

alinéa [alinea] *nm* [espace] indent ■ [paragraphe] paragraph.

alitement [alitmɑ̃] *nm* confinement *(to one's bed)*.

aliter [3] [alite] *vt* to confine to bed.
◆ **s'aliter** *vpi* to take to one's bed ■ **rester alité** to be confined to one's bed, to be bedridden.

alizé [alize] ◇ *adj m* [vent] trade *(modif)*.
◇ *nm* trade wind.

Allah [ala] *npr* Allah.

allaitement [alɛtmɑ̃] *nm* [processus] feeding, suckling *UK*, nursing *US* ■ [période] breast-feeding period ■ **~ maternel** *ou* **au sein** breast-feeding.

allaiter [4] [alete] *vt* to breastfeed ■ **à quelle heure est-ce tu l'allaites?** what time do you feed him?

allant, e [alɑ̃, ɑ̃t] *adj litt* cheerful, lively.
◆ **allant** *nm sout* energy, drive ■ **être plein d'~** to have ple[…] of drive.

alléchant, e [aleʃɑ̃, ɑ̃t] *adj* **1.** [plat, odeur] mouth-wateri[…] appetizing **2.** [proposition, projet, offre] enticing, tempting[…]

allécher [18] [aleʃe] *vt* **1.** [suj: odeur, plat] : **~ qqn** to give s[…] appetite ■ **l'odeur du pain chaud allèche les enfants** the sm[…] of hot bread makes the children's mouths water **2.** [su[…] fre, proposition, projet - gén] to tempt, to seduce, to enti[…] [- dans le but de tromper] to lure.

allée [ale] *nf* [à la campagne] footpath, lane ■ [dans un ja[…] alley ■ [dans un parc] walk, path ■ [en ville] avenue ■ [devant[…] maison, une villa] drive, driveway ■ [dans un cinéma, un t[…] aisle ■ **les ~s du pouvoir** the corridors of power.
◆ **allées et venues** *nfpl* comings and goings ■ **toutes[…] ~s et venues pour rien** all this running around *ou* about[…] nothing ■ **nous faisons des ~s et venues entre Québec et Toro[…]** we go *ou* we shuttle back and forth between Quebec […] Toronto.

allégation [alegasjɔ̃] *nf* allegation, (unsubstantia[…] claim.

allège [alɛʒ] *nf* **1.** CONSTR [d'une fenêtre] basement ■ [[…] dwarf wall **2.** NAUT barge, lighter.

allégé, e [aleʒe] *adj* low-fat.

allégeance [aleʒɑ̃s] *nf* HIST allegiance.

allègement [alɛʒmɑ̃] *nm* **1.** [diminution - d'un fardeau] li[…] ening ; [- d'une douleur] relief, alleviation, soothing **2.** ÉC[…] FIN reduction ■ **ils sont en faveur de l'~ des charges sociales p[…] les entreprises** they are in favour of reducing employers'[…] tional insurance contributions ◘ **~ fiscal** tax reduct[…] **3.** ÉDUC : **~ de l'effectif** reduction in class size ■ **~ des prog[…] mes** streamlining of the curriculum **4.** SPORT [des skis] lif[…] (the weight off the skis).

alléger [22] [aleʒe] *vt* **1.** [rendre moins lourd - malle, meuble[…] make lighter, to lighten ■ **il va falloir ~ le paquet de 10 g[…] mes** we'll have to take 10 grammes off the parcel **2.** ÉC[…] FIN [cotisation, contribution] to reduce ■ **~ les impôts de 10 […]** reduce tax by 10%, to take 10% off tax **3.** [soulager - dou[…] to relieve, to soothe ■ **je me suis senti allégé d'un grand p[…] ou fardeau** I felt (that) a great weight had been taken off[…] shoulders **4.** [faciliter - procédure, texte] to simplify, to t[…] (down) ■ **les formalités ont été allégées** some of the red t[…] was done away with **5.** ÉDUC : **~ le programme** to trim the […] riculum.

allégorie [alegɔri] *nf* allegory.

allégorique [alegɔrik] *adj* allegorical.

allégoriquement [alegɔrikmɑ̃] *adv* allegorically.

allègre [alɛgr] *adj* cheerful, light-hearted ■ **marcher d'un[…] ~** to walk with a light step.

allègrement [alɛgrəmɑ̃] *adv* **1.** [joyeusement] cheerf[…] light-heartedly **2.** *hum* [carrément] heedlessly, blithely.

allégresse [alegrɛs] *nf* cheerfulness, liveliness ■ **l'~ étai[…] nérale** there was general rejoicing.

alléguer [18] [alege] *vt* **1.** [prétexter] to argue ■ **~ comme[…] cuse/prétexte que** to put forward as an excuse/a pretext […] ■ **alléguant du fait que** arguing that **2.** *sout* [citer] to cite[…] quote.

alléluia [aleluja] *nm* alleluia, hallelujah.

Allemagne [almaɲ] *npr f* : **(l')~** Germany ■ **(l')~ de l'Est** E[…] Germany ■ **(l')~ de l'Ouest** West Germany.

allemand, e [almɑ̃, ɑ̃d] *adj* German.
◆ **Allemand, e** *nm, f* German ■ **Allemand de l'Est** East G[…] man ■ **Allemand de l'Ouest** West German.
◆ **allemand** *nm* LING German.
◆ **allemande** *nf* DANSE & MUS allemande.

aller[1] [ale] *nm* **1.** [voyage] outward journey ▪ **je suis passé les voir à l'~** I dropped in to see them on the way (there) ▪ **l'avion était en retard à l'~ et au retour** the flight was delayed both ways ▪ **un ~ (et) retour** a round trip ▪ **faire des ~s et retours** [personne, document] to go back and forth, to shuttle back and forth ▪ **ne faire qu'un** *ou* **que l'~ et retour : je vais à la banque mais je ne fais qu'un ~ et retour** I'm going to the bank, but I'll be right back **2.** [billet] : **~ (simple)** single (ticket) *UK*, one-way ticket *US* ▪ **~ (et) retour** return *UK ou* round-trip *US* (ticket) **3.** *fam* **~ et retour** [gifle] slap.

aller[2] [31] [ale] ◇ *v aux* **1.** *(suivi de l'infin)* [exprime le futur proche] to be going *ou* about to ▪ **tu vas tomber!** you're going to fall!, you'll fall! ▪ **attendez-le, il va arriver** wait for him, he'll be here any minute now ▪ **j'allais justement te téléphoner** I was just going to phone you, I was on the point of phoning you ▪ **il va être 5 h** it's going on 5 ‖ [pour donner un ordre] : **tu vas faire ce que je te dis, oui ou non?** will you do as I say or won't you? **2.** *(suivi de l'infin)* [en intensif] to go ▪ **ne va pas croire/penser que...** don't go and believe/think that... ▪ **tu ne vas pas me faire croire que tu ne savais rien!** you can't fool me into thinking that you didn't know anything! ▪ **que n'iront-ils pas s'imaginer!** God knows what they'll think! ▪ **où est-elle? – allez savoir!** where is she? – God knows! ▪ **allez expliquer ça à un enfant de 5 ans!** try and explain *ou* try explaining that to a 5-year-old! **3.** [exprime la continuité] *(suivi du gérondif)* **~ en : ~ en s'améliorant** to get better and better, to improve ▪ **~ en augmentant** to keep increasing ▪ **~ en diminuant : le bruit allait en diminuant** the noise was getting fainter and fainter ▪ *(suivi du p prés)* **~ croissant** [tension] to be rising ; [nombre] to be rising *ou* increasing.

◇ *vi*

A. EXPRIME LE MOUVEMENT
B. S'ÉTENDRE
C. PROGRESSER
D. ÊTRE DANS TELLE OU TELLE SITUATION
E. EXPRIME L'ADÉQUATION
F. LOCUTIONS

A. EXPRIME LE MOUVEMENT

1. [se déplacer] to go ▪ **qui va là?** who goes there? ▪ **va vite!** hurry up! ; [à un enfant] run along (now)! ▪ **vous alliez à plus de 90 km/h** [en voiture] you were driving at *ou* doing more than 90 km/h ▪ **~ (et) venir** [de long en large] to pace up and down ; [entre deux destinations] to come and go, to go to and fro ▪ **je n'ai fait qu'~ et venir toute la matinée** I was in and out all morning

2. [se rendre - personne] : **~ à** to go to ▪ **en allant à Limoges** on the way to Limoges ▪ **~ à la mer/à la montagne** to go to the seaside/mountains ▪ **~ à l'université** [bâtiment] to go to the university ; [institution] to go to university *ou* college ▪ **~ à la chasse/pêche** to go hunting/fishing ▪ **où vas-tu?** where are you going? ▪ **comment y va-t-on?** how do you get there? ▪ **y ~ : il y est allé en courant** he ran there ▪ **on y va!** let's go! ▪ **j'irai en avion/voiture** I'll fly/drive, I'll go by plane/car ▪ **~ chez : ~ chez un ami** to go to see a friend, to go to a friend's ▪ **tu n'iras plus chez eux, tu m'entends?** you will not visit them again, do you hear me? ▪ **~ dans : il a peur d'~ dans l'eau** he's afraid to go into the water ▪ **je vais dans les Pyrénées** I'm going to the Pyrenees ▪ **~ en : ~ en Autriche** to go *ou* to travel to Austria ▪ **~ en haut/bas** to go up/down ▪ **~ vers : j'allais vers le nord** I was heading *ou* going north

3. *(suivi de l'infin)* [pour se livrer à une activité] : **~ faire qqch** to go and do sthg, to go do sthg *US* ▪ **je vais faire mes courses tous les matins** I go shopping every morning ▪ **va ramasser les poires dans le jardin** go and pick the pears in the garden ⊙ **va voir là-bas si j'y suis!**[△] push off!, clear off! ▪ **va te faire voir**[△] *ou* **te faire foutre!**[▲] get lost! *ou UK* stuffed![△], go to hell!

4. [mener - véhicule, chemin] to go ▪ **cette rue va vers le centre** this street leads towards the city centre ⊙ **~ droit au cœur de qqn** to go straight to sb's heart

5. [fonctionner - machine] to go, to run ; [- moteur] to run ; [- voiture, train] to go

6. [se ranger - dans un contenant] to go, to belong ; [- dans un ensemble] to fit

7. [être remis] : **~ à** to go to ▪ **l'argent collecté ira à une œuvre** the collection will go *ou* be given to a charity

B. S'ÉTENDRE

1. [dans l'espace] : **~ de... à... : leur propriété va de la rivière à la côte** their land stretches from the river to the coast ▪ **le passage qui va de la page 35 à la page 43** the passage which goes from page 35 to page 43 ▪ **~ jusqu'à** [vers le haut] to go *ou* to reach up to ; [vers le bas] to go *ou* to reach down to ; [en largeur, en longueur] to go to, to stretch as far as

2. [dans le temps] : **~ de... à...** to go from... to... ▪ **~ jusqu'à** [bail, contrat] to run till

3. [dans une série] : **~ de... à...** to go *ou* to range from... to... ▪ **~ jusqu'à : les prix vont jusqu'à 8.000 euros** prices go as high as 8,000 euros

C. PROGRESSER

1. [se dérouler] : **~ vite/lentement** to go fast/slow ⊙ **plus ça va... : plus ça va, moins je comprends la politique** the more I see of politics, the less I understand it ▪ **plus ça va, plus je l'aime** I love her more each day

2. [personne] : **~ jusqu'à : j'irai jusqu'à 1.000 euros pour le fauteuil** I'll pay *ou* go up to 1,000 euros for the armchair ▪ **j'irais même jusqu'à dire que...** I would even go so far as to say that... ▪ **sans ~ jusque-là** without going that far ▪ **~ sur** *ou* **vers** [approcher de] : **il va sur** *ou* **vers la cinquantaine** he's getting on for *ou* going on 50 ▪ **elle va sur ses cinq ans** she's nearly *ou* almost five, she'll be five soon ⊙ **~ à la faillite/l'échec** to be heading for bankruptcy/failure ▪ **~ à sa ruine** to be on the road to ruin ▪ **où va-t-on** *ou* **allons-nous s'il faut se barricader chez soi?** what's the world coming to if people have to lock themselves in nowadays? ▪ **allons (droit) au fait** let's get (straight) to the point ▪ **~ au plus pressé** to do the most urgent thing first

D. ÊTRE DANS TELLE OU TELLE SITUATION

1. [en parlant de l'état de santé] : **bonjour, comment ça va? – ça va** hello, how are you? – all right ▪ **comment va la santé?, comment va?** *fam* how are you keeping? ▪ **ça va?** [après un choc] are you all right? ▪ **ça ne va pas du tout** I'm not at all well ▪ **~ bien : je vais bien** I'm fine *ou* well ▪ **ça va bien?** are you OK? ▪ **~ mieux : elle va beaucoup mieux** she's (feeling) much better ▪ **~ mal : il va mal** he's not at all well, he's very poorly ⊙ **ça va pas (bien)** *ou* **la tête!, ça va pas, non?** *fam* you're off your head!, you must be mad! ▪ **ça va? – on fait ~** *fam ou* **il faut faire ~** *fam* how are you? – mustn't grumble

2. [se passer] : **comment vont les affaires? – elles vont bien** how's business? – (it's doing) OK *ou* fine ▪ **ça va de moins en moins bien entre eux** things have gone from bad to worse between them ▪ **les choses vont** *ou* **ça va mal** things aren't too good *ou* aren't going too well ▪ **obéis-moi ou ça va mal ~ (pour toi)!** do as I say or you'll be in trouble! ▪ **comment ça va dans ton nouveau service?** how are you getting on *ou* how are things in the new department? ▪ **quelque chose ne va pas?** is there anything wrong *ou* the matter? ⊙ **ça ne va pas tout seul** *ou* **sans problème** it's not an *ou* it's no easy job ▪ **et le travail, ça va comme tu veux?** *fam* is work going all right?

E. EXPRIME L'ADÉQUATION

1. [être seyant] : **~ (bien) à qqn** [taille d'un vêtement] to fit sb ; [style d'un vêtement] to suit sb ▪ **le bleu lui va** blue suits her, she looks good in blue ▪ **ça ne te va pas de parler vulgairement** coarse language doesn't suit *ou* become you ▪ **ça te va bien de donner des conseils!** *iron* you're a fine one to give advice! ⊙ **cela te va à ravir** *ou* **à merveille** that looks wonderful on you, you look wonderful in that

2. [être en harmonie] : **~ avec : ~ avec qqch** to go with *ou* to match sthg ▪ **j'ai acheté un chapeau pour ~ avec ma veste** I bought a hat to go with *ou* to match my jacket ▪ **~ ensemble** [couleurs, styles] to go well together, to match ; [éléments d'une paire] to belong together ▪ **ils vont bien ensemble, ces deux-là!** those two make quite a pair! ▪ **je trouve qu'ils vont très mal ensemble** I think (that) they're an ill-matched couple *ou* they make a very odd pair

3. [convenir] : **la clé de 12 devrait ~** spanner number 12 should do (the job) ▪ **nos plats vont au four** our dishes are oven-proof ▪ **tu veux de l'aide? – non, ça ira!** do you want a hand? – no, I'll manage *ou* it's OK! ▪ **tu ne rajoutes pas de crème? – ça ira comme ça** don't you want to add some cream? – that'll do (as it is) *ou* it's fine like this ▪ **ça ira pour aujourd'hui** that'll be all for today, let's call it a day ▪ **pour un studio, ça peut ~** as far as bedsits *UK ou* studio apartments *US* go, it's not too bad ▪ ~

à qqn : on dînera après le spectacle – ça me va we'll go for dinner after the show – that's all right *ou* fine by me *ou* that suits me (fine)

F. LOCUTIONS

▶ **allez, un petit effort** come on, put some effort into it ■ **allez, je m'en vais!** right, I'm going now! ■ **zut, j'ai cassé un verre! – et allez (donc), le troisième en un mois!** damn! I've broken a glass! – well done, that's the third in a month! ■ **allez** *ou* **allons donc!** [tu exagères] go on *ou* get away (with you)!,come off it! ■ **allez-y!** go on!, off you go! ■ **allons-y!** let's go! ■ **allons-y, ne nous gênons pas!** *iron* don't mind me! ■ **allons bon, j'ai perdu ma clef maintenant!** oh no, now I've lost my key! ■ **allons bon, voilà qu'il recommence à pleurer!** here we go, he's crying again! ■ **c'est mieux comme ça, va!** it's better that way, you know! ■ **(espèce de) frimeur, va!** *fam* you show-off! ■ **va donc, eh minable!** *fam* get lost, you little creep! ■ **ça va** *fam*, **ça va bien** *fam*, **ça va comme ça** *fam* OK ■ **je t'aurai prévenu! – ça va, ça va!** don't say I didn't warn you! – OK, OK! ■ **ça va comme ça hein, j'en ai assez de tes jérémiades!** just shut up will you, I'm fed up with your moaning! ■ **y ~** *fam* **: une fois que tu es sur le plongeoir, il faut y ~!** once you're on the diving board, you've got to jump! ■ **quand faut y ~, faut y ~** when you've got to go, you've got to go ■ **y ~** [le faire] **: vas-y doucement, c'est fragile** gently *ou* easy does it, it's fragile ■ **vas-y mollo avec le vin!** *fam* go easy on the wine! ■ **comme tu y vas** *fam* **/vous y allez** *fam* **: j'en veux 30 euros – comme tu y vas!** I want 30 euros for it – isn't that a bit much? ■ **ça y va :** *fam* **ça y va, les billets de 10 euros!** 10 euro notes are going as if there was no tomorrow! ■ **y ~ de : aux réunions de famille, il y va toujours d'une** *ou* **de sa chansonnette** every time there's a family gathering, he sings a little song ■ **elle y est allée de sa petite larme** *hum* she had a little cry ■ **il** *ou* **cela** *ou* **ça va de soi (que)** it goes without saying (that) ■ **il** *ou* **cela** *ou* **ça va sans dire (que)** it goes without saying (that) ■ **il y va de : il y va de ta vie/carrière/ réputation** your life/ career/reputation is at stake ■ **il en va de... comme de... : il en va de la littérature comme de la peinture** it's the same with literature as with painting ■ **il en va de même pour : il n'en va pas de même pour toi** the same doesn't apply to you ■ **il en va autrement : il en irait autrement si ta mère était encore là** things would be very different if your mother was still here ■ **va pour le Saint-Émilion!** *fam* all right *ou* OK then, we'll have the Saint-Emilion! ■ **tout le monde est égoïste, si tu vas par là!** everybody's selfish, if you look at it like that!

◆ **s'en aller** *vpi* **1.** [partir - personne] to go ■ **je lui donnerai la clé en m'en allant** I'll give him the key on my way out ■ **va-t'en!** go away! ■ **tous les jeunes s'en vont du village** all the young people are leaving the village ■ **va-t'en de là!** get away from there! **2.** [se défaire, se détacher] to come undone **3.** *sout* [mourir - personne] to die, to pass away **4.** [disparaître - tache] to come off, to go (away) ; [- son] to fade away ; [- forces] to fail ; [- jeunesse] to pass ; [- lumière, soleil, couleur] to fade (away) ; [- peinture, vernis] to come off ■ **ça s'en ira au lavage/avec du savon** it'll come off in the wash/with soap ■ **leur dernière lueur d'espoir s'en est allée** their last glimmer of hope has gone *ou* vanished **5.** *(suivi de l'infin)* [en intensif] **: il s'en fut trouver le magicien** off he went to find the wizard ■ **je m'en vais lui dire ses quatre vérités!** *fam* I'm going to tell her a few home truths!

allergène [alɛrʒɛn] *nm* allergen.

allergie [alɛrʒi] *nf* **1.** MÉD allergy ■ **avoir** *ou* **faire une ~ à** to be allergic to **2.** *fam* [répugnance] allergy.

allergique [alɛrʒik] *adj* **1.** MÉD [réaction] allergic ■ **être ~ à qqch** to be allergic to sthg **2.** *fam fig* allergic ■ **je suis ~ au sport** I'm allergic to sport.

allergisant, e [alɛrʒizɑ̃, ɑ̃t] *adj* allergenic.

allergologie [alɛrgɔlɔʒi] *nf* diagnosis and treatment of allergies.

allergologue [alɛrgɔlɔg] *nmf* allergist.

alliage [aljaʒ] *nm* **1.** MÉTALL & TECHNOL alloy ■ **structure en ~ léger** alloy structure **2.** *litt* [ajout] adjunct.

alliance [aljɑ̃s] *nf* **1.** [pacte] alliance, pact, union ■ **l'~ entre socialistes et communistes** *ou* **les socialistes et les communistes** the alliance between *ou* of Socialists and Communists ■ **conclure une ~ avec un pays** to enter into *ou* to forge an alliance with a country ■ **conclure une ~ avec qqn** to ally o.s with sb ■ **l'Alliance française** *organization promoting French language and culture abroad* **2.** *sout* [mariage] union **3.** [combinaison] union, blending, combination ■ **~ de mots** LING oxymoron **4.** [bague] wedding ring **5.** RELIG covenant.

◆ **par alliance** *loc adj* by marriage.

allié, e [alje] ◇ *adj* allied.

◇ *nm, f* **1.** [pays, gouvernement] ally ■ **les Alliés** HIST the Allies **2.** DR relation by marriage **3.** [ami] ally, supporter.

allier [9] [alje] *vt* **1.** [unir - pays, gouvernements, chefs] to unite, to ally (together) ; [- familles] to relate *ou* to unite by marriage **2.** [combiner - efforts, moyens, qualités] to combine (together) ; [- sons, couleurs, parfums] to match, to blend (together) ■ **elle allie l'intelligence à l'humour** she combines intelligence and humour **3.** TECHNOL to (mix into an) alloy.

◆ **s'allier** *vpi* **1.** [pays] to become allied ■ **s'~ avec un pays** to ally o.s. to a country, to form an alliance with a country ■ *sout* [par le mariage - personnes] to marry ; [- familles] to become allied *ou* related by marriage ■ **s'~ à une famille** to marry into a family **2.** [se combiner - couleurs, sons, parfums] to match, to blend (together) ; [- qualités, talents, arts] to combine, to unite (together) **3.** TECHNOL to (become mixed into an) alloy.

alligator [aligatɔr] *nm* alligator.

allitération [aliterasjɔ̃] *nf* alliteration.

allô [alo] *interj* hello, hullo ■ **~, qui est à l'appareil?** hello, who's speaking?

allocataire [alɔkatɛr] *nmf* beneficiary.

allocation [alɔkasjɔ̃] *nf* **1.** [attribution] allocation ■ FIN [de parts] allotment, allotting **2.** SOCIOL [prestation] allowance benefit *UK*, welfare *US* ■ **avoir** *ou* **toucher des ~s** to be on benefit *UK ou* welfare *US* ▶ **~ (de) chômage** unemployment benefit ■ **~s familiales** family credit ■ **~ (de) logement, ~-logement** housing benefit *UK*, rent subsidy *ou* allowance *US* ■ **je touche une ~-logement** I get housing benefit *UK ou* a rent subsidy *US* ■ **~ (de) maternité** maternity allowance.

◆ **allocations** *nfpl fam* **les ~s** [service] social security *UK*, welfare *US* ; [bureau] the social security office.

allocutaire [alɔkytɛr] *nmf* addressee.

allocution [alɔkysjɔ̃] *nf* [discours] (formal) speech.

allogène [alɔʒɛn] ◇ *adj* [gén] foreign ■ [population] non-native.

◇ *nmf* alien.

allonge [alɔ̃ʒ] *nf* **1.** [rallonge - gén] extension ; [- d'une table] leaf **2.** [crochet] (butcher's) hook **3.** FIN rider **4.** SPORT reach ■ **avoir une bonne ~** to have a long reach.

allongé, e [alɔ̃ʒe] *adj* **1.** [long] long **2.** [couché] **: il était ~ sur le canapé** he was lying on the sofa ■ **il est resté ~ pendant trois mois** he was bedridden for three months.

allongement [alɔ̃ʒmɑ̃] *nm* **1.** [extension - d'une route, d'un canal] extension ; [- d'une distance] increasing, lengthening [- d'une durée, de la vie] lengthening, extension ; [- des jours] lengthening ■ **l'~ du temps de loisir** the increased time available for leisure pursuits **2.** TECHNOL [déformation] stretching ■ MÉTALL elongation **3.** LING lengthening.

allonger [17] [alɔ̃ʒe] ◇ *vt* **1.** [rendre plus long - robe, route, texte] to lengthen, to make longer ■ **la coupe vous allonge la silhouette** the cut of the garment makes you look thinner ■ **~ le pas** to take longer strides

2. [étirer - bras, jambe] to stretch out *(sép)* ■ **~ le cou** to stretch one's neck

3. [coucher - blessé, malade] to lay down *(sép)*

4. △ [donner - argent] to produce, to come up with ■ **cette fois ci, il a fallu qu'il les allonge** this time he had to cough up *ou* to fork out ■ **~ une taloche à qqn** to give sb a slap ■ **~ un coup à qqn** to fetch sb a blow

5. CULIN **: ~ la sauce** *pr* to make the sauce thinner ; *fig* to spin things out

6. ÉQUIT [allure] to lengthen.

◇ *vi* **: les jours allongent** the days are drawing out *ou* getting longer.

◆ **s'allonger** *vpi* **1.** [se coucher] to stretch out ▪ **allongez-vous!** lie down! ▪ **il/le chien s'allongea sur le tapis** he/the dog stretched out on the rug ▪ **allonge-toi un peu** have a little lie-down
2. [se prolonger - visite, récit] to drag on ; [- vie, période] to become longer
3. [se renfrogner] : **son visage s'allongea** her face fell, she pulled *UK OU* made *US* a long face.

allopathie [alɔpati] *nf* allopathy.

allopathique [alɔpatik] *adj* MÉD allopathic.

allophone [alɔfɔn] ◇ *adj* : **les résidents ~s** foreign-language speaking residents.
◇ *nmf person whose native language is not that of the community in which he/she lives.*

allouer [6] [alwe] *vt* **1.** [argent] to allocate ▪ [indemnité] to grant ▪ FIN [actions] to allot **2.** [temps] to allot, to allow ▪ **le temps alloué à ces activités** the time allotted *OU* allocated to these activities.

allumage [alymaʒ] *nm* **1.** [d'un feu, d'une chaudière] lighting ▪ [du gaz] lighting, turning on **2.** [d'une ampoule, d'un appareil électrique] turning *OU* switching on **3.** AUTO & MÉCAN ignition ▪ **régler l'~** to set *OU* to adjust the timing ▪ **avance/retard à l'~** advanced/retarded ignition **4.** ASTRONAUT ignition **5.** ARM firing *(of a mine).*

allume-cigares [alymsigar] *nm inv* cigarette lighter.

allume-feu [alymfø] *nm inv* **1.** [bois] kindling wood **2.** [à alcool] fire-lighter.

allume-gaz [alymgaz] *nm inv* gas lighter.

allumer [3] [alyme] *vt* **1.** [enflammer - bougie, réchaud, cigarette, torche, gaz] to light ; [- bois, brindille] to light, to kindle ; [- feu, incendie] to light, to start **2.** [mettre en marche - lampe, appareil] to turn *OU* to switch *OU* to put on *(sép)* ; [- phare] to put on, to turn on *(sép)* ▪ **j'ai laissé la radio allumée!** I forgot to turn off the radio! ▪ **le bureau est allumé** there's a light on in the office, the lights are on in the office ▪ *(en usage absolu)* **allume!** turn the light on! ▪ **comment est-ce qu'on allume?** how do you switch *UK OU* turn it on? ▪ **où est-ce qu'on allume?** where's the switch? **3.** *litt* [commencer - guerre] to start ; [- passion, haine] to stir up *(sép)* **4.** *fam* [sexuellement] to arouse, to turn on *(sép)*.

◆ **s'allumer** *vpi* **1.** [s'éclairer] : **leur fenêtre vient de s'~** a light has just come on at their window ▮ *fig* [visage, œil, regard] to light up **2.** [se mettre en marche - appareil, radio] to switch *OU* to turn on ; [- lumière] to come on **3.** [prendre feu - bois, brindille] to catch (fire) ; [- incendie] to start, to flare up **4.** *litt* [commencer - haine, passion] to be aroused ; [- guerre] to break out.

allumette [alymɛt] *nf* **1.** [pour allumer] match, matchstick ⊙ **~ suédoise** *OU* **de sûreté** safety match ▪ **être gros** *OU* **épais comme une ~** to be as thin as a rake ▪ **avoir des jambes comme des ~s** to have legs like matchsticks **2.** CULIN [gâteau - salé] allumette, straw ; [- sucré] allumette.

allumeur [alymœr] *nm* **1.** TECHNOL igniter **2.** AUTO (ignition) distributor **3.** [lampiste] : **~ de réverbères** lamp-lighter.

allumeuse [alymøz] *nf fam péj* tease.

allure [alyr] *nf* **1.** [vitesse d'un véhicule] speed ▪ **à grande/faible ~** at (a) high/low speed ▪ **rouler à petite ~** *OU* **à une ~ réduite** to drive at a slow pace *OU* slowly ▪ **aller** *OU* **rouler à toute ~** to go at (top *OU* full) speed **2.** [vitesse d'un marcheur] pace ▪ **il accélérait l'~** he was quickening his pace ▪ **marcher à vive ~** to walk at a brisk pace ▪ **à cette ~, tu n'auras pas fini avant demain** *fig* at that speed *OU* rate, you won't have finished before tomorrow **3.** [apparence - d'une personne] look, appearance ▪ **avoir de l'~** *OU* **grande ~** to have style ▪ **une femme d'~ élégante entra** an elegant-looking woman came in ▪ **avoir fière ~** to cut a fine figure ▪ **avoir piètre ~** to cut a shabby figure ▪ **il a une drôle d'~** he looks odd *OU* weird ▪ **un personnage à l'~** *OU* **d'~ suspecte** a suspicious-looking character ▪ **je n'aime pas l'~ qu'elle a** I don't like the look of her ▪ **le projet prend une mauvaise ~** the project is taking a turn for the worse ▪ **prendre des ~s de** to take on an air of.

allusif, ive [alyzif, iv] *adj* allusive ▪ **il est resté très ~** he wasn't very specific.

allusion [alyzjɔ̃] *nf* **1.** [référence] allusion, reference ▪ **faire ~ à qqch** to allude to sthg, to refer to sthg ▪ **il n'y a fait ~ qu'en passant** he only made a passing reference to it ▪ **par ~ à** alluding to **2.** [sous-entendu] hint ▪ **c'est une ~?** are you hinting at something? ▪ **l'~ m'échappe** I don't get it.

allusivement [alyzivmɑ̃] *adv* allusively.

alluvial, e, aux [alyvjal, o] *adj* alluvial.

alluvionnaire [alyvjɔnɛr] *adj* alluvial.

alluvionner [3] [alyvjɔne] *vi* to deposit alluvion *OU* alluvium.

alluvions [alyvjɔ̃] *nmpl* alluvion *(U)*, alluvium *(U)*.

almanach [almana] *nm* almanac.

aloès [alɔɛs] *nm* aloe.

aloi [alwa] *nm* : **de bon ~** [marchandise, individu] of sterling *OU* genuine worth ; [plaisanterie] in good taste ▪ **de mauvais ~** [marchandise] worthless ; [individu] worthless, no-good *(avant n)* ; [plaisanterie] in bad taste ; [succès] cheap.

alopécie [alɔpesi] *nf* alopecia.

alors [alɔr] *adv* **1.** [à ce moment-là] then ▪ **le cinéma d'~ était encore muet** films were still silent in those days ▪ **le Premier ministre d'~ refusa de signer les accords** the then Prime Minister refused to sign the agreement ▪ **jusqu'~** until then **2.** [en conséquence] so ▪ **il s'est mis à pleuvoir, ~ nous sommes rentrés** it started to rain, so we came back in **3.** [dans ce cas] then, so, in that case ▪ **je préfère renoncer tout de suite, ~!** in that case I'd just as soon give up straight away! ▪ **mais ~, ça change tout!** but that changes everything! **4.** [emploi expressif] : **il va se mettre en colère, et ~?** so what if he gets angry? ▪ **et ~, qu'est-ce qui s'est passé?** so what happened then? ▪ **~, tu viens oui ou non?** so are you coming or not?, are you coming or not, then? ▪ **dites-le-lui, ou ~ je ne viens pas** tell him, otherwise *OU* or else I'm not coming ▪ **~ là, il exagère!** he's going a bit far there! ▪ **~ là, je ne sais plus quoi dire!** well then, I don't know what to say! ▪ **ça ~, je ne l'aurais jamais cru!** my goodness, I would never have believed it! ▪ **non mais ~, pour qui vous vous prenez?** well really, who do you think you are?

◆ **alors que** *loc conj* **1.** [au moment où] while, when ▪ **l'orage éclata ~ que nous étions encore loin de la maison** the storm broke while *OU* when we were still a long way from the house **2.** [bien que, même si] even though ▪ **elle est sortie ~ que c'était interdit** she went out, even though she wasn't supposed to ▪ **~ même qu'il ne nous resterait que ce moyen, je refuserais de l'utiliser** *sout* even if this were the only means left to us I wouldn't use it **3.** [tandis que] while ▪ **il part en vacances ~ que je reste ici tout l'été** he's going on holiday while I stay here all summer.

alouette [alwɛt] *nf* **1.** ORNITH lark ▪ **il attend que les ~s lui tombent/il croit que les ~s vont lui tomber toutes cuites dans le bec** *fam* he's waiting for things to/he thinks that things will just fall into his lap **2.** CULIN : **~ sans tête** ≃ veal olive.

alourdir [32] [alurdir] *vt* **1.** [ajouter du poids à] to weigh down *(sép)*, to make heavy *OU* heavier ▪ **l'emballage alourdit le paquet de 200 grammes** the wrapping makes the parcel heavier by 200 grammes ▪ **alourdi par la fatigue** heavy with exhaustion **2.** [style, allure, traits] to make heavier *OU* coarser ▪ [impôts] to increase ▪ **cette répétition alourdit la phrase** the repetition makes the sentence unwieldy.

◆ **s'alourdir** *vpi* **1.** [grossir - personne] to put on weight ; [- taille] to thicken, to get thicker **2.** [devenir lourd] to become heavy *OU* heavier ▪ **ses paupières s'alourdissaient** his eyelids were beginning to droop *OU* were getting heavy ▪ **sa démarche s'est alourdie** he walks more heavily **3.** [devenir plus grossier] to get coarser ▪ **ses traits s'alourdissent** his features are getting coarser.

alourdissement [alurdismɑ̃] *nm* **1.** [d'un paquet, d'un véhicule] increased weight **2.** [d'un style] heaviness ▪ [des impôts] increase ▪ **seul l'~ de sa silhouette laissait deviner sa maladie** the only sign of her illness was that she had put on a little weight.

aloyau [alwajo] *nm* sirloin.

alpaga [alpaga] *nm* alpaca.

alpage [alpaʒ] *nm* **1.** [pâturage] high (mountain) pasture **2.** [saison] grazing season *(spent by livestock in high pastures)*.
◆ **d'alpage** *loc adj* [fromage, produit] mountain *(modif)*.

alpaguer [3] △ [alpage] *vt* **1.** [arrêter] to nab△, to bust△ *US* ■ **se faire ~** to get nabbed△ *ou* busted△ *US* **2.** [accaparer] to nab.

alpe [alp] *nf* (high) alpine pasture.

Alpes [alp] *npr fpl* : **les ~** the Alps ■ **les ~ du Sud** the Southern Alps.

alpestre [alpɛstr] *adj* alpine ■ **plante ~** alpine.

alpha [alfa] *nm* alpha ■ **l'~ et l'oméga de** *fig* the beginning and the end of.

alphabet [alfabɛ] *nm* **1.** [d'une langue] alphabet **2.** [abécédaire] spelling *ou* ABC book, alphabet **3.** [code] : **~ morse** Morse code ■ **~ phonétique** phonetic alphabet.

alphabétique [alfabetik] *adj* alphabetic, alphabetical.

alphabétiquement [alfabetikmɑ̃] *adv* alphabetically.

alphabétisation [alfabetizasjɔ̃] *nf* elimination of illiteracy ■ **campagne/taux d'~** literacy campaign/rate.

alphabétiser [3] [alfabetize] *vt* to teach to read and write.

alphabétisme [alfabetism] *nm* alphabetical writing (system).

alphanumérique [alfanymerik] *adj* alphanumeric.

alpin, e [alpɛ̃, in] *adj* **1.** BOT & GÉOL alpine **2.** SPORT [club] mountaineering *(modif)*, mountain-climbing *(modif)* ■ [ski] downhill.

alpinisme [alpinism] *nm* mountaineering, mountain-climbing ■ **faire de l'~** to climb, to go mountain-climbing.

alpiniste [alpinist] *nmf* mountaineer, climber.

Alsace [alzas] *npr f* : **(l')~** Alsace.

ALSACE

This administrative region includes the ***départements*** of Bas-Rhin and Haut-Rhin (capital: Strasbourg).

Alsace-Lorraine [alzaslɔrɛn] *npr f* : **(l')~** Alsace-Lorraine.

ALSACE-LORRAINE

This eastern part of France was the underlying cause of the longstanding conflict between Germany and France. Consisting of part of the two old French provinces of Alsace and Lorraine (today the ***départements*** of Haut Rhin, Bas Rhin and Moselle) it was seized by the Germans at the end of the Franco-Prussian war in 1871, becoming part of the German Reich. Reverting to France after the First World War, seized by Germany again in 1940, ***l'Alsace-Lorraine*** was finally restored to France at the end of the Second World War.

alsacien, enne [alzasjɛ̃, ɛn] *adj* Alsatian.
◆ **Alsacien, enne** *nm, f* Alsatian ■ **les Alsaciens** the people of Alsace.
◆ **alsacien** *nm* LING Alsatian.

altérabilité [alterabilite] *nf* alterability.

altérable [alterabl] *adj* alterable.

altération [alterasjɔ̃] *nf* **1.** [dégradation] alteration **2.** GÉOL weathering **3.** MUS [dièse] sharp (sign) ■ [bémol] flat (sign).

altercation [altɛrkasjɔ̃] *nf* ***sout*** quarrel, altercation ***sout*** ■ **j'ai eu une violente ~ avec elle** I had a violent quarrel *ou* a huge row with her.

altéré, e [altere] *adj* **1.** [modifié - aliments] adulterated ; [- couleurs] faded, altered ; [- faits] altered, falsified ; [- traits] drawn, distorted ; [- santé, amitié] impaired, affected **2.** [assoiffé] thirsty.

alter ego [alterego] *nm inv* **1.** ***hum*** [ami] alter ego **2.** [homologue] counterpart, alter ego.

altérer [18] [altere] *vt* **1.** [dégrader - couleur] to spoil ; [- denrée] to affect the quality of **2.** ***sout*** [falsifier - fait, histoire] to distort ; [- vérité] to distort, to twist **3.** [changer - composition, équilibre] to change, to alter, to modify ■ **les traits altérés par le chagrin/la fatigue/la maladie** her face pinched with grief/drawn with tiredness/drawn with illness ■ **la voix altérée par l'angoisse** her voice strained with anxiety **4.** *litt* [assoiffer] to make thirsty ■ **altéré de gloire** thirsting for glory **5.** MUS [accord] to alter ■ [note] to inflect.
◆ **s'altérer** *vpi* **1.** [se dégrader - denrée] to spoil ; [- sentiment, amitié] to deteriorate ; [- couleurs] to fade ; [- voix] to be distorted ■ **sa santé s'est altérée** her health has deteriorated **2.** [se transformer - substance, minéral] to alter, to (undergo a) change.

altérité [alterite] *nf* otherness.

altermondialiste [altɛrmɔ̃djalist] ◇ *adj* alterglobalist.
◇ *nmf* alterglobalist.

alternance [altɛrnɑ̃s] *nf* **1.** [succession] alternation ■ **l'~ des saisons** the alternating *ou* changing seasons ‖ AGRIC crop rotation **2.** POLIT : **~ (du pouvoir)** change-over of political power ■ **pratiquer l'~** to take turns running a country **3.** LING : **~ vocalique** vowel gradation **4.** CINÉ, MUS & THÉÂTRE alternating programmes ■ **une salle qui pratique l'~** a house that shows two alternating programmes.
◆ **en alternance** *loc adv* : **ils donnent** *ou* **programment "Manon" et "la Traviata" en ~** they're putting on "Manon" and "la Traviata" alternately ■ **jouer en ~ avec qqn** to alternate with another actor ■ **faire qqch en ~ avec qqn** to take turns to do sthg.

alternateur [altɛrnatœr] *nm* alternator.

alternatif, ive [altɛrnatif, iv] *adj* **1.** [périodique] alternate, alternating **2.** [à option] alternative ■ **modèle ~ de croissance** alternative model of growth ‖ SOCIOL alternative.
◆ **alternative** *nf* **1.** [choix] alternative, option ■ **se trouver devant une pénible alternative** to be faced with a difficult choice, to be in a difficult dilemma **2.** [solution de remplacement] alternative **3.** LOGIQUE alternative *ou* disjunctive (proposition).
◆ **alternatives** *nfpl* alternating phases.

alternativement [altɛrnativmɑ̃] *adv* (each) in turn, alternately.

alterné, e [altɛrne] *adj* **1.** TRANSP [stationnement] (authorized) on alternate sides of the street **2.** LITTÉR alternate **3.** MATH [application] alternate ■ [série] alternating.

alterner [3] [altɛrne] ◇ *vt* **1.** [faire succéder] to alternate **2.** AGRIC to rotate.
◇ *vi* [se succéder - phases] to alternate ; [- personnes] to alternate, to take turns ■ **faire ~** to alternate.

altesse [altɛs] *nf* Highness ■ **Son Altesse Royale** [prince] His Royal Highness ; [princesse] Her Royal Highness ■ **Son Altesse Sérénissime** [prince] His Most Serene Highness ; [princesse] Her Most Serene Highness.

altier, ère [altje, ɛr] *adj* haughty, arrogant ■ **avoir un port ~** to carry o.s. proudly.

altimètre [altimɛtr] *nm* altimeter.

altiport [altipɔr] *nm* (ski-resort) airfield.

altiste [altist] *nmf* viola player, violist.

altitude [altityd] *nf* altitude ■ **~ au-dessus du niveau de la mer** height above sea level ■ **à haute/basse ~** at high/low altitude ■ **prendre de l'~** to gain altitude, to climb ■ **perdre de l'~** to lose altitude.
◆ **en altitude** *loc adv* high up, at high altitude.

alto [alto] *nm* **1.** [instrument] viola **2.** [voix] contralto *ou* alto (voice) ■ [chanteuse] contralto, alto.

altruisme [altrɥism] *nm* altruism.

altruiste [altrɥist] ◇ *adj* altruistic.
◇ *nmf* altruist.

Altuglas® [altyglas] *nm* ≃ Perspex®.

alumine [alymin] *nf* alumina, aluminium *UK ou* aluminum *US* oxide.

aluminium [alyminjɔm] *nm* aluminium *UK*, aluminum *US*.

alun [alœ̃] *nm* alum.

alunir [32] [alynir] *vi* to land (on the moon).

alunissage [alynisaʒ] *nm* (moon) landing.

alvéolaire [alveɔlɛr] *adj* alveolar.

alvéole [alveɔl] *nf* **1.** [d'une ruche] cell, alveolus *spéc* **2.** ANAT : **~ dentaire** tooth socket, alveolus *spéc* ■ **~ pulmonaire** air cell, alveolus *spéc* **3.** GÉOL cavity, pit.

alvéolé, e [alveɔle] *adj* honeycombed, alveolate *spéc.*

amabilité [amabilite] *nf* [qualité] kindness, friendliness, amiability ■ **un homme plein d'~** a very kind man ■ **veuillez avoir l'~ de...** please be so kind as to...
◆ **amabilités** *nfpl* [politesses] polite remarks ■ **faire des ~s à qqn** to be polite to sb.

amadou [amadu] *nm* touchwood, tinder.

amadouer [6] [amadwe] *vt* **1.** [enjôler] to cajole ■ **elle essaie de l'~ pour qu'il accepte** she's trying to cajole *ou* to coax him into agreeing **2.** [adoucir] to mollify, to soften (up) ■ **c'est pour m'~ que tu me dis ça?** are you saying this to soften me up?

amaigri, e [amegri] *adj* [visage] gaunt ■ [trait] (more) pinched ■ **je le trouve très ~** he looks a lot thinner *ou* as if he's lost a lot of weight.

amaigrir [32] [amegrir] *vt* **1.** [suj: maladie, régime] to make thin *ou* thinner ■ **le visage amaigri par la maladie** his face emaciated from illness **2.** TECHNOL [épaisseur] to reduce ■ [pâte] to thin down *(sép).*
◆ **s'amaigrir** *vpi* to lose weight.

amaigrissant, e [amegrisɑ̃, ɑ̃t] *adj* slimming, reducing US.

amaigrissement [amegrismɑ̃] *nm* **1.** [perte de poids - du corps] weight loss ; [- des cuisses, de la silhouette] weight reduction **2.** TECHNOL [de l'épaisseur] reducing ■ [d'une pâte] thinning down.

amalgame [amalgam] *nm* **1.** MÉTALL amalgam **2.** [mélange] mixture, amalgam ■ **il ne faut pas faire l'~ entre ces deux questions** the two issues must not be confused **3.** HIST & MIL amalgamation.

amalgamer [3] [amalgame] *vt* **1.** MÉTALL to amalgamate **2.** [mélanger - ingrédients] to combine, to mix up *(sép)* **3.** [réunir - services, sociétés] to amalgamate.
◆ **s'amalgamer** *vpi* **1.** MÉTALL to amalgamate **2.** [s'unir] to combine, to amalgamate **3.** [se mélanger] to get mixed up.

amande [amɑ̃d] *nf* **1.** [fruit] almond ➊ **~ douce/amère** sweet/bitter almond **2.** [noyau] kernel.
◆ **d'amande(s)** *loc adj* almond.
◆ **en amande** *loc adj* [yeux] almond-shaped.

amandier [amɑ̃dje] *nm* almond tree.

amandine [amɑ̃din] *nf* almond tartlet.

amanite [amanit] *nf* amanita ■ **~ phalloïde** death cap ■ **~ tue-mouches** fly agaric.

amant [amɑ̃] *nm* (male) lover.
◆ **amants** *nmpl* lovers ■ **devenir ~s** to become lovers.

amante [amɑ̃t] *nf litt* lover, mistress.

amarante [amarɑ̃t] <> *adj inv* amaranthine.
<> *nf* amaranth.

amareyeur, euse [amarɛjœr, øz] *nm, f* oysterbed worker.

amarinage [amarinaʒ] *nm* **1.** [habitude] getting used to the sea, finding one's sea legs **2.** [remplacement] manning *(of a captured vessel).*

amariner [3] [amarine] *vt* **1.** [habituer à la mer] to accustom to life at sea **2.** [navire] to take over *(sép).*
◆ **s'amariner** *vpi* to find one's sea legs.

amarrage [amaraʒ] *nm* **1.** [dans un port] mooring **2.** [à un objet fixe] lashing **3.** AÉRON [d'un ballon] mooring ■ ASTRONAUT docking **4.** [amarres] ropes.
◆ **à l'amarrage** *loc adj* moored.

amarre [amar] *nf* mooring line *ou* rope ■ **larguer les ~s** *pr & fig* to cast off one's moorings ■ **rompre les ~s** *pr & fig* to break one's moorings.

amarrer [3] [amare] *vt* **1.** NAUT [cordages] to fasten, to make fast ■ [navire] to hitch, to moor **2.** [bagages] to tie down *(sép)* **3.** ASTRONAUT to dock.
◆ **s'amarrer** *vpi* **1.** NAUT [à une berge] to moor ■ [dans un port] to dock, to berth **2.** ASTRONAUT to dock.

amaryllis [amarilis] *nf* amaryllis.

amas [ama] *nm* **1.** [tas] heap, mass, jumble **2.** ASTRON cluster **3.** MINÉR mass.

amasser [3] [amase] *vt* **1.** [entasser - vivres, richesses] to amass, to hoard ■ **après avoir amassé un petit pécule** having got together a bit of money **2.** [rassembler - preuves, information] to amass.
◆ **s'amasser** *vpi* [foule, troupeau] to gather *ou* to mass (in large numbers) ■ [preuves] to accumulate, to pile up.

amateur, e [amatœr] <> *adj* **1.** *(avec ou sans trait d'union)* [non professionnel] amateur *(modif)* ■ **théâtre ~** amateur theatre ■ SPORT amateur, non-professional **2.** [friand, adepte] : **~ de : être ~ de qqch** to be very interested in sthg ■ **il est ~ de bonne chère** he's very fond of good food.
<> *nm, f* **1.** SPORT [non professionnel] amateur **2.** *péj* [dilettante] dilettante, mere amateur **3.** [connaisseur] : **~ de** connoisseur of ■ **~ d'art** art lover *ou* enthusiast **4.** *fam* [preneur] taker ■ **je ne suis pas ~** I'm not interested, I don't go in for that sort of thing.
◆ **d'amateur** *loc adj péj* amateurish ■ **c'est du travail d'~** it's a shoddy piece of work.
◆ **en amateur** *loc adv* non-professionally ■ **s'intéresser à qqch en ~** to have an amateur interest in sthg.

amateurisme [amatœrism] *nm* **1.** LOISIRS & SPORT amateurism, amateur sport **2.** *péj* [dilettantisme] amateurism, amateurishness ■ **c'est de l'~** it's amateurish.

amazone [amazon] *nf* **1.** [cavalière] horsewoman **2.** [tenue] (woman's) riding habit ■ [jupe] riding skirt **3.** △ *arg crime* [prostituée] *prostitute operating from a car.*
◆ **en amazone** *loc adv* : **monter en ~** to ride side-saddle.

Amazone [amazon] *npr f* **1.** MYTHOL Amazon **2.** GÉOGR : **l'~** the Amazon (river).

Amazonie [amazoni] *npr f* : **(l')~** the Amazon (Basin).

amazonien, enne [amazɔnjɛ̃, ɛn] *adj* Amazonian.

ambages [ɑ̃baʒ] ◆ **sans ambages** *loc adv sout* without beating about the bush.

ambassade [ɑ̃basad] *nf* **1.** [bâtiment] embassy ■ **l'~ du Canada** the Canadian embassy **2.** [fonction] ambassadorship **3.** [personnel] embassy (staff) **4.** [mission] mission.

ambassadeur, drice [ɑ̃basadœr, dris] *nm, f* **1.** [diplomate] ambassador ■ **c'est l'~ du Canada** he's the Canadian Ambassador ■ **~ auprès de** ambassador to ➊ **~ extraordinaire** ambassador extraordinary **2.** *fig* [représentant] representative, ambassador.
◆ **ambassadrice** *nf* [femme d'ambassadeur] ambassador's wife.

ambiance [ɑ̃bjɑ̃s] *nf* **1.** [atmosphère] mood, atmosphere ■ **l'~ qui règne à Paris** the general atmosphere *ou* mood in Paris ■ **l'~ générale du marché** the prevailing mood of the market **2.** [cadre] surroundings, ambiance *sout* ■ [éclairage] lighting effects **3.** *fam* [animation] : **il y a de l'~!** it's pretty lively in here!
◆ **d'ambiance** *loc adj* [éclairage] soft, subdued ■ [musique] mood *(modif).*

ambiant, e [ɑ̃bjɑ̃, ɑ̃t] *adj* [température] ambient ■ **les préjugés ~s** the reigning *ou* prevailing prejudices.

ambidextre [ɑ̃bidɛkstr] <> *adj* ambidextrous.
<> *nmf* ambidexter.

ambigu, ë [ɑ̃bigy] *adj* **1.** [à deux sens] ambiguous, equivocal ■ **de façon ~ë** ambiguously, equivocally **2.** [difficile à cerner] ambiguous.

ambiguïté [ɑ̃bigɥite] *nf* **1.** [équivoque] ambiguity ■ **réponse sans ~** unequivocal *ou* unambiguous answer ■ **répondre sans ~** to answer unequivocally *ou* unambiguously **2.** LING ambiguity.

ambitieux, euse [ɑ̃bisjø, øz] <> *adj* ambitious.
<> *nm, f* ambitious man (*f* woman).

ambition [ɑ̃bisjɔ̃] *nf* **1.** [désir] ambition, aspiration ■ **j'ai l'~** *ou* **mon ~ est de...** it's my ambition to... **2.** [désir de réussite] ambition ■ **avoir de l'~** to be ambitious.

ambitionner [3] [ɑ̃bisjɔne] *vt* [poste] to have one's heart set on ■ **~ de faire qqch : elle ambitionne de monter sur les planches** her ambition is to go on the stage.

ambivalence [ɑ̃bivalɑ̃s] *nf* ambivalence.

ambivalent, e [ɑ̃bivalɑ̃, ɑ̃t] *adj* ambivalent.

amble [ɑ̃bl] *nm* amble ■ **aller l'~** to amble.

ambre [ɑ̃br] <> *adj inv* amber.
<> *nm* : **~ (gris)** ambergris ■ **~ (jaune)** amber.

ambré, e [ɑ̃bre] *adj* [couleur] amber *(modif)* ■ [parfum] amber-scented.

ambrer [3] [ɑ̃bre] *vt* to scent with amber.

ambroisie [ɑ̃brwazi] *nf* ambrosia.

ambulance [ɑ̃bylɑ̃s] *nf* ambulance ■ **en ~** in an ambulance.

ambulancier, ère [ɑ̃bylɑ̃sje, ɛr] *nm, f* **1.** [chauffeur] ambulance driver **2.** [infirmier] ambulance man (*f* woman).

ambulant, e [ɑ̃bylɑ̃, ɑ̃t] *adj* itinerant, travelling ■ **c'est un dictionnaire ~** *fam* he's a walking dictionary.

ambulatoire [ɑ̃bylatwar] *adj* ambulatory.

âme [am] *nf* **1.** [vie] soul ■ **rendre l'~** to pass away
2. [personnalité] soul, spirit ■ **avoir** *ou* **être une ~ généreuse** to have great generosity of spirit ■ **avoir une ~ de chef** to be a born leader
3. [principe moral] : **en mon ~ et conscience** in all conscience
4. [cœur] soul, heart ■ **faire qqch avec/sans ~** to do sthg with/without feeling ■ **de toute mon ~** with all my heart *ou* soul ■ **c'est un artiste dans l'~** he's a born artist
5. [personne] soul ■ **un village de 500 ~s** a village of 500 souls ‖ *sout* [en appellatif] : **mon ~, ma chère ~** (my) dearest ⊃ **~ charitable, bonne ~** kind soul ■ **son ~ damnée** the person who does his evil deeds *ou* dirty work for him ■ **~ en peine : aller** *ou* **errer comme une ~ en peine** to wander around like a lost soul ■ **~ sensible** sensitive person ■ **~s sensibles, s'abstenir** not for the squeamish ■ **chercher/trouver l'~ sœur** to seek/to find a soulmate ■ **il n'y a pas ~ qui vive** there isn't a (living) soul around
6. *litt* [inspirateur] soul ■ **c'était elle, l'~ du groupe** *fig* she was the inspiration of the group
7. [centre - d'un aimant] core ; [- d'un câble] heart, core
8. [d'un violon] soundpost.

améliorable [ameljɔrabl] *adj* improvable, that can be improved.

amélioration [ameljɔrasjɔ̃] *nf* **1.** [action] improving, bettering **2.** [résultat] improvement ■ **apporter des ~s à qqch** to improve on sthg, to carry out improvements to sthg ■ **on observe une nette ~ de son état de santé** her condition has improved considerably ■ **~ des cours** BOURSE improvement in prices **3.** MÉTÉOR : **~ (du temps)** better weather ■ **pas d'~ prévue cet après-midi** no improvement expected in the weather this afternoon.
◆ **améliorations** *nfpl* DR improvements.

améliorer [3] [ameljɔre] *vt* **1.** [changer en mieux - sol] to improve ; [- relations] to improve, to make better ; [- productivité] to increase, to improve **2.** [perfectionner - technique] to improve, to better ■ **~ son anglais** to improve one's (knowledge of) English **3.** SPORT [record, score] to better, to improve on.
◆ **s'améliorer** *vpi* to improve ■ **l'état de la malade s'est un peu amélioré** there's been some improvement in the patient's condition ■ **le temps s'améliore** the weather's getting better, the weather's improving.

amen [amɛn] *nm inv* amen ■ **tu dis ~ à tout ce qu'elle fait** you agree with everything she does.

aménageable [amenaʒabl] *adj* **1.** [bureau, logement] convertible ■ **un espace ~ en garage** space which can be converted into a garage **2.** [emploi du temps] flexible.

aménagement [amenaʒmɑ̃] *nm* **1.** [d'une pièce, d'un local] fitting (out) ■ [d'un parc] laying out, designing ■ [d'un terrain] landscaping ■ **on prévoit l'~ d'un des bureaux en salle de réunion** we're planning to convert one of the offices into a meeting room **2.** ADMIN : **~ foncier** improvement of land ■ **~ rural** rural development *ou* planning ■ **~ du territoire** town and country planning, regional development ■ **~ urbain** urban planning **3.** [refonte - d'un texte] redrafting, adjusting **4.** [assouplissement] : **il a obtenu des ~s d'horaire** he managed to get his timetable rearranged.
◆ **aménagements** *nmpl* : **~s intérieurs** (fixtures and) fittings.

aménager [17] [amenaʒe] *vt* **1.** [parc] to design, to lay out *(sép)* ■ [terrain] to landscape **2.** [équiper] to fit out, to equip ■ **camping aménagé** fully-equipped camping site ■ **plage aménagée** beach with full amenities **3.** [transformer] : **~ qqch en : ~ une pièce en atelier** to convert a room into a workshop **4.** [installer] to install, to fit ■ **~ un placard sous un escalier** to fit *ou* to install a cupboard under a staircase **5.** [assouplir - horaire] to plan, to work out *(insép)* **6.** [refaire - texte] to adapt, to redraft.

amendable [amɑ̃dabl] *adj* **1.** [texte] amendable **2.** AGRIC improvable **3.** *Suisse* liable to be fined.

amende [amɑ̃d] *nf* fine ■ **une ~ de 100 euros** a 100-euro fine ■ **avoir une ~ de 100 euros** to be fined 100 euros ■ **'défense d'entrer sous peine d'~'** 'trespassers will be fined *ou* prosecuted' ⊃ **mettre qqn à l'~** *pr* to fine sb ; *fig* to penalize sb ■ **faire ~ honorable** to make amends.

amendement [amɑ̃dmɑ̃] *nm* **1.** DR & POLIT amendment **2.** AGRIC [incorporation] fertilizing, enrichment ■ [substance] fertilizer.

amender [3] [amɑ̃de] *vt* **1.** DR & POLIT to amend **2.** AGRIC to fertilize **3.** *litt* [corriger] to amend.
◆ **s'amender** *vpi* to mend one's ways, to turn over a new leaf.

amène [amɛn] *adj sout* affable, amiable ■ **d'une façon peu ~** in a very unpleasant manner.

amenée [amne] ◆ **d'amenée** *loc adj* supply *(modif)*.

amener [19] [amne] *vt* **1.** [faire venir - personne] to bring (along) ■ **~ qqn chez soi** to bring sb round to one's place, to bring sb home ■ **qu'est-ce qui vous amène?** what brings you here? ■ **~ des capitaux** to attract capital ■ **qu'est-ce qui vous a amené à la musique/à Dieu?** *fig* what got you involved with music/made you turn to God?
2. *fam* [apporter] to bring (along) ■ **j'amènerai mon travail** I'll bring some work along
3. [acheminer] to bring, to convey ■ [conduire - suj: véhicule, chemin] to take
4. [provoquer - perte, ruine] to bring about *(sép)*, to cause ; [- guerre, maladie, crise] to bring (on) *ou* about, to cause ; [- paix] to bring about
5. [entraîner] : **~ qqn à : mon métier m'amène à voyager** my job involves a lot of travelling
6. [inciter] : **~ qqn à faire qqch** to lead sb to do sthg ; [en lui parlant] to talk sb into doing sthg
7. [introduire - sujet] to introduce
8. JEUX to throw
9. NAUT [drapeau] to strike ■ MIL : **~ les couleurs** to strike the colours
10. PÊCHE to draw in *(sép)*.
◆ **s'amener** *vpi fam* to come along, to turn *ou* to show up ■ **alors, tu t'amènes?** are you coming or aren't you? ■ **elle s'est amenée avec deux types** she showed up with two blokes.

aménité [amenite] *nf sout* [caractère] amiability, affability ■ **sans ~** ungraciously, somewhat curtly.
◆ **aménités** *nfpl iron* insults, cutting remarks.

aménorrhée [amenɔre] *nf* amenorrhoea.

amenuisement [amənɥizmɑ̃] *nm* [de rations, de l'espoir] dwindling ■ [des chances] lessening.

amenuiser [3] [amənɥize] *vt* **1.** [amincir - planche, bande] to thin down *(sép)* **2.** [diminuer - économies, espoir] to diminish, to reduce.
◆ **s'amenuiser** *vpi* [provisions, espoir] to dwindle, to run low ▪ [chances] to grow *ou* to get slimmer ▪ [distance] to grow smaller.

amer[1] [amɛr] *nm* GÉOGR seamark.

amer[2]**, ère** [amɛr] *adj* [fruit] bitter ▪ *fig* [déception] bitter.
◆ **amer** *nm* [boisson] bitters.

amérasien, enne [amerazjɛ̃, ɛn] *adj* Amerasian.
◆ **Amérasien, enne** *nm, f* Amerasian.

amèrement [amɛrmɑ̃] *adv* bitterly.

américain, e [amerikɛ̃, ɛn] *adj* American.
◆ **Américain, e** *nm, f* American.
◆ **américain** *nm* LING American English.
◆ **américaine** *nf fam* [voiture] American car.
◆ **à l'américaine** *loc adj* **1.** ARCHIT American style **2.** CULIN à l'américaine *(cooked with tomatoes).*

américanisation [amerikanizasjɔ̃] *nf* Americanization.

américaniser [3] [amerikanize] *vt* to americanize.
◆ **s'américaniser** *vpi* to become americanized.

américanisme [amerikanism] *nm* **1.** [science] American studies **2.** [tournure] americanism.

américaniste [amerikanist] ◇ *adj* American studies *(modif).*
◇ *nmf* Americanist.

amérindien, enne [amerɛ̃djɛ̃, ɛn] *adj* Amerindian, American Indian.
◆ **Amérindien, enne** *nm, f* Amerindian, American Indian.

Amérique [amerik] *npr f* : **(l')~** America ▪ **l'~ centrale/latine/du Nord/du Sud** Central/Latin/North/South America.

amerlo [amɛrlo], **amerloque** [amɛrlɔk] *nmf fam* Yankee, Yank.

amerrir [32] [amerir] *vi* AÉRON to land (on the sea), to make a sea landing ▪ ASTRONAUT to splash down.

amerrissage [amerisaʒ] *nm* AÉRON sea landing ▪ ASTRONAUT splashdown.

amertume [amɛrtym] *nf* bitterness ▪ **avec ~** bitterly.

améthyste [ametist] *nf* amethyst.

ameublement [amœbləmɑ̃] *nm* **1.** [meubles] furniture ▪ **articles d'~** furnishings **2.** [installation] furnishing ▪ [décoration] (interior) decoration **3.** [activité] furniture trade.

ameublir [32] [amœblir] *vt* **1.** AGRIC to loosen, to break down *(sép)* **2.** DR & FIN to convert into personalty.

ameuter [3] [amœte] *vt* **1.** [attirer l'attention de] : **le bruit a ameuté les passants** the noise drew a crowd of passers-by ▪ **il a ameuté toute la rue** he got the whole street out ▪ **~ l'opinion sur qqch** to awaken public opinion to sthg ▪ **il faut ~ la presse** we must get the press onto this **2.** [chiens] to form into a pack.

ami, e [ami] ◇ *adj* [voix, peuple, rivage] friendly ▪ **dans une maison ~e** in the house of friends.
◇ *nm, f* **1.** [camarade] friend ▪ **c'est un de mes ~s/une de mes ~es** he's/she's a friend of mine ▪ **des ~s à nous** *fam* friends of ours ▪ **Tom et moi sommes restés ~s** I stayed friends with Tom ▪ **un médecin de mes ~s** *sout* a doctor friend of mine ▪ **un ~ de la famille** *ou* **maison** a friend of the family ▪ **je m'en suis fait une ~e** she became my friend *ou* a friend (of mine) ▪ **devenir l'~ de qqn** to become friends *ou* friendly with sb ▪ **ne pas avoir d'~s** to have no friends ▪ **nous sommes entre ~s (ici)** we're among *ou* we're all friends (here) ◐ **~s d'enfance** childhood friends ▪ **les ~s de mes ~s sont mes ~s** any friend of yours is a friend of mine
2. [amoureux] : **petit** *ou* *vieilli* **bon ~** boyfriend ▪ **petite** *ou* *vieilli* **bonne ~e** girlfriend
3. [bienfaiteur] : **l'~ des pauvres/du peuple** the friend of the poor/of the people ▪ **un ~ des arts** a patron of the arts
4. [partisan] : **club des ~s de Shakespeare** Shakespeare club *ou* society
5. *(comme interjection)* **mon pauvre ~!** you poor fool! ▪ **écoutez, mon jeune ~!** now look here, young man! ▪ **mon ~!** [entre amis] my friend! ; [entre époux] (my) dear!
6. *fam loc* **il a essayé de faire ~-~ avec moi** he came on all buddy-buddy with me.
◆ **en ami** *loc adv* [par amitié] as a friend ▪ **je te le dis en ~** I'm telling you as a friend *ou* because I'm your friend ▪ [en non-professionnel] as a friend, on a friendly basis.

amiable [amjabl] *adj* [accord, compromis] amicable, friendly.
◆ **à l'amiable** *loc adv* : **régler qqch à l'~** [gén] to reach an amicable agreement about sthg ; [sans procès] to settle sthg out of court.

amiante [amjɑ̃t] *nm* asbestos.

amiante-ciment [amjɑ̃tsimɑ̃] *(pl* **amiantes-ciments***)* *nm* asbestos cement.

amibe [amib] *nf* amoeba.

amibien, enne [amibjɛ̃, ɛn] *adj* amoebic.
◆ **amibien** *nm* member of the Amoebae.

amical, e, aux [amikal, o] *adj* friendly ▪ **peu ~** unfriendly.
◆ **amicale** *nf* association, club.

amicalement [amikalmɑ̃] *adv* in a friendly manner ▪ **bien ~** [en fin de lettre] (ever) yours.

amidon [amidɔ̃] *nm* starch.

amidonner [3] [amidɔne] *vt* to starch.

amincir [32] [amɛ̃sir] *vt* [amaigrir] to thin down *(sép)* ▪ [rendre svelte] to slim down *(sép)* ▪ **cette veste t'amincit** this jacket makes you look slimmer.
◆ **s'amincir** *vpi* to get thinner.

amincissant, e [amɛ̃sisɑ̃, ɑ̃t] *adj* slimming, reducing US.

amincissement [amɛ̃sismɑ̃] *nm* [d'une épaisseur] thinning down ▪ [de la taille, des hanches] slimming, reducing US.

aminé, e [amine] *adj* ▷ **acide**.

amiral, e, aux [amiral, o] *adj* : **vaisseau** *ou* **navire ~** flagship.
◆ **amiral, aux** *nm* admiral ▪ **~ de la flotte** Admiral of the Fleet.
◆ **amirale** *nf* admiral's wife.

amirauté [amirote] *nf* admiralty.

amitié [amitje] *nf* **1.** [sentiment] friendship ▪ **faire qqch par ~** to do sthg out of friendship ▪ **se lier d'~ avec qqn** to make friends *ou* to strike up a friendship with sb ▪ **prendre qqn en ~, se prendre d'~ pour qqn** to befriend sb, to make friends with sb ▪ **avoir de l'~ pour qqn** to be fond of sb **2.** [relation] friendship ▪ **lier** *ou* **nouer une ~ avec qqn** to strike up a friendship with sb ◐ **~ particulière** *euphém* homosexual relationship **3.** [faveur] kindness, favour ▪ **faites moi l'~ de rester** please do me the kindness *ou* favour of staying.
◆ **amitiés** *nfpl* [salutations, compliments] : **faites-lui** *ou* **présentez-lui mes ~s** give him my compliments *ou* best regards ▪ **(toutes) mes ~s** [en fin de lettre] best regards *ou* wishes ▪ **~s, Marie** love *ou* yours, Marie.

ammoniac, aque [amɔnjak] *adj* ammoniac ▪ **sel ~** salt ammoniac.
◆ **ammoniac** *nm* ammonia.
◆ **ammoniaque** *nf* ammonia (water), aqueous ammonia.

ammoniacal, e, aux [amɔnjakal, o] *adj* ammoniacal.

ammoniaque [amɔnjak] *f* ▷ **ammoniac**.

ammoniaqué, e [amɔnjake] *adj* ammoniated.

ammonite [amɔnit] *nf* ammonite.

ammonium [amɔnjɔm] *nm* ammonium.

amnésie [amnezi] *nf* amnesia.

amnésique [amnezik] ◇ *adj* amnesic.
◇ *nmf* amnesic, amnesiac.

amniocentèse [amnjɔsɛ̃tɛz] *nf* amniocentesis.

amniotique [amnjɔtik] *adj* amniotic.

amnistiable [amnistjabl] *adj* eligible for an amnesty.

amnistiant, e [amnistjɑ̃, ɑ̃t] *adj* amnestying.

amnistie [amnisti] *nf* amnesty ■ **l'~ des contraventions** *traditional waiving of parking fines by French president after a presidential election.*

AMNISTIE

Until 2002 parking fines were traditionally waived by the French president immediately after a presidential election. This is known as *l'amnistie des contraventions*.

amnistié, e [amnistje] ◇ *adj* amnestied.
◇ *nm, f* [prisonnier] amnestied prisoner ■ [exilé] amnestied exile.

amnistier [9] [amnistje] *vt* to amnesty.

amoché, e [amɔʃe] *adj fam* **1.** [voiture] wrecked **2.** [personne, visage] smashed *ou* messed up.

amocher [3] [amɔʃe] *vt fam* [meubles, vêtements] to ruin, to mess up *(sép)* ■ [voiture] to bash up *(sép)* ■ [adversaire, boxeur] to smash up *(sép)* ■ [visage, jambe] to mess up *(sép)* ■ **se faire ~** to get smashed up.
◆ **s'amocher** *vp (emploi réfléchi) fam* to get badly bashed ■ **il s'est salement amoché le genou en tombant de vélo** he fell off his bike and really messed up his knee.

amoindrir [32] [amwɛ̃drir] *vt* **1.** [faire diminuer - valeur, importance] to diminish, to reduce ; [- forces] to weaken ; [- autorité, faculté] to weaken, to lessen, to diminish ; [- réserves] to diminish **2.** [rendre moins capable] to weaken, to diminish ■ **il est sorti de son accident très amoindri** [physiquement] his accident left him physically much weaker ; [moralement] his accident left him psychologically impaired.
◆ **s'amoindrir** *vpi* [autorité, forces] to weaken, to grow weaker ■ [réserves] to diminish, to dwindle.

amoindrissement [amwɛ̃drismɑ̃] *nm* [d'une autorité, de facultés] weakening ■ [de forces] diminishing, weakening ■ [de réserves] reduction, diminishing.

amollir [32] [amɔlir] *vt* [beurre, pâte] to soften, to make soft ■ [volonté, forces] to weaken, to diminish ■ **~ qqn** [l'adoucir] to soften sb ; [l'affaiblir] to weaken sb.
◆ **s'amollir** *vpi* **1.** [beurre, pâte, plastique] to soften, to become soft ■ [jambes] to go weak **2.** [s'affaiblir - énergie, courage] to weaken.

amollissant, e [amɔlisɑ̃, ɑ̃t] *adj* enervating.

amonceler [24] [amɔ̃sle] *vt* **1.** [entasser - boîtes, livres, chaussures] to heap *ou* to pile up *(sép)* ; [- neige, sable, feuilles] to bank up *(sép)* ; [- vivres, richesses] to amass, to hoard ■ **~ une fortune** to build up *ou* to amass a fortune **2.** [rassembler - documents, preuves, informations] to amass.
◆ **s'amonceler** *vpi* [papiers, boîtes, feuilles] to heap *ou* to pile up ■ [preuves] to accumulate, to pile up ■ [dettes] to mount, to pile up ■ [neige, sable, nuages] to bank up.

amoncellement [amɔ̃sɛlmɑ̃] *nm* [d'objets divers, d'ordures] heap, pile ■ [de neige, de sable, de feuilles, de nuages] heap ■ [de richesses] hoard ■ **devant cet ~ de preuves** faced with this wealth of evidence.

amoncellerai *etc v* ▷ **amonceler**.

amont [amɔ̃] ◇ *nm* [d'une rivière] upstream water ■ [d'une montagne] uphill slope.
◇ *adj inv* [ski, skieur] uphill *(avant n).*
◆ **en amont** *loc adv pr & fig* upstream.
◆ **en amont de** *loc prép* [rivière] upstream from ■ [montagne] uphill from *ou* above ■ **les étapes en ~ de la production** *fig* the stages upstream of production, the pre-production stages.

amoral, e, aux [amɔral, o] *adj* amoral.

amoralisme [amɔralism] *nm* amorality.

amoralité [amɔralite] *nf* amorality.

amorçage [amɔrsaʒ] *nm* **1.** ARM & TECHNOL priming ■ ÉLECT [d'une dynamo] energizing ■ [d'un arc électrique] strikin **2.** PÊCHE baiting.

amorce [amɔrs] *nf* **1.** ARM [détonateur] primer, detonato ■ [d'un obus] percussion cap ■ [d'une balle] cap, primer ■ [p tard] cap **2.** PÊCHE bait **3.** [début] beginning ■ **l'~ d'une réform** the beginnings of a reform.

amorcer [16] [amɔrse] *vt* **1.** [commencer - travaux] to start, t begin ; [- réforme] to initiate, to begin ; [- discussion, réconcilia tion] to start, to begin, to initiate ; [- virage] to go into *(insép)* [- descente] to start, to begin ■ **les travaux sont bien amorcés** th work is well under way ■ **elle amorça un pas vers la porte** sh made as if to go to the door **2.** ARM & TECHNOL to prime ■ ÉLECT to energize **3.** PÊCHE to bait ■ *(en usage absolu)* **~ au pain** [u hameçon] to bait one's line with bread ; [répandre dans l'eau] t use bread as ground bait.
◆ **s'amorcer** *vpi* to begin.

amorceur [amɔrsœr] *nm* **1.** ÉLECTR igniter **2.** [d'une pomp primer.

amorphe [amɔrf] *adj* **1.** *fam* [indolent] lifeless, passive **2.** BI & MINÉR amorphous.

amorti [amɔrti] *nm* **1.** FOOTBALL : **faire un ~** to trap the ba **2.** TENNIS drop shot.

amortie [amɔrti] *nf* drop shot.

amortir [32] [amɔrtir] *vt* **1.** [absorber - choc] to cushion, to ab sorb ; [- son] to deaden, to muffle ; [- douleur] to deaden ■ SPO to trap the ball ■ **l'herbe a amorti sa chute** the grass broke hi fall ■ **~ le coup** *pr* to cushion *ou* to soften the blow ; *fig* to softe the blow **2.** [rentabiliser] : **il faudra louer cette machine pour en le coût** we'll have to rent out the machine to help cover c to recoup the cost **3.** FIN [dette] to pay off, to amortize ■ [équ pement] to depreciate ■ BOURSE to redeem ■ **~ des actions** t call in shares.
◆ **s'amortir** ◇ *vp (emploi passif)* : **un achat qui s'amortit e deux ans** ÉCON a purchase that can be paid off in two years BOURSE a purchase that can be redeemed in two years.
◇ *vpi* [s'affaiblir - bruit] to fade (away).

amortissable [amɔrtisabl] *adj* redeemable.

amortissement [amɔrtismɑ̃] *nm* **1.** [adoucissement - d'u choc] absorption, cushioning ; [- d'un coup] cushioning ; [- d'u son] deadening, muffling **2.** FIN [d'une dette] paying *ou* wri ing off ■ [d'un titre] redemption ■ [d'un emprunt] paying o amortization ■ **~ annuel** annual depreciation ■ **~ du capit** depreciation of capital.

amortisseur [amɔrtisœr] *nm* shock absorber.

amour [amur] *nm* **1.** [sentiment] love ■ **son ~ des** *ou* **pour l enfants** his love of *ou* for children ■ **l'~ de sa mère** [qu'elle pour lui] his mother's love ; [qu'il a pour elle] his love for h mother ■ **éprouver de l'~ pour qqn** to feel love for sb ■ **fai qqch par ~** to do sthg out of *ou* for love ■ **faire qqch par ~ po qqn** to do sthg for the love of *ou* out of love for sb ■ **ce n'e pas** *ou* **plus de l'~, c'est de la rage!** *fam* it's not so much love, it an obsession! ▶ **l'~ filial** [d'un fils] a son's love ; [d'une fille] daughter's love ■ **l'~ maternel/paternel** motherly/father love, a mother's/father's love
2. [amant] lover, love ■ **un ~ de jeunesse** an old flame
3. [liaison] (love) affair, romance
4. [acte sexuel] love-making ■ **faire l'~ à** *ou* **avec qqn** to mak love to *ou* with sb ■ **pendant/après l'~** while/after makin love
5. [vif intérêt] love ■ **faire qqch avec ~** to do sthg with lovir care *ou* love
6. [terme affectueux] : **mon ~** my love *ou* darling ■ **un ~ de peti fille** a delightful little girl ■ **apporte les glaçons, tu seras un** be a dear *ou* darling and bring the ice cubes
7. ART cupid.
◆ **amours** *nfpl* **1.** *hum* [relations amoureuses] love life ▶ **à v ~s!** [pour trinquer] cheers!, here's to you! ; [après un éternuemen bless you!
2. ZOOL courtship and mating.
◆ **d'amour** *loc adj* [chagrin, chanson] love *(modif).*

◆ **par amour** *loc adv* out of *ou* for love ■ **par ~ pour qqn** for the love of sb.
◆ **pour l'amour de** *loc prép* for the love *ou* sake of ■ **pour l'~ de Dieu!** [ton suppliant] for the love of God! ; [ton irrité] for God's sake! ■ **pour l'~ du ciel!** for heaven's sake! ■ **faire qqch pour l'~ de l'art** to do sthg for the sake of it.

Amour [amur] *npr m* **1.** GÉOGR : **l'~** the (River) Amur ■ **la Côte d'~** *the French Atlantic coast near la Baule* **2.** MYTHOL : **(le dieu) ~** Cupid, Eros.

amouracher [3] [amuraʃe] ◆ **s'amouracher de** *vp+prép* : **s'~ de qqn** to become infatuated with sb.

amourette [amurɛt] *nf* [liaison] casual love affair, passing romance *ou* fancy.

amoureusement [amurøzmɑ̃] *adv* lovingly ■ **il la regardait ~** he watched her lovingly *ou* with love in his eyes.

amoureux, euse [amurø, øz] ◇ *adj* **1.** [tendre - regard, geste] loving, tender ; [- vie, exploit] love *(modif)* ■ [épris] : **être ~ de qqn** to be in love with sb ■ **tomber ~ de qqn** to fall in love with sb ■ **être fou ~** to be madly in love **2.** [amateur] : **elle est amoureuse de la montagne** she has a passion for mountains.
◇ *nm, f* **1.** [amant] love, lover ■ **~ transi** lovesick hero **2.** [adepte] lover ■ **les ~ de la nature** nature-lovers.
◆ **en amoureux** *loc adv* : **si nous sortions en ~ ce soir?** how about going out tonight, just the two of us?

amour-propre [amurprɔpr] (*pl* **amours-propres**) *nm* pride.

amovible [amɔvibl] *adj* removable.

ampère [ɑ̃pɛr] *nm* ampere.

ampère-heure [ɑ̃pɛrœr] (*pl* **ampères-heures**) *nm* ampere-hour.

ampèremètre [ɑ̃pɛrmɛtr] *nm* ammeter, amperometer.

ampère-tour [ɑ̃pɛrtur] (*pl* **ampères-tours**) *nm* ampere turn.

amphétamine [ɑ̃fetamin] *nf* amphetamine.

amphi [ɑ̃fi] *nm fam* lecture hall *ou* theatre.

amphibie [ɑ̃fibi] ◇ *adj* AÉRON & MIL amphibious.
◇ *nm* amphibian.

amphibien [ɑ̃fibjɛ̃] *nm* amphibian.

amphithéâtre [ɑ̃fiteatr] *nm* **1.** ANTIQ amphitheatre ■ ÉDUC lecture hall *ou* theatre ■ [d'un théâtre] amphitheatre, (upper) gallery ■ [salle de dissection] dissection room **2.** GÉOL : **~ morainique** morainic cirque *ou* amphitheatre.

Amphitryon [ɑ̃fitrijɔ̃] *npr* Amphitryon.
◆ **amphitryon** *nm* host.

amphore [ɑ̃fɔr] *nf* amphora.

ample [ɑ̃pl] *adj* **1.** [vêtement, large - pull] loose, baggy ; [- cape, jupe] flowing, full **2.** [mouvement, geste] wide, sweeping **3.** [abondant - stock, provisions] extensive, ample ■ **de plus ~s renseignements** further details *ou* information.

amplement [ɑ̃pləmɑ̃] *adv* fully, amply ■ **gagner ~ sa vie** to make a very comfortable living ■ **ça suffit ~, c'est ~ suffisant** that's more than enough.

ampleur [ɑ̃plœr] *nf* **1.** [vêtement, largeur - d'un pull] looseness ; [- d'une cape, d'une jupe] fullness **2.** [rondeur - d'un mouvement, d'un geste] fullness **3.** [importance - d'un projet] scope ; [- d'un stock, de ressources] abundance ■ **l'~ des dégâts** the extent of the damages ■ **l'~ de la crise** the scale *ou* extent of the crisis ■ **des événements d'une telle ~** events of such magnitude.

ampli [ɑ̃pli] (*abr de* **amplificateur**) *nm fam* amp.

amplificateur, trice [ɑ̃plifikatœr, tris] *adj* ÉLECTR & PHYS amplifying ■ OPT magnifying ■ PHOTO enlarging.
◆ **amplificateur** *nm* **1.** ÉLECTR & RADIO amplifier **2.** PHOTO enlarger.

amplification [ɑ̃plifikasjɔ̃] *nf* **1.** ÉLECTR & PHYS amplification, amplifying ■ PHOTO [action] enlarging, enlargement ■ OPT magnifying **2.** [développement - de tensions, de revendications] increase ; [- d'échanges, de relations] development, expansion.

amplifier [9] [ɑ̃plifje] *vt* **1.** ÉLECTR & PHYS to amplify ■ OPT to magnify ■ PHOTO to enlarge **2.** [développer - courant, tendance] to develop, to increase ; [- conflit] to deepen ; [- hausse, baisse] to increase ; [- différence] to widen ; [- relations] to develop ■ *péj* [exagérer] to exaggerate, to magnify.
◆ **s'amplifier** *vpi* [augmenter - courant, tendance] to develop, to increase ; [- conflit] to deepen ; [- hausse, baisse] to increase ; [- différence] to widen.

ampliforme [ɑ̃plifɔrm] ◇ *adj* [soutien-gorge] padded.
◇ *nm* padded bra.

amplitude [ɑ̃plityd] *nf* **1.** ASTRON, MATH & PHYS amplitude **2.** MÉTÉOR range **3.** ÉCON : **~ des fluctuations** amplitude of fluctuations **4.** *litt* [étendue] magnitude, extent.

ampli-tuner [ɑ̃plitynɛr] (*pl* **amplis-tuners**) *nm* amplifier-tuner deck.

ampoule [ɑ̃pul] *nf* **1.** ÉLECTR bulb **2.** [récipient] phial ■ **~ autocassable** break-open phial **3.** MÉD blister.

ampoulé, e [ɑ̃pule] *adj péj* pompous, bombastic.

amputation [ɑ̃pytasjɔ̃] *nf* **1.** MÉD amputation **2.** *fig* [suppression] removal, cutting out ■ **ce texte a subi de nombreuses ~s** this text has been heavily cut.

amputé, e [ɑ̃pyte] *nm, f* amputee.

amputer [3] [ɑ̃pyte] *vt* **1.** MÉD [membre] to amputate, to remove ■ **elle a été amputée d'un pied** she had a foot amputated **2.** [ôter une partie de - texte] to cut (down), to reduce ; [- budget] to cut back *(sép)* ■ **l'article a été amputé d'un tiers** the article was cut by a third ■ **le palais a été amputé de son aile sud** the south wing of the palace was demolished.

Amsterdam [amstɛrdam] *npr* Amsterdam.

amuïr [32] [amɥir] ◆ **s'amuïr** *vpi* : **le "s" s'est amuï** the "s" became mute.

amulette [amylɛt] *nf* amulet.

amure [amyr] *nf* tack.

amusant, e [amyzɑ̃, ɑ̃t] *adj* **1.** [drôle] funny, amusing ■ **les gags ne sont même pas ~s** the jokes aren't even funny **2.** [divertissant] entertaining ■ **je vais t'apprendre un petit jeu ~** I'm going to teach you an entertaining little game.

amuse-gueule [amyzgœl] (*pl inv ou pl* **amuse-gueules**) *nm* appetizer, nibble *UK*.

amusement [amyzmɑ̃] *nm* **1.** [sentiment] amusement ■ **écouter qqn/sourire avec ~** to listen to sb with/to smile in amusement **2.** [chose divertissante] entertainment ■ **tu parles d'un ~!** *iron* this isn't exactly my idea of fun! ‖ [jeu] recreational activity, pastime.

amuser [3] [amyze] *vt* **1.** [faire rire] to make laugh, to amuse ■ **elle m'amuse** she makes me laugh ■ **cela ne m'amuse pas du tout** I don't find that in the least bit funny ➊ **~ la galerie** *fam* to play to the gallery **2.** [plaire à] to appeal to ■ **ça ne l'amuse pas de travailler chez eux** he doesn't enjoy *ou* like working there ■ **tu crois que ça m'amuse d'être pris pour un imbécile?** do you think I enjoy being taken for a fool? ■ **si ça t'amuse, fais-le** do it if that's what you want, if it makes you happy, do it **3.** [divertir] to entertain **4.** [détourner l'attention de] to divert, to distract **5.** *litt* [tromper] to delude, to deceive.
◆ **s'amuser** *vpi* **1.** [jouer - enfant] to play ■ **à cet âge-là, on s'amuse avec presque rien** at that age, they amuse themselves very easily ■ **s'~ avec** [manipuler] to fiddle *ou* to toy with **2.** [se divertir] to have fun ■ **ils se sont bien amusés** they really had a good time ■ **amusez-vous bien!** enjoy yourselves!, have a good time! ■ **qu'est-ce qu'on s'est amusés!** we had so much fun! ■ **on s'amusait comme des petits fous** *fam* we were having a whale of a time ■ **elles ont construit une hutte pour s'~** they built a hut, just for fun ■ **mais, papa, c'était pour s'~!** but, Dad, we were only having fun! ■ **ils ne vont pas s'~ avec le nouveau colonel** they won't have much fun with the new colonel ■ **s'~ aux dépens de qqn** to make fun of sb **3.** [perdre son temps] : **s'~ en route** *ou* **en chemin** *pr* to dawdle on the way ; *fig* to waste time needlessly ■ **on n'a pas le temps de s'~** there's no time for fooling around.

◆ **s'amuser à** *vp+prép* **1.** [jouer à] to play **2.** [s'occuper à] : **il s'amuse à faire des avions en papier en cours** he spends his time making paper planes in class **3.** [s'embêter à] : **si tu crois que je vais m'~ à ça!** if you think I have nothing better to do! ■ **si je dois m'amuser à tout lui expliquer, j'ai pas fini!** *fam* if I've got to go and explain everything to him, I'll still be here next week! **4.** [s'aviser de] : **ne t'amuse pas à toucher ce fil!** don't you (go and) touch *ou* go touching that wire!

amuseur, euse [amyzœr, øz] *nm, f* **1.** [artiste] entertainer **2.** *péj* [personne peu sérieuse] smooth talker.

amygdale [amidal] *nf* tonsil ■ **se faire opérer des ~s** to have one's tonsils removed *ou* out.

amygdalite [amidalit] *nf* tonsillitis.

amyotrophie [amjɔtrɔfi] *nf* MÉD amyotrophy, amyotrophia.

an [ɑ̃] *nm* **1.** [durée de douze mois] year ■ **dans un an** one year from now ■ **encore deux ans et je m'arrête** two more years before I stop ■ **j'ai cinq ans de métier** I have five years' experience in this field ■ **une amitié de vingt ans** a friendship of twenty years' standing ■ **un an plus tard** *ou* **après** one year *ou* twelve months later ■ **voilà deux ans qu'elle est partie** she's been gone for two years now ■ **deux fois par an** twice a year ■ **je gagne tant par an** I earn so much a year ■ **tous les ans** [gén] every *ou* each year ; [publier, réviser] yearly, on a yearly basis ➜ **bon an mal an** through good times and bad **2.** *(avec l'art déf)* [division du calendrier] (calendar) year ■ **l'an dernier** *ou* **passé** last year ■ **en l'an 10 après Jésus-Christ** in (the year) 10 AD ■ **en l'an 200 avant notre ère** in (the year) 200 BC ➜ **l'an Un/Deux de la Révolution** HIST Year One/Two of the (French) Revolution ■ **le jour** *ou* **le premier de l'an** New Year's day ■ **je m'en fiche** *ou* **moque comme de l'an quarante!** *fam* I don't give two hoots! **3.** [pour exprimer l'âge] : **à trois ans** at three (years of age) ■ **elle a cinq ans** she's five (years old) ■ **on fête ses vingt ans** we're celebrating his twentieth birthday ■ **un enfant de cinq ans** a five-year-old (child).
◆ **ans** *nmpl litt* advancing *ou* passing years.

anabaptiste [anabatist] *adj* & *nmf* Anabaptist.

anabolisant, e [anabɔlizɑ̃, ɑ̃t] *adj* anabolic.
◆ **anabolisant** *nm* anabolic steroid.

anabolisme [anabɔlism] *nm* anabolism.

anacardier [anakardje] *nm* cashew (tree).

anachorète [anakɔrɛt] *nm* anchorite.

anachronique [anakrɔnik] *adj* anachronistic, anachronic.

anachronisme [anakrɔnism] *nm* anachronism.

anacoluthe [anakɔlyt] *nf* anacoluthon.

anaconda [anakɔ̃da] *nm* anaconda.

anagramme [anagram] *nf* anagram.

anal, e, aux [anal, o] *adj* anal.

analeptique [analɛptik] *adj* & *nm* analeptic.

analgésie [analʒezi] *nf* analgesia.

analgésique [analʒezik] *adj* & *nm* analgesic.

analité [analite] *nf* anality.

anallergique [analɛrʒik] *adj* hypoallergenic.

analogie [analɔʒi] *nf* analogy ■ **trouver une ~ entre deux choses** to draw an analogy between two things.
◆ **par analogie** *loc adv* by analogy ■ **par ~ avec** by analogy with.

analogique [analɔʒik] *adj* **1.** [présentant un rapport] analogic, analogical **2.** INFORM analog.

analogue [analɔg] ◇ *adj* analogous, similar ■ **~ par la forme** analogous in shape ■ **une histoire ~ à une autre** a story similar to another one.
◇ *nm* analogue.

analphabète [analfabɛt] *adj* & *nmf* illiterate.

analphabétisme [analfabetism] *nm* illiteracy ■ **les problèmes liés à l'~** problems of literacy.

analysable [analizabl] *adj* **1.** [que l'on peut examiner] analys-able **2.** INFORM scannable.

analysant, e [analizɑ̃, ɑ̃t] *nm, f* analysand.

analyse [analiz] *nf* **1.** [étude] analysis ■ **cet argument ne résist pas à l'~** this argument doesn't stand up to analysis ■ **l'~ de faits montre que...** an examination of the facts show that... ➜ **~ de faisabilité** feasibility study ■ **~ de marché** mar ket survey *ou* research ■ **~ des postes de travail** job analysi ■ **~ des résultats** processing of results
2. ÉDUC analysis ■ **faire l'~ d'un texte** to analyse a text ■ **~ d texte** textual analysis ■ **~ logique/grammaticale** GRAMM sen tence/grammatical analysis ■ **faites l'~ grammaticale de cett phrase** parse this sentence
3. BIOL analysis ■ **~ de sang** blood analysis *ou* test
4. PSYCHOL analysis, psychoanalysis ■ **être en ~** to be in analy sis ■ **faire une ~** to undergo analysis
5. INFORM analysis ■ **~ fonctionnelle** functional *ou* system analysis ■ **~ numérique** numerical analysis ■ **~ organique** sys tems design ■ **~ des performances du système** system evalu ation ❙ ÉLECTRON scan, scanning
6. CHIM & MATH analysis
7. MIN essaying ■ **~ des minerais** ore essaying.

analysé, e [analize] *nm, f* PSYCHOL analysand.

analyser [3] [analize] *vt* **1.** [étudier] to analyse **2.** GRAMM t parse **3.** [résumer] to summarize, to make an abstract *ou* précis of **4.** BIOL & CHIM to analyse, to test **5.** PSYCHOL to ana lyse ■ **se faire ~** to undergo analysis.

analyseur [analizœr] *nm* **1.** INFORM analyser **2.** ÉLECTRO scanner, analyser **3.** ÉLECTR analyser **4.** CHIM analyst.

analyste [analist] *nmf* **1.** [gén] analyst **2.** PSYCHOL analys psychoanalyst.

analyste-programmeur, euse [analistprɔgramœ øz] *(mpl* **analystes-programmeurs**, *fpl* **analystes-program meuses**) *nm, f* systems analyst.

analytique [analitik] ◇ *adj* analytic, analytical.
◇ *nf* analytics *(U)*.

anamorphose [anamɔrfoz] *nf* ENTOM & OPT anamorphosis

ananas [anana(s)] *nm* pineapple.

anaphore [anafɔr] *nf* anaphora.

anaphorique [anafɔrik] *adj* anaphoric, anaphorical.

anar [anar] *nmf fam* anarchist.

anarchie [anarʃi] *nf* **1.** POLIT anarchy **2.** [désordre] anarchy

anarchique [anarʃik] *adj* anarchic, anarchical.

anarchisme [anarʃism] *nm* anarchism.

anarchiste [anarʃist] ◇ *adj* anarchist, anarchistic.
◇ *nmf* anarchist.

anarcho-syndicalisme [anarkosɛ̃dikalism] *(pl* **anarcho syndicalismes**) *nm* anarchosyndicalism.

anathématiser [3] [anatematize] *vt* **1.** *litt* [condamner] t censure **2.** RELIG to anathematize.

anathème [anatɛm] *nm* **1.** [condamnation] anathema ■ **jete l'~ sur** to pronounce an anathema upon, to anathematiz **2.** RELIG anathema.

Anatolie [anatɔli] *npr f* : **(l')~** Anatolia.

anatolien, enne [anatɔljɛ̃, ɛn] *adj* Anatolian.

anatomie [anatɔmi] *nf* **1.** SC [étude, structure] anatomy **2.** *fa* [corps] body ■ **dans la partie la plus charnue de son ~** *euphém* i his posterior.

anatomique [anatɔmik] *adj* anatomical ■ **faire l'étude d'un corps** to anatomize *ou* to dissect a body.

anatomiste [anatɔmist] *nmf* anatomist.

ancestral, e, aux [ɑ̃sɛstral, o] *adj* **1.** [venant des ancêtre ancestral **2.** [ancien - tradition, coutume] ancient, age-ol time-honoured.

ancêtre [ɑ̃sɛtr] *nmf* **1.** [ascendant] ancestor, forefather ■ **c'était mon ~** he/she was an ancestor of mine **2.** [précurseur - personne, objet] ancestor, forerunner, precursor **3.** *fam* [vieille personne] old boy (*f* old girl) *UK*, old timer *US*.
◆ **ancêtres** *nmpl* ancestors, forebears.

anche [ɑ̃ʃ] *nf* reed.

anchois [ɑ̃ʃwa] *nm* anchovy.

ancien, enne [ɑ̃sjɛ̃, ɛn] ◇ *adj* **1.** [vieux - coutume, tradition, famille] old, ancient, time-honoured ; [- amitié, relation] old, long-standing ; [- bague, châle] old, antique ■ **un meuble ~** an antique
2. ANTIQ [langue, histoire, civilisation] ancient ■ **la Grèce ~ne** ancient *ou* classical Greece
3. *(avant le n)* [ex - président, époux, employé] former, ex ; [- stade, église] former ■ **ses ~s camarades** his old *ou* former comrades ■ **mon ~ne école** my old school ■ **une ~ne colonie française** a former French colony ➔ **un ~ combattant** a (war) veteran, an ex-serviceman ■ **un ~ élève** an old boy *UK*, an alumnus *US* ■ **une ~ne élève** an old girl *UK*, an alumna *US*
4. [passé] former ■ **dans les temps ~s, dans l'~ temps** in former times, in olden *ou* bygone days
5. [qui a de l'ancienneté] senior ■ **vous n'êtes pas assez ~ dans la profession** you've not been in the job long enough
6. LING : **~ français** Old French.
◇ *nm, f* **1.** [qui a de l'expérience] old hand
2. [qui est plus vieux] elder
3. [qui a participé] : **un ~ de l'ENA** a former student of the ENA ■ **un ~ du parti communiste** an ex-member of the Communist Party ■ **un ~ de la guerre de Corée** a Korean war veteran, a veteran of the Korean war.
◆ **ancien** *nm* **1.** [objets] : **l'~** antiques ■ **meublé entièrement en ~** entirely furnished with antiques
2. [construction] : **l'~** old *ou* older buildings.
◆ **Anciens** *nmpl* ANTIQ & LITTÉR Ancients.
◆ **à l'ancienne** *loc adj* old-fashioned ■ **bœuf à l'~ne** beef in traditional style.
◆ **Ancien Régime** *nm* : **l'Ancien Régime** the Ancien Régime.
◆ **Ancien Testament** *nm* : **l'Ancien Testament** the Old Testament.

ANCIEN RÉGIME

The government and social structure of France before the Revolution of 1789 was an absolutist monarchy consisting of three estates: the nobility, the clergy (both enjoying institutional privileges), and the Third Estate, or commoners. The privileges which characterized the *Ancien Régime* were abolished the 4th of August 1789.

anciennement [ɑ̃sjɛnmɑ̃] *adv* previously, formerly.

ancienneté [ɑ̃sjɛnte] *nf* **1.** [d'une chose] oldness **2.** [d'une personne] length of service ■ **avoir de l'~ : elle a beaucoup d'~ chez nous** she's been with us for a long time ‖ [avantages acquis] seniority ■ **avancer** *ou* **être promu à l'~** to be promoted by seniority.

ancillaire [ɑ̃silɛr] *adj* [avec une servante] : **les amours ~s** love affairs with servants.

ancolie [ɑ̃kɔli] *nf* columbine, aquilegia.

ancrage [ɑ̃kraʒ] *nm* **1.** TECHNOL [fixation] anchorage **2.** NAUT [arrêt] moorage, anchorage ■ [droits] anchorage *ou* moorage *ou* berthing (dues) **3.** [enracinement] : **l'~ d'un parti dans l'électorat** a party's electoral base.

ancre [ɑ̃kr] *nf* NAUT : **~ (de marine)** anchor ■ **~ flottante** drag anchor ■ **~ de salut** *fig* last resort ■ **elle est mon ~ de salut** she's my last hope ■ **être à l'~** to ride *ou* to lie at anchor ■ **jeter l'~** *pr* to cast *ou* to drop anchor ; *fig* to put down roots ■ **lever l'~** *pr* to weigh anchor ■ **allez, on lève l'~!** *fam fig* come on, let's go!

ancrer [3] [ɑ̃kre] *vt* **1.** NAUT to anchor **2.** [attacher] to anchor **3.** *fig* to root ■ **la propagande a ancré le parti dans la région** propaganda has established the party firmly in this area ■ **c'est une idée bien ancrée** it's a firmly-rooted idea.
◆ **s'ancrer** *vpi* **1.** NAUT to drop *ou* to cast anchor **2.** [se fixer] to settle.

andalou, se [ɑ̃dalu, uz] *adj* Andalusian.

Andalousie [ɑ̃daluzi] *npr f* : **(l')~** Andalusia.

Andes [ɑ̃d] *npr fpl* : **les ~** the Andes.

andin, e [ɑ̃dɛ̃, in] *adj* Andean.

Andorre [ɑ̃dɔr] *npr f* : **(la principauté d)~** (the principality of) Andorra.

Andorre-la-Vieille [ɑ̃dɔrlavjɛj] *npr* Andorra la Vella.

andouille [ɑ̃duj] *nf* **1.** CULIN chitterlings sausage *(eaten cold)* **2.** *fam* [imbécile] dummy ■ **faire l'~** to fool around ■ **espèce d'~!** you great dummy! ■ **fais pas l'~, touche pas la prise!** watch out, don't touch the socket!

andouillette [ɑ̃dujɛt] *nf* chitterlings sausage *(for grilling)*.

André [ɑ̃dre] *npr* : **saint ~** Saint Andrew ■ **la Saint-~** Saint Andrew's Day.

androcéphale [ɑ̃drɔsefal] *adj* androcephalous.

androgène [ɑ̃drɔʒɛn] ◇ *adj* androgenic.
◇ *nm* androgen.

androgyne [ɑ̃drɔʒin] ◇ *adj* androgynous.
◇ *nm* androgyne.

androïde [ɑ̃drɔid] *nm* android.

Andromaque [ɑ̃drɔmak] *npr* Andromache.

Andromède [ɑ̃drɔmɛd] *npr* Andromeda.

andropause [ɑ̃drɔpoz] *nf* male menopause.

androstérone [ɑ̃drɔsteron] *nf* androsterone.

âne [an] *nm* **1.** ZOOL donkey, ass ■ **il est comme l'~ de Buridan** he can't make up his mind **2.** [imbécile] idiot, fool ■ **faire l'~** to play the fool ■ **c'est un ~ bâté** he's a complete idiot.

anéantir [32] [aneɑ̃tir] *vt* **1.** [détruire - armée, ville] to annihilate, to destroy, to wipe out *(sép)* ; [- rébellion, révolte] to quell, to crush ; [- espoir] to dash, to destroy ; [- succès, effort] to ruin, to wreck ; [- amour, confiance] to destroy **2.** [accabler - suj: nouvelle, événement] to overwhelm, to crush ■ **être anéanti par le chagrin** to be overcome by grief ■ **elle est anéantie** she's devastated ■ [épuiser] to exhaust ■ **elle est anéantie par la chaleur/fatigue** she's overwhelmed by the heat/utterly exhausted.
◆ **s'anéantir** *vpi* to disappear, to vanish ■ **tous nos espoirs se sont anéantis** all our hopes were dashed.

anéantissement [aneɑ̃tismɑ̃] *nm* **1.** [destruction] ruin, annihilation, destruction ■ **c'est l'~ d'un mois de travail** it's a whole month's work lost **2.** [accablement] prostration ■ **être dans l'~ le plus total** to be completely devastated.

anecdote [anɛkdɔt] *nf* anecdote ■ **tout cela, c'est de l'~** *péj* this is all trivial detail, this is just so much trivia.

anecdotique [anɛkdɔtik] *adj* **1.** [qui contient des anecdotes] anecdotal **2.** [sans intérêt] trivial *péj*.

anélastique [anelastik] *adj* unelastic.

anémie [anemi] *nf* **1.** MÉD anaemia **2.** *fig* **nous constatons une ~ de la production** we note that output has slowed to a trickle.

anémié, e [anemje] *adj* **1.** MÉD anaemic **2.** [affaibli] weakened, anaemic.

anémier [9] [anemje] *vt* **1.** MÉD to make anaemic **2.** [affaiblir] to weaken, to enfeeble *litt*.

anémique [anemik] *adj* **1.** MÉD anaemic **2.** [faible - personne] feeble, ineffectual ; [- plante] spindly, weedy ; [- économie, industrie] weak, slow, sluggish ■ **un texte plutôt ~** a rather colourless piece of writing.

anémomètre [anemɔmɛtr] *nm* anemometer.

anémone [anemɔn] *nf* **1.** BOT anemone **2.** ZOOL : **~ de mer** sea anemone.

ânerie [anri] *nf* **1.** [caractère stupide] stupidity ■ **tu es d'une ~!** you are so stupid!, you're such an idiot! **2.** [parole] stupid *ou* silly remark ■ **dire des ~s** to make stupid *ou* silly remarks, to talk rubbish **3.** [acte] stupid blunder *ou* mistake ■ **faire des ~s** to make stupid mistakes.

anéroïde [anerɔid] *adj* aneroid.

ânesse [anɛs] *nf* she-ass, jenny.

anesthésiant, e [anɛstezjɑ̃, ɑ̃t] = **anesthésique**.

anesthésie [anɛstezi] *nf* anaesthesia ■ **faire une ~ à qqn** to anaesthetize sb, to give sb an anaesthetic ■ **être sous ~** to be anaesthetized *ou* under an anaesthetic ➊ **~ locale/générale/péridurale** local/general/epidural anaesthesia.

anesthésier [9] [anɛstezje] *vt* **1.** MÉD to anaesthetize **2.** [insensibiliser - bras, jambe] to numb, to deaden ■ **le glaçon m'a anesthésié la gencive** the ice cube numbed *ou* took all the feeling out of my gum.

anesthésiologie [anɛstezjɔlɔʒi] *nf* anaesthetics *UK (U)*, anesthesiology *US*.

anesthésiologiste [anɛstezjɔlɔʒist] = **anesthésiste-réanimateur**.

anesthésique [anɛstezik] *adj* & *nm* anaesthetic ■ **un ~ local** a local anaesthetic.

anesthésiste-réanimateur [anɛstezistreanimatœr] (*pl* **anesthésistes-réanimateurs**) *nmf* anaesthetist *UK*, anesthesiologist *US*.

aneth [anɛt] *nm* dill.

anévrisme [anevrism] *nm* aneurysm.

anfractuosité [ɑ̃fraktyozite] *nf* **1.** [cavité] crevice, crack **2.** MÉD anfractuosity.

ange [ɑ̃ʒ] *nm* **1.** RELIG angel ■ **c'est mon bon ~** he's my guardian angel ■ **c'est mon mauvais ~** he's a bad influence on me ➊ **~ déchu/gardien** fallen/guardian angel ■ **un ~ passa** there was a pregnant pause *ou* an awkward lull in the conversation ■ **être aux ~s** to be beside o.s. with joy ■ **il riait** *ou* **souriait aux ~s dans son sommeil** he was smiling happily in his sleep **2.** [personne parfaite] angel ■ **passe-moi le pain, tu seras un ~** be an angel *ou* a dear and pass me the bread ‖ [en appellatif] : **mon ~** my darling *ou* angel **3.** ZOOL monkfish, angel shark.

angélique [ɑ̃ʒelik] ◇ *adj* RELIG & *fig* angelic ■ **un sourire ~** the sweet smile of an angel.
◇ *nf* BOT & CULIN angelica.

angélisme [ɑ̃ʒelism] *nm* otherworldliness.

angelot [ɑ̃ʒlo] *nm* cherub.

angélus [ɑ̃ʒelys] *nm* Angelus.

angevin, e [ɑ̃ʒvɛ̃, in] *adj* **1.** [d'Angers] from Angers **2.** [de l'Anjou] from Anjou.
➡ **Angevin, e** *nm, f* [habitant - d'Angers] *inhabitant of or person from Angers* ; [- de l'Anjou] *inhabitant of or person from Anjou* ■ **les Angevins** [d'Angers] the people of Angers ; [de l'Anjou] the people of Anjou.

angine [ɑ̃ʒin] *nf* **1.** [infection - des amygdales] tonsillitis ; [- du pharynx] pharyngitis ■ **avoir une ~** to have a sore throat **2.** [douleur cardiaque] angina ■ **~ de poitrine** angina (pectoris).

angineux, euse [ɑ̃ʒinø, øz] *adj* anginal, anginous.

angiographie [ɑ̃ʒjɔgrafi] *nf* angiography.

angiologie [ɑ̃ʒjɔlɔʒi] *nf* angiology.

angiome [ɑ̃ʒjom] *nm* angioma.

angiosperme [ɑ̃ʒjɔspɛrm] *nf* angiosperm.

anglais, e [ɑ̃glɛ, ɛz] *adj* [d'Angleterre] English ■ [de Grande-Bretagne] British ■ **l'équipe ~e** SPORT the England team.
➡ **Anglais, e** *nm, f* [d'Angleterre] Englishman (*f* Englishwoman) ■ [de Grande-Bretagne] Briton ■ **les Anglais** [d'Angleterre] English people, the English ; [de Grande-Bretagne] British people, the British.
➡ **anglais** *nm* LING English ■ **~ américain/britannique** American/British English.
➡ **anglaise** *nf* **1.** [écriture] italic longhand **2.** BOT morello cherry.
➡ **anglaises** *nfpl* ringlets ■ **elle était coiffée avec des ~es** her hair was in ringlets.
➡ **à l'anglaise** ◇ *loc adj* **1.** CULIN boiled **2.** HORT : **jardin/parc à l'~e** landscaped garden/park **3.** MENUIS : **escalier/limon à l'~e** open staircase/stringboard.
◇ *loc adv* : **se sauver** *ou* **filer à l'~e** to take French leave.

angle [ɑ̃gl] *nm* **1.** [coin - d'un meuble, d'une rue] corner ■ **la maison qui est à** *ou* **qui fait l'~** the house on the corner ■ **la statue est à l'~ de deux rues** the statue stands at a crossroads ➊ **meuble d'~** corner unit ■ **~ vif** sharp angle ■ **arrondir les ~s** to smooth things over
2. GÉOM angle ■ **~ aigu/droit/obtus** acute/right/obtuse angle ■ **la rue fait un ~ droit avec l'avenue** the street is at right angles to the avenue ■ **~ ouvert** wide angle ■ **~ plein** 360-degree angle
3. [aspect] angle, point of view ■ **je ne vois pas cela sous cet ~** I don't see it quite in that light *ou* from that angle ■ **vu sous l'~ économique/du rendement, cette décision se comprend** from an economic/a productivity point of view, the decision makes sense
4. OPT angle ■ **~ d'incidence/de réflexion/de réfraction** angle of incidence/of reflection/of refraction ■ **~ d'ouverture** aperture angle, beam width
5. TECHNOL angle.
➡ **angle mort** *nm* [en voiture] blind spot.
➡ **d'angle** *loc adj* **1.** CONSTR quoin *(modif)*, cornerstone *(modif)*
2. [table] corner *(modif)*.

Angleterre [ɑ̃glətɛr] *npr f* : **(l')~** England ; [Grande-Bretagne] (Great) Britain ■ **la bataille d'~** the Battle of Britain.

anglican, e [ɑ̃glikɑ̃, an] *adj* & *nm, f* Anglican.

anglicanisme [ɑ̃glikanism] *nm* Anglicanism.

angliche [ɑ̃gliʃ] *fam* ◇ *adj* [d'Angleterre] English ■ [de Grande-Bretagne] Brit.
◇ *nmf* [d'Angleterre] Englishman (*f* Englishwoman) ■ [de Grande-Bretagne] Brit.

anglicisation [ɑ̃glisizasjɔ̃] *nf* anglicization, anglicizing.

angliciser [3] [ɑ̃glisize] *vt* to anglicize.
➡ **s'angliciser** *vpi* to become anglicized.

anglicisme [ɑ̃glisism] *nm* anglicism.

angliciste [ɑ̃glisist] *nmf* **1.** [étudiant] student of English **2.** [enseignant] teacher of English **3.** [spécialiste] Anglicist, expert in English language and culture.

anglo- [ɑ̃glo] *préf* anglo-.

anglo-américain [ɑ̃gloamerikɛ̃, ɛn] (*mpl* **anglo-américains**, *fpl* **anglo-américaines**) *adj* Anglo-American.
➡ **Anglo-Américain, e** *nm, f* Anglo-American.
➡ **anglo-américain** *nm* LING American English.

anglo-français, e [ɑ̃glofrɑ̃sɛ, ɛz] (*mpl inv*, *fpl* **anglo-françaises**) *adj* Anglo-French.
➡ **Anglo-Français, e** *nm, f* : **c'est un Anglo-Français** he's half English and half French.

anglo-irlandais, e [ɑ̃gloirlɑ̃dɛ, ɛz] (*mpl inv*, *fpl* **anglo-irlandaises**) *adj* Anglo-Irish.
➡ **Anglo-Irlandais, e** *nm, f* : **c'est un Anglo-Irlandais** he's half English and half Irish ■ **les Anglo-Irlandais** the Anglo-Irish.

anglomane [ɑ̃glɔman] *nmf* Anglomaniac.

anglomanie [ɑ̃glɔmani] *nf* Anglomania.

anglo-normand [ɑ̃glonɔrmɑ̃, ɑ̃d] (*mpl* **anglo-normands**, *fpl* **anglo-normandes**) *adj* **1.** HIST Anglo-Norman **2.** GÉOGR of the Channel islands ■ **les îles ~es** the Channel Islands.
➡ **anglo-normand** *nm* LING Anglo-Norman.

anglophile [ɑ̃glɔfil] ◇ *adj* Anglophilic, Anglophiliac.
◇ *nmf* Anglophile.

anglophilie [ɑ̃glɔfili] *nf* Anglophilia.

anglophobe [ɑ̃glɔfɔb] ◇ *adj* Anglophobic.
◇ *nmf* Anglophobe.

anglophobie [ɑ̃glɔfɔbi] *nf* Anglophobia.

anglophone [ɑ̃glɔfɔn] *adj* & *nmf* Anglophone.

anglo-saxon, onne [ɑ̃glɔsaksɔ̃, ɔn] (*mpl* **anglo-saxons**, *fpl* **anglo-saxonnes**) *adj* **1.** [culture, civilisation] Anglo-American, Anglo-Saxon **2.** HIST Anglo-Saxon.
◆ **Anglo-Saxon, onne** *nm, f* Anglo-Saxon ■ **les Anglo-Saxons** [peuples] British and American people ; HIST the Anglo-Saxons.
◆ **anglo-saxon** *nm* LING Old English, Anglo-Saxon.

ANGLO-SAXON

The adjective *anglo-saxon* and the noun *Anglo-Saxon* are often used in French to refer to British and American people, culture, customs etc: *la musique anglo-saxonne, la littérature anglo-saxonne*.

angoissant, e [ɑ̃gwasɑ̃, ɑ̃t] *adj* [expérience] distressing, harrowing, agonizing ■ [nouvelle, livre, film] distressing, harrowing ■ **il a vécu trois jours très ~s** he lived through three harrowing days ‖ [sens affaibli] : **j'ai trouvé l'attente très ~e** the wait was a strain on my nerves.

angoisse [ɑ̃gwas] *nf* [inquiétude] anxiety ■ [tourment] anguish ■ **être** *ou* **vivre dans l'~** to live in (a constant state of) anxiety ■ **l'~ de : l'~ de la mort** the fear of death ■ **vivre dans l'~ de qqch** to live in dread of *ou* to dread sthg ▶ **~ existentielle** (existential) angst ■ **c'est l'~!** *fam* I dread the very idea!
◆ **angoisses** *nfpl* : **avoir des ~s** to suffer from anxiety attacks.

angoissé, e [ɑ̃gwase] ◇ *adj* [personne] anxious ■ [regard] haunted, anguished, agonized ■ [voix, cri] agonized, anguished ■ **être ~ avant un examen** to feel anxious before an exam.
◇ *nm, f* anxious person ■ **c'est un grand ~** he's the anxious type *ou* a terrible worrier.

angoisser [3] [ɑ̃gwase] ◇ *vt* : **~ qqn** [inquiéter] to cause sb anxiety, to cause anxiety to sb ; [tourmenter] to cause sb anguish.
◇ *vi fam* to worry ■ **j'angoisse à mort pour l'examen de demain** I'm worried sick about tomorrow's exam.
◆ **s'angoisser** *vpi fam* to get worked up.

Angola [ɑ̃gɔla] *npr m* : **(l')~** Angola.

angolais, e [ɑ̃gɔlɛ, ɛz] *adj* Angolan.
◆ **Angolais, e** *nm, f* Angolan.

angora [ɑ̃gɔra] ◇ *adj* angora.
◇ *nm* **1.** [chat, lapin] Angora **2.** [laine] angora.
◆ **en angora** *loc adj* angora *(modif)*.

angström [ɑ̃gstrœm] *nm* angstrom.

anguille [ɑ̃gij] *nf* ZOOL eel ■ **~ de mer/électrique** conger/electric eel ■ **souple comme une ~** supple as a reed ■ **il y a ~ sous roche** there's something fishy going on.

angulaire [ɑ̃gylɛr] *adj* angular.

anguleux, euse [ɑ̃gylø, øz] *adj* [objet] angular ■ [visage] bony, sharp-featured, angular ■ [personne] skinny, bony ■ [esprit, caractère] stiff, angular.

anhydre [anidr] *adj* anhydrous.

anicroche [anikrɔʃ] *nf* hitch, snag ■ **sans ~** smoothly, without a hitch.

ânier, ère [anje, ɛr] *nm, f* donkey driver.

animal, e, aux [animal, o] *adj* animal ▶ **échelle ~e** evolutionary ladder.
◆ **animal, aux** *nm* **1.** ZOOL animal ▶ **~ familier** *ou* **domestique** pet ■ **~ virtuel** cyberpet **2.** *fam* [personne] dope, oaf ■ **c'est qu'il a encore raison, cet ~-là** *ou* **l'~!** the beggar's right again!

animalerie [animalri] *nf* **1.** [de laboratoire] breeding farm *(for laboratory animals)* **2.** [magasin] pet shop.

animalier, ère [animalje, ɛr] *adj* [peintre, sculpteur] animal *(modif)* ■ **parc ~** wildlife park.
◆ **animalier** *nm* **1.** ART animalier **2.** [employé] animal keeper *(in a laboratory)*.

animalité [animalite] *nf* animality, animal nature.

animateur, trice [animatœr, tris] *nm, f* **1.** [responsable - de maison de jeunes, de centre sportif] youth leader, coordinator ; [- de groupe] leader ; [- d'entreprise, de service] coordinator **2.** RADIO & TV [gén] presenter ■ [de jeux, de variétés] host **3.** [élément dynamique] moving spirit, driving force **4.** CINÉ animator.

animation [animasjɔ̃] *nf* **1.** [entrain] life, liveliness, excitement ■ **mettre un peu d'~ dans une réunion** to liven up a meeting ■ **son arrivée a créé beaucoup d'~** his arrival caused a great deal of excitement **2.** [vivacité] liveliness, vivacity, animation ■ **elles discutaient de biologie avec ~** they were having a lively discussion about biology **3.** [d'un quartier, d'une ville] life ■ **il y a de l'~ dans les rues le soir** the streets are very lively *ou* full of life at night **4.** [coordination - d'un groupe] running ; [- d'un débat] chairing ■ **chargé de l'~ culturelle** in charge of cultural activities **5.** CINÉ animation.

animé, e [anime] *adj* **1.** [doué de vie] animate ■ **les êtres ~s** animate beings **2.** [doté de mouvement] moving, animated ■ **les vitrines ~es de Noël** moving *ou* animated window displays at Christmas **3.** [plein de vivacité - personne, discussion] lively, animated ; [- marché, ville, quartier] lively ■ **des rues ~es** bustling *ou* lively streets **4.** LING animate.

animer [3] [anime] *vt* **1.** [doter de mouvement - mécanisme, robot] to move, to actuate, to motivate ■ **le piston est animé d'un mouvement de va-et-vient** the piston is driven back and forth **2.** [inspirer] to prompt, to motivate ■ **c'est la générosité qui l'anime** he's prompted *ou* motivated by generous feelings ■ **être animé des meilleures intentions** to have the best of intentions ■ **être animé d'un nouvel espoir** to be buoyed up by new hope **3.** [égayer - soirée, repas] to bring life to, to liven up *(sép)* ; [- regard] to light up *(sép)* ■ **~ un personnage** to make a character come to life **4.** [présenter - débat] to chair ; [- émission d'actualité] to present ; [- émission de variétés] to host ■ [faire fonctionner - atelier] to run.
◆ **s'animer** *vpi* [personne, conversation] to become animated ■ [quartier, rue, visage, yeux] to come alive ■ [pantin, poupée] to come to life.

animisme [animism] *nm* animism.

animosité [animozite] *nf* animosity, hostility, resentment ■ **ressentir de l'~ contre qqn** to feel resentment *ou* hostility towards sb ■ **un regard plein d'~** a hostile look.

anion [anjɔ̃] *nm* anion.

anis [ani(s)] *nm* **1.** BOT anise **2.** CULIN aniseed ■ **à l'~** aniseed *(modif)*, aniseed-flavoured.

anisé [anize] *adj* anisated, aniseed-flavoured.

anisette [anizɛt] *nf* anisette.

Ankara [ɑ̃kara] *npr* Ankara.

ankylose [ɑ̃kiloz] *nf* **1.** MÉD ankylosis **2.** [engourdissement] stiffness, numbness.

ankylosé, e [ɑ̃kiloze] *adj* **1.** MÉD ankylotic **2.** [engourdi] numb.

ankyloser [3] [ɑ̃kiloze] *vt* to ankylose.
◆ **s'ankyloser** *vpi* **1.** MÉD to ankylose **2.** [devenir raide - bras, jambe] to become numb ; [- personne] to go stiff.

annal, e [anal] *adj* valid for one year, yearly.

annales [anal] *nfpl* annals ■ **rester dans les ~** to go down in history.

annaliste [analist] *nmf* annalist.

annamite [anamit] *adj* Annamese.
◆ **Annamite** *nmf* Annamese.

Annapurna [anapyrna] *npr m* : **l' ~** Annapurna.

anneau, x [ano] *nm* **1.** JOAILL ring ■ **un simple ~ d'or** a plain band of gold ■ **en forme d'~** annular *sout*, ring-shaped ▶ **~**

épiscopal/nuptial bishop's/wedding ring **2.** [pour rideaux] ring ■ [maillon] link ■ [boucle - de ficelle] loop **3.** MATH ring **4.** BOT & GÉOM annulus **5.** ZOOL [d'un ver] metamere, somatite ■ [d'un serpent] coil **6.** ANAT ring **7.** ASTRON ring ■ **les ~x de Saturne** the rings of Saturn **8.** SPORT : **~ de vitesse** [pour patinage] rink ; [pour bicyclette] racetrack **9.** OPT ring ■ **~x colorés** coloured rings.

◆ **anneaux** *nmpl* SPORT rings ■ JEUX hoopla.

◆ **en anneau** *loc adj* **1.** [gén] ring-shaped, annular *sout* **2.** ÉLECTRON ring *(modif)*.

année [ane] *nf* **1.** [division du calendrier] year ■ **~ bissextile** leap year ■ **~ civile** calendar *ou* civil year
2. [date] year ■ **~ de fabrication** date *ou* year of construction ■ **l'~ 1789** the year 1789
3. [durée] year ■ **l'~ de référence** the base year ■ **ce projet durera toute l'~** this project will last the whole year ■ **d'~ en ~** from year to year ■ **d'une ~ à l'autre** from one year to the next ■ **tout au long de l'~, toute l'~** all year long *ou* round ■ **j'ai encore deux ~s à faire** I have two more years to do ■ **j'ai cinq ~s de métier** I have five years' experience in this field ■ **entrer dans sa trentième ~** to enter one's thirtieth year ■ **les plus belles ~s de ma vie** the best years of my life ■ **première ~** UNIV first year *UK*, freshman year *US* ■ **dernière ~** UNIV final year ■ **c'est une étudiante de troisième ~** she's a third-year student *UK*, she's in her junior year *US* ■ **elle est en troisième ~ de médecine** she's in her third year at medical school ▶ **l'~ scolaire/universitaire/judiciaire** the school/academic/judicial year ■ **l'~ fiscale** the tax year, the fiscal year *US* ■ **une ~ sabbatique** a sabbatical (year) ■ **~s de vaches maigres/grasses** *fam* lean/prosperous years
4. [célébration] : **l'~ de** the Year of ■ **l'~ du Dragon** the Year of the Dragon ■ **l'~ de l'Enfance** the Year of the Child ■ **l'~ de la Femme** International Women's Year
5. [nouvel an] : **bonne ~!** happy New Year! ■ **souhaiter la bonne ~ à qqn** to wish sb a happy New Year ■ **carte/souhaits de bonne ~** New Year card/wishes.

◆ **années** *nfpl* : **les ~s 60/70** the sixties/seventies ▶ **les Années folles** the roaring twenties.

◆ **à l'année** *loc adv* [louer, payer] annually, on a yearly basis.

année-lumière [anelymjɛr] (*pl* **années-lumière**) *nf* light year ■ **à des années-lumière de** *fig* light years away from ■ **mon cousin et moi, nous sommes à des années-lumière l'un de l'autre** my cousin and I are poles apart.

annelé, e [anle] *adj* **1.** [gén] ringed **2.** ARCHIT & BOT annulate, annulated.

anneler [24] [anle] *vt* to ring.

annelet [anlɛ] *nm* **1.** [anneau] small ring **2.** ARCHIT annulet.

annexe [anɛks] ◇ *adj* **1.** [accessoire - tâche, détail, fait] subsidiary, related ■ [sans importance] minor ■ **des considérations ~s** side issues ■ **ne parlons pas de cela, c'est tout à fait ~** let's forget about this, it's very much a minor point *ou* it's not relevant to the matter in hand **2.** [dossier] additional ■ **les documents** *ou* **pièces ~s** the attached documents.
◇ *nf* **1.** [bâtiment] annexe **2.** [supplément] annexe ■ **mettre qqch en ~ à** to append sthg to ‖ [d'un bilan] schedule ■ [d'un dossier] appendix ■ DR [d'une loi] rider **3.** MÉD appendage.

annexer [4] [anɛkse] *vt* **1.** [joindre] to annex, to append ■ **~ un témoignage à un dossier** to append a testimony to a file **2.** HIST & POLIT to annex.

◆ **s'annexer** *vpt fam* **s'~ qqch** [le monopoliser] to hog sthg ; *euphém* [le voler] to filch sthg, to purloin sthg *hum*.

annexion [anɛksjɔ̃] *nf* annexation.

annexionnisme [anɛksjɔnism] *nm* annexationism.

annihiler [3] [aniile] *vt* [efforts, révolte] to annihilate, to destroy ■ [personne] to crush, to destroy *fig*.

anniversaire [anivɛrsɛr] ◇ *adj* anniversary *(modif)* ■ **le jour ~ de leur rencontre** the anniversary of the day they first met.
◇ *nm* **1.** [d'une naissance] birthday ■ **le jour de son ~** on his birthday ‖ [d'un mariage, d'une mort, d'un événement] anniversary **2.** [fête] birthday party.

annonce [anɔ̃s] *nf* **1.** [nouvelle] notice, notification ■ [fait de dire] announcement ■ **faire une ~** [gén] to make an announcement **2.** [texte publicitaire] advertisement ■ **mettre** *ou* **insérer une ~ dans un journal** to put *ou* to place an advertisement in a paper ▶ **~ judiciaire** legal notice ■ **~ publicitaire** advertisement ■ **les petites ~s** [location, vente] classified advertisements ; [courrier du cœur] personal column **3.** JEUX declaration ■ **faire une ~** to declare **4.** [présage] portent *litt*, sign ■ **cet incident était en fait l'~ de la guerre** this incident was really a portent of the forthcoming war.

annoncer [16] [anɔ̃se] *vt* **1.** [communiquer - décision, événement] to announce ; [- mauvaise nouvelle] to break, to announce ■ **je n'ose pas le lui ~** I daren't break it to her ■ **on annonce des réductions d'impôts** tax reductions have been announced ■ **on m'a annoncé sa mort** I was told *ou* informed of his death ■ **je vous annonce que je me marie** I'd like to inform you that I'm getting married ■ **je leur ai annoncé que je m'en allais** I told them I was leaving
2. [prédire] to forecast ■ **ils annoncent du soleil pour demain** sunshine is forecast for tomorrow, the forecast for tomorrow is sunny ■ **on annonce une hausse des taux d'intérêt** an increase in interest rates is predictedforecast
3. COMM [proposer] to quote ■ **~ un prix** to quote a price
4. [présenter - visiteur] to announce ; [- projet, changement] to introduce, to usher in *(sép)* ■ **qui dois-je ~?** what name shall I say? ■ **se faire ~** to give one's name ■ **elle est arrivée sans se faire ~** she came unannounced
5. [présager] to announce, to foreshadow, to herald *litt* ■ **ça n'annonce rien de bon** it doesn't bode well, it isn't a very good sign ‖ [être signe de] to be a sign *ou* an indication of
6. JEUX to declare ■ **~ la couleur** *fam* **: j'ai annoncé la couleur, ils savent que je démissionnerai s'il le faut** I've laid my cards on the table *ou* made no secret of it, they know I'll resign if I have to.

◆ **s'annoncer** ◇ *vp (emploi réfléchi)* [prévenir de sa visite] to notify *ou* to warn (that one will visit).
◇ *vpi* **1.** [se profiler] to be looming *ou* on the horizon ■ **une grave crise s'annonce** a serious crisis is looming
2. [dans des constructions attributives] : **la journée s'annonce très belle** it looks like it's going to be a beautiful day ■ **s'~ bien** cela s'annonce très bien, things are looking very promising *ou* good ■ **mes premiers oraux s'annoncent bien** I seem to have done all right in my first orals ■ **s'~ mal : cela s'annonce plutôt mal** it doesn't look very promising, the picture doesn't look *ou* isn't too good ■ **voilà un anniversaire qui s'annonce mal** it's an inauspicious start to *sout ou* a bad way to start a birthday.

annonceur, euse [anɔ̃sœr, øz] *nm, f* [présentateur] announcer.

◆ **annonceur** *nm* : **~ (publicitaire)** advertiser.

annonciateur, trice [anɔ̃sjatœr, tris] *adj* announcing, heralding, foreshadowing ■ **~ de : les secousses annonciatrices d'un tremblement de terre** the tremors that are the warning signs of an earthquake ■ **des nuages noirs ~s de pluie** black clouds which are the harbingers of rain.

◆ **annonciateur** *nm* **1.** ÉLECTRON signal **2.** TÉLÉCOM annunciator board.

Annonciation [anɔ̃sjasjɔ̃] *nf* **1.** BIBLE : **l'~** the Annunciation **2.** [fête] Annunciation *ou* Lady Day.

annotation [anɔtasjɔ̃] *nf* **1.** [note explicative] annotation **2.** [note personnelle] note.

annoter [3] [anɔte] *vt* **1.** [commenter] to annotate **2.** [de remarques personnelles] to write notes on ■ **un livre entièrement annoté** a book entirely covered with notes.

annuaire [anɥɛr] *nm* [recueil - d'une association, d'une société] yearbook, annual ■ **~ (téléphonique)** telephone directory *ou* book ■ **~ électronique** electronic directory.

annualisation [anɥalizasjɔ̃] *nf* calculation on a yearly basis.

annualiser [3] [anɥalize] *vt* to calculate on a yearly basis to annualize ■ **~ la durée du temps de travail** to annualize the work time.

annualité [anɥalite] *nf* yearly recurrence ■ **l'~ budgétaire** the yearly *ou* annual voting of the budget.

annuel, elle [anɥɛl] *adj* **1.** [qui revient chaque année] yearly, annual ■ **congé ~** annual leave **2.** [qui dure un an] annual ■ **une plante ~le** an annual.

annuellement [anɥɛlmɑ̃] *adv* annually, yearly, on a yearly basis.

annuité [anɥite] *nf* **1.** FIN annuity ■ **remboursement par ~s** repayment by annual payments *ou* yearly instalments *ou* annuities **2.** [année de service] year.

annulable [anylabl] *adj* **1.** [gén] cancellable, annullable **2.** DR [contrat] voidable, cancellable, revocable ■ [loi] revocable, repealable.

annulaire [anylɛr] <> *adj* **1.** [circulaire] annular *sout*, ring-shaped **2.** MÉD annular.
<> *nm* [doigt] third *ou* ring finger.

annulation [anylasjɔ̃] *nf* **1.** [d'un ordre, d'un rendez-vous] cancellation, calling off ■ [d'une réservation] cancellation ■ [d'une commande] cancellation, withdrawal ■ [d'une proposition] withdrawal **2.** DR [d'un décret, d'un acte judiciaire] cancellation, annulment ■ [d'un contrat] voidance, annulment ■ [d'un jugement] quashing, nullification ■ [d'un droit] defeasance ■ [d'une loi] revocation, rescindment.

annuler [3] [anyle] *vt* **1.** [ordre, rendez-vous, projet] to cancel, to call off *(sép)* ■ [réservation] to cancel ■ [commande] to cancel, to withdraw **2.** DR [contrat] to annul, to render null and void, to invalidate ■ [loi] to rescind, to revoke ■ [mariage] to annul ■ [testament] to set aside *(sép)*, to nullify ■ [jugement, verdict] to quash ■ **~ une subvention** to withdraw a subsidy **3.** INFORM to undo.
◆ **s'annuler** *vp (emploi réciproque)* to cancel each other out.

anobli, e [anɔbli] *adj* ennobled.

anoblir [32] [anɔblir] *vt* to ennoble, to confer a title on.

anoblissement [anɔblismɑ̃] *nm* ennoblement.

anode [anɔd] *nf* anode.

anodin, e [anɔdɛ̃, in] *adj* **1.** [inoffensif] harmless **2.** [insignifiant - personne, propos] ordinary, commonplace ; [- détail] trifling, insignificant ; [- événement] meaningless, insignificant.

anodique [anɔdik] *adj* anodic, anodal, anode *(modif)*.

anodiser [3] [anɔdize] *vt* to anodize.

anomal, e, aux [anɔmal, o] *adj* anomalous.

anomalie [anɔmali] *nf* **1.** [bizarrerie - d'une expérience, d'une attitude] anomaly ; [- d'une procédure, d'une nomination] irregularity **2.** ASTRON & LING anomaly **3.** BIOL abnormality.

ânon [ɑnɔ̃] *nm* (ass's) foal, young donkey *ou* ass.

ânonnement [ɑnɔnmɑ̃] *nm* **1.** [balbutiement] : **les ~s des enfants qui apprennent à lire** the faltering tones of children learning to read **2.** MÉD angophrasia.

ânonner [3] [ɑnɔne] <> *vi* to stammer out one's words ■ **il lisait en ânonnant** he read haltingly.
<> *vt* to stumble through ■ **~ sa leçon** to recite one's lesson falteringly.

anonymat [anɔnima] *nm* anonymity ■ **conserver** *ou* **garder l'~** to remain anonymous ■ **l'~ le plus total est garanti** confidentiality is guaranteed ■ **sous le couvert de** *ou* **en gardant l'~** anonymously.

anonyme [anɔnim] <> *adj* **1.** [sans nom - manuscrit, geste] anonymous ■ **rester ~** to remain unnamed *ou* anonymous **2.** [inconnu - auteur, attaquant] anonymous, unknown **3.** [sans personnalité - vêtement, meuble] drab, nondescript ; [- maison, appartement] anonymous, soulless, drab ■ **perdu dans la foule ~** lost in the crowd.
<> *nmf* anonym.

anonymement [anɔnimmɑ̃] *adv* anonymously.

anorak [anɔrak] *nm* anorak.

anorexie [anɔrɛksi] *nf* anorexia (nervosa).

anorexique [anɔrɛksik] *adj* & *nmf* anorexic.

anormal, e, aux [anɔrmal, o] <> *adj* **1.** [inhabituel - événement] abnormal, unusual ; [- comportement] abnormal, aberrant *sout* ■ **à son âge, c'est ~** it's not normal at his age **2.** [non réglementaire] irregular **3.** [injuste] unfair, unjustified **4.** [handicapé] mentally handicapped **5.** BIOL abnormal, anomalous.
<> *nm, f* mentally handicapped person.

anormalement [anɔrmalmɑ̃] *adv* **1.** [inhabituellement] unusually, abnormally **2.** BIOL abnormally, aberrantly.

anormalité [anɔrmalite] *nf* abnormality.

anovulatoire [anɔvylatwar] *adj* anovular.

anoxie [anɔksi] *nf* anoxia.

ANPE (*abr de* **Agence nationale pour l'emploi**) *npr f national employment agency* ■ **s'inscrire à l'~** to sign on.

anse [ɑ̃s] *nf* **1.** [poignée] handle **2.** GÉOGR cove, bight **3.** ANAT ansa, loop **4.** MÉD snare **5.** MATH compound curve.

antagonique [ɑ̃tagɔnik] *adj* antagonistic.

antagonisme [ɑ̃tagɔnism] *nm* antagonism.

antagoniste [ɑ̃tagɔnist] <> *adj* antagonistic ■ **les muscles ~s** antagonistic muscles.
<> *nmf* antagonist.

antalgique [ɑ̃talʒik] *adj* & *nm* analgesic.

antan [ɑ̃tɑ̃] ◆ **d'antan** *loc adj* of yesteryear ■ **mes amis d'~** my erstwhile friends, my friends from the old days.

antarctique [ɑ̃tarktik] *adj* Antarctic.
◆ **Antarctique** <> *npr m* [océan] : **l'Antarctique** the Antarctic (Ocean).
<> *npr f* [continent] : **(l')Antarctique** Antarctica.

antécédence [ɑ̃tesedɑ̃s] *nf* antecedence GEOL.

antécédent, e [ɑ̃tesedɑ̃, ɑ̃t] *adj* **1.** [précédent - élément] antecedent *sout* ; [- événement] prior, previous ■ **~ à** prior to **2.** GÉOL antecedent.
◆ **antécédent** *nm* **1.** GRAMM, LOGIQUE & MATH antecedent **2.** MÉD past *ou* previous (medical) history.
◆ **antécédents** *nmpl* **1.** [faits passés] antecedents, past *ou* previous history **2.** MÉD case history.

antéchrist [ɑ̃tekrist] *nm* Antichrist.

antédiluvien, enne [ɑ̃tedilyvjɛ̃, ɛn] *adj* **1.** BIBLE antediluvian **2.** *fam* [vieux] antiquated, ancient ■ **un frigo ~** a fridge (that looks like it's) out of the ark.

antémémoire [ɑ̃tememwar] *nf* INFORM cache (memory).

antenne [ɑ̃tɛn] *nf* **1.** ENTOM antenna, feeler ■ **avoir des ~s** *fam* [avoir de l'intuition] to be very intuitive ; [avoir des contacts] to know all the right people **2.** ÉLECTRON aerial, antenna ■ **~ parabolique** satellite dish **3.** RADIO & TV : **à vous l'~** over to you ■ **être à l'~** to be on (the air) ■ **garder l'~** to stay on the air ■ **rendre l'~** to hand back to the studio ■ **prendre l'~** to come on the air ■ **sur notre ~** RADIO on this frequency *ou* station ; TV on this channel ➲ **temps d'~** air time **4.** [agence, service] office ■ **notre ~ à Genève** our agent in Geneva, our Geneva office ➲ **~ chirurgicale** surgical unit.

antenne-relais (*pl* - **antennes-relais**) [ɑ̃tɛnrəlɛ] *nf* TÉLÉCOM mobile phone mast.

antépénultième [ɑ̃tepenyltjɛm] *sout* <> *adj* antepenultimate *sout* ■ **l'~ fois** the time before last.
<> *nf* antepenult.

antéposé, e [ɑ̃tepoze] *adj* word-initial, in a word-initial position.

antéposition [ɑ̃tepozisjɔ̃] *nf* word-initial position.

antérieur, e [ɑ̃terjœr] *adj* **1.** [précédent] anterior, prior ■ **la situation ~e** the previous *ou* former situation ■ **une vie ~e** a former life ■ **~ à** prior to, before ■ **c'était bien ~ à cette époque** it was long before that time **2.** [de devant] anterior **3.** LING front *(modif)*.
◆ **antérieur** *nm* foreleg, forelimb.

antérieurement [ɑ̃terjœrmɑ̃] *adv* previously.
◆ **antérieurement à** *loc prép* prior to, previous to, before.

antériorité [ɑ̃terjɔrite] *nf* **1.** [d'un événement] anteriority, antecedence, precedence **2.** GRAMM anteriority.

anthère [ɑ̃tɛr] *nf* anther.

anthologie [ɑ̃tɔlɔʒi] *nf* anthology.

anthracite [ɑ̃trasit] ◇ *adj inv* charcoal grey.
◇ *nm* anthracite, hard coal.

anthrax [ɑ̃traks] *nm* anthrax.

anthropocentrique [ɑ̃trɔpɔsɑ̃trik] *adj* anthropocentric.

anthropocentrisme [ɑ̃trɔpɔsɑ̃trism] *nm* anthropocentrism.

anthropoïde [ɑ̃trɔpɔid] ◇ *adj* anthropoid.
◇ *nm* anthropoid ape.

anthropologie [ɑ̃trɔpɔlɔʒi] *nf* anthropology.

anthropologique [ɑ̃trɔpɔlɔʒik] *adj* anthropological.

anthropologue [ɑ̃trɔpɔlɔg], **anthropologiste** [ɑ̃trɔpɔlɔʒist] *nmf* anthropologist.

anthropométrique [ɑ̃trɔpɔmetrik] *adj* anthropometric, anthropometrical.

anthropomorphe [ɑ̃trɔpɔmɔrf] *adj* anthropomorphous, anthropomorphic.

anthropomorphisme [ɑ̃trɔpɔmɔrfism] *nm* anthropomorphism.

anthropophage [ɑ̃trɔpɔfaʒ] ◇ *adj* cannibal *(modif)*, cannibalistic, anthropophagous *spéc.*
◇ *nmf* cannibal, anthropophagite *spéc.*

anthropophagie [ɑ̃trɔpɔfaʒi] *nf* cannibalism, anthropophagy *spéc.*

antiabolitionniste [ɑ̃tiabɔlisjɔnist] ◇ *adj* against the abolition of the death penalty.
◇ *nmf person opposed to the abolition of the death penalty.*

antiacarien [ɑ̃tiakarjɛ̃] ◇ *adj* anti-mite ▪ **traitement** *ou* **shampoing** anti-mite treatment *ou* shampoo.
◇ *nm* anti-mite treatment.

antiadhésif, ive [ɑ̃tiadezif, iv] *adj* [gén] antiadhesive *(avant n)* ▪ [poêle] nonstick.
◆ **antiadhésif** *nm* antiadhesive.

antiaérien, enne [ɑ̃tiaerjɛ̃, ɛn] *adj* antiaircraft.

anti-âge [ɑ̃tiaʒ] *adj* : **crème ~** anti-ageing cream.

antialcoolique [ɑ̃tialkɔlik] *adj* temperance *(modif)*, antialcohol *(avant n)*.

antialcoolisme [ɑ̃tialkɔlism] *nm* antialcoholism.

antiallergique [ɑ̃tialɛrʒik] ◇ *adj* antiallergenic.
◇ *nm* antiallergen.

anti-américain, e [ɑ̃tiamerikɛ̃, ɛn] *adj* anti-American.

antiapartheid [ɑ̃tiapartɛd] *adj* antiapartheid.

antiatomique [ɑ̃tiatɔmik] *adj* antiatomic, antiradiation.

antibactérien, enne [ɑ̃tibakterjɛ̃, ɛn] *adj* antibacterial.

antibiothérapie [ɑ̃tibjɔterapi] *nf* antibiotherapy.

antibiotique [ɑ̃tibiɔtik] *adj* & *nm* antibiotic.

antiblocage [ɑ̃tiblɔkaʒ] *adj* antilock *(avant n)*.

antibrouillage [ɑ̃tibrujaʒ] *nm* antijamming.

antibrouillard [ɑ̃tibrujar] *adj inv* fog *(modif)* ▪ **phare** *ou* **dispositif ~** fog lamp UK *ou* light US.

antibruit [ɑ̃tibrɥi] *adj inv* **1.** [matériau] soundproof **2.** ACOUST : **mur ~** antinoise barrier **3.** AUTO antidrumming, antisqueak.

antibuée [ɑ̃tibɥe] ◇ *adj inv* demisting, antimisting.
◇ *nm* **1.** [dispositif] demister **2.** [produit] antimist agent, clear vision agent.

anticalcaire [ɑ̃tikalkɛr] *adj* antiliming, antiscale *(avant n)*.

anticancéreux, euse [ɑ̃tikɑ̃serø, øz] *adj* **1.** [centre, laboratoire] cancer *(modif)* **2.** [médicament] anticancer *(avant n)*, carcinostatic *spéc.*

anticapitaliste [ɑ̃tikapitalist] *adj* anticapitalist.

antichambre [ɑ̃tiʃɑ̃br] *nf* anteroom, antechamber ▪ **dans les ~s du pouvoir** on the fringes of power ➊ **faire ~** to wait quietly (to be received).

antichar [ɑ̃tiʃar] *adj* antitank.

antichoc [ɑ̃tiʃɔk] *adj* shockproof.

anti-chute [ɑ̃tiʃyt] *adj* : **traitement ~** treatment to stop hair loss.

anticipation [ɑ̃tisipasjɔ̃] *nf* **1.** [prévision] anticipation **2.** COMM : **~ de paiement** [somme] advance payment ; [action] paying in advance **3.** [science-fiction] science fiction.
◆ **d'anticipation** *loc adj* [roman, film] science-fiction *(modif)*, futuristic.
◆ **par anticipation** ◇ *loc adj* FIN advance *(modif)* ▪ **paiement par ~** advance payment.
◇ *loc adv* [payer, régler] in advance.

anticipé, e [ɑ̃tisipe] *adj* **1.** [avant la date prévue - retraite, départ] early ▪ **faire le règlement ~ d'une facture** to pay a bill in advance **2.** [fait à l'avance] : **avec nos remerciements ~s** thanking you in advance *ou* anticipation.

anticiper [3] [ɑ̃tisipe] *vt* **1.** COMM & FIN : **~ un paiement** to pay *ou* to settle a bill in advance **2.** [prévoir] to anticipate ▪ **il a bien anticipé la réaction de son adversaire** he anticipated *ou* foresaw his opponent's reaction.
◆ **anticiper sur** *v+prép* : **~ sur ce qui va se passer** [deviner] to guess what's going to happen ; [raconter] to explain what's going to happen ▪ *(en usage absolu)* **mais j'anticipe!** but I'm getting ahead of myself! ▪ **n'anticipons pas!** let's just wait and see!, all in good time!

anticlérical, e, aux [ɑ̃tiklerikal, o] *adj* & *nm, f* anticlerical.

anticléricalisme [ɑ̃tiklerikalism] *nm* anticlericalism.

anticlinal, e, aux [ɑ̃tiklinal, o] *adj* anticlinal.
◆ **anticlinal, aux** *nm* anticline.

anticoagulant, e [ɑ̃tikoagylɑ̃, ɑ̃t] *adj* **1.** MÉD anticoagulating **2.** CHIM anticlotting.
◆ **anticoagulant** *nm* **1.** MÉD anticoagulant **2.** CHIM anticlotting agent.

anticolonialisme [ɑ̃tikɔlɔnjalism] *nm* anticolonialism.

anticolonialiste [ɑ̃tikɔlɔnjalist] *adj* & *nmf* anticolonialist.

anticommunisme [ɑ̃tikɔmynism] *nm* anticommunism.

anticommuniste [ɑ̃tikɔmynist] *adj* & *nmf* anticommunist.

anticonceptionnel, elle [ɑ̃tikɔ̃sɛpsjɔnɛl] *adj* contraceptive, birth-control *(modif)*.

anticonformisme [ɑ̃tikɔ̃fɔrmism] *nm* nonconformism.

anticonformiste [ɑ̃tikɔ̃fɔrmist] *adj* & *nmf* nonconformist.

anticonstitutionnel, elle [ɑ̃tikɔ̃stitysjɔnɛl] *adj* unconstitutional.

anticorrosif, ive [ɑ̃tikɔrozif, iv] *adj* anticorrosive ▪ **traitement ~** rustproofing.

anticorps [ɑ̃tikɔr] *nm* antibody.

anticorrosion [ɑ̃tikɔrozjɔ̃] *adj inv* anticorrosive, antistain.

anticyclone [ɑ̃tisiklon] *nm* anticyclone.

antidater [3] [ɑ̃tidate] *vt* to antedate, to predate.

antidémocratique [ɑ̃tidemɔkratik] *adj* antidemocratic.

antidépresseur [ɑ̃tidepresœr] *adj m* & *nm* antidepressant.

antidérapant, e [ɑ̃tiderapɑ̃, ɑ̃t] *adj* **1.** [surface, tapis] nonslip **2.** AUTO nonskid, antiskid.
◆ **antidérapant** *nm* slide preserver.

antidétonant, e [ɑ̃tidetɔnɑ̃, ɑ̃t] *adj* antiknock *(avant n).*
◆ **antidétonant** *nm* antiknock (compound).

antidiphtérique [ɑ̃tidifterik] *adj* diphtheria *(modif)* ■ **sérum ~** diphtheria serum.

antidiurétique [ɑ̃tidjyretik] *adj* & *nm* antidiuretic.

antidopage [ɑ̃tidɔpaʒ], **antidoping** [ɑ̃tidɔpiŋ] *adj inv* : **contrôle/mesure ~** drug detection test/measure.

antidote [ɑ̃tidɔt] *nm* antidote ■ **l'~ de l'arsenic** the antidote to arsenic ■ **un ~ contre la tristesse** a remedy for sadness.

antidrogue [ɑ̃tidrɔg] *adj inv* drug-prevention *(modif).*

antiéconomique [ɑ̃tiekɔnɔmik] *adj* contrary to economic principles, uneconomic.

anti-effraction [ɑ̃tiefraksjɔ̃] *adj inv* [dispositif] burglarproof.

anti-émeutes [ɑ̃tiemøt] *adj* [brigade] riot *(modif).*

antienne [ɑ̃tjɛn] *nf* **1.** RELIG antiphon **2.** *fig* refrain.

antiesclavagiste [ɑ̃tiɛsklavaʒist] ◇ *adj* antislavery ■ [aux États-Unis] abolitionist.
◇ *nmf* opponent of slavery ■ [aux États-Unis] abolitionist.

antiétatique [ɑ̃tietatik] *adj* opposed to state intervention, noninterventionist.

antifasciste [ɑ̃tifaʃist] *adj* & *nmf* antifascist.

antifongique [ɑ̃tifɔ̃ʒik] *adj* antifungal, fungicidal.

anti-g [ɑ̃tiʒe] *adj inv* anti-G.

antigang [ɑ̃tigɑ̃g] *adj* ▻ **brigade.**

antigel [ɑ̃tiʒɛl] *nm* **1.** AUTO antifreeze **2.** CHIM antigel.

antigène [ɑ̃tiʒɛn] *nm* antigen.

antigivrant, e [ɑ̃tiʒivrɑ̃, ɑ̃t] *adj* anti-ice *(modif).*
◆ **antigivrant** *nm* anti-icer.

Antigone [ɑ̃tigɔn] *npr* Antigone.

antigouvernemental, e, aux [ɑ̃tiguvɛrnəmɑ̃tal, o] *adj* antigovernment *(modif).*

antigrève [ɑ̃tigrɛv] *adj inv* antistrike *(avant n).*

antigrippal, e, aux [ɑ̃tigripal, o] *adj* [médicament, traitement] flu *(modif).*

Antigua [ɑ̃tigwa] *npr* Antigua ■ **~ et Barbuda** Antigua and Barbuda.

antihéros [ɑ̃tiero] *nm* antihero.

antihistaminique [ɑ̃tiistaminik] *nm* antihistamine.

antihygiénique [ɑ̃tiiʒjenik] *adj* unhygienic.

anti-impérialiste [ɑ̃tiɛ̃perjalist] (*pl* **anti-impérialistes**) *adj* & *nmf* anti-imperialist.

anti-inflammatoire [ɑ̃tiɛ̃flamatwar] (*pl* **anti-inflammatoires**) ◇ *adj* anti-inflammatory.
◇ *nm* anti-inflammatory agent.

anti-inflationniste [ɑ̃tiɛ̃flasjɔnist] (*pl* **anti-inflationnistes**) *adj* anti-inflationary.

antillais, e [ɑ̃tijɛ, ɛz] *adj* West Indian.
◆ **Antillais, e** *nm, f* West Indian.

Antilles [ɑ̃tij] *npr fpl* : **les ~** the Antilles, the West Indies ■ **aux ~** in the West Indies ■ **les ~ françaises/néerlandaises** the French/Dutch West Indies ■ **la mer des ~** the Caribbean Sea.

ANTILLES

The French West Indies include the overseas *départements* of Martinique and Guadeloupe, the latter including the islands of Désirade, Marie-Galante, Saint-Barthélemy (Saint-Barth), les Saintes and Saint-Martin.

antilope [ɑ̃tilɔp] *nf* antelope.

antimatière [ɑ̃timatjɛr] *nf* antimatter.

antimilitarisme [ɑ̃timilitarism] *nm* antimilitarism.

antimilitariste [ɑ̃timilitarist] *adj* & *nmf* antimilitarist.

antimissile [ɑ̃timisil] *adj inv* antimissile.

antimite [ɑ̃timit] ◇ *adj inv* : **boules ~** mothballs ■ **produit ~** moth repellent.
◇ *nm* mothproofing agent, moth repellent.

antimoine [ɑ̃timwan] *nm* antimony.

antimonarchique [ɑ̃timɔnarʃik] *adj* antimonarchical.

anti-mondialisation [ɑ̃timɔ̃djalizasjɔ̃] *adj inv* anti-globalization.

anti-mondialiste [ɑ̃timɔ̃djalist] *adj* anti-globalization.

antinataliste [ɑ̃tinatalist] *adj* : **une politique/décision ~** a policy/decision aimed at reducing the birth rate.

antinational, e, aux [ɑ̃tinasjɔnal, o] *adj* antinational.

antinazi, e [ɑ̃tinazi] *adj* & *nm, f* anti-Nazi.

antinévralgique [ɑ̃tinevralʒik] *adj* antineuralgic.

antinomie [ɑ̃tinɔmi] *nf* antinomy.

antinomique [ɑ̃tinɔmik] *adj* antinomic.

antinucléaire [ɑ̃tinykleɛr] *adj* antinuclear.

Antioche [ɑ̃tjɔʃ] *npr* Antioch.

Antiope® [ɑ̃tjɔp] *npr information system available via the French television network,* ≃ Teletext® UK.

antioxydant [ɑ̃tiɔksidɑ̃] *nm* antioxidant, oxidation inhibitor.

antipaludéen, enne [ɑ̃tipalydeɛ̃, ɛn], **antipaludique** [ɑ̃tipalydik] *adj* & *nm* antimalarial, antipaludal.

antipape [ɑ̃tipap] *nm* antipope.

antiparasite [ɑ̃tiparazit] ◇ *adj inv* anti-interference *(avant n).*
◇ *nm* interference suppressor, interference eliminator, noise blanker UK.

antiparlementaire [ɑ̃tiparləmɑ̃tɛr] *adj* antiparliamentary.

antiparlementarisme [ɑ̃tiparləmɑ̃tarism] *nm* antiparliamentarism.

antipathie [ɑ̃tipati] *nf* antipathy ■ **éprouver de l'~ pour qqn** to dislike sb.

antipathique [ɑ̃tipatik] *adj* unpleasant ■ **je le trouve assez ~, il m'est plutôt ~** I don't like him much.

antipatriotique [ɑ̃tipatriɔtik] *adj* unpatriotic.

antipelliculaire [ɑ̃tipɛlikylɛr] *adj* dandruff *(modif).*

antipersonnel [ɑ̃tipɛrsɔnɛl] *adj inv* antipersonnel.

antiphrase [ɑ̃tifraz] *nf* antiphrasis.
◆ **par antiphrase** *loc adv* paradoxically.

antipode [ɑ̃tipɔd] *nm* antipode ■ **la Nouvelle-Zélande est aux ~s de la France** New Zealand is at the opposite point of the globe from France ‖ *fig* **c'est aux ~s de ce que je pensais** it's light-years away from what I imagined.

antipoison [ɑ̃tipwazɔ̃] *adj inv* : **centre ~** emergency poisons unit.

antipoliomyélitique [ɑ̃tipɔljɔmjelitik] *adj* antipolio, polio *(modif).*

antipollution [ɑ̃tipɔlysjɔ̃] *adj inv* antipollution *(avant n)* ■ **contrôle/mesure ~** pollution control/measure.

antiprotéase [ɑ̃tiproteaz] *nf* MÉD protease inhibitor.

antiprotectionniste [ɑ̃tiprɔteksjɔnist] ◇ *adj* free trade *(modif)*.
◇ *nmf* antiprotectionist, free-trader.

antipsychiatrie [ɑ̃tipsikjatri] *nf* antipsychiatry.

antiquaille [ɑ̃tikaj] *nf* *péj* (worthless) antique, piece of bric-a-brac.

antiquaire [ɑ̃tikɛr] *nmf* antique dealer.

antique [ɑ̃tik] ◇ *adj* **1.** [d'époque - meuble, bijou, châle] antique, old **2.** *(avant le n)* [démodé] antiquated, ancient.
◇ *nm* : l'~ [œuvres] antiquities ; [art] classical art.

antiquité [ɑ̃tikite] *nf* **1.** [objet] antique ■ **des ~s** antiques ■ **sa voiture, c'est une ~!** *fig* & *hum* his car is an old wreck *OU* ancient! **2.** [période] : **l'~** ancient times, antiquity ■ **l'Antiquité (grecque et romaine)** Ancient Greece and Rome **3.** [ancienneté] great age.
◆ **antiquités** *nfpl* ART antique art.

antirabique [ɑ̃tirabik] *adj* anti-rabies *(avant n)*.

antirachitique [ɑ̃tiraʃitik] *adj* antirachitic.

antiracisme [ɑ̃tirasism] *nm* antiracism.

antiraciste [ɑ̃tirasist] *adj* & *nmf* antiracist.

antiradar [ɑ̃tiradar] *adj inv* antiradar.

antireflet [ɑ̃tirəflɛ] *adj inv* coated, bloomed *spéc* ■ **verre ~** non-reflecting glass.

antiréglementaire [ɑ̃tirɛgləmɑ̃tɛr] *adj* against regulations.

antireligieux, euse [ɑ̃tirəliʒjø, øz] *adj* antireligious.

antirépublicain, e [ɑ̃tirepyblikɛ̃, ɛn] *adj* & *nm, f* antirepublican.

antirides [ɑ̃tirid] *adj* anti-wrinkle *(avant n)*.

antiroman [ɑ̃tirɔmɑ̃] *nm* anti-novel.

antirouille [ɑ̃tiruj] ◇ *adj inv* antirust *(avant n)*, rust-resistant.
◇ *nm* rust preventive, rust inhibitor.

antiroulis [ɑ̃tiruli] *adj* anti-roll *(avant n)*.

antisèche [ɑ̃tisɛʃ] *nf* *arg scol* crib, cheat sheet *US*.

antiségrégationniste [ɑ̃tisegregasjɔnist] *adj* & *nmf* antisegregationist.

antisémite [ɑ̃tisemit] ◇ *adj* anti-Semitic.
◇ *nmf* anti-Semite.

antisémitisme [ɑ̃tisemitism] *nm* anti-Semitism.

antiseptique [ɑ̃tisɛptik] *adj* & *nm* antiseptic.

antisérum [ɑ̃tiserɔm] *nm* antiserum.

antisismique [ɑ̃tisismik] *adj* antiseismic.

antislash [ɑ̃tislaʃ] *nm* INFORM backslash.

antisocial, e, aux [ɑ̃tisɔsjal, o] *adj* antisocial.

antispasmodique [ɑ̃tispasmɔdik] *adj* & *nm* antispasmodic.

antisportif, ive [ɑ̃tispɔrtif, iv] *adj* [contraire à l'esprit sportif] unsporting, unsportsmanlike.

antistatique [ɑ̃tistatik] *adj* antistatic.

antisyndical, e, aux [ɑ̃tisɛ̃dikal, o] *adj* antiunion.

antitabac [ɑ̃titaba] *adj inv* antitobacco, anti-smoking.

antiterroriste [ɑ̃titɛrɔrist] *adj* antiterrorist.

antitétanique [ɑ̃titetanik] *adj* antitetanic.

antithèse [ɑ̃titɛz] *nf* antithesis.

antithétique [ɑ̃titetik] *adj* antithetical, antithetic.

antitoxine [ɑ̃titɔksin] *nf* antitoxin.

antitoxique [ɑ̃titɔksik] *adj* antitoxic.

antitranspirant, e [ɑ̃titrɑ̃spirɑ̃, ɑ̃t] *adj* anti-perspirant.

antitrust [ɑ̃titrœst] *adj inv* antitrust.

antituberculeux, euse [ɑ̃titybɛrkylø, øz] *adj* antitubercular, antituberculous.

antitussif, ive [ɑ̃titysif, iv] *adj* cough *(modif)* ■ **produit/comprimé ~** cough preparation/tablet.

antivariolique [ɑ̃tivarjɔlik] *adj* antivariolar.

antivénéneux, euse [ɑ̃tivenenø, øz] *adj* antidotal.

antivénérien, enne [ɑ̃tivenerjɛ̃, ɛn] *adj* antivenereal.

antivenimeux, euse [ɑ̃tivənimø, øz] *adj* antivenin.

antiviral, e, aux [ɑ̃tiviral, o] *adj* MÉD & INFORM anti-viral.
◆ **antiviral, aux** *nm* MÉD antiviral.

antivirus [ɑ̃tivirys] *nm* INFORM anti-virus software.

antivol [ɑ̃tivɔl] ◇ *adj inv* antitheft.
◇ *nm* **1.** AUTO theft protection ■ [sur la direction] steering (wheel) lock **2.** [de vélo] (bicycle) lock.

Antoine [ɑ̃twan] *npr* : **(Marc) ~** (Mark) Antony.

antonomase [ɑ̃tɔnɔmaz] *nf* antonomasia.

antonyme [ɑ̃tɔnim] *nm* antonym.

antre [ɑ̃tr] *nm* **1.** [abri] cavern, cave **2.** [repaire - d'un fauve, d'un ogre] lair, den ; [- d'un brigand] hideout **3.** *fig* den.

anus [anys] *nm* anus.

ANVAR [ɑ̃var] (*abr de* **Agence nationale de valorisation de la recherche**)*nf French public body that supports research and development in industry and commerce.*

Anvers [ɑ̃vɛr(s)] *npr* Antwerp.

anxiété [ɑ̃ksjete] *nf* anxiety, worry ■ **attendre qqch avec ~** to wait anxiously for sthg ■ **être en proie à l'~** to be distressed *OU* worried.

anxieusement [ɑ̃ksjøzmɑ̃] *adv* anxiously, worriedly ■ **ils se regardèrent ~** they exchanged worried *OU* anxious looks.

anxieux, euse [ɑ̃ksjø, øz] ◇ *adj* [inquiet - attente] anxious ; [- regard, voix, personne] anxious, worried ■ **~ de** anxious *OU* impatient to.
◇ *nm, f* worrier ■ **c'est un grand ~** he's the anxious type.

anxiogène [ɑ̃ksjɔʒɛn] *adj* anxiety-provoking.

anxiolytique [ɑ̃ksjɔlitik] ◇ *adj* anxiolitic.
◇ *nm* tranquillizer.

AOC = **appellation d'origine contrôlée**.

aorte [aɔrt] *nf* aorta.

Aoste [aɔst] *npr* Aosta.

août [u(t)] *nm* August ■ **la nuit du 4 ~ 1789** *the night during which feudal privileges were abolished by the 'Assemblée Constituante' (considered to be one of the starting points of the French Revolution)* ■ **le 15 ~** *feast of The Assumption, national holiday in France well-known as a time of heavy traffic congestion, voir aussi* **mars**.

aoûtat [auta] *nm* harvest mite, chigger *US*, redbug *US*.

aoûtien, enne [ausjɛ̃, ɛn] *nm, f* August holidaymaker *UK* *OU* vacationer *US*.

APA [apea] (*abr de* **Allocation personnalisée à l'autonomie**) *nf additional benefit awarded to an old-age pensioner for the purchase of certain particular goods or services.*

apache[1] [apaʃ] *adj* Apache.
◆ **Apache** *npr* Apache.

apache[2] [apaʃ] *nm* *vieilli* hooligan *(in turn-of-the century Paris)*.

apaisant, e [apɛzɑ̃, ɑ̃t] *adj* **1.** [qui calme la douleur] soothing **2.** [qui calme la colère] pacifying, mollifying.

apaisement [apɛzmɑ̃] *nm* [fait de calmer - soif, désir] quenching ; [- faim] assuaging ; [- chagrin] soothing, easing ■ [fait de se calmer] quietening down ■ **chercher l'~ auprès de qqn** to go to sb for reassurance.

apaiser [4] [apɛze] *vt* [calmer - opposants, mécontents] to calm down *(sép)*, to pacify, to appease ; [- douleur, chagrin] to soothe, to alleviate, to lessen ; [- faim] to assuage ▪ **~ les esprits** to calm things down.
◆ **s'apaiser** *vpi* [se calmer - personne] to calm down ; [- bruit, dispute, tempête, vent] to die down, to subside ; [- colère, chagrin, douleur] to subside ; [- faim] to be assuaged.

apanage [apanaʒ] *nm* prerogative, privilege ▪ **avoir l'~ de qqch** to have a monopoly on sthg ▪ **être l'~ de qqn** to be sb's privilege.

aparté [aparte] *nm* **1.** [discussion] private conversation **2.** THÉÂTRE aside.
◆ **en aparté** *loc adv* as an aside ▪ **dire qqch (à qqn) en ~ : il me l'a dit en ~** he took me aside to tell me.

apartheid [apartɛd] *nm* apartheid.

apathie [apati] *nf* apathy, listlessness.

apathique [apatik] *adj* apathetic, listless.

apatride [apatrid] ◇ *adj* stateless.
◇ *nmf* stateless person.

APD (*abr de* **aide publique au développement**) *nf* overseas development aid.

APEC [apɛk] (*abr de* **association pour l'emploi des cadres**) *nf employment agency for professionals and managers.*

Apennin [apenɛ̃] *npr m* **: l'~, les ~s** the Apennines.

apercevoir [52] [apɛrsəvwar] *vt* **1.** [voir brièvement] to glimpse, to catch sight of ▪ **il était pressé, je n'ai fait que l'~** he was in a hurry, so I just caught a glimpse of him **2.** [distinguer] to make out *(sép)* ▪ **on apercevait le phare au loin** you could (just) make out the lighthouse in the distance **3.** [remarquer] to see, to notice.
◆ **s'apercevoir** ◇ *vp (emploi réfléchi)* to catch sight of o.s.
◇ *vp (emploi réciproque)* to catch a glimpse of one another.
◆ **s'apercevoir de** *vp+prép* **1.** [remarquer] to notice, to see **2.** [comprendre] to become aware of, to realize ▪ **sans s'en ~** inadvertently, without realizing it ▪ **s'~ que** to realize *ou* to understand that.

aperçu [apɛrsy] *nm* outline, idea ▪ **un ~ de la situation** a fair idea *ou* an outline of the situation ▪ **un ~ du sujet en deux mots** a quick survey *ou* a brief outline of the subject.

aperçut *etc v* ▻ **apercevoir**.

apéritif, ive [aperitif, iv] *adj* **: faire une promenade apéritive** to take a walk to work up an appetite ▪ **prendre une boisson apéritive** to have an aperitif.
◆ **apéritif** *nm* drink, aperitif ▪ **venez à 19 h pour l'~** come round for drinks at 7 p.m.

apéro [apero] *nm fam* aperitif, drink *(before a meal)*.

apesanteur [apəzɑ̃tœr] *nf* weightlessness.

à-peu-près [apøprɛ] *nm inv* [approximation] approximation ▪ **dans votre devoir, on ne vous demande pas d'~** your homework answers should be very specific.

apeurer [5] [apœre] *vt* to frighten, to scare, to alarm.

apex [apɛks] *nm* **1.** ANAT, ASTRON & SC apex **2.** [accent] macron.

aphasie [afazi] *nf* aphasia.

aphasique [afazik] *adj* & *nmf* aphasic.

aphone [afɔn] *adj* **1.** [sans voix] hoarse ▪ **j'étais complètement ~** I'd lost my voice ▪ **il est devenu ~ tellement il a crié** he's shouted himself hoarse **2.** MÉD aphonic.

aphorisme [afɔrism] *nm* aphorism.

aphrodisiaque [afrɔdizjak] *adj* & *nm* aphrodisiac.

Aphrodite [afrɔdit] *npr* Aphrodite.

aphte [aft] *nm* mouth ulcer, aphtha *spéc.*

aphteux, euse [aftø, øz] *adj* aphthous.

API (*abr de* **alphabet phonétique international**) *nm* IPA.

à-pic [apik] *nm inv* steep rock face, sheer cliff.

apical, e, aux [apikal, o] *adj* apical.

apiculteur, trice [apikyltœr, tris] *nm, f* beekeeper, apiculturist *spéc*, apiarist *spéc.*

apiculture [apikyltyr] *nf* beekeeping, apiculture *spéc.*

apitoie *etc v* ▻ **apitoyer**.

apitoiement [apitwamɑ̃] *nm* pity, compassion.

apitoyer [13] [apitwaje] *vt* to arouse the pity of ▪ **il veut m'~** he's trying to make me feel sorry for him.
◆ **s'apitoyer sur** *vp+prép* **: s'~ sur qqn** to feel sorry for *ou* to pity sb ▪ **s'~ sur son sort** to wallow in self-pity.

ap. J.-C. (*abr écrite de* **après Jésus-Christ**) AD.

APL *nf* = **aide personnalisée au logement**.

aplanir [32] [aplanir] *vt* **1.** [niveler - terrain] to level (off), to grade ; [- surface] to smooth, to level off *(sép)* **2.** *fig* [difficulté] to smooth out *ou* over *(sép)*, to iron out *(sép)* ▪ [obstacle] to remove.
◆ **s'aplanir** *vpi* **1.** [surface] to level out *ou* off **2.** [difficulté, obstacle] **: les difficultés se sont peu à peu aplanies** the difficulties gradually smoothed themselves out.

aplat, à-plat [apla] (*pl* **à-plats**) *nm* [couleur] flat tint, solid colour.

aplati, e [aplati] *adj* flattened ▪ **la Terre est ~e aux pôles** the Earth is oblate.

aplatir [32] [aplatir] *vt* **1.** [rendre plat - tôle, verre, surface] to flatten (out) ; [- métal] to beat flat ; [- terre, sol] to roll, to crush ; [- rivet] to clench, to close ; [- couture, pli] to press (flat), to smooth (out) ; [- cheveux] to smooth *ou* to plaster down *(sép)* **2.** [écraser] to flatten, to squash, to crush ▪ **~ son nez contre la vitre** to flatten *ou* to squash one's nose against the window **3.** *fam* [vaincre] to crush, to flatten **4.** SPORT **: ~ le ballon** to touch the ball down ▪ **~ un essai** to score a try.
◆ **s'aplatir** *vpi* **1.** [être plat] to be flat ▪ [devenir plat] to flatten (out), to become flat **2.** [se coller] **: s'~ contre le mur** to flatten o.s. against the wall ▪ **sa voiture s'est aplatie contre un arbre** his car wrapped itself around a tree **3.** *fam* [s'humilier] to grovel, to fawn ▪ **s'~ devant qqn** to go crawling to sb ◐ **s'~ comme une carpette** to crawl, to creep *UK*.

aplatissement [aplatismɑ̃] *nm* **1.** [fait de rendre plat] flattening **2.** *fam* [servilité] crawling, fawning.

aplomb [aplɔ̃] *nm* **1.** [verticalité] perpendicularity ▪ **à l'~ de** [au-dessus de] directly above ; [au-dessous de] directly below **2.** [confiance en soi] aplomb ▪ **avoir de l'~** to be self-possessed, to be self-assured ▪ **répondre avec ~** to answer with self-assurance *ou* self-possession *ou* aplomb ▮ *péj* [insolence] nerve ▪ **avoir l'~ de faire qqch** to have the nerve to do sthg ▪ **il ne manque pas d'~** he really has a nerve.
◆ **aplombs** *nmpl* stand ÉQUIT.
◆ **d'aplomb** *loc adj* **1.** [vertical] perpendicular ▪ **être d'~** to be vertical ▪ **mettre qqch d'~** CONSTR to plumb sthg (up) ; [redresser] to straighten sthg up ▪ **ne pas être d'~** CONSTR to be out of plumb *ou* off plumb ; [en déséquilibre] to be askew ▪ **être bien d'~ sur ses jambes** to be steady on one's feet **2.** [en bonne santé] well ▪ **être d'~** to be well *ou* in good health ▪ **ne pas être d'~** to feel unwell *ou* out of sorts ▪ **remettre qqn d'~** to put sb back on his/her feet, to make sb better.

APN *nm* = **appareil photo numérique**.

apnée [apne] *nf* apnoea ▪ **descendre** *ou* **plonger en ~** to dive without breathing apparatus.

apocalypse [apɔkalips] *nf* **1.** [catastrophe] apocalypse ▪ **une ~ nucléaire** a nuclear holocaust **2.** RELIG **: l'Apocalypse** the Apocalypse, the (Book of) Revelation.
◆ **d'apocalypse** *loc adj* [vision] apocalyptic ▪ [récit] doom-laden ▪ **un paysage d'~** a scene of devastation.

apocalyptique [apɔkaliptik] *adj* apocalyptic, cataclysmic.

apocope [apɔkɔp] *nf* apocope.

apocryphe [apɔkrif] ◇ *adj* apocryphal.
◇ *nm* apocryphal text ▪ **les ~s (de la Bible)** the Apocrypha.

apogée [apɔʒe] *nm* **1.** ASTRON apogee **2.** [sommet] peak, summit, apogee ▪ **à l'~ de sa carrière** at the height *ou* at the peak of his career.

apolitique [apɔlitik] ◇ *adj* [sans convictions politiques] apolitical ▪ [non affilié] nonpolitical.
◇ *nmf* apolitical person.

apolitisme [apɔlitism] *nm* [refus de s'engager] apolitical stance ▪ [engagement sans affiliation] nonpolitical stance.

apollon [apɔlɔ̃] *nm* Adonis ▪ **c'est un véritable ~** he's like a Greek god.

Apollon [apɔlɔ̃] *npr* Apollo.

apologétique [apɔlɔʒetik] ◇ *adj* apologetic.
◇ *nf* apologetics *(U)*.

apologie [apɔlɔʒi] *nf* apologia ▪ **une ~ de** an apologia for ▪ **faire l'~ de qqch** to (seek to) justify sthg.

apologue [apɔlɔg] *nm* apologue.

apophyse [apɔfiz] *nf* apophysis.

apoplectique [apɔplɛktik] *adj* & *nmf* apoplectic.

apoplexie [apɔplɛksi] *nf* apoplexy.

apostasie [apɔstazi] *nf* apostasy.

apostat, e [apɔsta, at] ◇ *adj* apostate, renegade *(avant un nom)*.
◇ *nm, f* apostate, renegade.

a posteriori [apɔsterjɔri] ◇ *adj inv* a posteriori.
◇ *loc adv* afterwards ▪ **il est facile de juger ~** it's easy to be wise after the event.

apostille [apɔstij] *nf* apostil.

apostolat [apɔstɔla] *nm* **1.** RELIG apostolate, discipleship **2.** [prosélytisme] evangelism, proselytism **3.** [vocation] dedication, vocation ▪ **pour lui, l'enseignement c'est un ~** he is wholeheartedly devoted to teaching, teaching is his mission in life.

apostolique [apɔstɔlik] *adj* apostolic.

apostrophe [apɔstrɔf] *nf* **1.** [interpellation] invective **2.** GRAMM apostrophe ▪ **mis en ~** used in apostrophe **3.** [signe] apostrophe ▪ **"s" ~** "s" apostrophe.

APOSTROPHES

This former television book programme had a significant influence on the reading habits of people in France, and an invitation by its host Bernard Pivot was considered by authors to be a great honour. *Passer à Apostrophes* or *passer chez Pivot* became catchphrases.

apostropher [3] [apɔstrɔfe] *vt* to shout at.

apothéose [apɔteoz] *nf* **1.** [apogée] summit ▪ **ce concert a été l'~ du festival** the concert was the highlight of the festival **2.** THÉÂTRE (grand) finale ▪ **cela s'est terminé en ~** it ended in fine *ou* grand style **3.** ANTIQ apotheosis.

apothicaire [apɔtikɛr] *nm arch* apothecary.

apôtre [apotr] *nm* **1.** RELIG apostle, disciple **2.** [avocat] advocate ▪ **se faire l'~ d'une idée** to champion *ou* to speak for an idea ▶ **faire le bon ~** *péj* to be hypocritical.

Appalaches [apalaʃ] *npr mpl* : **les ~** the Appalachian Mountains, the Appalachians.

appalachien, enne [apalaʃjɛ̃, ɛn] *adj* Appalachian.

apparaître [91] [aparɛtr] *vi* **1.** [à la vue] to appear ▪ **après le bosquet, on voit ~ le village** after you pass the copse, the village comes into view ▪ **~ à qqn en songe** *ou* **rêve** to appear *ou* to come to sb in a dream ‖ [à l'esprit] to appear, to transpire, to emerge ▪ **la vérité m'est apparue un beau jour** the truth came to *ou* dawned on me one day ▪ **la voir dans un contexte professionnel la fait ~ sous un jour complètement nouveau** seeing her in a professional context shows her in a completely new light **2.** [surgir] to appear, to materialize **3.** [figurer] to appear, to feature **4.** [se manifester - symptôme, bouton] to appear ; [- maladie] to develop ; [- préjugé, habitude] to develop, to surface ▪ **faire ~** to reveal **5.** [sembler] to seem, to appear ▪ **cette histoire m'apparaît bien dérisoire aujourd'hui** the whole thing strikes me as being ridiculous now ▪ **il apparaît enfin tel qu'il est** he's showing his true self at last ▪ *(tournure impersonnelle)* **il apparaît que...** it appears *ou* emerges that...

apparat [apara] *nm* [cérémonie] pomp ▪ **en grand ~** with great pomp (and ceremony) ▪ **sans ~** without pomp, simply ▪ **costume/discours d'~** ceremonial dress/speech.

apparatchik [aparatʃik] *nm* apparatchik.

appareil [aparɛj] *nm* **1.** [dispositif] apparatus, device ▪ **~ de contrôle** tester ▪ **~ dentaire** [prothèse] dentures, (dental) plate ; [pour corriger] brace, plate ▪ **~ ménager** household appliance ▪ **~ de mesure** measuring device *ou* apparatus ▪ **~ photo** (still) camera ▪ **~ photo numérique** digital camera ▪ **~ de prothèse** surgical appliance ▪ **~ reflex** reflex camera ▪ **~ (téléphonique)** telephone ▪ **qui est à l'~?** who's speaking? ▪ **Berlot à l'~!** Berlot speaking! **2.** AÉRON craft, aircraft **3.** ANAT apparatus, system ▪ **~ digestif** digestive apparatus *ou* system ▪ **~ respiratoire** respiratory apparatus **4.** CONSTR bond **5.** [système] apparatus ▪ **l'~ du parti** the party apparatus *ou* machinery ▶ **~ critique** LITTÉR critical apparatus, apparatus criticus ▪ **~ idéologique d'État** POLIT ideological state apparatus ▪ **l'~ législatif** the machinery of the law **6.** *litt* [cérémonial] trappings.

appareillage [aparɛjaʒ] *nm* **1.** TECHNOL equipment **2.** MÉD prosthesis **3.** NAUT casting off.

appareiller [4] [aparɛje] ◇ *vt* **1.** ARCHIT to measure out **2.** MÉD to fit with a prosthesis **3.** [assortir] to match, to pair **4.** ZOOL to mate.
◇ *vi* NAUT to cast off, to get under way.

apparemment [aparamɑ̃] *adv* apparently ▪ **~, tout va bien** everything seems to be *ou* apparently everything's all right.

apparence [aparɑ̃s] *nf* [aspect - d'une personne] appearance ; [- d'un objet, d'une situation] appearance, look ▪ **avoir belle ~** to look impressive ▪ **sous l'~** *ou* **une ~ de libéralisme** in the guise *ou* behind a façade of liberalism ▪ **il va très bien, malgré les ~s** he's all right, contrary to all appearances ▪ **juger sur** *ou* **d'après les ~s** to judge *ou* to go by appearances ▪ **les ~s sont trompeuses, il ne faut pas se fier aux ~s** [en jugeant une personne] looks are deceptive ; [en jugeant une situation] there's more to it than meets the eye, appearances can be deceptive ▪ **faire qqch pour sauver les ~s** to do sthg for appearances' sake ▪ **heureusement pour nous, les ~s sont sauves** fortunately, we've been able to save face.
◆ **en apparence** *loc adv* apparently, by *ou* to all appearances ▪ **en ~ il travaille, mais comment le savoir vraiment?** to all appearances he works *ou* it would seem that he works, but how can one be sure?

apparent, e [aparɑ̃, ɑ̃t] *adj* **1.** [visible] visible ▪ **devenir ~** to become apparent, to surface, to emerge ▪ **avec poutres ~es** with exposed beams ▪ **couture ~e** topstitched seam **2.** [évident] obvious, apparent, evident ▪ **sans cause ~e** for no obvious *ou* apparent reason **3.** [superficiel] apparent ▪ **une tranquillité ~e** outward *ou* surface calm.

apparenté, e [aparɑ̃te] *adj* **1.** [parent] related **2.** [allié] allied ▪ **des listes ~es** grouped electoral lists *(in proportional elections)* ▪ **les socialistes et ~s** the socialists and their allies **3.** [ressemblant] similar.

apparentement [aparɑ̃tmɑ̃] *nm* **1.** [lien] link ▪ **son ~ à la bourgeoisie** his links to the bourgeoisie **2.** [alliance] alliance ▪ **~ de listes électorales** grouping of electoral lists *(in proportional elections)*.

apparenter [3] [aparɑ̃te] ◆ **s'apparenter** *vp (emploi réciproque)* POLIT to enter into an alliance.
◆ **s'apparenter à** *vp+prép* **1.** [ressembler à] to be like ▪ **cette histoire s'apparente à une aventure que j'ai vécue** this story is similar to *ou* is like an experience I once had **2.** [s'allier à] : **s'~ à un groupe** to join a group ▪ **s'~ à une famille** to marry into a family.

apparier [9] [aparje] *vt* **1.** [chaussures, gants] to match, to pair **2.** ZOOL to mate.
◆ **s'apparier** *vpi* to mate.

appariteur [aparitœr] *nm* **1.** [huissier] usher **2.** UNIV porter *UK*, campus policeman *US*.

apparition [aparisjɔ̃] *nf* **1.** [arrivée - d'une personne, d'une saison] arrival, appearance ■ **faire une ~** to put in *ou* to make an appearance ■ **faire son ~** [maladie] to develop ; [soleil] to come out **2.** [première manifestation] (first) appearance ■ **l'~ de la religion** the first appearance *ou* the birth of religion **3.** [vision] apparition, vision ■ **avoir une ~** to be visited by an apparition ■ **avoir des ~s** to have visions.

apparoir [aparwar] *v impers* : **il appert : il appert de ces témoignages que...** it appears *ou* it is evident from these statements that...

appart [apart] *nm fam* flat *UK*, apartment *US*.

appartement [apartəmɑ̃] *nm* flat *UK*, apartment *US* ■ **~ témoin** *ou* **modèle** show flat *UK*, model apartment *US*.

appartenance [apartənɑ̃s] *nf* **1.** [statut de membre] : **~ à un groupe/club** membership of a group/club ■ **~ à un parti** affiliation to *ou* membership of a party **2.** MATH membership.

appartenir [40] [apartənir] ◆ **appartenir à** *v+prép* **1.** [être la propriété de] to belong to ■ **cet argent m'appartient en propre** this money is my own **2.** [faire partie de - groupe] to belong to, to be part of ; [- professorat, syndicat] to belong to **3.** [dépendre de] : **la décision t'appartient** it's up to you, it's for you to decide ■ **pour des raisons qui m'appartiennent** for my own reasons ■ **l'éducation des enfants appartient aux deux parents** bringing up children is the responsibility of both parents ■ *(tournure impersonnelle)* **il appartient à chacun de faire attention** it's everyone's responsibility to be careful ■ **il ne vous appartient pas d'en décider** it's not for you to decide, the decision is not yours (to make) **4.** MATH to be a member of.
◆ **s'appartenir** *vpi* [être libre] : **avec tout ce travail, je ne m'appartiens plus** I have so much work, my time isn't my own any more.

apparu, e [apary] *pp* ▷ **apparaître**.

appas [apa] *nmpl litt* charms.

appât [apa] *nm* **1.** CHASSE & PÊCHE bait *(U)* **2.** [attrait] : **l'~ de** the lure of ■ **l'~ du gain** the lure *ou* attraction of money.

appâter [3] [apate] *vt* **1.** [attirer - poisson, animal] to lure ; [- personne] to lure, to entice **2.** [nourrir - oiseau] to feed **3.** [engraisser - volaille] to forcefeed.

appauvrir [32] [apovrir] *vt* [rendre pauvre - personne] to impoverish, to make poor ; [- pays] to impoverish, to drain ; [- terre] to impoverish, to drain, to exhaust ; [- sang] to make thin, to weaken ; [- langue] to impoverish.
◆ **s'appauvrir** *vpi* [personne, famille, pays] to get *ou* to grow poorer ■ [sol] to become exhausted ■ [sang] to become thin ■ [langue] to become impoverished, to lose it's vitality.

appauvrissement [apovrismɑ̃] *nm* impoverishment.

appeau, x [apo] *nm* **1.** [sifflet] birdcall **2.** [oiseau] decoy, stool pigeon.

appel [apɛl] *nm* **1.** [cri] call ■ **un ~ au secours** *ou* **à l'aide** *pr* a call for help ; *fig* a cry for help ■ **tu n'as pas entendu mes ~s?** didn't you hear me calling (out)? ◗ **l'~ du large** the call of the sea ■ **l'~ de la nature** the call of the wild ■ **~ aux armes** call to arms ■ **~ au peuple** appeal to the people ■ **~ au rassemblement** call for unity ■ **l'~ du 18 juin 1940** *General de Gaulle's radio appeal to the French people to resist the occupying Nazi forces* ■ **~ de détresse** NAUT distress call ; [d'une personne] call for help ■ **~ de phares : faire un ~ de phares (à qqn)** to flash one's lights (at sb) ■ **faire un ~ du pied à qqn** to make covert advances to sb ■ **~ radio** radio message
2. [coup de téléphone] : **~ (téléphonique)** (telephone *ou* phone) call ■ **~ interurbain** long-distance call ■ **~ en PCV** reverse charge call *UK*, collect call *US*
3. [sollicitation] appeal ■ **faire ~ à** [clémence, générosité] to appeal to ; [courage, intelligence, qualité, souvenirs] to summon (up) ■ **cela fait ~ à des notions complexes** it involves complex notions ■ **faire ~ à la force** to resort to force ■ **faire ~ à l'armée** to call in the army, to call the army out ■ **faire ~ à un spécialiste** to call in a specialist ■ **il a fait ~ à elle pour son déménagement** he asked for her help when he moved
4. ÉCON call ■ **~ de fonds** call for funds ■ **~ d'offres** invitation to tender ■ **répondre à un ~ d'offres** to make a bid
5. DR appeal ■ **en ~** on appeal ■ **faire ~** to appeal ■ **faire ~ d'un jugement** to appeal against a decision ■ **aller en ~** to appeal, to go to appeal ◗ **~ à témoins** appeal for witnesses (to come forward)
6. [liste de présence] roll call ■ MIL [mobilisation] call-up ■ **faire l'~** ÉDUC to take the register *UK*, to call (the) roll *US* ; MIL to call the roll ■ **répondre à l'~** to be present ■ **~ d'une classe** call-up *ou* calling up of a class
7. INFORM call ■ **~ par référence/valeur** call by reference/value ■ **programme/séquence d'~** call routine/sequence
8. JEUX : **faire un ~ à cœur/carreau** to signal for a heart/diamond
9. SPORT take-off ■ **prendre son ~** to take off
10. TECHNOL : **~ d'air** draught.
◆ **sans appel** *loc adj* **1.** DR without (the possibility of an) appeal
2. [irrévocable] irrevocable ■ **c'est sans ~** there's no going back on it, it's final ■ **sa décision est sans ~** his decision is final ■ **répondre d'un ton sans ~** to reply dismissively.

appelant, e [aplɑ̃, ɑ̃t] ◇ *adj* INFORM calling.
◇ *nm, f* DR appellant.

appelé, e [aple] *nm, f* : **il y a beaucoup d'~s et peu d'élus** many are called but few are chosen.
◆ **appelé** *nm* MIL conscript.

appeler [24] [aple] *vt* **1.** [interpeller] to call (out) to, to shout to ■ **appelle-le, il a oublié sa lettre** give him a shout, he's left his letter behind ■ **attendez que je vous appelle** wait till I call you ■ **~ qqn par la fenêtre** to call out to sb from the window ■ **~ le nom de qqn** to call out sb's name ■ **~ au secours** *pr* to shout "help", to call for help ; *fig* to call for help ■ *(en usage absolu)* **la pauvre, elle a appelé toute la nuit** the poor thing called out all night
2. [au téléphone] to call (up) ■ **appelez ce numéro en cas d'urgence** dial this number in an emergency ■ **on vous appelle de Bonn** there's a call for you from Bonn
3. [faire venir - médecin] to call, to send for *(insép)* ; [- police] to call ; [- renforts] to call up *ou* out *(sép)* ; [- ascenseur] to call ■ **~ du secours** to go for help ■ **~ qqn à l'aide** to call to sb for help ■ **~ un taxi** [dans la rue] to hail a taxi ; [par téléphone] to phone for *ou* to call a taxi ■ **~ le garçon** to call the waiter ■ **~ qqn à une fonction importante** to call *ou* to appoint sb to a high office ■ **être appelé sous les drapeaux** to be called up *ou* conscripted ■ **faire ~ qqn** to send for sb, to summon sb ■ **le devoir m'appelle!** *hum* duty calls! ■ **une affaire m'appelle en ville** I have to go to town on business
4. DR to summon ■ **être appelé à comparaître** to be summoned *ou* issued with a summons ■ **être appelé à la barre** to be called *ou* summoned to the witness stand ■ **être appelé devant le juge** to be called up before the magistrate
5. *sout* [désirer] : **~ qqch (de tous ses vœux)** to yearn (passionately) for
6. [nécessiter] to require, to call for *(insép)*
7. [entraîner] to lead to ■ **un coup en appelle un autre** one blow leads to another
8. [inviter] : **~ (des travailleurs) à la grève** to call a strike, to put out a strike call ■ **~ les gens à la révolte** to incite people to rebel ■ **~ aux armes** to call to arms ■ **il faut ~ les gens à voter** *ou* **aux urnes** people must be urged to vote
9. [destiner] : **être appelé à** to be bound to ■ **ce quartier est appelé à disparaître** this part of town is due to be demolished (eventually) ■ **il va être appelé à revenir souvent** he will have to come back often
10. [nommer] to call ■ **~ les choses par leur nom** to be blunt ■ **comment on appelle ça en chinois?** what's (the word for) this in Chinese? ■ **appelez-moi Jo** call me Jo ■ **elle se fait ~ Jaspe** she wants to be called Jaspe ◗ **se faire ~ Arthur** *fam* to get it in the neck *UK*, to catch it
11. INFORM [programme] to call (up) ■ [réseau] to dial.
◆ **en appeler à** *v+prép* to appeal to ■ **j'en appelle à vous en dernier recours** I'm coming to you as a last resort.

◆ **s'appeler** ◇ *vp (emploi passif)* to be called ■ **comment s'appelle-t-il?** what's his name?, what's he called? ■ **voilà ce qui s'appelle une gaffe!** that's what's called *ou* that's what I call putting your foot in it! ➤ **ça s'appelle revient** *fam* make sure you give it back.
◇ *vp (emploi réciproque)* to call one another ■ **vous vous appelez par vos prénoms?** are you on first-name terms?

appellatif, ive [apɛlatif, iv] *adj* appellative.
◆ **appellatif** *nm* appellative.

appellation [apɛlasjɔ̃] *nf* appellation, designation ■ **une ~ injurieuse** an insulting name ➤ **~ contrôlée** *government certification guaranteeing the quality of a French wine* ■ **~ d'origine** label of quality.

appelle *etc v* ▷ **appeler**.

appendice [apɛ̃dis] *nm* **1.** [note] appendix **2.** [prolongement] appendage **3.** *hum* [nez] snout **4.** ANAT appendix.

appendicectomie [apɛ̃disɛktɔmi] *nf* appendicectomy, appendectomy ■ **j'ai eu une ~** I had my appendix out.

appendicite [apɛ̃disit] *nf* appendicitis.

appendiculaire [apɛ̃dikylɛr] *adj* appendicular.

appentis [apɑ̃ti] *nm* **1.** [bâtiment] lean-to **2.** [toit] lean-to, sloping roof.

appert *v* ▷ **apparoir**.

appesantir [32] [apəzɑ̃tir] *vt* [rendre pesant - démarche] to slow down *(sép)* ; [- tête, corps] to weigh down *(sép)* ; [- facultés] to dull ■ **~ son bras** *ou* **autorité sur un pays** *fig* to strengthen one's authority over a country.
◆ **s'appesantir** *vpi* **1.** [devenir lourd - tête] to become heavier ; [- gestes, démarche] to become slower ; [- esprit] to grow duller **2.** [insister] : **s'~ sur un sujet** to concentrate on *ou* to dwell at length on a subject.

appétissant, e [apetisɑ̃, ɑ̃t] *adj* **1.** [odeur, mets] appetizing, mouthwatering ■ **peu ~** unappetizing **2.** *fam* [attirant] attractive ■ **une femme aux rondeurs ~es** a curvaceous woman.

appétit [apeti] *nm* **1.** [envie de manger] appetite ■ **avoir de l'~** *ou* **grand ~** *ou* **bon ~** to have a good *ou* hearty appetite ■ **manger avec ~** *ou* **de bon ~** to eat heartily ■ **la promenade m'a donné de l'~** *ou* **m'a ouvert l'~** *ou* **m'a mis en ~** the walk has given me an appetite ■ **quelques diapositives d'abord, pour vous ouvrir l'~** *fig* first, a few slides, to whet your appetite ■ **ça va te couper l'~** it'll spoil your appetite, it'll take your appetite away ■ **perdre l'~** to lose one's appetite ■ **bon ~!** enjoy your meal!, have a nice meal! ➤ **avoir un ~ d'oiseau** to eat like a bird ■ **avoir un ~ de loup** *ou* **d'ogre** to eat like a horse ■ **l'~ vient en mangeant** *prov & pr* eating whets the appetite ; *fig* the more you have, the more you want **2.** [désir] : **~ de** appetite for ■ **un insatiable ~ de vivre/de connaissances** an insatiable thirst for life/for knowledge.
◆ **appétits** *nmpl* [instincts] appetites.

applaudimètre [aplodimɛtr] *nm* clapometer *UK*, applause meter *US*.

applaudir [32] [aplodir] ◇ *vt* [personne] to applaud, to clap ■ [discours, pièce] to applaud ■ **et on l'applaudit encore une fois!** let's give him another big hand!, let's hear it for him one more time! ■ **il a longuement fait ~ le pianiste** he led a long round of applause for the pianist.
◇ *vi* to clap, to applaud ■ **~ à qqch** *fig* : **~ à une initiative** to praise *ou* to applaud an initiative ■ **~ des deux mains à qqch** to approve of *ou* to welcome sthg heartily ➤ **~ à tout rompre : les gens applaudissaient à tout rompre** there was thunderous applause.
◆ **s'applaudir de** *vp+prép* : **s'~ de qqch/d'avoir fait qqch** to congratulate o.s. on sthg/on having done sthg.

applaudissements [aplodismɑ̃] *nmpl* applause *(U)*, clapping *(U)* ■ **un tonnerre** *ou* **une tempête d'~** thunderous applause ■ **sous les ~** amidst *ou* in the midst of applause.

applicable [aplikabl] *adj* applicable ■ **loi ~ à partir du 1er mars** law to be applied as of March 1st ■ **règlement ~ immédiatement** ruling effective forthwith.

applicateur [aplikatœr] ◇ *adj m* applicator *(modif)*.
◇ *nm* applicator.

applicatif, ive [aplikatif, iv] *adj* INFORM application *(modif)*.

application [aplikasjɔ̃] *nf* **1.** [pose] application ■ **laisser sécher après l'~ de la première couche** allow to dry after applying the first coat of paint **2.** [mise en pratique - d'une loi] application, enforcement ; [- d'une sentence] enforcement ■ **mesures prises en ~ de la loi** measures taken to enforce the law, law-enforcement measures ■ **mettre qqch en ~** to put sthg into practice, to apply sthg **3.** SC & TECHNOL application **4.** [soin] application ■ **travailler avec ~** to work diligently, to apply o.s. (to one's work) **5.** MATH mapping, function **6.** inform application.

applique [aplik] *nf* **1.** [lampe] wall lamp **2.** COUT (piece of) appliqué work.

appliqué, e [aplike] *adj* **1.** [studieux] assiduous, industrious **2.** SC & UNIV applied.

appliquer [3] [aplike] *vt* **1.** [poser - masque, crème, ventouse] to apply ; [- enduit] to apply, to lay on *(sép)* ■ **~ son oreille contre la porte** to put one's ear to the door **2.** [mettre en pratique - décret] to enforce, to apply ; [- peine] to enforce ; [- idée, réforme] to put into practice, to implement ; [- recette, méthode] to use ; [- théorie, invention] to apply, to put into practice ■ **je ne fais qu'~ la consigne!** I don't make the rules, I'm just following orders! ■ **vous devez faire ~ le règlement** you must make sure the rules are applied **3.** [donner - sobriquet, gifle] to give ; [- baiser] to plant ■ **un coup de pied bien appliqué** a powerful kick **4.** [consacrer] : **~ qqch à** to devote sthg to ■ **~ toute son énergie à son travail** to devote all one's energy to one's work.
◆ **s'appliquer** ◇ *vp (emploi passif)* **1.** [se poser] : **s'~ sur** [suj: objet] to be laid *ou* to fit over ; [suj: enduit] to go over, to be applied on ■ **'s'applique sur toutes sortes de surfaces'** 'may be applied on many different surfaces' **2.** [être utilisé] to apply ■ **cela ne s'applique pas dans notre cas** it doesn't apply in *ou* it's not applicable to our case.
◇ *vpi* **1.** [être attentif - élève, apprenti] to take care (over one's work), to apply o.s. (to one's work) **2.** [s'acharner] : **s'~ à faire** to try to do ■ **je me suis appliqué à faire ce qu'on attendait de moi** I took pains to do what was expected of me.

appoint [apwɛ̃] *nm* **1.** [argent] : **faire l'~** to give the exact money *ou* change **2.** *litt* [aide] assistance, contribution.
◆ **d'appoint** *loc adj* : **radiateur d'~** extra radiator ■ **salaire d'~** extra income.

appointements [apwɛ̃tmɑ̃] *nmpl* salary.

appointer [3] [apwɛ̃te] *vt* **1.** [rémunérer] to pay a salary to **2.** TECHNOL to sharpen.

appontement [apɔ̃tmɑ̃] *nm* wharf, landing stage.

apponter [3] [apɔ̃te] *vi* to land *(on an aircraft carrier)*.

apport [apɔr] *nm* **1.** [action d'apporter] contribution ■ **un ~ d'argent frais** an injection of new money ■ **l'~ journalier en fer et en calcium** [fourni] the daily supply of iron and calcium ; [reçu] the daily intake of iron and calcium **2.** FIN & DR : **~s en communauté** goods contributed by spouses to the joint estate ■ **~s en numéraire/en nature** contribution in cash/in kind ■ **~s en société** capital invested.

apporter [3] [apɔrte] *vt* **1.** [objet] to bring ■ **apporte-le à papa dans la cuisine** take it to Dad in the kitchen ■ **je t'ai apporté un cadeau** I've brought you a present *ou* a present for you ■ **apportez vos livres avec vous** bring your books along, bring your books with you ■ **on lui apporte ses repas au lit** he has his meals brought to him in bed ➤ **~ sa pierre à l'édifice** to make one's contribution **2.** [fournir - message, nouvelle] to give ; [- preuve] to give, to provide, to supply ; [- résultat] to produce ; [- soulagement, satisfaction] to bring ; [- modification] to introduce ■ **~ de l'attention** *ou* **du soin à (faire) qqch** to exercise care in (doing) sthg ■ **vous avez des qualités à ~ à notre société** you have skills to contribute to our company ■ **~ de l'aide à qqn** to help sb.

apposer [3] [apoze] *vt* **1.** [ajouter - cachet, signature] to affix, to append ■ DR [insérer - clause] to insert **2.** [poser - affiche, plaque] to put up *(sép)* ■ **~ les scellés sur une porte** DR to affix the seals on a door.

apposition [apozisjɔ̃] *nf* **1.** [ajout] affixing, appending **2.** [pose] putting up ■ DR [des scellés] affixing **3.** GRAMM apposition.

appréciable [apresjabl] *adj* **1.** [perceptible - changement] appreciable, noticeable ■ **de manière ~** appreciably **2.** [considérable - somme, effort] appreciable.

appréciatif, ive [apresjatif, iv] *adj* **1.** [estimatif] evaluative ■ **état ~ du mobilier** evaluation *ou* estimate of the value of the furniture **2.** [admiratif] appreciative.

appréciation [apresjasjɔ̃] *nf* **1.** [estimation - d'un poids, d'une valeur] appreciation, estimate, assessment ; [- d'une situation] assessment, appreciation, grasp ■ **je laisse cela à votre ~** I leave it to your judgment **2.** [observation] remark, comment ■ **il a obtenu d'excellentes ~s** ÉDUC he got very good comments from his teachers *(in his report)* **3.** [augmentation - d'une devise] appreciation.

apprécier [9] [apresje] *vt* **1.** [évaluer - valeur] to estimate, to assess ; [- distance] to estimate, to judge ■ **je ne crois pas que tu l'apprécies/que tu apprécies son travail à sa juste valeur** I don't think you really appreciate what he/what his work is worth **2.** [discerner - ironie, subtilités] to appreciate **3.** [aimer] to appreciate ■ **~ qqn pour qqch** to appreciate sb for sthg, to like sb because of sthg ■ **j'ai beaucoup apprécié cette soirée** I really enjoyed the evening ■ **un vin très apprécié des connaisseurs** a wine much appreciated by connoisseurs ■ **je n'apprécie pas du tout ce genre de blagues** I don't care for *ou* like that sort of joke at all ■ **le sel dans son café, il n'a pas apprécié!** *fam* he was not amused when he found his coffee had salt in it! ■ **il a moyennement apprécié** he was not amused, he was none too pleased.

◆ **s'apprécier** *vpi* [monnaie] to appreciate (in value).

appréhender [3] [apreɑ̃de] *vt* **1.** [craindre - examen, réaction] to feel apprehensive about **2.** [comprendre] to comprehend *sout*, to grasp **3.** DR [arrêter] to arrest, to apprehend *sout*.

appréhension [apreɑ̃sjɔ̃] *nf* **1.** [crainte] fear, apprehension ■ **avoir** *ou* **éprouver de l'~** to feel apprehensive, to have misgivings **2.** PHILOS [compréhension] apprehension.

apprendre [79] [aprɑ̃dr] *vt* **1.** [s'initier à] to learn ■ **ils ont décidé de lui faire ~ l'anglais** they've decided that he should have English lessons ■ **~ qqch de qqn** to learn sthg from sb, to be taught sthg by sb ■ **~ qqch par cœur** to learn sthg (off) by heart *ou* rote ■ **~ à être patient** to learn patience, to learn to be patient ■ **~ à connaître qqn/une ville** to get to know sb/a town ■ *(en usage absolu)* **il apprend facilement/avec difficulté** learning comes/doesn't come easily to him ■ **~ lentement/vite** to be a slow/fast learner ■ **on apprend à tout âge** it's never too late to learn **2.** [enseigner] : **~ qqch à qqn** to teach sb sthg *ou* sthg to sb ■ **elle m'a appris le français/à nager** she taught me French/(how) to swim ■ **je t'apprendrai à fouiller dans mon sac!** I'll teach you to go through my bag! ■ **il/ça va lui apprendre à vivre!** he'll/it'll teach him a thing or two! ■ *(en usage absolu)* **ça lui apprendra!** that'll teach him! ➊ **on n'apprend pas à un vieux singe à faire la grimace** *prov* don't teach your grandmother to suck eggs **3.** [donner connaissance de] to tell ■ **~ qqch à qqn** to tell sb sthg ■ **vous ne m'apprenez rien!** tell me something new! **4.** [être informé de - départ, mariage] to learn *ou* to hear of *(insép)* ; [- nouvelle] to hear ■ **on apprend à l'instant qu'un prisonnier s'est échappé** we've just heard that a prisoner has escaped ■ **qu'est-ce que j'apprends, vous démissionnez?** what's this I hear about you resigning? ■ **apprenez** *ou* **vous apprendrez qu'ici on ne fait pas ce genre de choses** you'll have to learn that we don't do things like that here ■ **tiens, tiens, on en apprend des choses!** *fam* well, well, who'd have thought such a thing? ■ **on en apprend tous les jours!** *hum* you learn something new every day!

◆ **s'apprendre** *vp (emploi passif)* to be learnt ■ **le style, ça ne s'apprend pas** you can't learn style.

apprenti, e [aprɑ̃ti] *nm, f* apprentice ■ **~ maçon** builder's apprentice ➊ **jouer les ~s sorciers** *ou* **à l'~ sorcier** *fig* to play at being God.

apprentissage [aprɑ̃tisaʒ] *nm* **1.** [fait d'apprendre] : **l'~ des langues** language learning, learning languages ■ **faire l'~ de qqch** *fig* to learn one's first lessons in sthg **2.** [durée] (period of) apprenticeship.

◆ **d'apprentissage** *loc adj* [centre, école] training ■ [contrat] of apprenticeship.

◆ **en apprentissage** *loc adv* : **être en ~ chez qqn** to be apprenticed to *ou* to be serving one's apprenticeship with sb.

apprêt [aprɛ] *nm* **1.** [affectation] affectation, affectedness ■ **sans ~** unaffectedly, without affectation **2.** TECHNOL [préparation - du cuir, d'un tissu] dressing ; [- du papier] finishing ; [- d'un plafond, d'un mur] sizing ■ [produit - pour tissu] dressing ; [- pour papier] finish ; [- pour plafond, mur] size.

◆ **apprêts** *nmpl litt* [préparatifs] preparations.

apprêté, e [aprete] *adj* affected, fussy.

apprêter [4] [aprete] *vt* **1.** TECHNOL [peau, tissu] to dress, to finish ■ [plafond] to size **2.** *litt* [préparer - repas] to get ready, to prepare ■ [habiller] to get ready, to dress.

◆ **s'apprêter** *vp (emploi réfléchi) litt* to prepare *ou* to dress o.s.

◆ **s'apprêter à** *vp+prép* : **je m'apprêtais à te rendre visite** I was getting ready to call on you.

appris, e [apri, iz] *pp* ▻ **apprendre.**

apprivoisable [aprivwazabl] *adj* tameable, which can be tamed ■ **difficilement ~** difficult to tame.

apprivoisé, e [aprivwaze] *adj* tame.

apprivoiser [3] [aprivwaze] *vt* [animal] to tame, to domesticate ■ [enfant, peur] to tame.

◆ **s'apprivoiser** *vpi* [animal] to become tame ■ [personne] to become more sociable.

approbateur, trice [aprɔbatœr, tris] *adj* [regard, sourire] approving ■ [commentaire] supportive ■ **faire un signe de tête ~** to give an approving nod, to nod one's head in approval.

approbatif, ive [aprɔbatif, iv] *adj* approving.

approbation [aprɔbasjɔ̃] *nf* **1.** [assentiment] approval, approbation *sout* ■ **il sourit en signe d'~** he gave a smile of approval, he smiled approvingly ■ **rencontrer/gagner l'~ de qqn** to meet with/to win sb's approval ■ **donner son ~ à un projet** to approve a plan **2.** [autorisation] approval ■ **soumettre qqch à l'~ de qqn** to submit sthg to sb for approval.

approchable [aprɔʃabl] *adj* approachable, accessible ■ **une vedette difficilement ~** an inaccessible *ou* unapproachable star.

approchant, e [aprɔʃɑ̃, ɑ̃t] *adj* similar ■ **rien d'~** nothing like that ■ **il a dû le traiter d'escroc ou quelque chose d'~** he must have called him a crook or something like that *ou* something of the sort.

approche [aprɔʃ] *nf* **1.** [venue] approach ■ **l'~ des examens** the coming of the exams, the approaching exams **2.** [accès] approachability ■ **il est d'~ facile/difficile** he is approachable/unapproachable ■ **sa fiction est plus facile d'~ que son théâtre** her novels are more accessible than her plays **3.** [conception] approach ■ **une ~ écologique du problème** an ecological approach to the problem **4.** IMPR [espacement] spacing ■ [erreur] spacing error ■ [signe] close-up mark **5.** AÉRON approach **6.** SPORT approach (shot).

◆ **approches** *nfpl* : **les ~s de l'aéroport** the area surrounding the airport, the vicinity of the airport.

◆ **à l'approche de** *loc prép* **1.** [dans le temps] : **tous les ans, à l'~ de l'été** every year, as summer draws near ■ **à l'~ de la trentaine** as one nears *ou* approaches (the age of) thirty **2.** [dans l'espace] : **à l'~ de son père, il s'est enfui** he ran away as his father approached.

◆ **aux approches de** *loc prép* **1.** [dans le temps] : **tous les ans, aux ~s de l'été** every year, as summer draws near **2.** [dans l'espace] : **aux ~s de la frontière, il y avait davantage de soldats** there were more soldiers as we approached *ou* neared the border.

approché, e [aprɔʃe] *adj* [idée, calcul] approximate.

approcher [3] [aprɔʃe] ◇ *vt* **1.** [mettre plus près - lampe, chaise] to move *ou* to draw nearer, to move *ou* to draw closer ■ **approche la table du mur** move *ou* draw the table closer to the wall ■ **~ une tasse de ses lèvres** to lift *ou* to raise a cup to one's lips ■ **n'approche pas ta main de la flamme** don't put your hand near the flame **2.** [se mettre près de] to go *ou* to come near ■ **ne l'approchez/m'approchez surtout pas!** please don't go near him/come near me! **3.** [côtoyer - personnalité] to approach ■ **il n'est pas facile de l'~** she's not very approachable **4.** [établir un contact avec] to approach.
◇ *vi* **1.** [dans l'espace] to come *ou* to get nearer, to approach ■ **toi, approche!** you, come over here! ■ **on approche de Paris** we're getting near to *ou* we're nearing Paris ▮ *fig* to be close ■ **enfin nous approchons du but!** at last we're nearing our goal! ■ **~ de la perfection** to be *ou* to come close to perfection **2.** [dans le temps - nuit, aube] to draw near ; [- événement, saison] to approach, to draw near.
◆ **s'approcher** *vpi* : **approche-toi** come here *ou* closer ■ **elle le tira par la manche pour le faire s'~** she took him by the sleeve and pulled him closer.
◆ **s'approcher de** *vp+prép* **1.** [se mettre plus près de] : **s'~ d'une ville** to approach *ou* to near a town ■ **s'~ de qqn** to come close to sb, to come up to sb ■ **s'~ de qqch** to go near sthg **2.** [correspondre à] to be *ou* to come close to ■ **vos descriptions ne s'approchent pas du tout de la réalité** your descriptions bear no resemblance to the facts.

approfondi, e [aprɔfɔ̃di] *adj* thorough, detailed, extensive ■ **traiter qqch de façon ~e** to go into sthg thoroughly.

approfondir [32] [aprɔfɔ̃dir] *vt* **1.** [creuser - puits] to deepen, to dig deeper **2.** [détailler - sujet, étude] to go deeper *ou* more thoroughly into ■ **il faut ~ la question** the question needs to be examined in more detail ■ **sans ~** superficially **3.** [parfaire - connaissances] to improve, to deepen.

approfondissement [aprɔfɔ̃dismɑ̃] *nm* **1.** [d'un puits] increasing the depth of, deepening **2.** [des connaissances] extending ■ **l'~ de la question est réservé au deuxième volume** a more thorough examination of the issue will await volume two.

appropriation [aprɔprijasjɔ̃] *nf* DR [saisie] appropriation ■ **~ de fonds** misappropriation of funds, embezzlement.

approprié, e [aprɔprije] *adj* [solution, technique] appropriate, apposite *sout*, suitable ■ [tenue] proper, right ■ **peu ~** inappropriate ■ **un discours ~ aux circonstances** a speech appropriate *ou* suited to the circumstances.

approprier [10] [aprɔprije] *vt* [adapter] to adapt, to suit.
◆ **s'approprier** *vpt* [biens, invention] to appropriate ■ [pouvoir] to seize.

approuvable [apruvabl] *adj* approvable, commendable.

approuver [3] [apruve] *vt* **1.** [être d'accord avec - méthode, conduite] to approve of *(insép)* ■ **elle m'a approuvé de ne pas avoir cédé** she approved of my not giving in ■ **je vous approuve entièrement** I think you're entirely right ■ **la proposition a été approuvée par tout le monde** the proposition met with *ou* received general approval **2.** [autoriser - alliance, fusion] to approve, to agree to *(insép)* ; [- médicament, traitement] to approve ; [- contrat] to ratify ; [- projet de loi] to approve, to pass.

approvisionné [aprɔvizjɔne] *adj* : **bien ~** [magasin, rayon] well-stocked.

approvisionnement [aprɔvizjɔnmɑ̃] *nm* **1.** [action] supplying **2.** [provisions] supply, provision, stock **3.** COMM procurement.

approvisionner [3] [aprɔvizjɔne] *vt* **1.** [village, armée] to supply ■ **être approvisionné en électricité** to be supplied with electricity **2.** ARM to load **3.** BANQUE [compte] to pay (funds) into.
◆ **s'approvisionner** *vpi* [personne] to shop ■ [commerce, entreprise] to stock up ■ **s'~ en** [stocker] to stock up on.

approximatif, ive [aprɔksimatif, iv] *adj* [coût, évaluation] approximate, rough ■ [traduction] rough ■ [réponse] vague.

approximation [aprɔksimasjɔ̃] *nf* **1.** [estimation] approximation ■ **ce chiffre n'est qu'une ~** this is only an approximate figure *ou* a rough estimate **2.** *péj* [à-peu-près] generality, (vague) approximation **3.** MATH approximation ■ **calcul par ~s successives** calculus by continual approach.

approximativement [aprɔksimativmɑ̃] *adv* [environ] approximately, roughly ■ [vaguement] vaguely.

appt = **appartement**.

appui [apɥi] *nm* **1.** CONSTR [d'un balcon, d'un garde-fou] support ■ **~ de fenêtre** windowsill, window ledge **2.** [dans les positions du corps] : **prendre ~ sur** to lean (heavily) on ▮ [d'un alpiniste] press hold ■ **trouver un ~** [pied] to gain *ou* to get a hold ; [alpiniste] to get a purchase **3.** [soutien] support, backing ■ **apporter son ~ à une initiative** to back *ou* to support an initiative ■ **avoir l'~ de qqn** to have sb's support *ou* backing ▮ MIL support ■ **~ aérien/naval** air/naval support.
◆ **à l'appui** *loc adv* : **il a lu, à l'~, une lettre datée du 24 mai** in support of this *ou* to back this up, he read out a letter dated 24th May ■ **preuves à l'~** with supporting evidence.
◆ **à l'appui de** *loc prép* in support of, supporting ■ **à l'~ de ses dires** in support of *ou* to support what he was saying.
◆ **d'appui** *loc adj* [consonne] supporting ■ [voyelle] support *(modif)*.

appui-bras [apɥibra] (*pl* **appuis-bras**) *nm* armrest.

appuie *etc v* ▷ **appuyer**.

appuie-bras [apɥibra] *nm inv* = **appui-bras**.

appui(e)-tête [apɥitɛt] (*pl* **appuis-tête** *ou pl* **appuie-tête**) *nm* headrest.

appuyé, e [apɥije] *adj* [allusion] heavy, laboured ■ [regard] insistent.

appuyer [14] [apɥije] ◇ *vt* **1.** [faire reposer] to lean, to rest ■ **le vélo était appuyé contre la grille** the bicycle was resting *ou* leaning against the railings **2.** [étayer] to support ■ **mur appuyé sur des contreforts** wall supported by buttresses **3.** [donner son soutien à - candidat, réforme] to back, to support ■ **la police, appuyée par l'armée** the police, backed up *ou* supported by the army **4.** [fonder] to ground, to base ■ **~ son raisonnement sur des faits** to base one's argument on *ou* to ground one's argument in facts.
◇ *vi* **1.** [exercer une pression] to press, to push down ■ **il faut ~ de toutes ses forces** you have to press as hard as you can ■ **~ sur** [avec le doigt] to press, to push ; [avec le pied] to press down on ■ **~ sur la gâchette** to pull the trigger **2.** [insister] : **~ sur** [mot] to stress, to emphasize ; [note] to sustain **3.** AUTO : **~ sur la droite/la gauche** to bear right/left ■ **~ sur la pédale de frein** to brake ■ **~ sur la pédale** *fam* to put one's foot down *UK*, to step on the gas *US*.
◆ **s'appuyer**△ *vpt* to have to put up with.
◆ **s'appuyer à** *vp+prép* [physiquement] to lean *ou* to rest on.
◆ **s'appuyer contre** *vp+prép* to lean against ■ **s'~ contre la rampe** to lean against the banister.
◆ **s'appuyer sur** *vp+prép* **1.** [se soutenir sur] to lean on **2.** [s'en remettre à - ami] to lean *ou* to depend *ou* to rely on ; [- amitié, aide] to count *ou* to rely on ; [- témoignage] to rely on **3.** [se fonder sur] : **ce récit s'appuie sur une expérience vécue** this story is based on a real-life experience.

apr. = **après**.

âpre [apr] *adj* **1.** [âcre - goût] sour ; [- vin] rough **2.** [rude - voix, froid] harsh ■ [féroce - concurrence, lutte] bitter, fierce ■ **~ au gain** *péj* greedy, money-grabbing.

âprement [aprəmɑ̃] *adv* [sévèrement] bitterly, harshly ■ **cette victoire fut ~ disputée** it was a fiercely contested victory.

après [aprɛ] ◇ *prep* **1.** [dans le temps] after ■ **~ le départ de Paul** after Paul left ■ **~ (le) dîner** after dinner ■ **530 ~ Jésus-Christ** 530 AD ■ **c'était peu ~ 3 h** it was shortly *ou* soon after 3 o'clock ■ **c'était bien ~ son départ** it was a long time *ou* a good while after he left ■ **tu le contredis en public, et ~ ça tu t'étonnes qu'il s'énerve!** you contradict him publicly (and) then you're surprised to find that he gets annoyed! ■ **~ ça, il ne te reste plus qu'à aller t'excuser** the only thing you can do now is apologize ■ **~ quoi, nous verrons** then we'll see ■ **~ avoir dîné, ils**

bavardèrent after dining *ou* after dinner they chatted ■ **jour ~ jour** day after day ■ **page ~ page, le mystère s'épaissit** the mystery gets deeper with every page *ou* by the page
2. [dans l'espace] after ■ **la gare est ~ le parc** the station is past *ou* after the park ‖ *fam* [sur] : **son foulard est resté accroché ~ les ronces** his scarf got caught on the brambles
3. [dans un rang, un ordre, une hiérarchie] after ■ **~ vous, je vous en prie** after you ■ **vous êtes ~ moi** [dans une file d'attente] you're after me ■ **il était juste ~ moi dans la file** he was just behind me in the queue ■ **il fait passer ma carrière ~ la sienne** my career comes after his *ou* takes second place to his, according to him
4. [indiquant un mouvement de poursuite, l'attachement, l'hostilité] : **courir ~ qqn** to run after sb ■ **le chien aboie ~ les passants** the dog barks at the passers-by ■ **il est constamment ~ moi** [me surveille] he's always breathing down my neck ; [me harcèle] he's always nagging (at) *ou* going on at me ■ **ils sont ~ une invitation, c'est évident** it's obvious they're angling for *ou* they're after an invitation.
◇ *adv* **1.** [dans le temps] : **un mois ~** a month later ■ **bien ~** a long *ou* good while after, much later ■ **peu ~** shortly after *ou* afterwards ■ **garde tes forces pour ~** conserve your strength for afterwards *ou* later ■ **nous sommes allés au cinéma et ~ au restaurant** we went to the cinema and then to a restaurant ■ **~ on ira dire que je suis avare!** and then people will say I'm mean! ■ **~, tu ne viendras pas te plaindre!** don't come moaning to me afterwards! ◆ **et ~? qu'a-t-il fait?** and then what did he do? ■ **et ~? qu'est-ce que ça peut faire?** *fam* so what? who cares?
2. [dans l'espace] after
3. [dans un rang, un ordre, une hiérarchie] next ■ **qui est ~?** [dans une file d'attente] who's next?
◆ **après coup** *loc adv* afterwards, later ■ **il n'a réagi qu'~ coup** it wasn't until afterwards *ou* later that he reacted ■ **n'essaie pas d'inventer une explication ~ coup** don't try to invent an explanation after the event.
◆ **après que** *loc conj* after ■ **~ qu'il eut terminé...** after he had finished... ■ **je me suis couché ~ que tu aies téléphoné** I went to bed after you phoned.
◆ **après tout** *loc adv* **1.** [introduisant une justification] after all ■ **~ tout, ça n'a pas beaucoup d'importance** after all, it's not particularly important
2. [emploi expressif] then ■ **débrouille-toi tout seul, ~ tout!** sort it out yourself then!
◆ **d'après** ◇ *loc prép* **1.** [introduisant un jugement] according to ■ **d'~ moi** in my opinion ■ **alors, d'~ vous, qui va gagner?** so who do you think is going to win? ■ **d'~ les informations qui nous parviennent** from *ou* according to the news reaching us ■ **d'~ ce qu'elle dit** from what she says ■ **d'~ mon expérience** in my experience
2. [introduisant un modèle, une citation] : **d'~ Tolstoï** [adaptation] adapted from Tolstoy ■ **peint d'~ nature** painted from life ■ **d'~ une idée originale de...** based on *ou* from an original idea by...
◇ *loc adj* **1.** [dans le temps] following, next
2. [dans l'espace] next ■ **je descends à la station d'~** I'm getting off at the next station.

après-coup [aprɛku] (*pl* **après-coups**) *nm* after-effect PSYCHOL.

après-demain [aprɛdmɛ̃] *adv* the day after tomorrow ■ **~ matin/soir** the day after tomorrow in the morning/evening.

après-guerre [aprɛgɛr] (*pl* **après-guerres**) *nm ou nf* post-war era *ou* period ■ **le théâtre d'~** post-war drama.

après-midi [aprɛmidi] *nm inv ou nf inv* afternoon ■ **en début/fin d'~** early/late in the afternoon ■ **à 2 h de l'~** at 2 (o'clock) in the afternoon, at 2 p.m.

après-rasage [aprɛrazaʒ] (*pl* **après-rasages**) ◇ *adj inv* aftershave (*modif*).
◇ *nm* aftershave (lotion).

après-ski [aprɛski] (*pl* **après-skis**) *nm* [botte] snow boot.

après-soleil [aprɛsɔlɛj] (*pl* **après-soleils**) *nm* aftersun cream.

après-vente [aprɛvɑ̃t] *adj inv* after-sales.

âpreté [aprəte] *nf* **1.** [âcreté] sourness **2.** [dureté - d'un ton, d'une voix] harshness, roughness ; [- d'une saison] harshness, rawness ; [- d'un reproche] bitterness, harshness ■ **combattre avec ~** to struggle bitterly *ou* grimly.

a priori [aprijɔri] ◇ *loc adj inv* PHILOS a priori.
◇ *loc adv* on the face of it ■ **~, c'est une bonne idée** on the face of it *ou* in principle it's a good idea ■ **~, je ne vois pas d'inconvénient** in principle I can't see any reason why not.
◇ *nm inv* [préjugé] preconception, preconceived idea ■ **juger sans ~** to judge impartially, to be an unbiased judge.

à-propos [aprɔpo] *nm inv* aptness, relevance ■ **votre remarque manque d'~** your remark is not relevant *ou* to the point ■ **quelle que soit la situation, il réagit avec ~** whatever the situation, he always does *ou* says the right thing ■ **faire preuve d'~** to show presence of mind.

APS (*abr de* **Advanced Photo System**) *nm* APS.

apside [apsid] *nf* apsis.

apte [apt] *adj* : **~ à qqch** [par sa nature] fit for *ou* suited to sthg ; [par ses qualifications] qualified for sthg ; [par ses capacités] capable of sthg ■ **~ (au service militaire)** fit (for military service) ■ **~ à faire qqch** [par sa nature] suited to doing sthg ; [par ses qualifications] qualified to do sthg.

aptitude [aptityd] *nf* [capacité] ability, aptitude ■ **il n'a aucune ~ dans ce domaine** he has *ou* shows no aptitude in that direction.
◆ **aptitudes** *nfpl* : **~s (intellectuelles)** abilities ■ **avoir/montrer des ~s en langues** to have/to show a gift for languages.

aquaculture [akwakyltyr] *nf* aquaculture.

aquaplanage [akwaplanaʒ] = **aquaplaning**.

aquaplane [akwaplan] *nm* **1.** [activité] aquaplaning **2.** [planche] aquaplane.

aquaplaning [akwaplaniŋ] *nm* aquaplaning AUTO.

aquarelle [akwarɛl] *nf* [tableau] watercolour ■ **peindre à l'~** to paint in watercolours.

aquarelliste [akwarelist] *nmf* watercolourist.

aquarium [akwarjɔm] *nm* **1.** [décoratif] fish tank, aquarium **2.** [au zoo] aquarium ■ **~ d'eau de mer** oceanarium.

aquatique [akwatik] *adj* aquatic, water (*modif*).

aquavit [akwavit] *nm* aquavit.

aqueduc [akdyk] *nm* **1.** [conduit] aqueduct **2.** ANAT duct.

aqueux, euse [akø, øz] *adj* **1.** ANAT & CHIM aqueous **2.** [plein d'eau] watery.

aquifère [akɥifɛr] *adj* water-bearing, aquiferous *spéc*, ▷ **nappe**.

aquilin [akilɛ̃] *adj m* aquiline.

aquilon [akilɔ̃] *nm* *litt* north wind.

aquitain, e [akitɛ̃, ɛn] *adj* from Aquitaine, Aquitaine (*modif*).
◆ **Aquitaine** *npr f* : **(l')Aquitaine** Aquitaine.

AQUITAINE

This administrative region includes the *départements* of Dordogne, Gironde, Landes, Lot-et-Garonne and Pyrénées-Atlantiques (capital: Bordeaux).

AR[1] **1.** = **accusé de réception** **2.** = **arrière**.

AR[2]**, A-R** (*abr écrite de* **aller-retour**) R.

ara [ara] *nm* macaw.

arabe [arab] *adj* [cheval, pays] Arab, Arabian ▪ **chiffres ~s** Arabic numerals, Arabics.
◆ **Arabe** *nmf* Arab.
◆ **arabe** *nm* LING Arabic ▪ **~ dialectal/littéral** vernacular/written Arabic.

ARABE

Note that in a French context this word usually refers to people from North Africa (Algeria, Morocco, Tunisia).

arabesque [arabɛsk] *nf* ART & DANSE arabesque.

arabica [arabika] *nm* arabica.

Arabie [arabi] *npr f* : **(l')~** Arabia ▪ **(l')~ Saoudite** Saudi Arabia.

arabique [arabik] *adj* arabic.

arabisant, e [arabizɑ̃, ɑ̃t] ◇ *adj* Arabic.
◇ *nm, f* Arabist, Arabic scholar.

arabisation [arabizasjɔ̃] *nf* arabization.

arabisme [arabism] *nm* Arabism.

arable [arabl] *adj* arable.

arabophone [arabɔfɔn] ◇ *adj* Arabic-speaking.
◇ *nmf* Arabic speaker.

arachide [araʃid] *nf* peanut, groundnut *spéc.*

arachnéen, enne [arakneɛ̃, ɛn] *adj* **1.** *litt* [dentelle] gossamer *(modif)*, gossamery **2.** ZOOL arachnidan.

arachnide [araknid] *nm* arachnid.

araignée [areɲe] *nf* ZOOL spider ▪ **~ (de mer)** spider crab ▪ **avoir une ~ au plafond** *fam hum* to have bats in the belfry.

araire [arɛr] *nm* swing-plough.

arak [arak] *nm* arak, arrack.

Aral [aral] *npr* : **la mer d'~** the Aral Sea.

araméen, enne [arameɛ̃, ɛn] *adj* Aramaic, Aramean, Aramaean.
◆ **Araméen, enne** *nm, f* Aramean, Aramaean.
◆ **araméen** *nm* LING Aramaic.

Ararat [ararat] *npr* : **le mont ~** Mount Ararat.

arasement [arazmɑ̃] *nm* **1.** CONSTR [égalisation - d'un mur] levelling ; [- d'une planche] planing down ▪ [assise] levelling course **2.** GÉOL erosion.

araser [3] [araze] *vt* **1.** [égaliser - mur] to level, to make level *ou* flush ; [- planche] to plane down *(sép)* **2.** GÉOL to erode.

aratoire [aratwar] *adj* ploughing.

arbalète [arbalɛt] *nf* crossbow.

arbalétrier [arbaletrije] *nm* **1.** [soldat] crossbowman **2.** ORNITH black martin **3.** CONSTR rafter.

arbitrage [arbitraʒ] *nm* **1.** DR arbitration ▪ **recourir à l'~** to go to arbitration **2.** SPORT [gén] refereeing ▪ [au volley-ball, tennis, cricket] umpiring **3.** BOURSE arbitrage.

arbitraire [arbitrɛr] ◇ *adj* [choix, arrestation] arbitrary.
◇ *nm* arbitrariness, arbitrary nature.

arbitrairement [arbitrɛrmɑ̃] *adv* arbitrarily.

arbitral, e, aux [arbitral, o] *adj* **1.** DR arbitral **2.** SPORT : **décision ~e** referee's *ou* umpire's decision.

arbitre [arbitr] *nmf* **1.** DR arbiter, arbitrator ▪ **exercer un rôle d'~** to act as arbitrator, to arbitrate **2.** SPORT [gén] referee ▪ [au volley-ball, tennis, cricket] umpire **3.** PHILOS : **libre ~** free will.

arbitrer [3] [arbitre] *vt* **1.** [différend] to arbitrate, to settle by arbitration ▪ **il ne reste plus qu'à faire ~ votre différend par le directeur** the only option left is to ask the director to settle your dispute **2.** SPORT [gén] to referee ▪ [au volley-ball, tennis, cricket] to umpire **3.** BOURSE [valeurs] to carry out an arbitrage operation on.

arboré, e [arbɔre] *adj* planted with trees, wooded, arboreous *spéc.*

arborer [3] [arbɔre] *vt* **1.** [porter - veste, insigne] to sport, to wear ; [- drapeau] to bear, to display **2.** [afficher - sourire] to wear ; [- manchette, titre] to carry.

arborescence [arbɔresɑ̃s] *nf* [forme] arborescence ▪ tree (structure) ▪ [diagramme] tree diagram.

arborescent, e [arbɔresɑ̃, ɑ̃t] *adj* arborescent.

arboricole [arbɔrikɔl] *adj* **1.** HORT arboricultural **2.** ZOOL tree-dwelling, arboreal *spéc.*

arboriculteur, trice [arbɔrikyltœr, tris] *nm, f* tree grower, arboriculturist *spéc.*

arboriculture [arbɔrikyltyr] *nf* arboriculture ▪ **~ fruitière** cultivation of fruit trees.

arborisé, e [arbɔrize] *adj* *Suisse* **une plaine ~e** a plain dotted with trees.

arbouse [arbuz] *nf* arbutus berry.

arbousier [arbuzje] *nm* arbutus.

arbre [arbr] *nm* **1.** BOT tree ▪ **~ à caoutchouc** rubber tree ▪ **~ fruitier** fruit tree ▪ **~ généalogique** family tree ▪ **~ de Noël** Christmas tree ▪ **~ à pain** breadfruit ▪ **l'~ de la science du bien et du mal** BIBLE the tree of knowledge ▪ **les ~s cachent la forêt** you can't see the wood *UK ou* forest *US* for the trees **2.** MÉCAN shaft ▪ **~ moteur** *ou* **de couche** engine shaft ▪ **~ de transmission** drive *ou* propeller shaft.
◆ **arbre de vie** *nm* **1.** BOT thuya **2.** ANAT arbor vitae **3.** BIBLE tree of life.

arbrisseau, x [arbriso] *nm* shrub.

arbuste [arbyst] *nm* shrub, bush.

arc [ark] *nm* **1.** ARM bow **2.** MATH arc ▪ **~ de cercle** arc of a circle ▪ **être assis en ~ de cercle** to be seated in a semicircle **3.** ANAT arch **4.** PHYS : **~ électrique** electric arc **5.** ARCHIT arch ▪ **~ brisé** pointed arch ▪ **~ en fer à cheval/en plein cintre** horseshoe/semicircular arch ▪ **~ en ogive** ogee arch ▪ **l'~ de triomphe (de l'Étoile)** the Arc de Triomphe.
◆ **à arc** *loc adj* [lampe, soudure] arc *(modif).*

ARC [ark] (*abr de* **Association de Recherche sur le Cancer**) *nf* *French national cancer research charity.*

arcade [arkad] *nf* **1.** ARCHIT archway ▪ **des ~s** arches, an arcade **2.** ANAT arch ▪ **~ sourcilière** arch of the eyebrows ▪ **il s'est ouvert l'~ sourcilière** he was cut above the eye.

arcane [arkan] *nm* [secret] mystery, arcanum *litt* ▪ **les ~s de la politique/de la science** the mysteries of politics/of science.

arc-boutant [arkbutɑ̃] (*pl* **arcs-boutants**) *nm* flying buttress.

arc-bouter [3] [arkbute] *vt* [mur] to buttress.
◆ **s'arc-bouter** *vpi* to brace o.s. ▪ **s'~ contre un mur** to brace one's back against a wall.

arceau, x [arso] *nm* **1.** ARCHIT arch (of vault) **2.** MÉD cradle.

arc-en-ciel [arkɑ̃sjɛl] (*pl* **arcs-en-ciel**) *nm* rainbow.

archaïque [arkaik] *adj* **1.** [vieux] archaic, outmoded, antiquated **2.** ART & LING archaic.

archaïsant, e [arkaizɑ̃, ɑ̃t] ◇ *adj* archaistic.
◇ *nm, f* archaist.

archaïsme [arkaism] *nm* [mot] archaism, archaic term ▪ [tournure] archaism, archaic turn of phrase.

archange [arkɑ̃ʒ] *nm* archangel.

arche [arʃ] *nf* **1.** ARCHIT arch ▪ **la Grande Arche (de La Défense)** *large office block at La Défense near Paris, shaped like a square archway* **2.** RELIG ark ▪ **l'~ d'alliance** the Ark of the Covenant ▪ **l'~ de Noé** Noah's Ark.

archéologie [arkeɔlɔʒi] *nf* archeology, archaeology.

archéologique [arkeɔlɔʒik] *adj* archeological, archaeological.

archéologue [arkeɔlɔg] *nmf* archeologist, archaeologist.

archer [arʃe] *nm* archer, bowman.

archet [arʃɛ] *nm* MUS bow ■ **avoir un excellent coup d'~** to be an outstanding violonist.

archétypal, e, aux [arketipal] *adj* archetypal.

archétype [arketip] *nm* **1.** [symbole] archetype **2.** BIOL prototype.

archevêché [arʃəveʃe] *nm* **1.** [fonction, territoire] archbishopric **2.** [palais] archbishop's palace.

archevêque [arʃəvɛk] *nm* archbishop.

archi [arʃi] *fam* ◇ *nf* = **architecture.**
◇ *nmf* = **architecte.**

archidiacre [arʃidjakr] *nm* archdeacon.

archidiocèse [arʃidjɔsɛz] *nm* archdiocese.

archiduc [arʃidyk] *nm* archduke.

archiduchesse [arʃidyʃɛs] *nf* archduchess.

archiépiscopat [arʃiepiskɔpa] *nm* archiepiscopate.

Archimède [arʃimɛd] *npr* Archimedes.

archipel [arʃipɛl] *nm* archipelago.

archiplein, e [arʃiplɛ̃, ɛn] *adj fam* [train, salle] jam-packed.

archiprêtre [arʃiprɛtr] *nm* archpriest.

archiréussi, e [arʃireysi] *adj fam* : **c'était ~** it was a great success.

architecte [arʃitɛkt] *nmf* **1.** ARCHIT architect ■ **avoir un diplôme d'~** to have a degree in architecture ▶ **~ d'intérieur** interior designer ■ **~ naval** naval architect ■ **~ paysagiste** landscape architect ■ **~ urbaniste** town planner *UK*, city planner *US* **2.** *fig* [d'une réforme, d'une politique] architect.

architectonique [arʃitɛktɔnik] *nf* architectonics *(U)*.

architectural, e, aux [arʃitɛktyral, o] *adj* architectural.

architecture [arʃitɛktyr] *nf* **1.** [art, style] architecture ■ **~ d'intérieur** interior design **2.** [structure - d'une œuvre d'art] structure, architecture **3.** INFORM architecture.

architecturer [3] [arʃitɛktyre] *vt* to structure.

architrave [arʃitrav] *nf* architrave.

archivage [arʃivaʒ] *nm* filing *ou* storing (away).

archiver [3] [arʃive] *vt* **1.** [document, revue] to file *ou* to store (away) **2.** INFORM archive.

archives [arʃiv] *nfpl* **1.** [documents] archives, records ■ **~ familiales** family records ■ INFORM archive **2.** [lieu] record office ■ **les Archives départementales** the French Local Historical Archives ■ **les Archives nationales** the French Historical Archives, ≃ the Public Record Office *UK* ■ ≃ the National Archives *US*.
◆ **d'archives** *loc adj* library *(modif)* ■ **copie d'~** INFORM archive file.

LES ARCHIVES NATIONALES

The French Historical Archives, which house all legal documents concerning the history of France, were created in 1789. They are open to the public and located in the Marais in Paris.

LES ARCHIVES DÉPARTEMENTALES

The *Archives départementales* collect and make available documents issued by the local administration, notably registry documents from *communes*. They can be consulted by genealogists, historians, students and anybody interested.

archiviste [arʃivist] *nmf* archivist.

arçon [arsɔ̃] *nm* saddletree.

arctique [arktik] *adj* Arctic.
◆ **Arctique** *npr m* : **l'Arctique** the Arctic (Ocean).

ardéchois, e [ardeʃwa, az] *adj* from the Ardèche.

ardemment [ardamɑ̃] *adv* ardently, fervently, passionately ■ **désirer qqch ~** to yearn for *ou* to crave sthg.

ardennais, e [ardənɛ, ɛz] *adj* from the Ardennes.

ardeur [ardœr] *nf* **1.** [fougue] passion, ardour, fervour ■ **soutenir une cause avec ~** to support a cause ardently *ou* fervently *ou* passionately ■ **il n'a jamais montré une grande ~ au travail** he's never shown much enthusiasm for work ■ **modérez vos ~s!** *hum* control yourself! **2.** *litt* [chaleur] (burning) heat.

ardillon [ardijɔ̃] *nm* tongue *(of a belt buckle)*.

ardoise [ardwaz] *nf* **1.** [matière] slate ■ **toit d'~s** *ou* **en ~s** slate roof **2.** [objet] slate ■ **~ magique** magic slate **3.** *fam* [compte] bill, slate ■ **on a une ~ de 300 euros chez le boucher** we've run up a bill of 300 euros at the butcher's.

ardoisé, e [ardwaze] *adj* slate-grey.

ardu, e [ardy] *adj* [difficile - problème, question] tough, difficult ; [- tâche] arduous, hard.

are [ar] *nm* are, hundred square metres.

aréna [arena] *nm* **Québec** *sports centre with skating rink*, arena *US*.

arène [arɛn] *nf* **1.** [pour la corrida] bullring ■ **descendre** *ou* **entrer dans l'~** *fig* to enter the fray *ou* the arena **2.** [sable] arenite, sand.
◆ **arènes** *nfpl* ANTIQ amphitheatre.

arénicole [arenikɔl] ◇ *adj* sand-dwelling, arenicolous *spéc*.
◇ *nf* sandworm, lugworm.

aréopage [areɔpaʒ] *nm* learned assembly *ou* gathering ■ **l'Aréopage** ANTIQ the Areopagus.

arête [arɛt] *nf* **1.** [de poisson] (fish) bone ■ **enlever les ~s d'un poisson** to bone a fish ■ **poisson plein d'~s** fish full of bones, bony fish **2.** [angle - d'un toit] arris ; [- d'un cube] edge ; [- d'une voûte] groin **3.** ANAT : **l'~ du nez** the bridge of the nose **4.** GÉOGR crest, ridge **5.** BOT beard.

areu [arø] *interj langage enfantin* **~~!** goo-goo!

argent [arʒɑ̃] ◇ *nm* **1.** [métal] silver **2.** [monnaie] money ■ **avoir de l'~** to have money, to be wealthy ■ **une famille qui a de l'~** a well-to-do family ■ **(se) faire de l'~** to make money ■ **l'~ lui fond dans les mains** money just runs through his fingers ▶ **~ comptant : payer** *ou* **régler en ~ comptant** to pay cash ■ **accepter** *ou* **prendre qqch pour ~ comptant** to take sthg at face value ■ **~ liquide** ready cash *ou* money ■ **~ de poche** pocket money ■ **se faire de l'~ de poche** to make a bit of extra money ■ **l'~ sale** dirty money ■ **en avoir pour son ~ : tu en auras pour ton ~** you'll get your money's worth, you'll get value for money ■ **en être pour son ~** to end up out of pocket ■ **jeter l'~ par les fenêtres** to throw money down the drain, to squander money ■ **l'~ n'a pas** *ou* **point d'odeur** *prov* it's all money! ■ **l'~ ne fait pas le bonheur** *prov* money can't buy happiness ■ **l'~ (trouvé) n'a pas de maître** *prov* money knows no master ■ **le temps, c'est de l'~** *prov* time is money **3.** [couleur] silver colour **4.** HÉRALD argent.
◇ *adj inv* silver, silver-coloured.
◆ **d'argent** *loc adj* **1.** [en métal] silver *(modif)* **2.** [couleur] silver, silvery, silver-coloured **3.** [pécuniaire] money *(modif)* **4.** [intéressé] : **homme/femme d'~** man/woman for whom money matters.
◆ **en argent** *loc adj* silver *(modif)*.

argenté, e [arʒɑ̃te] *adj* **1.** [renard] silver *(modif)* ■ [tempes] silver, silvery **2.** [plaqué] silver-plated, silver *(modif)* ■ **métal ~** silver plate **3.** *fam* [fortuné] well-heeled ■ **on n'était pas très ~s à l'époque** we weren't very well-off *ou* we were rather hard up at the time.

argenter [3] [arʒɑ̃te] *vt* **1.** [miroir] to silver ■ [cuillère] to plate, to silver-plate **2.** *litt* [faire briller] : **la lune argentait la mer** the moon turned the sea silver.

argenterie [arʒɑ̃tri] *nf* silver, silverware.

argentier [arʒɑ̃tje] *nm* **1.** [meuble] silver cabinet **2.** *fam* **le Grand ~** [ministre] the Finance Minister.

argentifère [arʒɑ̃tifɛr] *adj* silver-bearing, argentiferous *spéc*.

argentin[1], e [arʒɑ̃tɛ̃, in] *adj* [son] silvery.

argentin², e [arʒɑ̃tɛ̃, in] *adj* GÉOGR Argentinian, Argentine.
◆ **Argentin, e** *nm, f* Argentinian, Argentine.

Argentine [arʒɑ̃tin] *npr f* : **(l')~** Argentina, the Argentine.

argentique [arʒɑ̃tik] *adj* traditional, non-digital.

argenture [arʒɑ̃tyr] *nf* silvering.

argile [arʒil] *nf* clay.

argileux, euse [arʒilø, øz] *adj* clayey, clayish.

argon [argɔ̃] *nm* argon.

argonaute [argɔnot] *nm* argonaut, paper nautilus.

Argonautes [argɔnot] *npr mpl* : **les ~** the Argonauts.

argot [argo] *nm* slang, argot ■ **~ de métier** jargon.

argotique [argɔtik] *adj* slang *(modif)*, slangy.

argotisme [argɔtism] *nm* [mot] slang word ■ [tournure] slang expression.

arguer [8] [arg(ɥ)e] *vt* **1.** [conclure] to deduce **2.** [prétexter] : **~ que...** to put forward the fact that... ■ **arguant qu'il avait une mauvaise vue** pleading his poor eyesight.
◆ **arguer de** *v+prép* to use as an excuse, to plead ■ **il s'en est tiré en arguant de son ignorance** he got away with it by putting forward *ou* using his ignorance as an excuse.

argument [argymɑ̃] *nm* **1.** [raison] argument ■ **ses ~s** his reasoning ■ **des ~s pour et contre** *ou* **dans les deux sens** pros and cons ■ **présenter ses ~s** to state one's case ■ **avoir de bons/solides ~s** to have a good/strong case **2.** COMM : **~ de vente** selling point **3.** LITTÉR [sommaire] general description, outline.

argumentaire [argymɑ̃tɛr] *nm* COMM promotion leaflet.

argumentation [argymɑ̃tasjɔ̃] *nf* **1.** [raisonnement] argumentation, rationale **2.** [fait d'argumenter] reasoning.

argumenter [3] [argymɑ̃te] ◇ *vi* **1.** [débattre] to argue ■ **~ en faveur de/contre qqch** to argue for/against sthg **2.** [ergoter] to be argumentative, to quibble.
◇ *vt* [texte, démonstration] to support with (relevant) arguments ■ **motion bien/mal argumentée** impressively/poorly argued motion.

argus [argys] *nm* **1.** PRESSE : **l'~ de l'automobile** the price guide for used cars **2.** ORNITH argus pheasant **3.** *litt* [gardien] guardian.

argutie [argysi] *nf* quibble ■ **~s** quibbling, hairsplitting.

aria [arja] ◇ *nf* MUS aria.
◇ *nm vieilli* [souci, tracas] nuisance.

Ariane [arjan] *npr* Ariadne ■ **le fil d'~** Ariadne's clew.

aride [arid] *adj* **1.** [sec - terre] arid, barren ; [- vent] dry ; [- cœur] unfeeling **2.** [difficile - sujet] arid, dull.

aridité [aridite] *nf* **1.** [du sol] aridity, barrenness ■ [du vent] dryness **2.** [d'un sujet] aridity *sout*, dullness.

ariégeois, e [arjeʒwa, az] *adj* from the Ariège.

aristo [aristo] *fam* ◇ *adj* aristocratic.
◇ *nmf* aristocrat ■ **les ~s** the upper crust.

aristocrate [aristɔkrat] ◇ *adj* aristocratic.
◇ *nmf* aristocrat ■ **une famille d'~s** an aristocratic family.

aristocratie [aristɔkrasi] *nf* aristocracy.

aristocratique [aristɔkratik] *adj* aristocratic.

Aristophane [aristɔfan] *npr* Aristophanes.

Aristote [aristɔt] *npr* Aristotle.

aristotélicien, enne [aristɔtelisjɛ̃, ɛn] *adj* & *nm, f* Aristotelian.

arithmétique [aritmetik] ◇ *adj* MATH [moyenne, progression] arithmetical.
◇ *nf* **1.** [matière] arithmetic **2.** [livre] arithmetic book.

Arizona [arizɔna] *npr m* : **l'~** Arizona.

Arkansas [arkɑ̃sas] *npr m* : **l'~** Arkansas.

arlequin [arlәkɛ̃] *nm* Harlequin.

Arlequin [arlәkɛ̃] *npr* Harlequin.

arlésien, enne [arlezjɛ̃, ɛn] *adj* from Arles.
◆ **Arlésien, enne** *nm, f inhabitant of or person from Arles* ■ **les Arlésiens** the people of Arles.
◆ **arlésienne** *nf fam* **sa copine/ce ministre, c'est l'~ne!** does this much talked-about girlfriend/minister REALLY exist?

armada [armada] *nf* **1.** [quantité] : **une ~ de touristes** an army of tourists **2.** HIST : **l'(Invincible) Armada** the Spanish Armada.

armagnac [armaɲak] *nm* Armagnac (brandy).

armailli [armaji] *nm Suisse* shepherd *(in Fribourg)*.

armateur [armatœr] *nm* [propriétaire - d'un navire] ship owner ; [- d'une flotte] fleet owner ■ [locataire] shipper.

armature [armatyr] *nf* **1.** [cadre - d'une tente, d'un abat-jour] frame ■ [structure - d'un exposé, d'une théorie] basis, framework **2.** CONSTR framework **3.** COUT underwiring ■ **soutien-gorge à ~** underwired bra **4.** MUS key signature.

arme [arm] *nf* **1.** [objet] weapon ■ **porter une ~ sur soi** to carry a weapon ■ **l'~ chimique/nucléaire** chemical/nuclear weapons ■ **~ blanche** knife ■ **~ à feu** firearm ■ **~ de poing** handgun ■ **~ de service** [d'un policier] service gun ■ **passer l'~ à gauche** *fam* to kick the bucket **2.** [armée] force, service ■ **l'~ de l'artillerie** the artillery **3.** [instrument] weapon ■ **une bonne ~ psychologique** a good psychological weapon ■ **~ à double tranchant** *fig* double-edged sword ■ **le pouvoir est une ~ à double tranchant** power is a double-edged sword ■ **tu lui as donné une ~ contre toi** you've given her a stick to beat you with.
◆ **armes** *nfpl* **1.** [matériel de guerre] arms, weapons, weaponry ■ **aux ~s!** to arms! ■ **porter les ~s** to be a soldier ■ **portez/présentez/reposez ~s!** shoulder/present/order arms! ■ **prendre les ~s** to take up arms ■ **régler** *ou* **résoudre qqch par les ~s** to settle sthg by force ➊ **~s conventionnelles** conventional weapons ■ **~s de guerre** weapons of war, weaponry ■ **passer qqn par les ~s** to send sb to the firing squad ■ **faire ses premières ~s** to start out, begin one's career ■ **mettre bas** *ou* **déposer** *ou* **rendre les ~s** to lay down one's arms ■ **partir avec ~s et bagages** to up sticks and leave **2.** ESCRIME fencing **3.** HÉRALD coat of arms.
◆ **à armes égales** *loc adv* on equal terms.
◆ **aux armes de** *loc prép* bearing the arms of HÉRALD.
◆ **d'armes** *loc adj* : **frère d'~s** brother-in-arms.

armé, e [arme] *adj* **1.** [personne] armed ■ **attention, il est ~** watch out, he's armed *ou* he's carrying a weapon! ■ **~ jusqu'aux dents** armed to the teeth ■ **~ de...** armed with... ■ **bien/mal ~ contre le froid** well-protected/defenceless against the cold ■ **mal ~ (pour lutter) contre la concurrence** defenceless in the face of the competition **2.** CONSTR reinforced.
◆ **armé** *nm* cock.
◆ **armée** *nf* **1.** MIL army ■ **être dans l'~e** to be in the army ■ **être à l'~e** to be doing one's military service ➊ **~e active** *ou* **régulière** regular army ■ **l'~e de l'air** the Air Force ■ **l'~e de mer** the Navy ■ **~e de métier** professional army ■ **~e nationale** conscript army ■ **~e d'occupation** army of occupation ■ **~e de réserve** reserves ■ **l'Armée rouge** the Red Army ■ **l'Armée du Salut** the Salvation Army ■ **l'~e de terre** the Army **2.** *fig* army, host ■ **une ~e de figurants/sauterelles** an army of extras/grasshoppers.

armement [armәmɑ̃] *nm* **1.** [militarisation - d'un pays, d'un groupe] arming **2.** NAUT commissioning, fitting-out **3.** [d'un appareil photo] winding (on) ■ [d'un pistolet] cocking **4.** [armes] arms, weapons, weaponry ■ **limitation** *ou* **réduction des ~s stratégiques** strategic arms limitation.

Arménie [armeni] *npr f* : **(l')~** Armenia.

arménien, enne [armenjɛ̃, ɛn] *adj* Armenian.
◆ **Arménien, enne** *nm, f* Armenian.
◆ **arménien** *nm* LING Armenian.

armer [3] [arme] *vt* **1.** MIL [guérilla, nation] to arm, to supply with weapons *ou* arms ■ **~ qqn chevalier** to knight sb, to dub sb a knight **2.** *fig* [préparer] to arm **3.** ARM to cock **4.** PHOTO to wind (on) *(sép)* **5.** NAUT to commission, to fit out *(sép)* **6.** CONSTR [béton, ciment] to reinforce **7.** TECHNOL [câble] to sheathe.

◆ **s'armer** *vp (emploi réfléchi)* [prendre une arme - policier, détective] to arm o.s. ; [- nation] to arm.
◆ **s'armer de** *vp+prép* **1.** [s'équiper de - arme] to arm o.s. with ; [- instrument] to equip o.s. with **2.** *fig* [prendre] : **s'~ de courage/patience** to muster *ou* summon up one's courage/patience.

armistice [armistis] *nm* armistice ▪ **(l'anniversaire de) l'Armistice** Armistice *ou* Remembrance Day *UK*, Veteran's Day *US*.

armoire [armwar] *nf* wardrobe, closet *US* ▪ **~ frigorifique** cold room *ou* store ▪ **~ à glace** *pr* mirrored wardrobe ▪ **c'est une véritable ~ à glace** *fig & hum* he's built like the side of a house ▪ **~ à linge** linen cupboard *ou* closet ▪ **~ normande** large wardrobe ▪ **~ à pharmacie** medicine cabinet *ou* chest.

armoiries [armwari] *nfpl* coat of arms, armorial bearings.
◆ **aux armoiries de** *loc prép* bearing the arms of.

armoricain, e [armɔrikɛ̃, ɛn] *adj* Armorican.

armorier [9] [armɔrje] *vt* to emblazon ▪ **~ qqch de** to emblazon sthg with.

Armorique [armɔrik] *npr f* : **(l')~** Armorica.

armure [armyr] *nf* **1.** HIST armour ▪ **vêtu de son ~** armour-clad **2.** [protection] defence.

armurerie [armyrri] *nf* **1.** [activité] arms trade **2.** [magasin] armourer's, gunsmith's **3.** [usine] arms factory.

armurier [armyrje] *nm* **1.** [fabricant] gunsmith, armourer **2.** MIL armourer.

ARN (*abr de* **acide ribonucléique**) *nm* RNA.

arnaque [arnak] *nf fam* swindle, rip-off.

arnaquer [3] [arnake] *vt fam* [duper] to rip off *(sép)* ▪ **~ qqn de 1 000 euros** to do sb out of 1,000 euros.

arnaqueur [arnakœr] *nm fam* swindler, rip-off merchant.

arnica [arnika] *nm ou nf* arnica.

arobase [arɔbaz] *nm* INFORM 'at', @ ▪ **l'~** the 'at' symbol *ou* sign.

aromate [arɔmat] *nm* [herbe] herb ▪ [condiment] spice ▪ **~s** seasoning.

aromathérapie [arɔmaterapi] *nf* MÉD aromatherapy.

aromatique [arɔmatik] ◇ *adj* aromatic, fragrant.
◇ *nm* CHIM aromatic compound.

aromatiser [3] [arɔmatize] *vt* to flavour ▪ **chocolat aromatisé au rhum** chocolate flavoured with rum, rum-flavoured chocolate.

arôme [arom] *nm* [parfum] aroma, fragrance ▪ [goût] flavour ▪ **~ artificiel** artificial flavouring.

arpège [arpɛʒ] *nm* arpeggio.

arpent [arpɑ̃] *nm arch* ≃ acre ▪ **un petit ~ de terre** a few acres *ou* a patch of land.

arpentage [arpɑ̃taʒ] *nm* land-surveying, land-measuring.

arpenter [3] [arpɑ̃te] *vt* **1.** [parcourir - couloir] to pace up and down **2.** [mesurer] to survey, to measure.

arpenteur [arpɑ̃tœr] *nm* : **~-géomètre** surveyor, land-surveyor.

arqué, e [arke] *adj* [sourcils] arched ▪ [nez] hooked ▪ [jambes] bandy, bow *(modif)* ▪ **aux jambes ~es** bandy-legged, bow-legged.

arquebuse [arkəbyz] *nf* arquebus, harquebus.

arquebusier [arkəbyzje] *nm* arquebusier, harquebusier.

arquer [3] [arke] *vt* [courber - planche] to bend, to curve ; [- dos] to arch.
◆ **s'arquer** *vpi* to bend, to curve.

arrachage [araʃaʒ] *nm* [d'une plante] pulling up, uprooting ▪ [de pommes de terre] lifting ▪ **l'~ des mauvaises herbes** weeding.

arraché [araʃe] *nm* SPORT snatch ▪ **gagner à l'~** *fig* to snatch a victory ▪ **une victoire à l'~** a hard-won victory.

arrache-clou [araʃklu] (*pl* **arrache-clous**) *nm* nail-wrench.

arrachement [araʃmɑ̃] *nm* **1.** [fait d'enlever - plante] uprooting, pulling out ; [- feuille, papier peint] ripping *ou* tearing out **2.** *fig* [déchirement] wrench ▪ **quitter notre pays fut un véritable ~** it was a wrench *ou* it was heart-rending to leave our country.

arrache-pied [araʃpje] ◆ **d'arrache-pied** *loc adv* [travailler] relentlessly.

arracher [3] [araʃe] *vt* **1.** [extraire - clou, cheville] to pull *ou* to draw out *(sép)* ; [- arbuste] to pull *ou* to root up *(sép)* ; [- betterave, laitue] to lift ; [- mauvaises herbes, liseron] to pull *ou* to root out *(sép)* ; [- poil, cheveu] to pull out *(sép)* ; [- dent] to pull out *(sép)*, to draw, to extract ▪ **se faire ~ une dent** to have a tooth out ▪ **il a eu un bras arraché dans l'explosion** he had an arm blown off in the explosion ▪ **ça arrache la gorge** *fam fig* it burns your throat ▪ **il t'aracherait les yeux s'il savait** he'd tear *ou* scratch your eyes out if he knew ▪ **~ son masque à qqn** to unmask sb
2. [déchirer - papier peint, affiche] to tear *ou* to rip off *(sép)* ; [- page] to tear out *(sép)*, to pull out *(sép)*
3. [prendre - sac, billet] to snatch, to grab ▪ **j'ai réussi à lui ~ le pistolet des mains** [très vite] I managed to snatch the gun away *ou* to grab the gun from him ; [après une lutte] I managed to wrest the gun from his grip ▪ [obtenir - victoire] to snatch ▪ **~ des aveux/une signature à qqn** to wring a confession/signature out of sb ▪ **~ des larmes à qqn** to bring tears to sb's eyes ▪ **~ un sourire à qqn** to force a smile out of sb ▪ **pas moyen de lui ~ le moindre commentaire** it's impossible to get him to say anything
4. [enlever - personne] : **~ qqn à son lit** to drag sb out of *ou* from his bed ▪ **comment l'~ à son ordinateur?** how can we get *ou* drag him away from his computer? ▪ **arraché très jeune à sa famille** torn from the bosom of his family at an early age *litt* ▪ **~ un bébé à sa mère** to take a child from its mother ▪ **~ qqn au sommeil** to force sb to wake up
5. [le sauver de] : **~ qqn à** to snatch *ou* to rescue sb from ▪ **~ qqn à la mort** to snatch sb from (the jaws of) death.
◆ **s'arracher** ◇ *vpt* **1.** [s'écorcher] : **je me suis arraché la peau du genou en tombant** I fell over and scraped my knee ▶ **c'est à s'~ les cheveux** *fam* it's enough to drive you crazy ▪ **s'~ les yeux** to scratch each other's eyes out
2. [se disputer - personne, héritage] to fight over *(insép)*.
◇ *vpi*^△ [partir] : **allez, on s'arrache!** come on, let's be off!
◆ **s'arracher à, s'arracher de** *vp+prép* to tear o.s. away from ▪ **s'~ au sommeil** to tear o.s. from sleep ▪ **s'~ à ses rêveries** to snap out of one's daydreams ▪ **s'~ à son travail/à son ordinateur/de son fauteuil** to tear o.s. away from one's work/computer/armchair.

arracheur [araʃœr] *nm arch* **~ de dents** tooth-puller.

arraisonnement [arɛzɔnmɑ̃] *nm* boarding (for inspection) NAUT.

arraisonner [3] [arɛzɔne] *vt* [navire] to board (for inspection) NAUT.

arrangeable [arɑ̃ʒabl] *adj* [difficulté] which can be settled ▪ [projet, voyage] which can be fixed *ou* arranged.

arrangeant, e [arɑ̃ʒɑ̃, ɑ̃t] *adj* accommodating, obliging.

arrangement [arɑ̃ʒmɑ̃] *nm* **1.** [fait de disposer] arrangement, laying out ▪ [résultat] arrangement, layout **2.** [accord] arrangement, settlement ▪ **parvenir à un ~** to reach an agreement, to come to an arrangement ▪ **~ à l'amiable** amicable settlement ▪ **nous avons un ~** we have an understanding ▪ **c'était un ~ entre nous** we'd agreed it between ourselves ▪ **sauf ~ contraire** unless otherwise agreed ▶ **~ de famille** DR family settlement *(in financial disputes)* **3.** MUS arrangement.

arranger [17] [arɑ̃ʒe] *vt* **1.** [mettre en ordre - chignon] to tidy up *(sép)* ; [- tenue] to straighten ; [- bouquet] to arrange ; [- chambre] to lay out *(sép)*, to arrange ▪ **il a bien arrangé son appartement** his appartment is nicely laid out

2. [organiser - rencontre, entrevue] to arrange, to fix ; [- emploi du temps] to organize ▪ **c'est Paul qui a arrangé la cérémonie/l'exposition** Paul organized the ceremony/put the exhibition together ▪ **~ qqch à l'avance** to prearrange sthg
3. [résoudre - dispute, conflit] to settle, to sort out *(sép)* ▪ **c'est arrangé, tu peux partir** it's all settled, you're free to leave now ▪ **et mes rhumatismes n'arrangent pas les choses** *ou* **n'arrangent rien à l'affaire** my rheumatism doesn't help matters either ▪ **voilà qui n'arrange pas mes affaires!** that's all I needed!
4. MUS to arrange
5. [convenir à] to suit ▪ **ce soir ou demain, comme ça t'arrange** tonight or tomorrow, as it suits you *ou* as is convenient for you ▪ **mardi? non, ça ne m'arrange pas** Tuesday? no, that's no good for me ▪ **on ne peut pas ~ tout le monde** you can't please everybody
6. *fam* [réparer - radio, réveil, voiture] to fix ; [- chaussures] to fix, to mend ; [- robe] to alter
7. [modifier - histoire, récit] to alter, to modify ▪ **je ne t'ai jamais rien promis, tu arranges l'histoire (à ta façon)** I never promised you anything, you're just twisting things
8. *fam* [maltraiter] to sort out *UK (sép)*, to work over *(sép)*.
➤ **s'arranger** ◇ *vp (emploi réfléchi)* **1.** [s'habiller, se maquiller] **: elle sait s'~** she knows how to make the best of herself
2. [se faire mal] **: tu t'es encore bien arrangé/bien arrangé la figure!** *fam iron* you've made a fine mess of yourself/your face again!
◇ *vp (emploi réciproque)* [se mettre d'accord] to come to an agreement.
◇ *vpi* **1.** [se débrouiller] to manage ▪ **s'~ pour : je me suis arrangé pour vous faire tous inviter** I've managed to get an invitation for all of you ▪ **il s'arrange toujours pour partir plus tôt** he always manages to leave early ▪ **on s'était arrangé pour que ce soit une surprise** we'd arranged it so that it would be a surprise
2. [s'améliorer - santé, temps] to improve, to get better ▪ **les choses s'arrangeront d'elles-mêmes** things'll sort themselves out *ou* take care of themselves ▪ **tout a fini par s'~** everything worked out fine in the end ▪ **tu ne t'arranges pas avec les années!** *hum* you're not getting any better in your old age!
3. [se dérouler] to turn out ▪ **comment ça s'est arrangé, tes histoires de bagnole?** *fam* what happened with your car then?
➤ **s'arranger avec** *vp+prép* to come to an agreement with ▪ **on s'est arrangé avec les voisins** we sorted something out with the neighbours ▪ **je m'arrangerai avec lui pour qu'il garde les enfants** I'll arrange for him to look after the children ▪ **il s'est arrangé à l'amiable avec ses créanciers** he came to an amicable agreement with his creditors ▪ **arrange-toi avec lui** you'll have to sort it out with him ▪ **je m'arrangerai avec ce que j'ai** I'll make do with what I've got.
➤ **s'arranger de** *vp+prép* to put up with, to make do with ▪ **ce n'est pas confortable, mais on s'en arrange** it's not comfortable, but we make do ▪ **il s'arrange de tout** he's very easygoing.

arrangeur [arɑ̃ʒœr] *nm* arranger.

arrdt = **arrondissement**.

arrérages [areraʒ] *nmpl* arrears.

arrestation [arɛstasjɔ̃] *nf* arrest ▪ **procéder à une ~** to make an arrest ▪ **être en état d'~** to be under arrest ▪ **se mettre en état d'~** to give o.s. up.

arrêt [arɛ] *nm* **1.** [interruption] stopping ▪ **~ momentané des programmes** temporary blackout ▪ **l'~ se fait automatiquement** it stops automatically ▪ **appuyer sur le bouton "~"** press the "stop" *ou* "halt" button ➊ **temps d'~** pause ▪ **marquer un temps d'~** to stop *ou* to pause for a moment ▪ **~ de travail** [grève] stoppage ; [congé] sick leave ; [certificat] doctor's *ou* medical certificate
2. TRANSP [pause] stop, halt ▪ **avant l'~ complet de l'appareil** before the aircraft has come to a complete stop *ou* standstill ▪ **ce train est sans ~ jusqu'à Arcueil** this train is non-stop *ou* goes straight through to Arcueil ▪ **en cas d'~ entre deux gares** if the train stops between stations ▪ **'~s fréquents'** 'slow deliveries' ▪ **'~ demandé'** 'stop requested' ‖ [lieu] **: ~ (d'autobus)** bus stop ▪ **je descends au prochain ~** I'm getting off at the next stop
3. SPORT **: faire un ~ du pied gauche** FOOTBALL to make a save with one's left foot ➊ **~ de jeu** stoppage ▪ **jouer les ~s de jeu** to play injury time
4. CINÉ & TV **: ~ sur image** freeze frame ▪ **faire un ~ sur image** to freeze a frame
5. MÉD **: ~ cardiaque** *ou* **du cœur** cardiac arrest, cardiac failure
6. COUT **: faire un ~** to fasten off
7. DR [décision] judgment, ruling ▪ **rendre un ~** to deliver *ou* to pronounce a judgment ➊ **~ de mort** death sentence ▪ **signer son ~ de mort** *fig* to sign one's own death warrant
8. [arrestation] arrest ▪ **faire ~ sur des marchandises** to seize *ou* to impound goods.
➤ **arrêts** *nmpl* MIL arrest ▪ **mettre qqn aux ~s** to place sb under arrest ➊ **~s forcés** *ou* **de rigueur** close arrest.
➤ **à l'arrêt** *loc adj* [véhicule] stationary ▪ **l'appareil est à l'~ sur la piste** the aircraft is at a standstill on the runway.
➤ **d'arrêt** *loc adj* **1.** TECHNOL [dispositif] stopping, stop *(modif)*
2. COUT **: point d'~** finishing-off stitch.
➤ **en arrêt** *loc adv* **: tomber en ~** [chien] to point ▪ **je suis tombé en ~ devant un magnifique vaisselier** I stopped short in front of a splendid dresser.
➤ **sans arrêt** *loc adv* [sans interruption] non-stop ▪ [à maintes reprises] constantly.

arrêté[1] [arete] *nm* **1.** [décret] order, decree ▪ **~ ministériel** ministerial order ▪ **~ municipal** ≃ by-law **2.** BANQUE **: ~ de compte** [bilan] statement of account ; [fermeture] settlement of account.

arrêté[2]**, e** [arete] *adj* [opinion] fixed, set ▪ [intention] firm.

arrêter [4] [arete] ◇ *vt* **1.** [empêcher d'avancer - passant, taxi] to stop ▪ **la circulation est arrêtée sur la N7** traffic is held up *ou* has come to a standstill on the N7 (road) ▪ **~ un ballon** SPORT to make a save, to save a goal ➊ **arrête ton char!** *fam hum* [je ne te crois pas] come off it! ; [arrête de te vanter] stop showing off!
2. [retenir - personne] to stop ; [- regard] to catch, to fix ▪ [interrompre] to interrupt ▪ **arrêtez-moi si je parle trop vite** stop me if I'm speaking too fast
3. [éteindre - radio, télévision] to turn off *(sép)* ; [- moteur] to stop, to switch off *(sép)*
4. [mettre fin à - élan] to stop, to check ; [- écoulement, saignement] to stem, to stop ; [- croissance, chute] to stop, to arrest, to bring to a halt ▪ **on n'arrête pas le progrès!** *fam hum* what will they think of next! ▪ **~ les frais** to stop messing about
5. [abandonner - construction, publication, traitement] to stop ; [- sport, chant] to give up *(sép)* ▪ [cesser de fabriquer] to discontinue (the manufacture of)
6. [suj: police] to arrest ▪ **se faire ~** to get *ou* be arrested
7. [déterminer - date, lieu] to appoint, to decide on *(insép)*, to fix ; [- plan, procédure] to decide on *(insép)*, to settle on *(insép)*, to settle upon *(insép)* ▪ **~ son choix** to make one's choice
8. [suj: médecin] **: ~ qqn** to put sb on sick leave ▪ **ça fait un mois que je suis arrêté** I've been on sick leave for a month
9. FIN **: ~ un compte** [le fermer] to close *ou* to settle an account ; [en faire un relevé] to draw up *ou* to make up a statement of account
10. COUT [point] to fasten off *(sép)* ▪ **~ les mailles** to cast off
11. [gibier] to point
12. INFORM [ordinateur] to shut down.
◇ *vi* **: arrête, tu me fais mal!** stop it, you're hurting me! ▪ **quatre albums en un an! mais vous n'arrêtez pas!** four albums in a year! you never stop *ou* you don't ever take a break, do you? ▪ **il a arrêté de travailler l'an dernier** he retired last year ▪ **j'ai arrêté de fumer** I've given up *ou* stopped smoking ▪ **~ de se droguer** to give up *ou* to come off drugs ▪ *(tournure impersonnelle)* **il n'a pas arrêté de neiger** it hasn't stopped snowing, it's been snowing non-stop.
➤ **s'arrêter** *vpi* **1.** [cesser - bruit, pluie, saignement] to stop ▪ **notre histoire ne s'arrête pas là** this isn't the end of our story ▪ **s'~ de** [cesser de] to stop ; [renoncer à] to give up, to stop ▪ **elle s'est arrêtée de jouer en me voyant** she stopped playing when she saw me ▪ **le monde ne va pas s'~ de tourner pour autant** that won't stop the world from turning
2. [s'immobiliser - montre] to stop ; [- ascenseur, véhicule] to stop, to come to a stop *ou* halt ▪ **une voiture vint s'~ à ma hauteur** a car pulled up alongside me ▪ **s'~ net** to stop dead *ou* short
3. [faire une halte, une pause] to stop ▪ **passer sans s'~ devant qqn** to pass by sb without stopping ▪ **on s'est arrêtés plusieurs fois**

en route we made several stops on the way ■ **s'~ chez qqn** to call at sb's ■ **tu peux t'~ chez l'épicier en venant?** could you stop off at the grocer's on your way here? ■ **nous nous étions arrêtés à la page 56** we'd left off at page 56
4. [se fixer] : **s'~ sur : son regard s'arrêta sur leur ami** his gaze fell on their friend ■ **notre choix s'est arrêté sur le canapé en cuir** we decided *ou* settled on the leather couch.
◆ **s'arrêter à** *vp+prép* [faire attention à] to pay attention to ■ **il ne faut pas s'~ aux apparences** one mustn't go by appearances ■ **s'~ à des vétilles** to pay attention to trifles.

arrêt-maladie [arɛmaladi] (*pl* **arrêts-maladies**) *nm* [congé] sick leave ■ [certificat] medical certificate.

arrhes [ar] *nfpl* deposit, earnest money ■ **verser des ~** to pay a deposit ■ **verser 300 euros d'~** to leave 300 euros as a deposit *ou* a deposit of 300 euros.

arrière [arjɛr] ◇ *adj inv* **1.** AUTO [roue, feu] rear ■ [siège] back **2.** SPORT backward.
◇ *nm* **1.** [d'une maison] back, rear ■ [d'un véhicule] rear (end), back (end) ■ **asseyez-vous à l'~** sit in the back **2.** SPORT [au basket-ball] guard ■ [au football, au rugby] back ■ [au volley-ball] rearline player ■ **la ligne des ~s, les ~s** the back line, the backs **3.** NAUT stern ■ **à l'~ de** at the stern of **4.** MIL : **les blessés ont été transportés à l'~** the wounded were carried behind the lines.
◇ *interj* : **~!** (stand) back!
◆ **arrières** *nmpl* MIL rear ■ **assurer** *ou* **protéger ses ~s** to protect one's rear ; *fig* to leave o.s. a way out *ou* an escape route.
◆ **en arrière** *loc adv* **1.** [regarder] back ■ [se pencher, tomber] backward, backwards ■ **revenir en ~** [sur une route] to retrace one's steps ; [avec un magnétophone] to rewind (the tape) ■ **se balancer d'avant en ~** to rock to and fro ■ **ramener ses cheveux en ~** to sweep one's hair back ■ **rester en ~** [d'un convoi, d'un défilé] to stay at the back *ou* rear **2.** [dans le temps] back ■ **revenir en ~** to go back in time ■ **cela nous ramène plusieurs mois en ~** this takes us back several months.
◆ **en arrière de** *loc prép* behind ■ **il reste en ~ des autres élèves** he's fallen behind the other pupils.

arriéré, e [arjere] ◇ *adj* **1.** [impayé - loyer, intérêt] overdue, in arrears ; [- dette] outstanding **2.** PSYCHOL & *vieilli* backward, (mentally) retarded **3.** [archaïque - idée, technologie] backward ■ **le pays est économiquement ~** the country is economically backward.
◇ *nm, f* PSYCHOL & *vieilli* retarded *ou* backward person.
◆ **arriéré** *nm* **1.** [dette] arrears *(pl)* ■ **avoir 2 000 euros d'~ de loyer/d'impôts** to be 2,000 euros in arrears with one's rent/taxes ■ **solder un ~** to pay off arrears **2.** [retard] backlog.

arrière-ban [arjɛrbɑ̃] (*pl* **arrière-bans**) *nm* HIST [levée] arrière-ban *(summons to the king's vassals to do military service)* ■ [vassaux] vassals.

arrière-bouche [arjɛrbuʃ] (*pl* **arrière-bouches**) *nf* back of the mouth.

arrière-boutique [arjɛrbutik] (*pl* **arrière-boutiques**) *nf* : **dans mon ~** at the back of my shop *UK ou* store *US*.

arrière-cour [arjɛrkur] (*pl* **arrière-cours**) *nf* backyard *UK*.

arrière-cuisine [arjɛrkɥizin] (*pl* **arrière-cuisines**) *nf* scullery.

arrière-garde [arjɛrgard] (*pl* **arrière-gardes**) *nf* rearguard.

arrière-gorge [arjɛrgɔrʒ] (*pl* **arrière-gorges**) *nf* back of the throat.

arrière-goût [arjɛrgu] (*pl* **arrière-goûts**) *nm* aftertaste ■ **le vin a un petit ~ de cassis** there's an aftertaste of blackcurrant to the wine.

arrière-grand-mère [arjɛrgrɑ̃mɛr] (*pl* **arrière-grands-mères**) *nf* great-grandmother.

arrière-grand-oncle [arjɛrgrɑ̃tɔ̃kl] (*pl* **arrière-grands-oncles**) *nm* great-great-uncle, great-granduncle.

arrière-grand-père [arjɛrgrɑ̃pɛr] (*pl* **arrière-grands-pères**) *nm* great-grandfather.

arrière-grands-parents [arjɛrgrɑ̃parɑ̃] *nmpl* great-grandparents.

arrière-grand-tante [arjɛrgrɑ̃tɑ̃t] (*pl* **arrière-grands-tantes**) *nf* great-great-aunt, great-grandaunt.

arrière-neveu [arjɛrnəvø] (*pl* **arrière-neveux**) *nm* great-nephew, grandnephew.

arrière-nièce [arjɛrnjɛs] (*pl* **arrière-nièces**) *nf* great-niece, grandniece.

arrière-pays [arjɛrpei] *nm inv* hinterland ■ **dans l'~** in the hinterland.

arrière-pensée [arjɛrpɑ̃se] (*pl* **arrière-pensées**) *nf* thought at the back of one's mind, ulterior motive ■ **sans ~s** without any ulterior motives.

arrière-petite-fille [arjɛrpətitfij] (*pl* **arrière-petites-filles**) *nf* great-granddaughter.

arrière-petit-fils [arjɛrpətifis] (*pl* **arrière-petits-fils**) *nm* great-grandson.

arrière-petits-enfants [arjɛrpətizɑ̃fɑ̃] *nmpl* great-grandchildren.

arrière-plan [arjɛrplɑ̃] (*pl* **arrière-plans**) *nm* background ■ **être à l'~** *fig* to remain in the background.

arrière-saison [arjɛrsɛzɔ̃] (*pl* **arrière-saisons**) *nf* end of the autumn *UK ou* fall *US*.

arrière-salle [arjɛrsal] (*pl* **arrière-salles**) *nf* inner room, back room.

arrière-train [arjɛrtrɛ̃] (*pl* **arrière-trains**) *nm* **1.** ZOOL hindquarters **2.** *hum* [fesses] hindquarters *hum*, behind.

arrimer [3] [arime] *vt* NAUT [ranger] to stow ■ [attacher] to secure.

arrimeur [arimœr] *nm* stevedore.

arrivage [arivaʒ] *nm* delivery, consignment ■ **'prix selon ~'** 'price according to availability'.

arrivant, e [arivɑ̃, ɑ̃t] *nm, f* newcomer, new arrival ■ **il y a dix nouveaux ~s** there are ten newcomers *ou* new arrivals.

arrivé, e [arive] *adj* [qui a réussi] successful.
◆ **arrivée** *nf* **1.** [venue - d'une saison, du froid] arrival, coming ; [- d'un avion, d'un ami] arrival ■ **on attend son ~e pour le mois prochain** we're expecting him to arrive *ou* he's expected to arrive next month ■ **à mon ~e à la gare** on *ou* upon my arrival at the station, when I arrived at the station ■ **quelques mois après son ~e au pouvoir** a few months after he came to power ■ **heure d'~e** [d'un train] time of arrival ; [du courrier] time of delivery **2.** SPORT finish **3.** TECHNOL : **~e d'air/de gaz** [robinet] air/gas inlet ; [passage] inflow of air/gas.

arriver [3] [arive] ◇ *vi (aux être)*

A. DANS L'ESPACE
B. DANS LE TEMPS

A. DANS L'ESPACE

1. [parvenir à destination - voyageur, véhicule, courrier] to arrive ■ **~ chez qqn** to arrive at sb's place ■ **~ chez soi** to get *ou* to arrive home ■ **~ au sommet** to reach the summit ■ **dès que je suis arrivé au Canada** as soon as I arrived in *ou* got to Canada ■ **on arrive à quelle heure?** what time do we get there? ■ **même en roulant vite ça nous fait ~ après minuit** even if we drive fast we won't get there before midnight ■ **nous sommes bientôt** *ou* **presque arrivés** we're almost there ■ **les invités vont bientôt ~** the guests will be arriving soon ■ **qui est arrivé après l'appel?** [en classe] who came in after I called the register *UK ou* called roll *US*? ■ **être bien arrivé** [personne, colis] to have arrived safely ■ **vous voilà enfin arrivés, je m'inquiétais** [ici] here you are *ou* you've arrived at last, I was getting worried ; [là-bas] you got there at last, I was getting worried ■ **par où es-tu arrivée?** [ici] which way did you come? ; [là-bas] which way did you go?

■ **ils arrivent de Tokyo** they've just arrived *ou* come from Tokyo ■ **j'arrive tout juste de vacances** I'm just back from my holidays
2. [finir - dans un classement] to come (in) ■ **~ le premier/dernier** [coureur] to come in first/last, to take first/last place ; [invité] to arrive first/last, to be the first/last to arrive
3. [venir] to come, to approach ■ **tu es prêt? – j'arrive tout de suite/dans une minute** are you ready? – I'm coming/I'll be with you in a minute ■ **j'arrive, j'arrive!** I'm coming! ■ **je n'ai pas vu la voiture ~** I didn't see the car (coming) ■ **ils sont arrivés en voiture** they came by car ■ **une odeur de chocolat arrivait de la cuisine** a smell of chocolate wafted in *ou* came from the kitchen

B. DANS LE TEMPS
1. [événement, jour, moment] to come ■ **Noël arrive bientôt** Christmas will soon be here *ou* with us ■ **le jour arrivera où...** the day will come when... ■ **la soixantaine/retraite est vite arrivée** sixty/retirement is soon here ■ **le grand jour est arrivé!** the big day's here at last! ■ **l'aube arriva enfin** dawn broke at last
2. [se produire] to happen ■ **comment est-ce arrivé?** how did it happen? ■ **un accident est si vite arrivé!** accidents will happen! ■ **ce sont des choses qui arrivent** these things happen ■ **il s'est fait renvoyer – ça devait lui ~** he got fired – it was bound to happen ■ **ça peut ~ à tout le monde de se tromper!** everybody makes mistakes! ■ **ça n'arrive pas qu'aux autres** it's easy to think it'll never happen to you ■ **ça ne t'arrive jamais d'être de mauvaise humeur?** aren't you ever in a bad mood? ■ **tu ne te décourages jamais? – si, ça m'arrive** don't you ever get discouraged? – yes, from time to time ■ **tu es encore en retard. Que cela ne t'arrive plus!** you're late again. Don't let it happen again!
◇ *v impers* **1.** [venir] : **il arrive un train toutes les heures** there's a train every hour **2.** [aventure, événement] : **il est arrivé un accident** there's been an accident ■ **comme il arrive souvent en pareilles circonstances** as is often the case in such circumstances ■ **il m'est arrivé une histoire incroyable!** something incredible happened to me! ■ **s'il m'arrivait quelque chose, prévenez mon père** if anything happens *ou* should anything happen to me, let my father know ■ **pourvu qu'il ne lui soit rien arrivé!** let's hope nothing's happened to her! **3.** [se produire parfois] : **il arrive que : ne peut-il pas ~ que l'ordinateur se trompe?** couldn't the computer ever make a mistake? ■ **il m'arrive parfois de le rencontrer dans la rue** sometimes I meet him in the street ■ **s'il arrivait que je sois** *ou* **fusse** *sout* **absent** if I happened to be absent.
◆ **arriver à** *v+prép* **1.** [niveau, taille, lieu] : **le bas du rideau arrive à 20 cm du sol** the bottom of the curtain is 20 cm above the ground ■ **le fil du téléphone n'arrive pas jusqu'à ma chambre** the phone cord doesn't reach *ou* isn't long enough to reach my bedroom ■ **des bruits de conversation arrivaient jusqu'à nous** the sound of chatter reached us ■ **ses cheveux lui arrivent à la taille** her hair comes down to her waist ■ **ma nièce m'arrive à l'épaule** my niece comes up to my shoulder ■ **la boue m'arrivait jusqu'aux genoux** the mud came up to my knees, I was knee-deep in mud **2.** [étape, moment, conclusion] to come to, to reach ■ **où (en) étions-nous arrivés la semaine dernière?** [dans une leçon] where did we get up to *ou* had we got to last week? ■ **j'arrive à un âge où...** I've reached an age when... ■ **et ses tableaux? – j'y arrive/arrivais** what about his paintings? – I'm/I was coming to that **3.** [rang, résultat] to get ■ [succès] to achieve ■ **tu as refait l'addition? – oui, j'arrive au même total que toi** did you redo the calculations? – yes, I get the same result as you ■ *(en usage absolu)* [réussir socialement] to succeed, to be successful ■ **si tu veux ~** if you want to get on *ou* to succeed in life **4.** [pouvoir, réussir à] : **~ à faire qqch** to manage to do sthg, to succeed in doing sthg ■ **tu n'arriveras jamais à la convaincre** you'll never manage to convince her, you'll never succeed in convincing her ■ **je n'arrive pas à m'y habituer** I just can't get used to it ■ **je n'arrive pas à comprendre son refus** I can't understand why he said no ■ **je parie que tu n'y arriveras pas!** I bet you won't be able to do it! ■ **tu m'aides? je n'y arrive pas!** can you help me? I can't do *ou* manage it! ■ **tu n'arriveras jamais à rien** you'll never get anywhere ■ **je n'arriverai jamais à rien avec lui!** I'll never be able to do anything with him! **5.** *loc* **(en) ~ à qqch** [en venir à] : **comment peut-on en ~ au suicide?** how can anybody get to the point of contemplating suicide? ■ **j'en arrive à penser que...** I'm beginning to think that... ■ **j'en arrive parfois à me demander si...** sometimes I (even) wonder if... ■ **en ~ là : depuis, je ne lui parle plus – c'est malheureux d'en ~ là** since then, I haven't spoken to him – it's a shame it has come to that.

arrivisme [arivism] *nm* pushiness, ambitiousness ■ **elle n'est entrée au comité que par ~** for her, joining the committee was just a way of furthering her career *ou* ambitions.

arriviste [arivist] ◇ *adj* self-seeking, careerist.
◇ *nmf* careerist.

arrogance [arɔgɑ̃s] *nf* arrogance ■ **parler avec ~** to speak arrogantly.

arrogant, e [arɔgɑ̃, ɑ̃t] ◇ *adj* arrogant.
◇ *nm, f* arrogant person.

arroger [17] [arɔʒe] ◆ **s'arroger** *vpt sout* to assume, to arrogate (to o.s.) *sout* ■ **s'~ le droit de faire qqch** to assume the right to do sthg.

Arromanches-les-Bains [arɔmɑ̃ʃlebɛ̃] *npr coastal town in the Calvados region famous for the Allied landings of June 1944.*

arrondi [arɔ̃di] *nm* **1.** COUT hemline **2.** [forme - d'une sculpture] rounded form *ou* shape ; [- d'un parterre] circular line *ou* design **3.** INFORM & MATH rounding.

arrondir [32] [arɔ̃dir] *vt* **1.** [rendre rond] to make into a round shape, to round (off) *(sép)* ■ [incurver] to round off *(sép)* **2.** [augmenter - capital, pécule] to increase ; [- patrimoine, domaine] to extend ■ **~ ses fins de mois** *fam* to make a little extra on the side **3.** MATH to round off *(sép)* ■ **~ un total à l'euro supérieur/inférieur** to round a sum up/down to the nearest euro **4.** COUT to level (off) *(sép)*.
◆ **s'arrondir** *vpi* **1.** [grossir - femme enceinte, ventre] to get bigger *ou* rounder ; [- somme] to mount up **2.** PHON to become rounded.

arrondissement [arɔ̃dismɑ̃] *nm* **1.** [dans une ville] *administrative subdivision of major French cities such as Paris, Lyons or Marseilles* **2.** [au niveau départemental] *administrative subdivision of a departement, governed by a 'sous-préfet'.*

arrosage [arozaʒ] *nm* **1.** [d'un jardin] watering ■ [de la chaussée] spraying **2.** *fam* [corruption] bribing.

arrosé, e [aroze] *adj* **1.** [pluvieux] : **la région est bien ~e** the area has a high rainfall **2.** [accompagné d'alcool] : **après un dîner un peu trop ~** *fam* after having had a bit too much to drink at dinner ➔ **café ~** coffee laced with alcohol.

arroser [3] [aroze] *vt* **1.** [asperger - jardin, pelouse] to water ■ **~ une voiture au jet** to hose down *ou* to spray a car ■ **arrête, tu m'arroses!** stop it, you're spraying water (all) over me *ou* I'm getting wet! ■ **se faire ~** *fam* [par la pluie] to get drenched *ou* soaked **2.** [inonder] to soak ■ **attention les enfants, vous allez ~ mon parquet!** careful, children, you'll get my floor all wet! ■ **~ qqn de qqch** to pour sthg over sb, to drench sb in sthg **3.** CULIN [gigot, rôti] to baste **4.** [repas] : **(bien) ~ son déjeuner** *fam* to drink (heavily) with one's lunch ■ **arrosé de : une mousse de saumon arrosée d'un bon sauvignon** a salmon mousse washed down with a fine Sauvignon **5.** *fam* [fêter] to drink to ■ **~ une naissance** to wet a baby's head *UK*, to drink to a new baby **6.** GÉOGR : **la Seine arrose Paris** the river Seine flows through Paris **7.** MIL [avec des bombes] to bomb ■ [avec des obus] to shell ■ [avec des balles] to spray **8.** *fam* [corrompre] to grease the palm of ■ **il avait arrosé des notables** he'd greased the palm of some VIPs.
◆ **s'arroser** *vp (emploi passif) fam* **la naissance de ta fille, ça s'arrose!** let's drink to your new baby daughter!

arroseur [arozœr] *nm* **1.** [personne] waterer ■ **c'est l'~ arrosé!** now the boot is on the other foot! **2.** [dispositif] sprinkler.

arroseuse [arozøz] *nf* water cart.

arrosoir [arozwar] *nm* watering can *UK ou* pot *US*.

arrt = **arrondissement**.

arsenal, aux [arsənal, o] *nm* **1.** MIL & NAUT arsenal ■ **ils ont découvert un véritable ~** [armes] they've stumbled on a major arms cache ; [bombes] they've stumbled on a bomb factory ▶ **~ maritime** naval dockyard **2.** *fam* [panoplie] equipment, gear ▪ **l'~ des lois, l'~ législatif** the might of the law.

Arsène Lupin [arsɛnlypɛ̃] *npr the gentleman thief in the detective novels of Maurice Leblanc (1864-1941).*

arsenic [arsənik] *nm* arsenic.

arsouille△ [arsuj] **vieilli** <> *adj* [allure, genre] loutish. <> *nmf* yob UK, roughneck US.

art [ar] *nm* **1.** ART art ▪ **l'~ pour l'~** art for art's sake ▶ **~ contemporain** contemporary art ▪ **~ déco** art deco ▪ **~ figuratif/abstrait** figurative/abstract art ▪ **Art nouveau** Art nouveau ▪ **~ pauvre** process art ▪ **cinéma** *ou* **salle d'~ et d'essai** art house ▪ **grand ~ : regardez cette pyramide de fruits, c'est du grand ~!** look at this pyramid of fruit, it's a work of art! ▪ **le Musée national d'~ moderne** *the Paris Museum of Modern Art, in the Pompidou Centre* **2.** [technique] art ▪ **découper un poulet, c'est tout un ~!** *fig* carving a chicken is quite an art! ▶ **l'~ culinaire** the art of cooking ▪ **l'~ dramatique** dramatic art, dramatics ▪ **cours d'~ dramatique** [classe] drama class ; [école] drama school ▪ **~ floral** flower arranging ▪ **l'~ de la guerre** the art of warfare ▪ **l'~ oratoire** public speaking ▪ **l'~ poétique** poetics ▪ **l'~ sacré, le grand ~** (the art of) alchemy **3.** [don] art, talent ▪ **il a l'~ de m'énerver** he has a knack of getting on my nerves ▶ **l'~ de vivre** the art of living ▪ **je voulais juste le prévenir! – oui, mais il y a l'~ et la manière** I didn't want to offend him, just to warn him! – yes, but there are ways of going about it.

➡ **arts** *nmpl* arts ▪ **être un ami des ~s** to be a friend of the arts ▶ **~s appliqués** ≃ art and design ▪ **~s décoratifs** decorative arts ▪ **~s graphiques** graphic arts ▪ **~s martiaux** martial arts ▪ **~s ménagers** ÉDUC home economics ▪ **les ~s et métiers** ÉDUC *college for the advanced education of those working in commerce, manufacturing, construction and design* ▪ **les ~s plastiques** the visual arts ▪ **les ~s du spectacle** the performing arts ▪ **~s et traditions populaires** arts and crafts ▪ **Arts Déco** *nickname of the École Nationale des arts décoratifs* ▪ **le musée des Arts d'Afrique et d'Océanie** *museum of African and Oceanian Art in Vincennes near Paris* ▪ **le musée des Arts décoratifs** *museum of decorative arts in the Louvre* ▪ **le musée des Arts et Traditions populaires** *museum of arts and crafts in the Bois de Boulogne.*

art. = article.

Artaban [artabɑ̃] *npr* : **fier comme ~** as proud as Punch.

Arte [arte] *npr Franco-German cultural television channel created in 1992.*

artefact [artefakt] *nm* artefact, artifact.

artère [artɛr] *nf* **1.** ANAT artery **2.** [avenue] (main) road *ou* street *ou* thoroughfare ▪ **les grandes ~s** the main roads.

artériel, elle [arterjɛl] *adj* arterial.

artériographie [arterjɔgrafi] *nf* arteriography.

artériole [arterjɔl] *nf* arteriole.

artériosclérose [arterjɔskleroz] *nf* arteriosclerosis.

artérite [arterit] *nf* arteritis.

artésien, enne [artezjɛ̃, ɛn] *adj* [langue, patois] from Artois.

arthrite [artrit] *nf* arthritis.

arthritique [artritik] <> *adj* arthritic. <> *nmf* arthritis sufferer.

arthropode [artrɔpɔd] *nm* arthropod ▪ **les ~s** the Arthropoda.

arthroscopie [artrɔskɔpi] *nf* arthroscopy.

arthrose [artroz] *nf* osteoarthritis, degenerative joint disease.

Arthur [artyr] *npr* Arthur ▪ **la légende du roi ~** Arthurian legend.

artichaut [artiʃo] *nm* (globe) artichoke.

article [artikl] *nm* **1.** COMM article, item ▪ **~s d'alimentation** foodstuffs ▪ **~s de bureau** office equipment and stationery ▪ **~s de luxe** luxury goods ▪ **~s de toilette** toiletries ▪ **~s de mode** fashion accessories ▪ **~s de voyage** travel goods ▪ **'~s en promotion'** 'special offers' ▶ **~ d'appel** loss leader ▪ **~s sans suite** discontinued line ▪ **faire l'~ pour** *pr* to do a sales pitch for ; *fig* to praise

2. PRESSE article ▪ **~ de fond** feature article ▮ [d'un dictionnaire, d'un guide] entry

3. [sujet] point ▪ **elle dit qu'on lui doit trois millions, et sur cet ~, tu peux lui faire confiance!** she says she's owed three millions, and on that score *ou* point, you can believe what she says!

4. RELIG : **~s de foi** articles of faith ▪ **le socialisme, pour moi, c'est un ~ de foi** *fig* socialism is an article of faith for me

5. [paragraphe] article, clause ▪ **les ~s de la Constitution** the articles *ou* clauses of the Constitution ▪ **l'~ 10 du contrat** point *ou* paragraph *ou* clause 10 of the contract ▶ **~ de loi** article of law

6. LING article

7. INFORM item

8. *loc* **à l'~ de la mort** at death's door, on the point of death.

articulaire [artikylɛr] *adj* articular ▪ **douleurs ~s** sore joints.

articulation [artikylasjɔ̃] *nf* **1.** ANAT & ZOOL joint ▪ **j'ai mal dans les ~s** my joints ache **2.** [prononciation] articulation **3.** [liaison] link, link-up ▪ **l'~ des deux parties** the link between the two parts **4.** DR enumeration, setting forth *ou* out **5.** MÉCAN connection, joint.

articuler [3] [artikyle] *vt* **1.** [prononcer] to articulate ▪ *(en usage absolu)* **articule, je ne comprends rien** speak more clearly, I don't understand ▪ **bien ~** to pronounce clearly **2.** [dire] to utter ▪ **j'étais si ému que je ne pouvais plus ~ un seul mot** I was so moved that I couldn't utter *ou* say a single word **3.** [enchaîner - démonstration, thèse] to link up *ou* together *(sép)* ; [- faits] to connect **4.** MÉCAN to joint **5.** DR [accusations] to enumerate, to set forth *ou* out *(sép)*.

➡ **s'articuler autour de** *vp+prép* to hinge *ou* to turn on.

➡ **s'articuler sur** *vp+prép* ANAT, MÉCAN & ZOOL to be articulated *ou* jointed with.

artifice [artifis] *nm* **1.** [stratagème] (clever) device *ou* trick ▪ **beauté sans ~s** artless beauty **2.** *litt* [adresse] skill ▪ **la scène est peinte avec tant d'~ que l'œil s'en trouve ébloui** the scene is depicted so skilfully that it is a wonder to behold **3.** [explosif] firework.

artificiel, elle [artifisjɛl] *adj* **1.** [colorant, fleur, lumière, intelligence, insémination] artificial ▪ [lac, soie] artificial, man-made ▪ [perle] artificial, imitation *(modif)* ▪ [dent] false ▪ [bras, hanche] replacement *(modif)* ▪ [mouche] artificial **2.** [factice - besoin, plaisir] artificial **3.** [affecté] artificial, false, insincere ▪ **le style est très ~** the style is very contrived *ou* unnatural **4.** [arbitraire] artificial.

artificiellement [artifisjɛlmɑ̃] *adv* artificially.

artificier [artifisje] *nm* **1.** [en pyrotechnie] fireworks expert **2.** MIL [soldat] blaster ▪ [spécialiste] bomb disposal expert.

artificieux, euse [artifisjø, øz] *adj* **litt** deceitful.

artillerie [artijri] *nf* artillery ▪ **ils ont envoyé la grosse ~** *ou* **l'~ lourde** *fig* they used drastic measures ▪ **pièce/tir d'~** artillery cannon/fire.

artilleur [artijœr] *nm* artilleryman.

artimon [artimɔ̃] *nm* mizzen, mizzenmast.

artisan, e [artizɑ̃, an] *nm, f* **1.** [travailleur] craftsman (*f* craftswoman), artisan ▪ **~ ébéniste** cabinet-maker **2.** [responsable] architect, author ▪ **l'~ de la paix** the peacemaker ▪ **être l'~ de sa propre chute/ruine** to bring about one's own downfall/ruin.

artisanal, e, aux [artizanal, o] *adj* **1.** [des artisans - classe, tradition] artisan *(modif)* **2.** [traditionnel - méthode, travail] traditional ▪ **un fauteuil fabriqué de façon ~e** a hand-made armchair ▪ **une bombe de fabrication ~e** a home-made bomb **3.** [rudimentaire] basic, crude.

artisanat [artizana] *nm* **1.** [profession] : **l'~** the craft industry, the crafts **2.** [ensemble des artisans] artisans **3.** [produits] arts and crafts ▪ **'~ d'art'** 'arts and crafts' ▪ **le travail du cuir fait partie de l'~ local** leatherwork is part of local industry.

artiste [artist] ◇ *adj* **1.** [personne] artistic **2.** [bohème - genre, vie] bohemian.
◇ *nmf* **1.** ART [créateur] artist ➲ ~ **peintre** painter **2.** CINÉ, LOISIRS & THÉÂTRE [interprète] performer ■ [comédien] actor ■ [chanteur] singer ■ [de music-hall] artiste, entertainer ■ **~ de cabaret** cabaret entertainer ■ **~ comique** comedian ■ **~ dramatique** actor (*f* actress) **3.** [personne habile] artist ■ **voilà ce que j'appelle un travail d'~!** that's what I call the work of an artist!

artistique [artistik] *adj* [enseignement, richesses] artistic ■ **elle a un certain sens ~** she has a certain feeling for art.

arum [arɔm] *nm* arum.

ARVA [arva] (*abr de* **appareil de recherche de victimes d'avalanches**) *nm equipment for searching for avalanche victims.*

aryen, enne [arjɛ̃, ɛn] *adj* Aryan.
◆ **Aryen, enne** *nm, f* Aryan.

arythmie [aritmi] *nf* arrhythmia.

as[1] [a] *v* ▷ **avoir.**

as[2] [as] *nm* **1.** JEUX [carte, dé, domino] ace ■ [aux courses] number one ■ **l'~ de cœur/pique** the ace of hearts/spades ■ **t'es fagoté** *ou* **ficelé** *ou* **fichu comme l'~ de pique** *fam* you look as if you've been dragged through a hedge backwards ■ **passer à l'~** *fam* : **et mon sandwich, alors, il passe à l'~?** what about my sandwich then? ■ **mon augmentation est passée à l'~** I might as well forget the idea of getting a pay increase **2.** *fam* [champion] ace, champ, wizard ■ **Delphine, t'es un ~!** Delphine, you're a marvel! ■ **un ~ de la route** *ou* **du volant** a crack driver.

AS *nf* = **association sportive**.

ASA, Asa [aza] *nf* ASA, Asa ■ **[unité de mesure] une pellicule 100 ~** a 100 ASA film.

asbeste [asbɛst] *nf* asbestos.

asc. = **ascenseur**.

ascendance [asɑ̃dɑ̃s] *nf* **1.** [ancêtres] ancestry **2.** [extraction] : **être d'~ allemande** to be of German descent ■ **être d'~ paysanne** to be of peasant origin **3.** ASTRON ascent, rising **4.** AÉRON & MÉTÉOR ascending current.

ascendant, e [asɑ̃dɑ̃, ɑ̃t] *adj* **1.** [mouvement] rising, ascending **2.** ANAT [aorte, côlon] ascending.
◆ **ascendant** *nm* **1.** [emprise] influence, ascendancy ■ **avoir de l'~ sur qqn** to have influence over sb ■ **subir l'~ de qqn** to be under the influence of sb **2.** ASTROL ascendant.
◆ **ascendants** *nmpl* DR [parents] ascendants, ancestors.

ascenseur [asɑ̃sœr] *nm* **1.** [in a building] lift *UK*, elevator *US* ■ **il habite au quatrième sans ~** he lives in a fourth-floor walk-up **2.** inform scroll bar.

ascension [asɑ̃sjɔ̃] *nf* **1.** [montée - d'un ballon] ascent **2.** [escalade - d'un alpiniste] ascent, climb ■ **faire l'~ d'un pic** to climb a peak **3.** [progression] ascent, rise ■ **ses affaires connaissent une ~ rapide** his business is booming **4.** RELIG : **l'Ascension** the Ascension ■ **le jour de l'Ascension** Ascension Day **5.** ASTRON ascension.

L'ASCENSION

In France many people take an extended weekend break after Ascension Day *le jeudi de l'Ascension*.

ascensionnel, elle [asɑ̃sjɔnɛl] *adj* upward.

ascèse [asɛz] *nf* asceticism, ascetic lifestyle.

ascète [asɛt] *nmf* ascetic ■ **vivre en ~** to live an ascetic life.

ascétique [asetik] *adj* ascetic.

ascétisme [asetism] *nm* asceticism.

ASCII [aski] (*abr de* **American Standard Code for Information Interchange**) *adj* ASCII *(modif)*.

ascorbique [askɔrbik] *adj* ascorbic.

ASE (*abr de* **Agence spatiale européenne**) *npr f* ESA.

asémantique [asemɑ̃tik] *adj* asemantic.

asepsie [asɛpsi] *nf* asepsis.

aseptique [asɛptik] *adj* aseptic.

aseptisation [asɛptizasjɔ̃] *nf* asepticization.

aseptisé, e [asɛptize] *adj* MÉD sterilized ■ *fig* [ambiance] impersonal ■ [discours, roman, univers] sanitized.

aseptiser [3] [asɛptize] *vt* to asepticize.

asexué, e [asɛksɥe] *adj* [plante, reproduction] asexual ■ [individu] sexless.

ashkénase [aʃkenaz] *adj* & *nmf* : **(juif) ~** Ashkenazi ■ **les ~s** the Ashkenazim.

asiatique [azjatik] *adj* **1.** [de l'Asie en général] Asian **2.** [d'Extrême-Orient] Oriental ■ **un restaurant ~** *a restaurant serving Oriental cuisine.*
◆ **Asiatique** *nmf* Asian.

ASIATIQUE

This word tends to refer to people from Far Eastern countries: China, Japan, Laos, etc.

Asie [azi] *npr f* Asia ■ **l'~ centrale** Central Asia ■ **l'~ Mineure** HIST Asia Minor ■ **l'~ du Sud-Est** Southeast Asia.

asile [azil] *nm* **1.** [abri] refuge ■ **chercher/trouver ~** to seek/to find refuge **2.** HIST & POLIT asylum ■ **demander l'~ diplomatique/politique** to seek diplomatic protection/political asylum **3.** [établissement - gén] home ■ **~ de nuit** night shelter.

asocial, e, aux [asɔsjal, o] ◇ *adj* asocial *sout*, antisocial.
◇ *nm, f* dropout, social outcast.

asparagus [asparagys] *nm* asparagus fern.

aspartam(e) [aspartam] *nm* aspartame ■ **yaourt à l'~** artificially sweetened yoghurt.

aspect [aspɛ] *nm* **1.** [apparence] appearance, look ■ **un bâtiment d'~ imposant** an imposing-looking building ■ **donner l'~ de qqch à qqn** to give sb the appearance of sthg, to make sb look like sthg ■ **prendre l'~ de qqch** [ressembler à qqch] to take on the appearance of sthg ; [se métamorphoser en qqch] to turn into sthg ■ **offrir** *ou* **présenter l'~ de qqch** to look like *ou* to resemble sthg **2.** [point de vue] aspect, facet ■ **envisager** *ou* **examiner une question sous tous ses ~s** to consider a question from all angles ■ **vu sous cet ~** seen from this angle *ou* point of view ■ **sous un ~ nouveau** in a new light **3.** ASTROL & LING aspect.
◆ **à l'aspect de** *loc prép* at the sight of, upon seeing.

asperge [aspɛrʒ] *nf* **1.** BOT asparagus **2.** *fam* [personne] : **une (grande) ~** a beanpole.

asperger [17] [aspɛrʒe] *vt* **1.** [légèrement] to sprinkle ■ **~qqn d'eau** *ou* **avec de l'eau** to spray sb with water **2.** [tremper] to splash, to splatter ■ **se faire ~** to get splashed ■ **~ qqn/qqch de qqch** to splash sb/sthg with sthg, to splash sthg on sb/sthg.
◆ **s'asperger** ◇ *vp (emploi réfléchi)* : **s'~ de qqch** to splash o.s. with sthg, to splash sthg on o.s.
◇ *vp (emploi réciproque)* to splash *ou* to spray one another.

aspergillus [aspɛrʒilys] *nm* aspergillus.

aspérité [asperite] *nf* **1.** [proéminence] rough bit ■ **les ~s d'une surface** the roughness of a surface **2.** *litt* [rudesse] asperity, harshness.

asperme [aspɛrm] *adj* seedless.

aspersion [aspɛrsjɔ̃] *nf* **1.** [d'eau] sprinkling, spraying **2.** RELIG sprinkling, aspersion.

aspersoir [aspɛrswar] *nm* **1.** RELIG [goupillon] aspersorium **2.** [pomme d'arrosoir] rose.

asphalte [asfalt] *nm* **1.** [bitume] asphalt **2.** *fam* [chaussée] street.

asphalter [3] [asfalte] *vt* to asphalt.

asphodèle [asfɔdɛl] *nm* asphodel.

asphyxiant, e [asfiksjɑ̃, ɑ̃t] *adj* **1.** [obus, vapeur] asphyxiating, suffocating **2.** [oppressant - ambiance] stifling, suffocating.

asphyxie [asfiksi] *nf* **1.** MÉD asphyxia ■ **~ par submersion** drowning **2.** *fig* paralysis ■ **la guerre conduit le pays à l'~** war is paralysing the country.

asphyxier [9] [asfiksje] *vt* **1.** [priver d'air] to suffocate ■ [faire respirer du gaz à] to asphyxiate ■ **mourir asphyxié** to die of asphyxiation **2.** *fig* [personne] to oppress ■ [pays, économie] to paralyse.
◆ **s'asphyxier** ◇ *vp (emploi réfléchi)* [volontairement, au gaz] to gas o.s.
◇ *vpi* [accidentellement] to suffocate.

aspic [aspik] *nm* **1.** ZOOL asp **2.** BOT & CULIN aspic.

aspirant, e [aspirɑ̃, ɑ̃t] ◇ *adj* sucking, pumping.
◇ *nm, f* candidate.
◆ **aspirant** *nm* officer cadet.

aspirateur [aspiratœr] *nm* **1.** [domestique] Hoover® *UK*, vacuum cleaner ■ **passer l'~** to do the hoovering *UK ou* vacuuming **2.** TECHNOL aspirator.

aspirateur-balai [aspiratœrbalɛ] (*pl* **aspirateurs-balais**) *nm* upright vacuum cleaner.

aspirateur-traîneau [aspiratœrtrɛno] (*pl* **aspirateurs-traîneaux**) *nm* cylinder-type vacuum cleaner.

aspiration [aspirasjɔ̃] *nf* **1.** [ambition] aspiration, ambition **2.** [souhait] yearning, longing, craving **3.** [absorption - d'air] inhaling ; [- d'un gaz, d'un fluide] sucking up **4.** MÉCAN induction **5.** PHON aspiration **6.** MÉD : **~ endo-utérine, IVG par ~** abortion by vacuum extraction.

aspiré, e [aspire] *adj* PHON aspirate.
◆ **aspirée** *nf* PHON aspirate.

aspirer [3] [aspire] *vt* **1.** [inspirer] to inhale, to breathe in *(sép)* **2.** [pomper] to suck up *(sép)* ■ **~ de l'air/des gaz d'une conduite** to pump air/gas out of a main ‖ [avec un aspirateur] to vacuum, to hoover *UK* **3.** PHON to aspirate.
◆ **aspirer à** *v+prép* [paix, repos] to long for *(insép)*, to yearn for *(insép)* ■ [rang, dignité] to aspire to *(insép)*.

aspirine [aspirin] *nf* aspirin ■ **un comprimé d'~** an aspirin.

assagir [32] [asaʒir] *vt litt* [apaiser - personne] to quieten down *(sép)* ; [- passion, violence] to soothe, to allay ■ **l'expérience l'a assagie** experience has made her a wiser person ■ [faire se ranger] to cause to settle down ■ **c'est un homme assagi maintenant** he's calmed down a lot.
◆ **s'assagir** *vpi* **1.** [personne] to settle down **2.** *fig* **la passion s'assagit avec l'âge** passion becomes calmer with age.

assaillant, e [asajɑ̃, ɑ̃t] *adj* [armée, troupe] assailing, assaulting, attacking.
◆ **assaillant** *nm* assailant, attacker.

assaillir [47] [asajir] *vt* MIL to attack, to assail *litt* ■ [esprit, imagination] to beset ■ **le bureau est assailli de demandes** the office is swamped *ou* besieged with inquiries.

assainir [32] [asenir] *vt* **1.** [nettoyer - quartier, logement] to clean up *(sép)* ; [- air] to purify **2.** [assécher - plaine, région] to improve the drainage of **3.** [épurer - situation] to clear up ; [- marché, monnaie] to stabilize ■ **~ le climat social** to put an end to social strife.
◆ **s'assainir** *vpi* to improve, to become healthier.

assainissement [asenismɑ̃] *nm* **1.** [nettoyage - d'une ville] improvement ; [- d'un appartement] cleaning up **2.** [assèchement] draining **3.** [d'une monnaie, d'un marché] stabilization, stabilizing.

assainisseur [asenisœr] *nm* air-freshener.

assaisonnement [asɛzɔnmɑ̃] *nm* **1.** [processus] dressing, seasoning **2.** [condiments] seasoning ■ [sauce] dressing.

assaisonner [3] [asɛzɔne] *vt* **1.** CULIN [plat, sauce] to season ■ [salade] to dress **2.** *fig* [agrémenter] : **~ qqch de** to spice *ou* to lace sthg with **3.** *fam* [malmener] : **~ qqn** to tell sb off ‖ [escroquer] to sting, to rip off *(sép)*.

assassin, e [asasɛ̃, in] *adj litt & hum* [œillade, regard] provocative ■ **lancer un regard ~** to look daggers at sb.
◆ **assassin** *nm* [gén] murderer, killer ■ [d'une personnalité connue] assassin ■ **à l'aide, à l'~!** help, murder!

assassinat [asasina] *nm* murder ■ [d'une personnalité connue] assassination.

assassiner [3] [asasine] *vt* **1.** [tuer - gén] to murder ; [- vedette, homme politique] to assassinate ■ **se faire ~** to be murdered **2.** *fam péj* [malmener - musique, symphonie] to murder, to slaughter.

assaut [aso] *nm* **1.** MIL assault, attack, onslaught ■ **aller** *ou* **monter à l'~** *pr* to attack, to storm ; *fig* to attack ■ **à l'~!** charge! ■ **donner l'~** to launch *ou* to mount an attack ■ **se lancer à l'~ d'une ville** to launch an attack *ou* to mount an onslaught on a town ■ **ils se sont lancés à l'~ du marché japonais** *fig* they set out to capture the Japanese market ■ **résister aux ~s de l'ennemi** to withstand enemy attacks ■ **prendre d'~ un palais** to storm a palace ■ **à la chute de la Bourse, les banques ont été prises d'~ par les petits porteurs** *fig* when the Stock Exchange crashed, the banks were stormed by small shareholders ■ **faire ~ de** *litt* : **elles font ~ de politesse/gentillesse** they're falling over each other to be polite/nice ➊ **troupes d'~** storm troops **2.** ESCRIME bout.

assèchement [asɛʃmɑ̃] *nm* draining, drying-up.

assécher [18] [aseʃe] ◇ *vt* [drainer - terre, sol] to drain (the water off) ■ [vider - étang, réservoir] to empty.
◇ *vi* [à marée basse] to become dry, to dry up.
◆ **s'assécher** *vpi* to become dry, to dry up.

ASSEDIC, Assedic [asedik] (*abr de* **Association pour l'emploi dans l'industrie et le commerce**) *npr French unemployment insurance scheme*, ≃ Unemployment Benefit Office *UK*, ≃ Unemployment Office *US* ■ **toucher les ~** to get unemployment benefit.

ASSEDIC

This is the government agency that provides unemployment insurance. Benefits are funded by a specific contribution paid by all employers and employees.

assemblage [asɑ̃blaʒ] *nm* **1.** [fait de mettre ensemble] assembling, constructing, fitting together ■ **procéder à l'~ de pièces** [gén] to assemble parts ; COUT to make up a garment **2.** AUTO & INDUST assembly **3.** [ensemble] assembly ■ CONSTR framework, structure ■ MENUIS joint **4.** ART assemblage **5.** IMPR gathering **6.** *péj* [amalgame] collection, concoction *péj* **7.** INFORM assembly.

assemblée [asɑ̃ble] *nf* **1.** [auditoire] gathering, audience ■ **en présence d'une nombreuse ~** in front of a large audience ■ **l'~ des fidèles** RELIG the congregation **2.** [réunion] meeting ■ **~ générale/annuelle** general/annual meeting ■ **la fédération a tenu son ~ annuelle à Lille** the federation held its annual meeting in Lille ■ **~ (générale) ordinaire/extraordinaire** ordinary/extraordinary (general) meeting **3.** POLIT [élus] : **l'Assemblée (nationale)** the (French) National Assembly ■ **la Haute Assemblée** the (French) Senate ➊ **~ constituante** constituent assembly ■ **~ fédérale** [en Suisse] (Swiss) federal assembly **4.** [bâtiment] : **l'Assemblée** ≃ the House.

L'ASSEMBLÉE NATIONALE

The National Assembly is the lower house of the French Parliaments. Its members (the *députés*) are elected in the *élections législatives* held every five years.

assembler [3] [asɑ̃ble] *vt* **1.** [monter] to assemble, to put *ou* to fit together *(sép)* ■ MENUIS to joint ■ **assemblez le dos et le devant du tricot** sew the back and the front of the sweater together ■ **~ deux pièces par collage/soudure** to glue/to solder two parts together **2.** [combiner - pensées] to gather (together) *(sép)* ; [- documents] to collate **3.** INFORM to assemble.
◆ **s'assembler** *vpi* to gather (together).

assembleur [asɑ̃blœr] *nm* **1.** INFORM assembler (language) **2.** [ouvrier] fitter.

assener [19], **asséner** [18] [asene] *vt* [coup] to deliver, to strike ■ **je lui ai asséné quelques vérités bien senties** *fig* I threw a few home truths at him.

assentiment [asɑ̃timɑ̃] *nm* assent, agreement ▪ **hocher la tête en signe d'~** to nod one's head (in agreement).

asseoir [65] [aswar] ◇ *vt* **1.** [mettre en position assise] : **~ qqn** [le mettre sur un siège] to sit sb down ; [le redresser dans son lit] to sit sb up ▪ **~ qqn sur le trône** [le couronner] to put sb on the throne ▪ **être assis : j'étais assise sur un tabouret** I was sitting on a stool ▪ **nous étions assis au premier rang** we were seated in the first row ▪ **êtes-vous bien assis?** are you sitting comfortably? ▪ **je préfère être assise pour repasser** I prefer doing the ironing sitting down ⊙ **être assis entre deux chaises** to be (caught) between two stools
2. *sout* [consolider] to establish ▪ **~ sa réputation sur qqch** to base one's reputation on sthg
3. [faire reposer - statue] to sit, to rest
4. *fam* [étonner] to stun, to astound
5. FIN [impôt, taxe] to base, to fix
6. ÉQUIT to sit.
◇ *vi* : **faire ~ qqn** to ask sb to sit down.
◆ **s'asseoir** *vpi* **1.** [s'installer] to sit down ▪ **asseyez-vous donc** please, do sit down ▪ **asseyons-nous par terre** let's sit on the floor ▪ **venez vous ~ à table avec nous** come and sit at the table with us ▪ **s'~ en tailleur** to sit cross-legged ▪ **il s'assit sur ses talons** he sat down on his heels
2. *loc* **s'~ dessus**△ **: ton opinion, je m'assois dessus** I couldn't give a damn about your opinion ▪ **votre dossier, vous pouvez vous ~ dessus** you know what you can do with your file.

assermenté, e [asɛrmɑ̃te] ◇ *adj* [policier] sworn, sworn in ▪ **expert ~** expert on *ou* under oath.
◇ *nm, f* person sworn in.

assermenter [3] [asɛrmɑ̃te] *vt* to swear in *(sép)*.

assertion [asɛrsjɔ̃] *nf* assertion.

asservir [32] [asɛrvir] *vt* [assujettir] to enslave ▪ **être asservi à une cause** to be in thrall to a cause.

asservissement [asɛrvismɑ̃] *nm* **1.** [sujétion] enslavement **2.** TECHNOL automatic control.

assesseur [asesœr] *nm* assessor.

asseyait *etc v* ▷ **asseoir**.

assez [ase] *adv* **1.** [suffisamment] enough ▪ **la maison est ~ grande pour nous tous** the house is big enough for all of us ▪ **j'ai ~ travaillé pour aujourd'hui** I've done enough work for today ▪ **c'est bien ~** that's plenty ▪ **c'est plus qu'~** that's more than enough ▪ **ça a ~ duré!** it's gone on long enough! ▪ **~ parlé, agissons!** that's enough talk *ou* talking, let's DO something! ▪ **en voilà** *ou* **c'(en) est ~!** that's enough!, enough's enough! ▪ *(en corrélation avec 'pour')* **elle est ~ grande pour s'habiller toute seule** she's old enough to dress herself **2.** [plutôt, passablement] quite, rather ▪ **j'aime ~ sa maison** I quite like his house ▪ **c'est un ~ bon exemple de ce qu'il ne faut pas faire** it's a pretty good example of what not to do ▪ **je suis ~ contente de moi** I'm quite pleased with myself ▪ **j'ai ~ peu mangé aujourd'hui** I haven't eaten much today.
◆ **assez de** *loc dét* enough ▪ **il y en a ~** there is/are enough ▪ **il n'a pas besoin de venir, nous sommes (bien) ~ de deux** he doesn't need to come, two of us will be (quite) enough ▪ *(en corrélation avec 'pour')* **j'ai ~ d'argent pour vivre** I have enough money to live on ⊙ **j'en ai (plus qu')~ de toutes ces histoires!** *fam* I've had (more than) enough of all this fuss!

assidu, e [asidy] *adj* **1.** [zélé] assiduous *sout*, diligent *sout*, hard-working ▪ **élève ~** hard-working pupil ▪ **il lui faisait une cour ~e** he courted her assiduously **2.** [constant] unflagging, unremitting, untiring ▪ **grâce à un travail ~** by dint of hard work ▪ **elle a fourni des efforts ~s** she made unremitting efforts **3.** [fréquent] regular, constant.

assiduité [asidɥite] *nf* **1.** [zèle] assiduity *sout* ▪ **travailler avec ~** to work assiduously *ou* zealously *sout* **2.** [régularité] assiduousness *sout* ▪ **l'~ aux répétitions est essentielle** regular attendance at rehearsals is vital.
◆ **assiduités** *nfpl* attentions ▪ **importuner** *ou* **poursuivre qqn de ses ~s** to force one's attentions upon sb.

assidûment [asidymɑ̃] *adv* **1.** [avec zèle] assiduously *sout* **2.** [régulièrement] assiduously *sout*, unremittingly, untiringly.

assied *etc v* ▷ **asseoir**.

assiégé, e [asjeʒe] *nm, f* besieged person ▪ **les ~s** the besieged.

assiégeant, e [asjeʒɑ̃, ɑ̃t] *adj* besieging.
◆ **assiégeant** *nm* besieger.

assiéger [22] [asjeʒe] *vt* **1.** MIL [ville, forteresse] to lay siege to *(insép)*, to besiege **2.** [se présenter en foule à] to besiege, to mob ▪ **les guichets ont été assiégés** the ticket office was stormed by the public.

assiéra *etc v* ▷ **asseoir**.

assiette [asjɛt] *nf* **1.** [récipient] plate ▪ **~ à dessert** dessert plate ▪ **~ creuse** *ou* **à soupe** soup dish ▪ **~ plate** (dinner) plate ▪ **grande ~** dinner plate ▪ **petite ~** dessert *ou* side plate ▪ **c'est l'~ au beurre** *fam* it's a cushy number ▌[contenu] plate, plateful ▪ **une (pleine) ~ de soupe** a (large) plateful of soup ▪ **finis d'abord ton ~** eat up what's on your plate first ⊙ **~ anglaise** assorted cold meats **2.** [assise] foundation, basis ▪ [d'une voie ferrée, d'une route] bed ▪ FIN [d'une hypothèque] basis ▪ **l'~ de l'impôt** the base (taxation) rate **3.** ÉQUIT seat **4.** *loc* **je ne suis pas** *ou* **je ne me sens pas dans mon ~** I don't feel too well, I'm feeling (a bit) out of sorts **5.** NAUT trim.

assiettée [asjete] *nf* [mesure] : **une ~ de** a plate *ou* plateful of.

assignable [asiɲabl] *adj* **1.** [attribuable] ascribable, attributable **2.** DR liable to be subpoenaed.

assignat [asiɲa] *nm* paper money *(issued during the French Revolution)*.

assignation [asiɲasjɔ̃] *nf* **1.** [de témoin] subpoena ▪ [d'un accusé] summons ▪ **~ à résidence** house arrest **2.** [de part, de rente] allocation.

assigner [3] [asiɲe] *vt* **1.** [attribuer - poste] to assign ; [- tâche] to allot, to allocate, to assign ▪ **~ un même objectif à deux projets** to set the same goal for two projects **2.** FIN [allouer] to allocate, to earmark ▪ **~ des crédits à la recherche** to allocate funds for *ou* to research **3.** DR : **~ un témoin (à comparaître)** to subpoena a witness ▪ **~ qqn à résidence** to put sb under house arrest ▪ **~ qqn (en justice) pour diffamation** to issue a writ for libel against sb.

assimilable [asimilabl] *adj* **1.** PHYSIOL assimilable, easily absorbed *ou* assimilated **2.** [abordable] easily acquired *ou* assimilated **3.** SOCIOL easily assimilated *ou* integrated **4.** [similaire] : **~ à** comparable to ▪ **son travail est souvent ~ à celui d'un médecin** his work can often be compared to that of a doctor.

assimilation [asimilasjɔ̃] *nf* **1.** PHYSIOL assimilation **2.** BOT : **~ chlorophyllienne** photosynthesis **3.** [fait de comprendre] : **avoir un grand pouvoir d'~** to acquire knowledge very easily ▪ **l'~ des connaissances se fait à un rythme différent selon les élèves** pupils assimilate knowledge at different rates **4.** [intégration] assimilation, integration **5.** [de statut] : **l'~ des postes de maîtrise à des postes de cadres** placing supervisory positions in the same category as executive positions **6.** PHON assimilation.

assimilé, e [asimile] *adj* comparable, similar ▪ **talc pour bébé et produits ~s** baby powder and similar products.
◆ **assimilé** *nm* : **cadres et ~s** executives and their equivalent.

assimiler [3] [asimile] *vt* **1.** PHYSIOL to assimilate, to absorb, to metabolize ▪ [digérer] to digest **2.** [comprendre] to assimilate, to take in *(sép)* ▪ **j'ai du mal à ~ les logarithmes** I have trouble mastering logarithms ▪ **c'est du freudisme mal assimilé** it's ill-digested Freudianism **3.** [intégrer] to assimilate, to integrate **4.** PHON to assimilate.
◆ **assimiler à** *v+prép* to compare to ▪ **être assimilé à un cadre supérieur** to be given equivalent status to an executive.
◆ **s'assimiler** *vp (emploi passif)* PHYSIOL to become absorbed *ou* metabolized ▪ [être digéré] to be assimilated *ou* digested.
◆ **s'assimiler à** *vp+prép* to compare o.s. to *ou* with.

assis, e [asi, iz] ◇ *pp* ▷ **asseoir**.
◇ *adj* **1.** [établi] stable ▪ **position bien ~e** well-established position **2.** [non debout] sitting (down) ▪ **rester ~ : je vous en prie,**

restez ~ please don't get up ■ **tout le monde est resté** ~ everyone remained seated ■ **se tenir** ~ to be sitting up ■ ~**!** [à un chien] sit!

◆ **assise** *nf* **1.** [fondement] foundation, basis **2.** CONSTR course ■ [d'une route] bed **3.** ANAT, BOT & GÉOL stratum.

◆ **assises** *nfpl* **1.** DR : **(cour d')~es** ≃ crown court *UK*, ≃ circuit court *US* **2.** [réunion] meeting, conference ■ **la fédération tient ses ~es à Nice** a meeting of the federation is being held *ou* taking place in Nice.

assistanat [asistana] *nm* **1.** ÉDUC (foreign) assistant exchange scheme **2.** UNIV assistantship **3.** [secours - privé] aid ; [- public] state aid.

assistance [asistɑ̃s] *nf* **1.** [aide] assistance ■ **prêter ~ à qqn** to lend *ou* give assistance to sb, to assist sb ■ **trouver ~ auprès de qqn** to get help from sb ◐ ~ **judiciaire** legal aid ■ **l'Assistance (publique)** [à Paris et Marseille] *authority which manages the social services and state-owned hospitals* ■ **c'est un enfant de l'Assistance** *vieilli* he was brought up in an institution ■ ~ **sociale** [aux pauvres] welfare ; [métier] social work ■ ~ **technique** technical aid **2.** [spectateurs - d'une pièce, d'un cours] audience ; [- d'une messe] congregation **3.** [présence] : **l'~ aux conférences n'est pas obligatoire** attendance at lectures is not compulsory.

assistant, e [asistɑ̃, ɑ̃t] *nm, f* **1.** [second] assistant **2.** ÉDUC (foreign language) assistant **3.** UNIV lecturer *UK*, assistant teacher *US* **4.** SOCIOL : ~ **maternel, ~e maternelle** [à son domicile] childminder *UK*, babysitter ; [en collectivité] crèche *UK ou* day-care center *US* worker ■ ~ **social, ~e sociale** social worker **5.** INFORM : ~ **numérique personnel** personal digital assistant, PDA.

◆ **assistante** *nf* : **~e de police** policewoman, WPC *UK (in charge of minors).*

assisté, e [asiste] ◇ *adj* **1.** TECHNOL [frein, direction] servo *(modif)* **2.** [aidé] : **enfants ~s** children in care *UK ou* in custody *US* ■ **être ~** ADMIN to receive state aid.

◇ *nm, f* ADMIN : **les ~s** recipients of state aid ■ **ils ont une mentalité d'~s** they expect everything to be done for them.

assister [3] [asiste] *vt* [aider] to assist, to aid ■ **le prêtre est assisté d'un enfant de chœur** the priest is attended by a choirboy ■ ~ **qqn dans ses derniers moments** *ou* **dernières heures** to comfort sb in his last hours ■ ~ **(qqn) d'office** DR to be appointed by the court (to defend sb).

◆ **assister à** *v+prép* **1.** [être présent à - messe, gala] to attend ; [- concert de rock, enregistrement de télévision] to be at **2.** [être témoin de] to witness, to be a witness to **3.** [remarquer] to note, to witness.

associatif, ive [asɔsjatif, iv] *adj* associative ■ **la vie associative** community life.

association [asɔsjasjɔ̃] *nf* **1.** [groupement] society, association ■ **protéger la liberté d'~** to protect freedom of association ◐ ~ **des anciens élèves** association of former pupils *UK ou* alumni *US* ■ ~ **de bienfaisance** charity, charitable organization ■ ~ **à but non lucratif** *ou* **sans but lucratif** non profit-making *UK ou* not-for-profit *US* organization ■ ~ **humanitaire** charity organization ■ ~ **de malfaiteurs** criminal conspiracy ■ ~ **de parents d'élèves** ≃ Parent-Teacher Association *UK*, ≃ Parent-Teacher Organization *US* **2.** [collaboration] partnership, association **3.** [d'images] association ■ [de couleurs] combination ◐ **~s (d'idées)** associations ■ **~s verbales** PSYCHOL free associations.

associé, e [asɔsje] ◇ *adj* associate.

◇ *nm, f* associate, partner.

associer [9] [asɔsje] *vt* **1.** [idées, images, mots] to associate ■ ~ **qqn/qqch à** to associate sb/sthg with, to connect sb/sthg with, to link sb/sthg with **2.** [faire participer] : ~ **qqn à : il m'a associé à son projet** he included me in his project **3.** [saveurs, couleurs] : ~ **qqch à** to combine sthg with.

◆ **s'associer** ◇ *vpi* **1.** [s'allier] to join forces ■ COMM to enter *ou* to go into partnership, to become partners *ou* associates ■ **la France et l'Allemagne se sont associées pour le projet Hermès** France and Germany are partners in the Hermes project **2.** [s'harmoniser] to be combined.

◇ *vpt* : **s'~ qqn** to take sb on as a partner.

◆ **s'associer à** *vp+prép* to share (in) ■ **je m'associe pleinement à votre malheur** I share your grief ■ **s'~ à une entreprise criminelle** to be an accomplice to *ou* to take part in a crime.

assoiffé, e [aswafe] *adj* thirsty ■ ~ **de sang** bloodthirsty.

assoiffer [3] [aswafe] *vt* to make thirsty.

assoit *etc v* ▻ **asseoir**.

assolement [asɔlmɑ̃] *nm* crop rotation.

assoler [3] [asɔle] *vt* [terres] to rotate crops on.

assombrir [32] [asɔ̃brir] *vt* **1.** [rendre sombre] to darken, to make dark *ou* darker ■ **le mur brun assombrit la pièce** the brown wall makes the room look darker **2.** [rendre triste] to cast a shadow *ou* cloud over, to mar.

◆ **s'assombrir** *vpi* **1.** [s'obscurcir] to darken, to grow dark ■ **à l'approche du cyclone, le ciel s'est assombri** with the approaching hurricane, the sky grew very dark **2.** [s'attrister - visage] to become gloomy, to cloud over ; [- personne, humeur] to become gloomy.

assombrissement [asɔ̃brismɑ̃] *nm litt* darkening.

assommant, e [asɔmɑ̃, ɑ̃t] *adj fam* **1.** [ennuyeux] boring, tedious **2.** [fatigant] : **tu es ~, à la fin, avec tes questions!** all these questions are getting really annoying!

assommer [3] [asɔme] *vt* **1.** [frapper] to knock out *(sép)*, to stun ■ **se faire ~** to be knocked out ■ [tuer] : ~ **un bœuf** to fell an ox **2.** *fam* [ennuyer] : ~ **qqn** to bore sb stiff ■ **ils m'assomment avec leurs statistiques** they bore me to tears with their statistics ■ [importuner] to harass, to wear down *(sép)* **3.** [abrutir] to stun.

Assomption [asɔ̃psjɔ̃] *nf* : **l'~** the Assumption.

L'ASSOMPTION

> Assumption, on the 15th of August, is a Catholic feast. It is a public holiday in France.

assonance [asɔnɑ̃s] *nf* assonance.

assorti, e [asɔrti] *adj* **1.** [en harmonie] : **un couple bien ~** a well-matched couple ■ **un couple mal ~** an ill-matched *ou* ill-assorted couple ■ **les deux couleurs sont très bien assorties** the two colours match (up) *ou* blend (in) perfectly ■ **pantalon avec veste ~e** trousers *UK ou* pants *US* with matching jacket **2.** [chocolats] assorted **3.** [approvisionné] : **un magasin bien ~** a well-stocked shop.

assortiment [asɔrtimɑ̃] *nm* **1.** [ensemble] assortment, selection ■ ~ **de charcuterie** selection of *ou* assorted cold meats ■ ~ **d'outils** set of tools, tool kit **2.** [harmonisation] arrangement, matching **3.** COMM [choix] selection, range, stock ■ **nous avons un vaste ~ de desserts** we offer a large selection *ou* a wide range of desserts.

assortir [32] [asɔrtir] *vt* **1.** [teintes, vêtements] to match ■ ~ **à : j'ai acheté le couvre-lit assorti au papier peint** I bought a bedspread to match the wallpaper ■ ~ **ses chaussures à sa ceinture** to match one's shoes with *ou* to one's belt **2.** [personnes] to match, to mix **3.** COMM [approvisionner] to supply **4.** [accompagner] : ~ **de : il a assorti son discours d'un paragraphe sur le racisme** he added a paragraph on racism to his speech.

◆ **s'assortir** *vpi* **1.** [s'harmoniser] to match, to go together well ■ **sa manière de s'habiller s'assortit à sa personnalité** the way he dresses matches *ou* reflects his personality **2.** [être complété] : **s'~ de : son étude s'assortit de quelques remarques sur la situation actuelle** his study includes a few comments on the present situation **3.** COMM to buy one's stock.

Assouan [aswɑ̃] *npr* Aswan, Assouan ■ **le barrage d'~** the Aswan (High) Dam.

assoupi, e [asupi] *adj* **1.** [endormi - personne] asleep, sleeping, dozing **2.** *litt* [sans animation - ville] sleepy.

assoupir [32] [asupir] *vt* **1.** [endormir] to make drowsy *ou* sleepy **2.** *litt* [atténuer - soupçon, douleur] to dull.

◆ **s'assoupir** *vpi* **1.** [s'endormir] to doze off, to fall asleep **2.** *litt* [s'affaiblir - crainte, douleur] to be dulled.

assoupissement [asupismɑ̃] *nm* **1.** [sommeil léger] doze ▪ [état somnolent] drowsiness ▪ **tomber dans un léger ~** to doze off **2.** *litt* [atténuation - des soupçons, de la douleur] dulling, numbing.

assouplir [32] [asuplir] *vt* **1.** [rendre moins dur - corps] to make supple, to loosen up *(sép)* ; [- linge, cuir] to soften ▪ **ajoutez du lait pour ~ la pâte** add milk until the dough is soft **2.** [rendre moins strict] to ease ▪ **~ ses positions** to take a softer line ▪ **l'âge n'a pas assoupli son caractère** age hasn't made her more tractable *OU* any easier ▪ **le règlement de l'école a été considérablement assoupli** the school rules have been considerably relaxed.
◆ **s'assouplir** *vpi* **1.** [devenir moins raide] to become looser *OU* more supple, to loosen up **2.** [caractère, règlement] to become more flexible.

assouplissant [asuplisɑ̃] *nm* (fabric) softener.

assouplissement [asuplismɑ̃] *nm* **1.** LOISIRS & SPORT limbering up, loosening up ▪ **des exercices** *OU* **une séance d'~** limbering-up exercises **2.** [d'un linge, d'un cuir] softening **3.** [d'une position] softening ▪ **demander l'~ d'un règlement** to ask for regulations to be relaxed **4.** ÉCON : **~ du crédit** easing of credit.

assouplisseur [asuplisœr] *nm* (fabric) softener.

assourdir [32] [asurdir] *vt* **1.** [personne] to deafen ▪ [bruit, son] to dull, to deaden, to muffle **2.** PHON to make voiceless *OU* unvoiced.
◆ **s'assourdir** *vpi* PHON to become voiceless *OU* unvoiced.

assourdissant, e [asurdisɑ̃, ɑ̃t] *adj* deafening, ear-splitting.

assouvir [32] [asuvir] *vt* *sout* [désir, faim] to appease, to assuage *sout* ▪ [soif] to quench.

assouvissement [asuvismɑ̃] *nm* *sout* [d'une passion, de la faim] appeasing, assuaging *sout* ▪ [de la soif] quenching.

assoyait *etc v* ▻ **asseoir**.

ASSU, Assu [asy] (*abr de* **Association du sport scolaire et universitaire**) *npr f former schools and university sports association.*

assujetti, e [asyʒeti] ◇ *adj* *litt* [population, prisonnier] subjugated.
◇ *nm, f* person liable for tax.

assujettir [32] [asyʒetir] *vt* **1.** [astreindre] to compel ▪ **être assujetti à un contrôle médical très strict** to be subjected to very strict medical checks ▪ **être assujetti à l'impôt** to be liable for taxation **2.** [arrimer] to fasten, to secure **3.** *litt* [asservir - nation, peuple] to subjugate, to hold under a yoke.
◆ **s'assujettir à** *vp+prép* to submit (o.s.) to.

assujettissement [asyʒetismɑ̃] *nm* **1.** *litt* [asservissement] subjection **2.** DR : **~ à l'impôt** liability to taxation.

assumer [3] [asyme] *vt* **1.** [endosser] to take on *(sép)*, to take upon o.s., to assume ▪ **j'en assume l'entière responsabilité** I take *OU* I accept full responsibility for it ▪ **nous assumerons toutes les dépenses** we'll meet all the expenses ▪ **elle assume à la fois les fonctions de présidente et de trésorière** she acts both as chairperson and treasurer ▪ **j'ai assumé ces responsabilités pendant trop longtemps** I held that job for too long **2.** [accepter] to accept ▪ **il assume mal ses origines** he's never been able to come to terms with his background ▪ *(en usage absolu)* **j'assume!** I don't care what other people think!
◆ **s'assumer** *vpi* : **il a du mal à s'~ en tant que père** he's finding it hard to come to terms with his role as father ▪ **il serait temps que tu t'assumes!** *fam* it's time you took responsibility for your actions!

assurance [asyrɑ̃s] *nf* **1.** COMM [contrat] insurance (policy) ▪ **placer des ~s** to sell insurance (policies) ▪ **~ contre l'incendie/les accidents** insurance against fire/(personal) accidents, fire/accident insurance ▪ **~ contre le vol** insurance against theft ▪ **les ~s** insurance companies ➋ **~ auto** *OU* **automobile** car *OU* automobile *US* insurance ▪ **~ chômage** unemployment insurance ▪ **~ maladie** health insurance ▪ **~ maternité** maternity benefit ▪ **~ mixte** endowment policy ▪ **~ personnelle** *OU* **volontaire** private health insurance *OU* cover ▪ **~ responsabilité civile** *OU* **au tiers** third party insurance ▪ **~ tous risques** comprehensive insurance ▪ **les ~s sociales** ≃ National Insurance *UK*, ≃ Welfare *US* ▪ **~ vieillesse** retirement pension
2. *sout* [promesse] assurance ▪ **j'ai reçu l'~ formelle que l'on m'aiderait financièrement** I was assured I would receive financial help
3. [garantie] : **une ~ de** a guarantee of ▪ **le retour à la démocratie constitue une ~ de paix pour le pays** the return of democracy will guarantee peace for the country
4. [aisance] self-confidence, assurance ▪ **manque d'~** insecurity, lack of self-confidence ▪ **manquer d'~** to be insecure, to have no self-confidence ▪ **s'exprimer avec ~** to speak with assurance *OU* confidently ▪ **elle a de l'~ dans la voix** she sounds confident
5. [certitude] : **avoir l'~ que** to feel certain *OU* assured that ▪ **j'ai l'~ qu'il viendra** I'm sure he'll come
6. [dans la correspondance] : **veuillez croire à l'~ de ma considération distinguée** yours faithfully *OU* sincerely, sincerely yours *US*.

assurance-crédit [asyrɑ̃skredi] (*pl* **assurances-crédits**) *nf* credit insurance.

assurance-décès [asyrɑ̃sdesɛ] (*pl* **assurances-décès**) *nf* life insurance *OU* assurance.

assurance-vie [asyrɑ̃svi] (*pl* **assurances-vie**) *nf* life insurance *OU* assurance.

assuré, e [asyre] ◇ *adj* **1.** [incontestable] certain, sure ▪ **succès ~ pour son nouvel album!** her new album is sure to be a hit! ▪ **discrétion ~e** confidentiality guaranteed **2.** [résolu] assured, self-confident ▪ **marcher d'un pas ~** to walk confidently ▪ **d'une voix mal ~e** quaveringly, in an unsteady voice ▪ **avoir un air ~** to look self-confident.
◇ *nm, f* **1.** [qui a un contrat d'assurance] insured person, policyholder ▪ **les ~s** the insured **2.** ADMIN : **~ social** ≃ contributor to the National Insurance scheme *UK* ▪ ≃ contributor to Social Security *US*.

assurément [asyremɑ̃] *adv* *sout* assuredly, undoubtedly, most certainly ▪ **~ non!** certainly *OU* indeed *sout* not! ▪ **~ (oui)!** yes, indeed!, (most) definitely!

assurer [3] [asyre] ◇ *vt* **1.** [certifier] to assure ▪ **il m'a assuré qu'il viendrait** he assured me he'd come ▪ **mais si, je t'assure!** yes, I swear! ▪ **il faut de la patience avec elle, je t'assure!** you need a lot of patience when dealing with her, I'm telling you!
2. [rendre sûr] to assure ▪ **laissez-moi vous ~ de ma reconnaissance** let me assure you of my gratitude
3. [procurer] to maintain, to provide ▪ **~ le ravitaillement des populations sinistrées** to provide disaster victims with supplies ▪ **une permanence est assurée le samedi après-midi** there is someone on duty on Saturday afternoons ▪ **pour mieux ~ la sécurité de tous** to ensure greater safety for all ▪ **~ une liaison aérienne/ferroviaire** to operate an air/a rail link ▪ **~ qqch à qqn : ~ à qqn un bon salaire** to secure a good salary for sb
4. [mettre à l'abri] to ensure, to secure ▪ **~ l'avenir** to make provision *OU* provide for the future ➋ **~ ses arrières** MIL to protect one's rear ; *fig* to leave o.s. a way out *OU* something to fall back on
5. [arrimer] to secure, to steady
6. COMM to insure ▪ **j'ai fait ~ mes bijoux** I had my jewels insured ▪ **être mal assuré contre le vol** to be under-insured in case of theft
7. SPORT to belay
8. NAUT [bout] to belay, to make fast.
◇ *vi* *fam* **il assure en physique/anglais** he's good at physics/English ▪ **elle a beau être nouvelle au bureau, elle assure bien** she may be new to the job but she certainly copes (well) ▪ **les femmes d'aujourd'hui, elles assurent!** modern women can do anything! ▪ **il va falloir ~!** we'll have to show that we're up to it!
◆ **s'assurer** ◇ *vp (emploi réfléchi)* COMM to insure o.s. ▪ **s'~ contre le vol/l'incendie** to insure o.s. against theft/fire ▪ **il est obligatoire pour un automobiliste de s'~** by law, a driver must be insured.
◇ *vpi* [s'affermir] to steady o.s.
◇ *vpt* [se fournir - revenu] to secure, to ensure.

◆ **s'assurer de** *vp+prép* [contrôler] : **assurez-vous de la validité de votre passeport** make sure your passport is valid ▪ **je vais m'en ~ immédiatement** I'll check right away ▪ **s'~ que** to make sure (that), to check (that) ▪ **assure-toi que tout va bien** make sure everything's OK.

assureur [asyrœr] *nm* insurer, underwriter.

Assyrie [asiri] *npr f* : **(l')~** Assyria.

assyrien, enne [asirjɛ̃, ɛn] *adj* Assyrian.
◆ **Assyrien, enne** *nm, f* Assyrian.

astérisque [asterisk] *nm* asterisk.

Astérix [asteriks] *npr* Asterix ▪ **le parc ~** *large theme park north of Paris.*

astéroïde [asterɔid] *nm* asteroid.

asthénique [astenik] ◇ *adj* asthenic.
◇ *nmf* asthenia sufferer.

asthmatique [asmatik] *adj & nmf* asthmatic.

asthme [asm] *nm* asthma ▪ **avoir de l'~** to suffer from asthma.

asticot [astiko] *nm* [ver] maggot ▪ PÊCHE gentle.

asticoter [3] [astikɔte] *vt fam* to bug.

astigmate [astigmat] *adj & nmf* astigmatic.

astiquer [3] [astike] *vt* to polish, to shine.

astragale [astragal] *nm* **1.** ANAT astragalus, talus **2.** ARCHIT astragal **3.** BOT astragalus.

astrakan [astrakɑ̃] *nm* astrakhan (fur) ▪ **un manteau en ~** an astrakhan coat.

astral, e, aux [astral, o] *adj* astral.

astre [astr] *nm* ASTROL & ASTRON star ▪ **l'~ du jour** *litt* the sun ● **beau comme un ~** radiantly handsome *ou* beautiful.

astreignait *etc v* ▻ **astreindre**.

astreignant, e [astrɛɲɑ̃, ɑ̃t] *adj* demanding, exacting ▪ **un programme ~** a punishing schedule.

astreindre [81] [astrɛ̃dr] *vt* : **~ qqn à qqch** to tie sb down to sthg ▪ **il est astreint à un régime sévère** he's on a very strict diet ▪ **~ qqn à faire qqch** to compel *ou* to force *ou* to oblige sb to do sthg.
◆ **s'astreindre à** *vp+prép* : **s'~ à faire qqch** to compel *ou* to force o.s. to do sthg ▪ **il s'astreint à un régime sévère** he sticks to a strict diet.

astreinte [astrɛ̃t] *nf* DR *daily penalty for delay in payment of debt.*

astringence [astrɛ̃ʒɑ̃s] *nf* astringency, astringence.

astringent, e [astrɛ̃ʒɑ̃, ɑ̃t] *adj* PHARM astringent ▪ [vin] sharp.

astrologie [astrɔlɔʒi] *nf* astrology.

astrologique [astrɔlɔʒik] *adj* astrological.

astrologue [astrɔlɔg] *nmf* astrologer.

astronaute [astrɔnot] *nmf* astronaut.

astronautique [astrɔnotik] *nf* astronautics *(U).*

astronef [astrɔnɛf] *nm vieilli* spaceship.

astronome [astrɔnɔm] *nmf* astronomer.

astronomie [astrɔnɔmi] *nf* astronomy.

astronomique [astrɔnɔmik] *adj* **1.** SC astronomic, astronomical **2.** *fam* [somme] astronomic, astronomical ▪ **ça a atteint des prix ~s!** it's become ridiculously expensive!

astrophysicien, enne [astrɔfizisjɛ̃, ɛn] *nm, f* astrophysicist.

astrophysique [astrɔfizik] *nf* astrophysics *(U).*

astuce [astys] *nf* **1.** [ingéniosité] astuteness, shrewdness ▪ **il est plein d'~** he's a shrewd individual **2.** *fam* [plaisanterie] joke, gag ▪ **je n'ai pas compris l'~!** I didn't get it! **3.** *fam* [procédé ingénieux] trick ▪ **en page 23, notre rubrique "~s"** our tips are on page 23 ▪ **je n'arrive pas à l'ouvrir – attends, il doit y avoir une ~** I can't open it – wait, there must be some knack (to it) ▪ **comment fais-tu tenir le loquet? – ah, ah, c'est l'~!** how do you get the latch to stay on? – aha, wouldn't you like to know! ▪ **les ~s du métier** the tricks of the trade.

astucieux, euse [astysjø, øz] *adj* shrewd, clever.

Asturies [astyri] *npr fpl* : **les ~** Asturias.

asymétrie [asimetri] *nf* asymmetry, lack of symmetry.

asymétrique [asimetrik] *adj* asymmetric, asymmetrical.

asynchrone [asɛ̃kron] *adj* asynchronous.

atavique [atavik] *adj* atavistic, atavic.

atavisme [atavism] *nm* atavism ▪ **ils sont prudents, c'est un vieil ~ paysan** they're very cautious, on account of their peasant origins ▪ **ça doit être par ~!** it must be in my/your *etc* blood!

atchoum [atʃum] *interj* atishoo.

atèle [atɛl] *nm* spider monkey.

atelier [atəlje] *nm* **1.** [d'un bricoleur, d'un artisan] workshop ▪ [d'un peintre, d'un photographe] studio ▪ COUT workroom **2.** [d'une usine] shop ▪ **l'~ s'est mis en grève** the shopfloor has gone on strike ● **~ d'assemblage** assembly shop ▪ **~ naval** shipyard ▪ **~ protégé** sheltered workshop **3.** [cours] workshop ▪ ART class ▪ **participer à un ~ de peinture sur soie** to take part in a silk painting workshop *ou* a workshop on silk painting **4.** [de francs-maçons] lodge.

atemporel, elle [atɑ̃pɔrɛl] *adj* timeless.

atermoie *etc v* ▻ **atermoyer**.

atermoiement [atɛrmwamɑ̃] *nm* procrastination *sout*, delaying.

atermoyer [13] [atɛrmwaje] *vi* to procrastinate *sout*, to delay ▪ **ayant atermoyé deux mois, ils ont fini par dire oui** having held back from making a decision for two months, they finally said yes.

athée [ate] ◇ *adj* atheistic, atheist *(modif).*
◇ *nmf* atheist.

athéisme [ateism] *nm* atheism.

Athéna [atena] *npr* Athena, Athene.

athénée [atene] *nm Belgique* high *ou* secondary school.

Athènes [atɛn] *npr* Athens.

athénien, enne [atenjɛ̃, ɛn] *adj* Athenian.
◆ **Athénien, enne** *nm, f* Athenian ▪ **c'est là que les Athéniens s'atteignirent** *hum* that was when things started to get complicated.

athérosclérose [ateroskleroz] *nf* atherosclerosis.

athlète [atlɛt] *nmf* athlete ▪ **un corps/une carrure d'~** an athletic body/build.

athlétique [atletik] *adj* athletic.

athlétisme [atletism] *nm* athletics *(sing).*

Atlantide [atlɑ̃tid] *npr f* : **l'~** Atlantis.

atlantique [atlɑ̃tik] *adj* Atlantic ▪ **la côte ~** the Atlantic coast ▪ **le Pacte ~** the Atlantic Charter.

Atlantique [atlɑ̃tik] *npr m* : **l'~** the Atlantic (Ocean).

atlas [atlas] *nm* **1.** [livre] atlas **2.** ANAT atlas.

Atlas [atlas] ◇ *npr* MYTHOL Atlas.
◇ *npr m* GÉOGR : **l'~** the Atlas Mountains.

atmosphère [atmɔsfɛr] *nf* **1.** GÉOGR atmosphere **2.** [ambiance] atmosphere, ambiance **3.** [air que l'on respire] air ▪ **l'~ humide du littoral** the dampness of the air on the coast **4.** PHYS atmosphere.

atmosphérique [atmɔsferik] *adj* [condition, couche, pression] atmospheric.

atoca [atɔka] *nm Québec* cranberry.

atoll [atɔl] *nm* atoll.

atome [atom] *nm* atom ■ **l'ère de l'~** the atomic age ➊ **avoir des ~s crochus avec qqn** *fam* to have things in common with sb ■ **je n'ai pas d'~s crochus avec elle** I don't have much in common with her.

atomique [atɔmik] *adj* [masse] atomic ■ [énergie] atomic, nuclear ■ [explosion] nuclear.

atomisé, e [atɔmize] <> *adj* PHYS atomized.
<> *nm, f* person suffering from the effects of radiation.

atomiser [3] [atɔmize] *vt* **1.** PHYS to atomize **2.** NUCL : ~ qqch to destroy sthg with an atom bomb, to blast sthg with a nuclear device **3.** *fig* to pulverize.

atomiseur [atɔmizœr] *nm* spray ■ **parfum en ~** spray perfume.

atomiste [atɔmist] <> *adj* **1.** PHYS atomic **2.** PHILOS atomistic, atomistical, atomist.
<> *nmf* **1.** PHYS atomic scientist **2.** PHILOS atomist.

atonal, e, aux [atɔnal, o] *adj* atonal.

atonalité [atɔnalite] *nf* atonality.

atone [atɔn] *adj* **1.** [expression, œil, regard] lifeless, expressionless **2.** PHON atonic, unaccented, unstressed **3.** MÉD atonic.

atonie [atɔni] *nf* **1.** [inertie] lifelessness **2.** MÉD atony.

atours [atur] *nmpl arch* attire, array ■ **elle avait revêtu ses plus beaux ~** *hum* she was dressed in all her finery.

atout [atu] *nm* **1.** JEUX trump ■ **jouer ~** to play a trump ; [en ouvrant le jeu] to lead trump *ou* trumps ■ **il a joué ~ carreau** diamonds were trumps ■ **l'~ est à pique** spades are trumps ■ **prendre avec de l'~** to trump ➊ **~ maître** *pr* master trump ; *fig* trump card **2.** [avantage] asset, trump *fig* ■ **il a tous les ~s dans son jeu** *ou* **en main** he has all the trumps *ou* all the winning cards.

ATP (*abr de* **Association des tennismen professionnels**) *npr f* ATP.

atrabilaire [atrabilɛr] *litt* <> *adj* cantankerous, atrabilious *litt*.
<> *nmf* cantankerous person.

âtre [atr] *nm litt* hearth.

atriau [atrijo] *nm Suisse circular forcemeat patty.*

Atrides [atrid] *npr mpl* : **les ~** the Atreids, the Atridae.

atrium [atrijɔm] *nm* atrium.

atroce [atrɔs] *adj* **1.** [cruel] atrocious, foul ■ **des scènes ~s** horrifying *ou* gruesome scenes ■ **leur vengeance fut ~** their revenge was awesome **2.** [insupportable] excruciating, dreadful, atrocious ■ **il est mort dans d'~s souffrances** he died in dreadful pain **3.** [en intensif] : **sa maison est d'un mauvais goût ~** his house is horribly tasteless **4.** *fam* [sens affaibli] atrocious, foul ■ **il est ~ avec son père** he's really awful to his father.

atrocement [atrɔsmɑ̃] *adv* **1.** [cruellement] atrociously, horribly ■ **~ mutilé** horribly *ou* hideously mutilated **2.** [en intensif] atrociously, dreadfully, horribly ■ **j'ai ~ froid** I'm frozen to death ■ **j'ai ~ faim** I'm starving ■ **j'ai ~ soif** I'm parched.

atrocité [atrɔsite] *nf* **1.** [caractère cruel] atrociousness ■ **le repentir n'excuse pas l'~ de ses crimes** repentance does not excuse the horror of his crimes **2.** [crime] atrocity.

atrophie [atrɔfi] *nf* atrophy.

atrophié, e [atrɔfje] *adj* atrophied.

atrophier [9] [atrɔfje] ◆ **s'atrophier** *vpi* to atrophy.

attabler [3] [atable] ◆ **s'attabler** *vpi* to sit down (at the table) ■ **tous les convives sont déjà attablés** all the guests are already seated at table ■ **venez donc vous ~ avec nous** do come and sit at our table.

ATTAC [atak] (*abr de* **Association pour la Taxation des Transactions pour l'Aide aux Citoyens**) *nf pressure group opposed to the dominance of the financial sphere in society, and which lobbies in favour of a tax on currency exchanges (Tobin tax).*

attachant, e [ataʃɑ̃, ɑ̃t] *adj* [personnalité] engaging, lovable ■ [livre, spectacle] captivating ■ **c'est un enfant très ~** he's such a lovable child.

attache [ataʃ] *nf* **1.** [lien - gén] tie ; [- en cuir, en toile] strap ; [- en ficelle] string ; [- d'un vêtement] clip, fastener ; [- d'un rideau] tie-back **2.** [ami] tie, friend ■ [parent] relative, family tie ■ **un homme sans ~s** [sans partenaire] an unattached man ; [sans relations] a man without family or friends ■ **tous les ans ils séjournaient à Monteau, ils s'y étaient fait des ~s** they went back to Monteau every year, they'd made friends there **3.** BOT tendril.
◆ **attaches** *nfpl* ANAT joints ■ **avoir des ~s fines** to be small-boned.
◆ **à l'attache** *loc adj* [chien, cheval] tied up.

attaché, e [ataʃe] <> *adj* attached ■ **~s avec un trombone** [documents] held together with a paperclip ■ **bien ~** firmly attached ■ **mal ~** poorly attached, loose.
<> *nm, f* attaché ■ **~ militaire/d'ambassade** military/embassy attaché ■ **~ d'administration** administrative assistant ■ **~ de presse** press attaché.

attachement [ataʃmɑ̃] *nm* **1.** [affection] affection, attachment ■ **son ~ pour sa mère** his affection for *ou* attachment to his mother ■ **avoir de l'~ pour qqn** to be fond of sb **2.** CONSTR daily statement *(to record progress and costs).*

attacher [3] [ataʃe] <> *vt* **1.** [accrocher] to tie, to tie up *(sép)* ■ **~ son chien** to tie up one's dog ■ **~ les mains d'un prisonnier** to tie a prisoner's hands together ■ **~ qqn/qqch à** to tie sb/sthg to ■ **~ un chien à une corde/à sa niche** to tie a dog to a rope/to his kennel ■ **pauvre bête, il l'a attachée à une chaîne** he's chained the poor thing up ■ **une photo était attachée à la lettre** [avec un trombone] a picture was clipped to the letter ; [avec une agrafe] a picture was stapled to the letter
2. [pour fermer] to tie ■ **~ un colis avec une ficelle** to tie up a parcel ■ **une simple ficelle attachait la valise** the suitcase was held shut with a piece of string
3. [vêtement] to fasten ■ **peux-tu m'aider à ~ ma robe?** can you help me do up my dress? ■ **~ ses lacets** to tie one's shoelaces ■ **attachez votre ceinture** fasten your seatbelt
4. [accorder] to attach ■ **j'attache beaucoup de prix** *ou* **de valeur à notre amitié** I attach great value to *ou* set great store by our friendship
5. [associer] to link, to connect ■ **le scandale auquel son nom est/reste attaché** the scandal with which his name is/remains linked ■ **plus rien ne l'attache à Paris** he has no ties in Paris now
6. *sout* [comme domestique, adjoint] : **~ qqn à** : **~ un apprenti à un maître** to apprentice a young boy to a master ■ **elle est attachée à mon service depuis dix ans** she has been working for me for ten years.
<> *vi* CULIN to stick ■ **le riz a attaché** the rice has stuck ■ **poêle/casserole qui n'attache pas** nonstick pan/saucepan.
◆ **s'attacher** <> *vp (emploi réfléchi)* to tie o.s.
<> *vp (emploi passif)* to fasten, to do up ■ **s'~ avec une fermeture Éclair®/des boutons** to zip/to button up.
<> *vpt* : **s'~ (les services de) qqn** to take sb on.
◆ **s'attacher à** *vp+prép* **1.** [se lier avec] to become fond of *ou* attached to ■ **s'~ aux pas de qqn** to follow sb closely
2. [s'efforcer de] to devote o.s. to ■ **je m'attache à le rendre heureux** I try (my best) to make him happy.

attaquable [atakabl] *adj* **1.** MIL open to attack **2.** [discutable] contestable ■ **son système/testament n'est pas ~** his system/will cannot be contested.

attaquant, e [atakɑ̃, ɑ̃t] <> *adj* attacking, assaulting, assailing.
<> *nm, f* attacker, assailant.
◆ **attaquant** *nm* SPORT striker.

attaque [atak] *nf* **1.** [agression] attack, assault ■ **passer à l'~** *pr* to attack ; *fig* to attack, to go on the offensive ➊ **~ aérienne** air attack *ou* raid ■ **~ à main armée** [contre une banque] armed robbery **2.** [diatribe] attack, onslaught ■ **il a été victime d'odieuses ~s dans les journaux** he was subjected to scurrilous attacks in the newspapers ■ **pas d'~s personnelles, s'il vous plaît**

let's not be personal please **3.** MÉD stroke, seizure ■ [crise] fit, attack **4.** MUS attack ■ **ton ~ n'est pas assez nette** your attack is too weak.

◆ **d'attaque** *loc adj fam* **se sentir d'~ : je ne me sens pas d'~ pour aller à la piscine** I don't feel up to going to the swimming pool ■ **te sens-tu d'~ pour un petit tennis?** do you feel up to a game of tennis? ■ **je ne me sens pas tellement d'~ ce matin** I don't really feel up to much this morning.

attaquer [3] [atake] *vt* **1.** [assaillir - ennemi, pays, forteresse] to attack, to launch an attack upon ; [- passant, touriste] to mug ■ **il s'est fait ~ par deux hommes** he was attacked *ou* assaulted by two men ■ **madame, c'est lui qui m'a attaqué!** please Miss, he started it! ■ **~ une place par surprise** to make a surprise attack on a fort ➋ **~ le mal à la racine** to tackle the root of the problem

2. [corroder] to damage, to corrode, to eat into *(insép)*

3. [critiquer] to attack, to condemn ■ **il a été attaqué par tous les journaux** he was attacked by all the newspapers ■ **j'ai été personnellement attaqué** I suffered personal attacks ‖ DR : **~ qqn en justice** to bring an action against sb, to take sb to court ■ **~ qqn en diffamation** to bring a libel action against sb ■ **~ un testament** to contest a will

4. [entreprendre - tâche] to tackle, to attack, to get started on *(insép)* ■ **prêt à ~ le travail?** ready to get *ou* to settle down to work?

5. *fam* [commencer - repas, bouteille] : **~ le petit déjeuner** *fam* to dig into breakfast ■ **on attaque le beaujolais?** *fam* shall we have a go at that Beaujolais?

6. MUS to attack ■ *(en usage absolu)* **quand l'orchestre attaque** when the orchestra strikes up

7. JEUX : **~ à l'atout** to lead trumps ■ **~ à carreau** to lead diamonds.

◆ **s'attaquer à** *vp+prép* **1.** [combattre] to take on, to attack ■ **s'~ aux préjugés** to attack *ou* to fight *ou* to tackle prejudice ■ **il s'est tout de suite attaqué au problème** he tackled the problem right away

2. [agir sur] to attack ■ **cette maladie ne s'attaque qu'aux jeunes enfants** only young children are affected by this disease ■ **les bactéries s'attaquent à vos gencives** bacteria attack your gums.

attardé, e [atarde] ◇ *adj* **1.** *vieilli* [anormal] backward, (mentally) retarded **2.** [démodé] old-fashioned.

◇ *nm, f vieilli* [malade] (mentally) retarded person.

attarder [3] [atarde] ◆ **s'attarder** *vpi* **1.** [rester tard - dans la rue] to linger ; [- chez quelqu'un] to stay late ; [- au bureau, à l'atelier] to stay on *ou* late ■ **ne nous attardons pas, la nuit va tomber** let's not stay, it's almost nightfall ■ **je me suis attardée près de la rivière** I lingered by the river ■ **rentre vite, ne t'attarde pas** be home early, don't stay out too late ■ **s'~ à faire qqch : elles s'attardaient à boire leur café** they were lingering over their coffee **2. s'~ sur** [s'intéresser à] to linger over, to dwell on ■ **s'~ sur des détails** to linger over details ■ **attardons-nous quelques minutes sur le cas de cette malade** let's consider the case of this patient for a minute ■ **l'image contenue dans la strophe vaut que l'on s'y attarde** the image in the stanza merits further consideration ■ **encore un mélodrame qui ne vaut pas que l'on s'y attarde** another forgettable melodrama.

atteindre [81] [atɛ̃dr] *vt* **1.** [lieu] to reach, to get to *(insép)* ■ **aucun son ne nous atteignait** no sound reached us ‖ RADIO & TV to reach ■ **des émissions qui atteignent un large public** programmes reaching a wide audience

2. [situation, objectif] to reach, to attain *sout* ■ **~ la gloire** to attain glory *sout* ■ **il a atteint son but** he's reached his goal *ou* achieved his aim ■ **leur propagande n'atteint pas son but** their propaganda misses its target ■ **les taux d'intérêt ont atteint un nouveau record** interest rates have reached a record high

3. [âge, valeur, prix] to reach ■ **~ 70 ans** to reach the age of 70 ■ **le sommet atteint plus de 4 000 mètres** the summit is over 4,000 metres high ■ **les dégâts atteignent neuf cent mille euros** nine hundred thousand euros' worth of damage has been done

4. [communiquer avec] to contact, to reach ■ **il est impossible d'~ ceux qui sont à l'intérieur de l'ambassade** the people inside the embassy are incommunicado

5. [toucher] to reach, to get at, to stretch up to *(insép)* ■ **je n'arrive pas à ~ le dictionnaire qui est là-haut** I can't reach the dictionary up there

6. ARM to hit ■ **~ la cible** to hit the target ■ **la balle/le policier l'a atteint en pleine tête** the bullet hit/the policeman shot him in the head ■ **atteint à l'épaule** wounded in the shoulder ‖ [blesser moralement] to affect, to move, to stir ■ **il peut dire ce qu'il veut à mon sujet, ça ne m'atteint pas** he can say what he likes about me, it doesn't bother me at all ■ **rien ne l'atteint** nothing affects *ou* can reach him

7. [affecter - suj: maladie, fléau] to affect ■ **les tumeurs secondaires ont déjà atteint le poumon** the secondary tumours have already spread to the lung ■ **être atteint d'un mal incurable** to be suffering from an incurable disease ■ **les pays atteints par la folie de la guerre** countries in the grip of war mania.

◆ **atteindre à** *v+prép litt* to achieve, to attain *sout*.

atteint, e [atɛ̃, ɛ̃t] *adj* **1.** [d'une maladie, d'un fléau] affected ■ **quand le moral est ~** when depression sets in **2.** *fam* [fou] : **il est plutôt ~** he's not quite right in the head.

◆ **atteinte** *nf* [attaque] attack ■ **~e aux bonnes mœurs** offence against public decency ■ **~e à la liberté individuelle** infringement of personal freedom ■ **~e aux droits de l'homme** violation of human rights ■ **~e à la sûreté de l'État** high treason ■ **~e à la vie privée** violation of privacy ■ **porter ~e au pouvoir de qqn** to undermine sb's power ■ **porter ~e à l'ordre public** to commit a breach of *ou* to disturb the peace ➋ **hors d'~e** out of reach.

◆ **atteintes** *nfpl* [effets nocifs] effects ■ **les premières ~es du mal se sont manifestées quand il a eu 20 ans** [épilepsie, diabète] he first displayed the symptoms of the disease at the age of 20 ; [alcoolisme, dépression] the first signs of the problem came to light when he was 20.

attelage [atlaʒ] *nm* **1.** [fait d'attacher - un cheval] harnessing ; [- un bœuf] yoking ; [- une charrette] hitching up **2.** [plusieurs animaux] team ■ [paire d'animaux] yoke **3.** [véhicule] carriage **4.** RAIL [processus] coupling ■ [dispositif] coupling.

atteler [24] [atle] *vt* **1.** [cheval] to harness ■ [bœuf] to yoke ■ [carriole] to hitch up *(sép)* **2.** RAIL to couple.

◆ **s'atteler à** *vp+prép* to get down to, to tackle ■ **il va falloir que tu t'attelles à ces révisions!** you'll have to get down to that revision!

attelle [atɛl] *nf* **1.** MÉD splint **2.** [pour un cheval] hame.

attellera *etc v* ▷ **atteler**.

attenant, e [atnɑ̃, ɑ̃t] *adj* adjoining, adjacent ■ **cour ~e à la maison** back yard adjoining the house.

attendre [73] [atɑ̃dr] ◇ *vt*

> **A.** IDÉE DE TEMPS, D'ATTENTE
> **B.** AVEC COMPLÉMENT INTRODUIT PAR 'QUE'
> **C.** AVEC COMPLÉMENT INTRODUIT PAR 'DE'

A. IDÉE DE TEMPS, D'ATTENTE

1. [rester jusqu'à la venue de - retardataire, voyageur] to wait for *(insép)* ■ **je l'attends pour partir** I'm waiting till he gets here before I leave, I'll leave as soon as he gets here ■ **il va falloir t'~ encore longtemps?** are you going to be much longer? ■ **(aller) ~ qqn à l'aéroport/la gare** to (go and) meet sb at the airport/the station ■ **le train ne va pas vous ~** the train won't wait (for you) ■ **l'avion l'a attendu** they delayed the plane for him ➋ **~ qqn au passage** *ou* **au tournant** *fig* to wait for a chance to pounce on sb ■ **elle se trompera, et je l'attends au tournant** she'll make a mistake and that's when I'll get her ■ **'En attendant Godot'** ***Beckett*** 'Waiting for Godot'

2. [escompter l'arrivée de - facteur, invité] to wait for *(insép)*, to expect ; [- colis, livraison] to expect, to await *sout* ; [- réponse, événement] to wait for *(insép)*, to await ■ **je ne t'attendais plus!** I'd given up waiting for you!, I'd given up on you ■ **~ qqn à** *ou* **pour dîner** to expect sb for dinner ■ **vous êtes attendu, le docteur va vous recevoir immédiatement** the doctor's expecting you, he'll see you straightaway ■ **qu'est-ce que tu attends?** [ton interrogatif ou de reproche] what are you waiting for? ■ **qu'est-ce qu'il attend pour les renvoyer?** why doesn't he just fire them? ■ **ils n'attendent que ça, c'est tout ce qu'ils attendent** that's exactly *ou* just what they're waiting for ■ **il attend le grand jour avec impatience** he's looking forward to the big day, he can't wait for the big day ■ **nous attendons des précisions** we're awaiting further details ■ **~ son tour** to wait one's turn ■ **~ son heure** to bide one's time ■ **~ le bon moment** to wait for the right moment (to come along) ■ **cela peut ~ demain** that can wait till *ou* until tomorrow ■ **je lui ai prêté 3 000 euros et je les attends toujours** I lent him 3,000 euros and I still haven't got it back ■ **se faire ~** to keep others waiting ■ **désolé de m'être fait ~** sorry to have kept you waiting ■ **les hors-d'œuvre se font ~** the starters are a long time coming ■ **la réforme se fait ~** the reform is taking a long time to materialize ■ **les résultats ne se sont pas fait ~** [après une élection] the results didn't take long to come in ; [conséquences d'une action] there were immediate consequences ➋ **alors, tu attends le dégel?** *fam* are you going to hang around here all day? ■ **~ qqn comme le Messie** to wait eagerly for sb

3. [suj: femme enceinte] : **~ un bébé** *ou* **enfant, ~ famille** *Belgique* to be expecting (a child), to be pregnant ■ **~ des jumeaux** to be pregnant with *ou* expecting twins ■ **j'attends une fille** I'm expecting a girl ■ **elle attend son bébé pour le 15 avril** her baby's due on 15 April ■ **~ un heureux événement** *euphém* to be expecting

4. [être prêt pour] to be ready for, to await *sout* ■ **la voiture vous attend** the car's ready for you, your car awaits *sout hum*

5. [suj: destin, sort, aventure] to await *sout*, to be *ou* to lie in store for ■ **une mauvaise surprise l'attendait** there was a nasty surprise in store for her ■ **une nouvelle vie vous attend là-bas** a whole new life awaits you there ■ **si tu savais** *ou* **tu ne sais pas ce qui t'attend!** you haven't a clue what you're in for, have you? ■ **avant de me porter volontaire, je voudrais savoir ce qui m'attend** before I volunteer, I'd like to know what I'm letting myself in for

6. [espérer] : **~ qqch de** to expect sthg from ■ **qu'attendez-vous de moi?** what do you expect of me? ■ **j'attendais mieux d'elle** I thought she'd do better, I was expecting better things from her ■ **nous attendons beaucoup de la réunion** we expect a lot (to come out) of the meeting

7. [avoir besoin de] to need ■ **le document attend encore trois signatures** the document needs another three signatures ■ **le pays attend encore l'homme qui sera capable de mettre fin à la guerre civile** the country is still waiting for the man who will be able to put an end to the civil war

B. AVEC COMPLÉMENT INTRODUIT PAR 'QUE'

~ que : nous attendrons qu'elle soit ici we'll wait till *ou* until she gets here *ou* for her to get here ■ **elle attendait toujours qu'il rentre avant d'aller se coucher** she would always wait up for him ■ **attends (un peu) que je le dise à ton père!** just you wait till *ou* until I tell your father!

C. AVEC COMPLÉMENT INTRODUIT PAR 'DE'

attends d'être grand wait til *ou* untill you're older ■ **nous attendions de sortir** we were waiting to go out ■ **j'attends avec impatience de la revoir** I can't wait to see her again, I'm really looking forward to seeing her again ■ **~ de voir la suite des événements** to wait to see what happens.

◇ *vi* **1.** [patienter] to wait ■ **les gens n'aiment pas ~** people don't like to be kept waiting *ou* to have to wait ■ **je passe mon temps à ~** I spend all my time waiting around ■ **il est en ligne, vous attendez?** he's on the other line, will you hold? ■ **faites-les ~** ask them to wait ■ **si tu crois qu'il va t'aider, tu peux toujours ~!** if you think he's going to help you, don't hold your breath! ■ **il peut toujours ~!** he'll have a long wait! ■ **mais enfin attends, je ne suis pas prêt!** wait a minute, will you, I'm not ready! ■ **elle s'appelle, attends, comment déjà?** her name is, wait a minute, now what is it? ■ **et attends, tu ne sais pas le plus beau!** wait (for it) *ou* hold on, the best part's yet to come! ■ **attendez voir, je crois me souvenir** let's see *ou* let me see *ou* think, I seem to remember ■ **attends voir, je vais demander** *fam* hold *ou* hang on, I'll ask ■ **attends voir, toi!** *fam* [menace] just you wait! ■ **tout vient à point à qui sait ~** *prov* everything comes to he who waits *prov* **2.** [suj: plat chaud, soufflé] to wait ■ [suj: vin, denrée] to keep ■ **les spaghetti ne doivent pas ~** spaghetti must be served as soon as it's ready **3.** [être reporté] to wait ■ **votre projet attendra** your plan'll have to wait.

◆ **attendre après** *v+prép fam* **1.** [avoir besoin de] : **~ après qqch** to be in great need of sthg **2.** [compter sur] : **~ après qqn** to rely *ou* to count on sb ■ **si tu attends après lui, tu n'auras jamais tes renseignements** if you're counting on him *ou* if you leave it up to him, you'll never get the information you want ■ **elle est assez grande, elle n'attend plus après toi!** she's old enough to get along (perfectly well) without you!

◆ **s'attendre** *vp (emploi réciproque)* to wait for each other ■ **on s'attend à l'entrée du cinéma** we'll wait for each other *ou* we'll meet outside the cinema.

◆ **s'attendre à** *vp+prép* to expect ■ **il faut s'~ à des embouteillages** traffic jams are expected ■ **il faut s'~ à tout** we should be prepared for anything ■ **s'~ au pire** to expect the worst ■ **savoir à quoi s'~** to know what to expect ■ **je ne m'attendais pas à cela de votre part** I didn't expect that from you ■ **nous ne nous attendions pas à ce que la grève réussisse** we weren't expecting the strike to succeed, we hadn't anticipated that the strike would succeed ■ **s'y ~ : il fallait s'y ~** that was to be expected ■ **comme il fallait s'y ~** as was to be expected, predictably enough ■ **je m'y attendais** I expected as much.

◆ **en attendant** *loc adv* **1.** [pendant ce temps] : **finis ton dessert, en attendant je vais faire le café** finish your dessert, and in the meantime I'll make the coffee **2.** *fam* [malgré cela] : **oui mais, en attendant, je n'ai toujours pas mon argent** that's as may be but I'm still missing my money ■ **ris si tu veux mais, en attendant, j'ai réussi à mon examen** you can laugh, but I passed my exam all the same.

◆ **en attendant que** *loc conj* until (such time as) ■ **en attendant qu'il s'explique, on ne sait rien** until (such time as) he's explained himself *ou* as long as he hasn't provided any explanations, we don't know anything.

attendri, e [atɑ̃dri] *adj* **1.** [ému] : **un regard ~** a look full of emotion **2.** [amolli - viande] tenderized.

attendrir [32] [atɑ̃drir] *vt* **1.** [émouvoir] to move to tears *ou* pity **2.** [apitoyer] : **~ qqn** to make sb feel compassion *ou* pity ■ **se laisser ~** to give in to pity **3.** [viande] to tenderize.

◆ **s'attendrir** *vpi* **1.** [être ému] to be moved *ou* touched ■ **ne nous attendrissons pas!** let's not get emotional! ■ **s'~ sur qqn/qqch** to be moved by sb/sthg, to be touched by sb/sthg **2.** [être apitoyé] to feel compassion ■ **s'~ sur le sort de qqn** to feel pity *ou* sorry for sb ■ **s'~ sur soi-même** to indulge in self-pity, to feel sorry for o.s.

attendrissant, e [atɑ̃drisɑ̃, ɑ̃t] *adj* moving, touching ■ **regarde-le essayer de s'habiller, c'est ~!** look at him trying to dress himself, how sweet!

attendrissement [atɑ̃drismɑ̃] *nm* **1.** [tendresse] emotion *(U)* ■ **pas d'~!** let's not get emotional! ‖ [élan] : **je ne suis pas porté aux ~s** I don't tend to get emotional, I'm not the emotive type **2.** [pitié] pity, compassion ■ **~ sur soi-même** self-pity.

attendrisseur [atɑ̃drisœr] *nm* tenderizer ■ **passer une viande à l'~** to tenderize meat.

attendu¹ [atɑ̃dy] *prep* considering, given.

◆ **attendu que** *loc conj* since, considering *ou* given that ■ DR whereas.

attendu² [atɑ̃dy] *nm* : **les ~s d'un jugement** the reasons adduced for a verdict.

attendu³, e [atɑ̃dy] ◇ *pp* ▷ **attendre**.

◇ *adj* : **très ~** eagerly-awaited.

attentat [atɑ̃ta] *nm* **1.** [assassinat] assassination attempt ■ **commettre un ~ contre qqn** to make an attempt on sb's life **2.** [explosion] attack ■ **~ à la bombe** bomb attack, bombing ■ **~ à la voiture piégée** car bomb explosion ■ **l'ambassade a été hier la cible d'un ~** the Embassy was bombed yesterday **3.** [atteinte] : **~ aux libertés constitutionnelles** violation of constitutional liberties ■ **~ contre la sécurité de l'État** acts harmful to State security ➋ **~ aux mœurs** DR indecent behaviour ■ **~ à la pudeur** act outraging public decency.

attentatoire [atɑ̃tatwar] *adj* : **~ à la dignité de l'homme** detrimental *ou* prejudicial to human dignity.

attentat-suicide [atɑ̃tasɥisid] (*pl* **attentats-suicides**) *nm* suicide attack ■ [à la bombe] suicide bombing.

attente [atɑ̃t] *nf* **1.** [fait d'attendre, moment] wait ▪ **l'~ est longue** it's a long time to wait ▪ **le plus dur, c'est l'~** the toughest part is the waiting ▪ **pendant l'~ du verdict/des résultats** while awaiting the sentence/results ▪ **deux heures d'~** a two-hour wait **2.** [espérance] expectation ▪ **répondre à l'~ de qqn** to come up to sb's expectations ▪ **si la marchandise ne répond pas à votre ~** should the goods not meet your requirements.
◆ **dans l'attente de** *loc prép* **1.** [dans le temps] : **être dans l'~ de qqch** to be waiting for *ou* awaiting *sout* sthg ▪ **il vit dans l'~ de ton retour** he lives for the moment when you return **2.** [dans la correspondance] : **dans l'~ de vous lire/de votre réponse/de vous rencontrer** looking forward to hearing from you/to your reply/to meeting you.
◆ **en attente** ◇ *loc adv* : **laisser qqch en ~** to leave sthg pending.
◇ *loc adj* : **les plans sont en ~** the plans have been shelved.

attenter [3] [atɑ̃te] ◆ **attenter à** *v+prép* **1.** [commettre un attentat contre] : **~ à la vie de qqn** to make an attempt on sb's life ▪ **~ à ses jours** *ou* **à sa vie** to attempt suicide **2.** [porter atteinte à] : **~ à l'honneur/à la réputation de qqn** to undermine sb's honour/reputation ▪ **~ aux libertés civiles** to violate civil rights.

attentif, ive [atɑ̃tif, iv] *adj* **1.** [concentré - spectateur, public, élève] attentive ▪ **soyez ~s!** pay attention! ▪ **écouter qqn d'une oreille attentive** to listen to sb attentively, to listen to every word sb says **2.** [prévenant - présence] watchful ; [- gestes, comportement, parole] solicitous *sout*, thoughtful **3.** [scrupuleux] : **un examen ~** a close *ou* careful examination **4.** : **~ à** [prêtant attention à] : **il était ~ au moindre bruit/mouvement** he was alert to the slightest sound/movement ▪ **être ~ à ce qui se dit** to pay attention to *ou* to listen carefully to what is being said ▪ **être ~ aux besoins de qqn** to be attentive to sb's needs ▪ **être ~ à sa santé** to be mindful of one's health ▪ **être ~ à son travail** to be careful *ou* painstaking in one's work ▪ **~ à** [soucieux de] : **~ à ne pas être impliqué** anxious not to be involved.

attention [atɑ̃sjɔ̃] ◇ *nf* **1.** [concentration] attention ▪ **appeler** *ou* **attirer l'~ de qqn sur qqch** to call sb's attention to sthg, to point sthg out to sb ▪ **mon ~ a été attirée sur le fait que...** it has come to my notice that... ▪ **consacrer toute son ~ à un problème** to devote one's attention to *ou* to concentrate on a problem ▪ **écouter qqn avec ~** to listen to sb attentively, to listen hard to what sb's saying ▪ **porter son ~ sur qqch** to turn one's attention to sthg ▪ **faites bien ~** [écoutez] listen carefully, pay attention ; [regardez] look carefully ▪ **faire ~ à** to pay attention to, to heed *sout* ▪ **fais particulièrement ~ au dernier paragraphe** pay special attention to the last paragraph ▪ **faites ~ à ces menaces** bear these threats in mind ▪ **faire ~ (à ce) que...** to make sure *ou* to ensure (that)...
2. [égard] attention *(U)*, attentiveness *(U)*, thoughtfulness *(U)* ▪ **je n'ai jamais droit à la moindre petite ~** nobody ever does nice things for me ▪ **entourer qqn d'~s, être plein d'~s pour qqn** to lavish attention on sb
3. [capacité à remarquer] attention ▪ **attirer l'~** to attract attention ▪ **tu vas attirer l'~!** [compliment] you'll make a few heads turn! ; [critique] you're too conspicuous! ▪ **attirer l'~ de qqn** to catch *ou* to attract sb's attention ▪ **faire ~ à : tu as fait ~ au numéro de téléphone?** did you make a (mental) note of the phone number? ▪ **quand il est entré, je n'ai d'abord pas fait ~ à lui** when he came in I didn't notice him at first ▪ **ne fais pas ~ à lui, il dit n'importe quoi** don't mind him *ou* pay no attention to him, he's talking nonsense
4. faire ~ à [surveiller, s'occuper de] : **faire ~ à sa santé** to take care of *ou* to look after one's health ▪ **faire ~ à soi** to look after *ou* to take care of o.s. ▪ **faire ~ à sa ligne** to watch one's weight ▪ **il ne fait pas assez ~ à sa femme** he doesn't pay enough attention to his wife
5. faire ~ [être prudent] to be careful *ou* cautious ▪ **fais bien ~ en descendant de l'escabeau** do be careful when you come off the stepladder ▪ **faire ~ à : fais ~ aux voitures** watch out for the cars ▪ **fais ~ à toi** take care ▪ **~ à la marche/porte** mind the step/door ▪ **~ au départ!** stand clear of the doors!
◇ *interj* **1.** [pour signaler un danger] watch *ou* look out ▪ **~, il est armé!** watch *ou* look out, he's got a gun! ▪ **~, ~, tu vas le casser!** gently *ou* easy (now), you'll break it! ▪ **'~ chien méchant'** 'beware of the dog' ▪ **'~ fragile'** 'handle with care' ▪ **'~ peinture fraîche'** 'wet paint' ▪ **'~ travaux'** 'men at work'
2. [pour introduire une nuance] : **~, ce n'est pas cela que j'ai dit** now look, that's not what I said.
◆ **à l'attention de** *loc prép* [sur une enveloppe] : **à l'~ de Madame Chaux** for the attention of Mme Chaux.

attentionné, e [atɑ̃sjɔne] *adj* thoughtful, solicitous *sout* ▪ **comme mari, il était très ~** he was an extremely caring husband.

attentisme [atɑ̃tism] *nm* wait-and-see policy.

attentiste [atɑ̃tist] ◇ *adj* : **attitude ~** wait-and-see attitude ▪ **politique ~** waiting game.
◇ *nmf* : **les ~s** those who play a waiting game.

attentive [atɑ̃tiv] *f* ⊳ **attentif.**

attentivement [atɑ̃tivmɑ̃] *adv* [en se concentrant] attentively, carefully, closely.

atténuant, e [atenɥɑ̃, ɑ̃t] *adj* [excuse, circonstance] mitigating.

atténuation [atenɥasjɔ̃] *nf* [d'une responsabilité] reduction, lightening *(U)* ▪ [d'une faute] mitigation ▪ [de propos] toning down *(U)* ▪ [d'une douleur] easing *(U)* ▪ [d'un coup] cushioning *(U)*, softening *(U)* ▪ **l'eau froide produit une petite ~ de la brûlure** cold water relieves the pain from the burn a little.

atténuer [7] [atenɥe] *vt* **1.** [rendre moins perceptible - douleur] to relieve, to soothe ; [- couleur] to tone down *(sép)*, to soften ; [- bruit] to muffle ▪ **le temps a atténué les souvenirs** memories have become fainter over time **2.** [rendre moins important, moins grave - responsabilité] to reduce, to lighten, to lessen ; [- accusation] to tone down *(sép)*.
◆ **s'atténuer** *vpi* [chagrin, cris, douleur] to subside, to die down ▪ [effet] to subside, to fade, to wane ▪ [lumière] to fade, to dim ▪ [bruit] to diminish, to tone down ▪ [couleur] to dim.

atterrant, e [aterɑ̃, ɑ̃t] *adj* appalling, shocking.

atterrer [4] [atere] *vt* to dismay, to appal ▪ **sa réponse m'a atterré** I was appalled at his answer ▪ **je l'ai trouvé atterré par la nouvelle** I found him reeling from the shock of the news ▪ **il les regarda d'un air atterré** he looked at them aghast *ou* in total dismay.

atterrir [32] [aterir] *vi* **1.** AÉRON to land, to touch down ▪ **~ en catastrophe** to make an emergency landing ▪ **~ sur le ventre** to make a belly landing **2.** *fam* [retomber] to land, to fetch *UK* *ou* to wind up ▪ **tous ses vêtements ont atterri dans la cour** all his clothes wound up in the yard **3.** *fam* [se retrouver] to end *ou* to wind *ou* to land up ▪ **~ en prison** to end up *ou* to land up in jail ▪ **mes lunettes, je me demande où elles ont bien pu ~!** where (on earth) could my glasses have got to?

atterrissage [aterisaʒ] *nm* landing ▪ **prêt à l'~** ready to touch down *ou* to land ▪ **~ en douceur** soft landing ▪ **~ sans visibilité/aux instruments/à vue** blind/instrument/visual landing.
◆ **d'atterrissage** *loc adj* landing *(modif)*.

attestation [atɛstasjɔ̃] *nf* **1.** [document] certificate ▪ **~ d'assurance** insurance certificate ▪ **~ de sortie du territoire** *card notifying parental consent for a minor to leave the country* **2.** ÉDUC [diplôme] certificate (of accreditation) **3.** DR attestation **4.** [preuve] proof ▪ **son échec est une nouvelle ~ de son incompétence** his failure further demonstrates his incompetence.

attesté, e [atɛste] *adj* LING attested.

attester [3] [atɛste] *vt* **1.** [certifier] to attest ▪ **ce document atteste que...** this is to certify that... **2.** [témoigner] to attest *ou* to testify to, to vouch for ▪ **cette version des faits est attestée par la presse** this version of the facts is borne out by the press.
◆ **attester de** *v+prép* to prove, to testify to, to show evidence of ▪ **ainsi qu'en attesteront ceux qui me connaissent** as those who know me will testify.

attiédir [32] [atjedir] *vt litt* **1.** [refroidir - air] to cool ; [- liquide] to make lukewarm **2.** [réchauffer] to warm (up) *(sép)* **3.** *fig* [sentiment] to cool.

◆ **s'attiédir** *vpi litt* **1.** [se refroidir] to cool (down), to become cooler **2.** [se réchauffer] to warm up, to become warmer **3.** *fig* [sentiment] to cool, to wane.

attifer [3] [atife] *vt fam péj* to get up *(sép)*, to rig out *(sép)*.
◆ **s'attifer** *vp (emploi réfléchi) fam péj* to get o.s. up, to rig o.s. out.

Attila [atila] *npr* Attila (the Hun).

attique [atik] ◇ *adj* attic.
◇ *nm* ARCHIT attic ■ **appartement en ~** penthouse.
◆ **Attique** *npr f* : **l'Attique** Attica.

attirail [atiraj] *nm* equipment ■ **~ de pêche** fishing tackle ■ **~ de plombier** plumber's tool kit ■ **on emporte l'ordinateur et tout son ~** *fam* let's take the computer with all the gear ■ **qu'est-ce que c'est que (tout) cet ~?** *fam péj* what's all this paraphernalia for?

attirance [atirɑ̃s] *nf* attraction ■ **l'~ entre nous deux a été immédiate** we were attracted to each other straight away ■ **éprouver de l'~ pour qqn/qqch** to feel attracted to sb/sthg ■ **l'~ du vice** the lure of vice.

attirant, e [atirɑ̃, ɑ̃t] *adj* attractive.

attirer [3] [atire] *vt* **1.** [tirer vers soi] to draw ■ **il m'a attiré vers le balcon pour me montrer le paysage** he drew me towards the balcony to show me the view ■ **l'aimant attire le fer/les épingles** iron is/pins are attracted to a magnet
2. [inciter à venir - badaud] to attract ; [- proie] to lure ■ **couvre ce melon, il attire les guêpes** cover that melon up, it's attracting wasps ■ **les requins, attirés par l'odeur du sang** sharks attracted *ou* drawn by the smell of blood ■ **~ qqn dans un coin/piège** to lure sb into a corner/trap
3. [capter - attention, regard] to attract, to catch ■ **~ l'attention de qqn sur qqch** to call sb's attention to sthg, to point sthg out to sb ■ **~ l'intérêt de qqn** to attract sb's interest
4. [plaire à] to attract, to seduce ■ **se sentir attiré par qqn** to feel attracted to sb ■ **il a une façon de sourire qui attire les femmes** women find the way he smiles attractive ■ **le jazz ne m'attire pas beaucoup** jazz doesn't appeal to me much
5. [avoir comme conséquence] to bring, to cause ■ **~ des ennuis à qqn** to cause trouble for sb, to get sb into trouble ■ **sa démission lui a attiré des sympathies** her resignation won *ou* earned her some sympathy ■ **~ sur soi la colère/haine de qqn** to incur sb's anger hatred
6. ASTRON & PHYS to attract.
◆ **s'attirer** ◇ *vp (emploi réciproque)* to attract one another.
◇ *vpt* : **s'~ des ennuis** to get o.s. into trouble, to bring trouble upon o.s. ■ **s'~ la colère de qqn** to incur sb's anger ■ **s'~ les bonnes grâces de qqn** to win *ou* to gain sb's favour.

attiser [3] [atize] *vt* **1.** [flammes, feu] to poke ■ [incendie] to fuel **2.** [colère, haine, désir] to stir up *(sép)*, to rouse.

attitré, e [atitre] *adj* **1.** [accrédité] accredited, appointed **2.** [habituel - fournisseur, marchand] usual, regular **3.** [favori - fauteuil, place] favourite.

attitude [atityd] *nf* **1.** [comportement] attitude ■ **son ~ envers moi/les femmes** his attitude towards me/women ■ **elle a eu une ~ irréprochable** her attitude was beyond reproach ‖ *péj* [affectation] attitude ■ **prendre une ~** to strike an attitude ■ **il prend des ~s de martyr** he puts on a martyred look ■ **il a l'air indigné, mais ce n'est qu'une ~** his indignation is only skin-deep **2.** [point de vue] standpoint ■ **adopter une ~ ambiguë** to adopt an ambiguous standpoint *ou* attitude **3.** [maintien] bearing, demeanour ■ **avoir une ~ gauche** to move clumsily ‖ [position] position, posture.

attouchement [atuʃmɑ̃] *nm* touching *(U)* ■ **se livrer à des ~s sur qqn** DR to fondle sb, to interfere with sb.

attractif, ive [atraktif, iv] *adj* **1.** PHYS attractive **2.** *sout* [plaisant] attractive, appealing.

attraction [atraksjɔ̃] *nf* **1.** ASTRON & PHYS attraction ■ **~ terrestre** earth's gravity ■ **~ universelle** gravity **2.** [attirance] attraction ■ **l'~ qu'il éprouve pour elle/la mort** his attraction to her/death ■ **exercer une ~ sur qqn/qqch** to attract sb/sthg **3.** [centre d'intérêt] attraction ■ **les ~s touristiques de la région** the area's tourist attractions **4.** LOISIRS attraction ■ **~ principale** *ou* **numéro un** star attraction ■ **il y aura des ~s pour les enfants** entertainment will be provided for children **5.** LING attraction.

attrait [atrɛ] *nm* **1.** [beauté - d'un visage, d'une ville, d'une idéologie] attraction, attractiveness ■ **elle trouve beaucoup d'~ à ses romans** she finds his novels very attractive ■ **village sans (grand) ~** rather charmless village **2.** [fascination] appeal, fascination ■ **éprouver un ~ pour qqch** to be fascinated by sthg.
◆ **attraits** *nmpl euphém & litt* charms ■ **sans qu'elle cherche à dissimuler ses ~s** making no attempt to hide what nature endowed her with.

attrape [atrap] *nf* catch, trick ■ **il doit y avoir une ~ là-dessous** there must be a catch in it somewhere.

attrape-couillon [atrapkujɔ̃] *(pl* **attrape-couillons***) nm fam* con trick.

attrape-mouche [atrapmuʃ] *(pl* **attrape-mouches***) nm* BOT flytrap.

attrape-nigaud [atrapnigo] *(pl* **attrape-nigauds***) nm* confidence trick.

attraper [3] [atrape] *vt* **1.** [prendre] to pick up *(sép)* ■ **la chatte attrape ses chatons par la peau du cou** the cat picks up her kittens by the scruff of the neck
2. [saisir au passage - bras, main, ballon] to grab ■ **~ qqn par le bras** to grab sb by the arm ■ **~ qqn par la taille** to grab sb round the waist ■ **attrape Rex, attrape!** come on Rex, get it!
3. [saisir par force, par ruse] to capture, to catch
4. [surprendre - voleur, tricheur] to catch ; [- bribe de conversation, mot] to catch ■ **attends que je t'attrape!** just you wait till I get hold of you! ■ **si tu veux le voir, il faut l'~ au saut du lit/à la sortie du conseil** if you want to see him, you must catch him as he gets up/as he comes out of the board meeting ■ **que je ne t'attrape plus à écouter aux portes!** don't let me catch you listening behind doors again!
5. [réprimander] to tell off *(sép)* ■ **se faire ~** to get a telling-off
6. [prendre de justesse - train] to catch
7. *fam* [avoir] to get ■ **~ un coup de soleil** to get sunburnt ■ **~ froid** *ou* **un rhume** *ou* **du mal** *vieilli* to catch *ou* to get a cold ■ **ferme la fenêtre, tu vas nous faire ~ un rhume!** close the window or we'll all catch cold! ■ **tiens, attrape!** [à quelqu'un qui vient d'être critiqué] that's one in the eye for you!, take that!
8. [tromper - naïf, gogo] to catch (out), to fool.
◆ **s'attraper** ◇ *vp (emploi passif)* [être contracté - maladie, mauvaise habitude] to be catching.
◇ *vp (emploi réciproque)* [se disputer] to fight, to squabble.

attrape-touristes [atrapturist] *nm inv* tourist trap.

attrape-tout [atraptu] *adj inv* catch-all *(avant n)* ■ **un parti politique ~** a catch-all political party.

attrayant, e [atrɛjɑ̃, ɑ̃t] *adj* [homme, femme] good-looking, attractive ■ [suggestion] attractive, appealing ■ **peu ~** unattractive, unappealing.

attribuable [atribɥabl] *adj* : **~ à** attributable to.

attribuer [7] [atribɥe] *vt* **1.** [distribuer - somme, bien] to allocate ; [- titre, privilège] to grant ; [- fonction, place] to allocate, to assign ; [- prix, récompense] to award ■ **nous ne sommes pas ici pour ~ des blâmes** it is not up to us to lay the blame ▶ **~ un rôle à qqn** THÉÂTRE to cast sb for a part ; *fig* to cast sb in a role **2.** [imputer] : **~ qqch à qqn** to ascribe *ou* to attribute sthg to sb ■ **~ la paternité d'un enfant/d'une œuvre à qqn** to consider sb to be the father of a child/author of a work ■ **un sonnet longtemps attribué à Shakespeare** a sonnet long thought to have been written by Shakespeare ■ **on attribue cette découverte à Pasteur** this discovery is attributed to Pasteur, Pasteur is accredited with this discovery ■ **j'attribue sa réussite à son environnement** I put her success down *ou* I attribute her success to her environment **3.** [accorder] : **~ de l'importance/de la valeur à qqch** to attach importance to/to find value in sthg ■ **~ de l'intérêt à qqch** to find sthg interesting.
◆ **s'attribuer** *vpt* : **s'~ qqch** to claim sthg for o.s. ■ **s'~ un titre** to give o.s. a title ■ **s'~ une fonction** to appoint o.s. to a function ■ **s'~ tout le mérite de qqch** to claim all the credit for sthg.

attribut [atriby] *nm* **1.** [caractéristique] attribute, (characteristic) trait ■ **~s (virils** *ou* **masculins)** *euphém* (male) genitals **2.** GRAMM predicate ■ **adjectif ~** predicative adjective.

attributaire [atribytɛr] *nmf* **1.** ÉCON allottee **2.** DR beneficiary **3.** [d'un prix] prize-winner, award-winner.

attributif, ive [atribytif, iv] *adj* **1.** GRAMM predicative, attributive **2.** DR assignment *(modif)*.

attribution [atribysjɔ̃] *nf* **1.** [distribution - d'une somme] allocation ; [- d'une place, d'une part] allocation, attribution ; [- d'un prix] awarding ■ ÉCON [d'actions] allotment **2.** [reconnaissance - d'une œuvre, d'une responsabilité, d'une découverte] attribution ■ **l'~ de la figurine à Rodin a été contestée** doubts have been cast on the belief that Rodin sculpted the figurine.
◆ **attributions** *nfpl* : **cela n'est pas** *ou* **n'entre pas dans mes ~s** this doesn't come within my remit *UK*.

attristant, e [atristɑ̃, ɑ̃t] *adj* saddening, depressing ■ **il est ~ de voir que...** it's such a pity to see that...

attrister [3] [atriste] *vt* to sadden, to depress ■ **cela m'attriste de voir que...** it makes me sad *ou* I find it such a pity to see that...
◆ **s'attrister de** *vp+prép* : **s'~ de qqch** to be sad about sthg.

attrition [atrisjɔ̃] *nf* MÉD & RELIG attrition.

attroupement [atrupmɑ̃] *nm* crowd.

attrouper [3] [atrupe] *vt* [foule] to gather, to draw, to attract.
◆ **s'attrouper** *vpi* [gén] to gather together ■ [en grand nombre] to flock together.

atypique [atipik] *adj* atypical.

au [o] ⊳ **à**.

aubade [obad] *nf* dawn serenade, aubade ■ **donner une ~ à qqn** to serenade sb (at dawn).

aubaine [obɛn] *nf* [argent] windfall ■ [affaire] bargain ■ [occasion] godsend, golden opportunity ■ **c'est une véritable ~ pour notre usine** it comes as *ou* it is a godsend to our factory ■ **profiter de l'~** to take advantage *ou* to make the most of a golden opportunity.

aube [ob] *nf* **1.** [aurore] dawn ■ **à l'~** at dawn, at daybreak ■ **l'~ d'une ère nouvelle** *fig* the dawn *ou* dawning of a new era **2.** RELIG alb **3.** NAUT paddle, blade **4.** [d'un moulin] vane ■ [pale] blade.

aubépine [obepin] *nf* hawthorn ■ **fleur d'~** may blossom.

auberge [obɛrʒ] *nf* inn ▶ **~ espagnole : les ordinateurs, c'est l'~** *ou* **c'est comme une ~ espagnole** you get out of computers what you put in them in the first place ■ **~ de jeunesse** youth hostel ■ **il n'est pas sorti/on n'est pas sortis de l'auberge** *fam* he's/we're not out of the woods yet.

aubergine [obɛrʒin] ◇ *nf* **1.** BOT aubergine *UK*, eggplant *US* **2.** *fam* [contractuelle] (female) traffic warden *UK*, meter maid *US*.
◇ *adj inv* [couleur] aubergine.

aubergiste [obɛrʒist] *nmf* inn-keeper.

aubier [obje] *nm* sapwood.

auburn [obœrn] *adj inv* auburn.

Aubusson [obysɔ̃] *npr town in central France famous as a centre for tapestry-making.*

aucun, e [okœ̃, yn] ◇ *adj indéf* **1.** [avec une valeur négative] : **il ne fait ~ effort** he doesn't make any effort ■ **~e décision n'a encore été prise** no decision has been reached yet ■ **~ article n'est encore prêt** none of the articles is ready yet ■ **il n'y a ~ souci à se faire** there is nothing to worry about ■ **ils n'eurent ~ mal à découvrir la vérité** they had no trouble (at all) finding out the truth ■ **je ne vois ~ inconvénient à ce que vous restiez** I don't mind your staying at all ■ **en ~e façon** in no way ■ **sans ~ doute** undoubtedly, without any doubt ■ **~e idée!** no idea! **2.** [avec une valeur positive] any ■ **il est plus rapide qu'~ autre coureur** he's faster than any other runner.
◇ *pron indéf* **1.** [avec une valeur négative] none ■ **je sais qu'~ n'a menti** I know that none *ou* not one of them lied ■ **je n'ai lu ~ de ses livres** I haven't read any of her books **2.** [servant de réponse négative] none **3.** [avec une valeur positive] any ■ **il est plus fort qu'~ de vos hommes** he's stronger than any of your men ■ **d'~s** *sout* some.

aucunement [okynmɑ̃] *adv* **1.** [dans des énoncés négatifs avec 'ne' ou 'sans'] in no way, not in the least *ou* slightest ■ **je n'ai ~ l'intention de me laisser insulter** I certainly have no *ou* I haven't the slightest intention of letting myself be insulted **2.** [servant de réponse négative] not at all.

AUD (*abr de* **Allocation unique dégressive**) *nf* unemployment benefit, jobseeker's allowance *UK (which decreases over time)*.

audace [odas] *nf* **1.** [courage] daring, boldness, audaciousness ■ **ils ont eu l'~ de nous attaquer par le flanc droit** they were bold enough to attack our right flank **2.** [impudence] audacity ■ **il a eu l'~ de dire non** he dared (to) *ou* he had the audacity to say no **3.** [innovation] innovation.

audacieux, euse [odasjø, øz] ◇ *adj* **1.** [courageux] daring, bold, audacious **2.** [impudent] bold, audacious, impudent **3.** [innovateur] bold, audacious, innovative.
◇ *nm, f* bold man (*f* woman) ■ **c'était un ~** he was very daring.

au-dedans [odədɑ̃] *adv* **1.** [à l'intérieur] inside **2.** [mentalement] inwardly ■ **elle a l'air confiante mais ~ elle a des doutes** she looks confident but deep within herself *ou* but inwardly she has doubts.
◆ **au-dedans de** *loc prép* inside, within ■ **~ d'elle-même, elle regrette son geste** *fig* deep down *ou* inwardly, she regrets what she did.

au-dehors [odəɔr] *adv* **1.** [à l'extérieur] outside **2.** [en apparence] outwardly ■ **elle est généreuse même si ~ elle paraît dure** she's generous even if she looks cold *ou* if she's outwardly cold.
◆ **au-dehors de** *loc prép* outside, without *litt* ■ **~ de ces murs, personne ne sait rien** nobody knows anything outside these walls.

au-delà [odəla] ◇ *nm* : **l'~** the hereafter, the next world.
◇ *loc adv* beyond ■ **~ il y a la mer** beyond *ou* further on there is the sea ■ **5 000 euro, et je n'irai pas ~** 5,000 euros and that's my final offer ■ **surtout ne va pas ~** [d'une somme] whatever you do, don't spend any more ■ **il a obtenu tout ce qu'il voulait et bien ~** he got everything he wanted and more.
◆ **au-delà de** *loc prép* [dans l'espace] beyond ■ [dans le temps] after ■ **~ de la frontière** on the other side of *ou* beyond the border ■ **~ de 500 euro, vous êtes imposable** above 500 euros you must pay taxes ■ **ne va pas ~ de 1 000 euro** don't spend more than 1,000 euros ■ **réussir ~ de ses espérances** to succeed beyond one's expectations ■ **~ de ses forces/moyens** beyond one's strength/means.

au-dessous [odsu] *adv* **1.** [dans l'espace] below, under, underneath ■ **il n'y a personne (à l'étage) ~** there's no one on the floor below **2.** [dans une hiérarchie] under, below ■ **enfants âgés de 10 ans et ~** children aged 10 and below ■ **taille ~** next size down ■ **un ton ~** MUS one tone lower.
◆ **au-dessous de** *loc prép* **1.** [dans l'espace] below, under, underneath ■ **elle habite ~ de chez moi** she lives downstairs from me **2.** [dans une hiérarchie] below ■ **~ du niveau de la mer** below sea level ■ **~ de zéro** below zero ■ **température ~ de zéro** sub-zero temperature ■ **~ de 65 ans** under 65 ■ **~ d'un certain prix** under *ou* below a certain price ■ **~ de sa condition** beneath one's condition ▶ **il est vraiment ~ de tout!** he's really useless! ■ **le service est ~ de tout** the service is an absolute disgrace.

au-dessus [odsy] *adv* **1.** [dans l'espace] above ■ **il habite ~** he lives upstairs ■ **il y a une croix ~** there's a cross above it ■ **là-haut, il y a le hameau des Chevrolles, et il n'y a rien ~** up there is Chevrolles village, and there's nothing beyond it **2.** [dans une hiérarchie] above ■ **les enfants de 10 ans et ~** children aged 10 and above ■ **la taille ~** the next size up ■ **un ton ~** MUS one tone higher.
◆ **au-dessus de** *loc prép* **1.** [dans l'espace] above ■ **le placard est ~ de l'évier** the cupboard is above the sink ■ **il habite ~ de chez moi** he lives upstairs from me ■ **un avion passa ~ de nos têtes** a plane flew overhead **2.** [dans une hiérarchie] above ■ **~**

du niveau de la mer above sea level ■ **10 degrés ~ de zéro** 10 degrees above zero ■ **~ d'un certain prix** above a certain price ■ **~ de 15 ans** over 15 years old ■ **vivre ~ de ses moyens** to live beyond one's means ■ **~ de tout soupçon** above all *ou* beyond suspicion ■ **elle est ~ de ça** she's above all that ■ **c'était ~ de mes forces** it was too much for *ou* beyond me ■ **se situer ~ des partis** to be politically neutral.

au-devant [odvɑ̃] ◆ **au-devant de** *loc prép* : **aller** *ou* **se porter ~ de qqn** to go and meet sb ■ **aller ~ des désirs de qqn** to anticipate sb's wishes ■ **il va ~ de graves ennuis/d'une défaite** he's heading for serious troubles/failure ■ **aller ~ du danger** to court danger.

audible [odibl] *adj* audible ■ **règle ton micro, tu es à peine ~** adjust your microphone, we can barely hear you.

audience [odjɑ̃s] *nf* **1.** [entretien] audience ■ **donner ~** *ou* **accorder une ~ à qqn** to grant sb an audience **2.** DR hearing **3.** [public touché - par un livre] readership ; [- par un film, une pièce, un concert] public ■ **une émission à large ~** a very popular programme ■ **cette proposition a trouvé ~ auprès de la population française** this proposal met with a favourable reception from the French population.

audiencer [16] [odjɑ̃se] *vt* to submit for hearing DR.

Audimat® [odimat] *nm device used for calculating viewing figures for French television, installed for a period of time in selected households.*

audimètre [odimɛtr] *nm* audience rating device ■ **victime de l'~** victim of the ratings.

audiocassette [odjɔkasɛt] *nf* (audio) cassette.

audioconférence [odjɔkɔ̃ferɑ̃s] *nf* audio conference.

audiofréquence [odjɔfrekɑ̃s] *nf* audio frequency.

audiogramme [odjɔgram] *nm* audiogram.

audioguide [odjɔgid] *nf* audio guide, headset.

audiomètre [odjɔmɛtr] *nm* audiometer.

audiométrie [odjɔmetri] *nf* audiometry.

audionumérique [odjɔnymerik] *adj* : **disque ~** compact disc.

audio-oral, e, aux [odjɔoral, o] *adj* ÉDUC audio-oral.

audioprothésiste [odjɔprɔtezist] *nmf* hearing aid specialist.

audiovisuel, elle [odjɔvizɥɛl] *adj* audiovisual.

◆ **audiovisuel** *nm* **1.** [matériel] : **l'~** [des médias] radio and television equipment ; [dans l'enseignement] audiovisual aids **2.** [médias] : **l'~** broadcasting **3.** [techniques] : **l'~** media techniques.

audit [odit] *nm* audit.

auditer [3] [odite] *vt* to audit.

auditeur, trice [oditœr, tris] *nm, f* **1.** [d'une radio, d'un disque] listener ■ **les ~s** the audience **2.** LING hearer **3.** ADMIN : **~ à la Cour des comptes** junior official at the Cour des comptes **4.** ÉDUC : **~ libre** unregistered student, auditor *US* ■ **j'y vais en ~ libre** I go to the lectures but I'm not officially on the course *UK*, I audit the lectures *US*.

auditif, ive [oditif, iv] *adj* hearing, auditory *spéc.*

audition [odisjɔ̃] *nf* **1.** DANSE, MUS & THÉÂTRE audition ■ **passer une ~** to audition ■ **faire passer une ~ à qqn** to audition sb **2.** DR : **pendant l'~ des témoins** while the witnesses were being heard **3.** PHYSIOL hearing **4.** [fait d'écouter] listening ■ **l'~ est meilleure dans cette salle** the sound is better in this room.

auditionner [3] [odisjɔne] ◇ *vt* : **~ qqn** to audition sb, to give sb an audition.

◇ *vi* to audition.

auditoire [oditwar] *nm* **1.** [public] audience **2.** *Belgique & Suisse* [salle de conférence] conference hall.

auditorium [oditɔrjɔm] *nm* auditorium.

auge [oʒ] *nf* **1.** CONSTR trough **2.** GÉOGR & GÉOL : **~ glaciaire, vallée en ~** U-shaped valley **3.** TECHNOL [d'un moulin] channel **4.** [mangeoire] trough ■ **passe ton ~** *fam hum* pass your plate.

augmentatif, ive [ogmɑ̃tatif, iv] *adj* augmentative.

augmenter [3] [ogmɑ̃te] ◇ *vt* **1.** [porter à un niveau plus élevé - impôt, prix, nombre] to put up *(sép)*, to increase, to raise ; [- durée] to increase ; [- tarif] to step up *(sép)* ; [- salaire] to increase, to raise ; [- dépenses] to increase ■ **~ le pain** *fam* *ou* **le prix du pain** to put up bread prices ■ **la crise a fait ~ le prix du pétrole** the crisis has pushed up the price of oil ■ **elle a été augmentée** *fam* she got a (pay) rise *UK* *ou* a raise *US* ■ **~ qqch de : ~ les impôts de 5 %** to put up *ou* to raise *ou* to increase taxes by 5% ■ **nous voulons ~ les ventes de 10 %** we want to boost sales by 10% ■ **ils ont augmenté les employés de 20 euros** *fam* they put up the employees' pay by 20 euros **2.** [intensifier - tension, difficulté] to increase, to step up *(sép)*, to make worse **3.** MUS to augment ■ **en augmentant** crescendo.

◇ *vi* **1.** [dette, population] to grow, to increase, to get bigger ■ [quantité, poids] to increase ■ [prix, impôt, salaire] to increase, to go up, to rise ■ **tout** *ou* **la vie augmente!** everything's going up! ■ **achetez maintenant, ça va ~!** buy now, prices are on the increase *ou* going up! ■ **la viande a augmenté** *fam*, **le prix de la viande a augmenté** meat's gone up, meat has increased in price **2.** [difficulté, tension] to increase, to grow ■ **la violence augmente dans les villes** urban violence is on the increase.

◆ **s'augmenter de** *vp+prép* : **la famille s'est augmentée de deux jumeaux** a pair of twins has joined the family.

augure [ogyr] *nm* **1.** ANTIQ augur ■ [voyant] prophet, soothsayer ■ **consulter les ~s** to consult the oracle **2.** [présage] omen ■ ANTIQ augury.

◆ **de bon augure** *loc adj* auspicious ■ **c'est de bon ~** it's auspicious, it augurs well, it bodes well.

◆ **de mauvais augure** *loc adj* ominous, inauspicious ■ **c'est de mauvais ~** it's ominous, it doesn't augur well, it bodes ill.

augurer [3] [ogyre] *vt* to foresee ■ **sa visite ne laisse pas ~ de progrès significatif** no significant progress can be expected as a result of his visit ■ **sa réponse augure mal/bien de notre prochaine réunion** his answer doesn't augur well/augurs well for our next meeting.

auguste [ogyst] ◇ *adj* **1.** [personnage] august **2.** [majestueux - geste, pas, attitude] majestic, noble.

◇ *nm* clown.

Auguste [ogyst] *npr* [empereur] Augustus.

augustin, e [ogystɛ̃, in] *nm, f* Augustinian.

Augustin [ogystɛ̃] *npr* : **saint ~** Saint Augustine.

augustinien, enne [ogystinjɛ̃, ɛn] *adj & nm, f* Augustinian.

aujourd'hui [oʒurdɥi] *adv* **1.** [ce jour] today ■ **le journal d'~** today's paper ■ **nous sommes le trois ~** today's the third ■ **ce sera tout pour ~** that'll be all for today ■ **il y a huit jours ~** a week ago today ➊ **qu'est-ce qu'il est paresseux! – c'est pas d'~!** *fam* he's so lazy! – tell me something new! ■ **alors! c'est pour ~ ou pour demain?** *fam* come on, we haven't got all day! **2.** [à notre époque] today, nowadays ■ **la France d'~** modern *ou* present-day France, the France of today.

aula [ola] *nf* *Suisse* hall.

aulne [on] *nm* alder.

aulx [o] *pl* ▻ **ail.**

aumône [omon] *nf* charity, alms ■ **faire l'~ à qqn** to give alms to sb ■ **demander l'~** to beg for alms ■ **je ne demande pas l'~, uniquement ce qui m'est dû** I'm not asking for any handouts, only for what's rightly mine ■ **vivre d'~s** to live on charity.

aumônerie [omonri] *nf* chaplaincy.

aumônier [omonje] *nm* chaplain.

aumônière [omonjɛr] *nf* purse.

aune [on] ◇ *nf* : **visage long** *ou* **tête longue d'une ~** face as long as a fiddle.

◇ *nm* = **aulne.**

auparavant [oparavɑ̃] *adv* **1.** [avant] before, previously **2.** [tout d'abord] beforehand, first.

auprès [oprɛ] *adv* nearby.
◆ **auprès de** *loc prép* **1.** [à côté de] close to, near, by ■ **rester ~ de qqn** to stay with *ou* close to sb **2.** [dans l'opinion de] : **il passe pour un fin connaisseur ~ de ses amis** he's considered a connoisseur by his friends **3.** [en s'adressant à] : **chercher du réconfort ~ d'un ami** to seek comfort from a friend ■ **faire une demande ~ d'un organisme** to make an application *ou* to apply to an organization **4.** [comparé à] compared with *ou* to ■ **ce n'est rien ~ de ce qu'il a gagné** it's nothing compared to *ou* with what he made **5.** [dans un titre] : **ambassadeur ~ du roi du Danemark** ambassador to the King of Denmark.

auquel [okɛl] *m* ▷ **lequel**.

aura [ora] *nf* aura.

Aurélien [oreljɛ̃] *npr* Aurelian.

auréole [oreɔl] *nf* **1.** ART halo ■ **ils aiment à se parer de l'~ du sacrifice** *fig* they like to wear the crown of sacrifice **2.** [tache] ring ■ **produit détachant qui ne laisse pas d'~** product that removes stains without leaving a mark **3.** ASTRON halo.

auréoler [3] [oreɔle] *vt* **1.** [parer] : **~ qqn de** : **~ qqn de toutes les vertus** to turn sb into a saint ■ **tout auréolée de ses victoires américaines, elle vient se mesurer aux basketteuses européennes** basking in the glory of her American victories, she's come to challenge the European basketball teams **2.** ART to paint a halo around the head of ■ **tête auréolée de cheveux roux** *fig* head with a halo of red hair.
◆ **s'auréoler de** *vp+prép* : **elle aime à s'~ de mystère** she likes to wreathe herself in mystery ■ **il s'était auréolé de gloire sur les champs de bataille** he had won his laurels on the battlefield.

auriculaire [orikylɛr] ◇ *adj* auricular.
◇ *nm* little finger.

aurifère [orifɛr] *adj* gold-bearing, auriferous *spéc.*

aurige [ɔriʒ] *nm* charioteer.

Aurigny [ɔriɲi] *npr* Alderney, *voir aussi* **île**.

aurique [orik] *adj* auric.

aurochs [orɔk] *nm* aurochs.

auroral, e, aux [ɔrɔral, o] *adj* **1.** *litt* [de l'aurore] dawn *(modif)* **2.** ASTRON & MÉTÉOR auroral.

aurore [ɔrɔr] ◇ *nf* **1.** [matin] daybreak, dawn ■ **nous voici à l'~ d'une ère nouvelle** *fig* we are witnessing the dawn *ou* dawning of a new era ■ **l'Aurore** PRESSE *former French newspaper* **2.** ASTRON aurora ■ **~ australe** aurora australis ■ **~ boréale** aurora borealis ■ **~ polaire** northern lights, aurora polaris.
◇ *adj inv* golden (yellow).
◆ **aux aurores** *loc adv* **hum** at the crack of dawn.

auscultation [oskyltasjɔ̃] *nf* auscultation.

ausculter [3] [oskylte] *vt* to listen to *ou* to sound the chest of, to auscultate *spéc* ■ **il t'a ausculté?** did he listen to your chest?

auspices [ospis] *nmpl* **1.** [parrainage] : **faire qqch sous les ~ de qqn** to do sthg under the patronage *ou* auspices of sb **2.** [présage] : **sous de bons/mauvais ~** under favourable/unfavourable auspices **3.** ANTIQ auspices.

aussi [osi] ◇ *adv* **1.** [également] too, also ■ **elle ~ travaille à Rome** she too works in Rome, she works in Rome as well ■ **il a faim, moi ~** he's hungry, and so am I *ou* me too ■ **elle parle russe, moi ~** SHE speaks Russian and so do I ■ **c'est ~ leur avis** they think so too ■ **joyeux Noël! – vous ~!** merry Christmas! – the same to you!
2. [en plus] too, also ■ **elle travaille ~ à Rome** she also works in Rome, she works in Rome too *ou* as well
3. [terme de comparaison] *(devant adj)* **il est ~ grand que son père** he's as tall as his father ■ **il est loin d'être ~ riche qu'elle** he's far from being as rich as she is *ou* as her ■ **elle est ~ belle qu'intelligente** *ou* **qu'elle est intelligente** she is as beautiful as she is intelligent ■ **ils sont ~ bons l'un que l'autre** they're both equally good ■ *(devant adv)* **il ne s'attendait pas à être payé ~ rapidement que cela** he didn't expect to be paid as quickly as that *ou* that quickly ■ **~ doucement que possible** as quietly as possible ■ **il ne s'est jamais senti ~ bien que depuis qu'il a arrêté de fumer** he's never felt so well since he stopped smoking ▶ **~ bien : je ferais ~ bien de partir** I might as well leave ■ **~ sec** *fam* right away
4. [tellement] so ■ [avec un adjectif épithète] such ■ **je n'ai jamais rien vu d'~ beau** I've never seen anything so beautiful ■ **une ~ bonne occasion ne se représentera plus** such a good opportunity won't come up again ■ *(antéposé au v)* **~ léger qu'il soit** *ou* **~ léger soit-il, je ne pourrai pas le porter** light as it is, I won't be able to carry it ■ **~ curieux que cela puisse paraître** strange as *ou* though it may seem.
◇ *conj* **1.** [indiquant la conséquence] therefore, and so ■ **il était très timide, ~ n'osa-t-il rien répondre** he was very shy, and so he didn't dare reply
2. [d'ailleurs] : **on ne lui a rien dit, ~ pourquoi n'a-t-il pas demandé?** we didn't tell him anything, but in any case, why didn't he ask?

aussitôt [osito] *adv* immediately ■ **~ après son départ** immediately *ou* right after he left ■ **je suis tombé malade ~ après avoir acheté la maison** right after buying *ou* as soon as I'd bought the house I was taken ill ■ **il est arrivé ~ après** he arrived immediately after *ou* afterwards ■ **~ rentré chez lui, il se coucha** as soon as he got home, he went to bed ▶ **~ dit, ~ fait** no sooner said than done.
◆ **aussitôt que** *loc conj* as soon as ■ **il l'appela ~ qu'il l'aperçut** he called out the moment *ou* as soon as he saw her.

austère [ostɛr] *adj* [architecture, mode de vie] austere, stark ■ [style] dry ■ [personnalité] stern, austere.

austérité [osterite] *nf* **1.** [dépouillement - d'une architecture, d'un mode de vie] austerity, starkness ; [- d'un style] dryness **2.** ÉCON : **mesures d'~** austerity measures ■ **politique d'~** policy of austerity.
◆ **austérités** *nfpl* RELIG : **les ~s** the austerities *sout.*

austral, e, als *ou* **aux** [ostral, o] *adj* [hémisphère] southern ■ [pôle] south ■ [constellation] austral.

Australasie [ostralazi] *npr f* : **(l')~** Australasia.

Australie [ostrali] *npr f* : **(l')~** Australia.

australien, enne [ostraljɛ̃, ɛn] *adj* Australian.
◆ **Australien, enne** *nm, f* Australian.

australopithèque [ostralɔpitɛk] *nm* Australopithecus.

austro-hongrois, e [ostroɔ̃grwa, az] *adj* Austro-Hungarian.
◆ **Austro-Hongrois, e** *nm, f* Austro-Hungarian.

autan [otɑ̃] *nm* southerly wind.

autant [otɑ̃] *adv* **1.** [marquant l'intensité] : **j'ignorais que tu l'aimais ~** I didn't know that you loved him so much ■ **s'entraîne-t-il toujours ~?** does he still train as much (as he used to)? ■ **pourquoi attendre ~?** why wait that *ou* so long? ■ *(en corrélation avec 'que')* as much as ■ **rien ne me déplaît ~ que d'être en retard** there's nothing I dislike so much as being late ■ **je l'aime ~ que toi** [que tu l'aimes] I like him as much as you do ; [que je t'aime] I like him as much as you
2. [indiquant la quantité] : **je ne pensais pas qu'ils seraient ~** I didn't think there would be so many of them ■ **elle boit toujours ~** she still drinks just as much (as she used to) ■ *(en corrélation avec 'que')* **ils sont ~ que nous** there are as many of them as (there are of) us ▶ **~ pour moi!** my mistake!
3. *(avec 'en')* [la même chose] : **tu devrais en faire ~** you should do the same ■ **il a fini son travail, je ne peux pas en dire ~** he's finished his work, I wish I could say as much *ou* the same ■ **j'en ai ~ à votre service!** *fam* same to you!, likewise!
4. *(avec l'infinitif)* [mieux vaut] : **~ revenir demain** I/you *etc* might as well come back tomorrow
5. [mieux] : **j'aurais ~ fait de rester chez moi** I'd have done as well to stay at home
6. *Belgique* [tant] : **il gagne ~ par mois** he earns so much a month.
◆ **autant... autant** *loc corrélative* : **~ il est cultivé, ~ il est nul en mathématiques** he's highly educated, but he's no good at mathematics ■ **~ j'aime le vin, ~ je déteste la bière** I hate beer as much as I love wine.
◆ **autant de** *loc dét* [avec un nom non comptable] as much ■ [avec un nom comptable] as many ■ **il y a ~ d'eau/de sièges ici**

there's as much water/there are as many seats here ■ **ces livres sont ~ de chefs-d'œuvre** every last one of these books is a masterpiece ■ **~ d'hommes, ~ d'avis** as many opinions as there are men ■ *(en corrélation avec 'que')* **il y a ~ de femmes que d'hommes** there are as many women as (there are) men ▶ **(c'est) ~ de gagné** *ou* **de pris** at least that's something ■ **c'est ~ de perdu** that's that (gone).

◆ **autant dire** *loc adv* in other words ■ **j'ai été payé 300 euros, ~ dire rien** I was paid 300 euros, in other words a pittance.

◆ **autant dire que** *loc conj* : **trois heures dans le four, ~ dire que le poulet était carbonisé!** after three hours in the oven, needless to say the chicken was burnt to a cinder! ■ **l'ambassade ne répond plus, ~ dire que tout est perdu** the embassy's phones are dead, a sure sign that all is lost.

◆ **autant que** *loc conj* **1.** [dans la mesure où] as far as ■ **~ que possible** as far as (is) possible ■ **~ que je me souvienne** as far as I can remember
2. [il est préférable que] : **~ que je vous le dise tout de suite...** I may as well tell you straightaway...

◆ **d'autant** *loc adv* : **si le coût de la vie augmente de 2 %, les salaires seront augmentés d'~** if the cost of living goes up by 2%, salaries will be raised accordingly ■ **cela augmente d'~ mon intérêt pour cette question** it makes me all the more interested in this question ■ **si l'on raccourcit la première étagère de cinq centimètres, il faudra raccourcir la deuxième d'~** if we shorten the first shelf by five centimetres, we'll have to shorten the second one by the same amount.

◆ **d'autant mieux** *loc adv* all the better, much better ■ **pars à la campagne, tu te reposeras d'~ mieux** you'll have a much better rest if you go to the country.

◆ **d'autant mieux que** *loc conj* : **il a travaillé d'~ mieux qu'il se sentait encouragé** he worked all the better for feeling encouraged.

◆ **d'autant moins que** *loc conj* : **je le vois d'~ moins qu'il est très occupé en ce moment** I see even less of him now that he's very busy.

◆ **d'autant moins... que** *loc corrélative* : **elle est d'~ moins excusable qu'on l'avait prévenue** what she did is all the less forgivable as she'd been warned.

◆ **d'autant plus** *loc adv* all the more reason.

◆ **d'autant plus que** *loc conj* especially as ■ **il vous écoutera d'~ plus qu'il vous connaît** he'll listen to you, especially as *ou* particularly as he knows you.

◆ **d'autant plus... que** *loc corrélative* : **c'est d'~ plus stupide qu'il ne sait pas nager** it's particularly *ou* all the more stupid given (the fact) that he can't swim.

◆ **d'autant que** *loc conj* [vu que, attendu que] especially as, particularly as ■ **c'est une bonne affaire, d'~ que le crédit est très avantageux** it's a good deal, especially as the terms of credit are very advantageous.

◆ **pour autant** *loc adv* : **la situation n'est pas perdue pour ~** the situation isn't hopeless for all that, it doesn't necessarily mean all is lost ■ **n'en perds pas l'appétit pour ~** don't let it put you off your food ■ **il t'aime bien, mais il ne t'aidera pas pour ~** just because he's fond of you (it) doesn't mean that he'll help you ■ **fais-le-lui remarquer sans pour ~ le culpabiliser** point it out to him, but don't make him feel guilty about it.

◆ **pour autant que** *loc conj* as far as ■ **pour ~ que je (le) sache** as far as I know ■ **pour ~ qu'on puisse faire la comparaison** inasmuch as a comparison can be made ■ **pour ~ qu'il ait pu être coupable** guilty though he might have been.

autarcie [otarsi] *nf* self-sufficiency, autarky *spéc* ■ **vivre en ~** to be self-sufficient.

autarcique [otarsik] *adj* autarkic.

autel [otel] *nm* RELIG altar ■ **conduire** *ou* **mener qqn à l'~** to take sb to the altar *ou* down the aisle.

Auteuil [otœj] *npr upper-class district of Paris, well-known for its racecourse.*

auteur [otœr] *nmf* **1.** [qui a écrit - un livre, un article, une chanson] writer, author ■ **~ de** [d'une toile] painter of ; [d'un décor, d'un meuble, d'un vêtement] designer of ; [d'un morceau de musique] composer of ; [d'une statue] sculptor of ; [d'un film, d'un clip] director of ■ **quelle jolie chanson, qui en est l'~?** what a lovely song, who wrote it? ■ **Léonard de Vinci a été l'~ de nombreuses inventions** Leonardo invented many contraptions ▶ **un ~ dramatique** a playwright ■ **un ~ à succès** a popular writer **2.** [responsable] : **l'~ de** : **l'~ du meurtre** the murderer ■ **les ~s de ce crime** those who committed that crime ■ **les ~s présumés de l'attentat** those suspected of having planted the bomb ■ **qui est l'~ de cette farce?** who thought up this practical joke? ■ **l'~ de la victoire/défaite** the person who brought about victory/defeat ■ **l'~ de mes jours** *litt ou hum* my progenitor *hum.*

auteur-compositeur [otœrkɔ̃pozitœr] (*pl* **auteurs-compositeurs**) *nm* composer and lyricist ■ **~ interprète** singer-songwriter ■ **je suis ~ interprète** I write and sing my own material.

authenticité [otɑ̃tisite] *nf* **1.** [d'un document, d'un tableau, d'un tapis] authenticity ■ [d'un sentiment] genuineness ■ **l'~ de son chagrin** his heartfelt grief **2.** DR authenticity.

authentifier [9] [otɑ̃tifje] *vt* to authenticate.

authentique [otɑ̃tik] *adj* **1.** [document, tableau, tapis, objet d'art] genuine, authentic ■ [sentiment] genuine, heartfelt **2.** DR authentic.

autisme [otism] *nm* autism.

autiste [otist] ◇ *adj* autistic.
◇ *nmf* autistic person.

autistique [otistik] *adj* autistic.

auto [oto] ◇ *nf* car, automobile *US* ■ **en ~, il faut être prudent** one should be careful when driving ▶ **~ tamponneuse** bumper car.
◇ *adj inv* ▷ **assurance**.

autoaccusateur, trice [otɔakyzatœr, tris] *adj* self-accusatory.

autoaccusation [otɔakyzasjɔ̃] *nf* self-accusation.

autoadhésif, ive [otɔadezif, iv] *adj* self-adhesive.

auto-alimenter [otɔalimɑ̃te] ◆ **s'auto-alimenter** *vp (emploi réfléchi)* to be self-perpetuating.

autoallumage [otɔalymaʒ] *nm* pre-ignition.

autoamorçage [otɔamɔrsaʒ] *nm* automatic priming.

autoanalyse [otɔanaliz] *nf* self-analysis.

autoberge [otɔbɛrʒ] *nf* : **(voie) ~** embankment road *UK*, expressway *US (along riverbank).*

autobiographie [otɔbjɔgrafi] *nf* autobiography.

autobiographique [otɔbjɔgrafik] *adj* autobiographical.

autobronzant, e [otɔbrɔ̃zɑ̃, ɑ̃t] *adj* tanning.
◆ **autobronzant** *nm* **1.** [crème] tanning cream **2.** [cachet] tanning pill.

autobus [otɔbys] *nm* bus ■ **~ à impériale** double-decker (bus) *UK.*

autocar [otɔkar] *nm* coach, bus ■ **~ pullman** luxury coach.

autocassable [otɔkasabl] *adj* ▷ **ampoule**.

autocélébrer [otɔselebre] ◆ **s'autocélébrer** *vp (emploi réfléchi)* to sing one's own praises, to blow one's own trumpet.

autocensure [otɔsɑ̃syr] *nf* self-censorship, self-regulation ■ **pratiquer l'~** to censor o.s.

autocensurer [3] [otɔsɑ̃syre] ◆ **s'autocensurer** *vp (emploi réfléchi)* to censor o.s.

autocentré, e [otɔsɑ̃tre] *adj* autocentric.

autochtone [otɔktɔn] ◇ *adj* native.
◇ *nmf* native ■ **les ~s sont arrivés en masse** *hum* the locals turned up in droves.

autocollant, e [otɔkɔlɑ̃, ɑ̃t] *adj* self-adhesive.
◆ **autocollant** *nm* sticker.

autoconsommation [otɔkɔ̃sɔmasjɔ̃] *nf* : **les légumes qu'ils cultivent sont destinés à l'~** the vegetables they grow are meant for their own consumption ■ **économie d'~** subsistence economy.

autocopiant, e [otɔkɔpjɑ̃, ɑ̃t] *adj* carbonless.

autocorrectif, ive [otɔkɔrɛktif, iv] *adj* self-correcting.

autocorrection [otɔkɔrɛksjɔ̃] *nf* self-correcting.

autocouchette [otɔkuʃɛt] *adj inv* = **autos-couchettes**.

autocrate [otɔkrat] *nm* autocrat.

autocratie [otɔkrasi] *nf* autocracy.

autocritique [otɔkritik] *nf* self-criticism ▪ **faire son ~** to make a thorough criticism of o.s.

autocuiseur [otɔkɥizœr] *nm* pressure cooker.

autodafé [otɔdafe] *nm* auto-da-fé ▪ **faire un ~ de livres** to burn books.

autodéfense [otɔdefɑ̃s] *nf* self-defence.
◆ **d'autodéfense** *loc adj* [arme] defensive ▪ **groupe d'~** vigilante group.

autodérision [otɔderizjɔ̃] *nf* self-mockery.

autodestructeur, trice [otɔdɛstryktœr, tris] *adj* self-destroying.

autodestruction [otɔdɛstryksjɔ̃] *nf* self-destruction.

autodétermination [otɔdetɛrminasjɔ̃] *nf* self-determination.

autodétruire [98] [otɔdetrɥir] ◆ **s'autodétruire** *vp (emploi réfléchi)* to self-destruct.

autodidacte [otɔdidakt] <> *adj* self-taught, self-educated.
<> *nmf* autodidact.

autodirecteur, trice [otɔdirɛktœr, tris] *adj* self-guiding.

auto-école [otɔekɔl] (*pl* **auto-écoles**) *nf* driving-school ▪ *(comme adj)* **voiture ~** driving-school car.

autoérotisme [otɔerɔtism] *nm* autoeroticism, onanism.

autofécondation [otɔfekɔ̃dasjɔ̃] *nf* self-fertilization, self-fertilizing.

autofinancement [otɔfinɑ̃smɑ̃] *nm* self-financing ▪ **capacité d'~** cash flow.

autofinancer [16] [otɔfinɑ̃se] ◆ **s'autofinancer** *vp (emploi réfléchi)* to be self-financing *ou* self-supporting.

autofocus [otɔfɔkys] <> *adj* autofocus.
<> *nm* **1.** [système] autofocus system **2.** [appareil] autofocus camera.

autogéré, e [otɔʒere] *adj* self-managed, self-run.

autogérer [18] [otɔʒere] *vt* [entreprise, commune] to self-manage.
◆ **s'autogérer** *vp (emploi réfléchi)* [collectivité] to be self-managing.

autogestion [otɔʒɛstjɔ̃] *nf* (workers') self-management ▪ **entreprise/université en ~** self-managed company/university.

autogestionnaire [otɔʒɛstjɔnɛr] <> *adj* based on workers' self-management.
<> *nmf* advocate of workers' self-management.

autographe [otɔgraf] <> *adj* handwritten, autograph *(modif)*.
<> *nm* autograph.

autogreffe [otɔgrɛf] *nf* autograft ▪ **faire une ~** to carry out an autograft.

autoguidage [otɔgidaʒ] *nm* guidance.

autoguidé, e [otɔgide] *adj* [avion] remotely-piloted ▪ [missile] guided.

auto-immunitaire [otɔimynitɛr] (*pl* **auto-immunitaires**) *adj* autoimmune.

auto-immunité [otɔimynite] (*pl* **auto-immunités**) *nf* autoimmunity.

auto-induction [otɔɛ̃dyksjɔ̃] (*pl* **auto-inductions**) *nf* self-induction.

auto-intoxication [otɔɛ̃tɔksikasjɔ̃] (*pl* **auto-intoxications**) *nf* self-poisoning, autointoxication.

autolyse [otɔliz] *nf* autolysis.

automate [otɔmat] *nm* **1.** [robot] automaton, robot **2.** *Suisse* [machine] vending machine ▪ [à billets] cash dispenser.

automaticien, enne [otɔmatisjɛ̃, ɛn] *nm, f* automation *ou* robotics specialist.

automaticité [otɔmatisite] *nf* automaticity.

automation [otɔmasjɔ̃] *nf* automation.

automatique [otɔmatik] <> *adj* automatic ▪ **de façon ~** automatically.
<> *nm* ARM automatic.
<> *nf* **1.** AUTO automatic (car) **2.** SC automation, cybernetics *(sing)*.

automatiquement [otɔmatikmɑ̃] *adv* automatically.

automatisation [otɔmatizasjɔ̃] *nf* automation.

automatiser [3] [otɔmatize] *vt* to automate.
◆ **s'automatiser** *vpi* to become automated.

automatisme [otɔmatism] *nm* automatism ▪ **j'éteins toutes les lampes, c'est un ~** I always switch lamps off, I do it without thinking *ou* it's automatic with me.

automédication [otɔmedikasjɔ̃] *nf* self-prescription *(of drugs)*.

automitrailleuse [otɔmitrajøz] *nf* armoured-car.

automnal, e, aux [otɔnal, o] *adj* autumnal *litt*, autumn *(modif)*, fall *US (modif)*.

automne [otɔn] *nm* autumn, fall *US* ▪ **l'~ de sa vie** *litt* the autumn of his life.

automobile [otɔmɔbil] <> *nf* **1.** [véhicule] motor car *UK*, automobile *US* **2.** SPORT driving, motoring *UK* **3.** [industrie] car industry.
<> *adj* **1.** MÉCAN [des voitures] car *(modif)* ▪ [bateau, engin] automotive, self-propelled **2.** ADMIN [vignette] car *(modif)* ▪ [assurance] car, automobile.

automobilisme [otɔmɔbilism] *nm* driving, motoring *UK*.

automobiliste [otɔmɔbilist] *nmf* driver, motorist *UK*.

automoteur, trice [otɔmɔtœr, tris] *adj* automotive, motorized, self-propelled.
◆ **automoteur** *nm* **1.** MIL self-propelled gun **2.** NAUT self-propelled barge.
◆ **automotrice** *nf* electric railcar.

automutilation [otɔmytilasjɔ̃] *nf* self-mutilation.

autoneige [otɔnɛʒ] *nf* *Québec* snowmobile.

autonettoyant, e [otɔnɛtwajɑ̃, ɑ̃t] *adj* self-cleaning.

autonome [otɔnɔm] *adj* **1.** [autogéré - territoire, gouvernement, organisme] autonomous, self-governing ▪ **gestion ~** managerial autonomy **2.** [non affilié - syndicat] independent **3.** [libre - caractère, personnalité] autonomous, independent ▪ **elle est très ~** she likes to make her own decisions.

autonomiste [otɔnɔmist] *adj & nmf* separatist.

autoportant, e [otɔpɔrtɑ̃, ɑ̃t] *adj* self-supporting.

autoportrait [otɔpɔrtrɛ] *nm* self-portrait ▪ **faire son ~** to paint a self-portrait ▪ **en réalité, dans cette nouvelle, elle fait son ~** this short story is in fact her self-portrait.

autopropulsé, e [otɔprɔpylse] *adj* self-propelled.

autopropulsion [otɔprɔpylsjɔ̃] *nf* self-propulsion.

autopsie [otɔpsi] *nf* **1.** MÉD autopsy ▪ **pratiquer une ~** to carry out an autopsy **2.** [analyse] critical analysis, autopsy ▪ **faire l'~ d'un conflit** to go into the causes of a conflict.

autopsier [9] [otɔpsje] *vt* to carry out an autopsy on.

autopunition [otɔpynisjɔ̃] *nf* self-punishment.

autoradio [otɔradjo] *nm* car radio.

autorail [otɔraj] *nm* railcar.

autoréglage [otɔreglaʒ] *nm* automatic control.

autorégulateur, trice [otɔregylatœr, tris] *adj* self-regulating.

autorégulation [otɔregylasjɔ̃] *nf* **1.** BIOL & PHYSIOL self-regulation **2.** TECHNOL automatic regulation.

auto-reverse [otɔrivœrs] *adj* auto-reverse.

autorisation [otɔrizasjɔ̃] *nf* **1.** [consentement - d'un parent] permission, consent ; [- d'un supérieur] permission, authorization ; [- d'un groupe] authorization ■ **donner son ~ à qqch** to consent to sthg ■ **donner à qqn l'~ de faire qqch** to give sb permission to do sthg **2.** ADMIN [acte officiel] authorization, permit ■ **~ de sortie** [d'un lycée] (special) pass ■ **~ de sortie du territoire** parental authorization *(permitting a minor to leave a country)* **3.** BANQUE : **une ~ de 1 000 euros** a temporary overdraft of up to 1,000 euros ■ **~ de crédit** credit line.

autorisé, e [otɔrize] *adj* **1.** PRESSE official ■ **de source ~e, le président aurait déjà signé l'accord** sources close to the President say that he's already signed the agreement **2.** [agréé - aliment, colorant] permitted **3.** [qui a la permission] : **personnes ~es** authorized persons.

autoriser [3] [otɔrize] *vt* **1.** [permettre - manifestation, réunion, publication] to authorize, to allow ; [- emprunt] to authorize, to approve **2.** [donner l'autorisation à] : **~ qqn à** to allow sb *ou* to give sb permission to ■ **je ne t'autorise pas à me parler sur ce ton** I won't have you talk to me like that ■ **~ qqn à faire** [lui en donner le droit] to entitle sb *ou* to give sb the right to do ■ **sa réponse nous autorise à penser que...** from his reply we may deduce *ou* his reply leads us to conclude that... **3.** [justifier] to permit of *sout*, to justify ■ **la jeunesse n'autorise pas tous les débordements** being young isn't an excuse for uncontrolled behaviour ■ **cette dépêche n'autorise plus le moindre espoir** this news spells the end of any last remaining hopes.
◆ **s'autoriser** *vpt* : **je m'autorise un petit verre de vin le soir** I allow myself a small glass of wine in the evening.
◆ **s'autoriser de** *vp+prép* [se servir de] : **elle s'autorise de sa confiance** she exploits his confidence in her.

autoritaire [otɔritɛr] *adj* authoritarian ■ **il est très ~** he's very overbearing.

autoritairement [otɔritɛrmɑ̃] *adv* in an authoritarian way, with (excessive) authority.

autoritarisme [otɔritarism] *nm* authoritarianism.

autorité [otɔrite] *nf* **1.** [pouvoir] authority, power ■ **par ~ de justice** by order of the court ■ **avoir de l'~ sur qqn** to be in *ou* to have authority over sb ■ **être sous l'~ de qqn** to be *ou* to come under sb's authority ■ **faire qqch de sa propre ~** to do sthg on one's own authority ■ **avoir ~ pour faire qqch** to have authority to do sthg ➊ **l'~ parentale** [droits] parental rights ; [devoirs] parental responsibilities **2.** [fermeté] authority ■ **faire preuve d'~ envers un enfant** to show some authority towards a child ■ **il a besoin d'un peu d'~** he needs to be taken in hand **3.** [compétence] authority ■ **parler de qqch avec ~** to talk authoritatively about sthg ■ **faire ~** authoritative edition ■ **version qui fait ~** definitive version ■ **essai qui fait ~** seminal essay ‖ [expert] authority, expert ■ **c'est une ~ en matière de...** he's an authority *ou* expert on... **4.** ADMIN : **l'~, les ~s** those in authority, the authorities ■ **l'~ militaire/religieuse** the military/religious authority ■ **s'adresser à l'~ compétente** to apply to the appropriate authority ■ **un agent** *ou* **représentant de l'~** an official ‖ [police] : **les ~s** the police force.
◆ **d'autorité** *loc adv* without consultation ■ **d'~, j'ai décidé de fermer la bibliothèque le mercredi** I decided on my own authority to close the library on Wednesdays.

autoroute [otɔrut] *nf* **1.** TRANSP motorway *UK*, freeway *US* ➊ **~ à péage** toll motorway *UK*, turnpike *US* ■ **l'~ du Soleil** *the motorway linking Paris, Lyons and Marseilles, famously congested during the 'grands départs' of July and August* **2.** INFORM : **~ électronique** information superhighway.

AUTOROUTE

In France, motorways are indicated with the letter *A* followed by a number. Many motorways are privately run and operate a toll system *(péage)*.

autoroutier, ère [otɔrutje, ɛr] *adj* motorway *UK (modif)* freeway *US (modif)*.
◆ **autoroutière** *nf car particularly suited to motorwa driving conditions* ■ **c'est une bonne autoroutière** it's ideal fo motorway driving.

autosatisfaction [otɔsatisfaksjɔ̃] *nf* self-satisfaction.

autos-couchettes [otɔkuʃɛt] *adj inv* : **train ~** car-sleepe train.

auto-stop [otɔstɔp] *nm sing* hitch-hiking, hitching ■ **fair de l'~** to hitch-hike, to hitch ■ **prendre qqn en ~** to give sb a lift *ou* ride.

auto-stoppeur, euse [otɔstɔpœr, øz] *(mpl* **auto-stop peurs**, *fpl* **auto-stoppeuses**) *nm, f* hitch-hiker ■ **prendre un ~** to pick up a hitch-hiker.

autosubsistance [otɔsybzistɑ̃s] *nf* (economic) self sufficiency.

autosuffisance [otɔsyfizɑ̃s] *nf* self-sufficiency.

autosuggestion [otɔsygʒɛstjɔ̃] *nf* autosuggestion.

auto tamponneuse [otɔtɑ̃pɔnøz] (*pl* **autos tamponneu ses**) *nf* bumper car, dodgem.

autotracté, e [otɔtrakte] *adj* self-propelled.

autotransformateur [otɔtrɑ̃sfɔrmatœr] *nm* autotrans former.

autour[1] [otur] *nm* goshawk.

autour[2] [otur] *adv* around, round ■ **il y avait un arbre et le enfants couraient (tout) ~** there was a tree and the childre were running round it ■ **une nappe avec des broderies tout ~** a tablecloth with embroidery all around it *ou* round the edges.
◆ **autour de** *loc prép* **1.** [dans l'espace] around ■ **il observai les gens ~ de lui** he looked at the people around him **2.** [in diquant une approximation] around ■ **ils sont arrivés ~ de 20 h** the arrived (at) around 8 p.m.

autovaccin [otɔvaksɛ̃] *nm* autogenous vaccine.

autre [otr] <> *dét (adj indéf)* **1.** [distinct, différent] : **un ~ homm** another *ou* a different man ■ **donnez-moi une ~ tasse, celle-c est ébréchée** give me another *ou* a new cup, this one's chip ped ■ **en d'~s lieux** elsewhere ■ **dans d'~s circonstances...** i other circumstances..., had the circumstances been differ ent... ■ **tu veux ~ chose?** do you want anything else? ■ **la vérit est tout ~** the truth is quite *ou* very *ou* altogether differen ■ **je me faisais une tout ~ idée de la question** I had quite a dif ferent concept of the matter ➊ **ça c'est une ~ histoire** *ou* **affaire** *ou* **paire de manches** *fam* that's something else al together, that's another story *ou* kettle of fish (altogether ■ **~s temps, ~s mœurs** other days, other ways
2. [supplémentaire] : **voulez-vous un ~ café?** would you like an other coffee? ■ **elle est partie sans ~s explications** she left with out further explanation ■ **il nous faut une ~ chaise** we nee one more *ou* an extra *ou* another chair ■ **essaie une ~ fois** tr again *ou* one more time
3. [devenu différent] different ■ **je me sens un ~ homme** I feel a different *ou* new man ■ **avec des fines herbes, ça a un tout ~ goût!** with some fines herbes, it has quite a different taste
4. [marquant la supériorité] : **leur ancien appartement avait un ~ ca chet!** their old flat had far more character! ■ **le Japon, ah c'es ~ chose!** Japan, now that's really something else! ■ **Marc es bon en maths, mais Jean c'est ~ chose!** Marc is good at maths but he's nowhere near as good as Jean!
5. [restant] other, remaining
6. [avec les pronoms 'nous' et 'vous'] : **nous ~s consommateurs...** w consumers... ■ **écoutez-le, vous ~s!** *fam* listen to him, you lot
7. [dans le temps] other ■ **on y est allés l'~ jour** we went ther the other day ■ **en d'~s temps** in other times ; [dans le passé in days gone by ■ **un ~ jour** some other day ■ **dans une ~ vi** in another life

8. [en corrélation avec 'l'un'] : **l'une et l'~ hypothèses sont valables** both hypotheses are valid ▪ **l'un ou l'~ projet devra être accepté** one of the two projects will have to be accepted ▪ **ni l'une ni l'~ explication n'est plausible** neither explanation is plausible.
◇ *pron* **1.** [désignant des personnes] : **un ~** someone else, somebody else ▪ **on n'attend pas les ~s?** aren't we going to wait for the others? ▪ **d'~s que moi vous donneront les explications nécessaires** others will give you the necessary explanations ▪ **plus que tout ~, tu aurais dû prévoir que...** you of all people should have foreseen that... ▪ **tout** *ou* **un ~ que lui aurait refusé** anyone else but him would have refused ▪ **quelqu'un d'~** someone else ▪ **aucun ~, nul ~** *sout* no one else, nobody else, none other *sout* ▪ **personne d'~** no one else, nobody else ǁ [désignant des choses] : **un ~** another one ▪ **d'~s** other ones, others ▪ **une maison semblable à une ~** a house like any other ▪ **ce livre ou l'~** this book or the other one ▪ **je n'en ai pas besoin d'~s** I don't need any more ▪ **rien d'~** nothing else ▶ **comme dit** *ou* **dirait l'~** as they say ▪ **à d'~s!** *fam* go on with you!, come off it! ▪ **et l'~ qui n'arrête pas de pleurer!** *fam* and that one who won't stop crying!
2. [en corrélation avec 'l'un'] : **l'une chante, l'~ danse** one sings, the other dances ▪ **l'un et l'~** both of them ▪ **l'un ou l'~** (either) one or the other, either one ▪ **ils marchaient l'un derrière l'~/l'un à côté de l'~** they were walking one behind the other/ side by side ▪ **ni l'un ni l'~ n'est venu** neither (of them) came ▪ **on les prend souvent l'un pour l'~** people often mistake one for the other ▪ **les uns le détestent, les ~s l'adorent** he's loathed by some, loved by others ▪ **aidez-vous les uns les ~s** help each other *ou* one another ▪ **n'écoute pas ce que disent les uns et les ~s** don't listen to what people say ▪ **l'un ne va pas sans l'~** you can't have one without the other ▪ **présente-les l'un à l'~** introduce them to each other ▪ **vous êtes des brutes les uns comme les ~s!** you're (nothing but) beasts, all of you! ▶ **l'un dans l'~** all in all, at the end of the day.
◇ *nm* PHILOS : **l'~** the other.

autrefois [otrəfwa] *adv* in the past, in former times *ou* days ▪ **je l'ai bien connu ~** I knew him well once ▪ **~ s'élevait ici un château médiéval...** there used to be a medieval castle here... ▪ **les maisons d'~ n'avaient aucun confort** in the past *ou* in the old days, houses were very basic.

autrement [otrəmɑ̃] *adv* **1.** [différemment] another *ou* some other way ▪ **la bouteille va se renverser, pose-la ~** that bottle will spill, stand it differently ▪ **la banque est fermée, je vais me débrouiller ~** the bank's closed, I'll find some other way (of getting money) ▪ **il est habillé ~ que d'habitude** he hasn't got his usual clothes on ▪ **en être ~ : comment pourrait-il en être ~** how could things be different? ▪ **il n'en a jamais été ~** things have always been this way *ou* have never been any other way *ou* have never been any different ▪ **faire ~ : nous ne les laisserons pas construire la route ici, il faudra qu'ils fassent ~** we won't let them build the road here, they'll have to find another *ou* some other way ▪ **il n'y a pas moyen de faire ~** there's no other way *ou* no alternative ▪ **faire ~ que : je n'ai pu faire ~ que de les entendre** I couldn't help but overhear them ▪ **il n'a pas pu faire ~ que de rembourser** he had no alternative but to pay the money back **2.** [sinon] otherwise, or else ▪ **payez car ~ vous aurez des ennuis** pay up or else you'll get into trouble ▪ **les gens sont désagréables, ~ le travail est intéressant** the people are unpleasant, but otherwise *ou* apart from that the work's interesting **3.** *(suivi d'un comparatif)* [beaucoup] far ▪ **c'est ~ plus grave cette fois-ci** it's far more serious this time.
◆ **autrement dit** *loc adv* in other words ▪ **~ dit tu me quittes?** in other words, you're leaving me?

Autriche [otriʃ] *npr f* : **(l')~** Austria.

autrichien, enne [otriʃjɛ̃, ɛn] *adj* Austrian.
◆ **Autrichien, enne** *nm, f* Austrian ▪ **l'Autrichienne** HIST (Queen) Marie-Antoinette.

autruche [otryʃ] *nf* ostrich ▪ **faire l'~** to bury one's head in the sand.

autrui [otrɥi] *pron indéf inv sout* others, other people ▪ **peu m'importe l'opinion d'~** other people's opinion *ou* the opinion of others means little to me ▶ **ne fais pas à ~ ce que tu ne voudrais pas qu'on te fît** *prov* do as you would be done by.

auvent [ovɑ̃] *nm* **1.** [en dur] porch roof **2.** [en toile] awning, canopy.

auvergnat, e [ovɛrɲa, at] *adj* from the Auvergne.
◆ **Auvergnat, e** *nm, f inhabitant of or person from the Auvergne* ▪ **les Auvergnats** the people of the Auvergne.

Auvergne [ovɛrɲ] *npr f* : **(l')~** the Auvergne.

AUVERGNE

This administrative region includes the ***départements*** of Allier, Cantal, Haute-Loire and Puy-de-Dôme (capital: Clermont-Ferrand).

aux [o] ⊳ **à**.

auxiliaire [oksiljɛr] ◇ *adj* **1.** LING auxiliary **2.** [annexe] assistant *(modif)*, auxiliary **3.** TECHNOL auxiliary, standby.
◇ *nmf* **1.** [employé temporaire] temporary worker ▪ **ce n'est qu'un ~** he's only temporary **2.** DR : **~ de justice** representative of the law **3.** MÉD : **~ médical** paramedic ▪ **les ~s médicaux** the paramedical profession **4.** [aide] helper, assistant.
◇ *nm* **1.** LING auxiliary **2.** [outil, moyen] aid ▪ **le magnétoscope est l'~ précieux de mon enseignement** I find a video-recorder to be an invaluable teaching aid.
◆ **auxiliaires** *nmpl* **1.** ANTIQ *foreign troops of the Roman Army* **2.** NAUT [moteurs] auxiliary engines ▪ [équipement] auxiliary equipment.

auxiliairement [oksiljɛrmɑ̃] *adv* **1.** LING : **verbe utilisé ~** verb used as an auxiliary **2.** [accessoirement] secondarily ▪ **~, cela peut servir d'abri** it can also, if necessary, be used as a shelter.

auxquelles, auxquels [okɛl] *fpl & mpl* ⊳ **lequel**.

av. = avenue.

AV ◇ *nm* = **avis de virement**.
◇ = **avant**.

avachi, e [avaʃi] *adj* **1.** [sans tenue - vêtement] crumpled, rumpled, shapeless ; [- cuir] limp ; [- sommier, banquette] sagging ; [- chaussure] shapeless, down-at-heel ; [- gâteau] soggy ; [- soufflé] collapsed ; [- chapeau] shapeless **2.** [indolent] flabby, spineless.

avachir [32] [avaʃir] ◆ **s'avachir** *vpi* **1.** [s'affaisser - vêtement] to become shapeless ; [- gâteau, forme] to collapse ; [- cuir] to go limp ; [- canapé] to start sagging **2.** [s'affaler] : **s'~ dans un fauteuil/sur une table** to slump into an armchair/over a table.

avachissement [avaʃismɑ̃] *nm* **1.** [perte de tenue - d'un tissu] becoming limp, losing (its) shape ; [- de chaussures] wearing out ; [- d'un canapé] starting to sag ; [- d'une forme] collapsing ; [- de ressorts, des muscles] slackening ▪ **lutter contre l'~ des tissus musculaires** to prevent the slackening of muscles ▪ [état déformé] limp *ou* worn-down appearance **2.** [perte de courage - physique] going limp ; [- moral] loss of moral fibre **3.** [état physique - temporaire] limpness ; [- permanent] flabbiness ▪ [découragement] loss of moral fibre ▪ [veulerie] spinelessness.

aval [aval] ◇ *nm* **1.** FIN endorsement, guarantee ▪ **donner son ~ à une traite** to guarantee *ou* to endorse a draft **2.** [soutien] support ▪ **donner son ~ à qqn** to back sb (up) **3.** [autorisation] authorization ▪ **avoir l'~ des autorités** to have (an) official authorization **4.** [d'une rivière] downstream water **5.** [d'une pente] downhill side *(of a slope)* ▪ **regardez vers l'~** look down the slope.
◇ *adj* : **ski/skieur ~** downhill ski/skier.
◆ **en aval de** *loc prép* **1.** [en suivant une rivière] downstream *ou* down-river from **2.** [en montagne] downhill from **3.** [après] following on from ▪ **les étapes qui se situent en ~ de la production** the post-production stages.

avalanche [avalɑ̃ʃ] *nf* **1.** GÉOGR avalanche **2.** *fig* [quantité - de courrier, de protestations, de compliments, de lumière] flood ; [- de coups, d'insultes] shower ▪ **il y eut une ~ de réponses** the answers came pouring in.

avalancheux, euse [avalɑ̃ʃø, øz] *adj* avalanche-prone.

avaler [3] [avale] *vt* **1.** [consommer - nourriture] to swallow ; [- boisson] to swallow, to drink ▪ **~ qqch de travers : j'ai dû ~**

quelque chose de travers something went down the wrong way ■ **je n'ai rien avalé depuis deux jours** I haven't had a thing to eat for two days ■ **~ du lait à petites gorgées** to sip milk ■ **~ sa salive** to swallow ■ **à midi, elle prend à peine le temps d'~ son déjeuner** at lunchtime, she bolts her meal ■ *(en usage absolu)* [manger, boire] to swallow
2. *fig* **~ les obstacles/kilomètres** to make light work of any obstacle/of distances ▶ **~ qqn tout cru** to eat sb alive ■ **~ son bulletin** *ou* **son acte de naissance** *ou* **sa chique** *fam* to kick the bucket, to go and meet one's maker *hum* ■ **comme quelqu'un qui aurait avalé son** *ou* **un parapluie** [raide] stiffly, with his back like a rod ; [manquant d'adaptabilité] stiffly, starchily
3. [inhaler - fumée, vapeurs] to inhale, to breathe in *(sép)*
4. [lire - roman, article] to devour
5. *fam* [croire - mensonge] to swallow, to buy ■ **je lui ai fait ~ que j'étais malade** I got him to believe that I was sick ■ **elle lui ferait ~ n'importe quoi** he believes anything she says
6. *fam* [accepter - insulte] to swallow ■ **pilule difficile à ~** *fig* hard *ou* bitter pill to swallow ▶ **~ la pilule** to swallow the bitter pill ■ **~ des couleuvres** [insultes] to swallow insults ; [mensonges] to be taken in ■ **faire ~ des couleuvres à qqn** [insultes] to humiliate sb ; [mensonges] to take sb in.

avaleur [avalœr] *nm* : **~ de sabres** sword swallower.

avaliser [3] [avalize] *vt* **1.** DR [effet] to endorse, to back ■ [signature] to guarantee **2.** [donner son accord à] to back, to condone, to support ■ **nous n'avalisons pas ces comportements barbares** we do not condone such barbaric behaviour.

à-valoir [avalwar] *nm inv* advance (payment).

avance [avɑ̃s] *nf* **1.** [par rapport au temps prévu] : **prendre de l'~ dans ses études** to get ahead in one's studies ■ **j'ai pris de l'~ sur le** *ou* **par rapport au planning** I'm ahead of schedule ■ **avoir de l'~ sur** *ou* **par rapport à ses concurrents** to be ahead of the competition *ou* of one's competitors ■ **arriver avec 10 minutes/jours d'~** to arrive 10 minutes/days early ■ **le maillot jaune a pris 37 secondes d'~** the yellow jersey's 37 seconds ahead of time
2. [d'une montre, d'un réveil] : **ta montre prend de l'~** your watch is fast ■ **ma montre a une minute d'~/prend une seconde d'~ toutes les heures** my watch is one minute fast/gains a second every hour
3. [avantage - d'une entreprise] lead ; [- d'une armée] progress ■ **l'~ prise par notre pays en matière de génétique** our country's lead in the field of genetics ■ **avoir 10 points d'~ sur qqn** to have a 10 point lead over sb ■ **avoir une demi-longueur d'~** to lead by half a length
4. [dans un approvisionnement] : **en avoir d'~, en faire d'~** : **prends ce beurre, j'en ai plusieurs paquets d'~** have this butter, I keep several packs in reserve ■ **de la sauce tomate? j'en fais toujours d'~** tomato sauce? I always make some in advance
5. [acompte] advance ■ **donner à qqn une ~ sur son salaire** to give sb an advance on his/her salary ■ **faire une ~ de 500 euros à qqn** to advance 500 euros to sb ▶ **~ bancaire** FIN (bank) overdraft ■ **~ de fonds** loan ■ **~ sur recette** loan to a producer *(to be recouped against box-office takings)* ■ **~ sur salaire** advance (on one's salary) ■ **~ sur titre** collateral loan
6. TECHNOL : **~ rapide** fast forward.
◆ **avances** *nfpl* [propositions - d'amitié, d'association] overtures, advances ; [- sexuelles] advances ■ **faire des ~s à qqn** [suj: séducteur] to make advances to sb ; [suj: entreprise] to make overtures to sb.
◆ **à l'avance** *loc adv* [payer] in advance, beforehand ■ **je n'ai été averti que deux minutes à l'~** I was only warned two minutes beforehand, I only got two minutes' notice ■ **réservez longtemps à l'~** book early.
◆ **d'avance, par avance** *loc adv* [payer, remercier] in advance ■ **savourant d'~ sa revanche** already savouring his revenge ■ **c'est joué d'~** it's a foregone conclusion ■ **c'est tout combiné d'~** *fam* it's a put-up job ■ **d'~ je peux te dire qu'il n'est pas fiable** I can tell you right away *ou* now that he's not reliable.
◆ **en avance** ◇ *loc adj* : **elle est en ~ sur le reste de la classe** she's ahead of the rest of the class ■ **être en ~ sur son temps** *ou* **époque** to be ahead of one's time.
◇ *loc adv* [avant l'heure prévue] early ■ **être en ~ de 10 minutes/jours** to be 10 minutes/days early ■ **je me dépêche, je ne suis pas en ~!** I must rush, I'm (rather) late!

avancé, e [avɑ̃se] *adj* **1.** [dans le temps - heure] late ■ **à un heure ~e** late at night ■ **la saison est ~e** it's very late in the sea son ■ **arriver à un âge ~** to be getting on in years **2.** [pourri poisson, viande] off *UK*, bad ; [- fruit] overripe **3.** [développé - in telligence, économie] advanced ■ **un garçon ~ pour son âge** a bo who's mature for *ou* ahead of his years ■ **à un stade peu ~** a an early stage ▶ **te voilà bien ~!** *iron* a (fat) lot of good that done you! **4.** MIL [division, élément] advance *(modif)* ■ **ouvrag ~** outwork.
◆ **avancée** *nf* **1.** [progression] progress **2.** [d'un toit] over hang.

avancement [avɑ̃smɑ̃] *nm* **1.** [promotion] promotion, ad vancement ■ **avoir** *ou* **obtenir de l'~** to get (a) promotion o promoted **2.** [progression] progress ■ **y a-t-il de l'~ dans les tra vaux?** is the work progressing? **3.** DR : **~ d'hoirie** advance ment.

avancer [16] [avɑ̃se] ◇ *vt* **1.** [pousser vers l'avant] to push c to move forward *(sép)* ■ [amener vers l'avant] to bring forwar *(sép)* ■ **tu es trop loin, avance ta chaise** you're too far awa move *ou* bring your chair forward ■ **~ un siège à qqn** to pu *ou* draw up a seat for sb
2. [allonger] : **~ la tête** to stick one's head out ■ **~ sa** *ou* **la ma vers qqch** [pour l'attraper] to reach towards sthg ; [pour qu'c vous le donne] to hold out one's hand for sthg
3. [dans le temps] to bring *ou* to put forward *(sép)*, to move u *US* ■ **l'heure du départ a été avancée de 10 minutes** the startin time was put forward 10 minutes ■ **la réunion a été avancée demain/lundi** the meeting has been brought forward to to morrow/Monday ■ **~ sa montre (d'une heure)** to put one watch forward (by an hour)
4. [proposer - explication, raison, opinion] to put forward *(sép)*, t suggest, to advance ; [- argument, théorie, plan] to put forwar ■ **être sûr de ce que l'on avance** to be certain of what one saying ■ **si ce qu'il avance est vrai** if his allegations are true
5. [faire progresser] : **je vais rédiger les étiquettes pour vous ~** I' write out the labels to make it quicker for you *ou* to hel you along ■ **trêve de bavardage, tout cela ne m'avance pas** that enough chatting, all this isn't getting my work done ■ **t'avance à quoi de mentir?** *fam* what do you gain by lying ■ **voilà à quoi ça t'avance de tricher** this is where cheating get you ■ **les insultes ne t'avanceront à rien** being abusive will g you nowhere
6. [prêter - argent, somme, loyer] to lend, to advance.
◇ *vi* **1.** [se déplacer dans l'espace] to move forward, to procee *sout*, to advance ■ MIL to advance ■ **~ d'un pas** to take one ste forward ■ **~ à grands pas** to stride along ■ **~ avec difficulté** plod along ■ **~ vers** *ou* **sur qqn d'un air menaçant** to advanc on sb threateningly ■ **avoir du mal à ~** to make slow progre ■ **le bus avançait lentement** the bus was moving slowly ■ **ne re tez pas là, avancez!** don't just stand there, move on!
2. [progresser - temps, action] to be getting on, to progres ■ **l'heure avance** time's *ou* it's getting on, it's getting lat ■ **l'été/l'hiver avance** we're well into the summer/winter ■ **a fur et à mesure que la nuit avançait** as the night wore on ■ **avance?** how's it going? ■ **les réparations n'avançaient pas/ava çaient** the repair work was getting nowhere/was makin swift progress ■ **le projet n'avance plus** the project's come t a halt *ou* standstill ■ **faire ~** [cause] to promote ; [connaissance to further, to advance ■ **faire ~ les choses** [accélérer une actio to speed things up ; [améliorer la situation] to improve matte
3. [faire des progrès] to make progress, to get further forwar ■ **j'ai l'impression de ne pas ~** I don't feel I'm getting anywhe *ou* I'm making any headway ■ **~ dans une enquête/son trava** to make progress in an investigation/one's work ■ **~ en âg** [enfant] to grow up, to get older ; [personne mûre] to be gettin on (in years) ■ **~ en grade** to be promoted, to get a promotic
4. [montre, réveil] : **votre montre avance** *ou* **vous avancez de 10 m nutes** your watch is *ou* you are 10 minutes fast ■ **pendule q avance d'une seconde toutes les heures** clock that gains a se ond every hour
5. [faire saillie - nez, menton] to jut *ou* to stick out, to protrude [- piton, promontoire] to jut *ou* to stick out.
◆ **s'avancer** *vpi* **1.** [approcher] to move forward *ou* close ■ **il s'avança vers moi** he came towards me
2. [prendre de l'avance] : **s'~ dans son travail** to make progre *ou* some headway in one's work

3. [prendre position] to commit o.s. ▪ **je ne voudrais pas m'~ mais il est possible que...** I can't be positive but it might be that... ▪ **je m'avance peut-être un peu trop en affirmant cela** it might be a bit rash of me to say this
4. [faire saillie] to jut *ou* to stick out, to protrude ▪ **la jetée s'avance dans la mer** the jetty sticks out into the sea.

avanie [avani] *nf* snub ▪ **subir des ~s** to be snubbed.

avant [avɑ̃] ◇ *prép* **1.** [dans le temps] before ▪ **il est arrivé ~ la nuit/le dîner** he arrived before nightfall/dinner ▪ **~ son élection** prior to her election, before being elected ▪ **200 ans ~ Jésus-Christ** 200 (years) BC ▪ **je ne serai pas prêt ~ une demi-heure** I won't be ready for another half an hour ▪ **nous n'ouvrons pas ~ 10 h** we don't open until 10 ▪ **le contrat sera signé ~ deux mois** the contract will be signed within two months ▪ **il faut que je termine ~ ce soir** I've got to finish by this evening ▪ **peu ~ les élections** a short while *ou* time before the elections **2.** [dans l'espace] before ▪ **vous tournez à droite juste ~ le feu** you turn right just before the lights **3.** [dans un rang, un ordre, une hiérarchie] before ▪ **vous êtes ~ moi** [dans une file d'attente] you're before me ▪ **il était juste ~ moi dans la file** he was just in front of me in the queue ▪ **leur équipe est maintenant ~ la nôtre dans le classement général** their team is now ahead of us in the league ▪ **je place le travail ~ tout le reste** I put work above *ou* before everything else ▪ **ta santé passe ~ ta carrière** your health is more important than *ou* comes before your career.
◇ *adv* **1.** [dans le temps] before ▪ **~, j'avais plus de patience avec les enfants** I used to be more patient with children ▪ **la maison est comme ~** the house has remained the same *ou* is the same as it was (before) ▪ **quand j'ai un rendez-vous, j'aime arriver un peu ~** when I'm due to meet someone, I like to get there a little ahead of time ▪ **bien** *ou* **longtemps ~** well *ou* long before ▪ **il est parti quelques minutes ~** he left a few minutes before *ou* earlier ▪ **très ~ dans la saison** very late in the season ▪ **discuter/lire bien ~ dans la nuit** to talk/to read late into the night **2.** [dans l'espace] : **vous voyez le parc? il y a un restaurant juste ~** see the park? there's a restaurant just before it *ou* this side of it ▪ **allons plus ~** let's go further ▪ **il s'était aventuré trop ~ dans la forêt** he'd ventured too far into the forest ▮ *fig* **sans entrer** *ou* **aller plus ~ dans les détails** without going into any further *ou* more detail ▪ **il est allé trop ~ dans les réformes** he went too far with the reforms **3.** [dans un rang, un ordre, une hiérarchie] : **est-ce que je peux passer ~?** can I go first?
◇ *adj inv* [saut périlleux, roulade] forward ▪ [roue, siège, partie] front.
◇ *nm* **1.** [d'un véhicule] front ▪ NAUT bow, bows ▪ **il s'est porté vers l'~ du peloton** he moved to the front of the bunch ▪ **montez à l'~** sit in the front ◐ **aller de l'~** *pr & fig* to forge ahead **2.** SPORT forward ▪ [au volley] frontline player ▪ **jouer ~ droit/gauche** to play right/left forward ▪ **la ligne des ~s, les ~s** the forward line, the forwards **3.** MIL : **l'~** the front.
◆ **avant de** *loc prép* before ▪ **~ de partir, il faudra...** before leaving, it'll be necessary to... ▪ **je ne signerai rien ~ d'avoir vu les locaux** I won't sign anything until *ou* before I see the premises.
◆ **avant que** *loc conj* : **ne dites rien ~ qu'il n'arrive** don't say anything until he arrives ▪ **je viendrai la voir ~ qu'elle (ne) parte** I'll come and see her before she leaves ▪ **~ qu'il comprenne, celui-là!** by the time he's understood!
◆ **avant que de** *loc prép litt* before.
◆ **avant tout** *loc adv* **1.** [surtout] : **c'est une question de dignité ~ tout** it's a question of dignity above all (else) **2.** [tout d'abord] first ▪ **~ tout, je voudrais vous dire ceci** first (and foremost), I'd like to tell you this.
◆ **avant toute chose** *loc adv* first of all ▪ **~ toute chose, je vais prendre une douche** I'll have a shower before I do anything else.
◆ **d'avant** *loc adj* : **le jour/le mois d'~** the previous day/month, the day/month before ▪ **je vais essayer de prendre le train d'~** I'll try to catch the earlier train ▪ **les locataires d'~ étaient plus sympathiques** the previous tenants were much nicer.
◆ **en avant** *loc adv* [marcher] in front ▪ [partir] ahead ▪ [se pencher, tomber, bondir] forward ▪ **en ~!** forward! ▪ **en ~, marche!** MIL forward march! ▮ *fig* **mettre qqn en ~** [pour se protéger] to use sb as a shield ; [pour le faire valoir] to push sb forward *ou* to the front ▪ **mettre qqch en ~** to put sthg forward.
◆ **en avant de** *loc prép* : **il marche toujours en ~ des autres** he always walks ahead of the others ▪ **le barrage routier a été installé en ~ de Dijon** the roadblock was set up just before Dijon.

avantage [avɑ̃taʒ] *nm* **1.** [supériorité] advantage ▪ **sa connaissance du danois est un ~ par rapport aux autres candidats** her knowledge of Danish gives her an advantage *ou* the edge over the other candidates ▪ **avoir un ~ sur qqn/qqch** to have an advantage over sb/sthg ▪ **cela vous donne un ~ sur eux** this gives you an advantage over them ▪ **garder/perdre l'~** to keep/to lose the upper hand ▪ **ils nous ont battus mais ils avaient l'~ du nombre** they defeated us but they had the advantage of numbers ▪ **j'ai sur toi l'~ de l'âge** I have age on my side ▪ **elle a l'~ d'avoir 20 ans/d'être médecin** she's 20/a doctor, which is an advantage
2. [intérêt] advantage ▪ **les ~s et les inconvénients d'une solution** the advantages and disadvantages *ou* pros and cons of a solution ▪ **cette idée présente l'~ d'être simple** the idea has the advantage of being simple ▪ **c'est (tout) à ton ~** it's in your (best) interest ▪ **exploiter une idée à son ~** to exploit an idea to one's own advantage ▪ **avoir ~ à faire** to be better off doing ▪ **tu as tout ~ à l'acheter ici** you'd be much better off buying it here ▪ **elle aurait ~ à se taire** she'd be well-advised to keep quiet ▪ **quel ~ as-tu à déménager?** what advantage is there in your moving house? ▪ **ne tirez pas ~ de sa naïveté** don't take advantage of his naivety ▪ **tirer ~ de la situation** to turn the situation to (one's) advantage ▪ **tourner à l'~ de : la réforme ne doit pas tourner à l'~ des privilégiés** the reform mustn't be allowed to work in favour of the wealthy
3. FIN [bénéfice] benefit ▪ **~s financiers** financial benefits ▪ **~s accessoires** fringe benefits ▪ **~s collectifs** social welfare ▪ **~s complémentaires** perks ▪ **~s en nature** payment in kind
4. *sout* [plaisir] : **je n'ai pas l'~ de vous avoir été présenté** I haven't had the privilege *ou* pleasure of being introduced to you ▪ **j'ai (l'honneur et) l'~ de vous annoncer que...** I am pleased *ou* delighted to inform you that.
5. SPORT advantage ▪ **~ (à) Rops!** advantage Rops!
6. *loc* **être à son ~** [avoir belle allure] to look one's best ; [dans une situation] to be at one's best ▪ **changer à son ~** to change for the better.

avantager [17] [avɑ̃taʒe] *vt* **1.** [favoriser] to advantage, to give an advantage to ▪ **ils ont été avantagés par rapport aux étudiants étrangers** they were given an advantage over the foreign students ▪ **être avantagé dès le départ par rapport à qqn** to have a head start on *ou* over sb ▪ **être avantagé par la nature** to be favoured by nature ▪ **elle n'a pas été avantagée par la nature!** nature hasn't been particularly kind to her! **2.** [mettre en valeur] to show off *(sép)*, to show to advantage ▪ **son uniforme l'avantage** he looks his best in (his) uniform ▪ **cette coupe ne t'avantage pas** this hairstyle isn't very flattering.

avantageusement [avɑ̃taʒøzmɑ̃] *adv* **1.** [peu cher] at *ou* for a good price **2.** [favorablement] : **il s'en est tiré ~** he got away lightly ▪ **vous pourriez ~ remplacer ces deux hommes par une machine** you could usefully replace these two operatives with a machine ▪ **l'opération se solde ~ pour elle** the transaction has worked to her advantage.

avantageux, euse [avɑ̃taʒø, øz] *adj* **1.** [contrat, affaire] profitable ▪ [prix] attractive ▪ [condition, situation] favourable ▪ **c'est une offre très avantageuse** it's an excellent bargain **2.** [flatteur - pose, décolleté, uniforme] flattering ▪ **prendre des airs ~** to look self-satisfied.

avant-bras [avɑ̃bra] *nm inv* forearm.

avant-centre [avɑ̃sɑ̃tr] (*pl* **avants-centres**) *nm* centre-forward.

avant-coureur [avɑ̃kurœr] (*pl* **avant-coureurs**) *adj m* precursory.

avant-dernier, ère [avɑ̃dɛrnje, ɛr] (*mpl* **avant-derniers**, *fpl* **avant-dernières**) ◇ *adj* next to last ▪ **l'avant-dernière fois** the time before last.
◇ *nm, f* last but one ▪ **arriver ~** to be last but one.

avant-garde [avɑ̃gard] (*pl* **avant-gardes**) *nf* **1.** MIL vanguard **2.** [élite] avant-garde ▪ **peinture/architecture d'~** avant-garde painting/architecture.

avant-gardiste [avɑ̃gardist] (*pl* **avant-gardistes**) ◇ *adj* avant-garde.
◇ *nmf* avant-gardist.

avant-goût [avɑ̃gu] (*pl* **avant-goûts**) *nm* foretaste.

avant-guerre [avɑ̃gɛr] (*pl* **avant-guerres**) *nm ou nf* pre-war years *ou* period ▪ **les voitures d'~** pre-war cars.

avant-hier [avɑ̃tjɛr] *adv* the day before yesterday.

avant-port [avɑ̃pɔr] (*pl* **avant-ports**) *nm* outer harbour.

avant-poste [avɑ̃pɔst] (*pl* **avant-postes**) *nm* **1.** MIL outpost **2.** [lieu de l'action] : **il est toujours aux ~s** he's always where the action is.

avant-première [avɑ̃prəmjɛr] (*pl* **avant-premières**) *nf* **1.** THÉÂTRE dress rehearsal **2.** CINÉ preview ▪ **présenter qqch en ~** to preview sthg.

avant-projet [avɑ̃prɔʒɛ] (*pl* **avant-projets**) *nm* pilot study.

avant-propos [avɑ̃prɔpo] *nm inv* foreword.

avant-scène [avɑ̃sɛn] (*pl* **avant-scènes**) *nf* **1.** [partie de la scène] apron THEAT, proscenium **2.** [loge] box THEAT.

avant-toit [avɑ̃twa] (*pl* **avant-toits**) *nm* : **l'~** the eaves.

avant-train [avɑ̃trɛ̃] (*pl* **avant-trains**) *nm* **1.** ZOOL forequarters **2.** AUTO front-axle unit **3.** MIL limber.

avant-veille [avɑ̃vɛj] (*pl* **avant-veilles**) *nf* two days before *ou* earlier ▪ **l'~ de son mariage** two days before he got married.

avare [avar] ◇ *adj* **1.** [pingre] mean, miserly, tight-fisted **2.** *fig* **elle est plutôt ~ de sourires** she doesn't smile much ▪ **il n'a pas été ~ de compliments/de conseils** he was generous with his compliments/advice.
◇ *nmf* miser ▪ **'l'Avare'** ***Molière*** 'The Miser'.

avarice [avaris] *nf* miserliness, avarice.

avaricieux, euse [avarisjø, øz] ◇ *adj* ***sout*** miserly, stingy.
◇ *nm, f* miser, skinflint.

avarie [avari] *nf* damage *(sustained by a ship)* ▪ **subir des ~s** to sustain damage ➊ **~s de mer** sea damage ▪ **~s de route** damage in transit.

avarié, e [avarje] *adj* **1.** [aliment, marchandise] spoilt, damaged ▪ **de la viande ~e** tainted meat ▪ **cette viande est ~e** this meat has gone off **2.** NAUT : **navire ~** damaged ship.
◆ **s'avarier** *vpi* [denrée alimentaire] to go off *UK ou* bad.

avatar [avatar] *nm* **1.** RELIG avatar **2.** [changement] change, metamorphosis **3.** [mésaventure] misadventure, mishap ▪ **les ~s de la vie politique** the vicissitudes of political life.

AVC (*abr de* **accident vasculaire cérébral**) *nm* CVA.

Ave [ave] *nm inv* Ave Maria, Hail Mary.

avec [avɛk] ◇ *prép* **1.** [indiquant la complémentarité, l'accompagnement, l'accord] with ▪ **je ne prends jamais de sucre ~ mon café** I never take sugar in my coffee ▪ **une maison ~ jardin** a house with a garden ▪ **un homme ~ une blouse blanche** a man in a white coat *ou* with a white coat on ▪ **tous les résidents sont ~ moi** all the residents support me *ou* are behind me *ou* are on my side ▪ **~ dans le rôle principal/dans son premier rôle, X** starring/introducing X ▪ **un film ~ Gabin** a film featuring Gabin ‖ [envers] : **être patient/honnête ~ qqn** to be patient/honest with sb ▪ **être gentil ~ qqn** to be kind *ou* nice to sb ▪ **se comporter bien/mal ~ qqn** to behave well/badly towards sb ‖ [en ce qui concerne] : **~ lui c'est toujours la même chose** it's always the same with him ▪ **~ lui tout est toujours simple** everything is always simple according to him ➊ **et ~ ceci?** anything else? ▪ **il est compétent et ~ ça il ne prend pas cher** he's very competent and he's cheap as well ▪ **et ~ ça il n'est pas content!** [en plus] and on top of that *ou* and what's more, he's not happy! ; [malgré tout] with all that, he's still not happy!
2. [indiquant la simultanéité] : **se lever ~ le jour** to get up at the crack of dawn ▪ **se coucher ~ les poules** to go to bed early ▪ **le paysage change ~ les saisons** the countryside changes with the seasons
3. [indiquant une relation d'opposition] with ▪ **être en guerre ~ un pays** to be at war with a country
4. [indiquant une relation de cause] with ▪ **~ le temps qu'il fait, je préfère ne pas sortir** I prefer not to go out in this weather ▪ **ils ne pourront pas venir, ~ cette pluie** they won't be able to come with (all) this rain ▪ **~ ce nouveau scandale, le ministre va tomber** this new scandal will mean the end of the minister's career ▪ **ils ont compris ~ le temps** in time, they understood
5. [malgré] : **~ ses airs aimables, c'est une vraie peste** despite his pleasant manner, he's a real pest
6. [indiquant la manière] with ▪ **faire qqch ~ plaisir** to do sthg with pleasure, to take pleasure in doing sthg ▪ **regarder qqn ~ passion/mépris** to look at sb passionately/contemptuously
7. [indiquant le moyen, l'instrument] with ▪ **fonctionner ~ des piles** to run on batteries, to be battery-operated ▪ **c'est fait ~ de la laine** it's made of wool.
◇ *adv fam* **ôtez vos chaussures, vous ne pouvez pas entrer ~** take off your shoes, you can't come in with them (on) ▪ **je vous mets les os ~?** shall I put the bones in for you?
◆ **d'avec** *loc prép* : **distinguer qqch d'~ qqch** to distinguish sthg from sthg ▪ **divorcer d'~ qqn** to divorce sb.

Ave Maria [avemarja] = **Ave**.

aven [avɛn] *nm* sinkhole, swallow hole *UK*.

avenant¹ [avnɑ̃] *nm* **1.** [gén] amendment ▪ **~ à un contrat** amendment to a contract **2.** [dans les assurances] endorsement, additional clause ▪ **~ d'augmentation de la garantie** endorsement for an increase in cover.
◆ **à l'avenant** *loc adv* : **un exposé sans intérêt et des questions à l'~** a boring lecture with equally boring questions.
◆ **à l'avenant de** *loc prép* in accordance with ▪ **ils se sont conduits à l'~ de leurs principes** they behaved according to their principles.

avenant², e [avnɑ̃, ɑ̃t] *adj* pleasant ▪ **une hôtesse ~e accueille les visiteurs** a gracious hostess greets the visitors ▪ **son visage arborait un air faussement ~** his face wore a deceptively welcoming look.

avènement [avɛnmɑ̃] *nm* **1.** [d'un souverain] accession ▪ [du Messie] advent ***sout***, coming **2.** [d'une époque, d'une mode] advent ▪ **l'~ d'une ère nouvelle** the advent of a new era.

avenir [avnir] *nm* **1.** [période future] future ▪ **dans un ~ proche/lointain** in the near/distant future ▪ **ce que nous réserve l'~** what the future holds (for us) ▪ **l'~ dira si j'ai raison** time will tell if I'm right ▪ **espérer dans/croire en un ~ meilleur** to hope for/to believe in a better future ▪ **les moyens de transport de l'~** the transport systems of the future ‖ [générations futures] future generations **2.** [situation future] future ▪ **tu as devant toi un brillant ~** you have a promising future ahead (of you) ‖ [chances de succès] future, (future) prospects ▪ **une invention sans ~** an invention with no future ▪ **les nouveaux procédés techniques ont de l'~** the new technical processes are promising *ou* have a good future ▪ **découverte d'un matériau d'~** discovery of a promising new material ▪ **les professions d'~** up-and-coming professions.
◆ **à l'avenir** *loc adv* in future.

avent [avɑ̃] *nm* : **l'~** Advent.

Aventin [avɑ̃tɛ̃] *npr* : **le mont ~** the Aventine Hill.

aventure [avɑ̃tyr] *nf* **1.** [incident - gén] experience, incident ; [- extraordinaire] adventure ▪ **il m'est arrivé une ~ singulière ce matin** a strange thing happened to me this morning ▪ **le récit d'une ~ en mer** the tale of an adventure at sea ▪ [risque] adventure, venture ▪ **adopter un tel projet c'est se lancer dans l'~** accepting such a project is a bit risky ▪ **se lancer dans une grande ~** to set off on a big adventure ➊ **dire la bonne ~ à qqn** to tell sb's fortune **2.** [liaison] (love) affair.
◆ **à l'aventure** *loc adv* at random, haphazardly ▪ **marcher/rouler à l'~** to walk/to drive aimlessly ▪ **partir à l'~** to go off in search of adventure.
◆ **d'aventure** *loc adj* [roman, film] adventure *(modif)*.

◆ **d'aventure, par aventure** *loc adv* by chance ■ **si d'~ tu le vois, transmets-lui mon message** if by any chance you see him, give him my message.

aventuré, e [avɑ̃tyre] *adj* [hypothèse, théorie] risky ■ [démarche] chancy, risky, venturesome *litt.*

aventurer [3] [avɑ̃tyre] *vt* **1.** [suggérer - hypothèse, analyse] to venture **2.** [risquer - fortune, réputation, bonheur] to risk, to chance.

◆ **s'aventurer** *vpi* [aller] to venture ■ **il n'avait pas peur de s'~ le soir dans des ruelles obscures** he wasn't afraid of venturing out into dark alleys at night.

◆ **s'aventurer à** *vp+prép* : **je ne m'aventure plus à faire des pronostics** I no longer venture *ou* dare to make any forecasts ■ **téléphone-lui si tu veux, moi je ne m'y aventurerais pas** ring her up if you like, I wouldn't chance it myself.

aventureux, euse [avɑ̃tyrø, øz] *adj* **1.** [hardi - héros] adventurous **2.** [dangereux - projet] risky, chancy.

aventurier [avɑ̃tyrje] *nm* **1.** [explorateur] adventurer ■ [aimant le risque] risk-taker **2.** *péj* [escroc] rogue.

aventurière [avɑ̃tyrjɛr] *nf péj* adventuress.

aventurine [avɑ̃tyrin] *nf* MINÉR aventurin, aventurine.

avenu, e [avny] *adj* : **nul et non ~** null and void.

avenue [avny] *nf* avenue ■ **sur l'~ Foch** on the Avenue Foch.

avéré, e [avere] *adj* [fait, information] known, established ■ **c'est un fait ~ que...** it is a known fact that...

avérer [18] [avere] *vt sout* [affirmer] : **~ un fait** to vouch for the accuracy of a fact.

◆ **s'avérer** *vpi* **1.** *sout* [être prouvé] to be proved (correct) **2.** *(suivi d'un adj ou d'une loc adj)* [se révéler] to prove ■ **la solution s'est avérée inefficace** the solution turned out *ou* proved (to be) inefficient **3.** *(tournure impersonnelle)* **il s'avère difficile d'améliorer les résultats** it's proving difficult to improve on the results ■ **il s'avère que mon cas n'est pas prévu par le règlement** it turns out *ou* it so happens that my situation isn't covered by the regulations.

averse [avɛrs] *nf* shower ■ **sous l'~** in the rain ■ **laisser passer l'~** *fig* to wait until the storm blows over ■ **une ~ d'injures s'abattit sur moi** I was assailed by a string *ou* stream of insults.

aversion [avɛrsjɔ̃] *nf* aversion, loathing ■ **il les a pris en ~** he took a violent dislike to them.

averti, e [avɛrti] *adj* [informé] informed, mature ■ [connaisseur] well-informed ■ **le consommateur est de plus en plus ~** consumers are better and better informed ■ **pour lecteurs ~s seulement** for adult readers only.

avertir [32] [avɛrtir] *vt* **1.** [informer] to inform, to tell ■ **avertis-moi dès que tu (le) sais** tell me *ou* let me know as soon as you know ■ **l'avez-vous averti de votre départ?** have you informed him that *ou* did you tell him that you are leaving? ■ **il faut l'~ que le spectacle est annulé** he must be informed *ou* told that the show's off **2.** [mettre en garde] to warn ■ **nous n'avons pas été avertis du danger** we were not warned about the danger ■ **je t'avertis que la prochaine fois la punition sera sévère** I'm warning you that the next time the punishment will be severe.

avertissement [avɛrtismɑ̃] *nm* **1.** [signe] warning, warning sign ■ **il est parti sans le moindre ~** he left without any warning **2.** [appel à l'attention] notice, warning ■ **il n'a pas tenu compte de mon ~** he didn't take any notice of my warning **3.** [blâme] warning, reprimand ■ ADMIN [lettre] admonitory letter *sout* ■ **donner un ~ à qqn** to give sb a warning, to warn sb ■ **premier et dernier ~!** I'm telling you now and I won't tell you again! **4.** [en début de livre] : **~ (au lecteur)** foreword **5.** RAIL warning signal.

avertisseur, euse [avɛrtisœr, øz] *adj* warning.

◆ **avertisseur** *nm* alarm, warning signal ■ **~ sonore** [gén] alarm ; AUTO horn ■ **~ visuel** indicator ■ **~ d'incendie** fire alarm.

aveu, x [avø] *nm* **1.** [confession] : **faire un ~** to acknowledge *ou* to confess *ou* to admit something ■ **je vais vous faire un ~, j'ai peur en voiture** I must confess that I'm scared in cars ■ **obtenir les ~x d'un criminel** to make a criminal confess ■ **recueillir les ~x d'un criminel** to take down a criminal's confession ■ **faire des ~x complets** [à la police] to make a full confession ; *fig & hum* to confess all ■ **passer aux ~x** *pr & fig* to confess ■ **faire l'~ de qqch** to own up to sthg **2.** *litt* [foi] : **sans ~** dishonourable **3.** *sout* [autorisation] permission, consent.

◆ **de l'aveu de** *loc prép* according to ■ **la tour ne tiendra pas, de l'~ même de l'architecte** the tower will collapse, even the architect says so ■ **de son propre ~** by his own reckoning.

aveuglant, e [avœglɑ̃, ɑ̃t] *adj* [éclat, lueur] blinding, dazzling ■ [évidence, preuve] overwhelming ■ [vérité] self-evident, glaring ■ **soudain, une vérité ~e lui est apparue** the truth came to her in a blinding flash.

aveugle [avœgl] ◇ *adj* **1.** [privé de la vue] blind, sightless ■ **un enfant ~ de naissance** a child born blind *ou* blind from birth ■ **devenir ~** to go blind ■ **l'accident qui l'a rendu ~** the accident which blinded him *ou* deprived him of his sight ■ **je ne suis pas ~, je vois bien tes manigances** I'm not blind, I can see what you're up to ■ **la passion la rend ~** she's blinded by passion **2.** [extrême - fureur, passion] blind, reckless **3.** [absolu - attachement, foi, soumission] blind, unquestioning **4.** CONSTR [mur, fenêtre] blind.

◇ *nmf* blind man (*f* woman) ■ **les ~s** the blind *ou* sightless.

◆ **en aveugle** *loc adv* : **se lancer en ~ dans une entreprise** to take a leap in the dark.

aveuglement [avœgləmɑ̃] *nm* blindness, blinkered state ■ **dans son ~ il est capable de tout** in his blindness, he's capable of anything.

aveuglément [avœglemɑ̃] *adv* [inconsidérément] blindly ■ **elle lui faisait ~ confiance** she trusted him utterly.

aveugle-né, e [avœgləne] (*mpl* **aveugles-nés**, *fpl* **aveugles-nées**) *nm, f person blind from birth* ■ **c'est un ~** he was born blind, he's been blind from birth.

aveugler [5] [avœgle] *vt* [priver de la vue] to blind ■ **l'accident qui l'a aveuglée** the accident which blinded her *ou* deprived her of her sight ■ [éblouir] to blind ■ **la haine l'aveugle** *fig* she's blinded by hatred.

◆ **s'aveugler sur** *vp+prép* to close one's eyes to ■ **ne vous aveuglez pas sur vos chances de réussite** don't overestimate your chances of success.

aveuglette [avœglɛt] ◆ **à l'aveuglette** *loc adv* **1.** [sans voir - conduire] blindly ■ **il m'a fallu marcher à l'~ le long d'un tunnel** I had to grope my way through a tunnel **2.** *fig* **je ne veux pas agir à l'~** I don't want to act without first weighing the consequences ■ **son projet n'a pas été entrepris à l'~** he did his homework before undertaking his project.

aveulir [32] [avølir] *vt litt* to weaken, to enervate *litt.*

aviateur, trice [avjatœr, tris] *nm, f* pilot, aviator *vieilli.*

aviation [avjasjɔ̃] *nf* **1.** TRANSP aviation ■ **~ civile/marchande** civil/commercial aviation **2.** [activité] flying ■ **elle était destinée à l'~** she was meant to fly **3.** MIL [armée de l'air] air force ■ [avions] aircraft, air force.

avicole [avikɔl] *adj* **1.** [ferme, producteur] poultry *(modif)*, bird *(modif)*, fowl *(modif)* **2.** [parasite] avicolous *spéc.*

aviculteur, trice [avikyltœr, tris] *nm, f* [éleveur - d'oiseaux] bird breeder *ou* farmer, aviculturist *spéc* ; [- de volailles] poultry breeder *ou* farmer.

aviculture [avikyltyr] *nf* [élevage - de volailles] poultry farming *ou* breeding ; [- d'oiseaux] aviculture *spéc*, bird breeding.

avide [avid] *adj* **1.** [cupide] greedy, grasping **2.** [enthousiaste] eager, avid ■ **écouter d'une oreille ~** to listen eagerly *ou* avidly ■ **~ de louanges** hungry for praise ■ **~ de nouveauté** eager *ou* avid for novelty ■ **~ de savoir** eager to learn, thirsty for knowledge ■ **~ de connaître le monde** eager *ou* anxious *ou* impatient to discover the world.

avidement [avidmɑ̃] *adv* **1.** [gloutonnement] greedily, ravenously ■ **boire ~** to drink thirstily ■ **manger ~** to eat hungrily **2.** [avec enthousiasme] eagerly, avidly, keenly **3.** [par cupidité] greedily, covetously.

avidité [avidite] *nf* **1.** [voracité] voracity, greed, gluttony *péj* **2.** [enthousiasme] eagerness, impatience **3.** [cupidité] greed, cupidity, covetousness.

Avignon [aviɲɔ̃] *npr* Avignon ■ **à** *ou* **en ~** in Avignon ■ **le festival d'~** the Avignon festival.

LE FESTIVAL D'AVIGNON

Founded by Jean Vilar in 1947 and held every summer in and around Avignon in the South of France, this arts festival is a showcase for new theatre and dance performances: ***sa nouvelle pièce sera donnée d'abord à/en Avignon.***

avilir [32] [avilir] *vt* **1.** [personne] to debase, to shame ■ **vos mensonges vous avilissent** your lies are unworthy of you **2.** *sout* [monnaie] to debase ■ [marchandise] to cause to depreciate ■ **l'inflation a avili l'euro** inflation has devalued the euro.
◆ **s'avilir** ◇ *vp (emploi réfléchi)* to demean *ou* to debase *ou* to disgrace o.s. ■ **il s'avilit dans l'alcoolisme** he's sunk into alcoholism.
◇ *vpi* [monnaie, marchandise] to depreciate.

avilissant, e [avilisɑ̃, ɑ̃t] *adj* degrading, demeaning ■ **mon métier n'a rien d'~** there is nothing shameful about my job.

avilissement [avilismɑ̃] *nm* **1.** [d'une personne] degradation, debasement ■ **le roman décrit l'~ d'un homme par le jeu** the novel describes a man's downfall through gambling **2.** *sout* [d'une monnaie] depreciation, devaluation.

aviné, e [avine] *adj* [qui a trop bu] drunken, intoxicated ■ [qui sent le vin - souffle] wine-laden ■ [altéré par la boisson - voix] drunken.

aviner [3] [avine] *vt* [fût, futaille] to season.

avion [avjɔ̃] *nm* **1.** [véhicule] plane, aeroplane *esp UK*, airplane *US* ■ **~ militaire/de chasse** military/fighter plane ■ **~ à hélices** propeller plane ■ **~ hôpital** hospital plane ■ **~ de ligne** airliner ■ **~ à réaction** jet (plane) **2.** [mode de transport] : **l'~** flying ■ **irez-vous en ~ ou en train?** are you flying or going by train? ■ **je déteste (prendre) l'~** I hate flying ■ **'par ~'** 'air mail' ➊ **courrier par ~** air mail.

avion-cargo [avjɔ̃kargo] (*pl* **avions-cargos**) *nm* air freighter.

avion-citerne [avjɔ̃sitɛrn] (*pl* **avions-citernes**) *nm* (air) tanker, supply plane.

avion-école [avjɔ̃ekɔl] (*pl* **avions-écoles**) *nm* training plane *ou* aircraft.

avionnerie [avjɔnri] *nf Québec* aircraft factory.

aviron [avirɔ̃] *nm* **1.** [rame] oar ■ **tirer sur les ~s** to row ■ **coup d'~** stroke **2.** [activité] rowing.

avis [avi] *nm* **1.** [point de vue] opinion, viewpoint ■ **avoir son** *ou* **un ~ sur qqch** to have views on sthg ■ **je n'ai pas d'~ sur la question** I have nothing to say *ou* no opinion on the matter ■ **j'aimerais avoir votre ~** I'd like to hear your views *ou* to know what you think (about it) ■ **demande** *ou* **prends l'~ d'un second médecin** ask the opinion of another doctor ■ **toi, je ne te demande pas ton ~!** I didn't ask for your opinion! ■ **donner son ~** to give *ou* to contribute one's opinion ■ **si vous voulez (que je vous donne) mon ~** if you ask me *ou* want my opinion ■ **donner** *ou* **émettre un ~ favorable** [à une demande] to give the go-ahead ; [à une proposition] to give a positive response, to come out in favour ■ **après ~ favorable, vous procéderez à l'expulsion** having obtained permission (from the authorities), you will start the eviction procedure ■ **à mon ~, c'est un mensonge** in my opinion, it's a lie, I think it's a lie ■ **à mon humble ~** *hum* in my humble opinion ■ **elle est d'~ qu'il est trop tard** she's of the opinion that it's too late ■ **je ne suis pas d'~ qu'on l'envoie en pension** I don't agree with his being sent away to boarding school ■ **de l'~ de** [selon] according to ■ **je suis de votre ~** I agree with you ■ **du même ~ (que)... : lui et moi ne sommes jamais du même ~** he and I don't see eye to eye *ou* never agree on anything ■ **je suis du même ~ que toi** I agree with you ■ **m'est ~ que...** *hum* it seems to me that..., methinks... ■ **sur l'~ de** on the advice *ou* at the suggestion of ■ **c'est sur leur ~ que j'ai fait refaire la toiture** I had the roof redone on their advice **2.** [information] announcement ■ [sommation - légale] notice ; [- fiscale] notice, demand ■ **jusqu'à nouvel ~** until further notice ■ **nous irons sauf ~ contraire** [de votre part] unless we hear otherwise *ou* to the contrary, we'll go ; [de notre part] unless you hear otherwise *ou* to the contrary, we'll go ➊ **~ au lecteur** foreword ■ **'~ au public'** 'public notice' ■ **~ de décès** death notice ■ **~ de domiciliation** notice of payment by banker's order ■ **~ de rappel** reminder ■ **~ de réception** acknowledgement of receipt ■ **~ de recherche** [d'un criminel] wanted (person) poster ; [d'un disparu] missing person poster ■ **il reste encore quelques parts de gâteau, ~ aux amateurs** there's still some cake left if anyone's interested.

avisé, e [avize] *adj* shrewd, prudent ■ **bien ~** well-advised ■ **mal ~** ill-advised.

aviser [3] [avize] ◇ *vt* **1.** [informer] to inform, to notify ■ **~ qqn de qqch** to inform *ou* to notify sb of sthg **2.** [voir] to notice, to glimpse, to catch sight of ■ **il avisa dans la foule un de ses amis** he caught sight of one of his friends in the crowd.
◇ *vi* to decide, to see (what one can do) ■ **maintenant nous allons devoir ~** we'll have to see what we can do now ■ **s'il n'est pas là dans une heure, j'aviserai** I'll have another think if he isn't here in an hour ■ **avisons au plus pressé** let's attend *ou* see to the most urgent matters.
◆ **s'aviser de** *vp+prép* **1.** [remarquer] to become aware of ■ **je me suis avisé de sa présence quand elle a ri** I suddenly noticed her presence when she laughed ■ **il s'est avisé trop tard (de ce) qu'il n'avait pas sa clé** he realized too late that he didn't have his key **2.** [oser] to dare to ■ **ne t'avise pas de l'interrompre quand elle parle** don't think of interrupting her while she's speaking ■ **et ne t'avise pas de recommencer!** and don't you dare do that again!

avitaillement [avitajmɑ̃] *nm* **1.** NAUT victualling, refuelling **2.** AÉRON refuelling *UK*, refueling *US*.

avitailleur [avitajœr] *nm* **1.** NAUT refuelling tanker *UK*, refueling tanker *US* **2.** AÉRON air tanker.

avitaminose [avitaminoz] *nf* vitamin deficiency, avitaminosis *spéc* ■ **~ C** vitamin C deficiency.

aviver [3] [avive] *vt* **1.** [intensifier - flammes] to fan, to stir up *(sép)* ; [- feu] to revive, to rekindle ; [- couleur] to brighten, to revive ; [- sentiment] to stir up ; [- désir] to excite, to arouse ; [- blessure] to irritate ; [- querelle] to stir up, to exacerbate ; [- crainte] to heighten **2.** MENUIS to square off **3.** MÉD to open up.

av. J.-C. (*abr écrite de* **avant Jésus-Christ**) BC.

avocaillon [avɔkajɔ̃] *nm fam péj* pettifogger, pettifogging lawyer.

avocasserie [avɔkasri] *nf fam vieilli* chicanery, pettifoggery.

avocat[1] [avɔka] *nm* BOT avocado (pear).

avocat[2]**, e** [avɔka, at] *nm, f* **1.** DR lawyer, barrister *UK*, attorney-at-law *US* ■ **mon ~** my counsel ■ **mes ~s** my counsel ■ **je lui mettrai mes ~s sur le dos!** *fam* I'll take him to court! ➊ **~ d'affaires** business lawyer ■ **~ consultant** ≃ counsel in chamber *UK*, ≃ consulting barrister *UK*, ≃ attorney *US* ■ **~ de la défense** counsel for the defence, ≃ defending counsel *UK*, ≃ defense counsel *US* ■ **~ général** ≃ counsel for the prosecution *UK*, ≃ prosecuting attorney *US* ■ **~ plaidant** court lawyer *UK*, trial attorney *US* **2.** [porte-parole] advocate, champion ■ **se faire l'~ d'une mauvaise cause** to advocate *ou* to champion a lost cause ■ **je serai votre ~ auprès de lui** I'll plead with him on your behalf ➊ **~ du diable** devil's advocate ■ **se faire l'~ du diable** to be devil's advocate.

avocatier [avɔkatje] *nm* avocado (tree).

avoine [avwan] *nf* [plante] oat ■ [grains] oats.

avoir[1] [avwar] *nm* **1.** COMM credit note ■ [en comptabilité] credit side ■ **la fleuriste m'a fait un ~** the florist gave me a credit note ■ **j'ai un ~ de 150 euros à la boucherie** I've got 150 euros credit at the butcher's ➊ **~ fiscal** FIN tax credit **2.** ÉCON & FIN : **~s** assets, holdings ■ **~s numéraires** *ou* **en caisse** cash holdings **3.** *litt* [possessions] assets, worldly goods ■ **vivre d'un petit ~ personnel** to live off a small personal income.

avoir² [1] [avwar] <> *v aux*

A.

1. [avec des verbes transitifs] : **as-tu lu sa lettre?** did you read *ou* have you read his letter? ■ **les deux buts qu'il avait marqués** the two goals he had scored ■ **j'aurais voulu vous aider** I'd have liked to help you ■ **non content de les ~ humiliés, il les a jetés dehors** not content with humiliating them, he threw them out
2. [avec des verbes intransitifs] : **j'ai maigri** I've lost weight ■ **as-tu bien dormi?** did you sleep well? ■ **tu as dû rêver** you must have been dreaming
3. [avec le verbe 'être'] : **j'ai été surpris** I was surprised ■ **il aurait été enchanté** he would've *ou* would have been delighted

B.

1. [exprime la possibilité] : **~ à : je n'ai rien à boire** I haven't got anything *ou* I have nothing *ou* I've got nothing to drink ■ **n'~ qu'à : ils n'ont qu'à écrire au directeur** [conseil] all they have to do *ou* all they've got to do is write to the manager ; [menace] just let them (try and) write to the manager ■ **s'il vous manque quelque chose, vous n'avez qu'à me le faire savoir** if you're missing anything, just let me know ■ **t'as qu'à leur dire!** *fam* why don't you (just) tell them!
2. [exprime l'obligation] : **~ à** to have to ■ **je n'ai pas à me justifier auprès de vous** I don't have to justify myself to you ■ **et voilà, je n'ai plus qu'à recommencer!** so now I've got to start all over again!
3. [exprime le besoin] : **~ à** to have to ■ **il a à te parler** he's got something to *ou* there's something he wants to tell you ■ **tu n'as pas à t'inquiéter** you shouldn't worry, you have nothing to worry about
4. *loc* **n'~ que faire de : je n'ai que faire de tes états d'âme** I couldn't care less about your moods.

<> *vt*

A.

1. [être propriétaire de - action, bien, domaine *etc*] to have, to own, to possess ; [- chien, hôtel, voiture] to have, to own ■ **~ de l'argent** to have money ■ **tu n'aurais pas un stylo en plus?** have you got *ou* do you happen to have a spare pen? ■ **je n'ai plus de sucre** I've run out of sugar ■ COMM to have ■ **nous avons plus grand si vous préférez** we have it in a larger size if you prefer
2. [ami, collègue, famille *etc*] to have ■ **il a encore sa grand-mère** his grandmother's still alive ■ **je n'ai plus ma mère** my mother's dead ■ **elle a trois enfants** she has three children ■ **~ un/une/des... qui : elle a un mari qui fait la cuisine** she's got the sort *ou* kind of husband who does the cooking ■ **~ son/sa/ses... qui** *fam* **: j'ai la chaîne de mon vélo qui est cassée** the chain on my bike is broken
3. [détenir - permis de conduire, titre] to have, to hold ; [- droits, privilège] to have, to enjoy ; [- emploi, expérience, devoirs, obligations] to have ; [- documents, preuves] to have, to possess ■ **quand nous aurons le pouvoir** when we're in power ■ **quelle heure avez-vous?** what time do you make it? ■ SPORT to have ■ **~ le ballon** to be in possession of *ou* to have the ball
4. [obtenir - amende, article] to get ; [- information, rabais, récompense] to get, to obtain ■ **je pourrais vous ~ des places gratuites** I could get you free tickets ■ [au téléphone] to get through to ■ **j'ai essayé de t'~ toute la journée** I tried to get through to you *ou* to contact you all day ■ **je l'ai eu au téléphone** I got him on the phone
5. [jouir de - beau temps, bonne santé, liberté, bonne réputation] to have, to enjoy ; [- choix, temps, mauvaise réputation] to have ■ **~ la confiance de qqn** to be trusted by sb ■ **~ l'estime de qqn** to be held in high regard by sb ■ **vous avez toute ma sympathie** you have all my sympathy ■ **j'ai une heure pour me décider** I have an hour (in which) to make up my mind ■ **il a tout pour lui et il n'est pas heureux!** he's got everything you could wish for and he's still not happy!
6. [recevoir chez soi] : **~ de la famille/des amis à dîner** to have relatives/friends over for dinner ■ **j'aurai ma belle-famille au mois d'août** my in-laws will be staying with me in August
7. RADIO & TV [chaîne, station] to receive, to get ■ **bientôt, nous aurons les chaînes européennes** soon, we'll be able to get the European channels
8. [attraper - otage, prisonnier] to have ■ **les flics ne l'auront jamais** *fam* the cops'll never catch him
9. [atteindre - cible] to get, to hit
10. [monter à bord de - avion, bus, train] to catch

B.

1. [présenter - tel aspect] to have (got) ■ **elle a un joli sourire** she's got *ou* she has a nice smile ■ **je cherche un acteur qui ait un grand nez** I'm looking for an actor with a big nose ■ **elle a une jolie couleur de cheveux** her hair's a nice colour ■ **elle a beaucoup de sa mère** she really takes after her mother ■ **~ tout de : il a tout de l'aristocrate** he's the aristocratic type ■ **la méthode a l'avantage d'être bon marché** this method has the advantage of being cheap ■ **ton père a le défaut de ne pas écouter ce qu'on lui dit** your father's weakness is not listening to what people tell him ■ [avec pour complément une partie du corps] to have ■ **~ l'estomac vide** to have an empty stomach ■ **j'ai le bras ankylosé** my arm's stiff ■ **~ le/la/les... qui : il a les yeux qui se ferment** he can't keep his eyes open ◗ **en ~**△ to have a lot of balls△
2. [porter sur soi - accessoire, vêtement, parfum] to have on *(sép)*, to wear ■ **tu vois la dame qui a le foulard?** do you see the lady with the scarf? ■ **faites attention, il a une arme** careful, he's got a weapon *ou* he's armed
3. [faire preuve de] : **~ de l'audace** to be bold ■ **~ du culot** *fam* to be cheeky, to have a nerve ■ **il a eu le culot de me le dire** *fam* he had the cheek *ou* the nerve to tell me ■ **~ du talent** to have talent, to be talented ■ **ayez la gentillesse de...** would you *ou* please be kind enough to... ■ **il a eu la cruauté de lui dire** he was cruel enough to tell him
4. [exprime la mesure] to be ■ **le voilier a 4 m de large** *ou* **largeur** the yacht is 4 m wide ■ **en ~ pour : j'en ai pour 500 euros** it's costing me 500 euros ■ **tu en as pour 12 jours/deux heures** it'll take you 12 days/two hours
5. [exprime l'âge] to be ■ **quel âge as-tu?** how old are you? ■ **j'ai 35 ans** I'm 35 (years old) ■ **nous avons le même âge** we're the same age ■ **il a deux ans de plus que moi** he's two years older than me ■ **il vient d'~ 74 ans** he's just turned 74

C.

1. [subir - symptôme] to have, to show, to display ; [- maladie, hoquet, mal de tête *etc*] to have ; [- accident, souci, ennuis] to have ; [- difficultés] to have, to experience ; [- opération] to undergo, to have ; [- crise] to have, to go through *(insép)* ■ **~ de la fièvre** to have *ou* to be running a temperature ■ **~ un cancer** to have cancer ■ **je ne sais pas ce que j'ai aujourd'hui** I don't know what's the matter *ou* what's wrong with me today ■ **sa sœur n'a rien eu** his sister escaped unscathed ■ **le car n'a rien eu du tout, mais la moto est fichue** *fam* there wasn't a scratch on the bus but the motorbike's a write-off ■ **qu'est-ce qu'elle a encore, cette voiture?** *fam* NOW what's wrong with this car? ■ **il a des souris chez lui** he's got mice ■ **un enfant/chaton qui a des vers** a child/kitten with worms
2. [émettre, produire - mouvement] to make ; [- ricanement, regard, soupir] to give ■ **~ un sursaut** to (give a) start ■ **elle eut cette phrase devenue célèbre** she said *ou* uttered those now famous words ■ **il eut une moue de dédain** he pouted disdainfully
3. [ressentir] : **~ faim** to be *ou* to feel hungry ■ **~ peur** to be *ou* to feel afraid ■ **~ des remords** to feel remorse ■ **~ du chagrin** to feel *ou* to be sad ■ **~ un pressentiment** to have a premonition ■ **~ de l'amitié pour qqn** to regard *ou* to consider sb as a friend ■ **je n'ai que mépris pour lui** I feel only contempt for him ■ **~ du respect pour qqn** to have respect for *ou* to respect sb ◗ **en ~ après** *ou* **contre qqn** *fam* to be angry with sb ■ **ce chien/cette guêpe en a après toi!** this dog/wasp has got it in for you! ■ **en ~ après** *ou* **contre qqch** to be angry about sthg
4. [élaborer par l'esprit - avis, idée, suggestion] to have ■ **j'ai mes raisons** I have my reasons ■ **elle a toujours réponse à tout** she's got an answer for everything

D.

1. [battre, surpasser] to get, to beat ■ **il va se faire ~ dans la dernière ligne droite** he's going to get beaten in the final straight
2. [escroquer] to have, to do, to con ■ **1 500 euros pour ce buffet? tu t'es fait ~!** 1,500 euros for that dresser? you were conned *ou* had *ou* done!
3. [duper] to take in *(sép)*, to take for a ride, to have ■ **tu t'es fait ~!** you've been had *ou* taken in *ou* taken for a ride! ■ **tu essaies de m'~!** you're having *ou* putting me on! ■ **n'essaie pas de m'~** don't try it on with me

E.

[devoir participer à - débat, élection, réunion] to have, to hold ; [- rendez-vous] to have ■ **j'ai (un) cours de chimie ce matin** I've got a chemistry lesson this morning.

◆ **il y a** *v impers* **1.** [dans une description, une énumération - suivi d'un singulier] there is ; [- suivi d'un pluriel] there are ■ **il n'y a pas de lit** there is no bed ■ **il y a du soleil** the sun is shining ■ **qu'est-ce qu'il y a dans la malle?** what's in the trunk? ■ **il n'y a qu'ici qu'on en trouve** this is the only place (where) you can find it/them ■ **il y a juste de quoi faire une jupe** there is just enough to make a skirt ■ **avoue qu'il y a de quoi être énervé!** you must admit it's pretty irritating! ⊙ **merci – il n'y a pas de quoi!** thank you – don't mention it *ou* you're welcome! ■ **il n'y a rien à faire, la voiture ne démarre pas** it's no good, the car won't start ■ **il n'y a pas à dire, il sait ce qu'il veut** there's no denying he knows what he wants ■ **il n'y a que lui pour dire une chose pareille!** trust him to say something like that! ■ **qu'est-ce qu'il y a? – il y a que j'en ai marre!** *fam* what's the matter? – I'm fed up, that's what! ■ **il y a voiture et voiture** there are cars and cars ■ **il n'y en a que pour lui!** *fam* he's the one who gets all the attention! ■ **il y en a** *ou* **il y a des gens, je vous jure!** *fam* some people, honestly *ou* really! **2.** [exprimant la possibilité, l'obligation *etc*] : **il n'y a qu'à lui dire** you/we *etc* just have to tell him ■ **il n'y a qu'à commander pour être servi** you only have to order to get served **3.** [indiquant la durée] : **il y a 20 ans de ça** 20 years ago ■ **il y a une heure que j'attends** I've been waiting for an hour **4.** [indiquant la distance] : **il y a bien 3 km d'ici au village** it's at least 3 km to the village **5.** *(à l'infinitif)* **il va y ~ de la pluie** there's going to be some rain ■ **il doit y ~ une raison** there must be a *ou* some reason.

avoisinant, e [avwazinɑ̃, ɑ̃t] *adj* neighbouring, nearby *(adj)* ■ **les quartiers ~s ont été évacués** the surrounding streets were evacuated.

avoisiner [3] [avwazine] *vt* **1.** [dans l'espace] to be near *ou* close to, to border on *(insép)* ■ **son attitude avoisine l'insolence** *fig* his attitude verges on insolence **2.** [en valeur] to be close on, to come close to.

Avoriaz [avɔrjaz] *npr* : **le festival d'~** *former festival of science-fiction and horror films held annually at Avoriaz in the French Alps.*

avorté, e [avɔrte] *adj* [réforme, tentative] failed, abortive ■ **une initiative ~e** an abortive move.

avortement [avɔrtəmɑ̃] *nm* MÉD & ZOOL abortion ■ **être contre l'~** to be against abortion ■ **l'~ d'une tentative** *fig* the failure of an attempt.

avorter [3] [avɔrte] ◇ *vi* **1.** MÉD to abort, to have an abortion ■ ZOOL to abort ■ **faire ~ qqn** to carry out an abortion on sb **2.** [plan] to fall through, to miscarry ■ [réforme] to fall through ■ [révolution] to fail, to come to nothing.
◇ *vt* to abort, to carry out an abortion on ■ **se faire ~** to have an abortion.

avorteur, euse [avɔrtœr, øz] *nm, f* abortionist.

avorton [avɔrtɔ̃] *nm* [chétif] runt ■ [monstrueux] freak, monster ■ **espèce de petit ~!** you little runt!

avouable [avwabl] *adj* worthy, respectable ■ **un motif ~** a worthy motive ■ **des mobiles peu ~s** disreputable motives.

avoué [avwe] *nm* ≃ solicitor UK, ≃ attorney US.

avouer [6] [avwe] *vt* **1.** [erreur, forfait] to admit, to confess (to), to own up to *(insép)* ■ **elle a avoué voyager sans billet/tricher aux cartes** she owned up to travelling without a ticket/to cheating at cards ■ *(en usage absolu)* **il a avoué** [à la police] he owned up, he made a full confession **2.** [doute, sentiment] to admit *ou* to confess to ■ **elle refuse d'~ ses angoisses/qu'elle a des ennuis** she refuses to acknowledge her anxiety/admit that she has problems ■ **je t'avoue que j'en ai assez** I must admit that I've had all I can take ■ **il lui a fallu du courage, j'avoue, mais...** what he did required courage, I grant you, but...
◆ **s'avouer** *vpi* : **elle ne s'avoue pas encore battue** she won't admit defeat yet ■ **je m'avoue complètement découragé** I confess *ou* admit to feeling utterly discouraged.

avril [avril] *nm* april ■ **en ~, ne te découvre pas d'un fil** *prov* ≃ ne'er cast a clout till May is out *prov, voir aussi* **mars**.

avunculaire [avɔ̃kylɛr] *adj* avuncular.

axe [aks] *nm* **1.** GÉOM axis ■ **~ des abscisses/des ordonnées** x-/y-axis ■ **~ optique** principal axis ■ **~ de symétrie** axis of symmetry **2.** [direction] direction, line ■ **deux grands ~s de développement** two major trends of development ■ **développer de nouveaux ~s de recherche** to open up new areas of research ■ **sa politique s'articule autour de deux ~s principaux** her policy revolves around two main themes *ou* issues ■ **il est dans l'~ du parti** [membre] he's in the mainstream of the party **3.** [voie] : **ils vont ouvrir un nouvel ~ Paris-Bordeaux** they're going to open up a new road link between Paris and Bordeaux ■ **l'~ Lyon-Genève** RAIL the Lyons-Geneva line ⊙ **(grand) ~** major road UK, main highway US ■ **tous les (grands) ~s routiers sont bloqués par la neige** all major roads are snowed up ■ **~ rouge** *section of the Paris road system where parking is prohibited to avoid congestion* **4.** MÉCAN axle **5.** HIST : **l'Axe** the Axis.
◆ **dans l'axe de** *loc prép* [dans le prolongement de] in line with ■ **la perspective s'ouvre dans l'~ du palais** the view opens out from the palace.

axer [3] [akse] *vt* : **il est très axé sur le spiritisme** he is very keen on spiritualism ■ **~ une campagne publicitaire sur les enfants** to build an advertising campaign around children ■ **le premier trimestre sera axé sur Proust** the first term will be devoted to Proust ■ **une modernisation axée sur l'importation des meilleures techniques étrangères** modernization based on importing the best foreign techniques.

axial, e, aux [aksjal, o] *adj* **1.** [d'un axe] axial **2.** [central] central ■ **éclairage ~** central overhead lighting *(in a street).*

axiologie [aksjɔlɔʒi] *nf* axiology.

axiome [aksjom] *nm* axiom.

axis [aksis] *nm* ANAT & ZOOL axis.

ay [aj] *nm* Champagne from Ay.

ayant *p prés* ▷ **avoir**.

ayant cause [ɛjɑ̃koz] (*pl* **ayants cause**) *nm* beneficiary, legal successor.

ayant droit [ɛjɑ̃drwa] (*pl* **ayants droit**) *nm* [gén] beneficiary ■ [à une propriété] rightful owner ■ [à un droit] eligible party.

ayatollah [ajatɔla] *nm* ayatollah.

ayons *etc v* ▷ **avoir**.

azalée [azale] *nf* azalea.

Azerbaïdjan [azɛrbajdʒɑ̃] *npr m* : **(l')~** Azerbaijan.

azeri [azeri] *adj* Azeri.
◆ **Azeri** *nmf* Azeri.

azimut [azimyt] *nm* azimuth ■ **partir dans tous les ~s** *fam* to be all over the place.
◆ **tous azimuts** *fam* ◇ *loc adj* all out, full scale.
◇ *loc adv* all over (the place) ■ **prospecter tous ~s** to canvass all over ■ **la jeune société se développe tous ~s** the new firm is really taking off.

azote [azɔt] *nm* nitrogen.

azoté, e [azɔte] *adj* nitrogenous, azotic.

AZT (*abr de* **azothymidine**) *nm* AZT.

aztèque [astɛk] *adj* Aztec.
◆ **Aztèque** *nmf* Aztec.

azur [azyr] ◇ *nm* **1.** [couleur] azure *litt*, sky-blue ■ **la Côte d'Azur** the French Riviera, the Côte d'Azur **2.** *litt* [ciel] skies.
◇ *adj inv* azure, sky-blue.

azuré, e [azyre] *adj litt* azure *litt*, sky-blue.

azuréen, enne [azyreɛ̃, ɛn] *adj* **1.** *litt* [bleu] azure *litt*, sky-blue **2.** [de la Côte d'Azur] of the Côte d'Azur *ou* French Riviera.

azurer [3] [azyre] *vt* to blue, to tinge with blue.

azyme [azim] *adj* ▷ **pain**.

B

b, B [be] *nm* b, B, *voir aussi* **g**.

B (*abr écrite de* **bien**) *good grade (as assessment of schoolwork),* ≃ B.

BA (*abr de* **bonne action**) *nf fam* *good deed* ▪ **faire une ~** to do a good deed.

baba [baba] ◇ *adj fam* : **être** *ou* **rester ~** to be flabbergasted.
◇ *nm* **1.** CULIN : **~ (au rhum)** (rum) baba **2.** *fam loc* **l'avoir dans le ~** to be let down ▪ **après ils partiront en congé et c'est toi qui l'auras dans le ~!** then they'll go off on holiday and you'll be left holding the baby!
◇ *nmf* = **baba cool**.

b.a.-ba [beaba] *nm* ABCs, rudiments ▪ **apprendre le ~ du métier** to learn the ABCs *ou* basics of the trade.

baba cool [babakul] (*pl* **babas cool**) *nmf fam* *person adopting hippie-like values and lifestyle.*

Babel [babɛl] *npr* ▷ **tour**.

babeurre [babœr] *nm* buttermilk.

babil [babil] *nm* [des enfants] prattle, babble ▪ [du ruisseau] murmuring, babble ▪ [des oiseaux] twittering.

babillage [babijaʒ] *nm* [des enfants] babble, babbling, prattle ▪ [d'un bavard] chatter.

babiller [3] [babije] *vi* [oiseau] to twitter ▪ [ruisseau] to murmur, to babble ▪ [enfant] to prattle, to babble, to chatter ▪ [bavard] to prattle (on), to chatter (away).

babines [babin] *nfpl* **1.** ZOOL chops **2.** *fam* [lèvres] lips ▪ **se lécher** *ou* **pourlécher les ~** to lick one's chops ▪ **à s'en lécher** *ou* **pourlécher les ~** scrumptious.

babiole [babjɔl] *nf* knick-knack, trinket ▪ **je voudrais lui acheter une ~ pour marquer son anniversaire** I would like to buy her a little something for her birthday.

bâbord [babɔr] *nm* port ▪ **à ~** on the port side.

babouche [babuʃ] *nf* (oriental) slipper.

babouin [babwɛ̃] *nm* baboon.

baby boom [bebibum] *nm* baby boom.

baby-foot [babifut] *nm inv* table football.

Babylone [babilɔn] *npr* Babylon.

babylonien, enne [babilɔnjɛ̃, ɛn] *adj* Babylonian.
◆ **Babylonien, enne** *nm, f* Babylonian.

baby-sitter [bebisitœr] (*pl* **baby-sitters**) *nmf* baby-sitter.

baby-sitting [bebisitiŋ] (*pl* **baby-sittings**) *nm* baby-sitting ▪ **faire du ~** to baby-sit.

bac [bak] *nm* **1.** NAUT (small) ferry *ou* ferryboat **2.** [dans un réfrigérateur] compartment, tray ▪ **~ à glace** ice-cube tray ▪ **~ à légumes** vegetable compartment ‖ [dans un bureau] : **~ mobile pour dossiers suspendus** filing trolley *UK*, movable file cabinet *US* ‖ [pour plantes] : **~ (à fleurs)** plant holder **3.** COMM [présentoir] dump bin **4.** [fosse, réserve - pour liquides] tank, vat ; [- pour stockage de pièces] container ▪ **~ à sable** [d'imprimante, de photocopieuse] paper tray ; [d'enfant] sandpit *UK*, sandbox *US* ; [pour routes] grit bin **5.** PHOTO [cuvette - vide] tray ; [- pleine] bath **6.** *fam* [diplôme] : **niveau ~ + 3** *3 years of higher education.*

BAC [bak] (*abr de* **brigade anticriminalité**) *nf* *police squad specializing in patrols to combat crime.*

baccalauréat [bakalɔrea] *nm* *final secondary school examination, qualifying for university entrance,* ≃ A-levels *UK*, ≃ high school diploma *US*.

BACCALAURÉAT

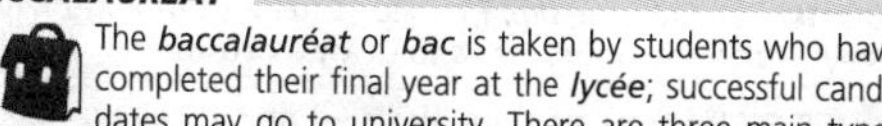

The *baccalauréat* or *bac* is taken by students who have completed their final year at the *lycée*; successful candidates may go to university. There are three main types *(filières)* of *bac*, each corresponding to a specific field: *bac L (littéraire)* being arts-oriented, *bac S (scientifique)* science-based and *bac ES (économique et social)* economics and social studies. Within each domain various obligatory and optional subjects can be combined to give up to eleven different types of diploma. There is also the *bac professionnel* which offers thirty-eight different specialist or vocational subjects.
The different levels of studies in France are referred to in terms of *Bac +* (*Bac + 2* for the *DEUG*, *Bac + 3* for the *licence*, *Bac + 4* for the *maîtrise*, *Bac + 5* for a *DEA* or a *DESS)* are used in job advertisements, CVs and day-to-day life in order to indicate one's level or years of studies.

baccara [bakara] *nm* baccara, baccarat.

baccarat [bakara] *nm* Baccarat (crystal).

Baccarat [bakara] *npr* *town in eastern France famous for its fine crystalware.*

bacchanale [bakanal] *nf litt* [débauche] drunken revel, bacchanal.
◆ **bacchanales** *nfpl* ANTIQ bacchanalia.

bacchante [bakɑ̃t] *nf* **1.** ANTIQ bacchante, bacchanal **2.** *litt & péj* [femme] bacchante *litt*.
◆ **bacchantes** *nfpl fam hum* moustache, whiskers *hum*.

Bacchus [bakys] *npr* Bacchus.

Bach [bak] *npr* : **Jean-Sébastien** *ou* **Johann Sebastian ~** Johann Sebastian Bach.

bâche [baʃ] *nf* transport cover, canvas sheet, tarpaulin ▪ **~s imperméables** waterproof tarpaulin.

bachelier, ère [baʃəlje, ɛr] *nm, f* *student who has passed the baccalauréat.*

bâcher [3] [baʃe] *vt* to cover over *(sép)*, to tarpaulin.

bachot [baʃo] *nm* **1.** [barque] wherry, skiff **2.** *vieilli* [diplôme] = **baccalauréat**.

bachotage [baʃɔtaʒ] *nm fam* cramming ▪ **faire du ~** to cram, to swot up *UK*, to bone up *US*.

bachoter [3] [baʃɔte] *vi fam* to cram, to swot up *UK*, to bone up *US* ▪ **il a été obligé de ~ dans toutes les matières** he had to cram all the subjects.

bacillaire [basilɛr] *adj* bacillar, bacillary ▪ **malade ~** tubercular patient.

bacille [basil] *nm* bacillus ▪ **~ de Koch** tubercle bacillus.

bacillose [basiloz] *nf* pulmonary tuberculosis.

bâclage [baklaʒ] *nm* [action] botching, skimping ▪ **cette toiture, c'est du ~!** they/you *etc* made a really shoddy job of that roof!

bâcler [3] [bakle] *vt* to skimp on *(insép)*, to botch ▪ **nous avons bâclé les formalités en deux jours** we pushed through the red tape in a couple of days ▪ **je vais ~ les comptes vite fait** *fam* I'll throw the accounts together in no time ▪ **c'est du travail bâclé** [réparation] it's a botched job ; [devoir] it's slapdash work.

bacon [bekɔn] *nm* [petit lard] bacon ▪ [porc fumé] smoked loin of pork, Canadian bacon.

bactéricide [bakterisid] ◇ *adj* bactericidal.
◇ *nm* bactericide.

bactérie [bakteri] *nf* bacterium.

bactérien, enne [bakterjɛ̃, ɛn] *adj* bacterial.

bactériologie [bakterjɔlɔʒi] *nf* bacteriology.

bactériologique [bakterjɔlɔʒik] *adj* bacteriological.

bactériologiste [bakterjɔlɔʒist] *nmf* bacteriologist.

badaboum [badabum] *interj* [bruit de chute] boom, crash (bang, wallop).

badaud, e [bado, od] *nm, f* [curieux] curious onlooker ▪ [promeneur] stroller ▪ **attirer les ~s** to draw a crowd.

baderne△ [badɛrn] *nf* : **une vieille ~** an old fogey, an old stick-in-the-mud.

badge [badʒ] *nm* **1.** [insigne] badge **2.** [autocollant] sticker **3.** [document d'identité] swipe card.

badger [17] [badʒe] *vi* [à l'entrée] to swipe in ▪ [à la sortie] to swipe out.

badgeuse [badʒøz] *nf* swipe card reader.

badiane [badjan] *nf* [arbre] Chinese anise tree ▪ [fruit] star anise.

badigeon [badiʒɔ̃] *nm* CONSTR [pour l'extérieur] whitewash ▪ [pour l'intérieur] distemper ▪ [pigmenté] coloured distemper, colourwash *UK* ▪ **passer qqch au ~** [pour l'extérieur] to whitewash sthg ; [pour l'intérieur] to distemper sthg.

badigeonner [3] [badiʒɔne] *vt* **1.** CONSTR [intérieur] to distemper ▪ [extérieur] to whitewash ▪ [en couleur] to paint with coloured distemper, to colourwash *UK* **2.** CULIN & MÉD to paint, to brush ▪ **~ la pâte de jaune d'œuf** brush the pastry with egg yolk.

badigoinces△ [badigwɛ̃s] *nfpl* lips ▪ **se lécher les ~** to lick one's lips *ou* chops.

badin[1] [badɛ̃] *nm* AÉRON airspeed indicator.

badin[2]**, e** [badɛ̃, in] *adj* [gai] light-hearted ▪ [plaisant] playful ▪ **répondre d'un ton ~** to answer playfully *ou* jokingly.

badinage [badinaʒ] *nm* banter, jesting, badinage *litt* & *hum*.

badine [badin] *nf* switch, stick.

badiner [3] [badine] *vi* to jest, to banter, to tease ▪ **~ avec : ne badine pas avec ta santé** don't trifle with your health ▪ **elle ne badine pas sur le chapitre de l'exactitude** she's very strict about *ou* she's a stickler for punctuality ▪ **'On ne badine pas avec l'amour'** *Musset* 'You Can't Trifle With Love'.

badinerie [badinri] *nf litt* jest, badinage *litt* & *hum*.

bad-lands [badlɑ̃ds] *nfpl* badlands GÉOGR.

badminton [badmintɔn] *nm* badminton.

BAFA, Bafa [bafa] (*abr de* **brevet d'aptitude aux fonctions d'animation**) *nm diploma for youth leaders and workers.*

baffe [baf] *nf fam* slap, clout, smack ▪ **coller une ~ à qqn** to give sb a smack in the face△.

baffle [bafl] *nm* AUDIO speaker ▪ TECHNOL baffle.

bafouer [6] [bafwe] *vt* [autorité, loi] to flout, to defy ▪ [sentiment] to ridicule, to scoff at *(insép)*.

bafouillage [bafujaʒ] *nm* **1.** [bredouillage] sputtering, stammering **2.** [propos - incohérents] gibberish ; [- inaudibles] mumblings.

bafouille△ [bafuj] *nf* letter, missive *hum*.

bafouiller [3] [bafuje] ◇ *vi* [bégayer] to stutter, to stammer ▪ **la peur le faisait ~** he was so frightened he couldn't talk properly ▪ **tellement embarrassé qu'il en bafouillait** stammering with embarrassment.
◇ *vt* to stammer ▪ **~ des propos incohérents** to talk (a lot of) gibberish.

bafouilleur, euse [bafujœr, øz] *nm, f* [bégayeur] stammerer ▪ [personne incohérente] mumbler.

bâfrer [3] △ [bafre] ◇ *vt* to gobble, to wolf (down) *(sép)* ▪ **elle a tout bâfré** she polished off the lot.
◇ *vi* to stuff one's face△, to pig o.s.△.

bâfreur, euse△ [bafrœr, øz] *nm, f* glutton, greedy-guts, chowhound *US*.

bagage [bagaʒ] *nm* **1.** [pour voyager] baggage, luggage ▪ **mes ~s** my luggage ▪ **il avait pour tout ~ un sac et un manteau** he was carrying only a bag and a coat ▪ **faire ses ~s** to pack one's bags ▪ **il a fait ses ~s sans demander son reste** *fig* he left without further ado ➊ **en ~ accompagné** [expédier, voyager] as registered baggage ▪ **un seul ~ de cabine est autorisé** only one piece of hand baggage is allowed ▪ **un ~ à main** a piece of hand-luggage ▪ **~s de soute** registered baggage *(in an aeroplane)* ▪ **soute à ~s** hold **2.** *(toujours sing)* [formation] background (knowledge).

bagagiste [bagaʒist] *nmf* **1.** [dans un hôtel] porter ▪ [dans un aéroport] baggage handler **2.** [fabricant] travel goods manufacturer.

bagarre [bagar] *nf* **1.** [échange de coups] fight, brawl ▪ **la ~ est devenue générale** the fight degenerated into a free-for-all ▪ **des ~s ont éclaté dans la rue** scuffles *ou* fighting broke out in the street **2.** *fig* battle, fight ▪ **se lancer dans la ~ politique** to join the political fray ▪ **la ~ a été très dure pendant la deuxième mi-temps/le deuxième set** SPORT it was a close fight during the second half/set.

bagarrer [3] [bagare] *vi* [physiquement] to fight ▪ [verbalement] to argue ▪ **elle a bagarré dur pour arriver là où elle est** she fought hard to get where she is ▪ **pour les convaincre, il faut ~** you have to work hard at convincing them.
◆ **se bagarrer** ◇ *vp (emploi réciproque)* **1.** [se combattre] to fight, to scrap **2.** [se quereller] to quarrel, to have a scene ▪ **mes parents se bagarraient** my parents used to quarrel.
◇ *vpi* **1.** [combattre] to fight, to scrap ▪ **il adore se ~** he loves a scrap **2.** *fig* to fight, to struggle ▪ **se ~ pour que justice soit faite** to fight *ou* to struggle in order to see justice done.

bagarreur, euse [bagarœr, øz] *adj fam* aggressive ▪ **elle a des enfants ~s** her kids are always ready for a scrap.

bagatelle [bagatɛl] *nf* **1.** [chose - sans valeur] trinket, bauble ; [- sans importance] trifle, bagatelle ▪ **se fâcher pour une ~** to take offence over nothing ▪ **ça m'a coûté la ~ de 700 euros** *iron* it cost me a mere 700 euros **2.** MUS bagatelle **3.** *fam* [sexe] : **il est porté/elle est portée sur la ~** he/she likes to play around.
◆ **Bagatelle** *npr* : **le parc de Bagatelle** *park in the Bois de Boulogne famous for its rose gardens.*

Bagdad [bagdad] *npr* Baghdad.

bagnard [baɲar] *nm* convict.

bagne [baɲ] *nm* [prison] prison ▪ HIST penal colony ▪ **c'est le ~, ici!** *fig* they work you to death in this place! ▪ **son travail, c'est pas le ~!** he's not exactly overworked!

bagnole [baɲɔl] *nf fam* car ▪ **une vieille ~** an old banger *UK OU* car.

bagou(t) [bagu] *nm fam* glibness ▪ **il a du ~** he has the gift of the gab, he can talk the hind legs off a donkey.

bagouze [baguz] *nf fam* big flashy ring.

bague [bag] *nf* **1.** JOAILL ring ▪ **passer la ~ au doigt à qqn** to marry sb **2.** [d'un champignon] ring ▪ [d'un cigare] band **3.** MÉCAN collar, ring.

baguenauder [3] [bagnode] *vi fam* to amble *OU* to stroll *OU* to drift along.
◆ **se baguenauder** *vpi fam* to amble *OU* to stroll *OU* to drift along.

baguer [3] [bage] *vt* **1.** [oiseau] to ring ▪ [doigt] to put a ring on **2.** TECHNOL to collar **3.** COUT to baste, to tack.

baguette [bagɛt] *nf* **1.** [petit bâton] switch, stick ▪ **~ de coudrier** hazel stick *OU* switch ▪ **~ magique** magic wand ▪ **d'un coup de ~ magique** as if by magic ▪ **~ de sourcier** divining rod ▪ **elle a les cheveux raides comme des ~s** her hair is dead straight **2.** CULIN [pain] French stick *UK OU* loaf, baguette ▪ [pour manger] chopstick ▪ **manger avec des ~s** to eat with chopsticks **3.** MUS [pour diriger] baton ▪ **sous la ~ du jeune chef** under the baton of the young conductor ▶ **~ de tambour** drumstick ▪ **mener *OU* faire marcher qqn à la ~** to rule sb with an iron hand *OU* a rod of iron **4.** [vêtement] [d'une chaussure] foxing ▪ [sur des bas, un collant] clock **5.** MENUIS length of beading ▪ **cacher les câbles avec des ~s** to bead in the wires.

bah [ba] *interj* **1.** [marque l'indifférence] pooh, who cares ▪ **~, on verra bien!** oh well, we'll have to see! **2.** [marque le doute] really, you don't say *US*.

Bahamas [baamas] *npr fpl* : **les ~** the Bahamas ▪ **aux ~** in the Bahamas.

Bahrayn [barajn], **Bahreïn** [barejn] *npr* Bahrain, Bahrein.

bahut [bay] *nm* **1.** [buffet] sideboard **2.** [coffre] trunk **3.** *fam* [collège, lycée] school **4.** *fam* [véhicule] car ▪ **le voilà, avec son gros ~** here he comes with his tank.

bai, e [bɛ] *adj* bay.

baie [bɛ] *nf* **1.** BOT berry **2.** ARCHIT opening ▪ **~ vitrée** picture *OU* bay window **3.** GÉOGR bay ▪ **la ~ d'Hudson** Hudson Bay ▪ **la ~ de San Francisco** San Francisco Bay.

baignade [bɛɲad] *nf* [activité] swimming, bathing *UK* ▪ **'~ interdite'** 'no swimming' ‖ [lieu] bathing *OU* swimming place ▪ **aménager une ~** to lay out an area for swimming ; [pour bébés] to lay out an area for paddling.

baigner [4] [bɛɲe] ◇ *vt* **1.** [pour laver] to bath *UK*, to bathe *US* ▪ [pour soigner] to bathe **2.** *litt* [suj: fleuve, mer] to wash, to bathe ▪ **un rayon de lumière baignait la pièce** light suffused the room, the room was bathed in light **3.** [mouiller] to soak, to wet ▪ **un visage baigné de larmes** a face bathed in tears ▪ **il était baigné de sueur après sa course** he was soaked with sweat after the race.
◇ *vi* **1.** [être immergé - dans l'eau, le lait] to soak ; [- dans l'alcool, le vinaigre] to steep ▪ **il faut que le tissu baigne complètement dans la teinture** the material must be fully immersed in the dye ‖ *litt* [être environné - de brouillard, de brume] to be shrouded *OU* swathed ▪ **le paysage baignait dans la brume** the countryside was shrouded in mist **2.** *fig* **nous baignons dans le mystère** we're deep in mystery ▪ **elle baigne dans la musique depuis sa jeunesse** she's been immersed in music since she was young **3.** *fam loc* : **ça *OU* tout baigne (dans l'huile)!** everything's great *OU* fine!
◆ **se baigner** ◇ *vp (emploi réfléchi)* : **se ~ les yeux/le visage** to bathe one's eyes/face.
◇ *vpi* [dans une baignoire] to have *OU* to take *US* a bath ▪ [dans un lac, dans la mer] to go swimming *OU* bathing *UK* ▪ **à quelle heure on se baigne?** what time shall we go for our swim?

baigneur, euse [bɛɲœr, øz] *nm, f* swimmer, bather *UK*.
◆ **baigneur** *nm* baby doll.

baignoire [bɛɲwar] *nf* **1.** [dans une salle de bains] bath *UK*, bathtub *US* ▪ **~ sabot** hip bath **2.** THÉÂTRE ground floor box **3.** MIL & NAUT conning tower.

Baïkal [baikal] *npr m* : **le (lac) ~** Lake Baikal.

bail, baux [baj, bo] *nm* **1.** [de location] lease ▪ **prendre qqch à ~** to take out a lease on sthg ▪ **faire/passer un ~** to draw up/to enter into a lease ▶ **~ commercial/professionnel/rural** commercial/professional/rural lease ▪ **~ à construction** construction lease ▪ **~ d'habitation** house-letting *UK*, rental lease *US* **2.** *loc* : **il y a *OU* ça fait un ~ que** *fam*... it's been ages since... ▪ **ça fait un ~ qu'il ne m'a pas téléphoné** it's been ages since he last phoned me, he hasn't phoned me for ages.

BAIL

In France, the usual duration of the *bail* or lease for private rented accommodation is three years. The expression *bail à céder*, often seen on signs in shop windows, means that the lease on the shop or office is for sale.

bâillement [bajmɑ̃] *nm* **1.** [action] yawn ▪ **des ~s** yawning *(U)* **2.** [ouverture] gap.

bailler [3] [baje] *vt arch* to give ▪ **la ~ belle *OU* bonne à qqn** to try to hoodwink sb.

bâiller [3] [baje] *vi* **1.** [de sommeil, d'ennui] to yawn ▪ **~ à s'en décrocher la mâchoire *OU* comme une carpe** to yawn one's head off **2.** [être entrouvert - porte, volet] to be ajar *OU* half-open ; [- col] to gape ▪ **son chemisier bâille aux emmanchures** her blouse gapes at the armholes.

bailleur, eresse [bajœr, bajrɛs], *nm, f* lessor ▪ **~ de fonds** backer, sponsor ▪ **~ de licence** licensor, licenser.

bailli [baji] *nm* bailiff HIST.

bailliage [bajaʒ] *nm* bailiwick.

bâillon [bajɔ̃] *nm* [sur une personne] gag ▪ **mettre un ~ à l'opposition** *fig* to gag *OU* to muzzle the opposition.

bâillonnement [bajɔnmɑ̃] *nm* gagging.

bâillonner [3] [bajɔne] *vt* [otage, victime] to gag ▪ [adversaire, opposant] to gag, to muzzle.

bain [bɛ̃] *nm* **1.** [pour la toilette] bath, bathing ▪ **donner un ~ à qqn** to bath sb, to give sb a bath ▪ **prendre un ~** to have *OU* to take a bath ▪ **vider/faire couler un ~** to empty/to run a bath ▶ **~ moussant/parfumé** bubble/scented bath ▪ **~ de bouche** mouthwash, mouth rinse ▪ **~ de boue** mudbath ▪ **~ de pieds** footbath ▪ **prendre un ~ de pieds** to soak *OU* to bathe one's feet (in warm soapy water) ▪ **~ de vapeur** steam bath ▪ **~ de siège** sitzbath, hip bath ▪ **être dans le ~** [s'y connaître] to be in the swing of things ; [être compromis] to be in it up to one's neck ▪ **quand on n'est plus dans le ~** when you've got out of the habit of things ▪ **être dans le même ~ (que)** to be in the same boat (as) ▪ **mettre qqn dans le ~** [l'initier] to put sb in the picture ; [le compromettre] to drag sb into it ▪ **se mettre *OU* se remettre dans le ~** to get (back) into the swing of things *OU* the routine
2. [baignoire] bath *UK*, bathtub *US* ▪ **~ à remous** Jacuzzi®
3. LOISIRS & SPORT [activité] bathing, swimming ▶ **~ de minuit** midnight swim *OU* dip
4. [bassin] : **grand ~** [bassin] big pool ; [côté] deep end ▪ **petit ~** [bassin] children's pool ; [côté] shallow end
5. *fig* [immersion] : **~ de culture** feast of culture ▪ **~ de foule** walkabout ▪ **prendre un ~ de foule** to go on a walkabout ▪ **~ de jouvence** rejuvenating *OU* regenerating experience ▪ **~ linguistique *OU* de langue** immersion in a language ▪ **la manifestation s'est terminée dans un ~ de sang** the demonstration ended in a bloodbath ▪ **~ de soleil** sunbathing ▪ **prendre un ~ de soleil** to sunbathe

6. [substance pour trempage] bath ■ **~ révélateur** *ou* **de développement** developing bath, developer ■ **~ de fixateur** fixing bath ■ **~ de friture** CULIN deep fat ‖ [cuve] vat.
◆ **bains** *nmpl* [établissement] baths ■ **~s douches** public baths (with showers) ■ **~s turcs** Turkish baths.
◆ **de bain** *loc adj* [sels, serviette] bath *(modif)*.

bain-marie [bɛ̃mari] (*pl* **bains-marie**) *nm* **1.** [processus] bain-marie cooking **2.** [casserole] bain-marie.
◆ **au bain-marie** *loc adv* in a bain-marie.

baïonnette [bajɔnɛt] *nf* bayonet ■ **~ au canon** fix bayonet.

baise▲ [bɛz] *nf* [sexe] : **la ~** sex.

baise-en-ville [bɛzɑ̃vil] *nm inv fam hum* overnight case *ou* bag.

baisemain [bɛzmɛ̃] *nm* : **faire le ~** to kiss a woman's hand.

baiser¹ [beze] *nm* kiss ■ **donner/envoyer un ~ à qqn** to give/to blow sb a kiss ▶ **~ de Judas** kiss of Judas.

baiser² [4] [beze] ◇ *vt* **1.** *litt* [embrasser] to kiss **2.** ▲ [coucher avec] to screw△, to fuck▲ **3.** ▲ [tromper] to shaft▲, to con ■ [vaincre] to outdo.
◇ *vi*▲ to fuck▲.

baiseur, euse▲ [bezœr, øz] *nm, f* : **c'est un sacré ~/une sacrée baiseuse** he/she screws around.

baisse [bɛs] *nf* **1.** [perte de valeur] fall, drop ■ **~ des taux d'intérêt** drop in interest rates ■ **le marché des obligations a connu une ~ sensible** the bond market has dropped considerably **2.** [perte d'intensité] decline, drop ■ **~ de prix** fall in prices ■ **~ de température** drop in temperature ■ **~ de pression** drop *ou* fall in pressure **3.** [perte de quantité] drop ■ **~ de la production** drop in production.
◆ **à la baisse** *loc adv* on the downswing *ou* downturn *ou* decline ■ **jouer à la ~** to speculate on the fall ■ **revoir à la ~** to revise downwards.
◆ **en baisse** *loc adj* [crédit, fonds] declining, decreasing ■ **les fonds sont en ~** funds are sinking *ou* decreasing.

baisser [4] [bese] ◇ *vt* **1.** [vitre de voiture] to lower, to wind *ou* to let down *(sép)* ■ [store] to lower, to take *ou* to let down *(sép)* ■ [tableau] to lower ■ **le rideau est baissé** THÉÂTRE the curtain's down ; [boutique] the iron curtain's down **2.** [main, bras] to lower ■ **~ les yeux** *ou* **paupières** to lower one's eyes, to look down, to cast one's eyes down ■ **faire ~ les yeux à qqn** to stare sb out *ou* down ■ **marcher les yeux baissés** [de tristesse] to walk with downcast eyes ; [en cherchant] to walk with one's eyes to the ground ■ **il gardait le nez baissé sur sa soupe** he was hunched over his soup ■ **~ son chapeau sur ses yeux** to pull *ou* to tip one's hat over one's eyes ■ **attention, baisse la tête!** look out, duck! ■ **en baissant la tête** [posture] with one's head down *ou* bent ; [de tristesse] head bowed (with sorrow) ■ **~ la tête** *ou* **le nez (de honte)** *fig* to hang one's head (in shame) ■ **~ les bras** to throw in the sponge *ou* towel *fig* **3.** [en intensité, en valeur] to lower, to turn down *(sép)* ■ **~ la voix** to lower one's voice ■ **~ un prix** to bring down *ou* to lower *ou* to reduce a price ■ **~ le ton** to calm down ■ **baisse le ton!** *fam* cool it!△, pipe down!
◇ *vi* [espoir, lumière] to fade ■ [marée] to go out ■ [soleil] to go down, to sink ■ [température] to go down, to drop, to fall ■ [prix, action boursière] to drop, to fall ■ [santé, faculté] to decline ■ [pouvoir] to wane, to dwindle, to decline ■ **le jour baisse** the daylight's fading ■ **la qualité baisse** the quality's deteriorating ■ **nos réserves de sucre ont baissé** our sugar reserves have run low, we're low on sugar ■ **ces mesures visent à faire ~ les prix du mètre carré** these measures are intended to bring down the price per square metre ■ **sa vue baisse** his eyesight's fading *ou* getting weaker *ou* failing ■ **sa mémoire baisse** her memory's failing ■ **~ dans l'estime de qqn** to go down in sb's estimation ‖ [réduire le prix] : **on l'a fait ~ à 200 euros** we beat him down to 200 euros.
◆ **se baisser** *vpi* **1.** [personne] to bend down ■ **se ~ pour éviter un coup** to duck in order to avoid a blow ▶ **il n'y a qu'à se ~ pour les prendre** *ou* **les ramasser** they're two a penny *UK ou* a dime a dozen *US* **2.** [store, vitre] to go down.

baissier, ère [besje, ɛr] ◇ *adj* bear *(modif)*, short, bearish.
◇ *nm, f* bear BOURSE.

bajoue [baʒu] *nf* ZOOL chop, chap.
◆ **bajoues** *nfpl hum* [gén] jowls ■ [de bébé] chubby cheeks ■ **il avait des ~s** he had great big jowls.

bakchich [bakʃiʃ] *nm fam* [pourboire] tip ■ [pot-de-vin] bribe, backhander *UK*.

Bakélite® [bakelit] *nf* Bakelite®.

baklava [baklava] *nm* baklava.

Bakou [baku] *npr* Baku.

bal, bals [bal] *nm* **1.** [réunion - populaire] dance ; [- solennelle] ball, dance ■ **~ en plein air** open-air dance ■ **aller au ~** to go dancing *ou* to a dance ▶ **~ costumé** fancy-dress ball ■ **~ masqué** masked ball ■ **~ populaire** *(local) dance open to the public* ■ **~ travesti** costume ball ■ **mener le ~** *pr* to lead off (at a dance) ; *fig* to have the upper hand **2.** [lieu] dance hall.

BAL, Bal [bal, beaɛl] (*abr de* **boîte aux lettres (électronique)**) *nf* E-mail, email.

balade [balad] *nf* **1.** [promenade - à pied] walk, stroll, ramble ; [- en voiture] drive, spin ; [- à cheval] ride ■ **faire une ~** [à pied] to go for a walk ; [en voiture] to go for a drive ; [à cheval] to go for a ride **2.** [voyage] jaunt, trip.

balader [3] [balade] *vt fam* **1.** [promener - enfant, chien] to take (out) for a walk ; [- touriste, visiteur] to take *ou* to show around *(sép)* ■ **je les ai baladés en voiture** I took them (out) for a drive **2.** [emporter] to carry *ou péj* to cart about.
◆ **se balader** *vpi fam* **1.** [se promener - à pied] to stroll *ou* to amble along ■ **se ~ sans but** to drift (aimlessly) along ■ **aller se ~ dans les rues** to go for a walk *ou* stroll through the streets ■ **aller se ~** [en voiture] to go for a drive ; [à cheval] to go for a ride **2.** [voyager] to go for a trip *ou* jaunt **3.** [traîner] to lie around.

baladeur, euse [baladœr, øz] *adj fam* **avoir la main baladeuse** to have wandering hands.
◆ **baladeur** *nm* **1.** AUDIO Walkman®, personal stereo **2.** MÉCAN sliding gear wheel.
◆ **baladeuse** *nf* [lampe] inspection *ou* portable lamp.

baladin [baladɛ̃] *nm arch* wandering player, travelling artist.

balafon [balafɔ̃] *nm* balafo.

balafre [balafr] *nf* **1.** [entaille] slash, gash, cut **2.** [cicatrice] scar.

balafré, e [balafre] ◇ *adj* scarred ■ **un visage ~** a scarred face.
◇ *nm, f* scarface.

balafrer [3] [balafre] *vt* to slash, to gash, to cut.

balai [balɛ] *nm* **1.** [de ménage] broom ■ **~ mécanique** carpet sweeper ▶ **du ~!** scram! **2.** ÉLECTR brush **3.** AUTO : **~ d'essuie-glace** windscreen *UK ou* windshield *US* wiper blade **4.** △ [année] year ■ **il a cinquante ~s** he's fifty.

balai-brosse [balɛbrɔs] (*pl* **balais-brosses**) *nm* (long-handled) scrubbing *UK ou* scrub *US* brush.

balaie *etc v* ▷ **balayer**.

balaise△ [balɛz] = **balèze**.

balance [balɑ̃s] *nf* **1.** [instrument de mesure] scales ■ **~ de ménage** kitchen scales ■ **~ de précision** precision balance ■ **~ romaine** steelyard ■ **jeter qqch dans la ~** *fig* to take sthg into account, to take account of sthg ■ **mettre tout son poids** *ou* **tout mettre dans la ~** *fig* to use (all of) one's influence to tip the scales ■ **tenir la ~ égale entre deux personnes/opinions** *fig* to strike a balance between two people/opinions
2. [équilibre] balance ■ ÉCON balance ■ **~ commerciale** balance of trade ■ **~ des comptes** balance of payments ■ **~ des paiements** balance of payments
3. PÊCHE crayfish net
4. ACOUST & ÉLECTR balance
5. △ *arg crime* [dénonciateur] squealer△, grass△ *UK*, rat *US*.

◆ **en balance** *loc adv* : **mettre deux arguments en ~** to balance two arguments ▪ **mettre en ~ les avantages et les inconvénients** to weigh (up) the pros and cons.

Balance [balɑ̃s] *npr f* **1.** ASTRON Libra **2.** ASTROL Libra ▪ **être ~** to be Libra *ou* a Libran.

balancé, e [balɑ̃se] *adj* : **être bien ~** *fam* to have a stunning figure ➜ **tout bien ~** all things considered, taking one thing with another.

balancelle [balɑ̃sɛl] *nf* **1.** [siège] swing chair **2.** TECHNOL swing tray.

balancement [balɑ̃smɑ̃] *nm* **1.** [mouvement - d'un train] sway, swaying ; [- d'un navire] pitching, roll, rolling ; [- de la tête] swinging ; [- des hanches] swaying ; [- d'une jupe] swinging **2.** [équilibre] balance, equilibrium, symmetry **3.** *litt* [hésitation] wavering, hesitation.

balancer [16] [balɑ̃se] ◇ *vt* **1.** [bras, hanches] to swing ▪ [bébé] to rock ▪ [personne - dans un hamac] to push **2.** [compenser] to counterbalance, to counteract, to cancel out *(sép)* **3.** *fam* [se débarrasser de - objet] to throw away *(sép)*, to chuck out *(sép)* ▪ **tout ~** to chuck it all in ▪ [se débarrasser de - personne] : **~ qqn** to get rid of sb **4.** *fam* [donner - coup] to give ▪ [lancer - livre, clefs] to chuck *ou* to toss (over) **5.** *fam* [dire - insulte] to hurl ▪ **elle n'arrête pas de me ~ des trucs vraiment durs** she's always making digs at me **6.** △ *arg crime* [dénoncer - bandit] to shop△ *UK*, to squeal on△ *(insép)* ; [- complice] to rat on *(insép)* **7.** FIN [budget, compte] to balance.

◇ *vi litt* [hésiter] to waver, to dither ➜ **entre les deux mon cœur balance** *hum* I can't choose between them.

◆ **se balancer** *vpi* **1.** [osciller - personne] to rock, to sway ; [- train] to roll, to sway ; [- navire] to roll, to pitch ; [- branche] to sway ▪ **se ~ d'un pied sur l'autre** to shift from one foot to the other ▪ **se ~ sur sa chaise** to tip back one's chair **2.** [sur une balançoire] to swing ▪ [sur une bascule] to seesaw ▪ [au bout d'une corde] to swing, to dangle **3.** [se compenser] to balance ▪ **profits et pertes se balancent** profits and losses cancel each other out, the account balances **4.** *fam loc* **s'en ~** [s'en moquer] : **je m'en balance** I don't give a damn.

balancier [balɑ̃sje] *nm* **1.** [de moteur] beam, rocker arm ▪ [d'horloge] pendulum ▪ [de montre] balance wheel ▪ [autour d'un axe] walking beam ➜ **retour de ~** backlash **2.** [de funambule] pole **3.** ZOOL balancer, haltere.

balançoire [balɑ̃swar] *nf* **1.** [suspendue] swing ▪ **faire de la ~** to have a (go on the) swing, to play on the swing **2.** [bascule] seesaw.

balayage [balɛjaʒ] *nm* **1.** [d'un sol, d'une pièce] sweeping ▪ [d'épluchures, de copeaux] sweeping up **2.** [avec un projecteur, un radar] scanning, sweeping **3.** [de la chevelure] highlighting **4.** ÉLECTRON scanning, sweep, sweeping **5.** INFORM scanning ▪ **~ télévision** raster scan.

balayer [11] [baleje] ◇ *vt* **1.** [nettoyer - plancher] to sweep ; [- pièce] to sweep (out) ; [- tapis] to brush, to sweep **2.** [pousser - feuilles, nuages] to sweep along *ou* away *ou* up ; [- poussière, copeaux, épluchures] to sweep up *(sép)* ▪ **balayé par le vent** windswept **3.** [parcourir - suj: vent, tir] to sweep (across *ou* over) ; [- suj: faisceau, regard] to sweep, to scan ; [- suj: caméra] to pan across *(insép)* **4.** [détruire - obstacles, préjugés] to sweep away *ou* aside *(sép)* ▪ **les ouragans balaient tout sur leur passage** hurricanes sweep away everything in their path **5.** ÉLECTRON to scan.

◇ *vi* to sweep up.

balayette [balɛjɛt] *nf* brush.

balayeur, euse [balɛjœr, øz] *nm, f* street *ou* road sweeper.

◆ **balayeuse** *nf* street cleaner.

balayures [balejyr] *nfpl* sweepings.

balbutiant, e [balbysjɑ̃, ɑ̃t] *adj* **1.** [hésitant] stuttering, stammering **2.** [récent] : **c'est une technique encore ~e** it's a technique that's still in its infancy.

balbutiement [balbysimɑ̃] *nm* stammer, stutter ▪ **~s** [d'un bègue] stammering, stuttering ; [d'un ivrogne] slurred speech ; [d'un bébé] babbling.

◆ **balbutiements** *nmpl* [d'une technique, d'un art] early stages, beginnings, infancy.

balbutier [9] [balbysje] ◇ *vi* **1.** [bègue] to stammer, to stutter ▪ [ivrogne] to slur (one's speech) ▪ [bébé] to babble ▪ **la timidité le fait ~** he's so shy he stammers **2.** [débuter] to be just starting *ou* in its early stages *ou* in its infancy.

◇ *vt* to stammer (out) ▪ **~ une prière** to mumble a prayer.

balcon [balkɔ̃] *nm* **1.** [plate-forme] balcony **2.** [balustrade] railings *(pl)*, railing **3.** THÉÂTRE balcony ▪ **premier ~** dress circle ▪ **deuxième ~** upper circle ▪ **dernier ~** gallery.

balconnet [balkɔnɛ] *nm* **1.** [balustrade] overhanging railing **2.** [soutien-gorge] : **Balconnet**® half-cup bra.

baldaquin [baldakɛ̃] *nm* **1.** [sur un lit] canopy, tester **2.** [sur un autel, un trône] canopy, baldachin, baldachino.

Bâle [bal] *npr* Basel, Basle.

Baléares [balear] *npr fpl* Baleares ▪ **les (îles) ~** the Balearic Islands.

baleine [balɛn] *nf* **1.** ZOOL whale ▪ **~ blanche/bleue/à bosse** white/blue/humpback whale ▪ **rire** *ou* **rigoler** *ou* **se tordre comme une ~** *fam* to split one's sides laughing **2.** [fanon] whalebone, baleen **3.** [de parapluie] rib **4.** [de corset - en plastique] bone, stay ; [- en métal] steel ; [- en fanon] (whalebone) stay **5.** [pour un col] collar stiffener.

baleineau, x [baleno] *nm* whale calf.

baleinier, ère [balenje, ɛr] *adj* whaling ▪ **industrie baleinière** whaling (industry).

◆ **baleinier** *nm* **1.** [navire] whaling ship, whaler **2.** [chasseur] whaler.

◆ **baleinière** *nf* **1.** NAUT lifeboat **2.** PÊCHE whaleboat, whaler, whale catcher.

balèze△ [balɛz] ◇ *adj* **1.** [grand] hefty, huge ▪ **un type ~** a great hulk (of a man) **2.** [doué] great, brilliant ▪ **~ en physique** dead good *UK ou* ace at physics.

◇ *nm* muscleman ▪ **un gros** *ou* **grand ~** a great hulk (of a man).

Bali [bali] *npr* Bali ▪ **à ~** in Bali.

balinais, e [balinɛ, ɛz] *adj* Balinese.

◆ **Balinais, e** *nm, f* Balinese ▪ **les Balinais** the Balinese.

balisage [balizaʒ] *nm* **1.** NAUT markers, beacons, buoyage ▪ **~ maritime** navigational markers ‖ AÉRON lights, markers ▪ **~ des bords de piste** runway lights ▪ **~ d'entrée de piste** airway markers ‖ [sur route] markers, road markers **2.** [pose - de signaux, de signes] marking out ▪ **~ par radars** beacon signalling **3.** INFORM tagging, mark-up.

balise [baliz] *nf* **1.** NAUT beacon, (marker) buoy ▪ **~ maritime** navigational marker ▪ **~ radio** (radio) beacon ‖ AÉRON marker, beacon ▪ **~ de guidage** radar beacon ‖ [sur route] road marker cone, police cone ▪ [sur sentier] waymark **2.** BOT canna fruit **3.** INFORM tag.

baliser [3] [balize] ◇ *vt* **1.** NAUT to mark out *(sép)*, to buoy **2.** AÉRON : **~ une piste** to mark out a runway with lights **3.** [trajet] to mark out *ou* off *(sép)* ▪ **~ une voie (pour l'interdire à la circulation)** to cone off a lane (from traffic) ➜ **sentier balisé** waymarked path **4.** INFORM to tag, to mark-up.

◇ *vi*△ to be scared stiff ▪ **ça me fait ~ rien que d'y penser** the very thought of it scares me stiff.

baliseur [balizœr] *nm* **1.** [navire] buoy keeper's boat, Trinity House boat *UK* **2.** [personne] buoy keeper.

balistique [balistik] ◇ *adj* ballistic.

◇ *nf* ballistics *(U)*.

baliveau, x [balivo] *nm* **1.** CONSTR scaffold *ou* scaffolding pole **2.** [arbre] sapling.

balivernes [balivɛrn] *nfpl* **1.** [propos] nonsense ▪ **dire des ~** to talk nonsense **2.** [bagatelles] trivia, trifles.

balkanique [balkanik] *adj* Balkan.

balkanisation [balkanizasjɔ̃] *nf* **1.** POLIT Balkanization **2.** [fragmentation] parcelling off into tiny units.

balkaniser [3] [balkanize] *vt* **1.** POLIT to balkanize **2.** [fragmenter] to parcel off into tiny units.

Balkans [balkɑ̃] *npr mpl* : **les ~** the Balkans.

ballade [balad] *nf* **1.** [poème lyrique, chanson] ballad **2.** [en prosodie, pièce musicale] ballade.

ballant, e [balɑ̃, ɑ̃t] *adj* [jambes] dangling ▪ [poitrine] wobbling ▪ **il était debout, les bras ~s** he stood with his arms dangling at his sides ▪ **ne reste pas là, les bras ~s** don't just stand there like an idiot.
◆ **ballant** *nm* looseness ▪ **donner du ~ à un câble** to give a cable some slack, to slacken off a cable.

ballast [balast] *nm* **1.** NAUT ballast tank *ou* container **2.** CONSTR & RAIL ballast.

balle [bal] *nf* **1.** ARM bullet ▪ **se tirer une ~ dans la bouche/tête** to shoot o.s. in the mouth/head ▪ **tué par ~s** shot dead ➊ **~ dum-dum/perdue/traçante** dum-dum/stray/tracer bullet ▪ **~ à blanc** blank ▪ **~ en caoutchouc** rubber bullet **2.** [pour jouer] ball ▪ **jouer à la ~** to play with a ball ➊ **~ de caoutchouc** rubber ball ▪ **~ de golf** golfball ▪ **~ de tennis** tennis ball ▪ **la ~ est dans son camp** *fig* the ball's in his court **3.** [point, coup] stroke, shot ▪ **faire des ~s** TENNIS to practice, to knock up *UK* ➊ **~ de jeu/match** TENNIS game/match point ▪ **~ nulle** no-ball **4.** [paquet] bale **5.** BOT & AGRIC : **la ~** the chaff, the husks **6.** *fam* [visage] face **7.** *fam* franc ▪ **t'as pas cent ~s?** have you got a hundred francs? ; [monnaie] can you spare some change?

ballerine [balrin] *nf* **1.** [danseuse] ballerina, ballet dancer **2.** [chaussure - de danse] ballet *ou* dancing shoe ; [- de ville] pump.

ballet [balɛ] *nm* **1.** [genre] ballet (dancing) **2.** [œuvre] ballet (music) ▪ [spectacle] ballet ▪ **~s roses/bleus** *euphém sexual orgies between adults and female/male minors* ▪ **~ diplomatique** *fig* : **l'incident a donné lieu à tout un ~ diplomatique** the incident has given rise to intense diplomatic activity **3.** [troupe] ballet company **4.** SPORT : **~ aquatique** aquashow, aquacade *US*.

ballon [balɔ̃] *nm* **1.** JEUX & SPORT ball ▪ **jouer au ~** to play with a ball ➊ **~ de foot** *ou* **football** football ▪ **~ de basket** basketball ▪ **~ de rugby** rugby ball ▪ **le ~ ovale** [le rugby] rugby ▪ **le ~ rond** [le foot] football *UK*, soccer **2.** [sphère] : **~ (de baudruche)** (party) balloon ▪ **~ d'hélium** helium balloon ▪ **~ d'oxygène** MÉD oxygen tank ; *fig* life-saver **3.** AÉRON (hot-air) balloon ➊ **~ captif/libre** captive/free balloon ▪ **~ d'essai** *pr* pilot balloon ; *fig* test ▪ **lancer un ~ d'essai** [se renseigner] to put out feelers ; [faire un essai] to do a trial run, to run a test **4.** CHIM round-bottomed flask ▪ [pour l'alcootest] (breathalyser) bag ▪ **souffler dans le ~** to be breathalysed **5.** [verre] (round) wine glass, balloon glass ▪ **~ de rouge** glass of red wine ‖ [contenu] glassful **6.** [réservoir] : **~ (d'eau chaude)** hot water tank **7.** GÉOGR ➊ **le ~ d'Alsace/de Guebwiller** the Ballon d'Alsace/de Guebwiller **8.** *Suisse* [petit pain] (bread) roll **9.** △ *loc* **avoir le ~** to have a bun in the oven△.

ballonné, e [balɔne] *adj* bloated ▪ **être ~** to feel bloated.

ballonnement [balɔnmɑ̃] *nm* **1.** MÉD distension *(U)*, flatulence *(U)* ▪ **j'ai des ~s** I feel bloated **2.** VÉTÉR bloat.

ballonner [3] [balɔne] *vt* to swell.

ballonnet [balɔnɛ] *nm* **1.** AÉRON ballonet **2.** JEUX small balloon.

ballon-sonde [balɔ̃sɔ̃d] (*pl* **ballons-sondes**) *nm* pilot balloon.

ballot [balo] *nm* **1.** [paquet] bundle, package **2.** *fam* [sot] nitwit, blockhead.

ballotin [balɔtɛ̃] *nm* sweet *UK ou* candy *US* box.

ballottage [balɔtaʒ] *nm* second ballot *ou* round ▪ **être en ~** to have to stand *UK ou* to run *US* again in a second round.

ballottement [balɔtmɑ̃] *nm* [d'un véhicule] rocking, swaying, shaking ▪ [d'un passager, d'un sac] rolling around ▪ [d'un radeau] tossing, bobbing about.

ballotter [3] [balɔte] ◇ *vt* [navire] to toss (about) ▪ [passager, sac] to roll around ▪ **les détritus ballottés par les vagues** refuse bobbing up and down in the waves ‖ *fig* **être ballotté entre deux endroits** to be shifted *ou* shunted around constantly from one place to the other ▪ **être ballotté par les événements** to be carried along by events.
◇ *vi* [tête] to loll, to sway ▪ [valise] to bang *ou* to shake about, to rattle around.

ballottine [balɔtin] *nf* stuffed and boned meat roll, ballottine.

ball-trap [baltrap] (*pl* **ball-traps**) *nm* **1.** [tir - à une cible] trapshooting, clay-pigeon shooting ; [- à deux cibles] skeet, skeet shooting **2.** [appareil] trap.

balluchon [balyʃɔ̃] *nm* bundle ▪ **faire son ~** *pr* & *fig* to pack one's bags.

balnéaire [balneɛr] *adj* seaside *(modif)*.

balnéothérapie [balneɔterapi] *nf* balneotherapy.

bâlois, e [balwa, az] *adj* from Basel.
◆ **Bâlois, e** *nm, f inhabitant of or person from Basel.*

balourd, e [balur, urd] ◇ *adj* awkward.
◇ *nm, f* awkward person.
◆ **balourd** *nm* MÉCAN unbalance.

balourdise [balurdiz] *nf* **1.** [caractère] awkwardness **2.** [parole, acte] blunder, gaffe ▪ **raconter des ~s** to say the wrong thing.

balsa [balza] *nm* balsa, balsa wood.

balsamine [balzamin] *nf* balsam, busy lizzie.

balsamique [balzamik] ◇ *adj* **1.** BOT & MÉD balsamic **2.** *litt* [odorant] fragrant, scented.
◇ *nm* balsam.

balte [balt] *adj* Baltic ▪ **les pays Baltes** the Baltic states ▪ **les républiques ~s** the Baltic republics.
◆ **Balte** *nmf* Balt.

Balthazar [baltazar] *npr* BIBLE Balthazar.

baltique [baltik] *adj* Baltic.
◆ **Baltique** *npr f* : **la (mer) Baltique** the Baltic (Sea).

baluchon [balyʃɔ̃] = **balluchon**.

balustrade [balystrad] *nf* [d'un balcon] balustrade ▪ [d'un pont] railing.

balustre [balystr] *nm* **1.** [pilier - de balustrade, de siège] baluster **2.** [compas] pair of compasses *(with spring bow dividers)*.

balzacien, enne [balzasjɛ̃, ɛn] *adj* : **une description ~ne** a description reminiscent of Balzac.

bambin [bɑ̃bɛ̃] *nm* toddler.

bamboche [bɑ̃bɔʃ] *nf fam vieilli* partying.

bambou [bɑ̃bu] *nm* bamboo ▪ **attraper un coup de ~** *fam* to get sunstroke ▪ **avoir le coup de ~** *fam* [devenir fou] to go crazy ; [être fatigué] to feel very tired ▪ **c'est le coup de ~ dans ce restaurant!** *fam* [très cher] this restaurant's a real rip-off!
◆ **en bambou** *loc adj* [meuble, cloison] bamboo *(modif)*.

bamboula△ [bɑ̃bula] *nf* : **faire la ~** to make whoopee.

ban [bɑ̃] *nm* **1.** [applaudissements] : **un ~ pour...!** three cheers *ou* a big hand for...! **2.** [roulement de tambour] drum roll ▪ **fermer le ~** *fig* to bring the proceedings to a close ▪ **ouvrir le ~** *fig* to open the proceedings ‖ [sonnerie de clairon] bugle call **3.** HIST [condamnation] banishment, banning ▪ [convocation] ban ▪ [vassaux] vassals ▪ **le ~ et l'arrière-ban** *fig* the world and his wife.
◆ **bans** *nmpl* banns ▪ **les ~s sont affichés** *ou* **publiés** the banns have been posted.
◆ **au ban de** *loc prép* : **être au ~ de la société** to be an outcast *ou* a pariah ▪ **mettre un pays au ~ des nations** to boycott a country.

banal, e, als [banal] *adj* **1.** [courant] commonplace, ordinary, everyday *(avant n)* ■ **ce n'est vraiment pas ~** it's most unusual, it's really strange **2.** [sans originalité - idée, histoire] trite, banal ; [- chose] commonplace ; [- argument] standard, well-worn ; [- vie] humdrum ; [- événement] everyday ■ **ce que je vais vous dire là est très ~** there's nothing original *OU* unusual about what I'm going to say **3.** INFORM general-purpose.

banalement [banalmɑ̃] *adv* in an ordinary way.

banalisation [banalizasjɔ̃] *nf* **1.** [généralisation] spread ■ *péj* [perte d'originalité] trivialization **2.** [d'un véhicule] : **la ~ des voitures de police** the use of unmarked police cars.

banalisé, e [banalize] *adj* **1.** [véhicule] unmarked **2.** INFORM general-purpose.

banaliser [3] [banalize] *vt* **1.** [rendre courant - pratique] to trivialize, to make commonplace ■ **maintenant que la téléphonie sans fil est banalisée** now that cordless phones have become commonplace **2.** *péj* [œuvre] to deprive *OU* to rob of originality ■ [idée] to turn into a commonplace **3.** [véhicule] to remove the markings from ■ [marque déposée] to turn into a household name.
◆ **se banaliser** *vpi* to become commonplace *OU* a part of (everyday) life ■ **la billetterie électronique s'est banalisée** electronic cash dispensing is now part of everyday life.

banalité [banalite] *nf* **1.** [d'une situation, d'un propos] triteness, banality, triviality ■ [d'une tenue] mundaneness **2.** [propos, écrit] platitude, commonplace, cliché.

banane [banan] ◇ *nf* **1.** BOT banana **2.** *fam* [coiffure] quiff *UK* **3.** *fam* [décoration] medal, gong *UK* **4.** [sac] bum-bag *UK*, waist-bag *US* **5.** ÉLECTR banana plug **6.** △ [idiot] nitwit, twit *UK*, dumbbell *US*.
◇ *adj inv* banana-shaped.

bananeraie [bananrɛ] *nf* banana plantation *OU* grove.

bananier, ère [bananje, ɛr] *adj* banana *(modif)*.
◆ **bananier** *nm* **1.** BOT banana, banana tree **2.** NAUT banana boat.

banc [bɑ̃] *nm*

A.

1. [gén] bench, seat ■ **(au) ~ des accusés** (in the) dock ■ **le ~ des avocats** the lawyers' bench ■ **sur le ~ des ministres** on the government bench ■ **(au) ~ des témoins** (in the) witness box *UK OU* stand *US* ■ **sur les ~s de l'école** in one's schooldays ■ **~ public** park bench
2. MENUIS & TECHNOL [établi] bench, workbench ■ [bâti] frame, bed
3. INFORM bank
4. NAUT (oarsman's) bench, thwart

B.

1. [de poissons] shoal, school ■ [zone] : **~ d'huîtres** [dans la mer] oyster bed ; [dans un restaurant] display of oysters
2. [amas] bank ■ **~ de neige** *Québec* snowdrift ■ **~ de sable** sandbank, sandbar
3. GÉOL [couche] bed, layer ■ [au fond de la mer] bank, shoal.
◆ **banc d'essai** *nm* INDUST test rig, test bed ■ INFORM benchmark ■ *fig* test ■ **faire un ~ d'essai** *pr* to test (an engine) ; *fig* to have a trial run ■ **mettre qqn au ~ d'essai** to give sb a test.

bancaire [bɑ̃kɛr] *adj* banking, bank *(modif)* ■ **chèque ~** cheque *UK*, check *US* ■ **commission ~** bank commission ■ **établissement ~** banking establishment, bank.

bancal, e, als [bɑ̃kal] *adj* **1.** [meuble] rickety, wobbly ■ [personne] lame **2.** [peu cohérent - idée, projet] unsound ; [- raisonnement] weak, unsound ■ **la proposition est un peu ~e** the proposal doesn't really stand up to examination.

bancassurance [bɑ̃kasyrɑ̃s] *nf* bancassurance.

banco [bɑ̃ko] *nm* banco ■ **faire ~** to go banco.

banc-titre [bɑ̃titr] (*pl* **bancs-titres**) *nm* rostrum camera.

bandage [bɑ̃daʒ] *nm* **1.** [pansement] bandage, dressing ◐ **~ herniaire** truss **2.** [fait de panser] bandaging, binding (up) **3.** [fait de tendre - un ressort] stretching, tensing ; [- un arc] bending, drawing **4.** AUTO & RAIL tyre.

bandana [bɑ̃dana] *nm* bandana, bandanna.

bandant, e▲ [bɑ̃dɑ̃, ɑ̃t] *adj* exciting ■ **elle est ~e** she's a real turn-on△ ‖ [sens affaibli] : **pas très ~ comme boulot!** *hum* this job's hardly the most exciting thing going!

bande [bɑ̃d] *nf*

A.

1. [groupe - de malfaiteurs] gang ; [- d'amis] group ; [- d'enfants] troop, band ; [- d'animaux] herd ; [- de chiens, de loups] pack ■ **faire partie de la ~** to be one of the group ◐ **~ armée** armed gang *OU* band
2. *loc* **faire ~ à part : il fait toujours ~ à part** he keeps (himself) to himself ■ **il a encore décidé de faire ~ à part** he's decided yet again to go it alone ■ **~ de** *péj* pack *OU* bunch of ■ **une ~ de menteurs/voleurs** a bunch of liars/crooks

B.

1. [d'étoffe, de papier *etc*] strip, band ■ **~ molletière** puttee, putty
2. [de territoire] strip ■ **~ de sable** strip *OU* spit *OU* tongue of sand ◐ **~ d'arrêt d'urgence** TRANSP emergency lane, hard shoulder
3. [sur une route] band, stripe ■ **~ blanche** white line ■ **~ de ralentissement** speed check
4. CINÉ reel ■ **~ sonore** soundtrack ■ **~ (magnétique)** AUDIO (magnetic) tape
5. ÉLECTRON & RADIO band ■ **~ de fréquence** frequency band ■ **sur la ~ FM** on FM ■ **~ passante** pass-band
6. INFORM : **~ perforée** punched paper tape *UK*, perforated tape
7. MÉD bandage ■ **~ Velpeau®** crepe bandage
8. ARCHIT band
9. LITTÉR & LOISIRS : **~ dessinée** [dans un magazine] comic strip, strip cartoon *UK* ; [livre] comic book ■ **la ~ dessinée** [genre] comic strips
10. [au billard] cushion
11. PHYS : **~ de fréquences** frequency band

C.

NAUT list, heel ■ **donner de la ~** to heel over, to list.
◆ **en bande** *loc adv* as *OU* in a group, all together ■ **ils ne se déplacent qu'en ~** they always move around in a gang.

bandé, e [bɑ̃de] *adj* **1.** [recouvert] bandaged ■ **avoir les yeux ~s** to be blindfolded ■ **pieds ~s** bound *OU* bound-up feet **2.** [tendu] stretched, tensed.

bande-annonce [bɑ̃danɔ̃s] (*pl* **bandes-annonces**) *nf* trailer.

bandeau, x [bɑ̃do] *nm* **1.** [serre-tête] headband **2.** [coiffure] coiled hair ■ **avoir les cheveux en ~, porter des ~x** to wear one's hair in coils **3.** [sur les yeux] blindfold ■ **avoir un ~ sur les yeux** *pr* to be blindfolded ; *fig* to be blind to reality ‖ [sur un œil] eye patch **4.** ARCHIT string *OU* belt course **5.** [espace publicitaire] AUTO advertising space *(in the shape of a band around a vehicle)* ; INFORM banner ad(vert), banner advertisement.

bandelette [bɑ̃dlɛt] *nf* [bande] strip ■ **les ~s d'une momie** the wrappings of a mummy.

bander [3] [bɑ̃de] ◇ *vt* **1.** [panser - main, cheville] to bandage (up) ■ **avoir les yeux bandés** MÉD to have one's eyes bandaged ; [avec un bandeau] to be blindfolded **2.** [tendre - arc] to draw, to bend ; [- ressort, câble] to stretch, to tense ■ *litt* [muscle] to tense, to tauten ■ **~ ses forces** to gather up *OU* to muster one's strength **3.** ARCHIT to arch, to vault.
◇ *vi*▲ to have a hard-on△ ■ [sens affaibli] : **ça me fait pas ~** it doesn't turn me on.

banderille [bɑ̃drij] *nf* banderilla.

banderole [bɑ̃drɔl] *nf* **1.** [bannière - sur un mât, une lance] banderole ; [- en décoration] streamer ; [- dans une manifestation] banner **2.** ARCHIT banderole.

bande-son [bɑ̃dsɔ̃] (*pl* **bandes-son**) *nf* soundtrack.

bande-vidéo [bɑ̃dvideo] (*pl* **bandes-vidéo**) *nf* videotape.

bandit [bɑ̃di] *nm* **1.** [brigand] bandit **2.** [escroc] crook, conman ■ [dit avec affection] : **~, va!** you rogue *OU* rascal!

banditisme [bɑ̃ditism] *nm* crime ■ **c'est du ~!** *fig* it's daylight robbery! ▶ **grand ~** organized crime.

bandonéon [bɑ̃dɔneɔ̃] *nm* bandoneon.

bandothèque [bɑ̃dɔtɛk] *nf* tape library.

bandoulière [bɑ̃duljɛr] *nf* **1.** ARM sling ■ [à cartouches] bandolier **2.** [d'un sac] shoulder strap.
◆ **en bandoulière** *loc adv* **: porter un sac en ~** to carry a shoulder bag.

bang [bɑ̃ŋ] ◇ *nm* [franchissement du mur du son] sonic boom.
◇ *interj* bang, crash.

Bangkok [bɑ̃kɔk] *npr* Bangkok.

bangladais, e [bɑ̃gladɛ, ɛz] *adj* Bangladeshi.
◆ **Bangladais, e** *nm, f* Bangladeshi.

Bangladesh [bɑ̃gladɛʃ] *npr m* **: le ~** Bangladesh.

banjo [bɑ̃(d)ʒo] *nm* banjo.

banlieue [bɑ̃ljø] *nf* suburb ■ **la ~** suburbia, the suburbs ■ **la maison est en ~** the house is on the outskirts of the town *ou* in the suburbs ▶ **~ pavillonnaire** *suburb with lots of little houses of uniform appearance* ■ **la ~ rouge** *towns in the Paris suburbs with Communist mayors* ■ **grande ~** outer suburbs, commuter belt ■ **proche ~** inner suburbs.

BANLIEUE

In France, the word *banlieue* is often associated with social problems such as delinquency.

banni, e [bani] ◇ *adj* banished, exiled.
◇ *nm, f* exile.

bannière [banjɛr] *nf* **1.** [étendard] banner ■ **la ~ étoilée** the star-spangled banner ■ **combattre** *ou* **lutter sous la ~ de qqn** to fight on sb's side **2.** INFORM banner(ad *ou* advert *ou* advertisement).

bannir [32] [banir] *vt* **1.** [expulser] to banish, to exile **2.** *litt* [éloigner] to reject, to cast out ■ **banni à jamais de mes relations** forever banished from my circle of friends **3.** [supprimer - idée, pensée] to banish ; [- aliment] to cut out *(sép)*.

bannissement [banismɑ̃] *nm* banishment.

banquable [bɑ̃kabl] *adj* [effet] bankable ■ **non ~** unbankable.

banque [bɑ̃k] *nf* **1.** [établissement] bank ■ **avoir/mettre une somme à la ~** to have/put some money in the bank ■ **passer à la ~** to go to the bank ▶ **~ d'affaires/de dépôt** merchant/deposit bank ■ **~ commerciale** commercial bank ■ **~ de compensation** clearing bank ■ **~ d'émission** issuing bank, issuing house ■ **la Banque d'Angleterre** the Bank of England ■ **la Banque centrale européenne** the European Central Bank ■ **la Banque de France** the Bank of France ■ **la Banque mondiale** the World Bank **2.** [profession] banking **3.** INFORM & MÉD bank ■ **~ du sang/du sperme/de données** blood/sperm/data bank ■ **~ d'images** picture library **4.** JEUX [réserve] bank ■ **tenir la ~** to be the banker, to keep the bank.

banquer△ [3] [bɑ̃ke] *vi* to fork out.

banqueroute [bɑ̃krut] *nf* **1.** [faillite] bankruptcy ■ **~ frauduleuse** fraudulent bankruptcy ■ **faire ~** to go bankrupt **2.** [échec] failure.

banquet [bɑ̃kɛ] *nm* banquet ▶ **'le Banquet'** ***Platon*** 'Symposium'.

banqueter [27] [bɑ̃kte] *vi* **1.** [bien manger] to feast, to eat lavishly **2.** [prendre part à un banquet] to banquet.

banquette [bɑ̃kɛt] *nf* **1.** [siège - de salon] seat, banquette US ; [- de piano] (duet) stool ; [- de restaurant] wall seat ; [- de voiture, de métro] seat ■ **~ avant/arrière** front/back seat **2.** ARCHIT window seat **3.** TRAV PUB berm **4.** RAIL track bench.

banquier, ère [bɑ̃kje, ɛr] *nm, f* banker.

banquise [bɑ̃kiz] *nf* [côtière] ice, ice shelf ■ [dérivante] pack ice, ice field *ou* floe.

bantou, e [bɑ̃tu] *adj* Bantu.
◆ **Bantou, e** *nm, f* Bantu.
◆ **bantou** *nm* LING Bantu.

banyuls [banjyls] *nm* Banyuls (wine).

baobab [baɔbab] *nm* baobab.

baptême [batɛm] *nm* **1.** RELIG baptism ■ [cérémonie] christening, baptism ■ **donner le ~ à qqn** to baptize *ou* to christen sb ■ **recevoir le ~** to be baptized *ou* christened **2.** [d'un bateau] christening, naming ■ [d'une cloche] christening, dedication **3.** [première expérience] **: ~ de l'air** first *ou* maiden flight ■ **~ du feu** MIL & *fig* baptism of fire.

baptiser [3] [batize] *vt* **1.** RELIG to christen, to baptize **2.** [nommer - personne, animal] to name, to call ■ [surnommer] to nickname, to christen, to dub **3.** [bateau] to christen, to name ■ [cloche] to christen, to dedicate **4.** *fam* [diluer - vin, eau] to water down *(sép)*.

baptismal, e, aux [batismal, o] *adj* baptismal.

baptisme [batism] *nm* Baptist doctrine.

baptiste [batist] *adj* & *nmf* Baptist.

baptistère [batistɛr] *nm* baptistery.

baquet [bakɛ] *nm* **1.** [récipient] tub **2.** [siège] bucket seat.

bar [bar] *nm* **1.** [café] bar ■ **~ à vin** wine bar **2.** [comptoir] bar ■ **le prix au ~ n'est pas le même que le prix en salle** drinks are more expensive if you sit at a table **3.** ZOOL bass **4.** PHYS bar.

baragouin [baragwɛ̃] *nm fam* **1.** [langage incompréhensible] jargon, gobbledegook, double Dutch UK **2.** *péj* [langue étrangère] lingo.

baragouinage [baragwinaʒ] *nm fam* **1.** [manière de parler] jabbering, gibbering **2.** [jargon] jargon, gobbledegook.

baragouiner [3] [baragwine] *fam* ◇ *vt* [langue] to speak badly ■ [discours] to gabble.
◇ *vi* [de façon incompréhensible] to jabber, to gibber, to talk gibberish ■ [dans une langue étrangère] to jabber away.

baragouineur, euse [baragwinœr, øz] *nm, f fam* jabberer, gabbler.

baraka [baraka] *nf* **1.** [dans l'Islam] baraka **2.** *fam* [chance] luck ■ **avoir la ~** to be lucky.

baraque [barak] *nf* **1.** [cabane - à outils] shed ; [- d'ouvriers, de pêcheurs] shelter, hut ; [- de forains] stall ; [- de vente] stall, stand, booth **2.** *fam* [maison] shack, shanty ■ **j'en ai marre de cette ~!** I've had enough of this place!

baraqué, e [barake] *adj fam* muscular, hefty, beefy *péj* ■ **un type ~** a great hulk of a man.

baraquement [barakmɑ̃] *nm* **1.** [baraques] shacks **2.** MIL camp.

baratin [baratɛ̃] *nm fam* **1.** [boniment] flannel ■ **faire du ~ à qqn** to spin sb a yarn, to flannel sb **2.** [vantardises] **: c'est du ~** it's just (a lot of) hot air.

baratiner [3] [baratine] *fam* ◇ *vi* **1.** [mentir] to flannel **2.** [se vanter] to shoot one's mouth (off) ■ **il baratine tout le temps** he's full of hot air.
◇ *vt* **: ~ qqn** [en vue d'un gain] to flannel sb ; [pour le séduire] to chat sb up UK, to give sb a line US ; [pour l'impressionner] to shoot one's mouth off to sb.

baratineur, euse [baratinœr, øz] *fam* ◇ *adj* **1.** [menteur] smooth-talking **2.** [vantard] big-mouthed.
◇ *nm, f* **1.** [séducteur] smooth talker **2.** [menteur] fibber **3.** [vantard] big mouth.

baratte [barat] *nf* churn.

baratter [3] [barate] *vt* to churn.

Barbade [barbad] *npr f* **: la ~** Barbados.

barbant, e [barbɑ̃, ɑ̃t] *adj fam* boring ■ **il est ~** he's a drag *ou* bore.

barbaque△ [barbak] *nf* [viande] meat ■ *péj* tough meat.

barbare [barbar] ◇ *adj* **1.** HIST [primitif] barbarian, barbaric **2.** [terme, emploi] incorrect **3.** [cruel] barbaric.

<> *nmf* barbarian.

barbaresque [barbarɛsk] *adj* Barbary *(modif)* ▪ **les États ~s** the Barbary states.

barbarisme [barbarism] *nm* barbarism.

barbe¹ [barb] *nm* [cheval] barb.

barbe² [barb] *nf* **1.** [d'homme - drue] (full) beard ; [- clairsemée] stubble ; [- en pointe] goatee ▪ **porter la ~** to have a beard ▪ **se faire la ~** to (have a) shave ▪ **se raser/se tailler la ~** to shave off/to trim one's beard ▪ **sans ~** [rasé] beardless, clean-shaven ; [imberbe] beardless, smooth-chinned ▪ **~ de deux jours** two days' stubble *ou* growth ➜ **~ à papa** candy floss *UK*, cotton candy *US* ▪ **fausse ~** false beard ▪ **femme à ~** bearded woman ▪ **rien que des vieilles ~s** *fam* a bunch of wrinklies *UK ou* greybeards *US* ▪ **c'est la ~!, quelle ~!** *fam* what a drag *ou* bore! ▪ **la ~!** *fam* [pour faire taire] shut up!, shut your mouth!△, shut your trap! △ ; [pour protester] damn!, hell!, blast! ▪ **parler dans sa ~** to mutter under one's breath ▪ **rire dans sa ~** to laugh up one's sleeve ▪ **faire qqch à la ~ de qqn** to do sthg under sb's very nose **2.** [d'animal] tuft of hairs, beard **3.** BOT beard, awn **4.** [filament - de plume] barb ; [- de coton] tuft ; [- de métal, de plastique] burr **5.** TECHNOL beard, bolt toe.
◆ **barbes** *nfpl* [de papier] ragged edge ▪ [d'encre] smudge.

barbeau, x [barbo] *nm* **1.** ZOOL barbel **2.** △ [souteneur] pimp **3.** BOT cornflower, bluebottle.

Barbe-Bleue [barbəblø] *npr* Bluebeard.

barbecue [barbəkju] *nm* **1.** [appareil] barbecue (set) ▪ **faire cuire de la viande au ~** to barbecue meat **2.** [repas] barbecue.

barbelé, e [barbəle] *adj* barbed.
◆ **barbelé** *nm* barbed wire, barbwire *US*.

barber [3] [barbe] *vt fam* **1.** [lasser] to bore ▪ **je vais lui écrire, mais ça me barbe!** I'll write to him, but what a drag! **2.** [importuner] to hassle.
◆ **se barber** *vpi* to be bored stiff *ou* to tears *ou* to death ▪ **qu'est-ce qu'on se barbe ici!** this place is so boring!

Barberousse [barbərus] *npr* Barbarossa.

Barbès [barbɛs] *npr district in north Paris with a large North African immigrant population.*

barbet, ette [barbɛ, ɛt] *nm, f* [chien] water spaniel.

barbichette [barbiʃɛt] *nf* (small) goatee.

barbier [barbje] *nm* barber ▪ **'le Barbier de Séville'** *Beaumarchais, Rossini* 'The Barber of Seville'.

barbiturique [barbityrik] <> *adj* barbituric.
<> *nm* barbiturate.

Barbizon [barbizɔ̃] *npr*: **l'école de ~** the Barbizon school *(landscape painters of the mid-19th century, including Millet, Corot and Diaz).*

barbon [barbɔ̃] *nm litt* [homme - âgé] old man, greybeard ; [- aux idées dépassées] (old) stick-in-the-mud.

barbotage [barbɔtaʒ] *nm* **1.** *fam* [baignade] paddling, splashing about **2.** CHIM bubbling (through a liquid).

barboter [3] [barbɔte] <> *vi* **1.** [s'ébattre] to paddle, to splash around *ou* about **2.** [patauger] to wade **3.** CHIM : **faire ~ un gaz** to bubble a gas (through a liquid).
<> *vt fam fam* [dérober] to pinch, to swipe.
◆ **barboter dans** *v+prép fam* [être impliqué dans] to have a hand in.

barbouillage [barbujaʒ] *nm* **1.** [application de couleur, de boue] daubing **2.** [fait d'écrire] scribbling, scrawling ▪ [écrit] scribble, scrawl **3.** [tableau - de mauvais artiste] daub *péj* ; [- d'enfant] scribbled picture ▪ **à l'âge des premiers ~s** when a child first learns to draw.

barbouiller [3] [barbuje] *vt* **1.** [salir] : **son menton était barbouillé de confiture** his chin was smeared with jam **2.** [peindre] to daub ▪ **~ des toiles** to mess about *ou* around with paint ▪ **~ qqch de peinture** to slap paint on sthg, to daub sthg with paint **3.** [gribouiller] to scrawl, to scribble ▪ **il barbouille du papier** *pr* he's scribbling away ; *fig & péj* he's just a scribbler **4.** *fam* [donner la nausée à] to nauseate ▪ **avoir l'estomac** *ou* **se sentir barbouillé** to feel queasy *ou* nauseated.

barbouilleur, euse [barbujœr, øz] *nm, f péj* [écrivain] scribbler ▪ [peintre] dauber.

barbouillis [barbuji] = **barbouillage**.

barbouze△ [barbuz] *nf* **1.** [espion] spy **2.** [garde du corps] heavy, minder ▪ [intermédiaire] minder **3.** [barbe] beard.

barbu, e [barby] *adj* bearded.
◆ **barbu** *nm* **1.** [homme] bearded man, man with a beard **2.** ZOOL barbet.

barbue [barby] *nf* ZOOL brill.

barcarolle [barkarɔl] *nf* barcarolle.

barcasse [barkas] *nf péj* boat, tub.

Barcelone [barsəlɔn] *npr* Barcelona.

barco® [barko] *nm* data projector.

barda [barda] *nm fam* **1.** MIL gear, kit *UK* **2.** [chargement] stuff, gear, paraphernalia.

bardage [bardaʒ] *nm* **1.** [revêtement de maison] weatherboarding *UK*, siding *US* **2.** [autour d'un tableau] (protective) boarding.

bardane [bardan] *nf* burdock.

barde [bard] <> *nm* [poète] bard.
<> *nf* CULIN bard.

bardeau, x [bardo] *nm* **1.** [pour toiture] shingle **2.** [pour façade] weatherboard *UK*, clapboard *US* **3.** [pour carrelage] lath **4.** = **bardot**.

barder [3] [barde] <> *vt* **1.** CULIN to bard **2.** *arch* [cuirasser] to bard **3.** *fig* **être bardé de** [être couvert de] to be covered in *ou* with ▪ **être bardé de diplômes** to have a string of academic titles.
<> *v impers fam fam* **quand il a dit ça, ça a bardé!** things really turned nasty when he said that! ▪ **si tu ne te dépêches pas, ça va ~!** you'll get it *ou* be for it if you don't hurry up!

bardot [bardo] *nm* hinny.

barème [barɛm] *nm* **1.** [tableau] ready reckoner **2.** [tarification] scale ▪ **~ des prix** price list, schedule of prices ▪ **~ des salaires** wage scale, variable sliding scale.

Barents [barɛ̃s] *npr* ▷ **mer**.

barge [barʒ] *nf* **1.** NAUT barge, lighter **2.** ZOOL godwit.

barguigner [3] [bargiɲe] *vi fam* **sans ~** without hesitation *ou* shillyshallying.

baril [baril] *nm* [de vin] barrel, cask ▪ [de pétrole] barrel ▪ [de lessive] pack ▪ **~ de poudre** powder keg.

barillet [barijɛ] *nm* **1.** [baril] small barrel *ou* cask **2.** ARM & TECHNOL cylinder.

bariolage [barjɔlaʒ] *nm* **1.** [action] daubing with bright colours **2.** [motif] gaudy colour-scheme.

bariolé, e [barjɔle] *adj* [tissu] motley, multicoloured, particoloured ▪ [foule] colourful.

barioler [3] [barjɔle] *vt* to cover with gaudy colours, to splash bright colours on.

barjo(t)△ [barʒo] *adj* nuts, bananas.

barmaid [barmɛd] *nf* barmaid.

barman [barman] (*pl* **barmans** *ou pl* **barmen** [- mɛn]) *nm* barman, bartender *US*.

bar-mitsva [barmitsva] *nf inv* Bar Mitzvah.

baromètre [barɔmɛtr] *nm* barometer, glass ▪ **le ~ est au beau fixe** the barometer is set *ou* reads fair ▪ **le ~ est à la pluie** the barometer is set on rain ▪ **~ de l'opinion publique** *fig* barometer *ou* indicator of public opinion.

barométrique [barɔmetrik] *adj* barometric.

baron, onne [barɔ̃, ɔn] *nm, f* **1.** [noble] baron (*f* baroness) **2.** [magnat] : **~ de la finance** tycoon.

baronet, baronnet [barɔnɛ] *nm* HIST baronet.

baroque [barɔk] <> *adj* **1.** ARCHIT, ART & LITTÉR baroque **2.** [étrange - idée] weird.
<> *nm* Baroque.

baroud [barud] *nm* ***fam*** fighting, battle ▪ **~ d'honneur** last stand.

baroudeur, euse [barudœr, øz] *nm, f* ***fam*** [qui aime le combat] fighter ▪ [qui a voyagé] : **il a un air de ~** he looks like he's been around a bit.

barouf△ [baruf] *nm* racket, din ▪ **faire du ~** [bruit] to kick up a racket ; [scandale] to make a fuss.

barque [bark] *nf* small boat ▪ **~ de pêcheur** small fishing boat ▪ **mener sa ~** ***fig*** to look after o.s. ▪ **il a bien/mal mené sa ~** he managed/didn't manage his affairs well.

barquette [barkɛt] *nf* **1.** CULIN *boat-shaped tartlet* **2.** [emballage] carton, punnet.

barracuda [barakuda] *nm* barracuda.

barrage [baraʒ] *nm* **1.** [réservoir] dam ▪ [régulateur] weir, barrage ▪ **~ (de retenue)** dam ▪ **~flottant** floating dam ▪ **faire ~ à** to stand in the way of, to obstruct, to hinder **2.** [dispositif policier] : **~ (de police)** police cordon ▪ **~ routier** roadblock **3.** SPORT : **(match de) ~** play-off.

barre [bar] *nf* **1.** [tige - de bois] bar ; [- de métal] bar, rod ▪ **j'ai une ~ sur l'estomac/au-dessus des yeux** [douleur] I have a band of pain across my stomach/eyes ➤ **~ de chocolat** chocolate bar ▪ **~ d'appui** handrail ▪ **~ de remorquage** tow bar ▪ **~ de torsion** AUTO torsion bar
2. SPORT : **~s asymétriques/parallèles** asymmetric/parallel bars ▪ **~ fixe** high *ou* horizontal bar ▌DANSE barre ▪ **exercices à la ~** barre work *ou* exercises
3. NAUT : **~ (de gouvernail)** [gén] helm ; [sur un voilier] tiller ; [sur un navire] wheel ▪ **prendre la ~** ***pr*** to take the helm ; ***fig*** to take charge ▪ **être à la ~** to be at the helm, to steer ; ***fig*** to be at the helm *ou* in charge
4. [trait] line ➤ **~ de soustraction/fraction** subtraction/fraction line ▪ **~ oblique** slash ▪ **avoir ~ sur qqn** to have a hold over *ou* on sb
5. [niveau] level ▪ **le dollar est descendu au-dessous de la ~ des 1 euro** the dollar fell below the 1 euro level ▪ **mettre** *ou* **placer la ~ trop haut** to set too high a standard
6. MUS : **~ (de mesure)** bar line
7. DR : **~ (du tribunal)** bar ▪ **~ des témoins** witness box *UK ou* stand *US* ▪ **appeler qqn à la ~** to call sb to the witness box
8. INFORM : **~ de défilement** scroll bar ▪ **~ d'espacement** space bar ▪ **~ d'état** status bar ▪ **~ de menu** menu bar ▪ **~ de navigation** navigation bar, navigation frame ▪ **~ d'outils** toolbar
9. GÉOGR [crête] ridge ▪ [banc de sable] sandbar ▪ [houle] race
10. HÉRALD bar.

barré, e [bare] *adj* **1.** [chèque] crossed ▪ **chèque non ~** open cheque **2.** ***fam loc*** **être bien/mal ~ : on est mal ~ pour y être à 8 h** we haven't got a hope in hell *ou* we don't stand a chance of being there at 8 ▪ **c'est mal ~** it's got off to a bad start.
◆ **barré** *nm* barré.

barreau, x [baro] *nm* **1.** [de fenêtre] bar ▪ [d'échelle] rung ▪ **~ de chaise** ***fam hum*** fat cigar **2.** DR : **le ~** the Bar ▪ **être admis** *ou* **reçu au ~** to be called to the Bar ▪ **être radié du ~** to be disbarred.

barrer [3] [bare] <> *vt* **1.** [bloquer - porte, issue] to bar ; [- voie, route] to block ▪ **la rue est temporairement barrée** the street has been temporarily closed ▪ **~ le passage à qqn** to block sb's way ➤ **~ la route à qqn** ***pr*** & ***fig*** to stand in sb's way **2.** [rayer - chèque] to cross ; [- erreur, phrase] to cross *ou* to score out *(sép)*, to strike out ▪ **un pli lui barrait le front** he had a deep line running right across his forehead **3.** NAUT to steer.
<> *vi* NAUT to steer, to be at the helm.
◆ **se barrer** *vpi* ***fam*** **1.** [partir] to beat it, to split, to clear off ▪ **barre-toi de là, tu me gênes!** shift, you're in my way! **2.** [se détacher] to come off.

barrette [barɛt] *nf* **1.** [pince] : **~ (à cheveux)** (hair) slide *UK*, barrette *US* **2.** COUT collar pin **3.** RELIG biretta ▪ **recevoir la ~** to be made a cardinal **4.** MIN helmet **5.** INFORM : **~de mémoire** memory module.

barreur, euse [barœr, øz] *nm, f* **1.** [gén] helmsman **2.** [en aviron] coxswain ▪ **avec ~** coxed ▪ **sans ~** coxless.

barricade [barikad] *nf* barricade ▪ **nous avons conquis ces libertés sur les ~s** we won those freedoms by going out in the streets and fighting for them ▪ **être de l'autre côté de la ~** to be on the opposite *ou* other side of the fence ▪ **les journées des Barricades** *insurrections where barricades are erected in the streets.*

barricader [3] [barikade] *vt* [porte, rue] to barricade.
◆ **se barricader** *vp (emploi réfléchi)* **1.** [se retrancher] to barricade o.s. **2.** [s'enfermer] to lock *ou* to shut o.s.

barrière [barjɛr] *nf* **1.** [clôture] fence ▪ [porte] gate ▪ **~ de passage à niveau** level *UK ou* grade *US* crossing gate ▪ **~ de dégel** *closure of road to heavy traffic during thaw* **2.** [obstacle] barrier ▪ **la ~ de la langue** the language barrier ▪ **dresser** *ou* **mettre une ~ entre...** to raise a barrier between... ▪ **faire tomber une ~/les ~s** to break down a barrier/the barriers ➤ **~s douanières** tariff *ou* trade barriers **3.** GÉOGR : **~ naturelle** natural barrier ▪ **la Grande Barrière** the Great Barrier Reef.

barrique [barik] *nf* barrel, cask.

barrir [32] [barir] *vi* [éléphant] to trumpet.

barrissement [barismɑ̃] *nm* trumpeting.

bartavelle [bartavɛl] *nf* rock partridge.

barycentre [barisɑ̃tr] *nm* barycentre.

baryton [baritɔ̃] *nm* [voix] baritone (voice) ▪ [chanteur] baritone.

baryum [barjɔm] *nm* barium ▪ **sulfate de ~** barium meal.

barzoï [barzɔj] *nm* borzoi, Russian wolfhound.

bas[1] [ba] *nm* [de femme] stocking ▪ **des ~ avec/sans couture** seamed/seamless stockings ▪ **~ fins** sheer stockings ▪ **~ de soie** silk stockings ▪ **~ de laine** ***pr*** woollen stocking ; ***fig*** savings, nest egg ▪ **~ (de) Nylon®** nylon stockings ▪ **~ résille** fishnet stockings ▪ **~ à varices** support stockings.

bas[2], **basse** [ba *(devant nm commençant par voyelle ou 'h' muet)* baz), bas] *adj*

A. DANS L'ESPACE
B. DANS UNE HIÉRARCHIE

A. DANS L'ESPACE

1. [de peu de hauteur - bâtiment, mur] low ; [- herbes] low, short ; [- nuages] low ▪ **attrape les branches basses** grasp the lower *ou* bottom branches
2. [peu profond] low ▪ **aux basses eaux** [de la mer] at low tide ; [d'une rivière] when the water level is low ; ***fig*** at a time of stagnation
3. [incliné vers le sol] : **marcher la tête basse** to hang one's head as one walks ▪ **le chien s'enfuit, la queue basse** the dog ran away with its tail between its legs
4. GÉOGR : **les basses terres** the lowlands ▪ **les basses Alpes** the foothills of the Alps ▪ **la basse vallée du Rhône** the lower Rhone valley

B. DANS UNE HIÉRARCHIE

1. [en grandeur - prix, fréquence, pression *etc*] low ▪ **à ~ prix** cheap, for a low price ▪ **à basse température** [laver] at low temperatures ▪ **son moral est très ~** he's down, he's in very low spirits
2. [médiocre - intérêt, rendement] low, poor ; [- dans les arts] inferior, minor, crude ▪ **le niveau de la classe est très ~** the (achievement) level of the class is very low ➤ **les ~ morceaux** [en boucherie] the cheap cuts
3. [inférieur dans la société] low, lowly ***litt***, humble ▪ **de basse condition** from a poor family ➤ **le ~ clergé** the minor clergy ▪ **le ~ peuple** the lower classes *ou* orders ***péj***
4. MUS [grave - note] low, bottom *(modif)* ; [- guitare, flûte] bass *(modif)*
5. [peu fort] low, quiet ▪ **parler à voix basse** to speak in a low *ou* quiet voice
6. ***péj*** [abject, vil - âme] low, mean, villainous ; [- acte] low, base, mean ; [- sentiment] low, base, abject ▪ **à moi toutes les basses besognes** I get stuck with all the dirty work ▪ [vulgaire - terme, expression] crude, vulgar

7. [le plus récent] : **le ~ Moyen Âge** the late Middle Ages.

◆ **bas** ◇ *adv* **1.** [à faible hauteur, à faible niveau] low ▪ **je mettrais l'étagère plus ~** I'd put the shelf lower down ▪ **les prix ne descendront pas plus ~** prices won't come down any further ▪ **leurs actions sont au plus ~** their shares have reached an all-time low ▪ **elle est bien ~** [physiquement] she's very poorly ; [moralement] she's very low *ou* down ▪ **vous êtes tombé bien ~** [financièrement] you've certainly gone down in the world ; [moralement] you've sunk really low ▪ **il est tombé bien ~ dans mon estime** he's gone down a lot in my estimation ▪ **plus ~, vous trouverez la boulangerie** [plus loin] you'll find the baker's a little further on ▮ [dans un document] : **voir plus ~** see below ▶ **~ les masques : je sais tout maintenant, alors ~ les masques** I know everything now, so you can stop pretending ▪ **~ les pattes!** *fam* hands off! **2.** ACOUST [d'une voix douce] in a low voice ▪ [d'une voix grave] in a deep voice ▪ **mets le son plus ~** turn the sound down ▶ **il dit tout haut ce que les autres pensent tout ~** he voices the thoughts which others keep to themselves **3.** MUS low **4.** VÉTÉR : **mettre ~** to give birth **5.** NAUT : **mettre pavillon ~** to lower *ou* to strike the colours.
◇ *nm* [partie inférieure - d'un pantalon, d'un escalier, d'une hiérarchie *etc*] bottom ; [- d'un visage] lower part ▪ **le ~ du dos** the small of the back.

◆ **basse** *nf* **1.** MUS [partie] bass (part) *ou* score ▪ **basse continue** basso continuo **2.** [voix d'homme] bass (voice) ▪ **basse chantante** basso cantante ▮ [chanteur] bass **3.** [instrument - gén] bass (instrument) ; [- violoncelle] (double) bass.

◆ **à bas** *loc adv* : **mettre qqch à ~** to pull sthg down ▪ **ils ont mis à ~ tout le quartier** they razed the whole district to the ground ▶ **à ~ la dictature!** down with dictatorship!

◆ **au bas de** *loc prép* : **au ~ des escaliers** at the foot *ou* bottom of the stairs ▪ **au ~ de la hiérarchie/liste** at the bottom of the hierarchy/list.

◆ **de bas en haut** *loc adv* from bottom to top, from the bottom up ▪ **regarder qqn de ~ en haut** to look sb up and down.

◆ **d'en bas** ◇ *loc adj* : **les voisins d'en ~** the people downstairs ▪ **la porte d'en ~ est fermée** the downstairs door is shut.
◇ *loc adv* [dans une maison] from downstairs ▪ [d'une hauteur] from the bottom ▪ **elle est partie d'en ~** *fig* she worked her way up, she started from nowhere.

◆ **du bas** *loc adj* **1.** [de l'étage inférieur] : **l'appartement du ~** the flat underneath *ou* below *ou* downstairs **2.** [du rez-de-chaussée] downstairs *(modif)* **3.** [de l'endroit le moins élevé] lower.

◆ **en bas** *loc adv* **1.** [à un niveau inférieur - dans un bâtiment] downstairs, down ▪ **la maison a deux pièces en ~ et deux en haut** the house has two rooms downstairs and two upstairs **2.** [dans la partie inférieure] : **prends le carton par en ~** take hold of the bottom of the box **3.** [vers le sol] : **je ne peux pas regarder en ~, j'ai le vertige** I can't look down, I feel dizzy ▪ **le village semblait si petit, tout en ~** the village looked so small, down there *ou* below ▪ **suspendre qqch la tête en ~** to hang sthg upside down.

◆ **en bas de** *loc prép* : **en ~ de la côte** at the bottom *ou* foot of the hill ▪ **signez en ~ du contrat** sign at the bottom of the contract.

basalte [bazalt] *nm* basalt.

basaltique [bazaltik] *adj* basaltic.

basané, e [bazane] ◇ *adj* **1.** [bronzé - touriste] suntanned ; [- navigateur] tanned, weather-beaten **2.** ▲ [connotation raciste] dark-skinned.
◇ *nm, f* ▲ *racist term used with reference to dark-skinned people,* ≃ darky *fam*.

bas-bleu [bablø] (*pl* **bas-bleus**) *nm péj* bluestocking.

bas-côté [bakote] (*pl* **bas-côtés**) *nm* [de route] side, verge ▪ [d'église] aisle.

basculant, e [baskylɑ̃, ɑ̃t] *adj* tip-up.

bascule [baskyl] *nf* **1.** [balance] weighing machine ▪ [pèse-personne] scales **2.** [balançoire] seesaw ▪ **mouvement de ~** seesaw motion ▪ **pratiquer une politique de ~** to change allies frequently **3.** TECHNOL bascule.

basculement [baskylmɑ̃] *nm* [d'une pile] toppling over ▪ [d'un récipient] tipping out *ou* over ▪ **pour empêcher le ~ de l'électorat vers les verts** to prevent a swing to the green party.

basculer [3] [baskyle] ◇ *vi* **1.** [personne] to topple, to fall over ▪ [vase] to tip over ▪ [benne] to tip up **2.** *fig* **son univers a basculé** his world collapsed ▪ **~ dans : la pièce bascule soudain dans l'horreur** the mood of the play suddenly switches to horror ▪ **~ dans l'opposition** to go over to the opposition.
◇ *vt* [renverser - chariot] to tip up *(sép)* ; [- chargement] to tip out *(sép)* ▪ **~ son vote sur** to switch one's vote to.

base [baz] *nf* **1.** [support] base ▪ **à la ~ du cou** at the base of the neck ▪ **~ de maquillage** make-up base
2. [fondement] basis, groundwork *(U)*, foundations ▪ **établir qqch/reposer sur une ~ solide** to set sthg up/to rest on a sound basis ▪ **établir** *ou* **jeter les ~s d'une alliance** to lay the foundations of *ou* for an alliance ▪ **quelle est votre ~ de départ?** what's *ou* where's your starting point?
3. MIL : **~ (aérienne/militaire/navale)** (air/army/naval) base ▪ **~ d'opérations/de ravitaillement** operations/supply base ▪ **rentrer à la ~** to go back to base
4. ASTRONAUT : **~ de lancement** launching site
5. POLIT : **la ~** the grass roots, the rank and file
6. FIN : **~ d'imposition** taxable amount
7. GÉOM, INFORM & MATH base ▪ **système de ~ cinq/huit** base five/eight system ▪ **~ de connaissances** knowledge base ▶ **~ de données** database ▪ **~ de données relationnelles** relational database
8. LING [en diachronie] root ▪ [en synchronie] base, stem ▪ [en grammaire générative] base component
9. CULIN [d'un cocktail, d'une sauce] basic ingredient
10. CHIM base
11. SPORT [détente] : **~ de loisirs** (outdoor) leisure *ou* sports complex.

◆ **bases** *nfpl* [fondations] foundations, basis ▪ [acquis] basic knowledge ▪ **avoir de bonnes ~s en arabe/musique** to have a good grounding in Arabic/in music.

◆ **à base de** *loc prép* : **à ~ de café** coffee-based.

◆ **à la base** *loc adv* **1.** [en son fondement] : **le raisonnement est faux à la ~** the basis of the argument is false
2. [au début] at the beginning, to begin *ou* to start off with.

◆ **de base** *loc adj* **1.** [fondamental - vocabulaire, industrie] basic ; [- principe] basic, fundamental ▪ **militant de ~** grass-roots militant
2. [de référence - salaire, traitement] basic
3. LING base *(modif)*.

base-ball [bɛzbol] (*pl* **base-balls**) *nm* baseball.

baser [3] [baze] *vt* **1.** [fonder] : **~ qqch sur (qqch)** to base sthg on (sthg) ▪ **tes soupçons ne sont basés sur rien** there are no grounds for your suspicions, your suspicions are groundless **2.** MIL & COMM [installer] to base ▪ **être basé à** to be based at *ou* in ▪ **aviation basée à terre** ground-based air force.

◆ **se baser sur** *vp+prép* to base one's judgment on ▪ **je me base sur les chiffres de l'année dernière** I've taken last year's figures as the basis for my calculations.

bas-fond [bafɔ̃] (*pl* **bas-fonds**) *nm* GÉOGR & NAUT shallow, shoal.

◆ **bas-fonds** *nmpl litt* **les ~s de New York** the slums of New York ▪ **les ~s de la société** the dregs of society.

basic [bazik] *nm* INFORM basic.

basicité [bazisite] *nf* basicity.

basilic [bazilik] *nm* **1.** BOT basil **2.** MYTHOL & ZOOL basilisk.

basilique [bazilik] *nf* basilica.

basique [bazik] *adj* basic CHIM.

basket [baskɛt] ◇ *nm ou nf* [chaussure] : **~s** trainers UK, sneakers US.
◇ *nm fam* = **basket-ball**.

basket-ball [baskɛtbol] (*pl* **basket-balls**) *nm* basketball.

basketteur, euse [baskɛtœr, øz] *nm, f* basketball player.

basmati [basmati] *nm* basmati (rice).

basquaise [baskɛz] *adj f* & *nf* Basque.

◆ **(à la) basquaise** *loc adj* CULIN basquaise, with a tomato and ham sauce.

basque[1] [bask] *nf* COUT basque ■ **s'accrocher** *OU* **se pendre aux ~s de qqn** to dog sb's footsteps, to stick to sb like glue.

basque[2] [bask] *adj* Basque ■ **le Pays ~** the Basque Country ■ **au Pays ~** in the Basque Country.
◆ **Basque** *nmf* Basque.
◆ **basque** *nm* LING Basque.

bas-relief [barəljɛf] (*pl* **bas-reliefs**) *nm* bas *OU* low relief.

basse [bas] *f* ▷ **bas.**

basse-cour [baskur] (*pl* **basses-cours**) *nf* **1.** [lieu] farmyard **2.** [volaille] : **(animaux de) ~** poultry ■ **toute la ~ était en émoi** the hens and chickens were extremely agitated.

bassement [basmɑ̃] *adv* [agir] basely, meanly ■ **question ~ intéressée, as-tu de quoi payer mon repas?** *hum* I hate to mention this, but have you got enough to pay for my meal?

Basse-Normandie [basnɔrmɑ̃di] *npr f* : **la ~** Basse-Normandie.

BASSE-NORMANDIE

This administrative region includes the *départements* of Calvados, Manche and Orne (capital: Caen).

bassesse [basɛs] *nf* **1.** [caractère vil] baseness ■ [servilité] servility **2.** [action - mesquine] base *OU* despicable act ; [- servile] servile act ■ **il ne reculera devant aucune ~** he will stoop to anything.

basset [basɛ] *nm* basset (hound).

bassin [basɛ̃] *nm* **1.** ANAT pelvis **2.** [piscine] pool ■ [plan d'eau] pond, ornamental lake **3.** [récipient] basin, bowl ■ **~ hygiénique** *OU* **de lit** bedpan **4.** GÉOGR basin ■ **~ houiller** coal basin ■ **~ sédimentaire** sedimentary basin ■ **le Bassin parisien** the Paris Basin **5.** NAUT dock.

bassinant, e [basinɑ̃, ɑ̃t] *adj fam* boring ■ **elle est vraiment ~e** she's a real pain in the neck.

bassine [basin] *nf* basin, bowl ■ **~ à confiture** preserving pan.

bassiner [3] [basine] *vt* **1.** [chauffer] to warm *(with a warming pan)* **2.** [humecter] to moisten **3.** *fam* [ennuyer] to bore ■ **tu nous bassines avec ça!** stop going on and on about it!

bassinet [basinɛ] *nm* **1.** ANAT renal pelvis **2.** HIST bascinet, basinet.

bassinoire [basinwar] *nf* **1.** [à lit] warming pan **2.** *fam* [importun] old bore, pain in the neck, crashing bore.

bassiste [basist] *nmf* **1.** [guitariste] bass guitarist **2.** [contrebassiste] double bass player.

basson [basɔ̃] *nm* **1.** [instrument] bassoon **2.** [musicien] bassoonist.

Bassora [basɔra] *npr* Basra, Basrah.

basta [basta] *interj fam* (that's) enough ■ **je la rembourse et puis ~!** I'll give her her money back and then that's it!

bastide [bastid] *nf* **1.** [maison] Provençal cottage ■ [ferme] Provençal farmhouse **2.** HIST walled town *(in southwest France).*

bastille [bastij] *nf* **1.** [fort] fortress **2.** [à Paris] : **la Bastille** [forteresse] the Bastille ; [quartier] Bastille, the Bastille area ■ **la prise de la Bastille** the storming of the Bastille ➋ **l'Opéra-Bastille** the Bastille opera house.

LA BASTILLE

The Bastille, a state prison and a symbol of *Ancien Régime* tyranny, fell to the people of Paris on 14th July 1789, marking the beginning of the Revolution. The square where the Bastille once stood is now the home of one of the Paris opera houses, known as *l'Opéra-Bastille*.

bastingage [bastɛ̃gaʒ] *nm* **1.** NAUT rail ■ **par-dessus le ~** overboard **2.** HIST bulwark.

bastion [bastjɔ̃] *nm* **1.** CONSTR bastion **2.** [d'une doctrine, d'un mouvement] bastion ■ **~ du socialisme** socialist stronghold, bastion of socialism.

baston△ [bastɔ̃] *nf* : **il y a eu de la ~** there was a bit of trouble.

bastonnade [bastɔnad] *nf* beating.

bastonner [bastɔne] *fam* ◆ **se bastonner** *vp (emploi réciproque)* to fight.

bastringue△ [bastrɛ̃g] *nm* **1.** [attirail] stuff, junk, clobber *UK* ■ **et tout le ~** and the whole bag of tricks, and all the whole shebang **2.** [bal] (sleazy) dance hall **3.** [orchestre] dance band.

bas-ventre [bavɑ̃tr] (*pl* **bas-ventres**) *nm* (lower) abdomen, pelvic area.

bat *etc v* ▷ **battre.**

bat. = **bâtiment.**

bât [ba] *nm* packsaddle ■ **cheval de ~** packhorse ■ **c'est là que** *OU* **où le ~ blesse** that's where the shoe pinches.

bataclan [bataklɑ̃] *nm fam* **et tout le ~** and the whole caboodle *OU* shebang.

bataille [bataj] *nf* **1.** [combat] battle, fight ■ **~ aérienne** [à grande échelle] air battle ; [isolée] dogfight ■ **~ aéronavale** sea-air battle ■ **~ de polochons** pillow fight ■ **~ de rue** street fight *OU* brawl ■ **~ rangée** pitched battle ■ **~ électorale** electoral contest ■ **arriver après la ~** *fig* to arrive when it's all over bar the shouting **2.** JEUX ≃ beggar-my-neighbour ■ **~ navale** battleships.
◆ **en bataille** *loc adj* **1.** MIL in battle order **2.** [en désordre] : **avoir les cheveux en ~** to have tousled hair ■ **avoir les sourcils en ~** to have bushy eyebrows, to be beetle-browed.

batailler [3] [bataje] *vi* **1.** [physiquement] to fight, to scuffle **2.** *fig* to struggle, to fight ■ **on a bataillé dur pour avoir ce contrat** we fought *OU* struggled hard to win this contract.

batailleur, euse [batajœr, øz] ◇ *adj* [agressif] quarrelsome, rowdy.
◇ *nm, f* fighter ■ **c'est un ~** [agressif] he's always spoiling *OU* ready for a fight.

bataillon [batajɔ̃] *nm* **1.** MIL battalion **2.** [foule] : **un ~ de** scores of, an army of.

bâtard, e [batar, ard] ◇ *adj* **1.** [enfant] illegitimate ■ [animal] crossbred ■ **chien ~** mongrel **2.** [genre, œuvre] hybrid ■ [solution] half-baked, ill thought-out.
◇ *nm, f* illegitimate child ■ *péj* bastard.
◆ **bâtard** *nm* [pain] *short French stick.*
◆ **bâtarde** *nf* slanting round-hand writing.

bâtardise [batardiz] *nf* illegitimacy, bastardy *péj & litt.*

batavia [batavja] *nf* batavia lettuce.

bâté, e [bate] *adj* : **âne ~** dunce, numskull.

bateau, x [bato] *nm* **1.** [navire, embarcation] boat, ship ■ **je prends le ~ à Anvers/à 10 h** I'm sailing from Antwerp/at 10 ■ **faire du ~** [en barque, en vedette] to go boating ; [en voilier] to go sailing ➋ **~ à moteur/rames** motor/rowing boat ■ **~ de pêche** fishing boat ■ **~ de plaisance** pleasure boat *OU* craft ■ **~ pneumatique** rubber boat, dinghy ■ **~ à voiles** yacht *OU* sailing boat ■ **mener** *OU* **conduire qqn en ~** *fam* to lead sb up the garden path, to take sb for a ride ■ **monter un ~ à qqn** *fam* to set sb up **2.** [charge] : **un ~ de charbon** a boatload of coal **3.** [sur le trottoir] dip (in the pavement), driveway entrance.
◆ **bateau** *adj inv* **1.** COUT : **col** *OU* **encolure ~** boat neck, bateau neckline **2.** [banal] hackneyed ■ **un sujet ~** an old chestnut.

bateau-bus [batobys] (*pl* **bateaux-bus**) *nm* riverbus ■ **prendre le~** to take the riverbus.

bateau-citerne [batositɛrn] (*pl* **bateaux-citernes**) *nm* tanker.

bateau-feu [batofø] (*pl* **bateaux-feux**) *nm* lightship.

bateau-lavoir [batolavwar] (*pl* **bateaux-lavoirs**) *nm* wash-house *(on a river).*

bateau-pilote [batopilɔt] (*pl* **bateaux-pilotes**) *nm* pilot ship *ou* boat.

bateau-pompe [batopɔ̃p] (*pl* **bateaux-pompes**) *nm* fireboat.

bateleur, euse [batlœr, øz] *nm, f* tumbler, street entertainer.

batelier, ère [batəlje, ɛr] ◇ *adj* inland waterways *(modif)*.
◇ *nm, f* [marinier] boatman (*f* boatwoman) ▪ [sur un bac] ferryman (*f* ferrywoman).

batellerie [batɛlri] *nf* **1.** [activité] inland waterways transport **2.** [flotte] inland *ou* river fleet.

bâter [3] [bate] *vt* to put a packsaddle on.

bath [bat] *adj inv fam vieilli* super, super-duper, great.

bathymètre [batimɛtr] *nm* bathometer, bathymeter.

bathyscaphe [batiskaf] *nm* bathyscaph, bathyscaphe.

bathysphère [batisfɛr] *nf* bathysphere.

bâti, e [bati] *adj* **1.** [personne] : **être bien ~** to be well-built ▪ **être ~ en force** to have a powerful build, to be powerfully built **2.** [terrain] built-up, developed.
◆ **bâti** *nm* **1.** COUT [technique] basting, tacking ▪ [fil] tacking **2.** [cadre] frame, stand ▪ **~ d'assemblage** assembly jig.

batifolage [batifɔlaʒ] *nm* **1.** [amusement] frolicking **2.** [flirt] flirting.

batifoler [3] [batifɔle] *vi* **1.** [s'amuser] to frolic **2.** [flirter] to flirt.

batik [batik] *nm* batik.

bâtiment [batimɑ̃] *nm* **1.** [édifice] building ▪ **les ~s d'exploitation** the sheds and outhouses (of a farm) **2.** [profession] : **le ~** the building trade, the construction industry ▪ **être dans le ~** to be a builder *ou* in the building trade **3.** NAUT ship, (seagoing) vessel ▪ **~ de guerre** warship ▪ **~ léger** light craft.

bâtir [32] [batir] *vt* **1.** CONSTR to build ▪ **se faire ~ une maison** to have a house built ▶ **~ (qqch) sur le sable** to build (sthg) on sand ▪ **~ des châteaux en Espagne** to build castles in the air **2.** [créer - fortune] to build up *(sép)* ; [- foyer] to build ▪ **bâtissons l'avenir ensemble** let's work together to build our future **3.** COUT to baste, to tack.
◆ **à bâtir** *loc adj* **1.** CONSTR [pierre, terrain] building *(modif)* **2.** COUT basting *(modif)*, tacking *(modif)*.

bâtisse [batis] *nf péj* building ▪ **une grande ~** a big barn of a place.

bâtisseur, euse [batisœr, øz] *nm, f* builder ▪ **~ d'empires** *fig* empire-builder.

batiste [batist] *nf* batiste, cambric.

bâton [batɔ̃] *nm* **1.** [baguette - gén] stick ; [- d'agent de police] truncheon *UK*, billy (club) *US* ; [- de berger] staff, crook ; [- de skieur] pole ▪ **~ de maréchal** *pr* marshal's baton ▪ **cette nomination, c'est son ~ de maréchal** *fig* this appointment is the high point of her career ▪ **~ de pèlerin** *pr* pilgrim's staff ▪ **être le ~ de vieillesse de qqn** to be the staff of sb's old age ▪ **mettre des ~s dans les roues à qqn** [continuellement] to impede sb's progress ; [en une occasion] to throw a spanner *UK ou* wrench *US* in the works for sb **2.** [barreau] : **~ de chaise** chair rung **3.** [de craie, de dynamite, de réglisse] stick ▪ **~ de rouge à lèvres** lipstick **4.** ÉDUC [trait] (vertical) line ▪ **faire des ~s** to draw vertical lines **5.** △ [dix mille francs] ten thousand francs ▪ **10 ~s** one hundred thousand francs.
◆ **à bâtons rompus** ◇ *loc adj* [conversation] idle.
◇ *loc adv* : **parler à ~s rompus** to make casual conversation.

bâtonnet [batɔnɛ] *nm* [petit bâton] stick ▪ **~ de manucure** orange stick.

bâtonnier, ère [batɔnje, ɛr] *nm, f* ≃ President of the Bar.

batracien [batrasjɛ̃] *nm* batrachian ▪ **les ~s** frogs and toads, batrachians *spécialiste*.

battage [bataʒ] *nm* **1.** [du blé] threshing ▪ [de l'or, d'un tapis] beating **2.** *fam* **faire du ~ autour d'un livre** to hype *ou US* to ballyhoo a book ▶ **~ médiatique** media hype.

battant, e [batɑ̃, ɑ̃t] ◇ *adj* : **porte ~e** [bruyante] banging door ; [laissée ouverte] swinging door ; [à battant libre] swing door ▪ **le cœur ~** with beating heart ▪ **sous une pluie ~e** in the driving *ou* pelting rain.
◇ *nm, f* fighter *fig* ▪ **c'est une ~e!** she's a real fighter!
◆ **battant** *nm* **1.** [d'une cloche] clapper, tongue **2.** [vantail, volet] flap ▪ **le ~ droit était ouvert** the right half (of the double door) was open.

batte [bat] *nf* **1.** SPORT bat ▪ **~ de base-ball/cricket** baseball/cricket bat **2.** CULIN : **~ à beurre** dasher **3.** [outil - maillet] mallet ; [- tapette] beater.

battement [batmɑ̃] *nm* **1.** [mouvement - des ailes] flapping ; [- des paupières] flutter ▪ **~ de mains** clapping, applause **2.** SPORT : **~ des jambes** leg movement **3.** [d'une porte] banging, beating ▪ **des ~s de tambour** drumbeats **4.** [rythme du cœur, du pouls] beating, throbbing, beat ▪ **je sens les ~s de son cœur** I can feel her heart beating ▶ **j'ai des ~s de cœur** [palpitations] I suffer from palpitations ; [émotion] my heart's beating *ou* pounding **5.** [pause] break ▪ **un ~ de 10 minutes** a 10-minute break ▌[attente] wait ▪ **j'ai une heure de ~ entre la réunion et le déjeuner** I have an hour between the meeting and lunch.

batterie [batri] *nf* **1.** MIL battery ▶ **~ antichars** antitank battery **2.** AUTO, ÉLECTR & PHYS battery ▪ **~ d'accumulateurs** battery of accumulators ▪ **~ de cellules solaires** solar-powered battery ▪ **recharger** *ou* **regonfler ses ~s** *fig* to recharge one's batteries **3.** MUS [en jazz, rock, pop] drums, drum kit ▪ [en musique classique] percussion instruments ▪ [roulement] drum roll ▪ **Harvey Barton à la ~** Harvey Barton on drums **4.** [série] battery ▪ **~ de piles** batteries ▪ **~ de tests/mesures** battery of tests/of measures ▶ **~ de cuisine** *pr* set of kitchen utensils ▪ **les officiers avec leur ~ de cuisine** *hum* the officers with all their gongs *UK ou* decorations **5.** AGRIC : **poulet de ~** battery hen, ▻ **élevage**, ▻ **élever 6.** DANSE batterie.

batteur [batœr] *nm* **1.** MUS drummer **2.** [appareil] : **~ (à œufs)** egg beater *ou* whisk **3.** [ouvrier] beater ▪ AGRIC thresher **4.** [au cricket] batsman ▪ [au base-ball] batter.

batteuse [batøz] *nf* AGRIC thresher, threshing machine.

battoir [batwar] *nm* [pour laver] beetle, battledore.
◆ **battoirs** *nmpl fam* (great) paws, mitts.

battre [83] [batr] ◇ *vt* **1.** [brutaliser - animal] to beat ; [- personne] to batter ▪ **~ qqn à mort** to batter sb to death ▶ **~ en brèche** [mur] to breach ; [gouvernement] to topple ; [politique] to drive a coach and horses through *UK*, to demolish ▪ **~ qqn comme plâtre** to beat sb severely
2. [vaincre - adversaire] to beat, to defeat ▪ **~ qqn aux échecs** to defeat *ou* to beat sb at chess ▪ **se tenir pour** *ou* **s'avouer battu** to admit defeat ▶ **~ qqn à plate couture** *ou* **plates coutures** to beat sb hollow
3. [surpasser - record] to beat ▪ **~ tous les records** *pr* & *fig* to set a new record ▪ **j'ai battu tous les records de vitesse pour venir ici** I must have broken the record getting here
4. [frapper - tapis, or] to beat (out) ; [- blé, grain] to thresh ▪ **~ qqch à froid** to cold-hammer sthg ▶ **~ froid à qqn** to cold-shoulder sb ▪ **~ la semelle** to stamp one's feet *(to keep warm)* ▪ **~ monnaie** to mint (coins) ▪ **il faut ~ le fer quand il est chaud** *prov* strike while the iron is hot *prov*
5. [remuer - beurre] to churn ; [- blanc d'œuf] to beat *ou* to whip (up), to whisk ▪ **~ l'air de ses bras** *fig* to beat the air with one's arms
6. [sillonner] : **~ le secteur** to scour *ou* to comb the area ▪ **~ les buissons** CHASSE to beat the bushes ▶ **~ la campagne** *ou* **le pays** *pr* to comb the countryside ; *fig* to be in one's own little world
7. JEUX : **~ les cartes** to shuffle the cards *ou* pack
8. MUS [mesure] to beat (out) ▪ MIL & MUS [tambour] to beat (on) ▪ **~ la générale** to sound the call to arms ▪ **~ le rappel** to drum up troops ▪ **~ le rappel de la famille/du parti** *fig* to gather the family/party round ▶ **~ (le) tambour** *ou* **la grosse caisse** *fam* to make a lot of noise ▪ **mon cœur bat la breloque** I've got a bad heart ▪ **mon cœur bat la chamade** my heart's racing
9. NAUT : **~ pavillon** to sail under *ou* to fly a flag
10. *loc* **~ son plein** [fête] to be in full swing.

◇ *vi* **1.** [cœur, pouls] to beat, to throb ■ [pluie] to lash, to beat down ■ [porte] to rattle, to bang ■ [store] to flap ■ **l'émotion faisait ~ mon cœur** my heart was beating *ou* racing with emotion
2. *loc* **~ en retraite** *pr* to retreat ; *fig* to beat a retreat.
◆ **battre de** *v+prép* : **~ des mains** to clap one's hands ■ **l'oiseau bat des ailes** *pr* [lentement] the bird flaps its wings ; [rapidement] the bird flutters its wings ▶ **~ de l'aile** to be in a bad way.
◆ **se battre** ◇ *vp (emploi réciproque)* to fight, to fight (with) one another ■ **se ~ à mains nues** to fight with one's bare hands ■ **se ~ à l'épée/au couteau** to fight with swords/knives ■ **se ~ en duel** to fight (each other in) a duel ■ **ne vous battez pas, il y en a pour tout le monde** *fig* don't get excited, there's enough for everyone ■ **surtout ne vous battez pas pour m'aider!** *iron* don't all rush to help me! ▶ **se ~ comme des chiffonniers** to fight like cats and dogs.
◇ *vpi* **1.** [lutter] to fight ■ **se ~ avec/contre qqn** to fight with/against sb ▶ **se ~ contre des moulins à vent** to tilt at windmills
2. *fig* to fight, to struggle ■ **je me suis battu pour qu'il accepte** I had a tough time getting him to accept ■ **nous nous battons pour la paix/contre l'injustice** we're fighting for peace/against injustice.
◇ *vpt* [frapper] : **se ~ les flancs** to struggle pointlessly.

battu, e [baty] *adj* **1.** [maltraité] battered **2.** [vaincu] beaten, defeated ■ **on est ~s d'avance** we've got no chance **3.** [or, fer] beaten.

battue [baty] *nf* **1.** CHASSE battue, beat **2.** [recherche] search *(through an area)*.

batture [batyr] *nf Québec* sand bar.

baud [bo] *nm* baud.

baudelairien, enne [bodlɛrjɛ̃, ɛn] *adj* of Baudelaire, Baudelairean.

baudet [bodɛ] *nm* [âne] donkey, ass.

baudrier [bodrije] *nm* **1.** [bandoulière] baldric **2.** SPORT harness.

baudroie [bodrwa] *nf* monkfish.

baudruche [bodryʃ] *nf* **1.** [peau] goldbeater's skin **2.** *fam* [personne] windbag.

bauge [boʒ] *nf* **1.** [du cochon, du sanglier] wallow **2.** [lieu sale] pigsty.

baume [bom] *nm* balsam, balm ■ **~ de benjoin** friar's balsam ■ **~ démêlant** hair conditioner ■ **~ du Pérou** Peru balsam, balsam of Peru ■ **~ du tigre** tiger balm ■ **mettre un peu de ~ au cœur de qqn** *fig* to soothe sb's aching heart.

baux [bo] *pl* COMM ▷ **bail.**

bauxite [boksit] *nf* bauxite.

bavard, e [bavar, ard] ◇ *adj* [personne] talkative ■ [roman, émission] wordy, long-winded ■ **elle n'était pas bien ~e ce soir** she hardly said a word *ou* she wasn't in a talkative mood tonight ▶ **il est ~ comme une pie** he's a real chatterbox.
◇ *nm, f* : **quelle ~e celle-là!** she's a real chatterbox! ■ **les ~s, on leur règle leur compte!** [délateurs] we know how to deal with informers!

bavardage [bavardaʒ] *nm* **1.** chatting, chattering ■ **puni pour ~** ÉDUC punished for talking in class **2.** INFORM chat.
◆ **bavardages** *nmpl* [conversation] chatter *(U)* ■ *péj* [racontars] gossip *(U)*.

bavarder [3] [bavarde] *vi* **1.** [parler] to chat, to talk ■ **~ avec qqn** to (have a) chat with sb ■ **on bavardait des heures au téléphone** we used to talk for hours on the phone **2.** *péj* [médire] to gossip.

bavarois, e [bavarwa, az] *adj* Bavarian.
◆ **bavaroise** *nf* CULIN Bavarian cream.

bavasser [3] [bavase] *vi fam péj* to natter, to yak.

bave [bav] *nf* [d'un bébé] dribble ■ [d'un chien] slobber, slaver ■ [d'un malade] foam, froth ■ [d'un escargot] slime ■ **la ~ du crapaud n'atteint pas la blanche colombe** *prov* sticks and stones may break my bones, but names will never hurt me.

baver [3] [bave] *vi* **1.** [bébé] to dribble, to drool, to slobber ■ [chien] to slaver, to slobber ■ [malade] to foam *ou* to froth at the mouth ■ **j'avais des bottes neuves, tous les copains en bavaient!** *fam fig* I had a pair of brand new boots, all my friends were green (with envy)! ■ **~ d'admiration devant qqn** to worship the ground sb walks on **2.** *fam loc* **en ~** [souffrir] to have a rough *ou* hard time of it ■ **on va t'en faire ~ à l'armée** they'll make you sweat blood *ou* they'll put you through it in the army ■ **en ~ des ronds de chapeau** [être étonné] to have eyes like saucers ; [souffrir] to go through the mill, to have a rough time of it **3.** [encre, stylo] to leak.

baveux, euse [bavø, øz] *adj* [bouche] drooling ■ [baiser] wet ■ [omelette] runny.

Bavière [bavjɛr] *npr f* : **(la) ~** Bavaria.

bavoir [bavwar] *nm* bib.

bavure [bavyr] *nf* **1.** IMPR smudge, ink stain **2.** INDUST burr **3.** [erreur] flaw, mistake ■ **un spectacle sans ~** a faultless *ou* flawless show ▶ **~ (policière)** police error ■ **il y a eu une ~** the police have made a serious blunder.

bayadère [bajadɛr] ◇ *nf* [danseuse] bayadere.
◇ *adj* [rayé] bayadere *(modif)*, striped.

bayer [3] [baje] *vi* : **~ aux corneilles** *pr* to stand gaping ; [être inactif] to stargaze.

bayou [baju] *nm* bayou.

bazar [bazar] *nm* **1.** [souk] bazaar, bazar ■ [magasin] general store, dime store *US* **2.** *fam* [désordre] clutter, shambles *(sing)* ■ **quel ~, cette chambre!** what a shambles *ou* mess this room is! **3.** *fam* [attirail] stuff, junk, clobber *UK* ■ **et tout le ~!** and (all that) stuff!
◆ **de bazar** *loc adj péj* [psychologie, politique] half-baked, two-bit *US (avant n)*.

bazarder [3] [bazarde] *vt fam* [jeter] to dump, to chuck (out).

bazooka [bazuka] *nm* bazooka.

BCBG (*abr de* **bon chic bon genre**) *adj inv term used to describe an upper-class lifestyle reflected especially in expensive but conservative clothes* ■ **elle est très ~** ≃ she's really sloany *fam UK* ■ **il est très ~** ≃ he's a real preppie type *fam US*.

BCE (*abr de* **Banque centrale européenne**) *nm* ECB.

BCG® (*abr de* **bacille Calmette-Guérin**) *nm* BCG.

bcp = **beaucoup.**

bd = **boulevard.**

BD *nf* = **bande dessinée.**

BD

A common abbreviation for *bande dessinée* or comic book. Considered a serious and important art form in France, the comic book has become popular among teenagers and intellectuals alike. An annual festival of comic book art is held in Angoulême.

bdc (*abr écrite de* **bas de casse**) lc.

beach-volley [bitʃvolɛ] (*pl* **beach-volleys**) *nm* beach volleyball ■ **jouer au ~** to play beach volleyball.

beagle [bigœl] *nm* beagle.

béant, e [beɑ̃, ɑ̃t] *adj* [gouffre] gaping, yawning ■ [plaie] gaping, open ■ **~ d'étonnement** gaping in surprise.

béarnais, e [bearnɛ, ɛz] *adj* from the Béarn.
◆ **Béarnais, e** *nmf sing inhabitant of or person from the Béarn.*
◆ **béarnaise** *nf* CULIN : **(sauce à la) ~e** béarnaise sauce.

béat, e [bea, at] *adj* [heureux] blissfully happy ■ *péj* [niais - air, sourire] vacuous ; [- optimisme] smug ; [- admiration] blind ■ **être ~ d'admiration** to be open-mouthed *ou* agape *litt* with admiration.

béatement [beatmɑ̃] *adv péj* [idiotement] : **il la regardait ~** he looked at her with a blissfully stupid expression.

béatification [beatifikasjɔ̃] *nf* beatification.

béatifier [9] [beatifje] *vt* to beatify.

béatitude [beatityd] *nf* **1.** RELIG beatitude ▪ **les ~s** the Beatitudes **2.** [bonheur] bliss, beatitude *litt.*

beatnik [bitnik] *nmf* beatnik ▪ **les ~s** the Beat Generation.

beau [bo] *(devant nm commençant par voyelle ou 'h' muet* **bel** [bɛl]*)* *(f* **belle** [bɛl], *mpl* **beaux** [bo], *fpl* **belles** [bɛl]*) adj*

A.

1. [bien fait, joli - femme] beautiful, good-looking ; [- homme] good-looking, handsome ; [- enfant, physique, objet, décor] beautiful, lovely ▪ **il est ~ garçon** *ou fam* **gosse** he's good-looking, he's a good-looking guy ▪ **ils forment un ~ couple** they make a lovely couple ▪ **se faire ~/belle** to get dressed up, to do o.s. up ▪ **ce n'était pas ~ à voir** *fam* it wasn't a pretty sight ▸ **il est ~ comme l'amour** *ou* **un ange** *ou* **un astre** *ou* **le jour** [homme] he's a very handsome *ou* good-looking man ; [petit garçon] he's a very handsome *ou* good-looking boy ▪ **il est ~ comme un dieu** he looks like a Greek god ▪ **elle est belle comme un ange** *ou* **le jour** she's a real beauty ▪ **sois belle et tais-toi!** *fam* just concentrate on looking pretty!
2. [attrayant pour l'oreille - chant, mélodie, voix] beautiful, lovely
3. [remarquable, réussi - poème, texte] fine, beautiful ; [- chanson, film] beautiful, lovely ▪ **de ~x vêtements** fine clothes ▪ **le boucher a de la belle marchandise** the butcher's got nice meat ▪ **il y a eu quelques ~x échanges** there were a few good *ou* fine rallies ▪ **nous avons fait un ~ voyage** we had a wonderful trip
4. MÉTÉOR fine, beautiful ▪ **la mer sera belle** the sea will be calm ▪ **temps froid mais ~ sur tout le pays** the whole country will enjoy cold but sunny weather ▪ **du ~ temps** nice *ou* good weather ▪ **les derniers ~x jours** the last days of summer

B.

1. [digne] noble, fine ▪ **une belle âme** a noble nature ▮ [convenable] nice ▪ **ce n'est pas ~ de mentir!** it's very naughty *ou* it's not nice to lie!
2. [brillant intellectuellement] wonderful, fine ▪ **c'est un ~ sujet de thèse** it's a fine topic for a thesis
3. [d'un haut niveau social] smart ▪ **faire un ~ mariage** [argent] to marry into money *ou* a fortune ; [classe] to marry into a very good family ▸ **le ~ monde** *ou fam* **linge** the upper crust, the smart set

C.

1. [gros, important - gains, prime, somme] nice, handsome, tidy ▪ **donnez-moi un ~ melon/poulet** give me a nice big melon/chicken ▪ **il a un bel appétit** he has a good *ou* hearty appetite ▪ **un ~ coup en Bourse** a spectacular deal on the Stock Exchange
2. [en intensif] : **je me suis fait une belle bosse** I got a great big bump ▪ **il y a eu un ~ scandale** there was a huge scandal ▪ **un bel hypocrite** a real hypocrite ▸ **il y a ~ temps : il y a ~ temps de ce que je te dis là** *fam* what I'm telling you now happened ages ago
3. [agréable] good ▪ **présenter qqch sous un ~ jour** to show sthg in a good light ▪ **c'est trop ~ pour être vrai** it's too good to be true ▪ **c'est ~ l'amour!** love's a wonderful thing!
4. [prospère] good ▪ **tu as encore de belles années devant toi** you still have quite a few good years ahead of you ▪ **avoir une belle situation** [argent] to have a very well-paid job ; [prestige] to have a high-flying job
5. [dans des appellations] : **venez, ma belle amie** do come along, darling ▪ **alors, (ma) belle enfant, qu'en dis-tu?** *fam* what do you think about that, my dear? ▪ **mon ~ monsieur, personne ne vous a rien demandé!** my friend, this is none of your business!
6. [certain] : **un ~ jour/matin** one fine day/morning

D.

iron **belle demande!** [saugrenue] what a question! ▪ **c'est du ~ travail!** a fine mess this is! ▪ **~x discours : ils ont oublié tous leurs ~x discours** they've forgotten all their fine *ou* fine-sounding words ▪ **garde tes belles promesses** *ou* **tes ~x serments!** you can keep your promises! ▸ **j'en ai appris** *ou* **entendu de belles sur toi!** I heard some fine *ou* right things about you! ▪ **il en a fait de belles quand il était petit!** he didn't half get up to some mischief when he was little! ▪ **nous voilà ~x!** we're in a fine mess now! ▪ **c'est bien ~ tout ça, mais...** that's all very fine *ou* well, but... ▪ **le plus ~** *fam* : **et tu ne sais pas le plus ~!** and you haven't heard the best part (yet)!, and the best part's still to come!

◆ **beau** ◇ *adv* **1.** MÉTÉOR : **il fait ~** the weather's *ou* it's fine ▪ **il fera ~ et chaud** it'll be warm and sunny ▪ **il n'a pas fait très ~ l'été dernier** the weather wasn't very nice *ou* good last summer **2.** *loc* **il ferait ~ voir qu'elle me donne des ordres!** her, boss me around? that'll be the day! ▸ **avoir ~ faire (qqch) : j'avais ~ tirer, la porte ne s'ouvrait pas** however hard I pulled, the door wouldn't open ▪ **j'ai eu ~ le lui répéter plusieurs fois, il n'a toujours pas compris** I have told him and told him but he still hasn't understood ▪ **on a ~ dire, on a ~ faire, les jeunes s'en vont un jour de la maison** *fam* whatever you do or say, young people eventually leave home ▪ **vous avez ~ dire, elle a quand même tout financé elle-même** say what you like *ou* you may criticize, but she's paid for it all herself ▪ **a ~ mentir qui vient de loin** *prov it's easy to lie when there's nobody around to contradict you* ▪ **tout ~ : alors, vous signez? – hé, tout ~ (tout ~)!** you will sign then? – hey, steady on *ou* not so fast!
◇ *nm* **1.** [esthétique] : **elle aime le ~** she likes beautiful things ▮ [objets de qualité] : **pour les meubles du salon, je veux du ~** I want really good *ou* nice furniture for the living room **2.** [homme] beau, dandy **3.** *loc* **au ~ : le temps est au ~** the weather looks fine ▪ **au ~ fixe : le temps/baromètre est au ~ fixe** the weather/barometer is set fair ▪ **nos relations sont au ~ fixe** *fam* things between us are looking rosy ▪ **il a le moral au ~ fixe** *fam* he's in high spirits ▪ **c'est du ~!** *fam* : **elle a dit un gros mot – c'est du ~!** she said a rude word! – how naughty! ▪ **faire le ~** [chien] to sit up and beg.

◆ **belle** *nf* **1.** [jolie femme] beauty ▪ [dame] lady ▪ **'la Belle et la Bête'** *Madame Leprince de Beaumont, Cocteau* 'Beauty and the Beast' ▪ **'la Belle au bois dormant'** *Perrault* 'Sleeping Beauty' **2.** *fam* [en appellatif] : **tu te trompes, ma belle!** you're quite wrong my dear! **3.** *hum & litt* [amie, amante] lady friend, beloved **4.** SPORT decider, deciding match ▪ JEUX decider, deciding game **5.** *fam loc* **(se) faire la belle** to do a runner *UK*, to cut and run *US*.

◆ **au plus beau de** *loc prép* : **au plus ~ de la fête** when the party was in full swing ▪ **au plus ~ du discours** right in the middle of the speech.

◆ **bel et bien** *loc adv* well and truly ▪ **elle s'est bel et bien échappée** she got away and no mistake.

◆ **bel et bon, bel et bonne** *loc adj* fine.

◆ **de plus belle** *loc adv* [aboyer, crier] louder than ever, even louder ▪ [frapper] harder than ever, even harder ▪ [taquiner, manger] more than ever, even more ▪ **il s'est mis à travailler de plus belle** he went back to work with renewed energy.

◆ **belle de Fontenay** *nf* Belle de Fontenay potato.

◆ **belle page** *nf* IMPR right-hand page ▪ **chaque chapitre commence en belle page** each chapter starts on the right-hand page.

Beaubourg [bobur] *npr name commonly used to refer to the Pompidou Centre.*

BEAUBOURG

This term officially refers to the area surrounding the Pompidou Centre but it has come to mean the museum itself. The very unusual design of the *Centre national d'art et de culture Georges Pompidou* was the subject of much controversy when it was built in 1977, but today it is the second most visited building in France. It houses a modern art gallery, a cinema, an open-stack library and other cultural exhibits.

beauceron, onne [bosrɔ̃, ɔn] *adj* from the Beauce area.
◆ **Beauceron, onne** *nm, f inhabitant of or person from the Beauce area.*

beaucoup [boku] *adv* **1.** [modifiant un verbe] a lot, a great deal ▪ [dans des phrases interrogatives ou négatives] much, a lot, a great deal ▪ **il travaille ~** he works a lot *ou* a great deal ▪ **je ne l'ai pas ~ vu** I didn't see much of him ▪ **je vous remercie ~** thank you very much (indeed) ▪ **ils ne s'apprécient pas ~** they don't like each other much **2.** [modifiant un adverbe] much, a lot ▪ **~ moins intéressant** much *ou* a lot less interesting ▪ **~ trop fort** much *ou* far too loud ▪ **il parle ~ trop** he talks far too much ▸ **en faire ~ trop** to overdo it **3.** [de nombreuses personnes] many, a lot ▪ [de nombreuses choses] a lot ▪ **il n'y en a pas ~ qui réussissent** not a lot of people *ou* not many succeed ▪ **nous étions ~ à le croire** many *ou* a lot of us believed it ➋ **c'est déjà ~ qu'il y soit allé!** at least he went! ▪ **il est pour ~ dans son succès** he played a large part in *ou* he had a great deal to do with her success ▪ **c'est ~ dire** that's a bit of an overstatement **4.** [modifiant un adjectif] : **imprudent, il l'est même ~** he's really quite careless.

◆ **beaucoup de** *loc dét* [suivi d'un nom comptable] many, a lot of ▪ [suivi d'un nom non comptable] much, a lot of, a great deal of ▪ **~ de monde** a lot of people ▪ **~ d'entre nous** many *ou* a lot of us ▪ **elle a ~ de goût** she has a lot of *ou* a great deal of taste ▪ **il ne nous reste plus ~ de temps** we've not got much time left ▪ **il y en a ~** there is/are a lot.

◆ **de beaucoup** *loc adv* **1.** [avec un comparatif ou un superlatif] by far ▪ **elle est de ~ la plus douée** she's the most talented by far, she is by far the most talented ▪ **il est mon aîné de ~** he's considerably older than I am **2.** [avec un verbe] : **il a gagné de ~** he won easily ▪ **il te dépasse de ~** he's far *ou* much taller than you ▪ **je préférerais de ~ rester** I'd much rather stay ▪ **as-tu raté ton train de ~?** did you miss your train by much? ▪ **je la préfère, et de ~** I much prefer her.

beauf△ [bof] *nm* **1.** [beau-frère] brother-in-law **2.** *péj* & *fig* *archetypal lower-middle-class Frenchman.*

beau-fils [bofis] (*pl* **beaux-fils**) *nm* **1.** [gendre] son-in-law **2.** [fils du conjoint] stepson.

beaufort [bofɔr] *nm* Beaufort cheese.

Beaufort [bofɔr] *npr* : **l'échelle de ~** the Beaufort scale.

beau-frère [bofrɛr] (*pl* **beaux-frères**) *nm* brother-in-law.

beaujolais [boʒɔlɛ] *nm* beaujolais (wine).

Beaujolais [boʒɔlɛ] *npr m* : **le ~** (the) Beaujolais (region).

beau-père [bopɛr] (*pl* **beaux-pères**) *nm* **1.** [père du conjoint] father-in-law **2.** [époux de la mère] stepfather.

beaupré [bopre] *nm* bowsprit.

beauté [bote] *nf* **1.** [d'une femme, d'une statue] beauty, loveliness ▪ [d'un homme] handsomeness ▪ **avoir la ~ du diable** to have a youthful glow **2.** [femme] beauty, beautiful woman ▪ **je vous offre un verre, ~?** can I get you a drink, darling? **3.** [élévation - de l'âme] beauty ; [- d'un raisonnement] beauty, elegance ▪ **pour la ~ du geste** *ou* **de la chose** for the beauty of it.

◆ **beautés** *nfpl* [d'un paysage] beauties, beauty spots ▪ [d'une œuvre] beauties.

◆ **de beauté** *loc adj* [concours, reine] beauty *(modif).*

◆ **de toute beauté** *loc adj* magnificent, stunningly beautiful.

◆ **en beauté** *loc adv* : **être en ~** to look stunning ▪ **finir en ~** to end with a flourish *ou* on a high note.

Beauvau [bovo] *npr* : **la place ~** *square in Paris where the Ministry of the Interior is situated.*

beaux-arts [bozar] *nmpl* **1.** [genre] fine arts ▪ **musée des Beaux-Arts** museum of fine art **2.** [école] : **les Beaux-Arts** *French national art school.*

beaux-parents [boparɑ̃] *nmpl* father-in-law and mother-in-law, in-laws.

bébé [bebe] <> *nm* **1.** [nourrisson] baby ▪ **attendre un ~** to be expecting a baby ▪ **faire le ~** *péj* to act like *ou* to be being a baby **2.** ZOOL baby ▪ **la lionne s'occupe de ses ~s** the lioness looks after her babies *ou* young *ou* cubs.

<> *adj inv péj* babyish *péj*, baby-like ▪ **elle est restée ~** she's still very much a baby.

◆ **bébé-éprouvette** *nm* test-tube baby.

bébé-bulle [bebebyl] (*pl* **bébés-bulles**) *nm* bubble baby.

bébête [bebɛt] *adj* silly ▪ **le Bébête Show** *satirical television puppet show in which French political figures were represented as animals.*

be-bop [bibɔp] *nm* bebop.

bec [bɛk] *nm* **1.** ZOOL beak, bill ▪ **donner des coups de ~ à** to peck (at) ▪ **nez en ~ d'aigle** hook nose ➋ **avoir ~ et ongles** to be well-equipped and ready to fight **2.** *fam* [bouche] mouth ▪ **ouvre le ~!** [en nourrissant un enfant] open wide! ▪ **ça lui a bouclé** *ou* **cloué** *ou* **clos le ~** it shut him up, it reduced him to silence ▪ **avoir toujours la cigarette/pipe au ~** to have a cigarette/pipe always stuck in one's mouth ➋ **être** *ou* **rester le ~ dans l'eau** to be left high and dry **3.** [d'une plume] nib **4.** [de casserole] lip ▪ [de bouilloire, de théière] spout **5.** MUS [de saxophone, de clarinette] mouthpiece **6.** GÉOGR bill, headland **7.** *fam Belgique, Suisse* & *Québec* [baiser] kiss **8.** [vêtement] : **faire un ~** to pucker **9.** *fam loc* **tomber sur un ~** to run into *ou* to hit a snag.

◆ **bec à gaz** *nm* gas burner.

◆ **bec de gaz** *nm* lamppost, gaslight.

◆ **bec fin** *nm* gourmet.

bécane [bekan] *nf fam* **1.** [moto, vélo] bike **2.** *hum* [machine] : **ma ~** [ordinateur] my micro ; [machine à écrire] my old typewriter.

bécarre [bekar] <> *adj* : **la ~** A natural.

<> *nm* natural sign.

bécasse [bekas] *nf* **1.** [oiseau] woodcock **2.** *fam* [sotte] twit *UK*, silly goose.

bécassine [bekasin] *nf* **1.** [oiseau] snipe **2.** *fam* [sotte] silly goose, nincompoop, ninny.

Bécassine [bekasin] *npr early cartoon character representing a naive but optimistic Breton housekeeper.*

bec-de-cane [bɛkdəkan] (*pl* **becs-de-cane**) *nm* **1.** [poignée] door handle **2.** [serrure] spring lock.

bec-de-lièvre [bɛkdəljɛvr] (*pl* **becs-de-lièvre**) *nm* harelip.

bec-de-perroquet [bɛkdəperɔkɛ] (*pl* **becs-de-perroquet**) *nm* osteophyte.

béchamel [beʃamɛl] *nf* : **(sauce) ~** white sauce, béchamel.

bêche [bɛʃ] *nf* spade.

bêcher [4] [beʃe] <> *vt* **1.** [sol] to dig (over) ▪ [pommes de terre] to dig (up *ou* out) **2.** *fam* [critiquer] to run down *(sép)*, to pull apart *ou* to pieces.

<> *vi* [faire le snob] to put on airs.

bêcheur, euse [bɛʃœr, øz] *nm, f fam* **1.** [critique] detractor **2.** *péj* [prétentieux] stuck-up person, snooty person.

bécot [beko] *nm fam* [bise] kiss, peck ▪ **gros ~** smacker.

bécoter [3] [bekɔte] *vt fam* to kiss.

◆ **se bécoter** *vp (emploi réciproque) fam* to smooch, to kiss (and cuddle).

becquée [beke] *nf* beakful ▪ **donner la ~** [oiseau] to feed.

becquerel [bɛkrɛl] *nm* becquerel.

becquet [bekɛ] *nm* **1.** AUTO spoiler **2.** [papier] slip *(of paper, to show the position of a query or addition in copy prepared for print)* **3.** THÉÂTRE *change made to a play by its author during rehearsals.*

becqueter [27] [bɛkte] *vt* **1.** [picoter] to peck (at) **2.** △ [manger] to eat ▪ **il n'y avait rien à ~** there was no grub.

bectance△ [bɛktɑ̃s] *nf* grub, nosh *UK*, chowder *US*.

becter [4] [bɛkte] = **becqueter** *(sens 2).*

bedaine [bədɛn] *nf* paunch ▪ **il a pris de la ~** he's developed a paunch *ou* a pot belly.

bédé [bede] *nf fam* **la ~** strip cartoons ▪ **une ~** a strip cartoon.

bedeau, x [bədo] *nm* beadle, verger.

bédéiste [bedeist] *nmf* comic strip artist.

bédéphile [bedefil] *nmf* comics fan.

bedon [bədɔ̃] *nm vieilli* [d'enfant] tummy ▪ [d'obèse] paunch.

bedonnant, e [bədɔnɑ̃, ɑ̃t] *adj* paunchy.

bedonner [3] [bədɔne] *vi* to get paunchy.

bédouin, e [bedwɛ̃, in] *adj* Bedouin, Beduin.

◆ **Bédouin, e** *nm, f* Bedouin, Beduin.

bée [be] *adj f* : **être bouche ~ devant qqn** to gape at sb ▪ **j'en suis restée bouche ~** I was flabbergasted.
beefsteak [biftɛk] = **bifteck.**
beeper [bipe] *vt* to beep.
béer [15] [bee] *vi* to be wide open ▪ **~ d'admiration** to gape with *ou* to be lost in admiration.
Beethoven [betɔvɛn] *npr* Beethoven.
beffroi [befrwa] *nm* belfry.
bégaie *etc v* ▻ **bégayer.**
bégaiement [begɛmɑ̃] *nm* [trouble de la parole] stammer, stutter ▪ **~s** [d'un bègue] stammering, stuttering ; [d'embarras, d'émotion] faltering ▪ **les premiers ~s d'une industrie nouvelle** *fig* the first hesitant steps of a new industry.
bégayer [11] [begeje] ◇ *vi* [hésiter - bègue] to stammer, to stutter ; [- ivrogne] to slur (one's speech) ▪ **la colère la faisait ~** she was so angry she was stammering.
◇ *vt* to stammer (out).
bégonia [begɔnja] *nm* begonia.
bègue [bɛg] ◇ *adj* stammering, stuttering ▪ **être ~** to (have a) stammer.
◇ *nmf* stammerer, stutterer.
bégueule [begœl] *fam* ◇ *adj* prudish, squeamish ▪ **elle n'est pas ~** she's no prude.
◇ *nf* prude.
béguin [begɛ̃] *nm* **1.** *fam* [attirance] : **avoir le ~ pour qqn** to have a crush on sb **2.** *fam* [amoureux] crush **3.** [coiffe] bonnet.
béhaviorisme [beavjɔrism] *nm* behaviourism.
béhavioriste [beavjɔrist] *adj* & *nmf* behaviourist.
Behring [beriŋ] = **Béring.**
beige [bɛʒ] *adj* & *nm* beige.
beigeasse [bɛʒas], **beigeâtre** [bɛʒatr] *adj péj* yellowish *ou* greyish beige.
beigne [bɛɲ] ◇ *nf*△ [gifle] slap, clout ▪ **filer une ~ à qqn** to slap sb, to give sb a smack.
◇ *nm Québec* [beignet] doughnut.
beignerie [bɛɲəri] *nf Québec snack bar serving doughnuts.*
beignet [bɛɲɛ] *nm* [gén] fritter ▪ [au sucre, à la confiture] doughnut ▪ **~ aux pommes** apple doughnut.
Beijing [bɛjʒiŋ] *npr* Beijing.
bel [bɛl] ◇ *adj* ▻ **beau.**
◇ *nm* ACOUST bel.
bêlant, e [bɛlɑ̃, ɑ̃t] *adj* **1.** [mouton] bleating **2.** [chevrotant - voix] bleating, shaky.
Bélarus [belarys] *npr* : **la république de ~** the Republic of Belarus.
bel canto [bɛlkɑ̃to] *nm* bel canto.
bêlement [bɛlmɑ̃] *nm* bleat ▪ **les ~s des moutons** the bleating of the sheep.
bêler [4] [bele] ◇ *vi* to bleat.
◇ *vt* [chanson] to bleat out *(sép).*
belette [bəlɛt] *nf* weasel.
belge [bɛlʒ] *adj* Belgian.
◆ **Belge** *nmf* Belgian.
belgicisme [bɛlʒisism] *nm* [mot] Belgian-French word ▪ [tournure] Belgian-French expression.
Belgique [bɛlʒik] *npr f* : **(la) ~** Belgium.
Belgrade [bɛlgrad] *npr* Belgrade.
bélier [belje] *nm* **1.** ZOOL ram **2.** TECHNOL hydraulic ram **3.** HIST battering ram.
Bélier [belje] *npr m* **1.** ASTRON Aries **2.** ASTROL Aries ▪ **je suis ~** I'm Aries *ou* an Arian.
Belize [beliz] *npr m* : **le ~** Belize ▪ **au ~** in Belize.
belladone [beladɔn] *nf* belladonna, deadly nightshade.
bellâtre [bɛlatr] *nm péj* fop.
belle [bɛl] *f* ▻ **beau.**
belle-de-jour [bɛldəʒur] *(pl* **belles-de-jour)** *nf* convolvulus, morning-glory.
belle-de-nuit [bɛldənɥi] *(pl* **belles-de-nuit)** *nf* **1.** BOT marvel-of-Peru, four-o'clock **2.** [prostituée] lady of the night.
belle-doche△ [bɛldɔʃ] *(pl* **belles-doches)** *nf* mother-in-law.
belle-famille [bɛlfamij] *(pl* **belles-familles)** *nf* : **sa ~** [de l'époux] her husband's family, her in-laws ; [de l'épouse] his wife's family, his in-laws.
belle-fille [bɛlfij] *(pl* **belles-filles)** *nf* **1.** [bru] daughter-in-law **2.** [fille du conjoint] stepdaughter.
bellement [bɛlmɑ̃] *adv* **1.** [joliment] nicely, finely **2.** [vraiment] well and truly, in no uncertain manner.
belle-mère [bɛlmɛr] *(pl* **belles-mères)** *nf* **1.** [mère du conjoint] mother-in-law **2.** [épouse du père] stepmother.
belles-lettres [bɛllɛtr] *nfpl* : **les ~** great literature, belles-lettres *sout.*
belle-sœur [bɛlsœr] *(pl* **belles-sœurs)** *nf* sister-in-law.
Belleville [bɛlvil] *npr area of Paris with a large immigrant population.*
belliciste [belisist] ◇ *adj* bellicose *sout*, warmongering.
◇ *nmf* warmonger.
belligérance [beliʒerɑ̃s] *nf* belligerence, belligerency.
belligérant, e [beliʒerɑ̃, ɑ̃t] ◇ *adj* belligerent, warring.
◇ *nm, f* belligerent ▪ **les ~s n'étaient que trois** there were only three warring parties.
belliqueux, euse [belikø, øz] *adj* [peuple] warlike ▪ [ton, discours] aggressive, belligerent ▪ [enfant, humeur] bellicose *sout*, quarrelsome.
belote [bəlɔt] *nf* belote ▪ **faire une ~** to play a game of belote.
belvédère [bɛlvedɛr] *nm* [pavillon] belvedere, gazebo ▪ [terrasse] panoramic viewpoint.
Belzébuth [bɛlzebyt] *npr* Beelzebub.
bémol [bemɔl] ◇ *adj* : **mi ~** E flat.
◇ *nm* flat ▪ **mettre un ~** [parler moins fort] to pipe down ; [modérer ses propos] to climb down.
ben [bɛ̃] *adv fam* **1.** [pour renforcer] : **~ quoi?** so what? ▪ **~ non** well, no ▪ **~ voyons (donc)!** what next! **2.** [bien] : **pt'êt ~ qu'oui, pt'êt ~ qu'non** maybe yes, maybe no.
bénédicité [benedisite] *nm* grace ▪ **dire le ~** to say grace.
bénédictin, e [benediktɛ̃, in] *adj* & *nm, f* Benedictine ▪ **les Bénédictins** the Benedictines.
◆ **Bénédictine**® *nf* [liqueur] Benedictine.
bénédiction [benediksjɔ̃] *nf* **1.** RELIG benediction, blessing ▪ **donner la ~ à qqn** to pronounce the blessing on *ou* to bless sb ▪ **la ~ nuptiale leur sera donnée à...** the marriage ceremony will take place *ou* the marriage will be solemnized *sout* at... **2.** [accord] blessing ▪ **il peut déguerpir dès demain, et avec ma ~!** *fam* he can get lost tomorrow, with my blessing! **3.** [aubaine] blessing, godsend.
bénef△ [benɛf] *nm* profit ▪ **c'est tout ~ pour elle** she gets quite a deal out of this.
bénéfice [benefis] *nm* **1.** ÉCON profit ▪ **~ avant/après impôt** pre-tax/after-tax profit ▪ **~ brut/net** gross/net profit ▪ **faire** *ou* **enregistrer un ~ brut/net de 5 000 euros** to gross/to net 5,000 euros ▪ **~ d'exploitation** operating profit ▪ **~s exceptionnels** windfall profit ▪ **c'est tout ~** *fam* : **à ce prix-là, c'est tout ~** at that price, you make a 100% profit on it
2. [avantage] benefit, advantage ▪ **tirer (un) ~ de qqch** to derive some benefit *ou* an advantage from sthg ▪ **c'est le ~ que l'on**

peut tirer de cette conduite that's the reward for such behaviour ▪ **le ~ du doute : laisser à qqn le ~ du doute** to give sb the benefit of the doubt
3. DR : **sous ~ d'inventaire** *without liability to debts beyond inherited assets* ▪ **j'accepte, sous ~ d'inventaire** *fig* everything else being equal, I accept
4. RELIG living, benefice
5. HIST benefice.
◆ **à bénéfice** *loc adv* [exploiter, vendre] at a profit.
◆ **au bénéfice de** *loc prép* **1.** [en faveur de] for (the benefit of)
2. DR : **au ~ de l'âge** by prerogative of age.

bénéficiaire [benefisjɛr] <> *adj* [opération] profitable, profit-making ▪ [marge] profit *(modif)*.
<> *nmf* [d'une mesure] beneficiary ▪ [d'un mandat, d'un chèque] payee, recipient ▪ **qui en seront les principaux ~s?** who will benefit by it most?

bénéficier [9] [benefisje] ◆ **bénéficier de** *v+prép* **1.** [avoir] to have, to enjoy ▪ **~ de conditions idéales/d'avantages sociaux** to enjoy ideal conditions/welfare benefits ▪ DR : **~ de circonstances atténuantes** to have the benefit of *ou* to be granted extenuating circumstances **2.** [profiter de] to benefit by *ou* from ▪ **~ d'une forte remise** to get a big reduction ▪ **~ d'une mesure** to benefit by *ou* to profit from a measure ▪ **faire ~ qqn de ses connaissances** to allow sb to benefit by *ou* to give sb the benefit of one's knowledge.

bénéfique [benefik] *adj* **1.** [avantageux] beneficial, advantageous **2.** ASTROL favourable.

Benelux [benelyks] *npr m* : **le ~** Benelux ▪ **les pays du ~** the Benelux countries.

benêt [bənɛ] *péj* <> *adj m* simple-minded, idiotic, silly.
<> *nm* simpleton ▪ **son grand ~ de fils** his great fool of a son.

bénévolat [benevɔla] *nm* [travail] voluntary help *ou* work ▪ [système] system of voluntary work.

bénévole [benevɔl] <> *adj* [aide, conseil] voluntary, free ▪ [association] voluntary ▪ [médecin] volunteer *(modif)*.
<> *nmf* volunteer, voluntary worker.

bénévolement [benevɔlmɑ̃] *adv* voluntarily ▪ **travailler ~ pour qqn** to do voluntary work for sb.

Bengale [bɛ̃gal] *npr m* : **le ~** Bengal ▪ **au ~** in Bengal ▪ **le golfe du ~** the Bay of Bengal.

bénigne [beniɲ] *f* ▷ **bénin**.

bénignité [beniɲite] *nf* **1.** MÉD [d'une maladie] mildness ▪ [d'une tumeur] non-malignant character **2.** *litt* [mansuétude] benignancy, kindness.

bénin, igne [benɛ̃, iɲ] *adj* **1.** MÉD [maladie] mild ▪ [tumeur] non-malignant, benign ▪ **une forme bénigne de rougeole** a mild form of measles **2.** [accident] slight, minor.

Bénin [benɛ̃] *npr m* : **(le) ~** Benin ▪ **au ~** in Benin.

béni-oui-oui [beniwiwi] *nmf péj* yes-man (*f* yes-woman).

bénir [32] [benir] *vt* **1.** RELIG [fidèles] to bless, to give one's blessing to ▪ [eau, pain] to consecrate ▪ [union] to solemnize **2.** [remercier] : **je bénis le passant qui m'a sauvé la vie** I'll be eternally thankful to the passer-by who saved my life ▪ **béni soit le jour où je t'ai rencontré** blessed be the day I met you ▪ **elle bénit le ciel de lui avoir donné un fils** she thanked God for giving her a son.

bénit, e [beni, it] *adj* consecrated, blessed.

bénitier [benitje] *nm* stoup, font.

benjamin, e [bɛ̃ʒamɛ̃, in] *nm, f* youngest child ▪ **mon ~** my youngest (child).

benjoin [bɛ̃ʒwɛ̃] *nm* benzoin, benjamin.

benne [bɛn] *nf* **1.** MIN tub, tram ▪ **~ basculante** tipper (truck) **2.** [à ordures] skip.

benoît, e [bənwa, at] *adj péj* [doucereux] bland, ingratiating.
◆ **benoîte** *nf* BOT herb bennet, wood avens.

Benoît [bənwa] *npr* : **saint ~** Saint Benedict.

benzène [bɛ̃zɛn] *nm* benzene.

benzine [bɛ̃zin] *nf* benzin, benzine.

benzol [bɛ̃zɔl] *nm* benzol, benzole.

béotien, enne [beɔsjɛ̃, ɛn] *adj* **1.** ANTIQ Boeotian **2.** *péj* [inculte] uncultured, philistine.
◆ **Béotien, enne** *nm, f* ANTIQ Boeotian.

BEP (*abr de* **brevet d'études professionnelles**) *nm vocational diploma (taken after two years of study at a 'lycée professionnel').*

BEPC (*abr de* **brevet d'études du premier cycle**) *nm former school certificate taken after four years of secondary education.*

béqueter [bekte] = **becqueter**.

béquille [bekij] *nf* **1.** [canne] crutch ▪ **marcher avec des ~s** to walk on *ou* with crutches **2.** [de moto] stand **3.** NAUT shore, prop **4.** ARM stand.

berbère [bɛrbɛr] *adj* Berber.
◆ **Berbère** *nmf* Berber.
◆ **berbère** *nm* LING Berber.

bercail [bɛrkaj] *nm* sheepfold ▪ **rentrer** *ou* **revenir au ~** [à la maison] to get back home ; RELIG to return to the fold.

berçante [bɛrsɑ̃t] *nf* **Québec (chaise) ~** rocking-chair.

berceau, x [bɛrso] *nm* **1.** [lit] cradle ▪ **on se connaît depuis le ~** we've known each other since we were babies ▪ **il/elle les prend au ~** *fam* [séducteur] he's/she's a cradle-snatcher **2.** [lieu d'origine] cradle, birthplace **3.** ARCHIT : **(voûte en) ~** barrel vault **4.** [tonnelle] arbour, bower.

bercement [bɛrsəmɑ̃] *nm* rocking *ou* swaying movement.

bercer [16] [bɛrse] *vt* **1.** [bébé] to rock, to cradle ▪ **les chansons qui ont bercé mon enfance** the songs I was brought up on **2.** [calmer - douleur] to lull, to soothe **3.** [tromper] : **~ qqn de** to lull sb with ▪ **~ qqn de paroles/promesses** to give sb fine words/empty promises.
◆ **se bercer de** *vp+prép* : **se ~ d'illusions** to delude o.s. with *ou* to nurse *ou* to entertain illusions.

berceur, euse [bɛrsœr, øz] *adj* lulling, soothing.

berceuse [bɛrsøz] *nf* **1.** [chanson d'enfant] lullaby ▪ MUS berceuse **2.** [fauteuil] rocking-chair **3.** **Québec = berçante**.

Bercy [bɛrsi] *npr* **1.** [ministère] *the French Ministry of Finance* **2.** [stade] *large sports and concert hall in Paris.*

BERD, Berd [bɛrd] (*abr de* **Banque européenne pour la reconstruction et le développement**) *npr f* EBRD.

béret [berɛ] *nm* : **~ (basque)** (French) beret.

Berezina [berezina] *npr f* : **la ~** *Napoleon's retreat over the River Berezina in Bielorussia in 1812* ▪ **c'était la ~** *fig* it was an absolute disaster.

Bergame [bɛrgam] *npr* Bergamo.

bergamote [bɛrgamɔt] *nf* bergamot orange.
◆ **à la bergamote** *loc adj* [savon] bergamot-scented ▪ [thé] with bergamot, bergamot-flavoured.

bergamotier [bɛrgamɔtje] *nm* bergamot (tree).

berge [bɛrʒ] *nf* **1.** [rive] bank GÉOGR : **route** *ou* **voie sur ~** [dans une grande ville] embankment road **2.** △ [an] year ▪ **à 25 ~s, elle a monté sa boîte** when she was 25, she set up her own business.

berger, ère [bɛrʒe, ɛr] *nm, f* [pâtre] shepherd (*f* shepherdess) ▪ **des histoires de ~s et de bergères** pastoral stories.
◆ **berger** *nm* ZOOL sheepdog ▪ **~ (allemand)** Alsatian, German shepherd ▪ **~ d'Écosse** collie (dog) ▪ **~ des Pyrénées** Pyrenean mountain dog.
◆ **bergère** *nf* [fauteuil] bergère.

bergerie [bɛrʒəri] *nf* **1.** AGRIC sheepfold **2.** ART [peinture] pastoral (painting) ▪ [tapisserie] pastoral tapestry ▪ LITTÉR [poème] pastoral.

bergeronnette [bɛrʒərɔnɛt] *nf* wagtail.

béribéri [beriberi] *nm* beriberi.

Béring [beriŋ] *npr* : **le détroit de ~** the Bering Strait.

berk [bɛrk] *interj fam* ugh, yuk.

Berlin [bɛrlɛ̃] *npr* Berlin ▪ **~-Est** East Berlin ▪ **~-Ouest** West Berlin ▪ **le mur de ~** the Berlin Wall.

berline [bɛrlin] *nf* **1.** AUTO saloon car *UK*, sedan *US* ▪ **moyenne ~** compact car **2.** HIST berlin, berline.

berlingot [bɛrlɛ̃go] *nm* **1.** [bonbon] ≃ boiled sweet *UK* ▪ ≃ hard candy *US* **2.** [emballage] carton.

berlinois, e [bɛrlinwa, az] *adj* from Berlin.
◆ **Berlinois, e** *nm, f* Berliner ▪ **~ de l'Est/l'Ouest** East/West Berliner.

berlue [bɛrly] *nf* : **avoir la ~** to be seeing things.

bermuda [bɛrmyda] *nm* : **un ~** (a pair of) Bermuda shorts, Bermudas.

Bermudes [bɛrmyd] *npr fpl* : **les ~** Bermuda ▪ **aux ~** in Bermuda ▪ **le triangle des ~** the Bermuda Triangle.

bernacle [bɛrnakl], **bernache** [bɛrnaʃ] *nf* barnacle goose.

bernardin, e [bɛrnardɛ̃, in] *nm, f* Bernardine.

bernard-l'ermite [bɛrnarlɛrmit] *nm inv* hermit crab.

berne [bɛrn] ◆ **en berne** *loc adv* at half-mast ▪ **mettre les drapeaux en ~** to half-mast the flags, to lower the flags to half-mast.

Berne [bɛrn] *npr* Bern.

berner [3] [bɛrne] *vt* [tromper] to fool, to dupe, to hoax ▪ **on s'est fait ~** we were taken in *OU* duped.

bernique [bɛrnik] ◇ *nf* limpet.
◇ *interj arch* nothing doing.

bernois, e [bɛrnwa, az] *adj* Bernese.
◆ **Bernois, e** *nm, f* Bernese.

béryl [beril] *nm* beryl.

berzingue [bɛrzɛ̃g] ◆ **à tout(e) berzingue** *loc adv fam* at full speed, double quick.

besace [bəzas] *nf* [sac] beggar's bag.

bésef△ [bezɛf] *adv (suivi d'un n non comptable)* much, a lot of ▪ *(suivi d'un n comptable)* many, a lot of ▪ **il n'y en avait pas ~, des clients** there weren't many *OU* a lot of customers.

bésicles [bezikl], **besicles** [bəzikl] *nfpl arch* spectacles ▪ *hum* specs.

bésigue [bezig] *nm* bezique.

besogne [bəzɔɲ] *nf* [travail] task, job, work ▪ **se mettre à la ~** to get down to work ▪ **c'est de la belle** *OU* **bonne ~** it's a fine piece of work, it's a neat job.

besogner [3] [bəzɔɲe] *vi péj* [travailler] to drudge, to slave away, to toil away.

besogneux, euse [bəzɔɲø, øz] ◇ *adj* **1.** *péj* [travailleur] hardworking **2.** *litt* [pauvre] needy, poor.
◇ *nm, f* drudge, hardworking man (*f* woman).

besoin [bəzwɛ̃] *nm* **1.** [nécessité] need ▪ **il a de gros ~s d'argent** he needs lots of money ▪ **nos ~s en pétrole/ingénieurs** our oil/engineering requirements ▪ **tous vos ~s seront satisfaits** all your needs will be answered *OU* satisfied ▪ **avoir** *OU* **sentir** *OU* **ressentir le ~ de faire qqch** to feel the need to do sthg ▪ **il n'est pas ~ de vous dire** you hardly need to be told ▪ **si ~ est** if necessary, if needs be ▪ **il n'est pas ~ de mentir** there's no need to lie ▪ **sans qu'il soit ~ de prévenir les parents** without it being necessary to let the parents know ▶ **~ (naturel), petit ~, ~ pressant** *euphém* call of nature ▪ **faire ses (petits) ~s** to attend to *OU* to answer the call of nature ▪ **être pris d'un ~ pressant** to be taken *OU* caught short ▪ **avoir un ~ pressant d'argent** to be pressed for money **2.** [pauvreté] need ▪ **dans le ~** in need ▪ **ceux qui sont dans le ~** the needy ▶ **c'est dans le ~ qu'on connaît le véritable ami** *OU* **ses vrais amis** *prov* a friend in need is a friend indeed *prov* **3.** *loc* **avoir ~ de qqch** to need sthg ▪ **avoir ~ de faire qqch** to need to do sthg ▪ **je n'en ai aucun ~** I have no need of it whatsoever ▪ **elle n'a pas ~ qu'on le lui répète** she doesn't need *OU* have to be told twice ▪ **je n'ai pas ~ de vous rappeler que...** I don't need to *OU* I needn't remind you that... ▪ **mon agenda a ~ d'être mis à jour** my diary *UK OU* agenda *US* needs updating *OU* to be updated ▪ **avoir bien** *OU* **grand ~ de qqch** to be in dire need of sthg, to need sthg badly ▪ **un pneu crevé! on en avait bien ~** *OU* **on avait bien ~ de ça!** *iron* a flat tyre, that's all we needed! ▪ **tu avais bien ~ de lui dire!** you WOULD have to go and tell him!, what did you (want to) tell him for?
◆ **au besoin** *loc adv* if necessary, if needs *OU* need be.
◆ **pour les besoins de** *loc prép* : **pour les ~s de la cause** for the purpose in hand.

bestiaire [bɛstjɛr] *nm* **1.** [recueil] bestiary **2.** ANTIQ gladiator.

bestial, e, aux [bɛstjal, o] *adj* [instinct, acte] bestial, brutish.

bestialité [bɛstjalite] *nf* **1.** [brutalité] bestiality, brutishness **2.** [zoophilie] bestiality.

bestiau [bɛstjo] *nm* beast, creature.

bestiaux [bɛstjo] *nmpl* [d'une exploitation] livestock ▪ [bovidés] cattle ▪ **traités/entassés comme des ~** treated/penned-in like cattle.

bestiole [bɛstjɔl] *nf* [insecte] creature *hum*.

best-seller [bɛstselœr] (*pl* **best-sellers**) *nm* best-seller.

bêta, asse [bɛta, as] *fam* ◇ *adj* [stupide] idiotic, silly, foolish.
◇ *nm, f* [idiot] blockhead, numskull ▪ **espèce de gros ~!** you blockhead!
◆ **bêta** ◇ *nm inv* [lettre] beta.
◇ *adj inv* GÉOL & ÉLECTRON beta *(modif)*.

bêtabloquant, e [bɛtablɔkɑ̃, ɑ̃t] *adj* beta-blocker *(modif)*.
◆ **bêtabloquant** *nm* beta-blocker.

bétail [betaj] *nm* : **le ~** [gén] livestock ; [bovins] cattle ▪ **100 têtes de ~** 100 head of cattle ▪ **traiter les gens comme du ~** to treat people like cattle ▶ **gros ~** (big) cattle.

bétaillère [betajɛr] *nf* cattle truck *UK*, stock car *US*.

bêtasse [bɛtas] *f* ⊳ **bêta**.

bête [bɛt] ◇ *adj* **1.** [peu intelligent] stupid, idiotic ▪ **il est plus ~ que méchant** he's not wicked, just (plain) stupid ▪ **mais non, cela ne me dérange pas, ce que tu peux être ~!** of course you're not putting me out, how silly (can you be *OU* of you)! ▪ **c'est encore moi qui vais payer, je suis bien ~, tiens!** I'll end up paying again, like an idiot! ▪ **mais oui, je me souviens maintenant, suis-je ~!** ah, now I remember, how stupid of me! ▪ **je ne suis pas ~ au point de...** I know better than to... ▪ **loin d'être ~** far from stupid ▪ **pas si ~, j'ai pris mes précautions** I took some precautions, since I'm not a complete idiot ▶ **être ~ comme ses pieds** *OU* **comme une cruche** *OU* **comme une oie** *OU* **à manger du foin** to be as thick as two short planks *UK*, to be as dumb as the day is long *US* ▪ **c'est ~ à pleurer** it's ridiculously stupid ▪ **je suis ~ et discipliné, moi, je fais ce qu'on me dit de faire!** I'm just carrying out orders!
2. [regrettable] : **je n'ai pas su le retenir, comme c'est ~!** I didn't know how to keep him, what a pity *OU* waste! ▪ **c'est ~ de ne pas y avoir pensé** it's silly *OU* stupid not to have thought of it ▪ **ce serait trop ~ de laisser passer l'occasion** it would be a pity not to take advantage of the occasion
3. [simple] : **c'est tout ~, il suffisait d'y penser!** it's so simple, we should have thought of it before! ▪ **ce n'est pas ~, ton idée!** that's quite a good idea you've got there! ▶ **c'est ~ comme tout** *OU* **chou** *fam* it's simplicity itself *OU* easy as pie *OU* easy as falling off a log
4. [stupéfait] : **en être** *OU* **rester tout ~** to be struck dumb *OU* dumbfounded.
◇ *nf* **1.** [animal - gén] animal ; [- effrayant] beast ▪ **jeté** *OU* **livré (en pâture) aux ~s** ANTIQ thrown to the lions ▶ **~ fauve** [gén] wild animal *OU* beast ; [félin] big cat ▪ **~ féroce** *OU* **sauvage** wild animal *OU* beast ▪ **~ de somme** *OU* **de charge** beast of burden ▪ **je ne veux pas être la ~ de somme du service** I don't want to do

all the dirty work in this department ■ ~ **de trait** draught *UK* *OU* draft *US* animal ■ **(petite)** ~ insect, creature *hum* ■ ~ **à bon Dieu** ladybird *UK*, ladybug *US*
2. [personne] : **grosse ~, va!** you silly fool! ■ **c'est une bonne** *OU* **brave** ~ *fam* [généreux] he's a good sort ; [dupe] he's a bit of a sucker ➲ ~ **à concours** *fam* swot *UK OU* grind *US (who does well at competitive exams)* ■ **ils nous regardaient comme des ~s curieuses** they were staring at us as if we'd come from Mars ■ **sa/ma ~ noire** his/my bugbear ■ **un ministre qui est la ~ noire des étudiants** a minister students love to hate ■ **le latin, c'était ma ~ noire** Latin was my pet hate ■ ~ **de scène/télévision** great live/television performer ■ **comme une ~ : malade comme une ~** sick as a dog ■ **travailler comme une ~** to work like a slave *OU* dog ■ **s'éclater comme une ~** *fam* to have a great time ■ **faire la ~ à deux dos** *arch & hum* to have sex ■ **se payer** *OU* **se servir sur la ~** to get one's payment in kind *(by docking it off a man's pay, or by demanding a woman's sexual favours)*
3. RELIG : **la ~ de l'Apocalypse** the beast of the Apocalypse.

bêtement [bɛtmɑ̃] *adv* **1.** [stupidement] foolishly, stupidly, idiotically ■ **rire ~** to giggle **2.** [simplement] : **tout ~** purely and simply, quite simply.

Bethléem [bɛtleɛm] *npr* Bethlehem.

Bethsabée [bɛtsabe] *npr* Bathsheba.

bêtifiant, e [betifjɑ̃, ɑ̃t] *adj* idiotic, stupid.

bêtifier [9] [betifje] *vi* to talk nonsense ■ **elle bêtifie quand elle parle à son enfant** she uses baby talk to her child.

bêtise [betiz] *nf* **1.** [stupidité] idiocy, foolishness, stupidity ■ **j'ai eu la ~ de ne pas vérifier** I was foolish enough not to check ■ **c'est de la ~ d'y aller seul** going there alone is sheer stupidity **2.** [remarque] silly *OU* stupid remark ■ **dire une ~** to say something stupid ■ **dire des ~s** to talk nonsense **3.** [action] stupid thing, piece of foolishness *OU* idiocy ■ **ne recommencez pas vos ~s** don't start your stupid tricks again ■ **faire une ~** to do something silly *OU* stupid ■ **je viens de faire une grosse ~** I've just done something very silly ■ **tu as fait une ~ en refusant** it was stupid *OU* foolish of you to refuse, you were a fool to refuse **4.** [vétille] trifle ■ **on se dispute toujours pour des ~s** we're always arguing over trifles *OU* having petty squabbles **5.** CULIN : **~s de Cambrai** humbug *UK*, (hard) mint candy *US*.

bêtisier [betizje] *nm* collection of howlers ■ **le ~ de la semaine** PRESSE gaffes of the week.

béton [betɔ̃] *nm* **1.** CONSTR concrete ➲ ~ **armé/précontraint** reinforced/prestressed concrete **2.** FOOTBALL : **faire le ~** to pack the defence **3.** *loc* **laisse ~!** *fam* forget it!, let it drop!
◆ **en béton** *loc adj* **1.** CONSTR concrete *(modif)* **2.** *fam* [résistant - estomac] cast-iron ; [- défense, garantie] watertight, surefire.

bétonnage [betɔnaʒ] *nm* **1.** CONSTR concreting **2.** FOOTBALL defensive play.

bétonner [3] [betɔne] ◇ *vt* CONSTR to concrete.
◇ *vi* FOOTBALL to pack the defence, to play defensively.

bétonnière [betɔnjɛr] *nf* cement mixer.

bette [bɛt] *nf* (Swiss) chard.

betterave [bɛtrav] *nf* : ~ **fourragère** mangelwurzel ■ ~ **rouge** beetroot *UK*, red beet *US* ■ ~ **sucrière** sugar beet.

beuglante [bøglɑ̃t] *nf fam* [chanson] song ■ [cri] yell ■ **pousser une ~** [chanter] to belt out a song ; [crier] to give a yell.

beuglement [bøgləmɑ̃] *nm* **1.** [cri - de la vache] moo ; [- du taureau] bellow ; [- d'une personne] bellow, yell ■ **des ~s** [de vache] mooing, lowing ; [de taureau] bellowing ; [d'une personne] bellowing, yelling, bawling **2.** [bruit - de la radio] blaring noise.

beugler [5] [bøgle] ◇ *vi* **1.** [crier - vache] to moo, to low ; [- taureau] to bellow ; [- chanteur, ivrogne] to bellow, to bawl **2.** [être bruyant - radio] to blare.
◇ *vt* [chanson] to bawl *OU* to bellow out *(sép)*.

beur [bœr] *adj born in France of North African parents.*
◆ **Beur** *nmf person born in France of North African immigrant parents.*

BEUR

The *verlan* word for *arabe* is not derogatory and is frequently used by second-generation Arabs in France.

Beurette [bœrɛt] *nf fam young woman born in France of North African immigrant parents.*

beurk [bœrk] *fam* = **berk**.

beurre [bœr] *nm* **1.** [de laiterie] butter ■ **au ~** (all) butter *(modif)* ■ **du ~ fondu** melted *UK OU* drawn *US* butter ➲ ~ **demi-sel** slightly salted butter ■ ~ **doux** unsalted butter ■ ~ **laitier** dairy butter ■ ~ **à la motte** loose butter ■ ~ **salé** salted butter ■ **entrer dans qqch comme dans du ~** to slice through sthg like a knife through butter ■ **faire son ~** *fam* to make money hand over fist ■ **ça met du ~ dans les épinards** *fam* it's a nice little earner ■ **vouloir le ~ et l'argent du ~** to want to have one's cake and eat it (too) **2.** [pâte] : ~ **d'arachide** *OU* **de cacahuètes** peanut butter ■ ~ **de cacao/de muscade** cocoa/nutmeg butter ■ ~ **d'anchois** anchovy paste ■ ~ **blanc/noir** white/black butter sauce ■ ~ **d'escargot** *flavoured butter used in the preparation of snails.*

beurré, e [bœre] *adj* **1.** CULIN : **tartine ~e** piece of bread and butter **2.** △ [ivre] plastered△, pissed△ *UK* ■ ~ **(comme un petit Lu)** pissed as a newt△ *UK*, stewed to the gills *US*.
◆ **beurré** *nm* butter-pear, beurré.
◆ **beurrée** *nf* **1.** △ [ivresse] : **prendre une ~e** to get plastered△, to get pissed△ *UK* **2.** *Québec* [tartine] piece of bread and butter ■ [substance] bread and butter (and jam) spread.

beurrer [5] [bœre] *vt* [tartine, moule] to butter.
◆ **se beurrer**△ *vpi* to get plastered△, to get pissed△ *UK*, to get sloshed.

beurrier, ère [bœrje, ɛr] *adj* [production] butter *(modif)* ■ [région] butter-producing.
◆ **beurrier** *nm* [récipient] butter dish.

beuverie [bœvri] *nf fam* drinking binge, bender.

bévue [bevy] *nf* [gaffe] blunder, gaffe ■ **commettre une ~** to blunder.

Beyrouth [berut] *npr* Beirut, Beyrouth ■ **de ~** Beiruti.

bézef△ [bezɛf] = **bésef**.

Biafra [bjafra] *npr* Biafra.

biais, e [bjɛ, bjɛz] *adj* [oblique] slanting.
◆ **biais** *nm* **1.** [obliquité] slant **2.** COUT [bande] piece (of material) cut on the bias ■ [sens] bias ■ **travailler dans le ~** to cut on the bias *OU* cross **3.** [moyen] way ■ **elle cherche un ~ pour se faire connaître** she is trying to find a way of making herself known ■ **par le ~ de** through, via, by means of **4.** [aspect] angle ■ **je ne sais pas par quel ~ le prendre** I don't know how *OU* from what angle to approach him **5.** [dans des statistiques] bias.
◆ **de biais** *loc adv* [aborder] indirectly, tangentially *sout* ■ **regarder qqn de ~** to give sb a sidelong glance.
◆ **en biais** *loc adv* sideways, slantwise, at an angle ■ **regarder qqn en ~** to give sb a sidelong glance ■ **traverser la rue en ~** to cross the street diagonally.

biaisé, e [bjeze] *adj* [statistiques, raisonnement] distorted.

biaiser [4] [bjeze] *vi* to prevaricate, to equivocate ■ **il va falloir ~ pour avoir des places pour l'opéra** we'll have to be a bit clever to get seats for the opera.

biathlon [biatlɔ̃] *nm* biathlon.

bibande [bibɑ̃d] *adj* dual-band.

bibelot [biblo] *nm* [précieux] curio, bibelot ■ [sans valeur] trinket, knick-knack.

biberon [bibrɔ̃] *nm* feeding *UK OU* baby *US* bottle ■ **donner le ~ à un bébé/agneau** to bottle-feed a baby/lamb ■ **enfant nourri** *OU* **élevé au ~** bottle-fed baby ■ **prendre son ~** to have one's bottle ■ **prendre qqn au ~** to start sb from the earliest possible age.

biberonner [3] [bibrɔne] *vi fam hum* to tipple, to booze.

bibi[1] [bibi] *nm fam* [chapeau] (woman's) hat.

bibi[2] [bibi] *pron fam hum* [moi] yours truly.

bibine [bibin] *nf fam* **c'est de la ~** [boisson, bière] it's dishwater; [c'est facile] it's a piece of cake.

bible [bibl] *nf* **1.** RELIG : **la Bible** the Bible **2.** [référence] bible.

bibliobus [biblijɔbys] *nm* mobile library *UK*, bookmobile *US*.

bibliographie [biblijɔgrafi] *nf* bibliography.

bibliographique [biblijɔgrafik] *adj* bibliographic.

bibliomanie [biblijɔmani] *nf* bibliomania.

bibliophile [biblijɔfil] *nmf* book-lover, bibliophile.

bibliothécaire [biblijɔtekɛr] *nmf* librarian.

bibliothèque [biblijɔtɛk] *nf* **1.** [lieu] library ■ [meuble] book-case ■ **~ municipale** public library ■ **la Bibliothèque nationale** *the French national library* ■ **~ de prêt** lending library ■ **~ universitaire** university library ‖ [collection] collection ■ **c'est une ~ ambulante** he's a walking encyclopedia ■ **~ de logiciels** software library ▶ **la Bibliothèque rose** *collection of books for very young children* ■ **la Bibliothèque verte** *collection of books for older children* **2.** COMM : **~ de gare** station bookstall *UK ou* newsstand *US*.

LA BIBLIOTHÈQUE NATIONALE

Situated in the rue de Richelieu in Paris, the *Bibliothèque nationale* or *BN* is a large copyright deposit library comparable to the British Library and the Library of Congress. At present it houses the library's collection of manuscripts, engravings, coins, medals and maps; the main bulk of the book collection has been transferred to the new François Mitterrand-Tolbiac complex in the 13th arrondissement.

biblique [biblik] *adj* biblical.

bibliste [biblist] *nmf* Biblist, Biblicist.

Bic® [bik] *nm* ball (point) pen, ≃ Biro® *UK*, ≃ Bic® *US*.

bicamérisme [bikamerism], **bicaméralisme** [bikameralism] *nm* two-chamber (political) system, bicameralism *sout*.

bicarbonate [bikarbɔnat] *nm* bicarbonate ■ **~ de soude** bicarbonate of soda.

bicentenaire [bisɑ̃tnɛr] *adj & nm* bicentenary, bicentennial.

bicéphale [bisefal] *adj* two-headed, bicephalous *sout*.

biceps [bisɛps] *nm* biceps ■ **avoir des ~** *fam* to have big biceps.

biche [biʃ] *nf* **1.** ZOOL doe, hind **2.** [en appellatif] : **ma ~** *fam* my darling.

bicher△ [3] [biʃe] *vi* to be tickled pink ■ *(tournure impersonnelle)* **ça biche?** how's it going?, how's things?

bichette [biʃɛt] *nf* **1.** ZOOL young hind *ou* doe **2.** *fam* [en appellatif] : **ma ~** my darling *ou* pet.

bichonner [3] [biʃɔne] *vt* [choyer] to pamper, to pet, to mollycoddle *péj* ■ **il aime se faire ~** he loves to be pampered. ◆ **se bichonner** *vp (emploi réfléchi)* [se pomponner] to spruce o.s. up.

bichromie [bikrɔmi] *nf* two-colour process.

bicolore [bikɔlɔr] *adj* two-coloured *UK*, two-colored *US*.

bicoque [bikɔk] *nf* shack.

bicorne [bikɔrn] *nm* cocked *ou* two-pointed hat.

bicot [biko] *nm* **1.** *fam* [biquet] kid ZOOL **2.** ▲ *racist term used to refer to North African Arabs.*

biculturalisme [bikyltyralism] *nm* biculturalism.

biculturel, elle [bikyltyrel] *adj* bicultural.

bicycle [bisikl] *nm* **1.** [à roues inégales] penny-farthing *UK*, ordinary *US* **2.** *Québec* bicycle.

bicyclette [bisiklɛt] *nf* **1.** [engin] bicycle ■ **faire de la ~** to ride a bicycle ■ **monter à ~** to ride a bicycle ■ **allons-y à ~** let's cycle, let's go there by bicycle **2.** LOISIRS & SPORT : **la ~** cycling.

bidasse [bidas] *nm fam* [soldat] private.

bide [bid] *nm fam* **1.** [ventre] belly, gut **2.** [échec] flop, washout ■ **ça a été** *ou* **fait un ~** it was a complete flop *ou* washout.

bidet [bidɛ] *nm* bidet.

bidoche△ [bidɔʃ] *nf* meat.

bidon [bidɔ̃] ◇ *adj inv fam* phoney.
◇ *nm* **1.** [récipient] can, tin ■ **~ de lait** milk-churn *UK*, milk can *US* ‖ MIL water bottle, canteen **2.** *fam* [ventre] belly, gut **3.** △ [mensonge] : **c'est du ~ tout ça** that's all baloney.

bidonnant, e [bidɔnɑ̃, ɑ̃t] *adj fam* side-splitting, screamingly funny ■ **c'était ~** it was a scream *ou* hoot.

bidonner [3] [bidɔne] ◆ **se bidonner** *vpi fam* to split one's sides laughing, to laugh one's head off ■ **qu'est-ce qu'on se bidonne avec eux!** it's a laugh a minute with them!

bidonville [bidɔ̃vil] *nm* shantytown.

bidouillage [bidujaʒ] *nm fam* messing around, fiddling, tampering.

bidouiller [3] [biduje] *vt fam* [serrure, logiciel] to fiddle (about) with, to tamper with.

bidule [bidyl] *nm fam* **1.** [objet] thingamajig, thingummy *UK*, contraption **2.** [personne] whatshisname (*f* whatshername) ■ **eh, Bidule, t'as pas vu ma sœur?** hey, Thingy *UK ou* buddy *US*, seen my sister?

bief [bjɛf] *nm* [de cours d'eau] reach ■ [de moulin] race.

bielle [bjɛl] *nf* connecting rod.

biélorusse [bjelɔrys] *adj* Belorussian, Byelorussian.
◆ **Biélorusse** *nmf* Belorussian, Byelorussian.

Biélorussie [bjelɔrysi] *npr f* : **(la) ~** Belarussia, Byelorussia.

bien [bjɛ̃] ◇ *adv* **1.** [de façon satisfaisante] well ■ **tout allait ~** everything was going well *ou* fine ■ **il cuisine ~** he's a good cook ■ **la pièce finit ~** the play has a happy ending ■ **la vis tient ~** the screw is secure *ou* is in tight ■ **il gagne ~ sa vie** he earns a good living ■ **ils vivent ~** they have a comfortable life ▶ **faire ~** to look good ■ **~ prendre qqch** to take sthg well ■ **il s'y est bien pris** he tackled it well ■ **il s'y est ~ pris pour interviewer le ministre** he did a good job of interviewing the minister ■ **vivre ~ qqch** to have a positive experience of sthg ■ **tiens-toi ~!** [à la rambarde] hold on tight! ; [sur la chaise] sit properly! ; [à table] behave yourself! ■ **tu tombes ~!** you've come at (just) the right time!
2. [du point de vue de la santé] : **aller** *ou* **se porter ~** to feel well *ou* fine ■ **il se porte plutôt ~!** *hum* he doesn't look as if he's starving!
3. [conformément à la raison, à la loi, à la morale] well, decently ■ **~ agir envers qqn** to do the proper *ou* right *ou* correct thing by sb ■ **tu as ~ fait** you did the right thing, you did right ■ **tu fais ~ de ne plus les voir** you're right not to see them any more ■ **tu fais ~ de me le rappeler** thank you for reminding me, it's a good thing you reminded me (of it) ■ **tu ferais ~ de partir plus tôt** you'd do well to leave earlier ■ **pour ~ faire, nous devrions partir avant 9 h** ideally, we should leave before 9 ■ **il faudrait lui acheter un cadeau pour ~ faire** we really ought to buy her a present
4. [sans malentendu] right, correctly ■ **ai-je ~ entendu ce que tu viens de dire?** did I hear you right?
5. [avec soin] : **écoute-moi ~** listen (to me) carefully ■ **as-tu ~ vérifié?** did you check properly? ■ **fais ~ ce que l'on te dit** do exactly *ou* just as you're told ■ **mélangez ~** stir well ■ **soigne-toi ~** take good care of yourself
6. *(suivi d'un adjectif)* [très] really, very ■ **c'est ~ agréable** it's really *ou* very nice ■ **tu es ~ sûr?** are you quite certain *ou* sure? ■ **bois un thé ~ chaud** have a nice hot cup of tea ■ *(suivi d'un adverbe)* **c'était il y a ~ longtemps** that was a very long time ago ■ **embrasse-le ~ fort** give him a big hug ■ **~ souvent** (very) often ■ **~ avant/après** well before/after ■ **~ trop tôt** far *ou* much too early

7. *(suivi d'un verbe)* [beaucoup] : **on a ~ ri** we had a good laugh, we laughed a lot
8. [véritablement] : **j'ai ~ cru que...** I really thought that... ■ **il a ~ failli se noyer** he very nearly drowned ■ **sans ~ se rendre compte de ce qu'il faisait** without being fully aware of *ou* without fully realizing what he was doing
9. [pour renforcer, insister] : **qui peut ~ téléphoner à cette heure-ci?** who could that be ringing at this hour? ■ **où peut-il ~ être?** where on earth is he? ■ **je sais ~ que tu dis la vérité** I know very well that you're telling the truth ■ **veux-tu ~ te taire?** will you please be quiet? ■ **ce n'est pas lui, mais ~ son associé que j'ai eu au téléphone** it wasn't him, but rather his partner I spoke to on the phone ■ **c'est ~ ça** that's it *ou* right ■ **c'est ~ ce que je disais/pensais** that's just what I was saying/thinking ■ **c'est ~ le moment d'en parler!** *iron* it's hardly the right time to talk about it! ■ **j'ai pourtant ~ entendu frapper** I'm sure I heard a knock at the door ■ **je le vois ~ médecin** I can (quite) see him as a doctor ▶ **tu vas lui dire? – je pense ~!** are you going to tell him? – you bet I am! ■ **je vais me plaindre – je comprends** *ou* **pense ~!** I'm going to complain – I should think so too! ■ **il ne m'aidera pas, tu penses ~!** he won't help me, you can be sure of that! ■ **c'est ~ de lui, ça!** that's typical of him!, that's just like him!
10. [volontiers] : **j'irais ~ avec toi** I'd really like to go with you ■ **je te dirais ~ quelque chose, mais je suis poli** I could say something rude but I won't ■ **je boirais ~ quelque chose** I could do with *ou* I wouldn't mind a drink
11. [au moins] at least
12. [exprimant la supposition, l'éventualité] : **tu verras ~** you'll see ■ **ils pourraient ~ refuser** they might well refuse ■ **ça se pourrait ~** it's perfectly possible
13. [pourtant] : **mais il fallait ~ le lui dire!** but he had to be told (all the same)! ■ **il faut ~ le faire** it's got to be done
14. [suivi d'un nom] : **~ de, ~ des** quite a lot of ■ **j'ai eu ~ du souci** I've had a lot to worry about ■ **elle a ~ du courage!** isn't she brave!, she's got a great deal of courage! ■ **~ des fois...** more than once... ■ **~ des gens** lots of *ou* quite a lot of *ou* quite a few people
15. [dans la correspondance] : **~ à toi** love ■ **~ à vous** yours.
◇ *adj inv* **1.** [qui donne satisfaction] good ■ **c'est ~ de s'amuser mais il faut aussi travailler** it's all right to have fun but you have to work too ■ **je recule? – non, vous êtes ~ là** *fam* shall I move back? – no, you're all right *ou* OK *ou* fine like that ■ **qu'est-ce qu'il est ~ dans son dernier film!** *fam* he's great *ou* really good in his new film! ■ ÉDUC [sur un devoir] good
2. [esthétique - personne] good-looking, attractive ; [- chose] nice, lovely ■ **tu es très ~ en jupe** [cela te sied] you look very nice in a skirt ; [c'est acceptable pour l'occasion] a skirt is perfectly all right ▶ **il est ~ de sa personne** he's a good-looking man
3. [convenable - personne] decent, nice ■ **c'est ~** [conduite, action] : **ce serait ~ de lui envoyer un peu d'argent** it'd be a good idea to send her some money ■ **ils se sont séparés et c'est ~ comme ça** they've split up and it's better that way ■ **ce n'est pas ~ de tirer la langue** it's naughty *ou* it's not nice to stick out your tongue ■ **ce n'est pas ~ de tricher** you shouldn't cheat
4. [en forme] well ■ **vous ne vous sentez pas ~?** aren't you feeling well? ; [mentalement] are you crazy? ■ **il n'est pas ~, celui-là!** *fam* he's got a problem, he has! ▶ **me/te/nous voilà ~!** NOW I'm/you're/we're in a fine mess!
5. [à l'aise] : **on est ~ ici** it's nice here ■ **on est vraiment ~ dans ce fauteuil** this armchair is really comfortable ■ **je suis ~ avec toi** I like being with you
6. [en bons termes] : **être ~ avec qqn** to be well in with sb ■ **ils sont ~ ensemble** they're happy together ■ **se mettre ~ avec qqn** to get in with sb, to get into sb's good books.
◇ *nm* **1.** PHILOS & RELIG : **le ~** good ■ **faire le ~** to do good
2. [ce qui est agréable, avantageux] : **c'est pour ton ~ que je dis ça** I'm saying this for your own good *ou* benefit ■ **c'est ton ~ que je veux** I only want what's best for you ■ **le ~ commun** *ou* **général** the common good ■ **c'est pour le ~ de tous/de l'entreprise** it's for the common good/the good of the firm ■ **pour le ~ public** in the public interest ■ **vouloir du ~ à qqn** to wish sb well ■ **dire/penser du ~ de** to speak/to think well of ■ **on ne m'a dit que du ~ de votre cuisine** I've heard the most flattering things about your cooking ■ **faire du ~ : continue à me masser, ça fait du ~** carry on massaging me, it's doing me good ■ **cela fait du ~ de se dégourdir les jambes** it's nice to be able to stretch your legs ■ **je me suis cogné l'orteil, ça fait pas du ~!** *fam* I bashed my toe, it's quite painful! ■ **faire du ~** *ou* **le plus grand ~ à qqn** [médicament, repos] to do sb good, to benefit sb ■ **le dentiste ne m'a pas fait du ~!** the dentist really hurt me! ■ **la séparation leur fera le plus grand ~** being apart will do them a lot *ou* a world of good ■ **grand ~ te/lui fasse!** *iron* much good may it do you/him! ▶ **~ m'en a pris** it was just as well I did it ■ **ça fait du ~ par où ça passe!** *fam* aah, I feel better for that!
3. [bienfait] good *ou* positive thing, benefit ■ **cette décision a été un ~ pour tout le monde** the decision was a good thing for all *ou* everyone concerned
4. [propriété personnelle] possession, (piece) *ou* item of property ■ [argent] fortune ■ **mon ~ t'appartient** what's mine is yours ■ **ils ont un petit ~ en Ardèche** *fam* they have a bit of land in the Ardèche ■ **la jeunesse est un ~ précieux** youth is a precious asset ■ **tous mes ~s** all my worldly goods, all I'm worth ▶ **avoir du ~ au soleil** *fam* to be well-off *ou* rich
5. DR & ÉCON : **~ de consommation courante** consumer good ■ **~s de consommation durables** consumer durables ■ **~s d'équipement** capital equipment *ou* goods ■ **~s privés/publics** private/public property.
◇ *interj* **1.** [indiquant une transition] OK, right (then)
2. [marquant l'approbation] : **je n'irai pas! – ~, n'en parlons plus!** I won't go! – very well *ou* all right (then), let's drop the subject! ■ **fort ~** fine ■ **~, ~, on y va** all right, all right *ou* OK, OK, let's go.
◆ **bien entendu** *loc adv* of course.
◆ **bien entendu que** *loc conj* of course ■ **~ entendu que j'aimerais y aller** of course I'd like to go.
◆ **bien que** *loc conj* despite the fact that, although, though ■ **~ que malade, il a tenu à y aller** although he was ill, he insisted on going.
◆ **bien sûr** *loc adv* of course.
◆ **bien sûr que** *loc conj* of course ■ **~ sûr qu'elle n'avait rien compris!** of course she hadn't understood a thing!

bien-aimé, e [bjɛ̃neme] (*mpl* **bien-aimés**, *fpl* **bien-aimées**) *adj & nm, f* beloved.

bien-être [bjɛ̃nɛtr] *nm inv* **1.** [aise] well-being **2.** [confort matériel] (material) well-being.

bienfaisance [bjɛ̃fəzɑ̃s] *nf* [charité] charity.
◆ **de bienfaisance** *loc adj* [bal] charity *(modif)* ■ [association, œuvre] charity *(modif)*, charitable ■ **travailler pour les œuvres de ~** to do charity work.

bienfaisant, e [bjɛ̃fəzɑ̃, ɑ̃t] *adj* **1.** [bénéfique - effet, climat] beneficial, salutary *sout* **2.** [indulgent - personne] beneficent *sout*, kind, kindly.

bienfait [bjɛ̃fɛ] *nm* **1.** *litt* [acte de bonté] kindness **2.** [effet salutaire] benefit ■ **les ~s d'un séjour à la montagne** the benefits *ou* beneficial effects of a stay in the mountains ■ **les ~s de la civilisation** the advantages *ou* benefits of civilisation.

bienfaiteur, trice [bjɛ̃fɛtœr, tris] *nm, f* benefactor (*f* benefactress) ■ **l'association fonctionne grâce à des ~s** the association keeps going *ou* running thanks to benefactors ▶ **~ du genre humain** great man (*f* woman).

bien-fondé [bjɛ̃fɔ̃de] (*pl* **bien-fondés**) *nm* [d'une revendication] rightfulness ■ [d'un argument] validity ■ **établir le ~ de qqch** to substantiate sthg.

bienheureux, euse [bjɛ̃nørø, øz] ◇ *adj* **1.** RELIG blessed **2.** [heureux - personne, vie] happy, blissful ; [- hasard] fortunate, lucky.
◇ *nm, f* RELIG : **les ~** the blessed *ou* blest.

biennal, e, aux [bjenal, o] *adj* biennial.
◆ **biennale** *nf* biennial arts festival.

Bienne [bjɛn] *npr* Biel.

bien-pensant, e [bjɛ̃pɑ̃sɑ̃, ɑ̃t] (*mpl* **bien-pensants**, *fpl* **bien-pensantes**) *péj* ◇ *adj* [conformiste] right-thinking, right-minded.
◇ *nm, f* right-thinking *ou* right-minded person.

bienséance [bjɛ̃seɑ̃s] *nf* decorum, propriety ■ **les ~s** the proprieties.

bienséant, e [bjɛ̃seɑ̃, ɑ̃t] *adj* decorous, proper, becoming ▪ **il n'est pas ~ d'élever la voix** it is unbecoming *OU* it isn't proper *OU* it isn't done to raise one's voice.

bientôt [bjɛ̃to] *adv* **1.** [prochainement] soon, before long ▪ **à (très) ~!** see you soon! ▪ **il sera ~ de retour** he'll soon be back, he'll be back before long ▪ **j'ai ~ fini** I've almost finished ▪ **il est ~ midi** it's nearly midday ▪ **c'est pour ~?** will it be long? ; [naissance] is it *OU* is the baby due soon? ▪ **c'est pas ~ fini ce vacarme?** *fam* have you quite finished (making all that racket)? **2.** *sout* [rapidement] soon, quickly, in no time ➲ **cela est ~ dit** that's easier said than done.

bienveillance [bjɛ̃vejɑ̃s] *nf* **1.** [qualité] benevolence, kindliness ▪ **parler de qqn avec ~** to speak favourably of sb **2.** [dans des formules de politesse] : **je sollicite de votre ~ un entretien** I beg to request an interview *sout.*

bienveillant, e [bjɛ̃vejɑ̃, ɑ̃t] *adj* [personne] benevolent, kindly ▪ [regard, sourire] kind, kindly, gentle.

bienvenu, e [bjɛ̃vny] <> *adj* opportune, apposite.
<> *nm, f* : **être le ~** to be welcome ▪ **cet argent était vraiment le ~** that money was most welcome.
◆ **bienvenue** *nf* welcome ▪ **souhaiter la ~e à qqn** to welcome sb ▪ **~e à toi, ami!** welcome to you, my friend!
◆ **de bienvenue** *loc adj* [discours] welcoming ▪ [cadeau] welcome *(modif).*

bière [bjɛr] *nf* **1.** [boisson] beer ▪ **~ blonde** lager ▪ **~ brune** brown ale *UK*, dark beer *US* ▪ **~ (à la) pression** draught *UK OU* draft *US* beer ▪ **c'est de la petite ~** *fam* it's small beer *OU* nothing **2.** [cercueil] coffin, casket *US* ▪ **mettre qqn en ~** to place sb in his/her coffin.

biffer [3] [bife] *vt* to cross *OU* to score *OU* to strike out *(sép).*

biffure [bifyr] *nf* crossing out, stroke ▪ **faire des ~s sur une lettre** to cross things out in a letter.

bifidus [bifidys] *nm* BIOL bifidus ▪ **yaourt au ~** live yoghurt.

bifocal, e, aux [bifɔkal, o] *adj* bifocal.

bifteck [biftɛk] *nm* **1.** [tranche] (piece of) steak ➲ **un ~ haché** a beefburger ▪ **défendre/gagner son ~** to look after/to earn one's bread and butter **2.** [catégorie de viande] steak ▪ **du ~ haché** (best) mince *UK*, lean ground beef *US.*

bifurcation [bifyrkasjɔ̃] *nf* **1.** [intersection] fork, junction, turn-off **2.** [changement] change (of course).

bifurquer [3] [bifyrke] *vi* **1.** TRANSP [route] to fork, to branch off, to bifurcate *sout* ▪ [conducteur] to turn off ▪ **on a alors bifurqué sur Lyon** we then turned off towards Lyons ▪ **~ à gauche** to take the left fork, to fork left, to turn left **2.** [changer] to branch off (into), to switch to ▪ **il a bifurqué vers la politique** he branched out into politics.

bigame [bigam] <> *adj* bigamous.
<> *nmf* bigamist.

bigamie [bigami] *nf* bigamy.

bigarré, e [bigare] *adj* [vêtement, fleur] variegated, multicoloured, parti-coloured ▪ [foule] colourful.

bigarreau, x [bigaro] *nm* bigarreau (cherry).

bigarrer [3] [bigare] *vt litt* [colorer] to variegate, to colour in many shades.

bigarrure [bigaryr] *nf* variegation, multicoloured effects.

big(-)bang [bigbɑ̃g] *nm* FIN & PHYS big bang.

bigler [3] [bigle] *fam* <> *vi* to squint.
<> *vt* [regarder] to (take a) squint at, to eye.
◆ **bigler sur** *v+prép fam* to eye (with greed).

bigleux, euse [biglø, øz] *fam* <> *adj* short-sighted.
<> *nm, f* short-sighted person.

bigophone [bigɔfɔn] *nm fam* [téléphone] phone, blower *UK*, horn *US* ▪ **passe-moi un coup de ~** give me a ring *UK OU* buzz.

bigorneau, x [bigɔrno] *nm* periwinkle, winkle.

bigorner [3]^△ [bigɔrne] *vt* [défoncer - moto] to smash up *(sép).*
◆ **se bigorner**^△ *vp (emploi réciproque)* to scrap, to fight.

bigot, e [bigo, ɔt] <> *adj* [dévot] sanctimonious, holier-than-thou.
<> *nm, f* (religious) bigot.

bigoterie [bigɔtri] *nf* (religious) bigotry.

bigouden [bigudɛn] <> *adj* from the Bigouden area (of Brittany).
<> *nm* Bigouden (woman's) headgear.
<> *nf* Bigouden woman.

bigoudi [bigudi] *nm* curler, roller ▪ **(se) mettre des ~s** to put one's hair into curlers *OU* rollers.

bigre [bigr] *interj vieilli* gosh, my.

bigrement [bigrəmɑ̃] *adv* [très] jolly *UK*, mighty *US* ▪ **il faut être ~ culotté** you have to have a hell of a nerve ▪ **ça a ~ changé** it has changed a heck of a lot.

biguine [bigin] *nf* beguine.

bihebdomadaire [biɛbdɔmadɛr] *adj* biweekly, semi-weekly.

bijection [biʒɛksjɔ̃] *nf* bijection.

bijou, x [biʒu] *nm* **1.** [parure] jewel ▪ **~x de famille** family jewels *OU* jewellery **2.** [fleuron] gem **3.** *fam* [en appellatif] : **bonjour, mon ~** hello precious *OU* my love.

bijouterie [biʒutri] *nf* **1.** [bijoux] jewels, jewellery **2.** [magasin] jeweller's (shop) *UK*, jeweler's (store) *US* **3.** [industrie] jewellery business **4.** [technique] jewellery-making.

bijoutier, ère [biʒutje, ɛr] *nm, f* jeweller.

Bikini® [bikini] *nm* bikini.

bilabiale [bilabjal] <> *adj f* bilabial.
<> *nf* bilabial (consonant).

bilan [bilɑ̃] *nm* **1.** ÉCON balance sheet, statement of accounts ▪ **dresser** *OU* **faire le ~** to draw up the balance sheet ▪ **porter un article au ~** to put an item into the balance **2.** [appréciation] appraisal, assessment ▪ **quand on fait le ~ de sa vie** when one takes stock of *OU* when one assesses one's (lifetime) achievements ▪ **quel est le ~ de ces discussions?** what is the end result of these talks?, what have these talks amounted to? ▪ **le ~ définitif fait état de 20 morts** the final death toll stands at 20 ▪ **un ~ économique positif** positive economic results **3.** MÉD : **~ (de santé)** (medical) check-up ▪ **se faire faire un ~ (de santé)** to have a check-up.

bilatéral, e, aux [bilateral, o] *adj* bilateral, two-way.

bilatéralité [bilateralite] *nf* bilateralism.

bilboquet [bilbɔkɛ] *nm* cup-and-ball game.

bile [bil] *nf* **1.** ANAT bile **2.** *fam loc* **décharger** *OU* **épancher sa ~ sur qqn** to vent one's spleen on sb ▪ **se faire de la ~** to fret ▪ **te fais pas de ~** don't you fret *OU* worry.

biler [3] [bile] ◆ **se biler** *vpi fam* [s'inquiéter] to fret, to worry o.s. sick ▪ **te bile pas!** no problem!

bileux, euse [bilø, øz] *adj fam* easily worried.

bilharziose [bilarzjoz] *nf* bilharziasis, schistosomiasis.

biliaire [biljɛr] *adj* biliary.

bilieux, euse [biljø, øz] *adj* **1.** [pâle - teint] bilious, sallow, yellowish **2.** [colérique - personne, tempérament] testy, irascible.

bilingue [bilɛ̃g] <> *adj* bilingual.
<> *nmf* bilingual speaker.

bilinguisme [bilɛ̃gɥism] *nm* bilingualism.

billard [bijar] *nm* **1.** [jeu] billiards *(sing)* ▪ **faire un ~** to play a game of billiards ➲ **~ américain** pool **2.** [salle] billiard room *UK*, poolroom *US* **3.** [meuble] billiard *UK OU* pool *US* table ▪ **~ électrique** [jeu] pinball ; [machine] pinball machine **4.** *fam* [table d'opération] : **monter** *OU* **passer sur le ~** to be operated (on), to have an operation.

bille [bij] *nf* **1.** JEUX [de verre] marble ▪ **placer ses ~s** to get o.s. in ▪ **reprendre ses ~s** to pull out *(of a deal)* ▪ **toucher sa ~ en** *fam* to be bloody^△ *UK OU* darned *US* good at ▌ [de billard] ball

2. INDUST & MÉCAN ball **3.** *fam* [tête] : **avoir une bonne ~** to look a good sort ■ **avoir une ~ de clown** to have a funny face **4.** [de bois] billet, log (of wood).

◆ **à bille** *loc adj* [crayon, stylo] ball-point *(modif)* ■ [déodorant] roll-on *(avant n)*.

◆ **bille en tête** *loc adv* straight, straightaway ■ **il est allé ~ en tête se plaindre à la direction** he went straight to the management with a complaint.

biller [3] [bije] *vt* to ball-test.

billet [bijɛ] *nm* **1.** LOISIRS & TRANSP ticket ■ **~ d'avion/de train/de concert/de loterie** plane/train/concert/lottery ticket ■ **voyageurs munis de ~s** ticket holders ■ **retenez** *ou* **réservez les ~s à l'avance** book ahead ◐ **~ aller** *ou* **simple** single ticket *UK*, single *UK*, one-way ticket *US* ■ **~ aller-retour** return *UK ou* roundtrip *US* ticket ■ **~ circulaire** day return (ticket) *UK*, roundtrip ticket *US* ■ **~ de faveur** complimentary ticket
2. FIN : **~ (de banque)** note *UK*, banknote *UK*, bill *US*, bankbill *US* ◐ **~ à ordre** promissory note, note of hand ■ **~ au porteur** bearer bill ■ **le ~ vert** the dollar, the US currency ■ **faux ~** forged banknote
3. [message] note ■ **~ doux** *ou* **galant** billet doux, love letter ■ **~ d'humeur** PRESSE column
4. MIL : **~ de logement** billet
5. *loc* **je te donne** *ou* **flanque** *fam ou* **fiche** *fam* **mon ~ que tu te trompes** I bet my bottom dollar *ou* my boots that you're wrong.

billetterie [bijɛtri] *nf* **1.** TRANSP & LOISIRS [opérations] ticket distribution ■ [guichet] ticket office ■ **~ automatique** ticket machine **2.** BANQUE [distributeur] cash dispenser.

billettiste [bijɛtist] *nmf* **1.** [vendeur] ticket seller **2.** [journaliste] columnist.

billevesées [bijvəze] *nfpl litt* nonsense, twaddle.

billion [biljɔ̃] *nm* **1.** [million de millions] billion *UK*, trillion *US* **2.** *vieilli* [milliard] milliard *UK*, billion *US*.

billot [bijo] *nm* [de bourreau, d'enclume] block ■ **finir** *ou* **périr sur le ~** to be beheaded.

bimbeloterie [bɛ̃blɔtri] *nf* **1.** [babioles] knick-knacks **2.** [commerce] fancy goods business.

bimensuel, elle [bimɑ̃sɥɛl] *adj* twice monthly, fortnightly *UK*, semimonthly *US*.

◆ **bimensuel** *nm* [revue] fortnightly *UK*, semimonthly *US*.

bimestriel, elle [bimɛstrijɛl] *adj* bimonthly.

◆ **bimestriel** *nm* [revue] bimonthly.

bimillénaire [bimilenɛr] *nm* bimillenary.

bimoteur [bimɔtœr] ◇ *adj m* twin-engined.
◇ *nm* twin-engined plane *ou* aircraft.

binaire [binɛr] *adj* INFORM & MATH binary.

binational, e, aux [binasjɔnal, o] *adj* with dual nationality.

biner [3] [bine] *vt* to harrow, to hoe.

binette [binɛt] *nf* **1.** AGRIC hoe **2.** *fam* [visage] mug **3.** *Québec* INFORM smiley.

bineuse [binøz] *nf* cultivator.

bing [biŋ] *onomat* thwack, smack.

biniou [binju] *nm* (Breton) bagpipes *(pl)*.

binoclard, e [binɔklar, ard] ◇ *adj* : **être ~** to wear specs.
◇ *nm, f fam* : **c'est une ~e** she wears specs *UK*.

binocle [binɔkl] *nm* [lorgnon] pince-nez.

◆ **binocles** *nmpl fam* [lunettes] specs *UK*, glasses.

binoculaire [binɔkylɛr] *adj* binocular.

binôme [binom] *nm* binomial.

binomial, e, aux [binɔmjal, o] *adj* binomial.

bintje [bintʃ] *nf* bintje potato.

bio [bjo] *adj inv* [nourriture, style de vie] organic.

biocarburant [bjɔkarbyrɑ̃] *nm* biomass fuel.

biochimie [bjɔʃimi] *nf* biochemistry.

biochimique [bjɔʃimik] *adj* biochemical.

biochimiste [bjɔʃimist] *nmf* biochemist.

bioclimat [bjɔklima] *nm* bioclimate.

biodégradable [bjɔdegradabl] *adj* biodegradable.

biodégradation [bjɔdegradasjɔ̃] *nf* biodegradation.

biodiversité [bjɔdivɛrsite] *nf* biodiversity.

bioénergétique [bjɔenɛrʒetik] *adj* bioenergetic.

bioénergie [bjɔenɛrʒi] *nf* bioenergetics.

bioéthique [bjɔetik] *nf* bioethics.

bio-feedback [bjɔfidbak] *nm* biofeedback.

biogenèse [bjɔʒənɛz] *nf* biogenesis.

biogénétique [bjɔʒenetik] *adj* biogenetic.

biographe [bjɔgraf] *nmf* biographer.

biographie [bjɔgrafi] *nf* biography.

biographique [bjɔgrafik] *adj* biographical.

biologie [bjɔlɔʒi] *nf* biology.

biologique [bjɔlɔʒik] *adj* **1.** BIOL biological **2.** [naturel - produit, aliment] natural, organic.

biologiste [bjɔlɔʒist] *nmf* biologist.

biomasse [bjɔmas] *nf* biomass.

biomatériau, x [bjɔmaterjo] *nm* biomaterial.

biomédical, e, aux [bjɔmedikal, o] *adj* biomedical.

biométrie [bjɔmetri] *nf* biometry, biometrics *(U)*.

biométrique [bjɔmetrik] *adj* biometric.

bionique [bjɔnik] ◇ *adj* bionic.
◇ *nf* bionics *(U)*.

biophysicien, enne [bjɔfizisjɛ̃, ɛn] *nm, f* biophysicist.

biophysique [bjɔfizik] *nf* biophysics *(U)*.

biopsie [bjɔpsi] *nf* biopsy.

biorythme [bjɔritm] *nm* biorhythm.

biosphère [bjɔsfɛr] *nf* biosphere.

biotechnologie [bjɔtɛknɔlɔʒi], **biotechnique** [bjɔtɛknik] *nf* biotechnology.

bioterrorisme [bjɔtɛrorism] *nm* bioterrorism.

biothérapie [bjɔterapi] *nf* biotherapy.

biotique [bjɔtik] *adj* biotic.

biotope [bjɔtɔp] *nm* biotope.

biotype [bjɔtip] *nm* biotype.

biovigilance [bjoviʒilɑ̃s] *nf* **1.** [en ce qui concerne les biotechnologies] GM monitoring **2.** [en ce qui concerne les prélèvements biologiques] *monitoring the health and safety of biological samples, removed organs etc.*

bioxyde [bjɔksid] *nm* dioxide.

bip [bip] *nm* **1.** [signal sonore] beep ■ **"parlez après le ~ (sonore)"** "please speak after the beep *ou* tone" ■ **émettre un ~** to bleep **2.** [appareil] pager, beeper.

bipale [bipal] *adj* twin-bladed.

biparti, e [biparti], **bipartite** [bipartit] *adj* **1.** BOT bipartite **2.** POLIT bipartite, two-party *(avant n)*.

bipartisme [bipartism] *nm* bipartism, two-party system.

bip-bip [bipbip] (*pl* **bips-bips**) *nm* bleep, bleeping sound *ou* tone ■ **faire ~** to bleep.

◆ **Bip-Bip** *npr* [personnage de dessin animé] Road Runner.

bipède [bipɛd] *adj* & *nm* biped.

biper [3] [bipe] *vt* to page.

biphasé, e [bifaze] *adj* diphasic, two-phase *(avant n)*.

biplace [biplas] ◇ *adj* two-seat *(avant n)*.
◇ *nm* two-seater.

biplan [biplɑ̃] *nm* biplane.

bipolaire [bipɔlɛr] *adj* bipolar.

bipolarisation [bipɔlarizasjɔ̃] *nf* bipolarization.

bipolarité [bipɔlarite] *nf* bipolarity.

bippeur [bipœr] *nm* = **bip** *(sens 2)*.

bique [bik] *nf* **1.** ZOOL nanny-goat **2.** *fam péj* [femme] : **vieille ~** old bag *ou* cow.

biquet, ette [bikɛ, ɛt] *nm, f* **1.** ZOOL kid **2.** [en appellatif] : **mon ~** *fam* my pet.

biquotidien, enne [bikɔtidjɛ̃, ɛn] *adj* twice-daily.

birbe [birb] *nm litt & péj* **vieux ~** old fuddy-duddy *ou* stick-in-the-mud.

BIRD [bœrd] (*abr de* **Banque internationale pour la reconstruction et le développement**) *npr f* IBRD.

biréacteur [bireaktœr] *nm* twin-engined jet.

birman, e [birmɑ̃, an] *adj* Burmese.
◆ **Birman, e** *nm, f* Burmese ▪ **les Birmans** the Burmese.

Birmanie [birmani] *npr f* : **(la) ~** Burma.

biroute [birut] *nf* **1.** AÉRON windsock, wind cone *ou* sleeve **2.** ▲ [pénis] cock▲, prick▲.

bis[1] [bis] ◇ *adv* **1.** MUS repeat, twice **2.** [dans une adresse] : **13 ~** 13 A.
◇ *interj* [à un spectacle] encore.

bis[2], **e** [bi, biz] *adj* [couleur] greyish-brown.

bisaïeul, e [bizajœl] *nm, f* great-grandfather (*f* great-grandmother).

bisannuel, elle [bizanɥɛl] *adj* [tous les deux ans] biennial.

bisbille [bizbij] *nf fam* tiff.
◆ **en bisbille** *loc adv fam* at loggerheads *ou* odds ▪ **on est longtemps restés en ~** we were at loggerheads for a long time.

biscornu, e [biskɔrny] *adj* **1.** [irrégulier - forme] irregular, misshapen **2.** [étrange - idée] cranky, queer, weird ; [- esprit, raisonnement] twisted, tortuous.

biscoteaux, biscotos [biskɔto] *nmpl fam* biceps.

biscotte [biskɔt] *nf* : **des ~s** *toasted bread sold in packets and often eaten for breakfast.*

biscuit [biskɥi] ◇ *nm* **1.** [gâteau sec] biscuit *UK*, cookie *US* ▪ **~ à la cuiller** ladyfinger, sponge finger ▪ **~ salé** savoury biscuit *UK*, cracker *US* **2.** [gâteau] : **~ de Savoie** sponge cake **3.** [porcelaine] biscuit, bisque.
◇ *adj inv* biscuit-coloured.

biscuiter [3] [biskɥite] *vt* INDUST to make into biscuit.

biscuiterie [biskɥitri] *nf* **1.** [usine] biscuit *UK ou* cookie *US* factory **2.** [industrie] biscuit *UK ou* cookie *US* trade.

bise [biz] ◇ *f* ▷ **bis** *(adj)*.
◇ *nf* **1.** GÉOGR North *ou* northerly wind **2.** [baiser] kiss ▪ **donne-moi *ou* fais-moi une ~** give me a kiss ▪ **se faire la ~** to give one another a kiss ▪ **grosses ~s** [dans une lettre] love and kisses.

biseau, x [bizo] *nm* bevel ▪ **en ~** bevelled.

biseauter [3] [bizote] *vt* **1.** [bois, verre] to bevel **2.** JEUX : **~ les cartes** to mark the cards.

bisexualité [bisɛksɥalite] *nf* bisexuality, bisexualism *US*.

bisexué, e [bisɛksɥe] *adj* bisexual.

bisexuel, elle [bisɛksɥɛl] *adj* bisexual.

bismuth [bismyt] *nm* MÉD & MÉTALL bismuth.

bison [bizɔ̃] *nm* **1.** [d'Amérique] American buffalo *ou* bison **2.** [d'Europe] European bison, wisent.

Bison Futé [bizɔ̃fyte] *npr organization giving details of road conditions, traffic congestion etc.*

bisou [bizu] *nm fam* kiss ▪ **donne-moi *ou* fais-moi un ~** give me a kiss.

bisque [bisk] *nf* bisque ▪ **~ de homard** lobster bisque.

bisquer [3] [biske] *vi fam* to be riled *ou* nettled ▪ **faire ~ qqn** to rile *ou* nettle sb.

bisse [bis] *nm Suisse* irrigation canal *(in the Valais region)*.

bissecteur, trice [bisɛktœr, tris] *adj* bisecting.
◆ **bissectrice** *nf* bisector, bisectrix.

bisser [3] [bise] *vt* [suj: spectateur] to encore ▪ [suj: artiste] to do again.

bissextile [bisɛkstil] *adj f* ▷ **année**.

bistouri [bisturi] *nm* lancet.

bistre [bistr] *adj inv & nm* bistre.

bistré, e [bistre] *adj* brownish.

bistrer [3] [bistre] *vt* to colour with bistre.

bistro(t) [bistro] *nm* ≃ café, ≃ pub *UK*, ≃ bar *US* ▪ *(comme adj inv)* **chaise/table ~** bistrot-style chair/table.

BISTROT

This word can refer either to a small café or to a cosy restaurant, especially one frequented by regulars. The *style bistrot* refers to a style of furnishing inspired by the chairs, tables and zinc countertops typical of the traditional *bistrot*.

bit [bit] *nm* INFORM bit ▪ **nombre de ~s par pouce/seconde** bits per inch/second.

BIT (*abr de* **Bureau international du travail**) *npr m* ILO.

bite▲ [bit] *nf* prick, cock.

bithérapie [biterapi] *nf* bitherapy, dual therapy.

bitte [bit] *nf* **1.** NAUT bitt **2.** ▲ [pénis] = **bite**.

bitter [bitɛr] *nm* bitters *(pl)*.

bitture△ [bityr] *nf* : **prendre une ~** to go on a bender, to get plastered.

bitturer [3] [bityre] ◆ **se bitturer**△ *vpi* to get plastered.

bitume [bitym] *nm* **1.** MIN bitumen **2.** TRAV PUB asphalt, bitumen **3.** *fam* [trottoir] pavement *UK*, sidewalk *US* ▪ **sur le ~** [sans abri] out on the street ; [sans ressources] on Skid Row.

bitumé, e [bityme] *adj* asphalted, bituminized.

bitumer [3] [bityme] *vt* to asphalt, to bituminize.

bitumineux, euse [bityminø, øz] *adj* bituminous.

biture△ [bityr] = **bitture**.

biturer [bityre] = **bitturer**.

bivalence [bivalɑ̃s] *nf* [gén - LOGIQUE] bivalence ▪ CHIM bivalency.

bivouac [bivwak] *nm* bivouac.

bivouaquer [3] [bivwake] *vi* to bivouac.

bizarre [bizar] ◇ *adj* [comportement, personne, idée, ambiance] odd, peculiar, strange ▪ **je l'ai trouvé ~ ce matin-là** I thought he was behaving oddly that morning ▪ **c'est un type vraiment ~** *fam* he's an odd bod *UK ou* a weirdo ▪ **se sentir ~** to feel (a bit) funny.
◇ *nm* : **le ~ dans l'histoire, c'est que...** what's really strange is that...

bizarrement [bizarmɑ̃] *adv* oddly, strangely, peculiarly ▪ **~, ce matin-là, il ne s'était pas rasé** for some strange reason, he hadn't shaved that morning.

bizarrerie [bizarri] *nf* **1.** [caractère bizarre] strangeness **2.** [action bizarre] eccentricity ▪ **ses ~s ne me surprennent plus** his eccentricities no longer surprise me.

bizarroïde [bizarɔid] *adj fam* odd, weird, bizarre.

bizou [bizu] *fam* = **bisou**.

bizut [bizy] *nm arg scol* fresher *UK*, freshman *US (liable to ragging)*.

bizutage [bizytaʒ] *nm arg scol practical jokes played on new arrivals in a school or college*, ≃ ragging UK, ≃ hazing US.

BIZUTAGE

In some French schools and colleges, students take to the streets in fancy-dress and play practical jokes on each other and on passers-by at the beginning of the school year. This is part of the traditional initiation ceremony known as *bizutage*.

bizuter [3] [bizyte] *vt arg scol* ≃ to rag UK, ≃ to haze US.

bla-bla(-bla) [blabla(bla)] *nm inv* blah, claptrap ▪ **c'est du ~** that's just a lot of waffle UK *ou* nonsense.

blackboulage [blakbulaʒ] *nm* blackballing.

blackbouler [3] [blakbule] *vt* [candidat] to blackball ▪ **il s'est fait ~ à son examen** they failed him at his exam.

black jack [blak(d)ʒak] *nm* blackjack.

black-out [blakaut] *nm inv* blackout.

blafard, e [blafar, ard] *adj* pallid, wan *litt*.

blague [blag] *nf* **1.** [histoire] joke ▪ **il est toujours à dire des ~s** he's always joking **2.** [duperie] hoax, wind-up UK ▪ **c'est une ~?** are you kidding?, you can't be serious! ▪ **vous allez arrêter, non mais, sans ~!** *fam* will you PLEASE give it a rest! ➲ **~ à part** kidding *ou* joking apart, in all seriousness **3.** [farce] (practical) joke, trick **4.** [maladresse] blunder, boob UK, blooper US ▪ [sottise] silly *ou* stupid thing (to do).

◆ **blague à tabac** *nf* tobacco pouch.

blaguer [3] [blage] *fam* ◇ *vi* to joke ▪ **j'aime bien ~** I like a joke.

◇ *vt* to tease.

blagueur, euse [blagœr, øz] *fam* ◇ *adj* [enfant, expression] joking, teasing.

◇ *nm, f* joker, prankster.

blair[△] [blɛr] *nm* nose, conk[△] UK, schnozz US.

blaireau, x [blɛro] *nm* **1.** ZOOL badger **2.** [pour se raser] shaving brush **3.** *fam péj* [homme] ≃ Essex man UK, ≃ Joe Sixpack US; [femme] ≃ Essex girl UK.

blairer[△] [3] [blɛre] *vt* : **personne ne peut le ~** no one can stand *ou* stick UK him.

blâmable [blamabl] *adj* blameworthy.

blâme [blam] *nm* **1.** [condamnation] disapproval *(U)* ▪ **rejeter le ~ sur qqn** to put the blame on sb **2.** ADMIN & ÉDUC reprimand ▪ **recevoir un ~** to be reprimanded ▪ **donner un ~ à qqn** to reprimand sb.

blâmer [3] [blame] *vt* **1.** [condamner] to blame ▪ **je ne le blâme pas d'avoir agi ainsi** I don't blame him for having acted that way **2.** ADMIN & ÉDUC [élève, fonctionnaire] to reprimand.

blanc, blanche [blɑ̃, blɑ̃ʃ] *adj* **1.** [couleur] white ▪ **avoir les cheveux ~s** to be white-haired *ou* snowy-haired *litt* ▪ **que tu es ~!** how pale you look! ▪ **être ~ de peau** to be white-skinned *ou* pale-skinned ➲ **être ~ comme un cachet d'aspirine** *fam hum* [non bronzé] to be completely white ▪ **~ comme un linge** white as a sheet ▪ **~ comme neige** *pr* snow-white, (as) white as snow, (as) white as the driven snow ; *fig* (as) pure as the driven snow ▪ **d'une voix blanche** in a monotone ▪ **le Mont Blanc** Mont Blanc

2. [race] white, Caucasian ▪ [personne] white, white-skinned, Caucasian

3. [vierge] blank ▪ **elle a remis (une) copie blanche** she handed in a blank sheet of paper ▪ **écrire sur du papier ~** to write on plain *ou* unlined paper ▪ **vote ~** blank vote

4. [examen] mock

5. [innocent] innocent, pure ▪ **il n'est pas sorti tout ~ de l'affaire** he hasn't come out of this business untarnished

6. CULIN [sauce, viande] white

7. [verre] plain

8. LITTÉR [vers] blank.

◆ **blanc** ◇ *nm* **1.** [couleur] white ▪ **le ~ lui va bien** she looks good in white ➲ **~ cassé** off-white

2. [matière blanche] ➲ **~ de baleine** spermaceti ▪ **~ d'Espagne** whiting

3. [cornée] : **~ de l'œil** white of the eye ▪ **regarder qqn dans le ~ des yeux** to look sb straight in the eye

4. CULIN : **~ d'œuf** egg white, white of an egg ▪ **~ de poulet** chicken breast

5. [linge] : **le ~** (household) linen ▪ **un magasin de ~** a linen shop ▪ **faire une machine de ~** to do a machine-load of whites

6. [vin] white wine ▪ **un ~ sec** a dry white wine ▪ **un petit ~** *fam* [verre] a glass of white wine ➲ **~ de ~s** blanc de blancs *(white wine from white grapes)* ▪ **~ cassis** kir *(made with blackcurrant cordial rather than crème de cassis)*

7. [espace libre] blank space, blank, space ▪ [dans une conversation] blank

8. BOT mildew.

◇ *adv* : **il a gelé ~ la semaine dernière** there was some white frost last week ➲ **voter ~** to return a blank vote ▪ **un jour il dit ~, l'autre il dit noir** one day he says yes, the next day he says no.

◆ **Blanc, Blanche** *nm, f* **1.** ANTHR white *ou* Caucasian man *(f* woman) ▪ **il a épousé une Blanche** he married a white woman ▪ **les Blancs** white people

2. HIST [en Russie] White Russian ▪ [en France] Bourbon supporter *(in post-revolutionary France)* ▪ **les Blancs et les Bleus** *Chouan insurgents and Republican soldiers during the French Revolution.*

◆ **blanche** *nf* **1.** MUS minim UK, half note US

2. [△] *arg crime* [héroïne] : **la blanche** smack[△]

3. [eau-de-vie] colourless spirit.

◆ **à blanc** ◇ *loc adj* [cartouche] blank ▪ **une balle à ~** a blank.

◇ *loc adv* **1.** ARM : **tirer à ~** to fire blanks

2. [à un point extrême] : **chauffer à ~** to make white-hot.

◆ **en blanc** ◇ *loc adj* **1.** [chèque, procuration] blank

2. [personne] : **une mariée en ~** a bride wearing white.

◇ *loc adv* [peindre, colorer] white ▪ [s'habiller, sortir] in white ▪ **laisser une ligne/page en ~** to leave a line/page blank ▪ **tu vas te marier en ~?** will you wear white?

blanc-bec [blɑ̃bɛk] *(pl* **blancs-becs***) nm* greenhorn ▪ **jeune ~** young whippersnapper.

blanchâtre [blɑ̃ʃatr] *adj* [mur] offwhite, whitish ▪ [nuage] whitish ▪ [teint] pallid.

blanche [blɑ̃ʃ] *f* ▻ **blanc**.

Blanche-Neige [blɑ̃ʃnɛʒ] *npr* Snow White ▪ **'~ et les sept nains'** *Grimm* 'Snow White and the Seven Dwarfs'.

blancheur [blɑ̃ʃœr] *nf* **1.** [couleur] whiteness ▪ **ces draps sont d'une ~ douteuse** these sheets aren't very white **2.** *litt* [pureté] purity, innocence.

blanchiment [blɑ̃ʃimɑ̃] *nm* **1.** [décoloration, nettoyage - d'un mur] whitewashing ; [- d'un tissu] bleaching **2.** [de l'argent] laundering **3.** [barbe, cheveux] ? **4.** HORT (industrial) blanching.

blanchir [32] [blɑ̃ʃir] ◇ *vt* **1.** [couvrir de blanc] to whiten, to turn white ▪ **~ à la chaux** to whitewash ‖ [décolorer] to turn white, to bleach **2.** [nettoyer - linge] to launder ▪ **être logé, nourri et blanchi** to get bed and board and to have one's laundry done **3.** [innocenter] to exonerate, to clear ▪ **il est sorti complètement blanchi des accusations portées contre lui** he was cleared of the charges laid against him ‖ [argent] : **~ l'argent de la drogue** to launder money made from drug trafficking **4.** CULIN to blanch **5.** IMPR [texte, page] to space, to space out *(sép)*.

◇ *vi* [barbe, cheveux] to turn white.

◆ **se blanchir** *vp (emploi réfléchi)* to exonerate o.s., to clear one's name ▪ **se ~ d'une accusation** to clear one's name of an allegation.

blanchissage [blɑ̃ʃisaʒ] *nm* **1.** [nettoyage] laundering ▪ **porter ses draps au ~** to take one's sheets to the laundry **2.** [raffinage] refining.

blanchissement [blɑ̃ʃismɑ̃] *nm* [nettoyage d'un tissu] cleaning, bleaching ▪ **~ à la chaux** whitewashing.

blanchisserie [blɑ̃ʃisri] *nf* laundry ■ **envoyer ses draps à la ~** to send one's sheets away to be laundered *ou* cleaned.

blanchisseur, euse [blɑ̃ʃisœr, øz] *nm, f* launderer, laundryman (*f* laundrywoman).

blanc-manger [blɑ̃mɑ̃ʒe] (*pl* **blancs-mangers**) *nm almond milk jelly.*

blanc-seing [blɑ̃sɛ̃] (*pl* **blancs-seings**) *nm* paper signed in blank ■ **donner son ~ à qqn** *pr & fig* to give sb carte blanche.

blanquette [blɑ̃kɛt] *nf* **1.** [vin] : **~ de Limoux** *sparkling white wine* **2.** CULIN blanquette ■ **~ de veau** blanquette of veal.

blase△ [blaz] *nm* **1.** [nom] handle△, moniker△ **2.** [nez] beak△, hooter *UK*△, schnozz *US*.

blasé, e [blaze] ◇ *adj* blasé.
◇ *nm, f* blasé person ■ **jouer les ~s** to act as if one's seen it all.

blaser [3] [blaze] *vt* to make blasé.
◆ **se blaser** *vpi* to become blasé.

blason [blazɔ̃] *nm* **1.** [écu] arms, blazon ■ **redorer son ~** [ses finances] to restore the family fortune *(by marrying into money)* ; [son prestige] to polish up one's image **2.** [héraldique] heraldry.

blasphémateur, trice [blasfematœr, tris] ◇ *adj* [personne] blaspheming ■ [acte, parole] blasphemous.
◇ *nm, f* blasphemer.

blasphématoire [blasfematwar] *adj* blasphemous.

blasphème [blasfɛm] *nm* blasphemy.

blasphémer [18] [blasfeme] ◇ *vi* to blaspheme.
◇ *vt litt* **~ le nom de Dieu** to take God's name in vain.

blastomycose [blastɔmikoz] *nf* blastomycosis.

blatérer [18] [blatere] *vi* [bélier] to bleat ■ [chameau] to bray.

blatte [blat] *nf* cockroach.

blazer [blazɛr] *nm* blazer.

blé [ble] *nm* **1.** BOT wheat ■ **~ noir** buckwheat ■ **~ en herbe** wheat in the blade ■ **~s** *litt* [champs] wheatfields **2.** △ [argent] dosh△ *UK*, dough△ *US*.

bled [blɛd] *nm* **1.** *fam* [petit village] small village ■ *péj* dump, hole ■ **un petit ~ paumé** a little place out in the sticks *ou* the middle of nowhere **2.** [en Afrique du Nord] : **le ~** the interior of the country.

blêmir [32] [blemir] *vi* to blanch, to (turn) pale ■ **~ de peur/rage** to go ashen-faced with fear/rage.

blêmissement [blemismɑ̃] *nm* paling, blanching.

blennorragie [blenɔraʒi] *nf* blennorrhagia, gonorrhoea.

blennorrhée [blenɔre] *nf* blennorrhoea.

blèsement [blɛzmɑ̃] *nm* lisping.

bléser [18] [bleze] *vi* to lisp.

blessant, e [blɛsɑ̃, ɑ̃t] *adj* wounding, hurtful ■ **se montrer ~ envers qqn** to hurt sb's feelings.

blessé, e [blese] ◇ *adj* **1.** [soldat] wounded ■ [accidenté] injured ■ **~ au genou** hurt in the knee **2.** [vexé - amour-propre, orgueil, personne] hurt.
◇ *nm, f* [victime - d'un accident] injured person ; [- d'une agression] wounded person ■ **les ~s de la route** road casualties ■ **~ léger/grave** slightly/severely injured person ➋ **grand ~** severely injured person ■ **~ de guerre** [en service] wounded soldier ; [après la guerre] wounded veteran.

blesser [4] [blese] *vt* **1.** [au cours d'un accident] to injure, to hurt ■ [au cours d'une agression] to injure, to wound ■ **il a été blessé par balle** he was hit by a bullet, he sustained a bullet-wound ■ **~ qqn avec un couteau** to inflict a knife-wound on sb ■ **elle est blessée à la jambe** she has a leg injury, her leg's hurt ■ **il a été blessé à la guerre** he was wounded in the war, he has a war-wound **2.** [partie du corps] to hurt, to make sore **3.** [offenser] to offend, to upset ■ **tes paroles m'ont blessé** I felt hurt by what you said ■ **~ qqn dans son amour-propre** to hurt sb's pride **4.** *litt* [aller contre - convenances, vérité] to offend ; [- intérêts] to harm.
◆ **se blesser** *vpi* to injure *ou* to hurt o.s. ■ **elle s'est blessée au bras** she injured *ou* hurt her arm.

blessure [blesyr] *nf* **1.** [lésion] wound, injury ■ **~ grave/légère/mortelle** severe/slight/fatal injury ■ **nettoyer une ~** to clean out a wound **2.** [offense] wound ■ **une ~ d'amour-propre** a blow to one's pride *ou* self-esteem.

blet, ette [blɛ, blɛt] *adj* mushy, overripe.
◆ **blette** *nf* = **bette**.

blettir [32] [bletir] *vi* to become mushy *ou* overripe.

blettissement [bletismɑ̃] *nm* : **pour empêcher le ~ des poires** to stop pears becoming mushy *ou* overripe.

bleu, e [blø] ◇ *adj* **1.** [coloré] blue ■ **avoir les yeux ~s** to have blue eyes, to be blue-eyed
2. [meurtri, altéré] blue, bruised ■ **il a les lèvres ~es** his lips are blue ■ **~ de froid** blue with cold
3. *loc* **avoir une peur ~e** to have the fright of one's life, to be terrified ■ **avoir une peur ~e de qqch/qqn** to be terrified *ou* scared stiff of sthg/sb
4. CULIN very rare.
◇ *nm, f fam* [gén] newcomer, greenhorn ■ MIL rookie, raw recruit.
◆ **bleu** *nm* **1.** [couleur] blue ■ **peindre un mur en ~** to paint a wall blue ■ **admirer le ~ du ciel/de la mer** to admire the blueness of the sky/sea ■ **~ clair** light blue ■ **~ foncé** dark blue ➋ **~ acier** steel blue ■ **~ ardoise** slate blue ■ **~ canard** peacock blue ■ **~ ciel** sky blue ■ **~ (de) cobalt** cobalt blue ■ **~ indigo** (indigo) blue ■ **~ lavande** lavender blue ■ **~ marine** navy blue ■ **~ de méthylène** MÉD methylene blue ■ **~ noir** blue black ■ **~ nuit** midnight blue ■ **~ outremer** ultramarine ■ **~ pastel** powder blue ■ **~ roi** royal blue ■ **~ turquoise** turquoise ■ **~ vert** blue green ■ **le grand ~** the blue depths of the sea
2. [ecchymose] bruise ■ **se faire un ~** to get a bruise ■ **se faire un ~ à la cuisse** to bruise one's thigh ■ **être couvert de ~s** to be black and blue, to be covered in bruises
3. [vêtement] : **~ (de travail)** (worker's denim) overalls
4. [fromage] blue cheese
5. HIST soldier of the Republic *(during the French Revolution).*
◆ **bleue** *nf* [mer] : **la grande ~e** the Mediterranean (sea).
◆ **au bleu** *loc adj* CULIN : **truite au ~** trout au bleu.
◆ **les Bleus** SPORT ■ *name of the French national teams.*

bleuâtre [bløatr] *adj* bluish, bluey.

bleuet [bløɛ] *nm* **1.** [fleur] cornflower **2.** *Québec* [fruit] blueberry, huckleberry.

bleuir [32] [bløir] ◇ *vi* to turn *ou* to go blue.
◇ *vt* to turn blue.

bleuissement [bløismɑ̃] *nm* : **empêcher le ~ des chairs** to stop the flesh turning *ou* going blue.

bleuté, e [bløte] *adj* [pétale, aile] blue-tinged ■ [lentille, verre] blue-tinted.

blindage [blɛ̃daʒ] *nm* **1.** [revêtement] armour plate *ou* plating ■ [fait de blinder] armouring **2.** ÉLECTR screening, shielding **3.** [d'une porte] reinforcing **4.** MIN timbering.

blindé, e [blɛ̃de] *adj* **1.** [voiture, tank, train] armoured, armour-clad, armour-plated ■ [brigade, division] armoured **2.** [renforcé - porte, paroi] reinforced **3.** *fam* [insensible] hardened **4.** △ [ivre] plastered△, sloshed△ *UK*.
◆ **blindé** *nm* MIL [véhicule] armoured vehicle ■ **les ~s** the armour ‖ [soldat] *member of a tank regiment.*

blinder [3] [blɛ̃de] *vt* **1.** [contre les agressions] to armour **2.** [renforcer - porte] to reinforce **3.** ÉLECTR to shield **4.** MIN to timber **5.** *fam* [endurcir] to toughen (up), to harden ■ **le genre d'éducation qui vous blinde pour la vie** the sort of education that gives you a thick skin for the rest of your life.
◆ **se blinder** *vpi* **1.** △ [s'enivrer] to drink o.s. into a stupor **2.** *fam* [s'endurcir] to toughen o.s. up.

blini [blini] *nm* blini.

blister [blistɛr] *nm* blister pack.

blizzard [blizar] *nm* blizzard.

bloc [blɔk] *nm* **1.** [masse - de pierre] block ; [- de bois, de béton] block, lump ■ **être tout d'un ~** [en un seul morceau] to be made of a single block ; [trapu] to be stockily built ; [direct] to be simple and straightforward ; [inflexible] to be unyielding **2.** [de papier] pad ■ **~ de bureau/papier** desk/writing pad ■ **~ calendrier** tear-off calendar ■ **~ à en-tête** headed notepad **3.** INFORM : **~ de calcul** arithmetic unit ■ **~ de mémoire** memory bank **4.** [installation] : **~ frigorifique** refrigeration unit ■ **~ opératoire** [salle] operating theatre ; [locaux] surgical unit **5.** [maisons] block **6.** [ensemble] block ■ **former un ~** [sociétés] to form a grouping ; [amis, alliés] to stand together ; [composants] to form a single whole ■ **faire ~** to form a block ■ **faire ~ avec/contre qqn** to stand (together) with/against sb ■ **le ~ des pays de l'Est** *ou* **soviétique** HIST the Eastern *ou* Soviet bloc ■ **le ~ des pays de l'Ouest** *ou* **occidental** the Western Alliance **7.** ÉCON & FIN : **~ monétaire** monetary bloc **8.** △ *arg crime* [prison] nick△ *UK*, slammer△.

◆ **à bloc** *loc adv* : **visser une vis à ~** to screw a screw down hard ■ **gonfler un pneu à ~** to blow a tyre right *UK ou* all the way *US* up ➲ **il est gonflé** *ou* **remonté à ~** *fam* he's on top form *ou* full of beans ■ **ne le provoque pas, il est remonté à ~ !** leave him alone, he's already wound up!

◆ **en bloc** *loc adv* as a whole ■ **j'ai tout rejeté en ~** I rejected it lock, stock and barrel, I rejected the whole thing ■ **condamner une politique en ~** to condemn a policy outright.

blocage [blɔkaʒ] *nm* **1.** [arrêt - des freins] locking, jamming on ; [- d'un écrou] tightening (up) ■ SPORT [- de la balle] blocking, trapping **2.** ÉCON [des loyers, des tarifs] freeze ■ **~ des prix et des salaires** freeze on wages and prices **3.** PSYCHOL block, blockage ■ **faire un ~ sur qqch** to block sthg off **4.** CONSTR rubble, infill.

blocaille [blɔkaj] *nf* rubble.

bloc-cuisine [blɔkkɥizin] (*pl* **blocs-cuisines**) *nm* kitchen unit.

bloc-évier [blɔkevje] (*pl* **blocs-éviers**) *nm* sink unit.

block [blɔk] *nm* RAIL block system.

blockhaus [blɔkos] *nm* blockhouse ■ [de petite taille] pillbox.

bloc-moteur [blɔkmɔtœr] (*pl* **blocs-moteurs**) *nm* engine block.

bloc-notes [blɔknɔt] (*pl* **blocs-notes**) *nm* notepad.

blocus [blɔkys] *nm* blockade ■ **faire le ~ d'une ville** to blockade a city ■ **le Blocus continental** HIST the Continental System.

blog [blɔg] *nm* INFORM blog.

blogueur, euse [blɔgœr, øz] *nm, f* INFORM blogger.

blond, e [blɔ̃, blɔ̃d] ◇ *adj* **1.** [chevelure] blond, fair ■ [personne] blond, fair-haired ■ **~ platine** *ou* **platiné** platinum blond ■ **~ ardent** *ou* **roux** *ou* **vénitien** light auburn ■ **~ cendré** ash blond ■ **~ filasse** flaxen-haired ■ **~ comme les blés** golden-haired **2.** [jaune pâle] pale yellow, golden, honey-coloured.
◇ *nm, f* blonde, fair-haired man (*f* woman) ■ **une ~e incendiaire** a bombshell ■ **une ~e décolorée** a peroxide blonde ■ **une ~e platine** a platinum blonde.

◆ **blond** *nm* [couleur - des cheveux] blond colour ; [- du sable] golden colour ■ **ses cheveux sont d'un ~ très clair** she has light blond hair.

◆ **blonde** *nf* **1.** [cigarette] Virginia cigarette **2.** [bière] lager **3.** *Québec* [amie] girlfriend.

blondasse [blɔ̃das] *adj péj* yellowish.

blondeur [blɔ̃dœr] *nf* fairness, blondness, blondeness.

blondinet, ette [blɔ̃dinɛ, ɛt] ◇ *adj* blond-haired, fair-haired.
◇ *nm, f* little blond-haired *ou* fair-haired child.

blondir [32] [blɔ̃dir] ◇ *vi* **1.** [personne, cheveux] to go fairer **2.** CULIN : **faire ~ des oignons** to fry onions gently until transparent **3.** *litt* [feuille, blé] to turn gold.
◇ *vt* : **~ ses cheveux** [à l'eau oxygénée] to bleach one's hair ; [par mèches] to put highlights in one's hair.

bloquer [3] [blɔke] *vt* **1.** [caler - table] to wedge, to stop wobbling ■ **bloque la porte** [ouverte] wedge the door open ; [fermée] wedge the door shut ■ **c'est le tapis qui bloque la porte** the carpet's jamming the door ■ **~ une roue** [avec une cale] to put a block under *ou* to chock a wheel ; [avec un sabot de Denver] to clamp a wheel
2. [serrer fort - vis] to screw down hard, to overtighten ; [- frein] to jam on, to lock
3. [entraver] : **~ le passage** *ou* **la route** to block *ou* to obstruct *sout* the way ■ **je suis bloqué à la maison avec un gros rhume** I'm stuck at home with a bad cold ■ **les pourparlers sont bloqués** the negotiations are at a standstill *ou* have reached an impasse
4. [empêcher l'accès à - ville, point stratégique] to block, to seal off *(sép)* ■ **bloqué par la neige** snowbound
5. *fam* [retenir - une personne] to hold up *(sép)*
6. ÉCON [loyers, prix, salaires] to freeze ■ FIN [compte] to freeze ■ [chèque] to stop ■ POLIT [mesure, vote] to block
7. [réunir] to group together ■ **on va ~ les activités sportives le matin** we'll have all sports events in the morning
8. PSYCHOL to cause *ou* to produce a (mental) block in ■ **ça la bloque** she has a mental block about it
9. SPORT : **~ la balle** [au basket] to block the ball ; [au football] to trap the ball
10. *Québec* [échouer à - examen] to fail, to flunk
11. CONSTR to fill (with rubble).

◆ **se bloquer** *vpi* **1.** [clef] to jam, to stick, to get stuck ■ [roue] to jam ■ [machine, mécanisme] to jam, to get stuck ■ [frein, roue] to jam, to lock
2. [personne - ne pas communiquer] to close in on o.s. ; [- se troubler] to have a mental block ■ **je me bloque quand on me parle sur ce ton** my mind goes blank *ou* I freeze when somebody speaks to me like that.

blottir [32] [blɔtir] *vt* **1.** [poser] : **~ sa tête contre l'épaule de qqn** to lay one's head on sb's shoulder **2.** *fig* **être blotti** : **ferme blottie au fond de la vallée** farmhouse nestling in the bottom of the valley.

◆ **se blottir** *vpi* to curl *ou* to cuddle *ou* to snuggle up ■ **blotti sous mes couvertures** snug in my blankets.

blousant, e [bluzɑ̃, ɑ̃t] *adj* loose, loose-fitting.

blouse [bluz] *nf* **1.** [à l'école] *smock formerly worn by French schoolchildren* ■ [pour travailler] overalls ■ [à l'ancienne, de paysan] smock ■ [corsage] blouse **2.** [d'un médecin] white coat ■ [d'un chimiste, d'un laborantin] lab coat ■ **les ~s blanches** doctors and nurses.

blouser [3] [bluze] ◇ *vt* **1.** *vieilli* [au billard] to pot, to pocket **2.** *fam* [tromper] to con, to trick.
◇ *vi* to be loose-fitting, to fit loosely ■ **faire ~ un chemisier** to pull a blouse out a bit at the waist.

blouson [bluzɔ̃] *nm* (short) jacket ■ **~ d'aviateur** bomber jacket ■ **les ~s noirs** *young louts in black leather jackets.*

blue-jean [bludʒin] (*pl* **blue-jeans**) *nm* (pair of) jeans.

blues [bluz] *nm* blues *(sing)* ■ **chanter le ~** to sing the blues.

bluet [blyɛ] *nm* cornflower ■ *Québec* blueberry.

bluff [blœf] *nm* bluff ■ **ne le crois pas, c'est du ~ !** don't believe him, he's just bluffing!

bluffer [3] [blœfe] *vt* & *vi* to bluff.

bluffeur, euse [blœfœr, øz] ◇ *adj* bluffing.
◇ *nm, f* bluffer.

blush [blœʃ] *nm* blusher.

blutage [blytaʒ] *nm* bolting, boulting.

BN *npr f* = **Bibliothèque nationale**.

boa [bɔa] *nm* **1.** ZOOL boa ■ **~ constricteur** boa constrictor **2.** [vêtement] boa.

boat people [botpipœl] *nm inv* (South East Asian) refugee ■ **les ~** the boat people.

bob [bɔb] *nm* **1.** [chapeau] sun hat **2.** = **bobsleigh**.

bobard [bɔbar] *nm fam* fib ■ **raconter des ~s** to fib△, to tell fibs.

bobèche [bɔbɛʃ] *nf* [d'un bougeoir] candle ring.

bobinage [bɔbinaʒ] *nm* **1.** [enroulage] winding, reeling **2.** ÉLECTR coil.

bobine [bɔbin] *nf* **1.** TEXT bobbin, reel, spool ■ **une ~ de fil** a reel of thread **2.** ÉLECTR coil **3.** CINÉ & PHOTO reel **4.** AUTO : **~ d'allumage** ignition coil **5.** *fam* [visage] face, mug.

bobinette [bɔbinɛt] *nf arch* wooden latch.

bobineur, euse [bɔbinœr, øz] *nm, f* winder, winding operative.
◆ **bobineur** *nm* [d'une machine à coudre] bobbin winder.
◆ **bobineuse** *nf* winding machine, coiler.

bobo [bobo] *nm langage enfantin* [égratignure] scratch ■ [bosse] bump ■ **faire ~ (à qqn)** to hurt (sb) ■ **se faire ~** to hurt o.s.

bobonne [bɔbɔn] *nf fam péj* wife, old girl *ou* lady ■ **sa femme, c'est une vraie ~** his wife's the housewife-in-curlers type.

bobsleigh [bɔbslɛg] *nm* bobsleigh, bobsled *US*.

bocage [bɔkaʒ] *nm* **1.** GÉOGR bocage *(countryside with small fields and many hedges)* **2.** *litt* [bois] copse, coppice, thicket.

bocager, ère [bɔkaʒe, ɛr] *adj* : **pays/paysage ~** country/landscape of small fields and hedges.

bocal, aux [bɔkal, o] *nm* **1.** [pour les conserves] jar, bottle ■ **mettre des haricots verts en bocaux** to preserve *ou* to bottle green beans **2.** [aquarium] fishbowl, bowl.

Boccace [bɔkas] *npr* Boccaccio.

boche△ [bɔʃ] *nmf vieilli & injur* Boche ■ **les ~s** the Boche.

Bochiman [bɔʃimɑ̃] *npr mpl* Bushman, Bushmen.

bock [bɔk] *nm* [récipient] ≃ (half-pint) beer glass ■ [contenu] glass of beer.

body [bɔdi] *nm* bodystocking, body.

bodybuildé, e [bɔdibilde] *adj fam fam* muscly.

body-building [bɔdibildiŋ] (*pl* **body-buildings**) *nm* : **le ~** body building.

Boer [bur] *npr m* : **les ~s** the Boers.

bœuf [bœf] *(pl* [bø]*)* ◇ *nm* **1.** ZOOL [de trait] ox ■ [de boucherie] bullock, steer ■ **comme un ~ : fort comme un ~** as strong as an ox ■ **saigner comme un ~** to bleed profusely ■ **souffler comme un ~** to wheeze *ou* to pant (heavily) **2.** CULIN beef ■ **~ bourguignon** bœuf *ou* beef bourguignon ■ **~ gros sel** ≃ boiled beef and vegetables (with sea salt) ■ **~ (à la) mode** beef à la mode **3.** *fam* MUS jam session ■ **faire un ~** to have a jam session, to jam.
◇ *adj inv fam* : **effet ~ : elle a fait un effet ~** she made quite a splash.

bof [bɔf] *interj term expressing lack of interest or enthusiasm* ■ **tu as aimé le film? – ~!** did you like the film? – it was all right I suppose ■ **la ~ génération** *in the seventies, the young who didn't seem to be interested in anything.*

BOF [bɔf, beoɛf] *(abr de* **Beurre, Œufs, Fromages***)* *nm* HIST *name given to black market profiteers during the Occupation of France.*

bogey [bɔgɛ] *nm* SPORT bogey.

Bogota [bɔgɔta] *npr* Bogota.

bogue [bɔg] ◇ *nf* BOT chestnut bur.
◇ *nm* INFORM bug ■ **~ de l'an 2000** millenium bug, Y2K.

bohème [bɔɛm] ◇ *adj* bohemian ■ **lui, c'est le genre ~** he's the artistic type.
◇ *nmf* bohemian.
◇ *nf* : **la ~** the bohemian *ou* artistic way of life.

Bohême [bɔɛm] *npr f* : **(la) ~** Bohemia.

bohémien, enne [bɔemjɛ̃, ɛn] *adj* Bohemian.
◆ **Bohémien, enne** *nm, f* **1.** [de Bohême] Bohemian **2.** *péj* [nomade] gipsy, traveller.

boille [bwaj] = **bouille** *(sens 2)*.

boire[1] [bwar] *nm* : **il en oublie** *ou* **perd le ~ et le manger** he's becoming totally distracted.

boire[2] **[108]** [bwar] ◇ *vt* **1.** [avaler] to drink ■ **~ un coup** *fam* *ou* **pot** *fam ou* **verre** to have a drink *ou* jar *UK* ■ **elle a tout bu d'un coup** she gulped it all down ■ **~ un coup de trop** *fam* to have one too many ■ **commander** *ou* **demander quelque chose à ~** to order a drink ■ *(en usage absolu)* **il buvait à petits coups** *ou* **à petites gorgées** he was sipping his drink ▶ **ça se boit comme du petit-lait** it goes down a treat *UK ou* like silk *US* ■ **~ du lait** *ou* **du petit-lait** to lap it up ■ **~ les paroles de qqn : il buvait ses paroles** he was lapping up everything she said ■ **~ la tasse** *fam* [en nageant] to swallow water ; [perdre de l'argent] to lose a lot of money ; [faire faillite] to go under **2.** [absorber] to absorb, to soak up *(sép)*.
◇ *vi* **1.** [s'hydrater] to drink, to take in a liquid ■ **fais-le ~** [malade, enfant, animal] give him a drink *ou* something to drink ■ **s'arrêter pour faire ~ les chevaux** to stop and water the horses ■ **tant qu'elle a de la fièvre, faites-la ~ abondamment** if she's feverish make sure she gets plenty of liquid ▶ **il y a à ~ et à manger là-dedans** [dans un verre] there are bits floating in the glass ; *fig* it's a bit of a mixed bag ■ **~ jusqu'à plus soif** to drink one's fill **2.** [pour fêter un événement] : **~ à** to toast ■ **nous buvons à ta santé** we're drinking to *ou* toasting your health **3.** [pour s'enivrer] to drink ■ **il boit trop** he has a drink problem ■ **il a toujours aimé ~** he's always enjoyed a drink ▶ **~ comme une éponge** *ou* **un tonneau** *ou* **un trou** *fam* to drink like a fish.
◆ **se boire** *vp (emploi passif)* : **se boit frais/chambré** should be drunk chilled/at room temperature.

bois [bwa] *nm* **1.** [de grands arbres] wood, wooded area ■ [de jeunes ou petits arbres] thicket, copse, coppice ■ [d'arbres plantés] grove ■ **un ~ de pins** a pine grove **2.** [matière] wood *(U)* ■ **en ~** wooden ▶ **~ à brûler** *ou* **de chauffage** firewood ■ **~ blanc** whitewood ■ **~ de charpente** timber ■ **~ debout** standing timber ■ **~ d'ébène** *pr* ebony ; *fig* black gold ■ **~ des îles** tropical hardwood ■ **~ de rose** rosewood ■ **~ mort** deadwood ■ **petit ~** kindling ■ **il est du ~ dont on fait les flûtes** he's very easy-going ■ **il est du ~ dont on fait les héros** he's got the stuff of heroes ■ **faire feu** *ou* **flèche de tout ~** to use all available means ■ **touchons** *ou* **je touche du ~** touch wood ■ **je vais leur montrer de quel ~ je me chauffe!** *fam* I'll show them what I'm made of! **3.** [d'une raquette] frame ■ [d'un club de golf] wood ■ **faire un ~** *fam* [au tennis] to hit the ball off the wood ■ **~ de lit** bedstead **4.** ART : **~ (gravé)** woodcut.
◆ **bois** *nmpl* ZOOL antlers ■ FOOTBALL goalposts ■ MUS woodwind section *ou* instruments.
◆ **de bois** *loc adj* **1.** [charpente, jouet, meuble] wooden **2.** [impassible] : **je ne suis pas de ~** I'm only human.

boisage [bwazaʒ] *nm* MIN [action] timbering ■ [soutènement] timber work.

boisé, e [bwaze] *adj* **1.** [région, terrain] wooded, woody **2.** CONSTR panelled.

boisement [bwazmɑ̃] *nm* afforestation.

boiser **[3]** [bwaze] *vt* **1.** AGRIC to afforest **2.** MIN to timber **3.** CONSTR to panel.

boiserie [bwazri] *nf* piece of decorative woodwork ■ **des ~s** panelling.

boisseau, x [bwaso] *nm* [mesure] bushel ■ **garder** *ou* **mettre** *ou* **tenir qqch sous le ~** to keep sthg hidden *ou* a secret.

boisson [bwasɔ̃] *nf* **1.** [liquide à boire] drink ■ **la consommation de ~s alcoolisées est interdite dans l'enceinte du stade** drinking alcohol is forbidden inside the stadium **2.** [alcool] : **la ~** drink, drinking ■ **c'est la ~ qui l'a tué** excessive drinking killed him.

boîte [bwat] *nf* **1.** [récipient - à couvercle, à fente] box ■ **~ d'allumettes** [pleine] box of matches ; [vide] matchbox ■ **~ à idées** suggestions box ■ **~ à ordures** dustbin *UK*, trash can *US* ■ **~ à outils** tool box, toolkit ■ **~ à ouvrage** sewing box ■ **et toi, ~ à malice?** *fam* what about you, you clever little monkey? ■ **~ de Pandore** Pandora's box
2. [pour aliments] : **~ (de conserve)** tin *UK*, can
3. [contenu - d'un récipient à couvercle, à fente] box, boxful ; [- d'une conserve] tinful *UK*, canful
4. [pour le courrier] : **~ (à)** *ou* **aux lettres** [dans la rue] pillar box *UK*, mailbox *US* ; [chez soi] letterbox *UK*, mailbox *US* ■ **mettre qqch à la ~** to post *UK ou* to mail *US* sthg ■ **servir de ~ aux lettres** to be a go-between ■ **~ postale** post box

5. AÉRON & AUTO : **~ noire** black box
6. *fam* [discothèque] : **~ de jazz** jazz club ■ **aller en ~** to go to a nightclub
7. *fam* [lieu de travail] office ■ **~ d'intérim** temping agency ■ **j'ai changé de ~** I got a job with a new firm ■ **il a été renvoyé de sa ~** he got the sack ‖ [lycée] school ■ **~ à bac** *OU* **bachot** *péj* crammer *UK*
8. ANAT : **~ crânienne** cranium
9. AUTO : **~ à gants** glove compartment ■ **~ de vitesses** gearbox
10. MUS : **~ à musique** musical box ■ **~ à rythmes** drum machine
11. INFORM : **~d'alerte** [avec 'OK'] warning box, alert box ; [avec 'oui' et 'non'] confirm box : **~ aux lettres (électronique)** electronic mailbox ■ **~ de dialogue** dialog box
12. TÉLÉCOM : **~ vocale** voicemail, message box.
◆ **en boîte** ◇ *loc adj* tinned, canned.
◇ *loc adv* **1.** INDUST & CULIN : **mettre des fruits en ~** to preserve *ou* to tin fruit
2. *fam loc* **mettre qqn en ~** to wind sb up *UK*, to pull sb's leg.

boitement [bwatmɑ̃] *nm* limp, limping ■ **être affecté d'un léger ~** to limp a little.

boiter [3] [bwate] *vi* **1.** [en marchant] to limp, to be lame ■ **~ du pied droit** *OU* **de la jambe droite** to have a game *OU* lame right leg **2.** [être bancal - chaise, table] to wobble, to be rickety **3.** [être imparfait - projet, raisonnement] to be shaky.

boiteux, euse [bwatø, øz] ◇ *adj* **1.** [cheval, personne] lame ■ [meuble, table] rickety ■ **il est ~** he walks with a limp, he limps **2.** [imparfait - paix, alliance] fragile, brittle, shaky ; [- comparaison, raisonnement] unsound, shaky ■ **ton premier paragraphe est ~** your first paragraph doesn't hang together.
◇ *nm, f* lame man (*f* woman).

boîtier [bwatje] *nm* **1.** [gén] case, casing ■ [d'une lampe de poche] battery compartment ■ **~ de montre** watchcase **2.** PHOTO camera body ■ **détacher l'objectif du ~** take the lens off (the camera).

boitillant, e [bwatijɑ̃, ɑ̃t] *adj* hobbling.

boitillement [bwatijmɑ̃] *nm* slight limp, hobble.

boitiller [3] [bwatije] *vi* to limp slightly, to be slightly lame, to hobble ■ **elle est rentrée/sortie en boitillant** she hobbled in/out.

boit-sans-soif [bwasɑ̃swaf] *nmf fam* drunk, lush *US*.

boivent *etc v* ▷ **boire**.

bol [bɔl] *nm* **1.** [récipient] bowl ■ **le Bol d'or** *French motorcycle racing trophy* **2.** [contenu] bowl, bowlful ■ **prendre un ~ d'air** [se promener] to (go and) get some fresh air ; [changer d'environnement] to get a change of air **3.** *fam* [chance] luck ■ **avoir du ~** to be a lucky devil **4.** *vieilli* [pilule] bolus.
◆ **au bol** *loc adj* [coupe de cheveux] pudding-bowl *(modif) UK*, bowl *(modif) US*.
◆ **bol alimentaire** *nm* bolus.

bolchevik, bolchevique [bɔlʃevik] *adj* & *nmf* Bolshevik, Bolshevist.

bolchevisme [bɔlʃevism] *nm* Bolshevism.

bolduc [bɔldyk] *nm type of flat linen or cotton ribbon used for gift wrapping.*

bolée [bɔle] *nf* : **~ de cidre** bowl *OU* bowlful of cider *(in N.W. France, cider is often served in bowls)*.

boléro [bɔlero] *nm* bolero.

bolet [bɔlɛ] *nm* boletus.

bolide [bɔlid] *nm* fast (racing) car ■ **entrer dans une/sortir d'une pièce comme un ~** to hurtle into a/out of a room.

bolivar [bɔlivar] *nm* bolivar.

Bolivie [bɔlivi] *npr f* : **(la) ~** Bolivia.

bolivien, enne [bɔlivjɛ̃, ɛn] *adj* Bolivian.
◆ **Bolivien, enne** *nm, f* Bolivian.

Bologne [bɔlɔɲ] *npr* Bologna.

bombage [bɔ̃baʒ] *nm* spray-painting.

bombance [bɔ̃bɑ̃s] *nf* feast ■ **faire ~** to feast.

bombarde [bɔ̃bard] *nf* **1.** MUS [jeu d'orgues] bombarde, bombardon ■ [de Bretagne] shawm **2.** ARM bombarde.

bombardement [bɔ̃bardəmɑ̃] *nm* **1.** MIL [avec des obus] shelling ■ [avec des bombes] bombing *(U)* ■ **~ aérien** aerial attack ; [raid] air raid ■ **les ~s aériens** [sur Londres] the Blitz **2.** [lancement de projectiles] showering, pelting ■ **~ atomique** PHYS atomic bombardment.

bombarder [3] [bɔ̃barde] *vt* **1.** MIL [avec des obus] to shell ■ [avec des bombes] to bomb **2.** [avec des projectiles] to shower, to pelt ■ PHYS to bombard ■ **~ qqn de questions** *fig* to bombard sb with questions **3.** *fam (suivi d'un n)* [promouvoir] : **il a été bombardé responsable du projet** he found himself catapulted into the position of project leader.

bombardier [bɔ̃bardje] *nm* **1.** AÉRON & MIL [avion] bomber ■ [pilote] bombardier **2.** ENTOM bombardier (beetle).

Bombay [bɔ̃bɛ] *npr* Bombay.

bombe [bɔ̃b] *nf* **1.** MIL & NUCL bomb ■ **~ A** *OU* **atomique** atom *OU* atomic bomb ■ **la ~ atomique** the Bomb ■ **~ à billes/fragmentation/neutrons** cluster/fragmentation/neutron bomb ■ **~ H** H bomb ■ **~ à hydrogène** hydrogen bomb ■ **~ incendiaire** firebomb ■ **~ à retardement** *pr* & *fig* time bomb ■ **arriver comme une ~** to come like a bolt out of the blue **2.** [aérosol] spray ■ **~ insecticide** fly *UK OU* bug *US* spray **3.** ÉQUIT riding hat *OU* cap **4.** CULIN : **~ glacée** bombe **5.** MÉD : **~ au cobalt** cobalt therapy unit **6.** *fam* [fête] feast, spree ■ **faire la ~** to whoop it up, to have a riotous old time.

bombé, e [bɔ̃be] *adj* **1.** [renflé - paroi] bulging ; [- front] bulging, domed ; [- poitrine, torse] thrown out, stuck out ; [- forme] rounded **2.** TRAV PUB cambered.

bombement [bɔ̃bmɑ̃] *nm* **1.** [renflement] bulge **2.** TRAV PUB camber.

bomber¹ [3] [bɔ̃be] ◇ *vt* **1.** TRAV PUB to camber **2.** [gonfler] : **~ le torse** *pr* to stick out one's chest ; *fig* to swagger about **3.** [slogan] to spray, to spray-paint.
◇ *vi* **1.** [route] to camber **2.** *fam* [se dépêcher] to belt along.

bomber² [bɔ̃bœr] *nm* bomber jacket.

bombyx [bɔ̃biks] *nm* bombyx ■ **~ du mûrier** silkworm moth.

bôme [bom] *nf* boom NAUT.

bon, bonne [bɔn, bɔ̃] *(devant nm commençant par voyelle ou 'h' muet* [bɔn], *f)* ◇ *adj*

A. QUI CONVIENT, QUI DONNE SATISFACTION
B. PLAISANT
C. JUSTE, ADÉQUAT
D. MORALEMENT
E. EN INTENSIF

A. QUI CONVIENT, QUI DONNE SATISFACTION

1. [en qualité - film, récolte, résultat, connaissance] good ■ **viande de bonne qualité** good-quality meat ■ **elle parle un ~ espagnol** she speaks good Spanish, her Spanish is good ■ **de bonnes notes** ÉDUC good *OU* high marks *UK OU* grades *US*
2. [qui remplit bien sa fonction - matelas, siège, chaussures, éclairage, freins] good ; [- cœur, veines, charpente, gestion, investissement] good, sound ■ **il a une bonne santé** he's in good health, his health is good ■ **une bonne vue, de ~s yeux** good eyesight ■ SPORT [au tennis] good ■ **la balle est bonne** the ball's in ■ **les bonnes vieilles méthodes** the good old methods
3. [qui n'est pas périmé - nourriture] all right ; [- document, titre de transport] valid ■ **le lait n'est plus ~** the milk's gone off *UK OU* has turned ■ **la colle n'est plus bonne** the glue isn't usable any more
4. [compétent] good ■ **~ père et ~ époux** a good father and husband ■ **en ~ professeur, il me reprend lorsque je fais des fautes** he corrects my mistakes, as any good teacher would ■ **être/ne pas être ~ en maths** to be good/bad at maths ■ **nos ~s clients** our good *OU* regular customers
5. [digne de] : **~ à : les piles sont bonnes à jeter** the batteries can go straight in the bin *UK OU* trash can *US* ■ **la table est tout juste**

bonne à faire du petit bois the table is just about good enough for firewood ➤ **à quoi ~?** what for? ▪ **je pourrais lui écrire, mais à quoi ~?** I could write to her but what would be the point? ▪ **il y a un restaurant là-bas – c'est ~ à savoir** there's a restaurant there – that's worth knowing *ou* that's good to know
6. [condamné à] : **~ pour : il est ~ pour 15 ans (de prison)** he's going to get 15 years in prison ▪ **je suis bonne pour recommencer** I'll have to do it (all over) again ▪ **on est ~s pour une amende** *fam* we're in for a fine

B. PLAISANT
1. [agréable - repas, odeur] good, nice ; [- soirée, vacances] good, nice, pleasant ▪ **ton gâteau était très ~** your cake was very good *ou* nice ▪ **l'eau du robinet n'est pas bonne** the tap water isn't very nice *ou* doesn't taste very nice ▪ **avoir une bonne odeur** to smell good *ou* nice ▪ **viens te baigner, l'eau est bonne!** come for a swim, the water's lovely and warm! ▪ **avoir une bonne tête** *ou* **bouille** *fam* to have a nice *ou* a friendly face ▪ **c'est si ~ de ne rien faire!** it feels so good to be doing nothing! ▪ **~ anniversaire!** happy birthday! ▪ **bonne (et heureuse) année!** happy new year! ▪ **bonne chance!** good luck! ▪ **bonne journée!** have a nice day! ▪ **~ voyage!** have a nice *ou* good trip! ▪ *(en intensif)* **un ~ grog bien chaud** *fam* a nice hot toddy ➤ **elle est bien bonne celle-là!** *iron* that's a good one! ; that's a bit much! ▪ **~ temps : prendre** *ou* **se donner** *ou* **se payer** *fam* **du ~ temps** to have fun, to have a great *ou* good time ▪ **le ~ vieux temps** the good old days
2. [favorable, optimiste - prévisions, présage, nouvelle] good ▪ **c'est (un) ~ signe** it's a good sign ▪ **la météo est bonne** the weather forecast is good

C. JUSTE, ADÉQUAT
1. [correct - numéro de téléphone] right ; [- réponse, solution] correct, right ▪ **c'est la bonne rue** it's the right street
2. [opportun] right, convenient, appropriate ▪ **l'héritage est arrivé au ~ moment pour elle** the inheritance came at the right time *ou* at a convenient time for her ▪ **je suis arrivé au ~ moment pour les séparer** I got there in time to separate them ▪ **juger** *ou* **trouver ~ de/que** to think it appropriate *ou* fitting to/that ▪ **elle n'a pas jugé ~ de s'excuser** she didn't find that she needed to *ou* she didn't see fit to apologize ▪ **il serait ~ de préciser l'heure de la réunion** it would be a good thing *ou* idea to give the time of the meeting ➤ **comme/où/quand/si ~ vous semble** as/wherever/whenever/if you see fit
3. [bénéfique, salutaire] good, beneficial ▪ **c'est ~ pour la santé** it's good for you, good for your health ▪ **le ~ air de la campagne** the good *ou* fresh country air
4. *fam loc* **c'est ~!** [c'est juste] that's right! ; [ça suffit] that'll do! ; [c'est d'accord] OK! ▪ **c'est ~?** OK?

D. MORALEMENT
1. [décent, honnête - conduite] good, proper ; [- influence, mœurs] good ▪ **avoir de bonnes lectures** to read the right kind of books ▪ **ils n'ont pas bonne réputation** they don't have much of a reputation
2. [bienveillant - personne] good, kind, kindly ▪ **Dieu est ~** RELIG God is merciful ▪ **je suis déjà bien ~ de te prêter ma voiture!** it's kind *ou* decent enough of me to lend you my car as it is! ➤ **~ cœur : avoir ~ cœur** to be kind-hearted ▪ **de ~ cœur** willingly ▪ **tenez, prenez, c'est de ~ cœur** please have it, I'd love you to ▪ **le Bon Dieu** the (good) Lord
3. [amical - relation] : **avoir de ~s rapports avec qqn** to be on good terms with sb
4. [brave] good ▪ **c'est une bonne petite** she's a nice *ou* good girl ▪ **et en plus ils boivent, mon ~ Monsieur!** and what's more they drink, my dear man!

E. EN INTENSIF
1. [grand, gros] good ▪ **une bonne averse** a heavy shower (of rain) ▪ **une bonne tranche** a thick slice ▪ **elle fait un ~ 42** she's a 14 or a 16, she's a large 14 ▪ **ça a duré une bonne minute** it lasted a good minute or so
2. [fort, violent] : **un ~ coup** [heurt] a hefty *ou* full blow ▪ **une bonne fessée** a good *ou* sound spanking ▪ **pleurer un ~ coup** *fam* to have a good cry
3. [complet, exemplaire] good ▪ **le mur a besoin d'un ~ lessivage** the wall needs a good scrub ▪ **arriver** *ou* **être ~ dernier** to bring up the rear ➤ **une bonne fois pour toutes** once and for all.

◇ *nm, f* **1.** [personne vertueuse] good person **2.** [personne idéale, chose souhaitée] right one ▪ **je crois que c'est enfin le ~** *fam* [lors d'un recrutement] I think we've got our man at last ; [lors d'une rencontre amoureuse] I think it's Mister Right at last.

◆ **bon** ◇ *nm* **1.** [dans les films] goody, goodie ▪ **les ~s et les méchants** the goodies and the baddies, the good guys and the bad guys **2.** [chose de qualité] : **n'acheter que du ~** to buy only good quality ➤ **il y a du ~ dans votre dissertation** there are some good points in your essay ▪ **avoir du ~** to have something good about it **3.** [ce qui est moral] : **le ~** good **4.** [coupon] coupon, voucher ▪ **~ d'achat** gift token ▪ **~ de caisse** cash voucher ▪ **~ de commande** order form ▪ **~ de garantie** guarantee ▪ **~ de livraison** delivery slip ▪ **~ de réduction** discount coupon **5.** FIN : **~ d'épargne** savings bond *ou* certificate ▪ **~ du Trésor** treasury bill.
◇ *adv* **1.** MÉTÉOR : **faire ~ : il fait ~ ici** it's nice and warm here **2.** *(suivi d'un infin)* **il ne faisait pas ~ être communiste alors** it wasn't advisable to be a communist in those days.
◇ *interj* **1.** [marque une transition] right, so, well now ▪ **~, où en étais-je?** well now *ou* right *ou* so, where was I? **2.** [en réponse] right, OK, fine ▪ **~ d'accord, allons-y** OK then, let's go.

◆ **bon à rien, bonne à rien** ◇ *loc adj* **1.** [inutile] : **je suis trop vieux, je ne suis plus ~ à rien** I'm too old, I'm useless *ou* no good now **2.** [incompétent] useless, hopeless.
◇ *nm, f* [personne sans valeur] good-for-nothing ▪ [personne incompétente] useless individual.

◆ **bon à tirer** *nm* final corrected proof ▪ **donner le ~ à tirer** to pass for press.

◆ **bonne femme** ◇ *nf fam* **1.** [petite fille] : **une petite bonne femme adorable** a lovely little girl **2.** [femme] woman ▪ **une vieille bonne femme** an old biddy.
◇ *loc adj* **1.** CULIN *cooking term used in the names of simple country dishes* **2.** COUT : **des rideaux bonne femme** *old-fashioned curtains with tie-backs and frilled edges.*

bonapartisme [bɔnapartism] *nm* Bonapartism.

bonapartiste [bɔnapartist] *adj & nmf* Bonapartist.

bonasse [bɔnas] *adj péj* easy-going, soft.

bonbon [bɔ̃bɔ̃] *nm* sweet UK, candy US ▪ **~ acidulé** acid drop ▪ **~ à la menthe** mint.

bonbonne [bɔ̃bɔn] *nf* [pour le vin] demijohn ▪ [pour des produits chimiques] carboy.

bonbonnière [bɔ̃bɔnjɛr] *nf* **1.** [boîte] sweet UK *ou* candy US box **2.** [appartement] bijou flat UK *ou* apartment US.

bond [bɔ̃] *nm* **1.** [d'une balle] bounce ▪ **prendre** *ou* **saisir une remarque au ~** to pounce on a remark ➤ **prendre** *ou* **saisir la balle au ~** *pr* to catch the ball on the bounce *ou* rebound ; *fig* to seize the opportunity **2.** [saut] jump, leap ▪ **faire un ~** [d'effroi, de surprise] to leap up ▪ **faire des ~s** *pr* to jump up and down ; *fig* to go up and down ▪ **faire un ~ en avant** [économie] to boom ; [prix, loyer] to soar ; [recherche] to leap forward ▪ **ne faire qu'un ~ : je n'ai fait qu'un ~ jusqu'à chez vous quand j'ai su la nouvelle** I rushed to your place when I heard the news ▪ **se lever d'un ~** to leap up ▪ **avancer** *ou* **progresser par ~s** to progress in leaps and bounds **3.** SPORT jump **4.** *loc* **faire faux ~ à qqn** [ne pas se présenter] to leave sb high and dry ; [décevoir] to let sb down.

bonde [bɔ̃d] *nf* **1.** [ouverture - d'un bassin] sluice gate ; [- d'un tonneau] bunghole ; [- d'un lavabo] plughole **2.** [bouchon - d'un tonneau] bung, stopper ; [- d'un lavabo] plug.

bondé, e [bɔ̃de] *adj* packed, jam-packed ▪ **le train était ~** the train was packed (with people).

bondieuserie [bɔ̃djøzri] *nf* **1.** [objet] religious trinket ▪ **des ~s** religious knick-knacks **2.** [bigoterie] religiosity.

bondir [32] [bɔ̃dir] *vi* **1.** [sauter] to bounce, to bound, to leap (up) ▪ **~ de : ~ de joie** to leap for joy ▪ **~ sur** [pour importuner, semoncer] to pounce on ▪ **faire ~** [d'indignation, de colère] : **ça va le faire ~** he'll hit the roof, he'll go mad **2.** [courir] to dash, to rush ▪ **quand il a appris l'accident, il a bondi jusqu'à l'hôpital/chez elle** when he heard about the accident, he rushed (over) to the hospital/her place.

bondissement [bɔ̃dismɑ̃] *nm litt* [d'un poulain] bouncing, bounding ■ [d'un agneau] gambolling.

bon enfant [bɔnɑ̃fɑ̃] *adj inv* [caractère] good-natured, easy-going ■ [atmosphère] relaxed, informal.

bonheur [bɔnœr] *nm* **1.** [chance] luck ■ **par ~** fortunately, luckily ■ **connaître son ~ : tu ne connais pas ton ~!** you don't know when you're lucky *ou* how lucky you are! ■ **porter ~ à qqn** to bring sb luck **2.** [contentement] happiness ■ **faire le ~ de qqn** [le contenter] to make sb happy, to bring sb happiness ■ **trouver le ~** to find happiness ■ **trouver son ~ : as-tu trouvé ton ~?** did you find what you were looking for?
◆ **au petit bonheur (la chance)** *loc adv* haphazardly.

bonheur-du-jour [bɔnœrdyʒur] (*pl* **bonheurs-du-jour**) *nm* escritoire, writing table.

bonhomie [bɔnɔmi] *nf* geniality, bonhomie.

bonhomme [bɔnɔm] (*pl* **bonshommes** [bɔ̃zɔm]) *fam* ◇ *nm* **1.** [homme] chap **2.** [partenaire] old man, fellow *vieilli* ■ [garçon] little chap *ou* lad ■ **allez viens, mon petit ~** come along, little man **3.** [figure] man ➊ **~ de neige** snowman **4.** *loc* **aller** *ou* **continuer son petit ~ de chemin** to go *ou* to carry on at one's own pace.
◇ *adj* [air, caractère] good-natured, good-tempered ■ [atmosphère] relaxed, informal.

boni [bɔni] *nm* **1.** [bonus] bonus **2.** [prime] bonus.

boniche [bɔniʃ] *fam péj* = **bonniche**.

bonification [bɔnifikasjɔ̃] *nf* **1.** AGRIC improvement **2.** SPORT [avantage] advantage, extra points **3.** [somme allouée] profit **4.** [rabais] discount, reduction **5.** ÉCON : **~ d'intérêts** interest relief.

bonifier [9] [bɔnifje] *vt* **1.** AGRIC to improve **2.** [adoucir - caractère] to improve, to mellow **3.** [payer] to pay as a bonus **4.** ÉCON to credit.
◆ **se bonifier** *vpi* [caractère] to mellow, to improve.

boniment [bɔnimɑ̃] *nm* **1.** COMM sales talk *ou* patter ■ **faire le ~** to deliver the sales patter *ou* spiel ■ **faire du ~ à** *fam* to sweet-talk, to soft-soap **2.** *fam* [mensonge] tall story ■ **tout ça, c'est des ~s** that's a load of claptrap *ou* guff ■ **arrête tes ~s** stop fibbing.

bonimenteur, euse [bɔnimɑ̃tœr, øz] *nm, f péj* [menteur] smooth talker.

bonite [bɔnit] *nf* bonito.

bonjour [bɔ̃ʒur] *nm* **1.** [salutation - gén] hello ; [- le matin] good morning ; [- l'après-midi] good afternoon ■ **vous lui donnerez le ~** *ou* **vous lui direz ~ de ma part** say hello for me ■ **vous avez le ~ de Martin** Martin sends his love ■ **bien le ~ chez vous** regards to everybody (back home) **2.** *fam* [exprime la difficulté] : **pour le faire aller à l'école, ~!** no way can you get him to go to school! ■ **je n'ai pas fait de gym depuis un mois, ~ les courbatures!** I haven't done any exercise for a month, I'm going to ache, let me tell you!

Bonn [bɔn] *npr* Bonn.

bonne [bɔn] ◇ *f* ▷ **bon**.
◇ *nf* **1.** [domestique] maid ■ **~ d'enfants** nanny *UK*, child's nurse *US* ■ **~ à tout faire** servant **2.** *fam* [chose plaisante] : **il m'en a dit** *ou* **raconté une bien ~** he told me a good one **3.** *loc* **avoir qqn à la ~** to like sb, to be in (solid) with sb *US* ■ **en avoir de ~s : tu en as de ~s!** are you kidding?

Bonne-Espérance [bɔnɛsperɑ̃s] *npr* : **le cap de ~** the Cape of Good Hope.

bonne-maman [bɔnmamɑ̃] (*pl* **bonnes-mamans**) *nf vieilli* grand-mama.

bonnement [bɔnmɑ̃] *adv* : **je lui ai dit tout ~ ce que je pensais** I quite simply told him what I thought.

bonnet [bɔnɛ] *nm* **1.** [coiffe - de femme, d'enfant] hat, bonnet ; [- de soldat, de marin] hat ■ **~ d'âne** dunce's cap ■ **~ de bain** swimming cap ■ **~ d'évêque** *fig* parson's nose ■ **~ de nuit** nightcap ; *fig & péj* wet blanket ■ **~ à poils** busby, bearskin ■ **~ phrygien** cap of liberty, Phrygian cap ■ **c'est ~ blanc et blanc ~** it's six of one and half a dozen of the other, it's all much of a muchness *UK* **2.** ZOOL reticulum **3.** [d'un soutien-gorge] cup.

bonneteau, x [bɔnto] *nm* three-card trick.

bonneterie [bɔnɛtri] *nf* **1.** [commerce] hosiery business *ou* trade **2.** [industrie] hosiery-making (industry).

bonnetier, ère [bɔntje, ɛr] *nm, f* **1.** [fabricant] hosier **2.** [ouvrier] hosiery worker.

bonniche [bɔniʃ] *nf fam péj* maid, skivvy *UK* ■ **faire la ~** to skivvy *UK*, to do all the dirty work.

bon-papa [bɔ̃papa] (*pl* **bons-papas**) *nm vieilli* grand-papa.

bonsaï [bɔnzaj] *nm* bonsai.

bonsoir [bɔ̃swar] *nm* **1.** [en arrivant] good evening ■ [en partant] good night **2.** *fam* [emploi expressif] : **ils paient les heures, mais pour les frais, ~!** they pay for your time, but when it comes to expenses, you might as well forget it! ■ **mais bon sang de ~, où est-il passé?** damn, where has he gone now?

bonté [bɔ̃te] *nf* [bienveillance] kindness, goodness ■ **elle l'a fait par pure ~ d'âme** she did it purely out of the goodness of her heart ■ **ayez la ~ de...** please be so kind as to... ➊ **~ divine!, ~ du ciel!** good gracious!
◆ **bontés** *nfpl litt* kindness, kindnesses.

bonus [bɔnys] *nm* [dans les assurances] no-claim *ou* no-claims bonus.

bonze [bɔ̃z] *nm* **1.** RELIG buddhist priest *ou* monk, bonze **2.** *fam péj & fig* big cheese ■ **un vieux ~** a pontificating old fool.

book [buk] *nm fam* pressbook, portfolio.

booké, e [buke] *adj fam* booked-up, busy.

bookmaker [bukmɛkœr] *nm* bookmaker.

booléen, enne [buleɛ̃, ɛn] *adj* Boolean.

boom [bum] *nm* **1.** [développement] boom, expansion ■ **le ~ de la natalité** the baby boom **2.** BOURSE boom.

boomer [bumœr] *nm* ACOUST woofer.

boomerang [bumrɑ̃g] *nm* boomerang ■ **faire ~** *fig*, **avoir un effet ~** *fig* to boomerang.

booster [3] [buste] *vt* to boost.

boots [buts] *nmpl* (desert) boots.

bop [bɔp] *nm* bop.

boqueteau, x [bɔkto] *nm* coppice, copse.

borate [bɔrat] *nm* borate.

borborygme [bɔrbɔrigm] *nm* **1.** [gargouillement] rumble, gurgle, borborygmus *spéc* **2.** *péj* [paroles] mumble.

borchtch [bɔrtʃ] *nm* borsch, borscht.

bord [bɔr] *nm* **1.** [côté - d'une forêt, d'un domaine] edge ; [- d'une route] side ■ **sur le ~ de** on the edge of ■ **sur le ~ de la route** by the roadside ■ **sur les ~s de : sur les ~s du fleuve** [gén] on the river bank ; [en ville] on the waterfront ■ **sur les ~s de Seine** on the embankment (in Paris), on the banks of the Seine ■ **regagner le ~** [de la mer] to get back to the shore *ou* beach ; [d'une rivière] to get back to the bank ; [d'une piscine] to get back to the side ■ **le ~ du trottoir** the kerb ➊ **le ~** *ou* **les ~s de mer** the seaside **2.** [pourtour - d'une plaie] edge ; [- d'une assiette, d'une baignoire] rim, edge ; [- d'un verre] rim ■ **remplir un verre jusqu'au ~** to fill a glass to the brim *ou* to the top **3.** COUT [non travaillé] edge ■ [replié et cousu] hem ■ [décoratif] border ■ **chapeau à larges ~s** wide-brimmed *ou* broad-brimmed hat **4.** NAUT [côté, bastingage] side ■ **jeter** *ou* **balancer** *fam* **qqch par-dessus ~** to throw *ou* to chuck sthg overboard ■ **tirer des ~s** to tack ‖ [navire] : **les hommes du ~** the crew **5.** [opinion] side ■ **nous sommes du même ~** we're on the same side.
◆ **à bord** *loc adv* AUTO on board ■ AÉRON & NAUT aboard, on board ■ **avant de monter à ~** before boarding *ou* going aboard.
◆ **à bord de** *loc prép* on board ■ **à ~ d'un navire/d'une voiture** on board a ship/car ■ **monter à ~ d'un bateau/avion** to board a boat/plane.

◆ **au bord de** *loc prép* **1.** [en bordure de] : **se promener au ~ de l'eau/la mer** to walk at the water's edge/the seaside ▪ **s'arrêter au ~ de la route** to stop by the roadside **2.** [à la limite de] on the brink *ou* verge of, very close to ▪ **au ~ des larmes/de la dépression** on the verge of tears/a nervous breakdown ➔ **être au ~ de l'abîme** to be on the verge of ruin.
◆ **bord à bord** *loc adv* edge to edge.
◆ **de bord** *loc adj* [journal, livre, commandant] ship's.
◆ **sur les bords** *loc adv* slightly, a touch ▪ **il est un peu radin sur les ~s** he's a bit tight-fisted.

bordage [bɔrdaʒ] *nm* **1.** COUT hedging, hemming **2.** NAUT [en bois] planking ▪ [en fer] plating ▪ **ajuster des ~s** [en bois] to adjust planks ; [en fer] to adjust plates **3.** *Québec* inshore ice.

bordé [bɔrde] *nm* **1.** NAUT [en bois] planking ▪ [en fer] plating **2.** COUT (piece of) trimming.

bordeaux [bɔrdo] <> *adj inv* [grenat] burgundy *(modif)*, claret *(modif)*.
<> *nm* Bordeaux (wine) ▪ **un ~ rouge** a red Bordeaux, a claret ▪ **un ~ blanc** a white Bordeaux.

Bordeaux [bɔrdo] *npr* Bordeaux.

bordée [bɔrde] *nf* **1.** NAUT [canons, salve] broadside ▪ [distance] tack ▪ **tirer des ~s** to tack ▪ **tirer une ~** *fam fig* to paint the town red ▮ [partie de l'équipage] watch **2.** *fig* [série] : **une ~ d'insultes** *fig* a torrent *ou* stream of abuse **3.** *Québec* **~ de neige** heavy snowfall.

bordel△ [bɔrdɛl] <> *nm* **1.** [hôtel de passe] brothel, whorehouse **2.** [désordre] shambles *(sing)*, mess ▪ **c'est toujours un vrai ~ chez toi!** your place is always a shambles! ▪ **mettre le ~ dans une pièce/réunion** to turn a room into a pigsty/a meeting into a shambles.
<> *interj* dammit, hell.

bordelais, e [bɔrdəlɛ, ɛz] *adj* **1.** [de Bordeaux] from Bordeaux **2.** [du Bordelais] from the Bordeaux area.
◆ **Bordelais, e** *nm, f inhabitant of or person from Bordeaux.*
◆ **bordelaise** *nf* **1.** [bouteille] Bordeaux bottle **2.** CULIN : **à la ~e** in shallots and red wine.

Bordelais [bɔrdəlɛ] *npr m* : **le ~** the Bordelais (region).

bordélique△ [bɔrdelik] *adj* [chambre] messy ▪ [écriture, esprit] chaotic ▪ **il est vraiment ~!** he leaves such a mess everywhere!

border [3] [bɔrde] *vt* **1.** [garnir] to edge, to trim ▪ **~ qqch de** to trim *ou* to edge sthg with **2.** [en se couchant] : **va te coucher, je viendrai te ~** go to bed, I'll come and tuck you in **3.** [délimiter] to line ▪ **la route est bordée de haies** the road is lined with hedges **4.** NAUT [de planches] to plank ▪ [de tôles] to plate ▪ [voile] to haul on.

bordereau, x [bɔrdəro] *nm* **1.** FIN & COMM note, slip ▪ **~ d'achat** purchase note ▪ **~ de caisse** cash statement ▪ **~ de salaire** salary advice, wages slip ▪ **~ de vente** sales slip ▪ **~ de versement** paying-in slip *UK*, deposit slip *US* **2.** DR : **~ des pièces** docket.

bordier, ère [bɔrdje, ɛr] *adj* **1.** NAUT : **navire ~** lop-sided ship, lopsider **2.** GÉOGR : **mer bordière** epicontinental sea **3.** *Suisse* [au bord de l'eau] waterside.
◆ **bordier** *nm* **1.** *Suisse* [riverain] local resident **2.** NAUT lop-sided ship, lopsider.

bordure [bɔrdyr] *nf* **1.** [bord - d'un évier] edge ; [- d'un verre] edge, brim ; [- d'une plate-bande] border, edge ; [- d'une cheminée] surround *UK*, border *US* ▪ **la ~ du trottoir** the kerb ▪ [bande décorative] border **2.** [vêtement] border, edge ▪ [d'un chapeau] brim.
◆ **en bordure de** *loc prép* : **habiter une maison en ~ de mer** to live in a house by the sea.

boréal, e, als *ou* **aux** [boreal, o] *adj* boreal, North *(modif)*.

borgne [bɔrɲ] <> *adj* **1.** [personne] one-eyed **2.** [fenêtre, mur] obstructed **3.** [mal fréquenté - hôtel] shady.
<> *nmf* one-eyed person, one-eyed man *(f* woman).

borique [bɔrik] *adj* boric ▪ **acide ~** boric acid.

bornage [bɔrnaʒ] *nm* boundary marking ▪ **procéder au ~ d'un terrain** to mark the boundaries of a plot.

borne [bɔrn] *nf* **1.** [pour délimiter] boundary stone, landmark ▪ **~ kilométrique** milepost ▪ **rester planté comme une ~ : ne reste pas là planté comme une ~!** don't just stand there! **2.** [point] : **~ d'appel d'urgence** emergency call box **3.** [pour marquer un emplacement] bollard **4.** *fam* [kilomètre] kilometre **5.** ÉLECTR terminal **6.** INFORM : ▪ **~ d'accès** [à Internet] acces point ▪ **~ interactive** *ou* **multimédia** electronic *ou* interactive kiosk, interactive terminal.
◆ **bornes** *nfpl fig* bounds, limits ▪ **dépasser** *ou* **passer les ~s** to go too far ▪ **son ambition n'a** *ou* **ne connaît pas de ~s** his ambition knows no bounds.

borné, e [bɔrne] *adj* [individu] narrow-minded ▪ [esprit] narrow ▪ **tu es vraiment ~** you're so narrow-minded!, you have such a limited outlook!

Bornéo [bɔrneo] *npr* Borneo ▪ **à ~** in Borneo.

borner [3] [bɔrne] *vt* **1.** [délimiter - champ, terrain] to mark off *ou* out *(sép)*, to mark the boundary of **2.** [restreindre] to limit, to restrict.
◆ **se borner à** *vp+prép* **1.** [se limiter à] to be limited *ou* restricted to ▪ **nos relations se sont bornées à quelques échanges sur le palier** our relationship was never more than the odd conversation on the landing **2.** [se contenter de] to limit *ou* to restrict o.s. to ▪ **bornez-vous à l'essentiel** don't stray from the essentials.

bortsch [bɔrtʃ] = **borchtch**.

boskoop [bɔskɔp] *nf* Boskoop apple.

bosniaque [bɔsnjak] *adj* Bosnian.
◆ **Bosniaque** *nmf* Bosnian.

Bosnie [bɔsni] *npr f* : **(la) ~** Bosnia.

Bosnie-Herzégovine [bɔsniɛrzegɔvin] *npr f* : **(la) ~** Bosnia-Herzegovina.

bosnien, enne [bɔsnjɛ̃, ɛn] = **bosniaque**.

Bosphore [bɔsfɔr] *npr m* : **le ~** the Bosphorus, the Bosporus.

bosquet [bɔskɛ] *nm* coppice, copse.

boss [bɔs] *nm fam* boss.

bosse [bɔs] *nf* **1.** [à la suite d'un coup] bump, lump ▪ **se faire une ~** to get a bump **2.** ANAT & ZOOL [protubérance] hump **3.** [du sol] bump ▪ [en ski] mogul ▪ **un terrain plein de ~s** a bumpy piece of ground **4.** *loc* **avoir la ~ des maths/du commerce** to be a born mathematician/businessman.
◆ **en bosse** *loc adj* ART embossed.

bosselage [bɔslaʒ] *nm* embossing.

bosseler [24] [bɔsle] *vt* **1.** ART to emboss **2.** [faire des bosses à] to dent.

bossellement [bɔsɛlmɑ̃] *nm* denting.

bossellera *etc v* ▷ **bosseler**.

bosselure [bɔslyr] *nf* (irregular) bumps.

bosser [3] [bɔse] *fam* <> *vi* to work ▪ **j'ai bossé toute la nuit pour cet examen** I stayed up all night working for that exam.
<> *vt* to swot up *(sép) UK*, to grind away at *US*.

bosseur, euse [bɔsœr, øz] *fam* <> *adj* : **être ~** to work hard, to be hardworking.
<> *nm, f* hard worker.

bossu, e [bɔsy] <> *adj* humpbacked, hunchbacked ▪ **être ~** to be humpbacked, to have a hump *ou* humpback.
<> *nm, f* humpback, hunchback ▪ **rire** *ou* **rigoler** *fam* *ou* **se marrer** *fam* **comme un ~** to laugh fit to burst, to laugh o.s. silly.

Boston [bɔstɔn] *npr* Boston.

bot, e [bo, bɔt] *adj* : **pied ~** club foot.

botanique [bɔtanik] <> *adj* botanical.
<> *nf* botany.

botaniste [bɔtanist] *nmf* botanist.

botte [bɔt] *nf* **1.** [chaussure] (high) boot ▪ **~s en caoutchouc** gumboots *UK*, wellington boots *UK*, rubber boots *US* ▪ **~s de sept lieues** seven-league boots ▪ **avoir qqn à sa ~** to have sb under one's thumb ▪ **cirer** *OU* **lécher les ~s de qqn** *fam* to lick sb's boots ▪ **sous la ~ de l'ennemi** beneath the enemy's heel **2.** [de fleurs, de radis] bunch ▪ [de paille] sheaf, bundle **3.** ESCRIME thrust ◐ **porter une ~ à qqn** *pr* to make a thrust at sb ; *fig* to hit out *OU* to have a dig at sb ▪ **~ secrète** secret weapon.

botteleur, euse [bɔtlœr, øz] *nm, f* trusser.

botter [3] [bɔte] *vt* **1.** [chausser - enfant] to put boots on ; [- client] to provide boots for, to sell boots to **2.** *loc* **ça me botte!** *fam* it's great! ▪ **~ le train** *fam* *OU* **les fesses** *fam* *OU* **le derrière** *fam* *OU* **le cul**△ **à qqn** to kick sb in the pants ▪ **se faire ~ les fesses** *OU* **le cul**△ to get a kick up the backside **3.** SPORT to kick ▪ **il a botté la balle en touche** he kicked the ball into touch **4.** *fig* **~ en touche** to stall, to play for time.

botteur [bɔtœr] *nm* SPORT kicker.

bottier [bɔtje] *nm* [fabricant - de bottes] bootmaker ; [- de chaussures] shoemaker.

bottillon [bɔtijɔ̃] *nm* ankle boot.

Bottin® [bɔtɛ̃] *nm* telephone directory, phone book ▪ **le ~ mondain** *directory of famous people,* ≃ Who's Who?

bottine [bɔtin] *nf* ankle boot.

boubou [bubu] *nm* boubou, bubu.

bouc [buk] *nm* **1.** ZOOL goat, he-goat, billy goat ▪ **sentir le ~, puer comme un ~** to stink to high heaven ▪ **~ émissaire** scapegoat **2.** [barbe] goatee.

boucan [bukɑ̃] *nm* *fam* din, racket ▪ **faire du ~** to kick up a din, to make a racket.

boucaner [3] [bukane] *vt* [viande] to smoke, to cure.

boucanier [bukanje] *nm* buccaneer.

bouchage [buʃaʒ] *nm* **1.** [d'une bouteille] corking **2.** [d'une fuite] plugging, stopping **3.** [d'un trou] filling up.

bouche [buʃ] *nf* **1.** ANAT & ZOOL mouth ▪ **ne parle pas la ~ pleine** don't talk with your mouth full ▪ **elle me donna sa ~** *litt* she offered me her lips ▪ **dans ta ~ le mot prend toute sa valeur** when you say it *OU* coming from you, the word takes on its full meaning ▪ **ce sont toutes les mères qui s'expriment par sa ~** she's speaking for all mothers ▪ **il a six ~s à nourrir** he has six mouths to feed (at home) ▪ **je n'ai pas l'intention de nourrir des ~s inutiles** I won't have loafers around here ◐ **ça c'est pour** *OU* **je le garde pour la bonne ~** [nourriture] I'm keeping this as a treat for later ; [nouvelle] I'm keeping the best until last ▪ **par le ~ à oreille** through the grapevine, by word of mouth ▪ **de ~ à oreille** confidentially ▪ **il m'a annoncé la ~ en cœur qu'il ne venait plus** he gaily announced to me that he was no longer coming ▪ **ouvrir la ~** *pr* to open one's mouth ▪ **elle n'a pas ouvert la ~ de la soirée** *fig* she didn't say a word all evening ▪ **il n'a que ce mot/nom à la ~** he only ever talks about one thing/person ▪ **son nom est sur toutes les ~s** her name is on everyone's lips, she's the talk of the town **2.** [orifice - d'un cratère] mouth ; [- d'un canon] muzzle ▪ **~ d'air chaud** *OU* **de chaleur** hot-air vent ▪ **~ d'eau** *OU* **d'incendie** fire hydrant ▪ **~ d'aération** air vent ▪ **~ d'arrosage** water pipe, standpipe ▪ **~ d'égout** manhole, inspection chamber ▪ **~ de métro** metro entrance, underground entrance.

◆ **bouches** *nfpl* [d'un fleuve, d'un détroit] mouth.

bouché, e [buʃe] *adj* **1.** [nez] blocked ▪ [oreilles] blocked up ▪ **j'ai le nez ~** my nose is blocked **2.** MÉTÉOR [ciel, horizon, temps] cloudy, overcast **3.** *fam* [idiot] stupid, thick *UK* **4.** [sans espoir - avenir] hopeless ; [- filière, secteur] oversubscribed **5.** [bouteille] corked ▪ [cidre, vin] bottled.

bouchée [buʃe] *nf* **1.** [contenu] mouthful ▪ **il n'a fait qu'une ~ du petit pain** he swallowed the roll whole ◐ **elle n'a fait qu'une ~ de ses rivales** she made short work of her rivals ▪ **mettre les ~s doubles** to work twice as hard, to put on a spurt ▪ **il a acheté ce tableau pour une ~ de pain** he bought this painting for next to nothing **2.** CULIN (vol-au-vent) case ▪ **~ à la reine** chicken vol-au-vent ‖ [friandise] : **~ (au chocolat)** chocolate bouchée.

bouche-à-bouche [buʃabuʃ] *nm inv* mouth-to-mouth resuscitation ▪ **faire du ~ à qqn** to give sb mouth-to-mouth resuscitation *OU* the kiss of life.

boucher[1] [3] [buʃe] *vt* **1.** [fermer - trou] to fill up *(sép)* ; [- fuite] to plug, to stop ; [- bouteille] to cork ▪ **~ un trou** *fig* to fill a gap ◐ **je parie que ça t'en bouche un coin!** *fam* I bet you're impressed! **2.** [entraver] to obstruct, to block ▪ **tu me bouches le passage** you're in *OU* blocking my way ▪ **la tour nous bouche complètement la vue** the tower cuts off *OU* obstructs our view totally.

◆ **se boucher** ◇ *vpi* **1.** [s'obstruer - tuyau, narine] to get blocked **2.** MÉTÉOR [temps] to become overcast.

◇ *vpt* : **se ~ le nez** to hold one's nose ▪ **se ~ les oreilles** *pr* to put one's fingers in *OU* to plug one's ears ; *fig* to refuse to listen.

boucher[2]**, ère** [buʃe, ɛr] *nm, f* butcher ▪ **ce chirurgien est un vrai ~** this surgeon is a real butcher.

boucherie [buʃri] *nf* **1.** [boutique] butcher's shop *UK* *OU* store *US* ▪ **~ chevaline** horse-butcher's (shop) **2.** [métier] butchery **3.** [massacre] slaughter, butchery.

bouche-trou [buʃtru] (*pl* **bouche-trous**) *nm* [personne] stand-in, stopgap ▪ [objet] makeshift replacement.

bouchon [buʃɔ̃] *nm* **1.** [en liège] cork ▪ [d'un bidon, d'une bouteille en plastique] cap ▪ [d'une bouteille en verre, d'une carafe] stopper ▪ **vin qui sent le ~** corked wine ◐ **un ~ de carafe** *fam* a huge diamond *OU* rock ▪ **tu pousses le ~ un peu loin** *fam* you're going a little too far *OU* pushing it a bit **2.** [bonde] plug ▪ **~ de cérumen** earwax plug **3.** [poignée de paille, de foin] wisp **4.** *fam* [embouteillage] traffic jam ▪ [à une intersection] gridlock **5.** PÊCHE float.

bouchonnage [buʃɔnaʒ] *nm* rubbing down *(of a horse)*.

bouchonné, e [buʃɔne] *adj* [vin] corked.

bouchonner [3] [buʃɔne] ◇ *vt* [cheval] to rub down *(sép)*.

◇ *vi* : **ça bouchonne à partir de 5 h** traffic is heavy from 5 p.m. onwards.

bouclage [buklaʒ] *nm* **1.** PRESSE [d'un article] finishing off ▪ [d'un journal] putting to bed ▪ **c'est mardi le ~** the paper's going to bed *OU* to press on Tuesday **2.** *fam* [d'un coupable] locking up ▪ [d'un quartier] surrounding, sealing off **3.** [d'une ceinture] fastening, buckling **4.** [des cheveux] curling.

boucle [bukl] *nf* **1.** [de cheveux] curl ▪ **Boucles d'or** LITTÉR Goldilocks **2.** [de ceinture] buckle ▪ [de lacet] loop ▪ [d'un cours d'eau] loop, meander ▪ **faire une ~ à un ruban** to loop a ribbon **3.** INFORM loop **4.** TÉLÉCOM : **~ locale (téléphonique)** local (telephone) loop ▪ : **~ locale (radio)** wireless local loop, WLL **5.** SPORT [en course] lap.

◆ **boucle d'oreille** *nf* earring.

bouclé, e [bukle] *adj* [cheveux, barbe] curly ▪ [personne] curly-haired.

bouclement [bukləmɑ̃] *nm* ringing *(of a bullock or a pig)*.

boucler [3] [bukle] ◇ *vt* **1.** [fermer - ceinture] to buckle, to fasten ◐ **~ sa valise** *pr* to shut one's suitcase ; *fig* to pack one's bags ▪ **la ~ : toi, tu la boucles!** *fam* not a word out of you! **2.** [dans une opération policière] : **~ une avenue/un quartier** to seal off an avenue/area **3.** *fam* [enfermer] to shut away *(sép)*, to lock up *(sép)* ▪ **je suis bouclé à la maison avec la grippe** I'm stuck at home with the flu ▪ **il s'est fait ~ pour six mois** he's been put away for six months **4.** [mettre un terme à - affaire] to finish off *(sép)*, to settle ; [- programme de révisions] to finish (off) ▪ **~ un journal/une édition** PRESSE to put a paper/an edition to bed **5.** [équilibrer] : **~ son budget** to make ends meet ▪ **il a du mal à ~ ses fins de mois** he's always in the red at the end of the month **6.** AÉRON : **~ la boucle** to loop the loop ◐ **la boucle est bouclée, on a bouclé la boucle** we're back to square one **7.** [cheveux, mèches] to curl.

◇ *vi* **1.** [cheveux] to curl, to be curly ▪ **il boucle naturellement** he has naturally curly hair **2.** INFORM to get stuck in a loop, to loop round and round.

◆ **se boucler** *vp (emploi réfléchi)* **se ~ chez soi** to shut o.s. away.

bouclette [buklɛt] *nf* **1.** [de cheveux] small curl **2.** *(comme adj)* TEXT [fil, laine] bouclé.

bouclier [buklije] *nm* **1.** [protection de soldat] shield ▪ [de policier] riot shield **2.** [protection] shield ▪ **~ atomique** atomic shield ▪ **~ humain** human shield **3.** GÉOL shield.

bouddha [buda] *nm* [statue] buddha.

Bouddha [buda] *npr* Buddha.

bouddhisme [budism] *nm* Buddhism.

bouddhiste [budist] *adj* Buddhist.

bouder [3] [bude] ◇ *vi* to sulk.
◇ *vt* [ami] to refuse to talk to ▪ [dessert, cadeau] to refuse to accept ▪ [élection] to refuse to vote ▪ [fournisseur] to stay away from ▪ **le public a boudé son film** hardly anyone went to see her film.

bouderie [budri] *nf* sulking *(U)* ▪ **je ne supporte plus ses ~s** I'm fed up with his sulking.

boudeur, euse [budœr, øz] ◇ *adj* sulky, sullen.
◇ *nm, f* sulky person.

boudiné, e [budine] *adj* [doigt, main] podgy *UK*, pudgy *US* ▪ **je me sens ~e dans cette robe** this dress is too tight for me.

boudiner [3] [budine] *vt* **1.** [suj: vêtement] : **cette jupe la boudine** that skirt makes her look fat **2.** INDUST [fil de métal] to coil ▪ TEXT to rove ▪ [tuyau] to extrude.
◆ **se boudiner** *vp (emploi réfléchi)* : **se ~ dans une jupe** to squeeze o.s. into a skirt (that is too tight).

boudoir [budwar] *nm* **1.** [pièce] boudoir **2.** [biscuit] sponge finger *UK*, ladyfinger *US*.

boue [bu] *nf* **1.** [terre détrempée] mud ▪ **couvert de ~** muddy **2.** [dépôt] sludge ▪ **~ d'épuration** sewage sludge.

bouée [bwe] *nf* **1.** [en mer] buoy **2.** [pour nager] rubber ring ▪ **~ de sauvetage** lifebelt, lifebuoy ▪ **il s'est raccroché à elle comme à une ~ de sauvetage** he hung onto her as if his life depended on it.

boueux, euse [buø, øz] *adj* **1.** [sale - trottoir] muddy ; [- tapis] mud-stained **2.** IMPR smudged.
◆ **boueux** *nm fam* bin man *UK*, garbage collector *US*.

bouffant, e [bufɑ̃, ɑ̃t] *adj* [cheveux] bouffant ▪ [manche] puffed out.

bouffarde [bufard] *nf fam* pipe.

bouffe [buf] ◇ *nf fam* food, grub, nosh ▪ **on se fait une ~?** do you fancy getting together for a meal? ▪ **aimer la bonne ~** to like one's food.
◇ *adj* : **opéra ~** comic opera.

bouffée [bufe] *nf* **1.** [exhalaison] puff ▪ **une ~ d'air frais** *pr & fig* a breath of fresh air ▪ **des odeurs de cuisine m'arrivaient par ~s** the smell of cooking wafted over to me **2.** [accès] fit, outburst ▪ **une ~ de colère** a fit of rage ➊ **avoir des ~s de chaleur** MÉD to have hot flushes *UK OU* flashes *US*.

bouffer [3] [bufe] ◇ *vt fam* **1.** [manger] to eat ▪ [manger voracement] to guzzle ▪ **je l'aurais bouffé!** *fig* I could have killed him! ▪ *(en usage absolu)* **~ au restaurant** to eat out ▪ **on a bien/mal bouffé** the food was great/terrible ▪ **je vais les faire ~ et on sera tranquilles** I'll give them something to eat and then we'll have some peace **2.** [gaspiller] to be heavy on, to soak up *(sép)* ▪ **~ de l'essence** to be heavy on petrol *UK OU* gas *US* **3.** [accaparer] : **les enfants me bouffent tout mon temps** the kids take up every minute of my time ▪ **tu te laisses ~ par ta mère** you're letting your mother walk all over you **4.** *loc* **~ du curé** to be a priest-hater ▪ **~ du communiste** to be a commie-basher.
◇ *vi* [gonfler] to puff (out).
◆ **se bouffer** *vp (emploi réciproque) fam* **se ~ le nez** [une fois] to have a go at one another ; [constamment] to be at daggers drawn.

bouffetance[△] [buftɑ̃s] = **bouffe** *(nf)*.

bouffi, e [bufi] *adj* [yeux] puffed-up, puffy ▪ [visage] puffed-up, puffy, bloated ▪ **être ~ d'orgueil** *fig* to be bloated with pride.
◆ **bouffi** *nm* [hareng] bloater.

bouffir [32] [bufir] ◇ *vt* **1.** [visage, yeux] to puff up **2.** [hareng] to bloat.
◇ *vi* to become swollen *OU* bloated, to puff up.

bouffissure [bufisyr] *nf* [d'un visage, d'un corps] puffy *OU* swollen state ▪ [d'un style] turgidness.

bouffon, onne [bufɔ̃, ɔn] *adj* [scène] comical, farcical.
◆ **bouffon** *nm* buffoon ▪ **le ~ du roi** HIST the king's jester.

bouffonnerie [bufɔnri] *nf* **1.** [acte] piece of buffoonery ▪ [parole] farcical remark **2.** [caractère] buffoonery.

bougainvillée [bugɛ̃vile], **bougainvillier** [bugɛ̃vilje] *nf OU nm* bougainvillaea.

bouge [buʒ] *nm* **1.** [logement] hovel **2.** [café] cheap *OU* sleazy bar.

bougeoir [buʒwar] *nm* candleholder, candlestick.

bougeotte [buʒɔt] *nf fam* fidgets ▪ **avoir la ~** [remuer] to have the fidgets ; [voyager] to have itchy feet.

bouger [17] [buʒe] ◇ *vi* **1.** [remuer] to move ▪ **rien ne bouge** nothing's stirring ▪ **j'ai une dent qui bouge** I have a loose tooth ▪ **rester sans ~** to stay still ▪ **le vent fait ~ les branches des arbres** the branches of the trees are swaying in the wind **2.** [se déplacer] to move ▪ **je n'ai pas bougé de la maison** I never stirred from the house **3.** [se modifier - couleur d'un tissu] to fade ▪ **les prix n'ont pas bougé** prices haven't changed *OU* altered **4.** [s'activer] to move, to stir.
◇ *vt* to move, to shift.
◆ **se bouger** *vpi fam* **si on se bougeait un peu?** come on, let's get moving *OU* let's get a move on! ▪ **tu ne t'es pas beaucoup bougé pour trouver un nouveau boulot** you didn't try very hard to find a new job.

bougie [buʒi] *nf* **1.** [en cire] candle **2.** AUTO sparking *UK OU* spark *US* plug.

bougnat [buɲa] *nm in Paris, owner of a small café who also sold coal.*

bougnoul(e)[▲] [buɲul] *nm racist term used with reference to North Africans.*

bougon, onne [bugɔ̃, ɔn] ◇ *adj* grouchy, grumpy.
◇ *nm, f* grumbler, grouch.

bougonnement [bugɔnmɑ̃] *nm* grouching, grumbling.

bougonner [3] [bugɔne] *vi* to grouch, to grumble.

bougre [bugr] *fam vieilli* ◇ *nm* **1.** [homme] chap, fellow ▪ **un pauvre ~** a poor bloke *UK OU* guy *US* **2.** *péj* **~ de : ~ d'imbécile** *OU* **d'andouille!** you stupid idiot!
◇ *interj* **1.** [marque la colère] damn, heck **2.** [marque la surprise] I'll be dashed, cripes.

bougrement [bugrəmɑ̃] *adv fam vieilli* damn, damned ▪ **il fait ~ froid** it's damn cold.

bougresse [bugrɛs] *nf fam vieilli* wretched woman.

boui-boui [bwibwi] (*pl* **bouis-bouis**) *nm fam* [restaurant] caff *UK*, greasy spoon ▪ **au ~ du coin** at the local caff.

bouillabaisse [bujabɛs] *nf* bouillabaisse.

bouillant, e [bujɑ̃, ɑ̃t] *adj* **1.** [qui bout] boiling ▪ [très chaud] boiling hot ▪ **j'aime boire mon café ~** I like my coffee to be boiling hot **2.** [ardent] fiery, passionate.

bouillasse [bujas] *nf fam* [boue] muck, mud ▪ [de neige] slush.

bouille [buj] *nf* **1.** *fam* [figure] face, mug ▪ **il a une bonne ~** [sympathique] he looks a nice bloke *UK OU* guy *US* **2.** *Suisse* churn *UK*, milk pail *US*.

bouilleur [bujœr] *nm* **1.** [distillateur] distiller ▪ **~ de cru** home distiller **2.** TECHNOL [d'une chaudière] heating *OU* fire tube.

bouilli, e [buji] *adj* [eau, lait, viande] boiled.

◆ **bouilli** *nm* [viande] boiled meat ▪ [bœuf] boiled beef.
◆ **bouillie** *nf* baby food *ou* cereal ➤ **c'est de la ~e pour les chats** it's a dog's breakfast.
◆ **en bouillie** *loc adj & adv* crushed ▪ **mettre qqn en ~e** to beat sb to a pulp.

bouillir [48] [bujir] ◇ *vi* **1.** [arriver à ébullition] to boil ▪ **faire ~ des légumes** to boil vegetables ➤ **faire ~ la marmite** to keep the pot boiling **2.** [s'irriter] to boil ▪ **ça me fait ~** it makes my blood boil ▪ **~ d'impatience/de colère** to seethe with impatience/anger.
◇ *vt* to boil ▪ **~ du linge** to boil washing.

bouilloire [bujwar] *nf* kettle ▪ **~ électrique** electric kettle.

bouillon [bujɔ̃] *nm* **1.** CULIN broth, stock ▪ **~ gras/maigre** meat/clear stock ▪ **~ cube** stock cube ▪ **~ de légumes** vegetable stock ▪ **~ de onze** *ou* **d'onze heures** poisoned drink ▪ **boire** *ou* **prendre un ~** *fam* [en nageant] to swallow water ; *fig* to suffer heavy losses, to take a bath
2. BIOL : **~ de culture** *pr* culture medium ▪ **ces quartiers sont un véritable ~ de culture pour la délinquance** *fig* these areas are a perfect breeding-ground for crime
3. [remous] : **éteindre le feu dès le premier ~** turn off the heat as soon as it boils ▪ **couler à gros ~s** to gush out *ou* forth ▪ **bouillir à gros ~s** to boil fast *ou* hard
4. COUT puff
5. PRESSE unsold copies.

bouillonnant, e [bujɔnɑ̃, ɑ̃t] *adj* bubbling, foaming, seething.

bouillonnement [bujɔnmɑ̃] *nm* bubbling, foaming, seething ▪ **~ d'idées** *fig* ferment of ideas.

bouillonner [3] [bujɔne] *vi* **1.** [liquide] to bubble ▪ [source] to foam, to froth ▪ **ils bouillonnent d'idées** *fig* they're full of ideas **2.** [s'agiter] : **~ d'impatience** to seethe with impatience.

bouillotte [bujɔt] *nf* hot-water bottle.

boul. = **boulevard**.

boulanger, ère [bulɑ̃ʒe, ɛr] *nm, f* baker.

boulangerie [bulɑ̃ʒri] *nf* **1.** [boutique] bakery, baker's (shop *UK ou* store *US*) ▪ **~ pâtisserie** baker's and confectioner's, bread and cake shop **2.** [industrie] bakery trade *ou* business.

boulangisme [bulɑ̃ʒism] *nm 19th-century movement supporting General Boulanger.*

boulangiste [bulɑ̃ʒist] ◇ *adj* [mouvement, parti] of General Boulanger.
◇ *nmf* supporter of General Boulanger.

boule [bul] *nf* **1.** [sphère] ball ▪ **~ de billard** billiard ball ▪ **~ de cristal** crystal ball ▪ **regarder dans sa ~ de cristal** to look into one's crystal ball ▪ **~ de feu** fireball ▪ **~ de gomme** gumdrop ▪ **~ de loto** lottery ball ▪ **~ de neige** snowball ▪ **faire ~ de neige** *fig* to snowball ▪ **~ de poils** [dans l'estomac d'un animal] hairball ▪ **une petite ~ de poils** [chaton] a little fluffy ball ▪ **~ puante** stinkbomb ▪ **~s Quiès®** earplugs ▪ **~ à thé** tea ball ▪ **avoir une ~ dans la gorge** to have a lump in one's throat **2.** *fam* [tête] : **il a la ~ à zéro** his head is completely shaven ▪ **coup de ~** headbutt ▪ **donner un coup de ~ à qqn** to headbutt *ou* nut sb **3.** JEUX : **~ (de pétanque)** (steel) bowl ▪ **jouer aux ~s** to play boules *(popular French game played on bare ground with steel bowls)* **4.** INFORM : **~ de commande** trackball.
◆ **boules**△ *nfpl* : **avoir les ~s** [être effrayé] to be scared stiff ; [être furieux] to be pissed off△ ; [être déprimé] to be feeling down.
◆ **en boule** *loc adj & loc adv* [en rond - animal] : **se mettre en ~** to curl up into a ball ▪ *fam* [en colère] : **être en ~** to be hopping mad, to be furious ▪ **ça me met en ~** it makes me mad, it really gets my goat.

bouleau, x [bulo] *nm* **1.** BOT birch ▪ **~ argenté** silver birch **2.** [bois] birch.

boule-de-neige [buldənɛʒ] (*pl* **boules-de-neige**) *nf* BOT [arbuste] guelder rose.

Boule-de-Suif [buldəsɥif] *npr the best known of Maupassant's tales, about the Franco-Prussian War.*

bouledogue [buldɔg] *nm* bulldog.

bouler [3] [bule] *vi* to roll along ▪ **~ au bas de l'escalier** to tumble down the stairs.

boulet [bulɛ] *nm* **1.** ARM cannonball ▪ [de prisonnier] ball (and chain) ▪ **tirer à ~s rouges sur qqn** to lay into sb **2.** MIN (coal) nut **3.** ZOOL fetlock.

boulette [bulɛt] *nf* **1.** CULIN : **~ (de viande)** meatball ▪ **~ empoisonnée** poison ball **2.** [de papier] pellet **3.** *fam* [erreur] blunder, blooper *US* ▪ **faire une ~** to blunder, to goof *US*.

boulevard [bulvar] *nm* **1.** [avenue] boulevard ▪ [à Paris] : **les grands ~s** the main boulevards *(with many theatres, restaurants and nightclubs)* ▪ **les ~s extérieurs** *ou* **des maréchaux** the outer boulevards *(following the old town wall)* ▪ **le ~ périphérique** the (Paris) ring road *UK ou* beltway *US* **2.** THÉÂTRE : **le ~** light comedy.
◆ **de boulevard** *loc adj* THÉÂTRE : **pièce de ~** light comedy.

bouleversant, e [bulvɛrsɑ̃, ɑ̃t] *adj* upsetting, distressing ▪ **témoignage ~** deeply moving testimony.

bouleversement [bulvɛrsəmɑ̃] *nm* upheaval, upset ▪ **le ~ de toutes mes habitudes** the disruption of my entire routine.

bouleverser [3] [bulvɛrse] *vt* **1.** [émouvoir] to move deeply ▪ **bouleversé par la naissance de son fils** deeply moved by his son's birth ▪ [affliger] to upset, to distress ▪ **bouleversé par la mort de son ami** shattered *ou* very distressed by the death of his friend **2.** [désorganiser - maison, tiroir] to turn upside down ; [- habitudes, vie, plan] to turn upside down, to disrupt, to change drastically.

boulgour [bulgur] *nm* bulgar *ou* bulgur wheat.

boulier [bulje] *nm* abacus.

boulimie [bulimi] *nf* compulsive eating, bulimia *spéc* ▪ **être atteint de ~, faire de la ~** to be a compulsive eater.

boulimique [bulimik] ◇ *adj* bulimic.
◇ *nmf* compulsive eater, bulimic *spéc.*

bouliste [bulist] *nmf* boules player.

boulle [bul] *nm inv* boulle furniture *(style of highly ornamented furniture associated with Henri-Charles Boulle [1642-1732]).*

boulocher [3] [bulɔʃe] *vi* to pill.

boulodrome [bulɔdrom] *nm* bowling alley.

Boulogne-Billancourt [bulɔɲbijɑ̃kur] *npr town in the Paris suburbs, the site until recently of the state-run Renault car factory, well-known for its enlightened approach to labour relations.*

boulon [bulɔ̃] *nm* bolt ▪ **~ avec écrou** nut and bolt ▪ **~ à vis** screw bolt ▪ **serrer les ~s** *fam fig* to tighten the screws ▪ **il lui manque un ~, à ce type!** *fam* this guy's got a screw loose!

boulonnage [bulɔnaʒ] *nm* bolting (on).

boulonner [3] [bulɔne] ◇ *vt* to bolt (on).
◇ *vi fam* to work, to plug away ▪ **il boulonne dur** he works really hard.

boulot[1] [bulo] *nm fam* **1.** [fait de travailler] : **le ~** work ➤ **elle est très ~ ~** *péj* she's a workaholic **2.** [ouvrage réalisé] piece of work, job ▪ **il s'est coupé les cheveux tout seul, t'aurais vu le ~!** he cut his own hair, you should have seen the mess! **3.** [travail à faire] : **du ~** a lot of work ▪ **il y a encore du ~ dessus!** it needs loads more work on it! ▪ **tout le monde au ~!** come on everybody, let's get cracking! **4.** [emploi, poste] job ▪ **un petit ~** casual work *(U)* **5.** [lieu] work ▪ **je déjeune au ~** I have lunch at work.

boulot[2]**, otte** [bulo, ɔt] *adj fam* plump, tubby.

boulotter [3] [bulɔte] *fam* ◇ *vt* [manger] to scoff.
◇ *vi* [travailler] *vieilli* to work, to slave away.

boum [bum] ◇ *interj* bang ▪ **faire ~** to go bang.

<> nm **1.** [bruit] bang **2.** *fam* [succès] : **le ~ des télécopieurs** the fax boom, the boom in fax machines ▶ **être en plein ~** [dans une boutique, une entreprise] to have a rush on ; [dans des préparations] to be rushed off one's feet, to be very busy.
<> *nf fam* party *(for teenagers)*.

boumer [3] [bume] *vi fam* **alors, ça boume?** so, how's tricks? ■ **ça boume pas très fort pour lui** he's having a rough time of it ■ **ça boume!** things are (going) fine!

bouquet [bukɛ] *nm* **1.** [fleurs - gén] bunch ; [- grand, décoratif] bouquet ; [- petit] sprig, spray **2.** [groupe - d'arbres] clump, cluster **3.** [dans un feu d'artifice] crowning *ou* final piece, the (grand) finale ■ **alors ça, c'est le ~!** *fam* that's the limit!, that takes the biscuit *UK ou* cake *US*! **4.** CULIN : **~ garni** bouquet garni **5.** ŒNOL bouquet, nose **6.** TV : **~ numérique** channel package channel bouquet **7.** ZOOL (common) prawn.

bouquetin [buktɛ̃] *nm* ibex.

bouquin [bukɛ̃] *nm* **1.** *fam* [livre] book **2.** [lapin] buck rabbit ■ [lièvre] male hare **3.** [bouc] (old) billy-goat.

bouquiner [3] [bukine] *vt & vi fam* to read.

bouquiniste [bukinist] *nmf* secondhand bookseller.

BOUQUINISTES

In Paris, this term can refer specifically to the people who sell books, prints, cards etc from small stalls along the banks of the Seine.

bourbe [burb] *nf* [gén] mud, mire *litt* ■ [dans l'eau] sludge.

bourbeux, euse [burbø, øz] *adj* muddy ■ **eau bourbeuse** muddy *ou* sludgy water.

bourbier [burbje] *nm* **1.** [marécage] quagmire **2.** *fig* [situation difficile] quagmire.

bourbon [burbɔ̃] *nm* bourbon.

Bourbon [burbɔ̃] *npr* Bourbon.

bourbonien, enne [burbɔnjɛ̃, ɛn] *adj* of the Bourbon dynasty.

bourde [burd] *nf* **1.** [bêtise] blunder, bloomer *UK*, blooper *US* ■ **faire une ~** [gaffer] to blunder, to put one's foot in it ; [faire une erreur] to make a mistake, to mess things up, to goof (up) *US* **2.** *vieilli* [mensonge] fib.

bourdon [burdɔ̃] *nm* **1.** ZOOL bumblebee, humblebee ■ **faux ~** drone **2.** MUS [jeu d'orgue] bourdon ■ [son de basse] drone **3.** [cloche] great bell **4.** IMPR omission, out **5.** [bâton] pilgrim's staff **6.** *loc* **avoir le ~** *fam* to feel down, to be down in the dumps.

bourdonnant, e [burdɔnɑ̃, ɑ̃t] *adj* [ruche, insecte] humming, buzzing, droning.

bourdonnement [burdɔnmɑ̃] *nm* [vrombissement - d'un insecte, d'une voix] hum, buzz, drone ; [- d'un ventilateur, d'un moteur] hum, drone ■ **avoir un ~ dans les oreilles** to have a ringing in one's ears.

bourdonner [3] [burdɔne] *vi* [insecte, voix] to hum, to buzz, to drone ■ [moteur] to hum ■ [oreille] to ring ■ [lieu] to buzz ■ **la salle bourdonnait du bruit des conversations** the room was buzzing with the sound of conversation.

bourg [bur] *nm* (market) town.

bourgade [burgad] *nf* (large) village, small town.

bourge [burʒ] *fam péj* <> *adj* upper-class.
<> *nmf* : **chez les ~s** in upper-class circles.

bourgeois, e [burʒwa, az] <> *adj* **1.** [dans un sens marxiste] of the bourgeoisie, bourgeois **2.** [dans un sens non marxiste] middle-class **3.** *péj* [caractéristique de la bourgeoisie] : **goûts ~** bourgeois tastes **4.** [aisé, confortable] : **intérieur ~** comfortable middle-class home ■ **quartier ~** comfortable residential area ‖ CULIN : **cuisine ~e** good plain home cooking.
<> *nm, f* **1.** [dans un sens marxiste] bourgeois **2.** [dans un sens non marxiste] member of the middle class ■ **grand ~** member of the upper-middle class **3.** HIST [au Moyen Âge] burgher ■ [avant la Révolution] member of the third estate **4.** *Suisse* [citoyen] citizen ■ **les ~** the townspeople **5.** *péj* [béotien] Philistine.
◆ **bourgeoise** *nf fam* **ma ~e** my old lady, the wife *UK*.

bourgeoisement [burʒwazmɑ̃] *adv* **1.** [conventionnellement] conventionally, respectably ■ **vivre ~** to lead a respectable life ■ **une maison meublée ~** a comfortably furnished house **2.** DR : **occuper ~ un local** to use premises for residential purposes only.

bourgeoisial, e [burʒwazjal] *adj Suisse* town *(modif)*.

bourgeoisie [burʒwazi] *nf* **1.** [dans un sens marxiste] bourgeoisie ■ **la petite ~** the petty bourgeoisie **2.** [classe aisée, professions libérales] middle class ■ **la petite/moyenne ~** the lower middle/the middle class ■ **la grande** *ou* **haute ~** the upper-middle class **3.** HIST [au Moyen Âge] burghers ■ [avant la Révolution] bourgeoisie, third estate.

bourgeon [burʒɔ̃] *nm* BOT & MÉD bud.

bourgeonnement [burʒɔnmɑ̃] *nm* BOT budding.

bourgeonner [3] [burʒɔne] *vi* **1.** BOT to bud **2.** [visage, nez] to break out in spots.

bourgmestre [burgmɛstr] *nm Belgique & Suisse* burgomaster.

bourgogne [burgɔɲ] *nm* Burgundy (wine).

Bourgogne [burgɔɲ] *npr f* : **(la) ~** Burgundy.

BOURGOGNE

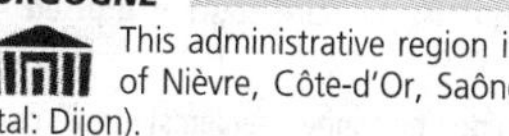

This administrative region includes the *départements* of Nièvre, Côte-d'Or, Saône-et-Loire and Yonne (capital: Dijon).

bourguignon, onne [burgiɲɔ̃, ɔn] *adj* **1.** GÉOGR & HIST Burgundian **2.** CULIN [sauce] bourguignonne.
◆ **bourguignonne** *nf* **1.** [bouteille] Burgundy wine bottle **2.** CULIN : **à la ~ne** with a bourguignonne sauce, cooked in red wine.

bourlinguer [3] [burlɛ̃ge] *vi* **1.** [voyager par mer] to sail (around) **2.** *fam* [se déplacer] to get around, to kick about ■ **elle a bourlingué dans le monde entier** she's been all over the world **3.** NAUT to labour.

bourlingueur, euse [burlɛ̃gœr, øz] *nm, f* **1.** [marin] old salt **2.** [aventurier] wanderer, rover ■ **c'est un ~** he's always on the move.

bourrache [buraʃ] *nf* borage.

bourrade [burad] *nf* [de la main] push, shove ■ [du coude] poke, dig.

bourrage [buraʒ] *nm* **1.** [remplissage - d'un coussin] stuffing ; [- d'une chaise] filling, padding ; [- d'une pipe, d'un poêle] filling ■ **~ de crâne** *fam* [propagande] brainwashing ; ÉDUC cramming **2.** TECHNOL : **~ (de cartes)** INFORM (card) jam ■ **~ du film** CINÉ piling up *ou* buckling of the film.

bourrasque [burask] *nf* **1.** [coup de vent] squall, gust *ou* blast (of wind) ■ **souffler en ~** to blow in gusts, to gust **2.** [incident] storm, crisis.

bourratif, ive [buratif, iv] *adj fam* filling, stodgy *péj* ■ **des aliments ~s** stodge *(U) péj*.

bourre[1] △ [bur] *nm arg crime* cop ■ **les ~s** the cops, the fuzz.

bourre[2] [bur] *nf* **1.** [rembourrage] filling, stuffing, wadding **2.** TEXT flock ■ **~ de papier** fluff **3.** BOT down **4.** ARM wad.
◆ **à la bourre** *loc adv fam* **être à la ~** to be in a rush ; [dans son travail] to be behind.

bourré, e△ [bure] *adj* pissed△ *UK*, bombed *US*.

bourrée [bure] *nf* DANSE bourrée.

bourreau, x [buro] *nm* **1.** [exécuteur - gén] executioner ; [- qui pend] hangman **2.** [tortionnaire] torturer ■ **~ d'enfant** child beater ■ **~ des cœurs** heartbreaker ■ **~ de travail** workaholic.

bourrelé, e [burle] *adj* : ~ **de remords** full of remorse, racked with guilt.

bourrelet [burlɛ] *nm* **1.** [isolant] weather strip, draught excluder *UK* **2.** [de graisse] fold ■ ~ **de chair** roll of flesh.

bourrelier [burəlje] *nm* saddler.

bourrellerie [burɛlri] *nf* saddlery.

bourrer [3] [bure] *vt* **1.** [rembourrer] to fill, to stuff **2.** [remplir - pipe] to fill ; [- poche] to fill, to cram, to stuff ; [- valise, tiroir] to cram (full), to pack tightly ■ **un texte bourré de fautes** a text full of *ou* riddled with mistakes ➋ ~ **le crâne** *ou* **le mou à qqn** *fam* to have *UK ou* to put *US* sb on ■ ~ **les urnes** to rig the vote *(by producing large numbers of false ballot papers)* **3.** [gaver - suj: aliment] to fill up ■ ~ **qqn de** to cram *ou* to stuff sb with ■ *(en usage absolu)* **les bananes, ça bourre** bananas are very filling *ou* fill you up **4.** [frapper] : ~ **qqn de coups** to beat sb (up).
◆ **se bourrer** *vp (emploi réfléchi)* **1.** *fam* [manger] to stuff o.s. *ou* one's face ■ **se ~ de** to stuff one's face with **2.** △ *loc* **se ~ la gueule** to get pissed△ *UK ou* bombed *US*.

bourriche [buriʃ] *nf* **1.** [panier] hamper, wicker case **2.** PÊCHE [filet] keepnet.

bourrichon [buriʃɔ̃] *nm fam* **monter le ~ à qqn** to have *UK ou* to put *US* sb on ■ **se monter le ~** to get (all) worked up.

bourricot [buriko] *nm* donkey, burro *US*.

bourrin [burɛ̃] *nm fam* (old) nag.

bourrique [burik] *nf* **1.** ZOOL donkey **2.** *fam* [personne obstinée] pig-headed individual **3.** *loc* **faire tourner qqn en ~** to drive sb crazy *ou* up the wall.

bourru, e [bury] *adj* **1.** [rude - personne, manières] gruff, rough ■ **d'un ton ~** gruffly **2.** TEXT rough **3.** [jeune - vin] fermented ; [- lait] raw.

bourse [burs] *nf* **1.** [porte-monnaie] purse ■ **sans ~ délier** without paying a penny *ou US* cent ■ **la ~ ou la vie!** stand and deliver!, your money or your life! **2.** ÉDUC & UNIV : ~ **(d'études)** [gén] grant ; [obtenue au mérite] scholarship ■ **avoir une ~** to have a grant *ou* scholarship.
◆ **bourses** *nfpl* scrotum.

Bourse [burs] *nf* **1.** [marché] stock exchange, stock market ■ **la ~ de Londres** the London Stock Exchange ■ **la ~ de Paris** the Paris Bourse *ou* Stock Exchange ➋ ~ **du commerce** *ou* **de marchandises** commodity exchange ■ ~ **maritime** *ou* **des frets** shipping exchange ■ ~ **du travail** *(local or regional) trade union centre* ■ ≃ trades' council *UK* ■ ~ **des valeurs** stock exchange **2.** [cours] market ■ **la ~ est calme/animée/en hausse** the market is quiet/is lively/has risen.
◆ **à la Bourse, en Bourse** *loc adv* on the stock exchange *ou* market ■ **jouer à la** *ou* **en ~** to speculate on the stock exchange *ou* market.

boursicotage [bursikɔtaʒ] *nm* dabbling (on the stock exchange).

boursicoter [3] [bursikɔte] *vi* to dabble (on the stock exchange).

boursicoteur, euse [bursikɔtœr, øz] *nm, f* small investor ■ **il était ~ à ses heures** he used to dabble from time to time on the stock exchange.

boursier, ère [bursje, ɛr] <> *adj* **1.** UNIV & ÉDUC : **un étudiant ~** a grant *ou* scholarship holder **2.** [de la Bourse] stock exchange *(modif)*, (stock) market *(modif)*.
<> *nm, f* **1.** UNIV & ÉDUC grant *ou* scholarship holder ■ **les ~s doivent remplir le formulaire ci-joint** students who receive a grant *ou* scholarship should fill in the accompanying form **2.** BOURSE operator.

boursouflage [bursuflaʒ] *nm* [gonflement - du visage] swelling, puffiness ; [- de la peinture] blistering.

boursouflé, e [bursufle] *adj* **1.** [gonflé - visage] swollen, puffy ; [- peinture] blistered ; [- plaie] swollen **2.** [ampoulé] bombastic, pompous, turgid.

boursouflement [bursufləmɑ̃] = **boursouflage**.

boursoufler [3] [bursufle] *vt* [gonfler - visage] to swell, to puff up *(sép)* ; [- peinture] to blister.
◆ **se boursoufler** *vpi* [visage] to become swollen *ou* puffy ■ [peinture] to blister ■ [surface] to swell (up).

boursouflure [bursuflyr] *nf* **1.** [bouffissure] puffiness ■ [cloque] blister **2.** [emphase] pomposity, turgidity.

bousculade [buskylad] *nf* **1.** [agitation] crush, pushing and shoving ■ **une ~ vers la sortie** a scramble *ou* stampede towards the exit ■ **j'ai perdu mon parapluie dans la ~** I lost my umbrella in the confusion **2.** *fam* [précipitation] rush.

bousculer [3] [buskyle] *vt* **1.** [pousser - voyageur, passant] to jostle, to push, to shove ; [- chaise, table] to bump *ou* to knock into ■ **se faire ~ par qqn** to be jostled by sb **2.** *fig* [changer brutalement] to upset, to turn on its head, to turn upside down ■ ~ **les habitudes de qqn** to upset sb's routine **3.** [presser] to rush, to hurry ■ **j'ai été très bousculé** I've had a lot to do *ou* a very busy time.
◆ **se bousculer** *vpi* **1.** [dans une cohue] to jostle, to push and shove **2.** [affluer] to rush ■ **les idées se bousculaient dans sa tête** his head was a jumble of ideas ➋ **ça se bouscule au portillon!** *fam* [il y a affluence] there's a huge crowd trying to get in!

bouse [buz] *nf* : ~ **(de vache)** [matière] cow dung ; [motte] cowpat.

bouseux, euse△ [buzø, øz] *nm, f péj* yokel, country bumpkin, hick *US*.

bousier [buzje] *nm* dung beetle.

bousillage [buzijaʒ] *nm* **1.** *fam* [gâchis] botch, botch-up **2.** CONSTR cob.

bousiller [3] [buzije] *vt fam* **1.** [mal faire] to bungle, to botch (up) **2.** [casser] to bust, to wreck ■ [gâcher] to spoil, to ruin **3.** △ [tuer] to bump off△ *(sép)*, to do in△ *(sép)*, to waste△.
◆ **se bousiller** *vpt fam* **se ~ les yeux/la santé** to ruin one's eyes/health.

boussole [busɔl] *nf* **1.** [instrument] compass **2.** *fam loc* **perdre la ~ : il a complètement perdu la ~** [vieillard] he's lost his marbles, he's gone gaga ; [fou] he's off his head *ou* rocker.

boustifaille△ [bustifaj] *nf* grub, nosh *UK*, chow *US*.

bout [bu] *nm* **1.** [extrémité - d'un couteau, d'un crayon] tip ; [- d'une botte, d'une chaussette] toe ; [- d'une table, d'une ficelle] end ■ **à ~s ronds** round-tipped ➋ ~ **du doigt** fingertip, tip of the finger ■ ~ **du nez** tip of the nose ■ ~ **du sein** nipple ■ ~ **filtre** filter tip ■ **à ~ filtre** filter-tipped ■ **le bon ~ : prendre qqn par le bon ~** to approach sb the right way ■ **plus que 40 pages à écrire, je tiens le bon ~** only another 40 pages to write, I can see the light at the end of the tunnel ■ **je ne sais pas par quel ~ le prendre** [personne] I don't know how to handle *ou* to approach him ; [article, travail] I don't know how to tackle *ou* to approach it ■ **aborder** *ou* **considérer** *ou* **voir les choses par le petit ~ de la lorgnette** to take a narrow view of things ■ **il a accepté du ~ des lèvres** he accepted reluctantly *ou* half-heartedly ■ **je l'ai sur le ~ de la langue** it's on the tip of my tongue ■ **sur le ~ des doigts** perfectly, by heart ■ **s'asseoir du ~ des fesses** *fam* to sit down gingerly ■ **s'en aller par tous les ~s** *fam* to fall *ou* to come to pieces ■ **en voir le ~ : enfin, on en voit le ~** at last, we're beginning to see the light at the end of the tunnel ■ **on n'en voit pas le ~** there's no end to it
2. [extrémité - d'un espace] end ■ **on voit enfin le ~ du tunnel** *fig* at last we can see the light at the end of the tunnel ■ **le ~ du monde** the back of beyong ■ **ce n'est pas le ~ du monde!** it won't kill you! ■ **ce serait bien le ~ du monde si ça prenait plus de deux jours** it'll take two days at the very most
3. [portion de temps] : **ça fait un bon ~ de temps de ça** *fam* it was quite a long time ago *ou* a while back ■ **il faudra attendre un bon ~ de temps** you'll have to wait for quite some time
4. [morceau] : ~ **de** [pain, bois, terrain] piece of ; [papier] scrap of ■ **un ~ de ciel bleu** a patch of blue sky ■ **donne-m'en un ~** give me some *ou* a piece *ou* a bit ■ **un (petit) ~ d'homme/de femme** *fam* a little man/woman ➋ ~ **de chou** *ou* **zan** *fam* [enfant] toddler ; [en appellatif] sweetie, poppet *UK* ■ ~ **d'essai** screen test ■ ~ **de rôle** THÉÂTRE & CINÉ walk-on *ou* bit part ■ **ça fait un bon ~ de chemin** it's quite some *ou* a way ■ **faire un ~ de chemin avec**

qqn to go part of the way with sb ▪ **faire un ~ de conduite à qqn** to walk sb part of the way ▪ **discuter** *ou* **tailler le ~ de gras** *fam* to chew the fat ▪ **mettre les ~s**△ to make o.s. scarce.
◆ **à bout** *loc adv* : **être à ~** to be at the end of one's tether ▪ **ma patience est à ~!** I've run out of patience! ▪ **mettre** *ou* **pousser qqn à ~** to push sb to the limit.
◆ **à bout de** *loc prép* **1.** [ne plus avoir de] : **être à ~ de : être à ~ de forces : il est à bout de forces** [physiquement] he's got no strength left in him ; [psychologiquement] he can't cope any more ▪ **être à ~ de nerfs** to be on the verge of a breakdown ▪ **être à ~ de patience** to have run out of patience
2. *loc* **à ~ de bras : porter un paquet à ~ de bras** to carry a parcel (in one's outstretched arms) ▪ **porter qqn/une entreprise à ~ de bras** *fig* to carry sb/a business ▪ **venir à ~ de** [adversaire, obstacle] to overcome ; [travail] to see the end of.
◆ **à bout portant** *loc adv* point-blank ▪ **tirer (sur qqn/qqch) à ~ portant** to shoot (sb/sthg) at point-blank range.
◆ **à tout bout de champ** *loc adv* all the time, non-stop.
◆ **au bout de** *loc prép* **1.** [après] after ▪ **au ~ d'un moment** after a while
2. [à la fin de] : **j'arrive au ~ de mon contrat** my contract's nearly up ▪ **pas encore au ~ de ses peines** not out of the woods yet
3. [dans l'espace] : **au ~ de la rue** at the bottom *ou* end of the road ⊙ **être au ~ de son** *ou* **du rouleau** [épuisé] to be completely washed out ; [presque mort] to be at death's door.
◆ **au bout du compte** *loc adv* at the end of the day, in the end.
◆ **bout à bout** *loc adv* end to end.
◆ **de bout en bout** *loc adv* [lire] from cover to cover ▪ **tu as raison de ~ en ~** you're completely *ou* totally right ▪ **elle a mené la course de ~ en ~** she led the race from start to finish.
◆ **d'un bout à l'autre** *loc adv* : **la pièce est drôle d'un ~ à l'autre** the play's hilarious from beginning to end *ou* from start to finish ▪ **il m'a contredit d'un ~ à l'autre** he contradicted me all the way.
◆ **d'un bout de... à l'autre** *loc corrélative* : **d'un ~ de l'année à l'autre** all year round ▪ **d'un ~ à l'autre du pays, les militants s'organisent** (right) throughout the country, the militants are organizing themselves.
◆ **en bout de** *loc prép* at the end of ▪ **en ~ de course** at the end of the race ▪ **le régime est en ~ de course** *fig* the regime is running out of steam.
◆ **jusqu'au bout** *loc adv* to the very end ⊙ **il va toujours jusqu'au ~ de ce qu'il entreprend** he always sees things to the very end ▪ **il est toujours soigné jusqu'au ~ des ongles** he's always immaculate ▪ **elle est artiste jusqu'au ~ des ongles** she's an artist through and through.

boutade [butad] *nf* [plaisanterie] joke, sally *sout.*

boute-en-train [butɑ̃trɛ̃] *nm inv* [amuseur] funny man, joker ▪ **le ~ de la bande** the life and soul of the group.

boutefas [butfa] *nm Suisse* pork sausage.

bouteille [butɛj] *nf* **1.** [récipient - pour un liquide] bottle ; [- pour un gaz] bottle, cylinder ▪ **une ~ de vin** [récipient] a wine bottle ▪ **un casier à ~s** a bottle rack ⊙ **~ Thermos**® Thermos® (flask *UK ou* bottle) ▪ **avoir de la ~** to be an old hand ▪ **prendre de la ~** *fam* to be getting *ou UK* knocking on a bit ▪ **c'est la ~ à l'encre** the whole thing's a muddle ▪ **jeter** *ou* **lancer une ~ à la mer** *pr* to send a message in a bottle ; *fig* to send out an SOS **2.** [contenu] bottle, bottleful ▪ **boire une bonne ~** to drink a good bottle of wine ⊙ **être porté sur** *ou* **aimer** *ou* **caresser la ~** to like one's drink.
◆ **bouteilles** *nfpl* NAUT heads, toilets.
◆ **en bouteille** ◇ *loc adj* [gaz, vin] bottled.
◇ *loc adv* : **mettre du vin en ~** to bottle wine ▪ **vieilli en ~** aged in bottle.

boutiquaire [butikɛr] *adj* : **niveau ~** [dans un aéroport] shopping level *ou* concourse.

boutique [butik] *nf* **1.** [magasin] shop *UK*, store *US* ▪ **~ de mode** boutique ▪ **~ franche** duty-free shop ▪ **tenir ~** to have a shop **2.** *fam* [lieu de travail] place, dump ⊙ **changer de ~** to get a new job ▪ **parler ~** to talk shop.

boutiquier, ère [butikje, ɛr] *nm, f* shopkeeper *UK*, storekeeper *US*.

boutis [buti] *nm* Marseilles embroidery, boutis, Provençal quilted embroidery.

boutoir [butwar] *nm* **1.** ZOOL snout **2.** *loc* **coup de ~** cutting remark.

bouton [butɔ̃] *nm* **1.** BOT bud ▪ **~ de rose** rosebud **2.** COUT button ▪ **~ de col** collar stud ▪ **~ de manchette** cuff link **3.** [poignée de porte, de tiroir] knob **4.** [de mise en marche] button ▪ **~ de sonnette** bellpush **5.** MÉD pimple, spot ▪ **avoir des ~s** [pustules] to have pimples ; [petits, rouges] to have a rash ⊙ **~ de fièvre** fever blister, cold sore **6.** INFORM : **~ radio** radio button.
◆ **en bouton** *loc adj* BOT in bud.

bouton-d'or [butɔ̃dɔr] (*pl* **boutons-d'or**) *nm* buttercup.

boutonnage [butɔnaʒ] *nm* **1.** [action de boutonner] buttoning (up) **2.** [mode de fermeture] buttons ▪ **à ~ de haut en bas** button-through *(modif)*.

boutonner [3] [butɔne] ◇ *vt* **1.** [vêtement] to button (up), to do up *(sép)* **2.** ESCRIME to button.
◇ *vi* BOT to bud (up).
◆ **se boutonner** ◇ *vp (emploi passif)* [se fermer] to button (up).
◇ *vp (emploi réfléchi) fam* [s'habiller] to button o.s. up.

boutonneux, euse [butɔnø, øz] *adj* [peau, visage, adolescent] spotty, pimply.

boutonnière [butɔnjɛr] *nf* **1.** COUT buttonhole **2.** MÉD buttonhole **3.** *fam* [blessure] gash.
◆ **à la boutonnière** *loc adv* on one's lapel.

bouton-pression [butɔ̃presjɔ̃] (*pl* **boutons-pression**) *nm* snap (fastener), press stud *UK*.

bouturage [butyraʒ] *nm* propagation by cuttings.

bouture [butyr] *nf* cutting ▪ **faire des ~s** to take cuttings.

bouturer [3] [butyre] ◇ *vt* **1.** [reproduire] to propagate (by cuttings) **2.** [couper] to take cuttings from.
◇ *vi* to grow suckers.

Bouvard et Pécuchet [buvarepekyʃe] *npr characters from a novel of the same name by Flaubert: two foolish men whose naïve quest for scientific knowledge leads them into comic situations.*

bouvier, ère [buvje, ɛr] *nm, f* bullock driver, cowherd.
◆ **bouvier** *nm* bouvier, sheepdog.

bouvreuil [buvrœj] *nm* bullfinch.

Bovary [bɔvari] *npr* : **Emma** *ou* **Madame ~** *heroine of Flaubert's novel 'Madame Bovary', after whom the term 'bovarysme' was coined to describe the feeling that romantic happiness is just round the corner.*

bovidé [bɔvide] *nm* bovid ▪ **les ~s** the Bovidae.

bovin, e [bɔvɛ̃, in] *adj* **1.** ZOOL [espèce] bovine ▪ [élevage] cattle *(modif)* **2.** *péj* [stupide] bovine.
◆ **bovin** *nm* bovine ▪ **les ~s** ZOOL the Bovini ; AGRIC cattle.

boviné [bɔvine] *nm* bovine ▪ **les ~s** the Bovini.

bowling [buliŋ] *nm* **1.** JEUX (tenpin) bowling ▪ **aller faire un ~** to go bowling **2.** [salle] bowling alley.

bow-window [bowindo] (*pl* **bow-windows**) *nm* bow window.

box[1] [bɔks] *nm inv* [cuir] box calf.

box[2] [bɔks] (*pl inv ou pl* **boxes**) *nm* **1.** [enclos - pour cheval] stall, loose box *UK* **2.** [garage] lock-up garage **3.** [compartiment - à l'hôpital, au dortoir] cubicle **4.** DR : **~ des accusés** dock ▪ **au ~ des accusés** *pr & fig* in the dock.

boxe [bɔks] *nf* boxing ▪ **faire de la ~** to box ⊙ **~ anglaise** boxing ▪ **~ française** kick *ou* French boxing.

boxer[1] [bɔksɛr] *nm* ZOOL boxer.

boxer[2] [3] [bɔkse] ◇ *vi* to box, to fight ▪ **~ contre qqn** to box with sb.
◇ *vt fam* to punch, to thump.

boxeur, euse [bɔksœr, øz] *nm, f* boxer.

box-office [bɔksɔfis] (*pl* **box-offices**) *nm* box office.

boxon△ [bɔksɔ̃] *nm* **1.** [maison close] brothel, whorehouse **2.** [désordre] godawful mess.

boy [bɔj] *nm* **1.** [serviteur] boy **2.** [danseur] (music-hall) dancer.

boyau, x [bwajo] *nm* **1.** CULIN length of casing **2.** MUS : **~ (de chat)** catgut, gut **3.** [passage - de mine] gallery, tunnel ▪ [souterrain] narrow tunnel ▪ [tranchée] trench ▪ [rue] narrow alleyway **4.** [chambre à air] inner tube.
◆ **boyaux** *nmpl* ZOOL guts, entrails ▪ [d'une personne] *fam* innards, guts.

boycott [bɔjkɔt], **boycottage** [bɔjkɔtaʒ] *nm* boycott.

boycotter [3] [bɔjkɔte] *vt* to boycott ▪ **les syndicats veulent faire ~ les élections** the unions want people to boycott the elections.

boycotteur, euse [bɔjkɔtœr, øz] ◇ *adj* boycotting *(avant n).*
◇ *nm, f* boycotter.

boy-scout [bɔjskut] (*pl* **boy-scouts**) *nm* **1.** *fam* [naïf] idealist **2.** *vieilli* [scout] boyscout, scout.

BP (*abr de* **boîte postale**) *nf* P.O. Box.

BPF (*abr écrite de* **bon pour francs**) *abbreviation printed on cheques and invoices before space for amount to be inserted.*

brabançon, onne [brabɑ̃sɔ̃, ɔn] *adj* from Brabant.

Brabançonne [brabɑ̃sɔn] *npr f Belgian national anthem.*

brabant [brabɑ̃] *nm* metal plough.

Brabant [brabɑ̃] *npr m* : **le ~** Brabant.

bracelet [braslɛ] *nm* **1.** [souple] bracelet ▪ [rigide] bangle ▪ **~ (de cheville)** anklet ▪ **~ (de montre)** watchstrap, watchband US **2.** [pour faire du sport] wristband ▪ **~ en éponge** sweatband **3.** [pour un condamné] : **~ électronique** electronic tag.
◆ **bracelets** *nmpl arg crime* [menottes] bracelets△, cuffs.

bracelet-montre [braslɛmɔ̃tr] (*pl* **bracelets-montres**) *nm* wristwatch.

brachial, e, aux [brakjal, o] *adj* brachial.

braconnage [brakɔnaʒ] *nm* poaching CHASSE.

braconner [3] [brakɔne] *vi* to poach CHASSE.

braconnier, ère [brakɔnje, ɛr] *nm, f* poacher CHASSE.

brader [3] [brade] *vt* to sell off *(sép)* cheaply.

braderie [bradri] *nf* **1.** [vente - en plein air, dans une salle] ≃ jumble sale UK, ≃ rummage sale US **2.** [soldes] clearance sale.

bradeur, euse [bradœr, øz] *nm, f* discounter.

braguette [bragɛt] *nf* flies UK, fly US *(on trousers).*

brahmane [braman] *nm* Brahman.

brahmanique [bramanik] *adj* Brahmanic.

brahmanisme [bramanism] *nm* Brahmanism.

braillard, e [brajar, ard] *péj* ◇ *adj* : **un bébé ~** a bawler.
◇ *nm, f* bawler, squaller.

braille [braj] *nm* Braille ▪ **apprendre le ~** to learn (to read) Braille.

braillement [brajmɑ̃] *nm* bawl, howl ▪ **les ~s d'un bébé** the crying *ou* howling of a baby.

brailler [3] [braje] ◇ *vi* **1.** [pleurer] to wail, to bawl, to howl **2.** [crier - mégère, ivrogne] to yell, to bawl ; [- radio] to blare (out) **3.** [chanter] to roar, to bellow.
◇ *vt* to bawl (out), to holler (out) US.

brailleur, euse [brajœr, øz] *péj* = **braillard.**

braiment [brɛmɑ̃] *nm* bray, braying.

brainstorming [brɛnstɔrmiŋ] *nm* brainstorming session.

brain-trust [brɛntrœst] (*pl* **brain-trusts**) *nm* brains trust UK, brain trust US.

braire [112] [brɛr] *vi* **1.** ZOOL to bray **2.** *fam* [crier] to yell, to bellow **3.** *fam loc* **tu me fais ~!** you're getting on my wick!

braise [brɛz] *nf* **1.** [charbons] (glowing) embers ▪ **un regard de ~** *fig* a smouldering look **2.** △ *arg crime* [argent] dough, moolah△.

braiser [4] [breze] *vt* to braise.

bramer [3] [brame] *vi* **1.** ZOOL to bell **2.** *fam* [pleurer] to wail.

brancard [brɑ̃kar] *nm* **1.** [civière] stretcher **2.** [limon d'attelage] shaft.

brancardier [brɑ̃kardje] *nm* stretcher-bearer.

branchage [brɑ̃ʃaʒ] *nm* [ramure] boughs, branches.
◆ **branchages** *nmpl* (cut) branches.

branche [brɑ̃ʃ] *nf* **1.** BOT [d'arbre] branch, bough ▪ [de céleri] stick ▪ **grosse ~** limb, large branch ➊ **vieille ~** *hum & vieilli* old chum *ou* buddy ▪ **s'accrocher** *ou* **se raccrocher aux ~s** *fam* to hang on by one's fingernails **2.** ANAT ramification **3.** ÉLECTRON leg, branch **4.** [tige - de lunettes] sidepiece UK, bow US ; [- d'un compas, d'un aimant] arm, leg ; [- de ciseaux] blade ; [- de tenailles] handle ; [- d'un chandelier] branch **5.** [secteur] field **6.** [d'une famille] side ▪ **par la ~ maternelle** on the mother's side (of the family) ▪ **la ~ aînée de la famille** the senior branch of the family.
◆ **en branches** *loc adj* [épinards] leaf *(modif).*

branché, e [brɑ̃ʃe] *fam* ◇ *adj* fashionable, trendy *péj.*
◇ *nm, f* : **tous les ~s viennent dans ce café** you get all the fashionable people *ou péj* trendies in this café.

branchement [brɑ̃ʃmɑ̃] *nm* **1.** CONSTR, ÉLECTR, TÉLÉCOM & TRAV PUB connection ▪ **~ d'appareil** [tuyau] connecting branch ; [liaison] connection, installation ▪ **~ au réseau électrique** network branch ▪ **~ électrique** electric power supply ▪ **faire un ~ au** *ou* **sur le réseau** to become connected to the mains (power supply) **2.** RAIL turnout.

brancher [3] [brɑ̃ʃe] ◇ *vt* **1.** CONSTR, ÉLECTR, TÉLÉCOM & TRAV PUB to connect ▪ **~ qqch sur une prise** to plug sthg in ▪ **être branché** [appareil] to be plugged in ; [canalisation] to be connected to the system **2.** *fam* [faire parler] : **~ qqn sur** to start sb off *ou* to get sb going on **3.** *fam* [mettre en rapport] : **~ qqn avec** to put sb in touch with **4.** *fam* [intéresser] : **ça me branche bien!** that's great! ▪ **il est très branché (sur les) voyages** he's really into travelling ▪ **ça vous brancherait d'y aller?** how do you fancy going there?
◇ *vi* to roost, to sit.
◆ **se brancher** ◇ *vp (emploi passif)* : **se ~ dans** to plug into.
◇ *vpi* : **se ~ sur** RADIO to tune in to ; [canalisation] to connect up to ▪ **il s'est branché sur l'informatique** *fam fig* he's got into computers.

branchies [brɑ̃ʃi] *nfpl* gills, branchiae *spéc.*

branchu, e [brɑ̃ʃy] *adj* branchy.

brandade [brɑ̃dad] *nf* brandade, salt cod puree.

brandebourg [brɑ̃dbur] *nm* COUT frog, frogging.

Brandebourg [brɑ̃dbur] *npr* Brandenburg.

brandebourgeois, e [brɑ̃dburʒwa, az] *adj* from Brandenburg.
◆ **Brandebourgeois, e** *nmf sing inhabitant of or person from Brandenburg.*

brandir [32] [brɑ̃dir] *vt* to brandish, to wave (about), to flourish.

brandon [brɑ̃dɔ̃] *nm* [pour allumer] firebrand ▪ **~ de discorde** [objet, situation] bone of contention ; [personne] troublemaker.

branlant, e [brɑ̃lɑ̃, ɑ̃t] *adj* **1.** [vieux - bâtiment, véhicule] ramshackle, rickety **2.** [instable - pile d'objets] unsteady, wobbly, shaky ; [- échelle, chaise] rickety, shaky ; [- démarche] tottering ; [- dent] loose ; [- résolution, réputation] shaky.

branle [brɑ̃l] *nm* [mouvement] pendulum motion ▪ [impulsion] impulsion, propulsion ▪ **être en ~** to be on the move ▪ **mettre en ~** [cloche] to set going ; [mécanisme, procédure] to set going *ou* in motion ▪ **se mettre en ~** [voyageur] to set off, to start out ; [mécanisme] to start going, to start moving ; [voiture] to start (moving).

branle-bas [brɑ̃lba] *nm inv* **1.** [agitation] pandemonium, commotion ▪ **~ de combat!** NAUT & *fig* action stations! **2.** NAUT clearing of the decks.

branlement [brɑ̃lmɑ̃] *nm* [dodelinement] wagging (of the head).

branler [3] [brɑ̃le] <> *vi* [échelle, pile d'objets] to be shaky *ou* unsteady ▪ [fauteuil] to be rickety ▪ [dent] to be loose ▪ **~ du chef** [de haut en bas] to nod ; [de droite à gauche] to shake one's head.
<> *vt*△ [faire] : **mais qu'est-ce qu'il branle?** [il est en retard] where the fuck is he?▲ ; [il fait une bêtise] what the fuck's he up to?▲.
◆ **se branler**△ *vpi* to (have a) wank▲ *UK*, to jerk off▲ *US* ▪ **je m'en branle** *fig* I don't give a shit▲ *ou* fuck▲.

branlette▲ [brɑ̃lɛt] *nf* wank ▪ **se faire une (petite) ~** to have a wank *UK*, to jerk off *US*.

branleur, euse△ [brɑ̃lœr, øz] *nm, f* wanker▲ *UK*, little shit▲.

brante [brɑ̃t] *nf* *Suisse grape-picker's basket.*

braquage [brakaʒ] *nm* **1.** AUTO (steering) lock **2.** AÉRON deflection **3.** *fam* [vol] holdup, stickup.

braque [brak] <> *adj fam* cracked, nuts ▪ **elle est complètement ~** she's as mad as a March hare *ou* a hatter, she's as crazy as a bedbug *US*.
<> *nm* ZOOL pointer.

braquer [3] [brake] <> *vt* **1.** [pointer - fusil] to point, to aim, to level ; [- projecteur, télescope] to train ▪ **~ son revolver sur qqn** to level *ou* to point one's gun at sb **2.** [concentrer] : **~ sur** to train *ou* to fix *ou* to turn on ▪ **son regard était braqué sur moi** she was staring straight at me, her gaze was fixed on me **3.** AUTO & AÉRON to lock **4.** [rendre hostile] to antagonize ▪ **~ qqn contre** to set sb against **5.** *fam* [attaquer - banque] to hold up *(insép)* ; [- caissier] to hold at gunpoint.
<> *vi* [voiture] to lock ▪ **~ à droite/gauche** to lock hard to the right/left ▪ **braque à fond!** wheel hard down!
◆ **se braquer** *vpi* to dig one's heels in.

braquet [brakɛ] *nm* transmission ratio.

braqueur, euse [brakœr, øz] *nm, f* holdup man *m*, holdup woman *f (in bank etc)*.

bras [bra] <> *nm* **1.** [membre] arm ▪ ANAT upper arm ▪ **son panier/épouse au ~** his basket/wife on his arm ▪ **porter un enfant dans les** *ou* **ses ~** to carry a child (in one's arms) ▪ **tomber dans les ~ de qqn** to fall into sb's arms ▪ **sous le ~** under one arm ▪ **prendre le ~ de qqn** to grab sb's arm ▪ **donner** *ou* **offrir son ~ à qqn** to offer sb one's arm ▪ **serrer qqn dans ses ~** to hold sb in one's arms, to hug sb ▪ **tendre** *ou* **allonger le ~** to stretch one's arm out ▪ **les ~ en croix** (with) arms outstretched *ou* outspread ▶ **~ droit** right hand man (*f* woman) ▪ **faire un ~ de fer avec qqn** *pr* to arm-wrestle with sb ; *fig* to have a tussle with sb ▪ **faire un ~ d'honneur à qqn** ≃ to give sb a V-sign *UK ou* the finger *US* ▪ **jouer les gros ~** to throw one's weight around ▪ **tomber à ~ raccourcis sur qqn** [gén] to lay into sb ; [physiquement] to beat sb to a pulp ▪ **avoir le ~ long** to be influential ▪ **se jeter dans les ~ de qqn** *pr* to throw o.s. into sb's arms ; *fig* to fall an easy prey to sb ▪ **les ~ lui en sont tombés** his jaw dropped *ou* fell ▪ **lever les ~** [d'impuissance] to throw up one's arms (helplessly) ▪ **lever les ~ au ciel** to throw up one's arms in indignation ▪ **tendre les ~ à qqn** *pr* to hold out one's arms to sb ; *fig* to offer sb (moral) support ▪ **tendre les ~ vers qqn** *pr* to hold out one's arms to sb ; *fig* to turn to sb for help **2.** ZOOL [du cheval] arm ▪ [tentacule] arm, tentacle **3.** [partie - d'une ancre, d'un électrophone, d'un moulin] arm ; [- d'une charrette] arm, shaft ; [- d'une grue] arm, jib ; [- d'un fauteuil] arm, armrest ; [- d'une brouette] handle ; [- d'une manivelle] web, arm ; [- d'un brancard] pole ; [- d'une croix] arm ▪ **~ de levier** lever arm *ou* crank ▪ **~ manipulateur** computer-operated arm **4.** [pouvoir] : **le ~ séculier** the secular arm ▪ **le ~ de la justice** the long arm of the law **5.** GÉOGR [d'un delta] arm ▪ **~ de mer** sound, arm of the sea **6.** NAUT (anchor) arm.
<> *nmpl* [main-d'œuvre] workers ▪ **on a besoin de ~** we're short-handed *ou* short-staffed.
◆ **à bras ouverts** *loc adv* [accueillir] with open arms.
◆ **au bras de** *loc prép* on the arm of, arm in arm with.
◆ **bras dessus, bras dessous** *loc adv* arm in arm.
◆ **sur les bras** *loc adv* : **avoir qqn/qqch sur les ~** to be stuck with sb/sthg ▪ **je me suis retrouvé avec le projet sur les ~** I got landed with the project ▪ **je n'ai plus mes enfants sur les ~** my children are off my hands now ▪ **le loyer m'est resté sur les ~** I was left with the rent to pay.

brasero [brazero] *nm* brazier.

brasier [brazje] *nm* **1.** [incendie] blaze, fire **2.** [tumulte] fire ▪ **le pays est maintenant un véritable ~** the whole country's ablaze.

Brasilia [brazilja] *npr* Brasilia.

bras-le-corps [bralkɔr] ◆ **à bras-le-corps** *loc adv* : **prendre qqn à ~** to catch hold of *ou* to seize sb around the waist ▪ **prendre un problème à ~** *fig* to tackle a problem head on.

brassage [brasaʒ] *nm* **1.** [de la bière] brewing ▪ [du malt] mashing **2.** [de liquides] mixing, swirling together ▪ [des cultures, des peuples] intermixing, intermingling.

brassard [brasar] *nm* armband ▪ **~ de deuil** black armband.

brasse [bras] *nf* **1.** SPORT breaststroke ▪ **elle traverse la piscine en 10 ~s** she can cross the swimming pool in 10 strokes *(doing the breaststroke)* ▶ **~ papillon** butterfly (stroke) **2.** [mesure] 5 feet ▪ NAUT fathom.

brassée [brase] *nf* armful.
◆ **par brassées** *loc adv* by the armful.

brasser [3] [brase] *vt* **1.** [bière] to brew ▪ [malt] to mash **2.** JEUX [cartes] to shuffle **3.** [populations] to intermingle **4.** [agiter - air] to fan ; [- feuilles mortes] to toss about *(sép)*, to stir **5.** [manier - argent, sommes] to handle ▪ **~ des affaires** to handle a lot of business.

brasserie [brasri] *nf* **1.** [fabrique de bière] brewery **2.** [café] *large café serving light meals.*

brasseur, euse [brasœr, øz] *nm, f* **1.** SPORT breaststroker ▪ **c'est un bon ~** he's good at the breaststroke **2.** [fabricant de bière] brewer.
◆ **brasseur d'affaires** *nm* big businessman.

brassière [brasjɛr] *nf* **1.** [vêtement] (baby's) vest *UK ou* undershirt *US* **2.** NAUT : **~ de sauvetage** life jacket **3.** *Québec* bra.

brasure [brazyr] *nf* **1.** [soudure] soldering joint *ou* surface *ou* seam **2.** [alliage] brazing alloy.

bravache [bravaʃ] <> *adj* swaggering, blustering.
<> *nm* braggart *litt*, swaggerer ▪ **faire le ~** to brag.

bravade [bravad] *nf* [ostentation] bravado ▪ [défi] defiance ▪ **faire qqch par ~** [ostentation] to do sthg out of bravado ; [défi] to do sthg in a spirit of defiance.

brave [brav] <> *adj* **1.** [courageux] brave, bold ▪ **faire le ~** to act brave **2.** *(avant le n)* [bon] good, decent ▪ **de ~s gens** good *ou* decent people ▪ **un ~ type** *fam* a nice bloke *UK ou* guy **3.** [ton condescendant] : **ma ~ dame/mon ~ monsieur, personne ne dit le contraire!** my dear lady/my dear fellow, nobody's saying anything to the contrary! ▪ **il est bien ~ mais il ne comprend rien** he means well but he doesn't understand a thing.
<> *nmf* [héros] brave man (*f* woman).
<> *nm* [guerrier indien] brave.

bravement [bravmɑ̃] *adv* **1.** [courageusement] bravely, courageously **2.** [sans hésitation] boldly, resolutely ▪ **il s'est ~ mis au travail** he set to work with a will.

braver [3] [brave] *vt* **1.** [affronter - danger, mort] to defy, to brave ; [- conventions] to go against, to challenge **2.** [défier - autorité] to defy, to stand up to *(insép)*.

bravo [bravo] <> *interj* **1.** [applaudissement] bravo **2.** [félicitations] well done, bravo.
<> *nm* bravo ▪ **un grand ~ pour nos candidats** let's have a big hand for our contestants.

bravoure [bravur] *nf* bravery, courage.

BRB *nf* = **brigade de répression du banditisme**.

break [brɛk] *nm* **1.** AUTO estate car *UK*, station wagon *US* **2.** [voiture à cheval] break **3.** MUS break.

brebis [brəbi] *nf* **1.** ZOOL ewe ■ **~ galeuse** black sheep **2.** RELIG sheep ■ **~ égarée** lost sheep.

brèche [brɛʃ] *nf* **1.** [ouverture] breach, gap, break **2.** MIL breach ■ **faire une ~ dans un front** to break open *ou* to breach an enemy line ⊙ **être toujours sur la ~** to be always on the go **3.** *fig* hole, dent ■ **faire une ~ à son capital** to make a hole *ou* dent in one's capital **4.** GÉOL breccia.

bréchet [breʃɛ] *nm* carina, keel.

brechtien, enne [brɛʃtjɛ̃, ɛn] *adj* Brechtian.

bredouille [brəduj] *adj* empty-handed ■ **rentrer ~** CHASSE & PÊCHE to come home empty-handed *ou* with an empty bag ; *fig* to come back empty-handed.

bredouillement [brədujmɑ̃] *nm* mumbling, muttering.

bredouiller [3] [brəduje] *vi* & *vt* to mumble, to mutter.

bref, brève [brɛf, brɛv] *adj* **1.** [court - moment, vision] brief, fleeting ■ [concis - lettre, discours] brief, short ■ **soyez ~** be brief **2.** PHON [syllabe, voyelle] short.
◆ **bref** ◇ *adv* in short, in a word ■ **enfin ~, je n'ai pas envie d'y aller** well, basically, I don't want to go ■ **~, ce n'est pas possible** anyway, it's not possible.
◇ *nm* RELIG (papal) brief.
◆ **brève** *nf* **1.** PHON [voyelle] short vowel ■ [syllabe] short syllable **2.** PRESSE, RADIO & TV brief ■ **brèves de comptoir** bar talk.
◆ **en bref** *loc adv* **1.** [en résumé] in short, in brief **2.** PRESSE, RADIO & TV : **en ~** news in brief.

brelan [brəlɑ̃] *nm three of a kind* ■ **~ de rois** three kings.

breloque [brəlɔk] *nf* [bijou] charm.

brème [brɛm] *nf* ZOOL bream.

Brésil [brezil] *npr m* : **le ~** Brazil.

brésilien, enne [breziljɛ̃, ɛn] *adj* Brazilian.
◆ **Brésilien, enne** *nm, f* Brazilian.
◆ **brésilien** *nm* LING Brazilian Portuguese.

Bretagne [brətaɲ] *npr f* : **(la) ~** Brittany ■ **la ~ bretonnante** LING the Breton-speaking part of Brittany ; [gén] the most typically Breton part of Brittany.

BRETAGNE

This administrative region includes the *départements* of Côtes-d'Armor, Finistère, Ille-et-Vilaine and Morbihan (capital: Rennes).

bretelle [brətɛl] *nf* **1.** [bandoulière] (shoulder) strap ■ **porter l'arme à la ~** to carry one's weapon slung over one's shoulder **2.** [de robe] shoulder strap ■ [de soutien-gorge] (bra) strap **3.** RAIL double crossover **4.** TRANSP slip road *UK*, access road ■ **~ d'accès** access road ■ **~ d'autoroute** motorway slip road *UK*, highway access road *US* ■ **~ de contournement** bypass ■ **~ de raccordement** motorway *UK ou* highway *US* junction ■ **~ de sortie** exit road.
◆ **bretelles** *nfpl* braces *UK*, suspenders *US* ■ **se faire remonter les ~s** *fig* to be told to pull one's socks up.

breton, onne [brətɔ̃, ɔn] *adj* Breton.
◆ **Breton, onne** *nm, f* Breton.
◆ **breton** *nm* LING Breton.

bretonnant, e [brətɔnɑ̃, ɑ̃t] *adj* Breton-speaking.

bretzel [brɛtzɛl] *nm* pretzel.

breuvage [brœvaʒ] *nm* **1.** [boisson] beverage, drink ■ **un drôle de ~** a strange concoction **2.** [potion] potion, beverage.

brève [brɛv] *f* ▷ **bref**.

brevet [brəvɛ] *nm* **1.** DR : **~ (d'invention)** patent ■ **titulaire d'un ~** patentee **2.** ÉDUC diploma ■ **le ~** *exam taken at 14 years of age* ⊙ **~ d'études professionnelles = BEP** ■ **~s militaires** ≃ staff college qualifications ■ **~ professionnel** *vocational diploma* ■ **~ de sécurité routière** proficiency test for riding a moped ■ **~ de technicien** *exam taken at 17 after 3 years' technical training* ■ **~ de technicien supérieur = BTS 3.** AÉRON : **~ de pilote** pilot's licence **4.** [certificat] certificate ■ **~ de secourisme** first-aid certificate ■ **décerner à qqn un ~ de moralité** to testify to *ou* to vouch for sb's character.

brevetable [brəvtabl] *adj* patentable.

breveté, e [brəvte] ◇ *adj* **1.** [diplômé] qualified **2.** [garanti] patented.
◇ *nm, f* patentee.

breveter [27] [brəvte] *vt* to patent ■ **faire ~ qqch** to take out a patent for sthg.

bréviaire [brevjɛr] *nm* breviary.

briard, e [brijar, ard] *adj* from the Brie region.
◆ **briard** *nm* Briard (sheepdog).

bribes [brib] *nfpl* **1.** [restes - d'un gâteau, d'un repas] scraps, crumbs **2.** [fragments - de discours] snatches, scraps ; [- d'information, de connaissance] scraps.
◆ **par bribes** *loc adv* in snatches, bit by bit ■ **je connais l'histoire par ~** I heard the story in snatches.

bric-à-brac [brikabrak] *nm inv* **1.** [tas d'objets] clutter, jumble, bric-à-brac **2.** [mélange d'idées] jumble of ideas, hotchpotch *UK ou* hodgepodge *US* of ideas **3.** [boutique] junk shop *UK*, secondhand store *US*.

bricelet [brislɛ] *nm* *Suisse thin crisp waffle*.

bric et de broc [brikedbrɔk] ◆ **de bric et de broc** *loc adv* haphazardly ■ **meublé de ~** furnished with bits and pieces.

bricolage [brikɔlaʒ] *nm* **1.** [travail manuel] do-it-yourself, DIY *UK* **2.** [réparation] makeshift repair ■ **c'est du bon ~** it's good work **3.** [mauvais travail] : **c'est du ~** it's just been thrown together.
◆ **de bricolage** *loc adj* [magasin, manuel, rayon] do-it-yourself *(modif)*, DIY *UK (modif)*.

bricole [brikɔl] *nf* **1.** [petit objet] : **des ~s** things, bits and pieces **2.** [article de peu de valeur] trifle ■ **je vais lui offrir une ~** I'm going to give her a little something ⊙ **...et des ~s** *fam* ...and a bit ■ **30 euros et des ~s** 30-odd euros **3.** [chose sans importance] piece of trivia ■ **des ~s** trivia **4.** *fam* [ennui] trouble **5.** [harnais] breast harness **6.** [bretelle] carrying girth *ou* strap **7.** PÊCHE double hook.

bricoler [3] [brikɔle] ◇ *vi* **1.** [faire des aménagements] to do DIY **2.** [avoir de petits emplois] to do odd jobs **3.** *fam péj* [mauvais artisan, praticien ou étudiant] to produce shoddy work.
◇ *vt* **1.** [confectionner] to make **2.** [réparer] to fix (up), to mend, to carry out makeshift repairs to **3.** [manipuler] to tinker *ou* to tamper with.

bricoleur, euse [brikɔlœr, øz] ◇ *nm, f* **1.** [qui construit ou répare soi-même] handyman (*f* handywoman), DIY enthusiast **2.** *péj* [dilettante] amateur, dilettante.
◇ *adj* : **il est très ~** he's good with his hands ■ **il n'est pas ~** he's no handyman.

bride [brid] *nf* **1.** ÉQUIT bridle ■ **tenir son cheval en ~** to curb *ou* to rein in a horse ■ **rendre la ~ à un cheval** to give a horse its head ⊙ **à ~ abattue, à toute ~** at full speed, like greased lightning ■ **avoir la ~ sur le cou** to be given a free hand ■ **laisser la ~ sur le cou à qqn** to give sb a free rein ■ **serrer** *ou* **tenir la ~ à qqn** to keep sb on a tight rein **2.** COUT bar ■ [en dentelle] bride, bar **3.** MÉD adhesion.

bridé, e [bride] *adj* : **avoir les yeux ~s** to have slanting eyes.

brider [3] [bride] *vt* **1.** ÉQUIT to bridle **2.** [serrer] to constrict ■ **ma veste me bride aux emmanchures** my jacket is too tight under the arms **3.** [émotion] to curb, to restrain ■ [personne] to keep in check **4.** COUT to bind **5.** CULIN to truss **6.** NAUT to lash together.

bridge [bridʒ] *nm* **1.** MÉD [dentisterie] bridge, bridgework **2.** JEUX bridge.

bridger [17] [bridʒe] *vi* to play bridge.

bridgeur, euse [bridʒœr, øz] *nm, f* bridge player.

brie [bri] *nm* Brie.

briefer [3] [brife] *vt* to brief.

briefing [brifiŋ] *nm* briefing.

brièvement [brijɛvmɑ̃] *adv* **1.** [pendant peu de temps] briefly, fleetingly, for a short time **2.** [avec concision] briefly, in a few words.

brièveté [brijɛvte] *nf* brevity, briefness.

brigade [brigad] *nf* **1.** MIL [détachement] brigade ■ **~ de gendarmerie** squad of gendarmes ‖ [régiments] brigade **2.** [équipe d'ouvriers] gang, team **3.** [corps de police] squad ■ **~ antigang** *ou* **de répression du (grand) banditisme** organized crime division ■ **~ des mineurs** juvenile squad ■ **~ des mœurs** vice squad ■ **~ des stupéfiants** *ou fam* **des stups** drug squad ■ **~ mobile** *ou* **volante** flying squad **4.** [en Italie] : **les Brigades rouges** the Red Brigades.

brigadier, ère [brigadje, ɛr] *nm, f* **1.** [de police] sergeant **2.** MIL corporal **3.** HIST brigadier.

brigadier-chef [brigadjeʃɛf] (*pl* **brigadiers-chefs**) *nm* lance-sergeant.

brigand [brigɑ̃] *nm* **1.** [bandit] bandit, brigand *litt* **2.** [escroc] crook, thief **3.** [avec affection] : **~, va!** *fam* you rogue *ou* imp *ou* rascal.

brigandage [brigɑ̃daʒ] *nm* **1.** [vol à main armée] armed robbery **2.** [acte malhonnête] : **c'est du ~** it's daylight robbery.

brigue [brig] *nf litt* intrigue ■ **avoir une place par (la) ~** to get a job by pulling strings.

briguer [3] [brige] *vt* [emploi] to angle for *(insép)* ■ [honneur] to seek, to pursue, to aspire to *(insép)* ■ [suffrage] to seek.

brillamment [brijamɑ̃] *adv* brilliantly, magnificently ■ **réussir ~ un examen** to pass an exam with flying colours.

brillant, e [brijɑ̃, ɑ̃t] *adj* **1.** [luisant - parquet] shiny, polished ; [- peinture] gloss *(modif)* ; [- cheveux, lèvres] shiny, glossy ; [- soie] lustrous ; [- toile, cristal] sparkling, glittering ; [- feuille, chaussure] glossy, shiny ; [- yeux] bright, shining ■ **~ de : yeux ~s de malice** eyes sparkling with mischief ■ **yeux ~s de fièvre** eyes bright with fever **2.** [remarquable - esprit, intelligence] brilliant, outstanding ; [- personne] outstanding ; [- succès, carrière, talent] brilliant, dazzling, outstanding ; [- conversation] brilliant, sparkling ; [- hommage] superb, magnificent ; [- représentation, numéro] brilliant, superb ■ **pas ~** it's not brilliant ■ **sa santé n'est pas ~e** he's not well, his health is not too good ■ **les résultats ne sont pas ~s** the results aren't too good *ou* aren't all they should be.

◆ **brillant** *nm* **1.** [éclat - d'un métal, d'une surface] gloss, sheen ; [- de chaussures] shine ; [- d'une peinture] gloss ; [- d'un tissu] sheen ; [- d'un diamant, d'un regard] sparkle **2.** [brio] brio, sparkle ■ **malgré le ~ de sa conversation/son œuvre** in spite of his brilliant conversation/impressive work **3.** JOAILL brilliant.

◆ **brillant à lèvres** *nm* [cosmétique] lip gloss.

brillantine [brijɑ̃tin] *nf* [pour les cheveux] brilliantine.

briller [3] [brije] *vi* **1.** [luire - chaussure, soleil, lumière, regard] to shine ; [- chandelle] to glimmer ; [- étoile] to twinkle, to shine ; [- diamant] to shine, to glitter, to sparkle ; [- dents] to sparkle ; [- eau] to shimmer, to sparkle ; [- feuille] to shine, to glisten ■ **j'ai le nez qui brille** I have a shiny nose ■ **faire ~ : faire ~ ses chaussures** to shine one's shoes ■ **faire ~ un meuble/l'argenterie** to polish a piece of furniture/the silver ■ **~ de : des yeux qui brillent de colère** eyes ablaze with anger ■ **des yeux qui brillent de plaisir/d'envie** eyes sparkling with pleasure/glowing with envy ■ **des yeux qui brillent de fièvre** eyes bright with fever ➤ **tout ce qui brille n'est pas (d')or** *prov* all that glitters is not gold *prov* **2.** [exceller] to shine, to excel, to be outstanding ■ **~ à un examen** to do very well in an exam ‖ [se distinguer] to stand out ■ **~ en société** to be a social success ■ **~ dans une conversation** to shine in a conversation ➤ **~ par son absence** to be conspicuous by one's absence.

brimade [brimad] *nf* **1.** [vexation] victimization, bullying ■ **faire subir des ~s à qqn** to victimize sb, to bully sb **2.** △ *arg scol* initiation ceremony.

brimborion [brɛ̃bɔrjɔ̃] *nm litt* bauble, trinket.

brimer [3] [brime] *vt* **1.** [tracasser] to victimize ■ **il se sent brimé** he feels victimized **2.** △ *arg scol* to initiate.

brin [brɛ̃] *nm* **1.** [filament] strand ■ **corde/laine à trois ~s** three-ply rope/wool ‖ TEXT fibre **2.** [tige - d'herbe] blade ; [- d'osier] twig ; [- de muguet, de persil] sprig ; [- de bruyère, d'aubépine] sprig **3.** [morceau - de laine, de fil] piece, length ■ **~ de paille** (piece of) straw **4.** [parcelle] : **un ~ de** a (tiny) bit of ■ **un ~ de génie** a touch of genius ■ **il n'a pas un ~ de bon sens** he hasn't an ounce *ou* a shred of common sense ■ **il n'y a pas un ~ de vent** there isn't a breath of wind ■ **il n'y a pas un ~ de vérité là-dedans** there isn't a grain of truth in it ■ **faire un ~ de : faire un ~ de causette (à)** *ou* **avec qqn** *fam* to have a quick chat (with sb) ■ **faire un ~ de cour à** to have a little flirt with ■ **faire un ~ de toilette** to have a quick wash **5.** *loc* **un beau ~ de fille** a good-looking girl.

◆ **un brin...** *loc adv fam* a trifle..., a touch... ■ **il était un ~ dépité** he was a trifle disappointed.

brindille [brɛ̃dij] *nf* twig.

bringue [brɛ̃g] *nf fam* **1.** [personne] *péj* **une grande ~** a bean-pole **2.** [noce] : **faire la ~** to live it up, to party.

bringuebaler [3] [brɛ̃gbale] ◇ *vt* to joggle, to shake.

◇ *vi* to rattle ■ **une voiture bringuebalante** a shaky old car.

bringuer [3] [brɛ̃ge] *Suisse* ◇ *vi* : **arrête de ~!** stop going on about it!

◇ *vt* to go on at *(insép)*.

◆ **se bringuer** *vpi* : **ils se bringuaient** they were having a row.

brinquebaler [brɛ̃kbale] = **bringuebaler**.

brio [brijo] *nm* brio, verve.

◆ **avec brio** *loc adv* : **s'en tirer avec ~** to carry sthg off with style.

brioche [brijɔʃ] *nf* **1.** CULIN brioche **2.** *fam* [ventre] paunch ■ **prendre de la ~** to be getting a paunch *ou* potbelly.

brioché, e [brijɔʃe] *adj* brioche-like.

brique [brik] ◇ *nf* **1.** CONSTR brick ■ **un mur de ~** *ou* **~s** a brick wall ➤ **~ réfractaire** firebrick ■ **bouffer des ~s**△ to have nothing to eat **2.** [morceau] piece ■ **~ de jeu de construction** building block **3.** [emballage - de lait, de jus de fruit] carton **4.** *fam* [million] *one million old francs (10,000 francs).*

◇ *adj inv* brick-red.

◆ **en brique** *loc adj* brick *(modif)*, made of brick.

briquer [3] [brike] *vt* [pont de navire] to scrub ■ *fam* [maison] to clean from top to bottom.

briquet [brikɛ] *nm* **1.** [appareil] lighter **2.** ZOOL beagle.

briquetage [briktaʒ] *nm* **1.** [maçonnerie] brickwork **2.** [enduit] imitation brickwork.

briqueter [27] [brikte] *vt* **1.** CONSTR [pavement, surface] to face in imitation brickwork **2.** [transformer en briquettes] to briquette.

briqueterie [brikɛtri] *nf* brickworks *(sing)*, brickyard.

briqueteur [briktœr] *nm* bricklayer.

briquetier [briktje] *nm* **1.** [ouvrier] brickmaker **2.** [dirigeant] brickyard manager.

briquette [brikɛt] *nf* **1.** CONSTR small brick **2.** [de combustible] briquette **3.** [conditionnement] carton.

bris [bri] *nm* **1.** [fragment] piece, fragment ■ **des ~ de glace** shards, fragments of glass ■ **être assuré contre les ~ de glace** to be insured for plate glass risk **2.** DR : **~ de clôture** breach of close ■ **~ de scellés** breaking of seals.

brisant, e [brizɑ̃, ɑ̃t] *adj* : **explosif ~** high explosive.

◆ **brisant** *nm* [haut-fond] reef, shoal.

◆ **brisants** *nmpl* [vagues] breakers.

briscard [briskar] *nm* **1.** MIL old soldier, veteran **2.** [vétéran] veteran, old hand.

brise [briz] *nf* breeze.

brisé, e [brize] *adj* **1.** [détruit] broken ■ **un homme ~** [par la fatigue] a run-down *ou* worn-out man ; [par les ennuis, le chagrin] a broken man **2.** GÉOM broken.
◆ **brisé** *nm* DANSE brisé.

brisées [brize] *nfpl* **1.** CHASSE broken branches *(to mark the way)* **2.** *loc* **aller** *ou* **marcher sur les ~ de qqn** to poach on sb's preserves.

brise-fer [brizfɛr] *nm inv fam vieilli* vandal.

brise-glace(s) [brizglas] *nm inv* **1.** NAUT icebreaker **2.** [pour un pont] icebreaker, ice apron *ou* guard **3.** [outil] hammer.

brise-jet [brizʒɛ] *nm inv* tap swirl.

brise-lames [brizlam] *nm inv* breakwater, groyne, mole.

brise-mottes [brizmɔt] *nm inv* harrow.

briser [3] [brize] *vt* **1.** [mettre en pièces - verre, assiette] to break, to smash ; [- vitre] to break, to shatter, to smash ; [- motte de terre] to break up *(sép)* ■ **~ qqch en mille morceaux** to smash sthg to pieces ■ **cela me brise le cœur** it breaks my heart ■ **~ les tabous** *fig* to break taboos **2.** [séparer en deux - canne, branche] to break, to snap ; [- liens, chaînes] to break ■ **~ la glace** to break the ice **3.** [défaire - réputation, carrière] to wreck, to ruin ; [- résistance, rébellion] to crush, to quell ; [- contrat] to break ; [- grève] to break (up) ■ **~ un mariage/une amitié/une famille** to break up a marriage/friendship/family ➤ **~ l'élan de qqn** *pr* to make sb stumble ; *fig* to clip sb's wings **4.** [soumettre] to break **5.** [épuiser - suj: soucis, chagrin] to break, to crush ; [- suj: exercice, voyage] to exhaust, to tire out *(sép)*.
◆ **briser avec** *v+prép* [ami, tradition] to break with.
◆ **se briser** *vpi* **1.** [se casser - verre] to shatter, to break ■ **son cœur s'est brisé** he was broken-hearted **2.** [être altéré - espoir] to shatter ; [- voix] to break, to falter **3.** [déferler - mer] to break **4.** [échouer - attaque, assaut] to fail.

briseur, euse [brizœr, øz] *nm, f* **1.** *litt* [casseur] wrecker **2.** *fig* **~ de grève** strikebreaker, scab.

brise-vent [brizvɑ̃] *nm inv* windbreak.

bristol [bristɔl] *nm* **1.** [carton] Bristol board, bristol **2.** [carte de visite] visiting *UK ou* calling *US* card **3.** [fiche] index card.

britannique [britanik] *adj* British.
◆ **Britannique** ◇ *adj* : **les îles Britanniques** the British isles.
◇ *nmf* Briton, Britisher *US* ■ **les Britanniques** the British.

broc [bro] *nm* [gén] pitcher ■ [pour la toilette] ewer.

brocante [brɔkɑ̃t] *nf* **1.** [objets] : **la ~** secondhand articles ■ **faire de la ~** to deal in secondhand goods **2.** [commerce] secondhand *ou* junk shop *UK*, used goods store *US*.

brocanter [3] [brɔkɑ̃te] *vi* to deal in secondhand goods.

brocanteur, euse [brɔkɑ̃tœr, øz] *nm, f* dealer in secondhand goods, secondhand *ou* junk shop owner *UK*, secondhand store keeper *US*.

brocart [brɔkar] *nm* brocade.

brochage [brɔʃaʒ] *nm* **1.** IMPR stitching, sewing **2.** TEXT brocade **3.** MÉCAN broaching.

broche [brɔʃ] *nf* **1.** CULIN spit, skewer, broach **2.** [bijou] broach **3.** [en alpinisme] piton **4.** ÉLECTRON & MÉD pin **5.** MÉCAN broaching tool, broach **6.** TECHNOL & TEXT spindle **7.** [d'une serrure] broach, hinge pin.
◆ **à la broche** *loc adv* on a spit ■ **cuit à la ~** roasted on a spit, spit-roasted.

broché, e [brɔʃe] *adj* **1.** TEXT brocaded, broché **2.** IMPR paperback *(modif)*.
◆ **broché** *nm* [tissu] brocade, broché *ou* swivel fabric.

brocher [3] [brɔʃe] *vt* **1.** IMPR to stitch, to sew **2.** MÉCAN to broach **3.** TEXT to brocade, to figure ■ **tissu broché d'or** material interwoven with raised gold threads.

brochet [brɔʃɛ] *nm* pike ZOOL.

brochette [brɔʃɛt] *nf* **1.** CULIN [broche] skewer ■ [mets] brochette, kebab **2.** [assemblée] lot ■ **une jolie ~ d'hypocrites** a fine lot of hypocrites **3.** [ribambelle] : **~ de décorations** row of decorations.

brocheur, euse [brɔʃœr, øz] *nm, f* **1.** IMPR stitcher, sewer **2.** TEXT brocade weaver.
◆ **brocheur** *nm* broché weaving machine.
◆ **brocheuse** *nf* IMPR binding machine.

brochure [brɔʃyr] *nf* **1.** IMPR stitched book, unbound book ■ [livret] pamphlet, booklet, brochure ■ **j'ai pris toutes les ~s sur Capri** I took all the brochures on Capri **2.** TEXT brocaded design, figured pattern.

brocoli [brɔkɔli] *nm* broccoli *(U)* ■ **des ~s** broccoli.

brodequin [brɔdkɛ̃] *nm* **1.** [chaussure] (laced) boot **2.** ANTIQ [bottine] brodekin, buskin.

broder [3] [brɔde] ◇ *vt* **1.** COUT to embroider ■ **brodé d'or** embroidered in gold thread **2.** *litt* [embellir] to embellish, to embroider *litt*.
◇ *vi* [exagérer] to use poetic licence.

broderie [brɔdri] *nf* **1.** COUT [technique] embroidery ■ **faire de la ~** to do embroidery *ou* needlework ➤ **~ anglaise** broderie anglaise **2.** [ouvrage] (piece of) embroidery, embroidery work **3.** [industrie] embroidery trade.

brodeur, euse [brɔdœr, øz] *nm, f* embroiderer.
◆ **brodeuse** *nf* embroidering machine.

Brogniart [brɔɲar] *npr* : **le palais ~** *name by which the Paris Stock Exchange is sometimes known.*

broie *etc v* ⊳ **broyer**.

bromure [brɔmyr] *nm* bromide ■ **~ de potassium** potassium bromide.

bronche [brɔ̃ʃ] *nf* bronchus ■ **les ~s** the bronchial tubes.

broncher [3] [brɔ̃ʃe] *vi* **1.** [réagir] to react, to respond ■ **le premier qui bronche...** the first one to move a muscle *ou* to budge... **2.** [cheval] to stumble.
◆ **sans broncher** *loc adv* without batting an eye *ou* eyelid, without turning a hair *ou* flinching.

bronchiole [brɔ̃ʃjɔl] *nf* bronchiole.

bronchique [brɔ̃ʃik] *adj* bronchial.

bronchite [brɔ̃ʃit] *nf* bronchitis.

bronchitique [brɔ̃ʃitik] ◇ *adj* bronchitic ■ **être ~** to have chronic bronchitis.
◇ *nmf* chronic bronchitis patient.

broncho-pneumonie [brɔ̃kopnømɔni] *(pl* **broncho-pneumonies)**, **broncho-pneumopathie** [brɔ̃kɔpnømopati] *(pl* **broncho-pneumopathies)** *nf* bronchopneumonia.

bronchoscopie [brɔ̃kɔskɔpi] *nf* bronchoscopy.

brontosaure [brɔ̃tɔzɔr] *nm* brontosaur, brontosaurus.

bronzage [brɔ̃zaʒ] *nm* **1.** [hâle] suntan, tan ■ **avoir un beau ~** to have a nice tan **2.** TECHNOL bronzing.

bronzant, e [brɔ̃zɑ̃, ɑ̃t] *adj* suntan *(avant n)*.

bronze [brɔ̃z] ◇ *nm* ART & MÉTALL bronze ■ **un homme au cœur de ~** *litt* a cold-hearted man.
◇ *adj inv* bronze, bronze-coloured.

bronzé, e [brɔ̃ze] *adj* **1.** [hâlé] suntanned, tanned **2.** TECHNOL bronze, bronzed.

bronzer [3] [brɔ̃ze] ◇ *vt* **1.** [hâler] to tan **2.** [donner l'aspect du bronze à] to bronze **3.** [fer] to blue.
◇ *vi* to tan, to go brown ■ **se faire ~** to sunbathe.

bronzette [brɔ̃zɛt] *nf fam* (bout of) sunbathing.

brossage [brɔsaʒ] *nm* **1.** [de chaussures, de vêtements] brushing **2.** [d'un cheval] brushing down.

brosse [brɔs] *nf* **1.** [ustensile] brush ■ **~ à chaussures** shoe brush ■ **~ à cheveux** hairbrush ■ **~ à dents** toothbrush ■ **~ à**

habits clothes brush ■ **~ à ongles** nailbrush ■ **~ en chiendent** scrubbing *UK ou* scrub *US* brush ■ **~ métallique** wire brush ■ **donner un coup de ~ à qqch** [pour dépoussiérer] to brush sthg ; [pour laver] to give sthg a scrub ■ **passer la ~ à reluire à qqn** *fam* to butter sb up, to soft-soap sb **2.** [pinceau] brush **3.** [coiffure] crew cut ■ **se faire couper les cheveux en ~** to have a crew cut *ou* a flat-top.

brosser [3] [brɔse] *vt* **1.** [épousseter - miettes] to brush (off) ; [- pantalon, jupe] to brush down **2.** [frictionner] to brush, to scrub ■ **~ un cheval** to rub a horse down **3.** ART [paysage, portrait] to paint ■ **il m'a brossé un tableau idéal de son travail** he painted me a glowing picture of his job.
◆ **se brosser** *vp (emploi réfléchi)* **1.** [se nettoyer] to brush o.s. (down) ■ **se ~ les dents/les cheveux** to brush one's teeth/hair **2.** *fam loc* **il peut toujours se ~, il n'aura jamais mon livre** he can whistle for my book.

brou [bru] *nm* BOT husk, shuck *US*.
◆ **brou de noix** *nm* walnut stain ■ **passer au ~ de noix** to stain with walnut.

brouet [bruɛ] *nm hum & litt* (coarse) gruel.

brouette [bruɛt] *nf* barrow, wheelbarrow.

brouettée [bruete] *nf* barrowful, wheelbarrowful.

brouetter [4] [bruete] *vt* to cart *(in a wheelbarrow)*, to barrow, to wheelbarrow.

brouhaha [bruaa] *nm* hubbub, (confused) noise.

brouillage [brujaʒ] *nm* [accidentel] interference ■ [intentionnel] jamming ■ **~ électronique** RADIO electronic jamming.

brouillard [brujar] *nm* **1.** MÉTÉOR [léger] mist ■ [épais] fog ■ **il y a du ~** it's misty, there's a mist ▶ **un ~ à couper au couteau** a very thick fog ■ **~ givrant** freezing fog ■ **~ matinal** early-morning fog ■ **il est dans le ~** he's not with it **2.** [voile] mist **3.** BOT gypsophila *spéc*, baby's breath **4.** [livre de comptes] day-book.

brouillasser [3] [brujase] *v impers* : **il brouillasse** it's drizzling.

brouille [bruj] *nf* tiff, quarrel ■ **leur ~ dure toujours** they're still not speaking *ou* on speaking terms.

brouillé, e [bruje] *adj* **1.** [terne] : **avoir le teint ~** to look off-colour **2.** [ciel] cloudy **3.** CULIN scrambled.

brouiller [3] [bruje] *vt* **1.** CULIN [œuf] to scramble **2.** [mélanger - cartes] to shuffle ■ **~ la cervelle** *fam ou* **le cerveau de qqn** to get sb muddled *ou* confused ■ **~ les cartes** *fig* to confuse the issue ■ **~ les pistes** [dans un roman] to confuse the reader ; [dans une poursuite] to cover one's tracks, to put sb off one's scent ; [dans un débat] to put up a smokescreen **3.** [dérégler] to jumble ■ **~ la combinaison d'un coffre** to jumble the combination of a safe **4.** [troubler - liquide] to cloud ■ **~ la vue** to cloud *ou* to blur one's eyesight ■ **il avait les yeux brouillés par les larmes** his eyes were blurred with tears **5.** RADIO [signal] to garble ■ [transmission, circuit] to jam **6.** [fâcher] to turn against, to alienate from ■ **ce professeur m'a brouillé avec les mathématiques** *fig* that teacher spoiled *ou* ruined mathematics for me.
◆ **se brouiller** ◇ *vp (emploi réciproque)* [se fâcher] to quarrel, to fall out (with one another).
◇ *vpi* **1.** [se mélanger - idées] to get confused *ou* muddled *ou* jumbled ■ [se troubler - vue] to blur, to become blurred **2.** MÉTÉOR [ciel] to become cloudy, to cloud over.
◆ **se brouiller avec** *vp+prép* to fall out with.

brouillerie [brujri] *nf* tiff.

brouilleur [brujœr] *nm* INFORM scrambler.

brouillon, onne [brujɔ̃, ɔn] ◇ *adj* **1.** [travail] untidy, messy **2.** [personne] muddleheaded, unmethodical ■ **avoir l'esprit ~** to be muddleheaded.
◇ *nm, f* muddler.
◆ **brouillon** *nm* (rough) draft ■ **faire un ~** to make a (rough) draft.

broussaille [brusaj] *nf* [touffe] clump of brushwood.
◆ **broussailles** *nfpl* [sous-bois] undergrowth ■ [dans un champ] scrub.
◆ **en broussaille** *loc adj* [cheveux] tousled, dishevelled ■ [sourcils, barbe] bushy, shaggy.

broussailleux, euse [brusajø, øz] *adj* **1.** [terrain] brushy, scrubby, covered with brushwood **2.** [sourcils, barbe] shaggy, bushy ■ [cheveux] tousled, dishevelled.

brousse [brus] *nf* **1.** GÉOGR [type de végétation] : **la ~** the bush **2.** [étendue] : **la ~** [en Afrique] the bush ; [en Australie] the outback ■ **vivre en pleine ~** *fam fig* to live in the backwoods *ou* out in the sticks *ou* in the boondocks *US*.
◆ **de brousse** *loc adj* **1.** [chaussures] desert *(modif)* **2.** [feux] bush *(modif)*.

brouter [3] [brute] ◇ *vt* **1.** [suj: bétail] to graze, to feed on *(insép)* ■ [suj: animal sauvage] to browse, to feed on *(insép)* ■ **~ des feuilles** to nibble at leaves **2.** △ *loc* **il nous les broute** he's being a pain in the neck *ou* arse.
◇ *vi* **1.** [bétail] to graze, to feed ■ [animal sauvage] to browse, to feed **2.** [machine-outil] to chatter, to judder *UK*, to jerk ■ [embrayage] to slip.

broutille [brutij] *nf* [chose futile] trifle, trifling matter ■ **il s'inquiète pour des ~s** he's worrying over nothing.

brownie [brɔni] *nm* CULIN brownie.

browser [brawzœr] *nm* browser.

broyer [13] [brwaje] *vt* **1.** [écraser - couleur, matériau friable, nourriture] to grind ; [- pierre, sucre, ail] to crush ; [- grain] to mill, to grind ; [- fibre] to break, to crush ; [- main, pied] to crush ■ **se faire ~** to be *ou* get crushed **2.** *loc* **~ du noir** to be in the doldrums, to think gloomy thoughts.

broyeur, euse [brwajœr, øz] ◇ *adj* grinding.
◇ *nm, f* grinder, crusher.
◆ **broyeur** *nm* [pulvérisateur - à minerai, à sable] grinder, crusher, mill ; [- à paille] bruiser ; [- à fibre] brake ; [- à déchets] disintegrator, grinder ■ **~ sanitaire** Saniflo®, macerator unit.

brrr [br] *interj* brrr.

bru [bry] *nf* daughter-in-law.

brucelles [brysɛl] *nfpl Suisse* (pair of) tweezers.

brucellose [bryseloz] *nf* brucellosis.

brugnon [bryɲɔ̃] *nm* (white) nectarine.

bruine [brɥin] *nf* drizzle.

bruiner [3] [brɥine] *v impers* : **il bruine** it's drizzling.

bruineux, euse [brɥinø, øz] *adj* drizzly.

bruire [105] [brɥir] *vi litt* [feuilles, vent] to rustle, to whisper ■ [eau] to murmur ■ [insecte] to hum, to buzz, to drone ■ **le vent faisait ~ les arbres** the trees were rustling in the wind.

bruissement [brɥismɑ̃] *nm* [des feuilles, du vent, d'une étoffe] rustle, rustling ■ [de l'eau] murmuring ■ [d'un insecte] hum, humming, buzzing ■ [des ailes, d'une voile] flapping.

bruissent, bruit *etc v* ▷ **bruire**.

bruit [brɥi] *nm* **1.** [son] sound, noise ■ **des ~s de pas** the sound of footsteps ■ **des ~s de voix** the hum of conversation ■ **les ~s de la maison/rue** the (everyday) sounds of the house/street ■ **un ~ sec** a snap ■ **un ~ sourd** a thud ■ **faire un ~** to make a sound *ou* noise ■ **il y a un petit ~** there's a slight noise ▶ **~ blanc** ACOUST white noise ■ **~ de fond** background noise ■ **en ~ de fond** in the background
2. [vacarme] : **j'ai horreur d'expliquer quelque chose dans le ~** I hate explaining something against a background of noise ■ **un ~ d'enfer** a huge racket ■ **faire du ~** to be noisy ■ **ne fais pas de ~** be quiet ■ **faire beaucoup de ~** *pr* to be very loud *ou* noisy ■ **il fait beaucoup de ~ mais il n'agit pas** *fig* he makes a lot of noise but he does nothing ■ **beaucoup de ~ pour rien** much ado about nothing
3. [retentissement] sensation, commotion, furore ■ **on a fait beaucoup de ~ autour de cet enlèvement** the kidnapping caused a furore
4. [rumeur] rumour, piece of gossip ■ **le ~ court que...** rumour has it *ou* it is rumoured that... ■ **se faire l'écho d'un ~** to bruit sthg abroad *sout* ▶ **des ~s de bottes** rumours of impending

war, the sound of jackboots ■ **c'est un ~ de couloir** it's a rumour ■ **faux ~** false rumour ■ **faire circuler des faux ~s** to spread false rumours
5. MÉD sound, bruit ■ **~ cardiaque** *ou* **du cœur** heart *ou* cardiac sound ■ **~ de souffle** (heart) murmur ■ **~ respiratoire** rattle
6. RADIO & TÉLÉCOM noise.
◆ **sans bruit** *loc adv* noiselessly, without a sound ■ **il s'avance sans ~** he moves forward without a sound.

bruitage [brɥitaʒ] *nm* sound effects.

bruiter [3] [brɥite] *vt* to make sound effects for.

bruiteur, euse [brɥitœr, øz] *nm, f* sound effects engineer.

brûlant, e [brylɑ̃, ɑ̃t] *adj* **1.** [chaud - lampe, assiette] burning (hot) ; [- liquide] burning *ou* boiling (hot), scalding ; [- nourriture] burning (hot), piping hot ; [- soleil, température] blazing (hot), scorching, blistering ; [- personne, front] feverish ■ **avoir les mains ~es** to have hot hands **2.** [animé] : **~ de : un regard ~ de désir** a look of burning desire **3.** [actuel, dont on parle] : **sujet** *ou* **dossier ~** burning issue ■ **c'est dire l'actualité ~e de ce livre** this shows how very topical this book is **4.** [ardent - regard, sentiment] ardent, impassioned ; [- imagination, récit, secret] passionate.

brûlé, e [bryle] ◇ *adj* [calciné] burnt.
◇ *nm, f* badly burnt person ■ **un grand ~** a patient suffering from third-degree burns ■ **service pour les grands ~s** burns unit.
◆ **brûlé** *nm* burnt part ■ **un goût de ~** a burnt taste ▶ **ça sent le ~** [odeur] there's a smell of burning ; *fam fig* fam there's trouble brewing.

brûle-gueule [brylgœl] *nm inv* (short) pipe.

brûle-parfum(s) [brylparfœ̃] (*pl* **brûle-parfums**) *nm* perfume vaporizer.

brûle-pourpoint [brylpurpwɛ̃] ◆ **à brûle-pourpoint** *loc adv* **1.** [sans détour] point-blank, without beating about the bush **2.** [inopinément] out of the blue ■ **demanda-t-elle à ~** she asked out of the blue.

brûler [3] [bryle] ◇ *vt* **1.** [détruire - feuilles, corps, objet] to burn, to incinerate ■ **~ qqn vif/sur le bûcher** to burn sb alive/at the stake ▶ **~ ce qu'on a adoré** to turn against one's former love *ou* loves ■ **~ le pavé** to tear along ■ **~ les planches** to give an outstanding performance ■ **~ ses dernières cartouches** to shoot one's bolt
2. [consommer - électricité, fioul] to burn (up), to use, to consume ■ **~ la chandelle par les deux bouts** to burn the candle at both ends ■ **elle brûle un cierge à la Vierge deux fois par an** *pr* she lights a candle to the Virgin Mary twice a year ■ **~ un cierge à qqn** *fig* to show one's gratitude to sb
3. [trop cuire] to burn
4. [trop chauffer - tissu] to burn, to scorch, to singe ; [- cheveux, poils] to singe ; [- acier] to spoil
5. [irriter - partie du corps] to burn ■ **la fumée me brûle les yeux** smoke is making my eyes smart *ou* sting ■ **le froid me brûle les oreilles** the cold is making my ears burn ■ **le piment me brûle la langue** the chili is burning my tongue ▶ **~ la cervelle à qqn** *pr* to blow sb's brains out ■ **l'argent lui brûle les doigts** money burns a hole in his pocket
6. [endommager - suj: gel] to nip, to burn ; [- suj: acide] to burn ■ **brûlé par le gel** frost-damaged
7. *fam* [dépasser] : **~ son arrêt** [bus, personne] to go past *ou* to miss one's stop ■ **~ un feu** to go through a red light ■ **~ un stop** to fail to stop at a stop sign ▶ **~ la politesse à qqn** [passer devant lui] to push in front of sb (in the queue) ; [partir sans le saluer] to leave without saying goodbye to sb ■ **~ les étapes** [progresser rapidement] to advance by leaps and bounds ; *péj* to cut corners, to take short cuts
8. [café] to roast
9. [animer] to burn ■ **le désir qui le brûle** the desire that consumes him
10. MÉD [verrue] to burn off *(sép)*
11. △ *arg crime* [tuer] to waste△.
◇ *vi* **1.** [flamber] to burn (up), to be on fire ■ [lentement] to smoulder ■ **~ sur le bûcher** to be burnt at the stake ■ **~ vif** to be burnt alive *ou* to death ■ **la forêt a brûlé** the forest was burnt down *ou* to the ground
2. [se consumer - charbon, essence] to burn ■ **laisser ~ la lumière** to leave the light burning *ou* on ■ **faire ~ le rôti** to burn the roast
3. [être chaud] to be burning ■ **avoir le front/la gorge qui brûle** to have a burning forehead/a burning sensation in the throat ■ **ça brûle** [plat, sol] it's boiling hot *ou* burning ; [eau] it's scalding ; [feu] it's burning ■ **les yeux me brûlent** my eyes are stinging *ou* smarting
4. JEUX to be close ■ **je brûle?** am I getting warm?
◆ **brûler de** *v+prép* **1.** [être animé de] : **~ de colère** to be burning *ou* seething with anger ■ **~ d'impatience/de désir** to be burning with impatience/desire
2. [désirer] to be dying *ou* longing to ■ **~ de parler à qqn** to be dying to talk to sb.
◆ **se brûler** *vp (emploi réfléchi)* to burn o.s. ■ **se ~ la main** to burn one's hand ▶ **se ~ la cervelle** *fam* to blow one's brains out ■ **se ~ les ailes** to get one's fingers burnt.

brûlerie [brylri] *nf* **1.** [pour le café] coffee roasting plant **2.** [pour l'eau-de-vie] distillery.

brûleur [brylœr] *nm* burner ■ **~ à gaz** gas burner *ou* ring.

brûlis [bryli] *nm* **1.** [mode de culture] slash-and-burn farming **2.** [terrain] patch of burn-baited land.

brûlot [brylo] *nm* **1.** [bateau] fireship **2.** [écrit] fierce *ou* blistering attack.

brûlure [brylyr] *nf* **1.** [lésion] burn ▶ **~ au premier/second/troisième degré** MÉD first-/second-/third-degree burn ■ **~ de cigarette** cigarette burn **2.** [sensation] burning sensation ■ **la ~ de la honte** *fig* the burning sensation of shame ▶ **~s d'estomac** heartburn **3.** [trace] burnt patch.

brumaire [brymɛr] *nm 2nd month of the French revolutionary calendar (from Oct 23 to Nov 21).*

brume [brym] *nf* **1.** [brouillard - de chaleur] haze ; [- de mauvais temps] mist ■ **~ de mer** sea mist **2.** NAUT fog **3.** [confusion] daze, haze ■ **il est encore dans les ~s du sommeil** he's still half asleep ■ **être dans les ~s de l'alcool** to be in a drunken stupor.

brumeux, euse [brymø, øz] *adj* **1.** MÉTÉOR misty, foggy, hazy **2.** [vague] hazy, vague ■ **un souvenir ~** a hazy *ou* dim recollection.

brun, brune [brœ̃, bryn] ◇ *adj* **1.** [au pigment foncé - cheveux] brown, dark ; [- peau] brown, dark ■ **~ cuivré** tawny **2.** [bronzé] brown, tanned.
◇ *nm, f* brown-haired *ou* dark-haired man (*f* woman), brunette.
◆ **brun** *nm* brown (colour).
◆ **brune** *nf* **1.** [cigarette] brown tobacco cigarette **2.** [bière] dark beer, ≃ brown ale *UK*.
◆ **à la brune** *loc adv litt* at dusk.

brunante [brynɑ̃t] *nf Québec* dusk.

brunâtre [brynatr] *adj* brownish.

brunch [brœntʃ] *nm* brunch.

Brunei [brynei] *npr m* : **le ~** Brunei ■ **au ~** in Brunei.

brunet, ette [brynɛ, ɛt] *nm, f* brown-haired lad (*f* lass).

bruni [bryni] *nm* burnish.

brunir [32] [brynir] ◇ *vi* **1.** [foncer - cheveux, couleur] to get darker, to darken ; [- peau] to get brown *ou* browner ■ **~ au soleil** to tan **2.** CULIN [sauce, oignons] to brown ■ [sucre] to darken ■ **faites ~ les oignons** brown the onions.
◇ *vt* **1.** [hâler] to tan **2.** [polir - métal] to burnish ; [- acier] to brown, to burnish.

brunissage [brynisaʒ] *nm* burnishing.

brunissement [brynismɑ̃] *nm* tanning.

Brushing® [brœʃiŋ] *nm* blow-dry ■ **faire un ~ à qqn** to blow-dry sb's hair.

brusque [brysk] *adj* **1.** [bourru - ton] curt, abrupt ; [- personne] brusque, blunt ; [- geste] abrupt, rough ■ **un mouvement ~** a jerk, a sudden movement **2.** [imprévu] abrupt, sudden ■ **une ~ baisse de température** a sudden drop in temperature.

brusquement [bryskəmɑ̃] *adv* [soudainement] suddenly, abruptly.

brusquer [3] [bryske] *vt* **1.** [malmener] to be rough with **2.** [hâter - dénouement] to rush ; [- adieux] to cut short ■ **~ les choses** to rush things.

brusquerie [bryskəri] *nf* **1.** [brutalité] abruptness, brusqueness, sharpness ■ **avec ~** abruptly **2.** [soudaineté] abruptness, suddenness.

brut, e [bryt] *adj* **1.** [non traité - pétrole, métal] crude, untreated ; [- laine, soie, charbon, brique] untreated, raw ; [- sucre] raw, coarse ; [- pierre précieuse] rough, uncut ; [- minerai] raw ; [- or] unrefined **2.** [émotion, qualité] naked, pure, raw ■ [donnée] raw ■ [fait] simple, plain ■ **à l'état ~** in the rough **3.** [sauvage] brute ■ **la force ~e** brute force **4.** ÉCON gross **5.** [poids] gross **6.** ŒNOL brut, dry.
◆ **brut** ◇ *adv* gross ■ **gagner 1 500 euros ~** to earn 1,500 euros gross.
◇ *nm* **1.** [salaire] gross income **2.** [pétrole] crude oil **3.** [champagne] brut *ou* dry champagne.

brutal, e, aux [brytal, o] ◇ *adj* **1.** [violent - personne] brutal, vicious ; [- enfant] rough ; [- choc] strong, violent ; [- force] brute ; [- jeu] rough **2.** [franc] brutal, blunt ■ **il a été très ~ en lui annonçant la nouvelle** he broke it to him very unfeelingly *ou* harshly **3.** [non mitigé] brutal, raw **4.** [soudain - changement] sudden, abrupt ; [- transition] abrupt.
◇ *nm, f* brute, violent individual.

brutalement [brytalmɑ̃] *adv* **1.** [violemment] brutally, violently, savagely **2.** [sèchement] brusquely, sharply, bluntly **3.** [tout d'un coup] suddenly ■ **s'arrêter ~** to come to an abrupt halt.

brutaliser [3] [brytalize] *vt* **1.** [maltraiter] to ill-treat ■ **~ qqn** to batter sb ■ **se faire ~ par la police** to be manhandled by the police **2.** [brusquer] to bully.

brutalité [brytalite] *nf* **1.** [violence] brutality, violence ■ **des ~s** brutalities, violent acts ■ **~s policières** police brutality **2.** [soudaineté] suddenness.

brute [bryt] *nf* **1.** [personne violente] bully ■ **comme une ~** with all one's might, like mad ■ **une grande *ou* grosse ~** a big brute (of a man) **2.** [personne fruste] boor, lout.

Bruxelles [brysɛl] *npr* Brussels.

bruxellois, e [brysɛlwa, az] *adj* from Brussels.
◆ **Bruxellois, e** *nm, f inhabitant of or person from Brussels.*

bruyamment [brɥijamɑ̃] *adv* [parler, rire, protester] loudly ■ [manger, jouer] noisily.

bruyant, e [brɥijɑ̃, ɑ̃t] *adj* [enfant, rue] noisy ■ **un rire ~** a loud laugh.

bruyère [brɥjɛr] *nf* **1.** BOT heather **2.** [lande] moor, heath.

BSR (*abr de* **brevet de sécurité routière**) *nm proficiency test for riding a moped.*

BT ◇ *nm* = **brevet de technicien**.
◇ *nf* (*abr de* **basse tension**) LT.

B to B [bitubi] (*abr de* **business to business**) *nm* business-to-business.

B to C [bitusi] (*abr de* **business to consumer**) *nm* business-to-consumer.

BTP (*abr de* **bâtiments et travaux publics**) *nmpl building and public works sector.*

BTS (*abr de* **brevet de technicien supérieur**) *nm advanced vocational training certificate (taken at the end of a 2-year higher education course).*

bu, e [by] *pp* ▷ **boire**.

BU *nf* = **bibliothèque universitaire**.

buanderie [byɑ̃dri] *nf* **1.** [pièce, local - à l'intérieur] laundry, utility room ; [- à l'extérieur] washhouse **2.** *Québec* [laverie] laundry.

bubon [bybɔ̃] *nm* bubo.

bubonique [bybɔnik] *adj* bubonic.

Bucarest [bykarɛst] *npr* Bucharest.

buccal, e, aux [bykal, o] *adj* mouth *(modif)*, buccal *spéc.*

bucco-dentaire [bykodɑ̃tɛr] *adj* mouth *(modif)* ■ **hygiène ~** oral hygiene.

bûche [byʃ] *nf* **1.** [morceau de bois] log **2.** *fam* [personne apathique] lump ■ **ne reste pas là comme une ~** don't just stand there like a lemon *UK ou* like a lump on a log *US* **3.** CULIN & HIST : **~ glacée** Yule log *(with an ice-cream filling)* ■ **~ de Noël** Yule log **4.** *fam loc* **prendre *ou* ramasser une ~** to take a tumble, to come a cropper *UK*.

bûcher [byʃe] *nm* **1.** [supplice] : **le ~** the stake ■ **être condamné au ~** to be sentenced to be burnt at the stake **2.** [funéraire] pyre **3.** [remise] woodshed.

bûcheron, onne [byʃrɔ̃, ɔn] *nm, f* woodcutter, lumberjack.

bûchette [byʃɛt] *nf* **1.** [petit bois] twig, stick **2.** [pour compter] stick.

bûcheur, euse [byʃœr, øz] *fam* ◇ *adj* hardworking.
◇ *nm, f* hardworking student, swot *UK péj*, grind *US péj.*

bucolique [bykɔlik] ◇ *adj* bucolic, pastoral.
◇ *nf* bucolic, pastoral poem ■ **'les Bucoliques' *Virgile*** 'The Eclogues', 'The Bucolics'.

Budapest [bydapɛst] *npr* Budapest.

budget [bydʒɛ] *nm* **1.** [d'une personne, d'une entreprise] budget ■ **avoir un petit ~** to be on a (tight) budget ■ **des prix pour les petits ~s** budget prices ➊ **~ temps** [délai] allowance ; SOCIOL time budget **2.** FIN & POLIT : **le Budget** ≃ the Budget ➊ **~ économique** ÉCON economic budget.

budgétaire [bydʒetɛr] *adj* budgetary.

budgétiser [3] [bydʒetize] *vt* to budget for.

buée [bɥe] *nf* condensation ■ **plein *ou* couvert de ~** misted *ou* steamed up.

Buenos Aires [bɥenozɛr] *npr* Buenos Aires.

buffer [bœfœr] *nm* INFORM buffer.

buffet [byfɛ] *nm* **1.** [de salle à manger] sideboard ■ **~ (de cuisine)** kitchen cabinet *ou* dresser **2.** [nourriture] : **il y aura un ~ pour le déjeuner** there will be a buffet lunch ➊ **~ campagnard** buffet *(mainly with country-style cold meats)* ■ **~ froid** (cold) buffet **3.** [salle] : **~ (de gare)** (station) café *ou* buffet *ou* cafeteria ‖ [comptoir roulant] refreshment trolley *UK ou* cart *US* **4.** [d'un orgue] case **5.** △ [ventre] belly ■ **se remplir le ~** to stuff one's face, to pig out.

buffle [byfl] *nm* **1.** ZOOL buffalo **2.** [pour polir] buffer.

buggy [bygi] *nm* buggy *(carriage).*

bugne [byɲ] *nf* CULIN *strip of fried dough sprinkled with sugar, speciality of the Lyon region.*

building [bildiŋ] *nm* tower block.

buis [bɥi] *nm* **1.** BOT box, boxtree **2.** MENUIS box, boxwood.

buisson [bɥisɔ̃] *nm* **1.** BOT bush **2.** CULIN : **~ d'écrevisses** crayfish en buisson **3.** RELIG : **~ ardent** burning bush.

buisson-ardent [bɥisɔ̃ardɑ̃] (*pl* **buissons-ardents**) *nm* BOT pyracantha.

buissonneux, euse [bɥisɔnø, øz] *adj* **1.** [terrain] shrub-covered **2.** [arbre, végétation] shrub-like.

buissonnière [bɥisɔnjɛr] *adj f* ▷ **école**.

bulbe [bylb] *nm* **1.** BOT bulb, corm **2.** ANAT : **~ pileux** hair bulb ■ **~ rachidien** medulla **3.** ARCHIT : **~ (byzantin)** onion dome **4.** NAUT bulb **5.** *(comme adj)* ÉLECTR : **groupe ~** bulb turbine generator set.

bulbeux, euse [bylbø, øz] *adj* BOT bulbous.

bulgare [bylgar] *adj* Bulgarian.

◆ **Bulgare** *nmf* Bulgarian.

Bulgarie [bylgari] *npr f* : **(la) ~** Bulgaria.

bulldozer [byldozɛr] *nm* **1.** [machine] bulldozer **2.** *fam* [fonceur] bulldozer ■ **c'est un ~, cette femme!** that woman bulldozes her way through life!

bulle [byl] ◇ *nf* **1.** [d'air, de gaz, de bain moussant] bubble ■ **~ de savon** soap bubble ■ **des ~s** bubbles, froth ■ **faire des ~s** [de savon] to blow bubbles ; [bébé] to dribble **2.** [de bande dessinée] balloon, speech bubble **3.** *arg scol* [zéro] nought, zero **4.** MÉD [enceinte stérile] bubble ■ *(comme adj)* **enfant ~** *child brought up in a sterile bubble* **5.** [emballage] blister **6.** RELIG bull **7.** INFORM : **~ d'aide** pop-up text, tooltip.
◇ *nm* : **(papier) ~** Manila paper.

buller△ [3] [byle] *vi* to bum about *ou* around.

bulletin [byltɛ̃] *nm* **1.** RADIO & TV bulletin ■ **~ d'informations** news bulletin ■ **~ météorologique** weather forecast *ou* report
2. ADMIN : **~ de naissance** birth certificate ■ **le Bulletin officiel** ADMIN *official listing of all new laws and decrees* ■ **~ de santé** medical report
3. ÉDUC : **~ (scolaire** *ou* **de notes)** (school) report *UK*, report card *US* ■ **~ mensuel/trimestriel** monthly/end-of-term report
4. BOURSE : **~ des oppositions** list of stopped bonds
5. POLIT : **~ de vote** ballot paper ■ **~ blanc** blank ballot paper ■ **~ secret** secret ballot
6. [revue] bulletin, annals
7. [ticket] : **~ de commande** order form ■ **~ de paie** *ou* **salaire** pay slip, salary advice ■ **~ de participation** entry form.

bulletin-réponse [byltɛ̃repɔ̃s] (*pl* **bulletins-réponse**) *nm* entry form.

bungalow [bœ̃galo] *nm* [maison - sans étage] bungalow ; [- de vacances] chalet.

bunker [bunkœr] *nm* **1.** SPORT bunker *UK*, sand trap *US* **2.** MIL bunker.

Bunsen [bœ̃zɛn] *npr* : **bec ~** Bunsen burner.

buraliste [byralist] *nmf* tobacconist *(licensed to sell stamps)*.

bure [byr] *nf* **1.** TEXT homespun **2.** [vêtement] frock, cowl ■ **la ~ du moine** monk's habit.

bureau, x [byro] *nm* **1.** [meuble - gén] desk ; [- à rabat] bureau ■ **~ à cylindre** roll-top desk **2.** [pièce d'une maison] study **3.** [lieu de travail] office ■ **aller au ~** to go to the office ■ **travailler dans un ~** to work in an office, to have an office job *ou* a desk job ■ **nos ~x sont transférés au 10, rue Biot** our office has *ou* our premises have been transferred to 10 rue Biot ➊ **~ d'accueil** reception ■ **~ paysager** open-plan office *(with plants)* ■ **employé de ~** office worker, clerk ■ **fournitures de ~** office supplies **4.** [agence] : **~ d'aide sociale** welfare office *ou* centre ■ **~ de change** [banque] bureau de change, foreign exchange office ; [comptoir] bureau de change, foreign exchange counter ■ **~ d'études** [entreprise] research consultancy ; [service] research department *ou* unit ■ **~ des objets trouvés** lost property *UK ou* lost-and-found *US* office ■ **~ de placement** employment agency *(for domestic workers)* ■ **~ de poste** post office ■ **~ de tabac** tobacconist's *UK*, tobacco dealer's *US* ■ **~ de tri** sorting office ■ **~ de vote** polling station **5.** [commission] committee ■ **le syndicat réuni en ~ confédéral** the union meeting at federal committee level ➊ **Bureau international du travail** International Labour Organization ■ **~ politique** Politburo **6.** INFORM desktop.

bureaucrate [byrokrat] *nmf* bureaucrat.

bureaucratie [byrokrasi] *nf* **1.** [système] bureaucracy **2.** [fonctionnaires] officials, bureaucrats **3.** [tracasseries] red tape, bureaucracy.

bureaucratique [byrokratik] *adj* bureaucratic, administrative.

bureaucratiser [3] [byrokratize] *vt* to bureaucratize.

Bureautique® [byrotik] ◇ *adj* : **système/méthode ~** system/method of office automation.
◇ *nf* **1.** [système] office automation **2.** [matériel] office equipment.

burette [byrɛt] *nf* **1.** [bidon] : **~ (d'huile)** oilcan **2.** CHIM burette **3.** RELIG cruet.

burger [bœrgœr] *nm* CULIN burger.

burin [byrɛ̃] *nm* **1.** MÉTALL cold, coldchise **2.** [outil de graveur] burin, graver **3.** [gravure] engraving, print.

buriné, e [byrine] *adj* [traits] strongly marked ■ [visage] craggy, furrowed.

buriner [3] [byrine] *vt* **1.** ART to engrave **2.** TECHNOL to chisel **3.** *litt* [visage] to carve deep lines into.

Burkina [byrkina] *npr m* : **le ~** Burkina-Faso ■ **au ~** in Burkina-Faso.

burkinabé [byrkinabe] *adj* from Burkina-Faso.

burlesque [byrlɛsk] ◇ *adj* **1.** [très drôle - accoutrement] comic, comical, droll ; [- plaisanterie] funny **2.** *péj* [stupide - idée] ludicrous, ridiculous **3.** CINÉ & LITTÉR burlesque.
◇ *nm* CINÉ & LITTÉR : **le ~** the burlesque.

burnous [byrnu] *nm* burnous, burnouse.

burundais, e [burundɛ, ɛz] *adj* Burundian.

Burundi [burundi] *npr m* : **le ~** Burundi ■ **au ~** in Burundi.

bus [bys] *nm* bus.

busard [byzar] *nm* harrier ■ **~ Saint-Martin** hen harrier.

buse [byz] *nf* **1.** ZOOL buzzard **2.** *fam péj* nitwit, dolt **3.** [conduit] duct **4.** AUTO : **~ de carburateur** choke tube.

business [biznɛs] *nm fam* [affaires] business.

busqué, e [byske] *adj* [nez] hook *(modif)*, hooked.

buste [byst] *nm* **1.** ANAT [haut du corps] chest ■ [seins] bust **2.** [sculpture] bust.

bustier [bystje] *nm* **1.** [soutien-gorge] strapless bra **2.** [corsage] bustier.

but [byt] *nm* **1.** [dessein] aim, purpose, point ■ **quel est le ~ de la manœuvre** *ou* **de l'opération?** what's the point of such a move? ■ **avoir pour ~ de** to aim to ■ **la réforme a un ~ bien précis** the purpose of the reform is quite precise ■ **dans le ~ de faire...** for the purpose of doing..., with the aim of doing... ■ **je lui ai parlé dans le seul ~ de t'aider** my sole aim in talking to him was to help you ■ **aller** *ou* **frapper droit au ~** to go straight to the point ■ **dans ce ~** with this end *ou* aim in view ■ **à ~ lucratif** profit-making ■ **à ~ non lucratif** non profit-making **2.** [ambition] aim, ambition, objective ■ **toucher au** *ou* **le ~** to be on the point of achieving one's aim **3.** [destination] : **le ~ de notre voyage leur était inconnu** our destination was unknown to them ■ **sans ~** aimlessly **4.** FOOTBALL [limite, point] goal ■ **gagner/perdre par 5 ~s à 2** to win/to lose by 5 goals to 2 ■ **marquer** *ou* **rentrer** *fam* **un ~** to score a goal ‖ [cible] target, mark **5.** GRAMM purpose.
◆ **de but en blanc** *loc adv* [demander] point-blank, suddenly ■ [rétorquer] bluntly ■ **demanda-t-elle de ~ en blanc** she suddenly asked.

butane [bytan] *nm* : **(gaz) ~** CHIM butane ; [dans la maison] Calor® gas.

buté, e [byte] *adj* mulish, stubborn.

butée [byte] *nf* **1.** TECHNOL stop ■ [de ski] toe-piece ■ MÉCAN stop block **2.** ARCHIT abutment.

buter [3] [byte] ◇ *vi* **1.** [trébucher] to stumble, to trip ■ **~ contre une pierre** to trip over a stone **2.** [cogner] : **~ contre qqch** to walk *ou* to bump into sthg **3.** [achopper] : **~ sur** : **~ sur une difficulté** to come *ou* to stumble across a problem ■ **~ sur un mot** [en parlant] to trip over a word ; [en lisant pour soi] to have trouble understanding a word **4.** CONSTR : **~ contre** to rest against, to be supported by.
◇ *vt* **1.** [braquer] : **~ qqn** to put sb's back up, to make sb dig his/her heels in **2.** △ *arg crime* [tuer] to bump off *(sép)*, to waste△ ■ **se faire ~** to be bumped off *ou* done in.
◆ **se buter** *vpi* **1.** [se braquer] to dig one's heels in, to get obstinate **2.** [se heurter] : **se ~ dans** *ou* **contre** to bump into.

buteur [bytœr] *nm* **1.** SPORT striker **2.** △ [assassin] killer.

butin [bytɛ̃] *nm* **1.** [choses volées - par des troupes] spoils, booty ; [- par un cambrioleur] loot **2.** [trouvailles] booty.

butiner [3] [bytine] <> *vi* [insectes] to gather nectar and pollen.
<> *vt* **1.** [pollen, nectar] to gather ▪ [fleurs] to gather pollen and nectar on **2.** [rassembler - idées] to glean, to gather.

butoir [bytwar] *nm* **1.** RAIL buffer **2.** [de porte] door stop **3.** FIN limit.

butor [bytɔr] *nm* **1.** *péj* [malotru] boor, lout **2.** ZOOL bittern.

buttage [bytaʒ] *nm* earthing *ou* banking up HORT.

butte [byt] *nf* **1.** [monticule] hillock, knoll ▪ **la Butte (Montmartre)** (the Butte) Montmartre **2.** MIL : **~ de tir** butts **3.** HORT mound.
◆ **en butte à** *loc prép* : **être en ~ à** to be exposed to, to be faced with.

butter [3] [byte] *vt* **1.** HORT to earth *ou* to bank up *(sép)* **2.** △ *arg crime* to bump off *(sép)*, to waste△.

Buttes-Chaumont [bytʃomɔ̃] *npr pl* : **le parc des** *ou* **les ~** *landscaped park in Paris.*

buvable [byvabl] *adj* **1.** [qui n'est pas mauvais à boire] drinkable **2.** PHARM [ampoule] to be taken orally.

buvait *etc v* ⊳ **boire**.

buvard [byvar] *nm* **1.** [morceau de papier] piece of blotting-paper ▪ [substance] blotting-paper **2.** [sous-main] blotter.

buvette [byvɛt] *nf* **1.** [dans une foire, une gare] refreshment stall ▪ **'buvette'** 'refreshments' **2.** [de station thermale] pump room.

buveur, euse [byvœr, øz] *nm, f* **1.** [alcoolique] drinker, drunkard ▪ **c'est un gros ~** he's a heavy drinker **2.** [client de café] customer **3.** [consommateur] : **~ de : nous sommes de grands ~s de café** we are great coffee drinkers.

BVA (*abr de* **Brulé Ville Associés**) *npr French market research company.*

BVP (*abr de* **Bureau de vérification de la publicité**) *npr m French advertising standards authority,* ≃ ASA *UK.*

by-pass [bajpas] *nm inv* **1.** ÉLECTR bypass **2.** MÉD bypass operation.

byronien, enne [bajrɔnjɛ̃, ɛn] *adj* Byronic.

Byzance [bizɑ̃s] *npr* **1.** GÉOGR Byzantium **2.** *fam loc* **c'est ~!** it's fantastic!

byzantin, e [bizɑ̃tɛ̃, in] *adj* **1.** HIST Byzantine **2.** *péj* & *sout* byzantine *péj.*
◆ **Byzantin, e** *nm, f* Byzantine.

BZH (*abr écrite de* **Breizh**) *Brittany (as nationality sticker on a car).*

C

c, C [se] *nm inv* [lettre] c, C, *voir aussi* **g**.

c 1. (*abr écrite de* **centime**) c **2.** = **centi**.

c' [s] ▷ **ce** *(pron dém)*.

ç' [s] ▷ **ce** *(pron dém)*.

C 1. (*abr écrite de* **Celsius, centigrade**) C **2.** (*abr écrite de* **coulomb**) C.

ca = **centiare**.

CA *nm* **1.** = **chiffre d'affaires 2.** = **conseil d'administration**.

ça[1] [sa] *nm* PSYCHOL id.

ça[2] [sa] *pron dém* **1.** [désignant un objet - proche] this, it ; [- éloigné] that, it ▪ **qu'est-ce que tu veux? – ça, là-bas** what do you want? – that, over there ▪ **il y avait ça entre moi et l'autobus** there was this *ou* that much between me and the bus ▶ **il ne m'a pas donné ça!** *fam* he didn't give me a thing *ou* a bean! ▪ **regarde-moi ça!** just look at that! ▪ **il ne pense qu'à ça!** *euphém* he's got a one-track mind! **2.** [désignant - ce dont on vient de parler] this, that ; [- ce dont on va parler] this ▪ **la liberté, c'est ça qui est important** freedom, that's what matters ▪ **il y a un peu de ça, c'est vrai** it's true, there's an element of *ou* a bit of that ▪ **il est parti il y a un mois/une semaine de ça** he left a month/a week ago ▪ **écoutez, ça va vous étonner...** this will surprise you, listen... **3.** [servant de sujet indéterminé] : **et ton boulot, comment ça se passe?** *fam* how's your job going? ▪ **ça souffle!** *fam* there's quite a wind (blowing)! ▪ **ça fait 2 kg/3 m** that's 2 kg/3 m ▪ **ça fait deux heures que j'attends** I've been waiting for two hours ▪ **qu'est-ce que ça peut faire?** what does it matter? ▪ **les enfants, ça comprend tout** children understand everything ▪ **et ça n'arrête pas de se plaindre!** *fam péj* and he is/they are *etc* forever complaining! ▶ **ça ira comme ça** that'll do ▪ **ça y est, j'ai fini!** that's it, I'm finished! ▪ **ça y est, ça devait arriver!** now look what's happened! ▪ **ça y est, c'est de ma faute!** that's it, it's all my fault! ▪ **c'est ça!** that's right ; *iron* right! ▪ **c'est ça, moquez-vous de moi!** that's right, have a good laugh at my expense! **4.** [emploi expressif] : **qui ça?** who?, who's that? ▪ **comment ça, c'est fini?** what do you mean it's over? ▪ **ah ça oui!** you bet! ▪ **ah ça non!** certainly not!

çà [sa] *adv* : **çà et là** here and there.

cabale [kabal] *nf* **1.** [personnes] cabal ▪ [intrigue] cabal, intrigue ▪ **monter une ~ contre qqn** to plot against sb **2.** HIST cabala, cabbala, kabbala.

cabaliste [kabalist] *nmf* cabalist, kabbalist.

cabalistique [kabalistik] *adj* [science] cabalistic.

caban [kabɑ̃] *nm* [longue veste] car coat ▪ [de marin] reefer jacket ▪ [d'officier] pea jacket.

cabane [kaban] *nf* **1.** [hutte] hut, cabin ▪ [pour animaux, objets] shed ▪ **~ de** *ou* **en rondins** log cabin ▶ **~ à lapins** *pr* rabbit hutch ; *fig* box ▪ **~ à outils** toolshed **2.** *fam* [maison] dump **3.** *fam* [prison] clink ▪ **il a fait 8 ans de ~** he did *ou* spent 8 years inside **4.** *Suisse* [refuge] mountain refuge **5.** *canadian english* **~ à sucre** sugar (and maple syrup) refinery, sap house.

cabanon [kabanɔ̃] *nm* **1.** [abri] shed, hut ▪ [en Provence] (country) cottage **2.** *vieilli* [pour fou] padded cell ▪ **il est bon pour le ~** *fam ou* **à mettre au ~** he should be put away.

cabaret [kabarɛ] *nm* **1.** [établissement] nightclub, cabaret **2.** [activité] : **le ~** cabaret ▪ **un spectacle de ~** a floorshow **3.** [meuble] liqueur cabinet **4.** *vieilli* [auberge] tavern.

cabaretier, ère [kabartje, ɛr] *nm, f vieilli* inn-keeper.

cabas [kaba] *nm* **1.** [pour provisions] shopping bag **2.** [pour figues, raisins] basket.

cabestan [kabɛstɑ̃] *nm* capstan.

cabillaud [kabijo] *nm* cod.

cabine [kabin] *nf* **1.** NAUT cabin **2.** AÉRON [des passagers] cabin **3.** [de laboratoire de langues] booth ▪ [de piscine, d'hôpital] cubicle ▪ **~ (de bain)** [hutte] bathing *ou* beach hut ; [serviette] beachtowel (for changing) ▪ **~ de douche** shower cubicle ▪ **~ d'essayage** changing *ou* fitting room *UK*, dressing room *US* ▪ **~ de projection** projection room **4.** TÉLÉCOM : **~ téléphonique** phone box *UK ou* booth **5.** TRANSP [de camion, de tracteur, de train] cab ▪ [de grue] cabin ▪ **~ (de téléphérique)** cablecar **6.** RAIL : **~ d'aiguillage** signal box, points control box.

cabinet [kabinɛ] *nm* **1.** [de dentiste] surgery *UK*, office *US* ▪ [de magistrat] chambers ▪ [d'avoué, de notaire] office ▪ **~ (médical** *ou* **de consultation)** (doctor's) surgery *UK ou* office *US*

2. [réduit] : **~ de débarras** boxroom *UK*, storage room *US* ▪ **~ noir** walk-in cupboard

3. [petite salle] : **~ de lecture** reading room ▪ **~ particulier** [de restaurant] private dining room ▪ **~ de toilette** bathroom ▪ **~ de travail** study

4. [clientèle - de médecin, de dentiste] practice ▪ **monter un ~** to set up a practice

5. [agence] : **~ d'affaires** business consultancy ▪ **~ d'architectes** firm of architects ▪ **~ d'assurances** insurance firm *ou* agency ▪ **~ conseil** consulting firm, consultancy firm ▪ **~ immobilier** estate agent's *UK ou* realtor's *US* office

6. POLIT [gouvernement] cabinet ▪ **faire partie du ~** to be in *ou* a member of the Cabinet ▪ **~ du Premier ministre** Prime Minister's departmental staff ▶ **~ fantôme** shadow cabinet ▪ **~ ministériel** minister's advisers, departmental staff

7. [d'un musée] (exhibition) room

8. [meuble] cabinet

9. [d'horloge] (clock) case.

◆ **cabinets** *nmpl fam* toilet, loo *UK*, bathroom *US*.

CABINET

In a French context this term refers to the team of civil servants who carry out advisory and administrative duties for a minister or a *préfet*. The Prime Minister's *cabinet* is made up not of ministers but of senior civil servants, including the *directeur de cabinet*, who has a political role as the Prime Minister's principal private secretary (and can deputize for him or her), and the *chef de cabinet*, whose function is largely administrative.

câblage [kablaʒ] *nm* **1.** TV [pose du réseau] cable TV installation, cabling ■ **le ~ d'une rue/ville** cabling a street/a town **2.** ÉLECTR [opération] wiring ■ [fils] cables **3.** [torsion] cabling.

câble [kabl] *nm* **1.** [cordage - en acier] cable, wire rope ; [- en fibres végétales] line, rope, cable ■ **~ de démarreur** *ou* **de démarrage** AUTO jump lead ■ **~ de frein** AUTO brake cable **2.** ÉLECTR cable ■ **~ électrique** electric cable ■ **~ hertzien** radio link *(by hertzian waves)* ■ **~ optique** optical fibre ■ **~ (à courant) porteur** carrier cable **3.** TV : **avoir le ~** to have cable TV ■ **transmettre par ~** to cablecast **4.** [télégramme] cable, cablegram **5.** INFORM : **~ d'imprimante** printer cable ■ **~ parallèle** parallel cable ■ **~ série** serial cable.

câblé, e [kable] *adj* **1.** TV [ville, région] with cable television ■ **réseau ~** cable television network **2.** INFORM hard-wired.
◆ **câblé** *nm* cord.

câbler [3] [kable] *vt* **1.** TV [ville, région] to link to a cable television network, to wire for cable ■ [émission] to cable **2.** ÉLECTR to cable **3.** [fils] to twist together (into a cable), to cable **4.** TÉLÉCOM [message] to cable.

câblerie [kabləri] *nf* cable *ou* cable-manufacturing plant.

câbleur, euse [kablœr, øz] *nm, f* cable-layer.

câblo-opérateur [kablooperatœr] (*pl* **câblo-opérateurs**) *nm* cable operator, cable company.

cabochard, e [kabɔʃar, ard] *fam* ◇ *adj* pigheaded, stubborn.
◇ *nm, f* : **c'est un ~** he's pigheaded *ou* as stubborn as a mule.

caboche [kabɔʃ] *nf* **1.** *fam* [tête] nut, noddle *UK* ■ **mets-toi (bien) ça dans la ~!** get that into your thick head! **2.** [clou] hobnail.

cabochon [kabɔʃɔ̃] *nm* **1.** JOAILL cabochon **2.** [clou] stud.

cabosser [3] [kabɔse] *vt* [carrosserie, couvercle] to dent ■ **voiture cabossée** battered car.

cabot [kabo] *nm* **1.** *fam* [chien] dog, mutt *péj* **2.** △ *arg mil* corporal **3.** [mulet] common grey mullet **4.** [acteur] ham (actor).

cabotage [kabɔtaʒ] *nm* coastal navigation ■ **petit/grand ~** inshore/seagoing navigation.

caboter [3] [kabɔte] *vi* [gén] to sail *ou* to ply along the coast ■ [ne pas s'éloigner] to hug the shore.

caboteur [kabɔtœr] *nm* [navire] coaster, tramp.

cabotin, e [kabɔtɛ̃, in] ◇ *adj* [manières, personne] theatrical.
◇ *nm, f* **1.** [personne affectée] show-off, poseur **2.** *péj* [acteur] ham (actor).

cabotinage [kabɔtinaʒ] *nm* [d'un poseur] affectedness, theatricality ■ [d'un artiste] ham acting ■ **faire du ~** to ham it up.

cabrer [3] [kabre] *vt* **1.** [cheval] : **il cabra son cheval** he made his horse rear up **2.** AÉRON to nose up *(sép)* **3.** [inciter à la révolte] : **~ qqn** to put sb's back up.
◆ **se cabrer** *vpi* **1.** [cheval] to rear up **2.** AÉRON to nose up **3.** [se rebiffer] to balk, to jib.

cabri [kabri] *nm* kid ZOOL.

cabriole [kabrijɔl] *nf* **1.** [bond - d'un enfant] leap ; [- d'un animal] prancing *(U)*, cavorting *(U)* ■ [acrobatie] somersault ■ **faire des ~s** [clown] to do somersaults ; [chèvre] to prance *ou* to cavort (about) ; [enfant] to dance *ou* to jump about **2.** [manœuvre] clever manoeuvre **3.** DANSE cabriole **4.** ÉQUIT capriole.

cabriolet [kabrijɔlɛ] *nm* **1.** [véhicule - automobile] convertible ; [- hippomobile] cabriolet **2.** [meuble] cabriole chair.

CAC, Cac [kak, sease] (*abr de* **cotation assistée en continu**) : **l'indice ~-40** *the French stock exchange shares index.*

caca [kaka] *nm fam* : **du ~ de chien** some dog dirt *ou* mess ■ **faire ~** to have a poo.
◆ **caca d'oie** *nm & adj inv* greenish-yellow.

cacahouète, cacahuète [kakawɛt] *nf* peanut.

cacao [kakao] *nm* **1.** BOT [graine] cocoa bean **2.** CULIN : **(poudre de) ~** cocoa (powder) ■ **au ~** cocoa-flavoured ‖ [boisson] cocoa.

cacaotier [kakaɔtje], **cacaoyer** [kakaɔje] *nm* cocoa tree.

cacaotière [kakaɔtjɛr], **cacaoyère** [kakaɔjɛr] *nf* cocoa plantation.

cacatoès [kakatɔɛs] *nm* cockatoo.

cachalot [kaʃalo] *nm* sperm whale.

cache [kaʃ] ◇ *nf* [d'armes, de drogue] cache.
◇ *nm* **1.** [pour œil, texte] cover card ■ [de machine à écrire] cover **2.** CINÉ & PHOTO mask.

caché, e [kaʃe] *adj* **1.** [dans une cachette - butin, or] hidden **2.** [secret - sentiment] secret ; [- signification] hidden, secret ; [- talent] hidden.

cache-cache [kaʃkaʃ] *nm inv* : **jouer à ~ (avec qqn)** *pr & fig* to play hide and seek (with sb).

cache-col [kaʃkɔl] *nm inv* scarf.

cache-cœur [kaʃkœr] *nm inv* wrapover top.

cachemire [kaʃmir] *nm* **1.** [tissu, poil] cashmere ■ **en ~** cashmere *(modif)* **2.** [châle] cashmere shawl ■ [pull-over] cashmere sweater ■ [gilet] cashmere cardigan **3.** *(comme adj)* [motif, dessin] paisley *(modif)*.

Cachemire [kaʃmir] *npr m* : **le ~** Kashmir ■ **au ~** in Kashmir.

cache-misère [kaʃmizɛr] *nm inv baggy outer garment worn to hide clothes underneath* ■ *fig* **cette réforme est un ~** it's just a token reform.

cache-nez [kaʃne] *nm inv* scarf, comforter *UK*.

cache-oreilles [kaʃɔrɛj] *nm inv* earmuffs.

cache-pot [kaʃpo] *nm inv* (flower *ou* plant) pot holder.

cache-prise [kaʃpriz] *nm inv* socket cover.

cacher[1] [kaʃɛr] = **kasher**.

cacher[2] [3] [kaʃe] *vt* **1.** [prisonnier, réfugié] to hide ■ [trésor, jouet] to hide, to conceal **2.** [accroc, ride] to hide, to conceal (from view) ■ **il cache son jeu** *pr* he's not showing his hand ; *fig* he's keeping his plans to himself, he's playing his cards close to his chest **3.** [faire écran devant] to hide, to obscure ■ **~ la lumière** *ou* **le jour à qqn** to be in sb's light ■ **tu me caches la vue!** you're blocking my view! **4.** [ne pas révéler - sentiment, vérité] to hide, to conceal, to cover up *(sép)* ■ **~ son âge** to keep one's age (a) secret ■ **~ qqch à qqn** to conceal *ou* to hide sthg from sb ■ **je ne cache pas que...** I must say *ou* admit that... ■ **je ne (te) cacherai pas que je me suis ennuyé** to be frank with you, (I must say that) I was bored ■ **il n'a pas caché son soulagement** his relief was plain for all to see.
◆ **se cacher** ◇ *vp (emploi réfléchi)* **1.** [suivi d'une partie du corps] : **je me cachais la tête sous les draps** I hid my head under the sheets ■ **cachez-vous un œil** cover one eye **2.** [au négatif] : **ne pas se ~ qqch** to make no secret of sthg, to be quite open about sthg ■ **il me plaît, je ne m'en cache pas!** I like him, it's no secret!
◇ *vpi* **1.** [aller se dissimuler - enfant, soleil] to hide ■ **se ~ de qqn** : **se ~ de ses parents pour fumer, fumer en se cachant de ses parents** to smoke behind one's parents' back **2.** [être dissimulé - fugitif] to be hiding ; [- objet] to be hidden.

cache-radiateur [kaʃradjatœr] *nm inv* radiator cover.

cache-sexe [kaʃsɛks] *nm inv* G-string.

cachet [kaʃɛ] *nm* **1.** PHARM tablet ■ **un ~ d'aspirine** an aspirin (tablet) **2.** [sceau] seal ■ [empreinte] stamp ■ **~ de la poste** postmark ■ **le ~ de la poste faisant foi** date of postmark will be taken as proof of postage **3.** [salaire] fee **4.** [charme - d'un édifice, d'une ville] character ; [- d'un vêtement] style ■ **avoir du ~** [édifice, village] to be full of character ; [vêtements] to be stylish.

cache-tampon [kaʃtɑ̃pɔ̃] (*pl inv ou pl* **cache-tampons**) *nm* JEUX ≃ hunt-the-thimble.

cacheter [27] [kaʃte] *vt* [enveloppe, vin] to seal ■ **~ un billet à la cire** to seal a letter with wax.

cachette [kaʃɛt] *nf* [d'un enfant] hiding place ■ [d'un malfaiteur, d'un réfugié] hideout ■ [d'un objet] hiding place.
◆ **en cachette** *loc adv* [fumer, lire, partir] secretly, in secret ■ [rire] to o.s., up one's sleeve ■ **en ~ de qqn** [boire, fumer] behind sb's back, while sb's back's turned ; [préparer, décider] without sb knowing, unbeknownst to sb.

cachettera *etc v* ▷ **cacheter**.

cachot [kaʃo] *nm* [de prisonnier] dungeon ■ **3 ans de ~** 3 years (locked away) in a dungeon.

cachotterie [kaʃɔtri] *nf* (little) secret ■ **faire des ~s à qqn** to keep secrets from sb.

cachottier, ère [kaʃɔtje, ɛr] *fam* ◇ *adj* secretive.
◇ *nm, f* : **c'est un ~** he's secretive.

cachou [kaʃu] *nm* **1.** [bonbon] cachou **2.** [substance, teinture] catechu, cachou, cutch.

cacique [kasik] *nm* **1.** [notable] cacique **2.** *arg scol* **le ~** [à un concours] *student graduating in first place (especially from the École normale supérieure)* **3.** *fam* [personne importante] big shot, bigwig.

cacochyme [kakɔʃim] *litt* ◇ *adj hum* doddery, doddering.
◇ *nmf* dodderer.

cacophonie [kakɔfɔni] *nf* cacophony.

cacophonique [kakɔfɔnik] *adj* cacophonous.

cactus [kaktys] *nm* cactus.

c.-à-d. (*abr écrite de* **c'est-à-dire**) i.e.

cadastral, e, aux [kadastral, o] *adj* cadastral.

cadastre [kadastr] *nm* [plans] cadastral register, ≃ land register.

cadastrer [3] [kadastre] *vt* ≃ to register with the land registry.

cadavérique [kadaverik] *adj* **1.** [du cadavre] of a corpse ■ **rigidité ~** rigor mortis **2.** [blancheur] deathly, cadaverous ■ [teint] deathly pale ■ [fixité] corpse-like.

cadavre [kadavr] *nm* **1.** [d'une personne - gén] corpse, body ; [- à disséquer] cadaver ■ [d'un animal] body, carcass ■ **c'est un ~ ambulant** he's a walking corpse **2.** *fam hum* [bouteille] empty bottle, empty.
◆ **cadavre exquis** *nm* [jeu] ≃ consequences ■ LITTÉR cadavre exquis.

caddie, caddy [kadi] *nm* [au golf] caddie, caddy.

Caddie® [kadi] *nm* [chariot] (supermarket) trolley *UK*, (grocery) cart *US*.

caddy [kadi] = **caddie**.

cadeau, x [kado] *nm* [don] present, gift ■ **faire un ~ à qqn** to give sb a present *ou* a gift ■ **faire ~ de qqch à qqn** [le lui offrir] to make sb a present of sthg, to give sb sthg as a present ■ **je te dois 15 euros – je t'en fais ~!** I owe you 15 euros – forget it! ■ **il ne m'a pas fait de ~** [dans une transaction, un match] he didn't do me any favours ; [critique] he didn't spare me ▶ **~ d'anniversaire/de Noël** birthday/Christmas present ■ **~ de noces** *ou* **de mariage** wedding present ■ **~ d'entreprise** giveaway *ou* free gift ■ **~ publicitaire** free gift ■ **ce n'est pas un ~!** *fam* [personne insupportable] he's a real pain! ; [personne bête] he's no bright spark! ■ **les petits ~x entretiennent l'amitié** *prov* gifts oil the wheels of friendship.

cadenas [kadna] *nm* padlock ■ **fermer au ~** to padlock.

cadenasser [3] [kadnase] *vt* **1.** [fermer] to padlock **2.** *fam* [emprisonner] to lock up *(sép)*, to put away *(sép)*.

cadence [kadɑ̃s] *nf* **1.** DANSE & MUS [rythme] rhythm ■ **marquer la ~** to beat out the rhythm ■ [accords] cadence ■ [passage de soliste] cadenza **2.** LITTÉR cadence **3.** [d'un marcheur, d'un rameur] pace ■ **à une bonne ~** at quite a pace **4.** INDUST rate ■ **~ de production** rate of production ■ **~ de travail** work rate **5.** MIL : **~ de tir** rate of fire.
◆ **à la cadence de** *loc prép* at the rate of.
◆ **en cadence** *loc adv* : **taper des mains en ~** to clap in time ■ **marcher en ~** to march.

cadencé, e [kadɑ̃se] *adj* [marche, musique] rhythmical ■ [gestes, démarche] swinging ■ **au pas ~** MIL in quick time.

cadencer [16] [kadɑ̃se] *vt* [vers, phrase] to give rhythm to ■ **~ son pas** to march in rhythm.

cadet, ette [kadɛ, ɛt] ◇ *adj* [plus jeune] younger ■ [dernier-né] youngest.
◇ *nm, f* **1.** [dans une famille - dernier-né] : **le ~, la ~te** the youngest child *ou* one ■ **son ~** [fils] his youngest son *ou* boy ; [frère] his youngest brother ■ [frère, sœur plus jeune] : **mon ~** my younger brother ■ **ma ~te** my younger sister **2.** [entre personnes non apparentées] : **être le ~ de qqn** to be younger than sb ■ **je suis son ~ de 4 ans** I'm 4 years his junior *ou* 4 years younger than he is **3.** SPORT junior *(between 13 and 16 years old)*.
◆ **cadet** *nm* **1.** MIL [élève] cadet **2.** HIST [futur militaire] cadet **3.** *loc* **c'est le ~ de mes soucis** it's the least of my worries.

cadmium [kadmjɔm] *nm* cadmium.

cadrage [kadraʒ] *nm* **1.** CINÉ & PHOTO centring **2.** MIN framing.

cadran [kadrɑ̃] *nm* [d'une montre, d'une pendule] face, dial ■ [d'un instrument de mesure, d'une boussole] face ■ [d'un téléphone] dial ■ **~ solaire** sun dial.

cadre [kadr] ◇ *nmf* **1.** [responsable - dans une entreprise] executive ; [- dans un parti, un syndicat] cadre ■ **un poste de ~** an executive *ou* a manager-ial post ■ **~ supérieur** *ou* **dirigeant** senior executive, member of (the) senior management ■ **~ moyen** middle manager ■ **femme ~** woman executive ■ **jeune ~ dynamique** *hum* whizz kid, ≃ yuppie
2. MIL officer, member of the officer corps
◇ *nm*

A.
1. ADMIN [catégorie] grade, category *(within the Civil Service)* ■ **le ~ (de la fonction publique)** [toutes catégories] the Civil Service
2. MIL corps

B.
1. [encadrement - d'un tableau, d'une porte, d'une ruche etc] frame ■ **~ de bicyclette** bicycle frame
2. [environnement] setting, surroundings ▶ **~ de vie** (living) environment
3. [portée, limites - d'accords, de réformes] scope, framework ▶ **loi ~** outline law ■ **plan ~** blueprint (project) ■ **réforme ~** general outline of reform
4. IMPR box, space ■ **'~ réservé à l'administration'** 'for official use only'
5. ÉLECTR [de radio] frame aerial
6. INFORM frame.
◆ **cadres** *nmpl* **1.** [contrainte] : **~s sociaux** social structures ■ **~s de la mémoire** structures of the memory **2.** ADMIN staff list ■ **être sur les ~s** to be a member of staff.
◆ **dans le cadre de** *loc prép* within the framework *ou* scope of ■ **dans le ~ de mes fonctions** as part of my job ■ **cela n'entre pas dans le ~ de mes fonctions** it falls outside the scope of my responsibilities.

CADRE

In French companies, employees are divided into two categories, *employés* and *cadres*. *Cadres*, who usually have a higher level of education and greater responsibilities, enjoy better salaries, more benefits and more prestige. They are also expected to work longer hours.

cadrer [3] [kadre] ◇ *vi* **1.** [correspondre - témoignages] to tally, to correspond ▪ **les deux notions ne cadrent pas ensemble** the two ideas don't go together ▪ **~ avec** to be consistent with **2.** [en comptabilité] : **faire ~ un compte** to square an account.
◇ *vt* CINÉ & PHOTO to centre.

cadreur, euse [kadrœr, øz] *nm, f* cameraman (*f* camerawoman).

caducée [kadyse] *nm* **1.** [de médecin, de pharmacien] caduceus, doctor's badge ▪ **avoir le ~ sur son pare-brise** to display a doctor's symbol on one's car **2.** MYTHOL Caduceus.

caducité [kadysite] *nf* deciduous nature *ou* character.

caduque [kadyk] *f* ▷ **caduc**.

cæcum [sekɔm] *nm* ANAT & VÉTÉR caecum.

CAF [kaf] ◇ *npr f* = **caisse d'Allocations familiales**.
◇ *adj inv* & *adv* (*abr de* **coût, assurance, fret**) cif.

cafard¹ [kafar] *nm* **1.** ENTOM cockroach **2.** *fam loc* **avoir le ~** to feel low, to feel down ▪ **donner le ~ à qqn** to get sb down ▪ **j'ai eu un coup de ~ hier** I felt a bit down yesterday.

cafard², e [kafar, ard] *nm, f fam* **1.** [dénonciateur] sneak, telltale **2.** [faux dévot] (religious) hypocrite.

cafardage [kafardaʒ] *nm fam* sneaking, taletelling.

cafarder [3] [kafarde] *fam* ◇ *vi* **1.** [rapporter] to sneak, to snitch **2.** [être déprimé] to feel depressed *ou* down ▪ **l'arrivée de l'automne me fait toujours ~** the arrival of autumn always depresses me.
◇ *vt* [quelqu'un] to sneak *ou* to snitch on *(insép)*.

cafardeur, euse [kafardœr, øz] *nm, f fam* sneak, telltale.

cafardeux, euse [kafardø, øz] *adj fam* [air, tempérament] gloomy ▪ **je suis** *ou* **je me sens ~ en ce moment** I'm feeling low *ou* down at the moment.

café [kafe] ◇ *nm* **1.** [boisson, graine] coffee ▪ **faire du ~** to make coffee ⊙ **~ frappé** *ou* **glacé** iced coffee ▪ **~ instantané** *ou* **soluble** instant coffee ▪ **~ noir** black coffee ▪ **~ crème** coffee with cream ▪ **~ filtre** filter coffee ▪ **~ en grains** coffee beans ▪ **~ au lait** white coffee *UK*, coffee with milk *US* ▪ **~ moulu** ground coffee ▪ **~ turc** Turkish coffee ▪ **~ viennois** Viennese coffee **2.** [fin du repas] coffee, coffee-time ▪ ***Belgique*** *early evening meal (served with coffee)*, ≃ high tea *UK* ▪ **au ~, il n'avait toujours pas terminé son histoire** he still hadn't finished his story by the time we got to the coffee ▪ **venez pour le ~** come and have coffee with us *(after the meal)* **3.** [établissement] : **~ (bar)** (licensed) café ▪ **c'est une discussion de ~ du Commerce** *péj* it's bar-room talk.
◇ *adj* coffee-coloured.
◆ **au café** *loc adj* [glace, entremets] coffee, coffee-flavoured ▪ **éclair au ~** coffee eclair.
◆ **café liégeois** *nm* coffee ice cream sundae.

CAFÉ

1. In French cafés, a small cup of strong black coffee is called *un (petit) café, un express* or, colloquially, *un petit noir*. This may be served *serré* (extra-strong), *léger* (weak) or *allongé* (diluted with hot water). An *express* with a tiny amount of milk added is called *une noisette*. A large cup of black coffee is *un grand café, un double express* or, colloquially, *un grand noir*. Coffee with frothy, steam-heated milk is called *un (grand/petit) crème*. The term *café au lait* is almost never used in cafés.
2. Parisian cafés have traditionally played an important part in the intellectual and artistic life of the city. For example, the Café de Flore was a favourite meeting place for the existentialists.

café-au-lait [kafeolɛ] *adj inv* coffee-coloured.

café-concert [kafekɔ̃sɛr] (*pl* **cafés-concerts**) *nm café where music-hall performances are given.*

caféier [kafeje] *nm* coffee tree.

caféine [kafein] *nf* caffeine.

cafetan [kaftɑ̃] *nm* caftan, kaftan.

cafétéria [kafeterja] *nf* cafeteria.

café-théâtre [kafeteatr] (*pl* **cafés-théâtres**) *nm* **1.** [café avec spectacle] *café where theatre performances take place* **2.** [petit théâtre] alternative theatre.

cafetier [kaftje] *nm vieilli* café owner.

cafetière [kaftjɛr] *nf* **1.** [machine] coffee maker ▪ [récipient] coffeepot **2.** *fam* [tête] nut, noddle *UK*.

cafouillage [kafujaʒ] *nm fam* **1.** [désordre] shambles, muddle ▪ **il y a eu un ~ devant les buts** there was a scramble in front of the goal **2.** AUTO misfiring.

cafouiller [3] [kafuje] *vi fam* **1.** [projet, service] to get into a muddle ▪ [décideur, dirigeant] to faff around *ou* about ▪ [présentateur, orateur] to get mixed up *ou* into a muddle ▪ **il a cafouillé dans ses explications** he got all confused (in his explanations) **2.** AUTO to misfire.

cafouilleur, euse [kafujœr, øz] *fam* ◇ *adj* [personne] : **il est ~** he's totally disorganised.
◇ *nm, f* bungler.

cafouilleux, euse [kafujø, øz] *adj fam* [explications] muddled ▪ [service] shambolic *UK*, chaotic ▪ **le départ de la course a été assez ~** there was chaos when the race started.

cafouillis [kafuji] *fam* = **cafouillage**.

caftan [kaftɑ̃] = **cafetan**.

cafter [3] [kafte] *fam vi* to sneak, to snitch.

cafteur, euse [kaftœr, øz] *nm, f fam* sneak, snitch.

cage [kaʒ] *nf* **1.** [pour animaux] cage ▪ **un animal en ~** a caged animal ▪ **mettre un animal en ~** to cage an animal ▪ **~ à lapins** *pr* rabbit hutch ▪ **habiter dans des ~s à lapins** *fig* to live in little boxes ▪ **~ à oiseau** *ou* **oiseaux** cage, birdcage ▪ **~ à poules** *pr* hen coop ▪ **vivre dans une ~ à poules** *fig* to live in cramped surroundings **2.** ANAT : **~ thoracique** rib cage **3.** CONSTR : **~ d'ascenseur** lift *UK ou* elevator *US* shaft ▪ **~ d'escalier** stairwell **4.** [structure, enceinte] : **~ d'écureuil** JEUX climbing frame ▪ **~ de Faraday** ÉLECTR Faraday cage **5.** MIN : **~ (d'extraction)** cage **6.** *fam* FOOTBALL goal **7.** *fam* [prison] nick *UK*, slammer.

cageot [kaʒo] *nm* **1.** [contenant] crate ▪ [contenu] crate, crateful **2.** *fam péj* [laideron] : **quel ~, sa femme!** his wife looks like the back of a bus *UK ou* Mack truck *US*!

cagette [kaʒɛt] *nf* crate.

cagibi [kaʒibi] *nm* boxroom *UK*, storage room *US*.

cagne [kaɲ] = **khâgne**.

cagneux, euse [kaɲø, øz] ◇ *adj* [jambes] crooked ▪ [cheval, personne] knock-kneed ▪ **genoux ~** knock knees.
◇ *nm, f* = **khâgneux**.

cagnotte [kaɲɔt] *nf* **1.** [caisse, somme] jackpot ▪ **la ~ est maintenant de 20 000 euros** the sum to be won is now 20,000 euros **2.** *fam* [fonds commun] kitty **3.** *fam* [économies] nest egg.

cagoule [kagul] *nf* **1.** [capuchon - d'enfant] balaclava ; [- de voleur] hood ; [- de moine] cowl ; [- de pénitent] hood, cowl **2.** [manteau] cowl.

cahier [kaje] *nm* **1.** ÉDUC notebook ▪ **~ de maths/géographie** maths/geography copybook ⊙ **~ de brouillon** roughbook *UK*, notebook *(for drafts)* ▪ **~ d'exercices** exercise book ▪ **~ de textes** [d'élève] homework notebook ; [de professeur] (work) record book ▪ **~ de travaux pratiques** lab (note) book **2.** [recueil] : **~ des charges** [de matériel] specifications ; [dans un contrat] remit ▪ **~ de revendications** claims register **3.** IMPR gathering.
◆ **cahiers** *nmpl* **1.** LITTÉR [mémoires] diary, memoirs **2.** HIST : **~s de doléances** book of grievances.

cahin-caha [kaɛ̃kaa] *loc adv* : **aller ~** [marcheur] to hobble along ; [entreprise, projet] to struggle along ▪ **comment va-t-il? – ~** how is he? – struggling along.

cahors [kaɔr] *nm* Cahors (wine).

cahot [kao] *nm* jolt, judder.

cahotant, e [kaɔtɑ̃, ɑ̃t] *adj* [chemin] bumpy, rough ▪ [voiture] jolting, juddering.

cahoter [3] [kaɔte] <> *vi* [véhicule] to jolt (along).
<> *vt* [passagers] to jolt, to bump about ■ [voiture] to jolt.

cahoteux, euse [kaɔtø, øz] *adj* bumpy, rough.

cahute [kayt] *nf* **1.** [abri] shack, hut **2.** *péj* [foyer] hovel.

caïd [kaid] *nm* **1.** *fam* [dans une matière] wizard ■ [en sport] ace ■ [d'une équipe] star **2.** *fam* [chef - de bande] gang leader ; [- d'une entreprise, d'un parti] big shot, bigwig ■ **jouer au ~, faire son ~** to act tough **3.** HIST caid, local governor *(of indigenous origin, under French rule).*

caillasse [kajas] *nf* **1.** [éboulis] loose stones, scree **2.** *fam péj* [mauvais sol] stones ■ **je ne peux rien planter, c'est de la ~** I can't plant anything, the ground's nothing but stones.

caille [kaj] *nf* **1.** ZOOL quail **2.** [en appellatif] : **ma (petite) ~** my pet.

caillé [kaje] <> *nm* curds.
<> *adj m* [lait] curdled.

caillebotis [kajbɔti] *nm* **1.** [grille] grating **2.** [plancher] duckboard.

cailler [3] [kaje] *vi* **1.** [lait] to curdle ■ [sang] to coagulate, to clot ■ **faire ~ du lait** to curdle milk **2.** △ [avoir froid] : **ça caille ici!** it's bloody UK OU goddam US freezing here!
◆ **se cailler**△ <> *vpi* to be cold.
<> *vpt* : **on se les caille dehors!** it's bloody UK OU goddam US freezing outside!

caillot [kajo] *nm* [de lait] (milk) curd ■ **~ (de sang)** bloodclot.

caillou, x [kaju] *nm* **1.** [gén] stone **2.** JOAILL stone **3.** *fam* [diamant] stone, sparkler **4.** MINÉR feldspar **5.** *fam* [crâne] : **il n'a plus un cheveu OU un poil sur le ~** he's as bald as a coot UK now.

caillouteux, euse [kajutø, øz] *adj* [chemin, champ] stony ■ [plage] pebbly, shingly.

caïman [kaimɑ̃] *nm* caiman, cayman.

Caïn [kaɛ̃] *npr* Cain.

Caire [kɛr] *npr* : **Le ~** Cairo ■ **au ~** in Cairo.

caisse [kɛs] *nf*

A.
1. [gén] box, case, chest ■ [à claire-voie] crate ➋ **~ d'emballage** packing crate ■ **~ à outils** toolbox
2. [boîte de 12 bouteilles] case
3. HORT box, tub

B.
1. [fût de tambour] cylinder ■ **~ claire** side OU snare drum ■ **~ de résonance** resonance chamber, resonating body ■ **grosse ~** [tambour] bass drum ; [musicien] bass drummer
2. [corps de violon] belly, sounding board
3. [d'horloge] case, casing

C.
1. [carrosserie] body
2. *fam* [voiture] car
3. RAIL water tank

D.
1. ANAT : **~ du tympan** middle ear, tympanic cavity *spéc*
2. *fam loc* **il part OU s'en va de la ~** it's his cough that'll carry him off *hum*

E.
1. [tiroir] till ■ [petit coffre] cashbox ■ **~ (enregistreuse)** till OU cash register ■ **tenir la ~** to be the cashier ■ **partir avec la ~** to run off with the takings ■ **faire une ~ commune** to put one's money together, to have a kitty ■ **les ~s de l'État** the coffers of the State
2. [lieu de paiement - d'un supermarché] check-out, till ; [- d'un cinéma, d'un casino, d'un magasin] cash desk ; [- d'une banque] cashier's desk ■ **passer à la ~** [magasin] to go to the cash desk ; [supermarché] to go through the check-out ; [banque] to go to the cashier's desk ; [recevoir son salaire] to collect one's wages ■ **après ce qu'il a dit au patron, il n'a plus qu'à passer à la ~!** *fam* after what he said to the boss, he'll be getting his cards UK OU pink slip US! ➋ **~ éclair** [distributeur] cashpoint ■ **~ rapide** [dans un supermarché] quick-service till, express checkout
3. [argent - d'un commerce] cash (in the till), takings ■ **faire la OU sa ~** to balance the till ➋ **~ noire** slush fund
4. BANQUE : **~ d'épargne** ≃ savings bank

F.
1. [organisme] office ■ **~ d'Allocations familiales** Child Benefit office UK, Aid to Dependent Children office US ■ **la Caisse des dépôts et consignations** *French funding body for public works and housing* ■ **~ de prévoyance** contingency fund ■ **~ primaire d'Assurance maladie** *French Social Security office in charge of medical insurance* ■ **~ de retraite** pension OU superannuation fund
2. [fonds] fund, funds.
◆ **en caisse** <> *loc adj* FIN : **argent en ~** cash.
<> *loc adv* : **avoir 3 000 euros en ~** to have 3,000 euros in the till ■ **je n'ai plus rien en ~** COMM my till's empty ; *fig* I'm broke.

caissette [kɛset] *nf* **1.** [contenant] small box **2.** [contenu] small boxful.

caissier, ère [kesje, ɛr] *nm, f* [d'une boutique, d'un casino, d'une banque] cashier ■ [d'un supermarché] check-out assistant UK OU clerk US ■ [de cinéma] cashier, box-office assistant UK.

caisson [kɛsɔ̃] *nm* **1.** TRAV PUB [pour fondation] caisson, cofferdam **2.** ARCHIT [pour plafond] coffer, caisson, lacunar **3.** NAUT caisson, cofferdam ■ **~ étanche OU de flottabilité** buoyancy tank **4.** SPORT : **~ hyperbare** bathysphere ■ **maladie OU mal des ~s** decompression sickness, the bends **5.** NUCL (nuclear reactor) casing **6.** HIST & MIL caisson, ammunition wagon.

cajoler [3] [kaʒɔle] *vt* [enfant] to cuddle.

cajolerie [kaʒɔlri] *nf* [manifestation de tendresse] cuddle ■ **faire des ~s à qqn** to cuddle sb.
◆ **cajoleries** *nfpl péj* [flatteries] flattery, cajolery.

cajoleur, euse [kaʒɔlœr, øz] <> *adj* **1.** [affectueux - parent, ton] affectionate, loving **2.** *péj* [flatteur] coaxing, wheedling.
<> *nm, f péj* [flatteur] wheedler, flatterer.

cajou [kaʒu] *nm* ▻ **noix.**

cajun [kaʒœ̃] *adj* Cajun.
◆ **Cajun** *nmf* Cajun.

cake [kɛk] *nm* fruit cake.

cal [kal] *nm* **1.** [durillon - à la main] callus ; [- au pied] corn **2.** BOT & MÉD callus.

calabrais, e [kalabrɛ, ɛz] *adj* Calabrian.

Calabre [kalabr] *npr f* : **(la) ~** Calabria.

Calais [kalɛ] *npr* Calais.

calamar [kalamar] = **calmar.**

calamine [kalamin] *nf* **1.** CHIM calamine **2.** AUTO carbon deposit.

calamite [kalamit] *nf* BOT calamite.

calamité [kalamite] *nf* **1.** [événement] calamity, catastrophe, disaster **2.** *fam hum* [personne] walking disaster.

calamiteux, euse [kalamitø, øz] *adj* calamitous, disastrous, catastrophic.

calandre [kalɑ̃dr] *nf* **1.** AUTO radiator grill **2.** TEXT [papeterie] calender.

calanque [kalɑ̃k] *nf* (Mediterranean) creek.

calcaire [kalkɛr] <> *adj* [roche, relief] limestone *(modif)* ■ [sol] chalky, calcareous *spéc* ■ [eau] hard.
<> *nm* **1.** GÉOL limestone **2.** [dans une casserole] fur UK, sediment US.

calcanéum [kalkaneɔm] *nm* calcaneum.

calcif [kalsif] *nm fam* pants UK, shorts US.

calcification [kalsifikasjɔ̃] *nf* calcification.

calcifié, e [kalsifje] *adj* calcified.

calciné, e [kalsine] *adj* [bois, corps, viande] charred, burned to a cinder ■ [mur, maison] charred.

calciner [3] [kalsine] *vt* **1.** [transformer en chaux] to calcine **2.** [brûler] to burn to a cinder, to char **3.** [chauffer - brique, minerai] to calcine.
◆ **se calciner** *vpi* **1.** [viande] to burn to a cinder **2.** [être chauffé - brique, minerai] to calcine.

calcite [kalsit] *nf* calcite.

calcium [kalsjɔm] *nm* calcium.

calcul [kalkyl] *nm*

A.

1. [suite d'opérations] calculation ■ **faire un ~** to do a calculation ■ **ça reviendra moins cher, fais le ~!** it'll be cheaper, just work it out! ■ **faire le ~ de qqch** to work sthg out, to calculate sthg ■ **le raisonnement est correct, mais le ~ est faux** the method's right but the calculations are wrong ▶ **~ différentiel/intégral/vectoriel** differential/integral/vector calculus ■ **~ algébrique** calculus ■ **~ des probabilités** probability theory
2. ÉDUC : **le ~** sums, arithmetic ▶ **~ mental** [matière] mental arithmetic ; [opération] mental calculation
3. [estimation] calculation, computation ■ **d'après mes ~s** according to my calculations ■ **un bon ~** a good move ■ **un mauvais** *ou* **faux ~** a bad move
4. *péj* [manœuvre] scheme ■ **par ~** out of (calculated) self-interest ■ **sans ~** without any *ou* with no ulterior motive

B.

MÉD stone, calculus *spéc* ■ **~ biliaire** gall stone ■ **~ urinaire** *ou* **rénal** kidney stone, renal calculus *spéc*.

calculabilité [kalkylabilite] *nf* calculability.

calculable [kalkylabl] *adj* [prix] calculable ■ [dégâts] estimable ■ **c'est ~ de tête** you can work it out *ou* calculate it in your head.

calculateur, trice [kalkylatœr, tris] ◇ *adj péj* calculating, scheming.
◇ *nm, f* **1.** [qui compte] : **c'est un bon/mauvais ~** he's good/bad at figures *ou* sums **2.** *péj* [personne intéressée] : **un fin ~** a shrewd operator ■ **un ignoble ~** a scheming character.
◆ **calculateur** *nm* AUTO : **~ embarqué** on-board computer.
◆ **calculatrice** *nf* [machine] calculator ■ **calculatrice de poche** pocket calculator.

calculer [3] [kalkyle] ◇ *vt* **1.** [dépenses, dimension, quantité etc] to calculate, to work out *(sép)* ■ **~ qqch de tête** *ou* **mentalement** to work sthg out in one's head ■ **~ vite** to be quick at figures, to calculate quickly **2.** [avec parcimonie - pourboire, dépenses] to work out to the last penny, to budget carefully **3.** [évaluer - avantages, inconvénients, chances, risque] to calculate, to weigh up *(sép)* ■ **mal ~ qqch** to miscalculate sthg ■ **~ que** to work out *ou* to calculate that **4.** [préparer - gestes, effets, efforts] to calculate, to work out *(sép)* ■ **j'ai tout calculé** I have it all worked out ▶ **~ son coup** *fam* to plan one's moves carefully ■ **tu as mal calculé ton coup!** you got it all wrong!
◇ *vi* to calculate ■ **il calcule vite et bien** he's quick at arithmetic.

calculette [kalkylɛt] *nf* pocket calculator.

Calcutta [kalkyta] *npr* Calcutta.

caldoche [kaldɔʃ] *adj* New Caledonian.
◆ **Caldoche** *nmf white inhabitant of New Caledonia.*

cale [kal] *nf*

A.

1. [pour bloquer - un meuble] wedge ; [- une roue] wedge, chock ■ **mettre une voiture sur ~s** to put a car on blocks
2. [d'ébéniste] : **~ à poncer** sanding block
3. [sur rails] chock

B.

1. NAUT hold
2. [d'un quai] slipway ■ **mettre sur ~s** to lay down ▶ **~ de construction** *ou* **de lancement** slip, slipway ■ **~ sèche** dry dock ■ **être en ~ sèche** to be in dry dock.

calé, e [kale] *adj fam* **1.** [instruit] : **il est ~ en histoire** he's brilliant at history **2.** [difficile - problème] tough.

calebasse [kalbas] *nf* **1.** [fruit, récipient] calabash, gourd **2.** *fam* [tête] nut, noddle *UK*.

calèche [kalɛʃ] *nf* barouche, calash ■ **une promenade en ~** a ride in a horse-drawn carriage.

caleçon [kalsɔ̃] *nm* **1.** [sous-vêtement] : **~ court, ~s courts** pair of (men's) underpants ■ **~ long, ~s longs** pair of long johns **2.** [pour nager] : **~ de bain** swimming trunks **3.** [pantalon] leggings.

calembour [kalɑ̃bur] *nm* play on words, pun ■ **faire des ~s** to play with words.

calendes [kalɑ̃d] *nfpl* **1.** ANTIQ calends **2.** *loc* **renvoyer** *ou* **remettre qqch aux ~ grecques** to put sthg off *ou* to postpone sthg indefinitely.

calendrier [kalɑ̃drije] *nm* **1.** [tableau, livret] calendar ■ **~ grégorien/républicain** Gregorian/Republican calendar ■ **~ perpétuel/à effeuiller** perpetual/tear-off calendar **2.** [emploi du temps] timetable, schedule ■ [plan - de réunions] schedule, calendar ; [- d'un festival] calendar ; [- d'un voyage] schedule ▶ **~ des rencontres** FOOTBALL fixture list *UK*, match schedule *US*.

CALENDRIER RÉPUBLICAIN

The Republican calendar was first used in 1793. The year began on 22nd September and was divided into twelve months of thirty days each, the remaining days being given over to celebrations. The names of the months were inspired by the changing seasons, the weather and the harvest: *vendémiaire, brumaire, frimaire, nivôse, pluviôse, ventôse, germinal, floréal, prairial, messidor, thermidor, fructidor*. The calendar was officially replaced by the Gregorian calendar in 1806.

cale-pied [kalpje] (*pl* **cale-pieds**) *nm* toe-clip.

calepin [kalpɛ̃] *nm* [carnet] notebook.

caler [3] [kale] ◇ *vt* **1.** [avec une cale - armoire, pied de chaise] to wedge, to steady with a wedge ; [- roue] to chock, to wedge ■ **~ une porte** [pour la fermer] to wedge a door shut ; [pour qu'elle reste ouverte] to wedge a door open **2.** [installer] to prop up *(sép)* ■ **~ qqn sur des coussins** to prop sb up on cushions ■ **bien calé dans son fauteuil** comfortably settled in his armchair **3.** *fam* [remplir] : **ça cale (l'estomac)** it fills you up, it's filling.
◇ *vi* **1.** AUTO [moteur, voiture] to stall ■ **j'ai calé** I've stalled **2.** [s'arrêter - devant un problème] to give up ; [- dans un repas] : **prends mon gâteau, je cale** have my cake, I can't eat anymore.
◆ **se caler** ◇ *vpi* [s'installer] : **se ~ dans un fauteuil** to settle o.s. comfortably in an armchair.
◇ *vpt fam loc* **se ~ les joues, se les ~** [bien manger] to stuff *ou* to feed one's face.

calfater [3] [kalfate] *vt* to calk, to caulk.

calfeutrage [kalføtraʒ], **calfeutrement** [kalføtrəmɑ̃] *nm* [d'une fenêtre, d'une porte] draught-proofing ■ [d'une ouverture] stopping up, filling.

calfeutrer [3] [kalføtre] *vt* [ouverture] to stop up *(sép)*, to fill ■ [fenêtre, porte - gén] to make draught-proof ; [- avec un bourrelet] to weatherstrip.
◆ **se calfeutrer** *vp (emploi réfléchi)* **1.** [s'isoler du froid] to make o.s. snug **2.** *fig* [s'isoler] to shut o.s. up *ou* away.

calibrage [kalibraʒ] *nm* **1.** [d'un obus, d'un tube] calibration **2.** COMM [de fruits] grading **3.** IMPR castoff.

calibre [kalibr] *nm* **1.** INDUST & MÉCAN gauge **2.** CONSTR & TRAV PUB template **3.** ARM & TECHNOL bore, calibre ■ **un canon de 70 ~s** a 70 millimetre gun ■ **de gros ~** large-bore ■ **de petit ~** small-bore **4.** COMM grade, (standardized *ou* standard) size **5.** △ *arg crime* [revolver] shooter△ *UK*, rod△ *US* **6.** *fig* [type] class, calibre ■ **de ce ~** of this calibre *ou* class ■ **il est d'un autre ~** he's not in the same league.

calibrer [3] [kalibre] *vt* **1.** [usiner - obus, revolver, tube] to calibrate **2.** COMM to grade **3.** IMPR to cast off *(sép)*.

calice [kalis] *nm* **1.** BOT & PHYSIOL calyx **2.** RELIG chalice.

calicot [kaliko] *nm* **1.** TEXT calico **2.** [bande] banner.

califat [kalifa] *nm* caliphate.

calife [kalif] *nm* caliph.

Californie [kalifɔrni] *npr f* : **(la)** ~ California.

californien, enne [kalifɔrnjɛ̃, ɛn] *adj* Californian.
◆ **Californien, enne** *nm, f* Californian.

califourchon [kalifurʃɔ̃] ◆ **à califourchon** *loc adv* astride ■ **être à ~ sur qqch** to bestride *ou* to be astride sthg ■ **monter** *ou* **s'asseoir** *ou* **se mettre à ~ sur qqch** to sit astride *ou* to straddle sthg.

Caligula [kaligyla] *npr* Caligula.

câlin, e [kalɛ̃, in] *adj* **1.** [regard, voix] tender **2.** [personne] affectionate.
◆ **câlin** *nm* cuddle ■ **faire un ~ à qqn** to give sb a cuddle ■ **faire des ~s à qqn** to (kiss and) cuddle sb.

câliner [3] [kaline] *vt* to (kiss and) cuddle, to pet ■ **se faire ~** to be cuddled.

câlinerie [kalinri] *nf* [qualité] tenderness ■ [geste] caress, cuddle ■ **faire des ~s à qqn** to kiss and cuddle sb.

calisson [kalisɔ̃] *nm* : **~ (d'Aix)** *lozenge-shaped sweet made of iced marzipan.*

calleux, euse [kalø, øz] *adj* **1.** [main, peau] callous, horny **2.** MÉD [ulcère] callous.

call-girl [kɔlgœrl] (*pl* **call-girls**) *nf* call girl.

calligramme [kaligram] *nm* calligramme.

calligraphe [kaligraf] *nmf* calligrapher.

calligraphie [kaligrafi] *nf* calligraphy.

calligraphier [9] [kaligrafje] *vt* **1.** ART to calligraph **2.** [écrire avec soin] : **~ qqch** to write sthg in a beautiful hand.

callosité [kalozite] *nf* callosity, callus.

calmant, e [kalmɑ̃, ɑ̃t] *adj* **1.** PHARM [contre l'anxiété] tranquillizing ■ [contre la douleur] painkilling **2.** [propos] soothing.
◆ **calmant** *nm* **1.** PHARM [contre l'anxiété] tranquillizer, sedative ■ **prendre des ~s** to be on tranquillizers **2.** [contre la douleur] painkiller.

calmar [kalmar] *nm* squid.

calme [kalm] ◇ *adj* **1.** [sans agitation - quartier, rue, moment] quiet, peaceful ; [- journée, ambiance] calm **2.** [sans mouvement - eau, étang, mer] still, calm ; [- air] still ■ **par temps ~** when there's no wind **3.** [maître de soi] calm, self-possessed **4.** [peu productif - marché] quiet, dull, slack.
◇ *nmf* [personne] calm *ou* placid person.
◇ *nm* **1.** [absence d'agitation] peace, quiet, calm ■ [de l'air, de l'eau] stillness ■ **avec ~** calmly ■ **du ~!** [ne vous agitez pas] keep quiet! ; [ne paniquez pas] keep cool! ■ **le ~** peace and quiet ■ **être au ~** to have *ou* to enjoy peace and quiet ■ **manifester dans le ~** to hold a peaceful demonstration ■ **ramener le ~** [dans une assemblée] to restore order ; [dans une situation] to calm things down ➊ **c'est le ~ avant la tempête** this is the calm before the storm **2.** [silence] silence ■ **faire qqch dans le ~** to do sthg quietly **3.** [sang-froid] composure, calm ■ **du ~!** calm down! ■ **une femme d'un grand ~** a very composed woman ■ **garder son ~** to keep calm ■ **perdre son ~** to lose one's composure ■ **retrouver son ~** to calm down, to regain one's composure **4.** [vent] calm ■ **c'est le ~ plat** [en mer] there's no wind ; [il ne se passe rien] there's nothing happening ; [à la Bourse] the Stock Exchange is in the doldrums.
◆ **calmes** *nmpl* : **~s équatoriaux** doldrums.

calmement [kalməmɑ̃] *adv* calmly, quietly.

calmer [3] [kalme] *vt* **1.** [rendre serein - enfant, opposant, foule] to calm down *(sép)* ■ **nous devons ~ les esprits** [dans un groupe] we must put everybody's mind at rest ; [dans la nation] we must put the people's minds at rest ■ **~ le jeu** SPORT to calm the game down ; *fig* to calm things down **2.** [dépassionner - mécontentement] to soothe, to calm ; [- colère] to calm, to appease ; [- querelle] to pacify, to defuse ; [- débat] to restore order to **3.** [diminuer - fièvre, inflammation] to bring down *(sép)* ; [- douleur] to soothe, to ease ; [- faim] to satisfy, to appease ; [- soif] to quench ; [- désespoir, crainte] to ease, to allay ; [- désir, passion, enthousiasme] to dampen ; [- impatience] to relieve ■ **ça devrait leur ~ les nerfs** that should soothe their (frayed) nerves.
◆ **se calmer** *vpi* **1.** [devenir serein] to calm down ■ **attends que les choses se calment** wait for things to calm down **2.** [se taire] to quieten *UK ou* to quiet *US* down **3.** [s'affaiblir - dispute, douleur] to die down *ou* away, to ease off *ou* up ; [- fièvre] to die *ou* to go down ; [- anxiété] to fade ; [- passion] to fade away, to cool ; [- faim, soif] to die down, to be appeased **4.** MÉTÉOR [averse] to ease off ■ [mer] to become calm ■ [vent] to die down, to drop.

calomniateur, trice [kalɔmnjatœr, tris] ◇ *adj* [parole] slanderous ■ [lettre] libellous.
◇ *nm, f* slanderer ■ [par écrit] libeller.

calomnie [kalɔmni] *nf* slander, calumny ■ **ce sont de pures ~s** it's all lies.

calomnier [9] [kalɔmnje] *vt* [dénigrer - personne] to slander, to calumniate *sout* ; [- par écrit] to libel.

calomnieux, euse [kalɔmnjø, øz] *adj* [propos] slanderous ■ [écrit] libellous, slanderous.

calorie [kalɔri] *nf* calorie ■ **ça apporte des ~s** [c'est nutritif] it'll help build you up ; [cela fait grossir] it's fattening ➊ **un régime basses ~s** a low-calorie diet.

calorifère [kalɔrifɛr] ◇ *adj* **1.** [produisant de la chaleur] heat-giving **2.** [transportant de la chaleur] heat-conveying.
◇ *nm* [poêle] stove.

calorifique [kalɔrifik] *adj* [perte] heat *(modif)* ■ [valeur] calorific.

calorifuge [kalɔrifyʒ] ◇ *adj* heat-insulating.
◇ *nm* heat insulator.

calorifuger [17] [kalɔrifyʒe] *vt* to insulate, to lag.

calorimètre [kalɔrimɛtr] *nm* calorimeter.

calorique [kalɔrik] *adj* PHYS & PHYSIOL calorific, caloric.

calot [kalo] *nm* **1.** [vêtement] cap **2.** MIL forage cap **3.** JEUX big marble.

calotin, e [kalɔtɛ̃, in] ◇ *adj* churchy.
◇ *nm, f* holy Joe.

calotte [kalɔt] *nf* **1.** [vêtement] skullcap ■ [de prêtre] calotte, skullcap ■ **la ~** *fam* the clergy **2.** *fam* [tape] box on the ear ■ **flanquer une ~ à qqn** to give sb a clip round the earhole ■ **(se) prendre** *ou* **recevoir une ~** to get a thick ear **3.** ANAT : **~ du crâne** *ou* **crânienne** top of the skull **4.** ARCHIT [voûte] calotte **5.** ASTRON : **~ polaire** polar region **6.** MATH : **~ sphérique** portion of a sphere **7.** GÉOGR : **~ glaciaire** icecap.

calotter [3] [kalɔte] *vt fam* **~ un enfant** to box a child around the ears.

calque [kalk] *nm* **1.** [feuille] piece of tracing paper ■ [substance] tracing paper **2.** [dessin] tracing, traced design ■ **prendre** *ou* **faire un ~ de** to trace **3.** [copie - d'un tableau, d'un texte] exact copy, replica **4.** [répétition - d'une attitude, d'une erreur] carbon copy **5.** LING calque, loan translation.

calquer [3] [kalke] *vt* **1.** [motif] to trace **2.** [imiter - manières, personne] to copy exactly **3.** LING to translate literally ■ **calqué sur** *ou* **de l'espagnol** translated literally from Spanish.

calumet [kalymɛ] *nm* peace pipe ■ **fumer le ~ de la paix** *pr* to smoke the pipe of peace ; *fig* to make peace.

calva [kalva] *fam* = **calvados.**

calvados [kalvados] *nm* Calvados, apple brandy.

calvaire [kalvɛr] *nm* **1.** RELIG [crucifixion] : **le Calvaire (de Jésus)** the suffering of Jesus on the Cross **2.** [monument - à plusieurs croix] calvary ; [- à une croix] wayside cross *ou* calvary **3.** ART calvary, road to Calvary **4.** [souffrance] ordeal ■ **sa maladie a été un long ~** his illness was a long ordeal.

calvinisme [kalvinism] *nm* Calvinism.

calvitie [kalvisi] *nf* **1.** [absence de cheveux] baldness ■ **~ précoce** premature baldness **2.** *fam* [emplacement] bald spot.

calypso [kalipso] *nm* calypso.

camaïeu, x [kamajø] *nm* **1.** [tableau] monochrome painting **2.** [gravure] monochrome engraving **3.** [technique] : **le ~** monochrome, monotint ■ **un ~ de bleus** a monochrome in blue **4.** [couleurs] shades.

camarade [kamarad] *nmf* **1.** [ami] friend ■ **~ de classe** classmate ■ **~ d'école** schoolmate ■ **~ de jeu** playmate ■ **~ de régiment** comrade (in arms) **2.** POLIT comrade.

camaraderie [kamaradri] *nf* [entre deux personnes] good fellowship, friendship ■ [dans un club, un groupe] companionship, camaraderie ■ **il n'y a que de la ~ entre eux** they're just (good) friends.

Camargue [kamarg] *npr f* : **la ~** the Camargue (area).

cambiste [kɑ̃bist] ◇ *adj* : **banquier ~** bank with a bureau de change *ou* foreign exchange counter.
◇ *nmf* **1.** BOURSE exchange broker **2.** [de bureau de change] bureau de change *ou* foreign exchange dealer.

Cambodge [kɑ̃bɔdʒ] *npr m* : **le ~** Cambodia ■ **au ~** in Cambodia.

cambodgien, enne [kɑ̃bɔdʒjɛ̃, ɛn] *adj* Cambodian.
◆ **Cambodgien, enne** *nm, f* Cambodian.

cambouis [kɑ̃bwi] *nm* dirty oil *ou* grease.

cambrage [kɑ̃braʒ] *nm* camber.

cambré, e [kɑ̃bre] *adj* [dos] arched ■ [pied] with a high instep ■ [personne] arched-back ■ [cheval] bow-legged.

cambrement [kɑ̃brəmɑ̃] = **cambrage**.

cambrer [3] [kɑ̃bre] *vt* **1.** [pied] to arch ■ **~ le dos** *ou* **les reins** to arch one's back **2.** TECHNOL [barre, poutre] to camber.
◆ **se cambrer** *vpi* to arch one's back.

cambriolage [kɑ̃brijɔlaʒ] *nm* **1.** [coup] burglary, break-in **2.** [activité] : **le ~** burglary, housebreaking.

cambrioler [3] [kɑ̃brijɔle] *vt* [propriété] to burgle *UK*, to burglarize *US* ■ [personne] to burgle ■ **se faire ~** to be burgled.

cambrioleur, euse [kɑ̃brijɔlœr, øz] *nm, f* burglar, housebreaker.

Cambronne [kɑ̃brɔn] *npr* : **le mot de ~** *euphemism for the word "merde".*

cambrousse [kɑ̃brus], **cambrouse** [kɑ̃bruz] *nf fam péj* country, countryside ■ **en pleine ~** in the middle of nowhere ■ **il arrive** *ou* **débarque de sa ~** he's just up from the backwoods *ou* sticks.

cambrure [kɑ̃bryr] *nf* **1.** [posture - du dos] curve ; [- du pied, d'une semelle] arch **2.** TECHNOL [d'une chaussée, d'une pièce de bois] camber **3.** [partie - du pied] instep ; [- du dos] small.

cambuse [kɑ̃byz] *nf* **1.** NAUT storeroom **2.** *fam péj* [chambre, maison] dump, tip *UK*.

came [kam] *nf* **1.** MÉCAN cam **2.** △ [drogue] junk△ **3.** △ [marchandises] stuff, junk.

camé, e△ [kame] ◇ *adj* high ■ **il est ~** he's on something.
◇ *nm, f* junkie.

camée [kame] *nm* JOAILL cameo.

caméléon [kameleɔ̃] *nm* ZOOL chameleon.

camélia [kamelja] *nm* camellia.

camelot [kamlo] *nm* **1.** [dans la rue] street peddler, hawker **2.** POLIT : **~ du roi** Royalist supporter *(in France).*

camelote [kamlɔt] *nf fam* **1.** [marchandise] stuff, goods **2.** *péj* [mauvaise qualité] : **c'est de la ~** it's junk *ou* trash ■ **leurs bagues, c'est de la ~** their rings are cheap and nasty.

camembert [kamɑ̃bɛr] *nm* **1.** [fromage] Camembert (cheese) **2.** [graphique] pie chart.

camer [3] [kame] ◆ **se camer**△ *vpi* to be a junkie ■ **se ~ à la cocaïne** to be on coke.

caméra [kamera] *nf* **1.** AUDIO, CINÉ & TV film *UK ou* movie *US* camera ■ **il s'est expliqué devant les ~s** he gave an explanation in front of the television cameras ➔ **~ invisible** candid camera ■ **~ portative** press camera ■ **~ sonore** sound camera ■ **~ super-8** super 8 camera ■ **~ vidéo** video camera **2.** OPT : **~ électronique** *ou* **électronographique** electronic camera.

cameraman [kameraman] (*pl* **cameramans** *ou pl* **cameramen** [-mɛn]) *nm* cameraman *m*, camera operator.

camériste [kamerist] *nf* **1.** [dame d'honneur] lady-in-waiting **2.** [femme de chambre] chambermaid.

Cameroun [kamrun] *npr m* : **le ~** Cameroon ■ **au ~** in Cameroon.

camerounais, e [kamrunɛ, ɛz] *adj* Cameroonian.
◆ **Camerounais, e** *nm, f* Cameroonian.

Caméscope® [kameskɔp] *nm* camcorder.

camion [kamjɔ̃] *nm* **1.** AUTO lorry *UK*, truck *US* ■ **'interdit aux ~s'** 'no HGVs' *UK*, 'no trucks' *US* ➔ **~ benne** dumper truck ■ **~ de déménagement** removal van *UK*, moving van *US* ■ **~ à remorque** lorry with trailer ■ **~ à semi-remorque** articulated lorry *UK*, trailer truck *US* **2.** [de peintre] (paint) pail.

camion-citerne [kamjɔ̃sitɛrn] (*pl* **camions-citernes**) *nm* tanker (lorry) *UK*, tank truck *US*.

camionnage [kamjɔnaʒ] *nm* (road) haulage.

camionner [3] [kamjɔne] *vt* to haul, to transport by lorry *UK ou* truck *US*.

camionnette [kamjɔnɛt] *nf* van.

camionneur, euse [kamjɔnœr, øz] *nm, f* **1.** [conducteur] lorry *UK ou* truck *US* driver **2.** [entrepreneur] (road) haulage contractor, (road) haulier *UK ou* hauler *US*.

camion-poubelle [kamjɔ̃pubɛl] (*pl* **camions-poubelles**) *nm* dustcart, (dust)bin lorry *UK*, garbage truck *US*.

camisard [kamizar] *nm* HIST Calvinist partisan *(in the Cévennes uprising of 1702).*

camisole [kamizɔl] *nf* **1.** [vêtement] camisole **2.** PSYCHOL : **~ de force** strait jacket.

camomille [kamɔmij] *nf* **1.** BOT camomile **2.** [infusion] camomile tea.

camouflage [kamuflaʒ] *nm* **1.** MIL [procédé] camouflaging ■ [matériel] camouflage **2.** [d'un message] coding **3.** ZOOL camouflage, mimicry.

camoufler [3] [kamufle] *vt* **1.** MIL to camouflage **2.** [cacher - passage, gêne] to conceal ; [- bavure] to cover up *(sép)* ; [- vérité] to hide, to conceal **3.** [déguiser] : **de nombreux crimes sont camouflés en suicides** murders are often made to look like suicide.
◆ **se camoufler** *vp (emploi réfléchi)* **1.** MIL to camouflage o.s. **2.** ZOOL to camouflage itself, to mimic its environment.

camouflet [kamuflɛ] *nm* **1.** *litt* [affront] snub, insult, affront **2.** MIL camouflet, stifler.

camp [kɑ̃] *nm* **1.** MIL (army) camp ■ **~ militaire/retranché** military/fortified camp ■ **~ de base** base camp ■ **~ de prisonniers** prisoner of war camp ■ **lever le ~** *pr* to break camp ; *fig* to make tracks
2. HIST & POLIT camp ■ **~ (de concentration)** concentration camp ■ **~ de déportation** deportation camp ■ **~ d'extermination** *ou* **de la mort** death camp ■ **~ de réfugiés** refugee camp ■ **~ de travail (forcé)** forced labour camp ■ **Camp David** HIST Camp David
3. LOISIRS campsite, camping site ■ **j'envoie les enfants en ~ cet été** I'm sending the children off to summer camp this year ➔ **~ de scouts** scout camp
4. JEUX & SPORT team, side
5. [faction] camp, side ■ **il faut choisir son ~** you must decide which side you're on ■ **passer dans l'autre ~, changer de ~** to change sides, to go over to the other side
6. *loc* **ficher le ~** *fam* to clear off ■ **foutre le ~**△ [personne] to bugger off *UK*, to take off *US* ■ **mon pansement fout le ~** my plaster's coming off ■ **tout fout le ~!** what is the world coming to?

campagnard, e [kɑ̃paɲar, ard] <> *adj* [accent, charme, style, vie] country *(modif)*, rustic.
<> *nm, f* countryman (*f* countrywoman).

campagne [kɑ̃paɲ] *nf* **1.** GÉOGR [habitat] country ■ [paysage] countryside ■ **une ~ plate** flat *ou* open country ■ **à la ~** in the country *ou* countryside **2.** [activité] campaign ■ **faire ~ pour/contre** to campaign for/against ▶ **~ de diffamation** smear campaign ■ **~ électorale** election campaign ■ **~ de presse** press campaign ■ **~ publicitaire** *ou* **de publicité** COMM advertising campaign **3.** MIL campaign ■ **faire ~** to campaign, to fight **4.** ARCHÉOL : **~ de fouilles** excavation plan.
◆ **de campagne** *loc adj* **1.** [rural - chemin, médecin, curé] country *(modif)* **2.** COMM [pain, saucisson] country *(modif)* **3.** MIL [tenue] field *(modif)*.
◆ **en campagne** *loc adv* in the field, on campaign ■ **être en ~** *fig* to be on the warpath ■ **entrer** *ou* **se mettre en ~** *pr* & *fig* to go into action.

campagnol [kɑ̃paɲɔl] *nm* vole.

campanile [kɑ̃panil] *nm* [d'une église] bell-tower ■ [isolé] campanile.

campanule [kɑ̃panyl] *nf* bellflower, campanula *spéc.*

campé, e [kɑ̃pe] *adj* : **bien ~** [robuste] well-built ■ **bien ~ sur ses jambes** standing firmly on his feet ■ **des personnages bien ~s** [bien décrits] well-drawn characters ; [bien interprétés] well-played characters.

campement [kɑ̃pmɑ̃] *nm* **1.** [installation] camp, encampment ■ [terrain] camping place *ou* ground ■ [de bohémiens] caravan site ■ **'~ interdit'** 'no camping' ■ **établir un ~** to set up camp **2.** MIL [détachement] detachment of scouts.

camper [3] [kɑ̃pe] <> *vi* **1.** LOISIRS to camp **2.** MIL to camp (out) ■ **~ sur ses positions** MIL to stand one's ground ; *fig* to stand one's ground, to stick to one's guns **3.** [habiter temporairement] : **je campe chez un copain en attendant** meanwhile, I'm camping (out) at a friend's.
<> *vt* **1.** THÉÂTRE [personnage] to play the part of **2.** [par un dessin - silhouette] to draw, to sketch out *(sép)* **3.** [par un écrit - personnage] to portray **4.** [placer] : **~ son chapeau sur sa tête** to stick one's hat on one's head **5.** MIL [troupes] to encamp.
◆ **se camper** *vpi* : **se ~ devant qqn** to plant o.s. in front of sb.

campeur, euse [kɑ̃pœr, øz] *nm, f* camper.

camphre [kɑ̃fr] *nm* camphor.

camphré, e [kɑ̃fre] *adj* camphorated.

camping [kɑ̃piŋ] *nm* **1.** [activité] camping ■ **on a fait du ~ l'été dernier** we went camping last summer ■ **j'aime faire du ~** I like camping ▶ **~ sauvage** [non autorisé] camping on non-authorized sites ; [en pleine nature] camping in the open, wilderness camping **2.** [terrain] camp *ou* camping site *UK*, campground *US* ■ [pour caravanes] caravan *UK ou* trailer *US* site.
◆ **de camping** *loc adj* camp *(modif)*, camping.

camping-car [kɑ̃piŋkar] (*pl* **camping-cars**) *nm* camper-van *UK*, camper *US*.

camping-caravaning [kɑ̃piŋkaravaniŋ] *nm inv* caravanning *UK*, camping in a trailer *US*.

Camping-Gaz® [kɑ̃piŋgaz] *nm inv* butane gas-stove.

campus [kɑ̃pys] *nm* campus ■ **sur le ~** on campus.

camus, e [kamy, yz] *adj* [nez] pug ■ [personne] pug-nosed.

Canada [kanada] *npr m* : **le ~** Canada ■ **au ~** in Canada.

Canadair® [kanadɛr] *nm* fire-fighting plane, tanker plane *US*.

canadianisme [kanadjanism] *nm* Canadianism.

canadien, enne [kanadjɛ̃, ɛn] *adj* Canadian.
◆ **Canadien, enne** *nm, f* Canadian.
◆ **canadienne** *nf* **1.** [tente] (ridge) tent **2.** [vêtement] fur-lined jacket **3.** [pirogue] (Canadian) canoe.

canaille [kanaj] <> *adj* **1.** [polisson] roguish **2.** [vulgaire] coarse, vulgar.
<> *nf* **1.** [crapule] scoundrel, crook **2.** [ton affectueux] : **petite ~!** you little devil *ou* rascal!

canaillerie [kanajri] *nf litt* **1.** [acte] low trick **2.** [malhonnêteté] crookedness **3.** [vulgarité] coarseness, vulgarity.

canal, aux [kanal, o] *nm* **1.** NAUT canal ▶ **~ maritime** *ou* **de navigation** ship canal ■ **le ~ du Midi** *canal linking the Garonne estuary to the Mediterranean* ■ **le ~ de Mozambique** the Mozambique Channel ■ **le ~ de Panama/Suez** the Panama/Suez Canal **2.** TRAV PUB duct, channel ■ **~ d'amenée** feed *ou* feeder channel **3.** AGRIC canal ■ **~ de drainage/d'irrigation** drainage/irrigation canal **4.** AUDIO & INFORM channel ■ **Canal +** *ou* **Plus** *French pay TV channel* ■ *Québec* [chaîne] (TV) channel **5.** ANAT & BOT duct, canal ■ **~ auditif** auditory canal ■ **~ biliaire** bile duct ■ **~ lacrymal** tear duct, lacrymal canal *spéc* **6.** ÉCON : **~ de distribution** distribution channel **7.** ARCHIT flute.
◆ **par le canal de** *loc prép* through, via.

CANAL +

Canal + is a private television channel. It broadcasts programmes that have to be unscrambled using a special decoding unit which is supplied to subscribers. Some of its programmes can be seen without this device.

canalisation [kanalizasjɔ̃] *nf* **1.** TRAV PUB [conduit] pipe ■ **~s** [système] pipes, pipework, piping **2.** ÉLECTR wiring **3.** [travaux - d'une rivière] channelling **4.** [rassemblement - d'énergies, d'une foule, de pensées] channelling.

canaliser [3] [kanalize] *vt* **1.** TRAV PUB [cours d'eau] to channel ■ [région] to provide with a canal system **2.** [énergies, foule, pensées, ressources] to channel.

canapé [kanape] *nm* **1.** [siège] settee, sofa ■ **~ clic-clac** *sofa bed operated by a spring mechanism* ■ **~ convertible** bed settee, sofa bed **2.** CULIN [pour cocktail] canapé ■ **caviar sur ~** canapé of caviar ‖ [pain frit] canapé, croûton *(spread with forcemeat, served with certain meats)*.

canapé-lit [kanapeli] (*pl* **canapés-lits**) *nm* bed settee, sofa bed.

canaque [kanak] *adj* Kanak.
◆ **Canaque** *nmf* Kanak.

canard [kanar] *nm* **1.** ZOOL duck ■ **~ mâle** drake ■ **~ sauvage** wild duck ■ **~ boiteux** *fig* lame duck **2.** CULIN duck ■ **~ laqué** Peking duck ■ **~ à l'orange** duck in orange sauce, duck à l'orange **3.** [terme affectueux] : **mon petit ~** sweetie, sweetie-pie **4.** *fam* [journal] paper, rag ■ **le Canard enchaîné** PRESSE *satirical French weekly newspaper* **5.** [informations] rumour **6.** [couac] false note ■ **faire un ~** to hit a false note, to go off key **7.** *fam* [sucre - au café] sugar lump dipped in coffee ; [- à l'eau-de-vie] sugar lump dipped in eau-de-vie ; [- au rhum] sugar lump dipped in rum **8.** MÉD [bol] feeding cup.

canardeau, x [kanardo] *nm* duckling.

canarder [3] [kanarde] <> *vt* [avec une arme à feu] to snipe at *(insép)*, to take potshots at *(insép)* ■ [avec des projectiles] to pelt ■ **se faire ~** [au fusil] to be sniped at.
<> *vi fam* [faire des fausses notes] to sing off key ■ [faire une fausse note] to hit a false note, to go off key.

canari [kanari] <> *nm* canary.
<> *adj inv* canary-yellow.

Canaries [kanari] *npr fpl* : **les (îles) ~** the Canary Islands, the Canaries ■ **aux ~** in the Canaries, *voir aussi* **île**.

canasson△ [kanasɔ̃] *nm* horse, nag *péj.*

Canberra [kɑ̃bɛra] *npr* Canberra.

cancan [kɑ̃kɑ̃] *nm* **1.** [cri du canard] quack **2.** [danse] (French) cancan **3.** [bavardage] piece of gossip ■ **des ~s** gossip.

cancaner [3] [kɑ̃kane] *vi* **1.** ZOOL to quack **2.** [médire] to gossip.

cancanier, ère [kɑ̃kanje, ɛr] <> *adj* gossipy.
<> *nm, f* gossip.

cancer [kɑ̃sɛr] *nm* **1.** MÉD cancer ■ **avoir un ~** to have cancer ■ **~ du foie/de la peau** liver/skin cancer **2.** [fléau] cancer, canker.

Cancer [kɑ̃sɛr] *npr m* **1.** ASTRON Cancer **2.** ASTROL Cancer ■ **être ~** to be Cancer *ou* a Cancerian.

cancéreux, euse [kɑ̃serø, øz] ◇ *adj* [cellule, tumeur] malignant, cancerous ■ [malade] cancer *(modif)*.
◇ *nm, f* cancer victim *ou* sufferer.

cancérigène [kɑ̃seriʒɛn] *adj* carcinogenic.

cancériser [3] [kɑ̃serize] ◆ **se cancériser** *vpi* to become cancerous *ou* malignant.

cancérogène [kɑ̃serɔʒɛn] = **cancérigène**.

cancérologie [kɑ̃serɔlɔʒi] *nf* cancerology.

cancérologue [kɑ̃serɔlɔg] *nmf* cancerologist.

cancoillotte [kɑ̃kwajɔt] *nf* Cancoillotte *(strong-tasting soft cheese, from the Franche-Comté region)*.

cancre [kɑ̃kr] *nm* dunce.

cancrelat [kɑ̃krəla] *nm* cockroach.

candélabre [kɑ̃delabr] *nm* **1.** [flambeau] candelabra **2.** [colonne ornementée] ornate column **3.** [réverbère] street lamp.

candeur [kɑ̃dœr] *nf* ingenuousness, naivety.

candi [kɑ̃di] *adj m* : **sucre ~** sugar candy, rock candy.

candida [kɑ̃dida] *nm* candida.

candidat, e [kɑ̃dida, at] *nm, f* **1.** POLIT candidate ■ **être ~ aux élections** to be a candidate in the elections, to stand *UK ou* to run in the elections ■ **être ~ à la présidence** to run for president, to stand for president *UK* **2.** [à un examen, à une activité] candidate ■ [à un emploi] applicant, candidate ■ **les ~s à l'examen d'entrée** entrance examination candidates ■ **être ~ à un poste** to be a candidate for a post ■ **se porter ~ à un poste** to apply for a post.

candidature [kɑ̃didatyr] *nf* **1.** POLIT candidature, candidacy ■ **poser sa ~** to stand *UK*, to declare o.s. a candidate ■ **retirer sa ~** to stand down ▶ **~ multiple** standing *UK ou* running for election in several constituencies ■ **~ officielle** standing *UK ou* running as official candidate **2.** [pour un emploi] application ■ **poser sa ~ (à)** to apply (for) ▶ **~ spontanée** prospective application.

candide [kɑ̃did] *adj* ingenuous, naive.

candidose [kɑ̃didoz] *nf* candidiasis.

cane [kan] *nf* (female) duck.

Canebière [kanbjɛr] *npr f* : **la ~** *large avenue in Marseilles.*

LA CANEBIÈRE

This name is sometimes used to refer to the city of Marseilles itself.

caner [3] △ [kane] *vi* **1.** [de peur] to chicken out **2.** [mourir] to kick the bucket.

caneton [kantɔ̃] *nm* ZOOL duckling.

canette [kanɛt] *nf* **1.** ZOOL duckling **2.** [bouteille] (fliptop) bottle **3.** [boîte] can ■ **~ (de bière)** bottle (of beer) **4.** [bobine] spool.

canevas [kanva] *nm* **1.** [d'un roman, d'un exposé] framework **2.** TEXT canvas **3.** [d'une carte] graticule.

caniche [kaniʃ] *nm* **1.** ZOOL poodle **2.** *péj* [personne] lapdog, poodle.

caniculaire [kanikylɛr] *adj* scorching, blistering.

canicule [kanikyl] *nf* **1.** [grande chaleur] scorching heat ■ **la ~** [en plein été] the midsummer heat ■ **quelle ~!** what a scorcher! **2.** ANTIQ caniculars, canicular days.

canif [kanif] *nm* penknife, pocketknife.

canin[1], e [kanɛ̃, in] *adj* canine ■ **exposition ~e** dog show.

canine[2] [kanin] *nf* canine tooth.

canisse [kanis] = **cannisse**.

caniveau, x [kanivo] *nm* **1.** [le long du trottoir] gutter **2.** [conduit] gutter, drainage channel.

cannabis [kanabis] *nm* [drogue, chanvre] cannabis.

cannage [kanaʒ] *nm* **1.** [activité] caning **2.** [produit] cane work.

canne [kan] *nf* **1.** [d'un élégant] cane ■ [d'un vieillard] walking-stick ▶ **~ (anglaise)** crutch ■ **marcher avec des ~s** to be on crutches ■ **~ blanche** white stick *UK ou* cane *US* **2.** PÊCHE : **~ à pêche** fishing-rod **3.** BOT : **~ à sucre** sugar cane **4.** [rotin] cane *(U)*.
◆ **cannes**△ *nfpl* [jambes] legs, pins ■ SPORT ski-poles, poles.

canné, e [kane] *adj* **1.** [en rotin] cane *(modif)* **2.** △ [mort] dead as a doornail.

canne-béquille [kanbekij] (*pl* **cannes-béquilles**) *nf* crutch.

canneberge [kanbɛrʒ] *nf* cranberry.

cannelé, e [kanle] *adj* **1.** [orné de cannelures] fluted **2.** OPT fluted **3.** [à gouttière] grooved.

canneler [24] [kanle] *vt* to flute.

cannelle [kanɛl] ◇ *nf* **1.** CULIN cinnamon **2.** [robinet] tap, faucet *US*, spigot *US*.
◇ *adj inv* pale brown, cinnamon-coloured.
◆ **à la cannelle** *loc adj* cinnamon-flavoured.

cannelloni [kanelɔni] (*pl inv ou pl* **cannellonis**) *nm* cannelloni.

cannelure [kanlyr] *nf* **1.** [d'un vase, d'un pilier] flute, fluting **2.** [d'une vis, d'une pièce de monnaie] groove, grooving **3.** BOT & GÉOL stria, striation.

canner [3] [kane] ◇ *vt* [tabouret] to cane.
◇ *vi*△ = **caner** *(sens 2)*.

Cannes [kan] *npr* Cannes ■ **le festival de ~** the Cannes film festival.

cannette [kanɛt] = **canette** *(sens 2 & 3)*.

cannibale [kanibal] *adj & nmf pr & fig* cannibal.

cannibalisme [kanibalism] *nm* **1.** [anthropophagie] cannibalism **2.** [férocité] cannibalism, savagery.

cannisse [kanis] *nf* rush fence.

cannois, e [kanwa, az] *adj* from Cannes.
◆ **Cannois, e** *nm, f inhabitant of or person from Cannes.*

canoë [kanɔe] *nm* canoe ■ **faire du ~** to go canoeing.

canoéiste [kanɔeist] *nmf* canoeist.

canoë-kayak [kanɔekajak] (*pl* **canoës-kayaks**) *nm* : **faire du ~** to go canoeing.

canon [kanɔ̃] *nm* **1.** ARM [pièce - moderne] gun ; [- ancienne] cannon ■ [tube d'une arme à feu] barrel ■ **à ~ double** double-barrelled ■ **à ~ scié** sawn-off *UK*, sawed-off *US* ■ **~ mitrailleur** heavy machine-gun **2.** ÉLECTRON : **~ électronique** *ou* **à électrons** electron gun **3.** AGRIC : **~ arroseur** irrigation cannon **4.** LOISIRS & SPORT : **~ à neige** snow-making machine **5.** [de clé, de serrure] barrel **6.** MUS canon ■ **~ à trois voix** canon for three voices ■ **chanter en ~** to sing a *ou* in canon **7.** ART canon **8.** *sout* [modèle] model, canon *sout* **9.** RELIG canon ■ *(comme adj m)* **droit ~** canonic law **10.** [de vin] glass (of wine) ■ [d'eau-de-vie] shot(of spirits).

cañon [kaɲɔn] *nm* canyon.

canonial, e, aux [kanɔnjal, o] *adj* RELIG **1.** [réglé par les canons] canonic, canonical **2.** [du chanoine] of a canon.

canonique [kanɔnik] ◇ *adj* **1.** [conforme aux règles] classic, canonic, canonical **2.** RELIG canonic, canonical **3.** MATH canonical.
◇ *nf* canon.

canonisation [kanɔnizasjɔ̃] *nf* canonization, canonizing.

canoniser [3] [kanɔnize] *vt* to canonize.

canonnade [kanɔnad] *nf* heavy gunfire, cannonade.

canonnier [kanɔnje] *nm* gunner.

canonnière [kanɔnjɛr] *nf* **1.** NAUT gunboat **2.** [meurtrière] loophole.

canopée [kanɔpe] *nf* ÉCOL canopy.

canot [kano] *nm* dinghy ▪ **~ automobile** motorboat ▪ **~ de pêche** fishing boat ▪ **~ pneumatique** pneumatic *ou* inflatable dinghy ▪ **~ de sauvetage** lifeboat.

canotage [kanɔtaʒ] *nm* boating.

canoter [3] [kanɔte] *vi* **1.** [se promener] to go boating **2.** [manœuvrer] to handle a boat.

canoteur, euse [kanɔtœr, øz] *nm, f* rower *(in a dinghy).*

canotier [kanɔtje] *nm* [chapeau] (straw) boater.

cantal [kɑ̃tal] *nm* Cantal cheese.

cantaloup [kɑ̃talu] *nm* cantaloup (melon).

cantate [kɑ̃tat] *nf* cantata.

cantatrice [kɑ̃tatris] *nf* [d'opéra] (opera) singer ▪ [de concert] (concert) singer ▪ **'la Cantatrice chauve'** ***Ionesco*** 'The Bald Primadonna'.

cantilène [kɑ̃tilɛn] *nf* cantilena.

cantine [kɑ̃tin] *nf* **1.** [dans une école] dining hall, canteen ▪ [dans une entreprise] canteen ▪ **les élèves qui mangent à la ~** pupils who have school meals *ou* school dinners **2.** [malle] (tin) trunk.

cantique [kɑ̃tik] *nm* canticle ▪ **le Cantique des ~s** The Song of Songs, The Song of Solomon.

canton [kɑ̃tɔ̃] *nm* **1.** [en France] division of an arrondissement, canton ▪ [en Suisse] canton ▪ [au Luxembourg] administrative unit, canton ▪ [au Canada] township **2.** RAIL section **3.** ARCHIT canton **4.** HÉRALD canton.

CANTON

This administrative unit in the French system of local government is administered by the local members of the *Conseil général*. There are between 11 and 70 *cantons* in each *département*. Each *canton* is made up of several *communes*.
Switzerland is a confederation of 23 districts known as *cantons*, three of which are themselves divided into *demi-cantons*. Although they are to a large extent self-governing, the federal government reserves control over certain areas such as foreign policy, the treasury, customs and the postal service.

cantonade [kɑ̃tɔnad] ◆ **à la cantonade** *loc adv* [sans interlocuteur précis] to all present, to the company at large ▪ **crier qqch à la ~** to call *ou* to shout sthg (out).

cantonais, e [kɑ̃tɔnɛ, ɛz] *adj* **1.** CULIN [cuisine] Cantonese ▪ **riz ~** (special) fried rice **2.** GÉOGR Cantonese.

cantonal, e, aux [kɑ̃tɔnal, o] *adj* local.
◆ **cantonales** *nfpl election held every six years for the 'conseil général',* ≃ local elections.

cantonnement [kɑ̃tɔnmɑ̃] *nm* **1.** [à une tâche, à un lieu] confinement, confining *(U)* **2.** MIL [lieu - gén] quarters ; [- chez l'habitant] billet **3.** MIL [action - gén] stationing ; [- chez l'habitant] billeting.

cantonner [3] [kɑ̃tɔne] <> *vt* **1.** [isoler] : **~ qqn dans un lieu** to confine sb to a place **2.** *fig* **~ qqch à** *ou* **dans** [activité, explication] to limit *ou* to confine sthg to **3.** MIL to billet ▪ **~ un soldat chez qqn** to billet a soldier on sb.
<> *vi* to be billeted ▪ **~ chez qqn** to be billeted on sb.
◆ **se cantonner à, se cantonner dans** *vp+prép* **1.** [s'enfermer] : **se ~ dans** [lieu] to confine o.s. to ▪ **il se cantonnait dans sa solitude** he took refuge in solitude **2.** [être limité] : **se ~ à** *ou* **dans** to be confined *ou* limited *ou* restricted to **3.** [se restreindre] : **se ~ à** *ou* **dans** [activité, explication] to confine *ou* to limit o.s. to.

cantonnier [kɑ̃tɔnje] *nm* **1.** [sur une route] roadman, road mender **2.** RAIL platelayer *UK*, trackman *US*.

Cantorbéry [kɑ̃tɔrberi] *npr* Canterbury.

canular [kanylar] *nm* **1.** [action] practical joke, hoax ▪ **faire un ~ à qqn** to play a hoax on sb **2.** [parole] hoax.

canule [kanyl] *nf* cannula.

canut, use [kany, yz] *nm, f* silk weaver *ou* worker *(in Lyons).*

canyon [kaɲɔn] = cañon.

CAO (*abr de* **conception assistée par ordinateur**) *nf* CAD.

caoutchouc [kautʃu] *nm* **1.** BOT (natural *ou* India) rubber **2.** CHIM (synthetic) rubber ▪ **~ Mousse®** foam rubber **3.** *fam* [élastique] rubber *ou* elastic band **4.** [soulier] galosh **5.** [ficus] rubber plant.
◆ **de caoutchouc, en caoutchouc** *loc adj* rubber *(modif).*

caoutchoutage [kautʃutaʒ] *nm* **1.** [processus] coating with rubber, rubberizing **2.** [enduit] rubberized coating.

caoutchouter [3] [kautʃute] *vt* to cover *ou* to overlay with rubber, to rubberize.

caoutchouteux, euse [kautʃutø, øz] *adj* [viande] rubbery, chewy ▪ [fromage] rubbery.

cap [kap] *nm* **1.** GÉOGR cape, headland, promontory ▪ **doubler** *ou* **passer un ~** to round a cape **2.** AÉRON, AUTO & NAUT course ▪ **~ au vent** head on to the wind ▪ **changer de** *ou* **le ~** to alter one's *ou* to change course ▪ **mettre le ~ sur** NAUT to steer *ou* to head for ; AUTO to head for ▪ **suivre un ~** to steer a course **3.** [étape] milestone, hurdle ▪ **passer** *ou* **franchir le ~ de** [dans une situation difficile] to get over, to come through ; [dans une gradation, des statistiques] to pass the mark of ▪ **il a passé le ~ de la cinquantaine** he's into his fifties ▪ **l'adolescence est un ~ difficile à passer** adolescence is a difficult time to live through ▪ **la revue a dépassé le ~ des deux mille lecteurs** the readership of the magazine has passed the two thousand mark.

CAP

le cap Blanc Cap Blanc ;
le cap Bon Cap Bon ;
le cap de Bonne-Espérance the Cape of Good Hope ;
cap Canaveral Cape Canaveral ;
le cap Horn Cape Horn ;
le cap Nord North Cape.

Cap [kap] *npr* : **Le ~** [ville] Cape Town ; [province] Cape Province ▪ **au ~** in Cape Town.

Cap. (*abr écrite de* **capitaine**) Capt.

CAP *nm* **1.** (*abr de* **certificat d'aptitude professionnelle**) *vocational training certificate (taken at secondary school),* ≃ City and Guilds examination *UK* **2.** (*abr de* **certificat d'aptitude pédagogique**) teaching diploma.

capable [kapabl] *adj* **1.** [compétent] capable, competent, able **2.** DR competent **3.** [résistant] : **être ~ de** [physiquement] to be able to, to be capable of ; [psychologiquement] to be capable of ▪ **~ de tout** capable of (doing) anything ▪ **il est ~ de nous oublier!** I wouldn't put it past him to forget us!

capacitaire [kapasitɛr] *nmf* **1.** [diplômé] *holder of the "capacité en droit" qualification* **2.** [étudiant] *student preparing for the "capacité en droit" examination.*

capacité [kapasite] *nf* **1.** [aptitude] ability, capability ▪ **avoir la ~ de faire qqch** to have the ability to do sthg, to be capable of doing sthg ▪ **avoir une grande ~ de travail** to be capable of *ou* to have a capacity for hard work **2.** [d'un récipient, d'une salle, d'un véhicule] capacity ▪ **sac d'une grande ~** roomy bag ➊ **~ vitale** *ou* **thoracique** ANAT & PHYSIOL vital capacity **3.** ÉLECTR capacitance **4.** INFORM & TÉLÉCOM capacity **5.** DR capacity ▪ **avoir ~ pour** to be (legally) entitled to ➊ **~ civile** civil capacity ▪ **~ électorale** (electoral) franchise **6.** [diplôme] : **~ en**

droit *law diploma leading to a law degree course* **7.** ÉCON : **~ de financement** financing capacity ▪ **~ productrice** maximum possible output *OU* capacity.
◆ **capacités** *nfpl* ability ▪ **~s intellectuelles** intellectual capacity.

caparaçonner [3] [kaparasɔne] *vt* **1.** [cheval] to caparison **2.** [protéger] to cover from top to bottom.
◆ **se caparaçonner** *vpi* to deck o.s. out, to bedeck o.s.

cape [kap] *nf* **1.** [pèlerine] cloak, cape **2.** [d'un cigare] wrapper, outer leaf **3.** [de torero] capa **4.** NAUT : **être à la ~** to lie to.
◆ **de cape et d'épée** *loc adj* cloak-and-dagger *(avant n)*.

capeline [kaplin] *nf* wide-brimmed hat, capeline.

capella [kapɛla] a capella.

CAPES, Capes [kapɛs] (*abr de* **certificat d'aptitude au professorat de l'enseignement du second degré**) *nm secondary school teaching certificate*, ≃ PGCE *UK*.

CAPES

Candidates who pass the competitive exam for the *CAPES* become *professeurs certifiés* and are entitled to teach in secondary schools.

capésien, enne [kapesjɛ̃, ɛn] *nm, f* **1.** [étudiant] student preparing to take the CAPES **2.** [diplômé] CAPES-holder.

Capet [kapɛ] *npr* : **Hugues ~** Hugues Capet.

CAPET, Capet [kapɛ] (*abr de* **certificat d'aptitude au professorat de l'enseignement technique**) *nm specialized teaching certificate*.

capharnaüm [kafarnaɔm] *nm* [chaos] shambles ▪ **leur maison est un vrai ~** their house is a real shambles.

Capharnaüm [kafarnaɔm] *npr* Capernaum.

cap-hornier [kapɔrnje] (*pl* **cap-horniers**) *nm* Cape Horner.

capillaire [kapilɛr] <> *adj* **1.** [relatif aux cheveux] hair *(modif)* **2.** [très fin - tube, vaisseau] capillary *(modif)*.
<> *nm* **1.** [vaisseau] capillary **2.** [tube] capillary (tube) **3.** BOT maidenhair (fern).

capillarité [kapilarite] *nf* PHYS capillarity, capillary action.
◆ **par capillarité** *loc adv* by *OU* through capillary action.

capilliculture [kapilikyltyr] *nf* hair care.

capitaine [kapitɛn] *nmf* **1.** NAUT [dans la marine marchande] captain, master ▪ [dans la navigation de plaisance] captain, skipper ▪ **oui, ~** yes, sir ◐ **~ de frégate** MIL commander ▪ **~ au long cours** master mariner ▪ **~ de port** ADMIN & NAUT harbour master ▪ **~ de vaisseau** MIL captain **2.** MIL [dans l'armée - de terre] captain ; [- de l'air] flight lieutenant *UK*, captain *US* ▪ *litt* leader of men, military commander ▪ **les ~s d'industrie** the captains of industry **3.** SPORT captain **4.** [des pompiers] chief fire officer *UK*, fire chief *US* **5.** ZOOL tread-fin.

capitainerie [kapitɛnri] *nf* harbour master's office.

capital[1], aux [kapital, o] *nm* **1.** FIN [avoir - personnel] capital *(U)* ; [- d'une société] capital *(U)*, assets ▪ **une société au ~ de 200 000 euros** a firm with assets of 200,000 euros ◐ **~ réel** *OU* **versé** paid-up capital ▪ **~ engagé** capital expenditure ▪ **~ d'exploitation** working capital ▪ **~ financier** finance capital ▪ **~ fixe** fixed *OU* capital assets ▪ **~ foncier** land ▪ **~ social** nominal capital ▪ **~ souscrit** subscribed capital ▪ **~ variable** ÉCON variable capital **2.** [compensation] : **~ décès** death benefit ▪ **~ départ** severance money *OU* pay **3.** [monde de l'argent, des capitalistes] : **le ~** capital ▪ **le grand ~** big business ▪ **'le Capital'** *Marx* 'Das Kapital' **4.** [accumulation] stock ▪ **notre ~ de confiance auprès des usagers** the stock of good-will we have built up among users ▪ **un ~ de connaissances** a fund of knowledge ▪ **le ~ culturel du pays** the nation's cultural wealth ▪ **n'entamez pas votre ~ santé** don't overtax your health.
◆ **capitaux** *nmpl* [valeurs disponibles] capital ▪ **circulation des capitaux** circulation of capital ▪ **fuite des capitaux** flight of capital ◐ **capitaux flottants** floating capital.

capital[2], e, aux [kapital, o] *adj* **1.** [detail] vital ▪ [question, aide] fundamental, crucial, vital **2.** [œuvre, projet] major **3.** [lettre - imprimée] capital ; [- manuscrite] (block) capital **4.** DR capital ▪ **la peine ~e** capital punishment, the death penalty.
◆ **capitale** *nf* **1.** POLIT & ADMIN capital (city) ▪ **la ~e** [Paris] the capital, Paris ◐ **~e régionale** regional capital **2.** [centre] : **la ~e de la mode** the capital of fashion **3.** IMPR capital (letter).
◆ **en capitales** *loc adv* IMPR in capitals, in block letters ▪ **écrivez votre nom en ~es (d'imprimerie)** write your name in block capitals, print your name.

capitalisation [kapitalizasjɔ̃] *nf* capitalization ▪ **~ boursière** capital stock.

capitaliser [3] [kapitalize] *vt* **1.** FIN [capital] to capitalize ▪ [intérêts] to add ▪ [revenu] to turn into capital ▪ **une fois que les intérêts ont été capitalisés** once the accrued interest has been calculated **2.** [amasser - argent] to save up *(sép)*, to accumulate **3.** [accumuler] to accumulate ▪ **~ des heures supplémentaires** to accrue *OU* to accumulate overtime ▪ **~ des connaissances** to accumulate knowledge.
◆ **capitaliser sur** *v+prép* to cash in on, to capitalize on.

capitalisme [kapitalism] *nm* capitalism.

capitaliste [kapitalist] <> *adj* capitalist, capitalistic.
<> *nmf* capitalist.

capital-risque [kapitalrisk] *nm* venture *OU* risk capital.

capital-risqueur (*pl* **capital-risqueurs**) [kapitalriskœr] *nm* venture capitalist.

capiteux, euse [kapitø, øz] *adj* **1.** [fort - alcool, senteur] heady **2.** [excitant - charme, blonde] sensuous.

Capitole [kapitɔl] *npr m* **1.** [à Toulouse] : **le ~** *nickname for the town of Toulouse* **2.** [à Rome] : **le ~** the Capitol **3.** [à Washington] : **le ~** Capitol Hill, the Capitol.

capiton [kapitɔ̃] *nm* **1.** [matériau] padding **2.** [section rembourrée] boss, padded section.

capitonnage [kapitɔnaʒ] *nm* padding.

capitonner [3] [kapitɔne] *vt* to pad.

capitulation [kapitylasjɔ̃] *nf* **1.** MIL [action] surrender, capitulation ▪ [traité] capitulation **2.** [fait de céder] surrendering.

capituler [3] [kapityle] *vi* **1.** MIL to surrender, to capitulate **2.** [céder] to surrender, to give in.

caporal, e, aux [kapɔral, o] <> *nm, f* **1.** [dans l'armée de terre] lance corporal *UK*, private first class *US* **2.** [dans l'armée de l'air] senior aircraftman (*f* aircraftwoman) *UK*, airman (*f* airwoman) first class *US*.
<> *nm*[tabac] Caporal tobacco.

caporal-chef, caporale-chef [kapɔralʃɛf] (*mpl* **caporaux-chefs** [kapɔroʃɛf], *fpl* **caporales-chefs**) *nm* corporal.

capot [kapo] <> *nm* **1.** AUTO bonnet *UK*, hood *US* **2.** NAUT [tôle] cover ▪ [ouverture] companion hatchway **3.** [d'une machine] hood.
<> *adj inv* CARTES : **être ~** to make no tricks at all.

capote [kapɔt] *nf* **1.** *fam* [préservatif] condom ▪ **~ anglaise** *vieilli* French letter *UK*, condom **2.** [d'une voiture] hood *UK*, top *US* **3.** [manteau] greatcoat **4.** [chapeau] bonnet.

capoter [3] [kapɔte] <> *vt* to fit with a hood.
<> *vi* **1.** [voiture] to overturn, to roll over ▪ [bateau] to turn turtle **2.** *fam* [projet] to fall through, to collapse ▪ [tractation] to fall through ▪ **il a tout fait ~** he messed everything up.

cappuccino [kaputʃino] *nm* cappuccino.

câpre [kapr] *nf* caper.

caprice [kapris] *nm* **1.** [fantaisie] whim, passing fancy ▪ **rien n'est réfléchi, il n'agit que par ~** he doesn't think things through, he just acts on impulse **2.** [colère] tantrum ▪ **faire des ~s** to throw tantrums ▪ **elle n'a pas mal, c'est un ~** she's not in pain, she's just being awkward *OU* difficult **3.** [irrégularité] : **c'est un véritable ~ de la nature** it's a real freak of nature **4.** [engouement] (sudden) infatuation **5.** MUS capriccio, caprice.

capricieusement [kaprisjøzmɑ̃] *adv* capriciously.

capricieux, euse [kaprisjø, øz] *adj* **1.** [coléreux] temperamental ■ **un enfant ~** an awkward child **2.** [fantaisiste] capricious, fickle **3.** [peu fiable - machine, véhicule] unreliable, temperamental ; [- saison, temps] unpredictable.

capricorne [kaprikɔrn] *nm* ZOOL capricorn beetle.

Capricorne [kaprikɔrn] *npr m* **1.** ASTRON Capricorn **2.** ASTROL Capricorn ■ **être ~** to be (a) Capricorn.

câprier [kaprije] *nm* caper (plant).

caprin, e [kaprɛ̃, in] *adj* goat *(modif)*, caprine *spéc.*
◆ **caprin** *nm* member of the goat family.

capsule [kapsyl] *nf* **1.** [d'un flacon] top, cap **2.** ASTRON : **~ (spatiale)** (space) capsule **3.** ARM cap, primer **4.** PHARM capsule **5.** BOT capsule **6.** ANAT capsule.

capsuler [3] [kapsyle] *vt* to put a cap *ou* top on.

captage [kaptaʒ] *nm* **1.** AUDIO & TÉLÉCOM picking up, receiving **2.** PHYS harnessing **3.** RAIL picking up (of current) **4.** ÉCOL arresting.

captateur, trice [kaptatœr, tris] *nm, f* inveigler.

captation [kaptasjɔ̃] *nf* **1.** DR inveiglement **2.** PHYS harnessing.

capter [3] [kapte] *vt* **1.** [attention, intérêt] to capture **2.** PHYS to harness **3.** ÉCOL to arrest **4.** AUDIO & TÉLÉCOM to pick up *(insép)*, to receive **5.** DR to inveigle.

capteur [kaptœr] *nm* **1.** ÉCOL : **~ (solaire)** solar panel **2.** [pour mesurer] sensor ■ [pour commander] probe.

captieux, euse [kapsjø, øz] *adj* specious *sout*, misleading.

captif, ive [kaptif, iv] ◇ *adj* **1.** COMM [marché] captive **2.** [emprisonné] captive.
◇ *nm, f litt* captive.

captivant, e [kaptivɑ̃, ɑ̃t] *adj* captivating, riveting, enthralling.

captiver [3] [kaptive] *vt* to captivate, to rivet.

captivité [kaptivite] *nf* captivity ■ **garder un animal en ~** to keep an animal in captivity.

capture [kaptyr] *nf* **1.** [de biens] seizure, seizing, confiscation ■ [d'un navire, d'un tank] capture **2.** [arrestation] capture ■ **après sa ~, il a déclaré...** after he was captured *ou* caught, he said... **3.** CHASSE & PÊCHE catching **4.** [biens ou animaux] catch, haul **5.** GÉOGR & PHYS capture **6.** [informatique] : **~ d'écran** [image] screenshot ; [action] screen capture.

capturer [3] [kaptyre] *vt* **1.** [faire prisonnier] to capture, to catch **2.** CHASSE & PÊCHE to catch **3.** [navire, tank] to capture.

capuche [kapyʃ] *nf* hood.

capuchon [kapyʃɔ̃] *nm* **1.** [vêtement - bonnet] hood ; [- manteau] hooded coat **2.** [d'un stylo] cap, top ■ [d'un dentifrice] top **3.** [d'une cheminée] cowl **4.** ANAT & ZOOL hood.
◆ **à capuchon** *loc adj* hooded.

capucin [kapysɛ̃] *nm* **1.** RELIG Capuchin (Friar) **2.** ZOOL capuchin (monkey) **3.** CHASSE hare.

capucine [kapysin] ◇ *nf* **1.** BOT nasturtium **2.** [danse] (children's) round **3.** RELIG Capuchin nun.
◇ *adj inv* orangey-red.

Cap-Vert [kapvɛr] *npr m* : **le ~** Cape Verde.

caquet [kakɛ] *nm* **1.** [gloussement] cackle, cackling **2.** *fam* [bavardage] yakking ■ **il a un de ces ~s!** he yaks on and on! ▶ **rabattre** *ou* **rabaisser le ~ à qqn** to take sb down a peg or two, to put sb in his/her place.

caquetage [kaktaʒ] *nm* [futile] prattle ■ [indiscret] gossip.

caqueter [27] [kakte] *vi* **1.** [poule] to cackle **2.** [tenir des propos - futiles] to prattle (on) ; [- indiscrets] to gossip.

car¹ [kar] (*abr de* **autocar**) *nm* bus, coach ■ **~ de police** police van ■ **~ de ramassage (scolaire)** school bus.

car² [kar] *conj* because, for *sout* ■ **il est efficace, ~ très bien secondé** he is efficient because he has very good back-up ■ **~ enfin, à quoi vous attendiez-vous?** I mean, what did you expect?

carabin [karabɛ̃] *nm fam* medic.

carabine [karabin] *nf* rifle ■ **~ à air comprimé** air rifle *ou* gun.

carabiné, e [karabine] *adj fam* [note à payer, addition] stiff, steep ■ [rhume] filthy, stinking ■ [migraine] blinding ■ **une grippe ~e** a dreadful dose of the flu.

carabinier [karabinje] *nm* **1.** [en Italie] carabiniere, policeman **2.** [en Espagne] carabinero, customs officer **3.** HIST carabineer, carabinier.

Carabosse [karabɔs] *npr* ▷ **fée.**

Caracas [karakas] *npr* Caracas.

caraco [karako] *nm* camisole.

caracoler [3] [karakɔle] *vi* **1.** [sautiller] to skip about, to gambol **2.** ÉQUIT to caracole.

caractère [karaktɛr] *nm* **1.** [nature] nature ■ **le ~ religieux de la cérémonie** the religious nature of the ceremony ■ **pour donner un ~ d'authenticité à son œuvre** to give his work a stamp of authenticity ■ **à ~ officiel** of an official nature
2. [tempérament] character, nature ■ **avoir un ~ passionné** to have a passionate nature, to be passionate ■ **ce n'est pas dans son ~ d'être agressif** it's not in character for him to be *ou* it's not in his nature to be aggressive ■ **quel ~!** what a temper! ■ **avoir bon ~** to be good-natured ■ **avoir mauvais ~** to be bad-tempered ■ **avoir un ~ de chien** *fam* *ou* **de cochon** *fam* to have a foul temper
3. [volonté, courage] character ■ **avoir du ~** to have character ■ **une femme de ~** a woman of character ■ **elle manque de ~** she's not very strong-willed
4. [trait] characteristic, feature, trait ■ **tous les ~s d'une crise économique** all the characteristics of an economic crisis
5. [originalité] character ■ **appartement/maison de ~** flat/house with character ■ **sans aucun ~** characterless
6. BIOL characteristic ■ **~ acquis/héréditaire** acquired/hereditary characteristic *ou* trait
7. IMPR & INFORM character ■ **le choix des ~s** the choice of type ▶ **en gros/petits ~s** in large/small print ■ **~s gras : en ~s gras** in bold (type) ■ **~s d'imprimerie** block letters.

caractériel, elle [karakterjɛl] ◇ *adj* **1.** PSYCHOL [adolescent] maladjusted, (emotionally) disturbed **2.** [d'humeur changeante] moody **3.** [du caractère] character *(modif)*.
◇ *nm, f* [enfant] problem child ■ [adulte] maladjusted person.

caractérisation [karakterizasjɔ̃] *nf* characterization.

caractérisé, e [karakterize] *adj* [méchanceté] blatant ■ [indifférence] pointed.

caractériser [3] [karakterize] *vt* **1.** [constituer le caractère de] to characterize ■ **avec la générosité qui le caractérise** with characteristic generosity **2.** [définir] to characterize, to define.
◆ **se caractériser par** *vp+prép* to be characterized by.

caractéristique [karakteristik] ◇ *adj* characteristic, typical ■ **c'est ~ de sa façon d'agir** it's typical of his way of doing things.
◇ *nf* **1.** [trait] characteristic, (distinguishing) feature *ou* trait **2.** MATH characteristic.

caractérologie [karakterɔlɔʒi] *nf* characterology.

carafe [karaf] *nf* **1.** [récipient - ordinaire] carafe ; [- travaillé] decanter **2.** [contenu] jugful ■ [de vin] carafe **3.** *fam* [tête] nut **4.** *loc* **rester** *ou* **tomber en ~** [véhicule] to break down ; [voyageur] to be stranded.

carafon [karafɔ̃] *nm* **1.** [récipient - ordinaire] small jug *ou* carafe ; [- travaillé] small decanter **2.** [contenu] (small) jugful ■ [de vin] small carafe **3.** *fam* [tête] nut ■ **il n'a rien dans le ~!** he's got no brains!

caraïbe [karaib] *adj* Caribbean.

Caraïbe [karaib] *npr f* : **la ~** the Caribbean ■ **la mer ~** the Caribbean Sea.

Caraïbes [karaib] *npr fpl* : **les (îles) ~** the Caribbean, the West Indies ▪ **la mer des ~** the Caribbean (Sea), *voir aussi* **île**, *voir aussi* **mer**.

carambolage [karɑ̃bɔlaʒ] *nm* **1.** [de voitures] pileup, multiple crash **2.** [au billard] cannon.

caramboler [3] [karɑ̃bɔle] ◇ *vi* to cannon.
◇ *vt* to crash into ▪ **11 voitures carambolées** a pileup of 11 cars.

carambouillage [karɑ̃bujaʒ] *nm*, **carambouille** [karɑ̃buj] *nf* fraudulent selling of goods bought on credit.

caramel [karamɛl] ◇ *nm* **1.** [pour napper] caramel **2.** [bonbon - dur] toffee, caramel ; [- mou] toffee, fudge.
◇ *adj inv* caramel colour.

caraméliser [3] [karamelize] *vt* **1.** [mets] to coat with caramel ▪ [boisson, glace] to flavour with caramel **2.** [sucre] to caramelize.
◆ **se caraméliser** *vpi* to caramelize.

carapace [karapas] *nf* **1.** ZOOL shell, carapace *spéc* **2.** *fig* (protective) shell.

carapater [3] [karapate] ◆ **se carapater** *vpi fam* to skedaddle, to scram, to make o.s. scarce.

carat [kara] *nm* [d'un métal, d'une pierre] carat ▪ **chaîne de 22 ~s** 22 carat (gold) chain.

Caravage [karavaʒ] *npr m* : **le ~** Caravaggio ▪ **un tableau du ~** a painting by Caravaggio.

caravanage [karavanaʒ] *nm* caravaning.

caravane [karavan] *nf* **1.** [véhicule - de vacancier] caravan *UK*, trailer *US* ; [- de nomade] caravan **2.** [convoi] caravan ▪ **~ publicitaire** following vehicles.

caravanier, ère [karavanje, ɛr] *nm, f* **1.** [conducteur] caravanner **2.** [vacancier] caravanner *UK*, camper *(in a trailer) US*.

caravaning [karavaniŋ] *nm* caravanning.

caravansérail [karavɑ̃seraj] *nm* caravanserai, caravansary.

caravelle [karavɛl] *nf* NAUT caravel.

Caravelle® [karavɛl] *nf* AÉRON Caravelle®.

carbonade [karbɔnad] *nf* carbonade, carbonnade.

carbonate [karbɔnat] *nm* carbonate.

carbone [karbɔn] *nm* **1.** [papier] (sheet of) carbon paper **2.** CHIM carbon ▪ **~ 14** carbon-14 ▪ **dater au ~ 14** to carbon-date, to date with carbon-14.

carboné, e [karbɔne] *adj* **1.** CHIM carbonaceous **2.** MINÉR carboniferous.

carbonique [karbɔnik] *adj* carbonic.

carboniser [3] [karbɔnize] *vt* **1.** [brûler - viande] to burn to a cinder ; [- édifice] to burn to the ground ▪ **des corps carbonisés** charred bodies **2.** [transformer en charbon] to carbonize, to turn into charcoal.

carbonnade [karbɔnad] = **carbonade**.

carburant [karbyrɑ̃] ◇ *adj m* : **mélange ~** mixture of air and petrol.
◇ *nm* fuel.

carburateur [karbyratœr] *nm* carburettor.

carburation [karbyrasjɔ̃] *nf* **1.** AUTO carburation **2.** MÉTALL carburization, carburizing.

carbure [karbyr] *nm* carbide.

carburé, e [karbyre] *adj* carburetted.

carburer [3] [karbyre] ◇ *vt* **1.** AUTO to carburate **2.** MÉTALL to carburize.
◇ *vi fam* **1.** [aller vite] : **fais tes valises, et que ça carbure!** pack your bags, and be quick about it! **2.** [travailler dur] to work flat out ▪ [réfléchir] : **ça carbure, ici!** brains are working overtime in here! **3.** [fonctionner] : **ça carbure?** how are things? ▪ **moi, je carbure au café** I can't do anything unless I have a coffee inside me.

carcan [karkɑ̃] *nm* **1.** HIST [collier] collar shackle ▪ **pris dans les règlements comme dans un ~** *fig* hemmed in by regulations **2.** [sujétion] yoke, shackles **3.** [pour bétail] yoke.

carcasse [karkas] *nf* **1.** [d'un animal] carcass **2.** *fam fig* **promener** *ou* **traîner sa (vieille) ~** to drag o.s. along **3.** [armature - d'un édifice] shell ; [- d'un meuble] carcass ; [- d'un véhicule] shell, body ; [- d'un parapluie] frame **4.** ÉLECTR yoke ring **5.** MÉTALL casing, frame **6.** [d'un pneu] carcass ▪ **~ radiale** radial-ply tyre.

carcéral, e, aux [karseral, o] *adj* prison *(modif)*.

carcinome [karsinom] *nm* carcinoma.

cardage [kardaʒ] *nm* carding.

cardan [kardɑ̃] *nm* : **(joint de) ~** universal joint.

carde [kard] *nf* edible part of a cardoon.

cardé [karde] *nm* **1.** [fil] carded yarn **2.** [étoffe] carded cloth.

carder [3] [karde] *vt* to card.

cardeur, euse [kardœr, øz] *nm, f* carder, carding operator.

cardiaque [kardjak] ◇ *adj* heart *(modif)*, cardiac ▪ **une maladie ~** a heart disease ▪ **elle est ~** she has a heart condition.
◇ *nmf* cardiac *ou* heart patient.

cardigan [kardigɑ̃] *nm* cardigan.

cardinal, e, aux [kardinal, o] *adj* **1.** ASTROL & MATH cardinal **2.** [essentiel] essential, fundamental ▪ **vertus ~es** cardinal virtues **3.** GÉOGR : **points cardinaux** points of the compass.
◆ **cardinal, aux** *nm* **1.** MATH cardinal number, cardinal **2.** RELIG cardinal **3.** ZOOL cardinal (grosbeak).

cardiogramme [kardjogram] *nm* cardiogram.

cardiographie [kardjografi] *nf* cardiography.

cardiologie [kardjolɔʒi] *nf* cardiology.

cardiologue [kardjolɔg] *nmf* heart specialist, cardiologist *spéc*.

cardiomyopathie [kardjomjɔpati] *nf* cardiomyopathy.

cardiopathie [kardjopati] *nf* heart disease, cardiopathy *spéc*.

cardio-pulmonaire [kardjopylmɔnɛr] (*pl* **cardio-pulmonaires**) *adj* cardio-pulmonary.

cardio-respiratoire [kardjorɛspiratwar] (*pl* **cardio-respiratoires**) *adj* cardiorespiratory ▪ **maladie ~** disease of the heart and respiratory system.

cardio-training [kardjotrɛniŋ] *nm inv* cardio-training, CV training.

cardio-vasculaire [kardjovaskylɛr] (*pl* **cardio-vasculaires**) *adj* cardiovascular.

cardon [kardɔ̃] *nm* cardoon.

carême [karɛm] *nm* **1.** RELIG : **le ~** [abstinence] fasting ; [époque] Lent ▪ **faire ~** to fast for *ou* to observe Lent ➤ **face** *ou* **figure de ~** sad *ou* long face **2.** [saison] dry season *(in the West Indies)*.

carénage [karenaʒ] *nm* **1.** NAUT careenage **2.** AÉRON & AUTO streamlined body.

carence [karɑ̃s] *nf* **1.** MÉD deficiency ▪ **~ en zinc** zinc deficiency ▪ **avoir une ~ alimentaire** to suffer from a nutritional deficiency **2.** [d'une administration, d'une œuvre, d'une méthode] shortcoming, failing **3.** PSYCHOL : **~ affective** emotional deprivation **4.** DR insolvency.

carencer [16] [karɑ̃se] *vt* to cause a nutritional deficiency in.

carène [karɛn] *nf* **1.** NAUT hull **2.** AÉRON & AUTO streamlined body **3.** BOT & ZOOL carina.

caréner [18] [karene] *vt* **1.** NAUT to careen **2.** AUTO & AÉRON to streamline.

carentiel, elle [karɑ̃sjɛl] *adj* deficiency-related.

caressant, e [karɛsɑ̃, ɑ̃t] *adj* **1.** [personne] affectionate, loving **2.** [voix, sourire] warm, caressing ▪ *litt* [vent] caressing.

caresse [karɛs] *nf* **1.** [attouchement] caress, stroke ▪ **faire des ~s à** [chat] to stroke ; [personne] to caress **2.** *litt* [d'un sourire] tenderness ▪ [du vent, du soleil] caress, kiss.

caresser [4] [karese] *vt* **1.** [toucher - affectueusement] to stroke ; [- sensuellement] to caress ▪ **~ un enfant** to pet a child ▪ **~ les cheveux de qqn** to stroke sb's hair ▪ **~ qqn des yeux** *OU* **du regard** to gaze lovingly at sb ▶ **il faut le ~ dans le sens du poil** don't rub him (up) the wrong way **2.** *litt* [effleurer - tissu, papier] to touch lightly **3.** [avoir, former] : **~ le dessein de faire** to be intent on doing ▪ **~ le rêve de faire qqch** to dream of doing sthg **4.** *fam* [battre] : **~ les oreilles à qqn** to clout sb round the ear.

car-ferry [karferi] (*pl* **car-ferries** [-ri]) *nm* ferry, car-ferry.

cargaison [kargɛzɔ̃] *nf* **1.** [marchandises] cargo, freight **2.** *fam* [quantité] : **une ~ de** a load of.

cargo [kargo] *nm* freighter.

cari [kari] *nm* **1.** [épice] curry powder **2.** [plat] curry.
◆ **au cari** *loc adj* : **poulet au ~** chicken curry, curried chicken.

cariatide [karjatid] = **caryatide**.

caribou [karibu] *nm Québec* caribou, reindeer.

caricatural, e, aux [karikatyral, o] *adj* **1.** [récit, explication] distorted **2.** [visage] grotesque **3.** [dessin, art] caricatural **4.** [exagéré] typical, caricature *(modif)*.

caricature [karikatyr] *nf* **1.** [dessin] caricature ▪ **~ politique** (political) cartoon **2.** [déformation] caricature **3.** [personne] : **c'est une vraie ~!** [physiquement] he looks grotesque! ; [dans son comportement] he's totally ridiculous!

caricaturer [3] [karikatyre] *vt* **1.** [dessiner] to caricature **2.** [déformer] to distort.

caricaturiste [karikatyrist] *nmf* caricaturist.

carie [kari] *nf* **1.** MÉD caries *spéc* ▪ **~ dentaire** tooth decay, dental caries *spéc* ▪ **elle n'a pas de ~s** she doesn't have amy bad teeth **2.** BOT [du blé] bunt, smut ▪ [des arbres] blight.

carié, e [karje] *adj* **1.** MÉD [dent] decayed, bad ▪ [os] carious **2.** [blé] smutty ▪ [arbre] blighted.

carier [9] [karje] *vt* to decay, to cause decay in.
◆ **se carier** *vpi* to decay.

carillon [karijɔ̃] *nm* **1.** [cloches] carillon **2.** [sonnerie - d'une horloge] chime ; [- d'entrée] chime **3.** [horloge] chiming clock **4.** MUS carillon.

carillonné, e [karijɔne] *adj* : **fête ~e** high festival.

carillonnement [karijɔnmɑ̃] *nm* [son] chiming.

carillonner [3] [karijɔne] ◇ *vi* **1.** [cloches] to ring, to chime **2.** [à la porte] to ring (the doorbell) loudly.
◇ *vt* **1.** *péj* [rumeur] to broadcast, to shout from the roof tops **2.** [festival] to announce with a peal of bells.

carillonneur, euse [karijɔnœr, øz] *nm, f* bell ringer.

carioca [karjɔka] *adj* from Rio de Janeiro, of Rio de Janeiro.
◆ **Carioca** *nmf* Cariocan, Carioca.

cariste [karist] *nmf* forklift truck driver *OU* operator.

caritatif, ive [karitatif, iv] *adj* charity *(modif)* ▪ **association caritative** charity.

carlingue [karlɛ̃g] *nf* **1.** AÉRON cabin **2.** NAUT keelson.

carmagnole [karmaɲɔl] *nf* MUS [vêtement] carmagnole.

carme [karm] *nm* Carmelite, White Friar.

carmel [karmɛl] *nm* **1.** [de carmélites] carmel, Carmelite convent ▪ [de carmes] carmel, Carmelite monastery **2.** [ordre] : **le ~** the Carmelite order.

carmélite [karmelit] *nf* Carmelite.

carmin [karmɛ̃] *nm* & *adj inv* crimson, carmine.

Carnac [karnak] *npr* **1.** [en Bretagne] Carnac ▪ **les alignements de ~** *lines of standing stones at Carnac* **2.** [en Égypte] Karnak.

carnage [karnaʒ] *nm* slaughter, carnage ▪ **à l'examen, ça a été le ~!** *fam fig* they went down like nine pins in the exam!

carnassier, ère [karnasje, ɛr] *adj* [animal] carnivorous ▪ [dent] carnassial.
◆ **carnassier** *nm* carnivore.
◆ **carnassière** *nf* **1.** [dent] carnassial **2.** [sac] gamebag.

carnation [karnasjɔ̃] *nf litt* [teint] complexion ▪ [en peinture] flesh tint.

carnaval [karnaval] *nm* **1.** [fête] carnival **2.** [mannequin] : **(Sa Majesté) Carnaval** King Carnival.

carnavalesque [karnavalɛsk] *adj* **1.** [de carnaval] of the carnival **2.** [burlesque] carnivalesque, carnival-like.

carne [karn] *nf* **1.** *fam* [viande] tough meat **2.** △ [terme d'injure] swine.

carné, e [karne] *adj* **1.** [en diététique] meat-based **2.** [rosé] flesh-toned, flesh-coloured.

carnet [karnɛ] *nm* **1.** [cahier] note-book **2.** [registre] : **~ d'adresses** address book ▪ **~ de bal** dance card ▪ **~ de bord** log book ▪ **~ de notes** school report *UK*, report card *US* ▪ **elle a eu un bon ~ (de notes)** she got a good report *UK OU* good grades *US* ▪ **~ de route** log book ▪ **~ de santé** child's health record **3.** [à feuilles détachables] : **~ de chèques** cheque book ▪ **~ à souches** counterfoil book ▪ **~ de tickets (de métro)** ten metro tickets ▪ **~ de timbres** book of stamps **4.** ÉCON : **~ de commandes** order book **5.** [rubrique] : **~ blanc** marriages column ▪ **~ mondain** court and social ▪ **~ rose** births column.

carnivore [karnivɔr] ◇ *adj* carnivorous.
◇ *nm* carnivore, meat-eater.

carnotset, carnotzet [karnotze] *nm Suisse* *room set aside for drinking with friends, usually in a cellar.*

Caroline [karɔlin] *npr f* : **(la) ~ du Nord** North Carolina ▪ **(la) ~ du Sud** South Carolina.

carolingien, enne [karɔlɛ̃ʒjɛ̃, ɛn] *adj* Carolingian, of Charlemagne.

carotène [karɔtɛn] *nm* carotene.

carotide [karɔtid] *nf* carotid.

carotte [karɔt] ◇ *nf* **1.** BOT carrot ▪ **les ~s sont cuites** *fam* the game's up **2.** *fam* [récompense] carrot ▪ **la ~ et le bâton** the carrot and the stick **3.** GÉOL & MIN core **4.** [tabac] plug **5.** [enseigne] tobacconist's sign.
◇ *adj inv* carroty *péj*, red, carrot-coloured.

carotter [3] △ [karɔte] *vt* [argent, objet] to nick *UK*, to pinch ▪ [permission] to wangle ▪ **~ qqch à qqn** to swindle *OU* to diddle sb out of sthg.

carotteur, euse [karɔtœr, øz], **carottier, ère** [karɔtje, ɛr] *nm, f* [escroc] crook.

caroube [karub] *nf* carob.

carpaccio [karpatʃjo] *nm* CULIN carpaccio.

Carpates [karpat] *npr fpl* : **les ~** the Carpathian Mountains *OU* Carpathians.

carpe [karp] ◇ *nf* carp.
◇ *nm* carpus.

carpette [karpɛt] *nf* **1.** [tapis] rug **2.** *fam péj* [personne] doormat, spineless individual ▪ **s'aplatir** *OU* **être (plat) comme une ~ devant qqn** to grovel in front of sb.

carquois [karkwa] *nm* quiver.

carrare [karar] *nm* Carrara marble.

carre [kar] *nf* **1.** SPORT [d'un ski, d'un patin à glace] edge ▪ **lâcher les ~s** to flatten the skis ▪ **reprendre de la ~** to go back on one's edges **2.** [d'une planche] crosscut **3.** [sur un pin] notch *(for extracting resin).*

carré, e [kare] *adj* **1.** [forme, planche] square ■ **avoir les épaules ~es** to be square-shouldered **2.** GÉOM & MATH square **3.** [sans détours] straight, straightforward ■ **être ~ en affaires** to have a forthright business manner **4.** NAUT [mât] square-rigged ■ [voile] square.
◆ **carré** *nm* **1.** [gén - GÉOM] square ■ **un petit ~ de ciel bleu** a little patch of blue sky ■ **~ blanc** *white square in the corner of the screen indicating that a television programme is not recommended for children* **2.** MATH square ■ **le ~ de six** six squared, the square of six ■ **élever un nombre au ~** to square a number **3.** HORT : **~ de choux** cabbage patch **4.** [vêtement] (square) scarf ■ **~Hermès®** *designer headscarf made by Hermès (a status symbol in France)* **5.** [coiffure] bob **6.** [viande] : **~ d'agneau/de mouton/de porc/de veau** loin of lamb/mutton/pork/veal **7.** JEUX [au poker] : **~ d'as** four aces **8.** MIL square **9.** NAUT wardroom **10.** ANAT quadrate muscle.
◆ **carrée** *nf fam* pad.

Carré [kare] *npr* : **virus de ~** canine distemper virus.

carreau, x [karo] *nm* **1.** [sur du papier] square ■ **papier à ~x** squared paper, graph paper ▮ [motif sur du tissu] check ■ **veste à ~x** check *ou* checked jacket ■ **draps à petits ~x** sheets with a small check design *ou* pattern **2.** [plaque de grès, de marbre] tile **3.** [sol] tiled floor ■ **se retrouver sur le ~** *fam* [par terre] to end up on the floor ; [pauvre] to wind up on Skid Row ■ **rester sur le ~** *fam* [être assommé] to be laid out ; [être tué] to be bumped off ; [échouer] to come a cropper *UK*, to take a spill *US* **4.** [vitre] window-pane ■ [fenêtre] window **5.** CARTES diamond **6.** *fam loc* **se tenir à ~ : tiens-toi à ~!** watch your step!
◆ **carreaux**△ *nmpl* [lunettes] specs.

carrefour [karfur] *nm* **1.** [de rues] crossroads *(sing)*, junction ■ **nous arrivons à un ~** *fig* we've come to a crossroads **2.** [point de rencontre] crossroads ■ **un ~ d'idées** a forum of ideas **3.** [rencontre] forum, symposium.

carrelage [karlaʒ] *nm* **1.** [carreaux] tiles, tiling ■ **poser un ~** to lay tiles *ou* a tiled floor **2.** [opération] tiling **3.** [sol] tiled floor.

carreler [24] [karle] *vt* [mur, salle de bains] to tile.

carrelet [karlɛ] *nm* **1.** ZOOL plaice **2.** [filet] square fishing net **3.** [aiguille] half-moon needle **4.** [règle] square ruler.

carreleur, euse [karlœr, øz] *nm, f* tiler.

carrelle *etc v* ▷ **carreler**.

carrément [karemɑ̃] *adv* **1.** [dire] straight out, bluntly ■ [agir] straight ■ **je vais le quitter! - ah, ~?** I'm going to leave him! - it's as serious as that, is it? **2.** *fam* [en intensif] pretty *(adv)*, downright ■ **on gagne ~ un mètre** you gain a whole metre ■ **c'est ~ du vol/de la corruption** it's daylight robbery/blatant corruption **3.** [poser] squarely, firmly.

carrer [3] [kare] ◆ **se carrer** *vpi* to settle, to ensconce o.s. *sout hum*.

carrier [karje] *nm* quarryman.

carrière [karjɛr] *nf* **1.** [d'extraction] quarry **2.** [profession] career ■ **la Carrière** [diplomatie] the diplomatic service **3.** [parcours professionnel] career ■ **faire ~ dans** to pursue a career in **4.** *litt* [de la vie, du soleil] course.
◆ **de carrière** *loc adj* [officier] regular ■ [diplomate] career *(modif)*.

carriérisme [karjerism] *nm* careerism.

carriériste [karjerist] *nmf* careerist, career-minded person.

carriole [karjɔl] *nf* **1.** [à deux roues] cart **2.** *Québec* car sleigh, carriole.

carrossable [karɔsabl] *adj* suitable for motor vehicles.

carrosse [karɔs] *nm* **1.** [véhicule] coach **2.** [panier] wine basket.

carrosser [3] [karɔse] *vt* [voiture] to fit a body to.

carrosserie [karɔsri] *nf* **1.** AUTO [structure] body ■ [habillage] bodywork **2.** [d'un appareil ménager] cover, case **3.** [métier] coachwork, coach-building.

carrossier [karɔsje] *nm* coachbuilder.

carrousel [karuzɛl] *nm* **1.** ÉQUIT carousel **2.** [de voitures, de personnes] merry-go-round **3.** [à valises] carousel **4.** AUDIO carousel.

carrure [karyr] *nf* **1.** [corps] build ■ **avoir une ~ d'athlète** to be built like an athlete **2.** [qualité] stature, calibre **3.** [vêtement] breadth across the shoulders.

carry [kari] = **cari**.

cartable [kartabl] *nm* [à bretelles] satchel ■ [à poignée] schoolbag.

carte [kart] *nf*

A.

1. [courrier] card ■ **~ d'anniversaire** birthday card ■ **~ d'invitation** invitation card ■ **~ de Noël** Christmas card ■ **~ postale** postcard ■ **~ de visite** [personnelle] visiting *UK ou* calling *US* card ; [professionnelle] business card ■ **~ de vœux** New Year greetings card
2. [de restaurant] menu ■ **la ~ des vins** the wine list ▮ [menu à prix non fixe] à la carte menu
3. [document officiel] card ■ **il a la ~ du parti écologiste** he's a card-carrying member of the green party ▶ **~ d'alimentation** *ou* **de rationnement** ration card ■ **~ d'abonnement** TRANSP season ticket *ou* pass ; MUS & THÉÂTRE season ticket ■ **~ d'adhérent** *ou* **de membre** membership card ■ **~ d'électeur** polling card *UK*, voter registration card *US* ■ **~ d'embarquement** boarding card ■ **~ d'étudiant** student card ■ **~ de famille nombreuse** discount card *(for families with at least three children)* ■ **~ de fidélité** loyalty card ■ **~ grise** car registration papers ■ **~ (nationale) d'identité** (national) identity card *ou* ID card ■ **~ (nationale) de priorité** *card giving priority in queues and on public transport* ■ **Carte Orange** season ticket *(on the Paris transport system)* ■ **~ de presse** presscard ■ **~ de séjour (temporaire)** (temporary) residence permit ■ **Carte Vermeil** *card entitling senior citizens to reduced rates in cinemas, on public transport etc* ■ **~ verte** green card *UK*, certificate of insurance *US* ■ **donner** *ou* **laisser ~ blanche à qqn** to give sb carte blanche *ou* a free hand
4. [moyen de paiement] : **Carte Bleue®** Visa Card® *(with which purchases are debited directly from the holder's current account)* ■ **~ de crédit** credit card *(to back up signatures on bills and to obtain cash from machines)* ■ **~ de paiement** credit card *(to effect automatic payment for goods and services)* ■ **~ de téléphone** *ou* **téléphonique** Phonecard® ■ **cabine à ~s** cardphone
5. INFORM (circuit) card *ou* board ■ **~ d'extension (mémoire)** add-in card ■ **~ graphique** graphics card ■ **~ magnétique** swipe card ■ **~ à mémoire** *ou* **à puce** smart card ■ **~ perforée** punch card

B.

GÉOGR & GÉOL map ■ ASTRON, MÉTÉOR & NAUT chart ■ **dresser une ~ de la région** to map (out) the area ▶ **~ du ciel** sky chart ■ **~ d'état-major** ≃ Ordnance Survey map *UK*, ≃ Geological Survey map *US* ■ **~ marine** nautical chart ■ **~ routière** road map ■ **~ topographique** contour map

C.

JEUX : **~ (à jouer)** (playing) card ■ **jeu de ~s** [activité] card game ; [paquet] pack of cards ■ **tirer** *ou* **faire** *fam* **les ~s à qqn** to read sb's cards ■ **se faire tirer les ~s** to have one's cards read ■ **jouons la ~ de l'honnêteté/la qualité** *fig* let's go for honesty/quality ▶ **~ maîtresse** *pr* master card ; *fig* master *ou* trump card ■ **montrer ses ~s** to show one's hand ■ **jouer ~s sur table** to lay one's cards on the table ■ **il n'a pas joué toutes ses ~s** *pr* he hasn't played his last card ; *fig* he still has a trick up his sleeve.
◆ **à la carte** ◇ *loc adj* **1.** [repas] à la carte **2.** [programme, investissement] customized ■ [horaire] flexible ■ **des séjours à la ~** tailor-made *ou* à la carte holidays.
◇ *loc adv* : **manger à la ~** to eat à la carte.

CARTE DE SÉJOUR

Foreign nationals living in France are required to carry this document. It is issued by their local *préfecture* as a certificate of residency.

cartel [kartɛl] *nm* **1.** ÉCON cartel **2.** POLIT coalition, cartel **3.** MIL cartel **4.** [pendule] (decorative) wall clock **5.** [plaque] name and title plaque *(on a painting, a statue)*.

carte-lettre [kartəlɛtr] (*pl* **cartes-lettres**) *nf* letter card.

carter [kartɛr] *nm* **1.** ÉLECTR case, casing **2.** AUTO : **~ d'engrenages** gearbox casing ■ **~ du moteur** crankcase ‖ [de vélo] chain guard.

carte-réponse [kartrepɔ̃s] (*pl* **cartes-réponse** *ou pl* **cartes-réponses**) *nf* reply card.

cartésianisme [kartezjanism] *nm* Cartesianism.

cartésien, enne [kartezjɛ̃, ɛn] *adj* & *nm, f* Cartesian.

Carthage [kartaʒ] *npr* Carthage.

carthaginois, e [kartaʒinwa, az] *adj* Carthaginian.
◆ **Carthaginois, e** *nm, f* Carthaginian.

cartilage [kartilaʒ] *nm* **1.** ANAT [substance] cartilage *(U)* **2.** [du poulet] piece of gristle.

cartilagineux, euse [kartilaʒinø, øz] *adj* **1.** ANAT cartilaginous **2.** [poisson] gristly.

cartographe [kartɔgraf] *nmf* cartographer.

cartographie [kartɔgrafi] *nf* cartography.

cartomancie [kartɔmɑ̃si] *nf* cartomancy, fortune-telling *(with cards)*.

cartomancien, enne [kartɔmɑ̃sjɛ̃, ɛn] *nm, f* fortune-teller *(with cards)*.

carton [kartɔ̃] *nm* **1.** [matière] cardboard **2.** [boîte - grande] cardboard box ; [- petite] carton ■ **~ à chapeaux** hatbox ■ **~ à chaussures** shoebox **3.** [contenu - d'une grande boîte] cardboard boxful ; [- d'une petite boîte] cartonful **4.** [rangement - pour dossiers] (box) file ; [- pour dessins] portfolio ■ **le projet est resté dans les ~s** *fig* the project never saw the light of day, the project was shelved **5.** ART sketch, cartoon **6.** GÉOGR insert map **7.** FOOTBALL : **~ jaune** yellow card ■ **~ rouge** red card **8.** *fam loc* **taper le ~** to play cards ■ **faire un ~** [au ball-trap] to take a pot-shot ; [réussir] to hit the jackpot ■ **faire un ~ sur qqn** to shoot sb down.
◆ **en carton** *loc adj* cardboard *(modif)*.

cartonnage [kartɔnaʒ] *nm* **1.** [reliure] boarding **2.** [boîte] cardboard box **3.** [empaquetage] cardboard packing **4.** [fabrication] cardboard industry.

cartonner [3] [kartɔne] ◇ *vt* [livre] to bind in boards.
◇ *vi fam* **1.** [réussir] to hit the jackpot **2.** *loc* **garé dans un couloir d'autobus, ça va ~!** he's parked in a bus lane, he's really going to catch it!

cartonneux, euse [kartɔnø, øz] *adj* cardboard-like.

carton-pâte [kartɔ̃pat] (*pl* **cartons-pâtes**) *nm* pasteboard.
◆ **de carton-pâte, en carton-pâte** *loc adj péj* [décor] cardboard *(modif)* ■ [personnage, intrigue] cardboard cut-out *(modif)*.

cartophilie [kartɔfili] *nf* picture postcard collecting.

cartothèque [kartɔtɛk] *nf* map library.

cartouche [kartuʃ] ◇ *nf* **1.** ARM [projectile, charge] cartridge **2.** COMM [recharge] cartridge ■ [emballage groupant plusieurs paquets] carton **3.** PHOTO cartridge, cassette, magazine **4.** ÉLECTR cartridge.
◇ *nm* **1.** ANTIQ & ART cartouche **2.** [sur un plan] box.

cartoucherie [kartuʃri] *nf* **1.** [fabrique] cartridge factory **2.** [dépôt] cartridge depot.

cartouchière [kartuʃjɛr] *nf* **1.** [de soldat] cartridge pouch **2.** [de chasseur] cartridge belt.

cary [kari] = **cari**.

caryatide [karjatid] *nf* caryatid.

cas [ka] *nm* **1.** [hypothèse] : **dans le premier ~** in the first instance ■ **dans le meilleur des ~** at best ■ **dans le pire des ~** at worst ■ **dans certains ~, en certains ~** in some *ou* certain cases ■ **en aucun ~** under no circumstances, on no account ■ **en pareil ~** in such a case ■ **auquel ~, en ce ~, dans ce ~** in which case, in that case, this being the case ▶ **envisageons ce ~ de figure** let us consider that possibility ■ **le ~ échéant** should this happen
2. [situation particulière] case, situation ■ **c'est également mon ~** I'm in the same situation ■ **ce n'est pas le ~** that's not the case ■ **c'est un ~ particulier, elle n'a pas de ressources** she's a special case, she has no income ■ **les ~ particuliers en grammaire russe** exceptions in Russian grammar ▶ **~ de conscience** matter of conscience ■ **poser un ~ de conscience à qqn** to put sb in a (moral) dilemma ■ **~ de force majeure** *pr* case of force majeure ; *fig* case of absolute necessity ■ **~ limite** borderline case ■ **c'est le ~ de le dire!** you've said it!
3. MÉD & SOCIOL case ■ **ce garçon est un ~!** *fam hum* that boy is something else *ou* a real case!
4. GRAMM case
5. *loc* **faire grand ~ de** [événement] to attach great importance to ; [argument, raison] to set great store by ; [invité, ami] to make a great fuss *ou* much of ■ **faire peu de ~ de** [argument, raison] to pay scant attention to ; [invité, ami] to ignore.
◆ **au cas où** *loc conj* in case ■ **au ~ où il ne viendrait pas** in case he doesn't come ■ *(comme adv)* **prends un parapluie au ~ où** *fam* take an umbrella just in case.
◆ **dans tous les cas** = **en tout cas**.
◆ **en cas de** *loc prép* in case of ■ **en ~ de besoin** in case of need ■ **en ~ de perte de la carte** should the card be lost.
◆ **en tout cas** *loc adv* in any case *ou* event, anyway.
◆ **cas social** *nm person needing social worker's assistance*.

casanier, ère [kazanje, ɛr] ◇ *adj* stay-at-home.
◇ *nm, f* stay-at-home type, homebody.

casaque [kazak] *nf* [d'un jockey] silks ■ [de mousquetaire] paletot *(with wide sleeves)* ■ [blouse] paletot ▶ **tourner ~** [fuir] to turn and run ; [changer d'opinion] to do a volte-face.

casbah [kazba] *nf* casbah, kasbah.

cascade [kaskad] *nf* **1.** [chute d'eau] waterfall, cascade *litt* **2.** [abondance] : **une ~ de** [tissu] a cascade of ; [compliments] a stream of ; [sensations] a rush of, a gush of ■ **des ~s d'applaudissements** thundering applause **3.** [acrobatie] stunt ■ **faire de la ~** to do stunts.
◆ **en cascade** ◇ *loc adj* **1.** [applaudissements] tumultuous ■ [rires] ringing **2.** ÉLECTR : **montage en ~** cascade *ou* tandem connection.
◇ *loc adv* : **ses cheveux tombaient en ~ sur ses épaules** her hair cascaded around her shoulders.

cascadeur, euse [kaskadœr, øz] *nm, f* stunt man (*f* woman).

case [kaz] *nf* **1.** [d'un damier] square ■ [d'une grille de mots croisés] square ■ [d'un formulaire] box ■ **~ départ : retournez** *ou* **retour à la ~ départ** return to go ■ **retour à la ~ départ!** *fig* back to square one! **2.** [d'un meuble, d'une boîte] compartment ■ **il a une ~ (de) vide** *fam ou* **en moins** *fam* he's not all there, he's got a screw loose **3.** INFORM box **4.** RADIO & TV slot **5.** [hutte] hut ■ **'la Case de l'oncle Tom'** ***Beecher-Stowe*** 'Uncle Tom's Cabin'.

caséine [kazein] *nf* casein.

casemate [kazmat] *nf* **1.** [d'une fortification] casemate **2.** [ouvrage fortifié] blockhouse.

caser [3] [kaze] *vt fam* **1.** [faire entrer] : **~ qqch dans qqch** to fit sthg in sthg **2.** [dire - phrase, histoire] to get in *(sép)* **3.** [loger - invités] to put up *(sép)* ■ **les enfants sont casés chez la grand-mère** the children are staying at their grandma's **4.** [dans un emploi] to fix up *(sép)* **5.** [marier] to marry off *(sép)* ■ **il est enfin casé** he's settled down at last.
◆ **se caser** *vpi fam* **1.** [dans un emploi] to get fixed up with a job **2.** [se marier] to settle down **3.** [se loger] to find somewhere to live.

caserne [kazɛrn] *nf* **1.** MIL barracks *(sing ou pl)* ■ **~ de pompiers** fire station ■ **des plaisanteries de ~** barrack-room *ou* locker-room jokes **2.** *péj* [logements] soulless high-rise flats *UK ou* apartments *US*.

casernement [kazɛrnəmɑ̃] *nm* **1.** [action] quartering in barracks **2.** [locaux] barrack buildings.

caserner [3] [kazɛrne] *vt* to barrack.

cash [kaʃ] *adv* cash ■ **payer ~** to pay cash ■ **je te le vends, mais ~!** *fam* I'll sell it to you but it's cash on the nail!

casher [kaʃɛr] = **kasher**.

cashmere [kaʃmir] *nm* cashmere.

casier [kazje] *nm* **1.** [case - ouverte] pigeonhole ; [- fermée] compartment ; [- dans une consigne, un gymnase] locker ■ **~ de consigne automatique** luggage locker **2.** [meuble - à cases ouvertes] pigeonholes ; [- à tiroirs] filing cabinet ; [- à cases fermées] compartment ; [- à cases fermant à clef] locker **3.** [pour ranger - des livres] unit ; [- des bouteilles] rack ; [- dans un réfrigérateur] compartment **4.** [pour transporter] crate **5.** ADMIN & DR record ■ **~ fiscal** tax record ■ **~ judiciaire** police *ou* criminal record ■ **un ~ judiciaire vierge** a clean (police) record **6.** PÊCHE pot.

casino [kazino] *nm* casino.

casoar [kazɔar] *nm* **1.** ZOOL cassowary **2.** [plumet] plume *(on hats worn by Saint-Cyr cadets)*.

Caspienne [kaspjɛn] *npr f* : **la (mer) ~** the Caspian Sea, *voir aussi* **mer**.

casque [kask] *nm* **1.** [pour protéger] helmet ■ [d'ouvrier] hard hat ▶ **~ colonial** pith helmet ■ **~ intégral** full face helmet ■ **~ de moto** crash helmet ■ **~ à pointe** spiked helmet ■ **les ~s bleus** the UN peace-keeping force, the blue berets **2.** AUDIO headphones, headset, earphones **3.** [de coiffeur] hood hairdrier **4.** ZOOL casque.

casqué, e [kaske] *adj* helmeted.

casquer [3] △ [kaske] *vi* to cough up, to come up with the cash.

casquette [kaskɛt] *nf* cap ■ **~ d'officier** officer's peaked cap.

cassable [kasabl] *adj* breakable.

Cassandre [kasɑ̃dr] *npr* Cassandra ■ **jouer les ~** to be a prophet of doom *ou* a real Jeremiah.

cassant, e [kasɑ̃, ɑ̃t] *adj* **1.** [cheveux, ongle] brittle ■ [métal] short **2.** [réponse] curt ■ **d'un ton ~** crisply **3.** *fam* [fatigant] : **c'est pas vraiment ~** it's not exactly tiring *ou* overtaxing.

cassate [kasat] *nf* cassata.

cassation [kasasjɔ̃] *nf* **1.** DR cassation **2.** MIL reduction to the ranks.

casse [kas] ◇ *nm fam* [d'une banque] bank robbery ■ [d'une maison] break-in.

◇ *nf* **1.** IMPR case ■ **bas/haut de ~** lower/upper case ■ **lettre bas-/haut- de-~** lower-case/upper-case letter **2.** [bris, dommage] breakage **3.** *fam* [bagarre] : **il va y avoir de la ~** there's going to be a bit of punch up *UK ou* a free-for-all *US* **4.** [de voitures] scrapyard ■ **mettre** *ou* **envoyer à la ~** to scrap ■ **une idéologie bonne pour la ~** *fig* an ideology fit for the scrapheap **5.** BOT cassia.

cassé, e [kase] *adj* ▷ **blanc**, ▷ **col**.

➤ **cassé** *nm* CULIN : **gros ~** large crack ■ **petit ~** small crack.

casse-cou [kasku] ◇ *adj inv* [personne] daredevil ■ [projet] risky.

◇ *nmf* daredevil.

casse-croûte [kaskrut] *nm inv fam* [repas léger] snack ■ [sandwich] sandwich.

Casse-Noisette [kasnwazɛt] *npr* : **'Casse-Noisette'** *Tchaïkovski* 'Nutcracker Suite'.

casse-noisettes [kasnwazɛt] *nm inv* nutcracker.

casse-noix [kasnwa] *nm inv* **1.** [instrument] nutcracker **2.** ZOOL nutcracker.

casse-pieds [kaspje] *adj inv fam* [ennuyeux] boring ■ [agaçant] annoying ■ **un peu ~ à préparer** a bit of a hassle to prepare.

casse-pipe(s) [kaspip] *nm inv* MIL & *fig* **aller au ~** *fam* to go to war.

casser [3] [kase] ◇ *vt* **1.** [mettre en pièces - table] to break (up) ; [- porte] to break down *(sép)* ; [- poignée] to break off *(sép)* ; [- noix] to crack (open) ■ **~ qqch en mille morceaux** to smash sthg to bits *ou* smithereens ■ **~ qqch en deux** to break *ou* to snap sthg in two ■ **un homme que la douleur a cassé** *fig* a man broken by suffering ■ **avoir envie de tout ~** to feel like smashing everything up ▶ **~ sa tirelire** to break into one's piggybank ■ **~ du sucre sur le dos de qqn** *fam* to knock sb when his/her back's turned ■ **un journal où on casse du coco**△ a commie-bashing paper ■ **~ la baraque** *fam* THÉÂTRE to bring the house down ; [faire échouer un plan] to ruin it all ■ **~ la croûte** *fam ou* **graine** *fam* to have a bite to eat ■ **~ sa pipe** *fam* to kick the bucket ■ **ça ne casse pas des briques** *fam* it's no great shakes *ou* no big deal ■ **il/ça ne casse pas trois pattes à un canard** *fam* he/it wouldn't set the world on fire

2. [interrompre - fonctionnement, déroulement, grève] to break ■ **~ l'ambiance** to spoil the atmosphere

3. [démolir] to demolish

4. [en parlant de parties du corps] to break ▶ **~ la figure** *fam ou* **gueule**△ **à qqn** to smash sb's face in ■ **~ les oreilles à qqn** *fam* [avec de la musique] to deafen sb ; [en le harcelant] to give sb a lot of hassle ■ **~ les pieds à qqn** *fam* to get on sb's nerves *ou* wick *UK* ■ **tu nous les casses**▲ you're a fucking pain (in the neck)

5. [abîmer - voix] to damage, to ruin

6. [annihiler - espoir] to dash, to destroy ; [- moral] to crush ■ **la religion, la famille, ils veulent tout ~** religion, family values, they want to smash everything

7. DR [jugement] to quash ■ [arrêt] to nullify, to annul

8. [rétrograder - officier] to break, to reduce to the ranks ; [- fonctionnaire] to demote

9. COMM : **~ les prix** to slash prices ■ **~ le métier** to operate at unfairly competitive rates

10. △ [cambrioler] to do a job on

11. *fam* [voiture] to take to bits *(for spare parts)*, to cannibalize.

◇ *vi* [verre, chaise] to break ■ [fil] to snap ■ [poignée] to break off ■ **la tige a cassé** [en deux] the stem snapped ; [s'est détachée] the stem snapped off ▶ **tout passe, tout lasse, tout casse** *prov* nothing lasts.

➤ **se casser** ◇ *vpi* **1.** [être mis en pièces - assiette] to break ; [- poignée] to break off ■ **se ~ net** [en deux] to snap into two ; [se détacher] to break clean off

2. △ [partir] to push *ou* to buzz off ■ **casse-toi!** get lost!, push off!

3. [cesser de fonctionner - appareil, véhicule] to break down

4. [être altéré - voix] to crack, to falter

5. [vêtement] to break (off).

◇ *vpt* to break ■ **se ~ le cou** *pr* to break one's neck ; *fig* to come a cropper *UK*, to take a tumble ■ **se ~ le cul**▲ *ou* **les reins** *fam* [au travail] to bust a gut, to kill o.s. ■ **se ~ la figure** *fam ou* **gueule**△ [personne] to come a cropper *UK*, to take a tumble ; [livre, carafe] to crash to the ground ; [projet] to bite the dust, to take a dive ■ **ne te casse pas la tête, fais une omelette** don't put yourself out, just make an omelette ■ **se ~ le nez** *fam* [ne trouver personne] to find no-one in ; [échouer] to come a cropper *UK*, to bomb *US* ■ **ça vaut mieux que de se ~ une jambe** *fam* it's better than a poke in the eye with a sharp stick.

➤ **à tout casser** *fam* ◇ *loc adj* [endiablé - fête] fantastic ; [- succès] runaway ■ **une soirée à tout ~** one hell of a party.

◇ *loc adv* [tout au plus] at the (very) most.

casserole [kasrɔl] *nf* **1.** [ustensile, contenu] saucepan **2.** *fam* [instrument de musique] flat *ou* off-key instrument **3.** CINÉ spot (light).

➤ **à la casserole** ◇ *loc adj* braised.

◇ *loc adv* : **faire** *ou* **cuire à la ~** to braise ▶ **passer à la ~** *fam* [être tué] to get bumped off ; [subir une épreuve] to go through it ■ **elle est passée à la ~**△ [sexuellement] she got laid△.

casse-tête [kastɛt] *nm inv* **1.** JEUX puzzle, brainteaser ■ **~ chinois** *pr* Chinese puzzle ■ **c'est un vrai ~ chinois** *fig* it's totally baffling ■ **organiser cette réception, c'était un vrai ~!** what a headache it was organizing that party! **2.** ARM club.

cassette [kasɛt] *nf* **1.** AUDIO & INFORM cassette **2.** [coffret] casket **3.** [trésor royal] privy purse.

casseur, euse [kasœr, øz] *nm, f* **1.** [dans une manifestation] rioting demonstrator **2.** *fam* [cambrioleur] burglar **3.** COMM scrap dealer, scrap merchant *UK*.

Cassiopée [kasjɔpe] *npr* MYTHOL & ASTRON Cassiopeia.

cassis [kasis] *nm* **1.** [baie] blackcurrant **2.** [plante] blackcurrant bush **3.** [liqueur] blackcurrant liqueur, cassis **4.** [dos d'âne] gully *(across a road)*.

cassolette [kasɔlɛt] *nf* **1.** CULIN small baking dish **2.** [brûle-parfum] incense-burner.

cassonade [kasɔnad] *nf* light brown sugar.

cassoulet [kasulɛ] *nm* cassoulet, haricot bean stew *(with pork, goose or duck)*.

cassure [kasyr] *nf* **1.** [fissure] crack **2.** [rupture dans la vie, le rythme] break **3.** [vêtement] fold ■ **la ~ de son pantalon** where his trousers rest on his shoes **4.** GÉOL break ■ [faille] fault.

castagnettes [kastaɲɛt] *nfpl* castanets ■ **ses dents jouaient des ~** his teeth were chattering ■ **ses genoux jouaient des ~** his knees were knocking.

caste [kast] *nf* ENTOM & SOCIOL caste.

castel [kastɛl] *nm litt* small castle.

castillan, e [kastijɑ̃, an] *adj* Castilian.
◆ **Castillan, e** *nm, f* Castilian.
◆ **castillan** *nm* LING Castilian.

Castille [kastij] *npr f* : **(la) ~** Castile.

casting [kastiŋ] *nm* casting CINÉ & THÉÂTRE : **passer un ~** to go to an audition.

castor [kastɔr] *nm* **1.** ZOOL beaver **2.** [fourrure] beaver.

castrat [kastra] *nm* MUS castrato.

castrateur, trice [kastratœr, tris] *adj* castrating.

castration [kastrasjɔ̃] *nf* **1.** [d'un homme, d'une femme] castration **2.** [d'un animal - mâle] castration, gelding ; [- femelle] castration, spaying.

castrer [3] [kastre] *vt* **1.** [homme, femme] to castrate ■ [cheval] to castrate, to geld ■ [chat] to castrate, to neuter, to spay **2.** BOT to castrate.

castrisme [kastrism] *nm* Castroism.

castriste [kastrist] ◇ *adj* Castroist.
◇ *nmf* Castroist, Castro supporter.

casuel, elle [kazɥɛl] *adj* **1.** [éventuel] fortuitous **2.** LING case *(modif)*.

casuiste [kazɥist] *nm* casuist.

casuistique [kazɥistik] *nf* casuistry.

CAT (*abr de* **Centre d'aide par le travail**) *nf day centre which helps disabled people to find work and become more independent.*

cataclysmal, e, aux [kataklismal, o] *adj* **1.** GÉOGR cataclysmal, cataclysmic **2.** [bouleversant] catastrophic, disastrous, cataclysmic.

cataclysme [kataklism] *nm* **1.** GÉOGR natural disaster, cataclysm **2.** [bouleversement] cataclysm, catastrophe, disaster.

cataclysmique [kataklismik] = **cataclysmal**.

catacombes [katakɔ̃b] *nfpl* catacombs.

catadioptre [katadjɔptr] *nm* **1.** AUTO reflector **2.** [sur une route] cat's eye.

catafalque [katafalk] *nm* catafalque.

catalan, e [katalɑ̃, an] *adj* Catalan.
◆ **Catalan, e** *nm, f* Catalan.
◆ **catalan** *nm* LING Catalan.

catalepsie [katalɛpsi] *nf* catalepsy.

cataleptique [katalɛptik] *adj* & *nmf* cataleptic.

catalogage [katalɔgaʒ] *nm* cataloguing.

catalogne [katalɔɲ] *nf* *Québec material woven from strips of coloured fabric.*

Catalogne [katalɔɲ] *npr f* : **(la) ~** Catalonia.

catalogue [katalɔg] *nm* **1.** [liste - de bibliothèque, d'exposition] catalogue ■ **faire le ~ des toiles exposées** to catalogue *ou* to itemize the exhibits ■ **~ raisonné** ART catalogue raisonné **2.** COMM [illustré] catalogue ■ [non illustré] price-list **3.** *péj* [énumération] (long) list.

cataloguer [3] [katalɔge] *vt* **1.** [livre] to list, to catalogue ■ [bibliothèque] to catalogue ■ [œuvre, marchandise] to put into a catalogue **2.** *fam* [juger] to label, to categorize ■ **il s'est fait ~ comme dilettante** he was labelled a dilettante.

catalyse [kataliz] *nf* catalysis.

catalyser [3] [katalize] *vt* **1.** [provoquer - forces, critiques] to act as a catalyst for **2.** CHIM to catalyse.

catalyseur [katalizœr] *nm* **1.** [personne, journal] catalyst ■ **il a été le ~ de...** he acted as a catalyst for... **2.** CHIM catalyst.

catalytique [katalitik] *adj* catalytic.

catamaran [katamarɑ̃] *nm* **1.** [voilier] catamaran **2.** [flotteurs] floats.

Cataphote® [katafɔt] *nm* reflector.

cataplasme [kataplasm] *nm* **1.** MÉD poultice, cataplasm **2.** *fam* [aliment] : **j'ai encore ce ~ sur l'estomac** I can still feel that lead weight in my stomach.

catapulte [katapylt] *nf* AÉRON, ARM & JEUX catapult.

catapulter [3] [katapylte] *vt* **1.** ARM & AÉRON to catapult **2.** [employé] to kick upstairs ■ **il a été catapulté directeur** he was pitchforked into the manager's job.

cataracte [katarakt] *nf* **1.** MÉD cataract ■ **se faire opérer de la ~** to have a cataract operation **2.** [chute d'eau] waterfall, cataract.

catarrhe [katar] *nm* catarrh.

catarrheux, euse [katarø, øz] ◇ *adj* catarrhous.
◇ *nm, f* catarrh sufferer.

catastrophe [katastrɔf] *nf* [désastre - en avion, en voiture] disaster ; [- dans une vie, un gouvernement] catastrophe, disaster ■ **éviter la ~** to avoid a catastrophe ■ **frôler la ~** to come close to disaster ■ **une ~, ce type!** *fam* that guy's a walking disaster! ■ **~, il nous manque deux chaises!** oh horrors, we're a couple of chairs short! ■ **~ naturelle** natural disaster ; [assurances] act of God.
◆ **en catastrophe** *loc adv* : **partir en ~** to rush off ■ **atterrir en ~** to make a forced *ou* an emergency landing.

catastropher [3] [katastrɔfe] *vt* to shatter, to stun ■ **un air catastrophé** a stunned look.

catastrophique [katastrɔfik] *adj* catastrophic, disastrous.

catastrophisme [katastrɔfism] *nm* catastrophism ■ **ne fais pas de ~!** don't be so pessimistic!

catch [katʃ] *nm* (all-in) wrestling ■ **faire du ~** to wrestle.

catcher [3] [katʃe] *vi* to wrestle.

catcheur, euse [katʃœr, øz] *nm, f* (all-in) wrestler.

catéchèse [kateʃɛz] *nf* catechesis.

catéchisation [kateʃizasjɔ̃] *nf* **1.** RELIG catechization, catechizing **2.** *péj* indoctrination.

catéchiser [3] [kateʃize] *vt* **1.** RELIG to catechize **2.** *péj* to indoctrinate.

catéchisme [kateʃism] *nm* **1.** RELIG [enseignement, livre] catechism ■ **aller au ~** to go to catechism, ≃ to go to Sunday school **2.** *fig* doctrine, creed ■ **cela fait partie de leur ~** it's Gospel truth to them.

catéchiste [kateʃist] *nmf* [gén] catechist ■ [pour enfants] Sunday-school teacher.

catéchumène [katekymɛn] *nmf* **1.** RELIG catechumen **2.** [que l'on initie] novice.

catégorie [kategɔri] *nf* **1.** [pour classifier - des objets, des concepts] category, class, type ; [- des employés] grade ■ **~ d'âge**

age group ■ ~ **sociale** social class ■ ~ **socio-économique** socio-economic class ■ ~ **socioprofessionnelle** socioprofessional group **2.** [qualité - dans les transports, les hôtels] class ■ **hotel de seconde** ~ second-class hotel ■ **morceau de première/deuxième/troisième** ~ [viande] prime/second/cheap cut **3.** SPORT class ■ **toutes ~s** for all comers **4.** PHILOS category.

catégoriel, elle [kategɔrjɛl] *adj* **1.** [d'une catégorie] category *(modif)* ■ **classement** ~ classification by category **2.** SOCIOL : **revendications ~les** sectional claims *(claims relating to one category of workers only)* **3.** LING & PHILOS category *(modif)*.

catégorique [kategɔrik] *adj* **1.** [non ambigu - refus] flat, categorical, point-blank **2.** [décidé] categorical ■ **là-dessus, je serai** ~ I'm not prepared to budge on that ■ **je suis** ~ [j'en suis sûr] I'm positive **3.** MATH & PHILOS categorical.

catégoriquement [kategɔrikmɑ̃] *adv* [nettement - affirmer] categorically ; [- refuser] categorically, flatly, point-blank.

catégoriser [3] [kategɔrize] *vt* [ranger] to categorize.

catelle [katɛl] *nf Suisse* ceramic tile.

caténaire [katenɛr] *nf Suisse* ceramic tile.

caténaire [katenɛr] ◇ *adj* catenary *(modif)*.
◇ *nf* catenary.

cathare [katar] *adj* Cathar.
◆ **Cathare** *nmf* Cathar.

catharsis [katarsis] *nf* PSYCHOL & THÉÂTRE catharsis.

cathartique [katartik] *adj* MÉD, PHYS & THÉÂTRE cathartic.

cathédral, e, aux [katedral, o] *adj* RELIG cathedral *(modif)*.
◆ **cathédrale** *nf* [édifice] cathedral.

Catherine [katrin] *npr* : **la Sainte-~** Saint Catherine's Day ■ **coiffer sainte** ~ *to be still unmarried by the age of 25* ■ ~ **d'Aragon** Catherine of Aragon ■ ~ **de Russie** Catherine the Great.

catherinette [katrinɛt] *nf woman who is still single and aged 25 on St Catherine's Day.*

cathéter [katetɛr] *nm* catheter.

cathode [katɔd] *nf* cathode.

cathodique [katɔdik] *adj* cathodic.

catholicisme [katɔlisism] *nm* (Roman) Catholicism.

catholicité [katɔlisite] *nf* RELIG [caractère] catholicity ■ [groupe] : **la** ~ [église] the (Roman) Catholic Church ; [fidèles] the (Roman) Catholic community.

catholique [katɔlik] ◇ *adj* **1.** RELIG (Roman) Catholic ■ **une institution** ~ a Catholic *ou* an RC school **2.** *fam loc* **pas très ~ comme façon de faire** [peu conventionnel] not a very orthodox way of doing things ; [malhonnête] not a very kosher way of doing things ■ **un individu pas très** ~ a rather shady individual.
◇ *nmf* (Roman) Catholic.

catimini [katimini] ◆ **en catimini** *loc adv* on the sly *ou* quiet ■ **arriver/partir en** ~ to sneak in/out.

catin [katɛ̃] *nf litt* trollop *vieilli*.

cation [katjɔ̃] *nm* cation.

catogan [katɔgɑ̃] *nm large bow holding the hair at the back of neck.*

Caton [katɔ̃] *npr* Cato.

Caucase [kokaz] *npr m* **1.** [montagnes] : **le** ~ the Caucasus **2.** [région] : **le** ~ Caucasia.

caucasien, enne [kokazjɛ̃, ɛn] *adj* Caucasian ■ **les langues ~nes** the Caucasian languages.
◆ **Caucasien, enne** *nmf sing* Caucasian.

cauchemar [kɔʃmar] *nm* **1.** [mauvais rêve] nightmare ■ **faire un** ~ to have a nightmare **2.** [situation] nightmare **3.** [personne assommante] nuisance.

cauchemarder [3] [kɔʃmarde] *vi* to have nightmares ■ **la perspective d'une semaine avec eux me fait** ~ the prospect of spending a week with them is a real nightmare.

cauchemardesque [kɔʃmardɛsk], **cauchemardeux, euse** [kɔʃmardø, øz] *adj* **1.** [sommeil] nightmarish **2.** *fig* [horrifiant] nightmarish, hellish.

caudal, e, aux [kodal, o] *adj* tail *(modif)*, caudal *spéc*.

causal, e, als *ou* **aux** [kozal, o] *adj* [lien] causal.

causalité [kozalite] *nf* causality.

causant, e [kozɑ̃, ɑ̃t] *adj fam* chatty ■ **il n'est pas très** ~ [coopératif] he's not exactly forthcoming.

cause [koz] *nf* **1.** [origine, motif] cause, reason, origin ■ ~ **de** : **la ~ profonde de sa tristesse** the underlying reason for his sadness ■ **être (la) ~ de qqch** to cause sthg ■ **le mauvais temps est ~ que je n'ai pu aller vous rendre visite** I wasn't able to come and see you on account of the bad weather ➊ **relation de ~ à effet** causal relationship ■ **à petite ~ grands effets** *prov* great oaks from little acorns grow *prov* ■ **et pour ~!** and for a very good reason! **2.** PHILOS cause ■ **la ~ première/seconde/finale** the prime/secondary/final cause **3.** DR [affaire] case, brief ■ ~ **célèbre** *pr* & *fig* cause célèbre ■ ~ **civile** civil action ■ ~ **criminelle** criminal proceedings ■ **un avocat sans ~s** a briefless barrister ■ **la ~ est entendue** *pr* each side has put its case ; *fig* there's no doubt about it ■ **plaider la ~ de qqn** *pr* & *fig* to plead sb's case ‖ [motif] : ~ **licite/illicite** just/unjust cause **4.** [parti que l'on prend] cause ■ **faire ~ commune avec qqn** to join forces with sb ■ **une ~ perdue** a lost cause ■ **pour la bonne** ~ [pour un bon motif] for a good cause ; *hum* [en vue du mariage] with honourable intentions ■ **je suis tout acquis à sa** ~ I support him wholeheartedly.
◆ **à cause de** *loc prép* **1.** [par la faute de] because *ou* on account of, due *ou* owing to **2.** [en considération de] because *ou* on account of, due *ou* owing to **3.** [par égard pour] for the sake *ou* because of.
◆ **en cause** ◇ *loc adj* **1.** [concerné] in question ■ **la voiture en ~ était à l'arrêt** the car involved *ou* in question was stationary ■ **la somme/l'enjeu en** ~ the amount/the thing at stake **2.** [que l'on suspecte] : **les financiers en** ~ the financiers involved ■ **certains ministres sont en** ~ some ministers are implicated **3.** [contesté] : **être en** ~ [talent] to be in question ‖ DR : **affaire en** ~ case before the court.
◇ *loc adv* **1.** [en accusation] : **mettre qqn en** ~ to implicate sb ■ **mettre qqch en** ~ to call sthg into question **2.** [en doute] : **remettre en** ~ [principe] to question, to challenge ■ **son départ remet tout en** ~ her departure reopens the whole question *ou* debate.
◆ **en tout état de cause** *loc adv* in any case, at all events, whatever happens.
◆ **pour cause de** *loc prép* owing to, because of ■ **'fermé pour ~ de décès'** 'closed owing to bereavement'.

causer [3] [koze] ◇ *vt* [provoquer - peine, problème] to cause ■ **cela m'a causé de graves ennuis** it got me into a lot of trouble.
◇ *vi fam* **1.** [bavarder] : ~ **(à qqn)** to chat (to sb) ■ **cause toujours (, tu m'intéresses)!** [je fais ce que je veux] yeah, yeah (I'll do what I like anyway)! ; [tu pourrais m'écouter] don't mind me! ■ **je l'avais prévenu, mais cause toujours!** I'd warned him but I might as well have been talking to the wall! **2.** [médire] to gossip, to prattle ■ **ça a fait ~ dans le quartier** it set tongues wagging in the district **3.** *(suivi d'un n sans article)* [parler] : ~ **politique** to talk about politics, to talk politics.

causerie [kozri] *nf* informal talk *(in front of an audience)*.

causette [kozɛt] *nf fam* **faire la ~ à qqn** to chat with sb ■ **faire un brin de** ~ to have a little chinwag *UK*, to chew the fat *US*.

causeur, euse [kozœr, øz] ◇ *adj* chatty, talkative.
◇ *nm, f* talker, conversationalist.
◆ **causeuse** *nf* love seat.

causticité [kostisite] *nf* CHIM & *fig* causticity.

caustique [kostik] ◇ *adj* **1.** CHIM caustic **2.** [mordant] caustic, biting, sarcastic.
◇ *nm* CHIM caustic.
◇ *nf* OPT caustic (curve).

cauteleux, euse [kotlø, øz] *adj litt* wily, cunning.

cautère [koter] *nm* cautery ■ **c'est un ~ sur une jambe de bois** it's as much use as a poultice on a wooden leg.

cautériser [3] [koterize] *vt* to cauterize.

caution [kosjɔ̃] *nf* **1.** [somme] bail ■ **payer la ~ de qqn** to post bail for sb, to bail sb out **2.** [garant] : **se porter ~ pour qqn** to stand security *ou* surety *ou* guarantee for sb **3.** [garantie morale] guarantee ■ [soutien] support, backing ■ **donner** *ou* **apporter sa ~ à** to support, to back ➊ **~ juratoire** guarantee given on oath **4.** COMM security, guarantee ■ **verser une ~ de 500 euros** to pay 500 euros as security, to put down a 500 euros deposit (as security).
◆ **sous caution** *loc adv* [libérer] on bail.

CAUTION

When renting accommodation in France, the future tenant is usually required to pay a *caution* or deposit (normally twice the monthly rent), repayable if the property is maintained in good condition. A *caution solidaire* is a statement signed by a third party guaranteeing payment of rent in the event of non-payment by the tenant. The term *caution parentale* is used when the guarantor is the tenant's mother or father.

cautionnement [kosjɔnmɑ̃] *nm* **1.** [contrat] surety *ou* security bond **2.** [dépôt - COMM] security, guarantee ■ DR bail ■ **~ réel** collateral security **3.** [soutien] support, backing.

cautionner [3] [kosjɔne] *vt* **1.** DR : **~ qqn** [se porter caution] to post bail for sb ; [se porter garant] to stand surety *ou* guarantee for sb **2.** [soutenir] to support, to back ■ **se faire ~ par ses parents pour la location d'un appartement** to provide a parental guarantee when renting a flat.

cavalcade [kavalkad] *nf* **1.** [défilé] cavalcade **2.** [course] stampede ■ **c'est tout le temps la ~** we're always in such a rush all the time.

cavalcader [3] [kavalkade] *vi* to scamper around.

cavale [kaval] *nf* **1.** *litt* [jument] mare ZOOL **2.** △ *arg crime* jailbreak ■ **être en ~** to be on the run.

cavaler [3] [kavale] *vi fam* **1.** [courir] to run *ou* to rush (around) ■ **je cavale tout le temps** I'm on the go the whole time **2.** [se hâter] to get a move on **3.** [à la recherche de femmes] to chase women ■ [à la recherche d'hommes] to chase men.
◆ **se cavaler** *vpi fam* to clear off.

cavalerie [kavalri] *nf* MIL cavalry ■ **~ légère** light (cavalry *ou* horse) brigade ■ **~ lourde, grosse ~** armoured cavalry ■ **la grosse ~** *fig* the run-of-the-mill stuff.

cavaleur, euse [kavalœr, øz] *adj fam* [homme] philandering ■ [femme] man-eating ■ **il est ~** he's a womanizer ■ **elle est cavaleuse** she'll go for anything in trousers.
◆ **cavaleur** *nm fam* philanderer, womanizer.
◆ **cavaleuse** *nf fam* man-eater.

cavalier, ère [kavalje, ɛr] ◇ *adj* **1.** ÉQUIT : **allée** *ou* **piste cavalière** bridle path, bridleway **2.** *péj* [désinvolte - attitude] offhand, cavalier ; [- réponse] curt, offhand ■ **agir de façon cavalière** to act in an offhand manner.
◇ *nm, f* **1.** ÉQUIT rider **2.** [danseur] partner.
◆ **cavalier** *nm* **1.** HIST Cavalier **2.** MIL cavalryman, mounted soldier **3.** BIBLE : **les (quatre) Cavaliers de l'Apocalypse** the (Four) Horsemen of the Apocalypse **4.** [pour aller au bal] escort ■ **faire ~ seul** [dans une entreprise] to go it alone ; POLIT to be a maverick **5.** JEUX [aux échecs] knight **6.** [sur un dossier] tab **7.** [clou] staple **8.** [surcharge] rider.

cavalièrement [kavaljɛrmɑ̃] *adv* casually, in a cavalier *ou* an offhand manner.

cave [kav] *nf* **1.** [pièce] cellar ■ **de la ~ au grenier** *fig* [ranger, nettoyer] from top to bottom **2.** [vins] (wine) cellar ■ **avoir une bonne ~** to keep a good cellar **3.** [cabaret] cellar *UK ou* basement *US* nightclub **4.** [coffret] : **~ à cigares** cigar box ■ **~ à liqueurs** cellaret **5.** JEUX [gén] stake ■ [au poker] ante.

caveau, x [kavo] *nm* **1.** [sépulture] vault, tomb, burial chamber **2.** [cabaret] club *(in a cellar)*.

caverne [kavɛrn] *nf* **1.** [grotte] cave, cavern ■ **une ~ de brigands** *fam* a den of thieves **2.** MÉD cavity.

caverneux, euse [kavɛrnø, øz] *adj* **1.** [voix] sepulchral **2.** MÉD [poumon] cavernulous ■ [souffle, râle] cavernous.

caviar [kavjar] *nm* **1.** CULIN caviar, caviare ■ **~ rouge** salmon roe ■ **~ d'aubergines** aubergine *UK ou* eggplant *US* puree **2.** IMPR blue pencil ■ **passer au ~** to blue-pencil, to censor.

caviarder [3] [kavjarde] *vt* to blue-pencil, to censor.

caviste [kavist] *nm* cellarman.

cavité [kavite] *nf* **1.** [trou] cavity **2.** ANAT cavity ■ **~ dentaire** pulp cavity **3.** ÉLECTRON : **~ résonante** resonant cavity, cavity resonator.

Cayenne [kajɛn] *npr* Cayenne.

CB [sibi] (*abr de* **citizen's band, canaux banalisés**) *nf* CB.

cc 1. (*abr écrite de* **cuillère à café**) tsp **2.** = **charges comprises**.

CCE (*abr de* **Commission des communautés européennes**) *npr f* ECC.

CCI (*abr de* **chambre de commerce et d'industrie**) *nf* CCI.

CCP (*abr de* **compte chèque postal, compte courant postal**) *nm post office account* ■ ≃ giro account *UK*, ≃ Post Office checking account *US*.

CD ◇ *nm* **1.** = **chemin départemental 2.** (*abr de* **Compact Disc**) CD ■ **~ vidéo** CD video, CDV **3.** = **comité directeur**.
◇ (*abr écrite de* **corps diplomatique**) CD.

CDD [sedede] (*abr de* **contrat à durée déterminée**) *nm* fixed term contract ■ **elle est en ~** she's on a fixed term contract.

CDI [sedei] *nm* **1.** (*abr de* **centre de documentation et d'information**) *school library* **2.** (*abr de* **contrat à durée indéterminée**) permanent employment contract ■ **elle est en ~** she's got a permanent employment contract.

CD-I (*abr de* **Compact Disc interactif**) *nm* interactive Compact Disc.

CD-Rom [sederɔm] (*abr de* **Compact Disc read only memory**) *nm inv* CD-Rom.

CDS (*abr de* **Centre des démocrates sociaux**) *npr m French political party*.

CDV (*abr de* **Compact Disc Video**) *nm* CVD.

ce[1] [sə] *(devant nm commençant par voyelle ou h muet* **cet** [sɛt]) (*f* **cette** [sɛt], *pl* **ces** [sɛ]) *dét (adj dém)* **1.** [dans l'espace - proche] this, these *pl* ; [- éloigné] that, those *pl* ■ **cet homme qui vient vers nous** the man (who's) coming towards us ■ **regarde de ce côté-ci** look over here
2. [dans le temps - à venir] this, these *pl* ; [- passé] last ■ **cette nuit nous mettrons le chauffage** tonight we'll turn the heating on ■ **cette nuit j'ai fait un rêve étrange** last night I had a strange dream ■ **cette semaine je n'ai rien fait** I haven't done a thing this *ou* this past *ou* this last week ■ **cette année-là** that year ■ **ces jours-ci** these days ■ **fait ce jour à Blois** witnessed by my hand this day in Blois
3. [désignant - ce dont on a parlé] this, these *pl*, that, those *pl* ; [- ce dont on va parler] this, these *pl*
4. [suivi d'une proposition relative] : **voici ce pont dont je t'ai parlé** here's the *ou* that bridge I told you about ■ **il était de ces comédiens qui...** he was one of those actors who...
5. [emploi expressif] : **cette douleur dans son regard!** such grief in his eyes! ■ **ce peuple!** *fam* what a crowd! ■ **cet enfant est un modèle de sagesse!** this *ou* that child is so well behaved! ■ **et ces douleurs/cette grippe, comment ça va?** *fam* how's the pain/ the flu doing? ■ **et pour ces messieurs, ce sera?** now what will the *ou* you gentlemen have?

ce[2] [sə] *(devant 'e' c' [s], devant 'a' ç' [s]) pron dém* **1.** [sujet du verbe 'être'] : **c'était hier** it was yesterday ■ **c'est un escroc** he's a crook ■ **ce sont mes frères** they are my brothers ■ **ce doit être son mari** it must be her husband ■ **dire oui, c'est renoncer à sa liberté** saying yes means *ou* amounts to giving up one's freedom ■ **c'est rare qu'il pleuve en juin** it doesn't often rain in June ■ **c'est encore loin, la mer?** is the sea still far away?, is it still a long way to the sea? ▪ **qui est-ce?, c'est qui?** *fam* who is it? ▪ **c'est à toi?** is this *ou* is it yours? ▪ **serait-ce que tu as oublié?** have you forgotten, by any chance?

2. [pour insister] : **c'est la robe que j'ai achetée** this is the dress (that) I bought ▪ **c'est l'auteur que je préfère** he's/she's my favourite writer ▪ **c'est à vous, monsieur, que je voudrais parler** it was you I wanted to speak to, sir ▪ **c'est à lui/à toi de décider** it's up to him/up to you to decide ▪ **c'est à pleurer de rage** it's enough to make you weep with frustration

3. ['c'est que' introduisant une explication] : **s'il ne parle pas beaucoup, c'est qu'il est timide** if he doesn't say much, it's because he's shy

4. [comme antécédent du pronom relatif] : **ce qui, ce que** what ▪ **ce qui m'étonne, c'est que...** what surprises me is that... ▪ **dis-moi ce que tu as fait** tell me what you did ‖ [reprenant la proposition] which ▪ **il dit en avoir les moyens, ce que je crois volontiers** he says he can afford it, which I'm quite prepared to believe ▪ **ce dont : ce dont je ne me souviens pas, c'est l'adresse** what I can't remember is the address ▪ **ce pour quoi : ce pour quoi j'ai démissionné** the reason (why) I resigned ▪ **ce en quoi : ce en quoi je croyais s'est effondré** the thing I believed in has collapsed ‖ [introduisant une complétive] : **de ce que : je m'étonne de ce qu'il n'ait rien dit** I'm surprised (by the fact that) he didn't say anything ▪ **à ce que : veille à ce que tout soit prêt** make sure everything's ready ▪ **sur ce que : il insiste sur ce que le travail doit être fait en temps voulu** he insists that the work must be done in the specified time

5. [emploi exclamatif] : **ce que tu es naïf!** you're so naive!, how naive you are! ▪ **tu vois ce que c'est que de mentir!** you see what happens when you lie!, you see where lying gets you! ▪ **ce que c'est (que) d'être instruit, tout de même!** it must be wonderful to be educated!

6. *loc* **ce me semble** *sout* & *hum* it seems to me, I think, methinks *litt hum* ▪ **ce faisant** in so doing ▪ **ce disant** so saying, with these words ▪ **et ce : il n'a rien dit, et ce malgré toutes les menaces** he said nothing, (and this) in spite of all the threats ▪ **sur ce : j'arrive et sur ce, le téléphone sonne** I arrive and just then the phone rings ▪ **sur ce, je vous salue** and now, I take my leave ▪ **sur ce, elle se leva** with that, she got up ▪ **pour ce faire** *sout* to this end.

CE ◇ *nm* **1.** = **comité d'entreprise 2.** (*abr de* **cours élémentaire**) ▪ **~1** *second year of primary school* ▪ **~2** *third year of primary school.*
◇ *npr f* (*abr de* **Communauté européenne**) EC.

CEA (*abr de* **Commissariat à l'énergie atomique**) *npr m French atomic energy commission,* ≃ AEA *UK,* ≃ AEC *US.*

céans [seɑ̃] *adv arch* here, within *ou* in this house.

CECA, Ceca [seka] (*abr de* **Communauté européenne du charbon et de l'acier**) *npr f* ECSC.

ceci [səsi] *pron dém* this ▪ **~ pour vous dire que...** (all) this to tell you that... ▪ **~ (étant) dit** having said this *ou* that ▪ **à ~ près que** except *ou* with the exception that ▪ **retenez bien ~...** now, remember this... ▪ **son rapport a ~ d'étonnant que...** her report is surprising in that... ▪ **~ n'explique pas cela** one thing doesn't explain the other.

cécité [sesite] *nf* blindness, cecity *sout* ▪ **~ nocturne/verbale/des neiges** night/word/snow blindness.

cédant, e [sedɑ̃, ɑ̃t] ◇ *adj* assigning, granting.
◇ *nm, f* assignor, grantor.

céder [18] [sede] ◇ *vt* **1.** [donner] to give (up) ▪ **il est temps de ~ l'antenne** our time is up ▪ **nous cédons maintenant l'antenne à Mélanie** we're now going to hand over to Mélanie ▪ **'cédez le passage'** 'give way *UK*, yield *US*' ▪ **~ le passage à qqn** to let sb through, to make way for sb ▶ **~ du terrain** MIL to give ground, to fall back ; *fig* to back down *ou* off ▪ **~ le pas à qqn** *pr* to give way to sb ; *fig* to let sb have precedence ▪ **il ne le cède à personne en ambition** *sout* as far as ambition is concerned, he's second to none ▪ **il ne le cède en rien à nos plus grands peintres** he can take his place alongside our greatest painters **2.** [vendre] to sell ▪ **'à ~'** 'for sale' ‖ [faire cadeau de] to give away *(sép)*, to donate.
◇ *vi* **1.** [à la volonté d'autrui] to give in ▪ **tu n'arriveras jamais à le faire ~** you'll never get him to back down **2.** MIL : **~ sous l'assaut de l'ennemi** to be overpowered *ou* overwhelmed by the enemy **3.** [casser - étagère, plancher] to give way ; [- câble, poignée] to break off ; [- couture] to come unstitched.
◆ **céder à** *v+prép* **1.** [ne pas lutter contre - sommeil, fatigue] to succumb to ; [- tentation, caprice] to give in *ou* to yield to ▪ **cette hypothèse cédera à la première analyse** this hypothesis won't stand up to analysis **2.** [être séduit par] : **~ à la facilité** to take the easy way out ▪ **~ à qqn** to give in to sb.

cédérom [sederɔm] *nm* INFORM CD-ROM.

cédétiste [sedetist] ◇ *adj* CFDT *(modif).*
◇ *nmf* member of the CFDT.

CEDEX, Cedex [sedɛks] (*abr de* **courrier d'entreprise à distribution exceptionnelle**) *nm accelerated postal service for bulk users.*

cédille [sedij] *nf* cedilla.

cédrat [sedra] *nm* citron.

cèdre [sɛdr] *nm* **1.** [arbre] cedar (tree), arborvitae *Canada* ▪ **~ du Liban** cedar of Lebanon **2.** [bois] cedar (wood).

cédrière [sedrijɛr] *nf Québec* cedar grove.

CEE [seøø] (*abr de* **Communauté économique européenne**) *npr f* EEC.

CEG (*abr de* **collège d'enseignement général**) *nm former junior secondary school.*

CEGEP [seʒɛp] (*abr de* **collège d'enseignement général et professionnel**) *nm Québec* ≃ college of further education.

cégépien, enne [seʒepjɛ̃, ɛn] *nm, f Québec student of a CEGEP.*

cégétiste [seʒetist] ◇ *adj* CGT *(modif).*
◇ *nmf* member of the CGT.

CEI [seøi] (*abr de* **Communauté des États indépendants**) *npr f* CIS.

ceindre [81] [sɛ̃dr] *vt litt* **1.** [entourer] : **un cercle de fer ceignait son front** he had a band of iron around his head ▪ **~ qqch de : ~ sa tête d'une couronne** to place a crown upon one's head ▪ **un château ceint de hautes murailles** a castle surrounded by high walls **2.** [porter] : **~ la couronne** to assume the crown ▪ **~ l'écharpe tricolore** to don the mayoral (tricolour) sash.
◆ **se ceindre** *vpt litt* **se ~ les reins** to gird one's loins.

ceinture [sɛ̃tyr] *nf* **1.** [vêtement en cuir, métal] belt ▪ [fine et tressée] cord ▪ [large et nouée] sash ▪ [gaine, corset] girdle ▪ **~ de chasteté** chastity belt ▪ **~ fléchée** *Québec* arrow sash ▪ **~ de sauvetage** life belt ▪ **~ de sécurité** seat *ou* safety belt ▪ **attachez votre ~** fasten your seat belt ▪ **faire ~** *fam*, **se serrer la ~** *fam* [se priver] to tighten one's belt ▪ **on a trop dépensé ces derniers temps, maintenant ~!** *fam* we've been overspending lately, we're going to have to tighten our belts now
2. SPORT [à la lutte] waistlock ▪ [au judo et au karaté] belt ▪ **elle est ~ blanche/noire** she is a white/black belt
3. [taille - COUT] waistband ▪ ANAT waist ▪ **de l'eau jusqu'à la ~** with water up to his waist ▪ **nu jusqu'à la ~** naked from the waist up ▪ **frapper au-dessous de la ~** *pr* & *fig* to hit below the belt
4. ZOOL : **~ pelvienne/scapulaire** pelvic/pectoral girdle
5. MÉD : **~ orthopédique** surgical corset ▪ **~ de grossesse** maternity girdle
6. TRANSP : **petite/grande ~** inner/outer circle
7. ARCHIT cincture
8. [enceinte] belt, ring ▶ **~ verte** green belt.

ceinturer [3] [sɛ̃tyre] *vt* **1.** [porter avec une ceinture] : **vous pouvez la ~** [robe] you can wear it with a belt **2.** [saisir par la taille] to grab round the waist ▪ SPORT to tackle **3.** [lieu] to surround, to encircle ▪ **les remparts ceinturent la ville** the town is surrounded by ramparts **4.** HORT to girdle.

ceinturon [sɛ̃tyrɔ̃] *nm* **1.** [vêtement] (broad) belt **2.** MIL [gén] belt ▪ [à cartouches] cartridge belt ▪ [à sabre] sword belt.

cela [səla] *pron dém* **1.** [désignant un objet éloigné] that **2.** [désignant - ce dont on vient de parler] this, that ; [- ce dont on va parler] this ▪ **~ (étant) dit...** having said this *ou* that... ▪ **qu'est-ce que ~?** what is that? ▪ **il est parti il y a un mois/une semaine de ~** he left a month/a week ago ■ **son histoire a ~ d'extraordinaire que...** her story is extraordinary in that... ➤ **c'est ~, moquez-vous de moi!** that's right, have a good laugh (at my expense)! ■ **je suis folle, c'est (bien) ~?** so I'm out of my mind, is that it *ou* am I? **3.** [dans des tournures impersonnelles] it ■ **~ ne fait rien** it doesn't matter ■ **~ fait une heure que j'attends** I've been waiting for an hour **4.** [emploi expressif] : **pourquoi ~?** why?, what for? ■ **qui ~?** who?, who's that? ■ **où ~?** where?, whereabouts?

céladon [seladɔ̃] ◇ *adj inv* pale green, celadon *litt.*
◇ *nm* celadon.

célébrant [selebrɑ̃] *nm* celebrant.

célébration [selebrasjɔ̃] *nf* celebration ■ **la ~ du mariage se fera à...** the marriage ceremony will take place at...

célèbre [selɛbr] *adj* famous, famed ■ **tristement ~** notorious ■ **~ dans le monde entier** world-famous.

célébrer [18] [selebre] *vt* **1.** [fête] to observe ■ [anniversaire, messe, mariage] to celebrate **2.** [glorifier - personne] to extol the virtues of ; [- exploit] to toast, to celebrate.

célébrité [selebrite] *nf* **1.** [gloire] fame, celebrity **2.** [personne] celebrity, well-known personality.

celer [25] [səle *ou* sele] *vt arch & litt* **~ qqch à qqn** to conceal sthg from sb.

céleri [sɛlri] *nm* celery ■ **~ en branches** celery ■ **~ rémoulade** celeriac salad.

céleri-rave [sɛlrirav] (*pl* **céleris-raves**) *nm* celeriac.

célérité [selerite] *nf litt* celerity *litt*, swiftness, speed ■ **avec ~** swiftly, rapidly.

céleste [selɛst] *adj* **1.** [du ciel] celestial **2.** [du paradis] celestial, heavenly **3.** [de Dieu] divine **4.** [surnaturel - beauté, voix, mélodie] heavenly, sublime **5.** HIST : **le Céleste Empire** the Celestial Empire.

célibat [seliba] *nm* [d'un prêtre] celibacy ■ [d'un homme] celibacy, bachelorhood ■ [d'une femme] spinsterhood, celibacy ■ **elle a choisi le ~** she decided to remain single *ou* not to marry ■ **vivre dans le ~** [homme] to remain a bachelor ; [femme] to remain single ; [prêtre] to be celibate.

célibataire [selibatɛr] ◇ *adj* **1.** [homme, femme] single, unmarried ■ [prêtre] celibate ■ **il est encore ~** he's still a single man *ou* a bachelor **2.** ADMIN single.
◇ *nm* single man ADMIN bachelor ■ **un ~ endurci** a confirmed bachelor ■ **un club pour ~s** a singles club.
◇ *nf* single woman.

celle [sɛl] *f* ▷ **celui.**

celle-ci [sɛlsi], **celle-là** [sɛlla] *f* ▷ **celui.**

cellier [selje] *nm* storeroom *(for wine or food)*, pantry.

Cellophane® [selɔfan] *nf* Cellophane® ■ **sous ~** cellophane-wrapped.

cellulaire [selylɛr] *adj* **1.** BIOL [de la cellule] cell *(modif)* ■ [formé de cellules] cellular **2.** TÉLÉCOM ▷ **téléphone 3.** MIN porous, poriferous **4.** TECHNOL [béton] cellular ■ [matériau, mousse] expanded **5.** [carcéral] : **emprisonnement** *ou* **régime ~** solitary confinement ■ **voiture ~** prison *ou* police van *UK*, police wagon *US*.

cellule [selyl] *nf* **1.** BIOL cell ■ **~ nerveuse/sanguine** nerve/blood cell ■ **~souche** stem cell **2.** [élément constitutif] basic element *ou* unit ■ **~ familiale** family unit *ou* group **3.** [d'une ruche] cell **4.** [d'un prisonnier, d'un religieux] cell ■ **deux par ~** two to a cell **5.** POLIT cell **6.** [groupe de travail] : **~ de crise** crisis centre ■ **~ de réflexion** think tank **7.** PHOTO : **~ (photoélectrique)** photoelectric cell **8.** TECHNOL : **~ photovoltaïque** photovoltaic cell **9.** AÉRON airframe **10.** ACOUST & INFORM cell ■ **~ (de) mémoire** storage cell.

cellulite [selylit] *nf* cellulitis.

celluloïd [selylɔid] *nm* celluloid.

cellulose [selyloz] *nf* cellulose.

Celsius [sɛlsjys] *npr* Celsius.

celte [sɛlt] *adj* Celtic.
➔ **Celte** *nmf* Celt.

celtique [sɛltik] *adj* Celtic ■ **les langues ~s** the Celtic languages.

celui [səlɥi] (*f* **celle** [sɛl], *mpl* **ceux** [sø], *fpl* **celles** [sɛl]) *pron dém*
1. [suivi de la préposition 'de'] : **le train de 5 h est parti, prenons ~ de 6 h** we've missed the 5 o'clock train, let's get the 6 o'clock ■ **j'ai comparé mon salaire avec ~ d'Eve** I compared my salary with Eve's ■ **ceux d'entre vous qui veulent s'inscrire** those of you who wish to register
2. [suivi d'un pronom relatif] : **~, celle** the one ■ **ceux, celles** those, the ones ■ **c'est celle que j'ai achetée** that's the one I bought ■ **c'est ~ qui a réparé ma voiture** he's the one who fixed my car
3. [suivi d'un adjectif, d'un participe] : **achetez celle conforme aux normes** buy the one that complies with the standard ■ **tous ceux désirant participer à l'émission** all those wishing *ou* who wish to take part in the show.
➔ **celui-ci** (*f* **celle-ci**, *mpl* **ceux-ci**, *fpl* **celles-ci**) *pron dém*
1. [désignant une personne ou un objet proches] : **~-ci, celle-ci** this one (here) ■ **ceux-ci, celles-ci** these ones, these (here) ■ **c'est ~-ci que je veux** this is the one I want, I want this one
2. [désignant ce dont on va parler ou ce dont on vient de parler] : **son inquiétude était celle-ci...** his worry was as follows... ■ **elle voulait voir Anne, mais celle-ci était absente** she wanted to see Anne, but she was out ■ **ah ~-ci, il me fera toujours rire!** now he always makes me laugh!
➔ **celui-là** (*f* **celle-là**, *mpl* **ceux-là**, *fpl* **celles-là**) *pron dém*
1. [désignant une personne ou un objet éloignés] : **~-là, celle-là** that one (there) ■ **ceux-là, celles-là** those ones, those (over there) ■ **c'est ~-là que je veux** that's the one I want, I want that one ■ **il n'y a aucun rapport entre les deux décisions, celle-ci n'explique pas celle-là** the two decisions are unconnected, the latter is no explanation for the former
2. [emploi expressif] : **il a toujours une bonne excuse, ~-là!** he's always got a good excuse, that one!

cément [semɑ̃] *nm* **1.** MÉTALL cement **2.** ANAT cement, cementum.

cendre [sɑ̃dr] *nf* **1.** [résidu - gén] ash, ashes ; [- de charbon] cinders ■ **~ de bois/de cigarette** wood/cigarette ash ■ **une viande au goût de ~** meat with a smoky taste ■ **mettre** *ou* **réduire en ~s** [maison] to burn to the ground **2.** GÉOL (volcanic) ash **3.** *littéraire* **~s** [dépouille] ashes, remains **4.** RELIG : **les Cendres, le mercredi des Cendres** Ash Wednesday.

cendré, e [sɑ̃dre] *adj* **1.** [gris] ashen, ash *(modif)*, ash-coloured **2.** [couvert de cendres] ash covered ■ **fromage ~** cheese matured in wood ash.
➔ **cendrée** *nf* **1.** CHASSE & PÊCHE dust shot **2.** [revêtement] cinder ■ [piste] cinder track.

cendreux, euse [sɑ̃drø, øz] *adj* **1.** [plein de cendres] full of ashes **2.** [gris - écorce, roche] ash-coloured ; [- teint] ashen, ashy **3.** MÉTALL grainy, granular ■ [sol] ashy.

cendrier [sɑ̃drije] *nm* [de fumeur] ashtray ■ [de fourneau] ash pit ■ [de poêle] ashpan ■ [de locomotive] ash box.

cendrillon [sɑ̃drijɔ̃] *nf litt* [servante] drudge.

Cendrillon [sɑ̃drijɔ̃] *npr* Cinderella.

cène [sɛn] *nf* **1.** [dernier repas] : **la Cène** the Last Supper **2.** [communion] Holy Communion, Lord's Supper.

cénobite [senɔbit] *nm* cenobite.

cénotaphe [senɔtaf] *nm* cenotaph.

cens [sɑ̃s] *nm* **1.** ANTIQ [recensement] census **2.** HIST : **~ électoral** poll tax ■ [féodal] quitrent.

censé, e [sɑ̃se] *adj* supposed to ■ **vous êtes ~ arriver à 9 h** [indication] you're supposed to arrive at 9 ; [rappel à l'ordre] we expect you to arrive at 9.

censément [sɑ̃semɑ̃] *adv* apparently, seemingly.

censeur [sɑ̃sœr] *nm* **1.** ÉDUC deputy headmaster *ou* head teacher *UK*, assistant principal *US* ■ **Madame le ~** the deputy headmistress *ou* head teacher *UK*, the assistant principal *US* **2.** [responsable de la censure] censor **3.** *sout* [critique] critic **4.** ANTIQ censor.

censitaire [sɑ̃sitɛr] *adj* poll-tax based.

censure [sɑ̃syr] *nf* **1.** [interdiction] censorship ▪ **face à la ~ paternelle** faced with his father's instruction that he shouldn't do it ▪ [commission] : **la ~** the censors ; [examen] censorship **2.** POLIT censure **3.** RELIG censure ▪ **les ~s de l'Église** the censure of the Church **4.** PSYCHOL & ANTIQ censorship.

censurer [3] [sɑ̃syre] *vt* **1.** [film, livre] to censor **2.** POLIT & RELIG to censure **3.** PSYCHOL to exercise censorship on **4.** *sout* [critiquer] to criticize, to censure.

cent [sɑ̃] ◇ *dét* **1.** a *ou* one hundred ▪ **~ mille** a hundred thousand ▪ **deux ~s filles** two hundred girls ▪ **trois ~ quatre rangs** three hundred and four rows ▶ **les Cent-Jours** HIST the Hundred Days ▪ **elle est aux ~ coups** [affolée] she's frantic ▪ **tu as ~ fois raison** you're a hundred per cent right ▪ **je préfère ~ fois celle-ci** I prefer this one a hundred times over ▪ **faire les ~ pas** to pace up and down ▪ **je ne vais pas attendre ~ sept ans** *fam* I'm not going to wait forever (and a day) ▪ **je m'embête** *fam ou* **m'emmerde**△ **à ~ sous de l'heure** I'm bored stiff *ou* to death **2.** [dans des séries] : **page deux ~ (six)** page two hundred (and six) ▪ **l'an neuf ~** the year nine hundred **3.** SPORT : **le ~ mètres** the hundred metres ▪ **le quatre ~ mètres haies** the four hundred metres hurdle *ou* hurdles ▪ **le ~ mètres nage libre** the hundred metres freestyle.
◇ *nm* **1.** [chiffre] : **j'habite au ~** I live at number one hundred **2.** [centaine] hundred **3.** [centime] cent BANQUE.

centaine [sɑ̃tɛn] *nf* **1.** [cent unités] hundred ▪ **la colonne des ~s** the hundreds column **2.** [environ cent] : **une ~ de** about a hundred, a hundred or so ▪ **plusieurs ~s de dollars** several hundred dollars ▪ **elle a traité des ~s de personnes** she treated hundreds of people **3.** [âge] : **j'espère atteindre la ~** I hope to live to be a hundred ▪ **dépasser la ~** to be over a hundred.
◆ **par centaines** *loc adv* by the hundreds ▪ **les gens arrivent par ~s** people are arriving by the hundreds *ou* in their hundreds.

centaure [sɑ̃tɔr] *nm* centaur.

centenaire [sɑ̃tnɛr] ◇ *adj* hundred-year old ▪ **plusieurs fois ~** several hundred years old.
◇ *nmf* [vieillard] centenarian.
◇ *nm* [anniversaire] centenary, centennial *US & Canada*.

centésimal, e, aux [sɑ̃tezimal, o] *adj* centesimal.

centième [sɑ̃tjɛm] ◇ *adj num* hundredth, *voir aussi* **cinquième**.
◇ *nm* **1.** [fraction] hundredth part **2.** *loc* **ce n'est pas le ~ de ce qu'il m'a fait** it doesn't even come close to what he did to me.
◇ *nf* THÉÂTRE hundredth performance.

centigrade [sɑ̃tigrad] *adj* centigrade.

centigramme [sɑ̃tigram] *nm* centigram.

centilitre [sɑ̃tilitr] *nm* centilitre.

centime [sɑ̃tim] *nm* **1.** [centième d'euro] (euro)cent ▪ **ça ne m'a pas coûté un ~** it didn't cost me a penny *UK ou* one cent *US* **2.** [centième de franc] centime **3.** FIN : **~s additionnels** additional tax.

centimètre [sɑ̃timɛtr] *nm* **1.** [unité de mesure] centimetre **2.** [ruban] tape measure, tape line *US*.

centrafricain, e [sɑ̃trafrikɛ̃, ɛn] *adj* Central African.
◆ **Centrafricain, e** *nm, f* Central African.

centrage [sɑ̃traʒ] *nm* centring.

central, e, aux [sɑ̃tral, o] *adj* **1.** [du milieu d'un objet] middle *(avant n)*, central ▪ **le trou ~** the central *ou* middle hole **2.** [du centre d'une ville] central **3.** ADMIN & POLIT central, national **4.** [principal] main, crucial ▪ **le point ~ de votre exposé** the main *ou* crucial *ou* key point in your thesis **5.** PHON centre *(modif)*.
◆ **central** *nm* **1.** TÉLÉCOM : **~ (téléphonique)** (telephone) exchange **2.** SPORT [de tennis] : **(court) ~** centre court.
◆ **centrale** *nf* **1.** [usine] power station ▪ **~e électrique/nucléaire/thermique** power/nuclear/thermal station **2.** POLIT : **~e ouvrière** trade *UK ou* labor *US* union confederation **3.** [prison] county jail, penitentiary *US*.
◆ **centrale d'achats** *nf* [groupement] central purchasing department ▪ [magasin] discount store.

Centrale [sɑ̃tral] *npr grande école training engineers.*

centralien, enne [sɑ̃traljɛ̃, ɛn] *nm, f student or ex-student of Centrale.*

centralisateur, trice [sɑ̃tralizatœr, tris] *adj* centralizing.

centralisation [sɑ̃tralizasjɔ̃] *nf* centralization, centralizing.

centraliser [3] [sɑ̃tralize] *vt* to centralize.

centralisme [sɑ̃tralism] *nm* centralism.

centraméricain, e [sɑ̃tramerikɛ̃, ɛn] *adj* Central American.
◆ **Centraméricain, e** *nm, f* Central American.

centre [sɑ̃tr] *nm* **1.** [milieu - gén] middle, centre ; [- d'une cible] bull's eye, centre ▪ **le ~** [d'une ville] the centre ▪ **elle était le ~ de tous les regards** all eyes were fixed on her ▶ **il se prend pour le ~ du monde** *ou* **de l'univers** he thinks the world revolves around him
2. [concentration] : **~ industriel** industrial area ▪ **~ urbain** town
3. [organisme] centre ▪ **~ d'accueil** reception centre ▪ **~ aéré** *holiday activity centre for schoolchildren* ▪ **~ commercial** shopping centre *ou UK* precinct, (shopping) mall *US* ▪ **~ de contrôle** [spatial] mission control ▪ **~ culturel** art *ou* arts centre ▪ **~ de dépistage du cancer/SIDA** centre for cancer/AIDS screening ▪ **~ de documentation** information centre ▪ **~ pour femmes battues** women's refuge ▪ **~ d'hébergement pour les sans-abri** hostel for the homeless ▪ **~ hospitalier** hospital (complex) ▪ **~ hospitalo-universitaire** teaching hospital ▪ **~ médical** clinic ▪ **~ social** social services office ▪ **~ de tri** sorting office
4. [point essentiel] main *ou* key point, heart, centre ▪ **être au ~ de** to be the key point of, to be at the heart *ou* centre of ▶ **~ d'intérêt** centre of interest
5. SC centre ▪ **~ de gravité** *pr & fig* centre of gravity ▪ **~ nerveux** nerve centre ▪ **~ vital** *pr* vital organs ; *fig* nerve centre
6. POLIT middle ground, centre ▶ **~ droit/gauche** moderate right/left ▪ **il est (de) ~ gauche** he's left-of-centre
7. SPORT [au basketball] post, pivot ▪ FOOTBALL centre pass
8. INDUST : **~ d'usinage** turning shop.
◆ **Centre** *npr m* : **le ~** Centre *(French region)*.

CENTRE

This administrative region includes the *départements* of Cher, Eure-et-Loire, Indre, Indre-et-Loire, Loir-et-Cher and Loiret (capital: Orléans).

centrer [3] [sɑ̃tre] *vt* **1.** [gén - PHOTO] [SPORT] to centre **2.** [orienter] : **centrons le débat** let's give the discussion a focus ▪ **être centré sur** to be centred *ou* focussed around ▪ **le documentaire était centré sur l'enfance de l'artiste** the documentary was focussed around the artist's childhood.

centreur [sɑ̃trœr] *nm plastic adaptor for singles on a record-player.*

centre-ville [sɑ̃trəvil] (*pl* **centres-villes**) *nm* town centre ▪ **aller au ~** to go into the centre (of town).

centrifuge [sɑ̃trifyʒ] *adj* centrifugal.

centrifuger [17] [sɑ̃trifyʒe] *vt* to centrifuge.

centrifugeuse [sɑ̃trifyʒøz] *nf* **1.** MÉD & TECHNOL centrifuge **2.** CULIN juice extractor, juicer *US*.

centripète [sɑ̃tripɛt] *adj* centripetal.

centrisme [sɑ̃trism] *nm* centrism.

centriste [sɑ̃trist] *adj & nmf* centrist.

centuple [sɑ̃typl] ◇ *adj* : **1 000 est un nombre ~ de 10** 1,000 is a hundred times 10.
◇ *nm* : **le ~ de 20 est 2 000** a hundred times 20 is 2,000 ▪ **il a gagné le ~ de sa mise** his bet paid off a hundredfold.
◆ **au centuple** *loc adv* a hundredfold.

centupler [3] [sɑ̃typle] ◇ *vt* to increase a hundredfold *ou* a hundred times, to multiply by a hundred.
◇ *vi* to increase a hundredfold ▪ **quelques placements heureux ont fait ~ sa fortune** a few lucky investments have increased his fortune one-hundredfold.

centurie [sɑ̃tyri] *nf* century.

centurion [sɑ̃tyrjɔ̃] *nm* centurion.

cep [sɛp] *nm* BOT : **~ (de vigne)** vine stock.

cépage [sepaʒ] *nm* vine.

cèpe [sɛp] *nm* **1.** BOT boletus **2.** CULIN cep.

cependant [səpɑ̃dɑ̃] *conj* however, nevertheless, yet ▪ **je suis d'accord avec vous, j'ai ~ une petite remarque à faire** I agree with you, however I have one small comment to make ▪ **il parle très bien, avec un léger accent ~** he speaks very well, but with a slight accent.
◆ **cependant que** *loc conj litt* while.

céphalée [sefale], **céphalalgie** [sefalalʒi] *nf* headache, cephalgia *spéc.*

céphalopode [sefalɔpɔd] *nm* cephalopod ▪ **les ~s** the Cephalopoda.

céphalo-rachidien, enne [sefalɔraʃidjɛ̃, ɛn] (*mpl* **céphalo-rachidiens,** *fpl* **céphalo-rachidiennes**) *adj* cerebrospinal, cephalorachidian *spéc.*

céramique [seramik] ◇ *adj* ceramic.
◇ *nf* **1.** [art] ceramics *(U)*, pottery **2.** [objet] piece of ceramic **3.** [matière] ceramic ▪ **des carreaux de ~** ceramic tiles **4.** MÉD [dentisterie] dental ceramics *ou* porcelain.

céramiste [seramist] *nmf* ceramist.

cérat [sera] *nm* cerate.

cerbère [sɛrbɛr] *nm litt* **1.** [concierge] ill-tempered doorkeeper **2.** [geôlier] jailer.

Cerbère [sɛrbɛr] *npr* MYTHOL Cerberus.

cerceau, x [sɛrso] *nm* [d'enfant, d'acrobate, de tonneau, de jupon] hoop ▪ [de tonnelle] half-hoop.

cerclage [sɛrklaʒ] *nm* **1.** [action de cercler] hooping **2.** MÉD cerclage **3.** [cercles d'une futaille] hooping.

cercle [sɛrkl] *nm* **1.** GÉOM circle ▪ [forme] circle, ring ▪ **décrire des ~s dans le ciel** [avion, oiseau] to fly around in circles, to wheel round, to circle ▪ **faire ~ autour de qqn** to stand *ou* to gather round sb in a circle ▪ **en ~** in a circle ➊ **~ vicieux** vicious circle
2. [gamme, étendue - d'activités, de connaissances] range, scope
3. [groupe] circle, group ▪ **le ~ de mes amis** my circle *ou* group of friends ➊ **~ de famille** family (circle) ▪ **~ littéraire** literary circle
4. [club] club ▪ **un ~ militaire** an officer's club
5. [objet circulaire] hoop
6. ASTRON & MATH circle
7. GÉOGR : **~ polaire** polar circle ▪ **~ polaire Arctique/Antarctique** Arctic/Antarctic Circle
8. ÉCON : **~ de qualité** quality circle.

cercler [3] [sɛrkle] *vt* **1.** [emballage] to ring ▪ [tonneau] to hoop ▪ **une caisse cerclée de fer** an iron-bound crate **2.** MÉD to wire.

cercueil [sɛrkœj] *nm* coffin *UK*, casket *US*.

céréale [sereal] *nf* **1.** BOT cereal **2.** CULIN : **des ~s** (breakfast) cereal.

céréaliculture [serealikyltyr] *nf* cereal farming.

céréalier, ère [serealje, ɛr] *adj* cereal *(modif)*.
◆ **céréalier** *nm* **1.** [producteur] cereal farmer *ou* grower **2.** [navire] grain ship.

cérébral, e, aux [serebral, o] ◇ *adj* **1.** ANAT cerebral **2.** MÉD brain *(modif)* **3.** [intellectuel - activité, travail] intellectual, mental ; [- film, livre] cerebral, intellectual.
◇ *nm, f* : **c'est un ~/une ~e** he's/she's an intellectual.

cérébro-vasculaire [serebrovaskylɛr] *adj* cerebrovascular.

cérémonial, als [seremɔnjal] *nm* [règles, livre] ceremonial.

cérémonie [seremɔni] *nf* **1.** RELIG ceremony **2.** [fête] ceremony, solemn *ou* formal occasion ▪ **~ d'ouverture/de clôture** opening/closing ceremony ▪ **~ nuptiale** wedding ceremony ▪ **la ~ de remise des prix** the award ceremony **3.** ANTHR ceremony, rites ▪ **~ d'initiation** initiation rites ▪ **~ du thé** tea ceremony.
◆ **cérémonies** *nfpl péj* [manières] fuss, palaver ▪ **ne fais pas tant de ~s** don't make such a fuss.
◆ **avec cérémonie** *loc adv* ceremoniously.
◆ **de cérémonie** *loc adj* [tenue] ceremonial.
◆ **en grande cérémonie** *loc adv* [apporter, présenter] with great formality, very ceremoniously.
◆ **sans cérémonie** *loc adv* **1.** [simplement] casually, informally ▪ **pas besoin de te changer, c'est sans ~** just come as you are, it's an informal occasion **2.** *péj* [abruptement] unceremoniously, without so much as a by-your-leave.

cérémonieux, euse [seremɔnjø, øz] *adj* ceremonious, formal.

cerf [sɛr] *nm* stag.

cerfeuil [sɛrfœj] *nm* chervil.

cerf-volant [sɛrvɔlɑ̃] (*pl* **cerfs-volants**) *nm* **1.** JEUX kite ▪ **jouer au ~** to fly a kite **2.** ZOOL stag beetle.

cerisaie [sərizɛ] *nf* cherry orchard.

cerise [səriz] ◇ *nf* [fruit] cherry ▪ **la ~ sur le gâteau** *fig* the icing on the cake.
◇ *adj inv* cherry, cherry-red, cerise.

cerisier [sərizje] *nm* **1.** [arbre] cherry (tree) **2.** [bois] cherry (wood).

CERN, Cern [sɛrn] (*abr de* **Conseil européen pour la recherche nucléaire**) *npr m* CERN.

cerne [sɛrn] *nm* **1.** [sous les yeux] shadow, (dark) ring ▪ **elle a des ~s** she's got dark rings under her eyes **2.** TEXT ring **3.** HORT (annual) ring **4.** ART outline.

cerné, e [sɛrne] *adj* : **avoir les yeux ~s** to have (dark) rings under one's eyes.

cerneau, x [sɛrno] *nm* (shelled) walnut.

cerner [3] [sɛrne] *vt* **1.** [entourer] to surround, to lie around ▪ **les lacs qui cernent la ville** the lakes dotted around the *ou* surrounding the town **2.** [assiéger - ville] to surround, to seal off *(sép)* ; [- armée, population] to surround ▪ **vous êtes cernés!** you are surrounded! **3.** [définir - question, problème] to define, to determine ▪ **ceci nous a permis de ~ le problème de près** this has enabled us to home in on the problem ▪ **il est difficile à ~** I can't make him out **4.** [ouvrir - noix] to crack open, to shell **5.** HORT to ring.

CERS (*abr de* **Commission européenne de recherches spatiales**) *nf* ESRO.

certain[1], e [sɛrtɛ̃, ɛn] *(devant nm commençant par voyelle ou h muet* [sɛrtɛn]*) adj* **1.** [incontestable - amélioration] definite ; [- preuve] definite, positive ; [- avantage, rapport] definite, clear ; [- décision, invitation, prix] definite ▪ **avec un enthousiasme ~** with real *ou* obvious enthusiasm ▪ **tenir qqch pour ~** to have no doubt about sthg ▪ **le projet a beaucoup de retard – c'est ~, mais...** the project is a long way behind schedule – that's certainly true but... ▪ **j'aurais préféré attendre, c'est ~** I'd have preferred to wait, of course ▪ **une chose est ~e** one thing's for certain *ou* sure **2.** [inéluctable - échec, victoire] certain ▪ **on nous avait présenté son départ comme ~** we'd been told he was certain to go **3.** [persuadé] : **être ~ de** : **être ~ de ce qu'on avance** to be sure *ou* certain about what one is saying ▪ **il n'est pas très ~ de sa décision** he's not sure he's made the right decision ▪ **si tu pars battu, tu es ~ de perdre!** if you think you're going to lose, (then) you're bound *ou* sure *ou* certain to lose! ▪ **êtes-vous sûr que c'était lui? – j'en suis ~!** are you sure it was him? – I'm positive! ▪ **ils céderont – n'en sois pas si ~** they'll give in – don't be so sure ▪ **si j'étais ~ qu'il vienne** if I knew (for sure) *ou* if I was certain that he was coming **4.** MATH & PHILOS certain.
◆ **certain** *nm* BOURSE fixed *ou* direct rate of exchange.

certain[2], e [sɛrtɛ̃, ɛn *(devant nm commençant par voyelle ou h muet)* sɛrtɛn] *dét (adj indéf)* **1.** [exprimant l'indétermination] : **à remettre à une ~e date** to be handed in on a certain date ▪ **à**

un ~ moment at one point ■ **un ~ nombre d'entre eux** some of them ■ **j'y ai cru un ~ temps** I believed it for a while ■ **d'une ~e façon** *ou* **manière** in a way ■ **dans** *ou* **en un ~ sens** in a sense **2.** [exprimant une quantité non négligeable] : **il a fait preuve d'une ~e intelligence** he has shown a certain amount of *ou* some intelligence ■ **il faut un ~ courage!** you certainly need some pluck! **3.** [devant un nom de personne] : **les dialogues sont l'œuvre d'un ~...** the dialogue is by someone called... *ou* by one... ■ **il voit souvent un ~ Robert** *péj* he sees a lot of some character called Robert.

◆ **certains, certaines** ◇ *dét (adj indéf pl)* [quelques] some, certain ■ **~es fois** sometimes, on some occasions ■ **~s jours** sometimes, on some days ■ **je connais ~es personnes qui n'auraient pas hésité** I can think of some *ou* a few people who wouldn't have thought twice about it.
◇ *pron indéf pl* [personnes] some (people) ■ [choses] some ■ [d'un groupe] some (of them) ■ **~s d'entre vous semblent ne pas avoir compris** some of you seem not to have understood.

certainement [sɛrtɛnmɑ̃] *adv* **1.** [sans aucun doute] certainly, surely, no doubt ■ **il va ~ échouer** he is bound to fail **2.** [probablement] surely, certainly ■ **il y a ~ une solution à ton problème** there must be *ou* there is surely a way to solve your problem ■ **elle va ~ t'appeler** she'll most likely call you ■ **tu te souviens ~ de Paul?** surely you remember Paul?, your remember Paul, surely? **3.** [dans une réponse] certainly ■ **je peux? – ~!** may I? – certainly *ou* of course!

certes [sɛrt] *adv sout* **1.** [assurément] certainly, indeed ■ **vous n'ignorez ~ pas quelle est la situation** I'm sure you are not unaware of the situation ■ **~, je ne pouvais pas lui dire la vérité** I certainly couldn't tell him the truth **2.** [servant de réponse] certainly ■ **m'en voulez-vous? – ~ non!** are you angry with me? – of course not *ou* certainly not! **3.** [indiquant la concession] of course, certainly ■ **~, sa situation n'est pas enviable, mais que faire?** his situation is certainly not to be envied, but what can be done?

certif [sɛrtif] *nm fam* = **certificat d'études (primaires)**.

certificat [sɛrtifika] *nm* **1.** [attestation] certificate ■ **~ de bonne vie et de bonnes mœurs** DR character reference ■ **~ médical** doctor's certificate ■ **~ de naissance** birth certificate ■ **~ d'origine** certificate of origin ■ **~ de sécurité** INFORM security certficate ■ **~ de scolarité** ÉDUC school attendance certificate ; UNIV university attendance certificate ■ **~ de travail** ≃ P 45 *UK*, attestation of employment ■ **~ de vaccination** vaccination certificate **2.** [diplôme] diploma, certificate ■ **~ d'aptitude professionnelle = CAP** ■ **~ d'aptitude au professorat de l'enseignement du second degré = CAPES** ■ **~ d'aptitude au professorat de l'enseignement technique = CAPET** ■ **~ d'études (primaires)** basic school-leaving qualification *(abolished in Metropolitan France in 1989)*.

certifié, e [sɛrtifje] ◇ *adj* holding the CAPES.
◇ *nm, f* CAPES holder.

certifier [9] [sɛrtifje] *vt* **1.** [assurer] to assure **2.** DR [garantir - caution] to guarantee, to counter-secure ; [- signature] to witness ; [- document] to certify ■ **certifié conforme : une copie certifiée conforme (à l'original)** a certified copy of the original document.

certitude [sɛrtityd] *nf* certainty, certitude *sout* ■ **avoir la ~ de qqch** to be convinced of sthg ■ **je sais avec ~ que...** I know for a certainty that...
Voir module d'usage

cérumen [serymɛn] *nm* earwax, cerumen *spéc.*

cerveau, x [sɛrvo] *nm* **1.** ANAT brain ■ **~ antérieur** forebrain ■ **~ moyen** midbrain ■ **~ postérieur** hindbrain ■ **il a le ~ malade** *fam ou* **dérangé** *fam ou* **fêlé** *fam* he's got a screw loose, he's cracked **2.** *fam* [génie] brainy person ■ **c'est un ~** he's got brains **3.** [instigateur] brains ■ **être le ~ de qqch** to be the brains behind sthg **4.** INFORM : **~ électronique** electronic brain.

cervelas [sɛrvəla] *nm* ≃ saveloy *(sausage)*.

cervelet [sɛrvəlɛ] *nm* cerebellum.

cervelle [sɛrvɛl] *nf* **1.** ANAT brain **2.** *fam* [intelligence] brain ■ **se mettre qqch dans la ~** to get sthg into one's head ■ **il n'a** *ou* **il n'y a rien dans sa petite ~** he's got nothing between his ears ■ **quand elle a quelque chose dans la ~** when she gets an idea into her head ▶ **avoir une ~ d'oiseau** *ou* **une tête sans ~** to be bird-brained **3.** CULIN brains ▶ **~ de canut** *fromage frais with herbs*.

cervical, e, aux [sɛrvikal, o] *adj* cervical.

cervidé [sɛrvide] *nm* cervid ■ **les ~s** the Cervidae *spéc.*

Cervin [sɛrvɛ̃] *npr m* : **le (mont) ~** the Matterhorn.

cervoise [sɛrvwaz] *nf* ale, barley wine.

ces [sɛ] *pl* ▷ **ce** *(dét, adj dém)*.

CES *nm* (*abr de* **collège d'enseignement secondaire**) *former secondary school.*

césar [sezar] *nm* **1.** [despote] tyrant, dictator **2.** CINÉ *French cinema award.*

César [sezar] *npr* Caesar ■ **rendez à ~ ce qui appartient à ~** render unto Caesar that which is Caesar's.

césarienne [sezarjɛn] *nf* Caesarean section.

cessant, e [sɛsɑ̃, ɑ̃t] *adj* ▷ **affaire**.

cessation [sɛsasjɔ̃] *nf* **1.** MIL : **~ des hostilités** cease-fire **2.** [d'une activité] cessation, stopping ■ **~ du travail** stoppage **3.** COMM : **~ de paiement** suspension of payments ■ **être en ~ de paiement** to have suspended (all) payments ■ **~ d'activité** termination of business ■ **pour cause de ~ de commerce** due to closure.

cesse [sɛs] *nf* : **n'avoir de ~ que** *sout* : **elle n'aura de ~ qu'elle n'ait trouvé la réponse** she will not rest until she finds the answer.
◆ **sans cesse** *loc adv* continually, constantly.

cesser [4] [sese] ◇ *vi* [pluie] to stop, to cease *sout* ■ [vent] to die down, to abate *sout* ■ [combat] to (come to a) stop ■ [bruit, mouvement] to stop, to cease *sout* ■ **~ de** *sout* to stop ■ **cesse de**

LA CERTITUDE

I'm sure it'll work. Je suis sûr que ça va marcher.

I'm absolutely certain it was him. Je suis sûr et certain que c'était lui.

He's definitely the man I saw. C'est lui que j'ai vu, j'en suis sûr.

There's no doubt about it, she's the guilty one. Aucun doute, c'est elle la coupable.

I know for a fact that he couldn't have done it. Je sais pertinemment que ça ne peut pas être lui.

There's no way she could have known. Elle ne pouvait absolument pas le savoir.

I'm convinced he was lying. Je suis convaincu qu'il mentait.

Take it from me, he's the right man for the job. Fais-moi confiance, c'est l'homme qu'il nous/vous faut.

Believe (you) me, it won't be easy. Ça ne va pas être facile, crois-moi.

I bet he changes his mind! Je parie qu'il va changer d'avis !

pleurer stop crying ■ **il n'a pas cessé de pleuvoir** it rained non-stop ■ **je ne cesse d'y penser** I cannot stop myself thinking about it.
◇ *vt* **1.** [arrêter] to stop, to halt ■ **~ le travail** to down tools, to walk out ■ **faire ~ qqch** to put a stop to sthg **2.** MIL : **~ le combat** to stop fighting ■ **~ le feu** to cease fire.

cessez-le-feu [seselfø] *nm inv* cease-fire.

cessible [sesibl] *adj* assignable, transferable.

cession [sɛsjɔ̃] *nf* DR transfer, assignment ■ **~ de bail** lease transfer.

cession-bail [sesjɔ̃baj] (*pl* **cessions-bails** *ou pl* **cessions-baux**) *nf* lease-back.

cessionnaire [sɛsjɔnɛr] *nmf* assignee, transferee.

c'est-à-dire [setadir] *loc adv* **1.** [introduisant une explication] that is (to say), i.e, in other words ■ [pour demander une explication] : **~?** what do you mean? **2.** [introduisant une rectification] or rather ■ **il est venu hier, ~ plutôt avant-hier** he came yesterday, I mean *ou* or rather the day before yesterday **3.** [introduisant une hésitation] : **tu penses y aller? – eh bien, ~...** are you thinking of going? – well, you know *ou* I mean...
◆ **c'est-à-dire que** *loc conj* **1.** [introduisant un refus, une hésitation] actually, as a matter of fact ■ **voulez-vous nous accompagner? – ~ que je suis un peu fatigué** do you want to come with us? – I'm afraid *ou* actually I'm a bit tired **2.** [introduisant une explication] which means **3.** [introduisant une rectification] or rather.

césure [sezyr] *nf* caesura.

cet [sɛt] *m* ▻ **ce (dét) (adj dém).**

cétacé [setase] *nm* cetacean ■ **les ~s** the Cetacea.

cette [sɛt] *f* ▻ **ce (dét) (adj dém).**

ceux [sø] *pl* ▻ **celui.**

ceux-ci [søsi], **ceux-là** [søla] *mpl* & *mpl* ▻ **celui.**

Ceylan [selɑ̃] *npr* Ceylon.

ceylanais, e [selanɛ, ɛz] *adj* Ceylonese.
◆ **Ceylanais, e** *nmf sing inhabitant of or person from Ceylon.*

cf. (*abr de* **confer**) cf.

CFA (*abr de* **Communauté financière africaine**) *npr* : **franc ~** *currency used in former French African colonies.*

CFAO (*abr de* **conception et fabrication assistées par ordinateur**) *nf* CADCAM.

CFC (*abr de* **chlorofluorocarbone**) *nm* CFC.

CFDT (*abr de* **Confédération française démocratique du travail**) *npr f French trade union.*

CFTC (*abr de* **Confédération française des travailleurs chrétiens**) *npr f French trade union.*

CGC (*abr de* **Confédération générale des cadres**) *npr f French management union.*

CGT (*abr de* **Confédération générale du travail**) *npr f major association of French trade unions (affiliated to the Communist Party).*

ch (*abr de* **cheval-vapeur**) hp.

ch. 1. = **charges 2.** = **chauffage 3.** = **cherche.**

CH (*abr écrite de* **Confédération helvétique**) *Swiss nationality sticker on a car.*

chablis [ʃabli] *nm* ŒNOL Chablis.

chablon [ʃablɔ̃] *nm Suisse* stencil.

chabrot [ʃabro] *nm* [dialecte] *country tradition of adding red wine to the last few spoonfuls of soup in one's bowl.*

chacal, als [ʃakal] *nm* **1.** ZOOL jackal **2.** *péj* [personne] vulture, wolf.

cha-cha-cha [tʃatʃatʃa] *nm inv* cha-cha, cha-cha-cha.

chacun, e [ʃakœ̃, yn] *pron indéf* **1.** [chaque personne, chaque chose] each ■ **~ à sa façon, ils ont raison** each one is right in his own way ■ **~ de** each (one) of ■ **~ des employés a une tâche à remplir** each employee has a job to do ■ **~ son tour : Madame, ~ son tour** please wait your turn, Madam ■ **alors comme ça tu pars en vacances? – eh oui, ~ son tour!** so you're off on holiday, are you? – well, it's my turn now! ■ **nous y sommes allés ~ à notre tour** we each went in turn **2.** [tout le monde] everyone, everybody ■ **à ~ ses goûts** to each his own ■ **à ~ son métier** every man to his own trade ■ **tout un ~** everybody, each and every person ▶ **à ~ sa ~e** *fam* every Jack has his Jill ■ **~ pour soi** every man for himself.

chafouin, e [ʃafwɛ̃, in] *adj péj* **un petit visage ~** a pinched *ou* foxy face.

chagrin[1] [ʃagrɛ̃] *nm* [peine] sorrow, grief ■ **causer du ~ à qqn** to cause distress to *ou* to distress sb ■ **avoir un ~ d'amour** to be disappointed in love.

chagrin[2] [ʃagrɛ̃] *nm* [cuir] shagreen.

chagrin[3]**, e** [ʃagrɛ̃, in] *adj litt* **1.** [triste] sad, sorrowful, woeful *litt* **2.** [revêche] ill-tempered, quarrelsome.

chagriner [3] [ʃagrine] *vt* **1.** [attrister] to grieve, to distress **2.** [contrarier] to worry, to bother, to upset **3.** [cuir] to shagreen, to grain.

chah [ʃa] = **shah.**

chahut [ʃay] *nm fam* rumpus, hullabaloo, uproar ■ **faire du ~** [élèves] to make a racket, to kick up a rumpus.

chahuter [3] [ʃayte] *fam* ◇ *vi* [être indiscipliné] to kick up a rumpus, to make a racket.
◇ *vt* **1.** [houspiller - professeur] to rag, to bait ; [- orateur] to heckle ■ **un professeur chahuté** a teacher who can't control his pupils ■ **se faire ~ : il se fait ~ en classe** he can't keep (his class in) order ■ **le Premier Ministre s'est fait ~ à l'Assemblée** the Prime Minister was heckled in parliament **2.** [remuer] to knock about, to bash around.

chahuteur, euse [ʃaytœr, øz] *fam* ◇ *adj* rowdy, boisterous.
◇ *nm, f* rowdy.

chai [ʃɛ] *nm* wine and spirits storehouse.

Chaillot [ʃajo] *npr* : **(le palais de) ~** *architectural complex built in 1937 on the site of the Trocadéro in Paris.*

chaînage [ʃɛnaʒ] *nm* INFORM chaining.

chaîne [ʃɛn] *nf* **1.** [attache, bijou] chain ■ **le chien était attaché à sa niche par une ~** the dog was chained to its kennel ■ **faire la ~** *fig* to form a (human) chain ▶ **~ de bicyclette** bicycle chain ■ **~ de sûreté** [sur un bijou] safety chain ; [sur une porte] (door) chain ■ **le peuple a brisé ses ~s** the people shook off their chains
2. [suite] chain, series ▶ **la ~ alimentaire** ÉCOL the food chain ■ **~ de montagnes** (mountain) range
3. TV channel ■ **je regarde la première ~** I'm watching channel one ■ **~ câblée** cable channel ■ **~ cryptée** pay channel *(for which one needs a special decoding unit)* ■ **une ~ payante** a subscription TV channel ■ **~ thématique** theme channel, dedicated channel
4. AUDIO : **~ hi-fi** hi-fi ■ **~ stéréo** stereo ■ **~ compacte** compact system ■ **~ laser** CD system
5. COMM [de restaurants, de supermarchés] chain
6. INDUST : **~ de montage/fabrication** assembly/production line
7. INFORM string ■ **~ vide/de caractères** nul/character string
8. CHIM & PHYS chain
9. TEXT warp
10. DANSE chain.
◆ **chaînes** *nfpl* AUTO (snow) chains.
◆ **à la chaîne** ◇ *loc adj* [travail] assembly-line *(modif)*, production-line *(modif)*.
◇ *loc adv* [travailler, produire] on the production line ■ **faire qqch à la ~** to mass-produce sthg.
◆ **en chaîne** *loc adj* : **des catastrophes en ~** a whole catalogue of disasters.

chaîner [4] [ʃene] *vt* **1.** CONSTR to chain, to tie **2.** [mesurer] to chain **3.** AUTO [pneu] to put chains on ■ [voiture] to fit with chains **4.** INFORM to chain.

chaînette [ʃɛnɛt] *nf* **1.** JOAILL small chain **2.** COUT : **(point de) ~** chain stitch **3.** [attache] : **~ de sûreté** safety chain.
◆ **en chaînette** *loc adj* ARCHIT & GÉOM catenary.

chaînon [ʃɛnɔ̃] *nm* **1.** [élément - d'une chaîne, d'un raisonnement] link ■ **le ~ manquant** *pr* & *fig* the missing link **2.** GÉOGR secondary chain *ou* range (of mountains) **3.** INFORM : **~ de données** data link.

chair [ʃɛr] ◇ *nf* **1.** [chez les humains, les animaux] : **la ~, les ~s** the flesh ➲ **~ à canon** cannon fodder ■ **~ fraîche : il aime la ~ fraîche** [ogre] he likes to eat children ; *hum* [séducteur] he's a bit of a cradle-snatcher ■ **avoir la ~ de poule** [avoir froid, avoir peur] to have goose pimples ■ **quelle horreur! ça me donne** *ou* **j'en ai la ~ de poule!** how awful! it gives me goose pimples! ■ **bien en ~** chubby ■ **un être de ~ et de sang** a creature of flesh and blood ■ **voir qqn en ~ et en os** to see sb in the flesh ■ **~ à saucisse** *pr* sausage meat ■ **je vais en faire de la ~ à saucisse** *ou* **à pâté!** *fam fig* I'm going to make mincemeat out of him! **2.** BOT flesh, pulp **3.** RELIG & *litt* **la ~ est faible** the flesh is weak ■ **la ~ de sa ~** his own flesh and blood.
◇ *adj inv* [couleur] flesh, flesh-coloured.
◆ **chairs** *nfpl* ART flesh parts *ou* tints.

chaire [ʃɛr] *nf* **1.** [estrade] rostrum ■ **monter en ~** *pr* to go up on the rostrum ; *fig* to start one's speech **2.** RELIG throne, cathedra ■ **la ~ apostolique** the Holy See **3.** UNIV chair ■ **être titulaire d'une ~ de linguistique** to hold a chair in linguistics.

chaise [ʃɛz] *nf* **1.** [siège] chair ■ **~ à bascule, ~ berçante** *Québec* rocking chair ■ **~ de cuisine/jardin** kitchen/garden chair ■ **~ haute** *ou* **d'enfant** *ou* **de bébé** highchair ■ **~ électrique** electric chair ■ **~ longue** [d'extérieur] deck *ou* canvas chair ; [d'intérieur] chaise longue ■ **faire de la ~ longue** to lounge about in a deck chair ■ **~ percée** commode ■ **~ pliante** folding chair ■ **~ à porteurs** sedan (chair) ■ **~ de poste** post chaise ■ **~ roulante** wheelchair **2.** JEUX : **~s musicales** musical chairs **3.** CONSTR wooden frame **4.** NAUT : **nœud de ~** bowline.

chaisier, ère [ʃɛzje, ɛr] *nm, f* **1.** [fabricant] chair maker **2.** [gardien] chair attendant *(in gardens or church)*.

chakra [ʃakra] *nm* chakra.

chaland[1] [ʃalɑ̃] *nm* NAUT barge.

chaland[2]**, e** [ʃalɑ̃, ɑ̃d] *nm, f arch* & COMM regular customer.

Chaldée [kalde] *npr f* : **(la) ~** Chaldea.

chaldéen, enne [kaldeɛ̃, ɛn] *adj* Chaldean.
◆ **Chaldéen, enne** *nmf sing* Chaldean.
◆ **chaldéen** *nm* LING Chaldee, Chaldean.

châle [ʃal] *nm* shawl.

chalet [ʃalɛ] *nm* [maison - alpine] chalet ; [- de plaisance] (wooden) cottage.

chaleur [ʃalœr] *nf* **1.** MÉTÉOR heat ■ **~ douce** warmth ■ **quelle ~!** what a scorcher! ■ **'craint** *ou* **ne pas exposer à la ~'** 'store in a cool place' **2.** PHYS heat ■ **~ massique** *ou* **spécifique** specific heat **3.** [sentiment] warmth ■ **il y avait une certaine ~ dans sa voix** his voice was warm (and welcoming) ■ **plaider une cause avec ~** to plead a case fervently *ou* with fervour ➲ **~ humaine** human warmth **4.** ART [d'une couleur] warmth.
◆ **chaleurs** *nfpl* **1.** MÉTÉOR : **les grandes ~s** the hottest days of the summer **2.** ZOOL heat ■ **la jument a ses ~s** the mare's on *UK ou* in *US* heat.
◆ **en chaleur** *loc adj* **1.** ZOOL on heat *UK*, in heat *US* **2.** ▲ [homme, femme] horny△.

chaleureusement [ʃalœrøzmɑ̃] *adv* warmly.

chaleureux, euse [ʃalœrø, øz] *adj* [remerciement] warm, sincere ■ [accueil] warm, cordial, hearty ■ [approbation] hearty, sincere ■ [voix] warm ■ [ami] warm-hearted.

châlit [ʃali] *nm* bedstead.

challenge [ʃalɑ̃ʒ, tʃalɛndʒ] *nm* **1.** [défi] challenge **2.** SPORT [épreuve] sporting contest ■ [trophée] trophy.

challenger [tʃalɛndʒœr] *nm* challenger.

chaloir [ʃalwar] *v impers arch* & *litt* **peu me** *ou* **peu m'en chaut** it matters (but) little to me.

chaloupe [ʃalup] *nf* [à moteur] launch ■ [à rames] rowing boat *UK*, rowboat *US*.

chaloupé, e [ʃalupe] *adj* **1.** [danse] gliding, swaying **2.** [démarche] rolling.

chalouper [3] [ʃalupe] *vi* **1.** [danser] to sway, to glide **2.** [marcher] to waddle.

chalumeau, x [ʃalymo] *nm* **1.** TECHNOL blowlamp *UK*, blowtorch *US* ➲ **~ oxhydrique/oxyacétylénique** oxyhydrogen/oxyacetylene torch **2.** MUS pipe **3.** [paille] straw.

chalut [ʃaly] *nm* trawl ■ **pêcher au ~** to trawl.

chalutier [ʃalytje] *nm* **1.** [pêcheur] trawlerman **2.** [bateau] trawler.

chamade [ʃamad] *nf* : **battre la ~** to beat *ou* to pound wildly.

chamaille [ʃamaj] *fam* = **chamaillerie.**

chamailler [3] [ʃamaje] ◆ **se chamailler** *vp (emploi réciproque) fam* to bicker, to squabble.
◆ **se chamailler avec** *vp+prép fam* to bicker with.

chamaillerie [ʃamajri] *nf fam* squabble, tiff ■ **~s** squabbling.

chamailleur, euse [ʃamajœr, øz] *fam* ◇ *adj* squabbling.
◇ *nm, f* bickerer, squabbler.

chaman, e [ʃaman] *nm, f* shaman.

chamanisme [ʃamanism] *nm* shamanism.

chamarrer [3] [ʃamare] *vt* to decorate, to adorn, to ornament ■ **un costume chamarré d'or** a costume decorated with gold.

chamarrures [ʃamaryr] *nfpl* trimmings, adornments ■ **elle adore les ~** she loves a glittery style of dress.

chambard [ʃɑ̃bar] *nm fam* din, racket, rumpus ■ **faire tout un ~** [faire du bruit] to kick up(a din), to make a rumpus ; [faire du désordre] to make a mess ; [protester] to kick up(a fuss), to raise a stink.

chambardement [ʃɑ̃bardəmɑ̃] *nm fam* upheaval ■ **le grand ~, le ~ général** the troubles.

chambarder [3] [ʃɑ̃barde] *vt fam* [endroit, objets] to mess up *(sép)*, to turn upside down *(sép)* ■ [projets] to upset, to overturn, to turn upside down.

chambellan [ʃɑ̃belɑ̃] *nm* chamberlain.

chamboulement [ʃɑ̃bulmɑ̃] *nm fam* **1.** [désordre] mess, shambles **2.** [changement] total change, upheaval ■ **il y a eu un ~ complet dans nos projets** our plans were turned upside down.

chambouler [3] [ʃɑ̃bule] *vt fam* [endroit, objets] to mess up *(sép)*, to turn upside down *(sép)* ■ [projets] to ruin, to upset, to mess up *(sép)* ■ **cette réunion imprévue a chamboulé mon emploi du temps** this last-minute meeting has messed up my schedule.

chambranle [ʃɑ̃brɑ̃l] *nm* [de cheminée] mantelpiece ■ [de porte] (door) frame *ou* casing ■ [de fenêtre] (window) frame *ou* casing.

chambre [ʃɑ̃br] *nf* **1.** [pièce] : **~ (à coucher)** (bed)room ■ **faire ~ à part** to sleep in separate rooms ■ **réserver une ~ d'hôtel** to book a hotel room ■ **~ individuelle** *ou* **pour une personne** single (room) ■ **~ double** *ou* **pour deux personnes** double room ■ **~ d'hôte** ≃ room in a guest house ■ **'~s à louer'** 'rooms available' ➲ **~ d'amis** guest *ou* spare room ■ **~ de bonne** *pr* maid's room ; [louée à un particulier] attic room *(often rented to a student)* ■ **~ d'enfant** child's room ; [pour tout-petits] nursery ■ **~ meublée** bedsit ■ **~ de service** servant's room
2. [local] : **~ de décontamination** decontamination chamber ■ **~ forte** strongroom ■ **~ froide** cold room ■ **~ à gaz** gas chamber
3. POLIT House, Chamber ■ **la Chambre des communes** the House of Commons ■ **la Chambre des députés** the (French) Chamber of Deputies ■ **la Chambre haute/basse** the Upper/Lower Chamber ■ **la Chambre des lords** *ou* **des pairs** the House of Lords ■ **la Chambre des représentants** the House of Representatives
4. DR [subdivision d'une juridiction] chamber ■ **première ~** upper chamber *ou* court ■ **deuxième ~** lower chamber *ou* court

■ [section] Court ■ **Chambre d'accusation** *ou* **des mises en accusation** Court of criminal appeal ■ **Chambre des appels correctionnels** District Court
5. [organisme] : **Chambre de commerce** Chamber of Commerce ■ **~ de compensation** clearing house ■ **Chambre des métiers** Guild Chamber ■ **Chambre syndicale** Employer's Syndicate
6. NAUT [local] : **~ de chauffe** stokehold
7. ARM chamber
8. MÉCAN, PHYS & TECHNOL chamber ■ **~ à air** inner tube ■ **~ de combustion** combustion chamber
9. PHOTO : **~ noire** darkroom
10. OPT : **~ claire/noire** camera lucida/obscura
11. ANAT : **~ antérieure** *ou* **de l'œil** anterior chamber of the eye.
◆ **en chambre** *loc adj hum* [stratège, athlète] armchair *(modif)*.

LA CHAMBRE DES DÉPUTÉS

This was the official name for the French parliamentary assembly until 1946, when the name *l'Assemblée nationale* was adopted.

chambrée [ʃɑ̃bre] *nf* MIL [pièce] (barrack) room ■ [soldats] : **toute la ~** all the soldiers in the barrack room.

chambrer [3] [ʃɑ̃bre] *vt* **1.** ŒNOL to allow to breathe, to bring to room temperature **2.** *fam* [se moquer de] to pull sb's leg ■ **arrête de me ~!** stop pulling my leg!

chambrette [ʃɑ̃brɛt] *nf* small room.

chameau, x [ʃamo] *nm* **1.** ZOOL camel **2.** *fam péj* **quel ~!** [homme] he's a real swine! ; [femme] she's a real cow! ■ **oh, le petit ~!** little tyke!

chamelier [ʃaməlje] *nm* camel driver.

chamelle [ʃamɛl] *nf* she-camel.

chamois [ʃamwa] ◇ *nm* **1.** ZOOL chamois **2.** SPORT *skiing proficiency grade* **3.** [couleur] buff, fawn.
◇ *adj inv* buff, fawn.

chamoiser [3] [ʃamwaze] *vt* to buff.

champ [ʃɑ̃] *nm* **1.** AGRIC field ■ **~ de blé** field of wheat ■ **~ de maïs** cornfield
2. [périmètre réservé] : **~ d'aviation** airfield ■ **~ de courses** racecourse ■ **~ de foire** fairground ■ **~ de tir** ARM [terrain] rifle range ; [portée d'une arme] field of fire
3. [domaine, étendue] field, range ➜ **avoir le ~ libre** to have a free hand ■ **laisser le ~ libre à qqn** to leave the field open for sb ■ **il a du ~ devant lui** he's got an open field in front of him ■ **prendre du ~** [pour observer] to step back ; [pour réfléchir] to stand back ; [pour sauter] to take a run-up
4. CINÉ & PHOTO : **être dans le ~** to be in shot ■ **sortir du ~** to go out of shot
5. ÉLECTR & PHYS field ■ **~ électrique/magnétique** electric/magnetic field
6. FOOTBALL : **~ (de jeu)** play area
7. HÉRALD field
8. INFORM : **~ d'action** sensitivity ■ **~ variable** variable field
9. LING & MATH field
10. MÉD field ■ **~ opératoire/visuel** field of operation/view
11. MIL ➜ **~ de bataille** *pr* battlefield, battleground ; *fig* mess ■ **la cuisine avait l'air d'un ~ de bataille** the kitchen looked like a bomb had hit it ■ **il est mort au ~ d'honneur** he died for his country ■ **~ de manœuvre** parade ground ■ **~ de mines** minefield
12. MYTHOL : **les ~s Élysées** *ou* **Élyséens** the Elysian Fields.
◆ **champs** *nmpl* [campagne] country, countryside ■ **la vie aux ~s** country life.
◆ **sur le champ** *loc adv* immediately, at once, right away.

champ' [ʃɑ̃p] *nm fam* champers.

champagne [ʃɑ̃paɲ] ◇ *nm* Champagne ■ **~ brut/rosé** extra dry/pink Champagne.
◇ *adj inv* **1.** [couleur] Champagne *(modif)* **2.** ŒNOL ▷ **fine** *(nf)*.

Champagne [ʃɑ̃paɲ] *npr f* : **(la) ~** Champagne.

Champagne-Ardenne [ʃɑ̃paɲardɛn] *npr f* : **la ~** Champagne-Ardenne.

CHAMPAGNE-ARDENNE

This administrative region includes the *départements* of Ardennes, Aube, Haute-Marne and Marne (capital: Châlons-en-Champagne).

champagniser [3] [ʃɑ̃paɲize] *vt* : **~ le vin** to make sparkling wine *(by using the Champagne method)* ■ **vins champagnisés** Champagne method wines.

Champ-de-Mars [ʃɑ̃dmars] *npr m* : **le ~** *the esplanade where the Eiffel Tower stands.*

champenois, e [ʃɑ̃pənwa, az] *adj* from Champagne ■ **méthode ~e** Champagne method.
◆ **Champenois, e** *nm, f inhabitant of or person from the Champagne region.*
◆ **champenoise** *nf bottle designed for Champagne.*

champêtre [ʃɑ̃pɛtr] *adj litt* [vie, plaisirs, travaux] country *(modif)*, rustic.

champignon [ʃɑ̃piɲɔ̃] *nm* **1.** BOT & CULIN mushroom, fungus SC : **~ de Paris** *ou* **de couche** button mushroom ■ **~ hallucinogène** magic mushroom ■ **grandir** *ou* **pousser comme un ~** [enfant] to grow (up) fast ; [ville, installations] to mushroom **2.** MÉD : **un ~, des ~s** a fungus, a fungal infection **3.** [nuage] : **~ (atomique)** mushroom cloud **4.** *fam* AUTO accelerator (pedal) ■ **mettre le pied** *ou* **appuyer sur le ~** to put one's foot down, to step on it.

champignonnière [ʃɑ̃piɲɔnjɛr] *nf* mushroom bed.

champion, onne [ʃɑ̃pjɔ̃, ɔn] ◇ *nm, f* **1.** SPORT champion ■ **le ~ du monde d'aviron** the world rowing champion ■ **c'est un ~ de la triche** *fam* he's a first-rate *ou* prize cheat **2.** [défenseur] champion ■ **se faire le ~ de qqch** to champion sthg.
◇ *adj fam* **pour les bêtises, il est ~!** he's a great one for getting up to stupid things! ■ **c'est ~!** it's terrific!

championnat [ʃɑ̃pjɔna] *nm* championship.

champlever [19] [ʃɑ̃ləve] *vt* [gravure] to cut away *(insép)* ■ [émail] to chase.

chançard, e [ʃɑ̃sar, ard] *fam* ◇ *adj* lucky, jammy *UK*.
◇ *nm, f* lucky dog *ou* devil, jammy devil *UK*.

chance [ʃɑ̃s] *nf* **1.** [aléa, hasard] luck ■ **souhaiter bonne ~ à qqn** to wish sb good luck **2.** [hasard favorable] (good) luck ■ **c'est une ~ que je sois arrivée à ce moment-là!** it's a stroke of luck that I arrived then! ■ **quelle ~ j'ai eue!** lucky me! ■ **avoir de la/ne pas avoir de ~** to be lucky/unlucky ■ **pas de ~!** bad luck! ■ **tenter sa ~** to try one's luck ■ **donner** *ou* **laisser sa ~ à qqn** to give sb his chance **3.** *(toujours sing)* [sort favorable] luck, (good) fortune ■ **la ~ lui sourit** luck favours him ■ **la ~ a voulu que sa lettre se soit égarée** luckily his letter got lost ■ **c'est ta dernière ~** it's your last chance ■ **négociations de la dernière ~** last-ditch negotiations ■ **jour de ~** lucky day ■ **sa ~ tourne** his luck is changing ■ **porter ~** to bring (good) luck ■ **pousser sa ~** to push one's luck **4.** [éventualité, probabilité] chance ■ **tu n'as pas une ~ sur dix de réussir** you haven't got a one-in-ten chance of succeeding ■ **ce qu'il dit a toutes les ~s d'être faux** the chances are that what he is saying is wrong ■ **il y a peu de ~s qu'on te croie** there's little chance (that) you'll be believed ■ **son projet a de fortes** *ou* **grandes ~s d'être adopté** his plan stands a good chance of being adopted ■ **n'hésite pas, tu as tes ~s** don't hesitate, you've got *ou* you stand a chance ■ **tu assisteras au débat? – il y a des ~s** *fam* will you be present at the debate? – maybe.
◆ **par chance** *loc adv* luckily, fortunately.

chancelant, e [ʃɑ̃slɑ̃, ɑ̃t] *adj* **1.** [vacillant - démarche, pas] unsteady, wobbling ; [- pile] tottering **2.** [faiblissant - santé] faltering, failing, fragile.

chanceler [24] [ʃɑ̃sle] *vi* **1.** [vaciller - personne] to totter, to wobble, to stagger ; [- pile d'objets] to be unsteady **2.** [faiblir - pouvoir, institution, autorité] to wobble, to totter ; [- santé] to be failing ■ **les émeutes ont fait ~ le pouvoir** the riots rocked the government.

chancelier, ère [ʃɑ̃səlje, ɛr] *nm, f* **1.** [d'ambassade] (embassy) chief secretary, chancellor *UK* ▪ [de consulat] first secretary **2.** POLIT [en Allemagne, en Autriche] chancellor ▪ [en Grande-Bretagne] : **~ de l'Échiquier** Chancellor of the Exchequer **3.** HIST chancellor.

chancelière [ʃɑ̃səljɛr] *nf* **1.** [épouse] chancellor's wife **2.** [chausson] foot muff.

chancelle *etc v* ▻ **chanceler.**

chancellerie [ʃɑ̃sɛlri] *nf* **1.** POLIT chancery, chancellery **2.** RELIG : **~ apostolique** Chancery.

chanceux, euse [ʃɑ̃sø, øz] ◇ *adj* lucky, fortunate, happy *litt.*
◇ *nm, f* lucky man (*f* woman).

chancre [ʃɑ̃kr] *nm* **1.** MÉD chancre ▪ **~ induré** *ou* **syphilitique** hard *ou* infective *ou* true chancre ▪ **~ mou** chancroid, soft chancre **2.** BOT canker **3.** *litt* [fléau] plague.

chandail [ʃɑ̃daj] *nm* pullover, sweater.

Chandeleur [ʃɑ̃dlœr] *nf* : **la ~** Candlemas.

chandelier [ʃɑ̃dəlje] *nm* [à une branche] candlestick ▪ [à plusieurs branches] candelabrum, candelabra.

chandelle [ʃɑ̃dɛl] *nf* **1.** [bougie] (tallow) candle ▪ **le jeu n'en vaut pas la ~** the game's not worth the candle ▪ **brûler la ~ par les deux bouts** to burn the candle at both ends ▪ **devoir une fière ~ à qqn** to be deeply indebted to sb ▪ **tenir la ~** to play gooseberry *UK* **2.** *fam* [morve] trickle of snot **3.** AÉRON chandelle ▪ **monter en ~** to chandelle **4.** [tir - RUGBY] up-and-under **5.** [position de gymnastique] : **faire la ~** to perform a shoulder stand **6.** CONSTR prop, stay.
◆ **aux chandelles** ◇ *loc adj* [dîner, repas] candlelit.
◇ *loc adv* [dîner] by candlelight.

chanfrein [ʃɑ̃frɛ̃] *nm* **1.** ZOOL snout, muzzle **2.** [pièce d'armure] chamfron, chamfrain **3.** ARCHIT chamfer, bevel edge.

change [ʃɑ̃ʒ] *nm* **1.** FIN [transaction] exchange ▪ [taux] exchange rate ▪ **faire le ~** to deal in foreign exchange ▪ **'~ (ouvert de 9 h à 11 h)'** 'bureau de change (open from 9 a.m. till 11 a.m.)' ◗ **donner le ~ à qqn** [le duper] to hoodwink sb, to put sb off the track ▪ **gagner/perdre au ~** *pr* to be better/worse off because of the exchange rate ; *fig* to come out a winner/loser on the deal ▪ **je perds au ~ du point de vue salaire** I'm worse off as far as my pay goes **2.** [couche] : **~ complet** disposable nappy *UK ou* diaper *US.*

changeant, e [ʃɑ̃ʒɑ̃, ɑ̃t] *adj* **1.** [moiré] shot **2.** [inconstant - fortune] fickle, unpredictable ; [- humeur] fickle, volatile, shifting **3.** MÉTÉOR [temps] unsettled, changeable ▪ **un ciel ~** changing skies.

changement [ʃɑ̃ʒmɑ̃] *nm* **1.** [substitution] change ▪ **~ de** change of ▪ **après le ~ d'entraîneur/de régime** after the new trainer/regime came in ◗ **~ d'adresse** change of address ▪ **'~ de propriétaire'** 'under new ownership'
2. [modification] change ▪ **apporter des ~s à qqch** to alter sthg ▪ **~ de : ~ de température/temps** change in temperature/(the) weather ◗ **~ de cap** *ou* **de direction** change of course ▪ **~ de programme** TV change in the (published) schedule ; *fig* change of plan *ou* in the plans
3. [évolution] : **le ~** change ▪ **pour le ~, votez Poblon!** for a new future, vote Poblon! ▪ **je voudrais bien un peu de ~** I'd like things to change a little ▪ **quand les enfants seront partis, ça fera du ~** things will be different after the children have gone
4. TRANSP change ▪ **j'ai trois ~s/je n'ai pas de ~ pour aller chez elle** I have to change three times/I don't have to change to get to her place ▮ [lieu] : **le ~ est au bout du quai** change (lines) at the end of the platform
5. THÉÂTRE : **~ à vue** set change in full view of the audience ▪ **~ de décor** *pr* scene change *ou* shift
6. SPORT : **~ de joueurs** change of players, changeover
7. AUTO : **~ de vitesse** [levier] gear lever, gear shift *US* ; [en voiture] gear change *ou* shift ; [à bicyclette] gear change.

changer [17] [ʃɑ̃ʒe] ◇ *vt (aux avoir)* **1.** [modifier - apparence, règlement, caractère] to change, to alter ; [- testament] to alter ▪ **je désire faire ~ l'ordre du jour de la réunion** I would like to propose some changes to the agenda of today's meeting ▪ **on ne le changera pas** he'll never change ▪ **cette coupe la change vraiment** that haircut makes her look really different ▪ **mais ça change tout!** ah, that makes a big difference! ▪ **qu'est-ce que ça change?** what difference does it make? ▪ **il ne veut rien ~ à ses habitudes** he won't alter his ways one jot *ou* iota
2. [remplacer - installation, personnel] to change, to replace ; [- roue, ampoule, drap *etc*] to change ▪ **ne change pas les assiettes** don't lay new plates ▪ **j'ai fait ~ les freins** I had new brakes put in
3. FIN [en devises, en petite monnaie] to change ▪ **~ un billet pour avoir de la monnaie** to change a note in order to get small change ▪ **~ des euros en dollars** to change euros into dollars
4. [troquer] : **~ qqch pour qqch** to change sthg for sthg ▪ *(en usage absolu)* **j'aime mieux ton écharpe, on change?** I like your scarf better, shall we swap?
5. [transformer] : **~ qqch en qqch** to turn sthg into sthg
6. [transférer] : **~ qqch de place** to move sthg ▪ **~ une cassette de face** to turn a cassette over ▪ **~ qqn de poste/service** to transfer sb to a new post/department ◗ **~ son fusil d'épaule** to have a change of heart
7. *fam* [désaccoutumer] : **pars en vacances, ça te changera un peu** *fam* you should go away somewhere, it'll be a change for you ▪ **enfin un bon spectacle, ça nous change des inepties habituelles!** *fam* a good show at last, that makes a change from the usual nonsense! ▪ **viens, ça te changera les idées** come along, it'll take your mind off things
8. [bébé] to change ▪ **~ un malade** to put fresh clothes on a sick person.
◇ *vi (aux avoir)* **1.** [se modifier - personne, temps, tarif *etc*] to change ▪ **~ en bien/mal** to change for the better/worse
2. TRANSP [de métro, de train] to change
3. [être remplacé] to change ▪ **le président change tous les trois ans** there's a change of chairperson every three years.
◇ *vi (aux être)* [malade, personnalité] to change.
◆ **changer de** *v+prép* : **~ d'adresse** [personne] to move to a new address ; [commerce] to move to new premises ▪ **~ de nom/nationalité** to change one's name/nationality ▪ **~ de partenaire** [en dansant, dans un couple] to change partners ▪ **~ de chaussettes** to change one's socks ▪ **~ de vêtements** to get changed ▪ **~ de coiffure** to get a new hairstyle ▪ **~ de style** to adopt a new style ▪ **~ de chaîne** [une fois] to change channels ; [constamment] to zap ▪ **je dois ~ d'avion à Athènes** I have to get a connecting flight in Athens ▪ **~ de vie** to embark on a new life ▪ **~ d'avis** *ou* **d'idée** to change one's mind ▪ **elle m'a fait ~ d'avis** she changed *ou* made me change my mind ▪ **tu vas ~ de ton, dis!** don't take that tone with me! ▪ **~ de direction** [gén] to change direction ; [vent] to change ▪ **~ de place** to move ▪ **changez de côté** [au tennis, au ping-pong] change *ou* switch sides ; [dans un lit] turn over ▪ **~ de vitesse** AUTO to change gear ◗ **~ d'air** to have a break ▪ **~ de décor** THÉÂTRE to change the set ▪ **j'ai besoin de ~ de décor** I need a change of scenery ▪ **~ d'avis comme de chemise** to keep changing one's mind ▪ **~ de cap** *pr* & *fig* to change course ▪ **~ de crémerie** *fam* to take one's custom *ou* business elsewhere ▪ **change de disque!** *fam* put another record on!
◆ **se changer** *vp (emploi réfléchi)* [s'habiller] to get changed.
◆ **se changer en** *vp+prép* to change *ou* to turn into ▪ **la grenouille se changea en princesse** the frog turned into a princess.
◆ **pour changer** *loc adv* for a change.
◆ **pour ne pas changer** *loc adv* as usual.

changeur [ʃɑ̃ʒœr] *nm* **1.** [personne] money changer **2.** [dispositif] : **~ de billets** change machine ▪ **~ de monnaie** money changer.

channe [ʃan] *nf Suisse* pewter jug.

chanoine [ʃanwan] *nm* canon.

chanoinesse [ʃanwanɛs] *nf* canoness.

chanson [ʃɑ̃sɔ̃] *nf* **1.** MUS song ▪ **mettre un texte en ~** to set a text to music ◗ **~ d'amour/populaire** love/popular song ▪ **~ à boire** drinking song ▪ **~ enfantine** children's song, nursery rhyme ▪ **~ de marins** shanty *UK*, chantey *US* ▪ *fig* **c'est toujours la même ~** it's always the same old story ▪ **ça va, on connaît la**

~ enough of that, we've heard it all before ■ **ça, c'est une autre ~** that's another story **2.** LITTÉR : ~ **de geste** chanson de geste, epic poem ■ **'la Chanson de Roland'** 'The Song of Roland'.

chansonnette [ʃɑ̃sɔnɛt] *nf* ditty, simple song.

chansonnier, ère [ʃɑ̃sɔnje, ɛr] *nm, f satirical cabaret singer or entertainer.*

◆ **chansonnier** *nm* **1.** *vieilli* songwriter **2.** [recueil] songbook.

chant [ʃɑ̃] *nm* **1.** [chanson] song ■ [mélodie] melody ■ ~ **grégorien** Gregorian chant ■ ~ **de Noël** Christmas carol ■ **son ~ du cygne** his swan song ■ **écouter le ~ des sirènes** to listen to the siren's *ou* mermaid's song **2.** [action de chanter] singing **3.** [art de chanter] singing ■ **prendre des leçons de ~** to take singing lessons **4.** [sons - d'un oiseau] singing, chirping ; [- d'une cigale] chirping ; [- d'un coq] crowing ■ **le ~ des vagues/de la source** *litt* the song of the waves/of the spring **5.** [forme poétique] ode, lyric ■ [division dans un poème] canto **6.** CONSTR edge.

◆ **au chant du coq** *loc adv* at cockcrow.

chantage [ʃɑ̃taʒ] *nm* blackmail ■ **faire du ~ à qqn** to blackmail sb.

chantant, e [ʃɑ̃tɑ̃, ɑ̃t] *adj* **1.** [langue] musical ■ [voix, accent] lilting **2.** [aisément retenu - air] tuneful ■ **un opéra très ~** an opera full of easily remembered tunes.

chanter [3] [ʃɑ̃te] ◇ *vi* **1.** [personne] to sing ■ ~ **juste/faux** to sing in tune/out of tune ▶ ~ **à tue-tête** to sing one's head off **2.** [oiseau] to sing, to chirp ■ [cigale] to chirp ■ [coq] to crow ■ *litt* [rivière, mer] to murmur ■ [bouilloire] whistle **3.** [être mélodieux - accent, voix] to lilt ■ **avoir une voix qui chante** to have a singsong voice **4.** *loc* **faire ~ qqn** to blackmail sb ■ **si ça te chante** if you fancy it ■ **viens quand ça te chante** come whenever you feel like it *ou* whenever the mood takes you.

◇ *vt* **1.** MUS [chanson, messe] to sing ■ **qu'est-ce que tu me chantes là?** *fig* what are you talking about? **2.** [célébrer] to sing (of) ■ ~ **victoire** to crow (over one's victory) ■ ~ **les louanges de qqn** to sing sb's praises.

chanterelle [ʃɑ̃trɛl] *nf* **1.** BOT chanterelle **2.** MUS E-string **3.** CHASSE decoy (bird).

chanteur, euse [ʃɑ̃tœr, øz] ◇ *nm, f* singer ■ ~ **de charme** crooner ■ ~ **folk** folk singer ■ ~ **de rock** rock singer ■ ~ **des rues** street singer.

◇ *adj* : **oiseau ~** songbird.

chantier [ʃɑ̃tje] *nm* **1.** [entrepôt] yard, depot **2.** [terrain] (working) site ■ **sur le ~** on the site **3.** CONSTR : ~ **(de construction)** building site ■ ~ **de démolition** demolition site *ou* area **4.** TRAV PUB roadworks **5.** NAUT : ~ **naval** shipyard **6.** *fam* [désordre] mess, shambles ■ **ta chambre, c'est un vrai ~** your bedroom is a total shambles *ou* looks like a bomb's hit it.

◆ **en chantier** ◇ *loc adj* : **la maison est en ~** they're still doing *ou* fixing *US* up the house.

◇ *loc adv* : **il a plusieurs livres en ~** he has several books on the stocks *ou* in the pipeline ■ **mettre un ouvrage en ~** to get a project started.

chantilly [ʃɑ̃tiji] ◇ *adj inv* ▷ **crème**.

◇ *nf inv* whipped cream Chantilly.

chantonner [3] [ʃɑ̃tɔne] *vt & vi* to hum, to croon, to sing softly.

chantre [ʃɑ̃tr] *nm* **1.** RELIG cantor ■ **grand ~** precentor **2.** *litt* **le ~ de** the eulogist of *ou* apologist for.

chanvre [ʃɑ̃vr] *nm* BOT & TEXT hemp ■ ~ **indien** BOT Indian hemp ; [drogue] marijuana.

chanvrier, ère [ʃɑ̃vrije, ɛr] ◇ *adj* hemp, hempen, hemplike.

◇ *nm, f* **1.** [cultivateur] hemp grower **2.** [ouvrier] hemp dresser.

chaos [kao] *nm* **1.** [confusion] chaos ■ **un ~ de ruines** a tangled heap of ruins **2.** RELIG : **le Chaos** Chaos.

chaotique [kaɔtik] *adj* chaotic.

chap. (*abr écrite de* **chapitre**) ch.

chapardage [ʃapardaʒ] *nm fam* petty theft ■ **des ~s répétés** pilfering *(U)*.

chaparder [3] [ʃaparde] *vt fam* to pinch, to swipe ■ **il s'est fait ~ sa montre** he had his watch pinched *ou* nicked *UK*.

chapardeur, euse [ʃapardœr, øz] *fam* ◇ *adj* inclined to (petty) theft.

◇ *nm, f* (casual) thief ■ **un ~ invétéré** a habitual pilferer.

chape [ʃap] *nf* **1.** RELIG [de prêtre] cope **2.** CONSTR screed ■ **comme une ~ de plomb** like a lead weight **3.** [d'un pneu] tread **4.** [d'une poulie] shell.

chapeau, x [ʃapo] *nm* **1.** [couvre-chef] hat ■ ~ **claque** opera hat ■ ~ **cloche** cloche (hat) ■ ~ **de feutre** felt hat ■ ~ **haut-de-forme** top hat ■ ~ **melon** bowler *ou* derby *US*(hat) ■ ~ **mou** trilby *UK*, fedora *US* ■ ~ **de paille** straw hat ■ **mettre** *ou* **porter la main au ~** to raise one's hat ■ **faire porter le ~ à qqn** to force sb to carry the can *UK*, to leave sb holding the bag *US* ■ **tirer son ~ à qqn** to take one's hat off to sb ■ **saluer qqn ~ bas** to doff one's hat to sb ■ **je te dis ~!** I'll take my hat off to you!, well done!, bravo! **2.** [d'un champignon] cap **3.** [de texte, d'article] introductory paragraph ■ RADIO & TV introduction **4.** [d'un tuyau de cheminée] cowl.

◆ **sur les chapeaux de roue** *loc adv* : **prendre un virage sur les ~x de roue** to take a turning on two wheels ▶ **démarrer sur les ~x de roue** *pr* to shoot off ; [film, réception, relation] to get off to a great start.

◆ **chapeau chinois** *nm* **1.** MUS crescent **2.** ZOOL limpet.

chapeauter [3] [ʃapote] *vt fam* [superviser] to oversee, to supervise ■ **il a décidé de faire ~ les deux services par un secrétaire général** he decided to put both departments under the control of a general secretary.

chapelain [ʃaplɛ̃] *nm* chaplain.

chapelet [ʃaplɛ] *nm* **1.** RELIG [collier] rosary, beads ■ [prières] rosary ■ **réciter** *ou* **dire son ~** to tell one's beads ▶ **débiter** *ou* **dévider son ~** *fam* to tell all **2.** [d'îles, de saucisses] string ■ [d'insultes] string, stream.

chapelier, ère [ʃapəlje, ɛr] ◇ *adj* [commerce, industrie] hat *(modif)*.

◇ *nm, f* hatter.

chapelle [ʃapɛl] *nf* **1.** RELIG chapel ■ ~ **ardente** chapel of rest **2.** [cercle] clique, coterie.

chapellerie [ʃapɛlri] *nf* **1.** [commerce] hat trade **2.** [industrie] hat *ou* hat-making industry.

chapelure [ʃaplyr] *nf* breadcrumbs ■ **passer qqch dans la ~** to coat sthg with breadcrumbs.

chaperon [ʃaprɔ̃] *nm* **1.** [surveillant] chaperon, chaperone ■ **servir de ~ à qqn** to chaperon *ou* to chaperone sb **2.** CONSTR [d'un mur] coping **3.** LITTÉR : **'le Petit Chaperon rouge'** *Perrault* 'Little Red Riding Hood'.

chaperonner [3] [ʃaprɔne] *vt* **1.** [jeune fille, groupe] to chaperon, to chaperone **2.** CONSTR to cope.

chapiteau, x [ʃapito] *nm* **1.** ARCHIT capital, chapiter **2.** [cirque] big top ■ **nous vous accueillons ce soir sous le plus grand ~ du monde** we welcome you tonight under the world's biggest top **3.** [d'un alambic] head.

chapitre [ʃapitr] *nm* **1.** [d'un livre] chapter **2.** FIN [d'un budget] item **3.** [question] matter, subject ■ **tu as raison, au moins sur un ~** you're right, at least on one score **4.** RELIG [assemblée] chapter ■ [lieu] chapterhouse.

chapitrer [3] [ʃapitre] *vt* [sermonner] to lecture ■ [tancer] to admonish ■ **je l'ai dûment chapitré sur ses responsabilités** I gave him the appropriate lecture about his responsibilities.

chapka [ʃapka] *nf* shapka *(round brimless fur hat worn in Russia)*.

chapon [ʃapɔ̃] *nm* capon.

chaponner [3] [ʃapɔne] *vt* to caponize.

chaptaliser [3] [ʃaptalize] *vt* to chaptalize.

chaque [ʃak] *dét (adj indéf)* **1.** [dans un groupe, une série] each, every ■ **je pense à elle à ~ instant** I think about her all the time ■ **~ chose en son temps!** all in good time! ▶ **à ~ jour suffit sa peine** *prov* sufficient unto the day (is the evil thereof) **2.** [chacun] each ■ **les disques sont vendus 18 euros ~** the records are sold at 18 euros each *ou* a piece.

char [ʃar] *nm* **1.** MIL tank ■ **~ d'assaut** *ou* **de combat** tank ■ **fait comme un ~ d'assaut** built like a tank **2.** LOISIRS float ■ **~ à voile** sand yacht ■ **faire du ~ à voile** to go sand yachting **3.** [voiture] : **~ à bancs** *open wagon with seats for passengers* ■ **~ à bœufs** ox cart ■ **~ funèbre** hearse **4.** ANTIQ chariot ■ **le ~ de l'État** the ship of State **5.** *fam Québec fam* car.

charabia [ʃarabja] *nm* gobbledegook, gibberish.

charade [ʃarad] *nf* **1.** [devinette] riddle **2.** [mime] (game of) charades.

charançon [ʃarɑ̃sɔ̃] *nm* weevil, snout beetle ■ **~ du blé/de la vigne** grain/vine weevil.

charançonné, e [ʃarɑ̃sɔne] *adj* weevilled, weevily.

charbon [ʃarbɔ̃] *nm* **1.** MIN coal ▶ **~ aggloméré** briquette ■ **~ de bois** charcoal ■ **aller au ~** *fam* to do one's bit ■ **être** *ou* **marcher sur des ~s ardents** to be on tenterhooks, to be like a cat on hot bricks *UK ou* a hot tin roof *US* **2.** ART [crayon] charcoal (pencil) ■ [croquis] charcoal drawing **3.** [maladie - chez l'animal, chez l'homme] anthrax ; [- des céréales] smut, black rust **4.** PHARM charcoal **5.** ÉLECTR carbon.

charbonnages [ʃarbɔnaʒ] *nmpl* coalmines, collieries *UK* ■ **les Charbonnages de France** the French Coal Board.

charbonner [3] [ʃarbɔne] ◇ *vt* **1.** ART [croquis, dessin] to (draw with) charcoal **2.** [noircir - visage] to charcoal.
◇ *vi* **1.** [mèche] to char **2.** NAUT to bunker, to coal.

charbonneux, euse [ʃarbɔnø, øz] *adj* **1.** [noir] coal-black, coal-like **2.** [souillé] sooty black ■ **avoir les yeux ~** *péj* to use heavy black eye makeup **3.** [brûlé] charred **4.** MÉD anthracoid **5.** BOT smutty.

charbonnier, ère [ʃarbɔnje, ɛr] ◇ *adj* [commerce, industrie] coal *(modif)* ■ **navire ~** coaler, collier.
◇ *nm, f* [vendeur] coaler, coalman ■ [fabricant de charbon de bois] charcoal-burner ■ **~ est maître dans sa maison** *ou* **chez soi** *prov* an Englishman's *UK ou* a man's *US* home is his castle *prov.*

charcutage [ʃarkytaʒ] *nm fam péj* [opération chirurgicale] butchering ■ [travail mal fait] hacking about ■ **~ électoral** gerrymandering.

charcuter [3] [ʃarkyte] *vt fam péj* **1.** [opérer] to butcher, to hack about ■ **se faire ~** to be hacked about **2.** [couper - volaille, texte] to hack to pieces *ou* about.
◆ **se charcuter** *vp (emploi réfléchi) fam* **je me suis charcuté un doigt/le pied** I mangled one of my fingers/my foot.

charcuterie [ʃarkytri] *nf* **1.** [magasin] delicatessen **2.** [produits] cooked meats **3.** [fabrication] cooked meats trade.

CHARCUTERIE

A *charcuterie* sells mainly food prepared with pork: sausages, pâtés, ham *etc*, also known collectively as *charcuterie*. Ready-prepared dishes to take away are also sold.

charcutier, ère [ʃarkytje, ɛr] *nm, f* **1.** [commerçant] pork butcher ■ **chez votre ~ habituel** ≃ at your local delicatessen **2.** *fam péj* [chirurgien] butcher.

chardon [ʃardɔ̃] *nm* **1.** BOT thistle **2.** [sur un mur] spike.

chardon(n)ay [ʃardɔnɛ] *nm* Chardonay *ou* Chardonnay (wine).

chardonneret [ʃardɔnrɛ] *nm* goldfinch.

charentais, e [ʃarɑ̃tɛ, ɛz] *adj* from the Charente.
◆ **charentaises** *nfpl* [pantoufles] slippers *(traditionally symbolising old-fashioned and home-loving attitudes in France).*

charge [ʃarʒ] *nf* **1.** [cargaison - d'un animal] burden ; [- d'un camion] load ; [- d'un navire] cargo, freight ▶ **~ utile** capacity load, payload ■ **~ à vide** empty weight
2. [gêne] burden, weight *fig*
3. [responsabilité] responsibility ■ **à qui revient la ~ de le faire?** who has *ou* carries the responsibility for doing it? ■ **toutes les réparations sont à sa ~** he will pay for the repair work, all the repair work will be done at his cost ■ **à ~ pour toi d'apporter le vin** you'll be responsible for bringing *ou* it'll be up to you to bring the wine ■ **prendre en ~ : nous prenons tous les frais médicaux en ~** we pay for *ou* take care of all medical expenses ■ **les frais d'hébergement sont pris en ~ par l'entreprise** accommodation is paid for by the company ■ **à ton âge, tu dois te prendre en ~** at your age, you should take responsibility for yourself *ou* you should be able to look after yourself ■ **avoir qqn à (sa) ~** [gén] to be responsible for supporting sb ; ADMIN to have sb as a dependant ■ **enfants à ~** dependent children ■ **ses enfants sont encore à sa ~** his children are still his dependants ■ **prendre des frais/un orphelin à sa ~** to take on the expenditure/an orphan
4. ADMIN [fonction] office ■ **~ élective** elective office ■ **~ de notaire** notary's office
5. ARM charge ▶ **~ d'explosifs** explosive charge
6. ÉLECTR : **mettre une batterie en ~** to charge a battery ▶ **~ électrique** electric charge ■ **~ négative/positive** negative/positive charge
7. PSYCHOL : **~ affective** *ou* **émotionnelle** emotional charge
8. DR [présomption] charge, accusation ■ **de très lourdes ~s pèsent contre lui** there are very serious charges hanging over him
9. [satire] caricature
10. MIL [assaut] charge ■ **donner la ~** to charge ■ **reculer devant une ~ de police** to retreat under a police charge ▶ **retourner** *ou* **revenir à la ~** *pr* to mount a fresh attack ; *fig* to go back onto the offensive ■ **je t'ai déjà dit non, ne reviens pas à la ~!** I've already said no, don't keep on at me!
◆ **charges** *nfpl* [frais] costs ■ **~s de famille** dependants ■ **~s (locatives)** maintenance charges ■ **~s salariales** wage costs ■ **~s sociales** social security contributions.
◆ **à charge de** *loc prép* : **j'accepte, à ~ de revanche** I accept, provided you'll let me do the same for you ■ **à ~ de preuve** pending production of proof.

CHARGES

Householders and tenants in blocks of flats are required to pay *charges*, a monthly sum for the general upkeep of the building. In estate agencies, rent is expressed either including this sum (*charges comprises* or *cc*) or excluding it (*hors charges* or *charges en sus*). Sometimes, the *charges* include heating costs.

chargé, e [ʃarʒe] *adj* **1.** [occupé - journée] busy, full **2.** [alourdi] intricate ■ **tissu/motif trop ~** overelaborate material/pattern **3.** *fig* **avoir la conscience ~e** to have a guilty conscience ■ **il a un casier judiciaire ~** he has a long (criminal) record **4.** MÉD : **estomac ~** overloaded stomach ■ **avoir la langue ~e** to have a furred tongue.
◆ **chargé** *nm* [responsable] : **~ d'affaires** chargé d'affaires ■ **~ de cours** ≃ part-time lecturer ■ **~ de famille** person supporting a family ■ **~ de mission** ≃ (official) representative.

CHARGÉ DE COURS

In French universities, *chargés de cours* supervise courses, though they do not hold full-time positions.

chargement [ʃarʒəmɑ̃] *nm* **1.** [marchandises - gén] load ; [- d'un navire] cargo, freight **2.** [fait de charger - un navire, un camion] loading ; [- une chaudière] stoking ; [- une arme] loading ■ **à ~ automatique** self-loading **3.** ÉLECTR charging (up).

charger [17] [ʃarʒe] *vt* **1.** [mettre un poids sur] to load ■ **tes livres chargent un peu trop l'étagère** the shelf is overloaded with your books ■ **être chargé** to be loaded ■ **il est entré, les bras chargés de cadeaux** he came in loaded down with presents ▶ **être chargé comme une bête** *ou* **un âne** *ou* **un baudet** to be weighed down
2. [prendre en charge - suj: taxi] to pick up *(sép)*

3. [alourdir, encombrer] to overload ■ **~ qqn de** to overload sb with
4. [arme, caméra, magnétoscope] to load (up) ■ ÉLECTR to charge (up)
5. [d'une responsabilité] : **~ qqn de qqch** to put sb in charge of sthg ■ **il m'a chargé de vous transmettre un message** he asked me to give you a message
6. [amplifier] to inflate, to put up *(sép)*
7. [exagérer - portrait] to overdo
8. [incriminer] : **~ qqn** to make sb appear guiltier ■ **certains témoins ont essayé de le ~ au maximum** some witnesses tried to strengthen the prosecution's case against him
9. [attaquer] to charge (at).
◆ **se charger de** *vp+prép* **1.** [obj: responsabilité] to take on, to take care of ■ **je me charge de lui remettre votre lettre** I'll see to it personally that he gets your letter
2. [obj: élève, invité] to take care of, to look after ■ **quant à lui, je m'en charge personnellement** I'll personally take good care of him.

chargeur [ʃarʒœr] *nm* **1.** PHOTO magazine **2.** ARM cartridge clip **3.** ÉLECTR charger **4.** [ouvrier] loader **5.** NAUT shipper.

chariot [ʃarjo] *nm* **1.** [véhicule - gén] wagon, waggon *UK* ; [- à bagages] trolley *UK*, cart *US* ; [- dans un supermarché] trolley *UK*, cart *US* ■ **~ élévateur** fork-lift truck ■ **~ élévateur à fourche** fork-lift truck **2.** ASTRON : **le Grand Chariot** the Great Bear *UK*, the Big Dipper *US* ■ **le Petit Chariot** the Little Bear *UK* *OU* Dipper *US* **3.** [de machine à écrire] carriage **4.** CINÉ & TV dolly.

charismatique [karismatik] *adj* **1.** RELIG charismatic **2.** [séduisant] charismatic ■ **être ~** to have charisma.

charisme [karism] *nm* **1.** RELIG charisma, charism **2.** [influence] charisma.

charitable [ʃaritabl] *adj* **1.** [généreux] charitable ■ **se montrer ~ envers qqn** to be charitable *OU* to exercise charity towards sb ■ **avis** *OU* **conseil ~** *iron* so-called friendly bit of advice **2.** [association, mouvement] charitable, charity *(modif)*.

charitablement [ʃaritabləmɑ̃] *adv* charitably, generously ■ **je lui ai ~ conseillé d'abandonner le chant** *hum* I advised her in the kindest possible way to give up singing.

charité [ʃarite] *nf* **1.** [altruisme] charity, love ■ **aurais-tu la ~ de leur rendre visite?** would you be kind enough to pay them a visit? ▶ **~ bien ordonnée commence par soi-même** *prov* charity begins at home *prov* **2.** [aumône] charity ■ **demander la ~** to beg (for charity) ■ **faire la ~ (à)** to give alms *vieilli* *OU* a handout (to) ■ **je n'ai nul besoin qu'on me fasse la ~** *fig* I don't need anybody's help, I'll manage on my own ■ **la ~, s'il vous plaît!** can you spare some change, please?
◆ **de charité** *loc adj* : **fête de ~** benefit event ■ **œuvres de ~** charities ■ **vente de ~** charity sale.

charivari [ʃarivari] *nm* hurly-burly, hullabaloo.

charlatan [ʃarlatɑ̃] *nm péj* charlatan.

charlatanerie [ʃarlatanri] *nf péj* = **charlatanisme**.

charlatanesque [ʃarlatanɛsk] *adj péj* **1.** [guérisseur] quackish **2.** [imposteur] phoney, bogus.

charlatanisme [ʃarlatanism] *nm péj* **1.** [d'un guérisseur] quackery **2.** [d'un imposteur] charlatanism.

Charlemagne [ʃarləmaɲ] *npr* Charlemagne.

Charles [ʃarl] *npr* : **~ Quint** Charles V, Charles the Fifth ■ **~ le Téméraire** Charles the Bold.

charleston [ʃarlɛstɔn] *nm* charleston.

charlot [ʃarlo] *nm fam* clown, joker ■ **jouer les ~s** to fool around.

Charlot [ʃarlo] *npr* CINÉ Charlie Chaplin.

charlotte [ʃarlɔt] *nf* CULIN charlotte ■ **~ aux pommes** apple charlotte.

charmant, e [ʃarmɑ̃, ɑ̃t] *adj* charming, delightful ■ **~e soirée!** *iron* what a great evening! ■ **c'est ~!** *iron* charming!

charme [ʃarm] *nm* **1.** [attrait] charm ■ **c'est ce qui fait tout son ~** that's what is so appealing *OU* charming about him **2.** [d'une femme, d'un homme] charm, attractiveness ■ **les femmes lui trouvent du ~** women find him attractive ▶ **faire du ~ à qqn** to try to charm sb **3.** [enchantement] spell ■ **être sous le ~ de** to be under the spell of ■ **tenir qqn/un public sous le ~** to hold sb/an audience spellbound **4.** BOT hornbeam **5.** *loc* **se porter comme un ~** to be in excellent health *OU* as fit as a fiddle.
◆ **charmes** *nmpl euphém* [d'une femme] charms ■ **vivre** *OU* **faire commerce de ses ~s** to trade on one's charms.
◆ **de charme** *loc adj* **1.** [tourisme] : **hôtel de ~** hotel **2.** *euphém* [érotique - presse] soft-porn ■ **hôtesse de ~** escort.

charmer [3] [ʃarme] *vt* **1.** [plaire à] to delight, to enchant ■ **son sourire l'a charmé** he was enchanted by her smile **2.** [envoûter - auditoire] to cast *OU* to put a spell on ; [- serpent] to charm **3.** [dans des formules de politesse] : **être charmé de : je suis charmé de vous revoir** I'm delighted to see you again ■ **charmé de vous avoir rencontré** (it's been) very nice meeting you.

charmeur, euse [ʃarmœr, øz] ◇ *adj* [air, sourire] charming, engaging, delightful.
◇ *nm, f* [séducteur] charmer ▶ **~ de serpents** snake charmer.

charmille [ʃarmij] *nf* **1.** [berceau de verdure] bower, arbour **2.** [allée] tree-covered walk *OU* path.

charnel, elle [ʃarnɛl] *adj* [sexuel] carnal.

charnellement [ʃarnɛlmɑ̃] *adv sout* carnally ■ **connaître qqn ~** to have carnal knowledge of sb.

charnier [ʃarnje] *nm* **1.** [fosse] mass grave **2.** [ossuaire] charnel house.

charnière [ʃarnjɛr] *nf* **1.** ANAT & MENUIS hinge **2.** [transition] junction, turning point ■ **Goethe est à la ~ du XVIIIe et du XIXe siècle** Goethe lived during the transition from 18th to the 19th century **3.** *(comme adj avec ou sans trait d'union)* **moment/siècle ~** moment/century of transition.

charnu, e [ʃarny] *adj* **1.** [corps] plump, fleshy ■ [lèvres] full, fleshy ■ [fruits] pulpy **2.** ANAT fleshy, flesh-covered ■ **la partie ~e de son anatomie** *hum* his posterior **3.** ŒNOL ropy.

charognard [ʃarɔɲar] *nm* **1.** ZOOL carrion feeder **2.** *fam* [exploiteur] vulture *fig*.

charogne [ʃarɔɲ] *nf* **1.** [carcasse] : **une ~** a decaying carcass ■ **ces animaux se nourrissent de ~** these animals feed off carrion **2.** △ [homme] bastard△ ■ [femme] bitch △ ■ **espèce de ~!** you bastard!△.

charolais, e [ʃarɔlɛ, ɛz] *adj* from the Charolais area.
◆ **charolais** *nm* Charolais bull ■ **les ~** Charolais cattle.
◆ **charolaise** *nf* Charolais cow.

Charon [karɔ̃] *npr* MYTHOL Charon.

charpente [ʃarpɑ̃t] *nf* **1.** CONSTR skeleton, framework ■ **~ en bois** timber work ■ **~ métallique** steel frame **2.** ANAT : **il a la ~ d'un boxeur** he's built like a boxer ▶ **~ osseuse** skeleton **3.** [schéma - d'un projet] structure, framework ; [- d'un roman] outline.

charpenté, e [ʃarpɑ̃te] *adj* : **bien** *OU* **solidement ~** [personne] well-built ; [film, argument] well-structured.

charpenter [3] [ʃarpɑ̃te] *vt* **1.** CONSTR to carpenter **2.** [structurer - œuvre] to construct, to structure.

charpentier, ère [ʃarpɑ̃tje, ɛr] *nm, f* [ouvrier] carpenter ■ [entrepreneur] (master) carpenter.

charpie [ʃarpi] *nf* [pansement] lint, shredded linen.
◆ **en charpie** *loc adv* : **mettre** *OU* **réduire qqch en ~** to tear sthg to shreds ■ **je vais le mettre** *OU* **réduire en ~** *fig* I'll make mincemeat (out) of him.

charretée [ʃarte] *nf* **1.** [contenu] cartful, cartload **2.** *fam* [grande quantité] : **une ~ d'insultes** loads *OU* a heap of insults.

charretier, ère [ʃartje, ɛr] ◇ *adj* [chemin, voie] cart *(modif)*.
◇ *nm, f* carter.

charrette [ʃarɛt] *nf* **1.** AGRIC cart **2.** HIST : **la ~ des condamnés** the tumbrel *ou* tumbril **3.** *loc* **~** [de licenciements] : **faire partie de la première/dernière ~** to be among the first/last group of people to be dismissed.

charriage [ʃarjaʒ] *nm* **1.** TRANSP carriage, haulage **2.** GÉOL overthrust.

charrié, e [ʃarje] *adj* GÉOL displaced *(as the result of an overthrust).*

charrier [9] [ʃarje] <> *vt* **1.** [suj: personne] to cart *ou* to carry (along) **2.** [suj: fleuve, rivière] to carry *ou* to wash along **3.** △ [railler] : **~ qqn** to take the mickey out of sb *UK*, to put sb on *US* ■ **se faire ~** to get ribbed.
<> *vi*△ [exagérer] to go too far *ou* (way) over the top ■ **10 euros d'augmentation, ils charrient!** 10 euros on the price, they've got a nerve! ■ **je veux bien aider mais faut pas ~** I don't mind lending a hand, but I don't like people taking advantage.

charroi [ʃarwa] *nm* carting.

charron [ʃarɔ̃] *nm* **1.** [fabricant] cartwright, wheelwright **2.** [réparateur] wheelwright.

charrue [ʃary] *nf* plough *UK*, plow *US* ■ **mettre la ~ avant les bœufs** to put the cart before the horse.

charte [ʃart] *nf* **1.** [document] charter ■ **la ~ des droits de l'homme** the Charter of Human Rights **2.** HIST charter ■ **la Grande Charte** Magna Carta **3.** [plan] : **~ d'aménagement** development plan.
◆ **chartes** *nfpl* ▷ **école.**

charter [ʃartɛr] *nm* [avion] chartered plane ■ [vol] charter flight.

chartiste [ʃartist] *nmf* **1.** POLIT [en Grande-Bretagne] Chartist **2.** UNIV *student or former student of the École des chartes.*

chartreux, euse [ʃartrø, øz] *nm, f* Carthusian monk.
◆ **chartreux** *nm* [chat] British blue (cat).
◆ **chartreuse** *nf* **1.** RELIG Charterhouse, Carthusian monastery, Carthusian convent ■ **'la Chartreuse de Parme'** *Stendhal* 'The Charterhouse of Parma' **2.** [liqueur] Chartreuse.

Charybde [karibd] *npr* Charybdis ■ **tomber de ~ en Scylla** to go from the frying pan into the fire.

chas [ʃa] *nm* eye *(of a needle).*

chasse [ʃas] *nf* **1.** [activité] hunting ■ [occasion] hunt ■ **~ au daim/renard/tigre** deer/fox/tiger hunt ■ **~ au lapin** (rabbit) shooting ■ **aller à la ~** [à courre] to go hunting ; [au fusil] to go shooting ➊ **~ à courre** [activité] hunting ; [occasion] hunt ■ **~ sous-marine** underwater fishing ■ **qui va à la ~ perd sa place** *prov* if somebody takes your place it serves you right for leaving it empty
2. [domaine - de chasse à courre] hunting grounds ; [- de chasse au fusil] shooting ground ■ **'~ gardée'** 'private, poachers will be prosecuted' ■ **laisse-la tranquille, c'est ~ gardée** *fam* leave her alone, she's spoken for
3. [butin] game ■ **la ~ a été bonne** we got a good bag
4. [poursuite] chase, hunt ■ **faire** *ou* **donner la ~ à un cambrioleur** to chase after a burglar ■ **prendre en ~ une voiture** to chase a car
5. [recherche] : **~ à** search for ■ **~ à l'homme** manhunt ■ **~ au trésor** treasure hunt ■ **~ aux sorcières** witch hunt ■ **faire la ~ à** to search for, to (try to) track down ■ **faire la ~ au mari** *fam* to go hunting for a husband ■ **se mettre en ~ pour trouver un emploi/une maison** to go job-hunting/house-hunting
6. AÉRON : **la ~** fighter planes
7. [d'eau] flush ■ **tirer la ~ (d'eau)** to flush the toilet.
◆ **en chasse** *loc adj* ZOOL on *UK ou* in *US* heat.

chassé [ʃase] *nm* chassé.

châsse [ʃas] *nf* **1.** RELIG [coffre] shrine **2.** [de lunettes] frames.

chasse-clou [ʃasklu] (*pl* **chasse-clous**) *nm* nail punch.

chassé-croisé [ʃasekrwaze] (*pl* **chassés-croisés**) *nm* **1.** [confusion] : **le ~ ministériel/de limousines** the comings and goings of ministers/of limousines **2.** DANSE set to partners.

chasselas [ʃasla] *nm* : **du ~** Chasselas grapes.

chasse-mouches [ʃasmuʃ] *nm inv* flyswatter.

chasse-neige [ʃasnɛʒ] *nm inv* **1.** [véhicule] snowplough *UK*, snowplow *US* **2.** [position du skieur] snowplough *UK*, snowplow *US* ■ **descendre/tourner en ~** to snowplough down/round.

chasser [3] [ʃase] <> *vt* **1.** CHASSE to hunt **2.** [expulser] to drive out *(sép)*, to expel ■ **il a été chassé de chez lui** he was made to leave home ■ **elle l'a chassé de la maison** she sent him packing **3.** [congédier - employé] to dismiss **4.** [faire partir] to dispel, to drive away *(sép)*, to get rid of ■ **sortez pour ~ les idées noires** go out and forget your worries ➊ **chassez le naturel, il revient au galop** the leopard can't change its spots **5.** [pousser] to drive (forward) ■ **le vent chasse le sable/les nuages** the wind is blowing the sand/the clouds along.
<> *vi* **1.** [aller à la chasse - à courre] to go hunting ; [- au fusil] to go shooting ■ **~ sur les terres d'autrui** *fig* to poach on somebody's preserve *ou* territory **2.** [déraper] to skid ■ **le navire chasse sur son ancre** NAUT the ship is dragging its anchor.

chasseresse [ʃasrɛs] <> *adj f* : **Diane ~** Diana the huntress.
<> *nf litt* huntress.

châsses△ [ʃas] *nmpl* peepers, eyes.

chasseur, euse [ʃasœr, øz] *nm, f* **1.** CHASSE hunter, huntsman (*f* huntress) ■ **un très bon ~** an excellent shot ■ **le Chasseur français** PRESSE *hunting magazine, whose small ads section is traditionally used by people looking for companionship* **2.** [chercheur] : **~ d'autographes** autograph hunter ■ **~ d'images** (freelance) photographer ■ **~ de prime** bounty hunter ■ **~ de têtes** *pr & fig* headhunter **3.** AÉRON & MIL fighter (plane) ■ **~-bombardier** fighter bomber **4.** MIL chasseur ■ **~ alpin** Alpine chasseur **5.** [dans un hôtel] messenger (boy), bellboy *US*.
◆ **chasseur** *adj inv* CULIN chasseur.

chassieux, euse [ʃasjø, øz] *adj* [œil] rheumy ■ [personne] rheumy-eyed ■ **avoir les yeux ~** to have rheumy eyes.

châssis [ʃasi] *nm* **1.** CONSTR frame **2.** ART stretcher ■ PHOTO (printing) frame ■ **~ d'imprimerie** IMPR chase **3.** AUTO chassis, steel frame **4.** △ [corps féminin] chassis, figure.

chaste [ʃast] *adj* chaste, innocent.

chastement [ʃastəmɑ̃] *adv* chastely, innocently.

chasteté [ʃastəte] *nf* chastity.

chasuble [ʃazybl] *nf* **1.** RELIG chasuble **2.** [vêtement] : **robe ~** pinafore dress.

chat, chatte [ʃa, ʃat] *nm, f* **1.** ZOOL [gén] cat ■ [mâle] tomcat ■ [femelle] she-cat ■ **un petit ~** a kitten ➊ **~ européen** *ou* **de gouttière** tabby (cat) ■ **~ persan/siamois** Persian/Siamese cat ■ **~ sauvage** [félin] wildcat ; *canadian english* [raton laveur] raccoon ■ **appeler un ~ un ~** to call a spade a spade ■ **avoir un ~ dans la gorge** to have a frog in one's throat ■ **il n'y a pas de quoi fouetter un ~** it's nothing to make a fuss about ■ **j'ai d'autres ~s à fouetter** I've got better things to do ■ **il n'y avait pas un ~** *fam* there wasn't a soul about ■ **il ne faut pas réveiller le ~ qui dort** *prov* let sleeping dogs lie *prov* ■ **quand le ~ n'est pas là, les souris dansent** *prov* when the cat's away, the mice will play *prov* ■ **à bon ~, bon rat** *prov* it's tit for tat *loc* ■ **~ échaudé craint l'eau froide** once bitten, twice shy *prov* **2.** LITTÉR : **'le Chat botté'** *Perrault* 'Puss in Boots' **3.** *fam* [terme d'affection] pussycat, sweetie, sweetheart **4.** JEUX : **jouer à ~** to play tag ■ **c'est Sonia le ~** Sonia's it ■ **jouer à ~ perché** to play off-ground tag ■ **jouer au ~ et à la souris avec qqn** *fig* to play cat-and-mouse with sb **5.** HIST & NAUT : **~ à neuf queues** cat-o'-nine-tails.
◆ **chatte**▲ *nf* pussy△, fanny△ *UK*.

chat [tʃat] *nm* INFORM chat.

châtaigne [ʃatɛɲ] *nf* **1.** BOT chestnut **2.** △ [coup] biff, clout ■ **il s'est pris une de ces ~s!** [il a été frappé] he got such a smack! ; [il s'est cogné] he gave himself a nasty knock!

châtaigneraie [ʃatɛɲərɛ] *nf* chestnut grove.

châtaignier [ʃateɲe] *nm* **1.** BOT chestnut tree **2.** [bois] chestnut.

châtain [ʃatɛ̃] ◇ *adj m* [cheveux] chestnut (brown) ■ **~ clair** light brown ■ **~ doré** *ou* **roux** auburn ■ **être ~** to have brown hair.
◇ *nm* chestnut brown.

château, x [ʃato] *nm* **1.** HIST castle ■ **~ fort** fortified castle **2.** [palais] castle, palace ■ [manoir] mansion, manor (house) ■ **ses illusions se sont écroulées comme un ~ de cartes** his illusions collapsed like a house of cards ■ **bâtir** *ou* **faire des ~x en Espagne** to build castles in the air [jeu de plage, attraction] : **~ gonflable** bouncy castle **3.** ŒNOL chateau ■ **mis en bouteilles au ~** chateau bottled.
◆ **château d'eau** *nm* water tower.

chateaubriand, châteaubriant [ʃatobrijɑ̃] *nm* Chateaubriand (steak).

Château-la-Pompe [ʃatolapɔ̃p] *npr m fam hum* water ■ **accompagné d'un verre de ~** washed down with a glass of good old tapwater *hum*.

châtelain, e [ʃatlɛ̃, ɛn] *nm, f* **1.** [propriétaire - gén] owner of a manor ; [- homme] lord of the manor ; [- femme] lady of the manor **2.** HIST (feudal) lord.
◆ **châtelaine** *nf* **1.** [chaîne de ceinture, bijou] chatelaine **2.** HIST [femme du châtelain] chatelaine, lady of the manor.

châtelet [ʃatlɛ] *nm* small (fortified) castle.

chat-huant [ʃaɥɑ̃] (*pl* **chats-huants**) *nm* tawny *ou* brown *ou* wood owl.

châtier [9] [ʃatje] *vt litt* **1.** [punir] to chastise, to castigate *litt* **2.** [affiner] to polish, to refine ■ **parler dans une langue châtiée** to use refined language.

chatière [ʃatjɛr] *nf* **1.** [pour un chat] cat door *ou* flap **2.** [dans un toit] ventilation hole.

châtiment [ʃatimɑ̃] *nm sout* chastisement *sout*, punishment.

chatoie *etc v* ▷ **chatoyer**.

chatoiement [ʃatwamɑ̃] *nm* [sur du métal, du verre] gleam, shimmer ■ [sur de la soie] (soft) glimmer.

chaton [ʃatɔ̃] *nm* **1.** ZOOL kitten **2.** BOT catkin, ament *spéc*, amentum *spéc* **3.** [poussière] ball of fluff **4.** [par affection] darling **5.** JOAILL [tête de la bague] bezel ■ [pierre enchâssée] stone.

chatouille [ʃatuj] *nf fam* tickle ■ **faire des ~s à qqn** to tickle sb ■ **elle craint les ~s** she's ticklish.

chatouillement [ʃatujmɑ̃] *nm* tickle ■ **je ressens encore un ~ dans les oreilles mais je n'ai plus mal** my ears still tickle but it doesn't hurt anymore.

chatouiller [3] [ʃatuje] *vt* **1.** [pour faire rire] to tickle **2.** [irriter] to tickle **3.** [exciter - odorat, palais] to titillate **4.** [heurter - amour-propre, sensibilité] to prick.

chatouilleux, euse [ʃatujø, øz] *adj* **1.** [physiquement] ticklish **2.** [pointilleux] sensitive, touchy ■ **~ sur** overparticular about.

chatouillis [ʃatuji] *nm fam* tickle ■ **faire des ~ à qqn** to tickle sb.

chatoyant, e [ʃatwajɑ̃, ɑ̃t] *adj* **1.** [brillant] gleaming, glistening, shimmering **2.** [luisant] glimmering.

chatoyer [13] [ʃatwaje] *vi* **1.** [briller] to gleam, to glisten, to shimmer ■ **la lumière des bougies faisait ~ les tissus précieux** the precious fabrics shimmered in the candlelight **2.** [luire] to glimmer.

châtrer [3] [ʃatre] *vt* **1.** [étalon, homme, taureau] to castrate ■ [verrat] to geld ■ [chat] to castrate, to fix *US* **2.** [article] to make innocuous.

chatte [ʃat] *f* ▷ **chat**.

chatterie [ʃatri] *nf* **1.** [câlinerie] coaxing ■ **faire des ~s à qqn** to pamper sb **2.** [friandise] delicacy.

chatterton [ʃatertɔn] *nm* adhesive insulating tape, friction tape.

chaud, e [ʃo, ʃod] *adj* **1.** [dont la température est - douce] warm ; [- élevée] hot ■ **une boisson ~e** a hot drink ■ **son front est tout ~** his forehead is hot ■ **au (moment le) plus ~ de la journée** in the heat of the day ● **marrons ~s** roast chestnuts ■ **~ devant!** [au restaurant] excuse me! *(said by waiters carrying plates to clear the way)*
2. [veste, couverture] warm
3. [qui n'a pas refroidi] warm ■ **la place du directeur est encore ~e** *fig* the manager's shoes are still warm
4. [enthousiaste] ardent, warm, keen ■ **je ne suis pas très ~ pour le faire** *fam* I'm not really eager to do it
5. [ardent - ambiance] warm ■ **avoir une ~e discussion sur qqch** to debate sthg heatedly
6. [agité, dangereux] hot ■ **les points ~s du monde** the danger spots in the world ■ **le mois de septembre sera ~** there will be (political) unrest in September ■ **l'alerte a été ~e** it was a near *ou* close thing
7. *fam* PRESSE hot (off the press) ■ **une nouvelle toute ~e** an up-to-the-minute piece of news
8. △ [sexuellement] hot, randy *esp UK*, horny ■ **~ lapin** randy devil
9. [couleur, voix] warm.
◆ **chaud** ◇ *adv* hot ■ **servir ~** serve hot ■ **bois-le ~** drink it (while it's) hot ■ **avoir ~** [douce chaleur] to feel warm ; [forte chaleur] to feel hot ■ **il fait ~** [douce chaleur] it's warm ; [forte chaleur] it's hot ● **on a eu ~!** *fam* that was a close *ou* near thing! ■ **ça ne me fait ni ~ ni froid** I couldn't care less.
◇ *nm* **1.** [chaleur] : **le ~** the heat *ou* hot weather
2. MÉD : **un ~ et froid** a chill.
◆ **chaude** *nf* MÉTALL heat, melt.
◆ **à chaud** *loc adv* **1.** [en urgence] : **l'opération s'est faite à ~** it was emergency surgery ■ **sonder à ~** to do a spot poll ■ **ne lui pose pas la question à ~** don't just spring the question on him in the midst of it all
2. MÉTALL : **souder à ~** to hot-weld ■ **étirer un métal à ~** to draw metal under heat.
◆ **au chaud** *loc adv* : **restez bien au ~** [au lit] stay nice and cosy *ou* warm in your bed ; [sans sortir] don't go out in the cold ■ **mettre** *ou* **garder des assiettes au ~** to keep plates warm.

chaudement [ʃodmɑ̃] *adv* **1.** [contre le froid] warmly ■ **se vêtir ~** to put on warm clothes **2.** [chaleureusement - gén] warmly, warmheartedly ; [- recommander] heartily ; [- féliciter] with all one's heart.

chaude-pisse▲ [ʃodpis] (*pl* **chaudes-pisses**) *nf* clap△.

chaud-froid [ʃofrwa] (*pl* **chauds-froids**) *nm* CULIN chaud-froid.

chaudière [ʃodjɛr] *nf* boiler ■ **~ à bois/charbon** wood-/coal-fired boiler ■ **~ à vapeur** steam boiler.

chaudron [ʃodrɔ̃] *nm* [en fonte] cauldron ■ [en cuivre] copper kettle *ou* boiler.

chaudronnerie [ʃodrɔnri] *nf* **1.** [profession] boilermaking, boilerwork **2.** [marchandises - de grande taille] boilers ; [- de petite taille] hollowware **3.** [usine] boilerworks.

chaudronnier, ère [ʃodrɔnje, ɛr] *nm, f* [gén] boilermaker ■ [sur du cuivre] coppersmith.

chauffage [ʃofaʒ] *nm* **1.** [d'un lieu] heating ■ **système de ~** heating system **2.** [installation, système] heating (system) ■ **installer le ~** to put heating in ■ **baisser/monter le ~** [dans une maison] to turn the heating down/up ; [en voiture] to turn the heater down/up ● **~ central/urbain** central/district heating ■ **~ électrique/solaire** electric/solar heating ■ **~ au gaz/au mazout** gas-fired/oil-fired heating.

chauffagiste [ʃofaʒist] *nm* heating specialist.

chauffant, e [ʃofɑ̃, ɑ̃t] *adj* [surface] heating.

chauffard [ʃofar] *nm* reckless driver ■ [qui s'enfuit] hit-and-run driver.

chauffe [ʃof] *nf* **1.** [opération] stoking **2.** [temps] heating time ■ **pendant la ~** [d'une machine] while the machine's warming up ; [d'une chaudière] while the boiler's heating.
◆ **de chauffe** *loc adj* boiler *(modif)*.

chauffe-assiettes [ʃofasjɛt] *nm inv* plate warmer, hostess tray.

chauffe-bain [ʃofbɛ̃] (*pl* **chauffe-bains**) *nm* water heater.

chauffe-biberon [ʃofbibrɔ̃] (*pl* **chauffe-biberons**) *nm* bottle warmer.

chauffe-eau [ʃofo] *nm inv* water heater ▪ **~ électrique** immersion heater.

chauffe-plats [ʃofpla] *nm inv* chafing dish.

chauffer [3] [ʃofe] ◇ *vi* **1.** [eau, plat, préparation] to heat up ▪ **mettre qqch à ~, faire ~ qqch** to heat sthg up ▪ **ça chauffe trop, baisse le gaz** it's overheating, turn the gas down **2.** [dégager de la chaleur to give out heat ▪ **en avril, le soleil commence à ~** in April, the sun gets hotter **3.** [avarie] [- surchauffer] to overheat ▪ **faire ~ sa voiture** [mise en route] to warm up one's car **4.** *fam* [être agité] : **ça commence à ~** things are getting hot ▪ **ça va ~!** there's trouble brewing! **5.** JEUX to get warm.
◇ *vt* **1.** [chambre, plat] to warm *ou* to heat up *(sép)* ▪ **~ une maison à l'électricité** to have electric heating in a house ▪ **piscine chauffée** heated swimming pool **2.** *loc* **tu commences à me ~ les oreilles** *fam* you're getting up my nose *UK*, you're starting to get my goat **3.** MÉTALL : **~ un métal à blanc/au rouge** to make a metal white-hot/red-hot **4.** *fam* [exciter] : **~ la salle** to warm up the audience.
◆ **se chauffer** *vpi* **1.** [se réchauffer] to warm o.s. (up) **2.** [dans un local] : **ils n'ont pas les moyens de se ~** they can't afford heating ▪ **se ~ à l'électricité** to have electric heating.

chaufferette [ʃofrɛt] *nf* [bouillotte, boîte] foot-warmer.

chaufferie [ʃofri] *nf* **1.** [local] boiler room **2.** NAUT & NUCL stokehold.

chauffeur [ʃofœr] *nm* **1.** [conducteur] driver ▪ **~ (routier), ~ de camion** lorry *UK ou* truck *US* driver ▪ **~ de taxi** taxi *ou* cab driver ▪ **~ du dimanche** *péj* Sunday driver **2.** [employé] : **location de voiture avec ~** chauffeur-driven hire-cars ▪ **j'ai fait le ~ de ces dames toute la journée** *fam* I drove the ladies around all day long ▪ **il est le ~ du président** he chauffeurs for the chairman ▶ **~ de maître** chauffeur **3.** [d'une locomotive] stoker.

chauffeuse [ʃoføz] *nf* low armless chair.

chauler [3] [ʃole] *vt* **1.** AGRIC to lime **2.** CONSTR to whitewash.

chaume [ʃom] *nm* **1.** [sur un toit] thatch ▪ **recouvrir un toit de ~** to thatch a roof **2.** AGRIC [paille] haulm ▪ [sur pied] stubble **3.** *litt* [champ] stubble field.

chaumer [3] [ʃome] ◇ *vt* [champs] to clear stubble from, to clear of stubble.
◇ *vi* to clear stubble.

chaumière [ʃomjɛr] *nf* ≃ cottage ▪ [avec un toit de chaume] thatched cottage ▪ **faire causer** *ou* **jaser dans les ~s** to give the neighbours something to talk about.

chaussant, e [ʃosɑ̃, ɑ̃t] *adj* [botte, soulier] well-fitting.

chaussée [ʃose] *nf* **1.** [d'une route] roadway, pavement *US* ▪ **'~ déformée'** 'uneven road surface' ▪ **'~ glissante'** 'slippery road, slippery when wet' **2.** [talus] dyke, embankment ▪ [voie surélevée] causeway ▪ **la Chaussée des Géants** the Giant's Causeway.

chausse-pied [ʃospje] (*pl* **chausse-pieds**) *nm* shoehorn.

chausser [3] [ʃose] ◇ *vt* **1.** [escarpins, skis, palmes] to put on *(sép)* ▪ **elle était chaussée de pantoufles de soie** she was wearing silk slippers **2.** [enfant, personne] : **viens ~ les enfants** come and put the children's shoes on for them **3.** [fournir en chaussures] to provide shoes for, to supply with shoes ▪ **je suis difficile à ~** it's hard for me to find shoes that fit **4.** [lunettes] to put *ou* to slip on *(sép)* **5.** AUTO : **la voiture est chaussée de pneus neige** the car has snow tyres on **6.** [arbre, plante] to earth up.
◇ *vi* : **voici un modèle qui devrait mieux ~** this style of shoe should fit better ▪ **du combien chausses-tu?** what size shoes do you take? ▪ **je chausse du 38** I take a size 38 shoe, I take size 38 in shoes.
◆ **se chausser** ◇ *vp (emploi réfléchi)* : **chausse-toi, il fait froid** put something on your feet, it's cold ▪ **se ~ avec un chausse-pied** to use a shoehorn.
◇ *vpi* [se fournir] : **je me chausse chez Lebel** I buy my shoes at *ou* I get my shoes from Lebel's.

chausses [ʃos] *nfpl* *arch* hose, chausses.

chausse-trap(p)e [ʃostrap] (*pl* **chausse-trap(p)es**) *nf pr & fig* trap.

chaussette [ʃosɛt] *nf* [vêtement] sock ▪ **en ~s** in one's stockinged feet ▪ **laisser tomber qqn comme une vieille ~** *fam* to ditch sb.

chausseur [ʃosœr] *nm* **1.** [fabricant] shoemaker **2.** [vendeur] shoemaker, footwear specialist.

chausson [ʃosɔ̃] *nm* **1.** [vêtement] [d'intérieur] slipper ▪ [de bébé] bootee **2.** [de danseuse] ballet shoe, pump ▪ [de gymnastique] soft shoe ▪ [dans la chaussure de ski] inner shoe **3.** CULIN turnover ▪ **~ aux pommes** ≃ apple turnover **4.** COUT : **point de ~** blind hem stitch.

chaussure [ʃosyr] *nf* **1.** [vêtement] shoe ▪ **acheter des ~s** to buy shoes ▶ **~s plates** flat shoes, flatties ▪ **~s à semelles compensées** platform shoes ▪ **~s à talon** (shoes with) heels ▪ **trouver ~ à son pied** *fig* to find a suitable match **2.** LOISIRS & SPORT : **~s de marche** walking *ou* hiking boots ▪ **~s de ski** ski boots ▪ **~s de sport** sports shoes, trainers *UK* **3.** COMM shoe trade ▪ [industrie] shoe *ou* shoe-manufacturing industry.

chaut *v* ⊳ **chaloir**.

chauve [ʃov] ◇ *adj* [crâne, tête] bald ▪ [personne] bald, baldheaded ▪ *litt* [montagne] bare ▪ **~ comme un œuf** *fam* as bald as a coot *UK ou* as an egg *US* ▪ **il devient ~** he's balding *ou* going bald.
◇ *nmf* bald person, bald man (*f* woman).

chauve-souris [ʃovsuri] (*pl* **chauves-souris**) *nf* bat.

chauvin, e [ʃovɛ̃, in] ◇ *adj* chauvinistic, jingoist, jingoistic.
◇ *nm, f* chauvinist, jingoist.

chauvinisme [ʃovinism] *nm* chauvinism, jingoism.

chaux [ʃo] *nf* lime ▪ **mur passé** *ou* **blanchi à la ~** whitewashed wall ▶ **~ vive** quicklime.

chavirer [3] [ʃavire] ◇ *vi* **1.** NAUT to capsize, to keel over, to turn turtle ▪ **faire ~** to capsize ▪ **arrête, tu vas faire ~ la barque!** stop it, you'll tip the boat over! **2.** [se renverser] to keel over, to overturn ▪ **tout chavire autour de moi** everything around me is spinning **3.** [tourner - yeux] to roll ▪ **avoir le cœur qui chavire** [de dégoût] to feel nauseated ; [de chagrin] to be heartbroken.
◇ *vt* **1.** [basculer] to capsize, to overturn **2.** [émouvoir] to overwhelm, to shatter ▪ **il a l'air tout chaviré** he looks devastated.

chèche [ʃɛʃ] *nm* scarf.

check-list [tʃɛklist] (*pl* **check-lists**) *nf* checklist.

check-up [tʃɛkœp] *nm inv* checkup.

chef [ʃɛf] ◇ *nm* **1.** [responsable - gén] head ; [- d'une entreprise] manager, boss ▪ **~ comptable** chief accountant ▪ **~ d'atelier** shop foreman ▪ **~ de bureau** head clerk ▪ **~ de cabinet** principal private secretary ▪ **~ de chantier** site foreman ▪ **~ d'établissement** ÉDUC headmaster (*f* headmistress), principal ▪ **~ de famille** head of the family ▪ **~ de l'État** Head of the State ▪ **~s d'État** heads of state ▪ **~ d'entreprise** company manager ▪ **~ d'équipe** foreman ▪ **~ de produit** product manager ▪ **~ de projet** project manager ▪ **~ de rayon** department manager ▪ **~ de service** section head ▪ **~ du personnel** personnel *ou* staff manager
2. MIL : **~ d'escadron** major ▪ **~ d'état-major** chief of staff ▪ **~ de patrouille** patrol leader
3. RAIL : **~ de gare** station master ▪ **~ mécanicien** chief mechanic
4. CULIN chef ▪ **la spécialité du ~ aujourd'hui** the chef's special today
5. MUS : **~ de pupitre** head of section ▪ **~ des chœurs** choirmaster
6. SPORT : **~ de nage** stroke
7. [leader] leader ▶ **~ de bande** gang leader ▪ **~ de file** leader ▪ **petit ~** *péj* [dans une famille] domestic tyrant ; [au bureau, à

l'usine] slave driver ▪ **une mentalité de petit ~** a petty-minded attitude to one's subordinates ▪ **elle s'est débrouillée comme un ~!** *fam* she did really well!
8. *(comme adj)* head *(modif)*, chief *(modif)* ▪ **infirmière ~** head nurse ▪ **ingénieur ~** chief engineer ▪ **médecin-~** ≃ senior consultant
9. *hum* [tête] head ▪ **opiner du ~** to nod
10. DR : **~ d'accusation** charge *OU* count (of indictment).
◇ *nf fam* [responsable] : **la ~** the boss.
◆ **au premier chef** *loc adv* above all, first and foremost ▪ **leur décision me concerne au premier ~** their decision has immediate implications for me.
◆ **de mon propre chef, de son propre chef** *etc loc adv* on my/his *etc* own authority *OU* initiative ▪ **j'ai agi de mon propre ~** I acted on my own initiative.
◆ **en chef** *loc adj* : **commandant en ~** commander-in-chief ▪ **ingénieur en ~** chief engineer.
◆ **chef d'orchestre** *nm* **1.** MUS conductor
2. *fig* [organisateur] organizer, orchestrator.

chef-d'œuvre [ʃɛdœvr] (*pl* **chefs-d'œuvre**) *nm* masterpiece.

chef-lieu [ʃɛfljø] (*pl* **chefs-lieux**) *nm* ADMIN *in France, administrative centre of a "département", "arrondissement" or "canton".*

cheftaine [ʃɛftɛn] *nf* [de louveteaux] cubmistress *UK*, den mother *US* ▪ [chez les jeannettes] Brown Owl *UK*, den mother *US* ▪ [chez les éclaireuses] captain.

cheik, cheikh [ʃɛk] *nm* sheik, sheikh.

chelem [ʃlɛm] *nm* JEUX & SPORT slam ▪ **grand ~** grand slam ▪ **petit ~** small *OU* little slam.

chemin [ʃəmɛ̃] *nm* **1.** [allée] path, lane ▪ **~ de ronde** covered way ▪ **~ de terre** dirt track ▪ **~ de traverse** *pr* path across the fields ; *fig* short cut ▪ **~ vicinal** *OU* **départemental** minor road ▪ **être toujours sur les (quatre) ~s** to be always on the move *OU* road ▪ **bandit** *OU* **voleur de grand ~** *OU* **grands ~s** highwayman ▪ **tous les ~s mènent à Rome** *prov* all roads lead to Rome *prov*
2. [parcours, trajet] way ▪ **faire** *OU* **abattre du ~** to go a long way ▪ **on s'est retrouvé à mi-~** *OU* **à moitié ~** we met halfway ▪ **demandons-lui notre ~** let's ask him how to get there ▪ **pas de problème, c'est sur mon ~** no problem, it's on my way ▪ **c'est le ~ le plus court/long** it's the shortest/longest way ▪ **nous avons fait tout le ~ à pied/en voiture** we walked/drove all the way ▪ **se frayer** *OU* **s'ouvrir un ~ dans la foule** to force one's way through the crowd ▪ **se mettre sur le ~ de qqn** to stand in sb's way ▪ **prendre le ~ de l'exil** to go into exile ▪ **prendre des ~s détournés pour faire qqch** *fig* to use roundabout means in order to do sthg ➊ **prendre le ~ des écoliers** to go the long way around ▪ **il voudrait devenir avocat, mais il n'en prend pas le ~** he'd like to be a lawyer, but he's not going about it the right way
3. *fig* [destinée, progression] way ▪ **se mettre sur le~ de qqn** to stand in sb's way ▪ **ouvrir/montrer le ~** to open/to lead the way ▪ **nos ~s se sont croisés autrefois** we met a long time ago ▪ **faire son ~** [personne] to make one's way in life ; [idée] to catch on ▪ **cet enfant fera du ~, croyez-moi!** this child will go far *OU* a long way, believe me! ▪ **se mettre sur le ~ de qqn** to stand in sb's way ▪ **trouver qqn sur son ~** [ennemi] to find sb standing in one's way ➊ **le ~ de Damas** BIBLE the road to Damascus ▪ **trouver son ~ de Damas** *fig* to see the light ▪ **ne t'arrête pas en si bon ~** don't give up now that you're doing so well ▪ **être/rester sur le droit ~** to be on/to keep to the straight and narrow ▪ **détourner qqn du droit ~** to lead sb astray
4. RELIG : **~ de croix** Way of the Cross
5. [napperon] : **~ de table** table runner
6. INFORM : **~ d'acces** path.
◆ **chemin faisant** *loc adv* on the way, on one's way.
◆ **en chemin** *loc adv* on the way *OU* one's way ▪ **nous en avons parlé en ~** we talked about it on the way *OU* on our way.

chemin de fer [ʃəmɛ̃dfɛr] (*pl* **chemins de fer**) *nm* RAIL railway *UK*, railroad *US* ▪ **voyager en ~** to travel by train ▪ **employé des ~s de fer** rail worker *UK*, railman.

chemineau, x [ʃəmino] *nm* *vieilli* tramp, vagrant, hobo *US*.

cheminée [ʃəmine] *nf* **1.** [gén] shaft ▪ [de maison] chimney (stack) ▪ [dans un mur] chimney ▪ [d'usine] chimney (stack), smokestack ▪ [de paquebot] funnel ▪ **~ d'aération** ventilation shaft **2.** [âtre] fireplace ▪ [chambranle] mantelpiece **3.** GÉOL [d'un volcan] vent ▪ **~ des fées** devil's chimney ▮ [d'un massif] chimney ▪ **~ des fées** devil's chimney.

cheminement [ʃəminmɑ̃] *nm* **1.** [parcours] movement **2.** *fig* [développement] development, unfolding ▪ **le ~ de sa pensée** the development of her thought **3.** MIL advance (under cover).

cheminer [3] [ʃəmine] *vi* **1.** *litt* [avancer - marcheur] to walk along ; [- fleuve] to flow ▪ **~ avec difficulté à travers bois** to struggle through the woods **2.** *fig* [progresser - régulièrement] to progress, to develop ; [- lentement] to make slow progress *OU* headway **3.** MIL to advance (under cover).

cheminot [ʃəmino] *nm* RAIL railwayman *UK*, railroad man *US*.

chemise [ʃəmiz] *nf* **1.** [vêtement] shirt ▪ **~ de nuit** [de femme] nightgown, nightdress ; [d'homme] nightshirt ▪ **en (bras** *OU* **manches de) ~** in shirt-sleeves ▪ **il donnerait jusqu'à sa ~** he'd give the shirt off his back ▪ **je m'en fiche** *fam* *OU* **soucie** *OU* **moque comme de ma première ~** I couldn't care less about it **2.** HIST : **Chemises brunes** Brownshirts ▪ **Chemises noires** Blackshirts ▪ **Chemises rouges** Redshirts **3.** [de carton] folder **4.** MÉCAN & TECHNOL [enveloppe - intérieure] lining ; [- extérieure] jacket.

chemiser [3] [ʃəmize] *vt* **1.** MÉCAN & TECHNOL [intérieurement] to line ▪ [extérieurement] to jacket **2.** CULIN to coat with aspic jelly.

chemiserie [ʃəmizri] *nf* **1.** [fabrique] shirt factory **2.** [boutique] gents' outfitter's *UK*, haberdasher's *US* **3.** [industrie] shirt trade.

chemisette [ʃəmizɛt] *nf* [pour femme] short-sleeved blouse ▪ [pour homme, pour enfant] short-sleeved shirt.

chemisier, ère [ʃəmizje, ɛr] *nm, f* shirtmaker *UK*, haberdasher *US*.
◆ **chemisier** *nm* blouse.

chenal, aux [ʃənal, o] *nm* **1.** [canal - dans les terres] channel ; [- dans un port] fairway, channel **2.** GÉOL [sous la mer] trench.

chenapan [ʃənapɑ̃] *nm* *hum* rascal, rogue, scoundrel.

chêne [ʃɛn] *nm* **1.** BOT oak ▪ **~ vert** holm oak, ilex ▪ **fort** *OU* **solide comme un ~** as strong as an ox **2.** MENUIS oak.

chéneau, x [ʃeno] *nm* gutter *(on a roof)*.

chêne-liège [ʃɛnljɛʒ] (*pl* **chênes-lièges**) *nm* cork oak.

chenet [ʃənɛ] *nm* andiron, firedog.

chenil [ʃənil] *nm* **1.** [établissement - pour la reproduction] breeding kennels ; [- pour la garde] boarding kennels ; [- pour le dressage] training kennels **2.** *Suisse* [bric-à-brac] (load of) junk.

chenille [ʃənij] *nf* **1.** ENTOM caterpillar ▪ **~ du bombyx** silk worm **2.** MÉCAN caterpillar ▪ **véhicule à ~s** tracked vehicle **3.** TEXT chenille.

chenillé, e [ʃənije] *adj* [engin, véhicule] tracked.

chenu, e [ʃəny] *adj* *litt* **1.** [vieillard] hoary **2.** [arbre] bald *OU* leafless (with age), glabrous *spéc.*

cheptel [ʃɛptɛl] *nm* **1.** [bétail] livestock ▪ **avoir un ~ de 1 000 têtes** to have 1,000 head of cattle ▪ **le ~ bovin de la France** the total number of cattle in France **2.** DR : **~ (vif)** livestock ▪ **~ mort** farm equipment.

chèque [ʃɛk] *nm* **1.** FIN cheque *UK*, check *US* ▪ **tirer/toucher un ~** to draw/to cash a cheque ▪ **faire un ~ de 100 euros à qqn** to write sb a cheque for 100 euros ▪ **~ bancaire** cheque ▪ **~ barré** crossed cheque ▪ **~ en blanc** blank cheque ▪ **~ en bois** *fam* *OU* **sans provision** dud cheque *UK*, bad check *US* ▪ **il a fait un ~ sans provision** his cheque bounced ▪ **~ à ordre** cheque to order ▪ **~ au porteur** bearer cheque ▪ **~ postal** *cheque drawn on the postal banking system* ▪ ≃ giro (cheque) *UK* ▪ **~ de voyage** traveller's cheque **2.** [coupon] : **~-cadeau** gift token ▪ **~ emploi-service** *special cheque used to pay casual workers such as part-time cleaners, babysitters, etc* ▪ **~-essence** petrol coupon *OU* voucher ▪ **~-repas** luncheon voucher.

Chèque-Restaurant® [ʃɛkrɛstɔrɑ̃] (*pl* **Chèques-Restaurants**) *nm* ≃ luncheon voucher.

chèque-service (*pl* **chèques-services**) [ʃɛksɛrvis] *nm* type of cheque that can be used to pay someone for their services, which automatically takes care of social-security contributions.

chèque-vacances (*pl* **chèques-vacances**) [sɛkvakɑ̃s] *nm* voucher that can be used to pay for holiday accommodation, activities, meals, *etc.*

chéquier [ʃekje] *nm* chequebook *UK*, checkbook *US*.

cher, chère [ʃɛr] *adj* **1.** [aimé] dear ▪ **ceux qui vous sont ~s** your loved ones, the ones you love ▪ **un être ~** a loved one **2.** [dans des formules de politesse] dear ▪ **mes bien** *ou* **très ~s amis** dearest friends ▪ **le ~ homme n'a pas compris** *hum* & *iron* the dear man didn't understand ▪ **mes bien** *ou* **très ~s frères** RELIG beloved brethren **3.** [précieux] dear, beloved ▪ **il est retourné à ses chères études** *hum* he's gone back to his ivory tower *ou* to his beloved books ▪ **la formule si chère aux hommes politiques** the phrase beloved of politicians, that favourite phrase of politicians ▪ **mon souhait le plus ~** my dearest *ou* most devout wish **4.** [onéreux] expensive, dear *UK* ▪ **c'est plus ~** it's dearer *UK ou* more expensive ▪ **c'est moins ~** it's cheaper *ou* less expensive ▪ **voilà un dîner pas ~!** now this is a cheap dinner!

◆ **cher** *adv* **1.** COMM : **coûter ~** to cost a lot, to be expensive ▪ **est-ce que ça te revient ~?** does it cost you a lot? ▪ **prendre ~** *fam* to charge a lot ▪ **il vaut ~** [bijou de famille] it's worth a lot *ou* valuable ; [article en magasin] it's expensive ▪ **je l'ai eu pour pas ~** *fam* I didn't pay much for it **2.** *loc* **donner ~ : je donnerais ~ pour le savoir** I'd give anything to know ▪ **je ne donne pas ~ de sa vie** I wouldn't give much for his chances of survival ▪ **il ne vaut pas ~** he's a good-for-nothing.

chercher [3] [ʃɛrʃe] *vt* **1.** [dans l'espace] to look *ou* to search for *(insép)* ▪ **~ qqn du regard** *ou* **des yeux** to look around for sb ▪ **~ qqn/qqch à tâtons** to fumble *ou* to grope for sb/sthg ➊ **~ la petite bête** *fam* to split hairs ▪ **~ des poux dans la tête de qqn** *fam* to try and pick a fight with sb ▪ **cherchez la femme** *Alexandre Dumas, père allus* cherchez la femme
2. [mentalement] to try to find, to search for *(insép)* ▪ *(en usage absolu)* **tu donnes ta langue au chat? – attends, je cherche** give up? – wait, I'm still thinking *ou* trying to think ➊ **~ des crosses** *fam ou* **des ennuis** *ou* **des histoires à qqn** to try and cause trouble for sb ▪ **~ chicane** *ou* **querelle à qqn** to try and pick a quarrel with sb ▪ **~ midi à quatorze heures** *fam* to look for complications (where there are none)
3. [essayer de se procurer] to look *ou* to hunt for *(insép)* ▪ **~ du travail** to look for work, to be job-hunting ▪ **il faut vite ~ du secours** you must get help quickly ▪ **il est parti ~ fortune à l'étranger** he went abroad to look for fame and fortune ▪ **~ refuge auprès de qqn** to seek refuge with sb
4. [aspirer à - tranquillité, inspiration] to look *ou* to search for *(insép)*, to seek (after) ▪ **il ne cherche que son intérêt** he thinks only of his own interests
5. *fam* [provoquer] to look for *(insép)* ▪ **tu l'as bien cherché!** you asked for it! ▪ **toujours à ~ la bagarre!** always looking *ou* spoiling for a fight! ▪ **quand** *ou* **si on me cherche, on me trouve** if anybody asks for trouble, he'll get it
6. [avec des verbes de mouvement] : **aller ~ qqn/qqch** to fetch sb/sthg ▪ **aller ~ les enfants à l'école** to pick the children up from school ▪ **allez me ~ le directeur** [client mécontent] I'd like to speak to the manager ➊ **aller ~** *fig* : **que vas-tu ~ là?** what on earth are you going on about? ▪ **où as-tu été ~ que j'avais accepté?** what made you think I said yes? ▪ **aller ~ dans les** *fam*, **aller ~ jusqu'à** *fam* : **ça va bien ~ dans les 200 euros** it's worth at least 200 euros ▪ **ça peut aller ~ jusqu'à dix ans de prison** it could get you up to ten years in prison ▪ **ça va ~ loin, cette histoire** *fam* this is a bad business.

◆ **chercher à** *v+prép* to try *ou* to attempt *ou* to seek to ▪ **cherche pas à comprendre** *fam* don't bother to try to *ou* and understand.

◆ **chercher après** *v+prép fam* to look for, to be *ou* to chase after.

◆ **se chercher** ◇ *vp (emploi réciproque)* **ils se sont cherchés pendant longtemps** they spent a long time looking for each other.
◇ *vpi* : **il se cherche** he's trying to sort himself out.

chercheur, euse [ʃɛrʃœr, øz] ◇ *adj* [esprit, mentalité] inquiring.
◇ *nm, f* **1.** UNIV researcher, research worker ▪ **travailler comme ~** to be a researcher, to do research **2.** [aventurier] : **un ~ de trésor** a treasure seeker ➊ **~ d'or** gold digger.

◆ **chercheur** *nm* ASTRON : **~ de comètes** finder.

chère [ʃɛr] *nf litt* & *hum* food, fare ➊ **faire bonne ~** to eat well.

chèrement [ʃɛrmɑ̃] *adv* **1.** [à un prix élevé] dearly, at great cost ▪ **la victoire fut ~ payée** the victory was won at great cost **2.** *litt* [tendrement] dearly, fondly.

chéri, e [ʃeri] ◇ *adj* darling, dear, beloved *sout.*
◇ *nm, f* **1.** *(en appellatif)* darling, dear, honey *US* ▪ **mon ~, je te l'ai dit cent fois** darling, I've already told you a hundred times **2.** [personne préférée] : **il a toujours été le ~ de ses parents** he was always the darling of the family ▪ **voilà le ~ de ces dames** *hum* here comes the ladykiller **3.** *fam* [amant] lover, boyfriend (*f* girlfriend).

chérir [32] [ʃerir] *vt litt* [aimer - personne] to cherish, to love (dearly) ; [- démocratie, liberté] to cherish ; [- mémoire, souvenir] to cherish, to treasure.

chérot [ʃero] *fam* ◇ *adj inv* pricey, on the pricey side.
◇ *adv* : **il vend plutôt ~!** his prices are on the stiff side!

cherra *v* ▷ **choir.**

cherry [ʃeri] (*pl* **cherrys** *ou pl* **cherries**) *nm* cherry brandy.

cherté [ʃɛrte] *nf* : **la ~ de la vie** the high cost of living.

chérubin [ʃerybɛ̃] *nm* **1.** RELIG cherub **2.** [enfant] cherub.

chétif, ive [ʃetif, iv] *adj* **1.** [peu robuste] sickly, puny **2.** BOT stunted **3.** *litt* [peu riche - récolte] meagre, poor ; [- existence] poor, wretched.

cheval, aux [ʃ(ə)val, o] *nm* **1.** ZOOL horse ▪ **~ de bataille** *fig* hobbyhorse, pet subject ▪ **~ de cirque** circus horse ▪ **~ de course** racehorse ▪ **~ de labour** plough horse ▪ **~ de manège** school horse ▪ **~ de selle** saddle horse ▪ **~ de trait** draught horse ▪ **à ~ donné on ne regarde pas la dent** *prov* don't look a gift horse in the mouth *prov* ▪ **monter sur ses grands chevaux** to get on one's high horse ▪ **ça ne se trouve pas sous le pas** *ou* **sabot d'un ~** it doesn't grow on trees
2. ÉQUIT (horseback) riding ▪ **faire du ~** to ride, to go riding
3. LOISIRS : **faire un tour sur les chevaux de bois** to go on the roundabout *ou* carousel ▪ **jouer aux petits chevaux** JEUX ≃ to play ludo
4. AUTO & FIN : **~ fiscal** horsepower *(for tax purposes)*
5. MIL : **~ de frise** cheval-de-frise
6. ANTIQ : **le ~ de Troie** the Trojan horse
7. [viande] horsemeat
8. *fam péj* [femme] : **grand ~** great horse of a woman.

◆ **à cheval** *loc adv* **1.** ÉQUIT on horseback ▪ **traverser une rivière à ~** to ride across a river
2. [à califourchon] : **être à ~ sur une chaise** to be sitting astride a chair ▪ **l'étang est à ~ sur deux propriétés** the pond straddles two properties ▪ **mon congé est à ~ sur février et mars** my period of leave starts in February and ends in March
3. *fam* [pointilleux] : **être à ~ sur** to be particular about ▪ **il est très à ~ sur les principes** he is a stickler for principles.

◆ **de cheval** *loc adj* **1.** CULIN horse *(modif)*, horsemeat *(modif)*
2. *fam* [fort] : **fièvre de ~** raging fever ▪ **remède de ~** drastic remedy
3. *péj* [dents] horsey *péj*, horselike.

cheval-d'arçons [ʃ(ə)valdarsɔ̃] *nm inv* vaulting horse.

chevaleresque [ʃ(ə)valrɛsk] *adj* **1.** [généreux] chivalrous ▪ **agir de façon ~** to behave like a gentleman **2.** [des chevaliers] : **l'honneur/le devoir ~** a knight's honour/duty.

chevalerie [ʃ(ə)valri] *nf* **1.** [ordre] knighthood **2.** [institution] chivalry.

chevalet [ʃ(ə)valɛ] *nm* **1.** [d'un peintre] easel **2.** [support] stand, trestle **3.** MUS bridge **4.** HIST [de torture] rack.

chevalier [ʃ(ə)valje] *nm* **1.** HIST knight ■ **il a été fait ~** he was knighted ▶ **~ errant** knight-errant ■ **~ d'industrie** wheeler-dealer ■ **~ servant** (devoted) escort ■ **les ~s de la Table ronde** the Knights of the Round Table **2.** ADMIN : **~ de la Légion d'honneur** chevalier of the Legion of Honour **3.** ORNITH sandpiper.

chevalière [ʃ(ə)valjɛr] *nf* signet ring.

chevalin, e [ʃ(ə)valɛ̃, in] *adj* **1.** [race] equine **2.** [air, allure, visage] horsey, horselike.

cheval-vapeur [ʃ(ə)valvapœr] (*pl* **chevaux-vapeur** [ʃəvovapœr]) *nm* horsepower.

chevauchée [ʃ(ə)voʃe] *nf* ride.

chevauchement [ʃ(ə)voʃmɑ̃] *nm* **1.** [superposition] overlap, overlapping ■ **pour éviter tout ~ dans l'emploi du temps des élèves** to avoid clashes *ou* overlaps between subjects in the students' timetable **2.** CONSTR spanning **3.** GÉOL thrust fault.

chevaucher [3] [ʃəvoʃe] *vt* **1.** [monter sur - moto, cheval, balai, vague] to ride ; [- âne, chaise] to sit astride *ou* astraddle **2.** [recouvrir en partie] to overlap.
◆ **se chevaucher** *vp (emploi réciproque)* **1.** [être superposé - dents] to grow into each other ; [- tuiles] to overlap ■ **mon cours et le sien se chevauchent** my lesson overlaps with hers **2.** GÉOL to overthrust.

chevau-léger [ʃ(ə)voleʒe] (*pl* **chevau-légers**) *nm* [soldat] soldier of the Household Cavalry.

chevelu, e [ʃəvly] <> *adj* **1.** [ayant des cheveux] hairy **2.** [à chevelure abondante] longhaired **3.** BOT comose, comate.
<> *nm, f péj* [personne] long-haired man (*f* woman).
◆ **chevelu** *nm* BOT root-hairs *(pl).*

chevelure [ʃəvlyr] *nf* **1.** [cheveux] hair ■ **son abondante ~** her thick hair **2.** ASTRON tail.

chevet [ʃ(ə)vɛ] *nm* **1.** [d'un lit] bedhead **2.** ARCHIT chevet.
◆ **au chevet de** *loc prép* at the bedside of.
◆ **de chevet** *loc adj* bedside *(modif).*

cheveu, x [ʃ(ə)vø] *nm* **1.** [poil] hair ■ **ses ~x** his hair ■ **une fille aux ~x courts** a girl with short hair, a short-haired girl ■ **avoir les ~x raides** to have straight hair ■ **les ~x en désordre** *ou* **bataille** with unkempt *ou* tousled hair ■ **(les) ~x au vent** with his/her *etc* hair blowing freely in the wind ■ **avoir le ~ rare** to be thinning (on top) ■ **s'il touche à un seul ~ de ma femme...** if he dares touch a hair on my wife's head... ▶ **en ~x** *vieilli* bareheaded ■ **une histoire à faire dresser les ~x sur la tête** a story that makes your hair stand on end ■ **il s'en est fallu d'un ~ qu'on y reste** we missed death by a hair's breadth ■ **il s'en est fallu d'un ~ qu'il ne soit renversé par une voiture** he very nearly got run over ■ **avoir un ~ sur la langue** to (have a) lisp ■ **se faire des ~x (blancs)** to worry o.s. sick ■ **venir** *ou* **arriver comme un ~ sur la soupe** to come at the wrong time ■ **c'est un peu tiré par les ~x** it's a bit far-fetched ■ **avoir mal aux ~x** *fam* to have a hangover **2.** [coiffure] hairstyle ■ **tu aimes mes ~x comme ça?** how do you like my haircut *ou* hairstyle?
◆ **à cheveux** *loc adj* hair *(modif).*
◆ **à un cheveu de** *loc prép* within a hair's breadth of.
◆ **cheveux d'ange** *nmpl* **1.** [guirlande] tinsel garland **2.** CULIN vermicelli.

cheville [ʃ(ə)vij] *nf* **1.** ANAT ankle ■ **ils avaient de la boue jusqu'aux ~s, la boue leur arrivait aux ~s** they were ankle-deep in mud, the mud came up to their ankles ▶ **son fils ne lui arrive pas à la ~** his son's hardly in the same league as him **2.** MENUIS [pour visser] plug ■ [pour boucher] dowel ■ **il est la ~ ouvrière du mouvement** *fig* he's the mainspring *ou* kingpin of the movement **3.** MUS peg **4.** LITTÉR cheville, expletive **5.** [de boucher] hook.
◆ **en cheville** *loc adv* : **être en ~ avec qqn** to be in cahoots with sb ■ **ils sont en ~ tous les deux** they're in it together.

cheviller [3] [ʃ(ə)vije] *vt* to peg ■ **l'armoire est chevillée** the wardrobe is pegged together.

chevillette [ʃ(ə)vijɛt] *nf* [clé] (wooden) peg.

chèvre [ʃɛvr] <> *nf* **1.** ZOOL [mâle] goat, billy-goat ■ [femelle] goat, she-goat, nanny-goat ■ **rendre qqn ~** *fam* to drive sb crazy **2.** [treuil] hoist ■ [chevalet] trestle.
<> *nm* goat's cheese.

chevreau, x [ʃəvro] *nm* **1.** ZOOL kid **2.** [peau] kid ■ **des gants de ~** kid gloves.

chèvrefeuille [ʃɛvrəfœj] *nm* honeysuckle.

chevrette [ʃəvrɛt] *nf* **1.** ZOOL [chèvre] kid, young nanny-goat *ou* she-goat ■ [femelle du chevreuil] roe, doe ■ [crevette] shrimp **2.** [fourrure] goatskin **3.** [trépied] tripod.

chevreuil [ʃəvrœj] *nm* **1.** ZOOL roe deer **2.** CULIN venison.

chevrier, ère [ʃəvrije, ɛr] *nm, f* goatherd.
◆ **chevrier** *nm* chevrier bean.

chevron [ʃəvrɔ̃] *nm* **1.** CONSTR rafter **2.** MIL chevron, V-shaped stripe **3.** [motif] chevron ■ **veste à ~s** [petits] herringbone jacket ; [grands] chevron-patterned jacket.

chevronné, e [ʃəvrɔne] *adj* seasoned, experienced, practised ■ **c'est un grimpeur ~** he's an old hand at climbing *ou* a seasoned climber.

chevrotant, e [ʃəvrɔtɑ̃, ɑ̃t] *adj* quavering.

chevroter [3] [ʃəvrɔte] *vi* [voix] to quaver.

chevrotin [ʃəvrɔtɛ̃] *nm* **1.** ZOOL fawn *(of roe deer)* **2.** CULIN [fromage] goat's cheese.

chevrotine [ʃəvrɔtin] *nf* piece of buckshot ■ **~s** buckshot.

chewing-gum [ʃwiŋgɔm] (*pl* **chewing-gums**) *nm* gum, chewing-gum ■ **un ~** a piece of gum.

Cheyenne [ʃejɛn] *nmf* Cheyenne ■ **les ~ s** the Cheyenne.

chez [ʃe] *prép* **1.** [dans la demeure de] : **rentrer ~ soi** to go home ■ **rester ~ soi** to stay at home *ou* in ■ **est-elle ~ elle en ce moment?** is she at home *ou* in at the moment? ■ **il habite ~ moi en ce moment** he's living with me *ou* he's staying at my place at the moment ■ **elle l'a raccompagné ~ lui** [à pied] she walked him home ; [en voiture] she gave him a lift home ■ **puis-je venir ~ vous?** may I come over (to your place)? ■ **les amis ~ qui j'étais ce week-end** the friends I stayed with this weekend ■ **ça s'est passé pas loin de/devant ~ nous** it happened not far from/right outside where we live ■ **~ M. Durand** [dans une adresse] care of Mr Durand ■ **fais comme ~ toi** make yourself at home ; *iron* do make yourself at home, won't you ■ **~ nous** [dans ma famille] in my *ou* our family ; [dans mon pays] in my *ou* our country ▶ **chacun ~ soi** everyone should look to his own affairs ■ **c'est une coutume/un accent bien de ~ nous** it's a typical local custom/accent
2. [dans un magasin, une société *etc*] : **aller ~ le coiffeur/le médecin** to go to the hairdresser's/the doctor's ■ **acheter qqch ~ l'épicier** to buy sthg at the grocer's ■ **je l'ai acheté ~ Denver & Smith** I bought it from Denver & Smith ■ **dîner ~ Maxim's** to dine at Maxim's ■ **une robe de ~ Dior** a Dior dress, a dress designed by Dior ■ **il a travaillé ~ IBM** he worked at *ou* for IBM ■ **il a fait ses études ~ les jésuites** he studied with the Jesuits *ou* at a Jesuit school
3. [dans un pays, un groupe] : **~ les Russes** in Russia ■ **~ les Grecs** in Ancient Greece ■ **cette expression est courante ~ les jeunes** this expression is widely used among young people ■ **~ l'homme/la femme** in men/women
4. [dans une personne] : **il y a quelque chose que j'apprécie particulièrement ~ eux, c'est leur générosité** something I particularly like about them is their generosity
5. [dans l'œuvre de] in.

chez-soi [ʃeswa] *nm inv* home ■ **avoir un ~** *ou* **son ~** to have a home of one's own.

chiader [3] △ [ʃjade] *vt* **1.** [perfectionner] to polish up *(sép)* ■ **c'est vachement chiadé comme bagnole!** this car's got the works! **2.** ÉDUC & UNIV to cram for, to swot (up) *UK.*

chialer [3] △ [ʃjale] *vi* to blubber, to bawl ■ **~ un bon coup** to bawl one's head off.

chiant, e△ [ʃjɑ̃, ɑ̃t] *adj* **1.** [assommant - personne, chose à faire, livre] boring ■ **ce que c'est ~ cette vérification!** having to check all this is a real drag! **2.** [difficile - chose à faire] : **c'est ~ à mettre en service, cette imprimante!** this printer is a real pain to install! **3.** [contrariant - personne, événement] annoying ■ **t'es ~e de**

pas répondre quand on te parle! why can't you answer me when I speak to you, it really pisses me off△ *UK ou* ticks me off! *US.*

chiard△ [ʃjar] *nm* brat.

chiasme [kjasm] *nm* **1.** [figure de style] chiasmus **2.** ANAT & ART chiasm, chiasma.

chiasse [ʃjas] *nf* **1.** ▲[diarrhée] : **avoir la ~** to have the trots△ *ou* runs△ **2.** △ [poisse] : **quelle ~!** what a drag!

chiatique△ [ʃjatik] *adj* : **t'es vraiment ~** you're a bloody *UK ou* damn pain△ ■ **c'est vraiment ~** it's a complete drag.

chibre [ʃibr] *nm Suisse popular Swiss card game.*

chic [ʃik] ◇ *adj inv fam* **1.** [élégant] stylish, smart, classy ■ **pour faire ~** in order to look smart *ou* classy **2.** [distingué] smart ■ **il paraît que ça fait ~ de...** it's considered smart (these days) to... **3.** [sympathique] nice ■ **être ~ avec qqn** to be nice to sb ■ **sois ~, donne-le-moi!** be an angel, give it to me!
◇ *nm* **1.** [élégance - d'une allure, d'un vêtement] style, stylishness, chic ■ **avoir du ~** to have style, to be chic ■ **s'habiller avec ~** to dress smartly ● **bon ~ bon genre** *fam* ≃ Sloaney *fam UK*, ≃ preppy *fam US* **2.** *fam loc* **avoir le ~ pour : il a le ~ pour dire ce qu'il ne faut pas** he has a gift for *ou* a knack of saying the wrong thing.
◇ *interj fam vieilli* **~ (alors)!** great!, smashing!

Chicago [ʃikago] *npr* Chicago.

chicane [ʃikan] *nf* **1.** [dans un procès] pettifogging *(U)*, chicanery *(U)* **2.** [querelle] squabble **3.** SPORT [de circuit] chicane ■ [de gymkhana] zigzag **4.** CARTES chicane.
◆ **en chicane** *loc adj* zigzag *(modif).*

chicaner [3] [ʃikane] ◇ *vt* : **~ qqn sur** to quibble with sb about.
◇ *vi* to quibble.

chicaneries [ʃikanri] *nfpl* quibbling *(U).*

chicaneur, euse [ʃikanœr, øz], **chicanier, ère** [ʃikanje, ɛr] ◇ *adj* quibbling.
◇ *nm, f* **1.** [au tribunal] pettifogger **2.** [ergoteur] quibbler.

chicano [ʃikano] *adj* Chicano.
◆ **Chicano** *nmf* Chicano.

chiche [ʃiʃ] *adj* **1.** [avare] mean ■ **être ~ de : il n'a pas été ~ de son temps/de ses efforts** he didn't spare his time/efforts ■ **il n'a pas été ~ de compliments** he was generous with his compliments **2.** [peu abondant - repas, dîner, récolte] scanty, meagre **3.** *fam* [capable] : **être ~ de : tu n'es pas ~ de le faire!** I'll bet you couldn't do it! ■ **elle est ~ de le faire!** she's quite capable of doing it! ■ **~!** want to bet? ■ **~ que je mange tout!** bet you I can eat it all! ■ **je vais lui dire ce que je pense! - allez, ~!** I'm going to give him a piece of my mind! - go on, I dare you!

chiche-kebab [ʃiʃkebab] (*pl* **chiches-kebabs**) *nm* kebab, shish kebab.

chichement [ʃiʃmɑ̃] *adv* **1.** [de façon mesquine] meanly, stingily **2.** [pauvrement] scantily ■ **vivre ~** to lead a meagre existence.

chichi [ʃiʃi] *nm fam* [simagrée] airs (and graces) ■ **faire des ~s** to put on airs ■ **ce sont des gens à ~s** these people give themselves airs ■ **un dîner sans ~s** an informal dinner ■ **ne fais pas tant de ~s pour une simple piqûre!** don't make such a fuss about a little injection!

chichiteux, euse [ʃiʃitø, øz] *fam* ◇ *adj* affected.
◇ *nm, f* show-off, poseur.

chicorée [ʃikɔre] *nf* **1.** [salade] endive **2.** [à café] chicory **3.** [fleur] (wild) chicory.

chicos [ʃikɔs] *adj fam* classy, smart, chic.

chicot [ʃiko] *nm* [d'une dent] stump ■ [d'un arbre] tree stump.

chié, e△ [ʃje] *adj* **1.** [réussi - soirée, livre] damn good **2.** [culotté] : **il est ~, lui!** he's got a nerve! **3.** [drôle] : **il est ~** he's a scream **4.** [difficile - tâche] hard ■ **alors là, c'est ~ comme question!** well, that's a hell of a question!

◆ **chiée**△ *nf* [grande quantité] : **une ~e de...** heaps *ou* a whole lot *ou* loads of...

chien, chienne [ʃjɛ̃, ʃjɛn] *nm, f* **1.** ZOOL dog (*f* bitch) ■ **~ d'arrêt** *ou* **couchant** pointer ■ **~ d'appartement** lapdog ■ **~ d'aveugle** guide dog ■ **~ de berger** sheepdog ■ **~ de chasse** retriever ■ **~ courant** hound ■ **~ errant** stray dog ■ **~ de garde** *pr* guard dog ; *fig* watchdog ■ **~ de meute** hound ■ **~ policier** police dog ■ **~ de race** pedigree dog ■ **~ de traîneau** husky ■ **'~ méchant'** 'beware of the dog' ■ **un regard de ~ battu** a hangdog expression ■ **(rubrique des) ~s écrasés** minor news items ■ **se regarder en ~s de faïence** to stare at one another ■ **ils sont comme ~ et chat** they fight like cat and dog ■ **comme un ~ savant** *péj* like a trained monkey ■ **arriver comme un ~ dans un jeu de quilles** to turn up at just the wrong moment ■ **ce n'est pas fait pour les ~s** *péj* it is there for a good reason ■ **merci mon ~!** *fam hum* I never heard you say thank you! ■ **je lui réserve** *ou* **garde un ~ de ma chienne** I've got something up my sleeve for him that he's not going to like one bit ■ **chienne de vie!** *fam* life's a bitch! ■ **bon ~ chasse de race** *prov* good breeding always tells ■ **il menace beaucoup, mais ~ qui aboie ne mord pas** *prov* his bark is worse than his bite ■ **les ~s aboient, la caravane passe** *prov* let the world say what it will **2.** △ [terme d'insulte] bastard△ *m*, bitch△ *f*.
◆ **chien** *nm* **1.** *fam loc* **avoir du ~ : elle a du ~** she's got sex-appeal **2.** ASTRON : **le Grand/Petit Chien** the Great/Little Dog **3.** ARM hammer, cock **4.** ZOOL : **~ de mer** dogfish.
◆ **chiens** *nmpl* (long) fringe.
◆ **à la chien** *loc adv* [coiffé] with a long fringe.
◆ **de chien** *loc adj fam* [caractère, temps] lousy, rotten ■ **avoir un mal de ~ à faire qqch** to find it terribly difficult to do sthg.
◆ **en chien de fusil** *loc adv* curled up.

chien-chien [ʃjɛ̃ʃjɛ̃] (*pl* **chiens-chiens**) *nm* doggy ■ **~ à sa mémère** *pr* Mummy's little doggie-woggie ; *fig* yes-man.

chiendent [ʃjɛ̃dɑ̃] *nm* couch grass ■ **ça pousse comme du ~** it grows at a phenomenal rate.

chienlit [ʃjɑ̃li] *nf fam* **1.** [désordre] mess, shambles ■ **c'est la ~** it's a shambles! **2.** [masque] mask **3.** [mascarade] masquerade.

chien-loup [ʃjɛ̃lu] (*pl* **chiens-loups**) *nm* Alsatian (dog), German shepherd.

chienne [ʃjɛn] *f* ▷ **chien.**

chier [9] ▲[ʃje] *vi* **1.** [déféquer] to (have *UK ou* take *US* a) shit▲ **2.** △ *loc* **ça chie (des bulles)** [ça fait du scandale] it's a bloody scandal▲ ; [entre deux personnes] they're having a real bloody go at each other▲ ■ **j'en ai chié pour le terminer à temps!** I've had a hell of a job getting this finished on time! ■ **faire ~ qqn** [l'importuner, le contrarier] to bug sb ; [l'ennuyer] to bore the pants off sb△ ■ **(ça) fait ~, ce truc!** this thing's a real pain in the arse *UK ou* ass *US*! △ ■ **qu'est-ce qu'on s'est fait ~ hier soir!** it was so damned boring last night! △ ■ **je vais pas me faire ~ à tout recopier!** I can't be arsed△ *UK ou* bothered with writing it all out again!, I'm not damned well writing it all out again!△ ■ **y a pas à ~, faut que j'aie fini ce soir!** I've damned well got to finish by tonight and that's that!△.
◆ **à chier**△ *loc adj* **1.** [très laid] : **son costard est à ~** his suit looks bloody awful△ *UK ou* godawful *US* **2.** [très mauvais] crap△ **3.** [insupportable] : **il est à ~, ce prof!** that teacher is a pain in the arse *UK ou* ass *US*! △.

chieur, euse△ [ʃjœr, øz] *nm, f* : **c'est un vrai ~/une vraie chieuse** he's/she's a real pain in the arse△ *UK ou* ass △ *US.*

chiffe [ʃif] *nf* : **c'est une vraie ~ molle** he's got no guts, he's totally spineless ■ **je suis une vraie ~ molle aujourd'hui** [fatigué] I feel like a wet rag today.

chiffon [ʃifɔ̃] *nm* **1.** [torchon] cloth ■ **~ à poussière** duster *UK*, dust cloth *US* **2.** [vieux tissu] rag ■ **parler ~s** to talk clothes *ou* fashion **3.** *péj* [texte] : **qui est l'auteur de ce ~?** who's responsible for this mess?
◆ **en chiffon** *loc adj* crumpled up (in a heap) ■ **toutes ses affaires sont en ~** his things are all crumpled up.

chiffonné, e [ʃifɔne] *adj* **1.** [froissé] crumpled **2.** [fatigué - visage] tired, worn.

chiffonner [3] [ʃifɔne] *vt* **1.** [vêtement] to rumple, to crumple ■ [papier] to crumple **2.** *fam* [préoccuper] to bother, to worry ■ **ça n'a pas eu l'air de la ~** it didn't seem to bother her.

chiffonnier, ère [ʃifɔnje, ɛr] *nm, f* rag dealer, rag-and-bone man *m*.
◆ **chiffonnier** *nm* [meuble] chiffonier, chiffonnier.

chiffrable [ʃifrabl] *adj* quantifiable.

chiffrage [ʃifraʒ] *nm* **1.** [d'un code] ciphering **2.** [évaluation] (numerical) assessment **3.** MUS figuring.

chiffre [ʃifr] *nm* **1.** MATH figure, number ■ **nombre à deux/trois ~ s** two/three digit number ■ **jusqu'à deux ~s après la virgule** up to two decimal points ■ **arrondi au ~ supérieur/inférieur** rounded up/down ■ **en ~s ronds** in round figures ⊙ **~ arabe/romain** Arabic/Roman numeral **2.** [montant] amount, sum ■ **le ~ des dépenses s'élève à 2 000 euros** total expenditure amounts to 2,000 euros **3.** [taux] figures, rate ■ **les ~s du chômage** the unemployment figures **4.** COMM : **~ d'affaires** turnover ■ **faire du ~** *fam* to run at a healthy profit **5.** INFORM digit ■ **~ binaire** bit, binary digit ■ **~ de contrôle** check digit **6.** TÉLÉCOM code, ciphering ■ [service] cipher (office) **7.** [d'une serrure] combination **8.** [initiales] initials ■ [à l'ancienne] monogram **9.** MUS figure.

chiffré, e [ʃifre] *adj* **1.** [évalué] assessed, numbered **2.** [codé] coded, ciphered **3.** MUS figured.

chiffrer [3] [ʃifre] <> *vt* **1.** [évaluer] to assess, to estimate ■ **~ des travaux** to draw up an estimate (of the cost of work) ■ **il est trop tôt pour ~ le montant des dégâts** it's too early to put a figure to the damage **2.** [numéroter] to number **3.** ADMIN, INFORM & MIL to cipher, to code, to encode **4.** [linge, vêtement - marquer de ses initiales] to mark *ou* to inscribe with initials ; [- marquer d'un monogramme] to monogram **5.** MUS to figure.
<> *vi fam* to cost a packet ■ **ça chiffre!** it mounts up!
◆ **se chiffrer** *vp (emploi passif)* **se ~ à** [se monter à] to add up *ou* to amount to ■ **se ~ en** *ou* **par** to amount to, to be estimated at.

chignole [ʃiɲɔl] *nf* **1.** [outil - à main] hand-drill ; [- électrique] electric drill **2.** *fam péj* [voiture] heap.

chignon [ʃiɲɔ̃] *nm* bun, chignon ■ **faire son ~** to coil up one's hair.

chihuahua [ʃiwawa] *nm* Chihuahua.

chiisme [ʃiism] *nm* Shiism.

chiite [ʃiit] *adj* Shiah, Shiite.
◆ **Chiite** *nmf* Shiite.

Chili [ʃili] *npr m* : **le ~** Chile ■ **au ~** in Chile.

chilien, enne [ʃiljɛ̃, ɛn] *adj* Chilean.
◆ **Chilien, enne** *nm, f* Chilean.

chimère [ʃimɛr] *nf* **1.** MYTHOL chimera **2.** [utopie] dream, fantasy ■ **je vous laisse à vos ~s** I'll leave you alone with your pipe dreams.

chimérique [ʃimerik] *adj* **1.** [illusoire] fanciful ■ **des espoirs ~s** fanciful hopes **2.** *litt* [utopiste] chimeric.

chimie [ʃimi] *nf* chemistry ⊙ **~ biologique** biochemistry ■ **~ minérale** inorganic chemistry ■ **~ organique** organic chemistry.

chimiothérapie [ʃimjɔterapi] *nf* chemotherapy.

chimiothérapique [ʃimjɔterapik] *adj* [méthode] chemotherapeutic ■ [traitement] drug-based, chemotherapeutic *spéc.*

chimique [ʃimik] *adj* **1.** [de la chimie] chemical **2.** *fam* [artificiel] chemical, artificial ■ **tous ces trucs ~s qu'on trouve dans la nourriture** all these additives you find in food.

chimiquement [ʃimikmɑ̃] *adv* chemically.

chimiquier [ʃimikje] *nm* chemical tanker.

chimiste [ʃimist] *nmf* chemist ■ **ingénieur ~** chemical engineer.

chimpanzé [ʃɛ̃pɑ̃ze] *nm* chimpanzee.

chinchilla [ʃɛ̃ʃila] *nm* **1.** [rongeur, fourrure] chinchilla **2.** [chat] chinchilla **3.** [lapin] chinchilla.

chine [ʃin] <> *nm* **1.** [porcelaine] china **2.** [papier] rice paper.
<> *nf* [brocante] secondhand goods trade.
◆ **à la chine** *loc adj* : **vente à la ~** hawking.

Chine [ʃin] *npr f* : **(la) ~** China ■ **~ communiste** Red *ou* Communist China ■ **~ populaire, République populaire de ~** People's Republic of China ■ **la mer de ~** the China Sea.

chiné, e [ʃine] *adj* [tissu] chiné, mottled ■ [laine] bicoloured wool.

chiner [3] [ʃine] <> *vt* **1.** TEXT to mottle **2.** *fam* [taquiner] to kid, to tease.
<> *vi* [faire les boutiques] to go round the second-hand shops.

chinetoque▲ [ʃintɔk] *adj* & *nmf racist term used with reference to Chinese people*, ≃ Chink△, ≃ Chinky△.

chinois, e [ʃinwa, az] *adj* **1.** [de Chine] Chinese **2.** *fam* [compliqué] twisted.
◆ **Chinois, e** *nm, f* Chinese ■ **les Chinois** the Chinese.
◆ **chinois** *nm* **1.** LING Chinese ■ **pour moi, c'est du ~** it's all Greek to me **2.** CULIN [passoire] (conical) strainer ■ **passer qqch au ~** to sieve sthg.

chinoiser [3] [ʃinwaze] *vi* to split hairs.

chinoiserie [ʃinwazri] *nf* **1.** *fam* [complication] complication ■ **~s administratives** red tape **2.** ART chinoiserie.

chiot [ʃjo] *nm* pup, puppy.

chiotte△ [ʃjɔt] *nf* [désagrément] drag, hassle ■ **quel temps de ~!** what godawful weather!
◆ **chiottes**△ *nfpl* bog△ *UK*, john△ *US* ■ **aux ~s!** [tu dis des bêtises] (what a load of) bullshit!△.

chiper [3] [ʃipe] *vt fam* to pinch, to swipe ■ **je me suis fait ~ mon stylo** someone's pinched *ou* nicked my pen.

chipie [ʃipi] *nf* minx.

chipolata [ʃipɔlata] *nf* chipolata.

chipotage [ʃipɔtaʒ] *nm fam* **1.** [en discutant] quibbling, hair-splitting **2.** [en mangeant] nibbling.

chipoter [3] [ʃipɔte] *vi fam* **1.** [discuter] to argue, to quibble ■ **~ sur les prix** to haggle over prices **2.** [sur la nourriture] to pick at one's food.

chipoteur, euse [ʃipɔtœr, øz] *fam* <> *adj* **1.** [en discutant] quibbling **2.** [en mangeant] finicky.
<> *nm, f* **1.** [ergoteur] fault-finder, quibbler **2.** [mangeur] picky eater.

chips [ʃips] *nfpl* (potato) crisps *UK ou* chips *US*.

chique [ʃik] *nf* **1.** [tabac] quid, chew (of tobacco) ■ **ça ne vaut pas une ~** *fam* it's not worth a bean **2.** [cocon de soie] *small, poor-quality silk cocoon.*

chiqué [ʃike] *nm fam péj* **~!** [dans un match] that's cheating! ■ **il n'a pas mal, c'est du** *ou* **il fait du ~** he's not in pain at all, he's putting it on *ou* just pretending.

chiquenaude [ʃiknod] *nf* **1.** [pichenette] flick **2.** [impulsion] push.

chiquer [3] [ʃike] <> *vt* to chew.
<> *vi* to chew tobacco.

chiromancie [kirɔmɑ̃si] *nf* chiromancy, palmistry.

chiromancien, enne [kirɔmɑ̃sjɛ̃, ɛn] *nm, f* chiromancer.

chiropracteur [kirɔpraktœr] = **chiropraticien**.

chiropractie [kirɔprakti] *nf* chiropractic.

chiropraticien, enne [kirɔpratisjɛ̃, ɛn] *nm, f* chiropractor.

chiropratique [kiropratik] *adj Québec* chiropractic.

chirurgical, e, aux [ʃiryrʒikal, o] *adj* **1.** MÉD surgical **2.** [précis] accurate.

chirurgie [ʃiryrʒi] *nf* surgery ▪ **~ esthétique** cosmetic surgery ▪ **~ non invasive** non invasive surgery ▪ **~ endoscopique** keyhole surgery.

chirurgien, enne [ʃiryrʒjɛ̃, ɛn] *nm, f* surgeon.

chirurgien-dentiste [ʃiryrʒjɛ̃dɑ̃tist] (*pl* **chirurgiens-dentistes**) *nm* dental surgeon.

chiure [ʃjyr] *nf* : **~ de mouche** fly speck.

ch-l = **chef-lieu**.

chleuh, e▲ [ʃlø] *adj & nm, f offensive term used with reference to German people* ▪ **les ~s** ≃ the Jerries, ≃ the Boche.

chlinguer [3] △ [ʃlɛ̃ge] *vi* to stink, to pong *UK* ▪ **ça chlingue, par ici!** it's a bit whiffy *UK* *OU* it sure stinks *US* around here!

chlore [klɔr] *nm* **1.** CHIM chlorine **2.** [Javel] bleach, bleaching agent.

chloré, e [klɔre] *adj* chlorinated.

chlorhydrate [klɔridrat] *nm* hydrochlorate.

chlorhydrique [klɔridrik] *adj* hydrochloric.

chlorofluorocarbone [klɔrɔflyɔrɔkarbɔn] *nm* CHIM chlorofluorocarbon.

chloroforme [klɔrɔfɔrm] *nm* chloroform.

chloroformer [3] [klɔrɔfɔrme] *vt* **1.** MÉD to administer chloroform to **2.** [abrutir] to stultify.

chlorophylle [klɔrɔfil] *nf* **1.** BOT chlorophyll **2.** [nature] : **les citadins avides de ~** city dwellers eager to breathe the fresh country air.

chlorure [klɔryr] *nm* chloride.

chnoque [ʃnɔk] = **schnock**.

chnouf [ʃnuf] = **schnouf**.

choc [ʃɔk] *nm* **1.** [collision - entre véhicules] crash ; [- entre personnes] collision ▪ [heurt] impact, shock ▪ **le ~ entre les deux voitures a été très violent** the two cars collided full on ▪ **résistant aux ~ s** shock-proof, shock-resistant ▪ **sous le ~** under the impact ▪ **sous le ~, l'avion se désintégra** the plane fell apart on impact ▪ **le verre n'a pas tenu le ~** the glass shattered on impact **2.** [bruit - métallique] clang ; [- sourd] thwack ; [- cristallin] clink, tinkle **3.** MIL [affrontement] clash **4.** [incompatibilité] clash, conflict ▪ **~ culturel** culture shock ▪ **le ~ des générations** the generation gap **5.** [émotion] shock ▪ **ça fait un ~!** it's a bit of a shock! ▪ **ça m'a fait un sacré ~ de les revoir** it was a great shock to me to meet them again **6.** ÉLECTR shock ▪ PHYS collision **7.** MÉD shock ▪ **~ allergique/anesthésique** allergic/anaesthesia shock ▪ **~ opératoire** post-operative trauma *OU* shock **8.** ÉCON : **~ pétrolier** oil crisis **9.** *(comme adj; avec ou sans trait d'union)* **argument/discours ~** hard-hitting argument/speech ▪ **des prix-~s** rock-bottom prices.

◆ **de choc** *loc adj* [unité, troupe, traitement] shock *(modif)* ▪ **être en état de ~** to be in a state of shock ▮ [patron] ultra-efficient.

◆ **sous le choc** *loc adj* : **être sous le ~** MÉD to be in shock ; [bouleversé] to be in a daze *OU* in shock.

chochotte [ʃɔʃɔt] *nf fam péj* **quelle ~ tu fais!** [mijaurée] don't be so stuck-up! ; [effarouchée] don't be so squeamish! ▪ **il ne supporte pas cette odeur, ~!** oh dear, his Lordship can't stand the smell!

chocolat [ʃɔkɔla] ◇ *nm* **1.** CULIN chocolate ▪ **~ blanc** white chocolate ▪ **~ à croquer** *OU* **noir** dark *OU* plain chocolate ▪ **~ au lait** milk chocolate ▪ **~ de ménage** cooking chocolate **2.** [friandise] chocolate ▪ **~ fourré à la fraise** chocolate filled with strawberry cream ▪ **~ glacé** choc ice **3.** [boisson] hot chocolate, cocoa.

◇ *adj inv* **1.** [couleur] chocolate brown **2.** *fam loc* **on est ~!** [dupés] we've been had! ; [coincés] we've blown it!

◆ **au chocolat** *loc adj* chocolate *(modif)*.

chocolaté, e [ʃɔkɔlate] *adj* chocolate *(modif)*, chocolate-flavoured.

chocolaterie [ʃɔkɔlatri] *nf* chocolate factory.

chocolatier, ère [ʃɔkɔlatje, ɛr] *nm, f* **1.** [fabricant] chocolate-maker **2.** [marchand] confectioner.

◆ **chocolatière** *nf* hot chocolate pot.

chocottes△ [ʃɔkɔt] *nfpl* : **avoir les ~** to be scared stiff ▪ **ça m'a donné** *OU* **filé les ~** it scared me out of my wits.

chœur [kœr] *nm* **1.** MUS [chorale] choir, chorus ▪ [morceau] chorus **2.** *fig* [ensemble] body, group **3.** ANTIQ chorus **4.** ARCHIT choir.

◆ **en chœur** *loc adv* **1.** MUS : **chanter en ~** to sing in chorus **2.** [ensemble] (all) together ▪ **parler en ~** to speak in unison.

choie *etc v* ⊳ **choyer**.

choir [72] [ʃwar] *vi sout* to fall ▪ **se laisser ~ sur une chaise/dans un fauteuil** to flop onto a chair/down in an armchair.

choisi, e [ʃwazi] *adj* **1.** [raffiné] : **une assemblée ~e** a select audience ▪ **en termes ~s** in a few choice phrases **2.** [sélectionné] selected, picked ▪ **bien ~** well-chosen, appropriate ▪ **mal ~** inappropriate.

choisir [32] [ʃwazir] *vt* **1.** [sélectionner] to choose, to pick ▪ **choisis ce que tu veux** take your choice *OU* pick ▪ **j'ai choisi les pommes les plus mûres** I selected the ripest apples ▪ **tu as choisi ton moment!** *iron* you picked a good time! ▪ **il a choisi la liberté** he chose freedom ▪ *(en usage absolu)* **bien ~** to choose carefully, to be careful in one's choice **2.** [décider] to decide, to choose, to elect *sout* ▪ **ils ont choisi de rester** they decided *OU* chose to stay ▪ *(en usage absolu)* **je n'ai pas choisi, c'est arrivé comme ça** it wasn't my decision, it just happened.

choix [ʃwa] *nm* **1.** [liberté de choisir] choice ▪ **donner le ~ à qqn** to give sb a *OU* the choice ▪ **avoir un** *OU* **le ~** to have a choice ▪ **ils ne nous ont pas laissé le ~** they left us no alternative *OU* other option ▪ **tu as le ~ entre rester et partir** you may choose either to stay or go ▪ **avoir le ~ des armes** *pr & fig* to have the choice of weapons **2.** [sélection] choice ▪ **faire un ~** to make a choice ▪ **arrêter son ~ sur** to decide on, to choose ▪ **mon ~ est fait** I've made up my mind ▪ **précisez votre ~ par téléphone** phone in your selection ▪ **la carrière de votre ~** your chosen career **3.** [gamme] : **un ~ de** a choice *OU* range *OU* selection of **4.** COMM : **premier ~** top quality ▪ **de premier ~** top-quality ▪ **viande** *OU* **morceaux de premier ~** prime cuts ▪ **de second ~** [fruits, légumes] standard, grade 2 ; [viande] standard ▪ **articles de second ~** seconds.

◆ **au choix** ◇ *loc adj* [question] optional.

◇ *loc adv* : **être promu au ~** to be promoted by selection ▪ **prenez deux cartes au ~** choose *OU* select (any) two cards ▪ **vous avez fromage ou dessert au ~** you have a choice of either cheeses or a dessert ▪ **répondre au ~ à l'une des trois questions** answer any one of the three questions.

◆ **de choix** *loc adj* **1.** [de qualité] choice *(avant n)*, selected **2.** [spécial] special ▪ **il gardera toujours une place de ~ dans nos cœurs** he will always have a special place in our hearts.

◆ **par choix** *loc adv* out of choice.

choléra [kɔlera] *nm* MÉD & VÉTÉR cholera.

cholestérol [kɔlɛsterɔl] *nm* cholesterol ▪ **avoir du ~** to have a high cholesterol level.

chômage [ʃomaʒ] *nm* **1.** [inactivité] unemployment ▪ **la montée du ~** the rise in unemployment ➊ **~ partiel** short-time working ▪ **~ technique : être mis au ~ technique** to be laid off **2.** *fam* [allocation] unemployment benefit, dole (money) *UK* ▪ **toucher le ~** to be on the dole.

◆ **au chômage** ◇ *loc adj* [sans emploi] unemployed, out of work ▪ **être au ~** to be unemployed *OU* out of work.

◇ *loc adv* : **s'inscrire au ~** to sign on *UK*, to register as unemployed.

chômé, e [ʃome] *adj* : **jour ~** public holiday.

chômedu [ʃomdy] *nm fam* unemployment ▪ **être au ~** to be out of work.

chômer [3] [ʃome] *vi* **1.** [être sans emploi] to be unemployed *OU* out of work **2.** [suspendre le travail - employé] to knock off work ; [- entreprise, machine] to stand idle, to be at a standstill **3.** [avoir du loisir] to be idle, to have time on one's hands ▪ **elle n'a pas le temps de ~** she hasn't got time to sit and twiddle her thumbs ▪ **il ne chôme pas** he's never short of something to do **4.** [être improductif] : **laisser ~ son argent** to let one's money lie idle.

chômeur, euse [ʃomœr, øz] *nm, f* [sans emploi] unemployed person ▪ **il est ~** he's unemployed *ou* out of work ▪ **le nombre des ~s est très élevé** the unemployment *ou* jobless figures are high ➲ **les ~s de longue durée** the long-term unemployed.

chope [ʃɔp] *nf* mug.

choper [3] [ʃɔpe] *fam vt* **1.** [contracter - maladie] to catch **2.** [intercepter] to catch, to get, to grab ▪ **tâche de la ~ à sa descente du train** try to grab her when she gets off the train ▪ **se faire ~** [gén] to get caught ; [par la police] to be nicked *UK ou* nabbed.

chopine [ʃɔpin] *nf* **1.** *fam* [bouteille] bottle **2.** *fam* [verre] glass ▪ **aller boire une ~** to go and have a jar *UK ou* a drink **3.** *Québec* [mesure] half-pint.

chopper [ʃɔpœr] *nm* **1.** ARCHÉOL chopper tool **2.** [moto] chopper **3.** ÉLECTRON chopper, vibrator.

choquant, e [ʃɔkɑ̃, ɑ̃t] *adj* **1.** [déplaisant - attitude] outrageous, shocking **2.** [déplacé - tenue] offensive, shocking ▪ **tu trouves sa tenue ~e?** do you find the way she's dressed offensive?

choqué, e [ʃɔke] *adj* shocked ▪ **il les regardait d'un air profondément ~** he looked at them, visibly shocked.

choquer [3] [ʃɔke] *vt* **1.** [heurter] to hit, to knock, to bump ▪ **~ des verres** to clink glasses **2.** [scandaliser] to shock, to offend ▪ **ça te choque qu'elle pose nue?** do you find it shocking *ou* offensive that she should pose in the nude? ▪ **être choqué (de qqch)** to be shocked (at sthg) ▪ *(en usage absolu)* **leur album a beaucoup choqué** their album caused great offence **3.** [aller contre] to go against, to be contrary to ▪ **ce raisonnement choque le bon sens** this line of argument is an insult to common sense **4.** [traumatiser] : **ils ont été profondément choqués par sa mort** they were devastated by his death ▪ **être choqué** MÉD to be in shock.
◆ **se choquer** *vpi* [être scandalisé] to be shocked.

choral, e, als *ou* **aux** [kɔral, o] *adj* choral.
◆ **choral, als** *nm* MUS & RELIG choral, chorale.
◆ **chorale** *nf* choir, choral society.

chorégraphe [kɔregraf] *nmf* choreographer.

chorégraphie [kɔregrafi] *nf* choreography ▪ **faire la ~ de** to choreograph.

choriste [kɔrist] *nmf* **1.** RELIG chorister **2.** THÉÂTRE chorus singer ▪ **les ~s** [au cabaret] the chorus line.

chorizo [(t)ʃɔrizo] *nm* chorizo.

chorus [kɔrys] *nm* : **faire ~** to (all) agree, to speak with one voice.

chose [ʃoz] ◇ *nf*

A. SENS CONCRET
B. PERSONNE
C. SENS ABSTRAIT

A. SENS CONCRET

1. [bien matériel, nourriture, vêtement] thing ▪ **il n'avait acheté que des bonnes ~s** he had only bought good things to eat ▪ **j'ai encore des ~s à lui chez moi** I still have a few of his things *ou* some of his belongings at home
2. [objet ou produit indéterminé] thing

B. PERSONNE

creature, thing ▪ **elle me prend pour sa ~** she thinks she can do what she wants with me

C. SENS ABSTRAIT

1. [acte, fait] : **une ~** a thing, something ▪ **j'ai encore beaucoup de ~s à faire** I've still got lots (of things) to do ▪ **ah, encore une ~, je ne viendrai pas demain** oh, one more thing, I won't be coming tomorrow ▪ **une ~ est sûre, il perdra** one thing's (for) sure, he'll lose ▪ **en avril, ce sera ~ faite** *ou* **la ~ sera faite** it will be done by April ▪ **ce n'est pas la même ~** [cela change tout] it's a different matter ▪ **je suis retourné à mon village, mais ce n'est plus la même ~** I went back to my village, but it's just not the same any more ▪ **la fidélité est une ~, l'amour en est une autre** faithfulness is one thing, love is quite another ▪ **ce n'est pas la ~ à dire/faire!** what a thing to say/do! ▪ **ce ne sont pas des ~s à faire en société** that's just not done in polite circles ▪ **~ extraordinaire/curieuse, il était à l'heure!** amazingly/strangely enough, he was on time! ▪ **ce sont des ~s qui arrivent** it's just one of those things ▪ **faire bien les ~s** [savoir recevoir] to do things in style ▪ **il ne fait pas les ~s à demi** *ou* **moitié** he doesn't do things by halves ▪ **~ promise ~ due** a promise is a promise
2. [parole] thing ▪ **il dit une ~ et il en fait une autre** he says one thing and does something else ▪ **je vais te dire une (bonne) ~, ça ne marchera jamais** let me tell you something, it'll never work ▪ **qu'a-t-il dit? – peu de ~s en vérité** what did he say? – very little *ou* nothing much, actually ▪ **bavarder** *ou* **parler de ~s et d'autres** to chat about this and that ➲ **dites-lui bien des ~s** give him my best regards
3. [écrit] thing ▪ **comment peut-on écrire des ~s pareilles!** how can anyone write such things!
4. [ce dont il est question] : **la ~ : comment a-t-il pris la ~?** how did he take it? ▪ **la ~ est entendue** we're agreed on this ▪ **laisse-moi t'expliquer la ~** let me explain what it's all about ➲ **être porté sur la ~** *euphém* to have a one-track mind
5. *sout* [affaires] : **la ~ publique** POLIT the state.
◇ *nm fam* **1.** [pour désigner un objet] thing, thingie **2.** [pour désigner une personne] : **Chose** [homme] What's-his-name, Thingie ; [femme] What's-her-name, Thingie.
◇ *adj fam* funny, peculiar ▪ **ton fils a l'air tout ~ aujourd'hui** your son looks a bit peculiar today.
◆ **choses** *nfpl* [situation] things ▪ **les ~s de la vie** the things that go to make up life ▪ **les ~s étant ce qu'elles sont** as things stand, things being as they are ▪ **au point où en sont les ~s** as things now stand ▪ **prendre les ~s comme elles viennent** to take life as it comes.
◆ **de deux choses l'une** *loc adv* : **de deux ~s l'une, ou tu m'obéis ou tu vas te coucher!** either you do as I tell you or you go to bed, it's up to you!

chosifier [9] [ʃozifje] *vt* to reify, to consider as a thing.

chou[1], x [ʃu] *nm* **1.** BOT : **~ (cabus)** white cabbage ▪ **~ de Bruxelles** Brussels sprout ▪ **~ frisé** (curly) kale ▪ **~ rouge** red cabbage **2.** CULIN : **(petit) ~** chou ▪ **~ à la crème** cream puff **3.** [ornement] round knot, rosette **4.** *fam loc* **être dans les ~x** to be in a mess ▪ **avec cette pluie, son barbecue est dans les ~x** it's curtains for his barbecue in this rain ▪ **faire ~ blanc** to draw a blank, to be out of luck ▪ **faire ses ~x gras de qqch** to put sthg to good use ▪ **rentrer dans le ~ à qqn** [en voiture] to slam into sb ; [agresser] to go for sb.

chou[2], choute [ʃu, ʃut] *nm, f fam* **1.** *(en appellatif)* honey, sugar, sweetheart ▪ **mon pauvre ~!** you poor little thing! **2.** [personne aimable] darling, love **3.** *(comme adj)* [gentil] nice, kind ▪ **tu es ~** [en demandant un service] there's a dear ; [pour remercier] you're so kind, you're an absolute darling ▮ [mignon] cute.

chouan [ʃwɑ̃] *nm* Chouan *(member of a group of counter-revolutionary royalist insurgents, one of whose leaders was Jean Chouan, in the Vendée (western France) from 1793 to 1800).*

chouannerie [ʃwanri] *nf* : **la ~** the Chouan uprising.

choucas [ʃuka] *nm* jackdaw.

chouchou, oute [ʃuʃu, ut] *nm, f fam péj* favourite ▪ **c'est le ~ du prof** she's the teacher's pet ▪ **le ~ de sa grand-mère** his grandmother's blue-eyed boy.

chouchouter [3] [ʃuʃute] *vt fam* [élève] to give preferential treatment to ▪ [enfant, ami] to mollycoddle, to pamper ▪ **se faire ~** to let o.s. be spoiled.

choucroute [ʃukrut] *nf* **1.** CULIN [chou] pickled cabbage ▪ [plat] sauerkraut ▪ **~ garnie** sauerkraut with meat **2.** *fam* [coiffure] beehive.

chouette[1] [ʃwɛt] *nf* **1.** ZOOL owl **2.** *fam péj* [femme] : **vieille ~** old bag.

chouette[2] [ʃwɛt] *fam* ◇ *adj* **1.** [agréable - soirée] fantastic, terrific ■ **elle est ~, ta sœur** your sister's really nice ■ **ben il est ~ avec ce chapeau!** *iron* doesn't he look great with that hat on? **2.** [gentil] kind ■ [coopératif] helpful ■ **il est très ~ avec nous** he's very good to us ■ **sois ~, prête-moi ta voiture** oh go on, lend me your car.
◇ *interj* great.

chou-fleur [ʃuflœr] (*pl* **choux-fleurs**) *nm* cauliflower ■ **oreille en ~** cauliflower ear.

chouia [ʃuja] *nm* **fam : un ~** a little *ou* wee *ou* tiny bit.

chouquette [ʃukɛt] *nf small chou bun coated with sugar.*

chou-rave [ʃurav] (*pl* **choux-raves**) *nm* kohlrabi.

chouraver [3] △ [ʃurave] *vt* to swipe, to pinch ■ **~ qqch à qqn** to pinch sthg from sb.

chow-chow [ʃoʃo] (*pl* **chows-chows**) *nm* chow (dog).

choyer [13] [ʃwaje] *vt* to pamper, to make a fuss of ■ **se faire ~** to be pampered.

CHR (*abr de* **centre hospitalier régional**) *nm regional hospital.*

chrême [krɛm] *nm* chrism, consecrated oil.

chrétien, enne [kretjɛ̃, ɛn] *adj* & *nm, f* Christian.

chrétiennement [kretjɛnmɑ̃] *adv* : **vivre ~** to live as a good Christian ■ **être enterré ~** to have a Christian burial.

chrétienté [kretjɛ̃te] *nf* Christendom.

Christ [krist] *npr m* : **le ~** Christ.
◆ **christ** *nm* [crucifix] (Christ on the) cross, crucifix.

christianisation [kristjanizasjɔ̃] *nf* Christianization, conversion to Christianity ■ **le pays avant la ~** the country before the spread of Christianity.

christianiser [3] [kristjanize] *vt* to evangelize, to convert to Christianity.

christianisme [kristjanism] *nm* Christianity.

chromatique [krɔmatik] *adj* **1.** MUS & OPT chromatic **2.** BIOL chromosomal.

chrome [krom] *nm* CHIM chromium.
◆ **chromes** *nmpl* [d'un véhicule] chrome *(U)*, chromium-plated parts ■ **faire les ~s d'une voiture/bicyclette** to polish up the chrome on a car/bicycle.

chromo [kromo] *nm péj* poor-quality colour print.

chromosome [kromozom] *nm* chromosome ■ **~ X/Y** X/Y chromosome ■ **jeu de ~s** set of chromosomes.

chromosomique [kromozomik] *adj* chromosomal, chromosome *(modif)*.

chronicité [krɔnisite] *nf* chronicity.

chronique [krɔnik] ◇ *adj* **1.** MÉD chronic **2.** [constant] chronic.
◇ *nf* **1.** PRESSE [rubrique] column ■ **faire la ~ de** to report on ➲ **~ littéraire** arts page ■ **~ mondaine** gossip column **2.** LITTÉR chronicle **3.** BIBLE : **les Chroniques** Chronicles.

chroniquement [krɔnikmɑ̃] *adv* **1.** MÉD chronically **2.** [constamment] chronically, perpetually.

chroniqueur, euse [krɔnikœr, øz] *nm, f* **1.** [journaliste] commentator, columnist ■ **~ mondain** gossip columnist **2.** [historien] chronicler.

chrono [krono] *fam* ◇ *nm* stopwatch.
◇ *adv* by the clock ■ **250 ~** recorded speed 250 kph.

chronobiologie [kronobjolɔʒi] *nf* chronobiology.

chronologie [krɔnɔlɔʒi] *nf* chronology, time sequence ■ **~ des événements** calendar of events.

chronologique [krɔnɔlɔʒik] *adj* chronological ■ **série ~** time series.

chronologiquement [krɔnɔlɔʒikmɑ̃] *adv* chronologically.

chronométrage [krɔnɔmetraʒ] *nm* timing, time-keeping.

chronomètre [krɔnɔmɛtr] *nm* stopwatch.

chronométrer [18] [krɔnɔmetre] *vt* to time *(with a stopwatch)*.

chronométreur, euse [krɔnɔmetrœr, øz] *nm, f* timekeeper.

chronométrique [krɔnɔmetrik] *adj* chronometric.

Chronopost® [krɔnɔpɔst] *nm express mail service.*

chrysalide [krizalid] *nf* chrysalis ■ **sortir de sa ~** *fig* to come out of one's shell.

chrysanthème [krizɑ̃tɛm] *nm* chrysanthemum.

CHS (*abr de* **centre hospitalier spécialisé**) *nm psychiatric hospital.*

ch'timi [ʃtimi] ◇ *adj* from the north of France.
◇ *nmf* northerner *(in France)*.

CHU *nm* = **centre hospitalo-universitaire**.

chuchotement [ʃyʃɔtmɑ̃] *nm* whisper ■ **des ~s** whispering *(U)*.

chuchoter [3] [ʃyʃɔte] ◇ *vi* to whisper.
◇ *vt* [mot d'amour, secret] to whisper ■ **~ qqch à qqn** to whisper sthg to sb ■ **il lui a chuchoté quelques mots à l'oreille** he whispered a few words in her ear.

chuchoteur, euse [ʃyʃɔtœr, øz] ◇ *adj* whispering.
◇ *nm, f* whisperer.

chuchotis [ʃyʃɔti] = **chuchotement**.

chuintant, e [ʃɥɛ̃tɑ̃, ɑ̃t] *adj* hushing.
◆ **chuintante** *nf* PHON palato-alveolar fricative.

chuintement [ʃɥɛ̃tmɑ̃] *nm* **1.** PHON *use of palato-alveolar fricatives instead of sibilants (characteristic of certain French regional accents)* **2.** [sifflement d'une bouilloire] hiss, hissing.

chuinter [3] [ʃɥɛ̃te] *vi* **1.** ZOOL to hoot **2.** [siffler] to hiss **3.** PHON to pronounce *ou* articulate sibilants as fricatives.

chut [ʃyt] *interj* hush, sh, shhh.

chute [ʃyt] *nf* **1.** [perte d'équilibre] fall ■ **faire une ~** to fall, to take a tumble ■ **faire une ~ de cheval** to come off a horse ■ **il a fait une ~ de neuf mètres** he fell nine metres ■ **il m'a entraîné dans sa ~** he dragged *ou* pulled me down with him ■ **'attention, ~ de pierres'** 'danger! falling rocks' ➲ **~ libre** free fall ■ **faire du saut en ~ libre** to skydive ■ **la livre est en ~ libre** *fig* the pound's plummetting
2. [perte] fall ■ **la ~ des cheveux** hair loss ■ **au moment de la ~ des feuilles** when the leaves fall
3. [baisse - des prix] drop, fall ■ **~ des ventes** COMM fall-off in sales ■ **~ de tension** MÉD drop in blood pressure ; ÉLECTR & PHYS voltage drop ■ **~ de pression** pressure drop
4. [effondrement - d'un gouvernement, d'une institution] collapse, fall ■ **entraîner qqn dans sa ~** to drag sb down with one
5. MIL fall
6. BIBLE : **la Chute** the Fall
7. MÉTÉOR : **~s de neige** snowfall ■ **~s de pluie** rainfall
8. [fin - d'une histoire] punch line ➲ **la ~ du jour** *litt* nightfall, the day's end
9. ANAT : **~ des reins** small of the back
10. [déchet - de tissu] scrap ; [- de bois, de métal] offcut, trimming ■ **~s de pellicule** film trims
11. CONSTR [d'un toit] pitch, slope.
◆ **chute d'eau** *nf* waterfall.

CHUTES

les chutes du Niagara (the) Niagara Falls ;
les chutes Victoria (the) Victoria Falls ;
les chutes d'Iguaçu (the) Iguaçu Falls.

chuter [3] [ʃyte] *vi* **1.** *fam* [tomber] to fall **2.** [ne pas réussir] to fail, to come to grief ■ **le candidat a chuté sur la dernière question** the candidate failed on the final question **3.** [baisser] to fall, to tumble ■ **faire ~ les ventes** to bring sales (figures) tumbling down **4.** JEUX to go down.

Chypre [ʃipr] *npr* Cyprus ■ **à ~** in Cyprus, *voir aussi* **île**.

chypriote [ʃiprijɔt] = **cypriote**.

ci [si] *pron dém inv* : **~ et ça** this and that.

-ci [si] *adv* **1.** [dans l'espace] : **celui~ ou celui-là?** this one or that one? **2.** [dans le temps - présent] : **à cette heure~ il n'y a plus personne** there's nobody there at this time of day ■ [dans le temps - futur] : **ils viennent dîner ce mercredi~** they're coming for dinner next Wednesday ■ [dans le temps - passé] : **je ne l'ai pas beaucoup vu ces temps~** I haven't seen much of him lately **3.** [pour insister] : **je ne t'ai pas demandé ce livre~** THAT's not the book I asked for ■ **cette fois~ j'ai compris!** NOW I've got it! ■ **c'est à cette heure~ que tu rentres?** what time do you call this?

Ci (*abr écrite de* **curie**) Ci.

CIA (*abr de* **Central Intelligence Agency**) *npr f* CIA.

ciao [tʃao] *interj fam* ciao.

ci-après [siaprɛ] *adv* hereafter, hereinafter, following ■ **les dispositions ~** the provisions set out below ■ **~ dénommé l'acheteur** hereinafter referred to as the Buyer.

cibiste [sibist] *nmf* CB user.

ciblage [siblaʒ] *nm* targeting.

cible [sibl] *nf* **1.** ARM & PHYS target ■ **~ fixe/mobile** stationary/moving target **2.** *fig* [victime] target ■ **prendre qqn pour ~** to make sb the target of one's attacks ■ **c'est toujours lui qu'on prend pour ~** he's always the scapegoat **3.** COMM target group ➲ **population ~** target population.

ciblé, e [sible] *adj* targeted.

cibler [3] [sible] *vt* [produit] to define a target group for ■ [public] to target.

ciboire [sibwar] *nm* RELIG ciborium.

ciboule [sibul] *nf* spring onion *UK*, scallion *US*.

ciboulette [sibulɛt] *nf* chives *(pl)*.

ciboulot [sibulo] *nm fam* head ■ **se creuser le ~** to rack one's brain ■ **elle en a dans le ~!** she's got a good head on her shoulders!

cicatrice [sikatris] *nf* **1.** MÉD scar **2.** *fig* [marque] mark, scar ■ **laisser des ~s** to leave scars **3.** BOT scar (of attachment) ■ **~ du haricot** hilum.

cicatrisant, e [sikatrizɑ̃, ɑ̃t] *adj* healing.
◆ **cicatrisant** *nm* healing agent, cicatrizant *spéc*.

cicatrisation [sikatrizasjɔ̃] *nf* **1.** MÉD scarring, cicatrization *spéc* ■ **la ~ se fait mal** the wound is not healing *ou* closing up properly **2.** [apaisement] healing.

cicatriser [3] [sikatrize] *vt* **1.** MÉD to heal, to cicatrize *spéc* ■ **cette pommade fera ~ la plaie plus vite** this cream will help the wound heal up more quickly **2.** [adoucir] to heal.
◆ **se cicatriser** *vpi* [coupure] to heal *ou* to close up ■ [tissus] to form a scar ■ *fig* to heal.

Cicéron [siserɔ̃] *npr* Cicero.

cicérone [siserɔn] *nm* guide, mentor.

ci-contre [sikɔ̃tr] *adv* opposite ■ **illustré ~** as shown (in the picture) opposite.

CICR (*abr de* **Comité international de la Croix-Rouge**) *npr m* IRCC.

Cid [sid] *npr m* : **le ~** El Cid ■ **'le ~'** *Corneille* 'Le Cid'.

ci-dessous [sidəsu] *adv* below.

ci-dessus [sidəsy] *adv* above ■ **l'adresse ~** the above address.

ci-devant [sidəvɑ̃] *nmf* HIST former aristocrat.

CIDEX, Cidex [sidɛks] (*abr de* **courrier individuel à distribution exceptionnelle**) *nm system grouping letter boxes in country areas.*

CIDJ (*abr de* **centre d'information et de documentation de la jeunesse**) *nm careers advisory service.*

cidre [sidr] *nm* cider ■ **~ bouché** bottled cider *(with a seal)* ■ **~ brut/doux** dry/sweet cider.

cidrerie [sidrəri] *nf* cider-house.

CIDUNaTI [sidynati] (*abr de* **Comité interprofessionnel d'information et de défense de l'union nationale des travailleurs indépendants**) *npr m union of self-employed craftsmen.*

Cie (*abr écrite de* **compagnie**) Co ■ **Johnson et ~** Johnson & Co.

ciel [sjɛl] (*pl* **cieux** [sjœ]) ◇ *nm* **1.** [espace] sky ■ **entre ~ et terre** in the air, in midair ■ **une explosion en plein ~** a midair explosion ➲ **lever les bras au ~** to throw up one's hands *(in exasperation, despair etc)* ■ **lever les yeux au ~** [d'exaspération] to roll one's eyes ■ **tomber du ~** [arriver opportunément] to be heaven-sent *ou* a godsend ; [être stupéfait] to be stunned
2. (*pl* ciels [sjɛl]) MÉTÉOR : **~ clair/nuageux** clear/cloudy sky
3. ASTRON sky
4. RELIG Heaven
5. *litt* [fatalité] fate ■ [providence] : **c'est le ~ qui t'envoie** you're a godsend ■ **le ~ soit loué** thank heavens ■ **que le ~ vous entende!** may heaven help you!
6. (*pl* ciels [sjɛl]) [plafond] : **~ de lit** canopy.
◇ *interj vieilli* **(juste) ~!** heavens above!, (good) heavens!
◆ **ciels** *nmpl litt* [temps] : **les ~s changeants de Bretagne** the changing skies of Brittany.
◆ **cieux** *nmpl litt* [région] climes, climate ■ **partir vers d'autres cieux** to be off to distant parts.
◆ **à ciel ouvert** *loc adj* **1.** MIN open-cast *UK*, open-cut *US* **2.** [piscine, stade] open-air.

cierge [sjɛrʒ] *nm* **1.** [bougie] altar candle ■ **~ magique** sparkler **2.** BOT cereus.

cieux [sjø] *pl* ▷ **ciel**.

cigale [sigal] *nf* cicada.

cigare [sigar] *nm* **1.** [à fumer] cigar **2.** *fam* [tête] head.

cigarette [sigarɛt] *nf* **1.** [à fumer] cigarette ■ **fumer une ~** to smoke a cigarette, to have a smoke ➲ **~ filtre** filter-tipped cigarette **2.** CULIN : **~ (russe)** *shortcrust biscuit shaped like a brandy snap.*

cigarillo [sigarijo] *nm* cigarillo.

ci-gît [siʒi] *adv* here lies.

cigogne [sigɔɲ] *nf* stork.

ciguë [sigy] *nf* : **(petite) ~** fool's-parsley ■ **grande ~** giant hemlock.

ci-inclus, e [siɛ̃kly, yz] (*mpl inv, fpl* **ci-incluses**) *adj (après le n)* enclosed.
◆ **ci-inclus** *adv* : **~ vos quittances** please find bill enclosed ■ **~ une copie du testament et les instructions du notaire** enclosures: one copy of the will and the solicitor's instructions.

CIJ (*abr de* **Cour internationale de justice**) *nf* ICJ.

ci-joint, e [siʒwɛ̃, ɛ̃t] (*mpl* **ci-joints**, *fpl* **ci-jointes**) *adj (après le n)* attached, enclosed.
◆ **ci-joint** *adv* : **~ photocopie** photocopy enclosed ■ **(veuillez trouver) ~ la facture correspondante** please find enclosed *ou* attached the invoice relating to your order.

cil [sil] *nm* **1.** ANAT eyelash, lash, cilium *spéc* **2.** BIOL : **~s vibratiles** cilia.

cilice [silis] *nm* hair shirt, cilice *spéc*.

cillement [sijmɑ̃] *nm* blinking, nictitation *spéc*.

ciller [3] [sije] *vi* **1.** [battre des cils] to blink **2.** [réagir] : **il n'a pas cillé** he didn't bat an eyelid *ou* turn a hair ■ **ils contemplaient le spectacle sans ~** they contemplated the sight with no visible sign of emotion.

cimaise [simɛz] *nf* **1.** ART picture rail ■ **pendre un tableau aux plus hautes ~s** to sky a painting **2.** ARCHIT cymatium.

cime [sim] *nf* **1.** GÉOGR peak, summit, top **2.** [haut d'un arbre] crown, top ■ **les singes vivent dans les ~s** monkeys live in the canopy of the forest.

ciment [simɑ̃] *nm* **1.** CONSTR cement ■ **~ à prise lente/rapide** slow-setting/quick-setting cement **2.** *sout* [lien] bond.

cimenter [3] [simɑ̃te] *vt* **1.** CONSTR to cement **2.** [renforcer] to consolidate.

cimenterie [simɑ̃tri] *nf* cement factory *ou* works.

cimeterre [simtɛr] *nm* scimitar.

cimetière [simtjɛr] *nm* cemetery, graveyard ■ [autour d'une église] churchyard ■ **~ de voitures** scrapyard *(for cars)*.

ciné [sine] *nm fam* **1.** [spectacle] : **le ~** the pictures ■ **se faire un ~** to go and see a film *UK ou* a movie *US* **2.** [édifice] cinema *UK*, movie theater *US*.

cinéaste [sineast] *nmf* film-director *UK*, movie director *US* ■ **~ amateur** amateur film-maker *UK ou* movie-maker *US*.

ciné-club [sineklœb] (*pl* **ciné-clubs**) *nm* film society *UK*, movie club *US*.

cinéma [sinema] *nm* **1.** [édifice] cinema *UK*, movie theater *US* ■ **~ d'art et d'essai** art house ■ **~ en plein air** [dans les pays chauds] open-air cinema ; [aux U.S.A.] drive-in (movie-theater) ■ **un ~ de quartier** a local cinema
2. [spectacle, genre] : **le ~** the cinema *UK*, the movies *US* ■ **des effets encore jamais vus au ~** effects never before seen on screen ▶ **le ~ d'animation** cartoons, animation ■ **le ~ d'art et d'essai** art films *UK ou* movies *US* ■ **le ~ muet** silent movies ■ **le ~ parlant** talking pictures, talkies
3. [métier] : **le ~** film-making *UK*, movie-making *US* ■ **faire du ~** [technicien] to work in films *UK ou* the movies *US* ; [acteur] to act in films *UK*, to be a screen actor ■ **étudiant en ~** student of film *UK ou* movies *US* ■ **école de ~** film *ou* film-making school *UK*, movie-making school *US*
4. [industrie] : **le ~** the film *UK ou* movie *US* industry
5. *fam loc* **c'est du ~** it's (all) playacting ■ **faire du** *ou* **tout un ~ (pour)** to kick up a huge fuss (about) ■ **arrête (de faire) ton ~!** [de mentir] stop putting us on! ; [de bluffer] stop shooting your mouth off! ■ **se faire du ~** to fantasize.
◆ **de cinéma** *loc adj* [festival, revue, vedette] film *UK (modif)*, movie *US (modif)* ■ [école] film-making *UK*, movie-making *US*.

Cinémascope® [sinemaskɔp] *nm* Cinemascope®.

cinémathèque [sinematɛk] *nf* film *UK ou* movie *US* library ■ **la Cinémathèque française** *the French film institute*.

LA CINÉMATHÈQUE FRANÇAISE

Founded in Paris in 1936, the *Cinémathèque* specializes in the conservation and restoration of films; it also screens films for public viewing.

cinématographe [sinematɔgraf] *nm* cinematograph.

cinématographie [sinematɔgrafi] *nf* cinematography.

cinématographique [sinematɔgrafik] *adj* cinematographic, film *UK (modif)*, movie *US (modif)* ■ **les techniques ~s** cinematic techniques ■ **une grande carrière ~** a great career in the cinema ■ **droits d'adaptation ~** film rights ■ **droits de reproduction ~** film printing rights.

cinématographiquement [sinematɔgrafikmɑ̃] *adv* cinematographically ■ **~ parlant** from a cinematic point of view.

ciné-parc [sinepark] (*pl* **ciné-parcs**) *nm Québec* drive-in cinema.

cinéphile [sinefil] ◇ *nmf* film *UK ou* movie *US* buff.
◇ *adj* : **être (très) ~** to be a film *UK ou* movie *US* buff.

cinéraire [sinerɛr] ◇ *adj* cinerary ■ **urne ~** funeral urn.
◇ *nf* cineraria.

cinétique [sinetik] ◇ *adj* kinetic.
◇ *nf* kinetics *(U)*.

cinghalais, e [sɛ̃galɛ, ɛz] *adj* Singhalese, Sinhalese.

cinglant, e [sɛ̃glɑ̃, ɑ̃t] *adj* **1.** [violent] bitter, biting ■ **une gifle ~e** a stinging slap **2.** [blessant] biting, cutting, stinging ■ **d'un ton ~** scathingly.

cinglé, e [sɛ̃gle] *fam* ◇ *adj* crazy, screwy, nuts.
◇ *nm, f* loony *UK*, screwball *US* ■ **les ~s du volant/jazz/cinéma** car/jazz/film fanatics.

cingler [3] [sɛ̃gle] ◇ *vi* NAUT : **~ vers** to sail (at full sail) towards, to make for.
◇ *vt* **1.** [fouetter] to lash **2.** [blesser] to sting.

cinoche [sinɔʃ] *nm fam* cinema *UK*, movies *US (pl)*.

cinq [sɛ̃k] ◇ *dét* **1.** five ■ **~ cents/mille étoiles** five hundred/thousand stars ■ **~ pour cent** five per cent ■ **~ dixièmes** five tenths ■ **~ fois mieux** five times better ■ **elle a ~ ans** [fillette] she's five (years old *ou* of age) ; [voiture] it's five years old ■ **une fille de ~ ans** a five-year old (girl) ▶ **les ~ lettres** *euphém* ≃ a four-letter word ■ **dire les ~ lettres à qqn** to tell sb where to go **2.** [dans des séries] five ■ **à la page ~** on page five ■ **au chapitre ~** in chapter five, in the fifth chapter ■ **il arrive le ~ novembre** he's arriving on November (the) fifth *ou* the fifth of November ■ **quel jour sommes-nous? – le ~ novembre** what's the date today? – the fifth of November **3.** [pour exprimer les minutes] : **trois heures ~** five past three ■ **trois heures moins ~** five to three ■ **elle est arrivée à ~** *fam* she arrived at five past ■ **~ minutes** [d'horloge] five minutes ; [un moment] a short while ■ **~ minutes plus tard, il a changé d'avis** a few minutes later he changed his mind ■ **j'en ai pour ~ minutes** it'll only take me a few minutes ■ **c'est à ~ minutes (d'ici)** it's not very far from here.
◇ *pron* five ■ **nous étions ~ dans la pièce** there were five of us in the room.
◇ *nm inv* **1.** MATH five ■ **~ et ~ font dix** five and five are ten ■ **deux fois ~** two times five, twice five **2.** [numéro d'ordre] number five ■ **c'est le ~ qui a gagné** number five wins ■ **allez au ~** [maison] go to number five **3.** JEUX five ■ **le ~ de carreau/pique** the five of diamonds/spades ■ [quille] kingpin **4.** [chiffre écrit] : **dessiner un ~** to draw a (figure) five **5.** TV : **La Cinq, La 5** *former French television channel.*
◆ **cinq sur cinq** *loc adv* : **je te reçois ~ sur ~** *pr & fig* I'm reading *ou* receiving you loud and clear ■ **t'as compris? – ~ sur ~!** got it? – got it!
◆ **en cinq sec** *loc adv fam* in no time at all, in the twinkling of an eye ■ **en ~ sec, c'était fait** it was done before you could say "Jack Robinson".

cinquantaine [sɛ̃kɑ̃tɛn] *nf* **1.** [nombre] : **une ~ de voitures** fifty or so cars, about fifty cars **2.** [d'objets] (lot of) fifty **3.** [âge] fifty ■ **il frise la ~** he's nearly fifty ■ **il a la ~ bien sonnée** he's well into his fifties.

cinquante [sɛ̃kɑ̃t] ◇ *dét* **1.** fifty ■ **~ et un** fifty-one ■ **~-deux** fifty-two ■ **~ et unième** fifty-first ■ **~ mille habitants** fifty thousand inhabitants ■ **deux billets de ~** *fam* two fifty-euro notes *ou* fifties ■ **dans les années ~** in the fifties ■ **la mode des années ~** fifties' fashions ■ **~ pour cent des personnes interrogées pensent que...** fifty per cent of *ou* half the people we asked think that... ■ **il est mort à ~ ans** he died at *ou* when he was fifty **2.** [dans des séries] fifty ■ **page/numéro ~** page/number fifty **3.** SPORT : **le ~ mètres** the fifty metres **4.** *loc* **des solutions, il n'y en a pas ~** *fam* there aren't that many ways to solve the problem ■ **je te l'ai dit ~ fois!** if I've told you once, I've told you a hundred times!
◇ *nm inv* **1.** MATH fifty ■ **deux fois ~** two times fifty **2.** [numéro d'ordre] number fifty ■ **c'est le ~ qui a gagné** number fifty wins ■ **allez au ~** [maison] go to number fifty **3.** [chiffre écrit] : **le ~ n'est pas lisible** the fifty is illegible.

cinquantenaire [sɛ̃kɑ̃tnɛr] ◇ *adj* fifty-year old.
◇ *nm* fiftieth anniversary, golden jubilee.

cinquantième [sɛ̃kɑ̃tjɛm] ◇ *adj num* fiftieth.
◇ *nm* fiftieth part, *voir aussi* **cinquième**.
◇ *nf* fiftieth performance.

cinquième [sɛ̃kjɛm] ◇ *adj num* fifth ■ **le vingt-~ concurrent** the twenty-fifth competitor ■ **la quarante-~ année** the forty-fifth year ■ **arriver ~** to come fifth ▶ **~ colonne** fifth column ■ **être la ~ roue du carrosse** *ou* **de la charrette** to be a fifth wheel.
◇ *nmf* **1.** [personne] fifth, fifth man (*f* woman) ■ **je suis ~** [dans une file] I'm fifth ; [dans un classement] I came fifth **2.** [objet] fifth (one) ■ **le ~ était cassé** the fifth (one) was broken.
◇ *nm* **1.** [étage] fifth floor *UK*, sixth floor *US* **2.** [arrondissement de Paris] fifth (arrondissement) **3.** MATH fifth ■ **les quatre ~s du total** four fifths of the total amount.
◇ *nf* **1.** ÉDUC second year *UK*, seventh grade *US* **2.** DANSE fifth (position).

cinquièmement [sɛ̃kjɛmmɑ̃] *adv* fifthly, in the fifth place.

cintrage [sɛ̃traʒ] *nm* **1.** MÉTALL bending **2.** ARCHIT centering.

cintre [sɛ̃tr] *nm* **1.** [portemanteau] coat-hanger **2.** ARCHIT arch **3.** MÉTALL bend, curve **4.** [d'un siège] crest **5.** THÉÂTRE rigging loft ▪ **les ~s** the flies.

cintré, e [sɛ̃tre] *adj* **1.** COUT close-fitting *(at the waist)*, waisted **2.** *fam* [fou] crazy, nuts, screwy.

cintrer [3] [sɛ̃tre] *vt* **1.** ARCHIT to arch, to vault **2.** [courber] to bend, to curve **3.** COUT to take in *(sép) (at the waist)*.

CIO (*abr de* **Comité international olympique**) *npr m* IOC.

cirage [siraʒ] *nm* [cire] shoe polish ▪ [polissage] polishing ▪ **être dans le ~** *fam* AÉRON to be flying blind ; *fig* to be groggy.

Circé [sirse] *npr* Circe.

circoncire [101] [sirkɔ̃sir] *vt* to circumcise.

circoncis [sirkɔ̃si] *adj* circumcised.

circoncisait *etc v* ▷ **circoncire**.

circoncision [sirkɔ̃sizjɔ̃] *nf* circumcision.

circonférence [sirkɔ̃ferɑ̃s] *nf* **1.** GÉOM circumference **2.** [tour] periphery.

circonflexe [sirkɔ̃flɛks] *adj* circumflex.

circonlocution [sirkɔ̃lɔkysjɔ̃] *nf péj* circumlocution ▪ **que de ~s!** what a roundabout way of putting it!

circonscription [sirkɔ̃skripsjɔ̃] *nf* **1.** ADMIN & POLIT area, district ▪ **~ électorale** constituency ▪ **~ consulaire** consular district **2.** GÉOM circumscription, circumscribing.

circonscrire [99] [sirkɔ̃skrir] *vt* **1.** [limiter - extension, dégâts] to limit, to control ▪ **~ un incendie** to bring a fire under control, to contain a fire **2.** [préciser] to define the limits *ou* scope of **3.** GÉOM to circumscribe.

circonspect, e [sirkɔ̃spɛ, ɛkt] *adj* [observateur, commentateur] cautious, wary ▪ [approche] cautious, circumspect *sout*.

circonspection [sirkɔ̃spɛksjɔ̃] *nf* caution, cautiousness, wariness ▪ **avec ~** cautiously, warily.

circonstance [sirkɔ̃stɑ̃s] *nf* **1.** [situation] : **étant donné les ~s** given the circumstances *ou* situation **2.** [conjoncture] circumstance, occasion ▪ **profiter de la ~** to seize the opportunity **3.** DR : **~s aggravantes/atténuantes** aggravating/extenuating circumstances.
◆ **de circonstance** *loc adj* **1.** [approprié] appropriate, fitting ▪ **vers de ~** occasional verse **2.** GRAMM : **complément de ~** adverbial phrase.
◆ **pour la circonstance** *loc adv* for the occasion.

circonstancié, e [sirkɔ̃stɑ̃sje] *adj* detailed ▪ **je ne vous ferai pas un rapport ~** I won't go into great detail.

circonstanciel, elle [sirkɔ̃stɑ̃sjɛl] *adj* GRAMM adverbial.

circonvenir [40] [sirkɔ̃vnir] *vt* [abuser - juge, témoin] to circumvent.

circonvolution [sirkɔ̃vɔlysjɔ̃] *nf* **1.** [enroulement] circumvolution **2.** ANAT convolution, gyrus.

circuit [sirkɥi] *nm* **1.** AUTO & SPORT circuit ▪ **~ automobile** racing circuit
2. [randonnée] tour, trip ▪ **faire le ~ des châteaux/vins** to do a tour of the chateaux/vineyards ▪ ≃ to go on a pub crawl *UK* ◆ **~ touristique** organized trip *ou* tour
3. [détour] detour, circuitous route
4. ÉLECTR & ÉLECTRON circuit ▪ **couper le ~** to switch off ◆ **~ imprimé** printed circuit ▪ **~ intégré** integrated circuit ▪ **~ logique** logical circuit
5. [parcours] progression, route
6. ÉCON channels ▪ **le ~ de distribution du pain** the distribution channels for bread
7. CINÉ network ▪ **le film est fait pour le ~ commercial** it's a mainstream film
8. [tuyaux] (pipe) system ▪ **~ de refroidissement** cooling system
9. [pourtour d'une ville] circumference
10. *loc* **elle est encore dans le ~** she's still around ▪ **quand je rentrerai dans le ~** when I'm back in circulation.
◆ **en circuit fermé** ◇ *loc adj* [télévision] closed-circuit *(modif)*.
◇ *loc adv* **1.** ÉLECTRON in closed circuit
2. [discuter, vivre] without any outside contact.

circulaire [sirkylɛr] ◇ *adj* **1.** [rond] circular, round **2.** [tournant - mouvement, regard] circular **3.** TRANSP return *UK (modif)*, round-trip *US (modif)* **4.** [définition, raisonnement] circular.
◇ *nf* circular.

circulairement [sirkylɛrmɑ̃] *adv* [marcher, rouler] in a circle.

circulation [sirkylasjɔ̃] *nf* **1.** TRANSP : **la ~ des camions est interdite le dimanche** lorries are not allowed to run on Sundays ▪ **il y a de la/peu de ~ aujourd'hui** the traffic is heavy/there isn't much traffic today ◆ **~ aérienne/ferroviaire/routière** air/rail/road traffic **2.** [du sang, de l'air, d'un fluide] circulation ▪ **avoir une bonne/mauvaise ~** to have good/bad circulation **3.** [déplacement] spread, movement ▪ **la libre ~ des marchandises** the free movement of goods ▪ **la ~ des capitaux** ÉCON the movement of capital **4.** [circuit] : **enlever** *ou* **retirer de la ~** COMM to take off the market ; *fig* to take out of circulation ▪ **être en ~** to be on the market ▪ **mettre en ~** [argent] to put into circulation ; COMM to bring out, to put on the market.

circulatoire [sirkylatwar] *adj* [appareil] circulatory.

circuler [3] [sirkyle] *vi* **1.** [se déplacer - personne] to move ▪ **circulez, il n'y a rien à voir** move along now, there's nothing to see ▪ **je n'aime pas que les enfants circulent dans toute la maison** I don't like the children to have the run of the whole house ▪ TRANSP [conducteur] to drive ▪ [flux de voitures] to move ▪ [train] to run **2.** [air, fluide] to circulate **3.** [passer de main en main] to be passed around *ou* round ▪ **le rapport circule** the report's being circulated **4.** [se propager] to circulate ▪ **faire ~ des bruits** to spread rumours ▪ **c'est une rumeur qui circule** it's a rumour that's going around ▪ **l'information ne circule pas** information is not getting around.

circumnavigation [sirkɔmnavigasjɔ̃] *nf* circumnavigation.

cire [sir] *nf* **1.** [encaustique] (wax) polish **2.** [dans une ruche] wax ▪ **~ d'abeille** beeswax ▪ **~ à cacheter** sealing wax **3.** [cérumen] earwax.
◆ **de cire** *loc adj* [poupée, figurine] wax *(modif)* ▪ **musée de ~, cabinet de ~** *vieilli* wax-works.

ciré, e [sire] *adj* waxed, polished.
◆ **ciré** *nm* **1.** [gén & vêtement] oilskin ▪ [de marin] sou'wester **2.** TEXT oilskin.

cirer [3] [sire] *vt* **1.** [faire briller - meuble, parquet] to wax, to polish ; [- chaussure] to polish ▪ **~ les bottes à qqn** *fam fig* to lick sb's boots **2.** *loc* **il en a rien à ~**△ he doesn't give a damn.

cireur, euse [sirœr, øz] *nm, f* [de rue] shoe shiner, shoeshine boy *(nm)*.
◆ **cireuse** *nf* floor polisher.

cireux, euse [sirø, øz] *adj* **1.** [comme la cire] waxy, wax-like, waxen *litt* **2.** [jaunâtre] waxen *litt*, wax-coloured.

cirque [sirk] *nm* **1.** LOISIRS [chapiteau] circus, big top ▪ [représentation] circus **2.** *fam* [agitation] : **c'est pas un peu fini ce ~?** will you stop fooling around? ▮ [lieu] : **c'est un vrai ~ ici!** it's chaos *ou* pandemonium in here! **3.** *fam* [scène] : **arrête un peu ton ~!** stop making a fuss! ▪ **faire son ~** to make a fuss **4.** GÉOGR cirque, corrie ▪ [sur la Lune] crater **5.** ANTIQ amphitheatre ▪ **les jeux du ~** the circus games.

cirrhose [siroz] *nf* cirrhosis.

cirrus [sirys] *nm inv* cirrus.

cisaille [sizaj] *nf* [outil] : **~, ~s** (pair of) shears ◆ **~ à lame** guillotine.

cisaillement [sizajmɑ̃] *nm* **1.** MÉTALL cutting **2.** HORT pruning.

cisailler [3] [sizaje] *vt* **1.** [barbelés, tôle] to cut **2.** [couper grossièrement] to hack (at).

cisalpin, e [sizalpɛ̃, in] *adj* Cisalpine ▪ **(la) Gaule ~e** Cisalpine Gaul.

ciseau, x [sizo] *nm* [outil] chisel ▪ **sculpter une figure au ~** to chisel out a figure.
◆ **ciseaux** *nmpl* **1.** [outil] : **(une paire de) ~x** (a pair of) scissors ▪ **(une paire de) grands ~x** (a pair of) shears ▪ **donner un coup de ~x dans un tissu** to cut a piece of material with scissors ▶ **~x à ongles** nail scissors **2.** SPORT : **saut en ~x** scissor jump.

ciseler [25] [sizle] *vt* **1.** MÉTALL [en défonçant] to engrave ▪ [en repoussant] to emboss ▪ **son nez délicatement ciselé** *fig* her finely chiselled nose **2.** *litt* [texte] to polish ▪ **un sonnet délicatement ciselé** a delicately crafted sonnet.

ciseleur [sizlœr] *nm* engraver.

ciselure [sizlyr] *nf* **1.** MÉTALL [en défoncé] engraving ▪ [en repoussé] embossing **2.** ART & MENUIS chiselling **3.** [de reliure] embossing.

Cisjordanie [sisʒɔrdani] *npr f* : **la ~** the West Bank.

cisjordanien, enne [sisʒɔrdanjɛ̃, ɛn] *adj* from the West Bank.
◆ **Cisjordanien, enne** *nm, f inhabitant of or person from the West Bank.*

cistercien, enne [sistɛrsjɛ̃, ɛn] *adj & nm, f* Cistercian.

citadelle [sitadɛl] *nf* **1.** CONSTR citadel ▪ **la ferme avait été transformée en ~** *fig* the farm had been made into a fortress **2.** [centre] stronghold.

citadin, e [sitadɛ̃, in] <> *adj* [habitude, paysage] city *(modif)*, town *(modif)*, urban ▪ [population] town-dwelling, city-dwelling, urban.
<> *nm, f* city-dweller, town-dweller.

citation [sitasjɔ̃] *nf* **1.** [extrait] quotation **2.** DR summons ▪ **~ à comparaître** [pour un témoin] subpoena ; [pour un accusé] summons ▪ **il a reçu une ~ à comparaître** [témoin] he was subpoenaed ; [accusé] he was summonsed **3.** MIL : **~ à l'ordre du jour** mention in dispatches.

cité [site] *nf* **1.** [ville] city ▪ [plus petite] town ▶ **la Cité interdite** the Forbidden City ▪ **la Cité de la Musique** *cultural centre devoted to music in the Parc de la Villette in Paris* ▪ **la ~ des Papes** Avignon ▪ **la ~ phocéenne** Marseille, Marseilles ▪ **la Cité des Sciences et de l'Industrie** *science and technology museum complex in the Parc de La Villette in Paris* **2.** [résidence] (housing) estate UK OU development US ▪ **les ~s de banlieue** suburban housing estates *(in France, often evocative of poverty and delinquency)* ▶ **~ ouvrière** ≃ council estate UK, ≃ housing project US ▪ **~ de transit** transit camp ▪ **~ universitaire** hall(s) of residence **3.** ANTIQ city-state.

cité-dortoir [sitedɔrtwar] (*pl* **cités-dortoirs**) *nf* dormitory town.

citer [3] [site] *vt* **1.** [donner un extrait de] to cite, to quote (from) **2.** [mentionner] to mention ▪ **~ qqn en exemple** to cite sb as an example **3.** [énumérer] to name, to quote, to list **4.** DR [témoin] to subpoena ▪ [accusé] to summons **5.** MIL to mention ▪ **~ un soldat à l'ordre du jour** to mention a soldier in dispatches.

citerne [sitɛrn] *nf* **1.** [cuve] tank ▪ [pour l'eau] water tank, cistern **2.** NAUT tank **3.** [camion] tanker **4.** RAIL tank wagon UK, tank car US.

cité U [sitey] *nf fam* = **cité universitaire**.

cithare [sitar] *nf* cithara.

citizen band [sitizənbɑ̃d] (*pl* **citizen bands**) *nf* Citizens' Band, CB.

citoyen, enne [sitwajɛ̃, ɛn] *nm, f* **1.** HIST & POLIT citizen **2.** *fam* [personnage] : **qu'est-ce que c'est que ce ~-là?** [inquiétant] he's a bit of a queer fish UK OU odd duck US ; [amusant] what an eccentric!

citoyenneté [sitwajɛnte] *nf* citizenship ▪ **prendre la ~ française** to acquire French citizenship.

citrique [sitrik] *adj* citric.

citron [sitrɔ̃] *nm* **1.** BOT lemon ▪ **~ pressé** freshly squeezed lemon juice ▪ **~ vert** lime **2.** *fam* [tête] nut **3.** ENTOM brimstone.
◆ **au citron** *loc adj* [lotion, savon] lemon *(modif)* ▪ [gâteau, sauce] lemon *(modif)*, lemon-flavoured ▪ **parfumé au ~** lemon-scented.

citronnade [sitrɔnad] *nf* lemonade.

citronné, e [sitrɔne] *adj* [gâteau] lemon-flavoured ▪ [pochette] lemon-scented ▪ [eau de toilette] lemon *(epith)*.

citronnelle [sitrɔnɛl] *nf* **1.** [mélisse] lemon balm **2.** [aromate tropical] lemongrass **3.** [baume] citronella oil **4.** [boisson] citronella liqueur.

citronnier [sitrɔnje] *nm* lemon tree.

citrouille [sitruj] *nf* **1.** [fruit] pumpkin **2.** *fam* [tête] nut.

cive [siv] *nf* chives *(pl)*.

civet [sivɛ] *nm* civet, stew ▪ **~ de lièvre, lièvre en ~** civet of hare, ≃ jugged hare.

civette [sivɛt] *nf* **1.** BOT chives *(pl)* **2.** [animal, parfum, fourrure] civet.

civière [sivjɛr] *nf* stretcher.

civil, e [sivil] *adj* **1.** [non religieux] civil **2.** [non militaire] civilian ▪ **porter des vêtements ~s** to wear civilian clothes **3.** ADMIN : **jour ~** civil OU calendar day **4.** [non pénal] civil **5.** *litt* [courtois] courteous, civil.
◆ **civil** *nm* DR civil action ▪ **porter une affaire au ~** to bring a case before the civil courts.
◆ **dans le civil** *loc adv* in civilian life.
◆ **en civil** *loc adj* : **être en ~** [soldat] to be wearing civilian clothes ▪ **policier en ~** plain clothes policeman.

civilement [sivilmɑ̃] *adv* **1.** DR : **se marier ~** to have a civil wedding ▪ **être ~ responsable** to be legally responsible **2.** *sout* [courtoisement] courteously.

civilisateur, trice [sivilizatœr, tris] <> *adj* civilizing.
<> *nm, f* civilizer.

civilisation [sivilizasjɔ̃] *nf* **1.** SOCIOL civilization **2.** [action de civiliser] civilization, civilizing **3.** [fait d'être civilisé] civilization **4.** *hum* [confort] civilization ▪ **nous sommes revenus à la ~ après dix jours sous la tente** we got back to civilization after ten days under canvas.

civilisé, e [sivilize] <> *adj* [nation, peuple] civilized ▪ **on est chez des gens ~s, ici!** *fam* we're not savages!
<> *nm, f* civilized person, member of a civilized society.

civiliser [3] [sivilize] *vt* to civilize, to bring civilization to.
◆ **se civiliser** *vpi* to become civilized.

civilité [sivilite] *nf litt* [qualité] politeness, polite behaviour, civility *sout* ▪ **la plus élémentaire ~ voudrait que l'on fasse OU serait de...** it would be only polite to...
◆ **civilités** *nfpl litt* [paroles] polite greetings.

civique [sivik] *adj* civic ▪ **avoir l'esprit ~** to be public-spirited ▶ **éducation OU instruction ~** civics *(U)*.

civisme [sivism] *nm* sense of citizenship, public-spiritedness.

cl (*abr écrite de* **centilitre**) cl.

clac [klak] *interj* [bruit - de fouet] crack ; [- d'une fenêtre] slam.

clafoutis [klafuti] *nm sweet dish made from cherries or other fruit and batter.*

claie [klɛ] *nf* **1.** [pour les fruits] rack **2.** [barrière] fence, hurdle **3.** [tamis] riddle, screen.

clair, e [klɛr] *adj* **1.** [lumineux - pièce, appartement] light, bright ▪ [ciel] clear ▪ **la pièce est très ~e le matin** the room gets a lot of light in the morning ▪ **une nuit ~e** a clear night ▪ **une ~e journée de juin** a fine OU bright day in June ▪ **par temps ~** in clear weather ▪ **il a le regard ~** he's got bright eyes
2. [limpide - eau, son] clear ▪ **d'une voix ~e** in a clear voice ▪ **teint ~** [frais] clear complexion ; [pâle] fair OU light complexion

3. [peu épais - sauce] thin ■ **une soupe ~e** a clear soup ■ [rare] sparse
4. [couleur] light ■ **porter des vêtements ~s** to wear light *ou* light-coloured clothes ■ **vert/rose ~** light green/pink
5. [précis - compte-rendu] clear ■ **il a été on ne peut plus ~** he was perfectly clear ■ **pourriez-vous être plus ~?** could you make yourself more clear?, could you elucidate? ■ **se faire une idée ~e de** to form a clear *ou* precise picture of ■ **cette affaire n'est pas très ~e** there's something fishy about all this ■ **je n'ai plus les idées très ~es** I can't think clearly any more
6. [évident] clear, obvious ➲ **c'est ~ et net** it's perfectly clear ■ **il n'a rien compris, c'est ~ et net** he clearly hasn't understood a thing ■ **c'est ~ comme le jour** *ou* **comme de l'eau de roche** *ou* **comme deux et deux font quatre** it's crystal clear
7. BIOL [œuf] unfertilized.
◆ **clair** ◇ *nm* **1.** [couleur] light colour ■ **les ~s et les ombres** ART light and shade
2. ASTRON : **~ de lune** moonlight ■ **au ~ de lune** in the moonlight
3. *loc* **le plus ~ de** the best part of ■ **passer le plus ~ de son temps à faire qqch** to spend most *ou* the best part of one's time doing sthg.
◇ *adv* : **il fait déjà ~ dehors** it's already light outside ➲ **parlons ~** let's not mince words! ■ **voir ~ : on n'y voit plus très ~ à cette heure-ci** the light's not very good at this time of the day ■ **y voir ~** [dans une situation] to see things clearly ■ **j'aimerais y voir ~** I'd like to understand ■ **y voir ~ dans le jeu de qqn** to see right through sb, to see through sb's little game.
◆ **au clair** *loc adv* : **mettre** *ou* **tirer qqch au ~** to clear sthg up, to clarify sthg ■ **il faut tirer cette affaire au ~** this matter must be cleared up, we must get to the bottom of this.
◆ **en clair** *loc adv* **1.** [sans code] : **envoyer un message en ~** to send an unscrambled message ■ **diffuser en ~** TV to broadcast unscrambled programmes ■ **'en ~ jusqu'à 20h'** 'can be watched by non-subscribers until 8 o'clock'
2. [en d'autres termes] to put it plainly.
◆ **claire** *nf* **1.** [bassin] oyster bed
2. [huître] fattened oyster.

clairement [klɛrmɑ̃] *adv* clearly ■ **il a répondu très ~** his answer was quite clear.

clairet, ette [klɛrɛ, ɛt] *adj* **1.** [léger - sauce, vin] light, thin *péj* **2.** [faible - voix] thin, reedy.
◆ **clairette** *nf light sparkling wine.*

claire-voie [klɛrvwa] (*pl* **claires-voies**) *nf* **1.** [barrière] lattice, open-worked fence **2.** ARCHIT clerestory, clearstory **3.** NAUT deadlight.
◆ **à claire-voie** *loc adj* open-work.

clairière [klɛrjɛr] *nf* [dans une forêt] clearing, glade.

clair-obscur [klɛrɔpskyr] (*pl* **clairs-obscurs**) *nm* **1.** ART chiaroscuro **2.** [pénombre] twilight, half-light.

clairon [klɛrɔ̃] *nm* MUS [instrument] bugle ■ [joueur] bugler ■ [orgue] clarion stop.

claironnant, e [klɛrɔnɑ̃, ɑ̃t] *adj* resonant, stentorian *litt.*

claironner [3] [klɛrɔne] ◇ *vi* to shout.
◇ *vt* to proclaim far and wide, to broadcast (to all and sundry).

clairsemé, e [klɛrsəme] *adj* [barbe, cheveux] sparse, thin ■ [arbres] scattered ■ [public] sparse ■ **il a eu quelques succès ~s au cours des 20 dernières années** he has had occasional successes over the last 20 years.

clairvoyance [klɛrvwajɑ̃s] *nf* **1.** [lucidité] clearsightedness ■ **faire preuve de ~** to be clearsighted **2.** [de médium] clairvoyance.

clairvoyant, e [klɛrvwajɑ̃, ɑ̃t] ◇ *adj* **1.** [lucide] clear-sighted, perceptive **2.** [non aveugle] sighted **3.** [médium] clairvoyant.
◇ *nm, f* **1.** [non aveugle] sighted person ■ **les ~s** the sighted **2.** [médium] clairvoyant.

clamer [3] [klame] *vt* **1.** [proclamer] : **~ son innocence** to protest one's innocence ■ **clamant leur mécontentement** making their dissatisfaction known **2.** [crier] to clamour, to shout.

clameur [klamœr] *nf* clamour (*U*) ■ **la ~ du marché montait** *ou* **les ~s du marché montaient jusqu'à nos fenêtres** the hubbub of the market could be heard from our windows.

clamser [3] △ [klamse] *vi* to kick the bucket.

clan [klɑ̃] *nm* **1.** SOCIOL clan **2.** *péj* [coterie] clan, coterie, clique.

clandestin, e [klɑ̃dɛstɛ̃, in] ◇ *adj* **1.** [secret] secret, underground, clandestine **2.** [illégal] illegal, illicit *sout.*
◇ *nm, f* [passager] stowaway ■ [immigré] illegal immigrant.

clandestinement [klɑ̃dɛstinmɑ̃] *adv* **1.** [secrètement] secretly, in secret, clandestinely **2.** [illégalement] illegally, illicitly *sout.*

clandestinité [klɑ̃dɛstinite] *nf* secrecy, clandestine nature.
◆ **dans la clandestinité** *loc adv* underground ■ **entrer dans la ~** to go underground.

clap [klap] *nm* CINÉ clapperboard.

clapet [klapɛ] *nm* **1.** TECHNOL [soupape] valve **2.** *fam* [bouche] : **elle a un de ces ~s!** she's a real chatterbox!, she can talk the hind legs off a donkey! ■ **ferme ton ~!** shut your mouth!

clapier [klapje] *nm* **1.** [à lapins] hutch **2.** *péj* [appartement] : **c'est un vrai ~ ici!** it's like living in a shoe box in this place!

clapir [32] [klapir] *vi* [lapin] to squeal.

clapotement [klapɔtmɑ̃] *nm* lapping.

clapoter [3] [klapɔte] *vi* [eau, vague] to lap.

clapotis [klapɔti] = **clapotement**.

clappement [klapmɑ̃] *nm* [de la langue] clicking ■ **des ~s de langue** clicks of the tongue.

clapper [3] [klape] *vi* to click one's tongue.

claquage [klakaʒ] *nm* MÉD [muscle] strained muscle ■ [ligament] strained ligament ■ **se faire** *ou* **avoir un ~** [muscle] to strain a muscle.

claquant, e [klakɑ̃, ɑ̃t] *adj fam* exhausting, killing.

claque [klak] ◇ *nm* [chapeau] opera hat.
◇ *nf* **1.** [coup] smack, slap ■ **une bonne ~** a stinger ■ **une ~ dans la gueule**△ *pr* a smack in the gob△ *UK ou* kisser *US* ; *fig* a slap in the face **2.** THÉÂTRE claque **3.** *Québec* [chaussure] rubber overshoe **4.** *fam loc* **j'en ai ma ~** [saturé] I've had it up to here ; [épuisé] I'm shattered *UK ou* bushed *US*.

claqué, e [klake] *adj* **1.** *fam* [éreinté] worn out, shattered *UK*, bushed *US* **2.** MÉD strained.

claquement [klakmɑ̃] *nm* [bruit violent] banging, slamming ■ **le ~ sec du fouet** the sharp crack of the whip ■ **un ~ de doigts** a snap of the fingers ■ **un ~ de langue** a clicking of the tongue ■ **entendre un ~ de portière** to hear a car door slam.

claquemurer [3] [klakmyre] *vt* to shut in (*sép*).
◆ **se claquemurer** *vp (emploi réfléchi)* to shut o.s. in *ou* away.

claquer [3] [klake] ◇ *vt* **1.** [fermer] to bang *ou* to slam (shut) ■ **~ la porte** *pr* to slam the door ; *fig* to storm out ■ **~ la porte au nez de qqn** *pr* to slam the door in sb's face ; *fig* to send sb packing **2.** [faire résonner] : **~ sa langue** to click one's tongue **3.** *fam* [dépenser] to spend ■ **j'ai tout claqué** I blew the lot **4.** *fam* [fatiguer] to wear out (*sép*) ■ **ça m'a claqué** it was absolutely shattering *UK*, it wiped me out *US* **5.** *fam* [gifler] to slap.
◇ *vi* **1.** [résonner - porte] to bang ; [- drapeau, linge] to flap ■ **un coup de feu a claqué** a shot rang out ■ **faire ~ ses doigts** to snap one's fingers ■ **le clocher fit ~ son fouet** the coachman cracked his whip **2.** *fam* [mourir] to peg out ■ [tomber en panne] to conk out ■ **le frigo va ~** the fridge is on the way out ■ **le projet lui a claqué dans les doigts** [il a échoué] his project fell through **3.** [céder avec bruit - sangle] to snap ; [- baudruche, chewing-gum] to pop.
◆ **claquer de** *v+prép* : **il claque des dents** his teeth are chattering ■ **~ des doigts** to snap one's fingers.
◆ **se claquer** ◇ *vpi fam* [se fatiguer] to wear o.s. out ■ **je me suis claqué pour rien** I worked myself into the ground for nothing.
◇ *vpt* : **se ~ un muscle** to strain *ou* to pull a muscle.

claquette [klakɛt] *nf* CINÉ clapperboard.
◆ **claquettes** *nfpl* **1.** DANSE tap-dancing ■ **faire des ~s** to tap-dance **2.** [tongs] flipflops.

clarification [klarifikasjɔ̃] *nf* [explication] clarification.

clarifier [9] [klarifje] *vt* **1.** [rendre limpide - suspension, beurre, sauce] to clarify ; [- vin] to settle **2.** [expliquer] to clarify, to make clear.
◆ **se clarifier** *vpi* **1.** [situation] to become clearer **2.** [suspension, sauce] to become clear **3.** CHIM to become clarified.

clarinette [klarinɛt] *nf* clarinet.

clarinettiste [klarinetist] *nmf* clarinettist, clarinet player.

clarisse [klaris] *nf* Clarisse ■ **les ~s** the Poor Clares.

clarté [klarte] *nf* **1.** [lumière] light ■ **la ~ du jour** daylight ▌[luminosité] brightness **2.** [transparence] clarity, limpidness, clearness **3.** [intelligibilité] clarity, clearness ■ **son raisonnement n'est pas d'une grande ~** his reasoning is not particularly clear.
◆ **clartés** *nfpl litt* knowledge.

clash [klaʃ] (*pl* **clashs** *ou pl* **clashes**) *nm fam* clash, conflict ■ **il y a eu un ~ entre nous (à propos de...)** we clashed (over...)

classable [klasabl] *adj* classable ■ **cette musique est difficilement ~** it's hard to classify this kind of music.

classe [klas] ◇ *nf*

> **A.** ÉDUCATION
> **B.** DANS UNE HIÉRARCHIE
> **C.** MILITAIRE

A. ÉDUCATION

1. [salle] classroom

2. [groupe] class ■ **camarade de ~** classmate ➜ **~ de neige** *residential classes in the mountains for schoolchildren* ■ **~ de mer** *residential classes at the seaside for schoolchildren* ■ **~ verte** *residential classes in the countryside for urban schoolchildren*

3. [cours] class, lesson ■ **~ de français** French class ■ **~ de perfectionnement** advanced class ■ **faire la ~** [être enseignant] to teach ; [donner un cours] to teach *ou* to take a class ■ **c'est moi qui leur fais la ~** I'm their teacher

4. [niveau] class, form *UK*, grade *US* ■ **dans les grandes/petites ~s** in the upper/lower forms *UK* ■ **monter de ~** to go on to the next form ■ **refaire** *ou* **redoubler une ~** to repeat a year ➜ **~s préparatoires** *schools specializing in preparing pupils to take Grandes Écoles entrance exams*

B. DANS UNE HIÉRARCHIE

1. [espèce] class, kind ■ MATH & SC class ■ [dans des statistiques] bracket, class, group ■ **~ d'âge** age group ■ **~ de revenus** income bracket

2. [rang] class, rank ■ **former une ~ à part** to be in a class *ou* league of one's own

3. POLIT & SOCIOL class ■ **~ sociale** social class ■ **les ~s populaires** *ou* **laborieuses** the working classes ■ **les ~s moyennes/dirigeantes** the middle/ruling classes ■ **l'ensemble de la ~ politique** the whole of the political establishment *ou* class

4. TRANSP class ■ **billet de première/deuxième ~** first-/second-class ticket ■ **voyager en première ~** to travel first class ■ **~ affaires/économique** AÉRON business/economy class

5. [niveau] quality, class ■ **de grande ~** top-quality ■ **de première ~** first-class ■ **un hôtel de ~ internationale** a hotel of international standing

6. [distinction] class, style ■ **avec ~** smartly, with elegance

7. LING class ■ **~ grammaticale** part of speech

C. MILITAIRE

annual contingent ■ **la ~ 70** the 1970 levy.

◇ *adj fam* **être ~** to be classy.
◆ **classes** *nfpl* : **faire ses ~s** MIL to go through training.
◆ **en classe** *loc adv* : **aller en ~** to go to school ■ **il a l'âge d'aller en ~** he's of school age ■ **rentrer en ~** [pour la première fois] to start school ; [à la rentrée] to go back to school, to start school again.

CLASSES PRÉPARATOIRES

> After the *baccalauréat* very successful students may choose to attend the ***classes préparatoires***, intensive courses organized in *lycées*. Students are completely immersed in their subject and do little else than prepare for the competitive *grandes écoles* entrance exams. If they do not succeed, two years of *prépas* are considered equivalent to a DEUG, and these students often continue at a university.

classé, e [klase] *adj* **1.** [terminé] closed, dismissed ■ **pour moi, c'est une affaire ~e** all that's over and done with *ou* the matter's closed as far as I'm concerned **2.** [protégé] listed ■ **monument/château ~** listed *ou* scheduled building/castle **3.** SPORT : **cheval non ~** also-ran.

classement [klasmɑ̃] *nm* **1.** [tri - de documents] classifying, ordering, sorting ; [- d'objets] sorting, grading ■ **faire un ~ de livres** to sort out *ou* to classify books ■ [rangement] filing **2.** CHIM grading **3.** [palmarès] ranking, placing ■ **avoir un mauvais/bon ~** to do badly/well ■ **donner le ~ d'un examen/d'une course** to give the results of an exam/of a race ■ **~ de sortie** pass list ■ **premier au ~ général** first overall **4.** INFORM sequencing **5.** ADMIN listing.

classer [3] [klase] *vt* **1.** [archiver - vieux papiers] to file (away) ; [- affaire] to close **2.** [agencer] to arrange, to classify, to sort ■ **~ qqch par ordre alphabétique** to put sthg in alphabetical order **3.** INFORM to sequence **4.** ADMIN [site] to list, to schedule **5.** [définir] : **~ qqn comme** to categorize *ou péj* to label sb as ■ **à sa réaction, je l'ai tout de suite classé** I could tell straight away what sort of person he was from his reaction.
◆ **se classer** *vpi* **1.** [dans une compétition] to finish, to rank ■ **se ~ troisième** to rank third **2.** [prendre son rang] : **se ~ parmi** to rank among.

classeur [klasœr] *nm* **1.** [chemise] binder, folder, jacket *US* ■ **~ à anneaux** ring binder ■ **~ à feuilles mobiles** loose-leaf binder **2.** [tiroir] filing drawer ■ [meuble] filing cabinet.

classicisme [klasisism] *nm* **1.** ART & LITTÉR classicism **2.** [conformisme] traditionalism.

classificateur, trice [klasifikatœr, tris] *adj* classifying.
◆ **classificateur** *nm* **1.** INFORM classifier **2.** CHIM screen, sizer.

classification [klasifikasjɔ̃] *nf* **1.** [répartition] classification **2.** [système] classification system ■ **~ décimale universelle** Dewey decimal system ■ **~ périodique des éléments** periodic table **3.** NAUT [mode d'identification] class logo **4.** BIOL classification.

classifier [9] [klasifje] *vt* **1.** [ordonner] to classify **2.** [définir] to label.

classique [klasik] ◇ *adj* **1.** ÉDUC classical ■ **faire des études ~s** to study classics **2.** LING & LITTÉR classical ■ **le français ~** seventeenth and eighteenth-century French ▌DANSE & MUS [traditionnel] classical ■ [dix-huitième siècle] classical, eighteenth-century ■ ANTIQ classical **3.** [conventionnel] conventional ■ **matériel/armement ~** conventional equipment/weapons ■ **vêtement de coupe ~** classically cut garment **4.** [connu - sketch, plaisanterie, recette] classic ■ **c'est le coup ~** [ça arrive souvent] that's typical! ; [une ruse connue] that's a well-known trick! **5.** ÉCON classic.
◇ *nm* **1.** LITTÉR [auteur] classical author ■ [œuvre] classic ■ **un ~ du genre** a classic of its kind ■ **connaître ses ~s** to be well-read ■ **c'est un des grands ~s de la littérature russe** it's one of the great classics of Russian literature **2.** MUS [genre] : **le ~** classical music ▌[œuvre - gén] classic ; [- de jazz] (jazz) standard **3.** [style - d'habillement, de décoration] classic style **4.** ÉQUIT classic.
◇ *nf* SPORT classic.

classiquement [klasikmɑ̃] *adv* **1.** [avec classicisme] classically **2.** [habituellement] customarily ■ **méthode ~ utilisée** customary *ou* classic method.

Claude [klod] *npr* [empereur romain] Claudius.

claudication [klodikasjɔ̃] *nf* limp, claudication *spéc.*

claudiquer [3] [klodike] *vi* to limp.

clause [kloz] *nf* **1.** DR clause, stipulation ▪ **~ de résiliation/retrait** termination/withdrawal clause ▪ **~ abusive** unfair clause ▪ **~ conditionnelle** proviso ▪ **~ dérogatoire** derogatory clause ▪ **~ pénale** penalty clause ▪ **~ de sauvegarde** safety clause ▪ **~ de style** *pr* standard *ou* formal clause ▪ **ce n'est qu'une ~ de style** *fig* it's only a manner of speaking **2.** POLIT [d'un traité] clause.

claustral, e, aux [klostral, o] *adj* **1.** [d'un cloître] claustral, cloistral **2.** [retiré] cloistered.

claustration [klostrasjɔ̃] *nf* confinement.

claustrer [3] [klostre] *vt* to confine ▪ **vivre claustré** to lead the life of a recluse.

◆ **se claustrer** *vp (emploi réfléchi)* to shut o.s. away ▪ **elle s'est claustrée** she has become a recluse.

claustrophobe [klostrɔfɔb] ◇ *adj* claustrophobic.
◇ *nmf* claustrophobe, claustrophobic.

claustrophobie [klostrɔfɔbi] *nf* claustrophobia.

clavecin [klavsɛ̃] *nm* harpsichord.

claveciniste [klavsinist] *nmf* harpsichordist, harpsichord player.

clavette [klavɛt] *nf* key, pin ▪ **~ de commande** actuating pin.

clavicule [klavikyl] *nf* collarbone, clavicle *spéc*.

clavier [klavje] *nm* **1.** [d'une machine] keyboard ▪ [d'un téléphone] keypad ▪ **~ numérique** *ou* **auxiliaire** keypad **2.** MUS [d'un piano] keyboard ▪ [d'un orgue] manual ▪ **~ main gauche** [d'un accordéon] fingerboard ▪ **~ de pédales** pedal board **3.** [registre] range.

claviste [klavist] *nmf* keyboard operator, keyboarder.

clayette [klɛjɛt] *nf* shelf, tray ▪ **~ coulissante d'un réfrigérateur** slide-out shelf in a fridge.

clé [kle] = **clef**.

clean [klin] *adj fam* [personne] wholesome-looking, clean-cut.

clébard△ [klebar], **clebs**△ [klɛps] *nm* dog, mutt.

clef[1] [kle] *nf* **1.** [de porte, d'horloge, de boîte de conserve] key ▪ [d'un tuyau de poêle] damper ▶ **prendre la ~ des champs** to get away ▪ **fausse ~** picklock ▪ **mettre la ~ sous la porte** *ou* **le paillasson** *pr* to shut up shop ; *fig* to disappear overnight
2. [outil] spanner *UK*, wrench *US* ▪ **~ anglaise** *ou* **à molette** monkey wrench ▪ **~ universelle** adjustable spanner
3. AUTO : **~ de contact** ignition key ▪ **mes ~s de voiture** my car keys
4. TÉLÉCOM : **~ d'appel** call button ▪ **~ de réponse** reply key ‖ INFORM : **~ d'accès** enter key ▪ **~ électronique** electronic key ▪ **~ de protection** data protection
5. MUS clef, key ▪ **~ de sol** key of G, treble clef ▪ **~ de fa** key of F, bass clef ▪ **~ d'ut** key of C, C clef ‖ [touche] key ▪ [d'un instrument - à vent] finger-plate ; [- à corde] peg ▪ **~s de tension** screws
6. [moyen] : **la ~ de** the key to ▪ **la ~ de la réussite** the key to success
7. [explication] clue, key ▪ **la ~ du mystère** the key to the mystery
8. [influence déterminante] : **la ~ de** the key to ▪ **Gibraltar est la ~ de la Méditerranée** he who holds Gibraltar holds the Mediterranean ▪ *(comme adj; avec ou sans trait d'union)* [essentiel] key *(avant n)* ▪ **mot/position ~** key word/post
9. [introduction] : **~s pour l'informatique/la philosophie** introduction to computer technology/philosophy
10. ARCHIT : **~ de voûte** *pr* keystone, quoin ; *fig* linchpin, cornerstone.

◆ **à clef** *loc adv* : **fermer une porte à ~** to lock a door.

◆ **à clefs** *loc adj* : **roman/film à ~s** novel/film based on real characters *(whose identity is disguised)*.

◆ **à la clef** *loc adv* **1.** MUS in the key signature ▪ **il y a un bémol/dièse à la ~** the key signature has a flat/sharp
2. [au bout du compte] : **avec... à la ~** [récompense] with... as a bonus ; [punition] with... into the bargain.

◆ **clef(s) en main** ◇ *loc adj* **1.** COMM : **prix ~** *ou* **~s en main** [d'un véhicule] on-the-road price ; [d'une maison] all-inclusive price
2. INDUST turnkey *(modif)*.
◇ *loc adv* **1.** COMM : **acheter une maison ~** *ou* **~s en main** to buy a house with vacant *ou* immediate possession ▪ **acheter une voiture ~** *ou* **~s en main** to buy a car ready to drive away
2. INDUST on a turnkey basis.

◆ **sous clef** *loc adv* **1.** [en prison] behind bars
2. [à l'abri] : **garder qqch sous ~** to lock sthg away, to put sthg under lock and key.

clef[2] [kle] *nm Suisse* garden gate.

clématite [klematit] *nf* clematis.

clémence [klemɑ̃s] *nf* **1.** MÉTÉOR mildness **2.** [pardon] leniency, mercy, clemency ▪ **s'en remettre à la ~ de qqn** to throw o.s. on sb's mercy.

clément, e [klemɑ̃, ɑ̃t] *adj* **1.** MÉTÉOR mild **2.** [favorable] : **à une époque moins ~e** in less happy times.

clémentine [klemɑ̃tin] *nf* clementine.

clenche [klɑ̃ʃ] *nf* **1.** [loquet] latch **2.** *Belgique* [poignée] door-handle.

Cléopâtre [kleɔpatr] *npr* Cleopatra.

clepsydre [klɛpsidr] *nf* clepsydra.

cleptomane [klɛptɔman] = **kleptomane**.

cleptomanie [klɛptɔmani] = **kleptomanie**.

clerc [klɛr] *nm* **1.** RELIG cleric **2.** *sout* scholar ▪ **il est grand ~ en la matière** he's an expert on the subject ▪ **point n'est besoin d'être grand ~ pour deviner la fin de l'histoire** you don't need to be a genius to guess the end of the story **3.** [employé] : **~ de notaire** clerk.

clergé [klɛrʒe] *nm* clergy, priesthood ▪ **~ régulier** regular clergy ▪ **le bas ~** the lower clergy.

clérical, e, aux [klerikal, o] *adj* [du clergé] clerical.

cléricalisme [klerikalism] *nm* clericalism.

CLES, Cles [klɛs] (*abr de* **contrat local emploi-solidarité**) *nm community work scheme for young unemployed people.*

clic [klik] *interj* & *nm* click.

clic-clac [klikklak] ◇ *nm inv* clickety-click.
◇ *adj inv* canapé.

cliché [kliʃe] *nm* **1.** PHOTO [pellicule] negative ▪ [photo] photograph, shot **2.** TECHNOL [plaque] plate **3.** INFORM format, layout **4.** *péj* [banalité] cliché ▪ **tous ses gags sont des ~s** his gags are all so corny.

client, e [klijɑ̃, ɑ̃t] *nm, f* [d'un magasin, d'un restaurant] customer ▪ [d'une banque, d'un salon de coiffure, d'un institut de beauté] customer, client ▪ [d'un avocat] client ▪ [d'un hôtel] guest ▪ [d'un taxi] passenger ▪ **je suis ~ chez eux** I'm one of their regular customers ▶ **chez eux, c'est à la tête du ~** they charge you what they feel like ▪ **ce professeur note à la tête du ~** the grades that teacher gives depend on whether he likes you or not ▪ **le Mexique est un gros ~ des États-Unis** the United States does a lot of trade with Mexico.

clientèle [klijɑ̃tɛl] *nf* **1.** [clients] clientele, customers ▪ **acheter une ~ à un confrère** to buy a practice from a colleague **2.** POLIT : **~ électorale** electorate, voters **3.** HIST patronage, protection.

clientélisme [klijɑ̃telism] *nm péj* populism.

clignement [kliɲmɑ̃] *nm* : **~ d'œil** *ou* **d'yeux** [involontaire] blink ; [volontaire] wink ▪ **des ~s d'œil** *ou* **d'yeux** blinking.

cligner [3] [kliɲe] ◇ *vt* [fermer] : **~ les yeux** to blink.
◇ *vi* [paupières, yeux] to blink.

◆ **cligner de** *v+prép* **1.** [fermer involontairement] : **~ des yeux** to blink **2.** [faire signe avec] : **~ de l'œil (en direction de qqn)** to wink (at sb).

clignotant, e [kliɲɔtɑ̃, ɑ̃t] *adj* [signal] flashing ▪ [lampe défectueuse] flickering ▪ [guirlande] twinkling, flashing.

◆ **clignotant** *nm* **1.** AUTO [lampe] indicator *UK*, turn signal *US* ▪ **mettre son ~** to indicate *UK*, to put on one's turn signal *US* **2.** [signal] warning light ▪ SPORT sequenced starting lights **3.** ÉCON [indice] (key) indicator.

clignotement [kliɲɔtmɑ̃] *nm* **1.** [lumière - d'une guirlande, d'une étoile] twinkling ; [- d'un signal] flashing ; [- d'une lampe défectueuse] flickering **2.** [mouvement - des paupières] flickering ; [- des yeux] blinking.

clignoter [3] [kliɲɔte] *vi* **1.** [éclairer - étoile, guirlande] to twinkle ; [- signal] to flash (on and off) ; [- lampe défectueuse] to flicker **2.** [automobiliste] to indicate *UK*, to put on one's turn signal *US*.

climat [klima] *nm* **1.** GÉOGR climate ▪ **sous d'autres ~s** in other countries ▪ **partir vers des ~s plus sereins** *sout* to travel to sunnier climes ➊ **~ artificiel** artificial climate **2.** [ambiance] climate, atmosphere ▪ **le ~ devient malsain!** things are turning nasty!

climatique [klimatik] *adj* **1.** MÉTÉOR weather *(modif)*, climatic **2.** LOISIRS : **centre/station ~** health centre/resort.

climatisation [klimatizasjɔ̃] *nf* **1.** [dans un immeuble] air conditioning **2.** [dans une voiture] heating and ventilation.

climatiser [3] [klimatize] *vt* to air-condition, to install air-conditioning in ▪ **restaurant climatisé** restaurant with air-conditioning.

climatiseur [klimatizœr] *nm* air-conditioner, air-conditioning unit.

climatologie [klimatɔlɔʒi] *nf* climatology.

clin [klɛ̃] ◆ **à clin** *loc adj* : **un pont à ~** a clapboard bridge.

clin d'œil [klɛ̃dœj] (*pl* **clins d'œil**) *nm* **1.** [clignement] wink ▪ **faire un ~ à qqn** to wink at sb **2.** [allusion] allusion, implied reference ▪ **un ~ à...** an allusion *OU* an implied reference to...
◆ **en un clin d'œil** *loc adv* in the twinkling of an eye, in less than no time, in a flash.

clinicien, enne [klinisjɛ̃, ɛn] *nm, f* **1.** MÉD clinical practitioner **2.** PSYCHOL clinical psychologist.

clinique [klinik] ◇ *adj* clinical ▪ **leçon ~** teaching at the bedside ▪ **les signes ~s de l'affection** the visible signs of the disease.
◇ *nf* **1.** [établissement] (private) clinic ▪ **~ d'accouchement** maternity hospital **2.** [service] teaching department *(of a hospital)*.

cliniquement [klinikmɑ̃] *adv* clinically.

clinquant, e [klɛ̃kɑ̃, ɑ̃t] *adj* **1.** [brillant] glittering, tinselly *péj* **2.** [superficiel - style] flashy ▪ **le monde ~ du show business** the razzmatazz of show business.
◆ **clinquant** *nm* **1.** [faux éclat] : **le ~ de leurs conversations** the superficial sparkle of their conversations **2.** [lamelle] tinsel.

clip [klip] *nm* **1.** [broche] clip, brooch **2.** [boucle d'oreille] clip-on earring **3.** [attache] clamp, clip ▪ **~s de fixation** holders **4.** [film] video.

cliquable [klikabl] *adj* clickable ▪ **plan ~** sensitive map.

clique [klik] *nf* **1.** [coterie] clique, gang, coterie **2.** MIL [fanfare] band.
◆ **cliques** *nfpl* : **prendre ses ~s et ses claques** *fam* [partir] to up and leave ; [emporter ses affaires] to pack one's bags (and go).

cliquer [3] [klike] *vi* to click.

cliquet [klike] *nm* **1.** [mécanisme] catch, dog, pawl ▪ **~ de retenue** holding-dog **2.** [outil] pawl ▪ **à ~** pawl *(modif)*.

cliqueter [27] [klikte] *vi* [clefs] to jangle ▪ [petite serrure] to click ▪ [grosse serrure] to clang, to clank ▪ [épées] to click ▪ [machine à écrire] to clack ▪ [assiettes] to clatter ▪ [verres] to clink.

cliquetis [klikti] *nm* [de clefs, de bijoux, de chaînes] jangling *(U)* ▪ [d'épées] rattling *(U)* ▪ [d'une machine à écrire] clacking *(U)* ▪ [d'assiettes] clatter, clattering *(U)* ▪ [de verres] clinking *(U)*.

cliquette *etc v* ▻ **cliqueter**.

clitoridien, enne [klitɔridjɛ̃, ɛn] *adj* clitoral.

clitoris [klitɔris] *nm* clitoris.

clivage [klivaʒ] *nm* **1.** [de roche, de cristal] cleavage, splitting **2.** [séparation] divide, division ▪ **~ social** social divide.

cliver [3] [klive] *vt* MINÉR to divide, to separate.
◆ **se cliver** *vpi* to split, to become divided.

cloaque [klɔak] *nm* **1.** [égout] cesspool, open sewer **2.** *litt* [lieu sale] cesspool, cloaca *litt* **3.** ZOOL cloaca.

clochard, e [klɔʃar, ard] *nm, f* tramp.

clochardisation [klɔʃardizasjɔ̃] *nf* : **on observe une ~ croissante chez les jeunes** more and more young people are turning into vagrants.

clochardiser [3] [klɔʃardize] *vt* to make destitute *OU* homeless.
◆ **se clochardiser** *vpi* to become destitute.

cloche [klɔʃ] ◇ *adj fam* [idiot] stupid.
◇ *nf* **1.** [instrument, signal] bell ➊ **(chapeau) ~** cloche hat ▪ **s'en mettre plein** *OU* **se taper la ~** *fam* to stuff one's face ▪ **déménager** *OU* **partir à la ~ de bois** to do a moonlight flit *UK*, to leave without paying the rent **2.** HORT cloche **3.** CULIN dome, dish-cover ▪ **~ à fromage** cheese dish *(with cover)*, cheese-bell **4.** NAUT : **~ de plongée** *OU* **à plongeur** diving-bell **5.** CHIM : **~ à vide** vacuum bell-jar **6.** *fam* [personne] idiot **7.** *fam* [vagabondage] : **être de la ~** to be of no fixed abode.
◆ **en cloche** *loc adj* bell-shaped.
◆ **sous cloche** *loc adv* : **mettre sous ~** HORT to put under glass, to cloche ; *fig* to mollycoddle.

cloche-pied [klɔʃpje] ◆ **à cloche-pied** *loc adv* : **sauter à ~** to hop.

clocher[1] [klɔʃe] *nm* **1.** [tour] bell-tower, church tower **2.** [village] : **son ~** the place where he was born.
◆ **de clocher** *loc adj* : **esprit de ~** parochialism, parish-pump mentality ▪ **querelles de ~** petty bickering.

clocher[2] [3] [klɔʃe] ◇ *vi fam* to be wrong ▪ **qu'est-ce qui cloche?** what's wrong *OU* up?
◇ *vt* HORT to (put under a) cloche.

clocheton [klɔʃtɔ̃] *nm* pinnacle turret.

clochette [klɔʃɛt] *nf* **1.** [petite cloche] small bell ▪ **~ à vache** cow-bell **2.** BOT [campanule] bell-flower.

clodo [klɔdo] *nmf fam* tramp, bum *US*.

cloison [klwazɔ̃] *nf* **1.** CONSTR partition ▪ **mur de ~** dividing wall **2.** AÉRON & NAUT bulkhead ▪ **~ étanche** watertight bulkhead **3.** ANAT & BOT dissepiment, septum ▪ **~ nasale** nasal septum.

cloisonné, e [klwazɔne] *adj* **1.** ANAT & BOT septated **2.** JOAILL cloisonné.
◆ **cloisonné** *nm* JOAILL cloisonné.

cloisonnement [klwazɔnmɑ̃] *nm* [division] division ▪ **le ~ des services dans une entreprise** the excessive compartmentalisation of departments in a firm.

cloisonner [3] [klwazɔne] *vt* **1.** CONSTR to partition off *(sép)* **2.** NAUT to bulkhead **3.** [séparer] to compartmentalise.

cloître [klwatr] *nm* **1.** [couvent] convent, monastery **2.** ARCHIT [d'un couvent] cloister ▪ [d'une cathédrale] close.

cloîtré, e [klwatre] *adj* [moine, religieuse] cloistered, enclosed ▪ [ordre] monastic.

cloîtrer [3] [klwatre] *vt* **1.** RELIG : **~ qqn** to shut sb up in a convent **2.** [enfermer] to shut up *OU* away ▪ **nous sommes cloîtrés toute la journée/dans notre atelier** we're shut up all day/in our workshop.
◆ **se cloîtrer** *vp (emploi réfléchi)* to shut o.s. away.

clonage [klonaʒ] *nm* cloning ▪ **~ thérapeutique** therapeutic cloning ▪ **~ reproductif** reproductive cloning.

clone [klon] *nm* clone.

cloner [3] [klone] *vt* to clone.

clope [klɔp] *nm & nf fam* fag *UK*, smoke *US*.

cloper [3] [klɔpe] *vi fam* to smoke.

clopin-clopant [klɔpɛ̃klɔpɑ̃] *adv* **1.** [en boitant] : **avancer ~** to hobble along **2.** [irrégulièrement] : **ça va ~** it has its ups and downs.

clopiner [3] [klɔpine] *vi fam* to hobble along.

clopinettes [klɔpinɛt] *nfpl fam* **gagner des ~** to earn peanuts ■ **des ~!** [refus] nothing doing!, no way!

cloporte [klɔpɔrt] *nm* **1.** ZOOL wood-louse **2.** *fam vieilli* [concierge] door-keeper, concierge.

cloque [klɔk] *nf* **1.** BOT & MÉD blister **2.** [défaut] raised spot, blister ■ **faire des ~s** to blister **3.** △ *loc* **être en ~** to have a bun in the oven△.

cloqué, e [klɔke] *adj* seersucker *(modif)*.

cloquer [3] [klɔke] *vi* **1.** [peinture, papier] to blister **2.** *fam* [peau] to come up in a blister.

clore [113] [klɔr] *vt* **1.** *sout* [fermer - porte, volet] to close, to shut ■ [entourer - parc] to shut off *(sép)* **2.** FIN : **~ un compte** to close an account **3.** [conclure] to conclude, to end, to finish ■ **les inscriptions seront closes le lundi 15** UNIV the closing date for enrolment is Monday 15th ■ **l'incident est ~** the matter is closed.

clos, e [klo, kloz] *adj* **1.** [fermé] closed, shut ■ **les yeux ~** with one's eyes shut ■ **trouver porte ~e** to find nobody at home **2.** PHON closed.
◆ **clos** *nm* enclosed garden *(often a vineyard)*.

closent *etc v* ▷ **clore**.

closerie [klozri] *nf* flower-garden.

clôt *etc v* ▷ **clore**.

clôture [klotyr] *nf* **1.** [barrière - en bois] fence ; [- en fil de fer] railings **2.** [fermeture] closing ■ **'~ annuelle'** 'annual closure' ■ **j'ai assisté à la ~** I attended the closing ceremony ‖ [fin] end ■ **~ des inscriptions le 20 décembre** UNIV the closing date for enrolment is December 20th **3.** BOURSE close ■ **à la ~** at the close **4.** [dans un monastère] enclosure.
◆ **de clôture** *loc adj* [séance, date] closing ■ **cours de ~** BOURSE closing price.
◆ **en clôture** *loc adv* BOURSE at closing ■ **combien valait l'euro en ~?** what was the closing price of the euro?, what did the euro close at?

clôturer [3] [klotyre] *vt* **1.** [fermer] to enclose, to fence (in) *(sép)* **2.** [terminer] to close, to end ■ **~ les débats** to close the debate **3.** FIN [compte] to close.

clou [klu] *nm* **1.** [pointe] nail ■ **~ d'ameublement** (upholstery) tack ■ **~ (de) tapissier** (carpet) tack ■ **~ sans tête** brad ■ **un ~ chasse l'autre** *prov* new enthusiasms chase out old ones **2.** [summum] : **le ~ de** the climax *ou* highlight of **3.** CULIN : **~ de girofle** clove **4.** *fam péj* [machine] : **vieux ~** [voiture] old banger *UK ou* crate *US* ; [bicyclette] old boneshaker *UK ou* bike **5.** *fam loc* **pas un ~ : ça ne vaut pas un ~** it's not worth a bean ■ **qu'est-ce qu'il a eu? – pas un ~!** what did he get? – not a sausage! *UK ou* zilch! *US* ■ **des ~s!** no way!, nothing doing! ■ **pour des ~** for nothing.
◆ **clous** *nmpl* pedestrian *ou* zebra crossing *UK*, crosswalk *US*.
◆ **à clous** *loc adj* [chaussure] hobnail *(modif)* ■ [pneu] studded.
◆ **au clou** *loc adv fam* in the pawnshop ■ **mettre qqch au ~** to pawn sthg, to hock sthg.

clouer [3] [klue] *vt* **1.** [fixer] to nail (down) **2.** [fermer] to nail shut ■ **~ le bec à qqn** *fam* to shut sb up **3.** [immobiliser - au sol] to pin down *(sép)* ■ **il est resté cloué au lit pendant trois jours** he was laid up in bed for three days ■ **la peur le clouait sur place** he was rooted to the spot with fear.

clouté, e [klute] *adj* **1.** [décoré] studded **2.** [renforcé - chaussure, semelle] hobnailed ; [- pneu] studded.

clouter [3] [klute] *vt* to stud.

Clovis [klɔvis] *npr* Clovis.

clovisse [klɔvis] *nf* clam.

clown [klun] *nm* clown ■ **faire le ~** to clown, to fool around ◐ **~ blanc** white-faced clown.

clownerie [klunri] *nf* **1.** LOISIRS : **des ~s** clown's antics **2.** *péj* [bêtise] (stupid) prank ■ **faire des ~s** to clown *ou* to fool around.

clownesque [klunɛsk] *adj* clownish, clownlike.

club [klœb] *nm* **1.** [groupe - de personnes] club ; [- de nations] group **2.** [centre] : **~ de gym** fitness centre, gym ■ **~ de sport** *ou* **sportif** sports club ■ **~ de vacances** holiday *UK ou* vacation *US* village **3.** [au golf] club.

cluse [klyz] *nf* cluse, transverse valley.

Clytemnestre [klitɛmnɛstr] *npr* Clytemnestra.

cm (*abr écrite de* **centimètre**) cm.

cm² (*abr écrite de* **centimètre carré**) sq.cm, cm².

cm³ (*abr écrite de* **centimètre cube**) cu.cm, cm³.

CM *nm* (*abr de* **cours moyen**) ■ **~1** *fourth year of primary school* ■ **~2** *fifth year of primary school.*

CMU (*abr de* **Couverture maladie universelle**) [seɛmy] *nf health insurance system for the less well-off,* ≃ Medicaid *US*.

CNAM [knam] *npr m* = **Conservatoire national des arts et métiers**.

CNC *npr m* **1.** (*abr de* **Conseil national de la consommation**) *consumer protection organization* **2.** (*abr de* **Centre national de la cinématographie**) *national cinematographic organization.*

CNCL (*abr de* **Commission nationale de la communication et des libertés**) *npr f former French TV and radio supervisory body.*

CNE (*abr de* **Caisse nationale d'épargne**) *npr f national savings bank.*

CNES, Cnes [knɛs] (*abr de* **Centre national d'études spatiales**) *npr m French national space research centre.*

CNIL [knil] (*abr de* **Commission nationale de l'informatique et des libertés**) *npr f board which enforces data protection legislation.*

CNIT, Cnit [knit] (*abr de* **Centre national des industries et des techniques**) *npr m trade centre at la Défense near Paris.*

Cnossos [knɔsos] *npr* Knossos.

CNPF (*abr de* **Conseil national du patronat français**) *npr m national council of French employers,* ≃ CBI *UK*.

CNRS (*abr de* **Centre national de la recherche scientifique**) *npr m national organization for scientific research,* ≃ SRC *UK*.

> ***CNRS***
> A state-supported agency comprising intellectuals, scientists and engineers set up to do original research. Being a member is a prestigious, often lifelong, position.

CNTS (*abr de* **Centre national de transfusion sanguine**) *npr m national blood transfusion centre.*

CNUCED, Cnuced [knysɛd] (*abr de* **Conférence des Nations unies pour le commerce et l'industrie**) *npr f* UNCTAD.

coaccusé, e [kɔakyze] *nm, f* codefendant.

coach [kotʃ] (*pl* **coachs** *ou pl* **coaches**) *nm* coach SPORT trainer.

coacquéreur [kɔakerœr] *nm* joint purchaser.

coadjuteur [kɔadʒytœr] *nm* coadjutor.

coadministrateur, trice [kɔadministratœr, tris] *nm, f* co-director.

coagulant, e [kɔagylɑ̃, ɑ̃t] *adj* coagulating.
◆ **coagulant** *nm* coagulant.

coagulation [kɔagylasjɔ̃] *nf* [du sang] coagulation, coagulating *(U)* ■ [du lait] curdling *(U)*.

coaguler [3] [kɔagyle] *vi* & *vt* [sang] to coagulate ■ [lait] to curdle.
◆ **se coaguler** *vpi* [sang] to coagulate ■ [lait] to curdle.

coalescence [kɔalesɑ̃s] *nf* coalescence, coalescing *(U)*.

coaliser [3] [kɔalize] *vt* to make into a coalition.
◆ **se coaliser** *vpi* to form a coalition.

coalition [kɔalisjɔ̃] *nf* POLIT coalition ■ *péj* conspiracy ■ **gouvernement de ~** coalition government.

coaltar [kɔltar] *nm* coaltar ■ **être dans le ~** *fam fig* to be in a daze.

coassement [kɔasmɑ̃] *nm* croaking.

coasser [3] [kɔase] *vi* **1.** [grenouille] to croak **2.** *péj* [commère] to gossip.

coassocié, e [kɔasɔsje] *nm, f* copartner.

coauteur [kootœr] *nmf* **1.** LITTÉR coauthor, joint author **2.** DR accomplice.

coaxial, e, aux [kɔaksjal, o] *adj* coaxial.

COB, Cob [kɔb] (*abr de* **Commission des opérations de Bourse**) *npr f commission for supervision of stock exchange operations,* ≃ SIB *UK,* ≃ SEC *US.*

cobalt [kɔbalt] *nm* cobalt.

cobaye [kɔbaj] *nm* guinea pig ■ **servir de ~** to be used as a guinea pig.

cobelligérant, e [kɔbeliʒerɑ̃, ɑ̃t] *adj* & *nm, f* cobelligerent.

cobol [kɔbɔl] *nm* Cobol, COBOL.

cobra [kɔbra] *nm* cobra ■ **~ royal** king cobra.

coca [kɔka] *nf* **1.** BOT coca **2.** PHARM coca extract.
◆ **Coca**® *nm inv fam* [boisson] Coke®.

Coca-Cola® [kɔkakɔla] *nm inv* Coca-Cola®.

cocagne [kɔkaɲ] ◆ **de cocagne** *loc adj* : **époque/pays de ~** years/land of plenty.

cocaïne [kɔkain] *nf* cocaine.

cocaïnomane [kɔkainɔman] *nmf* cocaine addict.

cocarde [kɔkard] *nf* **1.** [en tissu] rosette ■ HIST cockade **2.** [signe - militaire] roundel ; [- sur une voiture officielle] official logo.

cocardier, ère [kɔkardje, ɛr] <> *adj péj* chauvinistic, jingoistic.
<> *nm, f* chauvinist, jingoist.

cocasse [kɔkas] *adj* comical.

cocasserie [kɔkasri] *nf* [d'une situation] funniness ■ **c'était d'une ~!** it was a scream!

coccinelle [kɔksinɛl] *nf* **1.** ZOOL ladybird *UK,* ladybug *US* **2.** [voiture] beetle *UK,* bug *US.*

coccyx [kɔksis] *nm* coccyx.

coche [kɔʃ] <> *nf* [encoche] notch.
<> *nm* [voiture] stage coach ■ **manquer** *OU* **rater** *OU* **louper le ~** to miss the boat.

cochenille [kɔʃnij] *nf* **1.** [insecte] **2.** [teinture] cochineal.

cocher[1] [kɔʃe] *nm* coach driver ■ **~ de fiacre** cabman.

cocher[2] [3] [kɔʃe] *vt* to tick (off) *UK,* to check (off) *US.*

cochère [kɔʃɛr] *adj f* : **porte ~** carriage entrance, porte cochère.

Cochinchine [kɔʃɛ̃ʃin] *npr f* : **(la) ~** Cochin China.

cochon, onne [kɔʃɔ̃, ɔn] *fam* <> *adj* **1.** [sale] dirty, filthy, disgusting **2.** [obscène] smutty, dirty, filthy.
<> *nm, f* **1.** [vicieux] lecher **2.** [personne sale] (filthy) pig ■ **oh, le petit ~!** [à un enfant] you mucky pup!
◆ **cochon** *nm* **1.** ZOOL pig ■ **~ de lait** suckling pig ■ **sale comme un ~** filthy dirty ■ **manger comme un ~** to eat like a pig ■ **amis** *OU* **copains comme ~s** as thick as thieves **2.** [homme méprisable] dirty dog ■ **~ qui s'en dédit!** you've got a deal! ■ **ben mon ~!** *fam* well, I'll be damned!
◆ **de cochon** *loc adj* [temps] foul, filthy ■ [caractère] foul.
◆ **cochon d'Inde** *nm* guinea pig.

cochonceté [kɔʃɔ̃ste] *nf fam* **1.** [saleté] : **faire des ~s** to make a filthy mess **2.** [nourriture] junk food **3.** [obscénité] piece of smut ■ **dire des ~s** to say dirty things.

cochonnaille [kɔʃɔnaj] *nf* pork products ■ **des ~s pendaient au plafond** sausages and hams were hanging from the ceiling.

cochonner [3] [kɔʃɔne] <> *vt fam* [dessin, chambre] to make a mess of.
<> *vi* [truie] to pig.

cochonnerie [kɔʃɔnri] *nf fam* **1.** [chose médiocre] rubbish *(U) UK,* trash *(U) US* ■ [nourriture - mal préparée] pigswill *(U)* ; [- de mauvaise qualité] junk food *(U)* **2.** [saleté] mess *(U)* ■ **faire des ~s** to make a mess **3.** [obscénité] smut *(U)* ■ **dire des ~s** to say filthy things **4.** [action déloyale] dirty trick **5.** [dans des exclamations] : **~ de : ~ de voiture!/de brouillard!** damn this car!/this fog!

cochonnet [kɔʃɔnɛ] *nm* **1.** [aux boules] jack **2.** [porcelet] piglet.

cocker [kɔkɛr] *nm* cocker spaniel.

cockpit [kɔkpit] *nm* cockpit.

cocktail [kɔktɛl] *nm* **1.** [boisson] cocktail ■ [réception] cocktail party **2.** [mélange] mix, mixture **3.** ARM : **~ Molotov** Molotov cocktail.

coco [koko] *nm* **1.** *fam* [tête] nut ■ **il a rien dans le ~!** he's got nothing between the ears! **2.** *fam* [individu] : **un drôle de ~** *péj* a shady customer ■ **c'est un joli ~!** *iron* what a charming individual! **3.** *fam* [en appellatif - à un adulte] love *UK,* honey *US* ; [- à un enfant] sweetie **4.** *langage enfantin* [œuf] egg **5.** *fam péj* [communiste] commie **6.** TEXT coir.

cocoler [3] [kɔkɔle] *vt Suisse* to cosset.

cocon [kɔkɔ̃] *nm* cocoon ■ **vivre dans un ~** *fig* to live a cocooned *OU* sheltered existence, to live in a cocoon ■ **s'enfermer** *OU* **rester dans son ~** *fig* to stay in one's shell.

cocooning [kɔkuniŋ] *nm* cocooning *US* ■ **on a fait du ~ ce week-end** we had a quiet time at home this weekend.

cocorico [kɔkɔriko] *nm* **1.** *pr* cock-a-doodle-doo ■ **faire ~** to crow **2.** *fig expression of French national pride* ■ **~!** three cheers for France!

cocotier [kɔkɔtje] *nm* coconut palm.

cocotte [kɔkɔt] *nf* **1.** [casserole] casserole dish ■ **cuire à la ~** to casserole **2.** *langage enfantin* [poule] hen ■ **~ en papier** paper bird **3.** [en appellatif] darling, love *UK,* honey *US* **4.** *péj* [femme] tart ■ **sentir** *OU* **puer la ~** to stink of cheap perfume.
◆ **en cocotte** *loc adj* [œuf] coddled.

Cocotte-Minute® [kɔkɔtminyt] *nf* pressure cooker.
◆ **à la Cocotte-Minute**® <> *loc adj* pressure-cooked.
<> *loc adv* [cuit] in a pressure cooker.

cocotter [3] [kɔkɔte] *vi fam péj* to stink ■ **ça cocotte!** it stinks!

cocu, e [kɔky] *fam* <> *adj* : **il est ~** his wife's been unfaithful to him.
<> *nm, f* **1.** [conjoint trompé] deceived husband (*f* wife) ■ **elle l'a fait ~** she was unfaithful to him **2.** [dupe] sucker.

cocufier [3] [kɔkyfje] *vt fam* to be unfaithful to.

codage [kɔdaʒ] *nm* **1.** [chiffrement] coding **2.** LING encoding.

code [kɔd] *nm* **1.** [ensemble de lois] code ■ **le ~ (civil)** the civil code ■ **~ de commerce** commercial law ■ **~ maritime** navigation laws ■ **~ pénal** penal code ■ **~ de la route** Highway Code *UK,* rules of the road *US* ■ **~ du travail** labour legislation **2.** [normes] code ■ **~ de la politesse** code of good manners **3.** [ensemble de conventions] code ■ **~ international de signaux** NAUT International Code ■ **~ télégraphique** telegraphic code ■ **~ des transmissions** signal *OU* signalling code

4. [groupe de symboles] code ❯ ~ **alphanumérique/binaire** alphanumeric/binary code ▪ ~ **(à) barres** bar code ▪ ~ **confidentiel** [d'une carte de crédit] personal identification number, PIN ▪ ~ **d'entrée** [sur une porte] door code ▪ ~ **postal** post *UK OU* zip *US* code
5. [manuel] code-book ▪ ~ **de déchiffrement** code-book
6. LING language
7. SC : ~ **génétique** genetic code.
◆ **codes** *nmpl* AUTO dipped headlights *UK*, low beams *US*.
◆ **en code** *loc adv* **1.** [sous forme chiffrée] in code ▪ **mettre qqch en ~** to cipher *ou* to code sthg
2. AUTO : **se mettre en ~** to dip one's headlights *UK*, to put on the low beams *US*.

CODE POSTAL

A sequence of five numbers used for the automatic sorting of mail. The first two digits of a French postcode correspond to the code number of the ***département***.

codé, e [kɔde] *adj* encoded, coded ▪ **générateur d'impulsions ~es** pulse coder ▪ **message ~** cryptogram ▪ **langage ~** secret language.

code-barres [kɔdbar] (*pl* **codes-barres**) *nm* bar code.

codébiteur, trice [kɔdebitœr, tris] *nm, f* joint debtor.

codéine [kɔdein] *nf* codeine.

codemandeur, eresse [kɔdəmɑ̃dœr, drɛs] *nm, f* joint plaintiff.

coder [3] [kɔde] *vt* **1.** [chiffrer] to code, to encipher **2.** LING to encode.

codétenteur, trice [kɔdetɑ̃tœr, tris] *nm, f* joint holder.

codétenu, e [kɔdetny] *nm, f* fellow-prisoner.

codeur, euse [kɔdœr, øz] *nm, f* coder.
◆ **codeur** *nm* coding machine.

Codévi [kɔdevi] (*abr de* **compte pour le développement industriel**) *nm savings account, money from which is invested in industrial development.*

codex *nm* : ~ **pharmaceutique** pharmacopœia.

codicille [kɔdisil] *nm* DR codicil.

codificateur, trice [kɔdifikatœr, tris] ◇ *adj* codifying. ◇ *nm, f* codifier.

codification [kɔdifikasjɔ̃] *nf* **1.** [d'une profession, d'un système] codification **2.** DR classification of laws.

codifier [9] [kɔdifje] *vt* **1.** [pratique, profession] to codify **2.** DR to classify.

codirecteur, trice [kɔdirɛktœr, tris] *nm, f* joint manager.

codiriger [17] [kɔdiriʒe] *vt* : ~ **qqch** to manage sthg together *ou* jointly.

coéditer [3] [kɔedite] *vt* to copublish.

coéditeur, trice [kɔeditœr, tris] ◇ *adj* copublishing. ◇ *nm, f* copublisher.

coédition [kɔedisjɔ̃] *nf* copublication.

coefficient [kɔefisjɑ̃] *nm* **1.** MATH & PHYS coefficient ▪ ~ **multiplicateur** multiplying factor ▪ ~ **numérique** numerical coefficient **2.** [proportion] rating, ratio ▪ ~ **d'exploitation/de perte** operating/loss ratio **3.** [valeur] weight, weighting ▪ **l'anglais est affecté du ~ 3** English will be weighted at a rate equal to 300%.

COEFFICIENT

In *baccalauréat* examinations, the grade for each subject is multiplied by a ***coefficient*** which is determined by the type of *baccalauréat* chosen. For a *bac S*, which has a scientific bias, the coefficient for maths will be higher than the coefficient for philosophy, for example.

cœliochirurgie [seljɔʃiryrʒi] *nf* MÉD laparoscopic *ou* celioscopic surgery, celiosurgery.

cœlioscopie [seljɔskɔpi] *nf* coelioscopy.

coéquipier, ère [kɔekipje, ɛr] *nm, f* teammate.

coercitif, ive [kɔɛrsitif, iv] *adj* coercive.

coercition [kɔɛrsisjɔ̃] *nf* coercion.

cœur [kœr] *nm*

A. ORGANE
B. SYMBOLE DE L'AFFECTIVITÉ
C. PERSONNE
D. CENTRE
E. OBJET EN FORME DE CŒUR

A. ORGANE

1. ANAT heart ▪ **une balle en plein ~** a bullet through the heart ▪ **il est malade du ~** he's got a heart condition ❯ **ça m'a donné** *ou* **j'ai eu un coup au ~** it really made me jump ▪ **beau** *ou* **joli** *ou* **mignon comme un ~** as pretty as a picture ▪ **tenir qqn contre son ~** to hold sb to one's bosom *litt*
2. [estomac] : **avoir le ~ au bord des lèvres** to feel queasy *ou* sick ▪ **avoir mal au ~** to feel sick ▪ **ça me fait mal au ~** it breaks my heart ▪ **ça me ferait mal au ~de devoir le lui laisser!** *fam* I'd hate to have to leave it to him! ▪ **lever** *ou* **soulever le ~ à qqn** to sicken sb, to turn sb's stomach ▪ **un spectacle à vous lever** *ou* **soulever le ~** a nauseating *ou* sickening sight ▪ **pour voir ce reportage il faut avoir le ~ bien accroché** this report is not for the squeamish

B. SYMBOLE DE L'AFFECTIVITÉ

1. [pensées, for intérieur] heart ▪ **ouvrir son ~ à qqn** to open one's heart to sb ▪ **en avoir le ~ net : je veux en avoir le ~ net** I want to know *ou* to find out the truth
2. [énergie, courage] courage ▪ **le ~ lui a manqué** his courage failed him ▪ **tu n'aurais pas le ~ de la renvoyer!** you wouldn't have the heart to fire her! ❯ **il n'avait pas le ~ à l'ouvrage** his heart wasn't in it ▪ **avoir du ~ au ventre** to be courageous ▪ **elle adore son travail, elle y met du ~** she loves her work, she really puts her heart (and soul) into it ▪ **allez, haut les ~s!** come on, chin up!
3. [humeur] : **il est parti le ~ joyeux** *ou* **gai** he left in a cheerful mood ▪ **d'un ~ léger** light-heartedly ❯ **avoir le ~ à faire qqch** to be in the mood to do *ou* to feel like doing sthg ▪ **ils travaillent, mais le ~ n'y est pas** they're working but their hearts aren't in it ▪ **si le ~ t'en dit** if you feel like it, if the fancy takes you
4. [charité, bonté] : **avoir du** *ou* **bon ~** to be kind *ou* kind-hearted ▪ **tu n'as pas de ~!** you're heartless!, you have no heart! ▪ **ton bon ~ te perdra!** you're too kind-hearted for your own good! ▪ **c'était un homme au grand ~** *ou* **de ~** he was a good man ❯ **il a un ~ gros comme ça** *fam* he'd give you the shirt off his back ▪ **avoir le ~ sur la main** to be very generous ▪ **avoir un ~ d'or** to have a heart of gold ▪ **avoir le ~ dur** *ou* **sec, avoir un ~ de pierre** to have a heart of stone ▪ **à vot' bon ~ (M'sieurs-Dames)** spare us a few pence *UK ou* a dime *US*
5. [siège des émotions, de l'amour] heart ▪ **laisser parler son ~** to let one's feelings come through ▪ **venir du ~** to come (straight) from the heart ▪ **des mots venus du (fond du) ~** heartfelt words ▪ **aller droit au ~ : vos paroles me sont allées droit au ~** your words went straight to my heart ▪ **briser le ~ à qqn** to break sb's heart ▪ **cela me brise le ~ de le voir dans cet état** it breaks my heart to see him in such a state ▪ **c'était à vous briser** *ou* **fendre le ~** it was heartbreaking *ou* heartrending ▪ **cela chauffe** *ou* **réchauffe le ~** it warms the cockles of your heart, it's heartwarming ▪ **avoir le ~ serré** to have a lump in one's throat ❯ **histoire de ~** love affair ▪ **ses problèmes de ~** the problems he has with his love life ▪ **avoir le ~ gros** to feel sad, to have a heavy heart ▪ **je ne le porte pas dans mon ~** *fam* I'm not particularly fond of him

C. PERSONNE

1. [personne ayant telle qualité] : **c'est un ~ d'or** he has a heart of gold ▪ **c'est un ~ dur** *ou* **sec** *ou* **de pierre** he has a heart of stone, he's heartless ❯ **à ~ vaillant rien d'impossible** *prov* where there's a will there's a way *prov*
2. [terme d'affection] darling, sweetheart

D. CENTRE

1. [d'un chou, d'une salade, d'un fromage] heart ▪ [d'un fruit, d'un réacteur nucléaire] core ▪ [d'une ville] heart, centre ❯ ~ **de lai-**

tue lettuce heart ▪ ~ de palmier palm heart ▪ ~ d'artichaut *pr* artichoke heart ▪ c'est un vrai ~ d'artichaut *fig* he/she is always falling in love
2. [d'un débat] central point

E. OBJET EN FORME DE CŒUR
JEUX : du ~ hearts ▪ dame/dix de ~ queen/ten of hearts ▪ jouer à *ou* du ~ to play hearts.
◆ **à cœur** *loc adv* **1.** [avec sérieux] : prendre les choses à ~ to take things to heart ▪ elle prend vraiment son travail à ~ she really takes her job seriously ▪ tenir à ~ à qqn : ce rôle me tient beaucoup à ~ this part means a lot to me ▪ avoir à ~ de faire qqch to be very eager to do sthg **2.** CULIN : fromage fait à ~ fully ripe cheese.
◆ **à cœur joie** *loc adv* : s'en donner à ~ joie to have tremendous fun *ou* a tremendous time.
◆ **à cœur ouvert** ◇ *loc adj* [opération] open-heart *(modif)*.
◇ *loc adv* : parler à ~ ouvert à qqn to have a heart-to-heart (talk) with sb.
◆ **au cœur de** *loc prép* : au ~ de l'été at the height of summer ▪ au ~ de l'hiver in the depths of winter ▪ au ~ de la nuit in the *ou* at dead of night ▪ au ~ du Morvan in the heart of the Morvan region ▪ au ~ de la ville in the centre of town, in the town centre ▪ le sujet fut au ~ des débats this subject was central to the debate.
◆ **de bon cœur** *loc adv* [volontiers - donner] willingly ; [- rire, manger] heartily ; [- parler] readily ▪ il y est allé de bon ~ [en mangeant] he really tucked in ; [en travaillant] he really got stuck in *ou* he went at it with a will ▪ c'est de bon ~ : ne me remerciez pas, c'est de bon ~ (que je vous ai aidé) no need to thank me, it was a pleasure (helping you).
◆ **de tout cœur** *loc adv* wholeheartedly ▪ être de tout ~ avec qqn [condoléances] to sympathize wholeheartedly with sb ▪ je ne pourrai assister à votre mariage mais je serai de tout ~ avec vous I won't be able to attend your wedding but I'll be with you in spirit.
◆ **de tout mon cœur, de tout son cœur** *etc loc adv* **1.** [sincèrement - aimer, remercier] with all my/his *etc* heart, from the bottom of my/his *etc* heart ; [- féliciter] warmly, wholeheartedly ▪ rire de tout son ~ to laugh heartily *ou* one's head off **2.** [énergiquement] : y aller de tout son ~ *fam* to go at it hammer and tongs, to give it all one's got.
◆ **en cœur** *loc adj* [bouche, pendentif] heart-shaped.
◆ **par cœur** *loc adv* [apprendre, connaître] by heart ▪ connaître qqn par ~ to know sb inside out.
◆ **sans cœur** *loc adj* heartless.
◆ **sur le cœur** *loc adv* : la mousse au chocolat m'est restée sur le ~ *pr* the chocolate mousse made me feel sick ▪ ses critiques me sont restées *ou* me pèsent sur le ~ I still haven't got over the way she criticized me ▪ avoir qqch sur le ~ to have sthg on one's mind ▪ en avoir gros sur le ~ *fam* to be really upset.

coexistence [kɔɛgzistɑ̃s] *nf* coexistence ▪ ~ pacifique peaceful coexistence.

coexister [3] [kɔɛgziste] *vi* : ~ (avec) to coexist (with).

COFACE [kɔfas] (*abr de* **Compagnie française d'assurances pour le commerce extérieur**) *npr f export insurance company*, ≃ ECGD.

coffrage [kɔfraʒ] *nm* **1.** MIN & TRAV PUB coffering, lining **2.** CONSTR casing.

coffre [kɔfr] *nm* **1.** [caisse] box, chest ▪ ~ à jouets toybox **2.** NAUT locker ▪ ~ d'amarrage mooring buoy, trunk buoy **3.** AUTO boot *UK*, trunk *US* ▪ ~ de rangement [d'un camion] storage compartment ▪ ~ à bagages [d'un autocar] baggage *ou* luggage compartment **4.** [coffre-fort] safe, strongbox ▪ les ~s de l'État the coffers of the State ‖ BANQUE safe-deposit box ▪ ~ de nuit night safe **5.** ZOOL [poisson] coffer-fish **6.** *fam* [poitrine] chest ▪ [voix] (big) voice ▪ avoir du ~ [du souffle] to have a good pair of lungs.

coffre-fort [kɔfrəfɔr] (*pl* **coffres-forts**) *nm* safe, strongbox.

coffrer [3] [kɔfre] *vt* **1.** *fam* [emprisonner] to put behind bars ▪ se faire ~ to be sent down **2.** MIN to coffer **3.** CONSTR to form.

coffret [kɔfrɛ] *nm* **1.** [petit coffre] box, case ▪ dans un ~ cadeau in a gift box ➊ ~ à bijoux jewellery box **2.** [cabinet] cabinet.
◆ **en coffret** *loc adv* : présenté *ou* vendu en ~ sold in a box ▪ la présentation en ~ est ce qui fait le succès de ce produit this item sells so well because it comes in a presentation box.

cofinancer [16] [kɔfinɑ̃se] *vt* to cofinance, to finance jointly.

cofondateur, trice [kɔfɔ̃datœr, tris] *nm, f* cofounder.

cogérance [kɔʒerɑ̃s] *nf* joint management.

cogérant, e [kɔʒerɑ̃, ɑ̃t] *nm, f* joint manager (*f* manageress).

cogérer [18] [kɔʒere] *vt* to manage jointly.

cogestion [kɔʒɛstjɔ̃] *nf* joint management *ou* administration.

cogitation [kɔʒitasjɔ̃] *nf* **hum** cogitation *(U)*, pondering *(U)* ▪ je te laisse à tes ~s I'll leave you to think things over.

cogiter [3] [kɔʒite] *hum* ◇ *vi* to cogitate ▪ il faut que je cogite! I must put my thinking cap on!
◇ *vt* to ponder.

cognac [kɔɲak] *nm* [gén] brandy ▪ [de Cognac] Cognac.

cognassier [kɔɲasje] *nm* quince tree.

cognée [kɔɲe] *nf* axe, hatchet.

cogner [3] [kɔɲe] ◇ *vi* **1.** [heurter] to bang, to knock ▪ son cœur cognait dans sa poitrine his heart was thumping ▪ ~ à la fenêtre [fort] to knock on the window ; [légèrement] to tap on the window **2.** *fam* [user de violence] : ~ sur qqn to beat sb up ▪ ça va ~ things are going to get rough.
◇ *vt* **1.** [entrer en collision avec] to bang *ou* to knock *ou* to smash into **2.** *fam* [battre] to whack, to wallop.
◆ **se cogner** ◇ *vpi* **1.** [se faire mal] : je me suis cogné I banged into something **2.** *loc* il s'en cogne△ he doesn't give a damn *ou* monkey's△ *UK*.
◇ *vpt* : se ~ le coude to hit *ou* to bang one's elbow.

cognitif, ive [kɔgnitif, iv] *adj* cognitive.

cognition [kɔgnisjɔ̃] *nf* cognitive processes, cognition.

cohabitation [kɔabitasjɔ̃] *nf* **1.** [vie commune] cohabitation, cohabiting, living together **2.** POLIT *coexistence of an elected head of state and an opposition parliamentary majority.*

LA COHABITATION

Describes a situation whereby the French president represents one political party and the government another. This term was first used during the period 1986-1988, when the socialist president (François Mitterrand) had a right-wing prime minister (Jacques Chirac), following the victory of the RPR in the legislative elections.

cohabiter [3] [kɔabite] *vi* **1.** [partenaires] to cohabit, to live together ▪ [amis] to live together ▪ ~ avec qqn to live with sb **2.** [coexister] to coexist ▪ faire ~ deux théories to reconcile two theories.

cohérence [kɔerɑ̃s] *nf* [gén - OPT] coherence ▪ manque de ~ inconsistency.

cohérent, e [kɔerɑ̃, ɑ̃t] *adj* **1.** [logique] coherent **2.** [fidèle à soi-même] consistent ▪ être ~ to be true to o.s. **3.** OPT coherent.

cohéritier, ère [kɔeritje, ɛr] *nm, f* co-heir (*f* co-heiress).

cohésif, ive [kɔezif, iv] *adj* cohesive.

cohésion [kɔezjɔ̃] *nf* **1.** [solidarité] cohesion, cohesiveness ▪ la ~ du groupe the way the members of the group stick together **2.** [d'un corps, de molécules] cohesion.

cohorte [kɔɔrt] *nf* **1.** ANTIQ cohort **2.** *péj* [foule] : une ~ de hordes *ou* droves of **3.** SOCIOL population.

cohue [kɔy] *nf* **1.** [foule] crowd, throng **2.** [bousculade] : dans la ~ amidst the general pushing and shoving, in the (general) melee.

coi, coite [kwa, kwat] *adj* speechless ▪ **en rester ~** to be speechless ▪ **se tenir ~** to keep quiet.

coiffe [kwaf] *nf* **1.** [vêtement - de paysanne] (traditional) headdress ; [- de nonne] (nun's) headdress ; ▪ [garniture de chapeau] lining **2.** ASTRONAUT & BOT cap **3.** ANAT caul.

coiffer [3] [kwafe] *vt* **1.** [cheveux - avec un peigne] to comb ; [- avec une brosse] to brush ▪ **l'enfant coiffait la poupée** the child was combing *ou* brushing the doll's hair ▪ **elle était bien coiffée** her hair looked nice ▪ **tu es horriblement mal coiffé** your hair's all over the place ▪ **cheveux faciles/difficiles à ~** manageable/unmanageable hair **2.** [réaliser la coiffure de] : **elle s'est fait ~ par Paolo, c'est Paolo qui l'a coiffée** she had her hair done by Paolo **3.** [chapeauter] to cover the head of ▪ **il était coiffé d'une casquette** he was wearing a cap ▪ **il a coiffé la statue d'une casquette** he put a cap on the statue **4.** [mettre sur sa tête] to put on ▪ **~ la mitre** to be ordained a bishop **5.** *litt* [couvrir] : **la neige coiffait les sommets** the mountain-tops were covered in snow **6.** [diriger] to control ▪ **elle coiffe plusieurs services** she's in charge of several departments **7.** *loc* **~ qqn au** *ou* **sur le poteau** to pip sb at the post *UK*, to pass sb up *US* ▪ **se faire ~ au poteau** to be pipped at the post *UK*, to be nosed out.

se coiffer *vp (emploi réfléchi)* **1.** [se peigner] to comb one's hair ▪ [arranger ses cheveux] to do one's hair **2.** [mettre un chapeau] to put a hat on.

coiffeur, euse [kwafœr, øz] *nm, f* hairdresser, hair stylist ▪ **aller chez le ~** to go to the hairdresser's ➊ **~ pour hommes** gentlemen's hairdresser, barber ▪ **~ pour dames** ladies' hairdresser.

coiffeuse *nf* dressing-table.

coiffure [kwafyr] *nf* **1.** [coupe] hairdo, hairstyle ▪ **se faire faire une nouvelle ~** to have one's hair styled *ou* restyled ➊ **~ à la garçonne** Eton crop *UK*, urchin cut *US* ▪ **~ à la Jeanne d'Arc** pageboy haircut **2.** [technique] : **la ~** hairdressing **3.** [chapeau] headdress.

coin [kwɛ̃] *nm* **1.** [angle] corner ▪ **le ~ de la rue** the corner of the street ▪ **à un ~ de rue** on a street-corner ➊ **un ~ couloir/fenêtre** an aisle/a window seat ▪ **à chaque ~ de rue, à tous les ~s de rue** all over the place, everywhere ▪ **manger sur un ~ de table** to eat a hasty meal ▪ **au ~ du feu** *pr* by the fireside ▪ **rester au ~ du feu** *fig* to stay at home ▪ **au ~ d'un bois** *pr* somewhere in a wood ; *fig* in a lonely place

2. [commissure - des lèvres, de l'œil] corner ▪ **du ~ de l'œil** [regarder, surveiller] out of the corner of one's eye

3. [endroit quelconque] place, spot ▪ **dans un ~ de la maison** somewhere in the house ▪ **j'ai dû laisser mon livre dans un ~** I must have left my book somewhere or other ▪ **dans un ~ de sa mémoire** in a corner of his memory ▪ **bon ~ : il connaît les bons ~s** he knows all the right places ▮ [espace réservé] : **le ~ des bricoleurs** COMM the do-it-yourself department ▪ *(suivi d'un n; avec ou sans trait d'union)* **~ cuisine** kitchen recess ▪ **~ repas** *ou* **salle à manger** dining area ▮ [à la campagne] corner, place, spot ▪ **un petit ~ tranquille à la campagne** a quiet spot in the country ▪ **un ~ perdu** [isolé] an isolated spot ; [arriéré] a godforsaken place *péj* ➊ **chercher dans tous les ~s et les recoins** to look in every nook and cranny ▪ **connaître qqch dans les ~s** to know sthg like the back of one's hand ▪ **le petit ~** *fam euphém* the smallest room

4. [parcelle] patch, plot ▪ **il reste un ~ de ciel bleu** there's still a patch of blue sky

5. IMPR [forme] die ▪ [poinçon] stamp, hallmark

6. [cale] wedge.

au coin *loc adv* [de la rue] on *ou* at the corner ▪ **mettre un enfant au ~** to make a child stand in the corner (as punishment).

dans le coin *loc adv* [dans le quartier - ici] locally, around here ; [- là-bas] locally, around there ▪ **et Victor? – il est dans le ~** where's Victor? – somewhere around ▪ **je passais dans le ~ et j'ai eu envie de venir te voir** I was in the area and I felt like dropping in (on you).

dans son coin *loc adv* : **laisser qqn dans son ~** to leave sb alone ▪ **rester dans son ~** to keep oneself to oneself.

de coin *loc adj* [étagère] corner *(modif)*.

du coin *loc adj* [commerce] local ▪ **les gens du ~** [ici] people who live round here, the locals ; [là-bas] people who live there, the locals ▪ **désolé, je ne suis pas du ~** sorry, I'm not from around here.

en coin ◇ *loc adj* [regard] sidelong ▪ **un sourire en ~** a half-smile.

◇ *loc adv* [regarder, observer] sideways ▪ **sourire en ~** to give a half-smile.

coincé, e [kwɛ̃se] *adj fam* **1.** *péj* [inhibé] repressed, hung-up **2.** [mal à l'aise] tense, uneasy.

coincer [16] [kwɛ̃se] ◇ *vt* **1.** [immobiliser - volontairement] to wedge ; [- accidentellement] to stick, to jam ▪ **j'ai coincé la fermeture de ma robe** I got the zip of my dress stuck **2.** *fam* [attraper] to corner, to nab, to collar ▪ **se faire ~** to get nabbed **3.** *fam* [retenir] : **plus de trains? je suis coincé, maintenant!** the last train's gone? I'm in a real fix now! ▪ **elle est coincée entre ses convictions et les exigences de la situation** she's torn between her convictions and the demands of the situation **4.** [mettre en difficulté - par une question] to catch out *(sép) UK*, to put on the spot ▪ **là, ils t'ont coincé!** they've got you there!

◇ *vi* **1.** [être calé] : **c'est la chemise bleue qui coince au fond du tiroir** the blue shirt at the back is making the drawer jam **2.** [être entravé] to stick ▪ **les négociations coincent** the discussions have come to a sticking point ▪ **ça coince (quelque part)** *fam* there's a hitch somewhere.

se coincer ◇ *vpi* [se bloquer - clef, fermeture] to jam, to stick.

◇ *vpt* : **se ~ la main/le pied** to have one's hand/foot caught.

coïncidence [kɔɛ̃sidɑ̃s] *nf* **1.** [hasard] chance ▪ **quelle ~ de vous voir ici!** what a coincidence seeing you here! ▪ **c'est (une) pure ~** it's purely coincidental **2.** MATH coincidence.

par coïncidence *loc adv* coincidentally, by coincidence ▪ **par ~, il était là aussi** by coincidence *ou* chance, he was there as well.

coïncident, e [kɔɛ̃sidɑ̃, ɑ̃t] *adj* **1.** [dans l'espace] coextensive, coincident **2.** [dans le temps] concomitant, simultaneous.

coïncider [3] [kɔɛ̃side] *vi* **1.** [s'ajuster l'un sur l'autre] to line up, to coincide, to be coextensive *sout* ▪ **faites ~ les deux triangles** line up the two triangles (so that they coincide) **2.** [se produire ensemble] to coincide ▪ **nos anniversaires coïncident** our birthdays fall on the same day ▪ **j'ai essayé de faire ~ ma visite avec le début du festival** I tried to make my visit coincide with the beginning of the festival **3.** [concorder] to concord ▪ **les deux témoignages coïncident** the two statements are consistent.

coin-coin [kwɛ̃kwɛ̃] ◇ *nm inv* quacking.

◇ *onomat* quack quack.

coïnculpé, e [koɛ̃kylpe] *nm, f* co-defendant.

coing [kwɛ̃] *nm* quince.

coït [kɔit] *nm* coitus ▪ **~ interrompu** coitus interruptus.

coite [kwat] *f* ▻ **coi.**

coke [kɔk] ◇ *nm* coke.

◇ *nf fam* coke.

cokéfier [9] [kɔkefje] *vt* to coke.

cokerie [kɔkri] *nf* coking plant.

col [kɔl] *nm* **1.** COUT collar ▪ **~ blanc/bleu** white-collar/blue-collar worker ▪ **~ cassé** wing collar ▪ **~ châle** shawl collar ▪ **~ cheminée** turtleneck ▪ **~ chemisier** shirt collar ▪ **~ Claudine** Peter Pan collar ▪ **~ Mao** Mao collar ▪ **~ marin** sailor's collar ▪ **~ officier** mandarin collar ▪ **(pull à) ~ roulé** polo-neck sweater ▪ **se pousser du** *ou* **se hausser du** *ou* **se hausser le ~** *litt* to blow one's own trumpet ▪ **faux ~** *pr* detachable collar ; [de la bière] head **2.** [d'une bouteille] neck **3.** ANAT cervix, neck ▪ **~ du fémur** neck of the thighbone ▪ **~ de l'utérus** neck of the womb ▪ **cancer du ~ de l'utérus** cervical cancer **4.** GÉOGR pass, col.

col. = **colonne.**

Col. (*abr écrite de* **Colonel**) Col.

cola [kɔla] = **kola.**

colchique [kɔlʃik] *nm* colchicum ▪ **~ d'automne** autumn crocus.

cold-cream [kɔldkrim] (*pl* **cold-creams**) *nm* cold cream.

col-de-cygne [kɔldəsiɲ] (*pl* **cols-de-cygne**) *nm* swan-neck.

colégataire [kɔlegatɛr] *nmf* joint legatee.

coléoptère [kɔleɔptɛr] *nm* member of the Coleoptera.

colère [kɔlɛr] <> *nf* **1.** [mauvaise humeur] anger, rage ▪ **passer sa ~ sur qqn** to take out one's bad temper on sb ▪ **avec ~** angrily, in anger ◐ **~ bleue** *OU* **noire** towering rage ▪ **la ~ est mauvaise conseillère** *prov* anger and haste hinder good counsel **2.** [crise] fit of anger *ou* rage ▪ [d'un enfant] tantrum ▪ **piquer** *fam* *OU* **faire une ~** [adulte] to fly into a temper ; [enfant] to have *ou* to throw a tantrum ▪ **entrer dans une violente ~** to fly into a violent rage **3.** *litt* [des éléments, des dieux] wrath.
<> *adj* *vieilli* **être ~** to be bad-tempered.
◆ **en colère** *loc adj* angry, livid, mad ▪ **être en ~ contre qqn** to be angry with sb *UK OU* at sb *US* ▪ **mettre qqn en ~** to make sb angry ▪ **se mettre en ~** to flare up, to lose one's temper.

coléreux, euse [kɔlerø, øz], **colérique** [kɔlerik] *adj* [personne] irritable, quick-tempered ▪ **il a un caractère très ~** he's got quite a temper.

colibacille [kɔlibasil] *nm* colon bacillus.

colibacillose [kɔlibasiloz] *nf* colibacillosis.

colibri [kɔlibri] *nm* humming bird, colibri.

colifichet [kɔlifiʃɛ] *nm* knick-knack, trinket ▪ **vendre des ~s** to sell fancy goods.

colimaçon [kɔlimasɔ̃] *nm* snail.

colin [kɔlɛ̃] *nm* [lieu noir] coley *UK*, pollock *US* ▪ [lieu jaune] pollack ▪ [merlan] whiting ▪ [merlu] hake.

colin-maillard [kɔlɛ̃majar] (*pl* **colin-maillards**) *nm* blind man's buff.

colique [kɔlik] *nf* **1.** *fam* [diarrhée] diarrhoea ▪ **avoir la ~** to have diarrhoea **2.** MÉD [douleur] colic, stomach ache ▪ **~s néphrétiques** renal colic ; [chez le nourrisson] gripes **3.** △ [contrariété] hassle, drag.

colis [kɔli] *nm* package, packet, parcel ▪ **~ piégé** parcel *UK OU* package *US* bomb ▪ **~ postal** postal packet.

Colisée [kɔlize] *npr m* : **le ~** the Colosseum.

Colissimo® [kɔlisimo] *nm express parcel service run by the French Post Office.*

colistier, ère [kɔlistje, ɛr] *nm, f* fellow candidate *(on a list or platform).*

colite [kɔlit] *nf* colitis.

coll. 1. = **collection 2.** (*abr écrite de* **collaborateurs**) ▪ **et ~** et al.

collabo [kɔlabo] *nmf* *péj* & HIST collaborationist.

collaborateur, trice [kɔlabɔratœr, tris] *nm, f* **1.** [aide] associate **2.** [membre du personnel] member of staff **3.** *péj* & HIST collaborator, collaborationist.

collaboration [kɔlabɔrasjɔ̃] *nf* **1.** [aide] collaboration, co-operation, help ▪ **en ~ étroite avec** in close co-operation with **2.** HIST [politique] collaborationist policy ▪ [période] collaboration.

collaborer [3] [kɔlabɔre] *vi* **1.** [participer] to participate ▪ **~ à** to take part *ou* to participate in ; PRESSE to write for, to contribute to, to be a contributor to **2.** *péj* & HIST to collaborate.

collage [kɔlaʒ] *nm* **1.** [fixation] gluing, sticking ▪ **~ des affiches** billposting, bill sticking ▪ **~ du papier peint** paperhanging **2.** ART collage **3.** ŒNOL fining **4.** INDUST sizing.

collagène [kɔlaʒɛn] *nm* collagen.

collant, e [kɔlɑ̃, ɑ̃t] *adj* **1.** [adhésif] adhesive, sticking ▪ [poisseux] sticky **2.** [moulant] tightfitting **3.** *fam péj* [importun] limpet-like ▪ **qu'il est ~!** [importun] he just won't leave you alone! ; [enfant] he's so clinging!, he won't give you a minute's peace!
◆ **collant** *nm* **1.** [bas] (pair of) tights, pantyhose *US (U)* **2.** [de danse] leotard.
◆ **collante** *nf arg scol* [convocation] *letter asking a student to present himself for an exam.*

collatéral, e, aux [kɔlateral, o] *adj* [de chaque côté] collateral *sout.*
◆ **collatéral, aux** *nm* **1.** ARCHIT aisle **2.** DR collateral relative.

collation [kɔlasjɔ̃] *nf* **1.** [repas] light meal, snack **2.** RELIG collation, conferral, conferment **3.** [de textes] collation.

collationner [3] [kɔlasjɔne] *vt* to collate.

colle [kɔl] *nf* **1.** [glu] glue, adhesive ▪ **~ à bois** wood glue ▪ **~ végétale** vegetable size **2.** *fam* [énigme] trick question, poser, teaser ▪ **poser une ~ à qqn** to set sb a poser ▪ **là, vous me posez une ~!** you've got me there! **3.** *arg scol* [examen] oral test ▪ [retenue] detention ▪ **avoir une ~** to get detention, to be kept in *ou* behind (after school) ▪ **mettre une ~ à qqn** to keep sb behind (in detention).
◆ **à la colle** *loc adv fam* **ils sont à la ~** they've shacked up together.

collecte [kɔlɛkt] *nf* **1.** [ramassage] collection ▪ **faire la ~ du lait** to collect milk *(from farms for transportation to the local creamery)* **2.** INFORM : **~ des données** data collection *ou* gathering **3.** [quête] collection ▪ **faire une ~** to collect money, to make a collection ▪ **je fais une ~ pour lui acheter un cadeau de notre part à toutes** I've started a kitty to buy her a present from us all.

collecter [4] [kɔlɛkte] *vt* [argent] to collect ▪ [lait, ordures] to collect, to pick up *(sép).*

collecteur, trice [kɔlɛktœr, tris] <> *adj* collecting.
<> *nm, f* ADMIN : **~ d'impôts** tax collector.
◆ **collecteur** *nm* **1.** ÉLECTR [lames] commutator **2.** MÉCAN manifold ▪ **~ d'admission** intake manifold ▪ **~ d'air** ÉLECTRON air-trap ▪ **~ d'échappement** AUTO exhaust manifold **3.** CULIN drip cup, juice collector cup **4.** [égout] main sewer.

collectif, ive [kɔlɛktif, iv] *adj* **1.** [en commun] collective, common **2.** [de masse] mass *(modif)*, public ▪ **suicide ~** mass suicide ▪ **licenciements ~s** mass redundancies ▪ **viol ~** gang rape **3.** TRANSP group *(modif)* **4.** GRAMM collective.
◆ **collectif** *nm* **1.** GRAMM collective noun **2.** FIN : **~ budgétaire** interim budget, extra credits **3.** [équipe] collective ▪ **ouvrage rédigé par un ~ sous la direction de Jean Dupont** by Jean Dupont et al.

collection [kɔlɛksjɔ̃] *nf* **1.** [collecte] collecting ▪ **il fait ~ de timbres** he collects stamps **2.** [ensemble de pièces] collection **3.** COMM [série - gén] line, collection ; [- de livres] collection, series ▪ **dans la ~ jeunesse** in the range of books for young readers ▪ **la ~ complète des œuvres de Victor Hugo** the collected works of Victor Hugo **4.** [vêtement] collection ▪ **les ~s** [présentations] fashion shows **5.** MÉD gathering.

collectionner [3] [kɔlɛksjɔne] *vt* **1.** [tableaux, timbres] to collect **2.** *hum* [avoir en quantité] : **il collectionne les ennuis** he's never out of trouble.

collectionneur, euse [kɔlɛksjɔnœr, øz] *nm, f* collector.

collective [kɔlɛktiv] *f* ⊳ **collectif.**

collectivement [kɔlɛktivmɑ̃] *adv* collectively ▪ **ils se sont élevés ~ contre la nouvelle loi** they protested as a group against the new law.

collectivisation [kɔlɛktivizasjɔ̃] *nf* collectivization, collectivizing.

collectiviser [3] [kɔlɛktivize] *vt* to collectivize.

collectivisme [kɔlɛktivism] *nm* collectivism.

collectiviste [kɔlɛktivist] *adj* & *nmf* collectivist.

collectivité [kɔlɛktivite] *nf* **1.** [société] community ▪ **dans l'intérêt de la ~** in the public interest **2.** ADMIN : **les ~s locales** [dans un État] local authorities ; [dans une fédération] federal authorities ▪ **~ d'outre-mer** (French) overseas territories ▪ **~ territoriale** (partially) autonomous region.

collège [kɔlɛʒ] *nm* **1.** ÉDUC school ■ **~ privé/technique** private/technical school ■ **~ d'enseignement secondaire = CES** ■ **le Collège de France** the Collège de France ‖ RELIG private school *(run by a religious organization)* **2.** [corps constitué] college **3.** ADMIN body ■ **~ électoral** body of electors, constituency.

LE COLLÈGE DE FRANCE

This place of learning near the Sorbonne holds public lectures given by prominent academics and specialists. It is not a university and does not confer degrees, although it is controlled by the Ministry of Education.

collégial, e, aux [kɔleʒjal, o] *adj* collegial, collegiate ■ **exercer un pouvoir ~** to rule collegially.
◆ **collégiale** *nf* RELIG collegiate church.

collégialité [kɔleʒjalite] *nf* collegiality, collegial structure *ou* authority.

collégien, enne [kɔleʒjɛ̃, ɛn] *nm, f* schoolkid, schoolboy (*f* schoolgirl) ➊ **tu me prends pour un ~?** do you think I was born yesterday?

collègue [kɔlɛg] *nmf* **1.** [employé] colleague, fellow-worker ■ **~ de bureau : je l'ai prêté à un ~ de bureau** I lent it to somebody at the office **2.** [homologue] opposite number, counterpart.

coller [3] [kɔle] ◇ *vt* **1.** [fixer - étiquette, timbre] to stick (down) ; [- tissu, bois] to glue (on) ; [- papier peint] to paste (up) ; [- affiche] to post, to stick up *(sép)*, to put up *(sép)*
2. [fermer - enveloppe] to close up *(sép)*, to stick down *(sép)*
3. [emmêler] to mat, to plaster ■ **les cheveux collés par la pluie** his hair plastered flat by the rain
4. [appuyer] to press ■ **~ son nez à la vitre** to press one's face to the window ■ **~ qqn au mur** to put sb against a wall
5. *fam* [suivre] to follow closely, to tag along behind ■ **la voiture nous colle de trop près** the car's keeping too close to us
6. *fam* ÉDUC [punir] to keep in *(sép)* ■ **se faire ~** to get a detention ‖ [refuser] : **se faire ~ à un examen** to fail an exam
7. *fam* [mettre - chose] to dump, to stick ; [- personne] to put, to stick ■ **ils l'ont collée en pension/en prison** they stuck her in a boarding school/put her in jail ■ **je vais lui ~ mon poing sur la figure!** I'm going to thump him on the nose!
8. *fam* [imposer] to foist on, to saddle with ■ **~ qqch/qqn à qqn : ils m'ont collé le bébé pour la semaine** they've lumbered UK *ou* saddled me with the baby for a week ‖ [obliger à devenir] : **ils l'ont collé responsable de la rubrique sportive** they saddled him with the sports editorship
9. ŒNOL to fine
10. INDUST to size
11. INFORM to paste.
◇ *vi* **1.** [adhérer - timbre] to stick ■ **le caramel colle aux dents** toffee sticks to your teeth ■ [être poisseux] to be sticky ■ **avoir les doigts qui collent** to have sticky fingers ➊ **~ aux basques** *ou* **aux semelles de qqn** *fam* to stick to sb like glue ■ **~ au derrière** *fam ou* **aux fesses**△ **de qqn** *fig* to stick to sb like a limpet
2. [vêtement] to cling ■ **~ à la peau de qqn** *pr* to cling to sb ; *fig* to be inherent to *ou* innate in sb
3. *fam* [aller bien] : **ça colle!** it's OK!, right-ho! UK ■ **ça ne colle pas** it doesn't work, something's wrong ■ **ça ne colle pas pour demain soir** tomorrow night's off ■ **ça ne colle pas entre eux** they're not hitting it off very well ■ **ça ne colle pas avec son caractère** it's just not like him ■ **les faits ne collent pas les uns avec les autres** the facts don't make sense.
◆ **coller à** *v+prép* [respecter] to be faithful to ■ **~ à son sujet** to stick to one's subject ■ **~ à la réalité** to be true to life ■ **une émission qui colle à l'actualité** a programme that keeps up with current events.
◆ **se coller** ◇ *vpi* **1.** [se blottir] : **se ~ à qqn** to snuggle up *ou* to cling to sb, to hug sb ■ **se ~ à** *ou* **contre un mur pour ne pas être vu** to press o.s. up against a wall in order not to be seen
2. *fam* [s'installer] : **les enfants se sont collés devant la télé** the children plonked themselves down in front of the TV
3. *loc* **se ~ ensemble**△ [vivre ensemble] to shack up together ■ **s'y ~** *fam* [s'atteler à un problème, une tâche] to make an effort to do sthg, to set about doing sthg.
◇ *vpt fam* **se ~ qqch** to take sthg on ■ **il s'est collé tout Proust pour l'examen** he got through all of Proust for the exam.

collerette [kɔlrɛt] *nf* **1.** COUT collar, collarette ■ **~ de dentelle** lace collar ‖ HIST frill, ruff **2.** CULIN (paper) frill **3.** [sur une bouteille] neck-band label **4.** MÉCAN flange **5.** BOT annulus.

collet [kɔlɛ] *nm* **1.** [col] collar ■ **mettre la main au ~ de qqn** to get hold of sb, to collar sb ■ **prendre qqn au ~** *pr* to seize *ou* to grab sb by the neck ; *fig* to catch sb in the act ➊ **être ~ monté** to be straight-laced **2.** [piège] noose, snare ■ **prendre un lapin au ~** to snare a rabbit **3.** CULIN neck **4.** ANAT neck **5.** BOT annulus, ring.

colleter [27] [kɔlte] *vt* to seize by the collar ■ **se faire ~** to be collared *ou* nabbed.
◆ **se colleter** *vp (emploi réciproque)* to fight.
◆ **se colleter avec** *vp+prép* to struggle *ou* to wrestle with.

colleur, euse [kɔlœr, øz] *nm, f* : **~ d'affiches** billsticker, bill poster.
◆ **colleuse** *nf* **1.** CINÉ splicer, splicing unit **2.** IMPR pasting machine **3.** PHOTO mounting press.

collier [kɔlje] *nm* **1.** JOAILL necklace, necklet ■ **~ de perles** string of pearls **2.** [parure] collar ■ **~ de fleurs** garland of flowers **3.** [courroie - pour chien, chat] collar ■ **~ antipuces** flea collar ■ **~ de cheval** horse-collar ■ *fig* **donner un coup de ~** to make a special effort ■ **reprendre le ~** to get back into harness *ou* to the treadmill *péj* **4.** MÉCAN clip, collar, ring ■ **~ de fixation** bracket, clip ■ **~ de serrage** clamp collar **5.** [de plumes, de poils] collar, frill, ring ■ **~ (de barbe)** short *ou* clipped beard.

collimateur [kɔlimatœr] *nm* ASTRON & OPT collimator ■ ARM sight ■ **avoir qqn dans le ~** *ou* **son ~** to have one's eye on sb.

colline [kɔlin] *nf* hill ■ **les ~s** [au pied d'un massif] the foothills ■ **au sommet de la ~** up on the hilltop ■ **sur le versant de la ~** on the hillside.

collision [kɔlizjɔ̃] *nf* **1.** [choc] collision, impact ■ **entrer en ~ avec** to collide with ■ **~ entre les manifestants et la police** clash between demonstrators and police ‖ AUTO crash ■ **~ en chaîne** *ou* **série** (multiple) pile-up **2.** [désaccord] clash ■ **~ d'intérêts** clash of interests **3.** GÉOGR & PHYS collision.

collocation [kɔlɔkasjɔ̃] *nf* **1.** DR order of priority, ranking **2.** LING collocation.

colloïdal, e, aux [kɔlɔidal, o] *adj* colloidal.

colloïde [kɔlɔid] *nm* colloid.

colloque [kɔlɔk] *nm* conference, colloquium, seminar.

colloquer [3] [kɔlɔke] *vt* : **~ des créanciers** *to list creditors in bankruptcy proceedings in the order in which they should be paid.*

collusion [kɔlyzjɔ̃] *nf* collusion ■ **il y a ~ entre eux** they're in collusion.

collutoire [kɔlytwar] *nm* antiseptic throat preparation ■ **~ en aérosol** throat spray.

collyre [kɔlir] *nm* eyewash, antiseptic eye lotion.

colmatage [kɔlmataʒ] *nm* **1.** [réparation] filling-up, plugging ■ **après le ~ des brèches du barrage** after plugging the gaps in the dam **2.** MIL consolidation **3.** AGRIC warping **4.** [fait d'obstruer] clogging, choking.

colmater [3] [kɔlmate] *vt* **1.** [boucher] to fill in *(sép)*, to plug, to repair ■ **~ un déficit** to reduce a deficit ➊ **~ les brèches** *pr* & *fig* to close the gaps **2.** AGRIC to warp **3.** MIL to consolidate.

colo [kɔlo] *nf fam* (children's) holiday camp.

colocataire [kɔlɔkatɛr] *nmf* ADMIN co-tenant ■ [gen] flatmate.

colocation [kɔlɔkasjɔ̃] *nf* joint tenancy, joint occupancy.

Colomb [kɔlɔ̃] *npr* : **Christophe ~** Christopher Columbus.

colombage [kɔlɔ̃baʒ] *nm* frame wall, stud-work.
◆ **à colombages** *loc adj* half-timbered.

colombe [kɔlɔ̃b] *nf* dove ■ **les ~s et les faucons** POLIT the doves and the hawks.

Colombie [kɔlɔ̃bi] *npr f* : **(la) ~** Colombia.

colombien, enne [kɔlɔ̃bjɛ̃, ɛn] *adj* Columbian.
◆ **Colombien, enne** *nm, f* Columbian.

colombier [kɔlɔ̃bje] *nm* dovecot, dovecote, pigeon house.

colombin, e [kɔlɔ̃bɛ̃, in] *adj* reddish-purple.
◆ **colombin** *nm* ORNITH male pigeon.
◆ **colombine** *nf* AGRIC guano.

colombophile [kɔlɔ̃bɔfil] ◇ *adj* pigeon-fancying.
◇ *nmf* pigeon fancier.

colombophilie [kɔlɔ̃bɔfili] *nf* pigeon fancying.

colon [kɔlɔ̃] *nm* **1.** [pionnier] colonist, settler **2.** [enfant] boarder, camper *(at a "colonie de vacances")* **3.** △ *arg mil* colonel.

côlon [kolɔ̃] *nm* colon.

colonel, elle [kɔlɔnɛl] *nm, f* [de l'armée - de terre] colonel ; [- de l'air] group captain *UK*, colonel *US*.

colonelle [kɔlɔnɛl] *nf* colonel's wife.

colonial, e, aux [kɔlɔnjal, o] ◇ *adj* colonial ▪ **l'empire ~** the (colonial) Empire, the colonies.
◇ *nm, f* colonial ▪ **mon père était un ~** my father lived in the colonies.
◆ **coloniale** *nf* MIL : **la ~e** the colonial troops.

colonialisme [kɔlɔnjalism] *nm* colonialism.

colonialiste [kɔlɔnjalist] ◇ *adj* colonialistic.
◇ *nmf* colonialist.

colonie [kɔlɔni] *nf* **1.** [population] settlement **2.** POLIT [pays] colony ▪ [fondation] : **~ pénitentiaire** penal colony **3.** [communauté] community, (little) group ▪ **la ~ bretonne de Paris** the Breton community in Paris **4.** ZOOL colony group ▪ **des ~s de touristes marchaient vers la plage** crowds of tourists were marching along to the beach **5.** LOISIRS : **~ (de vacances)** *organized holidays for children* ▪ **l'été dernier, j'ai fait une** *OU* **je suis allé en ~** [enfant] I went to summer camp last year.

COLONIE DE VACANCES

The *colonie de vacances* or *colo* is an integral part of childhood for many French people.The *colonie* is a sort of summer camp; the children are supervised by *moniteurs* (group leaders), who organize games and activities.

colonisateur, trice [kɔlɔnizatœr, tris] ◇ *adj* colonizing.
◇ *nm, f* colonizer.

colonisation [kɔlɔnizasjɔ̃] *nf* **1.** [conquête] colonization **2.** [période] : **la ~** (the age of) colonization **3.** *péj* [influence] subjugation, colonization.

colonisé, e [kɔlɔnize] ◇ *adj* colonized.
◇ *nm, f* inhabitant of a colonized country ▪ **les ~s** colonized peoples.

coloniser [3] [kɔlɔnize] *vt* **1.** POLIT to colonize **2.** *fam* [envahir] to take over *(sép)*, to colonize ▪ **ne les laissez pas ~ nos plages!** don't let them take over our beaches!

colonnade [kɔlɔnad] *nf* ARCHIT colonnade.

colonne [kɔlɔn] *nf* **1.** ARCHIT column, pillar ▪ **~ dorique/ionique** Doric/Ionic column ▪ **~ Morris** *dark green ornate pillar used to advertise forthcoming attractions in Paris* **2.** CONSTR & TRAV PUB [poteau] column, post, upright ▪ [conduite] riser, pipe ▪ **~ de distribution** standpipe ▪ **~ montante** rising main, riser ▪ **~ sèche** dry riser **3.** ANAT : **~ (vertébrale)** backbone, spinal column *spéc* **4.** MÉCAN column ▪ **~ de direction** steering column **5.** [masse cylindrique] : **~ de liquide/mercure** liquid/mercury column **6.** [forme verticale] column, pillar ▪ **~ d'eau** column of water, waterspout ▪ **~ de feu/fumée** pillar of fire/smoke **7.** MIL column, line ▪ **~ d'assaut** attacking column ▪ **~ de ravitaillement** supply column **8.** [d'un formulaire, d'un texte, d'un tableau] column ▪ **~ des unités** unit column **9.** PRESSE column ▪ **dans les ~s de votre quotidien** in your daily paper.
◆ **en colonne** *loc adv* : **en ~ par trois/quatre** in threes/fours ▪ **les enfants étaient en ~ par deux** the children formed a line two abreast.

colonnette [kɔlɔnɛt] *nf* small column, colonnette.

colonoscopie [kɔlɔnɔskɔpi] *nf* colonoscopy.

colophane [kɔlɔfan] *nf* colophony, rosin.

coloquinte [kɔlɔkɛ̃t] *nf* **1.** BOT colocynth **2.** *fam* [tête] nut.

Colorado [kɔlɔrado] *npr m* **1.** [État] : **le ~** Colorado **2.** [fleuve] : **le ~** the Colorado (River).

colorant, e [kɔlɔrɑ̃, ɑ̃t] *adj* colouring.
◆ **colorant** *nm* colorant, dye, pigment ▪ **~ alimentaire** food colouring *(U)*, edible dye ▪ **'sans ~s'** 'no artificial colouring'.

colorature [kɔlɔratur] *nf* coloratura.

coloration [kɔlɔrasjɔ̃] *nf* **1.** [couleur] pigmentation, colouring **2.** [chez le coiffeur] hair tinting ▪ **se faire faire une ~** to have one's hair tinted **3.** [de la voix, d'un instrument] colour **4.** [tendance] : **~ politique** political colour *OU* tendency.

coloré, e [kɔlɔre] *adj* **1.** [teinté] brightly coloured ▪ **une eau ~e** [à la teinture] water with dye in it ; [avec du vin] water with just a drop of wine in it ▮ [bariolé] multicoloured **2.** [expressif] colourful, vivid, picturesque.

colorer [3] [kɔlɔre] *vt* **1.** [teinter - dessin, objet] to colour ; [- ciel, visage] to tinge, to colour ▪ **~ qqch en rouge/jaune** to colour sthg red/yellow **2.** [teindre - tissu] to dye ; [- bois] to stain, to colour **3.** [oignons, viande] to brown lightly.
◆ **se colorer** *vpi* [visage] to blush, to redden ▪ **se ~ de** *fig* to be tinged with.

coloriage [kɔlɔrjaʒ] *nm* **1.** [technique] colouring ▪ **faire du ~** *OU* **des ~s** to colour (a drawing) **2.** [dessin] coloured drawing.

colorier [9] [kɔlɔrje] *vt* to colour in ▪ **colorie le crocodile en vert** colour in the crocodile (in *OU* with) green.

coloris [kɔlɔri] *nm* [couleur] colour ▪ [nuance] shade ▪ **nous avons cette jupe dans d'autres ~** we have the same skirt in other colours.

colorisation [kɔlɔrizasjɔ̃] *nf* colourization *UK*, colorization *US*.

coloriser [3] [kɔlɔrize] *vt* to colourize *UK*, to colorize *US*.

coloriste [kɔlɔrist] *nmf* **1.** ART colourist **2.** IMPR colourer, colourist **3.** [coiffeur] hairdresser *(specializing in tinting)*.

colossal, e, aux [kɔlɔsal, o] *adj* huge, colossal.

colosse [kɔlɔs] *nm* **1.** [statue] colossus ▪ **un ~ aux pieds d'argile** an idol with feet of clay **2.** [homme de grande taille] giant ▪ **un ~ de l'automobile** *fig* a car manufacturing giant.

colportage [kɔlpɔrtaʒ] *nm* hawking, peddling.

colporter [3] [kɔlpɔrte] *vt* **1.** [vendre] to hawk, to peddle **2.** [répandre] to hawk about *(sép)* ▪ **qui a colporté la nouvelle?** who spread the news?

colporteur, euse [kɔlpɔrtœr, øz] *nm, f* hawker, pedlar ▪ **~ de mauvaises nouvelles** bringer of bad tidings ▪ **~ de ragots** scandalmonger.

colt [kɔlt] *nm* gun.

coltiner [3] [kɔltine] *vt* to carry ▪ **~ de lourdes charges** to carry heavy loads.
◆ **se coltiner** *vpt fam* **1.** [porter] : **se ~ une valise/boîte** to lug a suitcase/box around **2.** [supporter - corvée] to take on *(sép)*, to put up with *(insép)* ; [- personne indésirable] to put up with.

columbarium [kɔlɔ̃barjɔm] *nm* columbarium.

colvert [kɔlvɛr] *nm* mallard.

Colysée [kɔlize] *npr m* : **le ~** the Colosseum.

colza [kɔlza] *nm* colza, rape.

coma [kɔma] *nm* : **être/tomber dans le ~** to be in/to go *OU* to fall into a coma ▶ **être dans un ~ dépassé** to be brain dead.

Comanche [kɔmɑ̃ʃ] *nmf* Comanche.

comandant [komɑ̃dɑ̃] *nm* joint mandator.

comandataire [komɑ̃datɛr] *nmf* joint proxy.

comateux, euse [kɔmatø, øz] *adj* comatose.

combat [kɔ̃ba] ◇ *v* ▷ **combattre.**
◇ *nm* **1.** MIL battle, fight ■ **~ aérien/naval** air/sea battle ■ **~ d'arrière-garde** *pr & fig* rearguard action ■ **des ~s de rue** street fighting ■ **aller au ~ : il n'est jamais allé au ~** he never saw action ▶ **et le ~ cessa faute de combattants** *Corneille allus* and the combat ceased for want of fighters **2.** [lutte physique] fight ■ **~ corps à corps** hand-to-hand combat ■ **~ rapproché** close combat ■ **~ singulier** single combat ‖ SPORT contest, fight ■ **~ de boxe** boxing match ■ **~ de coqs** cockfight **3.** [lutte morale, politique] struggle, fight ■ **mener le bon ~** to fight for a just cause ■ **son long ~ contre le cancer** his long struggle against cancer ■ **~ d'intérêts** clash of interests.
◆ **de combat** *loc adj* **1.** MIL [zone] combat *(modif)* ■ [réserves] battle *(modif)*, war *(modif)* ■ **avion de ~** warplane, fighter plane ■ **navire de ~** battleship ■ **tenue de ~** battledress **2.** [de choc] militant.

combatif, ive [kɔ̃batif, iv] *adj* [animal] aggressive ■ [personne] combative, aggressive, pugnacious *litt* ■ **être d'humeur ~** to be full of fight.

combativité [kɔ̃bativite] *nf* combativeness, aggressiveness, pugnacity *litt.*

combattant, e [kɔ̃batɑ̃, ɑ̃t] ◇ *adj* fighting.
◇ *nm, f* MIL combatant, fighter, soldier ■ [adversaire] fighter.

combattre [83] [kɔ̃batr] ◇ *vt* **1.** MIL to fight (against) ■ **~ l'ennemi** to give battle to the enemy **2.** [s'opposer à - inflation, racisme] to combat, to fight, to struggle against ; [- politique] to oppose, to fight ■ **il est difficile de ~ son instinct** it's difficult to go against one's instincts ■ **il a longtemps combattu la maladie** he fought *ou* struggled against the disease for a long time **3.** [agir contre - incendie] to fight ; [- effets] to combat.
◇ *vi* **1.** MIL to fight **2.** [en politique, pour une cause] to fight, to struggle.

combe [kɔ̃b] *nf* combe, valley.

combien [kɔ̃bjɛ̃] ◇ *adv* **1.** [pour interroger sur une somme] how much ■ **c'est ~?, ça fait ~?** how much is it? ■ **~ coûte ce livre?** how much is this book?, how much does this book cost? ■ **à ~ doit-on affranchir cette lettre?** how much postage does this letter need? ■ **l'indice a augmenté de ~?** how much has the rate gone up by? ■ **de ~ est le déficit?** how large is the deficit?
2. [pour interroger sur le nombre] how many ■ **~ sont-ils?** how many of them are there?
3. [pour interroger sur la distance, la durée, la mesure *etc*] : **~ tu pèses?** how much do you weigh? ■ **~ tu mesures?** how tall are you? ■ **~ y a-t-il de Londres à Paris?** how far is it from London to Paris? ■ **~ dure le film?** how long is the film?, how long does the film last? ■ **il est arrivé ~?** where did he come? ■ **~ ça lui fait maintenant?** *fam* how old is he now? ■ **il y a ~ entre lui et sa sœur?** what's the age difference between him and his sister? ■ **de ~ votre frère est-il votre aîné?** how much older than you is your brother?
4. [en emploi exclamatif] how ■ **vous ne pouvez pas savoir ~ il est distrait!** you wouldn't believe how absent-minded he is! ■ **ces mesures étaient sévères mais ~ efficaces** these measures were drastic but extremely efficient ■ **c'est plus cher mais ~ meilleur!** it's more expensive but all the better for it! ■ **~ plus crédible était sa première version des faits!** his first version of the facts was so much more believable! ▶ **ô ~!** *litt & hum* : **elle a souffert, ô ~!** she suffered, oh how she suffered!
◇ *nm inv* : **le ~ sommes-nous?** what's the date (today)? ■ **le bus passe tous les ~?** how often does the bus come?
◆ **combien de** *loc dét* **1.** [pour interroger - suivi d'un nom non comptable] how much ; [- suivi d'un nom comptable] how many ■ **~ de fois** how many times, how often ■ **~ de temps resterez-vous?** how long will you be staying?
2. [emploi exclamatif] : **~ d'ennuis il aurait pu s'éviter!** he could have saved himself so much trouble!

combientième [kɔ̃bjɛ̃tjɛm] ◇ *adj interr* : **c'est ta ~ tasse de thé aujourd'hui?** just how many cups of tea have you drunk today? ■ **c'est la ~ fois que je te le dis?** how many times have I told you?, I must have told you umpteen times!, if I've told you once I've told you a hundred times!
◇ *nmf* **1.** [personne] : **c'est la ~ qui demande à être remboursée depuis ce matin?** how many does that make wanting their money back since this morning? **2.** [objet] : **prends le troisième – le ~?** have the third one – which one did you say? **3.** [rang] : **tu es le ~ en math?** how high are you *ou* where do you come in maths?

combinable [kɔ̃binabl] *adj* combinable.

combinaison [kɔ̃binɛzɔ̃] *nf* **1.** CHIM [action] combining ■ [résultat] combination ■ [composé] compound **2.** [d'un cadenas] combination **3.** INFORM : **~ de code** password **4.** MATH combination **5.** POLIT : **~ ministérielle** composition of a cabinet **6.** [vêtement, sous-vêtement] slip ■ [vêtement] : **~ anti-g** G suit ■ **~ de plongée** diving suit ■ **~ de ski** ski suit ■ **~ de travail** overalls ■ **~ de vol** flying suit **7.** [assemblage] : **la ~ des deux éléments est nécessaire** the two elements must be combined ■ **la ~ de l'ancien avec le moderne est très réussie** the combination *ou* mixture of ancient and modern is very successful.
◆ **combinaisons** *nfpl péj* [manigances] schemes, tricks.

combinard, e [kɔ̃binar, ard] *adj & nm, f fam péj* **c'est un vrai ~, il est vraiment ~** he's a real schemer, he always knows some dodge or other.

combinat [kɔ̃bina] *nm* (industrial) combine.

combinateur [kɔ̃binatœr] *nm* **1.** AUTO selector switch **2.** RAIL controller.

combinatoire [kɔ̃binatwar] ◇ *adj* **1.** [capable d'agencer] combinative **2.** LING combinatory **3.** MATH combinatorial.
◇ *nf* **1.** LING combinatorial rules **2.** MATH combinatorial mathematics *(sing).*

combine [kɔ̃bin] *nf fam* **1.** [astuce, truc] scheme, trick ■ **il a toujours des ~s, lui!** he always knows some trick or other ■ **j'ai une ~ pour entrer sans payer** I know a way of getting in for free ■ **c'est simple, il suffit de connaître la ~** it's easy when you know how ■ **être dans la ~** to be in on it ■ **mettre qqn dans la ~** to let sb in on it **2.** [vêtement] slip.

combiné, e [kɔ̃bine] *adj* joint, combined ■ **état-major ~** joint chief of staff.
◆ **combiné** *nm* **1.** [vêtement] corselet, corselette **2.** TÉLÉCOM receiver, handset **3.** CHIM compound **4.** SPORT [gén] athletics event ■ [en ski] combined competition ■ **~ alpin** alpine combined competition.

combiner [3] [kɔ̃bine] *vt* **1.** [harmoniser - styles] to combine, to match ; [- couleurs] to match, to harmonize, to mix ; [- sons] to harmonize, to mix ■ **~ son travail et ses loisirs** to combine business with pleasure **2.** [comprendre] to combine ■ **un appareil qui combine deux/diverses fonctions** a two-function/multi-function apparatus **3.** [planifier] to plan, to work out *(sép)* ■ **bien combiné** well planned **4.** *fam péj* [manigancer] to think up *(sép)* **5.** CHIM to combine.
◆ **se combiner** *vpi* **1.** [exister ensemble - éléments] to be combined ■ **en lui se combinent la sensibilité et l'érudition** he combines sensitivity with erudition **2.** [s'harmoniser - couleurs] to match, to harmonize, to mix ; [- sons] to harmonize, to mix **3.** CHIM : **se ~ avec** to combine with **4.** *fam* [se passer] : **ça se combine** *ou* **les choses se combinent bien** it's *ou* things are working out very well.

comble [kɔ̃bl] ◇ *adj* packed, crammed.
◇ *nm* **1.** [summum] : **le ~ de** the height *ou* epitome of ■ **le ~ du chic** the ultimate in chic ■ **du champagne et, ~ du luxe, du caviar** champagne and, oh, height of luxury, caviare ▶ **(c'est) un** *ou* **le ~!** that beats everything!, that takes the biscuit! *UK ou* takes the cake! *US* ■ **le comble, c'est que...** to crown *ou* to cap it all... ■ **les objectifs ne sont pas atteints, un ~ pour une usine-pilote!** they haven't fulfilled their objectives, which is just not on for a model factory! **2.** [charpente] roof timbers *ou* gable ■ **~ mansardé** mansard roof ■ **les ~s** the attic.
◆ **à son comble** *loc adv* at its height ■ **la panique était à son ~** the panic was at its height.
◆ **au comble de** *loc prép* at the height of, in a paroxysm of ■ **au ~ du bonheur** deliriously happy ■ **au ~ de la douleur** prostrate with *ou* in a paroxysm of grief.

◆ **pour comble de** *loc prép* : **et pour ~ de malchance, la voiture est tombée en panne** and then, to cap it all, the car broke down ■ **pour ~ d'hypocrisie, ils envoient leur fille chez les sœurs** then, to compound the hypocrisy, they send their daughter to a convent.

combler [3] [kɔ̃ble] *vt* **1.** [boucher - cavité, creux] to fill in *(sép)* **2.** [supprimer - lacune, vide] to fill ; [- silence] to break ; [- perte, déficit] to make up for **3.** [satisfaire - personne] to satisfy ; [- désir, vœu] to satisfy, to fulfil ■ **je suis vraiment comblée!** I have everything I could wish for!, I couldn't ask for anything more! ■ **voilà un père comblé!** there's a contented father! **4.** *fig* [couvrir, emplir] : **~ qqn de** : **~ un enfant de cadeaux** to shower a child with gifts ■ **~ qqn de joie** to fill sb with joy.
◆ **se combler** *vpi* [trou] to get filled in, to fill up.

comburant, e [kɔ̃byrɑ̃, ɑ̃t] *adj* combustive.
◆ **comburant** *nm* oxidant.

combustibilité [kɔ̃bystibilite] *nf* combustibility.

combustible [kɔ̃bystibl] ◇ *adj* combustible.
◇ *nm* fuel ■ **~ fossile** fossil fuel.

combustion [kɔ̃bystjɔ̃] *nf* combustion ■ **à ~ interne** internal-combustion *(modif)* ■ **à ~ lente** slow-burning.

Côme [kom] *npr* Como ■ **le lac de ~** Lake Como.

come-back [kɔmbak] *nm inv* comeback ■ **faire son** *ou* **un ~** to make *ou* to stage a comeback.

COMECON, Comecon [kɔmekɔn] (*abr de* **Council for Mutual Economic Assistance**) *npr m* COMECON.

comédie [kɔmedi] *nf* **1.** [art dramatique] : **jouer la ~** to act, to be an actor **2.** [pièce comique] comedy ■ **~ de caractères** character comedy ■ **~ de mœurs** comedy of manners ■ **~ de situation** situation comedy ➊ **~ musicale** musical ■ **'la Comédie humaine' *Balzac*** 'The Human Comedy' **3.** [genre] comedy ■ **acteur spécialisé dans la ~** comic actor **4.** [nom de certains théâtres] : **la Comédie du Nord** the Comédie du Nord **5.** *péj* [hypocrisie] act ■ **cette réception, quelle ~!** what a farce that party was! ■ **il n'est pas vraiment malade, c'est de la ~** *ou* **il nous joue la ~** he's only play-acting *ou* it's only an act, he's not really ill **6.** *fam* [caprice, colère] tantrum ■ **faire** *ou* **jouer la ~** to throw a tantrum, to make a fuss ■ **il m'a fait toute une ~ pour avoir le jouet** he kicked up a huge fuss to get the toy **7.** *fam* [histoire] : **c'est toute une ~ pour lui faire avaler sa soupe** you have to go through a whole rigmarole to get her to eat her soup ■ **pour avoir un rendez-vous, quelle ~!** what a palaver to get an appointment!
◆ **de comédie** *loc adj* comic, comedy *(modif)*.

Comédie-Française [kɔmedifrɑ̃sɛz] *npr f* : **la ~** *French national theatre company.*

LA COMÉDIE-FRANÇAISE

This state-subsidized company dates back to the seventeenth century; the theatre itself, officially called *le Théâtre-Français* or *le Français*, is situated in the rue de Richelieu in Paris. Its repertoire consists mainly of classical works, although modern plays are sometimes staged.

comédien, enne [kɔmedjɛ̃, ɛn] ◇ *adj* : **elle est ~ne** *fig* she's putting on an act, she's a phoney.
◇ *nm, f* **1.** [acteur - gén] actor (*f* actress) ; [- comique] comedian (*f* comedienne) **2.** [hypocrite] phoney ■ **quel ~!** he's putting it on!

comédon [kɔmedɔ̃] *nm* blackhead, comedo *spéc.*

COMES, Comes [kɔmɛs] (*abr de* **Commissariat à l'énergie solaire**) *npr m solar energy commission.*

comestible [kɔmɛstibl] *adj* edible ■ **non ~** inedible.
◆ **comestibles** *nmpl* food, foodstuffs.

comète [kɔmɛt] *nf* comet.

comice [kɔmis] *nf* [poire] comice pear.

comices [kɔmis] *nmpl* **1.** ANTIQ comitia **2.** AGRIC : **~ agricoles** agricultural fair.

comique [kɔmik] ◇ *adj* **1.** LITTÉR comic, comedy *(modif)* **2.** [amusant] comical, funny.
◇ *nmf* **1.** [artiste] comic, comedian (*f* comedienne) ■ **c'est un grand ~** he's a great comic actor **2.** [auteur] comic author, writer of comedies *ou* comedy.
◇ *nm* **1.** [genre] comedy ■ **le ~ de caractères/situation** character/situation comedy ■ **le ~ troupier** barrack-room comedy **2.** [ce qui fait rire] : **c'était du plus haut ~!** it was hysterically funny! ■ **le ~ de l'histoire, c'est que...** the funny part of it is that...

comiquement [kɔmikmɑ̃] *adv* comically, funnily.

comité [kɔmite] *nm* committee, board ■ **se constituer en ~** to form a committee ➊ **~ d'action** action committee ■ **~ central** central committee ■ **~ consultatif** advisory board ■ **~ directeur** steering committee ■ **~ électoral** POLIT electoral committee ■ **~ d'entreprise** works council ■ **~ exécutif** POLIT executive committee *ou* board ■ **~ de gestion** board of managers ■ **~ de lecture** supervisory committee.
◆ **en comité secret** *loc adv* secretly.
◆ **en petit comité, en comité restreint** *loc adv* as a select group ■ **on a dîné en petit ~** the dinner was just for a select group.

COMITÉ D'ENTREPRISE

In a company with more than 50 employees, the *CE* looks after the general welfare of company employees and organizes subsidized leisure activities, outings, holidays *etc.* It also deals with industrial problems.

commandant, e [kɔmɑ̃dɑ̃, ɑ̃t] *nm, f* **1.** MIL [de l'armée de terre] major ■ **~ d'armes** garrison commander ‖ [de l'armée de l'air] wing commander *UK*, lieutenant colonel *US* ■ [de la marine] commander ■ **~ en second** first lieutenant ‖ [de la marine marchande] captain ■ **~ en chef** commander in chief **2.** NAUT captain **3.** AÉRON : **~ (de bord)** captain ■ **~ en second** second in command.

commande [kɔmɑ̃d] *nf* **1.** COMM order ■ **passer/annuler une ~** to put in/to cancel an order ■ **passer ~ de 10 véhicules** to order 10 vehicles ■ **le garçon a pris la ~** the waiter took the order ‖ [marchandises] order, goods ordered **2.** TECHNOL control mechanism ■ **la ~ des essuie-glaces** the wiper mechanism ■ **~ à distance** remote control **3.** INFORM control ■ **~ numérique** numerical control ■ **~ de contact** contact operate ■ **~ d'interruption** break feature ■ **~ vocale** voice-operated.
◆ **commandes** *nfpl* [dispositif de guidage] controls ■ **être aux ~s** *pr* to be at the controls ; *fig* to be in charge ■ **prendre les** *ou* **se mettre aux ~s** *pr* to take over at the controls ; *fig* to take charge.
◆ **à la commande** *loc adv* : **payer à la ~** to pay while ordering ■ **payable à la ~** payment with order ■ **travailler à la ~** to work to order.
◆ **de commande** *loc adj* **1.** MÉCAN control *(modif)* **2.** *péj* [factice - enthousiasme, humour] forced, unnatural **3.** *litt* [indispensable] : **la plus grande circonspection/générosité est de ~** prudence/generosity is of the essence.
◆ **sur commande** *loc adv* COMM & *fig* to order.

commandement [kɔmɑ̃dmɑ̃] *nm* **1.** [ordre] command, order ■ **obéir aux ~s de qqn** to obey sb's orders ■ **à mon ~, prêt, partez!** on the word of command, ready, go! **2.** [fait de diriger] command ■ **prendre le ~ d'une section** to take over command of a platoon ■ **avoir le ~ de** [armée, pays] to be in command of, to lead **3.** [état-major] command ➊ **le haut ~** the High Command **4.** DR summons **5.** BIBLE commandment.

commander [3] [kɔmɑ̃de] ◇ *vt* **1.** [diriger - armée, expédition, soldats, équipe] to command ; [- navire] to be in command of ■ *(en usage absolu)* **tu dois lui obéir, c'est lui qui commande** you must obey him, he's in charge ■ **c'est moi qui commande ici!** I'm the one who gives the orders around here! **2.** [ordonner] : **~ la retraite aux troupes** to order the troops back *ou* to retreat ■ **~ à qqn de faire** *ou* **qu'il fasse** *sout* **qqch** to order sb to do sthg **3.** TECHNOL : **l'ouverture des portes est commandée par une manette** the doors open by means of a lever ■ **la télévision est commandée à distance** the television is remote-controlled **4.** COMM [tableau, ouvrage] to commission ■ [objet manufacturé, repas] to order ■ **~ une robe sur catalogue** to order a dress from a catalogue ▪ *(en usage absolu)* **c'est fait, j'ai déjà commandé** I've already ordered ▪ **vous avez commandé?** has somebody taken your order? **5.** *sout* [requérir] to demand ▪ **la prudence commande le silence absolu** prudence demands total discretion, total discretion is required for the sake of prudence **6.** *litt* [maîtriser] to control ▪ **il ne commande plus ses nerfs** he is no longer in control of his emotions **7.** INFORM to drive.

◇ *vi* [primer] : **le devoir commande!** duty calls! ▪ **le travail commande!** back to work!

◆ **commander à** *v+prép* **1.** [donner des ordres à - armée] to command **2.** *litt* [maîtriser] to control ▪ **on ne commande pas à ses désirs** desire cannot be controlled.

◆ **se commander** ◇ *vp (emploi passif) fam* [être imposé] : **je n'aime pas ces gens, ça ne se commande pas** I don't like those people, I can't help it ▪ **l'amour ne se commande pas** you can't make love happen.

◇ *vpi sout* [être relié - pièces] to be connected *ou* interconnected, to connect, to interconnect ▪ **toutes les pièces se commandent** all the rooms are interconnected.

commandeur [kɔmɑ̃dœr] *nm* **1.** RELIG commander **2.** [dans un ordre civil] commander ▪ **grand ~** Grand Commander.

commanditaire [kɔmɑ̃ditɛr] *nm* **1.** [d'une entreprise commerciale] sleeping *UK ou* silent *US* partner ▪ [d'un tournoi, d'un spectacle] backer, sponsor **2.** *(comme adj)* **associé ~** sleeping *UK ou* silent *US* partner.

commandite [kɔmɑ̃dit] *nf* share *(of limited partner)*.

commanditer [3] [kɔmɑ̃dite] *vt* [entreprise commerciale] to finance ▪ [tournoi, spectacle] to sponsor.

commando [kɔmɑ̃do] *nm* commando.

comme [kɔm] ◇ *conj* **1.** [introduisant une comparaison] as, like ▪ **c'est un jour ~ les autres** it's a day like any other ▪ **une maison pas ~ les autres** a very unusual house ▪ **ce fut ~ une révélation** it was like a revelation ▪ **il fait beau ~ en plein été** it's as hot as if it was the middle of summer ▪ **il a fait un signe, ~ pour appeler** he made a sign, as if to call out ▪ **c'est ~ ta sœur, elle ne téléphone jamais** your sister's the same, she never phones ▪ **je suis ~ toi, j'ai horreur de ça** I'm like you, I hate that kind of thing ▪ **fais ~ moi, ne lui réponds pas** do as I do, don't answer him ▪ **qu'est-ce que tu veux? – choisis ~ pour toi** what do you want? – get me the same as you ▪ **blanc ~ neige** white as snow ▪ **je l'ai vu ~ je vous vois** I saw it as sure as I'm standing here ⊙ **la voiture fait ~ un bruit** the car's making a funny noise ▪ **j'ai ~ l'impression qu'on s'est perdus!** I've got a feeling we're lost! ▪ **il y a ~ un défaut!** *fam* something seems to be wrong! ▪ **il ne m'a pas injurié, mais c'était tout ~** he didn't actually insult me, but it was close *ou* as good as

2. [exprimant la manière] as ▪ **fais ~ il te plaira** do as you like *ou* please ▪ **fais ~ je t'ai appris** do it the way I taught you ▪ **~ on pouvait s'y attendre, nos actions ont baissé** as could be expected, our shares have gone down ▪ **ça s'écrit ~ ça se prononce** it's written as it's pronounced ▪ **la connaissant ~ je la connais** knowing her as well as *ou* like I do ⊙ **je passerai vous prendre à 9 h ~ convenu** I'll pick you up at 9 as (we) agreed *ou* planned ▪ **~ dirait l'autre** *fam*, **~ dit l'autre** *fam* as the saying goes, to coin a phrase, as they say ▪ **~ on dit** as they say ▪ **~ il se doit en pareilles circonstances** as befits the circumstances, as is fitting in such circumstances ▪ **c'était ~ qui dirait un gémissement** it was a sort of moan ▪ **fais ~ bon te semble** do whatever you wish *ou* like ▪ **~ ci ~ ça** *fam* : **tu t'entends bien avec lui? – ~ ci ~ ça** do you get on with him? – sort of *ou* so-so

3. [tel que] like, such as ▪ **mince ~ elle est, elle peut porter n'importe quoi** being as slim as she is everything suits her, she is so slim that everything suits her ▪ **les arbres ~ le marronnier...** trees like *ou* such as the chestnut... ▪ **D ~ Denise** D for Denise

4. [en tant que] as ▪ **il vaut mieux l'avoir ~ ami que ~ ennemi** I'd sooner have him as a friend than as an enemy ▪ **je l'ai eu ~ élève** he was one of my students ▪ **qu'est-ce que vous avez ~ vin?** what (kind of) wine do you have? ▪ **c'est plutôt faible ~ excuse!** it's a pretty feeble excuse! ▪ **~ gaffeur, tu te poses là!** *fam* you really know how to put your foot in it!

5. [pour ainsi dire] : **il restait sur le seuil, ~ paralysé** he was standing on the doorstep, (as if he was) rooted to the spot ▪ **ta robe est ~ neuve!** your dress is as good as new! ▪ **il était ~ fou** he was like a madman

6. [et] : **l'un ~ l'autre aiment beaucoup voyager** they both love travelling ▪ **cette robe peut se porter avec ~ sans ceinture** you can wear this dress with or without a belt ▪ **le règlement s'applique à tous, à vous ~ aux autres** the rules apply to everybody, you included ▪ **un spectacle que les parents, ~ les enfants, apprécieront** a show which will delight parents and children alike ▪ **à la ville ~ à la scène** in real life as well as on stage

7. [indiquant la cause] since, as

8. [au moment où] as, when ▪ [pendant que] while.

◇ *adv* **1.** [emploi exclamatif] how ▪ **~ c'est triste!** how sad (it is)!, it's so sad! ▪ **~ tu es grande!** what a big girl you are now!, how big you've grown! ▪ **~ je te comprends!** I know exactly how you feel!

2. [indiquant la manière] : **tu sais ~ il est** you know what he's like *ou* how he is.

◆ **comme ça** ◇ *loc adj* **1.** [ainsi] like that ▪ **je suis ~ ça** I'm like that ▪ **il est ~ ça, on ne le changera pas!** that's the way he is, you won't change him! ▪ **j'ai fait pousser une citrouille ~ ça!** I grew a pumpkin THAT big!

2. [admirable] great.

◇ *loc adv* **1.** [de cette manière] like this *ou* that ▪ **qu'as-tu à me regarder ~ ça?** why are you staring at me like that? ▪ **c'est ~ ça, que ça te plaise ou non!** that's how *ou* the way it is, whether you like it or not! ▪ **il m'a répondu ~ ça qu'il était majeur** *fam* I'm old enough, he says to me

2. [en intensif] : **alors ~ ça, tu te maries?** (oh) so you're getting married? ▪ **où vas-tu ~ ça?** where are you off to?

3. [de telle manière que] that way, so that.

◆ **comme il faut** ◇ *loc adj* respectable, proper.

◇ *loc adv* **1.** [correctement] properly

2. *fam* [emploi exclamatif] : **il s'est fait battre, et ~ il faut (encore)!** he got well and truly thrashed!

◆ **comme quoi** *loc conj* **1.** [ce qui prouve que] which shows *ou* (just) goes to show that

2. *fam* [selon quoi] : **j'ai reçu des ordres ~ quoi personne ne devait avoir accès au dossier** I've been instructed not to allow anybody access to that file.

◆ **comme si** *loc conj* **1.** [exprimant la comparaison] as if ▪ **il se conduit ~ s'il était encore étudiant** he behaves as if he was still a student ⊙ **elle faisait ~ si de rien n'était** she pretended (that) there was nothing wrong, she pretended (that) nothing had happened ▪ **mais je n'y connais rien – fais ~ si!** but I don't know anything about it – just pretend!

2. [emploi exclamatif] as if, as though ▪ **c'est ~ si c'était fait!** it's as good as done! ▪ **~ s'il ne savait pas ce qu'il faisait!** as if *ou* as though he didn't know what he was doing!

◆ **comme tout** *loc adv* really, extremely, terribly ▪ **j'ai été malade ~ tout sur le bateau** I was (as) sick as a dog on the boat.

commedia dell'arte [kɔmedjadɛlarte] *nf* commedia dell'arte.

commémoratif, ive [kɔmemɔratif, iv] *adj* memorial *(modif)*, commemorative *sout* ▪ **une plaque commémorative** a commemorative plaque.

commémoration [kɔmemɔrasjɔ̃] *nf* commemoration ▪ **en ~ de** in commemoration of, in memory of.

commémorer [3] [kɔmemɔre] *vt* to commemorate, to celebrate the memory of.

commençant, e [kɔmɑ̃sɑ̃, ɑ̃t] *nm, f* beginner.

commencement [kɔmɑ̃smɑ̃] *nm* **1.** [première partie - de la vie, d'un processus] beginning, start, early stages ▪ **du ~ jusqu'à la fin** from start to finish, from beginning to end ▪ **~s** [période] beginnings, early *ou* initial stages ⊙ **c'est le ~ de la fin** *hum* it's the beginning of the end ▪ **il y a un ~ à tout** everybody has to learn to walk before they can run **2.** [essai] beginning, start, attempt ▪ **il y a eu un ~ d'émeute, vite réprimé** a riot started, but was soon brought under control ▪ **son texte ne comporte pas même le ~ d'une idée** there isn't even a vestige of an idea in his text **3.** DR : **~ d'exécution** *initial steps in the commission of a crime* ▪ **~ de preuve par écrit** prima facie evidence.

◆ **au commencement** *loc adv* in *ou* at the beginning.

◆ **au commencement de** *loc prép* at the beginning *ou* start of ▪ **au ~ de la période** DR when the period commences *sout*.

commencer [16] [kɔmɑ̃se] ◇ *vt* **1.** [entreprendre - ouvrage, jeu, apprentissage] to start, to begin ■ **il a commencé le repas** he's started eating ■ **allez, commence la vaisselle!** come on, get going on the dishes! ■ **vous commencez le travail demain** you start (work) tomorrow ■ **nous allons ~ notre descente vers Milan** we are beginning our descent towards Milan ■ *(en usage absolu)* **à quelle heure tu commences?** [au lycée] what time do you start school? ; [au travail] what time do you start work?
2. [passer au début de - journée, soirée] to start, to begin ■ **j'ai bien/mal commencé l'année** I've made a good/bad start to the year
3. [être au début de] to begin ■ **c'est son numéro qui commence le spectacle** her routine begins the show, the show begins with her routine.
◇ *vi* **1.** [débuter] to start ■ **ne commence pas!** don't start! ■ **ce n'est pas moi, c'est lui qui a commencé!** it wasn't me, HE started it! ■ **ça commence bien!** *pr & iron* things are off to a good start! ■ **~ à faire qqch** to start *ou* to begin doing sthg ■ **tu commences à m'énerver!** you're getting on my nerves! ■ **je commence à en avoir assez!** I'm getting fed up with all this! ■ **ça commence à bien faire!** *fam* enough is enough!, things have gone quite far enough! ■ **~ de** *litt* **: nous commencions de déjeuner** we had started luncheon ■ **~ par : la pièce commence par un dialogue** the play starts *ou* opens with a dialogue ■ **commençons par le commencement** let's begin at the beginning, first things first ■ **commence par enlever les couvertures** first, take the blankets off ■ **tu veux une moto? commence par réussir ton examen** if you want a motorbike, start by passing your exam ■ **je vais commencer par l'appeler** the first thing I'm going to do is call him ■ *(tournure impersonnelle)* **il commence à pleuvoir/neiger** it's started to rain/to snow ■ **il commence à se faire tard** *fam* it's getting late
2. [avoir tel moment comme point de départ] to start, to begin ■ **la séance commence à 20 h** the session starts *ou* begins at 8 p.m. ■ **le spectacle est commencé depuis un quart d'heure** the show started a quarter of an hour ago ■ **les vendanges ont commencé tard cette année** the grape harvest started *ou* is late this year ■ **les ennuis ont commencé quand il s'est installé au-dessous de chez moi** the trouble started *ou* began when he moved in downstairs ■ **on fait généralement ~ la crise après le premier choc pétrolier** the recession is generally said to have started after the first oil crisis
3. [se mettre à travailler] **: ~ dans la vie** to start off in life ■ **~ sur la scène/au cinéma** to make one's stage/screen debut ■ **j'ai commencé en 78 avec deux ouvrières** I set up *ou* started (up) in '78 with two workers
4. [dans un barème de prix] to start ■ **les pantalons commencent à/vers 50 euros** trousers start at/at around 50 euros.
➤ **à commencer par** *loc prép* starting with ■ **que tout le monde contribue, à ~ par toi!** let everyone give something, starting with you!
➤ **pour commencer** *loc adv* **1.** [dans un programme, un repas] first, to start with ■ **pour ~, du saumon** to start the meal *ou* as a first course, salmon
2. [comme premier argument] for a start, in the first place ■ **pour ~, tu es trop jeune, et ensuite c'est trop cher!** for a start you're too young, and anyway, it's too expensive!

commendataire [kɔmɑ̃datɛr] *adj* commendatory.

commensal, e, aux [kɔmɑ̃sal, o] *nm, f* **1.** *litt* [compagnon de table] table companion ■ [hôte] guest **2.** ZOOL commensal.

commensurable [kɔmɑ̃syrabl] *adj* commensurable, measurable.

comment [kɔmɑ̃] ◇ *adv* **1.** [de quelle manière] how ■ **~ lui dire que...?** how am I/are we *etc* going to tell him that...? ■ **~ t'appelles-tu?** what's your name? ■ **~ se fait-il qu'il n'ait pas appelé?** how come he hasn't called? ■ **~ faire?** what shall we do? ■ **~ tu parles!** *fam* what kind of language is that! ■ **~ allez-vous?** how are you? ■ **~ va?** *fam* how's things? ■ **et les enfants, ~ ça va?** and how are the children? **2.** [pour faire répéter] **: ~ ça va?** sorry?, what (was that)? **3.** [exprimant l'indignation, l'étonnement] **: ~, c'est tout ce que tu trouves à dire?** what! is that all you can say? ■ **~, ce n'est pas encore prêt?** you mean it's still not ready? ■ **~ ça, tu pars?** *fam* what do you mean, you're leaving? ▶ **le concert t'a plu? – et ~!** did you like the concert? – I certainly did! ■ **pouvons-nous entrer? – mais ~ donc!** can we come in? – of course! *ou* by all means!
◇ *nm* **: le ~** the how.

commentaire [kɔmɑ̃tɛr] *nm* **1.** [remarque] comment, remark, observation ■ **avez-vous des ~s?** any comments *ou* remarks? ■ **faire un ~** to make a remark *ou* a comment ■ **il n'a pas fait de ~s dans la marge** he didn't write any remarks in the margin ■ **je te dispense** *ou* **je me passe de tes ~s** I can do without your remarks ■ **c'est comme ça, et pas de ~!** *fam* that's how it is, and don't argue (with me)! ■ **cela se passe de ~** *ou* **~s** it speaks for itself ■ **sans ~!** no comment!
2. *péj* [critique] comment ■ **son mariage a suscité bien des ~s** her marriage caused a great deal of comment *ou* gossip ■ **avoir des ~s (à faire) sur : j'aurais des ~s à faire sur ton attitude d'hier soir** I'd like to say something about your attitude last night
3. RADIO & TV commentary ■ **~ de la rencontre, Pierre Pastriot** with live commentary from the stadium, Pierre Pastriot
4. ÉDUC **: un texte avec ~** an annotated text ■ **un ~ de la Bible** a biblical commentary, a biblical exegesis *sout* ▶ **~ de texte :** **faire un ~ de texte** to comment on a text ■ **un ~ composé** a written commentary
5. INFORM comment
6. LING comment, theme.

commentateur, trice [kɔmɑ̃tatœr, tris] *nm, f* **1.** ÉDUC & LITTÉR commentator, reviewer, critic **2.** [d'une cérémonie, d'un match] commentator ■ [d'un documentaire] presenter ■ **~ du journal télévisé** broadcaster, anchorman *US* ‖ [observateur] observer, critic.

commenter [3] [kɔmɑ̃te] *vt* **1.** [expliquer - œuvre] to explain, to interpret ■ **veuillez ~ ce dernier vers du poème** please write a commentary on the last line of the poem ■ **on leur fait ~ Dante dès la troisième année d'italien** they start doing literary criticism of Dante in the third year of Italian studies ■ **le directeur va maintenant ~ notre programme de fabrication** the manager will now explain our manufacturing schedule
2. [donner son avis sur] to comment on *(insép)*, to respond to, to give one's response to **3.** RADIO & TV [cérémonie, match] to cover, to do the commentary of *ou* for.

commérage [kɔmeraʒ] *nm* piece of gossip ■ **~s** gossip ■ **faire des ~s** to gossip ■ **ce ne sont que des ~s** it's only hearsay.

commerçant, e [kɔmɛrsɑ̃, ɑ̃t] ◇ *adj* **1.** [peuple, port, pays] trading *(modif)* ■ [rue, quartier] shopping *(modif)* **2.** [qui a le sens du commerce] **: ils en offrent deux pour le prix d'un, c'est très ~** they sell two for the price of one, that's good business sense ■ **il a l'esprit ~** he's a born salesman, he could sell you anything.
◇ *nm, f* shopkeeper *UK*, storekeeper *US* ■ **tous les ~s étaient fermés** all the shops *UK ou* stores *US* were closed ▶ **~ de détail** retail trader ■ **~ en gros** wholesale dealer ■ **les petits ~s** small *ou* retail traders.

commerce [kɔmɛrs] *nm* **1.** [activité] **: le ~** trade ■ **faire le ~ des céréales** to trade in cereals ■ **être dans le ~** to be in trade, to run a business ■ **faire du ~ avec qqn/un pays** to trade with sb/a country ▶ **le ~ extérieur/intérieur** foreign/domestic trade ■ **~ équitable** fair trade ■ **~ de détail** retail trade ■ **le ~ en gros** wholesale trade ■ **~ électronique** *ou* **en ligne** [gén] e-commerce ; [pour des achats] online shopping ■ **faire ~ de ses charmes** *euphém* to cash in on one's charms
2. [affaires] business ■ **cela fait marcher le ~** it's good for business ■ **le ~ marche mal** business is slow ■ **le monde du ~** the business world ▶ **le ~ dominical** Sunday trading ■ **~ intégré** corporate *ou* combined chain ■ **le petit ~** (small) business
3. [circuit de distribution] **: on ne trouve pas encore ce produit dans le ~** this item is not yet available on the market ■ **cela ne se trouve plus dans le ~** this item has gone off the market
4. [magasin] shop *UK*, store *US* ■ **tenir un ~** to run a business
5. *litt* [relation] **: entretenir un ~ d'amitié avec qqn** to keep company with sb ‖ [fréquentation] company.
➤ **de commerce** *loc adj* **1.** [opération] commercial, business *(modif)* ■ [acte] trade *(modif)* ■ [code, tribunal] commercial ■ [école] business *(modif)*
2. NAUT [marine, navire, port] trading, merchant *(modif)*.

commercer [16] [kɔmɛrse] *vi* to trade, to deal ■ **~ avec un pays** to trade with a country.

commercial, e, aux [kɔmɛrsjal, o] ◇ *adj* **1.** [activité] commercial ■ [relation] trade *(modif)* ■ **adressez-vous à notre service** *ou* **secteur ~** please apply to our sales department

■ **avoir des contacts commerciaux avec** to have trading *ou* trade links with ◗ **droit ~** business law ■ **l'anglais ~** business English ■ **un gros succès ~** [film, pièce] a big box-office success ; [livre] a best-selling book, a best-seller **2.** TV commercial ■ **les chaînes ~es** commercial channels **3.** *péj* [sourire] ingratiating ■ **c'est une chanson très ~e** it's a very commercial song.
◇ *nm, f* sales representative *ou* executive.
◆ **commerciale** *nf fam* AUTO commercial vehicle.

commercialement [kɔmɛrsjalmɑ̃] *adv* commercially ■ **~ parlant** from a business point of view.

commercialisable [kɔmɛrsjalizabl] *adj* marketable.

commercialisation [kɔmɛrsjalizasjɔ̃] *nf* marketing.

commercialiser [3] [kɔmɛrsjalize] *vt* **1.** COMM to market, to commercialize ■ **le modèle sera commercialisé en janvier** the model will be coming onto the market in January **2.** DR [dette, lettre de change] to market.

commère [kɔmɛr] *nf* **1.** [médisante] gossip **2.** [bavarde] chatterbox **3.** LITTÉR : **ma ~ la tortue** Mrs Tortoise.

commettre [84] [kɔmɛtr] *vt* **1.** [perpétrer - erreur] to make ; [- injustice] to perpetrate ; [- meurtre] to commit ■ **quand le crime a-t-il été commis?** when did the crime take place? ■ **~ une imprudence** to take an unwise step ■ **l'impatience lui a fait ~ une faute impardonnable** his impatience led him to make an inexcusable mistake **2.** DR [nommer - arbitre, avocat, huissier] to appoint ■ **commis d'office** appointed by the court **3.** *hum* & *péj* [produire - livre, émission] to perpetrate.
◆ **se commettre avec** *vp+prép litt* to associate with.

comminatoire [kɔminatwar] *adj* **1.** *litt* [menaçant] threatening **2.** DR *giving a warning that payment is due.*

commis, e [kɔmi, iz] *pp* ▷ **commettre**.
◆ **commis** *nm* **1.** DR agent **2.** [employé - de magasin] helper, assistant ; [- de banque] runner, junior clerk ; [- de ferme] lad, boy, farm hand ■ **~ greffier** assistant to the court clerk ■ **~ voyageur** *vieilli* travelling salesman **3.** ADMIN : **grand ~ de l'État** senior *ou* higher civil servant **4.** MIL & NAUT : **~ aux vivres** steward.

commisération [kɔmizerasjɔ̃] *nf* commiseration ■ **sans ~** ruthlessly, pitilessly.

commissaire [kɔmisɛr] *nmf* **1.** [membre d'une commission] commissioner **2.** SPORT steward **3.** ADMIN : **~ de la Marine/de l'Air** chief administrator in the Navy/the Air Force ■ **~ de la République** commissioner of the Republic ■ **~ du gouvernement** government commissioner ■ **~ de police** (police) superintendent *UK*, (police) captain *US*, precinct captain *US* ■ **bonjour, Monsieur le ~** good morning, Superintendent *UK ou* Captain *US* ■ **~ divisionnaire** chief superintendent *UK*, police chief *US* ■ **~ principal** chief superintendent *UK*, chief of police *US* **4.** FIN : **~ aux comptes** auditor **5.** NAUT : **~ de** *ou* **du bord** purser **6.** HIST [en URSS] commissar.

commissaire-priseur [kɔmisɛrprizœr] (*pl* **commissaires-priseurs**) *nm* auctioneer.

commissariat [kɔmisarja] *nm* **1.** [fonction] commissionership **2.** ADMIN : **~ de l'Air** Air Force staff ■ **~ de la Marine** Admiralty Board *UK*, Naval Command *US* **3.** FIN : **~ aux comptes** auditorship **4.** [local] : **~ (de police)** police station *ou* precinct *US*.

commission [kɔmisjɔ̃] *nf* **1.** [groupe] commission, committee ■ **~ d'arbitrage** arbitration committee ■ **~ du budget** budget committee ■ **~ de contrôle** supervisory committee ■ **~ d'enquête** board *ou* commission of enquiry ■ **la Commission Européenne** the European Commission ■ **~ d'examen** board of examiners ■ **~ paritaire** joint commission ■ **~ parlementaire** parliamentary committee *ou* commission ■ **~ permanente** standing committee ■ **être en ~** to be in committee ■ **renvoyer un projet de loi en ~** to commit a bill **2.** DR [pouvoir] commission ■ **~ rogatoire** letters rogatory **3.** MIL : **~ d'armistice** armistice council ■ **~ militaire** army exemption tribunal **4.** [pourcentage] commission, percentage ■ **toucher une ~ sur une vente** to get a commission *ou* percentage on a sale ■ **travailler à la ~** to work on a commission basis *ou* for a percentage **5.** [course] errand ■ **j'ai envoyé mon fils faire des ~s** I've sent my son off on some errands **6.** [message] : **n'oublie pas de lui faire la ~** don't forget to give him the message **7.** *fam euphém* **la petite/grosse ~** number one/two ■ **faire la petite/grosse ~** to do a wee-wee/poo.
◆ **commissions** *nfpl* [achats] shopping ■ **faire les ~s** to do some shopping.

commissionnaire [kɔmisjɔnɛr] *nmf* [intermédiaire] commission agent *UK*, broker, agent ■ **~ en douane** customs agent *ou* broker ■ **~ de transport** forwarding agent.

commissionner [3] [kɔmisjɔne] *vt* to commission.

commissure [kɔmisyr] *nf* **1.** [dans le cerveau] commissure **2.** [de la bouche] corner.

commode¹ [kɔmɔd] *adj* **1.** [pratique - moyen de transport] useful, convenient ; [- outil] useful, handy ■ **c'est bien ~ d'avoir un marché dans le quartier** it's very handy *ou* convenient having a market in the area **2.** [facile] easy ■ **ce n'est pas ~ à analyser** it's not easy to analyse ■ **ce n'est pas ~ de concilier deux activités** reconciling two different jobs is not easy *ou* a simple task ■ **c'est** *ou* **ce serait trop ~!** that would be too easy! **3.** [aimable] : **elle n'est pas ~ (à vivre)** she's not easy to live with ■ **son patron n'est pas ~** her boss isn't an easy person to get along with ■ **il est peu ~** he's awkward *ou* difficult.

commode² [kɔmɔd] *nf* chest of drawers.

commodément [kɔmɔdemɑ̃] *adv* [confortablement] comfortably.

commodité [kɔmɔdite] *nf* **1.** [facilité] convenience ■ **pour plus de ~** for greater convenience, to make things more convenient **2.** [aspect pratique] : **la ~ d'une maison** the comfort *ou* convenience of a house ■ **j'habite à côté de mon bureau, c'est d'une grande ~** I live next door to my office, it's extremely convenient.
◆ **commodités** *nfpl* [agréments] conveniences ■ *vieilli* [toilettes] toilet, toilets.

commotion [kɔmɔsjɔ̃] *nf* **1.** [choc] shock **2.** MÉD : **~ cérébrale** concussion **3.** *sout* [perturbation] upheaval, agitation.

commotionner [3] [kɔmɔsjɔne] *vt* to shake (up) *(sép)* ■ **la terrible nouvelle l'a commotionné** the appalling news gave him a shock.

commuable [kɔmɥabl] *adj* commutable.

commuer [7] [kɔmɥe] *vt* to commute ■ **~ une peine de prison en amende** to commute a prison sentence to a fine.

commun, e [kɔmœ̃, yn] *adj* **1.** [partagé - jardin, local] shared, communal ; [- ami] mutual ■ **hôtel avec salle de télévision ~e** hotel with public TV lounge ■ **~ à : une langue ~e à cinq millions de personnes** a language shared by five million people ■ **le court de tennis est ~ à tous les propriétaires** the tennis court is the common property of all the residents
2. [fait en collaboration - travail, politique] shared, common ; [- décision] joint ■ [en communauté] : **la vie ~e [conjugale]** conjugal life, the life of a couple ■ **ils vont reprendre la vie ~e** they're going to live together again
3. [identique - caractère, passion] similar ; [- habitude] common, shared ■ **nous avons des problèmes ~s** we share the same problems, we have similar problems ■ **il n'y a pas de ~e mesure entre...** there's no similarity whatsoever between... ■ **c'est sans ~e mesure avec...** there's no comparison with...
4. [courant - espèce, usage, faute] common, ordinary, run-of-the mill ■ **il est d'un courage peu ~** he's uncommonly *ou* exceptionally brave ■ **un nom peu ~** a very unusual name
5. *péj* [banal] common, coarse
6. LING common
7. MATH : **le plus grand dénominateur~** the highest common denominator.
◆ **commun** *nm* : **l'homme du ~** *vieilli* the common man ■ **un homme hors du ~** an exceptional *ou* unusual man ■ **cela sort du ~** this is very unusual ◗ **le ~ de : le ~ des mortels** the common run of people ■ **le ~ des lecteurs** the average reader.
◆ **communs** *nmpl* outbuildings, outhouses.
◆ **d'un commun accord** *loc adv* by mutual agreement, by common consent ■ **tous d'un ~ accord ont décidé que...** they decided unanimously that...

◆ **en commun** *loc adv* : **avoir qqch en ~ (avec)** to have sthg in common (with) ▪ **mettre qqch en ~** to pool sthg ▪ **nous mettons tout en ~** we share everything.

communal, e, aux [kɔmynal, o] *adj* **1.** ADMIN [en ville] ≃ of the urban district ▪ [à la campagne] ≃ of the rural district **2.** [du village - fête] local, village *(modif)*.
◆ **communale** *nf fam* primary *UK ou* grade *US* school.

communaliser [3] [kɔmynalize] *vt* ≃ to put under the jurisdiction of the local authority.

communard, e [kɔmynar, ard] ◇ *adj* HIST of the (Paris) Commune.
◇ *nm, f* HIST Communard, member of the (Paris) Commune.
◆ **communard** *nm red wine mixed with crème de cassis liqueur.*

communautaire [kɔmynotɛr] *adj* **1.** [vie, esprit] communal, community *(modif)* **2.** [du Marché commun] Common Market *(modif)*, Community *(modif)*.

communautarisme [kɔmynotarism] *nm* communitarianism.

communauté [kɔmynote] *nf* **1.** [similitude - de vues, de pensées] likeness, closeness ; [- d'intérêts] community ; [- de sentiments] commonness **2.** [groupe] community ▪ [de hippies] commune ▪ **~ linguistique** group of people speaking the same language ▪ **la ~ des fidèles** [d'une paroisse] the congregation ▪ **~ religieuse** religious community ➤ **la Communauté économique européenne** the European Economic Community ▪ **la Communauté des États indépendants** the Commonwealth of Independent States ▪ **la Communauté européenne du charbon et de l'acier** the European Coal and Steel Community ▪ **la Communauté européenne de l'énergie atomique** the European Atomic Energy Community ▪ **la Communauté européenne** the European Community ▪ **~ urbaine** *syndicate made up of a large town and surrounding "communes" responsible for the infrastructure of the area* **3.** [public] : **la ~** the general public **4.** DR joint estate.
◆ **en communauté** *loc adv* [vivre] communally, as a community.

commune [kɔmyn] ◇ *f* ▷ **commun.**
◇ *nf* **1.** [agglomération] commune ADMIN : **une jolie petite ~ rurale** a nice little country village ▪ **la ~ et ses alentours** [en ville] ≃ the urban district ; [à la campagne] ≃ the rural district **2.** [habitants] : **la ~** [en ville] people who live within the urban district ; [à la campagne] people who live within the rural district **3.** [administrateurs] : **c'est la ~ qui paie** the local authority *ou* the council *UK* is paying **4.** HIST : **la Commune (de Paris)** the (Paris) Commune **5.** [en Grande-Bretagne] : **les Communes** the House of Commons.

COMMUNE

A *commune* is an administrative district in France. There are 38,000 *communes*, some with less than 25 inhabitants. Each *commune* has an elected mayor and a town council.

LA COMMUNE

A revolutionary government set up in Paris from March 18th to May 28th 1871 after the Prussian siege was lifted. It was brutally put down by soldiers sent in by the Thiers government in Versailles and remains an important landmark in the history of European socialism.

communément [kɔmynemɑ̃] *adv* commonly, usually ▪ **la torture est encore ~ pratiquée là-bas** torture is still routinely practised there ▪ **la renoncule terrestre, ~ appelée bouton d'or** ranunculus, commonly known as *ou* usually called the buttercup.

communiant, e [kɔmynjɑ̃, ɑ̃t] *nm, f* communicant.

communicable [kɔmynikabl] *adj* **1.** [exprimable] communicable ▪ **c'est une impression difficilement ~** it's a feeling difficult to put into words **2.** [transmissible - données, informations] communicable ▪ **ces données ne sont pas ~s** this data is classified.

communicant, e [kɔmynikɑ̃, ɑ̃t] *adj* communicating ▪ **deux chambres ~es** two connecting *UK ou* adjoining *US* rooms.

communicatif, ive [kɔmynikatif, iv] *adj* **1.** [qui se répand - rire, bonne humeur] infectious **2.** [bavard] communicative, talkative ▪ **peu ~** not very communicative, quiet.

communication [kɔmynikasjɔ̃] *nf* **1.** [annonce] announcement, communication ▪ **donner ~ de qqch** to communicate sthg
2. [exposé - fait à la presse] statement ; [- fait à des universitaires, des scientifiques] paper ▪ **faire une ~ sur l'atome** to deliver a lecture on the atom
3. [transmission] communicating, passing on, transmission ▪ **pour éviter la ~ de ces maladies** to stop the spread of these diseases ▪ **avoir ~ d'un dossier** to get hold of a file, to have had a file passed on to one
4. [contact] communication, contact ▪ **être en ~ avec qqn** to be in contact *ou* touch with sb ▪ **vous devriez vous mettre en ~ avec elle** you should get in touch with her
5. [échange entre personnes] communication ▪ **il a des problèmes de ~ (avec les autres)** he has problems communicating with *ou* relating to people ▪ **il n'y a pas de ~ possible avec elle** it's impossible to relate to her ‖ [diffusion d'informations] : **la ~ : les techniques de la ~** media techniques ▪ **la ~ de masse** the mass media ▪ **~ interne** [dans une entreprise] interdepartmental communication
6. [moyen de liaison] (means of) communication
7. TÉLÉCOM : **~ téléphonique** (phone) call ▪ **je vous passe la ~** I'll put you through ▪ **je prends la ~** I'll take the call ▪ **il est en ~ avec...** he's speaking to..., he's on the phone to... ▪ **la ~ a été coupée** we were cut off ▪ **avoir la ~ : vous avez la ~** you're through ▪ **pour obtenir la ~, faites le 12** dial 12 in order to get through ▪ **~ interurbaine** inter-city *ou* city-to-city call ▪ **~ en PCV** reverse-charge call *UK*, collect call *US*
8. INFORM : **~ homme-machine** man-machine dialogue.
◆ **communications** *nfpl* MIL communications.
◆ **de communication** *loc adj* **1.** [porte, couloir] connecting
2. [réseau, satellite] communications *(modif)* ▪ **moyens de ~** means of communication
3. [agence] publicity *(modif)*.

communier [9] [kɔmynje] *vi* **1.** RELIG to communicate, to receive Communion **2.** *litt* [s'unir spirituellement] : **~ dans un même idéal** to be united in *ou* to share the same ideals ▪ **~ avec qqn** to share the same feelings as sb ▪ **~ avec la nature** to be at one *ou* to commune with nature.

communion [kɔmynjɔ̃] *nf* **1.** RELIG [communauté de foi] communion ▪ **Communion des saints** communion of saints ‖ [partie de la messe] : **Communion** (Holy) Communion ‖ [cérémonie] : **première ~** first communion ▪ **~ solennelle** solemn communion **2.** *litt* [accord] : **être en ~ avec qqn** to be at one *ou* to commune with sb ▪ **être en ~ d'idées** *ou* **d'esprit avec qqn** to share sb's ideas.

communiqué [kɔmynike] *nm* communiqué ▪ **un ~ de presse** a press release.

communiquer [3] [kɔmynike] ◇ *vt* **1.** [transmettre - information] to communicate, to give ; [- demande] to transmit ; [- dossier, message] to pass on *(sép)* ; [- savoir, savoir-faire] to pass on, to hand down *(sép)* ▪ **il s'est fait ~ le dossier** he asked for the file to be passed on to him **2.** PHYS [chaleur, lumière] to transmit ▪ [mouvement, impulsion] to impart **3.** [donner par contamination] to transmit ▪ **il leur a communiqué son fou rire/enthousiasme** he passed on his giggles/enthusiasm to them **4.** [annoncer] to announce, to impart, to communicate ▪ **j'ai une chose importante à vous ~** I have something important to say to you ▪ **selon une nouvelle qu'on nous communique à l'instant** according to news just in.
◇ *vi* **1.** [échanger des messages] to communicate ▪ **~ par téléphone/lettre** to communicate by phone/letter ‖ [échanger des sentiments] : **leur problème est qu'ils n'arrivent pas à ~ avec leurs parents** their problem is that they can't communicate with their parents ▪ **j'ai besoin de ~** I need to express my feelings (to others) **2.** [être relié] to interconnect ▪ **la chambre commu-**

nique avec la salle de bains there's a connecting door between the bathroom and the bedroom ▪ **une chambre avec salle de bains qui communique** a bedroom with bathroom en suite.

◆ **se communiquer** ◇ *vp (emploi passif)* [être transmis - don, savoir, savoir-faire] to be passed on, to be handed down ▪ **le vrai talent ne se communique pas** you can't teach people how to be talented.

◇ *vpi* [se propager - incendie] to spread ; [- maladie] to spread, to be passed on ▪ **se ~ à** to spread to ▪ **sa peur risque de se ~ à tout son entourage** he's likely to make everyone else as frightened as he is.

communisant, e [kɔmynizɑ̃, ɑ̃t] ◇ *adj* Communistic ▪ **un journal ~** a paper with Communist sympathies.

◇ *nm, f* Communist sympathizer, fellow traveller.

communisme [kɔmynism] *nm* Communism.

communiste [kɔmynist] ◇ *adj* Communist ▪ **le parti ~** the Communist party.

◇ *nmf* Communist.

commutateur [kɔmytatœr] *nm* ÉLECTR & ÉLECTRON [de circuits] changeover switch, commutator ▪ [interrupteur] switch ▪ **actionner un ~** [pour allumer] to switch on ; [pour éteindre] to switch off.

commutatif, ive [kɔmytatif, iv] *adj* **1.** MATH commutative **2.** LING commutable **3.** DR commutative.

commutation [kɔmytasjɔ̃] *nf* **1.** [substitution] commutation, substitution ▪ LING & MATH commutation **2.** DR : **~ de peine** commutation of a sentence **3.** ÉLECTR & ÉLECTRON commutation, switching ▪ **une ~ permet de passer automatiquement sur piles** it switches itself on to battery **4.** INFORM & TÉLÉCOM switch-over, switching ▪ **~ de bande/circuits** tape/circuit switching.

commuter [3] [kɔmyte] ◇ *vt* **1.** LING & MATH to commute **2.** ÉLECTR to commutate.

◇ *vi* **1.** MATH to commute **2.** LING to substitute, to commute.

Comores [kɔmɔr] *npr fpl* : **les ~** the Comoro Islands, the Comoros.

comorien, enne [kɔmɔrjɛ̃, ɛn] *adj* Comoran, Comorian.

◆ **Comorien, enne** *nmf sing* Comoran, Comorian.

compacité [kɔ̃pasite] *nf* compactness.

compact, e [kɔ̃pakt] *adj* **1.** [dense - matière] solid, dense ; [- foule] dense, packed ; [- poudre] pressed, compacted **2.** [ski] short **3.** AUDIO, AUTO & PHOTO compact **4.** MATH compact.

◆ **compact** *nm* **1.** [ski] short ski **2.** [disque] compact disc, CD ▪ **disponible en ~** available on CD **3.** [appareil photo] compact (camera).

Compact Disc® [kɔ̃paktdisk] (*pl* **Compact Discs**) *nm* compact disc, CD.

compacter [kɔ̃pakte] *vt* [gén] to compact ▪ INFORM [données] to compress.

compagne [kɔ̃paɲ] *nf* **1.** [camarade] (female) companion ▪ **~ de classe/jeux** (female) classmate/playmate ▪ **elle a été ma ~ d'infortune** she suffered with me, she was my companion in misery **2.** [épouse] wife ▪ [concubine] girlfriend **3.** [animal domestique] companion.

compagnie [kɔ̃paɲi] *nf* **1.** [présence] company ▪ **sa ~ m'est insupportable** I can't stand her company *ou* being with her ▪ **elle avait un chien pour toute ~** her dog was her only companion ▪ **être d'une ~ agréable/sinistre** to be a pleasant/ gloomy companion ▪ **être de bonne/mauvaise ~** to be good/ bad co mpany ▪ **être en bonne/mauvaise ~** to be in good/bad company ▪ **je te laisse en bonne ~** I leave you in good hands ▪ **tenir ~ à qqn** to keep sb company ▪ **tu sais, je me passerais bien de ~!** I could do with being left alone, you know!

2. [groupe] party, company, gang

3. COMM & INDUST company ▪ **~ aérienne** airline (company) ▪ **~ d'assurances** insurance company ▪ **Michel Darot et ~** *pr* Michel Darot and Company ▪ **tout ça, c'est mensonge/arnaque et ~** *fam fig* that's nothing but a pack of lies/a swindle

4. THÉÂTRE : **~ (théâtrale)** (theatre) group *ou* company *ou* troupe

5. ZOOL [de sangliers] herd ▪ [de perdreaux] covey, flock

6. MIL company ▪ **~ de chars** tank brigade

7. [dans des noms d'organisations] : **Compagnie de Jésus** Society of Jesus ▪ **Compagnies républicaines de sécurité** ≃ SAS *UK*, ≃ state troopers *US*.

◆ **de compagnie** *loc adj* [animal] domestic.

◆ **en compagnie de** *loc prép* accompanied by, (in company) with.

compagnon [kɔ̃paɲɔ̃] *nm* **1.** [camarade] companion ▪ **~ d'armes** brother *ou* comrade in arms ▪ **~ de cellule** cellmate ▪ **~ de jeux** playmate ▪ **~ de route** *ou* **voyage** travelling companion ▪ **~ d'infortune** companion in misfortune **2.** [époux] husband, companion ▪ [ami, concubin] boyfriend **3.** [animal] friend **4.** [franc-maçon] companion **5.** [ouvrier] : **Compagnon du Tour de France** journeyman, apprentice **6.** HIST : **Compagnon de la Libération** (French) Resistance fighter **7.** INDUST unskilled worker *ou* labourer.

compagnonnage [kɔ̃paɲɔnaʒ] *nm* HIST **1.** [chez un maître] ≃ apprenticeship **2.** [association] guild.

comparable [kɔ̃parabl] *adj* comparable, similar ▪ **comparons ce qui est ~** let's compare like with like ▪ **ce n'est pas ~** there's no comparison ▪ **je n'ai jamais rien goûté de ~** I've

LA COMPARAISON

They're (both) as lazy as each other. Ils sont aussi paresseux l'un que l'autre.

This book is not as good as his last one. Son dernier livre n'est pas aussi bon que le précédent.

He's nowhere near as good as her *ou* **as she is.** Il est loin d'être aussi doué qu'elle.

She's (much/a bit) taller than him. Elle est (bien/un peu) plus grande que lui.

His new film is far more interesting than the last one. Son dernier film est beaucoup plus intéressant que le précédent.

He eats much more/less than she does. Il mange beaucoup plus/moins qu'elle.

It's like this one, only smaller. Il est comme celui-ci, mais en plus petit.

Compared to his brother, he's a genius! Comparé à son frère, c'est un génie !

Unlike his father, Tony has always loved reading. Contrairement à son père, Tony a toujours aimé lire.

In comparison to *ou* **with London, Prague is quite small.** Par rapport à Londres, Prague est une assez petite ville.

Oxford is, by comparison, quite a peaceful city. Oxford, par comparaison, est une ville assez calme.

This year's results are pretty good compared with last year's. Les résultats de cette année sont plutôt bons comparés à ceux de l'année dernière.

There's not much to choose between them. Il n'y a pas une grande différence entre les deux.

Which do I prefer? Well, there's no comparison! Lequel je préfère ? C'est sans comparaison !

never tasted anything like it ■ **une fonction ~ à celle de comptable** a function comparable with *ou* similar to that of an accountant.

comparais *etc v* ▷ **comparaître.**

comparaison [kɔ̃parɛzɔ̃] *nf* **1.** [gén] comparison ■ **faire la** *ou* **une ~ entre deux qualités** to compare two qualities ■ **c'est sans ~ avec le mien** it cannot possibly be compared with mine ■ **elle est, sans ~, la plus grande chanteuse du moment** she's by far our best contemporary singer ■ **aucune ~!** there's no comparison! ■ **comment décider sans avoir un point de ~?** how can you possibly make up your mind without some means of comparison? ■ **supporter** *ou* **soutenir la ~ avec qqch** to bear *ou* to stand comparison with sthg **2.** [figure de style] comparison, simile ■ **adverbe de ~** comparative adverb.
◆ **en comparaison de, en comparaison avec** *loc prép* in comparison *ou* as compared with, compared to.
Voir module d'usage

comparaître [91] [kɔ̃parɛtr] *vi* to appear ■ **~ en justice** to appear before a court ■ **appelé** *ou* **cité à ~** summoned to appear ■ **faire ~ qqn devant un tribunal** to bring sb before a court.

comparatif, ive [kɔ̃paratif, iv] *adj* comparative.
◆ **comparatif** *nm* comparative ■ **~ de supériorité/d'infériorité** comparative of greater/lesser degree, *voir aussi* **pluriel.**

comparativement [kɔ̃parativmɑ̃] *adv* comparatively, by *ou* in comparison.

comparé, e [kɔ̃pare] *adj* [littérature] comparative.

comparer [3] [kɔ̃pare] *vt* **1.** [confronter] to compare ■ **~ un livre à** *ou* **avec un autre** to compare a book to *ou* with another ■ **il faut ~ ce qui est comparable** you must compare like with like **2.** [assimiler] : **~ qqch/qqn à** to compare sthg/sb to ■ **comme artiste, il ne peut être comparé à Braque** as an artist, he cannot compare with Braque.
◆ **se comparer** *vp (emploi passif)* : **ce sont deux choses qui ne se comparent pas** there can be no comparison between these two things.
◆ **se comparer à** *vp+prép* to compare o.s. with.
◆ **comparé à** *loc prép* compared to *ou* with, in comparison to *ou* with.

comparse [kɔ̃pars] *nmf* **1.** THÉÂTRE extra, walk-on ■ **un rôle de ~** a walk-on part **2.** *péj* [d'un brigand, d'un camelot] stooge.

compartiment [kɔ̃partimɑ̃] *nm* **1.** RAIL compartment ■ **~ de 1ère classe** first-class compartment **2.** [case - d'une boîte] compartment ; [- d'un sac] pocket **3.** NAUT tank **4.** INFORM : **~ protégé** hold area.
◆ **à compartiments** *loc adj* [tiroir, classeur] divided into compartments.

compartimentage [kɔ̃partimɑ̃taʒ], **compartimentation** [kɔ̃partimɑ̃tasjɔ̃] *nm* & *nf* [d'une caisse, d'une armoire] partitioning ■ [d'une administration, des connaissances] compartmentalization, fragmenting.

compartimenter [3] [kɔ̃partimɑ̃te] *vt* [caisse, armoire] to partition, to divide into compartments ■ [administration, connaissances] to compartmentalize, to split into small units.

comparu [kɔ̃pary] *pp* ▷ **comparaître.**

comparution [kɔ̃parysjɔ̃] *nf* appearance.

compas [kɔ̃pa] *nm* **1.** AÉRON & NAUT compass **2.** GÉOM (pair of) compasses ■ **~ d'épaisseur** spring-adjusting callipers ■ **~ à pointes sèches** dividers ■ **avoir le ~ dans l'œil** to be a good judge of distances/measurements *etc.*
◆ **au compas** *loc adv* **1.** NAUT by the compass **2.** [avec précision] with military precision.

compassé, e [kɔ̃pase] *adj* stiff, strait-laced.

compassion [kɔ̃pasjɔ̃] *nf* compassion, sympathy ■ **avec ~** compassionately.

compatibilité [kɔ̃patibilite] *nf* compatibility ■ **~ sanguine** blood-group compatibility *ou* matching.

compatible [kɔ̃patibl] ◇ *adj* [gén - CHIM] & TECHNOL compatible ■ **cela n'est pas ~ avec mon emploi du temps** this won't fit into my schedule.
◇ *nm* INFORM compatible.

compatir [32] [kɔ̃patir] ◆ **compatir à** *v+prép* : **je compatis à votre douleur** I sympathize with you in your grief, I share in your grief ■ *(en usage absolu)* **je compatis!** I sympathize! ; *iron* my heart bleeds!
Voir module d'usage

compatissant, e [kɔ̃patisɑ̃, ɑ̃t] *adj* sympathetic, compassionate.

compatriote [kɔ̃patrijɔt] *nmf* compatriot, fellow countryman (*f* countrywoman).

compensable [kɔ̃pɑ̃sabl] *adj* **1.** [perte] that can be compensated, compensable *US* **2.** [chèque] clearable.

compensateur, trice [kɔ̃pɑ̃satœr, tris] *adj* **1.** [indemnité] compensating, compensatory **2.** [pendule] compensation *(modif).*
◆ **compensateur** *nm* **1.** [appareil] compensator **2.** AÉRON (trim) tab.

compensation [kɔ̃pɑ̃sasjɔ̃] *nf* **1.** [dédommagement] compensation **2.** FIN [de dettes] offsetting ■ [de chèques] clearing **3.** DR : **~ des dépens** sharing of the costs *(among different parties)* **4.** MÉD & PSYCHOL compensation ■ **elle mange par ~** she eats for comfort **5.** NAUT correction, adjustment **6.** AÉRON tabbing **7.** MÉCAN & PHYS balancing.
◆ **en compensation** *loc adv* as a *ou* by way of (a) compensation.
◆ **en compensation de** *loc prép* by way of compensation *ou* as compensation *ou* to compensate for.

compensatoire [kɔ̃pɑ̃satwar] *adj* **1.** [qui équilibre] compensatory, compensating **2.** FIN countervailing.

compensé, e [kɔ̃pɑ̃se] *adj* **1.** MÉD compensated **2.** [semelle] : **chaussures à semelles ~es** platform shoes **3.** COMM : **publicité ~e** prestige advertising.

compenser [3] [kɔ̃pɑ̃se] *vt* **1.** [perte] to make up for *(insép)*, to offset ■ *(en usage absolu)* **pour ~, je l'ai emmenée au cinéma** to make up for it, I took her to the cinema **2.** DR : **~ les dépens** to order each party to pay its own costs **3.** MÉD to compensate, to counterbalance ■ PSYCHOL to compensate ■ *(en usage*

COMPATIR

I was so sorry to hear about (the death of) your father. J'ai été vraiment désolé d'apprendre le décès de ton père.

I'm so sorry. Je suis vraiment désolé.

Please accept my condolences. Sincères condoléances.

Our thoughts are with you. Nous sommes de tout cœur avec vous.

How awful for you! Ça doit être terrible pour toi !

You know where I am if you need me. Tu sais où me trouver si tu as besoin de moi.

If there's anything I can do... Si je peux faire quoi que ce soit...

You poor thing! Mon/Ma pauvre !

Poor you! Mon/Ma pauvre !

I sympathize. Je compatis.

Get well soon! Remets-toi vite !

There there. *(à un enfant).* Allez, ce n'est rien.

absolu) **elle mange pour ~** she eats for comfort **4.** MÉCAN & PHYS to balance **5.** NAUT to adjust, to correct **6.** FIN [dette] to offset, to balance out *(sép)*.

◆ **se compenser** *vp (emploi réciproque)* to make up for one another.

compère [kɔ̃pɛr] *nm* **1.** [complice - d'un camelot] accomplice ; [- d'un artiste] stooge **2.** LITTÉR : **(mon) ~ le lapin** Mister Rabbit.

compère-loriot [kɔ̃pɛrlɔrjo] *(pl* **compères-loriots***)* *nm* sty MÉD, stye.

compétence [kɔ̃petɑ̃s] *nf* **1.** [qualification, capacité] competence ■ **j'ai des ~s en informatique** I have computer skills ■ **avoir recours aux ~s d'un expert** to refer to an expert ■ **cela n'entre pas dans mes ~s, ce n'est pas de ma ~** [cela n'est pas dans mes attributions] this doesn't come within my remit ; [cela me dépasse] that's beyond my competence **2.** DR competence **3.** LING & MÉD competence.

compétent, e [kɔ̃petɑ̃, ɑ̃t] *adj* **1.** [qualifié] competent, skilful, skilled ■ **en cuisine, je suis assez ~e** I'm quite a good cook ■ **~ en la matière** [qui savent] : **les gens ~s en la matière** people who know about *ou* are conversant with *sout* this topic ■ **seul le maire est ~ en la matière** [habilité] only the mayor is competent to act in this matter **2.** [approprié - service] relevant.

compétiteur, trice [kɔ̃petitœr, tris] *nm, f* **1.** [rival] : **le ~ de qqn** sb's rival **2.** COMM & SPORT competitor.

compétitif, ive [kɔ̃petitif, iv] *adj* competitive ■ **leurs chaînes hi-fi sont à des prix ~s** their hi-fi equipment is competitively priced.

compétition [kɔ̃petisjɔ̃] *nf* **1.** [rivalité] competition, competing ■ **j'ai horreur de la ~** I hate having to compete (with others) **2.** [niveau d'activité sportive] competition ■ **faire de la ~** [athlétisme] to take part in competitive events ; AUTO & NAUT to race ■ **j'arrête la ~** I'm giving up competitive sports ■ *(comme adj inv)* **elle a le niveau ~ en aviron** she's a top-level oarswoman **3.** [concours - en athlétisme, en natation] competition, event ; [- au tennis] tournament ■ AUTO & NAUT competition, race.

◆ **de compétition** *loc adj* : **des skis de ~** [de descente] racing skis ; [de fond] eventing skis ➊ **sport de ~** competitive sport.

◆ **en compétition** *loc adv* SPORT at competition level.

◆ **en compétition avec** *loc prép* competing *ou* in competition with.

compétitivité [kɔ̃petitivite] *nf* competitiveness.

compilateur, trice [kɔ̃pilatœr, tris] *nm, f* **1.** *sout* [auteur] compiler **2.** *péj* [plagiaire] plagiarist.

◆ **compilateur** *nm* INFORM compiler.

compilation [kɔ̃pilasjɔ̃] *nf* **1.** [fait de réunir des textes] compiling ■ [ensemble de textes, de morceaux de musique] compilation **2.** *péj* [plagiat] plagiarizing, synthesizing ■ [ouvrage] (mere) compilation *ou* synthesis *péj* **3.** INFORM compilation.

compiler [3] [kɔ̃pile] *vt* **1.** [assembler] to put together *(sép)*, to assemble **2.** *péj* [suj: plagiaire] to borrow from **3.** INFORM to compile.

complainte [kɔ̃plɛ̃t] *nf* **1.** LITTÉR & MUS & *litt* lament, plaint **2.** DR complaint.

complaire [110] [kɔ̃plɛr] ◆ **complaire à** *v+prép litt* **~ à qqn** to please sb.

◆ **se complaire** *vpi* : **se ~ dans qqch** to revel *ou* to delight *ou* to take pleasure in sthg ■ **il se complaît dans son malheur** he wallows in his own misery ■ **se ~ à dire/faire qqch** to take great pleasure in saying/doing sthg.

complaisamment [kɔ̃plɛzamɑ̃] *adv* **1.** [avec amabilité] kindly, obligingly **2.** *péj* [avec vanité] smugly, complacently, with self-satisfaction.

complaisance [kɔ̃plɛzɑ̃s] *nf* **1.** [amabilité] kindness, obligingness ■ **avec ~** kindly, obligingly **2.** [vanité] complacency, smugness, self-satisfaction ■ **avec ~** smugly, complacently **3.** [indulgence - des parents] laxity, indulgence ; [- d'un tribunal, d'un juge] leniency, indulgence ; [- d'un mari] connivance.

◆ **complaisances** *nfpl* favours.

◆ **de complaisance** *loc adj* : **certificat** *ou* **attestation de ~** phoney certificate *(given to please the person concerned)* ■ **billet de ~** COMM accommodation bill.

◆ **par complaisance** *loc adv* out of sheer politeness, purely *ou* merely to be polite.

complaisant, e [kɔ̃plɛzɑ̃, ɑ̃t] *adj* **1.** [aimable] kind ■ [serviable] obliging, complaisant **2.** [vaniteux] smug, self-satisfied, complacent ■ **prêter une oreille ~e aux éloges** to lap up praise **3.** [indulgent - parents] lax, indulgent ; [- juge, tribunal] indulgent, lenient ■ **elle a un mari ~** her husband turns a blind eye to her infidelities.

complaisons *etc v* ⊳ **complaire**.

complément [kɔ̃plemɑ̃] *nm* **1.** [supplément] : **un ~ d'information est nécessaire** further *ou* additional information is required ■ **demander un ~ d'enquête** to order a more extensive inquiry **2.** [reste] rest, remainder **3.** MATH complement **4.** LING complement ■ **~ (d'objet) direct/indirect** direct/indirect object ■ **~ d'agent** agent ■ **~ circonstanciel** adverbial phrase **5.** ADMIN : **~ familial** means-tested family allowance *(for parents with three children above the age of three)*.

complémentaire [kɔ̃plemɑ̃tɛr] ◇ *adj* **1.** [supplémentaire - information] additional, further **2.** [industries, couleurs] complementary **3.** LING & MATH complementary **4.** ÉCON complementary **5.** ÉDUC : **cours ~** ≃ secondary modern school.

◇ *nm* MATH complementary.

complémentarité [kɔ̃plemɑ̃tarite] *nf* **1.** [fait de se compléter] complementarity ■ **la ~ du jaune et du violet** the complementary qualities of yellow and purple **2.** ÉCON complementarity.

complet, ète [kɔ̃plɛ, ɛt] *adj* **1.** [qui a tous ses éléments - série, collection, parure] complete, full ; [- œuvre] complete ➊ **change ~** disposable nappy UK *ou* diaper US **2.** [approfondi - compte-rendu, description] full, comprehensive ; [- analyse, examen] thorough, full **3.** [entier] full ■ **nous resterons un mois ~** we'll stay a full month ■ **le ticket est valable pour la journée complète** the ticket is valid for the whole day **4.** [bondé - bus, métro, stade] full ■ **'complet'** [hôtel] 'no vacancies' ; [parking] 'full' ■ **nous sommes ~s** [salle de concert, théâtre, restaurant] we're (fully) booked **5.** [parfait - homme, artiste] all-round *(avant n)*, complete **6.** [total, absolu - silence] total, absolute ; [- repos] complete ; [- échec] total ■ **ils vivent dans la pauvreté la plus complète** they live in utter *ou* absolute *ou* abject poverty ■ **un fiasco ~** a complete (and utter) disaster ➊ **c'est ~!** that's all we needed!, that's the last straw!, that caps it all! **7.** [fournissant tout le nécessaire] : **la natation est un sport ~** swimming is an all-round sport ■ **le lait est un aliment ~** milk is a complete food, milk contains all the necessary nutrients **8.** CULIN [pain, farine, spaghetti] wholemeal ■ [riz] brown **9.** BOT complete.

◆ **complet** *nm* [vêtement] : **~, ~-veston** (man's) suit.

◆ **au (grand) complet** *loc adj* : **(toute) l'équipe au ~** the whole team ■ **mes amis étaient là au ~** all my friends showed up ■ **les couverts ne sont pas au ~** there are some knives and forks missing.

complète [kɔ̃plɛt] *f* ⊳ **complet**.

complètement [kɔ̃plɛtmɑ̃] *adv* **1.** [totalement] completely, totally ■ **~ nu** stark naked ■ **le jeu les a ~ ruinés** gambling left them totally penniless **2.** [vraiment] absolutely ■ **elle est ~ folle** she's stark raving mad ■ **je suis ~ d'accord** I absolutely *ou* totally agree.

compléter [18] [kɔ̃plete] *vt* **1.** [ajouter ce qui manque à - collection, dossier] to complete ; [- somme, remboursement] to make up *(sép)* ■ **il a complété sa collection par un Van Gogh** he completed his collection with a painting by Van Gogh **2.** [approfondir - analyse, notes, formation] to complete ; [- enquête] to finish, to complete **3.** [constituer le dernier élément de] to complete, to finish *ou* to round off *(sép)* ■ **un index complète le guide** the guide is completed by an index ■ **pour ~ le tout** to cap *ou* to crown it all.

◆ **se compléter** ◇ *vp (emploi passif)* **ma collection se complète peu à peu** my collection will soon be complete.

◇ *vp (emploi réciproque)* [personnes, caractères] to complement (one another) ■ **le vin et le fromage se complètent parfaitement** wine complements cheese perfectly.

complétif, ive [kɔ̃pletif, iv] *adj* : **proposition complétive** noun clause.
◆ **complétive** *nf* noun clause.

complétude [kɔ̃pletyd] *nf sout* [fait d'être complet] completeness.

complexe [kɔ̃plɛks] ◇ *adj* **1.** [compliqué - processus, trajet] complicated ; [- caractère, personne] complex, complicated **2.** LING & MATH complex.
◇ *nm* **1.** PSYCHOL complex ■ **avoir des ~s** *fam* to be hung up ▶ **~ d'infériorité/de supériorité/d'Œdipe** inferiority/superiority/ Oedipus complex **2.** CONSTR & ÉCON complex ■ **~ hospitalier/ industriel** medical/industrial complex **3.** CHIM & MATH complex.
◆ **sans complexe(s)** ◇ *loc adj* **1.** [simple] natural **2.** *péj* [sans honte] uninhibited ■ **elle est sans ~, celle-là!** she's so brazen!
◇ *loc adv* **1.** [sans manières] quite naturally *ou* simply, uninhibitedly **2.** *péj* [avec sans-gêne] uninhibitedly ■ **elle s'est ruée sur le buffet sans ~** she went straight for the buffet quite unashamedly.

complexé, e [kɔ̃plɛkse] ◇ *adj* neurotic ■ **elle est ~e par son poids** she has a complex about her weight.
◇ *nm, f* : **c'est un ~** he has a lot of complexes.

complexer [4] [kɔ̃plɛkse] *vt* [personne] : **arrête, tu vas le ~** stop, you'll give him a complex.

complexifier [9] [kɔ̃plɛksifje] *vt* to complicate, to make more complex.

complexion [kɔ̃plɛksjɔ̃] *nf litt* constitution ■ **être de ~ robuste/délicate** to have a healthy/delicate constitution.

complexité [kɔ̃plɛksite] *nf* complexity.

complication [kɔ̃plikasjɔ̃] *nf* **1.** [problème] complication ■ **oui mais attendez, il y a une ~** yes but wait, it's more complicated than you think ■ **tu cherches des ~s là où il n'y en a pas** you're reading more into it than is justified ■ **pourquoi faire des ~s?** why make things more difficult than they need be? **2.** [complexité] complicatedness, complexity ■ **elle aime les ~s** she likes things to be complicated.
◆ **complications** *nfpl* MÉD complications.

complice [kɔ̃plis] ◇ *adj* [regard, sourire, silence] knowing ■ **être ~ de qqch** to be (a) party to sthg.
◇ *nmf* **1.** [malfrat] accomplice **2.** [ami, confident] partner, friend ■ **sa femme et ~ de tous les instants** his wife and constant companion **3.** [dans un spectacle, un canular] partner.

complicité [kɔ̃plisite] *nf* **1.** DR complicity ■ **avec la ~ de qqn** with the complicity of sb, with sb as an accomplice **2.** [entente, amitié] : **elle lui adressa un sourire de ~** she smiled at him knowingly, she gave him a knowing smile ■ **nous avons retrouvé ce très vieux film avec la ~ du réalisateur** we've unearthed this very old footage, with the kind help of the director.
◆ **en complicité avec** *loc prép* in collusion with.

compliment [kɔ̃plimɑ̃] *nm* **1.** [éloge] compliment ■ **faire un ~ à qqn** to pay sb a compliment, to pay a compliment to sb ■ **on m'a fait des ~s sur mon soufflé** I was complimented on my soufflé **2.** [félicitations] congratulations ■ **adresser des ~s au vainqueur** to congratulate the winner ■ **(je vous fais) mes ~s!** *iron* congratulations!, well done! **3.** [dans des formules de politesse] compliment ■ **mes ~s à votre épouse** my regards to your wife **4.** [discours] congratulatory speech.

complimenter [3] [kɔ̃plimɑ̃te] *vt* **1.** [féliciter] to congratulate ■ **~ qqn sur son succès** to congratulate sb on *ou* for having succeeded **2.** [faire des éloges à] to compliment ■ **Julie m'a complimentée sur** *ou* **pour ma robe** Julie complimented me on my dress.

compliqué, e [kɔ̃plike] ◇ *adj* **1.** [difficile à comprendre - affaire, exercice, phrase] complicated ; [- jeu, langue, livre, problème] difficult ; [- plan] intricate ■ **elle avait un nom ~** she had a real tongue-twister of a name ■ **c'est trop ~ à expliquer** it's too hard to explain ■ **regarde, ce n'est pourtant pas ~!** look, it's not so difficult to understand! **2.** [ayant de nombreux éléments - appareil, mécanisme] complicated, complex, intricate **3.** [qui manque de naturel - personne] complicated ; [- esprit] tortuous.
◇ *nm, f fam* : **ta sœur, c'est une ~e!** your sister certainly likes complications!

compliquer [3] [kɔ̃plike] *vt* to complicate, to make (more) difficult *ou* complicated ■ **il me complique la vie** he makes things *ou* life difficult for me.
◆ **se compliquer** ◇ *vpi* **1.** [devenir embrouillé] to become (more) complicated ■ **ça se complique!** things are getting complicated!, the plot thickens! *hum* **2.** MÉD to be followed by complications.
◇ *vpt* : **se ~ la vie** *ou* **l'existence** make life difficult for o.s.

complot [kɔ̃plo] *nm* **1.** POLIT plot ■ **le ~ des poudres** HIST the Gunpowder Plot **2.** [menées] plot, scheme.

comploter [3] [kɔ̃plɔte] ◇ *vt* to plot.
◇ *vi* to be part of a plot ■ **~ de tuer qqn** to conspire to kill sb, to plot sb's murder.

comploteur, euse [kɔ̃plɔtœr, øz] *nm, f* plotter.

complu [kɔ̃ply] *pp* ▷ **complaire**.

componction [kɔ̃pɔ̃ksjɔ̃] *nf* **1.** [gravité affectée] gravity, solemnity ■ **avec ~** with solemnity **2.** RELIG compunction, contrition.

comportement [kɔ̃pɔrtəmɑ̃] *nm* **1.** [attitude] behaviour **2.** AUTO & SC [d'un véhicule] performance, behaviour ■ [de pneus] performance ■ [d'une molécule] behaviour **3.** PSYCHOL behaviour.

comportemental, e, aux [kɔ̃pɔrtəmɑ̃tal, o] *adj* **1.** [relatif à la façon d'être] behaviour *(modif)*, behavioural **2.** PSYCHOL behaviourist.

comportementalisme [kɔ̃pɔrtəmɑ̃talism] *nm* behaviourism.

comporter [3] [kɔ̃pɔrte] *vt* **1.** [être muni de] to have, to include **2.** [être constitué de] to be made up *ou* to consist of ■ **la maison comporte trois étages** it's a three-storey house **3.** [contenir] to contain **4.** [entraîner] to entail, to imply ■ **c'est un voyage qui comporte des risques** it's a risky trip ■ **elle a choisi l'aventure, avec tout ce que cela comporte de dangers** she chose to lead a life of adventure with all the risks it entailed **5.** [permettre, admettre] to allow, to admit ■ **la règle comporte quelques exceptions** there are one or two exceptions to this rule.
◆ **se comporter** *vpi* **1.** [réagir - personne] to act, to behave ■ **tâche de bien te ~** try to behave (yourself *ou* well) ■ **se ~ en enfant/en adulte** to act childishly/like an adult **2.** [fonctionner - voiture, pneus] to behave, to perform ; [- molécule] to behave.

composant, e [kɔ̃pozɑ̃, ɑ̃t] *adj* **1.** [qui constitue] constitutive **2.** LING compound *(modif)*.
◆ **composant** *nm* **1.** [élément] component, constituent **2.** CONSTR, INDUST & LING component ■ **~ de base** base component.
◆ **composante** *nf* [gén - MATH] & PHYS component.

composé, e [kɔ̃poze] *adj* **1.** [formé d'un mélange - bouquet, salade] mixed, composite **2.** [affecté - attitude] studied ■ **un visage ~** a studied look **3.** BOT [feuille] compound ■ [inflorescence] composite ■ **fleur ~e** composite (flower) **4.** ARCHIT composite **5.** LING [temps] compound *(modif)* ■ **mot ~** compound (word) **6.** CHIM, ÉCON & MATH compound *(modif)*.
◆ **composé** *nm* **1.** [ensemble] : **~ de** mixture *ou* blend *ou* combination of **2.** CHIM & MATH compound **3.** LING compound (word).
◆ **composée** *nf* composite (flower) ■ **les ~es** the Compositae.

composer [3] [kɔ̃poze] ◇ *vt* **1.** [rassembler - équipe, cabinet] to form, to select (the members of) ; [- menu] to prepare, to put together *(sép)* ; [- bouquet] to make up *(sép)* **2.** [écrire - roman, discours] to write ; [- poème, symphonie] to compose ; [- programme] to draw up *(sép)*, to prepare **3.** [faire partie de] to (go to) make up *(insép)* ■ **être composé de** to be made up of, to consist of **4.** *litt* [apprêter, étudier - attitude] : **~ son personnage** to create an image for o.s. **5.** TÉLÉCOM [numéro de téléphone] to dial ■ [code] to key (in) **6.** IMPR to set.

◇ *vi* **1.** [transiger] to compromise ■ **tu ne sais pas ~** you're (too) uncompromising ■ **~ avec qqn/sa conscience** to come to a compromise with sb/one's conscience **2.** ÉDUC to take an exam ■ **~ en histoire** to take a history test *ou* exam **3.** MUS : **il ne compose plus depuis des années** he hasn't composed *ou* written anything for years.

◆ **se composer** *vpt* : **se ~ un visage de circonstance** to assume an appropriate expression.

◆ **se composer de** *vp+prép* to be made up *ou* composed of ■ **l'équipe se compose de onze joueurs** the team is made up of *ou* comprises eleven players.

composite [kɔ̃pozit] ◇ *adj* **1.** [mobilier, population] heterogeneous, mixed, composite ■ [foule, assemblée] mixed **2.** ARCHIT & TECHNOL composite.

◇ *nm* ARCHIT composite order.

compositeur, trice [kɔ̃pozitœr, tris] *nm, f* **1.** MUS composer **2.** IMPR compositor, typesetter.

composition [kɔ̃pozisjɔ̃] *nf* **1.** [fabrication, assemblage - d'un produit, d'un plat, d'un menu] making up, putting together ; [- d'un bouquet] making up, arranging ; [- d'une équipe, d'une assemblée, d'un gouvernement] forming, formation, setting up ■ **~ florale** flower arrangement **2.** [écriture - d'une symphonie] composition ; [- d'un poème, d'une lettre] writing ; [- d'un programme] drawing up **3.** [éléments - d'une assemblée, d'un gouvernement, d'un menu] composition ; [- d'un programme] elements ■ **quelle sera la ~ du jury?** who will the members of the jury be?, who will make up the jury? ■ CULIN, PHARM & CHIM composition ■ **des conservateurs entrent dans la ~ du produit** this product contains preservatives ■ **'~: eau, sucre, fraises'** 'ingredients: water, sugar, strawberries' **4.** ART & PHOTO [technique, résultat] composition ■ **avoir le sens de la ~** to have a good eye for composition **5.** IMPR typesetting, composition ■ **~ automatique** *ou* **programmée** automatic typesetting **6.** ÉDUC [dissertation] essay, composition ■ [examen] test, exam, paper ■ **~ française** French paper.

◆ **à composition** *loc adv sout* **amener qqn à ~** to lead sb to a compromise ■ **arriver** *ou* **venir à ~** to come to a compromise.

◆ **de bonne composition** *loc adj* accommodating, good-natured, easy-going.

◆ **de composition** *loc adj* [rôle] character *(modif)*.

◆ **de ma composition, de sa composition** *etc loc adj* : **il a chanté une petite chanson de sa ~** he sang a little song he'd written.

compost [kɔ̃pɔst] *nm* compost.

compostage [kɔ̃pɔstaʒ] *nm* **1.** [pour dater] date-stamping **2.** [pour valider] punching **3.** AGRIC composting.

composter [3] [kɔ̃pɔste] *vt* **1.** [pour dater] to date stamp **2.** [pour valider] to punch **3.** AGRIC to compost.

> ***COMPOSTER***
>
> Rail passengers in France are required to insert their ticket into a special punching machine ("composteur") on the platform before beginning their journey. The words "à composter" printed across the ticket mean that the passenger must do this before getting on the train.

composteur [kɔ̃pɔstœr] *nm* **1.** [dateur] datestamp **2.** [pour valider] ticket-punching machine **3.** INFORM : **~ de données** data cartridge.

compote [kɔ̃pɔt] *nf* CULIN : **~ (de fruits)** stewed fruit, compote ■ **~ de pommes** stewed apples, apple compote.

◆ **en compote** *loc adj* **1.** [fruits] stewed **2.** *fam* [meurtri, détruit] smashed up ■ **j'ai les pieds en ~** my feet are killing me ■ **il a la figure en ~** his face has been beaten to a pulp.

compotier [kɔ̃pɔtje] *nm* fruit bowl.

compréhensible [kɔ̃preɑ̃sibl] *adj* [intelligible] intelligible ■ [excusable, concevable] understandable.

compréhensif, ive [kɔ̃preɑ̃sif, iv] *adj* **1.** [disposé à comprendre] understanding **2.** PHILOS comprehensive.

compréhension [kɔ̃preɑ̃sjɔ̃] *nf* **1.** [fait de comprendre] comprehension, understanding ■ **des notes nécessaires à la ~ du texte** notes that are necessary to understand *ou* for a proper understanding of the text **2.** [bienveillance] sympathy, understanding ■ **être plein de ~** to be very understanding **3.** LING & MATH comprehension.

comprendre [79] [kɔ̃prɑ̃dr] *vt*

A.

1. [saisir par un raisonnement] to understand ■ **il comprend vite mais il faut lui expliquer longtemps!** *hum* he's a bit slow on the uptake! ■ **c'est à n'y rien ~** it's just baffling ■ **(c'est) compris?** [vous avez suivi] is it clear?, do you understand? ; [c'est un ordre] do you hear me! ■ **(c'est) compris!** all right!, OK! ■ **faire ~ qqch à qqn** [le lui prouver] to make sthg clear to sb ; [l'en informer] to give sb to understand sthg ■ **se faire ~ : est-ce que je me fais bien ~?** [mon exposé est-il clair?] is my explanation clear enough? ; [ton menaçant] do I make myself clear? ■ **quand j'ai vu la pile de dossiers, j'ai compris mon malheur** *ou* **ma douleur!** when I saw that great pile of files, I knew what I was in for! ■ *(en usage absolu)* **elle a fini par ~** [se résigner] she finally got the message ■ **ça va, j'ai compris, tu préfères que je m'en aille!** OK, I get the message, you want me to go!

2. [saisir grâce à ses connaissances - théorie, langue] to understand ■ **se faire ~** to make o.s. understood

3. [saisir par une intuition] to understand, to realize ■ **comprends-tu l'importance d'une telle décision?** do you realize how important a decision it is? ■ **je commence à ~ où il veut en venir** I'm beginning to realize what he's after

4. [admettre] to understand ■ **je comprends qu'on s'énerve dans les bouchons** it's quite understandable that people get irritable when caught in traffic jams ■ *(en usage absolu)* **elle n'a pas osé, il faut ~ (aussi)!** she didn't dare, you have to put yourself in her shoes!

DIRE QU'ON A COMPRIS/QU'ON N'A PAS COMPRIS

I see (what you mean now). Je vois (ce que vous voulez dire).

I understand. Je comprends.

I think I've got it now. Ça y est, je crois que j'ai compris.

I'm sorry, I don't follow you. Pardon, mais je ne vous suis pas.

I'm sorry, I still don't understand/it's still not very clear. Désolé, mais je ne comprends toujours pas/ce n'est toujours pas très clair.

I'm afraid you've lost me. Je ne vous suis plus.

5. [concevoir] to understand, to see ▪ **c'est ainsi que je comprends le rôle** this is how I understand *ou* see the part ▪ *(en usage absolu)* [pour établir un lien avec l'interlocuteur] : **tu comprends?, comprends-tu?** you see?, you know?
6. [avoir les mêmes sentiments que] to understand, to sympathize with ▪ **elle comprend les jeunes** she understands young people ▪ **je vous comprends, cela a dû être terrible** I know how you feel, it must have been awful ▪ **je la comprends, avec un mari pareil!** I don't blame her with the sort of husband she's got!
7. [apprécier] to have a feeling for, to understand ▪ **il ne comprend pas la plaisanterie** he can't take a joke

B.
1. [être composé entièrement de] to contain, to be made up *ou* to be comprised *ou* to consist of
2. [être composé en partie de] to include, to contain ▪ **l'équipe comprend trois joueurs étrangers** there are three foreign players in the team
3. [englober - frais, taxe] to include
4. *(au passif)* [se situer] : **l'inflation sera comprise entre 5 % et 8 %** inflation will be (somewhere) between 5% and 8% ▪ **la partie comprise entre la table et le mur** the section between the table and the wall.
◆ **se comprendre** ◇ *vp (emploi passif)* to be understandable ▪ **cela se comprend, ça se comprend** that's quite understandable.
◇ *vp (emploi réciproque)* to understand one another.
◇ *vp (emploi réfléchi)* *fam loc* **je me comprends!** I know what I'm getting at (even if others don't)!
Voir module d'usage

comprenette [kɔ̃prənɛt] *nf fam* **il n'a pas la ~ facile, il a la ~ dure** he's a bit slow (on the uptake).

comprennent, comprenons *etc v* ▻ **comprendre**.

compresse [kɔ̃prɛs] *nf* compress, pack.

compresser [4] [kɔ̃prese] *vt* [gén] to pack (tightly) in, to pack in tight ▪ [informatique] to compress.

compresseur [kɔ̃presœr] *nm* **1.** [d'un réfrigérateur] compressor **2.** MÉCAN supercharger **3.** TRAV PUB : **(rouleau) ~** steamroller.

compressibilité [kɔ̃presibilite] *nf* **1.** MÉCAN & PHYS compressibility **2.** *fig* [flexibilité] : **cela dépend de la ~ des dépenses** it depends on how much expenditure can be cut down *ou* reduced.

compressible [kɔ̃presibl] *adj* **1.** MÉCAN & PHYS compressible **2.** *fig* [réductible] reducible ▪ **commençons par les dépenses ~s** let's begin with expenses that can be cut down *ou* reduced.

compressif, ive [kɔ̃presif, iv] *adj* [bandage, appareil] compressive.

compression [kɔ̃presjɔ̃] *nf* **1.** MÉCAN & PHYS compression **2.** [des dépenses, du personnel] reduction, cutting down ▪ **procéder à une ~ des effectifs** to cut down the workforce ▪ **des ~s budgétaires** cuts *ou* reductions in the budget **3.** MÉD compression **4.** INFORM compression ▪ **~ des caractères** digit compression.
◆ **de compression** *loc adj* MÉCAN [pompe] compression *(modif).*

comprimé, e [kɔ̃prime] *adj* compressed.
◆ **comprimé** *nm* tablet.

comprimer [3] [kɔ̃prime] *vt* **1.** [serrer - air, vapeur, gaz] to compress ; [- objets] to pack (in) tightly ; [- foin, paille] to compact, to press tight ▪ **cette robe me comprime la taille** this dress is much too tight for me around the waist ▪ **les voyageurs étaient comprimés dans le train** the travellers were jammed *ou* packed tight in the train **2.** [diminuer - dépenses] to curtail, to trim, to cut down *(sép)* ; [- effectifs] to trim *ou* to cut down *(sép)* **3.** [contenir - colère, joie, rire] to hold back *(sép)*, to suppress, to repress ; [- larmes] to hold back *(sép)* **4.** INFORM to pack **5.** MÉD to compress.

compris, e [kɔ̃pri, iz] ◇ *pp* ▻ **comprendre**.
◇ *adj* **1.** [inclus - service, boisson] included ▪ **service non ~** service not included, not inclusive of the service charge ▪ **y ~** included, including ▪ **je travaille tous les jours y ~ le dimanche** I work every day including Sundays *ou* Sundays included ▪ [dans les dates] inclusive **2.** [pensé] : **bien ~** well thought-out.
◇ *interj fam* AÉRON & TÉLÉCOM : **~!** OK!
◆ **tout compris** *loc adv* net, all inclusive, all in *UK*.

compromets *etc v* ▻ **compromettre**.

compromettant, e [kɔ̃prɔmetɑ̃, ɑ̃t] *adj* [document, action] incriminating ▪ [situation] compromising ▪ **évitez toute relation ~e** avoid associating with anybody who might compromise you.

compromettre [84] [kɔ̃prɔmɛtr] ◇ *vt* **1.** [nuire à la réputation de] to compromise ▪ **compromis par une cassette** compromised *ou* incriminated because of a cassette ▪ **il est compromis dans l'affaire** he's implicated *ou* involved in the affair **2.** [mettre en danger - fortune, avenir, santé] to put in jeopardy, to jeopardize ▪ **s'il pleut, notre sortie est compromise** if it rains, our outing is unlikely to go ahead.
◇ *vi* DR to compromise.
◆ **se compromettre** *vp (emploi réfléchi)* to risk *ou* to jeopardize one's reputation, to be compromised.

compromis [kɔ̃prɔmi] *nm* [concession] compromise ▪ [moyen terme] compromise (solution) ▪ **faire des ~** to make compromises ▪ **trouver un ~** to reach *ou* to come to a compromise.

compromission [kɔ̃prɔmisjɔ̃] *nf* base action, (piece of) dishonourable behaviour ▪ **elle est prête à n'importe quelle ~ pour réussir** she will stoop to anything in order to succeed.

comptabilisation [kɔ̃tabilizasjɔ̃] *nf* FIN : **faire la ~ des recettes et des dépenses** to balance out credits and debits.

comptabiliser [3] [kɔ̃tabilize] *vt* **1.** FIN to list, to enter in the accounts **2.** [compter] to count ▪ **je n'ai pas comptabilisé ses allées et venues** I didn't keep a record of his comings and goings ▪ **~ les appels** to list *ou* to itemize phone calls.

comptabilité [kɔ̃tabilite] *nf* **1.** [profession] accountancy, accounting ▪ **faire de la ~** to work as an accountant **2.** [comptes] accounts, books ▪ **faire la ~ de qqn** to do sb's books *ou* book-keeping **3.** [technique] accounting, book-keeping ▪ **~ à partie double** double-entry book-keeping **4.** [service, bureau] accounts (department) **5.** ÉCON & FIN : **~ nationale** national auditing ▪ **~ publique** public finance.

comptable [kɔ̃tabl] ◇ *adj* **1.** FIN accounting *(modif)*, book-keeping *(modif)* **2.** LING count *(modif)*, countable.
◇ *nmf* accountant ▪ **~ du Trésor public** Treasury official.

comptage [kɔ̃taʒ] *nm* counting ▪ **faire le ~ de** to count.

comptant [kɔ̃tɑ̃] ◇ *adj m* : **je lui ai versé 250 euros ~s** I paid him 250 euros in cash.
◇ *adv* cash ▪ **payer ~** to pay cash ▪ **acheter/vendre ~** to buy/to sell for cash.
◆ **au comptant** *loc adv* cash *(adv)* ▪ **acheter/vendre au ~** to buy/to sell for cash.

compte [kɔ̃t] *nm*

A. CALCUL, SOMME CALCULÉE
B. DANS LE DOMAINE FINANCIER ET COMMERCIAL
C. LOCUTIONS

A. CALCUL, SOMME CALCULÉE
1. [opération] counting ▪ **faire le ~ (de)** [personnes] to count (up) ; [dépenses] to add up ▪ **faites le ~ vous-même** work it out (for) yourself ▪ **quand on fait le ~...** when you reckon it all up... ▶ **~ à rebours** *pr* & *fig* countdown
2. [résultat] (sum) total ▪ **j'ai le ~** I've got the right money ▪ **je vous remercie, monsieur, le ~ est bon** *ou* **y est!** thank you sir, that's right! ▪ **il n'y a pas le ~** [personnes] they're not all here *ou* there, some are missing ; [dépenses] it doesn't add up ▶ **~ rond : cela fait un ~ rond** that makes it a (nice) round sum *ou* figure ▪ **cela ne fait pas un ~ rond** it comes to an odd figure ▪ **comment fais-tu ton ~ pour te tromper à chaque fois/**

pour que tout le monde soit mécontent? how do you manage to get it wrong every time/manage it so (that) nobody's satisfied? ■ **mais comment a-t-il fait son ~?** but how did he make such a mess of it?
3. [avantage] : **j'y trouve mon ~** I do well out of it, it works out well for me ■ **il n'y trouvait pas son ~, alors il est parti** [il ne gagnait pas assez d'argent] he wasn't doing well enough out of it, so he left ; [dans une relation] he wasn't getting what he wanted out of it, so he left
4. [dû] : **demander son ~** to ask for one's wages ■ **donner son ~ à qqn** to give sb (his) notice ➜ **avoir son ~ (de)** to have more than one's fair share *ou* more than enough (of) ■ **je n'ai pas mon ~ de sommeil** I don't get all the sleep I need *ou* enough sleep ■ **il a déjà son ~** *fam* [il a beaucoup bu] he's had quite enough to drink already, he's had a skinful ■ **recevoir son ~** *pr* to get one's (final) wages ; *fam fig*fam to get the sack *UK ou* one's marching orders ■ **régler son ~ à qqn** *pr* to pay sb off ; *fam fig*fam to give sb a piece of one's mind ■ **régler ses ~s** [mettre en ordre ses affaires] to put one's affairs in order ■ **régler ses ~s avec qqn** [le payer] to settle up with sb ; [se venger] to settle a score with sb ■ **son ~ est bon** *fam* he's had it, he's done for

B. DANS LE DOMAINE FINANCIER ET COMMERCIAL
1. [de dépôt, de crédit] account ■ **~ bancaire** bank account ■ **~ courant** current *UK ou* checking *US* account ■ **~ de dépôt** deposit *UK ou* savings *US* account ■ **~ épargne** savings account ■ **~ épargne logement** savings account *(for purchasing a property)* ■ **~ joint** joint account ■ **~ numéroté** numbered account
2. [facture] bill, check *US* ■ **faites-moi** *ou* **préparez-moi le ~** may I have the bill, please?
3. [bilan] : **~ de profits et pertes** profit and loss account

C. LOCUTIONS
1. [argent] : **à mon/son** *etc* **~ : reprendre à son ~** [magasin] to take over in one's own name ; [idée, écrit] to adopt ■ **il a pris le repas à son ~** he paid for the meal ■ **être** *ou* **travailler à son ~** to be self-employed ■ **il est à son ~** he's his own boss, he's set up on his own ■ **à ~ d'auteur** at the author's own expense ■ **en ~ : passer** *ou* **porter une somme en ~** [recette] to credit a sum ; [dépense] to debit a sum ■ **nous sommes en ~, vous me réglerez tout à la fin** as we're doing business together, you may pay me in full at the end
2. [explication, compréhension] : **demander des ~s à qqn** to ask sb for an explanation of sthg, to ask sb to account for sthg ■ **rendre des ~s (à qqn)** to give *ou* to offer (sb) an explanation ■ **je n'ai pas de ~s à vous rendre** I don't have to justify myself to you ■ **rendre ~ de qqch à qqn** [s'en expliquer] to justify sthg to sb ; [faire un rapport] to give an account of sthg to sb ■ **devoir des ~s à qqn** to be responsible *ou* accountable to sb ■ **il ne te doit pas de ~s** he doesn't owe you any explanations ■ **prendre qqch en ~** [prendre en considération] to take sthg into account *ou* consideration ■ **se rendre ~ de qqch** to realize sthg ■ **te rends-tu ~ de ce que tu fais?** do you realize *ou* really understand what you're doing? ■ **on lui a collé une étiquette dans le dos mais il ne s'en est pas rendu ~** somebody stuck a label on his back but he didn't notice ■ **non mais, tu te rends ~!** *fam* [indignation] can you believe it? ■ **tenir ~ de qqch** to take account of sthg, to take sthg into account ■ **ne tenir aucun ~ de qqch** to disregard sthg ■ **elle n'a pas tenu ~ de mes conseils** she took no notice of *ou* ignored my advice ■ **~ tenu de** in view *ou* in the light of.

◆ **comptes** *nmpl* accounts, accounting ■ **faire/tenir les ~s** to do/to keep the accounts ➜ **faire des ~s d'apothicaire** to work things out to the last penny *ou* cent *US* ■ **les bons ~s font les bons amis** *prov* pay your debts and you'll keep your friends.
◆ **à bon compte** *loc adv* [acheter] cheap, cheaply ■ **s'en tirer à bon ~** [sans frais] to manage to avoid paying a fortune ; [sans conséquences graves] to get off lightly.
◆ **à ce compte, à ce compte-là** *loc adv* [selon ce raisonnement] looking at it *ou* taking it that way.
◆ **pour compte** *loc adv* : **laisser qqn pour ~** to neglect sb ■ **laisser des marchandises pour ~** to leave goods on a merchant's hands.
◆ **pour le compte** *loc adv* for the count.
◆ **pour le compte de** *loc prép* for ■ **elle travaille pour le ~ d'une grande société** she works for a large firm, she freelances for a large firm.
◆ **pour mon compte, pour son compte** *etc loc adv* for my/his *etc* part, as for me/him *etc*.
◆ **sur le compte de** *loc prép* **1.** [à propos de] on, about, concerning ■ **on a dit bien des bêtises sur son ~** people talked a lot of nonsense about him **2.** *loc* **mettre qqch sur le ~ de qqn** *pr* to put sthg on sb's bill ■ **mettre qqch sur le ~ de qqch** to put sthg down to sthg.
◆ **tout compte fait, tous comptes faits** *loc adv* [après tout] thinking about it, on second thoughts.

compte(-)chèques [kɔ̃tʃɛk] (*pl* **comptes-chèques** *ou pl* **comptes chèques**) *nm* current *UK ou* checking *US* account ■ **~ postal** *account held at the Post Office* ■ ≃ giro account *UK* ■ **les comptes-chèques postaux** *the banking service of the French Post Office* ■ ≃ the Giro Bank *UK*.

compte-gouttes [kɔ̃tgut] *nm inv* dropper.
◆ **au compte-gouttes** *loc adv* very sparingly ■ **payer qqn au ~** to pay sb off in dribs and drabs ■ **distribuer qqch au ~** to dole sthg out.

compter [3] [kɔ̃te] <> *vt* **1.** [dénombrer - objets, argent, personnes] to count ■ **on ne compte plus ses bévues** we've lost count of his mistakes ■ **on ne compte plus ses crimes** she has committed countless *ou* innumerable crimes ■ **j'ai compté qu'il restait 200 euros dans la caisse** according to my reckoning there are 200 euros left in the till ■ **~ les heures/jours** [d'impatience] to be counting the hours/days ■ **il m'a compté absent/présent** *fam* he marked me (down as) absent/present ➜ **~ les points** *pr & fig* to keep score ■ **on peut les ~ sur les doigts de la main** you can count them of the fingers of one hand ■ **on peut lui ~ les côtes** he's as thin as a rake
2. [limiter] to count (out) ■ **le temps lui est compté** [il va mourir] his days are numbered ; [pour accomplir quelque chose] he's running out of time ■ **ses jours sont comptés** his days are numbered ■ **il ne comptait pas sa peine/ses efforts** he spared no pains/effort ■ **tu es toujours à ~ tes sous!** you're always counting your pennies!
3. [faire payer] to charge for ■ **nous ne vous compterons pas la pièce détachée** we won't charge you *ou* there'll be no charge for the spare part ■ **le serveur nous a compté deux euros de trop** the waiter has overcharged us by two euros, the waiter has charged us 15 francs too much
4. [payer, verser] to pay ■ **il m'a compté deux jours à 90 euros** he paid me (for) two days at 90 euros
5. [inclure] to count (in), to include ■ **dans le total nous n'avons pas compté le vin** wine has not been included in the overall figure
6. [classer - dans une catégorie] : **~ qqch/qqn parmi** to count sthg/sb among, to number sthg/sb among
7. [prendre en considération] to take into account, to take account of ■ **et je ne compte pas la fatigue!** and that's without mentioning the effort! ■ **~ qqn/qqch pour : nous devons ~ sa contribution pour quelque chose** we must take some account of her contribution
8. [avoir - membres, habitants] to have ■ **nous sommes heureux de vous ~ parmi nous ce soir** we're happy to have *ou* to welcome you among us tonight ■ **il compte beaucoup d'artistes au nombre de** *ou* **parmi ses amis** he numbers many artists among his friends ■ **elle compte déjà cinq victoires dans des grands tournois** she's already won five big tournaments
9. [s'attendre à] to expect ■ **je compte recevoir les résultats cette semaine** I'm expecting the results this week
10. [avoir l'intention de] to intend ■ **~ faire qqch** to intend to do sthg, to mean to do sthg, to plan to do sthg
11. [prévoir] to allow ■ **il faut ~ entre 14 et 20 euros pour un repas** you have to allow between 14 and 20 euros for a meal ■ **je compte qu'il y a un bon quart d'heure de marche/une journée de travail** I reckon there's a good quarter of an hour's walk/ there's a day's work ■ *(en usage absolu)* **~ juste** to skimp ■ **~ large** to be generous ■ **il faudra deux heures pour y aller, en comptant large** it will take two hours to get there, at the most
12. SPORT [boxeur] to count out *(sép)*.
<> *vi* **1.** [calculer] to count, to add up ■ **~ jusqu'à 10** to count (up) to 10 ■ **~ sur ses doigts** to count on one's fingers ■ **~ avec une calculette** to add up with a calculator ■ **si je compte bien, tu me dois 345 francs** if I've counted right *ou* according to my calculations, you owe me 345 francs ■ **tu as dû mal ~** you must have got your calculations wrong, you must have miscalculated

2. [limiter ses dépenses] to be careful (with money)
3. [importer] to count, to matter ■ **ce qui compte, c'est ta santé/le résultat** the important thing is your health/the end result ■ **40 ans d'ancienneté, ça compte!** 40 years' service counts for something! ■ **une des personnes qui ont le plus compté dans ma vie** one of the most important people in my life ■ **tu comptes beaucoup pour moi** you mean a lot to me ■ **je prendrai ma décision seule! – alors moi, je ne compte pas?** I'll make my own decision! – so I don't count *ou* matter, then? ■ **tu as triché, ça ne compte pas** you cheated, it doesn't count ■ **à l'examen, la philosophie ne compte presque pas** philosophy is a very minor subject in the exam ■ **~ double/triple** to count double/triple ■ **~ pour quelque chose/rien** to count for something/nothing ■ **quand il est invité à dîner, il compte pour trois!** when he's invited to dinner he eats enough for three! ➤ **~ pour du beurre** *fam* to count for nothing
4. [figurer] : **~ parmi** to rank with, to be numbered among ■ **elle compte parmi les plus grands pianistes de sa génération** she is one of the greatest pianists of her generation.
◆ **compter avec** *v+prép* to reckon with ■ **désormais, il faudra ~ avec l'opposition** from now on, the opposition will have to be reckoned with.
◆ **compter sans** *v+prép* to fail to take into account, to fail to allow for ■ **il avait compté sans la rapidité de Jones** he had failed to take Jones' speed into account.
◆ **compter sur** *v+prép* [faire confiance à] to count *ou* to rely *ou* to depend on *(insép)* ■ [espérer - venue, collaboration, événement] to count on *(insép)* ■ **c'est quelqu'un sur qui tu peux ~** he's/she's a reliable person ■ **ne compte pas trop sur la chance** don't count *ou* rely too much on luck ■ **je vous le rendrai – j'y compte bien!** I'll give it back to you – I should hope so! ■ **je peux sortir demain soir? – n'y compte pas!** can I go out tomorrow night? – don't count *ou* bank on it! ■ **il ne faut pas trop y compter** don't count on it, I wouldn't count on it ■ **~ sur qqn/qqch pour : compte sur lui pour aller tout répéter au patron!** you can rely on him to go and tell the boss everything! ■ **si c'est pour lui jouer un mauvais tour, ne comptez pas sur moi!** if you want to play a dirty trick on him, you can count me out! ➤ **compte là-dessus (et bois de l'eau fraîche)!** *fam iron* you must be joking!, dream on!
◆ **se compter** ◇ *vp (emploi passif)* to be counted ■ **les détournements de fonds se comptent par dizaines** there have been dozens of cases of embezzlement ■ **ses succès ne se comptent plus** her successes are innumerable *ou* are past counting.
◇ *vp (emploi réfléchi)* **1.** [s'estimer] to count *ou* to consider o.s. ■ **je ne me compte pas parmi les plus malheureux** I count myself as one of the luckier ones
2. [s'inclure dans un calcul] to count *ou* to include o.s.
◆ **à compter de** *loc prép* as from *ou* of ■ **à ~ du 7 mai** as from *ou* of May 7th ■ **à ~ de ce jour, nous ne nous sommes plus revus** from that day on, we never saw each other again.
◆ **en comptant** *loc prép* including ■ **il faut deux mètres de tissu en comptant l'ourlet** you need two metres of material including *ou* if you include the hem.
◆ **sans compter** ◇ *loc adv* [généreusement] : **donner sans ~** to give generously *ou* without counting the cost ■ **se dépenser sans ~** to spare no effort.
◇ *loc prép* [sans inclure] not counting ■ [sans parler de] to say nothing of, not to mention.
◆ **sans compter que** *loc conj* quite apart from the fact that ■ **il est trop tôt pour aller dormir, sans ~ que je n'ai pas du tout sommeil** it's too early to go to bed, quite apart from the fact that I'm not at all sleepy.
◆ **tout bien compté** *loc adv* all things considered, all in all.

compte(-)rendu [kɔ̃trɑ̃dy] (*pl* **comptes rendus** *ou pl* **comptes-rendus**) *nm* [d'une conversation] account, report ■ [d'une séance, d'un match, d'une visite professionnelle] report ■ [d'un livre, d'un spectacle] review ■ **~ d'audience** court session record.

compte-tours [kɔ̃ttur] *nm inv* rev counter, tachometer *spéc.*

compteur [kɔ̃tœr] *nm* [appareil] meter ■ [affichage] counter ■ **relever le ~** to read the meter ■ **la voiture a 1 000 kilomètres au ~** the car has 1,000 kilometres on the clock ➤ **~ à gaz/d'eau/d'électricité** gas/water/electricity meter ■ **~ kilométrique** milometer *UK*, mileometer *UK*, odometer *US* ■ **~ de vitesse** speedometer.

comptine [kɔ̃tin] *nf* [chanson] nursery rhyme ■ [formule] counting-out rhyme.

comptoir [kɔ̃twar] *nm* **1.** [bar] bar ■ **j'ai pris un café au ~** I had a coffee at the bar *ou* counter **2.** COMM [table] counter **3.** HIST trading post **4.** ÉCON trading syndicate **5.** BANQUE bank branch **6.** *Suisse* [foire] fair *(where items are exhibited and sold)*.

compulser [3] [kɔ̃pylse] *vt* to consult, to refer to *(insép)*.

compulsif, ive [kɔ̃pylsif, iv] *adj* compulsive PSYCHOL.

compulsion [kɔ̃pylsjɔ̃] *nf* compulsion PSYCHOL.

computer [kɔ̃pjutœr], **computeur** [kɔ̃pytœr] *nm* computer.

comte [kɔ̃t] *nm* count, earl ■ **le Comte de Paris** *title of the present claimant to the French throne.*

comté [kɔ̃te] *nm* **1.** [territoire d'un comte] earldom **2.** [division géographique] county **3.** [fromage] comté (cheese).

comtesse [kɔ̃tɛs] *nf* countess.

con, conne[△] [kɔ̃, kɔn] ◇ *adj* **1.** [stupide] bloody[△] *UK ou* damn stupid ■ [irritant] bloody[△] *UK ou* damn irritating ■ **il n'est pas ~!** he's no fool! ■ **qu'est-ce qu'elle est conne!** God she's stupid! ➤ **~ comme un balai** *ou* **la lune** *ou* **un manche** thick as two short planks *UK*, as dumb as they come *US* ■ **se retrouver tout ~** to look an idiot, to end up looking stupid **2.** [regrettable] silly, stupid.
◇ *nm, f* [personne stupide] bloody *UK ou* goddam *US* fool[△] ■ **pauvre ~!** you prat[△] *UK ou* schmuck[△] *US!* ■ **pauvre conne!** silly bitch! ■ **bande de ~s!** (what a) load of jerks![△] ■ **le roi des ~s** a complete and utter prat[△] *UK ou* jerk[△] *US* ■ **jouer au ~, faire le ~** to arse around[△] *UK*, to screw around[△] *US*.
◆ **con**[▲] *nm* cunt.
◆ **à la con**[△] *loc adj* **1.** [stupide] bloody *UK ou* damn *US* stupid[△] **2.** [de mauvaise qualité] crappy[△], shitty[△].

conard[▲] [kɔnar] = **connard**.

conasse[▲] [kɔnas] = **connasse**.

concassé, e [kɔ̃kase] *adj* [poivre] coarse-ground ■ **blé ~** cracked wheat.

concasser [3] [kɔ̃kase] *vt* [pierre, sucre] to crush, to pound ■ [poivre] to grind.

concaténation [kɔ̃katenasjɔ̃] *nf* concatenation.

concave [kɔ̃kav] *adj* concave.

concavité [kɔ̃kavite] *nf* **1.** [fait d'être concave] concavity **2.** [creux] hollow, cavity.

concéder [18] [kɔ̃sede] *vt* **1.** [donner - droit, territoire] to concede, to grant **2.** [admettre] to admit, to grant ■ **elle parle bien, ça je te le concède** I must admit that she's a good speaker, she's a good speaker, I grant you **3.** SPORT [point, corner] to concede, to give away *(sép)*.

concentrateur [kɔ̃sɑ̃tratœr] *nm* INFORM concentrator.

concentration [kɔ̃sɑ̃trasjɔ̃] *nf* **1.** [attention] : **~ (d'esprit)** concentration ■ **faire un effort de ~** to try to concentrate **2.** [rassemblement] concentration ➤ **~ urbaine** conurbation **3.** CHIM, CULIN & PHARM concentration **4.** ÉCON : **~ horizontale/verticale** horizontal/vertical integration.

concentrationnaire [kɔ̃sɑ̃trasjɔnɛr] *adj* **1.** HIST : **l'univers ~** life in the (concentration) camps **2.** [rappelant les camps] concentration-like.

concentré, e [kɔ̃sɑ̃tre] *adj* **1.** [attentif] : **je n'étais pas assez ~** I wasn't concentrating hard enough **2.** CHIM, CULIN & PHARM concentrated **3.** [concis - style] compact, taut ■ **dans une lettre très ~e** in a letter that was very much to the point.
◆ **concentré** *nm* **1.** CULIN & PHARM [de jus de fruit] concentrate ■ [de parfum] extract ■ **~ de tomate** tomato purée **2.** [résumé] summary, boiled-down version *péj.*

concentrer [3] [kɔ̃sɑ̃tre] *vt* **1.** [rassembler - troupes, foule, élèves] to concentrate, to mass ■ **c'est là que l'on a concentré les malades** this is where all the sick people have been gathered together **2.** [intérêt, efforts] to concentrate, to focus ■ **~ (toute) son attention sur** to concentrate (all) one's attention on **3.** CHIM, CULIN & PHARM to concentrate **4.** OPT to focus.
◆ **se concentrer** *vpi* **1.** [être attentif] to concentrate ■ **se ~ sur qqch** to concentrate *ou* to focus on sthg **2.** [se réunir - foule] to gather, to cluster, to concentrate **3.** [se canaliser] to be concentrated *ou* focussed ■ **se ~ sur un seul problème** to concentrate on a single issue.

concentrique [kɔ̃sɑ̃trik] *adj* concentric.

concept [kɔ̃sɛpt] *nm* concept, notion.

concepteur, trice [kɔ̃sɛptœr, tris] *nm, f* designer ■ **c'est plutôt un ~ qu'un gestionnaire** he's more of an ideas man than a manager.

conception [kɔ̃sɛpsjɔ̃] *nf* **1.** [notion] idea, concept, notion ■ **elle a une ~ originale de la vie** she has an original way of looking at life **2.** *litt* [compréhension] understanding **3.** BIOL conception **4.** [élaboration - gén] design ; [- par une entreprise] product design ■ **produit de ~ française** French-designed product ■ **un ventilateur d'une ~ toute nouvelle** a fan with an entirely new design **5.** INFORM : **~ assistée par ordinateur** computer-aided design ■ **~ et fabrication assistées par ordinateur** computer-aided manufacturing.

conceptualisation [kɔ̃sɛptɥalizasjɔ̃] *nf* conceptualization.

conceptualiser [3] [kɔ̃sɛptɥalize] *vt* to conceptualize.

conceptuel, elle [kɔ̃sɛptɥɛl] *adj* conceptual.

concernant [kɔ̃sɛrnɑ̃] *prép* **1.** [relatif à] concerning, regarding **2.** [à propos de] regarding, with regard to.

concerner [3] [kɔ̃sɛrne] *vt* to concern ■ **cette histoire ne nous concerne pas** this business doesn't concern us *ou* is of no concern to us *ou* is no concern of ours ■ **les salariés concernés par cette mesure** the employees concerned *ou* affected by this measure ■ **se sentir concerné** to feel involved.
◆ **en ce qui concerne** *loc prép* concerning, as regards ■ **en ce qui me/le concerne** as far as I'm/he's concerned, from my/his point of view, as for me/him.

concert [kɔ̃sɛr] *nm* **1.** MUS concert ■ **~ rock/de musique classique** rock/classical (music) concert ■ **aller au ~** to go to a concert **2.** *fig* [ensemble] chorus ■ **~ de louanges/protestations** chorus of praises/protests **3.** *sout* [entente] entente.
◆ **de concert** *loc adv* together, jointly ■ **agir de ~ avec qqn** to act jointly *ou* in conjunction with sb.

concertant, e [kɔ̃sɛrtɑ̃, ɑ̃t] *adj* concertante.

concertation [kɔ̃sɛrtasjɔ̃] *nf* **1.** [dialogue] dialogue **2.** [consultation] consultation ■ **sans ~ préalable avec les syndicats** without consulting the unions.

concerté, e [kɔ̃sɛrte] *adj* **1.** [commun - plan, action] concerted, joint **2.** ÉCON : **fixation ~e des prix** common pricing, common price fixing.

concerter [3] [kɔ̃sɛrte] *vt* to plan *ou* to devise jointly.
◆ **se concerter** *vp (emploi réciproque)* to consult together, to confer.

concertiste [kɔ̃sɛrtist] *nmf* **1.** [gén] concert performer *ou* artist **2.** [soliste] soloist *(in a concerto)*.

concerto [kɔ̃sɛrto] *nm* concerto.

concessif, ive [kɔ̃sesif, iv] *adj* GRAMM concessive.

concession [kɔ̃sesjɔ̃] *nf* **1.** [compromis] concession ■ **faire des ~s** to make concessions **2.** DR [action de concéder] concession, conceding ■ **accorder une ~ à** to grant a concession to **3.** [terrain] concession ■ **~ minière/pétrolière** mining/oil concession ■ **~ funéraire** burial plot.

concessionnaire [kɔ̃sesjɔnɛr] <> *adj* concessionary.
<> *nmf* COMM dealer, franchise holder ■ **renseignez-vous auprès de votre ~ (automobile)** see your (car) dealer.

concessive [kɔ̃sesiv] *f* ⊳ **concessif.**

concevable [kɔ̃svabl] *adj* conceivable ■ **il n'est pas ~ que...** it's inconceivable that...

concevoir [52] [kɔ̃s(ə)vwar] *vt* **1.** [avoir une notion de] to conceive of *(insép)*, to form a notion of **2.** [imaginer] to imagine, to conceive of *(insép)* ■ **je ne conçois pas de repas sans vin** I can't imagine a meal without wine **3.** [comprendre] to understand, to see ■ **c'est ainsi que je conçois l'amour** this is my idea of love *ou* how I see love ■ **cela vous est difficile, je le conçois** I can (well) understand that it's difficult for you **4.** *litt* [ressentir - haine, amitié] to conceive, to develop **5.** [créer - meuble, décor, ouvrage] to design ; [- plan, programme] to conceive, to devise, to think up *(sép)* ■ **parc bien/mal conçu** well-/poorly-designed garden **6.** [rédiger - message, réponse] to compose, to couch ■ **une lettre conçue en ces termes** a letter written as follows *ou* couched in the following terms **7.** BIOL to conceive ■ *(en usage absolu)* **les femmes qui ne peuvent pas ~** women who cannot have children *ou* conceive.
◆ **se concevoir** *vp (emploi passif)* to be imagined ■ **une telle politique se conçoit en temps de guerre** such a policy is understandable in wartime.

conchyliculture [kɔ̃kilikyltyr] *nf* shellfish breeding.

concierge [kɔ̃sjɛrʒ] *nmf* **1.** [gardien - d'immeuble] caretaker, janitor US ; [- d'hôtel] porter UK, receptionist **2.** *fam péj* [bavard] gossip, blabbermouth.

CONCIERGE

In French apartment buildings, the *concierge* does general cleaning jobs, sees to it that no unwelcome visitors enter the building, and often also delivers mail to the occupants of the building. The concierge usually lives in a small flat (*la loge*) just inside the front entrance. The politically correct term for concierge is ***gardien/gardienne***.

conciergerie [kɔ̃sjɛrʒəri] *nf* **1.** [loge] caretaker's office, janitor's lodge US **2.** HIST : **la Conciergerie** the Conciergerie prison *(in Paris)*.

concile [kɔ̃sil] *nm* council ■ **~ de Trente** Council of Trent.

conciliable [kɔ̃siljabl] *adj* reconcilable, compatible ■ **des principes difficilement ~s** principles difficult to reconcile.

conciliabules [kɔ̃siljabyl] *nmpl* confab.

conciliant, e [kɔ̃siljɑ̃, ɑ̃t] *adj* [personne] conciliatory, accommodating ■ [paroles, ton] conciliatory, placatory.

conciliateur, trice [kɔ̃siljatœr, tris] <> *adj* conciliatory, placatory.
<> *nm, f* conciliator, arbitrator.

conciliation [kɔ̃siljasjɔ̃] *nf* **1.** [médiation] conciliation ■ **esprit de ~** spirit of conciliation **2.** DR conciliation, arbitration **3.** *litt* [entre deux personnes, deux partis] reconciliation.

conciliatoire [kɔ̃siljatwar] *adj* conciliatory.

concilier [9] [kɔ̃silje] *vt* **1.** [accorder - opinions, exigences] to reconcile ■ **~ travail et plaisir** to manage to combine work with pleasure **2.** [gagner - faveurs, sympathie] to gain, to win.
◆ **se concilier** *vpt* : **se ~ l'amitié de qqn** to gain *ou* to win sb's friendship ■ **se ~ les électeurs** to win the voters over.

concis, e [kɔ̃si, iz] *adj* [style] concise, tight ■ [écrivain] concise ■ **soyez plus ~** come to the point.

concision [kɔ̃sizjɔ̃] *nf* concision, conciseness, tightness ■ **avec ~** concisely.

concitoyen, enne [kɔ̃sitwajɛ̃, ɛn] *nm, f* fellow citizen.

conclave [kɔ̃klav] *nm* conclave.

concluant, e [kɔ̃klyɑ̃, ɑ̃t] *adj* [essai, démonstration] conclusive ■ **peu ~** inconclusive.

conclure [96] [kɔ̃klyr] <> *vt* **1.** [terminer - discussion, travail] to end, to conclude, to bring to a close *ou* conclusion ; [- repas] to finish *ou* to round off *(sép)* ■ *(en usage absolu)* **~ par** to end *ou* to conclude with ■ **maintenant, vous devez ~** now you must come to a conclusion **2.** [déduire] to conclude ■ **que peut-on**

~ de cette expérience? what conclusion can be drawn from this experience? **3.** [accord] to conclude ▪ [traité] to sign ▪ [cessez-le-feu] to agree to *(insép)* ▪ **marché conclu!** it's a deal!
◇ *vi* DR : **les témoignages concluent contre lui/en sa faveur** the evidence goes against him/in his favour.
◆ **conclure à** *v+prép* : **ils ont dû ~ au meurtre** they had to conclude that it was murder.
◆ **pour conclure** *loc adv* as a *ou* in conclusion, to conclude.

conclusif, ive [kɔ̃klyzif, iv] *adj* *sout* [paragraphe] closing, final.

conclusion [kɔ̃klyzjɔ̃] *nf* **1.** [fin] conclusion **2.** [déduction] conclusion ▪ **nous en sommes arrivés à la ~ suivante** we came to *ou* reached the following conclusion ▪ **tirer une ~ de qqch** to draw a conclusion from sthg ▪ **~, la voiture est fichue** *fam* the result is that the car's a write-off.
◆ **conclusions** *nfpl* [d'un rapport] conclusions, findings ▪ DR submissions ▪ **déposer** *ou* **signifier des ~s** to file submissions with a court.
◆ **en conclusion** *loc adv* as a *ou* in conclusion, to conclude.

concocter [3] [kɔ̃kɔkte] *vt* to concoct.

conçois, conçoivent *etc v* ▷ **concevoir**.

concombre [kɔ̃kɔ̃br] *nm* BOT cucumber.

concomitance [kɔ̃kɔmitɑ̃s] *nf* concomitance.

concomitant, e [kɔ̃kɔmitɑ̃, ɑ̃t] *adj* concomitant, attendant.

concordance [kɔ̃kɔrdɑ̃s] *nf* **1.** [conformité] agreement, similarity ▪ **la ~ des empreintes/dates** the similarity between the fingerprints/dates **2.** GRAMM : **~ des temps** sequence of tenses **3.** [index] concordance.
◆ **en concordance avec** *loc prép* in agreement *ou* keeping *ou* accordance with.

concordant, e [kɔ̃kɔrdɑ̃, ɑ̃t] *adj* [correspondant] : **les versions sont ~es** the stories agree *ou* match.

concordat [kɔ̃kɔrda] *nm* **1.** RELIG concordat **2.** COMM winding-up arrangement.

concorde [kɔ̃kɔrd] *nf* *litt* concord, harmony.

concorder [3] [kɔ̃kɔrde] *vi* [versions, chiffres] to agree, to tally ▪ [groupes sanguins, empreintes] to match ▪ **faire ~ qqch et** *ou* **avec qqch** to make sthg and sthg agree.

concourir [45] [kɔ̃kurir] *vi* **1.** [être en compétition] to compete ▪ **~ avec qqn** to compete with *ou* against sb **2.** GÉOM to converge **3.** DR to have concurrent claims.
◆ **concourir à** *v+prép* to contribute to ▪ **tout concourt à me faire croire qu'il ment** everything leads me to believe that he's lying.

concours [kɔ̃kur] *nm* **1.** [aide] aid, help, support ▪ **prêter son ~ à** to lend one's support to **2.** [combinaison] : **un heureux/un fâcheux ~ de circonstances** a lucky/an unfortunate coincidence **3.** [épreuve] competition, contest ▪ **~ de beauté/de chant** beauty/singing contest ▪ **~ agricole/hippique** agricultural/horse show **4.** ÉDUC competitive (entrance) exam ▪ **le ~ d'entrée à l'ÉNA** the entrance exam for ÉNA ➊ **le ~ de l'Eurovision** the Eurovision song contest ▪ **le ~ général** *competition in which the best pupils in the two upper forms at French lycées compete for prizes in a variety of subjects.*
◆ **avec le concours de** *loc prép* with the participation of, in association with.
◆ **par concours, sur concours** *loc adv* [recruter, entrer] on the results of a competitive entrance exam.

concouru [kɔ̃kury] *pp* ▷ **concourir**.

concret, ète [kɔ̃krɛ, ɛt] *adj* **1.** [palpable] concrete **2.** [non théorique] concrete, practical ▪ **faire des propositions concrètes** to make concrete *ou* practical proposals **3.** [s'appuyant sur l'expérience] concrete, empirical, experiential ▪ **un esprit ~** a practical mind **4.** LING & MUS concrete.
◆ **concret** *nm* : **ce qu'il nous faut, c'est du ~** we need something we can get our teeth into.

concrètement [kɔ̃krɛtmɑ̃] *adv* concretely, in concrete terms ▪ **je ne vois pas ~ ce que ça peut donner** I can't visualize what it would be like.

concrétion [kɔ̃kresjɔ̃] *nf* CHIM, GÉOL & MÉD concretion.

concrétisation [kɔ̃kretizasjɔ̃] *nf* concretization, materialization ▪ **la ~ d'un rêve** a dream come true.

concrétiser [3] [kɔ̃kretize] *vt* [rêve] to realize ▪ [idée, proposition] to make concrete.
◆ **se concrétiser** *vpi* [rêve] to come true, to materialize ▪ [proposition, idée] to be realized, to take concrete form *ou* shape.

conçu, e [kɔ̃sy] *pp* ▷ **concevoir**.

concubin, e [kɔ̃kybɛ̃, in] *nm, f* **1.** [amant] concubine, partner **2.** DR partner, cohabitee.

concubinage [kɔ̃kybinaʒ] *nm* **1.** [vie de couple] : **vivre en ~** to live as man and wife, to cohabit **2.** DR cohabitation, cohabiting ▪ **~ notoire** common-law marriage.

concupiscence [kɔ̃kypisɑ̃s] *nf* [envers les biens] greed ▪ [envers le sexe] lust, concupiscence *litt.*

concupiscent, e [kɔ̃kypisɑ̃, ɑ̃t] *adj* [envers les biens] greedy ▪ [envers le sexe] lustful, concupiscent *litt.*

concurremment [kɔ̃kyramɑ̃] *adv* at the same time, concurrently.
◆ **concurremment avec** *loc prép* **1.** [de concert avec] in conjunction *ou* concert *sout* with **2.** [en même temps que] concurrently with.

concurrence [kɔ̃kyrɑ̃s] *nf* **1.** [rivalité] competition ▪ **faire (de la) ~ à** to be in competition *ou* to compete with ➊ **~ déloyale** unfair competition *ou* trading **2.** [rivaux] : **la ~** the competition.
◆ **en concurrence** *loc adv* in competition ▪ **il est en ~ avec son frère** he's competing with his brother.
◆ **jusqu'à concurrence de** *loc prép* up to, to the limit of.

concurrencer [16] [kɔ̃kyrɑ̃se] *vt* to compete *ou* to be in competition with ▪ **ils nous concurrencent dangereusement** they're very dangerous *ou* serious competitors for us.

concurrent, e [kɔ̃kyrɑ̃, ɑ̃t] ◇ *adj* competing, rival *(avant n).*
◇ *nm, f* **1.** COMM & SPORT competitor **2.** ÉDUC candidate.

concurrentiel, elle [kɔ̃kyrɑ̃sjɛl] *adj* competitive ▪ **marchandises vendues à des prix ~s** competitively-priced goods.

concussion [kɔ̃kysjɔ̃] *nf* embezzlement, misappropriation of public funds.

conçut *etc v* ▷ **concevoir**.

condamnable [kɔ̃danabl] *adj* blameworthy, reprehensible.

condamnation [kɔ̃danasjɔ̃] *nf* **1.** [action] sentencing, convicting ▪ **il a fait l'objet de trois ~s pour vol** he's already had three convictions for theft, he's been convicted three times for theft ▮ [peine] sentence ▪ **~ aux travaux forcés** sentence of hard labour ▪ **~ à mort** death sentence ▪ **~ à la réclusion à perpétuité** life sentence, sentence of life imprisonment ▪ **~ par défaut/par contumace** decree by default/in absentia **2.** [blâme] condemnation, blame **3.** [fin - d'un projet, d'une tentative] end **4.** AUTO [blocage] locking ▪ [système] locking device.

condamné, e [kɔ̃dane] *nm, f* DR sentenced *ou* convicted person ▪ **~ à la réclusion perpétuelle** life prisoner, lifer ➊ **~ à mort** prisoner under sentence of death ▪ **la cigarette du ~** the condemned man's last cigarette.

condamner [3] [kɔ̃dane] *vt* **1.** DR [accusé] to sentence ▪ **~ qqn à mort/aux travaux forcés** to sentence sb to death/to hard labour ▪ **condamné à trois mois de prison pour...** sentenced to three months' imprisonment for... ▪ **condamné à une amende** fined ▪ **condamné aux dépens** ordered to pay costs ▪ **condamné pour meurtre** convicted of murder ▪ **~ qqn par défaut/par contumace** to sentence sb by default/in absentia ▪ **faire ~**

qqn to get *ou* to have sb convicted **2.** [interdire - magazine] to forbid publication of ; [- pratique] to forbid, to condemn ■ **la loi condamne l'usage de stupéfiants** the use of narcotics is forbidden by law **3.** [désapprouver - attentat, propos] to express disapproval of ■ **~ qqn pour avoir fait** *ou* **d'avoir fait qqch** to blame sb for having done sthg ■ **l'expression est condamnée par les puristes** the use of the phrase is condemned *ou* is disapproved of by purists **4.** [accuser] to condemn ■ **son silence la condamne** her silence condemns her **5.** [suj: maladie incurable] to condemn ■ **les médecins disent qu'il est condamné** the doctors say that there is no hope for him ■ **ce projet est condamné par manque d'argent** *fig* the project is doomed through lack of money **6.** [murer - porte, fenêtre] to block up *(sép)*, to seal off *(sép)* ; [- pièce] to close up *(sép)* ■ **~ toutes les fenêtres d'une maison** to board up the windows in a house ■ **~ sa porte** *fig* to bar one's door **7.** [obliger] : **je suis condamnée à rester alitée pendant dix jours** I'm confined to bed for ten days.

condensateur [kɔ̃dɑ̃satœr] *nm* **1.** ÉLECTR condenser, capacitor **2.** OPT : **~ optique** condenser.

condensation [kɔ̃dɑ̃sasjɔ̃] *nf* **1.** CHIM & PHYS condensation **2.** [buée] condensation ■ **une pièce où il y a beaucoup de ~** a very damp room **3.** [d'un texte] reducing.

condensé [kɔ̃dɑ̃se] *nm* digest, summary, abstract.

condenser [3] [kɔ̃dɑ̃se] *vt* **1.** CHIM & PHYS to condense **2.** [raccourcir - récit] to condense, to cut down.
◆ **se condenser** *vpi* to condense.

condenseur [kɔ̃dɑ̃sœr] *nm* **1.** CHIM, MÉTALL & PHYS condenser **2.** OPT condenser.

condescendance [kɔ̃desɑ̃dɑ̃s] *nf* condescension ■ **avec ~** condescendingly ■ **traiter qqn avec ~** to patronize sb.

condescendant, e [kɔ̃desɑ̃dɑ̃, ɑ̃t] *adj* [hautain - regard, parole] condescending, patronizing ■ **d'un air ~** patronizingly.

condescendre [73] [kɔ̃desɑ̃dr] ◆ **condescendre à** *v+prép* to condescend to ■ **elle a condescendu à me recevoir** *pr & hum* she condescended *ou* deigned to see me.

condiment [kɔ̃dimɑ̃] *nm* [épices] condiment ■ [moutarde] (mild) mustard.

condisciple [kɔ̃disipl] *nmf* ÉDUC classmate, schoolmate ■ UNIV fellow student.

condition [kɔ̃disjɔ̃] *nf* **1.** [préalable] condition ■ **une des ~s du progrès** one of the conditions of *ou* requirements for progress ■ **mettre une ~ à qqch** to set a condition before sthg can be done ■ **j'accepte mais à une ~** I accept but on one condition ◆ **~ nécessaire/suffisante** necessary/sufficient condition ■ **~ préalable** prerequisite ■ **~ requise** requirement ■ **une ~ sine qua non pour** an absolute prerequisite for **2.** [état] condition, shape ■ **~ physique/psychologique** physical/psychological shape ■ **être en bonne ~ physique** to be in condition, to be fit ■ **en grande** *ou* **excellente ~ physique** in excellent shape ■ **être en mauvaise ~ physique** to be in poor physical shape, to be unfit **3.** [position sociale] condition, rank, station ■ **une femme de ~ modeste** a woman from a modest background ■ **la ~ paysanne au XIXe siècle** the situation of peasants in the 19th century ■ **la ~ féminine** the lives of women, the female condition ■ **la ~ ouvrière** the condition of the working-class **4.** [destinée] : **la ~ humaine** the human condition **5.** GRAMM & DR condition.
◆ **conditions** *nfpl* **1.** [environnement] conditions ■ **~s climatiques/économiques** weather/economic conditions ■ **~s météo** weather conditions ◆ **~s de vie/travail** living/working conditions **2.** [termes] terms ■ **vos ~s seront les miennes** I'll go along with whatever conditions you wish to lay down ■ **quelles sont ses ~s?** what terms is he offering? ◆ **~s de vente/d'achat** terms of sale/purchase ■ **~s de paiement/de remboursement** payment/repayment terms.
◆ **à condition de** *loc prép* on condition that, providing *ou* provided (that).
◆ **à (la) condition que** *loc conj* on condition that, provided *ou* providing (that).
◆ **dans ces conditions** *loc adv* under these conditions ■ **dans ces ~s, pourquoi se donner tant de mal?** if that's the case, why go to so much trouble?
◆ **en condition** *loc adv* **1.** [en bonne forme] in shape ■ **mettre en ~** [athlète, candidat] to get into condition *ou* form ■ **se mettre en ~** to get (o.s.) fit *ou* into condition *ou* into shape **2.** [dans un état favorable] : **mettre le public en ~** to condition the public.
◆ **sans condition(s)** <> *loc adv* unconditionally.
<> *loc adj* unconditional.
◆ **sous condition** *loc adv* conditionally ■ **acheter sous ~** to buy on approval.
Voir module d'usage

conditionné, e [kɔ̃disjɔne] *adj* **1.** PSYCHOL conditioned **2.** [climatisé - bureau, autocar] air-conditioned **3.** COMM [marchandise] packaged.

conditionnel, elle [kɔ̃disjɔnɛl] *adj* **1.** [soumis à condition] conditional, tentative **2.** PSYCHOL conditioned **3.** GRAMM conditional.
◆ **conditionnel** *nm* GRAMM conditional (mood) ■ **~ présent/passé** present/perfect conditional tense, *voir aussi* **pluriel.**
◆ **au conditionnel** *loc adv* **1.** GRAMM in the conditional **2.** [comme une hypothèse] : **la nouvelle est à prendre au ~** the news has yet to be confirmed *ou* checked ■ **il faut l'annoncer au ~** it's not yet certain.

conditionnellement [kɔ̃disjɔnɛlmɑ̃] *adv* conditionally, tentatively.

conditionnement [kɔ̃disjɔnmɑ̃] *nm* **1.** [fait d'emballer, emballage] packaging **2.** TEXT conditioning **3.** INDUST processing **4.** PSYCHOL conditioning.

conditionner [3] [kɔ̃disjɔne] *vt* **1.** [emballer - marchandise, aliments] to package **2.** TEXT to condition **3.** INDUST to process **4.** [influencer] to condition, to influence ■ **notre départ est conditionné par son état de santé** our going away depends on *ou* is conditional on her state of health **5.** [climatiser] to air-condition.

LA CONDITION

If you leave now, you'll catch the last train. Si tu pars tout de suite, tu auras le dernier train.

If he does decide to go, let me know. S'il décidait vraiment de partir, prévenez-moi.

We'll go tomorrow, unless it rains. Nous irons demain, à moins qu'il ne pleuve.

The only way you'll pass is if you start working a bit harder. La seule façon de réussir, c'est de te mettre un peu plus sérieusement au travail.

I'll do it, but only on condition (that) you help me. Je ne le ferai qu'à la condition que tu m'aides.

What would you do if you won the lottery? Qu'est-ce que tu ferais, si tu gagnais au loto ?

If he had known, he would have told you. S'il avait su, il te l'aurait dit.

Had I thought about it, I would have acted differently. Si j'avais réfléchi à la question, j'aurais agi différemment.

Should he call *ou* **If he should call, tell him I'll phone back later.** Si jamais il téléphonait, dis-lui que je le rappellerai plus tard.

condoléances [kɔ̃dɔleɑ̃s] *nfpl* condolences ■ **lettre de ~** letter of condolence ■ **présenter ses ~** to offer one's condolences ■ **veuillez accepter mes plus sincères ~** please accept my deepest sympathy *ou* my most sincere condolences ■ **toutes mes ~, Paul** with deepest sympathy *ou* heartfelt condolences, Paul.

condom [kɔ̃dɔm] *nm* condom, sheath.

condominium [kɔ̃dɔminjɔm] *nm* condominium.

condor [kɔ̃dɔr] *nm* condor.

conducteur, trice [kɔ̃dyktœr, tris] ◇ *adj* **1.** ÉLECTR conductive **2.** *fig* [principal - principe, fil] guiding.
◇ *nm, f* **1.** TRANSP driver ■ **~ d'autobus** bus driver **2.** INDUST operator ■ **~ de travaux** foreman (*f* forewoman), clerk of works.
◆ **conducteur** *nm* PHYS conductor.

conductible [kɔ̃dyktibl] *adj* conductive, conductible.

conduction [kɔ̃dyksjɔ̃] *nf* conduction ■ **~ électrolytique** electrolysis.

conduire [80] [kɔ̃dɥir] *vt* **1.** [emmener - gén] to take ; [- en voiture] to drive, to take ■ **~ les enfants à l'école** to take *ou* to drive the children to school ■ **~ qqn jusqu'à la porte** to see sb to the door, to show sb the way out ■ **le policier l'a conduit au poste** the policeman took him down to the station ■ **il est obligé de se faire ~ au bureau par sa femme** he has to get his wife to drive him to work
2. [guider] to lead ■ **les empreintes m'ont conduit jusqu'au hangar** the footprints led me to the shed
3. [donner accès] : **~ à** to lead to *(insép)*, to open out onto *(insép)* ■ **cet escalier ne conduit nulle part** this staircase doesn't lead anywhere
4. [mener] : **~ qqn à : RAPPEL-ADRESSE/> qqn au désespoir** to drive sb to desperation ■ **ce qui nous conduit à la conclusion suivante** which leads *ou* brings us to the following conclusion ■ **~ qqn à la victoire** [entraîneur, entraînement] to lead sb (on) to victory ■ *(en usage absolu)* **cette filière conduit au bac technique** this stream allows you to go on to *ou* this stream leads to a vocational school-leaving qualification
5. TRANSP [véhicule] to drive ■ [hors-bord] to steer ■ *(en usage absolu)* **~ à droite/gauche** to drive on the right-/left-hand side of the road ■ **~ bien/mal/vite** to be a good/bad/fast driver
6. [diriger - État] to run, to lead ; [- affaires, opérations] to run, to conduct, to manage ; [- travaux] to supervise ; [- recherches, enquête] to conduct, to lead ; [- délégation, révolte] to head, to lead
7. [être en tête de] : **~ le deuil** to be at the head of the funeral procession, to be a chief mourner
8. MUS [orchestre, symphonie] to conduct
9. [faire passer - eau] to carry, to bring
10. PHYS [chaleur, électricité] to conduct, to be a conductor of.
◆ **se conduire** ◇ *vp (emploi passif)* [être piloté] to be driven, to drive.
◇ *vpi* [se comporter] to behave, to conduct o.s. ■ **se ~ bien** to behave (o.s.) well ■ **se ~ mal** to behave badly, to misbehave.

conduit, e [kɔ̃dɥi, it] *pp* ▷ **conduire.**
◆ **conduit** *nm* **1.** TECHNOL conduit, pipe ■ **~ d'aération** air duct ■ **~ de fumée** flue ■ **~ de ventilation** ventilation shaft **2.** ANAT canal, duct ■ **~ auditif** auditory canal ■ **~ lacrymal** tear *ou* lachrymal *spéc* duct.
◆ **conduite** *nf* **1.** [pilotage - d'un véhicule] driving ; [- d'un hors-bord] steering ▶ **la ~e à droite/gauche** driving on the right-/left-hand side of the road ■ **avec ~e à droite/à gauche** right-hand/left-hand drive *(modif)* ■ **~e accompagnée** *driving practice when accompanied by a qualified driver (authorized for learner drivers over 16 having passed their theoretical exam at a driving school)* ■ **~e en état d'ivresse** drink driving, drinking and driving ■ **faire un bout** *ou* **brin de ~e à qqn (jusqu'à)** *fam* to walk sb part of the way (to) **2.** [comportement] conduct, behaviour ■ **pour bonne ~e** [libéré, gracié] for good behaviour ■ **mauvaise ~e** misbehaviour, misconduct **3.** [direction - des affaires] management, conduct ; [- de la guerre] conduct ; [- d'un pays] running ; [- des travaux] supervision **4.** [voiture] : **~e intérieure** saloon (car) *UK*, sedan *US* **5.** TECHNOL pipe ■ [canalisation principale] main ■ **~e d'eau/de gaz** water/gas pipe ■ **~e forcée** pressure pipeline.

cône [kon] *nm* **1.** GÉOM cone ■ **en forme de ~** conical, cone-shaped **2.** BOT pine cone **3.** GÉOL : **~ volcanique** volcanic cone **4.** ZOOL cone shell **5.** [glace] cone, cornet.

conf. (*abr écrite de* **confort**) : **tt ~** mod. cons.

confection [kɔ̃fɛksjɔ̃] *nf* **1.** CULIN preparation, making **2.** COUT [d'une robe] making ■ [d'un veston] tailoring ■ **la ~** INDUST the clothing industry *ou* business.
◆ **de confection** *loc adj* ready-to-wear, off-the-peg *UK*.

confectionner [3] [kɔ̃fɛksjɔne] *vt* **1.** [préparer - plat, sauce] to prepare, to make **2.** COUT [robe] to make, to sew ■ [veston] to tailor ■ **c'est sa mère qui confectionne les costumes des enfants** it's her mother who runs up the children's costumes.

confédéral, e, aux [kɔ̃federal, o] *adj* confederal.

confédération [kɔ̃federasjɔ̃] *nf* **1.** [nation] confederation, confederacy ■ **la Confédération helvétique** the Swiss Confederation **2.** POLIT : **~ générale du travail = CGT.**

confédéré, e [kɔ̃federe] ◇ *adj* confederate.
◇ *nm, f Suisse person from another canton.*
◆ **confédérés** *nmpl* HIST : **les ~s** the Confederates.

confédérer [18] [kɔ̃federe] *vt* to confederate.

confer [kɔ̃fɛr] *vt* : **~ page 36** see page 36.

conférence [kɔ̃ferɑ̃s] *nf* **1.** [réunion] conference ■ **ils sont en ~** they are in a meeting ▶ **~ de presse** press conference ■ **~ au sommet** summit conference **2.** [cours] lecture ■ **il a fait une ~ sur Milton** he gave *ou* he delivered a lecture on Milton, he lectured on Milton **3.** BOT [poire] conference pear.

conférencier, ère [kɔ̃ferɑ̃sje, ɛr] *nm, f* speaker.

conférer [18] [kɔ̃fere] ◇ *vt* **1.** [décerner - titre, droit] to confer, to bestow ■ **~ une médaille à qqn** to confer a medal on *ou* upon sb **2.** *fig* [donner - importance, prestance] to impart.
◇ *vi* [discuter] to talk, to hold talks.

confesse [kɔ̃fɛs] *nf* [confession] : **aller à/revenir de ~** to go to/to come back from confession ▶ **chacun son tour, comme à ~** *hum* one at a time.

confesser [4] [kɔ̃fese] *vt* **1.** RELIG [péché] to confess (to) ■ [personne] to hear the confession of, to be the confessor of **2.** *fam* [faire parler] : **~ qqn** to make sb talk **3.** *litt* [foi, convictions] to proclaim **4.** [reconnaître, admettre] to admit, to confess.
◆ **se confesser** *vpi* to confess, to make one's confession ■ **se ~ à un prêtre** to confess to a priest.

confesseur [kɔ̃fesœr] *nm* RELIG confessor.

confession [kɔ̃fesjɔ̃] *nf* **1.** RELIG [aveu, rite] confession ■ **faire une ~** *pr & fig* to make a confession, to confess **2.** [appartenance] faith, denomination ■ **être de ~ luthérienne/anglicane** to belong to the Lutheran/Anglican faith **3.** *litt* [proclamation] proclaiming **4.** LITTÉR : **'Confessions'** *Rousseau* 'Confessions'.

confessionnal, aux [kɔ̃fesjɔnal, o] *nm* confessional.

confessionnel, elle [kɔ̃fesjɔnɛl] *adj* denominational.

confetti [kɔ̃feti] *nm* (piece of) confetti ■ **des ~s** confetti.

confiance [kɔ̃fjɑ̃s] *nf* **1.** [foi - en quelqu'un, quelque chose] trust, confidence ■ **avec ~** confidently ■ **~ excessive** overconfidence ■ **avoir ~ en qqn/qqch** to trust sb/sthg, to have confidence in sb/sthg ■ **faire ~ à qqn** to trust sb ■ **placer sa ~ en qqn** to put one's trust *ou* to place one's confidence in sb ■ **j'ai ~ en l'avenir de mon pays** I have faith in the future of my country **2.** POLIT : **voter la ~ au gouvernement** to pass a vote of confidence in the government ▶ **vote de ~** vote of confidence **3.** [aplomb] : **~ en soi** confidence, self-confidence, self-assurance ■ **manquer de ~ en soi** to lack self-confidence.
◆ **de confiance** *loc adj* : **poste de ~** position of trust ■ **personne de ~** reliable *ou* trustworthy person ■ **les hommes de ~ du président** the President's advisers.
◆ **en confiance** *loc adv* : **mettre qqn en ~** to win sb's trust ■ **se sentir** *ou* **être en ~ (avec qqn)** to feel safe (with sb).
◆ **en toute confiance** *loc adv* with complete confidence.

confiant, e [kɔ̃fjɑ̃, ɑ̃t] *adj* **1.** [qui fait confiance] trusting, trustful **2.** [qui exprime la confiance] trusting, confident **3.** [qui a confiance] : **être ~ dans** *ou* **en** to have confidence in ▪ **il est ~ (en lui-même)** he's self-assured *ou* self-confident.

confidence [kɔ̃fidɑ̃s] *nf* confidence ▪ **faire une ~ à qqn** to confide something to sb, to trust sb with a secret ▪ **faire des ~s à qqn** to confide in sb ▪ **mettre qqn dans la ~** to take sb into one's confidence, to let sb into the secret ◆ **~s sur l'oreiller** *hum* pillow talk.
◆ **en confidence** *loc adv* in (strict) confidence.

confident, e [kɔ̃fidɑ̃, ɑ̃t] *nm, f* confidant (*f* confidante).

confidentialité [kɔ̃fidɑ̃sjalite] *nf* confidentiality.

confidentiel, elle [kɔ̃fidɑ̃sjɛl] *adj* **1.** [secret - information] confidential ; [- entretien] private ▪ **à titre ~** in confidence, confidentially **2.** [limité] : **un tirage ~** a small print-run ▪ **un livre un peu ~** a book that only appeals to a limited readership.

confidentiellement [kɔ̃fidɑ̃sjɛlmɑ̃] *adv* confidentially, in (strict) confidence.

confier [9] [kɔ̃fje] *vt* **1.** [dire - craintes, intentions] to confide, to entrust ▪ **~ un secret à qqn** to confide *ou* to entrust a secret to sb, to share a secret with sb ▪ **il m'a confié qu'il voulait divorcer** he confided to me that he wanted to get a divorce **2.** [donner] to entrust ▪ **~ une mission à qqn** to entrust a mission to sb, to entrust sb with a mission ▪ **la garde de Marie a été confiée à sa mère** Marie has been put in her mother's care **3.** *litt* [livrer] to consign.
◆ **se confier** *vpi* [s'épancher] to confide ▪ **se ~ à qqn** to confide in sb ▪ **elle ne se confie pas facilement** she doesn't confide in people easily.
◆ **se confier à** *vp+prép* [s'en remettre à] to trust to ▪ **se ~ à sa bonne étoile** to trust to one's lucky star.

configuration [kɔ̃figyrasjɔ̃] *nf* **1.** [aspect général] configuration, general shape ▪ **la ~ des lieux** the layout of the place **2.** CHIM & INFORM configuration.

confiné, e [kɔ̃fine] *adj* [air] stale ▪ [atmosphère] stuffy ▪ **vivre ~ chez soi** to live shut up indoors.

confinement [kɔ̃finmɑ̃] *nm* **1.** [enfermement] confinement **2.** [d'une espèce animale] concentration *(in a particular area)*.

confiner [3] [kɔ̃fine] *vt* [reléguer] to confine ▪ **on le confine dans des rôles comiques** he's confined to comic parts.
◆ **confiner à** *v+prép* **1.** *sout* [être voisin de - pays, maison] to border on **2.** *fig* [être semblable à] to border *ou* to verge on ▪ **passion qui confine à la folie** passion bordering *ou* verging on madness.
◆ **se confiner** *vp (emploi réfléchi)* [s'enfermer] : **se ~ dans son bureau** to confine o.s. to one's study, to shut o.s. away in one's study.
◆ **se confiner à** *vp+prép* [se limiter à] to confine o.s. *ou* to limit o.s. *ou* to keep to.

confins [kɔ̃fɛ̃] *nmpl* [limites - d'un pays] borders ; [- d'un savoir, de l'intelligence] confines, bounds ▪ **les ~ de l'Europe et de l'Asie** the borders of Europe and Asia.
◆ **aux confins de** *loc prép* on the borders of.

confire [101] [kɔ̃fir] *vt* [dans du sucre] to preserve, to candy ▪ [dans du vinaigre] to pickle.

confirmation [kɔ̃firmasjɔ̃] *nf* **1.** [attestation] confirmation ▪ **donnez-nous ~ de votre rendez-vous** please give us confirmation of *ou* please confirm your appointment **2.** RELIG confirmation ▪ **recevoir la ~** to be confirmed **3.** DR upholding.

confirmé, e [kɔ̃firme] *adj* [professionnel] experienced.

confirmer [3] [kɔ̃firme] *vt* **1.** [rendre définitif - réservation, nouvelle] to confirm ▪ **cela reste à ~** it remains to be confirmed, it is as yet unconfirmed **2.** [renforcer - témoignage, diagnostic, impression] to confirm, to bear out *(insép)* ▪ **ceci confirme mes** *ou* **me confirme dans mes soupçons** this bears out *ou* confirms my suspicions **3.** [affermir - position, supériorité] to reinforce **4.** RELIG to confirm ▪ **se faire ~** to be confirmed.
◆ **se confirmer** *vpi* **1.** [s'avérer - rumeur] to be confirmed ▪ **son départ se confirme** it's been confirmed that he's leaving **2.** [être renforcé - tendance, hausse] to become stronger.

confisait *etc v* ▷ **confire.**

confiscable [kɔ̃fiskabl] *adj* liable to seizure *ou* to being seized, confiscable.

confiscation [kɔ̃fiskasjɔ̃] *nf* **1.** [saisie] confiscation, seizure, seizing **2.** DR forfeiture.

confiserie [kɔ̃fizri] *nf* **1.** [produit] sweet *UK*, candy *US* ▪ **acheter des ~s** to buy confectionery, to buy sweets *UK*, to buy candy *US* **2.** [industrie] confectionery (business *ou* trade) **3.** [magasin] confectioner's, sweet shop *UK*, candy store *US* **4.** [des olives, des sardines] pickling.

confiseur, euse [kɔ̃fizœr, øz] *nm, f* confectioner.

confisquer [3] [kɔ̃fiske] *vt* **1.** [retirer - marchandises, drogue] to confiscate, to seize ; [- sifflet, livre] to take away *(sép)*, to confiscate ▪ **~ qqch à qqn** to take sthg away from *ou* to confiscate sthg from sb **2.** DR to seize, to confiscate.

confit, e [kɔ̃fi, it] ◇ *pp* ▷ **confire.**
◇ *adj* **1.** [fruits] candied, crystallized ▪ [cornichons] pickled **2.** *fig* **être ~ en dévotion** to be steeped in piety.
◆ **confit** *nm* conserve ▪ **~ d'oie** goose conserve *(goose cooked in it's own fat to preserve it)*.

confiture [kɔ̃fityr] *nf* jam, preserve ▪ **~ de fraises/mûres** strawberry/blackberry jam ▪ **~ d'oranges** (orange) marmalade ◆ **donner de la ~ aux cochons** *fam* to cast pearls before swine.
◆ **en confiture** *loc adv* : **mettre qqch en ~** to reduce sthg to a pulp.

confiturerie [kɔ̃fityrri] *nf* jam factory.

conflagration [kɔ̃flagrasjɔ̃] *nf* **1.** [conflit] conflagration, conflict **2.** [bouleversement] major upheaval.

conflictuel, elle [kɔ̃fliktɥɛl] *adj* [pulsions, désirs] conflicting, clashing ▪ **situation/relation ~le** antagonistic situation/relationship.

conflit [kɔ̃fli] *nm* **1.** MIL conflict, war ◆ **~ armé** armed conflict *ou* struggle **2.** [heurt] : **entrer en ~ avec** to conflict with, to come into conflict with ▪ **il y a beaucoup de ~s internes** there's a lot of infighting ▪ **le ~ des générations** the clash between generations **3.** DR conflict ▪ **~ social** *ou* **du travail** labour *ou* industrial dispute ▪ **~ salarial** wage dispute.

confluence [kɔ̃flyɑ̃s] *nf* **1.** GÉOGR confluence **2.** [rencontre] confluence, convergence ▪ **à la ~ de** at the junction of.

confluent [kɔ̃flyɑ̃] *nm* **1.** GÉOGR confluence ▪ **au ~ du Rhône et de la Saône** at the confluence of the Saône and the Rhône **2.** [point de rencontre] junction **3.** ANAT confluence.

confluer [3] [kɔ̃flye] *vi* **1.** GÉOGR to meet, to merge **2.** *litt* [être réunis] to converge.

confondant, e [kɔ̃fɔ̃dɑ̃, ɑ̃t] *adj* astonishing, astounding.

confondre [75] [kɔ̃fɔ̃dr] *vt* **1.** [mêler - films, auteurs, dates] to confuse, to mix up *(sép)* ▪ **il a confondu la clef du garage et celle de la porte** he mistook the garage key for the door key, he mixed up the garage key and the door key ▪ **j'ai confondu leurs voix** I got their voices mixed up ▪ **~ qqn/qqch avec** to mistake sb/sthg for ▪ **tous âges confondus** irrespective of age ▪ *(en usage absolu)* **on ne se connaît pas, vous devez ~** we've never met, you must be making a mistake *ou* be mistaken ▪ **attention, ce n'est pas ce que j'ai dit, ne confondons pas!** hey, let's get one thing straight, that's not what I said **2.** [démasquer - menteur, meurtrier] to unmask, to expose **3.** *sout* [étonner] to astound, to astonish ▪ **être** *ou* **rester confondu devant** to be speechless in the face of *ou* astounded by.

◆ **se confondre** *vpi* **1.** [se mêler - fleuves] to flow together, to merge ; [- formes, couleurs] to merge **2.** [être embrouillé] to be mixed up *ou* confused.
◆ **se confondre en** *vp+prép* : **se ~ en excuses/remerciements** to be effusive in one's apologies/thanks, to apologize/thank profusely.

conformation [kɔ̃fɔrmasjɔ̃] *nf* **1.** [aspect physique] build ■ **un enfant qui a une mauvaise ~** a child with poor bone structure **2.** CHIM conformation, configuration.

conforme [kɔ̃fɔrm] *adj* **1.** [qui répond à une règle] standard ■ **ce n'est pas ~ à la loi** this is not in accordance with the law **2.** [conventionnel] conventional, standard **3.** [semblable] identical ■ **~ à l'original** true to the original ■ **ce n'est pas ~ à l'esquisse** it bears little resemblance to *ou* doesn't match the sketch ■ **une maison ~ à mes goûts** a house in keeping with my *ou* after my own tastes.

conformé, e [kɔ̃fɔrme] *adj* : **bien ~** [fœtus] well-formed ; [enfant] well-built ■ **mal ~** [fœtus] malformed ■ **un enfant mal ~** a child with poor bone structure.

conformément [kɔ̃fɔrmemɑ̃] ◆ **conformément à** *loc prép* in accordance with, according to.

conformer [3] [kɔ̃fɔrme] *vt* **1.** COMM [standardiser] to make standard, to produce according to the standards **2.** [adapter] : **~ qqch à** to adapt *ou* to match sthg to ■ **ils ont conformé leur tactique à la nôtre** they modelled their tactics on ours.
◆ **se conformer à** *vp+prép* [se plier à - usage] to conform to ; [- ordre] to comply with, to abide by ■ **se ~ à une décision** to abide by *ou* to comply with a decision.

conformisme [kɔ̃fɔrmism] *nm* conventionality, conformism.

conformiste [kɔ̃fɔrmist] ◇ *adj* **1.** [traditionnel] conformist, conventional **2.** HIST Conformist.
◇ *nmf* conformist, conventionalist.

conformité [kɔ̃fɔrmite] *nf* **1.** [ressemblance] similarity **2.** [obéissance] : **la ~ aux usages sociaux** conformity to social customs **3.** [conventionnalisme] conventionality.
◆ **en conformité avec** *loc prép* in accordance with, according to ■ **être en ~ avec** to conform to.

confort [kɔ̃fɔr] *nm* **1.** [commodités] : **le ~** [d'un appartement, d'un hôtel] modern conveniences ; [d'un aéroport] modern facilities ■ **un cinq-pièces tout ~** a five-room apartment with all mod cons UK *ou* modern conveniences US **2.** [aise physique] : **le ~** comfort ■ **j'aime (avoir) mon ~** I like my (creature) comforts ■ **son petit ~** his creature comforts ■ **améliorer le ~ d'écoute** to improve sound quality **3.** [tranquillité] : **le ~ intellectuel** self-assurance.

confortable [kɔ̃fɔrtabl] *adj* **1.** [douillet - lit, maison] comfortable, cosy, snug **2.** [tranquillisant - situation, routine] comfortable ■ **être dans une position peu ~** *pr & fig* to be in an awkward position **3.** [important - retraite, bénéfice] comfortable.

confortablement [kɔ̃fɔrtabləmɑ̃] *adv* comfortably ■ **vivre ~** [dans l'aisance] to lead a comfortable existence, to be comfortably off.

conforter [3] [kɔ̃fɔrte] *vt* [renforcer - position, avance] to reinforce, to strengthen ■ **cela la conforte dans la mauvaise opinion qu'elle a de moi** it confirms her poor opinion of me.

confraternel, elle [kɔ̃fratɛrnɛl] *adj* fraternal.

confraternité [kɔ̃fratɛrnite] *nf* fraternity *ou* brotherhood between colleagues.

confrère [kɔ̃frɛr] *nm* colleague.

confrérie [kɔ̃freri] *nf* **1.** [groupe professionnel] fraternity ■ **la ~ des journalistes sportifs** the fraternity of sports writers **2.** RELIG confraternity, brotherhood.

confrontation [kɔ̃frɔ̃tasjɔ̃] *nf* **1.** [face-à-face] confrontation **2.** DR confrontation **3.** [comparaison] comparison **4.** [conflit] confrontation ■ **~ armée** armed confrontation *ou* conflict ■ **il cherche toujours à éviter les ~s** *ou* **la ~** he always tries to avoid confrontation.

confronter [3] [kɔ̃frɔ̃te] *vt* **1.** [mettre face à face - accusés, témoins] to confront ■ **être confronté à** *ou* **avec qqn** to be confronted with sb ■ *fig* **être confronté à une difficulté** to be faced *ou* confronted with a difficulty **2.** [comparer - textes, points de vue] to compare.

confucéen, enne [kɔ̃fyseɛ̃, ɛn] *adj & nm, f* Confucian.

confucianisme [kɔ̃fysjanism] *nm* Confucianism.

Confucius [kɔ̃fysjys] *npr* Confucius.

confus, e [kɔ̃fy, yz] *adj* **1.** [imprécis - souvenir, impression] unclear, confused, vague ; [- idées] muddled ; [- situation, histoire] confused, involved ; [- explication] muddled, confused ■ **c'est un esprit ~** he is muddleheaded **2.** [désordonné - murmures, cris] confused ; [- amas] confused, disorderly **3.** [embarrassé] : **c'est un cadeau magnifique, je suis ~e** it's a splendid present, I'm quite overwhelmed *ou* I really don't know what to say ■ **~ de** ashamed at, embarrassed by ■ **je suis ~ de t'avoir fait attendre** I'm awfully *ou* dreadfully sorry to have kept you waiting.

confusément [kɔ̃fyzemɑ̃] *adv* **1.** [vaguement] confusedly, vaguely ■ **sentir ~ que** to have a vague feeling that **2.** [indistinctement] unintelligibly, inaudibly.

confusion [kɔ̃fyzjɔ̃] *nf* **1.** [méprise] mix-up, confusion **2.** [désordre] confusion, disarray, chaos ■ **semer** *ou* **répandre la ~ dans une assemblée** to throw a meeting into confusion ■ **il régnait une ~ indescriptible dans la gare** the station was in a state of indescribable confusion *ou* chaos ■ **jeter la ~ dans l'esprit de qqn** to sow confusion in sb's mind, to throw sb into confusion **3.** PSYCHOL : **~ mentale** mental confusion **4.** [honte] embarrassment, confusion ■ **rougir de ~** to blush (with shame) ■ **à ma grande ~** to my great embarrassment **5.** DR : **~ de dette** confusion **6.** POLIT : **~ des pouvoirs** nonseparation of legislative, executive and judiciary powers.

conga [kɔ̃ga] *nm* **1.** [danse] conga **2.** [tambour] conga drum.

congé [kɔ̃ʒe] *nm* **1.** [vacances] holiday UK, vacation US ■ ADMIN & MIL leave ■ **trois semaines de ~** three weeks off, three weeks' leave ■ **j'ai ~ le lundi** I have Mondays off, I'm off on Mondays, Monday is my day off ▶ **~ pour convenance personnelle** compassionate leave ■ **~ formation** *leave of absence to enable an employee to follow a training course* ■ **~ de maladie** sick leave ■ **~ (de) maternité** maternity leave ■ **~ de naissance** (three-day) paternity leave ■ **~ parental (d'éducation)** *parent's right to take time off without pay (after a birth or an adoption)* ■ **~ de paternité** paternity leave ■ **~s payés** *annual paid leave (at least 30 days per year in France)* ■ **~ sabbatique** sabbatical (leave) ■ **~s scolaires** school holidays UK *ou* vacation US ■ **~ sans solde** time off without pay, unpaid leave ■ **jour de ~** day off **2.** [avis de départ] notice ■ **donner son ~ à son patron** to hand in one's notice to the boss ■ **donner son ~ à son propriétaire** to give notice to one's landlord ■ **donner (son) ~ à un employé** to give notice to *ou* to dismiss an employee **3.** [adieu] : **donner ~ à qqn** to dismiss sb ■ **prendre ~** to (take one's) leave, to depart ■ **prendre ~ de** to take one's leave of.
◆ **en congé** *loc adv* : **être en ~** [soldat] to be on leave ; [écolier, salarié] to be on holiday UK *ou* vacation US ■ **je suis en ~ demain jusqu'à lundi** I'm off (from) tomorrow till Monday.

congédier [9] [kɔ̃ʒedje] *vt* [employé] to dismiss, to discharge ■ [locataire] to give notice to ■ [importun] *sout* to send away *(sép)* ■ **se faire ~** to be dismissed.

congelable [kɔ̃ʒlabl] *adj* freezable, suitable for freezing.

congélateur [kɔ̃ʒelatœr] *nm* deep freeze, freezer.

congélation [kɔ̃ʒelasjɔ̃] *nf* **1.** [technique] freezing ■ [durée] freezing time ▶ **sac de ~** freezer bag **2.** [passage à l'état de glace] freezing, turning to ice.

congeler [25] [kɔ̃ʒle] *vt* to freeze ■ **tarte/viande congelée** frozen pie/meat.
◆ **se congeler** ◇ *vp (emploi passif)* [dans un congélateur] to freeze ■ **la mayonnaise ne se congèle pas** you can't freeze mayonnaise (successfully), mayonnaise doesn't freeze well.
◇ *vpi* [eau] to freeze.

congénère [kɔ̃ʒenɛr] ◇ *adj* congeneric.
◇ *nmf* **1.** [animal] congener **2.** *péj* [personne] : **toi et tes ~s** you and your sort ■ **sans ses ~s, il se comporte correctement** away from his peers, he behaves well.

congénital, e, aux [kɔ̃ʒenital, o] *adj* congenital ■ **il est bête, c'est ~!** *fam hum* he was born stupid!

congère [kɔ̃ʒɛr] *nf* snowdrift.

congestif, ive [kɔ̃ʒɛstif, iv] *adj* congestive.

congestion [kɔ̃ʒɛstjɔ̃] *nf* congestion ■ **il a eu une ~** *fam* he has had a stroke ▶ **~ cérébrale** stroke ■ **~ pulmonaire** congestion of the lungs.

congestionné, e [kɔ̃ʒɛstjɔne] *adj* [visage] flushed ■ [route] congested.

congestionner [3] [kɔ̃ʒɛstjɔne] *vt* **1.** [partie du corps] to congest ■ [visage] to flush **2.** [encombrer - réseaux routiers] to congest, to clog up *(sép)*.
◆ **se congestionner** *vpi* **1.** [visage] to become flushed **2.** [être encombré] to become clogged up *ou* congested.

conglomérat [kɔ̃glɔmera] *nm* ÉCON & GÉOL conglomerate.

conglomération [kɔ̃glɔmerasjɔ̃] *nf* conglomeration.

conglomérer [18] [kɔ̃glɔmere] *vt* to conglomerate.

Congo [kɔ̃go] *npr m* : **le ~** [pays] the Congo ; [fleuve] the Congo River, the River Congo ■ **au ~** in the Congo.

congolais, e [kɔ̃gɔlɛ, ɛz] *adj* Congolese.
◆ **Congolais, e** *nm, f* Congolese ■ **les Congolais** the Congolese.
◆ **congolais** *nm* CULIN coconut cake.

congratulations [kɔ̃gratylasjɔ̃] *nfpl litt* felicitations.

congratuler [3] [kɔ̃gratyle] *vt litt* to congratulate.

congre [kɔ̃gr] *nm* conger (eel).

congrégation [kɔ̃gregasjɔ̃] *nf* **1.** [ordre] congregation, order **2.** [assemblée de prélats] congregation.

congrès [kɔ̃grɛ] *nm* [conférence, colloque] congress ■ **~ médical/scientifique** medical/scientific congress ▶ **le Congrès (américain)** Congress ■ **membre du Congrès** member of Congress, Congressman (*f* Congresswoman).

congressiste [kɔ̃gresist] *nmf* participant at a congress.

congru, e [kɔ̃gry] *adj* MATH congruent.

conifère [kɔnifɛr] *nm* conifer.

conique [kɔnik] *adj* **1.** [pointu] conical, cone-shaped **2.** MATH conic.

conjectural, e, aux [kɔ̃ʒɛktyral, o] *adj* conjectural.

conjecture [kɔ̃ʒɛktyr] *nf* conjecture, surmise ■ **se perdre en ~s** to be perplexed ■ **nous en sommes réduits aux ~s** we can only guess.

conjecturer [3] [kɔ̃ʒɛktyre] *vt sout* to conjecture *sout ou* to speculate about *(insép)* ■ **~ que** to surmise that ■ *(en usage absolu)* **~ sur** to make guesses about.

conjoint, e [kɔ̃ʒwɛ̃, ɛ̃t] ◇ *adj* **1.** [commun - démarche] joint **2.** [lié - cas, problème] linked, related **3.** [qui accompagne] : **note ~e** attached note **4.** MUS conjoint, conjunct.
◇ *nm, f* ADMIN spouse ■ **il faut l'accord des deux ~s** the agreement of both husband and wife is necessary ■ **les futurs ~s** the bride and groom, the future couple.

conjointement [kɔ̃ʒwɛ̃tmɑ̃] *adv* jointly ■ **~ avec mon associé** together with my associate ■ **vous recevrez ~ la facture et le catalogue** you'll find the invoice enclosed with the catalogue.

conjoncteur-disjoncteur [kɔ̃ʒɔ̃ktœrdisʒɔ̃ktœr] (*pl* **conjoncteurs-disjoncteurs**) *nm* circuit breaker.

conjonctif, ive [kɔ̃ʒɔ̃ktif, iv] *adj* **1.** GRAMM conjunctive **2.** ANAT connective.
◆ **conjonctive** *nf* **1.** GRAMM conjunctive clause **2.** ANAT conjunctiva.

conjonction [kɔ̃ʒɔ̃ksjɔ̃] *nf* **1.** [union] union, conjunction **2.** GRAMM conjunction ■ **~ de coordination/de subordination** coordinating/subordinating conjunction **3.** ASTRON conjunction.

conjonctivite [kɔ̃ʒɔ̃ktivit] *nf* conjunctivitis.

conjoncture [kɔ̃ʒɔ̃ktyr] *nf* **1.** [contexte] situation, conditions ■ **la ~ internationale actuelle** the current international context *ou* situation ■ **dans la ~ actuelle** under the present circumstances, at this juncture **2.** ÉCON economic situation *ou* trends ■ **de ~** conjunctural ■ **étude de ~** study of the (overall) economic climate ■ **crise de ~** economic crisis.

conjoncturel, elle [kɔ̃ʒɔ̃ktyrɛl] *adj* [chômage] cyclical ■ **crise ~le** economic crisis *(due to cyclical and not structural factors)*.

conjugable [kɔ̃ʒygabl] *adj* which can be conjugated.

conjugaison [kɔ̃ʒygɛzɔ̃] *nf* **1.** BIOL, CHIM & GRAMM conjugation **2.** [union] union, conjunction.

conjugal, e, aux [kɔ̃ʒygal, o] *adj* conjugal ■ **vie ~e** married life.

conjugalement [kɔ̃ʒygalmɑ̃] *adv* conjugally ■ **vivre ~** to live as a married couple *ou* as husband and wife.

conjugué, e [kɔ̃ʒyge] *adj* [uni - efforts] joint, combined.

conjuguer [3] [kɔ̃ʒyge] *vt* **1.** [verbe] to conjugate ■ **~ au futur** to conjugate in the future tense **2.** [unir - efforts, volontés] to join, to combine.
◆ **se conjuguer** ◇ *vp (emploi passif)* GRAMM to conjugate, to be conjugated.
◇ *vpi* [s'unir] to work together, to combine.

conjuration [kɔ̃ʒyrasjɔ̃] *nf* **1.** [complot] conspiracy **2.** [incantation] conjuration.

conjuré, e [kɔ̃ʒyre] *nm, f* conspirator, plotter.

conjurer [3] [kɔ̃ʒyre] *vt* **1.** *litt* [supplier] to beg, to beseech *litt* ■ **il la conjura de ne pas le dénoncer** he begged *ou* besought *litt* her not to give him away **2.** [écarter - mauvais sort, danger, crise] to ward off *(sép)*, to keep at bay **3.** *litt* [manigancer] to plot.

connais, connaissait *etc v* ▷ **connaître**.

connaissance [kɔnɛsɑ̃s] *nf* **1.** [maîtrise dans un domaine] knowledge ■ **une ~ approfondie de l'espagnol** a thorough knowledge *ou* good command of Spanish ▶ **la ~ de soi** self-knowledge
2. PHILOS : **la ~** knowledge
3. [fait d'être informé] : **il n'en a jamais eu ~** he never learnt about it, he was never notified of it ■ **prendre ~ des faits** to learn about *ou* to hear of the facts ■ **il est venu à notre ~ que...** it has come to our attention that...
4. [conscience] consciousness ■ **avoir toute sa ~** to be fully conscious ■ **il gisait là/il est tombé, sans ~** he was lying there/he fell unconscious ■ **perdre ~** to lose consciousness ■ **reprendre ~** to come to, to regain consciousness ■ **faire reprendre ~ à qqn** to bring sb to *ou* round
5. [rencontrer qqn] : **faire la ~ de qqn, faire ~ avec qqn** to make sb's acquaintance, to meet sb ■ **une fois que vous aurez mieux fait ~** once you've got to know each other better ■ **prendre ~ d'un texte** to read *ou* to peruse a text ■ **faire ~ avec qqch** [aborder qqch] to discover, to get to know
6. [ami] acquaintance ■ **c'est une simple ~** he's a mere *ou* nodding acquaintance ■ **faire de nouvelles ~s** to make new acquaintances, to meet new people.
◆ **connaissances** *nfpl* knowledge ■ **avoir des ~s** to be knowledgeable ■ **avoir de solides ~s en** to have a thorough knowledge of *ou* a good grounding in ■ **avoir des ~s sommaires en** to have a basic knowledge of, to know the rudiments of.
◆ **à ma connaissance, à sa connaissance** *etc loc adv* to (the best of) my/his *etc* knowledge, as far as I know/he knows *etc* ■ **pas à ma ~** not to my knowledge, not as far as I know, not that I know of.
◆ **de connaissance** *loc adj* : **être entre gens de ~** to be among familiar faces ■ **être en pays de ~** [dans un domaine] to be on familiar ground ; [dans un milieu] to be among familiar faces.

◆ **de ma connaissance, de sa connaissance** *etc loc adj*: **une personne de ma ~** an acquaintance of mine, somebody I know.

◆ **en connaissance de cause** *loc adv*: **faire qqch en ~ de cause** to do sthg with full knowledge of the facts ■ **et j'en parle en ~ de cause** and I know what I'm talking about.

connaisseur, euse [kɔnɛsœr, øz] ◇ *adj* [regard, air] expert *(avant n)*, knowledgeable.
◇ *nm, f* connoisseur ■ **un public de ~s** a knowledgeable audience, an audience of experts ■ **parler de qqch en ~** to speak knowledgeably about sthg ■ **être ~ en pierres précieuses** to be a connoisseur of *ou* knowledgeable about gems.

connaître [91] [kɔnɛtr] *vt*

> **A.** AVOIR UNE IDÉE DE
> **B.** IDENTIFIER, ÊTRE EN RELATION AVEC
> **C.** ÉPROUVER
> **D.** ADMETTRE

A. AVOIR UNE IDÉE DE

1. [avoir mémorisé - code postal, itinéraire, mot de passe] to know ■ **la cachette était connue d'elle seule** she was the only one who knew where the hiding place was
2. [être informé de - information, nouvelle] to know ■ **je suis impatient de ~ les résultats** I'm anxious to know *ou* to hear the results ■ **faire ~** [avis, sentiment] to make known ; [décision, jugement] to make known, to announce ■ **je vous ferai ~ ma décision plus tard** I'll inform you of my decision *ou* I'll let you know what I've decided later ■ **je ne lui connais aucun défaut** I'm not aware of her having any faults ■ **on ne lui connaissait aucun ennemi** he had no known enemies
3. [avoir des connaissances sur - langue, ville, appareil, œuvre] to know, to be familiar with ; [- technique] to know, to be acquainted with ; [- sujet] to know (about) ■ **je ne connais pas l'italien** I don't know *ou* can't speak Italian ■ **je connais un peu l'informatique** I have some basic knowledge of computing, I know a little about computing ■ **elle connaît tout sur tout** *pr & iron* she knows everything there is to know ■ **il connaît bien les Alpes** he knows the Alps well ■ **faire ~ : faire ~ un produit** to publicize a product ■ **son dernier film l'a fait ~ dans le monde entier** his latest film has brought him worldwide fame ■ **sa traduction a fait ~ son œuvre en France** her translation has brought his work to French audiences ■ **cette émission est destinée à faire ~ des artistes étrangers** this programme is aimed at introducing foreign artists ■ **ça me/le connaît** *fam*: **les bons vins, ça le connaît!** he knows a thing or two about *ou* he's an expert on good wine! ■ **connaît pas** *fam*: **à cet âge-là, la propreté, connaît pas** at that age they don't know the meaning of the word cleanliness ■ **y ~ quelque chose en** to have some idea *ou* to know something about ■ **ne rien y ~ : je n'y connais rien en biologie** I don't know a thing about biology ■ **je ne mange pas de cette horreur! – tu n'y connais rien!** I won't eat that horrible stuff! – you don't know what's good for you!

B. IDENTIFIER, ÊTRE EN RELATION AVEC

1. [par l'identité] to know ■ **~ qqn de vue/nom/réputation** to know sb by sight/name/reputation ■ **on la connaissait sous le nom de Louise Michel** she was known as Louise Michel ■ **se faire ~** [révéler son identité] to make o.s. known ; [devenir une personne publique] to make o.s. *ou* to become known ■ **notre auditeur n'a pas voulu se faire ~** our listener didn't want his name to be known *ou* wished to remain anonymous ■ **la connaissant, ça ne me surprend pas** knowing her, I'm not surprised ■ **tu me connais mal!** you don't know me! ■ **elle a bien connu ton oncle** she knew your uncle well ■ **je t'ai connue plus enjouée** I've known you to be chirpier ■ **je l'ai connu enfant** I knew him when he was a child ■ **si tu fais ça, je ne te connais plus!** if you do that, I'll have nothing more to do with you! ◗ **je te connais comme si je t'avais fait!** *fam* I know you as if you were my own *ou* like the back of my hand!
2. [rencontrer] to meet ■ **ah, si je t'avais connue plus tôt!** if only I'd met you earlier! ■ **je l'ai connu au cours du tournage** I got to know him while we were shooting the picture ■ **j'aimerais vous faire ~ mon frère** I would like to introduce you to my brother

C. ÉPROUVER

1. [peur, amour] to feel, to know, to experience
2. [faire l'expérience de] to experience ■ **la tour avait connu des jours meilleurs** the tower had seen better days ■ **ah, l'insouciance de la jeunesse, j'ai connu ça!** I was young and carefree once! ■ **ses promesses, je connais!** *fam* don't talk to me about his promises! ■ **faire ~ qqch à qqn** to introduce sb to sthg ‖ [obtenir - succès, gloire] to have, to experience ■ **enfin, elle connut la consécration** she finally received the highest accolade
3. [subir - crise] to go *ou* to live through *(insép)*, to experience ; [- épreuve, humiliation, guerre] to live through *(insép)*, to suffer, to undergo ■ **il a connu bien des déboires** he has had *ou* suffered plenty of setbacks

D. ADMETTRE

1. [suj: chose] to have ■ *(au nég)* to know ■ **son ambition ne connaît pas de bornes** *ou* **limites** her ambition is boundless *ou* knows no bounds
2. [suj: personne] : **ne pas ~ de** *litt* : **il ne connaît pas de maître** he knows no master ■ **ne ~ que : il ne connaît que le travail** work is the only thing he's interested in *ou* he knows ■ **contre les rhumes, je ne connais qu'un bon grog** there's nothing like a hot toddy to cure a cold.

◆ **se connaître** ◇ *vp (emploi réfléchi)* to know o.s., to be self-aware ■ **je n'oserai jamais, je me connais** I'd never dare, I know what I'm like ◗ **connais-toi toi-même** *Socrate allus* know thyself.
◇ *vp (emploi réciproque)* to be acquainted, to have met (before) ■ **vous vous connaissez?** have you met (before)? ■ **ils se connaissent bien** they know each other well.
◇ *vpi* : **s'y ~** [être expert] : **s'y ~ en architecture** to know a lot about architecture ■ **je m'y connais peu en informatique** I don't know much about computers ■ **ah ça, pour râler, il s'y connaît!** *fam* he's very good at grumbling! ■ **pour les gaffes, tu t'y connais!** *fam* when it comes to blunders, you take some beating! ■ **c'est un escroc, ou je ne m'y connais pas!** I know a crook when I see one!

connard▲ [kɔnar] *nm* wanker ▲ *UK*, arsehole▲ *UK*, asshole ▲ *US*.

connasse▲ [kɔnas] *nf* stupid cow *ou* bitch.

conne [kɔn] △ *f* ▷ **con**.

connectabilité [kɔnɛktabilite] *nf* INFORM connectivity.

connecter [4] [kɔnɛkte] *vt* to connect.

◆ **se connecter à** *vp+prép* INFORM to connect o.s. to.

connecteur [kɔnɛktœr] *nm* connector.

Connecticut [kɔnɛktikœt] *npr m* : **le ~** Connecticut.

connerie△ [kɔnri] *nf* **1.** [stupidité] stupidity **2.** [acte, remarque] stupid thing ■ **raconter des ~s** to talk rubbish ■ **elle a fait une ~** she's done sthg really bloody *UK ou* goddam stupid *US*.

connétable [kɔnetabl] *nm* HIST constable.

connexe [kɔnɛks] *adj* [idées, problèmes] closely related.

connexion [kɔnɛksjɔ̃] *nf* connection.

connivence [konivɑ̃s] *nf sout* connivance, complicity ■ **être de ~ avec** to be in connivance with, to connive with ■ **ils sont de ~** they're in league with each other ■ **un regard de ~** a conniving look.

connotation [kɔnɔtasjɔ̃] *nf* **1.** LING connotation **2.** [nuance] overtone.

connoter [3] [kɔnɔte] *vt* **1.** LING to connote **2.** PHILOS to connote, to imply, to have overtones of.

connu, e [kɔny] ◇ *pp* ▷ **connaître**.
◇ *adj* **1.** [découvert - univers] known **2.** [répandu - idée, tactique] well-known, widely known **3.** [célèbre - personnalité, chanteur] famous, well-known ■ **un de ses tableaux les moins ~s** one of his least well-known *ou* least-known paintings ■ **une blague ~e** *fam* an old joke ◗ **il est ~ comme le loup blanc** everybody knows him.

◆ **connu** *nm* : **le ~ et l'inconnu** the known and the unknown.

conque [kɔ̃k] *nf* **1.** ZOOL conch **2.** ANAT external ear, concha *spéc*.

conquérant, e [kɔ̃kerɑ̃, ɑ̃t] ◇ *adj* **1.** MIL & POLIT conquering **2.** [hautain - sourire] domineering ; [- démarche] swaggering ▪ **il entra d'un air ~** he swaggered in.
◇ *nm, f* conqueror.

conquérir [39] [kɔ̃kerir] *vt* **1.** MIL & POLIT to conquer **2.** [acquérir - espace, pouvoir] to gain control over, to capture, to conquer ▶ **se comporter comme en pays conquis** to act as if one owns the place **3.** [séduire - cœur, public] to win (over) *(sép)*, to conquer ▪ **~ un homme/une femme** to win a man's/a woman's heart ▪ **être conquis** to be entirely won over.

conquête [kɔ̃kɛt] *nf* **1.** [action] conquest ▪ **partir à la ~ de l'Amérique** to set out to conquer America **2.** [chose gagnée] conquest, conquered territory **3.** *fam* [personne] conquest ▪ **sa dernière ~ s'appelle Peter** her latest conquest is called Peter.

conquiert *etc v* ⊳ **conquérir.**

conquis [kɔ̃ki, iz] *pp* ⊳ **conquérir.**

conquistador [kɔ̃kistadɔr] *nm* conquistador.

consacré, e [kɔ̃sakre] *adj* **1.** RELIG [hostie] consecrated ▪ [terre] hallowed **2.** [accepté - rite, terme] accepted, established ▪ **c'est l'expression ~e** it's the accepted way of saying it **3.** [célèbre - artiste, cinéaste] established, recognized.

consacrer [3] [kɔ̃sakre] *vt* **1.** [réserver qqch à] : **~ qqch à** to devote *ou* to dedicate sthg to ▪ **as-tu dix minutes à me ~?** can you spare me ten minutes? **2.** RELIG [pain, autel, église, évêque] to consecrate ▪ **~ un temple à Jupiter** to consecrate *ou* to dedicate a temple to Jupiter **3.** [entériner - pratique, injustice] to sanction, to hallow ▪ **expression consacrée par l'usage** expression that has become established by usage ▪ **tradition consacrée par le temps** time-honoured tradition **4.** [couronner - artiste, acteur] to crown, to turn into a star ▪ **le jury l'a consacré meilleur acteur de l'année** the jury voted him best actor of the year.
◆ **se consacrer à** *vp+prép* to devote *ou* to dedicate o.s. to ▪ **je ne peux me ~ à mon fils que le soir** I can only find time for my son in the evenings.

consanguin, e [kɔ̃sɑ̃gɛ̃, in] ◇ *adj* : **sœur ~e** half-sister *(on the father's side)* ▪ **mariage ~** intermarriage, marriage between blood relatives.
◇ *nm, f* half-brother (*f* half-sister) *(on the father's side)* ▪ **les ~s** blood relations *ou* relatives.

consanguinité [kɔ̃sɑ̃ginite] *nf* **1.** [parenté] consanguinity **2.** [mariages consanguins] intermarriage.

consciemment [kɔ̃sjamɑ̃] *adv* consciously, knowingly.

conscience [kɔ̃sjɑ̃s] *nf* **1.** [connaissance] consciousness, awareness ▪ **avoir ~ de** to be conscious *ou* aware of ▪ **prendre ~ de qqch** to become aware of *ou* to realize sthg ▶ **~ de classe** class consciousness ▪ **~ collective/politique** collective/political consciousness ▪ **~ de soi** self-awareness **2.** [sens de la morale] conscience ▪ **agir selon sa ~** to act according to one's conscience ▪ **libérer** *ou* **soulager sa ~** to relieve one's conscience ▪ **avoir qqch sur la ~** to have sthg on one's conscience ▪ **sa ~ ne le laissera pas tranquille** *ou* **en paix** his conscience will give him no rest ▪ **avoir la ~ tranquille** to have an easy conscience ▪ **je n'ai pas la ~ tranquille de l'avoir laissé seul** I have an uneasy conscience *ou* I feel bad about having left him alone ▪ **avoir bonne ~** to have a clear conscience ▪ **tu dis ça pour te donner bonne ~** you're saying this to appease your conscience ▪ **avoir mauvaise ~** to have a guilty *ou* bad conscience ▶ **c'est une affaire** *ou* **un cas de ~** it's a matter of conscience ▪ **crise de ~** crisis of conscience ▪ **j'ai ma ~ pour moi** my conscience is clear **3.** [lucidité] consciousness ▪ **perdre ~** to lose consciousness ▪ **reprendre ~** to regain consciousness, to come to **4.** [application] : **~ professionnelle** conscientiousness ▪ **faire son travail avec beaucoup de ~ professionnelle** to do one's job very conscientiously, to be conscientious in one's work.
◆ **en (toute) conscience** *loc adv* in all conscience ▪ **je ne peux, en ~, te laisser partir seul** I can't decently let you go on your own.

consciencieusement [kɔ̃sjɑ̃sjøzmɑ̃] *adv* conscientiously.

consciencieux, euse [kɔ̃sjɑ̃sjø, øz] *adj* [élève] conscientious, meticulous ▪ [travail] meticulous.

conscient, e [kɔ̃sjɑ̃, ɑ̃t] *adj* **1.** [délibéré - geste, désir, haine] conscious **2.** [averti] aware ▪ **être ~ du danger** to be aware *ou* conscious of the danger **3.** [lucide - blessé] conscious.
◆ **conscient** *nm* : **le ~** the conscious (mind).

conscription [kɔ̃skripsjɔ̃] *nf* conscription, draft *US*.

conscrit [kɔ̃skri] *nm* conscript, draftee *US* ▪ **armée de ~s** conscript *ou* draft *US* army.

consécration [kɔ̃sekrasjɔ̃] *nf* **1.** RELIG consecration **2.** [confirmation - d'une coutume] establishment, sanctioning ; [- d'une injustice] sanctioning ; [- d'un artiste, d'une carrière] consecration, apotheosis, crowning point.

consécutif, ive [kɔ̃sekytif, iv] *adj* **1.** [successif] consecutive ▪ **c'est la cinquième fois consécutive qu'il remet le rendez-vous** this is the fifth time running *ou* in a row that he's postponed the meeting ▪ **~ à : l'infarctus est souvent ~ au surmenage** heart attacks are often the result of stress **2.** GRAMM & MATH consecutive.

consécution [kɔ̃sekysjɔ̃] *nf* [gén - LOGIQUE] consecution.

consécutivement [kɔ̃sekytivmɑ̃] *adv* consecutively ▪ **notre équipe a subi ~ quatre défaites** our team has suffered four consecutive defeats *ou* four defeats in a row ▪ **les accidents se sont produits ~** the accidents happened one after another *ou* the other.
◆ **consécutivement à** *loc prép* after, as a result of, following ▪ **~ à un incident technique** as a result of *ou* following a technical hitch.

conseil [kɔ̃sɛj] *nm* **1.** [avis] piece of advice, counsel *sout* ▪ **un ~ d'ami** a friendly piece of advice ▪ **des ~s** [d'ami] advice ; [trucs] tips, hints ▪ **agir sur/suivre le ~ de qqn** to act on/to take sb's advice, to ask sb's advice ▪ **demander ~ à qqn** to ask sb for advice ▪ **prendre ~ auprès de qqn** to take advice from sb **2.** [conseiller] adviser, consultant ▶ **~ conjugal** marriage-guidance counsellor ▪ **~ en publicité** advertising consultant ▪ **~ en organisation** organizational consultant ▪ **~ fiscal** tax consultant ▪ **~ juridique** legal adviser ▪ *(comme adj; avec ou sans trait d'union)* **ingénieur ~** consultant engineer ▪ **avocat ~** legal consultant **3.** [assemblée] board ▪ [réunion] meeting ▪ **tenir ~** to hold a meeting ▶ **~ d'administration** [d'une société] board of directors ; [d'une organisation internationale] governing body ▪ **~ de cabinet** cabinet council, council of ministers ▪ **le Conseil constitutionnel** *French government body ensuring that laws, elections and referenda are constitutional* ▪ **le Conseil économique et social** *consultative body advising the government on economic and social matters* ▪ **le Conseil d'État** the (French) Council of State ▪ **le Conseil de l'Europe** the Council of Europe ▪ **le Conseil européen** the European Council ▪ **~ de famille** board of guardians ▪ **~ général** ≃ county council ▪ **~ de guerre** [réunion] war council ≃ War Cabinet ; [tribunal] court-martial ▪ **passer en ~ de guerre** to be court-martialled ▪ **~ interministériel** interministerial council ▪ **le Conseil des ministres** ≃ the Cabinet ▪ **~ municipal** [en ville] ≃ town council ≃ local (urban) council ; [à la campagne] ≃ parish council *UK* ≃ local (rural) council ▪ **~ de prud'hommes** industrial arbitration court, ≃ ACAS *UK* ▪ **~ régional** regional council ▪ **~ de révision** MIL recruiting board, draft board *US* ▪ **le Conseil de sécurité** the Security Council ▪ **le Conseil supérieur de la magistrature** *French state body that appoints members of the judiciary* **4.** ÉDUC : **~ de classe** staff meeting *(concerning a class)* ▪ **~ de discipline** disciplinary committee ▪ **~ d'école** *committee responsible for internal organization of a primary school* ▪ **~ d'établissement** ≃ board of governors *UK*, ≃ board of education *US* ▪ **~ des maîtres** *teachers' committee at a primary school* ▪ **~ des professeurs** *termly meeting of teachers to discuss progress made by individual pupils* ▪ **~ d'UFR** departmental (management) committee ▪ **Conseil d'Université** ≃ university Senate *UK*, ≃ Board of Trustees *US*.
◆ **de bon conseil** *loc adj* : **un homme de bon ~** a man of sound advice, a wise counsellor ▪ **demande-lui, elle est de bon ~** ask her, she's good at giving advice.

LE CONSEIL CONSTITUTIONNEL

The *Conseil constitutionnel*, which ensures that new laws do not contravene the constitution, has nine members appointed for a nine-year period; it also includes the surviving former Presidents of France. The President of the Republic and any member of parliament can refer laws to the *Conseil constitutionnel* for scrutiny.

LE CONSEIL D'ÉTAT

The French Council of State acts both as the highest court to which the legal affairs of the state can be referred, and as a consultative body to which bills and rulings are submitted by the government prior to examination by the *Conseil des ministres*. It has 200 members.

CONSEIL DES MINISTRES

The President himself presides over the *Conseil des ministres*, which traditionally meets every Wednesday morning; strictly speaking, when ministers assemble in the sole presence of the Prime Minister, this is known as *le Conseil du cabinet*.

CONSEIL GÉNÉRAL

The body responsible for the administration of a *département*. Members are elected for a six-year term, with one councillor per *canton*, and are headed by the *président du conseil général*.

CONSEIL RÉGIONAL

The committee body for the administration of a *région*. Members are elected for a six-year term and are headed by the *président du conseil régional*. They decide on matters of planning, construction, regional development and education.

CONSEIL SUPÉRIEUR DE LA MAGISTRATURE

This state body advises on the appointment of members of the *magistrature*, and on specific points of law concerning the judiciary. It is also consulted when the president wishes to exercise his official pardon. It has ten members: the Minister of Justice and nine others appointed by the President of the Republic.

CONSEIL MUNICIPAL

The town council is elected during the *municipales* (local elections). Elected members, or *conseillers municipaux*, oversee the administration of a *commune* in conjunction with the mayor.

Voir module d'usage

conseiller¹ [4] [kɔ̃seje] *vt* **1.** [recommander - livre, dentiste] to recommend ▪ **~ qqch/qqn à qqn** to recommend sthg/sb to sb **2.** [donner son avis à - ami, enfant] to advise, to give advice to ▪ **on m'a bien/mal conseillé** I was given good/bad advice ▪ **~ à qqn de faire qqch** to advise sb to do sthg ▪ **il n'est pas conseillé de conduire par ce temps** it's not advisable to drive in this weather ▪ **beaucoup d'étudiants souhaitent se faire ~ dans le choix d'une filière** many students want to be advised about their choice of career.

conseiller², ère [kɔ̃seje, ɛr] *nm, f* **1.** [guide] adviser, counsellor *UK*, counselor *US* ▪ [spécialiste] adviser ▪ **~ économique/juridique** economic/legal adviser ▪ **~ conjugal** *ou* **matrimonial** marriage guidance counsellor **2.** ÉDUC : **~ d'éducation** *non-teaching staff member in charge of general discipline* ▪ **~ d'orientation** careers adviser *UK*, guidance counselor *US* ▪ **~ pédagogique** educational adviser **3.** [membre d'un conseil] councillor *UK*, councilor *US*, council member ▪ ADMIN : **~ d'État** member of the Conseil d'État ▪ **~ municipal** [en ville] ≃ local *ou* town councillor ; [à la campagne] ≃ local councillor ▪ **~ régional** regional councillor.

CONSEILLER MUNICIPAL

This term refers to any member of the *conseil municipal* or the mayor himself. The number of councillors depends on the size of the town, although there must be a minimum of six. Paris has 163 councillors, known as the *conseillers de Paris*.

conseilleur, euse [kɔ̃sejœr, øz] *nm, f péj* giver of advice ▪ **les ~s ne sont pas les payeurs** *prov* it's very easy to give advice when you're not going to suffer the consequences.

consens *etc v* ▻ **consentir.**

consensuel, elle [kɔ̃sɑ̃sɥɛl] *adj* [contrat] consensus *(modif)*, consensual ▪ **une politique ~le** a strategy of seeking the middle ground, consensus politics.

consensus [kɔ̃sɛ̃sys] *nm* consensus (of opinion).

consentant, e [kɔ̃sɑ̃tɑ̃, ɑ̃t] *adj* **1.** [victime] willing **2.** DR : **les trois parties sont ~es** the three parties are in agreement *ou* are agreeable ➊ **adultes ~s** consenting adults.

consentement [kɔ̃sɑ̃tmɑ̃] *nm* consent ▪ **donner son ~ à** to (give one's) consent to ➊ **~ exprès/tacite** DR formal/tacit consent ▪ **divorce par ~ mutuel** divorce by mutual consent.

consentir [37] [kɔ̃sɑ̃tir] *vt* [délai, réduction] to grant ▪ **~ qqch à qqn** to grant *ou* to allow sb sthg ▪ **on m'a consenti une remise de 10%/un délai supplémentaire de 15 jours** I was allowed a 10% discount/another two weeks.

◆ **consentir à** *v+prép* to consent *ou* to agree to ▪ **elle n'a pas consenti à m'accompagner** [n'a pas été d'accord pour le faire] she didn't agree to come with me ; [n'a pas daigné le faire] she didn't deign to *ou* stoop so low as to accompany me.

LES CONSEILS

Demander conseil

What should I do? Qu'est-ce que je dois faire ?

What would you do, if you were me? Qu'est-ce que tu ferais si tu étais moi ?

What would you do in my place? Qu'est-ce que tu ferais à ma place ?

Do you think I should tell him? Tu crois que je devrais le lui dire ?

I could do with *ou* **I need some advice.** J'aurais besoin d'un conseil.

Donner un conseil

Why don't you (just) tell her? Pourquoi ne pas le lui dire (carrément) ?

Take my advice and say nothing to her. Je te conseille de ne rien lui dire.

If I were you, I'd phone him. Si j'étais toi, je l'appellerais.

If you ask me, I think you should resign. Si tu veux mon avis, je pense que tu devrais démissionner.

Perhaps *ou* **Maybe you should warn him.** Peut-être que tu devrais le prévenir.

I'd think twice about going. Je réfléchirais à deux fois avant d'y aller.

You could always try writing to him. Ce serait peut-être pas mal de lui écrire.

It might be better to do it yourself. Ce serait peut-être mieux que tu le fasses toi-même.

Now listen to me: you really must go and see a doctor. Écoute, il faut absolument que tu ailles voir un médecin.

If you want my advice, you'll pretend it never happened. Si tu veux mon avis, fais comme si rien ne s'était passé.

I hope you won't take this the wrong way, but... Ne le prends pas mal, mais...

It's not really any of my business, but... Je sais que ça ne me regarde pas, mais...

conséquemment [kɔ̃sekamɑ̃] *adv* consequently ■ **~ à** as a result of, following (on *ou* upon).

conséquence [kɔ̃sekɑ̃s] *nf* consequence, repercussion ■ **lourd de ~s** with serious consequences ■ **ma gaffe a eu pour ~ de les brouiller** my blunder resulted in their falling out (with each other) ■ **cela ne tirera pas à ~** this won't have any repercussions *ou* will be of no consequence ■ **une déclaration sans ~** [sans importance] a statement of no *ou* little consequence ; [sans suite] an inconsequential statement.
◆ **de conséquence** *loc adj* : **personne de ~** person of consequence *ou* importance ■ **une affaire de ~** a matter of (some) consequence.
◆ **en conséquence** *loc adv* **1.** [par conséquent] consequently, therefore **2.** [comme il convient] accordingly.
◆ **en conséquence de** *loc prép* as a consequence *ou* result of ■ **en ~ de quoi** as a result of which.

conséquent, e [kɔ̃sekɑ̃, ɑ̃t] *adj* **1.** [cohérent] consistent ■ **être ~ avec soi-même** to be consistent **2.** *fam* [important - moyens, magasin] sizeable ; [- somme] tidy.
◆ **conséquent** *nm* **1.** PHILOS consequent **2.** MUS answer.
◆ **par conséquent** *loc adv* consequently, as a result.

conservateur, trice [kɔ̃sɛrvatœr, tris] ◇ *adj* **1.** [prudent - placement, gestion] conservative ■ **avoir un esprit ~** to be conservative-minded **2.** POLIT [gén] conservative ■ **le parti ~** [en Grande-Bretagne] the Conservative *ou* Tory Party ; [au Canada] the Progressive Conservative Party.
◇ *nm, f* POLIT [gén] conservative ■ [en Grande-Bretagne] Conservative, Tory.
◆ **conservateur** *nm* **1.** [additif] preservative **2.** [responsable - de musée] curator ; [- de bibliothèque] librarian ■ **~ des eaux et forêts** ≃ forestry commissioner ■ **~ des hypothèques** ≃ registrar of mortgages.

conservation [kɔ̃sɛrvasjɔ̃] *nf* **1.** [dans l'agroalimentaire] preserving ■ **~ par le froid** cold storage, ▷ **agent**, ▷ **durée 2.** [maintien en bon état] keeping, preserving, safeguarding **3.** BIOL & PHYS : **~ de l'énergie** conservation of energy **4.** [état] state of preservation **5.** ADMIN : **~ des eaux et forêts** ≃ Forestry Commission ■ **~ des hypothèques** ≃ Land Registry.

conservatisme [kɔ̃sɛrvatism] *nm* **1.** [prudence] conservatism **2.** POLIT [gén] conservatism ■ [en Grande-Bretagne] Conservatism.

conservatoire [kɔ̃sɛrvatwar] ◇ *adj* protective.
◇ *nm* [école] school, academy ■ **~ de musique** conservatoire ● **le Conservatoire (national supérieur d'art dramatique)** *national drama school in Paris* ■ **le Conservatoire (national supérieur de musique)** the Conservatoire *(in Paris and Lyon)* ■ **le Conservatoire national des arts et métiers** *science and technology school in Paris.*

conserve [kɔ̃sɛrv] *nf* item of tinned *UK ou* canned food ■ **les ~s** tinned *UK ou* canned food ■ **~s de fruits** conserves ■ **~s en bocaux** bottled preserves ■ **aliments en ~** tinned *UK ou* canned food ■ **mettre en ~** to tin *UK*, to can ■ **on ne va pas en faire des ~s!** *hum* we're not going to hang on to it forever!
◆ **de conserve** *loc adv* : **aller de ~** *fig* & *litt* to go (all) together ■ **agir de ~** *litt* to act in concert.

conservé, e [kɔ̃sɛrve] *adj* : **bien ~** well-preserved.

conserver [3] [kɔ̃sɛrve] *vt* **1.** [aliment - dans le vinaigre] to pickle ; [- dans le sel, par séchage, en congelant] to preserve ; [- dans le sucre] to preserve, to conserve ; [- dans des boîtes] to preserve, to tin *UK*, to can ; [- en bocal] to bottle
2. ARCHIT, CONSTR & ÉCOL [édifice, énergie] to preserve
3. [stocker] to keep, to store, to stock
4. [avoir en sa possession - photos, relations] to keep, to hang on to *(insép)* ■ **~ qqch précieusement** to treasure sthg
5. [garder - charme, force, illusion, calme] to keep, to retain ■ **~ (toute) sa tête** [rester calme] to keep one's head *ou* self-control ; [être lucide] to have all one's wits about one ■ **le sport, ça conserve** *fam* sport keeps you young ■ **~ son amitié à qqn** to stay friendly with sb
6. [à la suite d'une expérience] : **~ qqch de : j'en ai conservé un excellent souvenir** I've retained very good memories of it ■ **j'en ai conservé la peur du noir** it left me with a fear of the dark
7. MIL : **~ ses positions** to hold fast.
◆ **se conserver** ◇ *vp (emploi passif)* [être stocké] to be kept ■ **les pommes doivent se ~ sur des clayettes** apples must be stored on racks.
◇ *vpi* [durer - aliment] to keep ; [- poterie, parchemin] to survive ■ **les truffes au chocolat ne se conservent pas longtemps** (chocolate) truffles don't keep long.

conserverie [kɔ̃sɛrvəri] *nf* **1.** [industrie] canning industry **2.** [technique] canning **3.** [usine] canning factory.

considérable [kɔ̃siderabl] *adj* **1.** [important - somme, travail] considerable **2.** [éminent - personne] prominent ■ **une personnalité ~ dans le monde des lettres** a prominent figure in the world of literature.

considérablement [kɔ̃siderabləmɑ̃] *adv* considerably.

considération [kɔ̃siderasjɔ̃] *nf* **1.** [examen] consideration, scrutiny ■ **la question mérite ~** the question is worth considering **2.** [préoccupation] consideration, factor ■ **les ~s de temps** the time factor ■ **se perdre en ~s techniques** to get lost in technical considerations ■ **si l'on s'arrête à ce genre de ~s** if we pay too much attention to this kind of detail **3.** [respect] regard, esteem ■ **par ~ pour** out of respect *ou* regard for ■ **jouir d'une grande ~** to be highly considered *ou* regarded, to be held in great esteem ■ **manque de ~** disregard ● **veuillez agréer l'assurance de ma ~ distinguée** yours faithfully *UK*, yours sincerely *US*.
◆ **en considération** *loc adv* : **faire entrer qqch en ~** to bring sthg into play *ou* consideration ■ **prendre qqch en ~** to take sthg into account *ou* consideration ■ **toutes les candidatures seront prises en ~** all applications will be given careful consideration.
◆ **en considération de** *loc prép* : **en ~ de votre état de santé** because of *ou* given *ou* considering your health ■ **en ~ de vos services** in (full) recognition of your services.
◆ **sans considération de** *loc prép* : **sans ~ de personne** without taking individual cases into consideration *ou* account ■ **sans ~ du coût** regardless *ou* heedless of *ou* without considering (the) cost.

considérer [18] [kɔ̃sidere] *vt* **1.** [regarder] to gaze *ou* to stare at *(insép)* ■ **~ qqn avec hostilité** to stare at sb in a hostile manner ■ **considérons la droite AB** consider the line AB **2.** [prendre en compte - offre, problème] to consider, to take into consideration, to weigh up *(sép)* ■ **~ le pour et le contre** to weigh up the pros and cons ■ **il faut ~ que l'accusé est mineur** it must be taken into account *ou* be borne in mind that the defendant is underage **3.** [croire] to consider, to deem *sout* ■ **je la considère qualifiée pour ce travail** I consider her (to be) qualified for this job ■ **je considère que je n'en ai pas le droit** I consider that I don't have any right to do so **4.** [juger] : **~ bien/mal** to hold in high/low esteem ■ **elle me considère comme sa meilleure amie** she regards me as *ou* looks upon me as *ou* considers me to be her best friend **5.** [respecter] to respect, to hold in high esteem *ou* regard ■ **un spécialiste hautement considéré** a highly-regarded *ou* highly-respected expert.
◆ **se considérer** *vp (emploi réfléchi)* : **il se considère comme un très grand artiste** he considers himself (as) a great artist.
◆ **à tout bien considérer, tout bien considéré** *loc adv* [tout compte fait] on second thoughts *ou* further consideration.

consignataire [kɔ̃siɲatɛr] *nmf* **1.** COMM consignee **2.** NAUT consignee, forwarding agent **3.** DR depositary.

consignation [kɔ̃siɲasjɔ̃] *nf* **1.** COMM consignment ■ **en ~** on consignment **2.** DR deposit **3.** [d'un emballage] charging a deposit on ■ **la ~ est de 10 centimes** there's a 10-centime refund on return.

consigne [kɔ̃siɲ] *nf* **1.** [instruction] orders, instructions ■ **ils ont reçu pour ~ de ne pas tirer** they've been given orders not to shoot ■ **je n'ai pas (reçu) de ~s** I have received no instructions ■ **elle avait pour ~ de surveiller sa sœur** she'd been told to keep an eye on her sister **2.** [punition - MIL] confinement to barracks ■ ÉDUC detention **3.** RAIL left-luggage office *UK*, checkroom *US* ■ **~ automatique** (left-luggage *UK*) lockers **4.** COMM deposit.

consigné, e [kɔ̃siɲe] *adj* returnable ■ **non ~** non returnable.

consigner [3] [kɔ̃siɲe] *vt* **1.** [déposer - valise] to put in the left-luggage office *UK ou* checkroom *US* **2.** FIN [somme] to deposit **3.** [emballage] to put *ou* to charge a deposit on ▪ **la bouteille est consignée 50 centimes** there's a 50-centime deposit on the bottle **4.** [noter] to record, to put down *(sép)* ▪ **~ qqch par écrit** to put down sthg in writing *ou* on paper **5.** MIL to confine to barracks ▪ ÉDUC to keep in (detention) **6.** [interdire] : **~ sa porte à qqn** *sout* to bar one's door to sb, to refuse sb admittance ▪ **'consigné à la troupe'** 'out of bounds to troops' **7.** NAUT to consign.

consistance [kɔ̃sistɑ̃s] *nf* **1.** [état] consistency ▪ **~ crémeuse/dure** creamy/firm consistency ▪ **prendre ~** [sauce] to thicken ▪ **le projet prend ~** *fig* the project is taking shape ▪ **sans ~** *fig* [rumeur] groundless, ill-founded ; [personne] spineless ; [discours, raisonnement] woolly **2.** [cohérence] consistency.

consistant, e [kɔ̃sistɑ̃, ɑ̃t] *adj* **1.** [épais - sauce, peinture] thick **2.** [substantiel - plat, repas] substantial **3.** [bien établi - argument, rumeur] well-founded, well-grounded.

consister [3] [kɔ̃siste] ◆ **consister à** *v+prép* to consist in ▪ **son rôle consistait à claquer une porte** his part consisted in slamming a door.
◆ **consister dans, consister en** *v+prép* to consist of ▪ **en quoi consiste votre mission?** what does your mission consist of?, what is your mission all about?

consœur [kɔ̃sœr] *nf* **1.** [collègue] (female) colleague **2.** RELIG sister nun.

consolable [kɔ̃sɔlabl] *adj* consolable.

consolateur, trice [kɔ̃sɔlatœr, tris] ◇ *adj* comforting, consolatory.
◇ *nm, f* comforter.

consolation [kɔ̃sɔlasjɔ̃] *nf* **1.** [soulagement] consolation, comfort, solace *litt* ▪ **la compagnie de son chien était une maigre ~** his dog was of little comfort to him **2.** [personne ou chose qui réconforte] consolation.
◆ **de consolation** *loc adj* [épreuve, tournoi] runners-up *(modif)* ▪ [lot, prix] consolation *(modif)*.

console [kɔ̃sɔl] *nf* **1.** [table] console table **2.** CONSTR cantilever, bracket **3.** ARCHIT console **4.** MUS [d'un orgue] console ▪ [d'une harpe] neck **5.** INFORM console ▪ **~ de visualisation** (visual) display unit ▪ **~ de jeux** video game.

consoler [3] [kɔ̃sɔle] *vt* to console, to comfort ▪ **rien ne pouvait le ~** [enfant] nothing could cheer him up *ou* console him ▪ **si cela peut te ~** if it's any consolation.
◆ **se consoler** ◇ *vp (emploi réfléchi)* to console o.s. ▪ **se ~ dans l'alcool** to find solace in drink.
◇ *vpi* to console o.s., to be consoled ▪ **il ne s'est jamais consolé de la mort de sa femme** he never got over losing his wife.

consolidation [kɔ̃sɔlidasjɔ̃] *nf* **1.** [d'un édifice, d'un meuble] strengthening, reinforcement ▪ [d'un mur] bracing, buttressing, reinforcement **2.** [renforcement - d'une amitié, d'une position, d'un pouvoir] consolidation, strengthening ▪ **on assiste à la ~ de la dictature** the dictatorship is consolidating its power **3.** MÉD setting **4.** DR consolidation **5.** FIN consolidation **6.** GÉOL & TRAV PUB bracing, strengthening.

consolider [3] [kɔ̃sɔlide] *vt* **1.** [renforcer - édifice, meuble] to strengthen ; [- mur] to brace, to buttress **2.** [affermir - position, majorité, amitié] to consolidate, to strengthen **3.** MÉD to set, to reduce **4.** DR to consolidate **5.** FIN to consolidate ▪ **l'euro a consolidé son avance à la Bourse** the euro has strengthened its lead on the Stock Exchange.

consommable [kɔ̃sɔmabl] ◇ *adj* **1.** [nourriture] edible ▪ [boisson] drinkable **2.** CHIM consumable.
◇ *nm* consumable *(gén pl)*.

consommateur, trice [kɔ̃sɔmatœr, tris] ◇ *adj* : **système ~ d'électricité** electricity consuming system ▪ **les pays fortement ~s de pétrole** the countries that consume large quantities of crude oil.
◇ *nm, f* **1.** [par opposition à producteur] consumer **2.** [client - d'un service] customer, user.

consommation [kɔ̃sɔmasjɔ̃] *nf* **1.** [absorption - de nourriture] consumption **2.** [utilisation - de gaz, d'électricité] consumption ▪ **elle fait une grande ~ de parfum/papier** she goes through a lot of perfume/paper **3.** ÉCON : **la ~** consumption (of goods and services) ▪ **la ~ des ménages** household consumption ➔ **biens/société de ~** consumer goods/society **4.** AUTO : **une ~ de 4 litres aux 100 (km)** a consumption of 4 litres per 100 km **5.** [au café] drink ▪ **prendre une ~** [boire] to have a drink **6.** *litt* [accomplissement - d'un crime] perpetration ; [- d'un mariage] consummation.

consommé, e [kɔ̃sɔme] *adj sout* consummate.
◆ **consommé** *nm* clear soup, consommé.

consommer [3] [kɔ̃sɔme] *vt* **1.** [absorber - nourriture] to eat, to consume *sout* ; [- boisson] to drink, to consume *sout* ▪ **le pays où l'on consomme le plus de vin** the country with the highest wine consumption ▪ *(en usage absolu)* **toute personne attablée doit ~** anyone occupying a table must order a drink ▪ **'à ~ avant (fin)...'** 'best before (end)...' **2.** [utiliser - combustible] to use (up), to consume, to go through *(sép)* ▪ **une voiture qui consomme beaucoup/peu (d'essence)** a car that uses a lot of/that doesn't use much petrol **3.** DR [mariage] to consummate **4.** *litt* [accomplir - crime] to perpetrate ; [- ruine] to bring about the completion of.
◆ **se consommer** *vp (emploi passif)* : **ça se consomme froid** it's eaten cold, you eat it cold.

consomption [kɔ̃sɔ̃psjɔ̃] *nf vieilli* [amaigrissement] wasting ▪ [tuberculose] consumption.

consonance [kɔ̃sɔnɑ̃s] *nf* **1.** LITTÉR & MUS consonance **2.** [sonorité] sound ▪ **de ~ anglaise, aux ~s anglaises** English-sounding.

consonantique [kɔ̃sɔnɑ̃tik] *adj* **1.** [des consonnes] consonantal, consonant *(modif)* **2.** ACOUST consonant, resonant.

consonne [kɔ̃sɔn] *nf* consonant.

consort [kɔ̃sɔr] *adj* & *nm* consort.
◆ **consorts** *nmpl péj* **Paul et ~s** Paul and his kind, Paul and those like him.

consortial, e, aux [kɔ̃sɔrsjal, o] *adj relating to a consortium or a syndicate.*

consortium [kɔ̃sɔrsjɔm] *nm* consortium, syndicate ▪ **constituer un ~** to form a consortium.

conspirateur, trice [kɔ̃spiratœr, tris] *nm, f* conspirator, plotter, conspirer.

conspiration [kɔ̃spirasjɔ̃] *nf* conspiracy, plotting ▪ **la Conspiration des poudres** HIST the Gunpowder Plot.

conspirer [3] [kɔ̃spire] ◇ *vi* to conspire, to plot, to scheme ▪ **~ contre qqn** to conspire *ou* to plot *ou* to scheme against sb.
◇ *vt* to plot, to scheme.
◆ **conspirer à** *v+prép sout* to conspire to ▪ **tout conspire à la réussite de ce projet** everything conspires *ou* combines to make this project a success.

conspuer [7] [kɔ̃spɥe] *vt sout* to shout down *(sép)* ▪ **se faire ~** [orateur] to be shouted down ; [comédien] to be booed off the stage.

constamment [kɔ̃stamɑ̃] *adv* **1.** [sans interruption] continuously, continually **2.** [très fréquemment] constantly.

constance [kɔ̃stɑ̃s] *nf* **1.** [persévérance] constancy, steadfastness ▪ **vous avez de la ~!** you don't give up easily! **2.** *litt* [fidélité] constancy, fidelity, faithfulness **3.** PSYCHOL invariability, constancy.

constant, e [kɔ̃stɑ̃, ɑ̃t] *adj* **1.** [invariable] unchanging, constant ▪ **~ dans ses amitiés** faithful to one's friends *ou* in friendship ▪ **être ~ dans ses goûts** to be unchanging in one's tastes **2.** [ininterrompu] continual, continuous, unceasing **3.** MATH constant **4.** FIN constant.
◆ **constante** *nf* **1.** MATH & PHYS constant **2.** [caractéristique] stable *ou* permanent trait **3.** INFORM constant.

Constantin [kɔ̃stɑ̃tɛ̃] *npr* [empereur] Constantine.

Constantinople [kɔ̃stɑ̃tinɔpl] *npr* Constantinople.

constat [kɔ̃sta] *nm* **1.** [acte] certified statement *ou* report ▪ **~ d'accident** accident statement ▪ **faisons le ~** [après un accident] let's fill in the necessary papers (for the insurance) ▪ **~ à l'amiable** mutually-agreed accident report ▪ **~ d'huissier** process-server's affidavit **2.** [bilan] review ▪ **faire un ~ d'échec** to acknowledge *ou* to admit a failure.

CONSTAT

When there is a car crash, the drivers have to produce a report that explains the causes of the accident. It must be signed by both parties and is then used by the insurance companies to determine responsibilities. Insurance companies supply drivers with prepared *constats* which need to be filled out and sent within 5 days of the accident.

constatation [kɔ̃statasjɔ̃] *nf* **1.** [observation] noting, noticing **2.** [remarque] remark, comment, observation ▪ **ce n'est pas un reproche, c'est une simple ~** this isn't a criticism, it's just an observation *ou* I'm just stating a fact.
◆ **constatations** *nfpl* [d'une enquête] findings ▪ **procéder aux ~s** to establish the facts.

constater [3] [kɔ̃state] *vt* **1.** [remarquer] to note, to observe, to notice ▪ **je suis forcée de ~ que je ne peux te faire confiance** I am forced to the conclusion that I can't trust you ▪ *(en usage absolu)* **constatez par vous-même!** just see for yourself! **2.** [enregistrer - décès] to certify ; [- faits] to record, to list ▪ **l'expert est venu ~ les dégâts** the expert came to assess the damage.

constellation [kɔ̃stelasjɔ̃] *nf* **1.** ASTRON constellation **2.** [ensemble - de savants, de célébrités] constellation, galaxy.

consteller [4] [kɔ̃stele] *vt* to spangle, to stud ▪ **constellé de : un ciel constellé d'étoiles** a star-studded sky.

consternant, e [kɔ̃stɛrnɑ̃, ɑ̃t] *adj* distressing ▪ **d'une bêtise ~e** appallingly stupid ▪ **la pièce est ~e** the play's dire *ou* appallingly bad.

consternation [kɔ̃stɛrnasjɔ̃] *nf* consternation, dismay ▪ **la ~ était générale** everybody was appalled.

consterner [3] [kɔ̃stɛrne] *vt* to appall, to fill with consternation ▪ **consterné par une nouvelle** appalled by a piece of news ▪ **regarder qqch d'un air consterné** to look with consternation upon sthg.

constipation [kɔ̃stipasjɔ̃] *nf* constipation.

constipé, e [kɔ̃stipe] ◇ *adj* **1.** MÉD constipated **2.** *fam* [guindé] : **être** *ou* **avoir l'air ~** to look ill-at-ease *ou* uncomfortable.
◇ *nm, f* **1.** MÉD constipated person **2.** *fam* [personne guindée] repressed *ou* stuffy person.

constiper [3] [kɔ̃stipe] *vt* to constipate.

constituant, e [kɔ̃stitɥɑ̃, ɑ̃t] *adj* [élément] constituent.
◆ **constituant** *nm* **1.** DR & POLIT constituent ▪ HIST *member of the 1789 Constituent Assembly* **2.** CHIM component **3.** LING constituent.
◆ **Constituante** *nf* HIST : **la Constituante** the Constituent Assembly.

constitué, e [kɔ̃stitɥe] *adj* **1.** [personne] : **un homme normalement ~** a (physically) normal man ▪ **un individu solidement ~** a sturdily-built individual ▪ **bien ~** hardy **2.** POLIT [autorité] constituted.

constituer [7] [kɔ̃stitɥe] *vt* **1.** [créer - collection] to build up *(sép)*, to put together *(sép)* ; [- bibliothèque] to build *ou* to set up *(sép)* ; [- société anonyme, association, gouvernement] to form, to set up *(sép)* ; [- équipe, cabinet] to form, to select (the members of) ; [- dossier] to prepare **2.** [faire partie de] to form, to constitute, to (go to) make up ▪ **les timbres qui constituent sa collection** the stamps that make up his collection ▪ **l'eau est constituée de...** water consists *ou* is composed of... **3.** [être] to be, to represent ▪ **le vol constitue un délit** theft is *ou* constitutes an offence **4.** DR [nommer] to name, to appoint ▪ **~ qqn président** to appoint sb as *ou* to make sb chairman **5.** [établir] : **~ une dot/une rente à qqn** to settle a dowry/a pension on sb.
◆ **se constituer** ◇ *vpi* **1.** [être composé] : **se ~ de** to be made up of **2.** [se mettre en position de] : **se ~ prisonnier** to give o.s. up ▪ **se ~ partie civile** to file a civil action **3.** [se former] to form, to be formed ▪ **ils se sont constitués en association** they formed a society.
◇ *vpt* : **se ~ une vidéothèque** to build up a video library ▪ **se ~ un patrimoine** to amass an estate.

constitutif, ive [kɔ̃stitytif, iv] *adj* **1.** [qui compose] constituent, component ▪ **les éléments ~s de l'eau** the elements which make up *ou* the constituent elements of water **2.** [typique - propriété] constitutive **3.** DR constitutive.

constitution [kɔ̃stitysjɔ̃] *nf* **1.** [création - d'une collection] building up, putting together ; [- d'une bibliothèque] building up, setting up ; [- d'une association, d'une société, d'un gouvernement] forming, formation, setting up ; [- d'un dossier] preparation, putting together ; [- d'une équipe] selection **2.** [composition - d'un groupe] composition ; [- d'une substance] makeup, composition **3.** POLIT [lois] constitution ▪ [régime] : **~ républicaine** republic ▪ **~ monarchique** monarchy **4.** [santé] constitution, physique ▪ **une bonne/solide ~** a sound/sturdy constitution ▪ **être de ~ fragile** [souvent malade] to be susceptible to disease **5.** PHARM [en homéopathie] composition **6.** DR [d'une dot, d'une rente] settling, settlement ▪ [désignation] : **~ d'un avoué** appointment *ou* briefing of a lawyer ▪ **~ de partie civile** filing of a civil action.

constitutionnaliser [3] [kɔ̃stitysjɔnalize] *vt* to constitutionalize, to make constitutional.

constitutionnel, elle [kɔ̃stitysjɔnɛl] *adj* constitutional.

constitutionnellement [kɔ̃stitysjɔnɛlmɑ̃] *adv* constitutionally.

constricteur [kɔ̃striktœr] ◇ *adj m* ANAT & ZOOL constrictor.
◇ *nm* **1.** ANAT constrictor **2.** ZOOL boa constrictor.

constriction [kɔ̃striksjɔ̃] *nf* constriction.

constructeur, trice [kɔ̃stryktœr, tris] *adj* building, manufacturing.
◆ **constructeur** *nm* **1.** [d'édifices] builder **2.** [d'appareils, d'engins] manufacturer ▪ **~ automobile** car manufacturer ▪ **~ naval** shipbuilder **3.** INFORM handler, builder.

constructible [kɔ̃stryktibl] *adj* constructible ▪ **terrain** *ou* **parcelle ~** plot suitable for building on, building land.

constructif, ive [kɔ̃stryktif, iv] *adj* **1.** [qui fait progresser] constructive, positive **2.** CONSTR constructional, building *(modif)*.

construction [kɔ̃stryksjɔ̃] *nf* **1.** [édification] building, construction ▪ **la ~ de la tour a duré un an** it took a year to build *ou* to erect the tower **2.** [édifice] building, construction **3.** [fabrication] building, manufacturing ▪ **la ~ automobile** car manufacturing ▪ **appareil de ~ française** French-built machine ▮ [entreprise] : **~s navales** shipbuilding (industry) ▪ **~s aéronautiques** aircraft industry **4.** [structure - d'une œuvre] structure ; [- d'une phrase] construction, structure **5.** GRAMM construction **6.** MATH figure, construction.
◆ **de construction** *loc adj* **1.** [matériau] building *(modif)*, construction *(modif)* **2.** JEUX : **jeu de ~** set of building blocks.
◆ **en construction** *loc adv* under construction ▪ **la maison est encore en ~** the house is still being built *ou* still under construction.

constructivisme [kɔ̃stryktivism] *nm* constructivism.

construire [98] [kɔ̃strɥir] *vt* **1.** [route, barrage] to build, to construct ▪ [maison] to build ▪ **une maison récemment construite** a newly-built house ▪ **se faire ~ une maison** to have a house built ▪ **tous ensemble pour ~ l'Europe!** *fig* all united to build a new Europe! ▪ *(en usage absolu)* **leur rêve, c'est de pouvoir faire ~** they dream of having their own house built **2.** INDUST [fabriquer] to build, to manufacture **3.** [structurer - pièce, roman] to structure, to construct ; [- théorie, raisonnement] to build, to develop ; [- figure de géométrie] to draw, to construct ▪ **~ correctement une phrase** to construct a sentence properly **4.** GRAMM to construe ▪ **on construit "vouloir" avec le subjonctif** "vouloir" is construed with *ou* takes the subjunctive.

◆ **se construire** *vp (emploi passif)* **1.** [être édifié] to be built ▪ **ça se construit par ici!** ***fam*** a lot of stuff's going up *ou* a lot of building's going on around here! **2.** GRAMM : **se ~ avec** to be construed with, to take.

consubstantialité [kɔ̃sypstɑ̃sjalite] *nf* consubstantiality.

consul, e [kɔ̃syl] *nm, f* **1.** [diplomate] consul ▪ **le ~ de France** the French consul **2.** HIST Consul *(in France from 1799 to 1804).*

◆ **consul** *nm* ANTIQ consul.

consulaire [kɔ̃sylɛr] *adj* consular.

consulat [kɔ̃syla] *nm* **1.** [résidence, bureaux] consulate **2.** [fonction diplomatique] consulship **3.** HIST : **le Consulat** the Consulate *(in France from 1799 to 1804)* **4.** ANTIQ consulship.

consultable [kɔ̃syltabl] *adj* [ouvrage, fichier] which may be consulted, available for reference *ou* consultation.

consultant, e [kɔ̃syltɑ̃, ɑ̃t] ◇ *adj* ▷ **avocat**, ▷ **médecin**.

◇ *nm, f* consultant ▪ **~ en gestion** management consultant.

consultatif, ive [kɔ̃syltatif, iv] *adj* advisory.

consultation [kɔ̃syltasjɔ̃] *nf* **1.** [d'un plan, d'un règlement] consulting, checking ▪ **la ~ d'un dictionnaire** looking words up in a dictionary **2.** POLIT : **~ électorale** election **3.** [chez un professionnel] consultation ▪ **donner des ~s** [gén] to hold consultations ; [médecin] to have one's surgery *UK ou* office hours *US* ▪ **il est en ~** [médecin] he's with a patient ▪ **horaires de ~** [chez un médecin] surgery *UK ou* office *US* hours **4.** INFORM : **~ de table** table lookup ▪ **~ de fichier** file browsing *ou* browse.

consulter [3] [kɔ̃sylte] ◇ *vt* **1.** [médecin] to visit, to consult ▪ [avocat, professeur] to consult, to seek advice from ▪ [voyante] to visit ▪ **il ne m'a même pas consulté** he didn't even ask for my opinion ▪ **~ qqn du regard** to look questioningly at sb ▪ *(en usage absolu)* **se décider à ~** to decide to go to the doctor's **2.** [livre, dictionnaire] to refer to *(insép)* ▪ [plan, montre, baromètre, horaire] to look at *(insép)*, to check ▪ [horoscope] to read ▪ **~ ses notes** to go over one's notes **3.** *(au nég)* ***sout*** [prendre en compte] : **il ne consulte que son intérêt** he's guided only by self-interest **4.** INFORM to search.

◇ *vi* [docteur] to hold surgery, to see patients.

◆ **se consulter** *vp (emploi réciproque)* [discuter] to confer ▪ **se ~ du regard** to look questioningly at one another.

consumer [3] [kɔ̃syme] *vt* **1.** [brûler] to burn, to consume ▪ **les bûches consumées dans la cheminée** the charred logs in the fireplace **2.** ***litt*** [tourmenter] : **la jalousie la consume** she's consumed with jealousy ▪ **il est consumé de chagrin** *ou* **par le chagrin** he is racked with grief.

◆ **se consumer** *vpi* **1.** [brûler] to burn ▪ **laisser une cigarette se ~** to let a cigarette burn (out) **2.** ***litt*** [être tourmenté] : **il se consume de désespoir** he's wasting away in *ou* with despair ▪ **se ~ d'amour pour qqn** to pine for sb.

consumérisme [kɔ̃symerism] *nm* : **le ~** consumerism.

contact [kɔ̃takt] *nm* **1.** [toucher] touch, contact **2.** AUTO, ÉLECTR & RADIO contact, switch ▪ **le ~ ne se fait pas** there's no contact ▪ **il y a un mauvais ~** there's a loose connection somewhere ▪ **mettre/couper le ~** ÉLECTR to switch on/off ; AUTO to turn the ignition on/off ▪ **nous avons perdu le ~ radio avec eux** we're no longer in radio contact with them **3.** [lien] contact ▪ **avoir des ~s avec** to have contact with ▪ **prendre des ~s** to establish some contacts ▪ **prendre ~ avec qqn** to contact sb, to get in touch with sb ▪ **j'ai gardé le ~ avec mes vieux amis** I'm still in touch with my old friends **4.** [personne - dans les affaires, l'espionnage] contact, connection **5.** GÉOM : **(point de) ~ de deux plans** intersection *ou* meeting point of two planes **6.** PHOTO contact (print) **7.** ÉQUIT contact.

◆ **au contact de** *loc prép* : **au ~ de l'air** in contact with *ou* when exposed to the air ▪ **il a changé à mon ~** he's changed since he met me.

◆ **de contact** *loc adj* **1.** AUTO ignition *(modif)* **2.** RAIL [fil, ligne] contact *(modif)* **3.** OPT contact *(modif)*.

◆ **en contact** ◇ *loc adj* **1.** [reliés - personnes] in touch **2.** [adjacents - objets, substances] in contact **3.** ÉLECTR connected.

◇ *loc adv* : **rester en ~ avec qqn** to keep *ou* to stay *ou* to remain in touch with sb ▪ **entrer en ~ avec qqn** to contact sb, to get in touch with sb ; AÉRON & MIL to make contact with sb ▪ **mettre en ~** [personnes] to put in touch (with each other) ; [objets, substances] to bring into contact ; AÉRON to establish contact between.

contacter [3] [kɔ̃takte] *vt* to contact, to get in touch with ▪ **on peut me ~ par téléphone au bureau** you can reach me by phone at the office.

contagieux, euse [kɔ̃taʒjø, øz] ◇ *adj* [personne] contagious ▪ [maladie, rire] infectious, contagious ▪ **son virus/enthousiasme est ~** his virus/enthusiasm is catching.

◇ *nm, f* contagious patient.

contagion [kɔ̃taʒjɔ̃] *nf* **1.** MÉD contagion ▪ **pour éviter tout risque de ~** to avoid any risk of infection *ou* contagion **2.** [d'un rire, d'une peur] contagiousness, infectiousness.

container [kɔ̃tɛnɛr] = **conteneur**.

contaminateur, trice [kɔ̃taminatœr, tris] ◇ *adj* infectious.

◇ *nm, f* infectious carrier ▪ **chercher le ~ de qqn** to look for the contact who infected sb.

contamination [kɔ̃taminasjɔ̃] *nf* **1.** MÉD contamination **2.** [de l'environnement, des aliments] contamination ▪ **~ radioactive** radioactive contamination **3.** LING contamination **4.** ***litt*** [corruption] (moral) pollution.

contaminer [3] [kɔ̃tamine] *vt* **1.** MÉD to contaminate, to infect **2.** ÉCOL to contaminate **3.** ***litt*** [corrompre - personne] to corrupt.

conte [kɔ̃t] *nm* story, tale ▸ **~ de fées** ***pr & fig*** fairy tale.

contemplateur, trice [kɔ̃tɑ̃platœr, tris] *nm, f* contemplator.

contemplatif, ive [kɔ̃tɑ̃platif, iv] ◇ *adj* **1.** [pensif] thoughtful, contemplative, meditative **2.** RELIG contemplative.

◇ *nm, f* contemplative ▪ **c'est un ~** he likes to muse.

contemplation [kɔ̃tɑ̃plasjɔ̃] *nf* **1.** [méditation] contemplation, reflection ▪ **en ~ devant** lost in admiration of **2.** RELIG contemplation.

contempler [3] [kɔ̃tɑ̃ple] *vt* to look at ▪ **~ qqn avec amour** to gaze lovingly at sb.

contemporain, e [kɔ̃tɑ̃pɔrɛ̃, ɛn] ◇ *adj* **1.** [de la même époque] contemporary ▪ **être ~ de** to be contemporary with **2.** [moderne] contemporary, modern, present-day.

◇ *nm, f* contemporary ▪ **mon/son ~** my/his contemporary.

contempteur, trice [kɔ̃tɑ̃ptœr, tris] *nm, f* ***litt*** denigrator, despiser ▪ **ses ~s** those who derided him.

contenance [kɔ̃tnɑ̃s] *nf* **1.** [attitude] attitude, bearing ▪ **il essayait de prendre** *ou* **se donner une ~** he was trying to put on a brave face ▪ **faire bonne ~** to put up a bold *ou* good front ▪ **perdre ~** to lose one's composure **2.** [capacité - d'un tonneau, d'un réservoir] capacity ; [- d'un navire] (carrying *ou* holding) capacity.

contenant [kɔ̃tnɑ̃] *nm* container.

conteneur [kɔ̃tənœr] *nm* INDUST container ▪ **mise en ~** containerization.

contenir [40] [kɔ̃tnir] *vt* **1.** [renfermer] to contain, to hold ▪ **votre article contient beaucoup de paradoxes** your article is full of *ou* contains many contradictions **2.** [être constitué de] to contain ▪ **boissons qui contiennent de l'alcool** drinks containing alcohol **3.** [avoir telle capacité] to hold ▪ **véhicule pouvant ~ 35 personnes assises/debout** vehicle seating 35/with standing room for 35 people **4.** [réprimer - foule, larmes, sanglots] to hold back *(sép)* ; [- poussée, invasion] to contain ; [- rire, colère] to suppress.

◆ **se contenir** *vpi* to control o.s. ▪ **ils ne pouvaient plus se ~** [ils pleuraient] they couldn't hold back their tears any longer ; [ils riaient] they couldn't disguise their mirth any longer.

content, e [kɔ̃tɑ̃, ɑ̃t] *adj* **1.** [heureux] happy, glad, pleased ▪ **je suis ~ que tu aies pu venir** I'm glad that you could make it

■ **s'il n'est pas ~, c'est pareil!** *fam* he can like it or lump it! **2.** [satisfait] : **être ~ de qqch** to be satisfied with sthg ■ **je suis très ~ de moi** I'm very pleased with myself ■ **non ~ d'être riche, il veut aussi être célèbre** not content with being rich *ou* not satisfied with being rich, he wants to be famous as well.
◆ **content** *nm* *sout* **avoir (tout) son ~ de qqch** to have (had) one's fill of sthg ■ **laisse-les s'amuser tout leur ~** let them play as much as they like.

contentement [kɔ̃tɑ̃tmɑ̃] *nm* satisfaction, contentment ■ **avec ~** contentedly ➔ **~ de soi** self-satisfaction.

contenter [3] [kɔ̃tɑ̃te] *vt* **1.** [faire plaisir à] to please, to satisfy ■ **voilà qui devrait ~ tout le monde** this should satisfy *ou* please everybody **2.** [satisfaire] to satisfy.
◆ **se contenter de** *vp+prép* **1.** [s'accommoder de] to be content *ou* to content o.s. with, to make do with ■ **il se contente de peu** he's easily satisfied **2.** [se borner à] : **en guise de réponse, elle s'est contentée de sourire** she merely smiled in reply.

contentieux, euse [kɔ̃tɑ̃sjø, øz] *adj* contentious.
◆ **contentieux** *nm* **1.** [conflit] dispute, disagreement ■ **il y a un ~ entre eux** they're in dispute **2.** [service] legal department *ou* bureau **3.** [affaire] litigation ■ **~ administratif** procedure in contentious administrative matters ■ **~ fiscal** tax litigation.

contention [kɔ̃tɑ̃sjɔ̃] *nf* **1.** *litt* exertion, application **2.** MÉD [d'un os] setting, reduction ■ [d'un malade] restraint.

contenu, e [kɔ̃tny] *pp* ⊳ **contenir.**
◆ **contenu** *nm* **1.** [d'un récipient, d'un paquet] content, contents **2.** [teneur - d'un document] content, text **3.** LING (linguistic) content **4.** PSYCHOL : **~ latent** latent content.

conter [3] [kɔ̃te] *vt* *litt* to relate, to tell ➔ **~ fleurette à qqn** to murmur sweet nothings to sb ■ **en ~ : on m'en a conté de belles sur toi!** I've heard some fine things about you! ■ **elle ne s'en laisse pas ~** she's not easily taken in.

contestable [kɔ̃tɛstabl] *adj* debatable, questionable ■ **de manière ~** dubiously.

contestataire [kɔ̃tɛstatɛr] ◇ *adj* protesting *ou* revolting *(against established values)* ■ **un journal ~** an anti-establishment newspaper.
◇ *nmf* anti-establishment protester ■ **c'est un ~** he's always calling things into question.

contestation [kɔ̃tɛstasjɔ̃] *nf* **1.** [d'une loi, d'un testament, d'un document] contesting, opposing ■ [d'un récit, d'un droit] contesting, questioning ■ [d'une compétence] questioning, challenging, doubting ■ **sans ~ (possible)** beyond (all possible) dispute *ou* question **2.** [litige] dispute, controversy, debate **3.** POLIT : **la ~** protests, protesting, the protest movement.

conteste [kɔ̃tɛst] ◆ **sans conteste** *loc adv* indisputably, unquestionably.

contester [3] [kɔ̃tɛste] ◇ *vt* **1.** [testament] to contest, to object to ■ [récit, document] to dispute, to question ■ [compétence] to question, to dispute, to throw into doubt ■ **je ne conteste pas que votre tâche ait été difficile** I don't dispute *ou* doubt the fact that you had a difficult task ■ **je ne lui conteste pas le droit de...** I don't challenge *ou* question his right to... ■ **être contesté** to be a subject of controversy ■ **une personnalité très contestée** a very controversial personality **2.** POLIT to protest *ou* to rebel against.
◇ *vi* **1.** [discuter] : **obéir aux ordres sans ~** to obey orders blindly *ou* without raising any objections **2.** POLIT to protest.

conteur, euse [kɔ̃tœr, øz] *nm, f* **1.** [narrateur] narrator, storyteller **2.** [écrivain] storyteller.

contexte [kɔ̃tɛkst] *nm* **1.** [situation] context **2.** INFORM environment **3.** LING : **~ linguistique/de situation** linguistic/situational context.
◆ **en contexte** *loc adv* in context ■ **mettre qqch en ~** to put sthg into context, to contextualize sthg.

contextualiser [kɔ̃tɛkstyalize] *vt* to contextualize.

contextuel, elle [kɔ̃tɛkstɥɛl] *adj* contextual.

contient *etc v* ⊳ **contenir.**

contigu, ë [kɔ̃tigy] *adj* **1.** [bâtiments, terrains, objets] contiguous *sout*, adjacent, adjoining ■ **les maisons ~ës à la nôtre** [accolées] the houses joining on to ours **2.** *sout* [époques, sujets, domaines] close, contiguous *sout*.

contiguïté [kɔ̃tigɥite] *nf* **1.** [proximité - de bâtiments, de terrains, d'objets] contiguity *sout*, adjacency, proximity **2.** *sout* [de domaines, d'époques, de sujets] closeness, contiguousness *sout*, contiguity *sout* **3.** INFORM adjacency.

continence [kɔ̃tinɑ̃s] *nf* **1.** [abstinence] continence, (self-imposed) chastity **2.** [sobriété, discrétion] restraint **3.** MÉD continence.

continent[1] [kɔ̃tinɑ̃] *nm* **1.** GÉOGR continent ■ **l'Ancien/le Nouveau Continent** the Old/the New World **2.** [par opposition à une île] : **le ~** the mainland.

continent[2]**, e** [kɔ̃tinɑ̃, ɑ̃t] *adj* **1.** [chaste] continent, chaste ■ [discret] discreet, restrained, reserved **2.** MÉD continent.

continental, e, aux [kɔ̃tinɑ̃tal, o] ◇ *adj* **1.** [par opposition à insulaire] mainland *(modif)* **2.** GÉOGR [climat, température] continental.
◇ *nm, f* person who lives on the mainland ■ **les continentaux** people from the mainland.

contingence [kɔ̃tɛ̃ʒɑ̃s] *nf* MATH & PHILOS contingency.
◆ **contingences** *nfpl* contingencies, eventualities ■ **les ~s de la vie quotidienne** everyday happenings *ou* events ■ **prévoir toutes les ~s** to take unforeseen circumstances into consideration.

contingent[1] [kɔ̃tɛ̃ʒɑ̃] *nm* **1.** [quantité] (allotted) share **2.** [quota] quota **3.** [troupe] contingent ■ [ensemble des recrues] call-up *UK*, draft *US* ■ **le ~, les soldats du ~** those conscripted, the conscripts, the draft *US*.

contingent[2]**, e** [kɔ̃tɛ̃ʒɑ̃, ɑ̃t] *adj* **1.** PHILOS contingent **2.** *litt* [sans importance] incidental.

contingentement [kɔ̃tɛ̃ʒɑ̃tmɑ̃] *nm* **1.** ÉCON fixing of quotas, restriction **2.** COMM quota system, apportioning by quota.

contingenter [3] [kɔ̃tɛ̃ʒɑ̃te] *vt* **1.** ÉCON [importations] to limit, to fix a quota on ■ [produits de distribution] to restrict the distribution of **2.** COMM to distribute *ou* to allocate according to a quota.

contint *etc v* ⊳ **contenir.**

continu, e [kɔ̃tiny] *adj* **1.** [ininterrompu - effort, douleur, bruit] continuous, unremitting, relentless ; [- soins] constant ; [- ligne, trait] continuous, unbroken ; [- sommeil] unbroken **2.** ÉLECTR [courant] direct **3.** MATH continuous.
◆ **continu** *nm* MATH & PHILOS continuum.
◆ **en continu** *loc adv* continuously, uninterruptedly.

continuation [kɔ̃tinɥasjɔ̃] *nf* **1.** [suite] continuation, extension **2.** [fait de durer] continuing, continuance *sout* **3.** *fam loc* **bonne ~!** all the best!

continuel, elle [kɔ̃tinɥɛl] *adj* **1.** [ininterrompu] continual **2.** [qui se répète] constant, perpetual ■ **des pannes ~les** constant breakdowns.

continuellement [kɔ̃tinɥɛlmɑ̃] *adv* **1.** [de façon ininterrompue] continually **2.** [de façon répétitive] constantly, perpetually.

continuer [7] [kɔ̃tinɥe] ◇ *vt* **1.** [faire durer - exposé] to carry on *(insép)* ; [- conversation] to carry on *(insép)*, to maintain, to keep up *(sép)* ; [- études] to continue, to keep up *(sép)*, to go on with *(insép)* ■ **continuez le repas sans moi** go on with the meal without me **2.** [dans l'espace] to continue, to extend ■ **~ son chemin** [voyageur] to keep going ; [idée] to keep gaining momentum.
◇ *vi* **1.** [dans le temps] to go *ou* to carry on *(insép)* ■ **si tu continues, ça va mal aller!** if you keep this up, you'll be sorry! ■ **tu vois, continua-t-elle** you see, she went on ■ **une telle situation ne peut ~** this situation cannot be allowed to continue ■ **il continue de** *ou* **à pleuvoir** it keeps on raining ■ **ma plante continue de grandir** my plant keeps getting bigger **2.** INFORM [dans une boîte de dialogue] proceed **3.** [dans l'espace] to continue, to

carry on *(insép)*, to go on *(insép)* ■ **la route continue jusqu'au village** the road runs straight on to the village ■ **arrête-toi ici, moi je continue** you can stop right here, I'm going on ■ **continue!** [à avancer] keep going! ■ **continue tout droit jusqu'au carrefour** keep straight on to the crossroads.
◆ **se continuer** *vpi* **1.** [dans le temps] to carry on, to be carried on **2.** [dans l'espace] to extend.

continuité [kɔ̃tinɥite] *nf* **1.** [d'un effort, d'une tradition] continuity ■ [d'une douleur] persistence **2.** MATH continuity.

continuum [kɔ̃tinɥɔm] *nm* continuum ■ **~ espace-temps** space-time continuum.

contondant, e [kɔ̃tɔ̃dɑ̃, ɑ̃t] *adj* blunt.

contorsion [kɔ̃tɔrsjɔ̃] *nf* [d'acrobate] contortion, acrobatic feat *(involving twisting the body)* ■ **il a fait toutes sortes de ~s pour atteindre la boîte** he had to twist right round to reach the box.

contorsionner [3] [kɔ̃tɔrsjɔne] ◆ **se contorsionner** *vpi* to twist one's body, to contort o.s. ■ **se ~ comme un ver** to squirm *ou* to wriggle about like a worm.

contorsionniste [kɔ̃tɔrsjɔnist] *nmf* contortionist.

contour [kɔ̃tur] *nm* **1.** [d'un objet, d'une silhouette] contour, outline, shape ■ **~ d'un caractère** INFORM character outline **2.** [arrondi - d'un visage] curve ; [- d'une rivière, d'un chemin] winding part *ou* section.

contourné, e [kɔ̃turne] *adj* **1.** [avec des courbes] : **la balustrade ~e d'un balcon** the curved railing of a balcony **2.** [peu naturel] overelaborate.

contourner [3] [kɔ̃turne] *vt* **1.** [faire le tour de - souche, flaque] to walk around *(insép)* ; [- ville] to bypass, to skirt ■ **ayant contourné la forêt** [à pied] having walked round the forest ; [en voiture] having driven round the forest ■ MIL [position] to skirt **2.** [éluder - loi, difficulté] to circumvent, to get round *(insép)* **3.** *litt* [modeler - vase, piédestal] to fashion *ou* to shape (into complex curves).

contraceptif, ive [kɔ̃trasɛptif, iv] *adj* contraceptive.
◆ **contraceptif** *nm* contraceptive, method of contraception.

contraception [kɔ̃trasɛpsjɔ̃] *nf* contraception ■ **moyen de ~** means *(sing)* of contraception.

contractant, e [kɔ̃traktɑ̃, ɑ̃t] <> *adj* contracting.
<> *nm, f* : **les ~s** the contracting parties.

contracté, e [kɔ̃trakte] *adj* **1.** ANAT [muscle, voix] taut, tense ■ **il avait les mâchoires ~es** his jaw was stiff **2.** [nerveux - personne] tense.

contracter [3] [kɔ̃trakte] *vt* **1.** [se charger de - dette] to incur, to run up *(sép)* ; [- assurance] to take out *(sép)* ; [- obligation, engagement] to take on *(sép)* ■ **~ une alliance** to enter into an alliance **2.** [acquérir - manie, habitude] to develop, to acquire ; [- maladie] to contract *sout*, to catch **3.** [réduire - liquide, corps] to contract **4.** [raidir - muscle] to contract, to tighten, to tauten ; [- visage, traits] to tense (up), to tighten (up) ■ **le visage contracté par la peur** his/her face taut with fear **5.** [rendre anxieux] to make tense **6.** LING to contract.
◆ **se contracter** *vpi* **1.** [être réduit - liquide, corps] to contract, to reduce ; [- fibre] to shrink **2.** [se raidir - visage, traits] to tense (up), to become taut **3.** LING [mot] to contract, to be contracted.

contractile [kɔ̃traktil] *adj* contractile.

contraction [kɔ̃traksjɔ̃] *nf* **1.** [raidissement - d'un muscle] contracting, tensing ; [- du visage, des traits, de l'estomac] tensing, tightening (up) ; [- des mâchoires] clamping ■ [raideur - d'un muscle] tenseness, tautness ; [- de l'estomac] tightness ; [- des mâchoires] stiffness **2.** MÉD : **~ (utérine)** contraction **3.** LING contraction **4.** ÉDUC : **~ de texte** summary ■ **faire une ~ de texte** to summarize a text **5.** PHYS contraction.

contractualiser [3] [kɔ̃traktɥalize] *vt* **1.** [problème] to solve by a contract **2.** [employé] to hire as a public servant.

contractuel, elle [kɔ̃traktɥɛl] *adj* contractual, contract *(modif)*.
◆ **contractuel** *nm* ADMIN contract public servant ■ [policier] (male) traffic warden *UK ou* policeman *US*.
◆ **contractuelle** *nf* (female) traffic warden *UK*, traffic policewoman *US*.

contractuellement [kɔ̃traktɥɛlmɑ̃] *adv* contractually.

contracture [kɔ̃traktyr] *nf* **1.** MÉD contraction, cramp **2.** ARCHIT contracture.

contradicteur [kɔ̃tradiktœr] *nm* contradictor ■ **il y avait de bruyants ~s dans l'auditoire** there were some noisy hecklers in the audience.

contradiction [kɔ̃tradiksjɔ̃] *nf* **1.** [contestation] contradiction ■ **porter la ~ dans une discussion** to be a dissenter in a discussion **2.** [incompatibilité] contradiction, inconsistency ■ **il est plein de ~s** he's full of contradictions **3.** LOGIQUE contradiction **4.** DR allegation.
◆ **en contradiction avec** *loc prép* in contradiction with ■ **c'est en ~ avec sa façon de vivre** it goes against his style of life ■ **être en ~ avec soi-même** to be inconsistent.

contradictoire [kɔ̃tradiktwar] *adj* **1.** [opposé - théories, idées] contradictory, clashing ; [- témoignage] conflicting ■ **débat/réunion ~** open debate/meeting ■ **~ à** in contradiction to, at variance with **2.** LOGIQUE contradictory **3.** DR : **jugement ~** *judgment rendered in the presence of the parties involved.*

contradictoirement [kɔ̃tradiktwarmɑ̃] *adv* **1.** [de façon opposée] contradictorily **2.** DR *in the presence of the parties involved.*

contragestion [kɔ̃traʒɛstjɔ̃] *nf* emergency contraception.

contraignait *etc v* ▷ **contraindre**.

contraignant, e [kɔ̃trɛɲɑ̃, ɑ̃t] *adj* [occupation] restricting ■ [contrat] restrictive ■ [horaire] restricting, limiting.

contraindre [80] [kɔ̃trɛ̃dr] *vt* **1.** [obliger] : **~ qqn à : la situation nous contraint à la prudence** the situation forces us to be careful ■ **je suis contraint de rester à Paris** I'm obliged *ou* forced to stay in Paris **2.** *litt* [réprimer - désir, passion] to constrain *litt*, to restrain, to keep a check on **3.** *litt* [réprimer] : **~ une personne dans ses choix** to restrict sb's choice **4.** DR to constrain.
◆ **se contraindre** *vp (emploi réfléchi)* to force o.s.

contraint, e [kɔ̃trɛ̃, ɛ̃t] *adj* **1.** [emprunté - sourire] constrained, forced, unnatural ; [- politesse] unnatural **2.** [obligé] : **~ et forcé** under duress.
◆ **contrainte** *nf* **1.** [obligation] constraint, imposition ■ **les ~es sociales** social constraints **2.** [force] constraint ■ **céder sous la ~e** to give in under pressure **3.** [gêne] constraint, embarrassment ■ **parler sans ~e** to speak uninhibitedly **4.** DR : **~e par corps** imprisonment for non-payment of debts.

contraire [kɔ̃trɛr] <> *adj* **1.** [point de vue, attitude] opposite ■ **sauf avis ~** unless otherwise informed **2.** [inverse - direction, sens] : **dans le sens ~ à celui des aiguilles d'une montre** anticlockwise *UK*, counterclockwise *US* **3.** *sout* [défavorable, nuisible] contrary *sout*, unfavourable.
<> *nm* **1.** [inverse] : **le ~** the opposite ■ **j'avais raison, ne me dis pas le ~** I was right, don't deny it ■ **elle timide? c'est tout le ~!** her, shy? quite the opposite *ou* contrary! ■ **elle dit toujours le ~ de ce que disent les autres** she always says the opposite of what others say **2.** LING opposite, antonym.
◆ **au contraire, bien au contraire, tout au contraire** *loc adv* quite the reverse *ou* opposite.
◆ **au contraire de** *loc prép* unlike.
◆ **contraire à** *loc prép* : **c'est ~ à mes principes** it's against my principles.

contrairement [kɔ̃trɛrmɑ̃] ◆ **contrairement à** *loc prép* : **~ à ce qu'il m'a dit/aux prévisions** contrary to what he told me/to all expectations ■ **~ à son frère** unlike his brother.

contralto [kɔ̃tralto] *nm* contralto.

contrariant, e [kɔ̃trarjɑ̃, ɑ̃t] *adj* [personne] annoying ■ [nouvelle] annoying ■ **il n'est pas ~** he's really easy-going.

contrarié, e [kɔ̃trarje] *adj* [amour] frustrated, thwarted ■ [projet] disrupted ■ **tu as l'air ~** you look annoyed.

contrarier [9] [kɔ̃trarje] *vt* **1.** [ennuyer - personne] to annoy ■ **ça la contrarie de devoir arrêter de travailler** she's annoyed at having to stop work ■ **si cela ne te contrarie pas** if you don't mind **2.** [contrecarrer - ambitions, amour] to thwart ; [- mouvement, action] to impede, to bar ■ **~ un gaucher** *to force a left-handed person to use his right hand* **3.** [contraster] : **~ des couleurs** to use contrasting shades.
◆ **se contrarier** *vp (emploi réciproque)* **1.** [aller à l'encontre de - forces] to oppose one another **2.** [être en conflit - personnes] to clash **3.** [s'opposer - formes, couleurs] to contrast.

contrariété [kɔ̃trarjete] *nf* **1.** [mécontentement] annoyance, vexation ■ **éprouver une ~** to be annoyed *ou* upset **2.** *sout* [opposition] clash ■ **~ d'humeur** clash of personalities.

contraste [kɔ̃trast] *nm* contrast ■ **deux couleurs qui font ~** two contrasting shades.
◆ **en contraste** *loc adv* : **mettre deux choses en ~** to contrast two things.
◆ **en contraste avec** *loc prép* by contrast to *ou* with, in contrast to *ou* with.
◆ **par contraste** *loc adv* in contrast.
◆ **par contraste avec** *loc prép* by contrast to *ou* with, in contrast to *ou* with.

contrasté, e [kɔ̃traste] *adj* [couleurs, situations] contrasting ■ [photo, image] contrasty.

contraster [3] [kɔ̃traste] <> *vt* [caractères, situations, couleurs] to contrast ■ [photo] to show up the contrast in.
<> *vi* to contrast ■ **~ avec qqch** to contrast with sthg.

contrat [kɔ̃tra] *nm* **1.** [acte, convention] contract ■ **passer un ~ avec qqn** to enter into a contract with sb ■ **un ~ de deux ans** a two-year contract ➊ **~ administratif** public service contract ■ **~ d'assurance** insurance policy ■ **~ à durée déterminée/indéterminée** fixed-term/permanent contract ■ **~ d'insertion** [emploi] work placement (for an unemployed person) ; [formation] training bursary ≃ New Deal placement *UK* ■ **~ de louage** rental contract ■ **~ de mariage** marriage contract ■ **~ de qualification** training contract ■ **~ de travail** contract of employment ■ **~ de vente** bill of sale ■ **~ verbal** verbal contract *ou* undertaking ■ **remplir son ~** DR to fulfil the terms of one's contract ; *fig* [s'exécuter] to keep one's promise **2.** [entente] agreement, deal ■ **un ~ tacite** an unspoken agreement **3.** PHILOS : **~ social** social contract ■ **'Du ~ social'** *Rousseau* 'The Social Contract' **4.** *arg crime* [de tueur] contract **5.** CARTES contract ■ **réaliser son ~** to make one's contract.

contrat-type [kɔ̃tratip] (*pl* **contrats-types**) *nm* skeleton contract.

contravention [kɔ̃travɑ̃sjɔ̃] *nf* **1.** [amende] (parking) fine ■ [avis] (parking) ticket **2.** [infraction] contravention, infraction, infringement ■ **être en ~, se mettre en état de ~** to contravene *ou* to infringe the law.

contre [kɔ̃tr] <> *prép* **1.** [indiquant la proximité] against, on ■ **se frotter ~ qqch** to rub (o.s.) against *ou* on sthg ■ **se blottir ~ qqn** to cuddle up to sb ■ **joue ~ joue** cheek to cheek ■ **tenir qqn tout ~ soi** to hold sb close ■ **allongé tout ~ elle** lying right next to *ou* beside her ■ **un coup ~ la vitre** a knock on *ou* at the window ■ **je me suis cogné la tête ~ le radiateur** I hit my head on the radiator ■ **lancer une balle ~ le mur** to throw a ball against *ou* at the wall ■ **mettez-vous ~ le mur** stand (right) by the wall
2. [indiquant l'opposition] against ■ **nager ~ le courant** to swim upstream *ou* against the current ■ **notre équipe aura le vent ~ elle** our team will play into the wind ■ **être en colère ~ qqn** to be angry at *ou* with sb ■ **je suis ~ l'intervention** I'm opposed to *ou* against (the idea of) intervention ■ **voter ~ qqn/qqch** to vote against sb/sthg ■ **Durier ~ Chardin** DR Durier versus Chardin ■ **le match ~ le Brésil** the Brazil match, the match against *ou* with Brazil ■ **avoir qqch ~ qqn** to have sthg against sb ■ **pour une fois, j'irai ~ mon habitude** for once, I'll break my habit ■ **vous allez ~ l'usage/le règlement** you're going against accepted custom/the regulations
3. [pour protéger de] against ■ **pastilles ~ la toux** cough lozenges ■ **lutter ~ l'alcoolisme** to fight (against) alcoholism ■ **que faire ~ l'inflation?** what can be done about *ou* against *ou* to combat inflation? ■ **s'assurer ~ le vol** to take out insurance against theft
4. [en échange de] for, in exchange *ou* return for ■ **j'ai échangé mon livre ~ le sien** I swapped my book for hers ■ **elle est revenue sur sa décision ~ une promesse d'augmentation** she reconsidered her decision after being promised a rise
5. [indiquant une proportion, un rapport] against, to ■ **10 ~ 1 qu'ils vont gagner!** ten to one they'll win! ■ **156 voix ~ 34** 156 votes to 34 ■ **ils nous sont tombés dessus à trois ~ un** there were three of them for every one of us, they were three to one against us ■ **le dollar s'échange à 1,05 euros ~ 1,07 hier** the dollar is trading at 1.02 euros compared to *ou* (as) against 1.07 yesterday
6. [contrairement à] : **~ toute attente** contrary to *ou* against all expectations ■ **~ toute logique** against all logic.
<> *adv* **1.** [indiquant la proximité] : **il n'a pas vu le poteau, et sa tête a heurté ~** he didn't see the post, and he banged his head against *ou* on it
2. [indiquant l'opposition] against ■ **on partage? – je n'ai rien ~** shall we share? – I've nothing against it *ou* it's OK by me ■ **~? levez la main** hands up those against *UK*, all against, hands up *US*.
<> *nm* **1.** [argument opposé] : **le pour et le ~** the pros and cons **2.** SPORT & JEUX [au volley, au basket] block ■ [en escrime] counter ■ [au billard] kiss ■ [au bridge] double ■ **marquer sur un ~** FOOTBALL to score on a counter attack ■ **faire un ~** RUGBY to intercept the ball.
◆ **par contre** *loc adv* on the other hand ■ **il est très compétent, par ~ il n'est pas toujours très aimable** he's very competent, but on the other hand he's not always very pleasant ■ **il parle espagnol, par ~ son anglais laisse encore à désirer** his Spanish is good, but his English isn't all it might be.

contre-allée [kɔ̃trale] (*pl* **contre-allées**) *nf* [d'une avenue] service *ou* frontage *US* road ■ [d'une promenade] side track *ou* path.

contre-argument [kɔ̃trargymɑ̃] (*pl* **contre-arguments**) *nm* counterargument.

contre-attaque [kɔ̃tratak] (*pl* **contre-attaques**) *nf* **1.** MIL [gén] counterattack ■ [à l'explosif] counter-blast **2.** [dans une polémique] counterattack, counter-blast.

contre-attaquer [3] [kɔ̃tratake] *vt* to counterattack, to strike back *(sép)*.

contrebalancer [16] [kɔ̃trəbalɑ̃se] *vt* **1.** [poids] to counterbalance **2.** [compenser - inconvénients, efforts] to offset, to make up for *(insép)*, to compensate.
◆ **se contrebalancer** <> *vp (emploi réciproque)* [raisons, hypothèses] to counterbalance each other ■ [dépenses] to cancel each other out.
<> *vpi fam* [se moquer] : **je m'en contrebalance** I couldn't give a damn.

contrebande [kɔ̃trəbɑ̃d] *nf* **1.** [trafic] smuggling, contraband ■ **faire de la ~** to smuggle (in) goods **2.** [marchandises] contraband, smuggled goods ■ [alcool] bootleg ■ **~ de guerre** wartime smuggling.
◆ **de contrebande** *loc adj* smuggled, contraband *(modif)*.
◆ **en contrebande** *loc adv* : **faire entrer/sortir qqch en ~** to smuggle sthg in/out.

contrebandier, ère [kɔ̃trebɑ̃dje, ɛr] *nm, f* smuggler.

contrebas [kɔ̃trəba] ◆ **en contrebas** *loc adv* lower down, below *(adv)*.
◆ **en contrebas de** *loc prép* below.

contrebasse [kɔ̃trəbas] *nf* **1.** [instrument] (double) bass, contrabass **2.** [musicien] = **contrebassiste**.

contrebassiste [kɔ̃trəbasist] *nmf* (double) bass player, double bassist.

contre-braquer [3] [kɔ̃trəbrake] *vi* to drive into a skid.

contrecarrer [3] [kɔ̃trəkare] *vt* [personne] to thwart ■ [projet, initiative] to thwart, to block.

contrechamp [kɔ̃trəʃɑ̃] *nm* CINÉ reverse shot.

contre-chant [kɔ̃trəʃɑ̃] (*pl* **contre-chants**) *nm* counterpoint.

contrecœur [kɔ̃trəkœr] ◆ **à contrecœur** *loc adv* reluctantly, unwillingly, grudgingly.

contrecoup [kɔ̃trəku] *nm* [répercussion] repercussion, aftereffect ■ **subir le ~ de qqch** to suffer the aftershock *ou* aftereffects of sthg.

contre-courant [kɔ̃trəkurɑ̃] (*pl* **contre-courants**) *nm* countercurrent.
◆ **à contre-courant** *loc adv* **1.** [d'un cours d'eau] against the current, upstream **2.** [à rebours] : **aller à ~** to go against the grain.
◆ **à contre-courant de** *loc prép* : **aller à ~ de la mode** to go against the trend ■ **cela va à ~ de ce que je voulais faire** that is the (exact) opposite of what I wanted to do.

contredanse [kɔ̃trədɑ̃s] *nf* **1.** DANSE contredanse, contra danse **2.** *fam* [contravention] ticket ■ **avoir une ~** to get a ticket, to get booked.

contredire [103] [kɔ̃trədir] *vt* [personne, propos] to contradict ■ **sa version contredit la tienne** his version is at variance with *ou* contradicts yours.
◆ **se contredire** ◇ *vp (emploi réciproque)* **1.** [personnes] : **ils se contredisent (l'un l'autre)** they contradict each other **2.** [témoignages, faits] to be in contradiction (with each other), to contradict each other.
◇ *vp (emploi réfléchi)* : **il se contredit** he contradicts himself.

contredit [kɔ̃trədi] ◆ **sans contredit** *loc adv* unquestionably, undoubtedly.

contrée [kɔ̃tre] *nf litt* [pays] country, land *litt* ■ [région] region, area ■ **dans une ~ lointaine** in a faraway land.

contre-écrou [kɔ̃trekru] (*pl* **contre-écrous**) *nm* locknut.

contre-emploi [kɔ̃trɑ̃plwa] (*pl* **contre-emplois**) *nm* miscasting.

contre-enquête [kɔ̃trɑ̃kɛt] (*pl* **contre-enquêtes**) *nf* counterinquiry.

contre-épreuve [kɔ̃treprœv] (*pl* **contre-épreuves**) *nf* **1.** IMPR counterproof **2.** [contre-essai] repetition test, countercheck.

contre-espionnage [kɔ̃trɛspjɔnaʒ] (*pl* **contre-espionnages**) *nm* counterespionage.

contre-essai [kɔ̃tresɛ] (*pl* **contre-essais**) *nm* repetition *ou* second test, countercheck.

contre-exemple [kɔ̃trɛgzɑ̃pl] (*pl* **contre-exemples**) *nm* [illustration] counterexample.

contre-expertise [kɔ̃trɛkspɛrtiz] (*pl* **contre-expertises**) *nf* second expert evaluation *ou* opinion.

contrefaçon [kɔ̃trəfasɔ̃] *nf* **1.** [action d'imiter - une signature, une écriture, une monnaie] counterfeiting, forging ; [- un brevet] infringement **2.** [copie - d'un produit, d'un vêtement] imitation, fake ; [- d'une signature, d'une écriture, de monnaie] counterfeit, forgery.

contrefaire [109] [kɔ̃trəfɛr] *vt* **1.** [parodier] to mimic, to take off *(sép)* **2.** [signature, écriture, argent] to counterfeit, to forge ■ [brevet] to infringe **3.** [déformer - visage] to distort ; [- voix] to alter, to change, to distort.

contrefait, e [kɔ̃trəfɛ, ɛt] *adj* **1.** [déformé] deformed, misshapen **2.** [falsifié - signature, écriture, argent] counterfeit, forged.

contrefaites *v* ▷ **contrefaire**.

contrefera *etc v* ▷ **contrefaire**.

contrefiche [kɔ̃trəfiʃ] *nf* **1.** [étai] oblique prop *ou* stay **2.** ARCHIT [jambe de force] brace, strut.

contreficher [3] [kɔ̃trəfiʃe] ◆ **se contreficher de** *vp+prép fam* to be indifferent to ■ **je m'en contrefiche** I couldn't care less, who gives a damn?

contre-filet [kɔ̃trəfilɛ] (*pl* **contre-filets**) *nm* sirloin (steak).

contrefit, contrefont *etc v* ▷ **contrefaire**.

contrefort [kɔ̃trəfɔr] *nm* **1.** ARCHIT buttress, abutment **2.** [d'une chaussure] stiffener.
◆ **contreforts** *nmpl* GÉOGR foothills.

contrefoutre [116] [kɔ̃trəfutr] ◆ **se contrefoutre de**△ *vp+prép* : **je m'en contrefous** I don't give a shit△ *ou* toss△ *UK* (about it).

contre-indication [kɔ̃trɛ̃dikasjɔ̃] (*pl* **contre-indications**) *nf* **1.** MÉD contraindication **2.** [argument] counter-argument ■ **je ne vois pas de ~ à ce que nous construisions sur ce terrain** I see no reason why we shouldn't build on this piece of land.

contre-indiqué, e [kɔ̃trɛ̃dike] (*mpl* **contre-indiqués**, *fpl* **contre-indiquées**) *adj* **1.** MÉD contraindicated **2.** [déconseillé] inadvisable.

contre-indiquer [3] [kɔ̃trɛ̃dike] *vt* to contraindicate.

contre-interrogatoire [kɔ̃trɛ̃terɔgatwar] (*pl* **contre-interrogatoires**) *nm* cross-examination.

contre-jour [kɔ̃trəʒur] (*pl* **contre-jours**) *nm* **1.** [éclairage] back light **2.** [photo] contre-jour shot.
◆ **à contre-jour, en contre-jour** *loc adv* [être placé - personne] with one's back to the light ; [- objet] against the light *ou* sunlight ■ **une photo prise à ~** a contre-jour shot.

contre-la-montre [kɔ̃trəlamɔ̃tr] *nm inv* time trial.

contremaître [kɔ̃trəmɛtr] *nm* **1.** [dans un atelier] foreman, supervisor **2.** NAUT petty officer.

contre-manifestation [kɔ̃trəmanifɛstasjɔ̃] (*pl* **contre-manifestations**) *nf* counterdemonstration.

contremarche [kɔ̃trəmarʃ] *nf* [d'escalier] riser.

contremarque [kɔ̃trəmark] *nf* **1.** [billet - au spectacle] voucher *(exchanged for ticket at the entrance)* ; [- de transport] extra portion (of ticket) **2.** COMM & HÉRALD countermark.

contre-mesure [kɔ̃trəməzyr] (*pl* **contre-mesures**) *nf* [gén - MIL] countermeasure ■ **~ électronique** jamming device.

contre-nature [kɔ̃trənatyr] *adj inv* unnatural, contrary to nature.

contre-offensive [kɔ̃trɔfɑ̃siv] (*pl* **contre-offensives**) *nf* **1.** MIL counteroffensive **2.** [réplique] counteroffensive, counterblast.

contre-OPA [kɔ̃trɔpea] *nf inv* counter bid.

contrepartie [kɔ̃trəparti] *nf* **1.** [compensation] compensation ■ [financière] compensation, consideration ■ **vous aurez la ~ financière de la perte subie** you will be financially compensated for the loss incurred **2.** [registre comptable] duplicate register **3.** [d'une opinion] opposite view ■ [d'un argument] corollary, obverse, converse.
◆ **en contrepartie** *loc adv* **1.** [en compensation] in *ou* by way of compensation **2.** [en revanche] on the other hand **3.** [en retour] in return.
◆ **en contrepartie de** *loc prép* (as a *ou* in compensation) for ■ **service en ~ duquel vous devrez payer la somme de ...** for which services you will pay the sum of...

contre-pente [kɔ̃trəpɑ̃t] (*pl* **contre-pentes**) *nf* reverse slope.

contre-performance [kɔ̃trəpɛrfɔrmɑ̃s] (*pl* **contre-performances**) *nf* bad result, performance below expectation ■ **elle a eu** *ou* **fait une série de ~s** she's had a run of bad results.

contrepèterie [kɔ̃trəpetri] *nf* spoonerism.

contre-pied [kɔ̃trəpje] (*pl* **contre-pieds**) *nm* **1.** [d'une opinion] opposite (view) ■ [d'un argument] converse, obverse ■ **prendre le ~ d'une hypothèse** to oppose a hypothesis ■ **prenons le ~ de sa position** let's take the (exact) opposite position to hers **2.** SPORT : **prendre un adversaire à ~** to catch an opponent off balance, to wrong-foot an opponent **3.** CHASSE backscent.

contreplaqué [kɔ̃trəplake] *nm* plywood.

contre-plongée [kɔ̃trəplɔ̃ʒe] (*pl* **contre-plongées**) *nf* low-angle shot.
◆ **en contre-plongée** *loc adv* from below ▪ **prends-la en ~** get a low-angle shot of her, shoot her from below.

contrepoids [kɔ̃trəpwa] *nm* [gén] counterbalance, counterweight ▪ [d'une horloge] balance weight ▪ [d'un funambule] balancing pole ▪ **faire ~ (à qqch)** *pr* & *fig* to provide a counterweight (to sthg).

contre-poil [kɔ̃trəpwal] ◆ **à contre-poil** *loc adv* the wrong way ▪ **prendre qqn à ~** *fam* to rub sb up the wrong way.

contrepoint [kɔ̃trəpwɛ̃] *nm* LITTÉR & MUS counterpoint.
◆ **en contrepoint** *loc adv* **1.** LITTÉR & MUS contrapuntally **2.** *litt* [en même temps] at the same time, concurrently.
◆ **en contrepoint de** *loc prép* **1.** LITTÉR & MUS as counterpoint to **2.** [avec] as an accompaniment to.

contrepoison [kɔ̃trəpwazɔ̃] *nm* antidote.

contre-porte [kɔ̃trəpɔrt] (*pl* **contre-portes**) *nf* [d'isolation] inner door ▪ [de protection] screen door.

contre-pouvoir [kɔ̃trəpuvwar] (*pl* **contre-pouvoirs**) *nm* *challenge to established authority.*

contre-propagande [kɔ̃trəprɔpagɑ̃d] (*pl* **contre-propagandes**) *nf* counterpropaganda.

contre-proposition [kɔ̃trəprɔpozisjɔ̃] (*pl* **contre-propositions**) *nf* counterproposal.

contre-publicité [kɔ̃trəpyblisite] (*pl* **contre-publicités**) *nf* [qui concurrence] knocking copy ▪ [qui manque son objectif] anti-advertisement.

contrer [3] [kɔ̃tre] *vt* **1.** [s'opposer à] to block, to counter ▪ **elle me contre systématiquement** she tries to block everything I do **2.** JEUX to double **3.** SPORT [au volley] to block *(a smash)* ▪ [au rugby] to block *(a kick)* ▪ [à la boxe] to counter *(a punch)*.

contre-révolution [kɔ̃trərevɔlysjɔ̃] (*pl* **contre-révolutions**) *nf* counterrevolution.

contre-révolutionnaire [kɔ̃trərevɔlysjɔnɛr] (*pl* **contre-révolutionnaires**) *adj* & *nmf* counterrevolutionary.

contresens [kɔ̃trəsɑ̃s] *nm* **1.** [mauvaise interprétation] misinterpretation ▪ [mauvaise traduction] mistranslation ▪ **faire un ~** to mistranslate *(a word or a passage)* **2.** [aberration] sheer nonsense ▪ **la politique pétrolière de ce pays est un ~** this country's oil policy is an absurdity **3.** TEXT wrong way *(of fabric)*.
◆ **à contresens** *loc adv* **1.** [traduire, comprendre, marcher] the wrong way **2.** TEXT against the grain.

contresigner [3] [kɔ̃trəsiɲe] *vt* to countersign.

contretemps [kɔ̃trətɑ̃] *nm* **1.** [empêchement] hitch, mishap, setback ▪ **à moins d'un ~** unless there's a hitch, unless something unexpected crops up **2.** MUS offbeat.
◆ **à contretemps** *loc adv* **1.** [inopportunément] at the wrong time *ou* moment **2.** MUS off the beat.

contre-terrorisme [kɔ̃trətɛrɔrism] (*pl* **contre-terrorismes**) *nm* counterterrorism.

contre-ut [kɔ̃tryt] *nm inv* MUS top C, high C.

contrevenant, e [kɔ̃trəvnɑ̃, ɑ̃t] *nm, f* offender.

contrevenir [40] [kɔ̃trəvnir] ◆ **contrevenir à** *v+prép* to contravene, to infringe.

contrevenu [kɔ̃trəvny] *pp* ▻ **contrevenir**.

contrevérité [kɔ̃trəverite] *nf* falsehood, untruth.

contrevient, contrevint *etc v* ▻ **contrevenir**.

contre-voie [kɔ̃trəvwa] (*pl* **contre-voies**) *nf* parallel track *(going in the opposite direction)*.
◆ **à contre-voie** *loc adv* : **monter/descendre à ~** to get on/off on the wrong side of the train.

contribuable [kɔ̃tribɥabl] *nmf* taxpayer.

contribuer [7] [kɔ̃tribɥe] *vi* [financièrement] to contribute (money), to pay a share.
◆ **contribuer à** *v+prép* : **~ à l'achat d'un cadeau** to contribute to (buying) a present ▪ **~ au succès de** to contribute to *ou* to have a part in the success of ▪ **elle n'a pas contribué à la discussion** she took no part in the discussion ▪ **~ à faire qqch** to go towards doing sthg.

contribution [kɔ̃tribysjɔ̃] *nf* **1.** [argent apporté] contribution, sum contributed **2.** [aide] contribution, help ▪ **sa ~ au spectacle se limite à la rédaction du programme** his only contribution to the show was writing the programme **3.** [impôt] tax ▪ **~ indirecte** indirect taxation ▪ **les ~s sociales** social security contributions.
◆ **contributions** *nfpl* ≃ Inland Revenue *UK*, ≃ Internal Revenue Service *US*.
◆ **à contribution** *loc adv* : **mettre qqn à ~** to get sb involved ▪ **mets-le à ~** ask him to help.

contrit, e [kɔ̃tri, it] *adj* contrite, chastened.

contrition [kɔ̃trisjɔ̃] *nf* **1.** *litt* [repentir] contrition *litt*, remorse **2.** RELIG : **acte de ~** act of contrition.

contrôlable [kɔ̃trolabl] *adj* **1.** [maîtrisable] that can be controlled, controllable **2.** [vérifiable] that can be checked *ou* verified, checkable, verifiable.

contrôle [kɔ̃trol] *nm* **1.** [maîtrise] control ▪ **garder/perdre le ~ de sa voiture** to keep/to lose control of one's car ▪ **avoir le ~ de** [d'un secteur, de compagnies] to have (owning) control of ; [d'un pays, d'un territoire, d'un match] to be in control of ◐ **~ de soi-même** self-control ▪ **~ des naissances** birth control
2. [surveillance - de personnes, de travail] supervision, control ▪ **visite** *ou* **examen de ~** MÉD follow-up ◐ **~ aérien** flight control ▪ **~ budgétaire** budgeting control ▪ **~ des changes** exchange control ▪ **~ de gestion** management control ▪ **~ économique** *ou* **des prix** price control ▪ **~ judiciaire** ≃ probation ▪ **placé sous ~ judiciaire** ≃ put on probation ▪ **~ parental** parental control ▪ **~ de qualité** quality control ▪ **~ de vitesse** AUTO speed trap
3. [inspection - d'actes, de documents] control, check, checking ▪ **~ des comptes** *ou* **fiscal** audit ▪ **il a un ~ fiscal** ≃ the Inland Revenue *UK ou* IRS *US* is checking his returns ▪ **~ de douane** customs control ▪ **~ d'identité** *ou* **de police** identification check ▪ **~ des passeports** passport control ▪ **~ de routine** routine check-up ▪ **~ technique** AUTO test of roadworthiness, MOT (test) *UK*, inspection *US*
4. [bureau] check point
5. SPORT [de la balle] control
6. ÉDUC test ▪ **avoir un ~ en chimie** to have a chemistry test ◐ **~ continu (des connaissances)** continuous assessment
7. JOAILL [poinçon] hallmark ▪ [bureau] hallmark centre
8. MIL [liste] list, roll
9. INFORM : **~ carré** crosscheck ▪ **~ de la coupure de mot** hyphenation control ▪ **~ de parité** odd-even check
10. TÉLÉCOM monitoring.

contrôler [3] [kɔ̃trole] *vt* **1.** [maîtriser - émotions, sentiments] to control, to master, to curb ; [- respiration] to control ; [- discussion, match] to control, to master ; [- véhicule] to control, to be in control of ▪ **nous ne contrôlons plus la situation** the situation is out of our control **2.** [surveiller - personnes, travail] to supervise ▪ **nous sommes contrôlés toutes les semaines** a supervisor checks our work every week **3.** [vérifier - renseignement, exactitude] to check, to verify ; [- billet, papiers] to check, to inspect ; [- qualité] to control ; [- bon fonctionnement] to check, to monitor ; [- traduction] to check ▪ **se faire ~** [dans un bus, un train] to have one's ticket checked ; [par un agent de police] to have one's ID checked **4.** [avoir sous son autorité - affaires, secteur] to be in control of, to control ; [- territoire, zone] to control, to be in command of **5.** SPORT [ballon] to have control of **6.** JOAILL to hallmark **7.** TÉLÉCOM to monitor **8.** FIN [prix] to control ▪ [dépenses, comptes] to audit.
◆ **se contrôler** *vp (emploi réfléchi)* to control o.s., to be in control of o.s. ▪ **il ne se contrôlait plus** he'd lost his grip on himself, he was (totally) out of control.

contrôleur, euse [kɔ̃trolœr, øz] *nm, f* **1.** RAIL ticket inspector **2.** AÉRON : **~ aérien** air traffic controller **3.** ADMIN & FIN : **~ (de gestion)** auditor ▪ **~ (des impôts)** (tax) inspector *ou* assessor ▪ **~ des douanes** customs inspector.

◆ **contrôleur** *nm* **1.** INDUST regulator **2.** [horloge] telltale *UK*, time clock **3.** INFORM controller ▪ **~ interne de disques** internal storage control.

contrordre [kɔ̃trɔrdr] *nm* countermand, counterorder ▪ **il y a ~, vous ne partez plus** orders have been countermanded *ou* changed, you're not leaving ▪ **à moins d'un** *ou* **sauf ~** unless otherwise informed.

controverse [kɔ̃trɔvɛrs] *nf* [débat] controversy ▪ **donner lieu à ~** to be controversial.

controversé, e [kɔ̃trɔvɛrse] *adj* (much) debated *ou* disputed.

contumace [kɔ̃tymas] *nf* contumacy *sout*, refusal to appear in court, contempt of court.
◆ **par contumace** *loc adv* in absentia.

contusion [kɔ̃tyzjɔ̃] *nf* contusion *spéc*, bruise.

contusionner [3] [kɔ̃tyzjɔne] *vt* to bruise ▪ **visage contusionné** face covered in bruises.

conurbation [kɔnyrbasjɔ̃] *nf* conurbation.

convainc *etc v* ⊳ **convaincre.**

convaincant, e [kɔ̃vɛ̃kɑ̃, ɑ̃t] *adj* convincing, persuasive ▪ **un argument peu ~** a rather thin argument.

convaincre [114] [kɔ̃vɛ̃kr] *vt* **1.** [persuader] to convince, to persuade ▪ **~ qqn de faire qqch** to persuade sb to do sthg, to talk sb into doing sthg ▪ **votre dernier argument m'a convaincu** your last argument has won me over **2.** [prouver coupable] : **~ qqn de vol** to convict sb of theft, to find sb guilty of theft.
◆ **se convaincre** *vp (emploi réfléchi)* to realize, to accept ▪ **il est difficile de s'en ~** it's difficult to accept it.

convaincu, e [kɔ̃vɛ̃ky] ◇ *adj* convinced ▪ **être ~ de qqch** to be convinced of sthg ▪ **un partisan ~ du socialisme** a firm believer in socialism ▪ **parler d'un ton ~** to talk with conviction.
◇ *nm, f* firm *ou* great *ou* strong believer *(in an idea)*.

convainquait *etc v* ⊳ **convaincre.**

convalescence [kɔ̃valesɑ̃s] *nf* **1.** MÉD convalescence ▪ **être en ~** to be convalescing **2.** MIL *army convalescence leave.*

convalescent, e [kɔ̃valesɑ̃, ɑ̃t] *adj & nm, f* convalescent.

convecteur [kɔ̃vɛktœr] *nm* convector.

convenable [kɔ̃vnabl] *adj* **1.** [moment, lieu] suitable, appropriate **2.** [tenue] decent, respectable ▪ [comportement] seemly, correct ▪ **peu ~** improper ▪ **une famille très ~** a very respectable *ou* decent *ou* upstanding family **3.** [devoir] passable, adequate ▪ [logement, rémunération] decent, adequate.

convenablement [kɔ̃vnabləmɑ̃] *adv* **1.** [de façon appropriée] suitably, appropriately **2.** [décemment] decently, properly **3.** [de façon acceptable] : **gagner ~ sa vie** to earn a decent wage ▪ **il s'exprime très ~ en italien** he has a fairly good knowledge of Italian ▪ **on y mange ~** the food is quite adequate there.

convenance [kɔ̃vnɑ̃s] *nf litt* [adéquation] appropriateness, suitability ▪ **la ~ d'humeur** *ou* **de goût entre deux personnes** affinity of taste between two people.
◆ **convenances** *nfpl* propriety, decorum, accepted (standards of) behaviour ▪ **respecter les ~s** to respect *ou* to observe the proprieties.
◆ **à ma convenance, à sa convenance** *etc loc adv* as suits me/him *etc* (best).
◆ **pour convenance(s) personnelle(s)** *loc adv* for personal reasons.

convenir [40] [kɔ̃vnir] *vt* : **comme (cela a été) convenu** as agreed ▪ **~ que** to agree *ou* to accept *ou* to admit that.
◆ **convenir à** *v+prép* **1.** [être approprié à] to suit **2.** [plaire à] to suit ▪ **10 h, cela vous convient-il?** does 10 o'clock suit you? ▪ **ce travail ne lui convient pas du tout** this job's not right for him at all ▪ **la vie que je mène me convient parfaitement** the life I lead suits me perfectly ▪ **cette chaleur ne me convient pas du tout** this heat doesn't agree with me at all.
◆ **convenir de** *v+prép* **1.** [se mettre d'accord sur] to agree upon ▪ **nous avions convenu de nous retrouver à midi** we had agreed to meet at noon ▪ **~ d'un endroit** to agree upon a place ▪ **il est convenu avec la direction de...** it's agreed with the management to... ▪ **comme convenu** as agreed **2.** [reconnaître] : **~ de qqch** to admit sthg ▪ **je conviens d'avoir dit cela** I admit to having said that.
◆ **il convient de** *v impers* **1.** [il est souhaitable de] it is advisable *ou* a good idea to ▪ **il voudrait savoir ce qu'il convient de faire** he would like to know the right thing to do **2.** [il est de bon ton de] it is proper *ou* the done thing to.
◆ **se convenir** *vp (emploi réciproque)* to suit one another.

convention [kɔ̃vɑ̃sjɔ̃] *nf* **1.** [norme] convention ▪ **les ~s orthographiques** spelling conventions ▪ **un système de ~s** an agreed system **2.** [règle de bienséance] (social) convention ▪ **respecter les ~s** to conform to accepted social behaviour *ou* established conventions **3.** [accord - tacite] agreement, understanding ; [- officiel] agreement ; [- diplomatique] convention ➊ **~ collective (du travail)** collective agreement **4.** POLIT [assemblée - aux États-Unis] convention ; [- en France] assembly **5.** HIST : **la Convention** the French National Convention *(1792-1795)*.
◆ **de convention** *loc adj* conformist, conventional.
◆ **par convention** *loc adv* : **par ~, on symbolise la vitesse par un v** speed is usually symbolised by a v.

conventionné, e [kɔ̃vɑ̃sjɔne] *adj* **1.** [médecin, clinique] subsidized, designated by the health system, ≃ National Health *UK* ▪ **non ~** private **2.** [honoraires, prix] set ▪ **prêt ~** low-interest (subsidized) loan.

conventionnel, elle [kɔ̃vɑ̃sjɔnɛl] *adj* **1.** [conformiste] conventional, conformist ▪ **formules ~les** clichés, platitudes **2.** [arbitraire - signe, valeur] conventionally agreed **3.** POLIT : **accords ~s** agreements resulting from collective bargaining ▪ **politique ~le** policies relating to union-management agreements **4.** DR contractual **5.** ARM conventional.
◆ **conventionnel** *nm* [membre] member *(of a convention)*.

conventionner [3] [kɔ̃vɑ̃sjɔne] *vt* ≃ to link to the NHS *UK* *ou* a (public) medical care system.

convenu, e [kɔ̃vny] ◇ *pp* ⊳ **convenir.**
◇ *adj* : **style ~** conventional style ▪ **l'intrigue est très ~e** the plot is very obvious.

convergence [kɔ̃vɛrʒɑ̃s] *nf* **1.** [confluence - de chemins, de lignes] convergence, confluence ▪ **point de ~** *pr* point of convergence ; *fig* point of agreement **2.** [concordance] convergence ▪ **la ~ de nos efforts** our combined efforts **3.** MATH & OPT convergence.

convergent, e [kɔ̃vɛrʒɑ̃, ɑ̃t] *adj* convergent.

converger [17] [kɔ̃vɛrʒe] *vi* **1.** [confluer] to converge, to meet at a point **2.** [aboutir au même point] : **nos conclusions convergent** we tend toward the same conclusions **3.** MATH & OPT to converge.

conversation [kɔ̃vɛrsasjɔ̃] *nf* **1.** [discussion] discussion, conversation, talk ▪ **elle est en grande ~ avec son mari** she's deep in conversation with her husband ▪ **engager la ~ (avec qqn)** to start up a conversation (with sb) ▪ **suite à ma ~ téléphonique avec votre secrétaire** following my phone conversation with your secretary ▪ **détourner la ~** to change the subject ▪ **amener la ~ sur qqch** to steer the conversation towards sthg, to bring sthg up in the conversation ➊ **avoir de la ~** to be a good conversationalist **2.** [pourparlers] : **des ~s entre les syndicats et le patronat** talks between unions and management.

conversationnel, elle [kɔ̃vɛrsasjɔnɛl] *adj* interactive ▪ **en mode ~** in interactive *ou* conversational mode.

converser [3] [kɔ̃vɛrse] *vi* to converse, to talk.

conversion [kɔ̃vɛrsjɔ̃] *nf* **1.** [de chiffres, de mesures, de devises] conversion, converting ▪ **~ des miles en kilomètres** converting of miles to kilometres **2.** RELIG conversion **3.** [ralliement] conversion **4.** NAUT turning around **5.** [au ski] kick turn **6.** DR & SC conversion **7.** [formation] retraining.

converti, e [kɔ̃vɛrti] ◇ *adj* converted.
◇ *nm, f* convert.

convertibilité [kɔ̃vɛrtibilite] *nf* convertibility.

convertible [kɔ̃vɛrtibl] <> *adj* **1.** [transformable] convertible ■ ~ **en qqch** convertible into sthg ▶ **canapé ~** sofa bed, bedsettee *UK*, convertible sofa *US* ■ **fauteuil ~** convertible armchair **2.** FIN convertible.
<> *nm* **1.** [canapé] sofa bed, bedsettee *UK*, convertible sofa *US* **2.** AÉRON convertiplane, convertoplane.

convertir [32] [kɔ̃vɛrtir] *vt* **1.** [convaincre] to convert ■ ~ **qqn à** [religion] to convert sb to ; [opinion, mouvement] to win sb over *ou* to convert sb to **2.** FIN & MATH [mesure, grandeur, argent] to convert ■ ~ **des euros en dollars** to convert francs into dollars **3.** INFORM [données] to convert ■ ~ **en numérique** to digitize **4.** LOGIQUE to convert **5.** [transformer] : **ils ont converti la vieille gare en musée** they converted *ou* transformed the old railway station into a museum.
◆ **se convertir** *vpi* [athée] to become a believer ■ [croyant] to change religion ■ **se ~ à** [religion, mouvement] to be converted to, to convert to.

convertisseur, euse [kɔ̃vɛrtisœr, øz] *nm, f* RELIG converter.
◆ **convertisseur** *nm* **1.** MÉTALL converter **2.** ÉLECTR converter, convertor **3.** TV converter ■ ~ **d'images** image converter **4.** INFORM : ~ **numérique** digitizer ■ ~ **de signal** converter ■ ~ **tournant** motor generator (set) ■ ~ **série-parallèle** staticizer.

convexe [kɔ̃vɛks] *adj* convex.

conviction [kɔ̃viksjɔ̃] *nf* [certitude] conviction, belief ■ **j'ai la ~ que...** it's my belief that..., I'm convinced that... ■ **avec/sans ~** with/without conviction.
◆ **convictions** *nfpl* [credo] fundamental beliefs ■ **avoir des ~s politiques** to have political convictions.

convient *etc v* ▷ **convenir.**

convier [9] [kɔ̃vje] *vt litt* **1.** [faire venir] to invite ■ ~ **qqn à une soirée/un repas** to invite sb to a party/a meal **2.** [inciter] : ~ **qqn à faire qqch** to invite *ou* to urge sb to do sthg.

convint *etc v* ▷ **convenir.**

convive [kɔ̃viv] *nmf* guest *(at a meal).*

convivial, e, aux [kɔ̃vivjal, o] *adj* **1.** [ambiance, fête] convivial **2.** INFORM user-friendly.

convivialité [kɔ̃vivjalite] *nf* **1.** [d'une société] conviviality **2.** INFORM user-friendliness.

convocation [kɔ̃vɔkasjɔ̃] *nf* **1.** [d'une assemblée, de ministres] calling together, convening ■ [de témoins, d'un employé] summoning **2.** [avis écrit] notification ■ **vous recevrez bientôt votre ~** you'll be notified shortly ‖ DR summons *(sing).*

convoi [kɔ̃vwa] *nm* **1.** AUTO & NAUT convoy ■ **'~ exceptionnel'** 'wide *ou* dangerous load' **2.** RAIL train ■ ~ **postal** postal *UK ou* mail *US* train **3.** [cortège] convoy ▶ ~ **funèbre** funeral procession.
◆ **en convoi** *loc adv* in convoy.

convoie *etc v* ▷ **convoyer.**

convoiement [kɔ̃vwamɑ̃] *nm* [gén] escorting, convoying ■ AÉRON *shuttling of new planes to operational zones.*

convoiter [3] [kɔ̃vwate] *vt* **1.** [vouloir - argent, héritage, poste] to covet, to be after *(insép)* ■ **j'avais enfin le rôle tant convoité** at last, I had the role I had longed for **2.** *litt* [par concupiscence] to lust after *(insép).*

convoitise [kɔ̃vwatiz] *nf* **1.** [désir - d'un objet] desire, covetousness ; [- d'argent] greed, cupidity *sout* ■ **regarder qqch avec ~** to stare at sthg greedily **2.** *litt* [concupiscence] : ~ **(de la chair)** lust.

convoler [3] [kɔ̃vɔle] *vi arch* & *hum* : ~ **en secondes noces** to remarry ▶ ~ **en justes noces** to be wed.

convoquer [3] [kɔ̃vɔke] *vt* [assemblée, concile, ministres] to call together *(sép)*, to convene ■ [témoin] to summon to a hearing ■ [employé, postulant] to call in *(sép)* ■ [journalistes, presse] to invite ■ **ils m'ont convoqué pour passer un entretien** they've called *ou* asked me in for an interview ■ **elle est convoquée chez le proviseur** she's been summoned to the principal's office ■ **je suis convoqué à 9 h au centre d'examens** I have to be at the examination centre at 9.

convoyer [13] [kɔ̃vwaje] *vt* [accompagner] to escort ■ MIL to convoy.

convoyeur, euse [kɔ̃vwajœr, øz] <> *adj* escort *(modif).*
<> *nm, f* escort.
◆ **convoyeur** *nm* **1.** [transporteur] : ~ **de fonds** [entreprise] security firm *(transporting money)* ; [homme] security guard ≃ Securicor guard *UK* **2.** NAUT convoy (ship) **3.** [tapis roulant] conveyor belt.

convulser [3] [kɔ̃vylse] *vt* to convulse ■ **la peur convulsait son visage** her face was convulsed *ou* distorted with fear.
◆ **se convulser** *vpi* to be convulsed.

convulsif, ive [kɔ̃vylsif, iv] *adj* **1.** MÉD convulsive **2.** [brusque] : **un mouvement ~** a sudden *ou* uncontrolled movement.

convulsion [kɔ̃vylsjɔ̃] *nf* **1.** MÉD convulsion ■ **il fut soudain pris de ~s** he suddenly went into convulsion *ou* convulsions **2.** [agitation] convulsion, upheaval, disturbance.

convulsionner [3] [kɔ̃vylsjɔne] *vt* [visage] to convulse, to distort ■ [patient] to send into convulsion *ou* convulsions.

cooccupant, e [kɔɔkypɑ̃, ɑ̃t] *nm, f* co-occupier.

cooccurrence [kɔɔkyrɑ̃s] *nf* co-occurrence.

cookie [kuki] *nm* **1.** [petit gâteau] cookie *esp US*, biscuit *UK* **2.** INFORM cookie.

cool [kul] *fam* <> *adj inv* cool, laid-back, relaxed ■ **ils sont ~, ses parents** his parents are easy going.
<> *nm inv* MUS cool jazz.

coopérant, e [kɔɔperɑ̃, ɑ̃t] <> *adj* cooperative.
<> *nm, f* aid worker.
◆ **coopérant** *nm conscript doing National Service in a non-military capacity in a developing country.*

coopérateur, trice [kɔɔperatœr, tris] <> *adj* cooperative.
<> *nm, f* [collaborateur] cooperator, collaborator ■ [adhérent] member of a cooperative.

coopératif, ive [kɔɔperatif, iv] *adj* cooperative, helpful ■ **se montrer ~** to cooperate, to be cooperative.
◆ **coopérative** *nf* **1.** ÉCON cooperative, co-op **2.** ÉDUC : **coopérative scolaire** fund-raising group *(of pupils under the supervision of a teacher).*

coopération [kɔɔperasjɔ̃] *nf* **1.** [collaboration] cooperation ■ **il nous a offert sa ~** he offered to cooperate (with us) **2.** ÉCON & POLIT economic cooperation **3.** ADMIN & MIL *form of National Service in which the person works abroad on an aid project* ■ **le ministère de la Coopération et du Développement** *ministry promoting the development of Third World countries* **4.** ÉCON cooperation, cooperative action.

coopérer [18] [kɔɔpere] *vi* to cooperate ■ ~ **à qqch** to cooperate in (doing) sthg, to collaborate on doing sthg.

cooptation [kɔɔptasjɔ̃] *nf* co-option.

coordinateur, trice [kɔɔrdinatœr, tris] <> *adj* coordinating.
<> *nm, f* coordinator.

coordination [kɔɔrdinasjɔ̃] *nf* **1.** [d'une opération] coordination **2.** [des mouvements] coordination ■ **il n'a aucune ~** he is totally uncoordinated.

coordonné, e [kɔɔrdɔne] *adj* **1.** [harmonieux] coordinated **2.** LING : **propositions ~es** coordinate clauses **3.** [assorti] matching.
◆ **coordonnés** *nmpl* [vêtements] coordinates, (matching) separates ■ [linge] matched set.
◆ **coordonnées** *nfpl* **1.** GÉOGR & MATH coordinates **2.** *fam* [adresse] : **laissez-moi vos ~es** leave me your name, address and phone number.

coordonner [3] [kɔɔrdɔne] *vt* **1.** [organiser] to coordinate, to integrate ■ **il est là pour ~ les secours** his job is to act as coordinator for the emergency services **2.** [assortir] to match **3.** LING to coordinate.

copain, copine [kɔpɛ̃, kɔpin] *fam* ◇ *nm, f* [ami] mate *UK*, buddy *US*, friend ■ **un ~ d'école/de bureau** a school/an office chum ■ **être/rester bons ~s** to be/to remain good friends ➊ **petit ~** boyfriend ■ **petite copine** girlfriend.
◇ *adj* : **être très ~** *OU* **être ~-~** **avec** to be very pally with ■ **~s comme cochons** *fam* thick as thieves.

coparentalité [kɔparɑ̃talite] *nf* parenting as a couple ■ [après séparation] shared *OU* joint parenting.

copartage [kɔpartaʒ] *nm* coparcenary.

coparticipant, e [kɔpartisipɑ̃, ɑ̃t] ◇ *adj* in copartnership.
◇ *nm, f* copartner.

coparticipation [kɔpartisipasjɔ̃] *nf* copartnership.

copaternité [kɔpatɛrnite] *nf* joint responsibility *(for invention)*.

copeau, x [kɔpo] *nm* [de métal] (metal) chip ■ [de bois] (wood) chip ■ **des ~x** [de métal] chips, filings ; [pour l'emballage] woodwool.

Copenhague [kɔpənag] *npr* Copenhagen.

Copernic [kɔpɛrnik] *npr* Copernicus.

copiage [kɔpjaʒ] *nm péj* [plagiat] copying ■ ÉDUC cribbing.

copie [kɔpi] *nf* **1.** [reproduction légitime - d'un document] copy, duplicate ; [- d'une lettre] copy ■ **je vais en faire une ~** I'll go and make a copy (of it) ➊ **~ carbone** carbon copy, cc ■ **~ certifiée conforme (à l'original)** certified copy **2.** [reproduction frauduleuse - d'un tableau, d'une cassette, d'un produit] copy, imitation, reproduction **3.** [feuille] sheet ■ **des ~s simples/doubles** *single-/double-width sheets of squared paper used for schoolwork* **4.** ÉDUC [devoir] paper ➊ **rendre ~ blanche** *pr* to hand in a blank paper ; *fig* to fail to come up with the solution *(for a problem)* **5.** CINÉ, RADIO & TV copy **6.** PRESSE : **la ~** copy **7.** INFORM : **~ libre/en clair** blind/hard copy ■ **~ d'écran** screenshot.
◆ **pour copie conforme** *loc adv* certified accurate.

copier [9] [kɔpje] *vt* **1.** [modèle] to reproduce, to copy **2.** [bijou, tableau] to fake, to copy **3.** [transcrire - document, texte] to copy (out), to make a copy of ■ **~ un rapport au propre** to make a fair copy of a report ■ [punition] to copy out *(sép)* ■ INFORM to copy **4.** ÉDUC [pour tricher] to copy ■ **il a copié (l'exercice) sur moi/son livre** he copied (the exercise) from me/his book **5.** [attitude, personne] to copy, to imitate **6.** *fam loc* **tu me la copieras!, vous me la copierez!** that's something that's going to stick with me for a while!

copier-coller [3] [kɔpjekɔle] *vt* INFORM copy and paste.

copieur, euse [kɔpjœr, øz] *nm, f* [plagiaire] plagiarist ■ ÉDUC & UNIV cribber.
◆ **copieur** *nm* [de documents] copier.

copieusement [kɔpjøzmɑ̃] *adv* [manger] heartily ■ [annoter] copiously ■ [servir] generously ■ **après un repas ~ arrosé** after a meal washed down with generous amounts of wine ■ **il s'est fait ~ insulter par sa femme** *hum* he got quite a mouthful from his wife.

copieux, euse [kɔpjø, øz] *adj* [repas] copious, hearty, lavish ■ [ration] lavish, big, giant *US* ■ [notes] copious.

copilote [kɔpilɔt] *nmf* co-pilot.

copinage [kɔpinaʒ] *nm fam péj* (mutually profitable) chumminess ■ **par ~** through the old boy network *UK OU* one's connections.

copine [kɔpin] *f* ▷ **copain**.

copiner [3] [kɔpine] ◆ **copiner avec** *v+prép fam* to pal up with.

copiste [kɔpist] *nmf* copyist, transcriber.

coposséder [18] [kɔpɔsede] *vt* to own jointly, to have joint ownership of.

coprocesseur [kɔprɔsesœr] *nm* coprocessor.

coproducteur [kɔprɔdyktœr] *nm* co-producer.

coproduction [kɔprɔdyksjɔ̃] *nf* coproduction ■ **ce film est une ~ des télévisions française et italienne** this film has been coproduced by French and Italian television.

coproduire [80] [kɔprɔdɥir] *vt* to coproduce, to produce jointly.

copropriétaire [kɔprɔprijetɛr] *nmf* co-owner, joint owner, coproprietor.

copropriété [kɔprɔprijete] *nf* joint ownership.
◆ **en copropriété** *loc adj* jointly owned.

copte [kɔpt] *adj* Coptic.
◆ **Copte** *nmf* Copt.
◆ **copte** *nm* LING Coptic.

copulatif, ive [kɔpylatif, iv] *adj* copulative.

copulation [kɔpylasjɔ̃] *nf* copulation.

copule [kɔpyl] *nf* copula.

copuler [3] [kɔpyle] *vi* to copulate.

copyright [kɔpirajt] *nm* copyright.

coq [kɔk] ◇ *nm* **1.** [mâle - de la poule] cock, rooster *US* ; [- des gallinacés] cock, cockbird ■ **~ de bruyère** capercailie, capercaillie ■ **~ de combat** gamecock ■ **être comme un ~ en pâte** to be in clover ■ **passer** *OU* **sauter du ~ à l'âne** to jump from one subject to another **2.** [figure, symbole] : **~ de clocher** weathercock, weather vane ■ **~ gaulois** *French national symbol (a cockerel)* **3.** CULIN chicken ■ **~ au vin** coq au vin **4.** *fam* [fanfaron, séducteur] lady-killer **5.** NAUT (ship's) cook.
◇ *adj* SPORT [catégorie, poids] bantam *(modif)*.

LE COQ GAULOIS

The cockerel is the symbol of France. Its cry, *cocorico!*, is sometimes used to express national pride: *trois médailles d'or pour la France - cocorico!*

coq-à-l'âne [kɔkalan] *nm inv* **1.** [dans la conversation] sudden change of subject ■ **faire un ~** to go on to something completely different **2.** LITTÉR skit, satirical farce.

coquard, coquart [kɔkar] *nm fam* shiner, black eye.

coque [kɔk] *nf* **1.** [mollusque] cockle **2.** [de noix, de noisette, d'amande] shell **3.** [boucle - de ruban] loop, bow ; [- de cheveux] curl, lock **4.** [de chaussure de ski] shell **5.** *fam* [embarcation] : **~ (de noix)** skiff.
◆ **à la coque** *loc adj* [œuf] soft-boiled.

coquelet [kɔklɛ] *nm* young cockerel.

coquelicot [kɔkliko] *nm* poppy.

coqueluche [kɔklyʃ] *nf* **1.** MÉD whooping-cough, pertussis *spéc* **2.** *fam fig* **il est la ~ de l'école** he's the darling *OU* heartthrob of the school.

coquerel [kɔkrɛl] *nm Québec* cockroach.

coqueron [kɔkrɔ̃] *nm* **1.** NAUT peak **2.** *Québec* [logement] tumbledown house.

coquet, ette [kɔkɛ, ɛt] *adj* **1.** [qui s'habille bien] smartly dressed ■ [soucieux de son apparence] concerned about one's appearance **2.** [élégant - maison, mobilier] fashionable, stylish **3.** *vieilli* [qui cherche à séduire] coquettish, flirtatious **4.** *fam* [important - somme, indemnité] tidy, nice (little).
◆ **coquette** *nf* **1.** [femme] coquette, flirt **2.** THÉÂTRE stage coquette ■ **jouer les grandes ~tes** *pr* to specialize in stage coquette parts ; *fig* to be a coquette.

coquetier [kɔktje] *nm* **1.** [godet] eggcup **2.** [pêcheur] cockle gatherer **3.** *fam loc* **gagner** *OU* **décrocher le ~** to hit the jackpot.

coquettement [kɔkɛtmɑ̃] *adv* **1.** [décorer, meubler] elegantly, stylishly ■ [s'habiller] smartly, stylishly, elegantly **2.** [sourire, répondre] coquettishly, flirtatiously.

coquetterie [kɔkɛtri] *nf* **1.** [goût de la toilette] interest in one's looks, desire to look elegant **2.** *litt* [flirt] act of coquetry *ou* flirtatiousness **3.** *fam loc* **avoir une ~ dans l'œil** to have a cast in one's eye *ou* a slight squint.

coquillage [kɔkijaʒ] *nm* **1.** [mollusque] shellfish **2.** CULIN : **manger des ~s** to eat shellfish *ou* seafood **3.** [coquille] shell ▪ **collectionner des ~s** to collect sea-shells.

coquille [kɔkij] *nf* **1.** [de mollusque, d'œuf, de noix] shell ▪ **rentrer dans sa ~** *fig* to go *ou* to retire into one's shell ▪ **rester dans sa ~** *fig* to be introverted ▪ **sortir de sa ~** *fig* to come out of one's shell, to open up ▪ **~ Saint-Jacques** [mollusque] scallop ; [enveloppe] scallop shell **2.** [récipient] shell, scallop, scallop-shaped dish **3.** CULIN : **~ de beurre** butter curl ▪ **~ de poisson** fish served in a shell **4.** ARCHIT shell **5.** [bateau] : **~ de noix** *fam* cockleshell **6.** SPORT box **7.** MÉD spinal bed **8.** IMPR [en composition] misprint ▪ [d'une seule lettre] literal ▪ [en dactylographie] typo.
◆ **coquille d'œuf** *adj inv* eggshell.

coquillette [kɔkijɛt] *nf* : **des ~s** pasta shells.

coquin, e [kɔkɛ̃, in] ◇ *adj* **1.** [espiègle] mischievous ▪ **comme elle est ~e, cette petite!** what a little rascal *ou* devil she is! **2.** [grivois - histoire] risqué, naughty ▪ **une œillade ~e** a provocative glance **3.** [dialecte] : **~ de sort!** I'll be darned!
◇ *nm, f* [enfant] (little) rascal *ou* devil.
◆ **coquin** *nm* **1.** *arch* [voyou] rogue, scoundrel **2.** GÉOL nodule of phosphate of lime.
◆ **coquine** *nf arch* strumpet.

cor [kɔr] *nm* **1.** MUS horn ▪ **~ (de chasse)** hunting horn ▪ **~ anglais** cor anglais, English horn **2.** [au pied] corn.
◆ **à cor et à cri** *loc adv* : **réclamer qqch/qqn à ~ et à cri** to clamour for sthg/sb.

corail, aux [kɔraj, o] *nm* **1.** JOAILL & ZOOL coral ▪ **barrière de ~** coral reef **2.** CULIN coral.
◆ **corail** *adj inv* coral(-pink).
◆ **de corail** *loc adj* [rouge] coral(-pink).

corallien, enne [kɔraljɛ̃, ɛn] *adj* coralloid, coralline.

Coran [kɔrɑ̃] *nm* : **le ~** the Koran.

coranique [kɔranik] *adj* [texte, école] Koranic.

corbeau, x [kɔrbo] *nm* **1.** ORNITH crow **2.** *fam péj* [auteur anonyme] writer of poison-pen letters **3.** *vieilli* [escroc] shark.

corbeille [kɔrbɛj] *nf* **1.** [contenant, contenu] basket ▪ **~ à courrier** desk tray ▪ **~ à ouvrage** workbasket ▪ **~ à pain** breadbasket ▪ **~ à papier** wastepaper basket *ou* bin ▮ INFORM trash (can) **2.** THÉÂTRE dress circle **3.** ARCHIT bell **4.** BOURSE [à Paris] trading floor ▪ **à la ~** [en style journalistique] on the (Paris) Stock Exchange.
◆ **corbeille de mariage** *nf* [des invités] wedding presents ▪ [du marié] groom's wedding presents *(to the bride)* ▪ **mon père avait mis la voiture dans ma ~ de mariage** the car was a wedding present from my father.

corbillard [kɔrbijar] *nm* hearse.

cordage [kɔrdaʒ] *nm* **1.** [lien] rope ▪ **les ~s** ropes and cables **2.** [mesure] measuring by the cord **3.** [d'une raquette] strings ▪ [action de corder] stringing ▪ **faire refaire le ~ de sa raquette** to have one's racket re-strung.
◆ **cordages** *nmpl* NAUT rigging.

corde [kɔrd] *nf* **1.** [lien] rope ▪ **attaché au poteau par une ~** roped to the post ◐ **tirer (un peu trop) sur la ~** *fam* [profiter d'autrui] to push one's luck, to go a bit too far ; [abuser de sa santé, ses forces] to push o.s. to the limits, to overdo it ▪ **il tombe** *ou* **pleut des ~s** *fam* it's raining cats and dogs, it's bucketing down
2. [câble tendu] : **~ à linge** clothesline ▪ **~ raide** high wire, tightrope ▪ **être sur la ~ raide** *pr* to be on *ou* to walk the tightrope ; *fig* to walk a tightrope, to do a (difficult) balancing act
3. [pour pendre] rope ▪ **la ~** [supplice] the rope ▪ **passer la ~ au cou à qqn** to send sb to the gallows ◐ **se mettre** *ou* **se passer la ~ au cou** [se mettre à la merci de qqn] to put one's head in a noose ; [se marier] to saddle o.s. with a wife ▪ **il ne faut pas parler de ~ dans la maison d'un pendu** *prov* talk not of ropes in a hanged man's house
4. [matériau] cord, rope
5. ACOUST & MUS string ▪ **instruments à ~s** string instruments ▪ **toucher** *ou* **faire vibrer** *ou* **faire jouer la ~ sensible** to touch an emotional chord, to tug at the heartstrings
6. JEUX, LOISIRS & SPORT rope ▪ ÉQUIT rail ▪ **~ à nœuds** knotted climbing rope ▪ **~ à sauter** skipping rope ▪ **sauter à la ~** to skip ▪ **~ lisse** climbing rope
7. [d'une arbalète, d'une raquette] string ▪ **avoir plus d'une ~** *ou* **plusieurs ~s à son arc** to have more than one string to one's bow
8. ANAT cord ▪ **~s vocales** vocal cords ▪ **c'est dans ses ~s** it's right up her street, it's her line
9. TEXT thread ▪ **des manches qui montraient la ~** threadbare sleeves
10. [mesure] cord
11. MATH chord.
◆ **cordes** *nfpl* [instruments] strings, stringed instruments.
◆ **à la corde** *loc adv* AUTO & ÉQUIT : **être à la ~** to be on the inside ▪ **prendre un virage à la ~** to hug a bend.
◆ **dans les cordes** *loc adv* [d'un ring] on the ropes.
◆ **de corde, en corde** *loc adj* [semelle] cord *(modif)* ▪ [revêtement] whipcord *(modif)* ▪ [échelle] rope *(modif)*.

cordeau, x [kɔrdo] *nm* **1.** [fil] string, line ▪ **tiré au ~** [allée] perfectly straight, straight as a die **2.** [mèche] fuse.

cordée [kɔrde] *nf* roped party.

cordelette [kɔrdəlɛt] *nf* cord.

cordelière [kɔrdəljɛr] *nf* **1.** [corde] cord **2.** ARCHIT cable moulding, ropework.

corder [3] [kɔrde] *vt* **1.** [lier] to rope up *(sép)* **2.** [mettre en corde] to twist (into ropes *ou* a rope) **3.** [raquette] to string **4.** [mesurer - bois] to cord.

corderie [kɔrd(ə)ri] *nf* **1.** [industrie] ropemaking trade *ou* industry **2.** [usine] rope factory.

cordial, e, aux [kɔrdjal, o] *adj* warm, cordial, friendly ▪ **une haine/aversion ~e pour...** a heartfelt hatred of/disgust for...
◆ **cordial, aux** *nm* [boisson] tonic, pick-me-up.

cordialement [kɔrdjalmɑ̃] *adv* **1.** [saluer] warmly, cordially ▪ **ils se détestent ~** they heartily detest each other **2.** [dans la correspondance] : **~ vôtre** kind regards.

cordialité [kɔrdjalite] *nf* warmth, cordiality.

cordillère [kɔrdijɛr] *nf* mountain range, cordillera *spéc* ▪ **la ~ des Andes** the Andes (cordillera).

cordon [kɔrdɔ̃] *nm* **1.** [de rideaux] cord ▪ [d'un bonnet, d'un sac] string ▪ [de soulier] lace ▪ **~ de sonnette** bellpull ◐ **tenir les ~s de la bourse** to hold the purse strings **2.** [ligne - de policiers] row, cordon ; [- de peupliers] row, line ▪ **~ sanitaire** MÉD cordon sanitaire ; MIL cordon sanitaire, buffer zone **3.** ANAT : **~ ombilical** umbilical cord **4.** GÉOL : **~ littoral** offshore bar **5.** [insigne] sash ▪ **avoir** *ou* **recevoir le grand ~** to be awarded the grand-croix of the Légion d'honneur.

cordon-bleu [kɔrdɔ̃blø] (*pl* **cordons-bleus**) *nm* cordon bleu (cook), gourmet cook.

cordonnerie [kɔrdɔnri] *nf* **1.** [boutique - moderne] heel bar, shoe repair shop *UK ou* store *US* ; [- artisanale] cobbler's **2.** [activité] shoe repairing, cobbling.

cordonnet [kɔrdɔnɛ] *nm* **1.** [pour lier] (piece of) cord **2.** [pour orner] (piece of) braid.

cordonnier, ère [kɔrdɔnje, ɛr] *nm, f* [qui répare] shoe repairer, cobbler ▪ [qui fabrique] shoemaker ▪ **les ~s sont toujours les plus mal chaussés** *prov* the shoemaker's son always goes barefoot *prov*.

cordouan, e [kɔrdwɑ̃, an] *adj* from Cordoba.

Cordoue [kɔrdu] *npr* Cordoba.

Corée [kɔre] *npr f* Korea ▪ **(la) ~ du Nord/Sud** North/South Korea.

coréen, enne [kɔreɛ̃, ɛn] *adj* Korean.
◆ **Coréen, enne** *nm, f* Korean.

◆ **coréen** *nm* LING Korean.

coresponsable [kɔrɛspɔ̃sabl] <> *adj* jointly responsible. <> *nmf* person sharing responsibility ▪ **les ~s** those jointly responsible.

Corfou [kɔrfu] *npr* Corfu ▪ **à ~** in Corfu.

coriace [kɔrjas] *adj* **1.** [dur - viande] tough, chewy **2.** [problème, personne] tough ▪ **des taches ~s** tough stains, stains that won't come out.

coriandre [kɔrjɑ̃dr] *nf* [plante] (fresh) coriander ▪ [graines] coriander seeds.

coricide [kɔrisid] *nm* corn remover.

corinthien, enne [kɔrɛ̃tjɛ̃, ɛn] *adj* Corinthian.

cormoran [kɔrmɔrɑ̃] *nm* cormorant.

cornac [kɔrnak] *nm* elephant keeper, mahout.

corne [kɔrn] *nf* **1.** [d'un animal, d'un diable] horn ▪ **faire les ~s à qqn** to mock sb *(by making a gesture with one's fingers shaped like horns)* ▪ **avoir** *ou* **porter des ~s** *fam* to be a cuckold ▪ **faire porter des ~s à qqn** *fam* to cuckold sb **2.** [matériau] horn **3.** [outil] : **~ à chaussures** shoehorn **4.** MUS horn ▪ **~ de brume** fog horn **5.** [récipient] horn ▪ **~ d'abondance** [ornement] horn of plenty, cornucopia ; BOT horn of plenty **6.** [callosité] : **avoir de la ~** to have calluses **7.** [coin de page] dog-ear ▪ **faire une ~ à** to turn down the corner of **8.** [forme - d'un mont] peak ; [- d'un bois] (horn-shaped) corner ; [- de la Lune, d'un champ, d'une terre] horn **9.** CULIN : **~ de gazelle** *crescent-shaped cake, a North African Arab speciality.*

◆ **à cornes** *loc adj* **1.** [bête] horned **2.** [chapeau] cocked.

corné, e [kɔrne] *adj* [qui a l'apparence de la corne] corneous, horned.

cornée [kɔrne] *nf* ANAT cornea.

cornéen, enne [kɔrneɛ̃, ɛn] *adj* corneal.

corneille [kɔrnɛj] *nf* crow.

cornélien, enne [kɔrneljɛ̃, ɛn] *adj* [héros, vers] Cornelian, of Corneille ▪ **choix** *ou* **dilemme ~** conflict of love and duty.

cornemuse [kɔrnəmyz] *nf* (set of) bagpipes.

corner[1] [kɔrnɛr] *nm* FOOTBALL corner kick.

corner[2] [3] [kɔrne] <> *vt* **1.** [plier - par négligence] to dog-ear ; [- volontairement] to turn down the corner *ou* corners of **2.** *fam* [clamer - nouvelle] to blare out *(sép)* ▪ *(en usage absolu)* **~ aux oreilles de qqn** to deafen sb.
<> *vi* **1.** CHASSE to sound a horn **2.** AUTO & *arch* to hoot, to sound one's horn **3.** VÉTÉR to wheeze **4.** *loc* **les oreilles ont dû lui/te ~** his/your ears must have been burning.

cornet [kɔrnɛ] *nm* **1.** [papier] cornet ▪ [contenu] cornet, cornetful ▪ **un ~ de frites** a bag of chips *UK ou* French fries *US* ▪ **mettre sa main en ~** to cup one's hand to one's ear **2.** *Suisse* [sac en papier] paper bag ▪ [sac en plastique] plastic bag **3.** CULIN : **~ de glace** [gaufrette] cone ; [gaufrette et glace] ice cream cone, cornet *UK* **4.** [gobelet] : **~ à dés** dice cup **5.** MUS [d'un orgue] cornet stop ▪ [instrument] : **~ (à pistons)** cornet **6.** ACOUST : **~ acoustique** ear trumpet.

cornette [kɔrnɛt] *nf* [de religieuse] cornet.
◆ **cornettes** *nfpl Suisse cone-shaped Swiss pasta.*

corniaud [kɔrnjo] *nm* **1.** [chien] mongrel **2.** *fam* [imbécile] nitwit, nincompoop.

corniche [kɔrniʃ] *nf* **1.** GÉOGR [roche] ledge ▪ [neige] cornice **2.** [route] corniche (road) **3.** ARCHIT cornice.

cornichon [kɔrniʃɔ̃] *nm* **1.** [légume] gherkin ▪ [condiment] (pickled) gherkin **2.** *fam* [imbécile] nitwit, nincompoop.

cornouaillais, e [kɔrnwajɛ, ɛz] *adj* **1.** [de la Cornouaille] from Cornouaille **2.** [de la Cornouailles] Cornish.
◆ **Cornouaillais, e** *nm, f* Cornishman (*f* Cornishwoman).
◆ **cornouaillais** *nm* LING Cornish.

Cornouailles [kɔrnwaj] *npr f* : **(la) ~** Cornwall.

cornu, e [kɔrny] *adj* horned.
◆ **cornue** *nf* retort.

Corogne [kɔrɔɲ] *npr* : **La ~** La Coruña.

corollaire [kɔrɔlɛr] *nm* [conséquence] consequence ▪ LOGIQUE corollary ▪ **cela a pour ~ une inflation endémique** a consequence of this is endemic inflation, this results in endemic inflation.

corolle [kɔrɔl] *nf* corolla.

coron [kɔrɔ̃] *nm* [quartier] mining village ▪ [maison] miner's cottage.

coronaire [kɔrɔnɛr] <> *adj* coronary.
<> *nf* coronary artery.

coronarien, enne [kɔrɔnarjɛ̃, ɛn] *adj* coronary.

corporatif, ive [kɔrpɔratif, iv] *adj* [institution, système] corporative ▪ [image, esprit] corporate.

corporation [kɔrpɔrasjɔ̃] *nf* [groupe professionnel] corporate body ▪ **dans notre ~** in our profession.

corporatisme [kɔrpɔratism] *nm* **1.** POLIT corporatism **2.** *péj* [esprit de caste] professional protectionism.

corporatiste [kɔrpɔratist] *adj* & *nmf* corporatist.

corporel, elle [kɔrpɔrɛl] *adj* **1.** [douleur] physical ▪ [fonction] bodily ▪ [châtiment] corporal ▪ [hygiène] personal ▪ **soins ~s** care of *ou* caring for one's body **2.** PHILOS endowed with a (physical) body.

corps [kɔr] *nm* **1.** PHYSIOL body ▪ **tremblant de tout son ~** trembling all over ▪ **nationaliser? il faudra me passer sur le ~!** *fig* & *hum* nationalize? (it'll be) over my dead body! ▪ **elle te passerait sur le ~ pour obtenir le poste** *fig* she'd trample you underfoot to get the job ▶ **faire ~ avec** to be at *ou* as one with ▪ **près du ~** [vêtement] close-fitting, figure-hugging
2. [cadavre] body ▪ **porter un ~ en terre** to lay a body to rest
3. [élément, substance] body ▪ **~ simple/composé** simple/compound body ▪ **~ céleste** celestial *ou* heavenly body ▪ **~ étranger** foreign body ▪ **~ gras** fatty substance ▪ **~ noir** black body
4. [groupe, communauté] : **le ~ diplomatique** the diplomatic corps ▪ **le ~ médical** the medical profession ▪ **le ~ professoral** the teaching profession *(excluding primary school teachers)* ▪ **le ~ professoral de l'université** the teaching staff of the university, the Faculty *US* ▪ **le ~ électoral** the electorate, the body of voters ▪ **le ~ enseignant** the teaching profession ▪ **le ~ exécutif** the executive ▪ **~ législatif** legislative body ▪ **~ politique** body politic ▪ **un ~ d'état** *ou* **de métier** a building trade ▪ **le ~ de ballet** DANSE the corps de ballet ▪ **~ constitué** constituent body ▪ **grand ~ de l'État** *senior civil servants recruited through the École nationale d'administration*
5. MIL : **~ d'armée** army corps ▪ **~ de cavalerie** cavalry brigade ▪ **~ expéditionnaire** task force ▪ **~ de garde** [soldats] guards ; [local] guardroom ▪ **plaisanteries de ~ de garde** barrack-room jokes ▪ **~ de troupes** unit of troops
6. [partie principale - d'un texte] body ; [- d'une machine] main part ; [- d'un cylindre] barrel ▪ **~ de bâtiment** main body of a building ▪ **~ de logis** main building ▪ [majorité] bulk, greater part
7. [ensemble - de lois, de textes] body, corpus ; [- de preuves] body ▪ **le ~ du délit** corpus delicti
8. [consistance - d'un tissu, d'un arôme] body ▪ **donner ~ à une idée/un plan** to give substance to an idea/a scheme ▪ **prendre ~** [sauce] to thicken ; [projet] to take shape
9. ANAT : **~ caverneux** erectile tissue *(of the penis)* ▪ **~ vitré** vitreous body
10. RELIG : **le ~ mystique du Christ** the Body of Christ.
◆ **à corps perdu** *loc adv* with all one's might ▪ **se jeter** *ou* **se lancer à ~ perdu dans une aventure/entreprise** to throw o.s. headlong into an affair/a task.
◆ **à mon corps défendant, à son corps défendant** *etc loc adv* reluctantly.
◆ **corps et âme** *loc adv* body and soul.
◆ **corps et biens** *loc adv* NAUT : **perdu ~ et biens** lost with all hands ▪ **il s'est perdu ~ et biens** *fig* he's disappeared without trace.

corps à corps [kɔrakɔr] <> *nm pr* hand-to-hand combat *ou* fight ▪ *fig* hard struggle.
<> *loc adv* [lutter] hand to hand.

corps-mort [kɔrmɔr] (*pl* **corps-morts**) *nm* moorings, (mooring) buoys.

corpulence [kɔrpylɑ̃s] *nf* **1.** [volume corporel] build **2.** [obésité] stoutness, corpulence ■ **un monsieur d'une certaine ~** *euphém* a rather portly gentleman, a gentleman of ample girth.

corpulent, e [kɔrpylɑ̃, ɑ̃t] *adj* stout, corpulent, portly.

corpus [kɔrpys] *nm* **1.** [recueil] corpus, collection **2.** LING corpus.

corpusculaire [kɔrpyskylɛr] *adj* corpuscular.

corpuscule [kɔrpyskyl] *nm* ANAT & PHYS corpuscle.

corral, als [kɔral] *nm* corral.

correct, e [kɔrɛkt] *adj* **1.** [sans fautes - calcul, description] correct, accurate ; [- déroulement] correct, proper **2.** [tenue] proper, correct, decent **3.** [courtois] courteous, polite ■ **tu n'as pas été très ~ en partant sans prévenir** it was rather ill-mannered *ou* impolite of you to leave without warning **4.** [honnête - somme, offre] acceptable, fair **5.** [peu remarquable - repas, soirée] decent, OK.

correctement [kɔrɛktəmɑ̃] *adv* **1.** [sans fautes] correctly, accurately **2.** [selon la décence, la courtoisie] properly, decently **3.** [de façon peu remarquable] reasonably well.

correcteur, trice [kɔrɛktœr, tris] ◇ *adj* corrective.
◇ *nm, f* **1.** ÉDUC & UNIV examiner **2.** IMPR proofreader.
◆ **correcteur** *nm* **1.** [dispositif] corrector ■ **~ orthographique** *ou* **d'orthographe** spell checker ■ **~ grammatical** grammar checker **2.** [liquide] : **~ liquide** correction fluid.

correctif, ive [kɔrɛktif, iv] *adj* corrective.
◆ **correctif** *nm* **1.** [rectification] qualifying statement, corrective ■ **je voudrais apporter un ~ à ce qu'a dit mon collègue** I'd like to qualify what my colleague said **2.** [atténuation] toning down ■ **apporter un ~ à des mesures** to soften measures.

correction [kɔrɛksjɔ̃] *nf* **1.** [rectificatif] correction ■ **apporter une ~ à une déclaration** [mise au point] to qualify a statement ; [atténuation] to tone down a statement ‖ [action de rectifier] correction, correcting ■ **la ~ des troubles de la vue** correcting eye defects **2.** ÉDUC marking *UK*, grading *US* **3.** IMPR : **la ~** [lieu] the proofreading department ; [personnel] proofreaders, the proofreading department ◐ **~ d'auteur** author's corrections *ou* emendations ■ **~ d'épreuves** proofreading **4.** [punition] beating **5.** [conformité] accuracy **6.** [comportement] correctness, propriety.

correctionnel, elle [kɔrɛksjɔnɛl] *adj* : **tribunal ~** ≃ magistrate's *UK ou* criminal *US* court.
◆ **correctionnelle** *nf* : **la ~le** ≃ magistrate's *UK ou* criminal *US* court ■ **passer en ~le** to go before a magistrate *UK ou* judge.

Corrège [kɔrɛʒ] *npr m* : **le ~** Correggio.

corrélat [kɔrela] *nm* correlate.

corrélatif, ive [kɔrelatif, iv] *adj* LING & LOGIQUE correlative.
◆ **corrélatif** *nm* LING correlative.

corrélation [kɔrelasjɔ̃] *nf* **1.** [rapport] correlation ■ **il y a (une) ~ entre A et B** A and B are correlated ■ **il n'y a aucune ~ entre les deux** the two are unrelated ■ **mettre en ~** to correlate **2.** MATH correlation.

corrélativement [kɔrelativmɑ̃] *adv* correlatively.

correspondance [kɔrɛspɔ̃dɑ̃s] *nf* **1.** [lettres] post *UK*, mail *US*, correspondence *sout* ■ [échange de lettres] correspondence ■ **~ commerciale** business correspondence ■ **être en ~ avec** [par lettre] to correspond with ■ **cours par ~** correspondence courses **2.** PRESSE correspondence **3.** TRANSP connection ■ [train, bus] connection ■ [vol] connecting flight ■ **la ~ est au bout du quai** change trains at the end of the platform ■ **la ~ est assurée entre les aérogares** a shuttle service is provided between the air terminals **4.** [similitude] conformity ■ [rapport] correspondence **5.** MATH correspondence.

correspondant, e [kɔrɛspɔ̃dɑ̃, ɑ̃t] ◇ *adj* **1.** [qui s'y rapporte] corresponding, relevant ■ **une commande et la facture ~e** an order and the corresponding invoice *ou* the invoice that goes with it **2.** *sout* [qui écrit] corresponding.
◇ *nm, f* **1.** TÉLÉCOM *person one is calling* ■ **votre ~ est en ligne** you're through ■ **nous recherchons votre ~** we're trying to connect you *ou* put you through **2.** [épistolaire] correspondent ■ ÉDUC penfriend *UK*, pen pal **3.** [avec qui l'on traite] correspondent ■ **mon ~ était Butier** Butier was the person I was dealing with **4.** PRESSE : **~ (de presse)** (press) correspondent ■ **~ permanent/à l'étranger** permanent/foreign correspondent ■ **~ de guerre** war correspondent **5.** ÉDUC guardian *(of a boarder)*.

correspondre [75] [kɔrɛspɔ̃dr] *vi* [par lettre] to correspond *sout*, to write (letters to one another) ■ [par téléphone] to be in touch by telephone ■ **~ avec qqn** [par lettre] to correspond with sb *sout*, to write to sb ; [par téléphone] to stay in touch with sb ■ **l'entreprise correspond avec l'Allemagne** the firm has contacts in Germany.
◆ **correspondre à** *v+prép* **1.** [équivaloir à] to be equivalent to **2.** [être conforme à - désir] to correspond to ; [- vérité] to correspond to, to tally with ; [- besoin] to meet **3.** [être lié à] to correspond to.
◆ **se correspondre** *vp (emploi réciproque)* **1.** [communiquer - salles] to communicate, to connect **2.** [être en relation - idées, mots] to correspond.

corrida [kɔrida] *nf* **1.** [de taureaux] bullfight **2.** *fam* [agitation] carry-on *UK*, to-do.

corridor [kɔridɔr] *nm* **1.** [d'un bâtiment] corridor, passage **2.** [territoire] corridor.

corrigé [kɔriʒe] *nm* correct version ■ **faire un ~ de qqch** to give the correct version of sthg ■ **un ~ du problème de physique** a model answer to the physics problem.

corriger [17] [kɔriʒe] *vt* **1.** ÉDUC [copie] to mark *UK*, to grade *US* ■ [en cours] to correct, to give the correct version **2.** [rectifier - texte] to correct, to amend ; [- faute] to correct ■ IMPR to proofread **3.** [punir] to punish ■ **cet enfant mérite qu'on le corrige** that child deserves to be punished **4.** [modifier - vice] to cure ; [- mauvaise habitude] to break ; [- posture] to correct ; [- comportement] to improve **5.** [débarrasser] : **~ qqn de** [vice, mauvaise posture] to cure sb of ; [mauvaise habitude] to rid sb of **6.** [adoucir - agressivité] to mitigate ; [- parole dure] to soften **7.** ARM : **~ le tir** to adjust the firing.
◆ **se corriger** ◇ *vp (emploi réfléchi)* **1.** [élève, auteur] to correct one's (own) work ■ [orateur, présentateur] to correct o.s. **2.** [devenir - plus sage] to improve (one's behaviour) ; [- moins immoral] to mend one's ways **3.** [se guérir] : **se ~ de** [avarice, paranoïa] to cure o.s. of ; [mauvaise habitude] to rid o.s. of.
◇ *vp (emploi passif)* [être rectifié] to be put right ■ **la myopie se corrige avec une bonne paire de lunettes** short-sightedness can be corrected with a good pair of glasses.

corrigible [kɔriʒibl] *adj* rectifiable.

corroborer [3] [kɔrɔbɔre] *vt* to corroborate, to confirm.

corrodant, e [kɔrɔdɑ̃, ɑ̃t] *adj* corrosive.

corroder [3] [kɔrɔde] *vt* [métal] to corrode, to eat into *(insép)* ■ [amitié, bonheur] to corrode.
◆ **se corroder** *vpi* to corrode.

corrompre [78] [kɔrɔ̃pr] *vt* **1.** [vicier - denrée] to taint, to spoil ; [- sang] to taint, to rot ; [- air] to taint, to pollute **2.** [pervertir - innocent, enfant] to corrupt **3.** [soudoyer - fonctionnaire] to bribe **4.** *litt* [faire dévier - langue, sens] to distort, to debase **5.** *litt* [troubler - joie, bonheur] to mar, to taint *litt*, to spoil.

corrompu, e [kɔrɔ̃py] *adj* **1.** [en décomposition] rotting **2.** [vil] corrupted **3.** [vénal] venal ■ **des juges ~s** judges amenable to being bribed.

corrosif, ive [kɔrozif, iv] *adj* **1.** [satire, auteur] corrosive, biting, caustic **2.** [acide] corrosive.

corrosion [kɔrozjɔ̃] *nf* CHIM, GÉOL & MÉTALL corrosion.

corrupteur, trice [kɔryptœr, tris] ◇ *adj* corrupting.
◇ *nm, f* **1.** [qui soudoie] briber **2.** *litt* [qui débauche] corrupter.

corruptible [kɔryptibl] *adj* corruptible.

corruption [kɔrypsjɔ̃] *nf* **1.** [vénalité] corruption ▪ [fait de soudoyer] corruption, bribing ▶ **~ de fonctionnaire** bribery and corruption **2.** [avilissement - de la jeunesse, d'un innocent] corruption **3.** [putréfaction - d'un cadavre, d'une substance] corruption, decomposition, putrefaction **4.** *litt* [déviation - d'une langue, de termes] distortion, corruption, debasement *litt* ▪ **la ~ du jugement** distortion of judgement.

corsage [kɔrsaʒ] *nm* [blouse] blouse ▪ [d'une robe] bodice.

corsaire [kɔrsɛr] ◇ *nm* pirate, corsair ▪ **du temps des ~s** when pirates used to roam the high seas.
◇ *adj* : **pantalon ~** breeches.

corse [kɔrs] *adj* Corsican.
◆ **Corse** *nmf* Corsican.
◆ **corse** *nm* LING Corsican.

Corse [kɔrs] *npr f* : **(la) ~** Corsica.

LA CORSE

This administrative region includes the ***départements*** of Haute-Corse and Corse-du-Sud (capital: Ajaccio).

corsé, e [kɔrse] *adj* **1.** [café] full-flavoured ▪ [vin] full-bodied ▪ [mets] spicy ▪ **l'addition était plutôt ~e!** the bill was a bit steep! **2.** [scabreux] racy, spicy **3.** [difficile] : **il était ~, cet examen!** that exam was a real stinker!

corselet [kɔrsəlɛ] *nm* **1.** [d'une armure] corselet, corslet **2.** ENTOM [vêtement] corselet.

corser [3] [kɔrse] *vt* **1.** [compliquer - problème] to aggravate, to make harder to solve ; [- exercice] to complicate **2.** [rendre - plus intéressant] to liven up *(sép)* ; [- plus osé] to make racier **3.** CULIN to make spicier ▪ [boisson] to spike ▪ [vin] to strengthen.
◆ **se corser** *vpi* **1.** [se compliquer] to get complicated ▪ **l'affaire se corse** the plot thickens **2.** [devenir osé] to become spicy **3.** [devenir plus intéressant] to liven up.

corset [kɔrsɛ] *nm* **1.** [sous-vêtement] corset **2.** MÉD : **~ orthopédique** (orthopedic) corset **3.** *fig* [contrainte] straightjacket.

corseter [28] [kɔrsəte] *vt* **1.** [institution, jeunesse] to constrict ▪ **corseté de principes** hemmed about with principles **2.** [vêtement] to fit with a corset.

corsetier, ère [kɔrsətje, ɛr] *nm, f* corsetiere.

corso [kɔrso] *nm* procession of floats ▪ **~ fleuri** procession of flowered floats.

cortège [kɔrtɛʒ] *nm* **1.** [accompagnateurs] cortege ▪ [d'un roi] retinue **2.** [série] series, succession ▪ **un ~ d'échecs** a trail of failures ▪ **la guerre et son ~ de malheurs** the war and its attendant tragedies **3.** [défilé] procession ▪ **un ~ de manifestants** a march (of protesters) ▶ **~ funèbre** funeral cortege *ou* procession ▪ **~ nuptial** bridal procession.

cortex [kɔrtɛks] *nm* cortex.

corticoïde [kɔrtikɔid], **corticostéroïde** [kɔrtikɔsterɔid] *adj* & *nm* corticosteroid.

corticosurrénal, e, aux [kɔrtikɔsyrenal, o] *adj* adrenocortical.
◆ **corticosurrénale** *nf* adrenal cortex.

corticothérapie [kɔrtikɔterapi] *nf* corticotherapy.

cortisone [kɔrtizɔn] *nf* cortisone.

corvéable [kɔrveabl] *adj* & *nmf* HIST liable to the corvée.

corvée [kɔrve] *nf* **1.** [activité pénible] chore ▪ **repasser, quelle ~!** ironing's such a chore *ou* a drag! **2.** [service] duty ▪ MIL fatigue ▪ **être de ~** [soldat] to be on fatigue duty ▪ **on est de ~ de vaisselle** we're on dishwashing duty **3.** HIST corvée.

corvette [kɔrvɛt] *nf* corvette.

coryphée [kɔrife] *nm* ANTIQ coryphaeus.

coryza [kɔriza] *nm* coryza, head cold.

cosaque [kɔzak] *nm* cossack.

Cosette [kozɛt] *npr the persecuted girl in Hugo's 'les Misérables' who is saved by Jean Valjean. A symbol of innocence and vulnerability.*

cosignataire [kɔsiɲatɛr] *nmf* cosignatory.

cosigner [3] [kɔsiɲe] *vt* to cosign.

cosinus [kɔsinys] *nm* cosine.

cosmétique [kɔsmetik] *adj* & *nm* cosmetic.

cosmétologie [kɔsmetɔlɔʒi] *nf* cosmetology.

cosmique [kɔsmik] *adj* ASTRON cosmic.

cosmogonie [kɔsmɔgɔni] *nf* cosmogony.

cosmographie [kɔsmɔgrafi] *nf* cosmography.

cosmologie [kɔsmɔlɔʒi] *nf* cosmology.

cosmonaute [kɔsmɔnot] *nmf* cosmonaut.

cosmopolite [kɔsmɔpɔlit] ◇ *adj* **1.** [ville, foule] cosmopolitan, multi-ethnic **2.** [personne] cosmopolitan, international **3.** BOT & ZOOL ubiquitous.
◇ *nmf* cosmopolitan person.

cosmopolitisme [kɔsmɔpɔlitism] *nm* **1.** [d'une personne] cosmopolitanism, internationalism **2.** [d'un lieu] cosmopolitan air.

cosmos [kɔsmos] *nm* [univers] cosmos ▪ [espace] space, outer-space.

cossard, e[△] [kɔsar, ard] ◇ *adj* lazy.
◇ *nm, f* lazybones.

cosse [kɔs] *nf* BOT pod, husk.

cossu, e [kɔsy] *adj* [famille] affluent, well-off, wealthy ▪ [quartier] affluent, moneyed ▪ [maison, pièce] luxurious.

costal, e, aux [kɔstal, o] *adj* costal, rib *(modif)*.

costard [kɔstar] *nm fam* suit.

Costa Rica [kɔstarika] *npr m* : **le ~** Costa Rica ▪ **au ~** in Costa Rica.

costaud, e [kɔsto, od] *fam* ◇ *adj* **1.** [personne] hefty, beefy ▪ **elle est ~** *ou* **~e** she's pretty hefty ▪ **un type ~** a great hulk of a bloke *UK ou* guy *US* **2.** [meuble, arbre, tissu] strong, tough, resilient **3.** [problème] tough **4.** [alcool] strong, robust.
◇ *nm, f* beefy bloke *UK ou* fellow (*f* hefty lass).
◆ **costaud** *nm fam* : **c'est du ~** it's solid stuff.

costume [kɔstym] *nm* **1.** [complet] suit **2.** [tenue] costume ▪ **en ~ de cérémonie** in ceremonial costume *ou* dress ▶ **en ~ d'Adam/d'Ève** in his/her birthday suit ▪ **~ de bain** bathing costume *UK ou* suit **3.** HIST & THÉÂTRE costume.

costumé, e [kɔstyme] *adj* : **des enfants ~s** children in fancy dress ▪ **bal ~** fancy-dress ball.

costumier, ère [kɔstymje, ɛr] *nm, f* **1.** [vendeur, loueur] costumier, costumer **2.** THÉÂTRE wardrobe master (*f* mistress).

cosy [kɔzi] ◇ *adj inv* cosy.
◇ *nm vieilli bed with built-in shelves running along the headboard and down one side.*

cotation [kɔtasjɔ̃] *nf* BOURSE quotation.

cote [kɔt] *nf* **1.** BOURSE [valeur] quotation ▪ [liste] share (price) index ▪ **inscrit à la ~** [valeurs] listed **2.** COMM quoted value **3.** [estime] : **~ d'amour** *ou* **de popularité** [d'un homme politique] standing with the electorate *ou* (popular) rating *ou* popularity ; [d'un film, d'une idée] (popular) rating ▪ **avoir la ~** *fam* to be popular **4.** ARCHIT, CONSTR & TRAV PUB measurement **5.** GÉOGR height ▪ **~ d'alerte** *pr* flood *ou* danger level ; *fig* crisis *ou* flash point **6.** [dans une bibliothèque - sur un livre] shelf mark ; [- sur un périodique] serial mark **7.** ADMIN assessment ▪ **~ mobilière** property rate.

coté, e [kɔte] *adj* **1.** [quartier] sought-after ▪ [produit] highly rated ▪ **être bien/mal ~** to have a good/bad reputation **2.** BOURSE listed ▪ **valeurs ~es en Bourse** listed securities.

côte [kot] *nf* **1.** [hauteur] slope, incline ▪ [à monter, à descendre] hill ▪ **monter la ~** to go uphill ▪ **descendre la ~** to go downhill ▪ **en haut de la ~** on the top of the hill **2.** [rivage] coast ▪ [vu

d'avion, sur une carte] coastline **3.** ANAT rib ▪ **se tenir les ~s (de rire)** *fam* to be in stitches ▪ **caresser** *OU* **chatouiller les ~s à qqn** *fam* to give sb a good hiding **4.** [de porc, d'agneau, de veau] chop ▪ [de bœuf] rib **5.** ARCHIT, BOT & TEXT rib ▪ **point de ~s** ribbing stitch **6.** NAUT : **aller à la ~** to hug the coast.
◆ **côte-à-côte** *loc adv* [marcher, s'asseoir] side by side ▪ [travailler, lutter] side by side, shoulder to shoulder.

CÔTE

la Côte d'Amour the Atlantic coast near La Baule ;
la Côte d'Argent the Atlantic coast between the Gironde and Bidassoa estuaries ;
la Côte d'Azur the French Riviera ;
la Côte de Coromandel the Coromandel Coast ;
la Côte d'Émeraude part of the Northern French coast, near Saint-Malo ;
la Côte de Malabar the Malabar Coast ;
la Côte d'Opale the coast between Calais and Dieppe ;
la Côte Vermeille part of the Mediterranean coast, between Collioure and Cerbère.

côté [kote] *nm* **1.** [d'un tissu, d'une médaille] side
2. [d'un jardin, d'une pièce, d'une rue] side ▪ **allons de ce ~-ci** let's go this way ▪ **de ce/de l'autre ~ de la barrière** *pr* & *fig* on this side/on the other side of the fence ◐ **~ cour/jardin** THÉÂTRE stage left/right ▪ **~ sous le vent** NAUT leeward side ▪ **~ du vent** NAUT windward side ▪ **voir de quel ~ vient le vent** *fig* to see which way the wind blows *loc* ▪ **tomber du ~ où ça penche** to follow one's inclinations
3. [du corps] side ▪ **dormir sur le ~** to sleep on one's side
4. [parti] side ▪ **il s'est mis de mon ~** he sided with me ▪ **être aux ~s de qqn** to be by sb's side
5. [aspect] side ▪ **le ~ publicité** the advertizing side (of things) ▪ **~ travail** *fam* on the work front, workwise
6. [facette - d'une personnalité] side, facet ; [- d'une situation] side, aspect ▪ **elle a un ~ naïf** there's a naive side to her ▪ **chaque emploi a ses bons et ses mauvais ~s** every job has its good and bad sides *OU* points ▪ **prendre qqch du bon/mauvais ~** to take sthg in good/bad part ▪ **voir le bon ~ des choses** to look on the bright side ◐ **d'un ~** in a way, in some respects ▪ **d'un ~ ..., d'un autre ~ ...** on the one hand ..., on the other hand ...
◆ **à côté** *loc adv* **1.** [tout près] next door ▪ [pas très loin] nearby ▪ **les voisins d'à ~** the nextdoor neighbours
2. [mal] : **passer** *OU* **tomber à ~** to miss ▪ **elle a répondu à ~** [exprès] she avoided the question ; [involontairement] her answer was not to the point.
◆ **à côté de** *loc prép* **1.** [pas loin] next to ▪ **à ~ de la cible** off target ▪ **passer à ~ de** [chemin, difficulté, porte] to miss ; [occasion] to miss out on ◐ **à ~ de ça** on the other hand ▪ **être à ~ de la plaque** *fam* to have (got hold of) the wrong end of the stick
2. [par rapport à] by *OU* in comparison with ▪ **il fait plutôt avare à ~ de son frère** he seems rather mean compared to his brother.
◆ **de côté** *loc adv* **1.** [regarder] sideways ▪ [sauter, tomber] aside, to one side ▪ **la casquette posée de ~** the cap worn to *OU* on one side
2. [en réserve] aside, to one side ▪ **mettre qqch de ~** to put sthg aside *OU* by ▪ **laisser qqch de ~** to put sthg to one side ▪ **laisser qqn de ~** to leave sb out.
◆ **de mon côté, de son côté** *etc loc adv* **1.** [en ce qui concerne] for my/his *etc* part
2. [de la famille] on my/his *etc* side of the family.
◆ **de tous côtés** *loc adv* **1.** [partout - courir] everywhere, all over the place ; [- chercher] everywhere, high and low
2. [de partout] from all sides.
◆ **du côté de** *loc prép* **1.** [dans l'espace] : **elle est partie du ~ du village** she went towards the village ▪ **du ~ de chez toi** around where you live
2. [parmi] : **cherchons du ~ des auteurs classiques** let's look amongst classical authors.
◆ **d'un côté et de l'autre** *loc adv* here and there.

coteau, x [kɔto] *nm* **1.** [versant] hillside, slope **2.** [colline] hill.
◆ **coteaux** *nmpl* vineyards *(on a hillside)*.

Côte-d'Ivoire [kotdivwar] *npr f* : **(la) ~** the Ivory Coast.

côtelé, e [kotle] *adj* ribbed.

côtelette [kotlɛt] *nf* **1.** [de viande] : **~ d'agneau** lamb chop **2.** *fam* [d'une personne] rib.

coter [3] [kɔte] *vt* **1.** BOURSE to list (on the share index) ▪ **coté en Bourse** ≃ listed on the Stock Exchange **2.** COMM to price, to give a list price for **3.** [évaluer - œuvre d'art] to rate **4.** [dans une bibliothèque - livre] to assign a class *OU* shelf mark to ; [- périodique] to assign a serial mark to **5.** GÉOGR to write in the heights on.

coterie [kɔtri] *nf péj* set, clique *péj*, coterie *litt*.

cothurne [kɔtyrn] *nm* buskin, cothurnus.

côtier, ère [kotje, ɛr] *adj* [région, navigation] coastal ▪ [pêche] inshore ▪ [chemin] coast *(modif)* ▪ **un fleuve ~** a coastal river.

cotillon [kɔtijɔ̃] *nm* **1.** *hum* petticoat **2.** [farandole] cotillion, cotillon.
◆ **cotillons** *nmpl* party novelties.

cotisant, e [kɔtizɑ̃, ɑ̃t] ◇ *adj* contributing.
◇ *nm, f* [à une association] subscriber ▪ [à une assurance, à une fête] contributor.

cotisation [kɔtizasjɔ̃] *nf* [pour une fête] contribution ▪ [à une association] subscription, dues ▪ [pour la protection sociale] contributions ▪ **~ patronale** employer's contribution.

cotiser [3] [kɔtize] *vi* [par choix] to subscribe ▪ [par obligation] to pay one's contributions ▪ **~ à une caisse de retraite** to contribute to a pension fund.
◆ **se cotiser** *vpi* to club together ▪ **le groupe s'est cotisé** everyone in the group contributed.

côtoie *etc v* ▷ **côtoyer**.

côtoiement [kotwamɑ̃] *nm* contact ▪ **le ~ du danger** contact with danger.

coton [kɔtɔ̃] ◇ *nm* **1.** BOT [fibre, culture] cotton ▪ [plante] cotton plant **2.** TEXT [tissu] cotton ▪ [fil] (cotton) thread, piece of cotton **3.** [ouate] : **~ (hydrophile)** cotton wool *UK*, (absorbent) cotton *US* **4.** [tampon de ouate] cotton wool pad *UK*, cotton pad *US*.
◇ *adj fam* tough, tricky.

cotonnade [kɔtɔnad] *nf* cotton fabric, cottonade.

cotonneux, euse [kɔtɔnø, øz] *adj* **1.** BOT downy **2.** *litt* [vaporeux] fleecy **3.** [sourd - bruit] muffled.

cotonnier, ère [kɔtɔnje, ɛr] ◇ *adj* cotton *(modif)*.
◇ *nm, f* cotton spinner.
◆ **cotonnier** *nm* cotton (plant).

Coton-Tige® [kɔtɔ̃tiʒ] (*pl* **Cotons-Tiges**) *nm* cotton bud *UK*, Q-tip® *US*.

côtoyer [13] [kotwaje] *vt* **1.** [fréquenter] to mix with **2.** [être confronté à] to deal with ▪ **elle côtoie le danger tous les jours** she faces danger every day ▪ **ce travail me fait ~ des gens intéressants** I meet some interesting people in this job **3.** [suj: chemin] to skirt *OU* to run alongside ▪ [suj: fleuve] to flow *OU* to run alongside.

cotte [kɔt] *nf* **1.** ARM : **~ d'armes** coat of arms ▪ **~ de mailles** coat of mail **2.** [de travail] overalls *(pl)*, dungarees *(pl)*.

cotylédon [kɔtiledɔ̃] *nm* ANAT & BOT cotyledon.

cou [ku] *nm* **1.** ANAT neck ▪ **un pendentif autour du ~** a pendant round her neck ▪ **sauter** *OU* **se jeter au ~ de qqn** to throw one's arms around sb's neck ▪ **se casser** *OU* **se rompre le ~** *pr* to break one's neck ; *fig* to come a cropper *UK*, to take a tumble ◐ **il y est jusqu'au ~** he's up to his neck in it **2.** ZOOL neck **3.** [vêtement] neck **4.** [d'une bouteille, d'un vase] neck.

couac [kwak] ◇ *nm* [note] false note ▪ **faire un ~** to hit the wrong note.
◇ *onomat* arrk, quack.

couard, e [kwar, ard] *litt* ◇ *adj* cowardly.
◇ *nm, f* coward, poltroon *litt*.

couardise [kwardiz] *nf litt* cowardice.

couchage [kuʃaʒ] *nm* [matériel] bed ▪ [préparatifs] sleeping arrangements ▪ **matériel de ~** bedding.

couchant, e [kuʃɑ̃, ɑ̃t] *adj* ▷ **chien**, ▷ **soleil**.
◆ **couchant** *nm litt* [occident] west.

couche [kuʃ] *nf* **1.** [épaisseur - de neige, terre, maquillage] layer ; [- de peinture] coat ; CULIN layer ▪ **étaler qqch en ~s épaisses/fines** to spread sthg thickly/thinly ● **avoir** *ou* **en tenir une ~** *fam* to be (as) thick as a brick *UK ou* as two short planks *UK*, to be as dumb as they come *US* **2.** ASTRON & GÉOL layer, stratum ▪ **~ d'ozone** ozone layer ▪ **'préserve la ~ d'ozone'** 'ozone-friendly' **3.** SOCIOL level, social stratum **4.** HORT hotbed **5.** [de bébé] nappy *UK*, diaper *US* ▪ **~ jetable** disposable nappy **6.** *litt* [lit] bed.
◆ **couches** *nfpl* [accouchement] confinement ▪ **elle est morte en ~s** she died in childbirth.

couché, e [kuʃe] *adj* **1.** [allongé] lying down ▪ [au lit] in bed ▪ **~!** [à un chien] (lie) down! **2.** [écriture] slanting, sloping **3.** [pli] recumbent.

couche-culotte [kuʃkylɔt] (*pl* **couches-culottes**) *nf* disposable nappy *UK ou* diaper *US*.

coucher¹ [kuʃe] *nm* **1.** [action] going to bed ▪ **le ~ du roi** the king's going-to-bed ceremony **2.** [moment] bedtime ● **~ de soleil** sunset ▪ **au ~ du soleil** at sunset, at sundown *US*.

coucher² [3] [kuʃe] ◇ *vt* **1.** [mettre au lit] to put to bed ▪ [allonger] to lay down *(sép)* ▪ **~ qqn sur le carreau** *fam* to knock sb down, to lay sb out **2.** [héberger] to put up *(sép)*, to accommodate **3.** [poser - par terre] to lay down *(sép)* ▪ **~ une bouteille/moto** to lay a bottle/motorbike on its side ▪ **la pluie a couché les herbes** the rain flattened the grasses ▪ **le vent coucha le bateau** the wind made the boat keel over *ou* keeled the boat over ▪ **~ un fusil en joue** ARM to aim a gun **4.** *sout* [écrire] to set down (in writing) *ou* on paper ▪ **~ ses pensées sur le papier** to write down one's thoughts, to commit one's thoughts to writing *sout* ▪ **~ qqn sur son testament** to name sb in one's will.
◇ *vi* **1.** [aller dormir] to go to bed ▪ **cela va te faire ~ tard** that will keep you up late **2.** [dormir] to sleep ▪ **on couchera à l'hôtel** [une nuit] we'll spend the night *ou* we'll sleep in a hotel ; [plusieurs nuits] we'll stay in a hotel ▪ **~ à la belle étoile** to sleep out in the open ▪ **~ sous les ponts** to sleep rough **3.** △ [sexuellement] to sleep around.
◆ **coucher avec** *v+prép fam* to go to bed *ou* to sleep with.
◆ **se coucher** *vpi* **1.** [dans un lit] to go to bed ▪ **je vous empêche de vous ~?** am I keeping you up? ● **va te ~!** *fam* get lost *ou* knotted *UK* **2.** [s'allonger] to lie down ▪ **se ~ en chien de fusil** to lie curled up *ou* in the foetal position ▪ **se ~ à plat ventre** to lie face down **3.** [soleil, lune] to set, to go down **4.** NAUT to keel over.

coucherie [kuʃri] *nf fam* sleeping around.

couche-tard [kuʃtar] *nmf* night owl ▪ **c'est un ~** he's always late to bed, he's a night owl.

couche-tôt [kuʃto] *nmf*: **c'est un ~** he always goes to bed early.

couchette [kuʃɛt] *nf* [d'un train] couchette ▪ [d'un bateau] bunk.

coucheur, euse [kuʃœr, øz] *nm, f fam* **c'est un ~** he sleeps around, he's promiscuous ● **mauvais ~** awkward customer.

couci-couça [kusikusa] *loc adv fam* so-so.

coucou [kuku] ◇ *nm* **1.** ZOOL cuckoo ▪ **(pendule à) ~** cuckoo clock **2.** BOT cowslip **3.** *fam* [avion] crate, heap.
◇ *interj* [cri] hi.

coude [kud] *nm* **1.** ANAT elbow ▪ **~s au corps** elbows in ▪ **jusqu'au ~** up to one's elbow ● **jouer des ~s** *pr* to push and shove, to jostle ; *fig* to manoeuvre ▪ **~ à ~** [marcher, travailler] shoulder to shoulder, side by side ▪ **garder** *ou* **mettre** *ou* **tenir qqch sous le ~** to keep sthg shelved indefinitely, to keep sthg on the back burner ▪ **lever le ~** *fam* to booze ▪ **se serrer** *ou* **se tenir les ~s** to stick together **2.** [d'un vêtement] elbow ▪ [pièce en cuir, en tissu] elbow patch **3.** [d'un tuyau] bend, elbow ▪ [d'une route] bend ▪ **le couloir fait un ~** there's a sharp bend in the passage.

coudé, e [kude] *adj* bent, angled.
◆ **coudée** *nf* **1.** *loc* **avoir les ~es franches** to have elbow room **2.** *arch* [mesure] cubit.

cou-de-pied [kudpje] (*pl* **cous-de-pied**) *nm* instep.

couder [3] [kude] *vt* to bend (at an angle).

coudière [kudjɛr] *nf* elbow pad.

coudoie *etc v* ⊳ **coudoyer**.

coudoiement [kudwamɑ̃] *nm* : **le ~ de** mixing with.

coudoyer [13] [kudwaje] *vt* **1.** [fréquenter] to rub shoulders *ou* to mix with **2.** [frôler] to brush past **3.** [suj: réalité, image] to stand side by side with.

coudre [86] [kudr] *vt* **1.** COUT [robe] to make up *(sép)* ▪ [morceaux] to sew *ou* to stitch together *(sép)* ▪ [bouton] to sew on *(sép)* ▪ [semelle] to sew *ou* to stitch on *(sép)* ▪ **cousu (à la) machine** machined ▪ *(en usage absolu)* **j'aime ~** I enjoy sewing ▪ **~ à la main/machine** to sew by hand/machine ● **cousu (à la) main** hand-stitched ▪ **du cousu main** *fam* top-quality stuff ▪ **être (tout) cousu d'or** to be extremely wealthy ▪ **c'est cousu de fil blanc** it's plain for all to see ▪ **mensonge cousu de fil blanc** transparent lie **2.** [plaie] to stitch up *(sép)*, to sew up *(sép)* **3.** [livre] to stitch (together).
◆ **à coudre** *loc adj* sewing.

Coué [kwe] *npr* : **méthode ~** autosuggestion, Couéism.

couenne [kwan] *nf* [de porc] rind.

couette [kwɛt] *nf* **1.** [de cheveux] : **des ~s** bunches **2.** [édredon] duvet, (continental) quilt.

couffin [kufɛ̃] *nm* **1.** [pour bébé] Moses basket, bassinet *US* **2.** [cabas] (straw) basket.

cougouar [kugwar], **couguar** [kug(w)ar] *nm* cougar.

couic [kwik] *onomat* eek.

couille▲ [kuj] *nf* **1.** [testicule] nut△, ball▲, bollock▲ *UK* ● **avoir des ~s (au cul)** to have balls▲ ▪ **casser** *ou* **peler les ~s à qqn** to get on sb's tits△ *UK*, to break sb's balls *US* **2.** [échec, erreur] cock-up△ *UK*, ball-up▲ *US* **3.** [personne] : **une ~ molle** a wimp△.

couillon, onne△ [kujɔ̃, ɔn] ◇ *nm, f* [imbécile] wally△ *UK*, airhead ▪ [dupe] mug.
◇ *adj*△ damned stupid△.

couillonnade△ [kujɔnad] *nf* [histoire] damn stupid thing to say ▪ [action] damn stupid thing to do ▪ [objet] piece of junk ▪ **dire des ~s** to talk rubbish△.

couillonner [3] △ [kujɔne] *vt* to con ▪ **te laisse pas ~** don't let yourself be conned, don't be taken for a sucker ▪ **se faire ~** to be conned.

couinement [kwinmɑ̃] *nm* **1.** [d'une souris] squeak, squeaking ▪ [d'un lièvre, d'un porc] squeal, squealing **2.** [d'un enfant] whine, whining **3.** [d'un frein] squeal, squealing.

couiner [3] [kwine] *vi* **1.** [souris] to squeak ▪ [lièvre, porc] to squeal **2.** [enfant] to whine **3.** [frein] to squeal.

coulage [kulaʒ] *nm* [d'une statue] casting ▪ [d'un métal, de la cire, du verre] pouring.

coulant, e [kulɑ̃, ɑ̃t] *adj* **1.** *fam* [personne] easygoing, lax *péj* ▪ **elle est plus ~e avec toi** she lets you get away with more **2.** [style, prose] free, free-flowing **3.** [fromage] runny.

coulée [kule] *nf* **1.** [de sang, de peinture] streak **2.** [chute] : **~ de lave** lava flow ▪ **~ de neige** snowslide ▪ **~ de boue** mudslide **3.** MÉTALL [injection] casting ▪ [masse] casting.

coulemelle [kulmɛl] *nf* parasol mushroom.

couler [3] [kule] ◇ *vi* **1.** [fleuve, eau] to run, to flow ▪ [larmes] to run down, to flow ▪ **la sueur coulait sur son visage** [abondamment] sweat was pouring down his face ; [goutte à goutte] sweat was trickling down his face ▪ **le vin coulait à flots** wine flowed freely ▪ **le sable/l'argent coule entre ses doigts** sand/money trickles through her fingers ▪ **fais ~ l'eau** turn on the water ▪ **faire ~ un bain** to run a bath ▪ **fais ~ un peu d'eau dessus** pour a little water over it ▪ **avoir le nez qui coule** to have a runny nose ▪ **faire ~ de la salive** *fig* to cause some tongue-wagging, to set the tongues wagging ▪ **faire ~ beaucoup d'encre** *fig* to cause a lot of ink to flow ● **il coulera de l'eau sous**

les ponts avant que... there'll be a lot of water under the bridge before... **2.** [progresser facilement] to flow ▪ **le temps coule** *litt* time slips by ▶ **~ de source** to follow (on naturally) ▪ **cela coule de source** it's obvious ▪ **laisse ~!** *fam* don't bother!, just drop it! **3.** [avoir une fuite - robinet] to leak, to drip **4.** [se liquéfier - fromage, bougie] to run **5.** [sombrer - nageur] to go under ; [- bateau] to go down, to sink ▪ **~ à pic** to sink straight to the bottom ▪ [entreprise, politicien] to sink, to go down.
◇ *vt* **1.** [faire sombrer - bateau] to sink ; [- entreprise, concurrent] to sink, to bring down *(sép)* **2.** *litt* [passer] : **~ des jours heureux** to spend some happy days **3.** [ciment] to pour ▪ [métal] to cast **4.** [fabriquer - statue] to cast **5.** AUTO : **~ une bielle** to run a rod.
◆ **se couler** ◇ *vpi* [se glisser] : **se ~ dans** [lit, foule] to slip into ▪ **se ~ le long de** to slide alongside.
◇ *vpt* : **se la ~ douce** *fam* to have an easy time (of it).

couleur [kulœr] *nf* **1.** [impression visuelle] colour ▪ **de ~ vive** brightly-coloured ▪ **une jolie ~ verte** a pretty shade of green ▪ **je n'ai jamais vu la ~ de son argent** *fig* I've never seen the colour of his money ▶ **~s primaires** *ou* **fondamentales** primary colours ▪ **~s complémentaires** complementary colours ▪ **~ de muraille** stone grey ▪ **on en a vu de toutes les ~s** *fam* we've been through some hard times ▪ **en faire voir à qqn de toutes les ~s** to give sb a hard time
2. [pour les cheveux] tint, colour ▪ **se faire faire une ~** to have one's hair tinted, to have some colour put in one's hair
3. JEUX suit
4. [vivacité] colour ▶ **~ locale** local colour
5. [aspect - général] light, colour ▪ **l'avenir m'apparaissait sous les ~s les plus sombres/sous de belles ~s** the future presented itself (to me) in an unfavourable/favourable light ▪ **quelle sera la ~ politique de votre nouveau journal?** what will be the political colour of your new newspaper?
6. [d'une personne] shade, colour ▪ **changer de ~** to change colour ▪ **passer par toutes les ~s de l'arc-en-ciel** to go (through) all the colours of the rainbow ▮ [carnation] : **la ~ de la peau** skin colour
7. [linge] coloureds
8. HÉRALD & MUS colour.
◆ **couleurs** *nfpl* **1.** [linge] coloureds
2. [peintures] coloured paints
3. [bonne mine] (healthy) glow, colour ▪ **prendre des ~s** to get a tan *ou* a bit of colour in one's cheeks ▪ **avoir des ~s** to look well
4. SPORT [d'une équipe] colours ▪ [d'un jockey, d'un cheval] livery ▪ **elle a défendu les ~s de la France** she defended the French flag
5. HÉRALD colour.
◆ **aux couleurs de** *loc prép* : **aux ~s du parti** in party colours ▪ **aux ~s du propriétaire** [yacht] flying the owner's flag ; [cheval] in the owner's colours.
◆ **de couleur** *loc adj* coloured ▪ **une personne de ~** a coloured person, a nonwhite.
◆ **en couleur** *loc adv* in colour ▪ **tout en ~** in full colour ▶ **haut en ~** very lively *ou* colourful *ou* picturesque.

couleuvre [kulœvr] *nf* : **~ (à collier)** grass snake.

couleuvrine [kulœvrin] *nf* culverin.

coulis [kuli] *nm* **1.** CULIN purée, coulis **2.** [mortier] grout.

coulissant, e [kulisɑ̃, ɑ̃t] *adj* sliding.

coulisse [kulis] *nf* **1.** THÉÂTRE : **la ~, les ~s** the wings ▪ **les ~s du pouvoir** the corridors of power ▶ **dans les ~s, en ~** THÉÂTRE in the wings ; *fig* behind the scenes **2.** [glissière] runner **3.** COUT hem *(through which to pass tape)*.
◆ **à coulisse** *loc adj* sliding.

coulisser [3] [kulise] ◇ *vi* to slide.
◇ *vt* **1.** [volet] to provide with runners **2.** COUT to hem *(in order to run a tape through)*.

couloir [kulwar] *nm* **1.** [d'un bâtiment] corridor, passage ▪ [d'un wagon] corridor ▪ **les ~s du métro** the corridors of the tube *UK ou* subway *US* ▪ **intrigues de ~** backstage manoeuvring ▪ **bruits de ~s** rumours **2.** TRANSP : **~ (de circulation)** lane ▪ **~ aérien** air traffic lane **3.** [entre des régions, des pays] corridor **4.** GÉOGR gully, couloir *spéc* ▪ **~ d'avalanche** avalanche corridor **5.** [d'un appareil de projection] track **6.** SPORT lane ▪ TENNIS tramlines, alley *US*.

coulommiers [kulɔmje] *nm* Coulommiers cheese.

coulpe [kulp] *nf* : **battre sa ~** to beat one's breast.

coulure [kulyr] *nf* **1.** [traînée] streak **2.** MÉTALL run-out.

country [kuntri] *nm inv & nf inv* Country (and Western) music.

coup [ku] *nm*

> **A.** HEURT, DÉFLAGRATION
> **B.** GESTE, ACTION
> **C.** ACTE OU SITUATION EXCEPTIONNELS
> **D.** FOIS

A. HEURT, DÉFLAGRATION

1. [gén] blow, knock ▪ [avec le poing] punch, blow ▪ [avec le pied] kick ▪ **un ~ violent** a hard knock ▪ **elle a failli mourir sous ses ~s** he thrashed her to within an inch of her life, he nearly battered her to death ▪ **frapper à ~s redoublés** to hit twice as hard ▪ **donner un petit ~ à** *ou* **sur qqch** to tap sthg lightly ▪ **donner un ~ sec sur qqch** to give sthg a (hard *ou* smart) tap ▪ **il frappait sur la porte à grands ~s/à petits ~s** he banged on the door/he knocked gently at the door ▪ **donner un ~ sur la table** [avec le poing] to bang one's fist (down) on the table ▪ **en arriver** *ou* **en venir aux ~s** to come to blows ▪ **j'ai pris un ~ sur la tête** I got a knock *ou* a bang on the head ▪ **prendre des ~s** to get knocked about ▪ **recevoir un ~** to get hit ▪ **rendre ~ pour ~** *pr & fig* to hit back, to give as good as one gets ▶ **~s et blessures** DR grievous bodily harm ▪ **porter un ~ à qqn** *pr & fig* to deal sb a blow ▪ **les grandes surfaces ont porté un (rude) ~ au petit commerce** *fig* small traders have been dealt a (severe) blow by large retail chains ▪ **le ~ a porté** *pr & fig* the blow struck home
2. [attaque, choc] blow, shock ▪ **ça m'a fait un ~** [émotion] it gave me a shock ; [déception] it was a blow ▶ **sale ~ (pour la fanfare)!** *fam* that's a bit of a blow *ou* downer! ▪ **en prendre un ~** *fam* : **trois échecs d'affilée, son moral en a pris un ~** with three successive failures, her morale has taken a bit of a bashing ▪ **avec le krack boursier, l'économie en a pris un ~** the economy has suffered a great deal from the crash ▪ **tenir le ~ : j'ai trop de travail, je ne sais pas si je tiendrai le ~** I've got too much work, I don't know if I'll be able to cope
3. [en boxe] punch, blow ▪ **~ bas** *pr* blow *ou* punch below the belt ; *fig* blow below the belt ▪ **c'est un ~ bas** that's below the belt ▪ **tous les ~s sont permis** *pr & fig* (there are) no holds barred ▪ **compter les ~s** *pr & fig* to keep score
4. ARM shot, blast ▪ **un ~ de revolver** a shot, a gunshot ▪ **le ~ est parti** [revolver] the gun went off ; [fusil] the rifle went off ▪ **tirer un ~ de canon** to fire *ou* to blast a cannon ▶ **(revolver à) six ~s** six-shot gun ▪ **faire ~ double** CHASSE to do a right and left ; *fig* to kill two birds with one stone
5. [bruit - gén] knock ; [- sec] rap ▪ [craquement] snap ▪ **des ~s au carreau** knocking *ou* knocks on the window ▪ **un ~ de gong** a bang on a gong ▮ [heure sonnée] stroke
6. ▲ [éjaculation] : **tirer un** *ou* **son ~** to shoot one's load▲

B. GESTE, ACTION

1. [mouvement d'une partie du corps] : **un ~ de corne** a butt ▪ **un ~ de langue** a lick ▪ **elle nettoyait ses chatons à (grands) ~s de langue** she was licking the kittens clean ▶ **un ~ de bec** *pr* a peck ; *fig* cutting remark ▪ **un ~ de dent** *pr* a bite ; *fig* cutting remark ▪ **~ de griffe** *ou* **patte** *pr* swipe of the paw ; *fig* cutting remark
2. [emploi d'un instrument] : **donner un (petit) ~ de brosse/chiffon à qqch** to give sthg a (quick) brush/wipe ▪ **je vais me donner un ~ de peigne** I'll just comb my hair *ou* give my hair a (quick) comb ▪ **je viens pour un ~ de peigne** [chez le coiffeur] I just want a quick comb through ▪ **passe un ~ d'aspirateur au salon** give the living room a quick vacuum ▪ **passe un ~ d'éponge sur la table** give the table a wipe (with the sponge) ▪ **un ~ de marteau** a blow with a hammer ▪ **il s'est donné un ~ de marteau sur le doigt** he hit his finger with a hammer ▪ **en deux ~s de rame nous pouvons traverser la rivière** we can cross the river in a couple of strokes ▪ **passe un ~ dans la salle de bains** *fam* give the bathroom a going-over ▶ **en donner** *ou* **ficher** *fam* *ou* **mettre** *fam* **un ~** to get down to business ▪ **il a fallu qu'ils en mettent un sacré ~** they really had to pull out the stops
3. [au golf, au billard] stroke ▪ TENNIS shot, stroke ▪ **~ droit** (forehand) drive

4. *fam* [savoir-faire] knack ■ **ah, tu as le ~ pour mettre la pagaille!** you really have a gift *ou* a knack for creating havoc, don't you! ■ **une fois que tu auras pris le ~, ça ira tout seul!** you'll find it's very easy once you get used to it *ou* once you've got the knack!
5. MÉTÉOR : **~ de chaleur** heatwave ■ **~ de mer** heavy swell ■ **~ de vent** gust of wind
6. [effet soudain] wave ■ **j'ai un ~ de cafard** I feel down all of a sudden ■ **j'ai eu un ~ de fatigue** I suddenly felt tired, a wave of tiredness came over me ■ **il a eu un ~ de folie et a acheté une Rolls** he went mad and bought himself a Rolls-Royce ➲ **avoir un ~ de chaleur** to feel the beginnings of sunstroke
7. *fam* [boisson] drink ■ **j'ai le hoquet – bois un ~** I've got (the) hiccups – drink something *ou* have a drink ■ **tu me sers un ~ (à boire)?** could you pour me a drink? ■ **boire un ~ de trop** to have one too many ■ **un ~ de rouge** a glass of red wine
8. [lancer] throw ■ **elle a renversé toutes les boîtes de conserve en un seul ~** she knocked down all the cans in one throw ‖ [aux dés] throw (of the dice) ■ [action - JEUX] move ■ CARTES go ➲ **c'est un ~ pour rien** [essai] it's a trial run ; [échec] it's a failure

C. ACTE OU SITUATION EXCEPTIONNELS
1. *fam* [mauvais tour] trick ■ **il prépare un ~** he's up to something ■ **(faire) un mauvais** *ou* **sale ~ (à qqn)** (to play) a dirty trick (on sb) ■ **je parie que c'est un ~ de Julie!** I bet Julie's behind this! ■ **~ en traître** stab in the back ■ **monter un ~ contre qqn** to set sb up, to frame sb ■ **il nous a encore fait le ~** he's pulled the same (old) trick on us again ■ **faire le ~ de ... à qqn : il a essayé de me faire le ~ de la panne** he tried to pull the old running-out-of-petrol trick on me ■ **ne me fais pas le ~ de ne pas venir!** now don't stand me up, will you! ➲ **~ monté** put-up job, frame-up ■ **faire un ~ en douce : il fait toujours ses ~s en douce** he's always going behind people's backs
2. △ *arg crime* [vol, escroquerie] job
3. *fam* [affaire] : **je suis sur un ~** I'm onto something ■ **je veux l'acheter mais on est plusieurs sur le ~** I want to buy it but there are several people interested ■ **expliquer le ~ à qqn** to explain the situation *ou* set-up to sb ■ **être dans tous les ~s** to have a finger in every pie ■ **rattraper le ~** to sort things out ■ **il a manqué** *ou* **raté son ~** he didn't pull it off ■ **elle a réussi son ~** she pulled it off ■ **c'est un ~ à avoir un accident, ça!** that's the sort of thing that causes accidents! ■ **combien crois-tu que ça va coûter? – oh, c'est un ~ de 3 000 euros** how much do you think it will cost? – oh, about 3,000 euros ‖ [personne - sexuellement] ▲ **c'est un bon ~** he/she's a good lay△
4. [action remarquable, risquée] coup ■ **faire un beau** *ou* **joli ~** to pull a (real) coup ■ **quand il s'agit d'un gros ~, elle met la main à la pâte** when it's something really important, she lends a hand ■ **tenter le ~** to have a go, to give it a try ■ **c'est un ~ à faire** *ou* **tenter** it's worth trying *ou* a try
5. [circonstance marquante] : **marquer le ~** to mark the occasion ■ **un ~ de chance** *ou* **de pot** *fam* *ou* **de bol** *fam* a stroke of luck, a lucky break

D. FOIS
time, go ■ **du premier ~** first time, at the first attempt ■ **au prochain ~, tu vas y arriver** you'll do it next time *ou* at your next go ■ **essaie encore un ~** have another go ■ **ce ~-ci, on s'en va** this time, we're off ■ **pour un ~** *fam* just for (this) once ■ **un bon ~** *fam* : **c'est ça, pleure un bon ~** that's it, have a good cry ■ **vous devriez vous expliquer un bon ~!** you should have it out once and for all! ■ **un grand ~** *fam* [en se mouchant, sur des bougies] : **souffle un grand ~!** blow hard! ■ **respire un grand ~** take a deep breath.

◆ **à coups de** *loc prép* : **démoli à ~s de marteau** smashed to pieces with a hammer ■ **la productivité a été augmentée à ~s de primes spéciales** productivity was increased through *ou* by dint of special bonuses.

◆ **à coup sûr** *loc adv* undoubtedly, certainly, for sure ■ **elle ne s'engage qu'à ~ sûr** she only commits herself when she's certain of the outcome.

◆ **après coup** *loc adv* afterwards, later on ■ **son attitude, après ~, s'expliquait bien** it was easy to explain her attitude afterwards *ou* in retrospect.

◆ **à tous les coups** *loc adv fam* **1.** [chaque fois] every time ■ **ça marche à tous les ~s** it never fails **2.** [sans aucun doute] : **à tous les ~s, il a oublié** he's bound to have forgotten.

◆ **au coup par coup** *loc adv fam* bit by bit ■ **négocier au ~ par ~** to have piecemeal negotiations.

◆ **coup sur coup** *loc adv* one after the other, in quick succession.

◆ **dans le coup** *fam* ◇ *loc adj* : **elle est dans le ~** [complice] she's in on it *ou* involved in it ; [au courant] she knows all about it ; [à la page] she's hip *ou* with it ■ **moi, je ne suis plus dans le ~** [dans l'affaire] count me out *ou* leave me out of it ; [au courant] I'm a bit out of touch *ou* out of it.
◇ *loc adv* : **mettre qqn dans le ~** to let sb in on the act.

◆ **du coup** *loc adv* so, as a result ■ **elle ne pouvait pas venir, du ~ j'ai reporté le dîner** as she couldn't come, I put the dinner off, she couldn't come so I put the dinner off.

◆ **d'un (seul) coup** *loc adv* **1.** [en une seule fois] in one (go), all at once ■ **il a tout bu d'un ~** he drank the whole lot in one go, he downed it in one **2.** [soudainement] all of a sudden ■ **j'ai eu envie de pleurer/de le gifler, ça m'a pris d'un ~** *fam* I got a sudden urge to cry/to slap him.

◆ **pour le coup** *loc adv* : **pour le ~, je ne savais plus quoi faire** at that point, I didn't know what to do next ■ **j'ai aussi failli renverser le lait, c'est pour le ~ qu'il aurait été en colère!** *fam* I nearly spilt the milk as well, he really would have been furious then!

◆ **sous le coup de** *loc prép* : **faire qqch sous le ~ de la colère** to do sthg in anger ■ **sous le ~ de la colère, on dit des choses qu'on regrette après** you often say things in anger which you regret later ■ **il est encore sous le ~ de l'émotion** he still hasn't got over the shock ■ **tomber sous le ~ de qqch** to come within the scope of sthg ■ **tomber sous le ~ de la loi** to be punishable by law.

◆ **sur le coup** *loc adv* **1.** [mourir] instantly **2.** [à ce moment-là] straightaway, there and then ■ **je n'ai pas compris sur le ~** I didn't understand immediately *ou* straightaway.

◆ **sur le coup de** *loc prép* : **sur le ~ de 6 h/de midi** roundabout *ou* around 6 o'clock/midday.

◆ **coup d'aile** *nm* : **tous les moineaux se sont envolés d'un ~ d'aile** all the sparrows took wing suddenly ■ **Paris-Bruxelles en un ~ d'aile** *fig* Paris-Brussels in one short hop.

◆ **coup de balai** *nm* : **donner un ~ de balai** to sweep up ■ **je vais donner un ~ de balai dans la cuisine** I'm going to sweep (out) the kitchen ■ **la cuisine a besoin d'un bon ~ de balai** the kitchen needs a good sweep ■ **le comité aurait besoin d'un bon ~ de balai** *fig* the committee could do with a shake-up.

◆ **coup de barre** *nm fam* : **j'ai le ~ de barre** I feel tired all of a sudden.

◆ **coup de chapeau** *nm* praise ■ **donner un ~ de chapeau à qqn** to praise sb ■ **son livre mérite un ~ de chapeau** his book deserves some recognition.

◆ **coup de cœur** *nm* : **avoir un** *ou* **le ~ de cœur pour qqch** to fall in love with sthg, to be really taken with sthg ■ **voici nos ~s de cœur dans la collection de printemps** here are our favourite spring outfits ■ *(comme adj inv)* **des prix ~ de cœur** special offers.

◆ **coup de coude** *nm* : **donner un ~ de coude à qqn** [en signe] to nudge sb ; [agressivement] to dig one's elbow into sb.

◆ **coup d'éclat** *nm* feat ■ **faire un ~ d'éclat** to pull off a coup.

◆ **coup d'État** *nm* [putsch] coup (d'état).

◆ **coup de feu** *nm* **1.** [tir] shot ■ **tirer un ~ de feu** to fire a shot, to shoot ■ **on a entendu des ~s de feu** we heard shots being fired *ou* gunshots **2.** *fig* **c'est le ~ de feu** there's a sudden rush on.

◆ **coup de fil** = **coup de téléphone**.

◆ **coup de filet** *nm* [poissons] draught, haul ■ [suspects] haul.

◆ **coup de foudre** *nm* **1.** MÉTÉOR flash of lightning **2.** *fig* love at first sight ■ **ça a été le ~ de foudre** it was love at first sight.

◆ **coup de fouet** *nm* : **donner un ~ de fouet à qqn** *pr* to lash *ou* to whip sb ; *fig* to give sb a boost.

◆ **coup fourré** *nm fig* low trick.

◆ **coup franc** *nm* free kick.

◆ **coup de fusil** *nm* **1.** [acte] shot ■ [bruit] shot, gunshot ■ **on entendait des ~s de fusil** you could hear shooting *ou* shots being fired ■ **recevoir un ~ de fusil** to get shot **2.** *fig* **on y mange bien, mais après c'est le ~ de fusil!** it's a good restaurant, but the bill is a bit of a shock!

◆ **coup de grâce** *nm pr* & *fig* coup de grâce, deathblow.

◆ **coup du lapin** *nm* [coup] rabbit punch ▪ [dans un accident de voiture] whiplash *(U)*.

◆ **coup de main** *nm* **1.** [raid] smash-and-grab (attack) ▪ MIL coup de main **2.** [aide] : **donner un ~ de main à qqn** to give *ou* to lend sb a hand **3.** [savoir-faire] : **avoir le ~ de main** to have the knack *ou* the touch.

◆ **coup d'œil** *nm* **1.** [regard] look, glance ▪ **elle s'en rendit compte au premier ~ d'œil** she noticed straight away *ou* immediately *ou* at a glance ▪ **donner** *ou* **jeter un petit ~ d'œil à** to have a quick look *ou* glance at ▪ **d'un ~ d'œil, il embrassa le tableau** he took in the situation at a glance ▶ **avoir le ~ d'œil** to have a good eye ▪ **valoir le ~ d'œil** to be (well) worth seeing **2.** [panorama] view.

◆ **coup de pied** *nm* [d'une personne, d'un cheval] kick ▪ **le ~ de pied de l'âne** *fig* the parting shot ▪ **donner un ~ de pied à qqn/dans qqch** to kick sb/sthg.

◆ **coup de poing** ◇ *nm* punch ▪ **donner un ~ de poing à qqn** to give sb a punch, to punch sb ▪ **faire le ~ de poing** to brawl, to fight.

◇ *adj inv* : **'opération ~ de poing'** 'prices slashed'.

◆ **coup de poker** *nm* (bit of a) gamble ▪ **on peut tenter la chose, mais c'est un ~ de poker** we can try it but it's a bit risky.

◆ **coup de pompe** *nm fam* sudden feeling of exhaustion ▪ **j'ai un ~ de pompe** I suddenly feel completely shattered *UK ou* beat *US*.

◆ **coup de pouce** *nm* bit of help ▪ **donner un ~ de pouce à qqn** to pull (a few) strings for sb ▪ **donner un ~ de pouce à qqch** to give sthg a bit of a boost.

◆ **coup de sang** *nm* **1.** MÉD stroke **2.** *fig* angry outburst ▪ **elle a eu un ~ de sang** she exploded (with rage).

◆ **coup de soleil** *nm* sunburn *(U)* ▪ **prendre** *ou* **attraper un ~ de soleil** to get sunburnt.

◆ **coup du sort** *nm* [favorable] stroke of luck ▪ [défavorable] stroke of bad luck.

◆ **coup de téléphone** *nm* (phone) call ▪ **donner** *ou* **passer un ~ de téléphone** to make a call ▪ **donner** *ou* **passer un ~ de téléphone à qqn** to phone *ou* to call *ou* to ring *UK* sb ▪ **recevoir un ~ de téléphone** to receive *ou* to get a phone call.

◆ **coup de tête** *nm* **1.** [dans une bagarre] head butt ▪ **donner un ~ de tête à qqn** to head-butt sb **2.** SPORT header **3.** *fig* (sudden) impulse ▪ **sur un ~ de tête** on (a sudden) impulse.

◆ **coup de théâtre** *nm* THÉÂTRE coup de théâtre, sudden twist in the action ▪ *fig* sudden turn of events ▪ **et alors, ~ de théâtre, on lui demande de démissionner** and then, out of the blue, he was asked to resign.

◆ **coup de torchon** *nm fam* [bagarre] fist-fight ▪ [nettoyage] clear-out *UK*, cleanup.

◆ **coup de vent** *nm* **1.** [rafale] gust (of wind) **2.** *loc* **en ~ de vent** in a flash *ou* a whirl ▪ **entrer/partir en ~ de vent** to rush in/off ▪ **elle est passée par Lausanne en ~ de vent** she paid a flying visit to Lausanne ▪ **manger en ~ de vent** to grab something to eat.

coupable [kupabl] ◇ *adj* **1.** [fautif] guilty ▪ **prendre un air ~** to look sheepish *ou* guilty **2.** [responsable] guilty, culpable *sout* ▪ DR guilty **3.** *litt* [amour, rêve, pensée] sinful, reprehensible ▪ [action] culpable *sout*.

◇ *nmf* **1.** [élément responsable] culprit **2.** DR guilty party.

coupant, e [kupɑ̃, ɑ̃t] *adj* **1.** [tranchant - ciseaux] sharp ▪ **herbe ~e** grass you can cut yourself on **2.** [caustique - ton, remarque] cutting, biting.

◆ **coupant** *nm* cutting edge.

coup-de-poing [kudpwɛ̃] (*pl* **coups-de-poing**) ◇ *nm* : **~ américain** knuckle-duster.

◇ *adj* [argument, chanson] hard-hitting ▪ [politique] tough and uncompromising.

coupe [kup] *nf* **1.** [action] cutting (out) ▪ [coiffure] : **~ (de cheveux)** cut, haircut ▶ **~ au carré** (square) bob **2.** COUT [forme] cut ▪ [action] cutting ▪ [tissu] length **3.** [dessin] section ▪ **~ transversale** cross-section **4.** [au microscope] section **5.** JEUX [séparation] cut, cutting **6.** [sciage] cutting (down) ▪ [étendue] felling area ▪ [entaille] section ▪ **~ sombre** *pr* thinning out ; *fig* drastic cut ▪ **mettre en ~ réglée** *pr* to fell on a regular basis ; *fig* to bleed *ou* to drain systematically **7.** LING & LITTÉR break, caesura ▪ **~ syllabique** syllable break **8.** [verre, contenu - à boire] glass ; [- à entremets] dish ▪ **~ de glace/fruits** [dessert] ice cream/fruit *(presented in a dish)* ▶ **~ à glace** sundae dish ▪ **la ~ est pleine** the cup is full.

◆ **à la coupe** *loc adj* : **fromage/jambon à la ~** cheese cut/ham sliced at the request of the customer.

◆ **sous la coupe de** *loc prép* **1.** [soumis à] : **être sous la ~ de qqn** to be under sb's thumb ▪ **tomber sous la ~ de qqn** to fall into sb's clutches **2.** JEUX : **jouer sous la ~ de qqn** to lead after sb has cut.

coupé [kupe] *nm* AUTO & DANSE coupé.

coupe-choux [kupʃu] *nm inv fam* **1.** [sabre] sabre **2.** *hum* (cut-throat) razor.

coupe-cigares [kupsigar] *nm inv* cigar cutter.

coupe-circuit [kupsirkɥi] (*pl inv ou pl* **coupe-circuits**) *nm* cutout.

coupe-coupe [kupkup] *nm inv* machete.

coupe-faim [kupfɛ̃] *nm inv* **1.** [gén] snack **2.** MÉD appetite suppressant.

coupe-feu [kupfø] *nm inv* **1.** [espace] firebreak, fire line **2.** [construction] fireguard.

coupe-file [kupfil] (*pl* **coupe-files**) *nm* pass.

coupe-gorge [kupgɔrʒ] *nm inv* [quartier] dangerous area ▪ [bâtiment] death trap.

coupe-légumes [kuplegym] *nm inv* vegetable cutter, vegetable slicer.

coupelle [kupɛl] *nf* **1.** [petite coupe] (small) dish **2.** CHIM cupel.

coupe-ongles [kupɔ̃gl] *nm inv* (pair of) nail clippers.

coupe-papier [kuppapje] (*pl inv ou pl* **coupe-papiers**) *nm* paper knife.

couper [3] [kupe] ◇ *vt* **1.** [entailler - légèrement] to cut ; [- gravement] to slash ▪ **le vent lui coupait le visage** *fig* the wind stung her face ▶ **~ le souffle** *ou* **la respiration à qqn** to take sb's breath away ▪ **beau à ~ le souffle** breathtakingly beautiful ▪ **à ~ au couteau : il y avait un brouillard à ~ au couteau** the fog was so thick you couldn't see your hand in front of your face ▪ **un accent à ~ au couteau** a very strong accent ▪ **un silence à ~ au couteau** a silence you could cut with a knife

2. [membre] to cut off *(sép)* ▪ [tête] to cut off, to chop (off) ▪ **~ la tête** *ou* **le cou à un canard** to chop a duck's head off ▶ **~ bras et jambes à qqn** [surprise] to amaze sb ▪ **ça lui a coupé les jambes** [de fatigue] that's really tired him out

3. [mettre en morceaux - ficelle] to cut ; [- gâteau] to cut up *(sép)* ; [- saucisson] to cut up, to slice (up) ; [- bois] to chop (up) ▪ **~ en tranches** to cut up, to cut into slices, to slice ▪ **~ qqch en tranches fines/épaisses** to slice sthg thinly/thickly, to cut sthg into thin/thick slices ▶ **elle se ferait ~ en morceaux plutôt que de...** she'd rather die than... ▪ **~ la poire en deux** to meet half-way, to come to a compromise ▪ **~ les ponts avec qqn** to break all ties *ou* to break off relations with sb ▪ **~ les cheveux en quatre** to split hairs

4. [tailler - fleurs] to cut ; [- bordure] to cut off *(sép)* ; [- arbre] to cut *ou* to chop down *(sép)*, to fell ▪ **~ les cheveux à qqn** to cut *ou* to trim sb's hair ▪ **se faire ~ les cheveux** to have one's hair cut ▶ **~ le mal à la racine** to strike at the root of the evil

5. COUT [robe] to cut out *(sép)* ▪ [tissu] to cut

6. [écourter - film, texte] to cut ▪ [ôter - remarque, séquence] to cut (out), to edit out *(sép)*

7. [arrêter - crédit] to cut ▪ **~ l'eau** [par accident] to cut off the water ; [volontairement] to turn *ou* to switch off the water ▪ **son père va lui ~ les vivres** his father will stop supporting him *ou* will cut off his means of subsistence

8. [interrompre - relations diplomatiques, conversation] to break off ▪ **~ la parole à qqn** to cut sb short ▪ **~ l'appétit à qqn** to ruin *ou* spoil sb's appetite ▪ **~ qqn** *fam* to interrupt sb ▪ **je vais à la gym à midi, ça (me) coupe la journée** I go to the gym at lunchtime, it helps to break the day up ▶ **~ la chique** *ou* **le sifflet à qqn** *fam* to shut sb up ▪ **~ ses effets à qqn** to take the wind out of sb's sails

9. [barrer - route] to cut off *(sép)* ; [- retraite] to block off *(sép)*, to cut off ▪ **l'arbre nous coupait la route** the tree blocked our path

10. [diviser - surface] to cut ; [- ligne] to cut, to intersect ; [- voie] to cross, to cut across ■ **la voiture nous a coupé la route** the car cut across in front of us ■ **depuis, la famille est coupée en deux** *fig* since then, the family has been split in two ■ **~ qqn de qqch** to cut sb off from sthg ■ **je me sens coupé de tout** I feel cut off from everything *ou* totally isolated
11. [diluer - lait] to add water to, to thin *ou* to water down *(sép)* ■ **coupé d'eau** diluted, watered down ■ **~ du vin** [à l'eau] to water wine down ; [avec d'autres vins] to blend wine
12. CINÉ : **coupez!** cut!
13. TÉLÉCOM to cut off *(sép)*
14. JEUX [partager] to cut ■ [jouer l'atout] to trump
15. SPORT [balle] to slice.
◇ *vi* **1.** [être tranchant] to cut, to be sharp ■ **attention, ça coupe!** careful, it's sharp!
2. [prendre un raccourci] : **~ à travers champs** to cut across country *ou* the fields ■ **~ par une petite route** to cut through by a minor road ■ **~ au plus court** to take the quickest way
3. [interrompre] to cut in ■ **faux, coupa-t-elle** not true, she cut in.
◆ **couper à** *v+prép* : **~ court à qqch** [mettre fin à] to cut sthg short, to curtail sthg ■ **~ à qqch** to get out of sthg ■ **y ~ : on n'y a pas coupé, à son sermon!** sure enough we got a lecture from him! ■ **tu dois y aller, tu ne peux pas y ~!** you've got to go, there's no way you can get out of it!
◆ **se couper** ◇ *vp (emploi réfléchi)* to cut o.s. ■ **se ~ les ongles** to cut *ou* to trim one's nails ■ **se ~ le** *ou* **au front** to cut one's forehead ■ **se ~ les veines** to slit *ou* to slash one's wrists ▶ **se ~ en quatre pour qqn** [ponctuellement] to bend over backwards to help sb ; [continuellement] to devote o.s. utterly to sb.
◇ *vpi* **1.** [lignes, routes] to cut across one another, to intersect
2. *fam* [se contredire] to contradict o.s.

couper-coller [kupekɔle] *vt* & *vi* to cut-and-paste.

couperet [kuprɛ] *nm* **1.** [d'une guillotine] blade, knife **2.** [à viande] cleaver, chopper.

couperose [kuproz] *nf* red blotches (on the face), rosacea *spéc.*

couperosé, e [kuproze] *adj* blotchy and red, affected by rosacea *spéc.*

coupeur, euse [kupœr, øz] *nm, f* **1.** COUT cutter **2.** *loc* **un ~ de cheveux en quatre** a nitpicker.

coupe-vent [kupvɑ̃] *nm inv* **1.** [vêtement] windcheater *UK*, Windbreaker® *US* **2.** TRANSP V-shaped deflector.

couplage [kuplaʒ] *nm* ÉLECTR & MÉCAN coupling.

couple [kupl] *nm* **1.** [d'amoureux, de danseurs] couple ■ [de patineurs, d'animaux] pair ■ **leur ~ ne marche pas très fort** their relationship isn't going too well ■ **ils ont des problèmes de ~** they've got problems in their relationship **2.** MÉCAN & PHYS couple **3.** MATH pair.

couplé [kuple] *nm* [au tiercé] double.

coupler [3] [kuple] *vt* **1.** [mettre deux à deux] to couple together, to pair up *ou* off *(sép)* **2.** ÉLECTR & MÉCAN to couple.

couplet [kuplɛ] *nm* **1.** [strophe] verse ■ [chanson] song **2.** *péj* [discours] tirade ■ **il y allait de son ~ sur la jeunesse d'aujourd'hui** he gave his little set piece on the young people of today.

coupleur [kuplœr] *nm* **1.** ÉLECTR, RAIL & TRANSP coupler **2.** INFORM coupler.

coupole [kupɔl] *nf* ARCHIT dome ■ **la Coupole** [Académie] the Académie française ; [restaurant] *restaurant in Paris famous as a former meeting place for artists.*

coupon [kupɔ̃] *nm* **1.** TEXT remnant **2.** [de papier] coupon **3.** FIN [droit attaché à un titre] coupon **4.** TRANSP : **~ annuel/mensuel** yearly/monthly pass ■ *Belgique* rail *ou* train ticket.

coupon-réponse [kupɔ̃repɔ̃s] (*pl* **coupons-réponse**) *nm* reply coupon.

coupure [kupyr] *nf* **1.** [blessure] cut **2.** [trêve, repos] break **3.** ÉLECTR : **~ (de courant)** power cut, blackout ■ **il y a une ~ de gaz/d'eau** the gas/the water has been cut off **4.** [suppression - dans un texte] deletion **5.** [article] : **~ de journal/presse** newspaper/press cutting **6.** FIN note, bill *US* ■ **grosses ~s** large denominations.

couque [kuk] *nf Belgique* cake.

cour [kur] *nf* **1.** [d'immeuble] courtyard ■ [de ferme] yard, farmyard ■ **avec vue sur (la) ~** looking onto the inside of the building *ou* onto the courtyard ▶ **~ d'honneur** main courtyard ■ **~ de récréation** ÉDUC playground ■ **jouer dans la ~ des grands** *fig* to be up there with the leaders ■ **~ des Miracles** HIST *area in Paris where vagrants had the right of sanctuary* ■ **c'était la ~ des Miracles dans la salle d'attente** *fig* the waiting room was utter bedlam
2. [d'un roi] court ■ *fig* [admirateurs] following, inner circle (of admirers) ■ **être bien/mal en ~** to be in/out of favour
3. DR [magistrats] court ■ **Messieurs, la Cour!** all rise!, be upstanding in court! *UK* ❙ [tribunal] : **~ d'appel** Court of Appeal, appellate court *US* ■ **~ d'assises** ≃ Crown Court *UK* ■ ≃ Circuit court *US* ■ **Cour de cassation** final Court of Appeal ■ **Cour européenne des droits de l'homme** European Court of Human Rights ■ **Cour internationale de justice** International Court of Justice ■ **Haute ~** High Court *(for impeachment of president or ministers)*
4. ADMIN : **Cour des comptes** *the French audit office* ■ ≃ controller and auditor general *UK*, ≃ General Accounting Office *US*
5. *loc* **faire la ~ à qqn** to court sb, to woo sb.

COUR D'ASSISES

This is the court which hears criminal cases. It is made up of a president, two assessors, and a jury of laymen. Normally the court meets every three months in each *département.*

COUR DE CASSATION

The highest court of civil and criminal appeal in France. The court has the power to overturn the decisions of lower courts when it believes the law has been misinterpreted. It does not rehear cases but simply analyses the way the law was applied.

COUR DES COMPTES

A state body that supervises the financial affairs of public bodies and local authorities, and monitors the way public funds are used.

courage [kuraʒ] *nm* **1.** [bravoure] courage, bravery ■ **avec ~** courageously, bravely ■ **je n'ai pas eu le ~ de le lui dire** [mauvaise nouvelle] I didn't have the heart to tell him ■ **avoir le ~ de ses opinions** to have the courage of one's convictions ▶ **prendre son ~ à deux mains** to muster all one's courage **2.** [énergie] will, spirit ■ **travailler avec ~** to work with a will ■ **bon ~!** good luck!, hope it goes well! ■ **~, la journée est bientôt finie** keep it up, the day's nearly over ■ **un whisky pour te donner du ~** a whisky to buck you up ■ **prendre ~** to take heart ■ **perdre ~** to lose heart, to become discouraged ■ **je n'ai pas le ~ d'aller travailler/de le lui dire** I don't feel up to going to work/to telling her.

courageusement [kuraʒøzmɑ̃] *adv* **1.** [se battre, parler] courageously, bravely **2.** [travailler] with a will.

courageux, euse [kuraʒø, øz] *adj* courageous, brave ■ **~ mais pas téméraire** brave but not reckless *ou* foolhardy ■ **je ne me sens pas très ~ aujourd'hui** I don't feel up to much today.

couramment [kuramɑ̃] *adv* **1.** [bien] fluently ■ **elle parle le danois ~** she speaks Danish fluently *ou* fluent Danish **2.** [souvent] commonly ■ **l'expression s'emploie ~** the expression is in common usage ■ **ça se dit ~** it's a common *ou* an everyday expression ■ **cela se fait ~** it's common practice.

courant[1] [kurɑ̃] *nm* **1.** ÉLECTR : **~ (électrique)** (electric) current ■ **branché sur le ~** plugged into the mains ■ **couper le ~** to cut the power off ■ **mettre le ~** to switch the power on ■ **rétablir le ~** to put the power back on ▶ **~ alternatif/continu** alternating/direct current ■ **le ~ passe bien entre nous** we're on the same wavelength ■ **le ~ passe bien entre lui et le public** he comes across well to the public **2.** [dans l'eau] current, stream ■ **il y a trop de ~** the current is too strong ▶ **suivre le ~** *pr* to go with the current ; *fig* to follow the crowd, to go with the tide ■ **nager contre** *ou* **remonter le ~** *pr* to swim against the current ; *fig* to go against the tide **3.** [dans l'air] current ■ **~ (atmosphérique)** airstream, current ■ **~ d'air** draught ■ **il y a des ~s d'air** it's draughty ■ **se déguiser** *OU* **se transformer en ~ d'air** *hum* to vanish into thin air **4.** [tendance] current, trend ■ **les ~s de l'opinion** currents *OU* trends in public opinion ■ **un ~ d'optimisme** a wave of optimism **5.** [masse mouvante] movement, shift ■ **les ~s de population** shifts of population.

◆ **au courant** ◇ *loc adj* [informé] : **personne/journal bien au ~** well-informed person/paper ■ **il est parti mais les gens au ~ n'ont rien dit** he left but those who knew about it *OU* who were in the know kept quiet ■ **je ne suis pas au ~** I don't know anything about it.
◇ *loc adv* : **se tenir au ~** to keep abreast of things *OU* o.s. informed ■ **tiens-moi au ~** let me know how things are going ■ **mettre qqn au ~** to let sb know, to fill sb in ■ **tenir qqn au ~** to keep sb posted *OU* informed.

◆ **au courant de** *loc prép* **1.** [informé de] : **au ~ des nouvelles méthodes** well up on new methods ■ **tu es au ~ de la panne?** do you know about the breakdown? **2.** *litt* [au fil de] : **écrire qqch au ~ de la plume** [rapidement] to dash sthg off ; [sans effort] to pen sthg with ease.

◆ **dans le courant de** *loc prép* in *OU* during the course of.

courant[2], e [kurɑ̃, ɑ̃t] *adj* **1.** [quotidien - vie, dépenses] everyday ; [- travail] everyday, routine ■ **en anglais ~** in everyday *OU* conversational English **2.** [commun - problème, maladie] common ; [- incident] everyday **3.** [normal - modèle, pointure] standard **4.** [actuel] current ■ **votre lettre du 17 ~** your letter of the 17th instant *UK OU* the 17th of this month.

◆ **courante** *nf fam* [diarrhée] : **la ~e** the runs.

courbatu, e [kurbaty] *adj* aching (and stiff).

courbature [kurbatyr] *nf* ache ■ **plein de ~s** aching (and stiff) all over.

courbaturé, e [kurbatyre] *adj* aching (and stiff).

courbe [kurb] ◇ *adj* curving, rounded, curved.
◇ *nf* **1.** GÉOM curve, curved *OU* rounded line ■ **la route fait des ~s** the road curves **2.** [sur un graphique] curve ■ **tracer la ~ de** to plot the curve of, to graph **3.** GÉOGR : **~ de niveau** contour line.

courber [3] [kurbe] ◇ *vt* **1.** [plier] to bend **2.** [personne] : **~ la tête** to bow *OU* to bend one's head ■ **~ le front sur qqch** to bend over sthg ■ **marcher le dos courbé** to walk with a stoop ▶ **~ l'échine** *OU* **le dos devant qqn** to give in *OU* to submit to sb.
◇ *vi litt* **~ sous le poids** to be weighed down by a burden.

◆ **se courber** *vpi* **1.** [ployer - arbre, barre] to bend **2.** [personne - gén] to bend down ; [- de vieillesse] to stoop ; [- pour saluer] to bow (down) ; [- par soumission] : **se ~ devant qqch** to bow before sthg, to submit to sthg.

courbette [kurbɛt] *nf* **1.** [salut] low bow ■ **faire des ~s à qqn** *péj* to kowtow to sb, to bow and scrape to sb **2.** [d'un cheval] curvet.

courbure [kurbyr] *nf* curved line *OU* shape, curvature *sout.*

courette [kurɛt] *nf* [d'un immeuble] small yard *OU* courtyard, close ■ [d'une ferme] small yard *OU* farmyard.

coureur, euse [kurœr, øz] ◇ *adj* **1.** [cheval] racing **2.** *fam* [séducteur] : **il est très ~** he's a womanizer *OU* philanderer ■ **elle est très coureuse** she's always chasing men.
◇ *nm, f* **1.** SPORT runner ■ [sauteur de haies] hurdler ■ **~ de fond/demi-fond** long-distance/middle-distance runner ■ **~ cycliste** (racing) cyclist ■ **~ automobile** racing driver ■ **~ motocycliste** motorcycle *OU* motorbike driver **2.** *fam* [séducteur] womanizer (*f* maneater) ■ **~ de dot** dowry-hunter ■ **~ de jupons** womanizer, philanderer **3.** [amateur] : **un ~ de fêtes/musées** inveterate party-goer/museum-goer **4.** *Québec* **~ des bois** fur trader.

courge [kurʒ] *nf* **1.** CULIN (vegetable) marrow *UK*, squash *US* ■ [plante, fruit] gourd, squash **2.** *fam* [imbécile] idiot, dope, twit.

courgette [kurʒɛt] *nf* courgette *UK*, zucchini *US*.

courir [45] [kurir] ◇ *vi* **1.** [gén] to run ■ [sportif, lévrier] to run, to race ■ **entrer/sortir/traverser en courant** to run in/out/across ■ **monter/descendre l'escalier en courant** to run up/down the stairs ■ **partir en courant** to run off ■ **j'ai couru à fond de train** *OU* **à toutes jambes** I ran as fast as my legs could carry me ■ **~ tête baissée (vers)** to rush headlong (towards) ■ **~ après qqn** to run after sb ■ **elle a fait ~ son cheval dans le Grand Prix** she entered her horse in the Grand Prix ▶ **~ comme un lièvre** to run like a hare
2. [se déplacer - nuée] to race along *OU* by ; [- eau] to rush, to run ■ **ses doigts couraient sur les touches** his fingers ran up and down the keyboard ■ **laisser ~ sa plume** to let one's pen run freely
3. [se précipiter] to rush, to run ■ **j'y cours** I'll rush over ■ **j'ai couru toute la journée** I've been in a rush *OU* I've been run off my feet all day ■ **qu'est-ce qui le fait ~?** *fig* what drives him? ■ **la pièce qui fait ~ tout Paris** the play all Paris is flocking to see
4. [se propager - rumeur, idée] : **un bruit qui court** a rumour that's going round ■ **le bruit court que...** rumour has it that...
5. [temps] : **l'année qui court** the current year ■ **le contrat court jusqu'au 25** the contract runs until the 25th ■ **par les temps qui courent** nowadays
6. [s'étendre] : **~ le long de** [rivière, voie ferrée] to run *OU* to stretch along
7. FIN [intérêt] to accrue ■ **laisser ~ des intérêts** to allow interest to accrue
8. *loc* **tu peux (toujours) ~!** *fam* no way! ■ **l'épouser? il peut toujours ~!** *fam* marry her? he doesn't have a hope in hell! ■ **laisser ~** *fam* [abandonner] to give up ■ **laisse ~!** drop it!, forget it! ■ **~ sur le système**[△] *OU* **le haricot**[△] **à qqn** [l'énerver] to get up sb's nose *UK OU* on sb's nerves ■ **il commence à me ~!** *fam* he's beginning to get up my nose *UK OU* to tick me off *US*.
◇ *vt* **1.** SPORT [course] to compete in, to run
2. [sillonner - ville, mers] to roam, to rove ▶ **cela court les rues** [idée, style] it's run-of-the-mill ■ **quelqu'un comme ça, ça ne court pas les rues** people like that are hard to come by
3. [fréquenter] to go round ■ **elle court les musées** she's an inveterate museum-goer ■ **~ les filles/les garçons** to chase girls/boys ▶ **~ le jupon** *OU* **le cotillon** to be a womaniser ■ **~ la gueuse** *OU* **le guilledou** *OU* **la prétentaine** *hum & vieilli* to go wenching
4. [rechercher - honneurs, poste] to seek ■ [encourir] : **~ un risque** to run a risk ■ **faire ~ un risque** *OU* **danger à qqn** to put sb at risk ‖ [tenter] : **~ sa chance** to try one's luck
5. CHASSE to hunt ■ **il ne faut pas ~ deux lièvres à la fois** *prov* if you run after two hares you will catch neither *prov.*

◆ **courir à** *v+prép* [faillite, désastre] to be heading for ■ **elle court à sa perte** she's on the road to ruin.

◆ **courir après** *v+prép* [rechercher] : **~ après qqn** *fam* to bug sb ■ **~ après un poste** to be after a job ■ **~ après la célébrité** to strive for recognition ■ **il court toujours après le temps** he's always short of time ■ **elle ne court pas après l'argent** she's not after money.

◆ **courir sur** *v+prép* [approcher de] : **~ sur ses 60 ans** to be approaching 60.

◆ **se courir** *vp (emploi passif)* : **le tiercé se court à Enghien aujourd'hui** today's race is being run at Enghien.

couronne [kurɔn] *nf* **1.** [coiffure - d'un souverain] crown ; [- d'un pair] coronet ■ **~ de lauriers** crown of laurels, laurel wreath ■ **~ d'épines** crown of thorns ■ **~ royale** royal crown ▶ **~ mortuaire** (funeral) wreath ■ **porter la ~** *pr* to wear the crown
2. HIST & POLIT : **la Couronne d'Angleterre/de Belgique** the English/Belgian Crown ■ **prétendre à la ~** to lay claim to the throne
3. [cercle] crown, circle ■ **une ~ de nuages entourait la montagne** the mountain was surrounded by a ring of clouds
4. [périphérie] : **la petite ~** *the suburbs adjacent to Paris* ■ **la grande ~** *the outerlying Parisian suburbs*
5. [pain] ring *OU* ring-shaped loaf
6. [prothèse dentaire] crown
7. ARCHIT & ASTRON corona
8. [monnaie] crown ■ **~ danoise/norvégienne** krone ■ **~ suédoise** krona.

◆ **en couronne** *loc adj* **1.** [en rond] : **fleurs en ~** wreath of flowers ■ **nattes en ~** plaits (worn) in a crown
2. CULIN in a ring.

couronné, e [kurɔne] *adj* crowned.

couronnement [kurɔnmɑ̃] *nm* **1.** [cérémonie] coronation, crowning **2.** [réussite] crowning achievement **3.** [récompense] : **cette année a vu le ~ de ses efforts** this year her efforts were finally rewarded.

couronner [3] [kurɔne] *vt* **1.** [roi] to crown ■ **elle fut couronnée reine/impératrice** she was crowned queen/empress ‖ ANTIQ & HIST [orateur, soldat] to crown with a laurel wreath **2.** [récompenser - poète, chercheur] to award a prize to ; [- œuvre, roman] to award a prize for **3.** [conclure - carrière, recherches, vie] to crown ■ **sa nomination vient ~ sa carrière** her nomination is the crowning achievement of her career ■ **et pour ~ le tout** *fam* and to crown it all, and on top of all that **4.** [dent] to crown.
◆ **se couronner** *vpt* : **se ~ les genoux** to graze one's knees.

courrai *etc v* ▷ **courir.**

courre [kur] ▷ **chasse.**

courriel [kurjɛl] *nm* INFORM email.

courrier [kurje] *nm* **1.** [correspondance - reçue] mail, letters, post *UK* ; [- à envoyer] letters (to be sent) ■ **il y a du ~ pour moi aujourd'hui?** are there any letters for me *ou* have I got any mail *ou* is there any post *UK* for me today? ■ **avec la grève, il y a du retard dans le ~** with the strike, there are delays in mail deliveries ■ **faites partir ça avec le premier ~** send this first post today *UK*, send this by the first mail *US* **2.** [lettre] : **un ~** a letter **3.** ADMIN & POLIT [messager] courier **4.** [chronique] column ■ **~ du cœur** agony column, problem page ■ **~ des lecteurs** letters (to the editor) **5.** INFORM : **~ électronique** email **6.** TRANSP mail ■ HIST [homme] messenger.

courriériste [kurjerist] *nmf* columnist ■ **~ du cœur** agony aunt.

courroie [kurwa] *nf* **1.** [gén] belt strap **2.** TECHNOL belt ■ **~ de transmission** driving belt ■ **~ de ventilateur** AUTO fan belt.

courroucé, e [kuruse] *adj* wrathful.

courroucer [16] [kuruse] *vt sout* to anger, to infuriate.
◆ **se courroucer** *vpi sout* to become infuriated.

courroux [kuru] *nm sout* anger, ire *litt*, wrath *litt* ■ **les flots en ~** *litt* the raging sea.

cours [kur] *nm*

A. ÉCOULEMENT, SUCCESSION
B. DANS LE DOMAINE FINANCIER
C. DANS LE DOMAINE SCOLAIRE ET UNIVERSITAIRE

A. ÉCOULEMENT, SUCCESSION

1. GÉOGR [débit] flow ■ [parcours] course ■ **avoir un ~ lent** to be slow-flowing ■ **avoir un ~ rapide** to be fast-flowing ▶ **~ d'eau** [ruisseau] stream ; [rivière] river
2. [déroulement - des années, des saisons, de pensées] course ; [- d'événements] course, run ; [- de négociations, d'une maladie, de travaux] course, progress ■ **donner** *ou* **laisser (libre) ~ à** [joie, indignation] to give vent to ; [imagination, chagrin] to give free rein to ■ **suivre son ~** [processus] to continue ■ **reprendre son ~ : la vie reprend son ~** life goes on ■ **l'Histoire reprend son ~** history must take its course ■ **en suivant/remontant le ~ du temps** going forward/back in time
3. [dans des noms de rue] avenue

B. DANS LE DOMAINE FINANCIER

1. [de devises] rate ■ **~ des devises** *ou* **du change** foreign exchange rate *ou* rate of exchange ▶ **~ forcé** forced currency ■ **avoir ~** [monnaie] to be legal tender *ou* legal currency ; [pratique] to be common ■ **avoir ~ légal** to be legal tender *ou* a legal currency ■ **ne plus avoir ~** [monnaie] to be out of circulation, to be no longer legal tender *ou* a legal currency ; [pratique, théorie] to be obsolete ; [expression, terme] to be obsolete *ou* no longer in use
2. [d'actions] price, trading rate ■ **au ~ du marché** at the market *ou* trading price ■ **au ~ du jour** at today's rate ■ **~ limite** limit price ■ **premier ~, ~ d'ouverture** opening price ■ **dernier ~, ~ de clôture** closing price

C. DANS LE DOMAINE SCOLAIRE ET UNIVERSITAIRE

1. ÉDUC [classe] class, lesson ■ UNIV class, lecture ■ [ensemble des leçons] course ■ **aller en ~** to go to one's class ■ **être en ~** to be in class ■ **suivre des ~** to attend a course ■ **suivre un ~** *ou* **des ~ d'espagnol** to go to *ou* to attend a Spanish class ■ **prendre des ~** to take lessons *ou* a course ■ **elle prend des ~ au Conservatoire** she attends the Conservatoire ■ **j'ai ~ tout à l'heure** [élève, professeur] I have a class later ■ **j'ai ~ tous les jours** [élève, professeur] I have classes every day ■ **faire ~ : c'est moi qui vous ferai ~ cette année** I'll be teaching you this year ■ **les professeurs ne font pas ~ cet après-midi** there are no lessons this afternoon ■ **tu ne vas pas me faire un ~ sur la politesse?** are you going to give me a lecture on how to be polite? ▶ **~ par correspondance** correspondence course ; UNIV ≃ Open University course *UK* ■ **~ magistral** lecture ■ **donner/prendre des ~ particuliers** to give/to have private tuition ■ **~ de perfectionnement** proficiency course ■ **~ du soir** evening class
2. [manuel] course, coursebook, textbook ■ [notes] notes
3. [degré - dans l'enseignement primaire] : **~ préparatoire** ≃ first-year infants class *UK* ■ ≃ nursery school *US* ■ **~ élémentaire** ≃ second-year infants class *UK* ■ ≃ first grade *US* ■ **~ moyen** ≃ third-year infants class *UK* ■ ≃ second grade *US*
4. [établissement] school.
◆ **au cours de** *loc prép* during, in *ou* during the course of ■ **au ~ des siècles** over the centuries ■ **au ~ de notre dernier entretien** when we last spoke ■ **ça se décidera au ~ des prochaines semaines** it'll be decided in the weeks to come.
◆ **en cours** *loc adj* [actuel] : **l'année/le tarif en ~** the current year/price ■ **affaire/travail en ~** business/work in hand ■ **examen en ~** examination in progress ■ **être en ~** [débat, réunion, travaux] to be under way, to be in progress.
◆ **en cours de** *loc prép* in the process of ■ **en ~ de réparation** in the process of being repaired, undergoing repairs ■ **c'est en ~ d'étude** it's being examined ■ **en ~ de route** on the way.

course [kurs] *nf* **1.** SPORT [compétition] race ■ **épuisé par sa ~** exhausted from his running ■ **il a dû arrêter en pleine ~** he had to stop in the middle of the race ■ **faire la ~** to race ■ **faire la ~ avec qqn** to race (with) sb ■ **les enfants, on ne fait pas la ~!** children, no running! ■ **c'est toujours la ~ au bureau** *fig* we're always run off our feet at the office ▶ **~ attelée/handicap** harness/handicap race ■ **~ de fond** *ou* **d'endurance** long-distance race ■ **~ automobile** motor *ou* car race ■ **~ de chevaux** (horse) race ■ **~ cycliste** cycle race ■ **~ de demi-fond** middle-distance race ■ **~ d'obstacles** ÉQUIT steeplechase ■ **~ à pied** race ■ **~ de relais** relay race ■ **~ en sac** sack race ■ **~ de taureaux** bullfight ■ **~ de vitesse** sprint *UK*, dash *US* ■ **~ contre la montre** *pr* race against the clock, time-trial ; *fig* race against time ■ **être dans la ~** *fam* to be hip *ou* with it *vieilli* ■ **rester dans la ~** to stay in *ou* to be still in the race
2. [activité] : **la ~** [à pied] running ; [en voiture, à cheval] racing ■ **je fais de la ~ à pied tous les jours** I run every day ■ **la ~ à : la ~ aux armements** the arms race ■ **la ~ au pouvoir/à la présidence** the race for power/the presidency
3. [randonnée] : **faire une ~ en montagne** to go for a trek in the mountains
4. [d'un taxi - voyage] journey ; [- prix] fare
5. [commission] errand ■ **j'ai une ~ à faire** I've got to buy something *ou* to get something from the shops ‖ [d'un coursier] errand
6. [trajectoire - d'un astre, d'un pendule] course, trajectory ; [- d'un missile] flight ; [- d'un piston] stroke
7. *Suisse* [trajet] trip *(by train or boat)* ■ [excursion] excursion.
◆ **courses** *nfpl* **1.** [commissions] : **faire les/des ~s** to do the/some shopping
2. [de chevaux] races ■ **jouer aux ~s** to bet on the races *ou* on the horses.

course-poursuite [kurspursɥit] (*pl* **courses-poursuites**) *nf* **1.** SPORT track race **2.** [entre policiers et voleurs] car chase.

courser [3] [kurse] *vt fam* to chase, to run after *(insép)* ■ **elle s'est fait ~ par des voyous** she was chased by some thugs.

coursier, ère [kursje, ɛr] *nm, f* errand boy (*f* girl) ■ [à moto] dispatch rider.

◆ **coursier** *nm* **1.** [transporteur] : **envoyer qqch par ~** to send sthg by courier ▶ **~ international** courier company **2.** *litt* [cheval] steed.

coursive [kursiv] *nf* **1.** NAUT gangway **2.** CONSTR (raised) passageway.

court, e [kur, kurt] *adj*

> **A.** DANS L'ESPACE
> **B.** DANS LE TEMPS
> **C.** FAIBLE, INSUFFISANT

A. DANS L'ESPACE

1. [en longueur - cheveux, ongles] short ▪ **~ sur pattes** *fam* [chien] short-legged ; [personne] short ▪ **la jupe est trop ~e de trois centimètres** the skirt is three centimetres too short ▪ **il y a un chemin plus ~** there's a shorter *ou* quicker way
2. ANAT [os, muscle] short
3. RADIO [onde] short

B. DANS LE TEMPS

1. [bref, concis - discours, lettre, séjour, durée *etc*] short, brief ▪ **pendant un ~ instant** for a brief *ou* fleeting moment ▶ **cycle ~** *course of studies leading to qualifications exclusive of university entrance*
2. [proche] : **à ~ terme** short-term *(avant n)* ▪ **j'ai des projets à ~ terme** I have some plans in *ou* for the short term

C. FAIBLE, INSUFFISANT

1. [faible - avance, avantage] small ; [- majorité] small, slender ▶ **gagner d'une ~e tête** *pr & fig* to win by a short head
2. [restreint] : **avoir la respiration ~e** *ou* **le souffle ~** to be short of breath *ou* wind
3. *fam* [insuffisant - connaissances] slender, slim ; [- quantité, mesure] meagre, skimpy ▪ **deux bouteilles pour six, c'est un peu ~** two bottles for six people, that's a bit on the mean *UK ou* stingy side ▪ **l'avion décolle dans 30 minutes – c'est trop ~ pour l'avoir** the plane takes off in 30 minutes – we won't make it in time ▪ **plutôt ~ comme excuse!** (it's) a bit of a pathetic excuse! ▪ **à ~es vues** [personne] limited (in one's understanding) ; [explication] limited ▶ **avoir la vue ~e** *pr & fig* to be short-sighted *UK ou* nearsighted *US* ▪ **avoir la mémoire ~e** to have a short memory.

◆ **court** ◇ *adv* **1.** [en dimension] : **je me suis fait couper les cheveux ~** I had my hair cut short ▪ **elle s'habille ~** she wears her skirts short **2.** [en durée] : **pour faire ~** *fam* to cut a long story short **3.** [brusquement] : **s'arrêter ~** to stop short ▪ **tourner ~** [discussion, projet] to come to an abrupt end.
◇ *nm* **1.** [terrain] : **~ (de tennis)** tennis court ▪ **sur le ~** on (the) court **2.** COUT, vêtement [vêtement] : **le ~** short fashions *ou* hemlines *ou* styles **3.** *loc* **aller au plus ~** to take the quickest course of action ▪ **prendre par le** *ou* **au plus ~** [chemin, procédure] to take a short cut.

◆ **à court** *loc adv fam* short on cash, hard-up, a bit short.

◆ **à court de** *loc prép* : **être à ~ d'idées/de vivres** to have run out of ideas/food ▪ **nous étions presque à ~ d'eau** we were low on *ou* running short of water ▪ **être à ~ d'argent** to be short of money ▪ **elle n'est jamais à ~ d'arguments** she's never at a loss for an argument.

◆ **de court** *loc adv* : **prendre qqn de ~** [ne pas lui laisser de délai de réflexion] to give sb (very) short notice ; [le surprendre] to catch sb unawares *ou* napping.

◆ **tout court** *loc adv* : **appelez-moi Jeanne, tout ~** just call me Jeanne ▪ **cela indigne les chrétiens démocrates et même les chrétiens tout ~** this is shocking to Christian Democrats and even to Christians full stop *UK ou* period.

courtage [kurtaʒ] *nm* brokerage ▪ **vente par ~** selling on commission.

courtaud, e [kurto, od] *adj* [personne] short-legged, squat, dumpy.

court-bouillon [kurbujɔ̃] (*pl* **courts-bouillons**) *nm* court-bouillon ▪ **faire cuire au** *ou* **dans un ~** to cook in a court-bouillon.

court-circuit [kursirkɥi] (*pl* **courts-circuits**) *nm* ÉLECTR short circuit ▪ **faire ~** to short-circuit.

court-circuiter [3] [kursirkɥite] *vt* **1.** ÉLECTR to short, to short-circuit **2.** *fam* [assemblée, personnel] to bypass ▪ [procédure] to bypass, to short-circuit ▪ **court-circuite-le avant qu'il ne signe** grab him before he signs.

courtepointe [kurtəpwɛ̃t] *nf* duvet, counterpane.

courtier, ère [kurtje, ɛr] *nm, f* **1.** BOURSE broker **2.** COMM : **~ en assurances/vins** insurance/wine broker ▪ **~ maritime** ship *ou* shipping broker.

courtine [kurtin] *nf* curtain.

courtisan [kurtizɑ̃] *nm* **1.** HIST courtier **2.** *sout* [flatteur] flatterer, sycophant.

courtisane [kurtizan] *nf litt* courtesan.

courtiser [3] [kurtize] *vt* **1.** [femme] to court, to woo, to pay court to **2.** [pays, puissants] to woo ▪ **il le courtisait servilement** he fawned on him obsequiously.

court-jus [kurʒy] (*pl* **courts-jus**) *nm fam* short ÉLECTR.

court(-)métrage [kurmetraʒ] (*pl* **courts-métrages**) *nm* short film, short.

courtois, e [kurtwa, az] *adj* **1.** [poli - personne, manières] civil, courteous ▪ **de manière ~e** politely ▪ **d'un ton ~** civilly, courteously **2.** HIST & LITTÉR [amour] courtly ▪ [roman, littérature] about courtly love.

courtoisement [kurtwazmɑ̃] *adv* courteously.

courtoisie [kurtwazi] *nf* courteousness ▪ **avec ~** courteously.

court-vêtu, e [kurvety] (*mpl* **court-vêtus**, *fpl* **court-vêtues**) *adj* : **des femmes ~es** women in short skirts.

couru, e [kury] ◇ *pp* ▷ **courir**.
◇ *adj* **1.** [populaire] fashionable, popular ▪ [spectacle] popular **2.** *fam* [certain] : **c'est ~ (d'avance)!** it's a (dead) cert! *UK*, it's a sure thing! *US*.

cousait *etc v* ▷ **coudre**.

couscous [kuskus] *nm* couscous.

couscoussier [kuskusje] *nm* couscous steamer.

cousette [kuzɛt] *nf fam vieilli* dressmaker's apprentice.

cousin, e [kuzɛ̃, in] *nm, f* cousin ▪ **~ germain** first *ou* full cousin ▪ **petit ~, ~ au second degré** second cousin ▪ **~ éloigné** *ou* **à la mode de Bretagne** *hum* distant relation.

◆ **cousin** *nm* ENTOM (big) mosquito.

cousinage [kuzinaʒ] *nm vieilli* [parenté] cousinhood.

coussin [kusɛ̃] *nm* **1.** [de siège, de meuble] cushion ▪ *Belgique* [oreiller] pillow ▪ **un ~ de feuilles/mousse** a cushion of leaves/moss **2.** TECHNOL : **~ d'air** air cushion.

coussinet [kusinɛ] *nm* **1.** [petit coussin] small cushion **2.** ZOOL cushion.

cousu, e [kuzy] *pp* ▷ **coudre**.

coût [ku] *nm* **1.** [prix] cost, price ▪ **~ d'achat/de remplacement** purchase/replacement cost ▪ **~ du crédit** credit charges *ou* cost ▪ **~ de la main d'œuvre** labour costs ▪ **~ de production** production cost ▪ **~ de la vie** cost of living ▪ **~ salarial** cost of an employee for his employer **2.** *fig* **le ~ social de la privatisation** the social cost of privatization.

coûtant [kutɑ̃] *adj m* cost *(modif)*.

couteau, x [kuto] *nm* **1.** [à main] knife ▪ [d'une machine, d'un mixer] blade ▶ **~ à beurre/pain** butter/bread knife ▪ **~ de cuisine/de table** kitchen/table knife ▪ **~ économe** *ou* **éplucheur** *ou* **à éplucher** potato peeler ▪ **~ pliant** *ou* **de poche** pocket knife ▪ **~ de chasse** hunting knife ▪ **~ à cran d'arrêt** flick-knife ▪ **~ à désosser** boning knife ▪ **~ électrique** electric carving knife ▪ **~ à viande** carving knife ▪ **coup de ~** stab (with a knife) ▪ **donner un coup de ~ à qqn** to stab sb (with a knife) ▪ **prendre** *fam ou* **recevoir un coup de ~** to be knifed, to get stabbed ▪ **remuer** *ou* **retourner le ~ dans la plaie** to twist the knife in the wound ▪ **avoir le ~ sous la gorge** to have a gun pointed at one's head

■ **jouer les seconds ~x (dans une affaire)** to play a secondary role in a business, to play second fiddle ■ **être à ~x tirés avec qqn** to be at daggers drawn with sb
2. [d'une balance] knife edge
3. ART palette knife ■ **peinture au ~** knife painting
4. ZOOL razor shell *UK* *OU* clam *US*.

coutelas [kutla] *nm* **1.** [de cuisine] large kitchen knife **2.** ARM cutlass.

coutelier, ère [kutəlje, ɛr] *nm, f* cutler, cutlery specialist.

coutellerie [kutɛlri] *nf* **1.** [ustensiles] cutlery **2.** [lieu de fabrication] cutlery works **3.** [lieu de vente] kitchen-ware shop *UK* *OU* store *US* (specializing in cutlery) **4.** [industrie] cutlery industry.

coûter [3] [kute] *vt* **1.** [somme] to cost ■ **combien ça coûte?** *fam* how much is it?, how much does it cost? ■ **cela m'a coûté 20 euros** it cost me 20 euros ■ **je veux cette maison, ça coûtera ce que ça coûtera** I want that house no matter how much it costs ■ *(en usage absolu)* *fam* **une voiture, ça coûte!** *fam* a car is an expensive thing! ➲ **~ la peau des fesses** *fam* *OU* **une fortune** *OU* **les yeux de la tête** to cost a fortune *OU* the earth *OU* an arm and a leg ■ **~ cher** [produit, service] to be expensive, to cost a lot of money ■ **ça va lui ~ cher!** *fig* she's going to pay for this! ■ **cela ne coûte pas cher** it's cheap *OU* inexpensive **2.** [exiger - efforts] to cost ■ **ça ne coûte rien d'être aimable!** it doesn't cost anything to be kind! ■ **ça te coûterait beaucoup d'être poli/de me répondre?** would it be asking too much for you to be polite/to answer me? ■ **cette démarche lui a beaucoup coûté** it was a very difficult *OU* painful step for him to take ■ **tu peux bien l'aider, pour ce que ça te coûte!** it wouldn't be any trouble for you to help her! **3.** [provoquer - larmes] to cost, to cause **4.** [entraîner la perte de - carrière, membre, vote] to cost ■ **ça a failli lui ~ la vie** it nearly cost him his life ■ **un accident qui a coûté la vie à dix personnes** an accident which claimed the lives of ten people.
◆ **coûte que coûte** *loc adv* at all costs, whatever the cost, no matter what.

coûteux, euse [kutø, øz] *adj* **1.** [onéreux] expensive, costly ■ **peu ~** cheap **2.** [lourd de conséquences] costly ■ **des préjugés ~ pour l'avenir de l'homme** prejudices which prove costly for future generations.

coutil [kuti] *nm* [toile - gén] drill ; [- pour literie] ticking.

coutume [kutym] *nf* **1.** [tradition] custom ■ **comme c'est la ~ en Alsace** as is the custom *OU* is customary in Alsace ■ **d'après** *OU* **selon la ~** as custom dictates ■ **selon une ~ ancienne** according to an age-old tradition **2.** [habitude, manie] habit, custom ■ **avoir (pour) ~ de faire** to be in the habit of *OU* accustomed to doing ■ **il pleuvait, comme de ~** as usual, it was raining ■ **moins que de ~** less than usual, not as much as usual ■ **plus que de ~** more than usual **3.** DR customary.

coutumier, ère [kutymje, ɛr] *adj* **1.** [habituel] customary, usual **2.** [habitué à] : **~ de : j'ai oublié et pourtant je ne suis pas ~ du fait** I forgot, and yet it's not something I usually do.

couture [kutyr] *nf* **1.** [action de coudre, passe-temps, produit] : **j'ai de la ~ à faire** I've got some sewing to do ▌[confection] : **la ~ (artisanale)** dressmaking ■ **la haute ~** (haute) couture, fashion design **2.** [suite de points] seam ■ **faire une ~ à qqch** to seam sthg ■ **~ apparente** *OU* **sellier** top stitching, overstitching **3.** *litt* [cicatrice] scar ■ [points de suture] stitches **4.** [d'un moulage, d'une sculpture] seam.
◆ **à coutures** *loc adj* [bas, collant] seamed, with seams.
◆ **sans coutures** *loc adj* [bas, collant] seamless.
◆ **sous toutes les coutures** *loc adv* from every angle, very closely, under a microscope *fig*.

couturier, ère [kutyrje, ɛr] *nm, f* [fabricant - de complets] tailor ; [- de chemises] shirtmaker ; [- de robes] dressmaker ■ **j'ai besoin d'une couturière pour mes ravaudages** I need somebody to do some sewing (and mending) for me.
◆ **couturier** *nm* [de haute couture] : **(grand) ~** fashion designer.
◆ **couturière** *nf* THÉÂTRE *rehearsal preceding the final dress rehearsal, enabling last-minute alterations to costumes.*

couvaison [kuvɛzɔ̃] *nf* **1.** [période] incubation **2.** [action] brooding.

couvée [kuve] *nf* **1.** [œufs] clutch **2.** [oisillons] brood, clutch ■ **la nouvelle ~ de jeunes cinéastes** the new generation *OU* breed of young filmmakers **3.** *fam* [famille] : **sa ~** her brood.

couvent [kuvɑ̃] *nm* **1.** [de religieuses] convent ■ [de religieux] monastery ■ **entrer au ~** to enter a convent *OU* nunnery *vieilli* **2.** [pensionnat] convent school.

couver [3] [kuve] <> *vt* **1.** [suj: oiseau] to sit on *(insép)* ■ [suj: incubateur] to hatch, to incubate ■ *(en usage absolu)* **quand la mouette couve** when the seagull sits on its eggs *OU* broods *OU* is broody **2.** [protéger - enfant] to overprotect, to cocoon ■ **~ des yeux** *OU* **du regard** [personne aimée] to gaze fondly at ; [friandise, bijou] to look longingly at **3.** [maladie] to be coming down with ■ **je crois que je couve quelque chose** I can feel something coming on **4.** *litt* [vengeance, revanche] to plot.
<> *vi* **1.** [feu] to smoulder **2.** [rébellion] to be brewing (up) ■ [sentiment] to smoulder ■ **~ sous la cendre** to be brewing (up), to bubble under the surface.

couvercle [kuvɛrkl] *nm* [qui se pose, s'enfonce] lid, cover ■ [qui se visse] top, screw-top, cap.

couvert[1] [kuvɛr] *nm* **1.** [cuiller, fourchette, couteau] knife, fork and spoon ■ **des ~s en argent** silver cutlery ■ **~s à salade** salad servers ▌[avec assiette et verre] place setting ■ **mettre le ~** to lay *OU* to set the table ■ **j'ai mis trois ~s** I've laid three places *OU* the table for three **2.** [prix d'une place au restaurant] cover charge.

couvert[2]**, e** [kuvɛr, ɛrt] <> *pp* ▻ **couvrir**.
<> *adj* **1.** [abrité - allée, halle, marché] covered ; [- piscine] indoor *(avant n)* **2.** [vêtu - chaudement] warmly-dressed, (well) wrapped-up *OU* muffled-up ; [- décemment] covered (up) ■ **rester ~** [garder son chapeau] to keep one's hat on **3.** MÉTÉOR [temps] dull, overcast ■ [ciel] overcast, clouded-over ■ **attendez-vous à un après-midi ~** expect a cloudy afternoon.
◆ **couvert** *nm litt* leafy canopy.
◆ **à couvert** *loc adv* : **être à ~** [de projectiles] to be under cover ; [de critiques, de soupçons] to be safe ■ **se mettre à ~** [de projectiles] to get under *OU* to take cover ; [de critiques, de soupçons] to cover *OU* to safeguard o.s.
◆ **à couvert de** *loc prép* protected against ■ **ici, nous serons à ~ de la pluie** here, we'll be sheltered from the rain.
◆ **sous couvert de** *loc prép* in the guise of ■ **sous ~ de sollicitude, elle me suit partout** under the pretext of being concerned for me, she follows me around everywhere.
◆ **sous le couvert de** *loc prép* **1.** [sous l'apparence de] in the guise of **2.** [sous la responsabilité de] : **il l'a fait sous le ~ de son chef/frère** he did it using his boss/brother as a shield **3.** *litt* [à l'abri de] : **sous le ~ d'un bois** in the shelter of a wood.

couverture [kuvɛrtyr] *nf* **1.** [morceau de tissu] blanket ■ **sous les ~s** under the blankets *OU* covers ➲ **~ chauffante** electric blanket ■ **~ de survie** space *OU* survival blanket ■ **amener** *OU* **tirer la ~ à soi** [après un succès] to take all the credit ; [dans une transaction] to get the best of the deal **2.** CONSTR [activité] roofing ■ [ouvrage] (type of) roof **3.** PRESSE [activité] coverage ■ **assurer** *OU* **faire la ~ d'un événement** to give coverage of *OU* to cover an event ▌[d'un magazine] cover, front page ■ **mettre une photo en ~** to put a photo on the cover **4.** [d'un livre] cover **5.** [assurance] cover ■ **~ sociale** Social Security cover ■ **avoir une ~ sociale** to belong to a benefit scheme **6.** [prétexte] disguise, façade ■ **le financier/la société qui leur servait de ~** the financier/company they used as a front **7.** MIL cover ■ **~ aérienne** air cover.

couveuse [kuvøz] *nf* **1.** [poule] brooder, sitter **2.** [machine] : **~ (artificielle)** incubator.

couvrant, e [kuvrɑ̃, ɑ̃t] *adj* [peinture, vernis] that covers well.

couvre-chef [kuvrəʃɛf] (*pl* **couvre-chefs**) *nm hum* hat, headgear.

couvre-feu [kuvrəfø] (*pl* **couvre-feux**) *nm* curfew.

couvre-lit [kuvrəli] (*pl* **couvre-lits**) *nm* bedspread.

couvre-livre [kuvrəlivr] (*pl* **couvre-livres**) *nm* dust jacket.

couvre-pied(s) [kuvrəpje] (*pl* **couvre-pieds**) *nm* quilt.

couvreur [kuvrœr] *nm* roofer.

couvrir [34] [kuvrir] ◇ *vt* **1.** [d'une protection, d'une couche - meuble] to cover ; [- livre, cahier] to cover, to put a dust cover on ■ [d'un couvercle - poêle] to cover, to put a lid on ■ **~ le feu** to bank up the fire ■ **~ de** [surface] : **~ un mur de peinture** to paint a wall ■ **il avait couvert le mur de graffiti/posters** he'd covered the wall with graffiti/posters ■ **~ avec** *ou* **de** [protéger] to cover with ■ **~ qqn de** [lui donner en abondance] : **~ qqn de cadeaux/d'injures/de louanges/de reproches** to shower sb with gifts/insults/praise/reproaches ■ **~ qqn de caresses/baisers** to stroke/to kiss sb all over ■ **~ qqn de honte** to make sb feel ashamed ■ **~ qqn d'or** to shower sb with gifts **2.** [vêtir] to wrap *ou* to cover *ou* to muffle up *(sép)* ■ **couvre bien ta gorge!** make sure your throat is covered up! ■ [envelopper] to cover ■ **une mantille lui couvrait la tête** her head was covered with a mantilla, a mantilla covered her head **3.** [dissimuler - erreur] to cover up *(sép)* ■ [protéger - complice] to cover up for **4.** [voix] to drown (out) **5.** [assurer - dégâts, frais, personne, risque] to cover, to insure **6.** [inclure] to cover, to include **7.** [compenser] to cover ■ **nous couvrons nos frais maintenant** we're paying our way now **8.** MIL [retraite, soldat] to cover, to give cover ■ **~ ses arrières** to cover one's rear **9.** [parcourir] to cover **10.** [englober - dans l'espace] to cover ; [- dans le temps] to span **11.** [suj: émetteur, représentant] to cover **12.** PRESSE to cover, to give coverage to **13.** FIN [emprunt] to underwrite ■ [enchère] to bid higher than, to outbid **14.** VÉTÉR to cover **15.** JEUX [carte] to cover.
◇ *vi* : **cette peinture couvre bien** this paint covers well.
◆ **se couvrir** ◇ *vp (emploi réfléchi)* **1.** [se vêtir] to dress warmly, to wrap up (well) **2.** [mettre un chapeau] to put on one's hat **3.** SPORT to cover o.s. **4.** [se garantir] to cover o.s.
◇ *vpi* [ciel] to become overcast, to cloud over.
◆ **se couvrir de** *vp+prép* : **se ~ de fleurs/bourgeons/feuilles** to come into bloom/bud/leaf ■ **le champ s'est couvert de coquelicots** poppies have come up all over the field ■ **se ~ de ridicule** to make o.s. look ridiculous ■ **se ~ de honte/gloire** to cover o.s. with shame/glory.

cover-girl [kɔvœrgœrl] (*pl* **cover-girls**) *nf* cover girl.

covoiturage [kovwatyraʒ] *nm* car-pooling, car-sharing.

cow-boy [kɔbɔj] (*pl* **cow-boys**) *nm* cowboy ■ **jouer aux ~s et aux Indiens** to play (at) cowboys and Indians.

coyote [kɔjɔt] *nm* coyote.

CP (*abr de* **cours préparatoire**) *nm first year of primary school.*

CPAM (*abr de* **caisse primaire d'assurances maladie**) *nf national health insurance office.*

cps (*abr écrite de* **caractères par seconde**) cps.

cpt = **comptant**.

CQFD (*abr de* **ce qu'il fallait démontrer**) QED ■ **et voilà, ~!** and there you are!

crabe [krab] *nm* CULIN & ZOOL crab.
◆ **en crabe** *loc adv* : **marcher/se déplacer en ~** to walk/to move sideways.

crac [krak] *onomat* [bois, os] crack, snap ■ [biscuit] snap ■ [tissu] rip.

crachat [kraʃa] *nm* [salive] spit ■ **des ~s** spit, spittle.

craché, e [kraʃe] *adj fam* **tout ~** : **c'est son père tout ~!** he's the spitting image of his dad! ■ **ça, c'est du Maud tout ~!** that's just like Maud!, that's Maud all over!

crachement [kraʃmɑ̃] *nm* **1.** [fait de cracher] spitting ■ [crachat] mucus, sputum *spéc* ■ **avoir des ~s de sang** to spit blood **2.** [projection - de flammes, vapeur] burst, shower ; [- de scories, d'étincelles] shower **3.** [bruit - d'un haut-parleur] crackle, crackling.

cracher [3] [kraʃe] ◇ *vi* **1.** [personne] to spit ▶ **~ sur qqn** *pr* to spit at sb ; *fig* to spit on sb ■ **~ à la figure de qqn** *pr* & *fig* to spit in sb's face ■ **c'est comme si on crachait en l'air!** *fam* it's like whistling in the wind! ■ **il ne faut pas ~ dans la soupe** don't bite the hand that feeds you ■ **~ sur qqch** *fam* : **je ne cracherais pas sur 1 000 euros!** I wouldn't turn my nose up at *ou* say no to 1,000 euros! ■ **ce système a du bon, ne crache pas dessus!** there are things to be said for this system, don't knock it! ■ **~ au bassinet** to cough up **2.** [chat, marmotte] to spit, to hiss **3.** [fuir - stylo] to splutter ; [- robinet] to splutter, to splash **4.** [nasiller - haut-parleur, radio] to crackle.
◇ *vt* **1.** [rejeter - sang] to spit ; [- aliment] to spit out *(sép)* ■ **~ ses poumons** *fam* to cough up one's lungs **2.** [suj: volcan, canon] to belch (forth) *ou* out ■ [suj: fusil] to shoot a burst of, to spit ■ [suj: robinet] to spit *ou* to splutter out *(sép)* ■ **~ des flammes** *ou* **du feu** [dragon] to breathe fire **3.** [énoncer - insultes] to spit out *(sép)*, to hiss **4.** *fam* [donner - argent] to cough up *(sép)*, to fork out *(sép)*.

cracheur, euse [kraʃœr, øz] ◇ *adj* ZOOL spitting *(avant n)*.
◇ *nm, f* spitter ■ **~ (de feu)** fire-eater.

crachin [kraʃɛ̃] *nm* (fine) drizzle.

crachoir [kraʃwar] *nm* spittoon ■ **tenir le ~** *fam* to go on and on, to monopolize the conversation ■ **je n'ai pas envie de lui tenir le ~!** I don't feel like listening to her rambling on for hours!

crachotement [kraʃɔtmɑ̃] *nm* [d'une radio, d'un téléphone] crackle, crackling ■ [d'un robinet, d'une personne] splutter, spluttering.

crachoter [3] [kraʃɔte] *vi* [personne] to splutter, to sputter ■ [radio, téléphone] to crackle ■ [robinet] to splutter.

crack [krak] *nm* **1.** ÉQUIT crack **2.** *fam* [personne - gén] wizard ; [- en sport] ace ■ **c'est un ~ en ski** he's an ace skier ■ **c'est un ~ en latin** he's brilliant at Latin **3.** [drogue] crack.

cracra [krakra] *fam*, **cradingue**△ [kradɛ̃g], **crado** [krado] *fam adj inv* [personne, objet] filthy ■ [restaurant] grotty *UK*, lousy *US*.

craie [krɛ] *nf* chalk, limestone ■ **une ~** a stick of chalk ■ **écrire qqch à la ~** to chalk sthg, to write sthg with chalk.

craignait *etc v* ▷ **craindre**.

craignos△ [krɛɲos] *adj inv* : **c'est ~!** [louche] it's dodgy! *UK* ; [ennuyeux] it's a real pain!

craindre [80] [krɛ̃dr] *vt* **1.** [redouter - personne] to fear, to be frightened *ou* afraid of ; [- événement] to fear, to be afraid *ou* scared of ■ **~ Dieu** to go in fear of *ou* to fear God ■ **sa grosse voix le faisait ~ de tous ses élèves** his booming voice made all his pupils afraid of him ■ **elle sait se faire ~ de ses subordonnés** she knows how to intimidate her subordinates ■ **je ne crains pas les piqûres** I'm not afraid *ou* scared of injections ■ **~ le pire** to fear the worst ■ **ne crains rien** have no fear, never fear, don't be afraid ■ **il n'y a rien à ~** there's no cause for alarm

EXPRIMER SES CRAINTES

I'm frightened *ou* **scared of spiders.** J'ai peur des araignées.

I was terrified *ou* **petrified.** J'étais mort de peur.

I was scared out of my wits. J'étais mort de peur.

I'm dreading (the thought of) telling her. J'appréhende de le lui dire.

I'm not looking forward to telling her. La perspective de le lui dire ne m'enchante guère.

I'm afraid that he might get hurt *ou* **that he'll get hurt.** J'ai peur qu'il se blesse.

I'm worried about him. Je suis inquiète pour lui.

I'm concerned for *ou* **worried about her health.** Je m'inquiète pour sa santé.

sout, there's nothing to fear ■ **il y a tout à ~ d'une intervention militaire** one can expect the worst from a military intervention ■ **craignant de la réveiller, il a retiré ses chaussures** he took off his shoes, for fear of waking her up **2.** [tenir pour probable] to fear ■ **alors, je suis renvoyé? – je le crains** so, I'm fired? – I'm afraid so ■ **elle pourrait nous dénoncer – c'est à ~** she might give us away – unfortunately, (I think) it's likely ■ **je crains de l'avoir blessée** I'm afraid I've hurt her ■ **je crains fort qu'il (ne) soit déjà trop tard** I fear *ou* I'm very much afraid it's already too late ■ **je crains que oui/non** I fear *ou* I'm afraid so/not **3.** [être sensible à] : **ça craint le froid** [plante] it's sensitive to cold, it doesn't like the cold ■ **c'est une étoffe qui ne craint rien** it's a material that'll stand up to anything **4.** △ *loc* **ça craint** [c'est louche] it's dodgy *UK* ; [c'est ennuyeux] it's a real pain.
◆ **craindre pour** *v+prép* : **~ pour qqn/qqch** to fear for sb/sthg.

craint, e [krɛ̃, ɛ̃t] *pp* ▻ **craindre**.
◆ **crainte** *nf* [anxiété] fear ■ **la ~e de l'échec** fear of failure *ou* failing ■ **il vivait dans la ~e d'être reconnu** he lived *ou* went in fear of being recognized ■ **n'aie aucune ~e** *ou* **sois sans ~e, tout se passera bien** don't worry *ou* never fear, everything will be all right ■ **éveiller** *ou* **susciter les ~es de qqn** to alarm sb.
◆ **de crainte de** *loc prép (suivi de l'infin)* for fear of.
◆ **de crainte que** *loc conj (suivi du subj)* for fear of, fearing that ■ **de ~e qu'on (ne) l'accuse** for fear of being accused, fearing that she might be accused ■ **il faut agir vite, de ~e que la situation (n') empire** we must act quickly, lest *ou* in case the situation should get worse.
Voir module d'usage

craintif, ive [krɛ̃tif, iv] ◇ *adj* **1.** [facilement effarouché - personne] timid, shy ; [- animal] timid **2.** [qui reflète la peur - regard, geste] timorous, fearful.
◇ *nm, f* **1.** [timide] timid *ou* shy person **2.** [timoré] faint-hearted *ou* timorous person.

craintivement [krɛ̃tivmɑ̃] *adv* **1.** [timidement] timidly, shyly **2.** [avec peur] timorously, fearfully.

cramé, e [krame] *adj fam* [rôti] burnt, charred ■ [tissu] burnt, scorched ■ **la tarte est complètement ~e** the tart is burnt to a cinder.
◆ **cramé** *nm fam* **ça sent le ~** there's a smell of burning.

cramer [3] [krame] *fam* ◇ *vi* [immeuble] to be on fire ■ [rôti, tissu] to burn ■ [circuit électrique, prise] to burn out ■ **faire ~ qqch** to burn sthg.
◇ *vt* [rôti] to burn (to a cinder), to let burn ■ [vêtement] to burn, to scorch.

cramoisi, e [kramwazi] *adj* [velours] crimson ■ [visage] flushed, crimson ■ **il est devenu ~** [de honte, de timidité] he flushed crimson *ou* blushed ; [de colère] his face turned crimson ◗ **rouge ~** crimson red.
◆ **cramoisi** *nm* crimson.

crampe [krɑ̃p] *nf* MÉD cramp ■ **j'ai une ~ au pied** I have cramp *UK ou* a cramp *US* in my foot ■ **~ d'estomac** [gén] stomach cramp ; [de faim] hunger pang ■ **la ~ de l'écrivain** writer's cramp.

crampon [krɑ̃pɔ̃] *nm* **1.** [de chaussures - de sport] stud ; [- de montagne] crampon ■ [de fer à cheval] calk **2.** BOT [de plante grimpante] tendril ■ [d'algue] sucker **3.** [crochet] cramp **4.** *fam péj* [personne] : **c'est un/une ~** he/she sticks like a leech ■ *(comme adj)* **un enfant un peu ~** a clinging child.

cramponner [3] [krɑ̃pɔne] *vt* **1.** *fam* [s'accrocher à] to cling to ■ **ne cramponne pas tout le temps ton père!** just leave your father alone will you!, give your father a break! **2.** TECHNOL [pièces] to cramp together.
◆ **se cramponner** *vpi* **1.** [s'agripper] to hold on, to hang on ■ **se ~ à** [branche, barre] to cling (on) *ou* to hold on to ; [personne] to cling (on) to **2.** *fam* [s'acharner - malade] to cling *ou* to hang on ; [- étudiant] to stick with it ■ **se ~ à la vie/à un espoir** to cling to life/hope.

cran [krɑ̃] *nm* **1.** [entaille - d'une étagère, d'une crémaillère] notch ■ [trou - d'une ceinture] hole, notch ■ **il resserra/desserra sa ceinture d'un ~** he tightened/loosened his belt one notch ■ **baisser/monter d'un ~** [dans une hiérarchie] to come down/to move up a peg ; [voix] to fall/to rise slightly **2.** COUT [sur un ourlet] notch ■ [point de repère] nick **3.** [mèche] wave **4.** TECHNOL catch ■ **~ de sûreté** *ou* **sécurité** safety catch ■ **~ d'arrêt** *fam* [couteau] flick-knife **5.** *fam* [courage] : **avoir du ~** to have guts.
◆ **à cran** *loc adj fam* uptight, edgy, on edge.

crâne [kran] ◇ *nm* **1.** ANAT skull, cranium *spéc* **2.** *fam* [tête] : **avoir mal au ~** to have a headache ■ **mets-toi bien ça dans le ~!** get that into your head! ◗ **alors, ~ d'œuf!** hey, baldy!
◇ *adj litt* [courageux] bold, gallant.

crânement [kranmɑ̃] *adv litt* [fièrement] gallantly.

crâner [3] [krane] *vi fam* to show off, to swank *UK* ■ **tu crânes moins maintenant!** you aren't so sure of yourself now, are you!

crânerie [kranri] *nf litt* **1.** [bravoure] gallantry **2.** [vanité] conceit.

crâneur, euse [kranœr, øz] *fam péj* ◇ *adj* : **être ~** to be a bit of a show-off.
◇ *nm, f* show-off, hotshot *US* ■ **faire le ~** to show off, to swank *UK*.

crânien, enne [kranjɛ̃, ɛn] *adj* cranial.

cranté, e [krɑ̃te] *adj* [ourlet] notched ■ [lame de ciseaux] serrated ■ [cheveux] wavy.

crapahuter [3] △ [krapayte] *vi arg mil* to plough along.

crapaud [krapo] *nm* **1.** ZOOL toad ■ **~ de mer** angler-fish **2.** MINÉR flaw **3.** MUS baby grand piano **4.** [fauteuil] squat armchair.

crapule [krapyl] ◇ *nf* [individu] crook, villain ■ **petite ~!** you little rat!
◇ *adj* roguish.

crapuleux, euse [krapylø, øz] *adj* **1.** [malhonnête] crooked, villainous **2.** *litt* [débauché] dissolute.

craquage [krakaʒ] = **cracking**.

craquant, e [krakɑ̃, ɑ̃t] *adj* **1.** [croustillant - laitue] crisp ; [- céréales] crunchy **2.** *fam* [personne] gorgeous.

craque [krak] *nf fam* fib, whopper ■ **et me raconte pas de ~s!** and no lies!

craquelé, e [krakle] *adj* **1.** [fissuré] cracked ■ **j'ai la peau des mains toute ~e** my hands are badly chapped **2.** [décoré de craquelures] crackled.
◆ **craquelé** *nm* : **le ~** [procédé] crackling ; [verre] crackleware.

craquèlement [krakɛlmɑ̃] *nm* cracks, cracking.

craqueler [24] [krakle] *vt* [fendiller] to crack ■ [poterie] to crackle.
◆ **se craqueler** *vpi* [peinture, peau] to crack ■ [poterie] to crackle.

craquelure [kraklyr] *nf* **1.** [accidentelle] crack ■ **les ~s du tableau** ART the craquelure on *ou* cracks in the painting **2.** [artificielle] crackle.

craquement [krakmɑ̃] *nm* [de bois qui casse] snap, crack ■ [d'un plancher] creak ■ [d'herbes sèches] crackle ■ [de chaussures] squeak, creak.

craquer [3] [krake] ◇ *vi* **1.** [plancher] to creak ■ [bois qui casse] to snap, to crack ■ [cuir, soulier] to squeak, to creak ■ [herbes sèches] to crackle ■ **faire ~ ses doigts** to crack one's knuckles ■ **faire ~ une allumette** to strike a match **2.** [se fendre - couture, tissu] to split ; [- sac] to split open ; [- fil, lacets] to break, to snap off ; [- banquise] to crack, to split (up) ; [- collant] to rip **3.** *fam* [psychologiquement] to break down, to crack up ■ **ses nerfs ont craqué** she had a nervous breakdown, she cracked up ■ **ils ont essayé de me faire ~ en fumant devant moi** they tried to break my resolve by smoking in front of me **4.** *fam* [être séduit] to go wild ■ **il me fait ~** I'm wild about this guy ■ **j'ai craqué pour cette robe** I went wild over that dress **5.** *fam* [s'effondrer - institution, projet] to founder, to be falling apart, to be on the verge of collapse.
◇ *vt* **1.** [couture] to split, to tear **2.** [allumette] to strike **3.** *fam* [dépenser] to blow **4.** INDUST **du pétrole** to crack.

craqueter [27] [krakte] *vi* **1.** [brindille, sachet en plastique] to crackle **2.** [cigogne, grue] to screech ▪ [cigale] to chirp.

crash [kraʃ] *nm* **1.** [accident] crashing (to the ground) **2.** [atterrissage forcé] crash landing ▪ **faire un ~** to crash-land.

crasher [3] [kraʃe] ◆ **se crasher** *vpi fam* **1.** AÉRON [s'écraser] to crash ▪ [atterrir accidentellement] to crash-land **2.** [conducteur, véhicule] to crash ▪ **il s'est crashé contre un arbre** he smashed *ou* crashed into a tree.

crasse [kras] ◇ *nf* **1.** [saleté] filth **2.** *fam* [mauvais tour] dirty *ou* nasty trick ▪ **faire une ~ à qqn** to play a dirty *ou* nasty trick on sb **3.** TECHNOL : **la ~, les ~s** [scories] scum, dross, slag ; [résidus] scale.
◇ *adj fam* [stupidité] crass ▪ **d'une ignorance ~** abysmally ignorant, pig-ignorant.

crasseux, euse [krasø, øz] *adj* [mains, vêtements] filthy, grimy, grubby ▪ [maison] filthy, squalid ▪ [personne] filthy ▪ **une cuisinière toute crasseuse** a stove caked with dirt.

cratère [kratɛr] *nm* ANTIQ & GÉOGR crater.

cravache [kravaʃ] *nf* riding crop, horsewhip.
◆ **à la cravache** *loc adv* ruthlessly, with an iron hand.

cravacher [3] [kravaʃe] ◇ *vt* [cheval] to use the whip on ▪ [personne] to horsewhip.
◇ *vi fam* **1.** [en voiture] to belt along, to go at full tilt *ou* speed **2.** [travailler dur] to slog *UK ou* to plug *US* away.

cravate [kravat] *nf* tie, necktie *US* ▪ **en costume (et) ~** wearing a suit and a tie ⊃ **~ de chanvre** *fam* hangman's noose ▪ **s'en envoyer** *ou* **s'en jeter un derrière la ~** *fam* to knock back a drink.

cravater [3] [kravate] *vt* **1.** [vêtement d'homme] to put a tie on **2.** [attraper par le cou] to grab by the neck ▪ SPORT to get in a headlock, to put a headlock on **3.** △ [voler] to pinch, to swipe△ ▪ **je me suis fait ~ mes papiers** someone's pinched *ou* swiped△ my papers.
◆ **se cravater** *vp (emploi réfléchi)* to put on a tie.

crawl [krol] *nm* crawl ▪ **faire du** *ou* **nager le ~** to do *ou* to swim the crawl.

crawlé [krole] *adj* ▭ **dos**.

crawler [3] [krole] *vi* to do *ou* to swim the crawl.

crawleur, euse [krolœr, øz] *nm, f* crawl specialist *(swimmer)*.

crayeux, euse [krɛjø, øz] *adj* **1.** GÉOL chalky **2.** [teint] chalk-like.

crayon [krɛjɔ̃] *nm* **1.** [pour écrire, dessiner] pencil **2.** ART [œuvre] pencil drawing **3.** OPT : **~ optique** light pen **4.** PHARM : **~ (médicamenteux)** pencil ▪ **~ hémostatique** styptic pencil.
◆ **crayons** *nmpl fam* [cheveux] : **se faire tailler les ~s** to get a haircut.
◆ **au crayon** ◇ *loc adj* [ajout, trait] pencilled.
◇ *loc adv* [dessiner, écrire] in pencil ▪ **écrire/dessiner qqch au ~** to write/to draw sthg in pencil ▪ **faire ses yeux au ~** to outline one's eyes with eye pencil.

crayon-feutre [krɛjɔ̃føtr] *(pl* **crayons-feutres***)* *nm* felt-tip (pen).

crayon-lecteur [krɛjɔ̃lɛktœr] *(pl* **crayons-lecteurs***)* *nm* electronic *ou* light pen.

crayonner [3] [krɛjɔne] *vt* **1.** [dessiner rapidement] to sketch (in pencil) **2.** [gribouiller - feuille, mur] to scribble on *(insép)* ▪ **~ sur un bloc-notes** to doodle on a notepad **3.** [écrire - au crayon] to pencil ; [- rapidement] to jot down *(sép)*.

CRDP *(abr de* **centre régional de documentation pédagogique***)* *nm local centre for educational resources.*

CRDS [seɛrdeɛs] *(abr de* **contribution pour le remboursement de la dette sociale***)* *nf tax on earnings and investments that goes towards reducing the social-security deficit.*

créance [kreɑ̃s] *nf* **1.** FIN & DR [dette] claim, debt ▪ [titre] letter of credit ▪ **~ exigible** debt due ▪ **~ hypothécaire** debt secured by a mortgage ▪ **~ irrécouvrable** bad debt **2.** *litt* [foi] credence ▪ **donner ~ à** [ajouter foi à] to give *ou* to attach credence to ; [rendre vraisemblable] to lend credibility to.

créancier, ère [kreɑ̃sje, ɛr] *nm, f* creditor.

créateur, trice [kreatœr, tris] ◇ *adj* creative ▪ **imagination créatrice** creativity.
◇ *nm, f* designer.
◆ **Créateur** *nm* : **le Créateur** the Creator, our Maker.

créatif, ive [kreatif, iv] ◇ *adj* [esprit] creative, imaginative, inventive.
◇ *nm, f* [gén] creative person ▪ [de publicité] designer.

création [kreasjɔ̃] *nf* **1.** [œuvre originale - bijou, parfum, vêtement] creation ▪ COMM & INDUST new product ▪ **nos nouvelles ~s** our new range **2.** THÉÂTRE [d'un rôle] creation ▪ [d'une pièce] first production, creation ▪ **il y aura de nombreuses ~s au festival** a lot of new plays will be performed at the festival **3.** [fait de créer - une mode, un style] creation ; [- un vêtement] designing, creating ; [- une entreprise] setting up ; [- une association] founding, creating ; [- des emplois] creating, creation ▪ **il y a eu 3 000 ~s d'emplois en mai** 3,000 new jobs were created in May ▪ **il s'agit d'une ~ de poste** it's a newly created post **4.** BIBLE : **la ~** the Creation.

créative [kreativ] *f* ▭ **créatif**.

créativité [kreativite] *nf* **1.** [qualité] creativity, creativeness, creative spirit **2.** LING creativity.

créature [kreatyr] *nf* **1.** [personne ou bête créée] creature ▪ **les ~s de Dieu** God's creatures **2.** [femme] : **~ de rêve** gorgeous creature ▮ *péj* creature **3.** [personne soumise] slave, tool.

crécelle [kresɛl] *nf* rattle ▪ **jouer de la ~** to play the rattle.
◆ **de crécelle** *loc adj* : **une voix de ~** a grating *ou* rasping voice.

crèche [krɛʃ] *nf* **1.** [établissement préscolaire] crèche *UK*, day nursery *esp UK*, child-care center *US* ▪ [dans un centre sportif, un magasin] crèche *UK*, day-care center *US* **2.** [de la Nativité] : **~ (de Noël)** (Christ Child's) crib ▮ *litt* [mangeoire] manger, crib.

crèche△ [krɛʃ] *v* ▭ **crécher**.

crécher [18] △ [kreʃe] *vi* **1.** [habiter] to live **2.** [loger temporairement] to doss down *UK*, to crash ▪ **je peux ~ chez toi ce soir?** can I crash at your place tonight?

crédence [kredɑ̃s] *nf* **1.** [desserte d'église] credence (table), credenza **2.** [buffet] credenza.

crédibiliser [3] [kredibilize] *vt* to give credibility to.

crédibilité [kredibilite] *nf* credibility ▪ **perdre sa ~** to lose one's credibility.

crédible [kredibl] *adj* credible, believable.

CRÉDIF, Crédif [kredif] *(abr de* **Centre de recherche et d'étude pour la diffusion du français***)* *npr m official body promoting use of the French language.*

crédit [kredi] *nm* **1.** BANQUE [actif] credit ▪ [en comptabilité] credit, credit side ▪ **porter 100 euros au ~ de qqn** to credit sb *ou* sb's account with 100 euros, to credit 100 euros to sb *ou* sb's account ▪ **j'ai 2 890 euros à mon ~** I am 2,890 euros in credit **2.** COMM [paiement différé, délai] credit ▪ [somme allouée] credit ▪ **~ sur six mois** six months' credit ▪ **faire ~ à qqn** to give sb credit, to give credit to sb ▪ **'la maison ne fait** *ou* **nous ne faisons pas ~'** 'no credit' ▪ **accorder/obtenir un ~** to grant/to obtain credit ▪ **j'ai pris un ~ sur 25 ans pour la maison** I've got a 25-year mortgage on the house ⊃ **~ à long/court terme** long-term/short-term credit ▪ **~ gratuit/illimité** free/unlimited credit ▪ **~ bancaire** bank credit ▪ **~ à la consommation** consumer credit ▪ **~ documentaire** documentary credit ▪ **~ à l'exportation** export credit ▪ **~ d'impôt** tax rebate *ou* credit *(for bondholders)* ▪ **~ personnalisé** individual *ou* personal credit arrangement *ou* facility ▪ **~ public** public loan ▪ **~ relais, ~-relais** bridging loan **3.** *sout* [confiance, estime] credibility, esteem ▪ **jouir d'un grand ~ auprès de qqn** to be high in sb's esteem ▪ **connaître un grand ~** [idée, théorie] to be widely accepted *ou* held ▪ **il n'a plus aucun ~** he's lost all credibility ▪ **donner du ~ aux propos de qqn** to give credence to what sb says ▪ **trouver ~ auprès de qqn** [personne] to win sb's confidence ; [histoire] to find credence with *ou* to be believed by sb **4.** *Québec* UNIV credit.

◆ **crédits** *nmpl* [fonds] funds ■ **accorder des ~s** to grant *ou* to allocate funds ‖ [autorisation de dépenses] : **~s budgétaires** supplies ■ **voter des ~s** to vote supplies.
◆ **à crédit** ◇ *loc adj* ▷ **vente.**
◇ *loc adv* : **acheter à ~** to buy on credit ■ **vendre qqch à ~** to sell sthg on credit.
◆ **à mon crédit, à son crédit** *etc loc adv* to my/her *etc* credit ■ **c'est à mettre** *ou* **porter à son ~** one must credit him with it.
◆ **de crédit** *loc adj* [agence, établissement] credit *(modif).*

crédit-bail [kredibaj] (*pl* **crédits-bails**) *nm* leasing.

créditer [3] [kredite] *vt* **1.** BANQUE [somme] to credit ■ **mon compte a été crédité de 1 500 euros** 1,500 euros were credited to my account ■ **les intérêts seront crédités sur votre compte à la fin de chaque mois** the interest will be credited to your account at the end of every month **2.** SPORT to credit with **3.** *fig* **être crédité de** to be given credit *ou* to get the praise for ■ **c'est lui qui en sera crédité** he'll get (all) the credit for it.

créditeur, trice [kreditœr, tris] ◇ *adj* [solde] credit *(modif)* ■ **avoir un compte ~** to have an account in credit.
◇ *nm, f* customer in credit, creditworthy customer.

credo [kredo] *nm inv* **1.** [principe] credo, creed ■ **c'est mon ~** it's the thing I most fervently believe in **2.** RELIG : **le Credo** the (Apostles') Creed.

crédule [kredyl] *adj* gullible, credulous ■ **que tu es ~!** you'll believe anything!

crédulité [kredylite] *nf* gullibility, credulity.

créer [15] [kree] *vt* **1.** [inventer - personnage, style] to create ; [- machine] to invent ; [- vêtement] to create, to design ; [- mot] to invent, to coin **2.** THÉÂTRE [rôle] to create, to play for the first time ■ [pièce] to produce for the first time **3.** [occasionner, engendrer - emploi, différences, difficultés] to create ; [- poste] to create, to establish ; [- atmosphère] to create, to bring about *(insép)* ; [- tension] to give rise to ; [- précédent] to set ■ **~ des ennuis** *ou* **difficultés à qqn** to create problems for *ou* to cause trouble to sb ■ **elle a créé la surprise en remportant le match** she caused a sensation by winning the match **4.** [fonder - association, mouvement] to create, to found ; [- entreprise] to set up *(sép)* ; [- État] to establish, to create.
◆ **se créer** ◇ *vp (emploi passif)* [être établi] to be set up *ou* created.
◇ *vpt* : **il s'est créé un monde à lui** he's created a world of his own ■ **se ~ une clientèle** to build up a clientele.

crémaillère [kremajɛr] *nf* **1.** [de cheminée] trammel (hook) **2.** AUTO & MÉCAN rack **3.** RAIL rack.
◆ **à crémaillère** *loc adj* : **engrenage/direction à ~** rack (and pinion) gearing/steering ■ **chemin de fer à ~** rack railway.

crémation [kremasjɔ̃] *nf* cremation.

crématoire [krematwar] ◇ *adj* crematory.
◇ *nm* cremator *UK*, cinerator *US*.

crématorium [krematɔrjɔm] *nm* crematorium *UK*, crematory *US*.

crème [krɛm] ◇ *nf* **1.** CULIN [préparation] cream ■ [entremets] cream (dessert) ➜ **~ anglaise** custard ■ **~ au beurre** butter cream ■ **~ brûlée** crème brûlée ■ **~ (au) caramel** crème caramel ■ **~ Chantilly** sweetened chilled whipped cream ■ **~ fleurette** ≃ low-fat single cream ■ **~ fouettée** whipped cream ■ **~ fraîche** crème fraîche ■ **~ fraîche épaisse** double *UK ou* heavy *US* cream ■ **~ glacée** ice-cream ■ **~ du lait** top of the milk ■ **~ fraîche liquide** single cream ■ **~ pâtissière** confectioner's custard ■ **~ renversée** custard cream *UK*, cup custard *US* ■ **la ~ de** *fam* : **c'est la ~ des maris** he's the perfect husband **2.** [potage] : **~ de poireaux** cream of leek soup **3.** [boisson] : **~ de cassis** crème de cassis ■ **~ de cacao/menthe** crème de cacao/menthe **4.** [cosmétique] cream ■ **~ (de soins) pour les mains/le visage** hand/face cream ■ **~ antirides** anti-wrinkle cream ■ **~ de beauté** beauty *ou* skin cream ■ **~ décolorante** bleaching cream ■ **~ dépilatoire** hair removing cream ■ **~ hydratante** moisturizing cream, moisturizer ■ **~ à raser** shaving cream.
◇ *adj inv* off-white, cream, cream-coloured.
◇ *nm* **1.** [couleur] cream (colour) **2.** *fam* [café] white coffee *UK*, coffee with milk *ou* cream ■ **un grand/petit ~** a large/small cup of white coffee.
◆ **à la crème** *loc adj* [gâteau] cream *(modif)* ■ **framboises à la ~** raspberries and cream ■ **escalopes à la ~** escalopes with cream sauce.

crémerie [krɛmri] *nf* [boutique] *shop selling cheese and other dairy products.*

crémeux, euse [kremø, øz] *adj* **1.** [onctueux] creamy, unctuous, smooth **2.** [gras - fromage] soft.

crémier, ère [kremje, ɛr] *nm, f* dairyman (*f* dairywoman).

crémone [kremɔn] *nf* window catch.

créneau, x [kreno] *nm* **1.** ARCHIT [creux] crenel (embrasure), crenelle ■ [bloc de pierre] crenellation ■ **à ~x** crenellated ➜ **monter au ~** *fam* to step into the breach **2.** [meurtrière] slit, loophole ■ **~ de visée** aiming slit **3.** AUTO [espace] gap, (parking) space ■ **faire un ~** to reverse into a (parking) space *UK*, to parallel park *US* **4.** RADIO & TV [temps d'antenne] slot ■ **~ horaire/publicitaire** time/advertizing slot ‖ [dans un emploi du temps] slot, gap **5.** ÉCON gap (in the market), opening ■ **trouver un bon ~** to find a good opening (in the market).

crénelé, e [krɛnle] *adj* **1.** ARCHIT crenellated **2.** MÉTALL notched ■ [pièce de monnaie] milled.

créneler [24] [krɛnle] *vt* **1.** ARCHIT to crenellate **2.** MÉTALL to notch ■ [pièce de monnaie] to mill.

crénelure [krɛnlyr] *nf* **1.** ARCHIT crenellation **2.** MÉTALL notch.

crénom [krenɔ̃] *interj fam vieilli* **~ (de nom** *ou* **de Dieu)!** [d'impatience] for God's *ou* Pete's sake! ; [de colère] damn it! ; [de surprise] blimey! *UK*, holy cow! *US*.

créole [kreɔl] *adj* creole.
◆ **Créole** *nmf* Creole.
◆ **créole** *nm* LING creole.
◆ **créoles** *nfpl* hoop earrings.

crêpage [krɛpaʒ] *nm* **1.** [de tissu] crimping ■ [de papier] cockling *ou* crinkling (up) **2.** [des cheveux] backcombing ■ **~ de chignon** [coups] fight *ou* set-to *(between women).*

crêpe[1] [krɛp] *nm* **1.** TEXT crepe, crêpe ■ **~ de Chine** crepe de Chine ■ **~ de deuil** *ou* **noir** black mourning crepe ■ **porter un ~** [brassard] to wear a black armband ; [au revers de la veste] to wear a black ribbon ; [sur le chapeau] to wear a black hatband **2.** [caoutchouc] crepe rubber.
◆ **de crêpe** *loc adj* **1.** [funéraire] mourning ■ **voile de ~** mourning veil **2.** [chaussures, semelle] rubber *(modif).*

crêpe[2] [krɛp] *nf* CULIN pancake ■ **~ au beurre/sucre** pancake with butter/sugar ■ **~ au jambon et aux champignons** pancake filled with ham and mushrooms ➜ **~ dentelle** *light very thin pancake* ■ **~ Suzette** crêpe suzette.

crêpelé, e [krɛple] *adj* [ondulé] frizzy ■ [à l'africaine] afro.

crêper [4] [krepe] *vt* **1.** [cheveux] to backcomb **2.** TEXT to crimp, to crisp **3.** [papier] to cockle *ou* to crinkle (up).
◆ **se crêper** *vpt* : **se ~ les cheveux** to backcomb one's hair ➜ **se ~ le chignon** *fam* to have a go at each other *ou* a bust-up.

crêperie [krɛpri] *nf* [restaurant] pancake restaurant, creperie ■ [stand] pancake stall.

crépi, e [krepi] *adj* roughcast *(modif).*
◆ **crépi** *nm* roughcast.

crêpier, ère [krepje, ɛr] *nm, f* [d'un restaurant] pancake restaurant owner ■ [d'un stand] pancake maker *ou* seller.
◆ **crêpière** *nf* [poêle] pancake pan ■ [plaque] griddle.

crépine [krepin] *nf* ZOOL & CULIN caul.

crépinette [krepinɛt] *nf* CULIN flat sausage *(in a caul).*

crépir [32] [krepir] *vt* to roughcast.

crépitation [krepitasjɔ̃] *nf* MÉD : **~ osseuse** crepitation, crepitus.
◆ **crépitations** *nfpl* [d'un feu] crackle, crackling.

crépitement [krepitmɑ̃] *nm* [d'un feu] crackle, crackling ■ [d'une fusillade] rattle ■ [d'une friture] splutter ■ [de la pluie] pitter-patter ■ **les ~s de la grêle sur les feuilles** the pattering of hail on the leaves.

crépiter [3] [krepite] *vi* **1.** [feu, coups de feu] to crackle ■ [pluie] to patter ■ [friture] to splutter **2.** MÉD to crepitate.

crépon [krepɔ̃] *nm* **1.** [papier] crepe paper **2.** TEXT crepon, seersucker.

CREPS, Creps [krɛps] (*abr de* **centre régional d'éducation physique et sportive**) *nm regional sports centre.*

crépu, e [krepy] *adj* [cheveux] frizzy.

crépusculaire [krepyskylɛr] *adj* **1.** *litt* [lueur, moment] twilight *(modif)* ■ **une beauté ~** *fig* a fading beauty **2.** ZOOL crepuscular.

crépuscule [krepyskyl] *nm* **1.** [fin du jour] twilight, dusk **2.** ASTRON [lumière - du soir] twilight ; [- du matin] dawn light.
◆ **au crépuscule de** *loc prép litt* **au ~ de sa vie/du siècle** in the twilight of his life/the closing years of the century.

crescendo [kreʃɛndo, kreʃɛ̃do] ◇ *nm* **1.** MUS crescendo **2.** [montée] escalation.
◇ *adv* crescendo ■ **aller ~** [notes] to go crescendo ; [bruits, voix] to grow louder and louder ; [violence] to rise, to escalate ; [mécontentement] to reach a climax.

cresson [kresɔ̃] *nm* BOT & CULIN cress ■ **~ (d'eau** *ou* **de fontaine)** water cress.

crésus [krezys] *nm* Croesus, rich man.

Crésus [krezys] *npr* Croesus.

crêt [krɛt] *nm* hogsback.

Crète [krɛt] *npr f* : **(la) ~** Crete.

crête [krɛt] *nf* **1.** ORNITH [d'oiseau] crest ■ [de volaille] comb **2.** MIL [d'un casque] crest **3.** [d'une montagne, d'un toit] crest, ridge ■ [d'un mur] crest, top ■ [d'une vague] crest ■ **~ de plage** *ou* **prélittorale** GÉOGR watershed **4.** SC peak.

crête-de-coq [krɛtdəkɔk] (*pl* **crêtes-de-coq**) *nf* **1.** BOT cockscomb **2.** MÉD venereal papilloma.

crétin, e [kretɛ̃, in] ◇ *adj* moronic.
◇ *nm, f* **1.** [imbécile] moron, cretin **2.** MÉD & *vieilli* cretin.

crétinerie [kretinri] *nf* **1.** [comportement] stupidity, idiocy, moronic behaviour **2.** [acte] idiotic thing (to do) ■ [propos] idiotic thing (to say).

crétinisme [kretinism] *nm* **1.** [caractère] stupidity, idiocy **2.** MÉD & *vieilli* cretinism.

crétois, e [kretwa, az] *adj* Cretan.
◆ **Crétois, e** *nm, f* Cretan.

cretonne [krətɔn] *nf* cretonne.

creusement [krøzmɑ̃] *nm* [d'un trou] digging ■ [d'un canal] digging, cutting ■ [d'un puits] digging, sinking.

creuser [3] [krøze] *vt* **1.** [excaver - puits, mine] to dig, to sink ; [- canal] to dig, to cut ; [- tranchée] to dig, to excavate ; [- sillon] to plough ; [- passage souterrain, tunnel] to make, to bore, to dig ■ **~ un trou** [à la pelle] to dig a hole ; [en grattant] to scratch a hole ■ **la rivière a creusé son lit** the river has hollowed out its bed ■ **~ sa propre tombe** *fig* to dig one's own grave ■ **ça a creusé un abîme** *ou* **fossé entre eux** this has opened up a gulf between them ■ **~ sa tombe avec ses dents** to eat o.s. into an early grave **2.** [faire un trou dans - gén] to hollow (out) ; [- avec une cuillère] to scoop (out) ■ **~ la terre** to dig (a hole in) the earth **3.** [ployer] : **~ les reins** *ou* **le dos** to arch one's back ■ **~ la taille** to exaggerate one's waist **4.** [marquer - traits du visage] : **joues creusées par la souffrance** cheeks sunken with pain ■ **le visage creusé par la fatigue** his face hollow with fatigue **5.** *fam* [ouvrir l'appétit de] to make hungry ■ **la marche m'a creusé (l'estomac)** the walk gave me an appetite *ou* whetted my appetite *ou* made me feel hungry ■ *(en usage absolu)* **les émotions, ça creuse!** *hum* excitement gives you an appetite! **6.** [approfondir - idée] to look *ou* to go into *(insép)* ; [- problème, question] to look *ou* to delve into *(insép)* ■ *(en usage absolu)* **il paraît intelligent, mais il vaut mieux ne pas ~ (trop loin)** he seems intelligent, but it might be better not to go into it too deeply **7.** COUT [décolleté] to make deeper *ou* lower ■ [emmanchure] to make bigger.
◆ **se creuser** ◇ *vp (emploi réfléchi)* : **tu ne t'es pas beaucoup creusé pour écrire ce texte!** you didn't overtax yourself when you wrote this text! ➲ **se ~ la tête** *ou* **la cervelle** *fam* to rack one's brains.
◇ *vpi* **1.** [yeux, visage] to grow hollow ■ [joues] to grow gaunt *ou* hollow ■ [fossettes, rides] to appear ■ **la mer commence à se ~** the sea's starting to swell **2.** [augmenter - écart] to grow bigger ■ **le fossé entre eux se creuse** the gap between them is widening.

creuset [krøzɛ] *nm* **1.** PHARM & TECHNOL crucible, melting pot ■ [d'un haut-fourneau] crucible, hearth **2.** [rassemblement] melting pot, mixture ■ **~ de cultures** a melting pot of cultures.

creux, euse [krø, krøz] *adj* **1.** [évidé - dent, tronc] hollow ■ *fig* **j'ai le ventre ~** my stomach feels hollow, I feel hungry **2.** [concave - joues] hollow, gaunt ; [- visage] gaunt ; [- yeux] sunken, hollow ■ **un chemin ~** a sunken lane **3.** [qui résonne - voix] cavernous, hollow ; [- son] hollow **4.** *péj* [inconsistant - discours, phrases] empty, meaningless ; [- promesses] hollow, empty ; [- argumentation] weak **5.** [sans activité] : **périodes creuses** [au travail] slack periods ; [dans une tarification] off-peak periods ■ **pendant la saison creuse** [pour le commerce] during the slack season ; [pour les vacanciers] during the off-peak season ■ **heures creuses : la communication/le trajet aux heures creuses ne vous coûtera que 5 euros** the phone call/journey will cost you only 5 euros off-peak **6.** COUT [pli] inverted.
◆ **creux** ◇ *nm* **1.** [trou - dans un roc] hole, cavity ; [- d'une dent, d'un tronc] hollow (part), hole, cavity ■ **la route est pleine de ~ et de bosses** the road is bumpy *ou* is full of potholes ■ **avoir un ~ (à l'estomac)** *fam* to feel peckish *UK ou* a bit hungry **2.** [concavité - d'une main, d'une épaule] hollow ; [- de l'estomac] pit ■ **il a bu dans le ~ de ma main** it drank out of my hand ■ **j'ai mal dans le ~ du dos** *ou* **des reins** I've a pain in the small of my back **3.** [dépression - d'une courbe, d'une vague] trough **4.** [inactivité] slack period ■ **il y a un ~ des ventes en janvier** business slows down *ou* slackens off in January **5.** ART mould **6.** NAUT [d'une voile] belly.
◇ *adv* : **sonner ~** to give *ou* to have a hollow sound.
◆ **au creux de** *loc prép* : **au ~ de ses bras** (nestled) in his arms ➲ **au ~ de la vague** *pr* in the trough of the wave ■ **être au ~ de la vague** *fig* [entreprise, personne] to be going through a bad patch.

crevaison [krəvɛzɔ̃] *nf* puncture *UK*, flat *US* ■ **avoir une ~** to have a puncture *ou* a flat tyre *UK*, to have a flat *US*.

crevant, e [krəvɑ̃, ɑ̃t] *adj fam* **1.** [pénible - travail] exhausting, backbreaking ; [- enfant] exhausting **2.** [drôle - personne] killing, priceless ; [- histoire, spectacle] killing, side-splitting ■ **elle est ~e, sa gamine** her kid's a scream *ou* riot.

crevasse [krəvas] *nf* **1.** GÉOGR [dans le sol] crevice, fissure, split ■ [sur un roc] crack, crevice, fissure ■ [d'un glacier] crevasse **2.** [sur les lèvres, les mains] crack, split ■ **j'ai des ~s aux doigts** my fingers are badly chapped.

crevassé, e [krəvase] *adj* **1.** [sol] cracked, fissured **2.** [peau] chapped.

crevasser [3] [krəvase] *vt* **1.** [sol] to cause cracks *ou* fissures in **2.** [peau] to chap.
◆ **se crevasser** *vpi* **1.** [sol] to become cracked **2.** [peau] to become chapped.

crevé, e [krəve] *adj* **1.** [pneu] flat, punctured ■ [tympan] pierced ■ [yeux] gouged-out ■ [ballon] burst ■ **j'ai un pneu ~** I've got a puncture *UK ou* flat *US* **2.** [mort - animal] dead **3.** [fatigué] shattered *UK*, bushed *US*.
◆ **crevé** *nm* COUT slash.
◆ **à crevés** *loc adj* [chaussure, manche] slashed.

crève [krɛv] *nf fam* [rhume] bad cold ■ **tu vas attraper la ~** you'll catch your death (of cold).

crève-cœur [krɛvkœr] *nm inv* : **c'est un ~ de les voir** it's a heartbreaking *ou* heart-rending sight to see them.

crève-la-faim [krɛvlafɛ̃] *nm inv* half-starved wretch.

crever [19] [krəve] ◇ *vt* **1.** [faire éclater - abcès] to burst (open) ; [- bulle, ballon, sac] to burst ; [- pneu] to puncture, to burst ; [- tympan] to puncture, to pierce ▪ **un cri vint ~ le silence** a cry pierced *OU* rent the silence ▪ **~ un œil à qqn** [agression] to gouge *OU* to put out sb's eye ; [accident] to blind sb in one eye ▪ **cela crève le cœur** it's heartbreaking *OU* heart-rending ▪ **tu me crèves le cœur!** you're breaking my heart! ▶ **ça crève les yeux** *fam* [c'est évident] it's as plain as the nose on your face, it sticks out a mile ; [c'est visible] it's staring you in the face, it's plain for all to see ▪ **~ le plafond** [prix] to go through the roof ▪ **~ l'écran** [acteur] to have great presence (on the screen) **2.** *fam* [fatiguer] to wear out ▪ **~ sa monture** to ride one's horse to death **3.** *loc* **~ la faim** *fam* [par pauvreté] to be starving.
◇ *vi* **1.** [éclater - pneu] to puncture ; [- ballon, bulle, nuage] to burst ; [- abcès] to burst ▪ **on a crevé sur la rocade** *fam* we had a puncture *UK OU* a flat *US* on the bypass **2.** △ [mourir] to snuff it△ *UK*, to kick the bucket ▪ **qu'il crève!** to hell with him! ▪ **ils me laisseraient ~ comme un chien** they'd just let me die like a dog **3.** [mourir - animal, végétal] to die (off).
◆ **crever de** *v+prép* **1.** [éprouver] : **~ de faim** [par pauvreté] to be starving ; [être en appétit] to be starving *OU* famished ▪ **~ de soif** to be parched ▪ **je crève de chaud!** I'm baking *OU* boiling! ▪ **on crève de froid ici** it's freezing cold *OU* you could freeze to death here ▪ **~ de peur/d'inquiétude** to be scared/ worried to death **2.** [être plein de] : **~ de jalousie** to be eaten up with jealousy ▪ **~ d'orgueil** to be puffed up *OU* bloated with pride ▪ **je crève d'impatience de le voir** I can't wait to see him ▪ **~ d'envie de faire qqch** to be dying to do sthg.
◆ **se crever** *vp (emploi réfléchi)* : **se ~ au boulot** *OU* **à la tâche** to work o.s. to death ▶ **se ~ le cul**△ to bust a gut *UK*, to bust one's ass△ *US*.

crevette [krəvɛt] *nf* : **~ d'eau douce** (freshwater) shrimp ▪ **~ grise** shrimp ▪ **~ rose** (common) prawn.

crevettier [krəvɛtje] *nm* **1.** [filet] shrimping net **2.** [bateau] shrimper, shrimp boat.

CRF *npr f* = **Croix-Rouge française**.

cri [kri] *nm* **1.** [éclat de voix - gén] cry ; [- puissant] shout, yell ; [- perçant] shriek, scream ▪ **un petit ~ aigu** a squeak ▪ **~ de douleur** cry *OU* scream of pain ▪ **~ de joie** cry *OU* shout of joy ▪ **~ d'indignation** cry *OU* scream of indignation ▪ **~ d'horreur** shriek *OU* scream of horror ▪ **jeter** *OU* **pousser un ~** to cry out ▪ **pousser un ~ de joie/douleur** to cry out with joy/in pain ▶ **pousser des ~s** *pr* to cry out, to shout ; *fig* to make loud protests ▪ **jeter** *OU* **pousser des hauts ~s** to raise the roof, to raise a hue and cry, to kick up a fuss **2.** ZOOL [d'un oiseau] call ▪ [d'un petit oiseau] chirp ▪ [d'une chouette, d'un paon, d'un singe] screech ▪ [d'une mouette] cry ▪ [d'un dindon] gobble ▪ [d'un perroquet] squawk ▪ [d'un canard] quack ▪ [d'une oie] honk ▪ [d'une souris] squeak ▪ [d'un porc] squeal **3.** [parole] cry ▪ **~ d'amour** cry of love ▪ **~ de détresse** cry of distress ▪ **jeter** *OU* **lancer un ~ d'alarme** to warn against the danger ▪ **défiler au ~ de "des subventions!"** to march chanting "subsidies!" ▶ **~ du cœur** cri de coeur, cry from the heart.
◆ **à grands cris** *loc adv* : **appeler qqn à grands ~s** to shout for sb ▪ **demander** *OU* **réclamer qqch à grands ~s** to cry out *OU* to clamour for sthg.
◆ **dernier cri** ◇ *loc adj* [voiture, vidéo] state-of-the-art ▪ **il s'est acheté des chaussettes dernier ~** he bought the latest thing in socks.
◇ *nm inv* : **c'est le dernier ~** [vêtement] it's the (very) latest vogue *OU* fashion *OU* thing ; [machine, vidéo] it's state-of-the-art.

criaillement [kriajmɑ̃] *nm* ORNITH [d'une oie] honk ▪ [d'un paon] screech ▪ [d'un faisan] cry.
◆ **criaillements** *nmpl* [de dispute] screeching, shrieking.

criailler [3] [kriaje] *vi* **1.** *fam* [crier sans cesse] to screech, to shriek ▪ **~ après qqn** to shriek at sb **2.** ORNITH [faisan] to cry ▪ [oie] to honk ▪ [paon] to squawk, to screech.

criailleries [kriajri] *nfpl* [de dispute] screeching, shrieking.

criant, e [krijɑ̃, ɑ̃t] *adj* [erreur] glaring ▪ [mauvaise foi, mensonge] blatant, glaring, rank *(adj)* ▪ [parti pris] blatant ▪ [différence, vérité] obvious, striking ▪ [injustice] flagrant, blatant, rank ▪ [preuve] striking, glaring.

criard, e [krijar, ard] *adj* **1.** [voix] shrill, piercing ▪ **un enfant ~** a noisy child **2.** [couleur] loud, garish ▪ [tenue] garish, gaudy **3.** [urgent - dettes] pressing.

criblage [kriblaʒ] *nm* **1.** [tamisage - de sable, de grains] riddling, sifting ; [- de charbon] riddling, screening, sifting ; [- d'un minerai] screening, jigging **2.** [calibrage - de fruits, d'huîtres] grading.

crible [kribl] *nm* [pour des graines, du sable] riddle, sift ▪ [pour un charbon, un minerai] screen ▪ **passer au ~** [charbon] to riddle, to screen, to sift ; [grains, sable] to riddle, to sift ; [fruits, œufs] to grade ; [région] to go over with a fine-tooth comb, to comb ; [preuves] to sift *OU* to examine closely ; [document] to examine closely, to go over with a fine-tooth comb ; [candidat] to screen (for a job).

cribler [3] [krible] *vt* **1.** [tamiser - sable, grains] to riddle, to sift ; [- minerai] to screen, to jig ; [- charbon] to riddle, to screen **2.** [calibrer - fruits, œufs] to grade **3.** [trouer de] : **~ de** : **~ qqch de trous** to riddle sthg with holes ▪ **la façade est criblée d'impacts de balles** the facade is riddled with bullet holes **4.** [assaillir de] : **~ de** : **~ qqn de coups** to rain blows on sb ▪ **~ qqn de questions** to bombard sb with questions, to fire questions at sb ▪ **~ qqn de reproches** to heap reproaches on sb **5.** [accabler] : **être criblé de** to be covered in ▪ **être criblé de dettes** to be crippled with debt, to be up to one's eyes in debt.

cribleur [kriblœr] *nm* [personne] screener, sifter ▪ [machine] sifter, sifting machine.

cric[1] [krik] *onomat* [bruit de déchirement] rip, crack ▪ **~ (crac)!** [tour de clé] click!

cric[2] [krik] *nm* AUTO (car) jack ▪ **mettre une voiture sur** *OU* **élever une voiture avec un ~** to jack a car up ▶ **~ hydraulique/à vis** hydraulic/screw jack.

cricket [krikɛt] *nm* SPORT cricket ▪ **jouer au ~** to play cricket.

cricri [krikri] *nm* **1.** *fam* [grillon] cricket **2.** [cri du grillon] chirp, chirp-chirp.

criée [krije] *nf* fish market *(where auctions take place)*.
◆ **à la criée** ◇ *loc adj* ⊳ **vente**.
◇ *loc adv* by auction ▪ **vendre du thon à la ~** to auction off tuna.

crier [10] [krije] ◇ *vi* **1.** [gén] to cry (out) ▪ [d'une voix forte] to shout, to yell ▪ [d'une voix perçante] to scream, to screech, to shriek ▪ **ne fais pas ~ ta mère!** don't get your mother angry! ▪ **~ de douleur** to scream with *OU* to cry out in pain ▪ **~ de joie** to shout for joy ▪ **~ de plaisir** to cry out with pleasure ▶ **~ comme un sourd** *fam* to shout one's head off ▪ **~ comme un damné** *OU* **putois** *OU* **veau** *fam* [fort] to shout *OU* to yell at the top of one's voice ; [avec des sons aigus] to squeal like a stuck pig ; [protester] to scream blue murder ▪ **~ à** : **~ à l'injustice** to call it an injustice ▪ **~ au miracle** to hail it as a miracle ▪ **~ au scandale** to call it a scandal, to cry shame ▪ **~ à l'assassin** to cry blue murder ▪ **~ au loup** to cry wolf ▪ **~ au voleur** to cry (stop) thief ▪ **~ à l'aide** *OU* **au secours** to shout for help, to cry for help **2.** ZOOL [oiseau] to call ▪ [souris] to squeak ▪ [porc] to squeal ▪ [chouette, singe] to call, to screech ▪ [perroquet] to squawk ▪ [paon] to screech ▪ [oie] to honk **3.** [freins, pneu] to squeak, to screech ▪ [cuir, craie] to squeak ▪ [charnière] to creak.
◇ *vt* **1.** [dire d'une voix forte - avertissement] to shout *OU* to cry (out) ; [- insultes, ordres] to bawl *OU* to yell out *(sép)* ▪ **elle nous cria de partir** she shouted at us to go ▶ **sans ~ gare** [arriver] without warning ; [partir] without so much as a by-your-leave **2.** [faire savoir] : **~ son innocence** to proclaim *OU* to protest one's innocence ▪ **~ famine** to complain of hunger ▪ **~ misère** [se plaindre] to complain of hardship ▪ **~ victoire** to crow (over one's victory) ▪ **~ contre** to complain *OU* to shout about *(insép)* ▶ **~ qqch sur les toits** [le rendre public] to shout *OU* to proclaim sthg from the rooftops ; [s'en vanter] to let everyone know about sthg **3.** [demander] : **~ vengeance** to call for revenge ▶ **~ grâce** *pr* to beg for mercy ; *fig* to cry for mercy.
◆ **crier après** *v+prép fam* **1.** [s'adresser à] to shout *OU* to yell at **2.** [réprimander] to scold.

crieur, euse [krijœr, øz] *nm, f* **1.** [vendeur] : **~ (de journaux)** newspaper seller *OU* vendor **2.** [dans une criée] auctioneer **3.** HIST : **~ (public)** town crier.

crime [krim] *nm* **1.** DR [infraction pénale] crime, (criminal) offence ▪ **commettre un ~** to commit a crime ▸ **un ~ contre l'État** (high) treason *ou* a crime against the state ▪ **~ contre l'humanité** crime against humanity ▪ **~ contre la paix** crime against peace ▪ **~ de guerre** war crime ▪ **~ de lèse-majesté** *pr* act *ou* crime of lèse-majesté ▪ **~ politique** political offence **2.** [meurtre] murder ▪ **c'est le ~ parfait** it's the perfect crime ▪ **l'heure du ~** the time of the murder ▪ **le motif du ~** the motive for the murder ▪ **commettre un ~** to commit a murder ▸ **~ crapuleux** heinous crime ▪ **~ (à motif) sexuel** sex crime *ou* murder ▪ **~ passionnel** crime passionnel, crime of passion ▪ **l'arme du ~** the murder weapon **3.** [acte immoral] crime, act ▪ **c'est un ~ de démolir ces églises** it's a crime *ou* it's criminal to knock down these churches ▪ **ce n'est pas un ~!** it's not a crime! ▸ **~ contre nature** act *ou* crime against nature ▪ **'Crime et châtiment'** ***Dostoïevski*** 'Crime and Punishment' **4.** [criminalité] : **le ~** crime ▸ **le ~ ne paie pas** *prov* crime doesn't pay.

Crimée [krime] *npr f* : **(la) ~** (the) Crimea.

criminalisation [kriminalizasjɔ̃] *nf* criminalization.

criminaliser [3] [kriminalize] *vt* to criminalize.
◆ **se criminaliser** *vpi* to become criminalized.

criminalité [kriminalite] *nf* **1.** SOCIOL crime ▪ **la grande/petite ~** serious/petty crime **2.** *sout* [caractère criminel] criminality, criminal nature.

criminel, elle [kriminɛl] ◇ *adj* **1.** [répréhensible - action, motif] criminal ▪ **acte ~** criminal offence, crime ▪ **une organisation ~le** a criminal organization, a crime syndicate **2.** [relatif aux crimes - droit, enquête] criminal ; [- brigade] crime *(modif)* **3.** [condamnable - acte] criminal, reprehensible ▪ **c'est ~ de...** it's criminal to..., it's a crime to... ▪ **avoir des pensées ~les** to think wicked thoughts.
◇ *nm, f* [gén] criminal ▪ [meurtrier] murderer ▪ **~ de guerre** war criminal.
◆ **criminel** *nm* DR [juridiction criminelle] : **le ~** criminal law ▪ **avocat au ~** criminal lawyer ▪ **poursuivre qqn au ~** to institute criminal proceedings against sb.

criminellement [kriminɛlmɑ̃] *adv* **1.** [répréhensiblement] criminally **2.** DR : **poursuivre qqn ~** to institute criminal proceedings against sb.

criminologie [kriminɔlɔʒi] *nf* criminology.

crin [krɛ̃] *nm* **1.** [de cheval] hair **2.** [rembourrage] horse hair.
◆ **à tout crin, à tous crins** *loc adj* out-and-out, diehard ▪ **les conservateurs à tout ~** the diehard *ou* dyed-in-the-wool conservatives.
◆ **de crin, en crin** *loc adj* horsehair *(modif)*.

crincrin [krɛ̃krɛ̃] *nm fam* (squeaky) fiddle.

crinière [krinjɛr] *nf* **1.** ZOOL mane **2.** *fam* [chevelure] mane, mop *péj hum* **3.** [d'un casque] plume.

crinoline [krinɔlin] *nf* **1.** TEXT crinoline **2.** [vêtement] crinoline petticoat.
◆ **à crinoline** *loc adj* [robe] crinoline *(modif)*.

crique [krik] *nf* GÉOGR creek, inlet, (small) rocky beach.

criquet [krikɛ] *nm* locust ▪ **~ pèlerin** *ou* **migrateur** migratory locust.

crise [kriz] *nf* **1.** [période, situation difficile] crisis ▪ **traverser une ~** to go through a crisis *ou* a critical time ▪ **la ~ de la quarantaine** the midlife crisis ▪ **~ de confiance** crisis of confidence ▪ **~ de conscience** crisis of conscience ▪ **~ d'identité** identity crisis **2.** ÉCON & POLIT crisis ▪ **~ du logement/papier** housing/paper shortage ▪ **~ boursière** [grave] crisis *ou* panic on the Stock Exchange ; [passagère] blip on the Stock Exchange ▪ **~ économique** economic crisis *ou* slump, recession ▪ **~ politique** political crisis ▪ **la ~ de 1929** the 1929 slump **3.** [accès] outburst, fit ▪ **~ de colère** fit of temper ▪ **~ de rage** angry outburst ▪ **~ de larmes** fit of crying ▪ **~ de désespoir** fit of despair ▪ **~ de jalousie** fit of jealousy ▪ **quelle** *ou* **la ~ (de rire)!** *fam* what a scream *ou* hoot *ou* riot! ▪ **être pris d'une ~ de rire** to laugh uproariously ▮ [de colère] (fit of) rage ▪ **piquer une ~** *fam* to throw *ou* to have a fit ▪ **pas besoin de nous faire une ~ pour ça!** *fam* no need to kick up such a fuss! ▮ [besoin urgent] : **pris d'une ~ de rangement** feeling an urge to tidy things up **4.** MÉD : **~ d'appendicite/d'arthrose** attack of appendicitis/arthritis ▪ **~ épileptique** *ou* **d'épilepsie** epileptic fit ▸ **une ~ cardiaque** a heart attack ▪ **~ de foie** queasy feeling ▪ **tu vas attraper une ~ de foie à manger tous ces chocolats** *fam* you'll make yourself sick if you eat all these chocolates ▪ **~ de nerfs** fit of hysterics, attack of nerves ▪ **elle a fait une ~ de nerfs** she went into hysterics.
◆ **en crise** *loc adj* : **être en ~** to undergo a crisis.

crispant, e [krispɑ̃, ɑ̃t] *adj* [attente] nerve-racking ▪ [stupidité, personne] exasperating, irritating, infuriating ▪ [bruit] irritating ▪ **arrête de me dire comment jouer, c'est ~ à la fin!** stop telling me how to play, it's getting on my nerves!

crispation [krispasjɔ̃] *nf* **1.** [du visage] tension ▪ [des membres] contraction **2.** [tic] twitch ▪ **le médicament peut provoquer des ~s au niveau des mains** the drug can cause the hands to twitch **3.** [anxiété] nervous tension **4.** [du cuir] shrivelling ▪ [du papier] cockling.

crispé, e [krispe] *adj* **1.** [contracté - sourire, rire] strained, tense ; [- personne, visage, doigts] tense **2.** *fam* [irrité] irritated, exasperated.

crisper [3] [krispe] *vt* **1.** [traits du visage] to contort, to tense ▪ [poings] to clench ▪ **le visage crispé par la souffrance** his face contorted *ou* tense with pain **2.** *fam* [irriter] : **~ qqn** to get on sb's nerves **3.** [rider - cuir] to shrivel up *(sép)* ▪ [papier] to cockle up *(sép)*.
◆ **se crisper** *vpi* **1.** [se contracter - visage] to tense (up) ; [- personne] to become tense ; [- doigts] to contract ; [- sourire] to become strained *ou* tense ; [- poings] to clench **2.** *fam* [s'irriter] to get annoyed.

criss [kris] = **kriss**.

crissement [krismɑ̃] *nm* [de pneus, de freins] squealing, screeching ▪ [du cuir] squeaking ▪ [de neige, de gravillons] crunching ▪ [d'étoffe, de papier] rustling ▪ [d'une craie, d'une scie] grating.

crisser [3] [krise] *vi* [pneus, freins] to squeal, to screech ▪ [cuir] to squeak ▪ [neige, gravillons] to crunch ▪ [étoffe, papier] to rustle ▪ [craie, scie] to grate ▪ **la craie crissait sur le tableau** the chalk grated on the blackboard.

cristal, aux [kristal, o] *nm* **1.** MINÉR : **un ~, du ~** crystal ▸ **~ de roche** rock crystal **2.** [objet] piece of crystalware *ou* of fine glassware ▪ **des cristaux** crystalware, fine glassware ▮ [d'un lustre] crystal droplets.
◆ **de cristal** *loc adj* **1.** [vase] crystal *(modif)* **2.** [pur - eau] crystal-like, crystalline ; [- voix] crystal-clear, crystalline.

cristallerie [kristalri] *nf* **1.** [fabrication] crystal-making **2.** [usine] (crystal) glassworks **3.** [objets] : **de la ~** crystalware, fine glassware.

cristallin, e [kristalɛ̃, in] *adj* **1.** *litt* [voix] crystal-clear, crystalline ▪ [eau] crystalline **2.** MINÉR [massif, rocher] crystalline.
◆ **cristallin** *nm* ANAT crystalline lens.

cristallisation [kristalizasjɔ̃] *nf* crystallization, crystallizing.

cristallisé, e [kristalize] *adj* crystallized.

cristalliser [3] [kristalize] *vt* to crystallize.
◆ **se cristalliser** *vpi* to crystallize.

cristallographie [kristalɔgrafi] *nf* crystallography.

cristaux [kristo] *pl* ▻ **cristal**.

criste-marine [kristmarin] (*pl* **cristes-marines**) *nf* samphire.

critère [kritɛr] *nm* **1.** [principe] criterion ▪ **~ moral/religieux** moral/religious criterion ▪ **~s de sélection** selection criteria **2.** [référence] reference (point), standard ▪ **~ de convergence** convergence criteria.

critérium [kriterjɔm] *nm* SPORT [en cyclisme] rally ▪ [en natation] gala ▪ **le grand ~, le ~ des deux ans** ÉQUIT maiden race for two-year-olds.

critiquable [kritikabl] *adj* which lends itself to criticism ▪ **une décision peu ~** an uncontentious decision.

critique [kritik] <> *adj* **1.** [qui condamne - article, personne] critical ; *péj* [- personne] faultfinding ▪ **se montrer très ~ envers** *ou* **à l'égard de** to be very critical towards ▪ **voir qqch d'un œil (très) ~** to have (great) reservations about sthg **2.** [plein de discernement - analyse, œuvre, personne] critical ▪ **avoir l'esprit** *ou* **le sens ~** to have good judgement, to be discerning **3.** [crucial - étape, période] critical, crucial ; [- opération, seuil] critical **4.** [inquiétant - état de santé, situation] critical **5.** SC critical.
<> *nmf* [commentateur] critic, reviewer ▪ **~ d'art** art critic ▪ **~ de cinéma** film critic *ou* reviewer ▪ **~ littéraire** book reviewer, literary critic ▪ **~ musical** music critic ▪ **~ de théâtre** drama critic.
<> *nf* **1.** PRESSE review ▪ UNIV critique, appreciation ▪ **~ cinématographique** film review ▪ **~ littéraire** literary *ou* book review ▪ **~ musicale/théâtrale** music/drama review **2.** [activité] : **la ~ théâtrale** drama criticism ▪ **la ~ gastronomique** food writing ▪ **la ~ littéraire** literary criticism ▪ **faire la ~ de** PRESSE to review ; UNIV to write an appreciation *ou* a critique of **3.** [personnes] : **très bien/mal accueilli par la ~** acclaimed/panned by the critics ▪ **l'approbation/le mépris de la ~** critical acclaim/scorn **4.** [blâme] criticism ▪ **adresser** *ou* **faire une ~ à un auteur** to level criticism at an author **5.** [fait de critiquer] : **la ~** criticism, criticizing ⊳ **la ~ est aisée** *ou* **facile (mais l'art est difficile)** it's easy to be a critic (but hard to be an artist).

critiquer [3] [kritike] *vt* **1.** [blâmer - initiative, mesure, personne] to criticize, to be critical of ▪ **tu es toujours à me ~!** you find fault with everything I do! ▪ **il s'est déjà fait ~ pour sa négligence** he has already been criticized for his negligence **2.** [analyser] to critique, to criticize.

critiqueur, euse [kritikœr, øz] *nm, f péj* faultfinder ▪ **les ~s** those who carp *ou* who find fault.

croassement [krɔasmɑ̃] *nm* caw, cawing.

croasser [3] [krɔase] *vi* to caw.

croate [krɔat] *adj* Croat, Croatian.
◆ **Croate** *nmf* Croat, Croatian.
◆ **croate** *nm* LING Croat, Croatian.

Croatie [krɔasi] *npr f* : **(la) ~** Croatia.

croc [kro] *nm* **1.** ZOOL [de chien] tooth, fang ▪ [d'ours, de loup] fang ▪ **montrer les ~s** [animal] to bare its teeth *ou* fangs ▪ **la Prusse montrait les ~s** *fig* Prussia was showing its teeth **2.** *fam* [dent] (long) tooth ▪ **avoir les ~s : j'ai les ~s** I could eat a horse **3.** [crochet - de boucher] butcher's *ou* meat hook ; [- de marinier] hook, boathook ▪ **moustache en ~s** handlebar moustache.

croc-en-jambe [krɔkɑ̃ʒɑ̃b] (*pl* **crocs-en-jambe**) *nm* : **faire un ~ à qqn** *pr* & *fig* to trip sb up.

croche [krɔʃ] *nf* MUS quaver *UK*, eighth note *US* ▪ **double ~** semiquaver *UK*, sixteenth note *US*.

croche-patte [krɔʃpat] (*pl* **croche-pattes**), **croche-pied** [krɔʃpje] (*pl* **croche-pieds**) = **croc-en-jambe**.

crochet [krɔʃɛ] *nm* **1.** [attache, instrument] hook ▪ [pour volets] catch ▪ **~ d'arrêt** pawl, catch ▪ **~ d'attelage** coupling hook ▪ **~ à bottes** boot-hook ▪ **~ de boucher** *ou* **boucherie** meathook, butcher's hook ▪ **~ à boutons** buttonhook **2.** [de serrurier] picklock, lock pick **3.** COUT [instrument] crochet hook ▪ [technique] crochet ▪ [ouvrage] crochetwork ▪ **faire du ~** to crochet **4.** SPORT hook ▪ **il l'a envoyé à terre d'un ~ à la tête** he knocked him down with a hook to the head ▪ **~ du droit/gauche** right/left hook **5.** [détour] detour, roundabout way ▪ **faire un ~** to make a detour, to go a roundabout way **6.** [virage brusque - d'une voie] sudden *ou* sharp turn ; [- d'une voiture] sudden swerve ▪ **faire un ~** [rue] to bend sharply ; [conducteur] to swerve suddenly **7.** [concours] : **~ radiophonique** talent contest **8.** IMPR square bracket ▪ **entre ~s** in square brackets **9.** ZOOL [d'un serpent] fang ▪ [d'un chamois] horn ▪ ENTOM hook.
◆ **au crochet** <> *loc adj* [nappe, châle] crocheted.
<> *loc adv* : **faire un vêtement au ~** to crochet a garment.

crocheter [28] [krɔʃte] *vt* [serrure] to pick ▪ [porte] to pick the lock on.

crochu, e [krɔʃy] *adj* [nez] hooked, hook *(modif)* ▪ [doigts, mains] claw-like.

croco [krɔko] *nm fam* crocodile, crocodile-skin.
◆ **en croco** *loc adj fam* crocodile *(modif)*.

crocodile [krɔkɔdil] *nm* **1.** ZOOL crocodile **2.** [peau] crocodile, crocodile skin.
◆ **en crocodile** *loc adj* crocodile *(modif)*.

crocus [krɔkys] *nm* crocus.

croire [107] [krwar] <> *vt* **1.** [fait, histoire, personne] to believe ▪ **je te crois sur parole** I'll take your word for it ▪ **crois-moi, on n'a pas fini d'en entendre parler!** believe me, we haven't heard the last of this ▪ **je te crois!** *iron* I believe you! ▪ **je ne peux pas ~ pareille méchanceté de ta part** I can't believe (that) you could be so nasty ▪ **je n'en crois pas un mot** I don't believe a word of it ▪ **je te prie de ~ qu'il va entendre parler de nous!** believe me, we haven't finished with him! ▪ **tu ne me feras pas ~ que...** I refuse to believe that... ▪ **on lui a fait ~ que la réunion était annulée** they told him that the meeting had been cancelled ▪ **en ~** [se fier à] : **croyez-en ceux qui ont l'expérience** take it from those who know ▪ **à l'en ~** if he is to be believed ▪ **si j'en crois cette lettre** if I go by what this letter says ▪ **si vous m'en croyez** if you ask me *ou* want my opinion ▪ **je n'en crois pas mes yeux/oreilles** I can't believe my eyes/ears ⊳ **~ dur comme fer que** *fam* to be absolutely convinced that ▪ **ne va pas ~ ça!** don't you believe it! **2.** [penser] to believe, to think ▪ **je croyais pouvoir venir plus tôt** I thought *ou* assumed I could come earlier ▪ **à la voir on croirait sa sœur** to look at her, you'd think she was her sister ▪ **on croit rêver!** it's unbelievable! ▪ **tu ne crois pas si bien dire** you don't know how right you are ▪ **on l'a crue enceinte** she was believed *ou* thought to be pregnant ▪ **je ne suis pas celle que vous croyez** I'm not that kind of person ▪ **il faut ~ que tu avais tort** it looks like you were wrong ▪ **je crois que oui** I believe *ou* think so ▪ **il croit que non** he doesn't think so, he thinks not ▪ **on croirait qu'il dort** he looks as if he's asleep ⊳ **il faut ~, faut ~** *fam* (it) looks like it, it would seem so.
<> *vi* **1.** [sans analyser] to believe ▪ **on leur apprend à réfléchir et non à ~** they're taught to think and not simply to believe what they're told **2.** RELIG to believe ▪ **il croit** he's a believer ▪ **je ne crois plus** I've lost my faith.
◆ **croire à** *v+prép* **1.** [avoir confiance en] to believe in ▪ **il faut ~ à l'avenir** one must have faith in the future **2.** [accepter comme réel] to believe in ▪ **tu crois encore au Père Noël!** *fig* you're so naive! ▪ **c'est à n'y pas ~!** you just wouldn't believe *ou* credit it! ▪ **elle voulait faire ~ à un accident** she wanted it to look like an accident **3.** RELIG to believe in ▪ **~ à la vie éternelle** to believe in eternal life ▪ **il ne croit ni à Dieu ni au diable** he's a complete heathen **4.** [dans la correspondance] : **je vous prie de ~ à mes sentiments les meilleurs** yours sincerely ▪ **croyez à mon amitié toute dévouée** yours ever.
◆ **croire en** *v+prép* **1.** [avoir confiance en] to believe in **2.** RELIG : **~ en Dieu** to believe in God.
◆ **se croire** <> *vpt* [penser avoir] : **il se croit tous les droits** *ou* **tout permis** he thinks he can get away with anything.
<> *vpi* **1.** [se juger] : **il se croit beau/intelligent** he thinks he's handsome/intelligent ▪ **tu te crois malin?** think you're clever, do you? ▪ **elle se croit quelqu'un** she thinks she's something special ▪ **où te crois-tu?** where do you think you are? **2.** *fam loc* **se ~ sorti de la cuisse de Jupiter** to think one is God's gift (to mankind) ▪ **s'y ~ : il s'y croit!** he really thinks a lot of himself! ▪ **et ton nom en grosses lettres sur l'affiche, mais tu t'y crois déjà!** and your name in huge letters on the poster, you're letting your imagination run away with you!

croîs *etc v* ⊳ **croître**.

croisade [krwazad] *nf* **1.** HIST crusade ▪ **les ~s** the (Holy) Crusades **2.** *fig* [campagne] campaign, crusade ▪ **partir en ~ contre l'injustice** to go on a crusade *ou* to mount a campaign against injustice.

croisé, e [krwaze] *adj* **1.** [bras] folded ▪ [jambes] crossed ▪ **il était debout, les bras ~s** he was standing with his arms folded ▪ **ne reste pas là les bras ~s!** don't just stand there! ▪ **assis les jambes ~es** sitting cross-legged **2.** LITTÉR [rimes] alternate **3.** [hybride - animal, plante] crossbred **4.** [veste, veston] double-breasted **5.** ÉCON : **détention** *ou* **participation ~e** crossholding.
◆ **croisé** *nm* HIST crusader.
◆ **croisée** *nf* **1.** [intersection] crossing ▪ **être à la ~e des chemins** to be at the parting of the ways **2.** ARCHIT : **~e d'ogives** intersecting ribs **3.** [fenêtre] casement.

croisement [krwazmɑ̃] *nm* **1.** [intersection] crossroads, junction ▪ **au ~ de la rue et de l'avenue** at the intersection of the street and the avenue **2.** [hybridation] crossbreeding, crossing, interbreeding ▪ **faire des ~s (de races)** to crossbreed *ou* to interbreed (animals) ▪ **c'est un ~ entre un épagneul et un setter** it's a cross between a spaniel and a setter, it's a spaniel-setter crossbreed **3.** [rencontre] : **le ~ de deux voitures/navires** two cars/boats passing each other.

croiser [3] [krwaze] ◇ *vt* **1.** [mettre en croix - baguettes, fils] to cross ▪ **~ les jambes** to cross one's legs ▪ **~ les bras** to cross *ou* to fold one's arms ⊳ **~ le fer** *ou* **l'épée avec qqn** *pr* & *fig* to cross swords with sb **2.** [traverser] to cross, to intersect, to meet ▪ **là où la route croise la voie ferrée** where the road and the railway cross, at the junction of the road and the railway ⊳ **~ la route** *ou* **le chemin de qqn** *fig* to come across sb **3.** [rencontrer] to pass, to meet ▪ **ses yeux ont croisé les miens** her eyes met mine **4.** [hybrider] to cross, to crossbreed, to interbreed.
◇ *vi* **1.** [vêtement] to cross over **2.** NAUT to cruise.
◆ **se croiser** ◇ *vp (emploi réciproque)* **1.** [se rencontrer] to come across *ou* to meet *ou* to pass each other ▪ **leurs regards se sont croisés** their eyes met **2.** [aller en sens opposé - trains] to pass (each other) ; [- lettres] to cross ; [- routes] to cross, to intersect ▪ **nos chemins se sont croisés, nos routes se sont croisées** our paths met.
◇ *vpt* : **se ~ les bras** *pr* to fold one's arms ; *fig* [être oisif] to twiddle one's thumbs.
◇ *vpi* HIST to go off to the Crusades.

Croisette [krwazɛt] *npr f* : **(le boulevard de) la ~** *famous boulevard running along the seafront in Cannes.*

croiseur [krwazœr] *nm* MIL cruiser.

croisière [krwazjɛr] *nf* cruise ▪ **faire une ~ aux Bahamas** to go on a cruise to the Bahamas.

croisiériste [krwazjerist] *nmf* tourist on a cruise.

croisillon [krwazijɔ̃] *nm* [d'une fenêtre] cross bar ▪ [au dos d'un meuble] strengthener.

croissait *etc v* ⊳ **croître.**

croissance [krwasɑ̃s] *nf* **1.** PHYSIOL growth ▪ **elle est en pleine ~** she's growing fast **2.** [développement - d'une plante] growth ; [- d'un pays] development, growth ; [- d'une entreprise] growth, expansion ▪ **~ démographique** population growth ▪ **la ~ zéro** zero growth ▪ **notre entreprise est en pleine ~** our company is growing *ou* expanding.

croissant[1] [krwasɑ̃] *nm* **1.** CULIN croissant ▪ **~ aux amandes** almond croissant ▪ **~ au beurre** croissant made with butter ▪ **~ au fromage** cheese-filled croissant ▪ **~ ordinaire** croissant made without butter **2.** [forme incurvée] crescent **3.** ASTRON crescent ▪ **~ de lune** crescent moon **4.** HIST & GÉOGR : **le Croissant fertile** the Fertile Crescent.

croissant[2]**, e** [krwasɑ̃, ɑ̃t] *adj* growing, increasing ▪ **tension ~e dans le sud du pays** increasing tension in the south of the country.

croissanterie [krwasɑ̃tri] *nf* croissant shop *UK ou* store *US.*

Croissant-Rouge [krwasɑ̃ruʒ] *npr m* : **le ~** the Red Crescent.

croître [93] [krwatr] *vi* **1.** PHYSIOL to grow **2.** [augmenter - rivière] to swell ; [- lune] to wax ▪ **les jours ne cessent de ~** the days are growing longer ▪ **elle sentait ~ en elle une violente colère** she could feel a violent rage growing within her ▪ **ça ne fait que ~ et embellir** it's getting better and better ; *iron* it's getting worse and worse ▪ **~ en : ~ en beauté et en sagesse** to grow wiser and more beautiful ▪ **aller croissant** to be on the increase ▪ **le bruit allait croissant** the noise kept growing ⊳ **croissez et multipliez** *(Bible) allus* go forth and multiply.

croix [krwa] *nf* **1.** [gibet] cross ▪ **il est mort sur la ~** he died on the cross ⊳ **la (Sainte) Croix** RELIG the (Holy) Cross ▪ **porter sa ~** to have one's cross to bear
2. [objet cruciforme] cross ⊳ **c'est la ~ et la bannière pour le faire manger** it's an uphill struggle to get him to eat ▪ **~ de bois, ~ de fer, si je mens, je vais en enfer** cross my heart (and hope to die)
3. [emblème] cross ▪ **~ de Malte/St André** Maltese/St Andrew's cross ▪ **~ ansée** ansate cross ▪ **~ gammée** swastika ▪ **la ~ de Lorraine** the cross of Lorraine *(cross with two horizontal bars, the symbol of the Gaullist movement)*
4. [récompense] cross, medal ▪ [de la Légion d'honneur] Cross of the Legion of Honour ▪ **la ~ de guerre** the Military Cross
5. [signe écrit] cross ▪ **signer d'une ~** to sign with a cross ▪ **marquer qqch d'une ~** to put a cross on sthg ⊳ **c'est un jour à marquer d'une ~ blanche** it's a red-letter day ▪ **faire** *ou* **mettre une croix sur qqch** to forget *ou* to kiss goodbye to sthg
6. PRESSE : **la Croix (l'Événement)** *Catholic daily newspaper*
7. COUT : **point de ~** cross-stitch
8. ASTRON : **Croix du Sud** Southern Cross.
◆ **en croix** *loc adv* : **placer** *ou* **mettre deux choses en ~** to lay two things crosswise.

Croix-Rouge [krwaruʒ] *npr f* : **la ~** the Red Cross.

croquant, e [krɔkɑ̃, ɑ̃t] *adj* crisp, crunchy.

croque-au-sel [krɔkosɛl] ◆ **à la croque-au-sel** *loc adv* (raw) with salt ▪ **manger des artichauts à la ~** to eat raw artichokes dipped in salt.

croque-madame [krɔkmadam] *nm inv toasted cheese and ham sandwich with a fried egg on top.*

croque-mitaine [krɔkmitɛn] (*pl* **croque-mitaines**) *nm* bogeyman.

croque-monsieur [krɔkməsjø] *nm inv toasted cheese and ham sandwich.*

croque-mort [krɔkmɔr] (*pl* **croque-morts**) *nm* undertaker's assistant ▪ **il a vraiment une allure de ~** he has a really funereal look about him.

croquenot△ [krɔkno] *nm* clodhopper, beetlecrusher.

croquer [3] [krɔke] ◇ *vt* **1.** [pomme, radis, sucre d'orge] to crunch **2.** *fam* [dépenser - héritage] to squander **3.** [esquisser] to sketch ▪ [décrire] to outline ▪ **il est (joli)** *ou* **mignon à ~** *fam* he looks good enough to eat.
◇ *vi* to be crisp *ou* crunchy.
◆ **croquer dans** *v+prép* to bite into.

croquet [krɔkɛ] *nm* **1.** JEUX croquet **2.** CULIN almond biscuit *UK ou* cookie *US.*

croquette [krɔkɛt] *nf* CULIN croquette ▪ **~ de poisson** fishcake.
◆ **croquettes** *nfpl* [pour animal] dry food.

croqueur, euse [krɔkœr, øz] ◇ *adj* crisp, crunchy.
◇ *nm, f* devourer ▪ **croqueuse de diamants** *fam* gold-digger.

croquignolet, ette [krɔkinjɔlɛ, ɛt] *adj fam* sweet, cute.

croquis [krɔki] *nm* sketch ▪ **faire un ~ de qqch** to sketch sthg.

cross [krɔs], **cross-country** [krɔskuntri] (*pl* **cross-countrys** *ou pl* **cross-countries**) *nm* [à pied] cross-country running ▪ [à cheval] cross-country riding ▪ **faire du ~** [à pied] to go cross-country running ; [à cheval] to go cross-country riding.

crosse [krɔs] *nf* **1.** RELIG crosier, crozier **2.** SPORT [canne - de hockey] stick ; [- de golf] club ; [- du jeu de crosse] crosse **3.** *Québec* [jeu] lacrosse **4.** [extrémité - d'une canne] crook ; [- d'un violon] scroll **5.** ARM [d'un revolver] grip, butt ▪ [d'un fusil] butt ▪ [d'un canon] trail ▪ **ils l'ont tué à coups de ~** they beat him to death with their rifle butts **6.** BOT [d'une fougère] crosier **7.** ANAT [de l'aorte] arch.

crotale [krɔtal] *nm* rattlesnake.

crotte [krɔt] *nf* **1.** [d'un animal] dropping ▪ [d'un bébé] poo *(U)* ⊳ **~ (de bique)!** *fam* sugar! **2.** *fam péj* [chose ou personne méprisée] : **c'est de la ~ (de bique)** it's a load of rubbish *UK ou* garbage *US* ▪ **il se prend pas pour de la ~!** he really fancies himself! *UK*, he thinks he's God's gift! **3.** CULIN : **~ au chocolat** chocolate **4.** [morve] : **~ de nez** *fam* bogey.

crotté, e [krɔte] *adj* muddy, mucky ▪ **~ comme un barbet** covered in mud.

crotter [3] [krɔte] ◇ *vt* [chaussures, voiture] to dirty, to muddy.
◇ *vi fam* [chien] to do its business.

crottin [krɔtɛ̃] *nm* **1.** [de cheval] dung, manure **2.** CULIN *small round goat's milk cheese.*

croulant, e [krulɑ̃, ɑ̃t] ◇ *adj* crumbling, tumbledown ▪ **une vieille maison ~e** a tumbledown old house.
◇ *nm, f fam péj* old fogey.

crouler [3] [krule] *vi* **1.** [tomber - édifice] to collapse, to crumble, to topple ▪ **~ sous : l'étagère croule sous le poids des livres** the shelf is sagging under the weight of the books ▪ **un baudet qui croulait sous son chargement** a donkey weighed down with its load ▪ **~ sous le poids des ans/soucis** *fig* to be weighed down by age/worry ▪ **la salle croula sous les applaudissements** *fig* the auditorium thundered with applause **2.** [se désintégrer - empire, société] to be on the verge of collapse, to be crumbling.

croupe [krup] *nf* **1.** ZOOL croup, rump ▪ **monter en ~** to ride pillion **2.** *fam* ANAT behind **3.** [sommet - d'une colline] hilltop ; [- d'une montagne] mountain top.

croupetons [kruptɔ̃] ◆ **à croupetons** *loc adv* : **être à ~** to crouch, to squat ▪ **se mettre à ~** to squat down, to crouch (down).

croupi, e [krupi] *adj* [eau] stagnant, foul.

croupier, ère [krupje, ɛr] *nm, f* JEUX croupier.

croupion [krupjɔ̃] *nm* **1.** ORNITH rump **2.** CULIN parson's *UK* *ou* pope's *US* nose **3.** *fam* [fesses] bum *UK*, butt *US* **4.** *(comme adj avec ou sans trait d'union)* **parti ~** POLIT rump of a party ▪ **Parlement Croupion** HIST Rump Parliament.

croupir [32] [krupir] *vi* **1.** [eau] to stagnate, to grow foul **2.** *fig* [s'encroûter, moisir] : **je ne vais pas ~ ici toute ma vie** I'm not going to rot here all my life ▪ **~ dans l'ignorance** to wallow in one's ignorance.

croupissant, e [krupisɑ̃, ɑ̃t] *adj* [eau, mare] putrid, foul.

CROUS, Crous [krus] (*abr de* **Centre régional des œuvres universitaires et scolaires**) *npr m student representative body dealing with accommodation, catering etc.*

crousille [kruzij] *nf Suisse* piggybank.

croustade [krustad] *nf* croustade.

croustillant, e [krustijɑ̃, ɑ̃t] *adj* **1.** CULIN [biscuit, gratin] crisp, crunchy ▪ [baguette, pain] crusty **2.** [osé] saucy.

croustiller [3] [krustije] *vi* [biscuit, gratin] to be crisp *ou* crunchy ▪ [baguette, pain] to be crusty.

croûte [krut] *nf* **1.** [partie - du pain] crust ; [- du fromage] rind ▪ **une ~ de pain** a crust ▪ [préparation] pastry shell ▪ **~ de vol-au-vent** vol-au-vent case **2.** △ [nourriture] grub **3.** [dépôt] layer ▪ **~ de rouille/saleté** layer of rust/dirt **4.** GÉOL : **la ~ terrestre** the earth's crust **5.** MÉD scab ▪ **~s de lait** cradle cap **6.** *fam péj* [tableau] bad painting **7.** [de cuir] hide **8.** *péj* [personne] : **quelle ~!** *fam* what a stick-in-the-mud!

croûteux, euse [krutø, øz] *adj* scabby.

croûton [krutɔ̃] *nm* **1.** CULIN [frit] crouton ▪ [quignon] (crusty) end, crust **2.** *fam péj* [personne] : **vieux ~** fossil.

croyable [krwajabl] *adj* believable, credible ▪ **c'est à peine ~** it's hardly credible ▪ **son histoire n'est pas ~** his story is incredible *ou* unbelievable.

croyait *etc v* ▷ **croire.**

croyance [krwajɑ̃s] *nf* **1.** [pensée] belief ▪ **les ~s populaires** popular beliefs, conventional wisdom **2.** [fait de croire] faith ▪ **la ~ en Dieu** faith *ou* belief in God ▪ **la ~ à** *ou* **en la démocratie** belief in democracy **3.** [religion] faith, religion.

croyant, e [krwajɑ̃, ɑ̃t] ◇ *adj* : **il est/n'est pas ~** he's a believer/non-believer, he believes/he doesn't believe in God.
◇ *nm, f* believer.

CRS (*abr de* **compagnie républicaine de sécurité**) *nm* [policier] state security policeman ▪ **les ~ ont chargé les manifestants** the security police charged the demonstrators.

CRS

The *compagnie républicaine de sécurité* is a part of the Minister of the Interior's police force, whose primary responsibility is to ensure public order at demonstrations and riots. The CRS also monitors the safety of motorways, beaches and mountains.

cru[1] [kry] *nm* ŒNOL [terroir] vineyard ▪ [vin] vintage, wine ▪ **les grands ~s de Bourgogne** the great wines of Burgundy.
◆ **de mon cru, de son cru** *etc loc adj* : **une histoire de son ~** a story of his own invention.
◆ **du cru** *loc adj* : **un vin du ~** a local wine ▪ **les gens du ~** the locals.

cru[2], e [kry] *pp* = **croire.**

cru[3], e [kry] *adj* **1.** [non cuit - denrée] raw, uncooked ; [- céramique] unfired ▪ [non pasteurisé] : **beurre/lait ~** unpasteurized butter/milk **2.** [sans préparation - soie] raw ; [- minerai] crude ; [- bois] untreated **3.** [aveuglant - couleur] crude, harsh, glaring ; [- éclairage] harsh, blinding, glaring **4.** [net] blunt, uncompromising ▪ **c'est la vérité toute ~e** it's the pure, unadorned truth **5.** [osé] coarse, crude.
◆ **cru** ◇ *nm* CULIN : **le ~ et le cuit** the raw and the cooked.
◇ *adv* **1.** [sans cuire] : **manger qqch ~** to eat sthg raw ▶ **avaler** *ou* **manger qqn tout ~** to make mincemeat out of *ou* to wipe the floor with sb **2.** [brutalement] : **parler ~** to speak bluntly ▪ **je vous le dis tout ~** I'm telling you it as it is.
◆ **à cru** *loc adv* ÉQUIT bareback.

crû, ue [kry] *pp* ▷ **croître.**

cruauté [kryote] *nf* **1.** [dureté] cruelty ▪ **avec ~** cruelly **2.** [acte] cruel act, act of cruelty **3.** *litt* [rudesse] harshness, (extreme) severity, cruelty *litt.*

cruche [kryʃ] ◇ *nf* **1.** [récipient] pitcher, jug **2.** [contenu] jugful **3.** *fam péj* [personne] nitwit, dumbbell.
◇ *adj fam péj* dumb, stupid ▪ **ce que tu peux être ~!** you're so dumb!, you ninny!

crucial, e, aux [krysjal, o] *adj* crucial, vital.

crucifère [krysifɛr] ◇ *adj* cruciferous.
◇ *nf* crucifer ▪ **les ~s** the Cruciferea.

crucifié, e [krysifje] ◇ *adj* crucified.
◇ *nm, f* **1.** [victime] crucified person **2.** RELIG : **le Crucifié** Jesus Christ.

crucifier [9] [krysifje] *vt* **1.** [mettre en croix] : **~ qqn** to crucify sb **2.** *litt* [humilier] to crucify.

crucifix [krysifi] *nm* crucifix.

crucifixion [krysifiksjɔ̃] *nf* crucifixion.

cruciforme [krysifɔrm] *adj* cruciform *sout*, shaped like a cross.

cruciverbiste [krysivɛrbist] *nmf* crossword (puzzle) enthusiast.

crudité [krydite] *nf* **1.** [d'une couleur, de la lumière] harshness **2.** [brutalité - d'une réponse] bluntness **3.** [vulgarité] coarseness, crudeness.
◆ **crudités** *nfpl* CULIN raw vegetables ▪ [sur un menu] mixed salads, assorted raw vegetables.

crue [kry] *nf* **1.** [élévation de niveau] rise in the water level ▪ **la rivière en ~ a inondé la ville** the river burst its banks and flooded the town **2.** [inondation] : **la ~ des rivières au printemps** the swelling of the rivers in the spring ▪ **en période de ~** when there are floods.

cruel, elle [kryɛl] ◇ *adj* **1.** [méchant - personne] cruel ▪ [dur - propos] cruel, harsh **2.** [pénible - destin] cruel, harsh, bitter ; [- dilemme, choix] cruel, painful ; [- perte] cruel ▪ **être dans une ~le incertitude** to be horribly uncertain.
◇ *nm, f litt* cruel man (*f* woman).

cruellement [kryɛlmɑ̃] *adv* **1.** [méchamment] cruelly ▪ **traiter qqn ~** to be cruel to sb **2.** [péniblement] sorely ▪ **faire ~ défaut** to be sorely lacking.

crûment [krymɑ̃] *adv* **1.** [brutalement] bluntly **2.** [grossièrement] coarsely.

crustacé, e [krystase] *adj* crustaceous.
◆ **crustacé** *nm* **1.** ZOOL crustacean ▪ **les ~s** the Crustacea, the Crustaceans **2.** CULIN : **des ~s** seafood.

crut *etc v* ▷ **croire.**

crût *etc v* ▷ **croître.**

cryochirurgie [krijɔʃiryrʒi] *nf* cryosurgery.

cryogénie [krijɔʒeni] *nf* cryogenics *(sing).*

cryothérapie [krijɔterapi] *nm* MÉD cryotherapy ■.

cryptage [kriptaʒ] *nm* **1.** [d'un message] coding **2.** [d'une émission de télévision] coding, scrambling TV.

crypte [kript] *nf* ARCHIT & ANAT crypt.

crypté, e [kripte] *adj* **1.** [message] coded **2.** [émission de télévision] scrambled *(for non-subscribers)*, encrypted.

cryptogramme [kriptɔgram] *nm* cryptogram.

cryptographie [kriptɔgrafi] *nf* cryptography.

cryptologie [kriptɔlɔʒi] *nf* encryption.

cs (*abr écrite de* **cuillère à soupe**) tbs, tbsp.

CSA (*abr de* **Conseil supérieur de l'audiovisuel**) *npr m French broadcasting supervisory body.*

CSCE (*abr de* **Conférence sur la sécurité et la coopération en Europe**) *npr f* CSCE.

CSG (*abr de* **contribution sociale généralisée**) *nf income-related tax contribution.*

Cuba [kyba] *npr* Cuba ■ **à ~** in Cuba, *voir aussi* **île**.

cubage [kybaʒ] *nm* **1.** [évaluation] cubage, cubic content **2.** [volume] cubic volume, cubature, cubage.

cubain, e [kybɛ̃, ɛn] *adj* Cuban.
◆ **Cubain, e** *nm, f* Cuban.

cube [kyb] ◇ *adj* cubic ■ **centimètre ~** cubic centimetre.
◇ *nm* **1.** GÉOM & MATH cube ■ **quel est le ~ de 4?** what's 4 cubed *ou* the cube of 4? **2.** [objet cubique] cube **3.** JEUX (building) block **4.** *fam* [cylindrée] : **un gros ~** [moto] a big bike.

cuber [3] [kybe] ◇ *vt* to determine the cubic volume of.
◇ *vi* [contenir] : **le réservoir cube 100 litres** the tank has a cubic capacity of 100 litres.

cubique [kybik] ◇ *adj* **1.** [en forme de cube] cube-shaped, cube-like, cubic **2.** MATH & MINÉR cubic.
◇ *nf* MATH cubic.

cubisme [kybism] *nm* Cubism.

cubiste [kybist] ◇ *adj* Cubist, Cubistic.
◇ *nmf* Cubist.

Cubitainer® [kybitenɛr] *nm* plastic container *(for liquids)*.

cubitus [kybitys] *nm* ulna.

cucul [kyky] *adj inv fam* **~ (la praline)** silly, goofy.

cucurbitacée [kykyrbitase] *nf* cucurbit ■ **les ~s** the Cucurbitaceae.

cueillera *etc v* ▷ **cueillir**.

cueillette [kœjɛt] *nf* **1.** [ramassage - de fruits] gathering, picking ; [- de fleurs] picking **2.** [récolte] crop, harvest **3.** SOCIOL gathering ■ **une tribu qui vit de la ~** a tribe of gatherers.

cueilleur, euse [kœjœr, øz] *nm, f* [de fruits] picker, gatherer ■ [de fleurs] picker.

cueillir [41] [kœjir] *vt* **1.** [récolter - fruits] to gather, to pick ; [- fleurs] to pick, to pluck **2.** [trouver] to pick up *(sép)*, to collect ■ **il est venu me ~ chez moi** he came to pick me up at my place ■ **où es-tu allé ~ pareille idée?** where on earth did you get that idea? **3.** *fam* [surprendre] to catch, to grab ▶ **être cueilli à froid** to be caught off guard **4.** *fam* [arrêter] to nab, to collar **5.** [saisir au passage] to snatch, to grab ■ **~ un baiser** to snatch a kiss.

cui-cui [kɥikɥi] *nm inv* tweet-tweet ■ **faire ~** to tweet, to go tweet-tweet.

cuillère, cuiller [kɥijɛr] *nf* **1.** [instrument] spoon ■ **~ à café** *ou* **à moka** teaspoon ■ **~ à dessert** dessert spoon ■ **~ à soupe** tablespoon ■ **petite ~** teaspoon ■ **en deux** *ou* **trois coups de ~ à pot** *fam* in a jiffy, in no time at all **2.** [contenu] spoonful ■ **une ~ à café de sucre** a teaspoonful of sugar ■ **deux ~s à soupe de farine** two tablespoonfuls of flour **3.** PÊCHE spoon, spoonbait **4.** ARM [d'une grenade] safety catch **5.** △ [main] mitt, paw.
◆ **à la cuillère** ◇ *loc adj* : **pêche à la ~** spinning, trolling.
◇ *loc adv* **1.** [en mangeant] : **nourrir** *ou* **faire manger qqn à la ~** to spoon-feed sb **2.** PÊCHE : **pêcher la truite à la ~** to spin *ou* to troll for trout.

cuillerée [kɥijere] *nf* spoonful ■ **une ~ à café de** a teaspoonful of ■ **une ~ à soupe de** a tablespoonful of.

cuir [kɥir] *nm* **1.** [peau - traitée] leather ; [- brute] hide ■ **le ~** [vêtement] leather clothes ; COMM & INDUST leather goods ■ **un ~** *fam* a leather jacket ▶ **~ de Russie** Russia leather **2.** [peau humaine] skin ■ **~ chevelu** scalp ■ **tomber sur** *ou* **tanner le ~ à qqn** *fam* to tan sb's hide, to give sb a belting **3.** [lanière] : **~ à rasoir** strop **4.** *fam* [faute de liaison] incorrect liaison *(introducing an unwanted consonant between two words)*.
◆ **de cuir, en cuir** *loc adj* leather *(modif)*.

cuirasse [kɥiras] *nf* **1.** HIST [armure] breastplate, cuirass, corselet **2.** MIL [d'un char] armour **3.** [carapace] cuirass.

cuirassé, e [kɥirase] *adj* [char, navire] armoured, armour-plated.
◆ **cuirassé** *nm* battleship ■ **'le Cuirassé Potemkine'** ***Eisenstein*** 'The Battleship Potemkin'.

cuirasser [3] [kɥirase] *vt* **1.** MIL to armour, to armour-plate **2.** [endurcir] to harden ■ **son enfance difficile l'a cuirassé contre tout** his difficult childhood has made him very thick-skinned.
◆ **se cuirasser** *vpi* **1.** HIST to put on a breastplate **2.** [s'endurcir] to harden o.s.

cuire [98] [kɥir] ◇ *vt* **1.** CULIN [viande, légumes] to cook ■ [pain] to bake **2.** [brûler - peau] to burn.
◇ *vi* **1.** CULIN [aliment] to cook ■ **~ à feu doux** *ou* **petit feu** to simmer ■ **~ à gros bouillons** to boil hard ■ **poulet prêt à ~** oven-ready chicken ■ **faire ~ qqch** to cook sthg ■ **faire ~ à feu doux** to simmer ■ **faire ~ à feu vif** to cook over a high flame ■ **faire ~ qqch au four** to bake sthg ■ **j'ai trop fait ~ les légumes** I've overcooked the vegetables ■ **tu n'as pas fait assez ~ la viande** you've undercooked the meat ▶ **laisser qqn ~ dans son jus** *fam* to let sb stew in his/her own juice ■ **va te faire ~ un œuf!** *fam* get lost! ■ **je l'ai envoyé se faire ~ un œuf** *fam* I sent him packing **2.** *fam* [souffrir de la chaleur] : **on cuit dans cette voiture!** it's boiling hot in this car! **3.** [brûler] to burn, to sting ■ **les yeux me cuisent** my eyes are burning *ou* stinging **4.** *sout* **il vous en cuira** you'll regret it.
◆ **à cuire** *loc adj* : **chocolat à ~** cooking chocolate ■ **pommes à ~** cooking apples.

cuisant, e [kɥizɑ̃, ɑ̃t] *adj* **1.** [douleur, sensation] burning, stinging **2.** [affront, injure] stinging, bitter.

cuisine [kɥizin] *nf* **1.** [lieu] kitchen ■ **~ roulante** field kitchen **2.** [activité] cooking, cookery UK ■ **faire la ~** to cook ■ **elle fait très bien la ~** she's an excellent cook ■ **j'aime faire la ~** I enjoy cooking ■ **la ~ au beurre/à l'huile** cooking with butter/oil **3.** [ensemble de mets] cuisine, food, dishes ■ **~ fine et soignée** carefully prepared dishes *ou* food ■ **apprécier la ~ chinoise** to enjoy Chinese food ▶ **~ allégée, ~ minceur** cuisine minceur, lean cuisine
4. [cuisiniers] : **la ~** [dans un château] the kitchen staff ; [à la cantine] the catering *ou* kitchen staff
5. [meubles] kitchen (furniture) ■ **~ intégrée** fitted kitchen
6. *fam péj* [complications] complicated *ou* messy business ■ [malversations] wheeler-dealing.
◆ **cuisines** *nfpl* [au restaurant] kitchen ■ NAUT galley.
◆ **de cuisine** *loc adj* [table, couteau] kitchen *(modif)*.

cuisiné, e [kɥizine] *adj* ▷ **plat**.

cuisiner [3] [kɥizine] ◇ *vt* **1.** [plat, dîner] to cook **2.** *fam* [interroger - accusé, suspect] to grill ■ **il s'est fait ~ par la police** he was grilled by the police.
◇ *vi* to cook ■ **j'aime ~** I like cooking.

cuisinier, ère [kɥizinje, ɛr] *nm, f* cook.
◆ **cuisinière** *nf* stove, cooker UK ■ **cuisinière électrique** electric cooker ■ **cuisinière à gaz** gas cooker *ou* stove.

cuisons *etc v* ▷ **cuire**.

cuissardes [kɥisard] *nfpl* **1.** [de femme] thigh boots **2.** [de pêcheur] waders.

cuisse [kɥis] *nf* **1.** ANAT thigh ■ **avoir la ~ légère** *fam hum* to be free with one's favours, to put it about **2.** ZOOL leg **3.** CULIN leg ■ **~s de grenouille** frogs' legs ■ **~ de poulet** chicken leg.

cuissettes [kɥisɛt] *nfpl Suisse* (sports) shorts.

cuisson [kɥisɔ̃] *nf* CULIN [fait de cuire - le pain, les gâteaux] baking ; [- un rôti] roasting, cooking ■ **temps de ~** cooking time ■ [manière de cuire] cooking technique.

cuissot [kɥiso] *nm* [de gibier] haunch.

cuistot [kɥisto] *nm fam* cook, chef.

cuistre [kɥistr] *nm sout* **1.** [pédant] pedant, prig **2.** [rustre] lout, boor.

cuistrerie [kɥistrəri] *nf* pedantry, priggishness.

cuit, e [kɥi, kɥit] *adj* **1.** [aliment] cooked ■ **viande bien ~e** well-done meat ■ **viande ~e à point** medium rare meat ■ **trop ~** overcooked ◗ **jambon ~** cooked ham ■ **attendre que ça tombe tout ~ (dans le bec)** to wait for things to fall into one's lap **2.** [brûlé - peau] burnt, sunburnt ; [- jardin, champ] parched **3.** *fam* [usé] worn down, threadbare **4.** *fam* [perdu] **: je suis ~!** I'm done for!, I've had it! ■ **notre sortie de dimanche, c'est ~!** we can kiss our Sunday excursion goodbye! **5.** △ [ivre] loaded△, plastered△.

◆ **cuit** *nm* **1.** CULIN **: le ~** the cooked **2.** *loc* **du tout ~ : c'est du tout ~** it's as good as done (already) ■ **ça n'a pas été du tout ~** it was no walkover.

◆ **cuite** *nf*△ [beuverie] **: (se) prendre une ~e** to get plastered△.

cuiter [3] [kɥite] ◆ **se cuiter**△ *vpi* to get plastered△.

cuivre [kɥivr] *nm* **1.** MÉTALL copper ◗ **~ jaune** brass ■ **~ rouge** copper **2.** ART [planche] copperplate.

◆ **cuivres** *nmpl* **1.** [casseroles] copper (pots and) pans **2.** MUS brass instruments.

cuivré, e [kɥivre] *adj* **1.** ART copperplated **2.** [rouge] copper-coloured ■ **avoir le teint ~** *ou* **la peau ~e** [par le soleil] to be tanned ; [naturellement] to be swarthy ■ **des cheveux ~s** auburn hair.

cuivrer [3] [kɥivre] *vt* **1.** MÉTALL to copperplate, to coat *ou* to sheathe with copper **2.** [donner une teinte rougeâtre] to bronze, to tan.

cuivreux, euse [kɥivrø, øz] *adj* cuprous.

cul [ky] *nm* **1.** ▲ [fesses] arse△ *UK*, ass△ *US* ■ **un coup de pied au ~** a kick up the pants *ou* backside ◗ **avoir du ~** to be a jammy *UK ou* lucky bastard△ ■ **avoir** *ou* **être le ~ entre deux chaises** to have a foot in each camp ■ **on va lui foutre les flics au ~** let's get the cops on his tail ■ **comme ~ et chemise** as thick as thieves ■ **~ par-dessus tête** arse over tit△ *UK*, head over heels ■ **tu l'as dans le ~** you're screwed△ ■ **tu peux te le foutre** *ou* **mettre au ~!** go (and) fuck yourself!▲, up yours! ■ **j'en suis tombé** *ou* **ça m'a mis le ~ par terre** I was flabbergasted *ou* stunned ■ **mon ~!** my arse!△ ■ **en avoir plein le ~** to be totally pissed off△ ■ **pousser qqn au ~** to be on sb's back ■ **je suis sur le ~!** [fatigué] I'm knackered!△ *UK*, I'm bushed! *US* ; [surpris] I can't believe it! ■ **tomber sur le ~** to fall on one's arse△ ■ **(en) tomber** *ou* **rester sur le ~** to be flabbergasted **2.** ▲ [sexe] sex ■ **un film de ~** a porn film **3.** [fond d'une bouteille] bottom ◗ **faire ~ sec** *fam* to down a drink in one ■ **~ sec!** *fam* bottoms up! **4.** *loc* **gros ~** *fam* [camion] juggernaut *UK*, big truck *US* ■ **~ béni**△ religious bigot.

culasse [kylas] *nf* **1.** ARM breech **2.** MÉCAN cylinder head.

culbute [kylbyt] *nf* **1.** [pirouette] somersault ■ **faire des ~s** to do somersaults **2.** [chute] fall, tumble ■ **il a fait la ~ dans l'escalier** he fell head over heels down the stairs **3.** *fam* COMM & FIN collapse ■ **faire la ~** [faire faillite] to go bankrupt, to collapse ; [revendre] to double one's investment.

culbuter [3] [kylbyte] ◇ *vi* [à la renverse] to tumble, to fall (over backwards) ■ [en avant] to fall *ou* to tumble (headfirst).
◇ *vt* **1.** [faire tomber - personne] to knock over *(sép)* **2.** [venir à bout de - régime] to topple, to overthrow **3.** MIL **: ~ l'ennemi** to overwhelm the enemy **4.** △ [femme] to lay△.

culbuteur [kylbytœr] *nm* **1.** [jouet] tumbler **2.** MIN tippler, tipper **3.** AUTO rocker arm.

cul-de-jatte [kydʒat] (*pl* **culs-de-jatte**) *nmf* legless person.

cul-de-lampe [kydlɑ̃p] (*pl* **culs-de-lampe**) *nm* **1.** IMPR tailpiece **2.** ARCHIT [dans une église] cul-de-lampe, pendant ■ [dans une maison] bracket, corbel.

cul-de-poule [kydpul] ◆ **en cul-de-poule** *loc adj* **: une bouche en ~** a pouting little mouth.

cul-de-sac [kydsak] (*pl* **culs-de-sac**) *nm* **1.** [rue] dead end, cul-de-sac **2.** [situation] blind alley, no-win situation **3.** ANAT cul-de-sac.

culée [kyle] *nf* abutment pier.

culinaire [kylinɛr] *adj* culinary ■ **les délices ~s de la Bourgogne** the gastronomic delights of Burgundy.

culminant, e [kylminɑ̃, ɑ̃t] *adj* ▻ **point**.

culminer [3] [kylmine] *vi* **1.** GÉOGR **: les plus hauts sommets culminent à plus de 8 000 mètres** the highest peaks are more than 8,000 metres high ■ **l'Everest culmine à 8 848 mètres** Everest is 8,848 metres at its highest point **2.** [être à son maximum] to reach its peak, to peak **3.** ASTRON to culminate.

culot [kylo] *nm* **1.** *fam* [aplomb] cheek *UK*, nerve ■ **tu as un sacré ~!** you've got a nerve *ou* a cheek! **2.** [partie inférieure - d'une lampe] base, bottom ; [- d'une cartouche] base, cap ; [- d'une ampoule] base **3.** MÉTALL [résidu] residue, cinder, slag **4.** [d'une pipe] dottle.

◆ **au culot** *loc adv fam* **faire qqch au ~** to bluff one's way through sthg.

culotte [kylɔt] *nf* **1.** [sous-vêtement - de femme] (pair of) knickers *UK ou* panties *US* ; [- d'enfant] (pair of) knickers *UK ou* pants ■ **faire dans sa ~** *fam* to dirty one's pants ; [avoir peur] to be scared stiff **2.** [pantalon] trousers *UK*, pants *US* ■ HIST breeches ■ **~s courtes** shorts ■ **tu étais encore en ~ courte** *ou* **~s courtes** *fig* you were still in short pants ■ **porter la ~** to wear the trousers *UK ou* pants *US* ■ **~ de cheval** [vêtement] riding breeches, jodhpurs ; MÉD cellulite *(on the tops of the thighs)* ■ **(vieille) ~ de peau** Colonel Blimp *UK*, (old) military type **3.** [pièce de viande] rump **4.** [vêtement] **: une jupe-~** culottes.

culotté, e [kylɔte] *adj fam* [effronté] cheeky *UK*, sassy *US* ■ **il est drôlement ~ en affaires!** he's a businessman who takes risks!

culotter [3] [kylɔte] *vt* **1.** [vêtir] to put trousers *UK ou* pants *US* on **2.** [pipe] to season ■ [théière] to blacken ■ **culotté par la suie** sooty, covered in soot.

culpabilisant, e [kylpabilizɑ̃, ɑ̃t] *adj* guilt-provoking.

culpabilisation [kylpabilizasjɔ̃] *nf* **: la ~ des victimes** making the victims feel guilty, putting the burden of guilt on the victims.

culpabiliser [3] [kylpabilize] ◇ *vt* **: ~ qqn** to make sb feel guilty.
◇ *vi* to feel guilty, to blame o.s. ■ **je culpabilise à fond** *fam* I'm feeling so guilty.

◆ **se culpabiliser** *vp (emploi réfléchi)* to feel guilty, to blame o.s.

culpabilité [kylpabilite] *nf* **1.** PSYCHOL guilt, guilty feeling ■ **je ressens un certain sentiment de ~ à son égard** I feel rather guilty about her **2.** DR guilt.

culte [kylt] *nm* **1.** RELIG [religion] religion, faith ■ [cérémonie] service ■ [dans le protestantisme] **: assister au ~** to attend church ■ **célébrer le ~** to worship **2.** [adoration] cult, worship ■ **le ~ de la personnalité** personality cult ■ **vouer un ~ à qqn** to worship sb **3.** *(comme adj)* cult ■ **film ~** cult film *UK ou* movie *US*.

cul-terreux [kytɛrø] (*pl* **culs-terreux**) *nm fam péj* country bumpkin, redneck *US*.

cultivable [kyltivabl] *adj* [région, terre] arable, farmable.

cultivateur, trice [kyltivatœr, tris] *nm, f* farmer.

cultivé, e [kyltive] *adj* **1.** AGRIC cultivated ■ **passer dans les terres ~es** to walk across ploughed fields **2.** [éduqué] cultured, educated, well-educated.

cultiver [3] [kyltive] *vt* **1.** AGRIC [champ, terres] to cultivate, to farm ■ [plantes] to grow **2.** [conserver obstinément - accent] to cultivate ■ **elle cultive le paradoxe** she cultivates a paradoxical way of thinking **3.** [entretenir - relations, savoir] to keep up **4.** [protéger] to protect, to safeguard.

◆ **se cultiver** ◇ *vpi* to educate o.s. ▪ **elle s'est cultivée par elle-même** she's self-taught.
◇ *vpt* : **se ~ l'esprit** to cultivate the mind.

cultuel, elle [kyltɥɛl] *adj* [association, liberté] religious.

cultural, e, aux [kyltyral, o] *adj* [activité, méthode] farming.

culturalisme [kyltyralism] *nm* cultural anthropology.

culture [kyltyr] *nf* **1.** [production - de blé, de maïs] farming ; [- d'arbres, de fleurs] growing ➲ **~ associée** companion crop ▪ **~ biologique** organic farming ▪ **~ intensive/extensive** intensive/extensive farming ▪ **légumes de ~ biologique** organically grown vegetables ▪ **~ maraîchère** market gardening *UK*, truck farming *US*
2. [terrains] arable land ▪ **ne passe pas à travers les ~s** don't walk across fields with crops
3. [espèce] crop ▪ **introduire une nouvelle ~** to introduce a new crop
4. [connaissance] : **la ~** culture ▪ **parfaire sa ~** to improve one's mind ➲ **~ d'entreprise** corporate culture ▪ **~ générale** general knowledge ▪ **avoir une bonne ~ générale** [candidat] to be well up on general knowledge ; [étudiant] to have had a broadly-based education ▪ **~ de masse** mass culture
5. [civilisation] culture, civilization
6. BIOL culture ▪ **faire une ~ de cellules** to grow cells ➲ **~ microbienne** microbe culture ▪ **~ de tissus** tissue culture
7. *vieilli* & ÉDUC : **~ physique** physical education, PE.
◆ **en culture** *loc adv* [terres] under cultivation.

culturel, elle [kyltyrɛl] *adj* cultural.

culturellement [kyltyrɛlmɑ̃] *adv* culturally.

culturisme [kyltyrism] *nm* bodybuilding.

culturiste [kyltyrist] *nmf* bodybuilder.

cumin [kymɛ̃] *nm* **1.** [plante] cumin **2.** [condiment] caraway.

cumul [kymyl] *nm* **1.** [de plusieurs activités] multiple responsibilities *OU* functions ▪ [de plusieurs salaires] concurrent drawing ▪ **faire du ~** *fam* [directeur] to wear several hats ; [artisan] to moonlight ➲ **le ~ des fonctions** POLIT plurality of offices, pluralism **2.** DR plurality, combination ▪ **~ d'infractions** combination of offences ▪ **~ des peines** cumulative sentence.

cumulable [kymylabl] *adj* : **fonctions ~s** posts which may be held concurrently ▪ **retraites ~s** retirement pensions which may be drawn concurrently.

cumulard, e [kymylar, ard] *nm, f fam péj* **1.** POLIT politician with several mandates **2.** [directeur] *person making money as the head of several companies* **3.** [employé] holder of several jobs.

cumulatif, ive [kymylatif, iv] *adj* cumulative.

cumuler [3] [kymyle] *vt* **1.** [réunir - fonctions] to hold concurrently ; [- retraites, salaires] to draw concurrently **2.** [accumuler] to pile up *(sép)* ▪ **il cumule les erreurs depuis son arrivée** he's done nothing but make mistakes since he arrived **3.** DR to accrue ▪ **intérêts cumulés** accrued interest.

cumulo-nimbus [kymylonɛ̃bys] *nm inv* cumulonimbus.

cumulus [kymylys] *nm* **1.** MÉTÉOR cumulus **2.** [citerne] hot water tank.

cunéiforme [kyneifɔrm] *adj* & *nm* cuneiform.

cunnilingus [kynilɛ̃gys], **cunnilinctus** [kynilɛ̃ktys] *nm* cunnilingus.

cupide [kypid] *adj litt* grasping, greedy ▪ **il regardait l'argent d'un air ~** he was looking greedily at the money.

cupidité [kypidite] *nf litt* greed.

cupidon [kypidɔ̃] *nm* MYTHOL [ange] cupid.

Cupidon [kypidɔ̃] *npr* MYTHOL Cupid.

curable [kyrabl] *adj* curable, which can be cured.

curaçao [kyraso] *nm* curaçao, curaçoa.

curare [kyrar] *nm* curare, curari.

curatelle [kyratɛl] *nf* guardianship, trusteeship DR.

curateur, trice [kyratœr, tris] *nm, f* guardian, trustee DR.

curatif, ive [kyratif, iv] *adj* healing.

cure [kyr] *nf* **1.** MÉD [technique, période] treatment ▪ **~ d'amaigrissement** slimming *UK OU* weight-loss *US* course ▪ **~ de repos** rest cure ▪ **~ de sommeil** sleep therapy ▪ **~ thermale** treatment at a spa **2.** PSYCHOL : **la ~** the talking cure **3.** *fig* **faire une ~ de romans policiers** to go through a phase of reading nothing but whodunits **4.** *loc* **il n'a ~ de...** *litt* he cares nothing about... **5.** RELIG [fonction] cure ▪ [paroisse] parish ▪ [presbytère] vicarage.

CURE THERMALE

In certain cases the French *sécurité sociale* system provides for the cost of treatment at a spa.

curé [kyre] *nm* (Catholic) priest ▪ **aller à l'école chez les ~s** to be educated by priests.

cure-dent(s) [kyrdɑ̃] (*pl* **cure-dents**) *nm* toothpick.

curée [kyre] *nf* **1.** CHASSE quarry **2.** [ruée] (mad) scramble, rush ▪ **à son départ ça a été la ~ pour prendre sa place** people walked all over each other to get his job after he left.

cure-ongle(s) [kyrɔ̃gl] (*pl* **cure-ongles**) *nm* nail cleaner.

cure-oreille [kyrɔrɛj] (*pl* **cure-oreilles**) *nm* ear pick.

cure-pipe(s) [kyrpip] (*pl* **cure-pipes**) *nm* pipe cleaner.

curer [3] [kyre] *vt* to scrape clean.
◆ **se curer** *vpt* : **se ~ les ongles** to clean one's nails ▪ **se ~ les dents** to pick one's teeth (clean) ▪ **se ~ les oreilles** to clean (out) one's ears.

curetage [kyrtaʒ] *nm* **1.** MÉD curettage **2.** CONSTR renovation *(of a historical part of a town)*.

cureter [27] [kyrte] *vt* to curette.

cureton [kyrtɔ̃] *nm fam péj* priest.

curette [kyrɛt] *nf* curette, curet.

curie [kyri] *nf* **1.** ANTIQ curia **2.** RELIG curia, Curia **3.** PHYS [unité] curie.

curieusement [kyrjøzmɑ̃] *adv* **1.** [avec curiosité - regarder] curiously **2.** [étrangement - s'habiller] oddly, strangely ▪ **~, il n'a rien voulu dire** strangely *OU* funnily enough, he wouldn't say anything.

curieux, euse [kyrjø, øz] ◇ *adj* **1.** [indiscret] curious, inquisitive **2.** [étrange] curious, odd, strange ▪ **c'est un ~ personnage** he's a strange character **3.** [avide de savoir] inquiring, inquisitive ▪ **avoir un esprit ~** to have an inquiring mind ▪ **~ de : il est ~ d'entomologie** he has a keen interest in entomology ▪ **soyez ~ de tout** let your interests be wide-ranging.
◇ *nm, f* **1.** [badaud] bystander, onlooker **2.** [indiscret] inquisitive person.
◆ **curieux** *nm* **1.** [ce qui est étrange] : **c'est là le plus ~ de l'affaire** that's what's so strange **2.** △ *arg crime* examining magistrate, beak *UK*.
◆ **en curieux** *loc adv* : **je suis venu en ~** I just came to have a look.

curiosité [kyrjozite] *nf* **1.** [indiscrétion] inquisitiveness, curiosity ▪ **puni de sa ~** punished for being overinquisitive ▪ **par (pure) ~** out of (sheer) curiosity, just for curiosity's sake ➲ **la ~ est un vilain défaut** *prov* curiosity killed the cat *prov* **2.** [intérêt] curiosity **3.** [caractéristique] oddity, idiosyncrasy **4.** [objet] curio, curiosity, oddity ▪ **boutique** *OU* **magasin de ~s** bric-à-brac *OU* curiosity *vieilli* shop.
◆ **curiosités** *nfpl* : **les ~s de Nemours** interesting and unusual things to see in Nemours.

curiste [kyrist] *nmf person taking the waters at a spa* ▪ **les ~s viennent ici pour...** people come to this spa in order to...

curling [kœrliŋ] *nm* curling SPORT.

curriculum vitae [kyrikylɔmvite] *nm inv* curriculum vitae, CV, résumé *US*.

curry [kyri] = **cari**.

curseur [kyrsœr] *nm* cursor.

cursif, ive [kyrsif, iv] *adj* [écriture] cursive ▪ [lecture, style] cursory.
◆ **cursive** *nf* cursive.

cursus [kyrsys] *nm* degree course ▪ **~ universitaire** degree course.

curviligne [kyrviliɲ] *adj* curvilinear, curvilineal.

customiser [3] [kystɔmize] *vt* INFORM to customize.

cutané, e [kytane] *adj* cutaneous *spéc*, skin *(modif)*.

cuti [kyti] (*abr de* **cuti-réaction**) *nf fam* ▷ **virer**.

cuticule [kytikyl] *nf* ANAT, BOT & ZOOL cuticle.

cuti-réaction [kytireaksjɔ̃] (*pl* **cuti-réactions**) *nf* skin test *(for detecting TB or allergies)*.

cutter [kœtœr, kytɛr] *nm* Stanley® knife.

cuvage [kyvaʒ] *nm*, **cuvaison** [kyvɛzɔ̃] *nf* ŒNOL fermentation in vats.

cuve [kyv] *nf* **1.** [réservoir] tank, cistern **2.** [pour le blanchissage, la teinture] vat **3.** ŒNOL vat, tank ▪ **~ close** pressure tank.

cuvée [kyve] *nf* **1.** [contenu] tankful, vatful **2.** ŒNOL vintage ▪ **la ~ du patron** house wine ▪ **la ~ 1987 était excellente** the 1987 vintage was excellent ▪ **la dernière ~ de Polytechnique** *hum* the latest batch of graduates from the École Polytechnique.

cuver [3] [kyve] ◇ *vi* [vin] to ferment.
◇ *vt* : **~ son vin** to sleep off the booze ▪ *(en usage absolu)* **laisse-le ~ en paix** leave him to sleep it off.

cuvette [kyvɛt] *nf* **1.** [récipient - gén] basin, bowl, washbowl ; [- des WC] pan ; [- d'un lavabo] basin **2.** GÉOGR basin.

CV ◇ *nm* (*abr de* **curriculum vitae**) CV *UK*, résumé *US* ▪ **ça fera bien dans ton ~** it'll look good on your CV.
◇ (*abr écrite de* **cheval**) [puissance fiscale] *classification for scaling of car tax*.

cyanure [sjanyr] *nm* cyanide.

cybercafé [sibɛrkafe] *nm* cybercafé.

cybercash [sibɛrkaʃ] *nm* e-cash.

cybercitoyen, enne [sibɛrsitwajɛ̃, ɛn] *nmf* Net citizen, netizen.

cybercommerce [sibɛrkɔmɛrs] *nm* e-commerce.

cybercrime [sibɛrkrim] *nm* INFORM e-crime.

cyberculture [sibɛrkyltyr] *nf* cyberculture.

cyberentreprise [sibɛrɑ̃trəpriz] *nf* internet-based company.

cyberespace [sibɛrɛspas] *nm* cyberspace.

cybermagazine [sibɛrmagazin] *nm* e-zine.

cybermonde [sibɛrmɔ̃d] *nm* cyberworld.

cybernaute [sibɛrnot] *nm* cybernaut.

cybernéticien, enne [sibɛrnetisjɛ̃, ɛn] ◇ *adj* cybernetic.
◇ *nm, f* cyberneticist.

cybernétique [sibɛrnetik] *nf* cybernetics *(sing)*.

cyberpunk [sibɛrpœnk] *nm* cyberpunk.

cybersexe [sibɛrsɛks] *nm* INFORM cybersex.

cyborg [sibɔrg] *nm* cyborg.

cyclable [siklabl] *adj* cycle *(modif)*.

Cyclades [siklad] *npr fpl* : **les ~** the Cyclades, *voir aussi* **île**.

cyclamen [siklamɛn] *nm* cyclamen.

cycle [sikl] *nm* **1.** [série] cycle ▪ **le ~ des saisons** the cycle of the seasons ◗ **~ lunaire/solaire** ASTRON lunar/solar cycle **2.** [évolution] cycle ◗ **~ économique** ÉCON economic cycle **3.** ÉDUC & UNIV cycle ▪ **il suit un ~ court/long** ≃ he'll leave school at sixteen/go on to higher education ◗ **premier ~** ÉDUC lower secondary school years *UK*, junior high school *US* ; UNIV first and second years *UK*, freshman and sophomore years *US* ▪ **second ~** ÉDUC upper school *UK*, high school *US* ; UNIV last two years of a degree course ▪ **troisième ~** postgraduate studies ▪ **être en troisième ~** to be a postgraduate student **4.** LITTÉR cycle ▪ **le ~ d'Arthur** the Arthurian cycle **5.** [véhicule] cycle **6.** PHYSIOL : **~ œstral** oetrous cycle.

cyclique [siklik] *adj* cyclic, cyclical.

cyclisme [siklism] *nm* cycling ◗ **~ sur piste** track cycle racing ▪ **~ sur route** road cycle racing.

cycliste [siklist] ◇ *adj* : **coureur ~** racing cyclist, cycler *US* ▪ **course ~** cycle race.
◇ *nmf* cyclist, cycler *US*.
◇ *nm* [short] (pair of) cycling shorts.

cyclo-cross [siklɔkrɔs] *nm inv* cyclo-cross.

cyclomoteur [siklɔmɔtœr] *nm* small motorcycle, scooter.

cyclomotoriste [siklɔmɔtɔrist] *nmf* scooter rider.

cyclone [siklon] *nm* [dépression] cyclone ▪ [typhon] cyclone, hurricane.

cyclope [siklɔp] *nm* ZOOL cyclops.
◆ **Cyclope** *nm* Cyclops.

cyclopéen, enne [siklɔpeɛ̃, ɛn] *adj* **1.** ARCHÉOL Pelasgian, Pelasgic **2.** *litt* [gigantesque] Cyclopean, titanic, colossal.

cyclo-pousse [siklɔpus] *nm inv* ≃ (pedal-powered) rickshaw.

cyclothymique [siklɔtimik] *adj* & *nmf* cyclothymic, cyclothymiac.

cyclotourisme [siklɔturism] *nm* cycle touring ▪ **faire du ~** to go on a cycling holiday *UK* *OU* vacation *US*.

cyclotron [siklɔtrɔ̃] *nm* cyclotron.

cygne [siɲ] *nm* swan ▪ **~ mâle** cob ▪ **jeune ~** cygnet.
◆ **Cygne** *nm* ASTRON : **le Cygne** Cygnus, the Swan.

cylindre [silɛ̃dr] *nm* **1.** AUTO & GÉOM cylinder ▪ **un moteur à quatre/six ~s** a four-/six-cylinder engine ◗ **une six ~s** a six-cylinder car **2.** MÉCAN roller.

cylindrée [silɛ̃dre] *nf* cubic capacity, capacity displacement *US* ▪ **une petite ~** a small *OU* small-engined car.

cylindrer [3] [silɛ̃dre] *vt* **1.** TRAV PUB to roll **2.** TEXT to mangle.

cylindrique [silɛ̃drik] *adj* cylindric, cylindrical.

cymaise [simɛz] = **cimaise**.

cymbale [sɛ̃bal] *nf* cymbal ▪ **coup de ~s** crash of cymbals.

cymbalier, ère [sɛ̃balje, ɛr] *nm, f* = **cymbaliste**.

cymbaliste [sɛ̃balist] *nmf* cymbalist.

cymbalum [sɛ̃balɔm] *nm* cymbalo, dulcimer.

cynique [sinik] ◇ *adj* cynical.
◇ *nmf* **1.** [gén] cynic **2.** PHILOS Cynic.

cyniquement [sinikmɑ̃] *adv* cynically.

cynisme [sinism] *nm* **1.** [attitude] cynicism **2.** PHILOS Cynicism.

cyphose [sifoz] *nf* kyphosis.

cyprès [siprɛ] *nm* cypress.

cypriote [siprijɔt] *adj* [paysan, village] Cypriot, Cypriote ▪ [paysage] Cypriot, Cyprus *(modif)*.
◆ **Cypriote** *nmf* Cypriot, Cypriote.

cyrillique [sirilik] *adj* Cyrillic.

Cyrus [sirys] *npr* Cyrus.

cystite [sistit] *nf* cystitis.

Cythère [sitɛr] *npr* Cythera.

cytise [sitiz] *nm* laburnum.

cytobiologie [sitɔbjɔlɔʒi] *nf* cytobiology.

cytodiagnostic [sitɔdjagnɔstik] *nm* cytodiagnosis.

cytogénétique [sitɔʒenetik] *nf* cytogenetics *(sing)*.

cytologie [sitɔlɔʒi] *nf* cytology.

cytolyse [sitɔliz] *nf* cytolysis.

cytomégalovirus [sitɔmegalɔvirys] *nm* cytomegalovirus, CMV.

cytoplasme [sitɔplasm] *nm* cytoplasm.

czar [tsar] = **tsar**.

d, D [de] *nm* d, D, *voir aussi* **g**.

d *abr écrite de* **déci**.

d' [d] ▷ **de**.

da (*abr écrite de* **déca-**) da.

DAB [deabe, dab] (*abr de* **distributeur automatique de billets**) *nm* ATM.

d'abord [dabɔr] = **abord**.

d'ac [dak] *loc adv fam* OK ■ **on y va, ~?** we're going, OK?

Dacca [daka] *npr f* [jusqu'en 1982] Dacca ■ [depuis 1982] Dhaka.

d'accord [dakɔr] = **accord**.

dactyle [daktil] *nm* **1.** LITTÉR dactyl, dactylic **2.** BOT cocksfoot.

dactylo [daktilo] *nmf* typist.

dactylographe [daktilɔgraf] *nmf* typist.

dactylographie [daktilɔgrafi] *nf* typing, typewriting ■ **prendre des cours de ~** to learn how to type.

dactylographier [9] [daktilɔgrafje] *vt* to type (up).

dada [dada] <> *adj* Dadaist, Dadaistic.
<> *nm* **1.** ART & LITTÉR Dada, Dadaism **2.** *fam* [cheval] gee-gee *UK*, horsie **3.** *fam* [passe-temps] hobby ■ [idée] hobbyhorse ■ **le voilà reparti sur** *OU* **il a enfourché son ~** he's on his hobbyhorse again.

dadais [dadɛ] *nm* oaf ■ **grand ~** clumsy oaf.

dadaïsme [dadaism] *nm* Dada, Dadaism.

dadaïste [dadaist] <> *adj* Dadaist, Dadaistic.
<> *nmf* Dadaist.

dague [dag] *nf* **1.** ARM dagger **2.** ZOOL [du cerf] spike.

daguerréotype [dagereɔtip] *nm* daguerreotype.

dahlia [dalja] *nm* dahlia.

daigner [4] [deɲe] *vt* : **~ faire qqch** to deign to do sthg.

daim [dɛ̃] *nm* **1.** ZOOL (fallow) deer ■ **~ mâle** buck **2.** [cuir suédé] buckskin, doeskin.
◆ **de daim, en daim** *loc adj* suede *(modif)*.

dais [dɛ] *nm* canopy.

Dakar [dakar] *npr* Dakar.

Dakota [dakɔta] *npr m* : **le ~ du Nord/Sud** North/South Dakota.

dalaï-lama [dalailama] (*pl* **dalaï-lamas**) *nm* Dalai Lama.

dallage [dalaʒ] *nm* [action] paving ■ [surface] pavement.

dalle [dal] *nf* **1.** [plaque] flagstone ■ **~ de marbre/pierre** marble/stone slab ➊ **~ funéraire** tombstone **2.** CONSTR slab ■ **~ de béton** concrete slab ■ **~ de recouvrement** cover slab ■ **~ pleine** reinforced concrete slab **3.** *fam* [faim] : **avoir** *OU* **crever la ~** to be starving *ou* famished **4.** *fam loc* **avoir la ~ en pente** to be a boozer.
◆ **que dalle** *loc adv fam* damn all *UK*, zilch *US* ■ **on n'y voit que ~** you can't see a damn thing.

daller [3] [dale] *vt* to pave.

Dalloz [daloz] *npr* : **les ~** *series of law reference books*.

Dalmatie [dalmasi] *npr f* : **(la) ~** Dalmatia.

dalmatien [dalmasjɛ̃] *nm* Dalmatian ZOOL.

daltonien, enne [daltɔnjɛ̃, ɛn] <> *adj* daltonic *spéc*, colour-blind.
<> *nm, f* colour-blind person.

daltonisme [daltɔnism] *nm* daltonism *spéc*, colour blindness.

dam [dam] *nm* : **au grand ~ de qqn** *litt* [à son préjudice] to the detriment of sb ; [à son mécontentement] to the great displeasure of sb.

damas [dama(s)] *nm* **1.** TEXT damask **2.** BOT damson **3.** MÉTALL damask steel.

Damas [damas] *npr* Damascus.

damasquiner [3] [damaskine] *vt* to damascene.

damassé, e [damase] *adj* damask *(modif)*.
◆ **damassé** *nm* damask.

damasser [3] [damase] *vt* to damask.

dame [dam] <> *nf* **1.** [femme] lady ■ **ah, ma bonne** *OU* **pauvre ~** *fam*, **les temps ont bien changé!** ah, my dear, times have changed! ■ **qu'est-ce que je vous sers, ma petite ~?** *fam* what would you like, love *UK ou* miss? ➊ **~ de charité** Lady Bountiful ■ **~ de compagnie** lady's companion ■ **la Dame de fer** the Iron Lady ■ **~ patronnesse** patroness ■ **~ pipi** *fam* lavatory attendant ■ **'la Dame aux camélias'** *Dumas* 'The Lady of the Camellias'
2. *fam* [épouse] : **votre ~** your missus *ou* old lady
3. [titre] lady ■ **une grande ~** a (noble) lady ➊ **~ d'honneur** lady-in-waiting ■ **la première ~ de France** France's First Lady ■ **faire** *OU* **jouer les grandes ~s** *péj* to put on airs ■ **sa ~, la ~ de ses pensées** his ladylove
4. JEUX [aux dames] king ■ **aller à la** *OU* **mener un pion à ~** to crown a king ‖ [aux cartes et aux échecs] queen ■ **la ~ de cœur** the queen of hearts
5. NAUT : **~ de nage** rowlock *UK*, oarlock *US*
6. [outil de pavage] beetle, rammer.
<> *interj* [dialecte] *vieilli* of course, well ■ **~ oui!** yes, indeed!
◆ **dames** *nfpl* : **(jeu de) ~s** draughts *UK*, checkers *US*.
◆ **de dames, pour dames** *loc adj* [bicyclette] ladies'.

dame-jeanne [damʒan] (*pl* **dames-jeannes**) *nf* demijohn.

damer [3] [dame] *vt* **1.** [tasser - terre] to ram down *(sép)*, to pack down *(sép)* ; [- neige] to pack down ; [- piste] to groom **2.** JEUX [pion] to crown ▪ **~ le pion à qqn** *fig* to outwit sb.

damier [damje] *nm* JEUX draughtboard *UK*, checkerboard *US* ▪ **un tissu à** *ou* **en ~** checked material.

damnation [danasjɔ̃] *nf* **1.** RELIG damnation **2.** *arch* [juron] : **~!** damnation!

damné, e [dane] ◇ *adj* **1.** *fam péj* [maudit] cursed, damn, damned **2.** RELIG damned.
◇ *nm, f* RELIG damned person *ou* soul ▪ **les ~s** the damned ▪ **comme un ~** like a thing possessed.

damner [3] [dane] *vt* RELIG to damn ▪ **faire ~ qqn** *fam fig* to drive sb round the bend.
◆ **se damner** *vp (emploi réfléchi)* to damn o.s. ▪ **je me damnerais pour un chocolat** I'd give anything for a chocolate.

Damoclès [damɔklɛs] *npr* Damocles ▪ **l'épée de ~** the sword of Damocles.

damoiseau, x [damwazo] *nm* **1.** HIST [gentilhomme] (young) squire **2.** *hum* [jeune empressé] (dashing) young blade.

damoiselle [damwazɛl] *nf* HIST **1.** [fille noble] damsel *(title given to an unmarried noblewoman)* **2.** [femme de damoiseau] (young) squire's wife.

dan [dan] *nm* dan ▪ **premier/deuxième ~** first/second dan.

dancing [dɑ̃siŋ] *nm* dance hall.

dandiner [3] [dɑ̃dine] ◆ **se dandiner** *vpi* [canard, personne] to waddle ▪ **il est entré/sorti en se dandinant** he waddled in/out.

dandy [dɑ̃di] *nm* dandy.

Danemark [danmark] *npr m* : **le ~** Denmark ▪ **au ~** in Denmark.

danger [dɑ̃ʒe] *nm* danger ▪ **attention ~!** danger! ▪ **les ~s de la route** the hazards of the road ▪ **en grand ~ de** in great danger of ▪ **en ~ de mort** in danger of one's life ▪ **il y a un ~ d'inondation** there is a danger of flooding ▪ **pas de ~** *fam* : **il n'y a pas de ~ qu'il dise oui** it's not likely he'll say yes ▪ **moi, t'accompagner? pas de ~!** you mean I'd have to go with you? no way! ➊ **~ public** *fam* public menace.
◆ **en danger** *loc adj* : **être en ~** [personne] to be in danger ; [paix, honneur] to be jeopardized ▪ **la patrie est en ~** the nation is under threat ▪ **ses jours sont en ~** there are fears for his life ▪ **ses jours ne sont plus en ~** his condition is now stable ▪ **mettre qqn en ~** to put sb's life at risk ▪ **mettre un projet en ~** to jeopardize a project.
◆ **sans danger** ◇ *loc adj* [médicament] safe.
◇ *loc adv* safely ▪ **tu peux y aller sans ~** it's quite safe (to go there).

dangereusement [dɑ̃ʒrøzmɑ̃] *adv* dangerously, perilously.

dangereux, euse [dɑ̃ʒrø, øz] *adj* **1.** [risqué] dangerous, perilous, hazardous ▪ **zone dangereuse** danger area *ou* zone **2.** [nuisible] dangerous, harmful ▪ **les couleuvres ne sont pas dangereuses** grass snakes are harmless.

danois, e [danwa, az] *adj* Danish.
◆ **Danois, e** *nm, f* Dane.
◆ **danois** *nm* **1.** LING Danish **2.** ZOOL Great Dane.

dans [dɑ̃] *prép* **1.** [dans le temps - gén] in ; [- insistant sur la durée] during ; [- dans le futur] in ; [- indiquant un délai] within ▪ **~ son enfance** in *ou* during her childhood, when she was a child ▪ **c'était à la mode ~ les années 50** it was fashionable in *ou* during the 50's ▪ **je n'ai qu'un jour de libre ~ la semaine** I only have one day off during the week ▪ **~ dix ans, on ne parlera plus de son livre** in ten years *ou* years' time, his book will be forgotten ▪ **vous serez livré ~ la semaine** you'll get the delivery within the week *ou* some time this week ▪ **à consommer ~ les cinq jours** eat within five days of purchase
2. [dans l'espace - gén] in ; [- avec des limites] within ; [- avec mouvement] into ▪ **ils ont cherché partout ~ la maison** they looked through the whole house, they looked everywhere in the house ▪ **~ le métro** [wagon] on the underground ; [couloirs] in the underground ▪ **~ le train/l'avion** on the train/the plane ▪ **monte ~ la voiture** get in *ou* into the car ▪ **partout ~ le monde** all over the world, the world over ▪ **habiter ~ Paris** to live in (central) Paris ▪ **je suis bien ~ ces chaussures** I feel comfortable in these shoes, these shoes are comfortable ▪ **avoir mal ~ le dos** to have backache ▪ **ils se sont couchés ~ l'herbe** they lay down in *ou* on the grass ▪ **~ ces murs** within these walls ▪ **~ un rayon de 15 km** within a 15 km radius ▪ **entrer ~ une pièce** to go into a room ▪ **~ la brume/pénombre** in the mist/dark ▪ **je ne pouvais pas l'entendre ~ ce vacarme** I couldn't hear him in all that noise ▪ **~ Descartes** in (the works of) Descartes ▪ **c'est ~ le journal** it's in the paper
3. [à partir de - prendre, boire, manger] out of, from ▪ **boire ~ un verre** to drink out of *ou* from a glass ▪ **la phrase a été prise ~ mon discours** the quote was lifted from my speech
4. [à travers] through ▪ **un murmure a couru ~ la foule** a murmur ran through the crowd
5. [indiquant l'appartenance à un groupe] : **~ l'enseignement** in *ou* within the teaching profession ▪ **il est ~ le commerce** he's in business ▪ **il est ~ mon équipe** he's on *ou* in my team ▪ **~ nos rangs** within our ranks
6. [indiquant la manière, l'état] : **~ son sommeil** in his sleep ▪ **mettre qqn ~ l'embarras** to put sb in an awkward situation ▪ **je ne suis pas ~ le secret** I haven't been let in on *ou* I'm not in on the secret ▪ **je l'ai fait ~ ce but** I did it with this aim in mind ▪ **~ le but de** in order to, with the aim of ▪ **un contrat rédigé ~ les formes légales** a contract drawn out *ou* up in legal terms ▪ **c'est quelqu'un ~ ton genre** it's somebody like you
7. [indiquant une approximation] : **ça coûtera ~ les 200 euros** it'll cost around 200 euros ▪ **il était ~ les cinq heures du soir** it was around five pm ▪ **il doit avoir ~ les 50 ans** he must be about 50.

dansable [dɑ̃sabl] *adj* danceable.

dansant, e [dɑ̃sɑ̃, ɑ̃t] *adj* **1.** [qui danse] dancing **2.** [qui invite à danser] : **un rythme ~** a rhythm which makes you want to (get up and) dance **3.** [où l'on danse] : **soirée ~e** dance ▪ **thé ~** tea dance.

danse [dɑ̃s] *nf* **1.** [activité] dance ▪ **il aime la ~** he likes dancing ➊ **~ classique** ballet *ou* classical dancing ▪ **~ folklorique** folk dancing ▪ **~ sur glace** ice-dancing ▪ **~ paysanne** country dancing ▪ **~ de salon** ballroom dancing ▪ **~ du ventre** belly dancing ▪ **école de ~** [classique] ballet school ; [moderne] dance school ▪ **entrer dans la ~** *pr* to join in the dance ; *fig* to join in ▪ **conduire** *ou* **mener la ~** *pr* to lead the dance ; *fig* to call the tune **2.** [suite de pas - dans un ballet, au bal] dance ▪ **jouer une ~** to play a dance (tune) ▪ **la ~ des hirondelles dans les airs** swallows swooping back and forth in the sky **3.** [agitation] : **c'est la ~ des valeurs ce mois-ci à la Bourse** share values are fluctuating this month on the Stock Exchange **4.** MÉD : **~ de Saint-Guy** St Vitus' dance ▪ **tu as la ~ de Saint-Guy, ou quoi?** *fam* can't you stop fidgeting? **5.** △ [correction] hiding, thrashing, belting **6.** ART : **~ macabre** dance of death, danse macabre.

danser [3] [dɑ̃se] ◇ *vi* **1.** DANSE to dance ▪ **on danse?** shall we (have a) dance? ▪ **~ sur une corde raide** to walk a tightrope ▪ **faire ~ qqn** [suj: cavalier] to (have a) dance with sb ; [suj: musicien] to play dance tunes for sb ➊ **~ devant le buffet** *fam* : **chez nous, on dansait devant le buffet** at home, the cupboard was always bare **2.** [bouger - reflet, bouchon] to move, to bob up and down ; [- mots, lignes] to swim ▪ **le vent faisait ~ la flamme** the flame flickered in the wind.
◇ *vt* to dance ▪ **~ une valse/un tango** to (dance a) waltz/tango.

danseur, euse [dɑ̃sœr, øz] *nm, f* **1.** [gén] dancer ▪ [de ballet] ballet dancer ▪ **~ de claquettes** tap-dancer ▪ **~ de corde** tightrope walker ▪ **~ étoile** principal dancer ▪ **danseuse étoile** prima ballerina **2.** [cavalier] : **mon ~** my partner.
◆ **danseur** *nm* : **~ mondain** (male) escort.
◆ **en danseuse** *loc adv* : **monter la colline en danseuse** to cycle up the hill standing on the pedals.

dantesque [dɑ̃tɛsk] *adj* *litt* Dantean, Dantesque.

Danube [danyb] *npr m* : **le ~** the (River) Danube.

DAO (*abr de* **dessin assisté par ordinateur**) *nm* CAD.

dard [dar] *nm* **1.** ENTOM [d'une abeille, d'une guêpe] sting **2.** ARM & HIST javelin.

Dardanelles [dardanɛl] *npr fpl* : **le détroit des ~** the Dardanelles.

darder [3] [darde] *vt* **1.** [lancer] to shoot ▪ **le soleil du matin dardait ses rayons sur la plage** shafts of morning sunlight fell on the beach **2.** [dresser] to point.

dare-dare [dardar] *loc adv fam* double-quick, on the double ▪ **va chercher la boîte, et ~!** go and get the box, and get a move on!

darne [darn] *nf* fish steak, thick slice of fish *(cut across the body)*.

dartre [dartr] *nf* dartre ▪ **avoir des ~s** to have dry patches on one's skin.

darwinien, enne [darwinjɛ̃, ɛn] *adj* Darwinian.

darwinisme [darwinism] *nm* Darwinism.

darwiniste [darwinist] ◇ *adj* Darwinist, Darwinistic.
◇ *nmf* Darwinist.

DAT (*abr de* **digital audio tape**) *nm* DAT.

datable [databl] *adj* datable, dateable ▪ **ces rochers sont facilement/difficilement ~s** these rocks are easy to date/are not easily dated.

datage [dataʒ] *nm* : **le ~ de qqch** assigning a date to *ou* dating sthg.

DATAR, Datar [datar] (*abr de* **Délégation à l'aménagement du territoire et à l'action régionale**) *npr f regional land development agency*.

datation [datasjɔ̃] *nf* dating ▪ **il y a eu une erreur de ~ du fossile** the fossil was incorrectly dated ➊ **~ au carbone 14** carbon dating.

datcha [datʃa] *nf* dacha.

date [dat] *nf* **1.** [moment précis] date ▪ **une lettre sans ~** an undated letter ▪ **nous avons fixé la ~ de la conférence au 13 juin** we have decided to hold the conference on June 13th ▪ **se retrouver chaque année à ~ fixe** to meet on the same day every year ▪ **prenons ~** let's decide on *ou* let's fix a date ➊ **~ de départ** date of departure ▪ **~ limite** [pour un projet] deadline ▪ **~ limite de vente** best before date ▪ **~ limite de consommation** sell-by date ▪ **~ de naissance** date of birth ▪ **~ de péremption** [d'un aliment] sell-by date ; [d'un document] expiry date **2.** [période] date ▪ **à la ~ dont tu me parles, j'étais encore aux États-Unis** at the time you're talking about, I was still in the United States ▪ **les grandes ~s de notre histoire** the most important dates in our history ➊ **faire ~ : c'est une réalisation qui fera ~ (dans l'histoire)** it's an achievement which will stand out (in history) ▪ **de longue ~** long-standing ▪ **ils se connaissent de longue ~** they've known each other for a long time ▪ **c'est une amitié de fraîche ~** they haven't been friends for very long **3.** BANQUE : **~ de valeur** value date.
◆ **en date** *loc adv* : **quelle est sa dernière conquête en ~?** what is his latest conquest (to date)?
◆ **en date du** *loc prép* : **lettre en ~ du 28 juin** letter dated June 28th.

dater [3] [date] ◇ *vt* **1.** [inscrire la date] to date, to put a date on ▪ **carte datée de mardi** postcard dated Tuesday **2.** [déterminer l'âge de - fossile, manuscrit, édifice] to date.
◇ *vi* **1.** [compter] to stand out, to be a milestone ▪ **cet événement datera dans sa vie** this event will stand out in his life **2.** [être désuet - tenue] to look dated *ou* old-fashioned ; [- expression] to sound old-fashioned ; [- film] to show its age, to have aged, to be dated.
◆ **dater de** *v+prép* to date from, to go back to ▪ **un livre qui date du XVIIe siècle** a book dating back to the 17th century ▪ **de quand date votre dernière visite?** when was your last visit? ▪ **notre amitié ne date pas d'hier** we go *ou* our friendship goes back a long way ▪ **voilà une idée qui ne date pas d'hier** this idea's been around for quite some time.
◆ **à dater de** *loc prép* : **à ~ du 1er mars, vous ne faites plus partie du service** as of *ou* effective from March 1st, you are no longer on the staff.

dateur [datœr] ◇ *adj m* ▷ **timbre**.
◇ *nm* date stamp.

datif, ive [datif, iv] *adj* DR : **tuteur ~** guardian appointed by a court ▪ **tutelle dative** trusteeship *ou* guardianship ordered by a court.
◆ **datif** *nm* LING dative, *voir aussi* **pluriel**.

datte [dat] *nf* date.

dattier [datje] *nm* date palm.

daube [dob] *nf* CULIN stew ▪ **bœuf en ~** stewed beef.

dauber [3] [dobe] *litt* ◇ *vt* to jeer *ou* to scoff at.
◇ *vi* to jeer, to scoff.

dauphin [dofɛ̃] *nm* **1.** ZOOL dolphin **2.** HIST : **le ~** the dauphin **3.** [successeur] heir apparent, successor ▪ **qui est votre ~?** who's in line for your job?

dauphine [dofin] *nf* HIST : **la ~** the dauphine.

dauphinois, e [dofinwa, az] *adj* from the Dauphiné.

daurade [dɔrad] *nf* sea bream.

davantage [davɑ̃taʒ] *adv* **1.** [plus] more ▪ **donne-m'en ~** give me some more ▪ **je ne t'en dirai pas ~** I won't tell you any more ▪ **il a eu ~ de chance que les autres** he was luckier than the others **2.** [de plus en plus] : **chaque jour qui passe nous rapproche ~** each day that goes by brings us closer together **3.** [plus longtemps] : **je n'attendrai pas ~** I won't wait any longer.

David [david] *npr* BIBLE David.

Davis [devis] *npr* : **coupe ~** Davis Cup.

Dawha [doa] *npr* : **(al-) ~** Doha.

dB (*abr écrite de* **décibel**) dB.

DB *nf* = **division blindée**.

DCA (*abr de* **défense contre les aéronefs**) *nf* AA *(anti-aircraft)*.

DCT (*abr de* **diphtérie, coqueluche, tétanos**) *nm vaccine against diphtheria, tetanus and whooping cough.*

DDA (*abr de* **Direction départementale de l'agriculture**) *npr f local offices of the Ministry of Agriculture.*

DDASS, Ddass [das] (*abr de* **Direction départementale d'action sanitaire et sociale**) *npr f department of health and social security* ▪ **un enfant de la ~** a state orphan.

DDD (*abr de* **digital digital digital**) DDD.

DDE (*abr de* **Direction départementale de l'équipement**) *npr f local offices of the Ministry of the Environment.*

DDT (*abr de* **dichloro-diphényl-trichloréthane**) *nm* DDT.

DDTAB (*abr de* **diphtérie, tétanos, typhoïde, paratyphoïde A**) *nm vaccine against diphtheria, tetanus, typhoid and paratyphoid.*

de [də] *(devant voyelle ou h muet* d' [d], *contraction de 'de' avec 'le'* du [d], *contraction de 'de' avec 'les'* des [de]) ◇ *prép*

A. INDIQUANT L'ORIGINE, LE POINT DE DÉPART
B. DANS LE TEMPS
C. INDIQUANT LA CAUSE
D. INDIQUANT LE MOYEN, L'INSTRUMENT
E. INDIQUANT LA MANIÈRE
F. AVEC DES NOMBRES, DES MESURES
G. INDIQUANT L'APPARTENANCE
H. MARQUANT LA DÉTERMINATION
I. SERVANT DE LIEN SYNTAXIQUE

A. INDIQUANT L'ORIGINE, LE POINT DE DÉPART

1. [indiquant la provenance] from ▪ **il n'est pas d'ici** he's not from (around) here ▪ **il a sorti un lapin de son chapeau** he produced *ou* pulled a rabbit out of his hat
2. [à partir de] : **de quelques fleurs des champs, elle a fait un bouquet** she made a posy out of *ou* from a few wild flowers ▪ **faire un drame de rien** to make a fuss over nothing
3. [indiquant l'auteur] by
4. [particule] : **Madame de Sévigné** Madame de Sévigné ▪ **épouser un/une de quelque chose** *fam* to marry a man/woman with an aristocratic sounding name

B. DANS LE TEMPS
1. [à partir de] from ▪ **de ce jour** from that day
2. [indiquant le moment] : **de jour** during the *ou* by day ▪ **travailler de nuit** to work nights ▪ **il n'a pas travaillé de l'année** he hasn't worked all year ▪ **je ne le vois pas de la semaine** I don't see him at all during the week ▪ **le train de 9 h 30** the 9.30 train ▮ [depuis] : **de longtemps, on n'avait vu cela** such a thing hadn't been seen for a long time

C. INDIQUANT LA CAUSE
: **rougir de plaisir** to blush with pleasure ▪ **mourir de peur/de faim** to die of fright/of hunger ▪ **pleurer de joie** to cry for joy ▪ **souffrir de rhumatismes** to suffer from rheumatism ▪ **se tordre de douleur/de rire** to be doubled up in pain/with laughter

D. INDIQUANT LE MOYEN, L'INSTRUMENT
: **faire signe de la main** to wave ▪ **il voit mal de l'œil gauche** he can't see properly with his left eye

E. INDIQUANT LA MANIÈRE
: **manger de bon appétit** to eat heartily ▪ **de toutes ses forces** with all one's strength

F. AVEC DES NOMBRES, DES MESURES
1. [emploi distributif] : **50 euros de l'heure** 50 euros per *ou* an hour
2. [introduisant une mesure] : **un appartement de 60 m² ** a 60 m² flat ▪ **un homme d'1 m 80** a man who is 1 m 80 tall ▪ **une femme de 30 ans** a 30-year-old woman ▪ **un moteur de 15 chevaux** a 15 h.p. engine ▪ **un cadeau de 50 euros** a gift worth 50 euros ▪ **une équipe de 15 personnes** a team of 15
3. [indiquant une différence dans le temps, l'espace, la quantité] : **distant de cinq kilomètres** five kilometres away ▪ **ma montre retarde de 10 mn** my watch is 10 minutes slow ▪ **ce colis est trop lourd de 100 grammes** this parcel is 100 grammes too heavy

G. INDIQUANT L'APPARTENANCE
: **la maison de mes parents/Marie** my parents'/Marie's house ▪ **la porte du salon** the living room door ▪ **les pays de l'UE** the countries in the EU, the EU countries ▪ **pour les membres du club** for members of the club *ou* club members ▪ **les élèves de sa classe** the pupils in his class

H. MARQUANT LA DÉTERMINATION
1. [indiquant la matière, la qualité, le genre *etc*] : **un buffet de chêne** an oak dresser ▪ **un bonhomme de neige** a snowman ▪ **une réaction d'horreur** a horrified reaction ▪ **une pause de publicité** a commercial break ▪ **un livre d'un grand intérêt** a book of great interest ▪ **elle est d'un snob!** she is so snobbish!, she's such a snob!
2. [indiquant le contenu, le contenant] : **l'eau de la citerne** the water in the tank ▪ **un pot de fleurs** [récipient] a flowerpot ; [fleurs] a pot of flowers
3. [dans un ensemble] : **le plus jeune de la classe** the youngest pupil in the class ▪ **le plus jeune des deux** the younger of the two
4. [avec une valeur emphatique] : **l'as des as** the champ ▪ **le fin du fin** the very latest thing

I. SERVANT DE LIEN SYNTAXIQUE
1. [après un verbe] : **parler de qqch** to speak about *ou* of sthg ▪ **se séparer de qqn** to leave sb ▪ **se libérer du passé** to free o.s. from the past ▪ **instruire qqn de ses intentions** to notify sb of one's plans ▪ **ce champ est entouré d'une palissade** this field is surrounded by a fence
2. [après un substantif] : **l'amour de qqch** the love of sthg ▪ **troubles de l'audition** hearing problems
3. [après un adjectif] : **sûr de soi** sure of o.s. ▪ **il est facile de critiquer** it's easy to criticize
4. [après un pronom] : **rien de nouveau** nothing new ▪ **quoi de plus beau que la mer?** what is more beautiful than the sea?
5. [devant un adjectif, participe ou adverbe] : **c'est une heure de perdue** that's an hour lost ▪ **restez une semaine de plus** stay (for) one more *ou* an extra week
6. [introduisant un nom en apposition] : **le mois de janvier** the month of January ▪ **au mois de janvier** in January ▪ **cet imbécile de Pierre** that idiot Pierre
7. [indiquant le sujet d'un ouvrage] : **'De l'art d'être mère'** 'The Art of Being a Mother'
8. *litt* [introduisant un infinitif] : **et tous de rire** they all burst into laughter.

◇ *art partitif* **1.** [dans une affirmation] : **j'ai acheté de la viande** I bought (some) meat ▪ **c'est de la provocation/de l'entêtement!** it's sheer provocation/pig-headedness! ▪ **j'ai bu de ce vin** I drank some of that wine ▪ **manger de la viande** to eat meat ▪ **chanter du Fauré** to sing some Fauré *ou* a piece by Fauré ▮ [dans une interrogation] : **prends-tu du sucre dans ton café?** do you take sugar in your coffee? ▮ [dans une négation] : **il n'y a pas de place** there's no room, there isn't any room **2.** [exprimant une comparaison] : **il y a du prophète chez lui** he's a bit like a prophet ➊ **ça c'est du Julien tout craché** *ou* **du pur Julien** that's Julien all over, that's typical of Julien.
◇ *art déf* [dans une affirmation] : **il a de bonnes idées** he has *ou* he's got (some) good ideas ▮ [dans une négation] : **nous ne faisons pas de projets pour cet été** we are not making any plans for this summer.
◆ **de... à** *loc corrélative* **1.** [dans l'espace] from... to **2.** [dans le temps] from... to ▪ **d'un instant à l'autre** [progressivement] from one minute to the next ; [bientôt] any minute *ou* time now ▪ **d'ici à demain** by tomorrow **3.** [dans une énumération] from... to **4.** [dans une évaluation] : **ça vaut de 100 à 150 euros** it's worth between 100 and 150 euros.
◆ **de... en** *loc corrélative* **1.** [dans l'espace] from... to **2.** [dans le temps] : **de jour en jour** from day to day ▪ **l'espoir s'amenuisait d'heure en heure** hope dwindled as the hours went by ▪ **le nombre d'étudiants augmente d'année en année** the number of students is getting bigger by the year *ou* every year *ou* from one year to the next **3.** [dans une évolution] : **de déduction en déduction, il avait trouvé le coupable** he'd deduced who the culprit was ▪ **aller de déception en déception** to go from one disappointment to the next ▪ **un musée où vous irez de surprise en surprise** a museum where many surprises await you.

DE *adj* = **diplômé d'État**.

dé [de] *nm* **1.** JEUX die ▪ **des dés** dice ▪ **jouer aux dés** to play dice ➊ **coup de dé** *ou* **dés** throw of the dice ▪ **jouer qqch sur un coup de dés** to gamble sthg away ▪ **les dés (en) sont jetés** the die is cast **2.** CULIN cube ▪ **couper du lard en dés** to dice bacon **3.** COUT : **dé (à coudre)** thimble ▪ **je prendrai un dé à coudre de cognac** I'll have a tiny glass of cognac.

DEA (*abr de* **diplôme d'études approfondies**) *nm postgraduate diploma*.

deal [dil] *nm fam* [accord] deal.

dealer¹ [dilœr] *nm fam* pusher.

dealer² [dile] ◇ *vt fam* to push.
◇ *vi* to push drugs.

déambulateur [deɑ̃bylatœr] *nm* walking frame, Zimmer®.

déambulation [deɑ̃bylasjɔ̃] *nf litt* strolling, ambling (along).

déambulatoire [deɑ̃bylatwar] *nm* ambulatory.

déambuler [3] [deɑ̃byle] *vi* to stroll, to amble (along).

débâcher [3] [debaʃe] *vt* [camion, toit] to take the canvas sheet *ou* the tarpaulin off.

débâcle [debakl] *nf* **1.** [d'une rivière] breaking up (of ice) **2.** MIL rout **3.** [faillite - d'une institution, d'un système] collapse ▪ **c'est la ~!** it's absolute chaos!

déballage [debalaʒ] *nm* **1.** [des bagages] unpacking ▪ **le ~ de nos affaires nous a pris plusieurs heures** it took us several hours to unpack our things **2.** [éventaire] display **3.** *fam* [aveu] outpouring ▪ **un ~ de sentiments** an outpouring of feeling.

déballer [3] [debale] *vt* **1.** [bagages] to unpack **2.** [exposer - produits] to display ▪ *(en usage absolu)* **il déballe le dimanche aux Puces** he has a stall on Sundays at the flea market **3.** *fam* [sentiments] to unload.

débandade [debɑ̃dad] *nf* **1.** [déroute] rout **2.** [panique] panic, rush ▪ **ce fut la ~ générale** there was a mad rush.
◆ **à la débandade** *loc adv* : **les enfants sortent de l'école à la ~** children are piling out of school.

débander [3] [debɑ̃de] ◇ *vt* **1.** MÉD [plaie] to remove *ou* to take the bandages off ■ **~ les yeux d'un prisonnier** to remove the blindfold from a prisoner's eyes **2.** TECHNOL [arc] to unbend ■ [ressort] to slacken, to loosen.
◇ *vi* **1.** ▲ to lose one's hard-on▲ **2.** *fam loc* **sans ~** without letting up.

débaptiser [3] [debatize] *vt* [place, rue] to change the name of, to give another name to.

débarbouillage [debarbujaʒ] *nm* washing.

débarbouiller [3] [debarbuje] *vt* [enfant, visage] to wash.
◆ **se débarbouiller** *vp (emploi réfléchi) fam* to wash one's face ■ **débarbouille-toi avant de venir dîner** wash your face before dinner.

débarbouillette [debarbujɛt] *nf Québec* face flannel *UK*, washcloth *US*.

débarcadère [debarkadɛr] *nm* [de passagers] landing stage ■ [de marchandises] wharf.

débardeur [debardœr] *nm* **1.** [ouvrier] docker *UK*, longshoreman *US* **2.** [vêtement, tricot] tank top ■ [tee-shirt] sleeveless T-shirt.

débarqué, e [debarke] ◇ *adj* [passager] disembarked.
◇ *nm, f* disembarked passenger.

débarquement [debarkəmɑ̃] *nm* **1.** [déchargement - de marchandises] unloading ; [- de passagers] landing ■ **le ~ des marchandises prendra plusieurs jours** it will take several days to unload the goods **2.** HIST : **le (jour du) ~** D-day, the Normandy landings.
◆ **de débarquement** *loc adj* [quai] arrival *(modif)* ■ [navire, troupe, fiche] landing *(modif)*.

débarquer [3] [debarke] ◇ *vt* **1.** [décharger - marchandises] to unload ; [- voyageurs] to land **2.** *fam* [limoger] to fire, to sack *UK*, to can *US* ■ **il s'est fait ~** he got the sack *UK ou* boot.
◇ *vi* **1.** NAUT to disembark, to land ■ MIL to land **2.** [descendre] : **~ de** [train] to get off, to alight from **3.** *fam* [arriver] to turn *ou* to show up **4.** *fam* [être ignorant] : **tu débarques ou quoi?** where have you been? ■ **mets-moi au courant, je débarque** give me an update, I haven't a clue what's going on.

débarras [debara] *nm* **1.** [dépôt] storage room **2.** *fam loc* **bon ~!** good riddance!

débarrasser [3] [debarase] *vt* **1.** [nettoyer - table] to clear ■ [enlever - assiette] to clear (away) ■ **ne débarrasse pas les verres** leave the glasses on the table ➔ **~ le plancher** *fam* to clear *ou* to buzz off **2.** [désencombrer] : **~ qqn/qqch de : je vais te ~ de ta valise** I'll take your case ■ **il m'a demandé de le ~ de sa vieille table** he asked me to take his old table off his hands ■ **~ la ville de ses voyous** to rid the city of its hooligans, to flush the hooligans out of the city ■ **~ la cave de vieilles bouteilles** to clear old bottles out of the cellar ■ **je fais le nettoyage maintenant pour en être débarrassé (plus tard)** I'll do the cleaning now to get it out of the way ■ **~ qqn de ses mauvaises habitudes** to rid sb of his bad habits.
◆ **se débarrasser de** *vp+prép* **1.** [se défaire de] to get rid of **2.** [éloigner - importun] to get rid of ; [- serviteur] to get rid of, to dismiss **3.** [veste, gants] to take off, to remove ■ [sac à main, éventail] to put down ■ *(en usage absolu)* **débarrasse-toi tu vas avoir trop chaud** take your coat *ou* jacket off, you'll be too hot.

débat [deba] *nm* **1.** [controverse] debate, discussion **2.** [conflit intérieur] inner turmoil ■ **~ de conscience** moral dilemma.
◆ **débats** *nmpl* POLIT & DR proceedings.

débâtir [32] [debatir] *vt* COUT to unpick the basting from.

débattre [83] [debatr] *vt* [discuter - thème, question] to discuss, to thrash out *(sép)* ■ **ils ont longtemps débattu le prix** they haggled at length over the price.
◆ **débattre de, débattre sur** *v+prép* to debate, to discuss ■ **il faudra ~ de ces problèmes** these problems will have to be discussed.
◆ **se débattre** *vpi* **1.** [s'agiter - victime] to struggle ; [- poisson] to thrash about ■ **se ~ contre un voleur** to struggle with a thief **2.** [lutter] : **se ~ dans les problèmes financiers** to struggle against financial difficulties.
◆ **à débattre** *loc adj* : **'prix à ~'** open to offers, negotiable ■ **'30 euros à ~'** '30 euros or nearest offer' ■ **conditions à ~** conditions to be negotiated.

débauchage [deboʃaʒ] *nm* **1.** [renvoi] laying off, making redundant *UK* **2.** [détournement] : **le ~ des meilleurs cerveaux** luring away the best brains.

débauche [deboʃ] *nf* **1.** [dévergondage] debauchery ■ **inciter qqn à la ~** to debauch sb **2.** [profusion] : **une ~ de mets rares** an abundance of rare delicacies ■ **une ~ de couleurs** a riot of colours.
◆ **de débauche** *loc adj* [passé, vie] dissolute.

débauché, e [deboʃe] ◇ *adj* [personne] debauched ■ [vie] dissolute.
◇ *nm, f* debauched person, libertine.

débaucher [3] [deboʃe] *vt* **1.** [licencier] to lay off ■ *(en usage absolu)* **on débauche dans le textile** there are lay-offs in the textile industry **2.** [corrompre] to debauch **3.** *fam* [détourner] to lure *ou* to tempt away *(sép)* **4.** [inciter - à la grève] to incite to strike ; [- à quitter un emploi] to lure *ou* to tempt away *(sép)*, to poach.

débecter [4] △, **débéqueter** [28] △ [debɛkte] *vt* : **ça me débecte** it makes me sick *ou* want to puke△.

débile [debil] ◇ *adj* **1.** *fam* [inepte - livre, film, décision] stupid, daft *UK*, dumb *US* ; [- personne, raisonnement] stupid, moronic ■ **il est complètement ~** he's a complete idiot **2.** *litt* [faible - corps] frail, weak, feeble ; [- intelligence] deficient.
◇ *nmf* **1.** *fam* [idiot] moron, cretin, idiot **2.** PSYCHOL : **~ léger/moyen/profond** mildly/moderately/severely retarded person ■ **~ mental** *vieilli* retarded person.

débilitant, e [debilitɑ̃, ɑ̃t] *adj* **1.** [affaiblissant] debilitating, enervating **2.** *fam* [abrutissant] mindnumbing ■ **complètement ~, ce boulot!** that job's about as interesting as shelling peas!

débilité [debilite] *nf* **1.** *fam* [caractère stupide] stupidity, silliness, inanity **2.** PSYCHOL : **~ (mentale)** (mental) retardation.

débiliter [3] [debilite] *vt sout* **1.** [affaiblir] to debilitate, to enervate, to weaken **2.** [déprimer] to drag down *(sép)*, to dishearten, to demoralize.

débine△ [debin] *nf* poverty ■ **être dans la ~** to be hard up *ou* broke ■ **c'est la ~!** times are hard!

débiner [3] [debine] *vt fam* to run down *(sép)*.
◆ **se débiner** *vpi fam* **1.** [s'enfuir] to clear out ■ **te débine pas, j'ai à te parler** stick around, I want to talk to you ■ **n'essaie pas de te ~, je veux une réponse** *fig* don't try to change the subject, I want an answer **2.** [s'écrouler] to come *ou* to fall apart.

débit [debi] *nm* **1.** [d'eau, de passagers] flow ■ [de vapeur] capacity ■ [de gaz] output ■ [de marchandises, de clients] turnover ■ GÉOGR flow **2.** [élocution] (speed of) delivery ■ **il a un sacré ~** *fam* he talks nineteen to the dozen **3.** INFORM & TÉLÉCOM rate ■ **~ de traitement** data throughput *ou* speed ■ **~ de transmission** transmission rate **4.** ÉLECTR output ■ **~ de courant** power output, delivery rate **5.** COMM : **~ de boissons** bar ■ **~ de tabac** tobacconist *UK*, tobacco store *US* **6.** MÉD output, rate ■ **~ sanguin** circulation rate **7.** FIN debit ■ [sur un relevé] debit side **8.** COMM bill.
◆ **au débit de** *loc prép* : **inscrire une somme au ~ d'un compte** to charge an amount of money to sb's account ■ **porter une somme au ~ d'un compte** to debit an account ■ **240 euros à votre ~** 240 euros on the debit side (of your account).

débitable [debitabl] *adj* **1.** [bois] good *ou* ready for cutting up **2.** ÉCON : **compte ~** account one may draw money from, account with open access.

débitant, e [debitɑ̃, ɑ̃t] *nm, f* : **~ de boissons** publican *UK*, bar owner *US* ■ **~ de tabac** tobacconist *UK*, tobacco dealer *US*.

débiter [3] [debite] *vt* **1.** [couper - matériau, tissu, bœuf] to cut up *(sép)* ; [- bois] to cut *ou* to saw up *(sép)* ■ **~ du jambon en tranches** to slice ham **2.** COMM to retail, to sell (retail) **3.** IN-

DUST [machine, usine] to turn out *(sép)*, to produce **4.** [déverser - pompe] to discharge, to yield ; [- fleuve] to have a flow rate of **5.** *péj* [texte] to reel off *(sép)* ▪ [sermon] to deliver ▪ [banalité] to trot out ▪ **~ des mensonges** to come out with a pack of lies **6.** FIN to debit ▪ **votre compte sera débité à la fin du mois** your account will be debited at the end of the month.

débiteur, trice [debitœr, tris] ◇ *adj* [colonne, compte, solde] debit *(modif)* ▪ [personne, société] debtor *(modif)*.
◇ *nm, f* **1.** FIN debtor **2.** *sout* [obligé] : **être ~ de qqn** to be indebted to sb *ou* in sb's debt.

déblai [deblɛ] *nm* [dégagement] digging *ou* cutting (out).
◆ **déblais** *nmpl* [gravats] debris *(sing)*, excavated material, rubble ▪ [terre] (dug *ou* excavated) earth.
◆ **en déblai** *loc adj* sunken.

déblaie *etc v* ▷ **déblayer.**

déblaiement [deblɛmɑ̃] *nm* **1.** [d'un terrain, d'une ruine] clearing (out) ▪ **ils ont procédé au ~ de la forêt après l'accident aérien** they cleared the forest of wreckage after the plane crash **2.** MIN removing the overburden, stripping.

déblatérer [18] [deblatere] ◆ **déblatérer contre** *v+prép péj* to rant (and rave) about, to sound off about.

déblayage [deblɛjaʒ] = **déblaiement.**

déblayer [11] [debleje] *vt* **1.** [dégager - neige, terre] to clear away ; [- lieu] to clear out **2.** TRAV PUB to cut, to excavate, to dig **3.** *fig* [travail] to do the groundwork *ou* spadework on ▪ **~ le terrain** [se débarrasser des détails] to do the groundwork ▪ **allez, déblaie le terrain!** *fam* [va-t'en] go on, clear *ou* shove off!

déblocage [deblɔkaʒ] *nm* **1.** MÉCAN [d'un écrou, d'un dispositif] unblocking, releasing ▪ [de freins] unjamming **2.** [réouverture - d'un tuyau] clearing, freeing, unblocking ; [- d'une route] clearing **3.** ÉCON [des salaires, des prix] unfreezing ▪ BANQUE [d'un compte] freeing **4.** MIN haulage.

débloquer [3] [deblɔke] ◇ *vt* **1.** MÉCAN [écrou, dispositif] to release, to unblock, to free ▪ [freins] to unjam, to release **2.** [rouvrir - rue] to clear (of obstructions) ▪ **~ les discussions** *fig* to get the negotiations back on course ▪ **~ la situation** [après un conflit] to break the stalemate ; [la sortir de l'enlisement] to get things moving again **3.** ÉCON [prix, salaires] to unfreeze ▪ BANQUE [compte, crédit] to free, to unfreeze ▪ COMM [stock] to release **4.** *fam* [décontracter] : **ça m'a débloqué** it got rid of some of my inhibitions.
◇ *vi fam* **1.** [en parlant] to talk rubbish UK *ou* nonsense **2.** [être déraisonnable] to be nuts *ou* cracked ▪ **tu débloques!** you're out of your mind!

débobiner [3] [debɔbine] *vt* to unwind, to uncoil.

débogage [debɔgaʒ] *nm* debugging.

déboguer [debɔge] *vt* to debug.

débogueur [debɔgœr] *nm* debugger.

déboires [debwar] *nmpl* disappointments, setbacks, (trials and) tribulations ▪ **s'épargner** *ou* **s'éviter des ~** to spare o.s. a lot of trouble.

déboisement [debwazmɑ̃] *nm* deforestation, clearing (of trees).

déboiser [3] [debwaze] *vt* **1.** [couper les arbres de] to deforest, to clear of trees ▪ **il faudra ~ le terrain avant de construire** we'll have to clear the area of trees before we can start building **2.** MIN to draw the timbers of, to clear.

déboîtement [debwatmɑ̃] *nm* [luxation - de l'épaule, de la hanche] dislocation ; [- de la rotule] slipping.

déboîter [3] [debwate] ◇ *vt* **1.** [démonter - tuyau] to disconnect ; [- porte, fenêtre] to take off its hinges **2.** MÉD to dislocate, to put out *(sép)*.
◇ *vi* [véhicule] to pull out.
◆ **se déboîter** *vpt* : **se ~ le genou/l'épaule** to dislocate one's knee/shoulder.

débonnaire [debɔnɛr] *adj* [air] kindly, debonair ▪ [personne] good-natured, easy-going, debonair.

débordant, e [debɔrdɑ̃, ɑ̃t] *adj* [extrême - affection] overflowing ; [- activité] tireless ; [- imagination] wild, unbridled, boundless ▪ **d'un enthousiasme ~** bubbling with enthusiasm ▪ **être ~ de** to be full of ▪ **~ d'éloges/d'énergie** full of praise/of energy ▪ **~ de santé/de vie** bursting with health/with vitality.

débordé, e [deborde] *adj* **1.** [peu disponible] (very) busy **2.** [surmené] overworked.

débordement [debɔrdəmɑ̃] *nm* **1.** [écoulement - d'une rivière] overflowing ; [- d'un liquide] running over, overflowing **2.** [profusion - de paroles] rush, torrent ; [- d'injures] outburst, volley ; [- de joie] outburst, explosion **3.** [manœuvre] outflanking ▪ **il y a eu ~ des syndicats par la base** the rank and file have gone further than the union intended **4.** INFORM overflow.
◆ **débordements** *nmpl* [agitation] wild *ou* uncontrolled *ou* extreme behaviour ▪ *litt* [débauche] excesses.

déborder [3] [debɔrde] ◇ *vi* **1.** [rivière] to overflow ▪ [bouillon, lait] to boil over ▪ **le fleuve a débordé de son lit** the river has burst its banks ▪ **l'eau a débordé du lavabo** the sink has overflowed ▪ **les pluies ont fait ~ la rivière** the rain made the river burst its banks ▪ **son chagrin/sa joie débordait** she could no longer contain her grief/her delight ▪ **~ de** to overflow *ou* to be bursting with ▪ **~ de joie** to be bursting with joy **2.** [récipient] to overflow, to run over ▪ [tiroir, sac] to be crammed, to spill over ▪ **la casserole est pleine à ~** the saucepan's full to the brim *ou* to overflowing ▪ **laisser ~ la baignoire** to let the bath overflow ▪ **~ de : sac qui déborde de vêtements** bag overflowing with clothes **3.** [faire saillie] to stick *ou* to jut out, to project ▪ **la pile de gravats débordait sur l'allée** the heap of rubble had spilled out into the lane ▪ **~ en coloriant un dessin** to go over the edges while colouring in a picture.
◇ *vt* **1.** [dépasser] to stick *ou* to jut out from **2.** [s'écarter de] : **vous débordez le sujet** you've gone beyond the scope of the topic ▪ *(en usage absolu)* **nous débordons un peu, il est midi et deux minutes** we're going slightly over time, it's two minutes past twelve **3.** [submerger - troupe, parti, équipe] to outflank ▪ **être débordé : être débordé de travail** to be up to one's eyes in *ou* snowed under with work ▪ **être débordé par les événements** to let things get on top of one **4.** [tirer] : **~ les draps** to untuck the sheets.
◆ **se déborder** *vpi* : **se ~ en dormant** to come untucked *ou* to throw off one's covers in one's sleep.

débotté [debɔte] ◆ **au débotté** *loc adv litt* **prendre qqn au ~** to pounce on sb, to take sb unawares ▪ **répondre au ~** to answer off the cuff.

débotter [3] [debɔte] *vt* to remove the boots of.
◆ **se débotter** *vp (emploi réfléchi)* to take one's boots off.

débouché [debuʃe] *nm* **1.** [possibilité d'emploi] career prospect **2.** [perspective de vente] outlet, avenue for products ▪ [marché] market **3.** [issue] end ▪ **avoir un ~ sur la mer** to have an outlet to the sea.
◆ **au débouché de** *loc prép* at the end of ▪ **au ~ du défilé dans la vallée** where the pass opens out into the valley.

déboucher [3] [debuʃe] ◇ *vt* **1.** [ouvrir - bouteille de bière, tube] to uncap, to take the top off, to open ; [- bouteille de vin] to uncork, to open ; [- flacon] to unstop, to remove the stopper from **2.** [débloquer - pipe, trou, gicleur] to clear, to clean out *(sép)* ; [- lavabo] to unblock, to unstop, to clear ; [- tuyau, conduit] to clear, to unclog ; [- nez] to unblock ; [- oreille] to clean out *(sép)*.
◇ *vi* **1.** [aboutir] : **~ de** to emerge from, to come out of ▪ **~ sur** to open into, to lead to **2.** *fig* **~ sur** to lead to ▪ **des études qui ne débouchent sur rien** a course that doesn't lead anywhere ▪ **~ sur des résultats** to have positive results.
◆ **se déboucher** *vpt* : **se ~ le nez** to clear one's nose.

déboucheur [debuʃœr] *nm* **1.** [produit] drain clearing liquid **2.** [dispositif] : **~ à ventouse** plunger, plumber's friend US.

déboucler [3] [debukle] *vt* [détacher - ceinture] to unbuckle, to undo, to unfasten.

déboulé [debule] *nm* **1.** DANSE déboulé **2.** SPORT burst of speed **3.** CHASSE breaking of cover.
◆ **au déboulé** *loc adv* : **tirer un animal au ~** to shoot an animal as it breaks cover.

débouler [3] [debule] ◇ *vi* **1.** [surgir] to emerge suddenly ▪ **ils ont déboulé dans le couloir** they charged *ou* hurtled into the passage **2.** CHASSE to start, to bolt **3.** [tomber] to tumble down.
◇ *vt* : ~ **les escaliers** [en courant] to race *ou* to hurtle down the stairs ; [après être tombé] to tumble down the stairs.

déboulonner [3] [debulɔne] *vt* **1.** TECHNOL to unbolt, to remove the bolts (from) ▪ ~ **une statue** to take down a statue **2.** *fam* [évincer] to oust ▪ **se faire** ~ to get fired, to get the sack *UK ou* the boot.

débourber [3] [deburbe] *vt* **1.** [nettoyer - minerai, charbon] to wash, to clean, to clear (from mud) ; [- rivière] to dredge **2.** [sortir de la boue] to pull *ou* to drag *ou* to haul out of the mud.

débourrer [3] [debure] *vt* **1.** [trou] to clear **2.** [cheval] to break in *(sép)* **3.** TEXT to fettle, to strip.

déboursement [debursəmɑ̃] *nm* disbursement.

débourser [3] [deburse] *vt* to spend, to lay out *(sép)* ▪ **sans rien** ~ without spending *ou* paying a penny.

déboussoler [3] [debusɔle] *vt* to confuse, to disorientate, to bewilder ▪ **il est déboussolé depuis le départ de sa mère** his mother's departure has unsettled him.

debout [dəbu] *adv* **1.** [en parlant des personnes - en station verticale] standing up ▪ **manger** ~ to eat standing up ▪ ~**!** get *ou* stand up! ▪ **il était** ~ **sur la table** he was standing on the table ▪ **ils l'ont mis** ~ they helped him to his feet *ou* helped him up ▪ **se mettre** ~ to stand (up), to rise ▪ **je préfère rester** ~ I'd rather stand ▪ **je suis resté** ~ **toute la journée** I was on my feet all day ▪ **ne restez pas** ~ (please) sit down ▪ **bébé se tient** ~ baby can stand up ▪ **il ne tient plus** ~ [fatigué] he's dead on his feet ; [ivre] he's legless
2. [en parlant d'animaux] : **le poulain se tient déjà** ~ the foal is already up on its feet
3. [en parlant d'objets] upright, vertical ▪ **mettre une chaise** ~ to stand a chair up ▌ *fig* **mettre un projet** ~ to set up a project ▪ **ça ne tient pas** ~ it doesn't make sense ▪ **le raisonnement ne tient pas** ~ the argument doesn't hold water *ou* hold up
4. [éveillé] up ▪ ~**!** get up! ▪ **être** ~ **à 5 h** to be up at 5 o'clock ▪ **je reste** ~ **très tard** I stay up very late
5. [en bon état] standing ▪ **les murs sont encore** ~ the walls are still standing ▪ **la maison de mon enfance est encore** ~ the house where I lived as a child is still there ▪ **la république ne restera pas longtemps** ~ the republic won't hold out for long
6. [guéri] up on one's feet (again), up and about ▪ [sorti de chez soi, de l'hôpital] out and about
7. *litt* [dignement] uprightly, honourably.

débouter [3] [debute] *vt* to nonsuit, to dismiss ▪ **être débouté de sa plainte** to be nonsuited, to have one's suit dismissed.

déboutonner [3] [debutɔne] *vt* to unbutton.
◆ **se déboutonner** *vp (emploi réfléchi)* [pour se déshabiller] to unbutton (o.s.)

débraie *etc v* ▻ **débrayer**.

débraillé, e [debraje] *adj* [allure, vêtements, personne] slovenly, sloppy, scruffy ▪ [manières] slovenly ▪ [conversation] unrestrained.

débrancher [3] [debrɑ̃ʃe] *vt* **1.** [déconnecter - tuyau] to disconnect ; [- appareil électrique] to unplug **2.** RAIL [train] to split up.

débrayage [debrɛjaʒ] *nm* **1.** AUTO disengaging of the clutch **2.** [grève] stoppage, walkout.

débrayer [11] [debreje] ◇ *vt* **1.** AUTO to declutch *UK*, to disengage the clutch of **2.** [machine] to throw out of gear, to put out of operation.
◇ *vi* **1.** AUTO to declutch *UK*, to disengage the clutch ▪ **débrayez!** put the clutch in! **2.** [faire grève] to stop work, to come out *ou* to go on strike.

débridé, e [debride] *adj* unbridled, unrestrained, unfettered.

débrider [3] [debride] *vt* **1.** [cheval] to unbridle **2.** MÉD [abcès, blessure] to incise **3.** *loc* **sans** ~ nonstop, without stopping, at a stretch.

débris [debri] *nm* **1.** *(gén pl)* [fragment - de verre] piece, splinter, shard ; [- de vaisselle] (broken) piece *ou* fragment ; [- de roche] crumb, debris *(sing)* ; [- de métal] scrap ; [- de végétal] piece *ou* crumb of vegetable matter, debris *(sing)* **2.** *(gén pl)* [nourriture] scraps, crumbs ▪ *litt* [restes - d'une fortune, d'un royaume] last shreds, remnants ▪ [détritus] litter, rubbish *UK* **3.** △ [vieillard] : **(vieux)** ~ old codger△.

débrouillard, e [debrujar, ard] ◇ *adj* resourceful.
◇ *nm, f* resourceful person.

débrouillardise [debrujardiz] *nf* resourcefulness.

débrouille [debruj] *nf fam* : **s'en sortir par la** ~ to improvise one's way out of trouble ▪ **l'art de la** ~ the art of making do (with what's at hand).

débrouiller [3] [debruje] *vt* **1.** [démêler - fils] to unravel, to untangle, to disentangle ; [- énigme] to puzzle out *(sép)*, to untangle, to unravel ▪ ~ **les affaires de qqn** to sort out sb's business affairs **2.** *fam* [enseigner les bases à] to teach the basics to.
◆ **se débrouiller** *vpi* **1.** [faire face aux difficultés] to manage ▪ **débrouille-toi** you'll have to manage by yourself ▪ **comment vas-tu te** ~ **maintenant qu'elle est partie?** how will you cope now that she's gone? ▪ **elle se débrouille très bien dans Berlin** she really knows her way around Berlin ▪ **tu parles espagnol? – je me débrouille** do you speak Spanish? – I get by ▪ **j'ai dû me** ~ **avec le peu que j'avais** I had to make do *ou* manage with what little I had ▪ **se** ~ **pour se faire inviter par qqn** to wangle an invitation out of sb ➋ **donne cette casserole, tu te débrouilles comme un pied** *fam* give me that pan, you're all thumbs **2.** [subsister financièrement] to make ends meet, to manage.

débroussaillage [debrusajaʒ], **débroussaillement** [debrusajmɑ̃] *nm* **1.** [nettoyage] clearing **2.** [étude] : **le** ~ **d'un problème** the groundwork *ou* spadework *ou* preliminary work on a problem.

débroussailler [3] [debrusaje] *vt* **1.** [terrain] to clear (of brambles) **2.** *fig* [travail, problème] to do the groundwork *ou* spadework on.

débudgétiser [3] [debydʒetize] *vt* to remove from the budget, to debudget.

débuguer [3] [debyge] *vt* = **déboguer**.

débusquer [3] [debyske] *vt* **1.** CHASSE to start, to flush **2.** [découvrir] to hunt out *(sép)* ▪ **le logiciel débusque la moindre faute d'orthographe** the software can track down the slightest spelling mistake.

début [deby] *nm* **1.** [commencement] beginning, start ▪ **salaire de** ~ starting salary ▪ **un** ~ **: ce n'est pas mal pour un** ~ it's quite good for a first try *ou* attempt ▪ **ce n'est qu'un** ~ that's just the start *ou* beginning ▪ **il y a un** ~ **à tout** you have to start sometime ▪ **un** ~ **de : ressentir un** ~ **de fatigue** to start feeling tired ▪ **un** ~ **de grippe** the first signs of flu **2.** [dans l'expression des dates] : ~ **mars** at the beginning of *ou* in early March.
◆ **débuts** *nmpl* [dans une carrière] start ▪ [dans le spectacle] debut ▪ **il a eu des ~s difficiles** it wasn't easy for him at the start ▪ **mes ~s dans le journalisme** my first steps *ou* early days as a journalist ▪ **en être à ses ~s** [projet] to be in its early stages ; [personne] to have just started (out) ▌ [en société] debut ▪ **faire ses ~s** to make one's debut ▌ [première période] beginnings ▪ **le rock à ses ~s** early rock music.
◆ **au début** *loc adv* at first, to begin with.
◆ **au début de** *loc prép* : **au** ~ **du printemps/de l'année** at the beginning of spring/of the year ▪ **j'en suis encore au** ~ **du livre** I've only just started the book.
◆ **au tout début, tout au début** *loc adv* at the very beginning, right at the beginning.
◆ **dès le début** *loc adv* from the outset *ou* very start *ou* very beginning.
◆ **du début à la fin** *loc adv* [d'un livre, d'une histoire] from beginning to end ▪ [d'une course, d'un événement] from start to finish.

débutant, e [debytɑ̃, ɑ̃t] <> *adj* [dans un apprentissage] novice *(modif)* ■ [dans une carrière] young ■ **un professeur ~** a young teacher.
<> *nm, f sing* [dans un apprentissage] beginner, novice ■ [dans une carrière] beginner ■ **espagnol pour les ~s** beginner's Spanish ➊ **grand ~** absolute beginner ■ **se faire avoir comme un ~** *fam familier* to be taken in like a real greenhorn *fam*.
◆ **débutante** *nf* debutante.

débuter [3] [debyte] <> *vi* **1.** [commencer] to start, to begin ■ **~ par** to start (off) with **2.** [être inexpérimenté] to be a beginner, to begin ■ **elle débute dans le métier** she's new to the job **3.** [commencer à travailler] to start (out), to begin ■ **il a débuté comme serveur dans un restaurant** he started out as a waiter in a restaurant **4.** [artiste] to make one's debut **5.** [en société] : **~ (dans le monde)** to make one's debut, to come out.
<> *vt fam* : **c'est nous qui débutons le concert** we're on first, we're opening the show.

deçà [dəsa] *adv* : **~ (et) delà** *litt* hither and thither.
◆ **en deçà** *loc adv* on this side ■ **ne franchissez pas la rivière, restez en ~** don't cross the river, stay on this side.
◆ **en deçà de** *loc prép* **1.** [de ce côté-ci de] (on) this side of **2.** *fig* **en ~ d'un certain seuil** below a certain level ■ **rester en ~ de la vérité** to be short of the truth ■ **ce travail est en ~ de ses possibilités** this job doesn't exploit his potential to the full.

déca [deka] *nm fam* decaffeinated coffee, decaf.

déca- [deka] *préf* deca-.

décacheter [27] [dekaʃte] *vt* [ouvrir - en déchirant] to open, to tear open ; [- en rompant le cachet] to unseal, to break open.

décade [dekad] *nf* **1.** [série de dix] decade **2.** [dix jours] period of ten days **3.** [dix ans] decade.

décadenasser [3] [dekadnase] *vt* to remove the padlock from, to take the padlock off.

décadence [dekadɑ̃s] *nf* decadence, decline, decay ■ **la ~ de l'Empire romain** the decline *ou* fall of the Roman Empire.
◆ **en décadence** <> *loc adj* declining, decaying, decadent.
<> *loc adv* : **tomber** *ou* **entrer en ~** to become decadent, to start to decline.

décadent, e [dekadɑ̃, ɑ̃t] <> *adj* **1.** [en déclin] decadent, declining, decaying **2.** ART & LITTÉR decadent.
<> *nm, f* decadent.
◆ **décadents** *nmpl* : **les ~s** the Decadents.

décadrer [3] [dekadre] *vt* **1.** MIN to draw the timbers of, to remove the timbering of **2.** [décentrer] : **être décadré** INFORM [perforation] to be off-punch ; CINÉ to be off-cent.

décaféiné, e [dekafeine] *adj* decaffeinated.
◆ **décaféiné** *nm* decaffeinated coffee.

décagone [dekagɔn] *nm* decagon.

décaisser [4] [dekese] *vt* **1.** FIN to pay, to disburse *spéc* **2.** [déballer] to unpack, to take out of its container.

décalage [dekalaʒ] *nm* **1.** [dans l'espace] space, interval, gap **2.** [dans le temps] interval, time-lag, lag ■ **~ horaire** time difference ■ **souffrir du ~ horaire** to have jet lag **3.** [manque de concordance] discrepancy, gap **4.** AUDIO shift, displacement ■ **~ de l'image** image displacement ■ **~ son-image** pull-up sound advance, sound to image stagger **5.** ASTRON : **~ spectral** spectral shift **6.** INFORM shift.
◆ **en décalage** *loc adj* **1.** [dans le temps] : **nous sommes en ~ par rapport à Bangkok** there's a time difference between here and Bangkok **2.** [sans harmonie] : **on est en complet ~** we're on completely different wavelengths.

décalaminer [3] [dekalamine] *vt* **1.** [moteur] to decarbonize, to decoke, to decarburize **2.** MÉTALL to descale.

décalcification [dekalsifikasjɔ̃] *nf* decalcification, decalcifying.

décalcifier [9] [dekalsifje] *vt* to decalcify.
◆ **se décalcifier** *vpi* to become decalcified.

décalcomanie [dekalkɔmani] *nf* **1.** [image] transfer, decal, decalcomania *spéc* ■ **faire des ~s** to do transfers **2.** [procédé] transfer process, decal, decalcomania *spéc*.

décaler [3] [dekale] *vt* **1.** [dans l'espace] to pull *ou* to shift (out of line) ■ **les sièges sont décalés** the seats are staggered **2.** [dans le temps - horaire] to shift ■ **l'horaire a été décalé d'une heure** [avancé] the schedule was brought forward an hour ; [reculé] the schedule was brought *ou* moved one hour back ■ **essaie de faire ~ l'heure de ton départ** see if you can get your departure time changed **3.** [désorienter] : **être décalé par rapport à la réalité** to be out of phase with reality.
◆ **se décaler** *vpi* to move (out of line) ■ **décalez-vous d'un rang en avant/arrière** move forward/back a row.

décalitre [dekalitr] *nm* decalitre.

décalogue [dekalɔg] *nm* Decalogue.

décalotter [3] [dekalɔte] *vt* : **~ le pénis** to pull back the foreskin.

décalque [dekalk] *nm* tracing.

décalquer [3] [dekalke] *vt* to trace, to transfer.

Décaméron [dekamerɔ̃] *npr* : **'Décaméron'** *Boccace* 'The Decameron'.

décamètre [dekamɛtr] *nm* decametre.

décamper [3] [dekɑ̃pe] *vi* to make o.s. scarce, to buzz off ■ **décampe!** clear out!, beat it! ■ **faire ~ qqn** to chase *ou* to drive sb out.

décan [dekɑ̃] *nm* decan.

décaniller [3] [dekanije] *vi fam* to clear out *ou* off, to scram ■ **il n'y a pas moyen de les faire ~** there's no budging them.

décantage [dekɑ̃taʒ] *nm*, **décantation** [dekɑ̃tasjɔ̃] *nf* [d'un liquide] settling, clarification ■ [de l'argile] washing ■ [des eaux usées] clarification ■ [du vin] decantation, settling.

décanter [3] [dekɑ̃te] *vt* **1.** [purifier - liquide] to allow to settle, to clarify ; [- argile] to wash ; [- produit chimique] to decant **2.** [éclaircir] to clarify ■ **~ ses idées** to think things over.
◆ **se décanter** *vpi* **1.** [liquide] to settle **2.** [situation] to settle down ■ **il faut laisser les choses se ~** one must allow things to sort themselves out *ou* to settle down.

décapant, e [dekapɑ̃, ɑ̃t] *adj* **1.** [nettoyant] : **agent** *ou* **produit ~** stripper **2.** [incisif - remarque] caustic, vitriolic ; [- roman, article] corrosive ■ **elle avait un humour ~** she had a caustic sense of humour.
◆ **décapant** *nm* stripper CONSTR.

décaper [3] [dekape] *vt* **1.** [nettoyer - gén] to clean off *(sép)* ; [- en grattant] to scrape clean ; [- avec un produit chimique] to strip ; [- à la chaleur] to burn off *(sép)* ■ **~ un parquet** to sand (down) floorboards **2.** *fam* [racler] to burn through *(insép)*, to scour *péj* ■ **ça décape la gorge** it burns your throat **3.** GÉOL to clear of surface soil.

décapitation [dekapitasjɔ̃] *nf* beheading, decapitation.

décapiter [3] [dekapite] *vt* **1.** [personne] : **~ qqn** [le supplicier] to behead sb, to cut sb's head off, to decapitate sb ; [accidentellement] to cut sb's head off, to decapitate sb **2.** [arbre, fleur] to top, to cut the top off **3.** [entreprise, gouvernement] to decapitate, to deprive of leaders.

décapotable [dekapɔtabl] *adj* & *nf* convertible ■ **sa voiture est ~** her car has a folding top, she drives a convertible.

décapoter [3] [dekapɔte] *vt* **1.** [replier le toit de] to fold back the roof of *UK*, to lower the top of *US* **2.** [enlever le toit de] to remove the roof *UK* *ou* top *US* of.

décapsulage [dekapsylaʒ] *nm* opening.

décapsuler [3] [dekapsyle] *vt* to uncap, to take the top off.

décapsuleur [dekapsylœr] *nm* bottle opener.

décarcasser [3] [dekarkase] ◆ **se décarcasser** *vpi fam* to go through a lot of hassle, to sweat (blood).

décarreler [24] [dekarle] *vt* [sol] to take tiles up from ■ [mur] to strip tiles off.

décasyllabe [dekasilab], **décasyllabique** [dekasilabik] *adj* decasyllabic.
◆ **décasyllabe** *nm* decasyllable.

décathlon [dekatlɔ̃] *nm* decathlon.

décathlonien, enne [dekatlɔnjɛ̃, ɛn] *nm, f* decathlete.

décati, e [dekati] *adj* **fam** [personne] decrepit ■ [corps] decrepit, wasted ■ **un vieux tout ~** an old man gone all to seed *ou* pot.

décéder [18] [desede] *vi* **sout** to die, to pass away **euphém** ■ **personne décédée** deceased person ■ **s'il vient à ~** in the event of his death.

décelable [deslabl] *adj* **1.** [par analyse] detectable **2.** [par observation] discernible, detectable, perceivable.

déceler [25] [desle] *vt* **1.** [repérer - erreur] to detect, to spot, to discover ■ **je n'ai rien décelé d'anormal** I've found nothing wrong ■ [percevoir] to detect, to discern, to perceive **2.** [révéler] to reveal, to betray, to give away *(sép)*.

décélération [deselerasjɔ̃] *nf* deceleration, slowing down.

décélérer [18] [deselere] *vi* to decelerate, to slow down.

décembre [desɑ̃br] *nm* December, *voir aussi* **mars**.

décemment [desamɑ̃] *adv* **1.** [correctement] decently, properly **2.** [suffisamment] properly **3.** [raisonnablement] decently ■ **on ne peut pas ~ lui raconter ça** we can't very well *ou* we can hardly tell him that.

décence [desɑ̃s] *nf* decency ■ **avoir la ~ de** to have the (common) decency to.

décennat [desena] *nm* decade *(of leadership)*.

décennie [deseni] *nf* decade, decenium, decennary.

décent, e [desɑ̃, ɑ̃t] *adj* **1.** [convenable] decent ■ **il serait plus ~ de ne rien lui dire** it would be more fitting *ou* proper not to tell him anything **2.** [acceptable] decent, reasonable ■ **un prix ~** a reasonable *ou* fair price ■ **un repas ~** a decent meal.

décentralisation [desɑ̃tralizasjɔ̃] *nf* decentralization, decentralizing.

DÉCENTRALISATION

The shifting of a degree of administrative power from Paris to regional bodies, especially in the 1970s and 1980s, has been a key aspect of French domestic policy. This policy led to the creation of the 26 administrative regions in 1982 which are overseen by regional councils.

décentraliser [3] [desɑ̃tralize] *vt* to decentralize.

décentrer [3] [desɑ̃tre] *vt* to bring out of centre ■ **être décentré** to be off-centre.

déception [desɛpsjɔ̃] *nf* disappointment ■ **quelle ~!** what a disappointment!

décérébrer [18] [deserebre] *vt* to decerebrate, to pith.

décerner [3] [desɛrne] *vt* **1.** [prix, médaille] to award ■ [titre, distinction] to confer on **2.** DR to issue.

décerveler [24] [desɛrvəle] *vt* to brain.

décès [desɛ] *nm* DR & **sout** death.

décevant, e [desəvɑ̃, ɑ̃t] *adj* disappointing.

décevoir [52] [desəvwar] *vt* to disappoint ■ **elle l'a beaucoup déçu** he was quite disappointed in *ou* with her ■ **tu me déçois** I'm disappointed in you ■ **il ne va pas être déçu!** **iron** he's going to get a shock!

déchaîné, e [deʃene] *adj* [mer, vent] raging, wild ■ [passions] unbridled, raging ■ [personne] wild ■ [public] raving, delirious ■ [opinion publique] outraged ■ [foule] riotous, uncontrollable ■ **tu es ~, ce soir! fam** you're on top form tonight!

déchaînement [deʃɛnmɑ̃] *nm* [des éléments, de la tempête] raging, fury ■ [de colère, de rage] outburst ■ **rien ne justifie un tel ~** this outburst is totally unjustified.

déchaîner [4] [deʃene] *vt* **1.** [déclencher - violence, colère] to unleash, to arouse ; [- enthousiasme] to arouse ; [- rires] to trigger off *(sép)* ■ **~ l'hilarité générale** to set off a storm of laughter ■ **~ les passions : son article a déchaîné les passions** his article caused an outcry *ou* aroused strong passions **2.** [mettre en colère] : **il est déchaîné contre vous** he's ranting and raving against you.
◆ **se déchaîner** *vpi* **1.** [tempête, vent] to rage **2.** [hilarité, applaudissements] to break *ou* to burst out ■ [instincts] to be unleashed ■ **se ~ contre** to rave at *ou* against ■ **la presse s'est déchaînée contre le gouvernement** the press railed at the government ■ **elle s'est déchaînée contre son frère** she lashed out *ou* let fly at her brother.

déchanter [3] [deʃɑ̃te] *vi* to be disillusioned, to become disenchanted ■ **il croyait avoir trouvé l'amour mais il a déchanté** he thought he'd found love but the scales fell from his eyes.

décharge [deʃarʒ] *nf* **1.** ARM [tir] shot ■ **prendre** *ou* **recevoir une ~ en pleine poitrine** to get shot in the chest **2.** ÉLECTR discharge ■ **~ électrique** electric *ou* field discharge ■ **prendre une ~ fam** to get a shock **3.** [écrit, quittance] discharge paper, chit **4.** [dépotoir] dump, rubbish tip *UK*, garbage dump *US* ■ **'~ interdite'** 'no dumping' **5.** PHYSIOL rush ■ **~ d'adrénaline** rush of adrenaline.
◆ **à la décharge de** *loc prép* : **à sa ~, il faut dire que...** in his defence, it has to be said that...
◆ **de décharge** *loc adj* CONSTR [arc] relieving.

déchargement [deʃarʒəmɑ̃] *nm* **1.** [d'une arme, d'un véhicule] unloading **2.** ÉLECTRON dump.

décharger [17] [deʃarʒe] ◇ *vt* **1.** [débarrasser de sa charge - véhicule, animal] to unload ; [- personne] to unburden ■ **je vais te ~** [à un voyageur] let me take your luggage ; [au retour des magasins] let me take your parcels for you **2.** [enlever - marchandises] to unload, to take off *(sép)* ; [- passagers] to set down *(sép)* ■ **~ la cargaison/des caisses d'un navire** to unload the cargo/crates off a ship **3.** [soulager] to relieve, to unburden ■ **~ qqn de qqch** to relieve sb of sthg ■ **être déchargé de ses fonctions** to be discharged *ou* dismissed **4.** [disculper] to clear, to exonerate **5.** CONSTR to relieve, to discharge **6.** ARM [tirer avec] to fire, to discharge ■ **~ son arme sur qqn** to fire one's gun at sb ■ [ôter la charge de] to unload **7.** ÉLECTR to discharge **8.** ÉLECTRON to dump **9.** [laisser libre cours à] to vent, to give vent to ■ **~ sa bile** to vent one's spleen ■ **~ sa colère** to give vent to one's anger ■ **~ sa mauvaise humeur sur qqn** to vent one's temper on sb.
◇ *vi* **1.** [déteindre - étoffe] to run **2.** ▲ [éjaculer] to come▲.
◆ **se décharger** *vpi* **1.** ÉLECTR [batterie] to run down, to go flat ■ [accumulateur] to run down, to lose its charge **2.** [se débarrasser] : **se ~ (de qqch) sur : je vais essayer de me ~ de cette corvée sur quelqu'un** I'll try to hand over the chore to somebody else.

déchargeur [deʃarʒœr] *nm* [appareil] unloader.

décharné, e [deʃarne] *adj* [maigre - personne] emaciated, gaunt, wasted ; [- visage] emaciated, gaunt, haggard ; [- main] bony.

déchaussé, e [deʃose] *adj* **1.** [sans chaussures - pied] bare, shoeless, unshod ; [- personne] barefoot **2.** [branlant - dent] loose ; [- mur] laid bare **3.** [moine, nonne] discalced.

déchausser [3] [deʃose] *vt* **1.** [personne] : **~ qqn** to take off sb's shoes ■ [retirer] : **~ ses skis** to take off one's skis ■ *(en usage absolu)* to lose one's skis **2.** CONSTR [mur] to lay bare.
◆ **se déchausser** ◇ *vp (emploi réfléchi)* [personne] to take off one's shoes.
◇ *vpi* [dent] to get loose ■ **avoir les dents qui se déchaussent** to have receding gums.

dèche△ [dɛʃ] *nf* dire poverty ■ **être dans la ~** to be skint *UK ou* broke.

déchéance [deʃeɑ̃s] *nf* **1.** [avilissement] (moral) degradation ■ **tomber dans la ~** to go into (moral) decline **2.** [déclin social] lowering of social standing **3.** RELIG fall **4.** DR loss, forfeit ■ **~ de l'autorité parentale** loss of parental authority **5.** POLIT [d'un monarque] deposition, deposing ■ [d'un président] removal *(after impeachment)*.

déchet [deʃɛ] *nm* **1.** [portion inutilisable] : **dans un ananas il y a beaucoup de ~** there's a lot of waste in a pineapple **2.** *péj* [personne] (miserable) wretch **3.** COMM : **~ de route** losses in transit.
déchets *nmpl* **1.** [résidus] waste ■ **des ~s de nourriture** food scraps ■ **~s radioactifs/toxiques** radioactive/toxic waste **2.** PHYSIOL waste matter.

déchetterie [deʃɛtri] *nf* waste collection centre *(for sorting and recycling)*.

déchiffrable [deʃifrabl] *adj* decipherable ■ **écriture ~** legible handwriting.

déchiffrage [deʃifraʒ] *nm* sight-reading.

déchiffrer [3] [deʃifre] *vt* **1.** [comprendre - inscription, manuscrit] to decipher ; [- langage codé] to decipher, to decode ■ **je déchiffre à peine son écriture** I can barely make out her handwriting **2.** [lire] to spell out *(sép)* ■ **: apprendre à ~** to start spelling out words **3.** MUS to sight-read **4.** [élucider - énigme] to puzzle out *(sép)*, to make sense of.

déchiffreur, euse [deʃifrœr, øz] *nm, f* decipherer.

déchiqueté, e [deʃikte] *adj* **1.** [irrégulier - feuille] jagged ; [- montagne] jagged, ragged **2.** [tailladé] torn to bits, hacked about.

déchiqueter [27] [deʃikte] *vt* [papier, tissu] to rip (to shreds), to tear (to bits) ■ **les corps ont été déchiquetés par l'explosion** the bodies were torn to pieces by the explosion.

déchirant, e [deʃirɑ̃, ɑ̃t] *adj* [spectacle] heartbreaking, heartrending ■ [cri] agonizing, harrowing ■ [séparation] unbearably painful.

déchirement [deʃirmɑ̃] *nm* **1.** [arrachement] tearing, ripping, rending **2.** [souffrance] wrench **3.** [désunion] rift ■ **un pays en proie à des ~s politiques** a country torn apart by internal strife.

déchirer [3] [deʃire] *vt* **1.** [lacérer] to tear, to rip ■ **attention, tu vas ~ ton collant** mind not to rip your tights
2. [mettre en deux morceaux] to tear ■ **~ une page en deux** to tear a page into two ■ [mettre en morceaux] to tear up *ou* to pieces
3. [arracher] to tear off *(sép)*
4. [ouvrir] : **~ une enveloppe** to tear *ou* to rip open an envelope
5. [blesser] to tear (the skin *ou* flesh of), to gash ■ **un bruit qui déchire les tympans** an earpiercing *ou* earsplitting noise ■ **une douleur qui déchire la poitrine** a stabbing pain in the chest ■ **~ qqn** *ou* **le cœur de qqn** *litt* to break sb's heart, to make sb's heart bleed
6. *litt* [interrompre - nuit, silence] to rend, to pierce
7. [diviser] to tear apart ■ **le pays est déchiré par la guerre depuis 10 ans** the country has been torn apart by war for 10 years ■ **des familles déchirées par la guerre** war-torn families ■ **je suis déchiré entre eux deux** I'm torn between the two of them.
se déchirer ◇ *vp (emploi réciproque)* [se faire souffrir] to tear each other apart.
◇ *vp (emploi passif)* to tear ■ **ce tissu se déchire facilement** this material tears easily.
◇ *vpi* [vêtement, tissu, papier] to tear, to rip ■ [membrane] to break.
◇ *vpt* MÉD : **se ~ un muscle/tendon/ligament** to tear a muscle/tendon/ligament.

déchirure [deʃiryr] *nf* **1.** [accroc] tear, rip, split **2.** *litt* [souffrance] wrench **3.** MÉD tear ■ **~ musculaire** pulled muscle **4.** [trouée] crack, opening.

déchoir [71] [deʃwar] ◇ *vi* **1.** *(aux être)* **il est déchu de son rang** he has lost *ou* forfeited his social standing **2.** *(aux avoir) litt* [s'abaisser] to demean o.s. ■ [diminuer - fortune, prestige] to wane.
◇ *vt* [priver] : **~ qqn d'un droit** to deprive sb of a right.

déchristianisation [dekristjanizasjɔ̃] *nf* dechristianization, dechristianizing.

déchristianiser [3] [dekristjanize] *vt* to dechristianize.

déchu, e [deʃy] ◇ *pp* ▷ **déchoir**.
◇ *adj* [prince, roi] deposed, dethroned ■ [président] deposed ■ [ange, humanité] fallen.

déci [desi] *nm Suisse decilitre of wine*.

décibel [desibɛl] *nm* decibel.

décidé, e [deside] *adj* **1.** [résolu] resolute, determined, decided ■ **elle est entrée d'un pas ~** she strode resolutely into the room **2.** [réglé] settled.

décidément [desidemɑ̃] *adv* definitely, clearly ■ **~, ça ne marchera jamais** obviously it'll never work out ■ **~, c'est une manie** you're really making a habit of it, aren't you? ■ **j'ai encore cassé un verre – ~!** I've broken another glass – it's not your day, is it!

décider [3] [deside] *vt* **1.** [choisir] to decide (on) ■ **~ de faire** to decide *ou* to resolve to do ■ **ils ont décidé d'accepter/de ne pas accepter la proposition** they've decided in favour of/against the proposal ■ **~ que : il a décidé qu'il ne prendrait pas l'avion** he's decided not to *ou* that he won't fly ■ **~ combien/quoi/comment/si** to decide how much/what/how/whether ■ **c'est décidé** it's settled ■ *(en usage absolu)* **c'est toi qui décides** it's your decision, it's up to you ■ **c'est le temps qui décidera** it will depend on the weather **2.** [entraîner] : **~ qqn à** to convince *ou* to persuade sb to ■ **décide-la à rester** persuade her to stay **3.** *sout* [régler - ordre du jour] to decide, to set ; [- point de droit] to resolve, to give a ruling on, to decide on ■ *(en usage absolu)* **~ en faveur de qqn** to give a ruling in favour of sb.
décider de *v+prép* **1.** [influencer] to determine ■ **le résultat de l'enquête décidera de la poursuite de ce projet** the results of the survey will determine whether (or not) we carry on with the project **2.** [choisir - lieu, date] to choose, to determine, to decide on **3.** [juger] : **ta mère en a décidé ainsi!** your mother's decision is final! ■ **le sort en décida autrement** fate decreed otherwise.
se décider ◇ *vp (emploi passif)* to be decided (on) ■ **les choses se sont décidées très vite** things were decided very quickly.
◇ *vpi* [faire son choix] to make up one's mind ■ **se ~ pour** to decide on ■ **se ~ à : je me suis décidé à l'acheter** I decided *ou* resolved to buy it ■ **elle s'est décidée à déménager** she's made up her mind to move out ■ **je ne me décide pas à le jeter** I can't bring myself to throw it out ■ **la voiture s'est enfin décidée à démarrer** the car finally decided to start ■ *(tournure impersonnelle)* **il se décide à faire beau** it looks like the weather's trying to improve.

décideur, euse [desidœr, øz] *nm, f* decision-maker.

décigramme [desigram] *nm* decigramme, decigram.

décilitre [desilitr] *nm* decilitre.

décimal, e, aux [desimal, o] *adj* decimal ■ **fraction ~e** decimal, decimal fraction.
décimale *nf* decimal place ■ **nombre à trois ~es** number given to three decimal places.

décimaliser [3] [desimalize] *vt* to decimalize.

décime [desim] *nm* **1.** ADMIN 10% increase *(in tax)* **2.** HIST [dix centimes] tenth part of a franc, ten centimes.

décimer [3] [desime] *vt* to decimate.

décimètre [desimɛtr] *nm* decimetre.

décintrer [3] [desɛ̃tre] *vt* **1.** CONSTR to strike down *ou* to take down the center **2.** COUT to let out *(sép)*.

décisif, ive [desizif, iv] *adj* [déterminant - influence, intervention] decisive ; [- preuve] conclusive ; [- élément, coup] decisive, deciding ; [- coup] decisive ■ **il n'y a encore rien de ~** there's nothing conclusive *ou* definite yet ■ **il a eu un argument ~** what he said clinched the argument ■ **à un moment ~ de ma vie** at a decisive moment *ou* at a watershed in my life ■ **de façon** *ou* **manière décisive** decisively, conclusively.

décision [desizjɔ̃] *nf* **1.** [résolution] decision ■ **arriver à une ~** to come to *ou* to reach a decision ■ **prendre une ~** to make a decision ■ **je n'ai pas pris de ~ là-dessus** I haven't made up my mind about it ■ **qui a pris cette ~?** whose decision was it? ■ **la ~ t'appartient** the decision is yours, it's for you to decide ■ **soumettre qqch à la ~ d'un comité** to ask a committee to make a decision on sthg **2.** DR : **~ judiciaire** court ruling ■ **par**

~ **judiciaire** by order of the court **3.** [fermeté] decision ■ **agir avec ~** to be resolute ■ **avoir de la ~** to be decisive ■ **manquer de ~** to be hesitant *ou* irresolute **4.** INFORM decision.
◆ **de décision** *loc adj* [organe, centre] decision-making.

décisionnaire [desizjɔnɛr] *nmf* decision-maker.

décisionnel, elle [desizjɔnɛl] *adj* decision-making *(modif)*.

déclamateur, trice [deklamatœr, tris] *péj* ◇ *adj* bombastic.
◇ *nm, f* declaimer.

déclamation [deklamasjɔ̃] *nf* **1.** [art de réciter] declamation **2.** [emphase] declamation, ranting.

déclamatoire [deklamatwar] *adj* **1.** [art] declamatory **2.** *péj* [style] declamatory, bombastic.

déclamer [3] [deklame] *vt* to declaim.

déclaratif, ive [deklaratif, iv] *adj* **1.** DR declaratory **2.** GRAMM declarative.

déclaration [deklarasjɔ̃] *nf* **1.** [communication] statement ■ [proclamation] declaration ■ **faire une ~ à la presse** to issue a statement to the press ■ **je ne ferai aucune ~!** no comment! ■ **~ de guerre/d'indépendance** declaration of war/of independence ■ **la Déclaration des droits de l'homme et du citoyen** the Declaration of Human Rights *(of 1791)* ■ **~ de principe** declaration of principle **2.** [témoignage] statement ■ **faire une ~ aux gendarmes** to make a statement to the police ■ **selon les ~s du témoin** according to the witness's statement ■ **~ sous serment** sworn statement, statement under oath **3.** ADMIN declaration ■ **faire une ~ à la douane** to declare something at customs ■ **faire une ~ à son assurance** to file a claim with one's insurance company ■ **~ de perte : faire une ~ de perte de passeport à la police** to report the loss of one's passport to the police ▶ **~ de décès** *official registration of death (submitted to the Mairie)* ■ **~ d'impôts** tax return ■ **~ de naissance** birth registration ■ **~ de sinistre** damage claim **4.** [aveu] declaration ■ **faire une ~ d'amour** *ou* **sa ~ (à qqn)** to declare one's love (to sb) **5.** INFORM declaration.

DÉCLARATION D'IMPÔTS

People in France are required to declare their taxable earnings at the beginning of the year for the previous calendar year. Thrice-yearly tax payments (*tiers provisionnels*) are based on one third of the previous year's total, the final payment being adjusted according to the actual tax owed. It is also possible to pay tax on a monthly basis. This is known as *mensualisation*.

LA DÉCLARATION DES DROITS DE L'HOMME ET DU CITOYEN

Adopted by the National Assembly on 4th August 1789, the Declaration proclaims the inalienable natural right of all men to freedom, condemns the privileged class of the *Ancien Régime* and declares all citizens equal before the law. In 1793, the preface to the Constitution added the right to education, work and freedom of assembly to the text of 1789.

déclaré, e [deklare] *adj* [ennemi] declared, sworn ■ [intention, opinion] declared ■ **un fasciste ~** a professed *ou* self-confessed fascist ■ **un opposant ~** an avowed opponent.

déclarer [3] [deklare] *vt* **1.** [proclamer] to declare, to announce, to assert ▶ **~ forfait** SPORT to withdraw ; *fig* to throw in the towel ■ **~ la guerre à** *pr* & *fig* to declare war on **2.** *(avec un adj ou une loc adj)* [juger] : **~ qqn coupable** to find sb guilty ■ **on l'a déclaré incapable de gérer sa fortune** he was pronounced incapable of managing his estate **3.** [affirmer] to profess, to claim ■ **il déclare être innocent** he claims to be innocent *ou* protests his innocence ■ **il déclare être resté chez lui** he claims he stayed at home **4.** [révéler - intention] to state, to declare ■ **~ son amour** *ou* **sa flamme à qqn** *litt* to declare one's love to sb **5.** [dire officiellement] to declare ■ **~ ses revenus/employés** to declare one's income/employees ■ **~ un enfant à la mairie** to register the birth of a child ■ **~ un vol** to report a theft ■ **rien à ~** nothing to declare.

◆ **se déclarer** *vpi* **1.** [se manifester - incendie, épidémie] to break out ; [- fièvre, maladie] to set in **2.** [se prononcer] to take a stand ■ **se ~ pour/contre l'avortement** to come out in favour of/against abortion, to declare for/against abortion **3.** *(avec un adj ou une loc adj)* [se dire] to say ■ **il s'est déclaré ravi** he said how pleased he was **4.** *litt* [dire son amour] to declare one's love.

déclassé, e [deklase] ◇ *adj* **1.** SOCIOL déclassé **2.** [hôtel, joueur] downgraded.
◇ *nm, f* : **c'est un ~** he has lost his social status *ou* come down in the world.

déclassement [deklasmɑ̃] *nm* **1.** [dans la société] fall *ou* drop in social standing ■ [dans une hiérarchie] downgrading, loss of status **2.** [dévalorisation] depreciation **3.** [mise en désordre] putting out of order **4.** RAIL change to a lower class **5.** NAUT decommissioning.

déclasser [3] [deklase] *vt* **1.** [déranger] to put out of order **2.** [rétrograder] to downgrade **3.** [déprécier] to demean ■ **ce travail le déclassait** he was lowering *ou* demeaning himself in that job **4.** [changer de catégorie - hôtel] to downgrade ■ RAIL to change to a lower class **5.** NAUT & NUCL to decommission.
◆ **se déclasser** *vpi* **1.** SOCIOL to move one step down the social scale **2.** [dans un train] to change to a lower-class compartment ■ [dans un navire] to change to lower-class accommodation.

déclenchement [deklɑ̃ʃmɑ̃] *nm* **1.** [début - d'un événement] starting point, start, trigger ; [- d'une attaque] launching **2.** ÉLECTRON triggering **3.** MÉCAN release.

déclencher [3] [deklɑ̃ʃe] *vt* **1.** [provoquer - attaque] to launch ; [- révolte, conflit] to trigger (off), to bring about *(sép)* ; [- grève, émeute, rires] to trigger *ou* to spark off *(sép)* **2.** TECHNOL [mettre en marche - mécanisme, minuterie] to trigger, to activate ; [- sonnerie, alarme] to set off *(sép)* **3.** INFORM to trigger.
◆ **se déclencher** *vpi* **1.** [commencer - douleur, incendie] to start **2.** [se mettre en marche - sirène, sonnerie, bombe] to go off ; [- mécanisme] to be triggered off *ou* released.

déclencheur [deklɑ̃ʃœr] *nm* **1.** ÉLECTR release, circuit breaker **2.** PHOTO shutter release ■ **~ automatique** time release, self-timer **3.** TECHNOL release, tripping device.

déclic [deklik] *nm* **1.** [mécanisme] trigger, releasing mechanism **2.** [bruit] click **3.** [prise de conscience] : **il s'est produit un ~ et elle a trouvé la solution** things suddenly fell into place *ou* clicked and she found the answer.

déclin [deklɛ̃] *nm* **1.** [diminution] decline, waning ■ **le soleil à son ~** the setting sun **2.** *litt* [fin] close ■ **le ~ du jour** nightfall, dusk.
◆ **en déclin** *loc adj* on the decline ■ **un hebdomadaire en ~** a weekly paper with falling readership figures.
◆ **sur le déclin** *loc adj* [prestige, puissance] declining, on the wane ■ [malade] declining ■ **un acteur sur le ~** an actor who's seen better days.

déclinable [deklinabl] *adj* declinable ■ **une gamme d'ordinateurs ~ en plusieurs configurations** a range of computers enabling several different configurations.

déclinaison [deklinɛzɔ̃] *nf* **1.** GRAMM declension **2.** ASTRON & PHYS declination.

déclinant, e [deklinɑ̃, ɑ̃t] *adj* [force] declining, deteriorating ■ [influence, grandeur] declining, waning, fading ■ [société] declining, decaying.

décliner [3] [dekline] ◇ *vt* **1.** GRAMM to decline ■ **l'amour est décliné dans toutes les chansons** *fig* love is an ever-recurrent theme in songs **2.** [énoncer - identité] to give, to state **3.** [refuser - invitation] to decline, to refuse ; [- offre] to decline, to refuse, to reject ■ **~ toute responsabilité** to accept no responsibility.
◇ *vi* [soleil] to set ■ [vieillard] to decline ■ [malade] to decline, to fade ■ [santé, vue] to deteriorate ■ [prestige] to wane, to decline ■ [jour] to draw to a close.
◆ **se décliner** *vpi* : **une robe qui se décline dans différentes couleurs** a dress available in different colours.

déclivité [deklivite] *nf* **1.** [descente] downward slope, declivity *spéc*, incline **2.** [inclinaison - d'une route, d'un chemin de fer] gradient.

décloisonner [3] [deklwazɔne] *vt* to decompartmentalize.

déclouer [3] [deklue] *vt* [planche] to remove *ou* to pull the nails out of ▪ [couvercle] to prise *UK ou* to pry *US* open *(sép)*.
◆ **se déclouer** *vpi* to fall *ou* to come apart.

décocher [3] [dekɔʃe] *vt* **1.** [flèche] to shoot, to fire ▪ [coup] to throw ▪ **il m'a décoché un coup de pied** he kicked me ▪ **le cheval lui a décoché une ruade** the horse lashed out *ou* kicked at him **2.** [regard, sourire] to dart, to flash, to shoot ▪ [plaisanterie, méchanceté] to fire, to shoot **3.** [case] to check, to uncheck, to tick off *UK*.

décoction [dekɔksjɔ̃] *nf* decoction.

décodage [dekɔdaʒ] *nm* **1.** [d'un texte] decoding, deciphering **2.** INFORM & TV decoding, unscrambling.

décoder [3] [dekɔde] *vt* **1.** [texte] to decode **2.** INFORM & TV to decode, to unscramble.

décodeur [dekɔdœr] ◇ *adj m* decoding.
◇ *nm* decoder.

décoiffant, e [dekwafɑ̃, ɑ̃t] *adj fam* exciting.

décoiffer [3] [dekwafe] *vt* **1.** [déranger la coiffure de] : **~ qqn** to mess up sb's hair ▪ **elle est toute décoiffée** her hair's in a mess **2.** [ôter le chapeau de] : **~ qqn** to remove sb's hat **3.** *fam loc* **ça décoiffe** it takes your breath away.
◆ **se décoiffer** *vp (emploi réfléchi)* **1.** [déranger sa coiffure] to mess up *ou US* to muss up one's hair **2.** [ôter son chapeau] to remove one's hat.

décoincement [dekwɛ̃smɑ̃], **décoinçage** [dekwɛ̃saʒ] *nm* [déblocage - d'un objet] unjamming, freeing, loosening ; [- d'une vertèbre, d'une articulation] loosening up.

décoincer [16] [dekwɛ̃se] *vt* [débloquer - objet] to unjam, to free ; [- vertèbre, articulation] to loosen up *(sép)*.
◆ **se décoincer** *vpi* **1.** [objet] to unjam, to work loose **2.** *fam* [personne] to relax, to let one's hair down.

déçoit, déçoivent *etc v* ▷ **décevoir.**

décolérer [18] [dekɔlere] *vi* : **ne pas ~ : il n'a pas décoléré de la journée** he's been furious *ou* fuming all day ▪ **elle ne décolère jamais** she's permanently in a temper.

décollage [dekɔlaʒ] *nm* **1.** AÉRON takeoff ▪ ASTRONAUT lift-off, blast-off ▪ **au ~** AÉRON at *ou* on takeoff ; ASTRONAUT on takeoff *ou* lift-off **2.** [d'une enveloppe, d'un papier] unsticking **3.** ÉCON & SOCIOL takeoff.

décollé, e [dekɔle] *adj* : **avoir les oreilles ~es** to have ears that stick out.

décollement [dekɔlmɑ̃] *nm* **1.** [d'un papier] unsticking **2.** MÉD : **~ de la rétine** detachment *ou* separation of the retina.

décoller [3] [dekɔle] ◇ *vi* **1.** AÉRON to take off ▪ ASTRONAUT to take *ou* to lift *ou* to blast off **2.** [quitter le sol - skieur, motocycliste] to take off **3.** *fam* [partir] to leave **4.** [progresser - exportation, pays] to take off ▪ **ces mesures n'ont pas réussi à faire ~ l'économie** these measures failed to restart the economy **5.** [s'échapper] to escape.
◇ *vt* **1.** [détacher - papier] to unstick, to unglue, to peel off *(sép)* ▪ **~ à la vapeur** to steam off ▪ **~ dans l'eau** to soak off **2.** *fam* [faire partir] to tear *ou* to prise away *(sép)* ▪ **on ne peut pas le ~ de la télévision** there's no prising him away from the TV **3.** LOISIRS [au billard] to nudge away from the cushion.
◆ **se décoller** ◇ *vp (emploi passif)* to come off ▪ **ça se décolle simplement en tirant dessus** just pull it and it comes off.
◇ *vpi* **1.** [se détacher] to come *ou* to peel off **2.** MÉD to become detached.

décolleté, e [dekɔlte] *adj* **1.** [vêtement] low-cut, low-necked, décolleté ▪ **robe ~e dans le dos** dress cut low in the back **2.** [femme] décolleté, wearing a low-cut dress.
◆ **décolleté** *nm* **1.** [vêtement] low neckline ▪ **un ~ plongeant** a plunging neckline **2.** [d'une femme] cleavage.

décolleter [27] [dekɔlte] *vt* **1.** [robe] to give a low neckline to ▪ [personne] to reveal the neck and shoulders of **2.** AGRIC to top **3.** TECHNOL to cut off *(sép)*.

décolonisation [dekɔlɔnizasjɔ̃] *nf* decolonization.

LA DÉCOLONISATION

In a French context, the word refers to the period in the 40s and 50s when colonies progressively became independent of French colonial rule. In 1977, the last French colony was declared independent.

décoloniser [3] [dekɔlɔnize] *vt* to decolonize.

décolorant, e [dekɔlɔrɑ̃, ɑ̃t] *adj* **1.** [gén] decolorant, decolouring **2.** [pour cheveux] decolorizing *(avant n)*, decolorant, bleaching *(avant n)*.
◆ **décolorant** *nm* **1.** [gén] decolorant **2.** [pour cheveux] decolorizing agent, bleaching agent.

décoloration [dekɔlɔrasjɔ̃] *nf* **1.** [atténuation de la couleur] fading, discolouration **2.** [disparition de la couleur] bleaching, discolouring ▪ **~ d'une plante** bleaching of a plant **3.** [des cheveux] bleach treatment ▪ **faire une ~** to bleach someone's hair.

décoloré, e [dekɔlɔre] *adj* **1.** [fané] faded **2.** [blondi] bleached ▪ **une femme ~e** a peroxide *ou* bleached blonde **3.** [livide - visage, joue] ashen, pale.

décolorer [3] [dekɔlɔre] *vt* **1.** [affaiblir la couleur de] to fade **2.** [éclaircir - cheveux] to bleach ▪ **cheveux décolorés par le soleil** hair lightened *ou* bleached by the sun ▪ **elle se fait ~ (les cheveux)** she has her hair bleached.
◆ **se décolorer** ◇ *vp (emploi réfléchi)* [personne] to bleach one's hair.
◇ *vpi* **1.** [tissu, papier] to fade, to lose its colour **2.** [liquide] to lose its colour.

décombres [dekɔ̃br] *nmpl* **1.** [d'un bâtiment] debris *(sing)*, rubble, wreckage **2.** *litt* [d'une civilisation] ruins.

décommander [3] [dekɔmɑ̃de] *vt* [commande] to cancel ▪ [invitation, rendez-vous] to cancel, to call off *(sép)* ▪ [invité] to put off *(sép)*.
◆ **se décommander** *vpi* to cancel (one's appointment).

décompacter [dekɔ̃pakte] *vt* INFORM [données] to unpack.

décompartimentaliser [dekɔ̃partimɑ̃talize] *vt* to decompartmentalize.

décomplexer [4] [dekɔ̃plɛkse] *vt* to encourage, to reassure ▪ **ça m'a décomplexé** it made me feel more confident *ou* less inadequate.

décomposable [dekɔ̃pozabl] *adj* **1.** [corps chimique, matière] decomposable **2.** [texte, idée] analysable, that can be broken down **3.** MATH [équation] that can be factorized ▪ [polynôme] that can be broken up **4.** PHYS resoluble.

décomposer [3] [dekɔ̃poze] *vt* **1.** CHIM to decompose, to break down *(sép)* **2.** PHYS [force] to resolve ▪ [lumière] to disperse **3.** MATH to factorize ▪ **~ en facteurs premiers** to resolve into prime factors **4.** [analyser - texte, raisonnement] to break down *(sép)*, to analyse ; [- mouvement, processus] to decompose, to break up *(sép)* ; [- exercice, mélodie] to go through (step by step) *(insép)* ▪ **~ un pas de danse** to go through a dance step ▪ GRAMM [phrase] to parse **5.** [pourrir - terre, feuilles] to decompose, to rot **6.** [altérer] : **un visage décomposé par la peur** a face distorted with fear ▪ **être décomposé** to look stricken.
◆ **se décomposer** ◇ *vp (emploi passif)* : **le texte se décompose en trois parties** the text can be broken down *ou* divided into three parts ▮ GRAMM [phrase] to be parsed ▪ MATH to be factorized.
◇ *vpi* **1.** [pourrir] to decompose, to decay, to rot **2.** [s'altérer - visage] to become distorted ▪ **soudain son visage s'est décomposé** his face suddenly fell.

décomposition [dekɔ̃pozisjɔ̃] *nf* **1.** CHIM decomposition, breaking down **2.** PHYS [de la lumière] dispersion ▪ [d'une force] resolution **3.** MATH factorization **4.** [analyse] analysis, breaking down ▪ GRAMM parsing **5.** INFORM breakdown **6.** [pourrissement - de la matière organique] decomposition, decay, rot ; [- de la société] decline, decay, decadence ■ en (état de) ~ [cadavre] decomposing, decaying, rotting ; [société] declining, decaying **7.** [altération - des traits] contortion.

décompresser[1] [4] [dekɔ̃prese] *vi* **1.** [plongeur] to undergo decompression **2.** *fam* [se détendre] to relax, to unwind.

décompresser[2] [3] [dekɔ̃prese] *vt* INFORM to uncompress, to decompress.

décompresseur [dekɔ̃presœr] *nm* **1.** PHYS decompression device **2.** AUTO & MÉCAN decompressor.

décompression [dekɔ̃presjɔ̃] *nf* **1.** MÉD & TECHNOL decompression **2.** *fam* [détente] unwinding, relaxing **3.** AUTO & MÉCAN decompression.

décompte [dekɔ̃t] *nm* **1.** [calcul] working out, reckoning, calculation ■ **faire le ~ des voix** to count the votes ■ **faire le ~ des points** to add *ou* to reckon up the score **2.** [déduction] deduction.

décompter [3] [dekɔ̃te] <> *vt* **1.** [déduire] to deduct **2.** [dénombrer] to count.
<> *vi* to strike the wrong time.

déconcentration [dekɔ̃sɑ̃trasjɔ̃] *nf* **1.** ADMIN devolution **2.** ÉCON [décentralisation] decentralization, dispersion **3.** [dilution] dilution **4.** [manque d'attention] lack of concentration.

déconcentrer [3] [dekɔ̃sɑ̃tre] *vt* **1.** [transférer - pouvoir] to devolve **2.** [distraire] : **~ qqn** to distract sb's attention **3.** CHIM [diluer] : **~ une solution** to dilute a solution.
◆ **se déconcentrer** *vpi* to lose (one's) concentration.

déconcertant, e [dekɔ̃sɛrtɑ̃, ɑ̃t] *adj* disconcerting, off-putting.

déconcerter [3] [dekɔ̃sɛrte] *vt* to disconcert.

déconditionner [3] [dekɔ̃disjɔne] *vt* to decondition.

déconfit, e [dekɔ̃fi, it] *adj* crestfallen.

déconfiture [dekɔ̃fityr] *nf* **1.** [échec] collapse, defeat, rout ■ **tomber en ~** *litt & hum* to collapse **2.** DR insolvency.

décongélation [dekɔ̃ʒelasjɔ̃] *nf* defrosting, thawing.

décongeler [25] [dekɔ̃ʒle] *vt* to defrost, to thaw.

décongestionner [3] [dekɔ̃ʒɛstjɔne] *vt* **1.** [dégager - route] to relieve congestion in, to ease the traffic load in **2.** MÉD to decongest, to relieve congestion in *ou* the congestion of.

déconnecter [4] [dekɔnɛkte] *vt* **1.** [débrancher - tuyau, fil électrique] to disconnect, to cut off *(sép)* **2.** *fam fig* to disconnect, to cut off *(sép)* ■ **il est totalement déconnecté de la réalité** he's totally cut off from reality.

déconner [3]△ [dekɔne] *vi* **1.** [dire des bêtises] to talk rubbish *UK*, to bullshit△ **2.** [s'amuser] to horse *ou* to fool around **3.** [faire des bêtises] to mess around ■ **déconne pas!** stop messing about! **4.** [mal fonctionner] to be on the blink.

déconneur, euse△ [dekɔnœr, øz] *nm, f* clown.

déconnexion [dekɔnɛksjɔ̃] *nf* disconnection.

déconseiller [4] [dekɔ̃seje] *vt* to advise against ■ **c'est déconseillé** it's not (to be) recommended, it's to be avoided.

déconsidération [dekɔ̃siderasjɔ̃] *nf litt* discredit.

déconsidérer [18] [dekɔ̃sidere] *vt* to discredit ■ **ces révélations l'ont déconsidéré** these revelations have cast a slur on *ou* have discredited him.
◆ **se déconsidérer** *vp (emploi réfléchi)* to discredit o.s., to bring discredit upon o.s., to lose one's credibility.

déconstruction [dekɔ̃stryksjɔ̃] *nf* LITTÉR & PHILOS deconstruction.

décontamination [dekɔ̃taminasjɔ̃] *nf* decontamination ■ **~ d'un site nucléaire** decontaminating a nuclear site.

décontaminer [3] [dekɔ̃tamine] *vt* to decontaminate.

décontenancer [16] [dekɔ̃tnɑ̃se] *vt* to disconcert, to discountenance *sout.*
◆ **se décontenancer** *vpi* to lose one's composure.

décontracté, e [dekɔ̃trakte] *adj* **1.** [détendu - muscle, corps] relaxed ; [- caractère] easy-going, relaxed ; [- attitude] relaxed, composed, unworried ; [- style, vêtements] casual **2.** *péj* [désinvolte] casual, off-hand.

décontracter [3] [dekɔ̃trakte] *vt* [muscle] to relax, to unclench ■ **elle sait ~ les nouveaux venus** she knows how to put newcomers at ease.
◆ **se décontracter** *vpi* to relax.

décontraction [dekɔ̃traksjɔ̃] *nf* **1.** [relâchement, détente] relaxation, relaxing **2.** [aisance] coolness, collectedness.

déconvenue [dekɔ̃vny] *nf* disappointment.

décor [dekɔr] *nm* **1.** [décoration - d'un lieu] interior decoration, decor ; [- d'un objet] pattern, design **2.** [environs] setting ■ **la maison était située dans un ~ magnifique** the house stood in magnificent scenery *ou* surroundings **3.** CINÉ, THÉÂTRE & TV set, scenery, setting ■ **~ de cinéma** film *UK ou* movie *US* set ■ **~ de théâtre** stage set ■ **tourné en ~s naturels** shot on location ■ [toile peinte] backdrop, backcloth **4.** [apparence] façade, pretence.
◆ **dans le(s) décor(s)** *loc adv fam* **aller** *ou* **entrer** *ou* **valser dans le ~** [voiture, automobiliste] to go off the road ■ **d'un coup de poing, elle l'a envoyé dans le ~** she sent him flying against the wall with a punch.

décorateur, trice [dekɔratœr, tris] *nm, f* **1.** [d'appartement] interior decorator *ou* designer ■ **~ (de vitrines)** shopfitter **2.** THÉÂTRE [créateur] set designer *ou* decorator ■ [peintre] set painter.

décoratif, ive [dekɔratif, iv] *adj* decorative, ornamental.

décoration [dekɔrasjɔ̃] *nf* **1.** [ornement] decoration *(C)* **2.** [technique] decoration, decorating **3.** [médaille] medal, decoration.

décoré, e [dekɔre] <> *adj* [qui a reçu une distinction] decorated ■ [qui porte un insigne] wearing one's medals.
<> *nm, f person who has been awarded a decoration.*

décorer [3] [dekɔre] *vt* **1.** [orner - intérieur, vase, assiette] to decorate ; [- table, arbre] to decorate, to adorn **2.** [personne] to decorate ■ **être décoré de la Légion d'honneur** to be awarded the Legion of Honour.

décorner [3] [dekɔrne] *vt* **1.** [animal] to dehorn **2.** [page] to smooth out *(sép)*.

décorticage [dekɔrtikaʒ] *nm* **1.** [d'une crevette] peeling, shelling ■ [du grain] hulling, husking ■ [d'une noix] shelling **2.** [analyse] dissection, thorough analysis.

décortiquer [3] [dekɔrtike] *vt* **1.** [éplucher - crevette] to peel, to shell ; [- grain] to hull, to husk ; [- noix, amande] to shell ■ **riz non décortiqué** rice in the husk **2.** [analyser] to dissect, to analyse.

décorum [dekɔrɔm] *nm* **1.** [bienséance] decorum, propriety **2.** [protocole] etiquette, ceremonial.

décote [dekɔt] *nf* **1.** [réduction d'impôt] tax relief **2.** BOURSE below par rating.

découcher [3] [dekuʃe] *vi* to stay out all night ■ **elle a découché** she stayed out all night, she didn't sleep at home last night.

découdre [86] [dekudr] <> *vt* [vêtement, couture] to undo, to unpick ■ [point] to take out *(sép)* ■ [bouton] to take *ou* to cut off *(sép)*.
<> *vi* : **en ~** to fight ■ **vouloir en ~** to be spoiling for a fight ■ **en ~ avec qqn** to cross swords with sb.
◆ **se découdre** *vpi* [vêtement] to come unstitched ■ [bouton] to come off.

découler [3] [dekule] ◆ **découler de** *v+prép* to follow from ■ **...et tous les avantages qui en découlent**...and all the ensuing benefits ■ *(tournure impersonnelle)* **il découle de cette idée que...** it follows from this idea that...

découpage [dekupaʒ] *nm* **1.** [partage - d'un tissu, d'un gâteau] cutting (up) ; [- d'une volaille, d'une viande] carving ; [- en tranches] slicing (up) **2.** [image - à découper] figure *(for cutting out)* ; [- découpée] cut-out (picture) **3.** CINÉ shooting script **4.** INFORM : ~ **du temps** time slicing **5.** POLIT : ~ **électoral** division into electoral districts, apportionment *US* **6.** TECHNOL blanking, cutting.

découpe [dekup] *nf* **1.** COUT piece of appliqué work **2.** [de la viande] (type of) cut **3.** [tronçonnage] cutting (up).

découpé, e [dekupe] *adj* **1.** [irrégulier - côte] indented, ragged ; [- montagne] rugged, craggy, jagged ; [- feuille d'arbre] incised, serrate **2.** [en morceaux] cut.

découper [3] [dekupe] *vt* **1.** [détacher - image] to cut out *(sép)* ▪ ~ **des articles dans le journal** to take cuttings out of the newspaper **2.** [partager - gâteau, papier, tissu] to cut up *(sép)* ; [- viande, volaille] to carve ▪ **il a découpé le gâteau en parts égales** he cut the cake into equal parts ▪ **couteau à ~** carving knife **3.** [disséquer - texte, film] to dissect ; [- phrase] to parse.
◆ **se découper sur** *vp+prép* to be outlined against.

découpeur, euse [dekupœr, øz] *nm, f* cutting machine operator.

découplé, e [dekuple] *adj* : **bien ~** well-built, strapping.

découpler [3] [dekuple] *vt* **1.** CHASSE & ÉLECTR to uncouple **2.** ÉLECTRON to decouple.

découpure [dekupyr] *nf* **1.** [découpe] workmanship **2.** [bord - d'une dentelle, d'une guirlande] edge ; [- d'une côte] indentations.
◆ **découpures** *nfpl* [de papier] clippings, shavings, shreds ▪ [de tissu] cuttings, offcuts.

décourageant, e [dekuraʒɑ̃, ɑ̃t] *adj* **1.** [nouvelle, situation] discouraging, disheartening, depressing **2.** [personne] hopeless.

découragement [dekuraʒmɑ̃] *nm* discouragement, despondency, despondence ▪ **le ~ m'a envahi** I felt utterly discouraged *ou* dispirited.

décourager [17] [dekuraʒe] *vt* **1.** [abattre] to discourage, to dishearten ▪ ~ **qqn de faire qqch** to discourage sb from doing sthg ▪ **avoir l'air découragé** to look discouraged *ou* dispirited ▪ **ne te laisse pas ~** don't be discouraged **2.** [refuser - familiarité] to discourage.
◆ **se décourager** *vpi* to get discouraged, to lose heart ▪ **ne te décourage pas** don't give up.

découronner [3] [dekurɔne] *vt* **1.** [roi] to dethrone, to depose **2.** *litt* [ôter le sommet de] to cut the top off.

décousait *etc v* ▻ **découdre.**

décousu, e [dekuzy] ◇ *pp* ▻ **découdre.**
◇ *adj* **1.** COUT [défait - vêtement] undone, unstitched ; [- ourlet] undone **2.** [incohérent - discours] incoherent, disjointed ; [- conversation] desultory, disjointed ; [- style] disjointed, rambling ; [- idées] disjointed, disconnected, random ▪ **de manière ~e** disjointedly.

découvert, e [dekuvɛr, ɛrt] ◇ *pp* ▻ **découvrir.**
◇ *adj* [terrain, allée, voiture] open ▪ [tête, partie du corps] bare, uncovered.
◆ **découvert** *nm* **1.** [en comptabilité] deficit **2.** BANQUE overdraft ▪ **avoir un ~ de** to be overdrawn by **3.** BOURSE short (account).
◆ **à découvert** ◇ *loc adj* **1.** FIN [sans garantie] uncovered, unsecured **2.** BOURSE without cover ▪ **être à ~** to be caught short ➊ **vente à ~** short sale **3.** BANQUE overdrawn ▪ **être à ~** to be overdrawn, to have an overdraft.
◇ *loc adv* **1.** [sans dissimuler] openly **2.** [sans protection] without cover ▪ **sortir à ~** to break cover ▪ **la marée laisse ces rochers à ~** the tide leaves these rocks exposed.

découverte [dekuvɛrt] *nf* **1.** [détection] discovery, discovering ▪ [chose détectée] discovery, find **2.** [prise de conscience] discovery, discovering **3.** [personne de talent] discovery, find **4.** THÉÂTRE & TV backcloth **5.** MIN cutting.
◆ **à la découverte de** *loc prép* **1.** [en explorant] on a tour of ▪ **ils sont partis à la ~ de la forêt amazonienne** they went exploring in the Amazon rain forest **2.** [à la recherche de] in search of ▪ **aller à la ~ d'un trésor** to go in search of a treasure.

découvreur, euse [dekuvrœr, øz] *nm, f* discoverer.

découvrir [34] [dekuvrir] *vt* **1.** [dénicher] to discover, to find ▪ ~ **des armes dans une cache** to unearth a cache of weapons ▪ **on a découvert l'arme du crime** the murder weapon has been found ▪ ~ **du pétrole/de l'or** to strike oil/gold ▪ **j'ai découvert les lettres par accident** I came across the letters by accident ▪ ~ **l'Amérique** to discover America ▪ **elle m'a fait ~ la région** she took me around the area
2. [solution - en réfléchissant] to discover, to work out *(sép)* ; [- subitement] to hit on *ou* upon *(insép)*
3. [détecter] to discover, to detect ▪ ~ **qqch à qqn : on lui a découvert une tumeur** they found he had a tumour
4. [surprendre - voleur, intrus] to discover ; [- secret, complot] to discover, to uncover ▪ **et si l'on vous découvrait?** what if you were found out? ▪ **j'ai découvert que c'était faux** I found out (that) it wasn't true ➊ ~ **le pot aux roses** to discover the truth
5. [faire connaître] to uncover, to disclose, to reveal ▪ ~ **son jeu** to show one's hand
6. [apercevoir] to see ▪ **le rideau levé, on découvrit une scène obscure** the raised curtain revealed a darkened stage
7. [ôter ce qui couvre - fauteuil] to uncover ; [- statue] to uncover, to unveil ; [- casserole] to uncover, to take the lid off ▪ **il fait chaud dans la chambre, va ~ le bébé** it's hot in the bedroom, take the covers off the baby
8. [exposer - flanc, frontière] to expose
9. [mettre à nu - épaule, cuisse] to uncover, to bare, to expose ; [- mur, pierre] to uncover, to expose ▪ **sa robe lui découvrait le dos** her dress revealed her back.
◆ **se découvrir** ◇ *vp (emploi réfléchi)* **1.** [se déshabiller] to dress less warmly, to take a layer *ou* some layers off ▪ [au lit] to throw off one's bedclothes
2. [ôter son chapeau] to take off one's hat
3. [se connaître] to (come to) understand o.s.
4. [s'exposer] to expose o.s. to attack ▪ **un boxeur ne doit pas se ~** a boxer mustn't lower his guard.
◇ *vp (emploi passif)* to emerge, to be discovered ▪ **des scandales, il s'en découvre tous les jours** scandals come to light *ou* are discovered every day.
◇ *vp (emploi réciproque)* to discover each other.
◇ *vpt* : **se ~ qqch** [se trouver qqch] : **je me suis découvert une grosseur à l'aine** I discovered I had a lump in my groin ▪ **elle s'est découvert des amis partout** she discovered she had friends everywhere ▪ **il s'est découvert un don pour la cuisine** he found he had a gift for cooking.
◇ *vpi* : **ça se découvre** it's clearing up.
◆ **se découvrir à** *vp+prép litt* [se confier] to confide in, to open up to.

décrasser [3] [dekrase] *vt* **1.** [nettoyer - peigne, tête de lecture] to clean ; [- poêle, casserole] to scour, to clean out *(sép)* ; [- linge] to scrub ; [- enfant] to scrub (down), to clean up *(sép)* **2.** *fam* [dégrossir] to give a basic grounding, to teach the basics **3.** AUTO & INDUST to clean out *(sép)*, to decoke **4.** *fam* [remettre en forme] to get back into shape, to tone up ▪ **un peu d'exercice vous décrassera** some exercise will get you back into shape again.
◆ **se décrasser** *vp (emploi réfléchi)* [se laver] to clean up, to give o.s. a good scrub ▪ [se dérouiller] to get some exercise.

décrédibiliser [3] [dekredibilize] *vt* to discredit, to deprive of credibility, to take away the credibility of.

décrêper [4] [dekrepe] *vt* to straighten (out).

décrépir [32] [dekrepir] *vt* to strip the roughcast off.
◆ **se décrépir** *vpi* : **la façade se décrépit** the roughcast is coming off the front of the house.

décrépit, e [dekrepi, it] *adj* decrepit.

décrépitude [dekrepityd] *nf* **1.** [décadence] decay ▪ **tomber en ~** [civilisation] to decline, to decay ; [institution] to become obsolete **2.** [mauvais état] decrepitude, decrepit state.

decrescendo [dekreʃɛndo] ◇ *nm inv* decrescendo.

◇ *adv* : **jouer ~** to decrescendo ▪ **aller ~** *fig* to wane.

décret [dekrɛ] *nm* **1.** DR decree, edict ▪ **promulguer un ~** to issue a decree ➲ **~ d'application** *presidential decree affecting the application of a law* ▪ **~ ministériel** *order to carry out legislation given by the Prime Minister* **2.** RELIG decree.
◆ **décrets** *nmpl litt* **les ~s du destin/de la Providence** what fate/Providence has decreed ▪ **les ~s de la mode** the dictates of fashion.
◆ **par décret** *loc adv* : **gouverner par ~** to rule by decree.

décréter [18] [dekrete] *vt* **1.** [ordonner - nomination, mobilisation] to order ; [- mesure] to decree, to enact **2.** [décider] : **le patron a décrété qu'on ne changerait rien** the boss decreed *ou* ordained that nothing would change ▪ **quand il a décrété quelque chose, il ne change pas d'avis** when he's made up his mind about something, he doesn't change it.

décrier [10] [dekrije] *vt* [collègues, entourage] to disparage ▪ [livre, œuvre, théorie] to criticize, to censure, to decry *sout*.

décriminaliser [3] [dekriminalize] *vt* to decriminalize.

décrire [99] [dekrir] *vt* **1.** [représenter] to describe, to portray ▪ **son exposé décrit bien la situation** his account gives a good picture of the situation **2.** [former - cercle, ellipse] to describe, to draw ; [- trajectoire] to follow, to describe ▪ **~ des cercles dans le ciel** to fly in circles ▪ **la route décrit une courbe** the road curves *ou* bends.

décrispation [dekrispasjɔ̃] *nf* thaw, thawing ▪ **la ~ entre les deux pays** the easing of tension between the two countries.

décrisper [3] [dekrispe] *vt* **1.** [muscle] to relax, to untense **2.** [relations] to thaw ▪ [ambiance] to ease ▪ **pour ~ la situation** to ease the situation.
◆ **se décrisper** *vpi* to relax, to unwind.

décrit, e [dekri, it] *pp* ▷ **décrire**.

décrivait *etc v* ▷ **décrire**.

décrochage [dekrɔʃaʒ] *nm* **1.** [enlèvement - d'un rideau, d'un tableau] unhooking, taking down ; [- d'un wagon] uncoupling **2.** ÉLECTR pulling out of synchronism **3.** MIL disengagement **4.** AÉRON stall **5.** ASTRONAUT leaving orbit **6.** RADIO break in transmission **7.** *fam* [désengagement] : **le ~ par rapport à la réalité** being out of touch with reality.

décrochement [dekrɔʃmɑ̃] *nm* **1.** [fait de se décrocher] slipping **2.** ARCHIT [retrait] recess ▪ **faire un ~** [bâtiment] to form an angle ; [mur] to form *ou* to have a recess **3.** GÉOL thrust fault **4.** MÉD : **~ de la mâchoire** dislocation of the jaw.

décrocher [3] [dekrɔʃe] ◇ *vt* **1.** [dépendre] to unhook, to take down *(sép)* ▪ **~ un peignoir** to take a bathrobe off the hook *ou* peg ▪ **il a décroché ses gants de boxe** *fig* he went back to boxing *ou* into the ring again ➲ **~ la lune** to do the impossible ▪ **~ la timbale** *fam ou* **le coquetier** *fam ou* **le cocotier** *fam ou* **le pompon** *fam* to hit the jackpot **2.** [enlever - chaîne, laisse] to take off *(sép)* ; [- wagon] to uncouple **3.** TÉLÉCOM : **~ le téléphone** [le couper] to take the phone off the hook ; [pour répondre] to pick up the phone ▪ **tu décroches?** could you answer *ou* get it? **4.** *fam* [obtenir] to land, to get.
◇ *vi* **1.** *fam* [abandonner] to opt out ▪ **les étudiants qui décrochent** students who drop out **2.** *fam* [se déconcentrer] to switch off **3.** [être distancé] to drop *ou* to fall behind **4.** *fam* [se désintoxiquer] to kick the habit ▪ **~ de l'héroïne** to come off *ou* to kick heroin **5.** AÉRON to stall **6.** FIN : **le yen a décroché du dollar** the yen has lost against the dollar.
◆ **se décrocher** ◇ *vpi* : **le tableau s'est décroché** the painting came unhooked.
◇ *vpt* : **il s'est décroché la mâchoire** he dislocated his jaw.

décrocheur, euse [dekrɔʃœr, øz] *nm, f* **Québec** (high school) dropout.

décrois *etc v* ▷ **décroître**.

décroiser [3] [dekrwaze] *vt* : **~ les jambes/les bras** to uncross one's legs/one's arms.

décroissait *etc v* ▷ **décroître**.

décroissance [dekrwasɑ̃s] *nf* **1.** [diminution] decrease, fall, decline ▪ **une ~ rapide de la natalité** a sharp decline in the birth rate **2.** NUCL : **~ radioactive** radioactive decay.

décroissant, e [dekrwasɑ̃, ɑ̃t] *adj* **1.** MATH decreasing **2.** LING falling **3.** ASTRON waning, decreasing, decrescent.

décroître [94] [dekrwatr] *vi* **1.** [diminuer - nombre, intensité, force] to decrease, to diminish ; [- eaux] to subside, to go down ; [- fièvre] to abate, to subside, to decrease ; [- bruit] to die down, to lessen, to decrease ; [- son] to fade, to die down ; [- vent] to let up, to die down ; [- intérêt, productivité] to decline, to drop off ; [- vitesse] to slacken off, to drop ; [- taux d'écoute] to drop ; [- lumière] to grow fainter, to grow dimmer, to fade ; [- influence] to decline, to wane ▪ **les jours décroissent** the days are drawing in *ou* getting shorter ▪ **il voyait leurs silhouettes ~ à l'horizon** he could see their silhouettes getting smaller and smaller on the horizon ▪ **aller en décroissant** to be on the decrease **2.** ASTRON to wane.

décrotter [3] [dekrɔte] *vt* **1.** [nettoyer] to scrape the mud off **2.** *fam* [dégrossir] to refine, to take the rough edges off.

décrottoir [dekrɔtwar] *nm* [pour chaussures] (boot) scraper.

décru, e [dekry] *pp* ▷ **décroître**.
◆ **décrue** *nf* decrease *ou* dropping of the water level ▪ **attendre la décrue** [lors d'une inondation] to wait for the flood to subside ; [lors d'une crue] to wait for the water level to go down *ou* to drop *ou* to fall.

décryptage [dekriptaʒ], **décryptement** [dekriptəmɑ̃] *nm* **1.** [décodage] deciphering, decipherment, decoding **2.** [éclaircissement] elucidation, working out.

décrypter [3] [dekripte] *vt* **1.** [décoder - message, texte ancien] to decode, to decipher **2.** [éclaircir] to elucidate, to work out *(sép)*.

déçu, e [desy] ◇ *pp* ▷ **décevoir**.
◇ *adj* **1.** [personne] disappointed **2.** [amour] disappointed, thwarted ▪ [espoir] disappointed.

de cujus [dekyʒys] *nm* : **le ~** [qui a fait un testament] the testator ; [sans testament] the deceased.

déculottée△ [dekylɔte] *nf* thrashing, clobbering, hammering ▪ **prendre une ~** to get thrashed *ou* clobbered *ou* hammered.

déculotter [3] [dekylɔte] *vt* : **~ qqn** [lui enlever sa culotte] to take sb's pants UK *ou* underpants US off ; [lui enlever son pantalon] to take sb's trousers UK *ou* pants US off.
◆ **se déculotter** ◇ *vp (emploi réfléchi)* [enlever - sa culotte] to take one's pants UK *ou* underpants US down ; [- son pantalon] to drop one's trousers UK *ou* pants US.
◇ *vpi* **1.** *fam* [se montrer lâche] to lose one's nerve *ou* bottle UK **2.**△ [avouer] to squeal△.

déculpabilisation [dekylpabilizasjɔ̃] *nf* : **la ~ de la sexualité** removing the guilt attached to sexuality.

déculpabiliser [3] [dekylpabilize] *vt* : **~ qqn** to stop sb feeling guilty.
◆ **se déculpabiliser** *vp (emploi réfléchi)* to get rid of one's guilt.

déculturation [dekyltyrasjɔ̃] *nf* loss of cultural identity.

décuple [dekypl] *nm* : **le ~ de trois** ten times three.
◆ **au décuple** *loc adv* tenfold.

décuplement [dekypləmɑ̃] *nm* **1.** [d'une somme, d'un chiffre] tenfold increase **2.** [augmentation] : **ceci permettra le ~ de nos chances de succès** this will greatly increase our chances of success.

décupler [3] [dekyple] ◇ *vt* **1.** [rendre dix fois plus grand] to increase tenfold **2.** [augmenter] to increase greatly ▪ **la rage décuple les forces** rage greatly increases one's strength.
◇ *vi* to increase tenfold.

déçut *etc v* ▷ **décevoir**.

dédaignable [dedɛɲabl] *adj* : **ce n'est pas ~** it's not to be scoffed at.

dédaigner [4] [dedeɲe] *vt* **1.** [mépriser - personne] to look down on *(sép)*, to despise, to scorn ; [- compliment, richesse] to despise, to disdain **2.** [refuser - honneurs, argent] to despise, to disdain, to spurn ■ **une augmentation, ce n'est pas à ~** a salary increase is not to be sniffed at ■ **ne dédaignant pas la bonne chère** not being averse to good food **3.** [ignorer - injure, difficulté] to ignore, to disregard.
◆ **dédaigner de** *v+prép litt* **elle a dédaigné de parler** she didn't deign to speak ■ **il n'a pas dédaigné de goûter à ma cuisine** he was not averse to tasting my cooking.

dédaigneusement [dedɛɲøzmɑ̃] *adv* contemptuously, disdainfully.

dédaigneux, euse [dedɛɲø, øz] ◇ *adj* **1.** [méprisant - sourire, moue, remarque] contemptuous, scornful, disdainful ■ **d'un ton ~** contemptuously, scornfully, disdainfully **2.** *sout* **~ de** [indifférent à] disdainful *ou* contemptuous of ■ **je n'ai jamais été ~ de l'argent** I've never been one to spurn *ou* to despise money.
◇ *nm, f* disdainful *ou* scornful *ou* contemptuous person.

dédain [dedɛ̃] *nm* contempt, scorn, disdain ■ **avec ~** contemptuously, scornfully, disdainfully.
◆ **de dédain** *loc adj* scornful, contemptuous, disdainful.

dédale [dedal] *nm* maze ■ **dans le ~ des rues** in the maze of streets ■ **dans le ~ des lois** in the maze of the law.

Dédale [dedal] *npr* Daedalus.

dedans [dədɑ̃] ◇ *adv* [reprenant 'dans' + substantif] inside, in it/them *etc* ■ [par opposition à 'dehors'] inside, indoors ■ [à partir de - prendre, boire, manger] out of, from ■ **de ~, on ne voit rien** you can't see anything from inside ■ **il y a de l'anis ~** there's aniseed in it ■ **le tiroir était ouvert, j'ai pris l'argent ~** the drawer was open, I took the money out of *ou* from it ■ **il faut élargir l'ourlet et passer l'élastique ~** you must widen the hem and run the elastic band through it ■ **on n'apprécie pas le luxe quand on vit ~** you don't appreciate luxury when you've got it ◐ **ne me parle pas de comptes, je suis en plein ~** *fam* don't talk to me about the accounts, I'm right in the middle of them *ou* up to my eyeballs in them ■ **tu veux du mystère? on est en plein ~** you want mystery? we're surrounded by it ■ **mettre** *ou* **ficher qqn ~** *fam* [le tromper] to confuse *ou* to muddle sb ; [en prison] to put sb inside ■ **je me suis fichu ~** *fam* I got it wrong ■ **le piège, il est tombé en plein ~** he fell right into the trap.
◇ *nm* inside.
◆ **en dedans** *loc adv* : **c'est creux en ~** it's hollow inside ■ **marcher les pieds en ~** to be pigeon-toed.
◆ **en dedans de** *loc prép* : **en ~ d'elle-même, elle regrette son geste** deep down *ou* inwardly, she regrets what she did.

dédicace [dedikas] *nf* **1.** [formule manuscrite - d'un ami] (signed) dedication ; [- d'une personnalité] autograph, (signed) dedication **2.** [formule imprimée] dedication **3.** RADIO dedication **4.** RELIG [consécration] dedication, consecration ■ [fête] *celebration of the consecration of a place of worship.*

dédicacer [16] [dedikase] *vt* **1.** [ouvrage, photo] : **~ un livre à qqn** to autograph *ou* to sign a book for sb **2.** RADIO to dedicate.

dédié, e [dedje] *adj* INFORM dedicated ■ **ordinateur ~** dedicated computer.

dédier [9] [dedje] *vt* **1.** [livre, symphonie] to dedicate **2.** *litt* [vouer] : **dédiant toutes ses pensées à son art** dedicating *ou* devoting all her thoughts to her art.

dédifférencier [9] [dediferɑ̃sje] ◆ **se dédifférencier** *vpi* to undergo dedifferentiation.

dédire [103] [dedir] ◆ **se dédire** *vpi* **1.** [se rétracter - délibérément] to recant, to retract **2.** [manquer - à sa promesse] to go back on *ou* to fail to keep one's word ; [- à son engagement] to fail to honour one's commitment ■ **se ~ de** [promesse] to go back on, to fail to keep ; [engagement] to fail to honour.

dédit [dedi] *nm* **1.** *sout* [rétractation] retraction ■ [désengagement] failure to keep one's word ■ **un engagement qui ne tolère aucun ~** a binding commitment, a commitment which must be honoured **2.** DR [modalité] default ■ [somme] forfeit, penalty.

dédite [dedit] *nf Suisse* = **dédit**.

dédommagement [dedɔmaʒmɑ̃] *nm* compensation ■ **demander** *ou* **réclamer un ~** to claim compensation.
◆ **en dédommagement** *loc adv* as compensation.
◆ **en dédommagement de** *loc prép* as a *ou* in compensation for, to make up for.

dédommager [17] [dedɔmaʒe] *vt* **1.** [pour une perte] to compensate, to give compensation to ■ **~ qqn d'une perte** to compensate sb for a loss, to make good sb's loss ■ **fais-toi ~ pour le dérangement** claim compensation for the inconvenience ■ **j'ai réussi à me faire ~** [en argent] I managed to get reimbursed **2.** [pour un désagrément] to compensate.

dédouanage [dedwanaʒ], **dédouanement** [dedwanmɑ̃] *nm* [action] clearing through customs ■ [résultat] customs clearance.

dédouaner [3] [dedwane] *vt* **1.** ADMIN [marchandise] to clear through customs **2.** [personne] to clear (the name of).
◆ **se dédouaner** *vp (emploi réfléchi)* to make up for one's past misdeeds.

dédoublement [dedubləmɑ̃] *nm* **1.** [d'un groupe, d'une image] splitting *ou* dividing in two **2.** PSYCHOL : **~ de la personnalité** dual personality **3.** TRANSP putting on an extra train.

dédoubler [3] [deduble] *vt* **1.** [diviser - groupe] to split *ou* to divide in two ; [- brin de laine] to separate into strands **2.** TRANSP : **~ un train** to put on *ou* to run an extra train **3.** COUT to remove the lining of.
◆ **se dédoubler** *vpi* **1.** PSYCHOL : **sa personnalité se dédouble** he suffers from a split *ou* dual personality ■ **je cuisine, viens ici, je ne peux pas me ~!** *hum* I'm cooking, come here, I can't be everywhere at once! **2.** [se diviser - convoi, image] to be split *ou* divided in two ; [- ongle] to split.

dédramatiser [3] [dedramatize] *vt* [situation] to make less dramatic.

déductibilité [dedyktibilite] *nf* **1.** [d'une hypothèse] deducibility **2.** MATH deductibility.

déductible [dedyktibl] *adj* deductible ■ **non ~** nondeductible ■ **frais ~s des revenus** expenditure deductible against tax.

déductif, ive [dedyktif, iv] *adj* deductive.

déduction [dedyksjɔ̃] *nf* **1.** [d'une somme] deduction ■ **~ faite de** after deduction of, after deducting **2.** [conclusion] conclusion, inference **3.** [enchaînement d'idées] deduction ■ **faire une ~** to go through a process of deduction.
◆ **par déduction** *loc adv* by deduction, through a process of deduction.

déduire [98] [dedɥir] *vt* **1.** [frais, paiement] to deduct, to take off *(sép)* **2.** [conclure] to deduce, to infer.

déesse [deɛs] *nf* **1.** MYTHOL & RELIG goddess **2.** [femme] stunningly beautiful woman.
◆ **de déesse** *loc adj* [allure, port] majestic.

de facto [defakto] *loc adv* de facto.

défaillance [defajɑ̃s] *nf* **1.** [évanouissement] blackout ■ [malaise] feeling of faintness ■ **avoir une ~** [s'évanouir] to faint, to have a blackout ; [être proche de l'évanouissement] to feel faint ■ **des ~s dues à la chaleur** weak spells caused by the heat **2.** [faiblesse] weakness **3.** [lacune] lapse, slip ■ **une ~ de mémoire** a memory lapse ■ **les ~s du rapport** the weak spots in the report **4.** [mauvais fonctionnement] failure, fault ■ **en cas de ~ du système** in case of a failure in the system **5.** MÉD : **~ cardiaque/rénale** heart/kidney failure **6.** DR default **7.** [faillite] collapse.
◆ **sans défaillance** *loc adj* [mémoire] faultless ■ [attention, vigilance] unflinching.

défaillant, e [defajɑ̃, ɑ̃t] *adj* **1.** [près de s'évanouir] : **des spectateurs ~s** spectators about to faint *ou* on the verge of fainting **2.** [faible - santé] declining, failing ; [- cœur, poumon] weak, failing ; [- force, mémoire] failing ; [- détermination] weakening, faltering ; [- voix] faltering **3.** [qui ne remplit pas son rôle - appareil] malfunctioning ▪ **dû à l'organisation ~e du concert** due to the poor organization of the concert **4.** DR defaulting.

défaillir [47] [defajir] *vi litt* **1.** [être près de s'évanouir] to be about to faint *ou* on the verge of fainting **2.** [s'amollir] : **~ de plaisir** to swoon with pleasure **3.** [forces, mémoire] to fail ▪ [détermination] to weaken, to falter, to flinch.

défaire [109] [defɛr] *vt* **1.** [détacher - nœud] to untie, to unfasten ; [- fermeture] to undo, to unfasten ; [- cravate] to undo, to untie ▪ **~ les lacets d'une botte** to unlace a boot ▪ **~ ses cheveux** to let one's hair down *pr* ▪ **avec les cheveux défaits** [pas encore arrangés] with her hair undone, with tousled hair ; [que l'on a dérangés] with her hair messed up
2. [découdre - ourlet] to undo, to unpick
3. [démonter - décor de théâtre] to take down *(sép)*, to dismantle ; [- maquette] to take apart *(sép)*, to disassemble ; [- tente] to take down *(sép)*
4. [déballer - paquet] to open, to unwrap ▪ **~ ses valises** to unpack
5. [mettre en désordre] : **~ le lit** [pour changer les draps] to strip the bed ; [en jouant] to rumple the bedclothes ▪ **le lit défait** [pas encore fait] the unmade bed ▪ **le lit n'a pas été défait** the bed hasn't been slept in
6. [détruire] : **faire et ~ des gouvernements** to make and break governments
7. *litt* [délivrer] : **~ qqn de** to rid sb of
8. *litt* [armée] to defeat.
◆ **se défaire** *vpi* **1.** [se détacher - nœud] to come loose *ou* undone ; [- coiffure, paquet] to come undone ; [- tricot] to fray, to come undone, to unravel
2. [être détruit - gouvernement, amitié] to break ; [- destinée] to come apart
3. [se décomposer] : **son visage se défit** [de chagrin] he looked distraught ; [de déception] his face fell.
◆ **se défaire de** *vp+prép sout* [employé, dettes, meuble] to get rid of, to rid o.s. of *sout* ▪ [idée] to put out of one's mind ▪ [habitude] to break ▪ **il ne veut pas se ~ de son vieux chien** he won't get rid of his old dog.

défait, e [defɛ, ɛt] *adj* **1.** [accablé] : **être ~** to be broken **2.** [décomposé] : **il se tenait là, le visage ~** he stood there, looking distraught.

défaite [defɛt] *nf* MIL, POLIT & SPORT defeat.

défaites *v* ▷ **défaire**.

défaitisme [defetism] *nm* **1.** MIL defeatism **2.** [pessimisme] defeatism, negative attitude.

défaitiste [defetist] ◇ *adj* defeatist.
◇ *nmf* **1.** MIL defeatist **2.** [pessimiste] defeatist.

défalcation [defalkasjɔ̃] *nf* deduction ▪ **~ faite des frais** after deduction of expenses.

défalquer [3] [defalke] *vt* to deduct.

défasse *etc v* ▷ **défaire**.

défatiguer [3] [defatige] *vt* to refresh, to relax.

défaufiler [3] [defofile] *vt* to remove the tacking from.

défaut [defo] *nm* **1.** [imperfection - d'un visage, de la peau] blemish, imperfection ; [- d'un tissu, d'un appareil] defect, flaw ; [- d'un diamant, d'une porcelaine] flaw ; [- d'un projet] drawback, snag ▪ **le ~ de** *ou* **avec** *fam* **ton attitude, c'est que...** the trouble with your attitude is that... ▶ **~ d'élocution** *ou* **de prononciation** speech defect *ou* impediment ▪ **~ de fabrication** manufacturing defect ▪ **il y a comme un ~!** *fam hum* there's something wrong somewhere!
2. [tache morale] fault, failing
3. [manque] : **~ de** lack *ou* want of ▪ **~ de mémoire** memory lapse ▪ **~ d'attention** lapse in concentration ▪ **faire ~** to be lacking ▪ **l'argent faisant ~** [il y a peu d'argent] money being short ; [il n'y a pas d'argent] there being no money ▪ **ses forces lui ont fait ~** his strength failed him ▪ **le temps me fait ~** I don't have the time ▪ **l'imagination est loin de lui faire ~** he is far from lacking (in) imagination ▪ **notre fournisseur nous a fait ~** our supplier let us down
4. [bord, lisière] ▶ **le ~ de la cuirasse** *ou* **de l'armure** the chink in one's *ou* the armour
5. DR default ▪ **faire ~** to default ▶ **~ de paiement** default in payment, non-payment
6. INFORM default setting.
◆ **à défaut** *loc adv* if not, failing that ▪ **des roses ou, à ~, des tulipes** roses or, failing that, tulips.
◆ **à défaut de** *loc prép* for lack *ou* for want of ▪ **un voyage reposant à ~ d'être intéressant** a restful if not interesting trip.
◆ **en défaut** *loc adv* [en faute] : **être en ~** to be at fault ▪ **prendre qqn en ~** to catch sb out, to fault sb.
◆ **par défaut** *loc adv* **1.** [sans agir] by default
2. MATH : **calculé par ~** (worked out) to the nearest decimal point
3. DR by default
4. INFORM by default.
◆ **sans défaut** *loc adj* flawless.

défaveur [defavœr] *nf* discredit, disfavour ▪ **c'est tombé en ~** it's gone out of favour *ou* fashion ▪ **cela a tourné à ma ~** it worked against me in the end.

défavorable [defavɔrabl] *adj* unfavourable ▪ **voir qqch d'un œil ~** to view sthg unfavourably.

défavorablement [defavɔrabləmɑ̃] *adv* unfavourably.

défavorisé, e [defavɔrize] *adj* : **régions ~es** depressed areas ▪ **classes ~es** underprivileged social classes.

défavoriser [3] [defavɔrize] *vt* [dans un partage] to treat unfairly ▪ [dans un examen, une compétition] to put at a disadvantage.

défécation [defekasjɔ̃] *nf* PHYSIOL defecation.

défectif, ive [defɛktif, iv] *adj* defective GRAMM.

défection [defɛksjɔ̃] *nf* **1.** [fait de quitter] abandonment, abandoning ▪ **après la ~ de son père** after his father walked out **2.** [désistement - d'un allié, d'un partisan] withdrawal of support, defection ; [- d'un touriste, d'un client] cancellation ▪ **faire ~** [allié] to withdraw support ; [invité] to fail to appear.

défectueusement [defɛktɥøzmɑ̃] *adv* in a faulty manner.

défectueux, euse [defɛktɥø, øz] *adj* [appareil, produit] faulty, defective, substandard ▪ [loi] defective.

défectuosité [defɛktɥozite] *nf* **1.** [mauvaise qualité] substandard quality, defectiveness **2.** [malfaçon] imperfection, defect, fault.

défendable [defɑ̃dabl] *adj* **1.** MIL defensible **2.** [justifiable - position] defensible ; [- comportement] justifiable ; [- idée] tenable, defensible ▪ **des théories qui ne sont pas ~s** indefensible theories.

défendeur, eresse [defɑ̃dœr, drɛs] *nm, f* defendant.

défendre [73] [defɑ̃dr] *vt* **1.** [interdire] to forbid ▪ **~ l'accès au jardin** to forbid access to the garden ▪ **~ à qqn de faire qqch** to forbid sb to do sthg ▪ **~ qqch à qqn : l'alcool lui est défendu** he's not allowed to drink alcohol ▪ **c'est défendu** it's not allowed, it's forbidden **2.** MIL [pays, population] to defend ▪ [forteresse] to defend, to hold ▪ **~ chèrement sa vie** to fight for dear life **3.** [donner son appui à - ami] to defend, to protect, to stand up for ; [- idée, cause] to defend, to champion, to support ▪ **~ ses couleurs/son titre** to defend *ou* to fight for one's colours/title ▪ **je défends mon point de vue** I'm defending *ou* standing up for my point of view **4.** [préserver] : **~ qqn contre** *ou* **de qqch** to protect sb from *ou* against sthg **5.** DR to defend.
◆ **se défendre** ◇ *vp (emploi réfléchi)* **1.** [en luttant - physiquement] to defend o.s. ; [- verbalement] to stand up for *ou* to defend o.s. **2.** [se protéger] : **se ~ de** *ou* **contre** to protect o.s. from *ou* against.
◇ *vp (emploi passif)* [être plausible] to make sense.
◇ *vpi fam* [être compétent] to get by ▪ **il se défend bien en maths** he's quite good at maths ▪ **pour un débutant il ne se défend pas mal!** he's not bad for a beginner!
◆ **se défendre de** *vp+prép* **1.** [s'interdire de] : **se défendant de penser du mal d'elle** refusing to think ill of her ▮ [s'empêcher de] to refrain from **2.** [nier] : **se ~ de toute compromission** to deny being compromised ▪ **il se défend de vouloir la quitter** he won't admit that he wants to leave her.

défenestrer [3] [defənɛstre] *vt* to defenestrate, to throw out of the window.
◆ **se défenestrer** *vp (emploi réfléchi)* to jump out of the window.

défense [defɑ̃s] *nf* **1.** [interdiction] prohibition ▪ **malgré la ~ de sa mère** despite his mother having forbidden it ▪ **mais ~ expresse d'en parler!** but you're strictly forbidden to talk about it! ▪ **'~ d'entrer'** 'no admittance *ou* entry' ▪ **'danger, ~ d'entrer'** 'danger, keep out' ▪ **'~ d'afficher'** 'stick no bills' ▪ **'~ de fumer'** 'no smoking' ▪ **'~ de déposer des ordures'** 'no dumping'
2. [protection] defence ▪ **la ~ de la langue française** the defence of the French language ▪ **pour la ~ des institutions** in order to defend *ou* to safeguard the institutions ▮ [moyen de protection] defence ▪ **ne pas avoir de ~** to be unable to defend o.s.
3. [dans un débat] defence ▪ **prendre la ~ de qqn/qqch** to stand up for *ou* to defend sb/sthg
4. MIL defence ▪ **la Défense nationale** national defence ▪ **~ passive** civil defence ▪ **un secret Défense** a military secret
5. PHYSIOL & PSYCHOL defence
6. DR defence ▪ **présenter la ~** to put the case for the defence
7. SPORT : **la ~** the defence ▪ **jouer la ~** to play a defensive game
8. ZOOL tusk.
◆ **défenses** *nfpl* MIL defences.
◆ **de défense** *loc adj* **1.** MIL ▻ **ligne**
2. PSYCHOL defence *(modif).*
◆ **pour ma défense, pour sa défense** *etc loc adv* in my/his *etc* defence ▪ **je dirai pour ma ~ que...** I will say in my (own) defence that...
◆ **sans défense** *loc adj* **1.** [animal, bébé] defenceless, helpless
2. MIL undefended.
◆ **Défense** *npr f* : **la Défense** *ultra-modern business district west of Paris.*

défenseur [defɑ̃sœr] *nm* **1.** [partisan - de la foi] defender ▪ **les ~s de ces idées** advocates *ou* supporters of these ideas **2.** DR counsel for the defence *UK*, defense attorney *US* ▪ **l'accusé et son ~** the accused and his counsel **3.** SPORT defender.

défensif, ive [defɑ̃sif, iv] *adj* [armes, mesures] defensive.
◆ **défensive** *nf* : **être** *ou* **se tenir sur la défensive** to be (on the) defensive ▪ **ne sois pas toujours sur la défensive** don't be so defensive.

déféquer [18] [defeke] *vi* to defecate.

défera *etc v* ▻ **défaire.**

déférence [deferɑ̃s] *nf* respect, deference ▪ **avec ~** deferentially.

déférent, e [deferɑ̃, ɑ̃t] *adj* [employé, attitude, discours] deferential, respectful.

déférer [18] [defere] *vt* [affaire] to refer to a court ▪ [accusé] to bring before a court ▪ **~ qqn à la justice** to hand sb over to the law ▪ **il a été déféré au Parquet** he was sent to appear before the public prosecutor.
◆ **déférer à** *v+prép* to defer to.

déferlant, e [defɛrlɑ̃, ɑ̃t] *adj* [vague] breaking.
◆ **déferlante** *nf* [vague] breaker.

déferlement [defɛrləmɑ̃] *nm* **1.** [de vagues] breaking **2.** [invasion] : **~ de** [soudain] flood of ; [continu] stream of ▪ **on s'attend à un ~ de visiteurs** crowds of visitors are expected **3.** [accès] : **un ~ d'émotion** a surge *ou* wave of emotion.

déferler [3] [defɛrle] ◇ *vi* **1.** [vague] to break **2.** [se répandre] to rush into ▪ **ils déferlaient dans la rue** they flooded into the streets **3.** [fuser - émotion, applaudissements] to erupt.
◇ *vt* to unfurl, to stream NAUT.

déferrer [4] [defere] *vt* [cheval] to unshoe ▪ [coffre] to remove iron plates from.

défi [defi] *nm* **1.** [appel provocateur] challenge ▪ **jeter** *ou* **lancer un ~ à qqn** to throw down the gauntlet to sb, to challenge sb ▪ **relever un ~** to take up the gauntlet *ou* a challenge ▮ [attitude provocatrice] defiance ▪ **refuser par ~** to refuse out of defiance
2. [remise en question] : **c'est un ~ à ma position de chef de famille** it's a challenge to my position as head of the family ▪ **c'est un ~ au bon sens** it defies common sense.
◆ **au défi** *loc adv* : **mettre qqn au ~ (de faire)** to challenge sb (to do).
◆ **de défi** *loc adj* [attitude, air] defiant.

défiance [defjɑ̃s] *nf* **1.** [méfiance] mistrust, distrust ▪ **enfant sans ~** unsuspecting child ▪ **parler sans ~** to speak unsuspectingly **2.** [désapprobation] : **vote de ~** vote of no confidence.

défiant, e [defjɑ̃, ɑ̃t] *adj* [enfant, air] mistrustful, distrustful.

défibrillation [defibrijasjɔ̃] *nf* defibrillation.

déficeler [24] [defisle] *vt* [paquet] to untie, to take the string off ▪ [rôti] to remove the string from, to take the string off.

déficience [defisjɑ̃s] *nf* **1.** MÉD deficiency **2.** PSYCHOL : **~ mentale** mental retardation.

déficient, e [defisjɑ̃, ɑ̃t] *adj* **1.** MÉD deficient **2.** [insuffisant - théorie] weak, feeble.

déficit [defisit] *nm* **1.** ÉCON & FIN deficit ▪ **société en ~** company in deficit ➲ **~ budgétaire** budget deficit ▪ **~ commercial** trade deficit *ou* gap **2.** MÉD : **~ immunitaire** immunodeficiency ▪ **~ intellectuel** PSYCHOL mental retardation **3.** [manque] gap, lack.

déficitaire [defisitɛr] *adj* **1.** ÉCON & FIN in deficit ▪ **être ~** to be in deficit **2.** [insuffisant - production, récolte] poor.

défier [9] [defje] *vt* **1.** [dans un duel, un jeu] to challenge ▪ **~ qqn du regard** to give sb a challenging look ▪ **je te défie de trouver moins cher** I defy you to find a better price **2.** [affronter - danger] to defy, to brave ▪ **défiant les lois de l'équilibre** defying the laws of gravity ▪ **prix/qualité défiant toute concurrence** absolutely unbeatable prices/quality.
◆ **se défier de** *vp+prép litt* to mistrust, to distrust ▪ **elle se défie d'elle-même** she doesn't trust herself.

défigurer [3] [defigyre] *vt* **1.** [personne] to disfigure **2.** [ville, environnement] to blight, to ruin **3.** [caricaturer - vérité, faits] to distort.

défilé [defile] *nm* **1.** [procession - pour une fête] procession ; [- de militaires] march, parade ; [- de manifestants] march ▪ **~ aérien** flypast ▪ **un ~ de mode** a fashion show **2.** [multitude - d'invités, de pensées] stream ; [- de souvenirs] string ; [- d'images] succession **3.** GÉOGR defile, narrow pass.

défilement [defilmɑ̃] *nm* [d'un film, d'une bande] unwinding ▪ [d'un texte sur écran] scrolling.

défiler [3] [defile] ◇ *vi* **1.** [marcher en file MIL to march, to parade ; [- pour manifester] to march ▪ **~ dans la rue** to march through the streets ▪ **~ devant...** [gén] to file past ; [troupes, manifestants] to march past ▪ **les élèves défilaient devant la statue** the pupils filed past the statue ▪ **les mannequins défilaient** the models were parading up and down the catwalk **2.** [être nombreux] : **les journalistes ont défilé au ministère toute la journée** the journalists were in and out of the ministry all day ▪ **ses amis ont défilé à son chevet** his friends came to his bedside one after the other **3.** [se dérouler - bande magnétique] to unwind ; [- texte informatique] to scroll ; [- souvenirs, publicité] to stream past ▪ **faire ~** [données sur écran] to scroll ▪ **toute ma vie a défilé dans ma tête** my whole life flashed before my eyes.
◇ *vt* [perles] to unthread ▪ [collier] to unstring.
◆ **se défiler** *vpi fam* **1.** [fuir] to slip away **2.** [esquiver une responsabilité] : **n'essaie pas de te ~** don't try to get out of it.

défini, e [defini] *adj* **1.** [qui a une définition] defined ▪ [précis] precise ▪ **une utilisation bien ~e** a well-defined usage ▪ **mal ~** ill-defined **2.** GRAMM : **article ~** definite article ▪ **passé ~** preterite.

définir [32] [definir] *vt* **1.** [donner la définition de] to define ▪ **on définit le dauphin comme un mammifère** the dolphin is defined as a mammal **2.** [décrire - sensation] to define, to describe ; [- personne] to describe, to portray **3.** [circonscrire - objectif, politique, condition] to define ▪ **je définirais mon rôle comme étant celui d'un négociateur** I'd define *ou* describe my role as that of a negotiator.

définissable [definisabl] *adj* definable.

définitif, ive [definitif, iv] *adj* **1.** [irrévocable - décision] final ; [- acceptation] definitive ▪ **leur séparation est définitive** they're splitting up for good **2.** [qui fait autorité - œuvre] definitive ; [- argument] conclusive.
◆ **en définitive** *loc adv* **1.** [somme toute] finally, when all's said and done, in the final analysis **2.** [après tout] after all.

définition [definisjɔ̃] *nf* **1.** [d'une idée, d'un mot] definition **2.** LOGIQUE definition **3.** [de mots croisés] clue **4.** PHOTO & TÉLÉCOM definition.
◆ **par définition** *loc adv* by definition ▪ **pour elle les hommes sont égoïstes, par ~** as far as she is concerned men are, by definition, selfish.

définitivement [definitivmɑ̃] *adv* for good.

défiscalisation [defiskalizasjɔ̃] *nf* tax exemption.

défiscaliser [3] [defiskalize] *vt* to exempt from tax.

défit *etc v* ▻ **défaire**.

déflagration [deflagrasjɔ̃] *nf* **1.** [explosion] explosion ▪ [combustion] deflagration **2.** [conflit] clash ▪ **une ~ mondiale** a worldwide conflict.

déflation [deflasjɔ̃] *nf* FIN & GÉOL deflation.

déflationniste [deflasjɔnist] ◇ *adj* [principe] deflationist ▪ [mesure] deflationary.
◇ *nmf* deflationist.

déflecteur [deflɛktœr] *nm* AUTO quarter light *UK*, vent *US*.

déflocage [deflɔkaʒ] *nm* CONSTR asbestos removal, insulation removal, ≃.

défloration [deflɔrasjɔ̃] *nf* defloration.

déflorer [3] [deflɔre] *vt* **1.** [fille] to deflower **2.** *litt* [sujet] to corrupt, to spoil.

défoliant [defɔljɑ̃] *nm* defoliant.

défoliation [defɔljasjɔ̃] *nf* defoliation.

défonce△ [defɔ̃s] *nf* high *(n)* ▪ **son seul plaisir, c'est la ~** his only pleasure in life is getting high ▪ **~ aux amphétamines** taking speed, speeding.

défoncé, e [defɔ̃se] *adj* **1.** [cabossé - lit, sofa] battered ; [- chemin] rutted **2.** △ [drogué] stoned△, high ▪ **des mecs ~s** guys on drugs.

défoncer [16] [defɔ̃se] *vt* [démolir - porte] to smash in *(sép)*, to knock down *(sép)* ; [- mur] to smash *ou* to knock down *(sép)*, to demolish ; [- chaussée] to break up *(sép)* ; [- caisse, tonneau] to smash *ou* to stave in *(sép)* ▪ **le choc lui a défoncé trois côtes** the impact cracked three of her ribs ▪ **il a eu le crâne défoncé** his skull was smashed.
◆ **se défoncer** *vpi* **1.** *fam* [se démener - au travail] to work flat out ; [- en se distrayant] to have a wild time ▪ **il s'est défoncé sur scène hier soir** he gave it all he had on stage last night **2.** △ [se droguer] to get high ▪ **il se défonce à l'héroïne/à la colle** he does heroin/glue ▪ **moi je me défonce au café** *hum* coffee's MY drug.

défont *v* ▻ **défaire**.

déforestation [defɔrɛstasjɔ̃] *nf* deforestation ▪ **faire de la ~** to deforest.

déformant, e [defɔrmɑ̃, ɑ̃t] *adj* distorting.

déformation [defɔrmasjɔ̃] *nf* **1.** [changement de forme - gén] putting out of shape ; [- par torsion] bending out of shape ; [- en frappant] knocking out of shape ; [- par la chaleur] warping **2.** [travestissement - d'une pensée, de la réalité] distortion, misrepresentation ; [- d'une image] distortion, warping ➊ **~ professionnelle : elle pose toujours des questions, c'est une ~ professionnelle** she's always asking questions because she's used to doing it in her job ▪ **ne fais pas attention, c'est de la ~ professionnelle!** *hum* don't worry, it's just my job!

déformer [3] [defɔrme] *vt* **1.** [changer la forme de - planche] to warp ; [- barre] to bend (out of shape) ; [- pare-chocs] to knock out of shape, to buckle ; [- chaussure, pantalon] to put out of shape, to ruin the shape of **2.** [transformer - corps] to deform ; [- visage, voix] to distort ▪ **traits déformés par la haine** features contorted with hatred **3.** [changer le comportement de] : **l'enseignement l'a déformé** he's taken on all the mannerisms of the typical teacher **4.** [fausser - réalité, pensée] to distort, to misrepresent ; [- image] to distort ; [- goût] to warp ; [- paroles] to misquote.
◆ **se déformer** *vpi* [vêtement] to become shapeless, to go out of *ou* to lose its shape ▪ [planche] to become warped ▪ [barre] to become bent.

défoulement [defulmɑ̃] *nm* release ▪ **danser est un bon ~** dancing is a good way of unwinding.

défouler [3] [defule] ◆ **se défouler** *vpi* to let steam off, to unwind ▪ **rien de tel que le sport pour se ~** there's nothing like sport for letting off steam.

défourner [3] [defurne] *vt* [pain] to take out (of the oven) ▪ [poterie] to take out (of the kiln).

défragmenter [3] [defragmɑ̃te] *vt* INFORM to defragment,, to defrag *fam*.

défraîchi, e [defreʃi] *adj* : **des articles ~s** shopsoiled articles ▪ **les fleurs sont ~es** the flowers are past their best ▪ **des idées un peu ~es** *fig* rather stale ideas.

défraîchir [32] [defreʃir] *vt* [rideau] to give a worn look to ▪ [couleur] to fade.
◆ **se défraîchir** *vpi* [rideau, couleur] to fade ▪ [pantalon] to become worn.

défrayer [11] [defreje] *vt* **1.** [indemniser] : **~ qqn de** to meet sb's expenses for **2.** *loc* **~ la chronique** to be the talk of the town *loc*, to be widely talked about ▪ **~ la conversation** to be the main topic of conversation.

défrichage [defriʃaʒ] *nm* [d'un terrain] clearing.

défrichement [defriʃmɑ̃] = **défrichage**.

défricher [3] [defriʃe] *vt* **1.** [nettoyer - terrain] to clear ▪ **~ le terrain avant de négocier** *fig* to clear the way for negotiations **2.** [préparer - texte] to have a first look at ; [- enquête] to do the spadework for.

défricheur, euse [defriʃœr, øz] *nm, f* : **les premiers ~s** the people *ou* settlers who first cleared the land.

défriper [3] [defripe] *vt* to smooth out *(sép)*, to take the creases out of.

défriser [3] [defrize] *vt* **1.** [cheveux, moustache] to straighten out *(sép)*, to take the curl *ou* curls out of ▪ **se faire ~ (les cheveux)** to have one's hair straightened **2.** *fam* [contrarier] to bug.

défroisser [3] [defrwase] *vt* to smooth out *(sép)*, to take the creases out of.
◆ **se défroisser** *vpi* to lose its creases.

défroque [defrɔk] *nf* **1.** [vêtement] (old) rags **2.** [d'un religieux] effects.

défroqué, e [defrɔke] *adj* defrocked, unfrocked.
◆ **défroqué** *nm* [prêtre] defrocked priest ▪ [moine] defrocked monk.

défunt, e [defœ̃, œ̃t] *litt* ◇ *adj* **1.** [décédé - parent, mari] late **2.** [terminé - royauté] defunct ; [- espoir, amour] lost, extinguished.
◇ *nm, f* deceased person ▪ **le ~** the deceased ▪ **prière pour les ~s** prayer for the dead.

dégagé, e [degaʒe] *adj* **1.** [vue] open ▪ [pièce, passage] cleared **2.** [épaules] bare ▪ **je la préfère avec le front ~** I prefer her with her hair back **3.** [désinvolte - air, ton] casual ▪ **dit-elle d'un air ~** she said casually *ou* trying to look casual **4.** MÉTÉOR clear, cloudless.
◆ **dégagé** *nm* DANSE dégagé.

dégagement [degaʒmɑ̃] *nm* **1.** [émanation - d'odeur] emanation ; [- de chaleur] release, emission, emanation ▪ **un ~ de gaz** [accidentel] a gas leak ; [volontaire] a release of gas **2.** [espace - dans une maison] passage, hall ; [- dans une ville] open space ; [- dans un bois] clearing ▪ **un ~ d'un mètre entre le pont et le véhicule** one metre headroom between the bridge and the vehicle **3.** [déblaiement] opening out, digging out ▪ **le ~ du temple par les archéologues** excavation of the temple by the archaeologists **4.** MIL & POLIT disengagement **5.** [au mont-de-piété] redeeming *(from pawn)* **6.** SPORT [d'un ballon] clearance.

dégager [17] [degaʒe] *vt* **1.** [sortir] to free ▪ **il a essayé de ~ sa main de la mienne** he tried to pull his hand away *ou* to free his hand from mine
2. [enlever - arbres tombés, ordures] to remove, to clear ▪ **~ les branches de la route** to clear the branches off the road, to clear the road of branches
3. [désencombrer - couloir, table, salle] to clear (out) ; [- sinus] to clear, to unblock ; [- poitrine, gorge] to clear ; [- ouverture, chemin] to open ▪ **une coupe qui dégage la nuque** a hairstyle cut very short at the back ▪ **la robe dégage les épaules** the dress leaves the shoulders bare ▪ **dégagez la piste!** *fam fig* (get) out of the way!
4. FIN [crédit] to release ▪ **~ des bénéfices** to make a profit
5. [libérer] : **~ sa responsabilité** to deny responsibility ▪ **~ qqn de sa promesse** to release *ou* to free sb from their promise ▪ **~ qqn de ses dettes** to cancel sb's debt ▪ **il est dégagé des obligations militaires** he has completed his military service
6. [émettre - odeur] to give off *(insép)*, to emit ; [- gaz] to release, to emit
7. [manifester - quiétude] to radiate
8. [extraire - règle, principe] to draw ; [- vérité] to draw, to bring out *(sép)*, to extract
9. [du crédit municipal] to redeem *(from pawn)*
10. SPORT [ballon] to clear ▪ *(en usage absolu)* **~ en touche** to put *ou* kick the ball into touch
11. *fam (en usage absolu)* [partir] : **dégage!** clear off!, get lost!
◆ **se dégager** ◇ *vp (emploi passif)* [conclusion] to be drawn ▪ [vérité] to emerge, to come out ▪ **il se dégage du rapport que les torts sont partagés** it appears from the report that both sides are to blame.
◇ *vp (emploi réfléchi)* **1.** [s'extraire] : **se ~ d'un piège** to free o.s. from a trap ▪ **se ~ d'une étreinte** to extricate o.s. from an embrace ▪ **se ~ du peloton** to leave the bunch behind
2. [se libérer - d'un engagement] : **j'étais invité mais je vais me ~** I was invited but I'll get out of it ▪ **se ~ d'une affaire/d'une association** to drop out of a deal/an association ▪ **se ~ d'une obligation** to free o.s. from an obligation ▪ **se ~ de sa promesse** to break one's word.
◇ *vpi* **1.** [se déplacer] to move *ou* to step aside, to step back, to move out of the way
2. [se vider - route] to clear ; [- ciel] to clear ; [- sinus] to become unblocked, to clear
3. [émaner - odeur, gaz, fumée] to emanate, to be given off ▪ [se manifester - quiétude] to emanate, to radiate.

dégaine [degɛn] *nf fam* [démarche] (peculiar) gait ▪ [aspect ridicule] (gawky) look ▪ **tu parles d'une ~!** just look at that!

dégainer [4] [degene] *vt* **1.** ARM [épée] to unsheathe, to draw ▪ [revolver] to draw ▪ *(en usage absolu)* **avant que le gangster ait pu ~** before the gangster could draw his gun **2.** TECHNOL to unsheathe.

déganter [3] [degɑ̃te] ◆ **se déganter** *vp (emploi réfléchi)* to take off *ou* to remove one's glove *ou* gloves.

dégarni, e [degarni] *adj* **1.** [arbre, rayon, mur] bare ▪ **le placard est bien ~** the cupboard's rather empty *ou* bare **2.** [personne, crâne] balding ▪ **il a le front ~** he has a receding hairline.

dégarnir [32] [degarnir] *vt* **1.** [ôter les objets de - salon] to empty ; [- collection] to deplete **2.** [ôter l'argent de - portefeuille] to empty, to deplete ; [- compte en banque] to drain, to draw heavily on **3.** [ôter les feuilles de] to strip of its leaves.
◆ **se dégarnir** *vpi* **1.** [se vider - boîte, collection, rayonnage] to become depleted ; [- groupe] to become depleted, to thin out **2.** [devenir chauve] to go bald, to start losing one's hair ▪ **son front se dégarnit** his hairline is receding ▪ **son crâne se dégarnit** he's losing hair *ou* thinning on top **3.** [arbre] to lose its leaves ▪ [forêt] to become depleted *ou* thinner.

dégât [dega] *nm* damage *(U)* ▪ **il n'y a pas de ~s?** *fam* [après un accident] no harm done? ▪ **faire des ~s** to cause damage ➊ **~s des eaux** water damage ▪ **~s matériels** structural damage.

dégauchir [32] [degoʃir] *vt* **1.** [redresser] to straighten out *(sép)* **2.** MENUIS to plane.

dégazer [3] [degaze] ◇ *vt* MÉTALL to extract gas from.
◇ *vi* [pétrolier] to degas.

dégel [deʒɛl] *nm* **1.** MÉTÉOR thaw ▪ **au ~** when the thaw comes **2.** [après un conflit] thaw ▪ **une période de ~** POLIT a period of detente.

dégelée [deʒle] *nf fam* thrashing.

dégeler [25] [deʒle] ◇ *vt* **1.** [décongeler] to defrost **2.** [réchauffer - sol, étang] to thaw (out) ; [- tuyau] to unfreeze **3.** *fam* [mettre à l'aise] to thaw (out), to relax ▪ **je n'arrive pas à ~ mon collègue** I can't get my colleague to loosen up ▪ **elle sait ~ un auditoire** she knows how to warm up an audience **4.** [améliorer - relations diplomatiques] to thaw **5.** FIN [crédits] to unfreeze.
◇ *vi* **1.** [se réchauffer - banquise, étang] to thaw **2.** [décongeler] to defrost.
◆ **se dégeler** *vpi* **1.** [se décongeler] to defrost **2.** [se réchauffer - sol, étang] to thaw (out) **3.** *fam* [être moins timide] to thaw (out), to relax **4.** [s'améliorer - relations] to improve ▪ **les relations entre les deux pays se dégèlent** there is a thaw in relations between the two countries.

dégénératif, ive [deʒeneratif, iv] *adj* degenerative.

dégénéré, e [deʒenere] *adj & nm, f* degenerate.

dégénérer [18] [deʒenere] *vi* **1.** [perdre ses qualités - race, plante] to degenerate ▪ **ses gags ont beaucoup dégénéré** his jokes have really gone downhill **2.** [s'aggraver - situation] to worsen, to deteriorate ; [- discussion] to get out of hand ▪ MÉD [tumeur] to become malignant **3.** [se changer] : **~ en** to degenerate into ▪ **sa bronchite a dégénéré en pneumonie** his bronchitis developed into pneumonia.

dégénérescence [deʒeneresɑ̃s] *nf* **1.** BIOL degeneration **2.** *litt* [déclin] degeneration, becoming degenerate ▪ **~ morale** degeneration of moral standards.

dégingandé, e [deʒɛ̃gɑ̃de] *adj* gangling, lanky.

dégivrage [deʒivraʒ] *nm* [d'un congélateur] defrosting ▪ [d'une surface, d'un avion] de-icing ▪ **le ~ des vitres d'une voiture** de-icing the windows of a car.

dégivrer [3] [deʒivre] *vt* [congélateur] to defrost ▪ [surface] to de-ice ▪ **~ les vitres d'une voiture** to de-ice the windows of a car.

dégivreur [deʒivrœr] *nm* [d'un réfrigérateur] defroster.

déglaçage [deglasaʒ] *nm* **1.** CULIN deglazing **2.** [d'un bassin] melting of the ice, thawing **3.** [du papier] removal of gloss.

déglacer [16] [deglase] *vt* **1.** CULIN [poêle] to deglaze ▪ **déglacez au vin blanc** deglaze the pan with white wine **2.** [papier] to remove the gloss from **3.** [étang] to remove the ice from, to melt the ice on.

déglinguer [3] [deglɛ̃ge] *vt fam* **1.** [mécanisme] to break, to bust ▪ **un vélo tout déglingué** a bike which is coming apart *ou* falling to pieces **2.** [santé] to wreck.
◆ **se déglinguer** *vpi fam* **1.** [ne plus fonctionner] to be bust ▪ [mal fonctionner] to go on the blink ▪ [se détacher] to come *ou* to work loose **2.** [santé] to get worse ▪ [poumons, reins] to go to pieces ▪ **je me déglingue** *hum* I'm falling to pieces.

déglutir [32] [deglytir] *vi* to swallow, to gulp.

déglutition [deglytisjɔ̃] *nf* **1.** [de salive] swallowing, deglutition *spéc* **2.** [d'aliments] swallowing, deglutition *spéc.*

dégobiller [3] [degɔbije] *fam* ◇ *vt* to throw up *(sép)*.
◇ *vi* to throw up.

dégoiser [3] [degwaze] *fam péj* ◇ *vt* to spout, to come out with.
◇ *vi* to blather.

dégommer [3] [degɔme] *vt* **1.** [timbre] to remove the gum off *ou* from **2.** *fam* [renvoyer] to sack *UK*, to can *US*, to fire ▪ [destituer] to unseat.

dégonflage [degɔ̃flaʒ] *nm* **1.** [d'un ballon, d'une bouée, d'un pneu] letting air out of ▪ **ajuster la pression par ~** to adjust the pressure by letting air out **2.** *fam* [lâcheté] chickening *ou* bottling *UK* out.

dégonflé, e [degɔ̃fle] ◇ *adj* **1.** [ballon] deflated ▪ [pneu] flat **2.** *fam* [lâche] chicken *(modif).*
◇ *nm, f fam* chicken.

dégonfler [3] [degɔ̃fle] *vt* **1.** [ballon, bouée, pneu] to deflate, to let air out of **2.** MÉD [jambes, doigt] to bring down *ou* to reduce the swelling in **3.** [démystifier - prétention, mythe] to deflate, to debunk.
◆ **se dégonfler** *vpi* **1.** [ballon] to go down, to deflate **2.** MÉD [jambes, doigt] to become less swollen ▪ **ma cheville se dégonfle** the swelling in my ankle's going down **3.** *fam* [perdre courage] to chicken *ou* to bottle *UK* out.

dégorgement [degɔrʒəmɑ̃] *nm* **1.** [fait de déverser] disgorging **2.** [décharge - d'égout] discharging, overflow.

dégorger [17] [degɔrʒe] ◇ *vt* **1.** [déverser] to disgorge **2.** [débloquer - conduit] to unblock **3.** TEXT to clean, to cleanse **4.** ŒNOL to remove the sediment from *(a bottle).*
◇ *vi* **1.** TEXT to bleed **2.** CULIN [ris de veau, cervelle] to soak *(in cold water)* ▪ [concombre] to drain *(having been sprinkled with salt)* ▪ **faire ~** [ris de veau, cervelle] to (leave to) soak ; [concombre] to drain of water *(by sprinkling with salt)* ; [escargot] to clean *(by salting and starvation).*

dégoter [3], **dégotter** [3] [degɔte] *vt fam* [objet rare] to unearth ▪ [idée originale] to hit on *(insép).*

dégoulinade [degulinad] *nf* [coulée] trickle, drip.

dégoulinant, e [degulinɑ̃, ɑ̃t] *adj* dripping ▪ **les mains toutes ~es** with dripping wet hands.

dégoulinement [degulinmɑ̃] *nm* [en traînées] trickling ▪ [goutte à goutte] dripping.

dégouliner [3] [deguline] *vi* [peinture, sauce] to drip ▪ [larmes, sang] to trickle down ▪ **son maquillage dégoulinait** her make-up was running.

dégoupiller [3] [degupije] *vt* ARM to take the pin out of.

dégourdi, e [degurdi] *fam* ◇ *adj* : **être ~** to be smart *ou* on the ball ▪ **il n'est pas très ~** he's a bit slow on the uptake.
◇ *nm, f* : **c'est un petit ~!** there are no flies on him!

dégourdir [32] [degurdir] *vt* **1.** [ranimer - membres] to bring the circulation back to **2.** [réchauffer - liquide] to warm up *(sép)* **3.** *fam* [rendre moins timide] : **~ qqn** to teach sb a thing or two, to wise sb up.
◆ **se dégourdir** ◇ *vpt* [remuer] : **se ~ les jambes** to stretch one's legs ▪ **se ~ les doigts avant de jouer du piano** to warm up before playing the piano.
◇ *vpi fam* [devenir moins timide] to learn a thing or two, to wise up.

dégoût [degu] *nm* **1.** [aversion] disgust, distaste ▪ **éprouver du ~ pour qqch/qqn** to have an aversion to sthg/sb **2.** [lassitude] weariness.

dégoûtant, e [degutɑ̃, ɑ̃t] ◇ *adj* [sale] disgusting, disgustingly dirty ▪ [salace - film, remarque] disgusting, dirty ▪ **c'est ~!** [injuste] it's disgusting *ou* awful!
◇ *nm, f* **1.** [personne sale] : **petit ~!** you little pig! **2.** [vicieux] : **vieux ~!** you dirty old man! **3.** *fam* [personne injuste] : **quelle ~e!** that wretched woman!⚠ ▪ **quel ~!** the swine!

dégoûté, e [degute] ◇ *adj* **1.** [écœuré] repulsed, disgusted ▪ **prendre des airs ~s** to put on a look of disgust, to wrinkle one's nose ▪ **il n'est pas ~!** *hum* he's not very fussy! **2.** [indigné] outraged, revolted, disgusted.
◇ *nm, f* : **faire le ~** to be fussy, to make a fuss.

dégoûter [3] [degute] *vt* **1.** [écœurer] to disgust, to repel, to be repugnant to **2.** [indigner] to disgust, to outrage, to be (morally) repugnant to **3.** [lasser] to put off ▪ **il gagne toujours, c'est à vous ~!** he always wins, it's enough to make you sick! ▪ **la vie le dégoûtait** he was weary of life *ou* sick of living ▪ **~ qqn de qqch** to put sb off sthg ▪ **c'est à vous ~ d'être serviable** it's enough to put you (right) off being helpful.
◆ **se dégoûter** *vp (emploi réfléchi)* **je me dégoûte!** I disgust myself!
◆ **se dégoûter de** *vp+prép* : **se ~ de qqn/qqch** to get sick of sb/sthg.

dégouttant, e [degutɑ̃, ɑ̃t] *adj* dripping ▪ **toute ~e de pluie** dripping wet ▪ **les mains ~es de sang** hands dripping with blood.

dégoutter [3] [degute] *vi* to drip ▪ **son front dégoutte de sueur** his forehead is dripping with sweat, sweat is dripping off his forehead.

dégradable [degradabl] *adj* degradable.

dégradant, e [degradɑ̃, ɑ̃t] *adj* degrading.

dégradation [degradasjɔ̃] *nf* **1.** [destruction - d'un objet] wear and tear ; [- d'un bâtiment] dilapidation **2.** [détérioration - de rapports, d'une situation] deterioration, worsening ; [- de l'environnement] degradation **3.** [avilissement] degradation **4.** CHIM degradation **5.** PHYS : **~ de l'énergie** dissipation of energy **6.** INFORM : **~ de données** corruption of data **7.** [d'une couleur] toning down, gradation ▪ [de la lumière] gradation **8.** [d'un officier] ≃ dishonourable discharge ▪ **~ civique** loss of civil rights.

dégradé [degrade] *nm* **1.** [technique] shading off ▪ [résultat] gradation ▪ **un ~ de verts** greens shading off into each other **2.** [d'une coiffure] layered style.
◆ **en dégradé** *loc adj* : **tons en ~** colours shading off (into one another).

dégrader [3] [degrade] *vt* **1.** [abîmer] to damage **2.** [envenimer - rapports humains] to damage, to cause to deteriorate **3.** [avilir] to degrade **4.** [couleurs] to shade (into one another) ▪ [lumières] to reduce gradually **5.** [cheveux] to layer **6.** MIL : **~ un officier** to strip an officer of his rank.
◆ **se dégrader** *vpi* [meuble, bâtiment] to deteriorate ▪ [relation] to deteriorate ▪ [santé] to decline ▪ [langage] to deteriorate, to become debased ▪ [temps] to get worse.

dégrafer [3] [degrafe] *vt* [papiers] to unstaple ▪ [col, robe] to undo, to unfasten ▪ [ceinture] to undo ▪ [bracelet] to unclasp, to unhook ▪ **tu veux que je te dégrafe?** *fam* shall I undo your dress?
◆ **se dégrafer** ◇ *vp (emploi passif)* [robe] to undo.
◇ *vp (emploi réfléchi)* [ôter sa robe] to undo *ou* to unfasten one's dress ▪ [ôter son corset] to undo *ou* to unfasten one's corset.
◇ *vpi* [jupe] to come undone ▪ [papiers] to come unstapled ▪ [collier] to come unhooked.

dégraissage [degrɛsaʒ] *nm* **1.** [nettoyage] removal of grease marks **2.** *fam* [diminution du personnel] shedding staff **3.** *fam* [élimination du surplus] trimming ▪ **faire du ~ sur un manuscrit** to trim a manuscript down **4.** CULIN [d'un bouillon] skimming off the fat ▪ [d'une viande] trimming off the fat.

dégraissant, e [degrɛsɑ̃, ɑ̃t] *adj* [détachant] grease-removing.
◆ **dégraissant** *nm* [détachant] grease remover.

dégraisser [4] [degrese] *vt* **1.** [ôter les taches de] to remove grease marks from **2.** *fam* [entreprise] to make cutbacks in ▪ [personnel] to cut back *(sép)*, to shed ▪ *(en usage absolu)* **il va falloir ~** there will have to be cutbacks in staff **3.** *fam* [dissertation, manuscrit] to pare down *(sép)*, to trim down *(sép)* **4.** CULIN [sauce] to skim the fat off ▪ [viande] to cut *ou* to trim the fat off.

degré [dəgre] *nm* **1.** [échelon - d'une hiérarchie] degree ; [- d'un développement] stage ▪ **à un ~ avancé de** at an advanced stage of ▶ **le premier/second ~** ÉDUC primary/secondary education ▪ **second ~ : une remarque à prendre au second ~** a remark not to be taken at face value
2. [point] degree ▪ **un tel ~ de dévouement** such a degree of devotion ▪ **compréhensif jusqu'à un certain ~** understanding up to a point *ou* to a degree ▪ **courageux au plus haut ~** most courageous

3. [unité] degree ■ **du gin à 47,5 ~s** 83° proof gin, 47,5 degree gin *(on the Gay-Lussac scale)* ➊ **~ alcoolique** *ou* **d'alcool** alcohol content ■ **~ Baumé/Celsius/Fahrenheit** degree Baumé/ Celsius/Fahrenheit
4. ASTRON, GÉOM & MATH degree ■ **équation du premier/second ~** equation of the first/second degree
5. GRAMM degree
6. MUS degree
7. [de parenté] degree ■ **cousin au premier ~** first cousin
8. *(surtout au pl)* [d'un escalier] step ■ [d'une échelle] rung.
◆ **par degrés** *loc adv* by *ou* in degrees, gradually.

dégressif, ive [degresif, iv] *adj* [tarif] on a sliding scale ■ [impôt] on a sliding scale according to income.

dégrèvement [degrɛvmɑ̃] *nm* FIN : **~ fiscal** [d'une entreprise] tax relief ; [d'un produit] reduction of tax *ou* duty.

dégrever [19] [degrəve] *vt* **1.** FIN [contribuable, entreprise] to grant tax relief to ■ [produit] to reduce the tax *ou* duty on **2.** DR to lift a mortgage.

dégriffé, e [degrife] *adj* reduced *(and with the designer label removed)* ■ **robe ~e** *designer dress with the label removed sold at a reduced price.*
◆ **degriffé** *nm* reduced (and unlabelled) designer item.

dégringolade [degrɛ̃gɔlad] *nf* **1.** [chute] tumbling (down) **2.** [baisse - des prix] slump ; [- des cours] collapse ; [- d'une réputation] plunge ■ **l'industrie est en pleine ~** the industry is in the middle of a slump ■ **il était si admiré, quelle ~!** he was so admired, what a comedown!

dégringoler [3] [degrɛ̃gɔle] ◇ *vi* **1.** [chuter] to tumble down ■ [bruyamment] to crash down **2.** [baisser - prix] to slump, to tumble ; [- réputation] to plunge ■ **ça a fait ~ les prix** it sent prices plummetting **3.** [pleuvoir] : **ça dégringole!** it's tipping it down!
◇ *vt* : **~ l'escalier** [courir] to run *ou* to race down the stairs ; [tomber] to tumble down the stairs.

dégrippant [degripɑ̃] *nm* penetrating grease.

dégripper [3] [degripe] *vt* to release *(parts which are stuck).*

dégriser [3] [degrize] *vt* [désillusionner] to bring back down to earth, to sober up *(sép)* ■ [après l'ivresse] to sober up *(sép).*
◆ **se dégriser** *vpi* to sober up.

dégrossir [32] [degrosir] *vt* **1.** [apprenti, débutant] to polish, to smooth the rough edges of ■ **des jeunes gens mal dégrossis** uncouth young men **2.** [théorie, question] to do the groundwork on ■ [texte du programme] to have a first look at **3.** [bloc de pierre, de bois] to rough-hew.

dégrossissage [degrosisaʒ], **dégrossissement** [degrosismɑ̃] *nm* **1.** [d'une personne] polishing, smoothing the rough edges of **2.** [d'une théorie, d'une question] sorting out, doing the spadework on ■ **faire le ~ d'un projet** to do a first rough sketch for a project **3.** [d'un bloc de pierre, de bois] rough-hewing.

dégrouiller [3] [degruje] ◆ **se dégrouiller**△ *vpi* to get a move on, to hurry up.

dégrouper [3] [degrupe] *vt* [classe] to divide *ou* to split (up) ■ [objets] to split (up).

déguenillé, e [degənije] ◇ *adj* ragged, tattered.
◇ *nm, f* ragamuffin.

déguerpir [32] [degɛrpir] *vi* to run away, to decamp ■ **faire ~ un intrus** to drive away an intruder.

dégueu△ [degø] *adj inv* yucky ■ **c'est pas ~!** it's pretty good!

dégueulasse△ [degœlas] ◇ *adj* **1.** [sale] disgusting, filthy, yucky **2.** [injuste] disgusting, lousy **3.** [vicieux] disgusting, filthy **4.** [sans valeur] lousy, crappy△ ■ **c'est pas ~ comme cadeau** it's a pretty nice present, it's not a bad present.
◇ *nmf* **1.** [personne sale] filthy pig **2.** [pervers] : **un gros ~** a filthy lecher **3.** [personne immorale - homme] swine ; [- femme] bitch△.

dégueulasser [3]△ [degœlase] *vt* to muck UK *ou* to louse US up *(sép).*

dégueuler [5]△ [degœle] ◇ *vi* to throw up△, to puke△.
◇ *vt* to throw up *(sép)*△, to puke up *(sép)*△.

dégueulis△ [degœli] *nm* puke△.

déguisé, e [degize] *adj* **1.** [pour une fête] in fancy dress ■ [pour duper] in disguise, disguised **2.** *péj* [mal habillé] ridiculously dressed **3.** [changé - voix] disguised **4.** [caché - intention] disguised, masked, veiled ; [- agressivité] veiled.

déguisement [degizmɑ̃] *nm* **1.** [pour une fête] fancy dress, costume ■ [pour duper] disguise **2.** [d'une voix] disguising.

déguiser [3] [degize] *vt* **1.** [pour une fête] to dress up *(sép)* ■ **déguisé en : déguisé en pirate** dressed (up) as a pirate, wearing a pirate costume ■ [pour duper] to disguise **2.** [mal habiller] to dress ridiculously **3.** [changer - voix] to disguise **4.** [cacher - intention, vérité] to disguise, to mask ; [- honte] to conceal.
◆ **se déguiser** *vp (emploi réfléchi)* [pour une fête] to dress up ■ [pour duper] to put on a disguise, to disguise o.s. ■ **se ~ en courant d'air** *fam* to vanish, to do a disappearing act.

dégurgiter [3] [degyrʒite] *vt* [aliment] to bring (back) up *(sép).*

dégustateur, trice [degystatœr, tris] *nm, f* taster.

dégustation [degystasjɔ̃] *nf* **1.** [par un convive] tasting *(U)* ■ [par un dégustateur] tasting, sampling **2.** [dans une cave] (free) tasting ■ **~ (de vins)** wine-tasting **3.** [à un étalage, dans un restaurant] tasting *(C)* ■ **'~ de fruits de mer à toute heure'** 'seafood served all day'.

déguster [3] [degyste] ◇ *vt* **1.** [manger, boire - suj: convive] to taste ; [- suj: dégustateur professionnel] to taste, to sample **2.** [écouter, lire, regarder] to savour.
◇ *vi fam* [recevoir des coups] to get a bashing ■ [être mal traité] to have a rough time ■ [souffrir] to be in agony, to go through hell ■ **attends qu'il rentre, tu vas ~!** just wait till he gets home, you'll really catch it!

déhanché, e [deɑ̃ʃe] *adj* **1.** [balancé] swaying **2.** [boiteux] limping.

déhanchement [deɑ̃ʃmɑ̃] *nm* **1.** [démarche - séduisante] swaying walk ; [- claudicante] limp, lop-sided walk **2.** [posture] *standing with one's weight on one leg.*

déhancher [3] [deɑ̃ʃe] ◆ **se déhancher** *vpi* **1.** [en marchant] to sway (one's hips) **2.** [sans bouger] to stand with one's weight on one leg.

dehors[1] [dəɔr] ◇ *nm* **1.** [surface extérieure d'une boîte, d'un bâtiment] outside **2.** [plein air] outside ■ **les bruits du ~** the noises from outside **3.** [étranger] : **menace venue du ~** threat from abroad.
◇ *nmpl* [apparences] appearances ■ **sous des ~ égoïstes** beneath a selfish exterior.

dehors[2] [dəɔr] *adv* [à l'extérieur] outside ■ [en plein air] outside, outdoors, out of doors ■ [hors de chez soi] out ■ **on ne voit rien de ~** you can't see anything from the outside ■ **mettre qqn ~** *fam* to kick sb out ; [renvoyer] to sack sb.
◆ **en dehors** *loc adv* **1.** [à l'extérieur] outside **2.** [vers l'extérieur] : **avoir** *ou* **marcher les pieds en ~** to walk with one's feet turned out.
◆ **en dehors de** *loc prép* **1.** [excepté] apart from **2.** [à l'écart de] : **reste en ~ de leur dispute** don't get involved in *ou* stay out of their quarrel **3.** [au-delà de] outside (of), beyond.

déhoussable [deusabl] *adj* with loose *ou* removable covers, with a loose *ou* removable cover.

déictique [deiktik] *adj & nm* deictic.

déification [deifikasjɔ̃] *nf* deification.

déifier [9] [deifje] *vt* to deify, to turn into a god.

déisme [deism] *nm* deism.

déiste [deist] ◇ *adj* deistic, deistical.
◇ *nmf* deist.

déité [deite] *nf* deity, god.

déjà [deʒa] *adv* **1.** [dès maintenant, dès lors] already ■ **il doit être ~ loin** he must be far away by now ■ **il savait ~ lire à l'âge de 4**

ans he already knew how to read at the age of 4 ■ **enfant, il aimait ~ les fleurs** even as a child he liked flowers **2.** [précédemment] : **je vous l'ai ~ dit** I've told you already ■ **tu l'as ~ vu sur scène?** have you ever seen him on stage? ■ **il l'a ~ vue quelque part** he's seen her somewhere before **3.** [emploi expressif] : **il est d'accord sur le principe, c'est ~ beaucoup** he's agreed on the principle, that's something ■ **~ qu'il est en mauvaise santé** he's in poor health as it is ■ **elle est ~ assez riche** she's rich enough as it is ■ **ce n'est ~ pas si mal** you could do worse ■ **c'est ~ quelque chose** it's better than nothing ■ **donne un euro, ce sera ~ ça** give one euro, that'll be a start ■ **on a perdu une valise, mais ni l'argent ni les passeports, c'est ~ ça!** we lost a case, but not our money or passports, which is something at least! ■ **il faut ~ qu'il ait son examen** he needs to pass his exam first, before he does anything else he has to pass his exam **4.** *fam* [pour réitérer une question] again ■ **elle s'appelle comment ~?** what did you say her name was?, what's she called again?

déjanté, e [deʒɑ̃te] *adj fam* : **il est complètement ~** he's off his trolley *UK*△ *ou* out of his tree.

déjanter [3] [deʒɑ̃te] *vt* [pneu] to remove from its rim, to take the rim off.

déjà-vu [deʒavy] *nm inv* **1.** [banalité] commonplace ■ **c'est du ~ comme idée** that idea's a bit banal **2.** [sensation] : **(sensation** *ou* **impression de) ~** (feeling of) déjà vu.

déjection [deʒɛksjɔ̃] *nf* **1.** PHYSIOL [action] evacuation **2.** GÉOL [d'un volcan] : **~s** ejecta.
◆ **déjections** *nfpl* PHYSIOL faeces, dejecta *spéc.*

déjeté, e [deʒte] *adj* [dévié - mur, corps] lop-sided, crooked ; [- colonne vertébrale] twisted.

déjeuner¹ [5] [deʒœne] *vi* **1.** [le midi] to (have) lunch ■ **invite-le à ~** invite him for *ou* to lunch ■ **j'ai déjeuné d'une salade** I had a salad for lunch ■ **j'ai fait ~ les enfants plus tôt** I gave the children an early lunch **2.** [dialecte, le matin] to have breakfast.

déjeuner² [deʒœne] *nm* **1.** [repas de la mi-journée] lunch, luncheon *sout* ■ **prendre son ~** to have lunch ■ **un ~ d'affaires** a business lunch **2.** [dialecte: repas du matin] breakfast **3.** [tasse et soucoupe] (large) breakfast cup and saucer **4.** *loc* **~ de soleil** short-lived feeling, flash in the pan.

déjouer [6] [deʒwe] *vt* [vigilance] to evade, to elude ■ [complot, machination] to thwart, to foil ■ [plan] to thwart, to frustrate ■ [feinte] to outsmart.

de jure [deʒyre] *loc adv* de jure.

delà [dəla] *adv* ▻ **deçà.**

délabré, e [delabre] *adj* **1.** [en ruine - maison, mur] dilapidated, crumbling **2.** [qui n'est plus florissant - santé, réputation] ruined.

délabrement [delabrəmɑ̃] *nm* **1.** [d'un bâtiment] disrepair, ruin, dilapidation **2.** [d'un esprit, d'un corps] deterioration ■ **les patients étaient dans un état de ~ total** the patients were in a state of total neglect **3.** [d'une réputation] ruin ■ [d'une fortune] depletion.

délabrer [3] [delabre] *vt* **1.** [bâtiment, meuble] to ruin **2.** [santé] to ruin ■ [organe] to damage **3.** [réputation] to ruin.
◆ **se délabrer** *vpi* [bâtiment] to go to ruins ■ [meuble] to become rickety, to fall apart ■ [entreprise] to collapse.

délacer [16] [delase] *vt* [soulier, botte] to undo (the laces of) ■ [corset] to unlace.
◆ **se délacer** ◇ *vp (emploi réfléchi)* [ôter ses souliers] to undo *ou* to unlace one's shoes ■ [ôter ses bottes] to undo *ou* to unlace one's boots ■ [ôter son corset] to unlace one's corset ■ [ôter sa robe] to unlace one's dress.
◇ *vpi* [soulier] to become undone ■ [corset] to become unlaced.

délai [delɛ] *nm* **1.** [répit] extension (of time) ■ **donner** *ou* **accorder un ~ (supplémentaire) à qqn** to give *ou* grant sb an extension ■ **~ de réflexion** [avant réponse] time to think ; [avant de signer un contrat] cooling-off period ■ **laissez-moi un ~ de réflexion** give me time to think **2.** [temps fixé] time limit ■ **quel est le ~ à respecter?** what is the deadline? ◐ **~ de livraison** delivery time ■ **~ de paiement** repayment period ■ **~ de recouvrement** break-even period **3.** [période d'attente] waiting period ■ **il faut un ~ de trois jours avant que votre compte soit crédité** the cheque will be credited to your account after a period of three working days **4.** DR : **~ de carence** *period during which benefit is not paid* ■ **~ de grâce** period of grace ■ **un ~ de grâce de 10 jours** 10 days' grace.
◆ **dans les délais** *loc adv* within the (prescribed *ou* allotted) time limit, on time.
◆ **dans les meilleurs délais, dans les plus brefs délais** *loc adv* in the shortest possible time, as soon as possible ■ **j'y serai dans les plus brefs ~s** I'll be there very shortly.
◆ **dans un délai de** *loc prép* within (a period of) ■ **livrable dans un ~ de 30 jours** allow 30 days for delivery.
◆ **sans délai** *loc adv* without delay, immediately.

délai-congé [delɛkɔ̃ʒe] (*pl* **délais-congés**) *nm* DR term *ou* period of notice.

délaie *etc v* ▻ **délayer.**

délaissé, e [delese] *adj* [époux] deserted ■ [ami] forsaken, neglected ■ [parc] neglected.

délaissement [delɛsmɑ̃] *nm* **1.** *sout* [abandon - par un époux] desertion ; [- par un ami] neglecting **2.** DR [d'un bien] relinquishment ■ [d'un droit] relinquishment, renunciation.

délaisser [4] [delese] *vt* **1.** [quitter - époux] to desert ; [- ami] to neglect **2.** [ne plus exercer - temporairement] to neglect ; [- définitivement] to give up *(sép)* **3.** DR to relinquish.

délassant, e [delasɑ̃, ɑ̃t] *adj* [bain, lotion] relaxing, refreshing, soothing ■ [film] relaxing.

délassement [delasmɑ̃] *nm* **1.** [passe-temps] way of relaxing **2.** [état] relaxation, rest.

délasser [3] [delase] *vt* [physiquement] to relax, to refresh, to soothe ■ [mentalement] to relax, to soothe.
◆ **se délasser** *vpi* to relax.

délateur, trice [delatœr, tris] *nm, f sout & péj* informer *péj.*

délation [delasjɔ̃] *nf sout* denouncing, informing ■ **mais ce serait de la ~!** but that would be tantamount to denunciation!

délavé, e [delave] *adj* [tissu] faded ■ [aquarelle] toned down ■ [terres] waterlogged.

Delaware [dəlawar] *npr m* : **le ~** Delaware.

délayage [delɛjaʒ] *nm* **1.** [mélange - de farine, de poudre] mixing **2.** *fig & péj* [d'un exposé] toning down ■ [d'une idée] watering down ■ **faire du ~** to waffle *UK*, to spout off *US*.

délayer [11] [deleje] *vt* **1.** [diluer - poudre] to mix **2.** *péj* [une idée, un discours] to pad *ou* to spin out *(sép)* ■ [un exposé] to thin *ou* to water down *(sép)*.

Delco® [dɛlko] *nm* distributor AUTO.

délectable [delɛktabl] *adj litt* delectable, delightful.

délectation [delɛktasjɔ̃] *nf litt* delight, delectation *litt.*

délecter [4] [delɛkte] ◆ **se délecter** *vpi litt* **se ~ à qqch/à faire qqch** to take great delight in sthg/in doing sthg.

délégataire [delegatɛr] *nmf* delegatee.

délégation [delegasjɔ̃] *nf* **1.** [groupe envoyé] delegation ■ **envoyé en ~** sent as a delegation **2.** [commission] commission **3.** [fait de mandater] delegation ■ **agir par ~ pour qqn** to act on the authority of *ou* as a proxy for sb ◐ **~ de pouvoirs** delegation of powers ■ **~ de vote** proxy voting **4.** [dans des noms d'organismes] delegation.

délégué, e [delege] *nm, f* delegate ■ **~ de classe** *pupil elected to represent his or her class at 'conseils de classe'*, ≃ class rep ■ **~ des parents** parents' representative ■ **~ du personnel** staff representative ■ **~ syndical** union representative, shop steward.

déléguer [18] [delege] *vt* **1.** [envoyer - groupe, personne] to delegate ■ **j'ai délégué mon oncle pour voter à ma place** I have asked my uncle to cast my vote **2.** [transmettre - pouvoir] to delegate ■ *(en usage absolu)* **il faut savoir ~** you must learn to delegate.

délestage [delɛstaʒ] *nm* **1.** AÉRON & NAUT unballasting **2.** TRANSP relief ■ **itinéraire de ~** relief route **3.** ÉLECTR selective power cut.

délester [3] [delɛste] *vt* **1.** [décharger] : **~ qqn d'une valise/d'une obligation** to relieve sb of a suitcase/of an obligation **2.** AÉRON & NAUT to unballast **3.** TRANSP to relieve traffic congestion on **4.** ÉLECTR [secteur] to cut off power from, to black out *(sép)*.
◆ **se délester de** *vp+prép* to get rid of.

délétère [deletɛr] *adj* **1.** [gaz] noxious, deleterious *sout* **2.** *sout* [doctrine, pouvoir] deleterious *sout*, obnoxious.

Delhi [deli] *npr* Delhi.

délibératif, ive [deliberatif, iv] *adj* [fonction] deliberative.

délibération [deliberasjɔ̃] *nf* **1.** [discussion] deliberation ■ **le projet sera mis en ~** the project will be debated ■ **après ~ du jury** after due deliberation by the jury **2.** [réflexion] deliberation, thinking ■ **après (mûre) ~** after careful consideration.
◆ **délibérations** *nfpl* [décisions] resolutions, decisions.

délibéré, e [delibere] *adj* **1.** [intentionné] deliberate, wilful **2.** [décidé] resolute, determined, thought-out.
◆ **délibéré** *nm* deliberation of the court ■ **mettre en ~** to adjourn for further deliberation.

délibérément [deliberemɑ̃] *adv* **1.** [intentionnellement] deliberately, intentionally, wilfully **2.** [après réflexion] after thinking it over (long and hard), after due consideration.

délibérer [18] [delibere] *vi* **1.** [discuter] to deliberate ■ **~ de** to deliberate **2.** *litt* [réfléchir] to ponder, to deliberate.

délicat, e [delika, at] ◇ *adj* **1.** [fragile - tissu] delicate ; [- peau] sensitive ; [- santé] delicate, frail ; [- intestin, estomac] sensitive, delicate ; [- enfant, plante] fragile **2.** [sensible - palais] discerning **3.** [subtil - forme, aquarelle, nuance, travail] delicate, fine ; [- doigts, traits] delicate, dainty ; [- mets] dainty, delicate ; [- saveur, odeur] delicate ■ **il posa le vase d'un geste ~** he put the vase down delicately *ou* gently **4.** [difficile - situation] delicate, awkward, tricky ; [- opération chirurgicale, problème] difficult, tricky ; [- question] delicate, sensitive ■ **c'est ~** it's rather delicate *ou* awkward **5.** [courtois] thoughtful, considerate **6.** [difficile à contenter] fussy, particular ■ **être ~ sur la nourriture** to be fussy about one's food **7.** [scrupuleux - conscience, procédé] scrupulous.
◇ *nm, f* : **faire le ~** to be fussy ; [devant le sang, la malhonnêteté] to be squeamish.

délicatement [delikatmɑ̃] *adv* **1.** [sans brusquerie - poser, toucher] delicately, gently ; [- travailler, orner] delicately, daintily **2.** [agréablement et subtilement - peindre, écrire] delicately, finely ; [- parfumer] delicately, subtly **3.** [avec tact] delicately, tactfully.

délicatesse [delikatɛs] *nf* **1.** [subtilité - d'une saveur, d'un coloris] delicacy, subtlety ; [- d'une dentelle, d'un geste, d'un visage] delicacy, fineness, daintiness ; [- d'un travail artisanal] delicacy ; [- d'une mélodie] subtlety **2.** [fragilité - d'un tissu] delicate texture, fragility **3.** [honnêteté] scrupulousness, punctiliousness **4.** [tact] delicacy, tact, tactfulness ■ **il n'en a rien dit, par ~** he kept quiet out of tact, he tactfully said nothing ■ **quelle ~!** how tactful! **5.** [difficulté - d'une situation, d'une opération] delicacy, sensitiveness, trickiness.
◆ **délicatesses** *nfpl* *litt* [gestes aimables] kind attentions ■ **elle a eu des ~s à notre égard** she showed consideration towards us.

délice [delis] *nm* **1.** [source de plaisir] delight ■ **c'est un ~** [mets, odeur] it's delicious ; [d'être au soleil, de nager] it's sheer delight **2.** [ravissement] delight, (great) pleasure ■ **ses paroles la remplissaient de ~** his words filled her with delight.
◆ **délices** *nfpl* [plaisirs] delights, pleasures ■ **faire les ~s de qqn** to delight sb, to give sb great pleasure ■ **faire ses ~s de qqch** to take delight in sthg, to enjoy sthg greatly.
◆ **avec délice(s)** *loc adv* with great pleasure, with delight.

délicieusement [delisjøzmɑ̃] *adv* **1.** [agréablement] deliciously, delightfully, exquisitely ■ **elle était ~ parfumée** her perfume was delightful *ou* divine **2.** [en intensif] : **son repas était ~ bon** his meal was absolutely delicious ■ **elle était ~ bien dans ses bras** she was wonderfully happy in his arms.

délicieux, euse [delisjø, øz] *adj* **1.** [qui procure du plaisir - repas, parfum, sensation] delicious ; [- lieu, promenade, chapeau] lovely, delightful **2.** [qui charme - femme, geste] lovely, delightful ■ **votre sœur est délicieuse!** your sister's a delight (to be with)!

délictuel, elle [deliktɥɛl], **délictueux, euse** [deliktɥø, øz] *adj* *sout* criminal.

délié, e [delje] *adj* **1.** [sans épaisseur - écriture] fine ; [- cou] slender **2.** [agile - esprit] sharp ; [- doigt] nimble, agile ■ **avoir la langue ~e** to be chatty.
◆ **délié** *nm* upstroke.

délier [9] [delje] *vt* **1.** [dénouer - ruban, mains] to untie ; [- gerbe, bouquet] to undo **2.** [rendre agile] : **un exercice pour ~ les jambes/les doigts** an exercise to loosen the leg muscles/the fingers **3.** [délivrer] : **~ qqn de** [promesse, engagement] to free *ou* to release sb from **4.** RELIG to absolve.
◆ **se délier** ◇ *vpi* [langue] to loosen ■ **après quelques verres, les langues se délient** a few drinks help to loosen people's tongues.
◇ *vpt* [s'exercer] : **se ~ les jambes/les doigts** to relax one's leg muscles/one's fingers.
◆ **se délier de** *vp+prép* to release o.s. from ■ **se ~ d'une obligation** to free o.s. from an obligation.

délimitation [delimitasjɔ̃] *nf* **1.** [fait de circonscrire - un terrain] demarcation, delimitation ; [- un sujet, un rôle] defining, delineating, delimitation **2.** [limites] delimitation.

délimiter [3] [delimite] *vt* [espace, frontière] to demarcate, to delimit, to circumscribe ■ [sujet] to define, to delimit.

délinquance [delɛ̃kɑ̃s] *nf* : **la ~** criminality ▶ **la ~ juvénile** juvenile delinquency ■ **la petite ~** petty crime.

délinquant, e [delɛ̃kɑ̃, ɑ̃t] ◇ *adj* delinquent.
◇ *nm, f* offender ■ **jeune ~, ~ juvénile** juvenile delinquent ■ **~ primaire** first offender.

déliquescence [delikesɑ̃s] *nf* **1.** CHIM deliquescence **2.** [déclin] gradual decay, creeping rot.
◆ **en déliquescence** ◇ *loc adj* declining, decaying.
◇ *loc adv* : **tomber en ~** to be on the decline, to fall into decline.

déliquescent, e [delikesɑ̃, ɑ̃t] *adj* **1.** CHIM deliquescent **2.** [déclinant] declining, decaying, decrepit.

délirant, e [delirɑ̃, ɑ̃t] *adj* **1.** [malade] delirious ■ **fièvre ~e** delirious fever **2.** *fam* [insensé - accueil, foule] frenzied, tumultuous ; [- imagination] frenzied, wild ; [- luxe, prix] unbelievable, incredible ■ **c'est ~ de travailler dans de telles conditions** working in such conditions is sheer madness *ou* lunacy.

délire [delir] *nm* **1.** MÉD delirium, delirious state ▶ **~ de grandeur** PSYCHOL delusions of grandeur ■ **~ de persécution** persecution mania **2.** [incohérences] : **un ~ d'ivrogne** a drunkard's ravings **3.** *fam loc* **c'est le** *ou* **du ~ : partout où il se produit, c'est le** *ou* **du ~** wherever he performs, audiences go wild *ou* crazy ■ **demander aux gens de payer 50 % en plus, c'est du ~!** asking people to pay 50% over the odds is stark staring madness! ■ **ce n'est plus de la mise en scène, c'est du ~!** it's no longer stage production, it's sheer madness!
◆ **en délire** *loc adj* delirious, ecstatic.

délirer [3] [delire] *vi* [malade] to be delirious, to rave ■ **tu délires!** *fig* you're out of your mind!

delirium tremens [delirjɔmtremɛ̃s] *nm inv* delirium tremens ■ **avoir une crise de ~** to have an attack of delirium tremens.

délit [deli] *nm* **1.** DR [infraction] (nonindictable) offence *UK*, misdemeanor *US* ■ **~ d'adultère** adultery ■ **~ civil** tort ■ **~ de**

fuite failure to stop after causing a road accident ■ **être incarcéré pour ~ d'opinion** to be put in prison because of one's beliefs ■ **~ de presse** published provocation to commit an offence **2.** BOURSE : **~ d'initié** insider trading *ou* dealing.

délivrance [delivrɑ̃s] *nf* **1.** *litt* [libération - d'une ville] liberation, deliverance ; [- d'un captif] release **2.** [soulagement] relief ■ **attendre la ~** *euphém* to await death as a release from pain **3.** [d'un visa, d'un certificat] issue **4.** MÉD expulsion *ou* birth of the afterbirth.

délivrer [3] [delivre] *vt* **1.** [libérer - prisonnier] to release, to (set) free **2.** [soulager] to relieve ■ **se sentir délivré** to feel relieved ■ **ainsi délivré de ses incertitudes, il décida de...** thus freed from doubt, he decided to... **3.** [visa, titre] to issue ■ [ordonnance, autorisation] to give, to issue **4.** [faire parvenir - paquet, courrier] to deliver ; [- signal] to put out *(sép)*.

délocalisation [delɔkalizasjɔ̃] *nf* relocation.

délocaliser [3] [delɔkalize] *vt* to relocate.

déloger [17] [delɔʒe] ◇ *vt* **1.** [congédier - locataire] to throw *ou* to turn out *(sép)*, to oust **2.** [débusquer - lapin] to start.
◇ *vi* [décamper] to move out (hurriedly) ■ **il finira bien par ~** he'll clear off eventually ■ **faire ~ qqn** to throw sb out, to get sb to move.

déloyal, e, aux [delwajal, o] *adj* **1.** [infidèle - ami] disloyal, unfaithful, untrue *litt* **2.** [malhonnête - concurrence] unfair ; [- méthode] dishonest, underhand ; [- coup] foul, below-the-belt.

déloyauté [delwajote] *nf* **1.** [caractère perfide] disloyalty, treacherousness **2.** [action] disloyal act, betrayal ■ **commettre une ~ envers qqn** to play sb false, to be disloyal to sb.

Delphes [dɛlf] *npr* Delphi.

delta [dɛlta] ◇ *nm inv* [lettre] delta.
◇ *nm* GÉOGR : **~ (littoral)** delta ■ **le ~ du Nil** the Nile Delta.

deltaplane [dɛltaplan] *nm* **1.** [véhicule] hang-glider **2.** [activité] hang-gliding ■ **faire du ~** to go hang-gliding.

déluge [delyʒ] *nm* **1.** [averse] downpour, deluge **2.** BIBLE : **le Déluge** the Flood ➲ **ça remonte au ~** *fam* it's ancient history ■ **après moi le ~!** *Madame de Pompadour allus* what happens when I'm gone is none of my concern! **3.** [abondance - de paroles, de larmes, de plaintes] flood, deluge ; [- de coups] shower ■ **le standard est submergé par un ~ d'appels** the switchboard is deluged with calls.

déluré, e [delyre] ◇ *adj* **1.** [malin - enfant, air] quick, sharp, resourceful **2.** *péj* [effronté - fille] forward, brazen.
◇ *nm, f* : **un petit ~** a smart kid ■ **une petite ~e** a brazen little thing.

délurer [3] [delyre] *vt* [dévergonder] : **~ qqn** to open sb's eyes.
◆ **se délurer** *vpi* **1.** [devenir éveillé] to wake up *fig*, to become aware **2.** [se dévergonder] to become knowing ■ **vers 14 ans, ils se délurent** when they're about 14 they start learning the ways of the world.

démagnétiser [3] [demaɲetize] *vt* [carte] to demagnetize.
◆ **se démagnétiser** *vpi* to become demagnetized.

démagogie [demagɔʒi] *nf* demagogy, demagoguery.

démagogique [demagɔʒik] *adj* demagogic, demagogical.

démagogue [demagɔg] ◇ *adj* demagogic *sout*, rabble-rousing ■ **ils sont très ~s** they're real rabble-rousers.
◇ *nmf* demagogue.

démailler [3] [demaje] *vt* [défaire - tricot] to undo, to unravel ; [- chaîne] to unlink.
◆ **se démailler** *vpi* [tricot] to unravel, to fray, to come undone.

démailloter [3] [demajɔte] *vt* [bébé] to take the nappy *UK ou* diaper *US* off, to change ■ [doigt blessé] to take the bandage off ■ [momie] to unwrap.

demain [dəmɛ̃] *adv* **1.** [lendemain] tomorrow ■ **~ matin/après-midi** tomorrow morning/afternoon ■ **pendant la journée de ~** tomorrow ■ **les journaux de ~** tomorrow's papers ■ **~ en huit** a week tomorrow, tomorrow week *UK* ■ **~ en quinze** two weeks tomorrow ■ **salut, à ~!** bye, see you tomorrow! ■ **avance, sinon on y sera encore ~!** *fam* come on, let's not stay here all night! ➲ **~ il fera jour** tomorrow is another day ■ **ce n'est pas ~ la veille que le système changera** the system's not going to change overnight ■ **l'égalité des salaires n'est pas pour ~** equal pay isn't just around the corner **2.** [à l'avenir] in the future.
◆ **de demain** *loc adj* [futur] : **les architectes/écoles de ~** the architects/schools of tomorrow.

démancher [3] [demɑ̃ʃe] *vt* [couteau, marteau] to remove the handle of ■ [lame] to work out of its handle.
◆ **se démancher** *vpi* **1.** [balai] to lose its handle, to work loose in the handle **2.** *fam* [se démener] : **se ~ pour obtenir qqch** to move heaven and earth *ou* to bust a gut to get sthg.

demande [dəmɑ̃d] *nf* **1.** [requête] request ■ **~ d'argent** request for money ■ **adresser toute ~ de renseignements à...** send all inquiries to... ■ **accéder à/refuser une ~** to grant/to turn down a request ➲ **~ (en mariage)** (marriage) proposal ■ **faire sa ~ en mariage (auprès de qqn)** to propose (to sb) ■ **~ de rançon** ransom demand **2.** ADMIN & COMM application ■ **faire une ~ de bourse/visa** to apply for a scholarship/visa ■ **~ d'indemnité** claim for compensation ■ **remplir une ~** to fill in an application (form) ➲ **~ d'emploi** job application ■ **'~s d'emploi'** 'situations wanted' **3.** ÉCON demand ■ **~ excédentaire** excess demand ■ **la ~ des consommateurs** consumer demand ■ **il y a une forte ~ de traducteurs** translators are in great demand, translators are very much sought after **4.** DR : **~ en justice** petition

LES DEMANDES

Could you give me a hand with these bags? Tu pourrais m'aider à porter ces bagages ?

Certainly./With pleasure. Volontiers./Avec plaisir.

Could you possibly come back later? Vous serait-il possible de revenir plus tard ?

Yes, of course. When is it convenient? Oui, bien sûr. Quelle est l'heure qui vous convient le mieux ?

Can you tell him I'll phone back? Peux-tu lui dire que je le rappellerai ?

Yes, I'll tell him. Oui, je le lui dirai.

Will/Would you pass the salt, please. Tu peux/pourrais me passer le sel, s'il te plaît ?

Sure, here you are. Oui, voilà.

I was wondering whether you could lend me £10? Je me demandais si tu ne pourrais pas me prêter dix livres ?

I'm afraid not, I'm a bit short at the moment. Non, je regrette, je suis un peu juste en ce moment.

Would you mind getting me some stamps while you're out? Ça te dérangerait de m'acheter des timbres en passant ?

Not at all. How many do you want? Non, pas du tout, tu en veux combien ?

Please let me know if you're coming. Préviens-moi si tu viens.

Of course. I'll phone you. Oui, bien sûr. Je t'appellerai.

■ **~ en renvoi** request for transfer of a case (to another court) **5.** [expression d'un besoin] need ■ **la ~ doit venir du patient lui-même** the patient must express a need.

◆ **à la demande** *loc adj & loc adv* on demand.

◆ **à la demande générale** *loc adv* by popular request.

Voir module d'usage

demandé, e [dəmɑ̃de] *adj* sought-after, in demand ■ **le modèle B est très ~** model B is in great demand, demand for model B is high.

demander [3] [dəmɑ̃de] *vt* **1.** [solliciter - rendez-vous, conseil, addition] to ask for *(insép)*, to request ; [- emploi, visa] to apply for ■ **le cuisinier a demandé son samedi** the cook has asked to have Saturday off ■ **~ l'aumône** *ou* **la charité** to ask for charity, to beg for alms ■ **je ne demande pas la charité** *fig* I'm not asking for any favours ■ **~ le divorce** to petition *ou* to file for divorce ■ **~ la main de qqn** to ask for sb's hand (in marriage) ■ **~ qqn en mariage** to propose to sb ■ **~ grâce** to ask *ou* to beg for mercy ■ **~ pardon** to apologize ■ **je te demande pardon** I'm sorry ■ **il m'a demandé pardon de sa conduite** he apologized to me for his behaviour ■ **je vous demande pardon, mais c'est ma place** I beg your pardon, but this is my seat ■ **je vous demande pardon?** (I beg your) pardon? ■ **~ qqch à qqn : ~ une faveur** *ou* **un service à qqn** to ask sb a favour ■ **~ audience à qqn** to request an audience with sb ■ **je ne t'ai jamais demandé quoi que ce soit** I never asked you for anything ■ **~ à qqn de faire : il m'a demandé de lui prêter ma voiture** he asked me to lend him my car ■ *(en usage absolu)* **il suffisait de ~** you only had to *ou* all you had to do was ask
2. [exiger - indemnité, dommages] to claim, to demand ; [- rançon] to demand, to ask for ■ **~ l'impossible** to ask for the impossible ■ **~ justice** to demand justice *ou* fair treatment ■ **~ qqch à qqn** to ask sthg of sb ■ **en ~ : il ne faut pas trop m'en ~/lui en ~** you mustn't ask too much of me/him, you shouldn't expect too much of me/him ■ **il en demande 500 euros** he wants *ou* he's asking 500 euros for it ■ **~ que : tout ce que je demande, c'est qu'on me laisse seul** all I want *ou* ask is to be left alone ▶ **qui ne demande rien n'a rien** if you don't ask, you don't get ■ **je ne demande que ça** *ou* **pas mieux!** I'd be only too pleased! ■ **tu es riche et célèbre, que demande le peuple?** *fam* you're rich and famous, what more do you want? ■ **partir sans ~ son compte** *ou* **son reste** to leave without further ado *ou* without so much as a by-your-leave *hum*
3. [réclamer la présence de - gén] to want ; [- médecin] to send for *(insép)*, to call (for) ; [- prêtre] to ask for *(insép)* ■ **on te demande au téléphone/aux urgences** you're wanted on the telephone/in casualty ■ **il y a une demoiselle qui vous demande** there's a young lady wanting to see you ■ [au téléphone] **: qui demandez-vous?** who would you like to speak to? ■ **demandez-moi le siège à Paris/M. Blanc** get me the head office in Paris/Mr Blanc
4. [chercher à savoir] to ask ■ **~ qqch à qqn : ~ l'heure à qqn** to ask sb the time ■ **~ son chemin à qqn** to ask sb for directions ■ **je lui ai demandé la raison de son départ** I asked her why she (had) left ■ **~ des nouvelles de qqn** to ask after sb ■ **j'ai demandé de tes nouvelles à Marie** I asked for news of you from Marie, I asked Marie about you ■ **on ne t'a rien demandé (à toi)!** nobody asked YOU, nobody asked for YOUR opinion! ■ *(en usage absolu)* **demandez à votre agent de voyages** ask your travel agent ▶ **à quoi sert la police, je vous le demande** *ou* **je vous demande un peu!** *fam* what are the police for, I ask you?
5. [faire venir - ambulance, taxi] to send for *(sép)*, to call (for)
6. [chercher à recruter - vendeur, ingénieur] to want, to require ■ **'on demande un livreur'** 'delivery boy wanted *ou* required' ■ **on demande beaucoup de secrétaires** there's a great demand for secretaries, secretaries are in great demand
7. [nécessiter] to need, to require, to call for *(insép)* ■ **ça demande réflexion** it needs thinking about, it needs some thought.

◆ **demander à** *v+prép* to ask to ■ **je n'ai pas demandé à naître** I never asked to be born ■ **il demande à voir le chef de rayon** he wants to see the department supervisor ■ **je demande à voir!** *fam* I'll believe it when I see it! ▶ **je ne demande qu'à vous embaucher/aider** I'm more than willing to hire/help you.

◆ **demander après** *v+prép* **: ils ont demandé après toi** [ils t'ont réclamé] they asked for you ; [pour avoir de tes nouvelles] they asked how you were *ou* after you.

◆ **se demander** ◇ *vp (emploi passif)* **: cela ne se demande pas!** need you ask! *iron.*
◇ *vpi* to wonder, to ask o.s. ■ **on est en droit de se ~ pourquoi/comment/si...** one may rightfully ask o.s. why/how/whether...

demandeur¹, eresse [dəmɑ̃dœr, d(ə)rɛs] *nm, f* plaintiff, complainant ■ **~ en appel** appellant.

demandeur², euse [dəmɑ̃dœr, øz] ◇ *nm, f* **1.** TÉLÉCOM caller ■ **~, parlez** you're through, caller **2.** ADMIN **: ~ d'emploi** job seeker ■ **je suis ~ d'emploi** I'm looking for a job.
◇ *adj* **: les Français sont très ~s de ce produit** there is an enormous demand for this product in France.

démangeaison [demɑ̃ʒɛzɔ̃] *nf* **1.** [irritation] itch ■ **j'ai des ~s partout** I'm itching all over ■ **donner des ~s à qqn** to make sb itch **2.** *fam* [envie] itch.

démanger [17] [demɑ̃ʒe] *vt* to itch, to be itching ■ **ce pull me démange** that pullover makes me itch ■ **la langue le** *ou* **lui démangeait** *fam fig* he was itching *ou* dying to say something ■ **ça la** *ou* **lui démangeait de dire la vérité** she was itching *ou* dying to tell the truth.

démantèlement [demɑ̃tɛlmɑ̃] *nm* **1.** [démolition] demolition, pulling *ou* taking to pieces **2.** [d'un réseau, d'une secte] breaking up, dismantling.

démanteler [25] [demɑ̃tle] *vt* **1.** [démolir - rempart] to demolish, to tear down *(sép)* **2.** [désorganiser - réseau, secte] to break up *(sép)* ; [- entreprise, service] to dismantle.

démantibuler [3] [demɑ̃tibyle] *vt* to demolish, to take to bits *ou* pieces.

◆ **se démantibuler** *vpi fam* [se rompre] to fall apart, to come to pieces.

démaquillage [demakijaʒ] *nm* make-up removal ■ **le ~ dure deux heures** it takes two hours to remove *ou* to take off the make-up ■ **gel/lotion pour le ~ des yeux** eye make-up removing gel/lotion.

démaquillant, e [demakijɑ̃, ɑ̃t] *adj* **: crème/lotion ~e** cleansing cream/lotion.

◆ **démaquillant** *nm* cleanser, make-up remover ■ **~ pour les yeux** eye make-up remover.

démaquiller [3] [demakije] *vt* to remove the make-up from.

◆ **se démaquiller** *vp (emploi réfléchi)* to remove *ou* to take off one's make-up ■ **se ~ les yeux** to remove one's eye make-up.

démarcation [demarkasjɔ̃] *nf* **1.** [limite] demarcation, dividing line **2.** [fait de démarquer] boundary-defining, demarcating.

démarchage [demarʃaʒ] *nm* COMM door-to-door selling ■ **'~ interdit'** 'no hawkers' ▶ **~ électoral** POLIT canvassing.

démarche [demarʃ] *nf* **1.** [allure] gait, walk ■ **avoir une ~ gracieuse** to have a graceful gait, to walk gracefully **2.** [initiative] step, move ■ **faire toutes les ~s nécessaires** to take all the necessary steps ■ **faire une ~ auprès d'un organisme** to approach an organisation ■ **~s administratives/juridiques** administrative/legal procedures **3.** [approche - d'un problème] approach.

démarcher [3] [demarʃe] *vt* [client, entreprise] to visit.

démarcheur, euse [demarʃœr, øz] *nm, f* COMM door-to-door salesman (*f* saleswoman).

démarquage [demarkaʒ] *nm* **1.** COMM markdown, marking down **2.** [fait d'ôter la marque] **: le ~ des vêtements** [pour les vendre moins cher] removing the designer labels from clothes **3.** SPORT **: le ~ d'un joueur** escaping from a marker.

démarque [demark] *nf* **1.** COMM marking down, markdown ■ **~ inconnue** pilfering, shrinkage *(losses through shoplifting and pilfering)* **2.** SPORT freeing.

démarquer [3] [demarke] *vt* **1.** [enlever la marque de] : **~ des vêtements** to remove the designer labels from clothes **2.** COMM to mark down *(sép)* **3.** SPORT to free **4.** [plagier] to copy, to plagiarize.
◆ **se démarquer** *vp (emploi réfléchi)* SPORT to shake off one's marker.
◆ **se démarquer de** *vp+prép* to distinguish o.s. *ou* to be different from.

démarrage [demaraʒ] *nm* **1.** AUTO & MÉCAN [mouvement] moving off ▪ **~ en trombe** shooting off ▌[mise en marche] starting ▪ **le ~ de la voiture** starting the car ▪ **~ en côte** hill-start **2.** [commencement] start **3.** SPORT kick.

démarrer [3] [demare] <> *vt* to start.
<> *vi* **1.** AUTO & MÉCAN [se mettre à fonctionner] to start (up) ▪ [s'éloigner] to move off ▪ **je n'arrive pas à faire ~ la voiture** I can't get the car started **2.** [débuter] to start ▪ **le feuilleton démarre le 18 mars** the series starts on March 18th ▪ **faire ~ un projet** to get a project off the ground **3.** [dans une progression - économie] to take off, to get off the ground ▪ **les ventes ont bien démarré** sales have got off to a good start ▪ **l'association a mis du temps à ~** the association got off to a slow start **4.** SPORT [coureur] to put on a spurt, to pull away **5.** *fam* [s'en aller] to shift *UK*, to budge.

démarreur [demarœr] *nm* starter ▪ **~ automatique** self-starter.

démasquer [3] [demaske] *vt* **1.** [ôter le masque de] to unmask **2.** [confondre - traître, menteur] to unmask, to expose ▪ **se faire ~** to be unmasked **3.** [dévoiler - hypocrisie] to unmask, to reveal **4.** *loc* **~ ses batteries** *pr* to unmask one's guns ; *fig* to show one's hand.
◆ **se démasquer** *vp (emploi réfléchi)* **1.** [ôter son masque] to take off one's mask, to unmask o.s. **2.** *fig* to throw off *ou* to drop one's mask.

démâter [3] [demate] <> *vt* to dismast.
<> *vi* to lose its mast *ou* masts, to be dismasted.

démazouter [3] [demazute] *vt* to remove fuel oil from.

démêlage [demɛlaʒ] *nm* [des cheveux] disentangling, untangling.

démêlant, e [demɛlɑ̃, ɑ̃t] *adj* [baume] conditioning.
◆ **démêlant** *nm* hair conditioner.

démêlé [demele] *nm* [querelle] quarrel ▪ **avoir des ~s avec qqn** to have a bit of trouble *ou* a few problems with sb.

démêler [4] [demele] *vt* **1.** [cheveux] to untangle, to disentangle, to comb out *(sép)* ▪ [nœud, filet] to disentangle, to untangle **2.** [éclaircir - mystère, affaire] to clear up *(sép)*, to disentangle, to see through *(insép)* ▪ **~ la vérité du mensonge** *ou* **le vrai du faux** to disentangle truth from falsehood, to sift out the truth from the lies **3.** *litt* & *loc* **avoir quelque chose à ~ avec qqn** to have a bone to pick with sb.
◆ **se démêler** *vp (emploi passif)* [cheveux] to comb out, to be disentangled ▪ **ses cheveux se démêlent tout seuls** his hair combs out beautifully.

démembrement [demɑ̃brəmɑ̃] *nm* **1.** [partage] dismemberment, breaking up, carving up **2.** DR : **~ de la propriété** division of inherited property *(between heirs)*.

démembrer [3] [demɑ̃bre] *vt* **1.** [dépecer - carcasse] to dismember **2.** [désorganiser - association] to carve *ou* to split up *(sép)*, to dismantle.

déménagement [demenaʒmɑ̃] *nm* **1.** [changement de domicile] move ▪ **on les a aidés à faire leur ~** we helped them move house *UK ou* to move ➲ **camion de ~** removal *UK ou* moving *US* van ▪ **entreprise de ~** removal company *ou* firm *UK*, mover *US* **2.** [déplacement des meubles] : **le ~ du salon est fini** we've finished moving the furniture out of the living room.

déménager [17] [demenaʒe] <> *vt* [salon] to move the furniture out of, to empty of its furniture ▪ [piano, meubles] to move ▪ **j'ai tout déménagé dans ma chambre** I moved everything into my bedroom.
<> *vi* **1.** [changer de maison] to move (house *UK*) ▪ **il déménage, tu veux reprendre son appartement?** he's moving out, do you want to rent his flat? **2.** [changer de lieu] to move **3.** *fam* [partir] to clear off ▪ **il est dans mon bureau? je vais le faire ~ vite fait!** in my office, is he? I'll have him out of there in no time! **4.** △ [déraisonner] to be off one's nut△ *ou* rocker **5.** △ [faire de l'effet] : **t'as vu la blonde? elle déménage!** did you see that blonde? she's a knockout! ▪ **un rock qui déménage** a mind-blowing rock number△.

déménageur [demenaʒœr] *nm* [ouvrier] removal man *UK*, (furniture) mover *US* ▪ [entrepreneur] furniture remover *UK*, mover *US*.

déménageuse [demenaʒøz] *nf Suisse* removal *UK ou* moving *US* van.

démence [demɑ̃s] *nf* **1.** [gén] insanity, madness **2.** MÉD dementia ▪ **~ précoce** dementia praecox ▪ **~ présénile** presenile dementia **3.** *fam* [conduite déraisonnable] : **c'est de la ~!** it's madness!

démener [19] [demne] ◆ **se démener** *vpi* **1.** [s'agiter] to thrash about, to struggle ▪ **se ~ comme un beau diable** to thrash about, to struggle violently **2.** [faire des efforts] : **se ~ pour** to exert o.s. *ou* to go out of one's way (in order) to ▪ **je me suis démenée pour le retrouver** I went to great lengths to find him.

démens *etc v* ⊳ **démentir**.

dément, e [demɑ̃, ɑ̃t] <> *adj* **1.** [gén] mad, insane **2.** MÉD demented **3.** *fam* [remarquable] fantastic, terrific **4.** *fam péj* [inacceptable] incredible, unbelievable ▪ **c'est ~, tout ce qu'on lui demande de faire!** the amount she's being asked to do is sheer lunacy!
<> *nm, f* MÉD dementia sufferer, demented person.

démenti [demɑ̃ti] *nm* denial ▪ **publier un ~** to print a denial ▪ **opposer un ~ formel à une rumeur** to deny a rumour categorically ▪ **le témoignage reste sans ~** the testimony remains uncontradicted.

démentiel, elle [demɑ̃sjɛl] *adj* **1.** PSYCHOL insane **2.** MÉD dementia *(modif)* **3.** [excessif, extravagant] insane *fig*.

démentir [37] [demɑ̃tir] *vt* **1.** [contredire - témoin] to contradict **2.** [nier - nouvelle, rumeur] to deny, to refute ▪ **son regard démentait ses paroles** the look in his eyes belied his words.
◆ **se démentir** *vpi* : **son amitié pour moi ne s'est jamais démentie** his friendship has been unfailing ▪ **des méthodes dont l'efficacité ne s'est jamais démentie** methods that have proved consistently efficient.

démerdard, e△ [demɛrdar, ard] *adj* : **il est ~, il s'en sortira** he's always got some trick up his sleeve, he'll make it ▪ **il n'est pas ~ pour deux sous** he hasn't got a clue.

démerder [3] [demɛrde] ◆ **se démerder**△ *vpi* to get by, to manage ▪ **et moi, comment je vais me ~?** and how the hell am I supposed to cope?△.

démériter [3] [demerite] *vi sout* [s'abaisser] : **~ aux yeux de qqn** to come down in sb's esteem ▪ **il n'a jamais démérité** he has never proved unworthy of the trust placed in him.

démesure [deməzyr] *nf* [d'un personnage] excessiveness, immoderation ▪ [d'une passion, d'une idée] outrageousness ▪ **donner dans la ~** to (tend to) be excessive.

démesuré, e [deməzyre] *adj* **1.** [énorme - empire] vast, enormous ▪ **d'une longueur ~e** interminable **2.** [exagéré - orgueil] immoderate, inordinate ; [- appétit] huge, gross ▪ **cette affaire a pris une importance ~e** this affair has been blown up out of all proportion.

démesurément [deməzyremɑ̃] *adv* excessively, immoderately, inordinately ▪ **la plante avait poussé ~** the plant had grown inordinately tall.

Déméter [demetɛr] *npr* Demeter.

démettre [84] [demɛtr] *vt* **1.** MÉD [os, bras] to dislocate, to put out of joint **2.** [destituer] to dismiss ▪ **~ qqn de ses fonctions** to dismiss sb from his duties.
◆ **se démettre** <> *vpt* : **se ~ le poignet** to dislocate one's wrist, to put one's wrist out of joint.

◇ *vpi* to resign, to hand in one's resignation ▪ **se ~ de son poste** [directeur] to resign one's post *ou* from one's job ; [député, président] to resign from office.

demeurant [dəmœrɑ̃] ◆ **au demeurant** *loc adv* [du reste] for all that, notwithstanding ▪ **photographe de talent et très joli garçon au ~** a talented photographer and very good-looking with it.

demeure [dəmœr] *nf* **1.** [maison] residence **2.** *sout* [domicile] dwelling-place, abode **3.** DR delay ▪ **mettre qqn en ~ de payer** to give sb notice to pay ▪ **mettre qqn en ~ de témoigner/de s'exécuter** to order sb to testify/to comply.
◆ **à demeure** *loc adv* : **il s'est installé chez elle à ~** he moved in with her permanently *ou* for good.

demeuré, e [dəmœre] ◇ *adj* half-witted, backward.
◇ *nm, f* half-wit.

demeurer [5] [dəmœre] *vi* **1.** *(aux être)* [rester - dans tel état] to remain ▪ **~ silencieux/inconnu** to remain silent/unknown ▪ **en ~ là : l'affaire en est demeurée là** the matter rested there ▪ **il vaut mieux en ~ là pour aujourd'hui** we'd better leave it at that for today **2.** *(aux être)* [subsister] to remain, to be left ▪ **peu de traces demeurent** there are few traces left ▪ **cette épée nous est demeurée de notre père** this sword was left to us by our father **3.** *(aux avoir) sout* [habiter] to live, to stay.

demi, e [dəmi] ◇ *adj inv (devant le n, avec trait d'union)* **1.** [moitié de] half ▪ **une ~-pomme** half an apple ▪ **plusieurs ~-pommes** several halves of apple ▪ **une ~-livre de pommes** a half-pound of *ou* half a pound of apples **2.** [incomplet] : **cela n'a été qu'un ~-succès** it wasn't a complete *ou* it was only a partial success.
◇ *nm, f* [moitié] half ▪ **j'achète un pain? – non, un ~** shall I buy a loaf? – no, just (a) half.
◆ **demi** *nm* **1.** [bière] : **~ (de bière)** ≃ half *UK* ▪ ≃ half-pint *UK* **2.** SPORT : **~ droite** FOOTBALL right half *ou* halfback ▪ **~ de mêlée** RUGBY scrum half ▪ **~ d'ouverture** RUGBY fly *ou* stand-off half **3.** *Suisse* [vin] *half a litre of wine.*
◆ **demie** *nf* : **la ~e** half past ▪ **à la ~e de chaque heure** every hour on the half hour, at half past every hour ▪ **à la ~e de 4 h** at half past 4 ▪ **je te rappelle à la ~e** I'll call you back at half past.
◆ **à demi** *loc adv* **1.** *(avec un adjectif)* **à ~ mort** half-dead **2.** *(avec un verbe)* **ouvrir la porte à ~** to half-open the door ▪ **faire les choses à ~** to do things by halves.
◆ **et demi, et demie** *loc adj* **1.** [dans une mesure] and a half ▪ **ça dure deux heures et ~e** it lasts two and a half hours ▪ **boire une bouteille et ~e** to drink a bottle and a half **2.** [en annonçant l'heure] : **à trois heures et ~e** at three thirty, at half past three.

demiard [demjar] *nm Québec* [vin] *quarter of a pint of wine.*

demi-bouteille [dəmibutɛj] *(pl* **demi-bouteilles***) nf* half-bottle, half a bottle.

demi-canton [dəmikɑ̃tɔ̃] *(pl* **demi-cantons***) nm Suisse state of the Swiss confederation which is one half of a divided canton.*

demi-centre [dəmisɑ̃tr] *(pl* **demi-centres***) nm* SPORT centre-half.

demi-cercle [dəmisɛrkl] *(pl* **demi-cercles***) nm* half-circle, semicircle.
◆ **en demi-cercle** *loc adv* in a semicircle.

demi-deuil [dəmidœj] *(pl* **demi-deuils***) nm* [vêtement] half-mourning.

demi-dieu [dəmidjø] *(pl* **demi-dieux***) nm* demigod.

demi-douzaine [dəmiduzɛn] *(pl* **demi-douzaines***) nf* **1.** [six] half-dozen, half-a-dozen ▪ **deux ~s** two half-dozens ▪ **une ~ de tomates** a half-dozen *ou* half-a-dozen tomatoes **2.** *fam* [environ six] : **une ~ de gens attendaient** half-a-dozen people were waiting.

demi-fin, e [dəmifɛ̃, in] *(mpl* **demi-fins**, *fpl* **demi-fines***) adj* COMM : **petits pois ~s** garden peas ▪ **haricots ~s** green beans.

demi-finale [dəmifinal] *(pl* **demi-finales***) nf* semifinal ▪ **les ~s femmes/hommes** the women's/men's semifinals.

demi-finaliste [dəmifinalist] *(pl* **demi-finalistes***) nmf* semifinalist.

demi-fond [dəmifɔ̃] *nm inv* **1.** [activité] middle-distance running ▪ **faire du ~** to do middle-distance running **2.** [course] middle-distance race.

demi-frère [dəmifrɛr] *(pl* **demi-frères***) nm* half-brother.

demi-gros [dəmigro] *nm inv* wholesale *(dealing in retail quantities).*

demi-heure [dəmijœr] *(pl* **demi-heures***) nf* half-hour ▪ **une ~** half an hour ▪ **il y en a un toutes les ~s** there's one every half-hour.

demi-jour [dəmiʒur] *(pl* **demi-jours***) nm* [clarté] half-light ▪ [crépuscule] twilight, dusk.

demi-journée [dəmiʒurne] *(pl* **demi-journées***) nf* half-day, half-a-day ▪ **une ~ de travail** half a day's work, a half-day's work ▪ **je lui dois sa ~** I owe her half-a-day's pay *ou* for half-a-day's work.

démilitarisation [demilitarizasjɔ̃] *nf* demilitarization.

démilitariser [3] [demilitarize] *vt* to demilitarize.

demi-litre [dəmilitr] *(pl* **demi-litres***) nm* half-litre, half a litre ▪ **un ~ de lait, s'il vous plaît** half a litre of milk please.

demi-longueur [dəmilɔ̃gœr] *(pl* **demi-longueurs***) nf* half-length, half a length ▪ **une ~ d'avance** a half-length's lead.

demi-lune [dəmilyn] *(pl* **demi-lunes***) nf* [ouvrage fortifié] demi-lune, half-moon.
◆ **en demi-lune** *loc adj* half-moon *(modif)*, half-moon-shaped.

demi-mesure [dəmiməzyr] *(pl* **demi-mesures***) nf* **1.** [compromis] half measure ▪ **elle ne connaît pas les ~ s** *ou* **ne fait pas de** *fam* **~s** she doesn't do things by halves **2.** [moitié d'une mesure] half measure.

demi-mondaine [dəmimɔ̃dɛn] *(pl* **demi-mondaines***) nf* *arch* demimondaine.

demi-mot [dəmimo] ◆ **à demi-mot** *loc adv* : **il comprend à ~** he doesn't need to have things spelled out for him ▪ **on se comprend à ~** we know how each other's mind works.

déminage [deminaʒ] *nm* [sur la terre] mine clearance ▪ [en mer] mine sweeping.

déminer [3] [demine] *vt* to clear of mines.

déminéraliser [3] [demineralize] *vt* **1.** [eau] to demineralize **2.** PHYSIOL to deprive of minerals.
◆ **se déminéraliser** *vpi* [malade] to become deficient in essential minerals.

démineur [deminœr] ◇ *adj m* bomb-disposal *(modif).*
◇ *nm* bomb-disposal expert, member of a bomb-disposal unit.

demi-pause [dəmipoz] *(pl* **demi-pauses***) nf* minim *UK ou* half-note *US* rest.

demi-pension [dəmipɑ̃sjɔ̃] *(pl* **demi-pensions***) nf* [à l'hôtel] half-board ▪ **être en ~** ÉDUC to have school lunches *ou* dinners.

demi-pensionnaire [dəmipɑ̃sjɔnɛr] *(pl* **demi-pensionnaires***) nmf* pupil who has school dinners.

demi-portion [dəmipɔrsjɔ̃] *(pl* **demi-portions***) nf* **1.** [moitié de portion] half-helping **2.** *fam hum* [personne] half-pint, pipsqueak.

demi-queue [dəmikø] *(pl* **demi-queues***) adj & nm* : **un (piano) ~** a baby grand (piano).

démis, e [demi, iz] *pp* ▷ **démettre**.

demi-saison [dəmisɛzɔ̃] *(pl* **demi-saisons***) nf* [printemps] spring ▪ [automne] autumn, fall *US* ▪ **un temps de ~** the sort of mild weather you get in spring or autumn.

demi-sel [dəmisɛl] *nm inv* **1.** [beurre] slightly salted butter **2.** [fromage] Demi-sel *(slightly salted cream cheese)* **3.** △ *arg crime* [souteneur] small-time pimp ▪ [voyou] small-time gangster.

demi-siècle [dəmisjɛkl] *(pl* **demi-siècles***) nm* half-century.

demi-sœur [dəmisœr] *(pl* **demi-sœurs***) nf* half-sister.

demi-sommeil [dəmisɔmɛj] *(pl* **demi-sommeils***) nm* half-sleep, doze, drowsiness ▪ **dans mon ~, j'ai entendu...** while I was half asleep, I heard...

demi-soupir [dəmisupir] *(pl* **demi-soupirs***) nm* quaver *UK OU* eighth note *US* rest.

démission [demisjɔ̃] *nf* **1.** [départ] resignation ▪ **donner sa ~** to hand in *ou* to tender *sout* one's resignation, to resign **2.** [irresponsabilité] abdication of responsibility ▪ **à cause de la ~ des parents** because of the refusal of parents to shoulder their responsibilities.

démissionnaire [demisjɔnɛr] ◇ *adj* resigning, outgoing.
◇ *nmf* person resigning ▪ **les ~s** those who have resigned.

démissionner [3] [demisjɔne] ◇ *vi* **1.** [quitter son emploi] to resign, to hand in one's resignation *ou* notice ▪ **~ de son poste de directeur** to resign (one's position) as manager **2.** [refuser les responsabilités] to fail to shoulder one's responsibilities ▪ **~ devant qqn** to give in to sb ▪ **~ devant qqch** to give in when faced with sthg ▪ **c'est trop difficile, je démissionne** *fam* it's too hard, I give up.
◇ *vt fam* [renvoyer] : **~ qqn** to talk sb into resigning.

démit *etc v* ▷ **démettre**.

demi-tarif [dəmitarif] *(pl* **demi-tarifs***) nm* [billet] half-price ticket ▪ [carte] half-price card ▪ [abonnement] half-price subscription ▪ **voyager à ~** to travel at half-fare.

demi-teinte [dəmitɛ̃t] *(pl* **demi-teintes***) nf* halftone.
◆ **en demi-teinte** *loc adj* **1.** PHOTO halftone **2.** [subtil] subtle, delicate ▪ **sa musique/personnalité en ~** her subtle music/personality.

demi-ton [dəmitɔ̃] *(pl* **demi-tons***) nm* semitone *UK*, half step *US* ▪ **~ diatonique/chromatique** diatonic/chromatic semitone *UK OU* half step *US*.

demi-tour [dəmitur] *(pl* **demi-tours***) nm* **1.** [pivotement] about-face, about-turn ▪ **faire un ~** [gén - MIL] to about-face, to about-turn ▪ **~, droite!** MIL (right) about face! **2.** AUTO U-turn ▪ **faire un ~** to do *ou* to pull a U-turn ▪ **faire ~** [piéton] to retrace one's steps ; [conducteur] to turn back.

démiurge [demjyrʒ] *nm* demiurge, creator.

démobilisateur, trice [demɔbilizatœr, tris] *adj* [démotivant] demobilizing.

démobilisation [demɔbilizasjɔ̃] *nf* **1.** MIL demobilization ▪ **à la ~** when demobilization time came **2.** [démotivation] growing apathy ▪ **on constate une ~ de l'opinion publique sur ces questions** public opinion has become apathetic about *ou* has turned away from these issues.

démobiliser [3] [demɔbilize] *vt* **1.** MIL to demobilize **2.** [démotiver] to cause to lose interest, to demotivate.

démocrate [demɔkrat] ◇ *adj* **1.** [gén] democratic **2.** [dans des noms de partis] Democratic.
◇ *nmf* **1.** [gén] democrat **2.** [aux États-Unis] Democrat.

démocrate-chrétien, enne [demɔkratkretjɛ̃, ɛn] *(mpl* **démocrates-chrétiens**, *fpl* **démocrates-chrétiennes***) adj & nm, f* Christian Democrat.

démocratie [demɔkrasi] *nf* **1.** [système] democracy ▪ **~ directe/représentative** direct/representative democracy ▪ **~ populaire** people's democracy **2.** [pays] democracy, democratic country ▪ **vivre en ~** to live in a democracy ▪ **on est en ~, non?** *fam* this is a free country, as far as I know!

démocratique [demɔkratik] *adj* **1.** POLIT democratic **2.** [respectueux des désirs de tous] democratic ▪ **notre groupe est très ~** in our group, everyone gets a chance to have their say.

démocratiquement [demɔkratikmɑ̃] *adv* democratically.

démocratisation [demɔkratizasjɔ̃] *nf* **1.** POLIT democratization, making more democratic **2.** [mise à la portée de tous] : **la ~ du ski** putting skiing holidays within everyone's reach.

démocratiser [3] [demɔkratize] *vt* **1.** POLIT to democratize, to make more democratic **2.** [rendre accessible] to bring within everyone's reach ▪ **~ les voyages à l'étranger** to put foreign travel within everyone's reach.
◆ **se démocratiser** *vpi* **1.** POLIT to become more democratic **2.** [devenir accessible] to become available to anyone.

Démocrite [demɔkrit] *npr* Democritus.

démodé, e [demɔde] *adj* [style, technique] old-fashioned, outdated, out-of-date ▪ [parents] old-fashioned.

démoder [3] [demɔde] ◆ **se démoder** *vpi* to go out of fashion *ou* vogue, to become old-fashioned.

démographie [demɔgrafi] *nf* [science] demography ▪ [croissance de la population] population growth.

démographique [demɔgrafik] *adj* demographic, population *(modif)* ▪ **poussée/explosion ~** population increase/explosion.

demoiselle [dəmwazɛl] *nf* **1.** [jeune femme] young lady ▪ **~ d'honneur** bridesmaid ▪ **~ de compagnie** lady's companion **2.** *vieilli* [célibataire] maiden lady **3.** ZOOL dragonfly **4.** [outil] rammer.

démolir [32] [demɔlir] *vt* **1.** [détruire - immeuble, mur] to demolish, to pull *ou* to tear down *(sép)* ; [- jouet, voiture] to wreck, to smash up *(sép)* **2.** [anéantir - argument, théorie] to demolish ; [- projet] to ruin, to play havoc with ; [- réputation, autorité] to shatter, to destroy ▪ **l'alcool lui a démoli la santé** alcohol ruined *ou* wrecked his health **3.** *fam* [anéantir - auteur, roman] to pan **4.** *fam* [battre] to thrash, to beat up *(sép)* ▪ **~ le portrait à qqn** to beat *ou* to smash sb's face in **5.** *fam* [épuiser - physiquement] to do in *(sép)* ; [- moralement] to shatter.
◆ **se démolir** *vpt* : **se ~ la santé** to ruin one's health ▪ **se ~ la santé à faire qqch** *fam* to kill o.s. *ou* to bust a gut doing sthg.

démolisseur [demɔlisœr] *nm* **1.** [ouvrier] demolition worker, wrecker *US* **2.** [entrepreneur] demolition contractor **3.** [détracteur] destructive critic.

démolition [demɔlisjɔ̃] *nf* demolition, pulling *ou* tearing down.
◆ **de démolition** *loc adj* : **chantier/entreprise de ~** demolition site/contractors ▪ **une campagne de ~ systématique** *fig* a systematic campaign of destruction.
◆ **en démolition** *loc adj* being demolished, under demolition.

démon [demɔ̃] *nm* **1.** RELIG : **le ~** the Devil ▪ **être possédé du ~** to be possessed by the devil ⊙ **comme un ~** like a thing possessed **2.** MYTHOL daemon, daimon ▪ **son ~ intérieur** *fig* [mauvais] the evil *ou* demon within (him) ; [bon] the good spirit within (him) **3.** [tentation] demon ⊙ **le ~ de midi** *lust affecting a man in mid-life* **4.** [enfant turbulent] : **(petit) ~** (little) devil *ou* demon.

démonétiser [3] [demɔnetize] *vt* FIN to demonetize, to demonetarize.

démoniaque [demɔnjak] ◇ *adj* [ruse, rire] demonic *sout*, diabolical, fiendish.
◇ *nmf* person possessed by the devil.

démonstrateur, trice [demɔ̃stratœr, tris] *nm, f* COMM demonstrator, salesperson *(in charge of demonstrations)*.

démonstratif, ive [demɔ̃stratif, iv] *adj* **1.** [expressif] demonstrative, expressive, effusive ▪ **peu ~** reserved, undemonstrative **2.** [convaincant] demonstrative, conclusive **3.** GRAMM demonstrative.
◆ **démonstratif** *nm* [pronom] demonstrative pronoun ▪ [adjectif] demonstrative adjective.

démonstration [demɔ̃strasjɔ̃] *nf* **1.** LOGIQUE & MATH [preuve] demonstration, proof ▪ [ensemble de formules] demonstration ▪ **la ~ n'est plus à faire** *fig* it has been proved beyond all

doubt ➲ **~ par l'absurde** reductio ad absurdum **2.** COMM demonstration ▪ **faire la ~ d'un aspirateur** to demonstrate a vacuum cleaner **3.** [prestation] display, demonstration ▪ **~ aérienne** air display ▪ **faire une ~ de karaté** to give a karate demonstration **4.** [fait de manifester] demonstration, show ▪ **faire une ~ de force** to display one's strength.
◆ **démonstrations** *nfpl* [effusions] (great) show of feeling, gushing ▪ [crises] outbursts ▪ **~s de tendresse/joie/colère** show of tenderness/joy/anger ▪ **faire de grandes ~s d'amitié à qqn** to put on a great show of friendship for sb.

démontable [demɔ̃tabl] *adj* which can be dismantled *ou* taken to pieces.

démontage [demɔ̃taʒ] *nm* dismantling, taking to pieces ▪ **pour faciliter le ~** to make it easier to dismantle.

démonté, e [demɔ̃te] *adj* [mer] raging, stormy ▪ **par une mer ~e** in heavy seas.

démonte-pneu [demɔ̃tpnø] (*pl* **démonte-pneus**) *nm* tyre lever *UK*, tire iron *US*.

démonter [3] [demɔ̃te] *vt* **1.** [désassembler - bibliothèque, machine] to dismantle, to take down *(sép)* ; [- moteur] to strip down *(sép)*, to dismantle ; [- fusil, pendule] to dismantle, to take to pieces, to take apart *(sép)* ; [- manche de vêtement, pièce rapportée] to take off *(sép)* **2.** [détacher - pneu, store, persienne] to remove, to take off *(sép)* ; [- rideau] to take down *(sép)* **3.** [décontenancer] to take aback *(sép)* ▪ **ma question l'a démontée** she was taken aback *ou* flummoxed by my question ▪ **ne te laisse pas ~ par son ironie** don't be flustered by his ironic remarks **4.** ÉQUIT to unseat, to unhorse.
◆ **se démonter** ◇ *vp (emploi passif)* to be taken to pieces, to be dismantled ▪ **ça se démonte facilement** it can be easily dismantled.
◇ *vpi* [se troubler] to lose countenance, to get flustered.

démontrable [demɔ̃trabl] *adj* demonstrable, provable ▪ **c'est facilement ~** it's easy to prove.

démontrer [3] [demɔ̃tre] *vt* **1.** MATH to prove ➲ **~ qqch par A plus B** to prove sthg conclusively **2.** [montrer par raisonnement] to prove, to demonstrate ▪ **~ son erreur à qqn** to prove to sb that he/she's wrong, to prove sb wrong **3.** [révéler] to show, to reveal, to indicate.

démoralisant, e [demɔralizɑ̃, ɑ̃t] *adj* [remarque, nouvelle] demoralizing, disheartening, depressing ▪ **elle est ~e!** she's depressing!

démoralisateur, trice [demɔralizatœr, tris] *adj* demoralizing.

démoralisé, e [demɔralize] *adj* demoralized, down ▪ **il était complètement ~** he was completely demoralized, he's really down.

démoraliser [3] [demɔralize] *vt* to demoralize, to dishearten ▪ **il ne faut pas te laisser ~** you mustn't let it get you down.
◆ **se démoraliser** *vpi* to become demoralized, to lose heart.

démordre [76] [demɔrdr] ◆ **démordre de** *vp+prép* : **ne pas ~ de** to stick to, to stand by ▪ **il ne démord pas de son idée** he won't budge from his position ▪ **rien ne m'en fera ~** I'll stick to my guns come what may ▪ **elle n'en démord pas** she won't have it any other way.

démotivant, e [demɔtivɑ̃, ɑ̃t] *adj* demotivating, disheartening, dispiriting ▪ **c'est plutôt ~!** it's not exactly encouraging!

démotiver [3] [demɔtive] *vt* to demotivate, to discourage ▪ **les salaires les ont démotivés** the salary levels have discouraged *ou* demotivated them.

démoulage [demulaʒ] *nm* [d'une statuette] removal from the mould ▪ [d'un gâteau] turning out.

démouler [3] [demule] *vt* [statuette] to remove from the mould ▪ [gâteau] to turn out *(sép)* ▪ [tarte] to remove from its tin.

démultiplication [demyltiplikasjɔ̃] *nf* : **(rapport de) ~** reduction ratio.

démultiplier [10] [demyltiplije] *vt* **1.** MÉCAN to reduce, to gear down *(sép)* **2.** *fam* [multiplier] to increase ▪ **~ les pouvoirs de décision** to reinforce the executive through increased powers.

démuni, e [demyni] *adj* **1.** [pauvre] destitute **2.** [sans défense] powerless, resourceless.

démunir [32] [demynir] *vt* to deprive ▪ **~ qqn de qqch** to deprive *ou* to divest sb of sthg.
◆ **se démunir de** *vp+prép* to part with, to give up.

démuseler [24] [demyzle] *vt* [animal] to unmuzzle, to remove the muzzle from ▪ **~ la presse** to lift restrictions on the freedom of the press.

démystifiant, e [demistifjɑ̃, ɑ̃t] *adj* **1.** [qui détrompe] eye-opening **2.** [qui rend moins mystérieux] demystifying.

démystificateur, trice [demistifikatœr, tris] ◇ *adj* **1.** [qui détrompe] eye-opening **2.** [qui rend moins mystérieux] demystifying.
◇ *nm, f* demystifier.

démystification [demistifikasjɔ̃] *nf* **1.** [d'une dupe] opening the eyes of **2.** [d'un mystère, d'un phénomène] demystification.

démystifier [9] [demistifje] *vt* **1.** [détromper] to open the eyes of **2.** [rendre plus clair] to explain, to demystify.

démythifier [9] [demitifje] *vt* to demythologize, to make less mythical *ou* into less of a myth.

dénatalité [denatalite] *nf* fall *ou* drop in the birth rate.

dénationaliser [3] [denasjɔnalize] *vt* to denationalize.

dénaturaliser [3] [denatyralize] *vt* to denaturalize.

dénaturé, e [denatyre] *adj* **1.** [alcool] denatured **2.** [pervers - goût] unnatural, perverted.

dénaturer [3] [denatyre] *vt* **1.** [modifier - alcool] to adulterate, to denature ; [- saveur] to alter, to adulterate **2.** [fausser - propos, faits, intention] to distort, to misrepresent, to twist ▪ **vous dénaturez mes propos!** you're twisting my words *ou* putting words into my mouth!

dénégation [denegasjɔ̃] *nf* **1.** [contestation] denial ▪ **convaincu de son innocence par des ~s énergiques** persuaded of his innocence by his energetic denials **2.** PSYCHOL denial.
◆ **de dénégation** *loc adj* [geste, attitude] denying, of denial ▪ **en signe de ~** as a sign of disagreement.

déneiger [23] [deneʒe] *vt* to clear of snow, to clear snow from.

déni [deni] *nm* **1.** DR denial ▪ **~ de justice** denial of justice **2.** PSYCHOL : **~ de réalité** denial.

déniaiser [4] [denjeze] *vt* **1.** [dépuceler] : **~ qqn** to take away sb's innocence **2.** [rendre moins naïf] to open the eyes of.
◆ **se déniaiser** *vpi* [devenir moins naïf] to learn the ways of the world.

dénicher [3] [deniʃe] ◇ *vt* **1.** *fam* [trouver - collier, trésor] find, to unearth ; [- informations] to dig up *ou* out *(sép)* ; [- chanteur, cabaret] to discover, to spot ▪ **elle a l'art de ~ des antiquités intéressantes** she has a talent for hunting out interesting antiques **2.** [oiseau] to remove from the nest.
◇ *vi* [oiseau] to leave the nest, to fly away.

dénicheur, euse [deniʃœr, øz] *nm, f* **1.** [d'oiseaux] bird's nester **2.** [découvreur] : **~ de talents** talent scout *ou* spotter ▪ **~ de bibelots rares** curio-hunter.

denier [dənje] *nm* **1.** HIST [monnaie - romaine] denarius ; [- française] denier ▪ **j'en suis de mes ~s** I had to pay with my own money ➲ **le ~ du culte** contribution to parish costs ▪ **le ~ de Saint-Pierre** *annual diocesan gift made to the Pope (since 1849)* ▪ **les ~s publics** *ou* **de l'État** public money **2.** TEXT denier ▪ **bas de 20 ~s** 20-denier stockings.

dénier [9] [denje] *vt* **1.** [rejeter - responsabilité] to deny, to disclaim **2.** [refuser] to deny, to refuse ▪ **~ qqch à qqn** to deny *ou* to refuse sb sthg.

dénigrement [denigrəmɑ̃] *nm* denigration, disparagement ▪ **le mot ne s'emploie que par ~** the word is only used disparagingly.
◆ **de dénigrement** *loc adj* : **esprit/paroles de ~** disparaging spirit/remarks ▪ **campagne de ~** smear campaign.

dénigrer [3] [denigre] *vt* to disparage, to denigrate, to run down *(sép)*.

denim [dənim] *nm* denim.

dénivelé *nm* difference in level *ou* height.

dénivelée *nf* = **dénivelé**.

déniveler [24] [denivle] *vt* to make uneven.

dénivellation [denivelasjɔ̃] *nf*, **dénivellement** [denivɛlmɑ̃] *nm* **1.** [action] making uneven, putting out of level **2.** [pente] slope ▪ **les ~s de la route** the dips in the road.

dénivelle *etc* [denivɛl] *v* ▷ **déniveler**.

dénombrable [denɔ̃brabl] *adj* countable ▪ **non ~** uncountable.

dénombrement [denɔ̃brəmɑ̃] *nm* counting (out), count ▪ **faire un ~ de la population** to do a population count.

dénombrer [3] [denɔ̃bre] *vt* to count (out) ▪ **on dénombre 130 morts à ce jour** at the latest count there were 130 dead.

dénominateur [denɔminatœr] *nm* MATH denominator ▪ **~ commun** common denominator ▪ **plus grand ~ commun** highest common denominator.

dénomination [denɔminasjɔ̃] *nf* **1.** [fait de nommer] naming, denomination *sout* **2.** [nom] designation, denomination, name ▪ **~ sociale** company name.

dénommé, e [denɔme] *adj* : **le ~ Joubert** the man called Joubert ▪ **une ~e Madame Barda** a certain *ou* one Mrs Barda.

dénommer [3] [denɔme] *vt* **1.** [donner un nom à] to name, to call **2.** DR to name.

dénoncer [16] [denɔ̃se] *vt* **1.** [complice, fraudeur] to denounce, to inform on *(insép)* ▪ [camarade de classe] to tell on *(insép)* ▪ **~ qqn aux autorités** to denounce sb *ou* to give sb away to the authorities **2.** [condamner - pratiques, dangers, abus] to denounce, to condemn **3.** [annuler - armistice, traité] to renege on *(insép)* ; [- contrat] to terminate **4.** *sout* [dénoter] to indicate, to betray.
◆ **se dénoncer** *vp (emploi réfléchi)* to give o.s. up.

dénonciateur, trice [denɔ̃sjatœr, tris] ◇ *adj* denunciatory ▪ **lettre dénonciatrice** letter of denunciation.
◇ *nm, f* informer.

dénonciation [denɔ̃sjasjɔ̃] *nf* **1.** [accusation] denunciation ▪ **arrêté sur la ~ de son frère** arrested on the strength of his brother's denunciation ▶ **~ calomnieuse** false accusation **2.** [révélation - d'une injustice] exposure, denouncing, castigating **3.** [rupture - d'un traité] denunciation, reneging on ; [- d'un contrat] termination.

dénoter [3] [denɔte] *vt* **1.** LING & PHILOS to denote **2.** [être signe de] to denote, to indicate.

dénouement [denumɑ̃] *nm* [d'un film, d'une histoire, d'une pièce] dénouement ▪ [d'une crise, d'une affaire] outcome, conclusion ▪ **un heureux ~** a happy ending, a favourable outcome.

dénouer [6] [denwe] *vt* **1.** [défaire - ficelle, lacet] to undo, to untie, to unknot ; [- cheveux] to let down *(sép)*, to loosen **2.** [résoudre - intrigue] to unravel, to untangle.
◆ **se dénouer** ◇ *vpi* **1.** [cheveux] to come loose *ou* undone ▪ [lacet] to come undone *ou* untied **2.** [crise] to end, to be resolved.
◇ *vpt* : **se ~ les cheveux** to let down one's hair *pr*.

dénoyauter [3] [denwajote] *vt* to stone *UK*, to pit *US*.

dénoyauteur [denwajotœr] *nm* stoner *UK*, pitter *US*.

denrée [dɑ̃re] *nf* commodity ▪ **~s de première nécessité** staple foods, staples ▶ **~s alimentaires** foodstuffs ▪ **~s périssables** perishable goods, perishables ▪ **c'est une ~ rare que la générosité** generosity is hard to come by.

dense [dɑ̃s] *adj* **1.** [épais - brouillard, végétation] thick, dense **2.** [serré - foule] thick, tightly packed ; [- circulation] heavy ▪ **population peu ~** sparse population **3.** [concis - style] compact, condensed **4.** PHYS dense.

densément [dɑ̃semɑ̃] *adv* [cultivé] thickly, densely ▪ [peuplé] densely ▪ [écrit] tightly, tautly.

densification [dɑ̃sifikasjɔ̃] *nf* [du brouillard, de la foule] thickening ▪ **la ~ de la population sur le littoral** the increasing concentration of population along the coast.

densifier [9] [dɑ̃sifje] *vt* to make denser, to increase the density of.

densité [dɑ̃site] *nf* **1.** PHYS density ▪ **~ de charge/courant** ÉLECTR charge/current density **2.** [du brouillard, de la foule] denseness, thickness ▪ **selon la ~ de la circulation** depending on how heavy the traffic is ▶ **~ de population** population density ▪ **pays à faible/forte ~ de population** sparsely/densely populated country **3.** PHOTO density **4.** INFORM : **~ d'enregistrement** packing *ou* recording *ou* data density.

densitométrie [dɑ̃sitometri] *nf* densimetry, densitometry ▪ **densitométrie osseuse** MÉD bone densimetry *ou* densitometry.

dent [dɑ̃] *nf* **1.** ANAT tooth ▪ **faire** *ou* **percer ses ~s** to cut one's teeth, to teethe ▶ **~s du bas/haut** lower/upper teeth ▪ **~s de devant/du fond** front/back teeth ▪ **~ de lait** baby *ou* milk *UK* tooth ▪ **~ permanente** permanent *ou* second tooth ▪ **~ à pivot** post ▪ **~ de sagesse** wisdom tooth ▪ **fausses ~s** false teeth ▪ **avoir la ~** *fam* to be ravenous *ou* starving ▪ **avoir** *ou* **garder une ~ contre qqn** *fam* to have a grudge against sb, to bear sb a grudge ▪ **avoir les ~s longues** to fix one's sights high ▪ **être sur les ~s** *fam* [occupé] to be frantically busy ; [anxieux] to be stressed out ▪ **montrer les ~s** *pr* & *fig* to show one's teeth ▪ **parler entre ses ~s** to mutter ▪ **se faire les ~s** to cut one's teeth ▪ **l'escalade du mont Blanc, c'était juste pour se faire les ~s** climbing Mont Blanc was just for starters ▪ **on n'avait rien à se mettre sous la ~** we didn't have a thing to eat ▪ **tout ce qui lui tombe sous la ~** anything he can get his teeth into **2.** [de roue, d'engrenage] cog ▪ [de courroie] tooth **3.** [pointe - d'une scie, d'un peigne] tooth ; [- d'une fourchette, d'une herse] tooth, prong **4.** BOT serration **5.** GÉOGR jag **6.** ÉLECTRON : **~s de scie** sawtooth waveform.
◆ **à belles dents** *loc adv* : **mordre dans** *ou* **croquer** *ou* **manger qqch à belles ~s** *pr* to eat one's way through sthg ▪ **mordre dans** *ou* **croquer la vie à belles ~s** *fig* to live (one's) life to the full.
◆ **en dents de scie** *loc adj* [couteau] serrated ▪ **évolution en ~s de scie** uneven development.

dentaire [dɑ̃tɛr] ◇ *adj* [hygiène] oral, dental ▪ [cabinet, études, école] dental.
◇ *nf* **1.** *fam* ÉDUC dental school ▪ **faire ~** to study dentistry **2.** BOT toothwort.

dental, e, aux [dɑ̃tal, o] *adj* PHON dental.
◆ **dentale** *nf* dental (consonant).

dent-de-lion [dɑ̃dəljɔ̃] (*pl* **dents-de-lion**) *nf* dandelion.

denté, e [dɑ̃te] *adj* [courroie] toothed ▪ [feuille] serrate, dentate.

dentelé, e [dɑ̃tle] *adj* [contour] jagged, indented ▪ [feuille] dentate, serrate.

denteler [24] [dɑ̃tle] *vt* to indent the edge of, to give a jagged outline to ▪ **machine/ciseaux à ~** pinking machine/shears.

dentelle [dɑ̃tɛl] ◇ *nf* **1.** [tissu] lace, lacework ▪ **faire de la ~** to do lacework ▪ **des gants de** *ou* **en ~** lace gloves ▶ **~ à l'aiguille** *ou* **au point** lace, needlepoint ▪ **~ au fuseau** pillow lace ▪ **~ de papier** lacy paper ▪ **il ne fait pas dans la ~** *fam* he doesn't go in for subtleties **2.** [morceau de tissu] piece of lacework.
◇ *adj inv* **1.** [vêtement] : **bas ~** lace stocking **2.** CULIN : **crêpes ~** paper-thin pancakes.

dentellier, ère [dɑ̃təlje, ɛr] *nm, f* lacemaker, laceworker.

dentelure [dɑ̃tlyr] *nf* **1.** [découpe] serration, jagged edge **2.** ARCHIT denticulation **3.** [d'un timbre] perforations.

denticule [dɑ̃tikyl] *nm* ZOOL denticle.

◆ **denticules** *nmpl* ARCHIT row of dentils.

dentier [dɑ̃tje] *nm* denture, dentures, dental plate.

dentifrice [dɑ̃tifris] ◇ *adj* : **eau ~** mouthwash ■ **pâte ~** toothpaste ■ **poudre ~** tooth powder.
◇ *nm* toothpaste.

dentine [dɑ̃tin] *nf* dentin, dentine.

dentiste [dɑ̃tist] *nmf* dentist.

dentisterie [dɑ̃tistəri] *nf* dentistry.

dentition [dɑ̃tisjɔ̃] *nf* **1.** [dents] teeth, dentition *spéc* ■ **avoir une bonne ~** to have good teeth **2.** [poussée] tooth growth.

denture [dɑ̃tyr] *nf* **1.** ANAT & ZOOL set of teeth, dentition *spéc* **2.** TECHNOL teeth, cogs.

dénucléariser [3] [denyklearize] *vt* [région] to denuclearize.

dénudé, e [denyde] *adj* [dos, corps] bare, unclothed ■ [crâne] bald ■ [terrain] bare, bald ■ [fil électrique] bare.

dénuder [3] [denyde] *vt* [dos, épaules] to leave bare ■ [sol, câble, os, veine] to strip.
◆ **se dénuder** *vpi* **1.** [se déshabiller] to strip (off) **2.** [se dégarnir - crâne] to be balding ; [- arbre] to become bare ; [- fil électrique] to show through.

dénué, e [denɥe] *adj* : **~ de** lacking in, devoid of ■ **~ d'intérêt** utterly uninteresting, devoid of interest ■ **~ d'ambiguïté** unambiguous ■ **~ de sincérité** lacking in *ou* devoid of sincerity ■ **être ~ de tout** to be destitute.

dénuement [denymɑ̃] *nm* destitution ■ **être dans le ~ le plus complet** to be utterly destitute.

dénutri, e [denytri] ◇ *adj* malnourished.
◇ *nm, f person suffering from malnutrition.*

déodorant [deɔdɔrɑ̃] ◇ *adj m* deodorant *(modif)*.
◇ *nm* deodorant.

déontologie [deɔ̃tɔlɔʒi] *nf* professional code of ethics, deontology ■ **la ~ médicale** the medical code of ethics.

déontologique [deɔ̃tɔlɔʒik] *adj* ethical, deontological.

dépannage [depanaʒ] *nm* **1.** [réparation] fixing, repairing, repair job ■ **faire un ~** to fix a breakdown **2.** *fam* [aide] helping out.
◆ **de dépannage** *loc adj* : **voiture de ~** breakdown lorry *UK*, tow truck *US* ■ **service de ~** breakdown service.

dépanner [3] [depane] *vt* **1.** [réparer - voiture, mécanisme] to repair, to fix ■ **~ qqn sur le bord de la route** *fam* to help sb who's broken down on the side of the road ■ *(en usage absolu)* **nous dépannons 24 heures sur 24** we have a 24-hour breakdown service **2.** *fam* [aider] to help out *(sép)*, to tide over *(sép)* ■ **elle m'a dépanné en me prêtant sa voiture** she helped me out by lending me her car.

dépanneur, euse [depanœr, øz] *nm, f* [d'appareils] repairman (*f* repairwoman) ■ [de véhicules] breakdown mechanic.
◆ **dépanneur** *nm Québec* ≃ corner shop *UK*, ≃ convenience store *US*.
◆ **dépanneuse** *nf* breakdown lorry *UK*, tow truck *US*.

dépareillé, e [depareje] *adj* **1.** [mal assorti - serviettes, chaussettes] odd ■ **mes draps sont tous ~s** none of my sheets match ■ **articles ~s** oddments **2.** [incomplet - service, collection] incomplete **3.** [isolé] : **un volume ~ d'une collection** a single volume (that used to be part) of a collection.

dépareiller [4] [depareje] *vt* **1.** [désassortir] : **~ des draps** to put unmatched *ou* non matching sheets together **2.** [ôter des éléments à] to leave gaps in.

déparer [3] [depare] *vt* [paysage] to disfigure, to spoil, to be a blight on ■ [visage] to disfigure ■ **un compact qui ne dépare pas ma collection** a compact disc well worthy of my collection.

dépars *etc v* ▷ **départir**.

départ [depar] *nm* **1.** TRANSP departure ■ **le ~ du train est à 7 h** the train leaves at 7a.m ■ **le ~ est dans une heure** we're leaving in an hour ➤ **hall des ~s** RAIL (departure) concourse ; AÉRON & NAUT departure lounge
2. [fait de quitter un lieu] going ■ **on en a parlé après son ~** we discussed it after he went ➤ **les grands ~s** *the mass exodus of people from Paris and other major cities at the beginning of the holiday period, especially in August* ■ **le grand ~** *pr* the big move ; *fig* the passage into the great beyond ■ **être sur le ~** to be ready to go
3. [d'une course] start ■ **douze chevaux/voitures/coureurs ont pris le ~ (de la course)** there were twelve starters ➤ **prendre un bon/mauvais ~** *pr* & *fig* to get off to a good/bad start ■ **prendre un nouveau ~ dans la vie** to make a fresh start in life, to turn over a new leaf
4. [de son travail] departure ■ [démission] resignation ■ **au ~ du directeur** when the manager left *ou* quit (the firm) ■ **~ en préretraite** early retirement ■ **~ volontaire** voluntary redundancy
5. [origine] start, beginning ■ **au ~** at first, to begin with
6. COMM : **prix ~ usine** factory price, ex works price *UK*
7. *sout* [distinction] distinction, separation, differentiation ■ **faire le ~ entre** to draw a distinction between, to distinguish between.
◆ **au départ de** *loc prép* : **visites au ~ des Tuileries** tours departing from the Tuileries ■ **au ~ du Caire, tout allait encore bien entre eux** when they left Cairo, everything was still fine between them.
◆ **de départ** *loc adj* **1.** [gare, quai, heure] departure *(modif)* **2.** [initial] : **l'idée de ~** the initial *ou* original idea ■ **prix de ~** [dans une enchère] upset *ou* asking price ■ **salaire de ~** initial *ou* starting salary.

départager [17] [departaʒe] *vt* **1.** [séparer - ex-æquo] to decide between ■ **~ l'un de l'autre** to decide between one and the other **2.** ADMIN & POLIT to settle the voting, to give the casting vote.

département [departəmɑ̃] *nm* **1.** [du territoire français] département, department ■ **les ~s et régions d'outre-mer** French overseas departments **2.** [service] department, service, division ■ **le ~ du contentieux** the legal department **3.** [ministère] department, ministry ■ **~ ministériel** ministry ■ **le Département d'État** the State Department, the Department of State **4.** *Suisse administrative authority in a Swiss canton.*

DÉPARTEMENT

One of the three main administrative divisions in France. There are a hundred in all, four of which are overseas. Each is run by a ***conseil général***, which has its headquarters in the principal town of the ***département***.
Départements are numbered in alphabetical order (with a few exceptions in Île de France). The number is often used to refer to the department, particularly for the Paris area, and it is not uncommon to hear people say ***j'habite dans le 91*** meaning ***j'habite dans l'Essonne***.

départemental, e, aux [departəmɑ̃tal, o] *adj* **1.** [des départements français] of the département, departmental **2.** [dans une entreprise, une organisation] departmental, sectional **3.** [ministériel] ministerial.
◆ **départementale** *nf* [route] secondary road, ≃ B-road *UK*.

départementalisation [departəmɑ̃talizasjɔ̃] *nf* ADMIN conferring the statute of département on.

départementaliser [3] [departəmɑ̃talize] *vt* **1.** [territoire d'outre-mer] to confer the statute of département on, to make into a département **2.** [budget, responsabilité] to devolve to the départements.

départir [32] [departir] *vt litt* to assign, to apportion ■ **~ une tâche à qqn** to assign *ou* to apportion a task to sb.
◆ **se départir de** *vp+prép* : **se ~ de** to depart from, to abandon, to lose ■ **sans se ~ de sa bonne humeur** without losing his good humour ■ **elle ne se départit pas de son calme** she remained unruffled.

dépassé, e [depase] *adj* [mentalité, technique] outdated, old-fashioned ■ **c'est ~ tout ça!** all that's old hat! ■ **tu es ~, mon pauvre!** you're behind the times, my friend!

dépassement [depasmɑ̃] *nm* **1.** AUTO passing, overtaking *UK* **2.** [excès] exceeding, excess ■ **~ de coûts** cost overrun ■ **~ d'horaire de 15 minutes** overrun of 15 minutes ▶ **~ budgétaire** *ou* **de budget** FIN overspend ■ **être en ~ budgétaire** to be over budget **3.** [surpassement] : **~ (de soi-même)** surpassing o.s., transcending one's own capabilities **4.** ADMIN *charging, by a medical practitioner, of more than the standard fee recognized by the social services.*

dépasser [3] [depase] ◇ *vt* **1.** [doubler - voiture] to pass, to overtake *UK* ; [- coureur] to outrun, to outdistance ■ **se faire ~** [en voiture] to be overtaken
2. [aller au-delà de - hôtel, panneau] to pass, to go *ou* to get past ; [- piste d'atterrissage] to overshoot
3. [être plus grand que] to stand *ou* to be taller than ■ **elle me dépasse d'une tête** she's a head taller than me
4. [déborder sur] to go over *ou* beyond ■ **il a dépassé son temps de parole** he talked longer than had been agreed, he went over time ■ **votre renommée dépasse les frontières** your fame has spread abroad
5. [suivi d'une quantité, d'un chiffre] to exceed, to go beyond ■ **'ne pas ~ la dose prescrite'** 'do not exceed the stated dose' ■ **les socialistes nous dépassent en nombre** the socialists outnumber us, we're outnumbered by the socialists ■ **~ le budget de 15 millions** to go 15 million over budget ■ **je n'ai pas dépassé 60 km/h** I did not exceed *ou* I stayed below 60 km/h ■ **elle a dépassé la trentaine** she's turned thirty, she's over thirty ■ **ça dépasse mes moyens** it's beyond my means, it's more than I can afford
6. [surpasser - adversaire] to surpass, to be ahead of ■ **~ l'attente de qqn** to surpass *ou* to exceed sb's expectations ■ **cela dépasse tout ce que j'avais pu espérer** this is beyond all my hopes *ou* my wildest dreams ■ **~ qqn/qqch en : ~ qqn/qqch en drôlerie/stupidité** to be funnier/more stupid than sb/sthg ■ **ça dépasse tout ce que j'ai vu en vulgarité** for sheer vulgarity, it beats everything I've ever seen ■ **elle nous dépassait tous en musique** she was a far better musician than any of us
7. [outrepasser - ordres, droits] to go beyond, to overstep ■ **la tâche dépasse mes forces** the task is beyond me ■ **les mots ont dépassé ma pensée** I got carried away and said something I didn't mean ▶ **~ les bornes** *ou* **les limites** *ou* **la mesure** *ou* **la dose** *fam* to go too far, to overstep the mark
8. [dérouter] : **être dépassé par les événements** to be overtaken *ou* swamped by events ■ **une telle ignorance me dépasse** such ignorance defeats me ■ **les échecs, ça me dépasse!** chess is (quite) beyond me!
9. [surmonter] : **avoir dépassé un stade/une phase** to have gone beyond a stage/a phase.
◇ *vi* **1.** AUTO to pass, to overtake *UK* ■ **'interdiction de ~'** 'no overtaking *UK*, no passing *US*'
2. [étagère, balcon, corniche] to jut out, to protrude ■ **notre perron dépasse par rapport aux autres** our front steps stick out further than the others
3. [chemisier, doublure] to be hanging out *ou* untucked ■ **ton jupon dépasse!** your slip's showing! ■ **~ de** to be sticking out *ou* protruding *sout* from (under) ■ **pas une mèche ne dépassait de son chignon** her chignon was impeccable *ou* hadn't a hair out of place.
◆ **se dépasser** ◇ *vp (emploi réciproque)* to pass one another ■ **les voitures cherchent toutes à se ~** the cars are all jostling for position.
◇ *vpi* [se surpasser] to surpass *ou* to excel o.s.

dépassionner [3] [depasjɔne] *vt* [débat] to take the heat out of, to calm *ou* to cool down.

dépatouiller [3] [depatuje] ◆ **se dépatouiller** *vpi fam* to manage to get by ■ **qu'il se** *ou* **s'en dépatouille tout seul!** he can get out of this one by himself!

dépaver [3] [depave] *vt* to remove the cobblestones from.

dépaysant, e [depeizɑ̃, ɑ̃t] *adj* : **un voyage ~** a trip that gives you a complete change of scene.

dépaysement [depeizmɑ̃] *nm* **1.** [changement de cadre] change of scene *ou* scenery ■ **à Moscou, on a une extraordinaire impression de ~** when you're in Moscow everything feels totally unfamiliar **2.** [malaise] feeling of unfamiliarity ■ **les enfants n'aiment pas le ~** children don't like changes in environment.

dépayser [3] [depeize] *vt* **1.** [changer de cadre] to give a change of scenery *ou* surroundings to ■ **laissez-vous ~** treat yourself to a change of scene *ou* scenery **2.** [désorienter] to disorientate ■ **se sentir dépaysé** to feel like a stranger ■ **on fait tout pour que le touriste ne soit pas dépaysé** we do everything possible to make the tourist feel at home.

dépecer [29] [depəse] *vt* **1.** [démembrer - proie] to tear limb from limb ; [- volaille] to cut up *(sép)* **2.** [détruire - empire] to dismember, to carve up *(sép)*.

dépêche [depɛʃ] *nf* **1.** ADMIN dispatch ■ **~ diplomatique** diplomatic dispatch **2.** TÉLÉCOM : **~ (télégraphique)** telegram, wire ■ **envoyer une ~ à qqn** to wire *ou* to telegraph sb **3.** [nouvelle] news item *(sent through an agency)* ■ **une ~ vient de nous arriver** a news item *ou* some news has just reached us.

dépêcher [4] [depeʃe] *vt sout* [enquêteur] to send, to dispatch.
◆ **se dépêcher** *vpi* to hurry (up) ■ **pas besoin de se ~** (there's) no need to hurry ■ **mais dépêche-toi donc!** come on, hurry up! ■ **dépêche-toi de finir cette lettre** hurry up and finish that letter ■ **on s'est dépêchés de rentrer** we hurried home, we went back home in a hurry.

dépeignait *etc v* **1.** ▷ **dépeindre 2.** ▷ **dépeigner**.

dépeigner [4] [depeɲe] *vt* : **~ qqn** to mess up *ou* to muss *ou* to ruffle sb's hair ■ **elle est toujours dépeignée** her hair's always untidy *ou* dishevelled.

dépeindre [81] [depɛ̃dr] *vt* to depict, to portray.

dépenaillé, e [depənaje] *adj* [vêtement, rideau] scruffy, ragged, tattered ■ **un mendiant tout ~** a beggar in rags.

dépénalisation [depenalizasjɔ̃] *nf* : **la ~ d'un acte** decriminalizing an act.

dépénaliser [3] [depenalize] *vt* to decriminalize.

dépendance [depɑ̃dɑ̃s] *nf* **1.** [subordination] dependence ■ **vivre dans la ~** to be dependent, to lead a dependent life ■ [d'un drogué] addiction **2.** [annexe] outhouse, outbuilding **3.** [territoire] dependency.

dépendant, e [depɑ̃dɑ̃, ɑ̃t] *adj* **1.** [subordonné] dependent ■ **être ~ de qqn/qqch** to be dependent on sb/sthg **2.** [drogué] dependent.

dépendre [73] [depɑ̃dr] *vt* [décrocher - tableau, tapisserie] to take down *(sép)*.
◆ **dépendre de** *v+prép* **1.** [suj: employé, service] to be answerable to ■ **il dépend du chef de service** he's answerable *ou* he reports to the departmental head ■ **nous dépendons du Ministère** we're answerable to the Ministry **2.** [suj: propriété, domaine, territoire] to be a dependency of, to belong to ■ **le parc dépend du château** the park is part of the castle property **3.** [financièrement] to depend on *ou* upon, to be dependent on ■ **~ (financièrement) de qqn** to be financially dependent on *ou* upon sb ■ **je ne dépends que de moi-même** I'm my own boss ■ **~ d'un pays pour le pétrole** to be dependent on a country for one's oil supply **4.** [suj: décision, choix, résultat] to depend on ■ **notre avenir en dépend** our future depends *ou* rests on it ■ **ça ne dépend pas que de moi** it's not entirely up to me ■ *(en usage absolu)* **ça dépend!** it (all) depends! ■ *(tournure impersonnelle)* **il dépend de toi de rester ou de partir** it's up to you whether you stay or not.

dépens [depɑ̃] *nmpl* DR costs.
◆ **aux dépens de** *loc prép* at the expense of ■ **rire aux ~ de qqn** to laugh at sb's expense ■ **je l'ai appris à mes ~** I learnt it to my cost.

dépense [depɑ̃s] *nf* **1.** [frais] expense, expenditure ■ **occasionner de grosses ~s** to mean a lot of expense *ou* a big outlay ■ **je ne peux pas me permettre cette ~** I can't afford to lay out *ou* to spend so much money ■ **faire des ~s** to spend (money) ▶ **~s du ménage** household expenses ■ **~s publiques** public *ou* government spending ■ **~s et recettes** ÉCON & FIN expenditure and income **2.** [fait de dépenser] spending ■ **pousser qqn à la ~** to push *ou* to encourage sb to spend (money) ■ **regarder à la ~** to watch what one spends, to watch every penny ■ **ne regardez pas à la ~** spare no expense **3.** [consommation] consumption ■ **~ physique** physical exertion ■ **c'est une ~ de temps inutile** it's a waste of time ● **~ de carburant** fuel consumption.

dépenser [3] [depɑ̃se] *vt* **1.** [argent] to spend ■ **~ son salaire en cadeaux** to spend one's salary on gifts ■ **les enfants me font ~ beaucoup d'argent** I spend a lot because of the children ■ *(en usage absolu)* **~ sans compter** to spend (money) lavishly *ou* without counting the cost **2.** [consommer - mazout] to use **3.** [employer - temps] to spend ; [- énergie] to expend.

◆ **se dépenser** *vpi* **1.** [se défouler] to let off steam ■ **il se dépense beaucoup physiquement** he uses up a lot of energy ■ **elle a besoin de se ~** she needs an outlet for her (pent-up) energy **2.** [se démener] to expend a lot of energy, to work hard ■ **se ~ en efforts inutiles** to waste one's energies in useless efforts ■ **se ~ sans compter pour qqch** to put all one's energies into sthg, to give sthg one's all.

dépensier, ère [depɑ̃sje, ɛr] ◇ *adj* extravagant ■ **j'ai toujours été ~** I've always been a big spender, money has always slipped through my fingers.
◇ *nm, f* spendthrift ■ **un grand ~** a big spender.

déperdition [depɛrdisjɔ̃] *nf* [de chaleur, de matière] loss.

dépérir [32] [deperir] *vi* [malade] to fade *ou* to waste away ■ [de tristesse] to pine away ■ [plante] to wilt, to wither ■ [industrie] to decline.

dépérissement [deperismɑ̃] *nm* [affaiblissement] fading *ou* wasting *ou* pining away ■ [déclin] decline.

dépersonnalisation [depɛrsɔnalizasjɔ̃] *nf* [gén - PSYCHOL] depersonalization.

dépersonnaliser [3] [depɛrsɔnalize] *vt* [gén - PSYCHOL] to depersonalize.

◆ **se dépersonnaliser** *vpi* [individu] to become depersonalized, to lose one's personality ■ [lieu, œuvre] to become anonymous.

dépêtrer [4] [depetre] *vt* : **~ qqn/qqch de** to extricate sb/sthg from ■ **~ qqn d'une situation** to extricate sb from *ou* to get sb out of a situation.

◆ **se dépêtrer de** *vp+prép* **1.** [de filets, de pièges] to free o.s. from **2.** [d'un gêneur] to shake off *(sép)* ■ [d'une situation] to get out of ■ **il nous a dit tant de mensonges qu'il ne peut plus s'en ~** he's told us so many lies that he can no longer extricate himself from them ■ **j'ai tant de dettes que je ne peux plus m'en ~** I have so many debts I don't even know how to start paying them off.

dépeuplement [depœpləmɑ̃] *nm* **1.** SOCIOL depopulation **2.** [désertion] : **le ~ de la forêt** [déboisement] clearing *ou* thinning (out) the forest ; [absence d'animaux] the disappearance of animal life from the forest ■ **le ~ des rivières** [volontaire] destocking the rivers ; [par la pollution] the destruction of the fish stocks of the rivers.

dépeupler [5] [depœple] *vt* **1.** SOCIOL to depopulate **2.** [volontairement - étang] to empty (of fish), to destock ; [- forêt] to clear (of trees), to thin out the trees of ■ **~ l'étang/la forêt** [involontairement] to kill off the fish stocks in the pond/trees in the forest.

◆ **se dépeupler** *vpi* **1.** SOCIOL to become depopulated **2.** [rivière] to lose its stock ■ [forêt] to thin out.

déphasé, e [defaze] *adj* **1.** ÉLECTR out-of-phase **2.** [désorienté] disorientated ■ **être ~ par rapport à la réalité** to be out of touch with reality.

déphaser [3] [defaze] *vt* **1.** ÉLECTR to cause a phase difference in **2.** [désorienter] : **son séjour prolongé à l'hôpital l'a déphasé** his long stay in hospital made him lose touch with reality.

dépiauter [3] [depjote] *vt fam* **1.** [enlever la peau de - lapin, poisson] to skin, to take the skin off ; [- fruit] to peel **2.** [analyser] : **~ un texte** to dissect a text.

dépigmentation [depigmɑ̃tasjɔ̃] *nf* depigmentation, loss of pigmentation.

dépilation [depilasjɔ̃] *nf* **1.** MÉD hair loss **2.** [épilation] hair removal, removal of (unwanted) hair.

dépilatoire [depilatwar] ◇ *adj* depilatory.
◇ *nm* depilatory *ou* hair-removing cream.

dépistage [depistaʒ] *nm* **1.** MÉD screening ■ **le ~ du cancer** screening for cancer ■ **~ précoce** early screening ■ **le ~ du sida** AIDS testing **2.** [recherche] detection, unearthing.

dépister [3] [depiste] *vt* **1.** [criminel] to track down *(sép)* ■ [source, ruse] to detect, to unearth **2.** MÉD to screen for ■ **des techniques pour ~ le cancer** cancer screening techniques **3.** CHASSE [lièvre] to track down *(sép)* ■ [chien] to put off the scent **4.** [perdre - poursuivant] to throw off *(sép)*.

dépit [depi] *nm* pique ■ **faire qqch par ~** to do sthg in a fit of pique *ou* out of spite ■ **j'en aurais pleuré de ~** I was so vexed I could have cried ● **~ amoureux** heartache, unrequited love.

◆ **en dépit de** *loc prép* despite, in spite of ■ **faire qqch en ~ du bon sens** [sans logique] to do sthg with no regard for common sense ; [n'importe comment] to do sthg any old how.

dépité, e [depite] *adj* (greatly) vexed, piqued.

dépiter [3] [depite] *vt* to pique, to vex ■ **son refus m'a profondément dépité** I was greatly vexed *ou* piqued at his refusal.

déplacé, e [deplase] *adj* **1.** [malvenu - démarche, remarque, rire] inappropriate ■ **sa présence était ~e** his presence was uncalled-for **2.** [de mauvais goût - plaisanterie] indelicate, shocking **3.** SOCIOL displaced.

déplacement [deplasmɑ̃] *nm* **1.** [mouvement] moving, shifting ■ **le ~ de l'aiguille sur le cadran** the movement of the hands around the clock face ● **~ d'air** displacement of air **2.** [sortie] moving about ■ [voyage d'affaires] (business) trip ■ **Josie me remplace pendant mes ~s** Josie steps in for me when I'm away on business ■ **le docteur m'a interdit tout ~** the doctor said I mustn't move about ■ **merci d'avoir fait le ~** thanks for coming all this way ■ **joli panorama, ça vaut le ~!** *fam* what a lovely view, it's definitely worth going out of your way to see it! ■ **la soirée ne valait pas le ~** the party wasn't worth going to **3.** [mutation - d'un employé] transfer ■ **~ d'office** transfer **4.** NAUT displacement ■ **navire de 15 000 tonnes de ~** ship with a 15,000-ton displacement **5.** MÉD : **~ d'organe** organ displacement ■ **~ de vertèbre** slipped disc **6.** PSYCHOL displacement.

◆ **de déplacement** *loc adj* **1.** TRANSP : **moyen de ~** means *ou* mode of transport **2.** PSYCHOL displacement *(modif)*.

◆ **en déplacement** *loc adv* away ■ **Bordeaux est en ~ à Marseille** SPORT Bordeaux are playing away against Marseilles ■ **la directrice est en ~** the manager's away (on business) ■ **envoyer qqn en ~** to send sb away on a business trip.

déplacer [16] [deplase] *vt* **1.** [objet, pion, voiture] to move, to shift ■ **déplace-le vers la droite** move *ou* shift it to the right ● **~ de l'air** *fam hum* [en parlant] to talk big *ou* a lot of hot air **2.** [élève, passager] to move ■ [population] to displace **3.** [infléchir] : **ne déplacez pas le problème** *ou* **la question** don't change the question **4.** MÉD [os] to displace, to put out of joint ■ [vertèbre] to slip **5.** [muter - fonctionnaire] to transfer **6.** [faire venir - médecin, dépanneur] to send for ■ **ils ont déplacé l'ambulance pour cela?** did they really get the ambulance out for that? ■ **son concert a déplacé des foules** crowds flocked to his concert **7.** [dans le temps - festival, rendez-vous] to change, to shift, to move ■ **~ une date** [l'avancer] to move a date forward ; [la reculer] to put back a date **8.** NAUT to have a displacement of.

◆ **se déplacer** ◇ *vpi* **1.** [masse d'air, nuages] to move, to be displaced *spéc* ■ [aiguille d'horloge] to move **2.** [marcher] to move about *ou* around, to get about *ou* around ■ **se ~ à l'aide de béquilles** to get about on crutches ■ **avec notre messagerie, faites vos courses sans vous ~** do your shopping from home with our Teletext service ■ **cela ne vaut pas/vaut le coup de se ~** *fam* it's not worth/it's worth the trip **3.** [voyager] to travel, to get about.
◇ *vpt* : **se ~ une vertèbre** to slip a disc.

déplafonnement [deplafɔnmɑ̃] *nm* : **~ des cotisations** removal of the upper limit for contributions.

déplaire [110] [deplɛr] ◆ **déplaire à** *v+prép* **1.** [rebuter] to put off *(sép)* ■ **il m'a tout de suite déplu** I took an instant dislike to him ■ **je lui déplais tant que ça?** does he dislike me as much as that? ■ **un café? voilà qui ne me déplairait pas** *ou* **ne serait pas pour me ~** a coffee? I wouldn't say no! ■ **il m'a parlé franchement, ce qui n'a pas été pour me ~** he was frank with me, which I liked ■ **il ne lui déplairait pas de vivre à la campagne** he wouldn't object to living in the country **2.** [contrarier] to annoy, to offend ■ **ce que je vais dire risque de vous ~** I'm afraid you may not like what I'm going to say ■ **ne vous (en) déplaise** *litt* & *hum* whether you like it or not.

◆ **se déplaire** ◇ *vp (emploi réciproque)* [ne pas se plaire l'un à l'autre] to dislike each other *ou* one another.

◇ *vpi* [être mal à l'aise] to be unhappy *ou* dissatisfied ■ **je ne me suis pas déplu ici** I quite enjoyed *ou* liked it here.

déplaisant, e [deplɛzɑ̃, ɑ̃t] *adj* **1.** [goût, odeur, atmosphère] unpleasant, nasty **2.** [personne, comportement] unpleasant, offensive ■ **cette surveillance est assez ~e** being watched like this is rather unpleasant.

déplaisir [deplezir] *nm* **1.** *litt* [tristesse] unhappiness **2.** [mécontentement] displeasure, disapproval ■ **elle me verrait sans ~ accepter** she'd be quite pleased if I accepted ■ **je fais les corvées ménagères sans ~** I don't mind doing the housework ■ **à mon/son grand ~** much to my/his chagrin.

déplaisons *etc v* ▷ **déplaire**.

déplanter [3] [deplɑ̃te] *vt* [arbuste] to uproot, to take up *(sép)* ■ [jardin] to clear (of plants), to remove the plants from ■ [piquet] to dig out *(sép)*, to remove.

déplâtrer [3] [deplatre] *vt* **1.** CONSTR to strip of plaster, to remove the plaster from **2.** MÉD to take out of a plaster cast ■ **on le déplâtre demain** his plaster cast comes off tomorrow.

dépliant, e [deplijɑ̃, ɑ̃t] *adj* extendable, extensible.

◆ **dépliant** *nm* **1.** [brochure] brochure, leaflet ■ **~ publicitaire** advertising leaflet ■ **~ touristique** travel brochure **2.** IMPR foldout.

déplier [10] [deplije] *vt* **1.** [journal, lettre] to open out *ou* up *(sép)*, to unfold ■ **~ la pièce de tissu** to spread the cloth out ■ [bras, jambes] to stretch **2.** [mètre pliant, canapé] to open out.

◆ **se déplier** *vp (emploi passif)* **1.** [document] to unfold, to open out ■ **les cartes routières ne se déplient pas facilement** roadmaps aren't very easy to unfold **2.** [canapé, mètre pliant] to open out ■ **un canapé qui se déplie** a foldaway sofa-bed.

déplisser [3] [deplise] *vt* **1.** [enlever les plis de] to unpleat ■ **~ une jupe** to take the pleats out of a skirt **2.** [défriper] to smooth out *(sép)*.

◆ **se déplisser** *vpi* to come unpleated, to lose its pleats.

déploie *etc v* ▷ **déployer**.

déploiement [deplwamɑ̃] *nm* **1.** [des ailes d'un oiseau] spreading out, unfolding ■ NAUT unfurling **2.** MIL deployment ■ **un grand ~** *ou* **tout un ~ de police** a large deployment of police ▶ **~ en éventail** fan-shaped deployment **3.** [manifestation] : **~ de** show *ou* demonstration *ou* display of ■ **un grand ~ de force** a great show of strength ■ **un ~ d'affection** a display of affection ; *péj* a gush of affection.

déplomber [3] [deplɔ̃be] *vt* **1.** [dent] to remove the filling from **2.** [ouvrir] to take the seals off, to remove the seals from **3.** INFORM to break through the protection of, to hack into *(insép)*.

déplorable [deplɔrabl] *adj* **1.** [regrettable] deplorable, regrettable, lamentable **2.** [mauvais - résultat] appalling ; [- plaisanterie] awful, terrible, appalling ■ **elle s'habille avec un goût ~** she dresses with appallingly bad taste.

déploration [deplɔrasjɔ̃] *nf* **1.** MUS lament **2.** ART : **Déploration du Christ** Pietà.

déplorer [3] [deplɔre] *vt* **1.** *sout* [regretter] to object to, to regret, to deplore ■ **nous déplorons cet incident** we regret this incident ■ **je déplore que vous n'ayez pas compris** I find it regrettable that you didn't understand **2.** [constater] : **nous n'avons eu que peu de dégâts à ~** fortunately, we suffered only slight damage ■ **on déplore la mort d'une petite fille dans l'accident** sadly, a little girl was killed in the accident **3.** *litt* [pleurer sur] to lament *ou* to mourn for ■ **~ la mort d'un ami** to grieve over the death of a friend.

déployer [13] [deplwaje] *vt* **1.** [déplier] to spread out *(sép)*, to unfold, to unroll ■ **~ les voiles** NAUT to unfurl *ou* to extend the sails **2.** [faire montre de] to display, to exhibit ■ **elle a déployé toute son éloquence** she brought all her eloquence to bear ■ **il m'a fallu ~ des trésors de persuasion auprès d'elle** I had to work very hard at persuading her **3.** MIL to deploy.

◆ **se déployer** *vpi* **1.** NAUT to unfurl **2.** [foule] to extend, to stretch out **3.** MIL to be deployed.

déplu [deply] *pp* ▷ **déplaire**.

déplumé, e [deplyme] *adj* **1.** [sans plumes] moulting ■ **des tourterelles ~es** turtledoves that have lost their feathers **2.** *fam* [chauve] bald, balding.

déplumer [3] [deplyme] ◆ **se déplumer** *vpi* **1.** [perdre ses plumes] to lose *ou* to drop its feathers ■ **un vieux chapeau qui se déplume** an old hat that's losing its feathers **2.** *fam* [devenir chauve] : **il** *ou* **son crâne se déplume** he's going bald *ou* thinning on top.

déplut *etc v* ▷ **déplaire**.

dépoitraillé, e [depwatraje] *adj fam péj* bare-chested ■ **tout ~** with his shirt open almost down to his navel.

dépolariser [3] [depɔlarize] *vt* to depolarize.

dépoli, e [depɔli] *adj* frosted, ground.

dépolir [32] [depɔlir] *vt* to grind.

dépolissage [depɔlisaʒ] *nm* [du verre] grinding.

dépolitisation [depɔlitizasjɔ̃] *nf* [d'une personne, d'un thème] depoliticization.

dépolitiser [3] [depɔlitize] *vt* to depoliticize ■ **faut-il ~ le sport?** should politics be kept out of sport?

dépolluer [7] [depɔlɥe] *vt* to cleanse, to clean up *(sép)* ■ **~ les plages** to clean up the beaches.

dépollution [depɔlysjɔ̃] *nf* cleaning up, decontamination ■ **~ de l'eau** water purification.

dépopulation [depɔpylasjɔ̃] *nf* depopulation.

déportation [depɔrtasjɔ̃] *nf* **1.** HIST [exil] transportation, deportation **2.** [en camp] deportation, internment ■ **pendant mes années de ~** during my years in a concentration camp.

déporté, e [depɔrte] *nm, f* **1.** [prisonnier] deportee, internee **2.** HIST convict.

déportement [depɔrtəmɑ̃] *nm* [embardée] swerve, swerving.

déporter [3] [depɔrte] *vt* **1.** [exiler] to deport, to send to a concentration camp **2.** [déplacer] : **la voiture a été déportée sur la gauche** the car swerved to the left.

◆ **se déporter** *vpi* [doucement] to move aside ■ [brusquement] to swerve ■ **se ~ vers la droite/gauche** to veer (off) to the right/left.

dépose [depoz] *nf* taking out *ou* down ■ **~ gratuite de vos anciens appareils** your old appliances removed free of charge.

déposer [3] [depoze] ◇ *vt* **1.** [poser] to lay *ou* to put down *(sép)*

2. [laisser - gerbe] to lay ; [- objet livré] to leave, to drop off *(sép)* ; [- valise] to leave

3. [décharger - matériel] to unload, to set down *(sép)*

4. [conduire en voiture] to drop (off) ■ **je te dépose?** can I drop you off?, can I give you a lift?

5. [argent, valeurs] to deposit ■ **~ de l'argent en banque** to deposit money with a bank ■ **~ de l'argent sur son compte** to pay money into one's account, to deposit money in one's account ■ **~ des titres en garde** to deposit securities in safe custody

6. ADMIN : **~ son bilan** to file for bankruptcy, to go into (voluntary) liquidation ■ **~ un brevet** to file a patent application, to apply for a patent ■ **~ sa candidature** to apply ■ **~ une plainte** to lodge a complaint ■ **~ un projet de loi** to introduce *ou* to table a bill

7. [destituer - roi] to depose

8. *litt* [donner] : **~ un baiser sur le front de qqn** to kiss sb's forehead gently

9. [démonter - radiateur, étagère] to remove, to take out *ou* down *(sép)*.

◇ *vi* DR to give evidence, to testify.

◆ **se déposer** *vpi* to settle.

dépositaire [depozitɛr] *nmf* **1.** DR depositary, trustee ▪ **être le ~ d'une lettre** to hold a letter in trust **2.** COMM agent ▪ **~ exclusif** sole agent ▪ **~ d'une marque** agent for a brand ▪ **~ de journaux** newsagent **3.** *litt* [confident] repository ▪ **faire de qqn le ~ d'un secret** to entrust sb with a secret.

déposition [depozisjɔ̃] *nf* **1.** [témoignage] deposition, evidence, statement ▪ **faire une ~** to testify ▪ **recevoir une ~** to take a statement **2.** [destitution - d'un roi] deposition.

déposséder [18] [depɔsede] *vt* to dispossess ▪ **sa famille a été dépossédée** his family was stripped of all its possessions ▪ **~ qqn de** to deprive sb of.

dépossession [depɔsesjɔ̃] *nf* deprivation, dispossessing.

dépôt [depo] *nm* **1.** [remise - d'un rapport] handing in, submission ; [- d'un paquet, d'un télégramme] handing in
2. ADMIN [inscription] application, filing ▪ [enregistrement] filing, registration ▪ **~ d'une liste électorale** presentation of a list of candidates ⊳ **~ de bilan** petition in bankruptcy ▪ **~ de brevet** patent registration ▪ **~ légal** copyright deposit *(in France, copies of published or recorded documents have to be deposited at the Bibliothèque nationale)* ▪ **numéro de ~ légal** book number ▪ **~ d'une marque** registration of a trademark
3. FIN [démarche] depositing ▪ [somme] deposit ▪ **~ à terme/vue** open-access/restricted-access deposit ▪ **~ de garantie** deposit *(usually equivalent to two months' rent and refundable at end of lease)*
4. GÉOL deposit ▪ [couche] layer ▪ [sédiment] deposit, sediment ▪ **~ calcaire** *ou* **de tartre** layer of scale *ou* fur ▪ **~ alluvial/de cendres/de carbone** alluvial/ash/carbon deposit ▪ **~ glaciaire** glacial drift ▪ **~ marin** silt
5. ŒNOL sediment
6. [entrepôt] store, warehouse ▪ **~ des machines** engine house ⊳ **~ de charbon** coal depot ▪ **~ de matériel** storage yard ▪ **~ mortuaire** mortuary ▪ **~ d'ordures** rubbish dump *ou* tip *UK*, garbage dump *US*
7. MIL depot ▪ **~ de munitions** ammunition dump ▪ **~ de vivres** supply dump, commissary *US*
8. TRANSP depot, station *US*
9. [boutique] retail outlet ▪ **~ de pain** ≃ bread shop ▪ **l'épicier fait ~ de pain** the grocer sells bread
10. [prison] (police) cells *(in Paris)* ▪ **au ~** in the cells.
◆ **en dépôt** *loc adv* FIN in trust, in safe custody ▪ **confier qqch en ~ à qqn** to entrust sb with sthg ▪ **avoir en ~** to have on bond ▪ **mettre en ~** to bond.

dépoter [3] [depɔte] *vt* HORT to plant out *(sép)*, to transplant.

dépotoir [depɔtwar] *nm* **1.** [décharge] dump ▪ [usine] disposal plant, sewage works **2.** *péj* [lieu sale] pigsty ▪ **il faut empêcher la Manche de devenir un ~** we must prevent the Channel becoming an open sewer **3.** *fam* [débarras] dumping ground.

dépôt-vente [depovɑ̃t] (*pl* **dépôts-ventes**) *nm* second-hand shop ▪ **mettre qqch en ~** to put sthg on sale or return.

dépouille [depuj] *nf* **1.** [cadavre] : **~ (mortelle)** (mortal) remains ▪ **les ~s des victimes ont été rapatriées hier** the bodies of the victims were repatriated yesterday **2.** [peau - d'un mammifère] hide, skin ; [- d'un reptile] slough.
◆ **dépouilles** *nfpl* [trophée] booty, plunder, spoils.

dépouillé, e [depuje] *adj* **1.** [sans peau] skinned ▪ [sans feuilles] bare, leafless **2.** [sans ornement] plain, simple, uncluttered ▪ **un style ~** a concise *ou* terse style **3.** [dénué] : **~ de** lacking in.

dépouillement [depujmɑ̃] *nm* **1.** [analyse] breakdown, collection and analysis ▪ **~ des données** data reduction ▪ **~ d'un scrutin** tally *ou* counting of the votes **2.** [ouverture] : **~ du courrier** opening of the mail **3.** [simplicité - d'un décor] bareness, soberness **4.** [concision] conciseness, terseness **5.** [dénuement] dispossession, destitution.

dépouiller [3] [depuje] *vt* **1.** [lapin] to skin **2.** [câble] to strip ▪ **la bise a dépouillé les arbres de leurs feuilles** the north wind has stripped the trees bare *ou* of their leaves **3.** [voler] to dispossess, to despoil *litt* ▪ **~ qqn de** to deprive sb of ▪ **ils m'ont dépouillé de tout ce que j'avais sur moi** they stripped me of *ou* took everything I had on me ▪ **il s'est fait ~ de tous ses biens** he was robbed of everything he had **4.** [lire - journal, courrier, inventaire] to go through *(insép)* ▪ [analyser - questionnaire, réponses] to analyse, to study, to scrutinize ; [- données] to process ▪ **~ le scrutin** POLIT to count the votes **5.** *sout* [quitter] to cast aside *(sép)*, to strip off *(sép)* ▪ **les reptiles dépouillent leur peau** ZOOL reptiles slough off *ou* shed their skin.
◆ **se dépouiller** *vpi* **1.** [arbre, végétation] : **les arbres se dépouillent peu à peu** the trees are gradually losing *ou* shedding their leaves **2.** ZOOL to slough off its skin.
◆ **se dépouiller de** *vp+prép* **1.** [se défaire de] : **se ~ de ses vêtements** to strip off ▪ **se ~ de tous ses biens** to give away all one's property **2.** *litt* [se départir de] to cast off *(sép)*.

dépourvu, e [depurvy] *adj* **1.** [misérable] destitute **2.** [manquant] : **~ de** devoid of, lacking in ▪ **c'est ~ de tout intérêt** it is of *ou* holds no interest at all ▪ **totalement ~ de scrupules** totally unscrupulous ▪ **sa remarque n'était pas entièrement ~e de bon sens** his remark was not entirely devoid of common sense.
◆ **au dépourvu** *loc adv* : **prendre qqn au ~** to catch sb off guard *ou* unawares ▪ **ils ont été pris au ~ par cette information** the news caught them unawares.

dépoussiérage [depusjeraʒ] *nm* dust removal, dusting.

dépoussiérant, e [depusjerɑ̃, ɑ̃t] *adj* dust-removing ▪ **filtre ~** dust filter.
◆ **dépoussiérant** *nm* dust remover.

dépoussiérer [18] [depusjere] *vt* **1.** [nettoyer] to dust (off) **2.** [rajeunir] to rejuvenate, to give a new lease of life to.

dépravation [depravasjɔ̃] *nf* depravity, perversion, perverseness.

dépravé, e [deprave] ◇ *adj* immoral, depraved, perverted.
◇ *nm, f* degenerate, pervert.

dépraver [3] [deprave] *vt* [corrompre] to deprave, to corrupt, to pervert.

dépréciateur, trice [depresjatœr, tris] ◇ *adj* disparaging, deprecatory, depreciative.
◇ *nm, f* depreciator, disparager.

dépréciatif, ive [depresjatif, iv] *adj* derogatory, disparaging.

dépréciation [depresjasjɔ̃] *nf* depreciation, drop *ou* fall in value ▪ **la ~ des propriétés foncières** the drop in property values.

déprécier [9] [depresje] *vt* **1.** FIN to depreciate, to cause to drop in value **2.** [dénigrer] to run down *(sép)*, to belittle, to disparage.
◆ **se déprécier** ◇ *vp (emploi réfléchi)* [se déconsidérer] to belittle *ou* to disparage o.s., to run o.s. down.
◇ *vpi* FIN to depreciate.

déprédateur, trice [depredatœr, tris] ◇ *adj* depredatory *sout*, plundering.
◇ *nm, f* [pilleur] depredator *sout*, plunderer ▪ [escroc] swindler, embezzler.

déprédation [depredasjɔ̃] *nf* **1.** [dégâts] (wilful) damage **2.** [détournement] : **~ de biens** misappropriation of property ▪ **~ des finances publiques** embezzlement of public funds.

déprendre [79] [deprɑ̃dr] ◆ **se déprendre de** *vp+prép* *litt* to give up ▪ **se ~ de qqn** to fall out of love with sb.

dépressif, ive [depresif, iv] *adj* [personne] depressive, easily depressed out ▪ [caractère] depressive ▪ **avoir des tendances dépressives** to be depressive.

dépression [depresjɔ̃] *nf* **1.** MÉD & PSYCHOL depression, depressiveness ▪ **~ nerveuse** nervous breakdown ▪ **avoir** *ou* **faire** *fam* **une ~ (nerveuse)** to have a nervous breakdown **2.** GÉOGR depression **3.** [absence de pression] vacuum ▪ [différence de pression] suction **4.** MÉTÉOR cyclone, barometric depression, low **5.** ÉCON depression, slump.

dépressionnaire [depresjɔnɛr] *adj* **1.** ÉCON slump *(modif)* ▪ **le marché a des tendances ~s** the market's sliding towards a slump **2.** MÉTÉOR low pressure *(modif)*.

dépressurisation [depresyrizasjɔ̃] *nf* depressurization.

déprimant, e [deprimɑ̃, ɑ̃t] *adj* [démoralisant] depressing, disheartening, demoralizing.

déprime [deprim] *nf fam* **faire une ~** to be depressed ■ **il est en pleine ~** he's really down at the moment.

déprimé, e [deprime] *adj* [abattu] dejected, depressed ■ **je suis plutôt ~ aujourd'hui** I feel rather down today.

déprimer [3] [deprime] ◇ *vt* [abattre] to depress, to demoralize.
◇ *vi fam* to be depressed.

déprogrammer [3] [deprɔgrame] *vt* RADIO & TV to withdraw *ou* to remove from the schedule.

dépucelage [depyslaʒ] *nm* [d'une fille] defloration, deflowering ■ [d'un garçon] loss of virginity.

dépuceler [24] [depysle] *vt* to deflower ■ **c'est elle qui l'a dépucelé** he lost his virginity to her ■ **se faire ~** to lose one's virginity.

depuis [dəpɥi] ◇ *prép* **1.** [à partir d'une date ou d'un moment précis] since ■ **~ le 10 mars** since March 10th ■ **~ le début** from the very beginning, right from the beginning ■ **il nous suit ~ Tours** he's been following us since (we left) Tours ■ **je ne fais du golf que ~ cette année** I only started to play golf this year **2.** [exprimant une durée] for ■ **~ 10 ans** for 10 years ■ **~ longtemps** for a long time ■ **~ quelque temps** of late ■ **il ne joue plus ~ quelque temps** he hasn't been playing of late *ou* lately, he hasn't played for some time ■ **~ peu** recently, not long ago ■ **la piscine n'est ouverte que ~ peu** the pool opened only recently ■ **les hommes font la guerre ~ toujours** men have always waged war ■ **~ combien de temps le connais-tu?** how long have you known him for? ◗ **~ le temps : et tu ne sais toujours pas t'en servir ~ le temps!** and you still don't know how to use it after all this time! ■ **il me l'a rendu hier – ~ le temps!** he gave it back to me yesterday – it took him long enough *ou* and not before time!
3. [dans l'espace, un ordre, une hiérarchie] from ■ **il lui a fait signe ~ sa fenêtre** he waved to him from his window ■ **des matelas ~ 50 euros** mattresses from 50 euros (upwards).
◇ *adv* : **je ne l'ai rencontré qu'une fois, je ne l'ai jamais revu ~** I only met him once and I've not seen him again since (then).
◆ **depuis... jusqu'à** *loc corrélative* **1.** [dans le temps] from... to ■ **~ 12 h jusqu'à 20 h** from 12 to *ou* till 8 p.m
2. [dans l'espace, un ordre, une hiérarchie] from... to ■ **ils vendent de tout, ~ les parapluies jusqu'aux sandwiches** they sell everything, from umbrellas to sandwiches.
◆ **depuis le temps que** *loc conj* : **~ le temps que tu me le promets...** you've been promising me that for such a long time... ■ **~ le temps que tu le connais, tu pourrais lui demander** considering how long you've known him you could easily ask him.
◆ **depuis lors** *loc adv sout* since then ■ **il n'est pas retourné au village ~ lors** he hasn't been back to the village since then.
◆ **depuis quand** *loc adv* **1.** [pour interroger sur la durée] how long ■ **~ quand m'attends-tu?** how long have you been waiting for me?
2. [exprimant l'indignation, l'ironie] since when ■ **~ quand est-ce que tu me donnes des ordres?** since when do you give me orders?
◆ **depuis que** *loc conj* since ■ **je ne l'ai pas revu ~ qu'il s'est marié** I haven't seen him since he got married ■ **~ que j'ai arrêté de fumer, je me sens mieux** I feel better since I stopped smoking.

dépuratif, ive [depyratif, iv] *adj* cleansing, depurative.

députation [depytasjɔ̃] *nf* **1.** [envoi] deputation, mandating **2.** [groupe] delegation, deputation **3.** POLIT office of Deputy, membership of the Assemblée Nationale ■ **se présenter à la ~** to stand for the position of Deputy.

député, e [depyte] *nm, f* **1.** [représentant] delegate, representative **2.** POLIT [en France] deputy ■ [en Grande-Bretagne] member of Parliament ■ [aux États-Unis] Congressman (*f* Congresswoman) ■ **~-maire** *deputy who is also a mayor* ■ **femme ~** [en Grande-Bretagne] woman MP ; [aux États-Unis] Congresswoman.

députer [3] [depyte] *vt sout* to send, to delegate ■ **~ qqn auprès d'un ministre** to send sb (as delegate) *ou* to delegate sb to speak to the Minister.

déqualification [dekalifikasjɔ̃] *nf* deskilling.

déqualifier [9] [dekalifje] *vt* to deskill.

der [dɛr] *nm & nf inv* : **la ~ des ~** the war to end all wars.

déraciné, e [derasine] ◇ *adj* BOT & *fig* uprooted ■ **ils se sentent ~s** they feel cut off from their roots.
◇ *nm, f* person without roots.

déracinement [derasinmɑ̃] *nm* **1.** BOT uprooting **2.** [extirpation] eradication, suppression ■ **le ~ des préjugés** eradicating prejudice **3.** [exil] uprooting (from one's environment) ■ **ce fut pour eux un ~ complet** it was a complete change of environment for them.

déraciner [3] [derasine] *vt* **1.** BOT to uproot ■ **~ qqn** *fig* to uproot sb, to deprive sb of his roots **2.** [détruire - vice, racisme] to root out *(sép)* ■ **ces habitudes sont difficiles à ~** these habits die hard.

déraillement [derajmɑ̃] *nm* RAIL derailment ■ **il y a eu un ~ à Foissy** a train came off the track *ou* was derailed at Foissy.

dérailler [3] [deraje] *vi* **1.** RAIL to go off *ou* to leave the rails ■ **faire ~ un train** to derail a train **2.** *fam* [fonctionner mal] to be on the blink ■ **faire ~ les négociations** to derail the talks **3.** *fam* [déraisonner] to go off the rails ■ [se tromper] to talk through one's hat ■ **tu dérailles complètement!** you're talking utter nonsense!

dérailleur [derajœr] *nm* derailleur (gear).

déraison [derɛzɔ̃] *nf litt* foolishness, folly.

déraisonnable [derɛzɔnabl] *adj* foolish, senseless ■ **une attente/attitude ~** irrational expectation/behaviour ■ **il serait ~ de partir si tard** it wouldn't be wise to leave so late.

déraisonner [3] [derɛzɔne] *vi* **1.** [dire des sottises] to talk nonsense **2.** [divaguer] to rave.

déramer [3] [derame] *vt* to fan, to riffle.

dérangé, e [derɑ̃ʒe] *adj* **1.** *fam* [bizarre] crazy, old ■ **t'es pas un peu ~?** have you gone out of your mind? ■ **il a l'esprit un peu ~** his mind is going **2.** [malade] upset ■ **il a l'estomac** *ou* **il est ~** he's got an upset stomach **3.** [en désordre - coiffure] dishevelled, messed-up ; [- tenue] untidy.

dérangeant, e [derɑ̃ʒɑ̃, ɑ̃t] *adj* **1.** [qui fait réfléchir] thought-provoking **2.** [qui crée un malaise] distressing, upsetting, worrying.

dérangement [derɑ̃ʒmɑ̃] *nm* **1.** [désordre] disarrangement, disorder **2.** [gêne] trouble, inconvenience **3.** MÉD disturbance, upset ■ **~ de l'esprit** insanity, mental derangement ◗ **~ gastrique** *ou* **intestinal** *ou* **de l'intestin** stomach upset **4.** [déplacement] trip ■ **cela m'épargnera le ~** it'll save me having to go ■ **cela ne vaut pas/vaut le ~** it isn't/it's worth the trip.
◆ **en dérangement** *loc adj* out of order, faulty ■ **'en ~'** 'out of order' ■ **le circuit est en ~** there's a fault in the circuit.

déranger [17] [derɑ̃ʒe] ◇ *vt* **1.** [mettre en désordre] to mix *ou* to muddle up *(sép)*, to make a mess of ■ **ne dérange pas mes papiers!** don't get my papers mixed up *ou* in a muddle! ■ **~ la coiffure de qqn** to mess up sb's hair **2.** [gêner] to bother, to disturb ■ **'ne pas ~'** 'do not disturb' ■ **si cela ne vous dérange pas** if you don't mind ■ **est-ce que cela vous dérange si** *ou* **que...?** do you mind if...? ■ **ça ne te dérange pas de poster ma lettre?** would you mind posting my letter for me? ■ **et alors, ça te dérange?** *fam* so, what's it to you? ■ **ça te dérangerait d'être poli?** *fam* would it be too much trouble for you to be polite? **3.** [interrompre] to interrupt, to intrude upon ■ **allô, Marie, je te dérange?** hello Marie, is this a good time to call? ■ **désolé de vous ~** sorry to disturb you **4.** [perturber - projets] to interfere with, to upset ■ **ça lui a dérangé l'esprit** she was badly shaken up by it **5.** [estomac] to upset.
◇ *vi* : **ses livres dérangent** his books are challenging.
◆ **se déranger** *vpi* **1.** [venir] to come ■ [sortir] to go out ■ **il a refusé de se ~** he wouldn't come (out) ■ **je refuse de me ~** I refuse to go ■ **s'est-elle dérangée pour la réunion?** did she put in an appearance at the meeting? ■ **ce coup de fil m'a évité de**

me ~ that phone call saved me a useless journey ■ **se ~ pour rien** to have a wasted journey **2.** [se pousser] to move (aside) ■ **ne te dérange pas, je passe très bien** stay where you are, I can get through **3.** [se donner du mal] to put o.s. out ■ **ne vous dérangez pas, je reviendrai** please don't go to any trouble, I'll come back later.

dérapage [derapaʒ] *nm* **1.** SPORT [en ski] side-slipping ■ **faire du ~** to sideslip ‖ [en moto] skidding **2.** AÉRON & AUTO skid ■ **~ contrôlé** controlled skid **3.** [dérive] (uncontrolled) drifting ■ **le ~ des prix** the uncontrolled increase in prices **4.** [erreur] mistake, slip-up.

déraper [3] [derape] *vi* **1.** [gén] to skid **2.** [au ski] to sideslip **3.** AÉRON to skid sideways **4.** *fig* to go wrong ■ **ça a complètement dérapé** it went completely wrong ■ **la conversation a vite dérapé sur la politique** the conversation soon got round to politics.

dératé, e [derate] *nm, f* : **courir comme un ~** to run like lightning.

dératisation [deratizasjɔ̃] *nf* rodent control.

dératiser [3] [deratize] *vt* to clear of rats *ou* rodents.

derby [dɛrbi] (*pl* **derbys** *ou pl* **derbies**) *nm* **1.** ÉQUIT derby ■ **le ~ d'Epsom** the Derby **2.** [match] local derby **3.** [chaussure] derby shoe.

derechef [dərəʃɛf] *adv hum* once again, one more time.

déréglage [dereglaʒ] *nm* [gén] malfunction ■ RADIO & TV detuning.

dérèglement [derɛgləmɑ̃] *nm* [dérangement] disturbance, trouble ■ **~ des saisons** upsetting of the seasons.

◆ **dérèglements** *nmpl* [écarts] dissoluteness, debauchery.

déréglementation [dereglәmɑ̃tasjɔ̃] *nf* deregulation.

déréglementer [3] [dereglәmɑ̃te] *vt* to deregulate.

dérégler [18] [deregle] *vt* **1.** MÉCAN [mécanisme] to disturb, to put out (*sép*) ■ [carburateur] to put *ou* to throw out of tuning ■ **le compteur est déréglé** the meter's not working properly ■ **l'orage a déréglé la pendule électrique** the storm has sent the electric clock haywire **2.** [perturber] to unsettle, to upset ■ **~ son sommeil** to disturb one's sleep pattern.

◆ **se dérégler** *vpi* MÉCAN to go wrong, to start malfunctioning ■ **le carburateur s'est déréglé** the carburettor's out, the idling needs adjusting ■ **ma fixation s'est déréglée** my binding's come loose.

déréguler [3] [deregyle] *vt* to deregulate.

déréliction [dereliksjɔ̃] *nf* RELIG dereliction (*of man by God*).

déresponsabiliser [3] [derɛspɔ̃sabilize] *vt* : **~ qqn** [le priver de responsabilité] to deprive sb of responsibility ; [dans une entreprise] to give sb a less responsible job.

dérider [3] [deride] *vt* **1.** [détendre] to cheer up (*sép*) ■ **je n'ai pas réussi à le ~** I couldn't get a smile out of him **2.** [déplisser] to unwrinkle.

◆ **se dérider** *vpi* to brighten, to cheer up.

dérision [derizjɔ̃] *nf* **1.** [moquerie] derision, mockery ■ **tourner qqn/qqch en ~** to scoff at sb/sthg ■ **sur le ton de la ~** mockingly, derisively **2.** [ironie] irony ■ **quelle ~!** how ironic!

dérisoire [derizwar] *adj* **1.** [risible] ridiculous, laughable **2.** [piètre - salaire, prix] derisory, ridiculous **3.** [sans effet] inadequate, trifling, pathetic.

dérivatif, ive [derivatif, iv] *adj* **1.** [activité, occupation] derivative **2.** LING derivating.

◆ **dérivatif** *nm* distraction ■ **le travail sert de ~ à son chagrin** work is an outlet for his grief.

dérivation [derivasjɔ̃] *nf* **1.** [d'un cours d'eau] diversion **2.** ÉLECTR shunt, branch circuit **3.** CHIM, LING & MATH derivation ■ **~ régressive** LING back formation **4.** NAUT drift **5.** MÉD diversion.

dérive [deriv] *nf* **1.** [dérapage] drifting, drift ■ **la ~ de l'économie** the downward spiral of the economy ■ **aller à la ~** *pr* to drift, to go adrift ; *fig* to go downhill **2.** NAUT [déplacement] drift, drifting off course ■ [quille] centreboard, keel ■ **partir à la ~** to drift **3.** AÉRON [trajectoire] drift, drifting off course ■ [empennage] fin, stabilizer **4.** GÉOGR : **~ des continents** continental drift.

dérivé, e [derive] *adj* **1.** LING & MATH derived **2.** ÉLECTR diverted, shunt ■ **circuit ~** branch circuit.

◆ **dérivé** *nm* **1.** CHIM derivative **2.** LING derivation **3.** [sous-produit] by-product.

◆ **dérivée** *nf* MATH derivative.

dériver [3] [derive] ◇ *vi* NAUT to drift, to be adrift.
◇ *vt* **1.** [détourner - rivière] to divert (the course of) **2.** ÉLECTR to shunt **3.** CHIM & MATH to derive.

◆ **dériver de** *v+prép* **1.** [être issu de] to derive *ou* to come from **2.** CHIM to be produced from **3.** LING to stem *ou* to derive from ■ **mots français qui dérivent du latin** French words derived from Latin.

dériveur [derivœr] *nm* [bateau] sailing dinghy (*with a centreboard*).

dermabrasion [dɛrmabrasjɔ̃] *nf* dermabrasion.

dermato [dɛrmato] *nmf fam* dermatologist, skin-specialist.

dermatologie [dɛrmatɔlɔʒi] *nf* dermatology.

dermatologique [dɛrmatɔlɔʒik] *adj* dermatological, skin (*modif*).

dermatologiste [dɛrmatɔlɔʒist], **dermatologue** [dɛrmatɔlɔg] *nmf* dermatologist, skin-specialist.

dermatose [dɛrmatoz] *nf* dermatosis, skin disease ■ **~ professionnelle** industrial dermatosis.

derme [dɛrm] *nm* dermis.

dermique [dɛrmik] *adj* dermic, dermal.

dernier, ère [dɛrnje (*devant nm commençant par voyelle ou h muet* [dɛrnje], [dɛrnjɛr])] ◇ *adj*

> **A.** DANS LE TEMPS
> **B.** DANS L'ESPACE
> **C.** DANS UN CLASSEMENT, UNE HIÉRARCHIE
> **D.** EN INTENSIF

A. DANS LE TEMPS

1. (*avant le n*) [qui vient après tous les autres - avion, bus, personne] last ; [- détail, préparatif] final ■ **un ~ mot/point!** one final word/point! ■ **il vient de terminer ses ~s examens** [en fin de cycle d'études] he's just taken his final exams *ou* finals ■ **le ~ enchérisseur** the highest bidder ■ **un Warhol dernière période** a late Warhol ■ **les dernières années de sa vie** the last years of his life ■ **jusqu'à son ~ jour** to his dying day, until the day he died ■ **ce furent ses dernières paroles** these were his dying *ou* last words ■ **ses dernières volontés** his last wishes ➔ **~ arrivant** *ou* **arrivé** *ou* **venu** latecomer ■ **sa dernière demeure** her final resting place ■ **la dernière édition** the late edition ■ **la dernière séance** the last *ou* late performance ■ **avoir le ~ mot : il faut toujours qu'il ait le ~ mot** he always has to have the last word ■ **rendre les ~s devoirs** *ou* **honneurs** *ou* **un ~ hommage à qqn** to pay a final tribute *ou* one's last respects to sb

2. (*avant le n*) [arrêté, ultime] final ■ **c'est mon ~ prix** [vendeur] it's the lowest I'll go ; [acheteur] that's my final offer ■ **dans un ~ sursaut de rage** in a final burst of rage ■ **en dernière analyse** in the final *ou* last analysis, when all's said and done

3. [précédent] last, previous ■ **la nuit dernière** last night ■ **la dernière fois, la fois dernière** last time ■ **ces dix dernières années** these last ten years

4. (*avant le n*) [le plus récent] last, latest ■ **achète-moi la dernière biographie de Proust** get me the latest biography of Proust ■ **à la dernière minute, à la dernière seconde, au ~ moment : une décision prise à la dernière seconde** a last-minute decision ■ **je ferai mes valises au ~ moment** I'll pack at the last minute *ou* possible moment ■ **une nouvelle de dernière minute** a late newsflash ■ **on nous apprend/ils apprirent en dernière minute que...** we've just heard this minute/at the last minute they heard that... ■ **ces ~s temps** lately, of late ■ **les ~s temps de** the last stages *ou* days of, the end of ■ **tu connais la dernière nouvelle?** have you heard the latest? ■ **aux dernières nouvelles, le mariage aurait été annulé** according to the latest news, the wedding's been cancelled ■ **aux dernières nouvelles, elle était en Alaska** she was last heard of in Alaska ■ **de dernière heure** [changement] last-minute

B. DANS L'ESPACE

1. [du bas - étagère] bottom ■ **les chaussettes sont dans le ~ tiroir** the socks are in the bottom drawer
2. [du haut] top ■ **au ~ étage** on the top floor
3. [du bout] last ■ **un siège au ~ rang** a seat in the back (row)

C. DANS UN CLASSEMENT, UNE HIÉRARCHIE

1. [dans une série] last ■ **suite à la dernière page** continued on the back page
2. [le plus mauvais] last, bottom ■ **en dernière position** in last position, last ■ **le ~ élève de la classe** the pupil at the bottom of the class ■ **je suis ~ à l'examen** I came last *ou* bottom *UK* in the exam ■ **arriver bon ~** to come in last
3. [le meilleur] top, highest ■ **le ~ échelon** the highest level

D. EN INTENSIF

1. *(avant le n)* [extrême, sens positif] : **de la dernière importance** of paramount *ou* of the utmost importance ■ **du ~ chic** extremely smart ■ **atteindre le ~ degré de la perfection** to attain the summit of perfection
2. *(avant le n)* [extrême, sens négatif] : **un acte de la dernière lâcheté** the most cowardly of acts ■ **traiter qqn avec le ~ mépris** to treat sb with the greatest contempt ■ **c'est de la dernière effronterie/impolitesse** it's extremely cheeky/rude ■ **du ~ mauvais goût** in appalling bad taste ■ **c'est la dernière chose à faire** it's the last thing one should do ■ **il est la dernière personne à qui je penserais** he's the last person I'd have thought of! ■ **c'est le ~ métier qu'on puisse imaginer** it's the lowest job you could imagine ▶ **faire subir les ~s outrages à une femme** *euphém* to violate a woman.

◇ *nm, f* **1.** [dans le temps] last *ou* final one ■ **je suis partie la dernière** I left last, I was the last one to leave ■ **je suis arrivé dans les ~s** I was among the last *ou* final ones to arrive ‖ [dans une famille] youngest ■ **le ~** the youngest *ou* last (boy) ■ **la dernière** the youngest *ou* last (girl) ■ **ses deux ~s** his two youngest (children) ■ **le petit ~** the youngest son ■ **la petite dernière** the youngest daughter **2.** [dans l'espace - celui du haut] top one ; [- celui du bas] last *ou* bottom one ; [- celui du bout] last one ■ **son dossier est le ~ de la pile** her file is at the bottom of the pile **3.** [dans une hiérarchie - le pire] : **j'étais toujours le ~ en classe** I was always (at the) bottom of the class ■ **tu arrives le ~ avec 34 points** you come last with 34 points ■ **elle est la dernière à qui je le dirais** she's the last person I'd tell ■ **le ~ des ~s** *fam* the lowest of the low ■ **tu es le ~ des imbéciles** *fam* you're a complete idiot ■ **le ~ des lâches n'aurait pas fait ça** even the worst coward wouldn't have done that ■ **je serais vraiment le ~ des idiots!** I'd be a complete fool! ■ **c'est le ~ des maris** he's a terrible husband ■ [dans une série] last one ■ **allez, on en prend un ~!** [verre] let's have a last one (for the road)! ■ **ils les ont tués jusqu'au ~** every single one of them was killed **4.** [dans une narration] : **ce ~, cette dernière** [de deux] the latter ; [de plusieurs] this last, the last-mentioned ■ **il attendait la réponse de Luc, mais ce ~ se taisait** he was waiting for Luc's answer but the latter kept quiet.

◆ **dernier** *nm* **1.** [étage] top floor **2.** [dans une charade] : **mon ~ est/a...** my last is/has...

◆ **dernière** *nf* **1.** THÉÂTRE last performance **2.** *fam* [nouvelle] : **tu connais la dernière?** have you heard the latest?

◆ **au dernier degré, au dernier point** *loc adv* extremely, to the highest *ou* last degree ■ **j'étais excédé au ~ point** I was utterly furious ■ **c'est un alcoolique au ~ degré** he's a complete alcoholic ■ **drogué au ~ degré** drugged to the eyeballs.

◆ **au dernier degré de** *loc prép* in the utmost ■ **au ~ degré du désespoir** in the depths of despair.

◆ **dernier délai** *loc adv* at the latest.

◆ **en dernier** *loc adv* last ■ **entrer en ~** to go in last, to be the last one to go in ■ **son nom a été mentionné en ~** his name was mentioned last *ou* was the last one to be mentioned ■ **ajoute le sel en ~** add the salt last *ou* at the end.

dernièrement [dɛrnjɛrmɑ̃] *adv* lately, not long ago, (quite) recently.

dernier-né, dernière-née [dɛrnjene, dɛrnjɛrne] *(mpl* **derniers-nés**, *fpl* **dernières-nées)** *nm, f* **1.** [benjamin] last-born (child), youngest child **2.** COMM : **le ~ de notre gamme d'ordinateurs** the latest addition to our range of computers.

dérobade [derɔbad] *nf* **1.** *sout* [fuite] avoidance, evasion ■ **il a pris mon silence pour une ~** when I said nothing, he thought I was trying to avoid answering **2.** ÉQUIT jib, refusal.

dérobé, e [derɔbe] *adj sout* **1.** [caché] hidden, concealed, secret ■ **couloir/escalier ~** secret corridor/staircase **2.** [volé] stolen, purloined *litt.*

◆ **à la dérobée** *loc adv* secretly, on the sly, furtively ■ **regarder qqn à la ~e** to steal a glance at sb ■ **il la surveillait à la ~e** he was watching her furtively.

dérober [3] [derɔbe] *vt sout* **1.** [voler] to steal ■ **~ qqch à qqn** to steal sthg from sb ■ **on lui a dérobé son argent** he has been robbed of his money ■ **~ un baiser (à qqn)** *litt* to steal a kiss (from sb) **2.** [cacher] : **~ qqch à la vue** to hide *ou* to conceal sthg from view.

◆ **se dérober** *vpi* **1.** [éluder la difficulté] to shy away ■ **n'essaie pas de te ~** don't try to be evasive **2.** ÉQUIT to jib, to refuse ■ **se ~ devant l'obstacle** to refuse at the jump **3.** [s'effondrer] to collapse, to give way ■ **ses jambes se sont dérobées sous lui** his legs gave way under him.

◆ **se dérober à** *vp+prép* to avoid, to evade ■ **se ~ à ses obligations** to evade *ou* to shirk one's responsibilities.

dérogation [derɔgasjɔ̃] *nf* (special) dispensation *ou* exemption ■ **~ aux usages** departure from custom.

dérogatoire [derɔgatwar] *adj* dispensatory.

déroger [17] [derɔʒe] *vi sout* to demean o.s. ■ **en se mêlant à nous, il croirait ~** he thinks it's beneath him to associate with people like us.

◆ **déroger à** *v+prép* **1.** [manquer à] to depart from ■ **sans ~ à ses habitudes** without departing from one's usual practices **2.** HIST : **~ à son rang** to lose caste *(after working at a demeaning occupation).*

dérouillée△ [deruje] *nf* belting, thrashing.

dérouiller [3] [deruje] ◇ *vt* **1.** [enlever la rouille sur] to remove the rust from **2.** [assouplir - doigts, esprit] to loosen up *(sép)* ; [- jambes] to stretch.
◇ *vi fam* **1.** [être battu] to get it ■ **tu vas ~!** you're for it *ou* going to get it! **2.** [souffrir] to be in agony.

◆ **se dérouiller** *vpt* : **se ~ les doigts** to loosen up one's fingers ■ **se ~ les jambes** to stretch one's legs.

déroulement [derulmɑ̃] *nm* **1.** [débobinage] unreeling, unwinding **2.** [cours - d'une cérémonie, d'un discours] course ■ **le ~ des événements** the course *ou* sequence of events.

dérouler [3] [derule] *vt* **1.** [débobiner - câble] to unroll, to unwind, to uncoil ; [- tapis, rouleau] to unroll ■ **~ le tapis rouge pour qqn** *fig* to roll out the red carpet for sb **2.** MENUIS to cut *ou* to plane veneer from.

◆ **se dérouler** *vpi* **1.** [se déployer - câble, bande] to unwind, to uncoil, to unroll ■ **le paysage se déroule sous nos yeux** the landscape unfolds before our eyes **2.** [avoir lieu] to take place, to be going on ■ **les spectacles qui se déroulent en ce moment** the shows currently running ■ **les épreuves se sont déroulées conformément au règlement** the exams were conducted in accordance with the rules **3.** [progresser] to develop, to progress.

dérouleur [derulœr] *nm* **1.** [de papier, de bande] tape winder ■ **~ de bande magnétique** tape unit, magnetic tape drive ■ **~ de film magnétique** magnetic film handler **2.** [de cuisine] kitchen roll dispenser.

déroutant, e [derutɑ̃, ɑ̃t] *adj* perplexing, disconcerting, puzzling.

déroute [derut] *nf* **1.** MIL retreat, rout ■ **être en pleine ~** to be in full flight ■ **mettre qqn en ~** to disconcert sb ■ **l'armée a été aisément mise en ~** the army was easily routed **2.** [débâcle] ruin ■ **l'entreprise est en pleine ~** the firm's collapsing.

dérouter [3] [derute] *vt* **1.** [changer l'itinéraire de] to reroute **2.** [étonner] to disconcert, to perplex ■ **la question l'a dérouté** the question threw him off balance **3.** CHASSE to throw off the track.

derrick [derik] *nm* derrick.

derrière [dɛrjɛr] <> *prép* **1.** [en arrière de] behind ■ **ça s'est passé ~ chez moi** it happened behind my house ■ **il y a un chien ~ la grille** there's a dog (on) the other side of the gate ‖ *fig* **être ~ qqn** [le soutenir] to support sb ■ **ne sois pas toujours ~ moi!** [à me surveiller] stop watching everything I do all the time! ➲ **je sais bien ce qu'elle dit ~ mon dos** I'm quite aware of what she says behind my back ■ **il faut toujours être ~ lui** *ou* **~ son dos** he has to be watched all the time **2.** [à la suite de - dans un classement] behind **3.** [sous] beneath, under ■ **~ son indifférence apparente** beneath his apparent indifference ■ **qu'y a-t-il ~ tout ça?** what's the key to all this?, what's behind all this?, what's all this really about?
<> *adv* **1.** [en arrière] behind, the other side ■ **tu vois le bureau de poste? la bibliothèque est juste ~** do you see the post office? the library's just behind it ■ **passe ~, tu verras mieux** come through, you'll get a better view **2.** [du côté arrière] at the back ■ **tes cheveux sont trop longs ~** your hair's too long at the back ‖ [sur la face arrière] on the back ■ **écris le nom de l'expéditeur ~** write the sender's name on the back **3.** [dans le fond] at the rear *ou* back ■ **installe-toi ~** [dans une voiture] sit in the back **4.** *fig* behind ■ **elle est loin ~** she's a long way behind.
<> *nm* **1.** [d'un objet, d'un espace] back **2.** *fam* [fesses] bottom, posterior *hum* ■ **pousse ton ~!** shift your backside! ■ **avoir le ~ à l'air** to be bare-bottomed ➲ **coup de pied au ~** kick up the backside *ou* US in the pants ■ **être** *ou* **rester** *ou* **tomber le ~ par terre** to be stunned *ou* flabbergasted **3.** ZOOL rump ■ **le chien assis sur son ~** the dog sitting on its haunches.
◆ **de derrière** <> *loc adj* [dent, jardin, roue *etc*] back *(modif)* ■ **voici une vue de ~** here's a rear view.
<> *loc prép* **1.** [par l'arrière de] from behind **2.** *loc* **de ~ les fagots** very special.
◆ **par derrière** <> *loc adv* from behind ■ **il est passé par ~** [la maison] he went round the back ■ **dire du mal de qqn par ~** to criticize sb behind his/her back.
<> *loc prép* from behind ■ **je suis passé par ~ la maison** I went round the back of the house.

derviche [dɛrviʃ] *nm* dervish ■ **~ tourneur** whirling dervish.

des [de] <> *dét (art indéfini)* ⊳ **un.**
<> *prép* ⊳ **de.**

dès [dɛ] *prép* **1.** [dans le temps] from ■ **~ son retour, il faudra y penser** as soon as he comes back, we'll have to think about it ■ **~ le début** from the beginning ■ **prêt ~ 8 h** ready by 8 o'clock ■ **~ le quinzième siècle** as far back as the fifteenth century ■ **je vais le faire ~ aujourd'hui** I'm going to do it this very day ■ **vous pouvez réserver vos places ~ maintenant** booking is now open ■ **pouvez-vous commencer ~ maintenant?** can you start straight away? **2.** [dans un ordre, une hiérarchie] : **~ la seconde année** from the second year onwards ■ **~ sa nomination** as soon as he was appointed ■ **~ le deuxième verre, il ne savait plus ce qu'il disait** after his second glass he started talking nonsense **3.** [dans l'espace] : **~ la frontière** on reaching the border ■ **~ la sortie du village commence la forêt** the woods lie just beyond the village.
◆ **dès lors** *loc adv* **1.** [à partir de là] from then on, since (then) ■ **il a quitté la ville; ~ lors, on n'a plus entendu parler de lui** he left the town and he's never been heard of since **2.** [en conséquence] consequently, therefore.
◆ **dès lors que** *loc conj* **1.** [étant donné que] as, since ■ [du moment où] from the moment (that) ■ **~ lors qu'il a renoncé à ce poste, il ne peut prétendre à une augmentation** given that *ou* since *ou* as he refused that job, he can't expect a rise **2.** [dès que] as soon as ■ **~ lors que la loi entre en vigueur, il faut s'y conformer** as soon as the law comes into force, it must be respected.
◆ **dès que** *loc conj* **1.** [aussitôt que] as soon as ■ **~ que possible** as soon as possible ■ **~ que tu pourras** as soon as you can **2.** [chaque fois que] whenever ■ **~ qu'il peut, il part en vacances** whenever he can, he goes off on holiday.

désabonner [3] [dezabɔne] *vt* to cancel the subscription of.
◆ **se désabonner** *vp (emploi réfléchi)* to stop subscribing, to cancel *ou* to withdraw *ou* to discontinue one's subscription ■ **se ~ à une revue** to stop taking a magazine.

désabusé, e [dezabyze] *adj* **1.** [déçu] disillusioned, disenchanted **2.** [amer] embittered.

désaccord [dezakɔr] *nm* **1.** [litige] conflict, disagreement, dissension *(U)* ■ **s'il y a ~** if there's any disagreement **2.** [contraste] discrepancy, disharmony *litt.*
◆ **en désaccord** *loc adj* : **les parties en ~** the dissenting parties ■ **ils sont en ~ en ce qui concerne l'éducation de leurs enfants** they disagree about their children's education ■ **être en ~ avec qqn sur qqch** to be in conflict with sb over sthg ■ **sa conduite est en ~ avec ses principes** his behaviour is not consistent with his principles.
Voir module d'usage

désaccorder [3] [dezakɔrde] *vt* MUS to detune ■ **le piano est désaccordé** the piano's out of tune.
◆ **se désaccorder** *vpi* MUS to go out of tune.

désaccoutumance [dezakutymɑ̃s] *nf* **1.** [perte d'une habitude] loss of a habit **2.** MÉD & PSYCHOL end of a dependency ■ **la ~ du tabac** breaking tobacco dependency.

désaccoutumer [3] [dezakutyme] *vt* **1.** [déshabituer] to disaccustom, to cause to lose a habit **2.** MÉD & PSYCHOL : **~ qqn** to end sb's dependency.
◆ **se désaccoutumer de** *vp+prép* **1.** [se déshabituer] : **se ~ de faire** to get out of the habit of doing **2.** MÉD & PSYCHOL to lose one's dependency on ■ **se ~ du tabac** to kick the tobacco habit.

désacralisation [desakralizasjɔ̃] *nf* deconsecration.

désacraliser [3] [desakralize] *vt* to remove the sacred character from ■ *fig* to demythologize.

désactiver [3] [dezaktive] *vt* **1.** CHIM to deactivate, to make ineffective **2.** NUCL to decontaminate.

désadapté, e [dezadapte] <> *adj* : **un malade ~** a patient who's lost the ability to adapt *ou* to adjust (to normal life).
<> *nm, f* misfit ■ **les ~s** those who can't adapt *ou* adjust (to normal life) any more.

désaffectation [dezafɛktasjɔ̃] *nf* [d'une église] deconsecration, secularization, secularizing ■ [d'une gare] closing down, putting out of use *ou* commission.

désaffecté, e [dezafɛkte] *adj* [église] deconsecrated, secularized ■ [gare, entrepôt] disused.

LE DÉSACCORD

I'm sorry, but I can't agree with you there. Je regrette, mais je ne peux pas vous suivre sur ce point.
I don't agree/I disagree. Je ne suis pas d'accord.
I totally disagree. Je ne suis absolument pas d'accord.
I'm not convinced. Je ne suis pas convaincu.
I'm afraid I can't go along with you on that. Je crains de ne pas pouvoir vous suivre sur ce point.
With respect, I think you're forgetting one important point. Si je peux me permettre, je pense que vous oubliez un aspect important.
I don't think that's true. Je ne crois pas que ça soit vrai.
You have a point, but... Certes, mais...
That's all very well, but... Peut-être, mais...
Nonsense *ou* **Rubbish!** *fam* N'importe quoi !

désaffecter [4] [dezafɛkte] *vt* [église] to deconsecrate, to secularize ■ [entrepôt] to close down, to put out of use *ou* commission ■ **il a désaffecté son garage pour en faire un atelier** he turned his garage into a workshop.

désaffection [dezafɛksjɔ̃] *nf* disaffection, loss of interest ■ **manifester une certaine ~ pour qqch** to lose interest in *ou* to turn one's back on sthg.

désagréable [dezagreabl] *adj* **1.** [déplaisant] disagreeable, unpleasant ■ **~ à voir** unsightly ■ **une odeur ~** a nasty smell ■ **ce n'est pas ~** it's rather pleasant *ou* nice **2.** [peu sociable] bad-tempered, rude ■ **elle est ~ avec tout le monde** she's rude to everybody.

désagréablement [dezagreabləmɑ̃] *adv* unpleasantly, offensively ■ **un bruit qui résonne ~ aux oreilles** a noise that grates on the ears.

désagrégation [dezagregasjɔ̃] *nf* **1.** [d'un tissu, d'un béton] disintegration **2.** GÉOL weathering **3.** [d'une équipe] break-up, breaking *ou* splitting up, disbanding.

désagréger [22] [dezagreʒe] *vt* **1.** [effriter] to break up *(sép)*, to cause to disintegrate *ou* to crumble **2.** [désunir - équipe] to break up *(sép)*, to disband.
◆ **se désagréger** *vpi* **1.** [s'effriter] to powder ■ GÉOL to be weathered **2.** [groupe, équipe] to break up, to disband ■ **le club s'est désagrégé** the club disbanded.

désagrément [dezagremɑ̃] *nm* trouble *(U)*, inconvenience *(U)* ■ **causer des ~s à qqn** to cause trouble for sb, to inconvenience sb ■ **les voyages impliquent parfois quelques ~s** travelling sometimes involves inconvenience.

désalpe [dezalp] *nf* **Suisse** transhumance *(from the high pastures)*.

désaltérant, e [dezalterɑ̃, ɑ̃t] *adj* refreshing, thirst-quenching.

désaltérer [18] [dezaltere] *vt* to refresh, to quench the thirst of.
◆ **se désaltérer** *vpi* to quench *ou* to slake one's thirst.

désambiguïser [3] [dezɑ̃bigɥize] *vt* to disambiguate.

désamianter [dezamjɑ̃te] *vt* to remove the asbestos from.

désamorçage [dezamɔrsaʒ] *nm* **1.** ARM [d'une bombe] defusing ■ [d'une arme] unpriming **2.** ÉLECTR running down, de-energization **3.** MÉCAN air-binding.

désamorcer [16] [dezamɔrse] *vt* **1.** ARM [grenade] to defuse ■ [arme] to unprime **2.** ÉLECTR to run down *(sép)*, to de-energize **3.** MÉCAN : **~ une pompe** to draw off the water from a pump **4.** [contrecarrer] to defuse, to forestall, to inhibit ■ **des mesures d'urgence pour ~ la grève** emergency measures to defuse the strike.

désappointé, e [dezapwɛ̃te] *adj* **sout** disappointed, frustrated.

désappointement [dezapwɛ̃tmɑ̃] *nm* **litt** disappointment, dissatisfaction.

désappointer [3] [dezapwɛ̃te] *vt* **sout** to disappoint.

désapprendre [79] [dezaprɑ̃dr] *vt* to forget, to unlearn ■ **ce n'est pas facile de ~ à mentir** it's not easy to get out of the habit of lying.

désapprobateur, trice [dezaprɔbatœr, tris] *adj* censorious **sout**, disapproving ■ **d'un air ~** with a look of disapproval ■ **d'un ton ~** disapprovingly.

désapprobation [dezaprɔbasjɔ̃] *nf* disapproval ■ **exprimer ouvertement sa ~** to disapprove openly.
Voir module d'usage

désapprouver [3] [dezapruve] *vt* **1.** [condamner] to disapprove of ■ **un mariage civil? sachez que je désapprouve!** a registry office *UK ou* civil *US* wedding? let me say that I thoroughly disapprove *ou* I do not approve! **2.** [s'opposer à - projet, idée] to object to, to reject.

désarçonner [3] [dezarsɔne] *vt* **1.** ÉQUIT to unseat, to unhorse **2.** [déconcerter] to throw, to put off one's stride ■ **son intervention a désarçonné l'orateur** his remark threw the speaker off balance.

désargenté, e [dezarʒɑ̃te] *adj* **fam** penniless ■ **une famille ~e** a family fallen on hard times.

désargenter [3] [dezarʒɑ̃te] *vt* **1.** MIN to desilver **2.** [bijou, couvert] to wear off the silver plate of **3.** **fam** [priver d'argent] to deprive of cash.

désarmant, e [dezarmɑ̃, ɑ̃t] *adj* **1.** [touchant] disarming ■ **elle est ~e de gentillesse** she is disarmingly sweet **2.** [confondant] amazing, breathtaking.

désarmé, e [dezarme] *adj* **1.** ARM uncocked **2.** NAUT laid up **3.** [surpris] dumbfounded **4.** [privé de moyens] : **être ~ devant la vie/les mauvaises influences** to be ill-equipped to cope with life/to deal with bad influences.

désarmement [dezarməmɑ̃] *nm* MIL & POLIT disarmament.

désarmer [3] [dezarme] ◇ *vt* **1.** MIL & POLIT to disarm **2.** ARM to uncock **3.** [attendrir] to disarm ■ **être désarmé par la bonne volonté de qqn** to find sb's willingness disarming **4.** NAUT to lay up *(sép)*, to put out of commission.
◇ *vi* **1.** MIL to disarm **2.** **loc il ne désarme pas** he won't give in, he keeps battling on ■ **les journaux ne désarmeront pas** the press stories will go on and on.

désarroi [dezarwa] *nm* dismay, (utter) confusion ■ **être dans le ~ le plus profond** to be utterly dismayed, to be in utter confusion.

désarticulé, e [dezartikyle] *adj* dislocated, out of joint.

désarticuler [3] [dezartikyle] *vt* to disjoint, to dislocate.
◆ **se désarticuler** ◇ *vpi* [se contorsionner] to twist *ou* to contort o.s.
◇ *vpt* [par accident] : **se ~ un doigt/le genou** to put a finger/one's knee out of joint.

désastre [dezastr] *nm* **1.** [calamité] calamity, catastrophe, disaster ■ **ils ne purent que constater l'ampleur du ~** they could only record the extent of the damage **2.** [échec] disaster, failure ■ **le gâteau d'anniversaire fut un ~** the birthday cake was a complete failure.

désastreux, euse [dezastrø, øz] *adj* [résultat, effet] disastrous, awful, terrible ■ **des résultats ~ en physique** appalling results in physics ■ **le spectacle/pique-nique a été ~** the show/picnic was a complete disaster.

désatelliser [3] [desatelize] *vt* [pays] to free from dependence, to release from satellite status.

LA DÉSAPPROBATION

I don't approve *OU* **I disapprove of smoking.** Je suis contre le tabac.

I'm totally against it. Je m'y oppose complètement.

I don't think it's right to smack children. Je pense qu'il ne faut pas frapper les enfants.

I'm not happy about you staying out late. Ça ne me plaît pas que tu rentres tard.

She was wrong to *OU* **It was wrong of her to walk out on him like that.** Elle a eu tort de le quitter comme ça.

Frankly, that's no way to behave. Franchement, ce ne sont pas des façons de se comporter.

It's just not on! C'est inacceptable !

désavantage [dezavɑ̃taʒ] *nm* **1.** [inconvénient] disadvantage, drawback ▪ **avoir tous les ~s de qqch** to get the worst *ou* brunt of sthg **2.** [infériorité] disadvantage, handicap.
◆ **au désavantage de** *loc prép* : **c'est à ton ~** it's not to your advantage ▪ **se montrer à son ~** to show o.s. in an unfavourable light ▪ **tourner au ~ de qqn** to go against sb, to turn out to be a handicap for sb.

désavantager [17] [dezavɑ̃taʒe] *vt* [défavoriser] to (put at a) disadvantage, to penalize ▪ **il est désavantagé par son jeune âge** he is handicapped by his youth, his youth is against him ▪ **elle est désavantagée simplement parce que c'est une femme** she's at a disadvantage simply because she is a woman.

désavantageusement [dezavɑ̃taʒøzmɑ̃] *adv* disadvantageously.

désavantageux, euse [dezavɑ̃taʒø, øz] *adj* detrimental, disadvantageous ▪ **c'est ~ pour les petites entreprises** this works against the interests of small businesses.

désaveu, x [dezavø] *nm* **1.** [reniement] disavowal, retraction **2.** [condamnation] repudiation ▪ **il n'a pas supporté ce ~ public** he couldn't stand the idea of being condemned in public **3.** DR : **~ de paternité** repudiation of paternity **4.** PSYCHOL denial.

désavouer [6] [dezavwe] *vt* **1.** [renier - propos] to disavow, to repudiate ; [- dette] to repudiate ▪ **~ sa promesse** to go back on one's word, to break one's promise **2.** [refuser de reconnaître - représentant, candidat] to challenge the authority *ou* legitimacy of ▪ **elle avait un si bon accent qu'un autochtone ne l'aurait pas désavouée** her accent was so good that she could have passed for a native **3.** DR to disclaim, to repudiate.
◆ **se désavouer** *vpi* to retract.

désaxé, e [dezakse] ◇ *adj* **1.** MÉCAN out of alignment ▪ **roue ~e** dished wheel **2.** [dérangé] mentally deranged, unbalanced, unhinged.
◇ *nm, f* (dangerous) lunatic, psychopath.

désaxer [3] [dezakse] *vt* **1.** MÉCAN to offset, to throw out of alignment **2.** [perturber] to unhinge ▪ **ils ont été désaxés par la guerre** the war unhinged them *ou* left them psychologically disturbed.

desceller [4] [desele] *vt* **1.** [ouvrir] to unseal, to take the seal off **2.** [détacher] to loosen ▪ **les briques sont descellées** the bricks have worked loose *ou* are loose.

descendance [desɑ̃dɑ̃s] *nf* **1.** DR descent, lineage **2.** [progéniture] descendants.

descendant, e [desɑ̃dɑ̃, ɑ̃t] ◇ *adj* down *(avant n)*, downward, descending ▪ **escalator ~** down escalator ▪ **mouvement ~** downward movement.
◇ *nm, f* [dans une famille] descendant.
◆ **descendant** *nm* ASTROL descendant.

descendeur, euse [desɑ̃dœr, øz] *nm, f* [skieur] downhill skier, downhiller ▪ **~ en rappel** [alpiniste] abseiler.
◆ **descendeur** *nm* descender.

descendre [73] [desɑ̃dr] ◇ *vi (aux être)*

A.

1. [personne, mécanisme, avion - vu d'en haut] to go down ; [- vu d'en bas] to come down ▪ [oiseau] to fly *ou* to swoop down ▪ **j'ai rencontré la concierge en descendant** I met the caretaker on my way down ▪ **aide-moi à ~** help me down ▪ **je descends toujours par l'escalier** I always go down by the stairs *ou* take the stairs down ▪ **notre équipe est descendue à la huitième place** our team moved down *ou* dropped to eighth place ▪ **le premier coureur à ~ au-dessous de dix secondes au 100 mètres** the first runner to break ten seconds for the 100 metres ▪ **la pièce de monnaie ne voulait pas ~ (dans la fente)** the coin wouldn't go down (the slot) ▪ **son chapeau lui descendait jusqu'aux yeux** his hat came down over his eyes ▪ **mes chaussettes descendent** my socks are falling down *ou* slipping down ▪ **faire ~ : fais ~ la malade** help the patient down ▪ **ils ont fait ~ les passagers sur les rails** they made the passengers get down onto the tracks ▪ **ils nous ont fait ~ du train** they made us get off the train ▪ **c'est ce mécanisme qui fait ~ la plate-forme** this mechanism brings the platform down *ou* lowers the platform ▪ **~ de** [échafaudage, échelle] to come *ou* to climb down from, to get down from ; [arbre] to climb *ou* to come down out of ; [balançoire] to get off ◆ **~ dans la rue** [manifester] to take to the streets
2. [air froid, brouillard] to come down ▪ [soleil] to go down ▪ **la nuit** *ou* **le soir descend** night is closing in *ou* falling
3. [se rendre - dans un lieu d'altitude inférieure, dans le Sud, à la campagne] to go down ▪ **~ en ville** to go into town, to go downtown *US* ▪ **je suis descendu à Bordeaux en voiture** I drove down to Bordeaux
4. [poser pied à terre - d'un véhicule] to get off, to alight *sout* ▪ **'ne pas ~ avant l'arrêt complet du train'** 'please do not attempt to alight until the train has come to a complete standstill' ▪ **~ à terre** to go ashore ▪ **~ de bateau** to get off a boat, to land ▪ **~ de voiture** to get out of a car ▪ **~ de vélo** to get off one's bike ▪ **à quelle station descendez-vous?** where do you get off? ▪ **aider une vieille dame à ~** to help an old lady off
5. [faire irruption] : **la police est descendue chez elle/dans son bar** the police raided her place/her bar
6. [se loger] to stay ▪ **~ dans un hôtel** to put up at *ou* to stay at a hotel
7. *fam* [repas, boisson] to go *ou* to slip down ▪ **ton petit vin rouge descend bien** your red wine goes down very easily ▪ **bois un café pour faire ~ tout ça** have a coffee to wash it all down ◆ **avec lui, ça descend!** [il boit] he really knocks it back! ; [il mange] he can really tuck it away!
8. DANSE & THÉÂTRE to go downstage

B.

1. [cheveux, vêtement] : **~ à** *ou* **jusqu'à** to come down to ; [puits] to go down to ▪ **la jupe doit ~ jusqu'au-dessous du genou** the skirt must cover the knee
2. [suivre une pente - rivière] to flow down ; [- route] to go down *ou* downwards ; [- toit] to slope down ▪ **le sentier descendait parmi les oliviers** the path threaded its way down through the olive grove ▪ **le jardin descend en pente douce jusqu'à la plage** the garden slopes gently down to the beach ▪ **~ en pente raide** [route, terrain, toit] to drop sharply ▪ **la route descend brusquement** the road suddenly dips

C.

1. [baisser - marée, mer] to go out *(insép)*, to ebb ; [- prix] to go down, to fall ▪ **la température est descendue au-dessous de zéro** the temperature has dropped *ou* fallen below zero ▪ **les températures ne descendent jamais au-dessous de 10°** temperatures never fall below 10° ▪ **le thermomètre descend** *fam* the weather's *ou* it's getting colder ▪ **le cours du café est descendu à 800 dollars** the trading price of coffee has fallen down to 800 dollars ▪ **l'essence est descendue au-dessous de un euro** the price of petrol has fallen below the one euro mark ▪ **faire ~** [inflation, prix] to bring *ou* to push down *(sép)* ▪ **j'ai essayé de lui faire ~ son prix** I tried to get him to lower his price ▪ **faire ~ la fièvre** to bring down sb's temperature
2. [s'abaisser moralement] to stoop ▪ **~ dans l'estime de qqn** to go down in sb's estimation
3. MUS to go *ou* to drop down ▪ **~ d'une octave** to go down *ou* to drop an octave.

◇ *vt (aux avoir)* **1.** [parcourir - escalier, montagne] to go down *(insép)* ▪ **~ le courant** [détritus, arbre] to float downstream ▪ **~ un fleuve** [en nageant] to swim downstream ; [en bateau] to sail down a river ▪ **ils ont descendu le Mississippi en radeau** they went down the Mississippi on a raft ▪ **il a descendu tout le terrain balle au pied** FOOTBALL he ran the length of the field with the ball **2.** [placer plus bas - tableau] to lower ; [- store] to pull down *(sép)*, to lower ▪ **il faudrait ~ le cadre de deux centimètres** the frame should be taken down two centimetres **3.** [porter vers le bas - colis] to take down *(sép)*, to get down *(sép)* [- porter vers soi] to bring down *(sép)* ▪ **descendez les chaises en bas de la pelouse** carry the chairs down to the far end of the lawn ▪ **tu pourrais me ~ une veste, s'il te plaît?** could you bring me down a jacket please? ▪ **ils ont descendu le sauveteur au bout d'une corde** they lowered the rescuer on the end of a rope **4.** [amener en voiture] to take *ou* to drive down *(sép)* **5.** *fam* [abattre - gangster] to gun *ou* to shoot down *(sép)* ; [- avion] to bring *ou* to shoot down *(sép)* ▪ **se faire ~** to get shot **6.** *fam* [critiquer] to pan, to slate ▪ **il s'est fait ~ par le jury** he was slated by the jury **7.** *fam* [boire - bouteille] to down, to knock back *(sép)* **8.** MUS : **~ la gamme** to go down the scale.

◆ **descendre de** *v+prép* [être issu de] to be descended from ■ **le prince descendait des Habsbourg** the prince was descended from the Habsburgs.

descente [desɑ̃t] *nf* **1.** [pente] slope, hill ■ **courir/déraper dans la ~** to run/to skid down ■ **on ira vite, il n'y a que des ~s** we'll do it in no time, it's all downhill
2. [progression] going down ■ [chute] drop, fall
3. [sortie d'un véhicule] getting off, alighting ■ **à sa ~ d'avion** as he disembarked *ou* got off the aircraft ■ **à sa ~ du bateau** as he landed *ou* disembarked
4. [en ski] downhill race ■ SPORT [alpinisme] : **~ en rappel** abseiling
5. AÉRON descent ■ **~ en piqué** dive ■ **~ en spirale** spinning dive, spiral descent ■ **~ en vol plané** glide, gliding fall
6. MÉD : **~ d'organe** *ou* **d'organes** prolapse
7. [contrôle] inspection ■ [attaque] raid ■ **faire une ~** ADMIN to carry out a (surprise) inspection ; MIL to mount a raid ■ *fam* to make an unexpected visit ■ **faire une ~ sur qqch** *fig & hum* to raid ■ **il a encore fait une ~ sur le chocolat!** he's been raiding *ou* he's been at the chocolate again! ➊ **~ de police** police raid
8. *fam loc* **avoir une bonne ~** [boire beaucoup] to be able to take one's drink ; [manger beaucoup] to be a big eater.
◆ **descente de lit** *nf* **1.** [tapis] bedside rug
2. *fam péj* toady.

déscolariser [3] [deskɔlarize] *vt* to take out of the school system.

descriptible [dɛskriptibl] *adj* describable ■ **sa joie n'était pas ~** his joy was beyond description *ou* words.

descriptif, ive [dɛskriptif, iv] *adj* **1.** [présentation, texte] descriptive ■ **devis ~** specification **2.** ART, LING & LITTÉR descriptive **3.** GÉOM solid.
◆ **descriptif** *nm* [d'un appartement] description ■ [de travaux] specification.

description [dɛskripsjɔ̃] *nf* **1.** [fait de décrire] description ■ **faire la ~ de qqch** to describe sthg ■ **~ de poste** job description **2.** ART & LITTÉR description, descriptive passage **3.** LING descriptive analysis *ou* study.

déségrégation [desegregasjɔ̃] *nf* desegregation.

désembourber [3] [dezɑ̃burbe] *vt* to pull *ou* to get out of the mud.

désembouteiller [4] [dezɑ̃buteje] *vt* **1.** AUTO to unblock ■ **~ les grandes villes** to ease the traffic in the big cities **2.** TÉLÉCOM : **~ le standard** to remove the overload from *ou* to unjam the exchange.

désembrouiller [3] [dezɑ̃bruje] *vt* to disentangle, to unmesh, to make less complicated.

désembuer [7] [dezɑ̃bɥe] *vt* to demist.

désemparé, e [dezɑ̃pare] *adj* **1.** [perdu] : **être tout ~** to be lost ■ **sans argent dans cette ville étrangère, il était complètement ~** in a foreign town with no money, he had no idea what to do **2.** AÉRON & NAUT crippled.

désemparer [3] [dezɑ̃pare] *vi* : **sans ~** without a pause *ou* break.

désemplir [32] [dezɑ̃plir] *vi* : **leur maison ne désemplit pas** their house is always full.

désenchanté, e [dezɑ̃ʃɑ̃te] ◇ *adj* disenchanted, disillusioned.
◇ *nm, f* disenchanted *ou* disaffected person ■ **les ~s du socialisme** those who have become disenchanted with socialism.

désenchantement [dezɑ̃ʃɑ̃tmɑ̃] *nm* disillusionment, disenchantment, disillusion.

désenclaver [3] [dezɑ̃klave] *vt* to open to the outside world.

désencombrer [3] [dezɑ̃kɔ̃bre] *vt* to clear, to unblock.

désencrasser [3] [dezɑ̃krase] *vt* [ustensile, four] to clean out ■ [moteur] to decarbonize, to decoke.

désendettement [dezɑ̃dɛtmɑ̃] *nm* clearing of debts, debt-clearing.

désendetter [4] [dezɑ̃dete] *vt* : **~ qqn** to free sb of *ou* to release sb from debt.
◆ **se désendetter** *vp (emploi réfléchi)* to get out of debt, to clear one's debts.

désenfiler [3] [dezɑ̃file] ◆ **se désenfiler** *vpi* to come unthreaded.

désenfler [3] [dezɑ̃fle] ◇ *vt* to bring down *(sép)* *ou* to reduce the swelling of.
◇ *vi* to become less swollen ■ **ma cheville désenfle** the swelling in my ankle's going down ■ **la pommade a fait ~ ma cheville** the cream made my swollen ankle go down *ou* eased the swelling in my ankle.

désenfumer [3] [dezɑ̃fyme] *vt* to clear of smoke.

désengagement [dezɑ̃gaʒmɑ̃] *nm* disengagement, backing out.

désengager [17] [dezɑ̃gaʒe] *vt* to free *ou* to release from (a) commitment.
◆ **se désengager** *vp (emploi réfléchi)* **1.** [se dépolitiser] to give up one's political commitment **2.** [se décommander] to back out of a commitment.

désengorger [17] [dezɑ̃gɔrʒe] *vt* [tuyau, rue] to unblock, to clear ■ **~ le marché** ÉCON to reduce the overload on the market.

désenivrer [3] [dezɑ̃nivre] *vt* to sober up *(sép)*.
◆ **se désenivrer** *vpi* to sober up.

désensabler [3] [dezɑ̃sable] *vt* **1.** [extraire] to get out of *ou* to extract from the sand **2.** [nettoyer] to free *ou* to clear of sand.

désensibilisation [desɑ̃sibilizasjɔ̃] *nf* MÉD & PHOTO desensitizing, desensitization.

désensibiliser [3] [desɑ̃sibilize] *vt* **1.** MÉD & PHOTO to desensitize **2.** [désintéresser] : **~ qqn de qqch** to make sb less interested in sthg.

désensorceler [24] [dezɑ̃sɔrsəle] *vt* to free *ou* to release from a spell.

désentortiller [3] [dezɑ̃tɔrtije] *vt* **1.** [détordre] to untwist **2.** [démêler] to disentangle, to sort out *(sép)*.

désentraver [3] [dezɑ̃trave] *vt* to unchain.

désenvaser [3] [dezɑ̃vaze] *vt* **1.** [extraire] to get out of *ou* to extract from the mud **2.** [nettoyer] to clear (of mud).

désépaissir [32] [dezepesir] *vt* [sauce] to thin (down), to dilute ■ [cheveux] to thin (out).

déséquilibre [dezekilibr] *nm* **1.** [inégalité] imbalance ■ **il y a un ~ dans les programmes de la chaîne** the channel's schedule is unbalanced ❙ ÉCON disequilibrium, imbalance ■ **~ de la balance commerciale** unfavourable trade balance **2.** [perte d'équilibre] loss of balance **3.** PSYCHOL : **~ mental** *ou* **psychique** derangement **4.** PHYSIOL imbalance.
◆ **en déséquilibre** *loc adj* [mal posé] off balance ■ [branlant] unsteady, wobbly.

déséquilibré, e [dezekilibre] ◇ *adj* [personne, esprit] unbalanced, deranged.
◇ *nm, f* maladjusted person.

déséquilibrer [3] [dezekilibre] *vt* **1.** [faire perdre l'équilibre à] to throw off balance ■ [faire tomber] to tip over ■ **le vent l'a déséquilibré** the wind blew him off balance **2.** [déstabiliser - système, économie] to throw off balance, to destabilize **3.** [faire déraisonner] : **~ qqn** to disturb the balance of sb's mind.

désert, e [dezɛr, ɛrt] *adj* [abandonné] deserted, empty ■ [inhabité] desolate, uninhabited ■ **l'endroit était ~** the place was deserted, there was nobody around.
◆ **désert** *nm* **1.** GÉOGR desert **2.** [lieu inhabité] desert, wilderness, wasteland ■ **c'est le ~ ici!** it's deserted here! ■ **un ~ de béton** a concrete desert ➊ **il crie** *ou* **parle** *ou* **prêche dans le ~** his words fall on deaf ears **3.** *litt* [monotonie] vacuity ■ **le ~ de ma vie** my vacuous *ou* empty life.

DÉSERT

le désert de Gobi the Gobi Desert ;
le désert du Kalahari the Kalahari Desert ;
le désert de Libye the Libyan Desert ;
le désert du Namib the Namib Desert ;
le désert de Nubie the Nubian Desert ;
le désert du Sahara the Sahara Desert.

déserter [3] [dezɛrte] <> *vi* MIL to desert.
<> *vt* **1.** [quitter sans permission] to desert ■ **pour avoir déserté son poste** for having deserted his post **2.** [abandonner - parti, cause] to abandon, to give up on *(insép)* **3.** [suj: touristes, clients] to desert.

déserteur [dezɛrtœr] *nm* deserter.

désertification [dezɛrtifikasjɔ̃] *nf* GÉOGR desertification.

désertifier [9] [dezɛrtifje] ◆ **se désertifier** *vpi* to turn into a desert.

désertion [dezɛrsjɔ̃] *nf* **1.** MIL desertion **2.** [fait de quitter] : **la ~ des campagnes** the rural exodus **3.** [d'une cause, d'un parti] deserting, abandoning.

désertique [dezɛrtik] *adj* [du désert] desert *(modif)* ■ [sans végétation] infertile.

désescalade [dezɛskalad] *nf* de-escalation.

désespérant, e [dezɛsperɑ̃, ɑ̃t] *adj* **1.** [navrant] hopeless ■ **d'une paresse ~e** hopelessly lazy **2.** [très mauvais - temps] appalling, dreadful **3.** [douloureux] appalling, distressing, terrible.

désespéré, e [dezɛspere] <> *adj* **1.** [au désespoir] desperate, despairing **2.** [extrême - tentative] desperate, reckless ; [- mesure, situation] desperate **3.** [sans espoir] hopeless ■ **c'est un cas ~** [incorrigible] it's a hopeless case ; [gravement malade] the patient is critical ■ **être dans un état ~** [malade] to be in a critical condition **4.** [très déçu] deeply *ou* horribly disappointed.
<> *nm, f* **1.** [personne sans espoir] desperate person **2.** [suicidé] suicide.

désespérément [dezɛsperemɑ̃] *adv* **1.** [avec désespoir] desperately ■ **on entendait appeler ~ à l'aide** desperate cries for help could be heard **2.** [extrêmement] hopelessly, desperately.

désespérer [18] [dezɛspere] <> *vi* to despair, to give up hope ■ **il ne faut jamais ~!** never say die! *hum*, you should never give up hope!
<> *vt* **1.** [exaspérer] to drive to despair ■ **tu me désespères!** what am I going to do with you? **2.** [décourager] to drive *ou* to reduce to despair ■ **elle en a désespéré plus d'un** she'd driven more than one (suitor) to despair.
◆ **désespérer de** *v+prép* : **~ de qqch** to have lost faith in sthg ■ **~ de faire qqch** to despair of doing sthg ■ **je ne désespère pas d'obtenir le poste** I still think I may get *ou* I haven't yet given up on the idea of getting the job.
◆ **se désespérer** *vpi* to (be in) despair.

désespoir [dezɛspwar] *nm* despair ■ **faire le ~ de qqn** to drive *ou* to reduce sb to despair ■ **à mon grand ~, il n'a pu venir** to my despair, he was unable to come ■ **avec ~** despairingly, in despair.
◆ **au désespoir** <> *loc adj* : **être au ~** [être désespéré] to be desperate, to have lost all hope ■ **je suis au ~ de ne pouvoir vous aider** I'm deeply *ou* desperately sorry that I am unable to help you.
<> *loc adv* : **mettre qqn au ~** to drive *ou* to reduce sb to despair.
◆ **en désespoir de cause** *loc adv* in desperation, as a last resort ■ **en ~ de cause, elle essaya sa propre clef** as a last resort she tried her own key.

désexualiser [desɛksyalize] *vt* to desex.

déshabillage [dezabijaʒ] *nm* **1.** [d'une personne] undressing **2.** [dégarnissage - d'une pièce] emptying (of ornaments) ; [- d'un fauteuil] stripping of upholstery.

déshabillé [dezabije] *nm* négligé.

déshabiller [3] [dezabije] *vt* **1.** [dévêtir] : **~ qqn** to undress sb, to take sb's clothes off ■ **~ qqn du regard** to undress sb with one's eyes ■ **c'est ~ Pierre pour habiller Paul** it's robbing Peter to pay Paul **2.** [vider - pièce] to empty (of ornaments) ■ [dégarnir - fauteuil] to strip the upholstery from.
◆ **se déshabiller** *vp (emploi réfléchi)* **1.** [se dénuder] to strip (off), to take one's clothes off **2.** [ôter un vêtement] : **déshabille-toi** take off your coat.

déshabituer [7] [dezabitɥe] *vt* : **~ qqn du tabac** to make sb give up (using) tobacco ■ **~ qqn de faire qqch** to break sb of the habit of doing sthg.

désherbage [dezɛrbaʒ] *nm* weeding.

désherbant, e [dezɛrbɑ̃, ɑ̃t] *adj* weed-killing *(avant n)*.
◆ **désherbant** *nm* weedkiller.

désherber [3] [dezɛrbe] *vt* to weed.

déshérité, e [dezerite] <> *adj* **1.** [pauvre] underprivileged, deprived **2.** [région] poor *(lacking natural advantages)* **3.** [privé d'héritage] disinherited.
<> *nm, f* deprived person ■ **les ~s** the destitute.

déshériter [3] [dezerite] *vt* **1.** [priver d'héritage] to cut out of one's will, to disinherit ■ **si tu continues, je te déshérite!** *hum* carry on like this and I'll cut you off without a penny! **2.** [défavoriser] : **il se croit déshérité** he feels hard done by.

déshonneur [dezɔnœr] *nm* **1.** [perte de l'honneur] disgrace, dishonour *UK*, dishonor *US* ■ **vivre dans le ~** to live in dishonour **2.** [honte] disgrace ■ **c'est le ~ de sa famille** he's a disgrace to his family.

déshonorant, e [dezɔnɔrɑ̃, ɑ̃t] *adj* **1.** [qui prive de l'honneur] dishonourable, disgraceful **2.** [humiliant] degrading, shameful ■ **cela n'a rien de ~** there's nothing shameful about it.

déshonorer [3] [dezɔnɔre] *vt* **1.** [nuire à l'honneur de] to dishonour, to bring shame upon, to bring into disrepute **2.** *litt* [abuser de - femme, jeune fille] to ruin **3.** *litt* [lieu, monument] to spoil *ou* to ruin the look of.
◆ **se déshonorer** *vp (emploi réfléchi)* to bring disgrace upon o.s.

déshumanisé, e [dezymanize] *adj* **1.** [lieu] impersonal ■ [personne, ton] coldhearted, unsympathetic **2.** [fabrication, travail] automated.

déshumaniser [3] [dezymanize] *vt* to dehumanize.
◆ **se déshumaniser** *vpi* to become dehumanized.

déshumidificateur [dezymidifikatœr] *nm* dehumidifier.

déshydratant, e [dezidratɑ̃, ɑ̃t] *adj* demoisturizing.
◆ **déshydratant** *nm* desiccant.

déshydratation [dezidratasjɔ̃] *nf* **1.** PHYSIOL dehydration ■ **être dans un état de ~** to be dehydrated ❙ [de la peau] loss of moisture, dehydration **2.** TECHNOL dehydration, dewatering **3.** CHIM dehydration.

déshydraté, e [dezidrate] *adj* **1.** PHYSIOL dehydrated **2.** [aliment] desiccated, dehydrated.

déshydrater [3] [dezidrate] *vt* **1.** PHYSIOL to dehydrate ■ [peau] to dehydrate, to dry (out) **2.** TECHNOL to dehydrate, to dewater **3.** [aliment] to dehydrate, to desiccate **4.** CHIM to dehydrate.
◆ **se déshydrater** *vpi* [personne] to become dehydrated ■ [peau] to lose moisture, to become dehydrated.

désidérabilité [deziderabilite] *nf* ÉCON desirability, use-value.

desiderata [deziderata] *nmpl sout* requirements, wishes ■ **les ~ du personnel** the wishes of the staff.

design [dizajn] *nm* [création] design ■ **~ industriel** industrial design ■ *(comme adj inv)* designer *(modif)* ■ **mobilier ~** designer furniture.

désignation [deziɲasjɔ̃] *nf* **1.** DR : **~ du défendeur/requérant** name of the defendant/plaintiff **2.** [nomination] appointment, nomination.

désigné, e [dezine] *adj* : **tout ~ : c'est le porte-parole tout ~ des élèves** he's the ideal spokesperson for the students ■ **être tout ~ pour faire qqch** to be the right person to do sthg.

designer [dizajnœr] *nmf* designer.

désigner [3] [dezine] *vt* **1.** [montrer] to indicate, to point at *ou* to *(sép)*, to show ■ **~ qqn du doigt** to point at sb **2.** [choisir] to choose, to single out *(sép)* ■ **~ qqn comme héritier** to name sb as one's heir **3.** [nommer - expert, président] to appoint ; [- représentant] to nominate ■ [élire] to elect ■ **~ qqn pour un poste** to appoint sb to a post **4.** [s'appliquer à] to designate, to refer to ■ **le mot « félin » désigne de nombreux animaux** the word "feline" refers to many animals **5.** ADMIN [répertorier] to list, to set out *(sép)* ■ **les conditions désignées à l'annexe A** specifications set out in Annex A **6.** [exposer] : **~ qqn à : un geste qui vous désignera à sa fureur** a gesture which will surely unleash his fury on you.
◆ **se désigner** *vpi* [se proposer] to volunteer.
◆ **se désigner à** *vp+prép* : **se ~ à l'attention générale** to draw attention to o.s.

désillusion [dezilyzjɔ̃] *nf* disappointment, disillusionment, disillusion ■ **connaître des ~s** to be disillusioned *ou* disenchanted.

désillusionner [3] [dezilyzjɔne] *vt* to disillusion, to undeceive ■ **être désillusionné** to be disenchanted *ou* disillusioned.

désincarcération [dezɛ̃karserasjɔ̃] *nf* : **la ~ des détenus** the freeing of the prisoners ■ **sa ~ a pris une heure** it took an hour to free him.

désincarné, e [dezɛ̃karne] *adj* **1.** [sans corps] disembodied **2.** [irréel] insubstantial, unreal.

désincrustant, e [dezɛ̃krystɑ̃, ɑ̃t] *adj* **1.** [pour la peau] cleansing **2.** [détartrant] descaling.

désincruster [3] [dezɛ̃kryste] *vt* **1.** [peau] to cleanse **2.** [détartrer] to scale off *(sép)*.

désindexer [4] [dezɛ̃dɛkse] *vt* to stop indexation of ■ **ces pensions ont été désindexées** these retirement schemes are no longer index-linked.

désindustrialisation [dezɛ̃dystrijalizasjɔ̃] *nf* deindustrialization.

désinence [dezinɑ̃s] *nf* GRAMM inflection, ending.

désinfectant, e [dezɛ̃fɛktɑ̃, ɑ̃t] *adj* disinfecting *(avant n)*.
◆ **désinfectant** *nm* disinfectant.

désinfecter [4] [dezɛ̃fɛkte] *vt* to disinfect.

désinfection [dezɛ̃fɛksjɔ̃] *nf* disinfection, disinfecting.

désinflation [dezɛ̃flasjɔ̃] *nf* deflation, disinflation.

désinformation [dezɛ̃fɔrmasjɔ̃] *nf* disinformation.

désinformer [3] [dezɛ̃fɔrme] *vt* to disinform.

désinscrire [99] [desɛ̃skrir] ◆ **se désinscrire** *vp* INFORM to unsubscribe.

désinsectisation [dezɛ̃sɛktizasjɔ̃] *nf* insect control.

désinsertion [dezɛ̃sɛrsjɔ̃] *nf* : **~ sociale** dropping out.

désinstaller [3] [dezɛ̃stale] *vt* INFORM to uninstall.

désintégration [dezɛ̃tegrasjɔ̃] *nf* **1.** [d'un matériau, d'un groupe] disintegration, breaking-up, splitting **2.** NUCL disintegration ■ **~ radioactive** radioactive decay.

désintégrer [18] [dezɛ̃tegre] *vt* **1.** [matériau] to crumble, to disintegrate ■ [groupe, famille] to break up *(sép)*, to split (up) *(sép)* **2.** NUCL to disintegrate.
◆ **se désintégrer** *vpi* **1.** [exploser] to disintegrate **2.** [groupe, famille, théorie] to disintegrate, to collapse **3.** *hum* [disparaître] to vanish into thin air.

désintéressé, e [dezɛ̃terese] *adj* **1.** [conseil, jugement] disinterested, objective, unprejudiced **2.** [personne] selfless, unselfish.

désintéressement [dezɛ̃terɛsmɑ̃] *nm* **1.** [impartialité] disinterestedness, impartiality, absence of bias **2.** [générosité] selflessness **3.** [désintérêt] : **~ pour** lack of interest in, indifference to **4.** FIN buying out.

désintéresser [4] [dezɛ̃terese] *vt* [créancier] to pay off *(sép)* ■ [actionnaire] to buy out *(sép)*.
◆ **se désintéresser de** *vp+prép* : **se ~ de qqch** [ignorer] to be uninterested ; [perdre son intérêt pour] to lose interest in sthg.

désintérêt [dezɛ̃terɛ] *nm* indifference, lack of interest.

désintoxication [dezɛ̃tɔksikasjɔ̃] *nf* **1.** MÉD detoxification **2.** [contre-propagande] counteracting.

désintoxiquer [3] [dezɛ̃tɔksike] *vt* **1.** MÉD to detoxify ■ **se faire ~** to be weaned off drugs **2.** [informer] to counteract.
◆ **se désintoxiquer** *vpi* [drogué].

désinvestissement [dezɛ̃vɛstismɑ̃] *nm* **1.** ÉCON disinvestment **2.** PSYCHOL withdrawal of involvement.

désinvolte [dezɛ̃vɔlt] *adj* **1.** [sans embarras] casual, nonchalant **2.** *péj* [trop libre] offhand.

désinvolture [dezɛ̃vɔltyr] *nf* [légèreté] casualness ■ *péj* [sans-gêne] off-handedness ■ **avec ~** offhandedly.

désir [dezir] *nm* **1.** [aspiration] want, wish, desire ■ **j'ai toujours eu le ~ d'écrire** I've always wanted *ou* had a desire to write ■ **tu prends tes ~s pour des réalités!** wishful thinking! ▮ [souhait exprimé] wish ■ **selon le ~ de qqn** following sb's wishes ■ **il sera fait selon votre ~** it shall be done as you wish **2.** [motivation] desire, drive ■ **~ d'enfant** PSYCHOL wish to reproduce **3.** [appétit sexuel] desire ■ **rempli de ~** [personne] consumed with desire ; [regard] lustful.

désirable [dezirabl] *adj* **1.** [souhaitable] desirable ■ **peu ~** undesirable **2.** [séduisant] desirable, (sexually) exciting.

désirer [3] [dezire] *vt* **1.** [aspirer à - paix, bonheur] to wish for ■ **~ ardemment** to crave *ou* to long for ■ **il a tout ce qu'il peut ~** he has everything he could wish for ■ *(en usage absolu)* **tu ne peux ~ mieux** you couldn't wish for anything better ■ *(suivi d'un infin)* **elle a toujours désiré posséder un piano** she's always wanted to own a piano ■ **je désirerais savoir si...** I would like to know if... ➲ **se faire ~ : ton père se fait ~!** where could your father have got to? ■ **cette bière se fait ~!** how long's that beer going to take? ■ **laisser à ~** to leave something to be desired, to fail to come up to expectations **2.** [vouloir] : **~ faire** to want *ou* to wish to do ■ **il ne désirait pas vous faire de la peine** he didn't mean to hurt you ■ **~ que : je désire que tu restes** I want *ou* wish *sout* you to stay **3.** [dans un achat, une prestation de service] : **vous désirez?** can I help you? ■ **où désirez-vous aller?** where would you like to go? **4.** [sexuellement] to desire.

désireux, euse [dezirø, øz] *adj* : **~ de faire** inclined *ou* willing to do ■ **très ~ de faire** eager to do.

désistement [dezistəmɑ̃] *nm* POLIT withdrawal, standing down.

désister [3] [deziste] ◆ **se désister** *vpi* POLIT to stand down, to withdraw.

désobéir [32] [dezɔbeir] *vi* **1.** [être désobéissant] to be disobedient **2.** [enfreindre un ordre] to disobey ■ **~ à** to disobey, to fail to obey ■ **~ aux ordres/à ses parents** to disobey orders/one's parents ■ **~ aux lois** to break the law.

désobéissance [dezɔbeisɑ̃s] *nf* **1.** [manque de discipline] disobedience, rebelliousness **2.** [action] act of disobedience.

désobéissant, e [dezɔbeisɑ̃, ɑ̃t] *adj* [enfant] disobedient, rebellious ■ [chien] disobedient.

désobligeance [dezɔbliʒɑ̃s] *nf* disagreeableness.

désobligeant, e [dezɔbliʒɑ̃, ɑ̃t] *adj* [désagréable - personne] disagreeable, unkind ; [- propos] unkind.

désobliger [17] [dezɔbliʒe] *vt sout* to offend, to hurt, to upset ■ **sans vouloir vous ~** no offence (meant).

désodorisant, e [dezɔdɔrizɑ̃, ɑ̃t] *adj* deodorizing *(avant n)*.
◆ **désodorisant** *nm* deodorizer, air-freshener.

désodoriser [3] [dezɔdɔrize] *vt* to deodorize.

désœuvré, e [dezœvre] *adj* : **être ~** to have nothing to do.

désœuvrement [dezœvrəmɑ̃] *nm* idleness ■ **ils ne le font que par ~** they only do it because they have nothing better to do.

désolant, e [dezɔlɑ̃, ɑ̃t] *adj* **1.** [triste - spectacle] wretched, pitiful, awful **2.** [contrariant] annoying, irritating ■ **il n'a rien fait, c'est ~!** he didn't do anything, it's so annoying!

désolation [dezɔlasjɔ̃] *nf* **1.** [chagrin] desolation, grief ■ **être plongé dans la ~** to be disconsolate **2.** [cause de chagrin] : **cet enfant est ma ~** I despair of this child **3.** *litt* [d'un lieu, d'un paysage] desolation, desolateness, bleakness.

désolé, e [dezɔle] *adj* **1.** [contrit] apologetic, contrite ■ [pour s'excuser] sorry ■ **~ de vous déranger** sorry to disturb you ■ **~, j'étais là avant vous!** *iron* excuse me *ou* sorry, (but) I was here before you! **2.** *litt* [triste] disconsolate, sorrowful **3.** *litt* [aride] desolate, bleak.

désoler [3] [dezɔle] *vt* **1.** [attrister] to distress, to sadden **2.** [irriter] : **tu me désoles!** I despair!
◆ **se désoler** *vpi* to be sorry ■ **se ~ de qqch** to be disconsolate *ou* in despair about *ou* over sthg ■ **ses parents se désolent de la voir si malheureuse** it grieves her parents to see her so unhappy.

désolidariser [3] [desɔlidarize] ◆ **se désolidariser de** *vp+prép* to dissociate o.s. from.

désopilant, e [dezɔpilɑ̃, ɑ̃t] *adj* hilarious, hysterically funny.

désordonné, e [dezɔrdɔne] *adj* **1.** [désorganisé - dossier, esprit] confused, untidy **2.** [personne] disorderly **3.** [lieu] untidy, messy **4.** [irrégulier] helter-skelter *(modif)* ■ **courir de façon ~e** to run helter-skelter *ou* pell-mell ■ **le chien faisait des bonds ~s** the dog was leaping about all over the place **5.** *litt* [immoral] disorderly, disordered.

désordre [dezɔrdr] ◇ *nm* **1.** [fouillis] mess ■ **quel ~ là-dedans!** what a mess *ou* it's chaos in there! ■ **mettre le ~ dans une pièce** to mess up a room **2.** [manque d'organisation] muddle, confusion, disarray ■ **~ des idées** confused ideas **3.** [agitation] disorder, disturbance ■ **semer le ~** to cause a disturbance, to wreak havoc ➊ **~ sur la voie publique** DR disorderly conduct **4.** *litt* [immoralité] dissoluteness ■ **vivre dans le ~** to live a dissolute life **5.** JEUX : **gagner le tiercé dans le ~** to win a place bet in the wrong order.
◇ *adj* messy, untidy.
◆ **désordres** *nmpl* **1.** [émeutes] riots **2.** *litt* [débauche] dissolute *ou* disorderly behaviour.
◆ **en désordre** ◇ *loc adj* [lieu] messy, untidy ■ [cheveux] unkempt, dishevelled ■ **mon bureau était tout en ~** my desk was in a terrible mess.
◇ *loc adv* : **mettre en ~** to mess *ou* to muddle up.

désorganisé, e [dezɔrganize] *adj* disorganized.

désorganiser [3] [dezɔrganize] *vt* [service] to disorganize, to disrupt ■ [fiches] to disrupt the order of.

désorientation [dezɔrjɑ̃tasjɔ̃] *nf* [perplexité] disorientation, confusion.

désorienté, e [dezɔrjɑ̃te] *adj* **1.** [perplexe] confused, disoriented **2.** [égaré] lost.

désorienter [3] [dezɔrjɑ̃te] *vt* **1.** [faire s'égarer] to cause to become disoriented, to disorientate **2.** [déconcerter] to confuse, to throw into confusion *ou* disarray, to disorientate.

désormais [dezɔrmɛ] *adv* [à partir de maintenant] from now on, henceforth *sout* ■ [dans le passé] from that moment on, from then on, from that time (on) ■ **je ferai attention ~** I'll pay attention from now on.

désossé, e [dezɔse] *adj* [gigot, jambon] off the bone.

désosser [3] [dezɔse] *vt* [viande] to bone.
◆ **se désosser** *vpi* [se désarticuler] to contort o.s.

désoxyder [3] [dezɔkside] *vt* to deoxidize, to deactivate ■ **acier désoxydé** killed steel.

désoxyribonucléique [dezɔksiribɔnykleik] *adj* BIOL : **acide ~** deoxyribonucleic acid.

despote [dɛspɔt] *nm* **1.** POLIT despot, tyrant **2.** [personne autoritaire] tyrant, bully.

despotique [dɛspɔtik] *adj* **1.** POLIT despotic, tyrannical, dictatorial **2.** [autoritaire] despotic, domineering, bullying.

despotisme [dɛspɔtism] *nm* **1.** POLIT despotism ■ **~ éclairé** HIST enlightened despotism **2.** [autorité] tyranny, bullying.

desquamation [dɛskwamasjɔ̃] *nf* **1.** [de la peau] desquamation *spéc*, flaking ■ [des écailles] scaling off **2.** GÉOL : **~ en écailles** exfoliation.

desquamer [3] [dɛskwame] *vi* [peau] to flake, to desquamate *spéc* ■ [écailles] to scale off.
◆ **se desquamer** *vpi* [peau] to flake (off), to desquamate *spéc* ■ [écailles] to scale off.

desquels [dekɛl] *mpl* ▷ **lequel**.

desquelles *fpl* ▷ **lequel**.

DESS (*abr de* **diplôme d'études supérieures spécialisées**) *nm postgraduate diploma.*

dessaisir [32] [desezir] *vt* DR : **~ qqn de** to deny sb jurisdiction over.
◆ **se dessaisir de** *vp+prép* **1.** [se départir de] to part with, to relinquish **2.** DR : **se ~ d'une affaire** to decline (to exercise) jurisdiction over a case.

dessaler [3] [desale] ◇ *vt* **1.** [ôter le sel de] to desalinate, to remove the salt from ■ **~ du poisson** to freshen fish **2.** *fam* [dégourdir] to wise up *(sép)*, to educate in the ways of the world.
◇ *vi* NAUT to overturn, to capsize.
◆ **se dessaler** *vpi fam* to get wise, to wise up ■ **il s'est drôlement dessalé depuis qu'il travaille!** he's learnt a thing or two since he started working!

dessaouler [desule] = **dessoûler**.

desséchant, e [deseʃɑ̃, ɑ̃t] *adj* **1.** [asséchant] drying, withering ■ **un vent ~** a searing wind **2.** [activité, études] soul-destroying **3.** CHIM desiccating.

desséché, e [deseʃe] *adj* **1.** [pétale, feuille] withered, dried ■ [cheveux, peau] dry ■ [gorge] parched **2.** [décharné] emaciated, wasted **3.** [cœur, personne] hardened ■ **un vieux solitaire ~** a hardened old recluse.

dessèchement [desɛʃmɑ̃] *nm* **1.** [perte d'humidité] drying up **2.** [procédé] desiccation, drying (out) **3.** [stérilité - du cœur] hardening ; [- de la créativité] drying up.

dessécher [18] [deseʃe] *vt* **1.** [peau, cheveux] to dry out *(sép)* ■ [pétale, feuille] to wither ■ **la bouche desséchée par la peur** mouth dry *ou* parched with fear **2.** [amaigrir] to emaciate, to waste **3.** [endurcir] : **~ le cœur de qqn** to harden sb's heart.
◆ **se dessécher** *vpi* **1.** [peau, cheveux] to go dry **2.** [cœur] to harden.

dessein [desɛ̃] *nm litt* intention, goal, purpose ■ **son ~ est de prendre ma place** his intention is to *ou* he has determined to take my place ■ **former** *ou* **avoir le ~ de faire qqch** to determine to do sthg.
◆ **à dessein** *loc adv* deliberately, purposely.
◆ **dans le dessein de** *loc prép* in order *ou* with a view to.

desseller [4] [desele] *vt* to unsaddle.

desserrer [4] [desere] *vt* **1.** [vis, cravate, ceinture] to loosen **2.** [relâcher - étreinte, bras] to relax ■ [dents] to unclench ■ **il n'a pas desserré les dents** *ou* **lèvres** *fig* he didn't utter a word, he never opened his mouth **3.** [frein] to release.
◆ **se desserrer** *vpi* **1.** [se dévisser] to come loose **2.** [se relâcher - étreinte] to relax.

dessers [desɛr], **dessert** [desɛr] *v* ▷ **desservir**.

dessert [desɛr] *nm* dessert, pudding *UK*, sweet *UK* ■ **veux-tu un ~?** will you have some dessert? ■ **au ~** at the end of the meal.

desserte [desɛrt] *nf* **1.** [meuble] sideboard ■ [table roulante] tea-trolley *UK*, tea wagon *US* **2.** TRANSP service ■ **~ aérienne** air service ■ **la ~ du village est très mal assurée** the village is poorly served by public transport.

dessertir [32] [desɛrtir] *vt* to unset.
◆ **se dessertir** *vpi* to come unset.

desservir [38] [desɛrvir] *vt* **1.** [débarrasser] to clear (away) ■ *(en usage absolu)* **puis-je ~?** may I clear the table? **2.** [désavantager] to be detrimental *ou* harmful to, to go against ■ **son**

intervention m'a desservi he did me a disservice by intervening **3.** TRANSP to serve ■ **le village est mal desservi** public transport to the village is poor ■ **ce train dessert les stations suivantes** this train stops at the following stations **4.** RELIG [paroisse] to serve **5.** [donner accès à] to lead to ■ **un couloir dessert les chambres** a corridor leads off to the bedrooms.

dessiccation [desikasjɔ̃] *nf* [gén] desiccation, drying ■ [du bois] drying.

dessiller [3] [desije] *vt litt* **~ les yeux de** *ou* **à qqn** to cause the scales to fall from sb's eyes, to open sb's eyes.

◆ **se dessiller** *vpi litt* **mes yeux se dessillent** the scales have fallen from my eyes.

dessin [desɛ̃] *nm* **1.** [croquis] drawing ● **~ humoristique** *ou* **de presse** cartoon *(in a newspaper)* ■ **~ animé** cartoon ■ **~ à main levée** free hand drawing ■ **~ à la plume** pen and ink drawing ■ **~ au trait** outline drawing ■ **tu veux peut-être aussi que je te fasse un ~?** *fam* do you want me to spell it out for you? **2.** [art] : **le ~** drawing ■ **apprendre le ~** to learn (how) to draw **3.** [technique] : **la vigueur de son ~** the firmness of her drawing technique **4.** TECHNOL : **~ industriel** draughtsmanship, industrial design ■ **~ assisté par ordinateur** computer-aided design **5.** [forme, ligne] line, outline **6.** [ornement] design, pattern ■ **un tissu à ~s géométriques** a fabric with geometric patterns.

◆ **de dessin** *loc adj* : **cours/école de ~** art class/school.

dessinateur, trice [desinatœr, tris] *nm, f* **1.** [technicien] : **~ (industriel)** draughtsman **2.** [concepteur] designer **3.** ART : **il est meilleur ~ que peintre** he draws better than he paints ■ **~ humoristique** cartoonist.

dessiné, e [desine] *adj* : **bien ~** well-formed, well-defined.

dessiner [3] [desine] *vt* **1.** ART to draw ■ *(en usage absolu)* **il dessine bien** he's good at drawing ■ **~ à la plume/au crayon/au fusain** to draw in pen and ink/in pencil/in charcoal **2.** [former] to delineate ■ **bouche finement dessinée** finely drawn *ou* chiselled mouth **3.** TECHNOL [meuble, robe, bâtiment] to design ■ [paysage, jardin] to landscape **4.** [souligner] to show up the shape of.

◆ **se dessiner** *vpi* **1.** [devenir visible] to stand out ■ **un sourire se dessina sur ses lèvres** a smile formed on his lips **2.** [apparaître - solution] to emerge.

dessoûler [3] [desule] ◇ *vt* to sober up *(sép)* ■ **tu es dessoûlé maintenant?** are you sober now?

◇ *vi* to sober up ■ **il ne dessoûle pas de la journée** he's drunk all day.

dessous [dəsu] ◇ *adv* underneath ■ **les prix sont marqués ~** the prices are marked underneath ■ **mets-toi ~** get under it.

◇ *nm* [d'un meuble, d'un objet] bottom ■ [d'une feuille] underneath ■ **les gens du ~** the people downstairs, the downstairs neighbours ● **les ~ de la politique/de la finance** the hidden agenda in politics/in finance ■ **le ~ des cartes** *ou* **du jeu** the hidden agenda ■ **avoir le ~** to come off worst, to get the worst of it ■ **être dans le trente-sixième ~** to be down in the dumps.

◇ *nmpl* [sous-vêtements] underwear.

◆ **de dessous** *loc prép* from under, from underneath.

◆ **en dessous** *loc adv* underneath ■ **la feuille est verte en ~** the leaf is green underneath ■ **les gens qui habitent en ~, les gens d'en ~** *fam* the people downstairs, the people in the flat UK *ou* apartment US below ● **agir en ~** to act in an underhand way ■ **rire en ~** to laugh up one's sleeve ■ **regarder qqn par en ~** to steal a glance at sb.

◆ **en dessous de** *loc prép* below ■ **vous êtes très en ~ de la vérité** you're very far from the truth.

dessous-de-bouteille [dəsudbutɛj] *nm inv* coaster *(for a bottle)*.

dessous-de-bras [dəsudbra] *nm inv* dress shield.

dessous-de-plat [dəsudpla] *nm inv* table mat *(to protect the table from hot dishes)*, hot pad US.

dessous de table [dəsudtabl] *nm inv péj* bribe.

dessous-de-verre [dəsudvɛr] *nm inv* coaster.

dessus [dəsy] ◇ *adv* [placer, monter] on top ■ [marcher, écrire] on it/them *etc* ■ [passer, sauter] over it/them *etc* ■ **ils lui ont tiré/tapé ~** they shot at him/hit him ● **ne compte pas trop ~** don't count on it too much ■ **je suis ~ depuis un moment** [affaire, travail] I've been (working) on it for a while ; [appartement] I've been looking into it for a while ■ **ça nous est tombé ~ à l'improviste** it was like a bolt out of the blue ■ **il a fallu que ça me tombe ~!** it had to be me!

◇ *nm* **1.** [d'un objet, de la tête, du pied] top ■ [de la main] back ● **avoir/prendre le ~** to have/to get the upper hand ■ **reprendre le ~** [gagner] to get back on top (of the situation), to regain the upper hand ■ **elle a bien repris le ~** [après une maladie] she was soon back on her feet again ; [après une dépression] she got over it quite well ■ **le ~ du panier** [personnes] the cream, the elite ; [choses] the top of the pile *ou* heap **2.** [étage supérieur] : **les voisins du ~** the people upstairs, the upstairs neighbours ■ **l'appartement du ~** the flat above.

◆ **de dessus** *loc prép* : **enlève ça de ~ la table!** take it off the table!

◆ **en dessus** *loc adv* on top.

dessus de cheminée [dəsydʃəmine] *nm inv* mantleshelf runner.

dessus-de-lit [dəsydli] *nm inv* bedspread.

déstabilisant, e [destabilizɑ̃, ɑ̃t], **déstabilisateur, trice** [destabilizatœr, tris] *adj* [conflit, politique] destabilizing.

déstabiliser [3] [destabilize] *vt* [pays, régime] to destabilize.

déstalinisation [destalinizasjɔ̃] *nf* destalinization.

destin [dɛstɛ̃] *nm* **1.** [sort] fate, destiny ■ **le ~ a voulu que...** fate decreed that... ■ **un coup du ~** a blow from fate **2.** [vie personnelle] life, destiny, fate ■ **maître de son ~** master of his (own) fate **3.** [évolution] destiny, fate ■ **son roman a connu un ~ imprévu** her novel had an unexpected fate.

destinataire [dɛstinatɛr] *nmf* **1.** [d'une lettre] addressee ■ [de produits] consignee **2.** LING listener.

destination [dɛstinasjɔ̃] *nf* **1.** [lieu] destination ■ **arriver à ~** to reach one's destination **2.** [emploi] purpose, use.

◆ **à destination de** *loc prép* : **avion/vol à ~ de Nice** plane/flight to Nice ■ **les voyageurs à ~ de Paris** passengers for Paris, passengers travelling to Paris.

destinée [dɛstine] *nf* **1.** [sort] : **la ~** fate ■ **la ~ de qqn/qqch** the fate in store for sb/sthg **2.** [vie] destiny ■ **il tient ma ~ entre ses mains** he holds my destiny in his hands.

◆ **destinées** *nfpl sout* **les dieux qui président à nos ~s** the gods who decide our fate (on earth) ■ **promis à de hautes ~s** destined for great things.

destiner [3] [dɛstine] *vt* **1.** [adresser] : **~ qqch à qqn** to intend sthg for sb ■ **voici le courrier qui lui est destiné** here is his mail *ou* the mail for him **2.** [promettre] : **~ qqn à** to destine sb for ■ **rien ne/tout me destinait au violon** nothing/everything led me to become a violonist ■ **nous étions destinés l'un à l'autre** we were meant for each other ■ **on la destine à quelque gros industriel** her family wants to marry her off to some rich industrialist ■ **il était destiné à régner** he was destined to reign ■ **son idée était destinée à l'échec dès le départ** his idea was bound to fail *ou* doomed (to failure) from the very start **3.** [affecter] : **~ qqch à** to set sthg aside for.

◆ **se destiner à** *vp+prép* : **se ~ au journalisme** to want to become a journalist.

destituer [7] [dɛstitɥe] *vt* [fonctionnaire] to relieve from duties, to dismiss ■ [roi] to depose ■ [officier] to demote.

destitution [dɛstitysjɔ̃] *nf* [d'un fonctionnaire] dismissal ■ [d'un roi] deposition, deposal ■ [d'un officier] demotion.

déstocker [3] [destɔke] ◇ *vt* to take out of stock.

◇ *vi* to reduce stocks.

destrier [dɛstrije] *nm arch* charger, steed.

destroy [dɛstrɔj] *adj fam* [personne] wasted ■ **il a un look ~** he looks completely wasted *ou* a complete wreck.

destructeur, trice [dɛstryktœr, tris] ◇ *adj* destructive ■ **caractère ~** destructiveness.

◇ *nm, f* destroyer.

destructible [dɛstryktibl] *adj* destructible ■ **facilement ~** easy to destroy.

destructif, ive [dɛstryktif, iv] *adj* [action, croyance] destructive.

destruction [dɛstryksjɔ̃] *nf* **1.** [fait d'anéantir] destroying, destruction **2.** [dégâts] damage ▪ **les ~s causées par la tornade** the damage caused by the tornado.

déstructurer [3] [destryktyre] *vt* to remove the structure from.
◆ **se déstructurer** *vpi* to lose (its) structure, to become destructured.

désuet, ète [dezɥɛ, ɛt] *adj* [mot, vêtement] outdated, old-fashioned, out-of-date ▪ [technique] outmoded, obsolete ▪ **une chambre au charme ~** a room with old-fashioned charm.

désuétude [dezɥetyd] *nf* obsolescence ▪ **tomber en ~** [mot] to fall into disuse, to become obsolete ; [technique, pratique] to become obsolete.

désuni, e [dezyni] *adj* **1.** [brouillé - famille, ménage] disunited, divided **2.** ÉQUIT off his stride.

désunion [dezynjɔ̃] *nf* division, dissension *(U)*.

détachable [detaʃabl] *adj* [feuillet, capuchon] removable, detachable.

détachage [detaʃaʒ] *nm* [nettoyage] cleaning, dry-cleaning.

détachant, e [detaʃɑ̃, ɑ̃t] *adj* [produit] stain-removing.
◆ **détachant** *nm* stain remover.

détaché, e [detaʃe] *adj* **1.** [ruban] untied **2.** [air, mine] detached, casual, offhand **3.** ADMIN : **fonctionnaire ~** civil servant on secondment *UK ou* on a temporary assignment *US* **4.** MUS detached.

détachement [detaʃmɑ̃] *nm* **1.** [désintéressement] detachment **2.** [troupe] detachment **3.** ADMIN secondment *UK*, temporary assignment *US*.
◆ **en détachement** *loc adv* on secondment *UK*, on a temporary assignment *US* ▪ **en ~ auprès de** seconded to *UK*, on a temporary assignment with *US*.

détacher [3] [detaʃe] *vt* **1.** [libérer] to untie ▪ **~ ses cheveux** to untie one's hair, to let one's hair down ▪ **~ une guirlande** to take down a garland ▪ **~ une caravane** to unhitch *ou* to unhook a caravan
2. [séparer] : **~ une photo d'une lettre** [enlever le trombone] to unclip a picture from a letter ; [enlever l'agrafe] to unstaple a picture from a letter ▪ **~ une recette d'un magazine/un timbre d'un carnet** to tear a recipe out of a magazine/a stamp out of a book ▪ *(en usage absolu)* **~ suivant le pointillé** tear (off) along the dotted line
3. [défaire - ceinture] to unfasten ; [- col] to unfasten, to loosen
4. [détourner] : **~ ses yeux** *ou* **son regard de qqn** to take one's eyes off sb ▪ **~ son attention d'une lecture** to stop paying attention to one's reading ▪ [affectivement] : **~ qqn de** to take sb away from ▪ **être détaché de** to be detached from *ou* indifferent to
5. ADMIN to send on secondment *UK ou* on temporary assignment *US* ▪ **je vais être détaché auprès du ministre** I will be sent on secondment to the Ministry
6. [faire ressortir] to separate (out) ▪ **détachez bien chaque mot/note** make sure every word/note stands out (clearly)
7. [nettoyer] to clean ▪ **j'ai donné ton costume à ~** I took your suit to the cleaner's.
◆ **se détacher** ◇ *vp (emploi réfléchi)* [se libérer] to untie *ou* to free o.s.
◇ *vpi* **1.** [sandale, lacet] to come undone ▪ [étiquette] to come off ▪ [page] to come loose
2. SPORT [se séparer - du peloton] to break away
3. [se profiler] to stand out.
◆ **se détacher de** *vp+prép* **1.** [se décrocher de] to come off **2.** [s'éloigner de] : **il a eu du mal à se ~ d'elle** he found it hard to leave her behind ▪ **puis je me suis détachée de ma famille/de l'art figuratif** later, I grew away from my family/from figurative art.
◆ **à détacher** *loc adj* : **fiche/recette à ~** tear-off card/recipe.

détail [detaj] *nm* **1.** [exposé précis] breakdown, detailed account, itemization ▪ **faire le ~ de qqch** to break sthg down, to itemize sthg ▪ **faites-moi le ~ de ce qui s'est passé** tell me in detail what happened ▪ **il n'a pas fait le ~!** *fam* he was a bit heavy-handed! **2.** [élément - d'un récit, d'une information] detail, particular ▪ **je te passe les ~s** [ennuyeux] I won't bore you with the detail *ou* details ; [horribles] I'll spare you the (gory) details ▪ **jusque dans les moindres ~s** down to the smallest detail ▪ **pour plus de ~s, écrivez à...** for further details, write to... ▪ [point sans importance] detail, minor point ▪ **ne nous arrêtons pas à ces ~s** let's not worry about these minor details **3.** ART detail ▪ **Clemenceau, ~ d'un portrait par Manet** Clemenceau, a detail from a portrait by Manet **4.** COMM retail **5.** [petite partie - d'un meuble, d'un édifice] detail.
◆ **au détail** ◇ *loc adj* [vente] retail *(modif)*.
◇ *loc adv* : **vendre qqch au ~** to sell sthg retail, to retail sthg ▪ **vous vendez les œufs au ~?** do you sell eggs separately?
◆ **de détail** *loc adj* **1.** [mineur] : **faire quelques remarques de ~** to make a few minor comments **2.** COMM retail *(modif)*.
◆ **en détail** *loc adv* in detail ▪ **raconter une histoire en ~** to tell a story in detail.

détaillant, e [detajɑ̃, ɑ̃t] *nm, f* retailer.

détaillé, e [detaje] *adj* [récit] detailed ▪ [facture] itemized.

détailler [3] [detaje] *vt* **1.** COMM to sell retail **2.** [dévisager] to scrutinize, to examine ▪ **~ qqn de la tête aux pieds** to look sb over from head to foot, to look sb up and down **3.** [énumérer - faits, facture] to itemize, to detail.

détaler [3] [detale] *vi* [animal] to bolt ▪ [personne] to decamp, to cut and run *US* ▪ **les gamins ont détalé comme des lapins** the kids scattered like rabbits.

détartrage [detartraʒ] *nm* [des dents] scaling ▪ [d'une bouilloire] descaling ▪ **se faire faire un ~ (des dents)** to have one's teeth cleaned.

détartrant, e [detartrɑ̃, ɑ̃t] *adj* [produit, substance] descaling.
◆ **détartrant** *nm* descaling agent.

détartrer [3] [detartre] *vt* [dents] to scale ▪ [bouilloire] to descale.

détaxation [detaksasjɔ̃] *nf* : **la ~ des magnétoscopes** [réduction] the reduction of duty *ou* tax on videorecorders ; [suppression] the lifting of duty *ou* tax off videorecorders.

détaxe [detaks] *nf* **1.** [levée] : **la ~ des tabacs** [réduction] the reduction of duty *ou* tax on tobacco ; [suppression] the lifting of tax *ou* duty on tobacco **2.** [remboursement] : **cela m'a fait 500 euros de ~** the reduction of duty charges saved me 500 euros.

détaxer [3] [detakse] *vt* : **~ l'alcool** [en diminuant la taxe] to reduce the duty *ou* tax on alcohol ; [en supprimant la taxe] to lift the duty *ou* tax on alcohol.

détectable [detɛktabl] *adj* detectable ▪ **le signal est à peine ~** the signal is almost undetectable.

détecter [4] [detɛkte] *vt* to detect, to spot.

détecteur [detɛktœr] *nm* detector ▪ **~ de faux billets** forged banknote detector ▪ **~ de fumée** smoke detector, smoke alarm ▪ **~ d'incendie** fire detector ▪ **~ de mines** mine detector ▪ **~ de particules** particle detector.

détection [detɛksjɔ̃] *nf* [gén] detection, detecting, spotting.

détective [detɛktiv] *nmf* detective ▶ **~ privé** private detective *ou* investigator.

déteindre [81] [detɛ̃dr] ◇ *vi* **1.** [se décolorer] to run ▪ **~ au lavage** to run in the wash ▪ **le noir va ~ sur le rouge** the black will run into the red **2.** *fam* [humeur, influence] : **~ sur qqn** to rub off on sb, to influence sb.
◇ *vt* [linge] to discolour *UK*, to discolor *US* ▪ [tenture, tapisserie] to fade.

dételer [24] [detle] ◇ *vt* **1.** [cheval] to unharness, to unhitch ▪ [bœuf] to unyoke **2.** [caravane, voiture] to unhitch ▪ [wagon] to uncouple.
◇ *vi fam* [s'arrêter] to ease off.
◆ **sans dételer** *loc adv fam* without a break, non-stop.

détendre [73] [detɑ̃dr] *vt* **1.** [relâcher - corde] to ease, to loosen, to slacken ; [- ressort] to release **2.** [décontracter] to relax ▪ **il a réussi à ~ l'atmosphère avec quelques plaisanteries** he made things more relaxed by telling a few jokes **3.** [gaz] to depressurize.

◆ **se détendre** *vpi* **1.** [corde, courroie] to ease, to slacken **2.** [se décontracter] to relax ■ **détends-toi!** relax! **3.** [s'améliorer - ambiance] to become more relaxed **4.** [gaz] to be reduced in pressure.

détendu, e [detɑ̃dy] *adj* **1.** [calme] relaxed **2.** [corde, courroie] slack.

détenir [40] [detnir] *vt* **1.** [posséder - record] to hold, to be the holder of ; [- actions] to hold ; [- document, bijou de famille] to hold, to have (in one's possession) ; [- secret] to hold **2.** DR [emprisonner] to detain ■ **~ qqn préventivement** to hold sb on remand.

détente [detɑ̃t] *nf* **1.** [relaxation] relaxation ■ **j'ai besoin de ~** I need to relax **2.** POLIT : **la ~** détente **3.** [d'une horloge] catch ■ [d'un ressort] release mechanism **4.** ARM trigger **5.** SPORT spring **6.** [d'un gaz] expansion.

détenteur, trice [detɑ̃tœr, tris] *nm, f* holder ■ **être le ~ d'un record** to hold a record ■ **~ d'actions** shareholder.

détention [detɑ̃sjɔ̃] *nf* **1.** [emprisonnement] detention ■ **être maintenu en ~** to be detained ◆ **~ criminelle** imprisonment ■ **en ~ préventive** *ou* **provisoire** in detention awaiting trial, on remand ■ **mettre qqn en ~ préventive** to remand sb in custody **2.** [possession] possession ■ **arrêté pour ~ d'armes** arrested for illegal possession of arms.

détenu, e [detny] ◇ *pp* ▷ **détenir**.
◇ *adj* [accusé, prisonnier] imprisoned.
◇ *nm, f* prisoner ■ **les ~s manifestent** the prison inmates are demonstrating.

détergent, e [detɛrʒɑ̃, ɑ̃t] *adj* detergent *(modif)*.
◆ **détergent** *nm* [gén] detergent ■ [en poudre] washing powder ■ [liquide] liquid detergent.

détérioration [deterjɔrasjɔ̃] *nf* [de la santé, des relations] worsening, deterioration ■ [des locaux] deterioration.

détériorer [3] [deterjɔre] *vt* to cause to deteriorate, to damage, to harm.
◆ **se détériorer** *vpi* [temps, climat social] to deteriorate, to worsen.

déterminant, e [determinɑ̃, ɑ̃t] *adj* deciding, determining.
◆ **déterminant** *nm* **1.** MATH determinant **2.** LING determiner.

déterminatif, ive [determinatif, iv] *adj* determining.
◆ **déterminatif** *nm* determining adjective, determiner.

détermination [determinasjɔ̃] *nf* **1.** [ténacité] determination, resoluteness **2.** [résolution] determination, decision ■ **agir avec ~** to show determination **3.** [de causes, de termes] determining, establishing **4.** LING & PHILOS determination **5.** BIOL determination, determining ■ **~ des sexes** sex determination ■ **~ du groupe sanguin** blood typing.

déterminé, e [determine] *adj* **1.** [défini] determined, defined, circumscribed ■ **il n'a pas d'opinion ~e à ce sujet** he doesn't really have a strong opinion on the matter ■ **dans un but bien ~** for a definite reason ■ **à un prix bien ~** at a set price **2.** [décidé] determined, resolute **3.** LING & PHILOS determined.

déterminer [3] [determine] *vt* **1.** [définir] to ascertain, to determine **2.** [inciter] to incite, to encourage ■ **~ qqn à faire qqch** to encourage sb to do sthg **3.** [causer] to determine ■ **qu'est-ce qui détermine l'achat?** what determines whether somebody will buy or not? **4.** LING & PHILOS to determine **5.** BIOL [sexe] to determine ■ [groupe sanguin] to type.
◆ **se déterminer** *vpi* to decide, to make a decision, to make up one's mind ■ **se ~ à** to make up one's mind to.

déterminisme [determinism] *nm* determinism.

déterré, e [detere] *nm, f* : **avoir l'air d'un ~** *ou* **une mine de ~** *ou* **une tête de ~** to look deathly pale.

déterrer [4] [detere] *vt* **1.** [os, trésor] to dig up *(sép)*, to unearth **2.** [exhumer - cadavre] to dig up *(sép)*, to disinter **3.** [dénicher - secret, texte] to dig out *(sép)*, to unearth.

détersif, ive [detɛrsif, iv] = **détergent, e**.

détestable [detɛstabl] *adj* dreadful, detestable, foul.

détester [3] [detɛste] *vt* **1.** [personne] to hate, to detest, to loathe **2.** [viande, jazz, politique *etc*] to hate, to detest, to loathe ■ **il déteste devoir se lever tôt** he hates having to get up early ■ **je déteste qu'on me mente** I hate *ou* I can't stand being lied to ■ **je ne déteste pas une soirée tranquille à la maison** I'm quite partial to a quiet evening at home ■ **il m'a fait ~ les maths** he put me off maths completely.

déthéiné, e [deteine] *adj* decaffeinated.

détient, détint *etc v* ▷ **détenir**.

détonant, e [detɔnɑ̃, ɑ̃t] *adj* detonating.

détonateur [detɔnatœr] *nm* **1.** ARM detonator **2.** *fig* [déclencheur] detonator, trigger ■ **servir de ~ à qqch** to trigger off sthg.

détonation [detɔnasjɔ̃] *nf* **1.** [coup de feu - gén] shot ; [- d'un canon] boom, roar **2.** AUTO backfiring.

détoner [3] [detɔne] *vi* to detonate.

détonner [3] [detɔne] *vi* **1.** MUS to be out of tune *ou* off key **2.** [contraster - couleurs, styles] to clash ; [- personne] : **j'ai peur de ~ parmi ces gens-là** I'm afraid of being out of place among these people.

détordre [76] [detɔrdr] *vt* [câble, corde, linge] to untwist.

détour [detur] *nm* **1.** [tournant] bend, curve, turn ■ [méandre] wind, meander ■ **la route fait de nombreux ~s jusqu'au bout/ jusqu'en bas/jusqu'en haut de la vallée** the road winds all the way through/down/up the valley ■ **faire un brusque ~** to make a sharp turn **2.** [crochet] detour, diversion ■ **faire un ~ par un village** to make a detour through a village ■ **elle nous a fait faire un ~ pour venir ici** she brought us a roundabout way ■ **faisons un petit ~ par la psychanalyse** *fig* let's go off at a tangent for a minute and talk about psychoanalysis ◆ **valoir le ~** [restaurant, paysage] to be worth the detour **3.** [faux-fuyant] roundabout way ■ **un discours plein de ~s** a roundabout *ou* circumlocutory *sout* way of speaking.
◆ **au détour de** *loc prép* **1.** [en cheminant le long de] : **au ~ du chemin** as you follow the path **2.** [en consultant, en écoutant] : **au ~ de votre livre/œuvre, on devine vos préoccupations** leafing through your book/glancing through your work, one gets an idea of your main concerns ■ **au ~ de la conversation** in the course of the conversation.
◆ **sans détour** *loc adv* [parler, répondre] straightforwardly, without beating about the bush.

détourné, e [deturne] *adj* **1.** [route, voie] roundabout *(avant n)*, circuitous *sout* **2.** [façon, moyen] indirect, roundabout, circuitous *sout* ■ **apprendre qqch de façon ~e** to learn sthg indirectly ■ **agir de façon ~e** to behave deviously.

détournement [deturnəmɑ̃] *nm* **1.** [dérivation - d'une rivière] diverting, diversion **2.** AÉRON : **~ d'avion** hijacking ■ **faire un ~ d'avion** to hijack a plane **3.** FIN misappropriation ■ **~ de fonds** embezzlement **4.** DR : **~ de mineur** corruption of a minor ■ **~ de pouvoir** abuse of power *(especially by a local government body)*.

détourner [3] [deturne] *vt* **1.** TRANSP [circulation] to redirect, to divert, to reroute ■ [fleuve] to divert **2.** [avion, autocar] to hijack **3.** [éloigner - coup] to parry ; [- arme] to turn aside *ou* away *(sép)* ■ **~ les yeux** *ou* **le regard** to avert one's eyes, to look away ■ **~ la tête** to turn one's head away ■ **~ l'attention de qqn** to divert sb's attention ■ **~ les soupçons** to divert suspicion (away from o.s.) ■ **~ les soupçons sur qqn** to divert suspicion toward sb **4.** [déformer - paroles, texte] to distort, to twist **5.** [détacher] to take away *(sép)* ■ **~ qqn de son devoir** to divert sb from his/her duty ■ **~ qqn du droit chemin** to lead sb astray **6.** [extorquer] to misappropriate **7.** DR [mineur] to corrupt.
◆ **se détourner** *vpi* [tourner la tête] to turn (one's head), to look away.
◆ **se détourner de** *vp+prép* to turn away from ■ **en grandissant, je me suis détourné de la natation** I got tired of swimming as I grew older.

détracteur, trice [detraktœr, tris] ◇ *adj* disparaging, detractory.
◇ *nm, f* disparager, detractor ■ **tous ses ~s** all his critics *ou* those who have attacked him.

détraqué, e [detrake] ◇ *adj* **1.** [cassé] broken **2.** *fam* [dérangé] : **elle a les nerfs complètement ~s** she's a nervous wreck **3.** *fam* [désaxé] crazy, psychotic.
◇ *nm, f fam* maniac, psychopath ■ **~ sexuel** sex maniac.

détraquer [3] [detrake] *vt* **1.** [appareil] to damage **2.** *fam* [déranger] : **toutes ces études lui ont détraqué le cerveau** *hum* all that studying has addled his brain.
◆ **se détraquer** ◇ *vpi* [mal fonctionner] to go wrong ■ [cesser de fonctionner] to break down.
◇ *vpt fam* : **se ~ le foie/le système** to ruin one's liver/health.

détrempe [detrɑ̃p] *nf* **1.** MÉTALL softening, annealing **2.** [produit - à base de lait, d'eau] distemper ; [- à base d'œuf] tempera ■ [œuvre] distemper painting ■ **peindre un tableau à la** *ou* **en ~** to distemper a painting.

détremper [3] [detrɑ̃pe] *vt* **1.** MÉTALL to soften, to anneal **2.** [cuir] to soak, to soften **3.** [mouiller - chiffon, papier] to soak (through) ; [- chaux] to slake ; [- mortier] to mix with water **4.** ART to distemper.

détresse [detrɛs] *nf* **1.** [désespoir] distress, anxiety ■ **pousser un cri de ~** to cry out in distress **2.** [pauvreté] distress ■ **les familles dans la ~** families in dire need *ou* straits ■ **tomber dans une grande ~** to fall on hard times, to encounter hardship.
◆ **en détresse** *loc adj* [navire, avion] in distress.

détricoter [3] [detrikɔte] *vt* to unknit, to unravel.

détriment [detrimɑ̃] *nm litt* detriment.
◆ **au détriment de** *loc prép* to the detriment of, at the cost of.

détritus [detrity(s)] *nm* piece of rubbish UK *ou* garbage US ■ **des ~** refuse.

Detroit [detrwa] *npr* Detroit.

détroit [detrwa] *nm* **1.** GÉOGR strait ■ **les Détroits** the Dardanelles and the Bosphorus **2.** ANAT strait ■ **~ inférieur/supérieur du bassin** pelvic outlet/inlet.

DÉTROIT

le détroit de Béring the Bering Strait ;
le détroit de Cook the Cook Strait ;
le détroit des Dardanelles the Dardanelles ;
le détroit de Gibraltar the Strait of Gibraltar ;
le détroit d'Hormuz ou d'Ormuz the Strait of Hormuz *ou* Ormuz ;
le détroit de Magellan the Strait of Magellan ;
le détroit de Malacca the Strait of Malacca.

détromper [3] [detrɔ̃pe] *vt* to disabuse ■ **~ qqn** to put *ou* to set sb right.
◆ **se détromper** *vpi* : **détrompez-vous!** don't be so sure!

détrôner [3] [detrone] *vt* [roi] to dethrone, to depose ■ [personne, produit] to oust, to push into second position ■ **les compacts vont-ils ~ les cassettes?** will cassettes be ousted by CDs? ■ **se faire ~** *pr* to be dethroned.

détrousser [3] [detruse] *vt litt* to rob.

détruire [98] [detrɥir] *vt* **1.** [démolir, casser] to destroy ■ **ma vie est détruite** my life is in ruins **2.** [éliminer - population, parasites] to destroy, to wipe out *(sép)* ■ [tuer - ennemi] to kill ; [- animal malade, chien errant] to destroy **3.** [porter préjudice à - santé, carrière] to ruin, to destroy, to wreck ■ **tous ses espoirs ont été détruits en un instant** all her hopes were shattered in an instant.
◆ **se détruire** *vp (emploi réfléchi) vieilli* to do away with o.s.

dette [dɛt] *nf* **1.** [d'argent] debt ■ **avoir une ~** to have run up a debt ■ **avoir des ~s** to be in debt ■ **avoir des ~s vis-à-vis de qqn** to be in debt to sb ■ **être couvert** *ou* **criblé** *ou* **perdu de ~s** to be up to one's eyes UK *ou* ears US in debt ■ **faire des ~s** to get *ou* to run into debt ■ **je n'ai plus de ~s** I've cleared my debts ▶ **~ de l'État, ~ publique** national debt ■ **~ extérieure** external *ou* foreign debt ■ **~ d'honneur** debt of honour ■ **~ de jeu** gambling debt **2.** [obligation morale] debt ■ **régler sa ~ envers la société** to pay one's debt to society ■ **avoir une ~ de reconnaissance envers qqn** to be in sb's debt, to owe sb a debt of gratitude.

DEUG [dœg] (*abr de* **diplôme d'études universitaires générales**) *nm university diploma taken after 2 years.*

DEUG, DEUST

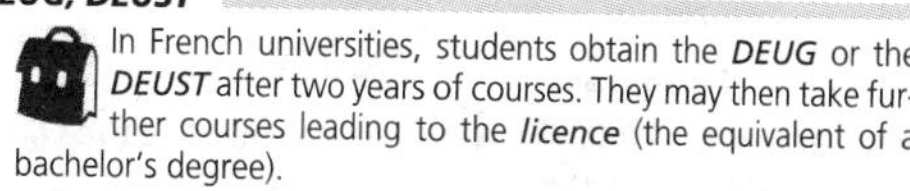

In French universities, students obtain the *DEUG* or the *DEUST* after two years of courses. They may then take further courses leading to the *licence* (the equivalent of a bachelor's degree).

deuil [dœj] *nm* **1.** [chagrin] grief, mourning ■ **faire son ~ de** *fam* : **j'en ai fait mon ~** I've resigned myself to not having it ■ **ta nouvelle voiture, tu peux en faire ton ~** you might as well kiss your new car goodbye **2.** [décès] bereavement **3.** [tenue conventionnelle] mourning ■ **porter/prendre le ~ (de qqn)** to be in/to go into mourning (for sb) **4.** [période] mourning **5.** [convoi] funeral procession ■ **conduire** *ou* **mener le ~** to be the chief mourner.
◆ **de deuil** *loc adj* [vêtement] mourning *(modif)* ■ **brassard de ~** black armband.
◆ **en deuil** *loc adj* bereaved ■ **une femme en ~** a woman in mourning.
◆ **en deuil de** *loc prép* : **être en ~ de qqn** to mourn for sb.

deus ex machina [deyseksmakina] *nm inv* deus ex machina.

deusio [døzjo] *adv fam* secondly, second.

DEUST [dœst] (*abr de* **diplôme d'études universitaires scientifiques et techniques**) *nm university diploma taken after 2 years of science courses.*

Deutéronome [døterɔnɔm] *npr m* Deuteronomy.

deuton [døtɔ̃] *nm* deuteron.

deux [dø] ◇ *dét* **1.** two ■ **eux/nous ~** both of them/us ■ **des ~ côtés** on both sides ■ **~ fois plus de livres** twice as many books ■ **~ fois moins de livres** half as many books ■ **j'ai ~ mots à te dire** I want a word with you ■ **~ ou trois** a couple, one or two ■ **~ ou trois livres/personnes** a couple of books/people, one or two books/people ■ **une personne à ~ visages** a two-faced individual ▶ **à ~ pas** close by, not far away ■ **à ~ pas de** close by, not far away from ■ **à ~ doigts de** close to, within an inch of ■ **j'ai été à ~ doigts de le renvoyer** I came very close to *ou* I was within inches of firing him ■ **entre ~ âges** middle-aged ■ **pris entre ~ feux** MIL exposed to crossfire ; *fig* caught in the crossfire ■ **nager entre ~ eaux** *fig* to sit on the fence ■ **je l'ai vu entre ~ portes** I only saw him briefly ■ **de ~ choses l'une, soit tu refuses, soit tu fais une proposition!** you've got a choice, you either say no or you suggest an alternative ■ **il n'a pas ~ sous de jugeote** he hasn't got a scrap of common sense ■ **en ~ temps trois mouvements** *fam* in no time at all, in a jiffy ■ **pour lui il y a ~ poids (et) ~ mesures** he has double standards ■ **~ avis valent mieux qu'un** two heads are better than one ■ **~ précautions valent mieux qu'un e** *prov* better safe than sorry ■ **de ~ maux, il faut choisir le moindre** one must choose the lesser of two evils **2.** [dans des séries] two, second ■ **à la page ~** on page two ■ **le ~ novembre** on November (the) second, on the second of November ■ **Henri II** Henry the Second, *voir aussi* **cinq**.
◇ *nm* **1.** [gén] two ■ **venez, tous les ~** come along, both of you ▶ **à nous ~!** right, let's get on with it! ■ **lui et le dessin, ça fait ~!** *fam* he can't draw to save his life! ■ **elle et la propreté, ça fait ~!** *fam* she doesn't know the meaning of the word "clean"! ■ **en moins de ~** in no time at all, in the twinkling of an eye **2.** JEUX : **le ~ de trèfle** the two of clubs.
◆ **à deux** *loc adv* [vivre] as a couple ■ [travailler] in pairs ■ **il faudra s'y mettre à ~** it'll take two of us.
◆ **deux à deux** *loc adv* in twos *ou* pairs.
◆ **deux par deux** *loc adv* in twos *ou* pairs ■ **les enfants, mettez-vous ~ par ~** children, get into twos *ou* pairs.

deuxième [døzjɛm] ◇ *adj num* second ■ **le Deuxième Bureau** POLIT the intelligence service.
◇ *nmf* second ■ **elle est la ~ sur la liste** she's second on the list.

deuxièmement [døzjɛmmɑ̃] *adv* secondly, in second place.

deux-mâts [døma] *nm inv* two-master.

deux-pièces [døpjɛs] *nm inv* **1.** [maillot de bain] two-piece **2.** [costume] two-piece **3.** [appartement] two-room flat UK *ou* apartment US.

deux-roues [døru] *nm inv* two-wheeled vehicle.

deux-temps [døtɑ̃] *nm inv* two-stroke ■ **un moteur ~** TECHNOL a two-stroke engine.

deuzio [døzjo] *adv fam* secondly, second.

dévaler [3] [devale] ◇ *vt* [en courant] to run *ou* to race *ou* to hurtle down ■ [en roulant] to tumble down.
◇ *vi* **1.** [personne] to hurry *ou* to hurtle down ■ [torrent] to gush down ■ [animal] to run down **2.** [s'abaisser - terrain] to fall *ou* to slope away **3.** [rouler] to tumble *ou* to bump down ■ **le chariot a dévalé tout seul** the trolley ran off on its own.

dévaliser [3] [devalize] *vt* **1.** [voler - banque, diligence] to rob ■ **il s'est fait ~** he was robbed **2.** *fam* [vider] to raid ■ **tous les marchands de glaces ont été dévalisés** all the ice-cream vendors have sold out.

dévaloir [devalwar] *nm Suisse* **1.** [à la montagne] *path through a mountain forest for transporting logs* **2.** [vide-ordures] rubbish *UK ou* garbage *US* chute.

dévalorisant, e [devalɔrizɑ̃, ɑ̃t] *adj* **1.** FIN depreciating **2.** [humiliant] humbling, humiliating.

dévalorisation [devalɔrizasjɔ̃] *nf* **1.** FIN depreciation **2.** [perte de prestige] devaluing, loss of prestige ■ **la ~ d'une profession/d'un diplôme** the loss of prestige of a profession/of a qualification.

dévaloriser [3] [devalɔrize] *vt* **1.** [discréditer - personne, talent] to depreciate, to devalue **2.** COMM to cause a drop in the commercial value of **3.** FIN to devalue.
◆ **se dévaloriser** ◇ *vp (emploi réfléchi)* [se discréditer] to lose credibility ■ **se ~ aux yeux de qqn** to lose credibility with sb.
◇ *vpi* FIN to become devalued.

dévaluation [devalɥasjɔ̃] *nf* devaluation, devaluing.

dévaluer [7] [devalɥe] *vt* **1.** FIN to devalue **2.** [déprécier] to devalue ■ **il l'a fait pour te ~ à tes propres yeux** he did it to make you feel cheap.
◆ **se dévaluer** *vpi* to drop in value.

devancement [dəvɑ̃smɑ̃] *nm* : **~ d'appel** enlistment before call-up.

devancer [16] [dəvɑ̃se] *vt* **1.** [dans l'espace - coureur, peloton] to get ahead of, to outdistance ■ **je la devançais de quelques mètres** I was a few metres ahead of her **2.** [dans le temps] to arrive ahead of ■ **elle m'avait devancé de deux jours** she had arrived two days before me ■ **~ l'appel** MIL to enlist before call-up ; *fig* to jump the gun **3.** [agir avant - personne] : **tu m'as devancé, c'est ce que je voulais lui offrir/lui dire** you beat me to it, that's just what I wanted to give her/to say to her ■ **il s'est fait ~ par les autres** the others got there before him **4.** FIN : **~ la date d'un paiement** to make a payment before it falls due.

devant [dəvɑ̃] ◇ *prép* **1.** [en face de] in front of ■ [avec mouvement] past ■ **il a déposé le paquet ~ la porte** he left the parcel outside the door ■ **toujours ~ la télé!** always glued to the TV! ■ **elle est passée ~ moi sans me voir** she walked right past (me) without seeing me
2. [en avant de] in front of ■ [en avance sur] ahead of ■ **nous passerons ~ lui pour lui montrer le chemin** we'll go ahead of him to show him the way ■ **l'ère de la communication est ~ nous** the age of communication lies ahead of *ou* before us ▶ **~ soi : aller droit ~ soi** to go straight on *ou* ahead ; *fig* to carry on regardless ■ **j'ai une heure ~ moi** I have an hour to spare ■ **elle avait une belle carrière ~ elle** she had a promising career ahead of her ■ **avoir quelques économies ~ soi** to have some savings put by
3. [en présence de] : **pleurer ~ tout le monde** [devant les gens présents] to cry in front of everyone ; [en public] to cry in public ■ **porter une affaire ~ la justice** to bring a case before the courts *ou* to court ■ **je jure ~ Dieu...** I swear to God...
4. [face à] in the face of, faced with ■ [étant donné] given ■ **son attitude ~ le malheur** his attitude in the face of *litt ou* to disaster ■ **égaux ~ la loi** equal before the law.
◇ *adv* **1.** [à l'avant] : **mettez les plus petits de la classe ~** put the shortest pupils at the *ou* in front ■ **installe-toi ~** sit in the front (of the car) ■ **ça se boutonne ~** it buttons up at the front ■ **faites passer la pétition ~** pass the petition forward ▶ **~ derrière** back to front, the wrong way round
2. [en face] : **tu es juste ~** it's right in front of you ■ **tu peux te garer juste ~** you can park (right) in front ■ **je suis passé ~ sans faire attention** I went past without paying attention
3. [en tête] : **elle est loin ~** she's a long way ahead ■ **passe ~, tu verras mieux** come *ou* go through you'll get a better view ■ **marche ~** walk in front.
◇ *nm* [gén] front ■ NAUT bow, bows, fore ■ **la jupe est plus longue sur le ~** the skirt is longer at the front ■ **sur le ~ de la scène** *fig* in the lime light ▶ **prendre les ~s** to make the first move, to be the first to act.
◆ **de devant** ◇ *loc adj* [dent, porte] front.
◇ *loc prép* : **va-t-en de ~ la fenêtre** move away from the window.

devanture [dəvɑ̃tyr] *nf* **1.** [vitrine] shop window *UK*, store window *US* **2.** [étalage] (window) display **3.** [façade] frontage, shopfront *UK*, storefront *US*.
◆ **en devanture** *loc adv* in the window.

dévastateur, trice [devastatœr, tris] *adj* devastating ■ **de manière dévastatrice** devastatingly.

dévastation [devastasjɔ̃] *nf* devastation, havoc.

dévaster [3] [devaste] *vt* **1.** [pays, ville] to devastate, to lay waste ■ [récolte] to ruin, to destroy ■ **des villages dévastés** destroyed villages **2.** *litt* [cœur] to ravage ■ **la souffrance a dévasté son visage** her looks have been ravaged by suffering.

déveine [deven] *nf* bad luck ■ **avec ma ~ habituelle** with my (usual) luck.

développé [devlɔpe] *nm* **1.** DANSE developpé **2.** SPORT press.

développement [devlɔpmɑ̃] *nm* **1.** [fait de grandir] development ■ **le ~ normal de l'enfant/du chêne** a child's/an oak's normal development ‖ [fait de progresser] development, growth ■ **pour aider au ~ du sens des responsabilités chez les jeunes** in order to foster a sense of responsibility in the young **2.** ÉCON : **le ~** development ■ **une région en plein ~** a fast-developing area ■ **~ durable** sustainable development **3.** [exposé] exposition ■ **entrer dans des ~s superflus** to go into unnecessary detail ‖ MUS development (section) **4.** [perfectionnement] developing ■ **nous leur avons confié le ~ du prototype** we asked them to develop the prototype for us **5.** PHOTO [traitement complet] processing, developing ■ [étape du traitement] developing **6.** MÉCAN gear ■ **bicyclette avec un ~ de six mètres** bicycle with a six metre gear **7.** MATH development **8.** [déploiement - d'une banderole] unrolling.
◆ **développements** *nmpl* [prolongements - d'une affaire] developments ■ **à la lumière des récents ~s** in the light of recent developments.

développer [3] [devlɔpe] *vt* **1.** [faire croître - faculté] to develop ; [- usine, secteur] to develop, to expand ; [- pays, économie] to develop ■ **pour ~ les muscles** for muscle development **2.** [exposer - argument, plan] to develop, to enlarge on **3.** [symptôme, complexe, maladie] to develop **4.** PHOTO [traiter] to process ■ [révéler] to develop ■ **faire ~ une pellicule** to have a film processed ■ **faire ~ des photos** to have some photos developed **5.** MATH to develop **6.** MÉCAN : **une bicyclette qui développe cinq mètres** a bicycle with a five metre gear **7.** [déballer - coupon] to unfold, to open out *(sép)* ; [- paquet] to unwrap ; [- banderole] to unroll.
◆ **se développer** *vpi* **1.** [croître - enfant, plante] to develop, to grow ; [- usine, secteur] to develop, to expand ; [- pays, économie] to develop, to become developed ■ **une région qui se développe** a developing area ■ **elle n'est pas très développée pour son âge** she's physically underdeveloped for her age **2.** [apparaître - membrane, moisissure] to form, to develop **3.** [se déployer - armée] to be deployed ; [- cortège] to spread out ; [- argument] to develop, to unfold ; [- récit] to develop, to progress, to unfold **4.** [se diversifier - technique, science] to improve, to develop **5.** [s'aggraver - maladie] to develop.

développeur [devlɔpœr] *nm* INFORM [entreprise] software development *ou* design company ■ [personne] software developer *ou* designer.

devenir[1] [dəvnir] *nm litt* **1.** [évolution] evolution **2.** [avenir] future.

◆ **en devenir** *loc adj litt* [société, œuvre] evolving, changing ▪ **en perpétuel ~** constantly changing, ever-changing.

devenir² [40] [dəvnir] *vi* **1.** [acquérir telle qualité] to become ▪ **~ professeur** to become a teacher ▪ **tu es devenue une femme** you're a woman now ▪ **~ réalité** to become a reality ▪ **~ vieux** to get *ou* to grow old ▪ **~ rouge/bleu** to go red/blue ▪ **l'animal peut ~ dangereux lorsqu'il est menacé** the animal can be dangerous when threatened ● **à (vous faire) ~ dingue** *fam*, **à (vous faire) ~ fou, à (vous faire) ~ chèvre** *fam* enough to drive you round the bend *ou* to make you scream **2.** [avoir tel sort] : **que sont devenus tes amis de jeunesse?** what happened to the friends of your youth? ▪ **que sont devenues tes belles intentions?** what has become of your good intentions? ▪ **et moi, qu'est-ce que je vais ~?** what's to become of me? ▪ **et moi, qu'est-ce que je deviens dans tout ça?** and where do I fit into all this? ▪ **je ne sais pas ce que je deviendrais sans toi** I don't know what I'd do without you **3.** *fam* [pour demander des nouvelles] : **que devenez-vous?** how are you getting on? ▪ **et lui, qu'est-ce qu'il devient?** what about him?, what's he up to these days? **4.** *(tournure impersonnelle)* **il devient difficile de...** it's getting difficult to... ▪ **il devient inutile de...** it's now pointless to...

dévergondage [devɛrgɔ̃daʒ] *nm* licentiousness, licentious *ou* immoral behaviour.

dévergondé, e [devɛrgɔ̃de] ◇ *adj* licentious, shameless.
◇ *nm, f* shameless person ▪ **quel ~!** he's a wild one!

dévergonder [3] [devɛrgɔ̃de] *vt* to corrupt, to pervert, to lead into a life of licentiousness ▪ **j'ai décidé de te ~, tu ne vas pas travailler aujourd'hui** *hum* I've decided to lead you astray, you're staying off work today.
◆ **se dévergonder** *vpi* to adopt a dissolute life style, to lead a life of licentiousness ▪ **dis donc, tu te dévergondes!** *hum* you're letting your hair down!

déverrouillage [devɛrujaʒ] *nm* **1.** ARM & INFORM unlocking **2.** [d'une porte] unbolting.

déverrouiller [3] [devɛruje] *vt* **1.** ARM & INFORM to unlock **2.** [porte] to unbolt.

déversement [devɛrsəmɑ̃] *nm* **1.** [écoulement] flowing **2.** [déchargement - d'eaux usées] pouring, discharging ; [- de passagers] offloading, discharging ; [- d'ordures] dumping, tipping *UK*.

déverser [3] [devɛrse] *vt* **1.** [répandre - liquide] to pour, to discharge **2.** [décharger] to discharge ▪ **les paysans ont déversé des tonnes de fruits sur la chaussée** the farmers dumped tons of fruit on the road **3.** [exprimer - chagrin, rage, plainte] to vent, to let *ou* to pour out ▪ **~ des flots d'injures** to come out with a stream of abuse.
◆ **se déverser** *vpi* **1.** [couler] to flow ▪ **se ~ dans la mer** to flow into the sea **2.** [tomber] : **le chargement s'est déversé sur la route** the load tipped over *ou* spilled onto the road.

déversoir [devɛrswar] *nm* [d'un barrage] spillway, wasteweir *UK*.

dévêtir [44] [devetir] *vt* to undress ▪ **dévêts-le** take his clothes off, undress him.
◆ **se dévêtir** *vp (emploi réfléchi)* to undress o.s., to get undressed, to take one's clothes off.

déviance [devjɑ̃s] *nf* deviance, deviancy.

déviant, e [devjɑ̃, ɑ̃t] *adj* & *nm, f* deviant.

déviation [devjasjɔ̃] *nf* **1.** TRANSP detour, diversion *UK* ▪ **'~ à 500 mètres'** 'diversion in 500 metres' **2.** [écart] swerving, deviating ▪ **il ne se permet aucune ~ par rapport à la ligne du parti** he will not deviate from *ou* be deflected away from the party line **3.** MÉD : **~ de la colonne vertébrale** curvature of the spine **4.** ÉLECTRON deflection **5.** NAUT [d'un compas] deviation.

déviationnisme [devjasjɔnism] *nm* deviationism.

dévider [3] [devide] *vt* **1.** TEXT to wind up, to reel, to spool (up) **2.** [dérouler - bobine] to unwind ; [- câble, corde] to uncoil ▪ **~ son rosaire** to say the rosary.

dévidoir [devidwar] *nm* **1.** TEXT reel, spool **2.** [de tuyau d'incendie] reel.

devient *etc v* ▻ **devenir.**

dévier [9] [devje] ◇ *vi* **1.** [s'écarter] to swerve, to veer ▪ **le bus a brusquement dévié sur la droite/gauche** the bus suddenly veered off to the right/left ▪ **~ de** to move away, to swerve from **2.** [dans un débat, un projet] to diverge, to deviate ▪ **faire ~ la conversation** to change the subject ▪ **l'association ne doit pas ~ par rapport à son but premier** the association must not be diverted from its original purpose *ou* must pursue its original goal unswervingly ▪ **~ de** to move away from, to stray off **3.** [se pervertir] : **la conversation dévie (sur un sujet scabreux)** the conversation is becoming a bit risqué.
◇ *vt* **1.** [balle, projectile] to deflect, to turn away *ou* aside *(sép)* ▪ [coup] to parry ▪ [circulation] to divert, to redirect, to reroute **2.** PHYS to refract **3.** [distraire - attention] to divert.

devin, devineresse [dəvɛ̃, dəvinrɛs] *nm, f* soothsayer ▪ **il n'est pas ~!** he's not a mind-reader! ▪ **(il n'y a) pas besoin d'être ~ pour comprendre** you don't need to be a genius to understand.

devinable [dəvinabl] *adj* **1.** [énigme] solvable ▪ [secret] guessable **2.** [prévisible - avenir] foreseeable.

deviner [3] [dəvine] *vt* **1.** [imaginer] to guess, to work out *(sép)*, to figure (out) *(sép)* ▪ **devine qui est là!** guess who's here! ▪ **je n'ai fait que ~** it was sheer guesswork **2.** [découvrir - énigme, mystère] : **il a tout de suite deviné ses intentions** he saw through her right away ▪ **tu ne devineras jamais ce qui m'est arrivé** you'll never guess what happened to me ▪ **~ que : j'ai deviné qu'il y avait quelque chose de bizarre** I guessed there was something strange **3.** [prédire - avenir] to foresee, to foretell **4.** [apercevoir] : **on devinait son soutien-gorge sous son chemisier** her bra showed through slightly under her blouse **5.** *litt* [percer à jour] : **~ qqn** to see through sb.
◆ **se deviner** *vp (emploi passif)* **1.** [être aperçu] to be made out ▪ **sa tête se devine derrière le rideau** you can just make out her head behind the curtain **2.** [transparaître - sentiment] to show (through).

devineresse [dəvinrɛs] *f* ▻ **devin.**

devinette [dəvinɛt] *nf* riddle ▪ **poser une ~ (à qqn)** to ask (sb) a riddle ▪ **jouer aux ~s** *pr* to play (at) riddles ; *fig* to speak in riddles.

devint *etc v* ▻ **devenir.**

déviriliser [3] [devirilize] *vt* [homme] to unman.

devis [dəvi] *nm* : **~ (estimatif)** estimate, quotation ▪ **faire** *ou* **établir un ~** to draw up an estimate ▪ **il a fait un ~ de 400 euros** he quoted 400 euros (in his estimate) ▪ **sur ~** on the basis of an estimate.

dévisager [17] [devizaʒe] *vt* to stare (persistently) at ▪ **on ne dévisage pas les gens** it's rude to stare.

devise [dəviz] *nf* **1.** HÉRALD device **2.** [maxime] motto ▪ **laisser faire les autres, c'est sa ~!** let the others do the work, that's his motto! **3.** FIN currency ▪ **acheter des ~s** to buy foreign currency ● **~ forte/faible** hard/soft currency ▪ **~ flottante** floating currency.

deviser [3] [dəvize] ◇ *vi litt* to converse *litt*, to talk.
◇ *vt Suisse* **~ qqn** to give sb an estimate.

dévisser [3] [devise] ◇ *vt* **1.** [desserrer - écrou, vis] to loosen ▪ [détacher] to undo, to unscrew, to screw off *(sép)* ▪ **dévissez le bouchon** unscrew the top off the bottle **2.** [tordre - bras, cou] to twist.
◇ *vi* [en montagne] to fall *ou* to come off.
◆ **se dévisser** ◇ *vp (emploi passif)* [se détacher] to unscrew, to undo ▪ **le bouchon se dévisse facilement** the top twists off the bottle easily.
◇ *vpt* : **se ~ le cou/la tête** to screw one's neck/one's head round.

de visu [devizy] *loc adv* : **je l'ai constaté ~** I saw it for myself *ou* with my own eyes.

dévitalisation [devitalizasjɔ̃] *nf* removal of a nerve *(from a tooth)*.

dévitaliser [3] [devitalize] *vt* to remove the nerve from, to devitalize *spéc* ▪ **se faire ~ une dent** to have a tooth devitalized.

dévitrifier [9] [devitrifje] *vt* to devitrify.

dévoie *etc v* ▷ **dévoyer**.

dévoilement [devwalmɑ̃] *nm* **1.** [d'une statue, d'un visage] unveiling **2.** [d'un secret, d'intentions] disclosing, revealing.

dévoiler [3] [devwale] *vt* **1.** [dénuder - visage, épaule, statue] to unveil, to uncover ▪ **~ ses charmes** *euphém* to reveal all **2.** [exprimer - intention, sentiment] to disclose, to reveal, to unveil ▪ **il a dévoilé ses pensées les plus secrètes** he laid bare his innermost thoughts.
◆ **se dévoiler** ◇ *vp (emploi réfléchi)* [ôter son voile] to unveil one's face *ou* o.s.
◇ *vpi* [se manifester] to be disclosed *ou* revealed, to show up, to come to light.

devoir¹ [dəvwar] *nm* **1.** ÉDUC assignment, exercise ▪ **~ de chimie** chemistry assignment *ou* exercise ▪ **~ de français** French essay ▪ **faire ses ~s** to do one's homework ▶ **~ sur table** (written) class test ▪ **~s de vacances** holiday *UK ou* vacation *US* homework **2.** [impératifs moraux] duty ▪ **le ~ m'appelle** duty calls ▪ **je ne l'ai prévenu que par ~** I warned him only because I thought it was my duty **3.** [tâche à accomplir] duty, obligation ▪ **faire** *ou* **accomplir** *ou* **remplir son ~** to carry out *ou* to do one's duty ▪ **avoir le ~ de** to have the duty to ▪ **se faire un ~ de faire qqch** to make it one's duty to do sthg ▪ **se mettre en ~ de faire qqch** to set about (doing) sthg ▶ **~ conjugal** conjugal duties.
◆ **devoirs** *nmpl* : **rendre les derniers ~s à qqn** to pay sb a final homage *ou* tribute ▪ **rendre ses ~s à qqn** to pay one's respects to sb.
◆ **de devoir** *loc adj* : **homme/femme de ~** man/woman with a (strong) sense of duty.
◆ **du devoir de** *loc prép* : **il est du ~ de tout citoyen de voter** it is the duty of every citizen to vote ▪ **j'ai cru de mon ~ de l'aider** I felt duty-bound to help him.

devoir² [53] [dəvwar] ◇ *v aux* **1.** [exprime l'obligation] : **il doit** he has to, he needs to, he must ▪ **dois-je être plus clair?** do I need *ou* have to be more explicit? ▪ **je dois admettre que...** I must admit that... ▪ **il ne doit pas** he must not, he musn't ▪ **on ne doit pas fumer** smoking is forbidden *ou* is not allowed **2.** [dans des conseils, des suggestions] : **il devrait** he ought to, he should ▪ **tu ne devrais pas boire** you shouldn't drink
3. [indique une prévision, une intention] : **il doit m'en donner demain** he's due to *ou* he should give me some tomorrow ▪ **c'est une pièce que l'on doit voir depuis un an!** it's a play we've supposedly been going to see *ou* we've been planning to see for a year! ‖ [dans le passé] : **il devait venir mais je ne l'ai pas vu** he was supposed to come *ou* to have come but I didn't see him
4. [exprime une probabilité] : **il/cela doit** he/it must, he's/it's got to ▪ **il doit être fatigué** he must be tired, he's probably tired ▪ **il ne devait pas beaucoup l'aimer pour écrire cela** he can't have really loved her to write this ▪ **il doit y avoir** *ou* **cela doit faire un an que je ne l'ai pas vu** it must be a year since I (last) saw him ▪ **une offre qui devrait les intéresser** an offer which should interest them
5. [exprime l'inévitable] : **nous devons tous mourir un jour** we all have to die one day ▪ **la maison où elle devait écrire "Claudine"** the house where she was to write "Claudine" ‖ [exprime une norme] : **un bon chanteur doit savoir chanter en direct** a good singer should be able to sing live ▪ **le four ne devrait pas faire ce bruit** the oven isn't supposed to *ou* shouldn't make that noise
6. *sout* **je l'aiderai, dussé-je aller en prison/y passer ma vie** I'll help him, even if it means going to prison/devoting my life to it.
◇ *vt* **1.** [avoir comme dette] to owe ▪ **~ qqch à qqn** to owe sb sthg, to owe sthg to sb ▪ **je te dois l'essence** I owe you for the petrol ▪ **je ne demande que ce qui m'est dû** I'm only asking for my due **2.** [être moralement obligé de fournir] : **~ qqch à qqn** to owe sb sthg ▪ **je te dois bien ça** that's the least I can do for you ▪ **traiter qqn avec le respect qu'on lui doit** to treat sb with due respect ▪ **selon les honneurs dus à sa fonction** with such pomp as befits her office
3. [être redevable de] : **~ qqch à qqn** to owe sthg to sb ▪ **c'est à Guimard que l'on doit cette découverte** we have Guimard to thank *ou* we're indebted to Guimard for this discovery ▪ **c'est à lui que je dois d'avoir trouvé du travail** it's thanks to him that I found a job ▪ **le son doit sa qualité à des enceintes très performantes** the good quality of the sound is due to excellent speakers ▪ **sa victoire ne doit rien au hasard** her victory has nothing to do with luck.
◆ **se devoir** *vp (emploi réciproque)* [avoir comme obligation mutuelle] : **les époux se doivent fidélité** spouses *ou* husbands and wives must be faithful to each other.
◆ **se devoir à** *vp+prép* : **tu te dois à ta musique** you must dedicate yourself to your music ▪ **je me dois à mon public** I must attend to my fans.
◆ **se devoir de** *vp+prép* to have it as one's duty to ▪ **tu es grand, tu te dois de donner l'exemple** you're a big boy now, it's your duty to show a good example.

dévoisé, e [devwaze] *adj* LING devoiced.

dévolu, e [devɔly] *adj* **1.** DR : **~ à** devolving on *ou* upon **2.** [destiné] : **argent ~ à cet usage** money allocated to that purpose.
◆ **dévolu** *nm loc* **jeter son ~ sur** [chose] to go for, to choose ; [personne] to set one's cap at.

dévolution [devɔlysjɔ̃] *nf* devolution.

dévorant, e [devɔrɑ̃, ɑ̃t] *adj* **1.** [faim] gnawing ▪ [soif] burning **2.** [amour, passion] consuming, all-consuming, burning, powerful ▪ **éprouver une jalousie ~e** to be consumed *ou* devoured by jealousy **3.** *litt* [feu] all-consuming.

dévorer [3] [devɔre] *vt* **1.** [manger - suj: animal, personne] to devour ▪ *(en usage absolu)* **il dévore!** he eats like a horse! ‖ *fig* **dévoré par les moustiques** eaten alive *ou* bitten to death by mosquitoes ▪ **une voiture qui dévore les kilomètres** a car which eats up the miles ▪ **~ qqch des yeux** *ou* **du regard** to stare hungrily *ou* to gaze greedily at sthg ▪ **~ qqn des yeux** *ou* **du regard** to stare hungrily *ou* to gaze greedily at sb ▪ **~ qqn de baisers** to smother sb with kisses **2.** [lire] to devour, to read avidly **3.** [consommer] to use (up) ▪ **dans mon métier, je dévore du papier/de la pellicule** in my job I use (up) huge quantities of paper/of film ▪ **ne te laisse pas ~ par ton travail** don't let your work monopolize your time **4.** [tenailler] to devour ▪ **l'ambition le dévore** he's eaten *ou* devoured by ambition ▪ **être dévoré par l'envie/la curiosité/les remords** to be eaten up with envy/curiosity/remorse.

dévoreur, euse [devɔrœr, øz] *nm, f fam* **~ de** : **c'est une dévoreuse de romans** she's an avid reader of novels.

dévot, e [devo, ɔt] ◇ *adj* devout.
◇ *nm, f* **1.** [qui croit] staunch believer **2.** *péj* [bigot] sanctimonious individual ▪ **faux ~** *péj* pharisee.

dévotement [devɔtmɑ̃] *adv* devoutly, religiously.

dévotion [devosjɔ̃] *nf* **1.** RELIG devoutness, religiousness, piety ▪ **fausse ~** *péj* false piety ▪ **~ à la Sainte Vierge** devotion to the Blessed Virgin ▪ **avec ~** [gén] devotedly ; RELIG devoutly **2.** *litt* [attachement] devotion ▪ **il voue une véritable ~ à sa mère** he worships his mother.
◆ **dévotions** *nfpl* [prières] devotions ▪ **faire ses ~s** to perform one's devotions.

dévoué, e [devwe] *adj* **1.** [fidèle] devoted, faithful ▪ **être ~ à ses amis** to be devoted to one's friends ▪ **nous vous remercions de votre appui ~** we thank you for your staunch support **2.** *sout* [dans des formules de politesse] : **votre ~ serviteur** your humble servant ▪ **je vous prie de croire à mes sentiments les plus ~s** Yours sincerely *ou US* truly.

dévouement [devumɑ̃] *nm* **1.** [abnégation] dedication, devotedness, devotion ▪ **soigner qqn avec ~** to look after sb devotedly ▪ **avoir l'esprit de ~** to be self-sacrificing **2.** [loyauté] devotion ▪ **son ~ à la cause** his devotion to the cause.

dévouer [6] [devwe] *vt litt* **~ qqch à** to dedicate *ou* to devote sthg to.
◆ **se dévouer** *vpi* [proposer ses services] : **allez, dévoue-toi pour une fois!** come on, make a sacrifice for once! ▪ **qui va se ~ pour faire le ménage?** who's going to volunteer to clean up? ▪ **finir la tarte? bon, je me dévoue!** *hum* you want me to finish up the tart? oh well, if I must!
◆ **se dévouer à** *vp+prép* [se consacrer à] to dedicate o.s. to.

dévoyé, e [devwaje] ◇ *adj* perverted, corrupted.
◇ *nm, f* corrupt individual.

dévoyer [13] [devwaje] *vt litt* to lead astray.

◆ **se dévoyer** *vpi* to go astray.

dextérité [dɛksterite] *nf* dexterity, deftness ▪ **avec ~** dexterously, deftly.

dézipper [3] [dezipe] *vt* INFORM to unzip.

dg (*abr écrite de* **décigramme**) dg.

DG (*abr de* **directeur général**) *nm* GM, CEO *US*.

DGI (*abr de* **Direction générale des impôts**) *npr f central tax office.*

DGSE (*abr de* **Direction générale de la sécurité extérieure**) *npr f the arm of the Defence Ministry in charge of international intelligence,* ≃ MI6 *UK*, ≃ CIA *US*.

DI *nf* = **division d'infanterie.**

diabète [djabɛt] *nm* diabetes ▪ **~ sucré** diabetes mellitus.

diabétique [djabetik] *adj* & *nmf* diabetic.

diabétologue [djabetɔlɔg] *nmf* diabetes specialist.

diable [djabl] ◇ *nm* **1.** RELIG devil ▪ **le ~** the Devil ➊ **aller au ~** to go to hell ▪ **envoyer qqn au ~** to send sb packing ▪ **au ~ les convenances!** to hell with propriety! ▪ **avoir le ~ au corps : ce gamin a le ~ au corps** *fam* this child's a real handful ▪ **comme un beau ~** [courir, sauter] like the (very) devil, like a thing possessed ; [hurler] like a stuck pig ▪ **comme un ~ dans un bénitier** like a cat on a hot tin roof ▪ **habiter au ~ vauvert** *OU* **vert** to live miles away ▪ **tirer le ~ par la queue** to live from hand to mouth ▪ **c'est le ~ qui bat sa femme et marie sa fille** *prov* it's rainy and sunny at the same time ▪ **ce serait bien le ~ s'il refusait!** I'd be very surprised if he refused! ▪ **ce n'est pourtant pas le ~!** it's really not that difficult! ▪ **c'est bien le ~ si je ne récupère pas mon argent!** I'll be damned if I don't get my money back! ▪ **le ~ soit de ces gens-là/tes principes** *arch* the devil take these people/your principles ▪ **(que) le ~ m'emporte si je mens!** the devil take me if I'm lying! **2.** [enfant] (little) devil ▪ [homme] : **un bon ~** a good sort ▪ **un grand ~** a great tall fellow ▪ **un mauvais ~** a bad sort ▪ **un pauvre ~** a wretched man, a poor wretch **3.** [chariot] trolley **4.** [jouet] jack-in-the-box **5.** [casserole] earthenware (cooking) pot.
◇ *adj* **1.** [espiègle] : **que tu es ~!** stop being such a little devil! **2.** CULIN [sauce] devilled.
◇ *adv* : **qui/que/comment ~?** who/what/how the devil?, who/what/how on earth?
◇ *interj* heck, my goodness, goodness me ▪ **~, voilà une histoire bien compliquée!** goodness me, what a complicated story!
◆ **à la diable** *loc adv* **1.** [vite et mal] : **un repas préparé à la ~** a meal thrown together quickly **2.** CULIN : **œuf à la ~** devilled eggs.
◆ **diable de** *loc adj* : **ce ~ de rhumatisme!** this damned rheumatism!
◆ **du diable, de tous les diables** *loc adj* : **faire un boucan de tous les ~s** *fam* to kick up a hell of a racket ▪ **il a eu un mal de tous les ~s pour finir à temps** he had a devil of a job to finish in time.
◆ **en diable** *loc adv sout* devilishly ▪ **jolie en ~** pretty as a picture ▪ **retors en ~** sly as a fox.

diablement [djabləmɑ̃] *adv fam vieilli* damned ▪ **cette pièce est ~ longue!** this play's interminable!

diablesse [djablɛs] *nf* **1.** RELIG she-devil **2.** [femme méchante] witch **3.** [fillette] : **petite ~!** you little devil!

diablotin [djablɔtɛ̃] *nm* **1.** MYTHOL small *OU* little devil **2.** [enfant] imp **3.** [pétard] cracker.

diabolique [djabɔlik] *adj* diabolic, diabolical, devilish ▪ **il a agi de façon ~** he acted diabolically.

diaboliquement [djabɔlikmɑ̃] *adv* diabolically, devilishly.

diabolo [djabɔlo] *nm* **1.** [jouet] diabolo **2.** CULIN : **~ menthe** *lemon soda with mint syrup.*

diachronie [djakrɔni] *nf* diachrony.

diaconat [djakɔna] *nm* diaconate.

diaconesse [djakɔnɛs] *nf* deaconess.

diacre [djakr] *nm* deacon.

diacritique [djakritik] *adj* & *nm* diacritic ▪ **(signe) ~** diacritic.

diadème [djadɛm] *nm* diadem.

diagnostic [djagnɔstik] *nm* diagnosis ▪ **~ prénatal** antenatal diagnosis.

diagnostiquer [3] [djagnɔstike] *vt* to diagnose ▪ **on lui a diagnostiqué un diabète** he's been diagnosed as suffering from diabetes.

diagonal, e, aux [djagɔnal, o] *adj* diagonal.
◆ **diagonale** *nf* diagonal (line).
◆ **en diagonale** *loc adv* **1.** [en biais] diagonally **2.** [vite] : **lire** *OU* **parcourir un livre en ~e** to skim through a book.

diagramme [djagram] *nm* **1.** [graphique] graph **2.** [croquis] diagram ▪ **~ en secteurs** pie chart.

dialectal, e, aux [djalɛktal, o] *adj* dialectal.

dialecte [djalɛkt] *nm* dialect.

dialectique [djalɛktik] ◇ *adj* dialectic, dialectical.
◇ *nf* dialectic, dialectics *(aussi sing).*

dialogue [djalɔg] *nm* **1.** [discussion] dialogue *UK*, dialog *US* ▪ **le ~ Est-Ouest** dialogue between East and West ▪ **entre eux, c'était un véritable ~ de sourds** they were not on the same wavelength at all **2.** CINÉ & THÉÂTRE dialogue ▪ **écrire les ~s d'un film** to write the dialogue for a film **3.** INFORM : **~ homme-machine** interactive use (of a computer).

dialoguer [3] [djalɔge] ◇ *vi* **1.** [converser] to converse **2.** [négocier] to have *OU* to hold talks ▪ **les syndicats vont de nouveau ~ avec le ministre** the unions are to resume talks *OU* their dialogue with the minister **3.** INFORM : **~ avec un ordinateur** to interact with a computer.
◇ *vt* [film, scénario] to write the dialogue for.

dialoguiste [djalɔgist] *nmf* dialogue writer.

dialyse [djaliz] *nf* dialysis ▪ **se faire faire une ~** to undergo dialysis ▪ **être sous ~** to be on dialysis.

dialysé, e [djalize] *nm, f* dialysis patient.

dialyser [3] [djalize] *vt* to dialyse.

diamant [djamɑ̃] *nm* diamond.

diamantaire [djamɑ̃tɛr] *nmf* **1.** [vendeur] diamond merchant **2.** [tailleur] diamond cutter.

diamétral, e, aux [djametral, o] *adj* diametral, diametric, diametrical.

diamétralement [diametralmɑ̃] *adv* diametrically ▪ **~ opposé** diametrically opposed.

diamètre [djamɛtr] *nm* diameter ▪ **le fût fait 30 cm de ~** the barrel is 30 cm across *OU* in diameter ▪ **couper le cercle dans son ~** cut the circle across.

diams [djams] *nmpl fam* ice, diamonds.

Diane [djan] *npr* MYTHOL Diana.

diantre [djɑ̃tr] *arch* ◇ *interj* ye gods *pr* & *hum.*
◇ *adv* : **qui ~ a dit cela?** who the deuce *OU* the devil said that?

diapason [djapazɔ̃] *nm* [instrument] tuning fork ▪ [registre] range, diapason.
◆ **au diapason** *loc adv* in tune ▪ *fig* **il n'est plus au ~** he's out of touch ▪ **se mettre au ~ (de qqn)** to fall *OU* to step into line (with sb).

diaphane [djafan] *adj* diaphanous.

diaphragme [djafragm] *nm* **1.** ANAT & TECHNOL diaphragm **2.** MÉD diaphragm *spéc*, (Dutch) cap **3.** PHOTO stop, diaphragm.

diapo [djapo] *nf fam* slide PHOTO.

diaporama [djaporama] *nm* slide show.

diapositive [djapozitiv] *nf* slide PHOTO.

diapré, e [djapre] *adj litt* mottled.

diarrhée [djare] *nf* diarrhoea ■ **avoir la ~** to have diarrhoea.

diaspora [djaspɔra] *nf* diaspora ■ **la ~ arménienne** the Armenian diaspora, Armenian communities throughout the world ■ **la Diaspora** the Diaspora.

diatonique [djatɔnik] *adj* diatonic.

diatribe [djatrib] *nf* diatribe *sout*, (vicious) attack.

dicastère [dikastɛr] *nm Suisse administrative division in the Swiss local government system.*

dichotomie [dikɔtɔmi] *nf* dichotomy.

dichotomique [dikɔtɔmik] *adj* dichotomous.

dico [diko] *nm fam* dictionary.

Dictaphone® [diktafɔn] *nm* Dictaphone®.

dictateur [diktatœr] *nm* dictator.

dictatorial, e, aux [diktatɔrjal, o] *adj* dictatorial.

dictature [diktatyr] *nf* dictatorship ■ **la ~ du prolétariat** the dictatorship of the proletariat ■ **la ~ de la mode** the edicts of fashion.

dictée [dikte] *nf* **1.** [à des élèves] dictation ■ **~ musicale** musical dictation **2.** [à une secrétaire, un assistant] dictating ■ **j'ai écrit le rapport sous sa ~** he dictated the report to me.

dicter [3] [dikte] *vt* **1.** ÉDUC to read out as dictation **2.** [courrier, lettre, résumé] to dictate **3.** [imposer - choix] to dictate, to impose, to force ; [- condition] to dictate ■ **on lui a dicté ses réponses** his replies had been dictated to him.

diction [diksjɔ̃] *nf* diction ■ **avoir une ~ parfaite** to speak with total clarity.
◆ **de diction** *loc adj* speech *(modif)*.

dictionnaire [diksjɔnɛr] *nm* **1.** [livre] dictionary ■ **~ bilingue** bilingual dictionary ■ **~ de la musique/des beaux-arts** dictionary of music/of art ■ **~ encyclopédique/de langue** encyclopedic/language dictionary **2.** INFORM dictionary.

dicton [diktɔ̃] *nm* dictum *sout*, (popular) saying ■ **comme dit le ~** as they say, as the saying goes.

didacticiel [didaktisjɛl] *nm* piece of educational software, teachware *US*.

didactique [didaktik] <> *adj* **1.** [de l'enseignement] didactic **2.** [instructif] didactic, educational **3.** PSYCHOL : **analyse ~** training analysis.
<> *nf* didactics *(sing)*.

dièdre [djɛdr] *nm* GÉOM dihedron.

diérèse [djerɛz] *nf* LING & LITTÉR diaeresis, dieresis.

dièse [djez] <> *adj* : **la ~** A sharp.
<> *nm* **1.** MUS sharp **2.** [symbole] hash ■ **appuyez sur la touche ~** press the hash key.

diesel [djezɛl] *nm* **1.** [moteur] diesel engine *ou* motor **2.** [véhicule] diesel **3.** [combustible] diesel (oil).

diète [djɛt] *nf* **1.** [régime] diet **2.** [absence de nourriture] fasting *(for health reasons)* **3.** HIST diet.
◆ **à la diète** *loc adv* **1.** [au régime] on a diet **2.** [sans nourriture] : **mettre qqn à la ~** to prescribe a fast for sb.

diététicien, enne [djetetisjɛ̃, ɛn] *nm, f* dietician, dietitian, nutrition specialist.

diététique [djetetik] <> *adj* [aliment] health *(modif)* ■ [boutique] health food *(modif)*.
<> *nf* nutrition science, dietetics *(sing) spéc* ■ **conseils de ~** nutritional advice.

dieu, x [djø] *nm* **1.** [divinité] god ■ **le ~ de la Guerre/l'Amour** the god of war/love ■ **il y a un ~ pour les ivrognes!** there must be a god who looks after drunks! ◐ **comme un ~** divinely, like a god ■ **jurer ses grands ~x** to swear to God **2.** [héros] god, idol **3.** [objet de vénération] god.
◆ **Dieu** *npr* **1.** [gén] God ■ **Dieu le père** God the father ■ **il se prend pour Dieu le père** *péj* he thinks he's God (Himself) ◐ **le bon Dieu** the good Lord ■ **c'est le bon Dieu qui t'a puni** you got your just deserts (for being bad) ■ **apporter le bon Dieu à un malade** to bring the Holy Sacrament to a sick person ■ **tous les jours** *ou* **chaque jour que (le bon) Dieu fait** every blessed day ■ **on lui donnerait le bon Dieu sans confession** he looks as if butter wouldn't melt in his mouth ■ **il vaut mieux s'adresser à Dieu qu'à ses saints** it's better to talk to the organ-grinder than the monkey ■ **si Dieu me prête vie** if I'm still alive (by then) **2.** [dans des exclamations] : **Dieu me damne** *ou* **maudisse (si...)!** *litt* may God strike me dead (if...)! ■ **Dieu m'est témoin** *litt* as God is my witness ■ **Dieu me pardonne!** *litt* (may) God forgive me! ■ **Dieu nous protège** god *ou* Lord protect us ■ **Dieu vous bénisse/entende!** *litt* may God bless/hear you! ■ **Dieu vous garde** *litt* God be with you ■ **c'est pas** *ou* **c'est-y Dieu possible!** *fam* it just can't be (true)! ■ **Dieu sait combien il l'a aimée!** God knows he loved her! ■ **Dieu seul le sait!** God (only) knows! ■ **à Dieu va** *ou* **vat!** *litt* it's in God's hands!, in God's hands be it! ■ **à Dieu ne plaise!** *litt* God forbid! ■ **bon Dieu!** *fam* for God's sake!, for Pete's sake! ■ **bon Dieu de...** *fam* blasted..., blessed... ■ **bon Dieu de bon Dieu!** for crying out loud! ■ **Dieu ait son âme!** *litt* God rest his soul! ■ **Dieu merci!** thank God *ou* the Lord! ■ **grand Dieu!** good God *ou* Lord! ■ **grands dieux!** good heavens *ou* gracious! ■ **mon Dieu!** my God!, my goodness!, good Lord! ■ **mon Dieu** [dans des prières] Lord, God ■ **vingt dieux!** *hum* struth!
◆ **des dieux** *loc adj* [festin] sumptuous, princely ■ [plaisir] divine, exquisite.

diffamant, e [difamɑ̃, ɑ̃t] *adj* [texte] defamatory, libellous ■ [geste, parole] slanderous ■ **des propos ~s** slander.

diffamateur, trice [difamatœr, tris] <> *adj* [texte] defamatory, libellous ■ [geste, parole] slanderous.
<> *nm, f* slanderer, defamer *litt*.

diffamation [difamasjɔ̃] *nf* **1.** [accusation - gén] defamation ; [- par un texte] libelling ; [- par des discours] slandering **2.** [texte] libel ■ [geste, parole] slander.
◆ **de diffamation** *loc adj* [campagne] smear *(modif)*.
◆ **en diffamation** *loc adj* : **intenter un procès en ~ à qqn** [pour un texte injurieux] to bring an action for libel against sb ; [pour des paroles injurieuses] to bring an action for slander against sb.

diffamatoire [difamatwar] *adj* [texte] defamatory, libellous ■ [geste, parole] slanderous ■ **parler/agir de façon ~** to speak/to act slanderously.

diffamer [3] [difame] *vt* [par écrit] to defame, to libel ■ [oralement] to slander.

différé, e [difere] *adj* **1.** [paiement, rendez-vous, réponse] deferred, postponed **2.** RADIO & TV prerecorded.
◆ **en différé** *loc adj* RADIO & TV prerecorded.

différemment [diferamɑ̃] *adv* differently ■ **il agit ~ des autres** he's not behaving like the others, he's behaving differently from the others.

différence [diferɑ̃s] *nf* **1.** [distinction] difference, dissimilarity ■ **faire la ~ entre** to make the distinction between, to distinguish between ■ **les électeurs indécis feront la ~** the don't-knows will tip the balance ■ **c'est ce qui fait toute la ~!** that's what makes all the difference! ■ **il s'est excusé – cela ne fait aucune ~** he apologized – it doesn't make any *ou* it makes no difference ■ **faire des ~s entre ses enfants** to treat one's children differently from each other **2.** [écart] difference ■ **~ d'âge** age difference *ou* gap ■ **~ de caractère** difference in characters ■ **il y a deux ans de ~ entre eux** there are two years between them **3.** [particularité - culturelle, sexuelle] : **revendiquer sa ~** to be proud to be different **4.** MATH [d'une soustraction] result ■ [ensemble] difference **5.** PHILOS difference.
◆ **à la différence de** *loc prép* unlike.
◆ **à cette différence (près) que, à la différence que** *loc conj* except that ■ **j'ai accepté son offre à cette ~ près que, cette fois, je sais ce qui m'attend** I accepted his offer but this time I know what to expect.

différenciateur, trice [diferɑ̃sjatœr, tris] *adj* differentiating.

différenciation [diferɑ̃sjasjɔ̃] *nf* **1.** [distinction] differentiation **2.** BIOL : **~ des sexes** sex determination.

différencier [9] [diferɑ̃sje] *vt* **1.** [distinguer] to distinguish, to differentiate ■ **rien ne les différencie** it's impossible to tell them apart ■ **ce qui nous différencie des animaux** that which sets us apart from animals **2.** BIOL to differentiate.
◆ **se différencier** *vpi* **1.** [se distinguer] to be different, to differ ■ **ils se différencient (l'un de l'autre) par leur manière de parler** they're different from one another by the way they speak **2.** BIOL to differentiate.

différend [diferɑ̃] *nm* disagreement, dispute ■ **avoir un ~ avec qqn** to be in dispute with sb.

différent, e [diferɑ̃, ɑ̃t] ◇ *adj* **1.** [distinct] different ■ **~ de** unlike, different from *UK ou* than *US* ■ **il n'est pas désagréable, il est timide, c'est ~** he isn't unpleasant, he's shy, there's a difference **2.** [original] different ■ **un week-end un peu ~** a weekend with a difference.
◇ *dét (adj indéf, devant un nom au pl)* different, various.

différentiel, elle [diferɑ̃sjɛl] *adj* differential.
◆ **différentiel** *nm* [pourcentage] differential.

différentier [9] [diferɑ̃sje] *vt* MATH to differentiate.

différer [18] [difere] ◇ *vt* [repousser - rendez-vous, réponse, réunion] to defer, to postpone ■ **~ le paiement d'une dette** to put off *ou* to delay paying a debt.
◇ *vi* **1.** [se différencier] to differ, to vary ■ **les coutumes diffèrent d'un endroit à un autre** customs vary from one place to another **2.** [s'opposer - dans un débat] to differ, to be at variance.

difficile [difisil] ◇ *adj* **1.** [route, montée] difficult, hard, tough **2.** [tâche] difficult, hard ■ **ce sera un livre ~ à vendre** this book will be hard to sell ■ **il s'en sortira? – ~ à dire** will he manage? – it's hard to say **3.** [douloureux] difficult, hard, tough ■ **il m'est ~ de lui parler de son père** it's difficult *ou* hard for me to talk to him about his father **4.** [personne - d'un tempérament pénible] difficult, demanding ; [- pointilleuse] particular, awkward, fussy ■ **être ~ (sur la nourriture)** to be fussy about one's food ■ **elle est très ~ sur le choix de ses amis** she's very particular about her friends ■ **il est si ~ à satisfaire!** he's so hard to please! **5.** [moralement] difficult, tricky ■ [financièrement] difficult, tough **6.** [impénétrable - œuvre, auteur] difficult, abstruse.
◇ *nmf* fusspot, fussbudget ■ **ne fais pas le ~!** don't be so awkward *ou* fussy!
◇ *nm* : **le ~ dans cette affaire est de plaire à tous** the difficult part of this business is knowing how to please everyone.

difficilement [difisilmɑ̃] *adv* with difficulty ■ **il s'endort ~** he has a hard time getting to sleep ■ **je peux ~ accepter** I find it difficult *ou* it's difficult for me to accept.

difficulté [difikylte] *nf* **1.** [caractère ardu] difficulty ■ **exercices d'une ~ croissante** increasingly difficult exercises ■ **chercher la ~** to look for problems ▮ [gêne] difficulty ■ **avoir de la ~ à faire qqch** to find it difficult to do sthg ■ **avoir de la ~ à marcher** to have difficulty walking, to walk with difficulty **2.** [problème] problem, difficulty ■ **faire des ~s** to create problems, to make a fuss ■ **avoir des ~s avec qqn** to have difficulties *ou* problems with sb ▮ [ennui - financier] : **avoir des ~s financières** to be in financial difficulties *ou* straits **3.** [point difficile] difficulty ■ **les ~s de ce requiem** the difficult passages in this requiem **4.** [impénétrabilité - d'une œuvre, d'un auteur] difficult *ou* abstruse nature.
◆ **en difficulté** *loc adj & loc adv* [nageur] in difficulties ■ [navire, avion] in distress ■ **un enfant en ~** [scolairement] a child with learning difficulties ; [psychologiquement] a child with behavioural problems ■ **un couple en ~** [sur le plan affectif] a couple who are having problems ; [financièrement] a couple with money problems ■ **mettre qqn en ~** to put sb in a difficult *ou* an awkward situation.
◆ **sans difficulté** *loc adv* easily, with no difficulty.

difforme [difɔrm] *adj* deformed, misshapen.

difformité [difɔrmite] *nf* deformity, misshapenness.

diffraction [difraksjɔ̃] *nf* diffraction.

diffus, e [dify, yz] *adj* [gén - BOT] diffuse.

diffusément [difyzemɑ̃] *adv* diffusely.

diffuser [3] [difyze] *vt* **1.** [répandre - chaleur, lumière] to spread, to disseminate *sout* **2.** AUDIO, RADIO & TV to broadcast ■ **émission diffusée en direct/différé** live/prerecorded broadcast ■ **de l'accordéon diffusé par haut-parleur** accordion music broadcast over a loud-speaker **3.** [propager - nouvelle, rumeur] to spread **4.** [distribuer - tracts] to hand out *(sép)*, to distribute ■ [dans l'édition] to distribute, to sell.

diffuseur [difyzœr] *nm* **1.** COMM distributing agent, distributor **2.** ACOUST, ÉLECTR & MÉCAN diffuser **3.** [de parfum] **4.** [conduit] diffuser.

diffusion [difyzjɔ̃] *nf* **1.** ACOUST diffusion, diffusivity **2.** PHYS [d'une particule] diffusion **3.** OPT diffusion **4.** MÉD spreading **5.** AUDIO, RADIO & TV broadcasting **6.** [propagation - du savoir, d'une théorie] spreading **7.** [distribution - de tracts] distribution, distributing ; [- de livres] distribution, selling **8.** [exemplaires vendus] number of copies sold, circulation.
◆ **en deuxième diffusion, en seconde diffusion** *loc adj* TV repeated, repeat *(modif)*.

digérer [18] [diʒere] *vt* **1.** PHYSIOL to digest ■ **je ne digère pas le lait** milk doesn't agree with me, I can't digest milk **2.** [assimiler - connaissances, lecture] to digest, to assimilate ■ **des notions de psychologie mal digérées** half-understood ideas on psychology **3.** *fam* [supporter] to stomach, to take.

digeste [diʒɛst] *adj* : **un aliment ~** an easily digested foodstuff.

digestif, ive [diʒɛstif, iv] *adj* digestive.
◆ **digestif** *nm* [alcool] digestif.

digestion [diʒɛstjɔ̃] *nf* digestion ■ **avoir une ~ lente** to digest one's food slowly ■ **ne te baigne pas pendant la ~** don't go swimming right after a meal.

digicode [diʒikɔd] *nm* door code *(for entrance to a building)*.

digital, e, aux [diʒital, o] *adj* **1.** ANAT digital **2.** [numérique] digital.

digitale [diʒital] *nf* foxglove, digitalis.

digitaline [diʒitalin] *nf* digitalin.

digitaliser [3] [diʒitalize] *vt* to digitalize, to digitize.

digne [diɲ] *adj* **1.** [noble] dignified ■ **d'un air très ~** in a dignified manner **2.** : **~ de** [qui mérite] worthy *ou* deserving of ■ **toute amie ~ de ce nom aurait accepté** a true friend would have accepted ■ **je n'ai pas eu de vacances ~s de ce nom depuis une éternité** I haven't had any holidays as such for ages ■ **~ de confiance** trustworthy ■ **~ de foi** credible ■ **~ d'être mentionné** worth mentioning **3.** [en conformité avec] : **~ de** worthy of ■ **ce n'est pas ~ de toi** it's unworthy of you.

dignement [diɲmɑ̃] *adv* **1.** [noblement] with dignity, in a dignified manner ■ **il s'en est allé ~** he left with dignity **2.** *litt* [justement] : **~ récompensé** justly rewarded.

dignitaire [diɲitɛr] *nm* dignitary.

dignité [diɲite] *nf* **1.** [noblesse] dignity ■ [maintien] poise **2.** [respect] dignity ■ **une atteinte à la ~ de l'homme** an affront to human dignity **3.** [fonction] dignity.

digression [digresjɔ̃] *nf* digression ■ **tomber** *ou* **se perdre dans des ~s** to digress (endlessly).

digue [dig] *nf* **1.** [mur] dyke, seawall ■ [talus] embankment ■ **~ de retenue** flood barrier **2.** *fig* [protection] safety valve, barrier.

diktat [diktat] *nm* diktat.

dilapidateur, trice [dilapidatœr, tris] ◇ *adj* spendthrift, wasteful.
◇ *nm, f* squanderer, spendthrift ■ **~ de fonds publics** embezzler of public funds.

dilapidation [dilapidasjɔ̃] *nf* wasting, frittering away, squandering ■ **~ de fonds publics** embezzlement of public funds.

dilapider [3] [dilapide] *vt* [gén] to waste, to fritter away *(sép)*, to squander ■ [fonds publics] to embezzle.

dilatateur, trice [dilatatœr, tris] *adj* dilatator *(modif)*, dilator *(modif)*.

dilatation [dilatasjɔ̃] *nf* **1.** PHYS expansion **2.** [des narines, des pupilles] dilation ▪ [de l'estomac] distension ▪ [du col de l'utérus] dilation, opening **3.** *litt* [du cœur, de l'âme] filling.

dilater [3] [dilate] *vt* **1.** PHYS to cause to expand **2.** [remplir d'air - tuyau, pneu] to inflate, to blow up *(sép)* **3.** [élargir - narine, pupille, veine] to dilate ; [- col de l'utérus] to dilate, to open ; [- poumons] to expand ▪ **~ la rate à qqn** *fam* to have sb in stitches.
◆ **se dilater** ◇ *vpi* **1.** PHYS to expand **2.** [être gonflé - tuyau, pneu] to blow up, to inflate **3.** [être élargi - narine, pupille, veine] to dilate ; [- col de l'utérus] to dilate, to open ; [- poumons] to expand.
◇ *vpt* : **se ~ les poumons** to fill one's lungs ▶ **se ~ la rate** *fam* to die laughing.

dilatoire [dilatwar] *adj* delaying, dilatory *sout*, procrastinating *sout* ▪ **user de moyens ~s** to play for time ▪ **donner une réponse ~** to answer evasively *(so as to play for time)*.

dilemme [dilɛm] *nm* dilemma ▪ **être devant un ~** to face a dilemma ▪ **être aux prises avec un ~** to be (caught) on the horns of a dilemma.

dilettante [dilɛtɑ̃t] ◇ *nmf* dilettante, dabbler.
◇ *adj* dilettantish, amateurish.
◆ **en dilettante** *loc adv* : **il fait de la peinture en ~** he dabbles in painting.

dilettantisme [dilɛtɑ̃tism] *nm* **1.** [attitude dilettante] dilettantism **2.** [amateurisme] amateurishness.

diligemment [diliʒamɑ̃] *adv litt* **1.** [soigneusement] scrupulously, conscientiously **2.** [rapidement] promptly, speedily, hastily.

diligence [diliʒɑ̃s] *nf* **1.** [véhicule] stagecoach **2.** *litt* haste, dispatch *litt* ▪ **avec ~** hastily, promptly, with dispatch *litt*.

diligent, e [diliʒɑ̃, ɑ̃t] *adj litt* **1.** [actif] prompt, speedy, active **2.** [assidu - soins] constant, assiduous ; [- élève] diligent ; [- employé] conscientious, scrupulous.

diluant [dilɥɑ̃] *nm* diluent.

diluer [7] [dilɥe] *vt* **1.** [allonger - d'eau] to dilute, to water down *(sép)* ; [- d'un liquide] to dilute **2.** [délayer] to thin down *(sép)* **3.** *péj* [discours, exposé] to pad *ou* to stretch out *(sép)* ▪ [idée, argument] to dilute.

dilution [dilysjɔ̃] *nf* **1.** [mélange de liquides] dilution, diluting ▪ [ajout d'eau] dilution, watering down **2.** [désépaississement] thinning down **3.** [dissolution - d'un comprimé] dissolving **4.** *péj* [d'un discours] padding *ou* stretching out.

diluvien, enne [dilyvjɛ̃, ɛn] *adj* **1.** BIBLE diluvial, diluvian **2.** [pluie] torrential.

dimanche [dimɑ̃ʃ] *nm* Sunday ▪ **le ~ de Pâques** Easter Sunday ▪ **le ~ des Rameaux** Palm Sunday.
◆ **du dimanche** *loc adj* **1.** [journal] Sunday **2.** *fam péj* [amateur] : **chauffeur du ~** Sunday driver.

dîme [dim] *nf* tithe ▶ **prélever une ~ (sur qqch)** *pr* to levy a tithe (on sthg) ; *fig* to take one's cut (of sthg).

dimension [dimɑ̃sjɔ̃] *nf* **1.** [mesure] dimension, measurement ▪ **prendre les ~s de qqch** to measure sthg (up) **2.** [taille] size, dimension ▪ **une pièce de petite/grande ~** a small-size(d)/large-size(d) room **3.** [importance] dimension ▪ **cela donne une nouvelle ~ au problème** this gives a new dimension to the problem ▪ **lorsque l'information prend les ~s d'une tragédie** when news assumes tragic proportions **4.** MATH & PHYS dimension.
◆ **à deux dimensions** *loc adj* two-dimensional.
◆ **à la dimension de** *loc prép* corresponding *ou* proportionate to ▪ **un salaire à la ~ du travail requis** wages proportionate to *ou* commensurate with *sout* the work involved.
◆ **à trois dimensions** *loc adj* three-dimensional.

dimensionner [3] [dimɑ̃sjɔne] *vt* to lay out *(sép)* ▪ **un appartement bien dimensionné** a well laid-out apartment.

diminué, e [diminɥe] *adj* **1.** [affaibli] : **il est très ~** [physiquement] his health is failing ; [mentalement] he's losing his faculties **2.** MUS diminished **3.** ARCHIT tapering **4.** [rang de tricot] decreased.

diminuer [7] [diminɥe] ◇ *vt* **1.** [réduire - prix, impôts, frais, ration] to reduce, to cut ; [- longueur] to shorten ; [- taille, effectifs, volume, vitesse, consommation] to reduce ▪ [atténuer - douleurs, souffrance] to alleviate, to lessen **2.** [affaiblir - personne] : **la maladie l'a beaucoup diminué** his illness has affected him very badly ▪ **sortir diminué d'une attaque** to suffer from the after-effects of an attack **3.** [humilier - personne] to belittle, to cut down to size ▪ **elle sort diminuée de cette affaire** her reputation has been badly damaged by this business ▪ [déprécier - qualité] : **cela ne diminue en rien votre mérite** this doesn't detract from *ou* lessen your merit at all **4.** [en tricot] to decrease **5.** MUS to diminish **6.** *fam* [employé] to cut the pay of.
◇ *vi* **1.** [pression] to fall, to drop ▪ [volume] to decrease ▪ [prix] to fall, to come down ▪ [chômage, accidents, criminalité] to decrease, to be on the decrease *ou* wane **2.** [s'affaiblir - forces] to ebb away, to wane, to lessen ; [- peur] to lessen ; [- intérêt, attention] to drop, to lessen, to dwindle **3.** [raccourcir] : **les jours diminuent** the days are getting shorter *ou* drawing in.

diminutif, ive [diminytif, iv] *adj* LING diminutive.
◆ **diminutif** *nm* **1.** [nom] diminutive ▪ **Greg est le ~ de Gregory** Greg is short for Gregory **2.** LING diminutive.

diminution [diminysjɔ̃] *nf* **1.** [réduction - de prix, d'impôts, des frais, des rations] reduction, cutting ; [- de longueur] shortening ; [- de taille] reduction, shortening ; [- de volume] decrease, decreasing ; [- de pression] fall ; [- de vitesse, de consommation, des effectifs] reduction ; [- du chômage, de la violence] drop, decrease ▪ **une ~ des effectifs** a reduction in the number of staff **2.** [affaiblissement - d'une douleur] alleviation ; [- des forces] waning, lessening ; [- de l'intérêt, de l'attention] lessening ; [- de l'appétit] decrease **3.** MUS diminution **4.** ARCHIT taper **5.** [en tricot] decrease ▪ **faire une ~** to decrease.

dinanderie [dinɑ̃dri] *nf* **1.** [technique] sheet metal craft **2.** [objets] objects made from sheet metal.

dinar [dinar] *nm* dinar.

dînatoire [dinatwar] *adj* : **buffet ~** buffet-dinner ▪ **goûter ~** early supper, (high) tea *UK*.

dinde [dɛ̃d] *nf* **1.** ORNITH turkey (hen) **2.** CULIN turkey **3.** [sotte] : **quelle petite ~!** what a stupid little goose!

dindon [dɛ̃dɔ̃] *nm* **1.** ORNITH turkey (cock) **2.** [sot] fool ▪ **être le ~ de la farce** [dupe] to be taken for a ride ; [victime de railleries] to end up a laughing stock.

dindonneau, x [dɛ̃dɔno] *nm* poult, young turkey.

dîner[1] [dine] *nm* **1.** [repas du soir] dinner ▪ **~ dansant** dinner dance **2.** *Belgique* & *Suisse* [déjeuner] lunch.

dîner[2] [3] [dine] *vi* **1.** [faire le repas du soir] to dine, to have dinner ▪ **dînons au restaurant** let's eat out, let's go out for dinner ▪ **avoir des amis à ~** to have friends to dinner *ou* round for dinner ▪ **nous avons dîné d'un simple potage** we just had soup for dinner ▪ **j'ai fait ~ les enfants plus tôt** I gave the children an early dinner **2.** [dialecte: déjeuner] to have lunch.

dîner-spectacle [dinespɛktakl] (*pl* **dîners-spectacles**) *nm* cabaret dinner.

dînette [dinɛt] *nf* **1.** [jouet] toy *ou* doll's tea set ▪ **jouer à la ~** to play (at) tea-parties **2.** *fam* [repas] light *ou* quick meal.

dîneur, euse [dinœr, øz] *nm, f* diner.

dingo [dɛ̃go] ◇ *adj fam* nuts, cracked ▪ **il est complètement ~** he's completely nuts, he's got a screw loose.
◇ *nmf fam* nutcase, loony, wack *US*.
◇ *nm* [chien] dingo.

dingue [dɛ̃g] *fam* ◇ *adj* **1.** [fou] nuts, crazy, screwy *US* **2.** [incroyable - prix, histoire] crazy, mad ▪ **c'est ~ ce qu'il peut faire chaud ici** it's hot as hell here.
◇ *nmf* nutcase, nutter, screwball *US* ▪ **c'est une maison de ~s!** this place is a real loony bin! ▪ **c'est un ~ de motos** he's a motorbike freak.

dinguer [3] [dɛ̃ge] *vi fam vieilli* **les assiettes dinguaient dans la cuisine!** plates were flying all over the kitchen!

dinosaure [dinozɔr] *nm* ZOOL & *fig* dinosaur.

diocésain, e [djɔsezɛ̃, ɛn] *adj* & *nm, f* diocesan.

diocèse [djɔsɛz] *nm* diocese.

diode [djɔd] *nf* diode.

Diogène [djɔʒɛn] *npr* Diogenes.

dionysiaque [djɔnizjak] *adj* Dionysiac, Dionysian.

Dionysos [djɔnizos] *npr* Dionysus, Dionysos.

dioptrie [djɔptri] *nf* dioptre *(unit)*.

dioxine [diɔksin] *nf* dioxin.

dioxyde [diɔksid] *nm* dioxide ▪ **~ de carbone** carbon dioxide.

diphasé, e [difaze] *adj* diphase, diphasic, two-phase *(avant n)*.

diphtérie [difteri] *nf* diphtheria.

diphtérique [difterik] ◇ *adj* diphtherial, diphtheric, diphtheritic.
◇ *nmf* diphtheria sufferer.

diphtongue [diftɔ̃g] *nf* diphthong.

diplodocus [diplɔdɔkys] *nm* ZOOL diplodocus.

diplomate [diplɔmat] ◇ *adj* diplomatic.
◇ *nmf* POLIT & *fig* diplomat.
◇ *nm* CULIN diplomat pudding.

diplomatie [diplɔmasi] *nf* **1.** POLIT [relations, représentation] diplomacy ▪ **la ~** [corps] the diplomatic corps *ou* service **2.** [tact] diplomacy, tact ▪ **avec ~** diplomatically, tactfully.

diplomatique [diplɔmatik] ◇ *adj* **1.** POLIT diplomatic **2.** [adroit] diplomatic, tactful, courteous ▪ **faire un mensonge ~** to tell a white lie.
◇ *nf* diplomatics *(U)*.

diplomatiquement [diplɔmatikmɑ̃] *adv* **1.** POLIT diplomatically **2.** [adroitement] diplomatically, courteously, tactfully.

diplôme [diplom] *nm* **1.** [titre] diploma, qualification ▪ **un ~ d'ingénieur** an engineering diploma ▪ **elle a des ~s** she's highly qualified ➊ **~ d'études approfondies = DEA** ▪ **~ d'études supérieures spécialisées = DESS** ▪ **~ d'études universitaires générales = DEUG** ▪ **~ universitaire de technologie = DUT** ▪ **~ d'études universitaires scientifiques et techniques = DEUST** **2.** [examen] exam **3.** HIST diploma.

diplômé, e [diplome] ◇ *adj* qualified.
◇ *nm, f* holder of a qualification ▪ **embaucher des ~s** to take on people with qualifications.

diptère [diptɛr] *nm* dipteran, dipteron.

diptyque [diptik] *nm* **1.** ART diptych **2.** [œuvre] *literary or artistic work in two parts.*

dircom (*abr de* **directeur ou directrice de la communication**) [dirkɔm] *nmf* director of communications.

dire¹ [dir] *nm* DR [mémoire] statement.
◆ **dires** *nmpl* statement ▪ **confirmer les ~s de qqn** to confirm what sb says ▪ **d'après** *ou* **selon les ~s de son père** according to his father *ou* to what his father said.
◆ **au dire de** *loc prép* : **au ~ de son professeur** according to his teacher *ou* to what his teacher says.

dire² [102] [dir] *vt*

> **A.** ARTICULER, PRONONCER
> **B.** EXPRIMER
> **C.** PENSER, CROIRE
> **D.** INDIQUER, DONNER DES SIGNES DE

A. ARTICULER, PRONONCER

1. [énoncer] to say ▪ **quel nom dis-tu? Castagnel?** what name did you say *ou* what's the name again? Castagnel? ▪ **il n'arrive pas à ~ ce mot** he cannot pronounce that word ▪ **vous avez dit "démocratie"?** "democracy", did you say? ▪ **je te dis merde!**△ [pour porter bonheur] break a leg! ; [pour insulter] get lost! ▪ **je ne dirais pas qu'il est distant, je dirais plutôt effarouché** I wouldn't say he's haughty, rather that he's been frightened off ▪ **une honte, que dis-je, une infamie!, une honte, pour ne pas ~ une infamie!** a shame, not to say an infamy! ▪ **qui dit... dit... : en ce temps-là, qui disait vol disait galère** in those days, theft meant the gallows ▪ **si (l')on peut ~** in a way, so to speak ▪ **disons-le, disons le mot** let's not mince words ▪ **~ non** to say no, to refuse ▪ **~ non au nucléaire** to say no to nuclear energy ▪ **tu veux un gin? – je ne dis pas non** would you like a gin? - I wouldn't say no ▪ **~ oui** [gén] to say yes ; [à une proposition] to accept ; [au mariage] to say I do ▪ **~ bonjour de la main** to wave (hello) ▪ **~ oui de la tête** to nod ▪ **~ non de la tête** to shake one's head ➊ **obéissant? il faut le ~ vite** *fam* obedient? I'm not so sure about that ▪ **déménager, c'est vite dit!** *fam* move? that's easier said than done ▪ **menteur! – c'est celui qui (le) dit qui y est** *ou* **qui l'est!** *fam* liar! – you're the liar!

2. [réciter - prière, table de multiplication] to say ; [- texte] to say, to recite, to read ; [- rôle] to speak ▪ **~ la/une messe** to say mass/a mass ▪ **~ des vers** to recite verse, to give a recitation ▪ *(en usage absolu)* **nul n'a oublié à quel point elle disait juste** nobody can forget how accurate her rendering was

B. EXPRIMER

1. [oralement] to say ▪ **que dis-tu là?** what did you say?, what was that you said? ▪ **tu ne sais pas ce que tu dis** you don't know what you're talking about ▪ **elle dit tout ce qui lui passe par la tête** she says anything that comes into her head ▪ **qu'est-ce que tu veux que je dise?** what do you expect me to say? ▪ **j'ai l'habitude de ~ ce que je pense** I always speak my mind *ou* say what I think ▪ **bon, bon, je n'ai rien dit!** OK, sorry I spoke! ▪ **pourquoi ne m'as-tu rien dit de tout cela?** why didn't you speak to me *ou* tell me about any of this? ▪ **il me dit comme ça, "t'as pas le droit"** *fam* so he says to me "you can't do that" ▪ **je suis un raté? tu sais ce qu'il te dit, le raté?** *fam* so I'm a loser, am I? well, do you want to hear what this loser's got to say to you? ▪ **faire ~ : ne me fais pas ~ ce que je n'ai pas dit!** don't put words into my mouth! ▪ **laisser qqn ~ qqch** to let sb say sthg ▪ **laissez-la ~!** let her speak! ▪ **pouvoir ~ : je peux ~ que tu m'as fait peur!** you certainly frightened me! ▪ **j'ai failli faire tout rater! – ça, tu peux le ~!** I nearly messed everything up – you can say that again! ▪ *(en usage absolu)* **c'est idiot – dis toujours** it's silly – say it anyway ▪ **j'ai une surprise – dis vite!** I have a surprise – let's hear it *ou* do tell! ▪ **comment ~** *ou* **dirais-je?** how shall I put it *ou* say? ▪ **bien dit!** well said! ➊ **dites donc, pour demain, on y va en voiture?** by the way, are we driving there tomorrow? ▪ **tu te fiches de moi, dis!** *fam* you're pulling my leg, aren't you? ▪ **merde!**△ **– dis donc, sois poli!** shit!△ – hey, (mind your) language! ▪ **je peux y aller, dis?** can I go, please? ▪ **vous lui parlerez de moi, dites?** you will talk to her about me, won't you? ▪ **tu es bien habillé, ce soir, dis donc!** my word, aren't you smart tonight! ▪ **il y a eu 60 morts – ben dites donc!** *fam* 60 people were killed – good God! ▪ **il nous faut, disons, deux secrétaires** we need, (let's) say, two secretaries ▪ **ce disant** with these words, so saying ▪ **ce qui est dit est dit** there's no going back on what's been said (before) ▪ **c'est (te/vous) ~ s'il est riche!** that gives you an idea how wealthy he is! ▪ **il ne m'a même pas répondu, c'est tout ~** he never even answered me, that says it all ▪ **pour tout ~** in fact, to be honest ▪ **je ne te/vous le fais pas ~** how right you are, I couldn't have put it better myself ▪ **il va sans ~ que...** needless to say (that)... ▪ **ça va sans ~** it goes without saying ▪ **ce n'est pas pour ~, mais à sa place j'aurais réussi** *fam* though I say it myself, if I'd been him I'd have succeeded ▪ **ce n'est pas pour ~ mais c'est bruyant** I don't mean to complain but it's noisy ▪ **il en est incapable, enfin (moi), ce que j'en dis...** he's not capable of it, at least that's what I'd say... ▪ **je ne dis pas** *fam* maybe ▪ **voici une confiture maison, je ne te dis que ça** here's some homemade jam that's out of this world ▪ **il y avait un monde, je te dis pas!** you wouldn't have believed the crowds!,

2. [symboliquement] to express, to tell of ▪ **je voudrais ~ mon espoir** I'd like to express my hope ▪ **vouloir ~** [signifier] to mean ▪ **un haussement d'épaules dans ce cas-là, ça dit bien ce que ça veut ~** in a situation like that, a shrug (of the shoulders) speaks volumes ➊ **est-ce à ~ que...?** *sout* does this mean that...? ▪ **vous partez, madame, qu'est-ce à ~?** Madam, what mean you by leaving?

3. [écrire] to say ▪ **dans sa lettre, elle dit que...** in her letter she says that...

4. [annoncer - nom, prix] to give ▪ **cela t'a coûté combien? – dis un prix!** how much did it cost you? – have a guess! ▪ **le général vous fait ~ qu'il vous attend** the general has sent me to tell you he's waiting for you ▪ **faire ~ à qqn de venir** to send for sb ▪ **je lui ai fait ~ qu'on se passerait de lui** I let him know that we'd manage without him
5. [prédire] to foretell, to tell ▪ **tu verras ce que je te dis!** you just wait and see if I'm right! ▪ **qui aurait dit que je l'épouserais?** who would have said that I'd marry him? ▪ **je te l'avais bien dit** I told you so ▪ **tu vas le regretter, moi je** *fam* *ou* **c'est moi qui** *fam* **te le dis!** you'll be sorry for this, let me tell you *ou* mark my words!
6. [ordonner] to tell ▪ **il m'a dit d'arrêter** he told me to stop ▶ **il ne se l'est pas fait ~ deux fois** he didn't have to be told twice ▪ [conseiller] to tell ▪ **tu me dis d'oublier, mais...** you tell me I must forget, but...
7. [objecter] to say, to object ▪ **sa mère ne lui dit jamais rien** her mother never tells her off ▪ **toi, on ne peut jamais rien te ~!** you can't take the slightest criticism! ▪ **mais, me direz-vous, il n'est pas majeur** but, you will object *ou* I hear you say, he's not of age ▪ **j'aurais des choses à ~ sur l'organisation du service** I have a few things to say *ou* some comments to make about the organization of the department ▪ **c'est tout ce que tu as trouvé à ~?** is that the best you could come up with? ▪ **Pierre n'est pas d'accord – il n'a rien à ~** Pierre doesn't agree – he's in no position to make any objections ▪ **il n'a rien trouvé à ~ sur la qualité** he had no criticisms to make about the quality ▪ **elle est maligne, il n'y a pas à** *ou* **on ne peut pas ~ (le contraire)** *fam* she's shrewd, there's no denying it *ou* and no mistake
8. [affirmer] to say, to state ▪ **si c'est vous qui le dites, si vous le dites, du moment que vous le dites** if you say so ▪ **puisque je vous le dis!** I'm telling you!, you can take it from me! ▪ **c'est le bon train? – je te dis que oui!** is it the right train? – yes it is! *ou* I'm telling you it is! ▪ **il va neiger – la météo a dit que non** it looks like it's going to snow – the weather forecast said it wouldn't ▪ **tu étais content, ne me dis pas le contraire!** you were pleased, don't deny it *ou* don't tell me you weren't! ▪ **on dit qu'il a un autre fils** rumour has it that *ou* it's rumoured that *ou* it's said that he has another son ▪ **loin des yeux, loin du cœur, dit-on** out of sight, out of mind, so the saying goes *ou* so they say ▪ **on le disait lâche** he was said *ou* alleged *ou* reputed to be a coward ▶ **je m'en moque – on dit ça** *fam* I don't care – that's what you say *ou* that's what they all say ▪ **elle trouvera bien une place – qu'elle dit** *fam* she'll find a job, no problem – that's what she thinks! ▪ **on dira ce qu'on voudra, mais l'amour ça passe avant tout** whatever people say, love comes before everything else ▪ **on ne dira jamais assez l'importance d'un régime alimentaire équilibré** I cannot emphasize enough the importance of a balanced diet
9. [prétendre] to claim, to allege ▪ **elle disait ne pas savoir qui le lui avait donné** she claimed *ou* alleged that she didn't know who'd given it to her ‖ [dans des jeux d'enfants] : **on dirait qu'on serait des rois** *fam* let's pretend we're kings
10. [admettre] to say, to admit ▪ **je dois ~ qu'elle est jolie** I must say *ou* admit she's pretty ▪ **il faut bien ~ qu'il n'est plus tout jeune** he's not young any more, let's face it ▪ **il faut ~ qu'elle a des excuses** (to) give her her due, there are mitigating circumstances ▪ **disons que...** let's say (that)...
11. [décider] : **il est dit que...** fate has decreed that... ▪ **il ne sera pas dit que...** let it not be said that... ▪ **rien n'est dit** [décidé] nothing's been decided yet ; [prévisible] nothing's for certain (yet) ▪ **tout est dit** [il n'y a plus à discuter] the matter is closed ; [l'avenir est arrêté] the die is cast ▪ **tout n'est pas encore dit** nothing's final yet ▪ **aussitôt dit, aussitôt fait** no sooner said than done ▪ *(en usage absolu)* **j'ai dit!** *hum* I have spoken!

C. PENSER, CROIRE
1. [penser] to say, to think ▪ **~ de : que dis-tu de ma perruque?** what do you think of *ou* how do you like my wig? ▪ **et comme dessert? – que dirais-tu d'une mousse au chocolat?** and to follow? – what would you say to *ou* how about a chocolate mousse? ▪ **~ que...** to think that...
2. [croire] : **on dirait** [introduit une comparaison, une impression] : **on dirait du thé** [au goût] it tastes like tea ; [à l'odeur] it smells like tea ; [d'apparence] it looks like tea ▪ **on dirait de la laine** [au toucher] it feels like wool ▪ **on dirait que je te fais peur** you behave as if *ou* as though you were scared of me ‖ [exprime une probabilité] : **on dirait sa fille, au premier rang** it looks like her daughter there in the front row

D. INDIQUER, DONNER DES SIGNES DE
1. [indiquer - suj: instrument] to say ; [- suj: attitude, regard] to say, to show ▪ **que dit le baromètre?** what does the barometer say? ▪ **un geste qui disait sa peur** a gesture that betrayed his fear ▪ **mon intuition** *ou* **quelque chose me dit qu'il reviendra** I have a feeling (that) he'll be back
2. [stipuler par écrit] to say ▪ **que dit la Bible/le dictionnaire à ce sujet?** what does the Bible/dictionary say about this?
3. [faire penser à] : **~ quelque chose : son visage me dit quelque chose** I've seen her face before, her face seems familiar ▪ **Lambert, cela ne vous dit rien?** Lambert, does that mean anything to you? ▪ **cela ne me dit rien de bon** *ou* **qui vaille** I'm not sure I like (the look of) it
4. [tenter] : **ta proposition me dit de plus en plus** your suggestion's growing on me ▪ **tu viens? – ça ne me dit rien** are you coming? – I'm not in the mood *ou* I don't feel like it ▪ **la viande ne me dit rien du tout en ce moment** I'm off meat at the moment ▪ **ça te dirait d'aller à Bali?** (how) would you like a trip to Bali?

◆ **se dire** ◇ *vp (emploi réciproque)* [échanger - secrets, paroles] to tell each other *ou* one another ▪ **nous n'avons plus rien à nous ~** we've got nothing left to say to each other ▪ **nous nous disions tout** we had no secrets from each other ▪ **qu'on se le dise** *arch* let this be known.
◇ *vp (emploi passif)* **1.** [être formulé] : **comment se dit "bonsoir" en japonais?** how do you say "goodnight" in Japanese?, what's the Japanese for "goodnight"? ▪ **il est vraiment hideux – peut-être, mais ça ne se dit pas** he's really hideous – maybe, but it's not the sort of thing you say ▪ **se dit de** [pour définir un terme] (is) said of, (is) used for, describes **2.** [être en usage] to be in use, to be accepted usage.
◇ *vpt* [penser] to think (to o.s.), to say to o.s. ▪ **maintenant, je me dis que j'aurais dû accepter** now I think I should have accepted ▪ **dis-toi bien que je ne serai pas toujours là pour t'aider** you must realize that *ou* get it into your head that I won't always be here to help you.
◇ *vpi* [estimer être] to say ▪ **il se dit flatté de l'intérêt que je lui porte** he says he's *ou* he claims to be flattered by my interest in him ‖ [se présenter comme] to say, to claim ▪ **ils se disent attachés à la démocratie** they claim to *ou* (that) they care about democracy.

direct, e [dirɛkt] *adj* **1.** [sans détour - voie, route, chemin] direct, straight **2.** TRANSP direct, without a change ▪ **c'est ~ en métro jusqu'à Pigalle** the metro goes direct to Pigalle ▪ **un vol ~ Paris-New York** a direct *ou* nonstop flight from Paris to New York ▪ **c'est un train ~ jusqu'à Genève** the train is nonstop to Geneva **3.** [franc - question] direct ; [- langage] straightforward ; [- personne] frank, straightforward **4.** [sans intermédiaire - cause, conséquence] immediate ; [- supérieur, descendant] direct ▪ **mettez-vous en relation ~e avec Bradel** get in touch with Bradel himself **5.** ASTRON, GRAMM & MÉCAN direct **6.** LOGIQUE positive.
◆ **direct** *nm* **1.** SPORT straight punch ▪ **un ~ du gauche** a straight left **2.** RAIL through *ou* nonstop train **3.** TV live ▪ **il préfère le ~ au playback** he prefers performing live to lip-synching.
◆ **en direct** *loc adj & loc adv* live.

directement [dirɛktəmɑ̃] *adv* **1.** [tout droit] straight **2.** [franchement] : **entrer ~ dans le sujet** to broach a subject immediately ▪ **allez ~ au fait** come straight to the point **3.** [inévitablement] straight, inevitably **4.** [sans intermédiaire] direct ▪ **adresse-toi ~ au patron** go straight to the boss ▪ **vendre ~ au public** to sell direct to the public ▪ **il descend ~ des du Mail** he's a direct descendant of the du Mail family **5.** [personnellement] : **adressez-moi ~ votre courrier** address your correspondence directly to me ▪ **cela ne vous concerne pas ~** this doesn't affect you personally *ou* directly ▪ **je me sens ~ visé** I feel singled out *ou* personally targeted.

directeur, trice [dirɛktœr, tris] ◇ *adj* **1.** [principal - force] controlling, driving ; [- principe] guiding ; [- idée, ligne] main, guiding **2.** AUTO [roue] front *(modif)*.
◇ *nm, f* **1.** [dans une grande entreprise] manager (*f* manageress), director ▪ [dans une petite entreprise] manager (*f* manageress) ▪ **~ d'agence** [dans une banque] bank manager ▪ **~ commercial** sales manager ▪ **~ financier/régional/du personnel**

financial/regional/personnel manager ▪ **~ général** managing director *UK*, chief executive officer *US* ▪ **~ général adjoint** assistant general manager ▪ **~ de prison** prison governor *UK* *ou* warden *US* **2.** ÉDUC : **~ d'école** head teacher *UK*, headmaster *UK*, principal *US* ▪ **directrice d'école** head teacher *UK*, headmistress *UK*, (lady) principal *US* **3.** UNIV [d'un département] head of department ▪ **~ de thèse** (thesis) supervisor **4.** CINÉ, THÉÂTRE & TV director ▪ **~ artistique** artistic director ▪ **~ de la photo** director of photography ▪ **~ du son** sound director.
◆ **directeur** *nm* **1.** HIST Director **2.** RELIG : **~ spirituel** *ou* **de conscience** spiritual advisor.
◆ **directrice** *nf* MATH directrix.

directif, ive [dirɛktif, iv] *adj* [entretien, méthode] directive.
◆ **directive** *nf* ADMIN, MIL & POLIT directive.
◆ **directives** *nfpl* orders, instructions.

direction [dirɛksjɔ̃] *nf* **1.** [fonction de chef - d'une entreprise] management, managing ; [- d'un orchestre] conducting, direction *US* ; [- d'un journal] editorship ; [- d'une équipe sportive] captaining ▪ **prendre la ~ de** [société, usine] to take over the running *ou* management of ; [journal] to take over the editorship of ▪ **se voir confier la ~ d'une société/d'un journal/d'un lycée** to be appointed manager of a firm/chief editor of a newspaper/head of a school ▪ **orchestre (placé) sous la ~ de** orchestra conducted by
2. [organisation - de travaux] supervision ; [- d'un débat] chairing, conducting ; [- de la circulation, des opérations] directing
3. [maîtrise, cadres] : **la ~ refuse toute discussion avec les syndicats** (the) management refuses to talk to the unions
4. [bureau] manager's office
5. [sens] direction, way ▪ **dans la ~ opposée** in the opposite direction ▪ **il a lancé la balle dans ma ~** he threw the ball towards me ▪ **vous allez dans quelle ~?** which way are you going?, where are you heading for? ▪ **prenez la ~ Nation** [dans le métro] take the Nation line ▪ **'toutes ~s'** 'all routes' ▪ **partir dans toutes les ~s** [coureurs, ballons] to scatter ; [pétards] to go off in all directions ; [conversation] to wander
6. CINÉ, THÉÂTRE & TV : **~ (d'acteurs)** directing, direction
7. AUTO & MÉCAN steering ▶ **~ assistée** power steering
8. ADMIN : **Direction départementale de l'équipement** *local government body responsible for public works.*
◆ **de direction** *loc adj* [équipe] managerial.
◆ **en direction de** *loc prép* in the direction of, towards ▪ **embouteillages en ~ de Paris** holdups for Paris-bound traffic ▪ **les trains/avions/vols en ~ de Marseille** trains/planes/flights to Marseilles ▪ **jeter un regard en ~ de qqn** to cast a glance at *ou* towards sb ▪ **il a tiré en ~ des policiers** he fired at the policemen.

directionnel, elle [dirɛksjɔnɛl] *adj* directional.

directive [dirɛktiv] *f* ▷ **directif**.

directivisme [dirɛktivism] *nm péj* authoritarianism.

directo [dirɛkto] *adv fam* straight, right ▪ **ça va ~ à la poubelle** it's going straight in the bin.

directoire [dirɛktwar] *nm* ADMIN & COMM directorate *(sing ou pl)*, board of directors.
◆ **Directoire** *npr m* : **le Directoire** the (French) Directory ▪ **meuble Directoire** piece of Directoire furniture.

directorat [dirɛktɔra] *nm* **1.** ADMIN, ÉDUC & THÉÂTRE directorate, directorship **2.** COMM managership.

directorial, e, aux [dirɛktɔrjal, o] *adj* **1.** [fonction, pouvoir] managerial, executive, directorial **2.** HIST Directory *(modif)*, of the Directory.

dirham [diram] *nm* dirham.

dirigeable [diriʒabl] ◇ *adj* dirigible.
◇ *nm* airship, dirigible.

dirigeant, e [diriʒɑ̃, ɑ̃t] ◇ *adj* ruling.
◇ *nm, f* POLIT [d'un parti] leader ▪ [d'un pays] ruler, leader ▪ **~ syndical** union leader.
◆ **dirigeants** *nmpl* COMM : **~s sociaux** managerial staff.

diriger [17] [diriʒe] *vt* **1.** [être à la tête de - usine, entreprise] to run, to manage ; [- personnel, équipe] to manage ; [- service, département] to be in charge of, to be head of ; [- école] to be head of ; [- orchestre] to conduct, to direct *US* ; [- journal] to edit ; [- pays] to run ; [- parti, mouvement] to lead ▪ **mal ~ une société** to mismanage a company ▪ *(en usage absolu)* **savoir ~** to be a (good) manager
2. [superviser - travaux] to supervise, to oversee ; [- débat] to conduct ; [- thèse, recherches] to supervise ; [- circulation] to direct ; [- opérations] to direct, to oversee
3. CINÉ, THÉÂTRE & TV to direct
4. [piloter - voiture] to steer ; [- bateau] to navigate, to steer ; [- avion] to fly, to pilot ; [- cheval] to drive ▪ [guider - aveugle] to guide ; [- dans une démarche] to direct, to steer ▪ **~ qqn vers la sortie** to direct sb to the exit ▪ **on vous a mal dirigé** you were misdirected ▪ **elle a été mal dirigée dans son choix de carrière** she had poor career guidance ▪ **~ un élève vers un cursus littéraire** to guide *ou* to steer a student towards an arts course
5. [acheminer - marchandises] to send ▪ **~ des colis sur** *ou* **vers la Belgique** to send parcels to Belgium ▪ **je fais ~ mes appels sur mon autre numéro** I have my calls redirected *ou* rerouted to my other number
6. [orienter - pensée] to direct ▪ **~ son regard vers qqn** to look in the direction of sb ▪ **tous les yeux étaient dirigés sur elle** everyone was staring at her ▶ **~ ses pas vers** *pr & fig* to head for
7. [adresser hostilement] to level, to direct ▪ **~ des accusations contre qqn** to level accusations at sb ▪ **leurs moqueries étaient dirigées contre lui** he was the butt of their jokes
8. [braquer] : **une antenne dirigée vers la tour Eiffel** an aerial trained on the Eiffel tower ▪ **lorsque la flèche est dirigée vers la droite** when the arrow points to the right ▮ ARM [tir] to aim ▪ **~ un canon vers** *ou* **sur une cible** to aim *ou* to level *ou* to point a cannon at a target.
◆ **se diriger** *vpi* **1.** [aller] : **se ~ sur** *ou* **vers** [frontière] to head *ou* to make for ▪ **se ~ vers la sortie** to make one's way to the exit ▪ **nous nous dirigeons vers le conflit armé** *fig* we're headed for armed conflict
2. [trouver son chemin] to find one's way ▪ **savoir se ~ dans une ville** to be able to find one's way round a city ▪ **on apprend aux élèves à se ~ dans leurs études** pupils are taught to take charge of their own studies.

dirigisme [diriʒism] *nm* state control, state intervention.

dirigiste [diriʒist] ◇ *adj* interventionist.
◇ *nmf* partisan of state control.

dirlo [dirlo] *nmf arg scol* head, principal.

disait *etc v* ▷ **dire**.

discal, e, aux [diskal, o] *adj* discal.

discernable [disɛrnabl] *adj* discernible, discernable, perceptible.

discernement [disɛrnəmɑ̃] *nm* **1.** [intelligence] (good) judgement, discernment *sout* ▪ **il a agi avec ~** he showed (good) judgement in what he did **2.** *sout* [discrimination] distinguishing, discrimination, discriminating.

discerner [3] [disɛrne] *vt* **1.** [voir] to discern, to distinguish, to make out *(insép)* **2.** [deviner] to discern, to perceive, to detect ▪ **~ les motivations de qqn** to see through sb **3.** [différencier] : **~ qqch de qqch** : **~ le bien du mal** to distinguish (between) right and wrong, to tell right from wrong.

disciple [disipl] *nm* **1.** RELIG & ÉDUC disciple **2.** [partisan] follower, disciple.

disciplinaire [disiplinɛr] *adj* disciplinary.

discipline [disiplin] *nf* **1.** [règlement] discipline **2.** [obéissance] discipline ▪ **avoir de la ~** to be disciplined ▶ **~ alimentaire** observance of one's diet ▪ **~ de vote** voting discipline **3.** ÉDUC & UNIV [matière] subject, discipline **4.** HIST discipline, whip, scourge.

discipliné, e [discipline] *adj* **1.** [personne] obedient, disciplined **2.** [cheveux] neat (and tidy), well-groomed.

discipliner [3] [discipline] *vt* **1.** [faire obéir - élèves, classe] to discipline, to (bring under) control **2.** [maîtriser - instincts] to control, to master ; [- pensée] to discipline, to train **3.** [endiguer - rivière] to control **4.** [coiffer - cheveux] to groom.
◆ **se discipliner** *vp (emploi réfléchi)* to discipline o.s.

disc-jockey [diskʒɔkɛ] *(pl* **disc-jockeys***)* *nmf* disc jockey.

disco [disko] ◇ *adj* disco ■ **musique ~** disco (music).
◇ *nm* [musique] disco (music) ■ [danse, chanson] disco number.
◇ *nf fam vieilli* [discothèque] disco.

discographie [diskɔgrafi] *nf* discography ■ **avoir une importante ~** to have made many recordings, to have recorded many pieces.

discontinu, e [diskɔ̃tiny] *adj* **1.** [ligne] broken ■ [effort] discontinuous, intermittent ■ **le bruit est ~** the noise occurs on and off **2.** LING & MATH discontinuous.

discontinuer [7] [diskɔ̃tinɥe] *vt & vi litt* to stop, to cease.
◆ **sans discontinuer** *loc adv* nonstop, continuously ■ **il peut parler des heures sans ~** he can talk for hours nonstop *ou* on end.

discontinuité [diskɔ̃tinɥite] *nf* [gén - MATH] discontinuity.

disconvenir [40] [diskɔ̃vnir] ◆ **disconvenir de** *v+prép sout* **vous avez raison, je n'en disconviens pas** I don't deny that you're right.

discordance [diskɔrdɑ̃s] *nf* **1.** MUS discord, discordance, disharmony **2.** [disharmonie - de couleurs, de sentiments] lack of harmony, clash ; [- entre des personnes, idées] clash, conflict, disagreement **3.** [écart] contradiction, inconsistency ■ **il existe certaines ~s entre les deux récits** the two stories contain several inconsistencies **4.** GÉOL discordance, discordancy, unconformability **5.** PSYCHOL dissociation.

discordant, e [diskɔrdɑ̃, ɑ̃t] *adj* **1.** MUS discordant ■ [criard] harsh, grating **2.** [opposé - styles, couleurs, avis, diagnostics] clashing ■ **ils ont présenté des témoignages ~s** their testimonies were at variance with each other.

discorde [diskɔrd] *nf* discord, dissension, dissention.

discothèque [diskɔtɛk] *nf* **1.** [collection] record collection **2.** [meuble] record case *ou* holder **3.** [établissement de prêt] record *ou* music library **4.** [boîte de nuit] disco, night club.

discount [disk(a)unt] ◇ *nm* **1.** [rabais] discount ■ **un ~ de 20%** (a) 20% discount, 20% off **2.** [technique] discount selling.
◇ *adj inv* discount *(modif)*.

discounter[1] [3] [disk(a)unte] *vt & vi* to sell at a discount.

discounter[2] [disk(a)untœr] *nm* discount dealer.

discoureur, euse [diskurœr, øz] *nm, f péj* speechifier.

discourir [45] [diskurir] *vi* **1.** *litt* [bavarder] to talk **2.** *péj* [disserter] to speechify ■ **~ à perte de vue sur l'avenir** to talk endlessly about the future.

discours [diskur] *nm* **1.** [allocution] speech, address ■ **faire un ~** to make a speech ▶ **~ de bienvenue** welcoming speech *ou* address ■ **~ d'inauguration** inaugural lecture *ou* speech ■ **~-programme** keynote speech ■ **~ du trône** POLIT inaugural speech *(of a sovereign before a Parliamentary session)*, *King's Speech, Queen's Speech* ■ **'Discours de la méthode'** ***Descartes*** 'Discourse on Method' **2.** *péj* [bavardage] chatter ■ **se perdre en longs ~** to talk *ou* to chatter endlessly ■ **tous ces (beaux) ~ ne servent à rien** all this fine talk doesn't get us anywhere **3.** LING [langage réalisé] speech ■ [unité supérieure à la phrase] discourse ■ **~ direct** GRAMM direct speech ■ **~ indirect** GRAMM reported *ou* indirect speech **4.** LOGIQUE discourse **5.** [expression d'une opinion] discourse ■ **le ~ des jeunes** the sorts of things young people say ■ **tenir un ~ de droite** to talk like a right-winger.

discourtois, e [diskurtwa, az] *adj* discourteous, impolite.

discourtoisie [diskurtwazi] *nf* discourtesy.

discouru [diskury] *pp* ▷ **discourir**.

discrédit [diskredi] *nm* discredit, disrepute ■ **jeter le ~ sur qqn/qqch** to discredit sb/sthg ■ **tomber dans le ~** to fall into disrepute.

discréditer [3] [diskredite] *vt* to discredit, to bring into disrepute.
◆ **se discréditer** ◇ *vp (emploi réfléchi)* [personne] to bring discredit upon o.s. ■ **se ~ auprès du public** to lose one's good name.
◇ *vpi* [idée, pratique] to become discredited.

discret, ète [diskrɛ, ɛt] *adj* **1.** [réservé - personne, attitude] reserved, discreet ■ **de manière discrète** discreetly **2.** [délicat - personne] tactful, discreet, diplomatic ■ **de manière discrète** tactfully, discreetly **3.** [qui sait garder un secret] discreet **4.** [dissimulé] : **sous emballage ~** in a plain wrapper **5.** [neutre - toilette, style] plain, sober, understated ; [- couleur] subtle ; [- lumière] subdued, soft ; [- parfum] subtle ; [- maquillage] light, subtle **6.** [isolé - lieu] quiet, secluded **7.** MATH discrete.

discrètement [diskrɛtmɑ̃] *adv* **1.** [sans être remarqué] quietly, discreetly, unobtrusively ■ **je lui en parlerai ~** I'll have a quiet word with him **2.** [se maquiller, se parfumer] discreetly, lightly, subtly ■ [s'habiller] discreetly, quietly, soberly.

discrétion [diskresjɔ̃] *nf* **1.** [réserve] discretion, tact, tactfulness **2.** [modestie] unobtrusiveness, self-effacement **3.** [sobriété - d'un maquillage] lightness, subtlety ; [- d'une toilette] soberness ■ **s'habiller avec ~** to dress soberly *ou* quietly **4.** [silence] discretion ■ **'~ assurée'** 'write in confidence'.
◆ **à discrétion** *loc adv* : **vous pouvez manger à ~** you can eat as much as you like.
◆ **à la discrétion de** *loc prép* at the discretion of.

discrétionnaire [diskresjɔnɛr] *adj* discretionary.

discriminant, e [diskriminɑ̃, ɑ̃t] *adj* distinguishing, discriminating.

discrimination [diskriminasjɔ̃] *nf* **1.** [ségrégation] : **~ raciale** racial discrimination **2.** *litt* [distinction] discrimination, distinction.

discriminatoire [diskriminatwar] *adj* discriminatory.

discriminer [3] [diskrimine] *vt* to distinguish.

disculper [3] [diskylpe] *vt* : **~ qqn de qqch** to exonerate sb from sthg.
◆ **se disculper** *vp (emploi réfléchi)* : **pour se ~ il invoqua l'ignorance** to vindicate *ou* to exonerate himself, he pleaded ignorance ■ **se ~ de qqch** to exonerate o.s. from sthg.

discursif, ive [diskyrsif, iv] *adj* **1.** [raisonné] discursive **2.** LING discourse *(modif)*.

discussion [diskysjɔ̃] *nf* **1.** [négociation] talk, discussion ■ [querelle] quarrel, argument ■ **pas de ~!** no arguing!, don't argue! **2.** [débat] debate, discussion ■ **la question de l'avortement donne matière** *ou* **est sujet à ~** the issue of abortion lends itself to debate **3.** [conversation] discussion, conversation.

discutable [diskytabl] *adj* [fait, théorie, décision] debatable, questionable ■ [sincérité, authenticité] questionable, doubtful ■ [goût] dubious.

discutailler [3] [diskytaje] *vi fam péj* to quibble.

discutailleur, euse [diskytajœr, øz] *adj fam péj* **il est très ~** he's a real quibbler.

discuté, e [diskyte] *adj* **1.** [débattu] debated, discussed ■ **très ~** hotly debated **2.** [contesté - nomination] controversial, disputed.

discuter [3] [diskyte] ◇ *vt* **1.** [débattre - projet de loi] to debate, to discuss ; [- sujet, question] to discuss, to argue, to consider ■ **~ le coup** *fam* to have a chat **2.** [contester - ordres] to question, to dispute ; [- véracité] to debate, to question ; [- prix] to haggle over ■ *(en usage absolu)* **inutile de ~, je ne céderai pas** it's no use arguing, I'm not going to give in.
◇ *vi* **1.** [parler] to talk, to have a discussion ■ **~ de** to talk about *(insép)*, to discuss ■ **~ de choses et d'autres** to talk about this and that **2.** [négocier] to negotiate.
◆ **se discuter** *vp (emploi passif)* **1.** [sujet, question] to be debated **2.** [point de vue] : **ça se discute** that's debatable.

dise *etc v* ▷ **dire**.

disert, e [dizɛr, ɛrt] *adj litt* articulate, eloquent, fluent.

disette [dizɛt] *nf* **1.** [pénurie - gén] shortage, dearth ; [- de nourriture] scarcity of food, food shortage **2.** *litt* [manque] : **~ d'argent** want *ou* lack of money.

diseur, euse [dizœr, øz] *nm, f* : **~ de bonne aventure** fortune-teller ■ **fin ~** fine talker ■ **les grands ~s ne sont pas les grands faiseurs** *prov* those who talk most aren't necessarily those who get things done.

disgrâce [disgras] *nf* **1.** *sout* [défaveur] disgrace, disfavour ■ **tomber en ~** to fall into disfavour, to fall from grace **2.** *litt* [manque de grâce] inelegance, awkwardness.

disgracier [9] [disgrasje] *vt litt* to disgrace.

disgracieux, euse [disgrasjø, øz] *adj* **1.** [laid - visage] ugly, unattractive ; [- geste] awkward, ungainly ; [- comportement] uncouth ; [- personne] unattractive, unappealing ; [- objet] unsightly **2.** *litt* [discourtois] ungracious, discourteous.

disjoindre [82] [disʒwɛ̃dr] *vt* **1.** [planches] to break up *(sép)* **2.** [causes, problèmes] to separate, to consider separately.
◆ **se disjoindre** *vpi* to come apart.

disjoint, e [disʒwɛ̃, ɛ̃t] *adj* **1.** [planches] loose **2.** MATH disjoint **3.** MUS disjunct.

disjoncter [3] [disʒɔ̃kte] *vi* to short-circuit ■ **ça a fait ~ tout le circuit** it blew the whole circuit.

disjoncteur [disʒɔ̃ktœr] *nm* circuit breaker, cutout (switch).

dislocation [dislɔkasjɔ̃] *nf* **1.** [d'une caisse] breaking up ■ [d'un empire] dismantling ■ [d'un parti] breaking up, disintegration ■ [d'une manifestation] breaking up, dispersal **2.** MÉD & PHYS dislocation.

disloquer [3] [dislɔke] *vt* **1.** [caisse] to take to pieces, to break up *(sép)* ■ [poupée] to pull apart *(sép)* ■ [corps] to mangle **2.** [faire éclater - empire] to dismantle ; [- parti] to break up *(sép)* **3.** MÉD to dislocate.
◆ **se disloquer** *vpi* **1.** [meuble] to come *ou* to fall apart, to fall to pieces **2.** [fédération] to disintegrate, to break up *(sép)* ■ [empire] to break up **3.** [se disperser - manifestation] to disperse, to break up **4.** MÉD to be dislocated **5.** [se contorsionner] to contort o.s.

disparaître [91] [disparɛtr] *vi* **1.** [se dissiper - peur, joie] to evaporate, to fade, to disappear ; [- douleur, problème, odeur] to disappear ; [- bruit] to stop, to subside ; [- brouillard] to clear, to vanish ■ **faire ~ qqch** [gén] to remove sthg ; [supprimer] to get rid of sthg ■ COMM : **'tout doit ~'** 'everything must go' **2.** [devenir invisible - soleil, lune] to disappear ; [- côte, bateau] to vanish, to disappear ■ **elle a disparu dans la foule** she vanished into the crowd **3.** [être inexplicablement absent] to disappear, to vanish ■ **son mari a disparu (sans laisser d'adresse)** her husband has absconded ■ **faire ~ qqn/qqch** to conceal sb/sthg ➲ **~ de la circulation** *ou* **dans la nature** *fam* to vanish into thin air **4.** [ne plus exister - espèce, race] to die out, to become extinct ; [- langue, coutume] to die out, to disappear ■ [mourir] to pass away, to die ■ **faire ~ qqn** *euphém* to eliminate sb, to have sb removed ■ **~ en mer** to be lost at sea.

disparate [disparat] *adj* **1.** [hétérogène - objets, éléments] disparate, dissimilar **2.** [mal accordé - mobilier] ill-assorted, nonmatching ; [- couple] ill-assorted, ill-matched ■ **deux chaises ~s** two chairs that don't match.

disparité [disparite] *nf* disparity ■ **~ de** [sommes d'argent] disparity in.

disparition [disparisjɔ̃] *nf* **1.** [du brouillard] lifting, clearing ■ [du soleil] sinking, setting ■ [d'une côte, d'un bateau] vanishing ■ [de la peur, du bruit] fading away ■ [du doute] disappearance ■ **frotter jusqu'à ~ des taches** rub until the stains disappear **2.** [absence - d'une personne, d'un porte-monnaie] disappearance **3.** [extinction - d'une espèce] extinction ; [- d'une langue, d'une culture] dying out, disappearance **4.** [mort] death, disappearance.

disparu, e [dispary] ◇ *pp* ▷ **disparaître**.
◇ *adj* **1.** [mort] dead ■ **porté ~** [soldat] missing (in action) ; [marin] lost at sea ; [passager, victime] missing believed dead **2.** [langue] dead ■ [coutume, culture] vanished, dead ■ [ère, époque] bygone.
◇ *nm, f* **1.** [défunt] dead person ■ **les ~s** the dead ■ **les ~s en mer** [marins] men lost at sea **2.** [personne introuvable] missing person.

dispatcher [3] [dispatʃe] *vt* to dispatch, to send around *(sép)*.

dispendieusement [dispɑ̃djøzmɑ̃] *adv litt* extravagantly, expensively.

dispendieux, euse [dispɑ̃djø, øz] *adj litt* expensive, costly.

dispensaire [dispɑ̃sɛr] *nm* clinic.

dispensateur, trice [dispɑ̃satœr, tris] *nm, f* dispenser.

dispense [dispɑ̃s] *nf* **1.** [exemption] exemption ■ **~ d'oral/du service militaire** exemption from an oral exam/from military service **2.** [certificat] exemption certificate **3.** [autorisation spéciale] : **~ d'âge** *special permission for people under or over the age limit* **4.** DR : **~ de peine** dismissal of charges **5.** RELIG dispensation.

dispenser [3] [dispɑ̃se] *vt* **1.** [exempter] : **~ qqn de qqch** to exempt sb from sthg ■ **se faire ~ de gymnastique** to be excused (from) gym ■ **je vous dispense de me rendre un rapport cette fois** I'll excuse you from writing me a report this time ■ **~ qqn de faire** to exempt sb from doing ■ **je te dispense de tes sarcasmes** spare me your sarcasm **2.** [donner - charité] to dispense, to administer ; [- parole] to utter ■ **~ des soins aux malades** to provide patients with medical care.
◆ **se dispenser de** *vp+prép* [obligation] to get out of ■ **je me dispenserais bien de cette corvée!** I could do without this chore! ■ **peut-on se ~ de venir à la répétition?** is it possible to skip the rehearsal?

dispersé, e [dispɛrse] *adj* **1.** [famille, peuple] scattered ■ [habitations] scattered, spread out **2.** *fig* **élève trop ~** [sur bulletin de notes] should pay more attention in class ■ **dans mon ancien poste j'étais trop ~** in my old job, I had too many different things to do **3.** PHYS disperse *(modif)*.

disperser [3] [dispɛrse] *vt* **1.** [répandre - cendres, graines] to scatter **2.** [brume, brouillard] to disperse, to lift **3.** [efforts] to dissipate ■ [attention] to divide **4.** [foule, manifestants] to disperse, to break up *(sép)*, to scatter ■ [collection] to break up, to scatter **5.** [troupes] to spread out *(sép)*.
◆ **se disperser** *vpi* **1.** [brume, brouillard] to lift, to disperse **2.** [manifestation, foule] to disperse, to break up **3.** [dans son travail] to tackle too many things at once ■ **la production s'est (trop) dispersée** the firm has overdiversified.

dispersion [dispɛrsjɔ̃] *nf* **1.** [de cendres, de débris] scattering **2.** [de la brume] dispersal, lifting **3.** [de troupes, de policiers] spreading out **4.** [d'une foule, de manifestants] dispersal **5.** [des forces, de l'énergie] waste ■ [de l'attention] dividing of attention ■ **une trop grande ~ de la production** overdiversification in manufacturing **6.** CHIM & PHYS dispersion **7.** [en statistiques] dispersion.

disponibilité [disponibilite] *nf* **1.** [d'une fourniture, d'un service] availability **2.** [liberté] availability *(for an occupation)* ■ **pour élever des enfants, il faut avoir une grande ~** to bring up children you need to have a lot of time to devote to them ➲ **~ d'esprit** open-mindedness, receptiveness **3.** ADMIN : **mise en ~** (extended) leave ■ **professeur en ~** teacher on (extended) leave ■ **se mettre en ~** to take (extended) leave **4.** DR [de bien] (owner's) free disposal of property.
◆ **disponibilités** *nfpl* available funds, liquid assets.

disponible [disponibl] ◇ *adj* **1.** [utilisable - article, service] available **2.** [libre - personnel, employé] free, available **3.** [ouvert - personne] receptive, open-minded **4.** ADMIN on (extended) leave.
◇ *nmf* ADMIN civil servant on (extended) leave of absence.
◇ *nm* COMM stock items.

dispos, e [dispo, oz] *adj* in good form *ou* shape.

disposé, e [dispoze] *adj* **1.** [arrangé] : **bien/mal ~** well-/poorly-laid out **2.** [personne] : **bien/mal ~** in a good/bad mood ■ **être bien/mal ~ à l'égard de qqn** to be well-disposed/ill-disposed towards sb.

disposer [3] [dispoze] ◇ *vt* **1.** [arranger - verres, assiettes] to lay, to set ; [- fleurs] to arrange ; [- meubles] to place, to arrange ■ **j'ai disposé la chambre autrement** I've changed the layout of the bedroom **2.** [inciter] : **~ qqn à** to incline sb to *ou* towards ■ **l'heure ne dispose pas aux confidences** this is not a suitable time for sharing secrets **3.** [préparer] : **~ qqn à** to prepare sb for ■ **être disposé à faire qqch** to feel disposed *ou* to be willing to do sthg ■ **être peu disposé à faire qqch** to be disinclined to do sthg ■ **j'étais en retard, ce qui l'a tout de suite mal disposé à mon égard** I was late, which put him off me straightaway.
◇ *vi* [partir] : **vous pouvez ~** you may leave *ou* go.
◆ **disposer de** *v+prép* **1.** [avoir] to have (at one's disposal *ou* available) **2.** [utiliser] to use ■ **disposez de moi comme il vous plaira** I am at your service **3.** DR : **~ de ses biens** to dispose of one's property.
◆ **se disposer à** *vp+prép* to prepare to.

dispositif [dispozitif] *nm* **1.** [appareil, mécanisme] machine, device ■ **~ d'alarme/de sûreté** alarm/safety device **2.** [mesures] plan, measure ■ **un important ~ policier sera mis en place** there will be a large police presence **3.** MIL plan **4.** CINÉ, THÉÂTRE & TV : **~ scénique** set **5.** DR [jugement] sentence ■ [acte, traité] purview.

disposition [dispozisjɔ̃] *nf* **1.** [arrangement - de couverts] layout ; [- de fleurs, de livres, de meubles] arrangement ■ **la ~ des pièces dans notre maison** the layout of the rooms in our house ■ **la ~ de la vitrine** the window display **2.** [fait d'arranger - des couverts] laying out, setting ; [- des meubles] laying out, arranging ; [- des fleurs] arranging **3.** [tendance - d'une personne] tendency ■ **avoir une ~ à la négligence/à grossir** to have a tendency to carelessness/to put on weight **4.** [aptitude] aptitude, ability, talent ■ **avoir une ~ pour** to have a talent for **5.** DR clause, stipulation ■ **les ~s testamentaires de...** the last will and testament of... ▌[jouissance] disposal ■ **avoir la ~ de ses biens** to be free to dispose of one's property **6.** ADMIN : **mise à la ~** secondment *UK*, temporary transfer *US*.
◆ **dispositions** *nfpl* **1.** [humeur] mood ■ **être dans de bonnes/mauvaises ~s** to be in a good/bad mood ■ **être dans de bonnes/mauvaises ~s à l'égard de qqn** to be well-disposed/ill-disposed towards sb **2.** [mesures] measures ■ **prendre des ~s** [précautions, arrangements] to make arrangements, to take steps ; [préparatifs] to make preparations.
◆ **à la disposition de** *loc prép* at the disposal of ■ **mettre** *ou* **tenir qqch à la ~ de qqn** to place sthg at sb's disposal, to make sthg available to sb ■ **se tenir à la ~ de** to make o.s. available for ■ **je suis à votre ~** I am at your service ■ **je suis** *ou* **me tiens à votre entière ~ pour tout autre renseignement** should you require further information, please feel free to contact me.

disproportion [disprɔpɔrsjɔ̃] *nf* disproportion ■ **~ de salaire entre deux personnes** discrepancy between two people's salaries.

disproportionné, e [disprɔpɔrsjɔne] *adj* **1.** [inégal] disproportionate ■ **un prix ~ avec** *ou* **à la qualité** a price out of (all) proportion to the quality **2.** [démesuré - cou, jambes] long ; [- mains, yeux] large.

dispute [dispyt] *nf* quarrel, argument.

disputer [3] [dispyte] *vt* **1.** [participer à - match, tournoi] to play ; [- combat] to fight ■ **~ le terrain** MIL to dispute every inch of ground ; *fig* to fight tooth and nail **2.** [tenter de prendre] : **~ qqch à qqn** to fight with sb over sthg ■ **~ la première place à qqn** to contend *ou* to vie with sb for first place **3.** *fam* [réprimander] to scold, to tell off *(sép)* ■ **tu vas te faire ~!** you're in for it! **4.** *litt* [contester] to deny **5.** *loc* **le ~ en... à qqn** *litt* : **nul ne le lui disputait en courage** nobody could rival his courage.
◆ **disputer de** *v+prép litt* to debate, to discuss.
◆ **se disputer** ◇ *vp (emploi passif)* [avoir lieu] to take place.
◇ *vp (emploi réciproque)* [se quereller] to quarrel, to argue, to fight.
◇ *vpt* : **se ~ qqch** to fight over sthg.
◆ **se disputer avec** *vp+prép* to have an argument *ou* a row with.

disquaire [diskɛr] *nmf* **1.** [commerçant] record dealer ■ **tu trouveras ça chez un ~** you'll find this in a record shop **2.** [vendeur] record salesman (*f* saleswoman).

disqualification [diskalifikasjɔ̃] *nf* disqualification ■ **risquer la ~** to risk being disqualified.

disqualifier [9] [diskalifje] *vt* **1.** SPORT to disqualify ■ **l'équipe s'est fait ~** the team was disqualified **2.** [discréditer] to discredit, to bring discredit on.
◆ **se disqualifier** *vp (emploi réfléchi)* to lose credibility.

disque [disk] *nm* **1.** [cercle plat] disc ■ **~ de stationnement** parking disc **2.** ANAT, ASTRON & MATH disc **3.** SPORT discus **4.** AUDIO record, disc ■ **~ compact** compact disc ■ **~ vidéo** videodisc **5.** INFORM disk ■ **~ analyseur/dur/magnétique** scanner/hard/magnetic disk ■ **~ optique compact** CD-Rom ■ **~ optique numérique** digital optical disk ■ **~ souple, mini ~** floppy disk.

disquette [diskɛt] *nf* floppy disk, diskette.

dissection [disɛksjɔ̃] *nf* **1.** MÉD dissection **2.** [analyse] (close *ou* minute) analysis, dissection.

dissemblable [disɑ̃blabl] *adj* different, dissimilar.

dissemblance [disɑ̃blɑ̃s] *nf sout* dissimilarity, difference.

dissémination [diseminasjɔ̃] *nf* [de graines] scattering ■ [de troupes] scattering, spreading, dispersion ■ [de maisons, des habitants] scattering.

disséminer [3] [disemine] *vt* [graines] to scatter.
◆ **se disséminer** *vpi* [graines] to scatter ■ [personnes] to spread (out).

dissension [disɑ̃sjɔ̃] *nf* disagreement, difference of opinion.

dissentiment [disɑ̃timɑ̃] *nm litt* disagreement.

disséquer [18] [diseke] *vt* **1.** MÉD to dissect **2.** [analyser] to dissect, to carry out a close *ou* minute analysis of.

dissertation [disɛrtasjɔ̃] *nf* **1.** ÉDUC & UNIV essay **2.** *péj* [discours] (long and boring) speech ■ **on a eu droit à une ~ sur la politesse** we were treated to a lecture on politeness.

disserter [3] [disɛrte] *vi* **1.** ÉDUC & UNIV : **~ sur** to write an essay on **2.** *fig* & *péj* to hold forth on *ou* about.

dissidence [disidɑ̃s] *nf* **1.** [rébellion] dissidence ■ **un mouvement de ~** a rebel movement **2.** [dissidents] dissidents, rebels **3.** [scission] scission.

dissident, e [disidɑ̃, ɑ̃t] ◇ *adj* **1.** [rebelle] dissident *(avant n)*, rebel *(avant n)* ■ **un groupe ~** a splinter *ou* breakaway group **2.** RELIG dissenting.
◇ *nm, f* **1.** [rebelle] dissident, rebel **2.** RELIG dissenter, nonconformist.

dissimilitude [disimilityd] *nf* dissimilarity.

dissimulateur, trice [disimylatœr, tris] ◇ *adj* dissembling.
◇ *nm, f* dissembler.

dissimulation [disimylasjɔ̃] *nf* **1.** [fait de cacher] concealment **2.** [hypocrisie] deceit, dissimulation, hypocrisy ■ [sournoiserie] dissembling, secretiveness **3.** DR : **~ d'actif** (unlawful) concealment of assets.

dissimulé, e [disimyle] *adj* **1.** [invisible - haine, jalousie] concealed ■ **non ~** open **2.** *péj* [fourbe] deceitful, hypocritical.

dissimuler [3] [disimyle] *vt* **1.** [cacher à la vue] to hide (from sight) **2.** [ne pas révéler - identité] to conceal ; [- sentiments, difficultés] to hide, to conceal, to cover up *(sép)* ; [- fait] to conceal, to disguise ■ **je ne vous dissimulerai pas que...** I won't hide from you (the fact) that... **3.** DR [revenus, bénéfices] to conceal.
◆ **se dissimuler** ◇ *vp (emploi réfléchi)* [se cacher] to hide *ou* to conceal o.s.
◇ *vpt* : **se ~ qqch** to hide sthg from o.s.

dissipateur, trice [disipatœr, tris] *litt* ◇ *adj* wasteful, spendthrift.
◇ *nm, f* squanderer, spendthrift.

dissipation [disipasjɔ̃] *nf* **1.** [de nuages] dispersal, clearing ▪ [du brouillard] lifting ▪ [de craintes] dispelling **2.** [d'un héritage] wasting, squandering **3.** *litt* [débauche] dissipation **4.** [indiscipline] lack of discipline, misbehaviour.

dissipé, e [disipe] *adj* **1.** [indiscipliné - classe] unruly, rowdy, undisciplined ▪ **élève ~** [sur bulletin de notes] this pupil doesn't pay enough attention in class **2.** [débauché] dissolute.

dissiper [3] [disipe] *vt* **1.** [nuages, brouillard, fumée] to disperse ▪ [malentendu] to clear up *(sép)* ▪ [crainte, inquiétude] to dispel **2.** [dilapider - héritage, patrimoine] to dissipate, to squander **3.** [distraire] to distract, to divert.
◆ **se dissiper** *vpi* **1.** [orage] to blow over ▪ [nuages] to clear away, to disperse ▪ [brouillard] to lift, to clear ▪ [fumée] to disperse **2.** [craintes] to disappear, to vanish ▪ [migraine, douleurs] to go, to disappear **3.** [s'agiter - enfant] to misbehave, to be undisciplined *ou* unruly.

dissociable [disɔsjabl] *adj* [questions, chapitres] separable.

dissociation [disɔsjasjɔ̃] *nf* [de questions, de chapitres, d'une famille] separation.

dissocier [9] [disɔsje] *vt* **1.** [questions, chapitres] to separate ▪ [famille] to break up *(sép)* ▪ **il doit apprendre à ~ ses désirs de ses besoins** he must learn to distinguish between his desires and his needs **2.** CHIM to dissociate.

dissolu, e [disɔly] *adj litt* dissolute.

dissolution [disɔlysjɔ̃] *nf* **1.** [d'un produit, d'un comprimé] dissolving ▪ **remuer jusqu'à ~ du sucre** stir until the sugar has dissolved **2.** [d'une société] dissolution ▪ [d'un groupe] splitting, breaking up **3.** DR [d'un mariage, d'une association] dissolution ▪ POLIT [d'un parlement] dissolution **4.** [pour pneus] rubber solution **5.** *litt* [débauche] dissoluteness, debauchery.

dissolvait *etc v* ▻ **dissoudre.**

dissolvant, e [disɔlvɑ̃, ɑ̃t] *adj* **1.** [substance] solvent **2.** *litt* [climat] enervating.
◆ **dissolvant** *nm* **1.** [détachant] solvent **2.** [de vernis à ongles] : **~ (gras)** nail polish remover.

dissonance [disɔnɑ̃s] *nf* **1.** [cacophonie] dissonance, discord **2.** *litt* [de couleurs, d'idées] discord *litt*, clash, mismatch **3.** MUS dissonance.

dissonant, e [disɔnɑ̃, ɑ̃t] *adj* **1.** [sons, cris] dissonant, discordant, jarring ▪ *litt* [couleurs] discordant *litt*, clashing **2.** MUS discordant.

dissoudre [87] [disudr] *vt* **1.** [diluer - sel, sucre, comprimé] to dissolve ▪ **faites ~ le comprimé** dissolve the tablet **2.** [désunir - assemblée, mariage] to dissolve ; [- parti] to break up *(sép)*, to dissolve ; [- association] to dissolve, to break up *(sép)*, to bring to an end.
◆ **se dissoudre** *vpi* **1.** [sel, sucre, comprimé] to dissolve **2.** [groupement] to break up, to come to an end.

dissuader [3] [disɥade] *vt* : **~ qqn de (faire) qqch** to dissuade sb from (doing) sthg.

dissuasif, ive [disɥazif, iv] *adj* **1.** [qui décourage] dissuasive, discouraging, off-putting *UK* **2.** MIL deterrent.

dissuasion [disɥazjɔ̃] *nf* dissuasion.
◆ **de dissuasion** *loc adj* [puissance] dissuasive.

dissymétrie [disimetri] *nf* dissymmetry.

dissymétrique [disimetrik] *adj* dissymmetrical.

distance [distɑ̃s] *nf* **1.** [intervalle - dans l'espace] distance ▪ **la ~ entre Pau et Tarbes** *ou* **de Pau à Tarbes** the distance between Pau and Tarbes *ou* from Pau to Tarbes ▪ **on les entend à une ~ de 100 mètres** you can hear them (from) 100 metres away *ou* at a distance of 100 metres ▪ **nous habitons à une grande ~ de la ville** we live far (away) from the city ▪ **il a mis une ~ respectueuse entre lui et le fisc** *hum* he made sure he stayed well out of reach of the taxman ⓘ **garder ses ~s** to stay aloof, to remain distant ▪ **prendre ses ~s** SPORT to space out ; MIL to spread out in *ou* to form open order ▪ **prendre ses ~s envers** *ou* **à l'égard de qqn** to hold o.s. aloof *ou* to keep one's distance from sb **2.** [parcours] distance ⓘ **tenir la ~** *pr & fig* to go the distance, to stay the course **3.** [intervalle - dans le temps] : **ils sont nés à deux mois de ~** they were born within two months of each other ▪ **il l'a revue à deux mois de ~** he saw her again two months later **4.** [écart, différence] gap, gulf, great difference ▪ **ce malentendu a mis une certaine ~ entre nous** we've become rather distant from each other since that misunderstanding.
◆ **à distance** *loc adv* **1.** [dans l'espace] at a distance, from a distance, from afar ▪ **cette chaîne peut se commander à ~** this stereo has a remote control ▪ **tenir qqn à ~** to keep sb at a distance *ou* at arm's length ▪ **se tenir à ~ (de)** to keep one's distance (from) **2.** [dans le temps] with time.
◆ **de distance en distance** *loc adv* at intervals, in places.

distancer [16] [distɑ̃se] *vt* SPORT to outdistance, to leave behind ▪ *fig* to outdistance, to outstrip ▪ **se laisser ~** SPORT to fall behind ; *fig* to be left behind ▪ **se faire ~ économiquement** to lag behind economically.

distanciation [distɑ̃sjasjɔ̃] *nf* [gén] detachment.

distancier [9] [distɑ̃sje] ◆ **se distancier de** *vp+prép* : **se ~ de qqch/qqn** to distance o.s. from sthg/sb.

distant, e [distɑ̃, ɑ̃t] *adj* **1.** [dans l'espace] far away, distant ▪ **être ~ de qqch** to be far *ou* some distance from sthg ▪ **les deux écoles sont ~es de 5 kilomètres** the (two) schools are 5 kilometres away from each other **2.** [dans le temps] distant **3.** [personne] aloof, distant ▪ [air, sourire] remote, distant ▪ [rapports] distant, cool.

distendre [73] [distɑ̃dr] *vt* **1.** [étirer - ressort] to stretch, to overstretch ; [- peau] to stretch, to distend *spéc* ; [- muscle] to strain **2.** [rendre moins intime - liens] to loosen.
◆ **se distendre** *vpi* **1.** [s'étirer - peau, ventre] to stretch, to become distended *spéc* **2.** [devenir moins intime - liens] to loosen.

distension [distɑ̃sjɔ̃] *nf* [étirage - de l'intestin, de l'estomac] distension ; [- d'un muscle] straining ; [- d'un ressort] slackening (off).

distillat [distila] *nm* distillate.

distillateur [distilatœr] *nm* [personne] distiller.

distillation [distilasjɔ̃] *nf* distillation, distilling.

distiller [3] [distile] *vt* **1.** [alcool, pétrole, eau] to distil **2.** *litt* [suc, venin] to secrete **3.** *litt* [ennui, tristesse] to exude.

distillerie [distilri] *nf* **1.** [usine, atelier] distillery **2.** [activité] distilling.

distinct, e [distɛ̃, ɛ̃kt] *adj* **1.** [clair, net] distinct, clear **2.** [différent] distinct, different ▪ **un résultat ~ du précédent** a result different from the previous one.

distinctement [distɛ̃ktəmɑ̃] *adv* distinctly, clearly.

distinctif, ive [distɛ̃ktif, iv] *adj* **1.** [qui sépare] distinctive, distinguishing **2.** LING distinctive.

distinction [distɛ̃ksjɔ̃] *nf* **1.** [différence] distinction ▪ **faire une ~ entre deux choses** to make *ou* to draw a distinction between two things **2.** [élégance, raffinement] refinement, distinction.
◆ **distinctions** *nfpl* [honneurs] honour.
◆ **sans distinction** *loc adv* indiscriminately, without exception.
◆ **sans distinction de** *loc prép* irrespective of.

distingué, e [distɛ̃ge] *adj* **1.** [élégant - personne] distinguished ; [- manières, air] refined, elegant, distinguished **2.** [brillant, éminent] distinguished, eminent **3.** [dans une lettre] : **veuillez croire en l'assurance de mes sentiments ~s** yours faithfully *ou* sincerely.

distinguer [3] [distɛ̃ge] *vt* **1.** [voir] to distinguish, to make out *(sép)* ▪ *(en usage absolu)* **on distingue mal dans le noir** it's hard to see in the dark **2.** [entendre] to hear, to distinguish, to make out *(sép)* **3.** [percevoir] : **je commence à ~ ses mobiles** I'm beginning to understand his motives ▪ **j'ai cru ~ une certaine colère dans sa voix** I thought I detected a note of anger in his voice **4.** [différencier] to distinguish ▪ **~ le vrai du faux** to distinguish truth from falsehood ▪ **je n'arrive pas à les ~**

I can't tell which is which, I can't tell them apart ▪ **je n'arrive pas à ~ ces deux arbres** I can't tell the difference between these two trees **5.** [honorer] to single out (for reward), to honour.

◆ **se distinguer** ◇ *vp (emploi passif)* **1.** [être vu] to be seen *ou* distinguished **2.** [différer] : **se ~ par : ces vins se distinguent par leur robe** you can tell these wines are different because of their colour.

◇ *vpi* **1.** [se faire remarquer] to distinguish o.s. ▪ **son fils s'est distingué en musique** his son has distinguished himself *ou* done particularly well in music **2.** [devenir célèbre] to become famous.

◆ **se distinguer de** *vp+prép* **1.** [différer de] : **le safran se distingue du curcuma par l'odeur** you can tell the difference between saffron and turmeric by their smell **2.** [être supérieur à] : **il se distingue de tous les autres poètes** he stands out from all other poets.

distinguo [distɛ̃go] *nm* distinction.

distordre [76] [distɔrdr] *vt* to twist.

◆ **se distordre** *vpi* to twist, to distort.

distorsion [distɔrsjɔ̃] *nf* **1.** [déformation] distortion **2.** [déséquilibre] imbalance.

distraction [distraksjɔ̃] *nf* **1.** [caractère étourdi] absent-mindedness ▪ **par ~** inadvertently ▮ [acte] lapse in concentration ▪ **excusez ma ~** forgive me, I wasn't concentrating **2.** [détente] : **il lui faut de la ~** he needs to have his mind taken off things ▮ [activité] source of entertainment ▪ **il n'y a pas assez de ~s le soir** there's not enough to do at night.

distraire [112] [distrɛr] *vt* **1.** [déranger] to distract ▪ **tu te laisses trop facilement ~** you're too easily distracted **2.** [amuser] to entertain, to divert **3.** [détourner] : **~ qqn de : ~ un ami de ses soucis** to take a friend's mind off his worries.

◆ **se distraire** *vpi* **1.** [s'amuser] to have fun, to enjoy o.s. **2.** [se détendre] to relax, to take a break.

◆ **se distraire de** *vp+prép* : **elle ne parvient pas à se ~ de son malheur** she can't take her mind off her grief.

distrait, e [distrɛ, ɛt] ◇ *adj* [gén] absent-minded.

◇ *nm, f* absent-minded person ▪ [élève] inattentive ▪ **avoir l'air ~** to look preoccupied ▪ **d'un air ~** abstractedly, absent-mindedly ▪ **excusez-moi, j'étais ~** sorry, I wasn't paying attention.

distraitement [distrɛtmɑ̃] *adv* absent-mindedly, abstractedly.

distrayait *etc v* ⊳ **distraire**.

distrayant, e [distrɛjɑ̃, ɑ̃t] *adj* amusing, entertaining.

distribué, e [distribɥe] *adj* **1.** [appartement] : **bien/mal ~** well/poorly laid-out **2.** [données, information] distributed.

distribuer [7] [distribɥe] *vt* **1.** [donner - feuilles, cadeaux, bonbons] to distribute, to give *ou* to hand out *(sép)* ; [- cartes] to deal ; [- courrier] to deliver ; [- vivres] to dispense, to share out *(sép)*, to distribute ; [- argent] to apportion, to distribute, to share out *(sép)* **2.** [attribuer - rôles] to allocate, to assign ; [- tâches, travail] to allot, to assign **3.** [répartir] to distribute, to divide (out) **4.** [approvisionner] to supply ▪ **l'eau est distribuée dans tous les villages** water is supplied *ou* carried to all the villages **5.** CINÉ & THÉÂTRE [rôle] to cast ▪ CINÉ [film] to distribute **6.** COMM & IMPR to distribute.

distributaire [distribytɛr] ◇ *adj* distributional.

◇ *nmf* recipient *(in a distribution)*.

distributeur, trice [distribytœr, tris] *nm, f* distributor.

◆ **distributeur** *nm* **1.** [non payant] dispenser ▪ **~ de savon/gobelets** soap/cup dispenser ▪ **~ automatique de billets** cash dispenser *ou* machine, cashpoint, automatic teller machine ▮ [payant] : **~ (automatique)** vending *ou* slot machine ▪ **~ de cigarettes/de timbres** cigarette/stamp machine **2.** COMM [vendeur] distributor ▪ [grande surface] retailer ▪ **~ en gros** wholesaler.

distributif, ive [distribytif, iv] *adj* distributive.

distribution [distribysjɔ̃] *nf* **1.** [remise - de vêtements, de cadeaux] distribution, giving *ou* handing out ; [- de cartes] dealing ; [- de secours] dispensing, distributing ; [- de tâches, du travail] allotment, assignment ; [- du courrier] delivery ▪ **assurer la ~ du courrier** to deliver the mail ➊ **la ~ des prix** ÉDUC prize-giving day **2.** [répartition dans l'espace - de pièces] layout ; [- de joueurs] positioning **3.** [approvisionnement] supply ▪ **~ d'eau/de gaz** water/gas supply **4.** BOT & SOCIOL [classement] distribution **5.** CINÉ & THÉÂTRE [des rôles] cast ▪ **c'est elle qui s'occupe de la ~** she's the one in charge of casting ▪ **~ par ordre d'entrée en scène** characters in order of appearance ▮ CINÉ [des films] distribution **6.** COMM distribution **7.** ÉCON, DR & MATH distribution **8.** AUTO timing **9.** LING (distributional) context.

district [distrikt] *nm* **1.** [région] district, region **2.** [d'une ville] district.

dit, e [di, dit] ◇ *pp* ⊳ **dire**.

◇ *adj* **1.** [surnommé] (also) known as **2.** [fixé] appointed, indicated ▪ **le jour ~** on the agreed *ou* appointed day.

◆ **dit** *nm* PSYCHOL : **le ~ et le non-dit** the spoken and the unspoken.

dites *v* ⊳ **dire**.

dithyrambe [ditirɑ̃b] *nm* **1.** ANTIQ dithyramb **2.** [panégyrique] panegyric, eulogy.

dithyrambique [ditirɑ̃bik] *adj* eulogistic, laudatory ▪ **un article ~ sur son exposition** an article praising her exhibition to the skies.

DIU [deiy] *(abr de* **dispositif intra-utérin***)* *nm* MÉD IUD.

diurétique [djyretik] *adj & nm* diuretic.

diurne [djyrn] *adj* diurnal.

diva [diva] *nf* diva, (female) opera singer.

divagations [divagasjɔ̃] *nfpl* ramblings, meanderings.

divaguer [3] [divage] *vi* **1.** [malade] to ramble, to be delirious ▪ **la soif le fait ~** he's delirious with thirst **2.** *fam péj* [déraisonner] to be off one's head.

divan [divɑ̃] *nm* **1.** [meuble] divan, couch **2.** HIST : **le ~** the divan.

divergence [divɛrʒɑ̃s] *nf* **1.** [différence] : **~ (d'idées** *ou* **de vues)** difference of opinion **2.** OPT & PHYS divergence.

divergent, e [divɛrʒɑ̃, ɑ̃t] *adj* **1.** [opinions, interprétations, intérêts] divergent, differing **2.** OPT & PHYS divergent.

diverger [17] [divɛrʒe] *vi* **1.** [intérêts, opinions] to differ, to diverge ▪ **~ de** to diverge *ou* to depart from **2.** OPT & PHYS to diverge ▪ **~ de** to diverge from.

divers, e [divɛr, ɛrs] ◇ *dét (adj indéf)* [plusieurs] various, several ▪ **en ~es occasions** on several *ou* various occasions ▪ **à usages ~** multipurpose *(avant n)*.

◇ *adj* **1.** [variés - éléments, musiques, activités] diverse, varied ▪ **nous avons abordé les sujets les plus ~** we talked about a wide range of topics ▪ **pour ~es raisons** for a variety of reasons ▪ **articles ~** COMM miscellaneous items **2.** [dissemblables - formes, goûts, motifs] different, various **3.** *sout* [multiple - sujet] complex ; [- paysage] varied, changing **4.** POLIT others ▪ **les ~ droite/gauche** other right/left-wing parties.

diversement [divɛrsəmɑ̃] *adv* **1.** [différemment] in different ways **2.** [de façon variée] in diverse *ou* various ways.

diversification [divɛrsifikasjɔ̃] *nf* diversification ▪ **une trop grande ~** overdiversification.

diversifier [9] [divɛrsifje] *vt* **1.** [production, tâches] to diversify **2.** [varier] to make more varied ▪ **dans sa deuxième période, l'artiste diversifie sa palette** in his second period, the artist uses a greater variety of colours.

◆ **se diversifier** *vpi* [entreprise, économie, centres d'intérêt] to diversify.

diversion [divɛrsjɔ̃] *nf* **1.** *sout* [dérivatif] diversion, distraction ▪ **faire ~** to create a distraction ▪ **faire ~ à la douleur de qqn** to take sb's mind off his/her suffering **2.** MIL diversion.

diversité [divɛrsite] *nf* [variété] diversity, variety ▪ **un paysage étonnant dans sa ~** an amazingly varied landscape ▮ [pluralité - de formes, d'opinions, de goûts] diversity.

divertir [32] [divɛrtir] *vt* **1.** [amuser - suj: clown, spectacle, lecture] to entertain, to amuse **2.** DR to divert, to misappropriate **3.** *litt* [éloigner] : ~ **qqn de** to turn sb away *ou* to distract sb from.

◆ **se divertir** *vpi* **1.** [se distraire] to amuse *ou* to entertain o.s. ▪ **que faire pour se ~ ici?** what do you do for entertainment around here? **2.** [s'amuser] to enjoy o.s., to have fun.

◆ **se divertir de** *vp+prép* : **se ~ de qqn** to make fun of sb.

divertissant, e [divɛrtisɑ̃, ɑ̃t] *adj* amusing, entertaining.

divertissement [divɛrtismɑ̃] *nm* **1.** [jeu, passe-temps] distraction ▪ [spectacle] entertainment **2.** [amusement] entertaining, distraction **3.** MUS [intermède] divertissement ▪ [divertimento] divertimento ▪ DANSE divertissement **4.** DR [de fonds] misappropriation.

dividende [dividɑ̃d] *nm* FIN & MATH dividend ▪ **toucher** *ou* **recevoir un ~** to receive *ou* to get a dividend ▪ **sans ~** ex-dividend.

divin, e [divɛ̃, in] *adj* **1.** RELIG divine ▪ **le ~ enfant** the Holy Child ▪ **'la Divine Comédie'** ***Dante*** 'The Divine Comedy' **2.** [parfait - beauté, corps, repas, voix] divine, heavenly, exquisite.

divinateur, trice [divinatœr, tris] <> *adj* divining, clairvoyant ▪ **puissance divinatrice** power of divination.
<> *nm, f* diviner.

divination [divinasjɔ̃] *nf* divination, divining.

divinatoire [divinatwar] *adj* divinatory.

divinement [divinmɑ̃] *adv* divinely, exquisitely.

diviniser [3] [divinize] *vt* to deify.

divinité [divinite] *nf* **1.** [dieu] deity, divinity **2.** [qualité] divinity, divine nature.

divisé, e [divize] *adj* **1.** [en désaccord - opinion, juges, parti] divided ▪ **être ~ sur** to be divided on (the question of) **2.** [fragmenté] divided.

diviser [3] [divize] *vt* **1.** [fragmenter - territoire] to divide up *(sép)*, to partition ; [- somme, travail] to divide up *(sép)* ; [- cellule, molécule] to divide, to split **2.** MATH to divide ▪ **9 divisé par 3 égale 3** 9 divided by 3 makes 3 ▪ **la classe est divisée en 3 groupes** the class is divided up into 3 groups **3.** [opposer] to divide, to set against each other ▪ **l'association est divisée en deux sur le problème de l'intégration** the association is split down the middle on the problem of integration ➊ **c'est ~ pour (mieux) régner** it's (a case of) divide and rule.

◆ **se diviser** <> *vp (emploi passif)* MATH to be divisible.
<> *vpi* **1.** [cellule] to divide *ou* to split (up) ▪ [branche, voie] to divide, to fork ▪ **le texte se divise en cinq parties** the text is divided into five parts **2.** [opposition, parti] to split.

diviseur [divizœr] *nm* MATH divisor ▪ **plus grand commun ~** highest common factor.

divisibilité [divizibilite] *nf* divisibility.

divisible [divizibl] *adj* divisible ▪ **8 n'est pas ~ par 3** 8 cannot be divided *ou* is not divisible by 3.

division [divizjɔ̃] *nf* **1.** MATH division ▪ **faire une ~** to do a division ➊ **~ à un chiffre** simple division ▪ **~ à plusieurs chiffres** long division **2.** [fragmentation - d'un territoire] splitting, division, partition ▪ **la ~ du travail** ÉCON the division of labour ▪ **~ cellulaire** BIOL cell division ▪ PHYS splitting **3.** [désaccord] division, rift **4.** FOOTBALL division ▪ **la première ~ du championnat** the first league division ▪ **un club de première/deuxième/troisième ~** a first/second/third division club ▪ **~ d'honneur** ≃ fourth division ▪ **en deuxième ~, X bat Y** in league division two, X beat Y ▮ [au baseball] league **5.** MIL & NAUT division ▪ **~ blindée** armoured division **6.** ADMIN division **7.** [graduation] gradation.

divisionnaire [divizjɔnɛr] <> *adj* ADMIN [service] divisional.
<> *nm* **1.** MIL major general **2.** [commissaire] ≃ chief superintendent *UK*, ≃ police chief *US*.

divorce [divɔrs] *nm* **1.** DR divorce ▪ **demander le ~** to ask *ou* to petition for a divorce ▪ **obtenir le ~ d'avec qqn** to get a divorce from sb ➊ **~ par consentement mutuel** divorce by mutual consent, no-fault divorce *US* **2.** *sout* [divergence] gulf.

divorcé, e [divɔrse] <> *adj* divorced.
<> *nm, f* divorcee.

divorcer [16] [divɔrse] *vi* DR to get a divorce, to get divorced ▪ **~ de qqn** *ou* **d'avec qqn** to get divorced from *ou* to divorce sb.

divulgateur, trice [divylgatœr, tris] *nm, f* divulger.

divulgation [divylgasjɔ̃] *nf* divulgation, disclosure.

divulguer [3] [divylge] *vt* to divulge, to disclose, to reveal.

dix [dis *(devant consonne)*, di *(devant voyelle ou h muet)*, diz] <> *dét* ten ▪ **il ne sait rien faire de ses ~ doigts** he can't do anything with his hands ➊ **les ~ commandements** BIBLE the Ten Commandments ▪ **'les Dix Commandements'** ***C.B. De Mille*** 'The Ten Commandments', *voir aussi* **cinq**.
<> *nm* ten.

dix-huit [dizɥit] *dét* & *nm inv* eighteen, *voir aussi* **cinq**.

dix-huitième [dizɥitjɛm] *adj num* & *nmf* eighteenth, *voir aussi* **cinquième**.

dixième [dizjɛm] *adj num* & *nmf* tenth, *voir aussi* **cinquième**.

dix-neuf [diznœf *(devant an, heure et homme)* diznœv] *dét* & *nm inv* nineteen, *voir aussi* **cinq**.

dix-neuvième [diznœvjɛm] *adj num* & *nmf* nineteenth, *voir aussi* **cinquième**.

dix-sept [disɛt] *dét* & *nm inv* seventeen, *voir aussi* **cinq**.

dix-septième [disɛtjɛm] *adj num* & *nmf* seventeenth, *voir aussi* **cinquième**.

dizaine [dizɛn] *nf* **1.** [dix] ten **2.** [environ dix] about *ou* around ten, ten or so.

DJ [didʒi, didʒe] *(abr de* **disc-jockey***)* *nm* DJ.

Djakarta [dʒakarta] *npr* Djakarta, Jakarta.

Djedda [dʒɛda] *npr* Jedda, Jidda.

Djibouti [dʒibuti] *npr* **1.** [État] Djibouti ▪ **à ~** in Djibouti **2.** [ville] Djibouti City.

djihad [dʒiad] *nm* jihad.

djinn [dʒin] *nm* jinn.

dm *(abr écrite de* **décimètre***)* dm.

DM *(abr écrite de* **Deutsche Mark***)* DM.

do [do] *nm inv* C ▪ [chanté] doh, *voir aussi* **fa**.

doberman [dɔbɛrman] *nm* Doberman (pinscher).

doc [dɔk] *(abr de* **documentation***)* *nf fam* literature, brochures ▪ **pouvez-vous me donner de la ~ sur cet ordinateur?** could you give me some literature about this computer?

DOC [dɔk] *nm* = **disque optique compact**.

docile [dɔsil] *adj* [animal] docile, tractable *sout* ▪ [enfant, nature] docile, obedient ▪ [cheveux] manageable.

docilement [dɔsilmɑ̃] *adv* docilely, obediently.

docilité [dɔsilite] *nf* [d'un animal, d'une personne] docility ▪ **avec ~** docilely.

dock [dɔk] *nm* **1.** [bassin] dock ▪ **~ de carénage/flottant** dry/floating dock **2.** [bâtiments, chantier] : **les ~s** the docks, the dockyard ➊ **les ~s de Londres** London's Docklands **3.** [entrepôt] warehouse.

docker [dɔkɛr] *nm* docker.

docte [dɔkt] *adj litt* learned, erudite.

doctement [dɔktəmɑ̃] *adv* knowledgeably.

docteur [dɔktœr] *nm* **1.** [médecin] : **le ~ Jacqueline R.** Dr Jacqueline R ▪ **faites venir le ~** send for the doctor ▪ **dites-moi, ~** tell me, Doctor ➊ **~ en médecine** doctor (of medicine) ▪ **'le Docteur Jivago'** ***Pasternak*** 'Doctor Zhivago' **2.** UNIV Doctor ➊ ~ **en histoire/physique** PhD in history/physics ▪ **Vuibert, ~ ès lettres** Vuibert, PhD **3.** RELIG : ~ **de l'Église** Doctor of the Church.

doctoral, e, aux [dɔktɔral, o] *adj* **1.** [pédant] pedantic **2.** UNIV doctoral.

doctoralement [dɔktɔralmɑ̃] *adv* pedantically.

doctorat [dɔktɔra] *nm* doctorate ▪ ~ **en droit/chimie** PhD in law/chemistry ▪ ~ **d'État** doctorate *(leading to high-level research)* ▪ ~ **de troisième cycle** doctorate *(awarded by a specific university), PhD.*

doctoresse [dɔktɔrɛs] *nf vieilli* (woman) doctor.

doctrinaire [dɔktrinɛr] ◇ *adj* doctrinaire, dogmatic. ◇ *nmf* doctrinaire.

doctrinal, e, aux [dɔktrinal, o] *adj* doctrinal.

doctrine [dɔktrin] *nf* doctrine.

document [dɔkymɑ̃] *nm* **1.** INFORM file **2.** [d'un service de documentation] document **3.** [de travail] document, paper **4.** [témoignage] document ▪ ~ **sonore** piece of sound archive **5.** DR document, paper ▪ **~s de transport** transport documents.

documentaire [dɔkymɑ̃tɛr] ◇ *adj* **1.** [qui témoigne - livre] documentary **2.** [de documentation] document *(modif).* ◇ *nm* CINÉ & TV documentary.

documentaliste [dɔkymɑ̃talist] *nmf* **1.** [gén] archivist **2.** ÉDUC (school) librarian.

documentariste [dɔkymɑ̃tarist] *nmf* documentary maker.

documentation [dɔkymɑ̃tasjɔ̃] *nf* **1.** [publicités] literature ▪ [instructions] instructions, specifications **2.** [informations] (written) evidence **3.** [opération] documentation **4.** [service] : **la ~** the research department.

documenté, e [dɔkymɑ̃te] *adj* : **bien** *ou* **très ~** [reportage, thèse] well-documented ; [personne] well-informed.

documenter [3] [dɔkymɑ̃te] *vt* [thèse] to document ▪ [avocat] to supply *ou* to provide with documents, to document.
◆ **se documenter** *vpi* to inform o.s. ▪ **se ~ sur** to gather information *ou* material about.

dodécaphonique [dɔdekafɔnik] *adj* dodecaphonic.

dodeliner [3] [dɔdəline] ◆ **dodeliner de** *v+prép* : **~ de la tête** to nod gently.

dodo [dodo] *nm langage enfantin* [sommeil] sleep, beddy-byes ▪ **faire ~** to go beddy-byes *ou* bybyes ▮ [lit] bed ▪ **va au ~** (time to) go to beddy-byes.

dodu, e [dɔdy] *adj* [oie] plump ▪ [personne, visage] plump, fleshy, chubby ▪ [bébé] chubby.

doge [dɔʒ] *nm* doge.

dogmatique [dɔgmatik] ◇ *adj* dogmatic. ◇ *nmf* dogmatic person. ◇ *nf* dogmatics *(U).*

dogmatiser [3] [dogmatize] *vi* to pontificate, to dogmatize.

dogmatisme [dɔgmatism] *nm* dogmatism.

dogme [dɔgm] *nm* dogma.

dogue [dɔg] *nm* mastiff ▪ ~ **allemand/anglais** German/English mastiff.

doigt [dwa] *nm* **1.** ANAT finger, digit *spéc* ▪ **le ~ sur la bouche** with one's finger on one's lips ▪ **lever le ~** to put one's hand up ▪ **manger avec ses ~s** to eat with one's fingers ▪ **mettre ses ~s dans** *ou* **se mettre les ~s dans le nez** to pick one's nose ▪ **mettre son ~ dans l'œil de qqn** to poke sb in the eye ➊ **le ~ de Dieu** the hand of God ▪ ~ **de pied** toe ▪ **les ~s de pied en éventail** *fam ou* **en bouquet de violettes** *fam* with one's feet up ▪ **~s de fée : couturière aux ~s de fée** very talented seamstress ▪ **petit ~** little finger ▪ **ils sont comme les (deux) ~s de la main** they're like brothers, they're as thick as thieves ▪ **glisser** *ou* **filer entre les ~s de qqn** to slip through sb's fingers ▪ **mettre le ~ dans l'engrenage** to get involved ▪ **se fourrer** *fam ou* **se mettre** *fam ou* **se foutre**△ **le ~ dans l'œil (jusqu'au coude)** to be barking up the wrong tree ▪ **mener** *ou* **faire marcher qqn au ~ et à l'œil** to have sb toe the line, to rule sb with a rod of iron ▪ **il lui obéit au ~ et à l'œil** she rules him with a rod of iron ▪ **les ~s dans le nez** *fam* **: tu pourrais le faire? – les ~s dans le nez!** could you do it? - standing on my head! ▪ **gagner les ~s dans le nez** to win hands down ▪ **mettre le ~ sur, toucher du ~** to identify precisely ▪ **tu as mis le ~ dessus!** that's precisely it!, you've put your finger on it! ▪ **là, nous touchons du ~ le problème principal** now we're getting to the crux of the problem ▪ **c'est mon petit ~ qui me l'a dit** a little bird told me ▪ **il ne bougera** *ou* **lèvera pas le petit ~ pour faire...** he won' t lift a finger to do... **2.** [mesure] little bit ▪ **servez-m'en un ~** just pour me out a drop.
◆ **à un doigt de, à deux doigts de** *loc prép* within an inch *ou* a hair's breadth of.

doigté [dwate] *nm* **1.** MUS [annotation, position] fingering ▪ [technique] fingering technique **2.** [adresse] dexterity ▪ **pour ouvrir un coffre-fort il faut beaucoup de ~** to open a safe you need a very fine touch **3.** [tact] tact, diplomacy ▪ **ne pas avoir de/avoir du ~** to be tactless/tactful.

doigtier [dwatje] *nm* fingerstall.

doit *etc* [dwa] *v* ▻ **devoir.**

doit [dwa] *nm* FIN debit ▪ ~ **et avoir** debit and credit.

doive *etc v* ▻ **devoir.**

Dolby® [dɔlbi] *nm* Dolby® ▪ **en ~ stéréo** in Dolby stereo.

doléances [dɔleɑ̃s] *nfpl* complaints, grievances.

dolent, e [dɔlɑ̃, ɑ̃t] *adj* **1.** *litt* [plaintif - personne] doleful, mournful ; [- voix] plaintive, mournful **2.** *péj* [sans énergie - personne] sluggish, lethargic.

doline [dɔlin] *nf* doline, dolina.

dollar [dɔlar] *nm* **1.** [en Amérique du Nord] dollar **2.** [dans l'Union européenne] : ~ **vert** green dollar.

dolmen [dɔlmɛn] *nm* dolmen.

Dolomites [dɔlɔmit] *npr fpl* : **les ~** the Dolomites.

DOM [dɔm] (*abr de* **département d'outre-mer**) *nm French overseas département.*

domaine [dɔmɛn] *nm* **1.** [propriété] estate, (piece of) property ▪ **mis en bouteille au ~** [dans le Bordelais] chateau-bottled ➊ **le ~ royal** ≃ Crown lands *ou* property ; HIST [en France] the property of the Kings of France ▪ ~ **skiable** area developed for skiing *(within a commune or across several communes)* ▪ ~ **vinicole** domaine
2. [lieu préféré] domain
3. DR : **le ~** State property ➊ ~ **privé** private ownership ▪ ~ **public** public ownership (of rights) ▪ **être dans le ~ public** to be out of copyright ▪ **tomber dans le ~ public** to come into the public domain
4. [secteur d'activité] field, domain, area ▪ **dans le ~ de la prévention, il y a encore beaucoup à faire** as far as preventive action is concerned, there's still a lot to do ▪ **dans tous les ~s** in every field *ou* domain ▪ **dans tous les ~s de la recherche** in all research areas ▮ [compétence, spécialité] field ▪ **l'art oriental, c'est son ~** she's a specialist in oriental art ▪ **l'électricité, c'est mon ~** I know quite a bit about electricity
5. [d'un dictionnaire] field ▪ [indication] field label
6. MATH & INFORM domain.
◆ **Domaines** *nmpl* ADMIN : **cet étang appartient aux Domaines** this pond is State property.

domanial, e, aux [dɔmanjal, o] *adj* **1.** [de l'État] national, state *(modif)* **2.** [privé] belonging to a private estate.

dôme [dom] *nm* **1.** [en Italie - cathédrale] cathedral ; [- église] church **2.** ARCHIT dome, cupola *spéc* **3.** *litt* [voûte] vault, canopy **4.** GÉOL dome.

domestication [dɔmɛstikasjɔ̃] *nf* [d'un animal, d'une plante] domestication ▪ [d'une énergie] harnessing.

domesticité [dɔmɛstisite] *nf* : **la ~** [dans une maison] the (domestic *ou* household) staff ▪ **avoir une nombreuse ~** to have a large staff *ou* many servants.

domestique [dɔmɛstik] ◇ *adj* **1.** [familial - problème, vie] family *(modif)* ; [- lieu] household *(modif)* **2.** [du ménage - affaires, devoirs, tâches] household *(modif)*, domestic ■ **les travaux ~s** household work, domestic chores ■ **personnel ~** domestic staff, (domestic) servants **3.** ÉCON [économie, marché] domestic, home *(modif)* **4.** [animal] domesticated ■ **les animaux ~s** pets.
◇ *nmf* domestic, servant ■ **les ~s** domestic staff, (domestic) servants, domestics ■ **il nous prend pour ses ~s** he thinks we're his servants.

domestiquer [3] [dɔmɛstike] *vt* [animal] to domesticate ■ [plante] to turn into a cultivated variety ■ [énergie] to harness.

domicile [dɔmisil] *nm* **1.** [lieu de résidence] home, place of residence *sout* ■ [adresse] (home) address ■ **être sans ~** [sans foyer] to be homeless ■ **sans ~ fixe** of no fixed abode *ou* address ▶ **~ fiscal/légal** address for tax/legal purposes ■ **~ conjugal** marital home ■ **~ permanent** permanent place of residence **2.** [d'une entreprise] registered address.
◆ **à domicile** ◇ *loc adj* : **soins à ~** domiciliary care, home treatment.
◇ *loc adv* [chez soi] at home ■ **travailler à ~** to work from home ■ **nous livrons à ~** we deliver to your home.

domiciliataire [dɔmisiljatɛr] *nmf* paying agent BANQUE.

domiciliation [dɔmisiljasjɔ̃] *nf* [d'une société] : **~ (bancaire)** domiciliation.

domicilié, e [dɔmisilje] *adj* : **être fiscalement ~ dans un pays** to be liable to pay tax in a country ■ **~ à Tokyo/en Suède** domiciled in Tokyo/in Sweden.

domicilier [9] [dɔmisilje] *vt* **1.** ADMIN to domicile ■ **je me suis fait ~ chez mon frère** I gave my brother's place as an accommodation address **2.** BANQUE & COMM to domicile.

dominance [dɔminɑ̃s] *nf* **1.** BIOL & PHYSIOL dominance, dominant nature **2.** ZOOL dominant behaviour.

dominant, e [dɔminɑ̃, ɑ̃t] *adj* **1.** [principal - facteur, thème, trait de caractère] dominant, main ; [- espèce] dominant ; [- couleur] dominant, main, predominant ; [- intérêt] main, chief ; [- idéologie] prevailing ; [- position] commanding **2.** BIOL [caractère, gène] dominant **3.** MÉTÉOR [vent] dominant, prevailing.
◆ **dominante** *nf* **1.** [aspect prépondérant] dominant *ou* chief *ou* main characteristic **2.** [teinte] predominant colour **3.** MUS dominant **4.** UNIV main subject *UK*, major *US*.

dominateur, trice [dɔminatœr, tris] ◇ *adj* **1.** [puissant - esprit, force, nation] dominating ; [- passion] ruling **2.** [autoritaire - personne] domineering, overbearing ; [- ton] imperious.
◇ *nm, f* **1.** POLIT ruler **2.** [personne autoritaire] tyrant, despot.

domination [dɔminasjɔ̃] *nf* **1.** [politique, militaire] domination, dominion, rule ■ **territoires sous ~ allemande** territories under German domination *ou* rule **2.** [prépondérance - d'un facteur] preponderance, domination **3.** [ascendant personnel, influence] domination, influence ■ **il exerçait sur eux une étrange ~** he had a strange hold over them ■ **subir la ~ de qqn** to be dominated by sb **4.** [contrôle - de sentiments] control ■ **~ de soi-même** self-control.

dominer [3] [dɔmine] *vt* **1.** POLIT [nation, peuple] to dominate, to rule **2.** [contrôler - marché] to control, to dominate ■ **ils ont dominé le match** they had the best of *ou* they controlled the match **3.** [influencer - personne] to dominate ■ **elle domine complètement son patron** she's got her boss under her thumb **4.** [surclasser] to outclass ■ **ils se sont fait ~ en mêlée** they were weaker in the scrums ■ **elle domine toutes les autres danseuses** she outclasses the other dancers **5.** [colère] to control ■ [complexe, dégoût, échec, timidité] to overcome ■ [passion] to master, to control ■ [matière, question] to master ■ **~ la situation** to be in control of the situation **6.** [prédominer dans - œuvre, style, débat] to predominate in, to dominate ■ *(en usage absolu)* [couleur, intérêt] to predominate, to be predominant ■ [caractéristique] to dominate, to be dominant ■ [idéologie, opinion] to prevail ■ **les femmes dominent dans l'enseignement** women outnumber men in teaching **7.** [surplomber] to overlook, to dominate ▶ **~ qqn de la tête et des épaules** *pr* to be taller than sb by a head ; *fig* to tower above sb, to be head and shoulders above sb.
◆ **se dominer** *vp (emploi réfléchi)* to control o.s. ■ **ne pas savoir se ~** to have no self-control.

dominicain, e [dɔminikɛ̃, ɛn] *adj* & *nm, f* RELIG Dominican.

dominicain, e [dɔminikɛ̃, ɛn] *adj* [de Saint-Domingue] Dominican.
◆ **Dominicain, e** *nm, f* Dominican.

dominical, e, aux [dɔminikal, o] *adj* Sunday *(modif)*, dominical *sout*.

dominion [dɔminjɔ̃] *nm* dominion.

Dominique [dɔminik] *npr f* : **la ~** Dominica ■ **à la ~** in Dominica.

domino [dɔmino] *nm* **1.** JEUX [vêtement] domino ■ **jouer aux ~s** to play dominoes **2.** ÉLECTR connecting block.

Domitien [dɔmisjɛ̃] *npr* Domitian.

Dom Juan [dɔ̃ʒɥɑ̃] *npr* = **Don Juan**.

dommage [dɔmaʒ] *nm* **1.** DR [préjudice] harm, injury ■ **causer un ~ à qqn** to cause *ou* to do sb harm ▶ **~ corporel** physical injury ■ **~s de guerre** war damage ■ **~s et intérêts, ~s-intérêts** damages **2.** *(gén pl)* [dégât matériel] : **~ matériel, ~s matériels** (material) damage ■ **causer des ~s à** to cause damage to ■ **en cas de ~s sur le véhicule** in case of damage to the vehicle **3.** [expression d'un regret] : **(c'est) ~!** what a shame *ou* pity! ■ **c'est vraiment ~ de devoir abattre ce chêne** it's a real shame to have to cut down this oak ■ **ça ne m'intéresse pas! – ~!** I'm not interested! – pity! ■ **~ que tu n'aies pas pu venir!** what a pity *ou* shame you couldn't come! ■ **je ne peux pas venir – ~ pour toi!** I can't come – too bad (for you)!

dommageable [dɔmaʒabl] *adj* detrimental, damaging ■ **~ à** detrimental to, damaging to.

domotique [dɔmɔtik] *nf* home automation.

domptable [dɔ̃tabl] *adj* tameable ■ **facilement/difficilement ~** easy/difficult to tame.

domptage [dɔ̃taʒ] *nm* taming.

dompter [3] [dɔ̃te] *vt* **1.** [animal] to tame **2.** *litt* [révoltés] to quash ■ [peuple] to subjugate **3.** [énergie, vent, torrent] to master ■ [rébellion] to break, to put down *(sép)*.

dompteur, euse [dɔ̃tœr, øz] *nm, f* tamer, liontamer.

DOM-TOM [dɔmtɔm] (*abr de* **départements et territoires d'outre-mer**) *npr formerly French overseas départements and territories.*

DOM-TOM

This is the abbreviation that is still commonly used for French overseas possessions, although the ***Départements d'Outre-Mer*** are now officially called ***DROM*** *(Départements et Régions d'Outre-Mer)* and the *Territoire d'Outre-mer* are now officially called ***COM*** *(Collectivités d'Outre-Mer)* or ***POM*** *(Pays d'Outre-Mer)*. Guadeloupe, Martinique, Guyane and La Réunion have ***département*** status, and their inhabitants are French citizens. The ***collectivités*** include Wallis and Futuna, French Polynesia, New Caledonia and French territories at the Poles. The territories are independent, though supervised by a French government representative.

don [dɔ̃] *nm* **1.** [aptitude naturelle] talent, gift ■ **avoir le ~ de voyance** to be clairvoyant ■ **elle a le ~ de trouver des vêtements pas chers** she has a flair for finding cheap clothes ■ **tu as le ~ d'envenimer les situations!** you have a knack for stirring up trouble! ■ **elle a un ~ pour la danse** she has a talent for dancing, she's a gifted dancer **2.** [cadeau] gift, donation ■ **la collection dont elle m'a fait ~** the collection she gave me as a present ■ **ceux qui ont fait ~ de leur vie pour leur pays** those who have laid down *ou* sacrificed their lives for their country ▶ **le ~ de soi** *ou* **de sa personne** self-denial, self-sacrifice ■ **~ en argent** cash donation ■ **~ en nature** donation in kind

3. DR donation ▪ **faire ~ d'un bien à qqn** to donate a piece of property to sb **4.** MÉD donation, donating ▪ **encourager les ~s d'organes** to promote organ donation **5.** [en Espagne] Don.

DON [dɔn] *nm* = **disque optique numérique**.

donataire [dɔnatɛr] *nmf* donee, recipient.

donateur, trice [dɔnatœr, tris] *nm, f* donor.

donation [dɔnasjɔ̃] *nf* [gén] donation, disposition ▪ [d'argent] donation ▪ **faire une ~ à un musée** to make a donation to a museum ➜ **~ entre vifs** donation inter vivos.

donation-partage [dɔnasjɔ̃partaʒ] (*pl* **donations-partages**) *nf* settlement *(laying out division of wealth between family members in the event of death)*.

donc [dɔ̃k] *conj* **1.** [par conséquent] so, therefore ▪ **je n'en sais rien, inutile ~ de me le demander** I don't know anything about it, so there's no use asking me ▪ **il faudra ~ envisager une autre solution** we should therefore think of another solution **2.** [indiquant une transition] so ▪ **nous disions ~ que...** so, we were saying that... **3.** [indiquant la surprise] so ▪ **c'était ~ toi!** so it was you! **4.** [renforçant une interrogation, une assertion, une injonction] : **mais qu'y a-t-il ~?** what's the matter, then? ▪ **fermez ~ la porte!** shut the door, will you! ▪ **viens ~ avec nous!** come on, come with us! ▪ **allons ~, vous vous trompez** come on (now), you're mistaken ▪ **allons ~, je ne te crois pas!** come off it, I don't believe you! ▪ **comment ~ est-ce possible?** how can that be possible? ▪ **eh ben dis ~!** well, really! ▪ **essaie ~!** go on, try! ▪ **essaie ~ pour voir!** *iron* just (you) try it!, go on then! ▪ **tiens ~!** well, well, well! ▪ **dites ~, pour qui vous vous prenez?** look here, who do you think you are? ▪ **dis ~, à propos, tu l'as vue hier soir?** oh, by the way, did you see her yesterday evening? ▪ **range ~ tes affaires!** why don't you put your things away?

dondon [dɔ̃dɔ̃] *nf fam péj* **une grosse ~** a big fat lump.

donjon [dɔ̃ʒɔ̃] *nm* keep, donjon.

don Juan [dɔ̃ʒɥɑ̃] (*pl* **dons Juans**) *nm* **1.** [séducteur] Don Juan, lady's man **2.** MUS & LITTÉR : **'Don Juan'** ***Mozart*** 'Don Giovanni' ▪ ***Byron*** 'Don Juan' ▪ ***Pouchkine*** 'The Stone Guest'.

donjuanesque [dɔ̃ʒɥanɛsk] *adj* [attitude, manières] of a Don Juan.

donjuanisme [dɔ̃ʒɥanism] *nm* donjuanism, philandering.

donne [dɔn] *nf* CARTES deal ▪ **il y a eu fausse** *ou* **mauvaise ~** there was a misdeal.

donné, e [dɔne] *adj* **1.** [heure, lieu] fixed, given ▪ **sur un parcours ~** on a given *ou* certain route **2.** [particulier, spécifique] : **sur ce point ~** on this particular point ▪ **à cet instant ~** at this (very) moment ▪ **à un moment ~** at one point **3.** [bon marché] : **c'est ~!** it's dirt cheap! ▪ **c'est pas ~!** it's hardly what you'd call cheap!

➜ **donné** *nm* PHILOS given.

➜ **donnée** *nf* **1.** INFORM, MATH & SC piece of data, datum *sout* ▪ **~es** data ▪ **fichier/saisie/transmission de ~es** data file/capture/transmission ▪ **en ~es corrigées des variations saisonnières** ÉCON with adjustments for seasonal variations, seasonally adjusted **2.** [information] piece of information ▪ **~es** facts, information ▪ **je ne connais pas toutes les ~es du problème** I don't have all the information about this question.

donner [3] [dɔne] <> *vt*

A. CÉDER, ACCORDER
B. CONFÉRER
C. GÉNÉRER
D. EXPRIMER, COMMUNIQUER

A. CÉDER, ACCORDER

1. [offrir] to give ▪ [se débarrasser de] to give away *(sép)* ▪ [distribuer] to give out *(sép)* ▪ **~ qqch à qqn** to give sthg to sb, to give sb sthg ▪ **~ qqch en cadeau à qqn** to make sb a present of sthg ▪ **~ qqch en souvenir à qqn** to give *ou* to leave sb sthg as a souvenir ▪ **il est joli, ce tableau! – je te le donne** what a lovely picture! – please have it ▪ **à ce prix-là, ma petite dame, je vous le donne!** at that price, dear, I'm giving it away! ▪ **c'était donné, l'examen, cette année!** *fam* the exam was a piece of cake this year! ▪ **dis donc, on te l'a donné, ton permis de conduire!** *hum* how on earth did you pass your driving test! ▪ **~ sa place à qqn dans le train** to give up one's seat to sb on the train ▪ **~ à boire à un enfant** to give a child a drink *ou* something to drink ▪ **~ à manger aux enfants/chevaux** to feed the children/horses ▪ *(en usage absolu)* to give ▪ **~ aux pauvres** to give to the poor ▪ **~ de son temps** to give up one's time ▪ **~ de sa personne** to give of o.s. ➜ **j'ai déjà donné!** *fam* I've been there *ou* through that already!

2. DR [léguer] to leave ▪ [faire don public de - argent, œuvre d'art, organe] to donate, to give

3. [accorder - subvention] to give, to hand out *(sép)* ; [- faveur, interview, liberté] to give, to grant ; [- prix, récompense] to give, to award ▪ **~ sa fille en mariage à qqn** to marry one's daughter to sb ▪ **~ la permission à qqn de faire qqch** to allow sb to do sthg, to give sb permission to do sthg ▪ **~ rendez-vous à qqn** ADMIN to make an appointment with sb ; [ami, amant] to make a date with sb ▪ **~ à qqn l'occasion de faire qqch** to give sb the opportunity to do sthg *ou* of doing sthg ▪ **~ son soutien à qqn** to give one's support to sb, to support sb ▪ *(tournure impersonnelle)* **il n'est pas donné à tout le monde de...** not everybody is fortunate enough to...

4. [laisser - délai] to give, to leave

5. [confier] to give, to hand, to pass ▪ **~ une tâche à qqn** to entrust sb with a job ▪ **elle m'a donné sa valise à porter** she gave me her suitcase to carry ▪ **~ ses enfants à garder** to have one's children looked after

6. [remettre - gén] to give ; [- devoir] to give, to hand in *(sép)* ▪ **donne la balle, Rex, donne!** come on Rex, let go (of the ball)! ▪ **donnez vos papiers** hand over your papers

7. [vendre - suj: commerçant] to give

8. [payer] to give ▪ **combien t'en a-t-on donné?** how much did you get for it? ▪ **je donnerais cher pour le savoir** I'd give a lot to know that ▪ **je donnerais n'importe quoi pour le retrouver** I'd give anything to find it again

9. [administrer - médicament, sacrement] to give, to administer *sout* ; [- bain] to give ▪ **~ 15 ans de prison à qqn** to give sb a 15-year prison sentence ▪ **~ une punition à qqn** to punish sb

10. [appliquer - coup, baiser] to give ▪ **~ une fessée à qqn** to smack sb's bottom, to spank sb ▪ **~ un coup de rabot/râteau/pinceau à qqch** to go over sthg with a plane/rake/paintbrush

11. [passer, transmettre] to give, to pass on *(sép)* ▪ **son père lui a donné le goût du théâtre** she got her liking for the theatre from her father

12. [organiser - dîner, bal] to give, to throw

13. *loc* **je vous le donne en cent** *ou* **mille** *fam* you'll never guess in a month of Sundays *ou* in a million years

B. CONFÉRER

1. [assigner] to give ▪ **~ un nom à qqn** to give sb a name, to name sb ▪ **je donne peu d'importance à ces choses** I attach little importance to these things

2. [attribuer] : **on ne lui donnerait pas son âge** he doesn't look his age ▪ **quel âge me donnez-vous?** how old would you say I am?

3. [prédire] to give ▪ **je ne lui donne pas trois mois** [à vivre] I give her less than three months to live ; [avant d'échouer] I'll give it three months at the most

C. GÉNÉRER

1. [suj: champ] to yield ▪ [suj: arbre fruitier] to give, to produce

2. [susciter, provoquer - courage, énergie, espoir] to give ; [- migraine] to give, to cause ; [- sensation] to give, to create ; [- impression] to give, to produce ▪ **~ du souci à qqn** to worry sb ▪ **les enfants donnent du travail** children are a lot of work ▪ **~ des boutons à qqn** to make sb come out in spots ▪ **faire la vaisselle me donne des boutons** *fig* I'm allergic to washing-up ▪ **ça donne la diarrhée** it gives you *ou* causes diarrhoea ▪ **~ chaud/froid/faim/soif à qqn** to make sb hot/cold/hungry/thirsty ▪ **~ mal au cœur à qqn** to make sb (feel) sick *ou* nauseous

3. [conférer - prestige] to confer, to give ; [- aspect, charme] to give, to lend ▪ **le grand air t'a donné des couleurs** the fresh air has brought colour to your cheeks ▪ **pour ~ plus de mystère à l'histoire** to make the story more mysterious

4. [aboutir à - résultats] to give, to yield ; [- effet] to result in ▪ **en ajoutant les impôts, cela donne la somme suivante** when you add (in) *ou* on the tax, it comes to the following amount ➜ **et ta candidature, ça donne quelque chose?** have you had anything about your application? ▪ **les recherches n'ont rien donné** the search was fruitless ▪ **la robe ne donne pas grand-chose comme**

cela, essaie avec une ceinture the dress doesn't look much like that, try it with a belt ▪ **j'ai ajouté du vin à la sauce – qu'est-ce que ça donne?** I've added some wine to the sauce – what is it like now?

D. EXPRIMER, COMMUNIQUER

1. [présenter, fournir - garantie, preuve, précision] to give, to provide ; [- explication] to give ; [- argument] to put forward *(sép)* ; [- ordre, consigne] to give ▪ **~ un conseil à qqn** to give sb a piece of advice, to advise sb ▪ **~ ses sources** to quote one's sources ▪ **~ une certaine image de son pays** to show one's country in a particular light ▪ **~ à entendre** *ou* **comprendre que** to let it be understood that ▪ **ces faits nous ont été donnés comme vrais** we were led to believe that these facts were true ▪ **~ qqch pour certain** to give sthg as a certainty ▪ **on le donnait pour riche** he was said *ou* thought to be rich
2. [dire] to give ▪ **~ des nouvelles à qqn** to give sb news ▪ **donnez-moi de ses nouvelles** tell me how he is ◆ **je te le donne pour ce que ça vaut** *fam* that's what I was told, anyway
3. [indiquer - suj: instrument] to give, to indicate, to show
4. *fam* [dénoncer] to give away *(sép)*, to rat on, to shop *UK*
5. [rendre public - causerie, cours] to give ; [- œuvre, spectacle] to put on ▪ **qu'est-ce qu'on donne au Rex?** what's on at the Rex?
◇ *vi* **1.** [produire - arbre] to bear fruit, to yield ; [- potager, verger, terre] to yield ▪ **la vigne a bien/mal donné cette année** the vineyard had a good/bad yield this year ▪ **dis donc, elle donne, ta chaîne hi-fi!** *fam* that's a mean sound system you've got there! ◆ **~ à plein** [radio] to be on full blast, to be blaring (out) ; [campagne de publicité, soirée] to be in full swing ▪ **le soleil donne à plein** the sun is beating down **2.** CARTES to deal ▪ **à toi de ~** your deal **3.** [attaquer] to charge ▪ **faire ~ la garde/troupe** to send in the guards/troops.

◆ **donner dans** *v+prép* **1.** [tomber dans] : **~ dans une embuscade** to be ambushed ▪ **sans ~ dans le mélodrame** without becoming too melodramatic **2.** [se cogner contre] : **l'enfant est allé ~ dans la fenêtre** the child crashed into the window **3.** [déboucher sur] to give out onto ▪ **l'escalier donne dans une petite cour** the staircase gives out onto *ou* leads to *ou* leads into a small courtyard.

◆ **donner de** *v+prép* **1.** [cogner avec] : **~ du coude/de la tête contre une porte** to bump one's elbow/one's head against a door **2.** [utiliser] : **~ du cor** to sound the horn ▪ **~ de la voix** to raise one's voice ◆ **~ de la tête** [animal] to shake its head ▪ **ne plus savoir où ~ de la tête** *fig* to be run off one's feet **3.** NAUT : **~ de la bande** to list **4.** *loc* **elle lui donne du "monsieur"** she calls him "Sir".

◆ **donner sur** *v+prép* **1.** [se cogner contre] : **la barque alla ~ sur le rocher** the boat crashed into the rock **2.** [être orienté vers] : **la chambre donne sur le jardin/la mer** the room overlooks the garden/the sea ▪ **chambre donnant sur la mer** room with a sea view.

◆ **se donner** ◇ *vp (emploi passif)* [film, pièce] to be on.
◇ *vpi* **1.** [employer son énergie] : **monte sur scène et donne-toi à fond** get on the stage and give it all you've got ▪ **se ~ à : se ~ à une cause** to devote o.s. *ou* one's life to a cause ▪ **elle s'est donnée à fond** *ou* **complètement dans son entreprise** she put all her effort into her business **2.** *sout* [sexuellement] : **se ~ à qqn** to give o.s. to sb.
◇ *vpt* **1.** [donner à soi-même] : **se ~ un coup de marteau sur les doigts** to hit one's fingers with a hammer ▪ **se ~ les moyens de faire qqch** to give o.s. the means to do sthg ▪ **se ~ du bon temps** [gén] to have fun ; *euphém* to give o.s. a good time ‖ [s'accorder - délai] to give *ou* to allow o.s. **2.** [échanger] to give one another *ou* each other ▪ **se ~ un baiser** to give each other a kiss, to kiss ▪ **ils se sont donné leurs impressions** they swapped views **3.** [se doter de] to give o.s. **4.** [prétendre avoir] : **il se donne trente ans** he claims to be thirty **5.** *loc* **s'en ~ à cœur joie, s'en ~ : les enfants s'en sont donné au square** the children had the time of their lives in the park.

◆ **se donner pour** *vp+prép* to pass o.s. off as, to claim to be.

◆ **donnant donnant** *loc adv* that's fair, fair's fair ▪ **d'accord, mais c'est donnant donnant** OK, but I want something in return.

donneur, euse [dɔnœr, øz] *nm, f* **1.** MÉD donor ▪ **~ d'organe/de sang** organ/blood donor ▪ **~ universel** universal blood donor **2.** JEUX dealer **3.** *loc* **~ de leçons : je ne veux pas me transformer en ~ de leçons, mais...** I don't want to lecture you, but... **4.** *fam* [délateur] squealer, informer.
◆ **donneur** *nm* **1.** ÉCON & FIN : **~ d'ordres** principal **2.** MÉD : **~ de sperme** sperm donor.

don Quichotte [dɔ̃kiʃɔt] *(pl* **dons Quichottes***) nm* **1.** [redresseur de torts] : **se poser en ~** to adopt a quixotic stance **2.** LITTÉR : **'Don Quichotte de la Manche'** *Cervantès* 'Don Quixote'.

donquichottisme [dɔ̃kiʃɔtism] *nm* quixotic attitudes.

dont [dɔ̃] *pron rel* **1.** [exprimant le complément du nom - personne] whose ; [- chose] whose, of which *sout* ▪ **le club ~ je suis membre** the club to which I belong *ou* of which I'm a member *sout*, the club I belong to **2.** [exprimant la partie d'un tout - personnes] of whom ; [- choses] of which ▪ **des livres ~ la plupart ne valent rien** books, most of which are worthless ▪ **deux personnes ont téléphoné, ~ ton frère** two people phoned, including your brother **3.** [exprimant le complément de l'adjectif] : **le service ~ vous êtes responsable** the service for which you are responsible ▪ **c'est la seule photo ~ je sois fier** it's the only photograph I'm proud of *ou* of which I'm proud **4.** [exprimant l'objet indirect] : **ce ~ nous avons discuté** what we talked about ▪ **une corvée ~ je me passerais bien** a chore (which) I could well do without **5.** [exprimant le complément du verbe - indiquant la provenance, l'agent, la manière *etc*] : **une personne ~ on ne sait rien** a person nobody knows anything about ▪ **cette femme ~ je sais qu'elle n'a pas d'enfants** that woman who I know doesn't have any children ▪ **la famille ~ je viens** the family (which) I come from ▪ **les amis ~ il est entouré** the friends he is surrounded by ▪ **les cadeaux ~ il a été comblé** the many presents (which) he received.

donzelle [dɔ̃zɛl] *nf fam hum* young lady *ou* thing.

dopage [dɔpaʒ] *nm* drug use *(in sport)*.

dopamine [dɔpamin] *nf* dopamine.

dopant, e [dɔpɑ̃, ɑ̃t] *adj* stimulant *(modif)*.
◆ **dopant** *nm* drug *(used as stimulant in competitions)*.

dope[△] [dɔp] *nf* dope.

doper [3] [dɔpe] *vt* **1.** [droguer] to dope *(in a competition)* ▪ **~ l'économie** to stimulate the economy artificially ▪ **~ les ventes** to boost sales **2.** CHIM to dope.
◆ **se doper** *vp (emploi réfléchi)* to take drugs *(in a competition)*.

doping [dɔpiŋ] = **dopage**.

Doppler [dɔplɛr] *npr* : **effet ~** Doppler effect.

dorade [dɔrad] = **daurade**.

Dordogne [dɔrdɔɲ] *npr f* : **la ~** [département] (the) Dordogne *(département in Aquitaine; chef-lieu: Périgueux, code: 24)* ; [rivière] the Dordogne (River).

doré, e [dɔre] *adj* **1.** [bouton, robinetterie] gilt, gilded ▪ **~ à la feuille** gilded with gold leaf ▪ **~ sur tranche** [livre] gilt-edged, with gilded edges **2.** [chevelure, lumière] golden ▪ [peau] golden brown ▪ **ses cheveux étaient d'un blond ~** he had golden hair ‖ [gâteau, viande] browned, golden brown **3.** [idéal - jours, rêves] golden **4.** [dans des noms d'animaux] golden.
◆ **doré** *nm* **1.** [dorure] gilt **2.** *Québec* ZOOL yellow *ou* wall-eyed pike.

dorénavant [dɔrenavɑ̃] *adv* [à partir de maintenant] from now on, henceforth *sout*, henceforward *sout* ▪ [dans le passé] from then on.

dorer [3] [dɔre] ◇ *vt* **1.** [couvrir d'or] to gild ▪ **faire ~ qqch** to have sthg gilded ◆ **~ la pilule à qqn** *fam* to sugar the pill for sb **2.** [brunir - peau] to give a golden colour to, to tan ; [- blés, poires] to turn gold ; [- paysage] to shed a golden light on **3.** CULIN : **~ une pâte à l'œuf/au lait** to glaze pastry with egg yolk/with milk.
◇ *vi* CULIN to turn golden ▪ **faites ~ les oignons** cook *ou* fry the onions until golden.
◆ **se dorer** *vp (emploi réfléchi)* [touriste] to sunbathe ◆ **se ~ la pilule** *fam* [bronzer] to lie in the sun getting o.s. cooked to a turn *hum* ; [ne rien faire] to do sweet FA *UK ou* zilch *US*.

doreur, euse [dɔrœr, øz] *nm, f* gilder.

dorien, enne [dɔrjɛ̃, ɛn] *adj* **1.** HIST & MUS Dorian **2.** LING Doric.
◆ **Dorien, enne** *nm, f* Dorian.

dorique [dɔrik] ◇ *adj* [ordre] Doric.
◇ *nm* : **le ~** the Doric order.

dorloter [3] [dɔrlɔte] *vt* to pamper, to cosset ■ **il adore se faire ~** he loves being looked after.

dormant, e [dɔrmɑ̃, ɑ̃t] *adj* **1.** [eau] still **2.** *litt* [passion, sensualité] dormant **3.** BIOL dormant, latent **4.** CONSTR [bâti, chassis] fixed **5.** DR & FIN.
◆ **dormant** *nm* **1.** CONSTR [bâti] fixed frame, casing *(C)* ■ [vitre] fixed **2.** NAUT standing end.

dormeur, euse [dɔrmœr, øz] ◇ *adj* [poupée, poupon] sleeping.
◇ *nm, f* sleeper ■ **c'est un grand** *ou* **gros ~** he likes his sleep.

dormir [36] [dɔrmir] *vi* **1.** PHYSIOL to sleep ■ [à un moment précis] to be asleep, to be sleeping ■ **tu as bien dormi?** did you sleep well? ■ **dors bien!** sleep tight! ■ **j'ai dormi tout l'après-midi** I was asleep *ou* I slept all afternoon ■ **il dort tard le dimanche** he sleeps in on Sundays ■ **on dort mal dans ce lit** you can't get a good night's sleep in this bed ■ **tu as pu ~ dans le train?** did you manage to get some sleep on the train? ■ **je n'ai pas dormi de la nuit** I didn't sleep a wink all night ■ **la situation m'inquiète, je n'en dors pas** *ou* **plus (la nuit)** the situation worries me, I'm losing sleep over it ■ **le thé m'empêche de ~** tea keeps me awake ■ **avoir envie de ~** to feel sleepy ■ **~ d'un sommeil léger** [habituellement] to be a light sleeper ; [à tel moment] to be dozing ■ **~ d'un sommeil profond** *ou* **lourd** *ou* **de plomb** [habituellement] to be a heavy sleeper ; [à tel moment] to be fast asleep, to be sound asleep, to be in a deep sleep ➊ **~ à poings fermés** to be fast asleep, to be sleeping like a baby ■ **~ comme un ange** [bébé] to be sound asleep ; [adulte] to sleep like a baby ■ **~ comme une bûche** *ou* **un loir** *ou* **une marmotte** *ou* **une souche** *ou* **un sabot** to sleep like a log ■ **~ debout : tu dors debout** you can't (even) keep awake, you're dead on your feet ■ **~ sur ses deux oreilles : tu peux dormir sur tes deux oreilles** there's no reason for you to worry, you can sleep soundly in your bed at night ■ **je ne dors que d'un œil** [je dors mal] I can hardly sleep, I hardly get a wink of sleep ; [je reste vigilant] I sleep with one eye open ■ **qui dort dîne** *prov* he who sleeps forgets his hunger **2.** [être sans activité - secteur] to be dormant *ou* asleep ; [- volcan] to be dormant ; [- économies personnelles] to lie idle ; [- économie nationale] to be stagnant ■ **ils ont laissé ~ le projet** they left the project on the back burner **3.** [être inattentif] : **ce n'est pas le moment de ~!** now's the time for action!

dormitif, ive [dɔrmitif, iv] *adj* **1.** *arch* [qui fait dormir] sleep-inducing, soporific **2.** *hum* [ennuyeux] soporific.

dorsal, e, aux [dɔrsal, o] *adj* ANAT & ZOOL dorsal, back *(modif)* ■ **la face ~e de la main** the back of the hand.
◆ **dorsal** *nm* ANAT : **grand ~, long ~** latissimus dorsi.
◆ **dorsale** *nf* **1.** ZOOL dorsal fin **2.** GÉOL [élévation] ridge ■ [montagne] mountain range.

dort *etc v* ▷ **dormir**.

dortoir [dɔrtwar] *nm* dormitory ■ **les ~s de la caserne** the sleeping quarters of the barracks ➊ **cité** *ou* **ville ~** dormitory town.

dorure [dɔryr] *nf* **1.** [en or] gilt **2.** [processus] gilding ■ **~ à la feuille/à la poudre** gold leaf/powder gilding ■ **~ sur tranches** [reliure] edge-gilding.

doryphore [dɔrifɔr] *nm* Colorado *ou* potato beetle.

dos [do] *nm* **1.** ANAT back ■ **le bas de son ~** the small of her back ■ **avoir le ~ rond** to be hunched up *ou* round-shouldered ■ **avoir le ~ voûté** to have a stoop ■ **j'ai mal au ~** my back hurts, I've got (a) backache ■ **j'avais le soleil dans le ~** the sun was behind me *ou* on my back ■ **être sur le ~** to be (lying) on one's back ■ **tourner le ~ à qqn** [assis] to sit with one's back to sb ; [debout] to stand with one's back to sb ; [l'éviter] to turn one's back on sb ■ **je ne l'ai vu que de ~** I only saw him from behind *ou* the back ■ **où est la gare? – vous lui tournez le ~** where is the station? – you're going away from it ■ **dès que j'ai le ~ tourné, il fait des bêtises** as soon as my back is turned, he gets into mischief ➊ **avoir bon ~ : comme d'habitude, j'ai bon ~!** as usual, I get the blame! ■ **avoir le ~ large : j'ai le ~ large mais il ne faut pas exagérer!** I can take a lot *ou* I may be resilient, but there are limits! ■ **avoir qqch sur le ~** *fam* : **ce gosse n'a rien sur le ~!** that kid's not dressed warmly enough! ■ **c'est moi qui ai tous les préparatifs sur le ~** I've been saddled with all the preparations ■ **faire qqch dans** *ou* **derrière le ~ de qqn** to do sthg behind sb's back ■ **être sur le ~ de** *fam* : **tu es toujours sur le ~ de ce gosse, laisse-le un peu!** you're always nagging that kid, leave him alone! ■ **vous aurez les syndicats sur le ~** the unions will be breathing down your necks ■ **faire le gros ~** [chat] to arch its back ; *fig* to lie low ■ **faire qqch sur le ~ de : ils ont bâti leur empire sur le ~ des indigènes** they built their empire at the expense of the natives ■ **l'avoir dans le ~** *fam* : **il l'a dans le ~!** he's been had *ou* done! ■ **se mettre qqn à ~** to put sb's back up ■ **il les avait tous à ~** they were all after him ■ **mettre qqch sur le ~ de qqn** *fam* [crime, erreur] to pin sthg on sb ■ **je n'ai rien/pas grand-chose à me mettre sur le ~** I have got nothing/virtually nothing to wear ■ **si le fisc lui tombe sur le ~, ça va lui coûter cher!** *fam* if the taxman gets hold of *ou* catches him, it'll cost him! ■ **avoir le ~ au mur** to have one's back to the wall **2.** [d'une fourchette, d'un habit] back ■ [d'un couteau] blunt edge ■ [d'un livre] spine ➊ **il n'y est pas allé avec le ~ de la cuillère!** *fam* [dans une action] he didn't go in for half-measures! ; [dans une discussion] he didn't mince words! **3.** SPORT : **~ crawlé** back crawl.
◆ **à dos de** *loc prép* on the back of ■ **aller à ~ d'âne/d'éléphant** to ride (on) a donkey/an elephant ■ **le matériel est transporté à ~ de lamas/d'hommes** the equipment is carried by llamas/men.
◆ **au dos** *loc adv* [d'une feuille] on the other side *ou* the back, overleaf.
◆ **au dos de** *loc prép* [d'une feuille] on the back of ■ **signer au ~ d'un chèque** to endorse a cheque.
◆ **dos à dos** *loc adv* with their backs to one another ■ **mettez-vous ~ à ~** *pr* stand back to back *ou* with your backs to one another ■ **mettre** *ou* **renvoyer deux personnes ~ à ~** *fig* to refuse to get involved in an argument between two people.

DOS, Dos [dɔs] (*abr de* **Disc Operating System**) *nm* DOS.

dosage [dozaʒ] *nm* **1.** [détermination] measurement of *ou* measuring a quantity ■ **faire un ~** to determine a quantity **2.** [dose précise de médicaments] (prescribed) dose **3.** [mélange] : **le ~ de ce cocktail est...** the (correct) proportions for this cocktail are... **4.** [équilibre] balance.

dos-d'âne [dodan] *nm inv* sleeping policeman UK, speed bump US ■ **pont en ~** humpback bridge.

dose [doz] *nf* **1.** PHARM dose ■ MÉD dose, dosage ■ **prendre une forte ~** *ou* **une ~ massive de sédatifs** to take an overdose of sedatives ■ **'respecter les ~s prescrites'** 'do not exceed the prescribed dose' **2.** COMM [quantité prédéterminée - gén] dose, measure ; [- en sachet] sachet ■ **une ~ de désherbant pour 10 ~s d'eau** one part weedkiller to 10 parts water **3.** [quantité - d'un aliment, d'un composant] amount, quantity ■ **~ de : ses documentaires ont tous une petite ~ d'humour** there's a touch of humour in all his documentaries ■ **il a une ~ de paresse peu commune** he's uncommonly lazy ■ **avec une petite ~ de bon sens/volonté** with a modicum of common sense/willpower ■ **j'ai eu ma ~ de problèmes!** *fam* I've had my (fair) share of problems! ■ **du moment qu'il a sa ~ journalière de télévision, il est content** as long as he gets his daily dose of television, he's happy **4.** *loc* **avoir sa ~** *fam* [lassé, ivre] : **il a sa ~** he's had a bellyful *ou* as much as he can stand ■ **en avoir sa ~** *fam* : **les problèmes, j'en ai ma ~!** *fam* don't talk to me about problems! ■ **il tient sa** *ou* **en a une bonne ~** *fam* he's as thick as two short planks UK, he's as dumb as they come US.
◆ **à faible dose** *loc adv* in small doses *ou* quantities.
◆ **à forte dose** *loc adv* in large quantities *ou* amounts.
◆ **à haute dose** *loc adv* in large doses *ou* quantities ■ **irradié à haute ~** having received a large level of radiation.
◆ **à petite dose, à petites doses** *loc adv* in small doses *ou* quantities ■ **j'aime bien le sport/ma sœur, mais à petites ~s** I like sport/my sister, but (only) in small doses.

doser [3] [doze] *vt* **1.** [médicament] to measure a dose of ■ [composant, ingrédient] to measure out *(sép)* **2.** [équilibrer -

cocktail, vinaigrette] to use the correct proportions for ▪ **sa collection de printemps dose admirablement fantaisie et rigueur** his spring collection is a wonderful combination of fantasy and severity **3.** [utiliser avec mesure] : **~ ses forces** *ou* **son effort** to pace o.s. ▪ **il faut savoir ~ ses critiques** you have to know how far you can go in your criticism **4.** MÉD [albumine] to determine the quantity of.

doseur [dozœr] *nm* measure ▪ *(comme adj)* **bouchon/gobelet ~** measuring cap/cup.

dossard [dosar] *nm* SPORT number *(worn by a competitor)* ▪ **portant le ~ numéro 3** wearing number 3.

dossier [dosje] *nm* **1.** [d'une chaise, d'un canapé] back **2.** [documents] file, dossier ▪ **avoir un ~ sur qqn** to keep a file on sb, to keep sb on file ▪ **constituer** *ou* **établir un ~ sur un suspect** to build up a file on a suspect ▪ **les élèves doivent faire un ~ sur un sujet de leur choix** the pupils must do a project on the subject of their choice ▮ DR [d'un prévenu] record ▪ [d'une affaire] case ▪ ADMIN [d'un cas social] case file ➲ **~ de candidature** application ▪ **~ d'inscription** UNIV registration forms ▪ **~ médical** medical file *ou* records ▪ **~ scolaire** ÉDUC school record *UK*, student file *US* **3.** PRESSE, RADIO & TV : **numéro spécial avec un ~ sur le Brésil** special issue with an extended report on Brazil ➲ **~ de presse** press pack **4.** [chemise cartonnée] folder, file ▪ INFORM folder.

Dostoïevski [dɔstɔjɛfski] *npr* Dostoevski, Dostoievsky.

dot [dɔt] *nf* [d'une mariée] dowry ▪ [d'une religieuse] (spiritual) dowry.

◆ **en dot** *loc adv* as dowry ▪ **apporter qqch en ~** to bring sthg as one's dowry, to bring a dowry of sthg.

dotation [dɔtasjɔ̃] *nf* **1.** [fonds versés - à un particulier, une collectivité] endowment ; [- à un service public] grant, funds **2.** [revenus - du président] (personal) allowance, emolument ; [- d'un souverain] civil list **3.** [attribution - de matériel] equipment ▪ **la somme est réservée pour la ~ du service en ordinateurs** the sum has been earmarked for providing *ou* equipping the department with computers ➲ **~ en personnel** *Québec* allocation of posts *(in the public service)*.

doter [3] [dɔte] *vt* **1.** [équiper] : **~ qqch de** to provide *ou* to equip sthg with **2.** [gratifier] : **pays doté d'une puissante industrie** country with a strong industrial base ▪ **quand on est doté d'une bonne santé** when you enjoy good health **3.** [donner une dot à] to give a dowry to **4.** [financer - particulier, collectivité] to endow ; [- service public] to fund.

◆ **se doter de** *vp+prép* to acquire.

douairière [dwɛrjɛr] *nf* **1.** [veuve] dowager (lady) **2.** *péj* [femme] rich old woman.

douane [dwan] *nf* **1.** [à la frontière] : **poste de ~** customs ▪ **passer à la ~** to go through customs **2.** [administration] : **la ~, les ~s, le service des ~s** [gén] the Customs (service) ; [en Grande-Bretagne] Customs and Excise (department) ▪ **entreposer qqch en ~** to put sthg in *ou* into bond ▪ **inspecteur des ~s** customs officer **3.** [taxe] : **(droits de) ~** customs duty *ou* dues ▪ **exempté de ~** duty-free, non-dutiable.

douanier, ère [dwanje, ɛr] ◇ *adj* [tarif, visite] customs *(modif)*.

◇ *nm, f* customs officer.

doublage [dublaʒ] *nm* **1.** CINÉ [d'un film] dubbing ▪ [d'un acteur] : **il n'y a pas de ~ pour les cascades** there's no stand-in for the stunts **2.** [habillage d'un coffre] lining **3.** COUT lining.

double [dubl] ◇ *adj* **1.** [deux fois plus grand - mesure, production] double ▪ **un ~ whisky** a double whisky ➲ **chambre/lit ~** double room/bed ▪ **disquette ~ densité/~ face** double-density/double-sided disk ▪ **~ menton** double chin **2.** [à deux éléments identiques] double ▪ **contrat en ~ exemplaire** contract in duplicate ➲ **~ deux/cinq** JEUX double two/five ▪ **~ allumage** dual ignition ▪ **en ~ aveugle** double-blind ▪ **~ commande** dual controls ▪ **faire un ~ débrayage** to double-declutch *UK*, to double-clutch *US* ▪ **~ faute** TENNIS double fault ▪ **en ~ file : stationner en ~ file** to double-park ▪ **je suis en ~ file** I'm double-parked ▪ **à ~ fond** [mallette] double-bottomed, false-bottomed ▪ **~ nœud** double knot ▪ **~ page** double page spread ▪ **~ vitrage** double glazing ▪ **faire ~ emploi** to be redundant ▪ **faire ~ emploi avec qqch** to replicate sthg **3.** [à éléments différents - avantage, objectif] double, twofold ; [- fonction, personnalité, tarification] dual ▪ **avoir la ~ nationalité** to have dual nationality ▪ **mener une ~ vie** to lead a double life ➲ **à ~ emploi** *ou* **usage** dual-purpose *(avant n)* ▪ **~ jeu** *fig* double-dealing ▪ **jouer** *ou* **mener (un) ~ jeu** to play a double game ▪ **coup ~ : faire coup ~** CHASSE to kill two animals with one shot ; *fig* to kill two birds with one stone.

◇ *nm* **1.** [en quantité] : **six est le ~ de trois** six is twice three *ou* two times three ▪ **coûter le ~ de** to cost twice as much as ▪ **j'ai payé le ~** I paid double that price *ou* twice as much ▪ **je croyais que ça coûtait 300 euros – c'est plus du ~** I thought it was 300 euros – it's more than twice that *ou* double that price **2.** [exemplaire - d'un document] copy ; [- d'un timbre de collection] duplicate, double ▪ **tu as un ~ de la clé?** have you got a spare *ou* duplicate key? ▪ **j'ai fait faire un ~ de la clé** I had a duplicate key made **3.** [sosie] double, doppelgänger **4.** SPORT : **jouer un ~** to play (a) doubles (match) ➲ **~ messieurs/dames/mixte** men's/women's/mixed doubles.

◇ *adv* [compter] twice as much, double ▪ [voir] double.

◆ **à double sens** ◇ *loc adj* : **une phrase à ~ sens** a double-entendre.

◇ *loc adv* : **on peut prendre la remarque à ~ sens** you can interpret *ou* take that remark two ways.

◆ **à double tranchant** *loc adj* [couteau, action] double-edged, two-edged ▪ **c'est un argument à ~ tranchant** the argument cuts both ways.

◆ **à double tour** *loc adv* : **fermer à ~ tour** to double lock ▪ **enfermer qqn à ~ tour** to lock sb up.

◆ **en double** *loc adv* : **les draps sont pliés en ~** the sheets are folded double *ou* doubled over ▪ **j'ai une photo en ~** I've got two of the same photograph ▪ **jouer en ~** SPORT to play (a) doubles (match).

doublé, e [duble] *adj* **1.** COUT lined ▪ **non ~** unlined **2.** CINÉ dubbed.

◆ **doublé** *nm* **1.** CHASSE right and left **2.** [succès] double **3.** MUS turn **4.** JOAILL rolled gold.

double-clic, doubles-clics [dublklik] *nm* INFORM double-click.

double-cliquer [3] [dublklike] *vt* INFORM to double-click on ▪ **double-cliquer sur l'image** to double-click on the picture.

double-crème [dubləkrɛm] (*pl* **doubles-crèmes**) *nm* ≃ cream cheese.

double-croche [dubləkrɔʃ] (*pl* **doubles-croches**) *nf* semiquaver *UK*, sixteenth note *US*.

double-décimètre [dublədesimɛtr] *nm* ruler.

doublement[1] [dubləmɑ̃] *nm* [d'une consonne] doubling.

doublement[2] [dubləmɑ̃] *adv* doubly ▪ **c'est ~ ironique** there's a double irony there ▪ **je suis ~ déçu/surpris** I'm doubly disappointed/surprised.

doubler [3] [duble] ◇ *vt* **1.** [dépasser - coureur, véhicule] to overtake *UK*, to pass ▪ **je me suis fait ~ par un cycliste** I was overtaken by a cyclist **2.** [porter au double - bénéfices, personnel, quantité] to double ▪ **~ l'allure** *ou* **le pas** to quicken one's pace ➲ **~ la mise** JEUX to double the stake ; *fig* to raise the stakes **3.** [garnir d'une doublure - coffret, jupe, tenture] to line **4.** CINÉ [voix] to dub ▪ [acteur] to stand in for, to double ▪ **il se fait ~ pour les cascades** he's got a stand-in for his stunts **5.** [mettre en double - corde, fil] to double ; [- couverture] to fold (in half), to double (over) **6.** *fam* [trahir] : **~ qqn** [le voler] to pull a fast one on sb *(and get something that was rightly his)* ; [le devancer] to pip sb at the post *UK*, to beat sb out *US* **7.** MUS [parties] to split **8.** NAUT [cap] to double, to round ▪ **~ le cap de la trentaine** *fig* to turn thirty ▪ **l'inflation a doublé le cap des 5 %** inflation has broken the 5% barrier **9.** ÉDUC to repeat.

◇ *vi* **1.** [bénéfices, poids, quantité] to double, to increase twofold **2.** TENNIS to double bounce.

◆ **se doubler de** *vp+prép* to be coupled with.

double-rideau [dublərido] (*pl* **doubles-rideaux**) *nm* double curtains.

doublet [dublɛ] *nm* JOAILL, LING & PHYS doublet.

doublon [dublɔ̃] *nm* **1.** [pièce] doubloon **2.** IMPR doublet.

doublure [dublyr] *nf* **1.** [garniture] lining *(C)* **2.** CINÉ stand-in ▪ THÉÂTRE understudy.

douceâtre [dusatr] *adj* [odeur, goût, saveur] sweetish ▪ [sourire, ton, voix] sugary.

doucement [dusmɑ̃] *adv* **1.** [avec délicatesse, sans brusquerie - caresser, poser, prendre] gently ; [- manier] gently, with care ; [- démarrer] smoothly ▪ **~** gently!, careful! ▪ **~ avec les verres!** careful *ou* go gently with the glasses! ▪ **~ avec le champagne/poivre!** (go) easy on the champagne/pepper! ▪ **vas-y ~, il est encore petit** go easy on *ou* with him, he's only a child **2.** [lentement - marcher, progresser, rouler] slowly **3.** [graduellement - augmenter, s'élever] gently, gradually **4.** [sans bruit - chantonner] softly ▪ **parle plus ~, il dort** lower your voice *ou* keep your voice down, he's sleeping ▪ **mets la radio, mais ~** put the radio on, but quietly **5.** *fam* [discrètement] : **ça me fait ~ rigoler, son projet de créer une entreprise** his idea of setting up a company is a bit of a joke **6.** [pour calmer, contrôler] : **~, ~, vous n'allez pas vous battre, tout de même!** calm down, you don't want a fight, do you? ▪ **~, je n'ai jamais dit ça!** hold on, I never said that! **7.** *fam* [moyennement] so-so.

doucereux, euse [dusrø, øz] *adj* [goût, liqueur] sweetish ▪ *péj* sickly sweet ▪ [voix, ton, paroles] sugary, honeyed ▪ [manières, personne] suave, smooth.

doucette [dusɛt] *nf* corn salad, lamb's lettuce.

doucettement [dusɛtmɑ̃] *adv* *fam* [marcher, progresser] slowly.

douceur [dusœr] *nf* **1.** [toucher - d'une étoffe, d'une brosse] softness ; [- des cheveux, de la peau] softness, smoothness ▪ [goût - d'un vin] sweetness ; [- d'un fromage] mildness **2.** [délicatesse - de caresses, de mouvements, de manières] gentleness ; [- d'une voix] softness ▪ **parler avec ~** to speak softly ▪ **prendre qqn par la ~** to use the soft approach with sb ▪ **la ~ de vivre** the gentle pleasures of life **3.** [bonté - d'une personne] sweetness, gentleness ; [- d'un regard, d'un sourire] gentleness **4.** [d'un relief] softness ; [- d'un regard, d'un sourire] gentleness **4.** [d'un relief] softness ▪ **la ~ de ses traits** his soft features **5.** TECHNOL [d'une eau] softness **6.** MÉTÉOR mildness **7.** [friandise] sweet.

◆ **douceurs** *nfpl* **1.** [agréments] pleasures ▪ **les ~s de la vie** the pleasures of life, the pleasant things in life **2.** [propos agréables] sweet words ▪ **les deux conducteurs échangeaient des ~s** *iron* the two drivers were swapping insults.

◆ **en douceur** ◇ *loc adj* [décollage, démarrage] smooth. ◇ *loc adv* [sans brusquerie - gén] gently ; [- démarrer, s'arrêter] smoothly ▪ **réveille-moi en ~ la prochaine fois** next time, wake me up gently.

douche [duʃ] *nf* **1.** [jet d'eau] shower ▪ **prendre une ~** to have *ou* to take a shower ▪ **il est sous la ~** he's in the shower ▶ **~ écossaise** *pr* hot and cold shower *(taken successively)* ▪ **c'est la ~ écossaise avec lui!** he blows hot and cold! **2.** [bac, cabine] shower unit ▪ **les ~s** the showers **3.** *fam* [averse] : **recevoir** *ou* **prendre une bonne ~** to get drenched *ou* soaked **4.** *fam* [choc, surprise] shock ▪ [déception] let-down, anticlimax ▪ **ça m'a fait l'effet d'une ~ (froide)** it came as a shock to me **5.** *fam* [reproches] telling-off, dressing-down.

doucher [3] [duʃe] *vt* **1.** [laver] to shower, to give a shower to ▪ **je me suis fait ~** *fam* [par la pluie] I got drenched *ou* soaked **2.** *fam* [décevoir] to let down **3.** *fam* [réprimander] : **~ qqn** to tell sb off, to give sb a good telling-off.

◆ **se doucher** *vp (emploi réfléchi)* to have *ou* to take a shower.

douchette [duʃɛt] *nf* bar-code reader *ou* scanner *(for bulky items)*.

doudou[1] [dudu] *nm* security blanket, comfort object.

doudou[2] [dudu] *nf* lovey.

doudoune [dudun] *nf* (thick) quilted jacket *ou* anorak.

doué, e [dwe] *adj* **1.** [acteur, musicien] gifted, talented ▪ **être ~ en dessin** to have a gift for *ou* to be good at drawing ▪ **être ~ pour tout** to be an all-rounder ▪ **tu es vraiment ~ pour envenimer les situations!** you've got a real knack for stirring things up! ▪ **je n'arrive pas à brancher le tuyau – tu n'es pas ~!** *fam* I can't connect the hose – you're hopeless! **2.** [doté] : **~ de** [obj: intelligence, raison] endowed with ; [obj: mémoire] gifted *ou* blessed *ou* endowed with.

douer [6] [dwe] *vt* : **la nature l'a doué de...** nature has endowed *ou* blessed him with...

douille [duj] *nf* **1.** [de cuisine] piping nozzle **2.** ARM (cartridge) case **3.** [d'une ampoule] (lamp) socket **4.** [de cylindre] casing.

douiller [3] △ [duje] *vi* to cough up, to fork out ▪ **la nourriture est super, mais ça douille** the food is great but it costs a packet *ou* an arm and a leg!

douillet, ette [dujɛ, ɛt] *adj* **1.** [très sensible à la douleur] oversensitive ▪ [qui a peur de la douleur] afraid of getting hurt ▪ **que tu es ~!** *péj* don't be so soft! **2.** [confortable - vêtement, lit] (nice and) cosy, snug.

◆ **douillette** *nf* **1.** [robe de chambre] quilted dressing gown **2.** [de prêtre] quilted overcoat.

douillettement [dujɛtmɑ̃] *adv* cosily, snugly ▪ **vous êtes ~ installé ici!** you're nice and cosy here!

douleur [dulœr] *nf* **1.** [physique] pain ▪ **une ~ fulgurante/sourde** a searing/dull pain ▪ **~s abdominales** stomachache ▪ **~s rhumatismales** rheumatic pains ▪ **j'ai une ~ à la cuisse** my thigh hurts, my thigh's sore, I've got a pain in my thigh ▪ **quand mes vieilles ~s se réveillent** when my old pains *ou* aches and pains return **2.** [psychologique] grief, sorrow, pain ▪ **nous avons la ~ de vous faire part du décès de...** it is with great *ou* deep sorrow (and regret) that we have to announce the death of...

douloureusement [dulurøzmɑ̃] *adv* **1.** [physiquement] painfully **2.** [moralement] painfully, grievously ▪ **~ touché par le départ de sa femme** wounded *ou* deeply hurt by his wife's leaving him.

douloureux, euse [dulurø, øz] *adj* **1.** [brûlure, coup, coupure] painful ▪ [articulation, membre] painful, sore ▪ **mes jambes sont très douloureuses le soir** my legs are very sore *ou* hurt a lot at night **2.** [humiliation, souvenirs] painful ▪ [circonstances, sujet, période] painful, distressing ▪ [nouvelle] grievous, painful, distressing ▪ [poème, regard] sorrowful.

◆ **douloureuse** *nf* *fam hum* [au restaurant] bill, check *US* ▪ [facture] bill.

doute [dut] *nm* **1.** [soupçon] doubt ▪ **avoir des ~s sur** *ou* **quant à** *ou* **au sujet de qqch** to have (one's) doubts *ou* misgivings about sthg ▪ **je n'ai pas le moindre ~ là-dessus** I haven't the slightest doubt about it ▪ **il n'y a aucun ~ (possible), c'est lui** it's him, (there's) no doubt about it ▪ **sa victoire ne faisait aucun ~** there was no doubt about her being the winner, her victory was certain ▪ **de gros ~s pèsent sur lui** heavy suspicion hangs over him ▪ **il y a des ~s quant à l'identité du peintre** there is some doubt as to the identity of the painter **2.** [perplexité, incertitude] doubt, uncertainty ▪ PHILOS doubt ▪ **il ne connaît pas le ~** he never has any doubts ▪ **jeter le ~ sur** to cast *ou* to throw doubt on ▪ **tu as semé** *ou* **mis le ~ dans mon esprit** you've made me doubtful.

◆ **dans le doute** *loc adv* : **être dans le ~** to be doubtful *ou* uncertain ▪ **laisser qqn dans le ~** [suj: personne, circonstances] to leave sb in a state of uncertainty.

◆ **en doute** *loc adv* : **mettre en ~** [suj: personne] to question, to challenge ; [suj: circonstances, témoignage] to cast doubt on ▪ **mettez-vous ma parole en ~?** do you doubt my word?

◆ **sans doute** *loc adv* **1.** [probablement] most probably, no doubt **2.** [assurément] : **sans aucun** *ou* **nul ~** without (a) doubt, undoubtedly, indubitably *sout* **3.** [certes] : **tu me l'avais promis – sans ~, mais...** you'd promised me – that's true *ou* I know, but...

douter [3] [dute] ◆ **douter de** *v+prép* **1.** [ne pas croire à - succès, victoire] to be doubtful of ; [- fait, éventualité] to doubt ▪ **on peut ~ de la sécurité du système** the safety of the system is open to doubt ▪ **tu viendras? – j'en doute fort** will you come? – I very much doubt it ▪ **elle ne doute de rien** she has no doubt about anything ▪ **je doute que le projet voie le jour** I have (my) doubts about the future of the project, I doubt whether the project will ever be realized **2.** [traiter avec défiance - ami, motivation] to have doubts about ▪ **~ de la parole de qqn** to doubt sb's word ▪ **~ de soi** [habituellement] to have doubts about *ou* to lack confidence in o.s. ; [à un moment] to have doubts about o.s. **3.** RELIG to have doubts about.

◆ **se douter de** *vp+prép* [s'attendre à] to know, to suspect ▪ **j'aurais dû m'en ~** I should have known ▪ **je me doutais un peu de sa réaction** I half expected him to react the way he did, his reaction didn't surprise me ▪ **comme tu t'en doutes sûrement** as you've probably guessed ▪ **il a eu très peur – je m'en doute** he got quite a fright – I can (well) imagine that ▪ **il faudra que tu viennes me chercher – je m'en doute!** [irritation] you'll have to come and fetch me – well, yes, I expected that! ▪ **j'ai raté le train – vu l'heure, on s'en serait douté!** I missed my train – given the time, that's pretty obvious! ▪ **se ~ de qqch** [soupçonner qqch] to suspect sthg ▪ **se ~ que : je ne me serais jamais douté que c'était possible** I'd never have thought it (was) possible ▪ **je lui ai proposé de travailler pour moi, tout en me doutant bien qu'il refuserait** I suggested he work for me, but I knew he wouldn't accept ▪ **j'étais loin de me ~ que...** little did I know that... ▪ **tu te doutes bien que je te l'aurais dit si je l'avais su!** you know very well that I would have told you if I'd known!

douteux, euse [dutø, øz] *adj* **1.** [non certain, non assuré - authenticité, fait] doubtful, uncertain, questionable ; [- avenir, issue, origine *etc*] doubtful, uncertain ; [- signature] doubtful ▪ **il est ~ que...** it's doubtful whether... **2.** *péj* [inspirant la méfiance - individu] dubious-looking ; [- comportement, manœuvres, passé *etc*] dubious, questionable ▪ **d'une manière douteuse** dubiously ▪ **le portrait/sa plaisanterie était d'un goût ~** the portrait/her joke was in dubious taste **3.** [sale, dangereux] dubious ▪ **du linge ~** clothes that are none too clean ▪ **l'installation électrique est douteuse** the wiring's none too safe.

douve [duv] *nf* **1.** ÉQUIT water jump **2.** [d'un château] moat **3.** [d'un fût] stave **4.** ZOOL fluke.

Douvres [duvr] *npr* Dover.

doux, douce [du, dus] ◇ *adj* **1.** [au toucher - cheveux, peau] soft, smooth ; [- brosse à dents] soft **2.** [au goût - vin] sweet ; [- fromage] mild **3.** [détergent, savon, shampooing] mild ▪ [énergie, technique] alternative ▪ [drogue] soft ▪ **médecines douces** alternative medicine **4.** [sans brusquerie - geste, caresse, personne] gentle ; [- pression] soft, gentle ; [- balancement, pente] gentle ; [- accélération] smooth ; [- véhicule] smooth-running ▪ **il a eu une mort douce** he died peacefully **5.** [bon, gentil - personne, sourire, tempérament, *etc*] gentle ▪ **~ comme un agneau** meek as a lamb **6.** [modéré - châtiment] mild ; [- reproche] mild, gentle ; [- éclairage, teinte] soft, subdued ; [- chaleur, campagne, forme] gentle **7.** MÉTÉOR [air, climat] mild ▪ [chaleur, vent] gentle **8.** [harmonieux - intonation, mélodie, voix] soft, sweet, gentle ▪ **quel ~ prénom!** what a sweet-sounding name! **9.** [plaisant - rêves, souvenir] sweet, pleasant ; [- paix, succès] sweet **10.** PHON soft.
◇ *nm, f* [par affection] **: ma douce** my sweet.
◆ **doux** *adv* **1.** [tiède] **: il fait ~** it's mild out **2.** *loc* **tout ~!** [sans brusquerie] gently (now)! ; [pour calmer] calm down!, easy now!
◆ **douce** *nf vieilli* & *hum* **sa douce** [sa fiancée] his beloved.
◆ **en douce** *loc adv fam* [dire, donner, partir, *etc*] on the quiet, sneakily.

doux-amer, douce-amère [duzamɛr, dusamɛr] (*mpl* **doux-amers**, *fpl* **douces-amères**) *adj* bittersweet.

douzaine [duzɛn] *nf* **1.** [douze] dozen **2.** [environ douze] **: une ~ de** a dozen, around twelve ▪ **une ~ d'escargots** a dozen snails ▪ **une ~ de pages** about *ou* roughly twelve pages.
◆ **à la douzaine** *loc adv* [acheter, vendre] by the dozen ▪ **des chanteurs comme lui, il y en a à la ~!** *fam* singers like him are two a penny!, you'll find dozens of singers like him!

douze [duz] *dét* & *nm inv* twelve, *voir aussi* **cinq**.

douzième [duzjɛm] *adj num* & *nmf* twelfth, *voir aussi* **cinquième**.

Dow Jones [dɔwdʒɔns] *nm* **: (indice) ~** Dow Jones (index).

doyen, enne [dwajɛ̃, ɛn] *nm, f* **1.** [d'un club, d'une communauté] most senior member ▪ [d'un pays] eldest *ou* oldest citizen ▪ [d'une profession] doyen (*f* doyenne) ▪ **~ (d'âge)** oldest person **2.** UNIV dean.
◆ **doyen** *nm* RELIG dean.

DPLG (*abr de* **diplômé par le gouvernement**) *adj certificate for architects, engineers etc.*

dr (*abr écrite de* **droite**) R, r.

Dr (*abr écrite de* **Docteur**) Dr.

dracher [3] [draʃe] *vi Belgique* to pour with rain.

drachme [drakm] *nf* drachma.

draconien, enne [drakɔnjɛ̃, ɛn] *adj* [mesure] drastic, draconian, stringent ▪ [règlement] harsh, draconian ▪ [régime] strict.

dragage [dragaʒ] *nm* [pour prélèvement] dragging, dredging ▪ [pour nettoyage] dredging ▪ **~ de mines** minesweeping.

dragée [draʒe] *nf* **1.** [confiserie] sugared almond ▪ PHARM (sugar-coated) pill ▪ **tenir la ~ haute à qqn** [dans une discussion, un match] to hold out on sb **2.** [balle] lead shot **3.** AGRIC dredge.

DRAGÉE

A small paper cone or box filled with sugared almonds is a traditional gift for guests at christenings and weddings in France.

dragéifié, e [draʒeifje] *adj* sugared, sugar-coated.

dragon [dragɔ̃] *nm* **1.** MYTHOL dragon **2.** [gardien] dragon **3.** *vieilli* [mégère] dragon **4.** ARM & HIST dragoon.

dragonne [dragɔn] *nf* [d'un bâton de ski, d'une cravache] wrist-strap, wrist-loop ▪ [d'une épée] swordknot.

drague [drag] *nf* **1.** TRAV PUB dredge **2.** PÊCHE dragnet **3.** *fam* [flirt] **: pour la ~, il est doué!** he's always on the pull *UK ou* on the make *US*.

draguer [3] [drage] ◇ *vt* **1.** [nettoyer - fleuve, canal, port] to dredge **2.** [retirer - mine] to sweep ; [- ancre] to drag (anchor) **3.** *fam* [fille, garçon] to chat up *(sép) UK*, to sweet-talk *US*, to try to pick up *(sép)* ▪ [en voiture] to cruise ▪ **je me suis fait ~ par le serveur** the waiter chatted me up *UK ou* was giving me a line *US*.
◇ *vi* to be on the pull *UK ou* on the make *US* ▪ **~ en voiture** to cruise.

dragueur, euse [dragœr, øz] *nm, f fam* **c'est un ~** he's always on the pull *UK ou* on the make *US* ▪ **sa sœur est une sacrée dragueuse** her sister's always chasing after boys.
◆ **dragueur** *nm* **1.** [navire] dredger ▪ **~ de mines** minesweeper **2.** [matelot] dredgerman **3.** PÊCHE dragnet fisherman.

drain [drɛ̃] *nm* ÉLECTRON, MÉD & TRAV PUB drain.

drainage [drɛnaʒ] *nm* **1.** [d'une plaie, d'un sol] drainage **2.** [de capital, de ressources] tapping **3.** [massage] **: ~ lymphatique** lymphatic draining.

drainer [4] [drene] *vt* **1.** [assécher] to drain **2.** [rassembler - capital, ressources] to tap **3.** [canaliser - foule] to channel **4.** GÉOGR **: la Seine draine les eaux de toute cette région** the waterways throughout the area flow towards *ou* drain into the Seine.

drakkar [drakar] *nm* NAUT & HIST drakkar.

dramatique [dramatik] ◇ *adj* **1.** THÉÂTRE [musique, œuvre] dramatic **2.** [grave - conséquences, issue, période, situation] horrendous, appalling ▪ **j'ai raté mon permis de conduire – ce n'est pas ~!** I've failed my driving test – it's not the end of the world! **3.** [tragique - dénouement, événement] dramatic.
◇ *nf* TV television play *ou* drama ▪ RADIO radio play *ou* drama.

dramatiquement [dramatikmɑ̃] *adv* tragically ▪ **encore un bal du samedi soir qui se termine ~** yet another Saturday night dance with a tragic ending.

dramatiser [3] [dramatize] *vt* **1.** [exagérer - histoire] to dramatize ▪ **ne dramatise pas!** don't make a drama out of it! **2.** THÉÂTRE [œuvre] to dramatize, to turn into a play.

dramaturge [dramatyrʒ] *nm* playwright, dramatist.

dramaturgie [dramatyrʒi] *nf* **1.** [art] dramatic art, drama **2.** [traité] treatise on dramatic art.

drame [dram] *nm* **1.** THÉÂTRE [œuvre] drama ■ [genre] drama **2.** RADIO & TV drama, play **3.** [événement] drama ■ **il l'a renversé, mais ce n'est pas un ~** he spilt it but it's not the end of the world ■ **faire un ~ de qqch** to make a drama out of sthg ■ **tourner** *OU* **virer au ~ : l'excursion a tourné** *OU* **viré au ~** the trip ended tragically ■ **~ de la jalousie hier à Lyon** jealousy caused a tragedy yesterday in Lyons.

drap [dra] *nm* **1.** [pour lit] : **~ (de lit)** (bed) sheet ■ **des ~s** sheets, bedlinen ■ **~ de dessus/dessous** top/bottom sheet ■ **dans de beaux** *OU* **vilains ~s : nous voilà dans de beaux** *OU* **vilains ~s!** we're in a fine mess! **2.** [serviette] : **~ de bain** bathtowel ■ **~ de plage** beach towel **3.** TEXT woollen cloth ■ **~ fin** broadcloth.

drapé [drape] *nm* [plis, tombé] : **la jupe a un beau ~** the skirt hangs beautifully.

drapeau, x [drapo] *nm* **1.** [pièce d'étoffe] flag ■ MIL flag, colours ▶ **le ~ blanc** the white flag, the flag of truce ■ **le ~ britannique** the British flag, the Union Jack ■ **le~ rouge** the red flag ■ **le ~ tricolore** the French flag, the tricolour (flag) ■ **combattre/se ranger sous le ~ de qqn** to fight under/to rally round sb's flag **2.** [patrie] : **pour le ~** *OU* **l'honneur du ~** *pr* & *hum* ≃ for King and country *UK* ■ ≃ for the red, white and blue *US* **3.** INFORM (flag) marker **4.** [au golf] pin.

◆ **sous les drapeaux** *loc adv* : **être sous les ~x** [au service militaire] to be doing one's military service ; [en service actif] to serve in one's country's armed forces.

draper [3] [drape] *vt* **1.** [couvrir - meuble] to drape, to cover with a sheet **2.** [arranger - châle, rideaux] to drape.

◆ **se draper** *vp (emploi réfléchi)* **se ~ dans un châle** to drape *ou* to wrap o.s. in a shawl ■ **se ~ dans sa dignité** to stand on one's dignity ■ **se ~ dans sa vertu** to cloak o.s. in virtue.

draperie [drapri] *nf* **1.** [tissu disposé en grands plis] drapery, hanging **2.** [industrie] cloth trade ■ [fabrique] cloth manufacture **3.** ART drapery.

drap-housse [draus] (*pl* **draps-housses**) *nm* fitted sheet.

drapier, ère [drapje, ɛr] ◇ *adj* : **marchand ~** draper *UK*, clothier *US*.

◇ *nm, f* [fabricant] cloth manufacturer ■ [vendeur] draper *UK*, clothier *US*.

drastique [drastik] *adj* **1.** [mesure] harsh, drastic ■ [règlement] strict **2.** PHARM drastic.

drave [drav] *nf* ***Québec*** drive *(of floating logs)*.

dravidien, enne [dravidjɛ̃, ɛn] *adj* Dravidian.

Dresde [drɛzd] *npr* Dresden.

dressage [drɛsaʒ] *nm* [d'un fauve] taming *(U)* ■ [d'un cheval sauvage] breaking in *(U)* ■ [d'un chien de cirque, de garde] training *(U)* ■ [d'un cheval de parade] dressage.

dressé, e [drese] *adj* **1.** [oreille, queue] (standing) erect **2.** [chien] trained.

dresser [4] [drese] *vt* **1.** [ériger - mât, pilier] to put up *(sép)*, to raise, to erect ; [- statue] to put up *(sép)*, to erect ; [- tente, auvent] to pitch, to put up *(sép)* **2.** [construire - barricade, échafaudage] to put up *(sép)*, to erect ; [- muret] to erect, to build ■ **~ des obstacles devant qqn** to put obstacles in sb's way, to raise difficulties for sb **3.** [installer - autel] to set up *(sép)* ■ **~ un camp** to set up camp ■ **~ le couvert** *OU* **la table** to lay *ou* to set the table ▶ **~ ses batteries** to lay one's plans **4.** [lever - bâton] to raise, to lift ; [- menton] to stick out ; [- tête] to raise, to lift ■ **~ les oreilles** [suj: chien] to prick up *ou* to cock its ears ■ **~ l'oreille** [suj: personne] to prick up one's ears **5.** [dompter - fauve] to tame ; [- cheval sauvage] to break in *(sép)* ; [- cheval de cirque, chien de garde] to train **6.** *fam* [mater - soldat] to drill, to lick into shape ■ **je vais le ~, moi!** I'll make him toe the line! **7.** [établir - liste, inventaire] to draw up *(sép)*, to make out *(sép)* ; [- bilan] to draw up, to prepare ■ **~ le bilan d'une situation** to take stock of a situation ■ **~ (une) contravention** to give a ticket *(for a driving offence)* **8.** [opposer] : **~ qqn contre qqn/qqch** to set sb against sb/sthg **9.** MENUIS to dress.

◆ **se dresser** *vpi* **1.** [se mettre debout] to stand up, to rise ■ **se ~ sur la pointe des pieds** to stand on tiptoe ■ **se ~ sur son séant** to sit up straight **2.** [oreille de chien] to prick up ▶ **c'est à vous faire ~ les cheveux sur la tête!** it makes your hair stand on end! **3.** [être vertical - montagne, tour] to stand, to rise ■ [dominer] to tower **4.** [surgir - obstacles] to rise, to stand ; [- objet] : **on vit soudain se ~ les miradors** the watchtowers loomed up suddenly.

◆ **se dresser contre** *vp+prép* to rise up *ou* to rebel against.

dresseur, euse [drɛsœr, øz] *nm, f* [de fauves] tamer ■ [de chiens de cirque, de garde] trainer ■ [de chevaux sauvages] horse-breaker.

dressing [drɛsiŋ] *nm* dressing room *(near a bedroom)*.

dressoir [drɛswar] *nm* sideboard.

drève [drɛv] *nf* ***Belgique*** tree-lined avenue.

Dreyfus [drɛfys] *npr* : **l'Affaire ~** the Dreyfus Affair.

L'AFFAIRE DREYFUS

Captain Alfred Dreyfus was wrongly convicted of passing military secrets to the Germans in 1894. His innocence was gradually established, notably by Zola's letter *J'accuse* published in *l'Aurore*. The affair, exacerbated by the fact that Dreyfus was Jewish, crystallized the opposition between left- and right-wing parties. The nation was divided between *dreyfusards*, calling for justice and favouring reformist and socialist trends, and the anti-Semitic *anti-dreyfusards*.

dreyfusard, e [drɛfyzar, ard] *nm, f* Dreyfus supporter.

DRH ◇ *nf* (*abr de* **direction des ressources humaines**) *personnel department*.

◇ *nm* (*abr de* **directeur des ressources humaines**) *personnel manager*.

dribble [dribl] *nm* SPORT dribble ■ **faire un ~** to dribble.

dribbler [3] [drible] *vi* to dribble SPORT.

drille [drij] *nm* ▷ **joyeux**.

drisse [dris] *nf* halyard.

drive [drajv] *nm* INFORM & SPORT drive.

driver[1] [drajvœr] *nm* ÉQUIT & golf driver.

driver[2] [3] [drajve] *vt* SPORT to drive.

drogue [drɔg] *nf* **1.** [narcotique] drug *(C)* ■ **la télévision est une ~ pour eux** they're television addicts ▶ **~ douce/dure** soft/hard drug **2.** [usage] : **la ~** drug-taking, drugs ■ **la ~ est un fléau** drugs are a scourge of society **3.** CHIM & PHARM drug *(C)*.

drogué, e [drɔge] *nm, f* drug addict ■ **les ~s du travail** *fam* workaholics.

droguer [3] [drɔge] *vt* **1.** [toxicomane] to drug **2.** [malade] to dose with drugs ■ **on m'a complètement drogué pendant deux semaines** I was given massive doses of drugs for two weeks **3.** [boisson] to drug, to lace with a drug ■ [repas] to put a drug in.

◆ **se droguer** *vpi* to take drugs, to be on drugs.

droguerie [drɔgri] *nf* **1.** [boutique] hardware shop *UK OU* store *US* **2.** [activité] hardware trade.

droguiste [drɔgist] *nmf* keeper of a hardware shop *UK OU* store *US*.

droit[1] [drwa] *nm* **1.** DR : **le ~** [lois, discipline] law ■ **faire son ~** to study law ■ **étudiant en ~** law student ■ **avoir le ~ pour soi** to have right *ou* the law on one's side ▶ **~ civil/commercial/constitutionnel** civil/commercial/constitutional law ■ **~ commun** *OU* **coutumier** common law ■ **~ international** international law ■ **~ pénal** criminal law ■ **~ privé/public** private/public law ■ **point de ~** point of law

2. [prérogative particulière] right ■ **avoir des ~s sur qqch** to have rights to sthg ■ **tu n'as aucun ~ sur moi** you have no power over me ▶ **~ d'aînesse** primogeniture ■ **~ d'asile** right of asylum ■ **~ d'association** right of (free) association ■ **~s civiques** civil rights ■ **~ de cuissage** HIST droit de seigneur ■ **dans cette entreprise, le ~ de cuissage est monnaie courante** sexual harassment is very common in this company ■ **de ~ divin** by divine right ■ **~ de grâce** right of reprieve ■ **~ de grève** right to strike ■ **les ~s de l'homme** human rights ■ **~ de passage** right of way *UK OU* easement *US* ■ **le ~ des peuples à disposer d'eux-mêmes** the right of peoples to self-determination ■ **~ de préemption**

pre-emptive right ■ ~ **de visite** right of access ■ ~ **de voirie** *tax paid by businesses who wish to place displays, signs etc on the public highway* ■ **le ~ de vote** (the) franchise, the right to vote ■ **avoir ~ de cité** [idéologie] to be established, to have currency ■ **ils se croient tous les ~s, ces gens-là!** these people think they can do what they like!
3. [autorisation sociale ou morale] right ■ **de quel ~ l'a-t-il lue?** what gave him the right to read it?, what right had he to read it? ■ **donner ~ à : le billet donne ~ à une consommation gratuite** the ticket entitles you to one free drink ■ **donner le ~ à qqn de faire qqch** to give sb the right to *ou* to entitle sb to do sthg ■ **être en ~ de faire** to be entitled *ou* to have the right to do ■ **je suis en ~ d'obtenir des explications** I'm entitled to an explanation ■ **reprendre ses ~s** [idée, habitude, nature] to reassert itself ■ **avoir ~ à** [explications] to be entitled to ; [bourse, indemnité] to be entitled to, to be eligible for ; [reconnaissance, respect] to deserve ■ **on a encore eu ~ à ses souvenirs de guerre!** we were regaled with his war memories as usual! ■ **on va avoir ~ à une bonne saucée!** *fam* we'll get well and truly soaked! ■ **avoir ~ de regard sur** [comptabilité, dossier] to have the right to examine *ou* to inspect ; [activités] to have the right to control ■ **avoir le ~ de faire** [gén] to be allowed *ou* to have the right to do ; [officiellement] to have the right *ou* to be entitled to do ■ **tu n'as pas le ~ de parler ainsi!** you've no right to talk like that! ■ **j'ai bien le ~ de me reposer!** I'm entitled to some rest, aren't I? ➊ **le ~ à la différence** the right to be different ■ ~ **de réponse** right of reply
4. [impôt, taxe] duty, tax ■ **exempt de ~s** duty-free ➊ ~ **au bail** *tax on rented accommodation (usually included in the rent)* ■ ~**s de douane** customs duties ■ ~**s de succession** death duties
5. [frais] fee ■ ~ **d'enregistrement** registration fee *(for legal documents)* ■ ~ **d'entrée** entrance fee ■ ~**s d'inscription** registration fee *ou* fees
6. *loc* **à qui de ~** to whom it may concern ■ **dans mon/son (bon) ~** within my/his rights ■ **de (plein) ~** by rights, as a right ■ **membre de plein ~** ex officio member.
◆ **droits** *nmpl* **1.** DR : **~s (d'auteur)** [prérogative] rights, copyright ; [somme] royalties ■ **avoir les ~s exclusifs pour** to have (the) sole rights for ■ **tous ~s (de reproduction) réservés** copyright *ou* all rights reserved
2. INFORM : ~ **d'accès** permissions.

droit[2], e [drwa, drwat] *adj* **1.** [rectiligne - allée, bâton, nez] straight ➊ **rentrer dans le ~ chemin** to mend one's ways ■ **rester dans le ~ chemin** to keep to the straight and narrow (path) **2.** [vertical, non penché - mur] upright, straight, plumb *spéc* ; [- dossier, poteau] upright, straight ■ **restez le dos bien ~** keep your back straight ■ **être** *ou* **se tenir ~** [assis] to sit up straight ; [debout] to stand up straight ➊ ~ **comme un cierge** *ou* **un i** *ou* **un piquet** (as) stiff as a poker *ou* a ramrod *ou* a post **3.** [d'aplomb] straight **4.** [loyal - personne] upright, honest **5.** [sensé - raisonnement] sound, sane **6.** [vêtement] : **manteau/veston ~** single-breasted coat/jacket ■ **col ~** stand-up collar ■ **jupe ~e** straight skirt.
◆ **droit** *adv* [écrire] in a straight line ■ [couper, rouler] straight *(adv)* ■ **après le carrefour, c'est toujours tout ~** after the crossroads, keep going straight on *ou* ahead ➊ **aller ~ à : j'irai ~ au but** I'll come straight to the point, I won't beat about the bush ■ **il est allé ~ à l'essentiel** *ou* **au fait** he went straight to the point ■ **aller ~ à la catastrophe/l'échec** to be heading straight for disaster/a failure ■ **ça m'est allé ~ au cœur** it went straight to my heart.
◆ **droite** *nf* GÉOM straight line.

droit[3], e [drwa, drwat] *adj* [ailier, jambe, œil] right ■ **le côté ~** the right-hand side.
◆ **droit** *nm* right ■ **crochet du ~** right hook.
◆ **droite** *nf* **1.** [côté droit] : **la ~e** the right (side), the right-hand side ■ **tenir sa ~e** AUTO to keep to the right ■ **de ~e et de gauche** from all quarters *ou* sides
2. POLIT : **la ~e** the right wing.
◆ **à droite** *loc adv* **1.** [du côté droit] : **conduire à ~e** to drive on the right-hand side ■ **tourne à ~e** turn right ■ **le poster est trop à ~e** the poster's too far to the right ■ **à ~e et à gauche** *fig* here and there, hither and thither *litt & hum*, all over the place
2. MIL : **à ~e, ~e!** right wheel!
3. POLIT : **être à ~e** to be right-wing *ou* on the right.
◆ **à droite de** *loc prép* to *ou* on the right of.
◆ **de droite** *loc adj* **1.** [du côté droit] : **la porte de ~e** the door on the right, the right-hand door
2. POLIT : **les gens de ~e** rightwingers, people on the right ■ **être de ~e** to be right-wing.

droitement [drwatmɑ̃] *adv* uprightly, honestly.

droit-fil [drwafil] (*pl* **droits-fils**) *nm* **1.** COUT straight grain **2.** *fig* **dans le ~ de** in line *ou* keeping with.

droitier, ère [drwatje, ɛr] ◇ *adj* right-handed.
◇ *nm, f* right-handed person, right-hander.

droiture [drwatyr] *nf* [d'une personne] uprightness, honesty ■ [d'intentions, de motifs] uprightness.

drôle [drol] ◇ *adj* **1.** [amusant - personne, film, situation *etc*] comical, funny, amusing ■ **le plus ~ c'est que...** the funny thing is that... ■ **ce n'est pas ~!** [pas amusant] it's not funny!, I don't find that funny *ou* amusing! ; [pénible] it's no joke! ■ **ce n'est pas toujours ~ au bureau!** life at the office isn't always a barrel of laughs! ■ **tu aurais dû le laisser faire – tu es ~, il se serait fait mal!** *fam* you should have let him – are you kidding? he'd have hurt himself! **2.** [étrange] strange, funny, peculiar ■ **(tout)/toute ~** *fam* : **ça me fait (tout) ~ de revenir ici** it feels really strange to be back ■ **se sentir (tout) ~** to feel (really) weird ■ **~ de : en voilà une ~ d'idée!** what a strange *ou* funny *ou* weird idea! ■ **ça fait un ~ de bruit** it makes a strange *ou* funny noise ■ **~s de gens!** what peculiar *ou* strange people! ■ **tu en fais une ~ de tête!** you look as if something's wrong! ■ **avoir un ~ d'air** to look strange *ou* funny ➊ **la ~ de guerre** HIST the phoney war **3.** [en intensif] : **~ de** *fam* : **il a de ~s de problèmes en ce moment** he hasn't half got some problems at the moment ■ **il faut un ~ de courage pour faire ça!** you need a hell of a lot of courage to do that! ■ **ça a de ~s d'avantages!** it's got terrific *ou* fantastic advantages!
◇ *nm litt* [voyou] rascal, rogue ■ [enfant déluré] little rascal *ou* rogue.
◆ **drôles** *nfpl fam* [histoires] : **il en a entendu/raconté de ~s!** he heard/told some very weird stories!

drôlement [drolmɑ̃] *adv* **1.** *fam* [vraiment] : **~ ennuyeux** awfully *ou* terribly boring ■ **ça sent ~ bon** it smells really great ■ **j'ai ~ eu peur** I had quite a fright ■ **je me suis ~ fait mal** I really hurt myself **2.** [bizarrement - regarder, parler] in a strange *ou* funny *ou* peculiar way **3.** [de façon amusante] amusingly, comically.

drôlerie [drolri] *nf* **1.** [d'une personne, d'un spectacle, d'une remarque] drollness, funniness, comicalness **2.** [acte] funny *ou* amusing *ou* comical thing (to do) ■ [remarque] funny *ou* amusing *ou* comical thing (to say).

drôlesse [drolɛs] *nf vieilli* [femme] (brazen) hussy.

dromadaire [drɔmadɛr] *nm* dromedary.

drosera [drɔzera] *nf* sundew.

dru, e [dry] *adj* [cheveux, végétation] dense, thick ■ [pluie] heavy.
◆ **dru** *adv* [croître, pousser] densely, thickly ■ [pleuvoir] heavily ■ **les mauvaises herbes ont poussé ~** there has been a thick growth of weeds.

drugstore [drœgstɔr] *nm* small shopping centre UK *ou* mall US.

druide [drɥid] *nm* druid.

druidisme [drɥidism] *nm* druidism.

drupe [dryp] *nf* drupe.

druze [dryz] *adj* Druzean, Druzian.
◆ **Druze** *nmf* Druze.

dry [draj] ◇ *adj inv* [apéritif, champagne] dry.
◇ *nm inv* dry Martini.

DS [deɛs] *nf* [voiture] *now legendary futuristic car produced by Citroën in the 1950s.*

DST (*abr de* **Direction de la surveillance du territoire**) *npr f internal state security department,* ≃ MI5 UK, ≃ CIA US.

DTP (*abr de* **diphtérie, tétanos, polio**) *nm vaccine against diphteria, tetanus and polio.*

du [dy] ▻ **de.**

dû, due [dy] ◇ *pp* ▻ **devoir.**
◇ *adj* [à payer] owed ▪ **quelle est la somme due?** what's the sum owed *ou* due?
◆ **dû** *nm* due ▪ **je ne fais que lui réclamer mon ~** I'm only asking for what he owes me.
◆ **en bonne et due forme** *loc adv* DR in due form.

dual, e, aux [dɥal, o] *adj* dual.

dualisme [dɥalism] *nm* dualism.

dualiste [dɥalist] ◇ *adj* dualistic.
◇ *nmf* dualist.

dualité [dɥalite] *nf* duality.

Dubayy [dybaj] *npr* Dubai.

dubitatif, ive [dybitatif, iv] *adj* dubious, sceptical.

Dublin [dyblɛ̃] *npr* Dublin.

dublinois, e [dyblinwa, az] *adj* from Dublin.
◆ **Dublinois, e** *nm, f* Dubliner.

duc [dyk] *nm* **1.** [titre] duke **2.** ZOOL horned owl.

ducal, e, aux [dykal, o] *adj* ducal ▪ **un titre ~** a duke's title.

ducasse [dykas] *nf* [dialecte] fair *(in Northern France).*

ducat [dyka] *nm* ducat.

duché [dyʃe] *nm* duchy, dukedom.

duchesse [dyʃɛs] *nf* **1.** [titre] duchess ▪ **faire la ~** *péj* to play the fine lady **2.** [poire] duchess pear **3.** [meuble] duchesse.

ductile [dyktil] *adj* ductile.

ductilité [dyktilite] *nf* ductility.

duègne [dɥɛɲ] *nf* duenna.

duel [dɥɛl] *nm* **1.** [entre deux personnes] duel ▪ **se battre en ~ avec un rival** to fight a duel *ou* to duel with a rival **2.** [conflit - entre États, organisations] battle ▶ **~ d'artillerie** artillery battle **3.** [compétition] : **~ oratoire** verbal battle **4.** LING dual.

duelliste [dɥelist] *nmf* duellist.

duettiste [dɥetist] *nmf* duettist.

duffle-coat (*pl* **duffle-coats**), **duffel-coat** (*pl* **duffel-coats**) [dœfœlkot] *nm* duffel coat.

dulcinée [dylsine] *nf* ***hum*** ladylove, dulcinea ***litt.***

dûment [dymɑ̃] *adv* duly ▪ **~ chapitré** told off in no uncertain terms.

dumping [dœmpiŋ] *nm* dumping ÉCON : **faire du ~** to dump (goods).

dune [dyn] *nf* dune.

Dunkerque [dœ̃kɛrk] *npr* Dunkirk.

duo [dyo] *nm* **1.** [spectacle - chanté] duet ; [- instrumental] duet, duo ▪ **chanter en ~** to sing a duet ▪ **un ~ comique** a (comic) double-act **2.** [dialogue] exchange **3.** MÉTALL two-high rolling mill.

duodécimal, e, aux [dɥɔdesimal, o] *adj* duodecimal.

duodénum [dyɔdenɔm] *nm* duodenum.

dupe [dyp] ◇ *nf* dupe ▪ **prendre qqn pour ~** to dupe sb, to take sb for a ride ▪ **jeu de ~s** fool's game.
◇ *adj* : **elle ment, mais je ne suis pas ~** she's lying but it doesn't fool me.

duper [3] [dype] *vt* ***litt*** to dupe, to fool.
◆ **se duper** *vp (emploi réfléchi)* to fool o.s.

duperie [dypri] *nf* dupery.

duplex [dyplɛks] *nm* **1.** : **(appartement en) ~** ≃ maisonnette UK, duplex (apartment) US **2.** TÉLÉCOM duplex ▪ **(émission en) ~** linkup.

duplexer [4] [dyplɛkse] *vt* to set up a linkup.

duplicata [dyplikata] *nm* duplicate.

duplicateur [dyplikatœr] *nm* duplicator.

duplication [dyplikasjɔ̃] *nf* **1.** [fait de copier] duplication, duplicating *(U)* **2.** AUDIO linking up **3.** BIOL doubling.

duplicité [dyplisite] *nf* duplicity, falseness, hypocrisy.

dupliquer [3] [dyplike] *vt* [document] to duplicate.

duquel [dykɛl] ▻ **lequel.**

dur, e [dyr] ◇ *adj* **1.** [ferme - viande] tough ; [- muscle] firm, hard ; [- lit, mine de crayon] hard ▶ **~ comme du bois** *ou* **le marbre** *ou* **le roc** rock-hard
2. [difficile] hard, difficult ▪ **la route est ~e à monter** it's a hard road to climb ▪ **c'est plutôt ~ à digérer, ton histoire!** ***fam*** your story's rather hard to take! ▪ **il est parfois ~ d'accepter la vérité** accepting the truth can be hard *ou* difficult ▪ **le plus ~ dans l'histoire, c'est de comprendre ce qui s'est passé** the hardest part of the whole business is understanding what really happened
3. [pénible à supporter - climat] harsh ▪ **les conditions de vie sont de plus en plus ~es** life gets harder and harder ▪ **le plus ~ est passé maintenant** the worst is over now ▪ **les temps sont ~s** these are hard times ▶ **plus ~e sera la chute** ***allus*** & BIBLE (the higher they come) the harder they fall ▪ **dur dur** ***fam*** **: pas de congé?/plus de café? dur dur !** no time off?/no coffee left? that's a blow!
4. [cruel] : **ne sois pas ~ avec lui** don't be nasty to *ou* tough on him
5. [rude, froid] harsh ▪ **d'une voix ~e** in a harsh voice ▪ **des yeux d'un bleu très ~** steely blue eyes
6. [endurci] tough ▪ **~ à : il est ~ à la douleur** he's tough, he can bear a lot of (physical) pain ▪ **il est ~ au travail** *ou* **à l'ouvrage** he's a hard worker ▶ **avoir le cœur ~** to have a heart of stone, to be hardhearted ▪ **il est ~ à cuire** ***fam*** he's a hard nut to crack ▪ **~ à la détente** ***fam*** tight-fisted ▪ **être ~ d'oreille** *ou* **de la feuille** ***fam*** to be hard of hearing
7. [intransigeant] hard ▪ **la droite/gauche ~e** the hard right/left
8. PHON & PHYS hard.
◇ *nm, f* ***fam*** **1.** [personne sans faiblesse] toughie, tough nut UK *ou* cookie US ▪ **un ~ en affaires** a hard-nosed businessman ▶ **c'est un ~ à cuire** he's a hard nut to crack
2. [voyou] tough guy, toughie ▪ **un ~ de ~** a real tough nut UK *ou* tough guy
3. POLIT hard-liner, hawk ▪ **les ~s du parti** the hard core in the party.
◆ **dur** *adv* **1.** [avec force] hard ▪ **il a tapé** *ou* **frappé ~** he hit hard ▪ **il travaille ~ sur son nouveau projet** he's working hard *ou* he's hard at work on his new project ▶ **il croit ~ comme fer qu'elle va revenir** he believes doggedly *ou* he's adamant that she'll come back
2. [avec intensité] : **le soleil tape ~ aujourd'hui** the sun is beating down today.
◆ **dures** *nfpl* ***fam*** [histoires, moments] : **il lui en a fait voir de ~es** he gave her a hard time ▪ **il nous en a dit de ~es** he told us some really nasty things.
◆ **à la dure** *loc adv* : **élever ses enfants à la ~e** to bring up one's children the hard way.
◆ **en dur** *loc adj* : **construction/maison en ~** building/house built with non-temporary materials.
◆ **sur la dure** *loc adv* : **coucher sur la ~e** to sleep on the ground.

durabilité [dyrabilite] *nf* [qualité] durableness, durability.

durable [dyrabl] *adj* **1.** [permanent] enduring, lasting, long-lasting ▪ **agriculture ~** durable agriculture **2.** ÉCON : **biens ~s** durable goods, durables.

durablement [dyrabləmɑ̃] *adv* durably, enduringly, for a long time ▪ **le beau temps devrait persister ~ dans notre pays** fine weather should persist over the country.

durant [dyrɑ̃] *prép* **1.** *(avant le n)* [au cours de] during, in the course of **2.** *(après le n)* [insistant sur la durée] for ▪ **il peut parler des heures ~** he can speak for hours (on end) ▪ **toute sa vie ~** his whole life through, throughout his whole life.

duratif, ive [dyratif, iv] *adj* LING durative.
◆ **duratif** *nm* LING durative.

durcir [32] [dyrsir] ◇ *vt* [rendre plus dur] to harden, to make firmer ▪ ***fig*** to harden, to toughen ▪ **cette coupe de cheveux lui durcit le visage** that haircut makes her look severe.

◇ *vi* [sol, plâtre] to harden, to go hard.
◆ **se durcir** *vpi* [personne] to harden o.s. ▪ [cœur] to become hard.

durcissement [dyrsismɑ̃] *nm* **1.** [raffermissement - du sol, du plâtre] hardening **2.** [renforcement] : **le ~ de l'opposition** the tougher stance taken by the opposition **3.** MIL stiffening (of enemy resistance).

durcisseur [dyrsisœr] *nm* hardener ▪ **~ pour ongles** nail hardener.

durée [dyre] *nf* **1.** [période] duration, length ▪ **pendant la ~ de** during, for the duration of ▪ **vente promotionnelle pour une ~ limitée** special sale for a limited period ▪ **la ~ hebdomadaire du travail est de 35 heures** the statutory working week is 35 hours ⊃ **disque longue ~** long playing record ▪ **~ de conservation** ≃ sell-by date **2.** [persistance] lasting quality **3.** MUS, PHON & LITTÉR length **4.** PSYCHOL perceived (passage of) time.
◆ **de courte durée** *loc adj* short-lived.
◆ **de longue durée** *loc adj* [chômeur, chômage] long-term.

durement [dyrmɑ̃] *adv* **1.** [violemment - frapper] hard **2.** [avec sévérité] harshly, severely ▪ **elle a élevé ses enfants ~** she brought up her children strictly **3.** [douloureusement] : **~ éprouvé par la mort de** deeply distressed by the death of ▪ **son absence est ~ ressentie** she's sorely missed **4.** [méchamment - répondre] harshly.

dure-mère [dyrmɛr] (*pl* **dures-mères**) *nf* dura mater.

Durendal [dyrɑ̃dal] *npr the holy and unbreakable sword of Roland in the medieval epic 'la Chanson de Roland'.*

durer [3] [dyre] *vi* **1.** [événement, tremblement de terre] to last, to go *ou* to carry on ▪ **la situation n'a que trop duré** the situation has gone on far too long ▪ **ça ne peut plus ~!** it can't go on like this! ▪ **ça durera ce que ça durera!** *fam* it might last and then it might not! **2.** [rester, persister] to last ▪ **ce soleil ne va pas ~** this sunshine won't last long ▪ **faire ~ : faire ~ les provisions** to stretch supplies, to make supplies last ▪ **faire ~ le plaisir** to spin things out **3.** [moteur, appareil] to last ▪ [œuvre] to last, to endure *sout* **4.** [peser] : **le temps me dure** time is lying heavy (on my hands) *ou* hangs heavily on me **5.** [vivre] to last.

dureté [dyrte] *nf* **1.** [du sol, du plâtre] hardness, firmness **2.** [du climat, de conditions] harshness **3.** [d'un maître, d'une règle] severity, harshness ▪ [d'une grève] bitterness, harshness ▪ **traiter qqn avec ~** to be harsh to *ou* tough on sb **4.** [d'une teinte, d'une voix, d'une lumière] harshness **5.** CHIM [de l'eau] hardness **6.** PHYS hardness.

durillon [dyrijɔ̃] *nm* callus.

Durit® [dyrit] *nf* flexible pipe.

dut *etc v* ▷ **devoir**.

DUT (*abr de* **diplôme universitaire de technologie**) *nm diploma taken after two years at an institute of technology.*

duvet [dyvɛ] *nm* **1.** [poils] down, downy hairs **2.** [plumes] down ▪ **un oreiller en ~** a down pillow **3.** [sac de couchage] sleeping bag ▪ [couette] duvet, quilt **4.** *Belgique* & *Suisse* eiderdown.

duveter [27] [dyvte] ◆ **se duveter** *vpi* to go *ou* to become downy, to get covered in down.

duveteux, euse [dyvtø, øz] *adj* downy.

DVD (*abr de* **Digital Video Disc** *ou* **Digital Versatile Disc**) *nm inv* DVD.

DVD-ROM [devederɔm] (*abr de* **Digital Video Disc-Read Only Memory** *ou* **Disc Versatile Disc-Read Only Memory**) *nm* DVD-ROM.

dynamique [dinamik] ◇ *adj* **1.** [énergique] dynamic, energetic **2.** [non statique] dynamic.
◇ *nf* **1.** MUS & SC dynamics *(sing)* **2.** [mouvement] dynamics *(sing)*, dynamic **3.** PSYCHOL : **~ de groupe** group dynamics.

dynamiquement [dinamikmɑ̃] *adv* dynamically.

dynamisation [dinamizasjɔ̃] *nf* [excitation] : **responsable de la ~ de l'équipe** responsible for injecting enthusiasm into the team.

dynamiser [3] [dinamize] *vt* [équipe] to dynamize, to inject enthusiasm into.

dynamisme [dinamism] *nm* **1.** [entrain] energy, enthusiasm **2.** PHILOS dynamism.

dynamitage [dinamitaʒ] *nm* blowing up *ou* blasting (with dynamite).

dynamite [dinamit] *nf* dynamite ▪ **c'est de la ~!** *fam fig* it's dynamite!

dynamiter [3] [dinamite] *vt* **1.** [détruire à l'explosif] to blow up *ou* to blast (with dynamite) **2.** [abolir - préjugé] to do away with, to sweep away.

dynamiteur, euse [dinamitœr, øz] *nm, f* **1.** [à l'explosif] dynamiter, dynamite expert **2.** [démystificateur] destroyer of received ideas.

dynamo [dinamo] *nf* dynamo, generator.

dynamomètre [dinamɔmɛtr] *nm* dynamometer.

dynastie [dinasti] *nf* **1.** [de rois] dynasty **2.** [famille] : **la ~ des Bach/Bruegel** the line of famous Bachs/Bruegels.

dysenterie [disɑ̃tri] *nf* dysentery.

dysfonctionnel, elle [disfɔ̃ksjɔnɛl] *adj* dysfunctional.

dysfonctionnement [disfɔ̃ksjɔnmɑ̃] *nm* malfunction, malfunctioning.

dysharmonie [dizarmɔni] *nf* dysharmony, discord.

dyslexie [dislɛksi] *nf* dyslexia.

dyslexique [dislɛksik] *adj* & *nmf* dyslexic.

dysménorrhée [dismenɔre] *nf* dysmenorrhoea *UK*, dysmenorrhea *US*.

dyspepsie [dispɛpsi] *nf* dyspepsia.

dystrophie [dystrɔfi] *nf* dystrophy ▪ **~ musculaire progressive** muscular dystrophy.

E

e, E [ø] *nm* **1.** [lettre] e, E ■ **e ouvert/fermé** open/close e ■ **e muet** silent e **2.** MATH & PHYS e.

E (*abr écrite de* **est**) E.

EAO (*abr de* **enseignement assisté par ordinateur**) *nm* CAL.

eau, x [o] *nf* **1.** [liquide incolore] water ■ **se mettre à l'~** [pour se baigner] to go in the water (for a swim) ■ **des légumes/melons pleins d'~** watery vegetables/melons ■ **prendre l'~** [chaussure, tente] to leak, to be leaky, to be leaking ⊙ **~ déminéralisée/distillée** demineralized/distilled water ■ **~ calcaire** *ou* **dure** hard water ■ **~ bénite** holy water ■ **~ courante** running water ■ **avoir l'~ courante** to have running water ■ **~ douce** fresh water ■ **d'~ douce** freshwater, river *(modif)* ■ **~ de jouvence** waters of youth ■ **~ de mer** seawater ■ **~ de pluie** rainwater ■ **~ de vaisselle** dish *ou* washing-up water ■ **jeu d'~** *ou* **d'~x** fountains ■ **comme l'~ et le feu** as different as chalk and cheese *UK ou* as night and day *US* ■ **ça doit valoir 150 euros, enfin, c'est dans ces ~x-là!** *fam* it costs around 150 euros more or less ■ **tu apportes de l'~ à mon moulin** you're adding weight to my argument ■ **il est passé/il passera beaucoup d'~ sous les ponts** a lot of water has gone/will flow under the bridge ■ **il y a de l'~ dans le gaz** *fam* there's trouble brewing ■ **j'en ai l'~ à la bouche** my mouth is watering
2. [boisson] water ⊙ **~ plate** still water ■ **~ gazeuse** soda *ou* fizzy water ■ **~ minérale** mineral water ■ **~ du robinet** tap water ■ **~ de Seltz** soda water ■ **~ de source** spring water ■ **point d'~** [pour les animaux] watering hole ; [dans un village] standpipe ■ **mettre de l'~ dans son vin** to climb down, to back off
3. CULIN water ■ **~ de cuisson** cooking water ■ **~ de fleur d'oranger** orange flower water ■ **finir** *ou* **partir** *ou* **tourner** *ou* **s'en aller en ~ de boudin** *fam* to peter *ou* to fizzle out
4. [parfum - PHARM] : **~ de Cologne** (eau de) Cologne ■ **~ dentifrice** mouthwash ■ **~ de parfum** perfume ■ **~ de rose** rose water ■ **~ de toilette** toilet water
5. CHIM : **~ écarlate** stain-remover ■ **~ de Javel** bleach, Clorox® *US* ■ **~ oxygénée** hydrogen peroxide
6. [limpidité - d'un diamant] water ■ **de la plus belle ~** *pr* & *fig* of the first water
7. NAUT : **faire de l'~** [s'approvisionner] to take on water ■ **faire ~** [avoir une fuite] to take on water ■ **faire ~ de toutes parts** *fig* to go under.

◆ **eaux** *nfpl* **1.** [masse] water ■ **les ~x se retirent** [mer] the tide's going out ; [inondation] the (flood) water's subsiding ⊙ **~x ménagères** waste water ■ **~x usées** sewage ■ **hautes/basses ~x** GÉOGR high/low water ■ **grandes ~x : les grandes ~x de Versailles** the fountains of Versailles ■ **on a eu droit aux grandes ~x (de Versailles)** *fam fig* she turned on the waterworks
2. NAUT [zone] waters ■ **~x internationales/territoriales** international/territorial waters ■ **~x côtières** inshore waters ■ **dans les ~x de** in the wake of
3. [d'une accouchée] waters
4. [thermes] : **prendre les ~x** to take the waters, to stay at a spa *(for one's health)*
5. ADMIN : **les Eaux et Forêts** ≃ the Forestry Commission.

◆ **à grande eau** *loc adv* : **laver à grande ~** [au jet] to hose down ; [dans un évier, une bassine] to wash in a lot of water ■ **rincer à grande ~** to rinse (out) thoroughly *ou* in a lot of water.

◆ **à l'eau** ◇ *loc adj* **1.** CULIN boiled
2. [perdu] : **mon week-end est à l'~** bang goes my weekend.
◇ *loc adv* **1.** CULIN : **cuire à l'~** [légumes] to boil ; [fruits] to poach
2. *loc* **se jeter** *ou* **se lancer à l'~** to take the plunge ■ **tomber à l'~** to fall through.

◆ **à l'eau de rose** *loc adj péj* sentimental.

◆ **de la même eau** *loc adj péj* of the same ilk.

◆ **en eau** *loc adj* sweating profusely ■ **ils étaient en ~** the sweat was pouring off them.

◆ **en eau profonde** *loc adv* NAUT in deep (sea) waters.

eau-de-vie [odvi] (*pl* **eaux-de-vie**) *nf* eau de vie.

eau-forte [ofɔrt] (*pl* **eaux-fortes**) *nf* **1.** CHIM aqua fortis **2.** ART etching.

ébahi, e [ebai] *adj* flabbergasted, stunned ■ **prendre un air ~** to look flabbergasted *ou* stunned.

ébahir [32] [ebair] *vt* to astound, to dumbfound, to stun.
◆ **s'ébahir de** *vp+prép* to marvel *ou* to wonder at.

ébahissement [ebaismɑ̃] *nm* amazement, astonishment.

ébarber [3] [ebarbe] *vt* **1.** MÉTALL to burr, to edge, to trim **2.** [feuilles de papier] to trim **3.** AGRIC to clip, to trim **4.** CULIN [poisson] to trim.

ébat *etc v* ▷ **ébattre**.

ébats [eba] *nmpl* frolics, frolicking ■ **~ amoureux** lovemaking.

ébattre [83] [ebatr] ◆ **s'ébattre** *vpi* to frolic.

ébaubi, e [ebobi] *adj* *hum* dumbfounded, flabbergasted, stunned.

ébauche [eboʃ] *nf* **1.** [première forme - d'un dessin] rough sketch *ou* draft ; [- d'un plan] outline ■ **projet à l'état d'~** project in its early stages **2.** [début] : **l'~ de : l'~ d'un sourire** the beginning of a *ou* an incipient smile ■ **une ~ de réconciliation** the first steps towards reconciliation.

ébaucher [3] [eboʃe] *vt* **1.** [esquisser - dessin, portrait] to rough *ou* to sketch out ; [- plan] to outline ■ **des formes vagues à peine ébauchées** a few indistinct shapes **2.** [commencer] to begin, to start ■ **~ des négociations/une réconciliation** to start the process of negotiation/reconciliation ■ **elle ébaucha un vague sourire/geste** she made as if to smile/to move.
◆ **s'ébaucher** *vpi* to (take) form, to start up.

ébène [ebɛn] *nf* ebony ■ **une table en ~** an ebony table ■ **noir d'~** ebony black.

ébénier [ebenje] *nm* ebony (tree).

ébéniste [ebenist] *nm* cabinetmaker.

ébénisterie [ebenistəri] *nf* **1.** [métier] cabinetmaking **2.** [placage] veneer ▪ **une table en ~** a veneered table.

éberlué, e [ebɛrlɥe] *adj* dumbfounded, stunned.

éblouir [32] [ebluir] *vt* **1.** [aveugler] to dazzle **2.** [impressionner] to dazzle, to stun ▪ **nous avons été éblouis par son talent** we were dazzled by her talent.

éblouissant, e [ebluisɑ̃, ɑ̃t] *adj* **1.** [aveuglant - couleur, lumière] dazzling **2.** [impressionnant - femme, performance] dazzling, stunning ▪ **~ de : mise en scène ~e d'ingéniosité** stunningly ingenious staging.

éblouissement [ebluismɑ̃] *nm* **1.** [fait d'être aveuglé] being dazzled **2.** [vertige] dizziness ▪ **avoir un ~** to have a dizzy spell **3.** [enchantement] dazzlement, bedazzlement.

ébonite [ebɔnit] *nf* ebonite, vulcanite.

éborgner [3] [ebɔrɲe] *vt* to blind in one eye.
◆ **s'éborgner** *vp (emploi réfléchi)* to put one's eye out.

éboueur [ebwœr] *nm* dustman *UK*, garbage collector *US*.

ébouillanter [3] [ebujɑ̃te] *vt* to scald.
◆ **s'ébouillanter** *vp (emploi réfléchi)* to scald o.s. ▪ **s'~ la main/le pied** to scald one's hand/foot.

éboulement [ebulmɑ̃] *nm* **1.** [chute] crumbling, subsiding, collapsing ▪ **un ~ de terrain** a landslide **2.** [éboulis - de terre] mass of fallen earth ; [- de rochers] mass of fallen rocks, rock slide ; [- en montagne] scree.

ébouler [3] [ebule] *vt* to break *ou* to bring down *(sép)*.
◆ **s'ébouler** *vpi* [petit à petit] to crumble, to subside ▪ [brutalement] to collapse, to cave in ▪ **le terrain s'est éboulé** there has been a landslide.

éboulis [ebuli] *nm* [de terre] mass of fallen earth ▪ [de rochers] mass of fallen rocks, rock slide ▪ [en montagne] scree.

ébouriffant, e [eburifɑ̃, ɑ̃t] *adj* breathtaking, staggering, stunning.

ébouriffé, e [eburife] *adj* tousled, dishevelled.

ébouriffer [3] [eburife] *vt* **1.** [décoiffer] to ruffle, to tousle **2.** *fam* [ébahir] to amaze, to dumbfound, to stun.

ébranlement [ebrɑ̃lmɑ̃] *nm* **1.** [départ - d'un cortège] moving *ou* setting off **2.** [tremblement - d'une vitre] tremor, shaking ▪ **causer l'~ du cabinet** *fig* to shake the Cabinet **3.** [choc] shock.

ébranler [3] [ebrɑ̃le] *vt* **1.** [faire trembler] to shake, to rattle **2.** [affaiblir] to shake, to weaken ▪ **~ la confiance de qqn** to shake *ou* to undermine sb's confidence ▪ **~ les nerfs de qqn** to make sb very nervous **3.** [atteindre moralement] to shake ▪ **très ébranlé par la mort de son fils** shattered by the death of his son.
◆ **s'ébranler** *vpi* [cortège, train] to move *ou* to set off, to pull away.

ébréché, e [ebreʃe] *adj* : **une assiette ébréchée** a chipped plate.

ébrécher [18] [ebreʃe] *vt* **1.** [assiette, vase] to chip ▪ [couteau, lame] to nick, to notch **2.** [fortune, héritage] to make a hole in, to deplete.

ébriété [ebrijete] *nf* *sout* intoxication ▪ **être en état d'~** to be under the influence (of drink).

ébrouer [3] [ebrue] ◆ **s'ébrouer** *vpi* **1.** [cheval] to snort **2.** [personne, chien] to shake o.s.

ébruitement [ebrɥitmɑ̃] *nm* disclosing, spreading.

ébruiter [3] [ebrɥite] *vt* to disclose, to spread.
◆ **s'ébruiter** *vpi* to spread.

ébullition [ebylisjɔ̃] *nf* boiling ▶ **point d'~** boiling point.
◆ **à ébullition** *loc adv* : **porter de l'eau/du lait à ~** to bring water/milk to the boil.
◆ **en ébullition** *loc adj* [liquide] boiling ▪ *fig* in turmoil ▪ **tout le pays est en ~ depuis qu'ils l'ont arrêté** the whole country has been in turmoil since they arrested him.

écaillage [ekajaʒ] *nm* **1.** [du poisson] scaling ▪ [des huîtres] opening **2.** [d'une peinture] flaking *ou* peeling *ou* scaling off ▪ [d'un vernis] chipping off.

écaille [ekaj] *nf* **1.** ZOOL [de poisson, de serpent] scale ▪ [matière] tortoiseshell ▪ **les ~s finiront par lui tomber des yeux** the scales will fall from his eyes **2.** [fragment - gén] chip ; [- de peinture] flake **3.** BOT scale.
◆ **en écaille** *loc adj* tortoiseshell *(modif)*.

écaillé, e [ekaje] *adj* [plâtre, vernis] chipped, flaking off ▪ [peinture] peeling.

écailler[1] [3] [ekaje] *vt* **1.** CULIN [poisson] to scale ▪ [huître] to open **2.** [plâtre, vernis] to cause to flake off *ou* to chip.
◆ **s'écailler** *vpi* [vernis, plâtre] to flake off ▪ [peinture] to peel off.

écailler[2], ère [ekaje, ɛr] *nm, f* [vendeur] oyster seller ▪ [dans un restaurant].

écale [ekal] *nf* husk.

écaler [3] [ekale] *vt* [noisette, noix] to husk.

écarlate [ekarlat] *adj* scarlet.

écarquiller [3] [ekarkije] *vt* : **~ les yeux** to open one's eyes wide, to stare (wide-eyed).

écart [ekar] *nm* **1.** [variation] difference, discrepancy ▪ **~ de poids/température** difference in weight/temperature ▶ **~ salarial** wage differential ▪ **~ type** standard deviation
2. [intervalle] gap, distance ▪ **un ~ de huit ans les sépare, il y a huit ans d'~ entre eux** there's an eight-year gap between them ▪ **réduire** *ou* **resserrer l'~ entre** to close *ou* to narrow the gap between
3. [déviation] swerving ▪ **faire un ~** [cheval] to shy ; [voiture, vélo] to swerve ▪ **j'ai fait un petit ~ aujourd'hui: j'ai mangé deux gâteaux** I broke my diet today: I ate two cakes
4. [excès] : **~ de conduite** misdemeanour, misbehaviour *(U)* ▪ **~s de langage** strong language
5. JEUX discard
6. DANSE & SPORT : **faire le grand ~** to do the splits ; *fig* to do a balancing act
7. [en comptabilité] margin ▪ [en statistiques] deviation
8. [hameau] hamlet.
◆ **à l'écart** *loc adv* **1.** [de côté] aside ▪ **mettre qqn à l'~** to put sb on the sidelines ▪ **prendre qqn à l'~** to take sb aside *ou* to one side/to draw sb aside *ou* to one side ▪ **tenir qqn à l'~** [éloigné] to hold *ou* keep sb back ; [empêcher de participer] to keep sb out of things ▪ **rester** *ou* **se tenir à l'~** [éloigné] to stand apart ; [ne pas participer] to stay on the sidelines *ou* in the background, to keep out of things
2. [loin des habitations] : **vivre à l'~** to live in a remote spot.
◆ **à l'écart de** *loc prép* : **nous sommes un peu à l'~ du village** we live a little way away from the village ▪ **il essaie de la tenir à l'~ de tous ses problèmes** he's trying not to involve her in all his problems ▪ **se tenir à l'~ de la vie politique** to keep out of politics.

écarté, e [ekarte] *adj* **1.** [isolé] isolated, remote **2.** [loin l'un de l'autre] : **gardez les bras ~s** keep your arms outspread ▪ **avoir les dents ~es** to be gap-toothed ▪ **avoir les yeux ~s** to have widely-spaced eyes.
◆ **écarté** *nm* JEUX écarté.

écartèlement [ekartɛlmɑ̃] *nm* [torture] quartering, tearing apart.

écarteler [25] [ekartəle] *vt* **1.** [torturer] to quarter, to tear apart *(sép)* **2.** [partager] to tear apart *(sép)* ▪ **écartelé entre le devoir et l'amour** torn between duty and love.

écartement [ekartəmɑ̃] *nm* **1.** RAIL : **~ (des rails** *ou* **de voie)** gauge **2.** AUTO : **~ des essieux** wheelbase ▪ **~ des roues** tracking **3.** [fait d'ouvrir] spreading (open), opening **4.** [évincement - d'un directeur] dismissing, removing.

écarter [3] [ekarte] *vt* **1.** [séparer - objets] to move apart *(sép)* ; [- personnes] to separate ▪ **ils écartèrent la foule pour passer** they pushed their way through the crowd ▪ [en parlant de parties du corps] : **~ les bras** to open *ou* to spread one's arms ▪ **~ les jambes/doigts/orteils** to spread one's legs/fingers/toes **2.** [éloigner] to move away *ou* aside *(sép)*, to pull away *ou* aside *(sép)* ▪ **écarte plus la table du mur** move the table further away from the wall **3.** [détourner] to divert ▪ **cette route vous écarte un peu** that road takes you a little bit out of your way **4.** [refuser - idée] to dismiss, to set aside *(sép)*, to rule out *(sép)* **5.** [tenir à distance] : **~ qqn de** [succession, conseil d'administration] to keep sb out of ▪ **~ qqn du pouvoir** [aspirant] to cut sb off from the road to power ; [homme d'État] to manoeuvre sb out of power **6.** JEUX to discard.

◆ **s'écarter** *vpi* to move away *ou* out of the way, to step *ou* to draw aside ▪ **s'~ de sa trajectoire** [fusée] to deviate from its trajectory ; [pilote] to deviate from one's course ▪ **s'~ du droit chemin** to go off the straight and narrow (path) ▪ **s'~ du sujet** to stray *ou* to wander from the subject.

écarteur [ekartœr] *nm* MÉD retractor.

ecchymose [ekimoz] *nf* bruise, ecchymosis *spéc.*

ecclésial, e, aux [eklezjal, o] *adj* ecclesial ▪ **biens ecclésiaux** church property.

Ecclésiaste [eklezjast] *nm* : **(le livre de) l'~** Ecclesiastes.

ecclésiastique [eklezjastik] <> *adj* [devoir] ecclesiastic, ecclesiastical ▪ [habitude] priestly, priestlike.
<> *nm* priest, ecclesiastic.

écervelé, e [esɛrvəle] <> *adj* scatterbrained.
<> *nm, f* scatterbrain.

échafaud [eʃafo] *nm* scaffold ▪ **monter sur l'~** to be executed.

échafaudage [eʃafodaʒ] *nm* **1.** CONSTR scaffolding **2.** [pile] heap, pile, stack **3.** [élaboration - de systèmes] elaboration, construction.

échafauder [3] [eʃafode] <> *vt* **1.** [entasser] to stack *ou* to heap *ou* to pile (up) **2.** [construire - systèmes, théories] to build up, to construct ▪ **~ des projets** to make plans.
<> *vi* CONSTR to put up scaffolding, to scaffold.

échalas [eʃala] *nm* **1.** [perche] pole, stake ▪ **être droit *ou* raide comme un ~** to be as stiff as a poker *ou* ramrod **2.** *fam* [personne] beanpole ▪ **c'est un grand ~** he's a real beanpole.

échalote [eʃalɔt] *nf* shallot.

échancré, e [eʃɑ̃kre] *adj* **1.** [vêtement] low-necked ▪ **une robe très ~e sur le devant** a dress with a plunging neckline **2.** BOT serrated **3.** GÉOGR [côte, littoral] indented, jagged.

échancrer [3] [eʃɑ̃kre] *vt* **1.** COUT to cut a low neckline in **2.** [entailler] to indent.

échancrure [eʃɑ̃kryr] *nf* **1.** [vêtement] low neckline **2.** BOT serration **3.** GÉOGR indentation.

échange [eʃɑ̃ʒ] *nm* **1.** [troc] swap, exchange ▪ **faire un ~** to swap, to do a swap ▪ **on fait l'~?** do you want to swap?, do you want to do a swap? ▪ **~ de prisonniers** exchange of prisoners ➊ **~ standard** replacement *(of a spare part)* **2.** ÉCON trade ➊ **~s internationaux** international trade **3.** [aller et retour] exchange ▪ **avoir un ~ de vues** to exchange opinions ▪ **~s culturels** cultural exchanges ➊ **c'est un ~ de bons procédés** one good turn deserves another **4.** [visite] : **~ (linguistique)** (language) exchange **5.** JEUX : **faire (un) ~** [aux échecs] to exchange pieces **6.** SPORT : **~ de balles** [avant un match] knocking up ; [pendant le match] rally **7.** BIOL : **~s gazeux** gaseous interchange **8.** DR exchange.

◆ **en échange** *loc adv* in exchange, in return.

◆ **en échange de** *loc prép* in exchange *ou* return for.

échangeable [eʃɑ̃ʒabl] *adj* exchangeable ▪ **nos articles sont ~s sur présentation d'un ticket de caisse** articles may be exchanged on production of a receipt.

échanger [17] [eʃɑ̃ʒe] *vt* **1.** [troquer] to exchange, to swap ▪ **~ un stylo contre *ou* pour un briquet** to exchange *ou* to swap a pen for a lighter **2.** [se donner mutuellement] to exchange ▪ **ils ont échangé des lettres** there was an exchange of letters between them ▪ **~ un regard/sourire** to exchange glances/smiles ▪ **~ quelques mots avec qqn** to exchange a few words with sb **3.** SPORT : **~ des balles** [avant le match] to knock up.

◆ **s'échanger** <> *vp (emploi passif)* [être troqué] to be swapped ▪ BOURSE to trade ▪ **le dollar s'échange aujourd'hui à un euro** today the dollar is trading at one euro.
<> *vp (emploi réciproque)* : **s'~ des disques** to swap records with each other.

échangeur [eʃɑ̃ʒœr] *nm* **1.** TRANSP [carrefour] interchange ▪ [donnant accès à l'autoroute] feeder **2.** PHYS : **~ (de chaleur)** heat exchanger.

échangisme [eʃɑ̃ʒism] *nm* [sexuel] partner swapping.

échangiste [eʃɑ̃ʒist] *adj* & *nmf* **1.** DR exchanger **2.** [sexuellement] swinger.

échanson [eʃɑ̃sɔ̃] *nm* HIST cupbearer ▪ *hum* wine waiter.

échantillon [eʃɑ̃tijɔ̃] *nm* **1.** COMM & SC sample, specimen ▪ **~ publicitaire** free sample **2.** [cas typique] example, sample **3.** [de population] cross-section.

échantillonnage [eʃɑ̃tijɔnaʒ] *nm* **1.** [action] sampling, selecting **2.** [de parfum] selection ▪ [de papier peint, de moquette] sample book **3.** INFORM & TÉLÉCOM sampling.

échantillonner [3] [eʃɑ̃tijɔne] *vt* **1.** COMM & SC to sample **2.** [population] to take a cross-section of.

échantillonneur [eʃɑ̃tijɔnœr] *nm* sampler MUS.

échappatoire [eʃapatwar] *nf* loophole, way out.

échappé, e [eʃape] *nm, f competitor who has broken away* ▪ **les ~s du peloton** runners breaking away from the rest of the field.

◆ **échappée** *nf* **1.** SPORT breakaway **2.** [espace ouvert à la vue] vista, view **3.** [dans un escalier] headroom **4.** [passage] space, gap ▪ **l'~e d'un garage** garage entrance **5.** [instant] : **une brève ~e de soleil** a brief sunny spell.

◆ **par échappées** *loc adv* every now and then, in fits and starts.

échappement [eʃapmɑ̃] *nm* **1.** [de gaz] exhaust ▪ **~ libre** cutout **2.** [d'horloge] escapement **3.** [d'un escalier] headroom.

échapper [3] [eʃape] <> *vt loc* **l'~ belle** to have a narrow escape.
<> *vi* **1.** [s'enfuir] : **faire ~** [animal] to let out ; [détenu] to help to escape ▪ **il a laissé ~ le chien** he let the dog loose **2.** [secret, paroles] : **pas un mot n'échappa de ses lèvres *ou* sa bouche** he didn't utter a single word ▪ **laisser ~** to let slip **3.** [glisser] to slip ▪ **le vase lui a échappé des mains** the vase slipped out of her hands **4.** [erreur, occasion] : **laisser ~ : j'ai pu laisser ~ quelques fautes** I may have overlooked a few mistakes ▪ **laisser ~ une occasion** to miss an opportunity.

◆ **échapper à** *v+prép* **1.** [se soustraire à] to avoid, to evade ▪ **~ à ses obligations** to evade one's duties **2.** [éviter] to escape from, to get away from ▪ **elle sent que sa fille lui échappe** she can feel (that) her daughter's drifting away from her **3.** [être dispensé de] : **~ à l'impôt** [officiellement] to be exempt from taxation ; [en trichant] to evade income tax **4.** [être oublié par] : **rien ne lui échappe** she doesn't miss a thing ▪ **ce détail m'a échappé** that detail escaped me ▪ **quelques erreurs ont pu m'~** I may have overlooked a few mistakes ▪ **son nom m'échappe** his name escapes me *ou* has slipped my mind ▪ **je me souviens de l'air mais les paroles m'échappent** I remember the tune but I forget the lyrics ▪ *(tournure impersonnelle)* **il ne m'a pas échappé qu'il avait l'air ravi** it was obvious to me that he looked delighted ▪ **il ne vous aura pas échappé que...** it will not have escaped your attention that... **5.** [être enlevé à] : **la victoire lui a échappé** victory eluded him **6.** [être prononcé par] : **si des paroles désagréables m'ont échappé, je te prie de m'excuser** if I let slip an unpleasant remark, I apologize ▪ **la phrase lui aura échappé** the remark must have slipped out.

◆ **s'échapper** *vpi* **1.** [s'enfuir] to escape, to get away ▪ **s'~ d'un camp** to escape from a camp **2.** [se rendre disponible] to get away ▪ **je ne pourrai pas m'~ avant midi** I won't be able to get away before noon **3.** [jaillir] to escape, to leak ▪ **des mèches s'échappaient de son foulard** wisps of hair poked out from underneath her scarf **4.** [disparaître] to disappear, to vanish **5.** SPORT [coureur] to break *ou* to draw away.

écharde [eʃard] *nf* splinter.

écharpe [eʃarp] *nf* **1.** [vêtement] scarf ▪ [d'un député, d'un maire] sash ▪ **l'~ tricolore** *sash worn by French mayors at civic functions* **2.** [pansement] sling.
◆ **en écharpe** *loc adv* : **avoir le bras en ~** to have one's arm in a sling.

écharper [3] [eʃarpe] *vt* to tear to pieces ▪ **il s'est fait ~ par sa femme quand il est rentré** his wife really laid into him when he got home.

échasse [eʃas] *nf* **1.** [bâton] stilt ▪ **marcher** *ou* **être monté sur des ~s** *fam* to have long legs **2.** ZOOL stilt.

échassier [eʃasje] *nm* wader, wading bird.

échauder [3] [eʃode] *vt* **1.** [ébouillanter - volaille] to scald ; [- vaisselle] to run boiling water over ; [- théière] to warm **2.** [décevoir] : **l'expérience de l'année dernière m'a échaudé** my experience last year taught me a lesson ▪ **il a déjà été échaudé une fois** he's had his fingers burned once already.

échauffement [eʃofmɑ̃] *nm* **1.** [réchauffement - du sol, d'une planète] warming (up) **2.** SPORT [processus] warming-up ▪ [exercices, période] warm-up **3.** [excitation] over-excitement **4.** MÉCAN overheating **5.** AGRIC fermenting.

échauffer [3] [eʃofe] *vt* **1.** [chauffer] to heat (up), to warm up *(sép)* **2.** [exciter] to heat, to fire, to stimulate ▪ **les esprits sont échauffés** feelings are running high ▶ **il m'échauffe la bile** *ou* **les oreilles** *fam* he really gets my goat *ou* on my nerves **3.** MÉCAN to overheat ▪ [fermenter] to cause fermentation **4.** SPORT to warm up *(sép)*.
◆ **s'échauffer** *vpi* **1.** SPORT to warm up **2.** [s'exciter] to become heated.

échauffourée [eʃofure] *nf* clash, skirmish.

échauguette [eʃogɛt] *nf* HIST watchtower.

échéance [eʃeɑ̃s] *nf* **1.** [date - de paiement] date of payment ; [- de maturité] date of maturity ; [- de péremption] expiry date ▪ **venir à ~** to fall due ▪ **payable à quinze jours d'~** payable at two weeks' date **2.** [somme d'argent] financial commitment **3.** [moment] term ▪ **nous sommes à trois mois de l'~ électorale** there are three months to go before the date set for the election ▪ **un mois avant l'~ de l'examen** one month before the exam (is due to take place).
◆ **à brève échéance, à courte échéance** ◇ *loc adj* short-term.
◇ *loc adv* in the short run.
◆ **à longue échéance** ◇ *loc adj* long-term.
◇ *loc adv* in the long run.

échéancier [eʃeɑ̃sje] *nm* **1.** [livre] bill book, tickler US **2.** [délais] schedule of repayments.

échéant, e [eʃeɑ̃, ɑ̃t] *adj* ▷ **cas**.

échec [eʃɛk] *nm* **1.** [revers] failure ▪ **la réunion s'est soldée par un ~** nothing came out of the meeting ▪ **faire ~ à** to foil, to prevent ▶ **l'~ scolaire** underperforming at school **2.** [défaite] defeat ▪ **son ~ au championnat** his defeat in the championship **3.** JEUX : **~ (au roi)!** check! ▪ **~ et mat!** checkmate! ▪ **faire ~** to check ▪ **faire ~ et mat** to checkmate.
◆ **échecs** *nmpl* chess *(U)* ▪ **jouer aux ~s** to play chess.
◆ **en échec** *loc adv* : **mettre/tenir qqn en ~** to put/to hold sb in check.

échelle [eʃɛl] *nf* **1.** [outil] ladder ▪ **monter dans l'~ sociale** *fig* to climb the social ladder ▶ **~ coulissante** extension ladder ▪ **~ de corde** rope ladder ▪ **~ double** (high) stepladder ▪ **~ d'incendie** fireman's ladder ▪ **~ de meunier** straight wooden staircase ▪ **faire la courte ~ à qqn** to give sb a leg up ▪ **il n'y a plus qu'à tirer l'~** *fam* we might as well just give up **2.** [mesure] scale ▪ **une carte à l'~ 1/10 000** a map on a scale of 1/10,000 ▪ **réduire l'~ d'un dessin** to scale a drawing down **3.** GÉOL scale ▪ **sur l'~ de Richter** on the Richter scale **4.** [dimension] scale ▪ **des événements à l'~ mondiale** world events ▪ **à l'~ nationale** nationwide ▪ **des villes à l'~ humaine** cities (built) on a human scale **5.** DR & ADMIN scale ▪ **~ des valeurs** scale of values ▪ **~ (mobile) des salaires** *ou* **traitements** (sliding) salary scale **6.** MUS scale ▪ **~ diatonique/chromatique** diatonic/chromatic scale.
◆ **à grande échelle** ◇ *loc adj* **1.** [dessin] large-scale **2.** [projet] ambitious.
◇ *loc adv* on a large scale.
◆ **à l'échelle** *loc adv* : **la façade n'est pas à l'~** the façade isn't (drawn) to scale ▪ **dessiner une carte à l'~** to draw a map to scale.
◆ **à l'échelle de** *loc prép* at the level *ou* on a scale of ▪ **à l'~ de la région/planète** on a regional/world(-wide) scale.

échelon [eʃlɔ̃] *nm* **1.** [barreau] rung **2.** ADMIN grade ▪ **grimper d'un ~** to go up one step *ou* grade **3.** [niveau] level ▪ **à l'~ local** at local level **4.** MIL echelon.
◆ **à l'échelon de** *loc prép* at the level of ▪ **à l'~ du ministère** at Ministry level.

échelonnement [eʃlɔnmɑ̃] *nm* **1.** [dans l'espace] spreading out, placing at regular intervals **2.** [dans le temps - d'un paiement] spreading (out) ; [- de congés] staggering **3.** [graduation - de difficultés] grading.

échelonner [3] [eʃlɔne] *vt* **1.** [dans l'espace - arbres, poteaux] to space out *(sép)*, to place at regular intervals **2.** [dans le temps - livraisons, remboursements, publication] to spread (out), to stagger, to schedule at regular intervals ▪ **paiements échelonnés** payments in instalments, staggered payments ▪ **faire ~ une dette** to arrange to pay back a debt in instalments **3.** [graduer - difficultés, problèmes] to grade, to place on a sliding scale **4.** MIL to echelon.
◆ **s'échelonner sur** *vp+prép* [suj: projet, travaux] to be spread out over.

écheveau, x [eʃvo] *nm* **1.** TEXT hank, skein **2.** [labyrinthe de rues] maze **3.** [embrouillamini] tangle ▪ **démêler l'~ d'une intrigue** to untangle a plot.

échevelé, e [eʃəvle] *adj* **1.** [ébouriffé] dishevelled, tousled **2.** [effréné] frantic, wild ▪ **une danse ~e** a wild dance.

écheveler [24] [eʃəvle] *vt litt* to tousle the hair of.

échevin [eʃvɛ̃] *nm* **1.** HIST deputy mayor of a town **2.** *Belgique* deputy burgmaster *ou* burgomaster.

échine [eʃin] *nf* **1.** ANAT & ZOOL backbone, spine ▪ **courber** *ou* **plier l'~ devant qqn** to submit to sb **2.** CULIN chine **3.** ARCHIT echinus.

échiner [3] [eʃine] ◆ **s'échiner à** *vp+prép* : **s'~ à faire qqch** to wear o.s. out doing sthg.

échiquier [eʃikje] *nm* **1.** JEUX chessboard ▪ **le rôle que nous jouons sur l'~ européen/mondial** *fig* the part we play on the European/world scene **2.** POLIT : **L'Échiquier** the (British) Exchequer.
◆ **en échiquier** *loc adv* in a check pattern.

écho [eko] *nm* **1.** ACOUST echo ▪ **il y a de l'~** there is an echo ▶ **~ multiple** reverberations ▪ **~ simple** echo **2.** *fig* **j'en ai eu des ~s** I heard something about it ▪ **sa proposition n'a pas trouvé d'~** his offer wasn't taken into consideration ▪ **aucun journal ne s'en est fait l'~** the story was not picked up by any newspaper **3.** TV ghosting **4.** [rubrique de journal] gossip column.
◆ **à tous les échos** *loc adv* in all directions.

échographie [ekɔgrafi] *nf* (ultrasound) scan ▪ **se faire faire une ~** to have a scan *ou* an ultrasound scan.

échographier [9] [ekɔgrafje] *vt* to scan *(with an ultrasound scan)*.

échoir [70] [eʃwar] *vi* FIN to fall due ▪ **intérêts à ~** accruing interest, interest falling due.
◆ **échoir à** *v+prép sout* **~ à qqn** to fall to sb ▪ **le sort qui lui est échu n'est guère enviable** one can hardly envy his lot ▪ *(tournure impersonnelle)* **c'est à moi qu'il échoit d'annoncer la mauvaise nouvelle** it falls to me to announce the bad news.

échoppe [eʃɔp] *nf* **1.** [outil] burin **2.** *vieilli* shop UK, store US.

échotier, ère [ekɔtje, ɛr] *nm, f* [journaliste] gossip columnist.

échouage [eʃwaʒ], **échouement** [eʃumɑ̃] *nm* [d'un navire] grounding, running aground.

échouer [6] [eʃwe] ◇ *vi* **1.** [rater - projet, tentative] to fail, to fall through ■ **ils ont échoué dans leur tentative de coup d'État** their attempted coup failed ■ **~ à un examen** to fail an exam ■ **faire ~** to foil, to frustrate **2.** *fam* [finir] to end *ou* to wind up **3.** NAUT to ground, to run aground.
◇ *vt* NAUT [accidentellement] to ground, to run aground ■ [volontairement] to beach.
◆ **s'échouer** *vpi* NAUT to run aground ■ **quelques caisses échouées sur la plage** a few boxes washed up *ou* stranded on the beach.

échu, e [eʃy] ◇ *pp* ▷ **échoir.**
◇ *adj* : **payer un loyer à terme ~** to pay at the end of the rental term.

écimer [3] [esime] *vt* to pollard.

éclabousser [3] [eklabuse] *vt* **1.** [asperger] to splash, to spatter ■ **éclaboussé de : éclaboussé de boue** mud-spattered **2.** [nuire à la réputation de] : **~ qqn** to malign sb, to tarnish sb's reputation **3.** *litt* [impressionner] : **~ qqn de son luxe/sa richesse** to flaunt one's luxurious lifestyle/one's wealth in sb's face.

éclaboussure [eklabusyr] *nf* **1.** [tache - de boue, de peinture] splash, spatter ■ **des ~s de sang** bloodstains **2.** [retombée] smear.

éclair [eklɛr] *nm* **1.** MÉTÉOR flash of lightning ■ **~s** lightning ■ **ses yeux jetaient** *ou* **lançaient des ~s** *fig* her eyes were flashing ■ **un ~ de colère passa dans ses yeux** anger flashed *ou* blazed in his eyes ▶ **le peloton est passé comme un ~** the pack of cyclists flashed past ■ **prompt** *ou* **rapide** *ou* **vif comme l'~** (as) quick as a flash **2.** [lueur - d'un coup de feu, d'un flash] flash **3.** [bref instant] : **dans un ~ de lucidité** in a flash of lucidity ■ **un ~ de génie** a flash of inspiration **4.** CULIN éclair **5.** *(comme adj)* lightning *(modif)* ■ **visite ~** lightning *ou* flying visit.
◆ **en un éclair** *loc adv* in a flash *ou* a trice *ou* an instant.

éclairage [eklɛraʒ] *nm* **1.** [illumination artificielle] lighting ▶ **~ indirect** indirect *ou* concealed lighting ■ **~ public** street lighting **2.** [intensité de lumière] light **3.** [installation] : **l'~, les ~s** the lighting ■ **~ aux projecteurs** floodlighting **4.** ART use of light ■ PHOTO light **5.** [aspect] light, perspective ■ **vu sous cet ~** seen in this light ■ **apporter à qqch un ~ nouveau** to throw new light on sthg **6.** MIL scouting expedition.

éclairagiste [eklɛraʒist] *nmf* **1.** CINÉ, THÉÂTRE & TV lighting engineer **2.** COMM dealer in lights and lamps.

éclairant, e [eklɛrɑ̃, ɑ̃t] *adj* **1.** [lumineux] lighting **2.** [édifiant - commentaire, conclusion] enlightening.

éclaircie [eklɛrsi] *nf* **1.** MÉTÉOR sunny spell, bright interval **2.** [amélioration] improvement **3.** [de forêt] clearing.

éclaircir [32] [eklɛrsir] *vt* **1.** [rendre moins sombre] to make lighter ■ **ce papier peint éclaircit la pièce** this wallpaper brightens up the room *ou* makes the room feel lighter ■ **~ ses cheveux** to make one's hair (look) lighter ; [par mèches] to put highlights in one's hair **2.** [rendre plus audible] : **des pastilles pour ~ la voix** *ou* **gorge** lozenges to clear the throat **3.** CULIN [sauce, soupe] to thin (down), to dilute **4.** [forêt] to thin (out) **5.** [élucider - affaire, mystère] to clear up ; [- situation] to clarify.
◆ **s'éclaircir** ◇ *vpi* **1.** MÉTÉOR to clear (up), to brighten up **2.** [pâlir - cheveux] to go lighter *ou* paler *ou* blonder **3.** [se raréfier] to thin (out) ■ **ses cheveux s'éclaircissent** his hair's getting thinner, he's going bald **4.** [être clarifié - mystère] to be solved ; [- situation] to become clearer.
◇ *vpt* : **s'~ la voix** *ou* **gorge** to clear one's throat.

éclaircissant, e [eklɛrsisɑ̃, ɑ̃t] *adj* [lotion, shampooing] lightening, highlighting.

éclaircissement [eklɛrsismɑ̃] *nm* **1.** [d'une peinture] lightening **2.** [explication] explanation ■ **je voudrais des ~s sur ce point** I would like some further clarification on this point.

éclairé, e [eklere] *adj* **1.** [lumineux] : **une pièce bien/mal ~e** a well-/badly-lit room **2.** [intelligent] enlightened.

éclairer [4] [eklere] ◇ *vt* **1.** [chemin, lieu] to light (up) ■ **~ un stade avec des projecteurs** to floodlight a stadium ■ **marchez derrière moi, je vais vous ~** walk behind me, I'll light the way for you **2.** [égayer] to brighten *ou* to light up *(sép)*, to illuminate ■ **le visage éclairé par un sourire** his face lit up by a smile **3.** [rendre compréhensible] to clarify, to throw light on **4.** [informer] to enlighten ■ **j'ai besoin qu'on m'éclaire sur ce point** I need sb to explain this point to me *ou* to enlighten me on this point ▶ **~ la lanterne de qqn** to put sb in the picture **5.** MIL to scout out.
◇ *vi* : **la lampe n'éclaire plus** the lamp's gone out ■ **cette ampoule éclaire bien/mal** this bulb throws out a lot of/doesn't throw out much light.
◆ **s'éclairer** ◇ *vp (emploi réfléchi)* : **s'~ à l'électricité** to have electric lighting ■ **s'~ à la bougie** to use candlelight ■ **tiens, prends ma lampe électrique pour t'~** here, take my flashlight to light your way.
◇ *vpi* **1.** [s'allumer] to be lit **2.** [visage, regard] to brighten *ou* to light up **3.** [se résoudre] to get clearer ■ **enfin, tout s'éclaire!** it's all clear (to me) now!

éclaireur, euse [eklɛrœr, øz] *nm, f* [scout] boy scout (*f* girl scout) ■ **les Éclaireurs de France** the (French) Scout Association.
◆ **éclaireur** *nm* MIL scout.
◆ **en éclaireur** *loc adv* : **envoyer qqn en ~** to send sb scouting ■ **partir en ~** to go (off) and scout around.

éclat [ekla] *nm* **1.** [fragment - de verre, de métal] splinter, shard ; [- de bois] splinter, sliver ■ **des ~s d'obus** shrapnel **2.** [bruit] burst ■ **~ de rire** burst *ou* roar of laughter ■ **on entendait des ~s de voix** loud voices could be heard **3.** [scandale] scandal ■ **faire un ~ en public** to cause a public scandal *ou* embarrassment **4.** [de la lumière, du jour] brightness ■ [du soleil, de projecteur] glare ■ **l'~ d'un diamant** the sparkle of a diamond **5.** [du regard, d'un sourire, d'une couleur] brightness ■ [du teint] radiance, bloom ■ **sans ~** dull ■ **elle a perdu tout son ~** she has lost all her bloom *ou* sparkle **6.** [splendeur] glamour, glitter ■ **donner de l'~ à** to make glamorous **7.** ASTRON : **~ absolu/apparent** true/apparent luminosity.

éclatant, e [eklatɑ̃, ɑ̃t] *adj* **1.** [soleil, couleur] dazzling, brilliant ■ [miroir, surface] sparkling ■ [dents] gleaming ■ **draps d'une blancheur ~e** *ou* **~s de blancheur** dazzling white sheets ■ **écharpe d'un rouge ~** bright red scarf ■ **un sourire ~** a dazzling smile **2.** [excellent - santé, teint] radiant, glowing ■ **~ de : ~e de beauté** radiantly beautiful **3.** [spectaculaire - revanche] spectacular ; [- triomphe, victoire] resounding **4.** [bruyant] loud, resounding ■ **on entendait son rire ~** his booming *ou* hearty laugh could be heard.

éclatement [eklatmɑ̃] *nm* **1.** [déflagration - d'une bombe] explosion ; [- d'un pneu, d'un fruit] bursting **2.** [rupture - d'un parti] breakup.

éclater [3] [eklate] *vi* **1.** [exploser] to explode, to blow up, to burst ■ **j'ai l'impression que ma tête/mon cœur/ma poitrine va ~** I feel as if my head/heart/chest is going to burst ■ **mon pneu a éclaté** my tyre burst **2.** [se fractionner] to split, to break up **3.** [retentir] : **l'orage a enfin éclaté** the thunderstorm finally broke ■ **un coup de tonnerre a soudain éclaté** there was a sudden thunderclap ■ **des coups de feu ont éclaté** shots rang out ■ **~ de : ~ de rire** to burst out laughing ■ **~ en : ~ en larmes/sanglots** to burst into tears/sobs ■ **~ en reproches** to let out a stream of reproaches **4.** [se déclencher - guerre, scandale] to break out **5.** [apparaître] to stand out **6.** [de colère] to explode **7.** [être célèbre] to be an instant success.
◆ **s'éclater** *vpi fam* to have a whale of a time *ou* a ball ■ **il s'éclate en faisant de la photo** he gets his kicks from photography.

éclectique [eklɛktik] ◇ *adj* [distraction, goût, opinion] eclectic, varied.
◇ *nmf* eclectic, person with eclectic tastes.

éclectisme [eklɛktism] *nm* eclecticism.

éclipse [eklips] *nf* **1.** ASTRON eclipse ■ **~ de Soleil/Lune** solar/lunar eclipse ■ **~ annulaire/totale/partielle** annular/total/partial eclipse **2.** [éloignement] eclipse, decline **3.** MÉD blackout.
◆ **à éclipses** *loc adj* : **phare/feu à ~s** intermittent beacon/light ■ **une carrière à ~s** *fig* a career progressing in fits and starts.

éclipser [3] [eklipse] *vt* **1.** ASTRON to eclipse **2.** [surclasser] to eclipse, to overshadow, to outshine ■ **éclipsé sur le marché des ordinateurs par...** overshadowed *ou* outclassed on the computer market by...
➡ **s'éclipser** *vpi fam* to slip away *ou* out, to sneak off.

éclisse [eklis] *nf* **1.** MÉD splint **2.** RAIL fishplate **3.** [claie à fromages] cheese tray.

éclopé, e [eklɔpe] ◇ *adj* lame, limping.
◇ *nm, f* person with a limp.

éclore [113] [eklɔr] *vi (aux être ou avoir)* **1.** [œuf, poussin] to hatch (out) ■ *litt* [fleur] to open out **2.** *litt* [apparaître - jour, amour] to dawn ; [- doute] to be born.

éclosion [eklozjɔ̃] *nf* **1.** [d'un œuf] hatching ■ **jusqu'à leur ~** until they hatch ‖ *litt* [d'une fleur] opening (out) **2.** *litt* [d'un amour] dawning.

écluse [eklyz] *nf* lock ■ **une porte d'~** a lock *ou* sluice gate ▸ **lâcher** *ou* **ouvrir les ~s** to turn on the waterworks.

écluser [3] [eklyze] ◇ *vt* **1.** NAUT [canal, voie d'eau] to lock ■ [bateau, péniche] to lock, to sluice **2.** △ [boire] to down, to knock back ■ **il avait déjà éclusé trois cognacs** *fam* he'd already downed three brandies.
◇ *vi*△ to booze, to knock back the booze.

éclusier, ère [eklyzje, ɛr] *nm, f* lockkeeper.

écodéveloppement [ekɔdevlɔpmɑ̃] *nm* ecodevelopment.

écœurant, e [ekœrɑ̃, ɑ̃t] *adj* **1.** [nauséeux] nauseating, cloying, sickly **2.** [indigne] disgusting **3.** *fam* [démoralisant] sickening, disheartening.

écœurement [ekœrmɑ̃] *nm* **1.** [nausée] nausea ■ **manger des chocolats jusqu'à ~** to make o.s. sick eating chocolates **2.** [aversion] disgust, aversion, distaste **3.** *fam* [découragement] discouragement.

écœurer [5] [ekœre] *vt* **1.** [donner la nausée] to sicken ■ **la vue de ce gâteau m'écœure** looking at that cake makes me feel sick **2.** [inspirer le mépris à] to disgust, to sicken ■ **sa mauvaise foi m'écœure** I'm disgusted by his bad faith **3.** *fam* [décourager] to dishearten, to discourage.

écoguerrier [ekɔgɛrje] *nm* eco-warrior.

écolage [ekɔlaʒ] *nm Suisse* school fees.

école [ekɔl] *nf* **1.** [établissement] school ■ **aller à l'~** to go to school ▸ **~ communale** local primary school ■ **~ élémentaire** *vieilli* primary school ■ **~ maternelle, petite ~** *fam* nursery school ■ **~ primaire, grande ~** *fam* primary school ■ **~ privée** private school ■ **~ publique** state school *UK*, public school *US* ■ **bateau-~** training ship ■ **voiture-~** driving-school car ■ **faire l'~ buissonnière** to play truant
2. [cours] school ■ **l'~ recommencera le 9 septembre** school will reopen on September 9th
3. [système] : **l'~ laïque** secular education ■ **l'~ libre** sectarian education ■ **l'~ obligatoire** compulsory schooling
4. [collège supérieur] : **~ de commerce** business school ■ **grande ~** *competitive-entry higher education establishment* ■ **École (centrale) des arts et manufactures, École centrale** *prestigious engineering school* ■ **École (nationale) des chartes** *grande école for archivists and librarians* ■ **École nationale d'administration = ENA** ■ **École nationale de la magistrature** *grande école for the judiciary* ■ **École normale d'instituteurs** *former primary teachers' training college* ■ **École normale supérieure** *prestigious grande école for teachers and researchers*, *voir aussi* **grand**
5. [lieu spécialisé] school ■ **~ de conduite** driving school ■ **~ de danse** ballet school ■ **~ de ski** skiing school ■ **~ de voile** sailing school
6. [pédagogie] : **l'~ active** the active method of teaching
7. [disciples] school ■ **l'~ de Pythagore** the Pythagorean school ■ **l'~ française du Louvre** the French collections at the Louvre ▸ **il est de la vieille ~** he's one of the old school *ou* guard ■ **faire ~** to attract a following
8. *fig* **une ~ de courage** a lesson in courage ▸ **être à bonne ~** to learn a lot ■ **être à rude ~** to learn the hard way.

L'ÉCOLE LAÏQUE

The separation of Church and State, which reflects the republican ideal and became law in 1905, is an important aspect of French culture. Since that date State education has been independent of the Church, and explicitly excludes religious instruction and religious ceremony.

écolier, ère [ekɔlje, ɛr] *nm, f* **1.** ÉDUC [garçon] schoolboy ■ [fille] schoolgirl **2.** [novice] beginner.

écolo [ekɔlo] *fam* ◇ *adj* green.
◇ *nmf* environmentalist.

écologie [ekɔlɔʒi] *nf* ecology.

écologique [ekɔlɔʒik] *adj* [gén] ecological ■ [politique, parti] green.

écologiquement [ekɔlɔʒikmɑ̃] *adv* ecologically.

écologisme [ekɔlɔʒism] *nm* ecology.

écologiste [ekɔlɔʒist] *nmf* **1.** [expert] ecologist, environmentalist **2.** [partisan] ecologist, green.

écomusée [ekɔmyze] *nm* ≃ heritage centre *(in rural area)*.

éconduire [98] [ekɔ̃dɥir] *vt* [importun, vendeur] to get rid of ■ [soupirant] to jilt, to reject.

économat [ekɔnɔma] *nm* **1.** [service - dans un collège, un hôpital] bursarship ; [- dans un club] stewardship **2.** [bureau - dans un collège, un hôpital] bursar's office ; [- dans un club] steward's office **3.** [coopérative] staff co-op.

économe [ekɔnɔm] ◇ *adj* **1.** [avec l'argent] thrifty ■ **être ~** to be careful with money **2.** [parcimonieux] : **être ~ de ses paroles/gestes** to be sparing with one's words/gestures ■ **être ~ de son temps** to give of one's time sparingly.
◇ *nmf* [d'une institution, d'un hôpital] bursar ■ [d'un club, d'un collège] steward.
◇ *nm* [couteau] (vegetable) peeler.

économie [ekɔnɔmi] *nf* **1.** [système] economy ■ **~ dirigée** *ou* **planifiée** planned economy ■ **~ libérale/socialiste** free-market/socialist economy ■ **~ de marché** market economy ■ **~ mixte** mixed economy ■ **~ parallèle** *ou* **souterraine** black economy **2.** [discipline] economics ■ **~ (politique)** economics ■ **~ d'entreprise** business economics **3.** [épargne] economy, thrift ■ **par ~, il y va à pied** he walks to save money ■ **une ~ de : nous avons réalisé une ~ de cinq euros par pièce produite** we made a saving of *ou* we saved five euros on each item produced ■ **les ~s d'énergie** energy conservation ■ **faire des ~s d'énergie** to conserve *ou* to save energy ■ **ce sera une ~ de temps/d'argent** it'll save time/money ■ **avec une grande ~ de moyens** with very limited means ■ **faire l'~ de** to save ■ **je ferai l'~ d'un voyage** it'll save me a trip ▸ **une ~** *ou* **des ~s de bouts de chandelles** *péj* cheeseparing **4.** [structure] : **nous n'approuvons pas l'~ générale du projet** we do not approve of the structure of the project.
➡ **économies** *nfpl* savings ■ **faire des ~s** to save money ■ **elle a quelques ~s** she has some savings ▸ **~s d'échelle** economies of scale ■ **il n'y a pas de petites ~s** *prov* take care of the pennies and the pounds will take care of themselves *prov*.

économique [ekɔnɔmik] ◇ *adj* **1.** ÉCON economic ■ **géographie ~** economic geography **2.** [peu coûteux] economical, cheap, inexpensive ■ **classe ~** economy class.
◇ *nm* : **l'~** the economic situation.

économiquement [ekɔnɔmikmɑ̃] *adv* **1.** [frugalement] frugally **2.** ÉCON economically, from an economic point of view ■ **les ~ faibles** the lower-income groups.

économiser [3] [ekɔnɔmize] ◇ *vt* **1.** [épargner - argent, temps] to save **2.** [ménager - force] to save ; [- ressources] to husband **3.** [énergie, électricité, denrée] to save, to conserve.
◇ *vi* to save money, to economize ■ **je n'arrive pas à ~** I just can't manage to save any money ■ **~ sur l'habillement** to cut down on buying clothes, to spend less on clothes.

économiseur [ekɔnɔmizœr] *nm* : **~ d'écran** screen saver.

économiste [ekɔnɔmist] *nmf* economist.

écope [ekɔp] *nf* bailer.

écoper [3] [ekɔpe] ◇ *vt* [barque, bateau] to bail out.
◇ *vi fam* [recevoir une sanction, une réprimande] to take the rap ▪ **c'est lui qui a écopé** he was the one who took the rap.
◆ **écoper de** *v+prép fam* to cop UK, to get ▪ **il a écopé de cinq ans de prison** he got five years inside.

écoproduit [ekɔprɔdɥi] *nm* green product.

écorce [ekɔrs] *nf* **1.** [d'un arbre] bark ▪ [d'un fruit] peel **2.** GÉOGR : **l'~ terrestre** the earth's crust **3.** [extérieur] exterior, outward appearance.

écorcer [16] [ekɔrse] *vt* [arbre] to bark ▪ [fruit] to peel ▪ [riz] to husk.

écorché, e [ekɔrʃe] *nm, f* : **c'est un ~ vif** he's hypersensitive.
◆ **écorché** *nm* **1.** ART écorché **2.** [dessin] cutaway.

écorcher [3] [ekɔrʃe] *vt* **1.** [animal] to skin **2.** [torturer] to flay ▪ **~ vif** to flay alive ▪ **il crie comme si on l'écorchait vif** he's squealing like a stuck pig **3.** [blesser] to scratch, to graze ▪ **ça t'écorcherait la bouche de dire merci/demander pardon?** *fam* it wouldn't actually hurt to say thank you/sorry, would it? ▪ **la musique lui écorchait les oreilles** the music grated on his ears ▪ **ce langage lui écorchait les oreilles** he found these words offensive **4.** [mal prononcer - mot] to mispronounce ▪ **il écorche toujours mon nom** he always mispronounces my name **5.** *fam* [escroquer] to fleece, to swindle.
◆ **s'écorcher** *vp (emploi réfléchi)* to scrape *ou* to scratch o.s. ▪ **je me suis écorché le pied** I scraped *ou* scratched my foot.

écorcheur [ekɔrʃœr] *nm* **1.** [d'animaux] flayer, skinner **2.** *fam* [escroc] swindler, crook.

écorchure [ekɔrʃyr] *nf* scratch, graze ▪ **se faire une ~** to scratch o.s.

écorecharge [ekɔrəʃarʒ] *nf* eco-refill.

écorner [3] [ekɔrne] *vt* **1.** [endommager - cadre, meuble] to chip a corner off ; [- livre, page] to fold down the corner of, to dog-ear ▪ **un livre tout écorné** a dog-eared book **2.** [fortune, héritage] to make a dent in.

écosphère [ekɔsfɛr] *nf* ecosphere.

écossais, e [ekɔsɛ, ɛz] *adj* **1.** GÉOGR [coutume, lande] Scottish ▪ **whisky ~** Scotch (whisky) **2.** TEXT tartan.
◆ **Écossais, e** *nm, f* Scot, Scotsman (*f* Scotswoman) ▪ **les Écossais** Scottish people, the Scots.
◆ **écossais** *nm* **1.** LING Scots Gaelic **2.** TEXT tartan.

Écosse [ekɔs] *npr f* : **(l')~** Scotland.

écosser [3] [ekɔse] *vt* [petits pois] to shell, to pod ▪ [fèves] to shell.

écosystème [ekɔsistɛm] *nm* ecosystem.

écot [eko] *nm* share ▪ **payer chacun son ~** to pay one's share.

écotaxe [ekɔtaks] *nf* green tax.

écotourisme [ekɔturism] *nm* eco-tourism.

écoulement [ekulmɑ̃] *nm* **1.** [déversement] flowing out, outflow ▪ **système d'~ des eaux** drainage system **2.** MÉD discharge **3.** [mouvement - de la foule] dispersal **4.** [passage] : **l'~ du temps** the passing of time **5.** [vente] selling, distributing.

écouler [3] [ekule] *vt* **1.** [vendre] to sell ▪ **~ entièrement son stock** to clear one's stock **2.** [se débarrasser de - fausse monnaie, bijoux volés] to dispose *ou* to get rid of.
◆ **s'écouler** *vpi* **1.** [se déverser - liquide] to flow (out) ; [- foule] to pour out ▪ **l'eau s'écoule peu à peu** the water trickles out **2.** [passer - année, temps] to go by, to pass (by).

écourter [3] [ekurte] *vt* **1.** [rendre plus court] to shorten, to cut short ▪ **nous avons dû ~ notre visite** we had to cut our visit short **2.** VÉTÉR to dock.

écoutant, e [ekutɑ̃, ɑ̃t] *nm, f* helpline volunteer, trained listener.

écoute [ekut] *nf* **1.** RADIO listening ▪ **heure** *ou* **période de grande ~** RADIO peak listening time ; TV peak viewing time, prime time ▪ **aux heures de grande ~** RADIO & TV in prime time **2.** [détection] listening (in) ▪ **~ clandestine** wiretapping ▪ **~ sous-marine** sonar ▪ **~s (téléphoniques)** phone tapping ▪ **mettre** *ou* **placer qqn sur ~s** to tap sb's phone ▪ **être sur ~s : elle est sur ~s** her phone's been tapped ▪ **poste d'~** listening post ▪ **table d'~** wiretapping set **3.** [attention] ability to listen ▪ **avoir une bonne ~** to be good at listening *ou* a good listener **4.** NAUT sheet.
◆ **à l'écoute de** *loc prép* **1.** RADIO : **restez à l'~ de nos programmes de nuit** stay tuned to our late night programmes ▪ **rester à l'~** to stay tuned **2.** [attentif à] : **il est toujours à l'~ (des autres)** he's always ready to listen (to others) ▪ **être à l'~ de l'actualité** to be well up on current affairs.
◆ **aux écoutes** *loc adv* : **être aux ~s** to be tuned in to what's going on.

écouter [3] [ekute] *vt* **1.** [entendre - chanson, discours, émission] to listen to *(insép)* ▪ **c'est un des jeux les plus écoutés en France** it's one of the most popular radio games in France ▪ **je vais te faire ~ un truc génial** I'm going to play you something really great ▪ *(en usage absolu)* **n'~ que d'une oreille : je n'écoutais que d'une oreille** I was only half listening ▪ **~ de toutes ses oreilles** to be all ears ▪ **~ aux portes** to eavesdrop **2.** [porter attention] to listen to ▪ **écoutez-moi avant de vous décider** listen to what I have to say before you make up your mind ▪ *(en usage absolu)* **il sait ~** he's a good listener ▪ **il n'a même pas voulu ~** he wouldn't even listen **3.** [obéir à] to listen to ▪ **n'écoutant que sa colère/sa douleur/son cœur** guided by his anger/pain/heart alone ▪ **~ la voix de la sagesse** to listen to the voice of reason **4.** [à l'impératif, à valeur d'insistance] : **écoutez, nous n'allons pas nous disputer!** listen *ou* look, let's not quarrel!
◆ **s'écouter** ◇ *vp (emploi passif)* : **c'est le genre de musique qui s'écoute dans le recueillement** this is the kind of music one should listen to with reverence.
◇ *vp (emploi réfléchi)* : **il s'écoute trop** he's a bit of a hypochondriac ▪ **si je m'écoutais, je le mettrais dehors** if I had any sense, I'd throw him out ➊ **s'~ parler** to love the sound of one's own voice.

écouteur [ekutœr] *nm* **1.** TÉLÉCOM earpiece **2.** AUDIO earphone.

écoutille [ekutij] *nf* hatch, hatchway.

écouvillon [ekuvijɔ̃] *nm* **1.** ARM & MÉD swab **2.** [goupillon] bottlebrush.

écrabouiller [3] [ekrabuje] *vt fam* to crush, to squash ▪ **le gâteau a été complètement écrabouillé** the cake was completely squashed.

écran [ekrɑ̃] *nm* **1.** [d'une console, d'un ordinateur] screen ▪ **~ cathodique** cathode screen ▪ **~ à cristaux liquides** liquid crystal display ▪ **~ plat** flat-faced screen ▪ **~ tactile** touch-sensitive screen
2. CINÉ cinema screen ▪ **à l'~** *ou* **sur les ~s, cette semaine** what's on this week 'at the cinema *ou* movies *US*) ▪ **porter un roman à l'~** to adapt a novel for the screen ▪ **vedettes de l'~** movie stars, stars of the big screen ➊ **le grand ~** the big screen
3. TV : **le petit ~** television
4. [protection] screen, shield ▪ **il se fit un ~ de sa main** he shielded his eyes with his hand ▪ **~ de fumée** *pr & fig* smoke screen ▪ **faire ~ à : les nombreuses citations font ~ à la clarté de l'article** the numerous quotations make the article difficult to understand ➊ **~ antibruit** noise-reduction screen ▪ **~ pare-fumée** smoke deflector ▪ **~ de protection** shield ▪ **~ solaire** sun screen ▪ **crème ~ total** total protection sun cream *ou* block
5. ART silk screen
6. RADIO & TV : **~ (publicitaire)** advertising slot.

écrasant, e [ekrazɑ̃, ɑ̃t] *adj* **1.** [insupportable - gén] crushing, overwhelming ; [- chaleur] unbearable ; [- responsabilité] weighty, burdensome **2.** [charge de travail, proportion] overwhelming ▪ **une majorité ~e en faveur de** an overwhelming majority in favour of.

écrasé, e [ekraze] *adj* squashed.

écrasement [ekrazmɑ̃] *nm* **1.** [de fruits, de graines] squashing, crushing, pulping ▪ [de pommes de terre] mashing **2.** [anéantissement - d'une révolte] crushing.

écraser [3] [ekraze] <> *vt* **1.** [appuyer sur] to crush ▪ **~ l'accélérateur** *OU* **le champignon** *fam* to step on it, to step on the gas *US* ▪ **~ le frein** to slam on the brake ▪ **~ les prix** to slash prices
2. [fruit, pomme de terre] to mash ▪ **~ un moustique** to swat a mosquito ▪ **~ une cigarette** to stub a cigarette out
3. [piéton, chat] to run over ▪ **il s'est fait ~** he was run over
4. [faire mal à] to crush, to squash ▪ **tu m'écrases les pieds** you're treading on my feet
5. [accabler] to crush ▪ **~ de : ~ un pays d'impôts** to overburden a country with taxes ▪ **être écrasé de fatigue** to be overcome by fatigue
6. [rendre plus petit] to dwarf
7. [anéantir] to crush ▪ **se faire ~ par l'équipe adverse** to get crushed by the opposing team
8. [dominer] to outdo ▪ **essayer d'~ qqn** to try and beat sb at his own game ▪ **il écrase tout le monde de son luxe** he flaunts his luxurious lifestyle everywhere.
<> *vi*△ **1.** [se taire] : **écrase, tu veux bien!** shut up, will you!
2. *loc* **en ~** to sleep like a log.
◆ **s'écraser** <> *vp (emploi passif)* to be crushed.
<> *vpi* **1.** [fruit, légume] to get crushed *OU* mashed *OU* squashed
2. [tomber - aviateur, avion] to crash ; [- alpiniste] to crash to the ground ▪ **s'~ contre un mur** to crash against a wall
3. *fam* [se presser] to be *OU* to get crushed ▪ **les gens s'écrasent pour entrer** there's a great crush to get in
4. △ [se taire] to shut up, to pipe down ▪ **il vaut mieux s'~** better keep quiet *OU* mum.

écraseur, euse [ekrazœr, øz] *nm, f fam* road hog.

écrémage [ekremaʒ] *nm* **1.** CULIN skimming, creaming **2.** MÉTALL & INDUST **du pétrole** skimming.

écrémer [18] [ekreme] *vt* **1.** CULIN to skim **2.** MÉTALL & PÉTR to skim **3.** [sélectionner] to cream off *(sép)* ▪ **~ une collection** to cream off the best pieces from a collection.

écrevisse [ekrəvis] *nf* crayfish, crawfish *US* ▪ **avancer** *OU* **marcher comme une ~** to take one step forward and two steps back.

écrier [10] [ekrije] ◆ **s'écrier** *vpi* to cry *OU* to shout (out), to exclaim ▪ **"j'arrive", s'écria-t-elle** "I'm coming", she cried.

écrin [ekrɛ̃] *nm* [gén] box, case ▪ [à bijoux] casket.

écrire [99] [ekrir] *vt* **1.** [tracer - caractère, mot] to write ▪ *(en usage absolu)* **mon crayon écrit mal** my pen doesn't write properly ▪ **tu écris mal** [illisiblement] your handwriting is bad ▪ **les enfants écrivaient dans le sable avec un bâton** the children were writing in the sand with a stick ◆ **~ comme un chat** to scrawl **2.** [rédiger - lettre, livre] to write ; [- chèque, ordonnance] to write (out) ▪ **~ une lettre à la machine/sur un traitement de texte** to type a letter on a typewriter/a word processor ▪ **c'est écrit noir sur blanc** *OU* **en toutes lettres** *fig* it's written (down) in black and white ▪ *(en usage absolu)* **~ pour demander des renseignements** to write in *OU* off for information ▪ **elle écrit bien/mal** [du point de vue du style] she's a good/bad writer ▪ **c'était écrit** it was bound to happen ▪ **il était écrit qu'ils se retrouveraient** they were bound *OU* fated to find each other again ◆ **ce qui est écrit est écrit** *allus* & BIBLE what is written is written **3.** [noter] to write down ▪ **écris ce qu'il te dicte** write down what he dictates to you ▪ *(en usage absolu)* **~ sous la dictée** to take a dictation ▪ **elle a écrit sous ma dictée** she took down what I dictated **4.** [épeler] to spell.
◆ **s'écrire** <> *vp (emploi passif)* [s'épeler] to be spelled ▪ **ça s'écrit comment?** how do you spell it?
<> *vp (emploi réciproque)* [échanger des lettres] to write to each other.

écrit, e [ekri, it] *adj* written ▪ **épreuves ~es d'un examen** written part of an examination.
◆ **écrit** *nm* **1.** [document] document **2.** [œuvre] written work **3.** ÉDUC [examen] written examination *OU* papers ▪ [partie] written part (of the examination).
◆ **par écrit** *loc adv* in writing ▪ **mettre qqch par ~** to put sthg down in writing.

écriteau, x [ekrito] *nm* board, notice, sign.

écritoire [ekritwar] *nf* **1.** [coffret] writing case **2.** [en Afrique] writing implement.

écriture [ekrityr] *nf* **1.** [calligraphie] writing ▪ [tracé] handwriting, writing ▪ **avoir une ~ élégante** to have elegant handwriting, to write (in) an elegant hand *sout* **2.** [système] writing ▪ **~ idéographique** ideographic writing **3.** [type de caractère] script ▪ **~ droite/en italique** upright/italic script ▪ TÉLÉCOM : **~ prédictive** predictive text **4.** [style] writing ▪ [création] writing **5.** FIN entry ▪ **passer une ~** to make an entry **6.** DR written document **7.** RELIG : **l'~ sainte, les Écritures** the Scriptures.
◆ **écritures** *nfpl* COMM accounts, entries ▪ **tenir les ~s** to do the bookkeeping ◆ **jeu d'~s** dummy entry.

écrivailler [3] [ekrivaje] *vi péj* to scribble.

écrivaillon [ekrivajɔ̃] *nm péj* [gén] scribbler ▪ [journaliste] hack.

écrivain [ekrivɛ̃] *nm* writer ▪ **elle est ~** she's a writer ◆ **~ public** public letter writer.

écrivait *etc v* ▻ **écrire.**

écrivassier, ère [ekrivasje, ɛr] *nm, f péj* scribbler.

écrou [ekru] *nm* **1.** MÉCAN nut **2.** DR committal.

écrouer [3] [ekrue] *vt* to imprison, to jail.

écroulement [ekrulmɑ̃] *nm* [d'un édifice, d'une théorie] collapse.

écrouler [3] [ekrule] ◆ **s'écrouler** *vpi* **1.** [tomber - mur] to fall (down), to collapse ; [- plafond, voûte] to cave in **2.** [être anéanti - empire, monnaie] to collapse ▪ **tous ses espoirs se sont écroulés** all her hopes vanished **3.** [défaillir - personne] to collapse ▪ **s'~ de sommeil/fatigue** to be overcome by sleep/weariness **4.** *fam loc* **s'~ (de rire)** to kill o.s. laughing ▪ **ils étaient écroulés** they were killing themselves laughing.

écru, e [ekry] *adj* **1.** TEXT raw **2.** [couleur] ecru.

ecsta [ɛksta] (*abr de* **ecstasy**) *nm* ecstasy, E.

ecstasy [ɛkstazi] *nm* ecstasy *(drug)*.

ectoplasme [ɛktɔplasm] *nm* BIOL ectoplasm.

écu [eky] *nm* **1.** HIST shield **2.** [ancienne monnaie] crown.

écubier [ekybje] *nm* hawsehole.

écueil [ekœj] *nm* **1.** NAUT reef **2.** *litt* [difficulté] pitfall, danger, hazard.

écuelle [ekɥɛl] *nf* bowl ▪ **une ~ de soupe** a bowful of soup.

éculé, e [ekyle] *adj* **1.** [botte, chaussure] down at heel, worn down at the heel **2.** [plaisanterie] hackneyed, well-worn.

écumant, e [ekymɑ̃, ɑ̃t] *adj litt* foamy, frothy ▪ **~ de rage** spitting with rage, foaming at the mouth (with rage).

écume [ekym] *nf* **1.** [de la bière] foam, froth ▪ [de la mer] foam, spume ▪ **ôter l'~ des confitures** to remove the scum from jam **2.** *litt* [de la société] scum, dross **3.** MÉTALL dross.

écumer [3] [ekyme] <> *vi* [cheval] to lather ▪ **~ (de rage** *OU* **colère)** to be foaming at the mouth (with rage), to foam with anger.
<> *vt* **1.** CULIN [confiture] to remove the scum from ▪ [bouillon] to skim **2.** MÉTALL to scum **3.** [piller] to plunder ▪ *fig* to go through ▪ **~ les mers** to scour the seas.

écumeur [ekymœr] *nm* HIST : **~ des mers** pirate.

écumeux, euse [ekymø, øz] *adj litt* foamy, frothy, spumy *litt.*

écumoire [ekymwar] *nf* skimmer, skimming laddle.

écureuil [ekyrœj] *nm* squirrel ▪ **l'Écureuil** *nickname for the Caisse d'épargne (whose logo is a squirrel).*

écurie [ekyri] *nf* **1.** [local à chevaux, mulets, ânes] stable ▪ **mettre à l'~** to stable ◆ **sentir l'~** to be in the home straight **2.** *fam* [endroit sale] pigsty **3.** [chevaux] stable ▪ **portant la casaque de l'~ Sarmantes** riding in the colours of the Sarmantes stable ▪ SPORT stable, team **4.** [dans une maison d'édition] (writing) team.

écusson [ekysɔ̃] *nm* **1.** [écu] badge **2.** HIST escutcheon, coat of arms **3.** HORT bud.

écuyer, ère [ekɥije, ɛr] *nm, f* **1.** [acrobate de cirque] circus rider **2.** [cavalier] rider.
◆ **écuyer** *nm* **1.** HIST [d'un chevalier] squire ▪ [d'un souverain] (royal) equerry **2.** [professeur d'équitation] riding teacher.

eczéma [ɛgzema] *nm* eczema.

eczémateux, euse [ɛgzematø, øz] *adj* eczema *(modif)*, eczematous *spéc.*

éd. (*abr écrite de* **édition**) ed, edit.

édam [edam] *nm* Edam (cheese).

edelweiss [edɛlvɛs] *nm* edelweiss.

éden [edɛn] *nm* **1.** BIBLE : **l'Éden** (the Garden of) Eden **2.** *litt* **un ~** an earthly paradise.

édenté, e [edɑ̃te] *adj* [vieillard, peigne, sourire] toothless.

édenter [3] [edɑ̃te] *vt* to break the teeth of.

EDF (*abr de* **Électricité de France**) *npr French national electricity company.*

édicter [3] [edikte] *vt* [loi] to decree, to enact.

édicule [edikyl] *nm* **1.** [petit édifice] small edifice **2.** [toilettes] public lavatory ▪ [abri] shelter.

édifiant, e [edifjɑ̃, ɑ̃t] *adj* **1.** [lecture] instructive, improving, edifying **2.** *hum* [révélateur] edifying, instructive.

édification [edifikasjɔ̃] *nf* **1.** [construction] erection, construction **2.** [instruction] edification, enlightenment ▪ **pour l'~ des masses** for the edification of the masses.

édifice [edifis] *nm* **1.** CONSTR edifice, building ▪ **~ public** public building **2.** [structure] structure, edifice, system ▪ **l'~ des lois** the legal system, the structure of the law **3.** [assemblage] heap, mound, pile.

édifier [9] [edifje] *vt* **1.** [construire - temple] to build, to construct, to erect **2.** [rassembler - fortune] to build up *(sép)*, to accumulate ; [- théorie] to construct, to develop **3.** [instruire] to edify, to enlighten ▪ **vous voilà édifiés sur ses intentions** now you know what his (true) intentions are.

édile [edil] *nm* **1.** ANTIQ aedile, edile **2.** *pr* & *hum* [magistrat municipal] town councillor, local worthy *ou* dignitary (on the town council).

Édimbourg [edɛ̃bur] *npr* Edinburgh.

édit [edi] *nm* edict, decree ▪ **l'~ de Nantes** the Edict of Nantes.

éditer [3] [edite] *vt* **1.** COMM [roman, poésie] to publish ▪ [disque] to produce, to release ▪ [meuble, robe] to produce, to present **2.** INFORM to edit.

éditeur, trice [editœr, tris] <> *adj* publishing ▪ **société éditrice** publishing company.
<> *nm, f* publisher, editor ▪ **~ de disques** record producer ▪ **~ de logiciels** software producer.
◆ **éditeur** *nm* INFORM : **~ de textes** text editor.

édition [edisjɔ̃] *nf* **1.** [activité, profession] publishing ▪ **le monde de l'~** the publishing world ▪ **travailler dans l'~** to be in publishing *ou* in the publishing business
2. [livre] edition ➊ **~ augmentée** enlarged edition ▪ **~ originale** first edition ▪ **~ de poche** paperback edition, pocket book *US* ▪ **~ revue et corrigée** revised edition
3. [disque - classique] edition, release ; [- de rock] release
4. [de journaux] edition ➊ **~ spéciale** [de journal] special edition ; [de revue] special issue ▪ **tu me l'as déjà dit, c'est la deuxième** *ou* **troisième ~!** *fam hum* that's the second *ou* third time you've told me that!
5. TV : **~ du journal télévisé** (television) news bulletin ▪ **dans la dernière ~ de notre journal** in our late news bulletin ➊ **~ spéciale en direct de Budapest** special report live from Budapest
6. INFORM editing ▪ **~ électronique** electronic publishing.

édito [edito] *nm fam* editorial.

éditorial, e, aux [editɔrjal, o] *adj* editorial.
◆ **éditorial** *nm* [de journal] editorial, leader *UK*.

éditorialiste [editɔrjalist] *nmf* leader *UK* *ou* editorial writer.

Édouard [edwar] *npr* [roi] Edward.

édouardien, enne [edwardjɛ̃, ɛn] *adj* Edwardian.

édredon [edrədɔ̃] *nm* eiderdown, quilt.

éducable [edykabl] *adj* teachable.

éducateur, trice [edykatœr, tris] <> *adj* educational, educative.
<> *nm, f* teacher, youth leader ▪ **~ spécialisé** teacher for special needs.

éducatif, ive [edykatif, iv] *adj* educational ▪ **le système ~** the education system.

éducation [edykasjɔ̃] *nf* **1.** [instruction] education ▪ **avoir reçu une bonne ~** to be well-educated ➊ **l'Éducation nationale** the (French) Education Department ▪ **~ permanente** continuing education ▪ **~ physique (et sportive)** physical education, PE ▪ **~ professionnelle** professional training ▪ **~ sexuelle** sex education ▪ **~ spécialisée** special education ▪ **~ surveillée** education in community homes *UK* *ou* reform schools *US* **2.** [d'un enfant] upbringing ▪ [bonnes manières] good manners ▪ **avoir de l'~** to be well-bred *ou* well-mannered ▪ **comment, tu ne connais pas, c'est toute une ~ à refaire!** *hum* what do you mean you've never heard of it, where on earth have you been?

éducationnel, elle [edykasjɔnɛl] *adj* educational.

édulcorant, e [edylkɔrɑ̃, ɑ̃t] *adj* sweetening.
◆ **édulcorant** *nm* sweetener, sweetening agent ▪ **~ de synthèse** artificial sweetener.

édulcorer [3] [edylkɔre] *vt* **1.** [sucrer] to sweeten **2.** *litt* [modérer - propos, compte rendu] to soften, to water down *(sép)* ; [- texte] to bowdlerize.

éduquer [3] [edyke] *vt* **1.** [instruire - élève, masses] to teach, to educate **2.** [exercer - réflexe, volonté] to train ▪ **~ le goût de qqn** to shape *ou* to influence sb's taste **3.** [élever - enfant] to bring up *(sép)*, to raise ▪ **être bien éduqué** to be well brought up *ou* well-bred *ou* well-mannered ▪ **être mal éduqué** to be badly brought up *ou* ill-bred *ou* ill-mannered.

EEE (*abr de* **Espace économique européen**) *nm* EEA.

effaçable [efasabl] *adj* erasable.

effacé, e [efase] *adj* **1.** [couleur] faded, discoloured **2.** [personne] self-effacing, retiring **3.** [épaules] sloping ▪ [poitrine] flat.

effacement [efasmɑ̃] *nm* **1.** [annulation - d'une faute] erasing ▪ [oubli - d'un cauchemar, d'un souvenir] erasing, blotting out, obliteration **2.** [modestie] : **~ de soi** self-effacement **3.** LING deletion **4.** AUDIO erasing, wiping out.

effacer [16] [efase] *vt* **1.** [ôter - tache, graffiti] to erase, to remove, to clean off *(sép)* ; [- mot] to rub out *UK (sép)*, to erase *US* ▪ [nettoyer - ardoise] to clean, to wipe ▪ **effacez avec un chiffon humide** wipe off with a damp cloth **2.** [cassette, disquette] to erase, to wipe off *(sép)* ▪ INFORM to delete **3.** [occulter - rêve, image] to erase ; [- bêtise] to erase, to obliterate ▪ **on efface tout et on recommence** [on se pardonne] let bygones be bygones, let's wipe the slate clean ; [on reprend] let's go back to square one, let's start afresh **4.** [éclipser - adversaire] to eclipse, to outshine.
◆ **s'effacer** <> *vp (emploi passif)* : **le crayon à papier s'efface très facilement** pencil rubs out easily *ou* is easily erased.
<> *vpi* **1.** [encre, lettres] to fade, to wear away ▪ [couleur] to fade **2.** [s'écarter] to move *ou* to step aside ▪ **s'~ pour laisser entrer qqn** to step aside (in order) to let sb in ▪ **il a dû s'~ au profit de son frère** he had to step aside in favour of his brother **3.** [disparaître - souvenir, impression] to fade, to be erased.

effaceur [efasœr] *nm* : **~ (d'encre)** ink rubber *UK* *ou* eraser *US*.

effarant, e [efarɑ̃, ɑ̃t] *adj* [cynisme, luxe] outrageous, unbelievable ▪ [étourderie, maigreur] unbelievable, stunning.

effaré, e [efare] *adj* **1.** [effrayé] alarmed **2.** [troublé] bewildered, bemused ▪ **elle le regarda d'un air ~** she looked at him with a bewildered air.

effarement [efarmɑ̃] *nm* **1.** [peur] alarm **2.** [trouble] bewilderment, bemusement.

effarer [3] [efare] *vt* **1.** [effrayer] to alarm **2.** [troubler] to bewilder, to bemuse.

effaroucher [3] [efaruʃe] *vt* [intimider] to frighten away *ou* off, to scare away *ou* off ■ **il s'approcha doucement pour ne pas ~ le cheval** he approached quietly so as not to frighten the horse.

◆ **s'effaroucher** *vpi* [prendre peur] to take fright ■ **s'~ de** to shy at, to take fright at.

effectif, ive [efɛktif, iv] *adj* [réel - travail, gain, participation] real, actual, effective ■ **l'armistice est devenu ~ ce matin** the armistice became effective *ou* took effect this morning ■ FIN effective.

◆ **effectif** *nm* [d'un lycée] size, (total) number of pupils ■ [d'une armée] strength ■ [d'un parti] size, strength ■ **réduction de l'~ des classes** reduction in the number of pupils per class ■ **nos ~s sont au complet** we are at full strength ■ **réduire ses ~s** to de-man, to downsize.

◆ **effectifs** *nmpl* MIL numbers, strength.

effectivement [efɛktivmɑ̃] *adv* **1.** [efficacement] effectively, efficiently **2.** [véritablement] actually, really ■ **c'est ~ le cas** this is actually the case **3.** [en effet] actually ■ **j'ai dit cela, ~** I did indeed say so ■ **on pourrait ~ penser que...** one may actually *ou* indeed think that...

effectuer [7] [efɛktɥe] *vt* [expérience, essai] to carry out *(sép)*, to perform ■ [trajet, traversée] to make, to complete ■ [saut, pirouette] to make, to execute ■ [service militaire] to do ■ [retouche, enquête, opération] to carry out *(sép)*.

◆ **s'effectuer** *vpi* [avoir lieu] to take place ■ **l'aller-retour s'effectue en une journée** the return trip *UK ou* round trip *US* can be made in one day.

efféminé, e [efemine] *adj* effeminate.

efféminer [3] [efemine] *vt litt* to make effeminate.

effervescence [efɛrvesɑ̃s] *nf* **1.** CHIM effervescence **2.** [agitation] agitation, turmoil.

◆ **en effervescence** *loc adj* bubbling *ou* buzzing with excitement.

effervescent, e [efɛrvesɑ̃, ɑ̃t] *adj* **1.** CHIM effervescent **2.** [excité] agitated.

effet [efɛ] *nm* **1.** [résultat] effect, result, outcome ■ **c'est un ~ de la pesanteur** it's a result of gravity ■ **c'est bien l'~ du hasard si...** it's really quite by chance that... ■ **avoir un ~ : cela n'a pas eu l'~ escompté** it didn't have the desired *ou* intended effect ■ **avoir pour ~ de : ton insistance n'aura pour ~ que de l'agacer** the only thing you'll achieve *ou* do by insisting is (to) annoy him ■ **faire un ~ : attends que le médicament fasse son ~** wait for the medicine to take effect ■ **tes somnifères ne m'ont fait aucun ~** your sleeping pills didn't work on me *ou* didn't have any effect on me ■ **être sans ~ : rester** *ou* **demeurer sans ~** to have no effect, to be ineffective ■ **mettre à ~** to bring into effect, to put into operation ■ **prendre ~ : prendre ~ à partir de** to take effect *ou* to come into operation as of ● **~ placebo** placebo effect ■ **~ en retour** blacklash ■ **~ secondaire** MÉD side-effect ■ **relation de cause à ~** cause and effect relationship

2. [impression] impression ■ **faire beaucoup d'~/peu d'~** to be impressive/unimpressive ■ **faire bon/mauvais/meilleur ~ : son discours a fait (très) bon/mauvais ~ sur l'auditoire** the audience was (most) favourably impressed/extremely unimpressed by his speech ■ **une jupe fera meilleur ~ qu'un pantalon** a skirt will make a better impression than a pair of trousers ■ **faire l'~ de : il me fait l'~ d'un jeune homme sérieux** he strikes me as (being) a reliable young man ■ **elle me fait l'~ d'un personnage de bande dessinée** she reminds me of a cartoon character ■ **faire un ~ : faire** *ou* **produire son petit ~** *fam* to cause a bit of a stir ■ **c'est tout l'~ que ça te fait?** *fam* you don't seem to be too impressed ■ **quel ~ cela t'a-t-il fait de le revoir?** how did seeing him again affect you? ■ **ça m'a fait un sale ~** it gave me a nasty turn

3. [procédé] effect ■ **~ de contraste/d'optique** contrasting/visual effect ■ **~ (de) domino** domino effect ■ **~ de style** stylistic effect ■ **~ de perspective** 3-D *ou* 3-dimensional effect ■ **rechercher l'~** to strive for effect ■ **manquer** *ou* **rater son ~** [magicien] to spoil one's effect ; [plaisanterie] to fall flat, to misfire ■ **créer un ~ de surprise** to create a surprise effect ■ **ça m'a coupé tous mes ~s** it stole my thunder ■ **faire des ~s de voix** to make dramatic use of one's voice ● **~ de lumière** THÉÂTRE lighting effect ■ **~s spéciaux** CINÉ special effects

4. FIN & COMM : **~ escomptable/négociable** discountable/negotiable bill ■ **~s à payer/recevoir** notes payable/receivable ■ **~ de commerce** bill of exchange ■ **~ à courte échéance** short *ou* short-dated bill ■ **~ à longue échéance** long *ou* long-dated bill ■ **~ au porteur** bill payable to bearer ■ **~ à vue** sight bill, demand bill *ou* draft ■ **~s publics** government securities

5. SC effect ■ **~ Doppler/Compton/Joule** Doppler/Compton/Joule-Thompson effect ■ **~ de serre** greenhouse effect

6. SPORT spin ■ **donner de l'~ à une balle** to put a spin on a ball.

◆ **effets** *nmpl* [affaires] things ■ [vêtements] clothes ■ **~s personnels** personal effects *ou* belongings.

◆ **à cet effet** *loc adv* to that effect *ou* end *ou* purpose.

◆ **en effet** *loc adv* **1.** [effectivement] : **oui, je m'en souviens en ~** yes, I do remember ■ **c'est en ~ la meilleure solution** it's actually *ou* in fact the best solution ■ **on peut en ~ interpréter l'événement de cette façon** it is indeed possible to interpret what happened in that way

2. [introduisant une explication] : **je ne pense pas qu'il vienne; en ~ il est extrêmement pris ces derniers temps** I don't think he'll come, he's really very busy these days ■ **il n'a pas pu venir; en ~, il était malade** he was unable to come since he was ill

3. [dans une réponse] : **drôle d'idée! – en ~!** what a funny idea! – indeed *ou* isn't it!

◆ **sous l'effet de** *loc prép* : **être sous l'~ d'un calmant/de l'alcool** to be under the effect of a tranquillizer/the influence of alcohol ■ **j'ai dit des choses regrettables sous l'~ de la colère** anger made me say things which I later regretted.

effeuillage [efœjaʒ] *nm* **1.** HORT thinning out of leaves **2.** *fam* [déshabillage] strip-tease.

effeuillaison [efœjɛzɔ̃] *nf*, **effeuillement** [efœjmɑ̃] *nm* shedding of leaves.

effeuiller [5] [efœje] *vt* [arbre] to thin out (the leaves of) ■ [fleurs] to pull the petals off ● **~ la marguerite** [fille] to play "he loves me, he loves me not" ; [garçon] to play "she loves me, she loves me not".

◆ **s'effeuiller** *vpi* [arbre] to shed *ou* to lose its leaves ■ [fleur] to shed *ou* to lose its petals.

efficace [efikas] *adj* **1.** [utile - politique, intervention] effective, efficient, efficacious *sout* **2.** [actif - employé] efficient ; [- médicament] effective, efficacious *sout*.

efficacement [efikasmɑ̃] *adv* effectively, efficiently, efficaciously *sout*.

efficacité [efikasite] *nf* effectiveness, efficiency, efficaciousness *sout* ■ **manque d'~** inefficiency.

efficience [efisjɑ̃s] *nf sout* efficiency.

efficient, e [efisjɑ̃, ɑ̃t] *adj sout* efficient.

effigie [efiʒi] *nf* effigy.

◆ **à l'effigie de** *loc prép* bearing the effigy of, in the image of.

◆ **en effigie** *loc adv* in effigy.

effilé, e [efile] *adj* **1.** [mince - doigt] slender, tapering ; [- main] slender ; [- cheveux] thinned ● **amandes ~es** CULIN split almonds **2.** [effiloché] frayed.

◆ **effilé** *nm* COUT fringe.

effiler [3] [efile] *vt* **1.** [tissu] to fray, to unravel **2.** [allonger - ligne, forme] to streamline ■ **~ sa moustache** to trim one's moustache into a point **3.** [cheveux] to thin.

◆ **s'effiler** *vpi* **1.** [s'effilocher] to fray, to unravel **2.** [s'allonger] to taper (off).

effilochage [efilɔʃaʒ] *nm* fraying.

effilocher [3] [efilɔʃe] *vt* to fray, to unravel.

◆ **s'effilocher** *vpi* to fray, to unravel.

efflanqué, e [eflɑ̃ke] *adj* [animal] raw-boned ■ [homme] lanky, tall and skinny.

effleurage [eflœraʒ] *nm* **1.** [du cuir] buffing (of leather) **2.** [massage] gentle massage.

effleurement [eflœrmɑ̃] *nm* **1.** [contact] light touch **2.** [caresse] light touch, gentle stroke *ou* caress.

effleurer [5] [eflœre] *vt* **1.** [frôler - cime, eau] to skim, to graze ; [- peau, bras] to touch lightly, to brush (against) ■ **la balle n'a fait qu'~ sa joue** the bullet only grazed his cheek **2.** [aborder - sujet] to touch on *ou* upon *(insép)* ■ **ça ne m'a même pas effleuré** it didn't even occur to me *ou* cross my mind **3.** [cuir] to buff.

effloraison [eflɔrezɔ̃] *nf* early flowering *ou* blooming.

efflorescence [eflɔresɑ̃s] *nf* **1.** BOT & CHIM efflorescence **2.** *litt* blooming, flowering.

efflorescent, e [eflɔresɑ̃, ɑ̃t] *adj* BOT & CHIM efflorescent.

effluent, e [eflyɑ̃, ɑ̃t] *adj* effluent.
◆ **effluent** *nm* [eaux - de ruissellement] drainage water ; [- usées] (untreated) effluent ■ **~ radioactif** effluent.

effluve [eflyv] *nm* **1.** [odeur] : **~s** [bonnes odeurs] fragrance, exhalations ; [mauvaises odeurs] effluvia, miasma **2.** PHYS : **~ électrique** discharge.

effondrement [efɔ̃drəmɑ̃] *nm* **1.** [chute - d'un toit, d'un pont] collapse, collapsing, falling down ; [- d'une voûte, d'un plafond] falling *ou* caving in **2.** [anéantissement - des prix, du dollar] collapse, slump ; [- d'un empire] collapse **3.** [abattement] dejection ■ **être dans un état d'~ complet** to be in a state of utter dejection.

effondrer [3] [efɔ̃dre] *vt* **1.** AGRIC to subsoil **2.** *fig* **être effondré : après la mort de sa femme, il était effondré** he was prostrate with grief after his wife's death.
◆ **s'effondrer** *vpi* **1.** [tomber - mur] to fall (down), to collapse ; [- plafond, voûte] to collapse, to fall *ou* to cave in **2.** [être anéanti - monnaie] to collapse, to plummet, to slump ; [- empire] to collapse, to crumble, to fall apart ; [- rêve, projet] to collapse, to fall through ; [- raisonnement] to collapse **3.** [défaillir] to collapse, to slump ■ **s'~ dans un fauteuil** to slump *ou* to sink into an armchair.

efforcer [16] [efɔrse] ◆ **s'efforcer** *vpi* : **s'~ de : s'~ de faire qqch** to endeavour to do sthg ■ **s'~ de sourire** to force o.s. to smile ■ **s'~ à : s'~ à l'amabilité** to try one's best to be polite.

effort [efɔr] *nm* **1.** [dépense d'énergie] effort ■ **~ physique/intellectuel** physical/intellectual effort ■ **avec ~** with an effort ■ **sans ~** effortlessly ■ **encore un (petit) ~!** one more try! ■ **fournir un gros ~** to make a great deal of effort ■ **tu aurais pu faire l'~ d'écrire/de comprendre** you could (at least) have tried to write/to understand ■ **faire un ~** to make an effort ■ **chacun doit faire un petit ~** everybody must do their share ■ **faire un ~ sur soi-même pour rester poli** to force o.s. to remain polite ■ **faire un ~ d'imagination** to try to use one's imagination ■ **faire un (gros) ~ de mémoire** to try hard to remember ■ **faire tous ses ~s pour obtenir qqch** to do one's utmost *ou* all one can to obtain sthg **2.** MÉCAN & TECHNOL stress, strain ■ **~ de cisaillement/torsion** shearing/torsional stress ■ **~ de rupture** breaking strain ■ **~ de traction** traction.

effraction [efraksjɔ̃] *nf* DR breaking and entering, housebreaking ■ **entrer par ~ dans une maison** to break into a house.

effraie[1] *etc* [efrɛ] *v* ▷ **effrayer.**

effraie[2] [efrɛ] *nf* : **(chouette) ~** barn owl.

effranger [17] [efrɑ̃ʒe] *vt* to fray into a fringe.
◆ **s'effranger** *vpi* to fray.

effrayant, e [efrɛjɑ̃, ɑ̃t] *adj* **1.** [qui fait peur] frightening, fearsome *sout* **2.** [extrême - chaleur, charge de travail] frightful, appalling ■ **c'est ~ ce qu'il peut être lent!** *fam* it's frightening how slow he can be!

effrayer [11] [efreje] *vt* **1.** [faire peur à] to frighten, to scare **2.** [décourager] to put *ou* to frighten off *(sép)* ■ **l'énormité de la tâche ne m'effrayait pas** the magnitude of the task didn't put me off.
◆ **s'effrayer** *vpi* **1.** [avoir peur] to become frightened, to take fright *sout* ■ **s'~ de qqch** to be frightened of sthg **2.** [s'alarmer] to become alarmed.

effréné, e [efrene] *adj* [poursuite, recherche] wild, frantic ■ [orgueil, curiosité, luxe] unbridled, unrestrained ■ [vie, rythme] frantic, hectic.

effritement [efritmɑ̃] *nm* **1.** [dégradation] crumbling away **2.** [affaiblissement] disintegration, erosion.

effriter [3] [efrite] *vt* to cause to crumble.
◆ **s'effriter** *vpi* **1.** [se fragmenter - roche, bas-relief] to crumble away, to be eroded **2.** [diminuer - majorité, popularité] to crumble, to be eroded ; [- valeurs, cours] to decline (in value).

effroi [efrwa] *nm* terror, dread ■ **inspirer de l'~ à qqn** to fill sb with terror ■ **regard plein d'~** frightened look ■ **un spectacle qui inspire l'~** an awe-inspiring sight.

effronté, e [efrɔ̃te] ◇ *adj* [enfant, manières, réponse] impudent, cheeky *UK* ■ [menteur, mensonge] shameless, barefaced, brazen.
◇ *nm, f* **1.** [enfant] impudent *ou* cheeky child ■ **petite ~e!** you cheeky *UK ou* sassy *US* little girl! **2.** [adulte] impudent fellow (*f* brazen hussy).

effrontément [efrɔ̃temɑ̃] *adv* impudently, cheekily *UK* ■ **mentir ~** to lie shamelessly *ou* barefacedly *ou* brazenly.

effronterie [efrɔ̃tri] *nf* [d'un enfant, d'une attitude] insolence, impudence, cheek *UK* ■ [d'un mensonge] shamelessness, brazenness ■ **il a eu l'~ de me répondre** he had the nerve to *ou* he was impudent enough to answer me back.

effroyable [efrwajabl] *adj* **1.** [épouvantable] frightening, appalling, horrifying **2.** [extrême - maigreur, misère] dreadful, frightful.

effroyablement [efrwajabləmɑ̃] *adv* awfully, terribly ■ **s'ennuyer ~** to be bored to death.

effusion [efyzjɔ̃] *nf* effusion, outpouring, outburst ■ **~ de sang** bloodshed ■ **sans ~ de sang** without any bloodshed ■ **~s de joie/tendresse** demonstrations of joy/affection ■ **remercier qqn avec ~** to thank sb effusively.

égaie *etc v* ▷ **égayer.**

égaiement [egɛmɑ̃] *nm* cheering up, enlivenment, brightening up.

égailler [3] [egaje] ◆ **s'égailler** *vpi* to disperse, to scatter.

égal, e, aux [egal, o] ◇ *adj* **1.** [identique] equal ■ **à prix ~, tu peux trouver mieux** for the same price, you can find something better ■ **à ~e distance de A et de B** equidistant from A and B, an equal distance from A and B ■ **la partie n'est pas ~e entre les deux joueurs** the players are unevenly matched ▶ **toutes choses ~es d'ailleurs** all (other) things being equal ■ **faire jeu ~** *pr* to have an equal score, to be evenly matched (in the game) ; *fig* to be neck and neck ■ **~ à lui-même/soi-même : être** *ou* **rester ~ à soi-même** to remain true to form, to be still one's old self ■ **~ à lui-même, il n'a pas dit un mot** typically, he didn't say a word **2.** MATH : **3 est ~ à 2 plus 1** 3 is equal to 2 plus 1 **3.** [régulier - terrain] even, level ; [- souffle, pouls] even, regular ; [- pas] even, regular, steady ; [- climat] equable, unchanging ■ **être de caractère ~** *ou* **d'humeur ~e** to be even-tempered **4.** *loc* **ça m'est (complètement) ~** [ça m'est indifférent] I don't care either way ; [ça ne m'intéresse pas] I don't care at all, I couldn't care less ■ **en train ou en avion, ça m'est ~** I don't care whether we go by train or plane ■ **c'est ~** *sout* all the same.
◇ *nm, f* [personne] equal ■ **nos égaux** our equals ■ **la femme est l'~e de l'homme** woman is equal to man ■ **il n'a pas son ~ pour animer une fête** he's second to none when it comes to livening up a party ■ **son arrogance n'a d'~e que sa sottise** *sout* his arrogance is only equalled by his foolishness.
◆ **à l'égal de** *loc prép litt* **je l'aimais à l'~ d'un fils** I loved him like a son.
◆ **d'égal à égal** *loc adv* [s'entretenir] on equal terms ■ [traiter] as an equal.
◆ **sans égal** *loc adj* matchless, unequalled, unrivalled.

égalable [egalabl] *adj* : **un exploit difficilement ~** a feat difficult to match.

également [egalmɑ̃] *adv* **1.** [autant] equally ■ **je crains ~ le froid et la chaleur** I dislike the cold as much as the heat **2.** [aussi] also, too, as well ■ **elle m'a ~ dit que...** she also told me that ...

égaler [3] [egale] *vt* **1.** [avoir la même valeur que] to equal, to match **2.** MATH : **3 fois 2 égale 6** 3 times 2 equals 6 **3.** *arch* [comparer] to rank **4.** [niveler] to level (out), to make flat.

égalisateur, trice [egalizatœr, tris] *adj* equalizing, levelling.

égalisation [egalizasjɔ̃] *nf* [nivellement - des salaires, d'un terrain] levelling.

égaliser [3] [egalize] ◇ *vt* [sentier] to level (out) ■ [frange] to trim ■ [conditions, chances] to make equal, to balance (out) ■ **se faire ~ les cheveux** to have one's hair trimmed.
◇ *vi* SPORT to equalize *UK*, to tie.
◆ **s'égaliser** *vpi* to become more equal, to balance out.

égaliseur [egalizœr] *nm* : **~ graphique** graphic equalizer.

égalitaire [egalitɛr] *adj* egalitarian.

égalitarisme [egalitarism] *nm* egalitarianism.

égalité [egalite] *nf* **1.** ÉCON & SOCIOL equality ■ **~ des salaires/droits** equal pay/rights ■ **politique/principe d'~ des chances** equal opportunities policy/principle **2.** MATH equality ■ **(signe d')~** equal *ou* equals sign **3.** GÉOM : **~ de deux triangles** isomorphism of two triangles **4.** TENNIS deuce ■ FOOTBALL draw, tie **5.** [uniformité - du pouls] regularity ; [- du sol] evenness, levelness ; [- du tempérament] evenness.
◆ **à égalité** *loc adv* TENNIS at deuce ■ [dans des jeux d'équipe] in a draw *ou* tie ■ **ils ont fini le match à ~** they tied ■ **ils sont à ~ avec Riom** they're lying equal with Riom.

égard [egar] *nm* [point de vue] : **à bien des ~s** in many respects ■ **à cet/aucun ~** in this/no respect.
◆ **égards** *nmpl* [marques de respect] consideration ■ **être plein d'~s** *ou* **avoir beaucoup d'~s pour qqn** to show great consideration for *ou* to be very considerate towards sb ■ **manquer d'~s envers qqn** to show a lack of consideration for *ou* to be inconsiderate towards sb.
◆ **à l'égard de** *loc prép* **1.** [envers] towards ■ **être dur/tendre à l'~ de qqn** to be hard on/gentle with sb ■ **ils ont fait une exception à mon ~** they made an exception for me *ou* in my case **2.** [à l'encontre de] against ■ **prendre des sanctions à l'~ de qqn** to impose sanctions against *ou* to apply sanctions to sb **3.** [quant à] with regard to ■ **elle émet des résistances à l'~ de ce projet** she's putting up some resistance with regard to the project.
◆ **à tous égards** *loc adv* in all respects *ou* every respect.
◆ **eu égard à** *loc prép sout* in view of, considering.
◆ **par égard pour** *loc prép* out of consideration *ou* respect for.
◆ **sans égard pour** *loc prép* with no respect *ou* consideration for, without regard for.

égaré, e [egare] *adj* **1.** [perdu - dossier, touriste] lost ; [- chat] lost, stray **2.** [affolé - esprit] distraught ; [- regard] wild, distraught ■ **avoir le regard ~** to be wild-eyed.

égarement [egarmɑ̃] *nm* **1.** [folie] distraction, distractedness ■ **dans son ~, il a oublié de...** he was so distraught he forgot to... **2.** [perte] loss.
◆ **égarements** *nmpl litt* : **les ~s de la passion** the follies of passion ■ **revenir de ses ~s** to see the error of one's ways.

égarer [3] [egare] *vt* **1.** [perdre - bagage, stylo] to lose, to mislay **2.** [tromper - opinion, lecteur] to mislead, to deceive ; [- jeunesse] to lead astray ■ **un électorat égaré par des promesses fallacieuses** voters misled by fraudulent promises **3.** *litt* [affoler] to make distraught, to drive to distraction ■ **la douleur vous égare** you're distraught with pain.
◆ **s'égarer** *vpi* **1.** [se perdre - promeneur] to lose one's way, to get lost ; [- dossier, clef] to get lost *ou* mislaid ■ **s'~ hors du droit chemin** to go off the straight and narrow **2.** [sortir du sujet] to wander ■ **ne nous égarons pas!** let's not wander off the point!, let's stick to the subject! **3.** *litt* [s'oublier] to lose one's self-control, to forget o.s.

égayer [11] [egeje] *vt* [convives] to cheer up *(sép)* ■ [chambre, robe, vie] to brighten up *(sép)* ■ [ambiance, récit] to brighten up *(sép)*, to liven up *(sép)*, to enliven.
◆ **s'égayer** *vpi sout* **s'~ aux dépens de qqn** to have fun at sb's expense.

Égée [eʒe] *npr* : **la mer ~** the Aegean Sea.

égéen, enne [eʒeɛ̃, ɛn] *adj* ANTIQ Aegean.

égérie [eʒeri] *nf* **1.** [inspiratrice] muse ■ **elle est l'~ du groupe** she's the driving force of the group **2.** ANTIQ : **Égérie** Egeria.

égide [eʒid] *nf* MYTHOL aegis.
◆ **sous l'égide de** *loc prép sout* under the aegis of ■ **prendre qqn sous son ~** to take sb under one's wing.

églantier [eglɑ̃tje] *nm* wild *ou* dog rose (bush) ■ **~ odorant** sweetbrier.

églantine [eglɑ̃tin] *nf* wild *ou* dog rose.

églefin [egləfɛ̃] *nm* haddock.

église [egliz] *nf* [édifice] church ■ **aller à l'~** [pratiquer] to go to church, to be a churchgoer ■ **se marier à l'~** to be married in church, to have a church wedding.

Église [egliz] *nf* : **l'~** the Church ■ **l'~ anglicane** the Church of England, the Anglican Church ■ **l'~ catholique** the (Roman) Catholic Church ■ **l'~ orthodoxe** the Orthodox Church ■ **l'~ protestante** the Protestant Church ■ **l'~ réformée** the Reformed Church ➲ **l'~ militante/triomphante** the Church militant/triumphant.
◆ **d'Église** *loc adj* : **homme d'~** clergyman ■ **gens d'~** priests, clergymen.

églogue [eglɔg] *nf* eclogue.

ego [ego] *nm* ego.

égocentrique [egɔsɑ̃trik] ◇ *adj* egocentric, self-centred.
◇ *nmf* egocentric *ou* self-centred person.

égocentrisme [egɔsɑ̃trism] *nm* egocentricity, self-centredness.

égoïsme [egɔism] *nm* selfishness.

égoïste [egɔist] ◇ *adj* selfish.
◇ *nmf* selfish man (*f* woman).

égoïstement [egɔistəmɑ̃] *adv* selfishly.

égorger [17] [egɔrʒe] *vt* to cut *ou* to slit the throat of.

égorgeur [egɔrʒœr] *nm* cutthroat.

égosiller [3] [egɔzije] ◆ **s'égosiller** *vpi* **1.** [crier] to shout o.s. hoarse **2.** [chanter fort] to sing at the top of one's voice.

égotisme [egɔtism] *nm* egotism.

égout [egu] *nm* sewer ➲ **~ collecteur** main sewer.

égoutter [3] [egute] ◇ *vt* [linge] to leave to drip ■ [vaisselle] to drain ■ **~ des légumes dans une passoire** to strain vegetables in a sieve.
◇ *vi* [vaisselle] to drain ■ [linge] to drip ■ **faire ~ les haricots** to strain the beans.
◆ **s'égoutter** *vpi* [linge] to drip ■ [légumes, vaisselle] to drain.

égouttoir [egutwar] *nm* **1.** [passoire] strainer, colander **2.** [pour la vaisselle] draining rack *ou* board, drainer.

égrainer [4] [egrene] = **égrener**.

égratigner [3] [egratiɲe] *vt* **1.** [jambe, carrosserie] to scratch, to scrape ■ [peau] to graze **2.** *fam* [critiquer] to have a dig *ou* a go at ■ **il s'est fait ~ par la presse à propos de sa dernière déclaration** the papers had a real go at him about his latest statement.
◆ **s'égratigner** *vp (emploi réfléchi)* : **s'~ le genou** to scrape *ou* to scratch *ou* to skin one's knee.

égratignure [egratiɲyr] *nf* **1.** [écorchure] scratch, scrape, graze ■ **il s'en est sorti sans une ~** he escaped without a scratch **2.** [rayure] scratch.

égrener [19] [egrəne] *vt* **1.** [blé] to shell ■ [pois] to shell, to pod ■ [coton] to gin ■ [ôter de sa tige - fruits] to take off the stalk **2.** [faire défiler] : **~ son chapelet** to tell one's beads, to say one's rosary ■ **~ un chapelet d'injures** to let out a stream of abuse.
◆ **s'égrener** *vpi* **1.** [grains de raisin] to drop off the bunch ■ [grains de blé] to drop off the stalk **2.** [se disperser - famille, foule] to scatter *ou* to disperse slowly, to trickle away **3.** *litt* [heures] to tick by ■ [notes] to be heard one by one.

égrillard, e [egrijar, ard] *adj* [histoire] bawdy, ribald ■ [personne] ribald.

Égypte [eʒipt] *npr f* : **(l')~** Egypt.

égyptien, enne [eʒipsjɛ̃, ɛn] *adj* Egyptian.
◆ **Égyptien, enne** *nm, f* Egyptian.
◆ **égyptien** *nm* LING Egyptian.

égyptologie [eʒiptɔlɔʒi] *nf* Egyptology.

eh [e] *interj* hey ■ **eh vous, là-bas!** hey you, over there! ■ **eh, eh! j'en connais un qui a fait une bêtise** who's done something silly then, eh?
◆ **eh bien** *loc adv* **1.** [au début d'une histoire] well, right **2.** [en interpellant] hey **3.** [pour exprimer la surprise] well, well.
◆ **eh non** *loc adv* well no.
◆ **eh oui** *loc adv* well (, actually,) yes ■ **c'est fini? – eh oui!** is it over? – I'm afraid so!

éhonté, e [eɔ̃te] *adj* [menteur, tricheur] barefaced, brazen, shameless ■ [mensonge, hypocrisie] brazen, shameless.

Eiffel [efɛl] *npr* : **la tour ~** the Eiffel Tower.

LA TOUR EIFFEL

Paris's most famous landmark was constructed out of steel on the Champ de Mars by Gustave Eiffel for the 1889 World Fair. At 320 m high, for half a century it was the tallest man-made structure in the world. It is now also used as a television transmitter.

Eire [ɛr] *npr f* : **(l')~** Eire.

éjaculateur, trice [eʒakylatœr, tris] *adj* ejaculatory.
◆ **éjaculateur** *nm* : **~ précoce** man who suffers from premature ejaculation.

éjaculation [eʒakylasjɔ̃] *nf* ejaculation ■ **~ précoce** premature ejaculation.

éjaculer [3] [eʒakyle] *vt & vi* to ejaculate.

éjecter [4] [eʒɛkte] *vt* **1.** ARM to eject **2.** AÉRON & AUTO to eject **3.** *fam* [renvoyer] to kick *ou* to chuck *ou* to boot out ■ **se faire ~ d'une boîte de nuit** to get kicked *ou* chucked *ou* booted out of a night club.
◆ **s'éjecter** *vp (emploi réfléchi)* AÉRON to eject.

éjection [eʒɛksjɔ̃] *nf* **1.** AÉRON, ARM & AUTO ejection **2.** *fam* [expulsion] kicking *ou* chucking *ou* booting out.

élaboration [elabɔrasjɔ̃] *nf* **1.** [d'une théorie, d'une idée] working out ■ **l'~ d'un projet de loi** drawing up a bill **2.** PHYSIOL elaboration **3.** PSYCHOL : **~ psychique** working out repressed emotions.

élaboré, e [elabɔre] *adj* **1.** [complexe - dessin] elaborate, intricate, ornate ■ [perfectionné - système] elaborate, sophisticated ■ [détaillé - carte, schéma] elaborate, detailed **2.** BOT [sève] elaborated.

élaborer [3] [elabɔre] *vt* **1.** [préparer - plan, système] to develop, to design, to work out *(sép)* **2.** PHYSIOL to elaborate.
◆ **s'élaborer** *vpi* [système, théorie] to develop.

élagage [elagaʒ] *nm* pruning.

élaguer [3] [elage] *vt* **1.** HORT to prune **2.** [rendre concis - texte, film] to prune, to cut down *(sép)* **3.** [ôter - phrase, scène] to edit out *(sép)*, to cut.

élagueur [elagœr] *nm* tree-trimmer.

élan [elɑ̃] *nm* **1.** [dans une course] run-up, impetus ■ **prendre son ~** to take a run-up ■ **saut avec/sans ~** running/standing jump
2. [énergie] momentum ■ **prendre de l'~** to gather speed *ou* momentum ▶ **être emporté par son propre ~** *pr & fig* to be carried along by one's own momentum ■ **emporté par son ~, il a tout raconté à sa mère** he got carried away and told his mother everything
3. [impulsion] impulse, impetus ■ **donner de l'~ à une campagne** to give an impetus to *ou* to provide an impetus for a campaign
4. [effusion] outburst, surge, rush ■ **~s de tendresse** surges *ou* rushes of affection ■ **~ de générosité** generous impulse ■ **contenir les ~s du cœur** to check the impulses of one's heart ■ **l'~ créateur** creative drive ■ **avec ~** eagerly, keenly, enthusiastically
5. PHILOS : **l'~ vital** the life force
6. ZOOL elk, moose US.

élancé, e [elɑ̃se] *adj* slim, slender ■ **à la taille ~e** slim-waisted.

élancement [elɑ̃smɑ̃] *nm* sharp *ou* shooting *ou* stabbing pain ■ **avoir des ~s dans la cuisse** to have a shooting *ou* sharp pain in the thigh.

élancer [16] [elɑ̃se] *vi* : **mon bras m'élance** I've got a shooting pain in my arm.
◆ **s'élancer** *vpi* **1.** [courir] to rush *ou* to dash forward ■ **s'~ à la poursuite de qqn** to dash after sb ■ **s'~ au secours de qqn** to rush to sb's aid, to rush to help sb ■ **s'~ vers qqn** to dash *ou* to rush towards sb **2.** SPORT to take a run-up **3.** [se dresser - tour, flèche] to soar upwards.

élargir [32] [elarʒir] ◇ *vt* **1.** [rendre moins étroit - veste] to let out *(sép)* ; [- chaussure] to stretch, to widen ; [- route] to widen ■ **le miroir élargit la pièce** the mirror makes the room look wider **2.** [débat] to broaden *ou* widen the scope of ■ **~ son horizon** to broaden *ou* to widen one's outlook **3.** [renforcer] : **le gouvernement cherche à ~ sa majorité** the government is seeking to increase its majority **4.** DR [libérer - détenu] to free, to release.
◇ *vi fam* to get broader, to get bigger *(across the shoulders)*.
◆ **s'élargir** *vpi* **1.** [être moins étroit - sentier, rivière] to widen, to get wider, to broaden (out) ; [- sourire] to widen **2.** [se relâcher - vêtement] to stretch **3.** [horizon, débat] to broaden out, to widen ■ **le cercle de mes amis s'est élargi** my circle of friends has broadened *ou* grown wider.

élargissement [elarʒismɑ̃] *nm* **1.** [agrandissement - d'une route] widening **2.** [extension - d'un débat] broadening, widening **3.** *sout* [libération] freeing, release.

élasticité [elastisite] *nf* **1.** [extensibilité] stretchiness, stretch, elasticity ■ **la ceinture a perdu toute son ~** there's no stretch left in the waistband **2.** ANAT elasticity **3.** [souplesse - d'un geste] suppleness ; [- d'un pas] springiness **4.** *fam péj* [laxisme - d'une conscience, d'un règlement] accommodating nature **5.** [variabilité] flexibility ■ **l'~ de l'offre/de la demande** the elasticity of supply/of demand.

élastique [elastik] ◇ *adj* **1.** [ceinture, cuir, tissu] stretchy, elastic ■ [badine] supple **2.** [agile - démarche] springy, buoyant ■ **elle a un corps ~** she's got a supple body **3.** *fam péj* [peu rigoureux - conscience, règlement] accommodating, elastic **4.** [variable - horaire] flexible ; [- demande, offre] elastic.
◇ *nm* **1.** [bracelet] elastic band **2.** [ruban] : **de l'~** elastic.

Élastiss® [elastis] *nm elasticated material.*

élastomère [elastɔmɛr] *nm* elastomer.

Elbe [ɛlb] ◇ *npr f* [fleuve] : **l'~** the (River) Elbe.
◇ *npr* : **l'île d'~** Elba.

eldorado [ɛldɔrado] *nm* Eldorado.

Eldorado [ɛldɔrado] *npr m* : **l'~** Eldorado.

électeur, trice [elɛktœr, tris] *nm, f* **1.** POLIT voter ■ **les ~s** the voters, the electorate ▶ **grands ~s** *body electing members of the (French) Senate* **2.** HIST Elector ■ **le Grand Électeur** the Great Elector.

électif, ive [elɛktif, iv] *adj* **1.** POLIT elective **2.** [douleur, traitement] specific.

élection [elɛksjɔ̃] *nf* **1.** [procédure] election, polls ■ **les ~s ont lieu aujourd'hui** it's election *ou* polling day today ■ **procéder à une ~** to hold an election ■ **se présenter aux ~s** to stand in the elections *UK*, to run for office *ou* as a candidate *US* ▶ **~s cantonales** *elections held every three years to elect half the members of the Conseil général* ■ **~s législatives** general elections *(held every five years)* ■ **~s municipales** local *ou* council *UK* elections *(held every six years)* ■ **~ partielle** by-election ■ **~ présidentielle** presidential election ■ **~s régionales** *elections held every six years to elect members of the Conseil régional* ■ **~s sénatoriales** *elections held every three years to elect one third of the members of the Sénat* **2.** [nomination] election ■ **son ~ à la présidence** her election as president *ou* to the presidency **3.** DR : **~ de domicile** choice of domicile.

◆ **d'élection** *loc adj* [choisi - patrie, famille] of one's own choice *ou* choosing, chosen.

ÉLECTIONS

All French citizens aged eighteen or over are entitled to vote in elections, after they have registered on the electoral rolls. Elections usually take place on a Sunday and polling stations are often set up in local schools. Voters go to a booth and put their voting slip in an envelope which is placed in the ballot box (*l'urne*) supervised by an *assesseur*, who then utters the words *a voté !*

électoral, e, aux [elɛktɔral, o] *adj* [liste] electoral ■ [succès] electoral, election *(modif)* ■ [campagne] election *(modif)* ■ **en période ~e** at election time ■ **nous avons le soutien ~ des syndicats** we can rely on the union vote.

électoralisme [elɛktɔralism] *nm péj* electioneering.

électoraliste [elɛktɔralist] *adj péj* [promesse, programme] vote-catching.

électorat [elɛktɔra] *nm* **1.** [électeurs] electorate ■ **l'importance de l'~ féminin/noir** the importance of the women's/the black vote ▶ **~ flottant** floating voters **2.** HIST electorate.

Électre [elɛktr] *npr* Electra.

électricien, enne [elɛktrisjɛ̃, ɛn] *nm, f* **1.** [artisan] electrician **2.** [commerçant] electrical goods dealer.

électricité [elɛktrisite] *nf* **1.** INDUST, SC & TECHNOL electricity ■ **~ statique** static (electricity) **2.** [installation domestique] wiring ■ **faire installer l'~ dans une maison** to have a house wired ■ **nous n'avons pas l'~ dans notre maison de campagne** there's no electricity in our country cottage ■ **allumer l'~** [au compteur] to switch on (at) the mains **3.** [consommation] electricity (bill) ■ **payer son ~** to pay one's electricity bill **4.** *fam* [tension] tension, electricity ■ **il y a de l'~ dans l'air!** there's a storm brewing!

électrification [elɛktrifikasjɔ̃] *nf* **1.** [d'une ligne de chemin de fer] electrification, electrifying **2.** [d'une région] : **l'~ des campagnes reculées** bringing electricity to remote villages.

électrifier [9] [elɛktrifje] *vt* **1.** [ligne de chemin de fer] to electrify **2.** [région] to bring electricity to.

électrique [elɛktrik] *adj* **1.** TECHNOL [moteur, radiateur, guitare] electric ■ [appareil, équipement] electric, electrical ■ [système, énergie] electrical ■ **atmosphère ~** *fig* highly-charged atmosphere ▶ **chaise ~** electric chair **2.** [par l'électricité statique] static ■ **elle a les cheveux ~s** *fam* her hair is full of static **3.** [couleur] : **bleu ~** electric-blue.

électriquement [elɛktrikmɑ̃] *adv* electrically ■ **commandé ~** working off electricity.

électrisant, e [elɛktrizɑ̃, ɑ̃t] *adj* **1.** TECHNOL electrifying **2.** [exaltant] electrifying, exciting.

électriser [3] [elɛktrize] *vt* **1.** TECHNOL to electrify, to charge **2.** *fam* [stimuler] to electrify, to rouse.

électroacoustique [elɛktrɔakustik] ◇ *adj* electroacoustic, electroacoustical.
◇ *nf* electroacoustics *(sing)*.

électroaimant [elɛktrɔɛmɑ̃] *nm* electromagnet.

électrocardiogramme [elɛktrɔkardjɔgram] *nm* electrocardiogram.

électrochimie [elɛktrɔʃimi] *nf* electrochemistry.

électrochoc [elɛktrɔʃɔk] *nm* electric shock *(for therapeutic purposes)* ■ **(traitement par) ~s** electroconvulsive *ou* electroshock therapy ■ **faire des ~s à qqn** to give sb electroconvulsive therapy.

électrocoagulation [elɛktrɔkɔagylasjɔ̃] *nf* electrocoagulation.

électrocuter [3] [elɛktrɔkyte] *vt* to electrocute.

◆ **s'électrocuter** *vp (emploi réfléchi)* to electrocute o.s., to be electrocuted ■ **il a failli s'~** he got a very bad electric shock.

électrocution [elɛktrɔkysjɔ̃] *nf* electrocution ■ **vous risquez l'~** you're at risk *ou* in danger of being electrocuted.

électrode [elɛktrɔd] *nf* electrode.

électroencéphalogramme [elɛktrɔɑ̃sefalɔgram] *nm* electroencephalogram.

électrogène [elɛktrɔʒɛn] *adj* **1.** ZOOL electric **2.** ÉLECTR electricity-generating.

électrolyse [elɛktrɔliz] *nf* electrolysis.

électromagnétisme [elɛktrɔmaɲetism] *nm* electromagnetism.

électromécanicien, enne [elɛktrɔmekanisjɛ̃, ɛn] *nm, f* electrical engineer.

électromécanique [elɛktrɔmekanik] ◇ *adj* electromechanical.
◇ *nf* electromechanical engineering.

électroménager [elɛktrɔmenaʒe] ◇ *adj* (domestic *ou* household) electrical.
◇ *nm* : **l'~** [appareils] domestic *ou* household electrical appliances ; [activité] the domestic *ou* household electrical appliance industry ■ **le petit ~** small household appliances.

électrométallurgie [elɛktrɔmetalyrʒi] *nf* electrometallurgy.

électromoteur, trice [elɛktrɔmɔtœr, tris] *adj* electromotive.

électron [elɛktrɔ̃] *nm* electron ■ **~ négatif** negatron ■ **~ positif** positron.

électronégatif, ive [elɛktrɔnegatif, iv] *adj* electronegative.

électronicien, enne [elɛktrɔnisjɛ̃, ɛn] *nm, f* electronics engineer.

électronique [elɛktrɔnik] ◇ *adj* **1.** INDUST & TECHNOL [équipement] electronic ■ [microscope] electron *(modif)* ■ [industrie] electronics *(modif)* **2.** [de l'électron] electron *(modif)* **3.** MUS electronic.
◇ *nf* electronics *(sing)*.

électrophone [elɛktrɔfɔn] *nm* record player.

électropositif, ive [elɛktrɔpozitif, iv] *adj* electropositive.

électrotechnicien, enne [elɛktrɔtɛknisjɛ̃, ɛn] *nm, f* electrotechnician.

électrothérapie [elɛktrɔterapi] *nf* electrotherapy.

élégamment [elegamɑ̃] *adv* [s'habiller] elegantly, smartly ■ [écrire, parler] stylishly, elegantly.

élégance [elegɑ̃s] *nf* **1.** [chic] elegance, smartness **2.** [délicatesse - d'un geste, d'un procédé] elegance ■ **savoir perdre avec ~** to be a good *ou* graceful loser **3.** [harmonie] grace, elegance, harmoniousness ■ **d'une grande ~ dans les proportions** very harmoniously proportioned **4.** [d'un style littéraire] elegance ■ [tournure] elegant *ou* well-turned phrase.

élégant, e [elegɑ̃, ɑ̃t] <> *adj* **1.** [chic - personne, mobilier] elegant, smart, stylish ■ **se faire ~** to smarten o.s. up **2.** [courtois - procédé, excuse] handsome, graceful **3.** [harmonieux - architecture, proportions] elegant, harmonious, graceful ; [- démonstration] elegant, neat.
<> *nm, f* [homme] dandy ■ [femme] elegant *ou* smart woman ■ **vouloir faire l'~** to try to look fashionable.

élégiaque [eleʒjak] *adj* **1.** LITTÉR elegiac **2.** *litt* [mélancolique] melancholy *(adj)*.

élégie [eleʒi] *nf* **1.** ANTIQ elegy **2.** [poème, œuvre] elegy, lament.

élément [elemɑ̃] *nm* **1.** [partie - d'un parfum, d'une œuvre] component, ingredient, constituent **2.** [donnée] element, factor, fact ■ **~s d'information** facts, information ■ **il n'y a aucun ~ nouveau** there are no new developments **3.** [personne] element ■ **~s indésirables** undesirables ■ **c'est un des meilleurs ~s de mon service** he's one of the best people in my department ■ **il y a de bons ~s dans ma classe** there are some good students in my class **4.** CHIM element ■ **~ radioactif** radioactive element **5.** ÉLECTR [de pile, d'accumulateur] cell ■ **batterie de cinq ~s** five-cell battery ‖ [de bouilloire, de radiateur] element **6.** [de mobilier] : **~ (de cuisine)** kitchen unit ■ **~s de rangement** storage units **7.** [milieu] element ■ **l'~ liquide** water ■ **les quatre ~s** the four elements ➊ **être dans son ~** to be in one's element ■ **je ne me sens pas dans mon ~ ici** I don't feel at home *ou* I feel like a fish out of water here **8.** MIL unit ■ **~s blindés/motorisés** armoured/motorized units.
◆ **éléments** *nmpl* [notions] elements, basic principles ■ **j'en suis resté aux premiers ~s de latin** I've never had more than an elementary knowledge of Latin ‖ [comme titre] : **"Éléments de géométrie"** "Elementary Geometry".

élémentaire [elemɑ̃tɛr] *adj* **1.** [facile - exercice] elementary ■ **c'est ~!** it's elementary! **2.** [fondamental - notion, principe] basic, elementary ■ **la plus ~ politesse aurait dû l'empêcher de partir** basic good manners *ou* common courtesy should have prevented him from leaving **3.** NUCL elementary **4.** CHIM elemental **5.** ÉDUC primary.

éléphant [elefɑ̃] *nm* elephant ■ **il a une démarche d'~** *hum & péj* he walks like an elephant ■ **~ femelle** cow elephant ➊ **~ d'Asie/d'Afrique** Indian/African elephant ■ **comme un ~ dans un magasin de porcelaine** like a bull in a china shop.
◆ **éléphant de mer** *nm* sea elephant, elephant seal.

éléphanteau, x [elefɑ̃to] *nm* baby *ou* young elephant.

éléphantesque [elefɑ̃tɛsk] *adj* gigantic, mammoth *(modif)*.

éléphantiasis [elefɑ̃tjazis] *nm* elephantiasis.

élevage [ɛlvaʒ] *nm* **1.** [activité] animal husbandry, breeding *ou* rearing *(of animals)* ■ **faire de l'~** to breed animals ■ **~ de poulets** *ou* **volaille** [intensif] battery-farming of chickens ; [extensif] rearing free-range chickens, free-range chicken-farming ■ **~ des abeilles** beekeeping ■ **~ intensif/en batterie** battery farming ■ **~ des bovins** cattle-rearing ■ **~ des chevaux** horse-breeding ■ **~ des lapins** rabbit-breeding ■ **~ des moutons** sheep-farming **2.** [entreprise] farm ■ **un ~ de vers à soie/de visons** a silkworm/mink farm.
◆ **d'élevage** *loc adj* **1.** [poulet] battery-reared **2.** [région] : **pays d'~** [bovin] cattle-rearing country ; [ovin] sheep-farming country.

élévateur, trice [elevatœr, tris] *adj* **1.** ANAT elevator *(modif)* **2.** TECHNOL [appareil, matériel] lifting.
◆ **élévateur** *nm* **1.** ANAT elevator **2.** [en manutention] elevator, hoist.

élévation [elevasjɔ̃] *nf* **1.** [augmentation] rise ■ **~ du niveau de vie** rise in the standard of living ■ **~ des températures** rise in temperatures **2.** MATH : **~ d'un nombre au carré** squaring of a number ■ **~ d'un nombre à une puissance** raising a number to a power **3.** ARCHIT [construction] erection, putting up ■ [plan] elevation **4.** [promotion] raising ■ **l'~ à la dignité de...** being elevated to the rank of. **5.** [noblesse - de style, des sentiments] elevation, nobility ■ **~ d'âme** *ou* **d'esprit** high-mindedness **6.** ARM elevation **7.** RELIG : **l'Élévation (de l'hostie)** [moment, geste] the Elevation *(of the Host)*.

élevé, e [elve] *adj* **1.** [fort - prix, niveau de vie] high ■ **taux peu ~** low rate **2.** [étage] high ■ [arbre] tall, lofty *litt* **3.** [important - position] high, high-ranking ; [- rang, condition] high, elevated **4.** *litt* [noble - inspiration, style] elevated, noble, lofty ■ **un sens ~ du devoir** a strong sense of duty ■ **avoir une âme ~e** to be high-minded **5.** [éduqué] : **bien ~** well-mannered, well-bred, well brought-up ■ **mal ~** bad-mannered, ill-mannered, rude ■ **c'est très mal ~ de répondre** it's very rude *ou* it's bad manners to answer back ‖ [grandi] : **avec des enfants ~s, je dispose de plus de liberté** now that my children are grown-up, I have more freedom.

élève [elɛv] *nmf* **1.** ÉDUC [enfant] pupil ■ [adolescent] student ■ **~ pilote** trainee pilot ■ **~ professeur** student *ou* trainee teacher **2.** [disciple] disciple, pupil **3.** MIL cadet ■ **~ officier** officer cadet *(in the Merchant Navy)* ■ **~ officier de réserve** military cadet.

élever [19] [elve] *vt* **1.** [éduquer - enfant] to bring up *(sép)*, to raise ■ **~ qqn dans du coton** to overprotect sb, to mollycoddle sb **2.** [nourrir - bétail] to breed, to raise ; [- moutons, chiens] to breed ; [- abeilles] to keep **3.** [hisser - fardeau] to raise, to lift (up) *(sép)* **4.** [ériger - statue, chapiteau] to erect, to raise, to put up *(sép)* **5.** [augmenter - prix, niveau, volume] to raise ■ **~ la voix** *ou* **le ton** to raise one's voice **6.** [manifester - objection, protestation] to raise ; [- critique] to make **7.** [promouvoir] to elevate, to raise ■ **~ qqn au grade d'officier** to promote *ou* to raise sb to (the rank of) officer **8.** [ennoblir] to elevate, to uplift ➊ **~ le débat** to raise the tone of the debate **9.** GÉOM : **~ une perpendiculaire** to raise a perpendicular ‖ MATH : **~ un nombre au carré/cube** to square/to cube a number ■ **~ un nombre à la puissance 3** to raise a number to the power of 3.
◆ **s'élever** *vpi* **1.** [augmenter - taux, niveau] to rise, to go up ■ **la température s'est élevée de 10 degrés** the temperature has risen by *ou* has gone up 10 degrees **2.** [se manifester] : **on entend s'~ des voix** you can hear voices being raised ■ **s'~ contre** [protester contre] to protest against ; [s'opposer à] to oppose **3.** [monter - oiseau] to soar, to fly *ou* to go up, to ascend ; [- cerf-volant] to go up, to soar **4.** [être dressé - falaise, tour] to rise ; [- mur, barricades] to stand **5.** *fig* [moralement, socialement] to rise ■ **s'~ au-dessus de** [jalousies, passions, préjugés] to rise above ■ **s'~ dans l'échelle sociale** to work one's way up *ou* to climb the social ladder ■ **s'~ à la force du poignet** to work one's way up unaided.
◆ **s'élever à** *vp+prép* [facture, bénéfices, pertes] to total, to add up to, to amount to ■ **le bilan s'élève à 10 morts et 12 blessés** the number of casualties is 10 dead and 12 injured.

éleveur, euse [elvœr, øz] *nm, f* stockbreeder ■ **~ de bétail** cattle breeder *ou* farmer, cattle rancher *US* ■ **~ de chiens** dog breeder ■ **~ de moutons/volaille** sheep/chicken farmer.

elfe [ɛlf] *nm* elf, spirit of the air.

élider [3] [elide] *vt* to elide *spéc*, to drop.
◆ **s'élider** *vp (emploi passif)* to elide *spéc*, to be dropped, to disappear.

Élie [eli] *npr* BIBLE Elijah.

éligibilité [eliʒibilite] *nf* POLIT eligibility.

éligible [eliʒibl] *adj* POLIT eligible.

élimé, e [elime] *adj* worn, threadbare ■ **un pantalon ~ aux genoux** trousers worn *ou* threadbare at the knees.

élimer [3] [elime] *vt* to wear thin.
◆ **s'élimer** *vpi* to wear thin, to become threadbare.

élimination [eliminasjɔ̃] *nf* **1.** PHYSIOL eliminating, voiding, expelling **2.** [exclusion] elimination, eliminating, excluding ■ **procéder par ~** to use a process of elimination.

éliminatoire [eliminatwar] <> *adj* [note, épreuve] eliminatory ■ [condition, vote] disqualifying.
<> *nf (souvent pl)* SPORT preliminary heat.

éliminer [3] [elimine] *vt* **1.** [se débarrasser de] to remove, to get rid of ■ PHYSIOL [déchets, urine] to eliminate ■ **pour ~ le tartre** to remove tartar ■ *(en usage absolu)* **il faut boire pour ~** you have to drink to clean out your system **2.** SPORT to eliminate, to knock out *(sép)* ■ **se faire ~** to be eliminated **3.** [rejeter - hypothèse, possibilité] to eliminate, to dismiss, to rule out *(sép)*

■ ~ **qqch de** to exclude sthg from ■ ~ **qqn d'un comité** to throw sb off a committee **4.** [tuer] to eliminate, to liquidate **5.** MATH to eliminate.

élire [106] [elir] *vt* **1.** POLIT to elect ■ **être élu à une assemblée** to be elected to an assembly ■ ~ **un nouveau président** to elect *ou* to vote in a new president ■ **se faire** ~ to be elected **2.** *litt* [choisir] to elect *litt*, to choose **3.** *loc* ~ **domicile à** to take up residence *ou* to make one's home in.

Élisabeth [elizabɛt] *npr* : **la reine** ~ Queen Elizabeth.

élisabéthain, e [elizabetɛ̃, ɛn] *adj* Elizabethan.

élisait *etc v* ▻ **élire**.

élision [elizjɔ̃] *nf* elision ■ **il y a** ~ **du "e"** the "e" elides.

élite [elit] *nf* [groupe] elite ■ **une** ~ an elite ■ **l'**~ **de** the elite *ou* cream of ■ **l'**~ **de la haute couture** top fashion designers.
◆ **d'élite** *loc adj* elite *(modif)*, top *(avant n)*.

élitisme [elitism] *nm* elitism.

élitiste [elitist] *adj* & *nmf* elitist.

élixir [eliksir] *nm* MYTHOL & PHARM elixir ■ ~ **d'amour/de longue vie** elixir of love/life ■ ~ **parégorique** paregoric (elixir).

elle [ɛl] *(pl* **elles***)* *pron pers f* **1.** [sujet d'un verbe - personne] she ; [- animal, chose] it ; [- animal de compagnie] she ■ ~**s** they **2.** [emphatique - dans une interrogation] : **ta mère est-**~ **rentrée?** has your mother come back? **3.** [emphatique - avec 'qui' et 'que'] : **c'est** ~ **qui me l'a dit** she's the one who told me, it was she who told me **4.** [complément - personne] her ; [- animal, chose] it ; [- animal de compagnie] her ■ **dites-le-lui à** ~ tell it to her, tell her it.

elle-même [ɛlmɛm] *pron pers* [désignant - une personne] herself ; [- une chose] itself ■ **elles-mêmes** themselves.

elles [ɛl] *fpl* ▻ **elle**.

ellipse [elips] *nf* **1.** MATH ellipse **2.** LING ellipsis ■ **parler par** ~**s** [allusivement] to hint at things, to express o.s. elliptically.

elliptique [eliptik] *adj* **1.** MATH elliptic, elliptical **2.** LING elliptical.

élocution [elɔkysjɔ̃] *nf* [débit] delivery ■ [diction] diction, elocution ■ **avoir une** ~ **claire** to have clear diction.

éloge [elɔʒ] *nm* **1.** [compliment] praise ■ **couvrir qqn d'**~**s** to shower sb with praise ■ **digne d'**~**s** praiseworthy ■ **faire l'**~ **de** to speak highly of *ou* in praise of ■ **faire son propre** ~ to sing one's own praises, to blow one's own trumpet *UK ou* horn *US* **2.** *litt* [panégyrique] eulogy ■ **faire l'**~ **d'un écrivain** to eulogize a writer ◐ **prononcer l'**~ **funèbre de qqn** to deliver a funeral oration in praise of sb.
◆ **à l'éloge de** *loc prép* (much) to the credit of ■ **elle a refusé, c'est tout à son** ~ she said no, (much) to her credit.

élogieusement [elɔʒjøzmɑ̃] *adv* highly, favourably ■ **il a décrit** ~ **leur demeure** he was full of praise for their house.

élogieux, euse [elɔʒjø, øz] *adj* laudatory, complimentary, eulogistic ■ **parler en termes** ~ **de** to speak very highly of, to be full of praise for.

éloigné, e [elwaɲe] *adj* **1.** [loin de tout - province, village] distant, remote, faraway **2.** [distant] : **les deux villes sont** ~**es de 50 kilomètres** the two towns are 50 kilometres apart ■ **maintenant que tout danger est** ~ now that there is no further risk, now that the danger is past ■ ~ **de** [à telle distance de] : **ce n'est pas très** ~ **de l'aéroport** it's not very far (away) from the airport ■ **se tenir** ~ **du feu** to keep away from the fire ■ **se tenir** ~ **de la politique** to keep away from *ou* to steer clear of politics ■ **rien n'est plus** ~ **de mes pensées** nothing could be *ou* nothing is further from my thoughts **3.** [dans le temps] distant, remote, far-off ■ **dans un passé/avenir pas si** ~ **que ça** in the not-too-distant past/future **4.** [par la parenté] distant **5.** [différent] : ~ **de** far removed *ou* very different from.

éloignement [elwaɲmɑ̃] *nm* **1.** [distance dans l'espace] distance, remoteness **2.** [retrait] : **l'**~ **de la vie politique m'a fait réfléchir** being away from politics made me do some thinking **3.** [mise à distance] taking away, removing, removal ■ **le tribunal a ordonné l'**~ **de mes enfants** the court has ordered that my children be taken away from me.

éloigner [3] [elwaɲe] *vt* **1.** [mettre loin] to move *ou* to take away *(sép)* ■ **ça nous éloignerait du sujet** that would take us away from the point **2.** [séparer] : ~ **qqn de** to take sb away from ■ **mon travail m'a éloigné de ma famille** my work's kept me away from my family ■ ~ **qqn du pouvoir** to keep sb out of power ■ **il a éloigné tous ses amis par son snobisme** his snobbish ways have alienated all his friends **3.** [repousser - insectes, mauvaises odeurs] to keep off *(sép)*, to keep at bay **4.** [dissiper - idée, souvenir] to banish, to dismiss ; [- danger] to ward off *(sép)* ■ ~ **les soupçons de qqn** to avert suspicion from sb **5.** [reporter - échéance] to postpone, to put off *(sép)*.
◆ **s'éloigner** *vpi* **1.** [partir - tempête, nuages] to pass, to go away ; [- véhicule] to move away ; [- personne] to go away ■ **les bruits de pas s'éloignèrent** the footsteps grew fainter ■ **s'**~ **à la hâte/à coups de rame** to hurry/to row away ■ **ne vous éloignez pas trop, les enfants** don't go too far (away), children ■ **éloignez-vous du bord de la falaise** move away *ou* get back from the edge of the cliff ■ **éloignez-vous de cette ville quelque temps** leave this town for a while ■ **s'**~ **du sujet** to wander away from *ou* off the point **2.** [s'estomper - souvenir, rêve] to grow more distant *ou* remote ; [- crainte] to go away ; [- danger] to pass **3.** [s'isoler] to move *ou* to grow away ■ **s'**~ **du monde des affaires** to move away from *ou* to abandon one's involvement with the world of business ■ **s'**~ **de la réalité** to lose touch with reality **4.** [affectivement] : **il la sentait qui s'éloignait de lui** he could feel that she was growing away from him *ou* becoming more and more distant ■ **peu à peu ils se sont éloignés l'un de l'autre** they gradually drifted apart **5.** [dans le temps] : **plus on s'éloigne de cette période...** the more distant that period becomes...

élongation [elɔ̃gasjɔ̃] *nf* **1.** MÉD [d'un muscle] strained *ou* pulled muscle ■ [d'un ligament] pulled ligament ■ **se faire une** ~ [d'un muscle] to strain *ou* to pull a muscle ; [d'un ligament] to pull a ligament **2.** PHYS displacement **3.** ASTRON elongation.

éloquence [elɔkɑ̃s] *nf* **1.** [art de parler] eloquence, fine oratory **2.** [expressivité] eloquence, expressiveness ■ **avec** ~ eloquently **3.** [persuasion] persuasiveness, eloquence.

éloquent, e [elɔkɑ̃, ɑ̃t] *adj* **1.** [parlant bien] eloquent ■ **il est très** ~ he's a fine speaker **2.** [convaincant - paroles] eloquent, persuasive ; [- chiffres, réaction] eloquent **3.** [expressif] eloquent, expressive ■ **le geste était très** ~ the gesture said it all ■ **ces images sont** ~**es** these pictures speak volumes *ou* for themselves.

élu, e [ely] ◇ *pp* ▻ **élire**.
◇ *adj* **1.** RELIG chosen **2.** POLIT elected.
◇ *nm, f* **1.** POLIT [député] elected representative ■ [conseiller] elected representative, councillor ◐ **les** ~**s locaux** local councillors **2.** *hum* [bien-aimé] : **qui est l'heureux** ~**?** who's the lucky man? ■ **l'**~ **de mon/ton cœur** my/your beloved **3.** RELIG : **les** ~**s** the chosen ones, the elect.

élucidation [elysidasjɔ̃] *nf* elucidation, clarification.

élucider [3] [elyside] *vt* [mystère] to elucidate, to explain, to clear up *(sép)* ■ [problème, texte] to elucidate, to clarify.

élucubrations [elykybrasjɔ̃] *nfpl péj* ravings, rantings.

éluder [3] [elyde] *vt* to elude, to evade.

élut *etc v* ▻ **élire**.

Élysée [elize] *npr m* **1.** MYTHOL Elysium **2.** POLIT : **(le palais de) l'**~ the Élysée Palace *(the official residence of the French President)*.

L'ÉLYSÉE

This eighteenth-century palace near the Champs-Élysées in Paris is the official residence of the French president. The name is often used to refer to the presidency itself.

élyséen, enne [elizeɛ̃, ɛn] *adj* **1.** MYTHOL Elysian **2.** POLIT from the Élysée Palace, presidential.

élytre [elitr] *nm* elytron, elytrum.

émacié, e [emasje] *adj* emaciated, wasted.

émacier [9] [emasje] *vt* to emaciate.
◆ **s'émacier** *vpi* to become emaciated *ou* wasted.

émail [emaj] (*pl* **émaux** [emo]) *nm* **1.** [matière] enamel **2.** [objet] piece of enamelware *ou* enamelwork **3.** (*pl* émails) ANAT enamel.
◆ **émaux** *nmpl* coloured enamels.
◆ **d'émail, en émail** *loc adj* enamel *(modif)*, enamelled.

e-mail [imel] *nm* INFORM email (message).

émailler [3] [emaje] *vt* **1.** [en décoration] to enamel **2.** [parsemer] to dot, to scatter, to speckle ■ **le pré est émaillé de coquelicots, les coquelicots émaillent le pré** the field is scattered *ou* dotted *ou* speckled with poppies ■ **~ un discours de citations** to pepper *ou* to sprinkle a speech with quotations ■ **un ciel émaillé d'étoiles** a star-studded sky.

émanation [emanasjɔ̃] *nf* [expression] expression ■ **ce journal est une ~ du pouvoir** this paper is a mouthpiece for the government.
◆ **émanations** *nfpl* [vapeurs] smells, emanations ■ **des ~s de gaz** a smell of gas ■ **~s pestilentielles** miasmas, foul emanations ■ **~s volcaniques** volatiles ■ **~s toxiques** toxic fumes.

émancipateur, trice [emɑ̃sipatœr, tris] ◇ *adj* emancipatory, liberating.
◇ *nm, f* emancipator, liberator.

émancipation [emɑ̃sipasjɔ̃] *nf* [libération - gén] emancipation ; [- de la femme] emancipation, liberation.

émancipé, e [emɑ̃sipe] *adj* [peuple] emancipated ■ [femme] emancipated, liberated.

émanciper [3] [emɑ̃sipe] *vt* **1.** [libérer - gén] to emancipate ; [- femmes] to emancipate, to liberate ■ **~ qqn de** to liberate *ou* to free sb from **2.** DR to emancipate.
◆ **s'émanciper** *vpi* **1.** [se libérer - gén] to become emancipated ; [- femme] to become emancipated *ou* liberated ■ **s'~ de** to become free from **2.** *péj* [devenir trop libre] to become rather free in one's ways.

émaner [3] [emane] ◆ **émaner de** *v+prép* [suj: odeur, lumière] to emanate *sout* *ou* to come from ■ [suj: demande, mandat] to come from, to be issued by ■ [suj: autorité, pouvoir] to issue from ■ **il émanait d'elle un charme mélancolique** she had an aura of melancholy charm.

émargement [emarʒəmɑ̃] *nm* **1.** [fait de signer] signing ■ **~ d'un contrat** initialling a contract **2.** [signature] signature.

émarger [17] [emarʒe] *vt* **1.** [signer] to sign ■ [annoter] to annotate **2.** [réduire la marge de] to trim.
◆ **émarger à** *v+prép* : **~ au budget de l'État** to be paid out of state funds.

émasculation [emaskylasjɔ̃] *nf* **1.** [castration] emasculation, emasculating **2.** *litt* [affaiblissement - gén] emasculation *litt*, weakening ; [- d'une œuvre] bowdlerization.

émasculer [3] [emaskyle] *vt* **1.** [castrer] to emasculate **2.** *litt* [affaiblir - politique, directive] to weaken ; [- œuvre] to bowdlerize.

émaux [emo] *pl* ▷ **émail**.

emballage [ɑ̃balaʒ] *nm* **1.** [gén] packaging ■ [papier] wrapper ■ [matière] wrapping *ou* packing materials ■ **~ consigné/perdu** returnable/non-returnable packing ■ **~ bulle** blister pack **2.** [processus] packing *ou* wrapping (up) **3.** *fam* SPORT final sprint.
◆ **d'emballage** *loc adj* [papier] packing, wrapping ■ **toile d'~** canvas wrapper.

emballant, e [ɑ̃balɑ̃, ɑ̃t] *adj* inspiring, thrilling, exciting ■ **une proposition ~e** an attractive *ou* exciting proposition.

emballé, e [ɑ̃bale] *adj* : **il était complètement ~ par l'idée** he was completely bowled over by the idea.

emballement [ɑ̃balmɑ̃] *nm* **1.** [d'un cheval] bolting ■ [d'un moteur] racing ■ **l'~ des cours à la Bourse** the Stock-Exchange boom **2.** [enthousiasme] sudden passion, flight *ou* burst of enthusiasm **3.** [emportement] : **dans un moment d'~** without thinking.

emballer [3] [ɑ̃bale] *vt* **1.** [empaqueter - marchandises] to pack (up) ; [- cadeau] to wrap (up) **2.** [moteur] to race **3.** *fam* [enthousiasmer - projet, livre] to grab, to thrill (to bits) ■ **ça n'a pas l'air de l'~** he doesn't seem to think much of the idea **4.** △ [arrêter - truand] to pull *ou* to run in *(sép)*, to nick△ *UK*, to bust△ *US* **5.** △ [séduire] to chat up, to pull△ *UK*.
◆ **s'emballer** *vpi* **1.** [cheval] to bolt ■ [moteur] to race ■ [cours, taux] to take off **2.** *fam* [s'enthousiasmer] to get carried away ■ **s'~ pour qqch** to get excited about sthg **3.** [s'emporter] to flare *ou* to blow up.

embarcadère [ɑ̃barkadɛr] *nm* landing stage, pier.

embarcation [ɑ̃barkasjɔ̃] *nf* (small) boat *ou* craft.

embardée [ɑ̃barde] *nf* [d'une voiture] swerve, lurch ■ [d'un bateau] yaw, lurch ■ **faire une ~** [voiture] to swerve, to lurch ; [bateau] to yaw, to lurch.

embargo [ɑ̃bargo] *nm* **1.** NAUT embargo ■ **mettre l'~ sur un navire** to lay *ou* to put an embargo on a ship, to embargo a ship **2.** ÉCON embargo ■ **mettre un ~ sur** to enforce an embargo on, to embargo ■ **lever l'~ sur les ventes d'armes** to lift *ou* to raise the embargo on arms sales.

embarquement [ɑ̃barkəmɑ̃] *nm* **1.** [de marchandises] loading **2.** [des passagers - d'un navire] embarkation, boarding ; [- d'un avion] boarding ■ **~ immédiat porte 16** now boarding at gate 16.

embarquer [3] [ɑ̃barke] ◇ *vt* **1.** TRANSP [matériel, troupeau] to load ■ [passagers] to embark, to take on board **2.** *fam* [emporter - voiture, chien] to cart off *ou* away *(sép)* ■ **m'embarque pas mon blouson!** don't walk *ou* waltz off with my jacket! **3.** *fam* [voler] to pinch, to filch, to nick *UK* **4.** *fam* [arrêter - gang, manifestant] to pull in ■ **se faire ~ par les flics** to get pulled in by the police **5.** *fam* [entraîner] to lug *ou* to take off *(sép)* ■ **c'est eux qui l'ont embarqué dans cette affaire** they're the ones who got him involved *ou* mixed up in this business **6.** *fam* [commencer] : **la réunion est bien/mal embarquée** the meeting's got off to a flying/lousy start.
◇ *vi* **1.** [aller à bord] to board, to go aboard *ou* on board **2.** [partir en bateau] to embark ■ **nous embarquons demain pour Rio** we're embarking *ou* sailing for Rio tomorrow.
◆ **s'embarquer** *vpi* [aller à bord] to embark, to go on board, to board.
◆ **s'embarquer dans** *vp+prép* to embark on *ou* upon, to begin, to undertake ■ **dans quelle histoire me suis-je embarqué!** what sort of a mess have I got myself into!

embarras [ɑ̃bara] *nm* **1.** [malaise] embarrassment, confusion ■ **à mon grand ~, il m'a embrassé** to my great embarrassment, he kissed me
2. [souci] : **l'~, les ~** trouble ■ **avoir des ~ financiers** *ou* **d'argent** to be in financial difficulties, to have money problems ■ **être dans l'~** [dans la pauvreté] to be short of money
3. [cause de souci] nuisance, cause of annoyance ■ **être un ~ pour qqn** to be a nuisance to sb
4. [position délicate] predicament, awkward position *ou* situation ■ **être dans l'~** [mal à l'aise] to be in a predicament *ou* in an awkward position ; [face à un dilemme] to be in *ou* caught on the horns of a dilemma ■ **mettre dans l'~ : ma question l'a mis dans l'~** my question put him on the spot ■ **tirer un ami d'~** to help a friend out of a predicament ● **l'~ du choix** an embarrassment of riches ■ **on les a en dix teintes, vous avez** *ou* **vous n'avez que l'~ du choix** they come in ten different shades, you're spoilt for choice ■ **on n'a pas l'~ du choix, il faut accepter** we don't have much of a choice, we have to accept
5. *péj* [simagrées] : **faire des ~** to make a fuss
6. MÉD : **~ gastrique** upset stomach, stomach upset
7. *vieilli* **les ~ de la circulation** traffic congestion.

embarrassant, e [ɑ̃barasɑ̃, ɑ̃t] *adj* **1.** [gênant - silence, situation] embarrassing, awkward **2.** [difficile - problème, question] awkward, thorny, tricky **3.** [encombrant - colis, vêtement] cumbersome.

embarrassé, e [ɑ̃barase] *adj* **1.** [gêné - personne] embarrassed ; [- sourire, regard] embarrassed, uneasy ■ **avoir l'air ~** to look embarrassed *ou* awkward **2.** [confus - explication] confused, muddled **3.** [encombré] : **avoir les mains ~es** to have one's hands full **4.** [pauvre] short (of money) **5.** MÉD : **avoir l'estomac ~** to have an upset stomach.

embarrasser [3] [ɑ̃barase] *vt* **1.** [mettre mal à l'aise] to embarrass ▪ **ça m'embarrasse de lui demander son âge** I'm embarrassed to ask her how old she is **2.** [rendre perplexe] : **ce qui m'embarrasse le plus c'est l'organisation du budget** what I find most awkward is how to organize the budget ▪ **je serais bien embarrassé de dire qui a raison** I'd be hard put *ou* at a loss to decide who was right **3.** [encombrer] to clutter up *(sép)*, to obstruct ▪ **laisse ta valise ici, elle va t'~** leave your suitcase here, it'll get in your way ▪ **si je t'embarrasse, dis-le moi** please tell me if I'm in your way **4.** MÉD : **~ l'estomac** to cause a stomach upset.

◆ **s'embarrasser dans** *vp+prép* : **s'~ dans sa traîne** to trip over one's train ▪ **s'~ dans ses mensonges/explications** to get tangled up in one's lies/explanations.

◆ **s'embarrasser de** *vp+prép* **1.** [s'encombrer de] to burden o.s. with **2.** [s'inquiéter de] to trouble o.s. with ▪ **sans s'~ de présentations** without bothering with the (usual) introductions.

embase [ɑ̃baz] *nf* ARCHIT & MENUIS base.

embauche [ɑ̃boʃ] *nf* hiring ▪ **il n'y a pas d'~ (chez eux)** they're not hiring anyone, there are no vacancies.

embaucher [3] [ɑ̃boʃe] *vt* to take on *(sép)*, to hire.

embauchoir [ɑ̃boʃwar] *nm* shoetree.

embaumer [3] [ɑ̃bome] <> *vt* **1.** [parfumer - air] to make fragrant ▪ **la lavande embaumait la salle** the scent of lavender filled the room **2.** [sentir - parfum] to be fragrant with the scent of ; [- odeur de cuisine] to be fragrant with the aroma of **3.** [momifier] to embalm.

<> *vi* [femme] to be fragrant ▪ [mets] to fill the air with a pleasant smell *ou* a delicious aroma ▪ [fleur, plante] to fill the air with a lovely fragrance *ou* a delicate scent.

embellie [ɑ̃beli] *nf* **1.** MÉTÉOR [de soleil] bright interval ▪ [du vent] lull **2.** [amélioration] : **une ~ dans sa vie** a happier period in her life ▪ **une ~ dans leurs rapports** an improvement in their relationship.

embellir [32] [ɑ̃belir] <> *vt* **1.** [enjoliver - rue] to make prettier ; [- pièce] to decorate, to adorn ▪ **~ une femme** to make a woman prettier *ou* more beautiful **2.** [exagérer - histoire] to embellish, to embroider on *(insép)*, to add frills to ▪ **~ la réalité** to make things seem more attractive than they really are.

<> *vi (aux avoir ou être)* to grow prettier *ou* more beautiful.

embellissement [ɑ̃belismɑ̃] *nm* **1.** [fait d'améliorer] embellishment, embellishing **2.** [apport - à un décor] embellishment ; [- à une histoire] embellishment, frill ▪ **il y a beaucoup d'~s dans son récit** there's a lot of poetic licence in his story.

emberlificoter [3] [ɑ̃bɛrlifikɔte] *vt fam* **1.** [tromper - personne] to soft-soap, to sweet-talk **2.** [compliquer] to muddle up *(sép)* ▪ **quelle histoire emberlificotée!** what a muddle *ou* mix-up of a story! **3.** [empêtrer] to tangle up *(sép)*.

◆ **s'emberlificoter** *vpt* : **s'~ les pieds dans** to get (one's feet) tangled up in.

◆ **s'emberlificoter dans** *vp+prép fam* **1.** [tissu, câbles] to get tangled up in **2.** [récit, calcul] to get muddled *ou* mixed up with.

emberlificoteur, euse [ɑ̃bɛrlifikɔtœr, øz] *fam* <> *adj* soft-soaping, sweet-talking.

<> *nm, f* sweet-talker.

embêtant, e [ɑ̃bɛtɑ̃, ɑ̃t] *adj fam* **1.** [lassant - travail] tiresome, boring **2.** [importun - enfant] annoying ▪ **tu es ~ avec tes questions** you're a nuisance with all these questions **3.** [gênant] tricky, awkward.

embêtement [ɑ̃bɛtmɑ̃] *nm fam* problem, hassle ▪ **~s** trouble ▪ **avoir des ~s : va les voir au commissariat, sinon tu peux avoir des ~s** go and see them at the police station or you could get into trouble ▪ **en ce moment, je n'ai que des ~s** it's just one damn thing after another at the moment.

embêter [4] [ɑ̃bete] *vt fam* **1.** [importuner] to annoy, to bother ▪ **se faire ~ par qqn** to be hassled by sb **2.** [lasser] to bore **3.** [mettre mal à l'aise] to bother, to annoy ▪ **cela m'embête d'avoir oublié** it annoys *ou* bothers me that I forgot.

◆ **s'embêter** *vpi fam* **1.** [s'ennuyer] to be bored ▪ **s'~ à mourir** to be bored to death *ou* tears **2.** *loc* **il s'embête pas!** [il est sans scrupules] he's got a nerve! ; [il est riche] he does pretty well for himself!

◆ **s'embêter à** *vp+prép* : **je ne vais pas m'~ à les éplucher** I'm not going to bother peeling them ▪ **et moi qui me suis embêtée à le refaire!** to think I went to (all) the trouble of doing it again!

emblée [ɑ̃ble] ◆ **d'emblée** *loc adv* straightaway, right away.

emblématique [ɑ̃blematik] *adj* emblematic.

emblème [ɑ̃blɛm] *nm* **1.** [blason] emblem **2.** [insigne] emblem, symbol ▪ **les ~s de la profession** the insignia of the trade.

embobeliner [ɑ̃bɔbline], **embobiner** [3] [ɑ̃bɔbine] *vt fam* **1.** [tromper] to take in *(sép)*, to hoodwink **2.** [manipuler] to get round *(insép)* ▪ **il sait t'~** he knows how to twist you round his little finger *ou* to get round you.

emboîtable [ɑ̃bwatabl] *adj* : **cubes/tuyaux ~s** cubes/pipes fitting into each other.

emboîtement [ɑ̃bwatmɑ̃] *nm* : **l'~ de deux tuyaux/os** the interlocking of two pipes/bones.

emboîter [3] [ɑ̃bwate] *vt* **1.** [ajuster - tuyaux] to fit together ; [- poupées russes] to fit into each other **2.** *loc* **~ le pas à qqn** *pr* to follow close behind sb ; *fig* to follow sb, to follow sb's lead.

◆ **s'emboîter** *vpi* to fit together *ou* into each other ▪ **des tables/poupées qui s'emboîtent les unes dans les autres** a nest of tables/dolls.

embolie [ɑ̃bɔli] *nf* embolism.

embonpoint [ɑ̃bɔ̃pwɛ̃] *nm* stoutness, portliness ▪ **prendre de l'~** to flesh out, to become stout, to put on weight.

embouché, e [ɑ̃buʃe] *adj* : **mal ~** *fam* [grossier] foulmouthed.

emboucher [3] [ɑ̃buʃe] *vt* **1.** MUS to put to one's mouth **2.** ÉQUIT : **~ un cheval** to put the bit in a horse's mouth.

embouchure [ɑ̃buʃyr] *nf* **1.** GÉOGR mouth **2.** MUS mouthpiece, embouchure **3.** ÉQUIT mouthpiece.

embourber [3] [ɑ̃burbe] *vt* [enliser] to stick.

◆ **s'embourber** *vpi* [dans la boue] to get bogged down *ou* stuck in the mud ▪ **s'~ dans ses mensonges/contradictions** to get bogged down in one's lies/contradictions.

embourgeoisement [ɑ̃burʒwazmɑ̃] *nm* [d'un groupe] becoming (more) bourgeois ▪ **l'~ des vieux quartiers rénovés** the gentrification of renovated inner city areas.

embourgeoiser [3] [ɑ̃burʒwaze] ◆ **s'embourgeoiser** *vpi* **1.** POLIT to become (more) bourgeois **2.** *péj* [gén] to become fonder and fonder of one's creature comforts ▪ [jeune couple] to settle down to a comfortable married life.

embout [ɑ̃bu] *nm* **1.** [d'un parapluie] tip, ferrule **2.** [bout - d'un tuyau] nozzle ; [- d'une seringue] adapter.

embouteillage [ɑ̃butɛjaʒ] *nm* **1.** AUTO traffic jam ▪ [à un carrefour] gridlock *US* ▪ **il y a de gros ~s** traffic is (jammed) solid **2.** *fam* TÉLÉCOM logjam(of calls).

embouteiller [4] [ɑ̃buteje] *vt* **1.** [mettre en bouteilles] to bottle **2.** AUTO to jam (up) *(sép)* ▪ **les routes sont embouteillées** the roads are congested *ou* jammed ▪ **~ un carrefour** to gridlock a junction *US*.

emboutir [32] [ɑ̃butir] *vt* **1.** [heurter] to crash into *(insép)* ▪ **je me suis fait ~ par un bus** I was hit by a bus ▪ **l'aile est toute emboutie** the wing's all dented **2.** MÉTALL to stamp.

embraie *etc v* ▷ **embrayer**.

embranchement [ɑ̃brɑ̃ʃmɑ̃] *nm* **1.** [carrefour - routier] fork ; [- ferroviaire] junction **2.** [voie annexe - routière] side road ; [- ferroviaire] branch line **3.** [d'égout] junction **4.** ZOOL & BOT phylum.

embrancher [3] [ɑ̃brɑ̃ʃe] ◆ **s'embrancher** *vpi* : **s'~ (sur)** to join (up with).

embrasement [ɑ̃brazmɑ̃] *nm litt* **1.** [incendie] blaze **2.** [rougeoiement] : **l'~ du couchant** the blaze of the setting sun **3.** [exaltation - de l'âme] kindling ; [- de l'imagination] firing.

embraser [3] [ɑ̃braze] *vt litt* **1.** [incendier] to set ablaze *ou* on fire, to set fire to **2.** [illuminer] to set ablaze *ou* aglow ▪ **le soleil levant embrasait le ciel** the rising sun set the sky aglow **3.** [rendre brûlant] to make burning hot **4.** [exalter - imagination] to fire ; [- âme] to kindle, to set aflame.
◆ **s'embraser** *vpi litt* **1.** [prendre feu] to catch fire, to blaze *ou* to flare up **2.** [s'illuminer] to be set ablaze **3.** [devenir brûlant] to become burning hot **4.** [s'exalter - âme, imagination] to be set on fire, to be kindled ; [- opprimés] to rise up ▪ **les esprits s'embrasaient** [par enthousiasme] imaginations were fired ; [par colère] passions were running high.

embrassade [ɑ̃brasad] *nf* : **une ~** a hug and a kiss ▪ **des ~s** hugging and kissing, hugs and kisses.

embrassements [ɑ̃brasmɑ̃] *nmpl* hugging and kissing, hugs and kisses.

embrasser [3] [ɑ̃brase] *vt* **1.** [donner un baiser à] to kiss ▪ **~ qqn sur la bouche** to kiss sb on the lips ▪ **embrasse Mamie, on s'en va!** kiss Granny goodbye! ▪ **vous embrasserez vos parents pour moi** (kind) regards to your parents ▪ **embrasse Lucie pour moi!** give Lucie a big kiss *ou* hug for me! ▪ **je t'embrasse** [dans une lettre] with love ; [au téléphone] kiss kiss! **2.** *litt* [serrer dans ses bras] to embrace, to hug ▪ **qui trop embrasse, mal étreint** *prov* he who grasps at too much loses all **3.** [adopter - idée, foi] to embrace, to take up *(sép)* ; [- carrière] to take up **4.** [saisir] : **~ du regard** to behold *litt* ▪ **~ d'un seul coup d'œil** to take in at a single glance **5.** [comprendre] to grasp **6.** [englober] to encompass, to embrace.
◆ **s'embrasser** *vp (emploi réciproque)* to kiss (one another).

embrasure [ɑ̃brazyr] *nf* **1.** [de porte] door-frame ▪ [de fenêtre] window-frame ▪ **se tenir dans l'~ d'une porte/fenêtre** to be framed in a doorway/window **2.** ARCHIT embrasure.

embrayage [ɑ̃brɛjaʒ] *nm* **1.** [mécanisme] clutch **2.** [pédale] clutch (pedal) **3.** [fait d'embrayer] putting in the clutch ▪ **voiture à ~ automatique** automatic car.

embrayer [11] [ɑ̃breje] ◇ *vt* AUTO to put in the clutch of.
◇ *vi* **1.** AUTO to put in *ou* to engage the clutch ▪ **embraye!** clutch in! **2.** *fam* [commencer] to get cracking, to go into action ▪ **~ sur** to get straight into.

embrigadement [ɑ̃brigadmɑ̃] *nm* **1.** MIL [dans une brigade] brigading ▪ [enrôlement forcé] being dragooned into the army *ou* pressed into service **2.** *péj* [adhésion forcée] press-ganging.

embrigader [3] [ɑ̃brigade] *vt* **1.** MIL [dans une brigade] to brigade ▪ [de force] to dragoon into the army, to press into service **2.** *péj* [faire adhérer] to press-gang ▪ **je ne veux pas être embrigadé dans leur mouvement** I won't let myself be press-ganged into joining their movement.

embringuer [3] [ɑ̃brɛ̃ge] *vt fam* **~ qqn dans** to drag sb into.

embrocation [ɑ̃brɔkasjɔ̃] *nf* embrocation.

embrocher [3] [ɑ̃brɔʃe] *vt* **1.** CULIN to spit, to spit-roast **2.** *fam* [transpercer] : **~ qqn avec qqch** to run sthg through sb.

embrouillamini [ɑ̃brujamini] *nm* (hopeless) muddle *ou* mix-up.

embrouille [ɑ̃bruj] *nf fam* **des ~s** shenanigans, funny business.

embrouillé, e [ɑ̃bruje] *adj* **1.** [fils, câbles] tangled up, entangled, snarled up **2.** [situation] muddled, confusing ▪ **avoir les idées ~es** to have muddled ideas, to be confused.

embrouillement [ɑ̃brujmɑ̃] *nm* : **tous ces incidents ont contribué à l'~ de la situation** all these incidents helped confuse the situation.

embrouiller [ɑ̃bruje] *vt* **1.** [emmêler] to tangle up ▪ **j'ai embrouillé les fils** I got the wires tangled up ▪ *fig* **~ qqn** to muddle sb, to confuse sb **2.** [compliquer] to complicate ▪ **~ la situation** *ou* **les choses** to confuse matters.
◆ **s'embrouiller** *vpi* to get muddled (up), to get confused.

embroussaillé, e [ɑ̃brusaje] *adj* [jardin] overgrown ▪ [cheveux] bushy ▪ [barbe] bushy, shaggy.

embrumer [3] [ɑ̃bryme] *vt* **1.** MÉTÉOR to cover in mist ▪ **la ligne embrumée des cimes** the misty mountain tops **2.** *litt* & *fig* to cloud.
◆ **s'embrumer** *vpi* **1.** MÉTÉOR to mist over **2.** [esprit, intelligence] to become clouded.

embruns [ɑ̃brœ̃] *nmpl* : **les ~** the sea spray *ou* spume.

embryologie [ɑ̃brijɔlɔʒi] *nf* embryology.

embryologiste [ɑ̃brijɔlɔʒist] *nmf* embryologist.

embryon [ɑ̃brijɔ̃] *nm* **1.** BIOL & BOT embryo **2.** *fig* [commencement] embryo, beginning ▪ **un ~ de projet** an embryonic project.

embryonnaire [ɑ̃brijɔnɛr] *adj* **1.** BIOL & BOT embryonic **2.** *fig* [non développé] embryonic, incipient ▪ **idée encore à l'état ~** idea still at the embryonic stage.

embûche [ɑ̃byʃ] *nf* **1.** [difficulté] pitfall, hazard **2.** [piège] trap ▪ **examen semé d'~s** exam paper full of trick questions.

embuer [7] [ɑ̃bɥe] *vt* to mist (up *ou* over) ▪ **des lunettes embuées** misted-up spectacles ▪ **les yeux embués de larmes** eyes misty with tears.

embuscade [ɑ̃byskad] *nf* ambush ▪ **se tenir en ~** to lie in ambush ▪ **tomber dans une ~** *pr* & *fig* to be caught in an ambush ▪ **tendre une ~ à qqn** *pr* & *fig* to set up an ambush for sb.

embusqué, e [ɑ̃byske] *nm, f* MIL & *péj* **les ~s de l'arrière** the troops that keep behind the lines.

embusquer [3] [ɑ̃byske] ◆ **s'embusquer** *vpi* **1.** [pour attaquer] to lie in ambush **2.** *péj* [pendant la guerre] to avoid active service.

éméché, e [emeʃe] *adj* tipsy ▪ **être (légèrement) ~** to be tipsy.

émécher [18] [emeʃe] *vt* to make tipsy.

émeraude [emrod] ◇ *nf* emerald.
◇ *adj inv* emerald *(modif)*, emerald-green.
◆ **Émeraude** *npr* : **la côte d'Émeraude** *part of the Northern French coast, near Saint-Malo.*

émergé, e [emɛrʒe] *adj* : **les terres ~es** the land above water level ▪ **la partie ~e de l'iceberg** the visible part of the iceberg.

émergence [emɛrʒɑ̃s] *nf* **1.** [apparition - d'une idée] (sudden) appearance *ou* emergence **2.** GÉOGR [d'une source] source.

émergent, e [emɛrʒɑ̃, ɑ̃t] *adj sout* [idée] emerging, developing.

émerger [17] [emɛrʒe] *vi* **1.** *fam* [d'une occupation, du sommeil] to emerge ▪ **~ de** to emerge from, to come out of **2.** [soleil] to rise, to come up **3.** [dépasser] : **~ de** [eau] to float (up) to the top of, to emerge from ▪ **une bonne copie/un bon élève qui émerge du lot** a paper/pupil standing out from the rest.

émeri [ɛmri] *nm* emery.

émérite [emerit] *adj* **1.** [éminent] (highly experienced and) skilled, expert *(avant n)* **2.** : **professeur ~** emeritus professor.

émerveillement [emɛrvɛjmɑ̃] *nm* **1.** [émotion] wonder, wonderment *litt* **2.** [chose merveilleuse] wonder.

émerveiller [4] [emɛrveje] *vt* to fill with wonder *ou* wonderment *litt* ▪ **elle fixait la poupée d'un regard émerveillé** she gazed at the doll in wonder.
◆ **s'émerveiller** *vpi* to be filled with wonder, to marvel ▪ **il s'émerveillait d'un rien** he marvelled at the smallest thing.

émet *etc v* ▷ **émettre.**

émétique [emetik] *adj* & *nm* emetic.

émetteur, trice [emetœr, tris] <> *adj* **1.** RADIO transmitting **2.** FIN issuing.
<> *nm, f* **1.** FIN drawer **2.** LING speaker.
◆ **émetteur** *nm* RADIO [appareil] transmitter ■ [élément] emitter.

émetteur-récepteur [emetœrresɛptœr] (*pl* **émetteurs-récepteurs**) *nm* transmitter-receiver, transceiver.

émettre [84] [emɛtr] <> *vt* **1.** [produire - rayon, son] to emit, to give out *(sép)* ; [- odeur] to give off *(sép)*, to produce **2.** [exprimer - hypothèse, opinion] to venture, to put forward, to volunteer ; [- doute, réserve] to express **3.** FIN [billet] to issue ■ [emprunt] to float **4.** RADIO & TV to broadcast, to transmit.
<> *vi* : **~ sur grandes ondes** to broadcast on long wave.

émeut *etc v* ▷ **émouvoir.**

émeute [emøt] *nf* riot ■ **il y a eu des ~s** there has been rioting ■ **tourner à l'~** to turn into a riot.

émeutier, ère [emøtje, ɛr] *nm, f* rioter.

émeuvent *etc v* ▷ **émouvoir.**

émiettement [emjɛtmɑ̃] *nm* [dispersion - des efforts] frittering away, dissipating ; [- du pouvoir] fragmentation.

émietter [4] [emjete] *vt* **1.** [mettre en miettes - gâteau] to crumble, to break up *(sép)*(into crumbs) **2.** [morceler - propriété] to break up *(sép)*.
◆ **s'émietter** *vpi* [pain] to crumble ■ [pouvoir] to ebb ■ [fortune] to gradually disappear, to be frittered away.

émigrant, e [emigrɑ̃, ɑ̃t] *nm, f* emigrant.

émigration [emigrasjɔ̃] *nf* emigration, emigrating *(U)*.

émigré, e [emigre] <> *adj* migrant.
<> *nm, f* emigrant ■ HIST emigré.

émigrer [3] [emigre] *vi* **1.** [s'expatrier] to emigrate **2.** ZOOL to migrate.

émincé [emɛ̃se] *nm* émincé ■ **~ de veau** émincé of veal, veal cut into slivers *(and served in a sauce)*.

émincer [16] [emɛ̃se] *vt* CULIN to slice thinly, to cut into thin strips.

éminemment [eminamɑ̃] *adv* eminently.

éminence [eminɑ̃s] *nf* **1.** GÉOGR hill, hillock, knoll **2.** ANAT protuberance **3.** *loc* **~ grise** éminence grise ■ **c'est l'~ grise du patron** he's the power behind the boss.

Éminence [eminɑ̃s] *nf* **1.** [titre] : **son ~ le cardinal Giobba** his Eminence Cardinal Giobba **2.** [cardinal] cardinal, Eminence.

éminent, e [eminɑ̃, ɑ̃t] *adj* eminent, prominent, noted ■ **mon ~ collègue** *sout* my learned colleague.

émir [emir] *nm* emir, amir.

émirat [emira] *nm* emirate ■ **les Émirats arabes unis** the United Arab Emirates.

émis, e [emi, iz] *pp* ▷ **émettre.**

émissaire [emisɛr] *nm* [envoyé] emissary, envoy.

émission [emisjɔ̃] *nf* **1.** PHYS [de son, de lumière, de signaux] emission **2.** RADIO & TV [transmission de sons, d'images] transmission, broadcasting ■ [programme] programme ■ **~ en direct/en différé** live/recorded broadcast **3.** FIN [de monnaie, d'emprunt] issuing **4.** [de sons articulés] : **~ de voix** utterance **5.** PHYSIOL emission.

emmagasiner [3] [ɑ̃magazine] *vt* **1.** COMM [marchandises - dans une arrière-boutique] to store ; [- dans un entrepôt] to warehouse **2.** [accumuler - connaissances] to store up *(sép)*, to accumulate ; [- provisions] to stock up on, to stockpile ■ **~ la chaleur** to keep in the heat.

emmailloter [3] [ɑ̃majɔte] *vt* [bébé] to swaddle ■ [membre] to wrap up *(sép)*.

emmanché, e▲ [ɑ̃mɑ̃ʃe] *nm, f* jerk△, dickhead△.

emmancher [3] [ɑ̃mɑ̃ʃe] *vt* [ajuster - tête de râteau, lame] to fit into a handle.
◆ **s'emmancher** *vpi fam* [commencer] : **l'affaire était mal emmanchée** the business got off to a bad start.

emmanchure [ɑ̃mɑ̃ʃyr] *nf* armhole.

Emmaüs [emays] *npr* Emmaus ■ **~ International** *charity organization to help the poor and homeless.*

emmêler [4] [ɑ̃mele] *vt* **1.** [mêler - cheveux, fils, brins de laine] to entangle, to tangle (up), to get into a tangle ■ **complètement emmêlé** all tangled up **2.** [rendre confus, confondre] to mix up *(sép)* ■ **j'emmêle les dates** I'm getting the dates confused ■ **des explications emmêlées** confused *ou* muddled explanations.
◆ **s'emmêler** <> *vpi* **1.** [être mêlé] to be tangled *ou* knotted *ou* snarled up **2.** [être confus - faits, dates] to get mixed up.
<> *vpt* : **s'~ les pieds dans** to get one's feet caught in ■ **s'~ les pieds** *ou* **pédales** *ou* **pinceaux** *ou* **crayons dans qqch** *fam fig* to get sthg all muddled up.

emménagement [ɑ̃menaʒmɑ̃] *nm* moving in.

emménager [17] [ɑ̃menaʒe] *vi* to move in.

emmener [19] [ɑ̃mne] *vt* **1.** [inviter à aller] to take along *(sép)* ■ **je t'emmène en montagne** I'll take you (with me) to the mountains ■ **~ qqn dîner** to take sb out to dinner **2.** [forcer à aller] to take away *(sép)* **3.** [accompagner] : **~ qqn à la gare** to take sb to the station ; [en voiture] to give sb a lift to *ou* to drop sb off at the station **4.** *fam* [emporter] to take (away) **5.** SPORT [sprint, peloton] to lead.

emment(h)al [emɛ̃tal] *nm* Emmenthal, Emmental.

emmerdant, e△ [ɑ̃mɛrdɑ̃, ɑ̃t] *adj* **1.** [importun] : **il est ~** he's a pain (in the neck) **2.** [gênant] bloody△ *UK ou* damn awkward ■ **c'est ~ d'avoir à laisser la porte ouverte** having to leave the door open is a real pain *ou* a bloody nuisance **3.** [ennuyeux] bloody *UK ou* godawful *US* boring△.

emmerde△ [ɑ̃mɛrd] *nf* hassle ■ **avoir des ~s : en ce moment j'ai que des ~s** it's just one frigging hassle after another at the moment△.

emmerdement△ [ɑ̃mɛrdəmɑ̃] *nm* hassle ■ **être dans les ~s jusqu'au cou** to be up the creek.

emmerder [3] △ [ɑ̃mɛrde] *vt* **1.** [gêner] to bug ■ **plus j'y pense, plus ça m'emmerde** the more I think about it, the more it bugs me ■ **d'y aller, ça m'emmerde!** it's a bloody *UK ou* goddam *US* nuisance having to go!△ ■ **se faire ~ par qqn** to be hassled by sb **2.** *(comme excl)* **je t'emmerde!** sod *UK ou* screw *US* you!△.
◆ **s'emmerder**△ *vpi* **1.** [s'ennuyer] to be bored stiff *ou* rigid ■ **on s'emmerde (à cent sous de l'heure) ici!** it's so bloody boring here! **2.** *loc* **il s'emmerde pas!** [il est sans scrupules] he's got a (bloody△) nerve! ; [il est riche] he does pretty well for himself!
◆ **s'emmerder à**△ *vp+prép* : **s'~ à faire** to be bothered doing ■ **et moi qui me suis emmerdé à tout recopier!** to think I went to the trouble of copying the whole bloody thing out!

emmerdeur, euse△ [ɑ̃mɛrdœr, øz] *nm, f* bloody△ *UK ou* damn pain.

emmitoufler [3] [ɑ̃mitufle] *vt* to wrap up (well) *(sép)*.
◆ **s'emmitoufler** *vp (emploi réfléchi)* to wrap up well ■ **s'~ dans une cape** to wrap o.s. up in a cape.

emmurer [3] [ɑ̃myre] *vt* **1.** [enfermer] to wall up *ou* in *(sép)* **2.** *fig* & *litt* [isoler] to immure.
◆ **s'emmurer dans** *vp+prép litt* **s'~ dans le silence** to retreat into silence.

émoi [emwa] *nm litt* [émotion] agitation ■ [tumulte] commotion ■ **elle était tout en ~** she was all in a fluster ■ **la population est en ~** there's great agitation among the population.

émollient, e [emɔljɑ̃, ɑ̃t] *adj* emollient.

émoluments [emɔlymɑ̃] *nmpl* [d'un employé] salary, wages ■ [d'un notaire] fees.

émonder [3] [emɔ̃de] *vt* [arbuste, buisson] to prune ■ [arbre] to trim (the top of).

émoticon [emotikɔ̃] *nm* INFORM emoticon, smiley.

émoticone [emotikon] *nf* ▷ **émoticon.**

émotif, ive [emɔtif, iv] <> *adj* [personne] emotional, sentimental ■ [trouble, choc] psychological.

<> *nm, f* : **c'est un grand ~** he's very emotional.

émotion [emosjɔ̃] *nf* **1.** [sensation] feeling ■ **~s fortes** strong feelings ■ **ils se sont quittés avec ~** they had an emotional parting ■ **sans ~** without emotion **2.** [affectivité] emotion, emotionality ■ **se laisser gagner par l'~** to become emotional **3.** [qualité - d'une œuvre] emotion.
◆ **émotions** *nfpl fam* : **des ~s** a (nasty) fright ■ **j'ai eu des ~s** I got a fright ■ **donner des ~s à qqn** to give sb a (nasty) turn *ou* a fright.

émotionnel, elle [emosjɔnel] *adj* [réaction] psychological.

émotionner [3] [emosjɔne] *vt fam* [émouvoir] to upset, to shake up *(sép)*.
◆ **s'émotionner** *vpi fam* [s'émouvoir] : **il s'émotionne pour un rien** he gets worked up about the slightest little thing.

émotivité [emɔtivite] *nf* emotionalism.

émoulu, e [emuly] *adj* ▷ **frais**.

émoussé [emuse] *adj* blunt.

émousser [3] [emuse] *vt* **1.** [rasoir, épée] to blunt, to take the edge off **2.** [affaiblir - appétit, goût, peine] to dull, to take the edge off ; [- curiosité] to temper.
◆ **s'émousser** *vpi* **1.** [couteau] to become blunt, to lose its edge **2.** [faiblir - appétit, peine] to dull ; [- curiosité] to become tempered.

émoustillant, e [emustijɑ̃, ɑ̃t] *adj* **1.** exhilarating **2.** [sexuellement] titillating.

émoustiller [3] [emustije] *vt* **1.** [animer] to excite, to exhilarate ■ **le champagne les avait tous émoustillés** they'd all got merry on champagne **2.** [sexuellement] to turn on *(sép)*.

émouvant, e [emuvɑ̃, ɑ̃t] *adj* moving, touching ■ **de façon ~e** movingly ■ **un moment ~** an emotional moment.

émouvoir [55] [emuvwar] *vt* **1.** [attendrir] to touch, to move ■ **ému jusqu'aux larmes** moved to tears **2.** [perturber] to disturb, to unsettle ■ **nullement ému par ces accusations** quite undisturbed *ou* unperturbed by these accusations ■ **se laisser ~** to let o.s. be affected.
◆ **s'émouvoir** *vpi* **1.** [s'attendrir] to be touched *ou* moved ■ **s'~ à la vue de** to be affected by the sight of **2.** [être perturbé] to be disturbed *ou* perturbed.
◆ **s'émouvoir de** *vp+prép* to pay attention to ■ **le gouvernement s'en est ému** it came to the notice *ou* attention of the government.

empaillé, e [ɑ̃paje] *nm, f fam péj* fat lump.

empailler [3] [ɑ̃paje] *vt* **1.** [animal] to stuff ■ **ils ont fait ~ un renard** they had a fox stuffed **2.** [chaise] to bottom with straw **3.** HORT to cover with straw.

empailleur, euse [ɑ̃pajœr, øz] *nm, f* **1.** [d'animaux] taxidermist **2.** [de chaises] chair caner.

empalement [ɑ̃palmɑ̃] *nm* impalement.

empaler [3] [ɑ̃pale] *vt* **1.** [supplicier] to impale **2.** [embrocher] to put on a spit.
◆ **s'empaler** *vpi* : **s'~ sur une fourche/un pieu** to impale o.s. on a pitchfork/stake.

empanacher [3] [ɑ̃panaʃe] *vt* to plume, to deck out *(sép) ou* to decorate with plumes ■ **casque empanaché** plumed helmet.

empanner [3] [ɑ̃pane] *vt* to wear NAUT.

empaqueter [27] [ɑ̃pakte] *vt* **1.** COMM to pack, to package **2.** [envelopper] to wrap up *(sép)*.

emparer [3] [ɑ̃pare] ◆ **s'emparer de** *vp+prép* **1.** [avec la main - gén] to grab (hold of), to grasp, to seize ; [- vivement] to snatch **2.** [prendre de force - territoire] to take over *(sép)*, to seize ; [- véhicule] to commandeer ■ **la grande industrie s'est emparée des médias** big business has taken over the media ■ **s'~ de la conversation** to monopolize the conversation **3.** [tirer parti de - prétexte, idée] to seize (hold of) **4.** [envahir] : **la colère s'est emparée d'elle** anger swept over her ■ **l'émotion s'est emparée d'elle** she was seized by a strong emotion ■ **le doute s'est emparé de moi** *ou* **mon esprit** I became a prey to *ou* my mind was seized with doubt.

empâté, e [ɑ̃pate] *adj* [langue, voix] slurred.

empâtement [ɑ̃patmɑ̃] *nm* **1.** [obésité] fattening out ■ [épaississement - des traits] coarsening ; [- de la taille] thickening **2.** ART impasto.

empâter [3] [ɑ̃pate] *vt* **1.** [bouffir] to make podgier ■ **les grossesses successives lui ont empâté la taille** she's grown fatter round the waist with each pregnancy **2.** [rendre pâteux] : **le vin lui a empâté la langue** his speech has become slurred from drinking wine **3.** ART impaste.
◆ **s'empâter** *vpi* to put on weight ■ **sa taille/figure s'est empâtée** he's grown fatter round the waist/fatter in the face.

empathie [ɑ̃pati] *nf sout* empathy.

empattement [ɑ̃patmɑ̃] *nm* **1.** CONSTR [de planches] tenoning ■ [d'un mur] footing ■ [d'une grue] base plate **2.** [d'un arbre, d'une branche] (wide) base **3.** AUTO wheelbase **4.** IMPR serif.

empêché, e [ɑ̃peʃe] *adj* : **il a été ~** [par un problème] he hit a snag ; [il n'est pas venu] he couldn't make it ; [il a été retenu] he was held up.

empêchement [ɑ̃pɛʃmɑ̃] *nm* **1.** [obstacle] snag, hitch, holdup ■ **si tu as un ~, téléphone** [si tu as un problème] if you hit a snag, phone ; [si tu ne viens pas] if you can't make it, phone ; [si tu es retenu] if you're held up, phone **2.** DR : **~ à mariage** impediment to a marriage.

empêcher [4] [ɑ̃peʃe] <> *vt* **1.** [ne pas laisser] : **~ qqn de faire qqch** to prevent sb (from) *ou* to keep sb from *ou* to stop sb (from) doing sthg ■ **pousse-toi, tu m'empêches de voir!** move over, I can't see! ■ **~ qqn d'entrer/de sortir/d'approcher** to keep sb out/in/away ■ **~ que qqn/qqch (ne) fasse** to stop sb/sthg from doing, to prevent sb/sthg from doing ◐ **le café m'empêche de dormir** *pr* coffee keeps me awake ■ **ce n'est pas ça qui va l'~ de dormir!** *fig* he's not going to lose any sleep over that! **2.** [pour renforcer une suggestion] to stop, to prevent ■ **cela ne t'empêche pas** *ou* **rien ne t'empêche de l'acheter à crédit** you could always buy it in instalments ■ **qu'est-ce qui nous empêche de le faire?** what's to prevent us (from) doing it?, what's to stop us? ■ **qu'est-ce qui vous empêche d'écrire à ses parents?** why don't you write to his parents? **3.** [prévenir - mariage, famine] to prevent, to stop ■ **~ l'extension d'un conflit** to stop a conflict spreading ◐ **ça n'empêche pas** *fam ou* **rien** *fam* **!** *fam* it makes no difference! **4.** [retenir] : **être empêché de faire** : **empêché de venir, il n'a pas pu voter** he couldn't vote, as he was (unavoidably) detained.
<> *v impers* : **il n'empêche qu'elle ne l'a jamais compris** the fact remains that she's never understood him ■ **il n'empêche que tu es encore en retard** maybe, but you're late again all the same.
◆ **s'empêcher de** *vp+prép* : **s'~ de faire** to refrain from *ou* to stop o.s. doing ■ **je ne peux pas m'~ de penser qu'il a raison** I can't help thinking he's right ■ **il n'a pas pu s'~ de le dire** he just had to say it.
◆ **n'empêche** *loc adv fam* all the same, though ■ **n'empêche, tu aurais pu (me) prévenir!** all the same *ou* even so, you could have let me know!
◆ **n'empêche que** *loc conj fam* **on ne m'a pas écouté, n'empêche que j'avais raison!** they didn't listen to me, even though I was right!

empêcheur, euse [ɑ̃pɛʃœr, øz] *nm, f* : **un ~ de danser** *ou* **tourner en rond** *fam* a spoilsport.

empeigne [ɑ̃pɛɲ] *nf* upper *(of a shoe)*.

empennage [ɑ̃pɛnaʒ] *nm* **1.** AÉRON empennage **2.** ARM [d'un obus, d'une bombe] tail fins ■ [d'une arbalète] feathers.

empereur [ɑ̃prœr] *nm* emperor ■ **l'Empereur** HIST Napoleon (Bonaparte *ou* the First).

empesé, e [ɑ̃pəze] *adj* **1.** [tissu] starched **2.** [discours, style] starchy.

empeser [19] [ɑ̃pəze] *vt* to starch.

empester [3] [ɑ̃pɛste] ◇ *vt* [pièce] to stink out *(sép)* UK, to make stink ■ [parfum] to stink of.
◇ *vi* to stink.

empêtré, e [ɑ̃petre] *adj* [air] awkward, self-conscious.

empêtrer [4] [ɑ̃petre] *vt* **1.** [entortiller - personne] to trap, to entangle ; [- jambes, chevilles] to trap, to catch ■ **empêtré dans ses couvertures** all tangled up in his blankets **2.** [embarrasser] to bog down *(sép)* ■ **être empêtré dans ses explications** to be bogged down *ou* muddled up in one's explanations ■ **être empêtré dans ses mensonges** to be caught in the web of *ou* trapped in one's own lies.
◆ **s'empêtrer** *vpi* **1.** [s'entortiller] to become tangled up *ou* entangled ■ **elle s'est empêtrée dans la corde** she got tangled up in the rope **2.** [s'enferrer] : **s'~ dans** [mensonges, explications] to get bogged down *ou* tied up in.

emphase [ɑ̃faz] *nf* **1.** *péj* [grandiloquence] pomposity, bombast ■ **un discours plein d'~** a pompous speech ■ **avec ~** pompously, bombastically **2.** LING emphasis.

emphatique [ɑ̃fatik] *adj* **1.** *péj* [grandiloquent] pompous, bombastic **2.** LING emphatic.

emphysème [ɑ̃fizɛm] *nm* emphysema.

empiècement [ɑ̃pjɛsmɑ̃] *nm* yoke TEXT.

empierrer [4] [ɑ̃pjere] *vt* **1.** [route] to gravel, to metal UK **2.** [pour le drainage] to line with stones.

empiétement [ɑ̃pjɛtmɑ̃] *nm* encroachment, encroaching *(U)*.

empiéter [18] [ɑ̃pjete] ◆ **empiéter sur** *v+prép* **1.** [dans l'espace, le temps] to encroach on *ou* upon *(insép)*, to overlap with *(insép)* **2.** [droit, liberté] to encroach on *ou* upon *(insép)*, to cut *ou* to eat into *(insép)*.

empiffrer [3] [ɑ̃pifre] ◆ **s'empiffrer** *vpi fam* to stuff o.s. ■ **s'~ de gâteaux** to stuff o.s. with cakes.

empilable [ɑ̃pilabl] *adj* stackable.

empilage [ɑ̃pilaʒ] *nm* [de boîtes] piling *ou* stacking up ■ [de chaises] stacking up.

empilement [ɑ̃pilmɑ̃] *nm* [ordonné] stack ■ [désordonné] heap, pile, mound.

empiler [3] [ɑ̃pile] *vt* **1.** [mettre en tas] to pile *ou* to heap up *(sép)* ■ [ranger en hauteur] to stack (up) **2.** [thésauriser] to amass (large quantities of).
◆ **s'empiler** ◇ *vp (emploi passif)* to be stacked up ■ **ces chaises s'empilent** the chairs are stackable.
◇ *vpi* [s'entasser] to pile up ■ **s'~ dans** [entrer nombreux dans] to pile *ou* to pack into.

empire [ɑ̃pir] *nm* **1.** [régime, territoire] empire ■ **je ne m'en séparerais pas pour (tout) un ~!** I wouldn't be without it for the world! ■ **l'~ d'Occident** the Western Empire ■ **l'~ d'Orient** [romain] the Eastern (Roman) Empire ; [byzantin] the Byzantine Empire ■ **l'~ du Soleil Levant** the Land of the Rising Sun **2.** MYTHOL & RELIG : **l'~ céleste** the kingdom of heaven ■ **l'~ des ténèbres** hell **3.** COMM & INDUST empire **4.** *sout* [influence] influence ■ **avoir de l'~ sur qqn** to have a hold on *ou* over sb.
◆ **sous l'empire de** *loc prép sout* [poussé par] : **sous l'~ de l'alcool** under the influence of alcohol ■ **sous l'~ de la jalousie** in the grip of jealousy.

Empire [ɑ̃pir] *npr m* : **l'~, le premier ~** the (Napoleonic) Empire ■ **sous l'~** during the Napoleonic era ■ **noblesse d'~** nobility created by Napoleon (Bonaparte) ■ **le second ~** the Second Empire ■ *(comme adj inv)* **meubles ~** Empire furniture, furniture in the French Empire style.

empirer [3] [ɑ̃pire] ◇ *vi* [santé] to become worse, to worsen, to deteriorate ■ [mauvais caractère] to become worse ■ [problème, situation] to get worse.
◇ *vt* to make worse, to cause to deteriorate.

empirique [ɑ̃pirik] *adj* **1.** PHILOS & SC empirical **2.** *péj* [non rigoureux] empirical, purely practical.

empirisme [ɑ̃pirism] *nm* **1.** PHILOS & SC empiricism **2.** *péj* [pragmatisme] empiricism, charlatanry.

empiriste [ɑ̃pirist] *adj* & *nmf* empiricist.

emplacement [ɑ̃plasmɑ̃] *nm* **1.** [position - d'un édifice, d'un monument] site, location ; [- d'une démarcation] position, place ■ **~ publicitaire** advertising space **2.** [pour véhicule] parking space.

emplâtre [ɑ̃platr] *nm* PHARM plaster.

emplette [ɑ̃plɛt] *nf* **1.** [fait d'acheter] : **faire ses/des ~ s** to do one's/some shopping **2.** [objet acheté] purchase.

emplir [32] [ɑ̃plir] *vt sout* [récipient] to fill (up) *(sép)* ■ [salle] to fill.
◆ **s'emplir** *vpi* to fill up ■ **s'~ de** to fill up with ■ **s'~ d'air** to inflate, to fill with air.

emploi [ɑ̃plwa] *nm* **1.** [travail] job ■ **il est sans ~** he is unemployed *ou* out of a job ■ **~ saisonnier** seasonal job **2.** [fait d'employer] employing **3.** ÉCON : **l'~** employment ■ **la situation de l'~** the job *ou* employment situation **4.** [au spectacle] part ➲ **avoir le physique** *ou* **la tête de l'~** to look the part **5.** [utilisation] use ■ **d'un ~ facile** easy to use ■ **faire mauvais ~ de son argent** to misuse one's money **6.** ÉDUC : **~ du temps** [de l'année] timetable ; [d'une journée, des vacances] timetable, schedule ■ **un ~ du temps chargé** a busy timetable *ou* schedule **7.** [cas d'utilisation - d'un objet] use ; [- d'une expression] use, usage **8.** [en comptabilité] entry.

emploie *etc v* ▷ **employer**.

employable [ɑ̃plwajabl] *adj* [personne] employable ■ [objet] usable.

employé, e [ɑ̃plwaje] *nm, f* employee ➲ **~ de banque** bank clerk ■ **~ de bureau** office worker ■ **j'attends un ~ du gaz** I'm expecting someone from the gas board UK *ou* company US ■ **~ de maison** servant ■ **~s de maison** domestic staff ■ **~ des postes** postal worker.

employer [13] [ɑ̃plwaje] *vt* **1.** [professionnellement] to employ ■ **~ qqn à faire qqch** [l'assigner à une tâche] to use sb to do sthg **2.** [manier - instrument, machine] to use **3.** [mettre en œuvre - méthode, ruse] to employ, to use ■ **~ la force** to use force ■ **~ son énergie à faire qqch** to devote *ou* to apply one's energy to doing sthg ■ **de l'argent bien employé** money well spent, money put to good use **4.** [expression] to use ■ **mal ~ un mot** to misuse a word, to use a word incorrectly **5.** [temps, journée] to spend ■ **bien ~ son temps** to make good use of one's time ■ **mal ~ son temps** to misuse one's time, to use one's time badly, to waste one's time **6.** [en comptabilité] to enter.
◆ **s'employer** *vp (emploi passif)* **1.** [mot] to be used ■ **ce verbe ne s'emploie plus** that verb is no longer in common usage **2.** [outil, machine] to be used.
◆ **s'employer à** *vp+prép* [se consacrer à] to devote *ou* to apply o.s. to ■ **je m'y emploie** I'm working on it.

employeur, euse [ɑ̃plwajœr, øz] *nm, f* employer.

emplumer [3] [ɑ̃plyme] *vt* to decorate with feathers.

empocher [3] [ɑ̃pɔʃe] *vt* **1.** [mettre dans sa poche] to pocket **2.** [s'approprier] to snap up *(sép)*.

empoignade [ɑ̃pwaɲad] *nf* **1.** [coups] brawl, set-to **2.** [querelle] row, set-to.

empoigne [ɑ̃pwaɲ] *nf* ▷ **foire**.

empoigner [3] [ɑ̃pwaɲe] *vt* [avec les mains] to grab, to grasp.
◆ **s'empoigner** *vp (emploi réciproque)* to set to ■ **ils se sont tous empoignés** there was a general mêlée *ou* free-for-all.

empois [ɑ̃pwa] *nm* starch.

empoisonnant, e [ɑ̃pwazɔnɑ̃, ɑ̃t] *adj fam* **1.** [exaspérant] annoying ■ **ce que tu peux être ~!** you can be so annoying *ou* you're such a pain sometimes! **2.** [ennuyeux] tedious, boring.

empoisonnement [ɑ̃pwazɔnmɑ̃] *nm* PHYSIOL poisoning.

empoisonner [3] [ɑ̃pwazɔne] *vt* **1.** [tuer] to poison **2.** ÉCOL to contaminate, to poison **3.** [mettre du poison sur - flèche] to poison **4.** [dégrader - rapports] to poison, to taint, to blight ; [- esprit] to poison ■ **~ l'existence à qqn** to make sb's life a misery **5.** [importuner] to bother ■ **tu m'empoisonnes avec tes questions!** you're being a real nuisance with your questions!

◆ **s'empoisonner** *vpi* **1.** PHYSIOL to get food poisoning **2.** *fam* [s'ennuyer] to be bored stiff.
◆ **s'empoisonner à** *vp+prép* [se donner du mal pour] : **je ne vais pas m'~ à coller toutes ces enveloppes!** I can't be bothered to seal all those envelopes!

empoisonneur, euse [ɑ̃pwazɔnœr, øz] *nm, f* **1.** *fam* [importun - qui lasse] nuisance, bore ; [- qui gêne] nuisance, pain (in the neck) **2.** [assassin] poisoner.

empoissonner [3] [ɑ̃pwasɔne] *vt* to stock with fish.

emporté, e [ɑ̃pɔrte] ◇ *adj* [coléreux - homme] quick-tempered ; [- ton] angry.
◇ *nm, f* quick-tempered person.

emportement [ɑ̃pɔrtəmɑ̃] *nm* **1.** [colère] anger *(U)* ■ [accès de colère] fit of anger ■ **avec ~** angrily **2.** *litt* [passion] transport ■ **aimer qqn avec ~** to love sb passionately.

emporte-pièce [ɑ̃pɔrtəpjɛs] *nm inv* punch TECHNOL.
◆ **à l'emporte-pièce** *loc adj* incisive.

emporter [3] [ɑ̃pɔrte] *vt* **1.** [prendre avec soi] to take ▶ **~ un secret dans la** *OU* **sa tombe** to take *OU* to carry a secret to the grave ■ **il ne l'emportera pas au paradis!** he's not getting away with that! **2.** [transporter - stylo, parapluie, chaton] to take ; [- bureau, piano, blessé] to carry (off *OU* away) ■ **emporte tout ça au grenier/à la cave** take these things (up) to the attic/(down) to the cellar **3.** [retirer - livre, stylo] to take (away), to remove ; [- malle, piano] to carry away *(sép)*, to remove ■ **feuilles emportées par le vent** leaves carried *OU* swept along by the wind ▶ **'Autant en emporte le vent'** ***Mitchell*** 'Gone With the Wind' **4.** [voler] to take, to go off with **5.** [endommager] to tear off ■ **il a eu le bras emporté par l'explosion** he lost an arm in the explosion, the explosion blew his arm off ■ **cette sauce emporte la bouche** this sauce takes the roof of your mouth off **6.** [émouvoir - suj: amour, haine] to carry (along) *(sép)* ; [- suj: élan] to carry away *(sép)* ■ **il s'est laissé ~ par son imagination** he let his imagination run away with him **7.** [tuer - suj: maladie] : **il a été emporté par un cancer** he died of cancer **8.** [gagner - victoire] to win, to carry off *(sép)* ■ **~ la décision** to win *OU* to carry the day ■ **~ l'adhésion de qqn** to win sb's support ▶ **~ le morceau** *fam* to have the upper hand ■ **l'~** [argument] to win *OU* to carry the day ; [attitude, méthode] to prevail ■ **le plus fort l'emportera** [boxeurs] the stronger man will win ; [concurrents] the best competitor will come out on top *OU* carry the day ■ **Cendrillon l'emportait en beauté (sur les autres)** Cinderella's beauty far outshone the others ■ **l'~ sur** to win *OU* to prevail over **9.** MIL [place] to take.
◆ **s'emporter** *vpi* **1.** [personne] to lose one's temper, to flare up **2.** [cheval] to bolt.
◆ **à emporter** *loc adj* to take away *UK*, to go *US* ■ **nous faisons des plats à ~** we have a takeaway *UK OU* takeout *US* service.

empoté, e [ɑ̃pɔte] *fam* ◇ *adj* clumsy, awkward.
◇ *nm, f* clumsy oaf.

empoter [3] [ɑ̃pɔte] *vt* to pot HORT.

empourprer [3] [ɑ̃purpre] *vt litt* [horizon] to (tinge with) crimson.
◆ **s'empourprer** *vpi litt* **1.** [horizon] to turn crimson **2.** [joues, personne] to flush (bright crimson).

empoussiérer [18] [ɑ̃pusjere] *vt* to cover with dust, to make dusty.

empreindre [81] [ɑ̃prɛ̃dr] *vt litt* [pensée] to mark, to stamp ■ [cœur, comportement] to mark ■ **empreint de : empreint d'un amour véritable** marked by true love ■ **ses manières sont empreintes de bonté** her ways are full of kindness ■ **d'un ton empreint de gravité** in a grave tone of voice.

empreinte [ɑ̃prɛ̃t] *nf* **1.** [du pas humain] footprint ■ [du gibier] track ■ **~s (digitales)** fingerprints **2.** [d'un sceau] imprint ■ [sur une médaille] stamp **3.** [d'une serrure] impression **4.** [influence] mark, stamp **5.** PSYCHOL imprint **6.** [d'une dent] impression **7.** GÉOL imprint **8.** BIOL : **~ génétique** genetic fingerprint.

empressé, e [ɑ̃prese] ◇ *adj* [fiancé] thoughtful, attentive ■ [serveuse, garde-malade] attentive ■ *péj* overzealous.
◇ *nm, f* : **faire l'~ auprès de qqn** to fawn over sb.

empressement [ɑ̃prɛsmɑ̃] *nm* **1.** [zèle] assiduousness, attentiveness ■ **montrer de l'~** to be eager to please **2.** [hâte] enthusiasm, eagerness, keenness ■ **il est allé les chercher avec ~/sans (aucun) ~** he went off to get them enthusiastically/(very) reluctantly ■ **son ~ à se déclarer coupable éveilla les soupçons** suspicions were aroused by the fact that he was so eager to admit his guilt.

empresser [4] [ɑ̃prese] ◆ **s'empresser** *vpi* : **s'~ autour** *OU* **auprès de qqn** [s'activer] to bustle around sb ; [être très attentif] to surround sb with attentions, to attend to sb's needs ■ **les hommes s'empressent autour d'elle** she always has men hovering around her.
◆ **s'empresser de** *vp+prép* : **s'~ de faire qqch** to hasten to do sthg.

emprise [ɑ̃priz] *nf* **1.** [intellectuelle, morale] hold ■ **l'~ du désir** the ascendancy of desire ■ **sous l'~ de la peur** in the grip of fear ■ **être sous l'~ de qqn** to be under sb's thumb **2.** ADMIN & DR expropriation.

emprisonnement [ɑ̃prizɔnmɑ̃] *nm* imprisonment ■ **condamné à 5 ans d'~** sentenced to 5 years in prison, given a 5-year sentence ▶ **~ à perpétuité** life imprisonment.

emprisonner [3] [ɑ̃prizɔne] *vt* **1.** [incarcérer - malfaiteur] to imprison, to put in jail, to put in prison **2.** [immobiliser] to trap ■ **le cou emprisonné dans une minerve** his neck tightly held in *OU* constricted by a surgical collar **3.** [psychologiquement] : **~ qqn dans une morale** to put sb in a moral straitjacket ■ **emprisonné dans des habitudes dont il ne peut pas se défaire** trapped in habits he is unable to break.

emprunt [ɑ̃prœ̃] *nm* **1.** FIN [procédé] borrowing ■ [argent] loan ■ **faire un ~** to borrow money, to take out a loan ■ **faire un ~ de 10 000 euros** to raise a loan of *OU* to borrow 10,000 euros ■ **~ à 11 %** loan at 11% ▶ **~ d'État/public** national/public loan **2.** [d'un vélo, d'un outil] borrowing **3.** LING [processus] borrowing ■ [mot] loan (word) **4.** [fait d'imiter] borrowing ■ [élément imité] borrowing.
◆ **d'emprunt** *loc adj* [nom] assumed.

emprunté, e [ɑ̃prœ̃te] *adj* [peu naturel - façon] awkward ; [- personne] awkward, self-conscious.

emprunter [3] [ɑ̃prœ̃te] *vt* **1.** FIN to borrow **2.** [outil, robe] to borrow **3.** [nom] to assume **4.** [imiter - élément de style] to borrow, to take **5.** [route] to take ■ [circuit] to follow ■ **vous êtes priés d'~ le souterrain** you are requested to use the underpass **6.** LING to borrow ■ **mot emprunté** loan (word).

emprunteur, euse [ɑ̃prœ̃tœr, øz] *nm, f* borrower.

empuantir [32] [ɑ̃pɥɑ̃tir] *vt* [salle] to stink out *(sép) UK*, to make stink ■ [air] to fill with a foul smell.

EMT (*abr de* **éducation manuelle et technique**) *nf practical sciences.*

ému, e [emy] ◇ *pp* ▷ **émouvoir**.
◇ *adj* [de gratitude, de joie, par une musique, par la pitié] moved ■ [de tristesse] affected ■ [d'inquiétude] agitated ■ [d'amour] excited ■ **~ jusqu'aux larmes** moved to tears ■ **parler d'une voix ~e** to speak with (a voice full of) emotion ■ **trop ~ pour parler** too overcome by emotion to be able to speak ■ **je garde d'elle un souvenir ~** I have fond memories of her.

émulateur [emylatœr] *nm* emulator.

émulation [emylasjɔ̃] *nf* **1.** [compétition] emulation **2.** INFORM emulation.

émule [emyl] *nmf* emulator ■ **le dictateur et ses ~s** the dictator and his followers.

émulsif, ive [emylsif, iv] *adj* emulsive.
◆ **émulsif** *nm* emulsifier.

émulsifiant, e [emylsifjɑ̃, ɑ̃t] = **émulsif**.

émulsion [emylsjɔ̃] *nf* CHIM, CULIN & PHOTO emulsion.

émulsionner [3] [emylsjɔne] *vt* **1.** [produit] to emulsify **2.** PHOTO to coat with emulsion.

émut *etc v* ▷ **émouvoir**.

en [ɑ̃] ◇ *prép*

A. DANS LE TEMPS
B. DANS L'ESPACE
C. INDIQUANT LE DOMAINE
D. INDIQUANT LA COMPOSITION
E. INDIQUANT LA MANIÈRE, LE MOYEN
F. AVEC LE GÉRONDIF
G. INTRODUISANT LE COMPLÉMENT DU VERBE

A. DANS LE TEMPS

[indiquant - le moment] in ; [- la durée] in, during ▪ **en soirée** in the evening ▪ **en deux heures c'était fini** it was over in two hours ▪ **en 40 ans de carrière...** in my 40 years in the job...

B. DANS L'ESPACE

1. [indiquant - la situation] in ; [- la direction] to ▪ **se promener en forêt/en ville** to walk in the forest/around the town ▪ **faire une croisière en Méditerranée** to go on a cruise around the Mediterranean ▪ **aller en Espagne** to go to Spain ▪ **partir en forêt** to go off into the forest

2. *fig* **en moi-même, j'avais toujours cet espoir** deep down *ou* in my heart of hearts, I still had that hope ▪ **trouver en soi la force de faire qqch** to find in o.s. the strength to do sthg ▪ **ce que j'apprécie en lui** what I like about him

C. INDIQUANT LE DOMAINE

1. [pour des connaissances] : **bon en latin/physique** good at Latin/ physics ▪ **je ne m'y connais pas en peinture** I don't know much about painting ▪ **il fait de la recherche en agronomie** he's doing research in agronomy

2. [dans une situation] : **je suis malheureux en amour** I'm unlucky in love ▪ **en cela** *ou* **ce en quoi il n'a pas tort** and I have to say he's right *ou* not wrong there

D. INDIQUANT LA COMPOSITION

[pour des objets] : **chaise en bois/fer** wooden/iron chair ▪ **c'est en quoi?** *fam* what's it made of?

E. INDIQUANT LA MANIÈRE, LE MOYEN

1. [marquant l'état, la forme, la manière] : **être en colère/en rage** to be angry/in a rage ▪ **être en forme** to be on (good) form ▪ **le pays est en guerre** the country is at war ▪ **se conduire en gentleman** to behave like a gentleman ▪ **en véritable ami, il m'a prévenu** good friend that he is *ou* being a true friend, he warned me ▪ **je suis venu en ami** I came as a friend ▪ **il m'a envoyé ces fleurs en remerciement** he sent me these flowers to say thank you ▪ **peint en bleu** painted blue ▪ **je la préfère en vert** I prefer it in green ▪ **il était en pyjama** he was in his pyjamas, he had his pyjamas on ▪ **couper qqch en deux** to cut sthg in two *ou* in half ▪ **en (forme de) losange** diamond-shaped ▪ **j'ai passé Noël en famille** I spent Christmas with my family ▪ **faire qqch en cachette/en vitesse/en douceur** to do sthg secretly/quickly/smoothly ▪ **du sucre en morceaux** sugar cubes ▪ **une rue en pente** a street on a slope *ou* a hill

2. [introduisant une mesure] in ▪ **je veux le résultat en dollars** I want the result in dollars ▪ **un tissu en 140 de large** 140 cm wide material ▪ **auriez-vous la même robe en 38 ?** do you have the same dress in a 38 ?

3. [indiquant une transformation] into ▪ **l'eau se change en glace** water turns into ice ▪ **se déguiser en fille** to dress up as a girl

4. [marquant le moyen] : **j'y vais en bateau** I'm going by boat ▪ **ils ont fait le tour de l'île en voilier** they sailed round the island (in a yacht) ▪ **en voiture/train** by car/train ▪ **avoir peur en avion** to be scared of flying ▪ **payer en liquide** to pay cash

F. AVEC LE GÉRONDIF

1. [indiquant la simultanéité] : **il est tombé en courant** he fell while running ▪ **nous en parlerons en prenant un café** we'll talk about it over a cup of coffee ▪ **c'est en le voyant que j'ai compris** when I saw him I understood ▪ **rien qu'en le voyant, elle se met en colère** she gets angry just seeing him, the mere sight of him makes her angry ▪ **tout en marchant, elles tentaient de trouver une réponse** while walking *ou* as they walked, they tried to find an answer

2. [indiquant la concession, l'opposition] : **en étant plus conciliant, il ne changeait toujours pas d'avis** whilst *ou* although he was more conciliatory, he still wouldn't change his mind

3. [indiquant la cause, le moyen, la manière] : **il marche en boitant** he walks with a limp ▪ **il est parti en courant** he ran off ▪ **retapez en changeant toutes les majuscules** type it out again and change all the capitals ▪ **ce n'est pas en criant que l'on résoudra le problème** shouting won't solve the problem

4. [introduisant une condition, une supposition] if ▪ **en prenant un cas concret, on voit que...** if we take a concrete example, we can see that... ▪ **en supposant que...** supposing that...

G. INTRODUISANT LE COMPLÉMENT DU VERBE

in ▪ **croire en qqn/qqch** to believe in sb/sthg.

◇ *pron*

A. COMPLÉMENT DU VERBE
B. EN COMPLÉMENT
C. LOCUTIONS

A. COMPLÉMENT DU VERBE

1. [indiquant le lieu] : **il faudra que tu ailles à la poste – j'en viens** you'll have to go to the post office – I've just got back from *ou* just been there

2. [indiquant la cause, l'agent] : **on en meurt** you can die of *ou* from it ▪ **je n'en dors plus** it's keeping me awake at nights ▪ **elle était tellement fatiguée qu'elle en pleurait** she was so tired (that) she was crying

3. [complément d'objet] : **voilà des fraises/du lait, donne-lui-en** here are some strawberries/here's some milk, give him some ▪ **passe-moi du sucre – il n'en reste plus** give me some sugar – there's none left ▪ **si tu n'aimes pas la viande/les olives, n'en mange pas** if you don't like meat/olives, don't eat any ▪ **tous les invités ne sont pas arrivés, il en manque deux** all the guests haven't arrived yet, two are missing ▪ **tu en as acheté beaucoup** you've bought a lot (of it/of them) ▪ **tu n'en as pas dit assez** you haven't said enough

4. [avec une valeur emphatique] : **tu en as de la chance!** you really are lucky, you are!

5. [complément d'objet indirect] about it ▪ **ne vous en souciez plus** don't worry about it any more

6. [comme attribut] : **les volontaires ? – j'en suis!** any volunteers ? – me!

B. EN COMPLÉMENT

1. [du nom ou du pronom] : **j'en garde un bon souvenir** I have good memories of it ▪ **écoute ces voix et admires-en la beauté** listen to these voices and admire their beauty

2. [de l'adjectif] : **sa maison en est pleine** his house is full of it/ them ▪ **tu en es sûr ?** are you sure (of that) ?

C. LOCUTIONS

[locutions verbales] : **il en va de même pour lui** the same goes for him ▪ **s'en prendre à qqn** to blame *ou* to attack sb ▪ **il n'en croit pas ses oreilles/yeux** he can't believe his ears/eyes.

ENA, Ena [ena] (*abr de* **École nationale d'administration**) *npr f prestigious grande école training future government officials.*

enamouré, e [ɑ̃namure] *adj* infatuated.

enamourer [3] [ɑ̃namure] ◆ **s'enamourer de** *vp+prép litt* to become enamoured with.

énarchie [enarʃi] *nf old-boy network of graduates of the ENA.*

énarque [enark] *nmf student or former student of the École nationale d'administration.*

encablure [ɑ̃kablyr] *nf* cable, 195 metres ▪ *fig* **à une ~ de** a stone's throw away from ▪ **à deux ~s de** not very far from.

encadré [ɑ̃kadre] *nm* box IMPR.

encadrement [ɑ̃kadrəmɑ̃] *nm* **1.** [mise sous cadre] framing ▪ [cadre] frame **2.** [embrasure - d'une porte] door frame ; [- d'une fenêtre] window frame ▪ **il apparut dans l'~ de la porte** he appeared (framed) in the doorway **3.** [responsabilité - de formation] training ; [- de surveillance] supervision ; [- d'organisation] backing ▪ [personnel] : **l'~** [pour former] the training staff ; [pour surveiller] the supervisory staff **4.** ÉCON : **~ des prix** price controls ▪ **~ des crédits** credit control.

encadrer [3] [ɑ̃kadre] *vt* **1.** [dans un cadre] to (put into a) frame **2.** [border] to frame, to surround ■ **un dessin encadré de bleu** a drawing with a blue border ■ **le visage encadré de boucles** her face framed with curls **3.** [flanquer] to flank ■ **deux potiches encadraient la cheminée** two large vases stood on either side of *ou* flanked the fireplace **4.** [surveiller, organiser] to lead, to organize, to supervise ■ **les scouts sont bien encadrés** the scout pack has responsible leaders **5.** *fam* [supporter - personne] to stand ■ **je ne peux pas l'~** I can't stand (the sight of) him.

encadreur, euse [ɑ̃kadrœr, øz] *nm, f* picture framer.

encagoulé, e [ɑ̃kagule] *adj* hooded, wearing a hood *ou* balaclava.

encaissable [ɑ̃kɛsabl] *adj* cashable.

encaisse [ɑ̃kɛs] *nf* cash in hand, cash balance ■ **~ métallique** gold and silver reserves.

encaissé, e [ɑ̃kese] *adj* [vallée] deep, steep-sided.

encaissement [ɑ̃kɛsmɑ̃] *nm* **1.** [d'une vallée] steep-sidedness **2.** FIN [d'argent] cashing in, receipt ■ [d'un chèque] cashing **3.** [de marchandises] boxing, packing.

encaisser [4] [ɑ̃kese] *vt* **1.** FIN [argent] to receive ■ [chèque] to cash **2.** *fam* [gifle, injure, échec] to take ■ **~ un coup** SPORT to take a blow ■ **il n'a pas encaissé que tu lui mentes/ce que tu lui as dit** he just can't stomach the fact that you lied to him/what you told him ■ *(en usage absolu)* **ne dis rien, encaisse!** take it, don't say anything! **3.** *fam* [tolérer] : **je ne peux pas l'~** I can't stand him **4.** [empaqueter] to box, to pack in boxes **5.** [planter - arbuste] to plant (out) in a box *ou* tub.

encaisseur, euse [ɑ̃kɛsœr, øz] *nm, f* debt collector.

encalminé, e [ɑ̃kalmine] *adj* becalmed NAUT.

encan [ɑ̃kɑ̃] *nm* : **vente à l'~** auction ■ **mettre qqch à l'~** *fig* & *litt* to sell sthg to the highest bidder.

encanailler [3] [ɑ̃kanaje] ◆ **s'encanailler** *vpi* **1.** [par snobisme] to mix with the riff-raff, to slum it *hum* **2.** [se dégrader] to go to the dogs.

encapuchonner [3] [ɑ̃kapyʃɔne] *vt* **1.** [personne, tête] to put a hood on ■ **la tête encapuchonnée** hooded **2.** [stylo] to put the cap on.

encart [ɑ̃kar] *nm* insert ■ **~ publicitaire** advertising insert.

en-cas, encas [ɑ̃ka] *nm inv* snack, something to eat ■ **j'ai un petit ~ dans mon sac** I have (a little) something to eat in my bag.

encastrable [ɑ̃kastrabl] *adj* built-in.

encastrement [ɑ̃kastrəmɑ̃] *nm* **1.** [d'un placard - action] building in, recessing ■ [placard, étagères] built-in fitting **2.** [d'un interrupteur - action] flushing in ■ [interrupteur] flush fitting.

encastrer [3] [ɑ̃kastre] *vt* **1.** [placard] to build in *(sép)*, to slot in *(sép)* ■ [interrupteur] to recess, to fit flush ■ [coffre-fort] to recess ■ **four encastré** built-in oven **2.** [dans un boîtier, un mécanisme] to fit.

encaustique [ɑ̃kostik] *nf* polish, wax.

encaustiquer [3] [ɑ̃kostike] *vt* to polish, to wax.

encaver [3] [ɑ̃kave] *vt* to cellar.

enceindre [81] [ɑ̃sɛ̃dr] *vt litt* **~ la ville de murs** to encircle *ou* to surround the city with walls.

enceinte[1] [ɑ̃sɛ̃t] *nf* **1.** [mur] : **(mur d)~** surrounding wall **2.** [ceinture] enclosure, fence ■ **protégé par une ~ de fossés** closed in by a circular moat **3.** ACOUST speaker.
◆ **dans l'enceinte de** *loc prép* within (the boundary of) ■ **dans l'~ du parc** within *ou* inside the park ■ **dans l'~ du tribunal** within the courtroom.

enceinte[2] [ɑ̃sɛ̃t] *adj f* [femme] pregnant ■ **~ de son premier enfant** expecting her first child ■ **~ de trois mois** three months pregnant.

encens [ɑ̃sɑ̃] *nm* **1.** [résine] incense ■ **bâtonnet d'~** incense stick, joss stick **2.** *fig* & *litt* sycophancy, flattery.

encensement [ɑ̃sɑ̃smɑ̃] *nm* **1.** [d'un écrivain] praising to the skies **2.** RELIG incensing.

encenser [3] [ɑ̃sɑ̃se] *vt* **1.** RELIG to incense **2.** [louer - mérites] to praise to the skies ; [- écrivain] to praise to the skies, to shower praise upon.

encensoir [ɑ̃sɑ̃swar] *nm* RELIG censer.

encéphale [ɑ̃sefal] *nm* encephalon.

encéphalogramme [ɑ̃sefalɔgram] *nm* encephalogram.

encéphalopathie [ɑ̃sefalɔpati] *nf* encephelopathy ■ **~ spongiforme bovine** bovine spongiform encephalopathy.

encercler [3] [ɑ̃sɛrkle] *vt* **1.** [marquer] to ring, to draw a ring round, to encircle ■ **encerclé d'un trait rouge** circled in red **2.** [entourer] to surround, to encircle, to form a circle around **3.** [cerner] to surround, to encircle, to hem in *(sép)* ■ **village encerclé par des soldats** village surrounded by troops.

enchaîné [ɑ̃ʃene] *nm* dissolve.

enchaînement [ɑ̃ʃɛnmɑ̃] *nm* **1.** [série] sequence, series *(sing)* ■ **un ~ de circonstances favorables** a series of favourable circumstances **2.** [lien] (logical) link ■ **faire un ~** [dans un raisonnement] to link up two ideas ; [dans un exposé] to link up two items **3.** [structure] structure, logical sequence **4.** DANSE enchaînement, linked-up steps **5.** SPORT linked-up movements ■ **faire un ~** to perform a sequence **6.** MUS : **~ des accords** chord progression.

enchaîner [4] [ɑ̃ʃene] <> *vt* **1.** [lier - personne] to put in chains, to chain ■ **~ à** to chain (up) to **2.** [attacher ensemble - prisonniers] to chain (up) together *(sép)* ; [- maillons] to link (up) *(sép)* **3.** [asservir - média] to trammel, to shackle ; [- personne] to enslave ; [- libertés] to put in chains *ou* shackles **4.** [relier - idées, mots] to link (up), to link *ou* to string together ■ **vos arguments ne sont pas bien enchaînés** your arguments aren't presented in logical sequence *ou* don't follow on from each other *UK* **5.** [dans une conversation] : **"c'est faux", enchaîna-t-elle** "it's not true," she went on **6.** DANSE to link ■ SPORT [mouvements] to run together *ou* into each other, to link up (together).
<> *vi* **1.** [poursuivre] to move *ou* to follow on ■ **~ sur : elle a enchaîné sur les élections** she went on to talk about the election **2.** RADIO & TV to link up two items of news ■ **enchaînons** let's go on to the next item **3.** CINÉ to fade ■ **~ sur une scène** to fade into a scene.
◆ **s'enchaîner** *vpi* [idées] to follow on (from one another) *UK*, to be connected ■ [images, épisodes] to form a (logical) sequence ■ [événements] to be linked together ■ **tes paragraphes s'enchaînent mal** your paragraphs don't hang together well *ou* are a bit disjointed.

enchanté, e [ɑ̃ʃɑ̃te] *adj* **1.** [magique] enchanted **2.** [ravi] delighted, pleased ■ **~!** pleased to meet you! ■ **je serais ~ de...** I'd be delighted *ou* very pleased to... ■ **~ de faire votre connaissance!** how do you do!, pleased to meet you!

enchantement [ɑ̃ʃɑ̃tmɑ̃] *nm* **1.** [en magie] (magic) spell, enchantment ■ **comme par ~** as if by magic **2.** [merveille] delight, enchantment ■ **la soirée fut un véritable ~** the evening was absolutely delightful *ou* enchanting.

enchanter [3] [ɑ̃ʃɑ̃te] *vt* **1.** [faire plaisir à] to enchant, to charm, to delight ■ **cela ne l'enchante pas (beaucoup)** *ou* **guère** he's none too pleased *ou* happy (at having to do it) **2.** [par la magie] to bewitch, to cast a spell on.

enchanteur, eresse [ɑ̃ʃɑ̃tœr, t(ə)rɛs] *adj* enchanting, bewitching, magical.
◆ **enchanteur** *nm* **1.** [magicien] enchanter, sorcerer **2.** [séducteur] charmer.
◆ **enchanteresse** *nf* **1.** [magicienne] enchantress, witch **2.** [séductrice] charmer, enchantress.

enchâssement [ɑ̃ʃasmɑ̃] *nm* JOAILL setting.

enchâsser [3] [ɑ̃ʃase] *vt* JOAILL to set.

enchère [ɑ̃ʃɛr] *nf* **1.** [vente] auction ▪ **vendre aux ~s** to sell by auction ▪ **mettre aux ~s** to put up for auction **2.** [offre d'achat] bid ▪ **faire monter les ~s** *pr* to raise the bidding ; *fig* to raise the stakes **3.** JEUX bid.

enchérir [32] [ɑ̃ʃerir] *vi litt* [devenir cher] to become dearer *ou* more expensive, to go up in price.
◆ **enchérir sur** *v+prép* [dans une enchère] : **~ sur une offre** to make a higher bid ▪ **~ sur une somme** to go over and above an amount ▪ **~ sur qqn** to bid higher than sb.

enchérisseur, euse [ɑ̃ʃerisœr, øz] *nm, f* bidder.

enchevêtrement [ɑ̃ʃəvɛtrəmɑ̃] *nm* **1.** [objets emmêlés] tangle, tangled mass ▪ **un ~ de branches** tangled branches, a tangle of branches **2.** [confusion] tangle, tangled state, confusion.

enchevêtrer [4] [ɑ̃ʃəvɛtre] *vt* **1.** [mêler - fils, branchages] to tangle (up), to entangle **2.** [embrouiller - histoire] to confuse, to muddle ▪ **une intrigue enchevêtrée** a complicated *ou* muddled plot.
◆ **s'enchevêtrer** *vpi* **1.** [être emmêlé - fils] to become entangled, to get into a tangle ; [- branchages] to become entangled **2.** [être confus - idées, événements] to become confused *ou* muddled.

enclave [ɑ̃klav] *nf* **1.** [lieu] enclave ▪ **une ~ de maisons isolées parmi les lotissements** an enclave of detached houses surrounded by housing developments **2.** [groupe, unité] enclave **3.** GÉOL inclusion, xenolith.

enclavement [ɑ̃klavmɑ̃] *nm* [d'une nation] setting up as an enclave ▪ [d'un jardin] enclosing, hemming in.

enclaver [3] [ɑ̃klave] *vt* **1.** [entourer - terrain] to enclose, to hem in *(sép)* **2.** [insérer] : **~ entre** to insert between **3.** [placer l'un dans l'autre] to fit into each other, to interlock.

enclenchement [ɑ̃klɑ̃ʃmɑ̃] *nm* **1.** [action] engaging ▪ [résultat] engagement ▪ **avant l'~ du loquet** before the catch engages **2.** [dispositif] interlock.

enclencher [3] [ɑ̃klɑ̃ʃe] *vt* **1.** MÉCAN to engage **2.** [commencer - démarche, procédure] to set in motion, to get under way, to set off *(sép)*.
◆ **s'enclencher** *vpi* **1.** MÉCAN to engage **2.** [démarche, procédure] to get under way, to get started.

enclin, e [ɑ̃klɛ̃, in] *adj* : **~ à qqch/à faire qqch** inclined to sthg/to do sthg ▪ **peu ~ à partager ses secrets** reluctant to share his secrets.

enclore [113] [ɑ̃klɔr] *vt* to enclose ▪ **enclos d'une haie** hedged in ▪ **enclos d'un mur** walled in.

enclos [ɑ̃klo] *nm* **1.** [terrain] enclosed plot of land ▪ [à moutons] pen, fold ▪ [à chevaux] paddock **2.** [muret] wall **3.** [grillage] (wire) fence.

enclosons *etc v* ▷ **enclore**.

enclume [ɑ̃klym] *nf* [du forgeron] anvil ▪ [du couvreur] (slater's) iron ▪ [du cordonnier] last ▪ **entre l'~ et le marteau** between the devil and the deep blue sea.

encoche [ɑ̃kɔʃ] *nf* **1.** [entaille] notch **2.** [d'une flèche] nock **3.** [d'un livre] thumb index ▪ **avec ~s** thumb-indexed, with thumb index.

encocher [3] [ɑ̃kɔʃe] *vt* **1.** [faire une entaille à] to notch **2.** [flèche] to nock.

encodage [ɑ̃kɔdaʒ] *nm* encoding.

encoder [3] [ɑ̃kɔde] *vt* to encode.

encodeur, euse [ɑ̃kɔdœr, øz] *nm, f* encoder.

encoignure [ɑ̃kwaɲyr, ɑ̃kɔɲyr] *nf* **1.** [angle] corner **2.** [table] corner table ▪ [placard] corner cupboard ▪ [siège] corner chair.

encollage [ɑ̃kɔlaʒ] *nm* pasting, sizing.

encoller [3] [ɑ̃kɔle] *vt* to paste, to size.

encolleuse [ɑ̃kɔløz] *nf* sizing machine.

encolure [ɑ̃kɔlyr] *nf* **1.** ANAT & ZOOL [vêtement] neck **2.** ÉQUIT neck ▪ **à une ~ du vainqueur** a neck behind the winner.

encombrant, e [ɑ̃kɔ̃brɑ̃, ɑ̃t] *adj* **1.** [volumineux] bulky, cumbersome ▪ **j'ai dû m'en débarrasser c'était trop ~** I had to get rid of it, it was taking up too much space *ou* it was getting in the way **2.** [importun] inhibiting, awkward ▪ **le jeune couple trouvait la petite sœur ~e** the young couple felt the little sister was in the way.
◆ **encombrants** *nmpl* bulky item.

encombre [ɑ̃kɔ̃br] ◆ **sans encombre** *loc adv* safely, without mishap ▪ **s'ils parviennent à revenir sans ~** if nothing untoward happens to them on their way back.

encombré, e [ɑ̃kɔ̃bre] *adj* **1.** [route] : **l'autoroute est très ~e** traffic on the motorway is very heavy, there is very heavy traffic on the motorway **2.** [plein d'objets] : **avoir les mains ~es** to have one's hands full ▪ **un salon ~** a cluttered living room **3.** [bronches] congested.

encombrement [ɑ̃kɔ̃brəmɑ̃] *nm* **1.** [embouteillage] traffic jam **2.** [fait d'obstruer] jamming, blocking ▪ **par suite de l'~ des lignes téléphoniques/de l'espace aérien** because the telephone lines are overloaded/the air space is overcrowded **3.** [entassement] clutter, cluttered state **4.** [dimension] size ▪ **meuble de faible ~** small *ou* compact piece of furniture **5.** MÉD : **~ des voies respiratoires** congestion of the respiratory system.

encombrer [3] [ɑ̃kɔ̃bre] *vt* **1.** [remplir] to clutter (up), to fill *ou* to clog up *(sép)* ▪ **~ qqch de** to clutter sthg (up) with **2.** [obstruer - couloir] to block (up) ; [- route] to block *ou* to clog up *(sép)* ; [- circulation] to hold up *(sép)* ▪ **une ville très encombrée** a congested city, a city choked with traffic **3.** [saturer] : **les logiciels encombrent le marché** there's a surplus *ou* glut of software packages on the market ▪ **une profession encombrée** an overcrowded profession **4.** [charger - d'un objet lourd] to load (down), to encumber ▪ **~ qqn de** to load sb down with **5.** [suj: objet gênant] : **tiens, je te donne ce vase, il m'encombre** here, have this vase, I don't know what to do with it ▪ **que faire de ces sacs qui nous encombrent?** what shall we do with these bags that are in the way? **6.** [gêner] to burden, to encumber ▪ **son enfant l'encombre** her child's a burden to her **7.** TÉLÉCOM to overload, to jam.
◆ **s'encombrer** ◇ *vpi* [avoir trop de bagages, de vêtements] to be loaded *ou* weighed down ▪ **laisse ta valise là si tu ne veux pas t'~** leave your case there if you don't want to be weighed down ▪ **s'~ de** *fig* to be overburdened with ▪ **il ne s'encombre pas de scrupules** he's not exactly overburdened with scruples.
◇ *vpt* : **s'~ l'esprit de** to fill one's mind *ou* to cram one's head with ▪ **s'~ la mémoire de** to fill *ou* to load one's memory with.

encontre [ɑ̃kɔ̃tr] ◆ **à l'encontre** *loc adv sout* in opposition.
◆ **à l'encontre de** *loc prép sout* : **aller à l'~ de** to go against, to run counter to ▪ **cette décision va à l'~ du but recherché** this decision is self-defeating *ou* counterproductive.

encorbellement [ɑ̃kɔrbɛlmɑ̃] *nm* corbelled construction ▪ **balcon en ~** corbelled balcony.

encorder [3] [ɑ̃kɔrde] *vt* to rope up *(sép)*.
◆ **s'encorder** *vpi* to rope up (together).

encore [ɑ̃kɔr] *adv* **1.** [toujours] still ▪ **ils en sont ~ à taper tout à la machine** they're still using typewriters
2. [pas plus tard que] only ▪ **ce matin ~, il était d'accord** only this morning he was in agreement
3. [dans des phrases négatives] : **pas ~** not yet ▪ **je n'ai pas ~ fini** I haven't finished yet ▪ **~ rien** still nothing, nothing yet ▪ **vous n'avez ~ rien vu!** you haven't seen anything yet! ▪ **je n'avais ~ jamais vu ça!** I'd never seen anything like it before!
4. [de nouveau] : **tu manges ~!** you're not eating again, are you! ▪ **je me suis coupé – ~!** I've cut myself – not again! ▪ **~ une fois, c'est non!** the answer's still no! ▪ **si tu fais ça ~ une fois...** if you do that again *ou* one more time *ou* once more... ▪ **~ de la glace?** some more *ou* a little more ice-cream? ▪ **je te sers ~ un verre?** will you have another drink? ▪ **quoi ~?** [dans une énumération] what else? ▪ *fam* [ton irrité] now what? ▪ **qu'est-ce qu'il y a ~?** what is it this time? ▪ **et puis quoi ~?** [dans une émunération] what else? ; *iron* will that be all? ; [marquant

l'incrédulité] whatever next? ▪ **elle est bien élevée, charmante, mais ~?** she's well brought-up and charming, and (apart from that)? ▪ **~ un qui ne sait pas ce qu'il veut!** another one who doesn't know what he wants!
5. [davantage] : **il va grandir ~** he's still got a bit more growing to do ▪ **réduisez-le ~** reduce it even more ▪ **il faudra ~ travailler cette scène** that scene still needs more work on it ‖ [devant un comparatif] : **il est ~ plus gentil que je n'imaginais** he is even nicer than I'd imagined (he'd be) ▪ **~ autant** as much again ▪ **~ pire** even *ou* still worse
6. [introduisant une restriction] : **c'est bien beau d'avoir des projets, ~ faut-il les réaliser** it's all very well having plans, but the important thing is to put them into practice ▪ **si ~ il** *ou* **~ s'il était franc, on lui pardonnerait** if only *ou* if at least he was honest you could forgive him ➊ **je t'en donne 100 euros, et ~!** I'll give you 100 euros for it, if that! ▪ **et ~, on ne sait pas tout!** and even then we don't know the half of it! ▪ **~ heureux!** thank goodness for that! ▪ **~ une chance qu'il n'ait pas été là!** thank goodness *ou* it's lucky he wasn't there!
◆ **encore que** *loc conj* : **j'aimerais y aller, ~ qu'il soit tard** I'd like to go even though it's late.

encorner [3] [ɑ̃kɔrne] ◇ *vt* to gore ▪ **se faire ~** to be gored.

encornet [ɑ̃kɔrnɛ] *nm* squid.

encourageant, e [ɑ̃kuraʒɑ̃, ɑ̃t] *adj* [paroles] encouraging ▪ [succès, résultat] encouraging, promising.

encouragement [ɑ̃kuraʒmɑ̃] *nm* encouragement, support ▪ **~s fiscaux** tax incentives ▪ **quelques mots d'~** a few encouraging words *ou* words of encouragement.

encourager [ɑ̃kuraʒe] *vt* **1.** [inciter] to encourage ▪ **~ qqn du geste** to wave to sb in encouragement ▪ **~ qqn de la voix** to cheer sb (on) ▪ **~ qqn à faire qqch** to encourage sb to do sthg **2.** [favoriser] to stimulate ▪ **un prix fondé pour ~ l'initiative** an award set up to stimulate *ou* to foster the spirit of enterprise.
◆ **s'encourager** ◇ *vp (emploi réfléchi)* to spur o.s. on. ◇ *vp (emploi réciproque)* to cheer each other on.

encourir [45] [ɑ̃kurir] *vt* [dédain, reproche, critique] to incur, to bring upon o.s.

encrage [ɑ̃kraʒ] *nm* inking.

encrassé [ɑ̃krase] *adj* [mécanisme] clogged.

encrassement [ɑ̃krasmɑ̃] *nm* [d'un filtre] clogging (up) ▪ [d'un tuyau] clogging (up), fouling (up) ▪ [d'une arme] fouling (up).

encrasser [3] [ɑ̃krase] *vt* **1.** [obstruer - filtre] to clog up *(sép)* ; [- tuyau] to clog *ou* to foul up *(sép)* ; [- arme] to foul up *(sép)* **2.** [salir] to dirty, to muck up *(sép)*.
◆ **s'encrasser** *vpi* **1.** [s'obstruer - filtre] to become clogged (up) ; [- tuyau] to become clogged (up), to become fouled up ; [- arme] to become fouled up **2.** [se salir] to get dirty.

encre [ɑ̃kr] *nf* **1.** [pour écrire] ink ▪ **écrire à l'~** to write in ink ➊ **~ de Chine** Indian ink ▪ **~ sympathique** invisible ink **2.** [style] : **écrire de sa plus belle ~** to write in one's best style **3.** ZOOL ink.

encrer [3] [ɑ̃kre] *vt* to ink.

encreur [ɑ̃krœr] *adj m* inking.

encrier [ɑ̃krije] *nm* [pot] inkpot ▪ [accessoire de bureau] inkstand ▪ [récipient encastré] inkwell.

encroûté, e [ɑ̃krute] *fam* ◇ *adj* : **être ~** [dans ses préjugés] to be a fuddy-duddy *ou* stick-in-the-mud ; [dans sa routine] to be stuck in a rut.
◇ *nm, f* **1.** [personne ayant des préjugés] : **un vieil ~** an old fuddy-duddy *ou* stick-in-the-mud **2.** [personne routinière] : **mener une vie d'~** to be in a rut.

encroûter [3] [ɑ̃krute] *vt* **1.** [couvrir - de terre, de sang] to encrust ; [- de calcaire] to fur up *(sép)* **2.** [rendre routinier] to get stuck in a rut **3.** *fam* [abêtir] to turn into a vegetable.
◆ **s'encroûter** *vpi* **1.** [s'encrasser - vêtement] to become encrusted ; [- bouilloire] to scale *ou* to fur up **2.** *fam* [devenir routinier] to be in a rut ▪ **il s'encroûte dans ses habitudes** he's got into a rut ▪ **il s'encroûte dans son métier** he's really in a rut in that job.

enculé, e▲ [ɑ̃kyle] *nm, f* bastard△, arsehole▲ *UK*, asshole▲ *US* ▪ **quelle bande d'~s!** what a load of wankers△ ! *UK ou* shits△ ! *US*.

enculer [3] ▲ [ɑ̃kyle] *vt* to bugger▲, to fuck ▪ **je t'encule!, va te faire ~!** fuck off!▲ ➊ **~ les mouches** to nit-pick.

encuver [3] [ɑ̃kyve] *vt* to vat.

encyclique [ɑ̃siklik] *adj & nf* encyclical.

encyclopédie [ɑ̃siklɔpedi] *nf* encyclopedia.

encyclopédique [ɑ̃siklɔpedik] *adj* **1.** [d'une encyclopédie] encyclopedic **2.** [érudit] : **un esprit/une mémoire ~** a mind/memory that retains every detail ‖ [connaissances] exhaustive, extensive, encyclopedic.

encyclopédisme [ɑ̃siklɔpedism] *nm* quest for all-round knowledge.

encyclopédiste [ɑ̃siklɔpedist] *nmf* **1.** [auteur] encyclopedist **2.** HIST : **les ~s** *ou* **Encyclopédistes** Diderot's Encyclopedists, the contributors to the Encyclopédie.

endémie [ɑ̃demi] *nf* endemic disease.

endémique [ɑ̃demik] *adj* [gén - MÉD] endemic ▪ **~ en Malaisie/dans notre société** endemic to Malaysia/our society.

endettement [ɑ̃dɛtmɑ̃] *nm* indebtedness ▪ **~ extérieur** foreign debt.

endetter [4] [ɑ̃dete] *vt* **1.** FIN to get into debt ▪ **il est lourdement endetté** he's heavily in debt **2.** *fig* **être endetté envers qqn** to be indebted to sb.
◆ **s'endetter** *vpi* to get *ou* to run into debt ▪ **je me suis endetté de 10 000 euros** I got 10,000 euros in debt.

endeuiller [5] [ɑ̃dœje] *vt* **1.** [famille, personne] to plunge into mourning **2.** [réception, course] to cast a tragic shadow over **3.** *litt* [tableau, paysage] to give a dismal aspect to.

endiablé, e [ɑ̃djable] *adj* **1.** [danse, musique, poursuite] wild, frenzied ▪ **se lancer dans une ronde ~e** to begin to dance wildly *ou* frenziedly in a circle **2.** [enfant] boisterous, unruly.

endiguement [ɑ̃digmɑ̃] *nm* **1.** [d'un cours d'eau] dyking (up) **2.** [d'émotions, d'un développement] holding back ▪ [du chômage, de dettes] checking, curbing.

endiguer [3] [ɑ̃dige] *vt* **1.** [cours d'eau] to dyke (up) **2.** [émotion, développement] to hold back *(sép)*, to check ▪ [chômage, excès] to curb.

endimanché, e [ɑ̃dimɑ̃ʃe] *adj* in one's Sunday best.

endive [ɑ̃div] *nf* chicory, French endive.

endocrine [ɑ̃dɔkrin] *adj* endocrine.

endocrinien, enne [ɑ̃dɔkrinjɛ̃, ɛn] *adj* endocrinal, endocrinous.

endocrinologie [ɑ̃dɔkrinɔlɔʒi] *nf* endocrinology.

endoctrinement [ɑ̃dɔktrinmɑ̃] *nm* indoctrination.

endoctriner [3] [ɑ̃dɔktrine] *vt* to indoctrinate.

endogamie [ɑ̃dɔgami] *nf* endogamy.

endogène [ɑ̃dɔʒɛn] *adj* BIOL & GÉOL endogenous.

endolori, e [ɑ̃dɔlɔri] *adj* painful, aching ▪ **le corps tout ~** aching all over ▪ **mon pied était ~** my foot hurt *ou* was aching.

endolorir [32] [ɑ̃dɔlɔrir] *vt* to make painful.

endommagement [ɑ̃dɔmaʒmɑ̃] *nm* damaging.

endommager [17] [ɑ̃dɔmaʒe] *vt* [bâtiment] to damage ▪ [environnement, récolte] to damage, to harm.

endomorphe [ɑ̃dɔmɔrf] *adj* endomorphic.

endormant, e [ɑ̃dɔrmɑ̃, ɑ̃t] *adj* **1.** [professeur, film] boring **2.** [massage, tisane] sleep-inducing.

endormeur, euse [ɑ̃dɔrmœr, øz] *nm, f litt* beguiler, enticer.

endormi, e [ɑ̃dɔrmi] <> *adj* **1.** [sommeillant] sleeping ▪ **il est ~** he's asleep *ou* sleeping ▪ **à moitié ~** half asleep **2.** [apathique] sluggish, lethargic **3.** [calme - ville] sleepy, drowsy **4.** [faible - désir] dormant ; [- vigilance] lulled.
<> *nm, f* [personne apathique] do-nothing, ne'er-do-well.

endormir [36] [ɑ̃dɔrmir] *vt* **1.** [d'un sommeil naturel] to put *ou* to send to sleep ▪ [avec douceur] to lull to sleep **2.** [anesthésier] to put to sleep **3.** [ennuyer] to send to sleep, to bore **4.** [tromper - électeurs, public] to lull into a false sense of security **5.** [affaiblir - douleur] to deaden ; [- scrupules] to allay ▪ **~ la vigilance de qqn** to get sb to drop his guard.
◆ **s'endormir** *vpi* **1.** [d'un sommeil naturel] to drop off *ou* to go to sleep, to fall asleep **2.** [sous anesthésie] to go to sleep **3.** [mourir] to pass away *ou* on **4.** [se relâcher] to let up, to slacken off ▶ **s'~ sur ses lauriers** to rest on one's laurels **5.** [devenir calme - maisonnée, pays] to grow calm **6.** [s'affaiblir - douleur] to subside, to die down ; [- scrupules] to be allayed ; [- vigilance] to slacken.

endormissement [ɑ̃dɔrmismɑ̃] *nm* : **qui aide à l'~** sleep-inducing.

endort *etc v* ▻ **endormir**.

endoscopie [ɑ̃dɔskɔpi] *nf* endoscopy.

endosquelette [ɑ̃dɔskəlɛt] *nm* endoskeleton.

endossable [ɑ̃dɔsabl] *adj* endorsable.

endossement [ɑ̃dosmɑ̃] *nm* BANQUE & FIN endorsement.

endosser [3] [ɑ̃dose] *vt* **1.** [revêtir] to put *ou* to slip on *(sép)*, to don *sout* **2.** [assumer] to assume ▪ **~ la responsabilité de qqch** to shoulder *ou* to assume the responsibility for sthg ▪ **il lui a fait ~ la responsabilité de l'accident** he made him take responsibility for the accident **3.** BANQUE & FIN to endorse **4.** [livre] to back.

endosseur [ɑ̃dosœr] *nm* endorser.

endroit [ɑ̃drwa] *nm* **1.** [emplacement] place ▪ **à quel ~ tu l'as mis?** where *ou* whereabouts did you put it? ▪ **ce n'est pas au bon ~** it's not in the right place ▪ **l'~ de la réunion** the place for *ou* the venue of the meeting **2.** [localité] place, spot ▪ **un ~ tranquille** a quiet place *ou* spot ▪ **l'~** the locality, the area **3.** [partie - du corps, d'un objet] place ; [- d'une œuvre, d'une histoire] place, point ▪ **cela fait mal à quel ~?** where does it hurt? ▪ **en plusieurs ~s** in several places ▪ **c'est l'~ le plus drôle du livre** it's the funniest part *ou* passage in the book ▶ **toucher qqn à un ~ sensible** *pr* to touch a sore spot ; *fig* to touch a nerve **4.** [d'un vêtement] right side.
◆ **à l'endroit** *loc adv* **1.** [le bon côté en haut] right side up **2.** [le bon côté à l'extérieur] right side out **3.** [le bon côté devant] right side round ▪ **remettre son pull à l'~** to put one's pullover on again the right way round **4.** [dans les explications de tricot] : **deux mailles à l'~** two plain, knit two ▪ **un rang à l'~** knit one row.
◆ **à l'endroit de** *loc prép litt* [personne] towards ▪ [événement, objet] regarding, with regard to, in regard to.
◆ **par endroits** *loc adv* in places, here and there.

enduire [98] [ɑ̃dɥir] *vt* **1.** [recouvrir] to coat *ou* to spread *ou* to cover with *(sép)* ▪ **~ de** : **~ de beurre le fond d'un plat** to smear the bottom of a dish with butter ▪ **~ qqch de colle** to apply glue to sthg **2.** CONSTR : **~ un mur** to plaster a wall over, to face a wall *(with finishing plaster)*.

enduit [ɑ̃dɥi] *nm* **1.** [revêtement] coat, coating, facing ▪ **~ au ciment** cement rendering **2.** [plâtre] plaster **3.** MÉD coating *(on the tongue, the stomach)*.

endurable [ɑ̃dyrabl] *adj* endurable, bearable.

endurance [ɑ̃dyrɑ̃s] *nf* **1.** [d'une personne] endurance, stamina **2.** [d'une matière, d'une machine] endurance, resilience **3.** SPORT endurance.

endurant, e [ɑ̃dyrɑ̃, ɑ̃t] *adj* resistant, tough.

endurci, e [ɑ̃dyrsi] *adj* **1.** [invétéré] hardened, inveterate ▪ **célibataire ~** confirmed bachelor **2.** [insensible - âme, caractère] hardened ▪ **des cœurs ~s** hard-hearted people.

endurcir [32] [ɑ̃dyrsir] *vt* **1.** [rendre résistant - corps, personne] to harden, to toughen ▪ **être endurci à** to be hardened to, to be inured to **2.** [rendre insensible] to harden.
◆ **s'endurcir** *vpi* **1.** [devenir résistant] to harden o.s., to become tougher ▪ **je me suis endurci avec l'âge** age has made me tougher *ou* has toughened me ▪ **s'~ à** to become hardened *ou* inured to **2.** [devenir insensible] to harden one's heart.

endurcissement [ɑ̃dyrsismɑ̃] *nm* **1.** [endurance] hardening, toughening **2.** [insensibilité] : **son ~ au fil des années** his increasing hard-heartedness over the years.

endurer [3] [ɑ̃dyre] *vt* to endure, to bear, to stand ▪ **il a dû ~ beaucoup d'épreuves** he had to put up with *ou* to suffer a lot of trials and tribulations.

Énée [ene] *npr* Aeneas.

Énéide [eneid] *nf* : **'l'~'** ***Virgile*** 'The Aeneid'.

énergétique [enɛrʒetik] <> *adj* **1.** ÉCOL & ÉCON energy *(modif)* **2.** [boisson, aliment] energy-giving ▪ [besoins, apport] energy *(modif)*.
<> *nf* energetics *(sing)*.

énergie [enɛrʒi] *nf* **1.** [dynamisme] energy, stamina, drive ▪ **se mettre au travail avec ~** to start work energetically ▪ **avoir de l'~** to have a lot of energy ▪ **donner de l'~ à qqn** to invigorate *ou* to energize sb ▪ **être sans** *ou* **manquer d'~** to have no energy, to lack energy ▪ **mettre toute son ~ à** to put all one's energy *ou* energies into **2.** [force] energy, vigour, strength ▪ **il faudrait dépenser trop d'~** it would be too much of an effort ▶ **avec l'~ du désespoir** with the strength born of despair **3.** SC & TECHNOL energy, power ▪ **~ atomique** atomic energy ▪ **~ électrique/solaire** electrical/solar energy ▪ **~ éolienne** wind power ▪ **~ hydraulique** water power ▪ **~ nucléaire** nuclear power *ou* energy ▪ **les ~s nouvelles** new sources of energy ▪ **source d'~** source of energy **4.** PSYCHOL : **~ psychique** psychic energy.
◆ **énergies** *nfpl* : **nous aurons besoin de toutes les ~s** we'll need all the help we can get.

énergique [enɛrʒik] *adj* **1.** [fort - mouvement, intervention] energetic, vigorous ; [- mesure] energetic, drastic, extreme ; [- paroles] emphatic ; [- traitement] strong, powerful **2.** [dynamique - personne, caractère] energetic, forceful, active ; [- visage] determined-looking.

énergiquement [enɛrʒikmɑ̃] *adv* [bouger, agir] energetically, vigorously ▪ [parler, refuser] energetically, emphatically.

énergisant, e [enɛrʒizɑ̃, ɑ̃t] *adj* energizing, energy-giving.
◆ **énergisant** *nm* energizer.

énergumène [enɛrgymɛn] *nmf* energumen *litt*, wild-eyed fanatic *ou* zealot.

énervant, e [enɛrvɑ̃, ɑ̃t] *adj* irritating, annoying, trying.

énervé, e [enɛrve] *adj* **1.** [irrité] irritated, annoyed **2.** [tendu] edgy **3.** [agité] agitated, restless.

énervement [enɛrvəmɑ̃] *nm* **1.** [agacement] irritation, annoyance ▪ **notre départ s'est fait dans l'~ général** everyone was getting irritated with everyone else when we left **2.** [tension] edginess **3.** [agitation] restlessness.

énerver [3] [enɛrve] *vt* **1.** [irriter] to annoy, to irritate ▪ **cette musique m'énerve** this music is getting on my nerves **2.** [agiter] to make restless, to excite, to overexcite.
◆ **s'énerver** *vpi* **1.** [être irrité] to get worked up *ou* annoyed *ou* irritated **2.** [être excité] to get worked up *ou* excited *ou* overexcited ▪ **il ne faut pas laisser les enfants s'~ avant de se coucher** the children mustn't get worked up *ou* excited before going to bed.

enfance [ɑ̃fɑ̃s] *nf* **1.** [période de la vie - gén] childhood ; [- d'un garçon] boyhood ; [- d'une fille] girlhood ▪ **dès son ~** from an early age ▪ **il retombe en ~** he's in his second childhood ▶ **la petite ~** infancy, babyhood, early childhood **2.** [enfants] children ▪ **l'~ délinquante/malheureuse** delinquant/unhappy children **3.** [commencement] infancy, start, early stage ▪ **c'est l'~ de l'art** it's child's play.
◆ **d'enfance** *loc adj* childhood *(modif)*.

enfant [ɑ̃fɑ̃] <> *adj* **1.** [jeune] : **il était encore ~ quand il comprit** he was still a child when he understood **2.** [naïf] childlike.
<> *nmf* **1.** [jeune - gén] child ; [- garçon] little boy ; [- fille] little girl ■ **un ~ à naître** an unborn child *ou* baby ■ **faire l'~** to act like a child ■ **ne fais pas l'~!** act your age!, don't be such a baby!, grow up! ■ **prendre qqn pour un ~** to treat sb like a child ▶ **~ bleu** blue baby ■ **~ de chœur** *pr* choirboy, altarboy ■ **ce n'est pas un ~ de chœur** *fig* he's no angel ■ **prendre qqn pour un ~ de chœur** to think sb is still wet behind the ears ■ **~ gâté** spoilt child ■ **l'~ Jésus** Baby Jesus ■ **~ naturel/légitime** illegitimate/legitimate child ■ **~ prodige** child prodigy ■ **~ sauvage** [vivant à l'état sauvage] wolf child ■ **~ terrible** enfant terrible ■ **~ trouvé** foundling ■ **grand ~** overgrown child, big kid ■ **petit ~** infant, little child, small child **2.** [descendant] child ■ **faire un ~** to have a child ■ **avoir de jeunes ~s/de grands ~s** to have a young family/grown-up children ■ **un couple sans ~s** a childless couple ■ **être en mal d'~** to be longing for a child ■ **décédé sans ~s** DR having died without issue ■ **un ~ de la crise/des années 80** a child of the depression/of the 80s ▶ **~ de l'amour** love child ■ **~ de la balle : je suis un ~ de la balle** [théâtre] I was born into the theatre ; [cirque] I was born under the big top ■ **~ du pays** [homme] son of the soil ; [femme] daughter of the soil ■ **l'~ prodigue** the prodigal son **3.** [en appellatif] child ■ **mon ~** my child ■ **belle ~** dear girl *ou* child ■ **alors, les ~s, encore un peu de champagne?** *fam* a bit more champagne, guys *ou* folks?
◆ **bon enfant** *loc adj inv* good-natured ■ **d'un ton bon ~** good-naturedly.
◆ **d'enfant** *loc adj* [des enfants - dessin, imagination] child's.

enfant-bulle [ɑ̃fɑ̃byl] *nm* MÉD *child who has to stay in a sterile tent.*

enfantement [ɑ̃fɑ̃tmɑ̃] *nm litt* **1.** [création] birth, bringing forth **2.** [accouchement] childbirth.

enfanter [3] [ɑ̃fɑ̃te] *vt litt* **1.** [produire] to give birth to, to create, to bring forth *(sép) litt* **2.** [suj: mère] to give birth to ■ **tu enfanteras dans la douleur** BIBLE in sorrow thou shalt bring forth children.

enfantillage [ɑ̃fɑ̃tijaʒ] *nm* **1.** [action, parole] piece of childishness ■ **arrête ces ~s!** don't be so childish!, do grow up! **2.** [chose sans importance] trifle, trifling matter.

enfantin, e [ɑ̃fɑ̃tɛ̃, in] *adj* **1.** [de l'enfance] childlike ■ **voix ~e** child's *ou* childlike voice ▌[adulte] childlike ■ **avoir un sourire ~** [homme] to have a boyish smile ; [femme] to have a girlish smile **2.** [simple] easy ■ **c'est ~** there's nothing to it, it's child's play **3.** [puéril] childish, infantile, puerile.

enfariné, e [ɑ̃farine] *adj* covered with white powder ■ **il est arrivé à 4 h, la gueule ~e** *ou* **le bec ~** he breezed in at 4 as if nothing was the matter.

enfer [ɑ̃fɛr] *nm* **1.** RELIG hell ■ **~ et damnation!** *hum* (hell and) damnation!, heck! ■ **l'~ est pavé de bonnes intentions** *prov* the road to hell is paved with good intentions *loc* **2.** [lieu, situation désagréable] hell ■ **sa vie est un véritable ~** his life is absolute hell ■ **l'~ de la guerre** the inferno of war **3.** [d'une bibliothèque] *section where books forbidden to the public are stored.*
◆ **enfers** *nmpl* MYTHOL : **les ~s** the underworld ■ **descendre aux ~s** to go down into the underworld.
◆ **d'enfer** *loc adj* **1.** [très mauvais - vie] hellish ; [- bruit] deafening ; [- feu] blazing, raging **2.** [très bien] great ■ **il est d'~ ton blouson!** what a brilliant *ou* wicked jacket!

enfermement [ɑ̃fɛrməmɑ̃] *nm* **1.** [action d'enfermer] shutting *ou* locking up **2.** [fait d'être enfermé] seclusion.

enfermer [3] [ɑ̃fɛrme] *vt* **1.** [mettre dans un lieu clos - personne, animal] to shut up *ou* in *(sép)*
2. [emprisonner - criminel] to lock up *ou* away *(sép)*, to put under lock and key ; [- fou] to lock up ■ **~ qqn dans une cellule** to shut sb up in a cell ■ **ce type-là, il faudrait l'~!** *fam* [dangereux] that guy ought to be locked up! ; [fou] that guy needs his head examined! ■ **faire ~ qqn** to have sb locked away
3. [ranger] to put *ou* to shut away *(sép)* ■ [en verrouillant] to lock up *ou* away *(sép)*
4. [confiner] to confine, to coop up *(sép)* ■ **ne restez pas enfermés, voilà le soleil!** don't stay indoors, the sun's come out! ■ **~ qqn dans un dilemme** to put sb in a dilemma ■ **~ qqn dans un rôle** *pr* & *fig* to typecast sb
5. [entourer] to enclose
6. [contenir - allusion, menace] to contain ■ **un triangle enfermé dans un cercle** a triangle circumscribed by *ou* in a circle
7. [maintenir - dans des règles] to confine, to restrict
8. SPORT to hem in *(sép)*.
◆ **s'enfermer** *vp (emploi réfléchi)* **1.** [se cloîtrer - dans un couvent] to shut o.s. up *ou* away
2. [verrouiller sa porte] to shut o.s. up *ou* in, to lock o.s. in ■ **s'~ dehors** to lock *ou* to shut o.s. out
3. [s'isoler] to shut o.s. away ■ **s'~ dans le silence** to retreat into silence ■ **s'~ dans ses contradictions** to become caught up in one's own contradictions ■ **s'~ dans un rôle** to stick to a role.

enferrer [4] [ɑ̃fere] *vt* [avec une lame] to run through *(sép)*, to transfix.
◆ **s'enferrer** *vpi* **1.** [s'enfoncer] to make matters worse ■ **s'~ dans ses explications** to get tangled *ou* muddled up in one's explanations ■ **s'~ dans ses mensonges** to be caught *ou* trapped in the mesh of one's lies **2.** [s'embrocher] to spike *ou* to spear o.s. **3.** PÊCHE [poisson] to hook itself.

enfiévrer [18] [ɑ̃fjevre] *vt* to fire, to stir up *(sép)* ■ **~ les esprits** to stir people up ■ **~ l'imagination** to fire the imagination ■ **une atmosphère enfiévrée** a feverish atmosphere.
◆ **s'enfiévrer** *vpi* to get excited.

enfilade [ɑ̃filad] *nf* **1.** [rangée] row, line ■ **une ~ de peupliers** a row of poplars **2.** MIL enfilade.
◆ **en enfilade** <> *loc adj* : **des pièces en ~** a suite of adjoining rooms.
<> *loc adv* : **prendre en ~** MIL to enfilade ■ **prendre les rues en ~** to follow along in a straight line from one street to the next.

enfilage [ɑ̃filaʒ] *nm* threading.

enfiler [3] [ɑ̃file] *vt* **1.** [faire passer] : **~ un élastique dans un ourlet** to thread a piece of elastic through a hem **2.** [disposer - sur un fil] to thread *ou* to string (on) *(sép)* ; [- sur une tige] to slip on *(sép)* ■ **~ une aiguille** to thread a needle ■ **elle enfila ses bagues** she slipped her rings on ▶ **~ des perles** *fam* to waste one's time with trifles **3.** [mettre - vêtement] to pull *ou* to slip on *(sép)*, to slip into *(sép)* ■ **~ son collant** to slip on one's tights **4.** [suivre] to take, to use ■ **la voiture a enfilé la rue jusqu'au carrefour** the car drove up the street to the crossroads **5.** ▲ [sexuellement] to screw▲.
◆ **s'enfiler** <> *vpi* : **s'~ dans** to go into ■ **s'~ sous un porche** to disappear into a doorway.
<> *vpt fam* **1.** [avaler - boisson] to knock back, to put away ; [- nourriture] to guzzle, to gobble up *(sép)*, to put away *(sép)* **2.** [faire - corvée] to get through *(insép)*.

enfin [ɑ̃fɛ̃] *adv* **1.** [finalement] at last ■ **~! depuis le temps!** and not before!, and about time too! ■ **~ seuls!** alone at last! ■ **un accord a été ~ conclu** an agreement has at last been reached
2. [en dernier lieu] finally ■ **~, j'aimerais vous remercier de votre hospitalité** finally, I would like to thank you for your hospitality
3. [en un mot] in short, in brief, in a word
4. [cependant] still, however, after all ■ **elle est triste, mais ~ elle s'en remettra** she's sad, but still, she'll get over it ■ **oui mais ~, c'est peut-être vrai** after all it might well be true
5. [avec une valeur restrictive] well, at least ■ **elle est jolie, ~, à mon avis** she's pretty, (or) at least I think she is
6. [emploi expressif] : **~! c'est la vie!** oh well, such is life! ■ **ce n'est pas la même chose, ~!** oh come on, it's not the same thing at all! ■ **~, reprends-toi!** come on, pull yourself together! ■ **~ qu'est-ce qu'il y a?** what on earth is the matter? ■ **c'est son droit, ~!** it's his right, after all! ■ **tu ne peux pas faire ça, ~!** you can't DO that!

enflammé, e [ɑ̃flame] *adj* **1.** [allumette, torche] lighted, burning ■ [bûche] burning **2.** *litt* [visage] burning ■ [regard] fiery **3.** [passionné - discours, déclaration] impassioned, fiery ; [- nature] fiery, hot-blooded **4.** MÉD inflamed.

enflammer [3] [ɑ̃flame] *vt* **1.** [mettre le feu à - bois] to light, to kindle, to ignite ; [- branchages] to ignite ; [- allumette] to light, to strike ; [- papier] to ignite, to set on fire, to set alight **2.** *litt* [rougir] to flush ▪ **la fièvre enflammait ses joues** his cheeks were burning *ou* flushed with fever **3.** [exalter - imagination, passion] to kindle, to fire ; [- foule] to inflame **4.** MÉD to inflame.

◆ **s'enflammer** *vpi* **1.** [prendre feu - forêt] to go up in flames, to catch fire, to ignite ; [- bois] to burst into flame, to light **2.** *litt* [rougir - visage, ciel] to flush ▪ **son visage s'enflamma de colère** his face was flushed with anger **3.** [s'intensifier - passion] to flare up **4.** [s'enthousiasmer] to be fired with enthusiasm.

enflé, e [ɑ̃fle] ◇ *adj* [cheville, joue] swollen.
◇ *nm, f*△ fathead, jerk△.

enfler [3] [ɑ̃fle] ◇ *vt* **1.** [gonfler - forme] to cause to swell, to make swell ; [- voix] to make louder, to raise **2.** [majorer - calcul, budget] to inflate **3.** *litt* [exagérer - difficulté, prestige] to overestimate.
◇ *vi* [augmenter de volume - cheville] to swell (up) ; [- voix] to boom (out).
◆ **s'enfler** *vpi* [voix] to boom (out) ▪ [voile] to billow *ou* to swell *ou* to fill out.

enflure [ɑ̃flyr] *nf* **1.** [partie gonflée] swelling **2.** [emphase] bombast, turgidity, pompousness ▪ **il donne dans l'~** he tends to be pompous **3.** △ [personne détestable] jerk△.

enfoiré, e△ [ɑ̃fware] *nm, f* bastard.

enfoncé, e [ɑ̃fɔ̃se] *adj* [yeux] sunken, deep-set.

enfoncement [ɑ̃fɔ̃smɑ̃] *nm* **1.** [destruction - d'un mur] breaking down ; [- d'une porte] breaking down, bashing in **2.** [cavité] depression, hollow **3.** MÉD fracture ▪ **~ de la boîte crânienne** skull fracture ▪ **~ du thorax** flail chest.

enfoncer [16] [ɑ̃fɔ̃se] ◇ *vt* **1.** [faire pénétrer - piquet, aiguille] to push in *(sép)* ; [- vis] to drive *ou* to screw in *(sép)* ; [- clou] to drive *ou* to hammer in *(sép)* ; [- épingle, punaise] to push *ou* to stick in *(sép)* ; [- couteau] to stick *ou* to thrust in *(sép)* ▪ **il a enfoncé le pieu d'un seul coup** he drove *ou* stuck the stake home in one ▶ **il faut ~ le clou** it's important to ram the point home **2.** [faire descendre] to push *ou* to ram (on) ▪ **il enfonça son chapeau jusqu'aux oreilles** he rammed his hat onto his head **3.** [briser - côte, carrosserie] to stave in *(sép)*, to crush ; [- porte] to break down *(sép)*, to bash in *(sép)*, to force open *(sép)* ; [- barrière, mur] to smash, to break down *(sép)* ▪ **la voiture a enfoncé la barrière** the car crashed through the fence ▶ **~ une porte ouverte** *ou* **des portes ouvertes** to labour UK *ou* to labor US the point **4.** [vaincre - armée, troupe] to rout, to crush ▪ **~ un adversaire** *fam* to crush an opponent **5.** [condamner] : **~ qqn : son témoignage n'a fait que l'~** he just dug himself into a deeper hole with that statement.
◇ *vi* to sink ▪ **~ dans la neige** to sink into the snow.
◆ **s'enfoncer** ◇ *vpi* **1.** [dans l'eau, la boue, la terre] to sink (in) ▪ **ils s'enfoncèrent dans la neige jusqu'aux genoux** they sank knee-deep into the snow ▪ **les vis s'enfoncent facilement dans le bois** screws go *ou* bore easily through wood **2.** [se lover] : **s'~ dans** to sink into ▪ **s'~ sous une couette** to burrow *ou* to snuggle under a quilt ▮ *péj* **s'~ dans son chagrin** to bury o.s. in one's grief **3.** [s'engager] : **s'~ dans** to penetrate *ou* to go into ▪ **le chemin s'enfonce dans la forêt** the path runs into the forest ▪ **plus on s'enfonce dans la forêt plus le silence est profond** the further you walk into the forest the quieter it becomes ▪ **ils s'enfoncèrent dans la nuit** they disappeared into the night **4.** [s'affaisser - plancher, terrain] to give way, to cave in **5.** [aggraver son cas] to get into deep *ou* deeper waters, to make matters worse.
◇ *vpt* : **s'~ une épine dans le doigt** to get a thorn (stuck) in one's finger ▪ **s'~ une idée dans la tête** *fam* to get an idea into one's head.

enfonceur, euse [ɑ̃fɔ̃sœr, øz] *nm, f* : **c'est un ~ de portes ouvertes** he's a great one for stating the obvious.

enfouir [32] [ɑ̃fwir] *vt* **1.** [mettre sous terre - os, trésor] to bury **2.** [blottir] to nestle ▪ **elle a enfoui sa tête dans l'oreiller** she buried her head in the pillow **3.** [cacher] to stuff, to bury.
◆ **s'enfouir** *vpi* **1.** [s'enterrer] to bury o.s. **2.** [se blottir] to burrow ▪ **s'~ dans un terrier/sous les couvertures** to burrow in a hole/under the blankets.

enfourcher [3] [ɑ̃furʃe] *vt* [bicyclette, cheval] to mount, to get on *(insép)* ▪ [chaise] to straddle ▪ **~ son cheval de bataille** *ou* **son dada** to get on one's hobbyhorse.

enfourner [3] [ɑ̃furne] *vt* **1.** [mettre dans un four] to put into an oven ▪ **~ des briques** to feed a kiln (with bricks) **2.** *fam* [entasser] to shove *ou* to cram *ou* to push (in) **3.** *fam* [manger] to put away *(sép)*, to wolf down *(sép)*.
◆ **s'enfourner** *vpt fam* : **s'~ qqch** [le manger] to wolf sthg down ▪ **s'~ qqch dans la bouche** to cram *ou* to stuff sthg into one's mouth.
◆ **s'enfourner dans** *vp+prép* [entrer dans] to rush *ou* to pile into ▪ **l'équipe s'enfourna dans le car** the team piled into the bus.

enfreindre [81] [ɑ̃frɛ̃dr] *vt* to infringe ▪ **~ la loi** to break *ou* to infringe the law ▪ **~ le règlement** to fail to comply with *ou* to break the rules.

enfuir [35] [ɑ̃fɥir] ◆ **s'enfuir** *vpi* to run away, to flee ▪ **s'~ avec qqn** [pour échapper à des sanctions] to run away *ou* off with sb ; [pour se marier] to elope with sb ▪ **s'~ de prison** to break out of *ou* to escape from jail ▪ **s'~ de chez soi** to run away from home ▪ **s'~ d'un pays** to flee a country.

enfumé, e [ɑ̃fyme] *adj* [pièce] smoky, smoke-filled ▪ [paroi] sooty.

enfumer [3] [ɑ̃fyme] *vt* **1.** [abeille, renard] to smoke out *(sép)* **2.** [pièce] to fill with smoke ▪ [paroi] to soot up *(insép)*.

enfuyait *etc v* ▻ **enfuir**.

engagé, e [ɑ̃gaʒe] ◇ *adj* **1.** [artiste, littérature] political, politically committed, engagé *sout* **2.** ARCHIT engaged **3.** [inscrit] : **les concurrents ~s dans la course** the competitors who are signed up to take part in the race.
◇ *nm, f* MIL volunteer.

engageant, e [ɑ̃gaʒɑ̃, ɑ̃t] *adj* [manières, sourire] engaging, winning ▪ [regard] inviting ▪ [perspective] attractive, inviting ▪ **un restaurant bien peu ~** a less than inviting restaurant.

engagement [ɑ̃gaʒmɑ̃] *nm* **1.** [promesse] commitment, undertaking, engagement *sout* ▪ **contracter un ~** to enter into a commitment ▪ **faire honneur à/manquer à ses ~s** to honour/to fail to honour one's commitments ▪ **passer un ~ avec qqn** to come to an agreement with sb ▪ **prendre l'~ de** to undertake *ou* to agree to ▪ **respecter ses ~s envers qqn** to fulfil UK *ou* to fulfill US one's commitments *ou* obligations towards sb ▪ **sans ~ de date** date subject to change ▪ **sans ~ de votre part** with no obligation on your part ; [dans une publicité] no obligation to buy **2.** [dette] (financial) commitment, liability ▪ **faire face à ses ~s** to meet one's commitments **3.** [embauche] appointment, hiring ▪ **~ à l'essai** appointment for a trial period ▮ CINÉ & THÉÂTRE job ▪ **acteur sans ~** out of work actor **4.** [début] beginning, start **5.** MIL [combat] engagement, action, clash ▪ [mise en action] : **~ d'une troupe** committing troops to action ▮ [recrutement] enlistment **6.** [prise de position] commitment **7.** [mise en gage] pawning **8.** MÉD engagement **9.** SPORT [participation] entry ▪ FOOTBALL kickoff.

engager [17] [ɑ̃gaʒe] *vt* **1.** [insérer - clef, disquette] to insert, to put *ou* to slot in *(sép)* ▪ **~ une vitesse** to put a car into gear ▪ [faire pénétrer] : **~ une péniche dans une écluse** to move a barge into a lock **2.** [lier] to bind, to commit ▪ **voilà ce que je pense, mais ça n'engage que moi** that's how I see it, but it's my own view ▪ **cela ne t'engage à rien** it doesn't commit you to anything **3.** [mettre en jeu - énergie, ressources] to invest, to commit ; [- fonds] to put in *(sép)* ▪ **~ sa parole** to give one's word (of) honour UK *ou* honor US ▪ **~ sa responsabilité** to accept responsibility **4.** [inciter] : **~ qqn à : je vous engage à la prudence/modération** I advise you to be prudent/moderate ▪ **~ qqn à faire qqch** to advise sb to do sthg **5.** [commencer] to open, to start, to begin ▪ **~ la conversation avec qqn** to engage sb in conversation, to strike up a conversation with sb ▪ **~ le débat** to start the discussion ▪ **l'affaire est mal engagée** the whole thing is off to a bad start ▪ **~ le match** FOOTBALL to kick off ; RUGBY to begin **6.** [embaucher] to take on *(sép)*, to hire **7.** MIL [envoyer] to commit to military action ▪ [recruter] to enlist **8.** [mettre en gage] to pawn.

◆ **s'engager** *vpi* **1.** [commencer - négociations, procédure, tournoi] to start, to begin **2.** [prendre position] to take a stand ▪ **s'~ contre la peine de mort** to campaign against *ou* to take a stand against the death penalty **3.** MIL to enlist ▪ **s'~ avant l'appel** to volunteer before conscription **4.** [auprès d'un employeur] to hire o.s. out ▪ **s'~ comme jeune fille au pair** to get a job as an au pair.
◆ **s'engager à** *vp+prép* : **s'~ à faire qqch** [promettre] to commit o.s. to doing sthg, to undertake to do sthg.
◆ **s'engager dans** *vp+prép* **1.** [avancer dans - suj: véhicule, piéton] to go *ou* to move into ▪ **la voiture s'est engagée dans une rue étroite** the car drove *ou* turned into a narrow street ▪ **s'~ dans un carrefour** to pull *ou* to draw out into a crossroads **2.** [entreprendre] to enter into, to begin ▪ **le pays s'est engagé dans la lutte armée** the country has committed itself to *ou* has entered into armed struggle **3.** SPORT : **s'~ dans une course/compétition** to enter a race/an event.

engazonner [3] [ɑ̃gazɔne] *vt* [par plaques] to turf ▪ [par semis] to grass.

engeance [ɑ̃ʒɑ̃s] *nf péj* scum, trash *US* ▪ **ils feraient n'importe quoi pour se procurer de l'argent, quelle (sale) ~!** they'd do anything for money, what scum!

engelure [ɑ̃ʒlyr] *nf* chilblain.

engendrer [3] [ɑ̃ʒɑ̃dre] *vt* **1.** [procréer] to beget BIBLE to father **2.** [provoquer - sentiment, situation] to generate, to create, to breed *péj* ▪ **il n'engendre pas la mélancolie** *hum* he's great fun **3.** LING & MATH to generate.

engin [ɑ̃ʒɛ̃] *nm* **1.** [appareil] machine, appliance ▪ **~ agricole** piece of farm machinery ▪ **~s de levage** lifting gears ▪ **~ de manutention** conveyor, handling equipment **2.** ASTRONAUT : **~ spatial** spacecraft **3.** MIL weaponry **4.** *fam* [chose] contraption, thingamabob, thingamajig **5.** △ [pénis] tool△.

engineering [ɛnʒiniriŋ] *nm* : **l'~** engineering.

englober [3] [ɑ̃glɔbe] *vt* **1.** [réunir] to encompass **2.** [inclure] to include ▪ **~ un texte dans un recueil** to include a piece in an anthology.

engloutir [32] [ɑ̃glutir] *vt* **1.** [faire disparaître] to swallow up *(sép)*, to engulf ▪ **une île engloutie par la mer** an island swallowed up by the sea **2.** [manger] to gobble up *(sép)*, to gulp *ou* to wolf down *(sép)* **3.** [dépenser] to squander ▪ **les travaux ont englouti tout mon argent** the work swallowed up all my money ▪ **il a englouti son capital dans son agence** he sank all his capital into his agency ▪ **ils ont englouti des sommes énormes dans la maison** they sank vast amounts of money into the house.
◆ **s'engloutir** *vpi* [vaisseau] to be swallowed up *ou* engulfed, to sink.

engloutissement [ɑ̃glutismɑ̃] *nm* **1.** [d'un navire, d'une ville] swallowing up, engulfment **2.** [d'une fortune] squandering.

engluer [3] [ɑ̃glye] *vt* **1.** CHASSE [oiseau, branche] to lime, to birdlime **2.** [rendre collant] to make sticky ▪ **des doigts englués de colle** fingers sticky with glue.
◆ **s'engluer** *vpi* **1.** [se couvrir de glu] to become gluey **2.** *fig* **s'~ dans qqch** to get bogged down in sthg.

engoncer [16] [ɑ̃gɔ̃se] *vt* to cramp, to restrict ▪ **être engoncé dans ses vêtements** to be restricted by one's clothes ▪ **tu as l'air (d'être) engoncé dans ce manteau** that coat looks too tight for you.

engorgement [ɑ̃gɔrʒəmɑ̃] *nm* [d'un tuyau] flooding ▪ [d'un sol] saturation ▪ **l'~ des grandes villes** congestion in the big cities ▪ **l'~ du marché automobile** saturation in the car industry, the glut of cars on the market.

engorger [17] [ɑ̃gɔrʒe] *vt* [canalisation] to flood ▪ [route] to congest, to jam ▪ [organe] to engorge ▪ [sol] to saturate ▪ [marché] to saturate, to glut.
s'engorger *vpi* to become blocked, to get blocked.

engouement [ɑ̃gumɑ̃] *nm* **1.** [pour une activité, un type d'objet] keen interest ▪ **un ~ pour le jazz** a keen interest in jazz **2.** [élan amoureux] infatuation ▪ **avoir un ~ pour** to be infatuated with.

engouer [6] [ɑ̃gwe] ◆ **s'engouer de, s'engouer pour** *vp+prép* [activité, objet] to have a craze *ou* a sudden passion for ▪ [personne] to become infatuated with.

engouffrer [3] [ɑ̃gufre] *vt* **1.** [avaler] to wolf *ou* to shovel (down), to cram (in) **2.** [entasser] to cram *ou* to stuff (in) **3.** [dépenser] to swallow up *(sép)*.
◆ **s'engouffrer** *vpi* [foule] to rush, to crush ▪ [personne] to rush, to dive ▪ [mer] to surge, to rush ▪ [vent] to blow, to sweep, to rush ▪ **s'~ dans un taxi** [seul] to dive into a taxi ; [à plusieurs] to pile into a taxi.

engoulevent [ɑ̃gulvɑ̃] *nm* nightjar ▪ **~ d'Amérique** nighthawk, bullbat.

engourdi, e [ɑ̃gurdi] *adj* **1.** [doigt, membre] numb, numbed ▪ **à force d'être resté dans cette position, j'ai la jambe ~e** I have been sitting like this so long that my leg has gone to sleep **2.** [esprit, imagination] slow, lethargic.

engourdir [32] [ɑ̃gurdir] *vt* **1.** [insensibiliser - doigt, membre] to numb, to make numb ; [- sens] to deaden ▪ **être engourdi par le froid** to be numb with cold ▪ **la chaleur a engourdi les élèves** the heat made the pupils drowsy *ou* sluggish **2.** [ralentir - esprit, faculté] to blunt, to dull ▪ **la fatigue lui engourdissait l'esprit** he was so tired he couldn't think straight.
◆ **s'engourdir** *vpi* to go numb.

engourdissant, e [ɑ̃gurdisɑ̃, ɑ̃t] *adj* [froid] numbing ▪ [chaleur] oppressive.

engourdissement [ɑ̃gurdismɑ̃] *nm* **1.** [insensibilité physique] numbness **2.** [affaiblissement - des facultés] blunting, blurring **3.** [torpeur] drowsiness, sleepiness.

engrais [ɑ̃grɛ] *nm* fertilizer ▪ **~ chimique** artificial fertilizer ▪ **~s verts** *ou* **végétaux** green *ou* vegetable manure ▪ **mettre une bête à l'~** to fatten (up) an animal.

engraissement [ɑ̃grɛsmɑ̃], **engraissage** [ɑ̃grɛsaʒ] *nm* fattening (up).

engraisser [4] [ɑ̃grese] ◇ *vt* AGRIC [bétail] to fatten up *(sép)* ▪ **~ une oie** to fatten a goose ▮ [terre] to feed.
◇ *vi* to grow fat *ou* fatter, to put on weight.
◆ **s'engraisser** *vpi* to get fat ▪ **il s'engraisse sur le dos de ses employés** *fig* he lines his pockets by underpaying his employees.

engrangement [ɑ̃grɑ̃ʒmɑ̃] *nm* **1.** AGRIC gathering in, storing **2.** [de documents] storing, collecting.

engranger [17] [ɑ̃grɑ̃ʒe] *vt* **1.** AGRIC to gather, to get in *(sép)* **2.** [documents] to store (up), to collect.

engrenage [ɑ̃grənaʒ] *nm* **1.** MÉCAN gear ▪ **les ~s d'une machine** the wheelwork *ou* train of gears *ou* gearing of a machine **2.** *fig* trap ▪ **être pris dans l'~** to be caught in a trap ▪ **être pris dans l'~ du jeu** to be trapped in the vicious circle of gambling.

engrener [19] [ɑ̃grəne] ◇ *vt* **1.** MÉCAN to gear, to mesh **2.** AGRIC to feed with grain, to fill with grain.
◇ *vi* to gear, to mesh.
◆ **s'engrener** *vpi* to gear, to mesh, to be in mesh.

engrosser [3] △ [ɑ̃grose] *vt* to knock up△ *(sép)* ▪ **se faire ~** to get oneself pregnant.

engueulade△ [ɑ̃gœlad] *nf* **1.** [réprimande] rollicking *UK*, bawling out *US* ▪ **recevoir une ~** to get a rollicking *UK ou* bawled out *US* **2.** [querelle] slanging match *UK*, run-in *US* ▪ **avoir une ~ avec qqn** to have a slanging match *UK ou* a run-in *US* with sb.

engueuler [5] △ [ɑ̃gœle] *vt* : **~ qqn** to give sb a rollicking *UK*, to bawl sb out *US* ▪ **se faire ~** to get a rollicking *UK*, to get chewed out *US*.

◆ **s'engueuler**△ ◇ *vp (emploi réciproque)* **on ne va tout de même pas s'~ pour ça** we're not going to fight over this, are we?
◇ *vpi* : **s'~ avec qqn** to have a row with sb.

enguirlander [3] [ɑ̃girlɑ̃de] *vt* **1.** [décorer] to garland, to deck with garlands **2.** *fam* [réprimander] to tick off *(sép)* *UK*, to chew out *(sép)* *US* ■ **se faire ~** to get a ticking-off *UK* *OU* a chewing-out *US*.

enhardir [32] [ɑ̃ardir] *vt* to embolden, to make bolder, to encourage.
◆ **s'enhardir** *vpi* : **l'enfant s'enhardit et entra dans la pièce** the child plucked up courage and went into the room.

enharmonie [ɑ̃narmɔni] *nf* enharmony.

énième [enjɛm] *adj* umpteenth, nth ■ **pour la ~ fois** for the umpteenth time.

énigmatique [enigmatik] *adj* enigmatic ■ **d'un air ~** enigmatically.

énigmatiquement [enigmatikmɑ̃] *adv* enigmatically.

énigme [enigm] *nf* **1.** [mystère] riddle, enigma, puzzle ■ **les enquêteurs tentent de résoudre l'~ de sa disparition** the police are trying to solve the riddle of his disappearance **2.** [devinette] riddle.

enivrant, e [ɑ̃nivrɑ̃, ɑ̃t] *adj* **1.** [qui rend ivre] intoxicating **2.** [exaltant] heady, exhilarating ■ **ce furent des moments ~s** those were heady days.

enivrement [ɑ̃nivrəmɑ̃] *nm* elation, exhilaration.

enivrer [3] [ɑ̃nivre] *vt* **1.** [soûler - suj: vin] to make drunk, to intoxicate **2.** [exalter] to intoxicate, to exhilarate, to elate ■ **le succès l'enivrait** he was intoxicated by his success.
◆ **s'enivrer** *vpi* to get drunk ■ **s'~ de** *fig* to become intoxicated with.

enjambée [ɑ̃ʒɑ̃be] *nf* stride ■ **avancer à grandes ~s dans la rue** to stride along the street ■ **faire de grandes ~s** to take long steps *OU* strides ■ **il a franchi le ruisseau en une ~** he crossed the stream in one stride.

enjambement [ɑ̃ʒɑ̃bmɑ̃] *nm* **1.** LITTÉR enjambment **2.** BIOL crossing-over.

enjamber [3] [ɑ̃ʒɑ̃be] *vt* [muret, rebord] to step over *(insép)* ■ [fossé] to stride across *OU* over *(insép)* ■ [tronc d'arbre] to stride *OU* to step over *(insép)* ■ **le pont enjambe le Gard** the bridge spans the river Gard.

enjeu [ɑ̃ʒø] *nm* JEUX stake, stakes ■ **c'est un ~ important** the stakes are high ■ **l'~ d'une guerre** the stakes of war.

enjoindre [82] [ɑ̃ʒwɛ̃dr] *vt litt* ~ **à qqn de faire qqch** to enjoin sb to do sthg.

enjôler [3] [ɑ̃ʒole] *vt* to cajole, to wheedle ■ **il a réussi à m'~** he managed to cajole me (into accepting).

enjôleur, euse [ɑ̃ʒolœr, øz] ◇ *adj* cajoling, wheedling ■ **un sourire ~** a wheedling smile.
◇ *nm, f* cajoler, wheedler.

enjolivement [ɑ̃ʒɔlivmɑ̃] *nm* embellishment, embellishing.

enjoliver [3] [ɑ̃ʒɔlive] *vt* **1.** [décorer - vêtement] to embellish, to adorn ■ **enjolivé de** adorned with **2.** [travestir - histoire, récit, vérité] to embellish, to embroider ■ **~ les faits** to embroider the facts.

enjoliveur [ɑ̃ʒɔlivœr] *nm* hubcap.

enjolivure [ɑ̃ʒɔlivyr] *nf* embellishment, ornament.

enjoué, e [ɑ̃ʒwe] *adj* [personne, caractère] cheerful, jolly, genial ■ [remarque, ton] playful, cheerful, jolly.

enjouement [ɑ̃ʒumɑ̃] *nm* cheerfulness, playfulness.

enkyster [3] [ɑ̃kiste] ◆ **s'enkyster** *vpi* to encyst, to turn into a cyst.

enlacement [ɑ̃lasmɑ̃] *nm* **1.** [entrecroisement] intertwining, interlacing, entwinement **2.** [embrassement] (lovers') embrace.

enlacer [16] [ɑ̃lase] *vt* **1.** [étreindre] to clasp ■ **~ qqn** to embrace sb (tenderly) ■ **ils étaient tendrement enlacés** they were locked in a tender embrace **2.** [mêler] to interweave, to intertwine, to interlace ■ **initiales enlacées** interwoven initials.
◆ **s'enlacer** *vp (emploi réciproque)* [amoureux] to embrace, to hug.

enlaidir [32] [ɑ̃ledir] ◇ *vt* to make ugly ■ **~ le paysage** to be a blot on the landscape *OU* an eyesore.
◇ *vi* to become ugly.
◆ **s'enlaidir** *vpi* to make o.s. (look) ugly.

enlaidissement [ɑ̃ledismɑ̃] *nm* : **les nouvelles constructions ont contribué à l'~ du quartier** the area has been disfigured partly by the new buildings.

enlevé, e [ɑ̃lve] *adj* [style, rythme] lively, spirited ■ **ses dialogues sont ~s** he writes quickfire dialogues.

enlèvement [ɑ̃lɛvmɑ̃] *nm* **1.** [rapt] abduction, kidnapping ■ **l'~ des Sabines** the rape of the Sabine women **2.** [fait d'ôter] removal, taking away ■ **l'~ d'une tache/d'un organe** the removal of a stain/of an organ **3.** [ramassage] : **l'~ des ordures a lieu le mardi** rubbish is collected on Tuesdays.

enlever [19] [ɑ̃lve] *vt* **1.** [ôter - couvercle, housse, vêtement] to remove, to take off *(sép)* ; [- étagère] to remove, to take down *(sép)* ■ **enlève ton manteau, mets-toi à l'aise** take your coat off and make yourself comfortable ■ **~ les pépins** to take the pips out ■ **ils ont enlevé le reste des meubles ce matin** they took away *OU* collected what was left of the furniture this morning
2. [arracher] to remove, to pull out ■ **~ un clou avec des tenailles** to prise *UK OU* to pry *US* a nail out with a pair of pliers
3. [faire disparaître] to remove ■ **~ une tache** [gén] to remove a stain ; [en lavant] to wash out a stain ; [en frottant] to rub out a stain ; [à l'eau de Javel] to bleach out a stain
4. MÉD [dentisterie] : **se faire ~ une dent** to have a tooth pulled out *OU* extracted ■ **se faire ~ un grain de beauté** to have a mole removed
5. [soustraire] : **~ qqch à qqn** to take sthg away from sb, to deprive sb of sthg ■ **ça m'enlève mes scrupules** it dispels *OU* allays *sout* my misgivings ■ **j'ai peur qu'on ne m'enlève la garde de mon enfant** I'm afraid they'll take my child away from me ■ **ne m'enlevez pas tous mes espoirs** don't deprive *OU* rob me of all hope
6. [obtenir - récompense] to carry off *(sép)*, to win ■ **il a enlevé la victoire** he ran away with the victory ■ **~ un marché** to get *OU* to secure a deal
7. [soulever] to lift ■ **~ 10 kilos sans effort** to lift 10 kilos easily
8. *litt* [faire mourir] to carry off *(sép)* ■ **c'est un cancer qui nous l'a enlevé** cancer took him from us
9. MIL to carry, to seize
10. [exécuter vite - sonate, chanson] to dash off *(sép)*
11. [kidnapper] to abduct, to kidnap, to snatch ■ **il a été enlevé à son domicile** he was snatched from his home ■ **se faire ~** to be kidnapped.
◆ **s'enlever** ◇ *vp (emploi passif)* **1.** [vêtement, étiquette] to come off ■ [écharde] to come out ■ **le costume s'enlève par le haut/par le bas** you slip the costume off over your head/step out of the costume ■ **comment ça s'enlève?** how do you take it off?
2. [s'effacer - tache] to come out *OU* off.
◇ *vpt* : **s'~ une écharde du doigt** to pull a splinter out of one's finger ■ **s'~ une épine du pied** *fig* to get rid of a niggling problem.

enlisement [ɑ̃lizmɑ̃] *nm* **1.** [enfoncement] sinking **2.** [stagnation] stagnation ■ **le manque de coopération a entraîné l'~ des pourparlers** due to a lack of cooperation, the talks have reached a stalemate.

enliser [3] [ɑ̃lize] *vt* : **~ ses roues** to get one's wheels stuck.

◆ **s'enliser** *vpi* **1.** [s'embourber] to get bogged down *ou* stuck, to sink ▪ **s'~ dans des sables mouvants** to sink *ou* to get sucked (down) into quicksand **2.** *fig* to get bogged down ▪ **s'~ dans la routine** to get *ou* to be bogged down in routine.

enluminer [3] [ɑ̃lymine] *vt* to illuminate.

enlumineur, euse [ɑ̃lyminœr, øz] *nm, f* illuminator.

enluminure [ɑ̃lyminyr] *nf* illumination.

ENM *npr f* = **École nationale de la magistrature**.

enneigé, e [ɑ̃neʒe] *adj* [champ, paysage] snow-covered ▪ [pic] snow-capped ▪ **les routes sont ~es** the roads are snowed up.

enneigement [ɑ̃nɛʒmɑ̃] *nm* snow cover ▪ **l'~ annuel** yearly *ou* annual snowfall ▪ **bulletin d'~** snow report.

enneiger [23] [ɑ̃neʒe] *vt* to cover with *ou* in snow.

ennemi, e [ɛnmi] ◇ *adj* **1.** MIL enemy *(modif)*, hostile **2.** [inamical] hostile, unfriendly ▪ [adverse] : **familles/nations ~es** feuding families/nations **3.** [opposé à] : **~ de : être ~ du changement** to be opposed *ou* averse to change.
◇ *nm, f* **1.** MIL enemy, foe *litt* ▪ **passer à l'~** to go over to the enemy **2.** [individu hostile] enemy ▪ **se faire des ~s** to make enemies ▪ **se faire un ~ de qqn** to make an enemy of sb ➊ **~ mortel** mortal enemy ▪ **~ public (numéro un)** public enemy (number one) **3.** [antagoniste] : **l'~ de : le bien est l'~ du mal** good is the enemy of evil.

ennoblir [32] [ɑ̃nɔblir] *vt* [personne] to ennoble ▪ [caractère, esprit] to ennoble, to elevate ▪ [physique] to lend dignity to.

ennoblissement [ɑ̃nɔblismɑ̃] *nm* **1.** [élévation] ennoblement, ennobling **2.** TEXT finishing, processing.

ennui [ɑ̃nɥi] *nm* **1.** [problème] problem, difficulty ▪ **des ~s** trouble, troubles, problems ▪ **attirer des ~s à qqn** to get sb into trouble ▪ **avoir des ~s : avoir de gros ~s** to be in bad trouble ▪ **tu vas avoir des ~s** you're going to get into trouble ▪ **avoir des ~s avec la police** to be in trouble with the police ▪ **des ~s de : avoir des ~s d'argent** to have money problems ▪ **avoir des ~s de voiture** to have problems with one's car ▪ **avoir des ~s de moteur** to have engine trouble ▪ **avoir des ~s de santé** to have health problems ▪ **faire des ~s à qqn** to get sb into trouble ▪ **l'~ : c'est ça l'~!** that's the hitch *ou* trouble! ▪ **l'~ c'est que...** the trouble is that... ➊ **un ~ ne vient jamais seul** *prov* it never rains but it pours *prov* **2.** [lassitude] boredom ▪ **c'était à mourir d'~** it was dreadfully *ou* deadly boring **3.** *litt* [mélancolie] ennui.

ennuyer [14] [ɑ̃nɥije] *vt* **1.** [contrarier] to worry, to bother ▪ **avoir l'air ennuyé** to look bothered *ou* worried ▪ **ça m'ennuie de les laisser seuls** I don't like to leave them alone ▪ **ça m'ennuie de te le dire mais...** I'm sorry to have to say this to you but... ▪ **cela m'ennuierait d'être en retard** I'd hate to be late **2.** [déranger] to bother, to trouble ▪ **si cela ne vous ennuie pas** if you don't mind ▪ **je ne voudrais pas vous ~ mais...** I don't like to bother *ou* trouble you but... **3.** [agacer] to annoy ▪ **tu l'ennuies avec tes questions** you're annoying him with your questions **4.** [lasser] to bore ▪ **les jeux de cartes m'ennuient** I find card games boring.
◆ **s'ennuyer** *vpi* to be bored ▪ **elle s'ennuie toute seule** she gets bored on her own ▪ **avec lui on ne s'ennuie pas!** *hum* he's great fun! ➊ **s'~ comme un rat mort** *fam* to be bored to death.
◆ **s'ennuyer de** *vp+prép* : **s'~ de qqn/qqch** to miss sb/sthg.

ennuyeux, euse [ɑ̃nɥijø, øz] *adj* **1.** [lassant - travail, conférencier, collègue] boring, dull ▪ **~ à mourir** *ou* **à périr** *ou* **comme la pluie** *ou* **comme la mort** (as) dull as ditchwater *UK ou* dishwater *US*, deadly boring **2.** [fâcheux] annoying, tiresome ▪ **c'est ~ qu'il ne puisse pas venir** [regrettable] it's a pity (that) he can't come ; [contrariant] it's annoying *ou* a nuisance that he can't come.

énoncé [enɔ̃se] *nm* **1.** [libellé - d'un sujet de débat] terms ; [- d'une question d'examen, d'un problème d'arithmétique] wording **2.** [lecture] reading, declaration ▪ **à l'~ des faits** when the facts were stated ▪ **écouter l'~ du jugement** to listen to the verdict being read out **3.** LING utterance.

énoncer [16] [enɔ̃se] *vt* [formuler] to formulate, to enunciate *sout*, to express ▪ **cela peut être énoncé plus simplement** it can be formulated *ou* expressed *ou* put in simpler terms.

énonciatif, ive [enɔ̃sjatif, iv] *adj* enunciative.

énonciation [enɔ̃sjasjɔ̃] *nf* **1.** [exposition] statement, stating **2.** LING enunciation.

enorgueillir [32] [ɑ̃nɔrgœjir] *vt litt* to make proud.
◆ **s'enorgueillir de** *vp+prép* to be proud of.

énorme [enɔrm] *adj* **1.** [gros] enormous, huge **2.** [important] huge, enormous, vast ▪ **10 euros, ce n'est pas ~** 10 euros isn't such a huge amount ▪ **elle n'a pas dit non, c'est déjà ~!** she didn't say no, that's a great step forward! **3.** [exagéré - mensonge] outrageous.

énormément [enɔrmemɑ̃] *adv* enormously, hugely ▪ **le spectacle m'a ~ plu** I liked the show very much indeed ▪ **s'amuser ~** to enjoy o.s. immensely *ou* tremendously ▪ **~ de** [argent, bruit] an enormous *ou* a huge *ou* a tremendous amount of ▪ **il y avait ~ de monde dans le train** the train was extremely crowded ▪ **ils ont mis ~ de temps à comprendre** it took them ages to understand.

énormité [enɔrmite] *nf* **1.** [ampleur - d'une difficulté] enormity ; [- d'une tâche, d'une somme, d'une population] enormity, size **2.** [extravagance] outrageousness, enormity **3.** [propos] piece of utter *ou* outrageous nonsense ▪ **vous dites des ~s** what you're saying is totally outrageous.

enquérir [39] [ɑ̃kerir] ◆ **s'enquérir de** *vp+prép sout* to inquire about *ou* after ▪ **s'~ de la santé de qqn** to inquire *ou* to ask after sb's health.

enquête [ɑ̃kɛt] *nf* **1.** [investigation] investigation, inquiry ▪ **faire** *ou* **mener sa petite ~** to make discreet inquiries ▪ **il a fait l'objet d'une ~** he was the subject of an investigation ▪ **mener une ~ sur un meurtre** to investigate a murder ▪ **ouvrir/conduire une ~** to open/to conduct an investigation ➊ **~ judiciaire (suite à un décès)** inquest ▪ **~ d'utilité publique** public inquiry **2.** [étude] survey, investigation ▪ **faire une ~** to conduct a survey **3.** PRESSE (investigative) report, exposé.

enquêté, e [ɑ̃kete] *nm, f* interviewee.

enquêter [4] [ɑ̃kete] *vi* to investigate ▪ **~ sur un meurtre** to inquire into *ou* to investigate a murder.

enquêteur, euse *ou* **trice** [ɑ̃kɛtœr, øz, tris] *nm, f* **1.** [de police] officer in charge of investigations, investigator **2.** [de sondage] pollster **3.** [sociologue] researcher.

enquiert *etc v* ▷ **enquérir**.

enquiquinant, e [ɑ̃kikinɑ̃, ɑ̃t] *adj fam* irritating ▪ **des voisins ~s** awkward neighbours.

enquiquinement [ɑ̃kikinmɑ̃] *nm fam* **des ~s** hassle ▪ **je n'ai eu que des ~s avec cette voiture** I've had nothing but hassle with this car.

enquiquiner [3] [ɑ̃kikine] *vt fam* **1.** [ennuyer] to bore (stiff) **2.** [irriter] to bug ▪ **je les enquiquine!** to hell with them! **3.** [importuner] : **se faire ~** to be hassled.
◆ **s'enquiquiner** *vpi fam* [s'ennuyer] to be bored (stiff).
◆ **s'enquiquiner à** *vp+prép fam* : **je ne vais pas m'~ à tout recopier** I can't be fagged *UK ou* bothered to copy it out again.

enquiquineur, euse [ɑ̃kikinœr, øz] *nm, f fam* pain, drag, nuisance.

enquis, e [ɑ̃ki, iz] *pp* ▷ **enquérir**.

enraciné, e [ɑ̃rasine] *adj* : **bien ~** [idée] firmly implanted *ou* entrenched ; [habitude] deeply ingrained ; [croyance] deep-seated, deep-rooted.

enracinement [ɑ̃rasinmɑ̃] *nm* **1.** BOT rooting **2.** *fig* [d'une opinion, d'une coutume] deep-rootedness.

enraciner [3] [ɑ̃rasine] *vt* **1.** BOT to root **2.** [fixer - dans un lieu, une culture] to root ▪ **se sentir profondément enraciné dans une culture** to feel deeply rooted in a culture **3.** [fixer dans l'esprit] to fix, to implant.

◆ **s'enraciner** *vpi* 1. BOT to root, to take root 2. [se fixer] to take root, to become firmly fixed ▪ **s'~ profondément dans une culture/l'esprit** to become deeply rooted in a culture/the mind.

enragé, e [ɑ̃raʒe] ◇ *adj* 1. MÉD rabid 2. [furieux] enraged, livid.
◇ *nm, f* 1. HIST [pendant la Révolution française] enragé ▪ [en 1968] militant student 2. [passionné] : **un ~ de : un ~ de football/ski/musique** a football/skiing/music fanatic.

enrageant, e [ɑ̃raʒɑ̃, ɑ̃t] *adj fam* maddening, infuriating.

enrager [17] [ɑ̃raʒe] *vi* [être en colère] to be furious *ou* infuriated ▪ **j'enrage de m'être laissé prendre** I'm enraged *ou* furious at having been caught ▪ **faire ~ qqn** [l'irriter] to annoy sb ; [le taquiner] to tease sb mercilessly.

enraie *etc v* ▷ **enrayer.**

enraiement [ɑ̃rɛmɑ̃], **enrayement** [ɑ̃rɛjmɑ̃] *nm* stopping, checking ▪ **l'~ d'une épidémie** checking the progress of an epidemic.

enrayage [ɑ̃rɛjaʒ] *nm* 1. ARM jamming 2. MÉCAN blocking.

enrayer [11] [ɑ̃reje] *vt* 1. ARM to jam 2. MÉCAN to block 3. [empêcher la progression de - processus] to check, to stop, to call a halt to ▪ **~ la crise** to halt the economic recession ▪ **~ l'inflation** to check *ou* to control *ou* to curb inflation ▪ **l'épidémie est enrayée** the epidemic has been halted.
◆ **s'enrayer** *vpi* to jam.

enrégimenter [3] [ɑ̃reʒimɑ̃te] *vt* to press-gang ▪ **~ qqn dans qqch** to press-gang sb into sthg.

enregistrable [ɑ̃rəʒistrabl] *adj* 1. ADMIN & DR receivable 2. AUDIO recordable.

enregistrement [ɑ̃rəʒistrəmɑ̃] *nm* 1. COMM [fait d'inscrire] booking ▪ [entrée] booking, entry 2. TRANSP [à l'aéroport] check-in ▪ [à la gare] registration 3. AUDIO recording ▪ **~ audio/vidéo/sur cassette** audio/video/cassette recording ▪ **~ numérique** digital recording 4. DR [fait de déclarer] registration, registering ▪ [entrée] entry 5. INFORM [informations] record ▪ [duplication] recording ▪ [consignation] logging 6. [diagramme] trace.
◆ **d'enregistrement** *loc adj* 1. COMM registration *(modif)* 2. INFORM [clef, tête, structure] format *(modif)* ▪ [densité, support] recording *(modif)* ▪ [unité] logging *(modif)*.

enregistrer [3] [ɑ̃rəʒistre] *vt* 1. [inscrire - opération, transaction, acte] to enter, to record ; [- déclaration] to register, to file ; [- note, mention] to log ; [- commande] to book (in) ▪ **~ un jugement** to enrol *UK ou* to enroll *US sout ou* to enter a judgement 2. [constater] to record, to note ▪ **l'entreprise a enregistré un bénéfice de...** the company showed a profit of... ▪ **on enregistre une baisse du dollar** the dollar has fallen in value 3. INFORM [fichier, dossier] to save 4. AUDIO [cassette audio, disque] to record, to tape ▪ [cassette vidéo] to record, to video, to video-tape ▪ **musique enregistrée** taped *ou* recorded music ▮ [pour commercialiser - disque, émission, dialogue] to record ▪ *(en usage absolu)* **ils sont en train d'~** they're doing *ou* making a recording 5. [afficher] to register, to record, to show ▪ **l'appareil n'a rien enregistré** nothing registered on the apparatus, the apparatus did not register anything 6. [retenir] to take in *(sép)* ▪ **d'accord, c'est enregistré** all right, I've got that ▪ *(en usage absolu)* **je lui ai dit mais il n'a pas enregistré** I told him but it didn't register *ou* he didn't take it in 7. TRANSP [à l'aéroport] to check in *(sép)* ▪ [à la gare] to register.

enregistreur, euse [ɑ̃rəʒistrœr, øz] *adj* recording *(modif)*.
◆ **enregistreur** *nm* recorder, recording device ▪ **~ de vol** flight recorder.

enrhumé, e [ɑ̃ryme] *adj* : **être ~** to have a cold.

enrhumer [3] [ɑ̃ryme] ◆ **s'enrhumer** *vpi* to catch cold, to get a cold.

enrichi, e [ɑ̃riʃi] *adj* 1. *péj* [personne] nouveau riche 2. [amélioré] enriched.

enrichir [32] [ɑ̃riʃir] *vt* 1. [rendre riche] to enrich, to make rich *ou* richer 2. [améliorer - savon, minerai, culture] to enrich ; [- esprit] to enrich, to improve ▪ **cette expérience m'a enrichi** I'm all the richer for that experience.
◆ **s'enrichir** ◇ *vpi* 1. [devenir riche] to grow rich *ou* richer, to become rich *ou* richer 2. [se développer - collection] to increase, to develop ; [- esprit] to be enriched, to grow.
◇ *vpt* : **s'~ l'esprit** to improve one's mind.

enrichissant, e [ɑ̃riʃisɑ̃, ɑ̃t] *adj* [rencontre] enriching ▪ [travail] rewarding ▪ [lecture] enriching, improving.

enrichissement [ɑ̃riʃismɑ̃] *nm* 1. [thésaurisation] becoming rich *ou* richer 2. [amélioration - d'un minerai, d'un sol, de l'esprit] improvement, improving 3. NUCL enrichment.

enrobage [ɑ̃rɔbaʒ] *nm* [d'un aliment] coating.

enrobé, e [ɑ̃rɔbe] *adj* [personne] plump, chubby.

enrober [3] [ɑ̃rɔbe] *vt* 1. [enduire] to coat ▪ **~ qqch de** to coat sthg with 2. [adoucir] to wrap *ou* to dress up *(sép)* ▪ **il a enrobé son reproche de mots affectueux** he wrapped his criticism in kind words.

enrochement [ɑ̃rɔʃmɑ̃] *nm* [gén] breakwater (made of loose boulders) ▪ TRAV PUB riprap.

enrôlé [ɑ̃role] *nm* enlisted private.

enrôlement [ɑ̃rolmɑ̃] *nm* 1. MIL enlistment 2. ADMIN & DR enrolment.

enrôler [3] [ɑ̃role] *vt* 1. MIL to enrol *UK*, to enroll *US*, to enlist ▪ *fig* **je vois que tu t'es fait ~ pour faire la vaisselle** I see you've been roped into doing the washing up 2. *fig* **~ qqn dans un parti/groupe** to recruit sb into a party/group 3. ADMIN & DR to enrol *UK*, to enroll *US*, to record.
◆ **s'enrôler** *vpi* to enrol *UK*, to enroll *US*, to enlist, to sign up.

enroué, e [ɑ̃rwe] *adj* : **je suis ~** I'm hoarse ▪ **d'une voix ~e** hoarsely.

enrouement [ɑ̃rumɑ̃] *nm* hoarseness.

enrouer [6] [ɑ̃rwe] ◆ **s'enrouer** *vpi* [de froid] to get hoarse ▪ [en forçant sa voix] to make o.s. hoarse.

enroulement [ɑ̃rulmɑ̃] *nm* 1. [mise en rouleau] rolling up, winding on 2. [volute] whorl, scroll 3. ÉLECTR [bobinage] winding ▪ [bobine] coil.

enrouler [3] [ɑ̃rule] *vt* 1. [mettre en rouleau - corde] to wind, to coil (up) ; [- ressort] to coil ; [- papier, tapis] to roll up *(sép)* ▪ **lierre enroulé autour d'un arbre** ivy twined *ou* wound round a tree 2. [envelopper] : **~ dans** to roll *ou* to wrap in.
◆ **s'enrouler** ◇ *vp (emploi réfléchi)* : **s'~ dans une couverture** to wrap o.s. up in a blanket.
◇ *vpi* [corde, fil] to be wound *ou* to wind (up) ▪ [serpent] to coil (itself).

enrouleur, euse [ɑ̃rulœr, øz] *adj* winding, coiling.
◆ **enrouleur** *nm* 1. [tambour] drum, reel 2. [galet] idle pulley, idler, roller ▪ **~ de ceinture automatique** automatic seat belt winder, inertia reel.
◆ **à enrouleur** *loc adj* self-winding.

enrubanner [3] [ɑ̃rybane] *vt* to decorate *ou* to adorn with ribbons.

ENS *npr f* = **École normale supérieure.**

ENSA [ɛnsa] *(abr de* **École nationale supérieure agronomique**) *nf one of five competitive-entry agricultural engineering schools.*

ensablement [ɑ̃sabləmɑ̃] *nm* [d'un bateau] running aground ▪ [d'un tuyau] choking (up) with sand ▪ [d'une route] sanding over ▪ [d'un port] silting up ▪ **il y a risque d'~** there is a risk of getting stuck in the sand.

ensabler [3] [ɑ̃sable] *vt* 1. [couvrir de sable] : **être ensablé** [port, estuaire] to be silted up ; [route, piste] to be covered in sand (drifts) 2. [enliser] : **une voiture ensablée** a car stuck in the sand.

◆ **s'ensabler** *vpi* **1.** [chenal] to silt up **2.** [véhicule] to get stuck in the sand **3.** [poisson] to bury itself in the sand.

ensacher [3] [ɑ̃saʃe] *vt* to bag, to sack.

ENSAD, Ensad [ɛnsad] (*abr de* **École nationale supérieure des arts décoratifs**) *npr f grande école for applied arts.*

ENSAM, Ensam [ɛnsam] (*abr de* **École nationale supérieure des arts et métiers**) *npr f grande école for engineering.*

ensanglanter [3] [ɑ̃sɑ̃glɑ̃te] *vt* **1.** [tacher] to bloody ■ **un mouchoir ensanglanté** a bloodstained handkerchief ■ **il entra, le visage ensanglanté** he came in with his face covered in blood **2.** [lieu, époque] to bathe in blood.

ENSBA (*abr de* **École nationale supérieure des Beaux-Arts**) *nf leading art school in Paris, knowed as "les Beaux-Arts".*

enseignant, e [ɑ̃sɛɲɑ̃, ɑ̃t] ◇ *adj* ▷ **corps.**
◇ *nm, f* teacher.

enseigne [ɑ̃sɛɲ] ◇ *nm* **1.** MIL : **~ de vaisseau 1ère classe** sub-lieutenant *UK*, lieutenant junior grade *US* ■ **~ de vaisseau 2e classe** midshipman *UK*, ensign *US* **2.** HIST [porte-drapeau] ensign.
◇ *nf* **1.** [panneau] sign ■ **~ lumineuse** *ou* **au néon** neon sign **2.** *litt* [étendard] ensign.

enseignement [ɑ̃sɛɲmɑ̃] *nm* **1.** [instruction] education ■ **~ assisté par ordinateur** computer-assisted learning ■ **~ par correspondance** correspondence courses **2.** [méthodes d'instruction] teaching (methods) **3.** [système scolaire] : **~ primaire/supérieur** primary/higher education ■ **~ privé** private education ■ **~ professionnel** vocational education ■ **~ public** state education *ou* schools ■ **l'~ du second degré** secondary education ■ **~ technique** technical education **4.** [profession] : **l'~** teaching, the teaching profession ■ **entrer dans l'~** to go into teaching ■ **travailler dans l'~** to work in education *ou* the teaching profession **5.** [leçon] lesson, teaching ■ **tirer un ~ de qqch** to learn (a lesson) from sthg.

enseigner [4] [ɑ̃seɲe] *vt* to teach ■ **~ qqch à qqn** to teach sb sthg *ou* sthg to sb ■ *(en usage absolu)* **elle enseigne depuis trois ans** she's been teaching for three years.

ensemble[1] [ɑ̃sɑ̃bl] *nm* **1.** [collection - d'objets] set, collection ; [- d'idées] set, series ; [- de données, d'informations, de textes] set, body, collection **2.** [totalité] whole ■ **la question dans son ~** the question as a whole ■ **l'~ de** : **l'~ des joueurs** all the players ■ **l'~ des réponses montre que...** the answers taken as a whole show that... ■ **il s'est adressé à l'~ des employés** he spoke to all the staff *ou* the whole staff **3.** [simultanéité] unity ■ **manquer d'~** to lack unity ■ **ils ont protesté dans un ~ parfait** they protested unanimously **4.** [groupe] group ◉ **~ instrumental** (instrumental) ensemble ■ **~ vocal** vocal group **5.** [vêtement] suit, outfit ■ **~ pantalon** trouser suit **6.** MATH set ■ **~ vide** empty set.
◆ **dans l'ensemble** *loc adv* on the whole, by and large, in the main.
◆ **d'ensemble** *loc adj* **1.** [général] overall, general ■ **mesures d'~** comprehensive *ou* global measures ■ **vue d'~** overall *ou* general view **2.** MUS : **faire de la musique d'~** to play in an ensemble.

ensemble[2] [ɑ̃sɑ̃bl] *adv* **1.** [l'un avec l'autre] together ■ **elles en sont convenues ~** they agreed (between themselves) ■ **nous en avons parlé ~** we spoke *ou* we had a talk about it ■ **aller bien ~** [vêtements, couleurs] to go well together ; [personnes] to be well-matched ■ **ils vont mal ~** [vêtements] they don't match ; [couple] they're ill-matched ■ **être bien/mal ~** to be on good/bad terms **2.** [en même temps] at once, at the same time.

ensemblier [ɑ̃sɑ̃blije] *nm* **1.** [décorateur] interior designer **2.** CINÉ & TV props assistant.

ensemencer [16] [ɑ̃səmɑ̃se] *vt* **1.** AGRIC to sow, to seed ■ **champ ensemencé de tournesols** field seeded *ou* sown with sunflowers **2.** PÊCHE to stock **3.** BIOL to culture.

enserrer [4] [ɑ̃sere] *vt* **1.** [agripper] to clutch, to grasp, to grip **2.** [être autour de - suj: col, bijou] to fit tightly around ■ **des fortifications enserrent la vieille ville** fortified walls form a tight circle around the old town.

ENSET, Enset [ɛnsɛt] (*abr de* **École nationale supérieure de l'enseignement technique**) *npr f grande école training science and technology teachers.*

ensevelir [32] [ɑ̃səvlir] *vt* **1.** *litt* [dans un linceul] to shroud, to enshroud *litt* ■ [dans la tombe] to entomb **2.** [enfouir] to bury ■ **l'éruption a enseveli plusieurs villages** the eruption buried several villages.
◆ **s'ensevelir dans** *vp+prép pr & fig* to bury o.s. in.

ensevelissement [ɑ̃səvlismɑ̃] *nm* **1.** *litt* [mise - dans un linceul] enshrouding ; [- au tombeau] entombment **2.** [disparition - d'une ruine, d'un souvenir] burying.

ENSI [ɛnsi] (*abr de* **École nationale supérieure d'ingénieurs**) *nf competitive-entry engineering institute.*

ensiler [3] [ɑ̃sile] *vt* to ensile, to silage.

ensileuse [ɑ̃siløz] *nf* silo filler.

en-soi [ɑ̃swa] *nm inv* : **l'~** the thing in itself.

ensoleillé, e [ɑ̃sɔleje] *adj* sunny, sunlit ■ **très ~** sun-drenched.

ensoleillement [ɑ̃sɔlɛjmɑ̃] *nm* (amount of) sunshine, insolation *spéc* ■ **l'~ annuel** the number of days of sunshine per year.

ensoleiller [4] [ɑ̃sɔleje] *vt* **1.** [donner du soleil à] to bathe in *ou* to fill with sunlight **2.** *fig* to brighten (up) ■ **cet enfant ensoleillait leur existence** that child was like a ray of sunshine in their lives.

ensommeillé, e [ɑ̃sɔmeje] *adj* sleepy, drowsy, dozy ■ **les yeux tout ~s** eyes heavy with sleep.

ensorcelant, e [ɑ̃sɔrsəlɑ̃, ɑ̃t] *adj* bewitching, entrancing, spellbinding.

ensorceler [24] [ɑ̃sɔrsəle] *vt* to bewitch, to cast a spell over ■ **elle m'a ensorcelé** I fell under her spell.

ensorceleur, euse [ɑ̃sɔrsəlœr, øz] ◇ *adj* bewitching, entrancing, spellbinding.
◇ *nm, f* **1.** [sorcier] enchanter (*f* enchantress), sorcerer (*f* sorceress) **2.** [charmeur] charmer.

ensorcelle *etc v* ▷ **ensorceler.**

ensorcellement [ɑ̃sɔrsɛlmɑ̃] *nm* bewitchment, enchantment ■ **elle ne pouvait résister à l'~ de ce pays étrange** she fell irresistibly under the spell of that strange country.

ensuit *v* ▷ **ensuivre.**

ensuite [ɑ̃sɥit] *adv* **1.** [dans le temps - puis] then, next ; [- plus tard] later, after, afterwards ■ **et ~, que s'est-il passé?** and what happened next?, and then what happened? ■ **ils ne sont arrivés qu'~** they didn't arrive until later ■ **ils se sont disputés, ~ de quoi on ne l'a jamais revu** they fell out, after which we didn't see him again **2.** [dans l'espace] then, further on.

ensuivre [89] [ɑ̃sɥivr] ◆ **s'ensuivre** *vpi* **1.** [en résulter] to follow, to ensue ■ **sa maladie et toutes les conséquences qui s'en sont suivies** his illness and all the ensuing consequences ■ *(tournure impersonnelle)* **il s'ensuit que** it follows that **2.** *litt* [venir après] to follow (on) **3.** *loc* **et tout ce qui s'ensuit** and so on (and so forth).

entablement [ɑ̃tabləmɑ̃] *nm* ARCHIT entablature.

entacher [3] [ɑ̃taʃe] *vt* **1.** [souiller] to sully, to soil **2.** [marquer] to mar ■ **une attitude entachée d'hypocrisie** an attitude marred by hypocrisy **3.** DR : **entaché de nullité** null.

entaille [ɑ̃taj] *nf* **1.** [encoche] notch, nick **2.** [blessure] gash, slash, cut ■ **petite ~** nick ■ **se faire une ~ au front** to gash one's forehead.

entailler [3] [ɑ̃taje] *vt* **1.** [fendre] to notch, to nick **2.** [blesser] to gash, to slash, to cut ■ **la lame lui a entaillé l'arcade sourcilière** the blade slashed his face above the eye.

entame [ɑ̃tam] *nf* **1.** [morceau - de viande] first slice *OU* cut ; [- de pain] crust **2.** JEUX opening.

entamer [3] [ɑ̃tame] *vt* **1.** [jambon, fromage] to start ▪ [bouteille, conserve] to open **2.** [durée, repas] to start, to begin ▪ [négociation] to launch, to start, to initiate ▪ [poursuites] to institute, to initiate **3.** [réduire - fortune, économies] to make a dent *OU* hole in ; [- résistance] to lower, to deal a blow to ; [- ligne ennemie] to break through **4.** [ébranler] to shake ▪ **rien ne peut ~ sa confiance en lui** nothing can shake *OU* undermine his self-confidence **5.** [user] to damage ▪ **l'acide entame le fer** acid eats into *OU* corrodes metal **6.** [écorcher - peau] to graze **7.** JEUX to open.

entartrage [ɑ̃tartraʒ] *nm* **1.** [d'une chaudière, d'un tuyau] scaling, furring (up) *UK* **2.** [d'une dent - processus] scaling ; [- état] scale, tartar deposit.

entartré [ɑ̃tartre] *adj* [fer à repasser] scaled ▪ [chauffe-eau] furred.

entartrer [3] [ɑ̃tartre] *vt* **1.** [chaudière, tuyau] to scale, to fur (up) *UK* **2.** [dent] to cover with tartar *OU* scale.
◆ **s'entartrer** *vpi* **1.** [chaudière, tuyau] to scale, to fur up *UK* **2.** [dent] to become covered in tartar *OU* scale.

entassement [ɑ̃tasmɑ̃] *nm* **1.** [amas] heap, pile, stack ▪ [mise en tas] heaping *OU* piling up, stacking **2.** [fait de s'agglutiner] crowding ▪ **l'~ des voyageurs dans le wagon** the crowding of passengers into the carriage.

entasser [3] [ɑ̃tase] *vt* **1.** [mettre en tas] to heap *OU* to pile *OU* to stack (up) ▪ **~ de la terre** to heap up *OU* to bank up earth **2.** [accumuler - vieilleries, journaux] to pile *OU* to heap (up) ▪ **elle entasse toutes ses affaires dans cette pièce** she piles up *OU* stores all her stuff in this room **3.** [thésauriser - fortune, argent] to pile up *(sép)*, to heap up *(sép)* **4.** [serrer] to cram *OU* to pack (in) ▪ **ils vivent entassés à quatre dans une seule pièce** the four of them live in one cramped room.
◆ **s'entasser** *vpi* [neige, terre] to heap *OU* to pile up, to bank ▪ [vieilleries, journaux] to heap *OU* to pile up ▪ [personnes] to crowd (in) *OU* together, to pile in ▪ **s'~ dans une voiture** to pile into a car.

ente [ɑ̃t] *nf* [greffon] scion ▪ [greffe] graft.

entendement [ɑ̃tɑ̃dmɑ̃] *nm* comprehension, understanding ▪ **cela dépasse l'~** it's beyond all comprehension *OU* understanding.

entendeur [ɑ̃tɑ̃dœr] *nm* : **à bon ~ salut** *prov* a word to the wise is enough *prov*.

entendre [73] [ɑ̃tɑ̃dr] *vt* **1.** [percevoir par l'ouïe] to hear ▪ **parlez plus fort, on n'entend rien** speak up, we can't hear a word (you're saying) ▪ **silence, je ne veux pas vous ~!** quiet, I don't want to hear a sound from you! ▪ **tu entends ce que je te dis?** do you hear me? ▪ **elle a dû m'~ le lui dire** she must have overheard me telling him ▪ **j'entends pleurer à côté** I can hear someone crying next door ▪ **~ dire** to hear ▪ **j'ai entendu dire qu'il était parti** I heard that he had left ▪ **c'est la première fois que j'entends (dire) ça** that's the first I've heard of it ▪ **je ne connais l'Islande que par ce que j'en ai entendu dire** I only know Iceland through what I've heard other people say about it ▪ **~ parler de** to hear about *OU* of ▪ **il ne veut pas ~ parler d'informatique** he won't hear of computers ▪ **je ne veux plus ~ parler de lui** I don't want to hear him mentioned again ▪ **on n'entend parler que de lui/de sa pièce** he's/his play's the talk of the town ▪ **vous n'avez pas fini d'en ~ parler!** you haven't heard the last of this! ▪ *(en usage absolu)* **j'entends mal de l'oreille droite** my hearing's bad in the right ear ▶ **on entendrait/on aurait entendu voler une mouche** you could hear/could have heard a pin drop ▪ **j'aurai tout entendu!** whatever next? ▪ **j'en ai entendu de belles** *OU* **de bonnes** *OU* **des vertes et des pas mûres sur son compte** *fam* I've heard a thing or two about him ▪ **ce qu'il faut ~!, ce qu'il faut pas ~!** *fam* the things some people come out with!, the things you hear! ▪ **il vaut mieux ~ ça que d'être sourd!** *fam* what a load of rubbish *UK OU* hogwash *US*!
2. [écouter] to hear, to listen to ▪ **essayer de se faire ~** to try to make o.s. heard ▪ **il ne veut rien ~** he won't listen ▶ **à l'~, à les ~ : à les ~ tout serait de ma faute** to hear them talk *OU* according to them it's all my fault ▪ **~ raison** to see sense ▪ **faire ~ raison à qqn** to make sb listen to reason, to bring sb to his/her senses ▪ **il va m'~!** I'll give him hell!
3. [accepter - demande] to agree to *(insép)* ; [- vœu] to grant ▪ **nos prières ont été entendues** our prayers were answered
4. RELIG : **~ la messe** to attend *OU* to hear mass ▪ **~ une confession** to hear *OU* to take a confession
5. DR [témoin] to hear, to interview
6. *sout* [comprendre] to understand ▪ **entend-il la plaisanterie?** can he take a joke? ▪ **il doit être bien entendu que...** it must be properly understood that... ▪ **donner qqch à ~** *OU* **laisser ~ qqch à qqn : elle m'a laissé** *OU* **donné à ~ que...** she gave me to understand that... ▪ **~ qqch à : y entendez-vous quelque chose?** do you know anything about it? ▪ *(en usage absolu)* **j'entends bien** I (do) understand ▶ **n'y ~ rien** *OU* **goutte** *vieilli* **: je n'y entends rien en politique** I don't understand a thing about politics ▪ **il ne l'entend pas de cette oreille** he won't have any of it
7. [apprendre] to hear
8. [vouloir dire] to mean ▶ **y ~ finesse** *OU* **malice** *vieilli* **: sans y ~ malice** without meaning any harm (by it)
9. [vouloir] to want, to intend ▪ **fais comme tu l'entends** do as you wish *OU* please ▪ **j'entends qu'on m'obéisse** I intend to *OU* I mean to *OU* I will be obeyed ▪ **il entend bien partir demain** he's determined to go tomorrow.
◆ **s'entendre** ◇ *vp (emploi passif)* **1.** [être perçu] to be heard ▪ **cela s'entend de loin** you can hear it *OU* it can be heard from far off ▮ [être utilisé - mot, expression] to be heard ▪ **cela s'entend encore dans la région** you can still hear it said *OU* used around here
2. [être compris] to be understood ▪ **ces chiffres s'entendent hors taxes** these figures do not include tax ▪ **(cela) s'entend** [c'est évident] obviously, it's obvious, that much is clear ▪ **après l'hiver, (cela) s'entend** when the winter is over, of course *OU* it goes without saying.
◇ *vp (emploi réciproque)* **1.** [pouvoir s'écouter] to hear each other *OU* one another
2. [s'accorder] to agree ▪ **s'~ sur un prix** to agree on a price ▪ **entendons-nous bien** let's get this straight
3. [sympathiser] to get on ▶ **s'~ comme chien et chat** to fight like cat and dog ▪ **s'~ comme larrons en foire** to be as thick as thieves.
◇ *vp (emploi réfléchi)* **1.** [percevoir sa voix] to hear o.s. ▪ **on ne s'entend plus tellement il y a de bruit** there's so much noise, you can't hear yourself think ▪ **tu ne t'entends pas!** you should hear yourself (talking)!, if (only) you could hear yourself!
2. *loc* **quand je dis qu'il est grand, je m'entends, il est plus grand que moi** when I say he's tall I really mean he's taller than myself.
◇ *vpi* : **s'y ~** [s'y connaître] : **il s'y entend en mécanique** he's good at *OU* he knows (a lot) about mechanics ▪ **s'y ~ pour** to know how to.
◆ **s'entendre avec** *vp+prép* **1.** [s'accorder avec] to reach an agreement with ▪ **parvenir à s'~ avec qqn sur qqch** to come to an understanding *OU* to reach an agreement with sb about sthg
2. [sympathiser avec] to get on with.

entendu, e [ɑ̃tɑ̃dy] *adj* **1.** [complice - air, sourire] knowing ▪ **hocher la tête d'un air ~** to nod knowingly **2.** [convenu] agreed ▪ **(c'est) ~, je viendrai** all right *OU* very well, I'll come.

entente [ɑ̃tɑ̃t] *nf* **1.** [harmonie] harmony ▪ **il y a une bonne ~ entre eux** they're on good terms (with each other) ▪ **vivre en bonne ~** to live in harmony **2.** POLIT agreement, understanding ▪ **arriver à une ~ sur** to come to an understanding *OU* agreement over ▮ ÉCON agreement, accord ▪ **~ entre producteurs** agreement between producers ▶ **~ industrielle** cartel, combine **3.** HIST : **l'Entente cordiale** the Entente Cordiale.
◆ **à double entente** *loc adj* ambiguous ▪ **c'est à double ~** it's ambiguous *OU* a double entendre.

enter [3] [ɑ̃te] *vt* **1.** CONSTR to scarf **2.** HORT to graft.

entérinement [ɑ̃terinmɑ̃] *nm* **1.** DR ratification **2.** [acceptation - d'un usage] confirmation, ratification, adoption ; [- d'un état de fait] acceptance, approval.

entériner [3] [ɑ̃terine] *vt* **1.** DR to ratify, to confirm **2.** [approuver - usage] to adopt ; [- état de fait, situation] to go along with, to assent to *sout.*

entérite [ɑ̃terit] *nf* enteritis.

enterrement [ɑ̃tɛrmɑ̃] *nm* **1.** [funérailles] funeral ▪ **cette soirée, c'était un ~ de première classe** it was like watching paint dry, that party **2.** [ensevelissement] burial **3.** [cortège] funeral procession **4.** [abandon - d'une idée, d'une dispute] burying ; [- d'un projet] shelving, laying aside.
◆ **d'enterrement** *loc adj* [mine, tête] gloomy, glum ▪ **faire une tête d'~** to wear a gloomy *ou* long expression.

enterrer [4] [ɑ̃tere] *vt* **1.** [ensevelir] to bury ▪ **être enterré vivant** to be buried alive **2.** [inhumer] to bury, to inter *sout* ▪ **vous nous enterrerez tous** you'll outlive us all ➊ **~ sa vie de garçon** to celebrate one's last night as a bachelor, to hold a stag party **3.** [oublier - scandale] to bury, to hush (up) ; [- souvenir, passé, querelle] to bury, to forget (about) ; [- projet] to shelve, to lay aside.
◆ **s'enterrer** *vp (emploi réfléchi) pr* to bury o.s. ▪ *fig* to hide o.s. away.

entêtant, e [ɑ̃tɛtɑ̃, ɑ̃t] *adj* heady.

en-tête [ɑ̃tɛt] *nm* **1.** [sur du papier à lettres] letterhead, heading **2.** IMPR head, heading **3.** INFORM header.
◆ **à en-tête** *loc adj* [papier, bristol] headed ▪ **papier à ~ de la compagnie** company notepaper.
◆ **en en-tête de** *loc prép* at the head *ou* top of ▪ **mettez l'adresse en ~ de la lettre** put the address at the top of the letter.

entêté, e [ɑ̃tete] ◇ *adj* obstinate, stubborn.
◇ *nm, f* stubborn *ou* obstinate person.

entêtement [ɑ̃tɛtmɑ̃] *nm* stubbornness, obstinacy.

entêter [4] [ɑ̃tete] *vt* to make dizzy ▪ **ce parfum m'entête** I find this perfume quite intoxicating.
◆ **s'entêter** *vpi* : **s'~ à faire** to persist in doing ▪ **s'~ dans : s'~ dans l'erreur** to persist in one's error.

enthousiasmant, e [ɑ̃tuzjasmɑ̃, ɑ̃t] *adj* exciting, thrilling.

enthousiasme [ɑ̃tuzjasm] *nm* enthusiasm, keenness ▪ **être plein d'~, déborder d'~** to be full of *ou* to be bubbling with enthusiasm ▪ **avec ~** enthusiastically.

enthousiasmer [3] [ɑ̃tuzjasme] *vt* to fill with enthusiasm ▪ **cela n'avait pas l'air de l'~** he didn't seem very enthusiastic (about it).
◆ **s'enthousiasmer** *vpi* : **il s'enthousiasme facilement** he's easily carried away ▪ **s'~ pour qqn/qqch** to be enthusiastic about sb/sthg.

enthousiaste [ɑ̃tuzjast] ◇ *adj* enthusiastic, keen ▪ **trop ~** overenthusiastic.
◇ *nmf* enthusiast.

entiché, e [ɑ̃tiʃe] *adj* : **être ~ de** to be wild about.

enticher [3] [ɑ̃tiʃe] ◆ **s'enticher de** *vp+prép* : **s'~ de qqn** [s'amouracher de qqn] to become infatuated with sb ▪ **s'~ de qqch** [s'enthousiasmer pour qqch] to become very keen on sthg.

entier, ère [ɑ̃tje, ɛr] *adj* **1.** [complet] whole, entire ▪ **une semaine entière** a whole *ou* an entire week ▪ **pendant des journées/des heures entières** for days/hours on end ▪ **dans le monde ~** in the whole world, throughout the world ▪ **payer place entière** to pay the full price ▪ **tout ~, tout entière : je le voulais tout ~ pour moi** I wanted him all to myself ▪ **tout ~ à, tout entière à : être tout ~ à son travail** to be completely wrapped up *ou* engrossed in one's work **2.** *(avant le n)* [en intensif] absolute, complete ▪ **donner entière satisfaction à qqn** to give sb complete satisfaction **3.** *(après le verbe)* [intact] intact ▪ **la difficulté reste entière** the problem remains unresolved **4.** [absolu - personne] : **c'est quelqu'un de très ~** she is someone of great integrity **5.** CULIN [lait] full-cream *UK*, whole **6.** MATH : **nombre ~** integer, whole number **7.** VÉTÉR entire.
◆ **entier** *nm* MATH [nombre] integer, whole number.
◆ **dans son entier** *loc adv* as a whole ▪ **l'industrie automobile dans son ~** the car industry as a whole.
◆ **en entier** *loc adv* : **manger un gâteau en ~** to eat a whole *ou* an entire cake ▪ **je l'ai lu en ~** I read all of it, I read the whole of it, I read it right through.

entièrement [ɑ̃tjɛrmɑ̃] *adv* entirely, completely ▪ **le bureau a été ~ refait** the office has been completely refitted ▪ **la maison avait été construite ~ en pierre de taille** the house had been made entirely of freestone ▪ **je l'ai ~ lu** I read all of it, I read the whole of it, I read it (all) through ▪ **tu as ~ raison** you're quite *ou* absolutely right ▪ **tu n'as pas ~ tort** there's some truth in what you say.

entièreté [ɑ̃tjɛrte] *nf* entirety.

entité [ɑ̃tite] *nf* [abstraction] entity.

entoiler [3] [ɑ̃twale] *vt* **1.** [renforcer] to mount on canvas **2.** [recouvrir] to cover with canvas.

entôler [3] △ [ɑ̃tole] *vt* to fleece.

entomologie [ɑ̃tɔmɔlɔʒi] *nf* entomology.

entomologiste [ɑ̃tɔmɔlɔʒist] *nmf* entomologist.

entonner [3] [ɑ̃tɔne] *vt* **1.** [hymne, air] to strike up *(insép)*, to start singing ▪ **~ les louanges de qqn** to start singing sb's praises **2.** [vin] to barrel.

entonnoir [ɑ̃tɔnwar] *nm* **1.** [ustensile] funnel **2.** GÉOGR sinkhole, swallow hole **3.** [trou d'obus] shell-hole, crater.

entorse [ɑ̃tɔrs] *nf* **1.** [foulure] sprain ▪ **se faire une ~ au poignet** to sprain one's wrist **2.** [exception] infringement (of) ▪ **faire une ~ au règlement** to bend the rules ▪ **faire une ~ à son régime** to break one's diet.

entortiller [3] [ɑ̃tɔrtije] *vt* **1.** [enrouler - ruban, mouchoir] to twist, to wrap **2.** [compliquer] : **être entortillé** to be convoluted **3.** *fam* [tromper] to hoodwink, to con ▪ **se faire ~** to be taken in.
◆ **s'entortiller** *vpi* **1.** [s'enrouler - lierre] to twist, to wind **2.** [être empêtré] to get caught *ou* tangled up ▪ **s'~ dans ses explications** to get tangled up in one's explanations.

entourage [ɑ̃turaʒ] *nm* [gén] circle ▪ [d'un roi, d'un président] entourage ▪ **~ familial** family circle ▪ **on dit dans l'~ du Président que...** sources close to the President say that...

entouré, e [ɑ̃ture] *adj* **1.** [populaire] : **une actrice très ~e** an actress who is very popular *ou* who is the centre of attraction **2.** [par des amis] : **heureusement, elle est très ~e** fortunately, she has a lot of friends around her.

entourer [3] [ɑ̃ture] *vt* **1.** [encercler - terrain, mets] to surround ▪ **~ qqch/qqn de : ~ un champ de barbelés** to surround a field with barbed wire, to put barbed wire around a field ▪ **~ un mot de *ou* en rouge** to circle a word in red ▪ **~ qqn de ses bras** to put *ou* to wrap one's arms around sb **2.** [environner] : **le monde qui nous entoure** the world around us *ou* that surrounds us **3.** [graviter autour de - suj: foule, conseillers] to surround, to be around **4.** [soutenir - malade, veuve] to rally round *(insép)* ▪ **~ un ami de son affection** to surround a friend with affection.
◆ **s'entourer de** *vp+prép* **1.** [placer autour de soi] to surround o.s. with, to be surrounded by ▪ *(en usage absolu)* **savoir s'~** to know all the right people **2.** [vivre au sein de] : **s'~ de mystère** to shroud o.s. in mystery ▪ **s'~ de beaucoup de précautions** to take elaborate precautions.

entourloupe [ɑ̃turlup], **entourloupette** [ɑ̃turlupɛt] *nf fam* nasty *ou* dirty trick ▪ **faire une ~ à qqn** to play a dirty trick on sb.

entournure [ɑ̃turnyr] *nf* armhole.

entracte [ɑ̃trakt] *nm* **1.** CINÉ & THÉÂTRE interval *UK*, intermission *US* ▪ **à *ou* pendant l'~** in the interval *UK*, during the intermission *US* **2.** [spectacle] interlude, entr'acte **3.** [pause] break, interlude.

entraide [ɑ̃trɛd] *nf* mutual aid ▪ **comité d'~** ADMIN support committee.

entraider [4] [ɑ̃trede] ◆ **s'entraider** *vp (emploi réciproque)* to help one another *ou* each other.

entrailles [ɑ̃traj] *nfpl* **1.** ANAT & ZOOL entrails, guts ▪ **être pris aux ~** [être ému] to be stirred to the depths of one's soul **2.** *litt* [ventre] womb **3.** [profondeur - de la terre] depths, bowels ; [- d'un piano, d'un navire] innards.

entrain [ɑ̃trɛ̃] *nm* **1.** [fougue] spirit ▪ **avoir beaucoup d'~, être plein d'~** to be full of life *ou* energy ▪ **retrouver son ~** to cheer *ou* to brighten up again **2.** [animation] liveliness ▪ **la fête manquait d'~** the party wasn't very lively.
◆ **avec entrain** *loc adv* with gusto, enthusiastically.
◆ **sans entrain** *loc adv* half-heartedly, unenthusiastically.

entraînable [ɑ̃trɛnabl] *adj* : **facilement ~** easily influenced.

entraînant, e [ɑ̃trɛnɑ̃, ɑ̃t] *adj* [chanson] catchy, swinging ▪ [rythme] swinging, lively ▪ [style, éloquence] rousing, stirring.

entraînement [ɑ̃trɛnmɑ̃] *nm* **1.** [d'un sportif] training, coaching ▪ [d'un cheval] training ▪ **séance d'~** training session ▪ **manquer d'~** to be out of training **2.** [habitude] practice ▪ **il ne faut pas de technique spéciale, juste un peu d'~** there's no need for any special skills, just some practice **3.** MÉCAN drive ▪ **~ à chaîne/par courroie** chain/belt drive.
◆ **d'entraînement** *loc adj* **1.** ÉQUIT & SPORT [séance, matériel] training *(modif)* ▪ **camp d'~ militaire** military training camp **2.** MÉCAN drive *(modif)*.

entraîner [4] [ɑ̃trene] *vt* **1.** [emporter] to carry *ou* to sweep along *(sép)* ▪ *fig* to carry away *(sép)* ▪ **entraînés par la foule** swept along by the crowd ▪ **se laisser ~ par la musique** to let o.s. be carried away by the music ▪ **cette discussion nous entraînerait trop loin** that discussion would carry *ou* take us too far ▮ [tirer - wagons] to pull, to haul ▪ [actionner - bielle] to drive ▪ **poulie entraînée par une courroie** belt-driven pulley **2.** [conduire] to drag (along) ▪ **c'est lui qui m'a entraîné dans cette affaire** he's the one who dragged me into this mess ▪ **ce sont les grands qui les entraînent à faire des bêtises** it's the older children who encourage them to be naughty ❯ **~ qqn dans sa chute** *pr* to pull *ou* to drag sb down in one's fall ; *fig* to pull sb down with one **3.** [occasionner] to bring about *(sép)*, to lead to *(insép)*, to involve ▪ **cela risque d'~ de gros frais** this is likely to involve heavy expenditure **4.** ÉQUIT & SPORT [équipe, boxeur] to train, to coach ▪ [cheval] to train.
◆ **s'entraîner** *vpi* SPORT to train ▪ **s'~ pour les** *ou* **en vue des jeux Olympiques** to be in training *ou* to train for the Olympic Games ▪ **s'~ à faire qqch** [gén] to teach o.s. to do sthg ; SPORT to train o.s. to do sthg.

entraîneur, euse [ɑ̃trɛnœr, øz] *nm, f* [d'un cheval] trainer ▪ [d'un sportif] trainer, coach ▪ **~ d'hommes** *fig* leader of men.
◆ **entraîneuse** *nf* : **~ (de bar)** hostess *(in a bar)*.

entrant, e [ɑ̃trɑ̃, ɑ̃t] ◇ *adj* incoming.
◇ *nm, f* **1.** SPORT substitute **2.** [celui qui entre] : **les ~s et les sortants** those who go in and those who come out.

entrapercevoir, entr'apercevoir [52] [ɑ̃trapɛrsəvwar] *vt* to catch a (fleeting) glimpse of.

entrave [ɑ̃trav] *nf* **1.** [obstacle] hindrance, obstacle ▪ **cette mesure est une ~ au libre-échange** this measure is an obstacle *ou* a hindrance to free trade **2.** [chaîne - d'esclave] chain, fetter, shackle ; [- de cheval] shackle, fetter ▪ **mettre des ~s à un cheval** to fetter a horse.
◆ **sans entraves** *loc adj* unfettered.

entravé, e [ɑ̃trave] *adj* **1.** [vêtement] hobble *(modif)* **2.** PHON checked.

entraver [3] [ɑ̃trave] *vt* **1.** [gêner - circulation] to hold up *(sép)* **2.** [contrecarrer - initiative, projet] to hinder, to hamper, to get in the way of ▪ **~ une négociation** to hamper negotiations **3.** [attacher - esclave] to put in chains ; [- cheval] to fetter, to shackle **4.** △ *arg crime* **j'y entrave rien** *ou* **que dalle** *ou* **que couic** I don't get this at all.

entre [ɑ̃tr] *prép* **1.** [dans l'espace] between ▪ [dans] in ▪ [à travers] through, between ▪ **Lyon est à la cinquième place, ~ Marseille et Bordeaux** Lyons is in fifth place, between Marseilles and Bordeaux ▪ **tenir qqch ~ ses mains** to hold sthg in one's hands ▪ **ce sont deux moitiés de génoise avec du chocolat ~** it's two halves of sponge cake with chocolate in between ▪ **il passa la main ~ les barreaux** he put his hand through the bars **2.** [dans le temps] between ▪ **~ le travail et le transport, je n'ai plus de temps à moi** between work and travel, I haven't any time left
3. [indiquant un état intermédiaire] : **une couleur ~ le jaune et le vert** a colour between yellow and green ▪ **elle était ~ le rire et les larmes** she didn't know whether to laugh or cry ▪ **le cidre est doux ou sec? – ~ les deux** is the cider sweet or dry? – it's between the two *ou* in between ▪ **c'était bien? – ~ les deux** *fam* was it good? – so-so
4. [exprimant une approximation] between ▪ **il y a ~ 10 et 12 km** it's between 10 and 12 kms ▪ **les températures oscilleront ~ 10° et 15°** temperatures will range from 10° to 15° ▪ **ils ont invité ~ 15 et 20 personnes** they've invited 15 to 20 people
5. [parmi] among ▪ **partagez le gâteau ~ les enfants** [entre deux] share the cake between the children ; [entre plusieurs] share the cake among the children ▪ **ceux d'~ vous qui désireraient venir** those among you *ou* of you who'd like to come ▪ **lequel est le plus âgé d'~ vous?** who is the oldest amongst you? ▪ **tu as le choix ~ trois réponses** you've got a choice of three answers ▪ **je me souvenais de ce jour ~ tous** I remembered that day above all others ▪ **je le reconnaîtrais ~ tous** [personne] I'd know him anywhere ; [objet] I couldn't fail to recognize it ▪ **brave ~ les braves** bravest of the brave
6. [dans un groupe] : **parle, nous sommes ~ amis** you can talk, we're among friends *ou* we're all friends here ▪ **on se réunit ~ anciens combattants** we've got together a gathering of veterans ▪ **nous ferons une petite fête, juste ~ nous** [à deux] we'll have a small party, just the two of us ; [à plusieurs] we'll have a party, just among ourselves ▪ **ils ont tendance à rester ~ eux** they tend to keep themselves to themselves ▪ **~ nous, il n'a pas tort** [à deux] between you and me, he's right ; [à plusieurs] between us, he's right ▪ **~ vous et moi** between you and me
7. [indiquant une relation] between ▪ **les clans se battent ~ eux** the clans fight (against) each other, there are fights between the clans ▪ **qu'y a-t-il ~ vous?** what is there between you?
◆ **entre autres** *loc adv* : **sa fille, ~ autres, n'est pas venue** his daughter, for one *ou* among others, didn't come ▪ **sont exposés, ~ autres, des objets rares, des œuvres de jeunesse du peintre, etc.** the exhibition includes, among other things, rare objects, examples of the artist's early work etc.

entrebâillement [ɑ̃trəbajmɑ̃] *nm* : **dans/par l'~ de la porte** in/through the half-open door.

entrebâiller [3] [ɑ̃trəbaje] *vt* [porte, fenêtre] to half-open ▪ **laisse la porte entrebâillée** leave the door half-open *ou* ajar.

entrebâilleur [ɑ̃trəbajœr] *nm* door chain.

entrechat [ɑ̃trəʃa] *nm* **1.** DANSE entrechat **2.** *hum* [bond] leap, spring.

entrechoquer [3] [ɑ̃trəʃɔke] *vt* to knock *ou* to bang together.
◆ **s'entrechoquer** *vp (emploi réciproque)* **1.** [se heurter - verres] to clink (together) ; [- épées] to clash (together) ; [- dents] to chatter **2.** [affluer - images, mots] to jostle together.

entrecôte [ɑ̃trəkot] *nf* entrecôte (steak) ▪ **~ minute** minute steak.

entrecoupé, e [ɑ̃trəkupe] *adj* [voix] broken.

entrecouper [3] [ɑ̃trəkupe] *vt* **1.** [interrompre] : **la conversation a été entrecoupée de sonneries de téléphone** the phone kept interrupting the conversation ▪ **une voix entrecoupée de sanglots** a voice broken by sobs **2.** [émailler] : **~ qqch de** to intersperse *ou* to pepper sthg with.
◆ **s'entrecouper** *vp (emploi réciproque)* to intersect.

entrecroisement [ɑ̃trəkrwazmɑ̃] *nm* intertwining, intersecting.

entrecroiser [3] [ɑ̃trəkrwaze] *vt* to intertwine.
◆ **s'entrecroiser** *vp (emploi réciproque)* to intersect.

entre-déchirer [3] [ɑ̃trədeʃire] ◆ **s'entre-déchirer** *vp (emploi réciproque)* *pr* & *fig* to tear one another to pieces.

entre-deux [ɑ̃trədø] *nm inv* **1.** [dans l'espace] space between, interspace **2.** [dans le temps] intervening period, period in between **3.** SPORT jump ball **4.** [meuble] console table *(placed between two windows)*.

entre-deux-guerres [ɑ̃trədøgɛr] *nm inv & nf inv* : **l'~** the interwar period.

entre-dévorer [3] [ɑ̃trədevɔre] ◆ **s'entre-dévorer** *vp (emploi réciproque) pr* to devour one another ■ *fig* to tear one another to pieces.

entrée [ɑ̃tre] *nf* **1.** [arrivée] entrance, entry ■ **à son ~, tout le monde s'est levé** everybody stood up as she walked in *ou* entered ■ **faire une ~ discrète** to enter discreetly ■ **il a fait une ~ remarquée** he made quite an entrance, he made a dramatic entrance ■ **faire son ~ dans le monde** [demoiselle] to come out, to make one's debut in society ■ **~ en** : **~ en action** coming into play ■ **dès son ~ en fonction, il devra...** as soon as he takes up office, he will have to... ■ **l'~ en guerre de la France** France's entry into *ou* France's joining the war ■ **~ en matière** [d'un livre] introduction ■ **l'~ en vigueur d'une loi** the implementation of a law ■ **date d'~ en vigueur** commencement **2.** THÉÂTRE entrance ■ **~ en scène** entrance ■ **au moment de mon ~ en scène** as I made my entrance *ou* as I walked on stage ■ **rater son ~** to miss one's cue
3. [adhésion] entry, admission ■ **l'~ de l'Espagne dans le Marché commun** Spain's entry into the Common Market ■ **au moment de l'~ à l'université** when students start university
4. [accès] entry, admission ■ **l'~ est gratuite pour les enfants** there is no admission charge for children ■ **'entrée'** 'way in' ■ **'~ libre'** [dans un magasin] 'no obligation to buy' ; [dans un musée] 'free admission' ■ **'~ interdite'** [dans un local] 'no entry', 'keep out' ; [pour empêcher le passage] 'no way in', 'no access' ; [dans un bois] 'no trespassing' ■ **'~ interdite à tout véhicule'** 'pedestrians only' ■ **'~ réservée au personnel'** 'staff only' ■ **avoir ses ~s** : **avoir ses ~s auprès de qqn** to have (privileged) access to sb ■ **avoir ses ~s dans un club** to be a welcome visitor to a club
5. [voie d'accès - à un immeuble] entrance (door) ; [- à un tunnel, une grotte] entry, entrance, mouth ■ **~ des artistes** stage door ■ **~ principale** main entrance ■ **~ de service** service *ou* tradesmen's entrance
6. [vestibule - dans un lieu public] entrance (hall), lobby ; [- dans une maison] hall, hallway
7. LOISIRS [billet] ticket ■ [spectateur] spectator ■ [visiteur] visitor ■ **le film a fait deux millions d'~s** two million people have seen the film
8. CULIN first course, starter ■ [dans un repas de gala] entrée
9. INFORM : **~ des données** [gén] inputting of data, data input ; [par saisie] keying in *ou* keyboarding of data
10. [inscription] entry ■ [dans un dictionnaire] headword, entry word *US* ■ **faire une ~ dans un registre** to enter an item into a register
11. TECHNOL : **~ d'air** air inlet
12. MUS entry.
◆ **entrées** *nfpl* [en comptabilité] receipts, takings.
◆ **à l'entrée de** *loc prép* **1.** [dans l'espace] at the entrance *ou* on the threshold of ■ **à l'~ de la grotte** at the entrance *ou* mouth of the cave
2. *litt* [dans le temps] at the beginning of.
◆ **d'entrée, d'entrée de jeu** *loc adv* from the outset, right from the beginning.

entrefaites [ɑ̃trəfɛt] *nfpl* : **sur ces ~** at that moment *ou* juncture.

entrefilet [ɑ̃trəfilɛ] *nm* short piece, paragraph *(in a newspaper)* ■ **l'affaire a eu droit à un ~** there was a paragraph *ou* there were a few lines in the newspaper about it.

entregent [ɑ̃trəʒɑ̃] *nm* : **avoir de l'~** to know how to handle people.

entr'égorger [17] [ɑ̃tregɔrʒe] ◆ **s'entr'égorger** *vp (emploi réciproque)* to cut one another's throats.

entrejambe [ɑ̃trəʒɑ̃b] *nm* crotch.

entrelacer [16] [ɑ̃trəlase] *vt* to intertwine, to interlace ■ **initiales entrelacées** intertwined initials.
◆ **s'entrelacer** *vp (emploi réciproque)* to intertwine, to interlace.

entrelacs [ɑ̃trəla] *nm* interlacing.

entrelardé, e [ɑ̃trəlarde] *adj* [rôti] larded ■ [tranche de poitrine] streaky.

entrelarder [3] [ɑ̃trəlarde] *vt* **1.** CULIN to lard **2.** [entrecouper] : **~ qqch de** to intersperse *ou* to interlard sthg with.

entremêler [4] [ɑ̃trəmele] *vt* **1.** [mêler - rubans, fleurs] to intermingle, to mix together *(sép)* **2.** [entrecouper] : **~ qqch de** : **paroles entremêlées de sanglots** words broken with sobs.
◆ **s'entremêler** *vp (emploi réciproque)* [fils, cheveux] to become entangled ■ [idées, intrigues] to become intermingled.

entremet *etc v* ▷ **entremettre.**

entremets [ɑ̃trəmɛ] *nm* entremets.

entremetteur, euse [ɑ̃trəmɛtœr, øz] *nm, f* **1.** *vieilli* [intermédiaire] mediator, go-between **2.** *péj* [dans des affaires galantes] procurer (*f* procuress).

entremettre [84] [ɑ̃trəmɛtr] ◆ **s'entremettre** *vpi* [à bon escient] to intervene ■ [à mauvais escient] to interfere.

entremise [ɑ̃trəmiz] *nf* intervention, intervening *(U)* ■ **offrir son ~** to offer to act as mediator.
◆ **par l'entremise de** *loc prép* through.

entremit *etc v* ▷ **entremettre.**

entrepont [ɑ̃trəpɔ̃] *nm* steerage.

entreposage [ɑ̃trəpozaʒ] *nm* [gén] storing *(U)*, storage.

entreposé [ɑ̃trəpoze] *adj* : **marchandises ~es** [en entrepôt] warehoused goods ; [en douane] bonded goods.

entreposer [3] [ɑ̃trəpoze] *vt* **1.** [mettre en entrepôt] to store, to put in a warehouse, to warehouse **2.** [déposer] to leave ■ **~ des livres chez un ami** to leave some books with a friend.

entrepôt [ɑ̃trəpo] *nm* warehouse ▶ **~ de douane** bonded warehouse ■ **ville d'~** entrepôt, free port.

entreprenait *etc v* ▷ **entreprendre.**

entreprenant, e [ɑ̃trəprənɑ̃, ɑ̃t] *adj* **1.** [dynamique] enterprising **2.** [hardi] forward.

entreprenaute [ɑ̃trəprənot] *nmf* INFORM internet entrepreneur.

entreprendre [79] [ɑ̃trəprɑ̃dr] *vt* **1.** [commencer - lecture, étude] to begin, to start (on) ; [- croisière, carrière] to set out on *ou* upon *(insép)* ; [- projet, démarche] to undertake, to set about *(insép)* ■ **~ des études de droit** to begin studying law, to undertake law studies **2.** [séduire - femme] to make (amorous) advances towards **3.** [interpeller - passant] to buttonhole ■ **~ qqn sur un sujet** to tackle sb about *ou* over a matter.

entrepreneur, euse [ɑ̃trəprənœr, øz] *nm, f* **1.** CONSTR : **~ en bâtiment** *ou* **construction** (building) contractor, builder **2.** [chef d'entreprise] entrepreneur ■ **petit ~** small businessman ■ **~ de transports** haulier *UK*, hauler *US* ■ **~ de pompes funèbres** funeral director, undertaker.

entreprennent, entreprenons *etc v* ▷ **entreprendre.**

entrepris, e [ɑ̃trəpri, iz] *pp* ▷ **entreprendre.**
◆ **entreprise** *nf* **1.** [société] firm, concern, business ■ **monter une ~e** to set up a business ▶ **~e commerciale/industrielle** business/industrial concern ■ **~e agricole** farm ■ **~e familiale** family business *ou* firm ■ **~e de pompes funèbres** funeral director's, undertaker's ■ **~e de transports** transport company ■ **~e de travaux publics** civil engineering firm ■ **~e d'utilité publique** public utility company ■ **junior ~e** *company set up by students to gain experience in business* ■ **petite/moyenne/grosse ~e** small/medium-sized/large firm **2.** [monde des affaires] : **l'~e** business, the business world **3.** [régime économique] enterprise *(U)* ■ **l'~e publique/privée** public/private enterprise **4.** [initiative] undertaking, initiative.
◆ **entreprises** *nfpl hum* [avances] (amorous) advances.
◆ **d'entreprise** *loc adj* [matériel, véhicule] company *(modif)*.

entrer [ɑ̃tre] <> *vi (aux être)*

A. PÉNÉTRER
B. DÉBUTER

A. PÉNÉTRER

1. [personne - gén] to enter ; [- vu de l'intérieur] to come in ; [- vu de l'extérieur] to go in ; [- à pied] to walk in ; [- à cheval, à bicyclette] to ride in ■ [véhicule] to drive in ■ **toc, toc! – entrez!** knock, knock! – come in! ■ **entrez, entrez!** do come in!, come on in! ■ **la cuisine est à droite en entrant** the kitchen is on the right as you come *ou* go in ■ **empêche-les d'~** keep them out, don't let them in ■ **entrez sans frapper** go (straight) in ■ **il m'invita à ~** he invited me in ■ **il me fit signe d'~** he beckoned me in ■ **les voleurs sont entrés par la porte de derrière** the burglars got in by the back door ■ **il n'a fait qu'~ et sortir** he just popped in for a moment ■ **~ en gare** to pull in (to the station) ■ **~ au port** to come into *ou* to enter harbour ■ **et voici les joueurs qui entrent sur le terrain/court** here are the players coming onto the field/court ■ **faites-la ~** [en lui montrant le chemin] show her in ; [en l'appelant] call her in ‖ [vent, eau] : **le vent entrait par rafales** the wind was blowing in in gusts ■ **par où entre l'eau?** how does the water penetrate *ou* get in? ■ **laisser ~ : ce genre de fenêtre laisse ~ plus de lumière** this kind of window lets more light in
2. [adhérer] : **~ à l'université** to go to university ■ **elle entre à la maternelle/en troisième année** she's going to nursery school/ moving up into the third year ■ **~ au service de qqn** to enter sb's service ■ **il a fait ~ sa fille comme attachée de presse** he got a job for his daughter as a press attaché
3. ÉCON [devises, produits] to enter ■ **faire ~ des marchandises** [gén] to get goods in ; [en fraude] to smuggle goods in
4. [tenir, trouver sa place] : **je peux faire ~ un autre sac sous le siège** [gén] I can fit another bag under the seat ; [en serrant] I can squeeze another bag under the seat
5. *fam* [connaissances, explication] to sink in ■ **la chimie n'entre pas du tout** I just can't get the hang of chemistry ■ **l'informatique, ça entre tout seul avec elle** learning about computers is very easy with her as a teacher
6. RELIG : **~ en religion** to enter the religious life ■ **~ au couvent** to enter a convent

B. DÉBUTER

[une action] : **~ en** : **~ en pourparlers** to start *ou* to enter negotiations ■ **~ en conversation avec qqn** to strike up a conversation with sb ■ **~ en concurrence** to enter into competition ■ **~ en ébullition** to reach boiling point, to begin to boil ■ **~ en guerre** to go to war.
<> *vt (aux avoir)* **1.** [produits - gén] to take in *(sép)*, to bring in *(sép)*, to import ; [- en fraude] to smuggle in *(sép)* **2.** [enfoncer] to dig **3.** [passer] : **entre la tête par ce trou-là** get your head through that hole **4.** INFORM to enter.
◆ **entrer dans** *v+prép* **1.** [pénétrer dans - obj: lieu] to enter, to come into, to go into ■ [à pied] to walk into ■ **~ dans l'eau** to get into the water ■ **y a-t-il un autre moyen d'~ dans cette pièce?** is there another way into this room? ■ **ils nous ont fait ~ dans une cellule** they got us into a cell ■ **il ne les laisse jamais ~ dans la chambre noire** he never lets *ou* allows them into the black room ■ **un rayon de soleil entra dans la chambre** a ray of sunlight entered the room **2.** [adhérer à - obj: club, association, parti] to join, to become a member of ; [- obj: entreprise] to join ■ **~ dans le monde du travail** to start work ■ **~ dans une famille** [par mariage] to marry into a family ■ **il l'a fait ~ dans la société** he got him a job with the firm **3.** [heurter - pilier, mur] to crash into, to hit ; [- voiture] to collide with **4.** [constituant] : **~ dans la composition de** to go into ■ **l'eau entre pour moitié dans cette boisson** water makes up 50% of this drink **5.** [se mêler de] to enter into ■ **je ne veux pas ~ dans vos histoires** I don't want to have anything to do with *ou* to be involved in your little schemes ‖ [se lancer dans] : **sans ~ dans les détails** without going into details **6.** [être inclus dans] : **c'est entré dans les mœurs** it's become accepted ■ **~ dans l'usage** [terme] to come into common use, to become part of everyday language ■ **elle est entrée dans la légende de son vivant** she became a living legend ■ **la TVA n'entre pas dans le prix** VAT isn't included in the price **7.** [s'enfoncer, pénétrer dans] : **la balle/flèche est entrée dans son bras** the bullet/arrow lodged itself in her arm ■ **faire ~ qqch de force dans** to force sthg into **8.** [tenir dans] to get in, to go in, to fit in ■ **tout n'entrera pas dans la valise** we won't get everything in the suitcase, everything won't fit in the suitcase ■ **faire ~** [en poussant] : **faire ~ des vêtements dans une valise** to press clothes in *ou* down in a suitcase **9.** [obj: période] to enter ■ **elle entre dans sa 97ᵉ année** she's entering her 97th year ■ **quand on entre dans l'âge adulte** when one becomes an adult **10.** [relever de - rubrique] to fall into, to come into ; [- responsabilités] to be part of ■ **cela n'entre pas dans mes attributions** this is not within my responsibilities ■ **j'espère ne pas ~ dans cette catégorie de personnes** I hope I don't belong to that category of people **11.** *fam* [obj: connaissances, explication] : **faire ~ qqch dans la tête de qqn** to put sthg into sb's head ; [à force de répéter] to drum *ou* to hammer sthg into sb's head ■ **tu ne lui feras jamais ~ dans la tête que c'est impossible** you'll never get it into his head *ou* convince him that it's impossible.

entresol [ɑ̃trəsɔl] *nm* mezzanine, entresol ■ **à l'~** on the mezzanine, at mezzanine level.

entre(-)temps [ɑ̃trətɑ̃] <> *adv* meanwhile, in the meantime.
<> *nm inv arch* **dans l'~** in the meantime.

entretenir [40] [ɑ̃trətnir] *vt* **1.** [tenir en bon état - locaux, château] to maintain, to look after *(insép)*, to see to the upkeep of ; [- argenterie, lainage] to look after *(insép)* ; [- matériel, voiture, route] to maintain ; [- santé, beauté] to look after *(insép)*, to maintain ■ **~ sa forme** *ou* **condition physique** to keep o.s. fit *ou* in shape **2.** [maintenir - feu] to keep going *ou* burning ; [- querelle, rancune] to foster, to feed ; [- enthousiasme] to foster, to keep alive *(sép)* ; [- espoirs, illusions] to cherish, to entertain ; [- fraîcheur, humidité] to maintain ■ **~ une correspondance avec qqn** to keep up *ou* to carry on a correspondence with sb **3.** [encourager] : **~ qqn dans : c'est ce qui m'a entretenu dans l'erreur** that is what kept me from seeing the mistake ■ **~ qqn dans l'idée que** to keep sb believing that **4.** [payer les dépenses de - enfants] to support ; [- maîtresse] to keep, to support ; [- troupes] to keep, to maintain ■ **entretenu à ne rien faire** paid to do nothing ■ **se faire ~ par qqn** to be kept by sb **5.** [lui parler de] : **~ qqn de** to converse with *sout ou* to speak to sb about.
◆ **s'entretenir** <> *vp (emploi réciproque)* to have a discussion, to talk ■ **ils se sont longuement entretenus de...** they had a lengthy discussion about...
<> *vp (emploi passif)* : **le synthétique s'entretient facilement** man-made fabrics are easy to look after.
◆ **s'entretenir avec** *vp+prép* to converse with, to speak to ■ **s'~ de qqch avec qqn** to have a discussion with sb about sthg.

entretenu, e [ɑ̃trətny] *adj* **1.** [personne] kept **2.** [lieu] : **maison bien ~e** [où le ménage est fait] well-kept house ; [en bon état] house in good repair ■ **maison mal ~e** [sale et mal rangée] badly kept house ; [en mauvais état] house in bad repair ■ **jardin bien/mal ~** well-kept/neglected garden.

entretien [ɑ̃trətjɛ̃] *nm* **1.** [maintenance] maintenance, upkeep ■ **sans ~** [appareil] maintenance-free **2.** [discussion - entre employeur et candidat] interview ■ [colloque] discussion ■ **solliciter/accorder un ~** to request/to grant an interview ▶ **~ d'embauche** job interview **3.** RADIO & TV [questions] interview.

entretient, entretint *etc v* ▷ **entretenir**.

entre-tuer [7] [ɑ̃trətɥe] ◆ **s'entre-tuer** *vp (emploi réciproque)* to kill one another.

entreverra, entrevit *etc v* ▷ **entrevoir**.

entrevoir [62] [ɑ̃trəvwar] *vt* **1.** [apercevoir] to catch sight *ou* a glimpse of **2.** [pressentir - solution, vie meilleure] to glimpse ; [- difficultés, issue] to foresee, to anticipate ■ **le directeur lui a fait ~ des possibilités de promotion** the director hinted at a possible promotion.

entrevue [ɑ̃trəvy] *nf* [réunion] meeting ■ [tête-à-tête] interview ■ **après son ~ avec le pape** after his meeting *ou* audience with the Pope.

entropie [ɑ̃trɔpi] *nf* entropy.

entrouvert, e [ɑ̃truvɛr, ɛrt] *adj* [porte] half-open, ajar.

entrouvrir [34] [ɑ̃truvrir] *vt* to half-open.

◆ **s'entrouvrir** *vpi* [porte] to half-open ■ [rideau] to draw back *(sép)* (slightly) ■ [lèvres] to part.

entuber [3] △ [ɑ̃tybe] *vt* to con, to rip off *(sép)* ■ **se faire ~** to be conned, to get ripped off.

enturbanné, e [ɑ̃tyrbane] *adj* turbaned.

énucléer [15] [enyklee] *vt* **1.** [œil] to enucleate **2.** [noyau] to stone, to pit.

énumératif, ive [enymeratif, iv] *adj* enumerative.

énumération [enymerasjɔ̃] *nf* **1.** [énonciation] enumeration, enumerating **2.** [liste] list, catalogue.

énumérer [18] [enymere] *vt* to enumerate, to list.

énurésie [enyrezi] *nf* enuresis *spéc*, bedwetting.

énurétique [enyretik] ◇ *adj* enuretic *spéc*, bedwetting *(modif)*.
◇ *nmf* enuresis sufferer *spéc*, bedwetter.

env. = environ.

envahir [32] [ɑ̃vair] *vt* **1.** [occuper - pays, palais] to invade, to overrun **2.** [se répandre dans] to overrun ■ **plate-bande envahie par les mauvaises herbes** border overrun with weeds ■ **jardin envahi par la végétation** overgrown garden **3.** [déranger] : **se laisser ~ par les tâches quotidiennes** to let o.s. be swamped by daily duties **4.** [suj: sensation, crainte] to sweep over *(insép)*, to seize ■ **le doute l'a envahi** he was seized with doubt.

envahissant, e [ɑ̃vaisɑ̃, ɑ̃t] *adj* **1.** [qui s'étend - végétation] overgrown ; [- ambition, passion] invasive **2.** [importun - voisin, ami] interfering, intrusive ■ **je commence à trouver ta famille un peu ~e** I'm beginning to find your family a bit too intrusive.

envahissement [ɑ̃vaismɑ̃] *nm* invasion.

envahisseur [ɑ̃vaisœr] *nm* invader.

envasement [ɑ̃vazmɑ̃] *nm* silting up.

envaser [3] [ɑ̃vaze] *vt* to silt up *(sép)*.
◆ **s'envaser** *vpi* [canal] to silt up ■ [barque] to get stuck in the mud.

enveloppant, e [ɑ̃vlɔpɑ̃, ɑ̃t] *adj* [voix, paroles] enticing, seductive.

enveloppe [ɑ̃vlɔp] *nf* **1.** [pour lettre] envelope ■ **prière de joindre une ~ affranchie** please enclose stamped addressed envelope *ou* s.a.e. *UK* ◗ **~ autoadhésive** self-sealing envelope ■ **~ à fenêtre** window envelope ■ **~ gommée** stick-down envelope ■ **~ de réexpédition** *special envelope used for forwarding several items at once* ■ **~ matelassée** *ou* **rembourrée** padded envelope, Jiffy bag® **2.** BOT [membrane] covering membrane ■ [cosse] husk **3.** [revêtement - d'un pneu] cover, casing ; [- d'un tuyau] lagging *(U)*, jacket **4.** FIN [don] sum of money, gratuity ■ [don illégal] bribe ■ [crédits] budget ■ **l'~ (budgétaire) du ministère de la Culture** the Arts budget ■ **il a touché une ~** [pot-de-vin] he got a backhander **5.** [aspect] exterior, outward appearance **6.** GÉOM envelope.
◆ **sous enveloppe** *loc adv* : **mettre/envoyer sous ~** to put/to send in an envelope ■ **envoyer un magazine sous ~** [pour le dissimuler] to send a magazine under plain cover.

enveloppement [ɑ̃vlɔpmɑ̃] *nm* **1.** [emballage] wrapping, packing *(U)* **2.** MIL encirclement, surrounding **3.** MÉD packing.

envelopper [3] [ɑ̃vlɔpe] *vt* **1.** [empaqueter] to wrap (up) ◗ **je vous l'enveloppe?** *hum* is that a deal? **2.** [emmailloter] to wrap (up) ■ **~ un enfant dans une couverture** to wrap a child in a blanket *ou* a blanket around a child **3.** [entourer] : **~ qqn de sa sollicitude** to lavish one's attention on sb ■ **~ du regard : il enveloppa le paysage du regard** he took in the landscape ■ **~ qqn du regard** to gaze at sb **4.** [voiler - suj: brume, obscurité] to shroud, to envelop **5.** MIL to encircle, to surround.
◆ **s'envelopper dans** *vp+prép* [vêtement] to wrap o.s. in.

envenimer [3] [ɑ̃vnime] *vt* **1.** MÉD to poison, to infect **2.** [aggraver - conflit] to inflame, to fan the flames of ; [- rapports] to poison, to spoil ■ **tu n'as fait qu'~ les choses** you've only made things *ou* matters worse.
◆ **s'envenimer** *vpi* **1.** MÉD to fester, to become septic **2.** [empirer - relation] to grow more bitter *ou* acrimonious ; [- situation] to get worse, to worsen.

envergure [ɑ̃vɛrgyr] *nf* **1.** [d'un oiseau, d'un avion] wingspan, wingspread **2.** NAUT breadth **3.** [importance - d'une manifestation, d'une œuvre] scale, scope ■ **de petite** *ou* **faible ~** small ■ **de grande ~** large-scale ■ **son entreprise a pris de l'~** her company has expanded **4.** [d'un savant, d'un président] calibre ■ **il manque d'~** he doesn't have a strong personality.

enverra *etc v* ⊳ **envoyer**.

envers [ɑ̃vɛr] ◇ *prép* [à l'égard de] towards, to ■ **elle est loyale ~ ses amis** she's loyal to her friends ■ **son attitude ~ moi** his attitude towards me ◗ **~ et contre tout** *ou* **tous** in the face of *ou* despite all opposition.
◇ *nm* **1.** [autre côté] : **l'~** [d'un papier] the other side, the back ; [d'une feuille d'arbre] the underside ; [d'une médaille, d'un tissu] the reverse side ; [d'une peau] the inside **2.** [mauvais côté] wrong side ■ **l'~ du décor** *ou* **tableau** the other side of the coin **3.** GÉOGR cold northern slope *(of valley)*.
◆ **à l'envers** *loc adv* **1.** [dans le mauvais sens] : **mettre à l'~** [chapeau] to put on the wrong way round, to put on back to front ; [chaussettes] to put on inside out ; [portrait] to hang upside down *ou* the wrong way up **2.** [mal, anormalement] : **tout va** *ou* **marche à l'~** everything is upside down *ou* topsy-turvy ■ **tu as tout compris à l'~** you misunderstood the whole thing ■ **il a l'esprit** *ou* **la tête à l'~** his mind is in a whirl, he doesn't know whether he's coming or going **3.** [dans l'ordre inverse] backwards, in reverse.

envi [ɑ̃vi] ◆ **à l'envi** *loc adv litt* **ils se sont déchaînés contre moi à l'~** they vied with one another in venting their rage on me ■ **trois sketches féroces à l'~** three sketches, each more corrosive than the last.

enviable [ɑ̃vjabl] *adj* enviable ■ **peu ~** unenviable.

envie [ɑ̃vi] *nf* **1.** [souhait, désir] desire ■ **l'~ de qqch/de faire qqch** the desire for sthg/to do sthg ■ **avoir ~ de : j'avais (très) ~ de ce disque** I wanted that record (very much) ■ **avoir ~ de rire/pleurer** to feel like laughing/crying ■ **avoir ~ de vomir** to feel sick ■ **je n'ai pas ~ de passer ma vie à ça** I don't want to spend the rest of my life doing that ■ **j'ai presque ~ de ne pas y aller** I have half a mind not to go ■ **il avait moyennement ~ de la revoir** he didn't really feel like seeing her again ■ **je le ferai quand j'en aurai ~** I'll do it when I feel like it ■ **mourir** *ou* **crever** *fam* **d'~ de faire qqch** to be dying to do sthg ■ **donner à qqn ~ de faire : ça m'a donné ~ de les revoir** it made me want to see *ou* feel like seeing them again ■ **avoir ~ que : elle n'a pas ~ que tu restes** she doesn't want you to stay ■ **faire ~ à qqn : un voyage au Brésil, ça ne te fait pas ~?** aren't you tempted by a trip to Brazil? ■ **l'~ lui prend de** *ou* **il lui prend l'~ de faire...** he feels like *ou* fancies doing... ■ **ôter** *ou* **faire passer à qqn l'~ de faire : voilà qui lui ôtera l'~ de revenir** this'll make sure he's not tempted to come back ◗ **~ de femme enceinte** (pregnant woman's) craving **2.** [désir sexuel] desire ■ **j'ai ~ de toi** I want you **3.** [besoin] urge ■ **être pris d'une ~ (pressante** *ou* **naturelle)** to feel the call of nature, to be taken short *UK* **4.** [jalousie] envy ■ **faire ~ à qqn : sa réussite me fait ~** I envy her success, her success makes me jealous ■ **tant de luxe, ça (vous) fait ~** such luxury makes one *ou* you envious ◗ **~ du pénis** PSYCHOL penis envy **5.** ANAT [tache] birthmark ■ [peau] hangnail.

envier [9] [ɑ̃vje] *vt* : **~ qqch à qqn** to envy sb (for) sthg ■ **vous n'avez rien à lui ~** you have no reason to be envious of her ■ **~ qqn d'avoir fait qqch** to envy sb for having done sthg.

envieux, euse [ɑ̃vjø, øz] ◇ *adj* envious ■ **être ~ de** to be envious of, to envy.
◇ *nm, f* envious person ■ **faire des ~** to arouse *ou* to excite envy.

environ [ɑ̃virɔ̃] *adv* about, around ■ **il y a ~ six mois** about six months ago ■ **il était ~ midi** it was around *ou* about 12 ■ **il habite à ~ 100 m** *ou* **à 100 m ~ d'ici** he lives about 100 m from here.

environnant, e [ɑ̃virɔnɑ̃, ɑ̃t] *adj* surrounding ■ **la campagne ~e** the surrounding countryside, the country round about.

environnement [ɑ̃virɔnmɑ̃] *nm* **1.** [lieux avoisinants] environment, surroundings, surrounding area **2.** [milieu] background ▪ **l'~ culturel/familial** the cultural/family background **3.** ÉCOL : l'~ the environment ▪ **défenseur de l'~** conservationist ▪ **un produit qui respecte l'~** an environment-friendly product ▪ **pollution/politique de l'~** environmental pollution/policy **4.** INFORM environment, platform.

environnemental, e, aux [ɑ̃virɔnmɑ̃tal, o] *adj* environmental.

environnementaliste [ɑ̃virɔnmɑ̃talist] *nmf* environmentalist.

environner [3] [ɑ̃virɔne] *vt* to surround, to encircle.
◆ **s'environner de** *vp+prép* to surround o.s. with.

environs [ɑ̃virɔ̃] *nmpl* surroundings, surrounding area ▪ **les ~ de Paris** the area around Paris.
◆ **aux environs de** *loc prép* **1.** [dans l'espace] near, close to ▪ **aux ~ de Nantes** in the vicinity of *ou* near Nantes **2.** [dans le temps] around, round about ▪ **aux ~ de midi** around noon, at noon or thereabouts.
◆ **dans les environs** *loc adv* in the local *ou* surrounding area.
◆ **dans les environs de** *loc prép* in the vicinity of, near.

envisageable [ɑ̃vizaʒabl] *adj* conceivable ▪ **ce n'est guère ~ à l'heure actuelle** it hardly seems possible at the present time, it's barely conceivable at present.

envisager [17] [ɑ̃vizaʒe] *vt* **1.** [examiner] to consider ▪ **~ tous les aspects d'un problème** to consider all the aspects of a problem **2.** [prévoir] to envisage, to contemplate, to consider ▪ **~ des licenciements/réparations** to consider lay-offs/repairs ▪ **j'envisage d'aller vivre là-bas** I'm contemplating going *ou* I'm thinking of going to live there.

envoi [ɑ̃vwa] *nm* **1.** [de marchandises, d'argent] sending ▪ **faire un ~** [colis] to send a parcel ; [lettre] to send a letter ▪ **~ contre remboursement** cash on delivery ▪ **contre ~ de** on receipt of **2.** [d'un messager, de soldats] sending in, dispatching, dispatch **3.** [colis] parcel, consignment ▪ [lettre] letter ▪ **~ franco de port** postage-paid consignment ▪ **~ recommandé** [colis] registered parcel ; [lettre] registered letter ▪ **~ recommandé avec accusé de réception** [colis] recorded delivery parcel *UK*, registered package with return receipt *US* ; [lettre] recorded delivery letter *UK*, registered letter with return receipt *US* ▪ **~ contre remboursement** guaranteed delivery ▪ **~ groupé** joint consignment ▪ **un ~ en nombre** a (mass) mailing **4.** SPORT : **coup d'~** kick-off ▪ **donner le coup d'~ d'un match** [arbitre] to give the sign for the match to start ; [joueur] to kick off ▪ **donner le coup d'~ d'une campagne** *fig* to get a campaign off the ground **5.** LITTÉR envoi.

envoie *etc v* ▷ **envoyer.**

envol [ɑ̃vɔl] *nm* **1.** [d'un oiseau] taking flight ▪ **l'aigle prit son ~** the eagle took flight **2.** AÉRON taking off *(U)*, takeoff.

envolée [ɑ̃vɔle] *nf* **1.** [élan] flight ▪ **~ lyrique** flight of lyricism ▪ **il s'est lancé dans une grande ~ lyrique** *hum* he waxed lyrical **2.** [augmentation] sudden rise ▪ **l'~ du mark** the sudden rise of the mark.

envoler [3] [ɑ̃vɔle] ◆ **s'envoler** *vpi* **1.** [oiseau] to fly off *ou* away **2.** AÉRON [avion] to take off **3.** [passer - temps] to fly **4.** [augmenter - cours, dollar] to soar **5.** [être emporté - écharpe] to blow off *ou* away ▪ **le vent a fait s'~ tous les papiers** the wind sent all the documents flying (everywhere) **6.** [disparaître - voleur, stylo] to disappear, to vanish (into thin air).

envoûtant, e [ɑ̃vutɑ̃, ɑ̃t] *adj* spellbinding, bewitching, entrancing.

envoûtement [ɑ̃vutmɑ̃] *nm* bewitchment, spell.

envoûter [3] [ɑ̃vute] *vt* to bewitch, to cast a spell on ▪ **être envoûté par une voix/femme** to be under the spell of a voice/woman.

envoûteur, euse [ɑ̃vutœr, øz] *nm, f* sorcerer (*f* sorceress).

envoyé, e [ɑ̃vwaje] *nm, f* [gén] messenger ▪ POLIT envoy ▪ PRESSE correspondent ▪ **de notre ~ spécial à Londres** from our special correspondent in London.

envoyer [30] [ɑ̃vwaje] *vt* **1.** [expédier - gén] to send (off) ; [- message radio] to send out *(sép)* ; [- marchandises] to send, to dispatch ; [- invitation] to send (out) ; [- vœux, condoléances] to send ; [- CV, candidature] to send (in) ; [- argent, mandat] to send, to remit ▪ **~ qqch par bateau** to ship sthg, to send sthg by ship ▪ **Fred t'envoie ses amitiés** Fred sends you his regards ▪ **~ un (petit) mot à qqn** to drop sb a line ▪ **tu peux te faire ~ la documentation** you can have the information sent to you ➊ **~ des fleurs à qqn** *pr* to send sb flowers ; *fig* to give sb a pat on the back
2. [personne] to send ▪ **~ un enfant à l'école** to send a child (off) to school ▪ **on m'a envoyé aux nouvelles** I've been sent to find out whether there's any news ▪ **~ des soldats à la mort** to send soldiers to their deaths ▪ *(suivi d'un infin)* **~ chercher qqn** to have sb picked up ▪ **je l'ai envoyé la chercher à la gare** I sent him to the station to pick her up *ou* to fetch her ▪ **~ chercher un médecin** to send for a doctor ➊ **~ dire : elle ne le lui a pas envoyé dire** she told him straight *ou* to his face ▪ **~ promener** *ou* **balader** *ou* **paître** *ou* **bouler qqn** *fam*, **~qqn au diable** *fam*, **~qqn sur les roses** *fam* to send sb packing ▪ **j'avais envie de tout ~ promener** *fam ou* **valser** *fam* I felt like chucking the whole thing in ▪ **~ dinguer qqn** *fam* [le repousser] to send sb sprawling ; [l'éconduire] to send sb packing
3. [projeter] : **~ un adversaire à terre** *ou* **au tapis** to knock an opponent down *ou* to the ground ▪ **~ une voiture dans le décor** *fam* to send a car skidding off the road
4. [lancer - projectile] to throw, to fling ; [- ballon] to throw ; [- balle de tennis] to send ▪ **~ sa fumée dans les yeux de qqn** to blow smoke into sb's eyes ▪ **~ des baisers à qqn** to blow sb kisses
5. [donner - coup] : **~ des gifles** *ou fam* **baffes** *fam* **àqqn** to slap sb (in the face) ▪ **~ des coups de pied/poing à qqn** to kick/to punch sb ➊ **il le lui a envoyé dans les dents** *fam ou* **gencives** *fam* he really let him have it
6. [hisser - pavillon] to hoist.
◆ **s'envoyer** ◇ *vp (emploi réciproque)* to send one another ▪ **s'~ des lettres** to write to one another.
◇ *vpt* **1.** *fam* [subir - corvée] to get saddled with
2. *fam* [consommer - bière, bouteille] to knock back *(sép)*, to down ; [- gâteau] to wolf down ▪ [sexuellement] △ **s'~ qqn** to get off with sb
3. [se donner] : **je m'enverrais des gifles** *ou fam* **baffes!** I could kick myself!
◇ *vpi loc* : **s'~ en l'air**△ to have it off.

envoyeur, euse [ɑ̃vwajœr, øz] *nm, f* sender.

enzyme [ɑ̃zim] *nf* ou *nm* enzyme.

éocène [eɔsɛn] ◇ *adj* eocene.
◇ *nm* Eocene (period).

Éole [eɔl] *npr* Aeolus.

éolien, enne [eɔljɛ̃, ɛn] *adj* aeolian *spéc*, wind *(modif)*.
◆ **éolienne** *nf* windmill, wind pump.

Éoliennes [eɔljɛn] *npr fpl* : **les (îles) ~** the Aeolian *ou* Lipari Islands, *voir aussi* **île**.

éolithe [eɔlit] *nm* eolith.

éosine [eɔzin] *nf* eosin, eosine.

épagneul [epaɲœl] *nm* spaniel ▪ **~ breton** Breton spaniel.

épais, aisse [epɛ, ɛs] *adj* **1.** [haut - livre, strate, tranche] thick ; [- couche de neige] thick, deep ▪ **une planche épaisse de 10 centimètres** a board 10 centimetres thick **2.** [charnu - lèvres, cheville, taille] thick ; [- corps] thickset, stocky ▪ **il n'est pas (bien) ~** *fam* he's thin (as a rake) **3.** [dense - fumée, sauce, foule] thick ; [- sourcil] thick, bushy **4.** [profond - silence, sommeil] deep ; [- nuit] pitch-black **5.** *péj* [non affiné - esprit, intelligence] dull, coarse.
◆ **épais** ◇ *nm* : **au plus ~ de la forêt** deep in the heart of the forest.
◇ *adv* [tartiner, semer] thick, thickly ▪ **il n'y en avait pas ~, de la viande** *fam* there wasn't much meat.

épaisseur [epɛsœr] *nf* **1.** [d'un mur, d'un tissu, d'une strate] thickness ▪ **un mur de 30 centimètres d'~** a wall 30 centimetres thick **2.** [couche] layer, thickness ▪ **plier un papier en quatre/cinq ~s** to fold a piece of paper in four/five **3.** [densité - du brouillard, d'une soupe, d'un feuillage] thickness **4.** [intensité - du silence, du sommeil] depth ; [- de la nuit] darkness, depth **5.** [substance] depth.

épaissir [32] [epesir] ◇ *vt* **1.** [sauce, enduit] to thicken (up) **2.** [grossir] to thicken ▪ **les traits épaissis par l'alcool** his features bloated with alcohol.
◇ *vi* **1.** [fumée, peinture, mayonnaise] to thicken, to get thicker **2.** [grossir - taille] to get thicker *ou* bigger ; [- traits du visage] to get coarser, to coarsen ▪ **il a beaucoup épaissi** he's put on a lot of weight.
◆ **s'épaissir** *vpi* **1.** [fumée, crème] to thicken, to get thicker **2.** [augmenter - couche de neige] to get thicker *ou* deeper ; [- pile de feuilles] to get bigger **3.** [grossir - traits] to get coarse *ou* coarser ; [- taille] to get thicker *ou* bigger ; [- personne] to grow stout *ou* stouter **4.** *fig* [mystère, ténèbres] to deepen ▪ **le mystère s'épaissit** [dans un fait divers] the mystery deepens ; [dans un roman] the plot thickens.

épaississant, e [epesisɑ̃, ɑ̃t] *adj* thickening *(avant n)*.

épanchement [epɑ̃ʃmɑ̃] *nm* **1.** [confidences] outpouring **2.** MÉD extravasation ▪ **~ de synovie** housemaid's knee.

épancher [3] [epɑ̃ʃe] *vt* [tendresse, craintes] to pour out *(sép)* ▪ [colère] to vent, to give vent to ▪ **~ son cœur** to open one's heart, to pour out one's feelings.
◆ **s'épancher** *vpi* **1.** [se confier] : **s'~ auprès d'un ami** to open one's heart to *ou* to pour out one's feelings to a friend **2.** *litt* [couler] to pour out.

épandage [epɑ̃daʒ] *nm* manure spreading, manuring.

épandre [74] [epɑ̃dr] *vt* to spread.

épanoui, e [epanwi] *adj* [rose, jeunesse] blooming ▪ [sourire] beaming, radiant ▪ [personne] radiant ▪ **son corps ~** her body in its prime.

épanouir [32] [epanwir] *vt* **1.** *litt* [fleur] to open (up) **2.** [détendre - visage] to light up *(sép)*.
◆ **s'épanouir** *vpi* **1.** [fleur] to bloom, to open **2.** [visage] to light up **3.** [personne] to blossom ▪ **une atmosphère où les enfants s'épanouissent** an atmosphere where children can develop.

épanouissant, e [epanwisɑ̃, ɑ̃t] *adj* fulfilling.

épanouissement [epanwismɑ̃] *nm* **1.** [d'une plante] blooming, opening up **2.** [d'un visage] lighting up ▪ [d'un enfant, d'une personnalité] fulfilment, self-fulfilment ▪ **une civilisation en plein ~** a civilization in full bloom.

épargnant, e [eparɲɑ̃, ɑ̃t] *nm, f* saver, investor ▪ **petits ~s** small investors.

épargne [eparɲ] *nf* **1.** [économies] : **l'~** savings **2.** [fait d'économiser] saving ▪ **~ salariale** employees' saving scheme *(with contributions deducted at source)*.

épargne-logement [eparɲlɔʒmɑ̃] *(pl* **épargnes-logements***)* *nf* : **plan d'~** home savings plan ▪ **prêt ~** home loan.

épargner [3] [eparɲe] ◇ *vt* **1.** [économiser - argent, essence, forces] to save ▪ **tu n'as pas épargné la chantilly!** *hum* you didn't skimp on the whipped cream! ▪ **n'~ ni sa peine ni son temps** to spare neither time nor trouble **2.** [éviter] : **tu m'as épargné un déplacement inutile** you spared *ou* saved me a wasted journey ▪ **je vous épargnerai les détails** I'll spare you the details **3.** [ménager - vieillard, adversaire] to spare ▪ **personne ne sera épargné** nobody *ou* no life will be spared.
◇ *vi* to save (money), to put money aside ▪ **~ sur qqch** *péj* to save on sthg.
◆ **s'épargner** *vpt* : **s'~ qqch** to save o.s. sthg

éparpillement [eparpijmɑ̃] *nm* **1.** [de papiers, de graines] scattering, dispersal **2.** [de la pensée, des efforts] dissipation.

éparpiller [3] [eparpije] *vt* **1.** [disperser - lettres, graines] to scatter ; [- troupes, famille] to disperse ▪ **éparpillés un peu partout dans le monde** scattered about the world **2.** [dissiper - attention, forces] to dissipate.
◆ **s'éparpiller** *vpi* **1.** [se disperser - foule, élèves] to scatter, to disperse **2.** [disperser son énergie] to dissipate one's energies.

épars, e [epar, ars] *adj* scattered.

épatant, e [epatɑ̃, ɑ̃t] *adj fam vieilli* splendid ▪ **c'est un type ~!** he's a splendid fellow!

épate [epat] *nf fam péj* showing off ▪ **faire de l'~** to show off.

épaté, e [epate] *adj* **1.** *fam* [étonné] amazed **2.** [aplati - nez, forme] flat, snub.

épatement [epatmɑ̃] *nm* [du nez] flatness.

épater [3] [epate] *vt fam* **1.** [étonner] to amaze ▪ **ça t'épate, hein?** how about that then? **2.** *péj* [impressionner] to impress ▪ **pour ~ la galerie** in order to cause a sensation ▪ **pour ~ le bourgeois** in order to shock *(middle-class values)*.
◆ **s'épater** *vpi* [s'élargir] to spread out.

épaule [epol] *nf* **1.** ANAT shoulder ▪ **être large d'~s** to be broad-shouldered ➊ **avoir les ~s tombantes** *ou fam* **en accent circonflexe** to be round-shouldered ▪ **donner un coup d'~ à qqn** to give sb a helping hand **2.** CULIN shoulder ▪ **~ d'agneau** shoulder of lamb.

épaulé-jeté [epoleʒəte] *(pl* **épaulés-jetés***)* *nm* clean-and-jerk.

épaulement [epolmɑ̃] *nm* **1.** CONSTR retaining wall **2.** GÉOGR escarpment.

épauler [3] [epole] *vt* **1.** [fusil] to raise (to the shoulder) **2.** [aider] to support, to back up *(sép)* ▪ **il a besoin de se sentir épaulé** he needs to feel that people are supporting him *ou* are behind him **3.** [vêtement] to put shoulder pads into ▪ **veste très épaulée** jacket with big shoulder pads.
◆ **s'épauler** *vp (emploi réciproque)* to help *ou* to support one another.

épaulette [epolɛt] *nf* **1.** MIL epaulette **2.** [vêtement] shoulder pad **3.** [bretelle] shoulder strap.

épave [epav] *nf* **1.** [débris] piece of flotsam (and jetsam) **2.** [véhicule, bateau] wreck **3.** [personne] (human) wreck.

épeautre [epotr] *nm* spelt (wheat).

épée [epe] *nf* **1.** ARM sword ▪ **l'~ de Damoclès** the sword of Damocles ▪ **c'est un coup d'~ dans l'eau** it's a waste of time **2.** [escrimeur] swordsman *(f* swordswoman).

épeler [24] [eple] *vt* [nom] to spell (out).
◆ **s'épeler** *vp (emploi passif)* : **comment ça s'épelle?** how do you spell it?, how is it spelt?

épépiner [3] [epepine] *vt* to seed, to de-seed.

éperdu, e [epɛrdy] *adj* **1.** [fou - regard, cri] wild, distraught ▪ **la quête ~e de la vérité** the frantic quest for truth ▪ **une fuite ~e** a headlong flight ▪ **~ de** overcome with ▪ **~ de joie** overcome with joy, overjoyed ▪ **~ de douleur** frantic *ou* distraught with grief **2.** [intense - gratitude] boundless ; [- besoin] violent, intense.

éperdument [epɛrdymɑ̃] *adv* **1.** [à la folie] madly, passionately **2.** [en intensif] : **je m'en moque** *ou* **fiche** *fam* **~** I couldn't care less *ou* give a damn.

éperlan [epɛrlɑ̃] *nm* smelt.

éperon [eprɔ̃] *nm* **1.** ÉQUIT & TRAV PUB spur **2.** BOT & GÉOGR spur ▪ **~ rocheux** rocky spur **3.** NAUT cutwater.

éperonner [3] [eprɔne] *vt* **1.** ÉQUIT to spur (on) **2.** [munir d'éperons] to put spurs on **3.** [stimuler] to spur on *(sép)* **4.** NAUT to ram.

épervier [epɛrvje] *nm* **1.** ORNITH sparrowhawk **2.** PÊCHE cast *ou* casting net.

éphèbe [efɛb] *nm* ANTIQ ephebe ▪ **(jeune) ~** *fig & hum* Adonis.

éphémère [efemɛr] ◇ *adj* [gloire, sentiment] short-lived, ephemeral, transient ▪ [mode] short-lived ▪ [regret] passing.
◇ *nm* ZOOL mayfly, dayfly, ephemera *spéc*.

éphéméride [efemerid] *nf* [calendrier] tear-off calendar.

◆ **éphémérides** *nfpl* ASTRON ephemeris.

Éphèse [efɛz] *npr* Ephesus.

épi [epi] *nm* **1.** [de fleur] spike ■ [de céréale] ear ■ **~ de maïs** corncob **2.** [de cheveux] tuft ■ **il a un ~** [toujours] his hair sticks out ; [en ce moment] his hair's sticking up.
◆ **en épi** *loc adv* : **voitures stationnées en ~** cars parked at an angle to the kerb.

épice [epis] *nf* spice.

épicé, e [epise] *adj* **1.** CULIN highly spiced, hot, spicy ■ **ce n'est pas très ~** it's quite mild, it's not very hot **2.** [grivois - histoire] spicy.

épicéa [episea] *nm* spruce.

épicentre [episɑ̃tr] *nm* epicentre.

épicer [16] [epise] *vt* **1.** CULIN to spice **2.** [corser - récit] to add spice to.

épicerie [episri] *nf* **1.** [magasin] grocery shop *UK ou* store *US* ■ **à l'~ du coin** at the local grocer's ■ **~ fine** delicatessen **2.** [profession] grocery trade **3.** [aliments] provisions, groceries.

épicier, ère [episje, ɛr] *nm, f* grocer.
◆ **d'épicier** *loc adj péj* [mentalité].

Épicure [epikyr] *npr* Epicurus.

épicurien, enne [epikyrjɛ̃, ɛn] <> *adj* **1.** PHILOS Epicurean **2.** [hédoniste] epicurean.
<> *nm, f* **1.** PHILOS Epicurean **2.** [bon vivant] epicure, bon viveur.

épicurisme [epikyrism] *nm* **1.** PHILOS Epicureanism **2.** [hédonisme] hedonism, epicureanism.

Épidaure [epidɔr] *npr* Epidaurus.

épidémie [epidemi] *nf* epidemic ■ **~ de typhus** epidemic of typhus, typhus epidemic ■ **c'est devenu une véritable ~** *pr & fig* it has reached epidemic proportions.

épidémiologie [epidemjɔlɔʒi] *nf* epidemiology.

épidémiologiste [epidemjɔlɔʒist] *nmf* epidemiologist.

épidémique [epidemik] *adj* epidemic.

épiderme [epidɛrm] *nm* skin, epidermis *spéc* ■ **avoir l'~ sensible** *pr* to have a sensitive *ou* a delicate skin ; *fig* to be thin-skinned *ou* touchy.

épidermique [epidɛrmik] *adj* **1.** ANAT epidermic *spéc*, epidermal *spéc*, skin *(modif)* ■ [blessure] surface *(modif)* ■ [greffe] skin *(modif)* **2.** [immédiat - sentiment, réaction] instant ■ **je ne peux pas le sentir, c'est ~** I don't know why, I just can't stand him.

épidural, e, aux [epidyral, o] *adj* epidural.

épier [9] [epje] *vt* **1.** [espionner] to spy on *(insép)* **2.** [réaction, mouvement] to watch closely ■ [bruit] to listen out for ■ [occasion] to be on the look-out, to watch for *(insép)*.

épieu, x [epjø] *nm* MIL pike ■ CHASSE hunting spear.

épigastre [epigastr] *nm* epigastrium.

épiglotte [epiglɔt] *nf* epiglottis.

épigone [epigɔn] *nm litt* epigone.

épigramme [epigram] *nf* [poème] epigram ■ [mot] witticism.

épigraphe [epigraf] *nf* epigraph.

épilation [epilasjɔ̃] *nf* hair removal ■ **l'~ des jambes** removal of hair from the legs.

épilatoire [epilatwar] *adj* depilatory, hair-removing *(avant n)*.

épilepsie [epilɛpsi] *nf* epilepsy.

épileptique [epilɛptik] *adj & nmf* epileptic.

épiler [3] [epile] *vt* [aisselles, jambes] to remove unwanted hair from ■ [sourcils] to pluck ■ **se faire ~ les jambes** to have one's legs waxed.
◆ **s'épiler** *vp (emploi réfléchi)* to remove unwanted hair ■ **s'~ les jambes à la cire** to wax one's legs.

épilogue [epilɔg] *nm* **1.** LITTÉR & THÉÂTRE epilogue **2.** [issue] conclusion, dénouement.

épiloguer [3] [epilɔge] *vi* : **c'est fini, on ne va pas ~!** it's over and done with, there's no point going on about it! ■ **~ sur qqch** to hold forth about *ou* to go over (and over) sthg.

épinard [epinar] *nm* spinach ■ **~s en branches** spinach leaves.

épine [epin] *nf* **1.** [de fleur] thorn, prickle ■ [de hérisson] spine, prickle ■ **tirer** *ou* **ôter une ~ du pied à qqn** to get sb out of a spot **2.** [buisson] thorn bush.
◆ **épine dorsale** *nf* backbone.

épinette [epinɛt] *nf* **1.** MUS spinet **2.** *Québec* [épicéa] spruce.

épineux, euse [epinø, øz] <> *adj* **1.** BOT thorny, prickly **2.** [délicat - problème, contexte] thorny, tricky.
<> *nm* thorn bush.

épingle [epɛ̃gl] *nf* COUT pin ■ **~ anglaise** *ou* **à nourrice** *ou* **de sûreté** safety pin ■ **~ à chapeau** hatpin ■ **~ à cheveux** hairpin ■ **~ à linge** clothes peg *UK ou* pin *US* ■ **monter qqch en ~** to highlight sthg ■ **tirer** *ou* **retirer son ~ du jeu** to pull out.

épingler [3] [epɛ̃gle] *vt* **1.** [attacher - badge, papier] to pin (on) ■ **~ une robe** [pour l'assembler] to pin a dress together ; [pour l'ajuster] to pin a dress up **2.** *fam* [arrêter] to nab ■ **se faire ~** to get nabbed.

épinoche [epinɔʃ] *nf* stickleback.

épiphanie [epifani] *nf* **1.** [fête] : **l'Épiphanie** Twelfth Night, the Epiphany **2.** [du Christ] : **l'~** Epiphany.

épiphénomène [epifenɔmɛn] *nm* epiphenomenon.

épiphyse [epifiz] *nf* [os] epiphysis ■ [glande] epiphysis (cerebri), pineal gland.

épique [epik] *adj* **1.** LITTÉR epic **2.** [extraordinaire - discussion, scène] epic ■ **pour retrouver sa trace, ça a été ~!** finding out where he was was quite a saga!

épiscopal, e, aux [episkɔpal, o] *adj* episcopal.

épiscopat [episkɔpa] *nm* episcopate, episcopacy.

épisiotomie [epizjɔtɔmi] *nf* episiotomy.

épisode [epizɔd] *nm* **1.** [partie] episode, instalment ■ **feuilleton en six ~s** six-part serial **2.** [circonstance] episode.
◆ **à épisodes** *loc adj* serialized ■ **sa vie est un roman à ~s** *fig* her life is a real saga.

épisodique [epizɔdik] *adj* **1.** [ponctuel] occasional **2.** [secondaire] minor, secondary.

épisodiquement [epizɔdikmɑ̃] *adv* occasionally.

épissure [episyr] *nf* splice NAUT.

épistémologie [epistemɔlɔʒi] *nf* epistemology.

épistémologiste [epistemɔlɔʒist], **épistémologue** [epistemɔlɔg] *nmf* epistemologist.

épistolaire [epistɔlɛr] *adj* [roman] epistolary ■ [style] letter-writing *(modif)* ■ **être en relations ~s avec qqn** *sout* to have a correspondence with sb.

épitaphe [epitaf] *nf* epitaph.

épithélium [epiteljɔm] *nm* epithelium.

épithète [epitɛt] <> *adj* attributive.
<> *nf* **1.** GRAMM attribute **2.** [qualificatif] epithet ■ **quelques ~s malsonnantes** *hum* a few choice adjectives *hum*.

épître [epitr] *nf* **1.** RELIG epistle ■ **l'Épître aux Corinthiens** the Epistle to the Corinthians ■ **Épîtres des Apôtres** Epistles **2.** LITTÉR epistle **3.** ANTIQ epistle.

éploré, e [eplɔre] *adj* [parent, veuve] tearful, weeping ■ [voix] tearful ■ [visage] bathed *ou* covered in tears.

épluchage [eplyʃaʒ] *nm* **1.** [de légumes] peeling **2.** [examen] dissection, critical examination.

épluche-légumes [eplyʃlegym] *nm inv* potato peeler.

éplucher [3] [eplyʃe] *vt* **1.** [peler - pomme] to peel ; [- poireau] to clean ■ **~ une laitue** to pick the best leaves out of a lettuce **2.** [analyser - texte] to dissect, to go over *(insép)* with a fine-tooth comb ; [- liste, statistiques] to go through *(insép)*.

épluchette [eplyʃɛt] *nf Québec* corn-husking party.

éplucheur, euse [eplyʃœr, øz] *nm, f* peeler.
◆ **éplucheur** *nm* [couteau] potato *ou* vegetable peeler.
◆ **éplucheuse** *nf* automatic potato *ou* vegetable peeler.

épluchure [eplyʃyr] *nf* piece of peeling ■ **~s de pommes** apple peelings.

éponge [epɔ̃ʒ] *nf* **1.** ZOOL sponge **2.** [pour nettoyer] sponge ■ **~ métallique** scouring pad, scourer ■ **effacer une tache d'un coup d'~** to sponge a stain out *ou* away ■ **jeter l'~** to throw in the sponge ■ **passer l'~ sur qqch** to forget all about sthg ■ **boire comme une ~, avoir une ~ dans le gosier** *ou* **l'estomac** to drink like a fish **3.** BOT : **~ végétale** loofah, vegetable sponge **4.** *fam* [poumon] lung.

éponger [17] [epɔ̃ʒe] *vt* **1.** [absorber - encre, vin] to soak *ou* to sponge (up) ■ **~ ses dettes** *fig* to pay off one's debts **2.** [nettoyer - table] to wipe, to sponge (down) ; [- visage] to sponge, to wipe.
◆ **s'éponger** *vpt* : **s'~ le front** to mop one's brow.

éponyme [epɔnim] *adj* eponymous.

épopée [epɔpe] *nf* [poème] epic (poem) ■ [récit] epic (tale).

époque [epɔk] *nf* **1.** [moment, date] time ■ **ça n'existait pas à l'~** it didn't exist at the time *ou* in those days ■ **à cette ~-là** at that time, in those days ■ **à l'~ où j'étais étudiant** when I was a student ■ **les jeunes de notre ~** the young people of today ■ **être de** *ou* **vivre avec son ~** to move with the times ■ **quelle ~!** what times we live in! ■ **on vit une drôle d'~** we live in strange times **2.** [période historique] age, era, epoch ■ **la Belle Époque** the Belle Epoque **3.** [style] period ■ **la Haute ~** [Moyen Âge] the Middle Ages ; [XVIème siècle] the High Renaissance **4.** GÉOL period **5.** ASTRON epoch.
◆ **d'époque** *loc adj* period *(modif)* ■ **la pendule est d'~** it's a period clock.

épouiller [3] [epuje] *vt* to delouse.

époumoner [3] [epumɔne] ◆ **s'époumoner** *vpi* to shout o.s. hoarse ■ **j'avais beau m'~, il n'entendait pas** even though I was yelling at the top of my voice, he still didn't hear me.

épousailles [epuzaj] *nfpl arch* nuptials.

épouse [epuz] *nf* wife, spouse *sout* ■ **voulez-vous prendre Maud Jolas pour ~?** do you take Maud Jolas to be your lawful wedded wife?

épousée [epuze] *nf arch* [dialecte] bride.

épouser [3] [epuze] *vt* **1.** [se marier avec] to marry ■ **~ une grosse dot** *ou* **fortune** to marry money *ou* into a rich family **2.** [adopter - idées] to espouse, to embrace ; [- cause] to take up *(sép)* **3.** [suivre] : **une robe qui épouse la forme du corps** a figure-hugging *ou* close-fitting dress.
◆ **s'épouser** *vp (emploi réciproque)* to marry, to get married.

époussetage [epustaʒ] *nm* dusting (off).

épousseter [27] [epuste] *vt* **1.** [nettoyer] to dust **2.** [enlever - poussière] to dust *ou* to flick off *(sép)*.

époustouflant, e [epustuflɑ̃, ɑ̃t] *adj fam* stunning, astounding, staggering.

époustoufler [3] [epustufle] *vt fam* to stun, to astound, to flabbergast.

épouvantable [epuvɑ̃tabl] *adj* **1.** [très désagréable] awful, horrible, terrible ■ **elle a un caractère ~** she has a foul temper **2.** [effrayant] frightening, dreadful.

épouvantablement [epuvɑ̃tabləmɑ̃] *adv* **1.** [en intensif] frightfully, terribly, dreadfully **2.** [de façon effrayante] frighteningly, dreadfully.

épouvantail [epuvɑ̃taj] *nm* **1.** [pour oiseaux] scarecrow **2.** [menace] bogey, bogeyman ■ **agiter l'~ de la drogue** to use the threat of drugs as a bogey **3.** *péj* [personne - laide] fright ; [- mal habillée] mess, sight.

épouvante [epuvɑ̃t] *nf* terror, dread ■ **être glacé d'~** to be terror-struck *ou* terror-stricken.
◆ **d'épouvante** *loc adj* [film, roman] horror *(modif)*.

épouvanter [3] [epuvɑ̃te] *vt* to terrify, to fill with terror *ou* dread.

époux [epu] *nm* husband, spouse *sout* ■ **voulez-vous prendre Paul Hilbert pour ~?** do you take Paul Hilbert to be your lawful wedded husband? ■ **les ~ Bertier** Mr and Mrs Bertier ■ **les futurs ~** the engaged couple ■ **les jeunes ~** the newly-weds.

éprendre [79] [eprɑ̃dr] ◆ **s'éprendre de** *vp+prép litt* **s'~ de qqn** to fall for sb, to become enamoured of sb *litt*.

épreuve [eprœv] *nf* **1.** [test] test ■ **l'~ du temps** the test of time ⓘ **~ de force** trial of strength **2.** [obstacle] ordeal, trial ■ **vie remplie d'~s** life of hardship ▮ *litt* [adversité] : **l'~** adversity, hardship **3.** ÉDUC & UNIV [examen] test, examination ■ **~ écrite** paper, written test ■ **~ orale** oral (test) ▮ [copie] paper, script ■ **corriger des ~s** to mark exam papers **4.** SPORT event ■ **~s d'athlétisme** track events ⓘ **~ éliminatoire** heat ■ **~ d'endurance** endurance trial ■ **~ contre la montre** time trial **5.** IMPR proof ■ **corriger** *ou* **revoir les ~s d'un livre** to proofread a book ⓘ **dernière/première ~** final/galley proof **6.** PHOTO print ■ **~s de tournage** CINÉ rushes **7.** HIST ordeal ■ **~s judiciaires** trial by ordeal ■ **l'~ du feu** ordeal by fire.
◆ **à l'épreuve** *loc adv* : **mettre qqn à l'~** to put sb to the test.
◆ **à l'épreuve de** *loc prép* proof against ■ **à l'~ des balles** bulletproof ■ **à l'~ du feu** fireproof.
◆ **à rude épreuve** *loc adv* : **mettre qqch à rude ~** to put sthg to the test ■ **mettre les nerfs de qqn à rude ~** to put sb's nerves to the test.
◆ **à toute épreuve** *loc adj* [mécanisme] foolproof ■ [patience, bonne humeur] unfailing.

épris, e [epri, iz] ◇ *pp* ▷ **éprendre**.
◇ *adj litt* **être ~ de qqn** to be in love with sb ■ **être ~ de liberté** to be in love with freedom.

éprouvant, e [epruvɑ̃, ɑ̃t] *adj* trying, testing ■ **un climat ~** a difficult climate.

éprouvé, e [epruve] *adj* [méthode, matériel] well-tested, tried and tested, proven ■ [compétence, courage] proven ■ [spécialiste] proven, experienced.

éprouver [3] [epruve] *vt* **1.** [ressentir - douleur, haine] to feel, to experience ■ **~ une grande honte/déception** to feel deeply ashamed/disappointed **2.** [tester - procédé] to try *ou* to test (out) ; [- courage, personne] to test ■ **~ la patience de qqn** to try sb's patience, to put sb's patience to the test **3.** [subir - pertes] to suffer, to sustain **4.** [faire souffrir] to try, to test ■ **son divorce l'a beaucoup éprouvée** her divorce was a very trying experience for her ■ **une région durement éprouvée par la crise** an area that has been hard-hit by the recession.

éprouvette [epruvɛt] *nf* test tube ■ **~ graduée** burette.

EPS (*abr de* **éducation physique et sportive**) *nf* PE.

epsilon [ɛpsilɔn] *nm* epsilon.

épuisant, e [epɥizɑ̃, ɑ̃t] *adj* exhausting.

épuisé, e [epɥize] *adj* **1.** [fatigué] exhausted, worn-out, tired-out **2.** COMM [article] sold-out ■ [livre] out of print ■ [stock] exhausted.

épuisement [epɥizmɑ̃] *nm* **1.** [fatigue] exhaustion **2.** COMM & INDUST exhaustion ■ **jusqu'à ~ des stocks** while stocks last.

épuiser [3] [epɥize] *vt* **1.** [fatiguer] to exhaust, to wear *ou* to tire out *(sép)* **2.** [exploiter - puits] to work dry *(sép)* ; [- gisement, veine] to exhaust, to work out *(sép)* ; [- sol, sujet] to exhaust **3.** [consommer - vivres, ressources] to exhaust, to use up *(sép)* ; [- stocks] to exhaust.
◆ **s'épuiser** *vpi* **1.** [être très réduit - provisions, munitions] to run out, to give out ; [- source] to dry up ; [- filon] to be worked

out **2.** [se fatiguer - athlète] to wear o.s. out, to exhaust o.s. ; [- corps] to wear itself out, to run out of steam ■ **s'~ à faire qqch** [s'évertuer à faire qqch] to wear o.s. out doing sthg.

épuisette [epɥizɛt] *nf* **1.** [filet] landing net **2.** [pelle] bailer.

épurateur [epyratœr] *nm* filter, purifier ■ **~ d'air** air filter ■ **~ d'eau** water filter.

épuration [epyrasjɔ̃] *nf* **1.** [de l'eau] purification, filtering **2.** [du style] refinement, refining **3.** POLIT purge ■ **l'Épuration** HIST *period after the Second World War during which collaborators were tried and punished.*

épure [epyr] *nf* [dessin fini] working drawing.

épurer [3] [epyre] *vt* **1.** [liquide] to filter ■ [pétrole] to refine **2.** [style, langue] to refine, to make purer **3.** POLIT [administration] to purge.

équarrir [32] [ekarir] *vt* **1.** [bois, pierre] to square (off) **2.** [animal] to cut up *(sép).*

équarrissage [ekarisaʒ] *nm* **1.** [du bois, de la pierre] squaring (off) **2.** [d'un animal] cutting up.

équarrisseur [ekarisœr] *nm* **1.** [de bois, de pierre] squarer **2.** [aux abattoirs] butcher *(at a slaughterhouse).*

équateur [ekwatœr] *nm* equator ■ **sous l'~** at the equator.

Équateur [ekwatœr] *npr m* : **(la république de) l'~** (the Republic of) Ecuador.

équation [ekwasjɔ̃] *nf* **1.** MATH equation ■ **~ du premier/second degré** simple/quadratic equation **2.** ASTRON : **~ du temps** equation of time **3.** CHIM : **~ chimique** chemical equation **4.** PSYCHOL : **~ personnelle** personal equation.

équatorial, e, aux [ekwatɔrjal, o] *adj* ASTRON & GÉOGR equatorial.
◆ **équatorial** *nm* equatorial *(telescope).*

équatorien, enne [ekwatɔrjɛ̃, ɛn] *adj* Ecuadoran, Ecuadorian.
◆ **Équatorien, enne** *nm, f* Ecuadoran, Ecuadorian.

équerre [ekɛr] *nf* : **~ à dessin** set square ■ **~ en T, double ~** T-square.
◆ **à l'équerre, d'équerre** *loc adj* [mur] straight ■ [pièce] square.
◆ **en équerre** *loc adj* T-shaped.

équestre [ekɛstr] *adj* [statue, peinture] equestrian ■ [exercice, centre] horseriding *(modif)* ■ **le sport ~** (horse) riding.

équeuter [3] [ekøte] *vt* [fruit] to pull the stalk off, to remove the stalk from.

équidé [ekide] *nm* member of the horse family *ou* of the Equidae.

équidistance [ekɥidistɑ̃s] *nf* equidistance.
◆ **à équidistance de** *loc prép* : **à ~ de Moscou et de Prague** half-way between Moscow and Prague.

équidistant, e [ekɥidistɑ̃, ɑ̃t] *adj* equidistant.

équilatéral, e, aux [ekɥilateral, o] *adj* equilateral.

équilibrage [ekilibraʒ] *nm* balancing, counterbalancing ■ **faire faire l'~ des roues** AUTO to have the wheels balanced.

équilibrant, e [ekilibrɑ̃, ɑ̃t] *adj* balancing *(modif).*

équilibre [ekilibr] *nm* **1.** [stabilité du corps] balance ■ **garder/perdre l'~** to keep/to lose one's balance ■ **faire perdre l'~ à qqn** to throw sb off balance *pr* **2.** [rapport de force] balance ■ **rétablir l'~** to restore the balance ■ **l'~ des forces** *ou* **du pouvoir** the balance of power ■ **l'~ de la terreur** the balance of terror ■ **l'~ naturel** the balance of nature **3.** ÉCON & FIN : **~ budgétaire** balance in the budget ■ **~ économique** economic equilibrium **4.** PSYCHOL : **manquer d'~** to be (mentally *ou* emotionally) unbalanced ⊃ **~ mental** (mental) equilibrium **5.** CHIM & PHYS equilibrium.
◆ **en équilibre** ⇔ *loc adj* [plateau, pile de livres] stable. ⇔ *loc adv* : **marcher en ~ sur un fil** to balance on a tightrope ■ **le clown tenait un verre en ~ sur son nez** the clown was balancing a glass on his nose ■ **mettre qqch en ~** to balance sthg.

équilibré, e [ekilibre] *adj* **1.** PSYCHOL balanced, stable **2.** [budget] balanced ■ [alimentation, emploi du temps] balanced, well-balanced ■ **mal ~** unbalanced, unstable.

équilibrer [3] [ekilibre] *vt* **1.** [contrebalancer - poids, forces] to counterbalance ■ **faire ~ ses roues** to have the wheels balanced **2.** [rendre stable - balance, budget] to balance ■ **~ son régime** to follow a balanced diet.
◆ **s'équilibrer** *vp (emploi réciproque)* to counterbalance each other *ou* one another, to even out.

équilibreur [ekilibrœr] *nm* stabilizer.

équilibriste [ekilibrist] *nmf* [acrobate] acrobat ■ [funambule] tightrope walker.

équinoxe [ekinɔks] *nm* equinox ■ **~ de printemps/d'automne** spring/autumn equinox.

équipage [ekipaʒ] *nm* **1.** AÉRON & NAUT crew ■ **membres de l'~** members of the crew, crew members **2.** *arch* [escorte - d'un prince] retinue, suite **3.** MIL [matériel] equipment.

équipe [ekip] *nf* **1.** [groupe - de chercheurs, de secouristes] team ■ **travailler en ~** to work as a team ■ **faire ~ avec qqn** to team up with sb **2.** INDUST : **~ de jour/nuit** day/night shift ■ **travailler en** *ou* **par ~s** [à l'usine] to work in shifts ; [sur un chantier] to work in gangs **3.** SPORT [gén] team ■ [sur un bateau] crew ■ **jouer en** *ou* **par ~s** to play in teams ■ **l'~ de France de rugby/hockey** the French rugby/hockey team ■ **l'Équipe** PRESSE *daily sports newspaper* **4.** [bande] crew, gang ■ **on formait une joyeuse ~** we were a happy lot.
◆ **d'équipe** *loc adj* **1.** [collectif] : **esprit d'~** team *ou* group spirit ■ **travail d'~** teamwork **2.** [sport, jeu] team *(modif).*

équipée [ekipe] *nf* **1.** [aventure] escapade ■ **une folle ~** a mad escapade **2.** *hum* [promenade] jaunt.

équipement [ekipmɑ̃] *nm* **1.** [matériel - léger] equipment, supplies ; [- lourd] equipment ■ **renouveler l'~ d'une usine** to refit a factory ⊃ **~ de bureau** office supplies ■ **~ électrique** electrical supplies ■ **~s spéciaux** AUTO [pneus] snow tyres ; [chaînes] chains **2.** [panoplie] kit, gear **3.** [infrastructure] : **~s collectifs** public amenities ■ **~s sportifs/scolaires** sports/educational facilities ■ **l'~ routier/ferroviaire du pays** the country's road/rail infrastructure ■ **(le service de) l'Équipement** *local government department responsible for road maintenance and issuing building permits* **4.** [fait de pourvoir] : **procéder à l'~ d'un terrain de jeu** to equip a playing field.

équiper [3] [ekipe] *vt* **1.** [pourvoir de matériel - armée, élève, skieur] to kit out *(sép)*, to fit out ; [- navire] to fit out *(sép)*, to commission ; [- salle] to equip, to fit out *(sép)* ; [- usine] to equip ■ **cuisine tout** *ou* **entièrement équipée** fully-equipped kitchen ■ **être bien équipé pour une expédition** to be all set up *ou* kitted out for an expedition ■ **~ qqch de** : **~ une maison d'un système d'alarme** to install a burglar alarm in a house **2.** [pourvoir d'une infrastructure] : **~ une ville d'un réseau d'égouts** to equip a town with a sewage system ■ **~ industriellement une région** to bring industry to a region.
◆ **s'équiper** *vp (emploi réfléchi)* to equip o.s., to kit o.s. out *UK.*

équipier, ère [ekipje, ɛr] *nm, f* team member.

équitable [ekitabl] *adj* [verdict, répartition] fair, equitable ■ [juge] fair, fair-minded, even-handed.

équitablement [ekitabləmɑ̃] *adv* fairly, equitably.

équitation [ekitasjɔ̃] *nf* horseriding, riding ■ **faire de l'~** to go horseriding.
◆ **d'équitation** *loc adj* [école, professeur] riding *(modif).*

équité [ekite] *nf* equity, fairness, fair-mindedness.
◆ **en toute équité** *loc adv* very equitably *ou* fairly.

équivalence [ekivalɑ̃s] *nf* **1.** [gén - LOGIQUE] & MATH equivalence **2.** UNIV : **faire une demande d'~, demander une ~** to request an equivalent rating of one's qualifications ■ **quels sont les diplômes étrangers admis en ~?** which foreign diplomas are recognized?

équivalent, e [ekivalɑ̃, ɑ̃t] *adj* [gén - MATH] equivalent ■ **le prix de vente est ~ au prix de revient** the selling price is equivalent to the cost price.
◆ **équivalent** *nm* [élément comparable] equivalent.

équivaloir [60] [ekivalwar] ◆ **équivaloir à** *v+prép* [être égal à] to be equal *ou* equivalent to ■ [revenir à] to amount to ■ **ça équivaut à s'avouer vaincu** it amounts to admitting defeat.
◆ **s'équivaloir** *vp (emploi réciproque)* to be equivalent.

équivoque [ekivɔk] <> *adj* **1.** [ambigu - terme, réponse] equivocal, ambiguous ; [- compliment] double-edged, backhanded **2.** [suspect - fréquentation, comportement] questionable, dubious ; [- personnage] shady.
<> *nf* **1.** [caractère ambigu] ambiguity *(U)* ■ **déclaration sans ~** unambiguous *ou* unequivocal statement **2.** [malentendu] misunderstanding *(C)* **3.** [doute] doubt ■ **pour lever** *ou* **dissiper l'~ sur mes intentions** so as to leave no doubt as to my intentions.

érable [erabl] *nm* maple.

éradication [eradikasjɔ̃] *nf* eradication, rooting out.

éradiquer [3] [eradike] *vt* to eradicate, to root out *(sép)*.

érafler [3] [erafle] *vt* **1.** [écorcher - peau, genou] to scrape, to scratch, to graze **2.** [rayer - peinture, carrosserie] to scrape, to scratch.
◆ **s'érafler** *vpt* : **s'~ les mains** to graze one's hands.

éraflure [eraflyr] *nf* scratch, scrape ■ **se faire une ~ au coude** to scrape *ou* to graze one's elbow.

éraillé, e [eraje] *adj* **1.** [rauque] rasping, hoarse ■ **avoir la voix ~e** to be hoarse **2.** [rayé - surface] scratched **3.** [injecté] : **avoir l'œil ~** to have bloodshot eyes.

érailler [3] [eraje] *vt* **1.** [surface] to scratch **2.** [voix] to make hoarse.
◆ **s'érailler** *vpt* : **s'~ la voix** to make o.s. hoarse.

Érasme [erasm] *npr* Erasmus.

ère [ɛr] *nf* **1.** [époque] era ■ **270 ans avant notre ~** 270 BC ■ **en l'an 500 de notre ~** in the year 500 AD, in the year of our Lord 500 ⊙ **l'~ chrétienne** the Christian era **2.** GÉOL era.

érectile [erɛktil] *adj* erectile.

érection [erɛksjɔ̃] *nf* **1.** PHYSIOL erection ■ **avoir une ~** to have an erection **2.** *litt* [édification] erection, raising *(U)*.

éreintage [erɛ̃taʒ] *nm* [critique] slating UK, panning.

éreintant, e [erɛ̃tɑ̃, ɑ̃t] *adj* gruelling, backbreaking.

éreintement [erɛ̃tmɑ̃] *nm sout* **1.** [d'un auteur] slating UK, panning **2.** [fatigue] exhaustion.

éreinter [3] [erɛ̃te] *vt* **1.** [épuiser] to exhaust, to wear out *(sép)* ■ **être éreinté** to be worn out **2.** [critiquer - pièce, acteur] to slate UK, to pan ■ **son spectacle s'est fait ~ par tous les critiques** all the critics slated *ou* panned his show.
◆ **s'éreinter** *vpi* to wear o.s. out ■ **s'~ à faire qqch** to wear o.s. out doing sthg.

érémiste [eremist] *nmf fam person receiving the RMI benefit.*

Érévan [erevɑ̃] *npr* Yerevan.

erg [ɛrg] *nm* GÉOGR & PHYS erg.

ergonomie [ɛrgɔnɔmi] *nf* ergonomics *(sing)*.

ergonomique [ɛrgɔnɔmik] *adj* ergonomic.

ergot [ɛrgo] *nm* **1.** [de coq] spur ■ [de chien] dewclaw ■ **monter** *ou* **se dresser sur ses ~s** to get on one's high horse **2.** BOT ergot.

ergotage [ɛrgɔtaʒ] *nm* quibbling.

ergoter [3] [ɛrgɔte] *vi* to quibble ■ **~ sur des détails** to quibble about details.

ergoteur, euse [ɛrgɔtœr, øz] *nm, f* quibbler.

ergothérapie [ɛrgɔterapi] *nf* occupational therapy.

Érié [erje] *npr* : **le lac ~** Lake Erie.

ériger [17] [eriʒe] *vt* **1.** [édifier - statue, temple] to erect, to raise **2.** [instituer - comité, tribunal] to set up *(sép)*, to establish **3.** [le transformer en] : **~ qqch/qqn en** : **le cynisme érigé en art** cynicism raised to the status of fine art.
◆ **s'ériger** *vpi* : **s'~ en moraliste/censeur** to set o.s. up as a moralist/a censor.

Érin [erin] *npr f litt* Erin.

ermitage [ɛrmitaʒ] *nm* **1.** [d'un ermite] hermitage **2.** [retraite] retreat.

ermite [ɛrmit] *nm* **1.** RELIG hermit **2.** [reclus] hermit, recluse ■ **vivre comme un ~** *ou* **en ~** to live like *ou* as a hermit, to lead the life of a recluse.

éroder [3] [erɔde] *vt* to erode.

érogène [erɔʒɛn] *adj* erogenous, erogenic.

éros [eros] *nm* PSYCHOL : **l'~** Eros.

Éros [eros] *npr* Eros.

érosif, ive [erozif, iv] *adj* erosive.

érosion [erozjɔ̃] *nm* **1.** GÉOGR & MÉD erosion **2.** [dégradation] erosion ■ **~ monétaire** erosion of the value of money.

érotique [erɔtik] *adj* erotic.

érotiquement [erɔtikmɑ̃] *adv* erotically.

érotisation [erɔtizasjɔ̃] *nf* eroticization, eroticizing.

érotiser [3] [erɔtize] *vt* to eroticize.

érotisme [erɔtism] *nm* eroticism ■ **d'un ~ torride** [film] steamy ; [situation] sexy, hot US.

érotomane [erɔtɔman] *nmf* erotomaniac.

errance [ɛrɑ̃s] *nf litt* wandering, roaming.

errant, e [ɛrɑ̃, ɑ̃t] *adj* wandering, roaming ■ **mener une vie ~e** to lead the life of a wanderer.

errata [erata] <> *pl* ▷ **erratum**.
<> *nm inv* [liste] list of errata.

erratique [eratik] *adj* **1.** GÉOL & MÉD erratic **2.** *sout* [variation] erratic.

erratum [eratɔm] *(pl* **errata** [erata]*)* *nm* erratum.

errements [ɛrmɑ̃] *nmpl litt* erring ways *litt*, bad habits.

errer [4] [ɛre] *vi* **1.** [marcher] to roam, to wander ■ **~ comme une âme en peine** to wander about like a lost soul **2.** [imagination] to wander, to stray ■ [regard] to wander, to rove **3.** *litt* [se tromper] to err.

erreur [ɛrœr] *nf* **1.** [faute] mistake, error ■ **il doit y avoir une ~** there must be a *ou* some mistake ■ **il y a ~ sur la personne** you've got the wrong person, it's a case of mistaken identity ■ **~!** wrong! ■ **c'est lui, pas d'~!** that's him all right! ■ **ce serait une ~ (que) de penser cela** it would be wrong *ou* a mistake to think that ■ **faire** *ou* **commettre une ~** to make a mistake *ou* an error ■ **faire ~** to be wrong *ou* mistaken ⊙ **~ de calcul** miscalculation ■ **~ typographique** *ou* **d'impression** misprint, printer's error ■ **l'~ est humaine** to err is human **2.** [errement] error ■ **des ~s de jeunesse** youthful indiscretions ■ **racheter ses ~s passées** to mend one's ways ■ **retomber dans les mêmes ~s** to lapse back into the same old bad habits **3.** DR : **~ judiciaire** miscarriage of justice.
◆ **par erreur** *loc adv* by mistake.
◆ **sauf erreur** *loc adv* : **sauf ~ de ma part, ce lundi-là est férié** unless I'm (very much) mistaken, that Monday is a public holiday.
◆ **sauf erreur ou omission** *loc adv* COMM & DR errors and omissions excepted.

erroné, e [ɛrɔne] *adj* erroneous, mistaken.

ersatz [ɛrzats] *nm* ersatz, substitute ■ **un ~ de café** ersatz coffee ■ **un ~ d'aventure/d'amour** a substitute for adventure/for love.

éructer [3] [erykte] <> *vi* to eruct *sout*, to belch.
<> *vt sout* : **~ des injures** to belch (forth) insults.

érudit, e [erydi, it] <> *adj* erudite, learned, scholarly.
<> *nm, f* scholar, erudite *ou* learned person.

érudition [erydisjɔ̃] *nf* erudition, scholarship.

éruption [erypsjɔ̃] *nf* **1.** ASTRON & GÉOL eruption ▪ **entrer en ~** to erupt ▪ **volcan en ~** erupting volcano **2.** MÉD outbreak ▪ **~ cutanée** rash ▪ **~ de boutons** outbreak of spots **3.** *fig* outbreak ▪ **~ de colère** fit of anger, angry outburst.

érythème [eritɛm] *nm* erythema ▪ **~ fessier** nappy rash.

Érythrée [eritre] *npr f* : **(l')~** Eritrea.

es *v* ▻ **être.**

E/S (*abr écrite de* **entrée/sortie**) I/O.

ès [ɛs] *prép* : **licencié ès lettres** ≃ Bachelor of Arts, ≃ BA ▪ **licencié ès sciences** ≃ Bachelor of Sciences, ≃ BSc ▪ **docteur ès lettres** ≃ Doctor of Philosophy, ≃ PhD.

esbroufe [ɛzbruf] *nf fam* bluff ▪ **faire de l'~** to bluff.
◆ **à l'esbroufe** *fam loc adv* : **il l'a fait à l'~** he bluffed his way through it.

escabeau, x [ɛskabo] *nm* **1.** [tabouret] stool **2.** [échelle] stepladder.

escadre [ɛskadr] *nf* **1.** NAUT squadron **2.** AÉRON wing.

escadrille [ɛskadrij] *nf* **1.** NAUT squadron **2.** AÉRON flight, squadron ▪ **~ de chasse** fighter squadron.

escadron [ɛskadrɔ̃] *nm* **1.** [dans la cavalerie] squadron ▪ [dans l'armée blindée] squadron ▪ [dans la gendarmerie] company ▪ **~ de la mort** POLIT death squad **2.** *fam hum* [groupe] bunch, gang.

escalade [ɛskalad] *nf* **1.** SPORT [activité] rock climbing *(U)* ▪ **faire de l'~** to go rock climbing ▮ [ascension] climb ▪ **~ artificielle** artificial climb **2.** [d'un mur, d'une grille] climbing *(U)*, scaling *(U)* ▪ DR illegal entry **3.** [aggravation] escalation ▪ **l'~ de la violence** the escalation of violence ▪ **l'~ des prix** the soaring of prices.

escalader [3] [ɛskalade] *vt* [portail] to climb, to scale, to clamber up *(insép)* ▪ [montagne] to climb ▪ [grille] to climb over ▪ [muret] to scramble up *(insép)*.

Escalator® [ɛskalatɔr] *nm* escalator, moving staircase.

escale [ɛskal] *nf* **1.** [lieu - NAUT] port of call ▪ AÉRON stop **2.** [halte - NAUT] call ▪ AÉRON stop, stopover ▪ **faire ~ à** [navire] to call at, to put in at ; [avion] to stop over at ➊ **~ technique** refuelling stop.
◆ **sans escale** *loc adj* nonstop, direct.

escalier [ɛskalje] *nm* staircase, (flight of) stairs ▪ **les ~s** the staircase *ou* stairs ▪ **en bas des ~s** downstairs ▪ **en haut des ~s** upstairs ▪ **être dans l'~** *ou* **les ~s** to be on the stairs ➊ **~ mécanique** *ou* **roulant** escalator ▪ **~ en colimaçon** *ou* **en vrille** spiral staircase ▪ **~ dérobé** hidden staircase ▪ **~ d'honneur** main staircase ▪ **~ de secours** fire escape ▪ **~ de service** backstairs, service stairs.
◆ **escaliers** *nmpl Belgique* [marches] steps.

escalope [ɛskalɔp] *nf* escalope ▪ **~ de veau/de poulet** veal/chicken escalope ➊ **~ panée** escalope in breadcrumbs.

escamotable [ɛskamɔtabl] *adj* [train d'atterrissage] retractable ▪ [lit, table] collapsible, foldaway.

escamotage [ɛskamɔtaʒ] *nm* **1.** [disparition] conjuring *ou* spiriting away *(U)* **2.** [vol] filching *(U)*.

escamoter [3] [ɛskamɔte] *vt* **1.** [faire disparaître - mouchoir, carte] to conjure *ou* to spirit away *(sép)* ; [- placard, lit] to fold away *(sép)* **2.** [voler] to filch **3.** [éluder - difficultés] to evade, to skirt round *(insép)* ; [- mot, note] to skip **4.** AÉRON to retract.

escampette [ɛskɑ̃pɛt] *nf* ▻ **poudre.**

escapade [ɛskapad] *nf* **1.** [fugue] : **faire une ~** to run off *ou* away **2.** [séjour] jaunt ▪ **une ~ de deux jours à Deauville** a two-day visit *ou* jaunt to Deauville.

escarbille [ɛskarbij] *nf* piece of soot.

escarboucle [ɛskarbukl] *nf* carbuncle.

escarcelle [ɛskarsɛl] *nf arch* moneybag ▪ **300 euros vont tomber** *ou* **rentrer dans mon ~** *hum* I'm about to have a little windfall of 300 euros.

escargot [ɛskargo] *nm* snail ▪ **avancer comme un ~** *ou* **à une allure d'~** to go at a snail's pace.

escarmouche [ɛskarmuʃ] *nf* skirmish.

escarpé, e [ɛskarpe] *adj* steep.

escarpement [ɛskarpəmɑ̃] *nm* [pente] steep slope.

escarpin [ɛskarpɛ̃] *nm* court shoe.

escarpolette [ɛskarpɔlɛt] *nf arch* [balançoire] swing.

escarre [ɛskar] *nf* scab.

Escaut [ɛsko] *npr m* : **l'~** the (River) Scheldt.

eschatologie [ɛskatɔlɔʒi] *nf* eschatology.

Eschyle [eʃil] *npr* Aeschylus.

escient [esjɑ̃] *nm* : **à bon ~** advisedly, judiciously ▪ **à mauvais ~** injudiciously, unwisely.

esclaffer [3] [ɛsklafe] ◆ **s'esclaffer** *vpi* to burst out laughing, to guffaw.

esclandre [ɛsklɑ̃dr] *nm* scene, scandal ▪ **faire un ~** to make a scene.

esclavage [ɛsklavaʒ] *nm* **1.** SOCIOL slavery ▪ **réduire qqn en ~** to reduce sb to slavery, to make a slave out of sb **2.** [contrainte] slavery, bondage *litt* **3.** [dépendance] : **vivre dans l'~ de** to be a slave to.

esclavagisme [ɛsklavaʒism] *nm* SOCIOL slavery.

esclavagiste [ɛsklavaʒist] *nmf* supporter of slavery.

esclave [ɛsklav] ◇ *adj* **1.** SOCIOL : **un peuple ~** an enslaved people **2.** *fig* **~ de** [assujetti à] : **ne sois pas ~ de ses moindres désirs** don't give in to her every whim ▪ **être ~ de l'alcool/du tabac** to be a slave to drink/to tobacco.
◇ *nm* **1.** SOCIOL slave **2.** *fig* slave ▪ **l'~ de** a slave to, the slave of.

escogriffe [ɛskɔgrif] *nm* : **un grand ~** a beanpole.

escomptable [ɛskɔ̃tabl] *adj* discountable.

escompte [ɛskɔ̃t] *nm* **1.** BANQUE : **faire un ~ à 2 %** to allow a discount of 2% **2.** COMM discount.

escompter [3] [ɛskɔ̃te] *vt* **1.** [espérer] : **~ qqch** to rely *ou* to count *ou* to bank on sthg ▪ **c'est mieux que ce que j'escomptais** it's better than what I expected **2.** BANQUE to discount.

escompteur [ɛskɔ̃tœr] *nm* discounter.

escorte [ɛskɔrt] *nf* **1.** AÉRON, MIL & NAUT escort **2.** [personne, groupe] escort ▪ **servir d'~ à qqn** to escort sb.
◆ **d'escorte** *loc adj* [escadron, avion] escort *(modif)*.
◆ **sous bonne escorte** *loc adv* : **être sous bonne ~** to be in safe hands ▪ **reconduit sous bonne ~ jusqu'à la prison** brought back to prison under heavy escort.

escorter [3] [ɛskɔrte] *vt* **1.** [ami, président, célébrité] to escort ▪ [femme] to escort, to be the escort of **2.** AÉRON, MIL & NAUT to escort.

escorteur [ɛskɔrtœr] *nm* escort ship.

escouade [ɛskwad] *nf* **1.** MIL squad **2.** [équipe - de balayeurs, de contrôleurs] squad, gang.

escrime [ɛskrim] *nf* fencing *(U)* ▪ **faire de l'~** to fence.

escrimer [3] [ɛskrime] ◆ **s'escrimer** *vpi* : **s'~ à faire qqch** to strive to do sthg ▪ **s'~ sur qqch** *fig* to plug away at sthg.

escrimeur, euse [ɛskrimœr, øz] *nm, f* fencer.

escroc [ɛskro] *nm* swindler, crook.

escroquer [3] [ɛskrɔke] *vt* **1.** [voler - victime, client] to swindle, to cheat ; [- argent, milliard] to swindle ▪ **~ de l'argent à qqn** to swindle money out of sb, to swindle sb out of (his/her) money **2.** [extorquer] : **~ une signature à qqn** to worm a signature out of sb.

escroquerie [ɛskrɔkri] *nf* **1.** [pratique malhonnête] swindle ▪ **100 euros le kilo, c'est de l'~!** 100 euros a kilo, it's daylight *UK* *ou* highway *US* robbery! **2.** DR fraud.

escudo [ɛskydo] *nm* escudo.

esgourde [ɛsgurd] *nf fam* earhole.

eskimo [ɛskimo] = **esquimau.**

Ésope [ezɔp] *npr* Aesop.

ésotérique [ezɔterik] *adj* esoteric.

ésotérisme [ezɔterism] *nm* esotericism.

espace[1] [ɛspas] *nm* **1.** [gén - ASTRON] : **l'~** space ■ **voyager dans l'~** to travel through space **2.** [place, volume] space, room ■ **manquer d'~** to be cramped ➲ **~ vital** living space **3.** [distance - physique] space, gap ; [- temporelle] gap, interval, space ■ **laissez un ~ d'un mètre entre les deux arbres** leave (a gap of) one metre between the two trees **4.** [surface] space, stretch ➲ **~ publicitaire** advertising space **5.** [lieu] : **~ de rangement** storage space ■ **un ~ vert** a park **6.** GÉOM & MATH space ■ **~ euclidien** Euclidean space **7.** AÉRON : **~ aérien** airspace.
◆ **dans l'espace de, en l'espace de** *loc prép* [dans le temps] within (the space of) ■ **malade cinq fois en l'~ d'un mois** sick five times within (the space of) a month.

espace[2] [ɛspas] *nf* IMPR space.

espacement [ɛspasmɑ̃] *nm* **1.** [dans le temps] spreading *ou* spacing out ■ **l'~ des paiements** staggering of payments **2.** [distance] space **3.** IMPR [entre deux lettres] space ■ [interligne] space (between the lines), spacing.

espacer [16] [ɛspase] *vt* **1.** [séparer - lignes, mots, arbustes] to space out *(sép)* **2.** [dans le temps] to space out ■ **vous devriez ~ vos rencontres** you should meet less often *ou* less frequently.
◆ **s'espacer** *vpi* **1.** [dans le temps - visites] to become less frequent **2.** [s'écarter - gymnastes] : **espacez-vous** move further away from each other.

espace-temps [ɛspastɑ̃] (*pl* **espaces-temps**) *nm* space-time (continuum).

espadon [ɛspadɔ̃] *nm* swordfish.

espadrille [ɛspadrij] *nf* espadrille.

Espagne [ɛspaɲ] *npr f* : **(l')~** Spain ■ **la guerre d'~** the Spanish Civil War.

espagnol, e [ɛspaɲɔl] *adj* Spanish.
◆ **Espagnol, e** *nm, f* Spaniard ■ **les Espagnols** the Spanish.
◆ **espagnol** *nm* LING Spanish.

espagnolette [ɛspaɲɔlɛt] *nf* window catch.

espalier [ɛspalje] *nm* **1.** HORT espalier **2.** SPORT gym ladder.

espèce [ɛspɛs] *nf* **1.** SC species *(sing)* ■ **l'~ humaine** the human race, mankind ■ **des ~s animales/végétales** animal/plant species ■ **~ en voie de disparition** endangered species **2.** [sorte] sort, kind ■ **rangez ensemble les livres de même ~** put books of the same kind together ■ **des escrocs de ton/son ~** crooks like you/him ■ **des gens de leur ~** their sort *péj*, the likes of them *péj* ■ **les gens de cette ~** that sort, people of that ilk ■ **de la pire ~** terrible ■ **c'est un menteur de la pire ~** he's the worst kind of liar, he's a terrible liar ■ **ça n'a aucune ~ d'importance!** that is of absolutely no importance! ➲ **une ~/l'~ de** *péj* : **c'était une ~ de ferme** it was a sort of farm *ou* a farm of sorts ■ **l'~ de malfrat barbu qui nous conduisait** the shady-looking fellow with a beard who was driving ■ **~ de** *fam péj* : **~ d'idiot!** you idiot! **3.** DR particular *ou* specific case.
◆ **espèces** *nfpl* **1.** FIN cash ■ **payer en ~s** to pay cash ➲ **~s sonnantes et trébuchantes** hard cash **2.** RELIG species.
◆ **en l'espèce** *loc adv* in this particular case ■ **j'avais de bons rapports avec mes employés mais en l'~ l'affaire a fini au tribunal** I always had good relations with my employees but in this instance, the matter finished up in court.

espérance [ɛsperɑ̃s] *nf* **1.** [espoir] hope, expectation **2.** [cause d'espoir] hope **3.** SOCIOL : **~ de vie** life expectancy **4.** RELIG hope.
◆ **espérances** *nfpl* **1.** [perspectives] prospects ■ **donner des ~s** to be promising ❚ [aspirations] hopes ■ **fonder ses ~s sur qqn** to pin one's hopes on sb **2.** *euphém* [espoir d'hériter] expectations, prospects of inheritance.
◆ **contre toute espérance** *loc adv* contrary to (all) *ou* against all expectations.

espérantiste [ɛsperɑ̃tist] *adj & nmf* Esperantist.

espéranto [ɛsperɑ̃to] *nm* Esperanto.

espérer [18] [ɛspere] <> *vt* **1.** [souhaiter] to hope ■ **~ le succès** to hope for success, to hope to succeed ■ **j'espère que vous viendrez** I hope (that) you will come ■ **j'espère vous revoir bientôt** I hope to see you soon ■ *(en usage absolu)* **j'espère (bien)!** I (do *ou* certainly) hope so! **2.** [escompter] to expect ■ **n'espère pas qu'elle te rembourse** don't expect her to pay you back ■ **je n'en espérais pas tant de lui** I didn't expect that much of him **3.** [attendre] to expect, to wait for *(insép)* ■ **on ne vous espérait plus!** we'd given up on you!
<> *vi* to hope ■ **~ en** *sout* to have faith in ■ **~ en Dieu** to have faith *ou* to trust in God ■ **il faut ~ en des temps meilleurs** we must live in hope of better times.

esperluette [ɛspɛrlɥɛt] *nf* ampersand.

espiègle [ɛspjɛgl] <> *adj* [personne] impish, mischievous ■ [regard, réponse] mischievous ■ **d'un air ~** mischievously.
<> *nmf* (little) rascal, imp.

espièglerie [ɛspjɛgləri] *nf* **1.** [caractère] impishness, mischievousness **2.** [farce] prank, trick, piece of mischief.

espiogiciel [ɛspjɔʒisjɛl] *nm* INFORM spyware.

espion, onne [ɛspjɔ̃, ɔn] *nm, f* spy.
◆ **espion** *nm (comme adj; avec ou sans trait d'union)* spy *(modif)* ■ **micro ~** bug ■ **satellite ~** spy satellite.

espionnage [ɛspjɔnaʒ] *nm* **1.** [action] spying **2.** [activité] espionage ■ **~ industriel** industrial espionage.
◆ **d'espionnage** *loc adj* [film, roman] spy *(modif)*.

espionner [3] [ɛspjɔne] *vt* to spy on *(insép)* ■ *(en usage absolu)* **elle est toujours là, à ~** she's always snooping (around).

esplanade [ɛsplanad] *nf* esplanade.

espoir [ɛspwar] *nm* **1.** [espérance] hope ■ **être plein d'~** to be very hopeful ■ **j'ai l'~ de le voir revenir** I'm hopeful that he'll return ■ **j'ai bon ~ qu'il va gagner** *ou* **de le voir gagner** I'm confident that he'll win ■ **il n'y a plus d'~** [il va mourir] there's no hope left ; [nous avons perdu] we've had it **2.** [cause d'espérance] hope ■ **tu es mon dernier ~** you're my last hope ■ **c'est un des ~s du tennis français** he's one of France's most promising young tennis players.
◆ **dans l'espoir de** <> *loc prép* in the hope of.
<> *loc conj* in the hope of ■ **dans l'~ de vous voir bientôt** hoping to see you soon.
◆ **sans espoir** *loc adj* hopeless.

esprit [ɛspri] *nm* **1.** [manière de penser] mind ■ **les voyages ouvrent l'~** travel broadens the mind ■ **avoir l'~ clair** to be a clear thinker ■ **avoir l'~ critique** to have a critical mind ■ **avoir l'~ étroit/large** to be narrow-minded/broad-minded ■ **avoir l'~ lent/vif** to be slow-witted/quick-witted ■ **avoir l'~ mal tourné** *fam* to have a dirty mind ■ **~ de : ~ d'analyse** analytical mind ■ **avoir l'~ d'aventure** to have a spirit of adventure ■ **avoir l'~ d'à-propos** to be quick off the mark, to have a ready wit ■ **avoir l'~ de contradiction** to be contrary *ou* argumentative ■ **~ de suite** consistency ■ **sans ~ de suite** inconsistently ■ **avoir l'~ de synthèse** to be good at drawing ideas together ➲ **avoir l'~ de l'escalier** to be slow off the mark
2. [facultés, cerveau] mind, head ■ **as-tu perdu l'~?** are you out of your mind?, have you completely lost your head? ■ **maintenant que j'ai fini le rapport, j'ai l'~ libre** now I've finished the report, I can relax ■ **où avais-je l'~?** what was I thinking of? ■ **j'ai l'~ ailleurs** I'm not concentrating ■ **il n'a pas l'~ à ce qu'il fait** his mind is elsewhere *ou* isn't on what he's doing ■ **ça m'a traversé l'~** it occurred to me, it crossed my mind ■ **une idée me vient à l'~** I've just thought of something ■ **dans son ~ nous devrions voter** according to him we should vote ■ **dans mon ~, la chambre était peinte en bleu** in my mind's eye, I saw the bedroom painted in blue ■ **dans mon ~, les enfants partaient avant nous** what I had in mind was for the children to go before us
3. [idée] sense ■ **il a eu le bon ~ de ne pas téléphoner** he had the sense not to call
4. [mentalité] spirit ■ **l'~ dans lequel cela a été fait** the spirit in which it was done ■ **avoir l'~ sportif** to be fond of sport ➲ **~ de chapelle** *ou* **clan** *ou* **clocher** *ou* **parti** parochial attitude ■ **avoir l'~ de clocher** to be parochial ■ **~ de caste** class consciousness ■ **~ de compétition/d'équipe** competitive/team spirit ■ **(avoir l')~ de corps** (to have) esprit de corps ■ **avoir l'~ d'entreprise** to be enterprising ■ **avoir l'~ de famille** to be family-minded ■ **~ de révolte** rebelliousness ■ **~ de sacrifice**

spirit of sacrifice ▪ **c'est du mauvais ~** he's/they're *etc* just trying to make trouble ▪ **faire preuve de mauvais ~** to be a troublemaker
5. [humeur] : **avoir l'~ à : je n'ai pas l'~ à rire** I'm not in the mood for laughing
6. [personne] mind ▪ **c'est un ~ tatillon** he's far too fussy ▪ **un des ~s marquants de ce siècle** one of the great minds *ou* leading lights of this century ▪ **~s chagrins** *péj* faultfinders ➊ **un ~ libre** a freethinker ▪ **un bel ~** a wit ▪ **les grands ~s se rencontrent** *hum* great minds think alike
7. [humour] wit ▪ **avoir de l'~** to be witty ▪ **faire de l'~** to try to be witty *ou* funny ▪ **une femme (pleine) d'~** a witty woman ▪ **une remarque pleine d'~** a witty remark, a witticism
8. RELIG spirit ▪ [ange] : **Esprit** Spirit ▪ **Esprit malin, Esprit des ténèbres** Evil Spirit, Evil One ▪ **l'Esprit Saint** the Holy Spirit *ou* Ghost
9. [fantôme] ghost, spirit ➊ **~ frappeur** poltergeist
10. LING breathing ▪ **~ doux/rude** smooth/rough breathing
11. CHIM [partie volatile] spirit ▪ **~ de sel, ~-de-sel** spirits of salt ▪ **~ de vin, ~-de-vin** spirits of wine, ethanol.
◆ **esprits** *nmpl* senses ▪ **reprendre ses ~s** [après un évanouissement] to regain consciousness, to come to ; [se ressaisir] to get a grip on o.s.
◆ **dans un esprit de** *loc prép* : **dans un ~ de conciliation** in an attempt at conciliation ▪ **dans un ~ de justice** in a spirit of justice, in an effort to be fair.

esquarre [ɛskar] = **escarre.**

esquif [ɛskif] *nm litt* skiff.

esquille [ɛskij] *nf* [de bois] splinter ▪ [d'os] bone splinter.

esquimau, aude, x [ɛskimo, od] *adj* Eskimo.
◆ **Esquimau, aude, x** *nm, f* Eskimo ▪ **les Esquimaux** the Eskimos.
◆ **esquimau** *nm* LING Eskimo.

Esquimau® [ɛskimo] *nm* choc-ice on a stick *UK*, Eskimo *US*.

esquinter [3] [ɛskɛ̃te] *vt fam* **1.** [endommager - chose] to ruin ; [- voiture] to smash up, to total *US & Canada* ; [- santé] to ruin ▪ **la moto est complètement esquintée** the bike is a wreck ▪ **sa voiture s'est fait ~ par les manifestants** his car was smashed up by the demonstrators **2.** [épuiser - personne] to exhaust, to knock out *(sép)* **3.** [dénigrer - livre, film] to pan, to slate *UK*.
◆ **s'esquinter** *vp (emploi réfléchi) fam* **1.** [s'épuiser] to kill o.s. **2.** [s'abîmer] : **s'~ la santé** to ruin one's health ▪ **tu vas t'~ les yeux avec cet écran** you'll strain your eyes with that screen.

esquisse [ɛskis] *nf* **1.** ART sketch **2.** [d'un projet, d'un discours, d'un roman] draft, outline **3.** [d'un sourire] hint, shadow, ghost ▪ [d'un geste] hint ▪ **sans l'~ d'un regret** with no regrets at all, without the slightest regret.

esquisser [3] [ɛskise] *vt* **1.** ART to sketch **2.** [projet, histoire] to outline, to draft **3.** [geste, mouvement] to give a hint of ▪ **il esquissa un geste d'approbation** he gave a slight nod of approval ▪ **~ un sourire** to give a faint *ou* slight smile.
◆ **s'esquisser** *vpi* [sourire] to appear, to flicker ▪ [solution, progrès] to appear.

esquive [ɛskiv] *nf* dodge, side step.

esquiver [3] [ɛskive] *vt* **1.** [éviter - coup] to dodge **2.** [se soustraire à - question] to evade, to avoid, to skirt ; [- difficulté] to skirt, to avoid, to side step ; [- démarche, obligation] to shirk, to evade.
◆ **s'esquiver** *vpi* to slip *ou* to sneak out (unnoticed).

essai [esɛ] *nm* **1.** [expérimentation - d'un produit, d'un appareil] test, testing, trial ; [- d'une voiture] test, testing, test-driving ▪ **faire l'~ de qqch** to try sthg (out) ➊ **~ sur route** AUTO test drive ▪ **période d'~** trial period **2.** [tentative] attempt, try ▪ **au deuxième ~** at the second attempt *ou* try ▪ **nous avons fait plusieurs ~s** we had several tries, we made several attempts ▪ **après notre ~ de vie commune** after our attempt at living together ➊ **coup d'~** first attempt *ou* try **3.** LITTÉR essay **4.** RUGBY try.
◆ **à l'essai** *loc adv* **1.** [à l'épreuve] : **mettre qqn/qqch à l'~** to put sb/sthg to the test **2.** COMM & DR : **engager** *ou* **prendre qqn à l'~** to appoint sb for a trial period ▪ **prendre qqch à l'~** to take sthg on approval.

essaie *etc v* ▷ **essayer.**

essaim [esɛ̃] *nm* **1.** ENTOM swarm **2.** [foule] : **un ~ de** [supporters, admirateurs] a throng *ou* swarm of ; [adolescentes] a gaggle of *péj*.

essaimer [4] [eseme] *vi* **1.** ENTOM to swarm **2.** *litt* [se disperser - groupe] to spread, to disperse ; [- firme] to expand.

essayage [esɛjaʒ] *nm* COUT [vêtement, séance] fitting ▪ [action] trying on.

essayer [11] [eseje] *vt* **1.** [tenter] : **~ de faire** to try to do, to try and do ▪ **~ que** *fam* : **j'essaierai que la soirée soit réussie** I'll do my best to make the party a success ▪ *(en usage absolu)* **essaie un peu!** *fam* just you try! **2.** [utiliser pour la première fois] to try (out) *(sép)* **3.** [mettre - vêtement, chaussures] to try on ▪ **faire ~ qqch à qqn** to give sb sthg to try on **4.** [expérimenter] to try, to test ▪ **~ un vaccin sur des animaux** to test a vaccine on animals ▪ **~ une voiture** [pilote, client] to test-drive a car.
◆ **s'essayer à** *vp+prép* : **s'~ à (faire) qqch** to try one's hand at (doing) sthg.

essayeur, euse [esɛjœr, øz] *nm, f* COUT fitter.

essayiste [esejist] *nmf* essayist, essay writer.

ESSEC, Essec [esɛk] (*abr de* **École supérieure des sciences économiques et commerciales**) *npr f grande école for management and business studies.*

essence [esɑ̃s] *nf* **1.** INDUST du pétrole petrol *UK*, gas *US*, gasoline *US* ▪ **~ ordinaire** two-star petrol *UK*, regular gas *US* ▪ **~ sans plomb** unleaded petrol *UK ou* gasoline *US* **2.** [solvant] spirit, spirits ▪ **~ de térébenthine** spirit *ou* spirits of turpentine, turps **3.** CULIN essence **4.** PHARM [cosmétique] (essential) oil, essence **5.** CHIM quintessence **6.** BOT species ▪ **le parc contient de nombreuses ~s différentes** the park contains many different species of trees **7.** PHILOS essence **8.** *sout* [contenu fondamental] essence, gist.
◆ **par essence** *loc adv sout* essentially, in essence.

essentiel, elle [esɑ̃sjɛl] *adj* **1.** [indispensable] essential ▪ **~ à : ~ à la vie** essential to life ▪ **condition ~le à la réussite du projet** condition which is essential for the success of the project **2.** [principal] main, essential **3.** PHILOS essential **4.** PHARM idiopathic.
◆ **essentiel** *nm* **1.** [l'indispensable] : **l'~** the basic essentials **2.** [le plus important] : **l'~ c'est que tu comprennes** the most important *ou* the main thing is that you should understand ▪ **l'~ de l'article se résume en trois mots** the bulk of the article can be summed up in three words **3.** [la plus grande partie] : **elle passe l'~ de son temps au téléphone** she spends most of her time on the phone.

essentiellement [esɑ̃sjɛlmɑ̃] *adv* **1.** [par nature] in essence, essentially **2.** [principalement] mainly, essentially.

esseulé, e [esœle] *adj litt* **1.** [délaissé] forsaken **2.** [seul] forlorn, lonely.

essieu, x [esjø] *nm* axle, axletree.

essor [esɔr] *nm* [d'un oiseau] flight ▪ [d'une entreprise, d'une industrie] rise, development ▪ **la sidérurgie connaît un nouvel ~** the steel industry has taken on a new lease of life ▪ **prendre son ~** [oiseau] to soar ; [adolescent] to fend for o.s., to become self-sufficient ; [économie, entreprise] to grow.

essorage [esɔraʒ] *nm* [à la machine] spinning ▪ [à l'essoreuse à rouleaux] mangling ▪ [à la main] wringing ▪ **'pas d'~'** 'do not spin' ▪ **l'~ de la salade** drying *ou* spin-drying lettuce.

essorer [3] [esɔre] *vt* [sécher] : **~ le linge** [à la machine] to spin-dry the laundry ; [à l'essoreuse à rouleaux] to put the laundry through the mangle ; [à la main] to wring the laundry ▪ **~ la salade** to dry *ou* to spin-dry the lettuce.

essoreuse [esɔrøz] *nf* **1.** [pour le linge] : **~ (à tambour)** spin-drier **2.** [pour la salade] salad drier.

essoufflement [esufləmɑ̃] *nm* breathlessness.

essouffler [3] [esufle] *vt* to make breathless ▪ **être essoufflé** to be breathless *ou* out of breath.

◆ **s'essouffler** *vpi* **1.** PHYSIOL to get breathless **2.** [s'affaiblir - moteur] to get weak ; [- production, économie] to lose momentum ; [- inspiration, écrivain] to dry up.

essuie *etc* [esɥi] *v* ▻ **essuyer.**

essuie-glace [esɥiglas] (*pl* **essuie-glaces**) *nm* windscreen *UK ou* windshield *US* wiper ■ **~ arrière** back wiper.

essuie-mains [esɥimɛ̃] *nm inv* hand towel.

essuie-tout [esɥitu] *nm inv* kitchen paper.

essuyage [esɥijaʒ] *nm* **1.** [séchage - de la vaisselle] wiping, drying up ; [- des mains, du sol, d'une surface] wiping, drying **2.** [nettoyage - d'un meuble] dusting (down) ; [- d'un tableau noir] wiping, cleaning ; [- d'une planche farinée, d'un mur plâtreux] wiping (down).

essuyer [14] [esɥije] *vt* **1.** [sécher - vaisselle] to wipe, to dry (up) ; [- sueur] to wipe, to mop up *(sép)*, to wipe (off) ; [- main] to dry, to wipe dry ; [- surface] to wipe (down) ; [- sol] to wipe, to dry ■ **~ une larme** to wipe away a tear ■ **~ les larmes de qqn** to dry sb's tears ➔ **~ les plâtres** *fam* to have to endure initial problems **2.** [nettoyer - surface poussiéreuse] to dust (down) ; [- tableau noir] to wipe (clean), to clean ■ **tes mains sont pleines de farine, essuie-les** wipe your hands, they're covered in flour ■ **essuie tes pieds sur le paillasson** wipe your feet on the doormat **3.** [subir - reproches] to endure ; [- refus] to meet with *(insép)* ; [- défaite, échec, pertes] to suffer ; [- tempête] to weather, to bear up against ■ **~ un coup de feu** to be shot at.

◆ **s'essuyer** *vp (emploi réfléchi)* [se sécher] to dry o.s. ■ **s'~ les mains** to dry *ou* to wipe one's hands.

est[1] [ɛ] *v* ▻ **être.**

est[2] [ɛst] ◇ *nm inv* **1.** [point cardinal] east ■ **~ nord-~** east-north-east ■ **~ sud-~** east-south-east ■ **nous allons vers l'~** we're heading eastward *ou* eastwards ■ **une terrasse exposée à l'~** an east-facing *ou* east terrace ■ **le soleil se lève à l'~** the sun rises in the east ■ **la bise souffle de l'~** it's a harsh eastern wind **2.** [partie d'un pays, d'un continent] east, eastern area *ou* regions ■ **l'Est** HIST & POLIT Eastern Europe, Eastern European countries ; [en France] the East (of France) ■ **l'Europe de l'Est** Eastern Europe ■ **les pays de l'Est** the Eastern Bloc.

◇ *adj inv* [façade] east *(modif)*, east-facing ■ [secteur, banlieue] east *(modif)*, eastern ■ **la côte ~ des États-Unis** the East coast *ou* Eastern seaboard of the United States.

◆ **à l'est de** *loc prép* (to the) east of.

establishment [ɛstabliʃmɛnt] *nm* : **l'~** [en GB] the Establishment ; [gén] the dominant *ou* influential group *ou* body.

estafette [ɛstafɛt] *nf* MIL courier.

estafilade [ɛstafilad] *nf* slash, gash.

est-allemand, e [ɛstalmɑ̃, ɑ̃d] *adj* East German.

estaminet [ɛstaminɛ] *nm* estaminet *litt*, seedy café *ou* bar.

estampe [ɛstɑ̃p] *nf* **1.** [image] engraving, print **2.** [outil] stamp.

estamper [3] [ɛstɑ̃pe] *vt* **1.** TECHNOL [façonner, marquer] to stamp **2.** *fam* [escroquer] to swindle, to con ■ **~ qqn de 100 euros** to con sb out of 100 euros.

estampillage [ɛstɑ̃pijaʒ] *nm* [d'un document] stamping ■ [d'une marchandise] marking.

estampille [ɛstɑ̃pij] *nf* [sur un document] stamp ■ [sur une marchandise] mark, trademark ■ **dans cette famille, ils sont tous marqués de la même ~** *fam* they're all tarred with the same brush in that family.

estampiller [3] [ɛstɑ̃pije] *vt* [document] to stamp ■ [marchandise] to mark.

est-ce que [ɛskə] *(devant voyelle ou 'h' muet est-ce qu'* [ɛsk]*)* *adv interr* **1.** *(suivi d'un verbe plein)* [au présent] : **~ vous aimez le thé?** do you like tea? ❙ [au passé] : **~ vous avez acheté la maison?** did you buy the house? ❙ [au futur] : **~ tu iras?** will you go? **2.** *(suivi d'un auxiliaire)* [au présent] : **~ tu as une enveloppe?** do you have *ou* have you got an envelope? ❙ [au passé] : **~ tu y étais?** were you there? ❙ [au futur] : **~ tu seras là?** will you be there? ❙ [au futur proche] : **~ tu vas lui téléphoner?** are you going to *ou* will you phone her? **3.** [avec un autre adverbe interrogatif] : **quand est-ce qu'il arrive?** when does he arrive?

ester[1] [ɛste] *vi* DR [seulement à l'infinitif] : **~ en justice** to go to court.

ester[2] [ɛstɛr] *nm* CHIM ester.

esthète [ɛstɛt] *nmf* aesthete ■ **cela ne plaira sûrement pas aux ~s** *péj* this will offend some people's aesthetic sense.

esthéticien, enne [ɛstetisjɛ̃, ɛn] *nm, f* [en institut de beauté] beautician.

esthétique [ɛstetik] ◇ *adj* **1.** ART & PHILOS aesthetic **2.** [joli] beautiful, lovely.

◇ *nf* **1.** ART & PHILOS [science] aesthetics *(sing)* ■ [code] aesthetic **2.** [harmonie] beauty, harmony **3.** INDUST : **~ industrielle** industrial design.

esthétiquement [ɛstetikmɑ̃] *adv* **1.** ART & PHILOS aesthetically **2.** [harmonieusement] harmoniously, beautifully **3.** [du point de vue de la beauté] aesthetically, from an aesthetic point of view ■ **~, ce n'est pas réussi** aesthetically, it's a failure.

esthétisant, e [ɛstetizɑ̃, ɑ̃t] *adj péj* mannered.

esthétisme [ɛstetism] *nm* aestheticism.

estimable [ɛstimabl] *adj* **1.** [digne de respect - personne] respectable **2.** [assez bon - ouvrage, film] decent.

estimatif, ive [ɛstimatif, iv] *adj* estimated.

estimation [ɛstimasjɔ̃] *nf* **1.** [évaluation - d'un vase] appraisal, valuation ; [- de dégâts] estimation, assessment ; [- d'une distance] gaging, gauging **2.** [montant] estimate, estimation ■ **nous sommes loin de l'~ de l'expert** we're not even close to the figure produced by the expert **3.** [prévision] projection.

estime [ɛstim] *nf* esteem, respect ■ **avoir de l'~ pour qqn/qqch** to have a great deal of respect for sb/sthg, to hold sb/sthg in high esteem ■ **baisser/monter dans l'~ de qqn** to go down/up in sb's esteem.

◆ **à l'estime** *loc adv* **1.** NAUT by dead reckoning **2.** [approximativement] roughly ■ **j'ai tracé les plans à l'~** I drew the plans blind.

estimé, e [ɛstime] *adj sout* [respecté] : **notre ~ collègue** our esteemed colleague ■ **une pneumologue très ~e** a highly regarded lung specialist.

estimer [3] [ɛstime] *vt* **1.** [expertiser - valeur, dégâts] to appraise, to evaluate, to assess ■ **les dégâts ont été estimés à mille euros** the damage was estimated at a thousand euros ■ **faire ~ un tableau** to have a painting valued **2.** [évaluer approximativement - quantité] to estimate ; [- distance] to gage, to gauge **3.** [apprécier - ami, écrivain, collègue] to regard with esteem *sout*, to esteem *sout*, to think highly of ■ **je l'estime trop pour ça** I respect him too for that much ■ **~ qqn à sa juste valeur** to judge sb correctly **4.** [juger] to think, to consider, to believe ■ **j'estime avoir mon mot à dire** I think I have the right to offer an opinion.

◆ **s'estimer** *vpi (suivi d'un adj)* **s'~ heureux** to count o.s. lucky ■ **s'~ satisfait de/que** to be happy with/that.

estival, e, aux [ɛstival, o] *adj* summer *(modif)*.

estivant, e [ɛstivɑ̃, ɑ̃t] *nm, f* summer tourist, holidaymaker *UK*, vacationer *US*.

estocade [ɛstɔkad] *nf* **1.** *litt* & *loc* **donner** *ou* **porter l'~ à qqn** to deal the death-blow to sb **2.** [lors d'une corrida] final sword thrust.

estomac [ɛstɔma] *nm* **1.** ANAT stomach ■ **j'ai mal à l'~** I have a stomach ache ■ **il a pris de l'~** *fam* he's developed a paunch *ou* potbelly ■ **avoir l'~ bien accroché** *fam* to have a strong stomach ➔ **ça m'est resté sur l'~** *fam pr* it weighed on my stomach ; *fig* it stuck in my craw ■ **avoir l'~ dans les talons** *fam* to be famished *ou* ravenous **2.** *fam* [hardiesse] : **avoir de l'~** to have a cheek *UK ou* a nerve ■ **manquer d'~** to lack guts.

◆ **à l'estomac** *loc adv fam* **ils y sont allés à l'~** they bluffed their way through it.

estomaquer [3] [ɛstɔmake] *vt fam* to stagger, to flabbergast.

estompe [ɛstɔ̃p] *nf* stump, tortillon.

estompé [ɛstɔ̃pe] *adj* : **les contours estompés des immeubles** the dim outline of buildings.

estomper [3] [ɛstɔ̃pe] *vt* **1.** ART to stump, to shade off *(sép)* **2.** [ride] to smoothe over *(sép)* ▪ [silhouette] to dim, to blur **3.** [souvenir, sentiment] to dim, to blur.
◆ **s'estomper** *vpi* **1.** [disparaître - contours] to become blurred **2.** [s'affaiblir - souvenir] to fade away ; [- douleur, rancune] to diminish, to die down.

Estonie [ɛstɔni] *npr f* : **(l')**~ Estonia.

estonien, enne [ɛstɔnjɛ̃, ɛn] *adj* Estonian.
◆ **Estonien, enne** *nm, f* Estonian.

estouffade [ɛstufad] *nf* CULIN : ~ **de bœuf** ≃ beef stew.

estourbir [32] [ɛsturbir] *vt fam vieilli* **1.** [assommer] to knock out *(sép)*, to lay out *(sép)* **2.** [tuer] to do in.

estrade [ɛstrad] *nf* [plancher] platform, rostrum, dais.

estragon [ɛstragɔ̃] *nm* tarragon.

estropié, e [ɛstrɔpje] ◇ *adj* crippled, maimed ▪ **il en restera** ~ he'll be left a cripple.
◇ *nm, f* cripple, disabled *ou* maimed person.

estropier [ɛstrɔpje] *vt* **1.** *pr* to cripple, to maim **2.** *fig* [en prononçant] to mispronounce ▪ [à l'écrit] to misspell ▪ [texte] to mutilate ▪ ~ **une citation** to misquote a text.

estuaire [ɛstɥɛr] *nm* estuary.

estudiantin, e [ɛstydjɑ̃tɛ̃, in] *adj litt* student *(avant n)*.

esturgeon [ɛstyrʒɔ̃] *nm* sturgeon.

et [e] *conj* **1.** [reliant des termes, des propositions] and ▪ **une belle et brillante jeune fille** a beautiful, clever girl ▪ **une robe courte et sans manches** a short sleeveless dress ▪ **toi et moi, nous savons ce qu'il faut faire** you and I know what should be done ▪ **il y a mensonge et mensonge** there are lies, and then there are lies ▪ **quand il pleut et qu'on s'ennuie** when it rains and you're feeling bored ▪ **il connaît l'anglais, et très bien** he speaks English, and very well at that
2. [exprimant une relation de simultanéité, de succession ou de conséquence] : **il s'est levé et il a quitté la pièce** he got up and left the room ▪ **j'ai bien aimé ce film, et toi ?** I really liked the film, how *ou* what about you ? ▪ **il travaille et ne réussit pas** he works but he's not successful
3. [reliant des propositions comparatives] : **plus ça va, et plus la situation s'aggrave** as time goes on, the situation just gets worse ▪ **moins je le vois et mieux je me porte!** the less I see him the better I feel!
4. [avec une valeur emphatique] : **et d'un, je n'ai pas faim, et de deux, je n'aime pas ça** for one thing I'm not hungry and for another I don't like it ▪ **j'ai dû supporter et les enfants et les parents!** I had to put up with both the parents and the children *ou* with the parents AND the children! ▪ **je l'ai dit et répété** I've said it over and over again, I've said it more than once ▪ **c'est fini et bien fini!** that's the end of that! ▪ **et les dix euros que je t'ai prêtés ?** and (what about) the ten euros I lent you ? ▪ **et si on lui disait tout?** what if we told him everything ? ▪ **et pourquoi pas?** (and) why not ? ▪ **et pourtant...** and yet *ou* still... ▪ **et voilà!** there you are!, there you go! ▪ **et moi je vous dis que je n'irai pas!** and I'm telling you that I won't go! ▪ **et voilà comment l'argent s'en va!** that's how money disappears! ▪ **et on a ri!** how we laughed! ▪ *litt* **et chacun d'exprimer sa satisfaction** whereupon each expressed his satisfaction
5. [dans les nombres composés, les horaires, les poids et les mesures] : **vingt et un** twenty one ▪ **vingt et unième** twenty-first ▪ **deux heures et demie** half past two ▪ **deux kilos et demi** two and a half kilos.

ét. (*abr écrite de* **étage**) fl.

ETA (*abr de* **Euskadi Ta Askatasuna**) *npr f* ETA.

étable [etabl] *nf* cowshed.

établi [etabli] *nm* workbench.

établir [32] [etablir] *vt* **1.** [duplex, liaison téléphonique] to set up *(sép)*, to establish **2.** [implanter - usine, locaux, quartier général] to establish, to set *ou* to put up *(sép)* ; [- filiale] to establish ▪ ~ **son domicile à Paris** to take up residence in Paris **3.** *vieilli* [pourvoir d'une situation] to set up *(sép)*(in business) ▪ [marier] to marry off *(sép)* **4.** [instaurer - règlement] to introduce, to promulgate *sout* ; [- usage] to pass ; [- pouvoir] to install, to implement ; [- ordre, relation] to establish ▪ **contester les coutumes établies** to challenge convention ▪ **une fois le silence établi** once calm has been established ▪ ~ **un précédent** to set a precedent ▪ ~ **des liens d'amitié** to establish friendly relations **5.** [bâtir - réputation] to establish ; [- empire] to build ▪ **avoir une réputation bien établie** to have a well established reputation **6.** [prouver] : ~ **l'innocence de qqn** to establish sb's innocence, to vindicate sb ▪ ~ **l'identité de qqn** to establish sb's identity **7.** [dresser - organigramme] to set out *(sép)* ; [- liste] to draw up *(sép)* ; [- devis] to provide ; [- chèque] to make out ; [- programme, prix] to fix **8.** SPORT : ~ **un record** to set a record.
◆ **s'établir** *vpi* **1.** [vivre] : **ils ont préféré s'**~ **en banlieue** they chose to live in the suburbs **2.** [professionnellement] to set (o.s.) up (in business) ▪ **s'**~ **à son compte** to set (o.s.) up in business, to become self-employed **3.** [être instauré] : **enfin, le silence s'établit** silence was finally restored ▪ **une relation stable s'est établie entre nous** a stable relationship has developed between the two of us.

établissement [etablismɑ̃] *nm*

A.
1. [institution] establishment, institution
2. COMM firm ▪ **les ~s Leroy** Leroy and Co ▪ **les ~s Fourat et fils** Fourat and Sons ▶ ~ **financier** financial institution ▪ ~ **d'utilité publique** public utility
3. ADMIN : ~ **public** state-owned enterprise

B.
1. [construction - d'un barrage, d'une usine] building, construction
2. [instauration - d'un empire] setting up, establishing ; [- d'un régime, d'une république] installing ; [- d'un usage] establishing
3. [préparation - d'un devis] drawing up, preparation ; [- d'une liste] drawing up ; [- d'un organigramme] laying out, drawing up
4. [installation] : **l'**~ **des Français en Afrique** the settlement of the French in Africa
5. *vieilli* [dans une profession] setting up ▪ [par le mariage] : **l'**~ **de sa fille** his marrying off his daughter
6. [preuve - de la vérité] establishment ▪ **rien n'est possible sans l'**~ **de son identité** nothing can be done if his identity cannot be established.

étage [etaʒ] *nm* **1.** [dans une maison] floor, storey *UK*, story *US* ▪ [dans un parking] level ▪ **au troisième** ~ [maison] on the third floor *UK*, on the fourth floor *US* ; [aéroport] on level three ▪ **habiter au premier/dernier** ~ to live on the first/top floor ▪ **elle est dans les ~s** she's upstairs somewhere ▪ **un immeuble de cinq ~s** a five-storey building
2. [division - d'une pièce montée] tier ; [- d'un buffet, d'une bibliothèque] shelf
3. GÉOL stage, layer.
◆ **étages** *nmpl* **1.** [escaliers] : **grimper/monter les ~s** to climb/to go upstairs ▪ **monter les ~s à pied/en courant** to walk/to run up the stairs ▪ **monter les ~s quatre à quatre** to take the stairs four at a time
2. BOT : **~s de végétation** levels of vegetation.
◆ **à l'étage** *loc adv* upstairs, on the floor above.
◆ **de bas étage** *loc adj péj* [vulgaire - cabaret] sleazy ; [- plaisanterie] cheap.

étagement [etaʒmɑ̃] *nm* [de collines, de vignobles] terracing.

étager [17] [etaʒe] *vt* to stack, to set out *ou* to range in tiers.
◆ **s'étager** *vpi* : **les maisons s'étageaient le long de la pente** the houses rose up the slope in tiers.

étagère [etaʒɛr] *nf* [planche] shelf ▪ [meuble] (set of) shelves ▪ ~ **encastrée** built-in shelves *ou* shelving.

étai [etɛ] *nm* **1.** NAUT stay **2.** [poutre] stay, prop, strut.

étaie *etc v* ▷ **étayer**.

étain [etɛ̃] *nm* **1.** [métal blanc] tin **2.** [vaisselle] piece of pewter ware ■ **des ~s** pewter (pieces).
◆ **en étain** *loc adj* pewter *(modif)*.

était *etc v* ⊳ **être**.

et al [ɛtal] *loc adv* et al.

étal, als [etal] *nm* **1.** [au marché] (market) stall **2.** [de boucher] block.

étalage [etalaʒ] *nm* **1.** [vitrine] (display) window ■ [stand] stall ■ **faire un ~** [vitrine] to dress a window ; [stand] to set up a stall **2.** *péj* [démonstration] : **un tel ~ de luxe suscite des jalousies** such a display *ou* show of wealth causes jealousy ■ **faire ~ de : faire ~ de ses succès** to show off one's success ■ **faire ~ de son argent** to flaunt one's wealth.

étalagiste [etalaʒist] *nmf* window dresser.

étale [etal] ◇ *adj* **1.** [mer, fleuve] slack ■ [navire] becalmed ■ [vent] steady **2.** [circulation] slack.
◇ *nm* slack (water).

étalement [etalmɑ̃] *nm* **1.** [déploiement - de papiers, d'objets] spreading (out) ; [- de marchandises] displaying **2.** [des vacances, des horaires, des paiements] staggering, spreading out **3.** [mise à plat] spreading out.

étaler [3] [etale] *vt* **1.** [exposer - marchandise] to display, to lay out *(sép)* **2.** [exhiber - richesse, luxe] to flaunt, to show off *(sép)* ■ **~ ses malheurs** to parade one's misfortunes ■ **~ ses connaissances** to show off one's knowledge **3.** [disposer à plat - tapis, tissu] to spread (out) ; [- plan, carte, journal] to open *ou* to spread (out) ; [- pâte à tarte] to roll out *(sép)* ■ **~ ses cartes** *ou* **son jeu** to show one's hand **4.** [appliquer en couche - beurre, miel] to spread ; [- pommade, fond de teint] to rub *ou* to smooth on ; [- enduit] to apply **5.** [dates, paiements, rendez-vous] to spread out *(sép)* ■ **les entreprises essaient d'~ les vacances de leurs employés** firms try to stagger their employees' holidays **6.** *arg scol* **se faire ~ (à un examen)** to flunk an exam.
◆ **s'étaler** ◇ *vp (emploi passif)* [s'appliquer] to spread ■ **une peinture qui s'étale facilement** a paint which goes on easily.
◇ *vpi* **1.** [s'étendre - ville, plaine] to stretch *ou* to spread out **2.** [être exhibé] : **son nom s'étale à la une de tous les journaux** his name is in *ou* is splashed over all the papers **3.** *fam* [tomber] to fall (down), to take a tumble **4.** *fam péj* [prendre trop de place] to spread o.s. out.
◆ **s'étaler sur** *vp+prép* [suj: vacances, paiements] to be spread over.

étalon [etalɔ̃] *nm* **1.** ZOOL [cheval] stallion ■ [âne, taureau] stud **2.** [référence] standard ■ **~-or** gold standard ■ **~ monétaire** monetary *ou* standard unit.

étalonnage [etalɔnaʒ], **étalonnement** [etalɔnmɑ̃] *nm* TECHNOL [graduation] calibration, calibrating ■ [vérification] standardization, standardizing.

étalonner [3] [etalɔne] *vt* **1.** TECHNOL [graduer] to calibrate ■ [vérifier] to standardize **2.** SC [test] to table, to grade.

étambot [etɑ̃bo] *nm* stern post.

étamine [etamin] *nf* **1.** BOT stamen **2.** COUT etamine, etamin ■ CULIN muslin.

étanche [etɑ̃ʃ] *adj* [chaussure, montre] waterproof ■ [réservoir] watertight ■ [surface] water-resistant, water-repellent ■ **~ à l'air** airtight ■ **rendre ~** to waterproof.

étanchéité [etɑ̃ʃeite] *nf* [d'une montre, de chaussures] waterproofness ■ [d'un réservoir] watertightness ■ [d'un revêtement] water-resistance ■ **~ à l'air** airtightness.

étancher [3] [etɑ̃ʃe] *vt* **1.** [rendre étanche] to make waterproof **2.** [arrêter - sang] to stanch, to staunch, to stem ; [- voie d'eau] to stop up *(sép)* ■ **~ sa soif** to quench *ou* to slake one's thirst.

étang [etɑ̃] *nm* pond.

étant[1] [etɑ̃] *p prés* ⊳ **être**.

étant[2] [etɑ̃] *nm* PHILOS being.

étant donné [etɑ̃dɔne] *loc prép* given, considering ■ **~ les circonstances** given *ou* in view of the circumstances.
◆ **étant donné que** *loc conj* since, given the fact that ■ **~ qu'il pleuvait...** since *ou* as it was raining...

étape [etap] *nf* **1.** [arrêt] stop, stopover ■ **nous avons fait ~ à Lille** we stopped off *ou* over at Lille **2.** [distance] stage ■ **voyager par (petites) ~s** to travel in (easy) stages **3.** SPORT stage **4.** [phase] phase, stage, step ■ **par ~s** in stages ■ **nous allons procéder par ~s** we'll do it in stages *ou* step by step.

état [eta] *nm*

> **A.** MANIÈRE D'ÊTRE PHYSIQUE
> **B.** MANIÈRE D'ÊTRE MORALE, PSYCHOLOGIQUE
> **C.** CONDITION SOCIALE
> **D.** DOCUMENT COMPTABLE OU LÉGAL

A. MANIÈRE D'ÊTRE PHYSIQUE

1. [d'une personne - condition physique] state, condition ; [- apparence] state ■ **le malade est dans un ~ grave** the patient's condition is serious ■ **tu t'es mis dans un drôle d'~!** look at the state of you! ■ **te voilà dans un triste ~!** you're in a sorry *ou* sad state! ■ **être dans un ~ second** [drogué] to be high ; [en transe] to be in a trance ■ **en ~ de : être en ~ d'ivresse** *ou* **d'ébriété** to be under the influence (of alcohol), to be inebriated ■ **être en ~ de faire qqch** to be fit to do sthg ■ **être hors d'~ de, ne pas être en ~ de** to be in no condition to *ou* totally unfit to ■ **mettre qqn hors d'~ de nuire** [préventivement] to make sb harmless ; [après coup] to neutralize sb ▶ **~ général** general state of health ■ **~ de santé** (state of) health, condition ■ **~ de veille** waking state

2. [d'un appartement, d'une route, d'une machine, d'un colis] condition, state ■ **être en bon/mauvais ~** [meuble, route, véhicule] to be in good/poor condition ; [bâtiment] to be in a good/bad state of repair ; [colis, marchandises] to be undamaged/damaged ■ **vendu à l'~ neuf** [dans petites annonces] as new ■ **réduit à l'~ de cendres/poussière** reduced to ashes/a powder ■ **en ~ de marche** in working order ■ **quand tu seras de nouveau en ~ de marche** *fam hum* when you're back on your feet again *ou* back in circulation ■ **en ~ de rouler** AUTO roadworthy ■ **en ~ de naviguer** NAUT seaworthy ■ **en ~ de voler** AÉRON airworthy ■ **être hors d'~ (de fonctionner)** to be out of order ■ **laisser une pièce en l'~** to leave a room as it is ■ **remettre en ~** [appartement] to renovate, to refurbish ; [véhicule] to repair ; [pièce de moteur] to recondition ■ **maintenir qqch en ~** [bâtiment, bateau, voiture] to keep sthg in good repair

3. [situation particulière - d'un développement, d'une technique] state ■ **dans l'~ actuel des choses** as things stand at the moment, in the present state of affairs ■ **l'~ de mes finances** my financial situation ■ **(en) ~ d'alerte/d'urgence** (in a) state of alarm/emergency ■ **être en ~ d'arrestation** to be under arrest ■ **je me suis renseigné sur l'~ d'avancement des travaux** I enquired about the progress of the work ▶ **~ de choses** state of things ■ **~ de fait** (established) fact ■ **~ de guerre** state of war ■ **être en ~ de siège** to be under siege

4. CHIM & PHYS : **~ gazeux/liquide/solide** gaseous/liquid/solid state ▶ **à l'~ brut** [pétrole] crude, unrefined, raw ■ **c'est de la bêtise à l'~ brut** it's plain stupidity ■ **à l'~ pur** [gemme, métal] pure ■ **c'est du racisme à l'~ pur** it's nothing more than racism

5. LING : **verbe d'~** stative verb

B. MANIÈRE D'ÊTRE MORALE, PSYCHOLOGIQUE

state ■ **être dans un ~ de grande excitation** to be in a state of great excitement *ou* very excited ■ **elle n'est pas dans son ~ normal** she's not her normal *ou* usual self ■ **ne te mets pas dans cet ~!** [à une personne inquiète, déprimée] don't worry! ; [à une personne énervée] don't get so worked up! ▶ **~ de conscience** state of consciousness ■ **~ d'esprit** state *ou* frame of mind ■ **~ limite** borderline state ■ **être dans tous ses ~s** [d'anxiété] to be beside o.s. with anxiety ; [de colère] to be beside o.s. (with anger) ■ **se mettre dans tous ses ~s** [en colère] to go off the deep end, to go spare

C. CONDITION SOCIALE

1. [profession] trade, profession ■ [statut social] social position, standing, station ▶ **il est cordonnier de son ~** he's a shoemaker by trade

2. ADMIN : **(bureau de l')~ civil** registry office

D. DOCUMENT COMPTABLE OU LÉGAL

1. [compte rendu] account, statement ▪ [inventaire] inventory ▪ **l'~ des dépenses/des recettes** statement of expenses/takings ▪ **~ appréciatif** evaluation, estimation ▪ **figurer sur les ~s d'une entreprise** to be on a company's payroll ▪ **~ de frais** bill of costs ▪ **~s de service** MIL service record ; [professionnellement] professional record ⊳ **~ des lieux** inventory (of fixtures) ▪ **dresser** *ou* **faire un ~ des lieux** *pr* to draw up an inventory of fixtures ; *fig* to take stock of the situation

2. *loc* **faire ~ de** [sondage, témoignages, thèse] to put forward *(sép)* ; [document] to refer to ; [fait] to mention ; [soucis] to mention.

◆ **état d'âme** *nm* mood ▪ **elle ne me fait pas part de ses ~s d'âme** she doesn't confide in me ▪ **j'en ai assez de leurs ~s d'âme!** I'm fed up with hearing about how THEY feel! ▪ **je me fiche de vos ~s d'âme!** I don't care whether you're happy about it or not! ▪ **avoir des ~s d'âme** to suffer from angst *hum.*

◆ **état de grâce** *nm* RELIG : **être en ~ de grâce** to be in a state of grace.

État [eta] *nm* **1.** POLIT [nation] state ▪ **l'~ français** the French state *ou* nation ▪ **l'~ de Washington** the State of Washington ▪ **les ~s membres** the member states ⊳ **l'~-patron** the State as an employer ▪ **l'~-providence** the Welfare state ▪ **un ~ dans l'~** a state within a state ▪ **l'~, c'est moi** *famous phrase attributed to Louis XIV proclaiming the absolute nature of the monarchy* **2.** ADMIN & ÉCON state ▪ **géré par l'~** state-run, publicly run ▪ **entreprise d'~** state-owned *ou* UK public company **3.** HIST : **les États généraux** the States *ou* Estates General

LES ÉTATS GÉNÉRAUX

A consultative assembly of representatives from the three estates of the *Ancien Régime*: clergy, nobility and the Third Estate, or commoners. It met for the last time in May 1789 in the *Jeu de Paume* in Versailles, where the Third Estate vowed not to disperse until they had established a constitution.

étatique [etatik] *adj* under state control, state-controlled.

étatisation [etatizasjɔ̃] *nf* **1.** [nationalisation] nationalization **2.** [dirigisme] state control.

étatiser [3] [etatize] *vt* to bring under state control ▪ **une firme étatisée** a state-owned company.

étatisme [etatism] *nm* state control.

étatiste [etatist] ◇ *adj* state-control *(modif).* ◇ *nmf* supporter of state control.

état-major [etamaʒɔr] (*pl* **états-majors**) *nm* **1.** MIL [officiers] general staff ▪ [locaux] headquarters **2.** [direction - d'une entreprise] management ; [- d'un parti politique] leadership ▪ **le président et son ~** the president and his advisers.

États-Unis [etazyni] *npr mpl* : **les ~ (d'Amérique)** the United States (of America) ▪ **aux ~** in the United States.

étau, x [eto] *nm* vice ▪ **être pris** *ou* **enserré (comme) dans un ~** *fig* to be caught in a vice ▪ **l'~ se resserre** *fig* the noose is tightening.

étayage [etɛjaʒ], **étayement** [etɛjmɑ̃] *nm* **1.** [d'un mur] propping-up, shoring-up **2.** [d'un raisonnement] support, supporting, shoring-up.

étayer [11] [eteje] *vt* **1.** [mur] to prop *ou* to shore up **2.** [raisonnement] to support, to back up.

◆ **s'étayer sur** *vp+prép* [s'appuyer sur] to be based on.

etc. (*abr écrite de* **et cetera**) etc.

et cetera, et cætera [ɛtsetera] *loc adv* et cetera, and so on (and so forth).

été[1] [ete] *pp* ⊳ **être.**

été[2] [ete] *nm* summer ⊳ **~ indien** Indian summer.

◆ **d'été** *loc adj* : **robe d'~** summer dress ▪ **nuit d'~** summer's night ▪ **l'heure d'~** daylight-saving time.

éteignoir [etɛɲwar] *nm* **1.** [instrument] extinguisher **2.** *fam* [rabat-joie] wet blanket, spoilsport, killjoy.

éteindre [81] [etɛ̃dr] *vt* **1.** [arrêter la combustion de - cigarette, incendie] to put out *(sép)*, to extinguish ; [- bougie] to put *ou* to blow out *(sép)* ; [- gaz, chauffage] to turn off *(sép)*

2. ÉLECTR [phare, lampe] to turn *ou* to switch off *(sép)* ▪ [radio, télévision] to turn off ▪ **va ~ (dans) la chambre** *fam* switch off the light in the bedroom ▪ **c'était éteint chez les voisins** the neighbours' lights were out ‖ INFORM to shut down

3. [faire perdre son éclat à] : **le chagrin avait éteint son regard** *litt* her eyes had been dulled by sorrow

4. [annuler - dette, rente] to wipe out *(sép)*

5. *litt* [soif] to quench, to slake *litt* ▪ [désirs, sentiments] to kill.

◆ **s'éteindre** *vpi* **1.** [feu, gaz, chauffage] to go out ▪ [bougie] to blow out ▪ [cigarette] to burn out ▪ [volcan] to die down

2. ÉLECTR [lampe] to go out ▪ [radio, télévision] to go off

3. *litt* [se dissiper - ardeur, amour] to fade away ; [- colère] to abate, to cool down

4. *euphém* [mourir - personne] to pass away

5. [race] to die out, to become extinct.

éteint, e [etɛ̃, ɛ̃t] *adj* **1.** [sans éclat - regard] dull, lacklustre ; [- visage, esprit] dull ; [- couleur] faded ▪ **d'une voix ~e** faintly ▪ **elle est plutôt ~e ces temps-ci** she's lost her spark recently **2.** [chaux] slaked.

étendard [etɑ̃dar] *nm* MIL standard ▪ **lever l'~ de la révolte** *fig* to raise the standard of revolt.

étendre [73] [etɑ̃dr] *vt* **1.** [beurre, miel] to spread ▪ [pommade, fond de teint] to rub *ou* to smooth on

2. [tapis, tissu] to unroll ▪ [plan, carte, journal] to open *ou* to spread (out) ▪ [pâte à tarte] to roll out *(sép)* ▪ **~ ses bras/jambes** to stretch (out) one's arms/legs

3. [faire sécher] : **~ du linge** [dehors] to put the washing out to dry, to hang out the washing ; [à l'intérieur] to hang up the washing

4. [allonger - personne] to stretch out *(sép)* ▪ **~ un blessé sur une civière** to place an injured person on a stretcher

5. [élargir - pouvoir] to extend ; [- recherches] to broaden, to extend ; [- cercle d'amis] to extend ▪ **~ son vocabulaire** to increase *ou* to extend one's vocabulary ▪ **~ qqch à : ~ une grève au secteur privé** to extend a strike to the private sector

6. [diluer - peinture] to dilute, to thin down *(sép)* ; [- sauce] to thin out *ou* down *(sép)*, to water down *(sép)* ; [- vin] to water down *(sép)*

7. *fam* [vaincre] to thrash ▪ **se faire ~** [à un match de boxe] to get knocked *ou* laid out ; [aux élections] to be trounced ; [à un examen] to be failed.

◆ **s'étendre** *vpi* **1.** [dans l'espace] to stretch ▪ **les banlieues s'étendaient à l'infini** the suburbs stretched out endlessly ▪ **s'~ à : son ambition s'étendait aux plus hautes sphères de la politique** his ambition extended to the highest echelons of politics ▪ **une loi qui s'étend à toutes les circonscriptions** a law that covers all districts

2. [dans le temps] : **la période qui s'étend du XVIIe au XIXe siècle** the period stretching from the 17th to the 19th century ▪ **les vacances s'étendent sur trois mois** the vacation stretches over three months

3. [se développer - épidémie, grève] to spread ; [- cercle d'amis] to widen ; [- pouvoir] to widen, to increase, to expand ; [- culture, vocabulaire] to increase, to broaden

4. [s'allonger - malade] to stretch out, to lie down.

◆ **s'étendre sur** *vp+prép* to enlarge on ▪ **je ne m'étendrai pas davantage sur ce sujet** I won't discuss this subject at any greater length.

étendu, e [etɑ̃dy] *adj* **1.** [vaste - territoire] big, wide, spread-out ; [- banlieue] sprawling ▪ **un panorama ~** a vast panorama **2.** [considérable - pouvoir, connaissances] extensive, wide-ranging ▪ **sa culture très ~e lui permettait de briller** his vast culture allowed him to shine **3.** [étiré] : **les bras ~s** with outstretched arms ▪ **les jambes ~es** with legs stretched out **4.** [dilué - vin, sauce] watered-down ; [- peinture, couleur] thinned-down.

◆ **étendue** *nf* **1.** [surface] area, stretch ▪ **une ~e désertique** a stretch of desert **2.** [dimension] area ▪ **un domaine d'une grande ~e** a large estate **3.** [durée] : **l'~e d'un discours** the length of a speech ▪ **sur une ~e de 10 ans** over a period of 10 years **4.** [ampleur] extent **5.** MUS range **6.** PHILOS extension.

éternel, elle [etɛrnɛl] *adj* **1.** PHILOS & RELIG eternal **2.** [sans fin] eternal, endless ■ **je lui voue une reconnaissance ~le** I'll be for ever *ou* eternally grateful to him ■ **cette situation ne sera pas ~le** this situation won't last for ever **3.** *(avant le n)* [invariable] : **c'est un ~ mécontent** he's perpetually discontented, he's never happy ■ **leurs ~les discussions politiques** their endless *ou* interminable political discussions ■ **son ~ cigare à la bouche** his inevitable cigar ▶ **l'~ féminin** womankind.
◆ **Éternel** *npr m* : **l'Éternel** the Eternal ▶ **grand voyageur/menteur devant l'Éternel** *fam* great *ou* inveterate traveller/liar.

éternellement [etɛrnɛlmɑ̃] *adv* eternally ■ **je ne l'attendrai pas ~** I'm not going to wait for him for ever.

éterniser [3] [etɛrnize] *vt* **1.** *péj* [prolonger - discussion, crise] to drag *ou* to draw out *(sép)* **2.** *litt* [perpétuer - nom, mémoire] to perpetuate.
◆ **s'éterniser** *vpi péj* **1.** [durer - crise, discussion] to drag on **2.** *fam* [s'attarder] : **on ne va pas s'~ ici** we're not going to stay here for ever ■ **j'espère qu'elle ne va pas s'~ chez moi** I hope she's not going to hang around here too long.

éternité [etɛrnite] *nf* **1.** PHILOS & RELIG eternity **2.** [longue durée] eternity ■ **il y avait une ~ que je ne l'avais vu** I hadn't seen him for ages *ou* an eternity ■ **la construction du stade va durer une ~** it will take forever to build the stadium.
◆ **de toute éternité** *loc adv litt* from time immemorial.

éternuement [etɛrnymɑ̃] *nm* sneeze ■ **être pris d'~s** to have a fit of sneezing.

éternuer [7] [etɛrnɥe] *vi* to sneeze ■ **ça me fait ~** it makes me sneeze.

êtes *v* ▷ **être**.

étêter [4] [etete] *vt* [arbre] to pollard ■ [poisson] to cut off the head of ■ [clou, épingle] to knock the head off.

éthanol [etanɔl] *nm* ethanol.

éther [etɛr] *nm* CHIM & *litt* ether.

éthéré, e [etere] *adj* CHIM & *litt* ethereal.

éthéromane [eterɔman] <> *adj* addicted to ether.
<> *nmf* ether addict.

éthéromanie [eterɔmani] *nf* addiction to ether.

éthicien, enne [etisjɛ̃, ɛn] *nm, f* ethicist.

Éthiopie [etjɔpi] *npr f* : **(l')~** Ethiopia.

éthiopien, enne [etjɔpjɛ̃, ɛn] *adj* Ethiopian.
◆ **Éthiopien, enne** *nm, f* Ethiopian.
◆ **éthiopien** *nm* LING Ethiopic.

éthique [etik] <> *adj* ethic, ethical.
<> *nf* **1.** PHILOS ethics *(sing)* **2.** [code moral] ethic.

ethnie [ɛtni] *nf* ethnic group.

ethnique [ɛtnik] *adj* ethnic.

ethnocentrisme [ɛtnɔsɑ̃trism] *nm* ethnocentrism.

ethnocide [ɛtnɔsid] *nm* ethnocide.

ethnographe [ɛtnɔgraf] *nmf* ethnographer.

ethnographie [ɛtnɔgrafi] *nf* ethnography.

ethnolinguistique [ɛtnɔlɛ̃gɥistik] <> *adj* ethnolinguistic.
<> *nf* ethnolinguistics *(sing)*.

ethnologie [ɛtnɔlɔʒi] *nf* ethnology.

ethnologique [ɛtnɔlɔʒik] *adj* ethnologic, ethnological.

ethnologue [ɛtnɔlɔg] *nmf* ethnologist.

éthologie [etɔlɔʒi] *nf* ethology.

éthylène [etilɛn] *nm* ethylene.

éthylique [etilik] <> *adj* ethyl *(modif)*.
<> *nmf* alcoholic.

éthylisme [etilism] *nm* alcoholism.

Étienne [etjɛn] *npr* : **saint ~** Saint Stephen.

étincelant, e [etɛ̃slɑ̃, ɑ̃t] *adj* **1.** [brillant - diamant, étoile] sparkling, gleaming, twinkling ; [- soleil] brightly shining ■ [bien lavé - vaisselle] shining, sparkling, gleaming ■ **la mer ~e** the sparkling sea **2.** [vif - regard, œil] twinkling ■ **les yeux ~s de colère/de haine** eyes glinting with rage/with hate **3.** [plein de brio - conversation, esprit, style] brilliant, sparkling.

étinceler [24] [etɛ̃sle] *vi* **1.** [diamant, étoile] to sparkle, to gleam, to twinkle ■ [soleil] to shine brightly ■ [vaisselle] to shine, to sparkle, to gleam ■ **la mer étincelait** the sea was sparkling **2.** [regard, œil] to sparkle, to glitter ■ **ses yeux étincelaient de colère/jalousie/passion** her eyes glittered with anger/jealousy/passion ■ **ses yeux étincelaient de bonheur/fierté** her eyes were sparkling with happiness/pride **3.** [conversation, style] to sparkle, to be brilliant.

étincelle [etɛ̃sɛl] *nf* **1.** [parcelle incandescente] spark ■ **~ électrique** electric spark ▶ **faire des ~s** *pr* to throw off sparks ; *fig* to cause a huge sensation, to be a big success ■ **c'est l'~ qui a mis le feu aux poudres** it was this which sparked everything off **2.** [lueur] spark, sparkle ■ **jeter des ~s** to sparkle ■ **ses yeux jettent des ~s** [de joie] his eyes shine with joy ; [de colère] his eyes flash with rage **3.** [bref élan] : **~ d'intelligence** spark of intelligence ■ **l'~ du génie** the spark of genius.

étincellement [etɛ̃sɛlmɑ̃] *nm* [d'un diamant, d'une lame] sparkle, glitter ■ [de la mer] glitter.

étincellera *etc v* ▷ **étinceler**.

étiolement [etjɔlmɑ̃] *nm* **1.** AGRIC & BOT bleaching, blanching, etiolation *spéc* **2.** [affaiblissement - d'une personne] decline, weakening ; [- d'un esprit] weakening.

étioler [3] [etjɔle] *vt* **1.** AGRIC & BOT to bleach, to blanch, to etiolate *spéc* **2.** [personne] to make weak *ou* pale *ou* sickly.
◆ **s'étioler** *vpi* **1.** AGRIC & BOT to blanch, to wither **2.** [s'affaiblir - personne] to decline, to fade away, to become weak ; [- esprit] to become lacklustre *ou* dull.

étiologie [etjɔlɔʒi] *nf* aetiology.

étique [etik] *adj litt* skinny, emaciated, scrawny.

étiquetage [etiktaʒ] *nm* [d'une marchandise] labelling ■ [d'un colis] ticketing, labelling.

étiqueter [27] [etikte] *vt* **1.** [marchandise] to mark, to label ■ [colis] to ticket, to label **2.** *péj* [cataloguer] to label ■ **j'ai été étiqueté comme écologiste** I was labelled as a green.

étiqueteur, euse [etiktœr, øz] *nm, f* labeller.
◆ **étiqueteuse** *nf* labelling machine.

étiquette [etikɛt] <> *v* ▷ **étiqueter**.
<> *nf* **1.** [marque - portant le prix] ticket ■ **~ autocollante** sticky label, sticker **2.** [appartenance] label ■ **mettre une ~ à qqn** to label sb ■ **sans ~ politique** [candidat, journal] independent **3.** INFORM label **4.** [protocole] : **l'~** etiquette ▶ **~ de Cour** court etiquette.

étirement [etirmɑ̃] *nm* [des membres, du corps] stretching.

étirer [3] [etire] *vt* **1.** [allonger - membres, cou] to stretch ; [- peloton, convoi] to stretch out *(sép)* **2.** [verre, métal] to draw (out) **3.** TEXT to stretch.
◆ **s'étirer** *vpi* **1.** [personne, animal] to stretch (out) **2.** [s'éterniser - journée, récit] to draw out.

Etna [ɛtna] *npr m* : **l'~, le mont ~** (Mount) Etna.

étoffe [etɔf] *nf* **1.** TEXT material, fabric ■ **des ~s somptueuses** rich fabrics **2.** [calibre - d'un professionnel, d'un artiste] calibre ■ **il est d'une autre/de la même ~** he's in a different/the same league ■ **il a l'~ d'un héros** he has the makings of a hero, he's the stuff heroes are made of ■ **avoir l'~ d'un chef** to be leadership material **3.** TECHNOL base-metal alloy.

étoffé, e [etɔfe] *adj* [roman, récit] full of substance, well-rounded ■ [voix] deep, sonorous.

étoffer [3] [etɔfe] *vt* **1.** [faire grossir] to put weight on ■ **son séjour à la campagne l'a étoffé** his spell in the country has made him fill out a bit **2.** [développer - roman, personnage] to flesh *ou* to fill out *(sép)*, to give substance to.
◆ **s'étoffer** *vpi* to fill out, to put on weight.

étoile [etwal] *nf* **1.** ASTRON star ■ **contempler** *ou* **observer les ~s** to stargaze ■ **ciel parsemé** *ou* **semé d'~s** starry sky, sky stud-

ded with stars ■ **une nuit sans ~s** a starless night ➊ **~ du matin/soir** morning/evening star ■ **~ du berger** morning star ■ **~ filante** shooting star ■ **~ Polaire** pole star ■ **carrefour en ~** multi-lane junction **2.** [insigne] star ■ **hôtel trois/quatre ~s** three-star/four-star hotel ➊ **l'~ jaune/rouge** the yellow/red star ■ **l'Étoile de David** the Star of David **3.** [destin] stars, fate ■ **c'est sa bonne ~** it's his lucky star **4.** *vieilli* [célébrité] star **5.** DANSE prima ballerina **6.** IMPR star, asterisk **7.** [au ski] badge (of achievement) ■ **première/deuxième/troisième ~** beginners/intermediate/advanced badge of proficiency *(at skiing)* **8.** ZOOL : **~ de mer** starfish **9.** MATH asterisk **10.** [à Paris] : **(place de) l'Étoile** place de l'Etoile *(in Paris)*.
◆ **à la belle étoile** *loc adv* [coucher, dormir] (out) in the open, outside.

étoilé, e [etwale] *adj* [ciel] starry, star-studded ■ [nuit] starry.

étoiler [3] [etwale] *vt* **1.** *litt* [parsemer - d'étoiles] to spangle with stars ■ **les vitres étoilées de givre** the window panes glittering with frost **2.** [fêler - vitre] to craze, to crack.
◆ **s'étoiler** *vpi* **1.** *litt* [ciel] to become starry **2.** [vitre] to crack.

étole [etɔl] *nf* COUT & RELIG stole.

étonnamment [etɔnamɑ̃] *adv* amazingly, astonishingly.

étonnant, e [etɔnɑ̃, ɑ̃t] *adj* **1.** [remarquable - personne, acteur, mémoire] remarkable, astonishing ; [- roman] great, fantastic ; [- voyage] fabulous **2.** [surprenant] surprising, amazing ■ **rien d'~ à ce qu'il ait divorcé** no wonder he got divorced ■ **ça n'a rien d'~** it's no wonder.

étonné, e [etɔne] *adj* astonished, amazed ■ **il avait l'air ~** he looked astonished *ou* amazed.

étonnement [etɔnmɑ̃] *nm* surprise, astonishment ■ **je fus frappé d'~ en apprenant la nouvelle** I was astonished when I heard the news.

étonner [3] [etɔne] *vt* to amaze, to surprise ■ **je suis étonné de ses progrès** I'm amazed at the progress he's made ■ **ça m'étonne qu'elle ne t'ait pas appelé** I'm surprised she didn't call you ■ **cela m'étonnerait** I'd be surprised ■ **ça ne m'étonne pas de toi!** you do surprise me! *iron* ■ **tu vas y aller? – tu m'étonnes!** *fam* are you going to go? – of course I am!
◆ **s'étonner** *vpi* to be surprised ■ **je ne m'étonne plus de rien** nothing surprises me anymore.

étouffant, e [etufɑ̃, ɑ̃t] *adj* **1.** [oppressant - lieu, climat, ambiance] stifling **2.** [indigeste - mets] stodgy, heavy.

étouffe-chrétien [etufkretjɛ̃] *nm inv fam* heavy *ou* stodgy food ■ *(comme adj)* heavy, stodgy ■ **c'est un peu ~, sa quiche** his quiche is a bit stodgy.

étouffée [etufe] ◆ **à l'étouffée** ◇ *loc adj* steamed *(in a tightly shut pot)*.
◇ *loc adv* : **cuire qqch à l'~** to steam sthg *(in a tightly shut steamer)*.

étouffement [etufmɑ̃] *nm* **1.** [asphyxie] suffocation **2.** [respiration difficile] breathlessness ■ **avoir une sensation d'~** to have a feeling of breathlessness *ou* suffocation ▌[crise] fit of breathlessness **3.** [répression - d'une révolte] quelling ; [- d'une rumeur] stifling ■ [camouflage - d'un scandale] hushing-up, covering-up.

étouffer [3] [etufe] ◇ *vt* **1.** [asphyxier - personne, animal] : **le bébé a été étouffé** [accident] the baby suffocated to death ; [meurtre] the baby was smothered ■ **mourir étouffé** to die of suffocation, to choke to death ■ **ne le serre pas si fort, tu l'étouffes!** *hum* don't hug him so hard, you'll smother him! ➊ **ce n'est pas la politesse qui l'étouffe** *fam hum* politeness isn't exactly his strong point ■ **ça t'étoufferait de dire bonjour/de ranger ta chambre?** would it kill you to say hello/to tidy your room? **2.** [oppresser - suj: famille, entourage] to smother ; [- suj: ambiance] to stifle **3.** [émouvoir fortement] : **la colère/l'émotion l'étouffe** he's choking with anger/emotion **4.** [arrêter, atténuer - feu] to put out *(sép)*, to smother ; [- bruit] to muffle, to deaden ; [- cris, pleurs, sentiment, rire] to stifle, to hold back *(sép)* ; [- voix] to lower ; [- révolte, rumeur] to quash ; [- scandale] to hush *ou* to cover up *(sép)*.
◇ *vi* **1.** [s'asphyxier] to suffocate, to choke ■ **j'ai failli ~ en avalant de travers** I almost choked on my food ■ **~ de : ~ de colère/jalousie** to choke with anger/jealousy **2.** [avoir chaud] to suffocate, to be gasping for air **3.** [être oppressé] to feel stifled.
◆ **s'étouffer** *vpi* to choke ■ **une sardine et une demi-tomate, on ne risque pas de s'~!** *hum* a sardine and half a tomato! there's no fear of us choking on that!

étouffoir [etufwar] *nm* **1.** [pour la braise] charcoal extinguisher **2.** MUS damper **3.** *fam* [lieu] oven ■ **c'est un ~ ici!** it's like an oven in here!

étoupe [etup] *nf* [lin, chanvre] tow.

étourderie [eturdəri] *nf* **1.** [faute] careless mistake **2.** [caractère] carelessness.
◆ **par étourderie** *loc adv* carelessly, without thinking.

étourdi, e [eturdi] ◇ *adj* [personne] careless ■ [acte, réponse] thoughtless.
◇ *nm, f* scatterbrain.

étourdiment [eturdimɑ̃] *adv* thoughtlessly, carelessly, foolishly.

étourdir [32] [eturdir] *vt* **1.** [assommer] to stun, to daze **2.** [griser - suj: vertige, sensation, alcool] to make dizzy *ou* lightheaded ; [- suj: odeur] to overpower ■ **le succès l'étourdissait** success had gone to his head ■ **cette perspective l'étourdissait** he was exhilarated at the prospect **3.** [abasourdir - suj: bruit] to deafen ■ **ces enfants m'étourdissent!** these children are making me dizzy (with their noise)! **4.** *litt* [calmer - douleur, chagrin] to numb, to deaden.
◆ **s'étourdir** *vpi* : **s'~ dans le plaisir** to live a life of pleasure ■ **s'~ de paroles** to get drunk on words.

étourdissant, e [eturdisɑ̃, ɑ̃t] *adj* **1.** [bruyant] deafening, ear-splitting **2.** [extraordinaire - beauté, créativité, activité] stunning ■ **être ~ d'esprit** to be very glib **3.** *litt* [grisant - adulation, passion] exciting, exhilarating.

étourdissement [eturdismɑ̃] *nm* **1.** [vertige] fit of giddiness *ou* dizziness, dizzy spell ■ MÉD fainting fit, blackout ■ **j'ai eu un léger ~ dû à la chaleur** I felt slightly dizzy on account of the heat **2.** *litt* [griserie] exhilaration.

étourneau, x [eturno] *nm* **1.** ORNITH starling **2.** *fam* [étourdi] birdbrain.

étrange [etrɑ̃ʒ] *adj* [personne] strange, odd ■ [chose, fait] strange, funny, odd ■ **chose ~, elle a dit oui** strangely enough, she said yes.

étrangement [etrɑ̃ʒmɑ̃] *adv* [bizarrement] oddly, strangely ■ **elle était ~ habillée** she was oddly dressed ▌[inhabituellement] strangely.

étranger, ère [etrɑ̃ʒe, ɛr] ◇ *adj* **1.** [visiteur, langue, politique] foreign **2.** [extérieur à un groupe] outside *(adj)* ■ **~ à : je suis ~ à leur communauté** I'm not a member of *ou* I don't belong to their community ■ **des personnes étrangères au service** non-members of staff **3.** [non familier - voix, visage, région, sentiment] unknown, unfamiliar **4.** [sans rapport avec] : **~ à : je suis complètement ~ à cette affaire** I'm in no way involved in *ou* I have nothing to do with this business ■ **ce sont là des considérations étrangères à notre discussion** those points are irrelevant *ou* extraneous *sout* to our discussion **5.** *sout* **~ à** [qui n'a pas le concept de] closed *ou* impervious to ■ **il est ~ à la pitié** he's completely lacking in compassion ■ **~ à** [inconnu de] unknown to ■ **ce sentiment/visage ne m'est pas ~** that feeling/face is not unknown to me.
◇ *nm, f* **1.** [habitant d'un autre pays] foreigner ADMIN alien ■ **'l'Étranger' *Camus*** 'The Stranger' **2.** [inconnu] stranger.
◆ **étranger** *nm* : **l'~** foreign countries ■ **ça vient de l'~** it comes from abroad.
◆ **à l'étranger** *loc adv* abroad.

étrangeté [etrɑ̃ʒte] *nf* **1.** [singularité - d'un discours, d'un comportement] strangeness, oddness **2.** *litt* [remarque] funny *ou* strange *ou* odd thing ■ [incident] strange *ou* odd fact.

étranglé, e [etrɑ̃gle] *adj* **1.** [rauque - voix, son] tight, strained **2.** [resserré - rue, passage] narrow.

étranglement [etrɑ̃ɡləmɑ̃] *nm* **1.** [strangulation] strangling, strangulation **2.** [étouffement, resserrement] tightening, constriction ■ **j'ai compris à l'~ de sa voix que...** the tightness in his voice told me that... **3.** [passage étroit] bottleneck ■ **grâce à l'~ du tuyau** owing to the narrower section of the pipe **4.** *litt* [restriction - des libertés] stifling **5.** MÉD strangulation.

étrangler [3] [etrɑ̃ɡle] *vt* **1.** [tuer - intentionnellement] to strangle ; [- par accident] to strangle, to choke **2.** [serrer] to choke, to constrict *sout* ■ **elle avait la taille étranglée par une grosse ceinture** she had a wide belt pulled in tight around the waist **3.** [faire balbutier - suj: colère, peur] to choke **4.** [ruiner] to decimate, to squeeze out of existence **5.** *litt* [restreindre - libertés] to stifle.

◆ **s'étrangler** *vpi* **1.** [personne] to choke ■ **s'~ avec un os** to choke on a bone ■ **s'~ de : s'~ de rire** to choke with laughter ■ **s'~ d'indignation** to be speechless with indignation **2.** [voix] to choke **3.** [chemin, rue, vallée] to form a bottleneck, to narrow (down).

étrangleur, euse [etrɑ̃ɡlœr, øz] *nm, f* strangler.

étrave [etrav] *nf* stem.

être[1] [2] [ɛtr] ◇ *vi*

> **A.** EXPRIME L'EXISTENCE, LA RÉALITÉ
> **B.** RELIE L'ATTRIBUT, LE COMPLÉMENT AU SUJET
> **C.** SUBSTITUT DE ALLER, PARTIR

A. EXPRIME L'EXISTENCE, LA RÉALITÉ

1. [exister] to be, to exist ■ **ne nie pas ce qui est** don't deny the facts ■ **si Dieu est** if God exists ■ **si cela est** if (it is) so ■ **mon fils n'est plus** *litt* my son is no more *litt ou* has died *ou* passed away ■ **la nounou la plus patiente qui soit** the most patient nanny that ever was *ou* in the world ■ **le plus petit ordinateur qui soit** the tiniest computer ever ▶ **~ ou ne pas ~** to be or not to be ■ **on ne peut pas ~ et avoir été** you only live once **2.** MATH : **soit une droite AB** let AB be a straight line

B. RELIE L'ATTRIBUT, LE COMPLÉMENT AU SUJET

1. [suivi d'un attribut] to be ■ **elle est professeur** she's a teacher ■ **je ne te le prêterai pas! – comment** *ou* **comme tu es!** *fam* I won't lend it to you! – you see what you're like! ■ **je suis comme je suis** I am what I am ■ **Bruno/ce rôle est tout pour moi** Bruno/this part means everything to me ■ **elle n'est plus rien pour lui** she no longer matters to him ■ **elle n'est plus ce qu'elle était** she's not what she used to be ■ **qui était-ce?** who was it? **2.** [suivi d'une préposition] : **~ à** [se trouver à] : **~ à l'hôpital** to be in hospital ■ **je suis à la gare** I'm at the station ■ **cela fait longtemps que je ne suis plus à Paris** I left Paris a long time ago ■ **j'y suis, j'y reste** here I am and here I stay ■ **je n'y suis pour personne** [à la maison] I'm not at home for anyone ; [au bureau] I won't see anybody ■ **je suis à vous dans un instant** I'll be with you in a moment ■ **je suis à vous** [je vous écoute] I'm all yours ■ **la Sardaigne est au sud de la Corse** Sardinia is (situated) south of Corsica ■ **tout le monde est à la page 15/au chapitre 9?** is everybody at page 15/chapter 9? ■ **vous êtes (bien) au 01.40.06.24.08** this is 01 40 06 24 08 ■ **nous ne sommes qu'au début du tournoi** the tournament has just started ■ **~ à** [appartenir à] : **ce livre est à moi** the book's mine ■ **~ à** [être occupé à] : **il est tout à son travail** he's busy with his work ■ **~ à** [être en train de] : **il est toujours à me questionner** he's always asking me questions ■ **~ de** [provenir de] to be from, to come from ■ **~ de** [dater de] : **l'église est du XVI**e the church is from *ou* dates back to the 16th century ■ **la lettre est du 12** the letter's dated the 12th ■ **les œufs sont d'hier** the eggs were laid yesterday ■ **~ de** [appartenir à] to belong to, to be a member of ■ **Bruno est de sa famille** Bruno is a member of her family *ou* is a relative of hers ■ **~ de** [participer à] : **je suis de mariage le mois prochain** I've got (to go to) a wedding next month ■ **qui est de corvée de vaisselle?** who's on washing-up duty? ■ **~ de** [se joindre à] : **acceptez-vous d'~ (un) des nôtres?** would you care to join us? ■ **~ en** [lieu] : **~ en prison/en France** to be in prison/in France ■ **~ en** [matériau] : **la table est en chêne** the table is made of oak ■ **~ en** [pour exprimer l'état] : **~ en bonne santé** to be in good health ■ **les dossiers qui sont en attente** the pending files ■ **~ sans : vous n'êtes pas sans savoir que...** I'm sure you're aware that... ■ **en ~ à : le projet n'en est qu'au début** the project has only just started ■ **où en es-tu avec Michel?** how is it going with Michel? ■ **j'en suis au moment où il découvre le trésor** I've got to the part *ou* the bit where he discovers the treasure ■ **où en étais-je?** [après une interruption dans une conversation] where was I ? ■ **où en sont les travaux?** how's the work coming along? ■ **en ~ à faire qqch : j'en suis à me demander si...** I'm beginning to wonder if... ■ **tu en es encore à lui chercher des excuses! – oh non, je n'en suis plus là!** you're still trying to find excuses for him! – oh no, I'm past that! ■ **ne plus savoir où l'on en est : je ne sais plus du tout où j'en suis dans tous ces calculs** I don't know where I am any more with all these calculations ■ **j'ai besoin de faire le point, je ne sais plus où j'en suis** I've got to take stock, I've completely lost track of everything ■ **y ~** [être prêt] : **tout le monde y est?** is everyone ready? ■ **y ~** [comprendre] : **tu te souviens bien de Marie, une petite brune! – ah, oui, j'y suis maintenant!** but you must remember Marie, a brunette! – oh yes, I'm with you now! ■ **je n'y suis pas du tout!** I'm lost! ■ **mais non, vous n'y êtes pas du tout!** you don't understand! ▶ **en ~** *fam*, **~ de ceux-là** *fam* [être homosexuel] to be one of them

3. [dans l'expression du temps] to be ■ **nous sommes le 8/jeudi** today is the 8th/Thursday ■ **quel jour sommes-nous?** what day is it today? ■ **on était en avril** it was April

C. SUBSTITUT DE ALLER, PARTIR

to go ■ **tu y as déjà été?** have you already been there? ■ **elle s'en fut lui porter la lettre** *litt* she went to take him the letter.

◇ *v impers* **1.** [exister] : **il est** [il y a] *(suivi d'un sing)* there is ■ *(suivi d'un pl)* there are ■ **il était une fois un prince...** once (upon a time) there was a prince... ■ **s'il en est : un escroc s'il en est** a crook if ever there was one **2.** [pour exprimer l'heure] : **il est 5 h** it's 5 o'clock ■ **quelle heure est-il?** what time is it? **3.** *sout* & *loc* **il en est ainsi de toutes les démocraties** that's how it is in all democracies ■ **on a dit que vous vouliez démissionner – il n'en est rien** it was rumoured you wanted to resign – that's not true ■ **il n'est que de : il n'est que de lire les journaux pour s'en rendre compte** you only have to read the newspapers to be aware of it.

◇ *v aux* **1.** [sert à former les temps composés] : **je suis/j'étais descendu** I came/had come down ■ **serais-tu resté?** would you have stayed? **2.** [sert à former le passif] : **des arbres ont été déterrés par la tempête** trees were uprooted during the storm **3.** [sert à exprimer une obligation] : **ce dossier est à préparer pour lundi** the file must be ready for Monday ■ **cela est à prouver** we have no proof of that yet.

◆ **cela étant** *loc adv* [dans ces circonstances] things being what they are ■ [cela dit] having said that.

être[2] [ɛtr] *nm* **1.** BIOL & PHILOS being ■ **l'~** PHILOS being ▶ **~ humain** human being ■ **~ de raison** rational being ■ **~ vivant** living thing **2.** RELIG : **l'être éternel** *ou* **infini** *ou* **suprême** the Supreme Being **3.** [personne] person ▶ **un ~ cher** a loved one **4.** [cœur, âme] being, heart, soul ■ **je le crois de tout mon ~** I believe it with all my heart.

étreindre [81] [etrɛ̃dr] *vt* **1.** [serrer entre ses bras - ami, amant, adversaire] to hug, to clasp *litt*, to embrace **2.** *sout* [oppresser - suj: émotion, colère, peur] to seize, to grip.

◆ **s'étreindre** *vp (emploi réciproque)* [amis, amants] to hug (each other), to embrace each other ■ [lutteurs] to grip each other, to have each other in a tight grip.

étreinte [etrɛ̃t] *nf* **1.** [embrassement] hug, embrace **2.** [d'un boa] constriction ■ [d'un lutteur] grip ■ **les troupes ennemies resserrent leur ~ autour de la ville** the enemy troops are tightening their grip *ou* stranglehold on the city **3.** *litt* [oppression] grip, grasp.

étrenne [etrɛn] *nf litt* & *loc* **avoir l'~ de qqch** to have the first use of sthg.

◆ **étrennes** *nfpl* [cadeau] New Year's Day present ■ **qu'est-ce que tu veux pour tes ~s?** what would you like as a present for New Year's Day? ‖ [pourboire] New Year's tip *(given to postmen, dustmen, delivery men etc in the weeks running up to the New Year)*, ≃ Christmas box UK, ≃ Christmas bonus US.

étrenner [4] [etrene] ◇ *vt* [machine] to use for the first time ■ [robe, chaussures] to wear for the first time.

◇ *vi* [souffrir] : **c'est toi qui vas ~!** YOU're going to get *ou* catch it!

étrier [etrije] *nm* **1.** ÉQUIT stirrup ■ **coup de l'~** stirrup cup, one for the road ■ **tenir l'~ à qqn** *pr* to help sb mount ; *fig* to give sb a leg up **2.** [d'escalade] étrier *UK*, stirrup *US*.

étrille [etrij] *nf* [peigne] currycomb.

étriller [3] [etrije] *vt* **1.** [cheval] to curry, to currycomb **2.** *fam* [vaincre] to crush, to trounce **3.** *fam* [critiquer] to pan, to slate *UK* **4.** *fam* [escroquer] to swindle, to con.

étriper [3] [etripe] *vt* **1.** [poisson] to gut ■ [volaille, gibier] to draw, to clean out *(sép)* **2.** *fam* [tuer] : **je vais l'~, celui-là!** I'm going to kill him *ou* to make mincemeat of him *ou* to have his guts for garters!
◆ **s'étriper** *vp (emploi réciproque) fam* to tear each other to pieces ■ **ils allaient s'~** they were at each other's throats.

étriqué, e [etrike] *adj* **1.** [trop petit - vêtement] skimpy **2.** [mesquin - vie, habitudes, caractère] mean, petty ■ **un point de vue très ~** a very narrow outlook.

étrivière [etrivjɛr] *nf* stirrup leather.

étroit, e [etrwa, at] *adj* **1.** [rue, bande, sentier] narrow ■ [vêtement] tight **2.** [mesquin - esprit] narrow ; [- idées] limited ■ **être ~ d'esprit** to be narrow-minded **3.** [liens, rapport, complicité, collaboration] close **4.** [surveillance] close, strict, tight ■ [acception, interprétation] narrow, strict.
◆ **à l'étroit** *loc adv* : **on est un peu à l'~ ici** it's rather cramped in here ■ **ils vivent** *ou* **sont logés à l'~** they haven't much living space.

étroitement [etrwatmɑ̃] *adv* **1.** [strictement - respecter] strictly ; [- surveiller] closely, strictly **2.** [intimement - relier] closely ■ **être ~ unis** to be closely allied, to have close links **3.** [à l'étroit] : **être ~ logé** to live in cramped conditions.

étroitesse [etrwatɛs] *nf* **1.** [d'une route, d'un couloir] narrowness **2.** [mesquinerie] : **~ d'esprit** *ou* **de vues** narrow-mindedness.

étron [etrɔ̃] *nm* piece of excrement.

Étrurie [etryri] *npr f* : **(l')~** Etruria.

étrusque [etrysk] *adj* Etruscan, Etrurian.
◆ **Étrusque** *nmf* Etruscan, Etrurian.

étude [etyd] *nf* **1.** [apprentissage] study ■ **l'~ des langues** the study of languages ■ **elle a le goût de l'~** she has a thirst for learning **2.** [analyse, essai] study, paper ➜ **~ de cas** case study ■ **~ de texte** ÉDUC textual analysis **3.** [travail préparatoire] study ■ **ce projet est à l'~** this project is under consideration *ou* being studied ➜ **~ de faisabilité** feasability study ■ **~ de marché** market research *(U)* **4.** ÉDUC [salle] study *ou* *UK* prep room ■ [période] study-time ■ **elle reste à l'~ le soir** she stays on to study in the evenings **5.** DR [charge] practice ■ [locaux] office **6.** MUS study, étude **7.** ART study.
◆ **études** *nfpl* ÉDUC & UNIV studies ■ **faire des ~s** to study ■ **elle fait des ~s d'histoire** she studies history ■ **arrêter ses ~s** [par choix] to give up studying ; [par rébellion] to drop out ■ **il a fait ses ~s à Bordeaux** he studied in Bordeaux ■ **payer ses ~s** to pay for one's education ➜ **~s supérieures** higher education.

étudiant, e [etydjɑ̃, ɑ̃t] ◇ *adj* student *(modif)*.
◇ *nm, f* [avant la licence] undergraduate, student ■ [après la licence] postgraduate, student ■ **~ en droit/médecine** law/medical student ■ **~ de première année** first year (student).

étudié, e [etydje] *adj* **1.** [bien fait - plan, dessin] specially *ou* carefully designed ; [- discours] carefully composed ; [- tenue] carefully selected **2.** COMM [prix] reasonable **3.** [affecté - gestes] studied ■ **avoir un comportement ~** to have a studied manner.

étudier [9] [etydje] ◇ *vt* **1.** [apprendre - matière] to learn, to study ; [- leçon] to learn ; [- piano] to learn (to play), to study ; [- auteur, période] to study ■ **~ l'histoire** ÉDUC to study history ; UNIV to study *ou* *UK* to read history ■ [observer - insecte] to study **2.** [examiner - contrat] to study, to examine ; [- proposition] to consider, to examine ; [- liste, inventaire] to go through *(insép)*, to check over *(insép)* ■ **~ le terrain** to survey the land **3.** [observer - passant, adversaire] to watch, to observe **4.** [concevoir - méthode] to devise ; [- modèle, maquette] to design ■ **être très étudié** to be specially designed ■ **c'est étudié pour** *fam* that's what it's for.
◇ *vi* **1.** [faire ses études] to study, to be a student **2.** [travailler] to study.
◆ **s'étudier** ◇ *vp (emploi réfléchi)* **1.** [se regarder soi-même] to gaze at *ou* to study o.s. **2.** *péj* [s'observer avec complaisance] to admire o.s.
◇ *vp (emploi réciproque)* [se regarder l'un l'autre] to observe each other.

étui [etɥi] *nm* [à lunettes, à cigares, de violon] case ■ **~ de revolver** holster.

étuve [etyv] *nf* **1.** [sauna] steamroom ■ **quelle ~** *ou* **c'est une vraie ~ ici!** it's steaming hot in here! **2.** TECHNOL [pour stériliser] sterilizer, autoclave ■ [pour sécher] drier.

étuvée [etyve] = **étouffée**.

étuver [3] [etyve] *vt* **1.** CULIN to steam **2.** [sécher] to dry, to heat **3.** TECHNOL to bake, to stove.

étymologie [etimɔlɔʒi] *nf* **1.** [discipline] etymology, etymological research **2.** [origine] etymology, origin ■ **l'~ d'un terme** the etymology *ou* origin of a term.

étymologique [etimɔlɔʒik] *adj* etymological.

étymologiquement [etimɔlɔʒikmɑ̃] *adv* etymologically.

étymologiste [etimɔlɔʒist] *nmf* etymologist.

eu, e [y] *pp* ▻ **avoir**.

E-U, E-U A *(abr de* **États-Unis (d'Amérique)**) *npr mpl* US, USA.

eucalyptus [økaliptys] *nm* eucalyptus.

eucharistie [økaristi] *nf* : **l'~** the Eucharist, Holy Communion.

eucharistique [økaristik] *adj* Eucharistic.

Euclide [øklid] *npr* Euclid.

euclidien, enne [øklidjɛ̃, ɛn] *adj* Euclidean, Euclidian.

eugénique [øʒenik] ◇ *adj* eugenic.
◇ *nf* = **eugénisme**.

eugénisme [øʒenism] *nm* eugenics *(sing)*.

euh [ø] *interj* er.

eunuque [ønyk] *nm* eunuch.

euphémisme [øfemism] *nm* euphemism ■ **je dis "mauvais" mais c'est un ~** I say "bad" but it's an understatement.
◆ **par euphémisme** *loc adv* euphemistically.

euphonie [øfɔni] *nf* euphony.

euphorie [øfɔri] *nf* euphoria.

euphorique [øfɔrik] *adj* euphoric ■ **rendre ~** to elate.

euphorisant, e [øfɔrizɑ̃, ɑ̃t] *adj* **1.** [médicament, drogue] euphoriant **2.** [atmosphère, succès] heady.
◆ **euphorisant** *nm* [médicament] anti-depressant ■ [drogue] euphoriant.

euphoriser [3] [øfɔrize] *vt* to make euphoric.

Euphrate [øfrat] *npr m* : **l'~** the (River) Euphrates.

eurafricain, e [ørafrikɛ̃, ɛn] *adj* Afro-European.

eurasiatique [ørazjatik] *adj* Eurasian.

Eurasie [ørazi] *npr f* : **(l')~** Eurasia.

eurasien, enne [ørazjɛ̃, ɛn] *adj* Eurasian.
◆ **Eurasien, enne** *nm, f* Eurasian.

eurêka [øreka] *interj* eureka.

Euripide [øripid] *npr* Euripides.

EURL [øyɛrɛl] *(abr de* **Entreprise unipersonnelle à responsabilité limitée**) *nf sole trader set up as a limited company.*

euro [ørɔ] *nm* euro.

eurocentrisme [ørɔsɑ̃trism] *nm* Eurocentrism.

eurochèque [ørɔʃɛk] *nm* Eurocheque.

eurocrate [ørɔkrat] *nmf* Eurocrat.

eurodéputé, e [ørɔdepyte] *nmf* Euro-MP.

eurodevise [ørɔdəviz] *nf* Eurocurrency.

eurodollar [ørɔdɔlar] *nm* Eurodollar.

euromissile [ørɔmisil] *nm* Euromissile.

euromonnaie [ørɔmɔnɛ] = **eurodevise**.

euro-obligation [ørɔɔbligasjɔ̃] (*pl* **euro-obligations**) *nf* Eurobond.

Europe [ørɔp] *npr f* **1.** GÉOGR : **(l')~** Europe ■ **(l')~ centrale** Central Europe ■ **(l')~ continentale** mainland Europe ■ **(l')~ de l'Est** East *ou* Eastern Europe ■ **(l')~ du Nord** Northern Europe ■ **(l')~ du Sud** Southern Europe ■ **l'~ verte** European (community) agriculture ■ **l'~ des douze** the Twelve, the twelve member states (of the EC) **2.** RADIO : **~ 1** *radio station broadcasting popular entertainment and general interest programmes* ■ **~ 2** *radio station broadcasting mainly music.*

européanisation [ørɔpeanizasjɔ̃] *nf* Europeanization, Europeanizing *(U)*.

européaniser [3] [ørɔpeanize] *vt* to Europeanize, to make European.

européen, enne [ørɔpeɛ̃, ɛn] *adj* European.
◆ **Européen, enne** *nm, f* European.
◆ **européennes** *nfpl* POLIT European elections, Euro-elections, elections to the European Parliament.

euroscepticisme [ørɔsɛptisism] *nm* Euroscepticism.

eurosceptique [ørɔsɛptik] *nmf* Eurosceptic.

Eurostar® [ørɔstar] *npr m* Eurostar®.

Eurotunnel® [ørɔtynɛl] *npr m* Eurotunnel®.

Eurovision [ørɔvizjɔ̃] *nf* Eurovision.

eusse *etc v* ▷ **avoir**.

eut *etc v* ▷ **avoir**.

euthanasie [øtanazi] *nf* euthanasia.

euthanasier [9] [øtanazje] *vt* [animal] to put down, to put to sleep ■ [personne] to practise euthanasia on, to help to die.

eux [ø] *pron pers* **1.** [sujet] they ■ **nous sommes invités, ~ pas** *ou* **non** we are invited but they aren't *ou* but not them ■ **ce sont ~ les responsables** they are the ones *ou* it is they who are responsible ■ **~ seuls connaissent la réponse** they alone *ou* only they know the answer ■ **~, voter? cela m'étonnerait** them? vote? I doubt it very much! **2.** [après une préposition] them ■ **avec ~, on ne sait jamais** you never know with them ■ *(en fonction de pronom réfléchi)* themselves ■ **ils ne pensent qu'à ~** they only think of themselves **3.** [suivi d'un nombre] : **~ deux** both *ou* the two of them.

eux-mêmes [ømɛm] *pron pers* themselves.

eV (*abr écrite de* **électron-volt**) eV.

EV (*abr écrite de* **en ville**) by hand.

évacuateur, trice [evakɥatœr, tris] *adj* evacuative, evacuation *(modif)*.

évacuation [evakɥasjɔ̃] *nf* **1.** PHYSIOL [de toxines] elimination, eliminating *(U)* ■ [du pus] draining off **2.** [écoulement] draining ■ **une conduite assure l'~ des eaux usées** the waste water drains out through a pipe **3.** [d'une ville, d'un lieu] evacuation **4.** [sauvetage] evacuation, evacuating ■ **organiser l'~ des habitants** to evacuate the local people.

évacué, e [evakɥe] ◇ *adj* : **personne ~e** evacuee.
◇ *nm, f* evacuee.

évacuer [7] [evakɥe] *vt* **1.** PHYSIOL [toxine] to eliminate ■ [excrément] to evacuate ■ [pus] to drain off *(sép)* **2.** [faire s'écouler] to drain **3.** MIL [terrain] to move off *(insép)* ■ [position] to retreat from *(insép)* ■ [place forte] to leave **4.** [navire, hôpital] to evacuate ■ **faire ~ un bâtiment** to evacuate *ou* to clear a building **5.** [personne, population] : **~ qqn de** to evacuate sb from.

évadé, e [evade] ◇ *adj* escaped.
◇ *nm, f* escaped prisoner ■ **un ~ de l'asile/de Fresnes** an escapee from the mental hospital/from Fresnes prison.

évader [3] [evade] ◆ **s'évader** *vpi* **1.** [s'enfuir] : **s'~ de** to escape from, to break out of **2.** [pour oublier ses soucis] to escape, to get away from it all.

évaluable [evalɥabl] *adj* appraisable, assessable ■ **difficilement ~** [dégâts, montant] hard to appraise *ou* to evaluate.

évaluation [evalɥasjɔ̃] *nf* **1.** [estimation] assessment, evaluation, valuation ■ **faire l'~ d'un tableau** to estimate the value of *ou* to evaluate a painting **2.** [quantité évaluée] estimation.

évaluer [7] [evalɥe] *vt* **1.** [estimer - bijou, tableau] to appraise, to assess ■ **faire ~ qqch** to have sthg valued ■ **la propriété a été évaluée à trois millions** the estate has been valued at *ou* the value of the estate has been put at three million **2.** [mesurer - dégâts, volume, débit] to estimate ■ **~ qqch à** to estimate *ou* to evaluate sthg at **3.** [estimer approximativement - distance] to gauge ■ **on évalue sa fortune à trois millions de dollars** his fortune is estimated at three million dollars **4.** [juger - qualité] to weigh up *(sép)*, to gauge, to assess ■ **mal ~ les risques** to miscalculate the risks.

évanescence [evanesɑ̃s] *nf litt* evanescence.

évanescent, e [evanesɑ̃, ɑ̃t] *adj litt* evanescent.

évangélique [evɑ̃ʒelik] *adj* **1.** [de l'Évangile] evangelic, evangelical **2.** [protestant] Evangelical.

évangélisateur, trice [evɑ̃ʒelizatœr, tris] ◇ *adj* evangelistic.
◇ *nm, f* evangelist.

évangélisation [evɑ̃ʒelizasjɔ̃] *nf* evangelization, evangelizing.

évangéliser [3] [evɑ̃ʒelize] *vt* to evangelize.

évangélisme [evɑ̃ʒelism] *nm* evangelism.

évangéliste [evɑ̃ʒelist] *nm* Evangelist.

évangile [evɑ̃ʒil] *nm* **1.** RELIG : **l'Évangile** the Gospel ■ **les Évangiles** the Gospels ■ **l'Évangile selon saint...** the Gospel according to Saint... **2.** [credo] gospel.

évanouir [32] [evanwir] ◆ **s'évanouir** *vpi* **1.** MÉD to faint, to pass out **2.** [disparaître - personne] to vanish (into thin air) ; [- craintes, illusions] to vanish, to disappear, to evaporate *litt* ■ **s'~ dans la nature** to fade into the background.

évanouissement [evanwismɑ̃] *nm* **1.** [syncope] fainting *(U)*, blackout ■ **avoir un ~** to (go into a) faint **2.** [disparition] disappearance, disappearing, vanishing **3.** TÉLÉCOM fading.

évaporation [evapɔrasjɔ̃] *nf* evaporation.

évaporé, e [evapɔre] ◇ *adj* scatterbrained, birdbrained.
◇ *nm, f* birdbrain, dimwit.

évaporer [3] [evapɔre] *vt* to evaporate.
◆ **s'évaporer** *vpi* **1.** [liquide] to evaporate **2.** [colère, crainte] to vanish, to disappear, to evaporate *litt* **3.** *fam* [disparaître] to vanish (into thin air) ■ **je me suis retourné et hop, il s'était évaporé!** I turned round and he'd gone, just like that!

évapotranspiration [evapɔtrɑ̃spirasjɔ̃] *nf* evapotranspiration.

évasé, e [evaze] *adj* [robe] flared ■ [ouverture, tuyau] splayed ■ [récipient] tapered ■ **la jupe a une jolie forme ~e** the skirt flares out nicely.

évasement [evazmɑ̃] *nm* [d'une ouverture, d'un tuyau] splay ■ [d'un entonnoir] widening-out.

évaser [3] [evaze] *vt* [jupe] to flare ■ [ouverture, tuyau] to splay.
◆ **s'évaser** *vpi* [chenal] to open out, to broaden ■ [forme, vêtement] to flare ■ [tuyau] to splay.

évasif, ive [evazif, iv] *adj* evasive, non-committal.

évasion [evazjɔ̃] *nf* **1.** [d'un prisonnier] escape **2.** [distraction] : **j'ai besoin d'~** I need to get away from it all **3.** FIN & DR : **~ fiscale** tax avoidance **4.** ÉCON : **~ de capitaux** flight of capital.
◆ **d'évasion** *loc adj* escapist.

évasivement [evazivmɑ̃] *adv* evasively ▪ **"qui sait", répondit-il ~** "who knows", was his vague reply *ou* he replied evasively.

Ève [ɛv] *npr* BIBLE Eve ▪ **je ne le connais ni d'~ ni d'Adam** I don't know him from Adam ▪ **en costume** *ou* **en tenue d'~** naked, in her birthday suit *hum*, in the altogether.

évêché [eveʃe] *nm* **1.** [territoire] bishopric, diocese **2.** [demeure] bishop's palace *ou* house **3.** [ville] cathedral town.

éveil [evɛj] *nm* **1.** *sout* [fin du repos] awakening *(C)* **2.** [déclenchement] : **l'~ de** the awakening *ou* early development *ou* first stirrings of ▪ **l'~ des sens/de la sexualité** the awakening of the senses/of sexuality ▪ **l'~ de qqn à qqch** sb's awakening to sthg ▪ **l'auteur raconte l'~ à l'amour d'une toute jeune fille** the author recounts the dawning of love in a young girl's heart **3.** ÉDUC : **activité** *ou* **matière d'~** early-learning *(U)* **4.** [alerte] : **donner l'~** to raise the alarm.
◆ **en éveil** *loc adv* **1.** [sur ses gardes] : **être en ~** to be on the alert **2.** [actif] : **à quatre ans, leur curiosité est en ~** by the time they're four, their curiosity is fully roused.

éveillé, e [eveje] *adj* **1.** [vif - enfant, esprit] alert, bright, sharp ; [- intelligence] sharp **2.** [en état de veille] awake ▪ **tout ~** wide awake ▪ **tenir qqn ~** to keep sb awake.

éveiller [4] [eveje] *vt* **1.** *litt* [tirer du sommeil] to awaken, to waken, to arouse *sout* **2.** [susciter - désir, jalousie, passion] to kindle, to arouse ; [- amour, méfiance] to arouse ; [- curiosité, soupçons] to arouse, to awaken ; [- espoir] to awaken ; [- attention, intérêt] to attract **3.** [stimuler - intelligence] to stimulate, to awaken.
◆ **s'éveiller** *vpi* **1.** [animal, personne] to awaken, to wake up, to waken **2.** *litt* [s'animer - campagne, village] to come to life, to wake up **3.** [se révéler - intelligence, talent] to reveal itself, to come to light **4.** [naître - curiosité, jalousie, méfiance] to be aroused ; [- amour] to dawn, to stir.
◆ **s'éveiller à** *vp+prép* : **s'~ à l'amour** to discover love.

événement, évènement [evɛnmɑ̃] *nm* **1.** [fait] event, occurrence, happening *(C)* ▪ **vacances pleines d'~s** eventful holidays ▪ **nous sommes débordés** *ou* **dépassés par les ~s** we have been overtaken by events **2.** POLIT : **les ~s d'Algérie** the Algerian War of Independence ▪ **les ~s de mai 68** the events of May 68 **3.** [fait important] event ▪ **leur rencontre est un ~ historique** their meeting is a historic event ▪ **~ sportif** sporting event ▪ **faire** *ou* **créer l'~** to be news *ou* a major event.

événementiel, elle, évènementiel, elle [evɛnmɑ̃sjɛl] *adj* purely descriptive.

éventail [evɑ̃taj] *nm* **1.** [accessoire] fan **2.** [gamme] range ▪ **l'~ de son répertoire** the range *ou* scope of his repertory ▪ **~ des salaires** salary range *ou* spread **3.** COMM range.
◆ **en éventail** *loc adj* [queue] spread-out.

éventaire [evɑ̃tɛr] *nm* **1.** [étalage] stall **2.** [plateau] (street vendor's) tray.

éventé, e [evɑ̃te] *adj* **1.** [altéré - bière, limonade] flat, stale ; [- parfum, vin] musty, stale **2.** [connu - complot] discovered.

éventer [3] [evɑ̃te] *vt* **1.** [avec un éventail, un magazine] to fan **2.** [grain] to aerate ▪ [mine] to ventilate **3.** [révéler - secret] to disclose, to give away *(sép)* **4.** CHASSE to scent, to get the scent of.
◆ **s'éventer** ◇ *vp (emploi réfléchi)* [pour se rafraîchir] to fan o.s. ▪ **s'~ avec un magazine** to fan o.s. with a magazine.
◇ *vp (emploi passif)* [être divulgué - plan d'attaque, secret] to get out, to become public knowledge.
◇ *vpi* [s'altérer - parfum, vin] to go musty *ou* stale ; [- limonade, eau gazeuse] to go flat *ou* stale.

éventrer [3] [evɑ̃tre] *vt* **1.** [personne - avec un couteau] to disembowel ▪ **il a été éventré par le taureau** he was gored by the bull **2.** [canapé, outre, oreiller, sac] to rip (open) ▪ [boîte en carton] to tear open ▪ [coffret] to break open **3.** [champ] to rip open *(sép)*, to rip holes in ▪ [immeuble] to rip apart *(sép)*.
◆ **s'éventrer** ◇ *vp (emploi réfléchi)* to disembowel o.s.
◇ *vpi* [se fendre - oreiller, sac] to burst open ▪ **la barque s'est éventrée sur un récif** the boat hit a reef, ripping a hole in its hull.

éventreur [evɑ̃trœr] *nm* ripper ▪ **Jack l'Éventreur** Jack the Ripper.

éventualité [evɑ̃tɥalite] *nf* **1.** [possibilité] possibility, contingency ▪ **cette ~ ne m'avait pas effleuré** this possibility hadn't occurred to me **2.** [circonstance] eventuality, possibility, contingency ▪ **pour parer** *ou* **être prêt à toute ~** to be ready for anything that might crop up ▪ **il faut envisager toutes les ~s** we must consider all the possibilities ▪ **dans cette ~** in such an *ou* in this event.
◆ **dans l'éventualité de** *loc prép* in the event of.

éventuel, elle [evɑ̃tɥɛl] *adj* [potentiel - client] potential, prospective ; [- bénéfice] possible, potential ; [- issue, refus, remplaçant *etc*] possible ▪ **à titre ~** as a possibility.

éventuellement [evɑ̃tɥɛlmɑ̃] *adv* : **tu me le prêterais? – ~** would you lend it to me? – maybe *ou* if need be ▪ **les entreprises qui pourraient ~ nous racheter** the companies which might *ou* could buy us out.

évêque [evɛk] *nm* bishop ▪ **~ suffragant** suffragan (bishop).

Everest [evrɛst] *npr m* : **l'~, le mont ~** Mount Everest.

évertuer [7] [evɛrtɥe] ◆ **s'évertuer à** *vp+prép* : **s'~ à faire qqch** to strive *ou* to endeavour to do sthg ▪ **je ne m'évertuerai pas à te convaincre** I won't waste energy trying to convince you.

éviction [eviksjɔ̃] *nf* **1.** DR eviction **2.** [expulsion] : **~ d'un poste** removal from a position ➜ **~ scolaire** expulsion, suspension.

évidemment [evidamɑ̃] *adv* **1.** [bien entendu] of course ▪ [manifestement] obviously ▪ **tu me crois? – ~!** do you believe me? – of course (I do)! **2.** [avec colère, irritation] needless to say, predictably enough ▪ **~, elle n'a rien préparé!** needless to say she hasn't prepared a thing! ▪ **j'ai oublié mes clés – ~!** [ton irrité] I've forgotten my keys – you would!

évidence [evidɑ̃s] *nf* **1.** [caractère certain] obviousness **2.** [fait manifeste] obvious fact ▪ **c'est une ~** it's obvious ▪ **il n'a dit que des ~s** *péj* he just stated the obvious **3.** [ce qui est indubitable] : **accepter** *ou* **se rendre à l'~** to face facts ▪ **c'est l'~ même!** it's quite obvious *ou* evident! ▪ **refuser** *ou* **nier l'~** to deny the facts *ou* obvious.
◆ **en évidence** *loc adv* [chose, personne] : **ses décorations bien en ~ sur le buffet** his medals lying conspicuously *ou* there for all to see on the sideboard ▪ **mettre en ~** [exposer] to display ; [détail, talent] to bring out ▪ **se mettre en ~** [se faire remarquer] to make o.s. conspicuous.
◆ **à l'évidence, de toute évidence** *loc adv* evidently, obviously.

évident, e [evidɑ̃, ɑ̃t] *adj* **1.** [manifeste - manque, plaisir] obvious, evident ; [- choix, raison] obvious, evident, self-evident **2.** [certain] obvious, certain ▪ **c'est ~!** of course!, obviously!, that's obvious! ▪ **il viendra? – pas ~!** will he come? – I wouldn't bet on it! ▪ **l'issue du match semblait ~e** it seemed fairly certain what the result of the match would be ▪ **il est ~ que...** it's obvious *ou* evident that... **3.** *fam loc* **ce n'est pas ~** [ce n'est pas facile] it's not that easy ; [ce n'est pas sûr] I wouldn't bank on it ▪ **ce n'est pas ~ qu'il réussisse** he may well not succeed.

évider [3] [evide] *vt* [rocher, fruit] to hollow *ou* to scoop out *(sép)*.

évier [evje] *nm* (kitchen) sink ▪ **~ à deux bacs** double sink.

évincement [evɛ̃smɑ̃] *nm* **1.** [d'un concurrent, d'un rival] ousting ▪ **elle a obtenu leur ~ du comité** she managed to have them ousted from *ou* thrown off the committee **2.** DR eviction.

évincer [16] [evɛ̃se] *vt* **1.** [concurrent, rival] to oust, to supplant ▪ **~ qqn d'un emploi** to oust sb from a job **2.** DR to evict.

éviscérer [18] [evisere] *vt* to eviscerate.

évitable [evitabl] *adj* [obstacle] avoidable ▪ [accident] preventable.

évitement [evitmɑ̃] *nm* RAIL shunting.
◆ **d'évitement** *loc adj* **1.** RAIL : **voie d'~** siding **2.** PSYCHOL [réaction] avoidance *(modif)*.

éviter [3] [evite] ◇ *vt* **1.** [ne pas subir - coup] to avoid ; [- danger] to avoid, to steer clear of ; [- corvée] to avoid, to shun ▪ **la catastrophe a été évitée de justesse** a catastrophe was averted by a hair's breadth ▪ **~ que : pour ~ que la mayonnaise (ne) tourne** to prevent the mayonnaise from *ou* to stop the mayonnaise curdling
2. [ne pas heurter - ballon] to avoid, to dodge, to stay out of the way of ; [- obstacle] to avoid
3. [regard, personne] to avoid, to shun
4. [lieu, situation] to avoid ▪ **j'évite les restaurants, ils sont trop enfumés** I avoid going into restaurants, they're too smoky ▪ **elle évite la foule** she shies away from crowds
5. [maladresse, impair] to avoid ▪ **évitez le franglais** try not to use franglais ▪ **~ de faire qqch** to avoid doing sthg, to try not to do sthg
6. [aliment] to avoid
7. [épargner] : **~ qqch à qqn** to spare sb sthg ▪ **évitons-lui tout souci** let's keep him from worrying (about anything) *ou* spare him any worries ▪ **cela lui évitera d'avoir à sortir** that'll save him having to go out.
◇ *vi* NAUT : **~ sur l'ancre** to swing at anchor.
◆ **s'éviter** ◇ *vp (emploi réciproque)* to avoid each other *ou* one another, to stay out of each other's way.
◇ *vpt* : **s'~ qqch** to save *ou* to spare o.s. sthg

évocateur, trice [evɔkatœr, tris] *adj* evocative, suggestive.

évocation [evɔkasjɔ̃] *nf* **1.** [rappel - du passé, d'une personne, d'un paysage *etc*] evocation, recalling ▪ **la simple ~ de cette scène la faisait pleurer** just recalling this scene made her weep ▪ **je commencerai par une brève ~ du passé de notre collège** I shall start with a brief recapitulation of the history of our college **2.** DR evocation.

évolué, e [evɔlɥe] *adj* **1.** [civilisé - peuple, société] advanced, sophisticated **2.** [progressiste - parents] broadminded ; [- idées] progressive **3.** [méthode, technologie] advanced, sophisticated.

évoluer [7] [evɔlɥe] *vi* **1.** [changer - maladie] to develop ; [- mœurs, circonstances] to change ▪ **la position du syndicat a évolué depuis hier** the union's position has changed since yesterday **2.** [progresser - pays] to develop ; [- civilisation, technique] to develop, to advance ; [- personne] to mature ▪ **ce stage l'a fait ~ de manière significative** the traineeship really brought him on **3.** [danseur] to perform ▪ [cerf-volant] to fly around ▪ [poisson] to swim (about) ▪ **ils évoluent sur scène en patins à roulettes** they move around the stage on roller-skates ▪ **les cercles dans lesquels elle évoluait** *fig* the circles in which she moved **4.** MIL & NAUT to manoeuvre **5.** BIOL to evolve.

évolutif, ive [evɔlytif, iv] *adj* **1.** [poste] with career prospects ▪ **une situation évolutive** a situation which keeps developing, a fluid situation **2.** MÉD [maladie] progressive.

évolution [evɔlysjɔ̃] *nf* **1.** [changement - de mœurs] change ; [- d'une institution, de la mode] evolution ; [- d'idées, d'événements] development **2.** [progrès - d'un pays] development ; [- d'une technique] development, advancement, evolution **3.** MÉD [d'une maladie] development, progression ▪ [d'une tumeur] growth ▪ **à ~ lente/rapide** slow/rapidly developing **4.** BIOL evolution **5.** *(souvent pl)* SPORT linked-up dance movements ▪ **les ~s** [d'un joueur, d'un patineur] movements ▪ **~s aquatiques** water ballet.

évolutionnisme [evɔlysjɔnism] *nm* evolutionism, evolutionary theory.

évolutionniste [evɔlysjɔnist] *adj & nmf* evolutionist.

évoquer [3] [evɔke] *vt* **1.** [remémorer - image, journée] to conjure up *(sép)*, to evoke ; [- souvenirs] to call up *(sép)*, to recall, to evoke ▪ **~ qqch à qqn** to remind sb of sthg ▪ **le nom ne lui évoquait rien** the name didn't ring any bells with *ou* meant nothing to him **2.** [recréer - pays, atmosphère] to call to mind, to conjure up *(sép)*, to evoke **3.** [rappeler par ressemblance] to be reminiscent of ▪ **un goût qui évoque un peu le romarin** a taste slightly reminiscent of rosemary ▪ **elle m'évoque un peu ma tante** she reminds me of my aunt a little **4.** [aborder - affaire, question] to refer to *(insép)*, to mention **5.** [appeler - démon, fantôme] to call up *(sép)* **6.** DR *to transfer (a case) from an inferior to a superior court.*

ex. = exemple.

ex- [ɛks] *préf* ex- ▪ **mon ~mari** my ex-husband *ou* former husband.

ex abrupto [ɛksabrypto] *loc adv* abruptly, without warning.

exacerbation [ɛgzasɛrbasjɔ̃] *nf* [d'une douleur] exacerbation, aggravation ▪ [d'une tension] heightening.

exacerbé, e [ɛgzasɛrbe] *adj* exaggerated ▪ **il est d'une susceptibilité ~e** he's extremely touchy.

exacerber [3] [ɛgzasɛrbe] *vt sout* [douleur, tension] to exacerbate *sout*, to aggravate, to sharpen ▪ [colère, curiosité, désir] to exacerbate, to heighten ▪ [mépris, remords] to deepen ▪ **des mesures qui vont ~ la concurrence** measures which will sharpen *ou* heighten competition.
◆ **s'exacerber** *vpi* to intensify ▪ **sa jalousie n'a fait que s'~** she has become even more jealous.

exact, e [ɛgzakt] *adj* **1.** [conforme à la réalité - description, information] exact, accurate ; [- copie, réplique] exact, true ; [- prédiction] correct, accurate ▪ **c'est ~, je t'avais promis de t'y emmener** quite right *ou* true *ou* correct, I'd promised I'd take you there ▪ **il est ~ que nous n'avions pas prévu son départ** true (enough), we hadn't anticipated (that) he'd leave **2.** [précis - mesure, poids] exact, precise ; [- expression, mot] exact, right ▪ **as-tu l'heure ~e?** have you got the right *ou* correct time? ▪ **pour être ~, disons que...** to be accurate, let's say that... ▪ MATH right, correct, accurate **3.** [fonctionnant avec précision - balance, montre] accurate **4.** [ponctuel] punctual, on time ▪ **être très ~** to be always on time *ou* very punctual.

exactement [ɛgzaktəmɑ̃] *adv* **1.** [précisément] exactly, precisely ▪ **ce n'est pas ~ ce que je cherchais** it's not exactly *ou* quite what I was looking for ▪ **mais c'est ~ le contraire!** but it's exactly *ou* precisely the opposite! ▪ **il est très ~ 2 h 13** it is 2.13 precisely **2.** [tout à fait] : **~!** exactly!, precisely!

exaction [ɛgzaksjɔ̃] *nf* exaction, extortion.
◆ **exactions** *nfpl sout* violent acts, acts of violence ▪ **se livrer à** *ou* **commettre des ~s** to perpetrate *ou* to commit acts of violence.

exactitude [ɛgzaktityd] *nf* **1.** [conformité à la réalité] exactness, accuracy ▪ **l'~ historique** historical accuracy **2.** [expression précise - d'une mesure] exactness, precision ; [- d'une localisation] exactness ▪ **je me souviens avec ~ des mots de sa lettre** I can remember the precise *ou* exact words she used in her letter **3.** [d'un instrument de mesure] accuracy **4.** [justesse - d'une traduction, d'une réponse] exactness, correctness **5.** [ponctualité] punctuality ▪ **être d'une parfaite ~** to be always perfectly on time ▶ **l'~ est la politesse des rois** *prov* punctuality is the politeness of kings **6.** *sout* [minutie] punctiliousness, meticulousness.

ex aequo [ɛgzeko] ◇ *loc adj* placed equal ▪ **être ~ (avec)** to tie *ou* to be placed equal (with) ▪ **on trouve Lille et Nantes ~ à la troisième place** Lille and Nantes come joint third ▪ **premiers ~, Maubert et Vuillet** [à un concours] the joint winners are Maubert and Vuillet ; ÉDUC top marks *UK ou* highest grades *US* have been awarded to Maubert and to Vuillet.
◇ *nmf* : **il y a deux ~ pour la troisième place** there's a tie for third place.

exagération [ɛgzaʒerasjɔ̃] *nf* **1.** [amplification] exaggeration, overstating *(U)* ▪ **tomber dans l'~** to exaggerate **2.** [écrit, parole] exaggeration, overstatement **3.** [outrance - d'un accent, d'une attitude] exaggeration.
◆ **sans exagération** *loc adv* : **tout le village a été détruit, sans ~** the whole village was destroyed, literally *ou* and that's no exaggeration.

exagéré, e [ɛgzaʒere] *adj* **1.** [excessif - dépense, prix] excessive ; [- éloge, critique] exaggerated, overblown ; [- optimisme, prudence] excessive, exaggerated ; [- hâte, mécontentement] undue ; [- ambition, confiance en soi] excessive, overweening ▪ **150 euros par personne, c'est un peu ~!** 150 euros per person, that's a bit much! ■ **il n'est pas ~ de parler de menace** it wouldn't be an overstatement to call it a threat **2.** [outré - accent, attitude] exaggerated, overdone ■ **en boitant de façon ~e** limping exaggeratedly.

exagérément [ɛgzaʒeremɑ̃] *adv* excessively, exaggeratedly ■ **~ méticuleux** over-meticulous.

exagérer [18] [ɛgzaʒere] ◇ *vt* **1.** [amplifier - importance, dangers, difficultés] to exaggerate, to overemphasize, to overstate ; [- mérites, pouvoir] to exaggerate, to overrate, to overstate ■ **tu exagères mon influence** you're crediting me with more influence than I have ■ **n'exagérons rien** let's not get carried away ■ *(en usage absolu)* **sans ~** without any exaggeration **2.** [outrer - accent, attitude] to overdo, to exaggerate.
◇ *vi* : **ça fait deux heures que j'attends, il ne faut pas ~!** I've been waiting for two hours, that's a bit much! ■ **j'étais là avant vous, faut pas ~!** *fam* I was there before you, you've got a nerve!
◆ **s'exagérer** *vpt* : **s'~ qqch** to make too much of sthg ■ **s'~ les mérites de qqn** to exaggerate sb's merits.

exaltant, e [ɛgzaltɑ̃, ɑ̃t] *adj* [expérience, perspective] exciting ■ [harangue] elating, stirring ■ **sa prestation n'est pas très ~e!** his performance isn't particularly exciting!

exaltation [ɛgzaltasjɔ̃] *nf* **1.** [excitation] (intense) excitement ■ [joie] elation **2.** [célébration - d'un talent, du travail] extolling, exalting, glorification.

exalté, e [ɛgzalte] ◇ *adj* **1.** [intense - désir, passion] inflamed **2.** [excité - personne] excited ; [- esprit] excited, inflamed ; [- imagination] wild.
◇ *nm, f péj* fanatic, hothead *péj*.

exalter [3] [ɛgzalte] *vt* **1.** [intensifier - désir] to excite, to kindle ; [- enthousiasme] to fire, to excite ; [- imagination] to fire, to stimulate, to stir up *(sép)* **2.** [exciter - foule, partisan] to excite ■ **exalté à l'idée de** carried away by the idea of **3.** *litt* [faire l'éloge de - beauté, bienfaits, talent] to glorify, to extol, to exalt *litt* **4.** *litt* [élever] to exalt, to ennoble.
◆ **s'exalter** *vpi* to become excited.

examen [ɛgzamɛ̃] *nm* **1.** ÉDUC & UNIV examination, exam ■ **tu as eu combien à l'~?** what did you get in the exam? ■ **passer un ~** [série d'épreuves] to take an exam ; [écrit] to sit *UK ou* to write *US* a paper ; [oral] to take a viva *UK ou* an oral (exam) ◗ **~ blanc** mock exam *UK*, practice test *US* ■ **~ écrit** written exam ■ **~ d'entrée** entrance exam ■ **~ de fin d'études** final examination ■ **~ oral** viva *UK*, oral (exam) ■ **~ partiel** midterm exam ■ **~ de passage** end-of-year *ou* sessional exam *UK*, final exam *US (for admission to the year above)* **2.** MÉD [auscultation] : **~ (médical)** (medical) examination ■ [analyse] test ■ **~s complémentaires** further tests ■ **~ neurologique/sérologique** neurological/serological test ■ **se faire faire un ~/des ~s** to have a test/some tests done ■ **je vais chercher mes ~s demain** I'll go and pick up my test results tomorrow **3.** [inspection] inspection, examination ■ **après ~ du corps de la victime** having examined the body of the victim **4.** [de documents, d'un dossier, d'un projet de loi] examination ■ [d'une requête] examination, consideration ■ [d'un texte] study ■ [d'une comptabilité] checking inspection ■ **son argumentation ne résiste pas à l'~** his arguments don't stand up to examination *ou* under scrutiny ◗ **~ de conscience** examination of (one's) conscience ■ **faire son ~ de conscience** [réfléchir] to do some soul-searching, to search one's conscience.
◆ **à l'examen** *loc adv* under consideration ■ **mettre une question à l'~** to put a topic on the table for discussion.

examinateur, trice [ɛgzaminatœr, tris] *nm, f* examiner ■ **les ~s** [jury] the examining panel ; [réunion] the board of examiners.

examiner [3] [ɛgzamine] *vt* **1.** [réfléchir sur - dossier, documents] to examine, to go through *(insép)* ; [- circonstances] to examine ; [- requête] to examine, to consider ; [- affaire] to investigate, to examine, to go into *(insép)* **2.** [regarder de près - meuble, signature *etc*] to examine ; [- personne] to look carefully at, to study ; [- appartement] to have a look around ■ **la police examine les lieux du crime** the police are examining the scene of the crime ◗ **~ qqch à la loupe** *pr* to look at sthg through a magnifying glass ; *fig* to have a very close look at, to scrutinize **3.** MÉD [lésion, malade] to examine ■ **se faire ~ les yeux** to have one's eyes tested **4.** ÉDUC & UNIV [candidat] to examine.
◆ **s'examiner** ◇ *vp (emploi réfléchi)* to examine o.s.
◇ *vp (emploi réciproque)* to scrutinize one another *ou* each other ■ **ils s'examinaient avec méfiance** they were eyeing each other up.

exaspérant, e [ɛgzasperɑ̃, ɑ̃t] *adj* exasperating, infuriating.

exaspération [ɛgzasperasjɔ̃] *nf* **1.** [colère] extreme annoyance, exasperation **2.** [d'un désir] exacerbation ■ [d'une émotion] heightening ■ [d'une douleur] aggravation, worsening.

exaspérer [18] [ɛgzaspere] *vt* **1.** [irriter] to infuriate, to exasperate ■ **être exaspéré contre qqn** to be exasperated with sb **2.** *sout* [intensifier - dépit, désir] to exacerbate ; [- douleur, tension] to aggravate.
◆ **s'exaspérer** *vpi* [désir, passion] to become exacerbated ■ [douleur] to worsen.

exaucement [ɛgzosmɑ̃] *nm* fulfilment, granting.

exaucer [16] [ɛgzose] *vt* **1.** [vœu] to grant, to fulfil ■ [prière] to answer, to grant **2.** [personne] to grant the wish of.

ex cathedra [ɛkskatedra] *loc adv* **1.** RELIG ex cathedra **2.** [doctement] solemnly, with authority.

excavateur, trice [ɛkskavatœr, tris] *nm, f* excavator, digger.

excavation [ɛkskavasjɔ̃] *nf* **1.** [trou - artificiel] excavation, hole ; [- naturel] hollow, cave ■ **~ minière** mine **2.** [creusement] excavation, excavating, hollowing out.

excaver [3] [ɛkskave] *vt* to excavate.

excédant, e [ɛksedɑ̃, ɑ̃t] *adj* exasperating, infuriating.

excédé, e [ɛksede] *adj* infuriated, exasperated.

excédent [ɛksedɑ̃] *nm* **1.** [surplus] surplus, excess ■ **~ de main-d'œuvre** labour surplus ■ **il y a un ~ de personnel dans le service** the department is overstaffed ■ **vous avez un ~ de bagages** your luggage is overweight **2.** ÉCON & FIN : **~ brut d'exploitation** gross operating profit ■ **~ de la balance commerciale** balance of trade surplus ■ **~s pétroliers** excess oil production.
◆ **en excédent** *loc adj* surplus *(modif)*, excess.

excédentaire [ɛksedɑ̃tɛr] *adj* [budget, balance commerciale] surplus *(modif)* ■ [solde] positive ■ [poids] excess ■ **cette année, la récolte est ~** this year, the crop exceeds requirements.

excéder [18] [ɛksede] *vt* **1.** [dépasser - poids, prix] to exceed, to be over, to be in excess of ; [- durée] to exceed, to last more than ; [- limite] to go beyond *(insép)* ■ **les recettes excèdent les dépenses** income is in excess of expenditure **2.** [outrepasser - pouvoirs, responsabilités] to exceed, to go beyond *(insép)*, to overstep ; [- forces, ressources] to overtax **3.** [exaspérer] to exasperate, to infuriate **4.** *litt* [épuiser] : **excédé de : excédé de fatigue** exhausted, overtired ■ **excédé de travail** overworked.

excellemment [ɛkselamɑ̃] *adv sout* excellently.

excellence [ɛkselɑ̃s] *nf* **1.** [qualité - d'une prestation, d'un produit] excellence **2.** [titre] : **Son/Votre Excellence** His/Your Excellency.
◆ **par excellence** *loc adv* par excellence *sout*, archetypal ■ **c'est le macho par ~** he's the archetypal male chauvinist, he's the male chauvinist par excellence.

excellent, e [ɛkselɑ̃, ɑ̃t] *adj* [très bon - artiste, directeur, nourriture] excellent, first-rate ; [- article, devoir, note] excellent ; [- santé] excellent, perfect ; [- idée] excellent.

exceller [4] [ɛksele] *vi* to excel, to shine ■ **elle excelle dans la pâtisserie** she excels at baking, she's an excellent pastry cook ■ **~ en : je n'excelle pas en latin** Latin isn't my strong point ■ **~ à faire** to be particularly good at doing.

excentré, e [ɛksɑ̃tre] *adj* **1.** MÉCAN thrown off centre, set over **2.** [quartier, stade] outlying ■ **c'est très ~** it's quite a long way out.

excentrer [3] [ɛksɑ̃tre] *vt* **1.** MÉCAN to throw off centre *(sép)*, to set over *(sép)* **2.** [bâtiment, stade] to build far from the town centre.

excentricité [ɛksɑ̃trisite] *nf* **1.** [attitude, acte] eccentricity ■ **qu'est-ce que c'est encore que ces ~s?** what's all this eccentric behaviour? **2.** ASTRON & MATH eccentricity.

excentrique [ɛksɑ̃trik] ◇ *adj* **1.** [bizarre] eccentric **2.** MATH eccentric **3.** [quartier, habitation] outlying.
◇ *nmf* [personne] eccentric.
◇ *nm* MÉCAN eccentric.

excepté[1], e [ɛksɛpte] *adj (après le n)* **elle ~e** except her, apart from her.

excepté[2] [ɛksɛpte] *prép* except, apart from ■ **il accepte tout, ~ d'avoir à me rendre des comptes** he accepts everything, except having to be accountable to me ■ **je viens avec toi, ~ si tu y vas en train** I'll come with you, so long as you're not going by train *ou* unless you're going by train.
◆ **excepté que** *loc conj* except for *ou* apart from the fact that.

excepter [4] [ɛksɛpte] *vt* to except ■ **si l'on excepte Marie, elles sont toutes là** with the exception of *ou* except for Marie they are all here ■ **toute son œuvre, sans ~ ses essais** all her work, including *ou* without excluding her essays.

exception [ɛksɛpsjɔ̃] *nf* **1.** [chose, être ou événement hors norme] exception ■ **cette règle admet des ~s** there are (some) exceptions to this rule ■ **ils sont tous très paresseux, à une ~/quelques ~s près** all of them with one exception/a few exceptions are very lazy ■ **faire ~** to be an exception ■ **être l'~** to be the *ou* an exception ■ **les collisions entre avions restent l'~** plane collisions are still very rare ▶ **l'~ confirme la règle** the exception proves the rule **2.** [dérogation] exception ■ **faire une ~ pour qqn/qqch** to make an exception for sb/sthg ■ **faire une ~ à** to make an exception to ■ **faire ~ de** [exclure] to make an exception of, to except **3.** DR plea ■ **~ péremptoire** peremptory plea ■ **~ d'illégalité/d'incompétence** plea of illegality/incompetence ■ **opposer une ~** to put in a demurrer *ou* plea.
◆ **à l'exception de, exception faite de** *loc prép* except, with the exception of.
◆ **d'exception** *loc adj* **1.** [mesure] exceptional ■ [loi] emergency *(modif)* **2.** [remarquable] remarkable, exceptional ■ **c'est un être d'~** [homme] he's an exceptional man ; [femme] she's an exceptional woman.
◆ **sans (aucune) exception** *loc adv* without (any) exception ■ **sortez tous, sans ~!** out, every (single) one of you!

exceptionnel, elle [ɛksɛpsjɔnɛl] *adj* **1.** [très rare - faveur, chance, circonstances] exceptional ; [- accident, complication] exceptional, rare ; [- mesure] exceptional, special ■ [unique - concert] special, one-off *UK* ■ **'ouverture ~le dimanche 22 décembre'** 'open Sunday 22nd December' **2.** [remarquable - intelligence, œuvre] exceptional ; [- personne] remarkable, exceptional **3.** POLIT [assemblée, conseil, mesures] special, emergency *(modif)*.

exceptionnellement [ɛksɛpsjɔnɛlmɑ̃] *adv* **1.** [beau, doué] exceptionally, extremely **2.** [contrairement à l'habitude] exceptionally ■ **notre magasin sera ouvert lundi ~** next week only, our shop will be open on Monday.

excès [ɛksɛ] ◇ *nm* **1.** [surabondance] surplus, excess ■ **~ de poids/calories** excess weight/calories ■ **~ de prudence/rigueur/sévérité** excessive care/rigour/harshness ■ **~ de zèle** overzealousness ■ **pas d'~ de zèle!** there's no need to be overzealous! **2.** TRANSP : **~ de vitesse** speeding ■ **faire un ~ de vitesse** to exceed *ou* to break the speed limit **3.** [abus] : **~ de langage** immoderate language ■ **se livrer à** *ou* **commettre des ~ de langage** to use strong language ■ **~ de pouvoir** DR abuse of power, action ultra vires *spéc* **4.** [manque de mesure] : **tomber dans l'~** to be extreme ■ **tomber dans l'~ inverse** to go to the opposite extreme ▶ **l'~ en tout est un défaut** *prov* moderation in all things *prov*.
◇ *nmpl* : **~ (de table)** overindulgence ■ **faire des ~** to eat and drink too much, to overindulge ‖ [violences] excesses ■ [débauche] excesses.
◆ **à l'excès** *loc adv* to excess, excessively ■ **critiquer à l'~** to be excessive in one's criticism.
◆ **avec excès** *loc adv* to excess, excessively, immoderately.
◆ **sans excès** *loc adv* with moderation, moderately.

excessif, ive [ɛksesif, iv] *adj* **1.** [chaleur, sévérité, prix] excessive ■ [colère] undue ■ [enthousiasme, optimisme] undue, excessive ■ **100 euros, ce n'est pas ~** 100 euros is quite a reasonable amount to pay **2.** [personne] extreme ■ **c'est quelqu'un de très ~** he's given to extremes of behaviour **3.** [grand] : **sans excessive gentillesse** without being especially pleasant.

excessivement [ɛksesivmɑ̃] *adv* **1.** [trop - raffiné] excessively ■ **~ cher** overpriced **2.** [extrêmement] : **il fait ~ froid** it's hideously cold.

excipient [ɛksipjɑ̃] *nm* excipient.

exciser [3] [ɛksize] *vt* to excise.

excision [ɛksizjɔ̃] *nf* excision.

excitable [ɛksitabl] *adj* **1.** [facilement irrité] : **il est très ~** he gets worked up quickly *ou* annoyed easily **2.** BIOL excitable.

excitant, e [ɛksitɑ̃, ɑ̃t] *adj* **1.** [stimulant - boisson] stimulating **2.** [aguichant - femme, homme, tenue] arousing **3.** [passionnant - aventure, projet, vie] exciting, thrilling ; [- film, roman] exciting ■ **le match devient un peu plus ~** the match is warming up.
◆ **excitant** *nm* stimulant.

excitation [ɛksitasjɔ̃] *nf* **1.** [exaltation] excitement ■ **en proie à une grande ~** very excited, in a state of great excitement ■ **dans l'~ du moment** in the heat of the moment **2.** [stimulation - d'un sens] excitation ; [- sexuelle] sexual arousal *ou* excitement **3.** PHYSIOL excitation, stimulation **4.** ÉLECTR & PHYS excitation.

excité, e [ɛksite] ◇ *adj* **1.** [enthousiasmé] excited, thrilled ■ **nous étions tout ~s à l'idée de la revoir** we were really excited at *ou* thrilled by the idea of seeing her again **2.** [stimulé - sens, curiosité, imagination] aroused, fired **3.** [agité - enfant, chien] excited, restless ; [- candidat] tense, excited **4.** [sexuellement - organe, personne] aroused.
◇ *nm, f péj* hothead ■ **les ~s du volant** dangerous drivers.

exciter [3] [ɛksite] *vt* **1.** [exalter] to excite, to exhilarate ■ **la vitesse l'excite** speed exhilarates her ■ **n'excite pas les enfants avant le coucher** don't get the children excited before bed **2.** [rendre agité - drogue, café] to make excited, to overstimulate, to stimulate **3.** [pousser] : **~ à** : **~ qqn à la révolte** to urge sb to rebel, to incite sb to rebellion ■ **~ un chien à l'attaque** to egg a dog on to attack ■ **~ qqn contre qqn** to work sb up against sb **4.** [attiser - admiration, envie] to provoke ; [- curiosité, intérêt, soupçons] to arouse, to stir up *(sép)* ; [- amour, jalousie] to arouse, to inflame, to kindle **5.** [intensifier - appétit] to whet ; [- rage] to whip up *(sép)* ; [- désir] to increase, to sharpen ; [- douleur] to intensify **6.** [sexuellement] to excite, to arouse **7.** *fam* [intéresser] to excite, to thrill, to get worked up ■ **cette perspective ne m'excite pas vraiment!** I can't say I'm thrilled *ou* wild about the idea! **8.** *fam* [mettre en colère] to annoy, to bug **9.** BIOL to stimulate **10.** ÉLECTR to excite.
◆ **s'exciter** *vpi* **1.** *fam* [se mettre en colère] to get worked up **2.** *fam* [s'acharner] : **j'ai commencé à m'~ sur la serrure** I was losing my patience with the lock **3.** [s'exalter] to get carried away *ou* excited *ou* overexcited.

exclamatif, ive [ɛksklamatif, iv] *adj* exclamatory ■ **proposition exclamative** exclamation.

exclamation [ɛksklamasjɔ̃] *nf* **1.** [cri] exclamation, cry ■ **des ~s de joie/surprise** cries of joy/surprise ■ **pousser une ~ de joie/surprise** to cry out with joy/in surprise **2.** LING exclamation.

exclamer [3] [ɛksklame] ◆ **s'exclamer** *vpi* to exclaim, to cry out ■ **s'~ sur** : **s'~ sur la beauté de qqch** to cry out in admiration over the beauty of sthg ■ **tous s'exclamaient sur le nouveau-né** they were all admiring the new-born baby.

exclu, e [ɛkskly] ◇ *adj* **1.** [non compris] excluded, left out ■ **du 15 au 30 ~** from the 15th to the 30th exclusive ■ **jusqu'à la ligne 22 ~e** up to line 21 inclusive, up to but excluding line 22 **2.** [rejeté - hypothèse, solution] ruled out, dismissed, rejec-

ted ■ **une victoire de la gauche n'est pas ~e** a victory for the left is not to be ruled out ■ **il est ~ que je m'y rende** my going there is totally out of the question ■ **il n'est pas ~ qu'on les retrouve** it's not impossible that they might be found **3.** [renvoyé - définitivement] expelled ; [- provisoirement] suspended.
◇ *nm, f* : **le grand ~ du palmarès à Cannes** the big loser in the Cannes festival.
◆ **exclus** *nmpl* : **les ~s** [gén] the underprivileged ; [SDF] the homeless.

exclure [96] [ɛksklyr] *vt* **1.** [expulser - membre, élève] to expel ; [- étudiant] to send down *UK (sép)*, to expel ; [- sportif] to ban ■ **elle a été exclue du comité** she was expelled from *ou* thrown off the committee ■ **elle s'est fait ~ de l'école pour 3 jours** she's been suspended from school for 3 days **2.** [écarter] to exclude ■ **les enfants sont exclus de la bibliothèque** the library is out of bounds to the children **3.** [mettre à part] to exclude, to leave aside *ou* out *(sép)* ■ **sont exclus tous les internes** this doesn't apply to boarders ■ **si l'on exclut le mois de mars** March excluded ■ **si l'on exclut de petits incidents techniques** apart from a few minor technical hitches **4.** [être incompatible avec] to exclude, to preclude ■ **l'un n'exclut pas l'autre** they're not mutually exclusive ■ **sa nomination exclut qu'elle vienne vous voir en octobre** her appointment will prevent her coming to see you in October **5.** [rejeter - hypothèse] to exclude, to rule out *(sép)*, to reject.
◆ **s'exclure** ◇ *vp (emploi réciproque)* [solutions, traitements] to exclude *ou* to preclude one another, to be incompatible *ou* mutually exclusive.
◇ *vp (emploi réfléchi)* [s'exposer au rejet] to cut o.s. off ■ **s'~ de** to cut o.s. off from ■ **l'enfant brutal s'exclut par son comportement** bullies cut themselves off from the other children because of the way they behave.

exclusif, ive [ɛksklyzif, iv] *adj* **1.** [droit, modèle, privilège] exclusive ■ [droits de reproduction, usage] exclusive, sole ■ [dépositaire, concessionnaire] sole ■ **vente exclusive en pharmacie** sold exclusively in pharmacies **2.** [incompatible avec] : **~ de** exclusive of, incompatible with ■ **les services proposés ne sont pas ~s l'un de l'autre** the services offered are not mutually exclusive **3.** [absolu - amour, relation] exclusive ■ **avoir un goût ~ pour** to like only ■ **dans le but ~ de** with the sole aim of **4.** [intolérant] blinkered **5.** [dossier, image, reportage] exclusive **6.** LING & MATH disjunctive.
◆ **exclusive** *nf sout* [exclusion] debarment ■ **frapper qqn/un pays d'exclusive** to debar sb/a country ■ **jeter** *ou* **prononcer l'exclusive contre qqn** to debar sb.

exclusion [ɛksklyzjɔ̃] *nf* **1.** [renvoi] expulsion ■ **demander l'~ de qqn** to ask for sb to be expelled ■ **son ~ du comité** his expulsion *ou* exclusion from the committee ⊙ **~ temporaire** suspension **2.** [mise à l'écart] exclusion ■ **l'~ des femmes de la scène politique** the exclusion of women from the world of politics **3.** SOCIOL exclusion ■ **les victimes de l'~ sociale** those rejected by society **4.** MATH exclusion.

◆ **à l'exclusion de** *loc prép* except, apart from, with the exception of ■ **tous les jours à l'~ de jeudi** every day apart from Thursday *ou* Thursday excluded.

exclusive [ɛksklyziv] *f* ▷ **exclusif.**

exclusivement [ɛksklyzivmɑ̃] *adv* **1.** [uniquement] exclusively, solely ■ **ouvert le lundi ~** open on Mondays only **2.** [non inclus] : **du 1er au 10 ~** from the 1st to the 10th exclusive **3.** [aimer] exclusively, in an exclusive way.

exclusivité [ɛksklyzivite] *nf* **1.** COMM [droit] exclusive rights ■ **avoir l'~ de** to have the exclusive rights for ■ **avoir l'~ d'une interview** to have (the) exclusive coverage of an interview **2.** [objet unique] : **ce modèle est une ~** this is an exclusive design ■ [article] exclusive (article) ■ [interview] exclusive interview **3.** CINÉ film *UK ou* movie *US* on general release **4.** [privilège exclusif] : **il n'a pas l'~ du talent** he doesn't have a monopoly on talent.
◆ **en exclusivité** *loc adv* **1.** COMM exclusively ■ **chemises Verpé en ~ chez Flakk** Flakk, sole authorized distributor for Verpé shirts **2.** [diffusé, publié] exclusively **3.** CINÉ : **en première ~** on general release.

excommunication [ɛkskɔmynikasjɔ̃] *nf* excommunication.

excommunié, e [ɛkskɔmynje] ◇ *adj* excommunicated.
◇ *nm, f* excommunicated person, excommunicate.

excommunier [9] [ɛkskɔmynje] *vt* to excommunicate ■ **se faire ~** to be excommunicated.

excrément [ɛkskremɑ̃] *nm* excrement ■ **~s** excrement, faeces.

excrétion [ɛkskresjɔ̃] *nf* PHYSIOL excretion.
◆ **excrétions** *nfpl* [substance] excreta.

excroissance [ɛkskrwasɑ̃s] *nf* **1.** MÉD growth, excrescence *spéc* **2.** *fig* excrescence *péj.*

excursion [ɛkskyrsjɔ̃] *nf* **1.** [voyage - en car] excursion, trip ; [- à pied] ramble, hike ; [- à bicyclette] ride, tour ; [- en voiture] drive ■ **faire une ~** [avec un véhicule] to go on an excursion ; [à pied] to go on *ou* for a hike ■ **~ d'un jour** day-trip ■ **~s de deux jours au pays de Galles** two-day tours *ou* trips to Wales **2.** [sortie - scolaire] outing, trip.

excursionniste [ɛkskyrsjɔnist] *nmf* **1.** [touriste en car, bateau] holiday-maker *UK*, vacationer *US* ■ [d'un jour] day-tripper **2.** [randonneur] hiker, rambler.

excusable [ɛkskyzabl] *adj* excusable, forgivable ■ **tu n'es pas ~** you have no excuse ■ **allons, c'est ~!** come on, it's understandable!

excuse [ɛkskyz] *nf* **1.** [motif allégué] excuse, pretext ■ **j'étais fatigué – ce n'est pas une ~!** I was tired – it's no excuse! ■ **tu**

LES EXCUSES

Présenter ses excuses

Sorry, I didn't see you there. Pardon, je ne vous avais pas vu.

Pardon me! *ou* **Excuse me!** *(après avoir éternué, par exemple).* Pardon ! *ou* Excusez-moi !

Sorry to interrupt, but could someone show me the way out? Désolé de vous interrompre, mais est-ce que quelqu'un pourrait m'indiquer la sortie ?

I'm sorry about *ou* **for the confusion this morning.** Je suis désolé pour le malentendu de ce matin.

I'm (terribly *ou* **awfully) sorry if I offended you the other day.** Si je t'ai vexé l'autre jour, je suis (vraiment) désolé.

I'm really sorry, but I can't come on Saturday. Je suis désolé, mais je ne peux pas venir samedi.

Pardon? What did you say? Pardon ? Vous disiez ?

I apologize for my behaviour last night. Je m'excuse pour hier soir.

I'm afraid we're going to have to cancel dinner next week. J'ai bien peur que nous devions annuler le dîner de la semaine prochaine.

Répondre à des excuses

That's *ou* **It's OK.** Ce n'est pas grave.

Don't worry (about it), it doesn't matter. Ne t'en fais pas, ça ne fait rien.

Let's say no more about it. N'en parlons plus.

There's no need to apologize. Ne vous excusez pas.

Apology accepted. N'en parlons plus.

n'as aucune ~ you have no excuse ■ **elle a donné pour ~ le manque d'argent** she used lack of money as an excuse ■ **trouver des ~s à qqn** to find excuses for *ou* to excuse sb ▶ **la belle ~!** *iron* what an *ou* that's some excuse! ■ **faites ~!** *hum* [regrets] I do apologize! ; [objection] excuse me! **2.** DR : **~ atténuante** extenuating excuse ■ **~ légale** legal excuse.

◆ **excuses** *nfpl* apology ■ **faire** *ou* **présenter ses ~s à qqn** to offer one's apologies *ou* to apologize to sb ■ **il vous fait ses plus plates ~s** he apologizes to you most humbly ■ **tu me dois des ~s** you owe me an apology.

Voir module d'usage

excuser [3] [ɛkskyze] *vt* **1.** [pardonner - conduite] to excuse, to forgive ; [- personne] to forgive ■ **excusez mon indiscrétion mais...** excuse my *ou* forgive me for being indiscreet but... ■ **excuse-moi d'appeler si tard** forgive me *ou* I do apologize for phoning so late ■ **excusez-moi** [regret] forgive me, I'm sorry, I do apologize ; [interpellation, objection, après un hoquet] excuse me ■ **oh, excusez-moi, je vous ai fait mal?** oh, sorry, did I hurt you? ■ **je vous prie de** *ou* **veuillez m'~** I (do) beg your pardon, I do apologize ■ **tu es tout excusé** you are forgiven, please don't apologize ▶ **excusez du peu!** *iron* is that all? **2.** [justifier - attitude, personne] to excuse, to find excuses *ou* an excuse for ■ **sa grossièreté ne peut être excusée** his rudeness is inexcusable, there is no excuse for his rudeness **3.** [accepter l'absence de] to excuse ■ **se faire ~** to ask to be excused **4.** [présenter les excuses de] : **excuse-moi auprès de lui** apologize to him for me.

◆ **s'excuser** *vpi* **1.** [demander pardon] to apologize ■ **tu pourrais t'~!** it wouldn't hurt you to say sorry! ■ **s'~ auprès de qqn** to apologize to sb ■ **je m'excuse de mon retard/de vous interrompre** sorry for being late/for interrupting you ▶ **qui s'excuse, s'accuse** *prov* he who apologises admits his guilt **2.** [ton indigné] : **je m'excuse (mais...)!** excuse me *ou* I'm sorry (but...)!

exécrable [ɛgzekrabl] *adj* **1.** [mauvais - dîner, goût, spectacle] abysmal, awful, foul ; [- temps] awful, rotten, wretched ; [- travail] abysmal ■ **il est d'une humeur ~ aujourd'hui** he's in a foul *ou* filthy mood today ■ **avoir un caractère ~** to be foul-tempered **2.** *sout* [crime] heinous *sout*.

exécration [ɛgzekrasjɔ̃] *nf sout* [dégoût, horreur] execration *sout* ■ **avoir qqch en ~** to loathe *ou* to abhor sthg.

exécrer [18] [ɛgzekre] *vt sout* to loathe, to abhor.

exécutable [ɛgzekytabl] *adj* possible, feasible ■ **ce n'est pas ~ en trois jours** it can't possibly be done in three days.

exécutant, e [ɛgzekytɑ̃, ɑ̃t] *nm, f* **1.** [musicien] performer **2.** *péj* [subalterne] subordinate, underling *péj* ■ **il a commandité l'assassinat, mais ce n'est pas lui l'~** he ordered the murder but did not carry it out.

exécuter [3] [ɛgzekyte] *vt* **1.** [mouvement, cabriole] to do, to execute **2.** [confectionner - maquette, statue] to make ; [- tableau] to paint **3.** [interpréter - symphonie] to perform, to play ; [- chorégraphie] to perform, to dance **4.** [mener à bien - consigne, ordre, mission] to carry out *(sép)*, to execute ; [- projet] to carry out ■ **~ un projet jusqu'au bout** to see a project through to the end **5.** [commande] to carry out *(sép)* **6.** [tuer - condamné] to execute, to put to death ; [- victime] to execute, to kill **7.** *fam* [vaincre - joueur] to slaughter, to trounce **8.** *fam* [critiquer] to slate *UK*, to pan **9.** DR [testament] to execute ■ [contrat] to fulfil the terms of ■ [arrêt, jugement, traité] to enforce ■ [débiteur] to distrain upon *(insép)* **10.** INFORM to run.

◆ **s'exécuter** *vpi* to comply, to do what one is told ■ **je lui demandai de sortir, il s'exécuta de mauvaise grâce** I asked him to go out, he did so *ou* complied reluctantly.

exécuteur, trice [ɛgzekytœr, tris] *nm, f* DR [d'un jugement] enforcer ■ [mandataire] : **~ testamentaire** [homme] executor ; [femme] executor, executrix.

◆ **exécuteur** *nm* : **~ des hautes œuvres** HIST executioner ; *hum* axeman.

exécutif, ive [ɛgzekytif, iv] *adj* executive ■ **le pouvoir ~** the executive (branch).

◆ **exécutif** *nm* : **l'~** the executive.

exécution [ɛgzekysjɔ̃] *nf* **1.** [d'une maquette] execution, making ■ [d'un tableau] execution, painting *(U)* **2.** [d'une symphonie, d'une chorégraphie] performance, performing **3.** [d'une menace, d'une décision] carrying out ■ [d'un projet] execution ■ **mettre qqch à ~** to carry sthg out ▶ **~!** MIL at the double! ■ **va ranger ta chambre, ~!** *hum* go and tidy up your bedroom, NOW *ou* on the double! **4.** [d'une commande] carrying out **5.** [d'un condamné] : **~ (capitale)** execution **6.** DR [d'un jugement, d'un traité] enforcement ■ [d'un contrat] fulfilment ■ BOURSE distraint, distress.

exécutoire [ɛgzekytwar] ◇ *adj* [jugement] enforceable ■ **formule ~** executory formula ■ **mesure ~** binding measure. ◇ *nm* writ of execution.

exégèse [ɛgzeʒɛz] *nf* exegesis ■ **faire l'~ de** to write a critical interpretation of.

exégète [ɛgzeʒɛt] *nmf* exegete.

exemplaire[1] [ɛgzɑ̃plɛr] *adj* **1.** [qui donne l'exemple - conduite] exemplary, perfect ; [- personne] exemplary, model ■ **d'une correction ~** perfectly correct **2.** [qui sert d'exemple - punition] exemplary.

exemplaire[2] [ɛgzɑ̃plɛr] *nm* **1.** [d'un document] copy ■ **~ gratuit** presentation copy ■ **en deux ~s** in duplicate ■ **en trois ~s** in triplicate ■ **le contrat est fait en quatre ~s** there are four copies of the contract ■ **le livre a été tiré à 10 000 ~s** 10,000 copies of the book were published ■ **le journal tire à 150 000 ~s** the newspaper has a circulation of 150,000 **2.** [d'un coquillage, d'une plante] specimen, example.

exemplarité [ɛgzɑ̃plarite] *nf* exemplariness, exemplarity.

exemple [ɛgzɑ̃pl] *nm* **1.** [d'architecture, d'un défaut, d'une qualité] example ■ [d'une situation] example, instance ■ **donner qqch en** *ou* **comme ~** to give sthg as an example ■ **citer qqch en ~** to quote sthg as an example **2.** [modèle] example, model ■ **elle est l'~ de la parfaite secrétaire** she's a model secretary ■ **il est l'~ type du yuppie** he's a typical yuppie ■ **donner l'~** to give *ou* to set the example ■ **faire un ~** to make an example ■ **prendre ~ sur qqn** to take sb as a model *ou* an example ■ **que cela vous serve d'~** let this be a warning to you ■ **suivre l'~ de qqn** to follow sb's example, to take one's cue from sb ■ **la France a dit non et d'autres pays ont suivi son ~** France said no and other countries followed suit **3.** GRAMM & LING (illustrative) example.

◆ **à l'exemple de** *loc prép* : **à l'~ de son maître** following his master's example.

◆ **par exemple** *loc adv* **1.** [comme illustration] for example *ou* instance **2.** [marque la surprise] : **(ça) par ~, c'est Pierre!** Pierre! well I never! ■ **ça par ~, le verre a disparu!** well, well, well, the glass has disappeared!

◆ **pour l'exemple** *loc adv* : **fusillé pour l'~** shot as an example (to others).

◆ **sans exemple** *loc adj* unprecedented.

exemplifier [9] [ɛgzɑ̃plifje] *vt* to exemplify.

exempt, e [ɛgzɑ̃, ɑ̃t] *adj* **1.** [dispensé] : **~ de** [d'une obligation] exempt from ■ **~ d'impôts** non taxable, exempt from tax ■ **produits ~s de taxes** duty-free *ou* non dutiable goods ■ **~ de port** carriage free **2.** [dépourvu] : **~ d'erreur** faultless ■ **son attitude n'était pas ~e d'un certain mépris** her attitude wasn't without contempt.

exempté, e [ɛgzɑ̃te] *adj* : **~ du service militaire** exempt from military service.

◆ **exempté** *nm* man exempt from military service.

exempter [3] [ɛgzɑ̃te] *vt* : **~ qqn de qqch : il a été exempté du service militaire** he has been exempted from doing military service ■ **il a réussi à se faire ~ du service militaire** he managed to get out of military service ■ **~ qqn d'impôts** to exempt sb from taxes.

exemption [ɛgzɑ̃psjɔ̃] *nf* **1.** [dispense] exemption ■ **bénéficier de l'~ d'une taxe** to be exempt from a tax **2.** MIL exemption from military service.

exercé, e [ɛgzɛrse] *adj* [oreille, œil] trained, keen ■ [personne] trained, experienced.

exercer [16] [ɛgzɛrse] *vt* **1.** [pratiquer - talent] to exercise ; [- profession] to exercise ; [- art] to practise ■ **quel métier exercez-vous?** what's your job? ■ **~ le métier de dentiste/forgeron** to work as a dentist/blacksmith ■ *(en usage absolu)* [suj: dentiste, avocat, médecin] to be in practice, to practise **2.** [autorité, influence] to exercise, to exert ■ [droit, privilège] to exercise ■ [sanctions] to carry out ■ **~ une action sur** to act on ■ **~ un attrait sur qqn** [personne] to be attractive to *ou* to attract sb ; [art, voyages] to appeal *ou* to be appealing to ■ **~ un contrôle sur** to control ■ **~ une pression sur qqch** to press sthg, to exert pressure on sthg ■ **~ une pression sur qqn** to put pressure on *ou* to pressurize sb ■ **~ des poursuites contre qqn** to bring an action against sb **3.** [entraîner - oreille, esprit, mémoire] to exercise, to train ■ **~ qqn à faire qqch** to train sb to do sthg **4.** *litt* [mettre à l'épreuve - patience] to try (sorely).

◆ **s'exercer** *vpi* **1.** [s'entraîner] to practise ■ **s'~ au piano** to practise (playing) the piano ■ **s'~ à faire des grimaces** to practise pulling faces **2.** [s'appliquer] : **s'~ sur** [force, pression] to be brought to bear on, to be exerted on.

exercice [ɛgzɛrsis] *nm* **1.** [mouvement] exercise ▶ **~s d'assouplissement/d'échauffement** stretching/warm-up exercises ■ **~s au sol** floor exercises ■ **faire des ~s** to exercise
2. [activité physique] : **l'~ (physique)** (physical) exercise ■ **faire de l'~** to take exercise, to exercise ■ **je manque d'~** I don't get enough exercise
3. ÉDUC exercise ■ **faire un ~** to do an exercise ■ **~ de chimie** chemistry exercise ▶ **sa dernière collection est un ~ de style** *fig* his latest collection is an exercise in style
4. MIL drill, exercise ■ **~s de tir** shooting drill *ou* practice
5. [usage] : **l'~ du pouvoir/d'un droit** exercising power/a right ■ **l'~ d'un métier** plying a trade ■ **condamné pour ~ illégal de la médecine** condemned for illegal practice of medicine ■ **dans l'~ de ses fonctions** in the exercise of her duties
6. FIN year ■ **les impôts pour l'~ 1993** taxes for the 1993 fiscal *ou* tax year ▶ **~ budgétaire** budgetary year.

◆ **à l'exercice** *loc adv* MIL on parade.

◆ **en exercice** *loc adj* [député, juge] sitting ■ [membre de comité] serving ■ [avocat, médecin] practising ■ **être en ~** [diplomate, magistrat] to be in *ou* to hold office.

exergue [ɛgzɛrg] *nm* **1.** [dans un livre] inscription ■ **mettre qqch en ~ : mettre une citation en ~ à un** *ou* **d'un texte** to head a text with quotation, to write a quotation as an epigraph to a text ■ **mettre un argument en ~** *fig* to underline *ou* to stress an argument **2.** [sur une médaille - espace] exergue ; [- inscription] epigraph.

exfoliant, e [ɛksfɔljɑ̃, ɑ̃t] *adj* exfoliative.

◆ **exfoliant** *nm* exfoliant.

exfolier [9] [ɛksfɔlje] *vt* to exfoliate.

exhalaison [ɛgzalɛzɔ̃] *nf sout* [odeur - agréable] fragrance ; [- désagréable] unpleasant odour ■ **les ~s fétides des égouts** the fetid fumes from the sewers.

exhalation [ɛgzalasjɔ̃] *nf* exhalation.

exhaler [3] [ɛgzale] *vt* **1.** [dégager - parfum] to exhale ; [- gaz, effluves, vapeur] to exhale, to give off *(sép)* **2.** [émettre - soupir] to breathe ; [- gémissement] to utter, to give forth *(insép) litt* **3.** *litt* [être empreint de] : **la maison exhalait la mélancolie/le bonheur** the house exuded melancholy/radiated happiness **4.** [en respirant] to exhale.

exhaustif, ive [ɛgzostif, iv] *adj* exhaustive.

exhaustivité [ɛgzostivite] *nf* exhaustiveness.

exhiber [3] [ɛgzibe] *vt* **1.** [afficher - décorations, muscles] to display, to show off *(insép)* ; [- richesses] to display, to make a (great) show of ; [- savoir] to show off **2.** [au cirque, à la foire] to show, to exhibit **3.** [document officiel] to produce, to show, to present.

◆ **s'exhiber** *vpi* [parader] to parade (around) ■ [impudiquement] to expose o.s.

exhibition [ɛgzibisjɔ̃] *nf* **1.** [comportement] piece of provocative behaviour ■ **après cette ~ ridicule, tu n'as plus qu'à t'excuser!** apologize after making such an absurd exhibition of yourself! **2.** *péj* [étalage] display **3.** [dans un concours] showing ■ **~ de bétail** cattle show ‖ [comme attraction] exhibiting ■ **~ d'animaux de cirque** exhibiting circus animals **4.** SPORT exhibition **5.** [présentation - de documents] presentation.

exhibitionnisme [ɛgzibisjɔnism] *nm* exhibitionism.

exhibitionniste [ɛgzibisjɔnist] *nmf* exhibitionist.

exhortation [ɛgzɔrtasjɔ̃] *nf* exhortation ■ **~s à la modération** calls for moderation.

exhorter [3] [ɛgzɔrte] *vt* to urge ■ **~ qqn à la prudence** to urge *ou* to exhort sb to be careful ■ **~ qqn à faire qqch** to exhort *ou* to urge sb to do sthg.

◆ **s'exhorter à** *vp+prép* : **s'~ à qqch : elle s'exhortait à la patience** she was exhorting herself to be patient ■ **s'~ à faire qqch** to exhort o.s. to do sthg.

exhumation [ɛgzymasjɔ̃] *nf* **1.** [d'un cadavre] exhumation ■ [d'objets enfouis] excavation, digging out **2.** *fig* [de sentiments] unearthing ■ [de vieux documents] digging out *ou* up.

exhumer [3] [ɛgzyme] *vt* **1.** [déterrer - cadavre] to exhume ; [- objets enfouis] to excavate, to dig out *(sép)* **2.** [sentiments] to unearth ■ [vieux documents] to dig out *ou* up *(sép)*, to rescue from oblivion.

exigeant, e [ɛgziʒɑ̃, ɑ̃t] *adj* **1.** [pointilleux - maître, professeur] demanding, exacting ; [- malade] demanding ; [- client] demanding, particular, hard to please ■ **je suis très ~ sur la qualité** I'm very particular about quality ■ **tu es trop ~e avec tes amis** you ask *ou* expect too much from your friends **2.** [revendicateur] : **ne sois pas trop ~, c'est ton premier emploi** don't be too demanding *ou* don't expect too much, it's your first job **3.** [ardu - métier] demanding, exacting.

exigence [ɛgziʒɑ̃s] *nf* **1.** [demande - d'un client] requirement ; [- d'un ravisseur] demand **2.** [nécessité] demand, requirement ■ **répondre aux ~s de qualité/sécurité** to meet quality/safety requirements **3.** [caractère exigeant - d'un client] particularity ; [- d'un professeur, d'un parent] strictness, exactingness ■ **devant l'~ de son client** faced with such a demanding customer.

◆ **exigences** *nfpl* [salaire] expected salary ■ **quelles sont vos ~s?** what salary do you expect?

exiger [17] [ɛgziʒe] *vt* **1.** [compensation, dû] to demand, to claim **2.** [excuse] to require, to demand, to insist on *(insép)* ■ **~ beaucoup/trop de qqn** to expect a lot/too much from sb **3.** [déclarer obligatoire] to require ■ **la connaissance du russe n'est pas exigée** knowledge of Russian is not a requirement ■ **le port du casque est exigé** hard hats must be worn ■ **aucun visa n'est exigé** no visa is needed **4.** [nécessiter] to require, to need ■ **un métier qui exige beaucoup de précision** a job requiring great accuracy ■ **le poste exige beaucoup de déplacements** the post involves a lot of travelling ■ **nous interviendrons si la situation l'exige** we'll intervene if it becomes necessary.

exigible [ɛgziʒibl] *adj* [impôt] due (for payment), payable ■ **cet impôt est ~ en septembre** payment of this tax falls due in September.

exigu, ë [ɛgzigy] *adj* [appartement, pièce] very small, tiny ■ [couloir] very narrow ■ **c'est un peu ~ pour ma famille** it's a bit cramped *ou* small for my family.

exiguïté [ɛgzigɥite] *nf* [d'une pièce] smallness ■ [d'un couloir] narrowness.

exil [ɛgzil] *nm* exile ■ **pendant son ~ londonien** while he was living in exile in London.

◆ **en exil** ◇ *loc adj* exiled.
◇ *loc adv* [vivre] in exile ■ **envoyer qqn en ~** to exile sb.

exilé, e [ɛgzile] ◇ *adj* exiled.
◇ *nm, f* exile.

exiler [3] [ɛgzile] *vt* to exile ■ **le dictateur a fait ~ tous les opposants au régime** the dictator had all the opponents of the regime sent into exile.

◆ **s'exiler** *vpi* **1.** [quitter son pays] to go into self-imposed exile **2.** [s'isoler] to cut o.s. off.

existant, e [ɛgzistɑ̃, ɑ̃t] *adj* [modèle, loi, tarif] existing, current, currently in existence.

existence [ɛgzistɑ̃s] *nf* **1.** [vie] life, existence ■ **que d'~s misérables!** so many wretched lives! ‖ [mode de vie] lifestyle ■ **j'en ai assez de cette ~** I've had enough of this (kind of) life **2.** [durée - d'une constitution, d'une civilisation] lifespan, lifetime

3. [réalité - d'un complot] existence ; [- d'une substance] presence, existence **4.** [présence - d'une personne] presence ■ **manifester** *OU* **signaler son ~** to make one's presence known.

existentialisme [ɛgzistɑ̃sjalism] *nm* existentialism.

existentialiste [ɛgzistɑ̃sjalist] *adj* & *nmf* existentialist.

existentiel, elle [ɛgzistɑ̃sjɛl] *adj* existential.

exister [3] [ɛgziste] *vi* **1.** [être réel] to exist, to be real ■ **ce personnage a bien existé, il vivait au XVIIe siècle** this character is real *OU* did exist, he lived in the 17th century ■ **le savon, ça existe!** *fam* there is such a thing as soap, you know! ■ **si elle n'existait pas, il faudrait l'inventer!** *hum* what would we do without her! **2.** [subsister] to exist ■ **l'hôtel existe toujours/n'existe plus** the hotel is still there/isn't there anymore ■ **la galanterie, ça n'existe plus** (the age of) chivalry is dead **3.** [être important] to matter ■ **seul son métier existe pour lui** his job's the only thing that matters to him **4.** [vivre - personne] to live ■ **fais comme si je n'existais pas** pretend I'm not here **5.** *(tournure impersonnelle)* **il existe** *(suivi d'un sing)* there is, there's ■ *(suivi d'un pl)* there are.

exit [ɛgzit] *adv* : **~ le Président** *fig* out goes the President.

ex-libris [ɛkslibris] *nm inv* ex-libris.

exode [ɛgzɔd] *nm* **1.** [départ] exodus ■ **l'~des cerveaux** the brain drain ■ **l'~des capitaux** the flight of capital ■ **l'~ rural** the drift from the land, the rural exodus ■ **l'~** HIST *the flight southward and westward of French civilians before the occupying German army in 1940* **2.** BIBLE : **l'Exode** the Exodus.

exonération [ɛgzɔnerasjɔ̃] *nf* exemption, exempting *(U)* ■ **~ fiscale** *OU* **d'impôt** tax exemption.

exonérer [18] [ɛgzɔnere] *vt* **1.** [contribuable, revenus] to exempt ■ **~ qqn d'impôts** to exempt sb from income tax ■ **marchandises exonérées** non-dutiable freight ■ **intérêt: 12 %, exonéré d'impôts** 12% interest rate, non-taxable *OU* free of tax **2.** *sout* [dégager] : **~ qqn de** [obligation] to free sb from ; [responsabilité] to exonerate *OU* to free sb from.

exorbitant, e [ɛgzɔrbitɑ̃, ɑ̃t] *adj* **1.** [trop cher - loyer] exorbitant, extortionate **2.** [démesuré - requête] outrageous ; [- prétention] absurd.

exorbité, e [ɛgzɔrbite] *adj* bulging ■ **les yeux ~s** with bulging eyes, with his eyes out on stalks *hum*.

exorciser [3] [ɛgzɔrsize] *vt* to exorcize.

exorcisme [ɛgzɔrsism] *nm* exorcism.

exorciste [ɛgzɔrsist] *nm* exorcist.

exosquelette [ɛgzɔskəlɛt] *nm* exoskeleton.

exotique [ɛgzɔtik] *adj* [produit, fruit, pays] exotic.

exotisme [ɛgzɔtism] *nm* exoticism.

expansé, e [ɛkspɑ̃se] *adj* [polystyrène] expanded.

expansible [ɛkspɑ̃sibl] *adj* expansible, liable to expand.

expansif, ive [ɛkspɑ̃sif, iv] *adj* **1.** [caractère, personne] expansive, exuberant, effusive ■ **il n'est pas très ~** he's never very forthcoming **2.** PHYS expansive.

expansion [ɛkspɑ̃sjɔ̃] *nf* **1.** ÉCON : **~ (économique)** (economic) growth ■ **l'Expansion** PRESSE *weekly business magazine* **2.** [augmentation - d'un territoire, de l'univers] expansion, expanding *(U)* **3.** [propagation - d'une idéologie, d'une influence] spread **4.** CHIM & PHYS expansion, expanding *(U)* **5.** *litt* [épanchement] expansiveness, effusiveness.

◆ **en (pleine) expansion** *loc adj* ÉCON expanding, booming.

expansionnisme [ɛkspɑ̃sjɔnism] *nm* expansionism.

expansionniste [ɛkspɑ̃sjɔnist] *adj* & *nmf* expansionist.

expansivité [ɛkspɑ̃sivite] *nf* expansiveness.

expatrié, e [ɛkspatrije] *adj* & *nm, f* expatriate.

expatrier [10] [ɛkspatrije] *vt* to expatriate.

◆ **s'expatrier** *vpi* to become an expatriate, to leave one's country (of origin).

expectative [ɛkspɛktativ] *nf* [attente - incertaine] state of uncertainty ; [- prudente] cautious wait ; [- pleine d'espoir] expectancy, expectation.

◆ **dans l'expectative** *loc adv* : **être dans l'~** [espérer] to be in a state of expectation ; [être incertain] to be in a state of uncertainty.

expectorant [ɛkspɛktɔrɑ̃] *nm* expectorant.

expectorer [3] [ɛkspɛktɔre] *vi* & *vt* to expectorate.

expédient, e [ɛkspedjɑ̃, ɑ̃t] *adj sout* expedient.

◆ **expédient** *nm* **1.** [moyen] expedient **2.** *loc* **user** *OU* **vivre d'~s** to live by one's wits.

expédier [9] [ɛkspedje] *vt* **1.** [envoyer - colis, lettre] to send, to dispatch ■ **~ par avion** to send by air mail ■ **~ par bateau** [lettre, paquet] to send surface mail ; [marchandises] to send by sea, to ship ■ **~ par la poste** to send through the post *UK OU* mail **2.** [personne] to send off *(sép)* ■ **je vais l'~ en colonie de vacances** I'm going to send her off to a summer camp ■ **~ qqn dans l'autre monde** *fam OU* **au cimetière** *fam* to send sb off to meet their maker **3.** [bâcler, finir sans soin - dissertation, lettre] to dash off *(sép)* ; [- corvée, travail] to make short work of, to dispatch ■ **elle a expédié le match en deux sets** she wrapped up the match in two sets **4.** [avaler vite - repas] to dispatch, to swallow ; [- verre de vin] to knock back *(sép)* **5.** DR to draw up *(sép)* **6.** *loc* **~ les affaires courantes** [employé] to deal with day-to-day matters (only) ; [président] to be a caretaker president.

expéditeur, trice [ɛkspeditœr, tris] ◇ *adj* [bureau, gare, société] dispatching, forwarding.

◇ *nm, f* sender, forwarder.

expéditif, ive [ɛkspeditif, iv] *adj* **1.** [efficace et rapide - procédé] expeditious *sout*, quick ; [- personne] expeditious *sout*, prompt ■ **elle est plutôt expéditive!** she certainly wastes no time! **2.** *péj* [trop rapide - procès, justice] hasty.

expédition [ɛkspedisjɔ̃] *nf* **1.** [voyage] expedition ■ **~ en Antarctique** expedition to the Antarctic ■ **partir en ~** to go on an expedition ■ **pour traverser la capitale, quelle ~!** *fam* it's quite an expedition to get across the capital! ‖ [équipe] (members of the) expedition **2.** MIL expedition **3.** [raid] : **~ punitive** punitive raid *OU* expedition **4.** [envoi] sending, dispatch, dispatching ■ **~ par bateau** [de marchandises] shipping **5.** [cargaison] : **une ~ de bananes** a consignment of bananas **6.** DR (exemplified) copy.

expéditionnaire [ɛkspedisjɔnɛr] ◇ *adj* MIL expeditionary.

◇ *nmf* COMM forwarding agent.

expéditive [ɛkspeditiv] *f* ⟶ **expéditif**.

expérience [ɛksperjɑ̃s] *nf* **1.** [connaissance] experience ■ **avoir de l'~ (en)** to have experience *OU* to be experienced (in) ■ **manquer d'~** to be inexperienced, to lack experience ■ **plusieurs années d'~ en gestion seraient souhaitables** several years' experience in management *OU* management experience would be desirable **2.** [apprentissage] experience ■ **ses ~s amoureuses** her love affairs ■ **ses premières ~s amoureuses** his first amorous experiences ■ **faire l'~ de la haine** to experience hatred ■ **je ne voudrais pas refaire l'~ d'une opération** I wouldn't like to go through an operation again **3.** [test] experiment ■ **~ de chimie** chemistry experiment ■ **faire des ~s (sur des rats)** to carry out experiments *OU* to experiment (on rats).

◆ **par expérience** *loc adv* from experience.

◆ **sans expérience** *loc adj* inexperienced.

expérimental, e, aux [ɛksperimɑ̃tal, o] *adj* **1.** [avion] trial *(modif)*, experimental **2.** [méthode, sciences] experimental ■ **à titre ~** experimentally, as an experiment.

expérimentalement [ɛksperimɑ̃talmɑ̃] *adv* experimentally.

expérimentation [ɛksperimɑ̃tasjɔ̃] *nf* experimentation.

expérimenté, e [ɛksperimɑ̃te] *adj* experienced, practised.

expérimenter [3] [ɛksperimɑ̃te] *vt* to try out *(sép)*, to test.

expert, e [ɛkspɛr, ɛrt] ◇ *adj* **1.** [agile] expert ■ **d'une main ~e** with an expert hand ■ **d'une oreille ~e** with a trained ear **2.** [savant] highly knowledgeable ■ **être ~ en la matière** to be a specialist in the subject ■ **être ~ en littérature chinoise** to be an expert on *ou* a specialist in Chinese literature.
◇ *nm, f* **1.** [chargé d'expertise] expert, specialist ■ [en bâtiments] surveyor ■ [en assurances] valuer ■ **~ judiciaire** legal expert ■ **~ maritime** surveyor ■ *(comme adj; avec ou sans trait d'union)* **chimiste ~** expert in chemistry ■ **médecin ~** medical expert **2.** [connaisseur] expert, connoisseur ■ **~ de** *ou* **en** expert on, specialist in.

expert-comptable, experte-comptable [ɛkspɛrkɔ̃tabl, ɛkspɛrtkɔ̃tabl] (*mpl* **experts-comptables**, *fpl* **expertes-comptables**) *nm* ≃ chartered accountant *UK*, ≃ certified public accountant *US*.

expertement [ɛkspɛrtəmɑ̃] *adv* expertly.

expertise [ɛkspɛrtiz] *nf* **1.** [examen - d'un meuble, d'une voiture] (expert) appraisal *ou* evaluation *ou* valuation ■ **faire faire une ~** [pour assurer un bien] to have a valuation done ■ **~ judiciaire** DR court-ordered appraisal ■ **~ médicale et psychiatrique** DR expert opinion *(by a doctor)* **2.** [document] expert's *ou* valuer's report.

expertiser [3] [ɛkspɛrtize] *vt* [véhicule] to value ■ [dommages, meuble, tableau] to appraise, to assess, to value ■ **faire ~ une voiture** [gén] to have a car valued ; [après un accident] to have the damage on a car looked at *(for insurance purposes)*.

expiable [ɛkspjabl] *adj* expiable.

expiation [ɛkspjasjɔ̃] *nf* : **~ de** expiation of, atonement for.

expiatoire [ɛkspjatwar] *adj* expiatory.

expier [9] [ɛkspje] *vt* [crime, péché] to expiate, to atone for *(insép)* ■ *sout* [erreur, faute] to pay *ou* to atone for *(insép)*.

expiration [ɛkspirasjɔ̃] *nf* **1.** [d'air] breathing out **2.** [fin] expiration, expiry ■ **le bail arrive à ~ le 30 août** the lease expires by August 30th ■ **date d'~** expiry date.
◆ **à l'expiration de** *loc prép* : **à l'~ du bail** when the lease expires ■ **à l'~ du délai** at the end of the stated period.

expirer [3] [ɛkspire] ◇ *vi* **1.** *sout* [mourir] to expire, to breathe one's last **2.** *litt* [s'évanouir - lueur, son] to expire, to die away **3.** *(aux avoir ou être)* [cesser d'être valide - abonnement, bail, délai] to expire, to end ; [- carte de crédit] to expire.
◇ *vt* [air] to breathe out *(sép)*.

explétif, ive [ɛkspletif, iv] *adj* expletive, expletory ■ **le "ne" ~** "ne" used as an expletive.

explicable [ɛksplikabl] *adj* explainable, explicable ■ **c'est un phénomène difficilement ~** it's a phenomenon which is difficult to explain *ou* which is not easily explained.

explicatif, ive [ɛksplikatif, iv] *adj* **1.** [brochure, lettre] explanatory ■ **notice** *ou* **note explicative** [sur un emballage] instructions *ou* directions for use ; [dans un dossier] explanatory note **2.** GRAMM : **proposition relative explicative** non-restrictive relative clause.

explication [ɛksplikasjɔ̃] *nf* **1.** [éclaircissement - d'un fait, d'une situation] explanation ■ **ça se passe d'~** it's self-explanatory **2.** [motif - d'une attitude, d'un retard] explanation ■ **donner l'~ de qqch** to give the reason for sthg, to explain sthg **3.** ÉDUC & UNIV [d'une œuvre] commentary, analysis ■ **~ de texte** critical analysis, appreciation of a text **4.** [discussion] discussion ■ [querelle] argument ■ **avoir une ~ avec qqn sur qqch** [discussion] to talk sthg over with sb ; [querelle] to have an argument with sb about sthg.
◆ **explications** *nfpl* [mode d'emploi] instructions *ou* directions (for use).
Voir module d'usage

explicitation [ɛksplisitasjɔ̃] *nf* **1.** [d'intentions] making explicit *ou* plain **2.** [d'un texte] clarifying, clarification.

explicite [ɛksplisit] *adj* explicit ■ **suis-je assez ~?** do I make myself plain (enough)?

explicitement [ɛksplisitmɑ̃] *adv* explicitly.

expliciter [3] [ɛksplisite] *vt* **1.** [intentions] to make explicit *ou* plain **2.** [phrase] to clarify, to explain.

expliquer [3] [ɛksplike] *vt* **1.** [faire comprendre - événement, réaction, fonctionnement, *etc.*] to explain ■ **~ qqch à qqn** to explain sthg to sb ■ **je me suis fait ~ la procédure** I asked *ou* got someone to explain the procedure to me **2.** [justifier - attitude, retard] to explain (away), to account for *(insép)* **3.** ÉDUC & UNIV [texte] to analyse, to make a critical analysis of, to comment on *(insép)*.
◆ **s'expliquer** ◇ *vp (emploi passif)* to be explained ■ **tout s'explique!** that explains it!
◇ *vp (emploi réciproque)* : **sors, on va s'~!** *fam* we'll talk this over outside!
◇ *vpi* [s'exprimer] to explain o.s., to make o.s. clear ■ **explique-toi mieux** make yourself clearer ■ **s'~ sur** [éclaircir] : **s'~ sur ses intentions** to make plain *ou* to explain one's intentions.
◇ *vpt* [comprendre] to understand ■ **je n'arrive pas à m'~ son silence** I can't understand why he remains silent.
◆ **s'expliquer avec** *vp+prép* **1.** [avoir une discussion avec] to talk things over with **2.** [se disputer avec] to have it out with.

exploit [ɛksplwa] *nm* **1.** [acte] exploit, feat ■ **~ sportif** remarkable sporting achievement ■ **~ technique** technical feat *ou* exploit ■ **ses ~s amoureux** his amorous exploits ■ **il ne s'est pas vanté de ses ~s!** he didn't have much to be proud of! ■ **avoir réussi à la convaincre relève de l'~!** it's no mean achievement to have convinced her! **2.** DR : **~ (d'huissier)** writ.

exploitable [ɛksplwatabl] *adj* [idée, mine, terre *etc*] exploitable, workable ■ [énergie] exploitable.

exploitant, e [ɛksplwatɑ̃, ɑ̃t] *nm, f* [d'une carrière, d'un cinéma] owner ■ **~ (agricole)** farmer ■ **petit ~** smallholder *UK*, small farmer ■ **~ forestier** forestry agent.

exploitation [ɛksplwatasjɔ̃] *nf* **1.** [entreprise] : **~ à ciel ouvert** open-cast mine ■ **~ agricole** farm (estate) ■ **petite ~ agricole** smallholding *UK*, small farm ■ **~ familiale** family holding ■ **~**

L'EXPLICATION

Demander une explication

Can you explain what this means? Peux-tu m'expliquer ce que cela veut dire ?

Explain yourself. Expliquez-vous.

What do you mean exactly? Qu'est-ce que tu veux dire au juste ?

What makes you say that? Qu'est-ce qui te fait dire ça ?

Why do you say that? Pourquoi est-ce que tu dis ça ?

How do you mean? Comment ça ?

Could you be a little more specific? Pourriez-vous être un peu plus précis ?

Fournir une explication

Let me explain:... Je m'explique :...

What I mean is/meant was... Ce que je veux/voulais dire, c'est...

What I'm trying to say is... Ce que j'essaie de dire, c'est...

The point I'm trying to make is... Ce que j'essaie de dire, c'est...

Let me put it another way:... En d'autres termes,...

The thing is,... Tu comprends,...

minière mine ▪ **~ vinicole** [vignes] vineyard ; [société] wine-producing establishment **2.** [d'un réseau ferroviaire] operating ▪ [d'un cinéma] running ▪ [d'une carrière, d'une forêt, d'une mine, d'un sol] exploitation, working ▪ **l'~ forestière** forestry, lumbering ▪ **mettre en ~** [carrière, mine, terres] to exploit, to work **3.** [utilisation - d'une idée, d'un talent] exploitation, exploiting *(U)*, utilizing *(U)* **4.** [fait d'abuser] exploitation, exploiting ▪ **leur ~ de la misère d'autrui** their exploitation of other people's wretchedness ▮ [de la main-d'œuvre] exploitation ▪ **l'~ de l'homme par l'homme** man's exploitation of man.
◆ **d'exploitation** *loc adj* FIN & INFORM operating.

exploité, e [ɛksplwate] *adj* **1.** [ferme, carrière, sous-sol] exploited **2.** [main-d'œuvre] exploited.

exploiter [3] [ɛksplwate] *vt* **1.** [mettre en valeur - forêt, mine, terre, *etc.*] to exploit, to work ▪ [faire fonctionner - cinéma] to run ; [- tunnel, réseau ferroviaire] to run, to operate **2.** [tirer avantage de - talent] to exploit, to make use of ; [- thème] to exploit ; [- situation] to exploit, to make capital out of, to take advantage of **3.** *péj* [abuser de] to exploit, to take (unfair) advantage of ▪ **~ la naïveté de qqn** to take advantage of sb's naivety ▮ [main-d'œuvre] to exploit ▪ **se faire ~** to be exploited.

exploiteur, euse [ɛksplwatœr, øz] *nm, f* exploiter.

explorateur, trice [ɛksplɔratœr, tris] *nm, f* explorer.

exploration [ɛksplɔrasjɔ̃] *nf* **1.** GÉOGR & MÉD exploration **2.** [analyse] exploration, examination.

exploratoire [ɛksplɔratwar] *adj* exploratory, tentative.

explorer [3] [ɛksplɔre] *vt* **1.** [voyager dans - contrée, île] to explore **2.** MÉD [voie respiratoire, tube digestif] to explore **3.** [examiner - possibilité] to explore, to examine.

exploser [3] [ɛksploze] *vi* **1.** [détoner - grenade, mine, maison] to explode, to blow up ; [- dynamite, gaz] to explode ▪ **faire ~ une bombe** to set off *ou* to explode *ou* to detonate a bomb **2.** [augmenter - population] to explode ; [- prix] to shoot up, to soar **3.** [se révéler soudain - mécontentement, joie] to explode ; [- rage] to explode, to burst out ; [- rires] to burst out ; [- artiste] to burst onto the scene ▪ **~ en : la salle explosa en applaudissements** the audience burst into thunderous applause **4.** *fam* [s'emporter] to flare up, to lose one's temper *ou* cool.

explosif, ive [ɛksplozif, iv] *adj* **1.** [mélange, puissance] explosive ▪ [obus] high-explosive **2.** [dangereux - situation, sujet] explosive, highly sensitive ; [- atmosphère] explosive, charged **3.** [fougueux - tempérament] fiery, explosive **4.** LING explosive.
◆ **explosif** *nm* ARM explosive.
◆ **explosive** *nf* LING explosive (consonant).

explosion [ɛksplozjɔ̃] *nf* **1.** [détonation - d'une bombe, d'une chaudière, d'une mine] explosion, blowing up ; [- d'un gaz] explosion ▪ **faire ~** [bombe] to go off, to explode ; [obus] to explode **2.** [manifestation] : **~ d'enthousiasme/d'indignation** burst of enthusiasm/indignation ▪ **~ de joie** outburst *ou* explosion of joy ▪ **ce fut une ~ de rire dans le public** the audience burst out into peals of laughter **3.** [accroissement] : **~ démographique** population boom *ou* explosion.

expo [ɛkspo] *nf fam* exhibition.

exponentiel, elle [ɛkspɔnɑ̃sjɛl] *adj* exponential ▪ **de manière ~le** exponentially.

exportable [ɛkspɔrtabl] *adj* exportable, which can be exported.

exportateur, trice [ɛkspɔrtatœr, tris] ◇ *adj* exporting ▪ **être ~ de** to be an exporter of, to export ▪ **les pays ~s de pétrole/céréales** oil/grain exporting countries.
◇ *nm, f* exporter.

exportation [ɛkspɔrtasjɔ̃] *nf* **1.** [sortie] export, exportation ▪ **réservé à l'~** for export only **2.** [marchandises] exports.
◆ **d'exportation** *loc adj* export *(modif)*.

exporter [3] [ɛkspɔrte] *vt* **1.** COMM & ÉCON to export **2.** [répandre à l'étranger - idées, culture] to export, to spread abroad.

exposant, e [ɛkspozɑ̃, ɑ̃t] *nm, f* **1.** [dans une galerie, une foire] exhibitor **2.** DR petitioner.
◆ **exposant** *nm* MATH exponent.

exposé, e [ɛkspoze] *adj* **1.** [orienté] : **ce balcon est bien/mal ~** the balcony gets a lot of sun/doesn't get much sun ▪ **la chambre est ~e au nord** the room faces north **2.** [non abrité] exposed, wind-swept **3.** [montré] on show, on display ▪ **objet ~** [dans une galerie, une foire] item on show, exhibit **4.** [par les médias] : **le ministre est toujours très ~** the Minister is always in the public eye *ou* gets a lot of media coverage.
◆ **exposé** *nm* **1.** [compte rendu] account, exposition *sout* ▪ **faire un ~ sur** to give an account of **2.** ÉDUC & UNIV [écrit] (written) paper ▪ [oral] talk, lecture ▪ **faire un ~ sur** [oral] to give a talk *ou* to read a paper on ; [écrit] to write a paper on **3.** DR : **~ des motifs** exposition of motives.

exposer [3] [ɛkspoze] *vt* **1.** [dans un magasin] to display, to put on display, to set out *(sép)* ▪ [dans une galerie, dans une foire] to exhibit, to show **2.** [soumettre] : **~ qqch à : ~ qqch aux radiations** to expose *ou* to subject sthg to radiation ▪ **~ qqn à** [critiques, ridicule] to lay sb open to, to expose sb to **3.** [mettre en danger - honneur, vie] to endanger, to put at risk **4.** [faire connaître - arguments, motifs] to expound, to put forward *(sép)* ; [- intentions] to set forth *ou* out *(sép)*, to explain ; [- revendications] to set forth, to put forward, to make known **5.** LITTÉR & MUS to set out *(sép)* ▪ [thème] to introduce ▪ **dialogue destiné à ~ l'action** expository dialogue **6.** PHOTO to expose.
◆ **s'exposer** *vp (emploi réfléchi)* **1.** [se compromettre] to leave o.s. exposed ▪ **s'~ à des poursuites judiciaires** to lay o.s. open to *ou* to run the risk of prosecution ▪ **s'~ à des représailles** to expose o.s. to retaliation **2.** [se placer] : **s'~ au soleil** to expose one's skin to the sun.

exposition [ɛkspozisjɔ̃] *nf* **1.** [d'œuvres d'art] show, exhibition ▪ [de produits manufacturés] exhibition, exposition ▪ **~ de peinture/photos** painting/photo exhibition ◗ **l'~ universelle** the World Fair **2.** [d'un corps] lying in state **3.** [d'arguments, de motifs] exposition, expounding *(U)* ▪ [d'une situation, d'une théorie] exposition **4.** LITTÉR & MUS exposition **5.** [soumission] : **~ à** [danger, radiation, risque] exposure to ▪ **éviter l'~ au soleil** do not stay in the sun **6.** [orientation] orientation, aspect ▪ **~ au sud** orientation to the south **7.** PHOTO exposure.
◆ **d'exposition** *loc adj* expository, introductory.

exposition-vente [ɛkspozisjɔ̃vɑ̃t] (*pl* **expositions-ventes**) *nf* [gén] exhibition *(where items are for sale)* ▪ [d'objets d'artisanat].

expo-vente [ɛkspovɑ̃t] = **exposition-vente**.

exprès[1] [ɛksprɛ] *adv* **1.** [délibérément] on purpose, intentionally, deliberately ▪ **faire ~ : tu l'as vexé – je ne l'ai pas fait ~** you've offended him – I didn't mean to *ou* it wasn't intentional ▪ **elle fait ~ de me contredire** she makes a point of contradicting me, she deliberately contradicts me ▪ **il y a du papier à l'intérieur – c'est fait ~** there's some paper inside – it's meant to be like that **2.** [spécialement] especially, specially.

exprès[2], **expresse** [ɛksprɛs] *adj* **1.** [avertissement, autorisation, ordre] express, explicit ▪ [recommandation] express, strict ▪ **défense expresse de fumer** smoking strictly prohibited **2.** [lettre, paquet] express UK, special delivery US *(modif)*.
◆ **en exprès, par exprès** *loc adv* : **envoyer qqch en ~** to send sthg by express post UK *ou* special delivery US.

express [ɛksprɛs] ◇ *adj inv* **1.** TRANSP ▻ **train 2.** [café] espresso.
◇ *nm* **1.** RAIL express *ou* fast train **2.** [café] espresso (coffee) **3.** PRESSE : **l'Express** *weekly news magazine.*

expressément [ɛksprɛsemɑ̃] *adv* **1.** [catégoriquement - défendre, ordonner] expressly, categorically ; [- conseiller, prévenir] expressly **2.** [spécialement] specially, specifically ▪ **je l'ai fait ~ pour toi** I did it specially for you.

expressif, ive [ɛksprɛsif, iv] *adj* **1.** [suggestif - style] expressive, vivid ; [- regard, visage] expressive, meaningful ; [- ton] expressive ▪ **sa mimique était expressive** the expression on her face said it all **2.** LING expressive.

expression [ɛksprɛsjɔ̃] *nf* **1.** [mot, tournure] expression, phrase, turn of phrase ▪ **avoir une ~ malheureuse** to use an unfortunate turn of phrase ▪ **passez-moi l'~** (if you'll) pardon the expression ▮ [dans la correspondance] : **veuillez croire à l'~ de ma considération distinguée** yours faithfully UK *ou* truly US ◗ **~**

familière colloquial expression, colloquialism ▪ ~ **figée** set phrase *ou* expression, fixed expression, idiom ▪ ~ **toute faite** [figée] set phrase *ou* expression ; [cliché] hackneyed phrase, cliché **2.** [fait de s'exprimer] expression, expressing *(U)*, voicing *(U)* **3.** [pratique de la langue] : **auteurs d'~ allemande** authors writing in German ➊ ~ **écrite/orale** written/oral expression **4.** [extériorisation - d'un besoin, d'un sentiment] expression, self-expression ▪ **trouver son ~ dans** to find (its) expression in ➊ ~ **corporelle** self-expression through movement **5.** [vivacité] expression ▪ **geste/regard plein d'~** expressive gesture/look **6.** [du visage] expression, look **7.** INFORM & MATH expression.
◆ **sans expression** *loc adj* expressionless, poker-faced.

expressionnisme [ɛksprɛsjɔnism] *nm* expressionism.

expressionniste [ɛksprɛsjɔnist] *adj* & *nmf* expressionist.

expressivité [ɛkspresivite] *nf* expressivity, expressiveness ▪ **avec beaucoup d'~** very expressively.

exprimable [ɛksprimabl] *adj* expressible ▪ **ma joie est difficilement ~** my joy is difficult to express.

exprimer [3] [ɛksprime] *vt* **1.** [dire - sentiment] to express ; [- idée, revendication] to express, to voice ▪ **comment vous ~ toute mon admiration?** how can I tell you how much I admire you? **2.** [manifester - mécontentement, surprise] to express, to show **3.** [pour chiffrer une quantité, une somme] to state, to express ▪ ~ **une quantité en kilos** to state a quantity in kilos **4.** [extraire - jus, pus] to express *sout*, to squeeze out *(sép)*.
◆ **s'exprimer** ◇ *vp (emploi passif)* [idée, sentiment] to be expressed, to express itself ▪ [opinion] to be heard.
◇ *vpi* **1.** [dire sa pensée] to express o.s. ▪ **chacun doit s'~** all opinions must be heard ▪ **vas-y, exprime-toi!** *hum* come on, out with it! ▪ **je me suis exprimée sur ce sujet** I've expressed myself *ou* made my opinions known on the subject ▪ **s'~ par signes** to use sign language **2.** [choisir ses mots] to express o.s. ▪ **exprime-toi clairement** express yourself clearly, make yourself clear ▪ **non, je me suis mal exprimé** no, I've put it badly ▪ **si je peux m'~ ainsi** if I can put it that way **3.** [manifester sa personnalité] to express o.s. ▪ **s'~ par la danse/musique** to express o.s. through dancing/music **4.** [se manifester - talent, sentiment] to express *ou* to show itself ▪ **laisse ton cœur s'~** let your heart speak.

expropriateur, trice [ɛksproprijatœr, tris] *adj* expropriating *(avant n)*.

expropriation [ɛksprɔprijasjɔ̃] *nf* **1.** [d'une personne] expropriation **2.** [d'une propriété] compulsory purchase.

exproprié, e [ɛksprɔprije] *adj* expropriated.

exproprier [10] [ɛksprɔprije] *vt* **1.** [personne] to expropriate ▪ **se faire ~** to have one's property expropriated, to have a compulsory purchase order placed on one's property *UK* **2.** [maison, terre] to expropriate, to place a compulsory purchase order on *UK*.

expulser [3] [ɛkspylse] *vt* **1.** [renvoyer - locataire] to evict, to throw out *(sép)* ; [- membre, participant] to expel ; [- immigrant] to expel, to deport ; [- joueur] to send off *(sép)* ▪ **la propriétaire a fait ~ ses locataires** the owner had the tenants thrown out **2.** MÉD to evacuate, to expel.

expulsion [ɛkspylsjɔ̃] *nf* **1.** [d'un locataire] eviction ▪ [d'un membre de comité] expulsion ▪ [d'un étudiant] sending down *UK*, expulsion *US* ▪ [d'un immigrant] expulsion, deportation ▪ [d'un joueur] sending off ▪ **décider l'~ d'un élève** [définitive] to decide to expel a pupil ; [temporaire] to decide to suspend a pupil **2.** MÉD expulsion, evacuation.

expurger [17] [ɛkspyrʒe] *vt* to expurgate, to bowdlerize.

exquis, e [ɛkski, iz] *adj* [saveur, vin, gentillesse *etc*] exquisite ▪ [personne] delightful.

exsangue [ɛksɑ̃g, ɛgzɑ̃g] *adj* **1.** *litt* [pâle - figure, lèvres] bloodless, livid **2.** [ayant perdu du sang - corps, victime] bloodless ▪ **après la guerre, notre industrie était ~** *fig* this country's industry was bled white by the war.

exsudation [ɛksydasjɔ̃] *nf* exudation.

extase [ɛkstaz] *nf* **1.** [exaltation] ecstasy, rapture ▪ **être** *ou* **rester en ~ devant** to be in raptures *ou* ecstasies over ▪ **tomber en ~ devant qqch/qqn** to go into ecstasies at the sight of sthg/sb **2.** RELIG ecstasy.

extasié, e [ɛkstazje] *adj* enraptured, ecstatic.

extasier [9] [ɛkstazje] ◆ **s'extasier** *vpi* : **s'~ devant** to go into raptures *ou* ecstasies over.

extatique [ɛkstatik] *adj* **1.** [de l'extase - vision, transport] ecstatic ▪ **état ~** ecstasy, trance **2.** [émerveillé] enraptured.

extenseur [ɛkstɑ̃sœr] ◇ *adj m* ANAT extensor.
◇ *nm* **1.** ANAT extensor **2.** [machine] chest expander.

extensibilité [ɛkstɑ̃sibilite] *nf* extensibility.

extensible [ɛkstɑ̃sibl] *adj* [organe] extensible ▪ [matière] tensible, extensible ▪ [tissu] stretch ▪ [liste] extendable ▪ **mon budget n'est pas ~** I can't stretch my budget any further, I can't make my budget go any further.

extensif, ive [ɛkstɑ̃sif, iv] *adj* **1.** AGRIC extensive **2.** PHYS [paramètre, force] extensive.

extension [ɛkstɑ̃sjɔ̃] *nf* **1.** [étirement - d'un élastique, d'un muscle] stretching ; [- d'une matière] extension ▪ MÉD traction, extension **2.** [agrandissement - d'un territoire] expansion, enlargement ; [- d'une entreprise, d'un marché, d'un réseau] expansion, extension ; [- de pouvoirs, d'un incendie, d'une infection] spreading ; [- de droits] extension ▪ **prendre de l'~** [territoire] to get bigger, to expand ; [secteur] to grow, to develop ; [infection] to spread, to extend ; [incendie] to spread **3.** [élargissement] : **on a décidé l'~ des mesures à toute la population** it has been decided to extend the scope of the measures to include the entire population **4.** [partie ajoutée - d'un bâtiment, d'un réseau] extension **5.** INFORM extension ▪ **carte d'~** expansion board **6.** LING & MATH extension.
◆ **en extension** *loc adj* **1.** [secteur] developing, expanding ▪ [production] increasing **2.** [muscle, ressort] stretched.
◆ **par extension** *loc adv* by extension.

extenso [ɛkstɑ̃so] ⊳ **in extenso**.

exténuant, e [ɛkstenɥɑ̃, ɑ̃t] *adj* exhausting.

exténuer [7] [ɛkstenɥe] *vt* to exhaust, to tire out *(sép)* ▪ **être exténué** to be worn out *ou* exhausted.
◆ **s'exténuer** *vpi* to exhaust o.s., to tire *ou* to wear o.s. out ▪ **s'~ à faire qqch** to exhaust o.s. doing sthg.

extérieur, e [ɛksterjœr] *adj* **1.** [escalier, bruit] outside ▪ [cour, poche, mur, orbite, bord] outer ▪ [porte] external, outer ▪ **les bruits ~s la gênent** outside noises *ou* noises from outside distract her ▪ **avoir des activités ~es** [hors du foyer] to have interests outside the home ; [hors du travail] to have interests outside of work **2.** [excentré - quartier] outlying, out-of-town *US* **3.** [non subjectif - monde, réalité] external **4.** [étranger à la personne, la chose considérée - influence, aide] outside, external ▪ ~ **à** outside (of) ▪ **personnes ~es à l'entreprise** persons not belonging to the staff **5.** [apparent] external, surface *(modif)*, outward ▪ **l'aspect ~** [d'un édifice, d'un objet] the outward appearance ; [d'une personne] the exterior **6.** *péj* [superficiel] superficial, surface *(modif)*, token *(modif)* **7.** ÉCON & POLIT [dette, politique] foreign, external **8.** GÉOM exterior **9.** TÉLÉCOM outside.
◆ **extérieur** *nm* **1.** : **l'~** [le plein air] the outside *ou* outdoors **2.** [à une personne] : **l'~** the outside (world) ▪ **être tourné vers l'~** to be outgoing ▪ **l'~** ÉCON & POLIT abroad **3.** [bord] : **l'~ de** : **l'~ de la chaussée** the outside (of the road) **4.** [apparence] outward appearance, exterior **5.** SPORT : **l'~** [d'une piste, d'un circuit] the outside **6.** CINÉ location shot ▪ **~s tournés à Rueil** shot on location in Rueil.
◆ **à l'extérieur** *loc adv* **1.** [en plein air] outside, outdoors ▪ **manger à l'~** [en plein air] to eat outside *ou* outdoors ; [hors de chez soi] to eat out **2.** [hors du système, du groupe] outside **3.** SPORT [sur une piste] on the outside ▪ [dans une autre ville] away ▪ **match joué à l'~** away match **4.** ÉCON & POLIT abroad **5.** TÉLÉCOM outside ▪ **téléphoner à l'~** to make an outside call.
◆ **à l'extérieur de** *loc prép* outside (of) ▪ **à l'~ de l'Afrique** outside Africa.

◆ **de l'extérieur** *loc adv* **1.** [dans l'espace] from (the) outside **2.** [dans un système] from the outside ■ **considérer un problème de l'~** to look at a problem from the outside ■ **des gens venus de l'~** outsiders.

extérieurement [ɛksterjœrmɑ̃] *adv* **1.** [au dehors] on the outside, externally **2.** [apparemment] outwardly.

extériorisation [ɛksterjɔrizasjɔ̃] *nf* **1.** [de sentiments] expression, show, display **2.** PSYCHOL exteriorization, externalization.

extérioriser [3] [ɛksterjɔrize] *vt* **1.** [montrer - sentiment] to express, to show ■ **: il n'extériorise pas assez (ses sentiments)** he doesn't show his feelings enough **2.** PSYCHOL to exteriorize, to externalize.
◆ **s'extérioriser** ◇ *vp (emploi passif)* [joie, mécontentement] to be expressed, to show.
◇ *vpi* [personne] to show one's feelings.

extériorité [ɛksterjɔrite] *nf* exteriority.

exterminateur, trice [ɛkstɛrminatœr, tris] ◇ *adj* exterminating.
◇ *nm, f* exterminator.

extermination [ɛkstɛrminasjɔ̃] *nf* extermination.

exterminer [3] [ɛkstɛrmine] *vt* **1.** [tuer - peuple, race] to exterminate ■ **se faire ~** to be wiped out **2.** *hum* [vaincre - adversaire] to annihilate.

externalisation [ɛkstɛrnalizasjɔ̃] *nf* outsourcing.

externaliser [3] [ɛkstɛrnalize] *vt* to outsource.

externat [ɛkstɛrna] *nm* **1.** ÉDUC [école] day school ■ [élèves] day pupils ■ [statut] non-residency ■ **pour mes enfants, je préfère l'~** I'd rather my children weren't boarders **2.** [en médecine] non-resident (medical) studentship.

externe [ɛkstɛrn] ◇ *adj* **1.** [cause, facteur] external **2.** [orbite, bord] outer, external.
◇ *nmf* **1.** ÉDUC day-pupil, non-boarder **2.** [en médecine] non-resident (medical) student *UK*, extern *US*.

exterritorialité [ɛksteritɔrjalite] *nf* exterritoriality, extraterritoriality.

extincteur, trice [ɛkstɛ̃ktœr, tris] *adj* extinguishing *(avant n)*.
◆ **extincteur** *nm* (fire) extinguisher.

extinction [ɛkstɛ̃ksjɔ̃] *nf* **1.** [arrêt - d'un incendie] extinction *sout*, extinguishment *sout*, putting out ■ **~ des feux** lights out **2.** [suppression - d'une dette] extinguishment ■ **espèce animale menacée** *ou* **en voie d'~** endangered animal species **3.** [affaiblissement] ◆ **~ de voix** MÉD loss of voice, aphonia *spéc* ■ **avoir une ~ de voix** to have lost one's voice.

extirper [3] [ɛkstirpe] *vt* **1.** [ôter - tumeur] to remove, to extirpate *spéc* ; [- épine, racine] to pull out *(sép)* ; [- plante] to root up *ou* out *(sép)*, to uproot, to pull up *(sép)* ■ **~ qqn d'un fauteuil/piège** to drag sb out of an armchair/a trap **2.** [détruire - préjugés, vice] to eradicate, to root out *(sép)*.
◆ **s'extirper** *vp (emploi réfléchi)* : **s'~ du lit** to drag *ou* to haul o.s. out of bed.

extorquer [3] [ɛkstɔrke] *vt* [fonds] to extort ■ **~ de l'argent à qqn** to extort money from sb ■ **~ une signature à qqn** to force a signature out of sb.

extorsion [ɛkstɔrsjɔ̃] *nf* extortion ■ **~ de fonds** extortion of money.

extra [ɛkstra] ◇ *adj inv* **1.** *fam* [exceptionnel - journée, personne, spectacle] great, terrific, super **2.** COMM **: poires (de qualité) ~** first class pears.
◇ *nm inv* **1.** [gâterie] (special) treat ■ **faire** *ou* **s'offrir un ~** to give o.s. a treat, to treat o.s. **2.** [frais] extra cost *ou* expenditure, incidental expenditure **3.** [emploi ponctuel] **: faire des ~ comme ouvreuse** to earn extra money by working (occasionally) as an usherette **4.** [serveur] help.

extrabudgétaire [ɛkstrabydʒetɛr] *adj* **: des dépenses ~s** extrabudgetary costs, costs that have not been budgeted for.

extraconjugal, e, aux [ɛkstrakɔ̃ʒygal, o] *adj* extramarital.

extracteur [ɛkstraktœr] *nm* **1.** ARM, CHIM & MÉD extractor **2.** [de fluides] extractor.

extractif, ive [ɛkstraktif, iv] *adj* extractive.

extraction [ɛkstraksjɔ̃] *nf* **1.** [origine] extraction *sout*, origin ■ **d'~ bourgeoise** from a bourgeois family **2.** MIN & PÉTR extraction ■ **~ à ciel ouvert** open cast mining ■ **l'~ de la pierre** quarrying (for stone) ■ **l'~ du charbon** coal extraction *ou* mining **3.** [d'une dent, d'une épine] pulling out, extraction **4.** CHIM & MATH extraction, extracting.
◆ **de basse extraction** *loc adj* of humble birth.
◆ **de haute extraction** *loc adj* highborn.

extrader [3] [ɛkstrade] *vt* to extradite.

extradition [ɛkstradisjɔ̃] *nf* extradition.

extrafin, e [ɛkstrafɛ̃, in] *adj* [haricots] extra(-)fine ■ [chocolats] superfine ■ **de qualité ~e** extra fine.

extrafort, e [ɛkstrafɔr, ɔrt] *adj* [carton] strong, stiff ■ [colle] extra-strong ■ [moutarde] hot.
◆ **extrafort** *nm* bias-binding.

extraire [112] [ɛkstrɛr] *vt* **1.** MIN & INDUST **du pétrole** [charbon] to extract, to mine ■ [pétrole] to extract ■ [pierre] to extract, to quarry **2.** [ôter - dent, écharde] to extract, to remove, to pull out *(sép)* ■ **~ qqch/qqn de : ~ une balle d'une jambe** to extract *ou* to remove a bullet from a leg ■ **~ un ticket de sa poche** to take *ou* to dig a ticket out of one's pocket ■ **ils ont eu du mal à l'~ de sa voiture accidentée** they had great difficulty extricating him from the wreckage of his car **3.** CHIM, CULIN & PHARM to extract ■ [en pressant] to squeeze out *(sép)* ■ [en écrasant] to crush out *(sép)* ■ [en tordant] to wring out *(sép)* **4.** MATH to extract ■ **~ la racine carrée/cubique d'un nombre** to extract the square/cube root of a number **5.** [citer - passage, proverbe] **: ~ de** to take *ou* to extract from.
◆ **s'extraire** *vp (emploi réfléchi)* **: s'~ de qqch** to climb *ou* to clamber out of sthg ■ **s'~ d'une voiture** [rescapé d'un accident] to extricate o.s. from (the wreckage of) a car ■ **s'~ d'un puits** to climb out of a well.

extrait [ɛkstrɛ] *nm* **1.** [morceau choisi - gén] extract ; [- de film, de livre] excerpt, extract ■ **un petit ~ de l'émission d'hier soir** a short sequence *ou* a clip from last night's programme **2.** ADMIN **: ~ (d'acte) de naissance** birth certificate ■ **~ de casier judiciaire** extract from police records **3.** BANQUE **: ~ de compte** abstract of accounts **4.** CULIN & PHARM extract, essence ■ **~ de violette** essence of violets ■ **~ de viande** meat extract *ou* essence.

extralucide [ɛkstralysid] *adj* & *nmf* clairvoyant.

extra-muros [ɛkstramyros] *loc adv* & *loc adj* outside the town, out of town.

extraordinaire [ɛkstraɔrdinɛr] *adj* **1.** [inhabituel - histoire] extraordinary, amazing ; [- cas, personnage, intelligence] extraordinary, exceptional ; [- talent, courage] extraordinary, exceptional, rare ; [- circonstances] extraordinary, special **2.** POLIT [mesures, impôt] special ■ [pouvoirs] special, emergency *(modif)* ■ **assemblée ~** special session, extraordinary meeting **3.** [remarquable - artiste, joueur, spectacle] remarkable, outstanding ; [- temps] wonderful ■ **le repas n'avait rien d'~** *ou* **n'était pas ~** there was nothing special about the meal **4.** [étrange] extraordinary, strange ■ **qu'y-a-t-il d'~ à cela?** what's so strange *ou* special about that?
◆ **par extraordinaire** *loc adv* **: si par ~ il arrivait que...** if by some unlikely chance it happened that... ■ **quand par ~ il me rendait visite** on those rare occasions when he would visit me.

extraordinairement [ɛkstraɔrdinɛrmɑ̃] *adv* **1.** [très] extraordinarily, extremely, exceptionally **2.** [bizarrement] extraordinarily, strangely, bizarrely.

extraplat, e [ɛkstrapla, at] *adj* extraflat, very slim, slimline ■ **une calculatrice ~e** a slimline calculator.

extrapolation [ɛkstrapɔlasjɔ̃] *nf* [gén - SC] extrapolation.

extrapoler [3] [ɛkstrapɔle] *vt* & *vi* [gén - SC] to extrapolate ▪ ~ **qqch d'un fait** to extrapolate sthg from a fact.

extrascolaire [ɛkstraskɔlɛr] *adj* out-of-school *(modif)*.

extrasensoriel, elle [ɛkstrasɑ̃sɔrjɛl] *adj* extrasensory.

extrasystole [ɛkstrasistɔl] *nf* MÉD extrasystole, premature beat.

extraterrestre [ɛkstratɛrɛstr] ◇ *adj* extraterrestrial. ◇ *nmf* extraterrestrial (being *ou* creature).

extraterritorialité [ɛkstratɛritɔrjalite] *nf* extraterritoriality.

extra-utérin, e [ɛkstrayterɛ̃, in] (*mpl* **extra-utérins**, *fpl* **extra-utérines**) *adj* extra-uterine.

extravagance [ɛkstravagɑ̃s] *nf* **1.** [outrance - d'une attitude, d'une personne, d'une réponse] extravagance ; [- d'une demande, de dépenses] extravagance, unreasonableness ; [- d'une tenue] extravagance, eccentricity **2.** [acte] extravagance ▪ [parole] foolish thing (to say) ▪ **faire des ~s** to behave extravagantly, to do eccentric things ▪ **dire des ~s** to talk wildly.

extravagant, e [ɛkstravagɑ̃, ɑ̃t] *adj* **1.** [déraisonnable - attitude, personne, tenue] extravagant, eccentric ; [- idée] extravagant, wild, crazy ▪ **raconter des histoires ~es** to tell wild stories **2.** [excessif - demande, exigence, dépenses] extravagant, unreasonable.

extraverti, e [ɛkstravɛrti] ◇ *adj* extroverted. ◇ *nm, f* extrovert.

extrayait *etc v* ▷ **extraire.**

extrême [ɛkstrɛm] ◇ *adj* **1.** [intense - confort, importance, soin *etc*] extreme, utmost ; [- froid] extreme, intense ▪ **d'une complexité/maigreur ~** extremely complex/skinny **2.** [radical - idée] extreme ; [- mesures] extreme, drastic ▪ **être ~ dans ses idées** to hold extreme views **3.** [exceptionnel - cas, exemple, situation] extreme **4.** [le plus éloigné] : **la limite ~, l'~ limite** the furthest point ▶ **l'~ droite/gauche** POLIT the extreme right/left. ◇ *nm* **1.** [cas limite] extreme ▪ **passer d'un ~ à l'autre** to go from one extreme to the other *ou* to another **2.** SC [terme] extreme.

◆ **à l'extrême** *loc adv* extremely, in the extreme ▪ **porter** *ou* **pousser les choses à l'~** to take *ou* to carry things to extremes.

extrêmement [ɛkstrɛmmɑ̃] *adv* extremely.

extrême-onction [ɛkstrɛmɔ̃ksjɔ̃] (*pl* **extrêmes-onctions**) *nf* extreme unction.

Extrême-Orient [ɛkstrɛmɔrjɑ̃] *npr m* : **(l')~** the Far East.

extrême-oriental, e, aux [ɛkstrɛmɔrjɑ̃tal, o] *adj* Far Eastern.

extremis [ɛkstremis] **in extremis.**

extrémisme [ɛkstremism] *nm* extremism.

extrémiste [ɛkstremist] *adj* & *nmf* extremist.

extrémité [ɛkstremite] *nf* **1.** [d'un bâtiment, d'une table, d'une jetée] end ▪ [d'un bâton] end, tip ▪ [d'un doigt, de la langue] tip ▪ [d'un champ] edge, end ▪ [d'un territoire] (furthest) boundary **2.** ANAT & MATH extremity **3.** [acte radical] extreme act ▪ **pousser qqn à des ~s** to drive sb to extremes **4.** *sout* [brutalité] act of violence **5.** *sout* [situation critique] plight, straits, extremity *sout* ▪ **être réduit à la dernière ~** to be in dire straits *ou* in a dreadful plight.

extrinsèque [ɛkstrɛ̃sɛk] *adj* extrinsic ▪ **valeur ~ d'une monnaie** face value of a currency.

extrusion [ɛkstryzjɔ̃] *nf* INDUST extrusion, extruding.

exubérance [ɛgzyberɑ̃s] *nf* **1.** [entrain] exuberance, joie de vivre ▪ **avec ~** exuberantly **2.** *litt* [action] exuberant behaviour *(U)* **3.** [énergie, vigueur - d'une végétation, d'un style] luxuriance ; [- d'une imagination] wildness, exuberance ; [- de figures, de formes] abundance, luxuriance.

exubérant, e [ɛgzyberɑ̃, ɑ̃t] *adj* **1.** [joyeux - attitude, personne] exuberant **2.** [vigoureux - végétation, style] luxuriant ; [- imagination] wild, exuberant.

exultation [ɛgzyltasjɔ̃] *nf litt* exultation *litt*, rejoicing.

exulter [3] [ɛgzylte] *vi* to exult, to rejoice ▪ **l'annonce de cette nouvelle la fit ~** when she heard the news she went wild with joy *ou* was over the moon.

exutoire [ɛgzytwar] *nm* **1.** [dérivatif] : **un ~ à** an outlet for **2.** [pour liquides] outlet.

ex-voto [ɛksvɔto] *nm inv* ex voto.

eye-liner [ajlajnœr] (*pl* **eye-liners**) *nm* eyeliner.

Ézéchiel [ezekjɛl] *npr* BIBLE Ezekiel.

F

f, F [ɛf] *nm* **1.** [lettre] f, F, *voir aussi* **g 2.** [appartement] : **un F3** ≃ a two-bedroomed flat *UK OU* apartment *US* ▪ **un F4** ≃ a three-bedroomed flat *UK OU* apartment *US*.

F 1. (*abr écrite de* **franc**) F ▪ **500 F** 500 francs, F 500, Ff 500 **2.** (*abr écrite de* **fahrenheit/farad**) F.

fa [fa] *nm inv* F ▪ **en fa majeur/mineur** in F major/minor ▪ **un fa bémol/dièse** an F flat/sharp ‖ [chanté] fa, fah.

FAB [fab] (*abr de* **franco à bord**) *adj inv & adv* FOB, fob.

fable [fabl] *nf* **1.** LITTÉR fable **2.** *péj* [invention] lie, invention ▪ **c'est une ~!** it's a fairytale! **3.** *litt* [légende] legend, tale.

fabliau, x [fablijo] *nm* fabliau.

fabricant, e [fabrikɑ̃, ɑ̃t] *nm, f* manufacturer, maker ▪ **~ de voitures** car manufacturer ▪ **~ de chaussures** shoemaker.

fabrication [fabrikasjɔ̃] *nf* **1.** INDUST manufacture, production ▪ **~ assistée par ordinateur** computer-aided manufacturing ▪ **~ en série** mass production **2.** [contrefaçon] counterfeiting, forging ▪ **~ de fausse monnaie** counterfeiting **3.** [production] workmanship ▪ **de ~ maison** home-made ▪ **c'est de ta ~?** did you make it yourself?
◆ **de fabrication** *loc adj* [coûts, procédés] manufacturing *(modif)* ▪ [numéro] serial *(modif)*.

fabrique [fabrik] *nf* INDUST factory, works, mill ▪ **~ de papier** paper mill.
◆ **de fabrique** *loc adj* [prix, secret] manufacturer's, trade *(modif)* ▪ [marque] trade *(modif)*.

fabriqué, e [fabrike] *adj* **1.** ÉCON [produit] manufactured **2.** [sans spontanéité - sentiment, réaction] lacking in spontaneity.

fabriquer [3] [fabrike] *vt* **1.** INDUST to make, to produce, to manufacture ▪ [gâteau, pull-over, guirlande] to make **2.** *fam* [faire] to do, to cook up *(sép)* ▪ **ça alors, qu'est-ce que tu fabriques par ici?** what on earth are you doing here? ▪ **qu'est-ce que tu as encore fabriqué avec mes clefs?** *péj* now what have you gone and done with my keys? ▪ **qu'est-ce qu'il fabrique, ce bus?** what's that bus up to? **3.** *péj* [histoire] to concoct ▪ [personnalité] to build up *(sép)* ▪ **~ qqch de toutes pièces** to make sthg up, to fabricate sthg.

fabulation [fabylasjɔ̃] *nf* fabrication.

fabuler [3] [fabyle] *vi* **1.** PSYCHOL to fabricate **2.** *péj* [mentir] to tell tales ▪ **des ours? – je crois qu'il fabule un peu** bears? – I think he's making it up.

fabuleusement [fabyløzmɑ̃] *adv* fabulously, fantastically.

fabuleux, euse [fabylø, øz] *adj* **1.** [de légende] fabulous, legendary **2.** [hors du commun] incredible, fabulous ▪ **un destin ~** an incredible fate **3.** [élevé - prix, somme] tremendous, astronomical ▪ **elle gagne des sommes fabuleuses** she earns a tremendous amount of money.

fabuliste [fabylist] *nmf* fabulist, writer of fables.

fac [fak] *nf fam* **en ~, à la ~** at university *OU* college.

façade [fasad] *nf* **1.** ARCHIT : **la ~ du château** the front of the palace ➊ **~ latérale** side (aspect) ▪ **~ principale** façade, (main) frontage **2.** [paroi] front wall *OU* panel **3.** [apparence] outward appearance, façade ▪ **ce n'est qu'une ~** it's all show *OU* a façade ‖ *péj* [faux-semblant] cover, pretence **4.** △ [visage] mug △, face ▪ **se refaire la ~** to touch up one's make-up ▪ **se faire refaire la ~** to have a face-lift **5.** GÉOGR : **la ~ atlantique** the Atlantic coast.
◆ **de façade** *loc adj* : **un optimisme de ~** apparent optimism ▪ **une générosité de ~** a show of magnanimity.

face [fas] *nf* **1.** [visage] face ▪ **les muscles de la ~** facial muscles ▪ **des lésions de la ~** lesions on the face ▪ **tomber ~ contre terre** to fall flat on one's face ➊ **arborer** *OU* **avoir une ~ de carême** to have a long face ▪ **perdre/sauver la ~** to lose/to save face ▪ **se voiler la ~** *litt* to avert one's gaze **2.** [aspect] : **changer la ~ de** to alter the face of ▪ **examiner un problème sous toutes ses ~s** to consider every aspect of a problem **3.** [côté - d'une médaille] obverse ; [- d'une monnaie] head, headside ; [- d'un disque] side ; [- d'une montagne] face ▪ **la ~ B d'un disque** the B-side *OU* flipside of a record ▪ **la ~ cachée d'un problème** *fig* the hidden side *OU* aspect of a problem ▪ **à double ~** double-sided ▪ **~!** heads! **4.** GÉOM & MÉCAN face, side ▪ **~ portante** bearing face **5.** INFORM : **disquette double ~** double-sided disk **6.** COUT : **tissu double ~** double-faced fabric **7.** *loc* **faire ~** to face up to things, to cope ▪ **faire ~ à** *pr* to stand opposite to, to face ; [danger] to face up to ; [obligations, dépense] to meet.
◆ **à la face de** *loc prép* **1.** [devant] : **à la ~ de son frère** to his brother's face **2.** [publiquement] : **à la ~ du monde** *OU* **de tous** openly, publicly ▪ **à la ~ de Dieu** before God.
◆ **de face** *loc adj* face *(modif)*, facing ▪ **photo/portrait de ~** ART & PHOTO full-face photograph/portrait ▪ **vue de ~** ARCHIT front view *OU* elevation ▪ **loge de ~** THÉÂTRE box facing the stage.
◆ **d'en face** *loc adj* : **ceux d'en ~** [adversaires] the opposition ; [voisins] the people opposite.
◆ **en face** *loc adv* [de front] : **avoir le soleil en ~** to have the sun (shining) in one's face ▪ **regarder qqn en ~** to look sb in the face ▪ **regarder la mort en ~** to face up to death ▪ **regarder les choses en ~** to face facts ▪ **je lui ai dit la vérité en ~** I told him the truth to his face.
◆ **en face de** *loc prép* : **juste en ~ de moi** right in front of me ▪ **sa maison est en ~ de l'église** his house is opposite *OU* faces the church ▪ **mettre qqn en ~ des réalités** to force sb to face reality ▪ **en ~ l'un de l'autre, l'un en ~ de l'autre** face to face.
◆ **face à** *loc prép* [dans l'espace] in front of ▪ **~ à l'ennemi/aux médias** faced with the enemy/media.

◆ **face à face** *loc adv* face to face ▪ **mettre qqn ~ à ~ avec** to bring sb face to face with.

face-à-face [fasafas] *nm inv* [conversation] (face-to-face) meeting ▪ [conflit] (one-to-one) confrontation ▪ **~ télévisé** television debate *(between two politicians)*.

face-à-main [fasamɛ̃] *(pl* **faces-à-main)** *nm* lorgnette.

facétie [fasesi] *nf* [plaisanterie] facetious remark, joke ▪ [trait d'esprit] witticism ▪ [farce] prank ▪ **se livrer à des ~s** to fool around.

facétieux, euse [fasesjø, øz] ◇ *adj* facetious, humorous.
◇ *nm, f* joker, prankster.

facette [fasɛt] *nf* **1.** ENTOM & JOAILL facet **2.** [aspect] facet, aspect, side ▪ **sa personnalité présente d'autres ~s** there are other sides to his personality.
◆ **à facettes** *loc adj* **1.** GÉOL & JOAILL multifaceted **2.** [personnalité, talent] multifaceted, many-sided.

fâché, e [faʃe] *adj* **1.** [contrarié] angry, cross ▪ **je suis ~ de l'avoir manqué** I'm really sorry I missed him ▪ *(au négatif)* **n'être pas ~ de : je ne serais pas ~ d'avoir une réponse** I wouldn't mind getting an answer ▪ **ils n'étaient pas ~s de se retrouver chez eux** they were rather pleased to be home again **2.** [brouillé] : **ils sont ~s** they're not on speaking terms **3.** *fig & hum* **être ~ avec qqch** [sans goût pour] : **je suis ~ avec les langues/les chiffres** languages/figures are not my line ▪ **il est ~ avec le savon** he's allergic to soap.

fâcher [3] [faʃe] *vt* [contrarier] to annoy, to vex ▪ **acceptez, le contraire les fâcherait** do come, they'd be offended *ou* they'd resent it if you didn't.
◆ **se fâcher** *vpi* **1.** [se brouiller] to fall out *ou* to quarrel (with one another) ▪ **se ~ avec qqn** to quarrel *ou* to fall out with sb **2.** [se mettre en colère] to get cross *ou* angry, to lose one's temper ▪ **tes parents se sont fâchés?** did your parents get angry? ▪ **se ~ tout rouge** to blow one's top ▪ **se ~ contre qqn** to get angry with sb.

fâcheusement [faʃøzmɑ̃] *adv* [malheureusement] unfortunately ▪ [désagréablement] unpleasantly.

fâcheux, euse [faʃø, øz] ◇ *adj* regrettable, unfortunate ▪ **une fâcheuse habitude** an unfortunate habit ▪ **c'est ~!** it's rather a pity!
◇ *nm, f litt* bore.

facho [faʃo] *adj & nmf fam péj* fascist.

facial, e, aux [fasjal, o] *adj* facial.

faciès [fasjɛs] *nm* **1.** [traits] facial aspect, features **2.** *péj* [visage] face ▪ **un ~ grimaçant derrière le carreau** a grimacing face behind the windowpane **3.** BOT & GÉOL facies.

facile [fasil] ◇ *adj* **1.** [aisé] easy ▪ **rien de plus ~** nothing easier ▪ **il ne m'est pas ~ d'expliquer la situation** it's not easy for me to explain the situation ▪ **~ à faire** easy to do, easily done ▪ **c'est ~ à dire (mais moins ~ à faire), c'est plus ~ à dire qu'à faire** easier said than done ▪ **~ d'accès** easy to reach, easily reached, readily accessible ▶ **~ comme bonjour** easy as pie **2.** [spontané, naturel] : **elle a la parole/plume ~** speaking/writing comes easily to her ▪ **avoir la larme ~** to be easily moved to tears **3.** [souple - caractère] easy, easy-going **4.** *péj* [libertin] : **une femme ~** *ou* **de mœurs ~s** a woman of easy virtue.
◇ *adv fam* **je te fais ça en deux heures ~** I can have it done for you in two hours, no problem ▪ **d'ici à la maison, il reste trente kilomètres ~** from here to the house, there's still a good thirty kilometres.

facilement [fasilmɑ̃] *adv* **1.** [sans difficulté] easily, readily **2.** [au moins] at least ▪ **je gagnerais ~ le double** I would easily earn twice as much.

facilité [fasilite] *nf* **1.** [simplicité] easiness, ease ▪ **selon le degré de ~ des exercices** depending on how easy the exercises are ▪ **céder à** *ou* **se laisser aller à** *ou* **choisir la ~** *péj* to take the easy way out *ou* the easy option **2.** [possibilité] opportunity ▪ **avoir toute ~** *ou* **toutes ~s pour faire qqch** to have every opportunity of doing sthg **3.** [aisance] gift, talent ▪ **~ de parole** fluency ▪ **avoir beaucoup de ~ pour** to have a gift for ▪ **avec ~** easily, with ease ▪ **avec une grande ~** with the greatest of ease ▪ **il n'a pas la ~ de son frère** things don't come as easily to him as they do to his brother.
◆ **facilités** *nfpl* **1.** [capacités] ability, aptitude **2.** FIN facilities ▪ **~s de caisse** overdraft facilities ▪ **~s de paiement** easy terms.

faciliter [3] [fasilite] *vt* to ease, to help along *(sép)*, to make easy ▪ **ça ne va pas ~ les choses entre eux** it won't make things easier *ou* smoother between them.

façon [fasɔ̃] *nf* **1.** [manière] manner, way ▪ **la phrase peut se comprendre de plusieurs ~s** the sentence can be interpreted in several ways ▪ **demande-lui de quelle ~ il compte payer** ask him how he wishes to pay ▪ **je n'aime pas la ~ dont il me parle** I don't like the way he talks *ou* his way of talking to me ▪ **pourquoi criez-vous de telle ~?** why are you shouting like that? ▪ **d'une ~ désordonnée** in a disorderly fashion ▪ **d'une ~ générale** generally speaking ▪ **de ~ systématique** systematically ▶ **sa ~ d'être** the way he is ▪ **ce n'est qu'une ~ de parler** *ou* **dire** it's just a manner of speaking ▪ **généreux, ~ de parler, il ne m'a jamais donné un centime!** *fam* generous, that's a funny way of putting it, he never gave me a penny! ▪ **je vais lui dire ma ~ de penser, moi!** I'll give him a piece of my mind! ▪ **ça dépend de ta ~ de voir les choses** it depends on your way of looking at things *ou* on how you lode at things ▪ **ils n'ont pas les mêmes ~s de voir** they see things differently
2. [moyen] way ▪ **pour obtenir son accord, il n'y a qu'une seule ~ de s'y prendre** there's only one way to get him to agree
3. [fabrication] making, fashioning ▪ [facture] craftsmanship, workmanship ▪ [main-d'œuvre] labour
4. COUT [vêtement] cut ▪ **de bonne ~** well-made, (beautifully) tailored
5. *(suivi d'un n)* [qui rappelle] : **une nappe ~ grand-mère** a tablecloth like Grandma used to have ▮ [imitant] : **~ marbre/bois** imitation marble/wood.
◆ **façons** *nfpl* [manières] manners, behaviour ▪ **en voilà des ~s!** manners!, what a way to behave! ▪ **faire des ~s** [se faire prier] to make a fuss ; [se pavaner] to put on airs ▪ **sans plus de ~s** without further ado.
◆ **à façon** *loc adj* [artisan] jobbing ▪ [travail] contract *(modif)* ▪ **centre de traitement** *ou* **travail à ~** INFORM data processing *ou* computer *ou* service bureau.
◆ **à la façon de** *loc prép* like, in the manner of ▪ **elle portait le paquet sur la tête, un peu à la ~ d'une Africaine** she was carrying the parcel on top of her head, much like an African woman would.
◆ **à ma façon, à sa façon** *etc* ◇ *loc adj* : **une recette à ma/ta ~** a recipe of mine/yours ▪ **un tour à sa ~** one of his tricks.
◇ *loc adv* : **chante-le à ta ~** sing it your way *ou* any way you like.
◆ **de cette façon** *loc adv* **1.** [comme cela] (in) this way, thus, in this manner
2. [par conséquent] that way.
◆ **de façon à** *loc prép* so as to, in order to ▪ **j'ai fermé la fenêtre de ~ à éviter les courants d'air** I shut the window in order to prevent draughts.
◆ **de façon (à ce) que** *loc conj* so that ▪ **il s'est levé de bonne heure de ~ à ce que tout soit prêt** he got up early so that everything would be ready in time.
◆ **de la même façon** *loc adv* in the same way.
◆ **de la même façon que** *loc conj* like, as, in the same (way) as.
◆ **de ma façon, de sa façon** *etc loc adj* : **une recette de ma/ta ~** a recipe of mine/yours ▪ **un tour de sa ~** one of his tricks.
◆ **de telle façon que** *loc conj* so that, in such a way that.
◆ **de toute façon, de toutes les façons** *loc adv* anyway, in any case.
◆ **d'une certaine façon** *loc adv* in a way, in a manner of speaking, so to speak.
◆ **d'une façon ou d'une autre** *loc adv* somehow.
◆ **sans façon(s)** ◇ *loc adj* [style] simple, unadorned ▪ [cuisine] plain ▪ [personne] simple.
◇ *loc adv* **1.** [familièrement] : **elle m'a pris le bras sans ~** *ou* **~s** she took my arm quite naturally
2. [non merci] no thank you.

faconde [fakɔ̃d] *nf litt & péj* fluency, flow of words ▪ **être doué d'une belle ~** to be a smooth talker.

façonnage [fasɔnaʒ] *nm* **1.** [mise en forme] shaping, working **2.** IMPR forwarding.

façonné [fasɔne] *nm* TEXT figured fabric.

façonnement [fasɔnmɑ̃] = **façonnage**.

façonner [3] [fasɔne] *vt* **1.** [modeler - argile] to shape, to fashion ; [- métal] to shape, to work ▪ **~ l'argile** to fashion clay **2.** *fig* [caractère] to mould, to shape **3.** [fabriquer] to manufacture, to produce, to make ▪ **façonné à la main** handmade.

fac-similé [faksimile] (*pl* **fac-similés**) *nm* **1.** [reproduction] facsimile **2.** TÉLÉCOM [technique] facsimile ▪ [document] facsimile, fax.

facteur[1] [faktœr] *nm* **1.** MATH & SC coefficient, factor ▪ **mettre en ~s** to factorize ⊳ **~ commun** common factor ▪ **~ premier** prime factor **2.** MÉD : **~ Rhésus** rhesus *ou* Rh factor **3.** [élément] element, factor ▪ **le ~ humain/temps** the human/time factor ▪ **~ de risque** risk factor ▪ **la courtoisie peut être un ~ de réussite** courtesy may be one of the ways to success **4.** MUS instrument maker ▪ **~ de pianos** piano maker ▪ **~ d'orgues** organ builder.

facteur[2]**, trice** [faktœr, tris] *nm, f* ADMIN postman *UK* (*f* postwoman), mailman *US* (*f* mailwoman) ▪ **est-ce que le ~ est passé?** has the postman been yet?

factice [faktis] *adj* **1.** [imité - diamant] artificial, false ; [- marchandise de présentation] dummy *(modif)* **2.** [inauthentique] artificial, simulated, false ▪ **une joie ~** simulated happiness.

factieux, euse [faksjø, øz] ◇ *adj* seditious.
◇ *nm, f* rebel.

faction [faksjɔ̃] *nf* **1.** [groupe] faction **2.** MIL sentry *ou* guard duty ▪ **être en** *ou* **de ~** to be on sentry *ou* guard duty ▪ **mettre une sentinelle de ~ devant la porte** to post a sentry in front of the door **3.** [dans une entreprise] (8-hour) shift.

factionnaire [faksjɔnɛr] ◇ *nm* MIL sentry, guard.
◇ *nmf* [ouvrier] shift worker.

factorisation [faktɔrizasjɔ̃] *nf* factorization, factorizing.

factotum [faktɔtɔm] *nm* factotum, handyman ▪ **je ne suis pas ton ~!** I'm not your servant!

factuel, elle [faktɥɛl] *adj* [gén - PHILOS] factual.

facturation [faktyrasjɔ̃] *nf* **1.** [action] invoicing, billing ⊳ **~ détaillée** itemized bill ▪ **~ séparée** INFORM unbundling **2.** [service] invoice department.

facture [faktyr] *nf* **1.** COMM invoice, bill ▪ **établir une ~** to make out an invoice ⊳ **~ pro forma** *ou* **provisoire** pro forma invoice ▪ **fausse ~** faked *ou* forged invoice ▪ **payer la ~** to pay the price **2.** MUS [de piano] making ▪ [d'orgues] building **3.** [technique] craftsmanship, workmanship.
◆ **de bonne facture** *loc adj* [meuble, piano] well-made, beautifully crafted ▪ [tableau] skilfully executed.

facturer [3] [faktyre] *vt* [article, service] : **~ qqch à qqn** to bill *ou* to invoice sb for sthg ▪ **~ séparément le matériel et le logiciel** INFORM to unbundle.

facturette [faktyrɛt] *nf* (credit card sales) receipt, record of charge form.

facturier, ère [faktyrje, ɛr] *nm, f* invoice clerk.

facultatif, ive [fakyltatif, iv] *adj* **1.** [au choix] optional ⊳ **épreuve facultative** optional subject **2.** [sur demande] : **arrêt ~** request stop.

facultativement [fakyltativmɑ̃] *adv* optionally, as an option.

faculté [fakylte] *nf* **1.** [capacité] ability, capability ▪ **~ d'adaptation** adaptability, ability to adapt **2.** [fonction] ability ▪ **les humains possèdent la ~ d'abstraire** mankind is capable of abstract thought **3.** *sout* [droit] freedom, right ▪ **avoir la ~ de** to have the right to *ou* the option of ▮ [autorité] power ▪ **avoir la ~ de** to be entitled to **4.** DR : **~s contributives** ability to pay **5.** UNIV [avant 1968] faculty ▪ **la ~ des sciences** the science faculty ▮ [depuis 1969] university, college ▪ **on s'est connu à la** *ou* **en ~** [étudiants] we met at university *ou* when we were students **6.** *hum* [médecins] : **la Faculté m'interdit/lui recommande de faire du sport** my doctors forbid me/his doctors encourage him to engage in sports.
◆ **facultés** *nfpl* [esprit] faculties, powers ▪ **avoir** *ou* **jouir de toutes ses ~s** to be of sound mind *ou* in full possession of one's faculties.
◆ **de faculté** *loc adj* [cours, professeur] university *(modif)* ▪ **des souvenirs de ~** memories of one's university *ou* student days.

fada [fada] *fam* ◇ *adj* cracked, nuts.
◇ *nmf* [fou] : **les ~s de la moto** motorbikes freaks.

fadaise [fadɛz] *nf* piece of nonsense ▪ **~s** drivel, nonsense, rubbish.

fadasse [fadas] *adj péj* **1.** [sans goût] insipid, tasteless, bland **2.** [sans éclat] dull ▪ **des couleurs ~s** washed-out colours.

fade [fad] *adj* **1.** [sans saveur] insipid, tasteless, bland **2.** [banal] dull, pointless, vapid *sout* ▪ **le compliment est plutôt ~** the compliment is rather flat.

fadeur [fadœr] *nf* **1.** [insipidité] blandness, lack of flavour **2.** [banalité] blandness, vapidity *sout.*

fading [fadiŋ] *nm* RADIO fade.

fagot [fago] *nm* **1.** [branches] bundle (of wood) ▪ **sentir le ~** [personne] to be a suspected heretic ; [opinion] to smack of heresy **2.** [en Afrique] firewood.

fagotage [fagɔtaʒ] *nm* **1.** *fam péj* [habillement] ridiculous getup **2.** [du bois] bundling (up).

fagoté, e [fagɔte] *adj fam péj* **mal ~** badly dressed.

fagoter [3] [fagɔte] *vt* **1.** [bois, branches] to bind together *(sép)*, to tie up *(sép)* in bundles **2.** *fam péj* [habiller] : **sa mère le fagote n'importe comment** his mother dresses him like nothing on earth.
◆ **se fagoter** *vp (emploi réfléchi) fam péj* **t'as vu comme elle se fagote!** have you seen some of the things she wears!

Fahrenheit [farɛnajt] *npr* : **degré/échelle ~** Fahrenheit degree/scale.

faiblard, e [fɛblar, ard] *adj fam* **1.** [vieillard, convalescent] weak, frail **2.** [excuse] feeble, lame ▪ [argument] feeble **3.** [lumière] weak.

faible [fɛbl] ◇ *adj* **1.** [malade, vieillard] weak, frail ▪ **se sentir ~** to feel weak ▮ [fonction organique] : **avoir la vue ~** to have weak *ou* poor eyesight ▪ **avoir le cœur/la poitrine ~** to have a weak heart/chest ▪ **avoir les reins ~s** to have kidney trouble ▪ **être de ~ constitution** to have a weak constitution
2. [étai, construction] weak, flimsy, fragile
3. [esprit] weak, deficient
4. [médiocre - étudiant, résultat] weak, poor, mediocre ▪ **elle est ~ en travaux manuels** she's not very good at handicrafts
5. [trop tempéré - style, argument, réforme] weak ; [- jugement] mild ; [- prétexte] feeble, flimsy ▪ **le mot est ~!** that's an understatement!
6. [complaisant] weak, lax ▪ [sans volonté] weak, spineless
7. [impuissant - nation, candidat] weak
8. COMM & ÉCON [demande] slack ▪ [marge] low ▪ [monnaie] weak ▪ [revenus] low ▪ [ressources] scant, thin
9. [léger - lumière] dim, faint ; [- bruit] faint ; [- brise] light ; [- odeur] faint
10. [peu important] low, small ▪ **aller à ~ vitesse** to proceed at low speed ▪ **de ~ encombrement** compact ▪ **à ~ teneur en alcool** low in alcohol ▪ **avoir de ~s chances de succès** to have slight *ou* slender chances of succeeding ▪ **donner une ~ idée de** to give a faint idea of
11. LING weak, unstressed.
◇ *nmf* weak-willed person ▪ **c'est un ~** he's weak-willed ▪ **~ d'esprit** simpleton.
◇ *nm* **1.** [préférence] : **avoir un ~ pour qqch** to be partial to sthg ▪ **avoir un ~ pour qqn** to have a soft spot for sb
2. *litt* [point sensible] weak spot ▪ **prendre qqn par son ~** to find sb's Achilles heel.

◆ **faibles** *nmpl* : les ~s the weak.

faiblement [fɛbləmɑ̃] *adv* **1.** [sans force] feebly, weakly **2.** [légèrement] faintly.

faiblesse [fɛblɛs] *nf* **1.** [manque de vigueur physique] weakness, frailty ■ **ressentir une grande ~** to feel very weak ■ **la ~ de sa constitution** his weak constitution **2.** [d'une construction] weakness, flimsiness, fragility ■ [d'une économie, d'un système] weakness, fragility, vulnerability ■ [d'une voix, d'un son] dimness, faintness ■ [de la vue, de la poitrine] weakness **3.** [médiocrité - d'un élève] weakness ; [- d'une œuvre, d'un argument] feebleness, weakness ▶ **~ d'esprit** feeblemindedness **4.** [insignifiance - d'une différence, d'un écart] insignificance ■ **la ~ des effectifs** [employés] a shortage of staff ; [élèves] insufficient numbers **5.** *litt* [lâcheté] weakness, spinelessness ■ **être d'une grande ~ envers qqn** [trop indulgent] to be overlenient with sb ■ **avoir la ~ de croire/dire** to be foolish enough to believe/to say ■ **avoir un moment de ~** to have a moment of weakness ■ **pour lui, l'amour filial est une ~** he considers that loving one's parents is a weakness **6.** [défaut] failing, flaw, shortcoming ■ **c'est là la grande ~ du scénario** this is the script's major flaw **7.** [préférence] weakness, partiality ■ **avoir une ~ pour** to have a weakness for, to be partial to **8.** *litt* [évanouissement] fainting fit, dizzy spell ■ **avoir une** *ou* **être pris de ~** to feel faint.

faiblir [32] [feblir] *vi* **1.** [perdre de sa force - personne, pouls] to get weaker ; [- mémoire, mécanisme] to fail ■ **chez elle, c'est la tête qui faiblit** she's going weak in the head **2.** [diminuer - vent, orage, bourrasque] to drop ; [- lumière] to dwindle ; [- enthousiasme, colère, intérêt] to wane, to dwindle ■ **le jour faiblit** it's getting dark ■ **le succès de la pièce ne faiblit pas** the play is still a great success **3.** [cesser d'être efficace - athlète, élève] to get weaker **4.** [plier - paroi, tige] to show signs of weakening ; [- résistance] to weaken **5.** *litt* [défaillir] to have a fainting fit.

faiblissant, e [fɛblisɑ̃, ɑ̃t] *adj* **1.** [vieillard, malade] weakening **2.** [lumière, vent] failing **3.** [économie, pouvoir d'achat] slackening.

faïence [fajɑ̃s] *nf* faience *spéc*, (glazed) earthenware ■ **~ fine** china.

faïencerie [fajɑ̃sri] *nf* **1.** [usine] pottery works **2.** [articles] (glazed) earthenware.

faïencier, ère [fajɑ̃sje, ɛr] *nm, f* potter, maker of (glazed) earthenware.

faignant, e [fɛɲɑ̃, ɑ̃t] = **feignant.**

faille[1] *etc* [faj] *v* ▷ **falloir.**

faille[2] [faj] *nf* **1.** GÉOL fault **2.** [faiblesse] flaw, weakness ■ [incohérence] inconsistency, flaw ■ **il y a une ~ dans votre démonstration** your demonstration is flawed **3.** TEXT faille.

◆ **sans faille** *loc adj* [logique] faultless, flawless ■ [fidélité, dévouement] unfailing, unwavering.

failli, e [faji] *adj* & *nm, f* bankrupt.

faillibilité [fajibilite] *nf* fallibility.

faillible [fajibl] *adj* fallible.

faillir [46] [fajir] *vi* **1.** [être sur le point de] : **j'ai failli rater la marche** I nearly missed the step ■ **tu l'as attrapé? – non, mais j'ai failli!** *fam* did you catch it? – not quite! ▶ **j'ai failli attendre** *hum* so you decided to come, did you? **2.** *litt* to fail in one's duty.

◆ **faillir à** *v+prép sout* **~ à une promesse** to fail to keep a promise ■ **~ à son devoir** to fail in one's duty.

◆ **sans faillir** *loc adv* unfailingly.

faillite [fajit] *nf* **1.** COMM bankruptcy, insolvency ■ **faire ~** to go bankrupt **2.** [échec] failure ■ **la ~ de ses espoirs** *litt* the end *ou* collapse of his hopes ■ **le spectacle a connu une ~ complète** the show was a total failure.

◆ **en faillite** ◇ *loc adj* bankrupt, insolvent ■ **être en ~** to be bankrupt.

◇ *loc adv* : **se mettre en ~** to file a petition for bankruptcy.

faim [fɛ̃] *nf* **1.** [appétit] hunger ■ **avoir ~** to be hungry ■ **j'ai une de ces ~s, je meurs de ~, je crève** *fam* **de ~** I'm famished *ou* starving ■ **merci, je n'ai plus ~** I've had enough, thank you ■ **ça me donne ~** it makes me hungry ■ **j'ai une petite ~** I'm feeling peckish ■ **manger à sa ~** to eat one's fill ▶ **j'ai une ~ de loup** *ou* **à dévorer les montagnes** I could eat a horse, I'm ravenous ■ **rester sur sa ~** *pr* to be still hungry ; *fig* to be left unsatisfied *ou* frustrated ■ **tromper sa ~** to stave off hunger ■ **la ~ chasse le loup (hors)** *ou* **fait sortir le loup du bois** *prov* hunger drives the wolf out of the wood **2.** [famine] : **la ~** hunger, famine ■ **souffrir de la ~** to be starving *ou* a victim of starvation ■ **mourir de ~** to starve to death, to die of starvation **3.** [envie] : **~ de : sa ~ de tendresse** his yearning for tenderness.

faine [fɛn] *nf* beechnut.

fainéant, e [feneɑ̃, ɑ̃t] ◇ *adj* idle, lazy.

◇ *nm, f* idler, layabout ■ **quel ~!** what a layabout!

fainéanter [3] [feneɑ̃te] *vi* to idle about *ou* around ■ **il passe des heures à ~** he spends hours twiddling his thumbs *ou* doing nothing.

fainéantise [feneɑ̃tiz] *nf* idleness, laziness.

faire [109] [fɛr] ◇ *vt*

> **A.** FABRIQUER, RÉALISER
> **B.** ACCOMPLIR, EXÉCUTER
> **C.** AVEC IDÉE DE DÉPLACEMENT
> **D.** AVEC IDÉE DE TRANSFORMATION
> **E.** INDIQUE UN RÉSULTAT
> **F.** INDIQUE UNE QUALITÉ, UNE FORME, UNE MESURE
> **G.** VERBE ATTRIBUTIF
> **H.** VERBE DE SUBSTITUTION

A. FABRIQUER, RÉALISER

1. [confectionner - objet, vêtement] to make ; [- construction] to build ; [- tableau] to paint ; [- film] to make ; [- repas, café] to make, to prepare ; [- gâteau, pain] to make, to bake ; [- vin] to make ; [- bière] to brew ■ [concevoir - thèse, dissertation] to do ■ **qu'as-tu fait (à manger) pour ce soir ?** what have you prepared for dinner ? ■ **c'est elle qui fait ses chansons** she writes her own songs ■ **il sait tout ~** he can turn his hand to anything ■ **grand-mère est super – oui, on n'en fait plus des comme ça!** *fam* grandma's great – yes, they broke the mould when they made her!

2. [produire, vendre] : **~ de l'élevage de bétail** to breed cattle ■ **~ du blé/de la vigne** to grow wheat/grapes ■ **~ une marque/un produit** to stock a make/an article ■ **je vous fais les deux à 350 euros** *fam* you can have both for 350 euros, I'll take 350 euros for both

3. [obtenir, gagner - bénéfices] to make ■ **~ de l'argent** to earn *ou* to make money

4. [mettre au monde] : **~ un enfant** to have a child ■ **il lui a fait deux enfants** he had two children with her ■ **la chatte a fait des petits** the cat has had kittens

5. PHYSIOL : **~ ses besoins** *euphém* to do one's business ■ *(en usage absolu)* **tu as fait ce matin ?** did you go to the toilet this morning ? ■ **il a fait dans sa culotte** *fam* he messed his pants

B. ACCOMPLIR, EXÉCUTER

1. [effectuer - mouvement, signe] to make ■ [saut périlleux, roue] to do ■ **fais-moi un bisou** *fam* **/un sourire** give me a kiss/a smile ▶ **~ la tête** *ou* **la gueule**△ to sulk

2. [accomplir - choix, erreur, réforme, proposition] to make ; [- inventaire] to do ; [- discours] to deliver, to make, to give ; [- conférence] to give ; [- exercice] to do ; [- recherches] to do, to carry out *(sép)* ; [- enquête] to carry out *(sép)* ■ **~ ses études** to study ■ **~ son devoir** to do one's duty ■ **~ une blague à qqn** to play a joke on sb ■ **~ son lit** to make one's bed ▶ **la ~ à qqn** *fam* [plaisanterie] : **on ne me la fait pas, à moi!** I won't be taken in! ■ **on me l'a déjà faite, celle-là** I know that one already

3. [étudier - matière, œuvre] to study, to do ■ [suivre les cours de] : **elle voulait ~ l'ENA** she wanted to go to the ENA

4. [pratiquer] : **~ de la poterie** to do pottery ■ **~ de la flûte/du violon** to play the flute/the violin ■ **~ de la danse** [cours] to go to dance classes ■ **il voulait ~ de la danse** he wanted to be a dancer ■ **~ de l'équitation/de la natation/de la voile** to go horse-riding/swimming/sailing ■ **~ du basket/du tennis** to play basketball/tennis

5. [écrire - lettre] to write ; [- contrat, testament] to write, to make

6. [dire] to say ■ **il fit oui/non de la tête** he nodded/he shook his head ■ **"non", fit-elle** "no", she said ■ **la vache fait "meuh!"** the cow goes "moo!"

7. [nettoyer - chambre, vitres] to clean, to do ; [- chaussures] to polish, to clean ▪ [tapisser, aménager - pièce, maison] to do, to decorate
8. [action non précisée] to do ▪ **que fais-tu dans la vie ?** what do you do (for a living) ? ▪ **je ne t'ai jamais rien fait!** I've never done you any harm! ▪ **ne ~ que : elle ne fait que se plaindre** she does nothing but complain ➡ **je ne veux rien avoir à ~ avec eux!** I don't want anything to do with them! ▪ **~ qqch de qqn/qqch : qu'ai-je fait de mes clefs ?** what have I done with *ou* where did I put my keys ? ▪ **que fais-tu de mes sentiments dans tout ça ?** what about my feelings ? ▪ **que vais-je ~ de toi ?** what am I going to do with you ? ▪ **donne-le moi! – non, rien à ~!** give it to me! – nothing doing *ou* no way! ▪ **tu lui as parlé ? – oui, mais rien à ~, il ne cédera pas** did you talk to him ? – yes, but it's no use, he won't give in ▪ **je vais vous raccompagner – n'en faites rien!** *sout* I'll take you back – there's really no need! ▪ **~ avec** *fam* to make do ▪ **j'apprécie peu sa façon de travailler mais il faut bien ~ avec!** I don't like the way he works but I suppose I'll just have to put up with it! ▪ **~ sans** *fam* to (make) do without ▪ **autant que ~ se peut** if possible, as far as possible ▪ **n'avoir que ~ de : je n'ai que ~ de tes conseils** I don't need your advice ▪ **mais bien sûr, tu n'as que ~ de ma carrière!** but of course, my career matters very little to you! *ou* you don't care about my career! ▪ **pour ce ~** for that ▪ **ce faisant** in so doing

C. AVEC IDÉE DE DÉPLACEMENT

1. [se déplacer à la vitesse de] : **le train peut ~ jusqu'à 400 km/h** the train can do 400 km/h
2. [couvrir - distance] : **le Concorde fait Paris-New York en moins de quatre heures** Concorde goes *ou* flies from Paris to New York in less than four hours ▪ **il y a des cars qui font Londres-Glasgow** there's a coach service between London and Glasgow
3. [visiter - pays, ville] to do, to go to, to visit ▪ [inspecter, passer au crible] : **j'ai fait tous les étages avant de vous trouver** I looked on every floor before I found you ▪ **j'ai fait tous les hôtels de la ville** [j'y suis allé] I did *ou* went to *ou* tried every hotel in town ; [j'ai téléphoné] I called *ou* did *ou* tried every hotel in town ▪ **~ les antiquaires** to go round the antique shops

D. AVEC IDÉE DE TRANSFORMATION

1. [nommer] : **elle l'a fait baron** she gave him the title of Baron, she made him a baron ▪ **elle l'a fait chevalier** she knighted him
2. [transformer en] : **~ qqch de qqn/qqch : des rats, la fée fit des laquais** the fairy changed the rats into footmen ▪ **ce feuilleton en a fait une vedette** this series made him a star ▪ **et ta robe bleue ? – j'en ai fait une jupe** what about your blue dress ? – I made it into a skirt ▪ **garde les restes, j'en ferai une soupe** keep the leftovers, I'll make a soup with them ▪ **c'était un tyran et votre livre en fait un héros!** he was a tyrant, and your book shows *ou* presents him as a hero!
3. [devenir] : **"cheval" fait "chevaux" au pluriel** the plural of "cheval" is "chevaux"
4. [servir de] : **une fois plié, le billard fait table** the billiard table, when folded, can be used *ou* can serve as a normal table ▪ **un canapé qui fait lit** a convertible settee ▪ **c'est un hôtel qui fait restaurant** it's a hotel with a restaurant
5. [remplir un rôle, une fonction] : **il fera un bon mari** he'll make *ou* be a good husband ▪ **il fait le Père Noël dans les rues** he goes around the streets disguised as Father Christmas ▮ CINÉ & THÉÂTRE to play the part of, to be ▪ [imiter - personne] to imitate, to take off, to impersonate ; [- automate, animal] to imitate ▪ **ne fais pas l'idiot** don't be stupid ▪ **ne fais pas l'innocent** don't play the innocent, don't come the innocent with me *UK* ▪ **il essayait de ~ son intéressant** he was showing off

E. INDIQUE UN RÉSULTAT

1. [provoquer] : **~ de la poussière** to raise dust ▪ **ce charbon fait beaucoup de fumée** this coal makes a lot of smoke ▪ **ça va ~ une marque/une auréole** it will leave a mark/a ring ▪ **l'accident a fait cinq morts** the accident left five dead *ou* claimed five lives ▪ **ce qui fait l'intérêt de son livre** what makes his book interesting ▪ **~ quelque chose à qqn** [l'émouvoir] to move sb, to affect sb ▪ **la vue du sang ne me fait rien** I don't mind the sight of blood, the sight of blood doesn't bother me ▪ **si cela ne vous fait rien** if you don't mind ▪ **~ que : la gravitation, force qui fait que les objets s'attirent** gravitation, the force which causes objects to be attracted towards each other ▪ **ce qui fait que je suis arrivé en retard** which meant I was late ▮ [pour exprimer un souhait] : **faites qu'il ne lui arrive rien!** please don't let anything happen to him!
2. [importer] : **qu'est-ce que cela peut ~?** what does it matter ?, so what? ▪ **qu'est-ce que cela peut te ~?** what's it to (do with) you ? ▪ **cela ne fait rien** it doesn't matter, never mind

F. INDIQUE UNE QUALITÉ, UNE FORME, UNE MESURE

1. [former] : **la route fait un coude** the road bends ▪ **le circuit fait un huit** the circuit is (in the shape of) a figure of eight ▪ **le tas fait une pyramide** the heap looks like a pyramid
2. [coûter] to be, to cost ▪ **ça fait combien ?** how much is it ?
3. [valoir, égaler] to be, to make ▪ **2 et 2 font 4** 2 and 2 are 4 ▪ **ça fait 23 en tout** that makes 23 altogether ▪ **on a dix euros, ça ne fait pas assez** we've got ten euros, that's not enough
4. [mesurer] : **il doit bien ~ 1 m 90** he must be 1 m 90 tall ▮ [taille, pointure] : **je fais du 38** I take size 38 ▮ [peser] : **je fais 56 kg** I weigh *ou* am 56 kg
5. [indique la durée, le temps] : **ça fait deux jours qu'il n'a pas mangé** he hasn't eaten for two days ▪ **elle a téléphoné, cela fait bien une heure** she phoned at least an hour ago

G. VERBE ATTRIBUTIF

1. [paraître] : **la broche fait bien** *ou* **joli** *ou* **jolie sur ta robe** the brooch looks nice on your dress ▪ **elle parle avec un léger accent, il paraît que ça fait bien!** she talks with a slight accent, it's supposed to be smart! ▪ **ça fait bizarre** it looks strange ▪ **il me faudrait un nom qui fasse artiste** I would need a name which sounds good for an artist ▪ **ça fait comment** *ou* **quoi de voir son nom sur une affiche?** what's it like to see your name on a poster ? ▪ **~ son âge** to look one's age
2. *fam* [devenir, embrasser la carrière de] to be ▪ **je veux ~ pompier** I want to be a fireman

H. VERBE DE SUBSTITUTION

(toujours en rappel du verbe utilisé) **range ta chambre – je l'ai déjà fait** go and tidy up your room – I've already done it ▪ **vous le lui expliquerez mieux que je ne saurais le ~** you'll explain it to her better than I could ▪ **tu lui écriras ? – oui, je le ferai** will you write to him ? – yes I will ▪ **puis-je prendre cette chaise ? – (mais) faites donc!** *sout* may I take this chair ? – please do *ou* by all means!

◇ *vi* [agir] to do ▪ **fais comme chez toi** [à l'arrivée de qqn] make yourself at home ▪ **fais comme chez toi, surtout!** *iron* you've got a nerve!, don't mind me! *iron* ▪ **faites comme vous voulez** do as you please ▪ **fais comme tu veux!** [ton irrité] suit yourself! ▪ **je le lui ai rendu – tu as bien fait!** I gave it back to him – you did the right thing *ou* you did right! ▪ **pourquoi l'as-tu acheté ? – je croyais bien ~!** why did you buy it ? – I thought it was a good idea! ▪ **tu ferais bien d'y réfléchir** you'd do well to *ou* you should *ou* you'd better think about it! ▪ **pour bien ~, il faudrait réserver aujourd'hui** the best thing would be to book today, ideally we should book today ▪ **ça commence à bien ~!** enough is enough!

◇ *v impers* **1.** MÉTÉOR : **il fait chaud/froid** it's hot/cold ▪ **il faisait nuit** it was dark ▪ **il fait (du) soleil** the sun is shining **2.** *loc* **c'en est fait de** *sout* : **c'en est fait de vous** you've had it, you're done for ▪ **c'est bien fait pour toi** it serves you right.

◇ *v aux* **1.** [provoquer une réaction] : **tu l'as fait rougir** you made her blush ▪ **ça me fait dormir** it puts *ou* sends me to sleep **2.** [forcer à] to make, to have ▪ **fais-moi penser à le lui demander** remind me to ask him ▪ **faites-le attendre** [pour qu'il s'impatiente] let him wait ; [en lui demandant] ask him to wait ▪ **n'essaie pas de me ~ croire que...** don't try to make *ou* to have me believe that... ▪ **ne me fais pas dire ce que je n'ai pas dit** don't put words into my mouth ▪ **il me faisait ~ ses dissertations** he had me write his essays for him **3.** [commander de] : **~~ qqch par qqn** to have sb do *ou* make sthg, to have sthg done *ou* made by sb ▪ **il fait ~ ses costumes sur mesure** he has his suits tailormade.

◆ **faire dans** *v+prép fam* **il ne fait pas dans le détail** he doesn't bother about details ▪ **son entreprise fait maintenant dans les produits de luxe** her company now produces luxury items.

◆ **se faire** ◇ *vp (emploi réfléchi)* **1.** [réussir] : **elle s'est faite seule** she's a self-made woman **2.** [se forcer à] : **se ~ pleurer/vomir** to make o.s.cry/vomit.

◇ *vp (emploi réciproque)* : **se ~ la guerre** to wage war on each other.

◇ *vp (emploi passif)* **1.** [être à la mode] to be fashionable, to be in fashion ▪ **les salopettes ne se font plus** dungarees are out of fashion **2.** [être convenable] : **ça ne se fait pas de demander son âge à une femme** it's rude *ou* it's not done to ask a woman her age **3.** [être réalisé] : **sans argent le film ne se fera pas** without money the film will never be made ■ **les choses se font petit à petit** things evolve gradually ■ **je dois signer un nouveau contrat, mais je ne sais pas quand cela va se ~** I'm going to sign a new contract, but I don't know when that will be ■ **tu pourrais me prêter 1 500 euros ? – ça pourrait se ~** could you lend me 1,500 euros ? – that should be possible ■ *(tournure impersonnelle)* **comment se fait-il que... ?** how come *ou* how is it that... ? ■ **il pourrait se ~ que...** it might *ou* may be that..., it's possible that... ■ **c'est ce qui se fait de mieux en papiers peints lavables** it's the best washable wallpaper available.

◇ *vpi* **1.** [se former] : **les couples se font et se défont** people get together and separate **2.** *(suivi d'un infin)* **se ~ opérer** to have an operation ■ **se ~ tuer** to get killed ■ **se ~ couper les cheveux** to have one's hair cut **3.** [devenir] to become ■ **sa voix se fit plus grave** his voice became deeper ■ **s'il arrive à l'heure, je veux bien me ~ nonne!** *fam* if he arrives on time, I'll eat my hat! ■ *(tournure impersonnelle)* **il se fait tard** it's getting late **4.** [s'améliorer - fromage] to ripen ; [- vin] to mature ■ **mes chaussures me serrent – elles vont se ~** my shoes feel tight – they'll stretch.

◇ *vpt* **1.** [fabriquer] : **elle se fait ses vêtements** she makes her own clothes **2.** [effectuer sur soi] : **il se fait ses piqûres seul** he gives himself his own injections ■ **je me suis fait une natte** I've plaited my hair ‖ [se maquiller] : **se ~ les ongles** to do one's nails ■ **se ~ les yeux** to make up one's eyes **3.** *fam* [gagner] : **elle se fait 4000 euros par mois** she earns 4,000 euros per month, she gets 4,000 euros every month **4.** *fam* [s'accorder] : **on se fait un film/un petit café ?** what about going to see a film/going for a coffee ? ■ **on s'est fait les trois musées dans la journée** we did the three museums in one day **5.** *fam* [supporter] : **il faut se la ~!** she's a real pain! **6.** △ *arg crime* [tuer] to kill, to bump off ■ [agresser] to beat up **7.** ▲ [posséder sexuellement] to screw▲, to lay▲.

◆ **se faire à** *vp+prép* to get used to.

◆ **s'en faire** *vpi* to worry ■ **je ne m'en fais pas pour lui** I'm not worried about him ■ **elle s'en souviendra, ne t'en fais pas!** she'll remember, don't you worry! ■ **encore au lit ? tu ne t'en fais pas!** still in bed ? you're taking it easy, aren't you ? ■ **tu as ouvert mon courrier ? faut pas t'en ~!** *fam* you've opened my mail ? you've got some nerve *ou* don't mind me!

faire-part [fɛrpar] *nm inv* [dans la presse] announcement ■ **~ de décès** death notice ■ **~ de mariage** wedding announcement ‖ [carte] *card sent to family or friends announcing a birth, wedding, death etc.*

faire-valoir [fɛrvalwar] *nm inv* **1.** THÉÂTRE stooge, straight man ■ **c'est lui le ~ de Robert** he acts as straight man to Robert **2.** AGRIC farming ■ **exploitation** *ou* **terres en ~ direct** owner farm.

fair-play [fɛrplɛ] ◇ *nm inv* fair play, fair-mindedness.
◇ *adj inv* fair-minded ■ **il est ~** [joueur] he plays fair ; *fig* he has a sense of fair play.

faisabilité [fəzabilite] *nf* feasibility.

faisable [fəzabl] *adj* [réalisable] feasible ■ [possible] possible ■ **ce n'est pas ~ par un enfant** no child could do it ■ **tu peux être là à 14 h? – c'est ~** can you come at 2 o'clock? – I should think so.

faisait *etc v* ▻ **faire.**

faisan [fəzɑ̃] *nm* **1.** ZOOL (cock) pheasant **2.** *fam péj* crook, con-man.

faisandé, e [fəzɑ̃de] *adj* **1.** CULIN gamy, high **2.** [goût, littérature] decadent.

faisander [3] [fəzɑ̃de] *vt* CULIN to hang.
◆ **se faisander** *vpi* **1.** CULIN to get high **2.** [pourrir] to rot.

faisane [fəzan] *adj f & nf* : **(poule) ~** (hen) pheasant.

faisant [fəzɑ̃] *p prés* ▻ **faire.**

faisceau, x [fɛso] *nm* **1.** [rayon] beam, ray ■ **~ cathodique** cathode ray ■ **~ électronique** electron beam ■ **~ hertzien** radio beam ■ **~ lumineux** light beam **2.** [gerbe] cluster, bundle ■ **~ aimanté** bunch of magnets ■ **~ de fils** wiring harness ■ **~ de preuves** *fig* accumulation of evidence **3.** MIL [pyramides d'armes] stack of arms ■ **former/rompre les ~x** to stack/to unstack arms **4.** ANAT & BOT fascicle **5.** RAIL : **~ de voies** group of sidings **6.** ANTIQ & HIST fasces ■ **les ~x consulaires** *ou* **des licteurs** the fasces of the consuls *ou* lictors.

faiseur, euse [fəzœr, øz] *nm, f* **1.** [artisan] maker ■ **le bon ~** a first-class tailor **2.** *péj* **faiseuse d'anges** back-street abortionist ■ **~ d'embarras** fusspot ■ **~ de miracles** miracle worker ■ **~ de vers** poetaster **3.** *péj* [escroc] swindler, dishonest businessman ■ [hâbleur] show-off, braggart.

faisselle [fɛsɛl] *nf* **1.** [récipient] cheese basket **2.** [fromage] fromage frais *(packaged in its own draining basket).*

fait[1] [fɛ] *nm* **1.** [action] act, deed ■ **l'erreur est de son ~** it was his mistake ▶ **~ d'armes** feat of arms ■ **~s de guerre** acts of war ■ **les ~s et gestes de qqn** everything sb says and does, sb's every move ■ **hauts ~s** heroic deeds ■ **prendre qqn sur le ~** to catch sb red-handed ■ **prendre ~ et cause pour qqn** to side with sb

2. [événement] event, fact, occurrence ■ **~ notoire** fact of common knowledge ■ **~ nouveau** new development ■ **au moment des ~s** at the time ■ **racontez-nous les ~s** tell us what happened ■ **les ~s qui lui sont reprochés** the charge laid against him ■ **de ce ~** thereby ■ **il est pénalisé par le seul ~ de son divorce** the very fact that he's divorced puts him at a disadvantage ■ **par le seul ~ que** (solely) because of, due (solely) to the fact that ▶ **~ (juridique)** DR fact ■ **~ concluant** DR conclusive evidence ■ **~s constitutifs de délit** DR factors that constitute an offence ■ **~ exprès : c'est (comme) un** *ou* **on dirait un ~ exprès** it's almost as if it was deliberate ■ **comme (par) un ~ exprès, il n'avait pas de monnaie** funnily enough, he had no change

3. [réalité] fact ■ **c'est un ~** it's a (matter of) fact ■ **le ~ est que nous étions en retard** the fact is we were late ▶ **placer** *ou* **mettre qqn devant le ~ accompli** to present sb with a fait accompli ■ **considérer qqch comme un ~ acquis** to take sthg for granted ■ **état de ~** (inescapable) fact ■ **le ~ est!** *fam* that's right!, you've said it!

4. [sujet, question] point ■ **aller (droit) au ~** to go straight to the point ■ **venons-en au ~** let's come *ou* get to the point

5. *loc* **dire son ~ à qqn** to give sb a piece of one's mind.

◆ **au fait** *loc adv* by the way, incidentally ■ **au ~, on pourrait peut-être y aller à pied?** by the way, couldn't we walk there?

◆ **au fait de** *loc prép* well aware of, fully informed about ■ **mettre qqn au ~ de la situation** to inform sb about the situation.

◆ **de fait** *loc adj* **1.** DR actual, de facto

2. [en affirmation] : **il est de ~ que** it is true *ou* a fact that.

◆ **de fait, en fait** *loc adv* in fact, actually, as a matter of fact ■ **en ~, il n'est pas mon père** actually *ou* in fact he isn't my father.

◆ **du fait de** *loc prép* because of, due to, on account of.

◆ **du fait que** *loc conj* because (of the fact that).

◆ **en fait de** *loc prép* **1.** [en guise de] by way of ■ **en ~ de nourriture, il n'y a qu'une boîte de sardines** there's only a can of sardines by way of food

2. [au lieu de] instead of ■ **en ~ de chien, c'était un loup** it wasn't a dog at all, it was a wolf.

fait[2]**, e** [fɛ, fɛt] ◇ *pp* ▻ **faire.**
◇ *adj* **1.** [formé] : **elle a la jambe bien ~e** she's got shapely *ou* nice legs ■ **une femme fort bien ~e** a very good-looking woman ▶ **~ au tour** shapely, well-turned **2.** [mûr] mature, ripe ■ **un fromage ~** a fully ripened cheese ■ **trop ~** over-ripe **3.** [maquillé] made-up ■ **elle a les yeux ~s** she's wearing eye make-up **4.** [prêt] : **tout ~** [vêtement] ready-made, ready-to-wear ; [tournure] set, ready-made ■ **une expression toute ~e** a set phrase, a cliché.

faîtage [fɛtaʒ] *nm* [poutre] ridgeboard, ridgepiece ■ [couverture] ridge tiling.

fait divers *(pl* **faits divers)**, **fait-divers** *(pl* **faits-divers)** [fɛdivɛr] *nm* **1.** [événement] news story, news item **2.** [rubrique] (news) in brief ■ [page] news in brief.

faîte [fɛt] *nm* **1.** GÉOGR crest, top **2.** [sommet] top, summit **3.** CONSTR ridgepiece **4.** [summum] climax, acme *sout* ▪ **le ~ de la gloire** the height of glory ▪ **atteindre le ~ de sa carrière** to reach the climax of one's career.

faites *v* ▻ **faire.**

faîtière [fɛtjɛr] <> *adj f* ▻ **lucarne,** ▻ **tuile.**
<> *nf* crest tile, ridge tile.

faitout *nm,* **fait-tout** *nm inv* [fɛtu] stewpot, cooking pot.

faix [fɛ] *nm litt* burden, load ▪ **ployer sous le ~** to bend beneath the load.

fakir [fakir] *nm* **1.** RELIG fakir **2.** [magicien] conjurer.

falafel [falafɛl] *nm* CULIN falafel.

falaise [falɛz] *nf* cliff ▪ **~ littorale** *ou* **vive** sea cliff.

falbalas [falbala] *nmpl péj* frills (and furbelows) ▪ **une architecture sans ~** an unadorned style of architecture.
◆ **à falbalas** *loc adj* [robe, rideau] flouncy, frilly.

Falkland [folklɑ̃d] *npr fpl* : **les (îles) ~** the Falkland Islands, the Falklands ▪ **aux îles ~** in the Falkland Islands.

fallacieux, euse [falasjø, øz] *adj* **1.** [trompeur] deceptive, misleading, fallacious ▪ **l'espoir ~ de les rencontrer** the illusory hope of meeting them ▪ **sous un prétexte ~** on some pretext **2.** [spécieux] insincere, specious.

falloir [69] [falwar] *v impers*

> **A.** EXPRIME LE BESOIN
> **B.** EXPRIME L'OBLIGATION
> **C.** DONNE UNE RAISON

A. EXPRIME LE BESOIN

1. [gén] : **pour ce tricot, il faut des aiguilles n°6** to knit this jumper, you need number 6 needles ▪ **il faut deux heures pour y aller** it takes two hours to get there ▪ **faut-il vraiment tout ce matériel?** is all this equipment really necessary? ▪ **il est inspecteur des impôts – il en faut!** *hum* he's a tax inspector – someone has to do it! ▪ **ajoutez de la moutarde, juste ce qu'il faut** add some mustard, not too much ▪ **je crois que nous avons trouvé l'homme qu'il nous faut** [pour un poste] I think we've found the right person for the job ▪ **c'est tout ce qu'il vous fallait?** [dans une boutique] anything else? ▪ **il me faudrait deux filets de cabillaud, s'il vous plaît** I'd like two cod fillets, please ▪ **j'ai plus d'argent qu'il n'en faut** I've got more money than I need ▪ **il ne lui en faut pas beaucoup pour se mettre en colère** it doesn't take a lot *ou* much to make her angry ● **il t'a fait ses excuses, qu'est-ce qu'il te faut de plus?** *fam* he apologized, what more do you want? ▪ **il n'est pas très beau – qu'est-ce qu'il te faut!** *fam* he's not really good-looking – you're hard to please! ▪ **ce n'est pas très cher – qu'est-ce qu'il te faut!** *fam* it's not very expensive – well, what do you call expensive then? ▪ **je suis satisfait de lui – il t'en faut peu!** *fam* I'm satisfied with him – you're not hard to please! ▪ **il faut ce qu'il faut!** *fam* well, you might as well do things in style!
2. *(suivi d'une complétive au subj)* **il faudrait que nous nous réunissions plus souvent** we should have more regular meetings

B. EXPRIME L'OBLIGATION

1. [gén] : **je lui ai dit – le fallait-il vraiment?** I told him – was it really necessary *ou* did you really have to? ▪ **il ne fallait pas** *fam* [en recevant un cadeau] you shouldn't have ▪ **s'il le faut** if I/we must, if necessary
2. *(suivi de l'infin)* **il faut m'excuser** please forgive me, you must forgive me ▪ **j'ai besoin d'aide – d'accord, que faut-il faire?** I need help – all right, what do you want me to do? ▪ **c'est un film qu'il faut voir (absolument)** this film's a must ▪ **il faut bien se souvenir/se dire que...** it has to be remembered/said that... ▪ **s'il fallait faire attention à tout ce que l'on dit!** if one had to mind one's Ps and Qs all the time! ▪ **il ne fallait pas commencer!** you shouldn't have started! ▪ **j'ai faim – il fallait le dire!** I'm hungry – why didn't you say so? ▪ **qui faut-il croire?** who is to be believed? ▪ **il me fallait lui mentir** *sout* I had to lie to him
3. *(suivi d'une complétive au subj)* **il a fallu que je m'absente** I had to go out for a while
4. *(au conditionnel, sens affaibli)* **il aurait fallu prévenir la police** the police should have been called ▪ **attention, il ne faudrait pas que tu te trompes!** careful, you'd better not make any mistakes! ▪ **il ne faudrait pas me prendre pour une idiote!** do you think I'm stupid?
5. [en intensif] : **il faut le voir pour le croire!** *fam* it has to be seen to be believed! ▪ **il faut le faire** *fam* [en regardant un acrobate, un magicien] : **il faut le faire!** that's amazing! ▪ **ne pas fermer sa voiture, faut le faire!** it takes a fool *ou* you've got to be completely stupid to leave your car unlocked! ▪ **ça représente un cheval – il fallait le deviner!** it's supposed to be a horse – I'd never have known! ▪ **il fallait l'entendre!** you should have heard him!

C. DONNE UNE RAISON

1. [fatalité] : **il a fallu que le téléphone sonne juste à ce moment-là!** the phone had to ring just then!
2. [pour justifier, expliquer] : **il faut que tu aies fait mal à Rex pour qu'il t'ait mordu!** you must have hurt Rex to make him bite you!
◆ **s'en falloir** *v impers* : **il s'en faut de beaucoup qu'il n'ait fini!** he's far from having finished! ▪ **peu s'en est fallu que je ne manque le train!** I very nearly *ou* almost missed the train! ▪ **il s'en est fallu de rien** *ou* **d'un cheveu** *fam ou* **d'un doigt** *fam* **qu'il ne fût décapité** he came within inches of having his head chopped off ● **tant s'en faut** far from it, not by a long way.

fallu [faly] *pp* ▻ **falloir.**

falot¹ [falo] *nm* lantern.

falot², e [falo, ɔt] *adj* colourless, bland, vapid *sout* ▪ **c'est un personnage assez ~** he's rather insipid.

falsifiable [falsifjabl] *adj* **1.** [signature, document] falsifiable, forgeable **2.** PHILOS which can be falsified.

falsificateur, trice [falsifikatœr, tris] *nm, f* falsifier, forger.

falsification [falsifikasjɔ̃] *nf* falsification, faking, forgery ▪ **~ des registres** tampering with registers.

falsifier [9] [falsifje] *vt* [vin, lait] to adulterate ▪ [document, signature] to forge, to falsify ▪ **les comptes ont été falsifiés** the accounts have been falsified.

falzar△ [falzar] *nm* trousers *UK,* pants *US.*

famé, e [fame] *adj* ▻ **mal famé, e.**

famélique [famelik] *adj* [chat] scrawny ▪ [prisonnier] half-starved.

fameusement [famøzmɑ̃] *adv fam* very, really ▪ **il est ~ rusé!** he's really crafty!

fameux, euse [famø, øz] *adj* **1.** [célèbre] famous, renowned, well-known **2.** *fam* [bon - gén] excellent, brilliant ; [- repas, mets] excellent, delicious ▪ **~, ton gâteau** your cake is delicious **3.** [en intensif] : **c'est un ~ mystère** it's quite a mystery ▪ **un ~ exemple de courage** an outstanding example of courage **4.** [dont on parle] famous ▪ **et où as-tu acheté ce ~ bouquin?** where did you buy the book you were talking about? **5.** *iron* so-called ▪ **c'est ça, ton ~ trésor?** is THAT your famous treasure?

familial, e, aux [familjal, o] *adj* **1.** [de famille] domestic, family *(modif)* ▪ **vie/réunion ~e** family life/meeting ▪ **une atmosphère ~e** a friendly atmosphere ▪ **querelles ~es** domestic quarrels ▪ **cet élève a des problèmes familiaux** this pupil has problems at home ▪ **maladie ~e** hereditary disease *ou* condition ● **la cuisine ~e** home cooking ▪ **quotient/revenu ~** family quotient/income **2.** COMM family-sized, economy *(modif)* ▪ **emballage ~** economy-size *ou* family pack.

familiarisation [familjarizasjɔ̃] *nf* familiarization.

familiariser [3] [familjarize] *vt* : **~ qqn avec** to make sb familiar *ou* to familiarize sb with, to get sb used to.
◆ **se familiariser avec** *vp+prép* to familiarize o.s. with ▪ **se ~ avec une technique/langue** to master a technique/language.

familiarité [familjarite] *nf* **1.** [désinvolture] familiarity, casualness **2.** [connaissance] : **il a une grande ~ avec l'œuvre de Proust** he has a close *ou* an intimate knowledge of the work of Proust.
◆ **familiarités** *nfpl* liberties, undue familiarity ■ **s'autoriser** *ou* **prendre des ~s avec qqn** to take liberties *ou* to be overfamiliar with sb.

familier, ère [familje, ɛr] *adj* **1.** [connu] familiar ■ **~ à : le problème m'est ~** I am familiar with the problem ■ **la maison lui était familière** he remembered the house quite clearly ■ **ce spectacle/bruit lui était ~** it looked/sounded familiar to him **2.** [habituel] usual ■ **une tâche familière** a routine task ■ **~ à : ce genre de travail leur est ~** they are used to this kind of work **3.** [apprivoisé] domestic, tame **4.** *péj* [cavalier] overfamiliar ■ **je n'aime pas leurs attitudes familières/les gens trop ~s** I don't like their offhand ways/people who are overfamiliar **5.** LING colloquial, informal.
◆ **familier** *nm* **1.** [ami] familiar, friend **2.** [client] habitué, regular ■ **les ~s de ce café** this café's regulars.

familièrement [familjɛrmɑ̃] *adv* **1.** [amicalement] familiarly, informally, casually **2.** [couramment] colloquially, in conversation ■ **la saxifrage, ~ appelée mignonnette** saxifrage, commonly named London pride.

famille [famij] *nf* **1.** [foyer] family ■ **la ~ Laverne** the Laverne family, the Lavernes ■ **revenu par ~** income per household ■ **il rentre dans sa ~ tous les week-ends** he goes back home every weekend ▶ **~ monoparentale** single-parent *ou* lone-parent family ■ **~ nombreuse, grande ~** *Suisse* large family ■ **~ nucléaire** nuclear family ■ **~ recomposée** blended family **2.** [enfants] family, children ■ **comment va la petite ~?** *fam* how are the children? **3.** [tous les parents] family, relatives ■ **ils sont de la même ~** they're related ■ **prévenir la ~** to inform sb's relatives ; DR to inform the next of kin ■ **c'est une ~ de danseurs** they're all dancers in their family, they're a family of dancers ■ **les 200 ~s** *the wealthiest families in France* **4.** BOT, LING & ZOOL family, group ■ **~ de langues** group of languages ■ **~ de mots/plantes** family of words/plants ▮ CHIM & PHYS chain, family ■ **~ de l'uranium** uranium series ▮ MATH & MUS family ■ **la ~ des instruments à vent** the wind family **5.** [idéologie] obedience, persuasion ■ **de la même ~ politique** of the same political persuasion.
◆ **de bonne famille** *loc adj* well brought up, from a good family.
◆ **de famille** ◇ *loc adj* [cercle, médecin, biens] family *(modif)*.
◇ *loc adv* : **c'est** *ou* **cela tient de ~** it runs in the family, it's in the blood.
◆ **des familles** *loc adj fam* cosy, nice (little).
◆ **en famille** *loc adv* **1.** [en groupe] : **passer Noël en ~** to spend Christmas with one's family *ou* at home **2.** [en confiance] : **se sentir en ~** to feel at home.

famine [famin] *nf* famine, starvation ■ **ils souffrent de la ~** they're victims of the famine, they're starving.

fan [fan] *nmf* fan ■ **c'est un ~ de jazz** he is a jazz fan.

fana [fana] *fam* ◇ *adj* enthusiastic, crazy ■ **il est ~ de sport** he is crazy about sport.
◇ *nmf* fan ■ **c'est une ~ de cinéma** she loves the cinema.

fanal, aux [fanal, o] *nm* lantern, lamp ■ **~ de locomotive** headlight.

fanatique [fanatik] ◇ *adj* **1.** RELIG & *péj* fanatical, bigoted, zealous **2.** [passionné] enthusiastic ■ **il est ~ des jeux vidéo** he's mad about video games ■ **je ne suis pas ~ de la bière** I'm not (that) keen on beer.
◇ *nmf* **1.** RELIG & *péj* zealot **2.** [partisan] fan, fanatic.

fanatiser [3] [fanatize] *vt* to fanaticize, to make fanatical ■ **suivi par une foule fanatisée** followed by a frenzied crowd.

fanatisme [fanatism] *nm* fanaticism.

fan-club [fanklœb] (*pl* **fans-clubs**) *nm* **1.** [d'un artiste] fan club **2.** *hum* admirers, supporters, fan club *fig.*

fane [fan] *nf* **1.** [de légumes] top ■ **~s de carotte/radis** carrot/radish tops **2.** [feuille morte] (dead *ou* fallen) leaf.

faner [3] [fane] ◇ *vi* **1.** AGRIC to make hay **2.** [se flétrir] to wither.
◇ *vt* **1.** AGRIC to ted, to toss **2.** [décolorer] to fade ■ **fané par le soleil** faded by the sun, sun-bleached ■ **des couleurs fanées** faded *ou* washed-out colours.
◆ **se faner** *vpi* **1.** BOT to fade, to wither **2.** [perdre son éclat] to wane, to fade ■ **sa beauté s'est fanée** her beauty has lost its bloom *ou* faded.

fanfare [fɑ̃far] *nf* [air] fanfare ■ [orchestre - civil] brass band ; [- militaire] military band.
◆ **en fanfare** *loc adv* [réveiller] noisily, brutally ■ **annoncer la nouvelle en ~** to trumpet the news.

fanfaron, onne [fɑ̃farɔ̃, ɔn] ◇ *adj* boastful, swaggering ■ **d'un air ~** boastfully.
◇ *nm, f* boaster, braggart, swaggerer ■ **faire le ~** to crow ■ **ah, tu ne fais plus le ~, maintenant?** ah, so you're not so pleased with yourself now?

fanfaronnade [fɑ̃farɔnad] *nf* **1.** [acte] bravado *(U)* ■ **par ~** out of (sheer) bravado **2.** [remarque] boast.

fanfaronner [3] [fɑ̃farɔne] *vi* to boast, to brag, to swagger.

fanfreluche [fɑ̃frəlyʃ] *nf* : **des ~s** frills (and furbelows).

fange [fɑ̃ʒ] *nf litt* mire ■ **vivre dans la ~** to live a life of degradation.

fanion [fanjɔ̃] *nm* flag, pennant.

fanon [fanɔ̃] *nm* **1.** [d'une baleine] whalebone plate **2.** [bajoue - d'un bœuf] dew-lap ; [- d'une dinde] lappet, wattle **3.** [d'un cheval] fetlock.

fantaisie [fɑ̃tezi] *nf* **1.** [imagination] imagination ■ **donner libre cours à sa ~** to give free rein to one's imagination ■ **être plein de ~** to be fanciful ■ **manquer de ~** [personne] to lack imagination, to be lacking in imagination ; [vie] to be monotonous *ou* uneventful ▮ *péj* fantasy ■ **vous interprétez le règlement avec beaucoup de ~** you have a rather imaginative interpretation of the rules ■ **le récit relève de la plus haute ~** the story is highly imaginative **2.** [lubie] whim ■ **c'est sa dernière ~** it's his latest whim ■ **et s'il lui prend la ~ de partir?** what if he should take it into his head to leave? ■ **s'offrir une ~** to give o.s. a treat, to treat o.s. ■ **cette (petite) ~ va vous coûter cher** *péj* you'll regret this little extravagance ■ **n'en faire qu'à sa ~** to do exactly as one pleases **3.** [bibelot] fancy ■ **un magasin de ~s** a novelty shop **4.** ART & LITTÉR (piece of) fantasy ■ MUS fantasy, fantasia **5.** *(comme adj inv)* [simulé] imitation ■ **bijou ~** piece of costume jewellery ▮ [peu classique] fancy ■ **des boutons ~** fancy buttons.
◆ **de fantaisie** *loc adj* [à bon marché] novelty *(modif)* ■ **article de ~** novelty.

fantaisiste [fɑ̃tezist] ◇ *adj* **1.** [farfelu] eccentric, unconventional **2.** [inventé] fanciful.
◇ *nmf* **1.** THÉÂTRE variety artist, sketcher **2.** *péj* [dilettante] joker, clown.

fantasmagorie [fɑ̃tasmagɔri] *nf* **1.** [féerie] phantasmagoria **2.** [effets de style] gothic effects.

fantasmagorique [fɑ̃tasmagɔrik] *adj* magical, phantasmagorical *litt.*

fantasmatique [fɑ̃tasmatik] *adj* fantasy *(modif)*.

fantasme [fɑ̃tasm] *nm* fantasy.

fantasmer [3] [fɑ̃tasme] *vi* to fantasize ■ **~ sur qqch/qqn** to fantasize about sthg/sb ■ **faire ~ qqn** [sexuellement] to turn sb on.

fantasque [fɑ̃task] *adj* **1.** [capricieux] capricious, whimsical **2.** *litt* [bizarre] odd, weird.

fantassin [fɑ̃tasɛ̃] *nm* foot soldier, infantry man.

fantastique [fɑ̃tastik] ◇ *adj* **1.** [fabuleux - animal, personnage] fantastical, fabulous, fantasy *(modif)* **2.** CINÉ & LITTÉR : **roman ~** gothic novel ■ **cinéma ~** science-fiction *ou* fantasy films **3.** *fam* [formidable] great, brilliant **4.** [étonnant] extraordinary, unbelievable ■ **il a un courage ~** he's incredibly courageous.

<> *nm* : **le ~** [l'étrange] the fantastic, the supernatural ; [genre] the gothic (genre).

fantoche [fɑ̃tɔʃ] *nm péj* puppet ■ *(comme adj)* **un gouvernement/souverain ~** a puppet government/king ■ **une armée ~** a non-existent army.

fantomatique [fɑ̃tɔmatik] *adj* phantom *(modif)*, ghostly.

fantôme [fɑ̃tom] *nm* **1.** [revenant] ghost, phantom, spirit **2.** *litt* [apparence] ghostly image *ou* shape, ghost ■ **un ~ de parti politique** a phantom political party **3.** *(comme adj)* **cabinet ~** shadow cabinet ■ **société ~** bogus company ■ **où est ce rapport ~?** where is this supposed report?

FAO <> *nf* (*abr de* **fabrication assistée par ordinateur**) CAM.
<> *npr f* (*abr de* **Food and Agricultural Organisation**) FAO.

faon [fɑ̃] *nm* fawn.

FAQ [fak] (*abr de* **Frequently Asked Questions**) *nf* FAQ.

faquin [fakɛ̃] *nm arch* knave.

far [far] *nm* : **~ (breton)** *Breton custard tart with prunes.*

farad [farad] *nm* farad.

faramineux, euse [faraminø, øz] *adj fam* [somme, fortune] huge, tremendous ■ **c'est ~ ce qu'elle a pu dépenser!** the amount of money she spent was incredible!

farandole [farɑ̃dɔl] *nf* **1.** DANSE farandole **2.** [au restaurant] : **et pour finir, la ~ des fromages/desserts** finally, choose from our cheese tray/dessert trolley.

faraud, e [faro, od] <> *adj* boastful ■ **il n'était pas si ~ pendant l'orage** he wasn't so cocky during the storm.
<> *nm, f* : **faire le ~** to show off.

farce[1] [fars] <> *nf* **1.** [tour] practical joke, prank, trick ■ **faire une ~ à qqn** to play a trick on sb ■ **la situation tournait à la ~** things were becoming farcical ■ **une mauvaise ~** a joke gone wrong **2.** LITTÉR & THÉÂTRE farce ■ **la vie n'est qu'une ~** life is nothing but a farce.
<> *adj vieilli* comical.
◆ **farces et attrapes** *nfpl* assorted tricks ■ **magasin de ~s et attrapes** joke shop.

farce[2] [fars] *nf* CULIN forcemeat, stuffing.

farceur, euse [farsœr, øz] <> *adj* mischievous ■ **il a l'œil ~** he has a waggish look ■ **ils sont ~s** they like playing tricks.
<> *nm, f* practical joker, prankster ■ **petit ~!** you rascal!

farci, e [farsi] *adj* CULIN stuffed.

farcir [32] [farsir] *vt* **1.** CULIN to stuff **2.** *fam* [remplir] : **~ qqch avec** *ou* **de** to fill sthg choc-a-block with, to cram sthg with ■ **elle avait la tête farcie de superstitions** her head was crammed full of superstitious beliefs.
◆ **se farcir** *vpt* : **se ~ qqn** *fam* [le subir] to have to put up with *ou* to have to take sb ; [sexuellement] ▲ to have it off△ with *UK* *ou* to screw△ sb ■ **se ~ qqch** *fam* [le subir] to have to put up with *ou* to have to take sthg ; [le boire] to knock sthg back, to down sthg ; [le manger] to stuff o.s. with sthg ■ **son beau-frère, faut se le ~!** his brother-in-law is a real pain!

fard [far] *nm* **1.** [produit] colour *(for make-up)* ■ **~ à joues** blusher ■ **~ à paupières** eyeshadow **2.** *vieilli* [maquillage] : **le ~** [gén] make-up ; THÉÂTRE greasepaint.
◆ **sans fard** <> *loc adj* straightforward, frank.
<> *loc adv* straightforwardly, frankly.

farde [fard] *nf Belgique* **1.** [cahier] exercise book **2.** [chemise] folder **3.** [cartouche] carton *(of cigarettes)*.

fardeau, x [fardo] *nm* **1.** [poids] burden, load **2.** [contrainte] burden, millstone.

farder [3] [farde] *vt* **1.** [maquiller] to make up *(sép)* **2.** [cacher] to conceal, to mask ■ **~ la réalité/ses sentiments** to disguise the truth/one's feelings **3.** COMM to camouflage.
◆ **se farder** *vp (emploi réfléchi)* to make up one's face, to put one's make-up on.

farfadet [farfadɛ] *nm* imp, elf, goblin.

farfelu, e [farfəly] *fam* <> *adj* crazy, strange, cranky.
<> *nm, f* oddball, weirdo, crackpot.

farfouiller [3] [farfuje] *fam* <> *vi* to grope *ou* to rummage about ■ **ils ont farfouillé dans tous les tiroirs** they've been rummaging about in all the drawers.
<> *vt* [chercher] : **qu'est-ce que tu farfouilles?** what are you after?

faribole [faribɔl] *nf litt* piece of nonsense ■ **~s!** nonsense!

farine [farin] *nf* **1.** CULIN flour ■ **~ d'avoine** oatmeal ■ **~ complète** wholemeal flour *UK*, wholewheat flour ■ **~ de froment/seigle** wheat/rye flour ■ **~ de maïs** cornflour ■ **~ animale** animal flour **2.** [poudre] powder.

fariner [3] [farine] *vt* to flour, to sprinkle flour over ■ **farinez le moule** dredge the tin with flour, flour the tin all over.

farineux, euse [farinø, øz] *adj* **1.** [fariné] floury, flour-covered **2.** [pâteux - poire] mealy ; [- pomme de terre] floury **3.** [au goût de farine] chalky, floury **4.** [féculent] farinaceous *spéc*, starchy.
◆ **farineux** *nm* starchy food ■ **évitez les ~ pendant quelque temps** avoid starch for a while.

farlouche [farluʃ] *nf Québec* *mixture of raisins and molasses used in tarts.*

farniente [farnjɛnte, farnjɑ̃t] *nm* idleness, laziness ■ **amateur de ~** idler.

farouche [faruʃ] *adj* **1.** [caractère] fierce, unflinching ■ [volonté] fierce **2.** [animal] wild ■ **un animal peu ~** a tame animal ‖ [personne] shy, coy **3.** [brutal] cruel, savage.

farouchement [faruʃmɑ̃] *adv* **1.** [ardemment] definitely, unquestionably ■ **je suis ~ contre!** I am definitely against it! ■ **il est toujours ~ décidé à ne pas bouger** he's still adamant he won't move **2.** [violemment] fiercely, savagely.

fart [far(t)] *nm* skiing wax.

farter [3] [farte] *vt* to wax *(skis)*.

Far-West [farwɛst] *nm* : **le ~** the Far West.

fascicule [fasikyl] *nm* **1.** [partie d'un ouvrage] instalment, part, section ■ **publié par ~s** published in parts **2.** [livret] booklet, manual.

fascinant, e [fasinɑ̃, ɑ̃t] *adj* captivating, fascinating.

fascination [fasinasjɔ̃] *nf* fascination ■ **exercer une ~ sur** to be fascinating to.

fasciner [3] [fasine] *vt* [charmer - suj: spectacle] to captivate, to fascinate ■ **elle est fascinée par ce garçon** she has been bewitched by that boy, she is under that boy's spell.

fascisant, e [faʃizɑ̃, ɑ̃t] *adj* fascist, fascistic, pro-fascist.

fascisme [faʃism] *nm* **1.** [gén] fascism **2.** HIST Fascism.

fasciste [faʃist] *adj & nmf* **1.** [gén] fascist **2.** HIST Fascist.

fasse *v* ▻ **faire**.

faste [fast] <> *adj* [favorable - année] good ; [- jour] good, lucky.
<> *nm* [luxe] sumptuousness, splendour ■ **avec ~** sumptuously, with pomp (and circumstance), munificently *sout* ■ **sans ~** simply, quietly, plainly.
◆ **fastes** *nmpl litt* pomp.

fast-food [fastfud] *nm* fast-food restaurant.

fastidieux, euse [fastidjø, øz] *adj* boring, tiresome, tedious.

fastoche [fastɔʃ] *adj fam* dead easy ■ **c'est ~** it's dead easy, it's a doddle.

fastueux, euse [fastɥø, øz] *adj* magnificent, munificent *sout*, sumptuous.

fat [fa(t)] *litt* <> *adj m* bumptious, conceited, self-satisfied ■ **prendre un air ~** to look smug.
<> *nm* smug person.

fatal, e, als [fatal] *adj* **1.** [fixé par le sort] fateful ■ **l'instant ~** the fatal moment **2.** [désastreux] disastrous, terrible **3.** [mortel - collision, blessure] fatal, mortal ▪ **porter un coup ~ à** [frapper] to deliver a deadly *ou* mortal blow to ; *fig* to administer the coup de grâce to **4.** [inévitable] inevitable.

fatalement [fatalmɑ̃] *adv* inevitably ▪ **il devait ~ perdre** he was bound to lose.

fatalisme [fatalism] *nm* fatalism.

fataliste [fatalist] ◇ *adj* fatalist, fatalistic ▪ **il est ~** he's resigned to his fate.
◇ *nmf* fatalist.

fatalité [fatalite] *nf* **1.** [sort] destiny, fate ▪ **poursuivi par la ~** pursued by fate ▪ **la ~ s'acharne contre eux** they're dogged by misfortune **2.** [circonstance fâcheuse] mischance ▪ **je le vois chaque fois que j'y vais, c'est une ~!** there must be a curse on me! every time I go there, I see him!

fatidique [fatidik] *adj* **1.** [marqué par le destin - date, jour] fated, fateful **2.** [important] crucial ▪ **c'est l'instant ~!** it's now or never!

fatigable [fatigabl] *adj* : **facilement ~** easily tired ▪ **difficilement ~** untiring.

fatigant, e [fatigɑ̃, ɑ̃t] *adj* **1.** [épuisant] tiring, wearing ▪ **c'est très ~** it's exhausting ▪ **la lumière vive est ~e pour les yeux** bright light is a strain on the eyes **2.** [agaçant] tiresome, tedious, annoying ▪ **ce que tu peux être ~!** you're a real nuisance!

fatigue [fatig] *nf* **1.** [lassitude] tiredness, weariness ▪ **je tombe** *ou* **je suis mort de ~** I'm dead on my feet **2.** [tension - physique] strain ; [- nerveuse] stress ▶ **~ musculaire** stiffness ▪ **~ nerveuse** nervous exhaustion ▪ **~ oculaire** eyestrain.

fatigué, e [fatige] *adj* **1.** [las] tired, weary ▪ **je suis très fatigué** I'm exhausted ▪ **~ de rester debout/d'attendre** tired of standing/waiting **2.** [usé - vêtement] worn ; [- livre] well-thumbed.

fatiguer [3] [fatige] ◇ *vt* **1.** [épuiser] to tire *ou* to wear out *(sép)* ▪ **si ça ne te fatigue pas trop** *hum* if you don't mind **2.** [lasser] to annoy ▪ **tu me fatigues avec tes critiques!** your constant criticism is getting on my nerves! **3.** [user - machine, moteur] to put a strain on **4.** [dialecte: remuer] : **~ la salade** to toss the (green) salad.
◇ *vi* **1.** [peiner] to grow tired, to flag ▪ **dépêche-toi, je fatigue!** hurry up, I'm getting tired! **2.** MÉCAN [faiblir] to become weakened ▪ [forcer] to bear a heavy strain **3.** NAUT to ride hard.
◆ **se fatiguer** ◇ *vpi* **1.** [s'épuiser] to get tired, to tire o.s. out ▪ **se ~ à : tu ne vas pas te ~ à tout nettoyer!** don't tire yourself out cleaning everything! **2.** [faire un effort] to push o.s. ▪ **ils ne se sont pas fatigués** they didn't exactly kill themselves **3.** [faire des efforts inutiles] : **ne te fatigue pas** don't waste your time ▪ **c'était bien la peine que je me fatigue!** I don't know why I bothered! ▪ **je me fatigue à le lui répéter** I wear myself out telling her.
◇ *vpt* : **se ~ la vue** *ou* **les yeux** to put a strain on *ou* to strain one's eyes.
◆ **se fatiguer de** *vp+prép* to get tired of.

fatma [fatma] *nf péj* North African woman.

fatras [fatra] *nm péj* **1.** [tas] clutter, jumble ▪ **tout un ~ de vieux papiers** a clutter of old papers **2.** [mélange] hotchpotch *UK*, hodgepodge *US* ▪ **un ~ de connaissances** a confused mass of knowledge.

fatuité [fatɥite] *nf* complacency, conceit, smugness.

faubourg [fobur] *nm* suburb ▪ **~ résidentiel** residential suburb ▪ **les ~s de la ville** the outskirts of the city ▪ **le ~ Saint-Antoine** *area in Paris famous for its furniture shops* ▪ **le ~ Saint-Honoré** *area of Paris well-known for its luxury shops.*

faubourien, enne [foburjɛ̃, ɛn] *adj* suburban ▪ **accent ~** working-class accent.

fauchage [foʃaʒ] *nm* cutting, reaping.

fauche [foʃ] *nf* **1.** *fam* [vol] thieving, (petty) theft ▪ [dans un magasin] shoplifting **2.** AGRIC & *vieilli* reaping.

fauché, e [foʃe] ◇ *adj* **1.** *fam* [sans argent] broke, skint *UK*, cleaned out ▪ **~ comme les blés** flat broke, stony broke *UK* **2.** AGRIC cut, reaped.
◇ *nm, f fam* penniless individual ▪ **ce sont tous des ~s** they haven't got a penny between them.

faucher [3] [foʃe] *vt* **1.** AGRIC to reap **2.** [renverser] to knock *ou* to mow down *(sép)* ▪ **les cyclistes ont été fauchés par un camion** the cyclists were knocked down by a lorry, a lorry ploughed into the cyclists **3.** [tuer] : **tous ces jeunes artistes fauchés à la fleur de l'âge** all these young artists struck down in the prime of life **4.** *fam* [voler] to pinch, to swipe ▪ **qui a fauché le sel?** who's got the salt? ▪ **je me suis encore fait ~ mon briquet!** my lighter's been pinched again!

faucheur, euse [foʃœr, øz] *nm, f* mower, reaper.
◆ **faucheuse** *nf* **1.** AGRIC mechanical reaper **2.** *litt* **la Faucheuse** the (grim) Reaper.

faucheux [foʃø] *nm* harvest spider, daddy-long-legs.

Fauchon [foʃɔ̃] *npr luxury food shop in Paris.*

faucille [fosij] *nf* sickle, reaping hook ▪ **la ~ et le marteau** the hammer and sickle.

faucon [fokɔ̃] *nm* ORNITH falcon, hawk ▪ **~ pèlerin** peregrine falcon.

fauconnerie [fokɔnri] *nf* **1.** [activité] hawking **2.** [abri] hawk-house.

fauconnier, ère [fokɔnje, ɛr] *nm, f* falconer.

faudra *etc v* ⊳ **falloir.**

faufil [fofil] *nm* basting *ou* tacking thread.

faufiler [3] [fofile] *vt* COUT to baste, to tack.
◆ **se faufiler** *vpi* to slip through, to edge ▪ **se ~ dans la foule** to weave through the crowd ▪ **se ~ entre les voitures** to weave one's way through the traffic ▪ **les enfants essayaient de se ~ au premier rang** the children were trying to sneak up to the front.

faune [fon] ◇ *nf* **1.** ZOOL fauna, animal life ▪ **la ~ et la flore** flora and fauna, wildlife **2.** *péj* [groupe] mob, bunch, crowd.
◇ *nm* MYTHOL faun.

faussaire [fosɛr] *nmf* faker, forger, falsifier.

fausse [fos] *f* ⊳ **faux.**

faussement [fosmɑ̃] *adv* **1.** [à tort] wrongfully **2.** [en apparence] falsely, spuriously ▪ **d'un air ~ ingénu** with a falsely innocent look, with feigned innocence.

fausser [3] [fose] *vt* **1.** [déformer - clef, lame] to bend, to put out of true ▪ [détériorer - serrure] to damage **2.** [réalité, résultat, fait] to distort ▪ [comptes] to falsify ▪ **faire une présentation qui fausse la réalité** to present a distorted vision of reality **3.** [diminuer la justesse de - esprit, raisonnement] to distort, to twist **4.** *loc* **~ compagnie à qqn** to give sb the slip.
◆ **se fausser** *vpi* [voix d'orateur] to become strained ▪ [voix de chanteur] to lose pitch.

fausset [fosɛ] *nm* **1.** MUS falsetto (voice) **2.** TECHNOL spigot.

fausseté [foste] *nf* **1.** [inexactitude] falseness, falsity ▪ **dénoncer la ~ d'une assertion** to expose the fallacy of an argument **2.** [duplicité] duplicity, treachery.

faut *v* ⊳ **falloir.**

faute [fot] *nf* **1.** [erreur] error, mistake ▪ **faire une ~** to make a mistake ▶ **~ d'étourderie** *ou* **d'inattention** careless mistake ▪ **~ de frappe** typing error ▪ **commettre une ~ de goût** to show a lack of taste ▪ **~ de grammaire** grammatical error *ou* mistake ▪ **~ d'impression** misprint ▪ **~ d'orthographe** spelling mistake
2. [manquement] misdeed, transgression ▪ **commettre une ~** to go wrong ▪ **il n'a commis aucune ~** he did nothing wrong ▶ **~ avouée est à moitié pardonnée** *prov* a fault confessed is half redressed *prov*
3. [responsabilité] fault ▪ **c'est (de) ma/ta ~** it's my/your fault ▪ **c'est bien sa ~ s'il est toujours en retard** it's his own fault that he's always late ▪ **tout ça, c'est ta ~!** it's all your fault! ▪ **à qui la ~?, la ~ à qui?** *fam* [question] who's to blame?, whose fault is

it? ; [accusation] you're the one to blame ▪ **imputer la ~ à qqn** to lay the blame at sb's door ▪ **la ~ en revient à l'inflation** it's because of inflation ▶ **c'est la ~ à pas de chance** *fam* it's just bad luck ▪ **c'est la ~ à Voltaire** *(allusion à Victor Hugo)* it must be somebody else's fault

4. ADMIN & DR offence ▶ **~ grave** serious offence, high misdemeanour ▪ **~ légère** minor offence ▪ **~ professionnelle** professional misconduct

5. *vieilli* [défaut] ▶ **ne pas se faire ~ de : ils ne se sont pas fait ~ de nous prévenir** they did warn us several times ▪ **je ne me suis pas fait ~ de lui rappeler sa promesse** I insisted on his keeping his promise

6. TENNIS fault ▪ FOOTBALL foul.

◆ **en faute** *loc adv* : **être en ~** to be at fault ▪ **prendre qqn en ~** to catch sb in the act.

◆ **faute de** *loc prép* for want of ▪ **~ de mieux** for want of anything better ▪ **~ de quoi** otherwise ▪ **~ de pouvoir aller au théâtre, il a regardé la télévision** since he couldn't go to the theatre he watched television (instead) ▶ **~ de grives, on mange des merles** *prov* half a loaf is better than no bread *prov*, beggars can't be choosers *prov*.

◆ **par la faute de** *loc prép* because of, owing to.

◆ **sans faute** ◇ *loc adj* faultless, offenceless ▪ **faire un parcours sans ~** ÉQUIT to get a clear round ; [coureur] to run a perfect race ; [dans un jeu télévisé] to get all the answers right ; [dans sa carrière] not to put a foot wrong.

◇ *loc adv* without fail.

fauter [3] [fote] *vi euphém & hum* to sin, to go astray ▪ **~ avec qqn** to be led astray by sb.

fauteuil [fotœj] *nm* **1.** [meuble] armchair, chair, seat ▪ **~ pivotant** *ou* **tournant** swivel chair ▪ **~ à bascule** rocking-chair ▪ **~ club** large leather armchair ▪ **~ de jardin** garden chair ▪ **~ pliant** folding chair ▪ **~ roulant** wheelchair **2.** THÉÂTRE : **~ de balcon** dress-circle seat ▪ **~ d'orchestre** seat in the stalls UK *ou* the orchestra US **3.** [à l'Académie française] *numbered seat occupied by a member of the Académie française.*

fauteur, trice [fotœr, tris] *nm, f* : **~ de troubles** troublemaker.

fautif, ive [fotif, iv] ◇ *adj* **1.** [défectueux - liste] incorrect ; [- citation] inaccurate **2.** [coupable] offending, responsible ▪ **se sentir ~** to feel guilty.

◇ *nm, f* offender ▪ **qui est le ~?** who's to blame?, who's the culprit?

fautivement [fotivmɑ̃] *adv* erroneously, by mistake.

fauve [fov] ◇ *adj* **1.** [couleur] fawn-coloured, tawny **2.** [âpre - odeur] musky.

◇ *nm* **1.** ZOOL big cat ▪ **les grands ~s** the big cats ▪ **ça sent le ~ dans cette pièce** this room stinks of sweat **2.** [couleur] fawn **3.** ART Fauve, Fauvist.

fauvette [fovɛt] *nf* warbler.

fauvisme [fovism] *nm* Fauvism.

faux[1] [fo] *nf* AGRIC scythe ▪ **couper de l'herbe à la ~** to scythe through grass.

faux[2], **fausse** [fo, fos] *adj*

> **A.** CONTRAIRE À LA VÉRITÉ, À L'EXACTITUDE
> **B.** CONTRAIRE AUX APPARENCES

A. CONTRAIRE À LA VÉRITÉ, À L'EXACTITUDE

1. [mensonger - réponse] wrong ; [- affirmation] untrue ; [- excuse, prétexte] false ; [- nouvelle, promesse, témoignage] false ▪ **condamné pour ~ serment** sentenced for perjury

2. [inexact - raisonnement] false, faulty ; [- calcul] wrong ; [- balance] faulty ▪ **t'as tout ~** *fam* you're completely wrong

3. [non vérifié - argument] false ; [- impression] mistaken, wrong, false ; [- espoir] false ▪ **tu te fais une fausse idée de lui** you've got the wrong idea about him ▪ **c'est un ~ problème** *ou* **débat** this is not the issue

4. MUS [piano, voix] out of tune

B. CONTRAIRE AUX APPARENCES

1. [dent, nez, barbe, poche] false ▪ [bijou, cuir, fourrure, marbre] imitation ▪ [plafond, poutre] false

2. [falsifié - monnaie] false, counterfeit, forged ; [- carte à jouer] trick ; [- papiers, facture] forged, false ; [- testament] spurious ▪ **fabriquer de la fausse monnaie** to counterfeit money ▪ **c'est un ~ Renoir** it's a fake Renoir

3. [feint - candeur, émotion] feigned

4. [pseudo - policier] bogus ; [- intellectuel] pseudo

5. [hypocrite - caractère, personne] false, deceitful ; [- regard] deceitful, treacherous.

◆ **faux** ◇ *adv* **1.** MUS [jouer, chanter] out of tune, off-key ▪ **sonner ~** [excuse] to have a hollow *ou* false ring ▪ **ça sonne ~** it doesn't ring true **2.** *loc* **porter à ~** [cloison] to be out of plumb *ou* true ; [objet] to be precariously balanced ; [argument, raisonnement] to be unfounded.

◇ *nm* **1.** DR [objet, activité] forgery ▪ **c'est un ~** [document, tableau] it's a fake *ou* a forgery ▶ **inculper qqn pour ~ et usage de ~** to prosecute sb for forgery and use of forgeries **2.** [imitation] : **c'est du cuir? – non, c'est du ~** is it leather? – no, it's imitation.

◆ **fausse alerte** *nf pr & fig* false alarm.

◆ **faux ami** *nm* false friend.

◆ **fausse couche** *nf* miscarriage ▪ **faire une fausse couche** to have a miscarriage.

◆ **faux-cul** ◇ *adj*△ **il est ~-cul** he's a two-faced bastard△.

◇ *nm* [vêtement] bustle.

◇ *nmf*△ two-faced bastard (*f* two-faced bitch).

◆ **faux départ** *nm pr & fig* false start.

◆ **faux frère** *nm* false friend.

◆ **faux jeton** *fam* ◇ *adj inv* hypocritical.

◇ *nmf* hypocrite.

◆ **faux pas** *nm* **1.** [en marchant] : **faire un ~ pas** to trip, to stumble **2.** [erreur] false move **3.** [maladresse] faux pas, gaffe.

faux-filet [fofilɛ] (*pl* **faux-filets**) *nm* sirloin.

faux-fuyant [fofɥijɑ̃] (*pl* **faux-fuyants**) *nm* excuse, subterfuge ▪ **répondre par des ~s** to give evasive answers ▪ **user de ~s** to prevaricate.

faux-monnayeur [fomɔnɛjœr] (*pl* **faux-monnayeurs**) *nm* forger, counterfeiter.

faux-semblant [fosɑ̃blɑ̃] (*pl* **faux-semblants**) *nm* : **ne vous laissez pas abuser par des ~s** don't let yourself be taken in by pretence.

faux-sens [fosɑ̃s] *nm inv* mistranslation.

favela [favɛla] *nf* favela, (Brazilian) shantytown.

faveur [favœr] *nf* **1.** [plaisir] favour ▪ **faire une ~ à qqn** to do sb a favour ▪ **faites-moi une ~** do me a favour ▪ **elle ne lui fit même pas la ~ d'un sourire** she didn't even favour him with a smile ▪ **nous ferez-vous la ~ de votre visite?** will you honour us with a visit? ▪ **faites-moi la ~ de m'écouter quand je parle** would you mind listening when I speak? **2.** [bienveillance] favour ▪ **il a la ~ du président** he's in the president's good books ▪ **elle a eu la ~ de la presse/du public** she found favour with the press/with the public **3.** [ruban] ribbon, favour.

◆ **faveurs** *nfpl sout* favours ▪ **accorder/refuser ses ~s à qqn** *euphém* to give/to refuse sb one's favours.

◆ **à la faveur de** *loc prép* owing to, with the help of ▪ **à la ~ de la nuit** under cover of darkness.

◆ **de faveur** *loc adj* preferential.

◆ **en faveur** *loc adv* : **être/ne pas être en ~** to be in/out of favour ▪ **être en ~ auprès de qqn** to be in favour with sb.

◆ **en faveur de** *loc prép* **1.** [à cause de] on account of **2.** [au profit de] to the benefit of, in favour of ▪ **en ma/votre ~** in my/your favour **3.** [favorable à] in favour of.

favorable [favɔrabl] *adj* **1.** [propice] favourable, right ▪ **saisir le moment ~** to take the opportunity **2.** [bien disposé] favourable ▪ **se montrer sous un jour ~** to show o.s. in a favourable light ▪ **regarder qqch d'un œil ~** to be favourable to sthg ▪ **je suis plutôt ~ à son départ** I'm rather in favour of his going ▪ **je suis ~ à cette décision/à vos idées** I approve of this decision/of your ideas.

favorablement [favɔrabləmɑ̃] *adv* favourably ▪ **répondre ~** to say yes ▪ **il a répondu ~ à mon invitation** he accepted my invitation ▪ **si les choses tournent ~** if things turn out all right.

favori, ite [favɔri, it] <> *adj* [mélodie, dessert] favourite ■ [idée, projet] favourite, pet *(modif)*.
<> *nm, f* **1.** SPORT favourite **2.** [parmi les enfants] favourite ■ **c'est elle la ~te** [dans la famille] she's their darling ; [en classe] she's the teacher's pet.
◆ **favori** *nm* HIST (king's *ou* royal) favourite.
◆ **favorite** *nf* HIST : **la ~te** the King's mistress.
◆ **favoris** *nmpl* sideboards, sideburns.

favorisé, e [favɔrize] *adj* fortunate ■ **les pays les plus ~s** the most favoured nations.

favoriser [3] [favɔrize] *vt* **1.** [traiter avantageusement] to favour, to give preferential treatment to **2.** [être avantageux pour] to favour, to be to the advantage of **3.** [faciliter] to further, to promote ■ **~ le développement de l'économie** to promote economic development.

favoritisme [favɔritism] *nm* favouritism.

fax [faks] *(abr de* **Téléfax***)* *nm* **1.** [machine] fax (machine) **2.** [message] fax ■ **par ~** by fax.

faxer [3] [fakse] *vt* to fax.

fayard [fajar] *nm Suisse* beech.

fayot [fajo] *nm fam* **1.** [haricot] bean **2.** *péj* [employé] toady, bootlicker ■ [élève] swot *UK*, apple-polisher *US*.

fayoter [3] [fajɔte] *vi fam* to lick sb's boots ■ **il est toujours à ~** he's always bootlicking.

FBI [ɛfbiaj] *(abr de* **Federal Bureau of Investigation***)* *npr m* FBI.

FCFA *(abr écrite de* **franc CFA***)* *currency used in former French colonies in Africa.*

fébrile [febril] *adj* **1.** MÉD febrile ■ **état ~** feverishness **2.** [agité] feverish, restless ■ **déployer une activité ~** to be in a fervent activity.

fébrilement [febrilmɑ̃] *adv* **1.** [avec inquiétude] feverishly **2.** [avec hâte] hastily.

fébrilité [febrilite] *nf* febrility *spéc*, feverishness.

fécal, e, aux [fekal, o] *adj* faecal.

fèces [fɛs] *nfpl* faeces.

fécond, e [fekɔ̃, ɔ̃d] *adj* **1.** BIOL fecund, fertile **2.** [prolifique - terre] rich, fertile ; [- écrivain, inventeur] prolific, productive ; [- imagination] lively, powerful ■ **une idée ~e** *litt* a rich idea ■ **~ en : terre ~e en fruits de toute sorte** *litt* land rich in every kind of fruit ■ **une journée ~e en événements** an eventful day.

fécondateur, trice [fekɔ̃datœr, tris] *adj litt* fertilizing.

fécondation [fekɔ̃dasjɔ̃] *nf* **1.** BIOL [des mammifères] fertilization, impregnation ■ [des ovipares] fertilization ■ **~ artificielle/in vitro** artificial/in vitro fertilization **2.** BOT fertilization, fertilizing.

féconder [3] [fekɔ̃de] *vt* **1.** BIOL [femme, femelle] to impregnate ■ [œuf] to fertilize **2.** *litt* [terre, champ] to make fertile.

fécondité [fekɔ̃dite] *nf* **1.** BIOL fecundity **2.** *litt* [d'une terre, d'un jardin] fruitfulness **3.** *litt* [d'un créateur] fertility.

fécule [fekyl] *nf* starch ■ **~ (de maïs)** cornflour *UK*, cornstarch *US* ■ **~ de pomme de terre** potato flour.

féculent, e [fekylɑ̃, ɑ̃t] *adj* [aliment] starchy.
◆ **féculent** *nm* starchy food, starch ■ **évitez les ~s** avoid starch *ou* starchy foods.

fedayin [fedajin] *nm* fedayee ■ **les ~s** the Fedayeen.

fédéral, e, aux [federal, o] *adj* **1.** POLIT federal **2.** *Suisse* federal *(relative to the Swiss Confederation)*.

fédéraliser [3] [federalize] *vt* to federalize, to turn into a federation.

fédéralisme [federalism] *nm* **1.** POLIT federalism **2.** *Suisse political tendency defending the independence of the Swiss cantons from federal authority.*

fédéraliste [federalist] <> *adj* federalist, federalistic.
<> *nmf* federalist, federal.

fédérateur, trice [federatœr, tris] <> *adj* federative, federating.
<> *nm, f* unifier.

fédératif, ive [federatif, iv] *adj* federative.

fédération [federasjɔ̃] *nf* **1.** POLIT [gén] federation ■ [au Canada] confederation ■ **la Fédération de Russie** the Federation of Russia **2.** [groupe] federation ■ **~ syndicale** trade union.

fédéraux [federo] *nmpl* ▻ **fédéral**.

fédéré, e [federe] *adj* federated.
◆ **fédéré** *nm* HIST federate.

fédérer [18] [federe] *vt* to federate, to form into a federation.
◆ **se fédérer** *vp (emploi réfléchi)* to federate.

fée [fe] *nf* fairy ■ **sa bonne ~** his good fairy, his fairy godmother ■ **la ~ Carabosse** the wicked fairy ■ **c'est une ~ du logis** she's a wonderful housewife.

feed-back [fidbak] *nm inv* TECHNOL feedback.

feeder [fidœr] *nm* feeder (pipe).

feeling [filiŋ] *nm fam* **: on va y aller au ~** we'll play it by ear ■ **j'ai un bon ~** I have a good feeling about it.

féerie [fe(e)ri] *nf* **1.** THÉÂTRE spectacular **2.** [merveille] enchantment ■ **une ~ de couleurs** a riot of colour.

féerique [fe(e)rik] *adj* **1.** MYTHOL fairy *(modif)*, magic, magical **2.** [beau - vue, spectacle] enchanting, magical.

feignait *etc v* ▻ **feindre**.

feignant, e [fɛɲɑ̃, ɑ̃t] *fam* <> *adj* lazy, idle.
<> *nm, f* loafer.

feindre [81] [fɛ̃dr] <> *vt* to feign ■ **~ la joie** to feign joy.
<> *vi* [dissimuler] to dissemble *litt*, to pretend ■ **elle feint de s'intéresser à cette histoire** she pretends she's interested in this story.

feinte [fɛ̃t] *nf* **1.** [ruse] ruse **2.** *litt* [dissimulation] dissembling *(U)*, dissimulation, pretence ■ **sans ~** frankly, without pretence **3.** SPORT [à la boxe et à l'escrime] feint ■ [au football, au rugby etc] dummy *UK*, fake *US* **4.** MIL feint, sham attack.

feinter [3] [fɛ̃te] <> *vt* **1.** SPORT : **~ l'adversaire** [à la boxe et à l'escrime] to feint at the opponent ■ **~ la passe** [au football et au rugby] to sell a dummy *UK*, to fake a pass *US* ■ *(en usage absolu)* to feint **2.** *fam* [duper] to fool, to take in *(sép)* ■ **feinté!** foiled again!
<> *vi* to dummy *UK*, to fake *US*.

fêlé, e [fele] <> *adj* **1.** [voix, son] hoarse, cracked **2.** *fam* [fou] nuts.
<> *nm, f fam* nut, loony ■ **tous des ~s!** they're all bonkers *ou* cracked.

fêler [4] [fele] *vt pr* to crack.
◆ **se fêler** *vpi* [tasse] to crack.

félicitations [felisitasjɔ̃] *nfpl* congratulation, congratulations ■ **(toutes mes) ~** congratulations! ■ **adresser** *ou* **faire ses ~ à qqn** to congratulate sb ■ **recevoir les ~ de qqn pour qqch** to be congratulated by sb on sthg ■ **avec les ~ du jury** UNIV with the examining board's utmost praise, summa cum laude.
Voir module d'usage

félicité [felisite] *nf litt* bliss, felicity *sout*.

féliciter [3] [felisite] *vt* to congratulate ■ **~ qqn de qqch** to congratulate sb on sthg ■ **permettez-moi de vous ~!** congratulations! ■ **je ne vous félicite pas!** you'll get no thanks from me!
◆ **se féliciter de** *vp+prép* **1.** [se réjouir de] : **se ~ de qqch** to be glad *ou* pleased about sthg **2.** [se louer de] : **je me félicite d'être resté calme** I'm pleased to say I remained calm.

félidé [felide] *nm* feline ■ **les ~s** the Felidae.

félin, e [felɛ̃, in] *adj* **1.** ZOOL feline **2.** [regard, démarche] feline, catlike.
◆ **félin** *nm* cat ■ **les ~s** the cat family.

fellaga, fellagha [felaga] *nm* fellagha *(name given by the French to Algerians fighting for independence).*

fellah [fela] *nm* fellah.

fellation [felasjɔ̃] *nf* fellatio, fellation ▪ **faire une ~ à qqn** to perform fellatio on sb.

félon, onne [felɔ̃, ɔn] *adj* **1.** *litt* [perfide] disloyal, treacherous, felonious *litt* **2.** HIST rebellious.
◆ **félon** *nm* **1.** *litt* [traître] traitor **2.** HIST felon.

félonie [felɔni] *nf* **1.** *litt* [traîtrise] disloyalty, treachery, act of betrayal **2.** HIST felony.

felouque [fəluk] *nf* felucca.

fêlure [felyr] *nf* **1.** [d'un objet] crack ▪ **il y a une ~ dans leur amitié** cracks are beginning to show in their friendship **2.** [de la voix] crack **3.** MÉD fracture.

femelle [fəmɛl] ◇ *adj* **1.** ZOOL female **2.** ORNITH hen **3.** BOT & ÉLECTR female ▪ **une prise ~** a socket.
◇ *nf* ZOOL female.

féminin, e [feminɛ̃, in] *adj* **1.** BIOL : **la morphologie ~e** the female body **2.** [composé de femmes] : **des craintes parmi la population ~e** fears among the female population ▪ **l'équipe ~e** the women's team **3.** [considéré comme typique de la femme] : **une réaction typiquement ~e** a typical female reaction ▪ **elle est très ~e** she's very feminine ▪ **il avait une voix ~e** he had a woman's voice **4.** [qui a rapport à la femme] : **le tennis ~** women's tennis **5.** GRAMM & LITTÉR [nom, rime] feminine.
◆ **féminin** *nm* **1.** GRAMM feminine (gender), *voir aussi* **pluriel 2.** ▷ **éternel**.

féminisant, e [feminizɑ̃, ɑ̃t] *adj* BIOL feminizing.

féminisation [feminizasjɔ̃] *nf* **1.** BIOL feminization, feminizing *(U)* **2.** SOCIOL : **la ~ d'une profession/d'un milieu** increased female participation in a profession/in a group.

féminiser [3] [feminize] *vt* **1.** BIOL to feminize **2.** GRAMM [mot] to put into the feminine gender **3.** [homme] to make effeminate **4.** SOCIOL : **il faut ~ ces professions** more women must be encouraged to enter those professions.
◆ **se féminiser** *vpi* **1.** BIOL to feminize **2.** [homme] to become effeminate **3.** SOCIOL : **notre profession se féminise** more and more women are entering our profession.

féminisme [feminism] *nm* [mouvement] feminism.

féministe [feminist] *adj* & *nmf* feminist.

féminité [feminite] *nf* femininity.

femme [fam] *nf* **1.** [personne] woman ▪ **~ ingénieur/soldat** woman engineer/soldier ▪ **une ~ à poigne/de parole** a tough/reliable woman ▪ **~ de ménage, ~ à journée** *OU Belgique* **d'ouvrage** cleaning lady, daily (woman) *UK*, maid *US* ▪ **~ d'affaires** businesswoman ▪ **~ de chambre** maid, chambermaid ▪ **~ écrivain** woman writer ▪ **~ de petite vertu** woman of easy virtue ▪ **~ policier** policewoman, WPC *UK* ▪ **une ~ enfant** a childlike woman ▪ **~ fatale** femme fatale **2.** [adulte] : **à treize ans elle fait déjà très ~** at thirteen she already looks very much a woman **3.** [ensemble de personnes] : **la ~, les ~s** woman, women ▪ **la libération/les droits de la ~** women's liberation/rights **4.** [épouse] wife ▪ **prendre qqn pour ~** to take sb as one's wife ▪ **prendre ~** *sout* to take a wife **5.** *(comme adj)* [féminine] : **être très ~** to be very feminine.

femmelette [famlɛt] *nf péj* [homme] sissy ▪ **pas de ~s chez nous!** we don't want any sissies around here!

femme-objet [famɔbʒɛ] *(pl* **femmes-objets***) nf woman seen or treated as an object.*

fémoral, e, aux [femɔral, o] *adj* femoral *spéc*, thigh *(modif).*

fémur [femyr] *nm* thigh bone, femur *spéc.*

FEN [fɛn] *(abr de* **Fédération de l'Éducation nationale***) npr f teachers' trade union,* ≃ NUT *UK.*

fenaison [fənɛzɔ̃] *nf* [récolte] haymaking ▪ [époque] haymaking time.

fendant[1] [fɑ̃dɑ̃] *nm* **1.** ESCRIME sword thrust **2.** [raisin] Fendant grape **3.** [vin] Fendant (wine).

fendant[2]**, e** [fɑ̃dɑ̃, ɑ̃t] *adj fam* hilarious, killing.

fendillé [fɑ̃dije] *adj* [miroir] cracked ▪ [poterie] crazed ▪ [bois] split ▪ **avoir les lèvres fendillées** to have chapped lips.

fendillement [fɑ̃dijmɑ̃] *nm* [d'un miroir, d'un mur, d'un tableau] cracking ▪ [du bois] splitting, springing ▪ [du verre, de l'émail, du vernis, de la porcelaine] crazing, crackling.

fendiller [3] [fɑ̃dije] *vt* [miroir, mur, tableau] to crack ▪ [bois] to split ▪ [émail, verre, vernis, poterie] to craze, to crackle.
◆ **se fendiller** *vpi* [miroir, mur, tableau] to crack ▪ [bois] to spring ▪ [verre, poterie, émail, vernis] to craze, to crackle.

fendre [73] [fɑ̃dr] *vt* **1.** [couper - bois, roche] to split, to cleave ; [- lèvre] to cut *OU* to split (open) ▪ **~ une bûche en deux** to split *OU* to chop a log down the middle ▪ **~ le crâne à qqn** to split sb's skull (open) ▪ **ça vous fend** *OU* **c'est à vous ~ le cœur** it breaks your heart, it's heartbreaking, it's heartrending **2.** [fissurer - terre, sol, mur] to crack **3.** COUT [veste, jupe, robe] to make a slit in **4.** [traverser - foule] to push *OU* to force one's way through ▪ **~ les flots/l'air/le vent** *litt* & *hum* to cleave through the seas/the air/the breeze.
◆ **se fendre** ◇ *vpi* **1.** [s'ouvrir - bois] to split ; [- terre, sol, mur] to crack **2.** *fam* [se ruiner] : **tu ne t'es pas trop fendu!** this really didn't ruin *OU* break you, did it! ▪ **se ~ de : se ~ de 100 euros** to fork out *OU* to shell out 100 euros **3.** ESCRIME to lunge.
◇ *vpt* : **se ~ qqch : elle s'est fendu la lèvre** she cut her lip (open) ▪ **se ~ le crâne** to crack one's skull (open) ▪ **se ~ la gueule**△ *OU* **pêche** *fam OU* **pipe** *fam OU* **poire** *fam* [rire] to split one's sides ; [s'amuser] to have a ball.

fendu, e [fɑ̃dy] *adj* [robe, jupe] slit ▪ [yeux] almond-shaped ▪ **une bouche ~e jusqu'aux oreilles** a broad grin *OU* smile.

fenêtre [fənɛtr] *nf* **1.** CONSTR window ▪ **regarder par la ~** to look out of the window ▪ **ouvrir une ~ sur** *fig* to open a window on ▶ **~ à coulisse** *OU* **à guillotine** sash window ▪ **~ mansardée** dormer window ▪ **~ à meneaux** mullioned window ▪ **~ à tabatière** skylight ▪ **fausse ~** blind window ▪ **une place côté couloir ou côté ~?** an aisle or a window seat? ▪ **'Fenêtre sur cour'**

LES FÉLICITATIONS

Congratulations! Félicitations !

Congratulations on your promotion! Félicitations pour votre promotion !

I hear congratulations are in order. Alors, il paraît qu'il faut te féliciter ?

Let me be the first to congratulate you. Laissez-moi vous féliciter.

That's great *OU* **wonderful (news)!** C'est formidable !

I'm so pleased *OU* **happy for you!** Je suis vraiment content pour toi !

Well done! *UK*, **Good job!** *US* Bravo !

Well played! Bien joué !

(Nice) shot! *(au tennis etc.)* Bien joué !

Hitchcock 'Rear Window' **2.** [d'une enveloppe] window **3.** INFORM window ▪ **~ de lecture-écriture** read-write slot **4.** [espace blanc] space, blank **5.** ANAT fenestra.

fenil [fənil] *nm* hayloft.

fennec [fenɛk] *nm* fennec.

fenouil [fənuj] *nm* fennel.

fente [fɑ̃t] *nf* **1.** [fissure - dans du bois] cleft, split ; [- dans un sol, un mur] crack, fissure ; [- dans une roche] cleft **2.** [ouverture - d'une jupe, des volets] slit ; [- dans une boîte, sur une vis] slot ; [- dans une veste] vent ; [- pour passer les bras] armhole **3.** ESCRIME lunge.

féodal, e, aux [feɔdal, o] *adj* feudal.
◆ **féodal** *nm* [propriétaire] landlord ▪ [seigneur] feudal lord.

féodalisme [feɔdalism] *nm* feudalism.

féodalité [feɔdalite] *nf* **1.** [système] feudal system **2.** *péj* [puissance] feudal power.

fer [fɛr] *nm* **1.** CHIM iron *(U)* **2.** MÉTALL iron *(U)* ▪ **~ doux** soft iron ▪ **~ forgé** wrought iron **3.** [dans les aliments] iron *(U)* **4.** [barre] (iron) bar **5.** [lame] blade ▪ **~ de lance** *pr & fig* spearhead ▪ **par le ~ et par le feu** by fire and sword **6.** [pour repassage] : **~ à repasser** iron ▪ **~ à vapeur** steam iron ▪ **~ électrique** (electric) iron ▪ **passer un coup de ~ sur un pantalon** to give a pair of trousers a quick iron ▪ **ton pantalon a besoin d'un petit coup de ~** your trousers could do with a quick iron **7.** [instrument] : **~ à dorer** gilding iron ▪ **~ à friser** curling tongs *UK ou* iron *US* ▪ **~ à gaufrer** goffering iron ▪ **~ à souder** soldering iron ▪ **~ rouge** brand **8.** [de chaussure] metal tip **9.** [de golf] iron *(C)* **10.** RAIL : **le ~** rail, the railway system, the railways **11.** *litt* [épée] blade.
◆ **fers** *nmpl* [chaînes] irons, shackles ▪ **mettre qqn aux ~s** to put sb in irons.
◆ **de fer** *loc adj* [moral, santé] cast-iron *(modif)* ▪ [discipline, volonté] iron *(modif)*.
◆ **fer à cheval** *nm* horseshoe ▪ **en ~ à cheval** [escalier, table] horseshoe-shaped, horseshoe *(modif)*.

fera *etc v* ▷ **faire.**

fer-blanc [fɛrblɑ̃] (*pl* **fers-blancs**) *nm* tin, tinplate.
◆ **en fer-blanc** *loc adj* tin *(modif)* ▪ **boîte en ~** can, tincan.

ferblanterie [fɛrblɑ̃tri] *nf* **1.** [manufacture] tinplate making **2.** [objets] tinware **3.** *péj* [décorations] medals.

ferblantier [fɛrblɑ̃tje] *nm* tinsmith.

feria [ferja] *nf* fair *(yearly, in Spain and Southern France)*.

férié, e [ferje] *adj* : **c'est un jour ~** it's a (public) holiday.

férir [ferir] *vt litt & loc* **sans coup ~** without any problem *ou* difficulty ▪ **conquérir une région sans coup ~** to conquer a region without bloodshed.

fermage [fɛrmaʒ] *nm* **1.** [location] tenant farming **2.** [redevance] farm rent.

ferme[1] [fɛrm] *nf* **1.** [maison] farmhouse ▪ [exploitation] farm **2.** DR : **prendre ~** to rent, to farm ▪ **donner à ~** to let **3.** ARCHIT truss.

ferme[2] [fɛrm] ◇ *adj* **1.** [dur - sol] solid, firm ; [- corps, chair, fruit, muscle] firm **2.** [stable] : **être ~ sur ses jambes** to stand steady on one's legs *ou* firm on one's feet **3.** [décidé - ton, pas] firm, steady ▪ **..., dit-elle d'une voix ~...,** she said firmly **4.** [inébranlable - volonté, décision] firm ; [- réponse] definite ▪ **des prix ~s et définitifs** firm *ou* definite prices **5.** ÉCON steady, firm ▪ **le dollar est resté ~** the dollar stayed firm **6.** COMM [achat, vente] firm.
◇ *adv* **1.** [solidement] : **tenir ~** [clou] to hold ; [personne, troupe] to stand firm, to hold on **2.** [beaucoup - travailler, boire] hard ▪ **il boit ~** he's a heavy *ou* a hard drinker **3.** [avec passion - discuter] with passion, passionately.

fermé, e [fɛrme] *adj* **1.** [passage] closed, blocked ▪ **'col ~'** 'pass closed to traffic' **2.** [porte, récipient] closed, shut ▪ **j'ai laissé la porte à demi ~e** I left the door ajar *ou* half-open ▪ **une boîte ~e** a box which is shut, a closed box ▪ [à clef] locked ▪ **~ à clef** locked ▪ **~ à double tour** double-locked **3.** [radiateur, robinet] off **4.** [bouche, œil] shut, closed (up) **5.** [magasin, bureau, restaurant] closed ▪ **~ le lundi** closed on Mondays, closing day Monday **6.** CHASSE & PÊCHE closed **7.** [méfiant - visage] closed, inscrutable, impenetrable ; [- regard] impenetrable ▪ **une personnalité ~e** a secretive *ou* an uncommunicative personality **8.** [exclusif - milieu, ambiance] exclusive, select **9.** PHON [syllabe, voyelle] closed **10.** SPORT [jeu] tight **11.** INFORM & MATH closed.

fermement [fɛrməmɑ̃] *adv* **1.** [avec force] firmly, solidly, steadily **2.** [résolument] firmly, strongly.

ferment [fɛrmɑ̃] *nm* **1.** CHIM ferment, leaven ▪ **~s lactiques** bacilli used in making yoghurt **2.** *litt* [facteur] : **leur présence est un ~ de haine** their presence stirs up hatred.

fermentation [fɛrmɑ̃tasjɔ̃] *nf* **1.** CHIM fermentation, fermenting **2.** *litt* [agitation] fermentation, commotion.
◆ **en fermentation** *loc adj* [raisin] fermenting.

fermenté, e [fɛrmɑ̃te] *adj* fermented.

fermenter [3] [fɛrmɑ̃te] *vi* **1.** CHIM to ferment **2.** *litt* [sentiment] to be stirred ▪ [esprit] to be in a ferment.

fermer [3] [fɛrme] ◇ *vt* **1.** [yeux] to shut, to close ▪ [poing, main] to close ▪ [enveloppe] to seal, to shut, to close ▪ [éventail] to fold, to close ▪ [col, jupe] to fasten, to do up *(sép)* ▪ [sac, valise, bocal, livre] to shut, to close ▪ [robinet] to turn off *(sép)* ▪ **~ les rideaux** to close *ou* draw the curtains ▪ **ferme le tiroir** shut the drawer ▶ **~ les yeux sur qqch** to turn a blind eye to sthg ▪ **je n'ai pas fermé l'œil de la nuit** I didn't get a wink (of sleep) all night ▪ **~ sa bouche** *fam ou* **sa gueule**△ *ou* **son bec** *fam* to shut up, to shut one's trap ▪ **la ~**△ : **je le savais mais je l'ai fermée** I knew it but I didn't let on ▪ **la ferme!**△ shut up!, shut your face!△
2. [porte] to close, to shut ▪ **~ une porte à clef** to lock a door ▪ **~ une porte à double tour** to double-lock a door ▪ **il a fermé la porte d'un coup de pied** he kicked the door shut ▪ **~ ses portes** [boutique, musée] to shut, to close ▪ *(en usage absolu)* **on ferme!** closing now!
3. *fam* [éteindre - électricité, lumière, compteur] to turn *ou* to switch off *(sép)* ; [- robinet] to turn off *(sép)*
4. [rendre inaccessible - rue, voie] to block, to bar, to obstruct
5. [interdire - frontière, port] to close ▪ **cette filière vous fermerait toutes les carrières scientifiques** this course would prevent you from following any scientific career
6. [faire cesser l'activité de] : **~ un restaurant/théâtre** [pour un congé] to close a restaurant/theatre ; [définitivement] to close a restaurant/theatre (down) ▪ **la police a fait ~ l'établissement** the police had the place closed down ▶ **~ boutique** [pour un congé] to shut up shop ; [pour cause de faillite] to stop *ou* to cease trading, to close down ; *fig* to give up
7. [rendre insensible] : **~ qqch à** : **~ son cœur à qqn** to harden one's heart to sb ▪ **~ son esprit à qqch** to close one's mind to sthg
8. [être à la fin de] : **~ la marche** to be at the back of the procession
9. [délimiter] : **les montagnes qui ferment l'horizon/la vue** the mountains which shut off the horizon/block the view
10. BANQUE & FIN [compte, portefeuille d'actions] to close
11. SPORT : **~ le jeu** to tighten up play.
◇ *vi* **1.** [se verrouiller - couvercle, fenêtre, porte] to close ▪ **le portail ferme mal** the gate is difficult to close *ou* won't close properly ▪ **le radiateur ferme mal** the radiator won't turn off properly
2. [cesser son activité - temporairement] to close ; [- définitivement] to close down.
◆ **se fermer** ◇ *vp (emploi passif)* [être attaché - col, robe, veste] to fasten, to do up.
◇ *vpi* **1.** [être verrouillé - porte, fenêtre] to close ▪ **se ~ à** [être inaccessible à] : **les sociétés occidentales se ferment à l'immigration** Western societies are closing their doors to immigrants ▪ **son cœur s'est fermé à la pitié** he has become impervious to pity
2. [se serrer, se plier - bras, fleur, huître, main] to close (up) ; [- aile] to fold ; [- bouche, œil, paupière, livre, rideau] to close ; [- blessure] to close (up), to heal ▪ **mes yeux se ferment tout seuls** I can't keep my eyes open
3. [être impénétrable] : **on ne peut pas lui parler, elle se ferme aussitôt** there's no talking to her, she just switches off *ou* freezes up.

fermeté [fɛrməte] *nf* **1.** [solidité - d'un objet] solidness, firmness ; [- d'un corps] firmness **2.** [assurance - d'un geste] assurance, steadiness ; [- d'une voix] firmness **3.** [autorité] firmness ▪ **faire preuve de ~ à l'égard de qqn** to be firm with sb ▪ **avec ~** firmly, resolutely, steadfastly ▪ **sans ~** irresolutely, waveringly **4.** BOURSE steadiness.

fermette [fɛrmɛt] *nf* **1.** [habitation] small farm *ou* farmhouse **2.** CONSTR small truss.

fermeture [fɛrmətyr] *nf* **1.** [obstruction] : **après la ~ du puits/tunnel** once the well/tunnel is blocked off ▪ **la ~ du coffre se fera devant témoins** the safe will be locked *ou* sealed in the presence of witnesses **2.** [rabattement] closing ▪ **la ~ des grilles avait lieu à midi** the gates were closed at noon ▪ **'ne pas gêner la ~ des portes'** 'please do not obstruct the doors' **3.** COMM [arrêt des transactions] : **au moment de la ~** [du bureau] at the end of the day's work ; [de la banque, du magasin, du café] at closing time ▪ **'~ annuelle'** 'closed for annual holiday' ▪ **~ définitive** closedown ▪ **à la ~** BOURSE at the close of trading ▮ ADMIN & FIN closing ⮞ **jour de ~** [hebdomadaire] closing day ; [férié] public holiday **4.** [fin - d'une session, d'un festival] close, closing ▪ CHASSE & PÊCHE closing **5.** [vêtement] : **~Éclair**® *ou* à glissière zip (fastener) UK, zipper US.

fermier, ère [fɛrmje, ɛr] *adj* **1.** ÉCON [compagnie, société] farm *(modif)* **2.** COMM : **poulet/œuf ~** free-range chicken/egg ▪ **lait/beurre ~** dairy milk/butter.
◆ **fermier** *nm* **1.** AGRIC [locataire] tenant farmer ▪ [propriétaire, agriculteur] farmer **2.** HIST : **~ général** farmer general.
◆ **fermière** *nf* **1.** [épouse] farmer's wife **2.** [cultivatrice] woman farmer.

fermoir [fɛrmwar] *nm* [de collier, de sac] clasp, fastener.

féroce [ferɔs] *adj* **1.** [brutal - tyran, soldat] cruel, bloodthirsty **2.** [acerbe - humour, examinateur] cruel, harsh, ferocious ▪ **dans une critique ~ qui vient de paraître** in a ferocious *ou* savage review just out **3.** [qui tue - animal, bête] ferocious **4.** [extrême - appétit] voracious.

férocement [ferɔsmɑ̃] *adv* **1.** [brutalement] cruelly **2.** [avec dureté] harshly, ferociously.

férocité [ferɔsite] *nf* **1.** [brutalité] cruelty, bloodlust **2.** [intransigeance] harshness, ferociousness ▪ **avec ~** ferociously **3.** [d'une bête] ferocity.

Féroé [ferɔe] *npr fpl* : **les (îles) ~** the Faeroes, the Faeroe Islands ▪ **aux ~** in the Faeroes, *voir aussi* **île**.

ferrage [fɛraʒ] *nm* **1.** [d'une roue] rimming ▪ [d'une canne] tipping with metal **2.** [d'un cheval, d'un bœuf] shoeing **3.** PÊCHE striking.

ferraillage [fɛrajaʒ] *nm* **1.** [action] framing with iron **2.** [armatures] iron framework.

ferraille [fɛraj] *nf* **1.** [débris] : **de la ~** scrap (iron) ▪ **un bruit de ~** a clanking noise **2.** [rebut] : **la ~ : bon pour la** *ou* **à mettre à la ~** ready for the scrapheap, good for scrap **3.** *fam* [monnaie] small change.

ferrailler [3] [fɛraje] *vi* **1.** ESCRIME to clash swords **2.** *fig* to clash, to cross swords ▪ **le gouvernement a ferraillé avec les syndicats** the government clashed with the unions.

ferrailleur [fɛrajœr] *nm* **1.** CONSTR ≃ building worker *(in charge of iron frameworks)* **2.** [commerçant] scrap merchant **3.** *arch* [duelliste] swashbuckler.

ferré, e [fɛre] *adj* **1.** [muni de fers - cheval] shod ; [- chaussure] hobnailed ; [- roue] rimmed ; [- lacets] tagged **2.** *fam loc* **être ~ sur qqch** to be a genius at sthg ▪ **être ~ en qqch** to be well up on sthg.

ferrer [4] [fɛre] *vt* **1.** [garnir - roue] to rim ; [- canne] to tip with metal **2.** [cheval, bœuf] to shoe **3.** PÊCHE to strike.

ferreux, euse [fɛrø, øz] *adj* ferrous.

ferrique [fɛrik] *adj* ferric.

ferronnerie [fɛrɔnri] *nf* **1.** [art] : **~ (d'art)** wrought-iron craft **2.** [ouvrage] : **une belle ~ du XVIII**[e] **siècle** a fine piece of 18th-century wrought ironwork *ou* wrought-iron work ▪ **des ~s, de la ~** wrought ironwork, wrought-iron work **3.** [atelier] ironworks *(sing ou pl)*.
◆ **de ferronnerie, en ferronnerie** *loc adj* wrought-iron *(modif)*.

ferronnier [fɛrɔnje] *nm* : **~ (d'art)** wrought-iron craftsman.

ferroutage [fɛrutaʒ] *nm* piggy back.

ferroviaire [fɛrɔvjɛr] *adj* [trafic, tunnel, réseau] rail *(modif)*, railway UK *(modif)*, railroad US *(modif)*.

ferrugineux, euse [fɛryʒinø, øz] *adj* ferrugineous, ferruginous.

ferrure [fɛryr] *nf* **1.** [garniture] metal hinge **2.** [fait de ferrer] shoeing *(U)* **3.** [fers] horseshoes.

ferry [fɛri] (*pl* **ferries**) *nm* [pour voitures] car-ferry, ferry ▪ [pour voitures ou trains] ferry, ferry-boat.

ferry-boat [fɛribot] (*pl* **ferry-boats**) *nm* ferry-boat.

fertile [fɛrtil] *adj* **1.** AGRIC & GÉOGR fertile, rich ▪ **~ en** rich in ▪ **région ~ en agrumes** area rich in citrus fruit **2.** *fig* **~ en** rich in ▪ **une année ~ en événements** a very eventful year **3.** BIOL [femelle, femme, couple] fertile **4.** NUCL fertile.

fertilisable [fɛrtilizabl] *adj* AGRIC fertilizable.

fertilisant, e [fɛrtilizɑ̃, ɑ̃t] *adj* AGRIC fertilizing.
◆ **fertilisant** *nm* fertilizer.

fertilisation [fɛrtilizasjɔ̃] *nf* AGRIC & BIOL fertilization, fertilizing.

fertiliser [3] [fɛrtilize] *vt* AGRIC to fertilize.

fertilité [fɛrtilite] *nf* **1.** AGRIC fertility, fruitfulness **2.** BIOL [d'un couple, d'une femme] fertility **3.** [d'un esprit, d'un cerveau] fertility ▪ **connu pour la ~ de son imagination** famous for his fertile imagination.

féru, e [fery] *adj* : **être ~ de qqch** to be keen on *ou* highly interested in sthg.

férule [feryl] *nf* **1.** [fouet] ferule, ferula **2.** *loc* **être sous la ~ de qqn** to be under sb's strict authority.

fervent, e [fɛrvɑ̃, ɑ̃t] ◇ *adj* fervent, ardent.
◇ *nm, f* devotee, enthusiast, addict ▪ **les ~s du rugby** rugby enthusiasts *ou* fans.

ferveur [fɛrvœr] *nf* fervour, ardour, enthusiasm ▪ **avec ~** with enthusiasm, fervently, enthusiastically.

Fès [fɛz] *npr* Fez.

fesse [fɛs] *nf* **1.** ANAT buttock ▪ **les ~s** the buttocks ▪ **montrer ses ~s à tout le monde** to be bare-bottomed ▪ **pose tes ~s!** *fam* sit yourself down! **2.** [sexualité] : **la ~**△ [intime] sex ; [la pornographie] pornography, the porn industry ▪ **raconter des histoires de ~s** *fam* to tell dirty jokes **3.** HIST & NAUT tuck.
◆ **aux fesses** *loc adv fam* **avoir qqn aux ~s** to have sb on one's back.

fessée [fese] *nf* spanking ▪ **donner une ~ à qqn** to spank sb.

fesser [4] [fese] *vt* to spank.

fessier, ère [fesje, ɛr] *adj* buttocks *(modif)*, gluteal *spéc*.
◆ **fessier** *nm* **1.** ANAT buttocks, gluteus *spéc* **2.** *fam* [postérieur] behind, bottom, bum UK.

fessu, e [fesy] *adj fam* big-bottomed.

festif, ive [fɛstif, iv] *adj sout* festive.

festin [fɛstɛ̃] *nm* feast, banquet ▪ **faire un ~** to have *ou* hold a feast.

festival, als [fɛstival] *nm* festival ▪ **un ~ de jazz** a jazz festival ▪ **un ~ de** *fig* a brilliant display of.

festivalier, ère [fɛstivalje, ɛr] ◇ *adj* festival *(modif)*.
◇ *nm, f* festival-goer.

festivités [fɛstivite] *nfpl* festivities.

fest-noz [fɛstnoz] *nm* [dialecte] *traditional Breton village festival.*

festoie *etc v* ▷ **festoyer**.

festoiement [fɛstwamɑ̃] *nm* feasting.

feston [fɛstɔ̃] *nm* **1.** [guirlande - ARCHIT] festoon **2.** COUT scallop ▪ **point de ~** blanket stitch, buttonhole stitch.

festonner [3] [fɛstɔne] *vt* **1.** ARCHIT to festoon **2.** *litt* [orner] to adorn, to embellish **3.** COUT : **~ un col** to trim a collar with fancy edging.

festoyer [3] [fɛstwaje] *vi* to feast.

feta [feta] *nf* feta (cheese).

fêtard, e [fɛtar, ard] *nm, f* party animal.

fête [fɛt] *nf* **1.** [célébration - civile] holiday ; [- religieuse] feast ▪ **demain c'est ~** tomorrow we have a day off ➊ **la ~ de l'Assomption** (the feast of) the Assumption ▪ **~ légale** public holiday ▪ **la ~ des Mères** Mother's Day, Mothering Sunday *UK* ▪ **la ~ des Morts** All Souls' Day ▪ **la ~ nationale** [gén] the national holiday ; [en France] Bastille Day ; [aux États-Unis] Independence Day ▪ **la ~ de Noël** (the celebration of) Christmas ▪ **la ~ des Pères** Father's Day ▪ **la ~ des Rois** Twelfth Night, Epiphany ▪ **la ~ du Travail** May Day
2. [d'un saint] saint's day, name day ▪ **souhaiter sa ~ à qqn** to wish sb a happy saint's *ou* name day ➊ **on va lui faire sa ~!** we're going to teach him a lesson he won't forget! ▪ **ça va être ta ~!** you'll cop it *UK ou* catch hell *US*
3. [réunion - d'amis] party ▪ **on donne** *ou* **organise une petite ~ pour son anniversaire** we're giving a party for his birthday, we're giving him a birthday party ▪ **le film est une vraie ~ pour l'esprit/les sens** the film is really uplifting/a real treat for the senses ➊ **une ~ de famille** a family celebration *ou* gathering ▪ **vous serez de la ~ ?** will you be joining us/them? ▪ **être à la ~ : il n'a jamais été à pareille ~** *fig* he's never had such a good time ▪ **que la ~ commence!** let the festivities begin!
4. [foire] fair ▪ [kermesse] fête, fete ▪ [festival] festival, show ▪ **(et) la ~ continue!** the fun's not over yet! ▪ **ce n'est pas tous les jours (la) ~!** it's not everyday you've got something to celebrate! ▪ **faire la ~** to have a party *ou* (some) fun *ou* a good time ➊ **la ~ de la bière** the beer festival ▪ **~ foraine** [attractions] funfair *UK*, carnival *US* ▪ **la ~ de l'Humanité** *ou* **de l'Huma** *fam annual festival organized by the Communist daily newspaper 'l'Humanité'* ▪ **la ~ de la Musique** *annual music festival organized on the 21st of June in the streets of large towns* ▪ **~ à Neu-Neu** *large funfair held in the Bois de Boulogne every summer* ▪ **~ patronale** *town or village festival marking the patron saint's name*
5. *loc* **faire (la) ~ à qqn** to greet sb warmly ▪ **mon chien m'a fait (la) ~ quand je suis revenu** my dog was all over me when I got back ▪ **se faire une ~ de** to look forward eagerly to.
◆ **fêtes** *nfpl* [gén] holidays ▪ [de Noël et du jour de l'an] the Christmas and New Year celebrations ▪ **les ~s juives/catholiques** the Jewish/Catholic holidays ➊ **~s galantes** ART fêtes galantes.
◆ **de fête** *loc adj* [air, habits] festive.
◆ **en fête** *loc adj* : **la ville/les rues en ~** the festive town/streets.

FÊTE

The French traditionally wish *bonne fête* to the person who has the same name as the saint commemorated on a particular day.

Fête-Dieu [fɛtdjø] (*pl* **Fêtes-Dieu**) *nf* : **la ~** Corpus Christi.

fêter [4] [fete] *vt* **1.** [célébrer - anniversaire, événement] to celebrate ▪ **une promotion? il faut ~ ça!** a promotion? that's worth celebrating! **2.** [accueillir - personne] to fête, to fete ▪ **ils l'ont fêté à son retour** they celebrated his return.

fétiche [fetiʃ] *nm* **1.** [objet de culte] fetish, fetich **2.** [porte-bonheur] mascot ▪ *(comme adj)* lucky ▪ **mon numéro ~** my lucky number **3.** PSYCHOL fetish.

fétichisme [fetiʃism] *nm* **1.** [culte] fetishism, fetichism **2.** PSYCHOL fetishism **3.** [admiration] worship, cult ▪ **le ~ des sondages électoraux** the obsession with pre-election polls.

fétichiste [fetiʃist] ◇ *adj* **1.** RELIG & PSYCHOL fetishistic **2.** [admiratif] worshipping.
◇ *nmf* RELIG & PSYCHOL fetishist, fetichist.

fétide [fetid] *adj* fetid.

fétidité [fetidite] *nf* fetidness.

fétu [fety] *nm* : **~ (de paille)** (wisp of) straw.

feu[1], **x** [fø] ◇ *nm* **1.** [combustion] fire ▪ **faire du** *ou* **un ~** to make a fire ▪ **allumer un ~** to light a fire ▪ **~ de bois** (wood) fire ▪ **~ de braises** (glowing) embers ▪ **~ de cheminée** chimney fire ▪ **mettre le ~ à une maison** to set a house on fire ▪ **au ~!** fire! ➊ **~ de camp** campfire ▪ **~ d'enfer** blazing fire ▪ **~ de joie** bonfire ▪ **~ de paille** flash in the pan ▪ **les ~x de la Saint-Jean** *bonfires lit to celebrate Midsummer's Day* ▪ **le ~, l'épreuve du ~** HIST ordeal by fire ▪ **prendre ~** *pr* to catch fire ▪ **avoir le ~ sacré** to burn with enthusiasm ▪ **il n'y a pas le ~ (au lac)!** *hum* what's the big hurry?, where's the fire? ▪ **elle n'a pas fait long ~ dans l'entreprise** she didn't last long in the company ▪ **jouer avec le ~** to play with fire ▪ **il n'y a vu que du ~** he never saw a thing, he was completely taken in ▪ **il se jetterait dans le ~ pour lui/eux** he'd do anything for him/them ▪ **avoir le ~ au derrière** *fam ou* **aux fesses** *fam ou* **au cul** ▲ [être pressé] to be in a tearing hurry ; [sexuellement] to be horny△
2. [brûleur] ring, burner ▪ **à ~ doux** [plaque] on a gentle *ou* slow heat ; [four] in a slow oven ▪ **mijoter** *ou* **faire cuire à petit ~** to cook slowly ▪ **tuer** *ou* **faire mourir qqn à petit ~** *fig* to kill sb slowly *ou* by inches ▪ **à ~ vif** on a fierce heat ▪ **avoir qqch sur le ~** to be (in the middle of) cooking sthg ▪ **j'ai laissé le lait sur le ~!** I've left the milk on! ▪ **un plat/ramequin qui va sur le ~** a fireproof dish/ramekin
3. [briquet] : **avez-vous du ~?** have you got a light? ▪ **il n'a jamais de ~** he's never got a light
4. [en pyrotechnie] : **~ d'artifice** [spectacle] fireworks display ▪ **son récital, un vrai ~ d'artifice!** *fig* his recital was a virtuoso performance! ▪ **des ~x d'artifice** fireworks ▪ **~ de Bengale** Bengal light
5. MIL [tir] fire, shooting ▪ [combats] action ▪ **ouvrir le ~ (sur)** to open fire (on), to start firing (at) ▪ **cesser le ~** to cease fire ▪ **faire ~** to fire, to shoot ▪ **~!** fire! ➊ **un ~ croisé, des ~x croisés** *pr* crossfire ▪ **pris dans le ~ croisé de leurs questions** *fig* caught in the crossfire of their questions ▪ **~ nourri** *pr* sustained fire ▪ **un ~ nourri de plaisanteries** *fig* a constant stream of jokes ▪ **~ roulant** *pr* constant barrage ▪ **un ~ roulant de commentaires** *fig* a running commentary ▪ **mettre le ~ aux poudres** *pr* to spark off an explosion ; *fig* to spark things off
6. TRANSP [signal] : **~ (tricolore** *ou* **de signalisation)** traffic lights ▪ **~ rouge/orange/vert** red/amber/green light ▪ **à droite au troisième ~ (rouge)** right at the third set of (traffic) lights ▪ **donner le ~ vert à qqn/qqch** *fig* to give sb/sthg the green light *ou* the go-ahead
7. AÉRON, AUTO & NAUT light ▪ **~ arrière** taillight ▪ **~x de brouillard** fog lamps ▪ **~ de position** sidelight ▪ **~ de recul** reversing light ▪ **~x de croisement** headlights ▪ **~x de détresse** warning lights ▪ **~x de navigation** sailing lights ▪ **~x de route** headlights on full beam
8. CINÉ & THÉÂTRE : **les ~x de la rampe** the footlights ▪ **être sous le ~ des projecteurs** *pr* to be in front of the spotlights ; *fig* to be in the limelight ▪ **il est sous les ~x de l'actualité** he's very much in the news at the moment
9. *litt* [ardeur] fire, passion, ardour
10. *litt* [éclat, lumière] fire, light ▪ **le ~ de son regard** her fiery eyes ▪ **les ~x de la ville** the city lights ▪ **les cristaux brillaient de tous leurs ~x** the crystals sparkled brightly ▪ **le ~ d'un diamant** the blaze *ou* fire of a diamond
11. [sensation de brûlure] burn ▪ **le ~ me monta au visage** I went *ou* turned red, my face *ou* I flushed ▪ **le ~ du rasoir** razor burn
12. *arch* [maison] house, homestead
13. *fam* [pistolet] gun, rod *US*.
◇ *adj inv* flame *(modif)*, flame-coloured.
◆ **à feu et à sang** *loc adv* : **mettre un pays à ~ et à sang** to ransack and pillage a country.
◆ **avec feu** *loc adv* passionately.
◆ **dans le feu de** *loc prép* in the heat of ▪ **dans le ~ de l'action** in the heat of the moment.
◆ **en feu** *loc adj* **1.** [incendié] on fire, burning
2. [brûlant] : **j'ai la bouche/gorge en ~** my mouth/throat is burning ▪ **il entra, les joues en ~** he came in, cheeks ablaze.
◆ **sans feu ni lieu** *loc adv litt* : **être sans ~ ni lieu** to have nowhere to lay one's head.

◆ **tout feu tout flamme** *loc adj* burning with enthusiasm.
◆ **feu follet** *nm* will-o'-the-wisp.

feu², e [fø] *adj sout (inv avant l'article ou le possessif)* late ▪ **~ la reine** the late Queen.

feuillage [fœjaʒ] *nm* **1.** [sur l'arbre] foliage *spéc*, leaves ▪ **là-haut dans le ~** [d'un arbre] up there amongst the leaves ; [de la forêt] up in the canopy **2.** [coupé] foliage *spéc*, greenery.

feuillaison [fœjɛzɔ̃] *nf* **1.** [phénomène] foliation **2.** [époque] foliation period ▪ **au moment de la ~** when trees foliate.

feuillantine [fœjɑ̃tin] *nf* **1.** CULIN feuillantine pastry, puff pastry cake **2.** RELIG Feuillant nun.

feuille [fœj] *nf* **1.** BOT leaf ▪ **~ morte** dead *ou* fallen leaf ▪ **les Feuilles Mortes** *one of the most famous French cabaret songs, by Joseph Kosma with words by Jacques Prévert* **2.** [morceau de papier] sheet ▪ **les ~s d'un cahier** the sheets *ou* leaves *ou* pages of a notebook ➤ **une ~ de papier** a sheet of paper, a piece of paper ▪ **~ volante** (loose) sheet of paper **3.** PRESSE : **~ à sensations** gossip sheet **4.** [imprimé] form, slip ▪ **~ de maladie** *ou* **de soins** *claim form for reimbursement of medical expenses* ▪ **~ de route** *ou* **de déplacement** MIL travel warrant ▪ **~ d'émargement** pay sheet ▪ **~ d'heures** time sheet ▪ **~ d'impôts** tax form, tax return ▪ **~ de paie** payslip ▪ **~ de présence** attendance sheet ▪ **~ de température** MÉD temperature chart **5.** [plaque] leaf, sheet ▪ **~ de métal/d'or** metal/gold leaf **6.** INFORM sheet.
◆ **feuille de chêne** *nf* [laitue] oakleaf.
◆ **feuille de chou** *nf* **1.** PRESSE rag **2.** *loc* **il a les oreilles en ~ de chou** *fam* his ears stick out.
◆ **feuille de vigne** *nf* **1.** BOT vine leaf **2.** ART fig-leaf **3.** CULIN : **~s de vigne farcies** dolmades, stuffed vine leaves.

feuille-à-feuille [fœjafœj] *adj inv* sheet-fed.

feuille-morte [fœjmɔrt] *adj inv* russet, yellowish-brown.

feuillet [fœjɛ] *nm* **1.** [d'un formulaire] page, leaf **2.** BIOL layer ▪ **~s embryonnaires** germ layers **3.** ZOOL third stomach of ruminants **4.** MENUIS thin sheet of wood.

feuilleté, e [fœjte] *adj* **1.** CULIN puff *(modif)* **2.** GÉOL foliated **3.** TECHNOL laminated.
◆ **feuilleté** *nm* **1.** [dessert] puff pastry **2.** [hors-d'œuvre] puff pastry case ▪ **~ aux asperges** asparagus in puff pastry.

feuilleter [27] [fœjte] *vt* **1.** [album, magazine] to leaf *ou* to flip *ou* to flick through *(insép)*, to skim (through) **2.** CULIN : **~ de la pâte** to work the dough (into puff pastry) by rolling and folding it.

feuilleton [fœjtɔ̃] *nm* **1.** PRESSE series *(sing)*, serial **2.** TV : **~ (télévisé)** [sur plusieurs semaines] TV serial, mini-series ; [sur plusieurs années] soap opera **3.** LITTÉR feuilleton **4.** *fig* saga.

feuilletoniste [fœjtɔnist] *nmf* feuilletonist, serial writer.

feuillette *etc v* ▷ **feuilleter.**

feuillu, e [fœjy] *adj* leafy.
◆ **feuillu** *nm* lobed-leaved tree.

feuillure [fœjyr] *nf* rabbet, rebate.

feulement [følmɑ̃] *nm* growl.

feuler [3] [føle] *vi* to growl.

feutrage [føtraʒ] *nm* felting.

feutre [føtr] *nm* **1.** TEXT [étoffe] felt ▪ **de** *ou* **en ~** felt **2.** [chapeau] felt hat, ≃ fedora **3.** [stylo] felt-tip (pen).

feutré, e [føtre] *adj* **1.** [pull, vêtement] felted **2.** [garni de feutre - bourrelet] felt *(modif)* **3.** [silencieux - salon, atmosphère] quiet ; [- voix] muffled ▪ **marcher à pas ~s** to creep stealthily.

feutrer [3] [føtre] ◇ *vt* **1.** TEXT to felt **2.** [garnir - selle] to pad *ou* to line (with felt).
◇ *vi* to felt, to become felted *ou* matted ▪ **l'eau trop chaude fait ~ les pulls** washing in very hot water makes jumpers lose their finish.
◆ **se feutrer** *vpi* to felt, to become felted *ou* matted.

feutrine [føtrin] *nf* felt.

fève [fɛv] *nf* **1.** BOT bean **2.** [des Rois] *lucky charm or token made of porcelain and hidden in a "galette des Rois".*

février [fevrije] *nm* February, *voir aussi* **mars.**

fez [fɛz] *nm* fez.

FF *(abr écrite de* **de franc français***)* FF.

FFA *(abr de* **Forces françaises en Allemagne***) npr fpl French forces in Germany.*

FFI *(abr de* **Forces françaises de l'intérieur***) npr fpl French Resistance forces during World War II.*

FFL *(abr de* **Forces françaises libres***) npr fpl free French Army during World War II.*

FFR *(abr de* **Fédération française de rugby***) npr f French rugby federation.*

fg = **faubourg.**

FGEN *(abr de* **Fédération générale de l'Éducation nationale***) npr f teachers' trade union.*

fi [fi] *interj* **1.** *hum* fi! pooh! **2.** *loc* **faire ~ de** [mépriser] to turn one's nose up at, to spurn ; [ignorer] to ignore.

fiabiliser [3] [fjabilize] *vt* [système] : **~ qqch** to safeguard sthg ‖ [document, label] to guarantee the accuracy of sthg.

fiabilité [fjabilite] *nf* [crédibilité] reliability.

fiable [fjabl] *adj* [crédible] reliable.

FIAC [fjak] *(abr de* **Foire internationale d'art contemporain***) npr f annual international contemporary art fair in Paris.*

fiacre [fjakr] *nm* fiacre, (horse-drawn) carriage.

fiançailles [fijɑ̃saj] *nfpl* **1.** [promesse] engagement ▪ **à quand tes ~?** when are you getting engaged? **2.** [cérémonie] engagement party **3.** [durée] engagement (period).

fiancé, e [fijɑ̃se] *nm, f* fiancé *(f* fiancée) ▪ **les ~s** the betrothed *litt & hum*, the engaged couple.

fiancer [16] [fijɑ̃se] *vt* to betroth *sout* ▪ **elle est fiancée à Paul** she's engaged to Paul, she and Paul are engaged.
◆ **se fiancer** *vpi* to get engaged ▪ **se ~ avec qqn** to get engaged to sb.

fiasco [fjasko] *nm* **1.** [entreprise, tentative] fiasco, flop ▪ [film, ouvrage] flop ▪ **faire ~** to flop, to be a (total) failure **2.** [échec sexuel] failure to perform.

fiasque [fjask] *nf* (Italian) wine flask.

fibre [fibr] *nf* **1.** [du bois] fibre, woodfibre ▪ **dans le sens de la ~** going with the grain (of the wood) **2.** OPT & TECHNOL fibre ▪ **~ de verre** fibreglass ▪ **~ optique** fibre optics *(sing)* **3.** TEXT : **une ~ textile** a fibre ▪ **les ~s naturelles/synthétiques** naturally-occurring/man-made fibres **4.** [dans un muscle] muscle fibre **5.** [sentiment] feeling ▪ **avoir la ~ commerçante** to be a born shopkeeper ▪ **avoir la ~ paternelle** to have strong paternal feelings ▪ **faire jouer** *ou* **vibrer la ~ patriotique de qqn** to play upon sb's patriotic feelings.

fibreux, euse [fibrø, øz] *adj* **1.** [dur - viande] stringy, tough **2.** [à fibres - tissu, muscle] fibrous.

fibrillation [fibrijasjɔ̃] *nf* fibrillation, fibrillating *(U)*.

fibrille [fibrij] *nf* [fibre - courte] short fibre ; [- fine] thin fibre.

fibrome [fibrom] *nm* [tumeur] fibroma ▪ [dans l'utérus] fibroid.

fibromyalgie [fibrɔmjalʒi] *nf* MÉD fibromyalgia (syndrome), fibrositis.

fibroscopie [fibrɔskɔpi] *nf* fibrescopy.

fibrose [fibroz] *nf* fibrosis.

ficelage [fislaʒ] *nm* tying up.

ficelé, e [fisle] *adj* : **bien ~** [histoire, scénario] tight, seamless ; [dossier] well put together.

ficeler [24] [fisle] *vt* to tie up *(sép)* ▪ **ficelé comme un saucisson** *fig* trussed up like a chicken.

ficelle [fisɛl] *nf* **1.** [corde] piece of string ■ **de la ~** string ◐ **la ~ est un peu grosse** *fig* it sticks out like a sore thumb ■ **connaître toutes les ~s du métier** to know the ropes ■ **ça, c'est une des ~s du métier** that's one of the tricks of the trade ■ **tirer les ~s** to pull the strings **2.** [pain] *very thin baguette* **3.** △ *arg mil* officer's stripe.

ficellera *etc v* ▷ **ficeler.**

fichage [fiʃaʒ] *nm* [mise sur fichier] filing, recording.

fiche[1] [3] [fiʃ] *vt fam* **1.** = **ficher 2.** *loc* **il n'en a rien à ~** he couldn't care less ■ **va te** *ou* **allez vous faire ~!** get lost!
◆ **se fiche** *fam* = **se ficher.**
◆ **se fiche de** *fam* = **se ficher de.**

fiche[2] [fiʃ] *nf* **1.** [carton] piece of (stiff) card, (index) card ■ **~ cuisine** recipe card ■ **mettre qqch sur ~** to index *ou* to card-index *UK* sthg **2.** [papier] sheet, slip ■ **~ de paie** pay slip ■ **~ signalétique** identification slip *ou* sheet ■ **~ technique** COMM product specification **3.** [formulaire] form ■ **mettre qqn en** *ou* **sur ~** to open a file on sb ◐ **remplir une ~ d'hôtel** to register (with a hotel), to fill in a (hotel) registration card **4.** JEUX counter **5.** INFORM : **~ suiveuse** route card **6.** CONSTR hinge **7.** ÉLECTR plug ■ **~ téléphonique** phone *ou* jack plug ■ **~ multiple** multiple adaptor *ou* adapter.

ficher[1] [3] [fiʃe] *vt* **1.** [enfoncer] to drive *ou* to stick (in) ■ **un couteau fiché entre les omoplates** a knife stuck right between the shoulderblades **2.** [information] to file, to put on file ■ [suspect] to put on file ■ **il est fiché** the police have got a file on him.

ficher[2] [3] [fiʃe] *vt* (*pp* **fichu**) *fam* **1.** [mettre] : **fiche-le à la porte!** throw *ou* kick him out! ■ **son patron l'a fichu à la porte** his boss fired him *ou* threw him out *ou* sacked *UK* him ■ **fiche ça dans le placard** throw *ou* stick it in the closet ■ **fiche-moi ça dehors!** get rid of this! ■ **je lui ai fichu mon poing dans la figure** I punched him in the face ■ **~ à plat : ce temps me fiche à plat** this weather really wipes me out ■ **~ dedans : c'est cette phrase qui m'a fichu dedans** it was that phrase that got me into trouble *ou* hot water ■ **~ en l'air : tu l'as fichue en l'air, sa lettre?** did you throw away his letter? ■ **ce contretemps fiche tout en l'air** this last-minute hitch really messes everything up ■ **~ en rogne : c'est le genre de remarque qui me fiche en rogne** that's the kind of remark that drives me mad ■ **~ par terre : fais attention sur ce vélo, tu vas te ~ par terre!** mind how you go on that bike or you'll fall off! ■ **si c'est fermé mardi, ça fiche tout par terre!** if it's closed on Tuesday, everything's ruined!
2. [faire] to do ■ **qu'est-ce que tu fiches ici?** what on earth *ou* the heck are you doing here? ■ **je n'ai rien fichu aujourd'hui** I haven't done a thing today ■ **bon sang, qu'est-ce qu'il fiche?** [où est-il] for God's sake, where on earth is he? ; [que fait-il] what the heck is he doing?
3. [donner] : **~ qqch à qqn : ça me fiche le cafard** it makes me feel down *ou* depressed ■ **ça m'a fichu la chair de poule/la trouille** it gave me the creeps/the willies ■ **fiche-moi la paix!** leave me alone! ■ **je t'en ficherai, moi, du champagne!** champagne? I'll give you champagne! ◐ **je te fiche mon billet que...** I'll bet my bottom dollar that...
◆ **se ficher** *vpi fam* [se mettre] : **ils se sont fichus dans un fossé** [en voiture] they drove into a ditch ; [pour passer inaperçus] they jumped into a ditch ■ **se ~ en l'air** to do o.s. in ■ **se ~ dedans** to land o.s. right in it.
◆ **se ficher de** *vp+prép fam* **1.** [railler] : **elle n'arrête pas de se ~ de lui** she keeps making fun of him, she's forever pulling his leg ■ **tu te fiches de moi ou quoi?** are you kidding me? ■ **300 euros pour ça ? il se fiche de toi!** 300 euros for this ? he's trying to swindle you *ou* he really takes you for a sucker ■ **eh bien, tu ne t'es pas fichu de nous!** well, you've really done things in style!
2. [être indifférent à] : **je me fiche de ce que disent les gens** I don't care what *ou* I don't give a damn about what people say ◐ **je m'en fiche comme de ma première chemise** *ou* **comme de l'an quarante** *ou* **complètement** I don't give a damn (about it), I couldn't care less.

fichier [fiʃje] *nm* **1.** [fiches] (card index) file, catalogue ■ **le ~ de nos clients** our file of customers **2.** [meuble] filing cabinet ■ [boîte] file **3.** INFORM file ■ **~ à accès limité** restricted file ■ **~ de détail/travail** detail/scratch file ■ **~ principal** main *ou* master file ■ **~ séquentiel** sequential file.

fichtre [fiʃtr] *interj fam vieilli* **~!** (my) gosh!, my (my)!

fichtrement [fiʃtrəmɑ̃] *adv fam vieilli* darn ■ **je n'en sais ~ rien!** how the heck should I know!

fichu[1] [fiʃy] *nm* (large) scarf.

fichu[2]**, e** [fiʃy] *adj fam* **1.** [perdu] : **il est ~** he's had it ■ **pour samedi soir, c'est ~** Saturday evening's up the spout *UK ou* down the drain *US* **2.** *(avant le n)* [mauvais] lousy, rotten ■ **quel ~ temps!** what lousy weather! **3.** *(avant le n)* [important] : **j'ai un ~ mal de dents** I've got one hell of a nasty toothache **4.** [capable] : **~ de : il n'est même pas ~ de prendre un message correctement** he can't even take a message properly **5.** *loc* **bien ~ : il est bien ~** he's got a nice body ■ **ce système est très bien ~** it's a very clever device ■ **mal ~** [de corps] : **il est mal ~** he hasn't got a very nice body ■ **leur manuel est mal ~** their handbook is lousy ■ **je suis mal ~ aujourd'hui** [malade] I feel lousy today.

fictif, ive [fiktif, iv] *adj* **1.** [imaginaire] imaginary, fictitious **2.** [faux - promesse] false **3.** FIN fictitious.

fiction [fiksjɔ̃] *nf* **1.** [domaine de l'imaginaire] : **la ~** fiction ■ **un livre de politique-~** a political novel **2.** [histoire] story, (piece of) fiction **3.** DR fiction *(C)* ■ **~ légale** *ou* **de droit** legal fiction.

fictivement [fiktivmɑ̃] *adv* fictitiously ■ **transposons-nous ~ au XVIII**[e] **siècle** let's imagine we're in the 18th century.

ficus [fikys] *nm* ficus ■ **~ elastica** rubber plant.

fidèle [fidɛl] ◇ *adj* **1.** [constant - ami] faithful, loyal, true ; [- employé, animal] loyal, faithful ; [- conjoint] faithful ; [- client] regular ■ **~ à : elle a été ~ à sa parole** *ou* **promesse** she kept her word ■ **être ~ à une idée** to stand by *ou* to be true to an idea ■ **être ~ à une marque/un produit** to stick with a particular brand/product ■ **~ à elle-même** true to herself ◐ **elle est toujours ~ au poste** you can always rely *ou* depend on her **2.** [conforme - copie, description] true, exact ; [- traduction] faithful, close ; [- historien, narrateur] faithful ; [- mémoire] reliable, correct ; [- balance] reliable, accurate ■ **~ à : livre ~ à la réalité** book which is true to life.
◇ *nmf* **1.** RELIG believer ■ **les ~s** [croyants] the believers ; [pratiquants] the faithful ; [assemblée] the congregation **2.** [adepte] devotee, follower ■ [client] regular ■ **je suis un ~ de votre émission** I never miss one of your shows.

fidèlement [fidɛlmɑ̃] *adv* **1.** [régulièrement] regularly **2.** [loyalement] faithfully, loyally ■ **suivre qqn ~** to follow sb faithfully **3.** [conformément] exactly, faithfully.
◆ **fidèlement vôtre** *loc adv* yours (ever).

fidélisation [fidelizasjɔ̃] *nf* : **~ des clients** *ou* **d'une clientèle** fostering of customer loyalty *(by a marketing policy).*

fidéliser [3] [fidelize] *vt* : **~ ses clients** *ou* **sa clientèle** to foster customer loyalty *(by a marketing policy)* ■ **~ un public** to maintain a regular audience *(by a commercial policy).*

fidélité [fidelite] *nf* **1.** [loyauté - d'un ami, d'un employé, d'un animal] faithfulness, loyalty ; [- d'un conjoint] faithfulness, fidelity ; [- d'un client] loyalty ■ **sa ~ à sa parole** *ou* **promesse** his faithfulness, his keeping faith **2.** [exactitude - d'un récit, d'une description] accuracy, faithfulness ; [- de la mémoire] reliability ; [- d'un instrument] accuracy, reliability.

Fidji [fidʒi] *npr fpl* : **les (îles) ~** Fiji, the Fiji Islands, *voir aussi* **île.**

fiduciaire [fidysjɛr] *adj* fiduciary.

fief [fjɛf] *nm* **1.** HIST fief **2.** [domaine réservé] fief, kingdom ◐ **un ~ électoral** a politician's fief.

fieffé, e [fjefe] *adj* **1.** HIST enfeoffed **2.** *fam péj* [extrême] complete, utter ■ **un ~ menteur/voleur** an arrant liar/thief.

fiel [fjɛl] *nm* **1.** [bile] gall, bile **2.** *litt* [amertume] rancour, bitterness, gall ■ [méchanceté] venom ■ **des propos pleins de ~** venomous words ■ **un sourire plein de ~** a twisted smile.

fielleux, euse [fjɛlø, øz] *adj litt* venomous, spiteful.

fiente [fjɑ̃t] *nf* : **de la ~** droppings.

fier[1] [9] [fje] ◆ **se fier à** *vp+prép* **1.** [avoir confiance en] to trust (in) ▪ **se ~ aux apparences** to go by *OU* on appearances ▪ **ne vous y fiez pas!** don't be fooled by it/him *etc* ! **2.** [compter sur] to rely on.

fier[2], **fière** [fjɛr] ◇ *adj* **1.** [satisfait] proud ▪ **il n'y a pas de quoi être ~** it's nothing to be proud of ▪ **~ de** proud of ▪ **j'étais ~ d'avoir gagné** I was proud (that) I won ▪ **je n'étais pas ~ de moi** I wasn't pleased with *OU* proud of myself **2.** [noble] noble, proud ▪ **une âme fière** *litt* a noble mind **3.** [arrogant - personnage] proud, arrogant, haughty ; [- regard] haughty, supercilious ▪ **quand il a fallu sauter, il n'était plus tellement ~** when it came to jumping, he didn't seem so sure of himself ▪ **avoir fière allure** to cut (quite) a dash ▶ **être ~ comme Artaban** *OU* **comme un coq** to be as proud as a peacock, to be puffed up with pride **4.** *fam (avant le n) fam* [extrême] : **tu as un ~ culot!** you've got some nerve!
◇ *nm, f* proud person ▪ **faire le ~** to put on airs and graces.

fier-à-bras [fjɛrabra] (*pl inv OU pl* **fiers-à-bras**) *nm* braggart.

fièrement [fjɛrmɑ̃] *adv* proudly.

fiérot, e [fjɛro, ɔt] *fam* ◇ *adj* proud.
◇ *nm, f* : **faire le ~** to show off.

fierté [fjɛrte] *nf* **1.** [dignité] pride ▪ **par ~, je ne lui ai pas parlé** my pride wouldn't let me talk to him ▪ **ravaler sa ~** to swallow one's pride ▪ **elle n'a pas beaucoup de ~** she hasn't much pride *OU* self-respect **2.** [arrogance] arrogance, haughtiness, superciliousness **3.** [satisfaction] (source of) pride ▪ **tirer ~** *OU* **une grande ~ de** to take (a) pride in, to pride o.s. on.
◆ **avec fierté** *loc adv* proudly.

fiesta [fjɛsta] *nf fam* (wild) party, rave-up *UK*, blowout *US* ▪ **faire la ~** to live it up.

fièvre [fjɛvr] *nf* **1.** MÉD fever, temperature ▪ **avoir de la ~** to have a temperature *OU* a fever ▪ **il a 40 de ~** his temperature is up to 40°, he has a temperature of 40° ▪ **pour faire baisser la ~** (in order) to get the temperature down ▶ **~ aphteuse** foot and mouth disease ▪ **~ jaune** yellow fever ▪ **~ de Malte** Malta fever ▪ **~ quinte** quintan fever ▪ **~ typhoïde** typhoid fever **2.** *sout* [agitation] excitement ▪ **elle parlait avec ~** she spoke excitedly ▪ **dans la ~ du moment** in the heat of the moment **3.** [désir] : **avoir la ~ de l'or** to have a passion for gold.

fiévreusement [fjevrøzmɑ̃] *adv* MÉD & *fig* feverishly.

fiévreux, euse [fjevrø, øz] *adj* MÉD & *fig* feverish, febrile.

FIFA [fifa] (*abr de* **Fédération internationale de football association**) *npr f* FIFA.

fifille [fifij] *nf fam* little girl.

fifre [fifr] *nm* **1.** [flûte] fife **2.** [joueur] fife player.

fifty-fifty [fiftififti] *loc adv fam* fifty-fifty, half-and-half ▪ **faisons ~** let's go halves.

fig. = **figure**.

Figaro [figaro] *npr m* : **le ~** PRESSE *French daily newspaper with a conservative bias.*

figé, e [fiʒe] *adj* set ▪ **dans une attitude ~e** motionless.

figer [17] [fiʒe] ◇ *vt* **1.** [coaguler - huile] to congeal ; [- sang] to coagulate, to clot ▪ **des cris à vous ~ le sang** bloodcurdling screams **2.** [immobiliser - personne] : **sa réponse m'a figé sur place** his answer struck me dumb.
◇ *vi* [huile] to congeal ▪ [sang] to coagulate, to clot.
◆ **se figer** *vpi* **1.** [être coagulé - huile] to congeal ; [- sang] to coagulate, to clot ▪ **mon sang s'est figé dans mes veines** my blood froze **2.** [s'immobiliser - attitude, sourire] to stiffen ; [- personne] to freeze ▪ **elle se figea sous l'effet de la terreur** she was rooted to the spot with fear.

fignolage [fiɲɔlaʒ] *nm* perfecting, touching up, polishing (up).

fignoler [3] [fiɲɔle] *vt* to perfect, to polish *OU* to touch up *(sép)* ▪ **un travail fignolé** a polished piece of work.

fignoleur, euse [fiɲɔlœr, øz] ◇ *adj* meticulous, finicky *péj.*
◇ *nm, f* meticulous *OU* *péj* finicky worker.

figue [fig] *nf* fig ▪ **~ de Barbarie** prickly pear.

figuier [figje] *nm* fig tree ▪ **~ de Barbarie** prickly pear, opuntia *spéc.*

figurant, e [figyrɑ̃, ɑ̃t] *nm, f* CINÉ extra ▪ THÉÂTRE extra, walk-on actor ▪ DANSE figurant ▪ **être réduit au rôle de ~** *OU* **à jouer les ~s** [dans une réunion] to be a mere onlooker ; [auprès d'une personne importante] to be a stooge.

figuratif, ive [figyratif, iv] *adj* [art] figurative, representational ▪ [artiste] representational ▪ [plan] figurative.
◆ **figuratif** *nm* representational artist.

figuration [figyrasjɔ̃] *nf* **1.** [métier] : **la ~** CINÉ being an *OU* working as an extra ; THÉÂTRE doing a walk-on part ; DANSE being a *OU* dancing as a figurant ▪ **faire de la ~** CINÉ to work as an extra ; THÉÂTRE to do walk-on parts ; DANSE to dance as a figurant **2.** [fait de représenter] representation, figuration.

figure [figyr] *nf* **1.** [visage] face ▪ [mine] face, features ▪ **faire triste** *OU* **piètre ~** to cut a sad figure, to be a sad *OU* sorry sight ▪ **faire bonne ~** to look contented ▪ **faire ~ de : parmi tous ces imbéciles, il fait ~ de génie!** all those idiots make him look like a genius! ▪ **prendre ~** to take shape ▶ **ne plus avoir ~ humaine** to be totally unrecognizable *OU* disfigured **2.** [personnage] figure ▪ **une grande ~ de la politique** a great political figure **3.** NAUT & *fig* **~ de proue** figurehead **4.** [illustration] figure, illustration ▪ [schéma, diagramme] diagram, figure ▪ **~ géométrique** geometrical figure **5.** JEUX picture card, face card *US* **6.** DANSE, MUS & SPORT figure ▪ **~s imposées** compulsory figures ▪ **~s libres** freestyle **7.** LING : **~ de rhétorique** rhetorical figure ▪ **~ de style** stylistic device.

figuré, e [figyre] *adj* LING [langage, sens] figurative.
◆ **au figuré** *loc adv* figuratively.

figurer [3] [figyre] ◇ *vt* **1.** [représenter] to represent, to show, to depict **2.** [symboliser] to symbolize.
◇ *vi* **1.** [apparaître] to appear ▪ **votre nom ne figure pas sur la liste** your name doesn't appear *OU* isn't on the list ▪ **~ au nombre des élus** to be among the successful candidates ▪ **j'ai oublié de faire ~ son nom sur l'affiche** I forgot to include his name on the poster **2.** CINÉ to be an extra ▪ THÉÂTRE to do a walk-on part.
◆ **se figurer** *vpt* **1.** [imaginer] to imagine **2.** [croire] to believe ▪ **figure-toi qu'il n'a même pas appelé!** he didn't even call, can you believe it! ▪ **eh bien figure-toi que moi non plus, je n'ai pas le temps!** surprising though it may seem, I haven't got the time either!

figurine [figyrin] *nf* figurine, statuette.

fil [fil] *nm* **1.** TEXT [matière - de coton, de soie] thread ; [- de laine] yarn *(U)* ▪ [brin - de coton, de soie] piece of thread ; [- de laine] strand ▪ **cachemire trois/quatre ~s** three-ply/four-ply cashmere ▶ **~ à bâtir/à coudre** basting/sewing thread ▪ **~ dentaire** dental floss ▪ **~ d'Écosse** lisle ▪ **~ de Nylon®** nylon thread ▪ **de ~ en aiguille** one thing leading to another ▪ **donner du ~ à retordre à qqn** to cause sb (no end of) trouble
2. [lin] linen ▪ **draps de ~** linen sheets
3. [filament - de haricot] string ▪ **haricots pleins de/sans ~s** stringy/stringless beans
4. [corde - à linge] line ; [- d'équilibriste] tightrope, high wire ; [- pour marionnette] string ▪ **~ d'Ariane** MYTHOL Ariadne's thread ▪ **~ conducteur** *OU* **d'Ariane** [d'une enquête] (vital) lead ; [dans une histoire] main theme ▪ **débrouiller** *OU* **démêler les ~s d'une intrigue** to unravel the threads *OU* strands of a plot ▪ **sa vie ne tient qu'à un ~** his life hangs by a thread ▪ **un ~ de la Vierge** a gossamer thread ▪ **avoir un ~ à la patte** to be tied down, to have one's hands tied
5. [câble] wire ▪ **~ de cuivre/d'acier** copper/steel wire ▶ **~ télégraphique/téléphonique** telegraph/telephone wire ▪ **~ de terre** earth *UK OU* ground *US* wire ▪ **~ à couper le beurre** cheesewire ▪ **~ électrique** wire ▪ **~ de fer** wire ▪ **~ de fer barbelé** barbed wire ▪ **clôture en ~ de fer** [gén] wire fence ; [barbelé] barbed wire fence ▪ **c'est un ~ de fer, ce type!** that guy's as thin as a rake! ▪ **~ à plomb** plumbline ▪ **~ à souder** soldering wire
6. *fam* [téléphone] : **au bout du ~** on the phone, on the line ▪ **à l'autre bout du ~** on the other end of the line

7. [tranchant] edge ▶ **passer qqn au ~ de l'épée** to put sb to the sword ■ **être sur le ~ du rasoir** to be on a knife-edge
8. [sens - du bois, de la viande] grain ■ **dans le sens contraire au ~, contre le ~** against the grain
9. [cours - de l'eau] current, stream ; [- de la pensée, d'une discussion] thread ■ **perdre/reprendre le ~ d'une histoire** to lose/to pick up the thread of a story ■ **le ~ des événements** the chain of events.
◆ **au fil de** *loc prép* **1.** [le long de] : **aller au ~ de l'eau** to go with the current *OU* stream
2. [au fur et à mesure de] : **au ~ du temps** as time goes by ■ **au ~ des semaines** as the weeks go by, with the passing weeks ■ **au ~ de la discussion je m'aperçus que...** as the discussion progressed I realized that...
◆ **sans fil** *loc adj* [télégraphie, téléphonie] wireless *(modif)* ■ [rasoir, téléphone] cordless.

fil-à-fil [filafil] *nm inv* pepper-and-salt cloth.

filage [filaʒ] *nm* **1.** TEXT spinning **2.** THÉÂTRE run-through.

filaire[1] [filɛr] [filɛr] *adj* telegraphic.

filaire[2] [filɛr] [filɛr] *nf* filaria.

filament [filamɑ̃] *nm* **1.** [fibre] filament **2.** TEXT thread **3.** ÉLECTR filament.

filamenteux, euse [filamɑ̃tø, øz] *adj* filamentous, filamentary.

filandreux, euse [filɑ̃drø, øz] *adj* **1.** [fibreux - viande] stringy **2.** *péj* [confus - style, discours] long-winded.

filant, e [filɑ̃, ɑ̃t] *adj* **1.** [qui file - liquide] free-running **2.** MÉD [pouls] (very) weak.

filasse [filas] ◇ *nf* tow.
◇ *adj inv* : **cheveux (blonds) ~** *péj* dirty blond hair.

filature [filatyr] *nf* **1.** TEXT [opérations] spinning ■ [usine] (spinning) mill **2.** [surveillance] shadowing, tailing ■ **prendre qqn en ~** to shadow *OU* to tail sb.

fildeferiste [fildəferist] *nmf* high wire acrobat.

file [fil] *nf* **1.** [suite - de véhicules] line, row ; [- de personnes] line ■ **se mettre en ~** to queue up *UK*, to line up, to stand in line ■ **prendre la ~** to join the line ▶ **~ d'attente** queue *UK*, line *US* ■ **en ~ indienne** in single file **2.** TRANSP lane ■ **la ~ de droite** the right-hand lane ■ **sur deux ~s** in two lanes **3.** MIL file of soldiers.
◆ **à la file** *loc adv* in a row, one after another *OU* the other ■ **il a bu trois verres à la ~** he drank three glasses in a row *OU* one after another.

filer [3] [file] ◇ *vt* **1.** TECHNOL & TEXT to spin ■ **~ un mauvais coton** *fam* [être malade] to be in bad shape ; [se préparer des ennuis] to be heading for trouble
2. ENTOM to spin
3. [dérouler - câble, amarre] to pay out *(sép)*, to release
4. [développer - image, métaphore] to draw *OU* to spin out *(sép)* ■ [tenir - note, son] to draw out *(sép)*
5. JEUX [carte] to palm off *(sép)* ■ **~ les cartes** [au poker] to show one's hand
6. [suivre - suj: détective] to tail, to shadow
7. [déchirer - collant, bas] to ladder *UK*, to run *US*
8. *fam* [donner] to give ■ **il m'a filé un coup de poing** he landed *UK OU* beaned *US* me one ■ **on m'a filé le sale boulot** they landed *UK OU* stuck *US* me with the rotten job ■ **elle m'a filé la grippe** she's given me the flu ■ **~ une gifle à qqn** to smack *OU* to slap sb in the face
9. *loc* **~ le parfait amour** to live a great romance.
◇ *vi* **1.** [liquide] to run, to flow ■ [fromage] to run
2. [flamme, lampe] to smoke
3. [se dérouler - câble] to run out
4. NAUT : **~ (à) 20 nœuds** to sail *OU* to proceed at 20 knots
5. [collants, bas] to ladder *UK*, to run ■ [maille] to run
6. [passer vite - coureur, véhicule] to dash ; [- nuage] to fly (past) ; [- temps] to fly ■ **~ à toute vitesse** [voiture] to bomb along ■ **il a filé dans sa chambre** [gén] he dashed *OU* flew into his bedroom ; [après une réprimande] he stormed off to his room ■ **bon, je file!** right, I'm off! ■ **l'argent lui file entre les doigts** money just slips through his fingers
7. *fam* [disparaître - cambrioleur] to scram, to scarper *UK*, to skedaddle *US* ■ **je t'ai assez vu, file!** I've had enough of you, scram! *OU* clear off! ▶ **~ à l'anglaise** to sneak off, to take French leave
8. *fam* [argent] to go, to disappear, to vanish
9. *loc* **~ doux** to behave o.s.

filet [filɛ] *nm* **1.** ANAT fibre
2. ARCHIT fillet
3. TECHNOL thread
4. IMPR rule
5. [petite quantité] : **un ~ de : un ~ d'eau** a trickle of water ■ **un ~ de bave** a dribble of saliva ■ **un ~ de sang** a trickle of blood ■ **un ~ d'air** a (light) stream of air ■ **un ~ de lumière** a (thin) shaft of light ■ **un ~ de citron/vinaigre** a dash of lemon/vinegar ■ **un (petit) ~ de voix** a thin (reedy) voice
6. CULIN [de viande, de poisson] fillet ■ **un morceau dans le ~** [de bœuf] ≃ a sirloin *OU* porterhouse steak ▶ **~ mignon** filet mignon
7. [ouvrage à mailles] net ■ **~ à cheveux/à papillons** hair/butterfly net ■ **~ (à bagages)** (luggage) rack ■ **~ à provisions** string shopping bag ■ **~ (de pêche)** (fishing) net ■ **attirer qqn dans ses ~s** *fig* to entrap *OU* to ensnare sb ■ **tendre un ~** [pour la chasse] to set a snare ; *fig* to lay a trap
8. SPORT [au football, au hockey, au tennis] net ■ [d'acrobate] safety net ■ **envoyer la balle dans le ~** to hit the ball into the net ▶ **monter au ~** to come to the net ■ **travailler sans ~** *pr* to perform without a safety net ; *fig* to take risks.

fileter [28] [filte] *vt* **1.** TECHNOL to thread **2.** CULIN to fillet.

fileur, euse [filœr, øz] *nm, f* spinner.

filial, e, aux [filjal, o] *adj* filial.
◆ **filiale** *nf* subsidiary (company).

filiation [filjasjɔ̃] *nf* **1.** [entre individus] line of descent, filiation *sout* ■ DR filiation **2.** [entre des mots, des idées] relationship.

filière [filjɛr] *nf* **1.** [procédures] procedures, channels ■ **passer par la ~ administrative** to go through administrative channels **2.** [réseau - de trafiquants, de criminels] network, connection ■ **remonter une ~** to trace a network back to its ringleaders **3.** ÉDUC & UNIV : **la ~ technique/scientifique** technical/scientific subjects **4.** MÉTALL : **~ (à machine)** [pour étirage] draw, drawing plate ; [pour tréfilage, filage] die **5.** ENTOM spinneret **6.** TEXT spinneret **7.** NAUT guardrail **8.** INDUST industry.

filiforme [filifɔrm] *adj* **1.** [maigre] lanky, spindly **2.** MÉD [pouls] thready.

filigrane [filigran] *nm* **1.** [d'un papier] watermark **2.** JOAILL filigree.
◆ **en filigrane** *loc adv* between the lines ■ **le problème du racisme apparaissait en ~ dans la discussion** the problem of racism was implicit in the discussion.

filigraner [3] [filigrane] *vt* **1.** [papier] to watermark ■ **du papier filigrané** watermarked paper **2.** JOAILL to filigree.

filin [filɛ̃] *nm* rope.

fille [fij] *nf* **1.** [enfant] girl ■ **c'est une belle/gentille ~** she's a good-looking/nice girl ■ **tu es une grande ~ maintenant** you're a big girl now ■ **c'est encore une petite ~** she's still a little girl
2. [jeune fille] girl ■ [femme] woman ■ **une ~ de la campagne** a country girl ■ **rester ~** *vieilli* to remain single *OU* unmarried ▶ **~ mère** unmarried mother
3. [descendante] daughter ▶ **une ~ de bonne famille** a respectable girl ■ **tu es bien la ~ de ton père!** you're just like your father!
4. [en appellatif] : **ma ~** (my) girl
5. *vieilli* [employée] : **~ de cuisine** kitchen maid ■ **~ de ferme** farm girl
6. *vieilli* [prostituée] whore ▶ **~ publique** *OU* **de joie** *OU* **des rues** *OU* **perdue** *litt* prostitute ■ **~ à soldats** camp follower
7. HIST : **~ d'honneur** maid of honour.

fillette [fijɛt] *nf* **1.** [enfant] little girl **2.** [bouteille] small bottle *(for wine)*.

filleul, e [fijœl] *nm, f* godchild, godson (*f* goddaughter) ■ **~ de guerre** MIL *soldier taken care of by a woman during a war.*

film [film] *nm* **1.** CINÉ [pellicule] film ■ [œuvre] film *UK*, movie *US* ■ **tourner un ~** to shoot a film ■ **les ~s d'aventures/d'épouvante** adventure/horror films ■ **~ doublé** dubbed film ▶ **~ en noir et blanc/en couleur** black and white/colour film ■ **~ d'actualités** newsreel ■ **~ d'animation** animated film ■ **~ d'auteur** art film ■ **~ catastrophe** disaster film *UK* ■ **~ culte** cult film ■ **~ documentaire** documentary (film) ■ **~ muet** silent film ■ **~ parlant** talking film, talkie ■ **~X** X *ou* adults-only film **2.** PHOTO film **3.** [couche] film ■ **un ~ d'huile** a film of oil **4.** [pour la cuisine] : **~ alimentaire** clingfilm **5.** [déroulement] sequence ■ **le ~ des événements** the sequence of events.

filmer [3] [filme] *vt* [scène, événement] to film, to shoot ■ [personnage] to film ■ **il a fait ~ toute la scène sans le dire** he got somebody to film the whole thing without telling anyone.

filmique [filmik] *adj* cinematic.

filmographie [filmɔgrafi] *nf* filmography.

filmothèque [filmɔtɛk] *nf* microfilm collection.

filocher [3] [filɔʃe] *fam* ◇ *vt* [suivre] : **~ qqn** to tail sb.
◇ *vi* [aller vite] to scarper *UK*, to skedaddle *US*.

filon [filɔ̃] *nm* **1.** GÉOL seam, vein ■ **ils ont déjà exploité ce ~** *fig* they have already exploited that goldmine **2.** *fam loc* **trouver le ~ pour gagner de l'argent** [moyen] : **il a trouvé un ~ facile pour gagner de l'argent** he found an easy way to make money ■ **trouver le ~** [situation lucrative] to strike it rich, to find the right connection *US* ■ **c'est un bon ~** it's a gold mine *ou* a money-spinner.

filou [filu] *nm* **1.** [voleur] crook, rogue **2.** [ton affectueux] rascal, scamp ■ **oh le ~, il a caché mon livre!** the little rascal's hidden my book!

filouter [3] [filute] *vt fam* **1.** [dérober] to pinch, to swipe **2.** [escroquer] to cheat, to swindle.

filouterie [filutri] *nf* DR fraud, swindle.

fils [fis] *nm* **1.** [enfant] son, boy ▶ **un ~ à papa** *fam* a daddy's boy ■ **il est bien le ~ de son père!** he's just like his father! ■ **un ~ de famille** a wealthy young man ■ **~ spirituel** spiritual son **2.** COMM : **Brunet @ Fils** Brunet @ Son *ou* Sons ■ **je voudrais parler à M. Picard ~** I'd like to talk to Mr Picard junior **3.** *litt* [descendant] descendant ■ [natif] son ■ **un ~ du terroir** a son of the land **4.** RELIG : **le Fils de l'homme** *ou* **de Dieu** the Son of man *ou* of God ■ **mon ~** my son **5.** *loc* **être ~ de ses œuvres** to be a self-made man.

filtrage [filtraʒ] *nm* [d'un liquide] filtering ■ [de l'information, de personnes] screening.

filtrant, e [filtrɑ̃, ɑ̃t] *adj* [matériau, dispositif] filtering *(avant n)* ■ [crème, huile solaire] sunscreen *(modif)* ■ [verre] filter *(modif)*.

filtrat [filtra] *nm* filtrate.

filtration [filtrasjɔ̃] *nf* filtration, filtering.

filtre [filtr] *nm* filter ■ **~ à café/huile** coffee/oil filter ■ **~ solaire** sunscreen ■ **~ à air** air filter ■ **filtre parental** INFORM internet filter, parental control filter.

filtrer [3] [filtre] ◇ *vt* **1.** [liquide, air, lumière] to filter **2.** [visiteurs, informations] to screen.
◇ *vi* **1.** [liquide] to seep *ou* to filter through ■ [lumière, bruit] to filter through **2.** [nouvelles] to filter through.

fin¹, e [fɛ̃, fin] *adj* **1.** [mince - sable, pinceau] fine ; [- cheveu, fil] fine, thin ; [- écriture] fine, small ; [- doigt, jambe, taille, main] slim, slender ■ [peu épais - papier, tranche] thin ; [- collant, bas] sheer ■ **pluie fine** drizzle ■ **haricots verts ~s** high quality green beans
2. [délicat - visage, traits] delicate
3. [aiguisé - pointe] sharp
4. [de qualité - aliments, produit] high-quality, top-quality ; [- mets, repas] delicate, exquisite, refined ; [- dentelle, lingerie] delicate, fine ; [- or, pierre, vin] fine
5. [subtil - observation, description] subtle, clever ; [- personne] perceptive, subtle ; [- esprit] sharp, keen, shrewd ; [- plaisanterie] witty ■ **ce n'était pas très ~ de ta part** it wasn't very smart *ou* clever of you ■ **c'est ~!** *fam iron* very clever! ■ **ne joue pas au plus ~ avec moi** don't try to outwit *ou* to outsmart me ▶ **c'est une fine mouche** he's a sharp customer
6. [sensible - ouïe, vue] sharp, keen, acute ; [- odorat] discriminating, sensitive
7. *(avant le n)* [extrême] : **dans le** *ou* **au ~ fond du placard** at the very back of the closet ■ **au ~ fond de la campagne** in the depths of the countryside, in the middle of nowhere *péj* ■ **le ~ mot de l'histoire c'est...** the best of it is... ■ **on ne connaîtra jamais le ~ mot de l'histoire** we'll never know what really happened *ou* the real story
8. *(avant le n)* [excellent] : **~ connaisseur** (great) connoisseur ■ **un ~ tireur** a crack shot ▶ **la fine équipe!** what a team! ■ **un ~ gourmet** a gourmet.

◆ **fin** *adv* **1.** [finement - moulu] finely ; [- taillé] sharply ■ **c'est écrit trop ~** it's written too small ■ **haché ~** [herbes] finely chopped
2. [tout à fait] : **être ~ prêt** to be ready ■ **être ~ saoul** *sout* to be blind drunk.

◆ **fine bouche** *nf* **1.** [gourmet] : **c'est une fine bouche** he's a gourmet
2. *loc* **tu ne vas pas faire la fine bouche!** don't be so choosy!

◆ **fine gueule** *nf fam* gourmet.

fin [fɛ̃] *nf* **1.** [terme - d'une période, d'un mandat] end ; [- d'une journée, d'un match] end, close ; [- d'une course] end, finish ; [- d'un film, d'un roman] end, ending *(C)* ■ **jusqu'à la ~ des temps** *ou* **des siècles** until the end of time ■ **par une ~ d'après-midi de juin** late on a June afternoon ■ **~ mai/1997** (at the) end of May/1997 ■ **se battre/rester jusqu'à la ~** to fight/to stay to the very end ■ **mener qqch à bonne ~** to pull *ou* to carry sthg off (successfully) ■ **mettre ~ à qqch** to put an end to sthg ■ **mettre ~ à ses jours** to put an end to one's life, to take one's own life ■ **prendre ~** to come to an end ■ **tirer** *ou* **toucher à sa ~** to come to an end, to draw to a close ▶ **~ de citation** end of quotation ■ **~ de semaine** weekend ■ **en ~ de semaine** at the end of the week ■ **faire une ~** to settle down, to get married ■ **on n'en voit pas la ~** there doesn't seem to be any end to it ■ **ça y est, j'en vois la ~!** at last, I can see the light at the end of the tunnel! ■ **avoir** *ou* **connaître des ~s de mois difficiles** to find it hard to make ends meet (at the end of the month)
2. [disparition] end ■ **la ~ de la civilisation inca** the end *ou* death of Inca civilization ■ **ce n'est quand même pas la ~ du monde!** it's not the end of the world, is it! ▶ **c'est la ~ de tout** *ou* **des haricots!** *fam hum* our goose is cooked!
3. [mort] death, end ■ **avoir une ~ tragique/lente** to die a tragic/slow death ■ **la ~ approche** the end is near
4. [objectif] end, purpose ■ **à cette ~** to this end, for this purpose, with that aim in mind ■ **à seule ~ de** with the sole aim of, (simply) for the sake of, purely in order to ■ **arriver** *ou* **parvenir à ses ~s** to achieve one's aim ■ **à des ~s personnelles** for personal *ou* private use ■ **à des ~s politiques/religieuses** to political/religious ends ▶ **~ en soi** end in itself ■ **la ~ justifie les moyens** *prov*, **qui veut la ~ veut les moyens** *prov* the end justifies the means *prov*
5. DR : **~ de non-recevoir** demurrer ■ **opposer une ~ de non-recevoir à qqn** *fig* to turn down sb's request bluntly
6. COMM : **~ courant** at the end of the current month ■ **~s de série** oddments.

◆ **à la fin** *loc adv* **1.** [finalement] in the end, eventually
2. *fam* [ton irrité] : **mais à la ~, où est-il?** where on earth is it? ■ **tu es énervant à la ~!** you're beginning to get on my nerves!

◆ **à la fin de** *loc prép* at the end *ou* close of.

◆ **à toutes fins utiles** *loc adv* **1.** [pour information] : **je vous signale à toutes ~s utiles que...** for your information, let me point out that...
2. [le cas échéant] just in case ■ **dans la boîte à gants j'avais mis à toutes ~s utiles une carte de France** I had put a map of France in the glove compartment just in case.

◆ **en fin de** *loc prép* : **en ~ de soirée/match** towards the end of the evening/match ■ **être en ~ de liste** to be *ou* to come at the end of the list ■ **être en ~ de course** [athlète, président] to be at the end of the road *fig* ■ **être en ~ de droit** to come to the end of one's entitlement *(to an allowance)*.

◆ **en fin de compte** *loc adv* in the end, when all is said and done.

◆ **fin de race** *loc adj* degenerate.

◆ **fin de siècle** *loc adj* decadent, fin de siècle.

◆ **sans fin** ◇ *loc adj* **1.** [interminable] endless, interminable, never-ending
2. TECHNOL endless.
◇ *loc adv* endlessly, interminably.

final, e, als *ou* **aux** [final, o] *adj* **1.** [qui termine] final, end *(modif)* **2.** LING & PHILOS final.
◆ **final, finale** *nm* DANSE & MUS finale.
◆ **finale** *nf* **1.** LING [syllabe] final syllable ■ [voyelle] final vowel **2.** SPORT final.

finalement [finalmɑ̃] *adv* **1.** [à la fin] finally, eventually, in the end **2.** [tout compte fait] after all, when all is said and done.

finaliser [3] [finalize] *vt* to finalize.

finalisme [finalism] *nm* finalism.

finaliste [finalist] ◇ *adj* **1.** SPORT : **l'équipe ~** the team of finalists ‖ JEUX : **candidat ~** finalist **2.** PHILOS finalistic.
◇ *nmf* JEUX, PHILOS & SPORT finalist.

finalité [finalite] *nf* **1.** [but] aim, purpose, end **2.** PHILOS finality.

finance [finɑ̃s] *nf* [profession] : **entrer dans la ~** to enter the world of finance ▶ **la haute ~** high finance.
◆ **finances** *nfpl* **1.** POLIT : **les Finances** ≃ the Exchequer *UK*, ≃ the Treasury Department *US* ▶ **~s publiques** public finance **2.** *fam* [budget] : **ça dépendra de mes ~s** it will depend on whether I can afford it or not ■ **mes ~s sont à zéro** my finances have hit rock-bottom.

financement [finɑ̃smɑ̃] *nm* financing *(U)*, finance.

financer [16] [finɑ̃se] *vt* [journal, projet] to finance, to back (financially), to put up the finance for ■ *(en usage absolu)* **une fois de plus, ce sont ses parents qui vont ~** *fam* once again, his parents will fork out.

financier, ère [finɑ̃sje, ɛr] *adj* **1.** [crise, politique] financial ■ **problèmes ~s** [d'un État] financial problems ; [d'une personne] money problems **2.** CULIN sauce financière, financière sauce *(made with sweetbreads, mushrooms etc).*
◆ **financier** *nm* CULIN financier *(rectangular sponge finger made with almonds).*
◆ **à la financière** *loc adj* à la financière, with financière sauce.

financièrement [finɑ̃sjɛrmɑ̃] *adv* financially.

finasser [3] [finase] *vi fam* to scheme.

finasserie [finasri] *nf fam* scheming.

finaud, e [fino, od] ◇ *adj* cunning, shrewd, wily.
◇ *nm, f* : **c'est un (petit) ~** he's a crafty *ou* sly one.

fine [fin] ◇ *f* ⊳ **fin.**
◇ *nf* **1.** [eau-de-vie] ≃ brandy ■ **~ champagne** *variety of Cognac*
2. [huître] : **~s de claire** *specially fattened greenish oysters.*

finement [finmɑ̃] *adv* **1.** [de façon fine - hacher, dessiner] finely **2.** [subtilement] subtly, with finesse.

finesse [finɛs] *nf* **1.** [délicatesse - d'un mets, d'un vin] delicacy ; [- d'une étoffe] delicacy, fineness ■ **un portrait d'une grande ~ d'exécution** a very delicately painted portrait **2.** [perspicacité] flair, finesse, shrewdness **3.** [subtilité] subtlety *(U)* ■ **une remarque pleine de ~** a very subtle remark ■ **~ d'esprit** intellectual refinement ■ **~ de goût** refined taste **4.** [acuité] sharpness, keenness **5.** [minceur - de la taille] slenderness, slimness ; [- des cheveux, d'une poudre] fineness ; [- du papier, d'un fil] thinness ■ **la ~ de ses traits** the fineness of her features ■ **des draps d'une grande ~** sheets of the finest cloth.
◆ **finesses** *nfpl* [subtilités] subtleties, niceties ■ **les ~s du français** the subtleties of the French language.

fini, e [fini] *adj* **1.** [perdu] finished ■ **c'est un homme ~** he's finished **2.** *péj* [en intensif] complete, utter ■ **un imbécile ~** a complete *ou* an utter fool **3.** MATH & PHILOS finite **4.** [accompli, terminé] finished, accomplished.
◆ **fini** *nm* **1.** [perfection] finish **2.** PHILOS : **le ~** that which is finite.

finir [32] [finir] ◇ *vt* **1.** [achever - tâche, ouvrage] to finish (off) ; [- guerre, liaison] to end ; [- études] to complete ; [- période, séjour] to finish, to complete ■ **il a fini ses jours à Cannes** he ended his days in Cannes ■ **~ la soirée au poste** to wind up in a police cell (at the end of a night out) ■ **mon travail est fini maintenant** my work's done now ■ **~ de faire qqch** to finish doing sthg ■ **finis de faire tes devoirs** finish your homework ■ *(en usage absolu)* **je n'ai pas fini!** I haven't finished (what I was saying)! ▶ **c'en est fini de** *sout* : **c'en est bien fini de mes rêves!** that's the end of all my dreams! ■ **en ~ : finissons-en** let's get it over with ■ **elle a voulu en ~** [se suicider] she tried to end it all ■ **il faut en ~, cette situation ne peut plus durer** we must do something to put an end to this situation ■ **en ~ avec : il veut en ~ avec la vie** he's had enough of life ■ **nous devons en ~ avec la crise économique** we must end the slump ■ **j'en aurai bientôt fini avec lui** I'll be done with him soon
2. [plat, boisson, *etc*] to finish (off *ou* up) ■ **finis ton assiette** *fam* eat up *ou* finish off what's on your plate ■ **il a fini le gâteau/la bouteille** he finished off the cake/the bottle
3. [en réprimande] : **vous n'avez pas fini de vous plaindre?** haven't you done enough moaning, can't you stop moaning? ■ **tu n'as pas bientôt fini!** will you stop it!
◇ *vi* **1.** [arriver à son terme] to finish, to end ■ **la route finit au pont** the road stops at the bridge ■ **la réunion a fini dans les hurlements** the meeting ended in uproar ■ **quand finit ton stage?** when's the end of your placement? ■ **je finirai sur ce vers de Villon** let me end with this line from Villon ■ **pour ~** in the end, finally ■ **~ par** *(suivi d'un infin)* : **il a fini par renoncer/réussir** he eventually *ou* finally gave up/succeeded ■ **ça finit par coûter cher** it costs a lot of money in the end ■ **ça a fini par des embrassades** it ended in a lot of hugging and kissing ▶ **fini de** *fam* : **et maintenant, fini de se croiser les bras!** and now let's see some action! ■ **en janvier, fini de rigoler, tu te remets au travail** come January there'll be no more messing around, you're going to have to get down to some work ■ **n'en pas ~, n'en plus ~ : cette journée/son discours n'en finit pas** there's no end to this day/his speech ■ **des plaintes à n'en plus ~** endless *ou* never-ending complaints ■ **~ en queue de poisson** *fam* to fizzle out
2. [avoir telle issue] : **elle a fini juge** she ended up a judge ■ **il a mal fini** [délinquant] he came to a bad end ■ **un roman qui finit bien/mal** a novel with a happy/sad ending ■ **comment tout cela va-t-il ~?** where *ou* how will it all end? ■ **ça va mal ~** no good will come of it, it will all end in disaster ▶ **tout est bien qui finit bien** *prov* all's well that ends well *prov*
3. [mourir] to die ■ **~ à l'hôpital** to end one's days *ou* to die in hospital.

finish [finiʃ] *nm inv* SPORT finish ■ **jouer un match/une partie au ~** (to play a) match/game to the finish ■ **je l'ai eu au ~** *fam fig* I got him in the end.

finissage [finisaʒ] *nm* finishing.

finissant, e [finisɑ̃, ɑ̃t] *adj litt* finishing ■ **au jour ~** at dusk.

Finistère [finistɛr] *npr m* : **le ~** Finistère *(département in Brittany; chef-lieu: Quimper, code: 29).*

finition [finisjɔ̃] *nf* **1.** [détail] : **la ~ de l'anorak est très bien faite** the anorak's nicely finished ■ **les ~s** the finishing touches **2.** [perfectionnement] finishing off *(U)* ■ **les travaux de ~ prendront plusieurs jours** it will take several days to finish off the work.

finitude [finityd] *nf* finiteness.

finlandais, e [fɛ̃lɑ̃dɛ, ɛz] *adj* Finnish.
◆ **Finlandais, e** *nm, f* Finn.
◆ **finlandais** *nm* LING Finnish.

Finlande [fɛ̃lɑ̃d] *npr f* : **(la) ~** Finland.

finnois, e [finwa, az] *adj* Finnish.
◆ **finnois** *nm* LING Finnish.

finno-ougrien, enne [finougrijɛ̃, ɛn] *(mpl* **finno-ougriens**, *fpl* **finno-ougriennes)** *adj* Finno-Ugric, Finno-Ugrian.
◆ **finno-ougrien** *nm* LING Finno-Ugric, Finno-Ugrian.

fiole [fjɔl] *nf* **1.** [bouteille] phial **2.**△ [tête] mug.

fioritures [fjɔrityr] *nfpl* **1.** [décorations] embellishments **2.** MUS fioritura.

◆ **sans fioritures** *loc adj* plain, unadorned.

fioul [fjul] *nm* fuel oil.

FIP [fip] (*abr de* **France Inter Paris**) *npr Paris radio station broadcasting continuous music and traffic information.*

firmament [firmamɑ̃] *nm litt* firmament *litt*, heavens.

firme [firm] *nf* firm, company.

FIS [fis] (*abr de* **Front islamique de salut**) *npr m* : **le ~** the FIS, the Islamic Salvation Front.

fisc [fisk] *nm* ≃ Inland *UK ou* Internal *US* Revenue ▪ **des problèmes avec le ~** problems with the taxman.

fiscal, e, aux [fiskal, o] *adj* fiscal, tax *(modif)* ▪ **dans un but ~** for the purpose of revenue ▶ **pression** *ou* **charge ~e** tax burden ▪ **l'administration ~e** the tax authorities ▪ **conseiller ~** tax adviser.

fiscalement [fiskalmɑ̃] *adv* fiscally, from the point of view of taxation ▪ **dans quel pays êtes-vous ~ domicilié?** in which country do you pay tax?

fiscalisation [fiskalizasjɔ̃] *nf* taxing, taxation.

fiscaliser [3] [fiskalize] *vt* to tax.

fiscalité [fiskalite] *nf* [système, législation] tax system.

fissible [fisibl], **fissile** [fisil] *adj* MINÉR & NUCL fissile.

fission [fisjɔ̃] *nf* fission ▪ **~ nucléaire** nuclear fission.

fissuration [fisyrasjɔ̃] *nf* fissuring *spéc*, cracking.

fissure [fisyr] *nf* **1.** [fente] crack, fissure *spéc* **2.** MÉD fissure **3.** *fig* [défaut] fissure, crack, chink ▪ **il y a des ~s dans son raisonnement** her argument doesn't hold water.

fissurer [3] [fisyre] *vt* [mur, paroi] to crack, to fissure *spéc*.

fiston [fistɔ̃] *nm fam* son.

fistule [fistyl] *nf* fistula.

fit *etc v* ▷ **faire**.

FIV [fiv] (*abr de* **fécondation in vitro**) *nf* IVF.

FIVETE, fivete [fivɛt] (*abr de* **fécondation in vitro et transfert d'embryon**) *nf* GIFT ▪ **une ~** a test-tube baby.

fixage [fiksaʒ] *nm* PHOTO fixing.

fixateur, trice [fiksatœr, tris] *adj* fixative.
◆ **fixateur** *nm* **1.** PHOTO fixer **2.** [pour les cheveux] setting lotion **3.** BIOL fixative **4.** ART fixative.

fixatif, ive [fiksatif, iv] *adj* fixative.
◆ **fixatif** *nm* fixative.

fixation [fiksasjɔ̃] *nf* **1.** [accrochage] fixing, fastening **2.** [établissement - d'un prix] setting ; [- d'un rendez-vous] making, fixing **3.** CHIM & BIOL fixation **4.** ART & PHOTO fixing **5.** PSYCHOL fixation, obsession ▪ **faire une ~ sur qqch** to be obsessed with *ou* by sthg **6.** [de ski] binding.

fixe [fiks] ◇ *adj* **1.** [invariable - repère] fixed ▪ **prendre un médicament à heure ~** to take (a) medicine at a set time ▶ **virgule ~** INFORM fixed point **2.** MIL : **(à vos rangs,) ~!** attention! **3.** [immobile - œil, regard] fixed, staring **4.** [durable - emploi] permanent, steady **5.** ÉCON, FIN & DR [droit] fixed duty *(modif)* ▪ [prix] set ▪ [revenu, salaire] fixed ▪ **assignation à jour ~** fixed summons.
◇ *nm* (fixed) *ou* regular salary.
◆ **au beau fixe** *loc adj* **1.** MÉTÉOR continuously sunny, set fair *spéc* **2.** [optimiste] : **humeur/moral au beau ~** permanently sunny mood/optimistic outlook.

fixement [fiksəmɑ̃] *adv* fixedly ▪ **elle le regarde ~** she's staring at him.

fixer [3] [fikse] *vt* **1.** [accrocher - gén] to fix ; [- par des épingles, des punaises] to pin (on) ; [- avec de l'adhésif] to tape (on) ; [- avec un fermoir, un nœud] to fasten **2.** [en regardant] to stare ▪ **~ qqn du regard** to stare at sb ▪ **tout le monde avait les yeux fixés sur elle** everybody was staring at her, all eyes were on her **3.** [concentrer] : **~ son attention/esprit sur qqch** to focus one's attention/mind on sthg ▪ **~ son choix sur qqch** to decide *ou* to settle on sthg **4.** [définir - date, lieu] to fix, to set, to decide on *(insép)* ▪ **~ le prix d'une réparation** to cost a repair job ▪ **~ un rendez-vous à qqn** to arrange a meeting with sb **5.** [informer] : **cette conversation m'a fixé sur son compte** that conversation set me straight about him ▪ **te voilà fixé!** now you know! **6.** [établir] : **~ son domicile à Paris** to take up (permanent) residence *ou* to settle (down) in Paris **7.** [stabiliser] to fix ▪ **~ la langue/l'orthographe** to standardize the language/the spelling **8.** ART, CHIM & PHOTO to fix.
◆ **se fixer** ◇ *vp (emploi passif)* [s'accrocher] to be fixed *ou* fastened ▪ **ça se fixe facilement sur le ski** it fastens easily onto the ski ▪ **ça se fixe avec une courroie** you attach it with a strap, you strap it on.
◇ *vpi* **1.** [s'installer] to settle ▪ **elle s'est fixée en Irlande** she settled (permanently) in Ireland **2.** [se stabiliser] to settle down ▪ **il s'est fixé après son mariage** he settled down after he got married.
◇ *vpt* : **il s'est fixé un but dans la vie, réussir** he has (set himself) one aim in life, to succeed.
◆ **se fixer sur** *vp+prép* [choisir] to decide on.

fixité [fiksite] *nf* [d'une disposition] fixity, unchangeableness ▪ [du regard] fixedness, steadiness.

fjord [fjɔrd] *nm* fjord.

flac [flak] *interj* splash.

flacon [flakɔ̃] *nm* [de parfum, de solvant] (small) bottle ▪ [de spiritueux] flask.

fla-fla [flafla] (*pl* **fla-flas**) *nm fam vieilli* **faire du ~** to make a huge fuss.
◆ **sans fla-flas** *loc adv fam* simply, without fuss.

flagada [flagada] *adj inv fam vieilli* pooped, washed-out.

flagellation [flaʒɛlasjɔ̃] *nf* flagellation.

flagelle [flaʒɛl] *nm* flagellum.

flageller [4] [flaʒɛle] *vt* [battre] to whip.

flageolant, e [flaʒɔlɑ̃, ɑ̃t] *adj* [jambe] shaking, trembling, wobbly.

flageoler [3] [flaʒɔle] *vi* [jambes] to shake, to tremble, to wobble ▪ **~ sur ses jambes** to sway to and fro.

flageolet [flaʒɔlɛ] *nm* **1.** BOT (flageolet) bean **2.** MUS flageolet.

flagorner [3] [flagɔrne] *vt litt* to fawn on *(insép)*.

flagornerie [flagɔrnəri] *nf litt* fawning, flattering, toadying.

flagorneur, euse [flagɔrnœr, øz] *nm, f litt* flatterer, toady.

flagrant, e [flagrɑ̃, ɑ̃t] *adj* **1.** [évident] blatant, obvious, flagrant ▪ **il apparaît de façon ~e que...** it is blatantly obvious that... **2.** DR : **~ délit** flagrante delicto ▪ **en ~ délit** in flagrante delicto ; *fig* in the act, red-handed ▪ **pris en ~ délit de mensonge** caught lying.

flair [flɛr] *nm* **1.** [odorat] scent **2.** [perspicacité] flair ▪ **il a du ~** he has flair.

flairer [4] [flɛre] *vt* **1.** [humer - suj: chien] to scent, to sniff at *(insép)* ; [- suj: personne] to smell **2.** [deviner] to sense ▪ **~ le danger** to have a sense of impending danger ▶ **~ le vent** to see which way *ou* how the wind blows.

flamand, e [flamɑ̃, ɑ̃d] *adj* Flemish.
◆ **Flamand, e** *nm, f* Fleming ▪ **les Flamands** the Flemish.
◆ **flamand** *nm* LING Flemish.

flamant [flamɑ̃] *nm* flamingo ▪ **~ rose** (pink) flamingo.

flambant, e [flɑ̃bɑ̃, ɑ̃t] *adj* **1.** *litt* [bois, fagot] burning, blazing ▪ MIN [houille] bituminous **2.** *loc* **~ neuf** brand new.
◆ **flambant** *nm* MIN bituminous coal.

flambard, flambart [flɑ̃bar] *nm fam vieilli* braggart.

flambé, e [flɑ̃be] *adj* **1.** CULIN flambéed **2.** *fam* [personne] ruined ▪ **être ~** to have gambled all one's money away.
◆ **flambée** *nf* **1.** [feu] blaze, fire ▪ **faire une bonne ~e** to get a roaring fire going **2.** *fig* [poussée] : **~e de : une ~e de colère** an outburst of anger ▪ **une ~e de violence** an outbreak *ou* a sudden wave of violence ▪ **la ~e des prix** the leap in prices.

flambeau, x [flɑ̃bo] *nm* **1.** [torche] torch ■ [chandelier] candlestick ■ *fig* torch ■ **marche** *ou* **retraite aux ~x** torchlit procession ■ **passer** *ou* **transmettre le ~** to pass on the torch ■ **se passer** *ou* **se transmettre le ~ (de génération en génération)** to pass the tradition down (from generation to generation) **2.** *litt* [lumière] : **le ~ du rationalisme/de la foi** the light of rationalism/faith.

flamber [3] [flɑ̃be] ◇ *vt* **1.** CULIN [lapin, volaille] to singe ■ [omelette] to flambé **2.** *fam* [dilapider] to blow, to throw away *(sép)*.
◇ *vi* **1.** [se consumer] to burn (brightly) **2.** [briller] to flash **3.** *fam* [augmenter - prix] to rocket, to soar ■ **les prix ont flambé** prices have rocketed *ou* soared **4.** *fam* [jouer] to gamble (for big stakes).

flambeur, euse [flɑ̃bœr, øz] *nm, f* big-time gambler.

flamboie *etc v* ⊳ **flamboyer**.

flamboiement [flɑ̃bwamɑ̃] *nm* [d'un incendie] blaze ■ [du regard] flashing.

flamboyant, e [flɑ̃bwajɑ̃, ɑ̃t] *adj* **1.** [brillant - foyer] blazing, flaming ; [- regard] flashing **2.** ARCHIT flamboyant *spéc* ■ **le gothique ~** high Gothic style.
◆ **flamboyant** *nm* BOT flamboyant.

flamboyer [13] [flɑ̃bwaje] *vi* **1.** [être en flammes] to blaze *ou* to flare (up) ■ **dans l'âtre qui flamboie** in the blazing hearth **2.** [briller - œil, regard] to flash.

flamenco, ca [flamɛnko, ka] *adj* flamenco.
◆ **flamenco** *nm* flamenco.

flamiche [flamiʃ] *nf* leek pie *ou* quiche.

flamingant, e [flamɛ̃gɑ̃, ɑ̃t] ◇ *adj* Flemish-speaking.
◇ *nm, f* **1.** LING Flemish speaker **2.** POLIT Flemish nationalist.

flamme [flam] *nf* **1.** [feu] flame ■ **faire une ~** to flare *ou* to blaze up ■ **cracher** *ou* **jeter** *ou* **lancer des ~s** [dragon] to breathe fire ; [canon] to flare ▶ **la ~ du tombeau du Soldat inconnu** the Eternal Flame **2.** *litt* [éclat] fire ■ **dans la ~ de son regard** in her fiery eyes **3.** [ferveur] fire ■ **discours plein de ~** impassioned speech **4.** *arch* & *litt* [amour] ardour **5.** [fanion - d'un navire de guerre] pennent, pennon ; [- de la cavalerie] pennon **6.** [sur une lettre] slogan **7.** ÉLECTR : **(ampoule) ~** candle bulb.
◆ **flammes** *nfpl* : **périr dans les ~s** to burn to death, to be burnt alive ▶ **les ~s éternelles** *ou* **de l'enfer** *fig* hell fire.
◆ **à la flamme de** *loc prép* by the light of ■ **lire une inscription à la ~ d'un briquet** to read an inscription by the light of a cigarette lighter.
◆ **avec flamme** *loc adv* passionately.
◆ **en flammes** ◇ *loc adj* burning, blazing.
◇ *loc adv* : **l'avion est tombé en ~s** the plane went down in flames ■ **descendre un auteur/une pièce en ~s** *fam* to pan an author/a play.

flammèche [flamɛʃ] *nf* (flying) spark.

flan [flɑ̃] *nm* **1.** CULIN (baked) egg custard ■ **~ à la vanille** vanilla *ou* vanilla-flavoured custard **2.** IMPR flong **3.** MÉTALL flan **4.** *fam loc* **c'est du ~!** it's a load of bunkum *ou* bunk! ■ **en rester comme deux ronds de ~** to be flabbergasted.

flanc [flɑ̃] *nm* **1.** ANAT [entre les côtes et le bassin] flank ■ [côté du corps] side **2.** ZOOL flank, side **3.** [côté - d'un navire] side ; [- d'une colline] side, slope **4.** MIL flank **5.** *litt* [ventre maternel] womb **6.** *loc* **tirer au ~** to be bone-idle.
◆ **à flanc de** *loc prép* : **à ~ de coteau** on the hillside.
◆ **sur le flanc** ◇ *loc adj* : **être sur le ~** [épuisé] to be exhausted ; [malade] to be laid up.
◇ *loc adv* [sur le côté] on one's side.

flancher [3] [flɑ̃ʃe] *vi* **1.** [faiblir] to give out, to fail ■ **j'ai la mémoire qui flanche** my memory's giving out on *ou* failing me **2.** [manquer de courage] to waver ■ **ce n'est vraiment pas le moment de ~** this is really no time for weakness.

Flandre [flɑ̃dr] *npr f* : **(la) ~, (les) ~s** Flanders ■ **en ~** *ou* **~s** in Flanders.

flanelle [flanɛl] *nf* TEXT flannel.

flâner [3] [flane] *vi* **1.** [se promener] to stroll *ou* to amble (along) **2.** *péj* [perdre son temps] to hang about, to lounge around, to idle ■ **on n'a pas le temps de ~ avant les examens** there's no time for hanging about before the exams.

flânerie [flanri] *nf* stroll, wander.

flâneur, euse [flanœr, øz] *nm, f* stroller.

flanquer [3] [flɑ̃ke] *vt* **1.** *fam* [lancer] to fling, to throw, to chuck ■ **~ qqn dehors** *ou* **à la porte** [l'expulser] to kick sb out ; [le licencier] to sack *UK ou* to can *US* sb ▶ **~ qqch par terre : il a flanqué les bouquins par terre** [volontairement] he chucked the books on the floor ; [par maladresse] he knocked the books onto the floor ■ **j'ai tellement voulu réussir et toi tu vas tout ~ par terre** *fig* I wanted to succeed so badly and now you're going to mess it all up (for me) **2.** *fam* [donner] : **~ un P-V à qqn** to give sb a ticket ■ **~ une gifle à qqn** to smack *ou* to slap sb ■ **~ un coup de poing à qqn** to punch sb ■ **~ un coup de pied à qqn** to kick sb ■ **~ la trouille** *ou* **frousse à qqn** to scare the pants off sb ■ **ça m'a flanqué le cafard** it really got me down **3.** [être à côté de] to flank **4.** *fam péj* [accompagner] : **être flanqué de : elle est arrivée, flanquée de ses deux frères** she came in with her two brothers at her side *ou* flanked by her two brothers **5.** MIL to flank.
◆ **se flanquer** ◇ *vpi fam* **se ~ par terre** to take a tumble.
◇ *vpt* : **je me suis flanqué une bonne indigestion** I gave myself a right dose of indigestion ▶ **se ~ la figure** *ou* **gueule**△ **par terre** to fall flat on one's face.

flapi, e [flapi] *adj fam* washed-out, worn-out.

flaque [flak] *nf* puddle ■ **une large ~ d'huile** a pool of oil.

flash [flaʃ] (*pl* **flashs** *ou pl* **flashes**) *nm* **1.** PHOTO [éclair] flash ■ [ampoule] flash bulb ■ **prendre une photo au ~** to take a picture using a flash ▶ **avoir un ~** *fam* to have a brainwave **2.** RADIO & TV : **~ (d'informations)** newsflash **3.** CINÉ & TV [plan] flash **4.** △ [d'un drogué] flash.

flash-back [flaʃbak] *nm inv* flashback ■ **elle utilise beaucoup les ~ dans ses romans** there are a lot of flashbacks in her novels.

flashball [flaʃbol] *nm* [arme] ≃ baton gun ■ [projectile] ≃ baton round.

flasher [3] [flaʃe] *vi* [clignoter] to flash (on and off).
◆ **flasher sur** *v+prép fam* to go crazy over.

flasque[1] [flask] *adj* **1.** [muscle, peau] flaccid, flabby **2.** [veule] spineless.

flasque[2] [flask] *nm* **1.** MÉCAN [d'une machine] flange, endplate **2.** ARM cheek *(of gun carriage)*.

flasque[3] [flask] *nf* [pour whisky] (hip) flask ■ [à mercure] flask.

flatter [3] [flate] *vt* **1.** [encenser] to flatter ■ **~ bassement qqn** to fawn upon sb **2.** [embellir] to be flattering to ■ **ce portrait la flatte plutôt** this portrait of her is rather flattering **3.** [toucher] to touch, to flatter ■ **il sera flatté de** *ou* **par tes remarques** he will be very touched by what you said **4.** *litt* [encourager] to encourage ■ **~ les caprices de qqn** to pander to sb's whims ■ **~ la vanité de qqn** to indulge sb's vanity **5.** [caresser - cheval, chien] to stroke **6.** [être agréable à - vue, odorat *etc*] to delight, to be pleasing to ■ **un vin qui flatte le palais** a (wonderfully) smooth wine.
◆ **se flatter** *vpi* : **sans vouloir me ~, je crois que j'ai raison** though I say it myself, I think I'm right ■ **elle se flatte de savoir recevoir** she prides herself on knowing how to entertain *ou* on her skills as a hostess.

flatterie [flatri] *nf* **1.** [adulation] flattery **2.** [propos] flattering remark ■ **~s** sweet talk.

flatteur, euse [flatœr, øz] ◇ *adj* flattering ■ **sans vouloir être ~ à ton égard, c'est vraiment du beau travail** without wishing to flatter you, you did a really nice job.
◇ *nm, f* flatterer.

flatteusement [flatøzmɑ̃] *adv* flatteringly.

flatulence [flatylɑ̃s] *nf* flatulence.

flatulent, e [flatylɑ̃, ɑ̃t] *adj* flatulent.

flatuosité [flatɥozite] *nf* flatus.

FLB *adj inv & adv* (*abr de* **franco long du bord**) FAS.

FLE, fle [flə] (*abr de* **français langue étrangère**) *nm French as a foreign language.*

fléau, x [fleo] *nm* **1.** [désastre] curse, plague **2.** *fam* [cause de désagréments] pain ■ **ces téléphones portables, quel ~!** mobiles phones are a real pain! **3.** [d'une balance] beam **4.** AGRIC flail **5.** ARM : **~ d'armes** flail.

fléchage [fleʃaʒ] *nm* marking (with arrows) ■ **le ~ de l'itinéraire bis n'est pas terminé** the alternative route hasn't been completely marked out (with arrows) yet.

flèche [flɛʃ] *nf* **1.** ARM [projectile] arrow ■ **partir comme une ~** to shoot off ‖ [d'un canon] trail **2.** [en balistique] : **~ d'une trajectoire** highest point of a trajectory **3.** [signe] arrow ■ **suivez la ~** follow the arrow **4.** ARCHIT [d'un arc] broach ■ [d'un clocher] spire **5.** [d'une balance] pointer **6.** MÉCAN [d'une grue] boom **7.** SPORT [au ski] *giant slalom proficiency test* **8.** *litt* [raillerie] broadside, jibe ➲ **la ~ du Parthe** the Parthian *ou* parting shot.

◆ **en flèche** *loc adv* **1.** [spectaculairement] : **monter** *ou* **grimper en ~** *pr* to go straight up (like an arrow), to shoot up ; *fig* to shoot up ■ **les tarifs montent en ~** prices are rocketing ■ **partir en ~** *pr* to go off like an arrow, to shoot off ; *fig* to shoot off **2.** [atteler] : **bœufs/chevaux attelés en ~** oxen/horses harnessed in tandem.

fléché, e [fleʃe] *adj* signposted ■ **suivez la déviation ~e** follow the detour signs.

flécher [18] [fleʃe] *vt* to mark with arrows, to signpost.

fléchette [fleʃɛt] *nf* dart.

fléchi, e [fleʃi] *adj* LING inflected.

fléchir [32] [fleʃir] ◇ *vt* **1.** [ployer] to bend, to flex ■ **~ le genou devant qqn** to bow the knee to sb **2.** [apitoyer - juge, tribunal] to move to pity ■ **se laisser ~** to relent.
◇ *vi* **1.** [se ployer] to bend ■ **elle sentait ses genoux ~ sous elle** she could feel her knees giving way **2.** [baisser] to fall ■ **le dollar a de nouveau fléchi** the dollar has fallen again **3.** [céder] to weaken ■ **nous ne fléchirons pas devant la menace** we will not give in to threats ■ **leur père ne fléchissait jamais** their father was utterly inflexible.

fléchissement [fleʃismɑ̃] *nm* **1.** [flexion - d'une partie du corps] flexing, bending **2.** [affaiblissement - des genoux] sagging ; [- de la nuque] drooping **3.** [baisse] fall ■ **~ de la demande** drop in demand ■ **~ de la production/natalité** fall in production/in the birthrate.

fléchisseur [fleʃisœr] ◇ *adj m* : **muscle ~** flexor.
◇ *nm* flexor.

flegmatique [flɛgmatik] ◇ *adj* phlegmatic.
◇ *nmf* phlegmatic person.

flegme [flɛgm] *nm* phlegm, composure ■ **perdre son ~** to lose one's composure.

◆ **avec flegme** *loc adv* coolly, phlegmatically.

flemmard, e [flɛmar, ard] *fam* ◇ *adj* idle, lazy, workshy.
◇ *nm, f* idler, loafer.

flemmarder [3] [flɛmarde] *vi fam* to loaf about.

flemmardise [flɛmardiz] *nf fam* idleness, laziness.

flemme [flɛm] *nf fam* idleness, laziness ■ **je me sens comme une grosse ~ ce matin** I feel like loafing around this morning ➲ **il tire une de ces ~s aujourd'hui!** he's been loafing around all day!

flétan [fletɑ̃] *nm* halibut.

flétrir [32] [fletrir] *vt* **1.** BOT to wither, to wilt **2.** *litt* [ôter l'éclat de - couleur] to fade ; [- teint] to wither **3.** *litt* [avilir - ambition, espoir] to sully, to corrupt, to debase **4.** *litt* [condamner] to condemn, to denounce.

◆ **se flétrir** *vpi* **1.** BOT to wither, to wilt **2.** *litt* [peau] to wither ■ [couleur, beauté] to fade.

flétrissure [fletrisyr] *nf* **1.** BOT wilting **2.** *litt* [altération - du teint, de la peau] withering *(U)* **3.** *litt* [déshonneur] stain ■ **l'ignoble ~ dont vous l'avez marquée** the foul stain you placed upon her honour.

fleur [flœr] *nf* **1.** BOT flower ■ [d'un arbre] blossom ■ **une robe à ~s** a flowery dress, a dress with a flower motif ➲ **~ de lotus** lotus blossom ■ **~ d'oranger** [fleur] orange flower ; [essence] orange flower water ■ **dites-le avec des ~s** *(slogan publicitaire)* *allus* say it with flowers ■ **'les Fleurs du mal'** ***Baudelaire*** 'The Flowers of Evil' **2.** *fig* **la ~ de** [le meilleur de] : **la ~ de l'âge** the prime of life ■ **~ de farine** fine wheat flour ■ **la ~ de la jeunesse** the full bloom of youth ■ **la fine ~ de** [l'élite de] : **c'est la fine ~ de l'école** he's the pride of his school ■ **la fine ~ de la canaille** a prize swine **3.** BIOL : **~ de vin/vinaigre** flower of wine/vinegar **4.** HÉRALD : **~ de lis** *ou* **lys** fleur-de-lis **5.** *vieilli* [virginité] virginity ■ **perdre sa ~** to lose one's virtue **6.** *loc* **faire une ~ à qqn** *fam* to do sb an unexpected favour *ou* a favour ■ **comme une ~ : arriver comme une ~** to turn up out of the blue ■ **faire qqch comme une ~** to do sthg almost without trying ■ **c'est passé comme une ~** it was as easy as pie.

◆ **fleurs** *nfpl* **1.** LITTÉR : **~s de rhétorique** flowers of rhetoric, rhetorical flourishes **2.** [louanges] : **couvrir qqn de ~s** to praise sb highly ■ **s'envoyer** *ou* **se jeter des ~s** *fam* [mutuellement] to sing one another's praises, to pat one another on the back ; [à soi-même] to pat o.s. on the back.

◆ **à fleur de** *loc prép* on the surface of ■ **à ~ d'eau** just above the surface (of the water) ■ **une sensibilité à ~ de peau** hypersensitivity.

◆ **en fleur(s)** *loc adj* [rose, pivoine] in flower *ou* bloom, blooming ■ [arbre, arbuste] blossoming, in blossom.

◆ **fleur bleue** *loc adj* sentimental.

fleurdelisé, e [flœrdəlize] *adj* decorated with fleurs-de-lis.

fleurer [5] [flœre] ◇ *vt litt* to smell of ■ **son histoire fleure le scandale** *fig* his story smacks of scandal.
◇ *vi* : **~ bon** to smell nice.

fleuret [flœrɛ] *nm* ESCRIME foil.

fleurette [flœrɛt] *nf* small flower, floweret, floret.

fleurettiste [flœrɛtist] *nmf* foilsman (*f* foilswoman).

fleuri, e [flœri] *adj* **1.** [arbre, arbuste] in bloom *ou* blossom ■ **un balcon ~** a balcony decorated with flowers **2.** [orné de fleurs] flowered, flowery **3.** *litt* [teint] florid **4.** [conversation, style] flowery, overornate.

fleurir [32] [flœrir] ◇ *vi* **1.** BOT [rose, pivoine] to flower, to bloom ■ [arbre, arbuste] to flower, to blossom **2.** [apparaître] to burgeon ■ **les antennes paraboliques qui fleurissent sur tous les toits** *fig* the satellite dishes mushrooming *ou* burgeoning all over every roof **3.** [se développer - affaire, commerce] to flourish, to thrive.
◇ *vt* to decorate with flowers ■ **~ la tombe de qqn** to put flowers on sb's grave.

fleuriste [flœrist] *nmf* **1.** [vendeur] florist **2.** [cultivateur] flower grower.

fleuron [flœrɔ̃] *nm* **1.** [ornement - de reliure] flower, fleuron ; [- en pierre] finial ■ **le (plus beau) ~ de...** *fig* the jewel of... ■ **on a volé le ~ de sa collection d'émeraudes** the finest emerald in his collection has been stolen **2.** BOT floret.

Fleury-Mérogis [flœrimerɔʒis] *npr town near Paris well-known for its prison.*

fleuve [flœv] *nm* **1.** [rivière] river *(flowing into the sea)* ■ **~ international** *river going across national borders* ➲ **~ côtier** coastal river ■ **le ~ Jaune** the Yellow River **2.** [écoulement] : **un ~ de : un ~ de boue** a river of mud, a mudslide ■ **un ~ de larmes** a flood of tears **3.** *(comme adj; avec ou sans trait d'union)* **une lettre ~** a very long letter.

flexibilité [flɛksibilite] *nf* **1.** [d'un matériau] pliability **2.** PSYCHOL flexible *ou* adaptable nature **3.** [d'un arrangement, d'un horaire] flexibility, adaptability ■ [d'un dispositif] versatility.

flexible [flɛksibl] ◇ *adj* **1.** [pliable] pliable, flexible **2.** PSYCHOL flexible, adaptable, amenable to change **3.** [variable - arrangement, horaire] flexible ; [- dispositif] versatile ■ **avoir des horaires ~s** to have a flexible schedule.
◇ *nm* **1.** [tuyau] flexible tube **2.** MÉCAN flexible shaft.

flexion [flɛksjɔ̃] *nf* **1.** [d'un arc, d'un ressort] bending *(U)*, flexion **2.** [des membres] flexing *(U)* ■ **~, extension!** bend, stretch! **3.** LING inflection ▶ **~ nominale** noun inflection.

flibuste [flibyst] *nf* : **la ~** [piraterie] freebooting ; [pirates] freebooters.

flibustier [flibystje] *nm* freebooter, buccaneer.

flic [flik] *nmf* ***fam*** cop.

flicaille△ [flikaj] *nf* ***péj*** **la ~** the pigs△ *OU* cops.

flic flac [flikflak] *onomat* splash splash, splish splosh.

flingue△ [flɛ̃g] *nm* piece△, gat△ *US*.

flinguer [3] △ [flɛ̃ge] *vt* to blow away△ *(sép)*, to waste△.
◆ **se flinguer**△ *vp (emploi réfléchi)* to blow one's brains out ■ **c'est à se ~, il y a de quoi se ~!** it's enough to drive you round the bend!

flippant, e△ [flipɑ̃, ɑ̃t] *adj* [déprimant] depressing ■ [inquiétant] worrying ■ **c'était ~** it was a real downer!

flipper[1] [flipœr] *nm* pinball machine.

flipper[2] [3] △ [flipe] *vi* **1.** [être déprimé] to feel down ■ **lui raconte pas tes malheurs, tu vas le faire ~** don't go telling him your troubles, it'll only get him down **2.** [paniquer] to flip△ **3.** [drogué] to have a bad trip△.

flirt [flœrt] *nm* ***vieilli*** **1.** [relation] (little) fling **2.** [ami] boyfriend ■ [amie] girlfriend ■ **un de ses anciens ~s** an old flame.

flirter [3] [flœrte] *vi* [badiner] to flirt ■ **elle aime ~** she's a flirt, she loves flirting ▶ **~ avec qqn** ***pr*** to have a little fling with sb ■ **il a longtemps flirté avec le socialisme** he had a long flirtation with socialism.

flirteur, euse [flœrtœr, øz] ◇ *adj* flirting.
◇ *nm, f* flirt.

FLN *(abr de* **Front de libération nationale***) npr m one of the main political parties in Algeria, established as a resistance movement, in 1954, at the start of the war for independence.*

FLNC *(abr de* **Front de libération nationale corse***) npr m Corsican liberation front.*

FLNKS *(abr de* **Front de libération nationale kanak et socialiste***) npr m Kanak independence movement in New Caledonia.*

floc [flɔk] *onomat* splash.

floche [flɔʃ] *adj* flossy ■ **fil/soie ~** floss thread/silk.

flocon [flɔkɔ̃] *nm* [parcelle - de laine, de coton] flock ; [- de neige] snowflake, flake ■ **~s d'avoine** oatmeal ■ **~s de maïs** cornflakes.

floconner [3] [flɔkɔne] *vi* to go fluffy.

floconneux, euse [flɔkɔnø, øz] *adj* fluffy.

flonflon [flɔ̃flɔ̃] *nm* oompah ■ **on entendait les ~s du bal** music could be heard coming from the dance.

flop [flɔp] *nm* ***fam*** flop ■ **faire un ~** to be a flop.

flopée [flɔpe] *nf* ***fam*** **une ~ de** a whole bunch of.

floraison [flɔrɛzɔ̃] *nf* **1.** BOT [éclosion] blooming, blossoming, flowering ■ [saison] flowering time ■ **quand les arbres sont en pleine ~** when the trees are in full bloom **2.** [apparition - d'artistes, d'œuvres] : **il y a actuellement une ~ de publicités pour des banques** at present there is something of a rash of advertisements for banks.

floral, e, aux [flɔral, o] *adj* [décor] floral ■ [exposition] flower *(modif)*.

floralies [flɔrali] *nfpl* flower show.

flore [flɔr] *nf* **1.** [végétation] flora **2.** [ouvrage] flora **3.** MÉD : **~ intestinale** intestinal flora.

floréal [flɔreal] *nm 8th month in the French Revolutionary calendar (from April 21 to May 20).*

Florence [flɔrɑ̃s] *npr* Florence.

florentin, e [flɔrɑ̃tɛ̃, in] *adj* Florentine.
◆ **Florentin, e** *nm, f* Florentine.
◆ **florentin** *nm* Florentine *(biscuit containing almonds and candied fruit with a chocolate base).*

florès [flɔrɛs] *nm* : **faire ~** ***litt*** to enjoy great success, to be a huge success.

floricole [flɔrikɔl] *adj* flower-dwelling.

floriculture [flɔrikyltyr] *nf* floriculture ***spéc***, flower-growing.

Floride [flɔrid] *npr f* : **(la) ~** Florida.

florifère [flɔrifɛr] *adj* floriferous ***spéc***, flowering.

florilège [flɔrilɛʒ] *nm* anthology.

florin [flɔrɛ̃] *nm* florin.

florissait *etc v* ▷ **fleurir** *(sens 3)*.

florissant, e [flɔrisɑ̃, ɑ̃t] ◇ *p prés* ▷ **fleurir** *(sens 3)*.
◇ *adj* [affaire, plante] thriving, flourishing ■ [santé] blooming.

flot [flo] *nm* **1.** [de larmes, de paroles] flood ■ [de boue] stream ■ **un ~ de gens** a stream of people ■ **un ~ de cheveux blonds** ***litt*** flowing blond hair ▶ **faire couler des ~s d'encre** to cause much ink to flow ■ **déverser des ~s de bile** to pour out one's gall **2.** [marée] : **le ~** the incoming *OU* rising tide.
◆ **flots** *nmpl* ***litt*** **les ~s** the waves.
◆ **à flot** *loc adv* **1.** NAUT : **mettre un navire à ~** to launch a ship ■ **remettre un bateau à ~** to refloat a boat **2.** [sorti de difficultés financières] : **je suis à ~ maintenant** I'm back on an even keel now ■ **remettre à ~** [personne, entreprise] to get back on an even keel.
◆ **à flots** *loc adv* in floods *OU* torrents ■ **la lumière du soleil entre à ~s dans la chambre** sunlight is flooding *OU* streaming into the bedroom ■ **le champagne coulait à ~s** champagne flowed like water.

flottabilité [flɔtabilite] *nf* buoyancy.

flottable [flɔtabl] *adj* [bois] buoyant ■ [fleuve] floatable.

flottage [flɔtaʒ] *nm* [du bois, du verre] floating.

flottaison [flɔtɛzɔ̃] *nf* **1.** [sur l'eau] buoyancy **2.** FIN floating.

flottant, e [flɔtɑ̃, ɑ̃t] *adj* **1.** [sur l'eau - épave, mine] floating **2.** [ondoyant - chevelure] flowing ; [- drapeau] billowing **3.** [hésitant - caractère, pensée] irresolute ■ **le raisonnement est un peu ~ dans le dernier chapitre** the line of argument loses its way slightly in the final chapter **4.** [variable] fluctuating, variable **5.** FIN floating **6.** ANAT [côte, rein] floating.
◆ **flottant** *nm* [vêtement] pair of baggy shorts.

flottation [flɔtasjɔ̃] *nf* flotation.

flotte [flɔt] *nf* **1.** AÉRON & NAUT fleet **2.** ***fam*** [pluie] rain ■ [eau] water ■ **on a eu de la ~ pendant un mois** it poured for a month.

flottement [flɔtmɑ̃] *nm* **1.** [incertitude] indecisiveness, wavering *(U)* ■ **on note un certain ~ dans ses réponses** his answers seem hesitant *OU* indecisive **2.** [imprécision] looseness, imprecision **3.** [ondoiement] flapping, fluttering **4.** [fluctuation - d'une monnaie] floating ; [- de chiffres] fluctuation **5.** MIL swaying.

flotter [3] [flɔte] ◇ *vi* **1.** [surnager] to float **2.** [être en suspension] to hang ■ **une bonne odeur de soupe flottait dans la cuisine** the kitchen was filled with a delicious smell of soup ■ **~ dans l'air** [idée, rumeur] to be going around **3.** [ondoyer - banderole] to flap, to flutter ■ **ses cheveux flottent au vent/sur ses épaules** her hair is streaming in the wind/hangs loose over her shoulders **4.** [être trop large] to flap (around) ■ [être au large] : **elle flotte dans sa robe** she's lost in that dress, her dress is too big for her **5.** ***litt*** [errer] to wander, to roam ■ **un vague sourire flottait sur ses lèvres** a faint smile crossed her lips **6.** FIN [monnaie] to float.
◇ *vt* [bois] to float.
◇ *v impers* ***fam*** [pleuvoir] to rain.

flotteur [flɔtœr] *nm* ball, float.

flottille [flɔtij] *nf* **1.** NAUT flotilla **2.** AÉRON squadron.

flou, e [flu] *adj* **1.** [imprécis - souvenir] blurred, hazy ; [- renseignements] vague **2.** CINÉ & PHOTO out of focus **3.** [souple - vêtement] ample, flowing, loose-fitting ; [- coiffure] soft.
◆ **flou** ◇ *nm* **1.** CINÉ & PHOTO blurredness, fuzziness ■ **~ artistique** *pr* soft-focus ■ **il entretient un certain ~ artistique** *fig* he's being fairly vague about it ■ **c'est un peu le ~ artistique en ce moment** things are very much up in the air at the moment **2.** [imprécision] vagueness.
◇ *adv* : **je vois ~** I can't focus properly.

flouer [3] [flue] *vt fam* to rook, to con ■ **il s'est fait ~** he was conned.

flouse△**, flouze**△ [fluz] *nm* dosh△ *UK*, dough△ *US*.

fluctuant, e [flyktɥɑ̃, ɑ̃t] *adj* fluctuating.

fluctuation [flyktɥasjɔ̃] *nf* fluctuation.

fluctuer [3] [flyktɥe] *vi* to fluctuate ■ **la production de pétrole fait ~ les cours mondiaux** oil production affects trading prices all over the world.

fluet, ette [flyɛ, ɛt] *adj* [personne] slender, slim ■ [voix] reedy.

fluide [flɥid] ◇ *adj* **1.** CHIM fluid **2.** [qui coule facilement] fluid, smooth ■ **la circulation est ~** *fig* there are no hold-ups (in the traffic) ■ **en un style ~** in a flowing style ■ **en une langue ~** fluently **3.** [fluctuant - situation] fluctuating, changeable ; [- pensée] elusive **4.** [flou - forme, blouse, robe] flowing.
◇ *nm* **1.** CHIM fluid **2.** [d'un médium] aura ■ **il a du ~** he has occult powers.

fluidifiant, e [flɥidifjɑ̃, ɑ̃t] *adj* MÉD expectorant.

fluidifier [9] [flɥidifje] *vt* to fluidize.

fluidité [flɥidite] *nf* **1.** [qualité - d'une crème, d'une sauce] smoothness, fluidity ■ **grâce à la ~ de la circulation** because there were no hold-ups in the traffic **2.** [flou - d'une forme, d'un vêtement] fluid *ou* flowing contours **3.** ÉCON flexibility.

fluo [flyo] *adj* fluorescent, Day-Glo®.

fluor [flyɔr] *nm* fluorine.

fluoré, e [flyɔre] *adj* fluoridated.

fluorescence [flyɔresɑ̃s] *nf* fluorescence.

fluorescent, e [flyɔresɑ̃, ɑ̃t] *adj* fluorescent.

fluorure [flyɔryr] *nm* fluoride.

flush [flœʃ, flɔʃ] (*pl* **flushs ou** *pl* **flushes**) *nm* JEUX flush ■ **~ royal** royal flush.

flûte [flyt] ◇ *nf* **1.** [instrument] flute ■ **~ à bec** recorder ■ **~ de Pan** panpipe ■ **~ traversière** flute ■ **petite ~** piccolo ■ **'la Flûte enchantée'** ***Mozart*** 'The Magic Flute' **2.** [verre] flute (glass) **3.** [pain] *thin loaf of French bread*.
◇ *interj fam* drat, bother.

flûté, e [flyte] *adj* [rire, voix] reedy.

flûtiau, x [flytjo] *nm* tin *ou* penny whistle.

flûtiste [flytist] *nmf* flautist.

fluvial, e, aux [flyvjal, o] *adj* [érosion] fluvial ■ [navigation] river *(modif)*.

fluvio-glaciaire [flyvjɔglasjɛr] (*pl* **fluvio-glaciaires**) *adj* fluvioglacial.

fluviométrique [flyvjɔmetrik] *adj* [mesure] fluviometric.

flux [fly] *nm* **1.** [marée] incoming tide ■ **le ~ et le reflux** the ebb and flow ■ **le ~ et le reflux de la foule** the ebbing and flowing of the crowd **2.** [écoulement - d'un liquide] flow ; [- du sang menstruel] menstrual flow **3.** [abondance] : **un ~ de : noyé dans un ~ de paroles** carried away by a stream of words ■ **devant ce ~ de recommandations** faced with this string of recommendations **4.** PHYS flux ■ **~ électrique** electric flux ■ **~ magnétique** magnetic flux **5.** COMM : **distribution à ~ tendus** just-in-time distribution **6.** MÉTALL flux **7.** FIN : **~ monétaire** flow of money **8.** SOCIOL : **~ migratoire** massive population movement.

fluxion [flyksjɔ̃] *nf* MÉD inflammation ■ **~ de poitrine** *vieilli* pneumonia.

FM (*abr de* **frequency modulation**) *nf* FM.

Fme = **femme**.

FMI (*abr de* **Fonds monétaire international**) *npr m* IMF.

FN *npr m* = **Front national**.

FNAC, Fnac [fnak] (*abr de* **Fédération nationale des achats des cadres**) *npr f chain of large stores selling hi-fi, books etc.*

FNE (*abr de* **Fonds national de l'emploi**) *nm state fund providing aid to jobseekers and workers who accept lower-paid work to avoid redundancy.*

FNEF, Fnef [fnɛf] (*abr de* **Fédération nationale des étudiants de France**) *npr f students' union*, ≃ NUS *UK*.

FNSEA (*abr de* **Fédération nationale des syndicats d'exploitants agricoles**) *npr f farmers' union*, ≃ NFU *UK*.

FO (*abr de* **Force ouvrière**) *npr f moderate workers' union (formed out of the split with Communist CGT in 1948).*

FOB [fɔb] (*abr de* **free on board**) *adj inv* & *adv* FOB.

foc [fɔk] *nm* jib ■ **grand ~** main *ou* outer jib ■ **petit ~** inner jib.

focal, e, aux [fɔkal, o] *adj* [central] : **point ~ d'un raisonnement** main *ou* central point in an argument.
◆ **focale** *nf* OPT & PHOTO focal distance *ou* length.

focalisation [fɔkalizasjɔ̃] *nf* **1.** OPT & PHYS focalization, focussing **2.** [concentration] focussing.

focaliser [3] [fɔkalize] *vt* **1.** OPT & PHYS to focus **2.** [concentrer] to focus.
◆ **se focaliser sur** *vp+prép* to be focussed *ou* to focus on.

fofolle [fɔfɔl] *f fam* ▷ **foufou**.

fœhn, föhn [føn] *nm* **1.** [vent] foehn, föhn **2.** *Suisse* hairdryer.

fœtal, e, aux [fetal, o] *adj* foetal, fetal.

fœtoscopie [fetɔskɔpi] *nf* foetoscopy.

fœtus [fetys] *nm* foetus.

foi [fwa] *nf* **1.** RELIG faith ■ **avoir la ~** to have faith ■ **il faut avoir la ~ pour travailler avec elle** *hum* you have to be really dedicated to work with her ➊ **faire sa profession de ~** *fig* to set out one's ideas and beliefs ■ **avoir la ~ du charbonnier** RELIG to have a naive belief in God ; *fig* to be naively trusting ■ **n'avoir ni** *ou* **être sans ~ ni loi** to fear neither God nor man ■ **il n'y a que la ~ qui sauve!** *hum* faith is a wonderful thing!
2. [confiance] faith, trust ■ **ajouter** *ou* **accorder ~ à des rumeurs** to give credence to rumours ■ **avoir ~ en** *ou* **dans qqn** to have faith in *ou* to trust (in) sb ■ **elle a une ~ aveugle en lui** she trusts him blindly
3. *litt* [parole] pledged word ■ **~ de : ~ d'honnête homme!** on my word of honour!
4. [preuve] : **il n'y a qu'une pièce officielle qui fasse ~** only an official paper is valid ■ **les coupons doivent être envoyés avant le 1er septembre, le cachet de la poste faisant ~** the coupons must be postmarked no later than September 1st
5. *loc* **en ~ de quoi** DR in witness whereof ■ **il avait dit qu'il viendrait, en ~ de quoi j'ai préparé un petit discours** *sout* he had said he would come, on the strength of which I have prepared a little speech ■ **ma ~!** well! ■ **viendrez-vous? – ma ~ oui!** will you come? – why, certainly! ■ **c'est ma ~ possible, qui sait?** it might be possible, who knows?
◆ **sous la foi de** *loc prép* : **sous la ~ du serment** on *ou* under oath.
◆ **sur la foi de** *loc prép* : **sur la ~ de ses déclarations/de sa réputation** on the strength of his statement/of his reputation.
◆ **bonne foi** *nf* : **être de bonne ~** to be sincere ■ **les gens de bonne ~** honest people, decent folk ■ **il a agi en toute bonne ~** he acted in good faith.
◆ **mauvaise foi** *nf* : **être de mauvaise ~** to be insincere ■ **écoutez-le, il est de mauvaise ~!** listen to him, he himself doesn't believe what he's saying!

foie [fwa] *nm* **1.** ANAT liver **2.** CULIN liver ■ **~ de génisse** cow's liver ■ **~ gras** foie gras ■ **~ de veau** calf's liver *(from a milk-fed animal)* ■ **~ de volaille** chicken liver.

◆ **foies**△ *nmpl* : **avoir les ~s** to be scared stiff.

foin [fwɛ̃] *nm* **1.** AGRIC hay ▪ **c'est la saison des ~s** it's haymaking season ▪ **faire les ~s** to make hay ➊ **chercher une aiguille** *ou* **une épingle dans une botte** *ou* **une meule de ~** to look for a needle in a haystack **2.** [d'un artichaut] choke **3.** *loc* **faire du ~** *fam* [être bruyant] to make a din ; [faire un scandale] to kick up a fuss.
◆ **foin de** *interj litt* **~ de l'argent et de la gloire!** the Devil take money and glory!

foire [fwar] *nf* **1.** [marché] fair ▪ **~ aux bestiaux** cattle fair *ou* market **2.** [exposition] trade fair **3.** [fête foraine] funfair ▪ **la ~ du Trône** *large annual funfair on the outskirts of Paris* **4.** *fam* [désordre] mess ▪ **c'est une vraie ~ dans cette maison!** this house is a real dump! ▪ **faire la ~** to live it up **5.** *loc* **~ d'empoigne** free-for-all.

foire-exposition [fwarɛkspozisjɔ̃] (*pl* **foires-expositions**) *nf* trade fair.

foirer [3] [fware] *vi* **1.** *fam* [rater] to fall through ▪ **tu as encore tout fait ~** you blew it again **2.** ARM to fail **3.** [vis] to slip.

foireux, euse [fwarø, øz] *adj fam* **1.** *péj* [mal fait] : **cette bagnole foireuse** this wreck of a car **2.** [poltron] yellow-bellied, chicken.

fois [fwa] *nf* **1.** [exprime la fréquence] : **une ~** once ▪ **deux ~** twice ▪ **trois ~** three times, thrice *litt* ▪ **payez en six ~** pay in six instalments ▪ **une autre ~ peut-être** [pour refuser une invitation] some other *ou* another time maybe ▪ **neuf ~ sur dix, quatre-vingt-dix-neuf ~ sur cent** nine times out of ten, ninety-nine times out of a hundred ▪ **par deux ~** *litt* twice ▪ **pour la énième ~** for the umpteenth time ▪ **pour une ~** for once ▪ **une (bonne) ~ pour toutes** once and for all ▪ **cette ~, je gagnerai** this time, I'll win ▪ **ça ira pour cette ~, mais ne recommencez pas** it's alright this once, but don't do it again ▪ **(à) chaque ~ que, toutes les ~ que** every *ou* each time ➊ **cent euros une ~, deux ~, trois ~, adjugé, vendu!** a hundred euros, going, going, gone! ▪ **une ~ n'est pas coutume** just the once won't hurt ▪ **il était une ~ un roi** once upon a time there was a king
2. [dans les comparaisons] time ▪ **c'est trois ~ plus grand** it's three times as big ▪ **il y a dix ~ moins de spectateurs que l'année dernière** there are ten times fewer spectators than last year
3. *(comme distributif)* **deux ~ par mois** twice a month ▪ **une ~ par semaine** once a week ▪ **trois ~ par an, trois ~ l'an** three times a year
4. MATH times ▪ **15 ~ 34** 15 times 34 ➊ **deux** *ou* **trois ~ rien** virtually nothing, hardly anything ▪ **ma maladie? trois ~ rien** my illness? it was nothing really
5. *loc* **une ~** *(suivi d'un pp)* : **une ~ nettoyé, il sera comme neuf** once *ou* after it's been cleaned, it'll be as good as new ▪ **tu n'as qu'à venir une ~ ton travail terminé** just come as soon as your work is finished ▪ **une ~ que** : **une ~ que tu auras compris, tout sera plus facile** once you've understood, you'll find everything's easier ▪ **des ~** *fam* [parfois] sometimes ▪ **non mais des ~!** honestly! ▪ **tu n'aurais pas vu mon livre, des ~?** you wouldn't happen to have seen my book anywhere, would you? ▪ **je préfère l'appeler, des ~ qu'elle aurait oublié** I'd rather call her in case she's forgotten.
◆ **à la fois** *loc adv* together, at a time, at the same time ▪ **pas tous à la ~!** one at a time!, not all at once!
◆ **(tout) à la fois** *loc adv* both ▪ **il rit et pleure (tout) à la ~** he's laughing and crying at (one and) the same time ▪ **elle est (tout) à la ~ auteur et traductrice** she's both an author and a translator.
◆ **une fois** *loc adv Belgique* indeed.

foison [fwazɔ̃] ◆ **à foison** *loc adv litt* galore, plenty ▪ **il y a de quoi boire à ~** there's drinks galore.

foisonnant, e [fwazɔnɑ̃, ɑ̃t] *adj* abundant.

foisonnement [fwazɔnmɑ̃] *nm* **1.** [de la végétation, d'idées] abundance, proliferation **2.** CHIM & TECHNOL expansion.

foisonner [3] [fwazɔne] *vi* **1.** [abonder] to abound ▪ **une œuvre où les idées foisonnent** a work rich in ideas ▪ **notre littérature foisonne en jeunes auteurs de talent** our literature abounds in *ou* is full of talented young authors **2.** CHIM & TECHNOL to expand.

fol [fɔl] *m* ▷ **fou**.

folâtre [fɔlatr] *adj* [enjoué] frisky, frolicsome ▪ **être d'humeur ~** to be in a playful mood.

folâtrer [3] [fɔlatre] *vi* to frolic, to fool around.

foldingue [fɔldɛ̃g] *adj* batty.

foliacé, e [fɔljase] *adj* foliaceous, foliate.

foliation [fɔljasjɔ̃] *nf* BOT & GÉOL foliation.

folichon, onne [fɔliʃɔ̃, ɔn] *adj fam* **pas ~** not much fun ▪ **un après-midi pas bien ~** a pretty dull afternoon ▪ **on ne peut pas dire que ses amis soient très ~s** his friends weren't exactly a bundle of laughs *ou* a laugh a minute.

folie [fɔli] *nf* **1.** MÉD [démence] madness ▪ **un accès** *ou* **une crise de ~** a fit of madness **2.** [déraison] madness, lunacy ▪ **c'est pure ~** it's utter madness *ou* sheer folly ▪ **elle a la ~ du jeu** she's got the gambling bug ➊ **c'est de la ~ douce que de vouloir la raisonner** it's sheer lunacy to try to reason with her ▪ **sortir par ce temps, c'est de la ~ furieuse!** it's (sheer) madness to go out in weather like this! ▪ **avoir la ~ des grandeurs** to suffer from *ou* to have delusions of grandeur **3.** [acte déraisonnable] crazy thing to do, folly *litt* ▪ **ce sont des ~s de jeunesse** those are just the crazy things you get up to when you're young ▪ **j'ai fait une ~ en achetant ce manteau** I was crazy *ou* mad to buy that coat ▪ **faire des ~s** [dépenser] to be extravagant **4.** HIST [maison] folly.
◆ **à la folie** *loc adv* passionately, to distraction ▪ **aimer qqn à la ~** to be madly in love with sb, to love sb to distraction.

folié, e [fɔlje] *adj* foliate.

folio [fɔljo] *nm* folio.

folioter [3] [fɔljɔte] *vt* to folio, to foliate.

folk [fɔlk] ◇ *adj* folk *(modif)*.
◇ *nm* folk music.

folklo [fɔlklo] *adj inv fam* weird ▪ **c'est un type plutôt ~** he's a bit of a weirdo.

folklore [fɔlklɔr] *nm* **1.** DANSE & MUS : **le ~** folklore **2.** *fam péj* **c'est du ~** it's a load of nonsense.

folklorique [fɔlklɔrik] *adj* **1.** DANSE & MUS folk *(modif)* **2.** *fam* [insolite, ridicule] bizarre, weird ▪ **tu l'aurais vu avec tous ses sacs en plastique, c'était ~!** you should have seen him with all those plastic bags, it was just too much!

folle [fɔl] ◇ *f* ▷ **fou**.
◇ *nf* PÊCHE wide-mesh fishing net.

follement [fɔlmɑ̃] *adv* **1.** [excessivement] madly ▪ **s'amuser ~** to have a great time ▪ **le prix en est ~ élevé** the price is ridiculously high ▪ **ce n'est pas ~ gai** it's not that much fun **2.** [déraisonnablement] madly, wildly.

follet [fɔlɛ] *adj m* ▷ **feu**.

folliculaire [fɔlikylɛr] = **folliculeux**.

follicule [fɔlikyl] *nm* ANAT & BOT follicle.

folliculeux *adj* follicular.

folliculine [fɔlikylin] *nf* oestrone.

fomenter [3] [fɔmɑ̃te] *vt litt* to foment *litt*, to cause.

foncé, e [fɔ̃se] *adj* dark, deep.

foncer [16] [fɔ̃se] ◇ *vi* **1.** [s'élancer] to charge ▪ **~ contre** *ou* **sur son adversaire** to rush at one's adversary ▪ **~ droit devant soi** to go straight ahead ➊ **~ dans le tas** *fam* to charge in, to pile in **2.** *fam* [se déplacer très vite] to speed along **3.** *fam* [se hâter] : **nous avons tous foncé pour boucler le journal** we all rushed to finish the newspaper in time ➊ **~ dans le brouillard** to forge ahead (without worrying about the consequences) **4.** [s'assombrir - cheveu] to go darker.
◇ *vt* **1.** [teinte] to make darker, to darken **2.** [mettre un fond à] to (fit with a) bottom **3.** CULIN [au lard] to line with bacon fat ▪ [avec de la pâte] to line with pastry **4.** MIN to bore, to sink.

fonceur, euse [fɔ̃sœr, øz] ◇ *adj* dynamic.
◇ *nm, f* dynamic type.

foncier, ère [fɔ̃sje, ɛr] *adj* **1.** ADMIN & FIN [impôt, politique, problème] land *(modif)* ▪ **biens ~s** (real) property, real estate ▪ **droit ~** ground law ▪ **propriétaire ~** landowner ▪ **propriété foncière** land ownership, ownership of land **2.** [fondamental] fundamental, basic.
◆ **foncier** *nm* land *ou* property tax.

foncièrement [fɔ̃sjɛrmɑ̃] *adv* **1.** [fondamentalement] fundamentally, basically **2.** [totalement] deeply, profoundly ▪ **il est ~ ignorant** he's profoundly ignorant.

fonction [fɔ̃ksjɔ̃] *nf* **1.** [emploi] office ▪ **entrer en ~** *ou* **~s** to take up one's post ▪ **faire ~ de** to act as ▪ **il a pour ~ d'écrire les discours du président** his job is to write the president's speeches ▪ **il occupe de hautes ~s** he has important responsibilities ▪ **est-ce que cela entre dans tes ~s?** is this part of your duties? ▪ **remplir ses ~s** to carry out one's job *ou* functions ▪ **se démettre de ses ~s** to resign one's post *ou* from one's duties ▪ **démettre qqn de ses ~s** to dismiss sb (from his duties) ▪ **prendre ses ~s** to take up one's post **2.** [rôle] function ▪ **~s de nutrition** nutritive functions ▪ **la pièce a pour ~ de maintenir l'équilibre de la balance** the part serves to keep the scales balanced ⊙ **la ~ crée l'organe** *Lamarck allus* necessity is the mother of invention **3.** [dépendre de] : **être ~ de : sa venue est ~ de son travail** whether he comes or not depends on his work **4.** CHIM, LING & MATH function ▪ **en ~ inverse de** in inverse ratio to.
◆ **de fonction** *loc adj* : **appartement** *ou* **logement de ~** tied accommodation *UK*, accommodation that goes with the job ▪ **voiture de ~** company car.
◆ **en fonction de** *loc prép* according to.
◆ **fonction publique** *nf* : **la ~ publique** the civil *ou* public service.

fonctionnaire [fɔ̃ksjɔnɛr] *nmf* civil servant ▪ **~ municipal** local government official ▪ **haut ~** senior civil servant ▪ **petit ~** minor official ▪ **avoir une mentalité de petit ~** *péj* to have a petty bureaucratic mentality.

FONCTIONNAIRE

This term covers a broader range of public service employees than the term "civil servant": from high-ranking members of the state administration to public-sector teachers and post-office workers.

fonctionnaliser [3] [fɔ̃ksjɔnalize] *vt* [ameublement, cuisine] to make more functional.

fonctionnalité [fɔ̃ksjɔnalite] *nf* functionality.

fonctionnariat [fɔ̃ksjɔnarja] *nm* employment by the state.

fonctionnariser [3] [fɔ̃ksjɔnarize] *vt* to make part of the civil service.

fonctionnel, elle [fɔ̃ksjɔnɛl] *adj* **1.** MATH, MÉD & PSYCHOL functional **2.** [adapté] practical, functional ▪ **des meubles ~s** functional furniture **3.** LING : **linguistique ~le** functional linguistics ▪ **mot ~** function word.

fonctionnement [fɔ̃ksjɔnmɑ̃] *nm* functioning, working ▪ **pour assurer le bon ~ de votre machine à laver** to keep your washing machine in good working order ▪ **ça vient d'un mauvais ~ de la prise** it's due to a fault in the plug.

fonctionner [3] [fɔ̃ksjɔne] *vi* [mécanisme, engin] to function, to work ▪ [métro, véhicule] to run ▪ **le moteur fonctionne mal/bien** the engine isn't/is working properly ▪ **mon cœur fonctionne encore bien!** my heart is still going strong! ▪ **faire ~ une machine** to operate a machine ▪ **les freins n'ont pas fonctionné** the brakes failed.

fond [fɔ̃] *nm* **1.** [d'un récipient] bottom ▪ [d'un placard] back ▪ [extrémité] bottom, far end ▪ [de la gorge] back ▪ [d'une pièce] far end, back ▪ [d'un jardin] far end, bottom ▪ **sans ~** bottomless ▪ **au fin ~ du désert** in the middle of the desert ▪ **il y a cinq mètres de ~** [de profondeur] the water is five metres deep *ou* in depth ▪ **aller par le ~** to sink ▪ **couler par 100 m de ~** to sink to a depth of 100 m ⊙ **~ de culotte** *ou* **de pantalon** seat (of one's pants) ▪ **le ~ d'œil** MÉD the back of the eye ▪ **faire un examen du ~ d'œil** MÉD to have an ophthalmoscopy ▪ **les grands ~s marins** the depths of the ocean ▪ **à ~ de cale** at rock bottom ▪ **gratter** *ou* **vider** *ou* **racler les ~s de tiroir** *fam fig* to scrape around *(for money, food etc)*
2. *fig* depths ▪ **toucher le ~ (du désespoir)** to reach the depths of despair ▪ **il connaît le ~ de mon cœur/âme** he knows what's in my heart/soul ▪ **je vous remercie du ~ du cœur** I thank you from the bottom of my heart
3. [cœur, substance] heart, core, nub ▪ **puis-je te dire le ~ de ma pensée?** can I tell you what I really think? ▪ **le ~ et la forme** LITTÉR substance and form ▪ **sur le ~, vous avez raison** you're basically right
4. [tempérament] : **il a un bon ~** he's basically a good *ou* kind person ▪ **elle n'a pas vraiment un mauvais ~** she's not really a bad person
5. [arrière-plan] background ⊙ **il y a un ~ de vérité dans ce que vous dites** there's some truth in what you're saying ▪ **~ sonore** background music ▪ **le ~ de l'air est frais** there's a chill *ou* nip in the air
6. [reste] drop ▪ **il reste un ~ de café** there's a drop of coffee left ⊙ **boire** *ou* **vider les ~s de bouteilles** to drink up the dregs ▪ **le ~ du panier** the leftovers
7. CULIN : **~ de sauce/soupe** basis for a sauce/soup ▪ **~ d'artichaut** artichoke heart ▪ **~ de tarte** pastry case
8. MIN : **travailler au ~** to work at the coal face ▪ **descendre au ~ de la mine** to go down the pit ⊙ **les mineurs de ~** the men in the pits.
◆ **à fond** *loc adv* in depth ▪ **respirer à ~** to breathe deeply ▪ **faire le ménage à ~ dans la maison** *fam* to clean the house thoroughly, to spring-clean ▪ **se donner à ~** to give one's all ▪ **se donner à ~ dans** *ou* **à qqch** to throw o.s. completely into sthg.
◆ **à fond de train** *loc adv* (at) full tilt.
◆ **à fond la caisse, à fond les manettes** *loc adv fam* = **à fond de train**.
◆ **au fond** *loc adv* basically ▪ **au ~, c'est mieux comme ça** it's better that way, really ▪ **au ~, on pourrait y aller en janvier** in fact, we could go in January.
◆ **au fond de** *loc prép* : **au ~ de soi-même** deep down ▪ **c'est au ~ du couloir/de la salle** it's at the (far) end of the corridor/of the hall ▪ **au ~ de la rivière** at the bottom of the river ▪ **regarder qqn au ~ des yeux** to look deeply into sb's eyes.
◆ **dans le fond** = **au fond**.
◆ **de fond** *loc adj* **1.** SPORT [épreuve, coureur, course] long-distance *(avant n)* ▪ **ski de ~** cross-country skiing
2. [analyse, remarque, texte] basic, fundamental.
◆ **de fond en comble** *loc adv* [nettoyer, fouiller] from top to bottom ▪ **revoir un texte de ~ en comble** *fig* to revise a text thoroughly.
◆ **fond de robe** *nm* slip.
◆ **fond de teint** *nm* (make-up) foundation.

fondamental, e, aux [fɔ̃damɑ̃tal, o] *adj* **1.** SC fundamental, basic ▪ **la recherche ~e** basic *ou* fundamental research **2.** [de base] elementary, basic **3.** [important] fundamental, essential, crucial **4.** PHYS [niveau] fundamental **5.** MUS fundamental.

fondamentalement [fɔ̃damɑ̃talmɑ̃] *adv* fundamentally ▪ **c'est ~ la même chose** it's basically the same thing ▪ **~ opposés** radically opposed.

fondamentalisme [fɔ̃damɑ̃talism] *nm* (religious) fundamentalism.

fondamentaliste [fɔ̃damɑ̃talist] ◇ *adj* fundamentalist, fundamentalistic.
◇ *nmf* fundamentalist.

fondant, e [fɔ̃dɑ̃, ɑ̃t] *adj* **1.** [glace, neige] melting, thawing **2.** [aliment] : **un rôti ~** a tender roast ▪ **un bonbon/chocolat ~** a sweet/chocolate that melts in the mouth.
◆ **fondant** *nm* **1.** CULIN [bonbon, gâteau] fondant **2.** MÉTALL flux.

fondateur, trice [fɔ̃datœr, tris] *nm, f* **1.** [gén] founder **2.** DR incorporator.

fondation [fɔ̃dasjɔ̃] *nf* **1.** [création - d'une ville, d'une société] foundation ; [- d'une bourse, d'un prix] establishment, creation **2.** [institution] foundation.
◆ **fondations** *nfpl* CONSTR foundations.

fondé, e [fɔ̃de] *adj* **1.** [argument, peur] justified ▪ **un reproche non ~** an unjustified reproach ▪ **mal ~** ill-founded **2.** *loc* **être ~ à** [avoir des raisons de] : **je serais ~ à croire qu'il y a eu malversation** I would be justified in thinking *ou* I would have grounds for believing that embezzlement has taken place.
◆ **fondé de pouvoir** *nm* proxy.

fondement [fɔ̃dmɑ̃] *nm* **1.** [base] foundation ▪ **jeter les ~s d'une nouvelle politique** to lay the foundations of a new policy **2.** *hum* derrière *hum*, behind, backside **3.** PHILOS fundament.
◆ **sans fondement** *loc adj* [crainte, rumeur] groundless, unfounded.

fonder [3] [fɔ̃de] *vt* **1.** [construire - empire, parti] to found ▪ **~ un foyer** *ou* **une famille** *sout* to start a family **2.** COMM to found, to set up ▪ **'maison fondée en 1930'** 'Established 1930' **3.** [appuyer] : **elle fondait tous ses espoirs sur son fils** she pinned all her hopes on her son **4.** [légitimer - réclamation, plainte] to justify.
◆ **se fonder sur** *vp+prép* **1.** [se prévaloir de] to base o.s. on ▪ **sur quoi te fondes-tu pour affirmer pareille chose?** what grounds do you have for such a claim? **2.** [remarque, théorie] to be based on.

fonderie [fɔ̃dri] *nf* **1.** [procédé] casting, founding **2.** [usine] smelting works **3.** [atelier] foundry.

fondeur, euse [fɔ̃dœr, øz] *nm, f* **1.** SPORT langläufer, cross-country skier **2.** [de bronze] caster ▪ [de l'or, de l'argent] smelter.

fondre [75] [fɔ̃dr] ◇ *vt* **1.** [rendre liquide] to melt ▪ **~ de l'or/de l'argent** to smelt gold/silver **2.** [fabriquer - statue, canon, cloche] to cast, to found **3.** [dissoudre] to dissolve **4.** [combiner - couleurs] to blend, to merge ; [- sociétés] to combine, to merge.
◇ *vi* **1.** [se liquéfier] to melt ▪ **la glace fond au-dessus de 0° C** ice thaws at 0° C ➊ **~ comme cire** *ou* **neige au soleil** to vanish into thin air **2.** [se dissoudre] to dissolve ▪ **faire ~ du sucre** to dissolve sugar ▪ **~ dans la bouche** to melt in the mouth **3.** [s'affaiblir - animosité, rage] to melt away, to disappear ▪ **il sent son cœur ~ quand il voit ses enfants** he can feel his heart melting when he sees his children ➊ **~ en larmes** to dissolve into tears **4.** *fam* [maigrir] to get thin ▪ **il fond à vue d'œil** the weight's dropping off him.
◆ **fondre sur** *v+prép* to sweep *ou* to swoop down on.
◆ **se fondre** *vpi* **1.** [se liquéfier] to melt **2.** [se mêler] to merge, to mix ▪ **se ~ dans la nuit/le brouillard** to disappear into the night/mist.

fondrière [fɔ̃drijɛr] *nf* **1.** [sur une route] pothole **2.** [marécage] bog, quagmire.

fonds [fɔ̃] ◇ *nm* **1.** [propriété] business ▪ **un ~ de commerce** a business **2.** FIN fund ▪ **~ commun de placement** unit trust, mutual fund *US* ▪ **~ d'amortissement** sinking fund ▪ **~ de réserve** reserve fund ▪ **~ de roulement** working capital ▪ **Fonds monétaire international** International Monetary Fund **3.** [ressources] collection.
◇ *nmpl* **1.** FIN funds ▪ **être en ~** to be in funds ▪ **rentrer dans ses ~** to recoup one's costs ▪ **mes ~ sont au plus bas** *hum* funds are low ▪ **prêter de l'argent à ~ perdus** to loan money without security ▪ **~ de pension** (private) pension fund ➊ **~ de prévoyance** contingency reserve ▪ **les ~ publics** public funds ▪ **les ~ propres** ÉCON shareholders' *ou* stockholders' equity ▪ **~ secrets** secret funds ▪ **collecte de ~** financial appeal, fund-raising *(U)* **2.** [argent] money.

fondu, e [fɔ̃dy] ◇ *pp* ▻ **fondre**.
◇ *adj* **1.** [liquéfié] melted ▪ MÉTALL molten ▪ **de la neige ~e** slush ➊ **fromage ~** cheese spread **2.** [ramolli] melted **3.** ART [teinte] blending.
◆ **fondu** *nm* **1.** CINÉ dissolve ▪ **les personnages apparaissent/disparaissent en ~** the characters fade in/out ▪ **~ enchaîné** fade-in fade-out **2.** ART blend.
◆ **fondue** *nf* CULIN : **~e bourguignonne** meat fondue ▪ **~e savoyarde** (Swiss) cheese fondue.

fongicide [fɔ̃ʒisid] ◇ *adj* fungicidal.
◇ *nm* fungicide.

font *v* ▻ **faire**.

fontaine [fɔ̃tɛn] *nf* **1.** [édifice] fountain ▪ **~ Wallace** *dark green ornate drinking fountain (typical of Paris)* **2.** [source] spring ▪ **il ne faut pas dire: ~ je ne boirai pas de ton eau** *prov* never say never *prov*.

fontainebleau [fɔ̃tɛnblo] *nm* CULIN *soft cheese whipped with cream.*

fontanelle [fɔ̃tanɛl] *nf* fontanelle.

fonte [fɔ̃t] *nf* **1.** MÉTALL cast iron **2.** [fusion - gén] melting ; [- du métal] smelting ; [- des neiges] thawing ▪ **à la ~ des neiges/glaces** when the snow/ice thaws **3.** IMPR fount, font *US* **4.** AGRIC & HORT : **~ des semis** damping off seedlings.

fonts [fɔ̃] *nmpl* : **~ (baptismaux)** (baptismal) font.

foot [fut] *nm fam* football *UK*, soccer ▪ **jouer au ~** to play football.

football [futbol] *nm* football *UK*, soccer ▪ **jouer au ~** to play football ▪ **~ américain** American football, football *US*.

footballeur, euse [futbolœr, øz] *nm, f* footballer *UK*, soccer player *US*.

footing [futiŋ] *nm* : **le ~** jogging ▪ **faire un ~** to go jogging, to go for a jog.

for [fɔr] *nm* : **en mon ~ intérieur** deep down *ou* inside, in my heart of hearts.

forage [fɔraʒ] *nm* [d'un puits de pétrole] boring, drilling ▪ [d'un puits, d'une mine] sinking.

forain, e [fɔrɛ̃, ɛn] ◇ *adj* [boutique] fairground *(modif)* ▪ **marchand ~** stallholder.
◇ *nm, f* stallholder.

forban [fɔrbɑ̃] *nm* **1.** [pirate] freebooter **2.** *péj* [escroc] crook.

forçat [fɔrsa] *nm* HIST [sur une galère] galley slave ▪ [dans un bagne] convict ▪ **travailler comme un ~** to work like a slave.

force [fɔrs] ◇ *nf* **1.** [puissance - d'une tempête, d'un coup] strength, force ; [- d'un sentiment] strength ; [- d'une idée, d'un argument] strength, power ▪ **avec ~** forcefully ▪ **un vent (de) ~ 7** MÉTÉOR a force 7 wind ➊ **les ~s du mal** the forces of evil ▪ **'la ~ tranquille'** *slogan used by François Mitterrand in his successful election campaign of 1981*
2. [vigueur physique] strength ▪ **avoir beaucoup de ~** to be very strong ▪ **avoir la ~ de faire qqch** to have the strength to do sthg ▪ **il sent sa ~ l'abandonner avec l'âge** he feels himself growing weaker with age ▪ **il est sans ~** he has no strength ▪ **reprendre des ~s** to regain one's strength ▪ **c'est au-dessus de mes ~s** it's beyond me ▪ **de toutes mes/ses ~s** with all my/his strength, with all my/his might ▪ **je le veux de toutes mes ~s** I want it with all my heart ➊ **être une ~ de la nature** to be a mighty force ▪ **être dans la ~ de l'âge** to be in the prime of life ▪ **les ~s vives de la nation** the nation's resources
3. [contrainte, autorité] force ▪ **vaincre par la ~** to win by (using) force ▪ **avoir recours à la ~** to resort to force ▪ **nous ne céderons pas à la ~** we will not yield to force ➊ **avoir ~ exécutoire** to be enforceable ▪ **avoir ~ de loi** to have the force of law ▪ **~ majeure** DR force majeure ▪ **c'est un cas de ~ majeure** it's completely unavoidable ▪ **il y a(cas de) ~ majeure** there are circumstances beyond my/our *etc* control ▪ **un coup de ~** POLIT & ÉCON a takeover by force
4. [puissance morale] strength ▪ **ce qui fait sa ~, c'est sa conviction politique** his political commitment is his strength ➊ **~ d'âme** spiritual strength ▪ **~ de caractère** strength of character ▪ [groupe de personnes] : **~ de vente** sales force
5. ADMIN & MIL : **la ~ nucléaire stratégique** *ou* **la ~ de frappe** *ou* **la ~ de dissuasion de la France** France's nuclear strike capacity ▪ **Force d'action rapide** *section of the French armed forces responding immediately in emergencies* ▪ **les ~s armées** the (armed) forces ▪ **~ d'intervention** task force ▪ **les ~s navales/aériennes** the naval/air forces ▪ **la ~ publique, les ~s de l'ordre** the police
6. [suprématie] strength, might ▪ **occuper une position de ~** to be in a position of strength
7. PHYS force ▪ **~ centrifuge/centripète** centrifugal/centripetal force ▪ **~ électromotrice** electromotive force ▪ **~ d'inertie** force of inertia

8. POLIT : **Force ouvrière** *trade union*
9. NAUT : **faire ~ de rames** to ply the oars ■ **faire ~ de voiles** to cram on sail
10. *loc* **~ est de** *sout* **: ~ est de constater que...** there is no choice but to accept that... ■ **par la ~ des choses/de l'habitude** by force of circumstance/of habit.
◇ *adv litt* & *hum* many ■ **je le lui ai expliqué avec ~ exemples** I explained it to him by giving numerous examples.
◆ **à force** *loc adv fam* **: tu vas le casser, à ~!** you'll break it if you go on like that! ■ **à ~, je suis fatigué** I'm getting tired.
◆ **à force de** *loc prép* by dint of ■ **à ~ de parler** by dint of talking.
◆ **à la force de** *loc prép* by the strength of ■ **grimper à la ~ des bras** to climb by the strength of one's arms ■ **s'élever à la ~ du poignet** *fig* to go up in the world by the sweat of one's brow.
◆ **à toute force** *loc adv* at all costs.
◆ **de force** *loc adv* by force ■ **il est entré de ~** he forced his way in ■ **on les a fait sortir de ~** they were made to leave.
◆ **en force** *loc adv* **1.** [en nombre] in force, in large numbers ■ **ils sont arrivés en ~** they arrived in force *ou* in great numbers
2. SPORT [sans souplesse] **: faire qqch en ~** to do sthg by brute force.
◆ **par force** *loc adv* **: par ~ nous nous sommes résignés à son départ** we were forced to accept *ou* we had to resign ourselves to his departure.

forcé, e [fɔrse] *adj* **1.** [obligé] forced ⊙ **atterrissage ~** emergency *ou* forced landing ■ **liquidation ~e** compulsory liquidation ■ **contraint et ~** under duress **2.** [inévitable] inevitable **3.** [sans spontanéité] strained ■ **rire ~** forced laugh ■ **comparaison ~e** artificial comparison.

forcement [fɔrsəmɑ̃] *nm* forcing.

forcément [fɔrsemɑ̃] *adv* inevitably, necessarily ■ **ça devait ~ arriver** it was bound to happen ■ **pas ~** not necessarily ■ **elle est très mince – ~, elle ne mange rien!** she's very slim – that's hardly surprising, she never eats a thing!

forcené, e [fɔrsəne] ◇ *adj* **1.** [passionné] fanatical, frenzied **2.** [violent] frenzied ■ **une haine ~e** a fanatical hatred.
◇ *nm, f* [fou] maniac.

forceps [fɔrsɛps] *nm* forceps.

forcer [16] [fɔrse] ◇ *vt* **1.** [obliger] to compel, to force ■ **~ qqn à faire qqch : il l'a forcée à quitter la société** he forced her out of the firm ■ **être forcé de faire qqch** to be forced to do sthg ■ **je suis forcée de rester au lit** I have (no choice but) to stay in bed ⊙ **on lui a forcé la main** he was made to do it, his hand was forced **2.** [ouvrir de force - tiroir, valise] to force (open) ; [- serrure, mécanisme] to force ■ **~ un coffre-fort** to force a safe open ■ **~ la porte de qqn** *fig* to barge *ou* to force one's way into sb's house **3.** [outrepasser] **: ~ la dose** PHARM to prescribe too large a dose ; *fig* to go too far **4.** *arch* [violer - personne] to violate **5.** [susciter] **: son courage a forcé l'admiration/le respect de tous** his courage commanded everybody's admiration/respect **6.** [influencer - destin, événements] to influence **7.** [presser] **: ~ le pas** to force the pace ■ **~ son cheval** ÉQUIT to overtax *ou* to override one's horse **8.** AGRIC & HORT to force **9.** [pousser trop loin] **: ~ sa voix** to strain one's voice ■ **~ sa nature** to go against one's true nature **10.** CHASSE to run down.
◇ *vi* to force, to strain ■ **ne force pas, tu vas casser le mécanisme** don't force the mechanism, you'll break it ■ **pliez la jambe sans ~** bend your leg very gently *ou* without straining.
◆ **forcer sur** *v+prép* to overdo ⊙ **~ sur la bouteille** *fam* to drink too much.
◆ **se forcer** *vp (emploi réfléchi)* [gén] to make an effort ■ [en mangeant] to force o.s. ■ **se ~ à lire/travailler** to force o.s. to read/to work.

forcing [fɔrsiŋ] *nm* SPORT pressure ■ **faire le ~** *pr* to put the pressure on ■ **faire du ~** *fam fig* to use fair means and foul.

forcir [32] [fɔrsir] *vi* to get bigger.

forclos, e [fɔrklo, oz] *adj* DR foreclosed.

forer [3] [fɔre] *vt* [puits de pétrole] to bore, to drill ■ [puits, mine] to sink.

forestier, ère [fɔrɛstje, ɛr] ◇ *adj* [chemin, code] forest *(modif).*
◇ *nm, f* forester.

foret [fɔrɛ] *nm* drill.

forêt [fɔrɛ] *nf* **1.** [arbres] forest ■ **~ vierge** virgin forest **2.** [multitude] **: une ~ de** a forest of.

Forêt-Noire [fɔrɛnwar] *npr f* **: la ~** the Black Forest.

foreur [fɔrœr] ◇ *adj m* [ingénieur, ouvrier] drilling *(modif).*
◇ *nm* TECHNOL driller.

foreuse [fɔrøz] *nf* drill.

forfaire [109] [fɔrfɛr] ◆ **forfaire à** *v+prép litt* to be false to.

forfait [fɔrfɛ] *nm* **1.** [abonnement - de transport, à l'opéra] season ticket ; [- au ski] pass, ski-pass ■ **~ train plus hôtel** package deal including train ticket and hotel reservation **2.** FIN **: être au ~** to be taxed on estimated income **3.** COMM **: payer qqn au ~** to pay sb a flat rate ■ **travailler au ~** to work for a flat rate **4.** SPORT [somme] withdrawal ■ **gagner par ~** to win by default **5.** *litt* [crime] infamy *litt*, (heinous) crime.

forfaitaire [fɔrfɛtɛr] *adj* inclusive ■ **somme** *ou* **montant ~** lump sum ■ **prix ~s** inclusive prices ■ **voyage à prix ~** package tour.

forfait-jour [fɔrfɛʒur] (*pl* **forfaits-jours**) *nm system of measuring working time, in days per year rather than hours per week.*

forfaiture [fɔrfetyr] *nf* **1.** DR abuse of authority **2.** HIST forfeiture.

forfait-vacances [fɔrfɛvakɑ̃s] (*pl* **forfaits-vacances**) *nm* package holiday.

forfanterie [fɔrfɑ̃tri] *nf litt* boastfulness.

forge [fɔrʒ] *nf* **1.** [atelier] forge, smithy **2.** [fourneau] forge.

forger [17] [fɔrʒe] *vt* **1.** TECHNOL to forge ⊙ **c'est en forgeant qu'on devient forgeron** *prov* practice makes perfect *prov* **2.** [inventer - alibi] to make up *(sép)* ; [- phrase] to coin ■ **une histoire forgée de toutes pièces** a fabricated story **3.** [fabriquer - document, preuve] to forge **4.** [aguerrir - personnalité, caractère] to form, to forge.
◆ **se forger** *vpt* **: se ~ une réputation** to earn o.s. a reputation ■ **se ~ un idéal** to build up an ideal for o.s. ■ **se ~ le caractère** to build up one's character.

forgeron [fɔrʒərɔ̃] *nm* blacksmith.

forgeur [fɔrʒœr] *nm litt* [de mots, de phrases] coiner ■ [de documents] forger.

formaliser [3] [fɔrmalize] *vt* [idée, théorie] to formalize.
◆ **se formaliser de** *vp+prép* to take offence at.

formalisme [fɔrmalism] *nm* **1.** [attitude] respect for etiquette ■ **faire preuve de ~** to be a stickler for etiquette **2.** ART, PHILOS & LITTÉR formalism.

formaliste [fɔrmalist] ◇ *adj* **1.** [guindé] strict about etiquette **2.** ART, LITTÉR & PHILOS formalistic.
◇ *nmf* **1.** [personne guindée] stickler for etiquette **2.** ART, LITTÉR & PHILOS formalist.

formalité [fɔrmalite] *nf* **1.** ADMIN formality ■ **~s administratives/douanières** administrative/customs formalities **2.** [acte sans importance] **: notre enquête n'est qu'une simple** *ou* **pure ~** we're just making routine enquiries ■ **cet examen n'est qu'une ~** this medical test is a mere formality **3.** [cérémonial] formality.

format [fɔrma] *nm* **1.** [dimension] size ■ **photo petit ~** small (format) print **2.** IMPR format ■ **livre en ~ de poche** paperback (book) ■ **~ tabloïd** tabloid ■ **papier ~ A4/A3** A4/A3 paper **3.** INFORM format.

formatage [fɔrmataʒ] *nm* formatting.

formater [3] [fɔrmate] *vt* to format INFORM.

formateur, trice [fɔrmatœr, tris] *adj* [rôle, influence] formative ▪ **ce stage a été très ~** this training course was very instructive.

formation [fɔrmasjɔ̃] *nf* **1.** [naissance] development, formation, forming **2.** [groupe] group ▪ **~ musicale** [classique] orchestra ; [moderne] band ▪ **~ politique** political group ▪ **~ syndicale** (trade) union **3.** ÉDUC [apprentissage] training *(U)* ▪ [connaissances] cultural background ▪ **elle a une bonne ~ littéraire/scientifique** she has a good literary/scientific background ▪ **il n'a aucune ~ musicale** he has no musical training ▪ **architecte de ~, elle est devenue cinéaste** having trained as an architect, she turned to making films ▶ **~ en alternance** sandwich course ▪ **~ continue** *ou* **permanente** *day release or night school education for employees provided by companies* ▪ **~ accélérée** intensive training ▪ **~ professionnelle** vocational training ▪ **~ professionnelle pour adultes** adult education **4.** MIL [détachement, disposition] formation **5.** DANSE & SPORT formation **6.** PHYSIOL puberty **7.** GÉOL formation **8.** LING : **la ~ du vocabulaire** vocabulary formation.

forme [fɔrm] *nf* **1.** [configuration] shape, form ▪ **un dessin de ~ géométrique** a geometrical pattern ▪ **la Terre a la ~ d'une sphère** the Earth is spherical ▪ **ne plus avoir ~ humaine** to be unrecognizable ▪ **mettre en ~ : mettez vos idées en ~** give your ideas some shape ▪ **mettre un écrit en ~** to structure a piece of writing ▪ **prendre la ~ de** to take (on) the form of, to assume the shape of ▪ **prendre ~** to take shape, to shape up
2. [état] form ▪ **se présenter sous ~ gazeuse** to come in gaseous form *ou* in the form of a gas ▪ **c'est le même sentiment sous plusieurs ~s** it's the same feeling expressed in several different ways ▪ **nous voulons combattre la misère sous toutes ses ~s** we want to fight poverty in all its forms
3. [silhouette] figure, shape
4. [type] form ▪ **des ~s de vie différentes sur d'autres planètes** different forms of life on other planets
5. [style] form ▪ **sacrifier à la ~** to put form above content
6. MUS form
7. LING form ▪ **mettre un verbe à la ~ interrogative/négative** to put a verb into the interrogative/in the negative (form) ▪ **la ~ progressive** the progressive
8. DR form ▪ **respecter la ~ légale** to respect legal procedures
9. [condition physique] form ▪ **~ physique** physical fitness ▪ **être en ~** to be on form ▪ **être au mieux** *ou* **sommet de sa ~, être en pleine ~** to be on top form ▪ **être en bonne ~ physique** to be fit ▪ **avoir** *ou* **tenir la ~** *fam* to be in great shape ▪ **je n'ai** *ou* **ne tiens pas la ~** I'm in poor shape ▪ **ayez la ~, pas les ~s** *(slogan publicitaire) allus* be fit not fat
10. [moule - pour chapeau] crown ; [- pour chaussure] last ; [- pour fromage] mould
11. PSYCHOL : **théorie de la ~** gestalt theory
12. IMPR forme.

◆ **formes** *nfpl* **1.** [physique] curves ▪ **avoir des ~s** to have a shapely figure
2. [convention] ▶ **y mettre les ~s** to be tactful ▪ **elle a toujours respecté les ~s** she has always respected convention.

◆ **dans les formes** *loc adv* according to form.

◆ **de pure forme** *loc adj* purely formal.

◆ **en bonne (et due) forme** ◇ *loc adj* [contrat] bona fide.
◇ *loc adv* [établir un document] in due form, according to the proper form.

◆ **en forme de** *loc prép* [ressemblant à] : **en ~ de poisson** shaped like a fish, fish-shaped.

◆ **pour la forme** *loc adv* for the sake of form, as a matter of form.

◆ **sans forme** *loc adj* shapeless.

◆ **sans autre forme de procès** *loc adv* without further ado.

◆ **sous forme de, sous la forme de** *loc prép* in the form of, as ▪ **un médicament qui existe sous ~ de comprimés** a drug available in tablet form.

formé, e [fɔrme] *adj* PHYSIOL fully-formed, fully-developed.

formel, elle [fɔrmɛl] *adj* **1.** [net - ordre, refus] definite ; [- identification, preuve] positive ▪ **le médecin a été ~, pas de laitages!** no milk products, the doctor was quite clear about that! **2.** [de la forme] formal **3.** [superficiel] : **leur protestation était purement ~le** their protest was purely for the sake of form **4.** PHILOS formal.

formellement [fɔrmɛlmɑ̃] *adv* **1.** [nettement] categorically ▪ **il m'a ~ interdit de fumer** he strictly forbade me to smoke **2.** [stylistiquement] formally **3.** PHILOS formally.

former [3] [fɔrme] *vt* **1.** [donner un contour à - lettre] to shape, to form ; [- phrase] to put together, to shape ▪ **Dieu forma l'homme à son image** BIBLE God made man in his own image **2.** [créer - gouvernement, association] to form ▪ **~ un train** to make up a train **3.** [se constituer en] to form ▪ **ils ont formé un cortège/attroupement** they formed a procession/a mob **4.** [dessiner] to form **5.** [constituer] to form ▪ **nous ne formions qu'un seul être** we were as one ▪ **ils forment un couple uni** they're a united couple ▪ **ils forment un couple étrange** they make a strange couple **6.** [faire apparaître] to make, to form **7.** *sout* [créer, faire par la pensée] : **~ un projet** to think up a plan ▪ **nous avons formé le dessein de nous marier** we are planning to marry ▪ **~ des vœux pour le succès de qqn/qqch** to wish sb/sthg success ▪ **tous les espoirs que nous formons pour eux** all the hopes we place in them **8.** LING to form **9.** ÉDUC & INDUST to train ▪ **~ les jeunes en entreprise** to give young people industrial training ▪ **~ son personnel à l'informatique** to train one's staff to use computers ▪ **formé à la gestion** trained in management (techniques) **10.** [développer - caractère, goût] to develop.

◆ **se former** ◇ *vpi* **1.** [apparaître - croûte, pellicule, peau] to form ; [- couche, dépôt] to form, to build up **2.** [se placer en] : **se ~ en** to form, to make ▪ **se ~ en carré** to form a square **3.** [se perfectionner] to train o.s. ▪ **se ~ sur le tas** to learn on the job *ou* as one goes along.
◇ *vpt* : **se ~ une opinion** to form an opinion.

Formica® [fɔrmika] *nm* Formica®.

formidable [fɔrmidabl] *adj* **1.** [imposant] tremendous ▪ *litt* formidable ▪ **elle a une volonté ~, elle réussira!** she has tremendous willpower, she'll succeed! **2.** *vieilli* [invraisemblable] incredible, unbelievable **3.** [admirable] great, wonderful.

formidablement [fɔrmidabləmɑ̃] *adv* tremendously ▪ **elle sait ~ bien s'occuper des enfants** she's great *ou* marvellous with children.

formol [fɔrmɔl] *nm* formalin.

Formose [fɔrmoz] *npr* Formosa ▪ **à ~** in Formosa.

formulable [fɔrmylabl] *adj* : **la proposition n'est pas encore ~** the proposal can't yet be formulated ▪ **~ en termes de droit** expressible in legal terms.

formulaire [fɔrmylɛr] *nm* form ADMIN.

formulation [fɔrmylasjɔ̃] *nf* formulation, wording ▪ **la ~ de votre problème est incorrecte** you formulated your problem incorrectly, the way you formulated your problem is incorrect.

formule [fɔrmyl] *nf* **1.** [tournure] expression, (turn of) phrase ▶ **elle a terminé sa lettre par une belle ~/une ~ toute faite** she ended her letter with a well-turned phrase/a ready-made phrase ▪ **~ consacrée** accepted expression ▪ **la ~ magique** the magic words ▪ **~ de politesse** [dans une lettre] letter ending
2. [imprimé] form
3. CHIM & MATH formula
4. PHARM formula, composition
5. [solution] formula, trick ▪ **ils ont (trouvé) la ~ pour ne pas avoir d'ennuis** they've found a way of not having any problems
6. [en langage publicitaire] way ▪ **une ~ économique pour vos vacances** an economical way to spend your holidays ▪ **nous vous proposons plusieurs ~s de crédit** we offer you several credit options ▪ **une nouvelle ~ de spectacle/restaurant** a new kind of show/restaurant ▪ **notre restaurant vous propose sa ~ à 16 euros ou sa carte** our restaurant offers you a set menu at 16 euros or an à la carte menu
7. AUTO formula
8. MÉD : **~ dentaire** dental formula.

formuler [3] [fɔrmyle] *vt* **1.** [exprimer - doctrine, revendication] to formulate, to express **2.** [rédiger - théorème] to formulate ; [- décret] to draw up *(sép)*.

fornicateur, trice [fɔrnikatœr, tris] *nm, f* *litt & hum* fornicator.

fornication [fɔrnikasjɔ̃] *nf* *litt & hum* fornication.

forniquer [3] [fɔrnike] *vi* *litt & hum* to fornicate.

FORPRONU [fɔrprɔny] (*abr de* **Forces de protection des Nations unies**) *nf* UN-profor.

fors [fɔr] *prép* *arch* except, save *arch* ■ **tout est perdu, ~ l'honneur François Ier** *allus* all is lost save honour.

forsythia [fɔrsisja] *nm* forsythia.

fort, e [fɔr, fɔrt] *adj*

> **A.** QUI A DE LA PUISSANCE, DE L'EFFET
> **B.** MARQUÉ
> **C.** HABILE

A. QUI A DE LA PUISSANCE, DE L'EFFET

1. [vigoureux - personne, bras] strong, sturdy ; [- vent] strong, high ; [- courant, jet] strong ; [- secousse] hard ; [- pluies] heavy ■ **mer ~e** MÉTÉOR rough sea ■ **~ comme un Turc** *OU* **un bœuf** as strong as an ox
2. [d'une grande résistance morale] : **une âme ~e** a steadfast soul ■ **rester ~ dans l'adversité** to remain strong *OU* to stand firm in the face of adversity
3. [autoritaire, contraignant - régime] strong-arm *(avant n)*
4. [puissant - syndicat, parti, économie] strong, powerful ; [- monnaie] strong, hard ; [- carton, loupe, tranquillisant] strong ■ **l'as est plus ~ que le roi** the ace is higher than the king ■ **colle (très) ~e** (super) *OU* extra strong glue ■ **c'est plus ~ que moi** I can't help it ■ **~ de : ~ de son expérience** with a wealth of experience behind him ■ **~ de leur protection** reassured by their protection ■ **une équipe ~e de 40 hommes** a 40-strong team ⊳ **l'homme ~ du parti** the strong man of the party
5. [de grand impact - œuvre, film] powerful ; [- argument] weighty, powerful, forcible

B. MARQUÉ

1. [épais, corpulent - jambes] big, thick ; [- personne] stout, large ; [- hanches] broad, large, wide ■ **avoir la taille ~e** to be big around the waist
2. [important quantitativement - dénivellation] steep, pronounced ; [- accent] strong, pronounced, marked ; [- fièvre, taux] high ; [- hausse] large ; [- somme] large, big ; [- concentration] high ; [- bruit] loud ; [- différence] great, big ■ **il est prêt à payer le prix ~** he's willing to pay the full price
3. [grand, intense - amour, haine] strong, intense ; [- douleur] intense, great ; [- influence] strong, big, great ; [- propension] marked ■ **il recherche les sensations ~es** he's after big thrills ■ **avoir une ~e volonté** to be strong-willed, to have a strong will ■ **elle a une ~e personnalité** she's got a strong personality
4. [café, thé, moutarde, tabac] strong ■ [sauce] hot, spicy ■ [odeur] strong
5. *fam loc* **et c'est moi qui devrais payer? alors ça c'est trop ~!** and I should pay? that's a bit much! ■ **le plus ~, c'est qu'il avait raison!** the best of it is that he was right!

C. HABILE

[compétent, doué] : **le marketing, c'est là qu'il est ~/que sa société est ~e** marketing is his/his company's strong point ■ **trouver plus ~ que soi** to meet one's match ■ **pour donner des leçons, elle est très ~e!** she's very good at lecturing people! ■ **~ en gymnastique/en langues** very good at gymnastics/at languages.

◆ **fort** ◇ *adv* **1.** [avec vigueur - taper, tirer] hard ■ **pousse plus ~** push harder ■ [avec intensité] : **sentir ~** to smell ■ **mets le gaz plus/moins ~** turn the gas up/down ■ **le gaz est trop ~** the gas is too high ⊳ **tu y vas un peu ~!** you're going a bit far! **2.** [bruyamment - parler] loudly, loud ■ **parle plus ~, on ne t'entend pas** speak up, we can't hear you ■ **parle moins ~** lower your voice ■ **mets le son plus/moins ~** turn the sound up/down **3.** *sout* [très] : **~ désagréable** most disagreeable ■ **~ joli** very pretty ■ **~ bien, partons à midi!** very well, let's leave at noon! ■ **j'en suis ~ aise!** *hum* I'm very pleased to hear it! **4.** *loc* **là, tu as fait très ~!** you've really excelled yourself!
◇ *nm* **1.** [physiquement, moralement] : **les ~s et les faibles** the strong and the weak ■ [intellectuellement] : **un ~ en thème** a swot **2.** [spécialité] forte ■ **la politesse n'est pas son ~!** politeness isn't his strongest point! **3.** [forteresse] fort.

◆ **au (plus) fort de** *loc prép* : **au (plus) ~ de l'hiver** in the depths of winter ■ **au (plus) ~ de l'été** in the height of summer.

forte [fɔrte] *adj & nm* MUS forte.

fortement [fɔrtəmɑ̃] *adv* **1.** [avec force] hard ■ **~ salé** heavily salted ■ **~ épicé** highly spiced **2.** [avec netteté] strongly **3.** [beaucoup] strongly ■ **il désire ~ vous rencontrer** he wishes very much to meet you ■ **être ~ tenté** to be sorely tempted ■ **être ~ intéressé par qqch** to be most interested in sthg.

forteresse [fɔrtərɛs] *nf* **1.** [citadelle] fortress **2.** [prison] fortress **3.** AÉRON : **~ volante** flying fortress.

fortiche [fɔrtiʃ] *adj* *fam* **elle est ~ en anglais!** she's dead *UK OU* real *US* good at English!

fortifiant, e [fɔrtifjɑ̃, ɑ̃t] *adj* **1.** [nourriture] fortifying ■ [climat] bracing, invigorating **2.** *litt* [édifiant] uplifting.
◆ **fortifiant** *nm* tonic.

fortification [fɔrtifikasjɔ̃] *nf* **1.** [mur] fortification, wall **2.** [action] : **la ~ d'une ville** the fortification of a town.

fortifier [9] [fɔrtifje] *vt* **1.** [affermir - muscle, santé] to fortify, to strengthen ; [- amitié, volonté, opinion] to strengthen ■ **ainsi fortifié dans ses préjugés, il reprit la lecture du journal** with his prejudices thus confirmed, he went back to reading the paper **2.** [protéger] to fortify ■ **une ville fortifiée** a walled *OU* fortified town.
◆ **se fortifier** ◇ *vp (emploi passif)* **la ville s'est fortifiée au XIIe siècle** the town was fortified *OU* walls were built around the town in the 12th century.
◇ *vpi* [muscle] to firm up, to grow stronger ■ [amitié, amour] to grow stronger.

fortin [fɔrtɛ̃] *nm* small fort.

fortiori [fɔrsjɔri] **a fortiori.**

fortuit, e [fɔrtɥi, it] *adj* [événement] fortuitous ■ **faire une rencontre ~e** to meet somebody by chance.

fortuitement [fɔrtɥitmɑ̃] *adv* fortuitously, by chance.

fortune [fɔrtyn] *nf* **1.** [biens] wealth, fortune ■ **ça lui a rapporté une (petite) ~** *fam* it brought him a nice little sum ■ **c'était une ~ à l'époque** it was a lot of money at the time ■ **voici 50 euros, c'est toute ma ~!** *hum* here's 50 euros, it's all my worldly wealth! ■ **faire ~** to make one's fortune **2.** *litt* [hasard] good fortune, luck ■ **il a eu la bonne** *OU* **l'heureuse ~ de la connaître** he was fortunate enough to know her ■ **il a eu la mauvaise ~ de tomber malade** he was unlucky enough *OU* he had the misfortune to fall ill ⊳ **faire contre mauvaise ~ bon cœur** to make the best of a bad job ■ **la ~ sourit aux audacieux** fortune favours the bold *prov* ■ **inviter qqn à la ~ du pot** to invite sb to take pot luck **3.** *litt* [sort] fortune ■ **leurs livres ont connu des ~s très diverses** their books had varying success.
◆ **de fortune** *loc adj* [lit] makeshift ■ [installation, réparation] temporary.
◆ **sans fortune** *loc adj* with no hope of an inheritance.

fortuné, e [fɔrtyne] *adj* **1.** [riche] rich, wealthy **2.** *litt* [heureux] fortunate, blessed *litt*.

forum [fɔrɔm] *nm* ANTIQ & ARCHIT forum ■ [débat] forum ■ **~ de discussion** INFORM newsgroup ■ **le Forum des Halles** *shopping complex at Les Halles in Paris.*

fosse [fos] *nf* **1.** [cavité] pit ■ **~ à purin** *OU* **fumier** manure pit ■ **~ (d'aisances)** cesspool ■ **~ aux lions** lions' den ■ **descendre dans la ~ aux lions** *fig* to enter the lions' den ■ **~ septique** septic tank **2.** AUTO & SPORT pit **3.** MUS : **~ d'orchestre** orchestra pit **4.** [tombe] grave ■ **~ commune** common grave **5.** ANAT fossa ■ **~s nasales** nasal fossae **6.** GÉOL trench **7.** MIN pit.

fossé [fose] *nm* **1.** [tranchée] ditch ▪ **finir** *ou* **se retrouver dans le ~** to end up in a ditch ▪ **~ antichar** MIL antitank ditch **2.** *fig* gulf, gap ▪ **~ culturel** culture gap ▪ **le ~ qui nous sépare** the gulf which divides us **3.** GÉOL trough.

fossette [fosɛt] *nf* dimple.

fossile [fosil] <> *adj pr* fossil *(modif)* ▪ *fig* fossil-like, fossilized.
<> *nm pr* & *fig* fossil.

fossilisation [fosilizasjɔ̃] *nf* fossilization.

fossiliser [3] [fosilize] *vt* to fossilize.
◆ **se fossiliser** *vpi* to become fossilized.

fossoyeur [foswajœr] *nm* gravedigger ▪ **les ~s de la révolution** *fig* & *litt* the destroyers *ou* gravediggers of the revolution.

fou [fu] *(devant nm commençant par voyelle ou h muet* **fol** [fɔl], *nf* **folle** [fɔl]*)* <> *adj* **1.** [dément] insane, mad ▪ **devenir ~** to go mad *ou* insane ▪ **un regard un peu ~** a somewhat crazed look ▪ **être ~ de bonheur/joie/douleur** to be beside o.s. with happiness/joy/grief ▪ **être ~ d'inquiétude** to be mad with worry ◐ **être ~ furieux** *ou* **à lier** to be (stark) raving mad
2. [déraisonnable] mad ▪ **ton projet est complètement ~** your plan is completely crazy *ou* mad ▪ **avoir de folles pensées** to have wild thoughts ◐ **pas folle, la guêpe!** *fam* he's/she's not stupid!
3. [hors de soi] wild, mad ▪ **rendre qqn ~** to drive *ou* to send sb mad
4. [passionné] : **être ~ de qqn/qqch** to be mad *ou* wild about sb/sthg
5. [intense] mad, wild ▪ **nous avons passé une folle soirée** we had a wild evening ▪ **entre eux, c'est l'amour ~** they're crazy about each other, they're madly in love
6. [incontrôlé] wild ▪ **se lancer dans une course folle** to embark on a headlong chase ▪ **camion/train ~** runaway truck/train ◐ **folle avoine** wild oats ▪ **avoir des mèches folles** to have wild *ou* straggly hair ▪ **~ rire** (uncontrollable) giggle *ou* giggles ▪ **avoir** *ou* **être pris d'un ~ rire** to have a fit of the giggles
7. *fam* [très important] tremendous ▪ **il y avait un monde ~** there was a huge crowd ▪ **un prix ~** an extortionate price ▪ **nous avons mis un temps ~ pour venir** it took us ages to get here ▪ **gagner un argent ~** to make piles *ou* a lot of money
8. [incroyable] incredible ▪ **c'est ~, ce qui lui est arrivé** what happened to him is incredible.
<> *nm, f* **1.** [dément] madman (*f* madwoman) ▪ **envoyer qqn chez les ~s** *vieilli* to have sb locked up *ou* put away ▪ **vous n'avez pas vu le feu rouge, espèce de ~?** didn't you see the red light, you stupid fool? ▪ **comme un ~** *pr* dementedly ; [intensément] like mad *ou* crazy
2. [excité] lunatic, fool ▪ **faire le ~** to act the fool *ou* idiot
3. [passionné] : **c'est un ~ de moto** he's mad on *ou* crazy about bikes.
◆ **fou** *nm* **1.** JEUX bishop
2. HIST : **~ (du roi)** (court) jester ▪ **plus on est de ~s plus on rit** the more the merrier *loc*
3. ORNITH : **~ (de Bassan)** gannet.
◆ **folle** *nf fam péj* [homosexuel] queen ▪ **grande folle** raving queen.

foucade [fukad] *nf litt* whim, passing fancy.

foudre[1] [fudr] *nm* **1.** [tonneau] tun **2.** MYTHOL thunderbolt.
◆ **foudre de guerre** *nm* **1.** [guerrier] great warrior **2.** *fig* **ce n'est pas un ~ de guerre** *hum* he wouldn't say boo to a goose.

foudre[2] [fudr] *nf* MÉTÉOR lightning ▪ **il est resté comme frappé par la ~** he looked as if he had been struck by lightning ◐ **prompt** *ou* **rapide comme la ~** (as) quick as lightning.
◆ **foudres** *nfpl litt* wrath, ire *litt* ▪ **il a tout fait pour s'attirer les ~s du public** he did everything to bring down the public's wrath upon him *ou* to incur the public's wrath.

foudroiement [fudrwamɑ̃] *nm* **1.** [fait de foudroyer] striking **2.** [fait d'être foudroyé] being struck.

foudroyage [fudrwajaʒ] *nm* MIN caving.

foudroyant, e [fudrwajɑ̃, ɑ̃t] *adj* **1.** [soudain] violent ▪ **une mort ~e** (an) instant death **2.** [extraordinaire] striking, lightning *(modif)* ▪ **la pièce a connu un succès ~** the play was a massive success ▪ **à une vitesse ~e** with lightning speed **3.** [furieux - regard] : **jeter des regards ~s à qqn** to look daggers at sb.

foudroyer [13] [fudrwaje] *vt* **1.** MÉTÉOR to strike ▪ **deux personnes ont été foudroyées hier pendant l'orage** two people were struck by lightning yesterday during the thunderstorm **2.** [tuer] to strike down *(sép)* ▪ **~ qqn du regard** *ou* **des yeux** *fig* to look daggers at sb **3.** [anéantir] to strike down *(sép)* ▪ **la mort de ses parents l'a foudroyé** he was crushed by his parents' death.

fouet [fwɛ] *nm* **1.** [instrument] whip **2.** CULIN whisk.

fouettard [fwɛtar] *adj m* ▷ **père**.

fouetté, e [fwete] *adj* [crème] whipped.
◆ **fouetté** *nm* DANSE fouetté.

fouettement [fwɛtmɑ̃] *nm* [de la pluie, de la grêle] lashing ▪ [d'une voile] flapping.

foufou, fofolle [fufu, fɔfɔl] *adj fam* daft, nutty, loopy.

fougasse [fugas] *nf flat loaf traditionally cooked in wood-ash and sometimes flavoured with olives or anchovies.*

fougère [fuʒɛr] *nf* fern ▪ **~ arborescente** tree fern.

fougue [fug] *nf* [ardeur] passion, spirit, ardour ▪ **un discours rempli** *ou* **plein de ~** a fiery speech ▪ **se battre avec ~** to fight with spirit, to put up a spirited fight ▪ **répondre avec ~** to answer with brio.

fougueusement [fugøzmɑ̃] *adv* ardently, with brio, with passion.

fougueux, euse [fugø, øz] *adj* [personne] ardent, fiery, impetuous ▪ [cheval] spirited ▪ [réponse, résistance] spirited, lively.

fouille [fuj] *nf* **1.** [d'un lieu] search ▪ **passer à la ~** to be searched ◐ **~ corporelle** [rapide] frisking ; [approfondie] body search **2.** AGRIC digging (up) **3.** MIN exploration, search ▪ **travail en ~** earth digging.
◆ **fouilles** *nfpl* ARCHÉOL dig, excavations ▪ **participer à des ~s** to take part in a dig.

fouillé, e [fuje] *adj* [enquête] thorough, wide-ranging ▪ [étude] detailed ▪ [détails] elaborate.

fouille-merde△ [fujmɛrd] *nmf* muckraker.

fouiller [3] [fuje] <> *vt* **1.** [explorer - tiroir] to search (through) ▪ **fouille un peu tes poches, tu vas sûrement le retrouver!** have a look in your pockets, you're sure to find it ▪ [au cours d'une vérification] to search, to go through *(insép)* ▪ **~ des voyageurs** [rapidement] to frisk travellers ; [de façon approfondie] to search travellers **2.** [creuser - suj: cochon, taupe] to dig ▪ **~ un site** ARCHÉOL to excavate a site **3.** [approfondir] to go deeply *ou* thoroughly ▪ **il aurait fallu ~ la question** the question should have been researched more thoroughly.
<> *vi* **1.** [creuser] to dig **2.** [faire une recherche] : **~ dans qqch** [légitimement] to go through sthg, to search sthg ; [par indiscrétion] to rifle through sthg *péj*, to go through sthg ▪ **~ dans sa mémoire** to search one's memory ▪ **~ dans son esprit** to rack one's brains ▪ **~ dans le passé de qqn** to delve into sb's past.
◆ **se fouiller** *vp (emploi réfléchi)* **se ~ les poches** to go through one's pockets ◐ **une participation? il peut se ~!** let him have a share in the profits? he can whistle for it *ou* not likely!

fouilleur, euse [fujœr, øz] *nm, f* **1.** ARCHÉOL excavator **2.** [policier] searcher.

fouillis [fuji] <> *nm* jumble ▪ **quel ~ dans ta chambre!** what a dump your room is! ▪ **le jardin n'est qu'un ~ de ronces** the garden's nothing but a mass of brambles ▪ **se perdre dans un ~ de détails** to get bogged down in (a mass of) details.
<> *adj* messy, untidy.
◆ **en fouillis** *fam* <> *loc adj* in a mess ▪ **une chambre en ~** a messy room ▪ **des dossiers en ~** muddled-up files.
<> *loc adv* : **laisser un lieu en ~** to leave a place in a mess.

fouinard, e [fwinar, ard] *adj fam* nosy, prying.
◆ **fouinard** *nm fam* busybody, nosy parker *UK*.

fouine [fwin] *nf* **1.** ZOOL stone marten ▪ **avoir un visage de ~** to be weasel-faced **2.** *fam* [fouineur] busybody, nosy parker *UK*.

fouiner [3] [fwine] *vi fam* **1.** [explorer] to go through ▪ **~ au marché aux puces** to go hunting for bargains at the flea market **2.** *péj* [être indiscret] to nose about *ou* around ▪ **il est toujours à ~ dans les affaires des autres** he keeps poking his nose into other people's business.

fouineur, euse [fwinœr, øz] *fam* ◇ *adj* nosy, prying. ◇ *nm, f* **1.** [indiscret] busybody, nosy parker *UK* **2.** [chez les brocanteurs] bargain hunter.

fouir [32] [fwir] *vt* to burrow, to dig.

fouisseur, euse [fwisœr, øz] *adj* burrowing *(avant n)*, fossorial *spéc.*
◆ **fouisseur** *nm* burrower, fossorial animal *spéc.*

foulant, e [fulɑ̃, ɑ̃t] *adj fam* [fatigant] backbreaking, exhausting ▪ **c'est pas ~!** it's not exactly backbreaking work!

foulard [fular] *nm* **1.** [vêtement] scarf **2.** TEXT foulard.

foule [ful] *nf* **1.** [gens] crowd, mob *péj* ▪ **il y a ~** *fam* there are crowds *ou* masses of people ▪ **il n'y a pas ~** *fam* there's hardly anyone around **2.** [masses populaires] : **la ~, les ~s** the masses ▪ **un président qui plaît aux ~s** a popular president **3.** [grand nombre] : **une ~ de** : **une ~ de gens** a crowd of people ▪ **une ~ d'amis** a host of friends ▪ **j'ai une ~ d'histoires à te raconter** I've got lots of stories to tell you ▪ **il m'a donné une ~ de détails** he gave me a whole mass of details.
◆ **en foule** *loc adv* [venir, se présenter] in huge numbers.

foulée [fule] *nf* stride ▪ **avancer à longues ~s** to stride along.
◆ **dans la foulée** *loc adv fam* : **dans la ~, j'ai fait aussi le repassage** I did the ironing while I was at it.
◆ **dans la foulée de** *loc prép* SPORT : **rester dans la ~ de qqn** to stay close on sb's heels.

fouler [3] [fule] *vt* **1.** [écraser - raisin] to press, to tread ; [- céréale] to tread **2.** [marcher sur] to tread *ou* to walk on *(insép)* ▪ **~ le sol natal** *litt* to tread the native soil ⊙ **~ qqch aux pieds** to trample on sthg **3.** [cuir, peau] to tan **4.** TEXT to full.
◆ **se fouler** ◇ *vpi fam* [se fatiguer] to strain o.s. ▪ **tu ne t'es pas beaucoup foulé** you didn't exactly strain *ou* overexert yourself, did you?
◇ *vpt* : **se ~ qqch** [se faire mal] : **se ~ la cheville** to sprain *ou* to twist one's ankle.

fouloir [fulwar] *nm* **1.** [pour le raisin] wine press **2.** TEXT fulling mill **3.** [de tanneur] tanning drum.

foulure [fulyr] *nf* sprain.

four [fur] *nm* **1.** CULIN oven ▪ **un plat allant au ~** an ovenproof dish ⊙ **~ à catalyse** self-cleaning oven ▪ **~ à chaleur tournante** fan-assisted oven ▪ **~ électrique/à gaz** electric/gas oven ▪ **~ à micro-ondes** microwave oven ▪ **~ à pain** baker's oven ▪ **~ à pyrolyse** self-cleaning oven ▪ **il fait chaud comme dans un ~** it's like an oven (in here) ▪ **avoir qqch au ~** *pr* to have sthg cooking (in the oven) ; *fig* to have sthg on the go *UK ou* in the pipeline ▪ **on ne peut pas être à la fois au ~ et au moulin** you can't be in two places at once **2.** TECHNOL furnace, kiln ▪ **~ à chaux** lime kiln ▪ **~ solaire** solar furnace **3.** HIST : **~ crématoire** (Hitler's) gas ovens **4.** *fam* [fiasco] flop ▪ **sa pièce a été** *ou* **a fait un ~** his play was a flop.

fourbe [furb] *litt* ◇ *adj* deceitful, treacherous.
◇ *nmf* cheat, treacherous *ou* false-hearted *litt* person.

fourberie [furbəri] *nf litt* **1.** [duplicité] treacherousness **2.** [acte] treachery.

fourbi [furbi] *nm fam* **1.** [ensemble hétéroclite] paraphernalia **2.** [truc] thingy.

fourbir [32] [furbir] *vt* **1.** [nettoyer] to polish (up) **2.** *litt & fig* **~ ses armes** to prepare for war.

fourbu, e [furby] *adj* **1.** [personne] exhausted **2.** [cheval] foundered.

fourche [furʃ] *nf* **1.** AGRIC fork **2.** [embranchement] fork ▪ **quitte le chemin là où il fait une ~** leave the path where it forks **3.** [d'une bicyclette, d'un arbre] fork **4.** [de cheveux] split end.

fourcher [3] [furʃe] *vi loc* **sa langue a fourché** he made a slip (of the tongue).

fourchette [furʃɛt] *nf* **1.** [pour manger] fork ▪ **~ à escargots** snail fork ▪ **elle a un bon coup de ~** she's a hearty eater **2.** [écart] bracket ▪ **une ~ comprise entre 100 et 150 euros** prices ranging from 100 to 150 euros ▪ **dans une ~ de prix acceptable** within an acceptable price range *ou* bracket **3.** ANAT : **~ sternale** jugular notch ▪ **~ vulvaire** fourchette **4.** ZOOL [du cheval] frog ▪ [de l'oiseau] wishbone, furcula *spéc.*

fourchu, e [furʃy] *adj* **1.** [cheveux] : **avoir les cheveux ~s** to have split ends **2.** [tronc, route] forked **3.** [pied] cloven-hoofed ▪ [sabot] cloven, cleft.

fourgon [furgɔ̃] *nm* **1.** [voiture] van ▪ **~ à bestiaux** cattle truck ▪ **~ cellulaire** police van *UK*, patrol *ou* police wagon *US* ▪ **~ de déménagement** removal *UK ou* moving *US* van ▪ **~ funèbre** *ou* **funéraire** *ou* **mortuaire** hearse ▪ **~ postal** mail van **2.** RAIL coach, waggon *UK* ▪ **~ à bagages** luggage van *UK*, baggage car *US* **3.** [tige de métal] poker.

fourgonnette [furgɔnɛt] *nf* (small) van.

fourguer [3] [furge] *vt* **1.** △ *arg crime* [vendre] to fence **2.** *fam péj* [donner] : **qui t'a fourgué ces vieilles nippes?** who palmed off those old clothes on you?

fouriérisme [furjerism] *nm* Fourierism.

fourme [furm] *nf hard cheese made in Central France* ▪ **~ d'Ambert** Fourme d'Ambert (blue) cheese.

fourmi [furmi] *nf* **1.** ENTOM ant ▪ **~ rouge** red ant **2.** [personne] busy bee **3.** *loc* **avoir des ~s dans les jambes** to have pins and needles in one's legs.
◆ **de fourmi** *loc adj* [travail] meticulous, painstaking.

fourmilier [furmilje] *nm* ZOOL anteater.

fourmilière [furmiljɛr] *nf* **1.** ENTOM anthill, antheap **2.** [lieu animé] hive of activity ▪ **l'aéroport s'est transformé en une véritable ~** the airport was bustling with activity.

fourmillement [furmijmɑ̃] *nm* **1.** [picotement] tingle ▪ **j'ai des ~s dans les doigts** I've got pins and needles in my fingers **2.** [foisonnement - de promeneurs] swarming ; [- d'idées] swarm.

fourmiller [3] [furmije] *vi* **1.** [s'agiter] to swarm **2.** [être abondant] to abound ▪ **~ de** [insectes, personnes] to swarm with ; [fautes, idées] to be full of, to be packed with **3.** [picoter] to tingle.

fournaise [furnɛz] *nf* **1.** *litt* [feu] blaze **2.** [lieu caniculaire] : **la ville est une ~ en été** the city's like an oven in the summer.

fourneau, x [furno] *nm* **1.** [cuisinière] stove ▪ **être aux** *ou* **derrière les ~x** to be cooking **2.** MÉTALL furnace **3.** [d'une pipe] bowl **4.** [pour explosif] mine chamber.

fournée [furne] *nf* **1.** [du boulanger] batch ▪ **faire deux ~s de pain dans la matinée** to bake two batches of bread in the morning **2.** *fam* [ensemble de personnes] lot.

fourni, e [furni] *adj* **1.** [touffu - cheveux] thick ; [- barbe] heavy, thick ; [- sourcils] bushy ; [- haie] luxuriant **2.** [approvisionné] : **abondamment** *ou* **bien ~** well supplied *ou* stocked.

fournil [furnil] *nm* bakehouse, bakery.

fournir [32] [furnir] *vt* **1.** [ravitailler] to supply ▪ **c'est eux qui me fournissent en pain** I buy (my) bread from them ▪ **il n'y a plus de quoi ~ les troupes** there's nothing left to feed the army ▪ **~ une entreprise en matières premières** to supply a firm with raw materials ▪ *(en usage absolu)* **je ne peux plus ~, moi!** *hum* I can't cope anymore! **2.** [procurer] to provide ▪ **c'est la France qui leur fournit des armes** it's France who is providing *ou* supplying them with weapons ▪ **~ un alibi à qqn** to provide sb with an alibi ▪ **la brochure vous fournira tous les renseignements nécessaires** the brochure will give you all the necessary information ▪ **fournissez-moi l'argent demain** let me have the money tomorrow **3.** [produire] to produce **4.** [accomplir] : **~ un effort** to make an effort **5.** JEUX : **~ la couleur demandée** to follow suit.

◆ **fournir à** *v+prép* : **~ aux besoins de qqn** to provide for sb's needs ▪ **~ à la dépense** to defray the cost.

◆ **se fournir** *vpi* : **se ~ chez qqn** to get one's supplies from sb ▪ **je me fournis toujours chez le même boucher** I always shop at the same butcher's, I get all my meat from the same place.

fournisseur [furnisœr] *nm* **1.** [établissement, marchand] supplier ▪ **~s de l'armée** army contractors **2.** INFORM : **~ d'accès Internet** Internet service provider.

fourniture [furnityr] *nf* [action] supplying, providing.

◆ **fournitures** *nfpl* [objets] materials ▪ **~s scolaires** school stationery.

fourrage [furaʒ] *nm* **1.** AGRIC fodder **2.** [vêtement, acte] lining ▪ [peau] lining fur.

fourrager[1] [17] [furaʒe] ◆ **fourrager dans** *v+prép* to rummage through *(insép)*.

fourrager[2]**, ère** [furaʒe, ɛr] *adj* fodder *(modif)*.

◆ **fourragère** *nf* **1.** MIL [décoration] fourragère **2.** [champ] field *(in which a fodder crop is grown)* **3.** [charrette] cart *(for fodder)*.

fourre [fur] *nf Suisse* [d'un oreiller] pillowcase ▪ [pour un édredon] quilt cover ▪ [d'un disque] sleeve ▪ [d'un livre] jacket.

fourré[1] [fure] *nm* [bois] thicket.

fourré[2]**, e** [fure] *adj* **1.** [doublé de fourrure] fur-lined ▪ **des chaussons ~s** lined slippers **2.** CULIN filled ▪ **bonbons ~s à la fraise** sweets *UK ou* candy *US* with strawberry-flavoured centres ▪ **des dates ~es à la pâte d'amandes** marzipan-filled dates, dates stuffed with marzipan ➊ **chocolats ~s** chocolate creams.

fourreau, x [furo] *nm* **1.** [d'une arme] sheath ▪ [d'un parapluie] cover ▪ **remettre son épée au ~** to sheathe one's sword **2.** [vêtement] sheath dress.

fourrer [3] [fure] *vt* **1.** [doubler de fourrure] to line with fur **2.** CULIN [fruit, gâteau] to fill **3.** *fam* [mettre] to stick, to shove ▪ **~ son doigt dans son nez** to stick one's finger up one's nose **4.** *fam* [laisser - papier, vêtement] to put, to leave ▪ **où as-tu fourré ce dossier?** where have you put *ou* left that file? **5.** *fam* [placer - personne, animal] to stick, to put ➊ **être toujours fourré dans** *ou* **chez : il est toujours fourré chez ses parents/à l'église** he's always at his parents'/in the church ▪ **ce chat/gosse, toujours fourré dans mes jambes!** that cat/childis always under my feet!

◆ **se fourrer** *fam* ◇ *vpi* **1.** [se mettre] : **se ~ au lit/sous les couvertures/dans son sac de couchage** to snuggle down in bed/ under the blankets/into one's sleeping bag ▪ **il ne savait plus où se ~** he wished the earth would open up and swallow him **2.** [s'engager] : **se ~ dans une sale affaire** to get mixed up in a nasty business ▪ **se ~ dans un (vrai) guêpier** to land o.s. in real trouble.

◇ *vpt* : **se ~ un doigt dans le nez** to stick one's finger up one's nose ▪ **se ~ une idée dans la tête** to get an idea into one's head.

fourre-tout [furtu] *nm inv* **1.** [pièce] junk room ▪ [placard] junk cupboard **2.** [sac léger] holdall *UK*, carryall *US* ▪ [trousse] pencil case **3.** *fig* jumble, ragbag ▪ **cette loi est un ~** this law is a real mess.

fourreur [furœr] *nm* furrier.

fourrier [furje] *nm* **1.** MIL & NAUT quartermaster **2.** *litt* **être le ~ de** to be a harbinger of **3.** HIST & MIL [responsable de la nourriture] quartermaster ▪ [responsable du logement] billeting officer.

fourrière [furjɛr] *nf* [pour chiens, voitures] pound ▪ **mettre une voiture en** *ou* **à la ~** to impound a car.

fourrure [furyr] *nf* **1.** [vêtement] fur ▪ **un manteau/une veste de ~** a fur coat/jacket ▪ **~ polaire** fleece **2.** [peau préparée] fur **3.** ZOOL fur, coat **4.** [commerce] : **la ~** the fur trade **5.** HÉRALD fur.

fourvoiement [furvwamɑ̃] *nm litt* going astray.

fourvoyer [13] [furvwaje] *vt litt* to lead astray, to mislead.

◆ **se fourvoyer** *vpi* to be in error, to make a mistake, to go astray ▪ **tu te fourvoies si tu crois qu'il va y renoncer** you're making a mistake if you think he'll give it up.

◆ **se fourvoyer dans** *vp+prép* to get o.s. involved in.

fous *etc v* ▷ **foutre**.

foutaise△ [futɛz] *nf* crap△, bull△ *US* ▪ **tout ça, c'est de la ~!** that's just a load of rubbish *UK ou* crap△!

foutoir△ [futwar] *nm* dump, tip *UK* ▪ **sa chambre est un vrai ~** her room is a complete tip.

foutre[1] △ [futr] *adv* : **je n'en sais ~ rien** I'm buggered△ *UK ou* the hell△ *US* if I know.

foutre[2] [116] [futr] ◇ *vt*△ **1.** [envoyer, mettre] : **fous-le dans la valise** bung it in the case ▪ **~ qqch par la fenêtre** to chuck sthg out of the window ▪ **~ qqn par terre** to throw sb to the ground ▪ **~ une pile de livres par terre** to knock a pile of books to the ground ▪ **~ un rêve/un projet par terre** *fig* to wreck a dream/a project ▪ **~ qqn à la porte** to throw *ou* to chuck sb out ▪ **~ qqch en l'air** to ruin sthg, to screw sthg up△ **2.** [donner] to give ▪ **~ une claque à qqn** to hit sb, to give sb a thump ▪ **~ la trouille à qqn** to give sb the creeps ▪ **~ le cafard à qqn** to get sb down ▪ **~ la paix à qqn** to leave sb alone, to get out of sb's hair ▪ **~ une raclée à qqn** *pr* to thump sb ▪ **il m'a foutu une raclée au tennis** he gave me a hiding at tennis **3.** [faire] to do ▪ **qu'est-ce que tu fous, on est pressés!** what the (bloody) hell△ are you doing, we're in a hurry! ➊ **qu'est-ce que ça peut te/lui ~?** what the hell does it matter to you/him?△ ▪ **rien à ~ : il en a rien à ~** he couldn't give a damn *ou* a toss△ *UK ou* monkey's△ *UK* **4.** *loc* **aller se faire ~**▲ : **va te faire ~** sod△ *UK ou* fuck▲ off ▪ **ça la fout mal** it looks pretty bad ▪ **en ~ un coup : il va falloir en ~ un coup si on veut avoir fini demain** we'll have to get a bloody△ *UK* move on if we want to be finished by tomorrow! ▪ **~ le camp : mon mec a foutu le camp** my man's buggered off (and left me)△ *UK ou* run out on me *US* ▪ **fous le camp de chez moi!** get the hell out of my house!△ ▪ **tout fout le camp!** this place is going to the dogs! ▪ **~ son billet à qqn que : je te fous mon billet qu'ils sont déjà partis** I'll bet you anything you like they've already left ▪ **rembourser? je t'en fous, il ne remboursera jamais!** you think he's going to pay you back? you'll be lucky ▪ **je t'en foutrai : je t'en foutrai, moi, du caviar!** caviar? I'll give you bloody caviar!

◇ *nm*▲ come.

◆ **se foutre**△ ◇ *vpi* : **il s'est foutu par terre** he fell flat, he came a cropper *UK* ➊ **se ~ dedans** to blow it.

◇ *vpt* : **il s'est foutu de la peinture sur son pantalon** he spilt paint all over his trousers ➊ **s'en ~ plein la lampe** to make a pig of o.s. ▪ **s'en ~ plein les poches** to line one's pockets.

◆ **se foutre de**△ *vp+prép* **1.** [se moquer de] to laugh at, to make fun of ▪ **tu te fous de moi ou quoi!** are you taking the piss? ▪ **ils se foutent du monde!** they really take people for idiots! **2.** [être indifférent à] not to give a damn△ *ou* a toss△ *UK* about.

foutrement△ [futrəmɑ̃] *adv* extremely, damn△ ▪ **c'est ~ bon** it's damn good△.

foutu, e△ [futy] ◇ *pp* ▷ **foutre**.

◇ *adj* **1.** [abîmé] buggered△ *UK*, screwed-up *US* ▪ [gâché] ruined ▪ **une voiture ~e** a write-off **2.** *(avant le n)* [considérable] bloody△ *UK*, damned△ ▪ **tu as eu une ~e chance** you were damned lucky△ ▪ **il lui a fallu une ~e volonté pour rester** he needed a hell of a lot of willpower to stay **3.** *(avant le n)* [détestable] bloody△ *UK*, god-awful ▪ **quel ~ caractère!** what a nasty individual! **4.** *loc* **bien ~ : cette machine est bien ~e** what a clever machine ▪ **une fille très bien ~e** a girl with a great figure ▪ **mal ~ : il est mal ~** [de corps] he's got an ugly body ; [malade] he feels awful ▪ **~ de** [en mesure de] : **pas ~ de planter un clou dans un mur!** can't even be bothered to hammer a nail into a wall! ▪ **il est ~ de réussir** he just might succeed.

fox [fɔks] = **fox-terrier**.

fox-hound [fɔksaund] (*pl* **fox-hounds**) *nm* foxhound.

fox-terrier [fɔkstɛrje] (*pl* **fox-terriers**) *nm* fox terrier.

fox-trot [fɔkstrɔt] *nm inv* fox-trot.

foyer [fwaje] *nm* **1.** [chez soi] home ➲ **~ conjugal** family home ▪ **femme au ~** housewife ▪ **être mère au ~** to be a housewife and mother ▪ **il est père au ~** he keeps house and looks after the children, he's a house husband
2. [résidence collective] hall ▪ **~ pour le troisième âge** retirement home ➲ **~ d'étudiants** (students) hall ▪ **~ d'immigrés** immigrant workers' hostel
3. [lieu de réunion - gén] hall ; [- pour le public d'un théâtre] foyer ▪ **~ socio-éducatif** ≃ community centre *UK ou* center *US*
4. [âtre] hearth
5. [dans une machine] firebox
6. [centre] seat, centre ▪ **un ~ d'incendie** a fire
7. MÉD : **~ infectieux** *ou* **d'infection** source of infection
8. OPT & PHYS focus, focal point ▪ **des lunettes à double ~** bifocals ▪ **lentilles à ~ variable** variable focus lenses
9. GÉOM focus
10. ADMIN : **~ fiscal** household.

FP (*abr de* **franchise postale**) PP.

FPA *nf* = **formation professionnelle pour adultes**.

FPLP (*abr de* **Front populaire de libération de la Palestine**) *npr m* PFLP.

frac [frak] *nm* tailcoat.

fracas [fraka] *nm* [bruit] crash, roar ▪ **le ~ de la circulation sur l'avenue** the roar of the traffic on the avenue.
◆ **à grand fracas** *loc adv* **1.** [bruyamment] with a great deal of crashing and banging **2.** [spectaculairement] with a lot of fuss.

fracassant, e [frakasɑ̃, ɑ̃t] *adj* **1.** [assourdissant] deafening, thunderous ▪ **la porte s'ouvrit avec un bruit ~** the door opened with a deafening bang **2.** [qui fait de l'effet] sensational, staggering.

fracasser [3] [frakase] *vt* to smash ▪ **~ qqch en mille morceaux** to smash sthg into pieces.
◆ **se fracasser** ◇ *vpi* to smash ▪ **se ~ contre** *ou* **sur** to smash into.
◇ *vpt* : **il s'est fracassé le crâne en tombant** he cracked his head when he fell.

fractal, e, aux [frakta, o] *adj* fractal.
◆ **fractale** *nf* fractal.

fraction [fraksjɔ̃] *nf* **1.** MATH fraction **2.** [partie] fraction, part ▪ **une large ~ de la population** a large proportion of the population ▪ **une ~ de seconde** a fraction of a second **3.** RELIG breaking of the bread.

fractionnaire [fraksjɔnɛr] *adj* MATH fractional.

fractionnement [fraksjɔnmɑ̃] *nm* **1.** CHIM fractionation **2.** [morcellement] splitting *ou* dividing up.

fractionner [3] [fraksjɔne] *vt* **1.** [diviser] to divide, to split up *(sép)* ▪ **vous pouvez ~ le remboursement** you may pay in instalments **2.** CHIM to fractionate.
◆ **se fractionner** *vpi* to split (up).

fracture [fraktyr] *nf* **1.** MÉD fracture ▪ **~ du crâne** fractured skull ▪ **il a eu une ~ du crâne** his skull was fractured ▪ **~ fermée** closed *ou* simple fracture ▪ **~ multiple** compound fracture ▪ **~ ouverte** open fracture **2.** GÉOL fracture **3.** SOCIOL : **la ~ sociale** social inequalities **4.** INFORM : **~ numérique** digital divide.

fracturer [3] [fraktyre] *vt* **1.** [briser] to break open *(sép)* ▪ **~ un coffre-fort à l'explosif** to blow a safe **2.** PETR to fracture.
◆ **se fracturer** *vpt* : **je me suis fracturé le bras/poignet** I fractured my arm/wrist.

fragile [fraʒil] *adj* **1.** [peu solide] fragile ▪ **'attention, ~'** 'fragile, handle with care' ▪ **c'est une pendule très ~** it's a very delicate clock **2.** [constitution] frail ▪ **il est de santé ~** his health is rather delicate ▪ **il a l'estomac très ~** he has a delicate stomach **3.** [personnalité] delicate **4.** [équilibre] fragile, frail.

fragiliser [3] [fraʒilize] *vt* **1.** PSYCHOL to weaken ▪ **la mort de son père l'a beaucoup fragilisé** his father's death left him very weak **2.** MÉTALL to embrittle.

fragilité [fraʒilite] *nf* **1.** [d'une horloge, d'une construction] fragility, weakness ▪ **l'effondrement de l'immeuble est dû à la ~ des fondations** the building collapsed because of weak foundations **2.** [d'un organe, d'un malade] weakness **3.** [d'un sentiment, d'une conviction, d'une victoire] fragility, frailty.

fragment [fragmɑ̃] *nm* **1.** [débris] chip, fragment, piece ▪ **des ~s de verre** bits of shattered glass, shards of glass **2.** [morceau - d'une œuvre en partie perdue] fragment ; [- d'un air, d'une conversation] snatch ▪ **il nous a lu quelques ~s de son dernier roman** he read a few extracts of his last novel for us ▪ **~ de vérité** shred of truth.

fragmentaire [fragmɑ̃tɛr] *adj* fragmentary, sketchy, incomplete.

fragmentation [fragmɑ̃tasjɔ̃] *nf* [fractionnement] division, splitting up.

fragmenter [3] [fragmɑ̃te] *vt* to divide, to split (up).
◆ **se fragmenter** *vpi* to fragment, to split.

fragrance [fragrɑ̃s] *nf litt* fragrance.

frai [frɛ] *nm* **1.** [œufs] spawn **2.** [poissons] fry **3.** [période] spawning season.

fraîche [frɛʃ] *f* ▷ **frais**.

fraîchement [frɛʃmɑ̃] *adv* **1.** [nouvellement] freshly, newly **2.** [froidement] coolly ▪ **il nous a reçus plutôt ~** he greeted us rather coolly **3.** *loc* **ça va plutôt ~ aujourd'hui** *fam* it's a bit chilly today.

fraîcheur [frɛʃœr] *nf* **1.** [température] coolness ▪ **dans la ~ du petit jour** in the cool of early dawn **2.** [bonne qualité] freshness **3.** [intensité - des couleurs] freshness, brightness ▪ **la robe n'est plus de la première ~** *fam* the dress isn't exactly brand new **4.** [éclat] freshness **5.** [indifférence] coolness.

fraîchir [32] [frɛʃir] *vi* **1.** [se refroidir] to get cooler ▪ **les jours fraîchissent, il faut vous couvrir** the weather is getting cooler, you'd better put on warm clothing **2.** NAUT [vent] to freshen, to get stronger.

fraie *etc v* ▷ **frayer**.

frais[1] [frɛ] *nmpl* **1.** [dépenses] expenditure, expense, costs ▪ **cela lui a occasionné des ~** it cost him a certain amount (of money) ▪ **les ~ du ménage** a family's everyday expenditure ▪ **faire des ~** to pay out a lot of money ▪ **faire des ~ de toilette** to spend money on clothes ▪ **à grands ~** with much expense, (very) expensively ▪ **à moindre ~** cheaper ▪ **à peu de ~** cheaply ➲ **~ de déplacement** *ou* **de mission** *ou* **de voyage** travelling expenses ▪ **~ d'entretien** maintenance costs ▪ **~ d'exploitation** operating costs ▪ **~ de garde** child-minding costs ▪ **~ de gestion** running costs ▪ **~ d'habillement** clothing expenses ▪ **~ de représentation** entertainment allowance ▪ **~ de production** production costs ▪ **~ professionnels** professional expenses ▪ **tous ~ payés** all expenses paid ▪ **en être pour ses ~** to waste one's time ▪ **faire les ~ de qqch** to pay the price for sthg ▪ **faire les ~ de la conversation** to be the centre of the conversation ▪ **rentrer dans ses ~** to break even, to recoup one's expenses ▪ **il en a été pour ses ~** *pr* he didn't even break even ; *fig* he was let down ▪ **se mettre en ~** to spend money ▪ **aux ~ de la princesse** *fam* : **hôtel cinq étoiles, restaurants de luxe, tout ça aux ~ de la princesse** *fam* five-star hotel, smart restaurants, all on expenses **2.** [en comptabilité] outgoings ▪ **~ bancaires** bank charges ▪ **~ divers** miscellaneous costs ▪ **~ d'envoi** *ou* **d'expédition** postage ▪ **~ généraux** overheads ▪ **~ réels** allowable expenses ▪ **~ variables** variable costs ▪ **faux ~** incidental costs **3.** DR : **~ (de justice)** (legal) costs ▪ **être condamné aux ~** to be ordered to pay costs **4.** ADMIN fees ▪ **~ de dossier** administrative charges ▪ **~ d'inscription** registration fee, membership fee ▪ **~ de scolarité** school fees.

frais[2], fraîche [frɛ, frɛʃ] ◇ *adj* **1.** [un peu froid] cool, fresh ▪ **l'air est ~ ce soir** it's chilly tonight **2.** [rafraîchissant] cooled, chilled ▪ **des boissons fraîches** cold drinks **3.** [récent - œuf, huître] fresh ; [- encre, peinture] wet ▪ **œufs ~ de ce matin** eggs newly laid this morning ▪ **il y avait des fleurs fraîches sur la table** there were freshly cut flowers on the table ▪ **j'ai reçu des nouvelles fraîches** I've got some recent news ▪ **la blessure** *ou* **la plaie est encore fraîche** the wound is still fresh ➲ **de fraîche date** recent, new **4.** [agréable] fresh, sweet ▪ **avoir la bouche** *ou* **l'haleine fraîche** to have sweet breath **5.** [reposé] fresh ▪ **je ne me**

sens pas trop ~ ce matin *fam* I don't feel too good *ou* well this morning ⊙ **être ~ comme un gardon** to be on top form ■ **~ et dispos, ~ comme une rose** as fresh as a daisy **6.** [éclatant] fresh **7.** [indifférent - accueil, réception] cool **8.** *fam* [en mauvais état] : **me voilà ~** I'm in a mess! **9.** ÉCON : **argent ~** ready cash.
◇ *adv* newly, freshly ■ **des fleurs ~coupées** freshly cut flowers.
◆ **frais** ◇ *adv* **1.** [nouvellement] newly ■ **~ émoulu : ~ émoulu de la faculté de droit** freshly graduated from law school **2.** [froid] : **il fait ~ dans la maison** it's chilly in the house ■ **boire ~** drink chilled ■ **servir ~** serve cold *ou* chilled.
◇ *nm* [air frais] : **le ~** the fresh air ■ **si on allait prendre un peu le ~ à la campagne?** how about going to the countryside for a breath of (fresh) air?
◆ **fraîche** *nf* **1.** [heure] cool (of evening) ■ **à la fraîche** in the cool evening air **2.** △ *arg crime* cash.
◆ **au frais** *loc adv* **1.** [dans un lieu froid] in a cool place **2.** △ *arg crime* [en prison] in the cooler△.

fraisage [frɛzaʒ] *nm* **1.** [usinage] milling **2.** [élargissement - d'un trou] reaming ; [- pour vis] countersinking.

fraise [frɛz] ◇ *nf* **1.** BOT strawberry ■ **~ des bois** wild strawberry ■ **aller aux ~s** to go (off) for a roll in the hay **2.** *fam* [visage] mug **3.** [pour couper] mill, cutter **4.** [pour faire - un trou] reamer ; [- un trou de vis] countersink (bit) **5.** MÉD [dentisterie] drill **6.** ORNITH wattle **7.** CULIN [de veau] caul **8.** [vêtement] ruff.
◇ *adj inv* strawberry (pink), strawberry-coloured.
◆ **à la fraise** *loc adj* strawberry *(modif)*, strawberry-flavoured.

fraiser [4] [frɛze] *vt* [usiner] to mill ■ [évaser - trou] to ream ; [- trou de vis] to countersink, to knead.

fraiseur, euse [frɛzœr, øz] *nm, f* milling machine operator.
◆ **fraiseuse** *nf* milling machine.

fraisier [frɛzje] *nm* **1.** BOT strawberry plant **2.** CULIN strawberry cream cake.

framboise [frɑ̃bwaz] *nf* **1.** BOT raspberry **2.** [alcool] raspberry liqueur.

framboisier [frɑ̃bwazje] *nm* **1.** BOT raspberry cane **2.** [gâteau] raspberry cream cake.

franc[1] [frɑ̃] *nm* [monnaie] franc ■ **ancien/nouveau ~** old/new franc **(in France)** ■ **~ symbolique** nominal sum.

franc[2]**, franche** [frɑ̃, frɑ̃ʃ] *adj* **1.** [honnête - réponse] frank, straightforward, honest ■ **un rire ~** an open laugh ■ **pour être ~ avec vous** to be honest with you ■ **il a l'air ~** he looks like an honest person, he has an honest look (about him) ⊙ **être ~ comme l'or** to be as honest as the day is long ■ **jouer ~ jeu** to play fair ■ **être ~ du collier** to be straightforward **2.** [pur] strong ■ **un rouge ~** a strong red **3.** *(avant le n) sout* & *péj* [parfait, extrême] utter ■ **un ~ scélérat, une franche canaille** a downright scoundrel ■ **l'ambiance n'était pas à la franche gaieté** the atmosphere wasn't exactly a happy one ■ **rencontrer une franche hostilité** to encounter outright hostility **4.** DR : **jour ~ : le jugement est exécutable au bout de trois jours ~s** the decision of the court to be carried out within three clear days **5.** COMM & FIN free ■ **port ~** free port ■ **ville franche** HIST free city ■ **zone franche** free zone.
◆ **franc** ◇ *adv* : **parlons ~** let's be frank.
◇ *adj m* : **~ de port (et d'emballage)** postage paid.

franc[3]**, franque** [frɑ̃, frɑ̃k] *adj* HIST Frankish.
◆ **Franc, Franque** *nm, f* Frank.

français, e [frɑ̃sɛ, ɛz] *adj* French.
◆ **Français, e** *nm, f* Frenchman (*f* Frenchwoman) ■ **les Français** [la population] French people, the French ; [les hommes] Frenchmen ■ **les Françaises** French women ■ **le Français n'aime pas...** the average Frenchman *ou* French person doesn't like...
◆ **français** *nm* LING French ■ **en bon ~** in proper French ■ **parler ~** to speak French.
◆ **à la française** ◇ *loc adj* [jardin, parquet] French, French-style.
◇ *loc adv* (in) the French way.

franc-bord [frɑ̃bɔr] (*pl* **francs-bords**) *nm* NAUT freeboard.

franc-comtois, e [frɑ̃kɔ̃twa, az] (*mpl* **francs-comtois**, *fpl* **franc-comtoises**) *adj* from Franche-Comté.

France [frɑ̃s] ◇ *npr f* : **(la) ~** France ■ **vivre en ~** to live in France ■ **la ~ profonde** grassroots France.
◇ *npr m* [navire] : **le ~** the 'France' *(French luxury liner)*.
◆ **vieille France** *loc adj inv* : **être** *ou* **faire (très) vieille ~** to be rather old-fashioned.

France 2 [frɑ̃sdø] *npr French state-owned television channel.*

France 3 [frɑ̃strwa] *npr French state-owned television channel.*

France-Culture [frɑ̃skyltyr] *npr radio station broadcasting mainly arts programmes.*

France-Dimanche [frɑ̃sdimɑ̃ʃ] *npr* PRESSE *popular Sunday newspaper.*

France-Infos [frɑ̃sɛ̃fo] *npr 24-hour radio news station.*

France-Inter [frɑ̃sɛ̃tɛr] *npr radio station broadcasting mainly current affairs programmes, interviews and debates.*

France-Musique [frɑ̃smyzik] *npr radio music station.*

France-Soir [frɑ̃sswar] *npr* PRESSE *daily newspaper with right-wing tendencies.*

France Télécom [frɑ̃stelekɔm] *npr state-owned company which runs all telecommunications services, until 1991 part of the PTT.*

Francfort [frɑ̃kfɔr] *npr* : **~ (sur-le-Main)** Frankfurt (am Main).

franche [frɑ̃ʃ] *f* ⊳ **franc** *(adj)*.

Franche-Comté [frɑ̃ʃkɔ̃te] *npr f* : **(la) ~** Franche-Comté.

FRANCHE-COMTÉ

This administrative region includes the ***départements*** of Doubs, Jura, Haute-Saône and Territoire de Belfort (capital: Besançon).

franchement [frɑ̃ʃmɑ̃] *adv* **1.** [sincèrement] frankly ■ **parlons ~** let's be frank ■ **pour vous parler ~, je ne sais pas de quoi il s'agit** to be honest with you, I don't know what it's all about ■ **~, je ne sais que faire** I honestly don't know what to do ■ **écoute, ~, tu crois vraiment qu'il le fera?** listen, do you honestly think he'll do it? **2.** [sans équivoque] clearly, definitely ■ **il a pris ~ parti pour son Premier ministre** he came down unequivocally on the side of his Prime Minister **3.** [résolument] boldly ■ **appuie ~ sur le bouton** press firmly on the button ■ **ils y sont allés ~** [dans un projet] they got right down to it ; [dans une conversation, une négociation] they didn't mince words **4.** [vraiment] really ■ **elle est devenue ~ jolie** she became really pretty ■ **il est ~ insupportable** he's downright unbearable.

franchir [32] [frɑ̃ʃir] *vt* **1.** [passer par-dessus - barrière, mur] to get over *(insép)* ■ **il a franchi le fossé d'un bond** he jumped over the ditch ⊙ **~ un obstacle** *fig* to get over an obstacle ■ **~ une difficulté** to overcome a difficulty **2.** [outrepasser - ligne, limite, date] to cross ■ **au moment de ~ le seuil, je m'arrêtai** I halted just as I was stepping across the threshold ■ **~ le mur du son** to break through the sound barrier ■ **il y a certaines limites à ne pas ~** there are certain limits which should not be overstepped ⊙ **~ un cap** *fig* to reach a milestone *ou* turning point ■ **~ le cap de la trentaine/cinquantaine** to turn thirty/fifty **3.** [dans le temps] to last through ■ **sa renommée a franchi les siècles** his reputation has lasted *ou* come down intact through the centuries.

franchisage [frɑ̃ʃizaʒ] *nm* franchising.

franchise [frɑ̃ʃiz] *nf* **1.** COMM & FIN [exploitation] franchise agreement ■ [exonération] exemption ⊙ **~ de bagages** baggage allowance ■ **~ douanière** exemption from customs duties ■ **en ~ postale** official paid **2.** [d'une assurance] excess *UK*, deductible *US* **3.** [honnêteté] frankness, straightforwardness ■ **avec ~** frankly, straightforwardly ■ **en toute ~** quite frankly, to be honest with you.

franchisé, e [frɑ̃ʃize] *nm, f* franchisee.

franchiseur [frɑ̃ʃizœr] *nm* franchisor.

franchissable [frɑ̃ʃisabl] *adj* : **un mur difficilement ~** a wall which is difficult to climb.

franchissement [frɑ̃ʃismɑ̃] *nm* [d'une barrière, d'un mur] getting over ■ [d'une rivière] crossing ■ [d'un obstacle, d'une difficulté] getting over, overcoming.

franchouillard, e [frɑ̃ʃujar, ard] *adj* **fam péj** typically French.

francilien, enne [frɑ̃siljɛ̃, ɛn] *adj* from the Île-de-France *(region around Paris).*

franciscain, e [frɑ̃siskɛ̃, ɛn] *adj* & *nmf* Franciscan.

franciser [3] [frɑ̃size] *vt* **1.** LING [mot, terme] to gallicize ■ **~ un nom propre** to give a proper name a French spelling **2.** NAUT [navire] to register as French.

francisque [frɑ̃sisk] *nf* francisc, francesque.

franc-jeu [frɑ̃ʒø] (*pl* **francs-jeux**) *nm* fair play.

franc-maçon, onne [frɑ̃masɔ̃, ɔn] (*mpl* **francs-maçons**, *fpl* **franc-maçonnes**) *nm, f* Freemason.

franc-maçonnerie [frɑ̃masɔnri] (*pl* **franc-maçonneries**) *nf* [société secrète] : **la ~** Freemasonry.

franc-maçonnique [frɑ̃masɔnik] *adj* Masonic.

franco [frɑ̃ko] ◇ *adj inv* & *adv* **1.** [dans un envoi] : **~ (de port)** postage paid **2.** COMM : **~ à bord = FAB** ■ **~ wagon** FOR.
◇ *adv* **fam** [franchement] : **y aller ~** to go straight *ou* right ahead.

franco- [frɑ̃ko] *préf* Franco-.

franco-britannique [frɑ̃kobritanik] (*pl* **franco-britanniques**) *adj* Franco-British.

franco-canadien, enne [frɑ̃kokanadjɛ̃, ɛn] (*mpl* **franco-canadiens**, *fpl* **franco-canadiennes**) *adj* French Canadian.
◆ **franco-canadien** *nm* LING Canadian French.

François [frɑ̃swa] *npr* Francis ■ **saint ~ (d'Assise)** Saint Francis (of Assisi) ■ **~ 1er** Francis I.

francophile [frɑ̃kɔfil] ◇ *adj* Francophil, Francophile.
◇ *nmf* Francophile.

francophilie [frɑ̃kɔfili] *nf* love of (all) things French.

francophobie [frɑ̃kɔfɔbi] *nf* Francophobia, dislike of (all) things French.

francophone [frɑ̃kɔfɔn] ◇ *adj* Francophone, French-speaking.
◇ *nmf* Francophone, French speaker.

francophonie [frɑ̃kɔfɔni] *nf* : **la ~** *French-speaking countries.*

FRANCOPHONIE

This is a wide-ranging cultural and political concept involving the promotion of the French language in French-speaking communities around the world.

franc-parler [frɑ̃parle] (*pl* **francs-parlers**) *nm* outspokenness ■ **il a son ~** he doesn't mince (his) words.

franc-tireur [frɑ̃tirœr] (*pl* **francs-tireurs**) *nm* **1.** MIL franc-tireur, irregular (soldier) **2.** [indépendant] maverick.

frange [frɑ̃ʒ] *nf* **1.** [de cheveux] fringe, bangs *US* **2.** [de tissu] fringe **3.** [minorité] fringe ■ **la ~ des indécis** the waverers **4.** [bordure] (fringed) edge.
◆ **à franges** *loc adj* fringed.

franger [17] [frɑ̃ʒe] *vt* [vêtement, tissu] to (edge with a) fringe.

frangin [frɑ̃ʒɛ̃] *nm* **fam** brother, bro.

frangine [frɑ̃ʒin] *nf* **fam** **1.** [sœur] sister, sis **2.** [femme] chick.

frangipane [frɑ̃ʒipan] *nf* **1.** CULIN [crème, gâteau] frangipane **2.** [fruit] frangipani.

frangipanier [frɑ̃ʒipanje] *nm* frangipani (tree).

franglais [frɑ̃glɛ] *nm* Franglais.

franque [frɑ̃k] *f* ▷ **franc** *(adj et histoire).*

franquette [frɑ̃kɛt] *nf* : **à la bonne ~** **fam** simply, informally ■ **recevoir qqn à la bonne ~** to have sb round for a simple meal (among friends).

franquisme [frɑ̃kism] *nm* Francoism.

franquiste [frɑ̃kist] ◇ *adj* pro-Franco.
◇ *nmf* Franco supporter.

fransquillon [frɑ̃skijɔ̃] *nm* **Belgique** **1.** **péj** [personne affectée] *Belgian who speaks French with an affected accent* **2.** [Flamand francophone] *French-speaking Flemish person.*

frappant, e [frapɑ̃, ɑ̃t] *adj* [ressemblance, exemple] striking.

frappe [frap] *nf* **1.** [d'une secrétaire, d'un pianiste] touch ■ **donner son texte à la ~** to give one's text (in) to be typed **2.** [copie] typed copy, typescript **3.** [d'une monnaie] minting **4.** SPORT [d'un footballeur] kick ■ [d'un boxeur] punch **5.** △ [voyou] hooligan, hoodlum ■ **une petite ~** a young hooligan **6.** MIL strike ■ **~ de précision** precision strike.

frappé, e [frape] *adj* **1.** [boisson] iced ■ **café ~** iced coffee ■ **servir bien ~** serve chilled **2.** TEXT embossed **3.** **fam** [fou] crazy ■ **il est un peu ~** he's a bit touched **4.** [bien exprimé] : **parole bien ~e** well-chosen word.

frapper [3] [frape] ◇ *vt* **1.** [battre - adversaire] to hit, to strike ■ **~ qqn à la tête** to aim for sb's head
2. [donner] to hit, to strike ■ **~ un grand coup** *ou* **un coup décisif** **fig** to strike a decisive blow ■ **~ les trois coups** *to give three knocks to announce the start of a theatrical performance*
3. [percuter] to hit ■ **~ les touches d'un clavier** to strike the keys on a keyboard ■ **~ la terre** *ou* **le sol du pied** to stamp (one's foot) ■ **être frappé d'une balle au front** to be hit *ou* struck by a bullet in the forehead ■ **être frappé par la foudre** to be struck by lightning
4. [affecter] to strike *ou* to bring down, to hit ■ **le deuil/mal qui nous frappe** the bereavement/pain we are suffering ■ *(en usage absolu)* **le voleur de parapluies a encore frappé!** **hum** the umbrella thief strikes again!
5. [s'appliquer à - suj: loi, sanction, taxe] to hit ■ **un châtiment qui frappe les coupables** a punishment which falls on the guilty
6. [surprendre] to strike ■ **ce qui me frappe chez lui, c'est sa désinvolture** what strikes me about him is his offhandedness ■ [impressionner] to upset, to shock ■ **j'ai été frappé de sa pâleur** I was shocked by his pallor ■ **être frappé de stupeur** to be stupefied *ou* struck dumb
7. [soumettre à] : **~ qqn/qqch de** : **~ qqn d'anathème** to put an anathema on sb ■ **~ qqn d'une interdiction de séjour** to ban sb ■ **~ l'alcool d'un impôt spécial** to put a special tax on alcohol
8. [vin] to chill
9. ART & TEXT to emboss
10. MÉTALL to stamp ■ **frappé au coin de** **fig** which bears the mark *ou* hallmark of.
◇ *vi* **1.** [pour entrer] to knock ■ **~ à la porte/fenêtre** to knock on the door/window ■ **on a frappé** someone knocked at the door ■ **~ à toutes les portes** **fig** to try every avenue ■ **~ à la bonne/mauvaise porte** **fig** to go to the right/wrong place
2. [pour exprimer un sentiment] : **~ dans ses mains** to clap one's hands ■ **~ du poing sur la table** to bang one's fist on the table ■ **~ du pied** to stamp one's foot
3. [cogner] to strike ➊ **~ dur** *ou* **sec** to strike hard ■ **~ fort** **pr** to hit hard ; **fig** to hit hard, to act decisively ■ **~ à la tête** to aim for the top.
◆ **se frapper** ◇ *vp (emploi réfléchi)* to hit o.s. ■ **se ~ la poitrine** to beat one's chest ■ **se ~ le front** to slap one's forehead.
◇ *vp (emploi réciproque)* to hit one another *ou* each other.
◇ *vpi* **fam** [s'inquiéter] to worry, to get (o.s.) worked up.

frasil [frazil] *nm* **Québec** frazil.

frasques [frask] *nfpl* escapades, pranks ■ **des ~ de jeunesse** youthful indiscretions.

fraternel, elle [fratɛrnɛl] *adj* brotherly, fraternal ■ **ils sont unis par des liens quasi ~s** they're almost as close as brothers.

fraternellement [fratɛrnɛlmɑ̃] *adv* brotherly, fraternally ■ **agir ~ envers qqn** to act in a brotherly way towards sb.

fraternisation [fratɛrnizasjɔ̃] *nf* fraternizing ■ **la ~ entre les peuples** fraternization between peoples.

fraterniser [3] [fratɛrnize] *vi* to fraternize.

fraternité [fratɛrnite] *nf* [lien] brotherhood, fraternity ▪ **~ d'armes** brotherhood of arms.

fratricide [fratrisid] ◇ *adj* [guerre, haine] fratricidal.
◇ *nmf* [meurtrier] fratricide.
◇ *nm* [meurtre] fratricide.

fratrie [fratri] *nf* siblings, brothers and sisters.

fraude [frod] *nf* **1.** [tromperie] fraud ▪ **la ~ aux examens** cheating at exams **2.** DR : **~ électorale** electoral fraud, vote *ou* ballot rigging ▪ **~ fiscale** tax evasion ▪ **~ sur les produits** fraudulent trading.
◆ **en fraude** *loc adv* [vendre] : **entrer/sortir en ~** to smuggle o.s. in/out ▪ **passer qqch en ~** to smuggle sthg in.

frauder [3] [frode] ◇ *vt* [état] to defraud ▪ **~ le fisc** to evade taxation.
◇ *vi* to cheat ▪ **~ à** *ou* **dans un examen** to cheat at an exam ▪ **~ sur le poids** to cheat on the weight, to give short measure.

fraudeur, euse [frodœr, øz] ◇ *adj* [attitude, tempérament] cheating.
◇ *nm, f* [envers le fisc] tax evader ▪ [à la douane] smuggler ▪ [à un examen] cheat ▪ **les ~s seront poursuivis** those guilty of fraud will be prosecuted.

frauduleusement [frodyløzmɑ̃] *adv* fraudulently ▪ **faire entrer/sortir qqch ~** to smuggle sthg in/out.

frauduleux, euse [frodylø, øz] *adj* fraudulent.

frayer [11] [frɛje] ◇ *vt* [route, voie] to clear ▪ **~ un chemin en abattant les arbres** to clear a path by felling the trees ▪ **~ la voie à qqch/qqn** *fig* to pave the way for sthg/sb.
◇ *vi* ZOOL to spawn.
◆ **frayer avec** *v+prép* to associate with *(sép)*.
◆ **se frayer** *vpt* : **se ~ un chemin** *ou* **un passage dans la foule** to force *ou* to push one's way through the crowd ▪ **se ~ un chemin** *ou* **une route vers la gloire** *fig* to work one's way towards fame.

frayeur [frɛjœr] *nf* fright ▪ **avoir des ~s nocturnes** to suffer from night terrors ▪ **faire une ~ à qqn** to give sb a fright.

fredaines [frədɛn] *nfpl* escapades, pranks ▪ **faire des ~** to get into *ou* up to mischief.

Frédéric [frederik] *npr* : **~ le Grand** Frederick the Great.

Frédéric-Guillaume [frederikgijom] *npr* Frederick William.

fredonnement [frədɔnmɑ̃] *nm* humming.

fredonner [3] [frədɔne] ◇ *vt* [air, chanson] to hum.
◇ *vi* to hum.

free-lance [frilɑ̃s] (*pl* **free-lances**) ◇ *adj inv* freelance.
◇ *nmf* freelance, freelancer.
◇ *nm* freelancing, freelance work ▪ **travailler** *ou* **être en ~** to work on a freelance basis *ou* as a freelancer.

freesia [frezja] *nm* freesia.

freezer [frizœr] *nm* freezer compartment.

frégate [fregat] *nf* **1.** ORNITH frigate bird **2.** NAUT frigate.

frein [frɛ̃] *nm* **1.** AUTO brake ▪ **mettre le ~** *fam* to pull on the handbrake ▶ **~ à disque** disc brake ▪ **~ à main** handbrake ▪ **~ moteur** engine brake ▪ **coup de ~ : donner un brusque coup de ~** to brake sharply *ou* suddenly ▪ **c'est un coup de ~ à l'économie** *fig* this will act as a brake on the economy ▪ **mettre un ~ à** to block **2.** ANAT fraenum, frenum.
◆ **sans frein** *loc adj* unbridled.

freinage [frɛnaʒ] *nm* braking.

freiner [4] [frene] ◇ *vt* **1.** [ralentir - véhicule] to slow down *(sép)* ; [- évolution] to check **2.** [amoindrir - impatience] to curb ; [- enthousiasme] to dampen.
◇ *vi* [conducteur, auto] to brake ▪ **ta voiture freine bien/mal** your car brakes are good/bad.

frelaté, e [frəlate] *adj* **1.** [nourriture, vin] adulterated **2.** *fig* & *litt* artificial ▪ **un mode de vie ~** an artificial way of life.

frelater [3] [frəlate] *vt* [lait, vin] to adulterate.

frêle [frɛl] *adj* **1.** [fragile - corps, santé] frail, fragile ; [- voix] thin, reedy ▪ **tout repose sur ses ~s épaules** everything rests on her frail shoulders **2.** [ténu - espoir] frail, flimsy.

frelon [frəlɔ̃] *nm* hornet.

freluquet [frəlykɛ] *nm* **1.** *fam* [homme chétif] pipsqueak, (little) runt **2.** *litt* [prétentieux] (young) whippersnapper.

frémir [32] [fremir] *vi* **1.** [trembler] to shiver, to shudder ▪ **~ de colère** to quiver with anger ▪ **~ d'impatience** to tremble with impatience ▪ **~ de plaisir** to quiver with pleasure **2.** *litt* [vibrer - tige, herbe] to quiver, to tremble ; [- surface d'un lac] to ripple **3.** [avant l'ébullition] to simmer.

frémissant, e [fremisɑ̃, ɑ̃t] *adj* **1.** [avant l'ébullition] simmering **2.** *litt* [feuilles] quivering, rustling ▪ [surface d'un lac] quivering **3.** [en émoi] quivering, trembling ▪ **une sensibilité ~e** a trembling sensitivity.

frémissement [fremismɑ̃] *nm* **1.** [d'indignation, de colère] quiver, shiver, shudder ▪ **un ~ d'impatience la parcourut** a thrill of impatience ran through her **2.** *litt* [des feuilles] rustling ▪ [de la surface d'un lac] rippling **3.** [avant l'ébullition] simmer, simmering.

french cancan [frɛnʃkɑ̃kɑ̃] (*pl* **french cancans**) *nm* (French) cancan.

frêne [frɛn] *nm* **1.** [arbre] ash (tree) **2.** [bois] ash.

frénésie [frenezi] *nf* frenzy ▪ **être pris d'une ~ de voyages** to have a strong urge to travel, to have the travel bug ▪ **avec ~** frantically, frenetically, wildly.

frénétique [frenetik] *adj* [agitation, hurlement] frantic ▪ [joie, passion] frenzied ▪ **des applaudissements ~s** frenzied applause.

frénétiquement [frenetikmɑ̃] *adv* frantically, frenetically, wildly.

fréquemment [frekamɑ̃] *adv* frequently, often.

fréquence [frekɑ̃s] *nf* **1.** [périodicité] frequency ▪ **quelle est la ~ des trains sur cette ligne?** how many trains a day run on this line? **2.** MÉD : **~ du pouls** fast pulse rate **3.** ACOUST frequency ▪ **basse/moyenne/haute ~** low/middle/high frequency ▮ TÉLÉCOM wavelength, (wave) band, frequency **4.** [en statistique] frequency.

fréquent, e [frekɑ̃, ɑ̃t] *adj* [répété] frequent.

fréquentable [frekɑ̃tabl] *adj* : **sa famille n'est guère ~** her family isn't exactly the kind you'd care to associate with ▪ **c'est un endroit bien peu ~** it's not the sort of place you'd like to be seen in.

fréquentatif, ive [frekɑ̃tatif, iv] *adj* LING frequentative.

fréquentation [frekɑ̃tasjɔ̃] *nf* **1.** [d'un lieu] frequenting **2.** COMM attendance **3.** [relation] acquaintance ▪ **avoir de mauvaises ~s** to keep bad company ▪ **ce garçon n'est pas une ~ pour toi** you shouldn't associate with this boy **4.** *litt* [lecture] : **la ~ des bons auteurs/de la littérature italienne** reading good books/Italian literature.

fréquenté, e [frekɑ̃te] *adj* : **un endroit bien/mal fréquenté** a place with a good/bad reputation ▪ **c'est un café très fréquenté par les jeunes** it's a café that's very popular with young people ▪ **un endroit peu ~** a place hardly anyone ever goes to.

fréquenter [3] [frekɑ̃te] *vt* **1.** [lieu] to frequent **2.** [personne] to see frequently, to associate with ▪ [courtiser] : **elle fréquente mon frère depuis un an** she's been going out with my brother for a year ▪ *(en usage absolu)* **il paraît qu'elle fréquente** *fam vieilli* there are rumours she's courting **3.** *litt* [lire] : **~ les bons écrivains/la littérature italienne** to read good books/Italian literature.
◆ **se fréquenter** *vp (emploi réciproque)* **ils se fréquentent depuis deux ans** they've been going out for two years ▪ **ils se fréquentent assez peu** they don't see much of each other.

frère [frɛr] *nm* **1.** [dans une famille] brother ▶ **~ aîné/cadet** older/younger brother ■ **~ jumeau** twin brother ■ **~ de sang** blood brother ■ **mon grand/petit ~** [de deux] my older/younger brother ; [de plusieurs] my oldest/youngest brother ■ **tu vas avoir un petit ~** you are going to have a little *ou* baby brother ■ **comme des ~s : se ressembler comme des ~s** to be like two peas (in a pod) ■ **ce sont des ~s ennemis** a friendly rivalry exists between them **2.** [compagnon] brother ■ **salut, vieux ~!** *fam* hello, old pal! ■ **j'ai un bougeoir qui a perdu son ~** *fam hum* I've got one candle holder but I've lost its companion ▶ **~s d'armes** brothers in arms **3.** RELIG brother, friar ■ **aller à l'école chez les ~s** to go to a Catholic boys' school **4.** [au sein d'une communauté] brother **5.** *(comme adj)* [groupe, parti, pays] sister *(modif)*.

frérot [frero] *nm fam* kid brother, little brother.

Fresnes [frɛn] *npr town in the Paris suburbs with a well-known prison.*

fresque [frɛsk] *nf* **1.** ART fresco ■ **peindre à ~** to paint in fresco **2.** [description] panorama, detailed picture.

fret [frɛ] *nm* **1.** [chargement - d'un avion, d'un navire] cargo, freight ; [- d'un camion] load ■ **donner à ~** to freight ■ **prendre à ~** to charter ▶ **~ aérien** air freight **2.** [prix - par air, mer] freight, freightage ; [- par route] carriage.

fréter [18] [frete] *vt* [avion] to charter ■ [navire] to freight ■ [camionnette] to hire.

fréteur [fretœr] *nm* freighter.

frétillant, e [fretijɑ̃, ɑ̃t] *adj* [ver, poisson] wriggling ■ [queue] wagging ■ **tout ~ d'impatience** *fig* quivering with impatience.

frétillement [fretijmɑ̃] *nm* [de la queue] wagging ■ [de vers, de poissons] wriggling.

frétiller [3] [fretije] *vi* [ver, poisson] to wriggle ■ [queue] to wag ■ **il frétille d'impatience** *fig* he's quivering with impatience.

fretin [frətɛ̃] *nm* fry.

freudien, enne [frødjɛ̃, ɛn] *adj & nm, f* Freudian.

freudisme [frødism] *nm* Freudianism.

friabilité [frijabilite] *nf* [d'une roche] friableness, friability ■ [d'un biscuit] crumbliness.

friable [frijabl] *adj* [roche] crumbly, friable ■ [biscuit] crumbly.

friand, e [frijɑ̃, ɑ̃d] *adj* : **~ de** [sucreries] fond of ■ **être ~ de compliments** to enjoy receiving compliments.
◆ **friand** *nm* **1.** [salé] ≃ meat pie (in puff pastry) **2.** [sucré] ≃ almond biscuit *UK ou* cookie *US*.

friandise [frijɑ̃diz] *nf* sweetmeat, (sweet) delicacy, titbit ■ **aimer les ~s** to have a sweet tooth.

fric [frik] *nm fam* cash, money ■ **il est bourré de ~** he's loaded.

fricadelle [frikadɛl] *nf Belgique* meatball.

fricandelle [frikɑ̃dɛl] *Belgique* = **fricadelle**.

fricasse [frikas] *nf Suisse* [grand froid] freeze.

fricassée [frikase] *nf* [ragoût] fricassee ■ **~ de museaux** *fam hum* exchange of kisses.

fricasser [3] [frikase] *vt* to fricassee ■ **faire ~ des champignons** to fricassee mushrooms.

fric-frac[△] [frikfrak] *nm inv* burglary, break-in.

friche [friʃ] *nf* **1.** AGRIC piece of fallow land, fallow **2.** INDUST : **~ industrielle** industrial wasteland **3.** [urbanisme] : **~ urbaine** brownfield site.
◆ **en friche** *loc adj* **1.** AGRIC : **terre en ~** plot of fallow land **2.** [inactif] unused.

frichti [friʃti] *nm fam* grub *UK*, chow *US*.

fricot [friko] *nm fam* **1.** [ragoût] ≃ stew **2.** [cuisine] : **faire le ~** to cook.

fricoter [3] [frikɔte] *vt fam* **1.** [cuisiner] to stew **2.** [manigancer] to cook up ■ **je me demande ce qu'il fricote** I wonder what he's up to *ou* what he's cooking up.
◆ **fricoter avec** *v+prép fam* **1.** [sexuellement] to knock around with **2.** [être complice de] to cook something up with.

fricoteur, euse [frikɔtœr, øz] *nm, f fam* fiddler.

friction [friksjɔ̃] *nf* **1.** [frottement] chafing **2.** [massage - gén] rub (down) ; [- du cuir chevelu] scalp massage **3.** [désaccord] friction ■ **il y a des ~s entre eux** they don't see eye to eye **4.** GÉOL & MÉCAN friction.

frictionner [3] [friksjɔne] *vt* to rub (down).
◆ **se frictionner** *vp (emploi réfléchi)* to rub o.s. ■ **frictionne-toi bien** give yourself a good rub down.

Frigidaire® [friʒidɛr] *nm* **1.** [portant la marque] Frigidaire®(refrigerator) **2.** [appareil quelconque] refrigerator, fridge ■ **mettre qqch au ~** *fig* to put sthg on the back burner, to shelve sthg.

frigide [friʒid] *adj* frigid.

frigidité [friʒidite] *nf* frigidity.

frigo [frigo] *nm fam* **1.** [réfrigérateur] fridge **2.** [chambre froide] cold room.

frigorifié, e [frigɔrifje] *adj fam fig* frozen stiff.

frigorifier [9] [frigɔrifje] *vt* to refrigerate ■ **la promenade m'a complètement frigorifié** *fam fig* I'm frozen stiff after that walk.

frigorifique [frigɔrifik] ◇ *adj* refrigerated.
◇ *nm* **1.** [établissement] cold store **2.** [appareil] refrigerator.

frileusement [friløzmɑ̃] *adv* : **s'envelopper ~ dans des couvertures** to wrap o.s. in blankets.

frileux, euse [frilø, øz] ◇ *adj* **1.** [qui a froid] sensitive to cold **2.** [prudent] timid, unadventurous.
◇ *nm, f person who is sensitive to cold.*

frimaire [frimɛr] *nm 3rd month in the French Revolutionary calendar (from Nov 22 to Dec 21).*

frimas [frima] *nm litt* hoarfrost.

frime [frim] *nf fam* put-on ■ **pour la ~** for show *ou* effect.

frimer [3] [frime] *vi fam* to show off, to put on an act.

frimeur, euse [frimœr, øz] *fam* ◇ *adj* [attitude, ton] showy.
◇ *nm, f* show-off.

frimousse [frimus] *nf* (sweet) little face.

fringale [frɛ̃gal] *nf fam* **1.** [faim] hunger ■ **j'ai une de ces ~s!** I'm starving! **2.** [désir] : **une ~ de** a craving for.

fringant, e [frɛ̃gɑ̃, ɑ̃t] *adj* **1.** [personne] dashing ■ **encore ~** (still) spry ■ **je ne me sens pas trop ~ aujourd'hui** I don't feel too good *ou* well today **2.** [cheval] frisky, spirited.

fringuer [3] [frɛ̃ge] *vt fam* to dress.
◆ **se fringuer** *vp (emploi réfléchi) fam* **1.** [s'habiller] to dress o.s. ■ **être bien/mal fringué** to be well/badly dressed **2.** [s'habiller bien] to do *ou* to get o.s. up.

fringues [frɛ̃g] *nfpl fam* gear, clobber *UK*, threads *US*.

fripe [frip] *nf* : **la ~, les ~s** secondhand clothes.

friper [3] [fripe] *vt* **1.** [chiffonner] to crumple *ou* to crease (up) ■ **son pantalon était tout fripé aux genoux** his trousers were all creased around the knee **2.** [rider] : **avoir un visage tout fripé** to have crease-marks all over one's face.
◆ **se friper** *vpi* to crumple, to get crumpled.

friperie [fripri] *nf* **1.** [boutique] secondhand clothes shop *UK ou* store *US* **2.** [vêtements] secondhand clothes.

fripier, ère [fripje, ɛr] *nm, f* secondhand clothes dealer.

fripon, onne [fripɔ̃, ɔn] ◇ *adj* [enfant] mischievous, roguish ■ [sourire] roguish.
◇ *nm, f* rogue ■ **tu n'es qu'un petit ~!** you little rogue *ou* scamp!

fripouille [fripuj] *nf* **1.** *péj* [scélérat] rascal, rogue **2.** [ton affectueux] : **(petite) ~!** you little rogue!

friqué, e [frike] *adj fam* [personne] loaded.

frire [115] [frir] <> *vt* CULIN to fry ■ [en friteuse, dans un bain d'huile] to deep-fry ■ **poisson frit** fried fish.
<> *vi* to fry ■ **faire ~ des poissons** to fry fish.

frisant, e [frizɑ̃, ɑ̃t] *adj* [lumière] oblique.

Frisbee® [frizbi] *nm* Frisbee®.

frise [friz] *nf* **1.** ARCHIT & ART frieze **2.** THÉÂTRE border.

Frise [friz] *npr f* : **(la) ~** Friesland.

frisé, e [frize] *adj* **1.** [barbe, cheveux] curly ■ [personne] curly-haired ■ **être ~ comme un mouton** to have curly *ou* frizzy hair **2.** [chicorée] curly.
◆ **frisée** *nf* [chicorée] curly endive ■ **~e aux lardons** *curly endive salad with fried bacon pieces.*

friser [3] [frize] <> *vt* **1.** [barbe, cheveux] to curl ■ **se faire ~ (les cheveux)** to have one's hair curled **2.** [effleurer] to graze, to skim **3.** [être proche de] : **elle doit ~ la quarantaine** she must be getting on for forty ■ **nous avons frisé la catastrophe** we came within an inch of disaster.
<> *vi* to have curly hair.

frisette [frizɛt] *nf* [de cheveux] small curl ■ **avoir des ~s** to have curly hair.

frison, onne [frizɔ̃, ɔn] *adj* Friesian, Frisian.
◆ **frisonne** *nf* [vache] : **~ne (pie noir)** Friesian *UK*, Holstein *US*.

frisottant, e [frizɔtɑ̃, ɑ̃t] *adj* [cheveux] frizzy.

frisotter [3] [frizɔte] <> *vt* to frizz.
<> *vi* to be frizzy ■ **la pluie fait ~ mes cheveux** the rain makes my hair go all frizzy.

frisquet, ette [friskɛ, ɛt] *adj fam* [temps, vent] chilly ■ **il fait plutôt ~ aujourd'hui** it's rather chilly *ou* there's a nip in the air today.

frisson [frisɔ̃] *nm* **1.** [de froid, de fièvre] shiver ■ [de peur] shudder ■ **ton livre m'a donné des ~s** your book gave me the shivers ■ **être pris *ou* saisi de ~s** to get the shivers **2.** *litt* [bruissement - de l'eau] ripple ; [- des feuilles] ripple.

frissonnant, e [frisɔnɑ̃, ɑ̃t] *adj* **1.** [eau] simmering **2.** [personne] shivering ■ **être ~ de froid/fièvre** to shiver with cold/a high temperature.

frissonnement [frisɔnmɑ̃] *nm* **1.** [de froid, de fièvre] shiver ■ [de peur] shudder ■ **un ~ lui parcourut le corps** a shiver ran through her body **2.** *litt* [de la surface d'un étang] ripple, rippling *(U)* ■ [des feuilles] rustling *(U)*.

frissonner [3] [frisɔne] *vi* **1.** [de froid, de fièvre] to shiver ■ [de peur] to shudder ■ [de joie] to quiver ■ **elle frissonnait de bonheur** she was trembling with happiness ■ **ça me fait ~ rien que d'y penser** the very thought of it gives me the creeps **2.** *litt* [feuilles] to rustle ■ [surface d'un étang] to ripple.

frisure [frizyr] *nf* curls ■ **elle a une ~ légère** her hair is slightly curly.

frit, e [fri, frit] <> *pp* ▷ **frire**.
<> *adj* fried.

frite [frit] *nf* **1.** CULIN chip *UK*, French fry *US* ■ **des ~s** chips *UK*, French fries *US* **2.** *loc* **avoir la ~** *fam* to be on top form.

friterie [fritri] *nf* [restaurant] ≃ fast-food restaurant ■ [ambulante] chip van *UK*, French fry vendor *US*.

friteuse [fritøz] *nf* deep fryer, chip pan *UK* ■ **~ électrique** electric fryer.

fritte [frit] *nf* frit.

fritter [3] [frite] *vt* to frit.

friture [frityr] *nf* **1.** [aliments frits] fried food ■ [poissons] fried fish ■ **acheter de la ~** to buy (small) fish for frying **2.** CULIN [cuisson] frying ■ [matière grasse] deep fat **3.** ACOUST static ■ **il y a de la ~** we're getting some interference **4.** *Belgique* [friterie] ≃ chip van *UK*, French fry vendor *US*.

fritz△ [frits] *nm vieilli & injur offensive term used with reference to Germans*, ≃ Kraut.

frivole [frivɔl] *adj* [personne] frivolous, shallow ■ [sujet] frivolous.

frivolement [frivɔlmɑ̃] *adv* frivolously.

frivolité [frivɔlite] *nf* **1.** [légèreté] frivolity, frivolousness ■ [manque de sérieux - d'un projet, d'une œuvre] triviality **2.** [vétille] trifle ■ **perdre son temps à des ~s** to waste time in frivolous pursuits *ou* frivolities.
◆ **frivolités** *nfpl vieilli* fancy goods, novelties.

froc [frɔk] *nm* **1.** *fam* [pantalon] trousers, pants *US* ■ **faire dans son ~**▲ to be scared shitless **2.** RELIG [habit] habit, frock ■ **jeter son ~ aux orties** to leave holy orders.

froid, e [frwa, frwad] *adj* **1.** [boisson, temps, moteur] cold ■ **un jour d'hiver ~ et sec** a crisp winter day ■ **par un matin très ~** on a raw morning **2.** [indifférent - personne] cold, insensitive, unfeeling ; [- tempérament] cold ; [- accueil] cold, chilly ; [- réponse] cold, cool ; [- attitude] cold, unfriendly ■ **ton/regard ~** hostile tone/stare ■ **devant ce spectacle, il est resté ~** he was unmoved by the sight ■ **ça me laisse ~** it leaves me cold ■ **style ~** bloodless *ou* cold style ⊃ **colère ~e** cold fury ■ **~ comme le marbre** as cold as marble **3.** [triste] cold, bleak ■ **des murs ~s et nus** cold bare walls **4.** [couleur] cold, cool **5.** [ancien] cold, dead ■ **la piste est ~e** the scent is cold, the trail's gone dead.
◆ **froid** <> *nm* **1.** [température] : **le ~** [climat] cold weather, the cold ; [air] the cold (air) ■ **par ce ~** in this cold ■ **conserver qqch au ~** to store sthg in a cold place ⊃ **coup de ~** cold spell *ou* snap ■ **il fait un ~ de canard *ou* sibérien** it's freezing *ou* bitterly cold **2.** [sensation] : **avoir ~** to be *ou* to feel cold ■ **j'ai ~ aux mains** my hands are cold ■ **attraper *ou* prendre ~** to get *ou* to catch a cold ■ **je meurs de ~** I'm freezing (cold) ⊃ **avoir ~ dans le dos** to feel one's blood run cold ■ **ça me donne ~ dans le dos** it makes my blood run cold, it sends shivers down my spine ■ **une histoire qui fait ~ dans le dos** a chilling *ou* creepy story ■ **il n'a pas ~ aux yeux** he's bold *ou* plucky **3.** [malaise] : **il y a un ~ entre eux** things have gone cool between them ⊃ **cela a jeté un ~** it cast a chill over the proceedings ■ **être en ~ avec qqn** to be on bad terms with sb.
<> *adv* : **il fait ~ dehors** it's cold out ■ **en janvier, il fait ~** the weather's cold in January ■ **boire ~** [habituellement] to drink cold drinks ■ **remuez et buvez ~** stir and chill before drinking.
◆ **à froid** <> *loc adj* ▷ **opération**.
<> *loc adv* **1.** [sans émotion] calmly, dispassionately **2.** [sans préparation] : **je ne peux pas répondre à ~** I can't answer off the top of my head ■ **prendre qqn à ~** to catch sb unawares *ou* off guard **3.** MÉTALL cold ■ **laminer à ~** to cold roll **4.** MÉD : **intervenir *ou* opérer à ~** to operate between attacks.

froidement [frwadmɑ̃] *adv* **1.** [avec réserve] coldly, coolly **2.** [lucidement] dispassionately ■ **raisonner ~** to use cold logic **3.** [avec indifférence] cold-bloodedly ■ **abattre qqn ~** to shoot down sb in cold blood **4.** *loc* **ça va ~!** *fam* I'm fine but a bit chilly!

froideur [frwadœr] *nf* **1.** [indifférence méprisante] coldness, cold indifference **2.** [manque de sensualité] coldness **3.** *litt* [au toucher] feel ■ **son front avait la ~ du marbre** his forehead was cold as marble.
◆ **avec froideur** *loc adv* coldly, indifferently ■ **accueillir qqn avec ~** to give sb a chilly welcome.

froidure [frwadyr] *nf* **1.** *litt* [temps] intense cold ■ [saison] cold season *ou* weather **2.** MÉD frostbite.

froissé [frwase] *adj* **1.** [chemise, tissu] creased **2.** [personne] hurt.

froissement [frwasmɑ̃] *nm* **1.** [plis - d'un papier, d'une étoffe] crumpling, creasing **2.** [bruit] rustling, rustle **3.** *litt* [vexation] hurt feelings **4.** MÉD straining *(U)*.

froisser [3] [frwase] *vt* **1.** [friper - tissu] to crease, to crumple ; [- papier] to crumple, to crease **2.** [carrosserie] to dent **3.** [blesser - orgueil] to ruffle, to bruise ; [- personne] to offend **4.** MÉD to strain.
◆ **se froisser** <> *vpi* **1.** [vêtement] to crush, to crease **2.** [personne] to get hurt, to take offence, to be offended.
<> *vpt* : **se ~ un muscle** to strain a muscle.

frôlement [frolmɑ̃] *nm* **1.** [frottement] brush, light touch ▪ **j'ai senti le ~ du chat contre ma jambe** I felt the cat brushing *ou* rubbing against my leg **2.** [bruit] rustle, swish, rustling sound.

frôler [3] [frole] *vt* **1.** [effleurer] to brush, to touch lightly, to graze ▪ **l'avion a frôlé les arbres** the plane skimmed *ou* grazed the treetops ▪ **il m'a frôlé la joue du doigt** he stroked my cheek lightly ▪ **la branche lui a frôlé les cheveux** the branch brushed against his hair **2.** [passer très près de] to come close to touching **3.** [échapper à] to come within a hair's breadth *ou* an ace of, to escape narrowly ▪ **~ la mort** to come within a hair's breadth of death *ou* dying.
◆ **se frôler** *vp (emploi réciproque)* to brush against *ou* to jostle each other.

frôleur, euse [frolœr, øz] *adj* [geste] stroking.
◆ **frôleur** *nm* pervert *(who likes to rub up against women in crowds).*

fromage [frɔmaʒ] *nm* **1.** [laitage] cheese ▪ **un ~** a cheese ▪ **du ~** cheese ▪ **prenez du ~** have some cheese ▪ **plusieurs sortes de ~s** several kinds of cheese ◐ **~ de vache/brebis/chèvre** cow's/sheep's/goat's milk cheese ▪ **~ blanc** fromage frais ▪ **~ frais** ≃ cream cheese ▪ **~ à pâte molle** soft cheese ▪ **~ à pâte pressée** hard cheese ▪ **~ à tartiner** cheese spread ▪ **en faire tout un ~** *fam* to kick up a (huge) fuss, to make a mountain out of a molehill **2.** *fam* [sinécure] cushy job *ou* number.
◆ **au fromage** *loc adj* [omelette, soufflé] cheese *(modif).*
◆ **fromage de tête** *nm* brawn *UK*, headcheese *US*.

fromager, ère [frɔmaʒe, ɛr] <> *adj* cheese *(modif).*
<> *nm, f* **1.** [commerçant] cheesemonger *UK*, cheese seller *US* **2.** [fabricant] cheese maker, dairyman (*f* dairywoman).
◆ **fromager** *nm* BOT kapok, silk-cotton tree, ceiba *spéc.*

fromagerie [frɔmaʒri] *nf* **1.** [boutique] cheese shop *UK ou* store *US* **2.** [fabrique] dairy.

froment [frɔmɑ̃] *nm* wheat.

frometon [frɔmtɔ̃] *nm fam* cheese.

fronce [frɔ̃s] *nf* [de tissu] gather ▪ **faire des ~s à un tissu** to gather a piece of material.
◆ **à fronces** *loc adj* gathered.

froncement [frɔ̃smɑ̃] *nm* : **~ de sourcils** frown.

froncer [16] [frɔ̃se] *vt* **1.** COUT to gather **2.** [rider] : **~ les sourcils** to knit one's brow, to frown ▪ **~ le nez** to wrinkle one's nose.

frondaison [frɔ̃dɛzɔ̃] *nf* **1.** [feuillage] foliage, leaves **2.** [époque] foliation.

fronde [frɔ̃d] *nf* **1.** ARM sling **2.** [lance-pierres] catapult *UK*, slingshot *US* **3.** *litt* [révolte] rebellion, revolt ▪ **la Fronde** HIST the Fronde rebellion **4.** BOT frond.

fronder [3] [frɔ̃de] *vt litt* to revolt against.

frondeur, euse [frɔ̃dœr, øz] <> *adj* insubordinate, rebellious.
<> *nm, f* **1.** HIST member of the Fronde, Frondeur **2.** [rebelle] rebel, troublemaker.

front [frɔ̃] *nm* **1.** ANAT forehead, brow ◐ **baisser le ~** *pr* to lower one's head ▪ **baisser** *ou* **courber le ~** *fig* to submit ▪ **relever le ~** to regain confidence ▪ **le ~ haut** proudly, with one's head held high **2.** [d'une montagne] face ▪ [d'un monument] frontage, façade ▪ **~ de mer** seafront **3.** [audace] : **avoir le ~ de faire** to have the audacity *ou* impudence to do **4.** POLIT front ▪ **le Front populaire** the Popular Front ▪ **le Front national** the National Front ▪ **~ uni** united front ▪ **faire ~** to form a united front, to close ranks ▪ **faire ~ devant l'adversaire** to present a united front to the enemy ▪ **faire ~ commun contre qqn/qqch** to make common cause against sb/sthg ▪ **je ne suis pas sûr qu'il puisse faire ~ seul** I'm not sure he'll be able to cope alone **5.** MIL [zone] front ▪ [ligne] front line **6.** MIN [gén] face ▪ [dans une houillère] coalface ▪ **~ de taille** working face **7.** MÉTÉOR front ▪ **~ froid/chaud** cold/warm front.
◆ **de front** *loc adv* **1.** [attaquer] head-on ▪ **aborder une difficulté de ~** to tackle a problem head-on **2.** [en vis-à-vis] head-on ▪ **se heurter de ~** [véhicules] to collide head-on ; [adversaires] to come into direct confrontation **3.** [côte à côte] abreast ▪ **on ne peut pas passer de ~** you can't get through side by side ▪ **nous marchions de ~** we were walking next to one another ▪ **rouler à trois voitures de ~** to drive three (cars) abreast **4.** [en même temps] at the same time, at a time.

LE FRONT POPULAIRE

The coalition of socialists, radicals and communists who came to power in 1936 under Léon Blum. Within a remarkably short period it established the forty-hour week and holidays with pay for commerce and industry, and passed a range of laws relating to the rights of trade unions.

frontal, e, aux [frɔ̃tal, o] *adj* **1.** ANAT & GÉOM frontal **2.** [conflit, attaque] head-on.
◆ **frontal** *nm* ANAT frontal bone.

frontalier, ère [frɔ̃talje, ɛr] <> *adj* border *(modif).*
<> *nm, f* cross-border commuter.

frontière [frɔ̃tjɛr] *nf* **1.** POLIT border ◐ **poste/ville/zone ~** border post/town/area **2.** [démarcation] boundary ▪ **la ~ entre la veille et le sommeil** the borderline between sleeping and waking ◐ **~ naturelle/linguistique** natural/linguistic boundary **3.** [limite] frontier **4.** MATH : **(point) ~** frontier.

frontispice [frɔ̃tispis] *nm* [titre, illustration] frontispiece.

fronton [frɔ̃tɔ̃] *nm* **1.** ARCHIT pediment **2.** SPORT [mur] fronton ▪ [court] pelota court.

frottement [frɔtmɑ̃] *nm* **1.** [friction] rubbing *(U)*, friction **2.** [bruit] rubbing *ou* scraping noise **3.** MÉD friction murmur ▪ **~ pleural** pleural rub.
◆ **frottements** *nmpl* [mésentente] dispute, disagreement ▪ **il y a des ~s entre eux** there is some friction between them.

frotter [3] [frɔte] <> *vt* **1.** [pour nettoyer] to rub, to scrub ▪ **~ une tache avec une brosse/avec du savon** to scrub a stain with a brush/with soap ▪ **~ une casserole** to scour a saucepan **2.** [pour enduire] to rub **3.** [mettre en contact] : **~ deux pierres l'une contre l'autre** to rub *ou* to scrape two stones together ▪ **~ une allumette** to strike a match **4.** [frictionner] to rub ▪ **~ le dos de qqn** to give sb's back a rub, to rub sb's back.
<> *vi* to scrape, to rub ▪ **il y a quelque chose qui frotte sous la voiture** there's something under the car making a scraping noise ▪ **le frein de mon vélo frotte** the brakes on my bike keep sticking.
◆ **se frotter** *vp (emploi réfléchi)* [se frictionner] to rub o.s. (down) ▪ **se ~ les yeux** to rub one's eyes ◐ **se ~ les mains** *pr* to rub one's hands (together) ; *fig* to rub one's hands.
◆ **se frotter à** *vp+prép* **1.** [effleurer] : **se ~ à** *ou* **contre** to rub (up) against ▪ **ne te frotte pas à lui quand il est en colère** *fig* steer clear of him when he's angry ◐ **s'y ~ : ne vous y frottez pas, c'est trop dangereux** don't interfere *ou* meddle, it's too dangerous ▪ **qui s'y frotte s'y pique** if you meddle you'll get your fingers burnt **2.** [se confronter à] to face **3.** [fréquenter] to rub shoulders with.

frottis [frɔti] *nm* **1.** MÉD smear ▪ **~ vaginal** cervical smear (test) ▪ **se faire faire un ~ (vaginal)** to have a smear test *ou* a cervical smear **2.** ART scumbling.

frottoir [frɔtwar] *nm* rough strip *(on a box of matches).*

froufrou, frou-frou [frufru] (*pl* **frous-frous**) *nm* [bruit] swish, rustle, froufrou.
◆ **froufrous, frous-frous** *nmpl* [vêtement] frills (and furbelows).

froufroutant, e [frufrutɑ̃, ɑ̃t] *adj* **1.** [bruissant] rustling, swishing **2.** [à volants - robe, jupe] frilly, flouncy.

froufroutement [frufrutmɑ̃] *nm* rustle, swish.

froufrouter [3] [frufrute] *vi* to rustle, to swish.

froussard, e [frusar, ard] *fam* <> *adj* cowardly, chicken, yellow-bellied.
<> *nm, f* coward, chicken, yellow-belly.

frousse [frus] *nf fam* fright ▪ **avoir la ~** to be scared ▪ **donner** *ou* **flanquer la ~ à qqn** to put the wind up *UK ou* to scare sb, to give sb the willies.

fructidor [fryktidɔr] *nm 12th month in the French Revolutionary calendar (from August 18/19 to September 17/18).*

fructifier [9] [fryktifje] *vi* **1.** AGRIC to be productive ■ BOT to bear fruit, to fructify *sout* **2.** ÉCON to yield a profit ■ **faire ~ son capital** to make one's capital yield a profit **3.** [produire des résultats] to bear fruit, to be productive *ou* fruitful.

fructose [fryktoz] *nm* fructose, fruit sugar.

fructueux, euse [fryktɥø, øz] *adj* **1.** [fécond] fruitful, productive ■ **vos recherches ont-elles été fructueuses?** were your investigations fruitful *ou* successful? **2.** [profitable] profitable.

frugal, e, aux [frygal, o] *adj* **1.** [simple] frugal **2.** [qui mange peu] frugal.

frugalement [frygalmɑ̃] *adv* frugally.

frugalité [frygalite] *nf* frugality.

fruit [frɥi] *nm* **1.** BOT : **un ~ : après ton fromage, veux-tu un ~?** would you like some fruit *ou* a piece of fruit after your cheese? ■ **des ~s** fruit ■ **manger des ~s** to eat fruit ■ **la tomate est un ~** the tomato is a (type of) fruit ➲ **~s des bois** fruits of the forest ■ **~ défendu** forbidden fruit ■ **~ de la passion** passion fruit ■ **un ~ sec** *pr* a piece of dried fruit ; *fig* a failure ■ **un ~ vert** *fig* an immature young girl ■ **~s confits** candied *ou* crystallized fruit ■ **~s déguisés** *prunes, dates etc, stuffed with almond paste* ■ **~s jumeaux** double fruits ■ **c'est au ~ qu'on connaît l'arbre** *prov* the tree is known by its fruit **2.** CULIN : **~s de mer** seafood **3.** [résultat] fruit ■ **le ~ de son travail** the fruit *ou* result of his labours ■ **le ~ de ses entrailles** *litt* the fruit of her womb ■ **cela a porté ses ~s** it bore fruit ■ **les ~s de la Terre** the fruits *ou* bounty of the Earth ■ **avec ~** *litt* fruitfully, profitably **4.** CONSTR batter.

fruité, e [frɥite] *adj* fruity ■ **ce vin est très ~** this wine is very fruity.

fruitier, ère [frɥitje, ɛr] ◇ *adj* fruit *(modif).*
◇ *nm, f* fruiterer, greengrocer *UK*, fruit seller *US*.
◆ **fruitier** *nm* **1.** [verger] orchard **2.** [arbre] fruit tree **3.** [local] storeroom (for fruit).
◆ **fruitière** *nf* cooperative cheese dairy.

frusques [frysk] *nfpl fam* togs, gear ■ **prends tes ~ et file!** take your things *ou* gear and get out!

fruste [fryst] *adj* **1.** [grossier - personne] uncouth, rough **2.** [sans élégance - style] unpolished, crude, rough **3.** MÉD mild.

frustrant, e [frystrɑ̃, ɑ̃t] *adj* frustrating.

frustration [frystrasjɔ̃] *nf* frustration.

frustré, e [frystre] ◇ *adj* frustrated.
◇ *nm, f* frustrated person ■ **'les Frustrés'** *cartoon characters created by Claire Bretécher in the late 70's & 80's, representing modern middle-class intellectuals.*

frustrer [3] [frystre] *vt* **1.** [décevoir] to frustrate, to thwart **2.** [priver] : **~ qqn de** to rob sb of **3.** PSYCHOL to frustrate **4.** DR : **~ qqn de** to defraud sb of.

FS (*abr de* **franc suisse**) SFr.

FTP (*abr de* **Francs-tireurs et partisans**) *nmpl Communist resistance during World War II.*

fuchsia [fyʃja] *nm* fuchsia.

fucus [fykys] *nm* wrack, fucus *spéc* ■ **~ vésiculeux** bladderwrack.

fuel [fjul], **fuel-oil** [fjulɔjl] (*pl* **fuel-oils**) *nm* (fuel *ou* heating) oil ■ **~ domestique** domestic heating oil.

fufute [fyfyt] *adj fam* bright, smart ■ **il n'est pas très ~** he's a bit thick, he's not very bright.

fugace [fygas] *adj* [beauté] transient, evanescent, ephemeral ■ [impression, souvenir, pensée] transient, fleeting.

fugacité [fygasite] *nf* transience, fleetingness.

fugitif, ive [fyʒitif, iv] ◇ *adj* **1.** [en fuite] runaway, fugitive **2.** [fugace - vision, idée] fleeting, transient ; [- bonheur] short-lived ; [- souvenir] elusive.
◇ *nm, f* runaway, fugitive.

fugue [fyg] *nf* **1.** MUS fugue **2.** [fuite] : **faire une ~** [de chez soi] to run away from home ; [d'une pension] to run away from boarding school ; [pour se marier] to elope.

fugué, e [fyge] *adj* fugato.

fuguer [1] [fyge] *vi* to run away, to do a bunk *UK*.

fugueur, euse [fygœr, øz] ◇ *adj* : **c'était un enfant ~** as a child, he used to run away repeatedly.
◇ *nm, f* runaway.

Führer [fyrœr] *npr m* : **le ~** the Führer.

fuir [35] [fɥir] ◇ *vi* **1.** [s'enfuir] to run away, to flee ■ **faire ~ qqn** to frighten sb away, to put sb to flight ■ **~ à toutes jambes** to run for dear *ou* one's life ■ **~ devant le danger** to flee in the face of danger **2.** [s'éloigner] to vanish, to recede ■ **des lignes qui fuient vers l'horizon** lines that converge towards the horizon ■ **le paysage fuyait par la vitre du train** the landscape flashed past the window of the train **3.** *litt* [passer] to fly, to slip away **4.** [se dérober] to run away ■ **~ devant ses responsabilités** to shirk *ou* to evade one's responsibilities **5.** [se répandre - eau] to leak ; [- gaz] to leak, to escape **6.** [perdre son contenu - tonneau, stylo] to leak, to be leaky.
◇ *vt* **1.** [abandonner] to flee (from) ■ **elle a fui le pays** she fled the country **2.** [éviter] to avoid, to shun ■ **~ les gens** to avoid contact with other people ■ **~ le regard de qqn** to avoid looking sb in the eye ■ **~ le danger** to keep away from *ou* to avoid danger **3.** [se soustraire à, s'éloigner de] to shirk, to evade ■ **~ la tentation** to flee from *ou* to avoid temptation **4.** [résister à] to elude ■ **le sommeil le fuyait** he couldn't sleep, sleep would not come to him.

fuite [fɥit] *nf* **1.** [départ] escape, flight ■ **prendre la ~** [prisonnier] to run away, to (make one's) escape ■ **être en ~** to be on the run ■ **mettre qqn/un animal en ~** to put sb/an animal to flight ➲ **~ en avant : l'action du gouvernement est considérée par certains comme une ~ en avant** some people accuse the government of rushing ahead without properly adressing the problem ■ **la ~ des cerveaux** the brain drain **2.** FIN : **~ de capitaux** flight of capital (abroad) ■ **~ devant l'impôt** tax evasion **3.** [écoulement - de liquide] leak, leakage ; [- de gaz] leak ; [- de courant] escape **4.** [d'un pneu] puncture ■ [d'une canalisation, d'un récipient] leak **5.** [indiscrétion] leak **6.** ART : **point de ~** vanishing point.

Fuji-Yama [fuʒijama] *npr m* : **le (mont) ~** the Fujiyama, Mount Fuji.

fulgurance [fylgyrɑ̃s] *nf litt* piercing *ou* blinding quality.

fulgurant, e [fylgyrɑ̃, ɑ̃t] *adj* **1.** [rapide - réponse] lightning *(modif)* ; [- idée] sudden ; [- carrière] dazzling ■ **j'ai eu une idée ~e** an idea flashed *ou* shot through my mind **2.** [intense - douleur] shooting, fulgurating *spéc* ; [- lumière] blinding, dazzling, fulgurant *sout* **3.** *litt* [éclatant - éclair] flashing ; [- regard] blazing, flashing ; [- beauté] dazzling.

fulguration [fylgyrasjɔ̃] *nf* **1.** MÉTÉOR heat lightning **2.** MÉD fulguration.

fuligineux, euse [fyliʒinø, øz] *adj* **1.** [qui produit de la suie] fuliginous *spéc*, sooty, smoky **2.** *fig & litt* fuliginous.

full [ful] *nm* JEUX full house.

fulminant, e [fylminɑ̃, ɑ̃t] *adj* **1.** *litt* [menaçant - regard] furious, enraged, irate ; [- lettre] venomous, vituperative *sout* **2.** CHIM fulminating.

fulminer [3] [fylmine] ◇ *vi litt* to fulminate, to rail ■ **~ contre le gouvernement** to fulminate *ou* to rail against the government.
◇ *vt* **1.** *litt* [proférer] to thunder, to roar, to utter **2.** RELIG to fulminate.

fumage [fymaʒ] *nm* **1.** CULIN smoking, curing **2.** AGRIC manuring, dunging.

fumant, e [fymɑ̃, ɑ̃t] *adj* **1.** [cheminée, feu] smoking, smoky ■ [cendres, décombres] smouldering **2.** [liquide, nourriture] steaming **3.** [furieux] fuming ▪ **être ~ de colère** to flare up with anger **4.** *fam* [remarquable] brilliant ▪ **un coup ~** a master-stroke **5.** CHIM fuming.

fumé, e [fyme] *adj* smoked.
◆ **fumé** *nm* [aliment] smoked food ▪ **évitez de consommer du ~** avoid smoked foods.

fume-cigare [fymsigar] *nm inv* cigar holder.

fume-cigarette [fymsigarɛt] *nm inv* cigarette holder.

fumée [fyme] *nf* **1.** [de combustion] smoke ▪ **partir** *ou* **s'en aller en ~** to go up in smoke ▪ **il n'y a pas de ~ sans feu** *prov* there's no smoke without fire **2.** [vapeur] steam.
◆ **fumées** *nfpl litt* stupor.

fumer [3] [fyme] ◇ *vt* **1.** [tabac] to smoke ▪ **~ la pipe** to smoke a pipe ▪ **~ cigarette sur cigarette** to chain-smoke ▶ **~ comme un pompier** *ou* **un sapeur** to smoke like a chimney **2.** CULIN to smoke **3.** AGRIC to manure, to dung, to fatten.
◇ *vi* **1.** [feu, cheminée] to smoke, to give off smoke ▪ [cendres, décombres] to smoke, to smoulder **2.** [liquide, nourriture] to steam, to give off steam ▪ **on voyait ~ les flancs des chevaux** you could see the steam coming *ou* rising off the horses' flanks **3.** CHIM to fume, to give off fumes **4.** *fam* [être furieux] to fume, to be mad US.

fumerie [fymri] *nf* opium den.

fumerolle [fymrɔl] *nf* fumarole.

fumet [fymɛ] *nm* **1.** [odeur - d'un plat] (pleasant) smell, aroma ; [- d'un vin] bouquet **2.** CULIN stock, fumet **3.** CHASSE scent.

fumette [fymɛt] *nf fam* smoking marijuana ▪ **se faire une ~** to get stored.

fumeur, euse [fymœr, øz] *nm, f* **1.** [adepte du tabac] smoker ▪ **un gros ~** a heavy smoker ▶ **compartiment ~s** smoking compartment *ou* car US **2.** INDUST curer.

fumeux, euse [fymø, øz] *adj* **1.** [confus] hazy ▪ **idée fumeuse** vague *ou* nebulous idea ▪ **il a l'esprit ~** his ideas are a bit woolly, he's woolly-minded **2.** [bougie, lampe] smoky.

fumier [fymje] *nm* **1.** AGRIC manure **2.**△ [personne] bastard△.

fumigateur [fymigatœr] *nm* **1.** AGRIC fumigator **2.** MÉD inhaler.

fumigation [fymigasjɔ̃] *nf* **1.** [pour un local] fumigation ▪ **faire des ~s de désinfectant** to fumigate with disinfectant **2.** AGRIC & MÉD fumigation.

fumigène [fymiʒɛn] ◇ *adj* smoke *(modif)*.
◇ *nm* smoke generator.

fumiste [fymist] ◇ *nm* **1.** [installateur] heating specialist **2.** [ramoneur] chimney sweep.
◇ *adj péj* lackadaisical.
◇ *nmf péj* shirker ▪ **c'est un ~** he doesn't exactly kill himself working.

fumisterie [fymistəri] *nf* **1.** *fam péj* humbug, sham, farce ▪ **une vaste ~** an absolute farce **2.** [métier - d'installateur] boiler installation *ou* fitting ; [- de ramoneur] chimney sweeping.

fumoir [fymwar] *nm* **1.** [pour fumeurs] smoking room, smoke room UK **2.** [pour aliments] smokehouse.

fumure [fymyr] *nf* **1.** [engrais] manure, fertilizer **2.** [fertilisation] manuring, fertilizing.

funambule [fynɑ̃byl] *nmf* tightrope walker, funambulist *sout*.

funboard [fœnbɔrd] *nm* funboard.

funèbre [fynɛbr] *adj* **1.** [relatif aux funérailles] funeral *(modif)* ▪ **cérémonie ~** funeral service ▪ **chant ~** dirge ▪ **veillée ~** death-watch, wake **2.** [lugubre] gloomy, lugubrious, funereal.

funérailles [fyneraj] *nfpl* funeral.

funéraire [fynerɛr] *adj* funeral *(modif)*, funerary *spéc* ▪ **urne/chambre ~** funerary urn/chamber.

funérarium [fynerarjɔm] *nm* funeral parlour, funeral home US.

funeste [fynɛst] *adj* **1.** [désastreux] disastrous, catastrophic ▪ **le jour ~ où je l'ai rencontré** that fateful *ou* ill-fated day when I met him ▪ **l'ignorance est souvent ~** ignorance is often dangerous *ou* harmful ▪ **suites ~s** tragic *ou* disastrous *ou* dire consequences ▪ **être ~ à qqn** to have terrible consequences for sb **2.** *litt* [triste] lugubrious ▪ **un récit ~** a sad tale **3.** *litt* [mortel] fatal, lethal.

funiculaire [fynikylɛr] ◇ *adj* funicular.
◇ *nm* funicular (railway).

funk [fœnk] *nm* : **le ~** funk.

funky [fœ̃nki] *nm* jazz funk.

furax [fyraks] *adj inv fam* livid, hopping mad.

furet [fyrɛ] *nm* **1.** ZOOL ferret ▪ **aller à la chasse au ~** to go ferreting **2.** JEUX pass the slipper.

fur et à mesure [fyreamzyr] ◆ **au fur et à mesure** *loc adv* gradually ▪ **donnez-les moi au ~** give them to me gradually *ou* as we go along ▪ **il s'adaptera au ~** he'll get used to it in time ▪ **je préfère faire mon travail au ~ plutôt que de le laisser s'accumuler** I prefer to do my work as and when it comes rather than letting it pile up.
◆ **au fur et à mesure de** *loc prép* as ▪ **au ~ de l'avance des travaux** as work proceeds ▪ **au ~ des besoins** as needed ▪ **je vous les enverrai au ~ de leur disponibilité** I'll send them to you as and when they are available.
◆ **au fur et à mesure que** *loc conj* as ▪ **l'eau s'écoule au ~ que je remplis l'évier** the water drains away as (soon as) I fill up the sink.

fureter [28] [fyrte] *vi* **1.** [fouiller] to ferret (around *ou* about), to snoop (around *ou* about) ▪ **les journalistes ont fureté dans mon passé** journalists pried into my past **2.** CHASSE to ferret.

fureteur, euse [fyrtœr, øz] *péj* ◇ *adj* prying.
◇ *nm, f* [indiscret] snooper.

fureur [fyrœr] *nf* **1.** [colère] rage, fury ▪ **accès de ~** fit of anger *ou* rage ▪ **~ noire** blind anger *ou* rage ▪ **se mettre dans une ~ noire** to fly into a rage **2.** [passion] passion ▪ **la ~ du jeu** a mania *ou* passion for gambling ▪ **la ~ de vivre** a lust for life ▶ **faire ~** to be all the rage **3.** *litt* [violence] rage, fury, wrath *litt*.
◆ **avec fureur** *loc adv* **1.** [colériquement] furiously **2.** [passionnément] passionately.
◆ **en fureur** ◇ *loc adj* furious, enraged.
◇ *loc adv* : **entrer en ~** to fly into a rage *ou* fury ▪ **mettre qqn en ~** to send sb wild with rage, to enrage sb.

furibard, e [fyribar, ard] *adj fam* hopping mad, livid.

furibond, e [fyribɔ̃, ɔ̃d] *adj* furious ▪ **être ~ contre qqn** to be furious with sb.

furie [fyri] *nf* **1.** [colère] fury, rage **2.** [mégère] fury ▪ **elle s'est jetée sur lui comme une ~** she flew at him like a fury **3.** MYTHOL : **Furie** Fury.
◆ **avec furie** *loc adv* **1.** [avec colère] furiously, angrily **2.** [ardemment] ardently, passionately, furiously ▪ **elle écrivait avec ~** she wrote furiously **3.** [violemment] furiously, wildly, savagely.
◆ **en furie** *loc adj* furious, enraged ▪ **les éléments en ~** *litt* the raging elements.

furieusement [fyrjøzmɑ̃] *adv* **1.** [avec colère] furiously, angrily **2.** [violemment] furiously, wildly, savagely **3.** [extrêmement] hugely, tremendously, extremely ▪ **avoir ~ envie de** to have a tremendous urge to.

furieux, euse [fyrjø, øz] ◇ *adj* **1.** [enragé - personne] furious, (very) angry ; [- geste, cri] furious ▪ **cela me rend ~** it makes me furious ▪ **d'un air ~** looking like thunder ▪ **être ~ contre qqn** to be furious with sb ▪ **~ de : être ~ de son échec** to be enraged *ou* infuriated at one's failure ▪ **il est ~ d'avoir attendu** he's furious at having been kept waiting **2.** *litt* [violent] raging, wild **3.** *litt* [passionné] furious **4.** [extrême] tremendous ▪ **avoir une furieuse envie de dormir** to have an overwhelming desire to go to sleep.

◇ *nm, f* madman (*f* madwoman), maniac.

furoncle [fyrɔ̃kl] *nm* boil, furuncle *spéc.*

furonculose [fyrɔ̃kyloz] *nf* furunculosis.

furtif, ive [fyrtif, iv] *adj* **1.** [comportement] furtive ▪ [geste, action] furtive, surreptitious, stealthy ▪ [regard] furtive, sly ▪ [sourire] quiet, secret ▪ [larme] hidden **2.** MIL anti-radar.

furtivement [fyrtivmɑ̃] *adv* stealthily, surreptitiously, furtively.

fusain [fyzɛ̃] *nm* **1.** BOT spindle (tree) **2.** ART [crayon] piece of charcoal ▪ [dessin] charcoal.
◆ **au fusain** ◇ *loc adj* charcoal *(modif).*
◇ *loc adv* [dessiner, illustrer] in charcoal.

fuseau, x [fyzo] *nm* **1.** [bobine] spindle ▪ **dentelle/ouvrage aux ~x** bobbin lace/needlework **2.** [vêtement] stirrup pants **3.** GÉOM lune.
◆ **en fuseau** ◇ *loc adj* tapered, spindle-shaped.
◇ *loc adv* : **tailler qqch en ~** to taper sthg.
◆ **fuseau horaire** *nm* time zone ▪ **changer de ~ horaire** to go into a different time zone.

fusée [fyze] *nf* **1.** ASTRONAUT rocket ▪ **~ à étages multiples** multiple-stage rocket ▪ **~ orbitale** orbital rocket ▪ **partir comme une ~** to be off like a shot, to shoot off **2.** [signal] rocket ▪ **~ de détresse** flare ▪ **~ éclairante** flare ▪ **~ de signalisation** signal (sky) rocket **3.** ARM rocket, missile ▪ **~ antiengin** antimissile missile ▪ [détonateur] fuse **4.** MÉD sinus *(of boil)* **5.** [de roue] stub axle **6.** HÉRALD fusil.

fuselage [fyzlaʒ] *nm* fuselage.

fuselé, e [fyzle] *adj* [doigt] slender, tapered, tapering ▪ [jambe] slender ▪ [muscle] well-shaped ▪ [colonne] tapered, tapering, spindle-shaped.

fuseler [24] [fyzle] *vt* **1.** [former en fuseau] to taper **2.** AÉRON, AUTO & NAUT to streamline.

fuser [3] [fyze] *vi* **1.** [jaillir - vapeur] to gush *ou* to spurt (out) ; [- liquide] to jet *ou* to gush *ou* to spurt (out) ; [- lumière] to stream out ; [- étincelle] to fly ▪ **un projectile a fusé dans l'espace** a missile shot through the air **2.** [retentir - rire, voix] to burst out **3.** [bougie] to melt ▪ [poudre] to burn slowly ▪ [sels] to crackle.

fusible [fyzibl] ◇ *adj* **1.** [qui peut fondre] fusible, meltable **2.** [à point de fusion bas] fusible.
◇ *nm* fuse ▪ **un ~ a grillé** a fuse blew ▪ **où sont les ~s?** where is the fuse box? ➊ **~ à cartouche** cartridge fuse.

fusil [fyzi] *nm* **1.** ARM gun, rifle ▪ **~ automatique/semi-automatique** automatic/semiautomatic rifle ▪ **~ à canon scié** sawn-off shotgun ▪ **~ de chasse** shotgun ▪ **~ à deux coups** double-barrelled gun ▪ **~ à lunette** rifle with telescopic sight ▪ **~ à répétition** repeating rifle ▪ **~ sous-marin** speargun **2.** [tireur] : **un bon ~** a good shot **3.** [affiloir] : **~ (à aiguiser)** steel.

fusilier [fyzilje] *nm* rifleman, fusilier *UK* ▪ **~ marin** marine.

fusillade [fyzijad] *nf* **1.** [bruit] shooting *(U)*, gunfire ▪ **j'ai entendu une ~** I heard a volley of shots **2.** [combat] gunfight, gun battle **3.** [exécution] shooting.

fusiller [3] [fyzije] *vt* [exécuter] to shoot ▪ **~ qqn du regard** to look daggers *ou* to glare at sb.

fusil-mitrailleur [fyzimitrajœr] (*pl* **fusils-mitrailleurs**) *nm* light machine gun.

fusion [fyzjɔ̃] *nf* **1.** MÉTALL fusion, melting **2.** MIN smelting **3.** [dissolution - du sucre, de la glace] melting **4.** NUCL : **~ (nucléaire)** fusion ▪ **~ du cœur** nuclear meltdown **5.** [union - d'idées, de sentiments] fusion ; [- de groupes] fusion, merging ; [- de peuples, de cultures] fusion, merging **6.** ÉCON merger, merging **7.** INFORM merge, merging.
◆ **en fusion** ◇ *loc adj* molten.
◇ *loc adv* : **mettre deux éléments en ~** to fuse two elements (together).

fusionnel, elle [fyʒjɔnɛl] *adj* [couple] inseparable, intense ▪ [relation] intense.

fusionnement [fyzjɔnmɑ̃] *nm* **1.** ÉCON amalgamation, merger **2.** [rassemblement - de groupes, de cultures] merging, fusion.

fusionner [3] [fyzjɔne] ◇ *vt* to merge.
◇ *vi* **1.** ÉCON to amalgamate, to merge **2.** INFORM to merge.

fusse *etc v* ▷ **être**.

fustiger [17] [fystiʒe] *vt litt* **1.** [battre] to thrash **2.** [critiquer - personne, attitude] to censure, to criticize harshly ; [- vice] to castigate *sout.*

fut *etc v* ▷ **être**.

fût [fy] *nm* **1.** [d'un arbre] bole **2.** [tonneau] cask **3.** [partie - d'une vis, d'un poteau] shaft ; [- d'une colonne] shaft, body **4.** [d'un canon] stock.

futaie [fytɛ] *nf* forest, (piece of) timberland *US* ▪ **haute** *ou* **vieille ~** established *ou* mature forest.

futaille [fytaj] *nf* cask, barrel.

futal [fytal], **fute** [fyt] *nm fam* trousers, pants *US.*

futé, e [fyte] ◇ *adj* sharp, smart, clever ▪ **il n'est pas très ~** he's not very bright.
◇ *nm, f* sharp person ▪ **hé, petit ~, comment tu l'enlèves maintenant?** hey, smarty-pants, now how are you going to get it off again?

futile [fytil] *adj* **1.** [frivole - raison] frivolous, trifling ; [- occupation, lecture, personne] frivolous **2.** [sans valeur - vie] pointless, futile ▪ **il serait ~ d'essayer** it would be futile *ou* pointless to attempt it.

futilité [fytilite] *nf* [caractère futile] triviality ▪ **il perd son temps à des ~s** he wastes his time in trivial pursuits ▪ **ils ne se racontaient que des ~s** their conversation consisted of nothing but trivialities.

futon [fytɔ̃] *nm* futon.

futur, e [fytyr] ◇ *adj* **1.** [à venir - difficulté, joie] future *(modif)* ▪ **les ~s emplois** the jobs to come ▪ **les générations ~es** future *ou* coming generations ▪ **la vie ~e** RELIG the afterlife **2.** *(avant le n)* **~e mère** mother-to-be ▪ **mon ~ époux** my future husband ▪ **un ~ client** a prospective client ▪ **un ~ mathématicien** a future *ou* budding mathematician.
◇ *nm, f hum* intended *hum*, husband-to-be (*f* wife-to-be).
◆ **futur** *nm* **1.** [avenir] : **le ~** the future ▪ **le ~ proche** the immediate future **2.** GRAMM future (tense) ▪ **~ antérieur** future perfect.

futurisme [fytyrism] *nm* futurism.

futuriste [fytyrist] ◇ *adj* **1.** [d'anticipation] futuristic **2.** ART & LITTÉR futurist.
◇ *nmf* futurist.

futurologie [fytyrɔlɔʒi] *nf* futurology.

futurologue [fytyrɔlɔg] *nmf* futurologist.

Futuroscope [fytyrɔskɔp] *npr m* : **le ~** *futuristic theme park near Poitiers.*

fuyait *etc v* ▷ **fuir**.

fuyant, e [fɥijɑ̃, ɑ̃t] *adj* **1.** [insaisissable - caractère] elusive ; [- regard] shifty, elusive **2.** [menton, front] receding ▪ **un homme au menton ~** a weak-chinned man **3.** ART vanishing ▪ **ligne ~e** converging line **4.** *litt* [fugitif] fleeting, transient.

fuyard, e [fɥijar, ard] *nm, f* runaway, fugitive.
◆ **fuyard** *nm* MIL retreating soldier.

G

g, G [ʒe] *nm* **1.** [lettre] g, G ■ **G majuscule** capital G ■ **g minuscule** small g ■ **ça commence par un g** it begins with g ■ **G comme Georges** G for George ■ **ça s'écrit avec deux g** it's spelt with a double g *ou* two g's **2.** (*abr écrite de* **gramme**) g **3.** (*abr écrite de* **gauss**) G **4.** (*abr écrite de* **giga**) G **5.** PHYS [accélération de l'appesanteur] g **6.** PSYCHOL : **facteur g** g factor.

g. (*abr écrite de* **gauche**) L, l.

G7 *npr m* : **le ~** G7 *(the seven most industrialised countries)*.

gabardine [gabardin] *nf* **1.** [tissu] gabardine, gaberdine **2.** [vêtement] gabardine (coat).

gabarit [gabari] *nm* **1.** [dimension] size ➊ **'hors ~'** 'heavy vehicles' **2.** *fam* [carrure] size, build ■ **c'est un tout petit ~** he/she is very slightly built ; [stature] he's a bit on the short side **3.** *fam fig* calibre ■ **elle a/n'a pas le ~** she is/isn't up to it ■ **ils sont bien du même ~** it's six of one and half a dozen of the other **4.** TECHNOL [pour mesure] gauge ■ [maquette] template ■ **~ de mise en page** IMPR (filmsetting) grid.

gabegie [gabʒi] *nf* : **la ~ administrative** bureaucratic waste.

Gabon [gabɔ̃] *npr m* : **le ~** Gabon ■ **au ~** in Gabon.

gabonais, e [gabɔnɛ, ɛz] *adj* Gabonese.
◆ **Gabonais, e** *nm, f* Gabonese ■ **les Gabonais** the Gabonese.

gâche [gaʃ] *nf* **1.** [de maçon] trowel **2.** [de verrou] keeper, strike ■ [de crémone] (espagnolette) plate ■ **~ automatique** remote control lock.

gâcher [3] [gaʃe] *vt* **1.** [gaspiller - argent, talent, temps] to waste **2.** [abîmer] to spoil, to ruin ■ **ne va pas me ~ le plaisir** *fam* don't go spoiling *ou* ruining it for me ■ **~ le métier** to spoil it for the others *(by undercutting prices or working for lower wages)* **3.** CONSTR [plâtre, ciment] to mix.

gâchette [gaʃɛt] *nf* [d'arme à feu] trigger ■ **appuyez sur la ~** pull the trigger ■ **avoir la ~ facile/rapide** to be trigger-happy/quick on the draw.

gâcheur, euse [gaʃœr, øz] ◇ *adj* wasteful.
◇ *nm, f* [gaspilleur] wasteful person, wastrel *sout* ■ [bâcleur] bungler, botcher.
◆ **gâcheur** *nm* CONSTR plasterer's mate *UK*, plasterer's helper *US*.

gâchis [gaʃi] *nm* **1.** [gaspillage] waste ■ **sa vie est un véritable ~** her life has been completely wasted **2.** [désordre] mess ■ **faire du ~** to make a mess ■ **~ politique** political muddle.

gadget [gadʒɛt] *nm* **1.** [appareil] gadget **2.** [idée, projet] gimmick **3.** *(comme adj; avec ou sans trait d'union)* **une mesure ~** a gimmicky measure ■ **une réforme ~** a token reform.

gadgétisé, e [gadʒetize] *adj* gadgety.

gadin△ [gadɛ̃] *nm* : **prendre** *ou* **ramasser un ~** to come a cropper *UK*, to fall flat on one's face.

gadoue [gadu] *nf fam* [boue] mud, muck.

gaélique [gaelik] ◇ *adj* Gaelic.
◇ *nm* LING Gaelic ■ **~ d'Écosse** Scots Gaelic ■ **~ d'Irlande** Irish.

gaffe [gaf] *nf* **1.** *fam* [bêtise - en paroles] gaffe ; [- en actions] blunder, boob *UK*, goof *US* ■ **tu as fait une ~ en le lui racontant** you put your foot in it *ou* you dropped a clanger *UK ou* you goofed *US* when you told her that **2.** *fam loc* **faire ~** [faire attention] to be careful **3.** NAUT boat-hook, hook **4.** PÊCHE gaff.

gaffer [3] [gafe] ◇ *vi fam* [en parlant] to drop a clanger *UK*, to make a gaffe ■ [en agissant] to put one's foot in it, to boob *UK*, to goof *US*.
◇ *vt* PÊCHE to gaff.

gaffeur, euse [gafœr, øz] *nm, f* blunderer ■ **c'est une gaffeuse née** she's always putting her foot in it.

gag [gag] *nm* gag, joke ■ **du coup j'ai laissé mes clefs à l'intérieur, c'est le ~!** now I've gone and locked myself out, what a farce this is! ➊ **~ à répétition** CINÉ running gag.

gaga [gaga] *fam* ◇ *adj* senile, gaga.
◇ *nmf* : **quel vieux ~!** what a doddering old fool!

gage [gaʒ] *nm* **1.** [caution] security, collateral *(U)* ■ [au mont-de-piété] pledge ■ **laisser qqch en ~** to leave sthg as security ■ **mettre qqch en ~** to pawn *ou US* to hock sthg **2.** *fig* [garantie] guarantee ■ **sa compétence sera le ~ d'une bonne gestion** his competence will guarantee *ou* secure good management **3.** [témoignage] proof, token ■ **en ~ de** as proof of ■ **en ~ de mon amour** as proof *ou* a pledge of my love ■ **en ~ de ma bonne volonté** as a token of my goodwill ■ **son premier film est le ~ d'un grand talent** his first film gives proof *ou* shows evidence of great talent **4.** JEUX forfeit.
◆ **gages** *nmpl vieilli* [salaire] wages, pay ■ **être aux ~s de qqn** to be in sb's employ (as a servant).

gagé, e [gaʒe] *adj* **1.** [objet] pledged, pawned **2.** [emprunt] secured ■ **~ sur l'or** backed by gold.

gager [17] [gaʒe] *vt* **1.** FIN [emprunt] to secure, to guarantee **2.** *litt* [parier] to wager ■ **gageons qu'il l'épousera** I wager he'll marry her.

gageure [gaʒyr] *nf sout* challenge ■ **pour le gouvernement, c'est une ~** the government is attempting the impossible ■ **soutenir la ~** to take up the challenge.

gagnant, e [gaɲɑ̃, ɑ̃t] ◇ *adj* [ticket, coupon] winning *(avant n)* ■ **il est donné ~** he is favourite *ou* has been tipped to win ■ **il fallait jouer Fleur de Lys ~** you should have backed Fleur

de Lys to win ■ **coup ~** TENNIS winner *(shot)* ■ **partir ~** *fig* **: elle part ~e** all the odds are in her favour ■ **jouer ~** *fig* to hold all the trump cards.
◇ *nm, f* winner ■ **c'est toi le grand ~ de l'histoire** you've come out on top, you've got the best of the bargain.

gagne [gaɲ] *nf fam* SPORT winning edge.

gagne-pain [gaɲpɛ̃] *nm inv* livelihood ■ **c'est mon seul ~** it's my only means of existence.

gagne-petit [gaɲpəti] *nmf* **1.** [qui gagne peu] : **les ~** the low-paid ■ **ce sont des ~** they work for a pittance **2.** *péj* [qui manque d'ambition] small-time operator, small-timer.

gagner [3] [gaɲe] ◇ *vt* **1.** [partie, match, élection, prix] to win ■ **ce n'est pas gagné d'avance** it's a bit early to start talking about success ■ **c'est gagné!** *iron* now you've got what you asked for! ▶ **~ le gros lot** *pr & fig* to win *ou* to hit the jackpot ■ **à tous les coups l'on** *ou* **on gagne!** everyone's a winner! ■ **c'est un pari gagné d'avance** it's in the bag
2. [argent - comme rémunération] to earn, to make ; [- comme récompense] to earn ; [- dans une transaction] to make a profit of, to make ■ **~ gros** *fam* to earn *ou* to make big money ■ **~ une fortune à la loterie** to win a fortune on the lottery ■ **allez, prends, tu l'as bien gagné!** go on, take it, you've earned it! ▶ **~ des mille et des cents** to earn a fortune ■ **~ sa vie** *ou* **son pain** *ou* **son bifteck** *fam ou* **sa croûte** *fam* to earn a living *ou* one's daily bread ■ **eh bien, j'ai gagné ma journée!** *fam iron* I should have stayed in bed today!
3. [avantage] to gain ■ **il y a tout à ~ à faire cette démarche** there's everything to gain *ou* to be gained from making this move ■ **et si j'accepte, qu'est-ce que j'y gagne?** and if I accept, what do I get out of it? ■ **qu'est-ce que tu gagnes à tout changer?** what's the point of changing everything? ▶ **c'est toujours ça de gagné!** that's something, anyway!
4. [économiser] to save ■ **~ de la place** to save space ■ **en enlevant la porte on gagne 10 cm** if you take the door off you gain an extra 10 cm ■ **~ du temps** [en allant très vite] to save time ; [en atermoyant] to play for time
5. ÉCON to gain ■ **l'indice a gagné deux points** the index has gone up by *ou* has gained two points
6. [conquérir - ami] to win ; [- partisan] to win over *(sép)* ■ **~ l'amitié/l'appui de qqn** to win sb's friendship/support ■ **~ qqn à une cause** to win sb over (to a cause)
7. [suj: sentiment, sensation] to overcome ■ **je sentais la panique me ~** I could feel panic coming *ou* creeping over me ‖ [suj: épidémie, feu, nuages] to spread to ■ **s'ils se laissent ~ par le froid, ils sont perdus** if they allow the cold to take a grip of *ou* to get to them, they are finished ■ **j'ai fini par me laisser ~ par son enthousiasme** I ended up being infected by her enthusiasm ▶ **~ du terrain** *pr & fig* to gain ground
8. [rejoindre] to reach, to get to ■ **il gagna la sortie** he made his way to the exit ■ **le ferry gagna le port/le large** the ferry reached port/got out into the open sea.
◇ *vi* **1.** [l'emporter] to win ■ **on a gagné (par) 3 buts à 2** we won (by) 3 goals to 2, we won 3-2 ■ **~ aux courses** to win at the races ■ **~ aux échecs** to win at chess ■ **à ce petit jeu, ce n'est pas toi qui gagneras** you're not going to beat me at that little game
2. [avancer - incendie, érosion] to gain ground ■ **~ sur** to gain *ou* to advance on ■ **~ en** to increase *ou* to gain in ■ **~ en longueur** to increase in length, to grow longer ■ **notre production gagne en qualité** the quality of our product is improving.
◆ **gagner à** *v+prép* : **elle gagne à être connue** once you get to know her a bit she grows on you ■ **vin qui gagne à vieillir** wine for laying down *ou* which improves with age ■ **ils gagneraient à ce que nul ne l'apprenne** it would be to their advantage if nobody found out ▶ **accepte, tu y gagnes** *ou* **tu gagnes au change** say yes, it's to your advantage.
◆ **se gagner** ◇ *vp (emploi passif)* : **l'argent ne se gagne pas si facilement** it isn't so easy to make money.
◇ *vpt* to win, to earn ■ **se ~ un adepte** to win over a follower.

gagneur, euse [gaɲœr, øz] *nm, f* winner, go-getter.

gai, e [gɛ] ◇ *adj* **1.** [mine, décor, personnalité] cheerful, happy ■ [musique] cheerful, jolly ■ [couleur] bright, cheerful ■ **sa vie n'a pas toujours été très ~e** his life hasn't always been much fun *ou* a happy one ■ **cette couleur rend la pièce plus ~e** this colour makes the room look more cheerful ■ **il pleut encore, c'est ~!** *iron* great, it's raining again! ▶ **~ comme un pinson** happy as a lark *ou* a sandboy *UK* **2.** [un peu ivre] merry, tipsy **3.** [homosexuel] = **gay**.
◇ *nm, f* = **gay**.

gaiement [gemɑ̃] *adv* **1.** [avec joie] cheerfully, cheerily **2.** [avec enthousiasme] cheerfully, heartily ■ **allons-y ~** let's get on with it!

gaieté [gete] *nf* **1.** [bonne humeur] cheerfulness, gaiety ■ **elle a retrouvé sa ~** she's cheered up again ■ **tu n'es pas d'une ~ folle ce matin** you're not exactly a bundle of fun this morning ■ **un accès de ~** a burst of merriment **2.** [d'une couleur] brightness, gaiety.
◆ **de gaieté de cœur** *loc adv* willingly, gladly ■ **je ne l'ai pas fait de ~ de cœur!** it's not something I enjoyed doing!

gaillard, e [gajar, ard] ◇ *adj* **1.** [grivois] bawdy, lewd **2.** [vigoureux] lusty ■ **il est encore ~** he is still sprightly *ou* lively.
◇ *nm, f* [personne forte] : **c'est un sacré ~!** [homme viril] he's a lusty *ou* red-blooded fellow! ; [costaud] he's a great strapping lad! ■ **c'est une (rude) ~e** she's no shrinking violet ■ **c'est une grande ~e** she's a big strapping girl *ou* lass *UK*.
◆ **gaillard** *nm fam* [avec menace] : **toi mon ~, tu n'as pas intérêt à bouger!** you'd better not move, mate! *UK ou* buddy! *US* ‖ [avec amitié] : **c'est un ~ qui promet** he's a promising lad *UK ou* boy.
◆ **gaillarde** *nf* DANSE & MUS galliard.

gaillardement [gajardəmɑ̃] *adv* **1.** [gaiement] : **elle accepte/supporte tout ça ~** she accepts/bears it all cheerfully **2.** [vaillamment] valiantly, gamely ■ **on se mit en marche ~** we set off boldly *ou* in good spirits ■ **elle va ~ sur ses 70 ans** she'll soon be a sprightly 70.

gaîment [gemɑ̃] *arch* = **gaiement**.

gain [gɛ̃] *nm* **1.** [succès] winning ■ **~ de cause : elle a eu** *ou* **obtenu ~ de cause** [dans un procès] she won the case ; *fig* it was agreed that she was in the right **2.** [économie] saving ■ **cela permet un (énorme) ~ de place/temps** it saves (a lot of) space/time **3.** [progrès] benefit ■ **un ~ de 30 sièges aux élections** a gain of 30 seats in the elections **4.** [bénéfice financier] profit, gain ■ **faire des ~s importants à la Bourse** to make a big profit on the stock exchange ‖ [rémunération] earnings ■ **~s illicites** illicit earnings ■ **l'amour du ~** the love of gain.

gaine [gɛn] *nf* **1.** [étui - de poignard] sheath ; [- de parapluie] cover **2.** ANAT & BOT sheath **3.** ARM priming tube **4.** ART [piédestal] plinth **5.** CONSTR [conduit vertical] shaft, duct ■ [de climatisation] duct ■ **~ d'aération** *ou* **de ventilation** ventilation shaft ■ **~ d'ascenseur** lift shaft *UK*, elevator shaft *US* **6.** ÉLECTRON jacket **7.** NAUT tabling **8.** NUCL can **9.** [vêtement] girdle.

gaine-culotte [gɛnkylɔt] (*pl* **gaines-culottes**) *nf* panty girdle.

gainer [4] [gene] *vt* [câble] to sheathe, to encase ■ [cylindre, tuyau] to lag ■ **flacon gainé de cuir** leather-cased flask.

gaîté [gete] *arch* = **gaieté**.

gala [gala] *nm* gala ■ **~ de charité** charity gala.
◆ **de gala** *loc adj* gala *(modif)*.

galactique [galaktik] *adj* galactic.

galamment [galamɑ̃] *adv* gallantly ■ **que c'est ~ dit!** there speaks a *ou* spoken like a true gentleman!

galant, e [galɑ̃, ɑ̃t] *adj* **1.** [courtois] gallant, gentlemanly ■ **sois ~, porte-lui son paquet** be a gentleman and carry her parcel for her ■ **un ~ homme** *sout* an honourable man, a gentleman **2.** *litt* [amoureux] : **un rendez-vous ~** a date, a rendezvous, a lover's tryst *vieilli* ■ **en ~e compagnie** in the company of the opposite sex.
◆ **galant** *nm vieilli* suitor, admirer.

galanterie [galɑ̃tri] *nf* **1.** [courtoisie] courteousness, gallantry, chivalry ■ **la ~ se perd!** the age of chivalry is dead! **2.** [compliment] gallant remark, gallantry.

galantine [galɑ̃tin] *nf* galantine.

Galapagos [galapagos] *npr fpl* : **les (îles) ~** the Galapagos islands.

galapiat [galapja] *nm fam vieilli* [polisson] rapscallion *arch*, rascal ▪ [vaurien] good-for-nothing.

galaxie [galaksi] *nf* galaxy ▪ **la Galaxie** the Galaxy.

galbe [galb] *nm* curve ▪ **des jambes d'un ~ parfait** shapely legs.

galbé, e [galbe] *adj* **1.** [commode, poterie] curved, with a curved outline ▪ **les pieds ~s d'une commode** the curved legs of a chest of drawers **2.** [mollet - de femme] shapely ; [- de sportif] muscular.

gale [gal] *nf* **1.** MÉD scabies ▪ **mauvais** *ou* **méchant comme la ~** wicked as sin **2.** *fam* [personne odieuse] rat, nasty piece of work *UK* **3.** VÉTÉR [du chien, du chat] mange ▪ [du mouton] scab **4.** BOT scab.

galéjade [galeʒad] *nf* [dialecte] tall story.

galène [galɛn] *nf* galena, galenite.

galénique [galenik] *adj* galenical ▪ **médicament ~** galenical.

galère [galɛr] <> *nf* **1.** [navire] galley ▪ **condamné** *ou* **envoyé aux ~s** sent to the galleys **2.** *fam* [situation pénible] hassle ▪ **c'est la ~ pour obtenir des places de théâtre** it's a real hassle getting theatre tickets ▪ **mais qu'allais-tu faire dans cette ~?** ***Molière allus*** why on earth did you have to get mixed up in this? <> *adj fam* **: il est vraiment ~, ce mec** he's nothing but trouble ▪ **c'est un peu ~** it's a bit of a hassle.

galérer [18] [galere] *vi fam* [avoir du mal] **: on a galéré 2 heures dans la banlieue** we wasted two whole hours driving around the suburbs ▪ **j'ai galéré toute la journée pour m'inscrire** I've been running around (like mad) all day sorting out my enrolment ▪ **elle a vraiment galéré avant d'être connue** she had a hard time of it before she made it.

galerie [galri] *nf* **1.** [local - d'expositions, de ventes] (art) gallery, private gallery ▪ **~ d'art** *ou* **de peinture** *ou* **de tableaux** art gallery **2.** [salle d'apparat] hall, gallery ▪ **la ~ des Glaces** the Hall of Mirrors **3.** [passage couvert] gallery ▪ [arcade] arcade ▪ **~ marchande** *ou* **commerciale** shopping arcade *UK*, shopping mall *US* **4.** THÉÂTRE **: la ~** the gallery, the balcony ➊ **les deuxièmes ~s** [qui ne sont pas les plus hautes] the dress circle ; [les plus hautes] the upper circle ▪ **jouer pour la ~** to play to the gallery ▪ **tout ce qu'il fait, c'est pour la ~** everything he does is calculated to impress ▪ **amuser la ~** to play to show off *ou* is calculated to impress ▪ **amuser la ~** to play for laughs **5.** [souterrain - de taupe] tunnel ; [- de termites] gallery **6.** MIN gallery, level **7.** AUTO roof rack.

galérien [galerjɛ̃] *nm* galley slave ▪ **travailler comme un ~** to work like a (galley) slave *ou* a horse *ou* a Trojan.

galet [galɛ] *nm* **1.** [caillou] pebble ▪ **sur les ~s** on the shingle *ou* the pebble beach **2.** [roue] roller ▪ MÉCAN roller.

galette [galɛt] *nf* **1.** [crêpe - épaisse] pancake, griddle cake ; [- de froment, de sarrasin] pancake ▪ [pain azyme] matzo bread ▪ [biscuit] shortbread ▪ **~ de maïs** corn bread *(U)* ➊ **la ~ des Rois** *pastry traditionally eaten on Twelfth Night (in France)* **2.** △ [argent] dough *US*, dosh△ *UK* ▪ **elle a de la ~** she's rolling in it.

Galice [galis] *npr f* **: (la) ~** Galicia.

Galicie [galisi] *npr f* **: (la) ~** Galicia.

Galilée [galile] <> *npr f* GÉOGR **: (la) ~** Galilee. <> *npr* HIST Galileo.

galiléen, enne [galileɛ̃, ɛn] *adj* GÉOGR & SC Galilean.
◆ **Galiléen, enne** *nm, f* Galilean.
◆ **Galiléen** *nm* **: le Galiléen** the Galilean.

galimatias [galimatja] *nm* gibberish *(U)*, gobbledegook *(U)*, nonsense *(U)*.

galipette [galipɛt] *nf* forward roll, somersault ▪ **les enfants dévalaient la colline en faisant des ~s** the children were tearing down the hill doing somersaults.

Galles [gal] *npr* **: le pays de ~** Wales ▪ **au pays de ~** in Wales.

gallicisme [galisism] *nm* LING [calque du français] gallicism ▪ [emprunt au français] French idiom, gallicism.

Galliera [galjera] *npr* **: le palais ~** *palace housing the Paris museum of fashion and costume.*

gallinacé, e [galinase] *adj* ZOOL gallinaceous, gallinacean.
◆ **gallinacé** *nm* gallinacean ▪ **les ~s** the chicken family, the Gallinaceae *spéc.*

gallois, e [galwa, az] *adj* Welsh.
◆ **Gallois, e** *nm, f* Welshman (*f* Welshwoman) ▪ **les Gallois** the Welsh.
◆ **gallois** *nm* LING Welsh.

gallon [galɔ̃] *nm* gallon ▪ **un ~ aux 30 miles** 30 miles to the *ou* per gallon ➊ **le ~ américain** the US gallon ▪ **le ~ impérial** the imperial *ou* British gallon.

gallo-romain, e [galɔrɔmɛ̃, ɛn] (*mpl* **gallo-romains**, *fpl* **gallo-romaines**) *adj* Gallo-Roman.
◆ **Gallo-Romain, e** *nm, f* Gallo-Roman.

galoche [galɔʃ] *nf* **1.** [chaussure] wooden-soled shoe, clog *(with leather uppers)* **2.** NAUT snatch block.

galon [galɔ̃] *nm* **1.** TEXT [ruban] braid *(U)*, trimming *(U)* ▪ **un ~ doré** a piece of gold braid **2.** MIL [insigne] stripe ➊ **prendre du ~** to take a step up the ladder, to get a promotion.

galonné [galɔne] *nm fam arg mil* officer, brass hat *UK* ▪ **les ~s** the top brass.

galonner [3] [galɔne] *vt* to braid, to trim (with braid) ▪ **col galonné de velours** velvet-trimmed collar.

galop [galo] *nm* **1.** ÉQUIT gallop ▪ **prendre le ~** to break into a gallop ▪ **~ d'essai** *pr* warm-up gallop ; *fig* dry run **2.** DANSE galop.
◆ **au galop** *loc adv* at a gallop ▪ **mettre sa monture au ~** to put one's horse into a gallop ▪ **il a descendu la colline au ~** he galloped down the hill ➊ **va m'acheter le journal, et au ~!** go and buy me the newspaper, and be quick about it! ▪ **au triple ~** *fig* at top speed.

galopade [galɔpad] *nf* **1.** [course] (mad) rush ▪ **on est arrivés à l'heure, mais après quelle ~!** we got there on time, but it was a real scramble *ou* dash! **2.** ÉQUIT lope.

galopant, e [galɔpɑ̃, ɑ̃t] *adj* [consommation, inflation] galloping ▪ [urbanisation] uncontrolled, unplanned.

galoper [3] [galɔpe] *vi* **1.** ÉQUIT to gallop ▪ **il faudrait faire ~ un peu la jument** the mare needs a good gallop **2.** [aller trop vite - idées, images] to race ; [- enfants] to charge ▪ **ne galopez pas dans les escaliers!** don't charge up and down the stairs! ▪ **~ après qqn/qqch** *fam* to chase (around) after sb/sthg.

galopin [galɔpɛ̃] *nm fam* (street) urchin, scamp ▪ **espèce de petit ~!** you little devil!, you little brat!

galvanisation [galvanizasjɔ̃] *nf* **1.** MÉD galvanization **2.** MÉTALL galvanization.

galvaniser [3] [galvanize] *vt* **1.** MÉD to galvanize **2.** MÉTALL to electroplate, to galvanize, to zinc-plate **3.** [stimuler] to galvanize *ou* to spur into action ▪ **~ les foules** to whip up *ou* to provoke the crowds ▪ **ça l'a galvanisé** [après une catastrophe] it galvanized *ou* spurred him into action ; [après une bonne nouvelle] it lifted his spirits.

galvaudé, e [galvode] *adj* [mot] hackneyed, commonplace, clichéd ▪ [plaisanterie] corny.

galvauder [3] [galvode] *vt* **1.** [réputation] to sully, to tarnish **2.** [don, qualité] to prostitute **3.** [mot, sens] to debase ▪ **le mot a été galvaudé** the word has become clichéd *ou* hackneyed through overuse.
◆ **se galvauder** *vpi* to demean *ou* to lower o.s.

gamba [gɑ̃ba, gɑ̃mba, *(pl)* gɑ̃bas, gɑ̃mbas] *nf type of large Mediterranean prawn.*

gambade [gɑ̃bad] *nf* [cabriole] leap, caper ▪ **faire des ~s** [chien] to frisk about ; [enfant] to skip about.

gambader [3] [gɑ̃bade] *vi* to gambol, to leap *ou* to caper about ▪ **les enfants gambadaient de joie autour de l'arbre de Noël** the children were gleefully capering around the Christmas tree.

gamberge△ [gɑ̃bɛrʒ] *nf* : **il est en pleine ~** [il combine quelque chose] he's plotting something ; [il rêvasse] he's daydreaming.

gamberger [17] △ [gɑ̃bɛrʒe] ◇ *vi* [penser] to think ■ **ça m'a fait ~, cette histoire** this business really made me think.
◇ *vt* [combiner] : **je me demande ce qu'il gamberge** I wonder what he's up to.

gambette [gɑ̃bɛt] *nf fam* [jambe] leg, pin *UK*, gam *US* ■ **jouer** *OU* **tricoter des ~s** to go off like a shot, to leg it.

Gambie [gɑ̃bi] *npr f* **1.** [pays] : **(la) ~** the Gambia **2.** [fleuve] : **la ~, le fleuve ~** the Gambia (River).

gambien, enne [gɑ̃bjɛ̃, ɛn] *adj* Gambian.
◆ **Gambien, enne** *nm, f* Gambian.

gamelle [gamɛl] *nf* **1.** [récipient - d'un soldat] mess tin ; [- d'un ouvrier] lunch box *UK OU* pail *US* **2.** MIL & NAUT mess **3.** *fam* CINÉ spot, spotlight **4.** △ *loc* **ramasser** *OU* **prendre une ~** to fall flat on one's face, to come a cropper *UK*.

gamète [gamɛt] *nm* gamete.

gamin, e [gamɛ̃, in] ◇ *nm, f* kid.
◇ *adj* [puéril] childish ■ [espiègle] childlike, impish, playful.

gaminerie [gaminri] *nf* [acte] childish *OU* silly prank ■ [comportement] childishness, infantile behaviour ■ **ses ~s m'exaspéraient** his childish ways were driving me mad.

gamma [gama] *nm* gamma.

gamme [gam] *nf* **1.** MUS scale, gamut *spéc* ■ **faire ses ~s** *pr* to play one's scales ; *fig* to go through the basics, to learn the ropes **2.** [de produits] range ■ [de sentiments] gamut **3.** COMM : **bas/haut de ~ : produits bas/haut de ~** down-market/up-market products ■ **un téléviseur haut de ~** an up-market *OU* a top-of-the-range TV.

gammée [game] *adj f* ▷ **croix**.

ganache [ganaʃ] ◇ *nf* **1.** *péj* **une (vieille) ~** an old codger **2.** [du cheval] lower jaw, cheek.
◇ *adj* ▷ **fauteuil**.

Gand [gɑ̃] *npr* Ghent.

gandin [gɑ̃dɛ̃] *nm sout* [dandy] dandy, fop.

gang [gɑ̃g] *nm* gang.

Gange [gɑ̃ʒ] *npr m* : **le ~** the (River) Ganges.

ganglion [gɑ̃glijɔ̃] *nm* MÉD ganglion ■ **~ lymphatique** lymph gland.

ganglionnaire [gɑ̃glijɔnɛr] *adj* ganglionic, ganglial.

gangrène [gɑ̃grɛn] *nf* **1.** MÉD gangrene **2.** [corruption] scourge, canker ■ **la ~ du terrorisme** the scourge of terrorism.

gangrener [19] [gɑ̃grəne] *vt* **1.** MÉD to cause to become gangrenous, to gangrene **2.** [corrompre] to corrupt, to rot.
◆ **se gangrener** *vpi* to become gangrenous ■ **la jambe risque de se ~** the leg may become gangrenous *OU* may get gangrene.

gangster [gɑ̃gstɛr] *nm* **1.** [bandit] gangster ■ **un film de ~s** a gangster film **2.** [escroc] cheat, swindler.

gangstérisme [gɑ̃gsterism] *nm* gangsterism.

gangue [gɑ̃g] *nf* **1.** MIN [d'une pierre précieuse, d'un minerai] gangue **2.** [couche] coating ■ **recouvert d'une ~ de glace** coated with ice **3.** *fig* **ils sont enfermés dans une ~ de préjugés** they are hidebound with prejudice.

ganse [gɑ̃s] *nf* COUT braid *OU* twine binding.

ganser [3] [gɑ̃se] *vt* [robe, tissu] to braid, to trim ■ [chapeau] to trim ■ **~ une couture** to pipe a seam.

gant [gɑ̃] *nm* [accessoire] glove ■ **~ de boxe/d'escrime** boxing/fencing glove ■ **~ de crin** massage glove ■ **~ de motard** motorcycle glove ■ **~ de toilette** flannel *UK*, washcloth *US*, facecloth *US* ■ **ça te/lui va comme un ~** it fits you/him like a glove ■ **mettre** *OU* **prendre des ~s avec qqn** to handle sb with kid gloves ■ **pour lui annoncer la nouvelle je te conseille de prendre des ~s** I'd advise you to break the news to him very gently ■ **jeter le ~ (à qqn)** to throw down the gauntlet (to sb) ■ **relever** *OU* **ramasser le ~** to take up the gauntlet, to accept the challenge.

gantelet [gɑ̃tlɛ] *nm* **1.** HIST & SPORT gauntlet **2.** INDUST gauntlet, hand leather.

ganter [3] [gɑ̃te] ◇ *vt* to glove ■ **ses mains étaient gantées de dentelle noire** her hands were gloved in black lace, she was wearing black lace gloves.
◇ *vi* : **vous gantez du combien?** what size gloves do you take?
◆ **se ganter** *vp (emploi réfléchi)* [mettre ses gants] to put on *OU* to slip on one's gloves.

ganterie [gɑ̃tri] *nf* **1.** [industrie] glove-making industry ■ [fabrique] glove factory **2.** [boutique] glove shop *UK OU* store *US*, glover's ■ [négoce] : **la ~** the glove trade.

gantier, ère [gɑ̃tje, ɛr] *nm, f* glover.

GAO (*abr de* **gestion assistée par ordinateur**) *nf* CAM, computer-aided management.

garage [garaʒ] *nm* **1.** [de voitures] garage ■ [de bateaux] boathouse ■ [de vélos] shed ■ [d'avions] shed, hangar ■ [de bus] garage, depot ■ **la voiture est au ~** the car is in the garage **2.** [atelier] garage, car repair shop *US* ■ **ma voiture est au ~** my car is at the garage **3.** RAIL siding.

garagiste [garaʒist] *nmf* [propriétaire] garage owner ■ [gérant] garage manager ■ [mécanicien] (garage) mechanic.

garance [garɑ̃s] ◇ *nf* **1.** BOT madder **2.** [teinture] madder (dye).
◇ *adj inv* [rouge] ruby red.

garant, e [garɑ̃, ɑ̃t] ◇ *adj* **1.** DR : **être ~ d'une dette** to stand guarantor *OU* surety for a debt **2.** [responsable] : **être/se porter ~ de** to vouch *OU* to answer for ■ **les pays ~s d'un traité** countries acting as guarantors of a treaty ■ **désormais, vous serez ~e de ses faits et gestes** from now on, you'll be answerable *OU* responsible for his conduct.
◇ *nm, f* **1.** [personne] : **tu es la ~e de notre réussite** thanks to you, we are assured of success **2.** [responsable] guarantor ■ **les membres du GATT sont les ~s de la liberté des échanges** the members of GATT are the guarantors of free trade.
◆ **garant** *nm* **1.** DR [personne] guarantor ■ [somme, bien, document] surety, security ■ **être le ~ de qqn** to stand surety for sb **2.** [garantie] guarantee, warranty **3.** NAUT (tackle) fall.

garanti [garɑ̃ti] *nm* DR guarantee.

garantie [garɑ̃ti] *nf* **1.** COMM [assurance] guarantee ➊ **contrat de ~** guarantee ■ **rupture de ~** breach of warranty **2.** DR [obligation] guarantee ■ **~ de paiement** guarantee of payment **3.** [gage] guarantee ■ **c'est sans ~!** I'm not promising *OU* guaranteeing anything! **4.** POLIT : **~ individuelle, ~s individuelles** guarantee of individual liberties.
◆ **sous garantie** *loc adj* under guarantee ■ **un appareil sous ~** an appliance under guarantee.

garantique [garɑ̃tik] *nf* [technique] computer security technology ■ [théorie] data protection.

garantir [32] [garɑ̃tir] *vt* **1.** [veiller sur] to guarantee, to safeguard **2.** [assurer - appareil] to guarantee **3.** [promettre] to guarantee, to assure ■ **suis mes conseils et je te garantis le succès** take my advice and I guarantee you'll succeed *OU* I guarantee you success ■ **il m'a garanti que ça serait livré demain, il m'a garanti la livraison pour demain** he assured me that it would be delivered tomorrow, he guaranteed delivery for tomorrow ■ **je te garantis que tu le regretteras!** I can assure you you'll regret it! **4.** [protéger] : **~ qqn de** to protect sb from **5.** DR : **~ qqn contre** to cover sb against **6.** FIN [paiement] to guarantee ■ [emprunt] to guarantee, to back ■ [créance] to secure.

garce△ [gars] *nf péj* bitch△ ■ **sale ~** you rotten bitch!

garçon [garsɔ̃] ◇ *nm* **1.** [enfant] boy ■ **grand ~ : un grand ~ comme toi, ça ne pleure pas** big boys like you don't cry ■ **petit ~** little boy ➊ **~ manqué** tomboy **2.** [homme] boy ➊ **~ d'honneur** best man ■ **il est plutôt joli ~** he's quite good-looking ■ **c'est un bon** *OU* **brave ~** he's a good sort ■ **c'est un mauvais ~** he's a bad lot *UK*, he's bad news **3.** [célibataire] bachelor

4. [employé] : **~ de bureau/courses** office/errand boy ■ **~ boucher** butcher's boy *OU* assistant **5.** [serveur] : **~ (de café** *OU* **de salle)** waiter **6.** *fam* [en appellatif] : **attention, mon ~!** watch it, sonny!
◇ *adj m* **1.** [célibataire] unmarried **2.** [qui a une apparence masculine] boyish.

garçonne [garsɔn] *nf* HIST : **les ~s des années vingt** the flappers.
◆ **à la garçonne** *loc adv* : **coiffée à la ~** with an Eton crop ■ **habillée à la ~** dressed like a (twenties) flapper.

garçonnet [garsɔnɛ] *nm* **1.** [petit garçon] (little) boy **2.** *(comme adj)* **rayon ~** boyswear (department).

garçonnier, ère [garsɔnje, ɛr] *adj* boyish ■ **des manières garçonnières** boyish ways.
◆ **garçonnière** *nf* bachelor pad.

garde[1] [gard] *nf*

A.
1. [surveillance - d'un bien, d'un lieu] : **je te confie la ~ du manuscrit** I am entrusting you with the manuscript, I am leaving the manuscript in your safekeeping *OU* care ■ **assurer la ~ d'un immeuble** [police] to guard a building ; [concierge] to look after a building, to be caretaker of a building ■ **faire bonne ~ : on te prête la maison pour le week-end, mais fais bonne ~** we'll let you use our house for the weekend, but look after it carefully ■ **affecté à la ~ du palais présidentiel** on guard duty at the presidential palace ■ **monter la ~** to stand guard
2. [protection - d'un enfant, d'un animal] care ■ **je confierai la ~ des enfants à ma tante** I will leave the children in the care of my aunt ■ **puis-je te confier la ~ de mon chien pendant deux jours?** would you take care of *OU* look after my dog for two days?
3. MÉD [service de surveillance] : **interne qui fait des ~s** locum *UK*, locum tenens *UK*, intern on duty *US* ▶ **~ de nuit** night duty
4. DR custody ■ **la ~ des enfants fut confiée à la mère** the mother was given custody of the children, the children were left in the custody of their mother ■ **~ alternée** divided *OU* alternated custody *(of the children)* ▶ **~ à vue** police custody ■ **droit de ~** (right of) custody

B.
SPORT guard ■ **tenir la ~ haute** to keep one's guard up ■ **baisser sa ~** to drop one's guard ■ **ne pas baisser sa ~ (devant qqn)** to remain on one's guard ▶ **n'avoir ~ de faire** *sout* : **je n'aurai ~ de vous contredire** I'll take good care not to contradict you ■ **prendre ~ : prends ~** watch out! ■ **prendre ~ à : prenez ~ à la marche** mind *UK OU* watch *US* the step ■ **prendre ~ de : prenez ~ de ne rien oublier** make sure *OU* take care you don't leave anything behind ■ **prendre ~ (à ce) que** *sout* : **prends ~ qu'on ne te voie pas** make sure nobody sees you

C.
1. [escorte, milice] guard ■ **~ (d'honneur)** guard of honour ■ **~ mobile** (State) security police ■ **la Garde républicaine** the Republican Guard *(on duty at French state occasions)* ■ **la vieille ~** the old guard *(of a political party)*
2. [soldats en faction] guard ■ **~ montante/descendante** relief/old guard

D.
ARM [d'une arme blanche] hilt ■ **jusqu'à la ~** *fig* up to the hilt ■ **il s'est enferré dans ses mensonges jusqu'à la ~** he got completely tangled up in his own lies.
◆ **gardes** *nfpl* guard *(civil militia, 1789-1871)* ■ **être/se tenir sur ses ~s** to be/to stay on one's guard.
◆ **de garde** *loc adj* **1.** ▷ **chien 2.** MÉD duty *(modif)* ■ **médecin de ~** duty doctor, doctor on duty ■ **elle est de ~ trois nuits par semaine** she's on duty three nights a week.
◆ **en garde** *loc adv* **1.** MIL & SPORT : **en ~** on (your) guard! ■ **mettez-vous en ~** take your guard **2.** [sous surveillance] : **ils prennent des animaux en ~ l'été** they board pets during the summer **3.** DR in care *UK*, in custody *US* **4.** *loc* **mettre qqn en ~** to warn sb ■ **je l'avais mise en ~ contre les dangers du tabac** I had warned her against the dangers of smoking.
◆ **sous bonne garde** *loc adv* : **le stade est sous bonne ~** the stadium is under (heavy) guard ■ **ton argent est sous bonne ~** your money is in safe hands.

garde[2] [gard] ◇ *nmf* [personne] : **la ~ des enfants est une jeune Allemande** the childminder *UK OU* baby-sitter is a young German girl.
◇ *nm* **1.** [surveillant] warden ■ **~ du corps** bodyguard ■ **~ forestier** forest warden *UK*, forest ranger *US* ■ **~ mobile** member of the (State) security police ■ **~ de nuit** night watchman ■ **~ républicain** Republican guardsman *(on duty at French state occasions)* ■ **~ des Sceaux** (French) Minister of Justice, ≃ Lord Chancellor *UK*, ≃ Attorney General *US* **2.** [soldat - en faction] guard ; [- en service d'honneur] guardsman ■ **~ rouge** Red Guard.
◇ *nf* MÉD nurse.

Garde [gard] *npr* ▷ **lac.**

garde-à-vous [gardavu] *nm inv* : **des soldats au ~** soldiers standing at *OU* to attention ■ **~, fixe!** attention!, 'shun! ■ **se mettre au ~** to stand to attention.

garde-barrière [gardəbarjɛr] (*pl* **gardes-barrière** *OU pl* **gardes-barrières**) *nmf* level-crossing keeper *UK*, grade-crossing keeper *US*.

garde-boue [gardəbu] *nm inv* mudguard.

garde-chasse [gardəʃas] (*pl* **gardes-chasse** *OU pl* **gardes-chasses**) *nm* gamekeeper.

garde-chiourme [gardəʃjurm] (*pl* **gardes-chiourme** *OU pl* **gardes-chiourmes**) *nm* **1.** HIST warder *(in charge of a gang of convicts)* **2.** *péj* [surveillant brutal] martinet, disciplinarian.

garde-corps [gardəkɔr] *nm inv* [balustrade] railing, handrail ■ [parapet] parapet.

garde-côtes [gardəkot] *nm inv* coastguard vessel.

garde-feu [gardəfø] (*pl inv OU pl* **garde-feux**) *nm* fireguard, fire screen.

garde-fou [gardəfu] (*pl* **garde-fous**) *nm* **1.** [barrière] railing, guardrail ■ [talus] (raised) bank **2.** *fig* [défense] : **servir de ~ contre** to safeguard against.

garde-frontière(s) [gardəfrɔ̃tjɛr] (*pl* **gardes-frontières**) *nm* border guard.

garde-malade [gardəmalad] (*pl* **gardes-malade** *OU pl* **gardes-malades**) *nmf* nurse.

garde-manger [gardəmɑ̃ʒe] *nm inv* [placard] food *OU* meat safe ■ [réserve] pantry, larder.

garde-meuble(s) [gardəmœbl] (*pl* **garde-meubles**) *nm* furniture depository *UK OU* storehouse ■ **mettre qqch au ~** to put sthg in storage.

Gardénal® [gardenal] *nm* phenobarbitone *UK*, phenobarbital *US*.

gardénia [gardenja] *nm* gardenia.

garden-party [gardɛnparti] (*pl* **garden-partys** *OU pl* **garden-parties**) *nf* garden party.

garde-pêche [gardəpɛʃ] (*pl* **gardes-pêche**) ◇ *nm* water bailiff *UK*, fish warden *US*.
◇ *nm inv* [en mer] fisheries protection vessel ■ [sur rivière] bailiff's boat *UK*, fish warden's boat *US*.

garder [3] [garde] *vt*

A.
1. [veiller sur - personne, animal] to look after *(insép)* ; [- boutique] to keep an eye on, to mind ■ **il doit faire ~ les enfants le soir** he has to get somebody to look after the children in the evening ■ **elle garde des enfants** she does some childminding *UK OU* baby-sitting ■ **les moutons sont gardés par des chiens** the sheep are guarded by dogs ▶ **on n'a pas gardé les cochons ensemble!** *fam* don't be so familiar!
2. [surveiller - personne, lieu] to guard
3. *litt* [prémunir] : **~ qqn de qqch** to protect *OU* to save sb from sthg
4. DR : **~ qqn à vue** to keep *OU* to hold sb in custody

B.

1. [suj: malade] : **~ le lit** to be confined to bed, to be laid up ▪ **elle garde la chambre** she is confined to her room *ou* staying in her room
2. MIL : **~ les arrêts** to remain under arrest

C.

1. [conserver - aliment] to keep
2. [ne pas se dessaisir de] to keep ▪ **j'ai gardé toutes ses lettres** I kept all his letters ▪ **garde-le, un jour il aura de la valeur** hold onto it *ou* keep it, one day it will be valuable
3. [conserver sur soi] to keep on *(sép)* ▪ **puis-je ~ mon chapeau/ manteau?** may I keep my hat/coat on?
4. [conserver en dépôt] to keep ▪ **la voisine garde mon courrier pendant mon absence** my neighbour keeps my mail for me when I'm away
5. [réserver] to save, to keep ▪ **ne te fatigue pas trop, il faut ~ des forces pour ce soir** don't overtire yourself, save some of your energy for tonight ▪ **attends que je termine mon histoire, j'ai gardé le meilleur pour la fin** wait for me to finish my story, I've kept the best bit until last ➲ **~ une poire pour la soif** to keep something for a rainy day
6. [retenir - personne] to keep ▪ **tu es pressé, je ne te garderai pas longtemps** as you're in a hurry I won't keep you long ▪ **~ qqn à dîner** to have sb stay for dinner ▪ **on les a gardés au commissariat** they were held at the police station ▪ **va-t-elle ~ le bébé?** [femme enceinte] is she going to keep the baby?
7. [ne pas révéler] to keep ▪ **~ le secret sur qqch** to keep sthg secret ▪ **tu ferais bien de ~ ça pour toi** you'd better keep that to yourself
8. [avoir à l'esprit] : **je n'ai pas gardé de très bons souvenirs de cette époque** my memories of that time are not very happy ones ▪ **~ qqch présent à l'esprit** to bear *ou* to keep sthg in mind
9. [maintenir - attitude, sentiment] to keep ▪ **~ l'anonymat** to remain anonymous ▪ **~ son calme** to keep calm *ou* cool ▪ **~ rancune à qqn de qqch** to bear *ou* to harbour a grudge against sb for sthg ▪ **~ son sérieux** to keep a straight face ▪ **~ le silence** to keep silent ▪ **~ la tête froide** to keep one's head *ou* a cool head ▪ **~ les yeux baissés** to keep one's eyes lowered
10. *sout* [observer, respecter - règle, loi] : **~ le jeûne** to observe a fast ▪ **~ ses distances** to keep one's distance
11. [ne pas perdre - qualité] : **le mot garde encore toute sa valeur** the word still retains its full meaning.

◆ **se garder** ◇ *vp (emploi passif)* [aliment] to keep ▪ **les framboises ne se gardent pas (longtemps)** raspberries do not keep (long).
◇ *vp (emploi réfléchi)* : **les enfants sont grands, ils se gardent tout seuls maintenant** the children are old enough to be left without a baby-sitter now.
◆ **se garder de** *vp+prép sout* **1.** [éviter de] : **je me garderai bien de lui en parler** I'll be very careful not to talk to him about it ▪ **garde-toi bien de le vexer** be very careful not to offend him **2.** [se méfier de] : **il faut se ~ des gens trop expansifs** one should beware *ou* be wary of over-effusive people.

garderie [gardəri] *nf* [de quartier] day nursery *UK*, day-care center *US* ▪ [liée à une entreprise] crèche *UK*, baby-sitting services *US*.

garde-rivière [gardərivjɛr] (*pl* **gardes-rivière** *ou pl* **gardes-rivières**) *nm* riverkeeper, river patrolman, waterways board official *UK*.

garde-robe [gardərɔb] (*pl* **garde-robes**) *nf* **1.** [vêtements] wardrobe ▪ **~ d'hiver** winter wardrobe ▪ **il serait temps que je renouvelle ma ~** it's high time I bought myself some new clothes **2.** [penderie] wardrobe.

gardeur, euse [gardœr, øz] *nm, f litt* **~ d'oies** gooseherd.

garde-voie [gardəvwa] (*pl* **gardes-voie** *ou pl* **gardes-voies**) *nm* (railway line *UK ou* railroad track *US*) patrolman.

gardian [gardjɑ̃] *nm* herdsman *(in the Camargue)*.

gardien, enne [gardjɛ̃, ɛn] *nm, f* **1.** [surveillant - d'une usine, d'une société] (security) guard ; [- d'un cimetière] caretaker ; [- d'un domaine] warden ; [- d'un zoo] keeper ▪ **~ d'immeuble** caretaker *UK*, porter *UK*, janitor *US* ▪ **~ de musée** museum attendant ▪ **~ de nuit** night watchman ▪ **~ de phare** lighthouse keeper ▪ **~ de prison** prison warder *UK*, prison guard *US* **2.** *fig* [protecteur] guardian, custodian.
◆ **gardien** *nm* : **~ de but** goalkeeper ▪ **~ de la paix** police officer.
◆ **gardienne** *nf* : **gardienne d'enfants** nursery help *ou* helper *UK*, day-care assistant *US*.

gardiennage [gardjɛnaʒ] *nm* : **assurer le ~ d'un entrepôt** to be in charge of security in a warehouse ▪ **société de ~** security firm ▪ **assurer le ~ d'une résidence** to be the caretaker *ou* porter in a block of flats *UK*, to be the doorman *ou* janitor in an apartment block *US*.

gardienne [gardjɛn] *f* ⊳ **gardien**.

gardon [gardɔ̃] *nm* ZOOL roach, ⊳ **frais**.

gare [gar] ◇ *nf* **1.** RAIL [installations et voies] station ▪ [hall] (station) concourse ▪ [bâtiments] station building *ou* buildings ▪ **le train de 14 h 30 à destination de Paris va entrer en ~ voie 10** the train now arriving at platform 10 is the two-thirty to Paris ➲ **~ frontière/maritime** border/harbour station ▪ **~ de passagers/marchandises** passenger/goods station ▪ **~ de triage** marshalling yard *UK*, switchyard *US* ▪ **romans de ~** cheap *ou* trashy novels **2.** [garage à bateaux] (river) basin ▪ [d'un canal] passing place **3.** TRANSP : **~ routière** [de poids lourds] haulage depot ; [de cars] bus station, coach station *UK*.
◇ *interj* : **~ à toi!, ~ à tes fesses!** *fam* you just watch it! ▪ **~ à vous si vous rentrez après minuit** if you come home after midnight, there'll be trouble!, you'd better be in by midnight, or else! ▪ **~ à tes doigts avec ce couteau** watch your fingers with that knife ▪ **~ dessous!** look out *ou* watch out down below!

garenne [garɛn] ◇ *nf* [lieu boisé] (rabbit) warren.
◇ *nm* ZOOL wild rabbit.

garer [3] [gare] *vt* **1.** [véhicule] to park ▪ **bien/mal garé** parked legally/illegally ▪ **garé en double file** double-parked **2.** TRANSP [canot] to dock, to berth ▪ [avion léger - dans un hangar] to put away *(sép)* ; [- sur la piste] to park **3.** RAIL to shunt, to move into a siding, to switch *US*.
◆ **se garer** *vpi* **1.** [en voiture] to park ▪ **trouver à se ~** to find a parking place *ou* space **2.** [s'écarter] : **gare-toi!** get out of the way!
◆ **se garer de** *vp+prép* [éviter] : **se ~ d'un danger** to steer clear of a danger.

gargantua [gargɑ̃tɥa] *nm* : **un (véritable) ~** a glutton.

Gargantua [gargɑ̃tɥa] *npr the giant in Rabelais' novel of the same name (1534)* ▪ **'(Vie inestimable du grand) ~'** *Rabelais* 'Gargantua and Pantagruel'.

gargantuesque [gargɑ̃tɥɛsk] *adj* gargantuan.

gargariser [3] [gargarize] ◆ **se gargariser** *vpi* to gargle.
◆ **se gargariser de** *vp+prép* to delight in *(insép)* ▪ **il se gargarise volontiers de mots à la mode/de noms célèbres** he delights in trotting out fashionable words/in dropping famous names.

gargarisme [gargarism] *nm* [rinçage] gargling ▪ [produit] mouthwash ▪ **faire des ~s** to gargle.

gargote [gargɔt] *nf péj* cheap restaurant.

gargouille [garguj] *nf* ARCHIT gargoyle.

gargouillement [gargujmɑ̃] *nm* **1.** [d'une fontaine] gurgling **2.** [de l'estomac] rumbling ▪ **j'ai des ~s dans le ventre** my stomach is rumbling.

gargouiller [3] [garguje] *vi* **1.** [liquide] to gurgle **2.** [estomac] to rumble.

gargouillis [garguji] = **gargouillement**.

garnement [garnəmɑ̃] *nm* brat, rascal.

garni, e [garni] *adj* **1.** CULIN [plat du jour, viande] with vegetables **2.** *vieilli* [chambre, logement, hôtel] furnished.
◆ **garni** *nm vieilli* furnished rooms *ou* accommodation.

Garnier [garnje] *npr* : **le palais ~** *the old Paris Opera House*.

garnir [32] [garnir] *vt* **1.** [décorer] : **ils ont garni la table de fleurs et de bougies** they decorated the table with flowers and candles **2.** [remplir] : **nous vendons la corbeille garnie de fruits** the basket is sold (complete) with an assortment of fruit ■ **il est bien garni, ton frigo!** your fridge is very well stocked! **3.** [équiper] : **les semelles sont garnies de pointes d'acier** the soles are steel-tipped ‖ AUTO & RAIL [aménager - intérieur d'un véhicule] to fit **4.** [de tissu - siège] to cover, to upholster ; [- vêtement, coffret] to line **5.** CULIN [remplir] to fill ■ [pour accompagner] : **toutes nos viandes sont garnies de pommes sautées** all our meat dishes come with *ou* are served with sautéed potatoes **6.** [remplir du nécessaire] to fill (up) ■ ~ **la chaudière pour la nuit** to stoke *ou* to fill (up) the boiler for the night.
◆ **se garnir** *vpi* **1.** [se remplir] to fill up **2.** [se couvrir] : **les murs du nouveau musée se garnissent peu à peu** the walls of the new museum are gradually becoming lined with exhibits.

garnison [garnizɔ̃] *nf* garrison ■ **le régiment est en ~ à Nancy** the regiment is garrisoned *ou* stationed in Nancy.
◆ **de garnison** *loc adj* garrison *(modif)*.

garnissage [garnisaʒ] *nm* **1.** [d'un chapeau] trim **2.** AUTO [intérieur d'un véhicule] (interior) trim **3.** TECHNOL [d'une chaudière] lining *(U)*.

garniture [garnityr] *nf* **1.** [ensemble] (matching) set ▶ ~ **de cheminée** (set of) mantelpiece ornaments ■ **une ~ de lit** a matching set of sheets and pillow-cases **2.** [ornementation] : **avec une ~ de dentelle** trimmed with lace ■ **la ~ d'une automobile** the interior trim *ou* the upholstery of a car **3.** [protection] : ~ **de frein/d'embrayage** brake/clutch lining ■ ~ **de porte** door liner **4.** CULIN [d'un feuilleté] filling ■ [accompagnement - décoratif] garnish ; [- de légumes] : **que servez-vous comme ~ avec le poisson?** what does the fish come with?, what is the fish served with? ■ **c'est servi sans ~** it is served without vegetables *ou* on its own.

garrigue [garig] *nf* scrubland, garigue.

garrot [garo] *nm* **1.** MÉD tourniquet ■ **mettre un ~** to apply a tourniquet **2.** [supplice] garrotte **3.** ZOOL withers.

garrotter [3] [garɔte] *vt* **1.** [attacher] to tie up *(sép)*, to bind **2.** *fig* [priver de liberté] to stifle, to muzzle ■ **tous les partis d'opposition ont été garrottés** the opposition parties have all been stifled *ou* muzzled **3.** [supplicier] to garrotte.

gars [ga] *nm fam* **1.** [garçon, fils] boy, lad *UK* ■ **qu'est-ce qui ne va pas, mon petit ~?** what's the matter, kid *ou* sonny? **2.** [jeune homme] boy, lad *UK*, guy *US* ■ **allons-y, les ~** let's go, boys ■ **c'est un ~ bizarre** he's a weird bloke *UK ou* guy *US* ■ **salut, les ~** hi, lads! *UK*, hi, guys! *US*.

Gascogne [gaskɔɲ] *npr f* : **(la) ~** Gascony ■ **le golfe de ~** the Bay of Biscay.

gascon, onne [gaskɔ̃, ɔn] *adj* Gascon.
◆ **Gascon, onne** *nm, f* Gascon ■ **une offre de Gascon** an empty promise.
◆ **gascon** *nm* LING Gascon (variety).

gas-oil (*pl* **gas-oils**), **gasoil** [gazɔjl, gazwal] = **gazole**.

gaspacho [gaspatʃo] = **gazpacho**.

Gaspar(d) [gaspar] *npr* BIBLE Caspar.

gaspillage [gaspijaʒ] *nm* waste ■ **évitez le ~ de nourriture/d'électricité** don't waste food/electricity.

gaspiller [3] [gaspije] *vt* [denrée, temps, talent] to waste ■ [économies] to squander ■ **arrête de me faire ~ mon temps** stop wasting my time.

gaspilleur, euse [gaspijœr, øz] ◇ *adj* wasteful.
◇ *nm, f* squanderer, spendthrift.

gastéropode [gasterɔpɔd] = **gastropode**.

Gaston Lagaf' [gastɔ̃lagaf] *npr clumsy youth in a strip cartoon of the same title.*

gastralgie [gastralʒi] *nf* stomach pains, gastralgia *spéc.*

gastrique [gastrik] *adj* gastric, stomach *(modif)* ■ **embarras/lésion ~** stomach trouble/lesion.

gastrite [gastrit] *nf* gastritis.

gastro-duodénal, e [gastrɔdyodenal] *adj* ANAT gastroduodenal.

gastro-entérite [gastrɔɑ̃terit] (*pl* **gastro-entérites**) *nf* gastroenteritis *(U)*.

gastro-entérologie [gastrɔɑ̃terɔlɔʒi] *nf* gastroenterology.

gastro-intestinal, e, aux [gastrɔɛ̃tɛstinal, o] *adj* gastrointestinal.

gastronome [gastrɔnɔm] *nmf* gastronome, gourmet.

gastronomie [gastrɔnɔmi] *nf* gastronomy ■ **ça ne va pas être de la haute ~, je fais un poulet rôti** don't expect anything fancy, I'm only doing roast chicken.

gastronomique [gastrɔnɔmik] *adj* gastronomic, gastronomical ■ **buffet ~** gourmet buffet.

gâteau, x [gato] *nm* **1.** CULIN [pâtisserie] cake ■ [biscuit] biscuit *UK*, cookie *US* ■ **donne-moi une petite part/tranche de ~** give me a small piece/slice of cake ▶ ~ **d'anniversaire** birthday cake ■ ~ **apéritif** savoury biscuit *UK*, cracker *US (to eat with drinks)* ■ ~ **marbré** marble cake ■ ~ **de riz/de semoule** ≃ rice/semolina pudding ■ ~ **de Savoie** sponge cake ■ ~ **sec** (sweet) biscuit *UK ou* cookie *US* ■ **ça n'est pas du ~** *fam* it isn't as easy as it looks ■ **c'est du ~** *fam* it's a piece of cake *ou* a walkover **2.** *Suisse* tart **3.** [masse pressée] cake ■ ~ **de miel** *ou* **de cire** honeycomb.
◆ **gâteau** *adj inv fam* **c'est un papa ~** he's a soft touch with his children ■ **j'ai eu un tonton ~** I had an uncle who spoilt me rotten.

gâter [3] [gate] *vt* **1.** [combler - ami, enfant] to spoil ■ **du champagne! vous nous avez gâtés!** champagne! you shouldn't have! ■ **tu n'es qu'une enfant gâtée!** a spoilt brat, that's what you are! ■ **quel beau temps, nous sommes vraiment gâtés** we're really lucky with the weather ■ **nous sommes gâtés avec cette pluie!** *iron* lovely weather for ducks! ■ **ne pas être gâté : tu as vu ce qu'il y a à la télé ce soir, on n'est pas gâtés!** *fam* have you seen what's on TV tonight, great, isn't it? *iron* ■ **il n'est pas gâté par la nature** nature wasn't very kind to him **2.** [abîmer] to spoil ■ **l'humidité gâte les fruits** moisture makes fruit go bad *ou* spoils fruit ■ **elle a beaucoup de dents gâtées** she's got a lot of bad teeth **3.** [gâcher] to spoil ■ **il est beau et riche, ce qui ne gâte rien** he's good-looking and wealthy, which does him no harm.
◆ **se gâter** *vpi* **1.** [pourrir - viande, poisson, lait] to go off *UK ou* bad ; [- fruit] to go bad **2.** [se carier - dent] to decay, to go rotten **3.** [se détériorer - situation] to go wrong ■ **voilà ses potes, attention ça va se ~** *fam* here come his mates, things are going to get nasty ■ **regarde le ciel, le temps se gâte** look at the sky, it's starting to cloud over *ou* the weather's changing for the worse.

gâterie [gatri] *nf* **1.** [cadeau] treat, present ■ **laisse-moi t'offrir une petite ~** let me treat you to a little something, let me buy you a little treat **2.** [friandise] treat, titbit.

gâte-sauce [gatsos] (*pl inv ou pl* **gâte-sauces**) *nm* kitchen help ■ *péj* bad cook.

gâteux, euse [gatø, øz] ◇ *adj* **1.** [sénile] doddering, doddery ■ **un vieillard ~** an old dodderer **2.** *fam* [stupide] gaga ■ **le bébé les rend tous ~** they are all completely besotted by the baby, they all go gaga over the baby.
◇ *nm, f* : **un vieux ~** *péj* a silly *ou* doddering old fool.

gâtifier [9] [gatifje] *vi fam* [devenir gâteux] to go soft in the head.

gâtisme [gatism] *nm* MÉD senility ■ **il se répète, c'est du ~!** *péj* he is repeating himself, he must be going senile!

GATT, Gatt [gat] (*abr de* **General Agreement on Tariffs and Trade**) *npr m* GATT.

gauche [goʃ] ◇ *adj* **1.** [dans l'espace] left ■ **la partie ~ du tableau est endommagée** the left *ou* left-hand side of the painting is damaged ■ **il est ailier ~** he plays on the left wing **2.** [maladroit - adolescent] awkward, gawky ; [- démarche] ungainly ; [- manières] awkward, gauche ; [- geste, mouvement] awkward, clumsy **3.** CONSTR warped.

◇ *nm* **1.** SPORT [pied gauche] : **marquer un but du ~** to score a goal with one's left (foot) ■ [poing gauche] : **il a un ~ imparable** he has an unstoppable left **2.** CONSTR warping.
◇ *nf* **1.** [côté gauche] : **la ~** the left *ou* left-hand side ■ **il confond sa droite et sa ~** he mixes up (his) right and left ■ **la page de ~** the left-hand page ■ **l'église est à ~ de l'hôtel** the church is to the left of the hotel ■ **la deuxième rue sur votre ~** the second street on your left **2.** POLIT left ■ **elle vote à ~** she votes (for the) left ■ **la ~ caviar** champagne Socialism.
◆ **à gauche** ◇ *interj* **1.** MIL : **à ~, ~!** left (turn)! **2.** NAUT : **à ~!** left! ■ **à ~ toute!** hard to port!
◇ *loc adv* **1.** [sur le côté gauche] on the left ■ **tournez à ~** turn left **2.** *fam loc* **mettre de l'argent à ~** to put *ou* to tuck some money away.
◆ **de gauche** *loc adj* left-wing ■ **être de ~** to be left-wing *ou* a left-winger.
◆ **jusqu'à la gauche** *loc adv fam* **on s'est fait arnaquer jusqu'à la ~** we got completely ripped off, they cheated us good and proper ■ **il est compromis jusqu'à la ~ dans cette affaire** he's involved right up to the hilt in this business.

gauchement [goʃmɑ̃] *adv* clumsily.

gaucher, ère [goʃe, ɛr] ◇ *adj* left-handed ■ **il n'est pas ~!** he is (rather) good with his hands!
◇ *nm, f* [gén] left-hander ■ [boxeur] southpaw.

gaucherie [goʃri] *nf* **1.** [attitude] clumsiness **2.** [acte, geste] awkwardness *(U)* ■ [expression] tactless *ou* insensitive statement ■ **bon exposé, malgré quelques ~s** a good essay, despite some clumsy turns of phrase **3.** MÉD [prévalence manuelle] left-handedness.

gauchir [32] [goʃir] ◇ *vt* **1.** CONSTR to warp, to buckle **2.** [altérer] to distort ■ **il accuse les journalistes d'avoir gauchi ses propos** he accuses the journalists of distorting *ou* misrepresenting his words.
◇ *vi* to warp.

gauchisant, e [goʃizɑ̃, ɑ̃t] POLIT ◇ *adj* : **être ~** to have left-wing tendencies.
◇ *nm, f* : **c'est un ~** he's on the left, he's got left-wing tendencies.

gauchisme [goʃism] *nm* POLIT [gén] leftism ■ [depuis 1968] New Leftism.

gauchissement [goʃismɑ̃] *nm* **1.** CONSTR warping **2.** *fig* distortion, misrepresentation.

gauchiste [goʃist] POLIT ◇ *adj* [gén] left ■ [depuis 1968] (New) Leftist.
◇ *nmf* [gén] leftist ■ [depuis 1968] (New) Leftist.

gaucho[1] [goʃo] *nm* [gardien de troupeaux] gaucho.

gaucho[2] [goʃo] *adj inv* & *nmf* *fam péj* & POLIT lefty, pinko.

gaudriole [godrijɔl] *nf fam* **1.** [plaisanterie] bawdy joke **2.** [sexe] : **il ne pense qu'à la ~** he's got a one-track mind.

gaufrage [gofraʒ] *nm* **1.** [relief - sur du cuir, du métal] embossing ; [- sur une étoffe] diapering **2.** [plissage d'un tissu] goffering **3.** IMPR goffering.

gaufre [gofr] *nf* **1.** CULIN waffle **2.** [de cire] honeycomb.

gaufrer [3] [gofre] *vt* **1.** [imprimer un relief sur - cuir, métal, papier] to emboss, to boss ; [- étoffe] to diaper **2.** [plisser - tissu] to goffer ; [- cheveux] to crimp ■ **elle s'est fait ~ les cheveux** she had her hair crimped.

gaufrerie [gofrəri] *nf Québec* waffle.

gaufrette [gofrɛt] *nf* wafer.

gaufrier [gofrije] *nm* waffle iron.

gaule [gol] *nf* **1.** [perche] pole **2.** PÊCHE fishing rod.

Gaule [gol] *npr f* : **la ~** Gaul.

gauler [3] [gole] *vt* **1.** [arbre] to beat ■ [fruit] to beat down *(sép)*(from the tree) **2.**△ *fam loc* **se faire ~** to be nicked *UK ou* busted *US*.

gaullien, enne [goljɛ̃, ɛn] *adj* of de Gaulle, de Gaulle's.

gaullisme [golism] *nm* Gaullism.

gaulliste [golist] *adj* & *nmf* Gaullist.

gaulois, e [golwa, az] *adj* **1.** HIST Gallic, Gaulish **2.** [grivois] bawdy ■ **l'humour ~** bawdy humour.
◆ **Gaulois, e** *nm, f* Gaul.
◆ **gaulois** *nm* LING Gaulish.
◆ **gauloise** *nf* [cigarette] Gauloise.

gauloiserie [golwazri] *nf* **1.** [plaisanterie] bawdy joke ■ [remarque] bawdy remark **2.** [attitude] bawdiness.

Gault et Millaut [goemijo] *nm* : **le ~** *annual guide to hotels and restaurants*.

gausser [3] [gose] ◆ **se gausser** *vpi litt* to mock ■ **vous vous gaussez!** you jest!

gavage [gavaʒ] *nm* **1.** AGRIC force-feeding, gavage ■ **le ~ des oies pour Noël** the fattening (up) of geese for Christmas **2.** MÉD tube-feeding.

gave [gav] *nm* (mountain) stream *(in SW France)*.

Gaveau [gavo] *npr* : **la salle ~** *concert hall in Paris*.

gaver [3] [gave] *vt* **1.** AGRIC to force-feed **2.** [bourrer] : **on l'a gavé d'antibiotiques** he has been stuffed with antibiotics ■ **la télévision nous gave de publicités** we get an overdose of commercials on television.
◆ **se gaver de** *vp+prép* to fill *ou* to stuff o.s. up with ■ **cet été je me suis gavé de romans policiers** *fig* this summer I indulged myself with detective stories.

gavroche [gavrɔʃ] ◇ *adj* [air, expression] mischievous, impish.
◇ *nm* : **un vrai petit ~** a typical Parisian urchin *(from a character in Victor Hugo's 'les Misérables')*.

gay [gɛ] *adj* & *nmf* gay ■ **il/elle est ~** he's/she's gay.

gaz [gaz] ◇ *nm inv* **1.** [pour le chauffage, l'éclairage] gas ■ **avoir le ~** to have gas, to be on gas *UK* ■ **employé du ~** gasman ▶ **~ de ville** town gas ■ **Gaz de France** *the French gas board* **2.** CHIM gas ■ **~ asphyxiant/hilarant/lacrymogène** asphyxiant/laughing/tear gas ■ **~ carbonique** carbon dioxide ■ **~ naturel** natural gas ■ **~ propulseur** propellant ■ **~ toxique** toxic gas **3.** MÉD [pour anesthésie] gas.
◇ *nmpl* **1.** PHYSIOL : **avoir des ~** to have wind *UK ou* gas *US* **2.** [carburant] : **~ brûlés** *ou* **d'échappement** exhaust fumes ■ **~ d'admission** air-fuel mixture ■ **mettre les ~** *fam* to put one's foot down *UK*, to step on the gas *US* ■ **on roulait (à) pleins ~** *fam* we were going flat out *ou* at full speed.

Gaza [gaza] *npr* Gaza ■ **la bande de ~** the Gaza Strip.

gaze [gaz] *nf* **1.** TEXT gauze **2.** MÉD gauze ■ **~ stérilisée** aseptic gauze.

gazé, e [gaze] ◇ *adj* gassed.
◇ *nm, f* (poison) gas victim.

gazéification [gazeifikasjɔ̃] *nf* **1.** CHIM gasification **2.** MIN : **~ souterraine** underground gasification **3.** [de l'eau] aeration ■ [avec du gaz carbonique] carbonation.

gazéifier [9] [gazeifje] *vt* **1.** CHIM to gasify **2.** [eau] to aerate ■ [avec du gaz carbonique] to carbonate.

gazelle [gazɛl] *nf* gazelle.

gazer [3] [gaze] ◇ *vt* **1.** [asphyxier] to gas ■ **il a été gazé** [dans une chambre à gaz] he died in a gas chamber ; [sur le champ de bataille] he was a victim of poison gas **2.** TEXT to singe.
◇ *vi fam* **1.** [aller bien] : **alors, ça gaze? – ça gaze!** how's things? *ou* how's it going? – great! ■ **ça ne gaze pas du tout en ce moment** things aren't too great at the moment **2.** [foncer] : **allez, gaze!** step on it!, get a move on!

gazetier, ère [gaztje, ɛr] *nm, f* **1.** *arch* gazette proprietor, gazetteer **2.** *péj* hack.

gazette [gazɛt] *nf arch* [journal] gazette, newspaper ■ **la Gazette de Lausanne** PRESSE *Swiss daily newspaper*.

gazeux, euse [gazø, øz] *adj* **1.** CHIM gaseous **2.** [boisson] fizzy, sparkling ■ [eau] sparkling, carbonated, fizzy ■ **eau gazeuse naturelle** naturally carbonated water **3.** MÉD gas *(modif)*.

gazier, ère [gazje, ɛr] *adj* gas *(modif)*.
◆ **gazier** *nm* **1.** [employé du gaz] gasman **2.** △ [individu] guy, bloke *UK*, dude *US*.

gazinière [gazinjɛr] *nf* gas stove, gas cooker *UK*.

gazoduc [gazɔdyk] *nm* gas pipeline.

gazole [gazɔl] *nm* **1.** [pour moteur Diesel] diesel (oil), derv *UK* **2.** [combustible] : **~ de chauffe** (domestic) fuel oil.

gazoline [gazɔlin] *nf* gasoline, gasolene.

gazomètre [gazɔmɛtr] *nm* gasholder, gasometer.

gazon [gazɔ̃] *nm* **1.** [herbe] : **du ~** turf **2.** [pelouse] lawn ▪ **~ anglais** well-kept lawn, smooth lawn.

gazonner [3] [gazɔne] *vt* to turf, to grass (over).

gazouillement [gazujmɑ̃] *nm* **1.** [d'oiseau] chirping *(U)*, warbling *(U)* **2.** [d'un bébé] babbling *(U)*, gurgling *(U)* **3.** *litt* [de l'eau] babbling ▪ **on n'entendait que le ~ d'une fontaine** all that could be heard was the gurgling *ou* babbling of a fountain.

gazouiller [3] [gazuje] *vi* **1.** [oiseau] to chirp, to warble **2.** [bébé] to babble, to gurgle **3.** *litt* [ruisseau, eau] to babble, to murmur, to gurgle.

gazouillis [gazuji] = **gazouillement**.

GB, G-B *(abr écrite de* **Grande-Bretagne***)* *npr f* GB.

gd = **grand**.

GDF *npr* = **Gaz de France**.

geai [ʒɛ] *nm* jay.

géant, e [ʒeɑ̃, ɑ̃t] ◇ *adj* **1.** [énorme] giant ▪ **une ville ~e** a gigantic town ▪ **un écran ~** a giant screen ▪ **une clameur ~e** an almighty clamour **2.** ASTRON giant **3.** *fam* [formidable] : **c'est ~!** it's wicked *ou* brill!
◇ *nm, f* **1.** [personne, chose de grande taille] giant ▶ **le projet avance à pas de ~** the project is coming on *UK ou* moving along *US* in leaps and bounds **2.** *fig* **les ~s de la littérature classique** the giants *ou* great names of classical literature ▪ **c'est un des ~s de l'électronique** ÉCON it's one of the giants of the electronics industry **3.** MYTHOL giant.

géhenne [ʒeɛn] *nf* BIBLE Gehenna.

Geiger [ʒeʒɛr] *npr* : **compteur (de) ~** Geiger counter.

geignait *etc v* ⊳ **geindre**.

geignard, e [ʒɛɲar, ard] *fam* ◇ *adj* [personne, voix] whining, whingeing *UK*, whiny *US* ▪ **et moi? dit-il d'une voix ~e** what about me? he whined.
◇ *nm, f* [enfant] crybaby ▪ [adulte] moaner, whinger *UK*, bellyacher *US*.

geignement [ʒɛɲəmɑ̃] *nm* moaning *(U)*, groaning *(U)*.

geindre [81] [ʒɛ̃dr] *vi* **1.** [gémir] to groan, to moan **2.** *fam* [pour des riens] to whine, to gripe **3.** *litt* [vent] to moan.

geisha [geʃa] *nf* geisha (girl).

gel [ʒɛl] *nm* **1.** MÉTÉOR frost ▪ **persistance du ~ sur toute la moitié ouest** it will stay frosty in the west **2.** [suspension] : **le ~ des opérations militaires** the suspension of military operations **3.** ÉCON freezing ▪ **le ~ des salaires** the wage freeze **4.** CHIM gel ▪ **~ coiffant** hair gel.

gélatine [ʒelatin] *nf* **1.** CULIN gelatine ▪ **~ de poisson** isinglass, fish glue **2.** PHOTO : **une plaque enduite de ~** a gelatine-coated plate.

gélatiné, e [ʒelatine] *adj* PHOTO : **papier ~** gelatine paper ▪ **plaque ~e** gelatinized plate.

gélatineux, euse [ʒelatinø, øz] *adj* **1.** [contenant de la gélatine] gelatinous ▪ **solution gélatineuse** gelatine solution **2.** [flasque] gelatinous, jellylike, flaccid.

gelé, e [ʒəle] *adj* **1.** AGRIC & MÉTÉOR [sol] frozen ▪ [pousse, bourgeon] frostbitten, frozen ▪ [arbre] frozen **2.** *fig* [glacé] frozen ▪ **des draps ~s** ice-cold sheets ▪ **être ~ jusqu'aux os** to be frozen to the bone, to be frozen stiff **3.** MÉD frostbitten **4.** ÉCON & FIN frozen **5.** [hostile] icy, stone-cold.

◆ **gelée** *nf* **1.** MÉTÉOR frost ▪ **~e blanche** white frost, hoarfrost **2.** CULIN jelly ▪ **~e de groseilles** redcurrant jelly *ou* preserve.
◆ **en gelée** *loc adj* in jelly ▪ **volaille en ~e** chicken in aspic *ou* jelly.
◆ **gelée royale** *nf* royal jelly.

geler [25] [ʒəle] ◇ *vt* **1.** [transformer en glace - eau, sol] to freeze **2.** [bloquer - tuyau, serrure] to freeze up *(sép)* **3.** [détruire - plante, tissu organique] to freeze **4.** [transir - visage] to chill, to numb ; [- membres] to freeze **5.** [paralyser - négociations] to halt ; [- projet] to halt, to block ; [- capitaux, salaires, prix] to freeze.
◇ *vi* **1.** [eau, liquide] to freeze ▪ [lac] to freeze over **2.** [tuyau, serrure] to freeze up **3.** [pousses, légumes] to freeze, to be nipped by the frost **4.** [personne] to freeze ▪ **je gèle** I'm frozen (stiff) ▪ **ferme la porte, on gèle ici** shut the door, it's freezing in here.
◇ *v impers* : **il gèle** it's freezing ▪ **il a gelé cette nuit** it was below freezing *ou* zero last night ▶ **il gèle à pierre fendre** it is freezing hard.
◆ **se geler** ◇ *vpi* [personne] : **je me suis gelé là-bas** I got (absolutely) frozen down there.
◇ *vpt* : **on se les gèle**△ it's damned cold△, it's brass monkey weather *UK*.

gélifiant, e [ʒelifjɑ̃, ɑ̃t] *adj* gelling.
◆ **gélifiant** *nm* gellant.

gélification [ʒelifikasjɔ̃] *nf* BOT & CHIM gelation, gelling.

gélifier [9] [ʒelifje] *vt* **1.** CHIM to gel **2.** CULIN to make into a jelly, to jellify.

gélule [ʒelyl] *nf* PHARM capsule.

gelure [ʒəlyr] *nf* frostbite *(U)*.

Gémeaux [ʒemo] *npr mpl* **1.** ASTRON Gemini **2.** ASTROL Gemini ▪ **les ~** Gemini ▪ **elle est ~** she's (a) Gemini.

gémellaire [ʒemelɛr] *adj* twin *(modif)*, gemellary *spéc* ▪ **grossesse ~** twin pregnancy.

géminé, e [ʒemine] *adj* **1.** [double] twin *(modif)*, geminate *spéc* ▪ **fenêtres ~es** paired *ou* gemel windows **2.** LING : **consonne ~e** geminate consonant.

gémir [32] [ʒemir] *vi* **1.** [blessé, malade] to moan, to groan **2.** [vent] to moan, to wail ▪ [parquet, gonds] to creak **3.** [se plaindre] to moan, to whine **4.** *litt* [souffrir] : **~ dans les fers** to languish in irons.

gémissant, e [ʒemisɑ̃, ɑ̃t] *adj* [blessé, malade] moaning, groaning ▪ *fig* **les accents ~s d'un violon** the wailing strains of a violin.

gémissement [ʒemismɑ̃] *nm* **1.** [gén] moan, groan ▪ **pousser un ~** to (utter a) groan ▪ **le ~ du vent** the moaning *ou* wailing of the wind ▪ **~s** [plaintes] whimpering, whining **2.** [de la tourterelle] cooing *(U)*.

gemme [ʒɛm] ◇ *nf* **1.** [pierre précieuse] gem **2.** [résine] (pine) resin.
◇ *adj* ⊳ **sel**.

gemmule [ʒɛmyl] *nf* gemmule.

gémonies [ʒemɔni] *nfpl* **1.** ANTIQ the Gemonies **2.** *loc* **traîner** *ou* **vouer qqn aux ~** to pillory sb ▪ **traîner** *ou* **vouer qqch aux ~** to hold sthg up to public ridicule.

gênant, e [ʒɛnɑ̃, ɑ̃t] *adj* **1.** [encombrant] in the way **2.** [ennuyeux] annoying ▪ **c'est ~ qu'elle ne soit pas là** it's annoying *ou* it's a bit of a nuisance that she's not here ▪ **ce n'est pas ~** it doesn't matter ▪ **est-ce que c'est ~?** does it matter? **3.** [embarrassant] awkward, embarrassing ▪ **c'est ~ d'y aller sans avoir été invité** I feel a bit awkward *ou* uncomfortable about going there without an invitation.

gencive [ʒɑ̃siv] *nf* ANAT gum ▪ **j'ai les ~s enflées** my gums are swollen ▪ **prendre un coup dans les ~s** *fam* to get socked in the jaw, to get a kick in the teeth.

gendarme [ʒɑ̃darm] *nmf* **1.** [policier] gendarme, policeman *(f* policewoman*)* ▪ **jouer au ~ et au voleur** *ou* **aux ~s et aux voleurs** to play cops and robbers **2.** *fam* [personne autoritaire] :

faire le ~ to lay down the law ▪ **leur mère est un vrai ~** their mother's a real *ou UK* right battle-axe **3.** *fam* [hareng] smoked herring **4.** [saucisse] *dry, flat sausage* **5.** [pointe rocheuse] gendarme.

gendarmer [3] [ʒɑ̃darme] ◆ **se gendarmer** *vpi* : **se ~ (contre)** [protester] to kick up a fuss (about) ; [s'indigner] to get on one's high horse (about).

gendarmerie [ʒɑ̃darməri] *nf* **1.** [corporation] gendarmerie, police force ▪ **~ mobile** riot police **2.** [bureaux] gendarmerie, police station ▪ [caserne] police *ou* gendarmerie barracks.

GENDARMERIE

In France, while the police are especially present in larger towns, a military institution called the *gendarmerie* patrols the road network, small towns and the countryside. The *gendarmes* fulfill the same role as police officers, ensuring law and order and recording declarations of theft.

gendre [ʒɑ̃dr] *nm* son-in-law.

gène [ʒɛn] *nm* gene.

gêne [ʒɛn] *nf* **1.** [matérielle] : **je resterais bien un jour de plus si ça ne vous cause aucune ~** I would like to stay for another day if it doesn't put you to any trouble *ou* if that's no bother ▪ **sa présence parmi nous est une ~** his being here with us is a bit awkward **2.** [morale] embarrassment ▪ **j'éprouvais une grande ~ à lui annoncer qu'il était renvoyé** I felt deeply embarrassed having to tell him that he was dismissed ▪ **il a accepté l'argent avec une certaine ~** he was uncomfortable about taking the money ▪ **un moment de ~** an awkward moment ➊ **où il y a de la ~, il n'y a pas de plaisir** there's no need to stand on ceremony ; [ton indigné] don't mind me *iron* **3.** [physique] difficulty, discomfort ▪ **éprouver** *ou* **avoir de la ~ à faire qqch** to find it difficult to do sthg **4.** [pauvreté] : **être dans la ~** to be in need.
◆ **sans gêne** *loc adj* inconsiderate.

gêné, e [ʒene] *adj* **1.** [personne, sourire] embarrassed ▪ **pourquoi prends-tu cet air ~?** why are you looking so embarrassed? ▪ **il n'est pas ~, lui!** *fam* he's got a nerve *ou UK* a cheek! **2.** [serré] ill at ease, uncomfortable ➊ **être ~ aux entournures** [mal à l'aise] to feel ill at ease *ou* self-conscious **3.** [financièrement] : **les personnes momentanément ~es peuvent demander une avance** people with temporary financial difficulties can ask for an advance.

généalogie [ʒenealɔʒi] *nf* **1.** [ascendance] ancestry ▪ **faire** *ou* **dresser sa ~** to trace one's ancestry *ou* family tree **2.** [science] genealogy.

généalogique [ʒenealɔʒik] *adj* genealogical.

généalogiste [ʒenealɔʒist] *nmf* genealogist.

génépi [ʒenepi], **genépi** [ʒənepi] *nm* **1.** BOT wormwood **2.** [liqueur] genipi *(absinthe liqueur)*.

gêner [4] [ʒene] *vt* **1.** [incommoder - suj: chose] to bother ▪ **mes lunettes me gênent pour mettre mon casque** my glasses get in the way when I put my helmet on ▪ **j'ai oublié mes lunettes, ça me gêne pour lire** I've left my glasses behind and I'm finding it difficult to read
2. [encombrer] to be in the way of ▪ **ne bougez pas, vous ne me gênez pas du tout** don't move, you're not in my *ou* the way at all ▪ *(en usage absolu)* **c'est le placard qui gêne pour ouvrir la porte** the door won't open because of the cupboard
3. [empêcher] : **la neige gênait la visibilité** visibility was hindered *ou* impaired by the snow ▪ **ce camion gêne la circulation** that lorry is holding up the traffic ▪ **je suis gêné dans mon métier par mes lacunes en mathématiques** the gaps in my knowledge of mathematics are a handicap *ou* a drawback in my line of business
4. [importuner - suj: personne] to put out *(sép)*, to bother, to inconvenience ▪ **ça ne le gênerait pas que j'arrive après minuit?** would it bother him *ou* put him out if I arrived after midnight? ▪ **ça vous gêne si j'ouvre la fenêtre?** do you mind if I open the window? ▪ **ça ne me gêne pas de le lui dire** I don't mind telling him (about it) ▪ **oui pourquoi, ça te gêne?** *fam* yes why, what's it to you *ou* got any objections? ▪ *(en usage absolu)* **ça ne gêne pas que tu viennes, il y a de la place** it'll be no bother *ou* trouble at all if you come, there's enough room
5. [intimider] to embarrass ▪ **les plaisanteries de son ami la gênaient** her friend's jokes embarrassed her *ou* made her feel uncomfortable
6. [mettre en difficulté financière] : **en ce moment, cela me gênerait un peu de vous prêter cet argent** I can't really afford to lend you the money at the moment.
◆ **se gêner** ◇ *vp (emploi réciproque)* : **la chambre est trop petite, on se gêne les uns les autres** the room is too small, we're in each other's way.
◇ *vpi fam* **je vais me ~, tiens!** just watch me! ▪ **tu aurais tort de te ~!** why should you worry *ou* care? ▪ **ne pas se ~ : continuez votre repas, ne vous gênez pas pour moi** go on with your meal, don't mind me ▪ **vous avez pris ma place, surtout ne vous gênez pas!** *iron* go on, take my seat, don't mind me! ▪ **il y en a qui ne se gênent pas!** some people have got a nerve!

général, e, aux [ʒeneral, o] *adj* **1.** [d'ensemble] general ▪ **la situation ~e** the general *ou* overall situation ▪ **le phénomène est ~** the phenomenon is widespread, it's a general phenomenon ▪ **le sens ~ d'un mot** the general *ou* broad meaning of a word ▪ **l'état ~ du malade est stationnaire** the patient's overall condition remains unchanged
2. [imprécis] general ▪ **il s'en est tenu à des remarques ~es** he confined himself to generalities *ou* to some general remarks
3. [collectif] general, common ▪ **le bien ~** the common good ▪ **à la demande ~e** by popular request ▪ **à la surprise/l'indignation ~e** to everybody's surprise/indignation
4. [total] general ▪ **amnistie ~e** general amnesty
5. ADMIN & POLIT [assemblée, direction] general ▪ **il a été nommé directeur ~** he's been appointed managing director
6. [discipline, science] general.
◆ **général, e, aux** *nm, f* MIL general ▪ **~ en chef** commander in chief ▪ **~ d'armée** general ▪ **~ de brigade** brigadier *UK*, brigadier general *US* ▪ **~ de corps d'armée** lieutenant general ▪ **~ de division** major general ▪ **~ de division aérienne** air vice-marshal *UK*, major general *US* ▪ **~ de corps aérien** air marshal *UK*, lieutenant general *US*
◆ **général, aux** *nm* **1.** RELIG general
2. *(toujours au sing)* general ▪ **aller du ~ au particulier** to move from the general to the particular.
◆ **générale** *nf* **1.** THÉÂTRE (final) dress rehearsal
2. MIL alarm call ▪ **battre** *ou* **sonner la ~e** to sound the alarm
3. [épouse du général] general's wife.
◆ **en général** *loc adv* **1.** [habituellement] generally
2. [globalement] : **on parlait de l'amour en ~** we were talking about love in general ▪ **tu parles en ~ ou (tu parles) de nous?** are you talking generally *ou* in general terms or (are you talking) about us? ▪ **est-ce que vous êtes d'accord avec ses propos? – en ~, non!** do you agree with what he says? – generally speaking, no!

généralement [ʒeneralmɑ̃] *adv* **1.** [habituellement] generally, usually **2.** [globalement] generally ▪ **~ parlant** generally speaking ▪ **on croit ~ que...** there is a widespread belief that..., it is widely believed that...

généralisable [ʒeneralizabl] *adj* : **l'expérience/la théorie est intéressante, mais est-elle ~?** it's an interesting experiment/theory, but can it be generalized *ou* applied more generally?

généralisateur, trice [ʒeneralizatœr, tris] *adj* : **c'est un livre trop ~** the book generalizes too much *ou* indulges in too many generalizations.

généralisation [ʒeneralizasjɔ̃] *nf* **1.** [propos, idée] generalization **2.** [extension] generalization ▪ **nous assistons à la ~ du conflit/de la maladie** the conflict/the disease is spreading.

généralisé, e [ʒeneralize] *adj* [cancer] general ▪ [conflit, crise] widespread, generalized.

généraliser [3] [ʒeneralize] *vt* **1.** [répandre] : **cette méthode/interdiction a été généralisée** this method/ban now applies to everybody ▪ **cette mesure a été généralisée en 1969** this measure was extended across the board in 1969 **2.** [globaliser] to generalize.
◆ **se généraliser** *vpi* [crise, famine] to become widespread ▪ **l'usage de la carte de crédit s'est généralisé** credit cards are now in general use.

généraliste [ʒeneralist] <> *adj* : **une chaîne de télévision ~** a general-interest TV channel ■ **le caractère ~ de l'entreprise** the diversity of the company's activities.
<> *nmf* MÉD general practitioner, GP.

généralité [ʒeneralite] *nf* **1.** [universalité] generality **2.** [majorité] : **dans la ~ des cas** in most cases.
◆ **généralités** *nfpl* [points généraux] general remarks ■ [banalités] generalities.

générateur, trice [ʒeneratœr, tris] *adj* **1.** [créateur] : **la nouvelle politique salariale sera génératrice d'emplois** the new wages policy will create jobs *ou* generate employment ■ **une industrie génératrice d'emplois** a job-creating industry ■ **un fanatisme ~ de violence** a fanaticism that breeds violence **2.** MATH : **ligne génératrice d'une surface** line which generates a surface.
◆ **générateur** *nm* **1.** ÉLECTR : **~ d'électricité** electricity generator ■ **~ de vapeur** steam generator **2.** INFORM : **~ de programmes** (program) generator ■ **~ automatique de programmes** report program generator ■ **~ de système expert** generic expert system tool ■ **~ de caractères** character generator.
◆ **génératrice** *nf* **1.** ÉLECTR generator **2.** MATH generatrix.

génératif, ive [ʒeneratif, iv] *adj* generative.

génération [ʒenerasjɔ̃] *nf* **1.** BIOL generation ➊ **~ spontanée** spontaneous generation **2.** [groupe d'âge] generation ■ **les jeunes de ma ~** young people my age *ou* of my generation ■ **des immigrés de la seconde ~** second-generation immigrants ■ **la ~ perdue** *fig* the lost generation ■ **entre le grand-père et le petit-fils il y a deux ~s** there are two generations between the grandfather and the grandson **3.** [d'une technique] generation ■ **les lecteurs de disques compacts de la quatrième ~** fourth-generation compact disc *ou* CD players ■ **~ de langage/machine/système** language/computer/system generation **4.** POLIT : **Génération Écologie** *one of the two green parties in France.*

générer [18] [ʒenere] *vt* to generate.

généreusement [ʒenerøzmɑ̃] *adv* **1.** [avec libéralité] generously **2.** [avec noblesse] generously **3.** [en grande quantité] : **se servir à manger ~** to help o.s. to a generous portion ■ **se verser ~ à boire** to pour o.s. a good measure.

généreux, euse [ʒenerø, øz] *adj* **1.** [prodigue] generous ■ **il a été très ~** he gave very generously, he was very generous **2.** [noble - geste, tempérament] noble ■ **des sentiments ~** unselfish *ou* noble sentiments **3.** [fertile - terre] generous, fertile **4.** [abondant - portion] generous ; [- repas] lavish **5.** [plantureux] : **aux formes généreuses** curvacious ■ **une femme à la poitrine généreuse** a woman with an ample bosom **6.** ŒNOL [riche - en alcool] high in alcohol ; [- en saveur] full-bodied.

générique [ʒenerik] <> *adj* generic.
<> *nm* **1.** CINÉ & TV credits ➊ **~ de début/fin** opening/final credits **2.** [indicatif musical] signature tune.

générosité [ʒenerɔzite] *nf* **1.** [largesse] generosity **2.** [bonté] generosity, kindness ■ **je l'ai fait dans un élan de ~** I did it in a sudden fit of kindness **3.** [d'un vin] full body ■ [des formes] opulence.
◆ **générosités** *nfpl* [cadeaux] gifts, liberalities *sout.*

Gênes [ʒɛn] *npr* Genoa.

genèse [ʒənɛz] *nf* **1.** [élaboration] genesis ■ **faire la ~ de qqch** to trace the evolution of sthg **2.** BIBLE : **la Genèse** (the Book of) Genesis.

genet [ʒənɛ] *nm* ZOOL jennet *(horse).*

genêt [ʒənɛ] *nm* BOT broom *(U).*

généticien, enne [ʒenetisjɛ̃, ɛn] *nm, f* geneticist.

génétique [ʒenetik] <> *adj* genetic.
<> *nf* genetics *(sing).*

génétiquement [ʒenetikmɑ̃] *adv* genetically.

gêneur, euse [ʒɛnœr, øz] *nm, f* : **il ne cesse de m'appeler, quel ~!** he keeps phoning me, what a nuisance (he is)!

Genève [ʒənɛv] *npr* Geneva ■ **le lac de ~** Lake Geneva.

genevois, e [ʒənvwa, az] *adj* Genevan, Genevese.
◆ **Genevois, e** *nm, f* Genevan, Genevese ■ **les Genevois** the Genevans, the Genevese.

genévrier [ʒənevrije] *nm* juniper.

Gengis Khan [ʒɛ̃ʒiskɑ̃] *npr* Genghis Khan.

génial, e, aux [ʒenjal, o] *adj* **1.** [qui a du génie] of genius **2.** [ingénieux] brilliant ■ **ce fut une invention ~e** it was a brilliant invention **3.** *fam* [sensationnel] brilliant, great, fantastic ■ **je n'ai pas trouvé cette exposition ~e** I didn't think much of that exhibition ■ **pas ~** not exactly brilliant ■ **elle est ~e, ta copine** your girlfriend is great *ou* fantastic ■ **~!** brilliant *ou* great!

génialement [ʒenjalmɑ̃] *adv* with genius, masterfully, brilliantly.

génie [ʒeni] *nm* **1.** [don] genius ■ **avoir du ~** to be a genius ■ **elle a le ~ des affaires** she has a genius for business ■ **tu as vraiment le ~ pour te mettre dans des situations impossibles!** you have a real gift for *ou* the knack of always getting into difficult situations! **2.** [personne] genius ■ **c'est loin d'être un ~** he's no genius ■ **à 15 ans, c'était déjà un ~ de l'électronique** at 15 he was already an electronics wizard **3.** [essence] genius ■ **le ~ de la langue française** the genius *ou* spirit of the French language **4.** LITTÉR & MYTHOL [magicien] genie ■ [esprit] spirit ➊ **être le bon/mauvais ~ de qqn** to be a good/bad influence on sb **5.** TECHNOL : **le Génie** engineering ■ **les officiers du Génie** ≃ the Royal Engineers *UK*, ≃ the (Army) Corps of Engineers *US* ➊ **~ atomique/chimique/civil/génétique** nuclear/chemical/civil/genetic engineering ■ **~ maritime/militaire** marine/military engineering ■ **~ logiciel** systems engineering.
◆ **de génie** *loc adj* [musicien, inventeur] of genius ■ [idée] brilliant.

genièvre [ʒənjɛvr] *nm* **1.** BOT [arbre] juniper ■ [fruit] juniper berry ■ **grain de ~** juniper berry **2.** [eau-de-vie] geneva.

génisse [ʒenis] *nf* heifer.

génital, e, aux [ʒenital, o] *adj* ANAT & PSYCHOL genital.

géniteur, trice [ʒenitœr, tris] *nm, f* *hum* progenitor.
◆ **géniteur** *nm* ZOOL sire.

génitif [ʒenitif] *nm* GRAMM genitive (case), *voir aussi* **pluriel**.

génito-urinaire [ʒenitɔyrinɛr] (*pl* **génito-urinaires**) *adj* genito-urinary.

génocide [ʒenɔsid] *nm* genocide.

génois, e [ʒenwa, az] *adj* Genoese, Genovese.
◆ **Génois, e** *nm, f* Genoese, Genovese ■ **les Génois** the Genoese, the Genovese.
◆ **génoise** *nf* CULIN sponge cake ■ **une ~e fourrée aux abricots** an apricot sponge (cake).

génome [ʒenom] *nm* genome.

génothérapie [ʒenɔterapi] *nf* MÉD gene therapy.

génotype [ʒenɔtip] *nm* genotype.

genou, x [ʒənu] *nm* **1.** ANAT knee ■ **on était dans la neige jusqu'aux ~x** we were knee-deep *ou* up to our knees in snow ■ **cette année les jupes s'arrêtent au ~** knee-length skirts are the fashion this year ■ **mon jean est troué aux ~x** my jeans have got holes at *ou* in the knees ■ **mettre un ~ à terre** to go down on one knee ■ **assis sur les ~x de sa mère** sitting on his mother's lap *ou* knee ➊ **faire du ~ à qqn** to play footsie with sb ■ **être sur les ~x** to be exhausted **2.** TECHNOL [joint] ball-and-socket joint **3.** COUT knee pad.
◆ **à genoux** *loc adv* **1.** [sur le sol] : **mets-toi à ~x** get down on your knees, kneel down **2.** *fig* **être à ~x devant qqn** [lui être soumis] to be on one's knees before sb ; [être en adoration devant lui] to worship sb ■ **c'est à tomber** *ou* **se mettre à ~x tellement c'est beau** it's so beautiful it bowls you over ■ **je ne vais pas me mettre à ~x devant lui** [le supplier] I'm not going to go down on my knees to him ■ **je te le demande à ~x** I beg of you.

genouillère [ʒənujɛr] *nf* **1.** [protection] knee pad **2.** [bandage] knee bandage *ou* support **3.** ARM knee piece, genouillère.

genre [ʒɑ̃r] *nm* **1.** [sorte, espèce] kind, sort, type ▪ **quel ~ de femme est-elle?** what kind of woman is she? ▪ **ce n'est pas le ~ à renoncer** she's not the sort to give up *ou* who gives up ▪ **partir sans payer, ce n'est pas son ~** it's not like him to leave without paying ▪ **dans le ~ vulgaire on ne fait pas mieux!** beat that for vulgarity! ▪ **il a exigé qu'on lui rembourse le dessert, tu vois le ~!** he had the dessert deducted from the bill, you know the sort! ▪ **un ~ de** [une sorte de] a kind *ou* sort of ▪ **elle m'a répondu quelque chose du ~ "je ne suis pas ta bonne"** she answered something along the lines of "I'm not here to wait on you"
2. [comportement, manières] type, style ▪ **le ~ intellectuel** the intellectual type ▪ **~ de vie** lifestyle ▪ **avoir un drôle de ~** to be an odd sort ▪ **avoir bon/mauvais ~ : leurs enfants ont vraiment bon ~** their children really know how to behave ▪ **elle a mauvais ~** she's a bit vulgar ▪ **il est romantique, tout à fait mon ~!** he's a romantic, just my type! ➋ **faire du ~, se donner un ~** to put on airs, to give o.s. airs
3. BIOL genus ▪ **le ~ humain** mankind, the human race
4. ART genre
5. GRAMM gender
6. LITTÉR genre ▪ **le ~ policier** the detective genre, detective stories ▪ **le ~ romanesque** the novel.
◆ **dans son genre** *loc adv* [à sa façon] in his/her (own) way.
◆ **en son genre** *loc adv* [dans sa catégorie] : **elle est unique en son ~** she's in a class of her own.
◆ **en tout genre, en tous genres** *loc adv* of all kinds ▪ **travaux en tous ~s** all kinds of work undertaken.

gens[1] [ʒɛ̃s] (*pl* **gentes** [ʒɛ̃tɛs]) *nf* [groupe de familles] gens ▪ **la ~ Cornelia** the gens Cornelia.

gens[2] [ʒɑ̃] *nmpl* & *nfpl* **1.** [personnes] *(adj au f si placé avant; adj au m si placé après)* people ▪ **les vieilles ~** old people, old folk ▪ **beaucoup de ~** many people, a lot of people ▪ **il y a des ~ qui demandent à vous voir** there are some people who want to see you ▪ **~ de la campagne** country folk *ou* people ▪ **les ~ d'ici** people from around here, the locals ▪ **les ~ du monde** society people ▪ **des ~ simples** ordinary folk *ou* people ▪ **les ~ de la ville** townspeople, townsfolk ▪ **petites ~** people of limited means ▪ **les bonnes ~ murmurent que...** people are saying *ou* whispering that... **2.** [corporation] : **comme disent les ~ du métier** as the experts *ou* the professionals say ➋ **les ~ d'Église** clergymen, the clergy, the cloth ▪ **~ de lettres** men and women of letters ▪ **~ de maison** servants, domestic staff ▪ **les ~ de robe** *litt* the legal profession ▪ **~ du spectacle** stage *ou* showbusiness people ▪ **les ~ du voyage** [artistes] travelling players *ou* performers ; [gitans] travellers.

gent [ʒɑ̃] *nf hum* [espèce] : **la ~ masculine/féminine** the male/female sex.

gentiane [ʒɑ̃sjan] *nf* **1.** [plante] gentian **2.** [liqueur] gentian bitters.

gentil, ille [ʒɑ̃ti, ij] *adj* **1.** [serviable] kind ▪ **ils sont ~s avec moi** they're kind *ou* nice to me ▪ **sois ~, apporte-moi mes lunettes** do me a favour and get my glasses for me ▪ **vous serez ~ de me prévenir de leur arrivée** be kind enough to let me know when they are arriving ▪ **merci, c'est ~** thanks, that's very kind of you **2.** [aimable] nice, sweet ▪ **elle a pris mon idée sans me le dire, ce n'est pas très ~** she stole my idea without telling me, that's not very nice (of her) **3.** [joli] nice, pretty, cute ▪ **un ~ petit minois** a cute little face **4.** [exprimant l'impatience] : **c'est bien ~ tout ça mais si on parlait affaires?** that's all very well but what about getting down to business? **5.** [obéissant] good ▪ **si tu es ~/~le** if you're a good boy/girl **6.** *(avant le n)* [considérable] : **une ~le somme** a tidy *ou* fair sum.
◆ **gentil** *nm* [non-juif] Gentile ▪ **les ~s** the Gentiles.

gentilhomme [ʒɑ̃tijɔm] (*pl* **gentilshommes** [ʒɑ̃tizɔm]) *nm* **1.** HIST nobleman, gentleman ▪ **~ de la garde** gentleman-at-arms ▪ **~ campagnard** (country) squire, country gentleman **2.** *litt* [gentleman] gentleman.

gentilhommière [ʒɑ̃tijɔmjɛr] *nf* country seat, manor house.

gentillesse [ʒɑ̃tijɛs] *nf* **1.** [d'une personne] kindness *(U)* ▪ **j'étais touché par la ~ de leur accueil** I was moved by their kind welcome **2.** [dans des formules de politesse] : **ayez la ~ de me prévenir à l'avance** be so kind as to let me know beforehand **3.** [parole] kind word ▪ **échanger des ~s** *iron* to exchange insults **4.** [acte] act of kindness ▪ **elle est toujours prête à toutes les ~s** she's always ready to help people out.

gentillet, ette [ʒɑ̃tijɛ, ɛt] *adj* **1.** [mignon] : **il est ~, leur appartement** they've got a lovely little flat *UK ou* apartment *US* **2.** *péj* **c'est un film ~, sans plus** it's a pleasant enough film, but that's about it.

gentiment [ʒɑ̃timɑ̃] *adv* **1.** [aimablement] kindly ▪ **les retardataires se sont fait ~ taper sur les doigts** the latecomers got a rap on the knuckles **2.** [sagement] : **on discutait ~ quand...** we were chatting away nicely *ou* quietly chatting away when...

gentleman [dʒɛntləman] (*pl* **gentlemen** [-mɛn]) *nm* gentleman ▪ **en parfait ~** like a true gentleman.

génuflexion [ʒenyflɛksjɔ̃] *nf* genuflection ▪ **faire une ~** to genuflect.

géochimie [ʒeɔʃimi] *nf* geochemistry.

géochimiste [ʒeɔʃimist] *nmf* geochemist.

géode [ʒeɔd] *nf* GÉOL & MÉD geode.

géodésie [ʒeɔdezi] *nf* geodesy, geodetics *(sing)*.

géodésique [ʒeɔdezik] ◇ *adj* **1.** MATH geodesic ▪ **point ~** triangulation point **2.** GÉOGR geodetic.
◇ *nf* **1.** MATH geodesic (line) **2.** GÉOGR geodesic (line).

géographe [ʒeɔgraf] *nmf* geographer.

géographie [ʒeɔgrafi] *nf* **1.** [science] geography ▪ **~ humaine/physique/politique** human/physical/political geography **2.** [livre] geography book.

géographique [ʒeɔgrafik] *adj* geographic, geographical.

geôle [ʒol] *nf litt* jail, gaol *UK*.

geôlier, ère [ʒolje, ɛr] *nm, f litt* jailer, gaoler *UK* ▪ **les lois ne doivent pas être les geôlières de la liberté** *fig* the law must not fetter liberty.

géologie [ʒeɔlɔʒi] *nf* geology.

géologique [ʒeɔlɔʒik] *adj* geologic, geological.

géologue [ʒeɔlɔg] *nmf* geologist.

géomètre [ʒeɔmɛtr] ◇ *nmf* **1.** MATH geometer, geometrician **2.** [arpenteur] land surveyor.
◇ *nm* ENTOM [chenille] measuring worm, looper ▪ [papillon] geometrid *ou* geometer moth.

géométrie [ʒeɔmetri] *nf* **1.** MATH geometry ▪ **~ euclidienne/non euclidienne** Euclidean/non-Euclidean geometry ▪ **~ plane/dans l'espace** plane/solid geometry **2.** [livre] geometry book.
◆ **à géométrie variable** *loc adj* **1.** [avion] swing-wing *(modif)* **2.** *fig* [susceptible d'évoluer] flexible, adaptable.

géométrique [ʒeɔmetrik] *adj* **1.** MATH geometric, geometrical ▪ **progression/suite ~** geometric progression/series **2.** ART geometric ▪ **abstraction ~** geometrical abstraction.

géométriquement [ʒeɔmetrikmɑ̃] *adv* geometrically.

géomorphologie [ʒeɔmɔrfɔlɔʒi] *nf* geomorphology.

géophysicien, enne [ʒeɔfizisjɛ̃, ɛn] *nm, f* geophysicist.

géophysique [ʒeɔfizik] ◇ *adj* geophysical.
◇ *nf* geophysics *(sing)*.

géopolitique [ʒeɔpɔlitik] ◇ *adj* geopolitical.
◇ *nf* geopolitics *(sing)*.

Georges [ʒɔrʒ] *npr* : **saint ~** Saint George.

Géorgie [ʒeɔrʒi] *npr f* : **(la) ~** Georgia.

georgien, enne [ʒɔrʒjɛ̃, ɛn] *adj* ARCHIT Georgian.

géorgien, enne [ʒeɔrʒjɛ̃, ɛn] *adj* GÉOGR Georgian.
◆ **Géorgien, enne** *nm, f* Georgian.
◆ **géorgien** *nm* LING Georgian.

géorgique [ʒeɔrʒik] *adj* LITTÉR georgic.

géosphère [ʒeɔsfɛr] *nf* geosphere.

géostationnaire [ʒeɔstasjɔnɛr] *adj* : **satellite ~** geostationary satellite.

géostatistique [ʒeɔstatistik] *nf* geostatistics *(sing)*.

géostratégie [ʒeɔstrateʒi] *nf* geostrategy.

gérable [ʒerabl] *adj* manageable ■ **un problème/une situation difficilement ~** a problem/a situation which is difficult to deal with *ou* to manage.

gérance [ʒerɑ̃s] *nf* management ■ **assurer la ~ de** to be (the) manager of, to manage ■ **prendre/reprendre un fonds en ~** to take on/to take over the management of a business ■ **mettre un fonds en ~** to appoint a manager to a business ▶ **~ libre** tenant management.

géranium [ʒeranjɔm] *nm* geranium.

gérant, e [ʒerɑ̃, ɑ̃t] *nm, f* manager (*f* manageress) ■ **~ d'immeubles** managing agent *(for an apartment block)* ■ **~ de société** managing director *(of a company)* ■ **~ de magasin** store manager.

gerbe [ʒɛrb] *nf* **1.** [de blé] sheaf ■ [de fleurs] wreath **2.** [de feu d'artifice] spray, gerbe *spéc* **3.** [jaillissement - d'eau] spray ; [- d'étincelles] shower ■ **une ~ de flammes** a blaze, a burst of flame **4.** ASTRON & PHYS shower.

gerber [3] [ʒɛrbe] ◇ *vt* **1.** [blé] to bind, to sheave, to bind into sheaves **2.** [fûts, paquets] to pile (up) *(sép)*, to stack (up) *(sép)*.
◇ *vi* **1.** △ [vomir] to throw up, to puke△ ■ **ça me fait ~** it makes me want to throw up *ou* puke△ **2.** [feu d'artifice] to shower, to fan out.

gerbier [ʒɛrbje] *nm* stack, rick.

gerboise [ʒɛrbwaz] *nf* jerboa.

gerce [ʒɛrs] *nf* **1.** MÉTALL crack **2.** [dans le bois] crack, flaw.

gercer [16] [ʒɛrse] ◇ *vi* **1.** [peau, mains, lèvres] to chap, to crack ■ **chaque hiver, j'ai les mains qui gercent** every winter I get chapped hands **2.** [bois, métal, enduit] to crack.
◇ *vt* to chap, to crack.
◆ **se gercer** *vpi* [peau, mains, lèvres] to chap, to get chapped, to crack ■ [terre] to crack.

gerçure [ʒɛrsyr] *nf* **1.** [des mains, des lèvres] crack, chapping *(U)* ■ **j'ai des ~s aux mains/lèvres** I've got chapped hands/lips **2.** TECHNOL [d'un métal, d'un enduit] hairline crack ■ [d'un diamant, du bois] flaw ■ [d'un tronc] shake.

géré, e [ʒere] *adj* **1.** [affaire, entreprise] : **bien ~** well managed ■ **mal ~** poorly managed **2.** INFORM : **~ par ordinateur** computer-assisted, computer-controlled ■ **~ par le système** system-maintained.

gérer [18] [ʒere] *vt* **1.** [budget, fortune] to administer, to manage ■ **mal ~ qqch** to mismanage sthg ■ **~ une tutelle** to administer the estate of a ward ■ **ils se contentent de ~ la crise** *fig* they're (quite) happy to sit out the crisis **2.** [entreprise, hôtel, magasin] to manage, to run ■ [stock, production] to control **3.** [ménage] to administer ■ [temps] to organize **4.** INFORM to manage ■ **~ des données/un fichier** to manage data/a file.

gerfaut [ʒɛrfo] *nm* gerfalcon, gyrfalcon.

gériatre [ʒerjatr] *nmf* geriatrician, geriatrist.

gériatrie [ʒerjatri] *nf* geriatrics *(sing)*.

gériatrique [ʒerjatrik] *adj* geriatric.

germain, e [ʒɛrmɛ̃, ɛn] *adj* **1.** [ayant un grand-parent commun] : **cousine ~e** first cousin **2.** [du même père et de la même mère] : **frère ~** full brother ■ **sœur ~e** full sister **3.** [d'Allemagne] Germanic, German.
◆ **Germain, e** *nm, f* German.

Germanie [ʒɛrmani] *npr f* HIST : **(la) ~** Germania.

germanique [ʒɛrmanik] ◇ *adj* **1.** HIST Germanic **2.** [allemand] Germanic ■ **à consonance ~** German-sounding.
◇ *nm* LING Germanic ■ HIST & LING Germanic, Proto-Germanic.

germanisant, e [ʒɛrmanizɑ̃, ɑ̃t] *nm, f* Germanist.

germaniser [3] [ʒɛrmanize] *vt* to Germanize.

germanisme [ʒɛrmanism] *nm* Germanism.

germaniste [ʒɛrmanist] *nmf* Germanist.

germanophile [ʒɛrmanɔfil] ◇ *adj* German-loving, Germanophile.
◇ *nmf* Germanophile.

germanophilie [ʒɛrmanɔfili] *nf* love of Germany, Germanophilia.

germanophobe [ʒɛrmanɔfɔb] ◇ *adj* German-hating, Germanophobic.
◇ *nmf* Germanophobe.

germanophobie [ʒɛrmanɔfɔbi] *nf* hatred towards Germany, Germanophobia.

germanophone [ʒɛrmanɔfɔn] ◇ *adj* German-speaking.
◇ *nmf* German speaker ■ **les ~s** German-speaking people *ou* peoples.

germe [ʒɛrm] *nm* **1.** ANAT, BIOL & MÉD germ ■ **~ dentaire** tooth bud **2.** [pousse] : **~ de pomme de terre** potato sprout ▶ **~ de blé** wheat germ ■ **~s de soja** (soya) bean sprouts **3.** [origine] : **le ~ d'une idée** the germ of an idea ■ **les ~s de la révolution** the seeds of revolution.
◆ **en germe** *loc adv* : **la théorie était déjà présente en ~ dans leur premier manifeste** the theory was already there in embryonic form in their first manifesto.

germé, e [ʒɛrme] *adj* [pomme de terre] sprouting ■ [blé] germinated.

germer [3] [ʒɛrme] *vi* **1.** AGRIC & HORT [graine] to germinate ■ [bulbe, tubercule] to shoot, to sprout ■ **faire ~ du blé** to germinate corn **2.** [idées] to germinate ■ **le concept a d'abord germé dans l'esprit des urbanistes** the notion first took shape in the minds of town planners.

germinal, e, aux [ʒɛrminal, o] *adj* germinal ■ **cellule ~e** reproductive *ou* germ cell.
◆ **germinal** *nm* Germinal *(7th month of the French Revolutionary calendar from March 22 to April 20)*.

germinatif, ive [ʒɛrminatif, iv] *adj* [du germe] germinative.

germination [ʒɛrminasjɔ̃] *nf* BIOL germination.

germoir [ʒɛrmwar] *nm* **1.** [pot] seed tray **2.** [bâtiment] germination area.

gérondif [ʒerɔ̃dif] *nm* [en latin] gerundive ■ [en français] gerund, *voir aussi* **pluriel**.

gérontocratie [ʒerɔ̃tɔkrasi] *nf* gerontocracy.

gérontologie [ʒerɔ̃tɔlɔʒi] *nf* gerontology.

gérontologue [ʒerɔ̃tɔlɔg] *nmf* gerontologist.

gésier [ʒezje] *nm* gizzard.

gésir [49] [ʒezir] *vi* **1.** [être étendu] to lie, to be lying **2.** [être épars] to lie.

Gestapo [gɛstapo] *npr f* : **la ~** the Gestapo.

gestation [ʒɛstasjɔ̃] *nf* **1.** BIOL gestation ■ **période de ~** gestation period **2.** *fig* [d'une œuvre] gestation (period).
◆ **en gestation** *loc adj* **1.** BIOL [fœtus] gestating **2.** *fig* **un roman en ~** a novel in preparation.

geste [ʒɛst] ◇ *nm* **1.** [mouvement] movement ■ [signe] gesture ■ **faire des ~s en parlant** to speak with one's hands ■ **d'un ~, elle le pria de sortir** she motioned to him (that she wanted him) to go out ■ **faire un ~ approbateur** to nod one's assent *ou* approval ■ **d'un ~ de la main, il refusa le whisky** he waved aside the glass of whisky ■ **congédier qqn d'un ~** to dismiss sb with a wave of the hand ■ **avoir un ~ malheureux** to make a clumsy gesture *ou* movement ■ **sans un ~** without moving ■ **pas un ~ ou je tire!** don't move or I'll shoot! ■ **il épie mes moindres ~s** *ou* **tous mes ~s** he watches my every move **2.** [action] gesture ■ **un ~ politique/diplomatique** a political/diplomatic gesture ■ **faire un beau ~** to make a noble gesture ■ **allez, fais un ~!** come on, do something! ■ **vous n'avez qu'un ~ à faire** you only

have to say the word ▪ **il a eu un ~ touchant, il m'a apporté des fleurs** a rather touching thing he did was to bring me some flowers.
◇ *nf* LITTÉR gest, geste.

gesticulation [ʒɛstikylasjɔ̃] *nf* gesticulation ▪ **cesse tes ~s!** stop gesticulating, stop waving your arms about!

gesticuler [3] [ʒɛstikyle] *vi* to gesticulate, to wave one's arms about.

gestion [ʒɛstjɔ̃] *nf* **1.** COMM & INDUST management ▪ **chargé de la ~ de l'hôtel** in charge of running *ou* managing the hotel ▪ **par une mauvaise ~** through bad management, through mismanagement ▪ **techniques de ~** management techniques *ou* methods ▪ **~ du stress** stress management ➊ **~ administrative** office management ▪ **~ d'affaires** (day-to-day) running of affairs *ou* business ▪ **~ assistée par ordinateur** computer-aided management ▪ **~ du changement** change management ▪ **~ prévisionnelle** forward planning ▪ **~ de la production** production management ▪ **~ de stock** inventory *ou* stock control **2.** INFORM management ▪ **système de ~ de base de données** database management system ▪ **~ de fichiers** file management ▪ **~ intégrée** integrated management ▪ **~ de périphérique** driver ▪ **~ des performances** performance monitoring *ou* tuning ▪ **~ des projets/travaux** project/job scheduling.

gestionnaire [ʒɛstjɔnɛr] ◇ *adj* administrative, managing, management *(modif)*.
◇ *nmf* **1.** ADMIN administrator **2.** COMM & INDUST manager, administrator.
◇ *nm* INFORM manager ▪ **~ de base de données** database administrator ▪ **~ de fichiers** file manager ▪ **~ de périphériques** driver ▪ **~ de tâches** task scheduler.

gestuel, elle [ʒɛstɥɛl] *adj* gestural ▪ **langage ~** gestural language.
◆ **gestuelle** *nf* **1.** [gén] non-verbal communication **2.** DANSE & THÉÂTRE gesture.

geyser [ʒezɛr] *nm* geyser.

Ghana [gana] *npr m* : **le ~** Ghana.

ghanéen, enne [ganeɛ̃, ɛn] *adj* Ghanaian, Ghanian.
◆ **Ghanéen, enne** *nm, f* Ghanaian, Ghanian.

ghetto [gɛto] *nm* ghetto.

ghettoïsation [gɛtoizasjɔ̃] *nf* ghettoisation.

gibecière [ʒibsjɛr] *nf* **1.** CHASSE gamebag **2.** *vieilli* [d'un écolier] satchel.

gibelin, e [ʒiblɛ̃, in] *adj* & *nm, f* Ghibelline.

gibelotte [ʒiblɔt] *nf* rabbit stew *(made with white wine)*.

giberne [ʒibɛrn] *nf* cartridge pouch.

gibet [ʒibɛ] *nm* **1.** [potence] gibbet, gallows **2.** RELIG : **le ~** the Rood.

gibier [ʒibje] *nm* **1.** [animaux] game *(U)* ▪ **gros/petit ~** big/small game ▪ **~ à plumes** game birds *ou* fowl *(U)* ▪ **~ à poil** game animals **2.** CULIN [viande] game **3.** *fam* [personne] quarry, prey ▪ **ces types-là, c'est du gros ~** these guys are in the big-time ▪ **un ~ de potence** a gallows bird.

giboulée [ʒibule] *nf* shower ▪ **~s de mars** April showers.

giboyeux, euse [ʒibwajø, øz] *adj* abounding *ou* rich in game, well stocked with game.

Gibraltar [ʒibraltar] *npr* Gibraltar ▪ **à ~** in Gibraltar ▪ **le détroit de ~** the strait of Gibraltar.

GIC ◇ *nm* = **grand invalide civil**.
◇ *npr m* = **Groupe interministériel de contrôle**.

giclée [ʒikle] *nf* **1.** [de liquide] jet, spurt, squirt **2.** △ [coup de feu] burst (of machine-gun fire).

gicler [3] [ʒikle] *vi* [liquide] to spurt, to squirt ▪ **arrête de faire ~ de l'eau!** stop splashing *ou* squirting water!

gicleur [ʒiklœr] *nm* AUTO (carburettor) jet ▪ **~ de pompe** pump nozzle.

GIE *nm* = **groupement d'intérêt économique**.

gifle [ʒifl] *nf* **1.** [coup] slap (in the face) ▪ **donner une ~ à qqn** to slap sb's face, to box sb's ears ▪ **une fameuse ~** a real smack in the face **2.** [humiliation] (burning) insult, slap in the face.

gifler [3] [ʒifle] *vt* **1.** [suj: personne] : **~ qqn** to slap sb's face *ou* sb in the face **2.** [suj: pluie, vent] to lash **3.** [humilier] to humiliate.

GIG (*abr de* **grand invalide de guerre**) *nm war invalid.*

gigantesque [ʒigɑ̃tɛsk] *adj* **1.** [animal, plante, ville] gigantic, giant *(modif)* **2.** [projet] gigantic, giant *(modif)* ▪ [erreur] huge, gigantic.

gigantisme [ʒigɑ̃tism] *nm* **1.** ANAT, BOT & ZOOL gigantism, giantism **2.** *fig* gigantic size ▪ **une ville atteinte de ~** a city that has grown to enormous proportions.

gigaoctet [ʒigaɔktɛ] *nm* INFORM gigabyte.

GIGN (*abr de* **Groupe d'intervention de la gendarmerie nationale**) *npr m special crack force of the gendarmerie,* ≃ SAS *UK,* ≃ SWAT *US.*

gigogne [ʒigɔɲ] *adj* ▷ **lit**, ▷ **poupée**, ▷ **table**.

gigolo [ʒigɔlo] *nm fam* gigolo.

gigot [ʒigo] *nm* CULIN leg ▪ **~ (d'agneau)** leg of lamb ▪ **~ de chevreuil** haunch of venison.

gigoter [3] [ʒigɔte] *vi* [bébé] to wriggle (about) ▪ [enfant] to fidget.

gigue [ʒig] *nf* **1.** DANSE gigue, jig ▪ **danser la ~** *fig* to wriggle about, to jig up and down **2.** MUS gigue **3.** *fam* [jambe] leg **4.** *fam* [personne] : **une grande ~** a beanpole **5.** CULIN : **~ de chevreuil** haunch of venison.

gilet [ʒilɛ] *nm* **1.** [vêtement - taillé] waistcoat *UK*, vest *US* ; [- tricoté] cardigan **2.** [sous-vêtement] vest *UK*, undershirt *US* **3.** [protection] : **~ pare-balles** bulletproof vest ▪ **~ de sauvetage** life jacket.

gin [dʒin] *nm* gin.

gingembre [ʒɛ̃ʒɑ̃br] *nm* ginger.

gingival, e, aux [ʒɛ̃ʒival, o] *adj* gingival *spéc*, gum *(modif)*.

gingivite [ʒɛ̃ʒivit] *nf* gum disease, gingivitis *spéc*.

gingko(-biloba) [ʒinkɔ(bilɔba)] *nm* gingko.

gin-rami [dʒinrami] (*pl* **gin-ramis**), **gin-rummy** [dʒinrœmi] (*pl* **gin-rummys**) *nm* gin rummy.

ginseng [ʒinsɑ̃g] *nm* ginseng.

gin-tonic [dʒintɔnik] (*pl* **gin-tonics**) *nm* gin and tonic.

girafe [ʒiraf] *nf* **1.** ZOOL giraffe **2.** *fam* [personne] beanpole **3.** *fam* CINÉ, RADIO & TV boom.

girafeau, x [ʒirafo], **girafon** [ʒirafɔ̃] *nm* baby giraffe.

giration [ʒirasjɔ̃] *nf* gyration.

giratoire [ʒiratwar] *adj* gyrating, gyratory, ▷ **sens**.

girl [gœrl] *nf* chorus *ou* show girl.

girofle [ʒirɔfl] *nm* clove.

giroflée [ʒirɔfle] *nf* BOT gillyflower.

giroflier [ʒirɔflije] *nm* clove (tree).

girolle [ʒirɔl] *nf* chanterelle.

giron [ʒirɔ̃] *nm* **1.** [d'une personne] lap ▪ **dans le ~ de sa mère** in his mother's lap **2.** *litt* [communauté] bosom ▪ **le ~ familial** the family fold ▪ **accepté dans le ~ de l'Église** accepted into the fold *ou* the bosom of the Church **3.** [d'une marche] tread **4.** HÉRALD giron, gyron.

girond, e [ʒirɔ̃, ɔ̃d] *adj fam vieilli* plump, buxom, well-padded ▪ **une femme plutôt ~e** a buxom *ou* plump woman.

Gironde [ʒirɔ̃d] *npr f* **1.** GÉOGR : **la ~** [département] the Gironde *(département in Aquitaine; chef-lieu: Bordeaux, code: 33)* ; [fleuve] the Gironde ; [estuaire] the Gironde estuary **2.** HIST : **la ~** the Girondist party.

girondin, e [ʒirɔ̃dɛ̃, in] *adj* **1.** GÉOGR from the Gironde **2.** HIST Girondist.
◆ **Girondin, e** *nm, f* **1.** GÉOGR *inhabitant of or person from the Gironde* **2.** HIST Girondist **3.** SPORT : **les Girondins (de Bordeaux)** *the Bordeaux football team.*

girouette [ʒirwɛt] *nf* **1.** [sur un toit] weathercock, weather vane **2.** NAUT (mast) **3.** *fam* [personne] weathercock ▪ **c'est une vraie ~!** he keeps changing his mind!, he's a real weathercock!

gis, gisait *etc v* ▷ **gésir.**

gisant, e [ʒizɑ̃, ɑ̃t] *adj litt* [corps] lifeless, motionless.
◆ **gisant** *nm* ART recumbent figure *ou* statue.

gisement [ʒizmɑ̃] *nm* GÉOL & MIN deposit ▪ **~ aurifère** *ou* **d'or** goldfield ▪ **~ houiller** [filon] coal deposit *ou* measures ; [bassin] coalfield ▪ **~ de pétrole** *ou* **pétrolifère** oilfield.

gît *v* ▷ **gésir.**

gitan, e [ʒitɑ̃, an] *adj* Gypsy *(modif).*
◆ **Gitan, e** *nmf* Gypsy.
◆ **gitane** *nf* Gitane (cigarette).

gîte [ʒit] ◇ *nm* **1.** [foyer] home ▪ **le ~ et le couvert** room and board ▶ **~ d'étape** [pour randonneurs] halt ▪ **~ rural** gîte **2.** chasse [de gibier] lair ▪ [de lièvre] form **3.** [viande] shin *UK ou* shank *US*(of beef) ▪ **~ à la noix** topside *UK*, round *US* **4.** MIN bed, deposit.
◇ *nf* NAUT list.

gîter [3] [ʒite] *vi* **1.** *sout* [voyageur] to stay **2.** [lapin] to couch ▪ [oiseau] to perch **3.** NAUT to list.

givrage [ʒivraʒ] *nm* **1.** AÉRON icing ▪ **à 9 000 mètres, on risque le ~** at 9,000 metres icing may occur **2.** [sur un verre] frosting.

givrant, e [ʒivrɑ̃, ɑ̃t] *adj* : **brouillard ~** freezing fog.

givre [ʒivr] *nm* **1.** [glace] frost ▪ **couvert de ~** frosted over **2.** JOAILL white fleck.

givré, e [ʒivre] *adj* **1.** [arbre] covered with frost ▪ [serrure] iced up **2.** [verre] frosted *(with sugar)* **3.** CULIN : **orange ~e** orange sorbet *UK ou* sherbet *US (served inside the fruit)* **4.** *fam* [fou] screwy, nuts.

givrer [3] [ʒivre] *vt* **1.** [avec du sucre] to frost **2.** [couvrir de givre] to cover with frost.
◆ **se givrer** *vpi* [se couvrir de givre] to frost *ou* to ice up.

glabre [glabr] *adj* **1.** [imberbe] smooth-chinned ▪ [rasé] clean-shaven ▪ **le visage ~** with a smooth face **2.** BOT glabrous, hairless.

glaçage [glasaʒ] *nm* **1.** [d'un tissu, du cuir, du papier, de photos] glazing ▪ INDUST [polissage] surfacing, burnishing **2.** CULIN [d'un gâteau] icing ▪ [de bonbons] sugar coating ▪ [de légumes, d'un poisson, d'une viande] glazing.

glaçant, e [glasɑ̃, ɑ̃t] *adj* [regard, attitude] cold, frosty.

glace [glas] *nf* **1.** [eau gelée] ice ▪ **rompre** *ou* **briser la ~** to break the ice **2.** [crème glacée] ice cream, ice *UK* ▪ [sucette] ice lolly *UK*, popsicle *US* ▪ [cône] ice cream (cone) ▪ **~ à la vanille/à l'abricot** vanilla/apricot ice cream **3.** CULIN icing ▪ **~ royale** royal icing ▪ [de viande] glaze **4.** [miroir] mirror ▪ **une ~ sans tain** a two-way mirror **5.** [vitre - d'un véhicule, d'une boutique] window **6.** TECHNOL sheet of plate glass ▪ **~ flottée** float glass **7.** JOAILL (white) fleck *ou* flaw **8.** INDUST : **~ sèche** *ou* **carbonique** dry ice.
◆ **glaces** *nfpl* [du pôle] ice fields ▪ [sur un fleuve] ice sheets ▪ [en mer] ice floes, drift ice ▪ **le navire est pris dans les ~s** the ship is icebound.
◆ **de glace** *loc adj* [accueil, visage, regard] icy, frosty ▪ **être** *ou* **rester de ~** to remain unmoved.

glacé, e [glase] *adj* **1.** [transformé en glace] frozen **2.** [lieu] freezing *ou* icy (cold) **3.** [personne] frozen, freezing cold ▪ **j'ai les pieds ~** my feet are frozen **4.** [hostile] frosty, icy **5.** CULIN [dessert, soufflé, café] iced ▪ [petit four] glacé ▪ [oignon, viande, poisson] glazed **6.** [brillant - photo] glossy ; [- papier] glazed ; [- cuir, soie] glazed, glacé.
◆ **glacé** *nm* glaze, gloss.

glacer [16] [glase] *vt* **1.** [transformer en glace] to freeze **2.** [refroidir - bouteille] to chill **3.** [transir] : **un froid qui vous glace jusqu'aux os** weather that chills you to the bone **4.** *fig* [pétrifier] : **son regard me glace** the look in his eye turns me cold ▪ **ça m'a glacé le sang (dans les veines)** it made my blood run cold ▪ **un hurlement à vous ~ le sang** a blood-curdling scream ▪ **ce souvenir me glace encore le cœur** the memory still sends shivers down my spine **5.** CULIN [petit four, oignon, poisson *etc*] to glaze ▪ [gâteau] to ice, to frost *US* **6.** INDUST & TECHNOL to glaze, to glacé.
◆ **se glacer** *vpi* : **leur sang se glaça dans leurs veines** their blood ran cold.

glacerie [glasri] *nf* **1.** [fabrication] ice-cream making **2.** [commerce] ice-cream trade.

glaciaire [glasjɛr] ◇ *adj* glacial.
◇ *nm* : **le ~** the Ice Age, the glacial period *ou* epoch.

glacial, e, als *ou* **aux** [glasjal, o] *adj* **1.** [climat] icy, freezing ▪ [vent] bitter, freezing ▪ [pluie] freezing (cold) **2.** [sourire] frosty ▪ [abord, personne] cold ▪ **elle est vraiment ~e** she's really cold *ou* a real iceberg.
◆ **glacial** *adv* : **il fait ~** it's freezing cold.

glaciation [glasjasjɔ̃] *nf* glaciation ▪ **pendant la ~** during the Ice Age.

glacier [glasje] *nm* **1.** GÉOL glacier ▪ **~ de vallée** valley *ou* Alpine glacier **2.** [confiseur] ice cream man *ou* salesman.

glacière [glasjɛr] *nf* **1.** [local] cold room **2.** [armoire] refrigerated cabinet ▪ [récipient] cool box ▪ **mon bureau est une ~!** *fig* my office is like a fridge *ou* an icebox!

glaciologie [glasjɔlɔʒi] *nf* glaciology.

glacis [glasi] *nm* **1.** HIST : **le ~ soviétique** the Soviet buffer zone **2.** ART glaze, scumble **3.** GÉOGR glacis ▪ **~ d'érosion** pediment.

glaçon [glasɔ̃] *nm* **1.** GÉOGR & MÉTÉOR [sur un fleuve] block of ice, ice floe ▪ [sur un étang] patch of ice ▪ [en mer] ice floe **2.** [pour boisson] ice cube ▪ **voulez-vous un ~?** would you like some ice? ▪ **servi avec des ~s** served with ice *ou* on the rocks **3.** *fig* **cette fille est un ~** that girl's a real cold fish.

gladiateur [gladjatœr] *nm* gladiator.

glaïeul [glajœl] *nm* gladiolus ▪ **des ~s** gladioli.

glaire [glɛr] *nf* **1.** PHYSIOL mucus ▪ **~ cervicale** cervical mucus **2.** [d'œuf] white **3.** [pour le cuir] glair.

glaise [glɛz] ◇ *nf* clay.
◇ *adj f* : **terre ~** (potter's) clay.

glaive [glɛv] *nm* glaive *arch*, broadsword ▪ **le ~ de la Justice** *litt* the sword of Justice.

gland [glɑ̃] *nm* **1.** [du chêne] acorn **2.** COUT tassel **3.** ANAT glans **4.** △ [imbécile] prat△ *UK*, jerk *US*.

glande [glɑ̃d] *nf* **1.** ANAT gland ▪ **~s endocrines/exocrines** endocrine/exocrine glands ▪ **~ lacrymale** tear gland ▪ **~ salivaire** salivary gland **2.** [ganglion] (neck) gland **3.** △ *loc* **foutre les ~s à qqn** to scare the hell out of sb△.

glander [3] △ [glɑ̃de] *vi* **1.** [ne rien faire] to loaf about ▪ **il a glandé pendant toute l'année** he's done nothing but loaf about all year **2.** [attendre] to hang around **3.** *loc* **j'en ai rien à ~** I don't give a damn△.

glandeur, euse△ [glɑ̃dœr, øz] *nmf* layabout.

glandouiller△ [glɑ̃duje] = **glander.**

glandulaire [glɑ̃dylɛr], **glanduleux, euse** [glɑ̃dylø, øz] *adj* glandular.

glaner [3] [glane] *vt* **1.** [ramasser - épis] to glean ; [- bois] to gather ; [- fruits] to gather, to pick up *(sép)* **2.** *fig* [renseignements, détails] to glean, to gather ▪ **il y a toujours quelque chose à ~ dans ses cours** there is always something to be got out of *ou* gleaned from his classes.

glaneur, euse [glanœr, øz] *nmf* gleaner.

glapir [32] [glapir] ◇ *vi* **1.** [renard] to bark ▪ [chiot] to yelp, to yap **2.** [personne] to yelp, to squeal.
◇ *vt* to shriek.

glapissement [glapismɑ̃] *nm* **1.** [du chien] yelp ▪ [du renard] bark **2.** [d'une personne] : **les enfants surexcités poussaient des ~s** the overexcited children were squealing.

glas [gla] *nm* knell ▪ **on sonne le ~ pour notre cousine** the bell is tolling *ou* they are tolling the knell for our cousin.

glaucome [glokom] *nm* glaucoma.

glauque [glok] *adj* **1.** *sout* [verdâtre] bluish-green, glaucous *litt* **2.** *fam* [lugubre] dreary.

glaviot [glavjo] *nm*△ gob of spit.

glissade [glisad] *nf* **1.** [jeu] sliding *(U)* **2.** DANSE glissade **3.** AÉRON : **~ sur l'aile** sideslip **4.** [glissoire] slide.

glissant, e [glisɑ̃, ɑ̃t] *adj* **1.** [sol] slippery ▪ **être sur une pente ~e/sur un terrain ~** to be on a slippery slope/on slippery ground **2.** [coulissant] sliding.

glisse [glis] *nf* [d'un ski] friction coefficient ▪ **sports de ~** *generic term referring to sports such as skiing, surfing, windsurfing etc.*

glissement [glismɑ̃] *nm* **1.** [déplacement] sliding *(U)* **2.** [évolution] shift ▪ **la politique du gouvernement a connu un net ~ à droite** there's been a marked shift to the right in government policy **3.** LING : **~ de sens** shift in meaning **4.** GÉOL : **~ de terrain** landslide, landslip.

glisser [3] [glise] ◇ *vi* **1.** [déraper - personne] to slip ; [- voiture] to skid ▪ **mon pied a glissé** my foot slipped ▪ **attention, ça glisse par terre** watch out, it's slippery underfoot *ou* the ground's slippery
2. [s'échapper accidentellement] to slip ▪ **ça m'a glissé des mains** it slipped out of my hands
3. [tomber] to slide ▪ **il se laissa ~ à terre** he slid to the ground
4. [avancer sans heurt - skieur, patineur] to glide along ; [- péniche, ski] to glide
5. [passer] : **son regard glissa de la fenêtre à mon fauteuil** his eyes drifted from the window to my chair ▪ **glissons sur ce sujet!** let's say no more about it ▪ **sur toi, tout glisse comme l'eau sur les plumes d'un canard** it's like water off a duck's back with you
6. *fig* [s'orienter] : **~ à** *ou* **vers** to shift to *ou* towards ▪ **une partie de l'électorat a glissé à gauche** part of the electorate has shifted *ou* moved to the left ▪ **il glisse vers le mélodrame** he is slipping into melodrama
7. DANSE to glissade
8. INFORM to drag.
◇ *vt* **1.** [introduire] to slip ▪ **~ une lettre sous la porte** to slip a letter under the door ▮ [dire furtivement] : **j'ai glissé ton nom dans la conversation** I managed to slip *ou* to drop your name into the conversation
2. [confier] : **~ un petit mot/une lettre à qqn** to slip sb a note/a letter ▪ **~ qqch à l'oreille de qqn** to whisper sthg in sb's ear
3. *loc* **~ un œil dans une pièce** to peep *ou* to peek into a room.
◆ **se glisser** *vpi* **1.** [se faufiler] : **se ~ au premier rang** [rapidement] to slip into the front row ▪ **glisse-toi là** [sans prendre de place] squeeze (yourself) in there
2. [erreur] : **des fautes ont pu se ~ dans l'article** some mistakes may have slipped *ou* crept into the article
3. [sentiment] : **le doute s'est peu à peu glissé en lui** little by little doubt crept into his mind.

glissière [glisjɛr] *nf* **1.** TECHNOL slide, runner ▪ **à ~** sliding ▪ **porte à ~** sliding door **2.** TRAV PUB : **~ de sécurité** crash barrier.

glissoire [gliswar] *nf* slide *(on ice).*

global, e, aux [glɔbal, o] *adj* [résultat, vision] overall, global ▪ **as-tu une idée ~e du coût?** have you got a rough idea of the cost? ◗ **revenu ~** total income.

globalement [glɔbalmɑ̃] *adv* all in all, overall ▪ **~, l'entreprise se porte bien** all in all *ou* by and large, the company is doing well.

globalisation [glɔbalizasjɔ̃] *nf* [d'un marché, d'un conflit] globalization.

globaliser [3] [glɔbalize] *vt* [réunir] : **le syndicat a globalisé ses revendications** the union is putting forward its demands en bloc.

globalité [glɔbalite] *nf* [ensemble] : **envisageons le processus dans sa ~** let's view the process as a whole ▪ **si l'on envisage les problèmes dans leur ~** if we look at all the problems together.

globe [glɔb] *nm* **1.** [sphère] globe ▪ **le ~** [la Terre] the globe, the world ▪ **sur toute la surface du ~** all over the globe ▪ **une région déshéritée du ~** a poor part of the world ◗ **~ céleste** celestial globe ▪ **le ~ terrestre** the terrestrial globe **2.** [d'une lampe] (glass) globe **3.** [pour protéger] glass dome ▪ **c'est une idée géniale, il faut la mettre sous ~!** *fig* that's a brilliant idea, we must make a note of it and keep it safe! **4.** ANAT globe ▪ **~ oculaire** eye.

globe-trotteur, euse [glɔbtrɔtœr, øz] (*mpl* **globe-trotteurs**, *fpl* **globe-trotteuses**) *nm* globe-trotter.

globulaire [glɔbylɛr] *adj* **1.** [sphérique] globular, globe-shaped **2.** BIOL & PHYSIOL corpuscular.

globule [glɔbyl] *nm* **1.** BIOL & PHYSIOL corpuscle ▪ **~ blanc** white corpuscle, white blood cell ▪ **~ rouge** red corpuscle, red blood cell **2.** PHARM (spherical) capsule.

globuleux, euse [glɔbylø, øz] *adj* **1.** [forme] globular, globulous **2.** [œil] protruding, bulging.

gloire [glwar] *nf* **1.** [renom] fame ▪ **connaître la ~** to find fame ▪ **au faîte** *ou* **sommet de sa ~** at the height *ou* pinnacle of his fame ▪ **ne t'attends pas à être payé, on fait ça pour la ~** don't expect payment, we're doing it for love **2.** [mérite] glory, credit ▪ **toute la ~ vous en revient** the credit is all yours ▪ **se faire ~ de** to boast about ◗ **c'est pas la ~** *fam* it's not exactly brilliant **3.** [éloge] praise ▪ **écrit à la ~ de...** written in praise of... ▪ **rendre ~ au courage de qqn** to praise sb's courage ▪ **~ à Dieu** praise be to *ou* glory to God **4.** [personne] celebrity **5.** ART [auréole] aureole ▪ [ciel décoré] glory **6.** RELIG glory ▪ **le séjour de ~** the Kingdom of Glory.

gloriette [glɔrjɛt] *nf* [pavillon] gazebo.

glorieux, euse [glɔrjø, øz] *adj* **1.** [remarquable] glorious ▪ **il a eu une mort glorieuse** he died a glorious death ▪ **une page peu glorieuse de notre histoire** an event in our history we can be less than proud of ▪ **ce n'est pas ~** *fam fig* it's not exactly brilliant **2.** *litt* [fier] : **~ de sa victoire** priding himself on his victory **3.** RELIG glorious.
◆ **Glorieuse** *nf* HIST : **les Trente Glorieuses** *the thirty years following the Second World War, now seen as a period of great economic and social progress* ▪ **les Trois Glorieuses** *the three-day Revolution in 1830 (27, 28 and 29 July).*

glorification [glɔrifikasjɔ̃] *nf sout* glorification.

glorifier [9] [glɔrifje] *vt* [exploit, qualité, héros] to glorify, to praise ▪ [Dieu] to glorify.
◆ **se glorifier de** *vp+prép* : **se ~ de qqch** to glory in sthg ▪ **se ~ d'avoir fait qqch** to boast of having done sthg.

gloriole [glɔrjɔl] *nf* vainglory ▪ **faire qqch par ~** to do sthg to show off *ou* for show.

glose [gloz] *nf* gloss.

gloser [3] [gloze] *vt* [annoter] to annotate, to gloss.
◆ **gloser sur** *v+prép* **1.** [discourir sur] : **~ sur qqch** to ramble on about sthg **2.** [jaser sur] : **~ sur qqch/qqn** to gossip about sthg/sb.

glossaire [glɔsɛr] *nm* glossary, vocabulary.

glotte [glɔt] *nf* ANAT glottis ▪ **coup de ~** LING glottal stop.

glouglou [gluglu] *nm* **1.** *fam* [d'une fontaine] gurgle, gurgling ▪ [d'une bouteille] glug-glug ▪ **faire ~** [fontaine] to gurgle ; [bouteille] to go glug-glug **2.** [du dindon] gobbling.

glouglouter [3] [gluglute] *vi* **1.** *fam* [fontaine] to gurgle ▪ [bouteille] to go glug-glug **2.** [dindon] to gobble.

gloussement [glusmɑ̃] *nm* **1.** [d'une personne] chuckle ▪ **~s** giggling **2.** [d'une poule] clucking.

glousser [3] [gluse] *vi* **1.** [personne] to chuckle **2.** [poule] to cluck.

glouton, onne [glutɔ̃, ɔn] ◇ *adj* greedy, gluttonous ■ **que ce bébé est ~!** what a greedy baby!
◇ *nmf* glutton.
◆ **glouton** *nm* ZOOL wolverine, glutton.

gloutonnerie [glutɔnri] *nf* gluttony.

glu [gly] *nf* **1.** [substance visqueuse] birdlime ■ **prendre des oiseaux à la ~** to lime birds **2.** *fam* [personne] : **c'est une vraie ~** she sticks to you like glue.

gluant, e [glyɑ̃, ɑ̃t] *adj* sticky, slimy ■ **riz ~** glutinous rice.

glucide [glysid] *nm* carbohydrate.

glucosamine [glykozamin] *nf* PHARM glucosamine.

glucose [glykoz] *nm* glucose.

gluten [glytɛn] *nm* gluten ■ **sans ~** gluten-free.

glycémie [glisemi] *nf* blood-sugar level, glycemia *spéc.*

glycérine [gliserin] *nf* glycerin, glycerine.

glycine [glisin] *nf* **1.** BOT wisteria **2.** CHIM glycine, glycocoll.

GMT (*abr de* **Greenwich Mean Time**) GMT.

gnangnan [ɲɑ̃ɲɑ̃] *fam* ◇ *adj inv péj* **1.** [personne] dopey **2.** [œuvre, style] : **j'ai vu le film, que c'était ~!** I saw the film, it was so soppy!
◇ *nm, f* wimp.

gnognot(t)e [ɲɔɲɔt] *nf fam* **c'est de la ~** [c'est facile] that's *ou* it's a cinch ; [c'est sans valeur] that's *ou* it's rubbish *UK ou* garbage *US*.

gnole△, **gnôle**△ [nol] *nf* hard stuff, hooch *US*.

gnome [gnom] *nm* **1.** [génie] gnome **2.** *sout* [nabot] dwarf, gnome.

gnon [ɲɔ̃] *nm fam* **1.** [coup] thump ■ **elle lui a flanqué un sacré ~** she gave him a real thump **2.** [enflure] bruise.

gnose [gnoz] *nf* gnosis.

gnosticisme [gnɔstisism] *nm* Gnosticism.

gnostique [gnɔstik] *adj* & *nmf* Gnostic.

gnou [gnu] *nm* wildebeest, gnu.

go [go] *nm inv* go ■ **le jeu de go** go.
◆ **tout de go** *loc adv fam* [dire, annoncer *etc*] straight out ■ **il est entré tout de go** he went straight in.

GO *nfpl* (*abr de* **grandes ondes**) LW.

goal [gol] *nm* [gardien] goalkeeper.

gobelet [gɔblɛ] *nm* **1.** [timbale] tumbler, beaker ■ **~ jetable** [en papier] paper cup ; [en plastique] plastic cup **2.** JEUX shaker.

Gobelins [gɔblɛ̃] *npr mpl* : **la manufacture des ~** *the factory in Paris where Gobelin tapestry is made.*

gobe-mouches [gɔbmuʃ] *nm inv* **1.** ORNITH flycatcher **2.** *fam vieilli* [naïf] gull.

gober [3] [gɔbe] *vt* **1.** [avaler - huître] to swallow ; [- œuf] to suck ; [- insecte] to catch (and eat) **2.** *fam* [croire] to swallow ■ **ils ont tout gobé!** they swallowed it (all), hook, line and sinker! **3.** *fam* [supporter] : **je n'ai jamais pu la ~!** I never could stand *ou* stick *UK* her! **4.** *fam loc* **ne reste pas là à ~ les mouches!** don't just stand there gawping!, don't just stand there like a lemon! *UK ou* lump! *US*.
◆ **se gober** *vpi fam* to think a lot of o.s.

goberger [17] [gɔbɛrʒe] ◆ **se goberger** *vpi fam* **1.** [festoyer] to have a ball, to whoop it up **2.** [se prélasser] to laze (about).

Gobi [gɔbi] *npr* : **le désert de ~** the Gobi Desert.

godailler [gɔdaje] = **goder**.

godasse [gɔdas] *nf fam* shoe.

godelureau, x [gɔdlyro] *nm hum* (young) Romeo, ladies' man.

godemiché [gɔdmiʃe] *nm* dildo.

godendart [godɑ̃dar] *nm Québec* two-handed saw.

goder [3] [gɔde] *vi* COUT to pucker, to be puckered.

godet [gɔdɛ] *nm* **1.** [petit récipient] jar ■ [verre] tumbler ■ **un ~ en étain** a pewter mug **2.** [pour peinture] pot **3.** [d'une pipe] bowl **4.** [nacelle - d'une noria] scoop ; [- d'une roue à eau, en manutention] bucket **5.** COUT [à ondulation] flare ■ [à découpe] gore ■ [défaut] pucker, ruck.

godiche [gɔdiʃ] *fam* ◇ *adj* [maladroit] oafish ■ [niais] silly, dumb *US* ■ **ce qu'il peut être ~!** he's such an oaf!
◇ *nf* [maladroite] clumsy thing ■ [niaise] silly thing.

godille [gɔdij] *nf* **1.** [rame] (stern-mounted) scull ■ **avancer à la ~** to scull **2.** [à ski] wedeln.

godiller [3] [gɔdije] *vi* **1.** NAUT to scull **2.** [au ski] to wedeln.

godillot [gɔdijo] *nm* **1.** [chaussure] clodhopper **2.** *fam* [personne] party-liner, yes-man.

goéland [gɔelɑ̃] *nm* seagull ■ **~ argenté/cendré** herring/common gull.

goélette [gɔelɛt] *nf* schooner.

goémon [gɔemɔ̃] *nm* wrack.

goglu [gogly] *nm Québec* bobolink.

gogo [gogo] *nm fam* sucker.
◆ **à gogo** *loc adv fam* galore.

goguenard, e [gɔgnar, ard] *adj* mocking, jeering ■ **un œil ~** a mocking look.

goguenardise [gɔgnardiz] *nf sout* mocking, jeering.

goguette [gɔgɛt] ◆ **en goguette** *loc adj* merry, a little tiddly ■ **des commerciaux en ~** some salesmen having a boozy get-together.

goïm [gɔjim] *pl* ▷ **goy**.

goinfre [gwɛ̃fr] *nmf fam* pig.

goinfrer [3] [gwɛ̃fre] ◆ **se goinfrer** *vpi fam* to pig *ou* to stuff o.s. ■ **se ~ de qqch** to stuff o.s. with sthg.

goinfrerie [gwɛ̃frəri] *nf fam* piggyness ■ **arrête de manger, c'est de la ~** stop eating, you're just being a pig *ou* making a pig of yourself.

goitre [gwatr] *nm* goitre.

goitreux, euse [gwatrø, øz] ◇ *adj* goitrous.
◇ *nm, f person with a goitre.*

golden [gɔldɛn] *nf* Golden Delicious.

golem [golɛm] *nm* golem.

golf [gɔlf] *nm* **1.** SPORT : **le ~** golf **2.** [terrain] (golf) links, golf course ■ **~ miniature** miniature golf, mini-golf.

golfe [gɔlf] *nm* gulf.

GOLFES

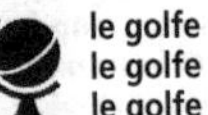

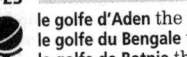

le golfe d'Aden the Gulf of Aden ;
le golfe du Bengale the Bay of Bengal ;
le golfe de Botnie the Gulf of Bothnia ;
le golfe de Californie the Gulf of California ;
le golfe de Gascogne the Bay of Biscay ;
le golfe du Lion the Gulf of Lions ;
le golfe du Mexique the Gulf of Mexico ;
le golfe Persique the Persian Gulf ;
le golfe de Thaïlande the Gulf of Siam.

Golfe [gɔlf] *npr m* : **le ~** the Gulf ■ **les États/la Guerre du ~** the Gulf States/War.

golfeur, euse [gɔlfœr, øz] *nmf* golfer.

Golgi [gɔlgi] *npr* : **appareil de ~** MÉD Golgi body *ou* apparatus.

Gomina® [gɔmina] *nf* brilliantine, ≃ Brylcreem®.

gominer [3] [gɔmine] ◆ **se gominer** *vp (emploi réfléchi)* to put Brylcreem® *ou* hair cream on.

gommage [gɔmaʒ] *nm* **1.** [effacement] erasing **2.** [de la peau] exfoliation ■ **se faire faire un ~** to have one's skin deep-cleansed **3.** [encollage] gumming.

gomme [gɔm] *nf* **1.** [pour effacer] rubber *UK*, eraser ▪ ~ **à encre** ink rubber *OU* eraser **2.** [substance] gum ▪ ~ **adragante** tragacanth ▪ ~ **arabique** gum arabic **3.** MÉD gumma **4.** [friandise] gum ▪ ~ **à mâcher** chewing-gum, bubble-gum **5.** *fam loc* **à la** ~ lousy ▪ **mettre (toute) la** ~ [en voiture] to step on it ; [au travail] to pull out all the stops.

gommé, e [gɔme] *adj* [papier] gummed.

gommer [3] [gɔme] *vt* **1.** [avec une gomme] to rub out *UK (sép)*, to erase **2.** [faire disparaître] to chase away *(sép)*, to erase **3.** [estomper] : ~ **les contours** to soften the outline **4.** [encoller] to gum.

Gomorrhe [gɔmɔr] *npr* ▻ **Sodome**.

Goncourt [gɔ̃kur] *npr* : **le prix** ~ *prestigious annual literary prize awarded by the Académie Goncourt.*

gond [gɔ̃] *nm* hinge ⊳ **sortir de ses ~s** to blow one's top, to fly off the handle.

gondolage [gɔ̃dɔlaʒ] *nm* [du bois] warping ▪ [d'une tôle] buckling ▪ [du papier] cockling.

gondolant, e△ [gɔ̃dɔlɑ̃, ɑ̃t] *adj* *vieilli* hysterical, side-splitting.

gondole [gɔ̃dɔl] *nf* COMM & NAUT gondola ▪ **tête de** ~ COMM gondola head.

gondolement [gɔ̃dɔlmɑ̃] = **gondolage**.

gondoler [3] [gɔ̃dɔle] ◇ *vi* [bois] to warp, to get warped ▪ [tôle] to buckle.
◇ *vt* to wrinkle, to crinkle ▪ **un disque gondolé** a warped record.
◆ **se gondoler** *vpi* **1.** [se déformer - bois] to warp ; [- papier] to wrinkle ; [- tôle] to buckle **2.** △ [rire] to fall about (laughing) ▪ **ils se sont tous gondolés quand je leur ai dit** when I told them they all fell about (laughing) *OU* they were all in stitches.

gondolier, ère [gɔ̃dɔlje, ɛr] *nmf* COMM merchandise assistant.
◆ **gondolier** *nm* [batelier] gondolier.

gonflable [gɔ̃flabl] *adj* [canot] inflatable ▪ [ballon, poupée] blow-up.

gonflage [gɔ̃flaʒ] *nm* **1.** [d'un pneu] inflating ▪ [d'un ballon] blowing up ▪ **vérifie le ~ des pneus** check the tyre pressure **2.** CINÉ enlargement.

gonflant, e [gɔ̃flɑ̃, ɑ̃t] *adj* **1.** [bouffant - jupon] full ; [- manche] puffed **2.**△ [irritant] : **c'est ~!** what a drag!
◆ **gonflant** *nm* [d'un tissu, d'une chevelure] volume.

gonflé, e [gɔ̃fle] *adj* **1.** [enflé] swollen, puffed up **2.** *fam loc* **t'es ~!** [effronté] you've got a nerve *OU* some cheek! ; [courageux] you've got guts! ▪ **être ~ à bloc** [en pleine forme] to be full of beans ; [plein d'ardeur] to be itching *OU* raring to go.

gonflement [gɔ̃fləmɑ̃] *nm* **1.** [grosseur] swelling **2.** [augmentation - des prix] inflation ; [- des statistiques] exaggeration ; [- des impôts] excessive increase **3.** AUTO blowing up, inflating.

gonfler [3] [gɔ̃fle] ◇ *vt* **1.** [remplir d'un gaz - bouée, pneu] to inflate, to blow up *(sép)* ; [- poumons] to fill ▪ **avoir le cœur gonflé de peine/de chagrin/de joie** to be heartbroken/grief-stricken/overjoyed **2.** [faire grossir - voiles] to fill ▪ **un abcès lui gonflait la joue** his cheek was swollen with an abscess ▪ **les yeux gonflés de sommeil/de larmes** eyes swollen with sleep/with tears **3.** [augmenter - prix, devis] to inflate, to push up *(sép)* ; [- frais, statistiques] to exaggerate, to inflate ; [- importance, impact] to exaggerate, to blow out of all proportion ; [- moteur] to soup up **4.** CINÉ to blow up *(sép)*, to enlarge **5.**△ [irriter] : ~ **qqn** to get on sb's nerves *OU UK* wick.
◇ *vi* **1.** CULIN [pâte] to rise ▪ [riz] to swell (up) **2.** [enfler] to be puffed up *OU* bloated ▪ **le bois a gonflé** the wood has warped ▪ **la bière fait ~ l'estomac** beer bloats the stomach.
◆ **se gonfler** ◇ *vp (emploi passif)* **ce matelas se gonfle à l'aide d'une pompe** this air bed can be blown up with a pump.
◇ *vpi* **1.** [voile] to swell ▪ [éponge] to swell up **2.** [se remplir de gaz] to inflate **3.** *fig* **son cœur se gonfle d'allégresse** her heart is bursting with joy.

gonflette [gɔ̃flɛt] *nf* *fam péj* **faire de la ~** to pump iron.

gonfleur [gɔ̃flœr] *nm* (air) pump.

gong [gɔ̃g] *nm* **1.** MUS gong **2.** SPORT bell.

gonocoque [gɔnɔkɔk] *nm* gonococcus ▪ **des ~s** gonococci.

gonorrhée [gɔnɔre] *nf* gonorrhoea.

gonzesse△ [gɔ̃zɛs] *nf* **1.** [femme] bird△ *UK*, chick *US* **2.** [homme] sissy, pantywaist△ *US*.

gordien [gɔrdjɛ̃] *adj m* ▻ **nœud**.

goret [gɔrɛ] *nm* **1.** [porcelet] piglet **2.** *fam* [personne] : **petit ~!** you grubby little pig!

gorge [gɔrʒ] *nf* **1.** [gosier] throat ▪ **avoir mal à la ~** to have a sore throat ⊳ **l'arête m'est restée en travers de la ~** *pr* the bone got stuck in my throat ▪ **son refus m'est resté en travers de la ~** *fig* his refusal stuck in my throat ▪ **avoir la ~ nouée** *OU* **serrée** to have a lump in one's throat ▪ **l'odeur/la fumée vous prenait à la ~** the smell/smoke made you gag ▪ **rire à ~ déployée** to roar with laughter ▪ **prendre qqn à la ~** *pr* to grab *OU* to take sb by the throat ▪ **pris à la ~, ils ont dû emprunter** *fig* they had a gun to their heads, so they had to borrow money ▪ **tenir qqn à la ~** *pr* to hold sb by the throat ; *fig* to have a strangle-hold on sb ▪ **faire rendre ~ à qqn** to force sb to pay *OU* to cough up ▪ **faire des ~s chaudes de qqn/qqch** to have a good laugh about sb/sthg **2.** *litt* [seins] bosom **3.** GÉOGR gorge **4.** ARCHIT groove, glyph, channel **5.** CONSTR [d'une cheminée] throat ▪ [d'une fenêtre] groove **6.** MÉCAN [d'une poulie] groove, score ▪ [d'une serrure] tumbler.

gorge-de-pigeon [gɔrʒdəpiʒɔ̃] *adj inv* dove-coloured.

gorgée [gɔrʒe] *nf* mouthful ▪ **à petites ~s** in little sips ▪ **à grandes ~s** in great gulps ▪ **d'une seule ~** in one gulp.

gorger [17] [gɔrʒe] *vt* : ~ **un enfant de sucreries** to stuff a child full of sweets ▪ **des champs gorgés d'eau** waterlogged fields.
◆ **se gorger de** *vp+prép* **1.** [se remplir de] : **au moment de la mousson, les rizières se gorgent d'eau** during the monsoon the rice paddies fill to overflowing with water **2.** [manger avec excès] : **se ~ de fruits** to gorge o.s. with fruit.

gorgone [gɔrgɔn] *nf* **1.** *litt* [femme] gorgon, virago **2.** ZOOL gorgonian.

gorgonzola [gɔrgɔ̃zɔla] *nm* Gorgonzola (cheese).

gorille [gɔrij] *nm* **1.** ZOOL gorilla **2.** *fam* [garde] bodyguard, gorilla.

Gorki [gɔrki] *npr* : **Maxime ~** Maxim Gorky.

gosette [gozɛt] *nf* *Belgique* *fruit-filled pastry.*

gosier [gozje] *nm* [gorge] throat, gullet ⊳ **ça m'est resté en travers du ~** *fam* it really stuck in my throat.

gospel [gɔspɛl] *nm* gospel (music).

gosse [gɔs] *nmf* *fam* **1.** [enfant] kid ▪ **sale ~!** you brat! ▪ **c'est une ~ de la rue** she grew up in the street **2.** [fils, fille] kid **3.** [jeune] : **il est beau ~** he's a good-looking chap.

Gotha [gɔta] *nm* [aristocratie] aristocracy ▪ [élite] elite ▪ **le ~ de l'édition** the leading lights of the publishing world ▪ **tout le ~ de la mode était là** (all) the big names in fashion were there.

gothique [gɔtik] ◇ *adj* **1.** ART & HIST Gothic **2.** LITTÉR Gothic.
◇ *nm* **1.** ART : **le ~** the Gothic style **2.** LITTÉR : **le ~** Gothic.
◇ *nf* Gothic (type).

Goths [go] *npr mpl* : **les ~** the Goths.

gouache [gwaʃ] *nf* gouache ▪ **peindre à la ~** to paint in *OU* with gouache.

gouaille [gwaj] *nf* *vieilli* cheeky humour.

gouailleur, euse [gwajœr, øz] *adj* *vieilli* mocking, cheeky.

gouape [gwap] *nf* *fam vieilli* hoodlum, hood△.

gouda [guda] *nm* Gouda (cheese) ▪ **vieux ~** mature Gouda.

goudron [gudrɔ̃] *nm* tar ▪ ~ **bitumineux** bitumen.
◆ **goudrons** *nmpl* (cigarette) tar.

goudronnage [gudrɔnaʒ] *nm* tarring, surfacing.

goudronné, e [gudrɔne] *adj* : **papier ~** tar-lined paper ■ **route ~e** tarred road.

goudronner [3] [gudrɔne] *vt* **1.** [route] to tar, to surface (with tar) **2.** [bateau] to pay.

goudronneux, euse [gudrɔnø, øz] *adj* tarry.
◆ **goudronneuse** *nf* [machine] tar tank *ou* spreader.

gouffre [gufr] *nm* GÉOL [dû à l'effondrement] trough fault (valley) ■ [dû à un fleuve] swallow hole ■ [abîme] chasm, abyss, pit ■ **cette affaire sera un ~ financier** this business will just swallow up money, we'll have to keep on pouring money into this business ■ **être au bord du ~** to be on the edge of the abyss.

gougnafier [guɲafje] *nm* ***fam vieilli*** good-for-nothing ■ **faire qqch comme un ~** to make a pig's ear of sthg *UK*, to foul sthg up.

gouille [guj] *nf* ***Suisse*** pond.

gouine△ [gwin] *nf* ***péj*** dyke△.

goujat [guʒa] *nm* ***sout*** boor.

goujaterie [guʒatri] *nf* ***sout*** boorishness, uncouthness ■ **quelle ~!** how uncouth!

goujon [guʒɔ̃] *nm* **1.** ZOOL gudgeon **2.** CONSTR [de bois] dowel ■ [de métal] gudgeon **3.** MÉCAN [de poulie] pin.

goujonner [3] [guʒɔne] *vt* **1.** CONSTR [bois] to dowel ■ [métal] to bolt **2.** MÉCAN to bolt (with gudgeons).

goulache [gulaʃ] *nm* goulash.

goulag [gulag] *nm* Gulag.

goulasch [gulaʃ] = **goulache**.

goulée [gule] *nf* **1.** [de liquide] gulp **2.** [d'air] : **prendre une ~ d'air** to take in a lungful of air.

goulet [gulɛ] *nm* **1.** [rétrécissement] narrowing ➤ **~ d'étranglement** bottleneck **2.** GÉOL gully, (narrow) gorge **3.** [chenal] channel.

gouleyant, e [gulejɑ̃, ɑ̃t] *adj* ŒNOL lively.

goulot [gulo] *nm* **1.** [de bouteille] neck ■ **boire au goulot** to drink straight from the bottle **2.** ***fig*** **~ d'étranglement** bottleneck.

goulu, e [guly] ◇ *adj* greedy, gluttonous.
◇ *nm, f* glutton.

goulûment [gulymɑ̃] *adv* greedily ■ **manger ~** to eat greedily, to gobble (down) one's food.

goupil [gupi] *nm* ***arch*** fox.

goupille [gupij] *nf* (joining) pin, cotter (pin).

goupiller [3] [gupije] *vt* **1.** TECHNOL to pin, to (fix with a) cotter **2.** ***fam*** [combiner] to set up *(sép)* ■ **elle avait bien goupillé son coup** she'd set it up neatly *ou* planned it just right.
◆ **se goupiller** *vpi* ***fam*** [se dérouler] to turn out ■ **ça s'est bien/mal goupillé** things turned out well/badly.

goupillon [gupijɔ̃] *nm* **1.** [brosse] bottle-brush **2.** RELIG aspersorium.

gourbi [gurbi] *nm* **1.** ***fam*** [taudis] slum **2.** [en Afrique du Nord] gourbi, shack.

gourd, e [gur, gurd] *adj* [engourdi] numb, stiff ■ **j'ai les doigts ~s** my fingers are numb *ou* stiff (with cold).

gourde [gurd] ◇ *adj* ***fam*** dopey, thick.
◇ *nf* **1.** [récipient - en peau] leather flask, wineskin ; [- en métal ou plastique] bottle, flask **2.** [courge] gourd **3.** ***fam*** [personne] blockhead, twit.

gourdin [gurdɛ̃] *nm* cudgel.

gourer [3] [gure] ◆ **se gourer** *vpi* ***fam*** [se tromper] : **je me suis gouré d'adresse** I made a slip-up with the address ■ **je me suis gouré dans les horaires** I got the times mixed up.

gourmand, e [gurmɑ̃, ɑ̃d] *adj* **1.** [personne] greedy ■ **~ de chocolat** fond of chocolate ‖ [gastronomique] : **notre page ~e** our food *ou* gastronomy page ■ **les petites recettes ~es de Julie** Julie's special *ou* tasty recipes **2.** [bouche] greedy ■ [lèvres] eager ■ [regard] greedy, eager **3.** [État, fisc] greedy.
◆ **gourmand** *nm* BOT sucker.

gourmander [3] [gurmɑ̃de] *vt* ***sout*** to rebuke, to castigate, to upbraid.

gourmandise [gurmɑ̃diz] *nf* **1.** [caractère] greediness, greed **2.** [sucrerie] delicacy.

gourme [gurm] *nf* **1.** [du cheval] strangles *(sing)*, equine distemper **2.** ***fam loc*** **jeter sa ~** ***vieilli*** to sow one's wild oats.

gourmet [gurmɛ] *nm* gourmet, epicure.

gourmette [gurmɛt] *nf* **1.** JOAILL (chain) bracelet **2.** [pour cheval] curb (chain).

gourou [guru] *nm* **1.** RELIG guru **2.** ***fig*** guru, mentor.

gousse [gus] *nf* [de haricot] pod, husk ■ [de petit pois] pod ■ [d'ail] clove ■ [de vanille] bean, pod.

gousset [gusɛ] *nm* **1.** COUT [de gilet] waistcoat pocket ■ [de pantalon] fob pocket **2.** CONSTR [traverse] support ■ [plaque] gusset, plate.

goût [gu] *nm* **1.** [sens] taste ■ **perdre le ~** to lose one's sense of taste
2. [saveur] taste ■ **avoir un drôle de ~** to taste funny ■ **ça a un ~ de miel/moutarde** it tastes of honey/mustard ■ **ce vin a un ~ de bouchon** this wine is corked ■ **ça n'a aucun ~** it's tasteless, it's got no taste ■ **ajoutez du sucre selon votre ~** add sugar to taste ➤ **je vais lui faire passer le ~ du mensonge** I'm going to put a stop to his lying once and for all
3. [préférence] taste ■ **un ~ marqué** *ou* **particulier pour...** a great liking *ou* fondness for... ■ **avoir des ~s de luxe** to have expensive tastes ■ **prendre ~ à qqch** to develop a taste for sthg ■ **c'est (une) affaire** *ou* **question de ~** it's a matter of taste ■ **à chacun son ~, chacun son ~** each to his own ➤ **tous les ~s sont dans la nature** it takes all sorts (to make a world) ■ **des ~s et des couleurs on ne discute pas** ***prov*** there's no accounting for taste
4. [intérêt] taste, liking ■ **il faut leur donner le ~ des maths** we've got to give them a taste *ou* a liking for maths ■ **ne plus avoir ~ à qqch** to have lost one's taste for sthg ■ **faire qqch par ~** to do sthg out of *ou* by inclination
5. [jugement esthétique] taste ■ **les gens de ~** people of taste ■ **elle a bon/mauvais ~** she has good/bad taste ■ **elle n'a aucun ~** she has no taste ■ **une décoration de bon ~** a tasteful decoration ■ **il serait de bon ~ de nous retirer** *ou* **que nous nous retirions** it would be proper to take our leave ■ **il a eu le (bon) ~ de se taire** he had the sense to remain silent ■ **cette plaisanterie est d'un ~ douteux** that joke is in poor *ou* doubtful taste ■ **une remarque de mauvais ~** a remark in poor *ou* bad taste
6. [mode] : **c'était le ~ de l'époque** it was the style of the time ■ **être au ~ du jour** to be in line with current tastes ■ **remettre qqch au ~ du jour** to update sthg ■ **dans ce ~-là : c'était une fourrure en renard, ou quelque chose dans ce ~-là** it was a fox fur, or something of the sort.
◆ **à mon goût, à son goût** *etc loc adj & loc adv* to my/his *etc* liking ■ **le décor est tout à fait à mon ~** the decor is exactly to my liking.
Voir module d'usage

goûter[1] [3] [gute] ◇ *vt* **1.** [aliment, boisson] to taste, to try ■ **voulez-vous ~ ma sauce?** would you like to taste *ou* try my sauce? ■ **fais-moi ~** let me have a taste, give me a taste ■ **ils m'ont fait ~ les spécialités de la région** they had me try the local delicacies **2.** ***sout*** [apprécier] to savour, to enjoy **3.** ***Belgique*** [avoir un goût de] to taste.
◇ *vi* **1.** [prendre une collation] to have an afternoon snack, to have tea *UK* ■ **venez ~, les enfants!** come and have your snack, children! **2.** ***Belgique*** [avoir bon goût] to taste nice.
◆ **goûter à** *v+prép* **1.** [manger] : **tu ne dois pas ~ au gâteau avant le dessert** you mustn't take any cake before the dessert ■ **goûtez donc à ces biscuits** do try some of these biscuits **2.** [faire l'expérience de] to have a taste of.
◆ **goûter de** *v+prép* **1.** [plat] to taste, to try **2.** [faire l'expérience de] to have a taste of ■ **il a goûté de la prison** he has had a taste of prison life.

goûter[2] [gute] *nm* [collation] *afternoon snack for children, typically consisting of bread, butter, chocolate, and a drink* ▪ [fête] children's party ▪ **invité à un ~ d'anniversaire** invited to a (children's) birthday party.

goûteur, euse [gutœr, øz] *nm, f* taster.

goutte [gut] *nf* **1.** [d'eau, de lait, de sang] drop ▪ [de sueur] drop, bead ▪ [de pluie] drop (of rain), raindrop ▪ **il est tombé une ~ (ou deux)** there was a drop (or two) of rain ▪ **~ de rosée** dewdrop ▪ **boire qqch jusqu'à la dernière ~** to drink every last drop of sthg ➲ **avoir la ~ au nez** to have a runny nose ▪ **c'est une ~ d'eau dans la mer** it's a drop in the ocean ▪ **c'est la ~ d'eau qui fait déborder le vase** it's the straw that broke the camel's back **2.** [petite quantité] : **une ~ de** a (tiny) drop of **3.** MÉD [maladie] gout **4.** ARCHIT drop, gutta.

◆ **gouttes** *nfpl* PHARM : **~s pour le nez/les oreilles/les yeux** nose/ear/eye drops.

◆ **goutte à goutte** *loc adv* drop by drop ▪ **tomber ~ à ~** to drip ▪ **ils laissent filtrer les informations ~ à ~** *fig* they are letting the news filter out bit by bit.

◆ **ne... goutte** *loc adv arch* **je n'y comprends** *ou* **entends ~** I can't understand a thing.

goutte-à-goutte [gutagut] *nm inv* MÉD drip *UK*, IV *US* ▪ **ils lui ont mis un ~** they've put him on a drip.

Goutte d'Or [gutdɔr] *npr* : **la ~** *working-class area of Paris with a large immigrant population.*

gouttelette [gutlɛt] *nf* droplet.

goutter [3] [gute] *vi* to drip.

goutteux, euse [gutø, øz] ◇ *adj* gouty.
◇ *nm, f* gout-sufferer.

gouttière [gutjɛr] *nf* **1.** CONSTR gutter ▪ **~ verticale** drainpipe **2.** MÉD (plaster) cast.

gouvernable [guvɛrnabl] *adj* governable ▪ **ce pays n'est pas ~** it's impossible to govern this country, this country is ungovernable.

gouvernail, s [guvɛrnaj] *nm* **1.** NAUT rudder ▪ **~ automatique/compensé** automatic/balanced rudder **2.** *fig* **être au** *ou* **tenir le ~** to call the tune.

gouvernant, e [guvɛrnɑ̃, ɑ̃t] ◇ *adj* ruling ▪ **les classes ~es** the ruling classes.
◇ *nm, f* man (*f* woman) in power ▪ **les ~s** the people in power, the Government.

◆ **gouvernante** *nf* **1.** [préceptrice] governess **2.** [dame de compagnie] housekeeper.

gouverne [guvɛrn] *nf* **1.** *sout* [instruction] : **pour ma/ta ~** for my/your information **2.** NAUT steering **3.** AÉRON control surface ▪ **~ de direction** (tail) rudder.

gouvernement [guvɛrnəmɑ̃] *nm* **1.** [régime] government ▪ **~ fantoche** puppet government ▪ **il est au ~ depuis 15 ans** he has been in government *ou* in power for 15 years **2.** [ensemble des ministres] Government ▪ **le Premier ministre a formé son ~** the Prime Minister has formed his government *ou* cabinet ▪ **le ~ a démissionné** the Government has resigned.

gouvernemental, e, aux [guvɛrnəmɑ̃tal, o] *adj* [parti] ruling, governing ▪ [presse] pro-government ▪ [politique, décision, crise] government *(modif)* ▪ **des dispositions ~es** measures taken by the government ▪ **l'équipe ~e** the Government *ou* Cabinet *UK ou* Administration *US*.

gouverner [3] [guvɛrne] ◇ *vt* **1.** POLIT to rule, to govern ▪ **le pays n'était plus gouverné** the country no longer had a government **2.** *litt* [maîtriser] to govern, to control ▪ **~ ses passions** to control one's passions ▪ **ne nous laissons pas ~ par la haine** let us not be governed *ou* ruled by hatred **3.** NAUT to steer **4.** GRAMM to govern.
◇ *vi* NAUT to steer.

◆ **se gouverner** *vp (emploi réfléchi)* to govern o.s. ▪ **le droit des peuples à se ~ eux-mêmes** the right of peoples to self-government.

gouvernés [guvɛrne] *nmpl* : **les ~** those who are governed.

gouverneur, euse [guvɛrnœr, øz] *nm, f* ADMIN & POLIT governor ▪ **le Gouverneur de la Banque de France** the Governor of the Bank of France ▪ **Gouverneur général** *Québec* Governor general.

goy [gɔj] (*pl* **goyim** *ou pl* **goïm** [gɔjim]) ◇ *adj* goyish.
◇ *nmf* goy ▪ **les goyim** goyim, goys.

goyave [gɔjav] *nf* guava.

goyim [gɔjim] *pl* ▻ **goy.**

GPL (*abr de* **gaz de pétrole liquéfié**) *nm* LPG.

GPS (*abr de* **global positionning system**) *nm* GPS.

GQG (*abr de* **grand quartier général**) *nm* GHQ.

gr = **grade.**

GR *nm* = **(sentier de) grande randonnée.**

Graal [gral] *npr m* : **le ~** the (Holy) Grail.

LES GOÛTS

Dire que l'on aime quelque chose ou quelqu'un

I like French food/reading in bed at night. J'aime la cuisine française/lire au lit la nuit.

I quite/really like her. Je l'aime bien/beaucoup.

I (really) love opera/swimming in the sea. J'adore l'opéra/nager dans la mer.

I like nothing better *ou* **There's nothing I like more than a hot bath.** Rien de tel qu'un bon bain chaud.

I think he's really nice. Je le trouve très sympa.

I have a soft spot for her. J'ai un faible pour elle.

I have a passion for sailing. J'adore la voile.

He's really into jazz *fam.* Il est très branché jazz.

You can't beat a nice cup of tea *fam.* Il n'y a rien de meilleur qu'une bonne tasse de thé.

Dire que l'on n'aime pas quelque chose ou quelqu'un

I don't (really) like him/rap. Je ne l'aime pas (vraiment)./Je n'aime pas (vraiment) le rap.

I don't like being told what to do. Je n'aime pas qu'on me dise ce que je dois faire.

The thing I don't like about him is his arrogance. Ce que je n'aime pas chez lui, c'est son arrogance.

I'm not too keen on classical music *UK*. Je n'aime pas trop la musique classique.

I hate him/football. Je le déteste/Je déteste le foot.

I hate having to get up early. Je déteste me lever tôt.

I can't stand (the sight of) her. Je ne peux pas la voir (en peinture).

If there's one thing I can't stand, it's hypocrisy. S'il y a une chose que je ne supporte pas, c'est bien l'hypocrisie.

Walking in the rain isn't my idea of fun. Marcher sous la pluie, ce n'est pas ce que j'appelle s'amuser.

He's not really into sport *fam.* Il n'est pas très branché sport.

Camping isn't really my (kind of) thing *fam.* Le camping, ce n'est pas tellement mon truc.

grabat [graba] *nm sout* pallet, litter.

grabataire [grabatɛr] ◇ *adj* bedridden.
◇ *nmf* (bedridden) invalid ■ **les ~s** the bedridden.

grabuge [grabyʒ] *nm* **fam il y avait du ~** there was a bit of a rumpus ■ **ça va faire du ~** that's going to cause havoc.

grâce [gras] ◇ *nf* **1.** [beauté - d'un paysage] charm ; [- d'une personne] grace ■ **avec ~** gracefully ■ **plein de ~** graceful ■ **sans ~** graceless **2.** [volonté] : **de bonne ~** with good grace, willingly ■ **avoir la bonne ~ de dire/faire** to have the grace to say/to do ■ **de mauvaise ~** with bad grace ■ **vous auriez mauvaise ~ à** *OU* **de vous plaindre** it would be ungracious of you to complain **3.** [faveur] favour ■ **être en ~ auprès de qqn** to be in favour with sb ■ **rentrer en ~ auprès de qqn** to come back into sb's favour ■ **fais-moi la ~ de m'écouter** do me the favour of listening to me ■ **trouver ~ aux yeux de qqn** to find favour with sb **4.** [sursis - de peine] pardon ; [- dans un délai] grace ■ **accorder sa ~ à qqn** to pardon sb ■ **crier** *OU* **demander ~** to beg for mercy ■ **faire ~ à qqn (de qqch) : je te fais ~ des centimes** I'll let you off the centimes ■ **je te fais ~ du récit complet** I'll spare you the full story ■ **une semaine/un mois de ~** one week's/month's grace ▶ **~ amnistiante** free pardon ■ **~ présidentielle** presidential pardon **5.** RELIG grace ■ **avoir la ~** to be inspired ■ **par la ~ de Dieu** by the grace of God ■ **à la ~ de Dieu** [advienne que pourra] come what may ; [n'importe comment] any old way ▮ [pour exprimer la reconnaissance] : **~ à Dieu!** thanks be to God! ■ **rendre ~** *OU* **~s à Dieu** to give thanks to God **6.** [titre] : **Sa Grâce** His/Her Grace.
◇ *interj arch* mercy ■ **de ~!** for God's *OU* pity's sake!
◆ **grâces** *nfpl* **1.** [faveurs] : **rechercher les bonnes ~s de qqn** to curry favour with sb, to seek sb's favour ■ **être/entrer dans les bonnes ~s de qqn** to be/to get in favour with sb ▮ [manières] : **faire des ~s** to put on airs (and graces) **2.** RELIG : **dire les ~s** to give thanks (after eating).
◆ **grâce à** *loc prép* thanks to.

Grâces [gras] *npr fpl* : **les trois ~** the three Graces.

graciable [grasjabl] *adj* pardonable.

gracier [9] [grasje] *vt* to reprieve.

gracieusement [grasjøzmɑ̃] *adv* **1.** [joliment] gracefully **2.** [aimablement] graciously, kindly ■ **il m'a accueilli le plus ~ du monde** he greeted me very amiably **3.** [gratuitement] free (of charge), gratis.

gracieux, euse [grasjø, øz] *adj* **1.** [joli] charming, graceful ■ **qu'elle est ~, cette danseuse!** graceful dancer! **2.** [aimable] affable, amiable, gracious **3.** [gratuit] free (of charge).

gracile [grasil] *adj litt* slender.

gracilité [grasilite] *nf litt* slenderness, slimness.

Gracques [grak] *npr mpl* : **les ~** the Gracchi.

gradation [gradasjɔ̃] *nf* **1.** [progression] : **il y a une ~ dans nos exercices** we grade our exercises ■ **avec une ~ lente** gradually, by degrees ▶ **~ ascendante/descendante** gradual increase/decrease **2.** [étape] stage.

grade [grad] *nm* **1.** [rang] rank ■ **avancer** *OU* **monter en ~** to be promoted ▶ **en prendre pour son ~** *fam* to get it in the neck *esp UK*, to get hauled over the coals **2.** [niveau] : **~ universitaire** degree **3.** GÉOM (centesimal) grade **4.** CHIM grade.

gradé, e [grade] ◇ *adj* : **militaire ~** non-commissioned officer, NCO.
◇ *nm, f* non-commissioned officer, NCO ■ **tous les ~s** all ranks.

gradient [gradjɑ̃] *nm* **1.** MÉTÉOR gradient **2.** MATH : **~ d'une fonction** gradient of a function **3.** ÉLECTR : **~ de potentiel** voltage gradient.

gradin [gradɛ̃] *nm* **1.** [dans un amphithéâtre] tier, (stepped) row of seats ■ [dans un stade] : **les ~s** the terraces **2.** GÉOGR step, terrace **3.** AGRIC terrace ■ **à ~s** terraced **4.** [d'un autel] gradin, gradine.

graduation [gradɥasjɔ̃] *nf* **1.** [repère] mark **2.** [échelle de mesure] scale ■ **la ~ va jusqu'à 20** the scale goes up to 20 **3.** [processus] graduating.

gradué, e [gradɥe] *adj* **1.** [à graduations] graduated **2.** [progressif] graded ■ **exercices ~s** graded exercises.

graduel, elle [gradɥɛl] *adj* gradual, progressive.
◆ **graduel** *nm* gradual.

graduer [7] [gradɥe] *vt* **1.** [augmenter] to increase gradually ■ **il faut ~ la difficulté des tests** the tests should become gradually more difficult **2.** [diviser] to graduate.

graff [graf] (*abr de* **graffiti**) *nm* (piece of) graffiti.

graffeur, euse [grafœr, øz] *nm, f* graffiti artist, graffitist.

graffiti [grafiti] (*pl inv OU pl* **graffitis**) *nm* **1.** [inscription] graffiti ■ **un ~** a piece of graffiti ■ **des ~s** graffiti *(U)* **2.** ARCHÉOL graffito.

grafigner [grafiɲe] *vt Québec* to scratch.

grailler [3] [graje] ◇ *vi* **1.** [corneille] to caw **2.** [personne] to speak hoarsely *OU* throatily **3.** △ [manger] to eat ■ **venez ~!** grub's up! *esp UK*, come chow down! *US*.
◇ *vt* △ to eat.

graillon [grajɔ̃] *nm* **fam** [friture] : **une odeur de ~** a smell of grease.

grain [grɛ̃] *nm* **1.** [de sel, de sable] grain, particle ■ [de riz] grain ■ [de poussière] speck ■ **fig un ~ de folie** a touch of madness ■ **il n'a pas un ~ de bon sens** he hasn't got an ounce *OU* a grain of common sense ▶ **mettre son ~ de sel** *fam* to stick one's oar in ■ **elle a un ~** *fam* she's got a screw loose△ **2.** [céréales] : **le ~, les ~s** (cereal) grain ▶ **alcool** *OU* **eau-de-vie de ~** grain alcohol **3.** [d'un fruit, d'une plante] : **~ de café** [avant torréfaction] coffee berry ; [après torréfaction] coffee bean ■ **~ de cassis/groseille** blackcurrant/redcurrant (berry) ■ **~ de poivre** peppercorn ■ **~ de raisin** grape **4.** [perle] bead ■ **un collier à ~s d'ambre** an amber necklace **5.** [aspect - de la peau] grain, texture ; [- du bois, du papier] grain ■ **à gros ~** coarse-grained ■ **à petit ~** close-grained, fine-grained ■ **aller/travailler dans le sens du ~** to go/to work with the grain **6.** MÉTÉOR squall **7.** PHOTO grain ■ **la photo a du ~** the photo is *OU* looks grainy.
◆ **en grains** *loc adj* [café, poivre] unground, whole ■ **moulu ou en ~s?** ground or not?, ground or whole?
◆ **grain de beauté** *nm* beauty spot, mole.

graine [grɛn] *nf* **1.** [semence] seed ■ **~ de lin** linseed ■ **~s (pour oiseaux)** birdseed *(U)* ■ **monter en ~** *pr* to go to seed ; *fig* to shoot up ■ **c'est de la mauvaise ~, ce garçon-là!** that boy is bad news! ■ **son frère, c'est de la ~ de voyou!** his brother has the makings of a hooligan! ■ **en prendre de la ~** *fam* : **ton frère a réussi tous ses examens, prends-en de la ~** your brother has passed all his exams, take a leaf out of his book **2.** [du ver à soie] silkworm eggs, graine.

grainer [4] [grɛne] ◇ *vi* AGRIC to seed.
◇ *vt* [rendre grenu] to grain.

graineterie [grɛntri] *nf* **1.** [commerce] seed trade **2.** [magasin] seed merchant's.

grainetier, ère [grɛntje, ɛr] ◇ *adj* : **le commerce ~** the seed trade.
◇ *nm, f* [marchand - de graines] seed merchant ; [- de grain] corn chandler.

graissage [grɛsaʒ] *nm* AUTO & MÉCAN [avec de l'huile] oiling, lubrication ■ [avec de la graisse] greasing, lubrication ■ **faire faire un ~** to have one's car lubricated.

graisse [grɛs] *nf* **1.** [corps gras] fat ■ **régime pauvre en ~s** low-fat diet ■ **prendre de la ~** *fam* to put on weight ▶ **~ animale/végétale** animal/vegetable fat ■ **~ de baleine/phoque** whale/seal blubber ■ **~ à chaussures** dubbin, dubbing ■ **~ de porc** lard **2.** MÉCAN grease **3.** ŒNOL ropiness **4.** IMPR thickness, boldness.

graisser [4] [grese] ◇ *vt* **1.** [enduire - moteur] to lubricate ; [- pièce, mécanisme] to grease, to oil ; [- fusil] to grease ; [- chaussures] to dub ; [- moule] to grease ■ **une crème qui ne graisse pas les mains** a non-greasy cream ▶ **~ la patte à qqn** to grease sb's palm ■ **il a graissé la patte aux témoins** he bribed the witnesses **2.** [tacher] to grease, to soil with grease.

◇ *vi* [devenir gras] : **ses cheveux graissent très vite** his hair gets greasy very quickly.

◆ **se graisser** *vpt* : **se ~ les mains avec une crème** to rub cream into one's hands.

graisseur, euse [grɛsœr, øz] *adj* greasing, lubricating.

◆ **graisseur** *nm* **1.** [gén] lubricator, oiler **2.** AUTO grease nipple.

graisseux, euse [grɛsø, øz] *adj* **1.** [cheveux, col] greasy **2.** [tumeur] fatty.

Gram [gram] *nm inv* SC Gram ■ **~ positif** Gram-positive ■ **~ négatif** Gram-negative.

graminée [gramine] *nf* grass ■ **les ~s** (the) grasses, the gramineae *spéc.*

grammaire [gramɛr] *nf* **1.** [règles] grammar ■ **la ~** grammar ■ **règle de ~** grammatical rule, rule of grammar ◐ **~ normative** normative grammar **2.** [livre] grammar (book) **3.** *fig* **la ~ du cinéma/dessin** the grammar of cinema/drawing.

grammairien, enne [gramɛrjɛ̃, ɛn] *nm, f* grammarian.

grammatical, e, aux [gramatikal, o] *adj* **1.** [de grammaire] grammatical ■ **exercice ~** grammar exercise ◐ **catégorie ~e** part of speech **2.** [correct] grammatical ■ **non ~** ungrammatical.

grammaticalement [gramatikalmɑ̃] *adv* grammatically.

grammaticaliser [3] [gramatikalize] *vt* to grammaticalize.

gramme [gram] *nm* gramme ■ **je n'ai pas pris un ~ pendant les fêtes!** I didn't put on an ounce over the Christmas holidays! ■ **pas un ~ de bon sens/de compassion** *fig* not an ounce of common sense/of compassion.

grand, e [grɑ̃ *(devant nm commençant par voyelle ou h muet)* grɑ̃t, grɑ̃d] ◇ *adj*

A. ASPECT QUANTITATIF
B. ASPECT QUALITATIF
C. EN INTENSIF

A. ASPECT QUANTITATIF

1. [de taille élevée - adulte] tall ; [- enfant] tall, big

2. [de grandes dimensions - objet, salle, ville] big, large ; [- distance] long ■ **~ A/B/C** capital A/B/C ■ **une ~e tour** a high *ou* tall tower ■ **un ~ fleuve** a long *ou* big river ■ **une statue plus ~e que nature** a large-scale statue ■ **de ~es jambes** long legs ■ **avoir de ~s pieds** to have big *ou* large feet ■ **ses ~s yeux bleus** her big blue eyes ■ **marcher à ~s pas** to walk with great *ou* long strides

3. [d'un certain âge - être humain] big ■ **tu es un ~ garçon maintenant** you're a big boy now ■ **tu es assez ~ pour comprendre** you're old enough to understand ■ [aîné - frère, sœur] big ■ [au terme de sa croissance - personne] grown-up ; [- animal] fully grown, adult ■ **quand je serai ~** when I'm grown-up *ou* big

4. [qui dure longtemps] long ■ **pendant un ~ moment** for quite some time

5. [intense, considérable] great ■ **les risques sont ~s** there are considerable risks ■ **de ~e diffusion** widely-distributed ■ **une ~e fortune** great wealth, a large fortune ■ **ils ont marié leur fille à ~s frais** they married off their daughter at great *ou* vast expense ■ **rincer à ~e eau** to rinse thoroughly ■ **les ~s froids** intense cold ■ **pendant les ~es chaleurs** in high summer, in *ou* at the height of summer ■ **nous avons fait un ~ feu** we made a big fire ■ **un ~ incendie** a major *ou* great fire ◐ **ce sont des articles de ~e consommation** they are everyday consumer articles ■ **(à l'époque des)~es marées** (at) spring tide ■ **au ~ jour** in broad daylight

6. [pour qualifier une mesure] large, great ■ **la ~e majorité de** the great *ou* vast majority of ■ **son ~ âge explique cette erreur** this mistake can be put down to her being so old ■ **ils plongent à une ~e profondeur** they dive very deep *ou* to a great depth ■ **un ~ nombre de passagers** a large number of passengers

7. [entier] : **une ~e cuillerée de sucre** a heaped spoonful of sugar ■ **elle m'a fait attendre une ~e heure/semaine** she made me wait a good hour/a good week

8. BOT great, greater

9. GÉOGR : **le Grand Canyon** the Grand Canyon ■ **les Grands Lacs** the Great Lakes

10. ZOOL : **les ~s animaux** (the) larger animals

B. ASPECT QUALITATIF

1. [important] great, major ■ **les ~s problèmes de notre temps** the main *ou* major *ou* key issues of our time

2. [acharné, invétéré] great, keen ■ **c'est un ~ travailleur** he's a hard worker, he's hard-working ■ **c'est une ~e timide** she's really shy ■ **ce sont de ~s amis** they're great *ou* very good friends ■ **~s fumeurs** heavy smokers ◐ **les ~s blessés/brûlés/invalides** the seriously wounded/burned/disabled ■ **les ~s handicapés** the severely handicapped

3. [puissant, influent - banque] top ; [- industriel] top, leading, major ; [- propriétaire, famille] important ; [- personnage] great

4. [dans une hiérarchie] : **les ~s dignitaires du régime** the leading *ou* important dignitaries of the regime ◐ **le Grand rabbin (de France)** the Chief Rabbi (of France) ■ **les ~s corps de l'État** the major public bodies

5. [noble] : **avoir ~ air** *ou* **~e allure** to carry o.s. well, to be imposing

6. [généreux] : **il a un ~ cœur** he's big-hearted, he has a big heart ■ **une ~e âme** a noble soul

7. [exagéré] big ■ **de ~s gestes** extravagant gestures ■ **~s mots** high-sounding words, high-flown language

8. [fameux, reconnu] great ■ **un ~ homme** a great man ■ **un ~ journaliste** a great *ou* top journalist ■ **les ~s textes classiques** the classics ■ **il ne descend que dans les ~s hôtels** he only stays in the best hotels *ou* the most luxurious hotels ■ **le ~ film de la soirée** tonight's big *ou* feature film ■ **le ~ jour** the big day ■ **les ~es dates de l'histoire de France** the great *ou* most significant dates in French history ■ **un ~ nom** a great name ■ **un ~ nom de la peinture contemporaine** one of today's great painters ◐ **les ~s couturiers** the top fashion designers

9. HIST : **la Grande Catherine** Catherine the Great

10. [omnipotent, suprême] great ■ **Dieu est ~** God is great

C. EN INTENSIF

: **avec une (très) ~e facilité** with (the greatest of) ease ■ **sans ~ enthousiasme/intérêt** without much enthusiasm/interest ■ **sa ~e fierté, c'est son jardin** he's very proud of *ou* he takes great pride in his garden ■ **c'était un ~ moment** it was a great moment ■ **un ~ merci à ta sœur** lots of thanks to *ou* a big thank you to your sister ■ **le ~ amour : c'est le ~ amour!** it's true love! ■ **Robert fut son ~ amour** Robert was the love of her life ■ **tu aurais ~ avantage à la prévenir** you'd be well advised to warn her ■ **cette cuisine a ~ besoin d'être nettoyée** this kitchen really needs *ou* is in dire need of a clean ■ **faire ~ bien : ça m'a fait le plus ~ bien** it did me a power of *ou* the world of good ■ **il en a pensé le plus ~ bien** he thought most highly of it ■ **~ bien lui fasse!** much good may it do her! ■ **faire ~ cas de** to set great store by ■ **toute la famille au ~ complet** the whole family, every single member of the family ■ **jamais, au ~ jamais je n'accepterai** never in a million years will I accept ■ **il n'y a pas ~ mal à demander des précisions** there's no harm in asking for further details ■ **il est parti de ~ matin** he left at the crack of dawn ■ **il n'y avait pas ~ monde à son concert** there weren't many people at his concert ■ **pour notre plus ~ plaisir** to our (great) delight ■ **prendre ~ soin de** to take great care of ■ **à sa ~e surprise** much to his surprise, to his great surprise ■ **il est ~ temps que tu le lises** it's high time you read it.

◇ *nm, f* **1.** [enfant - d'un certain âge] : **l'école des ~s** primary school ■ [en appellatif] : **merci mon ~!** thanks, son! ■ **allons, ma ~e, ne pleure pas!** come on now, love, don't cry! ◐ **comme un ~ : je me débrouillerai tout seul, comme un ~/toute seule, comme une ~e** I'll manage on my own, like a big boy/a big girl **2.** [adulte - gén] grown-up, adult ■ **un jeu pour petits et ~s** a game for young and old (alike) ■ [en appellatif] : **alors, ma ~e, tu as pu te reposer un peu?** well dear, did you manage to get some rest? ‖ [personne de grande taille] : **pour la photo, les ~s se mettront derrière** for the photo, tall people *ou* the taller people will stand at the back.

◆ **grand** ◇ *adv* **1.** [vêtement] : **chausser ~ : c'est un modèle qui chausse ~** this is a large-fitting shoe ■ **tailler ~ : ça devrait vous aller, ça taille ~** it should fit you, it's cut large **2.** *loc* **ils ont vu trop ~** they bit off more than they could chew ■ **elle voit ~ pour son fils** she's got great hopes for her son ■ **deux rôtis! tu**

as vu ~! two roasts! you don't do things by halves! **3.** [largement] : **~ ouvert** wide-open **4.** ART : **représenter qqch plus ~ que nature** to enlarge sthg.
◇ *nm* **1.** PHILOS ⊳ **infiniment 2.** [entrepreneur, industriel] : **un ~ de la mode** a leading light in the fashion business ▪ **les ~s de l'automobile** the major *ou* leading car manufacturers.
◆ **grands** *nmpl* ÉCON & POLIT : **les ~s** [les puissants] the rich (and powerful) ▪ **les ~s de ce monde** the people in (positions of) power *ou* in high places ▪ **les deux Grands** POLIT the two superpowers.
◆ **en grand** *loc adv* [complètement] on a large scale ▪ **il faut aérer la maison en ~** the house needs a thorough *ou* good airing ▪ **il a fait les choses en ~** *fig* he really did things properly.
◆ **grande école** *nf competitive-entrance higher education establishment.*
◆ **grand ensemble** *nm* housing scheme *UK*, housing project *US*.
◆ **grande surface** *nf* hypermarket.

GRANDE ÉCOLE

The *grandes écoles* are relatively small and highly respected higher education establishments. Admission is usually only possible after two years of intensive preparatory studies and a competitive entrance examination. Most have close links with industry. The *grandes écoles* include *l'École des hautes études commerciales* or *HEC* (management and business), *l'École polytechnique* or *l'X* (engineering) and *l'École normale supérieure* (teacher training).

grand-angle [grɑ̃tɑ̃gl] (*pl* **grands-angles** [grɑ̃zɑ̃gl]), **grand-angulaire** [grɑ̃tɑ̃gylɛr] (*pl* **grands-angulaires** [grɑ̃zɑ̃gylɛr]) *nm* wide-angle lens.

grand-chose [grɑ̃ʃoz] *pron indéf* : **pas ~** not much ▪ **je n'y comprends pas ~** I don't understand much of it ▪ **il ne me reste plus ~ à dire** there's not much more (left) to say.

grand-croix [grɑ̃krwa] (*pl* **grands-croix**) ◇ *nf inv* Grand Cross *(in various orders including the Légion d'honneur)*.
◇ *nmf* holder *ou* Knight of the Grand Cross.

grand-duc [grɑ̃dyk] (*pl* **grands-ducs**) *nm* **1.** [titre] grand duke **2.** [oiseau] eagle owl.

grand-ducal, e, aux [grɑ̃dykal, o] *adj* **1.** [du grand-duc] grand-ducal **2.** [du grand-duché] of the grand duchy.

grand-duché [grɑ̃dyʃe] (*pl* **grands-duchés**) *nm* grand duchy.

Grande-Bretagne [grɑ̃dbrətaɲ] *npr f* : **(la) ~** (Great) Britain.

grande-duchesse [grɑ̃ddyʃɛs] (*pl* **grandes-duchesses**) *nf* grand duchess.

grandement [grɑ̃dmɑ̃] *adv* **1.** [largement] absolutely ▪ **si c'est là votre opinion, vous vous trompez ~!** if that is what you believe, you are very much mistaken! ▪ **vous avez ~ raison/tort** you are quite right/wrong **2.** [beaucoup] a great deal, greatly ▪ **il m'a ~ aidée** he helped me a great deal, he's been a great help to me ▪ **être ~ reconnaissant à qqn de qqch** to be truly grateful to sb for sthg **3.** [généreusement] : **vous avez fait les choses ~!** you've done things in great style! ▪ **ils ne seront pas ~ logés** their accommodation will be nothing grand *ou* special.

grandeur [grɑ̃dœr] *nf* **1.** [taille] size ⊙ **(en)~ nature** life-size **2.** [noblesse] greatness ▪ **la ~ humaine** the greatness of man ▪ **avec ~** nobly ⊙ **~ d'âme** magnanimity **3.** [splendeur] greatness, splendour ▪ **~ et décadence de Byzance** rise and fall of Byzantium **4.** ASTRON magnitude **5.** MATH & SC : **chiffres de la même ~** figures of the same magnitude ⊙ **~ de sortie** output ▪ **~s énergétiques** energy consumption and supply.

grand-guignol [grɑ̃giɲɔl] *nm* : **c'est du ~** it's all blood and thunder.

grand-guignolesque [grɑ̃giɲɔlɛsk] (*pl* **grand-guignolesques**) *adj* blood-and-thunder.

grandiloquence [grɑ̃dilɔkɑ̃s] *nf* grandiloquence, pomposity *péj.*

grandiloquent, e [grɑ̃dilɔkɑ̃, ɑ̃t] *adj* grandiloquent, pompous *péj.*

grandiose [grɑ̃djoz] *adj* grandiose.

grandir [32] [grɑ̃dir] ◇ *vi* **1.** [devenir grand] to grow ▪ **sa fille a grandi de cinq centimètres** her daughter is five centimetres taller (than when I last saw her) ▪ **je te trouve grandie** you've grown *ou* you look taller since I last saw you ▪ **un enfant qui aurait grandi trop vite** a lanky child **2.** [mûrir] to grow up ▪ **j'ai compris en grandissant** I understood as I grew up *ou* older **3.** [s'intensifier - bruit] to increase, to grow louder ; [- influence] to increase **4.** [s'étendre - ville] to spread **5.** *fig* **~ en force/sagesse/beauté** to get stronger/wiser/more beautiful, to grow in strength/wisdom/beauty ▪ **il a grandi dans mon estime** he has gone up in my esteem.
◇ *vt* **1.** [faire paraître plus grand] : **ces talons hauts la grandissent encore** these high-heeled shoes make her (look) even taller **2.** [exagérer l'importance de] to exaggerate, to overstate **3.** [ennoblir] : **ils n'en sortent pas vraiment grandis** they don't come out of it terribly well, it hasn't done much for their reputation.
◆ **se grandir** *vp (emploi réfléchi)* [vouloir paraître - plus grand] to make o.s. (look) taller ; [- plus important] to show o.s. in the best possible light.

grandissant, e [grɑ̃disɑ̃, ɑ̃t] *adj* [effectifs, douleur, renommée] growing, increasing ▪ [vacarme] growing ▪ [pénombre] deepening.

grandissement [grɑ̃dismɑ̃] *nm* OPT magnification.

grandissime [grɑ̃disim] *adj* **hum** extraordinary, marvellous.

grand-livre [grɑ̃livr] (*pl* **grands-livres**) *nm* ledger ▪ **le ~ (de la dette publique)** the French National Debt.

grand-maman [grɑ̃mamɑ̃] (*pl* **grand-mamans** *ou pl* **grands-mamans**) *nf* granny, grandma.

grand-mère [grɑ̃mɛr] (*pl* **grand-mères** *ou pl* **grands-mères**) *nf* **1.** [aïeule] grandmother **2.** *fam* [vieille femme] old woman *péj*, little old lady.

grand-messe [grɑ̃mɛs] (*pl* **grand-messes** *ou pl* **grands-messes**) *nf* **1.** RELIG High Mass **2.** *fig* **la ~ du parti** the party jamboree.

grand-oncle [grɑ̃tɔ̃kl] (*pl* **grands-oncles** [grɑ̃zɔ̃kl]) *nm* great-uncle.

grand-papa [grɑ̃papa] (*pl* **grands-papas**) *nm* grandpa, grandad ▪ **le commerce/tourisme de ~** *fam fig* old-fashioned ways of doing business/of holidaying.

grand-peine [grɑ̃pɛn] ◆ **à grand-peine** *loc adv* with great difficulty.

grand-père [grɑ̃pɛr] (*pl* **grands-pères**) *nm* **1.** [parent] grandfather **2.** *fam* [vieil homme] grandad *UK*, old-timer *US*.

grand-route [grɑ̃rut] (*pl* **grand-routes**) *nf* main road.

grand-rue [grɑ̃ry] (*pl* **grand-rues**) *nf* high *ou* main street *UK*, mainstreet *US*.

grands-parents [grɑ̃parɑ̃] *nmpl* grandparents.

grand-tante [grɑ̃tɑ̃t] (*pl* **grand-tantes** *ou pl* **grands-tantes**) *nf* great-aunt.

grand-voile [grɑ̃vwal] (*pl* **grand-voiles** *ou pl* **grands-voiles**) *nf* mainsail.

grange [grɑ̃ʒ] *nf* barn.

granit(e) [granit] *nm* GÉOL granite ▪ **de ~** [indestructible] granitelike, made of granite ; [insensible] of stone.

granité, e [granite] *adj* granitelike.
◆ **granité** *nm* [sorbet] granita.

granitique [granitik] *adj* granitic, granite *(modif)*.

granivore [granivɔr] ◇ *adj* seed-eating, granivorous *spéc.*
◇ *nmf* seedeater, granivore *spéc.*

granny-smith [granismis] *nf inv* Granny Smith *(apple)*.

granulaire [granylɛr] *adj* granular, granulous.

granulation [granylasjɔ̃] *nf* **1.** [gén] graining, granulation **2.** MÉD granulation **3.** PHOTO grain, graininess.

granule [granyl] ◇ *nm* **1.** [particule] (small) grain, granule ■ [pour animaux] pellet **2.** PHARM (small) tablet, pill.
◇ *nf* ASTRON granule.

granulé, e [granyle] *adj* [surface] granular ■ [présentation] granulated.
◆ **granulé** *nm* granule.

granuler [3] [granyle] *vt* to granulate.

granuleux, euse [granylø, øz] *adj* **1.** [aspect] granular, grainy **2.** MÉD granular.

grape-fruit (*pl* **grape-fruits**), **grapefruit** [grɛpfrut] *nm* grapefruit.

graphe [graf] *nm* **1.** MATH graph **2.** INFORM graph.

graphie [grafi] *nf* written form.

graphique [grafik] ◇ *adj* **1.** [relatif au dessin] graphic **2.** [relatif à l'écriture] written **3.** INFORM : **informatique ~** computer graphics **4.** SC graphical.
◇ *nm* **1.** MATH [courbe] graph ■ [tracé] diagram, chart ■ **~ à bandes** bar chart ■ **~ circulaire** pie chart **2.** [de température] chart.
◇ *nf* graphics *(sing)*.

graphiquement [grafikmɑ̃] *adv* graphically.

graphisme [grafism] *nm* **1.** [écriture] handwriting **2.** [dessin] : **un ~ vigoureux** a vigorously executed drawing ■ **le ~ de Dürer** Dürer's draughtsmanship.

graphiste [grafist] *nmf* graphic artist.

graphite [grafit] *nm* graphite ■ **lubrifiant au ~** graphite lubricant.

graphologie [grafɔlɔʒi] *nf* graphology.

graphologique [grafɔlɔʒik] *adj* graphological.

graphologue [grafɔlɔg] *nmf* graphologist.

grappe [grap] *nf* [de fleurs, de fruit] : **~ de glycine** wisteria flowerhead ■ **~ de raisins** bunch of grapes ■ **~s humaines** *fig* clusters of people.
◆ **en grappe(s)** *loc adv* [tomber - fleurs] in bunches.

grappiller [3] [grapije] ◇ *vi* **1.** *litt* [après la vendange] *to gather grapes left after the harvest* **2.** [faire de petits profits] to be on the take *ou* the fiddle *UK*.
◇ *vt* **1.** *litt* [cerises, prunes] to pick ■ [brindilles] to gather ■ [fleurs] to pick, to gather **2.** *fam* [argent] to fiddle *UK*, to chisel *US* **3.** *fam* [temps] : **elle grappille tous les jours une demi-heure sur l'horaire** she sneaks off half an hour early every day **4.** *fam* [informations] to pick up *(sép)* ■ **on n'a pu ~ que quelques détails insignifiants** we could only pick up a few minor clues.

grappillon [grapijɔ̃] *nm* small bunch *ou* cluster.

grappin [grapɛ̃] *nm* **1.** NAUT [ancre] grapnel ■ [d'abordage] grappling iron **2.** [de levage] grab **3.** [pour grimper] grappler, climbing iron **4.** *fam loc* **mettre le ~ sur qqn : il m'a mis le ~ dessus à la sortie** he grabbed me on the way out ■ **attends que je lui mette le ~ dessus!** wait till I get my hands on him!

gras, grasse [gra, gras] *adj*

A.

1. CULIN fatty ■ **ne mettez pas trop de matière grasse** do not add too much fat ■ **fromage ~** full-fat cheese
2. [dodu] fat, plump ● **être ~ comme une caille** *ou* **un chanoine** *ou* **un cochon** *ou* **un moine, être ~ à lard** to be as round as a barrel
3. [huileux] greasy, oily ■ [taché] greasy
4. [vulgaire] crude, coarse
5. CHIM fatty
6. RELIG : **jours ~** meat days

B.

1. [terre, boue] sticky, slimy
2. [pavé] slippery
3. [voix, rire] throaty
4. *litt* [abondant - récompense] generous ; [- pâturage] rich ■ **ce n'est pas ~** *fam* [peu de chose] that's not much ; [profit médiocre] it's not a fortune
5. [épais - gén] thick ; [- trait] bold ; [- caractère] bold, bold-faced ■ **en ~** IMPR in bold (type)
6. MÉD [toux] phlegmy
7. ŒNOL [vin] ropy
8. *loc* **faire la grasse matinée** to stay in bed (very) late, to have a long lie-in *UK*.

◆ **gras** ◇ *nm* **1.** [d'une viande] fat ■ **le ~ de jambon** ham fat ■ **au ~** CULIN cooked with meat stock **2.** [du corps] fleshy part ■ **le ~ de la jambe** the calf **3.** [substance] grease ■ **des taches de ~** greasy stains.
◇ *adv* **1.** [dans l'alimentation] : **il mange trop ~** he eats too much fatty food **2.** RELIG : **faire ~** to eat meat **3.** [en grasseyant] : **parler ~** to speak coarsely *ou* gutturally **4.** *fam* [beaucoup] : **il n'y a pas ~ à manger** there's not much to eat.

gras-double [gradubl] (*pl* **gras-doubles**) *nm* CULIN (ox) tripe.

grassement [grasmɑ̃] *adv* **1.** [largement] handsomely ■ **il vit ~ de ses terres** *litt* he makes a handsome living from the land he owns **2.** [vulgairement] coarsely, crudely.

grasseyant, e [grasɛjɑ̃, ɑ̃t] *adj* : **avoir un parler/rire ~** to speak/to laugh from the back of one's throat.

grasseyement [grasɛjmɑ̃] *nm* : **le ~ des Parisiens** *the Parisian way of pronouncing Rs from the back of the throat* ; LING the uvular Parisian R.

grasseyer [12] [grasɛje] ◇ *vi* to pronounce one's Rs from the back of the throat, to use Parisian Rs.
◇ *vt* : **un R grasseyé** LING a uvular R.

grassouillet, ette [grasujɛ, ɛt] *adj* podgy *UK*, pudgy *US*.

gratifiant, e [gratifjɑ̃, ɑ̃t] *adj* gratifying, rewarding.

gratification [gratifikasjɔ̃] *nf* **1.** [pourboire] tip ■ [prime] bonus ■ **~ de fin d'année** Christmas bonus **2.** [satisfaction] gratification.

gratifier [9] [gratifje] *vt* **1.** [satisfaire] : **sa réussite a beaucoup gratifié ses parents** his success was very gratifying for his parents **2.** *iron* **~ qqn de qqch : elle m'a gratifié d'un sourire** she favoured me with a smile.

gratin [gratɛ̃] *nm* **1.** CULIN [plat - recouvert de fromage] gratin *(dish with a topping of toasted cheese)* ; [- recouvert de chapelure] *dish with a crispy topping* ■ **~ dauphinois** *sliced potatoes baked with cream and browned on top* ■ [croûte - de fromage] cheese topping ; [- de chapelure] crispy topping **2.** *fam* [élite] : **le ~** the upper crust ■ **tout le ~ parisien** everybody who's anybody in Paris.

gratiné, e [gratine] *adj* **1.** CULIN [doré] browned ■ [cuit au gratin] (cooked) au gratin **2.** *fam* [difficile] : **c'était un sujet d'examen ~!** it was a pretty tough exam question! ■ [intense] : **elle va avoir droit à un savon ~!** she's in for a real telling-off!
◆ **gratinée** *nf* French onion soup.

gratiner [3] [gratine] ◇ *vt* [cuire en gratin] to cook au gratin ■ [dorer] to brown ■ **faire ~ avant de servir** brown under the grill before serving.
◇ *vi* to brown.

gratis [gratis] *fam* ◇ *adv* free (of charge) ■ **il a fait la réparation ~** he repaired it for nothing.
◇ *adj* free.

gratitude [gratityd] *nf* gratitude, gratefulness.

gratos [gratɔs] *adj* & *adv fam* free.

grattage [grataʒ] *nm* scraping ■ **au ~ on s'aperçoit que la couche de peinture était très mince** when you scrape off the paint you can see that it was put on very thinly.

gratte [grat] *nf fam* **1.** [profit] : **faire de la ~** to make a bit on the side **2.** [guitare] guitar.

gratte-ciel [gratsjɛl] *nm inv* sky-scraper.

gratte-cul [gratky] *nm inv fam* rosehip.

gratte-dos [gratdo] *nm inv* back-scratcher.

grattement [gratmɑ̃] *nm* scratching ■ **elle entendit un léger ~ à la porte** she heard a gentle scratching at the door.

gratte-papier [gratpapje] *nm inv fam péj* penpusher.

gratte-pieds [gratpje] *nm inv* shoe scraper, metal doormat.

gratter [3] [grate] ◇ *vt* **1.** [avec des griffes, des ongles, une plume] to scratch ■ [avec un sabot] to paw **2.** [frotter - allumette] to strike ; [- métal oxydé] to scrape, to rub ; [- couche de saleté] to scrape *ou* to rub off *(sép)* **3.** [effacer] to scratch out *(sép)* **4.** [irriter] : **une chemise/un pull-over qui gratte (la peau)** a shirt/sweater which makes one itch ■ **ça (me) gratte** *fam* it's itchy ■ **un gros rouge qui gratte la gorge** *fam* a rough red wine which catches in the throat **5.** *fam* [grappiller] to fiddle *UK*, to chisel *US* **6.** *fam* [devancer] to overtake **7.** *fam* [jouer de] : **~ du violon** to scrape away at the violin.
◇ *vi* **1.** [plume] to scratch **2.** [tissu, laine, pull] to itch, to be itchy **3.** *fam* [travailler] to work, to do odd jobs.
◆ **se gratter** *vp (emploi réfléchi)* to scratch (o.s.), to have a scratch ■ **se ~ la tête/le bras** to scratch one's head/arm ● **tu peux toujours te ~!**△ you'll be lucky!

grattoir [gratwar] *nm* **1.** [de bureau] erasing-knife **2.** [de graveur] scraper **3.** [allumettes] striking surface **4.** ARCHÉOL grattoir.

gratuit, e [gratɥi, it] ◇ *adj* **1.** [non payant] free ■ **'entrée ~e'** 'free admission' ■ **c'est ~** it's free, there's no charge **2.** [sans fondement] unwarranted **3.** [absurde - violence] gratuitous ; [- cruauté] wanton, gratuitous **4.** [désintéressé] : **aide ~e** free help ■ **il est rare que les éloges soient ~s** praise is rarely disinterested.
◇ *nm* [magazine] free magazine.

gratuité [gratɥite] *nf* **1.** [accès non payant] : **nous voulons la ~ de l'enseignement/des livres scolaires** we want free education/schoolbooks **2.** [absence de motif - d'une accusation, d'un acte violent] gratuitousness ■ **la ~ d'un tel acte** the gratuitousness of such an act **3.** [désintéressement] disinterestedness.

gratuitement [gratɥitmɑ̃] *adv* **1.** [sans payer] free (of charge) **2.** [sans motif] gratuitously, for no reason ■ **vous l'agressez ~, elle ne vous a rien fait!** you're attacking her for no reason, she hasn't done you any harm!

gravats [grava] *nmpl* **1.** [décombres] rubble **2.** [de plâtre] (screening) oversize.

grave [grav] ◇ *adj* **1.** *(après le n)* [solennel] grave, solemn ■ **il la dévisageait, l'air ~** he stared at her gravely **2.** [sérieux - motif, problème, maladie, accident] serious ; [- opération] serious, major ■ **une faute ~** a grave error ■ **l'heure est ~** this is a critical moment ■ **ce n'est pas ~!** never mind!, it doesn't matter! ■ **elle a eu une ~ maladie** she's been seriously ill ■ **c'est ~, docteur?** is it serious, doctor? **3.** ACOUST & MUS [note] low ■ [voix] deep **4.** [accent] grave.
◇ *nm* MUS : **le ~** the low register ■ **les ~s et les aigus** low and high notes, the low and high registers.
◇ *nf* TRAV PUB aggregate.
◆ **graves** ◇ *nm* [vin] Graves (wine).
◇ *nmpl* ACOUST bass.
◇ *nfpl* [terrain] gravel beach *ou* strand.

graveleux, euse [gravlø, øz] *adj* **1.** [grivois] smutty **2.** [fruit] gritty.

gravement [gravmɑ̃] *adv* **1.** [solennellement] gravely, solemnly **2.** [en intensif] : **~ handicapé** severely handicapped ■ **~ malade** seriously ill ■ **tu t'es ~ trompé** you've made a serious *ou* big mistake ■ **vous êtes ~ coupable de l'avoir laissé sortir seul** the burden of guilt lies with you for having let him go out alone.

graver [3] [grave] *vt* **1.** [tracer - sur métal, sur pierre] to carve, to engrave ; [- sur bois] to carve **2.** *fig* **à jamais gravé (en lettres d'or) dans mon esprit/mon souvenir** indelibly printed on my mind/memory ■ **la souffrance était gravée sur son visage** suffering was written on his face **3.** ART to engrave ■ **~ à l'eau-forte** to etch **4.** [disque] to cut **5.** INFORM to burn.

graveur, euse [gravœr, øz] *nm, f* [personne] engraver, carver ■ **~ sur bois** wood engraver *ou* cutter ■ **~ à l'eau-forte** etcher.
◆ **graveur** *nm* **1.** [pour disques] cutter **2.** INFORM CD-RW drive, (CD-)burner.

gravide [gravid] *adj* MÉD pregnant, gravid *spéc* ■ **truie ~** sow in pig.

gravier [gravje] *nm* **1.** GÉOL grit, gravel **2.** [petits cailloux] gravel ■ **allée de ~** gravel path.

gravillon [gravijɔ̃] *nm* **1.** [caillou] piece of gravel *ou* grit **2.** [revêtement] grit, fine gravel ■ **'~s'** 'loose chippings'.

gravir [32] [gravir] *vt* **1.** *sout* [grimper] to climb ■ **~ une montagne/un escalier** to climb up a mountain/a staircase **2.** [dans une hiérarchie] : **il faut ~ (tous) les échelons** you must go up through the ranks.

gravissime [gravisim] *adj* very serious.

gravitation [gravitasjɔ̃] *nf* PHYS gravitation.

gravitationnel, elle [gravitasjɔnɛl] *adj* gravitational.

gravité [gravite] *nf* **1.** [sérieux, dignité] seriousness, solemnity ■ **l'enfant la dévisagea avec ~** the child stared at her solemnly **2.** [importance] seriousness, gravity **3.** [caractère alarmant] seriousness ■ [d'une blessure] severity ■ **un accident sans ~ s'est produit en gare d'Orléans** there was a minor accident at the station in Orléans ■ **une maladie sans ~** a minor ailment **4.** [pesanteur] gravity **5.** MUS lowness.

graviter [3] [gravite] *vi* **1.** ASTRON : **~ autour de** to revolve *ou* to orbit around **2.** *sout* [évoluer] : **il a toujours gravité dans les sphères gouvernementales** he has always moved in government circles.

gravure [gravyr] *nf* **1.** [tracé en creux] : **~ sur bois** [procédé] woodcutting ; [objet] woodcut ■ **~ sur pierre** stone carving ■ **~ sur verre** glass engraving **2.** IMPR [processus] engraving, imprinting ■ **~ sur cuivre** [procédé] copperplating ; [plaque] copperplate ■ **~ directe** hand cutting ■ **~ à l'eau-forte** etching ■ [image] engraving, etching ● **~ de mode** fashion plate ■ **habillé** *ou* **vêtu comme une ~ de mode** dressed like a model in a fashion magazine **3.** [d'un disque] cutting ■ **~ directe** direct cut ■ **disque à ~ universelle** *ou* **compatible** stereo compatible record.

gré [gre] *nm* **1.** [goût, convenance] : **prenez n'importe quelle chaise, à votre ~** sit down wherever you wish *ou* please ■ **il est trop jeune à mon ~** he's too young for my liking **2.** [volonté, accord] : **elle a toujours agi à son ~** she has always done as she pleased ■ **je suis venue de mon plein** *ou* **propre ~** I came of my own free will ■ **il la suivit de bon ~** he followed her willingly *ou* of his own accord ■ **on l'a fait signer contre son ~** they made her sign against her will ● **bon ~ mal ~ il faudra que tu m'écoutes** whether you like it or not you'll have to listen to me ■ **ramenez-le de ~ ou de force!** bring him back by fair means or foul! **3.** *sout* [gratitude] : **savoir ~ à qqn de qqch** to be grateful to sb for sthg ■ **on vous saura mauvais ~ d'avoir dit la vérité** you'll get little reward *ou* people won't thank you for having spoken the truth.
◆ **au gré de** *loc prép* : **le bail est renouvelable au ~ du locataire** the lease is renewable at the tenant's request ■ **au ~ des flots** *sout* at the mercy of the waves ■ **se laisser aller au ~ du courant** to let o.s. drift along with the current ■ **ballotté au ~ des événements** tossed about *ou* buffeted by events.
◆ **de gré à gré** *loc adv* DR by mutual agreement.

grec, grecque [grɛk] *adj* Greek ■ **profil ~** Grecian profile.
◆ **Grec, Grecque** *nm, f* Greek.
◆ **grec** *nm* LING Greek ■ **le ~ ancien** ancient Greek ■ **le ~ moderne** modern *ou* demotic Greek.
◆ **à la grecque** *loc adj* [champignons, oignons] (cooked) à la grecque *(in olive oil and spices)*.

Grèce [grɛs] *npr f* : **(la) ~** Greece ■ **la ~ antique** Ancient Greece.

Greco [greko] *npr* : **le ~** El Greco ■ **un tableau du ~** a painting by El Greco.

gréco-latin, e [grekɔlatɛ̃, in] *(mpl* **gréco-latins**, *fpl* **gréco-latines***) adj* Greco-Latin.

gréco-romain, e [grekɔrɔmɛ̃, ɛn] *(mpl* **gréco-romains**, *fpl* **gréco-romaines***) adj* Greco-Roman.

grecque [grɛk] ◇ *adj* ▻ **grec**.
◇ *nf* **1.** ▻ **grec 2.** ARCHIT (Greek) fret.

gredin, e [grədɛ̃, in] *nm, f* rascal, rogue.

gréement [gremɑ̃] *nm* [voilure] rigging, rig ■ [processus] rigging.

green [grin] *nm* [au golf] green.

Greenwich [grinwitʃ] *npr* Greenwich ■ **le méridien de ~** the Greenwich Meridian.

gréer [15] [gree] *vt* [navire] to rig.

greffage [grɛfaʒ] *nm* HORT grafting.

greffe [grɛf] ◇ *nm* DR clerk's office, clerk of the court's office ■ **~ du tribunal de commerce** commercial court.
◇ *nf* **1.** HORT [processus] grafting ■ [pousse] graft **2.** MÉD [organe, moelle osseuse] transplant ■ [os] graft ■ **~ de peau** skin graft.

greffé, e [grɛfe] *nm, f* transplant patient ■ **les ~s du cœur** heart-transplant patients.

greffer [4] [grɛfe] *vt* **1.** HORT to graft **2.** MÉD [os, peau] to graft ■ [organe, moelle osseuse] to transplant ■ **on lui a greffé une cornée** he had a cornea transplant, he was given a new cornea ■ **se faire ~ un rein** to have a kidney transplant.
◆ **se greffer sur** *vp+prép* : **puis d'autres problèmes sont venus se ~ là-dessus** then additional problems came along *ou* arose.

greffier [grɛfje] *nm* **1.** DR clerk (of the court), registrar **2.** *fam* [chat] puss, pussy.

greffon [grɛfɔ̃] *nm* **1.** HORT graft, scion *spéc* **2.** MÉD [tissu] graft ■ [organe] transplant.

grégaire [gregɛr] *adj* gregarious ■ **l'instinct ~** the herd instinct.

grégarisme [gregarism] *nm* gregariousness, herd instinct.

grège [grɛʒ] ◇ *adj* [soie] raw, unbleached, undyed.
◇ *adj inv* [couleur] dove-coloured.
◇ *nm* greyish-beige, beigey-grey.

Grégoire [gregwar] *npr* : **~ de Tours** Gregory of Tours ■ **~ le Grand** Gregory the Great.

grégorien, enne [gregɔrjɛ̃, ɛn] *adj* Gregorian.
◆ **grégorien** *nm* Gregorian chant.

grêle [grɛl] ◇ *adj* **1.** [mince et long] spindly, thin **2.** [aigu - voix] reedy.
◇ *nf* **1.** MÉTÉOR hail ■ **une averse de ~** a hailstorm **2.** *fig* **une ~ de coups** a shower of blows ■ **une ~ d'insultes** a volley of insults.

grêlé, e [grele] *adj* [peau, visage] pockmarked, pitted.

grêler [4] [grele] ◇ *v impers* : **il grêle** it's hailing.
◇ *vt* : **l'orage a grêlé les vignes** the vines suffered hail damage in the storm.

grêleux, euse [grelø, øz] *adj* : **le temps est souvent ~ en mars** it often hails in March.

grêlon [grɛlɔ̃] *nm* hailstone.

grelot [grəlo] *nm* [clochette] (small sleigh *ou* jingle) bell.

grelottant, e [grəlɔtɑ̃, ɑ̃t] *adj* [tremblant] shivering ■ **~ de froid** shivering with cold ■ **tout ~** shivering all over.

grelottement [grəlɔtmɑ̃] *nm* [tremblement] shivering.

grelotter [3] [grəlɔte] *vi* **1.** [avoir froid] : **ferme la fenêtre, on grelotte** shut the window, it's freezing in here **2.** [trembler] : **~ de froid** to shiver *ou* to tremble with cold ■ **~ de peur** to shake with fear ■ **~ de fièvre** to shiver with fever **3.** *sout* [cloche] to jingle.

grenade [grənad] *nf* **1.** ARM grenade ■ **~ fumigène/incendiaire/lacrymogène** smoke/incendiary/teargas grenade ■ **~ à fusil/main** rifle/hand grenade ■ **~ sous-marine** depth charge **2.** [écusson militaire] grenade ornament **3.** BOT pomegranate.

Grenade [grənad] ◇ *npr f* [île] : **la ~** Grenada ■ **à la ~** in Grenada.
◇ *npr* [ville d'Espagne] Granada.

grenadier [grənadje] *nm* **1.** MIL grenadier **2.** BOT pomegranate tree.

grenadine [grənadin] *nf* [sirop] grenadine *(bright red fruit syrup used in making drinks)* ■ **une ~** [boisson] a (glass of) grenadine.

grenaille [grənaj] *nf* **1.** MÉTALL shot, steel grit ■ **en ~** grained, granulated **2.** [plomb de chasse] shot ■ **~ de plomb** lead shot.

grenat [grəna] ◇ *nm* [pierre, couleur] garnet.
◇ *adj inv* garnet, garnet-coloured.

greneler [24] [grɛnle] *vt* to grain.

grenier [grənje] *nm* **1.** [combles] attic ■ **~ aménagé** converted loft **2.** [à grain] loft ■ **~ à foin** hayloft ■ **le ~ à blé de la France** *fig* the granary of France.

Grenoble [grənɔbl] *npr* Grenoble.

grenoblois, e [grənɔblwa, az] *adj* from Grenoble.
◆ **Grenoblois, e** *nm, f inhabitant of or person from Grenoble.*

grenouille [grənuj] *nf* ZOOL frog ■ **~ verte/rousse** edible/common frog ■ **c'est une vraie ~ de bénitier** *fam* she's very churchy.

grenouiller [3] [grənuje] *vi fam* to plot, to scheme, to connive.

grenouillère [grənujɛr] *nf* **1.** [vêtement] sleepsuit, sleeping-suit **2.** [lieu] frog pond.

grenu, e [grəny] *adj* **1.** [surface] grainy, grained **2.** GÉOL granulose.

grès [grɛ] *nm* **1.** GÉOL sandstone **2.** [vaisselle] : **~ (cérame)** stoneware ■ **des assiettes en ~** stoneware plates.

grésil [grezil] *nm* fine hail.

grésillement [grezijmɑ̃] *nm* **1.** [de l'huile] sizzling ■ [du téléphone] crackling ■ **il y a des ~s sur la ligne** there's some interference on the line, the line's crackling **2.** [cri du grillon] chirping.

grésiller [3] [grezije] ◇ *v impers* : **il grésille** it's hailing.
◇ *vi* **1.** [huile] to sizzle ■ [feu, téléphone] to crackle ■ **ça grésille** it's all crackly **2.** [grillon] to chirp.

gressin [gresɛ̃] *nm* grissino ■ **des ~s** grissini.

GRETA, Greta [greta] *(abr de* **groupements d'établissements pour la formation continue***) npr m state body organizing adult training programmes.*

greubons [grøbɔ̃] *nmpl Suisse leftover fat from cooked meat, fried and used as an accompaniment to some Swiss dishes.*

grève [grɛv] *nf* **1.** [cessation d'une activité] strike ■ **être en ~, faire ~** to be on strike, to strike ■ **se mettre en ~** to go on strike ➊ **~ bouchon** disruptive strike ■ **~ de la faim** hunger strike ■ **~ générale** general strike ■ **~ partielle** partial *ou* localized strike ■ **~ perlée** go-slow *UK*, slowdown *US* ■ **~ sauvage** *ou* **illégale** wildcat strike ■ **~ de solidarité** sympathy strike ■ **ils font une ~ de solidarité** they've come out in sympathy ■ **~ surprise** lightning strike ■ **~ sur le tas** sit-down strike ■ **~ tournante** staggered strike ■ **~ du zèle** work-to-rule **2.** *litt* [plage] shore, strand *litt* ■ [rive] bank, strand *litt*.

grever [19] [grəve] *vt* **1.** *sout* [économie] to put a strain on ■ **l'inflation a grevé le pouvoir d'achat** inflation has restricted *ou* put a squeeze on purchasing power ■ **les vacances ont grevé mon budget** the holidays have put a severe strain on my finances **2.** DR : **sa propriété est grevée d'hypothèques** he's mortgaged up to the hilt.

Grévin [grevɛ̃] *npr* : **le musée ~** *wax museum in Paris.*

gréviste [grevist] ◇ *nmf* striker, striking worker ▪ **~ de la faim** hunger striker.
◇ *adj* striking.

GRH (*abr de* **gestion des ressources humaines**) *nf personnel management.*

gribouillage [gribujaʒ] *nm* **1.** [dessin] doodle ▪ **faire des ~s** to doodle **2.** [écriture illisible] scrawl, scribble.

gribouiller [3] [gribuje] ◇ *vt* to scribble.
◇ *vi* to doodle, to scribble.

gribouilleur, euse [gribujœr, øz] *nm, f* scribbler.

gribouillis [gribuji] = **gribouillage**.

grief [grijɛf] *nm litt* grievance ▪ **faire ~ à qqn de qqch** to hold sthg against sb ▪ **on lui a fait ~ d'avoir épousé un banquier** they resented her marrying a banker.

grièvement [grijɛvmɑ̃] *adv* [blessé] severely, seriously ▪ **quinze blessés dont trois ~** fifteen wounded, three of them seriously.

griffe [grif] *nf* **1.** ZOOL claw ▪ **il fait ses ~s** it's sharpening its claws ▪ **rentrer/sortir ses ~s** to draw in/to show one's claws ➲ **le voilà qui montre ses ~s** now he's showing his teeth ▪ **tomber dans les ~s de qqn** to fall into sb's clutches ▪ **il faut l'arracher des ~s de sa mère** he needs to be rescued from his mother's clutches ▪ **donner un coup de ~ à qqn** *pr* to scratch *ou* to claw sb ▪ **elle a reçu de nombreux coups de ~s** *fig* she was the victim of quite a bit of back-biting **2.** [d'un couturier] label, signature ▪ [d'un auteur] stamp **3.** BOT [de l'asperge] crown ▪ [du lierre] tendril **4.** JOAILL claw.

griffé, e [grife] *adj* [vêtement] designer *(modif).*

griffer [3] [grife] *vt* **1.** [suj: personne, animal] to scratch **2.** [suj: couturier] to put one's label on.
◆ **se griffer** *vp (emploi réfléchi)* to scratch o.s. ▪ **je me suis griffé au rosier** I scratched myself on the rosebush.

griffon [grifɔ̃] *nm* **1.** MYTHOL griffin **2.** [chien] griffon **3.** ORNITH griffon (vulture).

griffonnage [grifɔnaʒ] *nm* **1.** [écrit] scribbling **2.** [dessin] rough sketch.

griffonner [3] [grifɔne] ◇ *vt* **1.** [noter - adresse] to scribble (down) ; [- plan] to sketch roughly, to do a quick sketch of **2.** [mal écrire] to scribble.
◇ *vi* to scribble ▪ **les pages étaient toutes griffonnées au crayon noir** the pages were all scribbled over in black pencil.

griffu, e [grify] *adj* clawed.

griffure [grifyr] *nf* [d'une personne, d'une ronce] scratch ▪ [d'un animal] scratch, claw mark.

grignotage [griɲɔtaʒ] *nm* wearing away, erosion ▪ **le ~ des voix par l'opposition** the gradual loss of votes to the opposition.

grignotement [griɲɔtmɑ̃] *nm* nibbling, gnawing.

grignoter [3] [griɲɔte] ◇ *vt* **1.** [ronger] to nibble (at *ou* on) **2.** *fig* [amoindrir] to erode **3.** [acquérir] to acquire gradually.
◇ *vi* to nibble ▪ **ne grignotez pas entre les repas** don't eat between meals.

grignoteuse [griɲɔtøz] *nf* nibbling machine.

grigou [grigu] *nm* skinflint ▪ **quel vieux ~!** what an old skinflint *ou* Scrooge!

gri-gri (*pl* **gris-gris**), **grigri** [grigri] *nm* grigri.

gril [gril] *nm* CULIN grill, broiler *US* ▪ **faire cuire du poisson sur le ~** to grill fish, to broil fish *US* ▪ **être sur le ~** *fig* to be on tenterhooks.

grill [gril] *nm* [restaurant] grill-room, grill.

grillade [grijad] *nf* grill, grilled meat.

grillage [grijaʒ] *nm* **1.** [matériau] wire netting *ou* mesh **2.** [clôture] wire fence *ou* fencing **3.** [d'une fenêtre] wire screen **4.** CULIN roasting **5.** TEXT singeing.

grillager [17] [grijaʒe] *vt* **1.** [fenêtre] to put wire mesh *ou* netting on **2.** [terrain] to surround with a wire fence.

grille [grij] *nf* **1.** [porte] (iron) gate ▪ [barrière] railing ▪ [d'une fenêtre] bars **2.** [d'un égout, d'un foyer] grate ▪ [d'un parloir, d'un comptoir, d'un radiateur] grill, grille **3.** [programme] schedule **4.** JEUX : **une ~ de mots croisés** a crossword grid *ou* puzzle ▪ **la ~ du Loto** Loto card **5.** TRAV PUB (frame) grate **6.** DR & ÉCON : **~ des salaires** payscale ▪ **~ indiciaire** [de la fonction publique] wage index.

grillé, e [grije] *adj* **1.** [amandes, noisettes] roasted ▪ [viande] grilled ▪ **une tartine ~e** a piece of toast **2.** *fam* [personne] : **il est ~** his cover's blown.

grille-pain [grijpɛ̃] *nm inv* toaster.

griller [3] [grije] ◇ *vt* **1.** CULIN [pain] to toast ▪ [cacahuète, café] to roast ▪ [poisson, viande] to grill, to broil *US* **2.** [cultures, végétation] : **grillé par la chaleur** scorched by the heat ▪ **grillé par le froid** killed by the cold **3.** *fam* [ampoule, fusible] to blow ▪ [moteur] to burn out **4.** TEXT to singe **5.** *fam* [dépasser] : **~ un feu rouge** to go through a red light ▪ **~ quelques étapes** to jump a few stages ▪ **~ qqn (à l'arrivée)** to pip sb at the post *UK*, to beat sb out *US* **6.** *fam* [fumer] : **~ une cigarette, en ~ une** to have a smoke **7.** *fam* [compromettre] : **il nous a grillés auprès du patron** he's really landed us in it with the boss **8.** [fermer d'une grille] to put bars on.
◇ *vi* **1.** CULIN : **faire ~ du pain** to toast some bread ▪ **faire ~ du café** to roast coffee beans ▪ **faire ~ de la viande** to grill meat, to broil meat *US* **2.** *fam* [avoir trop chaud] to roast, to boil ▪ **ouvre la fenêtre, on grille ici** open the window, it's boiling in here ▪ [brûler] : **la ferme a entièrement grillé** the farmhouse was burnt to the ground **3.** *fig* **je grille (d'envie** *ou* **d'impatience) de la rencontrer** I'm itching *ou* dying to meet her.
◆ **se griller** ◇ *vp (emploi réfléchi)* [se démasquer] : **il s'est grillé en disant cela** he gave himself away by saying that.
◇ *vpt* : **se ~ les orteils devant la cheminée** to toast one's feet in front of the fire.

grilloir [grijwar] *nm* grill, broiler *US*.

grillon [grijɔ̃] *nm* cricket.

grill-room [grilrum] = **grill**.

grimaçant, e [grimasɑ̃, ɑ̃t] *adj* [sourire] painful ▪ [bouche] twisted ▪ [visage] contorted ▪ [clown, gargouille] grimacing.

grimace [grimas] *nf* **1.** [expression - amusante] funny face ; [- douloureuse] grimace ▪ **une ~ de dégoût** a disgusted look ▪ **faire la ~** to make a face **2.** [vêtement] pucker.
◆ **grimaces** *nfpl litt* [manières] airs.

grimacer [16] [grimase] *vi* **1.** [de douleur] to grimace, to wince ▪ [de dégoût] to make a face **2.** [pour faire rire] to make a funny face **3.** [robe] to pucker.

grimacier, ère [grimasje, ɛr] *adj* **1.** [grotesque] grimacing **2.** *litt* [maniéré] affected.

grimage [grimaʒ] *nm* make-up *(of a clown).*

grimer [3] [grime] *vt* to make up *(sép)* ▪ **grimé en vieillard/chat** made up as an old man/a cat.
◆ **se grimer** *vp (emploi réfléchi)* : **se ~ en** to make o.s. up as.

grimoire [grimwar] *nm* **1.** [livre de sorcellerie] book of magic spells **2.** *sout* [écrit illisible] illegible scrawl *ou* scribble.

grimpant, e [grɛ̃pɑ̃, ɑ̃t] *adj* [arbuste] climbing ▪ [fraisier] creeping.

grimpée [grɛ̃pe] *nf* [pente, montée] stiff *ou* steep climb.

grimper [3] [grɛ̃pe] ◇ *vi* **1.** [personne, animal, plante] to climb ▪ **~ à une échelle/un mur** to climb up a ladder/wall ▪ **~ à un arbre** to climb (up) a tree ; [en s'aidant des jambes] to shin up a tree ▪ **~ sur une table** to climb on (to) a table ▪ **grimpe dans la voiture** get into the car ▪ **le lierre grimpe le long du mur** the ivy climbs up the wall **2.** [s'élever en pente raide] to climb ▪ **ça grimpe!** it's steep! ▪ **ça grimpe à cet endroit-là** there's a steep climb at that point **3.** [température, inflation] to soar.
◇ *vt* [escalier, pente] to climb (up) *(insép).*
◇ *nm* SPORT rope-climbing.

grimpette [grɛ̃pɛt] *nf fam* steep *ou* stiff climb.

grimpeur, euse [grɛ̃pœr, øz] ◇ *adj* ORNITH scansorial.
◇ *nm, f* **1.** SPORT climber **2.** ORNITH : **les ~s** scansorial birds.

grinçant, e [grɛ̃sɑ̃, ɑ̃t] *adj* **1.** [porte, parquet] squeaking, creaking **2.** [voix, musique] grating **3.** [humour] sardonic.

grincement [grɛ̃smɑ̃] *nm* [bruit] grating, creaking ▪ **dans un ~ de freins** with a squeal of brakes ▪ **il y a eu des ~s de dents** *fig* there was much gnashing of teeth.

grincer [16] [grɛ̃se] *vi* **1.** [bois] to creak ▪ [frein] to squeal ▪ [métal] to grate ▪ [ressort] to squeak **2.** [personne] : **~ des dents** *pr* to gnash one's teeth ▪ **le bruit de la craie sur le tableau me fait ~ des dents** *fig* the noise the chalk makes on the board sets my teeth on edge.

grincheux, euse [grɛ̃ʃø, øz] ◇ *adj* grumpy, grouchy.
◇ *nm, f* grumbler ▪ **un vieux ~** an old grouch *ou* moaner.

gringalet [grɛ̃galɛ] *nm* [enfant] puny child ▪ [adulte] puny man.

gringue△ [grɛ̃g] *nm* : **faire du ~ (à qqn)** to sweet-talk(sb), to chat (sb) up *UK*.

griotte [grijɔt] *nf* BOT morello (cherry).

grippage [gripaʒ] *nm* MÉCAN jamming, seizing (up) ▪ **pour éviter le ~ du piston** to stop the piston from seizing up *ou* jamming.

grippal, e, aux [gripal, o] *adj* flu *(modif)*, influenzal *spéc* ▪ **état ~** influenza, flu.

grippe [grip] *nf* MÉD flu, influenza *spéc* ▪ **avoir la ~** to have (the) flu ▪ **ce n'est qu'une petite ~** it's just a touch of flu ◐ **~ asiatique** Asian flu ▪ **~ intestinale** gastric flu ▪ **prendre qqn/qqch en ~** to take a (strong) dislike to sb/sthg.

grippé, e [gripe] *adj* **1.** MÉD : **être ~** to have (the) flu ▪ **elle est un peu ~e** she's got a touch of the flu **2.** MÉCAN seized (up), jammed.

gripper [3] [gripe] ◇ *vt* to block, to jam.
◇ *vi* to jam, to seize up ▪ **les rouages de l'État commencent à ~** *fig* the wheels of state are beginning to seize up.
◆ **se gripper** *vpi* to jam, to seize up.

grippe-sou [gripsu] (*pl inv ou pl* **grippe-sous**) *fam* ◇ *nm* skinflint ▪ **un vieux ~** an old Scrooge.
◇ *adj inv* money-grabbing.

gris, e [gri, griz] *adj* **1.** [couleur] grey *UK*, gray *US* ▪ **~ acier/anthracite/ardoise/argent/fer/perle** steel/charcoal/slate/silver/iron/pearl grey ▪ **~ bleu/vert** bluish/greenish grey ▪ **une robe ~ foncé** a dark grey dress ▪ **~ pommelé** dapple-grey ▪ **~ souris** mouse-colour ▪ **avoir les cheveux ~** to have grey hair, to be grey-haired **2.** MÉTÉOR overcast ▪ **ciel ~ sur tout le pays** skies will be grey *ou* overcast over the whole country ▪ **nous sommes partis par un matin ~** we left on a dull (grey) morning **3.** [terne] dull, grey *UK*, gray *US* ▪ **en apprenant la nouvelle, il a fait ~e mine** his face fell when he heard the news **4.** *fam* [ivre] tipsy **5.** ŒNOL : **vin ~** rosé (wine).
◆ **gris** ◇ *adv* : **il a fait ~ toute la journée** it's been grey *ou* dull all day.
◇ *nm* **1.** [couleur] grey *UK*, gray *US* **2.** [tabac] *French caporal tobacco in grey packet*, ≃ shag **3.** [cheval] grey *UK ou* gray *US*(horse).

grisaille [grizaj] *nf* **1.** [morosité] dullness, greyness **2.** MÉTÉOR dull weather ▪ **encore de la ~ pour aujourd'hui** today will again be dull (and overcast) **3.** ART grisaille.

grisailler [3] [grizaje] ◇ *vt* to paint in grisaille.
◇ *vi* to turn *ou* to become grey.

grisant, e [grizɑ̃, ɑ̃t] *adj* **1.** [enivrant] intoxicating, heady **2.** [excitant] exhilarating.

grisâtre [grizatr] *adj* [couleur] greyish.

grisbi△ [grizbi] *nm arg crime* dough△, cash.

grise [griz] *f* ▷ **gris.**

grisé [grize] *nm* grey tint.

griser [3] [grize] *vt* **1.** [colorer] to tint **2.** [enivrer] to intoxicate **3.** [étourdir, exciter] to intoxicate, to fascinate ▪ **grisé par la vitesse** intoxicated by speed ▪ **le luxe ambiant l'a grisé** the luxuriousness of the place went to his head.
◆ **se griser** ◇ *vp (emploi réfléchi)* to get drunk.
◇ *vpi* : **se ~ de** to get drunk on.

griserie [grizri] *nf* **1.** [ivresse] intoxication **2.** [exaltation] : **se laisser porter par la ~ du succès** to let success go to one's head.

grisette [grizɛt] *nf vieilli* grisette.

grison, onne [grizɔ̃, ɔn] *adj* from the Graubünden, of the Graubünden.
◆ **Grison, onne** *nm, f inhabitant of or person from the Graubünden.*

grisonnant, e [grizɔnɑ̃, ɑ̃t] *adj* greying ▪ **elle est ~e, elle a les cheveux ~s** she's going grey ▪ **avoir les tempes ~es** to be greying at the temples.

grisonnement [grizɔnmɑ̃] *nm* greying.

grisonner [3] [grizɔne] *vi* [barbe, cheveux] to be going grey.

Grisons [grizɔ̃] *npr mpl* : **les ~** the Graubünden ▪ **viande des ~** *thinly sliced dried beef, traditionally served with raclette.*

grisou [grizu] *nm* firedamp ▪ **coup de ~** firedamp explosion.

grive [griv] *nf* thrush.

grivelé, e [grivle] *adj* speckled.

griveler [24] [grivle] *vi to eat a meal or to stay at a hotel and deliberately leave without paying.*

grivèlerie [grivɛlri] *nf offence of leaving a restaurant or a hotel without having paid.*

grivois, e [grivwa, az] *adj* risqué, bawdy.

grivoiserie [grivwazri] *nf* **1.** [caractère] bawdiness **2.** [histoire] bawdy story.

grizzli, grizzly [grizli] *nm* grizzly (bear).

Groenland [grɔɛnlɑ̃d] *npr m* : **le ~** Greenland ▪ **au ~** in Greenland.

groenlandais, e [grɔɛlɑ̃dɛ, ɛz] *adj* from Greenland, Greenland *(modif)*.
◆ **Groenlandais, e** *nm, f* Greenlander.

grog [grɔg] *nm* hot toddy ▪ **~ au rhum** rum toddy.

groggy [grɔgi] *adj inv* **1.** [boxeur] groggy **2.** *fam* [abruti] stunned, dazed.

grognard [grɔɲar] *nm* HIST *soldier of Napoleon's Old Guard.*

grognasse△ [grɔɲas] *nf* old bag, old bat.

grogne [grɔɲ] *nf* dissatisfaction, discontent.

grognement [grɔɲmɑ̃] *nm* **1.** [d'une personne] grunt, growl **2.** [d'un cochon] grunt, grunting *(U)* ▪ [d'un chien] growl, growling *(U)*.

grogner [3] [grɔɲe] ◇ *vi* **1.** [personne] to grumble, to grouse **2.** [cochon] to grunt ▪ [chien] to growl.
◇ *vt* [réponse, phrase] to grunt (out).

grognon, onne [grɔɲɔ̃, ɔn] *adj fam* grumpy, crotchety ▪ **un air ~** a surly look.
◆ **grognon** *nmf fam* grumbler, moaner.

groin [grwɛ̃] *nm* **1.** [d'un porc] snout **2.** *fam* [visage laid] mug.

grol(l)e△ [grɔl] *nf* shoe ▪ **mets des ~s** put something on your feet.

grommeler [24] [grɔmle] ◇ *vi* **1.** [personne] to grumble, to mumble **2.** [sanglier] to snort.
◇ *vt* to mutter.

grommellement [grɔmɛlmɑ̃] *nm* **1.** [du sanglier] snorting **2.** [d'une personne] muttering ▪ **quelques ~s indistincts** a few vague mutters *ou* mutterings.

grommellera *etc v* ▷ **grommeler.**

grondement [grɔ̃dmɑ̃] *nm* **1.** [du tonnerre, du métro] rumbling ▪ **le ~ de la foule se fit de plus en plus fort** the angry murmur of the crowd grew louder and louder **2.** [d'un chien] growling.

gronder [3] [grɔ̃de] <> *vi* **1.** [rivière, tonnerre, métro] to rumble **2.** [chien] to growl **3.** *litt* [révolte] to be brewing.
<> *vt* [réprimander] to scold, to tell off *(insép)* ▪ **se faire ~** to get told off.

gronderie [grɔ̃dri] *nf* scolding, telling-off.

grondeur, euse [grɔ̃dœr, øz] *adj* [personne, voix] scolding, grumbling ▪ **d'un ton ~** in a tone of reproof.

grondin [grɔ̃dɛ̃] *nm* gurnard.

groom [grum] *nm* [employé d'hôtel] bellboy.

gros, grosse [gro *(devant nm commençant par voyelle ou h muet* groz), gros] <> *adj* **1.** [grand] large, big ▪ [épais, solide] big, thick ▪ **une grosse boîte de haricots** a large *ou* big can of beans ▪ **le paquet est/n'est pas (très) ~** the parcel is/isn't (very) big ▪ **prends-le par le ~ bout** pick it up by the thick *ou* thicker end ▪ **de grosses chaussures** heavy shoes ▪ **~ drap** coarse linen ▪ **de grosses lèvres** thick lips ▪ **un ~ pull** a thick *ou* heavy jumper ▪ **~ trait de crayon** thick pencil mark ▪ **une grosse tranche** a thick slice
2. [corpulent] big, fat ▪ **un homme grand et ~** a tall fat man ▪ **de grosses jambes** fat *ou* stout legs
3. [en intensif] : **un ~ appétit/mangeur** a big *ou* hearty appetite/eater ▪ **~ bêta!** you great ninny! ▪ **un ~ bisou** *fam* a big kiss ▪ **un ~ bruit** a loud *ou* big noise ▪ **un ~ buveur** a heavy drinker ▪ **par les grosses chaleurs** in the hot season ▪ **un ~ soupir** a big *ou* heavy sigh
4. [abondant] heavy ▪ **une grosse averse** a heavy shower ▪ **son usine a de ~ effectifs** his factory employs large numbers of people *ou* has a large workforce
5. [important] big ▪ **le ~ avantage des supermarchés** the big *ou* major advantage of supermarkets ▪ **de ~ dégâts** extensive *ou* widespread damage ▪ **une grosse entreprise** a large *ou* big company ▪ **de ~ frais** heavy expenses ▪ **avoir de ~ moyens** to have a large income *ou* considerable resources ▪ **de ~ profits** big *ou* fat profits ▪ **une grosse somme** a large sum of money ▪ **il y a de ~ travaux à faire dans cette maison** that house needs a lot (of work) done to it ▪ **une grosse angine** a (very) sore throat ▪ **un ~ rhume** a bad *ou* heavy cold ▪ **de ~ ennuis** serious trouble, lots of trouble ▪ **une grosse journée (de travail)** a hard day's work ▪ **de grosses pertes** heavy losses ➋ **~ œuvre** structural work, carcass *spéc*
6. [prospère] big ▪ **un ~ producteur d'Hollywood** a big Hollywood producer ▪ **les ~ actionnaires** the major shareholders
7. [rude] : **une grosse voix** a rough *ou* gruff voice ▪ **un ~ rire** coarse laughter ▪ **l'astuce/la supercherie était un peu grosse** the trick/the hoax was a bit obvious ▪ **grosse blague** crude joke ‖ [exagéré] : **j'ai trouvé ça un peu ~!** I thought it was a bit much! ▪ **tout de suite, les grosses menaces!** *fam* so it's threats already, is it?
8. MÉTÉOR : **par ~ temps/grosse mer** in heavy weather/seas ▪ **~ vent** gale
9. *sout* [rempli] : **~ de** : **un ciel ~ d'orage** stormy skies ▪ **un cœur ~ de tendresse** a heart full of tenderness.
<> *nm, f* fat person ▪ **un petit ~** a fat little man ▪ **ça va, mon ~?** *fam* all right, son *ou* old boy?
◆ **gros** <> *nm* **1.** [majorité] : **le ~ de** : **le ~ des étudiants** most of the students ▪ **le ~ de l'hiver est passé** the worst of the winter is over ▪ **le ~ du chargement** the bulk of the cargo
2. COMM : **le ~** the wholesale business.
<> *adv* : **couper ~** to cut in thick slices ▪ **écrire ~** to write big ▪ **coûter/gagner ~** to cost/to win a lot (of money) ▪ **ça va vous coûter ~** *pr & fig* it'll cost you dear ▪ **jouer ~** *pr* to play for high stakes ▪ **jouer** *ou* **miser** *ou* **risquer ~** *fig* to take *ou* to run a big risk, to stick one's neck out ▪ **elle donnerait ~ pour savoir** she'd give her right arm *ou* a lot to find out.
◆ **de gros** *loc adj* [commerce, prix] wholesale.
◆ **en gros** <> *loc adj* bulk *(modif)* ▪ **vente en ~** wholesaling.
<> *loc adv* **1.** [approximativement] roughly ▪ **je sais en ~ de quoi il s'agit** I know roughly what it's about
2. [en lettres capitales] : **c'est imprimé en ~** it's printed in big letters
3. COMM wholesale ▪ **acheter en ~** to buy wholesale.
◆ **gros bonnet** *nm fam* bigwig, big shot.
◆ **grosse légume** *nf fam* [personne influente] bigwig, big shot ▪ [officier] brass (hat) ▪ **les grosses légumes du régiment** the top brass (of the regiment).

groseille [grozɛj] <> *nf* : **~ rouge** redcurrant ▪ **~ blanche** white currant ▪ **~ à maquereau** gooseberry.
<> *adj inv* light red.

groseillier [grozeje] *nm* currant bush ▪ **~ rouge** redcurrant bush ▪ **~ blanc** white currant bush ▪ **~ à maquereau** gooseberry bush.

gros-grain [grogrɛ̃] (*pl* **gros-grains**) *nm* grosgrain.

gros-porteur [grопɔrtœr] (*pl* **gros-porteurs**) *nm* jumbo, jumbo jet.

grosse [gros] *f* ⊳ **gros**.

grossesse [grosɛs] *nf* pregnancy ▪ **pendant ma ~** when I was pregnant ➋ **~ extra-utérine** ectopic pregnancy ▪ **~ nerveuse** phantom pregnancy.

grosseur [grosœr] *nf* **1.** [taille] size ▪ **de la ~ d'une noix** the size of a walnut **2.** *sout* [obésité] weight, fatness **3.** MÉD lump.

grossier, ère [grosje, ɛr] *adj* **1.** [impoli] rude, crude ▪ **... et il est devenu ~...** and then he started getting abusive ‖ [vulgaire] vulgar, uncouth ▪ **(quel) ~ personnage!** what a rude *ou* vulgar individual! **2.** [peu raffiné] coarse, rough ▪ **des traits ~s** coarse features **3.** [approximatif] rough, crude *péj* ▪ **c'est du travail ~** it's shoddy work ▪ **je n'ai qu'une idée grossière de l'endroit où il se trouve** I've only got a rough idea (of) where he is **4.** [flagrant - erreur] gross, stupid ; [- manœuvre, procédé] unsubtle.

grossièrement [grosjɛrmɑ̃] *adv* **1.** [approximativement] roughly (speaking) ▪ **j'ai évalué ~ les frais** I made a rough estimate of the costs **2.** [sans délicatesse] roughly **3.** [injurieusement] rudely **4.** [beaucoup] : **tu te méprends ~** you're grossly *ou* wildly mistaken.

grossièreté [grosjɛrte] *nf* **1.** [impolitesse] coarseness, rudeness **2.** [manque de finesse - d'une personne] coarseness ; [- d'une chose] crudeness, coarseness **3.** [gros mot] coarse remark ▪ **je me suis retenu pour ne pas lui dire des ~s** I had to bite my tongue to avoid swearing at him ‖ [obscénité] rude joke.

grossir [32] [grosir] <> *vi* **1.** [prendre du poids] to put on weight ▪ **elle a beaucoup grossi** she's put on a lot of weight ▪ **j'ai grossi d'un kilo** I've put on a kilo ▪ **ça fait ~** it's fattening **2.** [augmenter en taille - tumeur, entreprise, somme, troupeau] to grow, to get bigger ; [- vague, nuages] to get bigger ; [- effectifs] to increase ; [- rumeur] to grow ▪ **les bourgeons/ruisseaux grossissent** the buds/streams are swelling ▪ **le bruit grossit** the noise is getting louder ▪ **le malaise qui règne dans le groupe grossit** there is a growing sense of unease within the group.
<> *vt* **1.** [faire paraître gros] : **ta robe te grossit** your dress makes you look fatter **2.** [augmenter] to raise, to swell ▪ **des pluies diluviennes ont grossi la rivière** the river has been swollen by torrential rain ▪ **~ le nombre/les rangs des manifestants** to join the growing numbers of demonstrators, to swell the ranks of the demonstrators **3.** [exagérer] to exaggerate, to overexaggerate ▪ **on a grossi l'affaire** the affair was blown up out of all proportion **4.** [à la loupe] to magnify, to enlarge.

grossissant, e [grosisɑ̃, ɑ̃t] *adj* **1.** [verre] magnifying **2.** *litt* [qui s'accroît] growing, swelling.

grossissement [grosismɑ̃] *nm* **1.** [d'une tumeur] swelling, growth **2.** [avec une loupe] magnifying **3.** [exagération] exaggeration.

grossiste [grosist] *nmf* wholesaler.

grosso modo [grosomodo] *loc adv* roughly, more or less ▪ **laisse-moi t'expliquer l'histoire ~** let me give you a rough idea of the story.

grotesque [grɔtɛsk] <> *adj* **1.** [burlesque] ridiculous **2.** [absurde] ridiculous, ludicrous ▪ **son livre est d'un ~!** his book is ludicrous!
<> *nm* **1.** ART & LITTÉR : **le ~** the grotesque **2.** [absurdité] ludicrousness, preposterousness.
◆ **grotesques** *nfpl* ART grotesques.

grotte [grɔt] *nf* **1.** GÉOL cave **2.** ARCHIT grotto.

grouillant, e [grujɑ̃, ɑ̃t] *adj* swarming, teeming ▪ **les rues ~es de monde** the streets swarming *ou* teeming with people.

grouillement [grujmɑ̃] *nm* : **un ~ d'insectes** a swarm of insects ▪ **un ~ de vers** a wriggling mass of worms ▪ **le ~ de la foule** the bustling *ou* milling *ou* seething crowd.

grouiller [3] [gruje] *vi* **1.** [clients, touristes] to mill *ou* to swarm about ▪ **la foule grouille sur les boulevards** the boulevards are bustling with people ‖ [asticots] : **les vers grouillent sur la viande** the meat is crawling with maggots **2.** [être plein de] : **~ de** to be swarming *ou* crawling with ▪ **ce texte grouille de termes techniques** *fig* this text is crammed with technical terms **3.** △ [se dépêcher] : **allez, grouillez, ça commence dans cinq minutes** come on, get cracking *ou* get a move on, it starts in five minutes.
◆ **se grouiller** *vpi fam* to get a move on ▪ **grouille-toi, on est en retard** get a move on, we're late.

groupage [grupaʒ] *nm* **1.** COMM bulking ▪ **le ~ des commandes** bulk ordering **2.** MÉD (blood) grouping.

groupe [grup] *nm* **1.** [de gens, d'objets] group ▪ **ils sont venus par ~s de quatre ou cinq** they came in groups of four or five *ou* in fours and fives ▶ **~ hospitalier/scolaire** hospital/school complex ▪ **~ familial** family group ▪ **~ parlementaire** parliamentary group ▪ **~ de parole** support group ▪ **~ de pression** pressure group ▪ **~ de rock** rock band *ou* group ▪ **~ de travail** working group *ou* party
2. ÉCON group ▶ **~ de presse** press consortium *ou* group
3. ART group
4. ÉLECTR set ▪ **~ électrogène** generator
5. LING : **~ consonantique** consonant cluster ▪ **~ de mots** word group ▪ **~ du verbe** *ou* **verbal** verbal group ▪ **~ du nom** *ou* **nominal** nominal group
6. MATH group
7. MÉD : **~ sanguin** blood group
8. MIL group
9. BOT & ZOOL [classification] group.
◆ **de groupe** *loc adj* group *(modif)* ▪ **psychologie/psychothérapie de ~** group psychology/therapy.
◆ **en groupe** *loc adv* in a group.

groupé, e [grupe] *adj* **1.** COMM ▷ **achat 2.** INFORM blocked **3.** SPORT ▷ **saut.**

groupement [grupmɑ̃] *nm* **1.** [association] group ▪ **~ d'achat (commercial)** bulk-buying group ▪ **~ d'intérêt économique** intercompany management syndicate **2.** [rassemblement] : **on a procédé au ~ des commandes** all the orders have been grouped together.

grouper [3] [grupe] *vt* **1.** [réunir - personnes] to group together *(sép)* ; [- ressources] to pool **2.** [classer] to put *ou* to group together *(sép)* **3.** COMM [paquets] to bulk **4.** MÉD to determine the blood group of.
◆ **se grouper** *vpi* **1.** [dans un lieu] to gather **2.** [dans une association] to join together ▪ **se ~ autour d'un chef** to join forces under one leader.

groupie [grupi] *nmf* **1.** [d'un chanteur] groupie **2.** [inconditionnel] avid follower, groupie.

groupuscule [grupyskyl] *nm* POLIT & *péj* small group ▪ **les ~s gauchistes** tiny ultra-left (splinter) groups.

grouse [gruz] *nf* (red) grouse.

gruau [gryo] *nm* groats ▪ **farine de ~** fine wheat flour.

grue [gry] *nf* **1.** TECHNOL crane ▪ **~ automotrice** motor-driven crane ▪ **~ flottante** floating crane ▪ **~ de levage** wrecking crane ▪ **~ à portique** gantry crane **2.** CINÉ & TV crane **3.** ORNITH crane **4.**△ *vieilli* [prostituée] tart UK, hooker △ US **5.** *fam vieilli* [femme stupide] silly goose.

gruger [17] [gryʒe] *vt* **1.** *litt* [tromper] to deceive, to swindle ▪ **se faire ~** to get swindled **2.** TECHNOL to shape the edges of.

grumeau, x [grymo] *nm* lump ▪ **plein de ~x** lumpy ▪ **sans ~x** smooth.

grumeler [24] [grymle] ◆ **se grumeler** *vpi* [sauce] to go lumpy.

grumeleux, euse [grymlø, øz] *adj* **1.** [sauce] lumpy **2.** [peau] uneven ▪ [surface] granular **3.** [fruit] gritty.

grumelle *etc v* ▷ **grumeler.**

grunge [grʌnʒ] *adj* grunge.

grutier [grytje] *nm* crane driver *ou* operator.

gruyère [gryjɛr] *nm* : **~, fromage de Gruyère** Gruyere (cheese).

guacamole [gwakamol(e)] *nm* guacamole.

Guadeloupe [gwadlup] *npr f* : **la ~** Guadeloupe ▪ **à la** *ou* **en ~** in Guadeloupe.

guadeloupéen, enne [gwadlupeɛ̃, ɛn] *adj* Guadeloupean.
◆ **Guadeloupéen, enne** *nm, f* Guadeloupean.

guano [gwano] *nm* guano.

Guatemala [gwatemala] *npr m* : **le ~** Guatemala ▪ **au ~** in Guatemala.

guatémaltèque [gwatemaltɛk] *adj* Guatemalan.
◆ **Guatémaltèque** *nmf* Guatemalan.

gué [ge] *nm* [passage] ford ▪ **passer un ruisseau à ~** to ford a stream.

guéguerre [gegɛr] *nf fam* (little) war, squabble ▪ **se faire la ~** to squabble, to bicker.

guenilles [gənij] *nfpl* rags (and tatters) ▪ **être vêtu de ~** to wear old rags.

guenon [gənɔ̃] *nf* **1.** ZOOL female monkey, she-monkey **2.** △ *péj* [femme] dog.

guépard [gepar] *nm* cheetah.

guêpe [gɛp] *nf* ZOOL wasp.

guêpier [gepje] *nm* **1.** [nid de guêpes] wasp's nest **2.** [situation périlleuse] sticky situation ▪ **il s'est fourré** *ou* **mis dans un beau ~** he got himself into a sticky situation **3.** ORNITH bee eater.

guêpière [gepjɛr] *nf* basque.

guère [gɛr] *adv sout* **1.** [employé avec 'ne'] : **il n'est ~ aimable** he's not very nice ▪ **je n'aime ~ cela** I don't much like that, I don't like that much ▪ **elle n'y voit plus ~** she can hardly see anymore ▪ **il n'est ~ plus aimable qu'elle** he's not much nicer than she is ▪ **il n'y a ~ de monde** there's hardly anyone ▪ **le beau temps ne dura ~** the fine weather lasted hardly any time at all *ou* didn't last very long ▪ **il ne vient ~ nous voir** he hardly ever comes to see us ▪ **il n'y a plus ~ de noyers dans la région** there are hardly *ou* scarcely any walnut trees left in this area ▪ **il n'a ~ plus de vingt ans** he is barely *ou* scarcely twenty years old ▪ **je ne suis plus ~ qu'à une heure de Paris** I'm only an hour away from Paris ▪ **il ne se déplace plus ~ qu'avec une canne** he can hardly walk without a stick anymore **2.** [dans une réponse] : **aimez-vous l'art abstrait? – ~** do you like abstract art? – not really ▪ **comment allez-vous? – ~ mieux** how are you? – not much better *ou* hardly any better.

guéridon [geridɔ̃] *nm* [table] occasional table.

guérilla [gerija] *nf* **1.** [guerre] guerrilla warfare ▪ **~ urbaine** urban guerrilla warfare **2.** [soldats] group of guerrillas, guerrilla unit.

guérillero [gerijero] *nm* guerrilla.

guérir [32] [gerir] ◇ *vt* **1.** MÉD [malade, maladie] to cure ▪ [blessure] to heal **2.** *fig* **je vais le ~ de cette manie** I'll cure him of that habit ▪ **le temps seul guérit les grands chagrins** only time can heal deep grief.
◇ *vi* **1.** MÉD [convalescent] to recover, to be cured ▪ **elle est guérie de sa rougeole** she's cured of *ou* recovered from her measles ▪ **ma mère est guérie** my mother's better *ou* recovered ‖ [blessure] to heal, to mend **2.** *fig* **il est guéri de sa timidité** he is cured of *ou* he has got over his shyness ▪ **l'amour, il en est guéri!** you won't catch him falling in love again!
◆ **se guérir** ◇ *vp (emploi réfléchi)* to cure o.s.
◇ *vpi* **1.** [maladie] : **est-ce que ça se guérit facilement?** is it easy to cure? **2.** [personne] : **il ne s'est jamais guéri de sa jalousie** he never got over his jealousy.

guérison [gerizɔ̃] *nf* **1.** MÉD [d'un patient] recovery ▪ [d'une blessure] healing ▪ **il est maintenant en voie de ~** he's now on the road to recovery **2.** *fig* **la ~ sera lente après une telle déception** it'll take a long time to get over such a disappointment.

guérissable [gerisabl] *adj* MÉD [patient, mal] curable.

guérisseur, euse [gerisœr, øz] *nm, f* healer ▪ *péj* quack.

guérite [gerit] *nf* **1.** [sur un chantier] site office **2.** MIL sentry box.

Guernesey [gɛrnəzɛ] *npr* Guernsey ▪ **à ~** on Guernsey, *voir aussi* île.

guernesiais, e [gɛrnəzjɛ, ɛz] *adj* from Guernsey, Guernsey *(modif)*.

guerre [gɛr] *nf* **1.** [conflit] war ▪ **en temps de ~** in wartime ▪ **être en ~ (contre)** to be at war (with) ▪ **des pays en ~** countries at war, warring countries ▪ **entrer** *ou* **se mettre en ~ (contre)** to go to war (with) ▪ **déclarer la ~ (à)** to declare war (against *ou* on) ▪ **maintenant, entre Jeanne et moi c'est la ~** Jeanne and I are at each others' throats all the time now ▶ **~ atomique/nucléaire** atomic/nuclear war ▪ **la ~ de Cent Ans** the Hundred Years War ▪ **~ civile** civil war ▪ **la ~ de Corée** the Korean War ▪ **la ~ de Crimée** the Crimean War ▪ **~ d'embuscade** guerrilla war ▪ **la ~ des étoiles** Star Wars ▪ **la ~ froide** the cold war ▪ **~ des gangs** gang warfare ▪ **la ~ du Kippour** the Yom Kippur War ▪ **~ mondiale** world war ▪ **~ des nerfs** war of nerves ▪ **~ à outrance** all-out war ▪ **~ ouverte** open war ▪ **la ~ presse-bouton** push-button warfare ▪ **~ de religion** war of religion ▪ **~ sainte** Holy War ▪ **la ~ de Sécession** the American Civil War ▪ **la ~ des sexes** t he battle of the sexes ▪ **la ~ des Six Jours** the Six-Day War ▪ **la ~ de 70** the Franco-Prussian War ▪ **~ totale** total war ▪ **la ~ de Troie** the Trojan War ▪ **~ d'usure** war of attrition ▪ **la Grande Guerre, la Première Guerre (mondiale), la ~ de 14** the Great War, the First World War, World War I ▪ **la Seconde Guerre mondial e, la ~ de 40** World War II, the Second World War ▪ **faire la ~ (à)** *pr* to wage war (against) ; *fig* to battle (with) ▪ **il a fait la ~ en Europe** he was in the war in Europe ▪ **je fais la ~ aux moustiques/fumeurs** I've declared war on mosquitoes/smokers ▪ **elle lui fait la ~ pour qu'il mange plus lentement** she's always (nagging) on at him to eat more slowly ▪ **mes chaussures/gants ont fait la ~** *fam* my shoes/gloves have been in the wars ▪ **partir en ~ (contre)** *pr* to go to war (against) ; *fig* to launch an attack (on) ▪ **à la ~ comme à la ~** *fam* well, you just have to make the best of things ▪ **c'est de bonne ~** all's fair in love and war *prov* ▪ **de ~ lasse je l'ai laissé sortir** in the end I let him go out just to have some peace (and quiet) ▪ **'Guerre et Paix'** ***Tolstoï*** 'War and Peace' **2.** [technique] warfare ▪ **~ biologique/chimique** biological/chemical warfare ▪ **~ bactériologique** germ warfare ▪ **~ éclair** blitzkrieg ▪ **~ des ondes** radio propaganda warfare ▪ **~ psychologique** psychological warfare ▪ **~ de tranchées** trench warfare.

guerrier, ère [gɛrje, ɛr] ◇ *adj* [peuple] warlike ▪ **un chant ~** a battle song *ou* chant.
◇ *nm, f* warrior.

guerroyer [13] [gɛrwaje] *vi sout* to (wage) war.

guet [gɛ] *nm* watch ▪ **faire le ~** to be on the lookout.

guet-apens [gɛtapɑ̃] (*pl* **guets-apens** [gɛtapɑ̃]) *nm* ambush, trap ▪ **tendre un ~ à qqn** to set a trap *ou* an ambush for sb ▪ **tomber dans un ~** to fall into a trap, to be ambushed.

guêtre [gɛtr] *nf* **1.** [bande de cuir] gaiter **2.** [en tricot] leggings.

guetter [4] [gete] *vt* **1.** [surveiller] to watch **2.** *fig* [menacer] : **la mort le guette** death is lying in wait for him ▪ **les ennuis la guettent** there's trouble in store for her **3.** [attendre] to watch out for *(insép)* ▪ **le chat guette la souris** the cat is watching for the mouse ▪ **il guette le facteur** he is on the lookout for the postman ▪ **~ l'occasion propice** to watch out for the right opportunity.

guetteur [getœr] *nm* **1.** MIL lookout ▪ HIST watch, watchman **2.** [gén] lookout.

gueulante△ [gœlɑ̃t] *nf* : **pousser une ~** to raise the roof.

gueulard, e△ [gœlar, ard] ◇ *adj* **1.** [personne] loud, loudmouthed ▪ [radio, chanson] noisy, bawling **2.** [couleur] loud.
◇ *nm, f* [adulte] loudmouth ▪ [bébé] bawler.
◆ **gueulard** *nm* MÉTALL (blast furnace) throat *ou* shaft.

gueule [gœl] *nf* **1.** △ [bouche] gob△ *UK*, yap△ *US* ▪ **se soûler la ~** to get pissed△ *UK ou* juiced△ *US* ▪ **pousser un coup de ~** to yell out ▪ **c'est une grande ~** *ou* **un fort en ~** he's a big mouth *ou* a loudmouth, he's always shooting his mouth off△ ▪ **(ferme) ta ~!** shut your mouth *ou* trap△ ! **2.** △ [visage] mug△, face ▪ **quelle sale ~ (il a)!** [il est laid] what an ugly mug he's got!△ ; [il est malade] he looks terrible! ▪ **il va faire une sale ~ quand il saura la vérité** he's going to be mad *ou* livid when he finds out the truth ▪ **j'en ai pris plein la ~** I got a right mouthful ▪ **avoir** *ou* **faire une drôle de ~** to look funny *ou* weird ▪ **elle a fait une de ces ~s en trouvant la porte fermée!** you should have seen her face when she saw the door was shut! ▶ **~ cassée** WW1 veteran *(with bad facial injuries)* ▪ **~ noire** miner ▪ **faire la ~ : il nous fait la ~ depuis notre arrivée** he's been in a huff *ou* in a bad mood with us ever since we arrived **3.** *fam* [apparence] : **cette pizza a une sale ~** that pizza looks disgusting **4.** △ [charme] : **il a de la ~, ce type** that guy's really got something ▪ **leur maison a vraiment de la ~** their house really has got style **5.** [d'un animal] mouth ▪ **se jeter dans la ~ du loup** to throw o.s. into the lion's mouth *ou* jaws **6.** [d'un canon] muzzle ▪ [d'un four] mouth.
◆ **gueule de bois** *nf fam* hangover.

gueule-de-loup [gœldəlu] (*pl* **gueules-de-loup**) *nf* BOT snapdragon.

gueulement△ [gœlmɑ̃] *nm* bawl, yell ▪ **pousser des ~s** to yell, to bawl.

gueuler [5] [gœle] *fam* ◇ *vi* **1.** [personne - de colère] to shout ; [- de douleur] to yell out ▪ **faudrait ~!** we should kick up a fuss! ▪ **~ sur qqn** to shout at sb **2.** [radio, haut-parleur] to blare out *(insép)* ▪ **faire ~ sa radio** to turn the radio up full blast **3.** [chien] to howl.
◇ *vt* to bellow out *(sép)*, to bawl out *(sép)*.

gueules [gœl] *nm* HÉRALD gules.

gueuleton△ [gœltɔ̃] *nm* [repas] nosh-up *UK*, blowout.

gueuletonner [3] [gœltɔne] *vi fam* to have a blowout, to have a nosh-up *UK*.

gueuse [gøz] ◇ *f* ▻ **gueux**.
◇ *nf* [bière] = **gueuze**.

gueux, gueuse [gø, gøz] *nm, f arch & litt* beggar ▪ **les ~** the wretched.
◆ **gueuse** *nf* **1.** MÉTALL pig (mould) **2.** *arch & litt* harlot, painted lady **3.** HIST : **la Gueuse** *name given to the French Republic by Royalists during the Third Republic.*

gueuze [gøz] *nf* gueuze (beer).

gugusse [gygys] *nm fam* clown, twit *UK* ▪ **faire le ~** to fool around.

gui [gi] *nm* **1.** BOT mistletoe **2.** NAUT boom.

guibol(l)e△ [gibɔl] *nf* pin *UK*, gam *US* ▪ **j'en ai plein les ~s** my legs have had it.

guiche [giʃ] *nf* [mèche de cheveux] kiss curl *UK*, spit curl *US*.

guichet [giʃɛ] *nm* **1.** [d'une banque] counter ▪ [d'un théâtre] ticket office ▪ [d'une poste] counter, window ▪ **'~ fermé'** 'position closed' ▶ **~ automatique** autobank, cash dispenser ▪ **jouer à ~s fermés** to play to packed houses **2.** [porte] hatch, wicket **3.** [judas] judas ▪ [d'un confessionnal] shutter.

guichetier, ère [giʃtje, ɛr] *nm, f* counter clerk.

guidage [gidaʒ] *nm* guiding ▪ **~ de missile** missile guidance *ou* tracking.

guide [gid] ◇ *nmf* **1.** SPORT : **~ (de haute montagne)** mountain guide **2.** [pour touristes] (tour) guide.
◇ *nm* **1.** [personne] guide, leader **2.** [principe] guiding principle **3.** [livre] guidebook ▪ **Guide Bleu®** *detailed tourist guide* ▪ **~ de conversation** phrasebook ▪ **~ touristique** guidebook ▪ **Guide Vert®** Michelin guide **4.** TÉLÉCOM : **~ d'ondes** (wave) guide.
◇ *nf* **1.** [scout] girl guide *UK*, girl scout *US* **2.** [rêne] rein.

guider [3] [gide] *vt* **1.** [diriger] to guide **2.** [conseiller] to guide ▪ **guidée par son expérience** guided by her experience ▪ **nous**

sommes là pour vous ~ dans vos recherches we're here to help you find what you're looking for ▪ **j'ai besoin d'être guidé** I need some guidance.
◆ **se guider** *vpi* : **il s'est guidé sur le soleil** he used the sun as a guide ▪ **il s'est guidé sur l'exemple de son maître** he modelled himself on his master.

guidon [gidɔ̃] *nm* **1.** [d'un vélo] handlebars **2.** MIL & NAUT guidon **3.** ARM foresight.

guigne [giɲ] *nf* **1.** BOT sweet cherry ▪ **il se soucie de son avenir comme d'une ~** *fam* he doesn't care two hoots about his future **2.** *fam* [malchance] bad luck ▪ **il porte la ~ à toute sa famille** he's the bane of his family ▪ **avoir la ~** to be jinxed, to have rotten luck.

guigner [3] [giɲe] *vt* to sneak a look at ▪ **il guigne l'argent de son oncle depuis des années** *fig* he has had his eye on his uncle's money for years.

guignol [giɲɔl] *nm* **1.** [pantin] (glove) puppet ▪ [théâtre] puppet theatre ▪ [spectacle] Punch and Judy show ▪ **on va au ~** we're off to see Punch and Judy **2.** *fam fig* **faire le ~** to clown around ▪ **ce nouveau ministre est un ~** that new minister is a (real) clown.
◆ **Guignol** *npr* (Mister) Punch ▪ **les Guignols (de l'info)** *satirical television programme with puppets representing political figures and well-known personalities.*

guilde [gild] *nf* guild.

guili-guili [giligili] *nm inv langage enfantin* tickle ▪ **faire ~** to tickle.

guillaume [gijom] *nm* MENUIS rabbet plane.

Guillaume [gijom] *npr* : **~ le Conquérant** William the Conqueror ▪ **~ le Roux** William Rufus ▪ **~ Tell** William Tell.

guilledou [gijdu] *nm* ⊳ **courir.**

guillemet [gijmɛ] *nm* quotation mark, inverted comma *UK* ▪ **ouvrir/fermer les ~s** to open/to close (the) inverted commas ▪ **entre ~s** in inverted commas *UK*, in quotation marks, in quotes ▪ **tu connais son sens de la "justice", entre ~s** you know his so-called sense of justice.

guilleret, ette [gijrɛ, ɛt] *adj* jolly, cheerful ▪ **d'un air ~** jauntily.

guillotine [gijɔtin] *nf* guillotine.

guillotiné, e [gijɔtine] ◇ *adj* guillotined.
◇ *nm, f* guillotined person.

guillotiner [3] [gijɔtine] *vt* to guillotine.

guimauve [gimov] *nf* **1.** BOT & CULIN marshmallow **2.** *fig & péj* **ses chansons, c'est de la ~** his songs are all soppy *OU* schmaltzy.

guimbarde [gɛ̃bard] *nf* **1.** *fam* [voiture] (old) banger *UK*, jalopy *US* **2.** MUS jew's-harp.

Guimet [gimɛ] *npr* : **le musée ~** *museum of Far Eastern art in Paris.*

guindaille [gɛ̃daj] *nf Belgique fam student party.*

guindé, e [gɛ̃de] *adj* [personne] stiff, starchy ▪ [discours] stilted ▪ **d'un air ~** starchily, stiffly ▪ **prendre un ton ~** to speak in a stilted manner.

guinder [3] [gɛ̃de] *vt* **1.** [personne] : **son costume le guinde** he looks very stiff and starchy in that suit **2.** TECHNOL to hoist.

guinée [gine] *nf* [monnaie] guinea.

Guinée [gine] *npr f* : **(la) ~** Guinea ▪ **(la) ~-Bissau** Guinea-Bissau ▪ **(la) ~-Équatoriale** Equatorial Guinea.

guinéen, enne [gineɛ̃, ɛn] *adj* Guinean.
◆ **Guinéen, enne** *nm, f* Guinean.

guingois [gɛ̃gwa] ◆ **de guingois** ◇ *loc adj* : **l'affiche est de ~** the poster is lop-sided.
◇ *loc adv* [de travers] : **marcher de ~** to walk lop-sidedly.

guinguette [gɛ̃gɛt] *nf open-air café or restaurant with dance floor.*

guipure [gipyr] *nf* TEXT guipure (lace).

guirlande [girlɑ̃d] *nf* **1.** [de fleurs] garland **2.** [de papier] paper garland ▪ **~ de Noël** (length of) tinsel **3.** [de lumières] : **~ électrique** [de Noël] Christmas tree lights, fairy lights ; [pour une fête] fairy lights **4.** *sout* [de personnes] string.

guise [giz] ◆ **à ma guise, à ta guise, etc** *loc adv* as I/you *etc* please ▪ **il n'en fait qu'à sa ~** he just does as he pleases *OU* likes.
◆ **en guise de** *loc prép* by way of ▪ **en ~ de dîner, nous n'avons eu qu'un peu de soupe** for dinner, we just had a little soup.

guitare [gitar] *nf* guitar ▪ **avec Christophe Banti à la ~** with Christophe Banti on guitar ➊ **~ basse/électrique** bass/electric guitar ▪ **~ hawaïenne/sèche** Hawaiian/acoustic guitar.

guitariste [gitarist] *nmf* guitar player, guitarist.

Gulf Stream [gœlfstrim] *npr m* : **le ~** the Gulf Stream.

guru [guru] = **gourou.**

gus(se) [gys] *nm fam* guy, bloke *UK*.

gustatif, ive [gystatif, iv] *adj* gustatory, gustative.

gustation [gystasjɔ̃] *nf* tasting, gustation *spéc.*

Gustave [gystav] *npr* [roi] Gustav ▪ **~ Adolphe** Gustavus Adolphus.

guttural, e, aux [gytyral, o] *adj* **1.** [ton] guttural ▪ [voix] guttural, throaty **2.** PHON guttural.
◆ **gutturale** *nf* PHON guttural.

Guyana [gɥijana] *npr f & npr m* : **(la** *OU* **le) ~** Guyana.

guyanais, e [gɥijanɛ, ɛz] *adj* **1.** [région, département] Guianese, Guianian **2.** [république] Guyanan, Guyanese.
◆ **Guyanais, e** *nm, f* **1.** [région, département] Guianese, Guianian ▪ **les Guyanais** the Guianese, the Guianians **2.** [république] Guyanan, Guyanese ▪ **les Guyanais** the Guyanans, the Guyanese.

Guyane [gɥijan] *npr f* : **la ~, les ~s** Guiana, the Guianas ▪ **(la) ~ française** French Guiana ▪ **(la) ~ hollandaise** Dutch Guiana.

guyot [gɥijo] ◇ *nm* GÉOL guyot.
◇ *nf* BOT guyot pear.

gym [ʒim] *nf* [à l'école] PE ▪ [pour adultes] gym ▪ **aller à la ~** to go to gym class ▪ **faire de la ~** to do exercises.

gymkhana [ʒimkana] *nm* **1.** SPORT rally ▪ **~ motocycliste** scramble *UK*, motorcycle rally **2.** *fam fig* obstacle course.

gymnase [ʒimnaz] *nm* **1.** [salle] gym, gymnasium **2.** *Suisse* [lycée] secondary school *UK*, high school *US*.

gymnasial [ʒimnazjal] *adj Suisse* secondary school *(modif) UK*, high school *(modif) US*.

gymnaste [ʒimnast] *nmf* gymnast.

gymnastique [ʒimnastik] *nf* **1.** SPORT physical education, gymnastics *(sing)* ▪ **professeur de ~** gymnastics *OU* PE teacher ▪ **faire de la ~** to do exercises ➊ **~ corrective** remedial gymnastics ▪ **~ rythmique** eurhythmics *(sing)* ▪ **au pas (de) ~** at a jog trot **2.** *fig* gymnastics *(sing)* ▪ **~ mentale** *OU* **intellectuelle** mental gymnastics ▪ **ça a été toute une ~ pour obtenir des billets** getting tickets was a real hassle.

gymnique [ʒimnik] *adj* gymnastic.

gynécée [ʒinese] *nm* gynaeceum *spéc.*

gynéco [ʒineko] (*abr de* **gynécologue**) *nmf fam* gynecologist.

gynécologie [ʒinekɔlɔʒi] *nf* gynecology.

gynécologique [ʒinekɔlɔʒik] *adj* gynecological.

gynécologue [ʒinekɔlɔg] *nmf* gynecologist.

gypse [ʒips] *nm* gypsum.

gyrophare [ʒirɔfar] *nm* rotating light *OU* beacon.

gyroscope [ʒirɔskɔp] *nm* gyroscope.

h, H [aʃ] *nm* h, H ■ **h aspiré/muet** aspirate/silent h.

h **1.** (*abr écrite de* **heure**) hr **2.** (*abr écrite de* **hecto**) h.

H = **homme**.

ha[1] (*abr écrite de* **hectare**) ha.

ha[2] ['a] *interj* **1.** [surprise] : **ha, vous partez déjà?** what, (are you) leaving already? ❙ [ironie, suspicion] : **ha, ha, je t'y prends!** aha! caught you! **2.** [rire] : **ha, ha, que c'est drôle!** ha-ha, very funny!

hab. = **habitant**.

habeas corpus [abeaskɔrpys] *nm inv* : **l'~** habeas corpus.

habile [abil] *adj* **1.** [adroit] skilful ■ **être ~ de ses mains** to be good *ou* clever with one's hands **2.** [intelligent, fin - personne] clever, bright ; [- ouvrage] clever **3.** [rusé] clever, cunning.

habilement [abilmɑ̃] *adv* [travailler] cleverly, skilfully ■ [répondre] cleverly ■ **les négociations ont été ~ menées** the negotiations were conducted with skill.

habileté [abilte] *nf* **1.** [dextérité] skill, dexterity *sout* ■ **un orfèvre d'une grande ~** a very skilful goldsmith, a goldsmith of great skill **2.** [ingéniosité] cleverness, smartness ■ **son ~ en affaires est bien connue** his business sense *ou* flair is well-known.

habilitation [abilitasjɔ̃] *nf* **1.** DR capacitation **2.** UNIV accreditation, habilitation *sout*.

habilité, e [abilite] *adj* DR : **~ à** fit to ■ **toute personne ~e à signer** any person who is entitled to sign.

◆ **habilité** *nf* DR fitness, entitlement.

habiliter [3] [abilite] *vt* **1.** DR to entitle, to empower **2.** UNIV to accredit, to authorize, to habilitate *sout*.

habillage [abijaʒ] *nm* **1.** [revêtement - d'une machine] casing ; [- d'un produit] packaging ; [- d'un ordinateur] cabinetry ■ AUTO [- d'un siège] covering ; [- d'un plafond] lining ; [- d'un intérieur] trim **2.** CULIN dressing ■ **l'~ d'un poulet** cleaning and trussing a chicken **3.** [d'un acteur] dressing.

habillé, e [abije] *adj* [vêtements] smart, dressy ■ **dîner ~** dinner in evening dress.

habillement [abijmɑ̃] *nm* **1.** [vêtements] clothes, clothing ■ [action d'habiller] dressing, clothing ■ **il a de grosses dépenses d'~** his clothing expenses are very high **2.** COMM clothing trade *UK*, garment industry *US*.

habiller [3] [abije] *vt* **1.** [vêtir] to dress ■ **toujours habillé de** *ou* **en vert** always dressed in green ■ **il est mal habillé** [sans goût] he's badly dressed **2.** [équiper - famille, groupe] to clothe ; [- skieur, écolier] to kit out *(sép)* ■ **j'habille toute la famille** I make clothes for all the family ■ **la somme devrait suffire à ~ toute la famille** the money should be enough to keep the entire family in clothes ■ [suj: couturier, tailleur] to design clothes for ■ **elle est habillée par un grand couturier** she gets her clothes from a top designer **3.** [déguiser] : **elle a habillé sa fille en Zorro** she dressed her daughter up as Zorro **4.** [décorer, recouvrir] to cover ■ **~ un mur de toile de jute** to cover a wall with hessian **5.** [en marketing] to package (and present) **6.** CULIN [volaille] to clean and truss.

◆ **s'habiller** *vp (emploi réfléchi)* **1.** [se vêtir] to get dressed, to dress ■ **il s'habille tout seul maintenant** he's able to dress himself now ■ **tu devrais t'~ plus jeune** you should wear younger clothes ■ **tu t'habilles mal** you have no dress sense ■ **habille-toi chaudement** wrap up well *ou* warm ■ **il s'habille chez un jeune couturier** he buys his clothes from a young fashion designer ■ **s'~ sur mesure** to have one's clothes made *ou* tailor-made ■ **s'~ en** [se déguiser en] to dress up as **2.** [se parer] to dress up ■ **s'~ pour le dîner** to dress for dinner.

habilleur, euse [abijœr, øz] *nm, f* CINÉ, THÉÂTRE & TV dresser.

habit [abi] *nm* **1.** [déguisement] costume, outfit ■ **un ~ de fée/sorcière** a fairy/witch outfit ■ **~ d'arlequin** Harlequin suit *ou* costume **2.** [vêtement de cérémonie] tails ■ **en ~** wearing tails ■ **se mettre en ~** to wear tails ◐ **~ de cour** court dress ■ **l'~ de lumière** the bullfighter's outfit ■ **l'~ vert** *regalia worn by members of the Académie française* ■ **porter l'~ vert** to be a member of the Académie française **3.** RELIG habit ■ **l'~ ecclésiastique** ecclesiastical dress ■ **prendre l'~** [femme] to take the veil ; [homme] to go into holy orders ■ **quitter l'~** to leave orders ◐ **l'~ ne fait pas le moine** *prov* you can't judge a book by its cover *prov*.

◆ **habits** *nmpl* clothes ■ **mettre ses ~s du dimanche** to put on one's Sunday best.

habitabilité [abitabilite] *nf* **1.** [d'un véhicule] capacity **2.** [d'un lieu] habitability.

habitable [abitabl] *adj* : **la maison est tout à fait ~** the house is perfectly fit to live in.

habitacle [abitakl] *nm* **1.** AÉRON cockpit **2.** AUTO passenger compartment **3.** NAUT binnacle.

habitant, e [abitɑ̃, ɑ̃t] *nm, f* **1.** [d'une ville, d'un pays] inhabitant ■ [d'un immeuble] occupant ■ [d'un quartier] inhabitant, resident ■ **nous avons dormi chez l'~** we stayed with a family **2.** *(gén pl)* *litt* [animal] denizen **3.** *(gén pl)* *sout* [être humain] dweller ■ **les ~s des cavernes** cave-dwellers ■ **les ~s de la terre** earthlings **4.** farmer *Canada*.

habitat [abita] *nm* **1.** BOT & ZOOL habitat **2.** ANTHR & SOCIOL settlement ■ **~ dispersé** open settlement ■ **amélioration de l'~** home improvement.

habitation [abitasjɔ̃] *nf* **1.** [immeuble] house, building ■ **groupe d'~s** housing estate *UK ou* development *US* ■ **~ à loyer modéré** = **HLM** **2.** [domicile] residence ■ **~ principale** main residence **3.** [action d'habiter] living ■ **les conditions d'~ sont très difficiles** living *ou* housing conditions are very hard.

habité, e [abite] *adj* [maison] occupied ▪ [planète] inhabited ▪ **engin spatial ~** manned spacecraft.

habiter [3] [abite] ◇ *vt* **1.** [maison, ville, quartier] to live in ▪ [ferme] to live on **2.** *fig* & *sout* to inhabit, to be *ou* to dwell in ▪ **les craintes/démons qui l'habitent** the fears/demons within him **3.** *sout* [animaux] to inhabit.
◇ *vi* to live ▪ **~ à l'hôtel** to live *ou* to stay in a hotel ▪ **vous habitez chez vos parents?** do you live at home?

habitude [abityd] *nf* **1.** [manière d'agir] habit ▪ **avoir l'~ de : j'ai l'~ de me coucher tôt** I normally *ou* usually go to bed early ▪ **je n'ai pas l'~ d'attendre!** I am not in the habit of being kept waiting! ▪ **elle a l'~ de la conduite sur circuit** she's used to race track driving ▪ **prendre l'~ de faire qqch** to get into the habit of doing sthg ▪ **elle a ses petites ~s** she's got her own (little) ways *ou* habits ▪ **ce n'est pas dans mes ~s d'insister ainsi** I don't usually insist on things like that ▪ **à** *ou* **selon** *ou* **suivant son ~** as is his wont, as usual ▪ **tu n'as rien préparé, comme à ton ~!** you didn't get a thing ready, as usual *ou* as always! ➊ **l'~ est une seconde nature** *prov* habits are just like instincts **2.** [usage] custom ▪ **c'est l'~ chez nous** it's a custom with us *ou* our custom.
◆ **d'habitude** *loc adv* usually ▪ **comme d'~** as usual.
◆ **par habitude** *loc adv* out of habit.

habitué, e [abitɥe] *nm, f* regular ▪ **ça va déplaire aux ~s** the regulars won't like it.

habituel, elle [abitɥɛl] *adj* **1.** [traditionnel] usual, regular **2.** [ordinaire, courant] usual ▪ **au sens ~ du terme** in the everyday sense of the term.

habituellement [abitɥɛlmɑ̃] *adv* usually, normally ▪ **~ il se lève à 8 h** he usually *ou* generally gets up at 8.

habituer [7] [abitɥe] *vt* to accustom ▪ **~ qqn à qqch** to get sb used to sthg, to accustom sb to sthg ▪ **on l'a habitué à se taire** he's been taught to keep quiet ▪ **il est habitué** [il a l'habitude] he's used to it ▪ **c'est facile quand on est habitué** it's easy once you're used to it *ou* once you get used to it.
◆ **s'habituer à** *vp+prép* to get *ou* to grow *ou* to become used to.

hâblerie ['ablәri] *nf sout* [parole] boast ▪ **ce n'était qu'une ~ de sa part** he was only bragging.

hâbleur, euse ['ablœr, øz] *sout* ◇ *adj* boastful.
◇ *nm, f* boaster, braggart.

Habsbourg ['abzbur] *npr* Hapsburg, Habsburg.

hache ['aʃ] *nf* **1.** [instrument tranchant] axe ▪ **abattre un arbre à la ~** to chop a tree down ➊ **~ de guerre** tomahawk ▪ **enterrer la ~ de guerre** *pr* & *fig* to bury the hatchet ▪ **déterrer la ~ de guerre** *pr* & *fig* to be on the warpath (again) **2.** *fig* **fait** *ou* **taillé à coups de ~** [ouvrage] rough-hewn, crudely worked ; [visage] rough-hewn, rugged.

haché, e ['aʃe] *adj* **1.** CULIN [légume, amandes] chopped ▪ [viande] minced *UK*, ground *US* **2.** [style, tirade] jerky ▪ **son début était trop ~** his delivery was too jerky.
◆ **haché** *nm* mince *UK*, ground meat *US*.

hache-légumes ['aʃlegym] *nm inv* vegetable chopper.

hacher [3] ['aʃe] *vt* **1.** [légumes, fines herbes] to chop (up) ▪ **~ de la viande** to mince *UK ou* to grind *US* meat ▪ **le persil doit être haché menu** the parsley should be chopped finely ➊ **je vais le ~ menu comme chair à pâté** I'll make mincemeat (out) of him ▪ **se faire ~ (menu** *ou* **en morceaux) : il se ferait ~ plutôt que de reconnaître ses torts** he'd die (screaming) rather than admit he was wrong **2.** [saccader] to break up *(insép)*.

hachette ['aʃɛt] *nf*, **hachereau, x** ['aʃro] *nm* [outil] hatchet.

hache-viande ['aʃvjɑ̃d] *nm inv* mincer *UK ou* grinder *US*.

hachis ['aʃi] *nm* [de viande] mince *UK*, ground meat *US* ▪ [pour farce] (meat) stuffing, forcemeat ▪ [de légumes] chopped vegetables ▪ **~ Parmentier** CULIN hachis Parmentier *(dish similar to shepherd's pie)*.

hachisch ['aʃiʃ] = **haschisch**.

hachoir ['aʃwar] *nm* **1.** [couteau] chopping knife, chopper **2.** [planche] chopping board ▪ [machine] (meat) mincer *UK ou* grinder *US*.

hachure ['aʃyr] *nf* **1.** [en cartographie et dessin industriel] hachure **2.** [dessin, gravure] hatching *(U)*.

hachurer [3] ['aʃyre] *vt* **1.** TECHNOL to hachure **2.** [dessin, gravure] to hatch.

hacienda [asjɛnda] *nf* hacienda.

HAD [aʃade] *(abr de* **Hospitalisation à domicile***)* *nm* MÉD homecare *(for seriously ill patients)*.

haddock ['adɔk] *nm* smoked haddock.

Hadrien [adrijɛ̃] *npr* Hadrian.

Haendel ['ɛndɛl] *npr* Handel.

hagard, e ['agar, ard] *adj* wild, crazed ▪ **il me regardait avec des yeux ~s** he was looking at me with wild *ou* staring eyes ▪ **avoir l'air ~** to look crazed, to have a wild look in one's eyes.

hagiographe [aʒjɔgraf] *nmf* hagiographer.

hagiographie [aʒjɔgrafi] *nf* **1.** RELIG hagiography **2.** *fig* flattering biography.

Hague ['ag] *npr* : **la ~** la Hague.

LA HAGUE

Note that *la Hague* is a peninsula in Normandy well-known for its nuclear waste processing plants; it is not to be confused with *La Haye* (= The Hague, in the Netherlands).

haï, e ['ai] *pp* ▻ **haïr**.

haie ['ɛ] *nf* **1.** HORT hedge ▪ **~ vive** quickset hedge **2.** SPORT hurdle ▪ **courir le 400 mètres ~s** to run the 400 metres hurdles ‖ ▪ ÉQUIT fence ▪ **course de ~s** hurdles race **3.** [file de gens] line, row ▪ **les spectateurs ont fait une ~ pour laisser passer les coureurs** the spectators all drew back to let the runners go through ➊ **~ d'honneur** guard of honour.

haillons ['ajɔ̃] *nmpl* rags, torn and tattered clothes ▪ **être en ~** to be in rags.

Hainaut ['ɛno] *npr m* : **le ~** Hainaut.

haine ['ɛn] *nf* hatred, hate ▪ **sa ~ de la guerre** his hatred of war ➊ **être plein de ~ envers qqn** to be full of hatred *ou* filled with hatred for sb ▪ **prendre qqn/qqch en ~** to take an immense dislike to sb/sthg ▪ **sans ~** without hatred, with no hatred ▪ **avoir la ~** *fam* to be full of hatred.
◆ **par haine de** *loc prép* out of hatred for.

haineusement ['ɛnøzmɑ̃] *adv* with hatred.

haineux, euse ['ɛnø, øz] *adj* full of hatred *ou* hate.

haïr [33] ['air] *vt* **1.** [personne] to hate ▪ **il me hait de lui avoir menti** he hates me for having lied to him **2.** [attitude, comportement] to hate, to detest.

haïssable ['aisabl] *adj sout* [préjugé, attitude, personne] hateful, loathsome, detestable.

haïssait *etc v* ▻ **haïr**.

Haïti [aiti] *npr* Haiti ▪ **à ~** in Haiti.

haïtien, enne [aisjɛ̃, ɛn] *adj* Haitian.
◆ **Haïtien, enne** *nm, f* Haitian.

halage ['alaʒ] *nm* [traction] hauling ▪ [remorquage] warping, towing.

hâle ['al] *nm* suntan, tan.

hâlé, e ['ale] *adj* suntanned, tanned.

haleine [alɛn] *nf* **1.** [mouvement de respiration] breath, breathing ▪ **hors d'~** out of breath ▪ **reprendre ~** to get one's breath back ➊ **tenir qqn en ~** to keep sb in suspense *ou* on tenterhooks ▪ **courir à perdre ~** to run until one is out of breath **2.** [air expiré] breath ▪ **avoir mauvaise ~** to have bad breath.
◆ **de longue haleine** *loc adj* long-term ▪ **des recherches de longue ~** long-term research.

haler [3] ['ale] *vt* [tirer] to haul ■ [remorquer] to warp, to tow.

hâler [3] ['ale] *vt* **1.** [peau, corps] to tan **2.** TEXT to sundry.

haletant, e ['altɑ̃, ɑ̃t] *adj* [chien] panting ■ **il est entré, tout ~** he came in, all out of breath.

halètement ['alɛtmɑ̃] *nm* **1.** [respiration saccadée] panting *(U)* **2.** *sout* [rythme saccadé] : **le ~ de la locomotive** the puffing of the locomotive.

haleter [28] ['alte] *vi* **1.** [chien] to pant ■ [asthmatique] to gasp for breath ■ [pendant l'accouchement] to breathe hard, to pant ■ **~ d'émotion** to be breathless with emotion ■ **~ de colère** to choke with anger **2.** *sout* [faire un bruit saccadé] to sputter.

haleur, euse ['alœr, øz] *nm, f* [personne] tower, hauler.
◆ **haleur** *nm* [remorqueur] tug.

hall ['ol] *nm* [d'un hôtel] hall, lobby, foyer ■ [d'une banque] lobby, hall ■ **~ de gare** concourse ■ **je t'attendrai dans le ~ de la gare** I'll wait for you inside the station ■ **~ d'exposition** exhibition hall.

hallali [alali] *nm* : **l'~** [sonnerie] the mort.

halle ['al] *nf* **1.** [édifice] (covered) market ■ **~ au blé** corn exchange ■ **elle fait ses courses aux ~s** she goes to the central food market to do her shopping **2.** [le quartier] : **les Halles** *the Paris food market until 1968 (now a shopping centre).*

LES HALLES

The central Paris food markets, dating from the Second Empire. Once a tourist attraction and also a source of traffic congestion, they were moved to the outskirts, mainly to Rungis, near Orly, in the 1960s. After much delay and controversy, the site was redeveloped in the late 1970s with a metro station and a modernistic shopping centre, the *Forum des Halles.*

hallebarde ['albard] *nf* **1.** ARM halberd, halbert **2.** *fam loc* **il pleut** *ou* **il tombe des ~s** it's raining cats and dogs.

hallebardier ['albardje] *nm* halberdier.

hallier ['alje] *nm* thicket, (brush) covert.

hallucinant, e [alysinɑ̃, ɑ̃t] *adj* **1.** [frappant] staggering, incredible **2.** [qui rend fou] hallucinatory.

hallucination [alysinasjɔ̃] *nf* hallucination ■ **avoir des ~s** to hallucinate ■ **j'ai des ~s (ou quoi)!** *fam* I must be seeing things!

hallucinatoire [alysinatwar] *adj* hallucinatory.

halluciné, e [alysine] ◇ *adj* [regard] wild-eyed, crazed.
◇ *nm, f* visionary, lunatic *péj* ■ **comme un ~** like a madman.

halluciner [3] [alysine] ◇ *vi* **1.** PSYCHOL to hallucinate, to suffer from *ou* to have hallucinations **2.** *fam fig* **mais j'hallucine ou quoi?** I don't believe this!
◇ *vt litt* **halluciné par le manque de sommeil** seeing double through lack of sleep.

hallucinogène [alysinɔʒɛn] ◇ *adj* hallucinogenic.
◇ *nm* hallucinogen.

halo ['alo] *nm* **1.** ASTRON halo, corona **2.** PHOTO halo **3.** *litt* aureole, halo ■ **un ~ de lumière/de gloire** a halo of light/of glory.

halogène [alɔʒɛn] ◇ *adj* halogenous.
◇ *nm* **1.** CHIM halogen **2.** [éclairage] : **(lampe à) ~** halogen lamp.

halte ['alt] ◇ *nf* **1.** [arrêt] stop, break ■ **faire ~** to halt, to stop ■ **faire une ~** to have a break, to pause **2.** [lieu] stopping *ou* resting place ■ RAIL halt *UK.*
◇ *interj* stop ■ MIL halt ■ **~ à la pollution!** no more pollution! ■ **~, qui va là?** halt, who goes there? ■ **~-là, ne t'emballe pas trop** hold on, don't get carried away.

halte-garderie ['altəgardəri] (*pl* **haltes-garderies**) *nf* ≃ day nursery.

haltère [altɛr] *nm* **1.** [avec des sphères] dumbbell ■ [avec des disques] barbell ■ **faire des ~s** to do weight-lifting **2.** ANTIQ halterer.

haltérophile [alterɔfil] *nmf* weight-lifter.

haltérophilie [alterɔfili] *nf* weight-lifting.

hamac ['ama(k)] *nm* hammock.

hamamélis [amamelis] *nm* witch hazel *(U).*

Hambourg ['ɑ̃bur] *npr* Hamburg.

hambourgeois, e ['ɑ̃burʒwa, az] *adj* from Hamburg.
◆ **Hambourgeois, e** *nm, f inhabitant of or person from Hamburg.*

hamburger ['ɑ̃bœrgœr] *nm* hamburger.

hameau, x ['amo] *nm* hamlet.

hameçon [amsɔ̃] *nm* (fish) hook.

hammam ['amam] *nm* Turkish *ou* steam bath, hammam.

hampe ['ɑ̃p] *nf* **1.** [d'un drapeau] pole **2.** ARM & PÊCHE shaft **3.** [d'une lettre - vers le haut] upstroke ; [- vers le bas] downstroke **4.** [d'un pinceau] handle.

hamster ['amstɛr] *nm* hamster.

han ['ɑ̃] *nm inv* oof ■ **pousser des ~** to grunt (with effort).

hanap ['anap] *nm* hanap *arch,* goblet.

hanche ['ɑ̃ʃ] *nf* **1.** ANAT hip ■ **avoir des ~s larges /étroites** to have wide/narrow hips, to be wide-/narrow-hipped ■ **mettre les mains** *ou* **les poings sur les ~s** to put one's hands on one's hips **2.** ZOOL haunch, hindquarter **3.** ENTOM coxa.

handball ['ɑ̃dbal] *nm* handball.

handballeur, euse ['ɑ̃dbalœr, øz] *nm, f* handball player.

handicap ['ɑ̃dikap] *nm* **1.** [gén - SPORT] handicap ■ **son poids est un grand ~** her weight is a great handicap **2.** *(comme adj; avec ou sans trait d'union)* handicap *(modif).*

handicapant, e ['ɑ̃dikapɑ̃, ɑ̃t] *adj* : **c'est (très) ~** it's a (great) handicap.

handicapé, e ['ɑ̃dikape] ◇ *adj* handicapped ■ **enfants ~s mentaux** mentally handicapped children.
◇ *nm, f* handicapped *ou* disabled person ■ **les ~s** the disabled ◗ **un ~ moteur** a spastic.

handicaper [3] ['ɑ̃dikape] *vt* to handicap ■ **ça l'a handicapé dans sa carrière** it was a handicap to his career.

handicapeur ['ɑ̃dikapœr] *nm* (official) handicapper.

handisport ['ɑ̃dispɔr] *adj* : **activité ~** sport for the disabled.

hangar ['ɑ̃gar] *nm* [gén] shed ■ [pour avions] (aircraft) hangar ■ **~ à bateaux** boathouse ■ **un ~ à charbon** a coal shed.

hanneton ['antɔ̃] *nm* cockchafer, maybug.

Hannibal [anibal] *npr* Hannibal.

Hanoi [anɔj] *npr* Hanoi.

Hanovre ['anɔvr] *npr* Hanover.

Hanse ['ɑ̃s] *npr f* : **(la) ~** Hanse.

hanséatique ['ɑ̃seatik] *adj* Hanseatic.

hanté, e ['ɑ̃te] *adj* [maison, forêt] haunted.

hanter [3] ['ɑ̃te] *vt* to haunt ■ **ce souvenir le hante** he's haunted by the memory.

hantise ['ɑ̃tiz] *nf* obsession, obsessive fear ■ **avoir la ~ de la mort** to be haunted *ou* obsessed by the fear of death ■ **sa ~ d'un accident l'empêche de conduire** his obsessive fear of accidents stops him from driving ■ **chez lui, c'est une ~** he's obsessed by it, it's an obsession with him.

happement ['apmɑ̃] *nm* snapping *(with the mouth).*

happening ['apniŋ] *nm* [spectacle] happening.

happer [3] ['ape] *vt* **1.** [avec le bec ou la bouche] to snap up ■ [avec la main ou la patte] to snatch, to grab **2.** [accrocher violemment] to strike *ou* to hit violently ■ **être happé par un train/une voiture** to be mown down *ou* hit by a train/car.

happy end ['apiɛnd] (*pl* **happy ends**) *nm* happy ending.

hara-kiri ['arakiri] (*pl* **hara-kiris**) *nm* hara-kiri ▪ **(se) faire ~** to commit hara-kiri ▪ **: Hara-Kiri** PRESSE *former monthly satirical magazine.*

harangue ['arɑ̃g] *nf* **1.** [discours solennel] harangue **2.** *péj* [sermon] sermon.

haranguer [3] ['arɑ̃ge] *vt* to harangue.

haras ['ara] *nm* stud farm.

harassant, e ['arasɑ̃, ɑ̃t] *adj* exhausting, wearing.

harassé, e ['arase] *adj* exhausted, worn out ▪ **avoir l'air ~** to look exhausted.

harassement ['arasmɑ̃] *nm litt* exhaustion, fatigue.

harasser [3] ['arase] *vt* to exhaust, to wear out *(sép).*

harcelant, e ['arsəlɑ̃, ɑ̃t] *adj* **1.** [obsédant] haunting **2.** [importun] harassing, pestering.

harcèlement ['arsɛlmɑ̃] *nm* harassing, pestering ▪ **~ sexuel** sexual harassment ▪ **~ moral** bullying *(in the workplace).*

harceler [25] ['arsəle] *vt* to harass ▪ **~ qqn de questions** to plague *ou* to pester sb with questions ▪ **cesse de me ~!** stop pestering *ou* bothering me! ▪ **~ l'ennemi** to harass *ou* to harry the enemy.

hard ['ard] *fam* **1.** = **hard-core 2.** = **hard-rock**.

hard-core ['ardkɔr] <> *adj inv* hard-core ▪ **un film ~** a hard-core (porn) movie.
<> *nm inv* [genre] hard-core porn.

harde ['ard] *nf* **1.** [d'animaux sauvages] herd **2.** CHASSE [lien] leash ▪ [chiens liés] set (of coupled hounds).

hardes ['ard] *nfpl litt & péj* rags, tatters.

hardi, e ['ardi] *adj* **1.** [intrépide] bold, daring ▪ **l'hypothèse est un peu ~e** *fig* the supposition is a bit rash *ou* hasty **2.** [licencieux] daring, bold.
◆ **hardi** *interj arch* **~, les gars!** go to it, boys!

hardiesse ['ardjɛs] *nf* **1.** [intrépidité] boldness, daring, audacity *sout* ▪ **avoir la ~ de faire qqch** to be forward *ou* daring enough to do sthg **2.** [acte, parole] **: ~ de langage** bold turn of phrase ▪ **des ~s de langage** [propos crus] bold language ; [effets de style] daring stylistic effects **3.** [indécence] boldness, raciness ▪ **la ~ de certaines scènes peut choquer** you may find the explicitness of some of the scenes offensive.

hardiment ['ardimɑ̃] *adv* boldly, daringly, fearlessly.

hard-rock ['ardrɔk] *nm inv* MUS hard rock, heavy metal.

hardware ['ardwɛr] *nm* INFORM hardware.

harem ['arɛm] *nm* harem.

hareng ['arɑ̃] *nm* CULIN & ZOOL herring ▪ **~ fumé** kipper ▪ **~ saur** smoked herring, kipper.

hargne ['arɲ] *nf* aggressiveness ▪ **avec ~** aggressively, cantankerously.

hargneusement ['arɲøzmɑ̃] *adv* aggressively, cantankerously.

hargneux, euse ['arɲø, øz] *adj* **1.** [caractère] aggressive, quarrelsome ▪ **un vieil homme ~** a cantankerous old man **2.** [ton] scathing, caustic ▪ **des paroles hargneuses** scathing remarks **3.** [animal] vicious.

haricot ['ariko] *nm* **1.** [légume] bean ▪ **~ blanc** white (haricot) bean ▪ **~ mange-tout** runner *ou* string bean ▪ **~ rouge** red *ou* kidney bean ▪ **~ vert** French *UK ou* green *american english ou* string bean ▪ **~s fins/extrafins** high-quality/superfine French *UK ou* green *american english* beans **2.** CULIN [ragoût] **: ~ de mouton** mutton haricot *ou* stew **3.** MÉD [cuvette] kidney tray *ou* dish.
◆ **haricots** *nmpl fam* **des ~s** not a thing, zilch△ *esp US.*

harissa ['arisa] *nf* harissa (sauce).

harki ['arki] *nm Algerian who fought for the French during the Franco-Algerian War and who was subsequently given French nationality.*

harmattan [armatɑ̃] *nm* harmattan.

harmonica [armɔnika] *nm* harmonica, mouth organ ▪ **~ de verres** glass harmonica.

harmonie [armɔni] *nf* **1.** [élégance] harmony ▪ **l'~ du corps humain** the beauty of the human body **2.** [entente] harmony **3.** MUS [accords] harmony ▪ [instruments à vent et percussions] wind section (with percussion) ▪ [fanfare] brass band **4.** LING **: ~ vocalique** vowel harmony ▪ **~ consonantique** consonant drift.
◆ **en harmonie** <> *loc adv* in harmony, harmoniously ▪ **en parfaite ~** in perfect harmony.
<> *loc adj* in harmony ▪ **le tapis n'est pas en ~ avec les meubles** the carpet doesn't go with *ou* match the furniture.

harmonieusement [armɔnjøzmɑ̃] *adv* harmoniously, in harmony.

harmonieux, euse [armɔnjøøz] *adj* **1.** [mélodieux - son, instrument] harmonious ; [- voix] harmonious, tuneful, melodious **2.** [équilibré] harmonious, balanced ▪ **des teintes harmonieuses** well-matched colours ▪ **un visage ~** well-balanced features.

harmonique [armɔnik] <> *adj* ACOUST, MATH & MUS harmonic ▪ **série/progression ~** harmonic series/progression ▪ **son ~** harmonic.
<> *nm* **1.** ACOUST & MUS harmonic **2.** PHYS harmonic, overtone.

harmonisation [armɔnizasjɔ̃] *nf* **1.** [mise en accord] harmonization ▪ **réclamer l'~ des salaires du public et du privé** to demand that public sector salaries be brought into parity *ou* line with those in the private sector **2.** MUS harmonizing.

harmoniser [3] [armɔnize] *vt* MUS to harmonize ▪ [styles, couleurs] to match ▪ **~ les salaires du public et du privé** to bring public and private sector salaries into line.
◆ **s'harmoniser** *vpi* **: s'~ avec** to harmonize with ▪ **ces couleurs s'harmonisent bien entre elles** these colours go together well.

harmoniste [armɔnist] *nmf* **1.** [spécialiste de l'harmonie] harmonist **2.** TECHNOL tuner.

harmonium [armɔnjɔm] *nm* harmonium.

harnachement ['arnaʃmɑ̃] *nm* **1.** [équipement] harness ▪ [action] harnessing **2.** *hum* [accoutrement] outfit, get-up ▪ [attirail] paraphernalia.

harnacher [3] ['arnaʃe] *vt* **1.** [cheval] to harness **2.** *hum* [accoutrer] to deck *ou* to rig out *(sép)* ▪ [équiper] to kit out *(sép).*
◆ **se harnacher** *vp (emploi réfléchi)* [s'équiper] to get kitted out ▪ **ils s'étaient harnachés de cordes et de piolets pour l'ascension** they were kitted out with ropes and ice axes for the climb.

harnais ['arnɛ] *nm* **1.** [d'un cheval] harness **2.** [sangles] **: ~ (de sécurité)** (safety) harness ▪ **mettre le ~ (de sécurité) à qqn** to strap sb in **3.** TECHNOL backgear **4.** TEXT healds, harness.

haro ['aro] *nm* **: crier ~ sur qqn** to raise a hue and cry against sb ▪ **on a crié ~ sur le baudet** there was a hue and cry.

harpagon [arpagɔ̃] *nm litt* Scrooge, skinflint *(from the main character in Molière's 'l'Avare').*

harpe ['arp] *nf* **1.** MUS harp ▪ **~ éolienne** wind *ou* aeolian harp **2.** ZOOL [mollusque] harp (shell) **3.** CONSTR [pierre en saillie] toothing (stone).

harpie ['arpi] *nf* **1.** [mégère] shrew, harpy **2.** HÉRALD harpy **3.** ORNITH harpy eagle.

harpiste ['arpist] *nmf* harpist.

harpon ['arpɔ̃] *nm* **1.** PÊCHE harpoon **2.** CONSTR (wall) staple **3.** ARCHÉOL harping iron, harpoon.

harponnage ['arpɔnaʒ], **harponnement** ['arpɔnmɑ̃] *nm* **1.** PÊCHE harpooning **2.** CONSTR stapling.

harponner [3] ['arpɔne] *vt* **1.** PÊCHE to harpoon **2.** *fam* [arrêter] to nab, to collar ▪ **les flics l'ont harponné à la sortie du club** the cops collared him outside the club.

harponneur ['arpɔnœr] *nm* harpooner.

hasard ['azar] *nm* **1.** [providence] chance, fate ■ **s'il gagne, c'est le ~** if he wins it's luck *ou* it's by chance ■ **s'en remettre au ~** to leave it to chance, to trust to luck ■ **ne rien laisser au ~** to leave nothing to chance ■ **le ~ a voulu que je sois à l'étranger** as luck would have it I was abroad ■ **le ~ fait bien les choses** there are some lucky coincidences ■ **le ~ faisant bien les choses, ils se retrouvèrent quelques années plus tard** as chance would have it, they met again some years later **2.** [incident imprévu] : **quel heureux ~!** what a stroke of luck *ou* piece of good fortune! ■ **un ~ malheureux** a piece of bad luck **3.** [coïncidence] : **quel heureux ~!** what a fantastic coincidence! ■ **c'est un (pur) ~ que vous m'ayez trouvé chez moi à cette heure-ci** it's sheer luck that you've found me in at this time of day ■ **par un curieux ~, il était né le même jour** by a strange coincidence he was born on the same day ■ **par quel ~ étiez-vous là ce jour-là?** how come you happened to be there that day? ■ **par le plus grand des ~s** by the most extraordinary *ou* incredible coincidence ■ **tu n'aurais pas, par le plus grand des ~s, vu mes lunettes?** you wouldn't by any chance have happened to see my glasses, would you? **4.** JEUX : **jeu de ~** game of chance **5.** [statistiques] chance ■ **échantillonnage/nombres au ~** random sampling/numbers.

◆ **hasards** *nmpl* **1.** [aléas] : **les ~s de la vie** life's ups and downs, life's vicissitudes *sout* **2.** *litt* [périls] hazards, dangers.

◆ **à tout hasard** *loc adv* on the off chance, just in case.

◆ **au hasard** *loc adv* at random ■ **j'ai ouvert le livre au ~** I opened the book at random ■ **aller** *ou* **marcher au ~** [par indifférence] to walk aimlessly ; [par plaisir] to go where one's fancy takes one ■ **tirez** *ou* **piochez une carte au ~** pick a card (, any card).

◆ **au hasard de** *loc prép* : **je me suis fait des amis au ~ de mes voyages** I made friends with people I happened to meet on my travels.

◆ **de hasard** *loc adj* chance *(avant n)* ■ **des amours de ~** brief encounters.

◆ **par hasard** *loc adv* by chance *ou* accident ■ **si par ~ vous la voyez** if by any chance you should see her, should you happen to see her ■ **je suis entré par ~ et je l'ai pris la main dans le sac** I went in quite by chance and caught him red-handed ■ **comme par ~!** *iron* that's a surprise, surprise, surprise! ■ **comme par ~, elle n'a rien entendu** surprisingly enough, she didn't hear a thing!

hasardé, e ['azarde] = **hasardeux.**

hasarder [3] ['azarde] *vt* [opinion, démarche] to hazard, to venture, to risk.

◆ **se hasarder** *vpi* [s'aventurer] to venture ■ **il se hasarda dans l'obscurité** he ventured into the darkness ■ **se ~ à : la nouvelle élève se hasarda à répondre** the new student plucked up courage to answer ■ **je ne m'y hasarderais pas** I wouldn't risk it *ou* chance it.

hasardeux, euse ['azardøøz] *adj* **1.** [douteux] dubious ■ **l'issue en est hasardeuse** the outcome of all this is uncertain **2.** [dangereux] hazardous, dangerous ■ **une affaire hasardeuse** a risky business.

hasch ['aʃ] *nm fam* hash.

haschi(s)ch ['aʃiʃ] *nm* hashish.

hâte ['at] *nf* **1.** [précipitation] haste, hurry, rush ■ **dans sa ~, il a oublié ses clés** he was in such a hurry *ou* rush (that) he left his keys behind ■ **avec ~** hastily, hurriedly ■ **sans ~** at a leisurely pace, without hurrying ■ **sans grande ~** with no great haste, unhurriedly **2.** [être impatient de] : **avoir ~ de : avoir ~ de faire qqch** to be looking forward to doing sthg ■ **j'ai ~ que vous veniez/Noël arrive** I can't wait for you to come/Christmas to come round ■ **pourquoi avez-vous ~ de partir?** why are you in (such) a hurry *ou* rush to leave? ■ **il n'a qu'une ~, c'est d'avoir un petit-fils** he's dying to have a grandson.

◆ **à la hâte** *loc adv* hurriedly, hastily, in a rush ■ **faire qqch à la ~** to do sthg hastily.

◆ **en hâte, en grande hâte, en toute hâte** *loc adv* hurriedly, in (great) haste ■ **envoyez votre réponse en toute ~ à l'adresse suivante** send your reply without delay *ou* rush your reply to the following address.

hâter [3] ['ate] *vt* **1.** [accélérer] to speed up, to hasten *sout* ■ **~ le pas** to quicken one's pace *sout*, to walk quicker **2.** *sout* [avancer - date] to bring forward ; [- naissance, mort, mariage] to precipitate ■ **je dois ~ mon départ** I must go sooner than I thought.

◆ **se hâter** *vpi sout* to hurry (up), to hasten *sout*, to make haste *sout* ■ **hâtez-vous de me répondre** answer me posthaste *sout* ■ **elle s'est hâtée de répandre la nouvelle** she hastened to spread the news.

hâtif, ive ['atif, iv] *adj* **1.** [rapide - travail, repas] hurried, rushed ; [- décision] hasty, rash **2.** [précoce - croissance] early.

hâtivement ['ativmɑ̃] *adv* hastily, hurriedly, in a rush ■ **le livre a été écrit un peu ~** the book was written in somewhat of a rush.

hauban ['obɑ̃] *nm* **1.** AÉRON & NAUT shroud **2.** TECHNOL stay.

hausse ['os] *nf* **1.** [augmentation] rise, increase ■ **la ~ du coût de la vie** the rise in the cost of living **2.** [élévation] rise **3.** ARM back-sight **4.** [d'une ruche] superhive.

◆ **à la hausse** *loc adv* **1.** [au maximum] : **réviser le budget à la ~** to increase the budget **2.** BOURSE : **jouer à la ~** to speculate on the rising market *ou* on the bull market ■ **vendre à la ~** to sell in a rising market, to contrary sell *spéc* ■ **le marché évolue** *ou* **est à la ~** there is an upward trend in the market.

◆ **en hausse** *loc adj* increasing, rising ■ **être en ~** to be on the increase, to be rising ■ **les vols de voitures sont en ~ de 30% sur l'année dernière** car thefts are up 30% on last year.

haussement ['osmɑ̃] *nm* : **avec un ~ d'épaules** with a shrug (of his shoulders) ■ **avec un ~ de sourcils** with raised eyebrows.

hausser [3] ['ose] *vt* **1.** ÉCON to raise, to increase, to put up *(sép)* ■ **le prix a été haussé de 10 %** the price has been increased *ou* has gone up by 10% ■ **~ ses prétentions** to aim higher **2.** CONSTR & TRAV PUB to raise ■ **~ qqn au niveau de** *fig* to raise sb up to the level of **3.** [partie du corps] : **~ les épaules** to shrug (one's shoulders) ■ **~ le sourcil** to raise one's eyebrows **4.** [intensifier] : **~ la voix** *ou* **le ton** to raise one's voice.

◆ **se hausser** *vpi* **1.** [se hisser] to reach up ■ **se ~ sur la pointe des pieds** to stand on tiptoe **2.** [atteindre un degré supérieur] : **elle est parvenue à se ~ au niveau de la classe** she managed to reach the level of the other students in her class.

haussier, ère ['osje, ɛr] ◇ *adj* BOURSE : **un marché ~** a rising *ou* bull market.
◇ *nm, f* BOURSE bull.

Haussmann [osman] *npr* : **un immeuble ~** *a building designed by Baron Haussmann.*

HAUSSMANN

Georges Eugène Haussmann (1809-1891) was responsible during the Second Empire for redesigning the centre of Paris, demolishing whole areas of old housing and creating the wide boulevards of the present-day city.

haut, e ['o, 'ot] *(devant nm commençant par voyelle ou 'h' muet* ['ot]*)* *adj* **1.** [de grande dimension] high, tall ■ **les ~es colonnes du temple** the lofty *ou* towering columns of the temple ■ **les pièces sont ~es de plafond** the rooms have high ceilings ‖ BOT [tige, tronc] tall ■ [qui a poussé] high **2.** [d'une certaine dimension] : **la maison est ~e de trois mètres** the house is three metres high **3.** [situé en hauteur] high ■ **le soleil est ~ dans le ciel** the sun is high (up) in the sky ■ **la partie ~e de l'arbre** the top of the tree ➊ **le Haut Nil** the upper (reaches of the) Nile **4.** [extrême, intense] high ■ **c'est de la plus ~e importance** it's of the utmost *ou* greatest importance ■ **à ~ risque** high-risk ➊ **~ débit** INFORM & TELEC broadband ■ **~e fréquence** high frequency ■ **~e technologie** high technology **5.** [dans une hiérarchie] high, top *(avant n)* ■ **de ~ niveau** top-level, high-level ■ **des gens de ~ niveau** high-fliers ■ **de ~s dignitaires** eminent dignitaries ➊ **la ~e coiffure** haute coiffure, designer hairdressing ■ **la ~e cuisine** haute cuisine ■ **de ~es études commerciales/militaires** advanced business/military studies ■ **les ~s fonctionnaires** top *ou* top-ranking civil servants ■ **les ~s salaires** the highest *ou* top salaries **6.** [dans une échelle de valeurs] high ■ **d'une ~e intelligence** highly intelligent ■ **tenir qqn/qqch**

en ~e estime to hold sb/sthg in high esteem **7. BOURSE & COMM** high **8. MUS & PHON** high **9. HIST : le ~ Moyen Âge** the Early Middle Ages **10.** *litt* [noble] lofty, high-minded.

◆ **haut** ◇ *adv* **1.** [dans l'espace] high ■ **levez ~ la jambe** raise your leg (up) high *ou* high up **2.** [dans le temps] far (back) ■ [dans un livre] : **voir plus ~** see above **3.** [fort, avec puissance] : **(tout) ~** aloud ■ **parlez plus ~** speak up, speak louder ■ **dites-le ~ et clair** *ou* **bien ~** tell (it to) everyone, say it out loud **4. MUS** high **5.** [dans une hiérarchie] high ■ **être ~ placé** to be highly placed, to hold high office ■ **des amis ~ placés** friends in high places ■ **nous l'avons toujours placé très ~ dans notre estime** *fig* we've always held him in high regard **6. BOURSE & COMM** high.
◇ *nm* **1.** [partie supérieure] top ■ [sur une caisse, un emballage] : **'haut'** '(this way *ou* side) up' **2.** [vêtement & gén] top ■ [de robe] bodice **3.** [hauteur] : **un mur d'un mètre de ~** a one metre (high) wall ■ **tomber de tout son ~** [chuter] to fall headlong ; [être déçu] to come down (to earth) with a bump ; [être surpris] to be flabbergasted.

◆ **hauts** *nmpl* **1.** [dans des noms de lieux] heights **2.** *loc* **avoir** *ou* **connaître des ~s et des bas** to have one's ups and downs.

◆ **haute** *nf fam* **la ~e** the upper crust ■ **les gens de la ~e** upper crust people.

◆ **de haut** *loc adv* **1.** [avec détachement] casually, unconcernedly ■ **prendre** *ou* **regarder** *ou* **voir les choses de ~** to look at things with an air of detachment **2.** [avec mépris] : **prendre qqch de ~** to be high and mighty about sthg ■ **regarder qqn de ~** to look down on sb ■ **traiter qqn de ~** to treat sb high-handedly **3.** *loc* **tomber de ~** [être surpris] to be flabbergasted ; [être déçu] to come down (to earth) with a bump.

◆ **de haut en bas** *loc adv* **1.** [sans mouvement] from top to bottom **2.** [avec mouvement, vers le bas] from top to bottom, downwards **3.** [avec mépris] : **regarder** *ou* **considérer qqn de ~ en bas** to look sb up and down.

◆ **d'en haut** *loc adv* **1.** [depuis la partie élevée] from above ■ **d'en ~ on voit la mer** you can see the sea from up there **2.** *fig* from on high ■ **le bon exemple doit venir d'en ~** people in positions of authority must give the lead.

◆ **du haut** *loc adj* : **les gens du ~** [de la partie haute du village] the people up the top end (of the village) ; [des étages supérieurs] the people upstairs ■ **les chambres du ~** the upstairs bedrooms.

◆ **du haut de** *loc prép* **1.** [depuis la partie élevée de - échelle, colline] from the top of **2.** *fig* **il nous regarde du ~ de sa grandeur** he looks down his nose at us.

◆ **en haut** *loc adv* **1.** [à l'étage supérieur] upstairs **2.** [dans la partie élevée] at the top ■ **nous sommes passés par en ~** [par la route du haut] we came along the high road **3.** [en l'air] up in the sky.

◆ **en haut de** *loc prép* at the top of ■ **tout en ~ d'une colline** high up on a hill ■ **regarde en ~ de l'armoire** look on top of the wardrobe.

hautain, e ['otɛ̃, ɛn] *adj* haughty ■ **d'une façon ~e** haughtily.

hautbois ['obwa] *nm* **1.** [instrument] oboe **2.** [instrumentiste] oboe (player).

hautboïste ['obɔist] *nmf* oboist, oboe (player).

haut-commissaire ['okɔmisɛr] (*pl* **hauts-commissaires**) *nm, f* high commissioner.

haut-commissariat ['okɔmisarja] (*pl* **hauts-commissariats**) *nm* **1.** [fonction] high commissionership **2.** [bureaux] high commission.

haut-de-chausse(s) ['odʃos] (*pl* **hauts-de-chausse** *ou pl* **hauts-de-chausses**) *nm* knee-breeches, breeches, trunk-hose.

haut-de-forme ['odfɔrm] (*pl* **hauts-de-forme**) *nm* top hat.

haute-contre ['otkɔ̃tr] (*pl* **hautes-contre**) ◇ *nf* [voix] countertenor (voice).
◇ *nm* [chanteur] countertenor.

haute-fidélité ['otfidelite] (*pl* **hautes-fidélités**) *nf* **1. TECH** high fidelity, hi-fi **2.** *(comme adj)* high-fidelity *(avant n)*, hi-fi.

hautement ['otmɑ̃] *adv* **1.** *sout* [fortement] highly, extremely ■ **ce qu'elle dit est ~ sujet à caution** you should be extremely wary of what she says **2.** [ouvertement] openly.

Haute-Normandie ['otnɔrmɑ̃di] *npr f* : **la ~** Haute-Normandie.

HAUTE-NORMANDIE

This administrative region includes the *départements* of Eure and Seine-Maritime (capital: Rouen).

hauteur ['otœr] *nf* **1.** [mesure verticale] height ■ **il est tombé de toute sa ~** he fell headlong ■ **de faible ~** low ■ **la pièce fait trois mètres de ~ (sous plafond)** the ceiling height in the room is three metres ‖ ▮ **CONSTR** height ■ **COUT** length ‖ ■ **GÉOM : la ~ d'un triangle** the perpendicular height of a triangle **2.** [altitude] height, altitude ■ **prendre de la ~** to gain altitude *ou* height ■ **n'étant plus mandaté, je me permets de voir les choses avec (une certaine) ~** as I'm no longer in office, I can afford to look upon things with a certain detachment **3. MUS & PHON** height, pitch **4.** *sout* [noblesse] nobility **5.** [arrogance] haughtiness, arrogance **6. SPORT : la ~** the high jump.

◆ **hauteurs** *nfpl* heights ■ **il y a de la neige sur les ~s** there's snow on the higher slopes ■ **l'aigle s'envola vers les ~s** the eagle soared high up (into the sky *ou* air).

◆ **à hauteur de** *loc prép* [jusqu'à] : **à ~ des yeux** at eye level ■ **à ~ d'homme** about six feet off the ground ■ **vous serez remboursé à ~ de 4 000 euros** you'll be reimbursed up to 4,000 euros.

◆ **à la hauteur** *loc adj fam* **tu ne t'es pas montré à la ~** you weren't up to it *ou* equal to the task ■ **elle a été (tout à fait) à la ~** she coped beautifully.

◆ **à la hauteur de** *loc prép* **1.** [à côté de] : **arrivé à sa ~, je m'aperçus qu'il parlait tout seul** when I was *ou* drew level with him, I noticed he was talking to himself ■ **elle habite à la ~ de l'église** she lives near the church *ou* up by the church ■ **arrivés à la ~ du cap** when we were in line with *ou* when we were off the cape ■ **il y a des embouteillages à la ~ de l'échangeur de Rocquencourt** there are traffic jams at the Rocquencourt interchange **2.** [digne de] worthy of ■ **une carrière à la ~ de ses ambitions** a career commensurate with her ambitions ■ **être à la ~ d'une situation** to be equal to *ou* up to a situation.

◆ **en hauteur** *loc adv* **1.** [debout] upright ■ **mettez-le en ~** put it on its end **2.** [dans un endroit élevé] : **range ces cartons en ~** put these boxes up out of the way ■ **ça ne vous ennuie pas d'habiter en ~?** doesn't living high up bother you?

Haute-Volta ['otvɔlta] *npr f* : **(la) ~** Upper Volta.

haut-fond ['ofɔ̃] (*pl* **hauts-fonds**) *nm* shallow, shoal.

haut-fourneau ['ofurno] (*pl* **hauts-fourneaux**) *nm* blast furnace.

Haut-Karabakh ['okarabak] *npr m* Nagorno-Karabakh.

haut-le-corps ['olkɔr] *nm inv* start, jump ■ **avoir un ~** to start, to jump.

haut-le-cœur ['ol(ə)kœr] *nm inv* **1.** [nausée] : **avoir un** *ou* **des ~** to retch **2.** *fig* **une attitude aussi lâche me donne des ~** such cowardly behaviour makes me (feel) sick.

haut-parleur ['oparlœr] (*pl* **haut-parleurs**) *nm* loudspeaker, speaker ■ **~ d'aigus** tweeter.

haut-relief ['orəljɛf] (*pl* **hauts-reliefs**) *nm* high relief.

hauturier, ère ['otyrje, ɛr] *adj* deep-sea ■ **navigation hauturière** ocean navigation.

havanais, e ['avanɛ, ɛz] *adj* from Havana.

◆ **Havanais, e** *nm, f inhabitant of or person from Havana.*

◆ **havanaise** *nf* habanera.

havane ['avan] ◇ *nm* **1.** [tabac] Havana **2.** [cigare] Havana.
◇ *adj inv* Havana brown.

Havane ['avan] *npr f* : **La ~** Havana.

hâve ['av] *adj sout* haggard.

haveuse ['avøz] *nf* **MIN** cutting machine, cutter.

havre ['avr] *nm litt* haven, harbour ■ **~ de paix** haven of peace.

Havre ['avr] *npr m* : **Le ~** Le Havre ■ **au ~** in Le Havre.

havresac ['avrəsak] *nm* [de campeur] haversack, knapsack ■ [de militaire] haversack, kitbag.

hawaïen [awajɛ̃] = **hawaiien.**

Hawaii [awaj] *npr* Hawaii ▪ **à ~** in Hawaii.

hawaiien, enne [awajɛ̃, ɛn] *adj* Hawaiian.
◆ **Hawaiien, enne** *nm, f* Hawaiian.
◆ **hawaiien** *nm* LING Hawaiian.

Haydn [ajdən] *npr* Haydn.

Haye ['ɛ] *npr f* : **La ~** The Hague.

hayon ['ajɔ̃] *nm* **1.** AUTO tailgate ▪ **véhicule à ~ arrière** hatchback (car) **2.** TECHNOL : **~ élévateur** (fork) lift.

HB, hdb = **heures de bureau.**

hé ['e] *interj* **1.** [pour interpeller quelqu'un] hey ▪ **~, vous, là!** hey! you! **2.** [d'étonnement] hey, well (well, well) ▪ **hé, la voilà qui arrive!** hey, here she comes!

heaume ['om] *nm* HÉRALD & HIST helm, helmet.

hebdo [ɛbdo] *nm* PRESSE weekly.

hebdomadaire [ɛbdɔmadɛr] *adj* & *nm* weekly.

hebdomadairement [ɛbdɔmadɛrmɑ̃] *adv* weekly, once a week.

hébergement [ebɛrʒəmɑ̃] *nm* **1.** [lieu] lodgings, accommodation **2.** [action] lodging ▪ **l'~ est en chalet** chalet accommodation is provided **3.** INFORM : **~ de site Web** website hosting.

héberger [17] [ebɛrʒe] *vt* [pour une certaine durée] to lodge, to accommodate ▪ [à l'improviste] to put up *(sép)* ▪ [réfugié, vagabond] to take in *(sép)*, to shelter ▪ [criminel] to harbour, to shelter ▪ **notre bâtiment hébergera le secrétariat pendant les travaux** the secretarial offices will be housed in our building during the alterations ▮ INFORM : **~ un site Web** to host a website.

hébété, e [ebete] *adj* dazed, in a daze ▪ **il avait un air ~** he looked dazed.

hébétement [ebɛtmɑ̃] *nm* stupor ▪ **son ~ est dû à l'alcool** he's in a drunken stupor.

hébéter [18] [ebete] *vt* to daze ▪ **hébété par l'alcool/la drogue** in a drunken/drug-induced stupor.

hébétude [ebetyd] *nf* **1.** *litt* stupor, stupefaction *litt* **2.** PSYCHOL hebetude.

hébraïque [ebraik] *adj* Hebraic, Hebrew *(modif).*

hébraïsme [ebraism] *nm* Hebraism.

hébreu, x [ebrø] *adj m* Hebrew.
◆ **Hébreux** *nmpl* : **les Hébreux** the Hebrews.
◆ **hébreu** *nm* **1.** LING Hebrew **2.** *fam loc* **pour moi, c'est de l'~** I can't make head or tail of it, it's all Greek to me.

Hébrides [ebrid] *npr fpl* : **les (îles) ~** the Hebrides ▪ **aux ~** in the Hebrides.

HEC (*abr de* **Hautes études commerciales**) *npr grande école for management and business studies.*

hécatombe [ekatɔ̃b] *nf* **1.** [carnage] slaughter, massacre ▪ **l'~ annuelle des blessés de la route** the carnage that occurs every year on the roads **2.** *fig* **les jeux Olympiques ont été une véritable ~ pour leurs athlètes** the Olympics have been disastrous for their athletes **3.** ANTIQ hecatomb.

hectare [ɛktar] *nm* hectare.

hectique [ɛktik] *adj* : **fièvre ~** hectic fever.

hecto [ɛkto] *nm fam* **1.** (*abr de* **hectogramme**) hectogramme, hectogram **2.** (*abr de* **hectolitre**) hectolitre.

hectogramme [ɛktɔgram] *nm* hectogram, hectogramme.

hectolitre [ɛktɔlitr] *nm* hectolitre ▪ **un ~** a hundred litres, a hectolitre.

hectomètre [ɛktɔmɛtr] *nm* hectometre ▪ **un ~** a hundred metres, a hectometre.

hectopascal [ɛktɔpaskal] (*pl* **hectopascals**) *nm* hectopascal.

hectowatt [ɛktɔwat] *nm* hectowatt ▪ **un ~** a hundred watts, a hectowatt.

hédonisme [edɔnism] *nm* hedonism.

hédoniste [edɔnist] ◇ *adj* hedonist, hedonistic.
◇ *nmf* hedonist.

hégélianisme [egeljanism] *nm* Hegelianism.

hégélien, enne [egeljɛ̃, ɛn] *adj* & *nm, f* Hegelian.

hégémonie [eʒemɔni] *nf* hegemony.

hégémonique [eʒemɔnik] *adj* hegemonic.

hégémonisme [eʒemɔnism] *nm* hegemonic tendencies.

hégire [eʒir] *nf* : **l'~** the Hegira *ou* Hejira.

hein ['ɛ̃] *interj fam* **1.** [quoi] : **~?** eh?, what? **2.** [n'est-ce pas] eh ▪ **c'est drôle, ~!** funny, eh *ou* isn't it! **3.** [exprimant la colère] OK, right ▪ **on se calme, ~!** cool it, will you!, that's enough, OK?

hélas ['elas] *interj* unfortunately, unhappily, alas *litt*.

héler [18] ['ele] *vt* to call out to *(insép)*, to hail ▪ **~ un taxi/porteur** to hail a cab/porter.

hélianthe [eljɑ̃t] *nm* sunflower, helianthus *spéc*.

hélice [elis] *nf* **1.** MÉCAN & NAUT propeller, screw, screw-propeller **2.** ARCHIT & MATH helix.

hélico [eliko] *nm fam* AÉRON chopper.

hélicoïdal, e, aux [elikɔidal, o] *adj* **1.** [en forme de vrille] helical, spiral ▪ **escalier ~** spiral staircase **2.** MATH & MÉCAN helicoid, helicoidal.

hélicoptère [elikɔptɛr] *nm* helicopter.

héliocentrique [eljɔsɑ̃trik] *adj* heliocentric.

héliographie [eljɔgrafi] *nf* heliography.

héliogravure [eljɔgravyr] *nf* photogravure, heliogravure.

héliomarin, e [eljɔmarɛ̃, in] *adj* [cure] involving sunshine and sea air therapy ▪ [établissement] offering heliotherapy.

Hélios [eljos] *npr* Helios.

héliothérapie [eljɔterapi] *nf* heliotherapy.

héliotrope [eljɔtrɔp] *nm* BOT & MINÉR heliotrope.

héliport [elipɔr] *nm* heliport.

héliportage [elipɔrtaʒ] *nm* helicopter transportation.

héliporté, e [elipɔrte] *adj* **1.** [transporté par hélicoptère] helicoptered ▪ **troupes ~es** airborne troops *(brought in by helicopter)* **2.** [exécuté par hélicoptère] : **une opération ~e** a helicopter mission.

hélitransporté, e [elitrɑ̃spɔrte] *adj* transported by helicopter, helicoptered.

hélitreuiller [3] [elitrœje] *vt* to winch up *(sép) (into a helicopter in flight).*

hélium [eljɔm] *nm* helium.

hellénique [elenik] *adj* Hellenic.

hellénisant, e [elenizɑ̃, ɑ̃t] *nm, f* Hellenist.

helléniser [3] [elenize] *vt* to hellenize.

hellénisme [elenism] *nm* **1.** [civilisation] Hellenism **2.** LING Hellenism, Graecism.

helléniste [elenist] = **hellénisant.**

hellénistique [elenistik] *adj* Hellenistic.

hello ['ɛlo] *interj* hello.

Héloïse [elɔiz] *npr* : **~ et Abélard** Heloïse and Abelard.

Helsinki ['ɛlsinki] *npr* Helsinki.

helvète [ɛlvɛt] *adj* Helvetian, Swiss.
◆ **Helvète** *nmf* Helvetian, Swiss.

Helvétie [ɛlvesi] *npr f* HIST : **(l')~** Helvetia.

helvétique [ɛlvetik] *adj* Swiss, Helvetian.

helvétisme [ɛlvetism] *nm* LING *characteristic word or expression used by French-speaking Swiss.*

hem ['ɛm] *interj* **1.** [exprimant - le doute] hum, ahem, mmm ; [- une hésitation] hum, er **2.** [pour attirer l'attention] ahem.

hématie [emasi] *nf* erythrocyte.

hématite [ematit] *nf* haematite.

hématologie [ematɔlɔʒi] *nf* haematology.

hématologique [ematɔlɔʒik] *adj* haematological, haematologic.

hématologiste [ematɔlɔʒist], **hématologue** [ematɔlɔg] *nmf* haematologist.

hématome [ematom] *nm* bruise, haematoma *spéc.*

hématose [ematoz] *nf* haematosis.

héméralopie [emerabpi] *nf* night blindness, nyctalopia *spéc.*

hémicycle [emisikl] *nm* **1.** [espace en demi-cercle] semicircle ■ **l'abside de l'église est un ~** the apse of the church is semicircular **2.** [salle garnie de gradins] semicircular amphitheatre ■ **l'~** POLIT [salle] the benches *ou* chamber of the French National Assembly ; [Assemblée] the French National Assembly.

hémiplégie [emipleʒi] *nf* hemiplegia.

hémiplégique [emipleʒik] *adj* & *nmf* hemiplegic.

hémisphère [emisfɛr] *nm* hemisphere ■ **l'~ Nord/Sud** the Northern/Southern hemisphere.

hémisphérique [emisferik] *adj* hemispheric, hemispherical.

hémistiche [emistiʃ] *nm* hemistich.

hémoglobine [emɔglɔbin] *nf* **1.** BIOL haemoglobin **2.** *fam* [sang] gore, blood and guts.

hémopathie [emɔpati] *nf* blood disease.

hémophile [emɔfil] *adj* & *nmf* haemophiliac.

hémophilie [emɔfili] *nf* haemophilia.

hémorragie [emɔraʒi] *nf* **1.** MÉD haemorrhage, bleeding *(U)* ■ **~ cérébrale** cerebral haemorrhage ■ **~ interne/externe** internal/external haemorrhage ■ **faire une ~** to haemorrhage **2.** *fig* [perte] drain ■ **l'~ des capitaux** the drain *ou* haemorrhage of capital.

hémorragique [emɔraʒik] *adj* haemorrhagic.

hémorroïdaire [emɔrɔidɛr] <> *adj* haemorrhoidal ■ [malade] suffering from haemorrhoids.
<> *nmf* haemorrhoids sufferer.

hémorroïdal, e, aux [emɔrɔidal, o] *adj* haemorrhoidal.

hémorroïdes [emɔrɔid] *nfpl* haemorrhoids ■ **avoir des ~** to suffer from haemorrhoids, to have piles.

hémostatique [emɔstatik] *adj* & *nm* haemostatic.

henné ['ene] *nm* henna ■ **les cheveux teints au ~** hennaed hair.

hennin ['enɛ̃] *nm* hennin.

hennir [32] ['enir] *vi* **1.** [cheval] to neigh, to whinny **2.** [personne] to bray.

hennissant, e ['enisɑ̃, ɑ̃t] *adj* **1.** [cheval] neighing **2.** [rire] braying.

hennissement ['enismɑ̃] *nm* **1.** [d'un cheval] neigh, whinny **2.** [d'une personne] braying *(U)*.

Henri [ɑ̃ri] *npr* [roi de France] Henri ■ [roi d'Angleterre] Henry.

hep ['ɛp] *onomat* hey ■ **~! taxi!** hey! taxi!

hépatique [epatik] <> *adj* hepatic, liver *(modif).*
<> *nmf person suffering from liver ailments.*
<> *nf* BOT liverwort, hepatic.

hépatite [epatit] *nf* hepatitis ■ **~ A/B/C** hepatitis A/B/C ■ **~ virale** viral hepatitis.

Héphaïstos [efaistos] *npr* Hephaestus.

heptagonal, e, aux [ɛptagɔnal, o] *adj* heptagonal.

heptagone [ɛptagɔn] *nm* heptagon.

heptathlon [ɛptatlɔ̃] *nm* heptathlon.

Héra [era] *npr* Hera.

Héraclès [eraklɛs] *npr* Heracles.

Héraclite [eraklit] *npr* Heraclitus.

héraldique [eraldik] <> *adj* heraldic.
<> *nf* heraldry.

héraldiste [eraldist] *nmf* heraldry specialist, heraldist.

héraut ['ero] *nm* **1.** HIST herald ■ **~ d'armes** officer *ou* herald of arms **2.** *fig* & *litt* herald, messenger.

herbacé, e [ɛrbase] *adj* herbaceous.

herbage [ɛrbaʒ] *nm* [prairie] grazing land, pasture (land).
◆ **herbages** *nmpl* PÊCHE coral fishing nets.

herbager, ère [ɛrbaʒe, ɛr] *nm, f* grazier.

herbe [ɛrb] *nf* **1.** [plante, gazon] grass ■ **laisser un champ en ~** to leave a field under grass ➲ **~ à chats** catmint, catnip ■ **~s folles** wild grass ■ **~s marines** seaweed ■ **une mauvaise ~** a weed ■ **comme de la mauvaise ~** like wildfire ■ **couper** *ou* **faucher l'~ sous le pied à qqn** to cut the ground *ou* to pull the rug from under sb's feet ■ **l'~ du voisin est toujours plus verte** *prov* the grass is always greener on the other side of the fence **2.** *fam* [marihuana] grass.
◆ **herbes** *nfpl* : **fines ~s** CULIN herbs, fines herbes ■ **~s (médicinales)** PHARM medicinal herbs.
◆ **en herbe** *loc adj* BOT green ■ *fig* in the making ■ **c'est un musicien en ~** he has the makings of a musician, he's a budding musician.

herbeux, euse [ɛrbø, øz] *adj* grassy.

herbicide [ɛrbisid] <> *adj* herbicidal.
<> *nm* weedkiller, herbicide *spéc.*

herbier [ɛrbje] *nm* **1.** [collection] herbarium *spéc* **2.** GÉOGR aquatic plant habitat.

herbivore [ɛrbivɔr] <> *adj* herbivorous.
<> *nm* herbivore.

herboriser [3] [ɛrbɔrize] *vi* to botanize, to collect plants.

herboriste [ɛrbɔrist] *nmf* herbalist, herb doctor.

herboristerie [ɛrbɔristəri] *nf* herbalist's (shop).

herbu, e [ɛrby] *adj* grassy.

hercule [ɛrkyl] *nm* **1.** [homme fort] Hercules **2.** LOISIRS : **~ (de foire)** strong man.

Hercule [ɛrkyl] *npr* MYTHOL Hercules.

herculéen, enne [ɛrkyleɛ̃, ɛn] *adj* [tâche] Herculean ■ [force] Herculean, superhuman.

hercynien, enne [ɛrsinjɛ̃, ɛn] *adj* Hercynian.

hère ['ɛr] *nm* **1.** *litt* **un pauvre ~** a poor wretch **2.** ZOOL (yearling) stag.

héréditaire [ereditɛr] *adj* **1.** DR hereditary **2.** BIOL inherited, hereditary ■ **il est toujours grincheux, c'est ~!** *hum* he's always moaning, it's congenital!, he was born moaning!

héréditairement [ereditɛrmɑ̃] *adv* hereditarily, through heredity.

hérédité [eredite] *nf* **1.** BIOL heredity ■ **elle a une ~ chargée** *ou* **une lourde ~** her family history has a lot to answer for **2.** DR : **action en pétition d'~** *claim to succeed to an estate held by a third party.*

hérésie [erezi] *nf* **1.** [erreur] sacrilege, heresy ■ **une table Régence dans la cuisine, c'est de l'~!** a Regency table in the kitchen, that's (a) sacrilege! **2.** RELIG heresy.

hérétique [eretik] <> *adj* heretical.
<> *nmf* heretic.

hérissé, e ['erise] *adj* **1.** [cheveux, poils - naturellement raides] bristly ; [- dressés de peur] bristling, standing on end ■ **un chien à l'échine ~e** a dog with its hackles up **2.** [parsemé] : **~ de** full of, stuffed with ■ **un texte ~ de difficultés** a text bristling with *ou* full of difficult points **3.** BOT spiny.

hérisser [3] ['erise] *vt* **1.** [dresser] : **le chat hérissait ses poils** the cat's fur was bristling ■ **le perroquet hérissait ses plumes** the parrot was ruffling its feathers **2.** [irriter] : **cette question le hérisse** *ou* **lui hérisse le poil** that question gets his back up *ou* really makes his hackles rise.
◆ **se hérisser** *vpi* **1.** [se dresser - pelage] to bristle ; [- cheveux] to stand on end **2.** [dresser son pelage] : **le chat se hérisse** the cat's coat is bristling **3.** [s'irriter] to bristle ■ **elle se hérisse facilement** she's easily ruffled.

hérisson ['erisɔ̃] *nm* **1.** ZOOL hedgehog ■ **~ de mer** sea urchin **2.** *fam* [personne] : **c'est un vrai ~** he's really prickly **3.** MIL cheval-de-frise **4.** CONSTR [pointes] spiked wall strip ■ [fondation] placed foundation (stone) **5.** TRAV PUB cobblestone road foundation **6.** [égouttoir] bottle drainer **7.** [brosse] flue brush, chimney sweep's brush **8.** AGRIC [d'un épandeur] beater **9.** TEXT urchin.

héritage [eritaʒ] *nm* **1.** DR [destiné à - une personne] inheritance ; [- une institution] bequest ■ **faire un ~** to inherit ■ **faire un gros ~** to come into a fortune ■ **elle m'a laissé ses bijoux en ~** she left me her jewels ■ **avoir eu qqch en ~** to have inherited sthg **2.** *fig* heritage, legacy ■ **nos problèmes sont l'~ de la décennie précédente** our problems are the legacy of the previous decade.

hériter [3] [erite] ◇ *vi* to inherit ■ **~ de qqch** [recevoir en legs] to inherit sthg ■ **nous héritons d'une longue tradition humaniste** *fig* we are the inheritors of a long-standing tradition of humanism ■ **comment as-tu hérité de cette toile?** how did you come into possession of *ou* come by *ou* acquire this canvas?
◇ *vt* **1.** [bien matériel] to inherit ■ *(en usage absolu)* **~ de qqn** to inherit from sb ■ **elle a hérité de sa mère** she received an inheritance *ou* a legacy from her mother **2.** [trait physique ou moral] : **~ qqch de qqn : elle a hérité sa bonne humeur de sa famille paternelle** she inherited her even temper from her father's side of the family.

héritier, ère [eritje, ɛr] *nm, f* **1.** DR heir (*f* heiress) ■ **l'~ d'une fortune/d'une grosse entreprise** the heir to a fortune/to a big firm ■ **l'unique** *ou* **le seul ~** the sole heir ◗ **l'~ apparent/présomptif** the heir apparent/presumptive ■ **l'~ naturel** the heir-at-law ■ **~ testamentaire** devisee, legatee **2.** *fam* [enfant] heir ■ [fils] son and heir ■ [fille] daughter **3.** [disciple] heir, follower.

hermaphrodisme [ɛrmafrɔdism] *nm* hermaphroditism.

hermaphrodite [ɛrmafrɔdit] ◇ *adj* hermaphrodite, hermaphroditic.
◇ *nmf* hermaphrodite.

herméneutique [ɛrmenøtik] ◇ *adj* hermeneutic, hermeneutical.
◇ *nf* hermeneutics *(U)*.

Hermès [ɛrmɛs] *npr* Hermes.

hermétique [ɛrmetik] *adj* **1.** [étanche - gén] hermetically sealed, hermetic *sout* ; [- à l'eau] watertight ; [- à l'air] airtight **2.** [incompréhensible] abstruse **3.** [impénétrable - visage] inscrutable, impenetrable ■ **son expression était parfaitement ~** his face was totally expressionless **4.** [insensible] : **être ~ à** to be unreceptive *ou* impervious to ■ **je suis complètement ~ à l'art moderne** modern art is a closed book to me.

hermétiquement [ɛrmetikmɑ̃] *adv* hermetically ■ **fermer un bocal ~** to hermetically seal a jar.

hermétisme [ɛrmetism] *nm* **1.** [doctrine] alchemy **2.** *sout* [caractère incompréhensible] abstruseness, reconditeness *sout*.

hermine [ɛrmin] *nf* **1.** ZOOL [brune] stoat ■ [blanche] ermine **2.** [fourrure] ermine *(U)* ■ [sur une robe de magistrat] ermine **3.** HÉRALD ermine.

herniaire ['ɛrnjɛr] *adj* hernial.

hernie ['ɛrni] *nf* **1.** MÉD hernia, rupture ■ **~ discale** prolapsed invertebral disc *spéc*, slipped disc ■ **~ étranglée/hiatale** strangulated/hiatus hernia **2.** [d'un pneu] bulge.

Hérode [erɔd] *npr* Herod ■ **vieux comme ~** as old as Methuselah *ou* the hills.

héroïne [erɔin] *nf* **1.** [drogue] heroin **2.** [femme] ⊳ **héros**.

héroïnomane [erɔinɔman] *nmf* heroin addict.

héroïnomanie [erɔinɔmani] *nf* heroin addiction.

héroïque [erɔik] *adj* **1.** [courageux] heroic ■ **je lui ai opposé un refus ~** *hum* I heroically refused his offer **2.** LITTÉR heroic **3.** [mémorable] : **l'époque ~ des machines volantes** the pioneering *ou* great days of the flying machines ◗ **les temps ~s, l'âge ~** ANTIQ the heroic age.

héroïquement [erɔikmɑ̃] *adv* heroically.

héroïsme [erɔism] *nm* heroism ■ **épouser un homme comme ça, mais c'est de l'~!** *hum* marrying a man like that is nothing short of heroic!

héron ['erɔ̃] *nm* heron ■ **~ cendré** (grey *ou* common) heron.

héros, héroïne ['ero, erɔin] *nm, f* hero (*f* heroine) ■ **il est mort en ~** he died a hero's death *ou* like a hero ■ **tu ne t'es pas comporté en ~** you weren't exactly heroic.
◆ **héros** *nm* ANTIQ : **les dieux et les ~ grecs** the gods and heroes of Greece.

herpès [ɛrpɛs] *nm* herpes *(U)* ■ **avoir de l'~ à la bouche** to have a cold sore (on one's mouth).

herse ['ɛrs] *nf* **1.** AGRIC harrow ■ **~ roulante** revolving harrow **2.** [d'un château] portcullis ■ [pour barrer la route] cheval-de-frise **3.** THÉÂTRE batten **4.** RELIG candleholder.

herser [3] ['ɛrse] *vt* AGRIC to harrow.

hertz ['ɛrts] *nm* hertz.

hertzien, enne ['ɛrtsjɛ̃, ɛn] *adj* Hertzian.

Hésiode [ezjɔd] *npr* Hesiod.

hésitant, e [ezitɑ̃, ɑ̃t] *adj* **1.** [indécis] hesitant ■ **je suis encore un peu ~** I haven't quite made up my mind yet **2.** [peu assuré] hesitant, faltering.

hésitation [ezitasjɔ̃] *nf* **1.** [atermoiement] hesitation ■ **après quelques minutes d'~** after hesitating for a few minutes *ou* a few minutes' hesitation **2.** [arrêt] pause ■ **marquer** *ou* **avoir une ~** to pause, to hesitate **3.** [doute] doubt ■ **pas d'~, c'est lui!** it's him, no doubt about it *ou* without a doubt!
◆ **sans hésitation** *loc adv* unhesitatingly, without hesitation ■ **je préfère le ciné à la télé, sans ~** I prefer cinema to television any day.

hésiter [3] [ezite] *vi* **1.** [être dans l'incertitude] to hesitate ■ **sans ~** without hesitating *ou* hesitation ■ **il n'y a pas à ~** why wait? ■ **elle hésite encore sur la pointure** she's still not sure about the size **2.** [être réticent] : **~ à** to hesitate to ■ **n'hésitez pas à m'appeler** don't hesitate to call me ■ **j'hésite à lui dire** I'm not sure whether to tell him **3.** [marquer un temps d'arrêt] to pause, to falter ■ **il a hésité en prononçant le nom** he faltered *ou* stumbled over the name.

Hespérides [ɛsperid] *npr fpl* **1.** [nymphes] : **les ~** the Hesperides **2.** [îles] : **les ~** the Hesperides, the Islands of the Blessed.

hétaïre [etair] *nf* **1.** ANTIQ hetaera, hetaira **2.** *litt* courtesan.

hétéro [etero] *adj* & *nmf* *fam* hetero, straight.

hétéroclite [eterɔklit] *adj* disparate ■ **tout le mobilier est ~** none of the furniture matches.

hétérodoxe [eterɔdɔks] *adj* **1.** RELIG heterodox **2.** *sout* [non conformiste] heterodox *sout*, unorthodox.

hétérodoxie [eterɔdɔksi] *nf* heterodoxy.

hétérogamie [eterɔgami] *nf* **1.** BIOL heterogamy **2.** SOCIOL : **l'~ est fréquente** mixed marriages are common.

hétérogène [eterɔʒɛn] *adj* **1.** [mêlé] heterogeneous *sout*, mixed **2.** CHIM heterogeneous.

hétérogénéité [eterɔʒeneite] *nf* heterogeneousness, heterogeneity.

hétérosexualité [eterɔsɛksyalite] *nf* heterosexuality.

hétérosexuel, elle [eterɔsɛksyɛl] *adj & nm, f* heterosexual.

hétérozygote [eterɔzigɔt] <> *adj* heterozygous.
<> *nmf* heterozygote.

hêtraie [ˈɛtrɛ] *nf* beech grove.

hêtre [ˈɛtr] *nm* **1.** BOT beech (tree) **2.** MENUIS beech (wood).

heu [ˈø] *interj* **1.** [exprime le doute] h'm, um, er **2.** [exprime l'hésitation] er, um ▪ **~, ~, je ne sais pas** er, er, I don't know.

heur [œr] *nm sout* good fortune ▪ **je n'ai pas eu l'~ de lui plaire** I did not have the good fortune to please him.

heure [œr] *nf* **1.** [unité de temps] hour ▪ **j'attends depuis une bonne** *ou* **grande ~** I've been waiting for a good hour ▪ **revenez dans une petite ~** be back in less than *ou* in under an hour ▪ **à 45 km à l'~** at 45 km an *ou* per hour ▪ **24 ~s sur 24** round-the-clock, 24 hours a day ▪ **pharmacie ouverte 24 ~s sur 24** all-night *ou* 24-hour chemist ⊃ **d'~ en ~** by the hour
2. [durée d'un trajet] hour ▪ **à deux ~s (de voiture** *ou* **de route) de chez moi** two hours' (drive) from my home ▪ **il y a trois ~s de marche/vol** it's a three hour walk/flight
3. [unité de travail ou de salaire] hour ▪ **un travail (payé) à l'~** a job paid by the hour ▪ **quinze euros de l'~** fifteen euros an *ou* per hour ▪ **une ~ de travail** an hour's work, an hour of work ▪ **sans compter les ~s de main-d'œuvre** excluding labour (costs) ▪ **une ~ de chimie** ÉDUC a chemistry period *ou* class ⊃ **une ~ supplémentaire** an *ou* one hour's overtime ▪ **des ~s supplémentaires** overtime *(U)*
4. [point précis de la journée] time ▪ **15 h ~ locale** 3 p.m. local time ▪ **elle est passée sur le coup de huit ~s** *fam* she dropped in at about eight ▪ **c'est l'~!** [de partir] it's time (to go)! ; [de rendre sa copie] time's up! ▪ **l'~, c'est l'~** on time is on time ▪ **quand c'est l'~, c'est l'~!** *fam* when you've got to go, you've got to go! ▪ **avant l'~** before time ▪ **avant l'~, c'est pas l'~, après l'~ c'est plus l'~** there's a right time for every thing ▪ **quelle ~ est-il?** what time is it?, what's the time? ▪ **vous avez l'~?** do you have the time? ▪ **quelle ~ avez-vous?** what time do you make it? ▪ **tu as vu l'~ (qu'il est)?** have you any idea what time it is? ▪ **il ne sait pas encore lire l'~** he can't tell the time yet ▪ **il y a une ~ pour tout, chaque chose à son ~** there's a time (and a place) for everything ▪ **il n'y a pas d'~ pour les braves!** when a man's got to go, a man's got to go! ▪ **il n'a pas d' ~, avec lui il n'y a pas d'~** *fam* [il n'est pas ponctuel] he just turns up when it suits him ⊃ **l'~ d'été** British Summer Time *UK*, daylight (saving) time *US* ▪ **passer à l'~ d'été/d'hiver** to put the clocks forward/back ▪ **l'~ de Greenwich** Greenwich Mean Time, GMT ▪ **l'~ H** zero hour
5. [moment] time ▪ **à une ~ indue** at some ungodly *ou* godforsaken hour ▪ **ce doit être ma tante qui appelle, c'est son ~** that must be my aunt, this is her usual time for calling ▪ **ton ~ sera la mienne** (you) choose *ou* name a time ▪ **elle est romancière à ses ~s** she writes the odd novel (now and again) ▪ **l'~ d'aller au lit** bedtime ▪ **l'~ du déjeuner** lunchtime ⊃ **les ~s d'affluence** the rush hour ▪ **~s de bureau** office hours ▪ **les ~s creuses** [sans foule] off-peak period ; [sans clients] slack period
6. [période d'une vie] hour ▪ **son ~ de gloire** his moment of glory ▪ **l'~ est grave** things are serious ▪ **l'~ est à l'action** now is the time for action ▪ **c'est sa dernière ~** his time is near ▪ **dis-toi que ce n'était pas ton ~** don't worry, your time will come ⊃ **l'~ de vérité** the moment of truth
7. INFORM : **~s machine** computer time
8. ASTRON hour.

◆ **heures** *nfpl* RELIG hours ▪ **livre d'~s** Book of Hours.

◆ **à la bonne heure** *loc adv* good ▪ **elle est reçue, à la bonne ~!** so she passed, good *ou* marvellous!

◆ **à l'heure** <> *loc adj* **1.** [personne] on time **2.** [montre] : **la montre est à l'~** the watch is keeping good time.
<> *loc adv* : **mettre sa montre/une pendule à l'~** to set one's watch/a clock right ⊃ **le Japon à l'~ anglaise** the Japanese go British.

◆ **à l'heure de** *loc prép* in the era *ou* age of.

◆ **de bonne heure** *loc adv* [tôt] early ▪ [en avance] in good time.

◆ **pour l'heure** *loc adv* for now *ou* the time being *ou* the moment.

◆ **sur l'heure** *loc adv litt* straightaway, at once.

◆ **tout à l'heure** *loc adv* **1.** [dans un moment] later, in a (short *ou* little) while ▪ **à tout à l'~!** see you later!
2. [il y a un moment] earlier (today).

heure-homme [œrɔm] *nf* man-hour.

heureusement [œrøzmɑ̃] *adv* **1.** [par chance] fortunately, luckily ▪ **je le surveillais, et ~!** I was keeping an eye on him, and just as well *ou* and a good thing too! ▪ **il a freiné à temps – oh, ~!** he braked in time – thank God *ou* goodness for that! ▪ **il m'a remboursé et s'est même excusé – eh bien, ~!** he paid me back and even apologized – I should hope *ou* think so too! ▪ **~ que : la soirée fut une catastrophe, ~ que tu n'es pas venu** the party was a total flop, (it's a) good thing you didn't come **2.** *sout* [avec succès] successfully **3.** [favorablement] well **4.** [dans le bonheur] happily.

heureux, euse [œrø, øz] <> *adj* **1.** [qui éprouve du bonheur] happy ▪ **rendre qqn ~** to make sb happy ▪ **elle a tout pour être heureuse** she has everything going for her ▪ **~ en ménage** happily married ▪ **~ (celui) qui...** *sout* happy is he who... ⊃ **ils vécurent ~ et eurent beaucoup d'enfants** they lived happily ever after
2. [satisfait] happy, glad ▪ **être ~ de** to be happy with ▪ **il était trop ~ de partir** he was only too glad to leave ▪ **(très) ~ de faire votre connaissance** pleased *ou* nice to meet you
3. [chanceux] lucky, fortunate ▪ **il est ~ que...** it's fortunate *ou* it's a good thing that... ⊃ **l'~ élu** the lucky man *(to be married or recently married)* ▪ **l'heureuse élue** the lucky girl *(to be married or recently married)* ▪ **~ au jeu, malheureux en amour** *prov* lucky at cards, unlucky in love
4. [bon] good ▪ **un ~ événement** *euphém* a happy event ▪ **bonne et heureuse année!** happy new year!
5. [réussi] good, happy, felicitous *sout & hum* ▪ **c'est un choix ~** it's well-chosen ▪ **ce n'est pas très ~ comme prénom pour une fille** it's a rather unfortunate name for a girl.
<> *nm, f* happy man (*f* woman) ▪ **faire des ~** to make some people happy.

heuristique [øristik] *adj & nf* heuristic.

heurt [ˈœr] *nm* **1.** [choc - léger] bump, knock, collision ; [- violent] crash, collision **2.** *sout* [contraste] clash **3.** [conflit] clash, conflict ▪ **il y a eu des ~s entre le président et le secrétaire** the chairman and the secretary crossed swords ▪ **le concert/débat s'est déroulé sans ~s** the concert/debate went off smoothly.

heurté, e [ˈœrte] *adj* **1.** [style] jerky, abrupt **2.** [mouvement] halting, jerky.

heurter [3] [ˈœrte] *vt* **1.** [cogner] to strike, to hit, to knock ▪ **en descendant du train, je l'ai heurté avec mon sac** I caught him with my bag *ou* I bumped into him with my bag as I got off the train ▪ **son front a violemment heurté le carrelage** she banged her forehead on the tiled floor **2.** [aller à l'encontre de] to run counter to *sout*, to go against ▪ **son discours risque de ~ l'opinion publique** his speech is likely to go against public opinion **3.** [choquer] to shock, to offend ▪ **~ la sensibilité de qqn** to hurt sb's feelings.

◆ **heurter à** *v+prép litt* [porte] to knock at.

◆ **heurter contre** *v+prép* to bump into ▪ **le voilier a heurté contre un récif** the sailing boat struck a reef.

◆ **se heurter** *vp (emploi réciproque)* **1.** [passants, véhicules] to collide, to bump *ou* to run into each other **2.** [être en désaccord] to clash (with each other) ▪ **nous nous sommes heurtés à la dernière réunion** we crossed swords *ou* clashed at the last meeting.

◆ **se heurter à** *vp+prép* [rencontrer] to come up against ▪ **il s'est heurté à un refus catégorique** he met with a categorical refusal.

heurtoir [ˈœrtwar] *nm* **1.** [de porte] (door) knocker **2.** MÉCAN stop, stopper **3.** RAIL buffer.

hévéa [evea] *nm* hevea.

hexaèdre [ɛgzaɛdr] <> *adj* hexahedral.
<> *nm* hexahedron.

hexagonal, e, aux [ɛgzagɔnal, o] *adj* **1.** GÉOM & SC hexagonal **2.** *fig* [français] French ▪ *péj* chauvinistically French.

hexagone [ɛgzagɔn] *nm* **1.** GÉOM hexagon **2.** *fig* **l'Hexagone** [la France] (metropolitan) France.

hexamètre [ɛgzamɛtr] ◇ *adj* hexametric, hexametrical. ◇ *nm* hexameter.

HF (*abr écrite de* **hautes fréquences**) HF.

hi ['i] *interj* : **hi hi ha ha** ▪ **hi, hi, que c'est drôle!** ha ha, that's funny!

hiatal, e, aux [jatal, o] *adj* hiatal.

hiatus [jatys] *nm* **1.** [interruption] break, hiatus *sout*, gap **2.** LING hiatus **3.** MÉD hiatus.

hibernal, e, aux [ibɛrnal, o] *adj* **1.** BOT hibernal **2.** ZOOL winter *(modif)*.

hibernant, e [ibɛrnɑ̃, ɑ̃t] *adj* hibernating.

hibernation [ibɛrnasjɔ̃] *nf* **1.** ZOOL hibernation ▪ **l'industrie textile est en état d'~** *fig* the textile industry is in the doldrums **2.** MÉD : **~ artificielle** induced hypothermia.
◆ **en hibernation** *loc adj fig* in mothballs ▪ **mettre un projet en ~** to shelve *ou* to mothball a project.

hiberner [3] [ibɛrne] *vi* to hibernate.

hibiscus [ibiskys] *nm* hibiscus.

hibou, x ['ibu] *nm* owl.

hic ['ik] *nm inv fam* snag ▪ **c'est bien là** *ou* **voilà le ~** there's the rub, that's the trouble.

hic et nunc [ikɛtnɔ̃k] *loc adv* here and now.

hidalgo [idalgo] *nm* hidalgo.

hideur ['idœr] *nf litt* hideousness.

hideusement ['idøzmɑ̃] *adv* hideously.

hideux, euse ['idø, øz] *adj* hideous.

hier [ijɛr] *adv* **1.** [désignant le jour précédent] yesterday ▪ **~ (au) soir** yesterday evening ▪ **le journal d'~** yesterday's paper ▪ **j'y ai consacré la journée/l'après-midi d'~** I spent all (day) yesterday/all yesterday afternoon doing it **2.** [désignant un passé récent] : **~ encore on ignorait tout de cette maladie** until very recently, this disease was totally unknown.

hiérarchie ['jerarʃi] *nf* **1.** [structure] hierarchy ▪ **la ~ des salaires** the wage ladder **2.** *fam* [supérieurs] : **la ~** the top brass **3.** INFORM : **~ de mémoire** memory hierarchy, hierarchical memory structure.

hiérarchique ['jerarʃik] *adj* hierarchic, hierarchical ▪ **passer par la voie** *ou* **le canal ~** to go through official channels.

hiérarchiquement ['jerarʃikmɑ̃] *adv* hierarchically ▪ **dépendre ~ de qqn** to report to sb.

hiérarchisation ['jerarʃizasjɔ̃] *nf* [action] establishment of a hierarchy ▪ [structure] hierarchical structure.

hiérarchisé, e ['jerarʃize] *adj* [gén - INFORM] hierarchical.

hiérarchiser [3] ['jerarʃize] *vt* **1.** ADMIN to organize along hierarchical lines ▪ **~ les salaires** to introduce wage differentials **2.** [classer - données] to structure, to classify ; [- besoins] to grade *ou* to assess according to importance.

hiératique [jeratik] *adj* hieratic.

hiéroglyphe ['jerɔglif] *nm* hieroglyph.
◆ **hiéroglyphes** *nmpl hum* [écriture illisible] hieroglyphics.

hiéroglyphique ['jerɔglifik] *adj* **1.** ARCHÉOL hieroglyphic, hieroglyphical **2.** [illisible] scrawled, illegible.

hi-fi ['ifi] *nf inv* hi-fi.

high-tech ['ajtɛk] *nm inv* & *adj inv* high tech.

hi-han ['iɑ̃] *onomat* & *nm inv* hee-haw.

hi-hi ['i'i] *interj* **1.** [rire - gén] tee-hee ; [- méchant] snigger snigger **2.** [pleurs] boo-hoo.

hilarant, e [ilarɑ̃, ɑ̃t] *adj* hilarious.

hilare [ilar] *adj* laughing, smiling, joyful ▪ **un visage ~** a laughing *ou* merry face.

hilarité [ilarite] *nf* hilarity, mirth, gaiety.

Himalaya [imalaja] *npr m* : **l'~** the Himalayas.

himalayen, enne [imalajɛ̃, ɛn] *adj* Himalayan.

hindi ['indi] *nm* LING Hindi.

hindou, e [ɛ̃du] *adj* hindu.
◆ **Hindou, e** *nm, f* Hindu.

hindouisme [ɛ̃duism] *nm* Hinduism.

Hindoustan [ɛ̃dustɑ̃] *npr m* : **(l')~** Hindostan, Hindustan.

hinterland [intɛrlɑ̃d] *nm* GÉOGR hinterland.

hip ['ip] *interj* : **hip, hip, hip, hourra!** hip, hip, hooray!

hippie ['ipi] *adj* & *nmf* hippie, hippy.

hippique [ipik] *adj* horse *(modif)* ▪ **concours ~** horse trials *ou* show ▪ **course ~** horse race *ou* racing ▪ **sport ~** equestrian sports.

hippisme [ipism] *nm* equestrian sports, equestrianism *sout*.

hippocampe [ipɔkɑ̃p] *nm* ZOOL sea horse.

Hippocrate [ipɔkrat] *npr* Hippocrates ▪ **le serment d'~** the Hippocratic oath.

hippodrome [ipɔdrom] *nm* **1.** [champ de courses] racecourse **2.** ANTIQ hippodrome.

hippogriffe [ipɔgrif] *nm* hippogriff, hippogryph.

hippomobile [ipɔmɔbil] *adj* horsedrawn.

hippophagique [ipɔfaʒik] *adj* : **boucherie ~** horsemeat butcher's.

hippopotame [ipɔpɔtam] *nm* **1.** ZOOL hippopotamus **2.** *fam* [personne] elephant ▪ **c'est un vrai ~!** what an elephant!

hippopotamesque [ipɔpɔtamɛsk] *adj fam* hippo-like.

hippy ['ipi] = **hippie**.

hirondelle [irɔ̃dɛl] *nf* **1.** ORNITH swallow ▪ **~ de mer** tern ▪ **une ~ ne fait pas le printemps** *prov* one swallow doesn't make a summer *prov* **2.** *fam vieilli* [policier] bobby *UK*, cop *US*.

Hiroshima [irɔʃima] *npr* Hiroshima.

hirsute [irsyt] *adj* **1.** [échevelé] bushy-haired ▪ [touffu - sourcils] bushy ; [- barbe, cheveux] unkempt **2.** BIOL hirsute, hairy.

hirsutisme [irsytism] *nm* hirsutism.

hispanique [ispanik] *adj* **1.** [gén] Hispanic **2.** [aux États-Unis] Spanish-American.
◆ **Hispanique** *nmf* [aux États-Unis] Spanish American.

hispanisant, e [ispanizɑ̃, ɑ̃t] *nm, f* Hispanicist.

hispanisme [ispanism] *nm* Hispanism, Hispanicism.

hispaniste [ispanist] = **hispanisant**.

hispano-américain, e [ispanɔamerikɛ̃, ɛn] (*mpl* **hispano-américains**, *fpl* **hispano-américaines**) *adj* Spanish-American.
◆ **Hispano-Américain, e** *nm, f* Spanish American.

hispano-arabe [ispanɔarab] (*pl* **hispano-arabes**) *adj* Hispano-Moorish.

hispano-mauresque (*pl* **hispano-mauresques**), **hispano-moresque** (*pl* **hispano-moresques**) [ispanɔmɔrɛsk] = **hispano-arabe**.

hispanophone [ispanɔfɔn] ◇ *adj* Spanish-speaking. ◇ *nmf* Spanish speaker.

hisse ['is] *interj* : **ho ~!** heave!, heave-ho!

hisser [3] ['ise] *vt* **1.** [lever - drapeau] to run up *(sép)* ; [- voile] to hoist ; [- ancre] to raise ; [- épave] to raise, to haul up *(sép)* ▪ [soulever - personne] to lift up *(sép)* ▪ **~ qqn sur ses épaules** to lift sb onto one's shoulders **2.** *fig* **~ qqn au poste de directeur** to raise sb to the position of manager.

◆ **se hisser** *vpi* **1.** [s'élever] to hoist o.s. ■ **se ~ sur la pointe des pieds** to stand up on tiptoe ■ **se ~ sur une balançoire** to heave *ou* to hoist o.s. (up) onto a swing **2.** *fig* **elle s'est hissée au poste d'adjointe de direction** she worked her way up to the position of assistant manager.

histogenèse [istɔʒənɛz] *nf* histogenesis.

histogramme [istɔgram] *nm* histogram.

histoire [istwar] *nf* **1.** [passé] history ■ **un lieu chargé d'~** a place steeped in history
2. [mémoire, postérité] history ■ **rester dans l'~** to go down in history *ou* in the history books ■ **l'~ dira si nous avons eu raison** history will tell whether we were right
3. [période précise] history ■ **l'~ et la préhistoire** history and prehistory
4. [discipline] : **l'Histoire avec un grand H** History with a capital H ■ **l'~ de l'art/la littérature** art/literary history ■ **l'~ ancienne/du Moyen Âge** Ancient/Medieval History ■ **tout ça, c'est de l'~ ancienne** *fig* that's all ancient history ■ **l'~ contemporaine** contemporary history ■ **~ naturelle** BIOL & *vieilli* natural history ■ **l'Histoire sainte** Biblical history ■ **licence d'~** ≃ History degree *UK*, ≃ BA in History ■ **pour la petite ~** for the record ■ **sais-tu, pour la petite ~, qu'il est né au Pérou?** do you know that he was born in Peru, by the way?
5. [récit, écrit] story ■ **elle a écrit une ~ du village** she wrote a history of the village ■ **je leur raconte une ~ tous les soirs** every night I tell them a story ■ **l'~ de la pièce** the plot *ou* story of the play ■ **c'est une ~ vraie** it's a true story ■ **nous avons vécu ensemble une belle ~ d'amour** we had a wonderful romance ■ **attends, je ne t'ai pas encore dit le plus beau** *ou* **le meilleur de l'~!** wait, the best part *ou* bit is still to come! ➲ **une ~ drôle** a joke, a funny story ■ **~ à dormir debout** *fam* cock and bull story, tall story
6. [mensonge] : **tout ça, c'est des ~s** *fam* that's a load of (stuff and) nonsense, that's all hooey *ou* baloney *US* ■ **raconter des ~s** to tell tall stories ■ **allez, tu me racontes des ~s!** come on, you're pulling my leg!
7. *fam* [complications] trouble, fuss ■ **faire des ~s** to make a fuss ■ **ça va faire toute une ~** there'll be hell to pay ■ **c'est toute une ~ tous les matins pour la coiffer** what a palaver *ou* struggle doing her hair every morning ■ **elle en a fait (toute) une ~** she kicked up a (huge) fuss about it ■ **sans faire d'~** *ou* **d'~s** without (making) a fuss
8. [ennuis] trouble ■ **faire des ~s (à qqn)** to cause *ou* to make trouble (for sb) ■ **si tu ne veux pas avoir d'~s** if you want to keep *ou* to stay out of trouble ■ **tu vas nous attirer** *ou* **nous faire avoir des ~s** you'll get us into trouble ■ **taisez-vous toutes les trois, j'en ai assez de vos ~s!** shut up you three, I've had enough of you going on like that!
9. [question, problème] : **pourquoi démissionne-t-elle? – oh, une ~ de contrat** why is she resigning? – oh, something to do with her contract ■ **se fâcher pour une ~ d'argent** to fall out over a question of money ■ **ne pensons plus à cette ~** let's forget the whole thing *ou* business ■ **qu'est-ce que c'est que cette ~?** what's this I hear?, what's all this about? ■ **c'est toujours la même ~** it's always the same (old) story ■ **c'est une (toute) autre ~** that's quite a different matter
10. *fam loc* **~ de** [afin de] just to ■ **on va leur téléphoner, ~ de voir s'ils sont là** let's ring them up, just to see if they're there ■ **~ de dire quelque chose** for the sake of saying something.
◆ **sans histoires** *loc adj* [gens] ordinary ■ [voyage] uneventful, trouble-free.

histologie [istɔlɔʒi] *nf* histology.

histologique [istɔlɔʒik] *adj* histologic, histological.

historicité [istɔrisite] *nf* historicity.

historié, e [istɔrje] *adj* **1.** [manuscrit] storiated, historiated **2.** ARCHIT historied.

historien, enne [istɔrjɛ̃, ɛn] *nm, f* **1.** [spécialiste] historian ■ **se faire l'~ d'un village/d'une institution** to tell the story of a village/an institution **2.** [étudiant] history student.

historiette [istɔrjɛt] *nf* anecdote.

historiographie [istɔrjɔgrafi] *nf* historiography.

historique [istɔrik] ◇ *adj* **1.** [relatif à l'histoire - méthode, roman] historical ; [- fait, personnage] historical **2.** [célèbre] historic **3.** [mémorable] historic.
◇ *nm* background history, (historical) review ■ **faire l'~ des jeux Olympiques** to trace the (past) history of the Olympic Games.

historiquement [istɔrikmɑ̃] *adv* historically ■ **le fait n'est pas ~ prouvé** it's not a historically proven fact.

histrion [istrijɔ̃] *nm* **1.** ANTIQ histrion **2.** HIST [jongleur] wandering minstrel, troubadour.

histrionique [istrijɔnik] *adj* **1.** *litt* thespian **2.** PSYCHOL histrionic.

hit ['it] *nm* [succès] hit song.

hitlérien, enne [itlerjɛ̃, ɛn] ◇ *adj* Hitlerian, Hitlerite.
◇ *nm, f* Hitlerite.

hitlérisme [itlerism] *nm* Hitlerism.

hit-parade ['itparad] (*pl* **hit-parades**) *nm* **1.** MUS charts ■ **ils sont premiers au ~** they're (at the) top of *ou* they're number one in the charts **2.** *fig* [classement] : **placé au ~ des hommes politiques** among the top *ou* leading politicians.

hittite ['itit] *adj* Hittite.
◆ **Hittite** *nmf* : **les Hittites** the Hittites.

HIV (*abr de* **human immunodeficiency virus**) *nm* HIV ■ **être atteint du virus ~** to be HIV-positive.

hiver [ivɛr] *nm* **1.** [saison] winter ■ **en ~** *ou* **l'~, on rentre les géraniums** we bring in the geraniums in (the) winter ■ **l'~ dernier** last winter ■ **l'~ prochain** next winter ■ **l'~ fut précoce/tardif** winter came early/late ■ **tout l'~** all winter long, all through the winter ■ **au cœur de l'~** in the middle of winter, in midwinter ➲ **~ nucléaire** nuclear winter **2.** *fig* & *litt* **à l'~ de sa vie** in the twilight *ou* evening of his life.
◆ **d'hiver** *loc adj* [ciel, paysage] wintry ■ [quartiers, vêtements, fruits] winter *(modif)*.

hivernage [ivɛrnaʒ] *nm* **1.** AGRIC [activité] winter feeding, wintering ■ [fourrage] winter fodder **2.** MÉTÉOR winter season *(in tropical regions)* **3.** NAUT wintering **4.** [des abeilles] wintering.

hivernal, e, aux [ivɛrnal, o] *adj* [propre à l'hiver] winter *(modif)* ■ [qui rappelle l'hiver] wintry ■ **un temps ~** wintry weather.

hivernant, e [ivɛrnɑ̃, ɑ̃t] *adj* wintering.

hiverner [3] [ivɛrne] ◇ *vi* [passer l'hiver] to winter.
◇ *vt* AGRIC to winter.

hl (*abr écrite de* **hectolitre**) hl.

HLM (*abr de* **habitation à loyer modéré**) *nm ou nf low rent, state-owned housing*, ≃ council house/flat *UK*, ≃ public housing unit *US*.

hm (*abr écrite de* **hectomètre**) hm.

ho ['o] *interj* **1.** [de surprise] oh **2.** [pour interpeller] hey.

hobby ['ɔbi] (*pl* **hobbys** *ou pl* **hobbies**) *nm* hobby.

hobereau, x ['ɔbro] *nm* **1.** HIST [gentilhomme] squireling **2.** ORNITH hobby.

hochement ['ɔʃmɑ̃] *nm* : **~ de tête** [approbateur] nod ; [désapprobateur] shake of the head.

hochequeue [ɔʃkø] *nm* wagtail.

hocher [3] ['ɔʃe] *vt* : **~ la tête** [pour accepter] to nod ; [pour refuser] to shake one's head.

hochet ['ɔʃɛ] *nm* **1.** [jouet] rattle **2.** *fig* & *litt* gewgaw.

hockey ['ɔkɛ] *nm* hockey ■ **~ sur glace** ice hockey ■ **~ sur gazon** hockey *UK*, field hockey *US*.

hockeyeur, euse ['ɔkɛjœr, øz] *nm, f* hockey player.

Hodgkin ['ɔdʒkin] *npr* : **maladie de ~** Hodgkin's disease.

hoirie [wari] *nf* **1.** [legs] : **avancement d'~** advancement *(of an inheritance)* **2.** *Suisse* [héritage] joint legacy ■ [ensemble des héritiers] : **l'~** the legatees.

holà ['ɔla] ◇ *interj* hey, whoa.
◇ *nm* : **mettre le ~ à qqch** to put a stop to sthg.

holding ['ɔldiŋ] *nm ou nf* holding company.

hold-up ['ɔldœp] *nm inv* raid, hold-up ■ **un ~ à la banque/poste** a bank/post office raid.

hollandais, e ['ɔlɑ̃dɛ, ɛz] *adj* Dutch.
◆ **Hollandais, e** *nm, f* Dutchman (*f* Dutchwoman) ■ **les Hollandais** the Dutch.
◆ **hollandais** *nm* LING Dutch.
◆ **hollandaise** *nf* **1.** CULIN hollandaise (sauce) **2.** [vache] Friesian.

hollande ['ɔlɑ̃d] ◇ *nm* **1.** CULIN Dutch cheese *(Edam or Gouda)* **2.** [papier] Dutch paper.
◇ *nf* **1.** CULIN Dutch potato **2.** TEXT holland **3.** [porcelaine] Dutch porcelain.

Hollande ['ɔlɑ̃d] *npr f* : **(la) ~** Holland ■ **en ~** in Holland.

hollywoodien, enne ['ɔliwudjɛ̃, ɛn] *adj* [de Hollywood] Hollywood *(modif)* ■ [évoquant Hollywood] Hollywood-like ■ **un luxe ~** Hollywood-style *ou* ostentatious luxury.

holocauste [ɔlɔkost] *nm* **1.** HIST : **l'~, l'Holocauste** the Holocaust **2.** [massacre] holocaust, mass murder **3.** RELIG burnt offering ■ **offrir un animal en ~** to offer an animal in sacrifice.

hologramme [ɔlɔgram] *nm* hologram.

holographe [ɔlɔgraf] *nm* holograph.

holographie [ɔlɔgrafi] *nf* holography.

holophrastique [ɔlɔfrastik] *adj* holophrastic.

homard ['ɔmar] *nm* lobster ■ **~ à la nage** CULIN lobster cooked in court-bouillon.

home ['om] *nm* [centre d'accueil] : **~ d'enfants** residential leisure centre (for children).

homélie [ɔmeli] *nf* **1.** RELIG homily **2.** *sout* [sermon] lecture, sermon ■ **suivit une longue ~ sur les dangers du tabac** there then followed a long lecture on the dangers of smoking.

homéopathe [ɔmeɔpat] ◇ *nmf* homoeopath, homoeopathist.
◇ *adj* : **médecin ~** homoeopathic doctor.

homéopathie [ɔmeɔpati] *nf* homoeopathy.

homéopathique [ɔmeɔpatik] *adj* homoeopathic.

homéostasie [ɔmeɔstazi] *nf* homeostasis.

homéostat [ɔmeɔsta] *nm* homeostat.

Homère [ɔmɛr] *npr* Homer.

homérique [ɔmerik] *adj* **1.** LITTÉR Homeric **2.** [phénoménal] Homeric.

home-trainer ['omtrɛnœr] (*pl* **home-trainers**) *nm* exercise bicycle.

homicide [ɔmisid] ◇ *adj litt* homicidal.
◇ *nmf litt* [personne] homicide.
◇ *nm* **1.** [acte] killing *(U)* **2.** DR homicide ■ **~ involontaire** *ou* **par imprudence** involuntary manslaughter *ou* homicide ■ **~ volontaire** murder.

hominidé [ɔminide] *nm* hominid ■ **les ~s** the Hominidae.

hominien [ɔminjɛ̃] *nm* ANTHR hominoid.

hommage [ɔmaʒ] *nm* **1.** [marque de respect] tribute, homage *sout* ■ **rendre ~ à qqn/qqch** to pay homage *sout ou* (a) tribute to sb/sthg **2.** [don] : **~ de l'éditeur** complimentary copy **3.** HIST homage.
◆ **hommages** *nmpl sout* **être sensible aux ~s** to appreciate receiving compliments ■ **(je vous présente) mes ~s, Madame** my respects, Madam ■ **veuillez agréer, Madame, mes ~s respectueux** *ou* **mes respectueux ~s** yours faithfully *UK*, yours truly *US*.
◆ **en hommage à** *loc prép* in tribute *ou* homage *sout* to.

hommasse [ɔmas] *adj péj* mannish, masculine.

homme [ɔm] *nm* **1.** [individu de sexe masculin] man ■ **sors si t'es un ~!** step outside if you're a man! ■ **le service militaire en a fait un ~** national service made a man of him ■ **il est ~ à démissionner si besoin est** he's the sort (of man *ou* person) who'll resign if necessary ■ **trouver son ~** [pour un travail] to find one's man ■ **si vous voulez quelqu'un de tenace, Lambert est votre ~** if you want somebody who'll stick at it, then Lambert's just the person ■ **une double page sur l'~ du jour** a two-page spread on the man of the moment ■ **c'est lui qui est l'~ fort de l'alliance** he is the kingpin in the partnership ■ **une discussion d'~ à ~** a man-to-man talk ■ *(comme adj)* **je n'ai que des professeurs ~s** all my teachers are male *ou* men ▶ **~ d'action** man of action ■ **~ d'affaires** businessman ■ **~ d'Église** man of the Church *ou* cloth ■ **~ d'État** statesman ■ **~ à femmes** lady's *ou* ladies' man, womanizer *péj* ■ **~ de loi** lawyer ■ **~ de main** henchman ■ **c'est un parfait ~ du monde** he's a real gentleman ■ **~ de paille** man of straw ■ **~ de peine** labourer ■ **~ de science** scientist, man of science ■ **~ à tout faire** jack-of-all-trades ■ **les ~s du Président** the President's men ■ **un magazine pour ~s** a men's magazine ■ **comme un seul ~** as one man ■ **un ~ averti en vaut deux** *prov* forewarned is forearmed *prov* ■ **les ~s naissent libres et égaux en droit** ***Déclaration des droits de l'homme et du citoyen*** *allus* ≃ all men are born equal ■ **le musée de l'Homme** *the Paris Museum of Mankind, in the Palais de Chaillot*
2. [être humain] man ■ **l'~** man, mankind, humankind ■ **les ~s** man, mankind, human beings ▶ **l'~ des cavernes** caveman ■ **depuis l'~ de Cro-Magnon** since Cro-Magnon man ■ **l'~ de Neandertal** Neanderthal man ■ **l'~ propose, Dieu dispose** *prov* man proposes, God disposes *prov* ■ **l'~ de la rue** the man in the street
3. *fam* [amant, époux] : **mon/son ~** my/her man ▶ **l'~ idéal** Mr Right ■ **elle a rencontré l'~ de sa vie** she's met the love of her life
4. NAUT [marin] : **~ de barre** helmsman ■ **~ d'équipage** crew member, crewman ■ **~ de quart** man *ou* sailor on watch ■ **~ de vigie** lookout ■ **un ~ à la mer!** man overboard!
5. MIL : **les officiers et leurs ~s** the officers and their men ▶ **~ de troupe** private
6. HIST : **~ d'armes** man-at-arms ■ **~ lige** liege (man)
7. AÉRON crewman, crew member.

homme-grenouille [ɔmgrənuj] (*pl* **hommes-grenouilles**) *nm* frogman, diver.

homme-orchestre [ɔmɔrkɛstr] (*pl* **hommes-orchestres**) *nm* **1.** MUS one-man band **2.** *fig* jack-of-all-trades.

homme-sandwich [ɔmsɑ̃dwitʃ] (*pl* **hommes-sandwichs**) *nm* sandwich man.

homo [ɔmo] *adj & nmf fam* [homosexuel] gay.

homocentrique [ɔmɔsɑ̃trik] *adj* homocentric.

homogène [ɔmɔʒɛn] *adj* **1.** [substance, liquide] homogeneous ■ **ayant obtenu une pâte bien ~** when you have a nice smooth mixture **2.** [gouvernement, classe] uniform, consistent, coherent **3.** CHIM & MATH homogeneous.

homogénéisation [ɔmɔʒeneizasjɔ̃] *nf* **1.** [d'une substance] homogenization **2.** *fig* [uniformisation] standardization ■ **on constate une ~ des modes de paiement** payment methods are being standardized.

homogénéiser [3] [ɔmɔʒeneize] *vt* [substance, liquide] : **~ qqch** to homogenize sthg, to make sthg homogeneous.

homogénéité [ɔmɔʒeneite] *nf* **1.** [d'une substance] homogeneity, homogeneousness **2.** [d'une œuvre, d'une équipe] coherence, unity.

homographe [ɔmɔgraf] ◇ *adj* homographic.
◇ *nm* homograph.

homologation [ɔmɔlɔgasjɔ̃] *nf* **1.** [de conformité] accreditation **2.** DR [entérinement] ratification, approval **3.** SPORT ratification ■ **l'~ d'un record** the ratification of a record.

homologie [ɔmɔlɔʒi] *nf* MATH & SC homology.

homologue [ɔmɔlɔg] <> *adj* **1.** [équivalent] homologous, homologic, homological ■ **amiral est le grade ~ de général** an Admiral is equal in rank to a General **2.** BIOL & MÉD homologous **3.** MATH homologous, homologic, homological.
<> *nmf* [personne] counterpart, opposite number.
<> *nm* CHIM homologue.

homologuer [3] [ɔmɔlɔge] *vt* **1.** [déclarer conforme] to approve, to accredit ■ **prix homologué** authorized price **2.** DR [entériner] to sanction, to ratify **3.** SPORT to ratify.

homoncule [ɔmɔ̃kyl] = **homuncule**.

homonyme [ɔmɔnim] <> *adj* homonymous.
<> *nmf* [personne, ville] namesake.
<> *nm* LING homonym.

homonymie [ɔmɔnimi] *nf* homonymy.

homoparental, e, aux [ɔmɔparɑ̃tal, o] *adj* relating to gay parenting, homoparental.

homoparentalité [ɔmɔparɑ̃talite] *nf* gay parenting.

homophobe [ɔmɔfɔb] *adj* homophobe.

homophobie [ɔmɔfɔbi] *nf* homophobia.

homophone [ɔmɔfɔn] <> *adj* **1.** LING homophonous **2.** MUS homophonic.
<> *nm* LING homophone.

homophonie [ɔmɔfɔni] *nf* LING & MUS homophony.

homosexualité [ɔmɔsɛksɥalite] *nf* homosexuality.

homosexuel, elle [ɔmɔsɛksɥɛl] *adj* & *nm, f* homosexual, gay.

homosphère [ɔmɔsfɛr] *nf* homosphere.

homothétie [ɔmɔtesi] *nf* homothetic transformation.

homozygote [ɔmɔzigɔt] <> *adj* homozygous.
<> *nmf* homozygote.

homuncule [ɔmɔ̃kyl] *nm* [en alchimie] homunculus.

Honduras ['ɔ̃dyras] *npr m* : **le ~** Honduras ■ **(le) ~ britannique** British Honduras.

hondurien, enne ['ɔ̃dyrjɛ̃, ɛn] *adj* Honduran.
◆ **Hondurien, enne** *nm, f* Honduran.

Hongkong, Hong Kong ['ɔ̃gkɔ̃g] *npr* Hong Kong.

hongre ['ɔ̃gr] <> *adj m* gelded.
<> *nm* gelding.

Hongrie ['ɔ̃gri] *npr f* : **(la) ~** Hungary.

hongrois, e ['ɔ̃grwa, az] *adj* Hungarian.
◆ **Hongrois, e** *nm, f* Hungarian.
◆ **hongrois** *nm* LING Hungarian, Magyar.

honnête [ɔnɛt] *adj* **1.** [scrupuleux - vendeur, associé] honest **2.** [franc] honest ■ **il faut être ~, elle n'a aucune chance de réussir** let's face it *ou* we might as well face facts, she hasn't got a hope of succeeding **3.** [acceptable - prix] fair, reasonable ; [- résultat] decent, reasonable ; [- repas] decent ■ **12 sur 20, c'est ~** 12 out of 20, that's not bad **4.** [respectable] honest, respectable, decent ■ **des gens ~s** respectable people ■ **un ~ homme** *litt* ≃ a gentleman.

honnêtement [ɔnɛtmɑ̃] *adv* **1.** [sincèrement] honestly, frankly, sincerely ■ **~, je ne la connais pas!** honestly, I don't know her! ■ **non mais, ~, tu la crois?** come on now, be honest, do you believe her? **2.** [décemment] fairly, decently ■ **elle a terminé ~ son année scolaire** she finished the year with reasonable marks **3.** [de façon morale] honestly ■ **vivre ~** to live *ou* to lead an honest life ■ **c'est de l'argent ~ gagné** it's money honestly earned ■ **il a relaté les faits ~** he told the story honestly *ou* candidly.

honnêteté [ɔnɛt(ə)te] *nf* **1.** [franchise] honesty, candour ■ **avec ~** honestly, candidly **2.** [intégrité - d'une conduite] honesty, decency ; [- d'une personne] integrity, decency.
◆ **en toute honnêteté** *loc adv* **1.** [avec sincérité] in all honesty, frankly ■ **répondez en toute ~** give an honest answer **2.** [pour être honnête] to tell the truth, to be perfectly honest.

honneur [ɔnœr] *nm* **1.** [dignité] honour ■ **l'~ est sauf** my/his *etc* honour is saved *ou* intact ■ **c'est une question d'~** it's a matter of honour ■ **mettre un point d'~ à** *ou* **se faire un point d'~ de faire qqch** to make a point of honour of doing sthg ■ **venger l'~ de qqn** to avenge sb's honour ■ **se faire ~ de** to pride o.s. on *ou* upon
2. [mérite] : **c'est tout à son ~** it's entirely to his credit ■ **l'~ vous en revient** the credit is yours ■ **faire ~ à qqn** to do sb credit ■ **ces sentiments ne lui font pas ~** these feelings do him no credit
3. [marque de respect] honour ■ **vous me faites trop d'~** you're being too kind (to me) ■ **c'est lui faire trop d'~** he doesn't deserve such respect ■ **à vous l'~!** after you! ■ **~ aux dames!** ladies first! ‖ *sout* [dans des formules de politesse] privilege, honour ■ **c'est un ~ pour moi de vous présenter...** it's a great privilege for me to introduce to you... ■ **j'ai l'~ de solliciter votre aide** I would be most grateful for your assistance ■ **nous avons l'~ de vous informer que...** we have the pleasure of informing you that... ■ **faites-nous l'~ de venir nous voir** would you honour us with a visit? ■ **faites-moi l'~ de m'accorder cette danse** may I have the honour of this dance? ■ **à qui ai-je l'~?** to whom do I have the honour (of speaking)?
4. [titre] : **votre/son Honneur** Your/His Honour
5. *loc* **faire ~ à qqch** : **faire ~ à ses engagements/sa signature** to honour one's commitments/signature ■ **ils ont fait ~ à ma cuisine/mon gigot** they did justice to my cooking/leg of lamb.
◆ **honneurs** *nmpl* **1.** [cérémonie] honours ■ **les ~s dus à son rang** the honours due to his rank ◗ **~s funèbres** last honours ■ **enterré avec les ~s militaires** buried with (full) military honours ■ **rendre les ~s à qqn** to pay sb one's last respects ■ **les ~s de la guerre** MIL the honours of war ■ **avec les ~s de la guerre** *fig* honourably
2. [distinction] : **briguer** *ou* **rechercher les ~s** to seek public recognition ■ **avoir les ~s de la première page** to get a write-up on the front page ◗ **faire à qqn les ~s de qqch** to show sb round sthg
3. CARTES honours.
◆ **à l'honneur** *loc adj* : **être à l'~** to have the place of honour ■ **les organisateurs de l'exposition ont voulu que la sculpture soit à l'~** the exhibition organizers wanted sculpture to take pride of place.
◆ **d'honneur** *loc adj* [invité, place, tour] of honour ■ [membre, président] honorary ■ [cour, escalier] main.
◆ **en honneur** *loc adj* in favour ■ **mettre qqch en ~** to bring sthg into favour.
◆ **en l'honneur de** *loc prép* in honour of ■ **une fête en mon/son ~** a party for me/him ■ **en quel ~?** *fam* why, for goodness' sake? ■ **ce regard noir, c'est en quel ~?** *fam hum* what's that frown in aid of? *UK*, what's that frown for?
◆ **sur l'honneur** *loc adv* upon *ou* on one's honour ■ **jurer sur l'~** to swear on one's honour.

honnir [32] ['ɔnir] *vt litt* to despise ■ **honni soit qui mal y pense** honi soit qui mal y pense, shame be to him who thinks evil of it.

honorabilité [ɔnɔrabilite] *nf* respectability.

honorable [ɔnɔrabl] *adj* **1.** [digne de respect] respectable, honourable **2.** *hum* [avant le nom] : **mon ~ collègue** my esteemed colleague **3.** [satisfaisant] fair, decent ■ **son bulletin scolaire est tout à fait ~/est ~ sans plus** her school report is quite satisfactory/is just satisfactory.

honorablement [ɔnɔrabləmɑ̃] *adv* **1.** [de façon respectable] decently, honourably **2.** [de façon satisfaisante] creditably, honourably ■ **gagner ~ sa vie** to earn an honest living.

honoraire [ɔnɔrɛr] *adj* **1.** [conservant son ancien titre] : **professeur ~** professor emeritus **2.** [ayant le titre mais non les fonctions] honorary.

honoraires [ɔnɔrɛr] *nmpl* fee, fees ■ **il demande des ~ raisonnables** he charges reasonable fees *ou* a reasonable fee.

honoré, e [ɔnɔre] *adj* **1.** [honorable] : **mes chers et ~s confrères** most honourable and esteemed colleagues **2.** [lors de présentations] : **très ~!** I'm (greatly) honoured!
◆ **honorée** *nf* COMM : **par votre ~e du 20 avril** by your letter of the 20th April.

honorer [3] [ɔnɔre] *vt* **1.** [rendre hommage à] to honour **2.** [respecter, estimer] to honour ■ **tu honoreras ta famille** you will respect your family **3.** [contribuer à la réputation de] to honour, to be a credit *ou* an honour to ■ **votre sincérité vous honore**

your sincerity does you credit **4.** [gratifier] to honour ▪ **votre présence m'honore** you honour me with your presence **5.** [payer] : **~ un chèque** to honour a cheque **6.** RELIG : **~ Dieu** to honour *ou* to praise God.
◆ **s'honorer de** *vp+prép* to be proud of, to take pride in, to pride o.s. upon.

honorifique [ɔnɔrifik] *adj* honorary ▪ **c'est un poste ~** it's an honorary position.

honoris causa ['ɔnɔriskoza] *loc adj* : **être docteur ~** to be the holder of an honorary doctorate.

honte ['ɔ̃t] *nf* **1.** [sentiment d'humiliation] shame ▪ **avoir ~ (de qqn/qqch)** to be *ou* to feel ashamed (of sb/sthg) ▪ **vous devriez avoir ~!** you should be ashamed! ▪ **j'ai ~ d'arriver les mains vides** I feel *ou* I'm ashamed at arriving empty-handed ▪ **faire ~ à qqn** to make sb (feel) ashamed, to shame sb *sout* ▪ **il fait ~ à son père** [il lui est un sujet de mécontentement] his father is ashamed of him ; [il lui donne un sentiment d'infériorité] he puts his father to shame ⊃ **toute ~ bue : trois ans plus tard, toute ~ bue, il recommençait son trafic** three years later, totally lacking in any sense of shame, he started up his little racket again
2. [indignité, scandale] disgrace, (object of) shame ▪ **être la ~ de sa famille** to be a disgrace to one's family ▪ **la société laisse faire, c'est une ~!** it's outrageous *ou* it's a crying shame that society just lets it happen!
3. [déshonneur] shame, shamefulness ▪ **essuyer** *ou* **subir la ~ d'un refus** to suffer the shame of a rebuff ▪ **à ma grande ~** to my shame ▪ **~ à celui/celle qui...** shame on him/her who... ▪ **il n'y a pas de ~ à être au chômage** being unemployed is nothing to be ashamed of
4. [dialecte: peur] fear ▪ **tu as ~ de venir me dire bonjour?** are you afraid to come and say hello?
5. [pudeur] : **fausse ~** bashfulness.
◆ **sans honte** *loc adv* shamelessly, without shame, unashamedly ▪ **vous pouvez parler sans ~** you may talk quite openly.

honteusement ['ɔ̃tøzmɑ̃] *adv* **1.** [avec gêne] shamefully, ashamedly ▪ **elle cacha ~ son visage dans ses mains** she hid her face in shame **2.** [scandaleusement] shamefully, disgracefully.

honteux, euse ['ɔ̃tø, øz] *adj* **1.** [déshonorant] shameful, disgraceful ⊃ **maladie honteuse** venereal disease **2.** [scandaleux - exploitation, politique] disgraceful, outrageous, shocking ▪ **c'est ~ de lui prendre le peu qu'elle a** it's disgraceful *ou* a disgrace to take from her the little she has **3.** [qui a des remords] ashamed ▪ **je suis ~ de ce que j'ai fait** I'm ashamed of what I did.

hooligan ['uligan] = **houligan**.

hop ['ɔp] *interj* : **allez, ~!** [à un enfant] come on, upsadaisy! ▪ **et** *ou* **allez ~, on s'en va!** (right,) off we go!

hôpital, aux [ɔpital, o] *nm* **1.** [établissement] hospital ▪ **~ de jour** day hospital *UK*, outpatient clinic *US* ▪ **~ psychiatrique** psychiatric hospital ▪ **c'est l'~ qui se moque de la Charité** *prov* it's the pot calling the kettle black *prov* **2.** *(comme adj; avec ou sans trait d'union)* hospital *(modif)* ▪ **navire ~** hospital ship.

hoquet ['ɔkɛ] *nm* **1.** [spasme] hiccup, hiccough ▪ **avoir le ~** to have the hiccups **2.** [d'un appareil] chug, gasp.

hoqueter [27] ['ɔkte] *vi* **1.** [personne] to hiccup, to have (the) hiccups **2.** [appareil] to judder ▪ **le moteur hoqueta puis s'arrêta** the engine juddered to a halt.

Horace [ɔras] *npr* [poète] Horace.
◆ **Horaces** *npr mpl* [frères romains] : **les ~s** the Horatii.

horaire [ɔrɛr] ◇ *adj* hourly.
◇ *nm* **1.** [de travail] schedule, timetable ▪ **nous n'avons pas les mêmes ~s** we don't work the same hours ▪ **je n'ai pas d'~** I don't have any particular schedule ⊃ **~ individualisé** *ou* **souple** *ou* **à la carte** flexible working hours, flexitime *UK* ▪ **nous avons un ~ à la carte** we work flexitime *UK*, we have flexible working hours **2.** [de train, d'avion] schedule, timetable ▪ **je ne connais pas l'~ des trains** I don't know the train times.

horde ['ɔrd] *nf* horde ▪ **des ~s de gens affamés assaillaient les trains** hordes *ou* throngs of hungry people mobbed the trains.

horizon [ɔrizɔ̃] *nm* **1.** [ligne] horizon ▪ **à l'~** *pr & fig* on the horizon ▪ **le soleil disparaît à l'~** the sun is disappearing below the horizon ▪ **rien à l'~** *pr & fig* nothing in sight *ou* view **2.** [paysage] horizon, view, vista ▪ **changer d'~** to have a change of scene *ou* scenery **3.** [domaine d'activité] horizon ▪ **élargir ses ~s** to broaden one's horizons **4.** [perspectives d'avenir] : **notre ~ est janvier 2002** our objective is *ou* we are working towards January 2002 ▪ **les prévisions à l'~ 2010** the forecast for 2010 ▪ **ouvrir des ~s** to open up new horizons *ou* prospects ⊃ **~ économique/politique** ÉCON economic/political prospects **5.** ASTRON (celestial) horizon **6.** ART : **ligne/plan d'~** horizon line/plane.

horizontal, e, aux [ɔrizɔ̃tal, o] *adj* horizontal ▪ **mettez-vous en position ~e** lie down (flat) ▪ **le un ~** [aux mots croisés] one across.
◆ **horizontale** *nf* horizontal.
◆ **à l'horizontale** *loc adv* horizontally, in a horizontal position ▪ **placer qqch à l'~e** to lay sthg down (flat).

horizontalement [ɔrizɔ̃talmɑ̃] *adv* horizontally ▪ **pose l'échelle ~** lay the ladder down flat ▪ **~: un, en six lettres, oiseau** one across, six letters, bird.

horizontalité [ɔrizɔ̃talite] *nf* horizontalness, horizontality.

horloge [ɔrlɔʒ] *nf* [pendule] clock ▪ **~ atomique** atomic clock ▪ **~ interne** *ou* **biologique** body *ou* biological clock ▪ **~ normande** grandfather *ou* longcase *UK* clock ▪ **~ parlante** speaking clock *UK*, time (telephone) service *US* ▪ **~ pointeuse** time clock.

horloger, ère [ɔrlɔʒe, ɛr] ◇ *adj* clock-making ▪ **la production horlogère** clock and watch making.
◇ *nm, f* watchmaker, clockmaker ▪ **~ bijoutier** jeweller.

horlogerie [ɔrlɔʒri] *nf* **1.** [technique, métier] clock (and watch) *ou* timepiece making ▪ **pièce d'~** [interne] clock component ; [horloge] timepiece **2.** [boutique] watchmaker's, clockmaker's ▪ **~ (bijouterie)** jewellery shop *UK*, jewelry store *US*.

hormis ['ɔrmi] *prép litt* save (for) ▪ **le stade était vide, ~ quelques rares spectateurs** the stadium was empty, save for *ou* apart from a handful of spectators.
◆ **hormis que** *loc conj litt* except *ou* save that.

hormonal, e, aux [ɔrmɔnal, o] *adj* [gén] hormonal ▪ [traitement, crème] hormone *(modif)*.

hormone [ɔrmɔn] *nf* hormone ▪ **~ de croissance/sexuelle** growth/sex hormone.

hormonothérapie [ɔrmɔnɔterapi] *nf* MÉD hormone therapy ▪ [pour femmes ménopausées] hormone replacement therapy.

Hormuz [ɔrmuz] *npr* : **le détroit d'~** the strait of Hormuz.

Horn ['ɔrn] *npr* : **le cap ~** Cape Horn.

horodaté, e [ɔrɔdate] *adj* stamped *(with the date and time)* ▪ **stationnement ~** pay and display parking zone.

horodateur, trice [ɔrɔdatœr, tris] *adj* time-stamping.
◆ **horodateur** *nm* [administratif] time-stamp ▪ [de parking] ticket machine.

horokilométrique [ɔrɔkilɔmetrik] *adj* : **rendement ~** time-distance ratio.

horoscope [ɔrɔskɔp] *nm* horoscope.

horreur [ɔrœr] *nf* **1.** [effroi] horror ▪ **saisi** *ou* **rempli d'~** horror-stricken, filled with horror ▪ **hurler/reculer d'~** to cry out/to shrink away in horror ▪ **avoir qqch en ~** [dégoût] to have a horror of *ou* to loathe sthg ▪ **avoir qqn en ~** to loathe sb ▪ **avoir ~ de** to loathe, to hate ▪ **j'ai ~ qu'on me dérange** I hate *ou* I can't stand being disturbed ▪ **faire ~ à qqn** to horrify *ou* to terrify sb, to fill sb with horror ▪ **film d'~** horror film **2.** [cruauté] horror, ghastliness ▪ **il décrit la guerre des tranchées dans toute son ~** he describes trench warfare in all its

horror **3.** *fam* [chose ou personne laide] **: c'est une ~** [personne] he's/she's repulsive ; [objet] it's hideous ▪ **jette-moi toutes ces vieilles ~s** throw away all these horrible old things **4.** [dans des exclamations] **: oh, quelle ~!** that's awful *ou* terrible! ▪ **quelle ~, cette odeur!** what a disgusting *ou* vile smell!
◆ **horreurs** *nfpl* **1.** [crimes] horrors ▪ **les ~s de la guerre** the horrors of war ▪ **les ~s dont il est responsable** the horrible *ou* dreadful deeds he is responsible for **2.** [calomnies] **: on m'a raconté des ~s sur lui** I've heard horrible things about him.

horrible [ɔribl] *adj* **1.** [effroyable - cauchemar] horrible, dreadful ; [- mutilation, accident] horrible, horrific ; [- crime] horrible, ghastly ; [- cri] horrible, frightful **2.** [laid - personne] horrible, hideous, repulsive ; [- vêtement] ghastly, frightful ; [- décor, style] horrible, hideous, ghastly **3.** [méchant] horrible, nasty, horrid ▪ **être ~ avec qqn** to be nasty *ou* horrible to sb ▪ **raconter des histoires ~s sur qqn** to say horrible *ou* nasty things about sb **4.** [infect] horrible, disgusting, frightful **5.** [temps] terrible ▪ [douleur] terrible, awful.

horriblement [ɔribləmɑ̃] *adv* **1.** [en intensif] horribly, terribly, awfully ▪ **je suis ~ confus** I'm terribly sorry ▪ **faire qqch ~ mal** to do sthg very badly indeed ▪ **~ mal habillé** appallingly dressed ▪ **ça fait ~ mal** it hurts terribly **2.** [atrocement] horribly.

horrifiant, e [ɔrifjɑ̃, ɑ̃t] *adj* horrifying, terrifying.

horrifier [9] [ɔrifje] *vt* **: ~ qqn** to horrify sb, to fill sb with horror ▪ **être horrifié par** to be horrified at ▪ **elle recula, horrifiée** she shrank back in horror.

horrifique [ɔrifik] *adj litt* horrific, horrendous, horrifying.

horripilant, e [ɔripilɑ̃, ɑ̃t] *adj fam* infuriating, exasperating, irritating ▪ **il est ~, avec sa manie de jeter les journaux!** he gets on my nerves, always throwing out the papers!

horripiler [3] [ɔripile] *vt* **1.** *fam* [exaspérer] to exasperate ▪ **ses petites manies m'horripilaient** his annoying little habits were getting on my nerves **2.** MÉD to horripilate *spéc*.

hors ['ɔr] *prép* **1.** *litt* [hormis] except (for), save (for) *sout* **2.** *loc* **~ antenne** off the air ▪ **~ barème** off-scale, unquoted ▪ **~ cadre** ADMIN seconded, on secondment ▪ **~ catégorie** outstanding, exceptional ▪ **~ circuit : mettre une lampe ~ circuit** to disconnect a lamp ▪ **être ~ circuit** *fig* to be out of circulation ▪ **~ commerce** not for sale to the general public ▪ **il est ~ concours** [exclu] he's been disqualified ; *fig* he is in a class of his own ▪ **le film a été présenté ~ concours** the film was presented out of competition ▪ **être ~-course** to be out of touch ▪ **il est ~ jeu** SPORT he's offside ▪ **~ la loi : mettre qqn ~ la loi** to declare sb an outlaw, to outlaw sb ▪ **se mettre ~ la loi** to place o.s. outside the law ▪ **~ les murs** [festival] out of town ▪ **~ normes** nonstandard ▪ **~ pair, ~ ligne** exceptional, outstanding ▪ **~ saison** off-season ▪ **louer ~ saison** to rent in the off-season ▪ **~ série** [remarquable] outstanding, exceptional ; [personnalisé] custom built, customized ▪ **numéro ~ série** [public atio n] special issue ▪ **~ service** out of order ▪ **~ sujet** irrelevant, off the subject ▪ **~ taxe** *ou* **taxes** excluding tax ; [à la douane] duty-free ▪ **planche ~ texte** plate ▪ **~ tout** overall.
◆ **hors de** *loc prép* **1.** [dans l'espace - à l'extérieur de] out of, outside ; [- loin de] away from ◐ **~ de ma vue** out of my sight ▪ **~ d'ici!** *sout* get out of here!
2. [dans le temps] **: ~ de saison** out of season ▪ **~ du temps** timeless ▪ **elle est** *ou* **elle vit ~ de son temps** she lives in a different age
3. *loc* **~ de portée (de)** [trop loin] out of reach *ou* range (of) ; *fig* out of reach (of) ▪ **être ~ d'affaire** to have come *ou* pulled through ▪ **être ~ de combat** SPORT to be knocked out *ou* hors de combat *sout* ; *fig* to be out of the game *ou* running ▪ **~ du commun** outstanding, exceptional ▪ **ici, vous êtes ~ de danger** you're safe *ou* out of harm's reach here ▪ **la victime n'est pas encore ~ de danger** the victim isn't out of danger yet ▪ **il est ~ de doute que** it's beyond doubt that ▪ **il est ~ d'état de nuire** he's been rendered harmless ; *euphém* [tué] he's been taken care of ▪ **~ de prix** prohibitively *ou* ruinously expensive ▪ **~ de propos** inopportune, untimely ▪ **c'est ~ de question** it's out of the question ▪ **~ de soi : il était ~ de lui** he was beside himself ▪ **elle m'a mis ~ de moi** she infuriated me, she made me furious *UK ou* mad *US* ▪ **~ d'usage** out of service.

hors-bord ['ɔrbɔr] *nm inv* **1.** [moteur] outboard motor **2.** [bateau] speedboat, outboard.

hors-cote ['ɔrkɔt] ◇ *adj inv* BOURSE unlisted.
◇ *nm inv* [marché] unlisted securities market.

hors-d'œuvre ['ɔrdœvr] *nm inv* **1.** CULIN starter, hors d'œuvre *sout* ▪ **~ variés** (assorted) cold meats and salads **2.** *fig* **et ce n'était qu'un ~** and that was just the beginning.

hors-jeu ['ɔrʒø] ◇ *adj inv* offside ▪ **le joueur est ~** the player is offside.
◇ *nm inv* offside.

hors-la-loi ['ɔrlalwa] *nmf inv* outlaw.

hors-piste(s) ['ɔrpist] ◇ *nm inv* **: faire du ~** to ski off piste.
◇ *adj inv* **: le ski ~** off-piste skiing.

hors-série [ɔrseri] ◇ *adj inv* special.
◇ *nm* (*pl* **hors-séries**) special issue *ou* edition.

hors-sol [ɔrsɔl] *adj* [culture] non-soil ▪ [piscine] aboveground, raised ▪ **élevage ~** battery farming.

hors-texte ['ɔrtɛkst] *nm inv* IMPR plate.

hortensia [ɔrtɑ̃sja] *nm* hydrangea.

horticole [ɔrtikɔl] *adj* horticultural.

horticulteur, trice [ɔrtikyltœr, tris] *nm, f* horticulturist.

horticulture [ɔrtikyltyr] *nf* horticulture.

hosanna [ozana] *nm* hosanna.

hospice [ɔspis] *nm* **1.** [asile] **: ~ (de vieillards)** (old people's) home **2.** RELIG hospice.

hospitalier, ère [ɔspitalje, ɛr] ◇ *adj* **1.** ADMIN [frais, service, personnel] hospital *(modif)* ◐ **établissement ~** hospital **2.** [accueillant - personne, peuple, demeure] hospitable, welcoming ▪ *sout* [- rivage, île] inviting **3.** RELIG [frère, sœur, ordre] Hospitaller.
◇ *nm, f* member of hospital staff ▪ **les ~s** hospital staff *ou* workers.
◆ **hospitalier** *nm* Knight Hospitaller.

hospitalisation [ɔspitalizasjɔ̃] *nf* hospitalization ▪ **son état nécessite une ~ immédiate** in her state, she should be admitted to hospital immediately ▪ **pendant mon ~** while I was in hospital ◐ **~ à domicile** home care.

hospitalisé, e [ɔspitalize] *nm, f* hospital patient.

hospitaliser [3] [ɔspitalize] *vt* to hospitalize ▪ **se faire ~** to be admitted *ou* taken to hospital ▪ **elle est hospitalisée à La Salpêtrière** she's in hospital at La Salpêtrière.

hospitalité [ɔspitalite] *nf* **1.** [hébergement] hospitality ▪ **offrir/donner l'~ à qqn** to offer/to give sb hospitality **2.** [cordialité] **: nous vous remercions de votre ~** [après un séjour, un repas] thank you for making us (feel) welcome.

hospitalo-universitaire [ɔspitaloyniversitɛr] (*pl* **hospitalo-universitaires**) *adj* **: centre ~** teaching *ou* university hospital ▪ **enseignement ~** clinical teaching.

hostellerie [ɔstɛlri] *nf arch* inn, hostelry.

hostie [ɔsti] *nf* RELIG host.

hostile [ɔstil] *adj* **1.** [inamical] hostile, unfriendly **2.** [opposé] hostile ▪ **être ~ à qqn** to be hostile to *ou* opposed to *ou* against sb **3.** ÉCOL hostile.

hostilement [ɔstilmɑ̃] *adv* hostilely, with hostility.

hostilité [ɔstilite] *nf* hostility ▪ **manifester de l'~ envers qqn/qqch** to show hostility to *ou* towards sb/sthg.
◆ **hostilités** *nfpl* MIL **: les ~s** hostilities ▪ **reprendre les ~s** to reopen *ou* to resume hostilities.

hosto [ɔsto] *nm fam* [hôpital] hospital.

hot ['ɔt] ◇ *adj inv* [jazz] hot.
◇ *nm inv* hot jazz.

hôte, hôtesse [ot, otɛs] *nm, f sout* [personne qui reçoit] host (*f* hostess).
◆ **hôte** *nm* **1.** [invité] guest ▪ [client dans un hôtel] patron, guest ▪ **un ~ de marque** an important guest ◐ **~ payant** paying guest **2.** *litt* [habitant] **: les ~s des bois/lacs** the denizens of the woodlands/lakes **3.** BIOL host **4.** INFORM host (computer).

◆ **hôtesse** *nf* [responsable de l'accueil - dans un hôtel] receptionist ; [- dans une exposition] hostess ▪ **hôtesse d'accueil** receptionist ▪ **hôtesse de l'air** air hostess *UK*, stewardess.

hôtel [otɛl] *nm* **1.** COMM & LOISIRS hotel ▪ **~ tout confort** hotel with all mod cons ▪ **~ de tourisme** basic *ou* tourist hotel ➤ **~ de passe** *hotel used for prostitution* **2.** [bâtiments administratifs] : **l'~ Drouot** *sale rooms in Paris where auctions are held* ▪ **l'~ des Invalides** *building constructed by Louis XIV for wounded soldiers, now housing a military museum; the tomb of Napoleon I lies under the dome* ▪ **l'~ de la Monnaie** *the former French Mint,* ≃ the Mint *UK*, ≃ the (Federal) Mint *US* ▪ **l'~ de Sens** *historic building, now a museum, in the Marais district of Paris, a fine example of late medieval architecture famous for its associations with Marguerite de Valois* ▪ **l'~ de Soubise** *eighteenth-century house in the Marais district of Paris, home of the national archives since 1808* ▪ **~ des ventes** sale room *ou* rooms, auction room *ou* rooms ▪ **~ de ville** town *ou* city hall.
◆ **hôtel particulier** *nm* (private) mansion, town house.

L'HÔTEL DE LA MONNAIE

Legal tender is no longer minted at the *hôtel de la Monnaie* in Paris, although medals are still made there. Money is now minted at Pessac near Bordeaux.

hôtel-Dieu [otɛldjø] (*pl* **hôtels-Dieu**) *nm* general hospital.

hôtelier, ère [otəlje, ɛr] ◇ *adj* [relatif à l'hôtellerie] hotel *(modif)* ▪ **l'infrastructure hôtelière** hotel facilities.
◇ *nm, f* COMM & LOISIRS hotelier, hotel manager *ou* owner.
◆ **hôtelier** *nm* RELIG hospitaller.

hôtellerie [otɛlri] *nf* **1.** COMM & LOISIRS hotel trade *ou* business *ou* industry **2.** RELIG hospice.

hôtel-restaurant [otɛlrɛstɔrɑ̃] (*pl* **hôtels-restaurants**) *nm* hotel and restaurant.

hôtesse [otɛs] *f* ⊳ **hôte**.

hotte [ˈɔt] *nf* **1.** [de cheminée, de laboratoire] hood ▪ **~ aspirante** *ou* **filtrante** [de cuisine] extractor hood **2.** [de vendangeur] basket ▪ **la ~ du Père Noël** Father Christmas's sack.

hottentot, e [ɔtɑ̃to, ɔt] *adj* Hottentot.
◆ **Hottentot, e** *nm, f* Hottentot.

hou [ˈu] *interj* [pour effrayer] boo ▪ [pour faire honte] shame.

houblon [ˈublɔ̃] *nm* BOT hop (plant) ▪ [de bière] hops.

houe [ˈu] *nf* HORT hoe ▪ AGRIC (drag) hoe ▪ **~ rotative** rotary (motor) hoe.

houille [ˈuj] *nf* **1.** MIN coal ▪ **~ flambante** bituminous coal ▪ **~ maigre/grasse** lean/bituminous coal **2.** ÉLECTR : **~ blanche** hydroelectric power *(from waterfalls)* ▪ **~ bleue** wave and tidal power ▪ **~ verte** hydroelectric power *(from rivers)*.

houiller, ère [ˈuje, ɛr] *adj* [bassin, production] coal *(modif)* ▪ [sol, roche] coal-bearing, carboniferous *spéc.*
◆ **houiller** *nm* [en Europe] Upper Carboniferous ▪ [aux États-Unis] Pennsylvanian.
◆ **houillère** *nf* coalmine.

houle [ˈul] *nf* [mouvement de la mer] swell ▪ **grosse** *ou* **grande ~** heavy swell ▪ **il y a de la ~** the sea's rough.

houlette [ˈulɛt] *nf* **1.** [d'un berger] crook **2.** HORT trowel.
◆ **sous la houlette de** *loc prép* under the leadership *ou* direction *ou* aegis *sout* of.

houleux, euse [ˈulø, øz] *adj* **1.** [mer] rough, choppy **2.** [débat, réunion] stormy.

houligan [ˈuligan] *nm* (football) hooligan.

houmous [umus] *nm* houmous, hummus.

houppe [ˈup] *nf* **1.** [à maquillage] powder puff **2.** [de cheveux] tuft (of hair) **3.** [décorative] tassel **4.** ORNITH tuft.

houppelande [ˈuplɑ̃d] *nf* mantle.

houppette [ˈupɛt] *nf* powder puff.

hourra [ˈura] ◇ *interj* hurrah, hooray.
◇ *nm* cheer (of joy) ▪ **pousser des ~s** to cheer.

house, house music [(a)ws, awsmjusik] *nf* : **la ~ (music)** house music.

houspiller [3] [ˈuspije] *vt* to tell off *(sép)* ▪ **se faire ~** to get told off.

housse [ˈus] *nf* **1.** [de machine à écrire] dust cover ▪ [de couette, de coussin] cover ▪ [de meubles - pour protéger] dustsheet ; [- pour décorer] cover *UK*, slipcover *US* ▪ [de vêtements] suit sack **2.** TECHNOL rough casting.

houx [ˈu] *nm* holly.

HS (*abr de* **hors service**) *adj* *fam* [appareil] out of order ▪ [personne] shattered ▪ **la télé est complètement ~** the telly's on the blink.

HT ◇ *adj* (*abr de* **hors taxe**) *not including tax* ▪ **300 euros ~** ≃ 300 euros plus VAT.
◇ *nf* (*abr de* **haute tension**) HT.

HTML (*abr de* **Hypertext Mark-up Language**) *nm* HTML.

huard, huart [ˈyar] *nm Québec* ORNITH (black-throated) diver *UK ou* loon *US*.

hublot [ˈyblo] *nm* [de bateau] porthole ▪ [d'avion] window ▪ [de machine à laver] (glass) door ▪ **mes ~s** *fam* my specs.

huche [ˈyʃ] *nf* chest ▪ **~ à pain** bread bin.

Hudson [ytsɔn] ◇ *npr m* : **l'~** the Hudson River.
◇ *npr* ⊳ **baie**.

hue [ˈy] *interj* gee up ▪ **allez ~, cocotte!** gee up!, giddy up!
◆ **à hue et à dia** *loc adv* : **tirer à ~ et à dia** to pull *ou* to tug in opposite directions (at once).

huée [ˈɥe] *nf* CHASSE hallooing, halloos.
◆ **huées** *nfpl* boos, booing *(U)* ▪ **il quitta la scène sous les ~s** he was booed *ou* hissed off stage.

huer [7] [ˈɥe] ◇ *vt* **1.** [par dérision] to boo **2.** CHASSE to halloo.
◇ *vi* [hibou] to hoot ▪ [héron] to croak.

huguenot, e [ˈygno, ɔt] *adj* & *nm, f* Huguenot.

huilage [ˈɥilaʒ] *nm* oiling, lubrication.

huile [ɥil] *nf* **1.** CULIN oil ▪ **à l'~ : pommes à l'~** potatoes (done) in an oil dressing ➤ **~ d'arachide/de coco/de colza/d'olive/de maïs/de noix/de tournesol** groundnut/coconut/rapeseed *ou* colza/olive/corn/walnut/sunflower oil ▪ **~ de cuisson** cooking oil ▪ **~ de cade** oil of cade ▪ **~ de table** (salad) oil ▪ **~ végétale** vegetable oil ▪ **~ vierge** unrefined *ou* virgin oil ▪ **jeter** *ou* **mettre** *ou* **verser de l'~ sur le feu** to add fuel to the flames
2. [pour chauffer, pour lubrifier] oil ▪ **~ de chauffage** *Québec* domestic fuel ▪ **~ de coude** *fam* elbow grease ▪ **~ (pour) moteur** engine oil ▪ **~ de vidange** waste (lubricating) oil
3. PHARM : **~ d'amandes douces/amères** sweet/bitter almond oil ▪ **~ essentielle** *ou* **volatile** essential oil ▪ **~ de lin/ricin** linseed/castor oil ▪ **~ de vaseline** *ou* **paraffine** paraffin oil ▪ **~ de foie de morue** cod-liver oil
4. RELIG : **les saintes ~s** the holy oils
5. ART [œuvre] oil (painting)
6. *fam* [personne importante] bigwig, VIP, big shot ▪ **les ~s du régiment** the regimental (top) brass *ou* big shots.
◆ **d'huile** *loc adj* [mer] glassy ▪ **la mer était d'~** the sea was like glass *ou* a mill pond.

huilé, e [ɥile] *adj* **1.** [enduit d'huile] oiled **2.** [qui fonctionne] : **bien ~** well-oiled.

huiler [3] [ɥile] *vt* to oil, to lubricate.

huilerie [ɥilri] *nf* [fabrique] oil works *ou* factory.

huileux, euse [ɥilø, øz] *adj* **1.** [substance] oily **2.** [cheveux, doigts] oily, greasy.

huilier, ère [ɥilje, ɛr] *adj* oil *(modif)*.
◆ **huilier** *nm* **1.** [ustensile de table] oil and vinegar set ▪ [avec moutardier] cruet (stand), condiment set **2.** [fabricant] oil manufacturer.

huis [ɥi] *nm litt* door.

huis clos [ˈɥiklo] *nm* : **demander le ~** to ask for proceedings to be held in camera ➤ **'Huis clos'** *Sartre* 'In Camera'.

◆ **à huis clos** *loc adv* : **le procès se déroulera à ~** the trial will be held in camera ▪ **avoir une discussion à ~** to have a discussion behind closed doors.

huisserie [ɥisri] *nf* [de porte] (door) frame ▪ [de fenêtre] (window) frame.

huissier [ɥisje] *nm* **1.** [gardien, appariteur] usher **2.** DR : **~ (de justice)** ≃ bailiff.

huit [ˈɥit, ˈɥi *(devant consonne)*] ◇ *dét* eight ▪ **~ jours** [une semaine] a week.
◇ *nm inv* **1.** [nombre] eight ▪ **nous avons rendez-vous le ~ (mars)** we are meeting on the eighth (of March) ▪ **jeudi en ~** a week on *UK ou* from Thursday **2.** [dessin] figure of eight **3.** SPORT [en patinage] figure of eight ▪ [en aviron] : **~ (barré)** eight **4.** LOISIRS : **le grand ~** rollercoaster *(in figure of eight)*.

huitaine [ˈɥitɛn] *nf* : **une ~** about eight, eight or so ▪ **une ~ (de jours)** about a week, a week or so ▪ **sous ~** within a week ▪ **remis à ~** postponed for a week.

huitante [ˈɥitɑ̃t] *adj num card inv Suisse* eighty.

huitième [ˈɥitjɛm] ◇ *adj num ord* eighth ▪ **le ~ art** television ▪ **la ~ merveille du monde** the eighth wonder of the world, *voir aussi* **cinquième**.
◇ *nmf* : **il est arrivé ~** he finished eighth.
◇ *nm* eighth ▪ **les ~s de finale** SPORT the round before the quarterfinals.

huître [ɥitr] *nf* ZOOL oyster ▪ **~ plate** flat *ou* native oyster.

huîtrier, ère [ɥitrije, ɛr] *adj* oyster *(modif)*.
◆ **huîtrier** *nm* ORNITH oystercatcher.
◆ **huîtrière** *nf* [banc] oyster bed ▪ [parc] oyster farm *ou* bed.

hulotte [ˈylɔt] *nf* tawny *ou* brown owl.

hululement [ˈylylmɑ̃] *nm* hooting.

hululer [3] [ˈylyle] *vi* to hoot.

hum [ˈœm] *interj* **1.** [marquant le doute] er, um, h'mm **2.** [pour signaler sa présence] ahem.

humain, e [ymɛ̃, ɛn] *adj* **1.** [propre à l'homme - corps, race, condition] human ▪ **il cherche à se venger, c'est ~** he's looking for revenge, it's only human ▪ **une ville nouvelle aux dimensions ~es** a new town planned with people in mind *ou* on a human scale **2.** [bienveillant] humane ▪ **il est très ~** he's very understanding ▪ **être ~ avec qqn** to act humanely towards sb, to treat sb humanely.
◆ **humain** *nm* **1.** [être] : **un ~** a human (being) ▪ **les ~s** mankind, humans, human beings **2.** *litt* **l'~** [nature] human nature ; [facteur] the human element *ou* factor.

humainement [ymɛnmɑ̃] *adv* **1.** [avec bienveillance] humanely **2.** [par l'homme] humanly ▪ **faire tout ce qui est ~ possible** to do everything that is humanly possible.

humanisation [ymanizasjɔ̃] *nf* humanization ▪ **aujourd'hui, on vise à une ~ des rapports dans l'entreprise** today, the aim is to make relationships in the company more human.

humaniser [3] [ymanize] *vt* [environnement] to humanize, to adapt to human needs ▪ [personne] to make more human.
◆ **s'humaniser** *vpi* to become more human ▪ **l'environnement industriel s'est humanisé** the industrial environment has a more human face.

humanisme [ymanism] *nm* humanism.

humaniste [ymanist] ◇ *adj* humanist, humanistic.
◇ *nmf* humanist.

humanitaire [ymanitɛr] *adj* humanitarian.
◆ **humanitaire** *nm* : **l'~** [organisations] humanitarian organizations ; [actions] humanitarian relief ▪ **travailler dans l'~** to work for a humanitarian organization.

humanitarisme [ymanitarism] *nm* humanitarianism.

humanitariste [ymanitarist] *adj & nmf* humanitarian.

humanité [ymanite] *nf* **1.** [êtres] : **l'~** humanity, mankind, humankind **2.** [compassion] humanity, humaneness ▪ **traiter qqn avec ~** to treat sb humanely **3.** PRESSE : **l'Humanité** *French daily newspaper representing the views of the French Communist Party.*
◆ **humanités** *nfpl* **1.** *Belgique the three years leading to the baccalaureat examination in Belgium* **2.** UNIV : **les ~s** *vieilli* the classics.

humanoïde [ymanɔid] *adj & nmf* humanoid.

humble [œbl] *adj* **1.** [effacé - personne] humble, meek ▪ **d'un ton ~** humbly, meekly **2.** [par déférence] humble ▪ **à mon ~ avis** in my humble opinion **3.** [pauvre, simple - demeure, origine] humble ; [- employé] humble, lowly, obscure.

humblement [œbləmɑ̃] *adv* **1.** [gén] humbly **2.** [sans richesse] humbly ▪ **vivre ~** to live modestly *ou* humbly.

humecter [4] [ymɛkte] *vt* [linge] to dampen ▪ [visage - avec un liquide] to moisten ; [- avec un linge mouillé] to dampen ▪ **la sueur humectait son front** his forehead was damp with perspiration.
◆ **s'humecter** *vpt* : **s'~ les lèvres** to moisten one's lips.

humer [3] [ˈyme] *vt* [sentir] to smell ▪ [inspirer] to inhale, to breathe in *(sép)*.

humérus [ymerys] *nm* humerus.

humeur [ymœr] *nf* **1.** [état d'esprit] mood ▪ **être d'~ à faire qqch** to be in the mood to do sthg *ou* for doing sthg ▪ **être de bonne/mauvaise ~** to be in a good/bad mood ▶ **être d'une ~ noire** to be in a foul mood **2.** [caractère] temper ▪ **être d'~ chagrine** to be bad-tempered *ou* sullen ▪ **être d'~ égale/inégale** to be even-tempered/moody **3.** *litt* [acrimonie] bad temper, ill humour ▪ **répondre avec ~** to answer testily *ou* moodily ▶ **accès/mouvement d'~** outburst/fit of temper **4.** [caprice] : **il a ses ~s** he has his whims **5.** MÉD : **~ aqueuse/vitrée** aqueous/vitreous humour.
◆ **humeurs** *nfpl arch* humours.

humide [ymid] *adj* [linge, mur] damp ▪ [éponge] damp, moist ▪ [cave] damp, dank ▪ [chaussée] wet ▪ [chaleur, air, climat] humid, moist ▪ [terre] moist ▪ **j'ai les mains ~s** my hands are wet ▪ **temps chaud et ~** muggy weather.

humidificateur [ymidifikatœr] *nm* humidifier.

humidification [ymidifikasjɔ̃] *nf* **1.** [de l'air] humidification *spéc*, humidifying, moisturizing **2.** [du linge] dampening, moistening.

humidifier [9] [ymidifje] *vt* **1.** [air] to humidify, to moisturize **2.** [linge] to dampen, to moisten.

humidité [ymidite] *nf* [de l'air chaud] humidity, moisture ▪ [de l'air froid, d'une terre] dampness ▪ [d'une cave] dampness, dankness ▪ **il y a des taches d'~ au plafond** there are damp patches on the ceiling.

humiliant, e [ymiljɑ̃, ɑ̃t] *adj* humiliating ▪ **critique ~e** galling *ou* mortifying criticism.

humiliation [ymiljasjɔ̃] *nf* humiliation ▪ **infliger une ~ à qqn** to humiliate sb.

humilié, e [ymilje] *adj* humiliated.

humilier [9] [ymilje] *vt* to humiliate, to shame.
◆ **s'humilier** *vp (emploi réfléchi)* : **s'~ devant qqn/qqch** to humble o.s. before sb/sthg.

humilité [ymilite] *nf* **1.** [d'une personne] humility, humbleness, modesty ▪ **avec ~** humbly **2.** *litt* [d'une tâche] humbleness, lowliness.
◆ **en toute humilité** *loc adv sout* in all humility.

humoriste [ymɔrist] *nmf* humorist.

humoristique [ymɔristik] *adj* [récit, ton] humorous.

humour [ymur] *nm* humour ▪ **avec ~** humorously ▪ **sans ~** humourless ▪ **plein d'~** humorous ▪ **avoir de** *ou* **le sens de l'~** to have a sense of humour ▶ **~ noir** black humour.

humus [ymys] *nm* humus.

Hun [ˈœ̃] *nmf* Hun ▪ **les ~s** (the) Hun.

hune [ˈyn] *nf* NAUT top.

huppe [ˈyp] *nf* ORNITH **1.** [oiseau] hoopoe **2.** [plumes] crest ▪ [chez certains pigeons] tuft, tufts.

huppé, e ['ype] *adj* **1.** *fam* [personne, restaurant, soirée] posh *UK*, smart ■ **les gens ~s** the upper crust **2.** ORNITH crested.

hurlant, e ['yrlɑ̃, ɑ̃t] *adj* [foule] yelling, howling.

hurlement ['yrləmɑ̃] *nm* **1.** [humain] yell, roar ■ **des ~s de joie** whoops of joy ■ **des ~s d'indignation** howls of indignation ■ **pourquoi tous ces ~s?** what is all this shouting about? **2.** [d'un chien, d'un loup] howl **3.** *litt* [de la tempête] roar ■ [du vent] howling, screaming ■ [d'une sirène] howl.

hurler [3] ['yrle] ◇ *vi* **1.** [crier] to yell, to scream ■ **~ de douleur** to howl with pain ■ **~ de joie** to whoop *ou* to shout with joy ■ **~ de rage** to howl with rage ■ **ça me fait ~ d'entendre ça!** it makes me so mad to hear things like that! ■ **il me fait ~ de rire!** *fam* he creases me up! **2.** [parler fort] to shout, to bellow **3.** [singe] to howl, to shriek ■ [chien, loup, sirène] to howl ■ **~ à la mort** to bay at the moon ■ **~ avec les loups** to follow the pack **4.** [jurer - couleur] to clash.
◇ *vt* **1.** [ordre] to bawl out *(sép)*, to yell out *(sép)* **2.** [douleur, indignation, réponse] to howl out *(sép)*.

hurleur, euse ['yrlœr, øz] *nm, f* howler, bawler.

hurluberlu, e [yrlybɛrly] *nm, f fam* crank, weirdo.

huron, onne ['yrɔ̃, ɔn] *adj* Huron.
◆ **Huron, onne** *nm, f* Huron.
◆ **Huron** *npr* : **le lac Huron** Lake Huron.

hurrah ['ura] = **hourra**.

hussard ['ysar] *nm* hussar.

hussarde ['ysard] *nf* : **à la ~** roughly, brutally.

hutte ['yt] *nf* hut, cabin.

hyacinthe [jasɛ̃t] *nf* **1.** BOT hyacinth **2.** MINÉR hyacinth, jacinth.

hybridation [ibridasjɔ̃] *nf* hybridization.

hybride [ibrid] ◇ *adj* **1.** BOT, ZOOL & LING hybrid **2.** [mêlé] hybrid, mixed ■ **une architecture ~** a patchwork of architectural styles.
◇ *nm* hybrid.

hybridité [ibridite] *nf* hybridity.

hydrant [idrɑ̃] *nm Suisse* fire hydrant.

hydratant, e [idratɑ̃, ɑ̃t] *adj* **1.** [crème, lotion] moisturizing **2.** CHIM hydrating.
◆ **hydratant** *nm* moisturizer.

hydratation [idratasjɔ̃] *nf* **1.** [de la peau] moisturizing **2.** CHIM hydration.

hydrate [idrat] *nm* hydrate ■ **~ de carbone** carbohydrate.

hydrater [3] [idrate] *vt* **1.** [peau] to moisturize **2.** CHIM to hydrate.
◆ **s'hydrater** *vpi* **1.** [peau] to become moisturized **2.** CHIM to become hydrated, to hydrate.

hydraulique [idrolik] ◇ *adj* hydraulic.
◇ *nf* hydraulics *(sing)*.

hydravion [idravjɔ̃] *nm* seaplane, hydroplane.

hydre [idr] *nf* ZOOL hydra.

Hydre [idr] *npr f* MYTHOL : **l'~ de Lerne** the Lernean Hydra.

hydrobase [idrɔbaz] *nf* seaplane *ou* hydroplane base.

hydrocarbure [idrɔkarbyr] *nm* hydrocarbon.

hydrocéphale [idrɔsefal] ◇ *adj* hydrocephalic, hydrocephalous.
◇ *nmf* hydrocephalic.

hydrocortisone [idrɔkɔrtizɔn] *nf* hydrocortisone.

hydrocuté, e [idrɔkyte] *nm, f* drowned person *(after syncope induced by cold water)*.

hydrocution [idrɔkysjɔ̃] *nf* drowning *(after syncope induced by cold water)*.

hydrodésulfuration [idrɔdesylfyrasjɔ̃] *nf* hydrodesulphurization.

hydrodynamique [idrɔdinamik] ◇ *adj* hydrodynamic.
◇ *nf* hydrodynamics *(sing)*.

hydroélectricité [idrɔelɛktrisite] *nf* hydroelectricity.

hydroélectrique [idrɔelɛktrik] *adj* hydroelectric.

hydrofuge [idrɔfyʒ] ◇ *adj* waterproof, water-repellent.
◇ *nm* water-repellent.

hydrogel [idrɔʒɛl] *nm* hydrogel.

hydrogène [idrɔʒɛn] *nm* **1.** [élément] hydrogen ■ **~ lourd** heavy hydrogen, deuterium **2.** *(comme adj)* hydrogen *(modif)*.

hydrogéner [8] [idrɔʒene] *vt* to hydrogenate.

hydroglisseur [idrɔglisœr] *nm* hydroplane (boat).

hydrographe [idrɔgraf] *nmf* hydrographer.

hydrographie [idrɔgrafi] *nf* hydrography.

hydrographique [idrɔgrafik] *adj* hydrographic, hydrographical.

hydrologie [idrɔlɔʒi] *nf* hydrology.

hydrolyse [idrɔliz] *nf* hydrolysis.

hydromel [idrɔmɛl] *nm* [non fermenté] hydromel *arch* ■ [fermenté] mead.

hydromètre [idrɔmɛtr] ◇ *nm* [pour densité] hydrometer ■ [de réservoir] depth gauge.
◇ *nf* ENTOM water measurer.

hydrométrie [idrɔmetri] *nf* hydrometry.

hydrophile [idrɔfil] ◇ *adj* CHIM hydrophilic.
◇ *nm* ENTOM scavenger beetle.

hydrophobe [idrɔfɔb] *adj* CHIM & TEXT hydrophobic.

hydropneumatique [idrɔpnømatik] *adj* hydropneumatic.

hydroptère [idrɔptɛr] *nm* hydrofoil.

hydrosol [idrɔsɔl] *nm* hydrosol.

hydrosoluble [idrɔsɔlybl] *adj* water-soluble.

hydrosphère [idrɔsfɛr] *nf* hydrosphere.

hydrostatique [idrɔstatik] ◇ *adj* hydrostatic.
◇ *nf* hydrostatics *(sing)*.

hydrothérapie [idrɔterapi] *nf* **1.** [cure] hydrotherapy **2.** [science] hydrotherapeutics *(sing)*.

hydroxyde [idrɔksid] *nm* hydroxide.

hyène [jɛn] *nf* ZOOL hyena, hyaena ■ **~ tachetée** spotted hyena.

Hygiaphone® [iʒjafɔn] *nm* speaking grill.

hygiène [iʒjɛn] *nf* **1.** [principes] hygiene ● **~ alimentaire/corporelle** food/personal hygiene ■ **~ mentale/publique** mental/public health ■ **avoir une bonne ~ de vie** to live healthily **2.** [science] hygienics *(sing)*, hygiene **3.** DR : **~ et sécurité du travail** industrial hygiene and safety.

hygiénique [iʒjenik] *adj* hygienic ■ **ce n'est pas ~** it's unhygienic ■ **un mode de vie ~** a healthy life style ● **une promenade ~** a constitutional.

hygromètre [igrɔmɛtr] *nm* hygrometer.

hygrométrie [igrɔmetri] *nf* hygrometry.

hygrométrique [igrɔmetrik] *adj* hygrometric.

hymen [imɛn] *nm* **1.** ANAT hymen **2.** *litt* (bonds of) marriage.

hyménée [imene] *nm litt* (ties *ou* bonds of) marriage.

hyménoptère [imenɔptɛr] *nm* hymenopteran, hymenopteron ■ **les ~s** the Hymenoptera.

hymne [imn] *nm* **1.** LITTÉR & RELIG hymn ■ **~ national** national anthem **2.** *litt* [glorification] hymn.

hyper [ipɛr] *fam* = **hypermarché**.

hyper- [ipɛr] *préf* **1.** SC hyper- **2.** [en intensif] : **techniques ~spécialisées** highly specialized techniques ■ **elle est ~riche/~sympa** *fam* she's dead rich/dead nice.

hyperactif, ive [ipɛraktif, iv] *adj* hyperactive.

hyperactivité [ipɛraktivite] *nf* hyperactivity.

hyperbare [ipɛrbar] *adj* hyperbaric.

hyperbole [ipɛrbɔl] *nf* **1.** [figure de style] hyperbole **2.** GÉOM hyperbola.

hyperbolique [ipɛrbɔlik] *adj* **1.** [expression, compliments] hyperbolic **2.** GÉOM hyperbolic.

hypercholestérolémie [ipɛrkɔlɛsterɔlemi] *nf* hypercholesteraemia, hypercholesterolaemia.

hypercorrection [ipɛrkɔrɛksjɔ̃] *nf* hypercorrection.

hyperémotivité [iperemɔtivite] *nf* hyperemotivity, hyperemotionality.

hyperfocal, e, aux [ipɛrfɔkal, o] *adj* hyperfocal.

hyperglycémie [ipɛrglisemi] *nf* hyperglycaemia.

hyperlien [ipɛrljɛ̃] *nm* hyperlink.

hypermarché [ipɛrmarʃe] *nm* hypermarket.

hypermétrope [ipɛrmetrɔp] ◇ *adj* farsighted, longsighted, hypermetropic *spéc.*
◇ *nmf* farsighted *ou* hypermetropic *spéc* person.

hypermétropie [ipɛrmetrɔpi] *nf* farsightedness, longsightedness, hypermetropia *spéc.*

hypernerveux, euse [ipɛrnɛrvø, øz] ◇ *adj* overexcitable.
◇ *nm, f* overexcitable person.

hypernervosité [ipɛrnɛrvozite] *nf* overexcitability, hyperexcitability *spéc.*

hyperplasie [ipɛrplazi] *nf* hyperplasia.

hyperréalisme [iperrealism] *nm* hyperrealism.

hypersensibilité [ipɛrsɑ̃sibilite] *nf* hypersensitivity, hypersensitiveness.

hypersensible [ipɛrsɑ̃sibl] ◇ *adj* hypersensitive.
◇ *nmf* hypersensitive (person).

hypertendu, e [ipɛrtɑ̃dy] ◇ *adj* suffering from hypertension *spéc ou* high blood pressure.
◇ *nm, f* hypertensive.

hypertension [ipɛrtɑ̃sjɔ̃] *nf* high blood pressure, hypertension *spéc.*

hypertexte [ipɛrtɛkst] *nm* hypertext.

hyperthyroïdie [ipɛrtirɔidi] *nf* hyperthyroidism *spéc* ■ **faire de l'~** to have an overactive thyroid.

hypertrophie [ipɛrtrɔfi] *nf* **1.** MÉD hypertrophia, hypertrophy **2.** *fig* exaggeration ■ **une ~ de l'amour-propre** an inflated sense of self-importance.

hypertrophié, e [ipɛrtrɔfje] *adj* hypertrophied *spéc*, abnormally enlarged.

hypertrophier [9] [ipɛrtrɔfje] *vt* to enlarge abnormally, to hypertrophy *spéc.*
◆ **s'hypertrophier** *vpi* to become abnormally large, to hypertrophy *spéc.*

hypertrophique [ipɛrtrɔfik] *adj* abnormally enlarged, hypertrophic *spéc.*

hypervitaminose [ipɛrvitaminoz] *nf* hypervitaminosis.

hypnose [ipnoz] *nf* hypnosis ■ **sous ~** under hypnosis.

hypnotique [ipnɔtik] ◇ *adj* MÉD hypnotic.
◇ *nm* hypnotic (drug).

hypnotiser [3] [ipnɔtize] *vt* **1.** MÉD to hypnotize **2.** [fasciner] to fascinate.
◆ **s'hypnotiser sur** *vp+prép* to become obsessed with.

hypnotiseur, euse [ipnɔtizœr, øz] *nm, f* hypnotist.

hypnotisme [ipnɔtism] *nm* hypnotism.

hypoallergénique [ipɔalɛrʒenik] = **hypoallergique** *(adj).*

hypoallergique [ipɔalɛrʒik] *adj* & *nm* hypoallergenic.

hypocalcémie [ipɔkalsemi] *nf* hypocalcaemia.

hypocalorique [ipɔkalɔrik] *adj* [régime] low-calorie.

hypocentre [ipɔsɑ̃tr] *nm* hypocentre.

hypocondriaque [ipɔkɔ̃drijak] ◇ *adj* hypochondriac, hypochondriacal.
◇ *nmf* hypochondriac.

hypocondrie [ipɔkɔ̃dri] *nf* hypochondria.

hypocrisie [ipɔkrizi] *nf* **1.** [attitude] hypocrisy **2.** [action] hypocritical act ■ **assez d'~s** let's stop this pretence.

hypocrite [ipɔkrit] ◇ *adj* **1.** [sournois - personne] hypocritical, insincere **2.** [mensonger - attitude, regard] hypocritical ; [- promesse] hollow.
◇ *nmf* hypocrite.

hypocritement [ipɔkritmɑ̃] *adv* hypocritically.

hypoderme [ipɔdɛrm] *nm* PHYSIOL hypodermis.

hypodermique [ipɔdɛrmik] *adj* hypodermic.

hypogastrique [ipɔgastrik] *adj* hypogastric.

hypoglycémie [ipɔglisemi] *nf* hypoglycaemia.

hypokhâgne [ipɔkaɲ] *nf* **arg scol** *1st year of a two-year Arts course, preparing for entrance to the École normale supérieure.*

hyponyme [ipɔnim] *nm* hyponym.

hypophyse [ipɔfiz] *nf* hypophysis, pituitary gland.

hypoplasie [ipɔplazi] *nf* hypoplasia.

hypostase [ipɔstaz] *nf* hypostasis.

hypotendu, e [ipɔtɑ̃dy] ◇ *adj* hypotensive.
◇ *nm, f* hypotensive (person).

hypotenseur [ipɔtɑ̃sœr] *nm* hypotensive (drug).

hypotension [ipɔtɑ̃sjɔ̃] *nf* low blood pressure, hypotension *spéc.*

hypoténuse [ipɔtenyz] *nf* hypotenuse.

hypothalamus [ipɔtalamys] *nm* hypothalamus.

hypothécable [ipɔtekabl] *adj* mortgageable.

hypothécaire [ipɔtekɛr] *adj* mortgage *(modif).*

hypothèque [ipɔtɛk] *nf* **1.** DR mortgage ■ **prendre une ~** to take out a mortgage ■ **lever une ~** to raise a mortgage ▶ **~ légale** legal mortgage **2.** *fig* **prendre une ~ sur l'avenir** to count one's chickens before they're hatched ■ **lever l'~** to remove the stumbling block *ou* the obstacle.

hypothéquer [18] [ipɔteke] *vt* **1.** [propriété] to mortgage **2.** *fig* **~ son avenir** to mortgage one's future.

hypothermie [ipɔtɛrmi] *nf* hypothermia.

hypothèse [ipɔtɛz] *nf* **1.** [supposition] hypothesis, assumption ■ **dans la meilleure des ~s** at best ■ **dans l'~ où il refuserait, que feriez-vous?** supposing he refuses, what would you do? ■ **dans l'~ d'un tremblement de terre** in the event of an earthquake ■ **ce n'est pas une simple ~ d'école** it's not just a speculative hypothesis ▶ **~ de travail** working hypothesis **2.** LOGIQUE hypothesis.
◆ **en toute hypothèse** *loc adv* in any event, whatever the case.

hypothétique [ipɔtetik] *adj* **1.** [supposé] hypothetical, assumed **2.** [peu probable] hypothetical, unlikely, dubious ■ **c'est très ~** it's extremely doubtful **3.** LOGIQUE hypothetical.

hypothyroïdie [ipɔtirɔidi] *nf* hypothyroidism *spéc* ■ **faire de l'~** to have an underactive thyroid.

hypotrophie [ipɔtrɔfi] *nf* hypotrophy.

hypovitaminose [ipɔvitaminoz] *nf* hypovitaminosis.

hystérectomie [isterɛktɔmi] *nf* hysterectomy.

hystérie [isteri] *nf* hysteria ■ **~ collective** mass hysteria.

hystérique [isterik] ◇ *adj* hysterical.
◇ *nmf* hysteric.

hystérographie [isterɔgrafi] *nf* hysterography, uterography.

Hz (*abr écrite de* **hertz**) Hz.

I

i, I [i] *nm* i ■ **mettre les points sur les i** *fig* to dot the i's and cross the t's, *voir aussi* **g**.

IA (*abr de* **intelligence artificielle**) *nf* AI.

IAC (*abr de* **insémination artificielle entre conjoints**) *nf* AIH.

IAD (*abr de* **insémination artificielle par donneur extérieur**) *nf* AID.

iambe [jɑ̃b] *nm* iamb, iambus.
◆ **iambes** *nmpl* [pièce satirique] iambic.

iambique [jɑ̃bik] *adj* iambic.

IAO (*abr de* **ingénierie assistée par ordinateur**) *nf* CAE.

ibère [ibɛr] *adj* Iberian.
◆ **Ibère** *nmf* Iberian.

ibérique [iberik] *adj* Iberian.

ibid. (*abr écrite de* **ibidem**) ibid.

ibidem [ibidɛm] *adv* ibidem.

ibis [ibis] *nm* ibis.

Icare [ikar] *npr* Icarus.

iceberg [ajsbɛrg] *nm* **1.** GÉOGR iceberg **2.** *fig* **la partie immergée de l'~** the hidden aspects of the problem.

icelle [isɛl] *arch* ◇ *pron dém f* [personne] she ■ [objet] it.
◇ *adj dém f* this.

icelui [isəlɥi] (*pl* **iceux** [isø]) *arch* ◇ *pron dém m* [personne] he ■ [objet] it.
◇ *adj dém m* this.

ichtyologie [iktjɔlɔʒi] *nf* ichthyology.

ichtyosaure [iktjɔsɔr] *nm* ichtyosaurus.

ici [isi] *adv* **1.** [dans ce lieu, à cet endroit] here ■ [dans un écrit, un discours] here, at this point ■ **vous ~!** what are you doing here? ■ **vous êtes ~ chez vous** make yourself at home ■ **pour toute demande, s'adresser ~** please enquire within ■ **c'est ~ que j'ai mal** this is where it hurts ■ **il y a 11 km d'~ au village** it's 11 km from here to the village ■ **les gens d'~** the locals, the people from around here
2. [dans le temps] : **d'~ (à) lundi, on a le temps** we've got time between now and Monday ■ **d'~ demain ce sera terminé** it will be finished by tomorrow ■ **d'~ peu** before (very) long ■ **d'~ là, tout peut arriver!** in the meantime *ou* until then *ou* between now and then anything can happen! ■ **vous serez guéri d'~ là** you'll be better by then ■ **d'~ à ce qu'il se décide** *fam* by the time he makes up his mind ■ **d'~ à ce qu'il change d'avis, il n'y a pas loin!** it won't be long before he changes his mind again! ➊ **je vois ça d'~!** I can just see that!
3. [au téléphone, à la radio] : **allô, ~ Paul** hello, (it's) Paul here *ou* Paul speaking ■ **~ France Culture** this is *ou* you are listening to France Culture.
◆ **par ici** *loc adv* **1.** [dans cette direction] this way ■ **elle est passée par ~ avant d'aller à la gare** she stopped off here on her way to the station ■ **par ~ la monnaie!** *fam hum* come on now, cough up!
2. [dans les environs] around here.

ici-bas [isiba] *adv* here below, on earth ■ **d'~** in this life *ou* world.

Ici-Paris [isipari] *npr* PRESSE *popular Sunday newspaper*.

icône [ikon] *nf* icon.

iconifier [9] [ikɔnifje] *vt* INFORM to iconize.

iconiser [3] [ikɔnize] *vt* INFORM to iconize.

iconoclasme [ikɔnɔklasm] *nm* iconoclasm.

iconoclaste [ikɔnɔklast] ◇ *adj* iconoclastic.
◇ *nmf* iconoclast.

iconographe [ikɔnɔgraf] *nmf* iconographer.

iconographie [ikɔnɔgrafi] *nf* **1.** [étude théorique] iconography **2.** [illustrations] artwork.

iconographique [ikɔnɔgrafik] *adj* iconographical.

iconologie [ikɔnɔlɔʒi] *nf* iconology.

iconothèque [ikɔnɔtɛk] *nf* **1.** [dans un musée] iconography department *(of a museum)* **2.** [dans une bibliothèque] photo *ou* picture library.

ictère [iktɛr] *nm* icterus *spéc*, jaundice.

id. (*abr écrite de* **idem**) id.

Idaho [idao] *npr m* : **l' ~** Idaho.

idéal, e, als *ou* **aux** [ideal, o] *adj* **1.** [demeure, société, solution] ideal, best, perfect ■ **ce n'est pas le comédien ~ pour le rôle de Falstaff** he's not the ideal actor for playing Falstaff **2.** [pureté, bonheur] absolute **3.** MATH ideal.
◆ **idéal, als** *ou* **aux** *nm* **1.** [modèle parfait] ideal **2.** [valeurs] ideal, ideals ■ **tous ces jeunes sans ~** *ou* **qui n'ont pas d'~!** all these young people with no ideal in life! **3.** [solution parfaite] : **l'~ serait de/que...** the ideal *ou* best solution would be to/if... **4.** MATH ideal.

idéalement [idealmɑ̃] *adv* ideally ■ **~ situé à proximité de la plage** ideally situated *ou* situated in an ideal position close to the beach.

idéalisation [idealizasjɔ̃] *nf* idealization.

idéaliser [3] [idealize] *vt* to idealize.

idéalisme [idealism] *nm* [gén - PHILOS] idealism.

idéaliste [idealist] ◇ *adj* **1.** [gén] idealistic **2.** PHILOS idealist.
◇ *nmf* idealist.

idée [ide] *nf* **1.** [pensée] idea, thought ▪ **se faire à l'~** to get used to the idea ▪ **j'ai ~ que...** *fam* I've got the feeling that... ▪ **rien qu'à l'~ de la revoir, je tremble** the mere thought *ou* the very idea of seeing her again makes me nervous ▪ **heureusement qu'il a eu l'~ d'éteindre le gaz** luckily he thought of turning the gas off *ou* it occurred to him to turn the gas off ▪ **je me faisais une autre ~ de la Tunisie/de sa femme** I had imagined Tunisia/his wife to be different ▪ **il a eu la bonne ~ de ne pas venir** *hum* he was quite right not to come ▪ **moi, t'en vouloir? en voilà une ~!** me, hold it against you? where did you get that idea (from)? ▪ **se faire des ~s** to imagine things ▪ **s'il croit obtenir le rôle, il se fait des ~s** if he thinks he's going to get the part, he's deceiving himself ▪ **se faire des ~s sur qqn** to have the wrong idea about sb ▪ **donner des ~s à qqn** to give sb ideas *ou* to put ideas in *ou* into sb's head ◗ **avoir une ~ derrière la tête** to be up to sthg ▪ **avoir des ~s noires** to be down in the dumps, to have the blues
2. [inspiration, création] idea ▪ **qui a eu l'~ du barbecue?** whose idea was it to have *ou* who suggested having a barbecue? ▮ [imagination] ideas, imagination ▪ **avoir de l'~** to be quite inventive ▪ **pas mal ce dessin, il y a de l'~** *fam* not bad this drawing, it's got something
3. [gré, convenance] : **fais à ton ~** do as you see fit *ou* as you please
4. *(toujours sing)* [esprit] : **avoir dans l'~ que...** to have an idea that..., to think that... ▪ **avais-tu dans l'~ d'acheter des actions?** were you thinking of buying shares? ▪ **tu la connais, quand elle a dans l'~ de faire quelque chose!** you know her, when she's got it into her head to do something *ou* when she's set her mind on doing something! ▪ **t'est-il jamais venu à l'~ que...?** has it never occurred to you *ou* entered your head that...? ▪ **il ne me viendrait jamais à l'~ de le frapper** it would never cross my mind to hit him ▪ **on va au concert ce soir? ça m'était complètement sorti de l'~** *fam* we're going to the concert tonight? it had gone clean *ou* right out of my mind
5. [point de vue] : **avoir des ~s bien arrêtées sur** to have set ideas *ou* definite views about ▪ **je préfère me faire moi-même une ~ de la situation** I'd rather assess the situation for myself ▪ **changer d'~** to change one's mind ◗ **~ fixe** idée fixe *sout*, obsession ▪ **c'est une ~ fixe chez toi!** it's an obsession with you! ▪ **~ reçue** commonplace, received idea *sout*, idée reçue *sout* ▪ **~s préconçues** preconceived ideas, preconceptions ▪ **avoir les ~s larges/étroites** to be broad-/narrow-minded ▪ **avoir une haute ~ de qqn/qqch** to have a high opinion of sb/sthg, to think highly of sb/sthg
6. [aperçu, impression] idea ▪ **donnez-moi une ~ du prix que ça va coûter/du temps que ça va prendre** give me a rough idea *ou* some idea of the price/of the time it will take ▪ **tu n'as pas ~ de son entêtement!** you have no idea *ou* you can't imagine how stubborn he is! ▪ **je n'en ai pas la moindre ~** I haven't the slightest *ou* faintest idea ▪ **aucune ~!** I haven't got a clue!, no idea!
7. *(en composition; avec ou sans trait d'union)* **une ~-cadeau** a gift idea.

idée-force [idefɔrs] (*pl* **idées-forces**) *nf* [point principal] crux, nub, mainstay ▪ [point fort] strong point.

idem [idɛm] *adv* idem, ditto.

identifiable [idɑ̃tifjabl] *adj* identifiable ▪ **difficilement ~** difficult to identify ▪ **aisément ~ à son plumage bleuté** easily identified by its bluish feathers.

identifiant [idɑ̃tifjɑ̃] *nm* INFORM user name, login name.

identificateur [idɑ̃tifikatœr] *nm* INFORM identifier.

identification [idɑ̃tifikasjɔ̃] *nf* **1.** [assimilation] identification ▪ **~ à** identification with ▪ **~ d'appel** caller identification, caller ID **2.** [d'un cadavre] identification ▪ [d'un tableau] identification, attribution.

identifier [9] [idɑ̃tifje] *vt* **1.** [reconnaître] to identify ▪ **il a été identifié comme étant le voleur** he was identified as the robber **2.** [assimiler] : **~ qqn/qqch à** to identify sb/sthg with.
◆ **s'identifier à** *vp+prép* : **s'~ à qqn/qqch** to identify o.s. with sb/sthg ▪ **elle s'est complètement identifiée à son personnage** she's got right into the part.

identique [idɑ̃tik] *adj* identical ▪ **~ à qqn/qqch** identical to sb/sthg ▪ **elle reste ~ à elle-même** she's still the same as she always *ou* ever was.

identiquement [idɑ̃tikmɑ̃] *adv* identically.

identitaire [idɑ̃titɛr] *adj* : **crise ~** identity crisis ▪ **repli ~** exaggerated sense of identity, recourse to identity politics ▪ **démarche/revendication ~** assertion of (one's) identity ▪ **discours ~** discourse of identity ▪ **tentation ~** (attractions of) identity politics.

identité [idɑ̃tite] *nf* **1.** [personnalité, état civil] identity ▪ **sous une fausse ~** under an assumed name ▪ **établir son ~** to prove one's identity ▪ **l'~ des victimes n'a pas été révélée** the names of the victims haven't been released ◗ **contrôle** *ou* **vérification d'~** (police) identity check **2.** [similitude] identity, similarity **3.** LOGIQUE, MATH & PSYCHOL identity **4.** DR : **Identité judiciaire** ≃ Criminal Record Office.

idéogramme [ideɔgram] *nm* ideogram.

idéographie [ideɔgrafi] *nf* ideography.

idéologie [ideɔlɔʒi] *nf* ideology.

idéologique [ideɔlɔʒik] *adj* ideological.

idéologue [ideɔlɔg] *nmf* ideologist.

ides [id] *nfpl* ides ▪ **les ~ de mars** the ides of March.

IDHEC [idɛk] (*abr de* **Institut des hautes études cinématographiques**) *npr m former French film school.*

idiolecte [idjɔlɛkt] *nm* idiolect.

idiomatique [idjɔmatik] *adj* idiomatic ▪ **une expression** *ou* **une tournure ~** an idiom, an idiomatic expression.

idiome [idjom] *nm* LING idiom.

idiosyncrasie [idjɔsɛ̃krazi] *nf* idiosyncrasy.

idiot, e [idjo, ɔt] ◇ *adj* **1.** [stupide - individu, réponse] idiotic, stupid ; [- sourire] idiotic ; [- accident, mort] stupid ▪ **un ricanement ~** a silly *ou* foolish snigger ▪ **ce serait vraiment ~ de ne pas en profiter** it would be foolish *ou* stupid not to take advantage of it **2.** MÉD & *vieilli* idiotic.
◇ *nm, f* **1.** [imbécile] idiot ▪ **arrête de faire l'~!** [de faire le pitre] stop fooling around *ou* about! ; [à un enfant] stop being stupid! ; [à un simulateur] stop acting stupid! **2.** MÉD & *vieilli* idiot ▪ **l'~ du village** the village idiot.

idiotement [idjɔtmɑ̃] *adv* idiotically, stupidly ▪ **ricaner ~** to snigger like an idiot.

idiotie [idjɔsi] *nf* **1.** [caractère] idiocy, stupidity **2.** [acte, parole] stupid thing ▪ **arrête de dire des ~s** stop talking nonsense ▪ **il y en a des ~s à la télé!** they show such a lot of nonsense on TV!

idiotisme [idjɔtism] *nm* idiom, idiomatic phrase, idiomatic expression.

idoine [idwan] *adj litt* appropriate ▪ **jusqu'à ce que nous trouvions la solution ~** until we find the appropriate solution.

idolâtre [idɔlatr] ◇ *adj* **1.** RELIG idolatrous **2.** [fanatique] adulatory.
◇ *nmf* **1.** RELIG idolater (*f* idolatress) **2.** [fanatique] devotee.

idolâtrer [3] [idɔlatre] *vt* **1.** RELIG to idolize **2.** [adorer] to idolize.

idolâtrie [idɔlatri] *nf* **1.** RELIG idolatry, idol worshipping **2.** [fanatisme] : **il l'aime jusqu'à l'~** he idolizes her.

idole [idɔl] *nf* **1.** RELIG idol **2.** [personne] idol ▪ **mon frère était mon ~** I used to idolize my brother.

IDS (*abr de* **initiative de défense stratégique**) *nf* SDI.

idylle [idil] *nf* **1.** [poème] idyll **2.** [amourette] romantic idyll.

idyllique [idilik] *adj* **1.** LITTÉR idyllic **2.** [amour, couple, paysage] idyllic, perfect ▪ **se faire une idée ~ de qqch** to have an idealized view of sthg.

Iéna [jena] *npr* Jena.

if [if] *nm* **1.** BOT yew (tree) **2.** MENUIS yew.

IFOP, Ifop [ifɔp] (*abr de* **Institut français d'opinion publique**) *npr m French market research institute.*

igloo *nm* igloo.

IGN (*abr de* **Institut géographique national**) *npr m French national geographical institute,* ≃ Ordnance Survey UK.

IGN

Created in 1940, this state agency is responsible for the official map of France. It keeps a geographical database and publishes large scale maps. It is organized into regional offices and sponsors a school which trains 200 students a year.

Ignace [iɲas] *npr* : ~ **de Loyola** Ignatius Loyola.

igname [iɲam] *nf* yam.

ignare [iɲar] ◇ *adj* ignorant, uncultivated.
◇ *nmf* ignoramus.

igné, e [igne] *adj* **1.** PHYS heat-engendered ■ CHIM pyrogenic ■ GÉOL igneous **2.** *litt* [en feu] fiery, burning, flaming.

ignifuge [ignifyʒ] ◇ *adj* [qui ne brûle pas] fireproof ■ [qui brûle difficilement] fire-retardant.
◇ *nm* [pour protéger du feu] fireproof substance ■ [pour ralentir la propagation] fire-retardant substance.

ignifuger [17] [ignifyʒe] *vt* to fireproof.

ignition [ignisjɔ̃] *nf* PHYS ignition.

ignoble [iɲɔbl] *adj* **1.** [vil - individu] low, base ; [- crime] infamous, heinous ; [- accusation] shameful ; [- conduite] unspeakable, disgraceful, shabby **2.** *fam* [bâtisse] hideous ■ [nourriture] revolting, vile ■ [logement] squalid ■ **d'~s taudis** squalid hovels.

ignoblement [iɲɔbləmɑ̃] *adv* vilely, disgracefully.

ignominie [iɲɔmini] *nf* **1.** [caractère vil] ignominy, infamy ■ [déshonneur] ignominy, (public) disgrace *ou* dishonour ■ **se couvrir d'~** to disgrace o.s. **2.** [action] ignominy, disgraceful act ■ **commettre une ~** to behave ignominiously *ou* disgracefully ‖ [parole] ignominy ■ **dire des ~s** to say disgraceful *ou* hateful things.

ignominieux, euse [iɲɔminjø, øz] *adj litt* ignominious.

ignorance [iɲɔrɑ̃s] *nf* ignorance ■ **être dans l'~ de qqch** to be unaware of sthg ■ **tenir qqn dans l'~ de qqch** to keep sb in ignorance of sthg ■ **pécher par ~** to err through ignorance.

ignorant, e [iɲɔrɑ̃, ɑ̃t] ◇ *adj* **1.** [inculte] ignorant, uncultivated **2.** [incompétent] : **il est ~ en informatique** he doesn't know anything about computers **3.** [pas au courant] : **~ de** ignorant *ou* unaware of.
◇ *nm, f* ignoramus ■ **ne fais pas l'~** don't pretend you don't know.

ignoré, e [iɲɔre] *adj* **1.** [cause, événement] unknown ■ **être ~ de qqn** to be unknown to sb **2.** [artiste] unrecognized.

ignorer [3] [iɲɔre] *vt* **1.** [cause, événement etc] to be unaware of ■ **j'ignore son adresse/où il est/quand elle revient** I don't know her address/where he is/when she's coming back ■ **il ignorait tout de son passé/d'elle** he knew nothing about her past/her ■ **j'ignorais qu'il était malade** I was unaware that he was ill **2.** [personne, regard] to ignore, to take no notice of ■ [avertissement, panneau] to ignore, to take no heed of ■ [ordre, prière] to ignore **3.** *sout* [faim, pauvreté] to have had no experience of ■ **il ignore la peur** he knows no fear, he doesn't know the meaning of fear.
◆ **s'ignorer** ◇ *vp (emploi réciproque)* to ignore each other.
◇ *vpi* : **c'est un comédien qui s'ignore** he is unaware of his talent as an actor, he's an actor without knowing it.

IGP [iʒepe] (*abr de* **Indication géographique de provenance**) *nm* Geographical Indication of Origin *(on food label).*

IGS (*abr de* **Inspection générale des services**) *npr f police disciplinary body for Paris,* ≃ Metropolitan Police Commission UK.

iguane [igwan] *nm* iguana.

il [il] (*pl* **ils**) *pron pers m* **1.** [sujet d'un verbe - homme] he ; [- animal, chose] it ; [- animal de compagnie] he ■ **ils** they **2.** [sujet d'un verbe impersonnel] : **il pleut** it's raining ■ **il faut patienter** you/we have to wait ‖ [dans des tournures impersonnelles] : **il manque deux élèves** two pupils are missing **3.** [emphatique - dans une interrogation] : **ton père est-il rentré?** has your father come back?

île [il] *nf* **1.** GÉOGR island, isle *litt* ■ **une petite ~** an islet ■ **les habitants de l'~** the islanders ■ **vivre sur** *ou* **dans une ~** to live on an island ■ **aller sur une ~** to go to an island ● **l'~ de la Cité** *island on the Seine in Paris where Notre-Dame stands* ■ **~ déserte** desert island ■ **l'~ de Beauté** Corsica ■ **les ~s de la mer Égée** the Aegean *ou* Greek Islands **2.** *litt & vieilli* [colonie] : **les îles** the Caribbean (Islands), the West Indies **3.** CULIN : **~ flottante** floating island.

ÎLE

les îles Aléoutiennes the Aleutian Islands ;
les îles Anglo-Normandes the Channel Islands ;
les îles Australes the Tubuai *ou* Austral Islands ;
les îles Bahrayn *ou* **Bahreïn** the Bahrain *ou* Bahrein Islands ;
les îles Baléares the Balearic Islands ;
les îles Britanniques the British Isles ;
les îles Canaries the Canary Islands ;
les îles du Cap Vert the Cape Verde Islands ;
les îles Carolines the Caroline Islands ;
l'île Christmas Christmas Island ;
les îles Comores the Comoros ;
l'île d'Elbe Elba ;
les îles Éoliennes the Aeolian Islands ;
les îles Falkland the Falkland Islands, the Falklands ;
les îles Féroé the Faeroes ;
les îles Fidji the Fiji Islands ;
les îles Galapagos the Galapagos Islands ;
les îles Hébrides the Hebrides ;
les îles Ioniennes the Ionian Islands ;
les îles Kouriles the Kuril *ou* Kurile Islands ;
les îles Maldives the Maldives ;
les îles Malouines the Falkland Islands, the Falklands ;
l'île de Man the Isle of Man ;
les îles Mariannes the Mariana Islands ;
les îles Marquises the Marquesas Islands ;
les îles Marshall the Marshall Islands ;
l'île Maurice Mauritius ;
les îles Moluques the Molucca Islands, the Moluccas ;
l'île du Nord North Island ;
l'île d'Ouessant (the Isle of) Ushant ;
l'île de Pâques Easter Island ;
l'île du Prince-Édouard Prince Edward Island ;
les îles Salomon the Solomon Islands ;
l'île de Sein the Ile de Sein ;
les îles Shetland the Shetland Islands, the Shetlands ;
les îles de la Sonde the Sunda Islands ;
les îles Sorlingues the Scilly Islands ;
les îles Sous-le-Vent (aux Antilles) the Netherlands (and Venezuelan) Antilles; (en Polynésie) the Leeward Islands, the Western Society Islands; ;
l'île du Sud South Island ;
l'île de la Trinité Trinidad ;
les îles Turks et Caicos the Turks and Caicos Islands ;
l'île Vancouver Vancouver Island ;
les îles du Vent (aux Antilles) the Windward Islands; (en Polynésie) the Eastern Society Islands; ;
les îles Vierges the Virgin Islands ;
l'île de Wight the Isle of Wight.

Île-de-France [ildəfrɑ̃s] *npr f* : **l'~** the Île-de-France ■ **en ~** in the Île-de-France region.

ÎLE-DE-FRANCE

This administrative region includes the *départements* of Paris, Seine-St-Denis, Val-de-Marne, Val-d'Oise, Essonne, Yvelines, Seine et Marne.

Iliade [iljad] *npr f* : **'l'~'** ***Homère*** 'The Iliad'.

iliaque [iljak] *adj* iliac ■ **artère ~** iliac artery ■ **fosses ~s** iliac fossae ■ **os ~** hip bone.

illégal, e, aux [ilegal, o] *adj* [contre la loi] illegal, unlawful ■ [sans autorisation] illicit ■ **de façon ~e** illegally ■ **détention ~e** unlawful detention.

illégalement [ilegalmɑ̃] *adv* illegally, unlawfully.

illégalité [ilegalite] *nf* **1.** [caractère] illegality, unlawfulness ▪ **être dans l'~** to be in breach of the law ▪ **vivre dans l'~** to live outside the law, to be an outlaw **2.** [délit] illegal *ou* unlawful act.

illégitime [ileʒitim] *adj* **1.** DR [enfant, acte] illegitimate **2.** [requête, prétention] illegitimate ▪ [frayeur] groundless.

illégitimement [ileʒitimmɑ̃] *adv* **1.** DR illegitimately, unlawfully **2.** [injustement] unwarrantedly, unjustifiably.

illégitimité [ileʒitimite] *nf* **1.** DR [d'un enfant, d'un acte] illegitimacy **2.** [injustice] unwarrantedness, unfoundedness.

illettré, e [iletre] ◇ *adj* **1.** [analphabète] illiterate **2.** [ignorant] uncultivated, uneducated.
◇ *nm, f* **1.** [analphabète] illiterate **2.** [ignorant] uncultivated *ou* uneducated person.

illettrisme [iletrism] *nm* illiteracy.

illicite [ilisit] *adj* illicit ▪ **pratiques/gains ~s** unlawful activities/gains.

illicitement [ilisitmɑ̃] *adv* illicitly.

illico [iliko] *adv* : **~ (presto)** right away, pronto.

illimité, e [ilimite] *adj* **1.** [en abondance - ressources, espace] unlimited ; [- patience, bonté] boundless, limitless **2.** [non défini - durée] unlimited, indefinite ▪ **en congé ~** on indefinite leave **3.** MATH unrestricted ▪ GÉOM unbounded **4.** INFORM : **accès ~** unrestricted access.

Illinois [ilinwa] *npr m* : **l' ~** Illinois.

illisible [ilizibl] *adj* **1.** [écriture] illegible, unreadable **2.** [écrivain, roman] unreadable.

illogique [ilɔʒik] *adj* illogical ▪ **de façon ~** illogically.

illogisme [ilɔʒism] *nm* illogicality, absurdity.

illumination [ilyminasjɔ̃] *nf* **1.** [d'un monument] floodlighting **2.** [lumière] illumination, lighting (up) **3.** [idée] flash of inspiration *ou* understanding ▪ [révélation] illumination.
◆ **illuminations** *nfpl* illuminations, lights ▪ **les ~s de Noël** the Christmas lights.

illuminé, e [ilymine] ◇ *adj* [monument] lit up, floodlit, illuminated ▪ [rue] lit up, illuminated.
◇ *nm, f* **1.** [visionnaire] visionary, illuminate *arch* **2.** *péj* [fou] lunatic.

illuminer [3] [ilymine] *vt* **1.** [ciel - suj: étoiles, éclairs] to light up *(sép)* ▪ [monument] to floodlight ▪ [pièce] to light **2.** [visage, regard] to light up *(sép)* ▪ **un sourire illumina son visage** a smile lit up her face.
◆ **s'illuminer** *vpi* **1.** *sout* [ciel, regard, visage] to light up ▪ **~ de** to light up with **2.** [vitrine] to be lit up ▪ [guirlande] to light up.

illusion [ilyzjɔ̃] *nf* **1.** [idée fausse] illusion ▪ **ne lui donne pas d'~s** don't give him (any) false ideas ▪ **perdre ses ~s** to lose one's illusions ▪ **se faire des ~s** to delude o.s. ▪ **se bercer d'~s** to delude o.s., to harbour illusions **2.** [erreur de perception] illusion, trick ▪ **le miroir donne une ~ de profondeur** the mirror gives an illusion of depth ▪ **en donnant** *ou* **créant une ~ de stabilité** with an outward show of stability ▪ **faire ~ : c'est un vieux manteau mais il fait ~** it's an old coat but you wouldn't think so to look at it ▪ **son aisance fait ~** his apparent ease is deceptive ▶ **~ d'optique** optical illusion.

illusionner [3] [ilyzjɔne] *vt* to delude.
◆ **s'illusionner** *vpi* to delude *ou* to deceive o.s. ▪ **tu t'illusionnes sur ses intentions** you're deluding yourself *ou* you're mistaken about his intentions ▪ **ne t'illusionne pas sur sa détermination** make no mistakes about his firmness.

illusionnisme [ilyzjɔnism] *nm* **1.** ART illusionism **2.** [prestidigitation] conjuring tricks ▪ [truquage] illusionism.

illusionniste [ilyzjɔnist] *nmf* conjurer, illusionist.

illusoire [ilyzwar] *adj* [promesse] deceptive, illusory ▪ [bonheur, victoire] illusory, fanciful ▪ **il serait ~ de croire que...** it would be wrong *ou* mistaken to believe that...

illustrateur, trice [ilystratœr, tris] *nm, f* illustrator.

illustratif, ive [ilystratif, iv] *adj* illustrative.

illustration [ilystrasjɔ̃] *nf* **1.** [image, activité] illustration ▪ [ensemble d'images] illustrations ▪ **l'~ de cette édition est somptueuse** this book is lavishly illustrated **2.** *fig* [démonstration] illustration ▪ [exemple] illustration, example.

illustre [ilystr] *adj* illustrious ▶ **l'~ compagnie** *sout* the Académie française ▪ **~ inconnu, ~ inconnue** *hum* : **quel est cet ~ inconnu?** who is this famous person I've never heard of!

illustré, e [ilystre] *adj* illustrated.
◆ **illustré** *nm* pictorial, illustrated magazine.

illustrer [3] [ilystre] *vt* **1.** [livre] to illustrate **2.** [définition, théorie] to illustrate.
◆ **s'illustrer** *vpi* to become renowned *ou* famous ▪ **les Français se sont illustrés en natation** the French distinguished themselves at swimming.

illustrissime [ilystrisim] *adj* *hum* most illustrious.

îlot [ilo] *nm* **1.** GÉOGR small island, islet **2.** [espace] island ▪ **dans l'~ de calme où je travaille** in the island *ou* oasis of peace where I work ▶ **~ de résistance** pocket of resistance **3.** [pâté de maisons] block ▪ [pour surveillance policière] patrol area, beat **4.** [dans un magasin] (island) display unit **5.** NAUT island.

îlotage [ilɔtaʒ] *nm* [d'un quartier] community policing, policing on the beat.

ilote [ilɔt] *nm* ANTIQ Helot.

îlotier, ère [ilɔtje, ɛr] *nm* community policeman (*f* community policewoman).

ils [il] *pl* ⊳ **il.**

IMA [ima] *npr m* = **Institut du Monde Arabe**.

image [imaʒ] *nf* **1.** [représentation] picture ▪ **livre d'~s** picture book ▪ **elle était l'~ du malheur/de la bonne santé** *fig* she was the very picture of tragedy/health ▶ **~ de la mère/du père** mother/father figure ▪ **~ d'Épinal** *popular 19th-century print showing idealized scenes of French and foreign life, well-known characters or heroic events* ▪ **c'est une véritable ~ d'Épinal** *fig* it's a very stereotyped image ▪ **~ pieuse** holy image
2. [réflexion] image, reflection ▪ PHYS image ▪ **~ réelle/virtuelle** real/virtual image
3. TV image ▪ CINÉ frame ▪ **25 ~s par seconde** 25 frames per second ▪ **l'~ est floue** [télévision] the picture is fuzzy ▪ **il n'y a plus d'~** there's nothing on screen
4. LITTÉR image
5. [idée] image, picture ▪ **quelle ~ te fais-tu de lui?** how do you picture him? ▪ **donner une fausse ~ de qqch** to misrepresent sthg, to give a false impression of sthg ▶ **~ mentale** PSYCHOL mental image
6. MATH image
7. INFORM [imprimée] hard copy ▪ [sur l'écran] image ▪ **~ mémoire** dump.
◆ **à l'image de** *loc prép* : **Dieu créa l'homme à son ~** God created man in his own image ▪ **ce jardin est à l'~ de son propriétaire** this garden is the reflection of its owner.
◆ **image de marque** *nf* [d'un produit] brand image ▪ [d'une entreprise] corporate image ▪ [d'une personnalité, d'une institution] (public) image.

imagé, e [imaʒe] *adj* full of imagery ▪ **elle a un langage très ~** she uses colourful imagery ▪ **parler de façon ~e** to use picturesque speech.

imagerie [imaʒri] *nf* **1.** [ensemble d'images] prints, pictures ▪ **l'~ napoléonienne** the imagery of the Napoleonic era **2.** [commerce] coloured print trade ▪ [fabrication] printing **3.** MÉTÉOR satellite photography **4.** MÉD : **~ médicale** medical imaging **5.** INFORM imagery.

imaginable [imaʒinabl] *adj* imaginable, conceivable ▪ **c'est difficilement ~** it's hard to imagine ▪ **ce n'est plus ~ à notre époque** it's just unthinkable nowadays.

imaginaire [imaʒinɛr] ◇ *adj* **1.** [fictif - pays, personnage] imaginary **2.** MATH imaginary.
◇ *nm* imagination ▪ **le domaine de l'~** the realm of fancy ▶ **l'~ collectif** PSYCHOL the collective imagination.

imaginatif, ive [imaʒinatif, iv] *adj* imaginative, fanciful.

imagination [imaʒinasjɔ̃] *nf* **1.** [faculté] imagination ■ **c'est de l'~ pure et simple** it's sheer *ou* pure imagination ■ **essaie d'avoir un peu d'~** try to use your imagination ■ **avoir beaucoup d'~** to have a lot of imagination, to be very imaginative **2.** [chimère] : **~s que tout cela!** those are just imaginings!

imaginer [3] [imaʒine] *vt* **1.** [concevoir] to imagine ■ **la maison est plus grande que je l'imaginais** the house is bigger than I imagined it (to be) ■ **tu imagines sa tête quand je lui ai dit ça!** you can imagine *ou* picture his face when I told him that! ■ **tu n'imagines tout de même pas que je vais céder?** you don't really think *ou* imagine I'm going to give in, do you? **2.** [supposer] to imagine, to suppose ■ **tu veux de l'argent, j'imagine!** you want some money, I suppose! **3.** [inventer - personnage] to create, to imagine ; [- gadget, mécanisme] to devise, to think up *(sép)*.

◆ **s'imaginer** ◇ *vp (emploi réfléchi)* to imagine o.s. ■ **j'ai du mal à m'~ grand-mère** I have a hard job picturing *ou* seeing myself as a grandmother.
◇ *vpt* [se représenter] to imagine, to picture ■ **s'~ que** to imagine *ou* to think that ■ **tu t'imagines bien que je n'ai pas vraiment apprécié** as you can imagine, I wasn't too pleased ■ **si je m'imaginais te rencontrer ici!** fancy meeting you here!

imago [imago] ◇ *nm* ENTOM imago.
◇ *nf* PSYCHOL imago.

imam [imam] *nm* imam.

imbattable [ɛ̃batabl] *adj* unbeatable.

imbécile [ɛ̃besil] ◇ *adj* [niais] stupid.
◇ *nmf* **1.** [niais] idiot, fool ■ **ne fais pas l'~** [ne fais pas le pitre] stop fooling about *ou* around ; [ne simule pas] stop acting stupid *ou* dumb ■ **le premier ~ venu peut comprendre ça** *fam* any (old) fool can understand that ▶ **espèce d'~ heureux!** *fam* you twit *ou* stupid idiot! **2.** MÉD & *vieilli* imbecile.

imbécillité [ɛ̃besilite] *nf* **1.** [caractère] stupidity, idiocy **2.** [parole] nonsense *(U)* ■ [acte] stupid behaviour *(U)* ■ **avec ses ~s il va finir par se faire prendre** his foolish behaviour is going to land him in trouble one of these days **3.** MÉD & *vieilli* imbecility.

imberbe [ɛ̃bɛrb] *adj* beardless.

imbibé, e [ɛ̃bibe] *adj* *fam* sozzled *UK*, soused *US*.

imbiber [3] [ɛ̃bibe] *vt* to soak ■ **~ une éponge d'eau** to soak a sponge with water ■ **la terre est imbibée d'eau** the earth is completely waterlogged.

◆ **s'imbiber** *vpi* **1.** [s'imprégner] to become soaked ■ **s'~ de** [suj: gâteau] to become soaked with *ou* in ; [suj: terre] to become saturated with **2.** *fam* [boire] to booze.

imbrication [ɛ̃brikasjɔ̃] *nf* **1.** [d'écailles, de pièces, de tuiles] imbrication *spéc*, overlapping **2.** [de considérations, d'hypothèses] interweaving, overlapping **3.** INFORM interleaving, nesting.

imbriqué, e [ɛ̃brike] *adj* **1.** [écailles, pièces] imbricated ■ [cercles] overlapping **2.** [questions] interlinked.

imbriquer [3] [ɛ̃brike] *vt* [pièces] to fit into *ou* over each other ■ [tuiles] to overlap ■ **il faut ~ les différents morceaux les uns dans les autres** the different pieces have to be fitted into each other.

◆ **s'imbriquer** *vpi* **1.** CONSTR [pièces] to fit into *ou* over each other ■ [tuiles, feuilles, écailles] to overlap, to imbricate *spéc* **2.** [être lié] to be interlinked *ou* closely linked ■ **des questions pratiques sont venues s'~ dans les considérations esthétiques** practical problems began to interfere with the purely aesthetic considerations ■ **le scénariste a fait s'~ les vies de tous les personnages** the screenwriter linked the lives of all his characters together.

imbroglio [ɛ̃brɔljo] *nm* imbroglio.

imbu, e [ɛ̃by] *adj* : **être ~ de sa personne** *ou* **de soi-même** to be full of o.s., to be full of a sense of one's own importance *sout*.

imbuvable [ɛ̃byvabl] *adj* **1.** [boisson] undrinkable **2.** *fam* [individu] unbearable.

imitable [imitabl] *adj* imitable ■ **difficilement ~** hard to imitate.

imitateur, trice [imitatœr, tris] *nm, f* imitator ■ [de personnalités connues] impersonator, mimic ■ [de cris d'animaux] imitator, mimic.

imitatif, ive [imitatif, iv] *adj* imitative, mimicking.

imitation [imitasjɔ̃] *nf* **1.** [parodie] imitation, impersonation ■ **elle a un talent d'~** she's a talented mimic **2.** ART imitation, copy ■ LITTÉR imitation **3.** [matière artificielle] imitation ■ **~ marbre** imitation marble **4.** MUS & PSYCHOL imitation.

◆ **à l'imitation de** *loc prép* in imitation of.

imiter [3] [imite] *vt* **1.** [copier - bruit, personne] to imitate ; [- mouvements, façon de parler] to imitate, to mimic ■ **~ la signature de qqn** to imitate sb's signature ; [à des fins criminelles] to forge sb's signature **2.** [suivre l'exemple de] to imitate, to copy ■ **si elle démissionne, d'autres l'imiteront** if she resigns, others will do the same *ou* follow suit *ou* do likewise **3.** [ressembler à] to look like ■ **c'est une matière qui imite le liège** it's imitation cork.

immaculé, e [imakyle] *adj* *sout* [blanc, neige] immaculate ■ [réputation] immaculate, unsullied, spotless ■ **une nappe ~e** an immaculately *ou* spotlessly clean cloth ▶ **l'Immaculée Conception** RELIG the Immaculate Conception.

immanence [imanɑ̃s] *nf* immanence.

immanent, e [imanɑ̃, ɑ̃t] *adj* immanent.

immangeable [ɛ̃mɑ̃ʒabl] *adj* uneatable, inedible.

immanquable [ɛ̃mɑ̃kabl] *adj* **1.** [inévitable] inevitable **2.** [infaillible] sure, reliable, infallible.

immanquablement [ɛ̃mɑ̃kabləmɑ̃] *adv* definitely.

immatérialité [imaterjalite] *nf* immateriality.

immatériel, elle [imaterjɛl] *adj* **1.** PHILOS immaterial **2.** *litt* [léger] ethereal **3.** COMM intangible.

immatriculation [imatrikylasjɔ̃] *nf* registration ■ **numéro d'~** registration number *UK*, license number *US*.

IMMATRICULATION

The last two numbers on French number plates refer to the *département* where the vehicle was registered. When moving to a new *département*, the vehicle is issued with new number plates. However the system is due to change in 2008, when vehicles will be registered with a number 'for life' regardless of a change of owner or *département*.

immatriculer [3] [imatrikyle] *vt* : **(faire) ~** to register ■ **car immatriculé à Paris** coach with a Paris registration *UK ou* license *US* number ■ **je ne suis plus immatriculé 92** *fam* my registration *UK ou* license *US* number no longer ends in 92.

immature [imatyr] *adj* immature.

immaturité [imatyrite] *nf* immaturity.

immédiat, e [imedja, at] *adj* **1.** [avenir] immediate ■ [réponse] immediate, instantaneous ■ [effet] immediate, direct ■ [soulagement] immediate, instant ■ **sa mort fut ~e** he died instantly **2.** [voisins] immediate, next-door *(avant n)* ■ [environs] immediate ■ **dans mon voisinage ~** in close proximity to *ou* very near where I live ■ **supérieur ~** direct superior **3.** SC & PHILOS immediate.

◆ **dans l'immédiat** *loc adv* for the time being, for the moment, for now ■ **nous n'effectuerons pas de changement dans l'~** we will introduce no immediate changes.

immédiatement [imedjatmɑ̃] *adv* **1.** [dans le temps] immediately, at once, forthwith *sout hum* **2.** [dans l'espace] directly, immediately.

immédiateté [imedjatte] *nf* **1.** *sout* [instantanéité] immediacy, immediateness **2.** PHILOS immediacy.

immémorial, e, aux [imemɔrjal, o] *adj* age-old, immemorial ■ **de temps ~** from time immemorial.

immense [imɑ̃s] *adj* [forêt, bâtiment, plaine] vast, huge ■ [talent] immense, towering ■ [soulagement, impact] immense, great, tremendous ■ [sacrifice, dévotion] immense, boundless.

immensément [imɑ̃semɑ̃] *adv* immensely, hugely.

immensité [imɑ̃site] *nf* **1.** [d'un lieu] immensity, vastness ▪ [de la mer] immensity ▪ **dans l'~** *litt* in infinity, in infinite space **2.** [d'une tâche, d'un problème] enormity ▪ [d'un talent, d'un chagrin] immensity.

immergé, e [imɛrʒe] *adj* [au-dessous de l'eau] submerged ▪ **la majeure partie d'un iceberg est ~e** the bulk of an iceberg is underwater ▪ **l'épave est ~e par 500 m de fond** the wreck is lying 500 m underwater *ou* under 500 m of water ◐ **plante ~e** aquatic plant ▪ **terres ~es** submerged areas of land.

immerger [17] [imɛrʒe] *vt* [oléoduc, bombes] to lay under water, to submerge ▪ [produits radioactifs] to dump *ou* to deposit at sea ▪ [cadavre] to bury at sea.
◆ **s'immerger** *vpi* [sous-marin] to dive, to submerge.

immérité, e [imerite] *adj* undeserved, unmerited.

immersion [imɛrsjɔ̃] *nf* **1.** [d'un sous-marin] diving, submersion ▪ [d'un oléoduc, de bombes] underwater laying, submersion ▪ [de déchets] dumping at sea ▪ [d'un cadavre] burying at sea **2.** ASTRON & RELIG immersion.

immettable [ɛ̃metabl] *adj* [abîmé] no longer fit to wear ▪ [indécent] unwearable.

immeuble [imœbl] <> *adj* DR immovable, real ▪ **biens ~s** immovables, real estate.
<> *nm* **1.** CONSTR [gén] building ▪ : **~ de bureaux** office block *esp UK ou* building ▪ **~ commercial** rented office block *esp UK ou* building ▪ **~ d'habitation** residential building, block of flats *UK*, apartment building *US* ▪ **~ de rapport** investment property ▪ **~ à usage locatif** [résidentiel] block of rented flats *UK*, rental apartment building *US* **2.** DR real estate.

immigrant, e [imigrɑ̃, ɑ̃t] *adj & nm, f* immigrant.

immigration [imigrasjɔ̃] *nf* immigration.

immigré, e [imigre] <> *adj* immigrant ▪ **travailleur ~** immigrant worker, guest worker.
<> *nm, f* immigrant.

immigrer [3] [imigre] *vi* to immigrate ▪ **~ en France/aux États-Unis** to immigrate to France/to the (United) States.

imminence [iminɑ̃s] *nf* imminence.

imminent, e [iminɑ̃, ɑ̃t] *adj* imminent, impending ▪ **c'est ~** it's imminent, it won't be long (now).

immiscer [16] [imise] ◆ **s'immiscer dans** *vp+prép* **1.** [intervenir dans] : **s'~ dans une affaire** to interfere with *ou* in a matter **2.** DR : **s'~ dans une succession** to enter into *ou* to assume a succession.

immixtion [imiksjɔ̃] *nf* **1.** interference, interfering **2.** DR assumption.

immobile [imɔbil] *adj* **1.** [mer, surface] still, calm ▪ [nuit, air] still ▪ [feuillage, animal, personne] still, motionless ▪ [visage] immobile **2.** *litt* [temps] immobile.

immobilier, ère [imɔbilje, ɛr] *adj* COMM & DR [marché, opération] property *(modif)* ▪ [action] real ▪ [fortune] real estate *(modif)* ▪ **biens ~s** immovables, real estate ▪ **crédit ~** mortgage.
◆ **immobilier** *nm* : **l'~** COMM the property *ou* real estate business, realty.

immobilisation [imɔbilizasjɔ̃] *nf* **1.** [d'un adversaire, de forces armées] immobilization ▪ **le manque à gagner dû à l'~ des machines** losses through downtime **2.** FIN [de capitaux] tying up **3.** DR conversion *(of personalty into realty)* **4.** SPORT hold **5.** MÉD immobilization.
◆ **immobilisations** *nfpl* fixed assets.

immobiliser [3] [imɔbilize] *vt* **1.** [membre] to strap up *(sép)*, to immobilize ▪ [adversaire, forces armées] to immobilize ▪ [balancier] to stop ▪ [circulation] to bring to a standstill *ou* to a halt ▪ **il est resté immobilisé au lit pendant cinq semaines** he was laid up in bed for five weeks **2.** FIN [des capitaux] to tie up *(sép)*, to immobilize **3.** DR to convert *(personalty into realty)*.
◆ **s'immobiliser** *vpi* [personne] to stand still *ou* stock-still ▪ [véhicule] to come to a halt, to pull up.

immobilisme [imɔbilism] *nm* [gén] opposition to change ▪ POLIT immobilism.

immobiliste [imɔbilist] <> *adj* conservative, immobilist *spéc* ▪ **la politique ~ du gouvernement** the government's conservative policies.
<> *nmf* conservative, upholder of the status quo.

immobilité [imɔbilite] *nf* [d'un lac, d'une personne] stillness, motionlessness ▪ [d'un regard] immobility, steadiness ▪ **je suis contraint à l'~ totale** I've been confined to bed.

immodéré, e [imɔdere] *adj* immoderate, inordinate.

immodérément [imɔderemɑ̃] *adv* immoderately, excessively.

immodeste [imɔdɛst] *adj sout* immodest.

immolateur [imɔlatœr] *nm litt* immolator.

immolation [imɔlasjɔ̃] *nf sout* immolation.

immoler [3] [imɔle] *vt* **1.** RELIG [sacrifier] to immolate ▪ **~ qqn à** to sacrifice sb to **2.** *litt* [exterminer] to kill **3.** *fig & litt* [renoncer à] to sacrifice.
◆ **s'immoler** *vp (emploi réfléchi) litt* to sacrifice o.s. ▪ **il s'immola par le feu** he set fire to himself.

immonde [imɔ̃d] *adj* **1.** RELIG [impur] unclean, impure **2.** [sale] foul, filthy, obnoxious **3.** [ignoble - crime, pensées, propos] sordid, vile, base ; [- individu] vile, base, obnoxious.

immondices [imɔ̃dis] *nfpl* refuse, rubbish *UK*, trash *US*.

immoral, e, aux [imɔral, o] *adj* immoral.

immoralement [imɔralmɑ̃] *adv* immorally.

immoraliste [imɔralist] *adj & nmf* immoralist.

immoralité [imɔralite] *nf* immorality.

immortaliser [3] [imɔrtalize] *vt* to immortalize.

immortalité [imɔrtalite] *nf* immortality ▪ **son œuvre lui a assuré l'~** her work won her everlasting fame *ou* immortality.

immortel, elle [imɔrtɛl] <> *adj* [dieu] immortal ▪ [bonheur, gloire] immortal, everlasting, eternal.
<> *nm, f* **1.** MYTHOL Immortal **2.** *fam* [académicien] : **les Immortels** *the members of the Académie française.*
◆ **immortelle** *nf* BOT everlasting (flower), immortelle.

immuable [imɥabl] *adj* [principes, vérités, amour] immutable *sout*, unchanging ▪ [sourire] unchanging, fixed ▪ [politesse] eternal, unfailing ▪ [opinion] unwavering, unchanging.

immuablement [imɥabləmɑ̃] *adv* eternally, perpetually, immutably *sout* ▪ **ville ~ brumeuse** perpetually foggy town.

immun, e [imœ̃, yn] *adj* MÉD immune.

immunisation [imynizasjɔ̃] *nf* immunization.

immuniser [3] [imynize] *vt* MÉD to immunize ▪ **~ qqn contre qqch** to immunize sb against sthg ▪ **depuis le temps qu'elle me critique, je suis immunisé!** she's been criticizing me for so long, I'm immune to it now! ▪ **son échec l'a immunisé contre l'aventurisme politique** his failure has cured him of political adventurism.

immunitaire [imynitɛr] *adj* immune ▪ **système ~** immune system.

immunité [imynite] *nf* **1.** DR immunity ▪ **~ diplomatique** diplomatic immunity ▪ **~ parlementaire** parliamentary privilege **2.** MÉD immunity ▪ **acquérir une ~ (à)** to become immune (to) *ou* immunized (against).

immunodéficience [imynɔdefisjɑ̃s] *nf* immunodeficiency.

immunodéficitaire [imynɔdefisitɛr] *adj* immunodeficient.

immunodépresseur [imynɔdeprɛsœr] *nm* immunosuppressive.

immunogène [imynɔʒɛn] *adj* immunogenic.

immunoglobuline [imynɔglɔbylin] *nf* immunoglobulin.

immunologie [imynɔlɔʒi] *nf* immunology.

immunologique [imynɔlɔʒik] *adj* immunological.

immunothérapie [imynɔterapi] *nf* immunotherapy.

impact [ɛ̃pakt] *nm* **1.** [choc - de corps] impact, collision ; [- de projectiles] impact ▪ **au moment de l'~** on impact ➔ **point d'~** point of impact **2.** [influence, effet - de mesures] impact, effect ; [- d'un mouvement, d'un artiste] impact, influence ➔ **étude d'~** ÉCOL environmental impact assessment.

impair, e [ɛ̃pɛr] *adj* **1.** [chiffre] odd, uneven ▪ **les jours ~s** odd *ou* odd-numbered days ▪ **le côté ~** [dans la rue] the uneven numbers **2.** LITTÉR [vers] irregular *(having an odd number of syllables)* **3.** RAIL [voie, train] down.

◆ **impair** [ɛ̃pɛr] *nm* **1.** [bévue] blunder ▪ **faire** *ou* **commettre un ~** to (make a) blunder **2.** JEUX : **l'~** odd numbers ; [à la roulette] impair.

impalpable [ɛ̃palpabl] *adj* impalpable, intangible.

impaludation [ɛ̃palydasjɔ̃] *nf* malarial infection ▪ **~ thérapeutique** malaria therapy.

impaludé, e [ɛ̃palyde] *adj* : **région ~e** malaria-infested *ou* malarious region.

imparable [ɛ̃parabl] *adj* **1.** [coup, ballon] unstoppable **2.** [argument] unanswerable ▪ [logique] irrefutable.

impardonnable [ɛ̃pardɔnabl] *adj* [erreur, oubli] unforgivable, inexcusable ▪ **tu es ~ d'avoir oublié son anniversaire** it's unforgivable of *ou* inexcusable for you to have forgotten her birthday.

imparfait, e [ɛ̃parfɛ, ɛt] *adj* **1.** [incomplet] imperfect, partial ▪ **guérison ~e** incomplete recovery **2.** [personne] imperfect **3.** [inexact] inaccurate.

◆ **imparfait** *nm* LING : **l'~** the imperfect (tense) ▪ **l'~ du subjonctif** the imperfect subjunctive ▪ **à l'~** in the perfect.

imparfaitement [ɛ̃parfɛtmɑ̃] *adv* imperfectly.

imparité [ɛ̃parite] *nf* imparity, oddness.

impartageable [ɛ̃partaʒabl] *adj* [expérience] which cannot be shared ▪ [domaine] indivisible.

impartial, e, aux [ɛ̃parsjal, o] *adj* impartial, unprejudiced, unbiased.

impartialement [ɛ̃parsjalmɑ̃] *adv* impartially, without prejudice *ou* bias.

impartialité [ɛ̃parsjalite] *nf* impartiality, fairness ▪ **juger avec ~** to judge impartially.

impartir [32] [ɛ̃partir] *vt* **1.** [temps] : **~ un délai à qqn** to grant sb an extension ▪ **le temps qui vous était imparti est écoulé** you have used up the time allotted to you **2.** *litt* [pouvoir] : **en vertu des pouvoirs qui me sont impartis** by virtue of the powers (that are) vested in me.

impasse [ɛ̃pas] *nf* **1.** [rue] dead end, cul-de-sac ▪ **'impasse'** 'no through road' **2.** [situation] impasse, blind alley ▪ **il faut absolument faire sortir les négociations de l'~** we must break the deadlock in the negotiations ➔ **~ budgétaire** FIN budget deficit **3.** *arg scol* **j'ai fait une ~ sur la Seconde Guerre mondiale** I missed out *UK ou* skipped (over) *US* World War II in my revision **4.** JEUX finesse ▪ **j'ai fait l'~ au roi** I finessed against the king.

impassibilité [ɛ̃pasibilite] *nf* impassiveness, impassivity, composure ▪ **être d'une grande ~** to show great composure.

impassible [ɛ̃pasibl] *adj* impassive, imperturbable.

impatiemment [ɛ̃pasjamɑ̃] *adv* impatiently ▪ **nous attendons ~ le résultat** we eagerly await the result.

impatience [ɛ̃pasjɑ̃s] *nf* impatience ▪ **avec ~** impatiently, with impatience ▪ **sans ~** patiently.

impatient, e [ɛ̃pasjɑ̃, ɑ̃t] *adj* [personne, geste] impatient ▪ **~ de commencer** impatient to start ▪ **êtes-vous ~ de rentrer?** are you anxious *ou* eager to get home?

◆ **impatiente** *nf* BOT impatiens *spéc*, balsam, busy lizzie *UK*.

impatienter [3] [ɛ̃pasjɑ̃te] *vt* to annoy, to irritate ▪ **son entêtement a fini par m'~** his stubbornness made me lose my patience in the end, I finally lost patience with his stubbornness.

◆ **s'impatienter** *vpi* [dans une attente] to grow *ou* to become impatient ▪ [dans une discussion] to lose one's patience ▪ **s'~ de qqch** to get impatient with sthg ▪ **s'~ contre qqn** to get impatient with sb ▪ *(en usage absolu)* **j'ai fini par m'~** I lost patience in the end.

impavide [ɛ̃pavid] *adj litt* impassive, unruffled, composed.

impayable [ɛ̃pɛjabl] *adj fam* priceless ▪ **il est vraiment ~!** he's priceless *ou* a scream!

impayé, e [ɛ̃pɛje] *adj* [facture] unpaid ▪ [dette] outstanding ▪ **tous les effets ~s le 8 mai** all bills not settled by May 8th.

◆ **impayé** *nm* [somme] unpaid *ou* dishonoured bill ▪ **'les ~s'** 'payments outstanding'.

impec [ɛ̃pɛk] *adj fam* perfect.

impeccable [ɛ̃pekabl] *adj* **1.** [propre et net - intérieur, vêtement] spotless, impeccable ; [- coiffure, ongles] impeccable **2.** [parfait - manières, travail] impeccable, flawless, perfect ▪ **10 heures, ça te va? – oui, ~!** *fam* would 10 o'clock suit you? – yes, great *ou* perfect! **3.** RELIG impeccable.

impeccablement [ɛ̃pekabləmɑ̃] *adv* impeccably ▪ **elle parle ~ russe** she speaks impeccable *ou* perfect Russian.

impénétrabilité [ɛ̃penetrabilite] *nf* impenetrability.

impénétrable [ɛ̃penetrabl] *adj* impenetrable.

impénitent, e [ɛ̃penitɑ̃, ɑ̃t] *adj* **1.** RELIG impenitent, unrepentant **2.** [buveur, fumeur] inveterate.

impensable [ɛ̃pɑ̃sabl] *adj* [inconcevable] unthinkable, inconceivable ▪ [incroyable] unbelievable ▪ **ç'aurait été ~ il y a dix ans** it would have been unthinkable ten years ago.

imper [ɛ̃pɛr] *nm* raincoat, mac *UK*.

impératif, ive [ɛ̃peratif, iv] *adj* **1.** [qui s'impose - mesure, intervention] imperative, urgent, vital ; [- besoin, date] imperative ▪ **il est ~ de...** it is imperative *ou* essential to... **2.** [de commandement - appel, geste, voix] imperative, peremptory **3.** LING imperative.

◆ **impératif** *nm* **1.** *(souvent pl)* [exigence] requirement, necessity ▪ **les ~s de la mode** the dictates of fashion ▪ **les ~s du direct** *fam* the constraints of live broadcasting **2.** LING : **l'~** the imperative (mood) ▪ **verbe à l'~** imperative verb, verb in the imperative.

impérativement [ɛ̃perativmɑ̃] *adv* : **il faut que je termine ~ pour ce soir** it's essential that I should finish tonight.

impératrice [ɛ̃peratris] *nf* empress.

imperceptibilité [ɛ̃pɛrsɛptibilite] *nf* imperceptibility.

imperceptible [ɛ̃pɛrsɛptibl] *adj* imperceptible ▪ **de manière ~** imperceptibly.

imperceptiblement [ɛ̃pɛrsɛptibləmɑ̃] *adv* imperceptibly.

imperdable [ɛ̃pɛrdabl] ◇ *adj* : **ce match est ~!** this is a match you can't lose!

◇ *nf Suisse* safety pin.

imperfection [ɛ̃pɛrfɛksjɔ̃] *nf* **1.** [défaut - d'un tissu, d'un cuir] imperfection, defect ; [- d'une personne] imperfection, shortcoming ; [- d'un style, d'une œuvre] imperfection, weakness ; [- d'un système] shortcoming ▪ **toutes les petites ~s de la peau** all the small blemishes on the skin **2.** [état] imperfection.

impérial, e, aux [ɛ̃perjal, o] *adj* **1.** HIST & POLIT imperial **2.** *fig* [allure, manières] imperial, majestic **3.** COMM imperial, of superior quality.

◆ **impériale** *nf* **1.** [étage] top deck ▪ **bus/rame à ~e** double-decker bus/train **2.** [dais] crown ▪ [de lit] (domed) tester **3.** JEUX royal flush **4.** [barbe] imperial.

impérialisme [ɛ̃perjalism] *nm* imperialism.

impérialiste [ɛ̃perjalist] *adj* & *nmf* imperialist.

impérieusement [ɛ̃perjøzmɑ̃] *adv* **1.** [impérativement] absolutely **2.** [autoritairement] imperiously, peremptorily.

impérieux, euse [ɛ̃perjø, øz] *adj* **1.** [irrésistible - désir] urgent, compelling, pressing ■ **un besoin ~** a pressing need **2.** [de commandement - appel, personne, voix] imperious, peremptory ■ **d'un ton ~** in a commanding tone.

impérissable [ɛ̃perisabl] *adj sout* [vérité] eternal, imperishable *sout* ■ [splendeur] undying ■ [souvenir] enduring ■ **garder un souvenir ~ de qqch** to have an enduring memory of sthg.

imperméabilisant, e [ɛ̃pɛrmeabilizɑ̃, ɑ̃t] *adj* waterproofing.
◆ **imperméabilisant** *nm* waterproofing (substance).

imperméabilisation [ɛ̃pɛrmeabilizasjɔ̃] *nf* waterproofing.

imperméabiliser [3] [ɛ̃pɛrmeabilize] *vt* to (make) waterproof *ou* rainproof.

imperméabilité [ɛ̃pɛrmeabilite] *nf* **1.** GÉOL & TEXT [vêtement] impermeability **2.** *sout* [incompréhension] imperviousness.

imperméable [ɛ̃pɛrmeabl] ◇ *adj* **1.** GÉOL impermeable **2.** [combinaison de plongée] waterproof ■ [enduit intérieur] waterproof, water-resistant *spéc* ■ [vêtement, chaussure, enduit extérieur] waterproof, rainproof **3.** *sout* [insensible] : **être ~ à** to be impervious to.
◇ *nm* [vêtement] raincoat.

impersonnalité [ɛ̃pɛrsɔnalite] *nf* impersonality.

impersonnel, elle [ɛ̃pɛrsɔnɛl] *adj* **1.** [atmosphère, décor, ton] impersonal, cold ■ **de manière ~le** impersonally **2.** [approche, texte] impersonal **3.** LING impersonal.

impersonnellement [ɛ̃pɛrsɔnɛlmɑ̃] *adv* impersonally.

impertinence [ɛ̃pɛrtinɑ̃s] *nf* **1.** [caractère] impertinence, impudence, effrontery **2.** [parole] impertinence, impertinent remark **3.** *sout* [manque d'à-propos] irrelevance, inappropriateness.

impertinent, e [ɛ̃pɛrtinɑ̃, ɑ̃t] ◇ *adj* **1.** [impudent] impertinent, impudent **2.** *sout* [question, remarque] irrelevant.
◇ *nm, f* impertinent person.

imperturbable [ɛ̃pɛrtyrbabl] *adj* imperturbable.

imperturbablement [ɛ̃pɛrtyrbabləmɑ̃] *adv* imperturbably.

impétigo [ɛ̃petigo] *nm* impetigo.

impétrant, e [ɛ̃petrɑ̃, ɑ̃t] *nm, f* recipient.

impétueux, euse [ɛ̃petɥø, øz] *adj* **1.** [personne] impetuous, rash, impulsive ■ [tempérament] fiery, impetuous **2.** *litt* [flot, rythme] impetuous, wild.

impétuosité [ɛ̃petɥozite] *nf* **1.** [d'une personne, d'un tempérament] impetuousness, impetuosity, foolhardiness **2.** *litt* [des flots, d'un rythme] impetuosity, impetuousness.

impie [ɛ̃pi] *sout* ◇ *adj* impious ■ **des paroles ~s** blasphemy.
◇ *nmf* impious *ou* ungodly person.

impiété [ɛ̃pjete] *nf* **1.** [caractère] impiety, ungodliness **2.** [parole, acte] impiety.

impitoyable [ɛ̃pitwajabl] *adj* [juge, adversaire] merciless, pitiless ■ [haine, combat] merciless, relentless.

impitoyablement [ɛ̃pitwajabləmɑ̃] *adv* mercilessly, ruthlessly, pitilessly.

implacable [ɛ̃plakabl] *adj* **1.** [acharné, inflexible] implacable *sout* **2.** *litt* [inéluctable] relentless, implacable *sout* ■ **avec une logique ~** with relentless logic.

implacablement [ɛ̃plakabləmɑ̃] *adv* implacably, mercilessly, relentlessly.

implant [ɛ̃plɑ̃] *nm* implant ■ **~ dentaire** (dental) implant.

implantation [ɛ̃plɑ̃tasjɔ̃] *nf* **1.** [établissement] establishment, setting up ■ **l'~ d'une usine a permis la création de cent emplois** the setting up of a factory has led to the creation of one hundred jobs **2.** [des cheveux] hairline **3.** MÉD (lateral) implantation ■ [en odontologie] implant **4.** ÉLECTRON implantation.

implanté, e [ɛ̃plɑ̃te] *adj* : **une tradition bien ~e** a well-established tradition ■ **notre société est ~e dans 10 pays** our company operates in 10 countries.

implanter [3] [ɛ̃plɑ̃te] *vt* **1.** [bâtiment] to locate ■ [entreprise] to set up, to establish, to locate ■ [idées] to implant ■ [coutumes, mode] to introduce ■ [parti politique] to establish ■ **~ un produit sur le marché** to establish a product on the market **2.** MÉD to implant **3.** CONSTR [tracer] to stake out *(sép)*.
◆ **s'implanter** *vpi* [entreprise, ville] to be set up *ou* located *ou* established ■ [peuple] to settle.

implication [ɛ̃plikasjɔ̃] *nf* **1.** [participation] involvement, implication **2.** PHILOS & MATH implication.
◆ **implications** *nfpl* implications, consequences.

implicite [ɛ̃plisit] *adj* **1.** [tacite] implicit **2.** INFORM [option, valeur] default *(modif)*.

implicitement [ɛ̃plisitmɑ̃] *adv* **1.** [tacitement] implicitly **2.** INFORM : **toutes les variables prennent ~ la valeur 0** all the variables have the default value 0.

impliqué *adj* : **être ~ dans qqch** to be involved in sthg.

impliquer [3] [ɛ̃plike] *vt* **1.** [compromettre] to implicate, to involve ■ **~ qqn dans qqch** to implicate sb in sthg **2.** [supposer - suj: terme, phrase] to imply **3.** [entraîner - dépenses, remaniements] to imply, to involve, to entail **4.** MATH : **p implique q** if p then q.
◆ **s'impliquer dans** *vp+prép* : **s'~ dans qqch** to get (o.s.) involved in sthg.

implorant, e [ɛ̃plɔrɑ̃, ɑ̃t] *adj sout* [voix, regard, geste] imploring, beseeching ■ **d'un ton ~** imploringly, beseechingly.

imploration [ɛ̃plɔrasjɔ̃] *nf sout* entreaty.

implorer [3] [ɛ̃plɔre] *vt* **1.** [solliciter] to implore, to beseech ■ **~ le pardon de qqn** to beg sb's forgiveness **2.** *sout* [supplier] : **~ qqn de faire qqch** to implore *ou* to beg sb to do sthg.

imploser [3] [ɛ̃ploze] *vi* to implode.

implosif, ive [ɛ̃plozif, iv] *adj* PHON implosive.

implosion [ɛ̃plozjɔ̃] *nf* PHON & PHYS implosion.

impoli, e [ɛ̃pɔli] ◇ *adj* impolite, rude, uncivil ■ **être ~ envers qqn** to be impolite *ou* rude to sb.
◇ *nm, f* impolite *ou* ill-mannered person.

impoliment [ɛ̃pɔlimɑ̃] *adv* impolitely, rudely.

impolitesse [ɛ̃pɔlitɛs] *nf* **1.** [caractère] impoliteness, rudeness ■ **il est d'une ~!** he's so rude! **2.** [acte, parole] impolite thing ■ **commettre une ~** to do something rude *ou* impolite.

impondérable [ɛ̃pɔ̃derabl] ◇ *adj* imponderable.
◇ *nm (gén pl)* unknown quantity, imponderable.

impopulaire [ɛ̃pɔpylɛr] *adj* [mesure, dirigeant] unpopular.

impopularité [ɛ̃pɔpylarite] *nf* unpopularity.

importable [ɛ̃pɔrtabl] *adj* **1.** ÉCON importable **2.** [habit] unwearable.

importance [ɛ̃pɔrtɑ̃s] *nf* **1.** [qualitative - d'une décision, d'un discours, d'une personne] importance, significance ■ **avoir de l'~** to be of importance, to matter ■ **sans ~** [personne] unimportant, insignificant ; [fait] of no importance, irrelevant ; [somme] insignificant, trifling ■ **que disais-tu? – c'est sans ~** what were you saying? – it's of no importance *ou* it doesn't matter ■ **accorder** *ou* **attacher trop d'~ à qqch** to attach too much importance *ou* significance to sthg ■ **se donner de l'~** to act important **2.** [quantitative - d'un effectif, d'une agglomération] size ; [- de dégâts, de pertes] extent ■ **prendre de l'~** to expand ■ **une entreprise d'~ moyenne** a medium-sized business.
◆ **d'importance** *loc adj* important.

important, e [ɛ̃pɔrtɑ̃, ɑ̃t] ◇ *adj* **1.** [qualitativement - découverte, témoignage, rencontre, personnalité] important ; [- date, changement] important, significant ; [- conséquence] important, serious, far-reaching ; [- position] important, high ■ **peu**

~ [petit] small ; [insignifiant] unimportant ■ **c'est ~ pour moi de connaître la vérité** finding out the truth matters *ou* is important to me **2.** [quantitativement - collection, effectif] sizeable, large ; [- augmentation, proportion] substantial, significant, large ; [- somme] substantial, considerable, sizeable ; [- retard] considerable ; [- dégâts] considerable, extensive **3.** [présomptueux] : **prendre** *ou* **se donner des airs ~s** to act important, to give o.s. airs.
◇ *nm, f* [personne] : **faire l'~** to act important.
◆ **important** *nm* : **l'~, c'est de...** the important thing is to..., the main thing is to...

importateur, trice [ɛ̃pɔrtatœr, tris] ◇ *adj* importing ■ **les pays ~s de pétrole** oil-importing countries.
◇ *nm, f* importer.

importation [ɛ̃pɔrtasjɔ̃] *nf* **1.** ÉCON importation, importing ■ **produit d'~** imported product, import **2.** [d'un mouvement, d'une invention] introduction, importation ■ [d'un animal] importing.
◆ **importations** *nfpl* COMM imports ■ **nos ~s dépassent nos exportations** we import more than we export.

importer [3] [ɛ̃pɔrte] ◇ *vt* **1.** [marchandises, main-d'œuvre, brevets] to import ■ [mode] to introduce, to import ■ [animal, végétal] to import, to introduce into the country ■ [idée] to import, to bring in *(sép)* ■ **musique importée des États-Unis** music imported from the United States **2.** INFORM to import.
◇ *vi* [avoir de l'importance] to matter ■ **peu importe** it doesn't matter ■ **qu'importe!** what does it matter! ■ **ce qui importe avant tout c'est que tu sois heureuse** the most important thing *ou* what matters most is your happiness ■ **peu m'importe!** it doesn't matter to me! ■ *(tournure impersonnelle)* **il importe de partir/qu'elle vienne** it is necessary to leave/for her to come.

import-export [ɛ̃pɔrɛkspɔr] (*pl* **imports-exports**) *nm* import-export ■ **il travaille dans l'~** he works in the import-export business.

importun, e [ɛ̃pɔrtœ̃, yn] ◇ *adj* [question] importunate *sout*, untimely ■ [visite, visiteur] unwelcome, importunate *sout* ■ **je crains d'être ~ en restant** *sout* I would not wish to outstay my welcome.
◇ *nm, f* pest, nuisance.

importunément [ɛ̃pɔrtynemɑ̃] *adv litt* **1.** [fâcheusement] irritatingly, importunately *sout* **2.** [mal à propos] inopportunely.

importuner [3] [ɛ̃pɔrtyne] *vt sout* [suj: musique, insecte] to bother, to disturb, to annoy ■ [suj: personne] to importune *sout*, to bother ■ **de crainte de les ~ avec mes problèmes** for fear of bothering them with my problems.

importunité [ɛ̃pɔrtynite] *nf sout* [d'une question, d'une arrivée] untimeliness, importunity *sout*.

imposable [ɛ̃pozabl] *adj* taxable ■ **non ~** nontaxable.

imposant, e [ɛ̃pozɑ̃, ɑ̃t] *adj* imposing, impressive.

imposé, e [ɛ̃poze] ◇ *adj* **1.** SPORT ▷ **figure 2.** COMM ▷ **prix**.
◇ *nm, f* [contribuable] taxpayer.

imposer [3] [ɛ̃poze] *vt* **1.** [fixer - règlement, discipline] to impose, to enforce ; [- méthode, délai, corvée] to impose ■ **~ qqch à qqn** to force sthg on sb ■ **~ le silence à qqn** to impose silence on sb ■ **~ un effort à qqn** to force sb to make an effort ■ **~ sa volonté/son point de vue** to impose one's will/one's ideas ■ **~ sa loi (à qqn)** to lay down the law (to sb)
2. [provoquer] : **~ l'admiration/le respect** to command admiration/respect ■ **cette affaire impose la prudence/la discrétion** this matter requires prudence/discretion
3. [rendre célèbre] : **~ son nom** [personne] to make o.s. known ; [entreprise] to become established
4. ÉCON to tax ■ **imposé à 33 %** taxed at 33%
5. *loc* **en ~** to be impressive ■ **en ~ à qqn** to impress sb ■ **s'en laisser ~** to let o.s. be impressed
6. IMPR to impose.
◆ **s'imposer** ◇ *vpi* **1.** [se faire accepter de force] to impose o.s. ■ **de peur de s'~** for fear of being in the way *ou* of imposing
2. [se faire reconnaître] to stand out ■ **s'~ dans un domaine** to make a name for o.s. in a field ■ **elle s'impose par son talent** her talent makes her stand out
3. [être inévitable] to be necessary ■ **cette dernière remarque ne s'imposait pas** that last remark was unnecessary *ou* uncalled for.
◇ *vpt* [se fixer] : **~ qqch** to impose sthg on o.s. ■ **s'~ un effort/un sacrifice** to force o.s. to make an effort/a sacrifice.

imposition [ɛ̃pozisjɔ̃] *nf* **1.** ÉCON [procédé] taxation ■ [impôt] tax **2.** IMPR imposition **3.** RELIG : **~ des mains** laying on *ou* imposition *sout* of hands.

impossibilité [ɛ̃pɔsibilite] *nf* impossibility ■ **être dans l'~ de faire qqch** to be unable to do sthg.

impossible [ɛ̃pɔsibl] ◇ *adj* **1.** [infaisable] impossible ■ **il est ~ de...** it's impossible *ou* not possible to... ■ **il m'est ~ de te répondre** it's impossible for me to give you an answer, I can't possibly answer you ■ **désolé, cela m'est ~** I'm sorry but I can't (possibly) ■ **il n'est pas ~ que je vienne aussi** I might (just) *ou* there's a chance I might come too ➲ **~ n'est pas français** *prov* there's no such word as "can't" **2.** [insupportable - personne] impossible, unbearable ; [- situation, vie] impossible, intolerable **3.** *fam* [extravagant] impossible, ridiculous, incredible ■ **à des heures ~s** at the most ungodly hours ■ **un nom ~** a preposterous name.
◇ *nm* : **ne me demande pas l'~** don't ask me to do the impossible *ou* to perform miracles ■ **nous ferons l'~** we will do our utmost, we will move heaven and earth ➲ **à l'~ nul n'est tenu** *prov* nobody is expected to do the impossible.
◆ **par impossible** *loc adv* : **si par ~** if by any (remote) chance *ou* by some miracle.

imposteur [ɛ̃pɔstœr] *nm* impostor.

imposture [ɛ̃pɔstyr] *nf litt* fraud, (piece of) trickery, deception.

impôt [ɛ̃po] *nm* **1.** [prélèvement] tax ■ **l'~** taxation, taxes ■ **les ~s** income tax ■ **payer des ~s** to pay (income) tax ■ **payer 1 000 euros d'~** to pay 1,000 euros in taxes *ou* (in) tax ■ **c'est déductible des ~s** it's tax-deductible ■ **écrire/aller aux ~s** *fam* [à l'hôtel des impôts] to write to/to go and see the tax people ■ **financé par l'~** paid for out of taxes *ou* with the taxpayers' money ➲ **~ sur le capital** capital tax ■ **~ sur le chiffre d'affaires** turnover *ou* cascade *UK* tax ■ **~ direct/indirect** direct/indirect tax ■ **~ foncier** property tax ■ **~ forfaitaire** basic-rate tax ■ **~ sur les grandes fortunes** *former wealth tax* ■ **~s locaux** ≃ council tax *UK*, ≃ local property tax *US* ■ **~ sur les plus-values** capital gains tax ■ **~ progressif** graduated tax ■ **~ sur le revenu** income tax ■ **~ de solidarité sur la fortune** wealth tax ■ **~ sur le transfert des capitaux** capital transfer tax **2.** *fig & litt* **l'~ du sang** the duty to serve one's country.

IMPÔTS LOCAUX

These are taxes levied to finance local, departmental or regional governments. The best-known are the *taxe d'habitation* (paid by rent-paying tenants), the *taxe foncière* (paid by homeowners) and the *taxe professionnelle* (levied on businesses). The rate of each tax is decided at local level.

impotence [ɛ̃pɔtɑ̃s] *nf* loss of mobility *(through old age)*, infirmity.

impotent, e [ɛpɔtɑ̃, ɑ̃t] ◇ *adj* [personne] infirm ■ [membre] withered.
◇ *nm, f* [personne] cripple.

impraticable [ɛ̃pratikabl] *adj* **1.** [col] inaccessible, impassable ■ [fleuve] unnavigable ■ [aérodrome] unfit for use ■ [route] impassable **2.** *litt* [méthode, idée] unfeasible, unworkable, impracticable.

imprécation [ɛ̃prekasjɔ̃] *nf litt* imprecation *litt*, curse ■ **proférer des ~s à l'encontre de qqn** to call down curses upon sb's head, to inveigh against sb *litt*.

imprécatoire [ɛ̃prekatwar] *adj sout* imprecatory *litt*.

imprécis, e [ɛ̃presi, iz] *adj* **1.** [témoignage, souvenir] imprecise, vague **2.** [appareil, instrument] imprecise, inaccurate.

imprécision [ɛ̃presizjɔ̃] *nf* **1.** [d'un souvenir, d'un témoignage] vagueness, imprecision **2.** [d'un appareil, d'un instrument] inaccuracy, lack of precision.

imprégnation [ɛ̃preɲasjɔ̃] *nf* **1.** [d'une matière] impregnation, saturation ■ [d'un esprit] impregnation, inculcation, imbuing ■ **~ alcoolique** blood alcohol level **2.** CONSTR treating, impregnation **3.** MENUIS steeping, impregnation *spéc* **4.** MÉTALL & TRAV PUB impregnation **5.** ZOOL imprinting.

imprégner [18] [ɛ̃preɲe] *vt* **1.** [imbiber] to soak, to impregnate ■ **être imprégné de** to be soaked in, to be impregnated with **2.** [être présent dans] to permeate, to pervade, to fill ■ **l'odeur du tabac imprègne ses vêtements** his clothes reek of tobacco.
◆ **s'imprégner de** *vp+prép* [éponge, bois] to become soaked *ou* impregnated with ■ [air] to become permeated *ou* filled with ■ [personne, esprit] to become immersed in *ou* imbued with.

imprenable [ɛ̃prənabl] *adj* **1.** MIL [ville] impregnable ■ [position] unassailable **2.** [gén] : **vue ~ sur la baie** uninterrupted view of the bay.

imprésario, impresario [ɛ̃presarjo] (*pl* **impresarii** [-ri]) *nm* impresario.

imprescriptible [ɛ̃prɛskriptibl] *adj* **1.** DR imprescriptible, indefeasible **2.** *sout* [éternel] eternal.

impression [ɛ̃presjɔ̃] *nf* **1.** [effet, réaction] impression ■ **faire bonne/mauvaise ~** to make a good/a bad impression ■ **faire une forte** *ou* **grosse ~** to make quite a strong impression ■ **il donne l'~ de s'ennuyer** he seems to be bored
2. [sensation] : **avoir l'~** [croire] : **j'ai l'~ qu'elle ne viendra plus** I have a feeling (that) she won't come ■ **j'ai comme l'~ qu'il mentait** *fam* I have a hunch he was lying ■ **j'ai l'~ d'avoir déjà vécu cette scène** I've got a strong sense of déjà vu
3. [empreinte] impression, mark
4. [motif, dessin] pattern
5. IMPR printing ■ **envoyer un manuscrit à l'~** to send a manuscript off to press *ou* the printer's
6. PHOTO exposure
7. [en peinture] priming, ground.

impressionnable [ɛ̃presjɔnabl] *adj* **1.** [émotif] impressionable ■ **c'est quelqu'un de facilement ~** he's very impressionable **2.** PHOTO (photo) sensitive.

impressionnant, e [ɛ̃presjɔnɑ̃, ɑ̃t] *adj* **1.** [imposant - œuvre, personnalité] impressive ; [- portail, temple] awe-inspiring ; [- exploit] impressive, stunning, sensational ; [- somme] considerable **2.** *sout* [bouleversant] disturbing, upsetting.

impressionner [3] [ɛ̃presjɔne] *vt* **1.** [frapper] to impress ■ **être impressionné par qqch** to be impressed by sthg ■ **se laisser ~** to let o.s. be impressed **2.** [bouleverser] to distress, to upset **3.** PHOTO to expose.

impressionnisme [ɛ̃presjɔnism] *nm* impressionism.

impressionniste [ɛ̃presjɔnist] <> *adj* **1.** ART impressionist **2.** [subjectif] impressionistic.
<> *nmf* impressionist.

imprévisibilité [ɛ̃previzibilite] *nf* unpredictability.

imprévisible [ɛ̃previzibl] *adj* unpredictable, unforeseeable.

imprévision [ɛ̃previzjɔ̃] *nf* lack of foresight.

imprévoyance [ɛ̃prevwajɑ̃s] *nf* [gén] lack of foresight ■ [financière] improvidence.

imprévoyant, e [ɛ̃prevwajɑ̃, ɑ̃t] <> *adj* [gén] lacking (in) foresight ■ [financièrement] improvident.
<> *nm, f* improvident person ■ **les ~s** spendthrifts.

imprévu, e [ɛ̃prevy] *adj* [inattendu] unexpected, unforeseen ■ **de manière ~e** unexpectedly.
◆ **imprévu** *nm* **1.** [les surprises] : **l'~** : **j'adore l'~!** I love surprises! **2.** [événement] unexpected event ■ **sauf ~** *ou* **à moins d'un ~, je serai à l'heure** unless anything unforeseen happens *ou* barring accidents, I'll be on time ■ **les ~s de la vie** life's little surprises **3.** [dépense] unforeseen *ou* hidden expense.

imprimante [ɛ̃primɑ̃t] *nf* printer ■ **~ matricielle** *ou* **par points** (dot) matrix printer ■ **~ (ligne) par ligne** line printer ■ **~ (à) laser** laser printer ■ **~ à bulles d'encre** bubblejet printer ■ **~ à jet d'encre** ink jet printer ■ **~ à impact** impact printer ■ **~ à marguerite** daisywheel printer ■ **~ photo** photo printer.

imprimé [ɛ̃prime] *nm* **1.** [brochure, livre] printed book *ou* booklet ■ **'~s'** 'printed matter' **2.** [formulaire] (printed) form **3.** [étoffe] printed fabric *ou* material.

imprimer [3] [ɛ̃prime] *vt* **1.** IMPR [fabriquer] to print (out) *(sép)* ■ [publier] to print, to publish **2.** TEXT to print **3.** [transmettre] to transmit, to impart, to give ■ **~ un mouvement à qqch** to impart *ou* to transmit a movement to sthg **4.** *litt* [marquer] to imprint ■ **il voulait ~ tous ces détails dans sa mémoire** he wanted to impress all these details on his memory.
◆ **s'imprimer** *vpi* to be printed.

imprimerie [ɛ̃primri] *nf* **1.** [technique] printing **2.** [établissement] printing works *(sing)*, printer's ■ [atelier] printing office *ou* house ■ PRESSE print room ➲ **l'Imprimerie nationale** *the French government stationery office* **3.** [matériel] printing press *ou* machines ■ [jouet] printing set **4.** [industrie] : **l'~** the printing industry.

L'IMPRIMERIE NATIONALE

The *Imprimerie nationale* prints official state documents for the various government departments. It also offers a highly qualified printing service especially when foreign alphabets or special printing techniques are required.

imprimeur [ɛ̃primœr] *nm* [industriel] printer ■ [ouvrier] printer, print worker.

improbabilité [ɛ̃prɔbabilite] *nf* improbability.

improbable [ɛ̃prɔbabl] *adj* unlikely, improbable.

improductif, ive [ɛ̃prɔdyktif, iv] <> *adj* unproductive.
<> *nm, f* unproductive person ■ **les ~s** the nonproductive members of society.

improductivité [ɛ̃prɔdyktivite] *nf* unproductiveness, nonproductiveness.

impromptu, e [ɛ̃prɔ̃pty] *adj* [improvisé] impromptu, unexpected, surprise *(modif)* ■ **faire un discours ~** to give an impromptu *ou* off-the-cuff speech.
◆ **impromptu** *nm* LITTÉR & MUS impromptu.

imprononçable [-ɛprɔnɔ̃sabl] *adj* unpronounceable.

impropre [ɛ̃prɔpr] *adj* **1.** [personne, produit] unsuitable, unsuited, unfit ■ **il est ~ à ce type de travail** he's unsuited to *ou* unsuitable for this kind of work ➲ **produits ~s à la consommation** products not fit *ou* unfit for human consumption **2.** [terme] inappropriate.

improprement [ɛ̃prɔprəmɑ̃] *adv* incorrectly, improperly.

impropriété [ɛ̃prɔprijete] *nf* **1.** [caractère] incorrectness, impropriety *sout* **2.** [terme] mistake, impropriety *sout*.

improvisateur, trice [ɛ̃prɔvizatœr, tris] <> *adj* improvisational, improvising.
<> *nm, f* improviser, improvisor.

improvisation [ɛ̃prɔvizasjɔ̃] *nf* **1.** [gén] improvisation, improvising **2.** MUS & THÉÂTRE improvisation ■ **faire de l'~** to improvise.

improvisé, e [ɛ̃prɔvize] *adj* [discours] improvised, extempore *sout* ■ [explication] off-the-cuff, ad hoc ■ [mesure, réforme] hurried, makeshift, improvised ■ [décision] snap ■ **un repas ~** a makeshift meal.

improviser [3] [ɛ̃prɔvize] <> *vt* to improvise ■ **~ une explication** to give an off-the-cuff explanation ■ **on l'a improvisé trésorier** they set him up as treasurer ad hoc.
<> *vi* **1.** [parler spontanément] to improvise **2.** MUS to improvise.
◆ **s'improviser** <> *vp (emploi passif)* to be improvised ■ **l'orthographe, ça ne s'improvise pas** you can't just make spelling up as you go along.
<> *vpi* : **s'~ journaliste/photographe** to act as a journalist/photographer ■ **on ne s'improvise pas peintre** you don't become a painter overnight *ou* just like that.

improviste [ɛ̃prɔvist] ◆ **à l'improviste** *loc adv* unexpectedly, without warning ▪ **arriver à l'~** to turn up unexpectedly *ou* without warning.

imprudemment [ɛ̃prydamɑ̃] *adv* recklessly, carelessly, imprudently ▪ **agir ~** to act foolishly *ou* unwisely.

imprudence [ɛ̃prydɑ̃s] *nf* **1.** [caractère] imprudence, carelessness, foolhardiness **2.** [acte] careless act *ou* action ▪ **commettre une ~** to do something stupid *ou* thoughtless *ou* careless ▪ **il a commis l'~ d'en parler aux journalistes** he was stupid enough to talk to the press about it ▪ **pas d'~s!** be careful!, don't do anything silly!

imprudent, e [ɛ̃prydɑ̃, ɑ̃t] ◇ *adj* **1.** [conducteur] careless ▪ [joueur] reckless **2.** [acte, comportement] unwise, imprudent ▪ [remarque] foolish, careless, unwise ▪ [projet] foolish, ill-considered ▪ [décision] rash, unwise, ill-advised.
◇ *nm, f* [personne] careless *ou* reckless person.

impubère [ɛ̃pybɛr] *adj* prepubescent, preadolescent.

impubliable [ɛ̃pyblijabl] *adj* unpublishable, unprintable.

impudemment [ɛ̃pydamɑ̃] *adv* impudently, insolently, brazenly.

impudence [ɛ̃pydɑ̃s] *nf* **1.** [caractère] impudence, insolence, brazenness **2.** [action] impudent act ▪ [remarque] impudent remark.

impudent, e [ɛ̃pydɑ̃, ɑ̃t] ◇ *adj* impudent, insolent, brazen.
◇ *nm, f* impudent person.

impudeur [ɛ̃pydœr] *nf* **1.** [immodestie] immodesty, shamelessness **2.** [impudence] brazenness, shamelessness.

impudique [ɛ̃pydik] *adj* **1.** [immodeste] immodest, shameless **2.** [indécent] shameless, indecent.

impuissance [ɛ̃pɥisɑ̃s] *nf* **1.** [faiblesse] powerlessness, helplessness **2.** [incapacité] inability, powerlessness ▪ **~ à faire qqch** inability to do sthg **3.** MÉD & PSYCHOL impotence.

impuissant, e [ɛ̃pɥisɑ̃, ɑ̃t] *adj* **1.** [vain] powerless, helpless ▪ **être ~ à faire qqch** to be powerless to do sthg **2.** MÉD & PSYCHOL impotent.
◆ **impuissant** *nm* MÉD & PSYCHOL impotent (man).

impulsif, ive [ɛ̃pylsif, iv] ◇ *adj* impulsive.
◇ *nm, f* impulsive person.

impulsion [ɛ̃pylsjɔ̃] *nf* **1.** MÉCAN & PHYS impulse ▪ ÉLECTRON pulse, impulse **2.** *fig* [dynamisme] impetus, impulse ▪ **donner une ~ au commerce** to give an impetus to *ou* to boost trade ▪ **sous l'~ des dirigeants syndicaux** spurred on by the union leaders **3.** [élan] impulse ▪ **céder à une ~** to give in to an impulse ▪ **sous l'~ de la haine** spurred on *ou* driven by hatred ▪ **sur *ou* sous l'~ du moment** on the spur of the moment **4.** ARM impulse **5.** PSYCHOL impulsion.

impulsivement [ɛ̃pylsivmɑ̃] *adv* impulsively.

impulsivité [ɛ̃pylsivite] *nf* impulsiveness.

impunément [ɛ̃pynemɑ̃] *adv* with impunity.

impuni, e [ɛ̃pyni] *adj* unpunished.

impunité [ɛ̃pynite] *nf* impunity ▪ **en toute ~** with impunity.

impur, e [ɛ̃pyr] *adj* **1.** *sout* [pensée, sentiment] impure, unclean ▪ [air, eau] impure, foul ▪ [style] impure ▪ [race] mixed, mongrel **2.** MÉTALL impure.

impureté [ɛ̃pyrte] *nf* **1.** [caractère] impurity, foulness **2.** [élément] impurity ▪ **l'eau contient de nombreuses ~s** the water contains numerous impurities **3.** *litt* [impudicité] lewdness **4.** ÉLECTRON impure atom.

imputable [ɛ̃pytabl] *adj* **1.** [attribuable] : **~ à** imputable *ou* ascribable *ou* attributable to **2.** FIN : **~ sur** [crédit] chargeable *ou* to be credited to ; [débit] to be debited from.

imputation [ɛ̃pytasjɔ̃] *nf* **1.** [accusation] charge, imputation *sout* **2.** FIN charging.

imputer [3] [ɛ̃pyte] *vt* **1.** [attribuer] : **~ un crime à qqn** to impute a crime to sb ▪ **~ ses échecs à la malchance** to put one's failures down to bad luck **2.** FIN : **~ des frais à un budget** [déduire] to deduct expenses from a budget ▪ **~ une somme à un budget** to allocate a sum to a budget.

imputrescible [ɛ̃pytresibl] *adj* rot-resistant, antirot.

in [in] *adj inv fam* in, trendy.

INA [ina] (*abr de* **Institut national de l'audiovisuel**) *npr m national television archive.*

inabordable [inabɔrdabl] *adj* [lieu] inaccessible ▪ **l'île/le port est ~ par mauvais temps** the island/the harbour is inaccessible in bad weather ▮ [personne] unapproachable, inaccessible ▪ [prix] exorbitant ▪ [produit, service] exorbitantly priced.

inabouti, e [inabuti] *adj* unsuccessful, failed.

inabrogeable [inabrɔʒabl] *adj* unrepealable.

inaccentué, e [inaksɑ̃tɥe] *adj* [voyelle] unstressed ▪ [syllabe] unstressed, unaccentuated ▪ [pronom] atonic.

inacceptable [inaksɛptabl] *adj* [mesure, proposition] unacceptable ▪ [propos, comportement] unacceptable, intolerable, inadmissible.

inaccessibilité [inaksesibilite] *nf* inaccessibility.

inaccessible [inaksesibl] *adj* **1.** [hors d'atteinte - sommet] inaccessible, out-of-reach, unreachable ▪ [irréalisable - objectif, rêve] unfeasible, unrealizable ▪ [inabordable - personne] unapproachable, inaccessible ▪ [obscur - ouvrage] inaccessible, opaque **2.** [indifférent] : **être ~ à la pitié** to be incapable of feeling pity.

inaccompli, e [inakɔ̃pli] *adj* **1.** [inachevé] unaccomplished **2.** LING imperfective.
◆ **inaccompli** *nm* LING imperfective.

inaccoutumé, e [inakutyme] *adj* unusual, unaccustomed ▪ **~ à obéir** unused *ou* unaccustomed to obeying.

inachevé, e [inaʃve] *adj* [non terminé] unfinished, uncompleted ▪ [incomplet] incomplete.

inachèvement [inaʃɛvmɑ̃] *nm* incompletion.

inactif, ive [inaktif, iv] ◇ *adj* **1.** [personne - oisive] inactive, idle ; [- sans travail] non-working **2.** [traitement, produit] ineffective **3.** BOURSE & COMM slack, slow **4.** OPT (optically) inactive **5.** GÉOL : **volcan ~** dormant volcano.
◇ *nm, f* : **les ~s** SOCIOL the non-working population, those not in active employment.

inaction [inaksjɔ̃] *nf* [absence d'activité] inaction ▪ [oisiveté] idleness, lethargy.

inactiver [3] [inaktive] *vt* to inactivate.

inactivité [inaktivite] *nf* inactivity ▪ **une période d'~** a slack period ▪ **en ~** ADMIN & MIL not in active service.

inadaptation [inadaptasjɔ̃] *nf* maladjustment ▪ **~ à la vie scolaire** failure to adapt to school life ▪ **l'~ du réseau routier aux besoins actuels** the inadequacy of the road system to cope with present-day traffic.

inadapté, e [inadapte] ◇ *adj* **1.** [enfant] with special needs, maladjusted ▪ **enfants ~s au système scolaire** children who fail to adapt to the educational system ➊ **enfance ~e** children with special needs **2.** [outil, méthode] : **~ à** unsuited *ou* not adapted to.
◇ *nm, f* [adulte] person with social difficulties, social misfit *péj* ▪ [enfant] child with special needs, maladjusted child.

inadéquat, e [inadekwa, at] *adj sout* inadequate, inappropriate ▪ **~ à qqch** inadequate to *ou* for sthg.

inadéquation [inadekwasjɔ̃] *nf sout* inadequacy, inappropriateness.

inadmissible [inadmisibl] *adj* inadmissible, intolerable, unacceptable.

inadvertance [inadvɛrtɑ̃s] *nf sout* oversight, slip (up), inadvertence.
◆ **par inadvertance** *loc adv* inadvertently, by mistake.

inaliénable [inaljenabl] *adj* inalienable, unalienable.

inaltérable [inalterabl] *adj* **1.** [métal] stable ■ [couleur] permanent, fast ■ **~ à l'air** air-resistant ◉ **peinture ~** non-fade paint **2.** [amitié] steadfast ■ [haine] eternal ■ [espoir] unfailing, steadfast ■ [humeur, courage] unfailing ■ [optimisme] steadfast, unshakeable ■ **bonne humeur ~** unfailing good humour.

inaltéré, e [inaltere] *adj* **1.** [bois] unwarped **2.** [sentiment] unchanged.

inamical, e, aux [inamikal, o] *adj* unfriendly, inimical.

inamovible [inamɔvibl] *adj* **1.** ADMIN [fonctionnaire] permanent, irremovable **2.** [fixé] fixed.

inanimé, e [inanime] *adj* **1.** [mort] lifeless ■ [évanoui] unconscious **2.** LING inanimate ■ **objets ~s** inanimate objects.

inanité [inanite] *nf* futility, pointlessness.

inanition [inanisjɔ̃] *nf* [faim] starvation ■ [épuisement] total exhaustion, inanition *spéc* ■ **tomber/mourir d'~** *pr* to faint/to die with hunger ; *fig & hum* to be starving.

inapaisable [inapɛzabl] *adj litt* [soif] unquenchable ■ [faim] voracious, insatiable ■ [chagrin, souffrance] unappeasable.

inapaisé, e [inapeze] *adj litt* [soif] unquenched ■ [faim] unsatiated ■ [chagrin, souffrance] unappeased.

inaperçu, e [inapɛrsy] *adj* unnoticed ■ **passer ~** to go unnoticed.

inapplicable [inaplikabl] *adj* inapplicable, not applicable.

inappliqué, e [inaplike] *adj* **1.** [loi, règlement] not applied **2.** [personne] lacking in application.

inappréciable [inapresjabl] *adj* **1.** [précieux] invaluable, priceless **2.** [difficile à évaluer] inappreciable, imperceptible.

inapprochable [inaprɔʃabl] *adj* : **il est vraiment ~ en ce moment** you can't say anything to him at the moment.

inapproprié, e [inaprɔprije] *adj* inappropriate ■ **~ à qqch** inappropriate to *ou* unsuitable for sthg.

inapte [inapt] ◇ *adj* **1.** [incapable] unsuitable ■ **être ~ à qqch** to be unsuitable *ou* unfit for sthg ■ **être ~ à faire qqch** to be unfit to do sthg **2.** MIL : **~ (au service militaire)** unfit (for military service).
◇ *nmf* MIL army reject.

inaptitude [inaptityd] *nf* **1.** [incapacité - physique] incapacity, unfitness ; [- mentale] (mental) inaptitude ■ **~ à qqch** unfitness for sthg ■ **~ à faire qqch** unfitness for doing *ou* to do sthg **2.** MIL unfitness (for military service).

inarticulé, e [inartikyle] *adj* inarticulate.

inassimilable [inasimilabl] *adj* [substance] indigestible, unassimilable *spéc* ■ [connaissances] impossible to take in ■ [population] which cannot become integrated.

inassouvi, e [inasuvi] *adj sout* **1.** [soif] unquenched ■ [faim] unappeased, unsatiated **2.** [passion] unappeased, unsatiated ■ [désir] unfulfilled.

inattaquable [inatakabl] *adj* **1.** [personne] beyond reproach *ou* criticism ■ [conduite] unimpeachable, irreproachable ■ [argument, preuve] unassailable, irrefutable, unquestionable ■ [forteresse, lieu] impregnable **2.** MÉTALL corrosion-resistant.

inattendu, e [inatɑ̃dy] *adj* [personne] unexpected ■ [réflexion, événement] unexpected, unforeseen ■ **c'est assez ~ de votre part** I didn't quite expect this from you.

inattentif, ive [inatɑ̃tif, iv] *adj* inattentive ■ **vous êtes trop ~ (à)** you don't pay enough attention (to).

inattention [inatɑ̃sjɔ̃] *nf* lack of attention *ou* concentration, inattentiveness ■ **un moment** *ou* **une minute d'~** a momentary lapse of concentration ■ **faute** *ou* **erreur d'~** careless mistake.

inaudible [inodibl] *adj* **1.** [imperceptible] inaudible **2.** [insupportable] unbearable.

inaugural, e, aux [inogyral, o] *adj* [discours, cérémonie] opening *(modif)*, inaugural ■ [voyage] maiden *(modif)*.

inauguration [inogyrasjɔ̃] *nf* **1.** [cérémonie] inauguration **2.** [commencement] beginning, inauguration, initiation.

inaugurer [3] [inogyre] *vt* **1.** [route, monument, exposition] to inaugurate ■ *fig* [système, méthode] to initiate, to launch **2.** [marquer le début de] to usher in ■ **le changement de gouvernement inaugurait une ère de liberté** the change of government ushered in an era of freedom.

inauthentique [inotɑ̃tik] *adj* inauthentic.

inavouable [inavwabl] *adj* unmentionable, shameful.

inavoué, e [inavwe] *adj* secret, unconfessed.

INC (*abr de* **Institut national de la consommation**) *npr m consumer protection body.*

inca [ɛ̃ka] *adj* Inca.
◆ **Inca** ◇ *nmf* Inca ■ **les Incas** the Inca, the Incas.
◇ *nm* [souverain] Inca.

incalculable [ɛ̃kalkylabl] *adj* **1.** [considérable] incalculable, countless ■ **un nombre ~ de** a countless number of **2.** [imprévisible] incalculable.

incandescence [ɛ̃kɑ̃desɑ̃s] *nf* incandescence ■ **être en ~** to be incandescent ■ **porté à ~** heated until glowing, incandescent.

incandescent, e [ɛ̃kɑ̃desɑ̃, ɑ̃t] *adj* incandescent.

incantation [ɛ̃kɑ̃tasjɔ̃] *nf* incantation.

incantatoire [ɛ̃kɑ̃tatwar] *adj* incantatory *sout* ■ **formule ~, paroles ~s** incantation.

incapable [ɛ̃kapabl] ◇ *adj* **1.** [par incompétence] incapable, incompetent, inefficient ■ **~ de : être ~ de faire qqch** to be incapable of doing sthg ■ **elle était ~ de répondre** she was unable to answer, she couldn't answer ■ **je serais bien ~ de le dire** I really wouldn't know, I really couldn't tell you **2.** [par nature] : **~ de : être ~ de qqch** to be incapable of sthg ■ **elle est ~ d'amour** she's incapable of loving *ou* love ■ **elle est ~ de méchanceté** there's no malice in her ■ **être ~ de faire** to be incapable of doing **3.** DR incapable.
◇ *nmf* **1.** [incompétent] incompetent **2.** DR person under disability.

incapacité [ɛ̃kapasite] *nf* **1.** [impossibilité] incapacity, inability ■ **être dans l'~ de faire qqch** to be unable to do sthg ■ **son ~ à se décider** his incapacity *ou* inability to make up his mind **2.** [incompétence] incapacity, incompetence, inefficiency **3.** MÉD disablement, disability ■ **~ permanente** permanent disablement *ou* disability ■ **~ de travail** industrial disablement **4.** DR (legal) incapacity.

incarcération [ɛ̃karserasjɔ̃] *nf* imprisonment, incarceration *sout*.

incarcérer [18] [ɛ̃karsere] *vt* to incarcerate *sout* ■ **faire ~ qqn** to have sb put in prison ■ **se faire ~** to be put in prison.

incarnat, e [ɛ̃karna, at] *adj* crimson.
◆ **incarnat** *nm* strong red, crimson.

incarnation [ɛ̃karnasjɔ̃] *nf* **1.** MYTHOL & RELIG incarnation **2.** [manifestation] embodiment ■ **elle est l'~ de la bonté** she's the embodiment *ou* personification of goodness.

incarné, e [ɛ̃karne] *adj* **1.** [personnifié] incarnate, personified ■ **le diable ~** the devil incarnate **2.** MÉD : **un ongle ~** an ingrowing *ou* ingrown toenail.

incarner [3] [ɛ̃karne] *vt* **1.** [symboliser] to embody, to personify **2.** [interpréter - personnage] to play.

◆ **s'incarner** *vpi* **1.** RELIG to become incarnate **2.** [se matérialiser] to be embodied **3.** MÉD : **un ongle qui s'incarne** an ingrowing toenail.

incartade [ɛ̃kartad] *nf* **1.** [écart de conduite] misdemeanour, escapade ■ **à la moindre ~, vous serez puni** put one foot wrong and you'll be punished **2.** [d'un cheval] swerve.

incassable [ɛ̃kasabl] *adj* unbreakable.

incendiaire [ɛ̃sɑ̃djɛr] ◇ *adj* **1.** ARM incendiary **2.** [propos] incendiary, inflammatory.
◇ *nmf* fire-raiser *UK*, arsonist.

incendie [ɛ̃sɑ̃di] *nm* **1.** [feu] fire ■ **maîtriser un ~** to bring a fire *ou* blaze under control ▶ **~ criminel** (act of deliberate) arson ■ **~ de forêt** forest fire **2.** *litt* [lumière] blaze, glow **3.** *fig* [violence] fire ■ **l'~ de la révolte** the frenzy of revolt.

incendié, e [ɛ̃sɑ̃dje] ◇ *adj* **1.** [ville, maison] burnt (down), destroyed by fire ■ **les familles ~es seront dédommagées** the families affected by the fire will be given compensation ■ **les bâtiments ~s** the buildings gutted by fire **2.** *litt* [éclairé] ablaze, aglow.
◇ *nm, f* fire victim.

incendier [9] [ɛ̃sɑ̃dje] *vt* **1.** [mettre le feu à] to set fire to, to set on fire **2.** *fam* [invectiver] : **~ qqn** to give sb hell ■ **tu vas te faire ~!** you'll be in for it! **3.** *fig* [brûler] to burn **4.** [esprit, imagination] to stir **5.** *litt* [illuminer] to light up ■ **le soleil couchant incendiait les champs** the setting sun gave the fields a fiery glow.

incertain, e [ɛ̃sɛrtɛ̃, ɛn] *adj* **1.** [peu sûr - personne] uncertain, unsure ■ **être ~ de qqch** to be uncertain *ou* unsure of sthg **2.** [indéterminé - durée, date, quantité] uncertain, undetermined ; [- fait] uncertain, doubtful **3.** [aléatoire - gén] uncertain ; [- temps] unsettled **4.** [vague - contour] indistinct, vague, blurred ; [- lumière] poor **5.** [mal équilibré - démarche, appui] unsteady, uncertain, hesitant.
◆ **incertain** *nm* BOURSE : **coter l'~** to quote in a foreign currency.

incertitude [ɛ̃sɛrtityd] *nf* **1.** [doute, précarité] uncertainty ■ **nous sommes dans l'~** we're uncertain, we're not sure ■ **il est seul face à ses ~s** he's left alone with his doubts **2.** MATH & PHYS uncertainty.
Voir module d'usage

incessamment [ɛ̃sesamɑ̃] *adv* shortly, soon ■ **il doit arriver ~** he'll be here any minute now.

incessant, e [ɛ̃sesɑ̃, ɑ̃t] *adj* [effort] ceaseless, continual ■ [bruit, bavardage] incessant, ceaseless, continual ■ [douleur, pluie] unremitting, constant.

incessible [ɛ̃sesibl] *adj* DR [privilège] non-transferable ■ [droit] inalienable, indefeasible.

inceste [ɛ̃sɛst] *nm* incest.

incestueux, euse [ɛ̃sɛstɥø, øz] *adj* **1.** [personne, relation] incestuous **2.** [né d'un inceste] : **enfant ~** child born of an incestuous relationship.

inchangé, e [ɛ̃ʃɑ̃ʒe] *adj* unchanged, unaltered.

inchavirable [ɛ̃ʃavirabl] *adj* non-capsizing, self-righting.

inchiffrable [ɛ̃ʃifrabl] *adj* unquantifiable, immeasurable ■ **les dégâts sont ~s** it's impossible to put a figure on the damage.

incidemment [ɛ̃sidamɑ̃] *adv* [accessoirement] incidentally, in passing ■ [par hasard] by chance.

incidence [ɛ̃sidɑ̃s] *nf* **1.** [répercussion] effect, repercussion, impact ■ **avoir une ~ sur** to affect ▶ **~ fiscale** ÉCON fiscal effect **2.** AÉRON & PHYS incidence.

incident[1] [ɛ̃sidɑ̃] *nm* **1.** [événement] incident, event ■ [accrochage] incident ■ **sans ~** safely ■ **~ diplomatique/de frontière** diplomatic/border incident ■ **~ technique** technical hitch *ou* incident ▶ **avoir un ~ de parcours** to come across a hitch (on the way) ■ **sa démission n'est qu'un ~ de parcours** his resignation is only a minor incident ■ **l'~ est clos** the matter is (now) closed **2.** DR : **~ (de procédure)** objection (on a point of law) **3.** LITTÉR (little) episode.

incident[2], e [ɛ̃sidɑ̃, ɑ̃t] *adj* **1.** [accessoire - remarque] incidental **2.** LING interpolated, parenthetical **3.** PHYS incident **4.** DR incidental ■ **demande ~e** accessory claim.
◆ **incidente** *nf* GRAMM parenthetical clause.

incinérateur [ɛ̃sineratœr] *nm* incinerator.

incinération [ɛ̃sinerasjɔ̃] *nf* [de chiffons, de papiers] incineration ■ [de cadavres] cremation.

incinérer [18] [ɛ̃sinere] *vt* [linge, papier] to incinerate ■ [cadavre] to cremate.

incise [ɛ̃siz] *nf* **1.** LING interpolated clause **2.** MUS phrase.

inciser [3] [ɛ̃size] *vt* **1.** MÉD to incise, to make an incision in ■ [abcès] to lance **2.** HORT to incise, to cut (a notch into) ■ [pour extraire la résine] to tap.

incisif, ive [ɛ̃sizif, iv] *adj* [ironie, remarque, ton] cutting, incisive, biting ■ [regard] piercing.

incision [ɛ̃sizjɔ̃] *nf* **1.** MÉD cut, incision *spéc* **2.** HORT notch, incision *spéc* ■ **~ annulaire** ringing.

incisive [ɛ̃siziv] ◇ *f* ▷ **incisif.**
◇ *nf* incisor.

incitateur, trice [ɛ̃sitatœr, tris] ◇ *adj* inciting, incentive.
◇ *nm, f* inciter.

incitation [ɛ̃sitasjɔ̃] *nf* [encouragement] incitement, encouragement ■ **c'est une ~ à la violence** it's incitement to *ou* it encourages violence ■ **~ fiscale** ÉCON tax incentive.

inciter [3] [ɛ̃site] *vt* **1.** [encourager] : **~ qqn à faire qqch** to prompt *ou* to encourage sb to do sthg ■ **~ qqn à qqch : cela vous incite à la réflexion/prudence** it makes you stop and think/makes you cautious **2.** DR to incite.

incivil, e [ɛ̃sivil] *adj* *sout* uncivil, impolite.

L'INCERTITUDE

I'm not sure whether it'll work (or not). Je ne suis pas sûr que ça va marcher.

I'm not at all sure (that) I want to go. Je ne suis pas sûr du tout d'avoir envie d'y aller.

It's still not sure whether the contract will be signed. Il y a encore une incertitude sur la signature du contrat.

He doesn't know whether she's coming (or not). Il ne sait pas si elle vient ou pas.

I'm still in two minds about going. Je ne sais toujours pas si je vais y aller.

Nothing has been decided yet. Rien n'est encore sûr.

I doubt (that) he'll pass. Je doute qu'il réussisse.

Who knows why she did it? Va savoir pourquoi elle l'a fait.

It's anyone's guess when they'll get here. Dieu seul sait quand ils arriveront.

incivilité [ɛ̃sivilite] *nf* **1.** [manque de courtoisie] rudeness, disrespect **2.** [fraude] petty crime ▪ [insultes, vandalismes] antisocial behaviour.

incivique [ɛ̃sivik] *adj vieilli* lacking in civic *ou* public spirit, lacking in public-mindedness ▪ **il tient des propos ~s** what he says isn't very public-spirited.

inclassable [ɛ̃klasabl] *adj* unclassifiable.

inclément, e [ɛ̃klemɑ̃, ɑ̃t] *adj litt* **1.** [qui manque d'indulgence] merciless, pitiless **2.** [rigoureux - climat] inclement.

inclinable [ɛ̃klinabl] *adj* reclining, tilting.

inclinaison [ɛ̃klinɛzɔ̃] *nf* **1.** [d'un plan] incline, slant ▪ [d'un avion] tilt, tilting ▪ [d'un toit, des combles, d'un pignon] pitch, slope ▪ [d'un navire] list, listing ▪ **la faible/forte ~ du jardin** the gentle slope/the steepness of the garden ▪ **l'~ de la voie** RAIL & TRAV PUB the gradient, the incline **2.** [d'une partie du corps] : **l'~ de la tête** the tilt of the head **3.** GÉOM inclination, angle **4.** ASTRON declination.

inclination [ɛ̃klinasjɔ̃] *nf* **1.** [tendance] inclination, tendency ▪ [goût] inclination, liking ▪ **avoir une ~ pour la musique** to have a liking for music, to be musically inclined ▪ **une ~ à douter** a tendency to doubt things ▪ **suivre son ~** to follow one's (natural) inclination **2.** [mouvement - de la tête] bow, inclination ; [- du corps] bow ▪ [signe d'acquiescement] nod **3.** *litt* [attirance] : **avoir de l'~ pour qqn** to have a liking for sb ▪ **un mariage d'~** a love match.

incliné, e [ɛ̃kline] *adj* [en pente] sloping ▪ [penché - mur] leaning ; [- dossier, siège] reclining.

incliner [3] [ɛ̃kline] *vt* **1.** [courber] to bend ▪ **~ la tête** *ou* **le front** to bow *ou* to incline *litt* one's head ; [pour acquiescer ou saluer] to nod (one's head) ▪ **~ le corps (en avant)** to bend forward ; [pour saluer] to bow ▪ [pencher - dossier, siège] to tilt ▪ **être incliné** AÉRON to tilt ; NAUT to list
2. *sout* [inciter] : **~ qqn à faire** to encourage *ou* to prompt sb to do ▪ **cette information m'incline à revoir mon point de vue** this news leads me *ou* makes me inclined to reconsider my position ▪ **~ qqn à la rigueur** to encourage sb to be strict.
◆ **incliner à** *v+prép* to tend to *ou* towards, to incline towards ▪ **j'incline à penser qu'elle a tort** I tend *ou* I'm inclined to think she's wrong.
◆ **s'incliner** *vpi* **1.** [être penché - mur] to lean (over) ; [- toit, route] to slope ; [- avion] to tilt, to bank ; [- navire] to list ; [- siège] to tilt ▪ [se courber - personne] to bend forward ; [- personne qui salue] to bow ; [- cime d'arbre] to bend (over)
2. *fig* [se soumettre] : **s'~ devant le talent** to bow before talent ▪ **s'~ devant les faits** to submit to *ou* to accept the facts ▪ **s'~ devant la supériorité de qqn** to yield to sb's superiority ▪ **le Racing s'est incliné devant Toulon par 15 à 12** SPORT Racing Club lost *ou* went down to Toulon 15 to 12
3. [se recueillir] : **s'~ devant la dépouille mortelle de qqn** to pay one's last respects to sb.

inclure [96] [ɛ̃klyr] *vt* **1.** [ajouter] to include, to add, to insert **2.** [joindre] to enclose **3.** [comporter] to include ▪ [impliquer] : **cet accord inclut une autre condition** the agreement includes a further condition.

inclus, e [ɛ̃kly, yz] *adj* **1.** [contenu] enclosed **2.** [compris] included ▪ **le service est ~** service is included ▪ **du 1er au 12 juin ~** from June 1st to June 12th inclusive, from June 1 through June 12 *US* ▪ **jusqu'au dimanche ~** up to and including Sunday ▪ **dimanche ~** including Sundays **3.** MATH : **l'ensemble X est ~ dans l'ensemble Z** the set X is included in the set Z *ou* is a subset of Z **4.** MÉD : **dent ~e** impacted tooth.

inclusif, ive [ɛ̃klyzif, iv] *adj* inclusive ▪ **prix ~** all-inclusive price.

inclusion [ɛ̃klyzjɔ̃] *nf* **1.** [action] inclusion **2.** MÉD impaction **3.** MÉTALL inclusion.

inclusivement [ɛ̃klyzivmɑ̃] *adv* up to and including, through *US*.

incoagulable [ɛ̃kɔagylabl] *adj* non-coagulating.

incoercible [ɛ̃kɔɛrsibl] *adj* irrepressible, uncontrollable, incoercible *sout*.

incognito [ɛ̃kɔɲito] ◇ *adv* incognito.
◇ *nm* incognito ▪ **garder l'~** to remain anonymous *ou* incognito.

incohérence [ɛ̃kɔerɑ̃s] *nf* **1.** [manque d'unité] inconsistency, incoherence **2.** [contradiction] inconsistency, contradiction, discrepancy.

incohérent, e [ɛ̃kɔerɑ̃, ɑ̃t] *adj* **1.** [confus, décousu] incoherent, inconsistent ▪ **de manière ~e** incoherently **2.** [disparate] divided.

incoiffable [ɛ̃kwafabl] *adj* [cheveux] unmanageable.

incollable [ɛ̃kɔlabl] *adj* **1.** CULIN : **riz ~** non-stick rice **2.** *fam* [connaisseur] unbeatable ▪ **elle est ~ en géographie** you can't trip her up in geography.

incolore [ɛ̃kɔlɔr] *adj* **1.** [transparent - liquide] colourless ; [- vernis, verre] clear ; [- cirage] neutral **2.** *fig* [terne - sourire] wan ; [- style] colourless, bland, nondescript ▪ **~, inodore et sans saveur** deadly dull.

incomber [3] [ɛ̃kɔ̃be] ◆ **incomber à** *v+prép* **1.** [revenir à] : **les frais de déplacement incombent à l'entreprise** travelling expenses are to be paid by the company ▪ **à qui en incombe la responsabilité?** who is responsible for it? ▪ **cette tâche vous incombe** this task is your responsibility ▪ *(tournure impersonnelle)* **il vous incombe de la recevoir** it's your duty *ou* it's incumbent *sout* upon you to see her **2.** DR [être rattaché à] : **cette pièce incombe au dossier Falon** this document belongs in the Falon file.

incombustibilité [ɛ̃kɔ̃bystibilite] *nf* incombustibility.

incombustible [ɛ̃kɔ̃bystibl] *adj* non-combustible.

incommensurable [ɛ̃kɔmɑ̃syrabl] *adj* **1.** [énorme] immeasurable **2.** MATH incommensurable.

incommodant, e [ɛ̃kɔmɔdɑ̃, ɑ̃t] *adj* [chaleur] unpleasant, uncomfortable ▪ [bruit] irritating, irksome ▪ [odeur] offensive, nauseating.

incommode [ɛ̃kɔmɔd] *adj* **1.** [peu pratique - outil] impractical, awkward ; [- livre] unwieldy, impractical ; [- maison] inconvenient **2.** [inconfortable - position] uncomfortable, awkward ; [- fauteuil] uncomfortable.

incommoder [3] [ɛ̃kɔmɔde] *vt* to bother ▪ **la chaleur commence à m'~** the heat is beginning to bother me *ou* to make me feel uncomfortable.

incommodité [ɛ̃kɔmɔdite] *nf* [d'un outil] inconvenience, impracticability, unsuitability ▪ [d'un meuble, d'une posture, d'un trajet] uncomfortableness, discomfort.

incommunicable [ɛ̃kɔmynikabl] *adj* incommunicable.

incommutabilité [ɛ̃kɔmytabilite] *nf* non-transferability.

incommutable [ɛ̃kɔmytabl] *adj* non-transferable.

incomparable [ɛ̃kɔ̃parabl] *adj* **1.** [très différent] not comparable, unique, singular ▪ **nos deux situations sont ~s** you can't compare our two situations **2.** [inégalable] incomparable, matchless, peerless.

incomparablement [ɛ̃kɔ̃parabləmɑ̃] *adv* incomparably ▪ **il est ~ plus beau que moi** he's incomparably *ou* infinitely more handsome than me.

incompatibilité [ɛ̃kɔ̃patibilite] *nf* **1.** [opposition] incompatibility ▪ **~ d'humeur** mutual incompatibility ▪ **il y a une totale ~ entre eux** they are totally incompatible **2.** BOT, MÉD & PHARM incompatibility.

incompatible [ɛ̃kɔ̃patibl] *adj* incompatible ▪ **ces deux solutions sont ~s** these two solutions are mutually exclusive.

incompétence [ɛ̃kɔ̃petɑ̃s] *nf* **1.** [incapacité] incompetence **2.** [ignorance] ignorance, lack of knowledge **3.** DR incompetence, incompetency, (legal) incapacity.

incompétent, e [ɛ̃kɔ̃petɑ̃, ɑ̃t] ◇ *adj* **1.** [incapable] incompetent, inefficient **2.** [ignorant] ignorant ▪ **je suis ~ en la matière** I'm not qualified *ou* competent to speak about this **3.** DR & POLIT incompetent.

◇ *nm, f* incompetent.

incomplet, ète [ɛ̃kɔ̃plɛ, ɛt] *adj* [fragmentaire] incomplete ▪ [inachevé] unfinished.

incomplètement [ɛ̃kɔ̃plɛtmɑ̃] *adv* incompletely, not completely.

incompréhensibilité [ɛ̃kɔ̃preɑ̃sibilite] *nf* incomprehensibility.

incompréhensible [ɛ̃kɔ̃preɑ̃sibl] *adj* incomprehensible, impossible to understand.

incompréhensif, ive [ɛ̃kɔ̃preɑ̃sif, iv] *adj* unsympathetic, unfeeling.

incompréhension [ɛ̃kɔ̃preɑ̃sjɔ̃] *nf* lack of understanding *ou* comprehension ▪ **leur ~ était totale** they found it totally impossible to understand.

incompréhensive [ɛ̃kɔ̃preɑ̃siv] *f* ▷ **incompréhensif**.

incompressibilité [ɛ̃kɔ̃presibilite] *nf* **1.** PHYS incompressibility **2.** [de dépenses, d'un budget] irreducibility.

incompressible [ɛ̃kɔ̃presibl] *adj* **1.** PHYS incompressible **2.** [dépenses] which cannot be reduced ▪ **notre budget est ~** we can't cut down on our budget **3.** DR : **peine ~** irreducible sentence.

incompris, e [ɛ̃kɔ̃pri, iz] ◇ *adj* **1.** [méconnu] misunderstood **2.** [énigmatique] impenetrable ▪ **un texte qui jusqu'à ce jour était resté ~** a text which had not been understood until today.

◇ *nm, f* : **je suis un éternel ~** *hum* nobody ever understands me.

inconcevable [ɛ̃kɔ̃svabl] *adj* inconceivable, unthinkable, unimaginable ▪ **avec un aplomb ~** with an incredible *ou* amazing nerve.

inconciliable [ɛ̃kɔ̃siljabl] *adj* [incompatible] incompatible, irreconcilable ▪ **~ avec qqch** incompatible with sthg.

inconditionnel, elle [ɛ̃kɔ̃disjɔnɛl] ◇ *adj* **1.** [appui] unconditional, wholehearted ▪ [reddition] unconditional **2.** PHILOS unconditioned.

◇ *nm, f* : **un ~ de** a fan of ▪ **pour les ~s de l'informatique** for computer buffs *ou* enthusiasts.

inconditionnellement [ɛ̃kɔ̃disjɔnɛlmɑ̃] *adv* unconditionally, unreservedly, wholeheartedly.

inconduite [ɛ̃kɔ̃dɥit] *nf* *sout* [dévergondage] loose living ▪ [mauvaise conduite] misconduct.

inconfort [ɛ̃kɔ̃fɔr] *nm* [d'une maison] lack of comfort ▪ [d'une posture] discomfort ▪ [d'une situation] awkwardness.

inconfortable [ɛ̃kɔ̃fɔrtabl] *adj* **1.** [maison, siège] uncomfortable **2.** [situation, posture] uncomfortable, awkward.

incongru, e [ɛ̃kɔ̃gry] *adj* [remarque, réponse] incongruous, out of place ▪ [bruit] unseemly, rude ▪ [personne] uncouth.

incongruité [ɛ̃kɔ̃grɥite] *nf* **1.** [caractère incongru] incongruity, incongruousness **2.** [parole] unseemly remark.

incongrûment [ɛ̃kɔ̃grymɑ̃] *adv* *sout* in an unseemly manner.

inconnu, e [ɛ̃kɔny] ◇ *adj* **1.** [personne - dont on ignore l'existence] unknown ; [- dont on ignore l'identité] : **il est né de père ~** the name of his father is not known ▪ **'~ à cette adresse'** 'not known at this address' **2.** [destination] unknown **3.** [étranger] unknown ▪ **ce visage ne m'est pas ~** I've seen that face before ▸ **~ au bataillon** *fam* never heard of him **4.** [sans notoriété] unknown.

◇ *nm, f* **1.** [étranger] unknown person, stranger **2.** [personne sans notoriété] unknown person.

➡ **inconnu** *nm* : **l'~** the unknown.

➡ **inconnue** *nf* **1.** [élément ignoré] unknown quantity *ou* factor ▪ **il y a trop d'~es pour que je prenne une décision** there are too many unknown factors for me to decide **2.** MATH unknown.

inconsciemment [ɛ̃kɔ̃sjamɑ̃] *adv* [machinalement] unconsciously, unwittingly ▪ [dans l'inconscient] unconsciously.

inconscience [ɛ̃kɔ̃sjɑ̃s] *nf* **1.** [insouciance] recklessness, thoughtlessness ▪ [folie] madness, craziness **2.** [perte de connaissance] unconsciousness.

inconscient, e [ɛ̃kɔ̃sjɑ̃, ɑ̃t] ◇ *adj* **1.** [ignorant] : **être ~ de qqch** to be unaware of sthg **2.** [insouciant] reckless, rash ▪ [irresponsable] thoughtless, careless **3.** [automatique] mechanical, unconscious ▪ PSYCHOL unconscious **4.** [évanoui] unconscious.

◇ *nm, f* reckless *ou* thoughtless *ou* crazy person.

➡ **inconscient** *nm* PSYCHOL : **l'~** the unconscious ▪ **l'~ collectif** the collective unconscious.

inconséquence [ɛ̃kɔ̃sekɑ̃s] *nf* [manque - de cohérence] incoherence, inconsistency ; [- de prudence] thoughtlessness, carelessness, recklessness.

inconséquent, e [ɛ̃kɔ̃sekɑ̃, ɑ̃t] *adj* [incohérent] incoherent, inconsistent ▪ [imprudent] thoughtless, unthinking, reckless.

inconsidéré, e [ɛ̃kɔ̃sidere] *adj* thoughtless, rash, foolhardy.

inconsidérément [ɛ̃kɔ̃sideremɑ̃] *adv* rashly, thoughtlessly, unwisely.

inconsistance [ɛ̃kɔ̃sistɑ̃s] *nf* **1.** [d'un roman, d'un argument] flimsiness, shallowness ▪ [d'une personne] shallowness, superficiality **2.** [de la boue, de la vase] softness ▪ [d'une crème] thinness, runniness ▪ [d'une soupe] wateriness.

inconsistant, e [ɛ̃kɔ̃sistɑ̃, ɑ̃t] *adj* **1.** [roman, argument] flimsy, weak, shallow ▪ [personne, caractère] shallow, superficial, indecisive **2.** [crème, enduit] thin, runny ▪ [soupe] watery.

inconsolable [ɛ̃kɔ̃sɔlabl] *adj* inconsolable.

inconsolé, e [ɛ̃kɔ̃sɔle] *adj* [peine, chagrin] unconsoled ▪ [personne] disconsolate.

inconsommable [ɛ̃kɔ̃sɔmabl] *adj* unfit for consumption.

inconstance [ɛ̃kɔ̃stɑ̃s] *nf* **1.** [infidélité, variabilité] inconstancy, fickleness **2.** *litt* **l'~ du succès** the fickleness of fortune.

inconstant, e [ɛ̃kɔ̃stɑ̃, ɑ̃t] ◇ *adj* **1.** [infidèle, d'humeur changeante] inconstant, fickle ▪ **être ~ en amour** to be fickle **2.** *litt* [changeant - temps] changeable, unsettled.

◇ *nm, f* fickle person.

inconstitutionnel, elle [ɛ̃kɔ̃stitysjɔnɛl] *adj* unconstitutional.

inconstructible [ɛ̃kɔ̃stryktibl] *adj* : **zone ~** site without development approval, permanently restricted zone *US*.

incontestable [ɛ̃kɔ̃tɛstabl] *adj* incontestable, indisputable, undeniable ▪ **il a fait un gros effort, c'est ~** there's no denying the fact that he put in a lot of effort.

incontestablement [ɛ̃kɔ̃tɛstabləmɑ̃] *adv* indisputably, undeniably, beyond any shadow of (a) doubt ▪ **~ coupable** unquestionably guilty.

incontesté, e [ɛ̃kɔ̃tɛste] *adj* uncontested, undisputed ▪ **c'est un expert ~** he's an unchallenged *ou* undisputed expert.

incontinence [ɛ̃kɔ̃tinɑ̃s] *nf* **1.** MÉD incontinence ▪ **~ nocturne** bed-wetting **2.** *litt* [débauche] debauchery **3.** [dans le discours] : **~ verbale** logorrhoea, verbal diarrhoea *hum*.

incontinent, e [ɛ̃kɔ̃tinɑ̃, ɑ̃t] *adj* **1.** MÉD incontinent **2.** *litt* [débauché] debauched.

➡ **incontinent** *adv* *litt* forthwith, straightaway, directly.

incontournable [ɛ̃kɔ̃turnabl] *adj* : **c'est un problème ~** this problem can't be ignored ▪ **son œuvre est ~** her work cannot be overlooked.

incontrôlable [ɛ̃kɔ̃trolabl] *adj* **1.** [sentiment, colère] uncontrollable, ungovernable, wild ▪ [personne] out of control **2.** [non vérifiable - affirmation] unverifiable, unconfirmable.

incontrôlé, e [ɛ̃kɔ̃trole] *adj* **1.** [bande, groupe] unrestrained, unruly, out of control ▪ **des éléments ~s** unruly elements **2.** [non vérifié - nouvelle] unverified, unconfirmed.

inconvenance [ɛ̃kɔ̃vnɑ̃s] *nf* **1.** [caractère] impropriety, indecency ▪ **vous avez été d'une ~ choquante** you behaved in a most unseemly manner **2.** [parole] impropriety, rude remark ▪ [acte] impropriety, rude gesture.

inconvenant, e [ɛ̃kɔ̃vnɑ̃, ɑ̃t] *adj* [déplacé] improper, indecorous, unseemly ▪ [indécent] indecent, improper ▪ **rien d'~ ne s'est passé entre eux** nothing improper *ou* untoward passed between them.

inconvénient [ɛ̃kɔ̃venjɑ̃] *nm* [désagrément] disadvantage, drawback, inconvenience ▪ [danger] risk ▪ **je ne vois pas d'~ à ce que tu y ailles** I can see nothing against your going ▪ **y voyez-vous un ~?** [désagrément] can you see any difficulties *ou* drawbacks in this? ; [objection] do you have any objection to this?, do you mind?

inconvertible [ɛ̃kɔ̃vɛrtibl] *adj* **1.** FIN inconvertible **2.** RELIG unconvertable.

incoordination [ɛ̃kɔɔrdinasjɔ̃] *nf* **1.** [incohérence - de la pensée, d'un discours] lack of coordination **2.** [des mouvements] uncoordination, lack of coordination, ataxia *spéc.*

incorporable [ɛ̃kɔrpɔrabl] *adj* **1.** MIL recruitable *UK*, draftable *US* **2.** [parcelle, matériau] incorporable.

incorporation [ɛ̃kɔrpɔrasjɔ̃] *nf* **1.** MIL recruitment, conscription *UK*, induction *US* ▪ **j'attends mon ~** I'm waiting to be called up **2.** PSYCHOL incorporation **3.** [d'un produit] blending, incorporating, mixing ▪ [d'un territoire] incorporation.

incorporé, e [ɛ̃kɔrpɔre] *adj* built-in, integrated ▪ **avec cellule ~e photoélectrique** with built-in light meter.
◆ **incorporé** *nm* recruit, inductee *US.*

incorporel, elle [ɛ̃kɔrpɔrɛl] *adj* **1.** [intangible] insubstantial, incorporeal **2.** DR : **bien ~** intangible property ▪ **propriété ~le** incorporeal hereditaments.

incorporer [3] [ɛ̃kɔrpɔre] *vt* **1.** [mêler] to blend, to mix ▪ **incorporez le sucre peu à peu** gradually mix in the sugar **2.** MIL to recruit *UK*, to draft *US*, to induct *US* **3.** [intégrer] to incorporate, to integrate.

incorrect, e [ɛ̃kɔrɛkt] *adj* **1.** [erroné] incorrect, wrong ▪ **l'emploi ~ d'un mot** the improper use of a word **2.** [indécent] improper, impolite, indecent ▪ **dans une tenue ~e** improperly dressed **3.** [impoli] rude, discourteous, impolite **4.** [irrégulier] underhand, irregular, unscrupulous ▪ **il a été très ~ avec ses concurrents** he behaved quite unscrupulously towards his competitors.

incorrectement [ɛ̃kɔrɛktəmɑ̃] *adv* wrongly, incorrectly ▪ **mots orthographiés ~** wrongly spelt words.

incorrection [ɛ̃kɔrɛksjɔ̃] *nf* **1.** [caractère incorrect] impropriety, indecency **2.** [propos] impropriety, improper remark ▪ [acte] improper act ▪ **c'est une ~ de...** it's not proper to... **3.** [emploi fautif] impropriety.

incorrigible [ɛ̃kɔriʒibl] *adj* **1.** [personne] incorrigible ▪ **c'est un ~ paresseux** he's incorrigibly lazy **2.** [défaut] incorrigible.

incorruptibilité [ɛ̃kɔryptibilite] *nf* **1.** [honnêteté] incorruptibility **2.** [inaltérabilité - d'un métal] stability ; [- d'un bois] incorruptibility, rot-resistance.

incorruptible [ɛ̃kɔryptibl] <> *adj* **1.** [honnête] incorruptible ▪ **on la sait ~** everybody knows she wouldn't take a bribe **2.** [inaltérable - métal] stable ; [- bois] non-decaying.
<> *nmf* incorruptible ▪ **c'est un ~** he's incorruptible.

incrédibilité [ɛ̃kredibilite] *nf* incredibleness, incredibility.

incrédule [ɛ̃kredyl] <> *adj* **1.** [sceptique] incredulous, disbelieving ▪ **d'un air ~** incredulously, in disbelief **2.** [incroyant] unbelieving.
<> *nmf* [incroyant] nonbeliever, unbeliever.

incrédulité [ɛ̃kredylite] *nf* **1.** [doute] incredulity, disbelief, unbelief ▪ **avec ~** incredulously, in disbelief **2.** [incroyance] lack of belief, unbelief.

incrémenter [3] [ɛ̃kremɑ̃te] *vt* INFORM to increment.

incrémentiel, elle [ɛ̃kremɑ̃sjɛl] *adj* INFORM incremental.

increvable [ɛ̃krəvabl] *adj* **1.** [pneu, ballon] puncture-proof **2.** *fam* [personne] tireless ▪ **cette voiture est ~** this car will last for ever.

incriminable [ɛ̃kriminabl] *adj litt* condemnable.

incrimination [ɛ̃kriminasjɔ̃] *nf* incrimination, accusation.

incriminer [3] [ɛ̃krimine] *vt* **1.** [rejeter la faute sur] to put the blame on, to incriminate **2.** [accuser - décision, négligence] to (call into) question ; [- personne] to accuse ▪ **il avait déjà été incriminé dans une affaire de drogue** he'd previously been implicated in a drugs case.

incroyable [ɛ̃krwajabl] <> *adj* **1.** [peu vraisemblable] incredible, unbelievable ▪ **il est ~ que** it's incredible *ou* hard to believe that **2.** [étonnant] incredible, amazing ▪ **tu es vraiment ~, pourquoi ne veux-tu pas venir?** you're unbelievable, why don't you want to come? ▪ **d'une bêtise ~** incredibly stupid ▪ **c'est quand même ~, ce retard!** this delay is getting ridiculous!
<> *nmf* HIST Incroyable, dandy.

incroyablement [ɛ̃krwajabləmɑ̃] *adv* incredibly, unbelievably, amazingly.

incroyance [ɛ̃krwajɑ̃s] *nf* unbelief.

incroyant, e [ɛ̃krwajɑ̃, ɑ̃t] <> *adj* unbelieving.
<> *nm, f* unbeliever.

incrustation [ɛ̃krystasjɔ̃] *nf* **1.** [décoration] inlay ▪ [procédé] inlaying **2.** GÉOL [action] encrusting ▪ [résultat] incrustation **3.** COUT insertion **4.** TV (image) inlay, cut-in.

incruster [3] [ɛ̃kryste] *vt* **1.** [orner] to inlay ▪ **~ qqch de** to inlay sthg with ▪ **un bracelet incrusté d'émeraudes** a bracelet inlaid with emeralds **2.** [recouvrir - gén] to incrust, to coat ; [- de calcaire] to fur up **3.** CONSTR [pierre] to insert.
◆ **s'incruster** *vpi* **1.** [se couvrir de calcaire] to become incrusted, to become covered in scale, to fur up **2.** [adhérer] to build up **3.** *fam* [personne] : **ne t'incruste pas** don't stick around too long.

incubateur, trice [ɛ̃kybatœr, tris] *adj* incubating.
◆ **incubateur** *nm* incubator.

incubation [ɛ̃kybasjɔ̃] *nf* **1.** [d'œufs] incubation **2.** [d'une maladie] incubation ▪ **l'~ dure trois jours** the incubation period is three days.

incuber [3] [ɛ̃kybe] *vt* [œuf] to incubate.

inculcation [ɛ̃kylkasjɔ̃] *nf litt* inculcation, instilling.

inculpation [ɛ̃kylpasjɔ̃] *nf* indictment, charge ▪ **être sous le coup d'une ~ (pour)** to be indicted (for) *ou* on a charge (of).

inculpé, e [ɛ̃kylpe] *nm, f* : **l'~** the accused.

inculper [3] [ɛ̃kylpe] *vt* to charge ▪ **inculpé de meurtre** charged with murder.

inculquer [3] [ɛ̃kylke] *vt* to inculcate ▪ **~ qqch à qqn** to inculcate sthg in sb.

inculte [ɛ̃kylt] *adj* **1.** [campagne, pays] uncultivated **2.** [esprit, intelligence, personne] uneducated, uncultured, uncultivated ▪ **ils sont complètement ~s** they're totally ignorant **3.** [cheveux] unkempt, dishevelled ▪ [barbe] untidy.

incultivable [ɛ̃kyltivabl] *adj* unworkable, uncultivable ▪ **des terres ~s** wasteland.

incultivé, e [ɛ̃kyltive] *adj litt* [région, terre] uncultivated.

inculture [ɛ̃kyltyr] *nf* [d'une personne] lack of culture *ou* education.

incurable [ɛ̃kyrabl] <> *adj* **1.** MÉD incurable **2.** [incorrigible - personne, défaut] incurable, inveterate.
<> *nmf* incurable.

incurablement [ɛ̃kyrabləmɑ̃] *adv* **1.** MÉD incurably **2.** [irrémédiablement] incurably, desperately, hopelessly.

incurie [ɛ̃kyri] *nf sout* carelessness, negligence.

incursion [ɛ̃kyrsjɔ̃] *nf* **1.** [exploration] foray, incursion **2.** MIL foray, raid.

incurver [3] [ɛ̃kyrve] *vt* to curve (inwards), to make into a curve.
◆ **s'incurver** *vpi* **1.** [trajectoire] to curve (inwards *ou* in), to bend **2.** [étagère] to sag.

Inde [ɛ̃d] *npr f* : (l')~ India.

indéboulonnable [ɛ̃debulɔnabl] *adj hum* : **il est ~!** they'll never be able to sack him!

indécemment [ɛ̃desamɑ̃] *adv* indecently.

indécence [ɛ̃desɑ̃s] *nf* **1.** [manque de pudeur] indecency **2.** [propos, acte] indecency, impropriety.

indécent, e [ɛ̃desɑ̃, ɑ̃t] *adj* **1.** [honteux] indecent ▪ **c'est un gaspillage presque ~** the waste is almost obscene **2.** [licencieux] indecent, obscene.

indéchiffrable [ɛ̃deʃifrabl] *adj* **1.** [code] undecipherable, indecipherable ▪ **aucun code n'est ~** there's no code that can't be broken *ou* cracked **2.** [écriture] illegible, unreadable **3.** [visage, mystère, pensée] inscrutable, impenetrable.

indéchirable [ɛ̃deʃirabl] *adj* tear-resistant.

indécis, e [ɛ̃desi, iz] <> *adj* **1.** [flou] vague, indistinct **2.** [incertain] undecided, unsettled ▪ **le temps est ~** the weather is unsettled **3.** [hésitant] undecided, unsure, uncertain ▪ [irrésolu] indecisive, irresolute ▪ **je suis ~ (sur la solution à choisir)** I'm undecided (as to the best solution), I can't make up my mind (which solution is the best).
<> *nm, f* indecisive person ▪ [électeur] floating voter, don't-know ▪ **le vote des ~** the floating vote.

indécision [ɛ̃desizjɔ̃] *nf* [caractère irrésolu] indecisiveness ▪ [hésitation] indecision ▪ **être dans l'~ (quant à)** to be undecided *ou* unsure (about).

indécollable [ɛ̃dekɔlabl] *adj* [gén] non-removable ▪ [revêtement] permanent.

indécrottable [ɛ̃dekrɔtabl] *adj fam* hopeless ▪ **c'est un ~ imbécile!** he's hopelessly stupid! ▪ **un ~ réactionnaire** an out-and-out reactionary.

indéfectible [ɛ̃defɛktibl] *adj* [amitié, soutien] staunch, unfailing, unshakeable ▪ [confiance] unshakeable ▪ **une ~ volonté** staunch determination.

indéfendable [ɛ̃defɑ̃dabl] *adj* **1.** [condamnable - personne, comportement] indefensible **2.** [insoutenable - théorie, opinion] indefensible, untenable.

indéfini, e [ɛ̃defini] *adj* **1.** [sans limites] indefinite, unlimited ▪ **un temps ~** an undetermined length of time **2.** [confus] ill-defined, vague **3.** LING indefinite.

indéfiniment [ɛ̃definimɑ̃] *adv* indefinitely, for ever.

indéfinissable [ɛ̃definisabl] *adj* indefinable.

indéformable [ɛ̃defɔrmabl] *adj* [chapeau, vêtement] which cannot be pulled out of shape ▪ [semelle] rigid.

indéfrichable [ɛ̃defriʃabl] *adj* [sol, terre] unclearable.

indélébile [ɛ̃delebil] *adj* **1.** [ineffaçable - encre] indelible, permanent ; [- tache] indelible **2.** [indestructible - souvenir] indelible.

indélébilité [ɛ̃delebilite] *nf* indelibility.

indélicat, e [ɛ̃delika, at] *adj* **1.** [grossier] coarse, indelicate, rude **2.** [véreux] dishonest, unscrupulous.

indélicatesse [ɛ̃delikatɛs] *nf* **1.** [des manières] indelicacy, coarseness **2.** [caractère malhonnête] dishonesty, unscrupulousness **3.** [acte malhonnête] dishonest *ou* unscrupulous act.

indémaillable [ɛ̃demajabl] *adj* [bas, collant] runproof, ladderproof *UK* ▪ [pull, tissu] run-resistant, runproof.

indémêlable [ɛ̃demelabl] *adj* [cheveux] hopelessly entangled ▪ [intrigue] inextricable, entangled.

indemne [ɛ̃dɛmn] *adj* **1.** [physiquement] unhurt, unharmed ▪ **ma sœur est sortie ~ de la collision** my sister was unhurt in the collision **2.** [moralement] unscathed.

indemnisable [ɛ̃dɛmnizabl] *adj* [propriétaire, réfugié] entitled to compensation, compensable *US*.

indemnisation [ɛ̃dɛmnizasjɔ̃] *nf* **1.** [argent] compensation, indemnity ▪ **il a reçu 100 000 euros d'~** he received 100,000 euros compensation **2.** [procédé] compensating.

indemniser [3] [ɛ̃dɛmnize] *vt* **1.** [après un sinistre] to compensate, to indemnify ▪ **se faire ~** to receive compensation **2.** [après une dépense] : **être indemnisé de ses frais** to have one's expenses paid for *ou* reimbursed.

indemnitaire [ɛ̃dɛmnitɛr] <> *adj* compensative, compensatory.
<> *nmf* **1.** [recevant une allocation] recipient of an allowance **2.** [après un sinistre] person awarded compensation.

indemnité [ɛ̃dɛmnite] *nf* **1.** [après un sinistre] compensation ▪ [dommages et intérêts] damages **2.** [allocation] allowance ▪ **~ journalière** sickness benefit ▪ **~ de licenciement** redundancy payment ▪ **~ parlementaire** ≃ MP's salary *UK* ▪ **~ de transport** travel allowance *ou* expenses ▪ **~ viagère de départ** *severance money for retiring farmers.*

indémodable [ɛ̃demɔdabl] *adj* perenially fashionable.

indémontable [ɛ̃demɔ̃tabl] *adj* [jouet, serrure] which cannot be taken apart *ou* dismantled ▪ [étagère] fixed.

indémontrable [ɛ̃demɔ̃trabl] *adj* **1.** LOGIQUE & MATH indemonstrable **2.** [non prouvable] unprovable.

indéniable [ɛ̃denjabl] *adj* undeniable.

indéniablement [ɛ̃denjabləmɑ̃] *adv* undeniably.

indénombrable [ɛ̃denɔ̃brabl] *adj* innumerable, uncountable.

indentation [ɛ̃dɑ̃tasjɔ̃] *nf* indentation ▪ **les ~s du littoral** the ragged coastline.

indépendamment [ɛ̃depɑ̃damɑ̃] *adv* **1.** [séparément] independently ▪ **~ l'un de l'autre** independently of one another **2.** [outre, mis à part] : **~ de** apart from.

indépendance [ɛ̃depɑ̃dɑ̃s] *nf* **1.** [d'un pays, d'une personne] independence ▪ **prendre son ~** to assume one's independence ⊙ **le jour de l'Indépendance** Independence Day **2.** [absence de relation] independence.

indépendant, e [ɛ̃depɑ̃dɑ̃, ɑ̃t] <> *adj* **1.** [gén - POLIT] independent ▪ **pour des raisons ~es de notre volonté** for reasons beyond our control **2.** [distinct] : **ces deux problèmes sont ~s l'un de l'autre** these two problems are separate *ou* distinct from each other ▪ **une chambre ~e** a self-contained room ▪ **avec salle de bains ~e** with own *ou* separate bathroom **3.** LING & MATH independent.
<> *nm, f* POLIT independent.
◆ **en indépendant** *loc adv* : **travailler en ~** to work on a freelance basis.

indépendantisme [ɛ̃depɑ̃dɑ̃tism] *nm* : **l'~** the independence *ou* separatist movement.

indépendantiste [ɛ̃depɑ̃dɑ̃tist] <> *adj* : **mouvement ~** independence *ou* separatist movement.
<> *nmf* separatist.

indéracinable [ɛ̃derasinabl] *adj* **1.** [préjugé, habitude] entrenched, ineradicable *sout* **2.** [personne] : **deux ou trois poivrots ~s** *fam* two or three drunks who couldn't be shifted.

indéréglable [ɛ̃dereglabl] *adj* [mécanisme, montre] extremely reliable.

Indes [ɛ̃d] *npr fpl* Indies ▪ **les ~ occidentales/orientales** HIST the West/East Indies ▪ **la Compagnie des ~ orientales** HIST the East India Company.

indescriptible [ɛ̃dɛskriptibl] *adj* indescribable.

indésirable [ɛ̃dezirabl] <> *adj* undesirable, unwanted. <> *nmf* undesirable ■ **on nous traite comme des ~s** we are treated as though we were not wanted.

indestructibilité [ɛ̃dɛstryktibilite] *nf* indestructibility, indestructibleness.

indestructible [ɛ̃dɛstryktibl] *adj* [bâtiment, canon] indestructible, built to last ■ [amour, lien] indestructible.

indétectable [ɛ̃detɛktabl] *adj* undetectable.

indéterminable [ɛ̃detɛrminabl] *adj* indeterminable ■ **sa date de naissance est ~** his date of birth cannot be determined (with any certainty).

indétermination [ɛ̃detɛrminasjɔ̃] *nf* **1.** [approximation] vagueness **2.** [indécision] indecision, uncertainty **3.** MATH indeterminacy **4.** PHILOS indetermination.

indéterminé, e [ɛ̃detɛrmine] *adj* **1.** [non défini] indeterminate, unspecified ■ **à une date ~e** at an unspecified date ■ **l'origine du mot est ~e** the origin of the word is uncertain *ou* not known **2.** MATH indeterminate.

indéterminisme [ɛ̃detɛrminism] *nm* indeterminism.

index [ɛ̃dɛks] *nm* **1.** [doigt] index finger, forefinger **2.** [repère] pointer **3.** [liste] index **4.** HIST : **l'Index** the Index ➊ **mettre qqch à l'~** to blacklist sthg **5.** INFORM (fixed) index.

indexage [ɛ̃dɛksaʒ] *nm* indexing, indexation.

indexation [ɛ̃dɛksasjɔ̃] *nf* indexation, indexing.

indexé, e [ɛ̃dɛkse] *adj* ÉCON [loyer, prix] indexed ■ [salaire] indexed, index-linked ■ INFORM [valeur] indexed.

indexer [4] [ɛ̃dɛkse] *vt* **1.** [gén - ÉCON] to index ■ **~ les salaires sur le coût de la vie** to index salaries to the cost of living **2.** [ouvrage, mot] to index **3.** INFORM to index.

Indiana [indjana] *npr m* : **l'~** Indiana.

Indianapolis [indjanapɔlis] *npr* Indianapolis.

indic [ɛ̃dik] *nm fam* (police) informer.

indicateur, trice [ɛ̃dikatœr, tris] <> *adj* indicative. <> *nm, f* [informateur] (police) informer *ou* spy.
◆ **indicateur** *nm* **1.** [plan, liste] : **~ des rues** street guide *ou* directory ■ **~ des chemins de fer** railway *UK ou* railroad *US* timetable **2.** [appareil] indicator, gauge ■ **~ de pression** pressure gauge ■ **~ de vitesse** speedometer **3.** [indice] indicator, pointer ■ **~ économique** economic indicator ■ **~ de tendance** BOURSE market indicator **4.** CHIM & LING indicator **5.** NUCL (radioactive) indicator *ou* tracer.

indicatif, ive [ɛ̃dikatif, iv] *adj* [état, signe] indicative ■ GRAMM [mode] indicative.
◆ **indicatif** *nm* **1.** GRAMM indicative **2.** RADIO & TV theme *ou* signature tune **3.** TÉLÉCOM [de zone] (dialling) code ■ **~ du pays** international dialling code **4.** INFORM : **~ de tri** sort key.

indication [ɛ̃dikasjɔ̃] *nf* **1.** [recommandation] instruction ■ **les ~s du mode d'emploi** the directions for use ■ **~s scéniques** stage directions **2.** [information, renseignement] information *(U)*, piece of information **3.** [signe] sign, indication **4.** [aperçu] indication ■ **c'est une excellente ~ sur l'état de l'économie** it's an excellent indication of the state of the economy **5.** MÉD & PHARM : **sauf ~ contraire du médecin** unless otherwise stated by the doctor ■ **~ thérapeutique** indication **6.** COMM : **~ d'origine** label of origin.

indice [ɛ̃dis] *nm* **1.** [symptôme - d'un changement, d'un phénomène] indication, sign ; [- d'une maladie] sign, symptom ■ **aucun ~ ne laissait présager le drame** there was no hint of the coming tragedy ■ **la presse s'accorde à y voir l'~ de proches négociations** all the papers agree that this is evidence *ou* a sign that negotiations are imminent **2.** [d'une enquête policière] clue ■ [d'une énigme] clue, hint **3.** ÉCON, OPT & PHYS index ■ BOURSE index, average ■ **~ du coût de la vie** cost of living index ■ **l'~ de l'INSEE** ≃ the retail price index ■ **~ des prix (à la consommation)** (consumer) price index ■ **~ de rémunération** *ou* **traitement** ADMIN salary grading **4.** RADIO & TV : **l'~ d'écoute** the audience rating, the ratings **5.** PHOTO : **~ de lumination** exposure value *ou* index **6.** MATH index ■ **b ~ 3** b subscript *ou* index 3 **7.** LING index.

indiciaire [ɛ̃disjɛr] *adj* **1.** ÉCON index-based **2.** ADMIN grade-related.

indicible [ɛ̃disibl] *adj* indescribable, unutterable *sout.*

indiciblement [ɛ̃disibləmɑ̃] *adv* ineffably.

indien, enne [ɛ̃djɛ̃, ɛn] *adj* Indian ■ **l'océan Indien** the Indian Ocean.
◆ **Indien, enne** *nm, f* **1.** [de l'Inde] Indian **2.** [amérindien] : **~ (d'Amérique)** American Indian, Native American.
◆ **indienne** *nf* **1.** TEXT printed (Indian) cotton *UK*, printed calico *US* **2.** [nage] overarm stroke.

indifféremment [ɛ̃diferamɑ̃] *adv* **1.** [aussi bien] : **elle joue ~ de la main droite ou de la main gauche** she plays equally well with her right or left hand ■ **la radio marche ~ avec piles ou sur secteur** the radio can run on batteries or be plugged into the mains **2.** [sans discrimination] indiscriminately.

indifférence [ɛ̃diferɑ̃s] *nf* [détachement - envers une situation, un sujet] indifference, lack of interest ; [- envers qqn] indifference ■ **son roman est paru dans la plus grande ~** the publication of his novel went completely unnoticed.
Voir module d'usage

indifférenciation [ɛ̃diferɑ̃sjasjɔ̃] *nf* **1.** PHYSIOL absence of differentiation ■ **pendant l'~ sexuelle de l'embryon** while the embryo is still sexually undifferentiated **2.** MÉD anaplasia.

indifférencié, e [ɛ̃diferɑ̃sje] *adj* **1.** PHYSIOL [organisme] undifferentiated ■ [cellule] unspecialized **2.** MÉD anaplastic.

indifférent, e [ɛ̃diferɑ̃, ɑ̃t] <> *adj* **1.** [insensible, détaché] indifferent ■ **laisser ~ : leur divorce me laisse ~** their divorce is of no interest to me *ou* is a matter of indifference to me ■ **elle ne le laisse pas ~** he's not blind *ou* indifferent to her charms ■ **être ~ à la politique** to be indifferent towards politics **2.** [d'intérêt égal] indifferent, immaterial ■ [dans les petites annonces] : **'âge ~'** 'age unimportant *ou* immaterial' ■ **'religion/race ~e'** 'religion/race no barrier' **3.** [insignifiant] indifferent, uninteresting, of no interest ■ **parler de choses ~es** to talk about this and that ■ **ça m'est ~** it's (all) the same to me *ou* I don't care either way ■ **il lui était ~ de partir (ou non)** it didn't matter *ou* it was immaterial to him whether he left or not ■ **la suite des événements m'est ~e** what happens next is of no concern *ou* interest to me.
<> *nm, f* indifferent *ou* apathetic person ■ **il fait l'~** *ou* **joue les ~s** he's feigning indifference.

indifférer [18] [ɛ̃difere] ◆ **indifférer à** *v+prép* **1.** [n'inspirer aucun intérêt à] : **il m'indiffère complètement** I'm totally indifferent to him, I couldn't care less about him ■ **tout l'indiffère** she takes no interest in anything **2.** [être égal à] to be of

L'INDIFFÉRENCE

Chocolate? I can take it *ou* **leave it.** Le chocolat ? Je n'en raffole pas.
I don't mind either way. Ça m'est égal.
I'm not bothered either way. Ça m'est égal.
I don't care one way or the other. Ça m'est égal.
I don't mind, you choose. Peu importe, choisis.
You decide, it's all the same to me. Choisis, je n'ai pas de préférence particulière.

no importance to ■ **le prix m'indiffère** the price is of no importance (to me) ■ **ça m'indiffère** I don't mind, it's all the same to me.

indigence [ɛ̃diʒɑ̃s] *nf* **1.** [matérielle] poverty, indigence *sout* ■ **vivre dans l'~** to be destitute **2.** [intellectuelle] paucity, poverty.

indigène [ɛ̃diʒɛn] ◇ *adj* **1.** [d'avant la colonisation - droits, pratique] native, indigenous **2.** [autochtone - population] native, indigenous **3.** BOT & ZOOL indigenous, native ■ **la faune ~ de ces régions** the fauna indigenous to these regions.
◇ *nmf* **1.** [colonisé] native **2.** [autochtone] native **3.** BOT & ZOOL indigen, indigene, native.

indigent, e [ɛ̃diʒɑ̃, ɑ̃t] ◇ *adj* **1.** [pauvre] destitute, poor, indigent *sout* **2.** [insuffisant] poor.
◇ *nm, f* pauper ■ **les ~s** the destitute, the poor.

indigeste [ɛ̃diʒɛst] *adj* **1.** [nourriture] indigestible, heavy ■ **je trouve la choucroute très ~** I find sauerkraut very heavy on the stomach **2.** [livre, compte-rendu] heavy-going.

indigestion [ɛ̃diʒɛstjɔ̃] *nf* **1.** MÉD indigestion *(U)* ■ **avoir une ~** to have (an attack of) indigestion **2.** *fig* **avoir une ~ de** to get a surfeit *ou* an overdose of.

indignation [ɛ̃diɲasjɔ̃] *nf* indignation ■ **protester avec ~** to protest indignantly ■ **un regard d'~** an indignant look.
Voir module d'usage

indigne [ɛ̃diɲ] ◇ *adj* **1.** [honneur, confiance] : **~ de** unworthy of ■ **un mensonge/une corvée ~ de lui** a lie/chore unworthy of him ■ **des médisances ~s d'une sœur** malicious gossip one doesn't expect from a sister ■ **il est ~ de succéder à son père** he's not fit to take his father's place **2.** [choquant - action, propos] disgraceful, outrageous, shameful ■ **avoir une attitude ~** to behave shamefully *ou* disgracefully ■ [méprisable - personne] unworthy ■ **c'est une mère ~** she's not fit to be a mother ■ **un fils ~** an unworthy son **3.** DR : **être ~ d'hériter** to be judicially debarred from inheriting.
◇ *nmf* (judicially) disinherited person.

indigné, e [ɛ̃diɲe] *adj* indignant, shocked, outraged.

indignement [ɛ̃diɲəmɑ̃] *adv* disgracefully, shamefully.

indigner [3] [ɛ̃diɲe] *vt* to make indignant, to incense, to gall.
◆ **s'indigner** *vpi* [se révolter] to be indignant ■ **s'~ de** to be indignant about ■ **s'~ contre l'injustice** to cry out *ou* to inveigh against injustice.

indignité [ɛ̃diɲite] *nf* **1.** [caractère indigne] unworthiness, disgracefulness **2.** [acte] shameful *ou* disgraceful act **3.** DR : **~ successorale** judicial debarment from succession **4.** HIST : **~ nationale** loss of citizenship rights *(for having collaborated with Germany during WW II).*

indigo [ɛ̃digo] ◇ *nm* indigo.
◇ *adj inv* indigo (blue).

indiqué, e [ɛ̃dike] *adj* **1.** [recommandé - conduite] advisable **2.** [approprié - personne, objet] : **tout ~** : **tu es tout ~ pour le rôle** you're exactly the right person *ou* the obvious choice for the part ■ **ce médicament est/n'est pas ~ dans ce cas** this drug is appropriate/inappropriate in this case **3.** [date, jour] agreed ■ [endroit] agreed, appointed ■ [heure] appointed.

indiquer [3] [ɛ̃dike] *vt* **1.** [montrer d'un geste - chose, personne, lieu] to show, to point out *(sép)* ■ **~ qqch de la tête** to nod towards sthg, to indicate sthg with a nod ■ **~ qqch de la main** to point out *ou* to indicate sthg with one's hand ■ **~ qqn/qqch du doigt** to point to sb/sthg **2.** [musée, autoroute, plage] to show the way to ■ [chemin] to indicate, to show ■ **pouvez-vous m'~ (le chemin de) la gare?** could you show me the way to *ou* direct me to the station? **3.** [suj: carte, enseigne, pancarte, statistiques] to show, to say, to indicate ■ [suj: flèche, graphique] to show ■ [suj: horaire] to show, to say, to give ■ [suj: dictionnaire] to say, to give ■ **l'horloge indique 6 h** the clock says *ou* shows that it's 6 o'clock **4.** [noter - date, prix] to note *ou* to write (down) ; [- repère] to mark, to draw ■ **ce n'est pas indiqué dans le contrat** it's not written *ou* mentioned in the contract **5.** [conseiller - ouvrage, professionnel, restaurant] to suggest, to recommend ; [- traitement] to prescribe, to give ■ **une auberge qu'elle m'avait indiquée** an inn she'd told me about **6.** [dire - marche à suivre, heure] to tell ■ [fixer - lieu de rendez-vous, jour] to give, to name **7.** [être le signe de - phénomène] to point to *(insép)*, to indicate ; [- crainte, joie] to show, to betray ■ **tout indique que nous allons vers une crise** everything suggests that we are heading towards a crisis **8.** ART to sketch out.

indirect, e [ɛ̃dirɛkt] *adj* **1.** [approche] indirect, roundabout ■ [influence] indirect ■ **faire allusion à qqch de façon ~e** to refer obliquely *ou* indirectly to sthg ■ **elle m'a fait des reproches ~s** she told me off in a roundabout way **2.** DR : **héritier ~** collateral heir **3.** GRAMM : **complément ~** [d'un verbe transitif] indirect complement ; [d'un verbe intransitif] prepositional complement ■ **discours** *ou* **style ~** indirect *ou* reported speech.

indirectement [ɛ̃dirɛktəmɑ̃] *adv* indirectly ■ **je l'ai su ~** I heard about it indirectly *ou* in a roundabout way.

indiscernable [ɛ̃disɛrnabl] *adj* indiscernible.

indiscipline [ɛ̃disiplin] *nf* [dans un groupe] lack of discipline, indiscipline ■ [d'un enfant] disobedience ■ [d'un soldat] insubordination ■ **faire preuve d'~** [écoliers] to be undisciplined ; [militaires] to defy orders.

indiscipliné, e [ɛ̃disipline] *adj* [dans un groupe] undisciplined, unruly ■ [enfant] unruly, disobedient ■ [soldat] undisciplined, insubordinate ■ **cheveux ~s** unmanageable hair ■ **mèches ~es** flyaway wisps (of hair).

indiscret, ète [ɛ̃diskrɛ, ɛt] ◇ *adj* **1.** [curieux - personne] inquisitive ; [- demande, question] indiscreet ; [- regard] inquisitive, prying ■ **sans (vouloir) être ~, combien est-ce que ça vous a coûté?** could I possibly ask you how much you paid for it? ■ **loin des oreilles indiscrètes** far from *ou* out of reach of eavesdroppers **2.** [révélateur - propos, geste] indiscreet, telltale ; [- personne] indiscreet, garrulous.
◇ *nm, f* **1.** [personne curieuse] inquisitive person **2.** [personne bavarde] indiscreet person.

indiscrètement [ɛ̃diskrɛtmɑ̃] *adv* **1.** [sans tact] indiscreetly **2.** [avec curiosité] inquisitively.

L'INDIGNATION

How dare she call me a liar! Comment ose-t-elle me traiter de menteur !

Who does he think he is! Pour qui est-ce qu'il se prend !

Are you accusing me of cheating? Vous m'accusez de tricher ?

I beg your pardon! Pardon !

I don't see why I should have to apologize! Je ne vois pas pourquoi je devrais m'excuser !

What business is it of yours, anyway? Qu'est-ce que ça peut te faire, de toute façon ?

Nobody should have to put up with this kind of treatment. Ce n'est une façon de traiter les gens.

It's about time something was done about this. Il serait temps que quelqu'un fasse quelque chose.

indiscrétion [ɛ̃diskresjɔ̃] *nf* **1.** [d'une personne] inquisitiveness, curiosity ■ [d'une question] indiscreetness, tactlessness ■ **pardonnez mon ~** forgive me for asking ■ **sans ~, avez-vous des enfants?** do you mind if I ask you if you've got any children? **2.** [révélation] indiscretion ■ **commettre une ~** to commit an indiscretion, to say something one shouldn't.

indiscutable [ɛ̃diskytabl] *adj* indisputable, unquestionable.

indiscutablement [ɛ̃diskytabləmɑ̃] *adv* indisputably, unquestionably.

indiscuté, e [ɛ̃diskyte] *adj* undisputed ■ **ses vertus curatives sont ~es** its curative powers are unquestioned.

indispensable [ɛ̃dispɑ̃sabl] ◇ *adj* [fournitures, machine] essential, indispensable ■ [mesures] essential, vital, indispensable ■ [précautions] essential, required, necessary ■ [personne] indispensable ■ **cette entrevue est-elle vraiment ~?** is this interview really necessary?, do I really have to go through with this interview? ■ **tes réflexions n'étaient pas ~s!** we could have done without your remarks! ■ **il est ~ de/que...** it's essential to/that... ■ **son fils lui est ~** he can't do without his son ■ **~ à tous les sportifs!** essential *ou* a must for all sportsmen! ■ **ce document m'est ~ pour continuer mes recherches** this document is absolutely vital *ou* essential if I am to carry on my research.
◇ *nm* : **l'~** [le nécessaire] the essentials.

indisponibilité [ɛ̃dispɔnibilite] *nf* **1.** [d'une machine] downtime *spéc* ■ [d'une marchandise, d'une personne] non-availability, unavailability **2.** DR inalienability.

indisponible [ɛ̃dispɔnibl] *adj* **1.** [marchandise, personne] not available, unavailable ■ **je suis ~ jusqu'à 19 h** I'm not free until 7 o'clock **2.** DR inalienable.

indisposé, e [ɛ̃dispoze] *adj* **1.** [légèrement souffrant] unwell, indisposed *sout* **2.** *sout* [mal disposé] ill-disposed, hostile.
◆ **indisposée** *adj f euphém* **je suis ~e** it's the time of the month.

indisposer [3] [ɛ̃dispoze] *vt* **1.** [irriter] to annoy ■ **~ qqn contre** to set sb against **2.** [rendre malade] to upset, to make (slightly) ill, to indispose *sout*.

indisposition [ɛ̃dispozisjɔ̃] *nf* **1.** [malaise] discomfort, ailment, indisposition *sout* ■ **j'ai eu une ~ passagère** I felt slightly off colour for a little while **2.** *euphém* [menstruation] period.

indissociable [ɛ̃disɔsjabl] *adj* indissociable, inseparable.

indissolubilité [ɛ̃disɔlybilite] *nf* indissolubility.

indissoluble [ɛ̃disɔlybl] *adj* [lien, union] indissoluble.

indistinct, e [ɛ̃distɛ̃(kt), ɛ̃kt] *adj* [chuchotement] indistinct, faint ■ [forme] indistinct, unclear, vague ■ **prononcer des paroles ~es** to mumble inaudibly.

indistinctement [ɛ̃distɛ̃ktəmɑ̃] *adv* **1.** [confusément - parler] indistinctly, unclearly ; [- se souvenir] indistinctly, vaguely **2.** [sans distinction] indiscriminately ■ **recruter ~ hommes et femmes** to recruit people regardless of sex.

individu [ɛ̃dividy] *nm* **1.** [personne humaine] individual **2.** [quidam] individual, person ■ **un drôle d'~** a strange character ■ **un sinistre ~** a sinister individual **3.** BIOL, BOT & LOGIQUE individual.

individualisation [ɛ̃dividɥalizasjɔ̃] *nf* **1.** [d'une espèce animale, d'une langue] individualization ■ [d'un système] adapting to individual requirements **2.** DR : **~ de la peine** *sentencing depending upon the individual requirements or characteristics of the defendant.*

individualisé, e [ɛ̃dividɥalize] *adj* **1.** [enseignement] individualized **2.** [méthode, caractère] distinctive ■ [groupe] separate, distinct.

individualiser [3] [ɛ̃dividɥalize] *vt* [système] to adapt to individual needs, to tailor.
◆ **s'individualiser** *vpi* to acquire individual characteristics.

individualisme [ɛ̃dividɥalism] *nm* individualism.

individualiste [ɛ̃dividɥalist] ◇ *adj* individualistic.
◇ *nmf* individualist.

individualité [ɛ̃dividɥalite] *nf* **1.** [caractère - unique] individuality ; [- original] originality **2.** [style] : **une forte ~** a strong personal *ou* individual style.

individuel, elle [ɛ̃dividɥɛl] ◇ *adj* **1.** [personnel] individual, personal **2.** [particulier] individual, private ■ **chambre ~le** (private) single room ■ **cas ~** individual case ● **ligne ~le** TÉLÉCOM private line **3.** SPORT : **épreuve ~le** individual event.
◇ *nm, f* SPORT [gén] individual sportsman (*f* sportswoman) ■ [athlète] individual athlete.

individuellement [ɛ̃dividɥɛlmɑ̃] *adv* **1.** [séparément] individually, separately, one by one **2.** [de façon personnelle] individually, personally.

indivis, e [ɛ̃divi, iz] *adj* joint, undivided.
◆ **en indivis, par indivis** *loc adv* DR in common ■ **posséder une propriété en ~** to own a property jointly.

indivisibilité [ɛ̃divizibilite] *nf* indivisibility.

indivisible [ɛ̃divizibl] *adj* indivisible.

indivision [ɛ̃divizjɔ̃] *nf* joint ownership ■ **propriété/biens en ~** jointly-owned property/goods.

Indochine [ɛ̃dɔʃin] *npr f* : **(l')~** Indochina ■ **la guerre d'~** the Indochinese War.

indochinois, e [ɛ̃dɔʃinwa, az] *adj* Indo-Chinese.
◆ **Indochinois, e** *nm, f* Indo-Chinese.

indocile [ɛ̃dɔsil] ◇ *adj* disobedient, recalcitrant, indocile *sout*.
◇ *nmf* rebel.

indocilité [ɛ̃dɔsilite] *nf* disobedience, recalcitrance.

indo-européen, enne [ɛ̃dɔœrɔpeɛ̃, ɛn] (*mpl* **indo-européens**, *fpl* **indo-européennes**) *adj* Indo-European.
◆ **Indo-Européen, enne** *nm, f* Indo-European.
◆ **indo-européen** *nm* LING Indo-European.

indolence [ɛ̃dɔlɑ̃s] *nf* **1.** [mollesse - dans le travail] indolence, apathy, lethargy ; [- dans l'attitude] indolence, languidness ■ **une pose pleine d'~** a languid posture **2.** MÉD benignancy.

indolent, e [ɛ̃dɔlɑ̃, ɑ̃t] *adj* **1.** [apathique] indolent, apathetic, lethargic **2.** [languissant] indolent, languid **3.** MÉD benign.

indolore [ɛ̃dɔlɔr] *adj* painless.

indomptable [ɛ̃dɔ̃tabl] *adj* **1.** [qu'on ne peut dompter] untamable, untameable **2.** *fig* [courage, volonté] indomitable, invincible.

indompté, e [ɛ̃dɔ̃te] *adj* **1.** [sauvage] untamed, wild ■ **cheval ~** unbroken horse **2.** *fig* [qui ne se soumet pas] untamed ■ **nation ~e** unsubjugated nation.

Indonésie [ɛ̃dɔnezi] *npr f* : **(l')~** Indonesia.

indonésien, enne [ɛ̃dɔnezjɛ̃, ɛn] *adj* Indonesian.
◆ **Indonésien, enne** *nm, f* Indonesian.

indu, e [ɛ̃dy] *adj* **1.** [inopportun] undue, excessive **2.** DR [non fondé - réclamation] unjustified, unfounded.
◆ **indu** *nm* DR sum not owed.

indubitable [ɛ̃dybitabl] *adj* undoubted, indubitable, undisputed ■ **c'est ~** it's beyond doubt *ou* dispute.

indubitablement [ɛ̃dybitabləmɑ̃] *adv* undoubtedly, indubitably.

inducteur, trice [ɛ̃dyktœr, tris] *adj* ÉLECTR inductive.
◆ **inducteur** *nm* ÉLECTR inductor.

inductif, ive [ɛ̃dyktif, iv] *adj* PHILOS & PHYS inductive.

induction [ɛ̃dyksjɔ̃] *nf* PHILOS & PHYS induction ■ **procéder** *ou* **raisonner par ~** to employ inductive reasoning, to induce.

induire [98] [ɛ̃dɥir] *vt* **1.** [inciter] : **~ qqn en erreur** to mislead sb ■ **~ qqn à mentir** *sout* to induce sb to lie **2.** [avoir pour conséquence] to lead to **3.** ÉLECTR, PHILOS & NUCL to induce.
◆ **induit** *nm* ÉLECTR armature ■ [rotor] rotor.

indulgence [ɛ̃dylʒɑ̃s] *nf* **1.** [clémence] leniency, tolerance, indulgence *sout* ■ **je fais appel à votre ~** I'm asking you to make allowances **2.** RELIG indulgence.
◆ **sans indulgence** ◇ *loc adj* [traitement, critique] severe, harsh ■ [regard] stern, merciless.
◇ *loc adv* [traiter, critiquer] severely, harshly ■ [regarder] sternly, mercilessly.

indulgent, e [ɛ̃dylʒɑ̃, ɑ̃t] *adj* **1.** [qui pardonne] lenient, forgiving ■ **soyons ~s** let's forgive and forget **2.** [sans sévérité - personne] indulgent, lenient ; [- verdict] lenient ■ **tu es trop ~ avec eux** you're not firm enough with them ■ **sois ~ avec elle** go easy on her.

indûment [ɛ̃dymɑ̃] *adv* unjustifiably, without due *ou* just cause ■ **tu te l'es ~ approprié** you had no right to take it.

induré, e [ɛ̃dyre] *adj* GÉOL & MÉD indurate.

indurer [3] [ɛ̃dyre] *vt* GÉOL & MÉD to indurate.
◆ **s'indurer** *vpi* GÉOL & MÉD to become indurate.

industrialisation [ɛ̃dystrijalizasjɔ̃] *nf* industrialization.

industrialisé, e [ɛ̃dystrijalize] *adj* [pays] industrialized ■ [agriculture] industrial.

industrialiser [3] [ɛ̃dystrijalize] *vt* **1.** [doter d'industries] to industrialize **2.** [mécaniser] to mechanize, to industrialize.
◆ **s'industrialiser** *vpi* **1.** [se doter d'industries] to industrialize, to become industrialized **2.** [se mécaniser] to become mechanized *ou* industrialized.

industrie [ɛ̃dystri] *nf* **1.** [secteur de production] industry ■ **~ extractive** *ou* **minière** mining industry ■ **~ alimentaire** food (processing) industry ■ **~ automobile** car *UK ou* automobile *US* industry ■ **~ légère** light industry ■ **~ lourde** heavy industry ■ **~ de luxe** luxury goods industry ■ **~ de pointe** hightech industry ■ **~ de précision** precision tool industry ■ **~ textile** textile industry **2.** [secteur commercial] industry, trade, business ■ **l'~ hôtelière** the hotel industry *ou* trade *ou* business ■ **l'~ du spectacle** the entertainment business ■ **l'~ des loisirs** the leisure industry ■ **l'~ du crime** organized crime **3.** [équipements] plant, industry **4.** [entreprise] industrial concern.

industriel, elle [ɛ̃dystrijɛl] *adj* **1.** [procédé, secteur, zone, révolution, société] industrial ■ [pays] industrial, industrialized **2.** [destiné à l'industrie - véhicule, équipement, rayonnages] industrial, heavy, heavy-duty **3.** [non artisanal] mass-produced, factory-made ■ **des crêpes ~les** ready-made *ou* factory-made pancakes.
◆ **industriel** *nm* industrialist, manufacturer.

industriellement [ɛ̃dystrijɛlmɑ̃] *adv* industrially ■ **fabriqué ~** factory-made, mass-produced.

industrieux, euse [ɛ̃dystrijø, øz] *adj* industrious.

inébranlable [inebrɑ̃labl] *adj* **1.** [ferme] steadfast, unshakeable, unwavering ■ **ma décision est ~** my decision is final ■ **elle a été ~** there was no moving her, she was adamant **2.** [solide - mur] immovable, (rock) solid.

inécoutable [inekutabl] *adj* : **de la musique ~** music which is impossible to listen to.

inécouté, e [inekute] *adj* : **rester ~** to remain unheeded *ou* ignored.

INED, Ined [inɛd] (*abr de* **Institut national d'études démographiques**) *npr m national institute for demographic research.*

inédit, e [inedi, it] *adj* **1.** [correspondance, auteur] (hitherto) unpublished ■ **ce film est ~ en France** this film has never been released in France **2.** [jamais vu] new, original.
◆ **inédit** *nm* **1.** [œuvre] unpublished work **2.** [nouveauté] : **c'est de l'~ pour nos trois alpinistes** it's a first for our three climbers.

ineffable [inefabl] *adj* **1.** [indicible] ineffable, indescribable **2.** [amusant] hilarious.

ineffaçable [inefasabl] *adj* [marque] indelible ■ [souvenir, traumatisme] unforgettable, enduring.

inefficace [inefikas] *adj* [méthode, médicament] ineffective ■ [personne] inefficient, ineffective.

inefficacité [inefikasite] *nf* [d'une méthode] inefficacy, ineffectiveness ■ [d'une personne] inefficiency, ineffectiveness ■ **d'une totale ~** totally ineffective.

inégal, e, aux [inegal, o] *adj* **1.** [varié - longueurs, salaires] unequal, different ■ [mal équilibré] uneven, unequal ■ **le combat était ~** the fight was one-sided **2.** [changeant - écrivain, élève, pouls] uneven, erratic ; [- humeur] changeable, uneven ■ **la qualité est ~e** it varies in quality ■ **le livre est ~** the book is uneven **3.** [rugueux] rough, uneven, bumpy.

inégalable [inegalabl] *adj* incomparable, matchless, peerless.

inégalé, e [inegale] *adj* unequalled, unmatched, unrivalled.

inégalement [inegalmɑ̃] *adv* **1.** [différemment] : **~ remplis** unequally filled **2.** [irrégulièrement] unevenly.

inégalitaire [inegalitɛr] *adj* non-egalitarian, elitist.

inégalité [inegalite] *nf* **1.** [disparité] difference, disparity ■ **~ entre deux variables/nombres** difference between two variables/numbers ■ **l'~ des salaires** the difference *ou* disparity in wages ■ **l'~ des chances** the lack of equal opportunities ■ **combattre les ~s sociales** to fight social injustice **2.** [qualité variable - d'une surface] roughness, unevenness ; [- d'un travail, d'une œuvre] uneven quality, unevenness ; [- du caractère] changeability **3.** MATH inequality.

inélégamment [inelegamɑ̃] *adv sout* inelegantly.

inélégance [inelegɑ̃s] *nf sout* **1.** [d'allure] inelegance, ungainliness, gracelessness ■ [d'une méthode] inelegance, unwieldiness ■ **le procédé était d'une grande ~** his behaviour was most ungracious **2.** [acte, tournure] impropriety.

inélégant, e [inelegɑ̃, ɑ̃t] *adj sout* **1.** [qui manque d'élégance - allure] inelegant, ungainly ; [- manières] inelegant **2.** [indélicat] indelicate, inelegant ■ **ce fut très ~ de ta part** that was very indelicate of you.

inéligible [ineliʒibl] *adj* DR ineligible.

inéluctable [inelyktabl] *adj* inevitable, unavoidable, ineluctable *litt.*

inéluctablement [inelyktabləmɑ̃] *adv* inevitably, inescapably, unavoidably.

inemployable [inɑ̃plwajabl] *adj* **1.** [ressources, matériaux] unusable ■ [méthode] useless, unserviceable **2.** [travailleur] unemployable.

inemployé, e [inɑ̃plwaje] *adj* [ressources, talent] dormant, untapped ■ [énergie] untapped, unused.

inénarrable [inenarabl] *adj* hilarious ■ **si tu avais vu le tableau, c'était ~ !** I wish you'd seen it, I can't tell you how funny it was!

inentamé, e [inɑ̃tame] *adj* [économies] intact, untouched ■ [bouteille, boîte] unopened.

inepte [inɛpt] *adj* [personne] inept, incompetent ■ [réponse, raisonnement] inept, foolish ■ [plan] inept, ill-considered.

ineptie [inɛpsi] *nf* **1.** [caractère d'absurdité] ineptitude, stupidity **2.** [acte, parole] piece of nonsense ■ **dire des ~s** to talk nonsense.

inépuisable [inepɥizabl] *adj* **1.** [réserves] inexhaustible, unlimited ■ [courage] endless, unlimited **2.** [bavard] inexhaustible ■ **elle est ~ sur mes imperfections** once she gets going about my faults, there's no stopping her.

inépuisé, e [inepɥize] *adj* not yet used up *ou* exhausted.

inéquation [inekwasjɔ̃] *nf* inequation *spéc*, inequality.

inéquitable [inekitabl] *adj* inequitable, unjust, unfair.

inerte [inɛrt] *adj* **1.** [léthargique] inert, apathetic, lethargic **2.** [semblant mort] inert, lifeless **3.** CHIM & PHYS inert.

inertie [inɛrsi] *nf* **1.** [passivité] lethargy, inertia, passivity **2.** MATH, MÉD, PHOTO & PHYS inertia.

inescomptable [inɛskɔ̃tabl] *adj* FIN undiscountable.

inespéré, e [inɛspere] *adj* unhoped-for ■ **c'est pour moi un bonheur ~** it's a pleasure I hadn't dared hope for.

inesthétique [inɛstetik] *adj* unsightly, unattractive.

inestimable [inɛstimabl] *adj* **1.** [impossible à évaluer] incalculable, inestimable ■ **les dégâts sont ~s** it's impossible to work out the extent of the damage **2.** [précieux] inestimable, invaluable, priceless.

inévitable [inevitabl] <> *adj* **1.** [auquel on ne peut échapper] unavoidable, inevitable ■ **c'était ~!** it was bound to happen *ou* inevitable! **2.** *(avant le n)* [habituel] inevitable.
<> *nm* : **l'~** the inevitable.

inévitablement [inevitabləmɑ̃] *adv* inevitably, predictably ■ **et ~, elle se décommanda à la dernière minute** and predictably *ou* sure enough, she cancelled at the last minute.

inexact, e [inɛgza(kt), akt] *adj* **1.** [erroné] inexact, incorrect, inaccurate ■ **le calcul est ~** there's a mistake in the calculations ■ **il serait ~ de dire...** it would be wrong *ou* incorrect to say... **2.** [en retard] unpunctual, late ■ **il est très ~** he's always late.

inexactitude [inɛgzaktityd] *nf* **1.** [d'un raisonnement] inaccuracy, imprecision ■ [d'un récit] inaccuracy, inexactness ■ [d'un calcul] inaccuracy, inexactitude **2.** [erreur] inaccuracy, error **3.** [manque de ponctualité] unpunctuality, lateness.

inexaucé, e [inɛgzose] *adj* [demande] unanswered ■ [vœu] unfulfilled.

inexcusable [inɛkskyzabl] *adj* [action] inexcusable, unforgivable ■ [personne] unforgivable.

inexécutable [inɛgzekytabl] *adj* [plan, programme] unworkable, impractical ■ [tâche] unfeasible, impossible ■ [musique] unplayable ■ [pas de danse] undanceable ■ **des ordres ~s** orders which are impossible to carry out *ou* to execute.

inexécuté, e [inɛgzekyte] *adj* [ordre, travaux] not (yet) carried out *ou* executed.

inexécution [inɛgzekysjɔ̃] *nf* [d'un contrat] nonfulfilment ■ **~ des travaux** failure to carry out work.

inexercé, e [inɛgzɛrse] *adj* [recrue, novice] untrained, inexperienced ■ [oreille, main] unpractised, untrained, untutored.

inexigible [inɛgziʒibl] *adj* [dette, impôt] inexigible *sout*, unrecoverable.

inexistant, e [inɛgzistɑ̃, ɑ̃t] *adj* **1.** [très insuffisant] nonexistent, inadequate ■ **les structures de base sont ~es** the basic structures are lacking, there are hardly any basic structures **2.** [irréel - monstre, peur] imaginary.

inexistence [inɛgzistɑ̃s] *nf* **1.** [de Dieu] nonexistence ■ [de preuves, structures] lack, absence ■ **l'~ de structures économiques** the complete lack *ou* absence of economic structure **2.** [manque de valeur] uselessness **3.** ADMIN & DR nullity.

inexorable [inɛgzɔrabl] *adj* **1.** [inévitable] inexorable, inevitable **2.** *sout* [intransigeant] inexorable.

inexorablement [inɛgzɔrabləmɑ̃] *adv* [inévitablement] inexorably, inevitably.

inexpérience [inɛksperjɑ̃s] *nf* lack of experience.

inexpérimenté, e [inɛksperimɑ̃te] *adj* **1.** [sans expérience] inexperienced ■ **un pilote ~** an inexperienced pilot **2.** [non testé] (as yet) untested.

inexpert, e [inɛkspɛr, ɛrt] *adj* inexpert, untrained ■ **confié à des mains ~es** placed in the hands of a novice.

inexpiable [inɛkspjabl] *adj* [inexcusable] inexpiable ■ **un crime ~** an unpardonable crime.

inexpié, e [inɛkspje] *adj* unexpiated.

inexplicable [inɛksplikabl] <> *adj* [comportement] inexplicable ■ [raison, crainte] inexplicable, unaccountable.
<> *nm* : **l'~** the inexplicable.

inexplicablement [inɛksplikabləmɑ̃] *adv* inexplicably, unaccountably.

inexpliqué, e [inɛksplike] *adj* [décision] unexplained ■ [phénomène] unexplained, unsolved ■ [agissements, départ] unexplained, mysterious ■ **une disparition restée ~e jusqu'à ce jour** a disappearance that remains a mystery to this day.

inexploitable [inɛksplwatabl] *adj* [ressources] unexploitable ■ [mine] unworkable ■ [idée] impractical, unfeasible.

inexploité, e [inɛksplwate] *adj* [richesses] undeveloped, untapped ■ [idée, talent] untapped, untried ■ [technique] unexploited, untried ■ **laisser un don ~** to fail to exploit a latent talent.

inexploré, e [inɛksplɔre] *adj* unexplored ■ **cette branche de la science est encore ~e** this branch of science is still unexplored.

inexpressif, ive [inɛkspresif, iv] *adj* [visage, regard] inexpressive, expressionless, blank ■ **il a gardé un visage ~ pendant tout le match** his face remained impassive throughout the match.

inexprimable [inɛksprimabl] *adj* inexpressible, ineffable, indescribable.

inexprimé, e [inɛksprime] *adj* unspoken ■ **une rancœur ~e** unspoken resentment.

inexpugnable [inɛkspygnabl] *adj litt* [forteresse] unassailable, impregnable ■ [vertu] inexpugnable.

inextensible [inɛkstɑ̃sibl] *adj* [appareil, câble] non-stretchable, inextensible TECHNOL ■ [tissu] non-stretch.

in extenso [inɛkstɛ̃so] *loc adv* in full, in extenso *sout* ■ **recopie le paragraphe ~** copy out the paragraph in full *ou* the whole paragraph.

inextinguible [inɛkstɛ̃gibl] *adj* **1.** *litt* [feu] inextinguishable **2.** *sout* [soif, désir] inextinguishable, unquenchable ■ [amour] undying **3.** *sout* [rire] uncontrollable.

in extremis [inɛkstremis] *loc adv* **1.** [de justesse] at the last minute, in the nick of time, at the eleventh hour ■ **réussir qqch ~** to (only) just manage to do sthg **2.** [avant la mort] in extremis *sout* ■ **baptiser un enfant/un adulte ~** to christen a child before he dies/an adult on his deathbed.

inextricable [inɛkstrikabl] *adj* inextricable ■ **tu t'es mise dans une situation ~** you've got yourself into an impossible position.

inextricablement [inɛkstrikabləmɑ̃] *adv* inextricably.

infaillibilité [ɛ̃fajibilite] *nf* [gén - RELIG] infallibility.

infaillible [ɛ̃fajibl] *adj* **1.** [efficace à coup sûr] infallible **2.** [certain] infallible, reliable, guaranteed ■ **c'est la marque ~ d'une forte personnalité** it's a sure sign of a strong personality **3.** [qui ne peut se tromper] infallible ■ **nul n'est ~** no-one is infallible, everyone makes mistakes.

infailliblement [ɛ̃fajibləmɑ̃] *adv* **1.** [inévitablement] inevitably, without fail **2.** *litt* [sans se tromper] infallibly.

infaisable [ɛ̃fəzabl] *adj* [choix] impossible ■ **c'est ~** [projet] it can't be done.

infalsifiable [ɛ̃falsifjabl] *adj* [carte d'identité] forgery-proof.

infamant, e [ɛ̃famɑ̃, ɑ̃t] *adj* **1.** *sout* [déshonorant - acte, crime] heinous, infamous, abominable ■ **tu peux réclamer ton argent, ce n'est pas ~** you can go and ask for your money, there's no shame in that **2.** DR ▻ **peine.**

infâme [ɛ̃fam] *adj* **1.** [vil - crime] despicable, loathsome, heinous ; [- criminel] vile, despicable ; [- traître] despicable **2.** [répugnant - odeur, nourriture] revolting, vile, foul ; [- endroit] disgusting, revolting ■ **une ~ odeur de putréfaction** a foul stench of rotting.

infamie [ɛ̃fami] *nf sout* **1.** [déshonneur] infamy, disgrace ▪ **il a couvert sa famille d'~** he has brought infamy upon his family **2.** [caractère abject - d'une action, d'une personne] infamy, vileness **3.** [acte révoltant] infamy, loathsome deed **4.** [propos] piece of (vile) slander, smear.

infant, e [ɛ̃fɑ̃, ɑ̃t] *nm, f* infante (*f* infanta).

infanterie [ɛ̃fɑ̃tri] *nf* infantry ▪ **~ aéroportée/motorisée** airborne/motorized infantry ▪ **~ légère** light infantry.

infanticide [ɛ̃fɑ̃tisid] ◇ *nm* infanticide.
◇ *nmf* [personne] child killer DR infanticide *litt*.

infantile [ɛ̃fɑ̃til] *adj* **1.** MÉD & PSYCHOL child *(modif)*, infantile *spéc* **2.** *péj* [puéril] infantile, childish ▪ **se comporter de façon ~** to behave like a child.

infantiliser [3] [ɛ̃fɑ̃tilize] *vt* to infantilize.

infantilisme [ɛ̃fɑ̃tilism] *nm* **1.** *péj* [puérilité] infantilism, immaturity ▪ **elle a refusé! – c'est de l'~!** she said no! – how childish! **2.** MÉD & PSYCHOL infantilism.

infarctus [ɛ̃farktys] *nm* infarct ▪ **avoir un ~** to have a heart attack *ou* a coronary ▶ **~ du myocarde** myocardial infarction.

infatigable [ɛ̃fatigabl] *adj* **1.** [toujours dispos] tireless, untiring, indefatigable *sout* **2.** [indéfectible - énergie, courage] inexhaustible, unwavering, unflagging ; [- détermination] dogged, unflagging ; [- dévouement] unstinting, unflagging ▪ **elle a mené une lutte ~ contre l'injustice** she fought tirelessly against injustice.

infatigablement [ɛ̃fatigabləmɑ̃] *adv* tirelessly, untiringly, indefatigably *sout*.

infatué, e [ɛ̃fatɥe] *adj litt* **1.** [vaniteux] self-satisfied, conceited, bumptious ▪ **~ de sa personne** self-important, full of o.s. **2.** [entiché] : **~ de qqn/qqch** infatuated with sb/sthg.

infatuer [7] [ɛ̃fatɥe] ◆ **s'infatuer** *vpi litt* [être content de soi] to be conceited.
◆ **s'infatuer de** *vp+prép litt* [s'enticher de] to become infatuated with.

infécond, e [ɛ̃fekɔ̃, ɔ̃d] *adj litt* **1.** [sol, femme] infertile, barren *litt* **2.** *fig* [pensée] sterile, barren, unproductive.

infécondité [ɛ̃fekɔ̃dite] *nf litt* **1.** [d'un sol, d'une femme] infertility, infecundity *sout*, barrenness *litt* **2.** *fig* [d'une pensée] sterility, barrenness, unproductiveness.

infect, e [ɛ̃fɛkt] *adj* **1.** [répugnant - repas] rotten, revolting, disgusting ; [- odeur] foul, rank, putrid ▪ **il est ~, leur vin** their wine's awful *ou* disgusting **2.** *fam* [très laid, très désagréable] foul, appalling, lousy ▪ **c'est un type ~** he's a revolting individual ▪ **les enfants ont été ~s ce matin** the kids were terrible *ou* awful this morning ▪ **être ~ avec qqn** to be rotten to sb.

infecter [4] [ɛ̃fɛkte] *vt* **1.** PHYSIOL & INFORM to infect ▪ **plaie infectée** septic wound **2.** [rendre malsain] to contaminate, to pollute **3.** *litt* [empester] : **l'usine infecte toute la région** the factory pollutes the whole area.
◆ **s'infecter** *vpi* to become infected, to go septic.

infectieux, euse [ɛ̃fɛksjø, øz] *adj* [maladie] infectious ▪ **un sujet ~** a carrier.

infection [ɛ̃fɛksjɔ̃] *nf* **1.** MÉD infection **2.** [puanteur] (foul) stench ▪ **c'est une ~, ce marché!** this market stinks (to high heaven)!

inféoder [3] [ɛ̃feɔde] *vt* **1.** HIST to enfeoff **2.** [soumettre] to dominate.
◆ **s'inféoder à** *vp+prép* POLIT to become subservient *ou* subjected to.

inférer [18] [ɛ̃fere] *vt sout* to infer ▪ **que pouvons-nous en ~?** what can we infer *ou* gather from this?

inférieur, e [ɛ̃ferjœr] ◇ *adj* **1.** [du bas - étagères, membres] lower ; [- lèvre, mâchoire] lower, bottom *(avant n)* ▪ [situé en dessous] lower down, below ▪ **c'est à l'étage ~** it's on the floor below *ou* on the next floor down ▪ **la couche ~e** the layer below *ou* beneath ▪ **être ~ à** to be lower than *ou* below **2.** [moins bon - niveau] lower ; [- esprit, espèce] inferior, lesser ; [- qualité] inferior, poorer ▪ **les gens d'un rang ~** people of a lower rank *ou* lower in rank ▪ **se sentir ~ (par rapport à qqn)** to feel inferior (to sb) ▪ **~ à** inferior to, poorer than ▪ **en physique il est très ~ à sa sœur** he's not nearly as good as his sister at physics
3. [plus petit - chiffre, salaire] lower, smaller ; [- poids, vitesse] lower ; [- taille] smaller ▪ **nous (leur) étions ~s en nombre** there were fewer of us (than of them) ▪ **~ à** [chiffre] lower *ou* smaller *ou* less than ; [rendement] lower than, inferior to ▪ **des températures ~es à 10° C** temperatures below 10°C *ou* lower than 10°C
4. [dans une hiérarchie - le plus bas] lower ▪ **animaux/végétaux ~s** BOT & ZOOL lower animals/plants
5. ASTRON inferior
6. GÉOGR [cours, région] lower.
◇ *nm, f* [gén] inferior ▪ [subalterne] inferior, subordinate, underling *péj*.

inférieurement [ɛ̃ferjœrmɑ̃] *adv* [moins bien] less well ▪ **~ entretenu/approvisionné/conçu** less well-maintained/-stocked/-designed.

inférioriser [3] [ɛ̃ferjɔrize] *vt* **1.** [dévaloriser] : **~ qqn** to make sb feel inferior **2.** [minimiser] to minimise the importance of.

infériorité [ɛ̃ferjɔrite] *nf* **1.** [inadéquation - en grandeur, en valeur] inferiority ; [- en effectif] (numerical) inferiority **2.** [handicap] weakness, inferiority, deficiency ▪ **être en situation d'~** to be in a weak position.

infernal, e, aux [ɛ̃fɛrnal, o] *adj* **1.** *fam* [insupportable] infernal, hellish, diabolical ▪ **cet enfant est ~!** that child's a real terror! ▪ **ils mettent de la musique toute la nuit, c'est ~** they've got music on all night, it's absolute hell **2.** *litt* [de l'enfer] infernal **3.** [diabolique - engrenage, logique] infernal, devilish, diabolical ▪ **cycle ~** vicious circle.

infertile [ɛ̃fɛrtil] *adj litt* **1.** [terre] infertile, barren **2.** [imagination, esprit] infertile, uncreative, sterile.

infertilité [ɛ̃fɛrtilite] *nf litt* **1.** [de la terre, de l'imagination] infertility *sout* **2.** [d'une femme] infertility, barrenness *sout*.

infestation [ɛ̃fɛstasjɔ̃] *nf* **1.** [infection] infection **2.** [de parasites, de moustiques] infestation.

infester [3] [ɛ̃fɛste] *vt* **1.** [suj: rats] to infest, to overrun ▪ [suj: pillards] to infest ▪ **la région est infestée de sauterelles/moustiques** the area is infested with locusts/mosquitoes **2.** MÉD to infest.

infibulation [ɛ̃fibylasjɔ̃] *nf* infibulation.

infidèle [ɛ̃fidɛl] ◇ *adj* **1.** [gén] disloyal, unfaithful ▪ [en amour] unfaithful, untrue *litt* ▪ [en amitié] disloyal ▪ **être ~ à sa parole** to go back on one's word **2.** [inexact - témoignage, texte] inaccurate, unreliable ; [- mémoire] unreliable ▪ **une traduction ~** an unfaithful *ou* inaccurate translation **3.** RELIG infidel.
◇ *nmf* RELIG infidel.
◇ *nf* LITTÉR : **belle ~** *well-turned but inaccurate translation (term used in 17th-century literature).*

infidèlement [ɛ̃fidɛlmɑ̃] *adv* [inexactement] inaccurately, unfaithfully.

infidélité [ɛ̃fidelite] *nf* **1.** [inconstance] infidelity, unfaithfulness ▪ [aventure adultère] infidelity, affair ▪ **faire une ~ à qqn** to be unfaithful to sb ▪ **j'ai fait une ~ à mon coiffeur** *hum* I deserted my usual hairdresser **2.** [déloyauté] disloyalty, unfaithfulness ▪ **l'~ à la parole donnée** being untrue to *ou* breaking one's word **3.** [caractère inexact] inaccuracy, unreliability ▪ [erreur] inaccuracy, error.

infiltration [ɛ̃filtrasjɔ̃] *nf* **1.** MÉD injection ▶ **~ anesthésique** infiltration anesthesia **2.** [gén - PHYSIOL] infiltration ▪ **il y a des ~s dans le plafond** there are leaks in the ceiling, water is leaking *ou* seeping through the ceiling ▶ **eaux d'~** GÉOGR percolated water **3.** [d'une idée] penetration, percolation *litt* ▪ [d'un agitateur] infiltration.

infiltrer [3] [ɛ̃filtre] *vt* **1.** MÉD to infiltrate *spéc*, to inject **2.** [organisation, réseau] to infiltrate.

◆ **s'infiltrer** *vpi* [air, brouillard, eau] to seep ▪ [lumière] to filter in ▪ **s'~ dans : quand l'eau s'infiltre dans le sable** when the water seeps (through) into the sand ▪ **s'~ dans les lieux** to get into the building ▪ **s' ~ dans un réseau d'espions** to infiltrate a spy network.

infime [ɛ̃fim] *adj* [quantité, proportion] infinitesimal, minute, tiny ▪ [détail] minor.

infini, e [ɛ̃fini] *adj* **1.** [étendue] infinite, vast, boundless ▪ [ressources] infinite, unlimited **2.** [extrême - générosité, patience, reconnaissance] infinite, boundless, limitless ; [- charme, douceur] infinite ; [- précautions] infinite, endless ; [- bonheur, plaisir] infinite, immeasurable ; [- difficulté, peine] immense, extreme ▪ **mettre un soin ~ à faire qqch** to take infinite pains to do sthg **3.** [interminable] never-ending, interminable, endless ▪ **j'ai dû attendre un temps ~** I had to wait interminably **4.** MATH infinite.

◆ **infini** *nm* **1.** MATH, OPT & PHOTO infinity ▪ **faire la mise au point sur l'~** PHOTO to focus to infinity **2.** PHILOS : **l'~** the infinite ▪ **l'~ de cette vaste plaine** *litt* the immensity of this endless plain.

◆ **à l'infini** *loc adv* **1.** [discuter, reproduire] endlessly, ad infinitum ▪ [varier] infinitely ▪ [s'étendre] endlessly **2.** MATH to *ou* towards infinity.

infiniment [ɛ̃finimɑ̃] *adv* **1.** [extrêmement - désolé, reconnaissant] extremely, infinitely ; [- généreux] immensely, boundlessly ; [- agréable, douloureux] immensely, extremely ; [- long, grand] infinitely, immensely ▪ **je vous remercie ~** thank you so much ▪ **c'est ~ mieux/pire que la dernière fois** it's infinitely better/worse than last time ▪ **elle est ~ plus brillante** she's far *ou* infinitely brighter ▪ **avec ~ de patience/de précautions** with infinite patience/care **2.** MATH infinitely ▪ **l'~ grand** the infinite, the infinitely great ▪ **l'~ petit** the infinitesimal.

infinité [ɛ̃finite] *nf* **1.** [très grand nombre] : **une ~ de** an infinite number of ▪ **on me posa une ~ de questions** I was asked endless *ou* a great many questions **2.** *litt* **l'~ de l'espace** the infinity of space.

infinitésimal, e, aux [ɛ̃finitezimal, o] *adj* infinitesimal.

infinitif, ive [ɛ̃finitif, iv] *adj* infinitive.

◆ **infinitif** *nm* infinitive (mood) ▪ **~ de narration** infinitive of narration, *voir aussi* **pluriel**.

infirmatif, ive [ɛ̃firmatif, iv] *adj* invalidating.

infirmation [ɛ̃firmasjɔ̃] *nf* invalidation.

infirme [ɛ̃firm] <> *adj* disabled, crippled.

<> *nmf* disabled person ▪ **les ~s** the disabled ⊙ **~ moteur cérébral** person suffering from cerebral palsy, spastic *vieilli*.

infirmer [3] [ɛ̃firme] *vt* **1.** [démentir] to invalidate, to contradict **2.** DR [arrêt] to revoke ▪ [jugement] to quash.

infirmerie [ɛ̃firməri] *nf* [dans une école, une entreprise] sick bay *ou* room ▪ [dans une prison] infirmary ▪ [dans une caserne] infirmary, sick bay ▪ [sur un navire] sick bay.

infirmier, ère [ɛ̃firmje, ɛr] <> *nm, f* male nurse (*f* nurse) ▪ **elle fait un stage d'infirmière** she's on *UK ou* in *US* a nursing course ⊙ **~ en chef, infirmière en chef** charge nurse *UK*, head nurse *US* ▪ **~ militaire** medical orderly ▪ **~ de nuit** night nurse ▪ **infirmière diplômée d'État** Registered Nurse *UK* ▪ **infirmière visiteuse** district nurse.

<> *adj* nursing *(modif)*.

infirmité [ɛ̃firmite] *nf* **1.** [invalidité] disability, handicap ⊙ **~ motrice cérébrale** cerebral palsy **2.** *litt* [faiblesse] failing, weakness.

inflammable [ɛ̃flamabl] *adj* **1.** [combustible] inflammable, flammable ▪ **gaz ~** flammable gas ▪ **matériaux ~s** inflammable materials **2.** *litt* [impétueux] inflammable.

inflammation [ɛ̃flamasjɔ̃] *nf* MÉD inflammation ▪ **j'ai une ~ au genou** my knee is inflamed.

inflammatoire [ɛ̃flamatwar] *adj* MÉD inflammatory.

inflation [ɛ̃flasjɔ̃] *nf* **1.** ÉCON inflation ▪ **~ par la demande/les coûts** demand-pull/cost-push inflation ▪ **~ galopante/larvée** galloping/creeping inflation ▪ **des investissements à l'abri de l'~** inflation-proof investments **2.** [accroissement - des effectifs] : **l'~ du nombre des bureaucrates** the inflated *ou* swelling numbers of bureaucrats.

inflationniste [ɛ̃flasjɔnist] <> *adj* [tendance] inflationary ▪ [politique] inflationist.

<> *nmf* inflationist.

infléchi, e [ɛ̃fleʃi] *adj* [phonème] inflected.

infléchir [32] [ɛ̃fleʃir] *vt sout* **1.** [courber] to bend, to inflect **2.** [influer sur] to modify, to influence ▪ **~ le cours des événements** to affect *ou* to influence the course of events.

◆ **s'infléchir** *vpi* **1.** [décrire une courbe] to bend, to curve (round) **2.** *fig* [changer de but] to shift, to change course ▪ **la politique du gouvernement s'infléchit dans le sens du protectionnisme** government policy is shifting *ou* veering towards protectionism.

infléchissement [ɛ̃fleʃismɑ̃] *nm* shift, change of course ▪ **~ d'une politique** change of emphasis *ou* shift in policy.

inflexibilité [ɛ̃flɛksibilite] *nf* **1.** [d'un matériau] inflexibility, rigidity **2.** [d'une personne] inflexibility, firmness.

inflexible [ɛ̃flɛksibl] *adj* **1.** [matériau] rigid, inflexible **2.** [personne] inflexible, rigid, unbending ▪ **il est resté ~** he wouldn't change his mind **3.** [loi, morale] rigid, hard-and-fast ▪ [règlement, discipline] strict.

inflexiblement [ɛ̃flɛksibləmɑ̃] *adv sout* inflexibly, rigidly.

inflexion [ɛ̃flɛksjɔ̃] *nf* **1.** [modulation - de la voix] inflection, modulation **2.** [changement de direction] shift, change of course **3.** LING & MATH inflection **4.** [inclination] : **avec une gracieuse ~ de la tête** with a graceful nod ▪ **une ~ du buste** a bow.

infliger [17] [ɛ̃fliʒe] *vt* : **~ une punition/une défaite/des souffrances/des pertes à qqn** to inflict a punishment/a defeat/sufferings/losses on sb ▪ **~ une amende/corvée à qqn** to impose a fine/chore on sb ▪ **~ une humiliation à qqn** to put sb down, to humiliate sb ▪ **tel est le châtiment infligé aux traîtres** such is the punishment meted out to traitors ▪ **~ sa compagnie** *ou* **présence à qqn** to inflict one's company *ou* presence on sb.

influençable [ɛ̃flyɑ̃sabl] *adj* : **elle est beaucoup trop ~** she's far too easily influenced *ou* swayed.

influence [ɛ̃flyɑ̃s] *nf* **1.** [marque, effet] influence ▪ **cela n'a eu aucune ~ sur ma décision** it didn't influence my decision at all, it had no bearing (at all) on my decision **2.** [emprise - d'une personne, d'une drogue, d'un sentiment] influence ▪ **avoir une bonne ~ sur** to be *ou* to have a good influence on ▪ **j'ai beaucoup d'~ sur lui** I've got a lot of influence over him ▪ **subir l'~ de qqn** to be influenced by sb ▪ **être sous l'~ de la boisson/drogue** to be under the influence of drink/drugs **3.** PSYCHOL influence **4.** [poids social ou politique] influence ▪ **avoir de l'~** to have influence, to be influential **5.** ÉLECTR static induction.

influencer [16] [ɛ̃flyɑ̃se] *vt* to influence ▪ **ne te laisse pas ~ par la publicité** don't let advertising influence you, don't let yourself be influenced by advertising.

influent, e [ɛ̃flyɑ̃, ɑ̃t] *adj* influential ▪ **c'est une personne ~e** she's a person of influence *ou* an influential person.

influer [3] [ɛ̃flye] ◆ **influer sur** *v+prép* to have an influence on, to influence, to affect.

influx [ɛ̃fly] *nm* : **~ nerveux** nerve impulse.

info [ɛ̃fo] *nf fam* info *(U)* ▪ **c'est lui qui m'a donné cette ~** I got the info from him.

◆ **infos** *nfpl fam* **les ~s** the news *(U)*.

Infographie® [ɛ̃fografi] *nf* computer graphics.

infographique [ɛ̃fɔgrafik] *adj* computer graphics *(modif)*.

in-folio [infɔljo] <> *adj inv* folio.

<> *nm inv* folio ▪ **des ~** folios.

infondé, e [ɛ̃fɔ̃de] *adj* unfounded, groundless.

informateur, trice [ɛ̃fɔrmatœr, tris] *nm, f* informer.

informaticien, enne [ɛ̃fɔrmatisjɛ̃, ɛn] *nm, f* [dans une entreprise] data processor ■ [à l'université] computer scientist ■ **son fils est ~** his son works in computers.

informatif, ive [ɛ̃fɔrmatif, iv] *adj* informative.

information [ɛ̃fɔrmasjɔ̃] *nf* **1.** [indication] piece of information ■ **des ~s** (some) information ■ **demander des ~s sur** to ask (for information) about, to inquire about ■ **je vais aux ~s** I'll go and find out
2. [diffusion de renseignements] information ■ **réunion d'~** briefing session ■ **l'~ circule mal entre les services** there's poor communication between departments ■ **nous demandons une meilleure ~ des consommateurs sur leurs droits** we want consumers to be better informed about their rights ■ **pour ton ~, sache que...** for your (own) information you should know that...
3. PRESSE, RADIO & TV news item, piece of news ■ **voici une ~ de dernière minute** here is some last minute news ■ **des ~s de dernière minute semblent indiquer que le couvre-feu est intervenu** latest reports seem to indicate that there has been a ceasefire ■ **des ~s économiques** economic news, news about the economy ■ **l'~** the news ■ **la liberté d'~** freedom of information ■ **place à l'~** priority to current affairs ▶ **journal d'~** quality newspaper
4. INFORM : **l'~, les ~s** data, information ▶ **les sciences de l'~** information sciences, informatics ■ **protection de l'~** data protection ■ **traitement de l'~** data processing
5. DR [instruction] : **ouvrir une ~** to set up a preliminary inquiry ▶ **~ judiciaire** preliminary investigation *ou* inquiry.
◆ **informations** *nfpl* RADIO & TV [émission] : **les ~s** the news (bulletin) ■ **~s télévisées/radiodiffusées** television/radio news ■ **c'est passé aux ~s** it was on the news.

informatique [ɛ̃fɔrmatik] <> *adj* computer *(modif)* ■ **un système ~** a computer system.
<> *nf* [science] computer science, information technology ■ [traitement des données] data processing ■ **faire de l'~** to work *ou* to be in computing ▶ **~ documentaire** (electronic) information retrieval ■ **~ familiale** home *ou* domestic computing ■ **~ de gestion** [dans une administration] administrative data processing ; [dans une entreprise] business data processing, business applications ■ **~ grand public** mass (consumer) computing.

informatisable [ɛ̃fɔrmatizabl] *adj* computerizable.

informatisation [ɛ̃fɔrmatizasjɔ̃] *nf* computerization.

informatisé, e [ɛ̃fɔrmatize] *adj* [secteur, système] computerized ■ [enseignement] computer-based ■ [gestion] computer-aided, computer-assisted.

informatiser [3] [ɛ̃fɔrmatize] *vt* to computerize.
◆ **s'informatiser** *vpi* to become computerized ■ **la bibliothèque s'est informatisée** the library catalogue has been computerized ■ **depuis que je me suis informatisé** since I got a computer.

informative [ɛ̃fɔrmativ] *f* ▷ **informatif.**

informe [ɛ̃fɔrm] *adj* **1.** [inesthétique - vêtement, sculpture] shapeless **2.** [qui n'a plus de forme - chaussure] shapeless, battered **3.** [sans contours nets] formless, shapeless ■ **une masse ~ de cellules** an amorphous mass of cells **4.** [ébauché] rough, unfinished, undeveloped.

informé, e [ɛ̃fɔrme] *adj* well-informed, informed ■ **de source bien ~e** from a well-informed *ou* an authoritative source ■ **c'est son amant – tu m'as l'air bien** *ou* **très ~!** he's her lover – you seem to know a lot! ■ **nous sommes mal ~s** [peu renseignés] we don't get enough information, we're not sufficiently informed ; [avec de fausses informations] we're being misinformed ■ **se tenir ~ de** to keep o.s. informed about ■ **tenir qqn ~ (de qqch)** to keep sb informed (of sthg).
◆ **informé** *nm* (judicial *ou* legal) inquiry ■ **jusqu'à plus ample ~** pending further information.

informel, elle [ɛ̃fɔrmɛl] *adj* **1.** [non officiel, décontracté] informal **2.** ART informal.
◆ **informel** *nm* informal artist.

informer [3] [ɛ̃fɔrme] <> *vt* **1.** [aviser] : **~ qqn de** to inform *ou* to tell *ou* to advise *sout* sb of ■ **si le notaire téléphone, vous voudrez bien m'en ~** if the lawyer phones, will you please let me know *ou* inform me ■ **~ qqn que** to inform *ou* to tell sb that ■ **l'a-t-on informé qu'il est muté?** has he been informed *ou* notified of his transfer? ■ **nous informons Messieurs les voyageurs que...** passengers are informed that... **2.** [renseigner] to inform, to give information to **3.** PHILOS to inform.
<> *vi* DR : **~ contre qqn** to start investigations concerning sb.
◆ **s'informer** *vpi* : **où puis-je m'~?** where can I get some information *ou* ask *ou* inquire? ■ **je me suis informé auprès de mon avocat/de la mairie** I asked my lawyer/at the town hall ■ **s'~ de** [droit, horaire, résultats] to inquire *ou* to ask about ■ **s'~ de la santé de qqn** to inquire after sb's health ■ **s'~ sur** to inform o.s. about ■ **je vais m'~ sur la marche à suivre** I'm going to find out what the procedure is.

informulé, e [ɛ̃fɔrmyle] *adj* unformulated, unspoken.

infortune [ɛ̃fɔrtyn] *nf litt* **1.** [événement] misfortune **2.** [malheur] misfortune ■ **dans son ~, elle a au moins une consolation** she has at least one consolation in the midst of her misfortune ▶ **~ conjugale** *euphém* infidelity.

infortuné, e [ɛ̃fɔrtyne] *litt* <> *adj (avant le n)* [malchanceux - gén] unfortunate, luckless ; [- mari] hapless, wretched.
<> *nm, f* (unfortunate) wretch.

infra [ɛ̃fra] *adv* : **voir ~** see below.

infraction [ɛ̃fraksjɔ̃] *nf* **1.** DR breach of the law, offence ■ **~ au code de la route** driving offence ■ **être en ~** to be in breach of the law ■ **je n'ai jamais été en ~** I've never committed an *ou* any offence ▶ **~ politique** ≃ offence *ou* offences against the state **2.** [transgression] infringement, transgression ■ **~ à** breach of, transgression against.

infranchissable [ɛ̃frɑ̃ʃisabl] *adj* **1.** [col] impassable ■ [rivière] which cannot be crossed **2.** [difficulté] insuperable, insurmountable.

infrarouge [ɛ̃fraruʒ] <> *adj* infrared.
<> *nm* infrared (radiation).

infrason [ɛ̃frasɔ̃] *nm* infrasound.

infrasonore [ɛ̃frasɔnɔr] *adj* infrasonic.

infrastructure [ɛ̃frastryktyr] *nf* **1.** [ensemble d'équipements] infrastructure **2.** CONSTR substructure.

infréquentable [ɛ̃frekɑ̃tabl] *adj* : **ils sont ~s** they're not the sort of people you'd want to associate with ■ **tu es ~!** you're a disgrace!

infroissable [ɛ̃frwasabl] *adj* crease-resistant.

infructueux, euse [ɛ̃fryktɥø, øz] *adj* fruitless.

infuse [ɛ̃fyz] *adj f* ▷ **science.**

infuser [3] [ɛ̃fyze] <> *vt* **1.** [faire macérer - thé] to brew, to infuse ; [- tisane] to infuse **2.** *litt* [insuffler] : **~ qqch à qqn** to infuse *ou* to inject sb with sthg, to infuse *ou* to inject sthg into sb.
<> *vi (aux être ou avoir)* [macérer - thé] to brew, to infuse ; [- tisane] to infuse ■ **laissez ~ quelques minutes** leave to infuse for a few minutes.

infusion [ɛ̃fyzjɔ̃] *nf* **1.** [boisson] herbal tea, infusion *sout* **2.** [macération - de thé] brewing, infusion ; [- de tisane] infusion, infusing ■ **le thé n'a pas besoin d'être passé après ~** the tea doesn't need straining after brewing.

ingambe [ɛ̃gɑ̃b] *adj litt* nimble, spry, sprightly ■ **il est resté ~ jusqu'à la fin** he remained very active to the end.

ingénier [9] [ɛ̃ʒenje] ◆ **s'ingénier à** *vp+prép* to try hard *ou* to endeavour *ou* to strive to ■ **s'~ à trouver une solution** to work hard at finding *ou* to do all one can to find a solution ■ **s'~ à plaire** to strive to please ■ **on dirait qu'il s'ingénie à me nuire** it's as if he's going out of his way to do me down.

ingénierie [ɛ̃ʒeniri] *nf* engineering ■ **~ assistée par ordinateur** computer-assisted engineering ■ **~ génétique** genetic engineering ■ **~ de systèmes** systems engineering.

ingénieur [ɛ̃ʒenjœr] *nm* engineer ■ **~ agronome** agricultural engineer ■ **~ commercial** sales engineer ■ **~ électricien** electrical engineer ■ **~ du génie civil** civil engineer ■ **~ informaticien** computer engineer ■ **~ mécanicien** mechanical engineer ■ ~ **des ponts et chaussées** civil engineer ■ ~ **du son** sound engineer ■ ~ **système** systems engineer ■ ~ **des travaux publics** construction engineer.

ingénieur-conseil [ɛ̃ʒenjœrkɔ̃sɛj] (*pl* **ingénieurs-conseils**) *nm* (engineering) consultant, consulting engineer.

ingénieusement [ɛ̃ʒenjøzmɑ̃] *adv* ingeniously.

ingénieux, euse [ɛ̃ʒenjø, øz] *adj* [personne] ingenious, clever, inventive ■ [plan, appareil, procédé] ingenious.

ingéniosité [ɛ̃ʒenjozite] *nf* ingenuity, inventiveness.

ingénu, e [ɛ̃ʒeny] ◇ *adj* ingenuous, naive.
◇ *nm, f* ingenuous *ou* naive person.
◆ **ingénue** *nf* THÉÂTRE ingenue *ou* ingénue (role) ■ **cesse de jouer les ~es** *fig* stop acting *ou* playing the innocent.

ingénuité [ɛ̃ʒenɥite] *nf* ingenuousness, naivety.

ingénument [ɛ̃ʒenymɑ̃] *adv* ingenuously, naively.

ingérable [ɛ̃ʒerabl] *adj fam* unmanageable.

ingérence [ɛ̃ʒerɑ̃s] *nf* interference ■ POLIT interference, intervention.

ingérer [18] [ɛ̃ʒere] *vt* to absorb, to ingest.
◆ **s'ingérer dans** *vp+prép* to interfere in ■ **s'~ dans la vie privée de qqn** to meddle in sb's private life.

ingestion [ɛ̃ʒɛstjɔ̃] *nf* ingestion.

ingouvernable [ɛ̃guvɛrnabl] *adj* ungovernable.

ingrat, e [ɛ̃gra, at] ◇ *adj* **1.** [sans grâce - visage] unattractive, unpleasant, coarse ■ **avoir un physique ~** to be unattractive *ou* graceless **2.** [tâche, travail] unrewarding, thankless ■ [terre] unproductive **3.** [sans reconnaissance] ungrateful ■ **être ~ avec** *ou* **envers qqn** to be ungrateful towards sb.
◇ *nm, f* ungrateful person.

ingratitude [ɛ̃gratityd] *nf* **1.** [d'une personne] ingratitude, ungratefulness ■ **faire preuve d'~** to behave with ingratitude **2.** [d'une tâche] thanklessness.

ingrédient [ɛ̃gredjɑ̃] *nm* **1.** [dans une recette, un mélange] ingredient **2.** *fig* [élément] ingredient ■ **les ~s du bonheur** the recipe for happiness.

inguérissable [ɛ̃gerisabl] *adj* MÉD incurable.

ingurgiter [3] [ɛ̃gyrʒite] *vt fam* **1.** [avaler - aliments] to wolf *ou* to gulp down *(sép)* ; [- boisson] to gulp down *(sép)*, to knock back *(sép)* **2.** *fig* to take in *(sép)* ■ **avec tout ce qu'on leur fait ~ avant l'examen!** with all the stuff they have to cram (into their heads) before the exam! ■ **faire ~ des faits/dates à qqn** to stuff sb's head full of facts/dates.

inhabile [inabil] *adj sout* **1.** [sans aptitude] inept, unskilful ■ **~ à** unfit for **2.** [maladroit - mouvement] clumsy, awkward ; [- propos, méthode] inept, clumsy ■ **une déclaration ~** a bungling statement **3.** DR (legally) incapable ■ **~ à témoigner** incompetent to stand as a witness.

inhabileté [inabilte] *nf litt* ineptitude, ineptness, clumsiness.

inhabilité [inabilite] *nf* (legal) incapacity.

inhabitable [inabitabl] *adj* [maison, grenier] uninhabitable ■ [quartier] unpleasant to live in.

inhabité, e [inabite] *adj* [maison, chambre] uninhabited, unoccupied ■ [contrée] uninhabited ■ **de vastes contrées ~es s'étendent vers le nord** vast empty tracts of land lie to the north.

inhabituel, elle [inabitɥɛl] *adj* unusual, odd.

inhalateur, trice [inalatœr, tris] *adj* inhaling, breathing.
◆ **inhalateur** *nm* **1.** [pour inhalations] inhaler **2.** AÉRON oxygen mask.

inhalation [inalasjɔ̃] *nf* **1.** [respiration] breathing in, inhalation *spéc* **2.** [traitement] (steam) inhalation ■ **je (me) fais des ~s avec ce produit** I use this product as an inhalant.

inhaler [3] [inale] *vt* to inhale, to breathe in *(sép)*.

inhérence [inerɑ̃s] *nf* inherence.

inhérent, e [inerɑ̃, ɑ̃t] *adj* inherent ■ **~ à** inherent in.

inhibé, e [inibe] ◇ *adj* inhibited, repressed.
◇ *nm, f* inhibited *ou* repressed person.

inhiber [3] [inibe] *vt* to inhibit.

inhibiteur, trice [inibitœr, tris] *adj* inhibitive, inhibitory.
◆ **inhibiteur** *nm* inhibitor.

inhibition [inibisjɔ̃] *nf* PHYSIOL & PSYCHOL inhibition ■ **le traumatisme a provoqué une ~ de la parole chez l'enfant** the child had speech difficulties after the shock.

inhospitalier, ère [inɔspitalje, ɛr] *adj* inhospitable.

inhumain, e [inymɛ̃, ɛn] *adj* inhuman.

inhumainement [inymɛnmɑ̃] *adv* inhumanly, inhumanely.

inhumanité [inymanite] *nf litt* inhumanity.

inhumation [inymasjɔ̃] *nf* burial, interment *sout*, inhumation *sout*.

inhumer [3] [inyme] *vt* to bury, to inter.

inimaginable [inimaʒinabl] *adj* unimaginable ■ **un paysage d'une beauté ~** an unbelievably beautiful landscape.

inimitable [inimitabl] *adj* inimitable.

inimité, e [inimite] *adj* which has still to be imitated, unique.

inimitié [inimitje] *nf sout* enmity, hostility ■ **regarder qqn avec ~** to look at sb hostilely.

ininflammable [inɛ̃flamabl] *adj* [produit] non-flammable ■ [revêtement] flame-proof.

inintelligence [inɛ̃tɛliʒɑ̃s] *nf sout* **1.** [stupidité] lack of intelligence **2.** [incompréhension] incomprehension, lack of understanding ■ **une profonde ~ des difficultés** a total lack of insight into the problems.

inintelligent, e [inɛ̃tɛliʒɑ̃, ɑ̃t] *adj sout* unintelligent.

inintelligibilité [inɛ̃teliʒibilite] *nf* unintelligibility.

inintelligible [inɛ̃teliʒibl] *adj* unintelligible, impossible to understand.

inintelligiblement [inɛ̃teliʒibləmɑ̃] *adv* unintelligibly.

inintéressant, e [inɛ̃terɛsɑ̃, ɑ̃t] *adj* uninteresting.

ininterrompu, e [inɛ̃tɛrɔ̃py] *adj* [série, flot] unbroken, uninterrupted ■ [bruit] continuous ■ [tradition] continuous, unbroken ■ [effort] unremitting, steady ■ [bavardage] continuous, ceaseless ■ **une nuit de sommeil ~** a night of unbroken sleep ■ **nous diffusons aujourd'hui cinq heures de musique ~e** today we are broadcasting five hours of non-stop *ou* uninterrupted music.

inique [inik] *adj sout* iniquitous *sout*, unjust, unfair.

iniquité [inikite] *nf sout* iniquity *sout*, injustice ■ **commettre des ~s** to commit wrongs.

initial, e, aux [inisjal, o] *adj* initial ◐ **cellules ~es** BOT initial cells.
◆ **initiale** *nf* [première lettre] initial ■ **une trousse à vos ~es** a pencil-case with your initials.

initialement [inisjalmɑ̃] *adv* initially, at first, originally.

initialisation [inisjalizasjɔ̃] *nf* INFORM initialization.

initialiser [3] [inisjalize] *vt* INFORM to initialize.

initiateur, trice [inisjatœr, tris] ◇ *adj* initiatory.
◇ *nm, f* **1.** [maître] initiator ■ **elle a été son initiatrice en amour/musique** it was thanks to her that he discovered love/music **2.** [novateur] pioneer ■ **les ~s de la biologie/du structuralisme** the founders of biology/of structuralism.

initiation [inisjasjɔ̃] *nf* **1.** [approche] initiation, introduction ■ **~ à la psychologie/au russe** introduction to psychology/to Russian **2.** CHIM & PHYS initiating, setting off **3.** ANTHR initiation.

initiatique [inisjatik] *adj* initiatory, initiation *(modif)*.

initiative [inisjativ] *nf* **1.** [esprit de décision] initiative ■ **avoir de l'~** to have initiative *ou* drive ■ **manquer d'~** to lack initiative ■ **esprit d'~** initiative **2.** [idée] initiative ■ **à** *ou* **sur l'~ de qqn** on sb's initiative ■ **les négociations ont été organisées à l'~ du Brésil** the negotiations were initiated by Brazil *ou* organized on Brazil's initiative ■ **prendre l'~ de qqch** to initiate sthg, to take the initiative for sthg ▶ **~ gouvernementale** governmental prerogative to propose legislation ■ **~ parlementaire** parliamentary prerogative to legislate ■ **~ privée** ÉCON private initiative ; DR & POLIT initiative **3.** [action spontanée] initiative ■ **faire qqch de sa propre ~** to do sthg on one's own initiative ■ **prendre des ~s** to show initiative ■ **elle nous laisse prendre des ~s** she allows us freedom of action ■ **prendre l'~ de faire qqch** to take the initiative in doing sthg ▶ **~ de paix** POLIT peace initiative *ou* overture.

initiatrice [inisjatris] *f* ▷ **initiateur**.

initié, e [inisje] ◇ *adj* initiated.
◇ *nm, f* **1.** [connaisseur] initiated person, initiate *sout* ■ **les ~s** the initiated ■ **pour les ~s** not for the uninitiated **2.** ANTHR initiate.

initier [9] [inisje] *vt* **1.** [novice] to initiate ■ **~ qqn à qqch** to initiate sb into sthg, to introduce sb to sthg **2.** ANTHR to initiate **3.** [faire démarrer] to initiate, to get going.
◆ **s'initier à** *vp+prép* to learn the basics of, to get to know ■ **j'ai besoin de deux semaines pour m'~ au traitement de texte** I need two weeks to teach myself *ou* to learn how to use a word processor.

injecté, e [ɛ̃ʒɛkte] *adj* **1.** [rougi] : **yeux ~s de sang** bloodshot eyes **2.** MÉD injected **3.** TECHNOL injection-moulded.

injecter [4] [ɛ̃ʒɛkte] *vt* **1.** CONSTR, GÉOL & MÉD to inject **2.** [introduire] to inject, to infuse, to instil ■ **~ des millions dans une affaire** to inject *ou* to pump millions into a business **3.** MÉCAN to inject **4.** ASTRONAUT : **~ un engin sur orbite** to inject a spacecraft (into its orbit).
◆ **s'injecter** *vpi* [yeux] to become bloodshot.

injecteur, trice [ɛ̃ʒɛktœr, tris] *adj* injection *(modif)*.
◆ **injecteur** *nm* injector.

injection [ɛ̃ʒɛksjɔ̃] *nf* **1.** CONSTR, GÉOL & MÉD injection **2.** ÉCON [apport - d'argent] injection **3.** TECHNOL ▷ **moulage 4.** MÉCAN injection ■ **à ~** (fuel) injection *(modif)* **5.** ASTRONAUT & MATH injection.

injoignable [ɛ̃ʒwaɲabl] *adj* : **j'ai essayé de l'appeler toute la matinée mais il était ~** I tried to phone him all morning, but I couldn't get through (to him) *ou* get hold of him.

injonction [ɛ̃ʒɔ̃ksjɔ̃] *nf* **1.** *sout* [ordre] order ■ **sur l'~ de qqn** at sb's behest **2.** DR injunction, (judicial) order ■ **~ de payer** order to pay.

injouable [ɛ̃ʒwabl] *adj* unplayable ■ **la sonate est ~** the sonata is impossible to play ■ **la balle est ~** the ball is unplayable.

injure [ɛ̃ʒyr] *nf* **1.** [insulte] insult, abuse *(U)* ■ **un chapelet d'~s** a stream of abuse *ou* insults ■ **il se mit à lâcher des ~s** he started hurling abuse ■ **accabler** *ou* **couvrir qqn d'~s** to heap abuse on sb ▶ **~ publique** DR ≃ slander without special damage **2.** *sout* [affront] affront, insult ■ **c'est une ~ à la nation** it's an insult to our country ■ **il m'a fait l'~ de refuser mon invitation** he insulted me by refusing my invitation.

injurier [9] [ɛ̃ʒyrje] *vt* **1.** [adresser des insultes à] to insult, to abuse **2.** *litt* [offenser moralement] to be an insult to.
◆ **s'injurier** *vp (emploi réciproque)* to insult each other ■ **les chauffeurs de taxi se sont injuriés** the taxi drivers hurled insults at each other *ou* swore at one another.

injurieux, euse [ɛ̃ʒyrjø, øz] *adj* abusive, insulting, offensive ■ **des propos ~** abusive *ou* offensive language ■ **être ~ envers qqn** to be abusive *ou* insulting to sb.

injuste [ɛ̃ʒyst] *adj* **1.** [décision] unjust, unfair **2.** [personne] unfair, unjust ■ **ne sois pas ~!** be fair!, don't be unfair! ■ **être ~ envers qqn** to do sb an injustice.

injustement [ɛ̃ʒystəmɑ̃] *adv* **1.** [avec iniquité] unfairly, unjustly ■ **punir ~** to punish unjustly **2.** [sans raison] without reason.

injustice [ɛ̃ʒystis] *nf* **1.** [caractère inique] injustice, unfairness ■ **l'~ sociale** social injustice **2.** [acte inique] injustice, wrong ■ **commettre une ~ envers qqn** to do sb wrong *ou* an injustice ■ **c'est une ~!** that's unfair!

injustifiable [ɛ̃ʒystifjabl] *adj* unjustifiable.

injustifié, e [ɛ̃ʒystifje] *adj* [critique, punition] unjustified, unwarranted ■ [crainte] unfounded, groundless ■ [absence] unexplained.

inlassable [ɛ̃lasabl] *adj* [infatigable - personne] indefatigable, tireless, untiring ; [- énergie] tireless ■ **elle est d'un dévouement ~** her devotion is untiring.

inlassablement [ɛ̃lasabləmɑ̃] *adv* indefatigably, tirelessly, untiringly ■ **elle répétait ~ le même mot** she kept repeating the same word over and over again.

inné, e [ine] *adj* **1.** [don] inborn, innate **2.** PHILOS innate.

innerver [3] [inɛrve] *vt* to innervate.

innocemment [inɔsamɑ̃] *adv* innocently.

innocence [inɔsɑ̃s] *nf* **1.** [gén] innocence ■ **en toute ~** in all innocence, quite innocently **2.** RELIG innocence ■ **en état d'~** in a state of innocence **3.** DR innocence ■ **établir** *ou* **prouver l'~ de qqn** to establish *ou* to prove sb's innocence.

innocent, e [inɔsɑ̃, ɑ̃t] ◇ *adj* **1.** [non responsable - inculpé, victime] innocent ■ **déclarer qqn ~** DR to find sb innocent *ou* not guilty ■ **être ~ de qqch** to be innocent of sthg **2.** [plaisanterie, question, plaisirs] innocent, harmless ■ [baiser, jeune fille] innocent **3.** [candide - enfant, âge] innocent **4.** [niais] innocent, simple.
◇ *nm, f* **1.** [personne non coupable] innocent person **2.** [personne candide] innocent ■ **faire l'~** to play *ou* to act the innocent ■ **ne joue pas l'~** *ou* **les ~s avec moi!** don't come the innocent with me! ■ **c'est un grand ~!** he's a bit naive! **3.** [niais] simpleton.

Innocent [inɔsɑ̃] *npr* [pape] Innocent.

innocenter [3] [inɔsɑ̃te] *vt* **1.** DR [suj: jury] to clear, to find innocent *ou* not guilty ■ [suj: témoignage, document] to prove innocent, to show to be innocent ■ **il réussit à faire ~ son client** he managed to get his client cleared **2.** [excuser] to excuse.

innocuité [inɔkɥite] *nf* harmlessness, innocuousness *sout*.

innombrable [inɔ̃brabl] *adj* innumerable, countless ■ **une foule ~** a vast *ou* huge crowd.

innomé, e [inɔme] *adj* **1.** [sans nom] unnamed **2.** ANTIQ & DR : **contrat ~** innominate contract.

innommable [inɔmabl] *adj* unspeakable, loathsome, nameless.

innovateur, trice [inɔvatœr, tris] ◇ *adj* innovative, innovatory.
◇ *nm, f* innovator.

innovation [inɔvasjɔ̃] *nf* **1.** [créativité] innovation **2.** [changement] innovation **3.** COMM innovation ■ **~ technologique** technological innovation.

innover [3] [inɔve] *vi* to innovate ■ **~ en (matière de)** to break new ground *ou* to innovate in (the field of).

inobservation [inɔpsɛrvasjɔ̃] *nf* *litt* & DR inobservance, breach ■ **~ d'une loi/d'un contrat** non-compliance with a law/with a contract.

inoccupé, e [inɔkype] *adj* **1.** [vide - maison, local] unoccupied, empty **2.** [vacant - poste] unoccupied, vacant, available ; [- taxi, fauteuil] empty, free **3.** [inactif] inactive, unoccupied, idle ■ **elle est longtemps restée ~e** for a long time she had nothing to do.

inoculable [inɔkylabl] *adj* inoculable.

inoculation [inɔkylasjɔ̃] *nf* **1.** MÉD [vaccination] inoculation ■ [contamination] infection **2.** MÉTALL inoculation.

inoculer [3] [inɔkyle] *vt* **1.** MÉD to inoculate ■ **on inocule le virus à un cobaye** a guinea pig is injected with the virus **2.** [transmettre - enthousiasme, manie] to infect, to pass on to.

inodore [inɔdɔr] *adj* **1.** [sans odeur] odourless ■ **peinture ~** odourless paint **2.** [sans intérêt] uninteresting, commonplace.

inoffensif, ive [inɔfɑ̃sif, iv] *adj* [personne] harmless, inoffensive ■ [animal] harmless ■ [remarque] innocuous.

inondable [inɔ̃dabl] *adj* liable to flooding.

inondation [inɔ̃dasjɔ̃] *nf* **1.** [d'eau] flood, flooding, inundation *sout* **2.** *fig* flood, deluge ■ **on assiste à une ~ du marché par des voitures étrangères** foreign cars are flooding *ou* inundating the market.

inondé, e [inɔ̃de] <> *adj* **1.** [champ, maison, cave] flooded **2.** *fig* **être ~ de réclamations/de mauvaises nouvelles** to be inundated with complaints/with bad news ■ **une pièce ~e de soleil** a room flooded with *ou* bathed in sunlight.
<> *nm, f* flood victim.

inonder [3] [inɔ̃de] *vt* **1.** [champs, maison, ville] to flood, to inundate *sout* ■ **tu ne peux donc pas prendre un bain sans tout ~?** can't you have a bath without flooding the bathroom? **2.** [tremper] to soak ■ **les yeux inondés de pleurs** his eyes full of *ou* swimming with tears ■ **le front inondé de sueur** his forehead bathed in sweat ■ **elle avait inondé ses vêtements de parfum** her clothes were soaked with perfume **3.** *fig* [envahir - marché] to flood, to inundate, to swamp ; [- suj: foule] to flood into, to swarm ; [- suj: lumière] to flood *ou* to pour into, to bathe ■ **ils inondent le marché de leurs produits** they're flooding *ou* inundating the market with their products ■ **ses fans l'inondent de lettres** she is inundated with fan mail.
◆ **s'inonder de** *vp+prép* : **chaque matin il s'inonde d'eau de Cologne** every morning he douses himself with eau de Cologne.

inopérable [inɔperabl] *adj* inoperable.

inopérant, e [inɔperɑ̃, ɑ̃t] *adj* inoperative, ineffective.

inopiné, e [inɔpine] *adj* [inattendu] unexpected.

inopinément [inɔpinemɑ̃] *adv* unexpectedly.

inopportun, e [inɔpɔrtœ̃, yn] *adj* ill-timed, inopportune, untimely ■ **sa remarque était plutôt ~e** he timed his remark rather badly.

inopportunément [inɔpɔrtynemɑ̃] *adv litt* inopportunely.

inopportunité [inɔpɔrtynite] *nf litt* inopportuneness, untimeliness.

inorganique [inɔrganik] *adj* inorganic.

inorganisation [inɔrganizasjɔ̃] *nf* lack of organization, disorganization.

inorganisé, e [inɔrganize] <> *adj* **1.** [désordonné] disorganized, unorganized **2.** [non syndiqué] unorganized **3.** BIOL unorganized.
<> *nm, f* [travailleur non syndiqué] non-union member, unorganized worker.

inoubliable [inublijabl] *adj* unforgettable, never to be forgotten.

inouï, e [inwi] *adj* **1.** [incroyable] incredible, amazing, unbelievable ■ **c'est ~ ce que cet enfant peut faire comme dégâts!** you wouldn't believe how much havoc that child can cause! **2.** *litt* [sans précédent - prouesse, performance] unheard of, unprecedented.

Inox® [inɔks] *nm inv* stainless steel ■ **couverts en ~** stainless steel cutlery.

inoxydable [inɔksidabl] <> *adj* MÉTALL stainless.
<> *nm* stainless steel.

in petto [inpeto] *loc adv litt* privately, in petto *litt*.

input [input] = **intrant**.

inqualifiable [ɛ̃kalifjabl] *adj* unspeakable ■ **un acte ~** an unspeakable act ■ **ce que tu as fait est ~** there are no words for what you've done.

inquiet, ète [ɛ̃kjɛ, ɛt] <> *adj* **1.** [personne] worried, anxious, concerned ■ [regard] worried, uneasy, nervous ■ [attente] anxious ■ **je suis ~ de l'avoir laissé seul** I'm worried *ou* uneasy about having left him alone ■ **être ~ de qqch** to be worried about sthg ■ **je suis ~ de son silence** I'm worried about not having heard from her **2.** *litt* [activité, curiosité] restless.
<> *nm, f* worrier.

inquiétant, e [ɛ̃kjetɑ̃, ɑ̃t] *adj* worrying, disturbing ■ **la situation est ~e** the situation is worrying *ou* gives cause for concern.

inquiéter [18] [ɛ̃kjete] *vt* **1.** [troubler - suj: personne, situation] to worry, to trouble ■ **son silence m'inquiète beaucoup** I find her silence quite disturbing *ou* worrying ■ **qu'est-ce qui t'inquiète?** what are you worried about?, what's worrying you? ■ **il n'est pas encore arrivé? tu m'inquiètes!** hasn't he arrived yet? you've got me worried now! ■ *(en usage absolu)* **ces nouvelles ont de quoi ~** this news is quite disturbing *ou* worrying *ou* alarming **2.** [ennuyer, harceler] to disturb, to bother, to harass ■ **le magistrat ne fut jamais inquiété par la police** the police never troubled the magistrate ■ **ils ont vidé les coffres sans être inquiétés** they were able to empty the safes without being disturbed *ou* interrupted ■ **il n'a jamais inquiété le champion du monde** he's never posed any threat to the world champion.
◆ **s'inquiéter** *vpi* [être soucieux] to worry, to be worried ■ **il y a de quoi s'~** that's something to be worried about, there's real cause for concern ■ **s'~ au sujet de** *ou* **pour qqn** to be worried *ou* concerned about sb ■ **ne t'inquiète pas pour elle!** don't (you) worry about her! ■ **je m'inquiète beaucoup de le savoir seul** it worries *ou* troubles me a lot to know that he's alone.
◆ **s'inquiéter de** *vp+prép* **1.** [tenir compte de] to bother *ou* to worry about **2.** [s'occuper de] to see to sthg ■ **et son cadeau? – je m'en inquiéterai plus tard** what about her present? – I'll see about that *ou* take care of that later ■ **t'es-tu inquiété de réserver les places?** did you think of booking? ● **où tu vas? – t'inquiète!** *fam* where are you off to? – mind your own business! *ou* what's it to you? **3.** [se renseigner sur] to inquire *ou* to ask about.

inquiétude [ɛ̃kjetyd] *nf* worry, anxiety, concern ■ **un sujet d'~** a cause for concern *ou* anxiety ■ **n'ayez aucune ~, soyez sans ~** rest easy, have no fear ■ **avoir des ~s** to be worried *ou* concerned.

inquisiteur, trice [ɛ̃kizitœr, tris] *adj* inquisitive, prying.

inquisition [ɛ̃kizisjɔ̃] *nf* **1.** HIST : **la (Sainte) Inquisition** the (Holy) Inquisition **2.** *sout* & *péj* [ingérence] inquisition.

inquisitoire [ɛ̃kizitwar] *adj* DR inquisitorial.

inquisitorial, e, aux [ɛ̃kisitɔrjal, o] *adj* **1.** *sout* [méthode] inquisitorial, high-handed **2.** HIST inquisitorial, Inquisition *(modif)*.

INR (*abr de* **Institut national de radiodiffusion**) *npr m Belgian broadcasting company.*

INRA, Inra [inra] (*abr de* **Institut national de la recherche agronomique**) *npr m national institute for agronomic research.*

inracontable [ɛ̃rakɔ̃tabl] *adj* [trop grivois] unrepeatable ■ [trop compliqué] too complicated for words ■ **je me suis débattu avec le fisc, c'est ~!** I can't even begin to tell you what a struggle I had with the tax people!

insaisissable [ɛ̃sezisabl] *adj* **1.** [imprenable - terroriste, voleur] elusive **2.** [imperceptible] imperceptible, intangible **3.** [fuyant] unfathomable, elusive **4.** DR exempt from seizure.

insalissable [ɛ̃salisabl] *adj* dirtproof.

insalubre [ɛ̃salybr] *adj* [immeuble] insalubrious ■ [climat] insalubrious, unhealthy.

insalubrité [ɛ̃salybrite] *nf* [d'un immeuble] insalubrity ■ [du climat] insalubrity, unhealthiness.

insanité [ɛ̃sanite] *nf* **1.** [folie] insanity **2.** [remarque] insane *ou* nonsensical remark ■ [acte] insane act, insane thing to do ■ **proférer des ~s** to say insane things ■ **tu n'es pas forcé d'écouter ses ~s** you don't have to listen to his ravings.

insatiabilité [ɛ̃sasjabilite] *nf* insatiability.

insatiable [ɛ̃sasjabl] *adj* insatiable.

insatiablement [ɛ̃sasjabləmɑ̃] *adv* insatiably.

insatisfaction [ɛ̃satisfaksjɔ̃] *nf* dissatisfaction.

insatisfaisant, e [ɛ̃satisfəzɑ̃, ɑ̃t] *adj* unsatisfactory.

insatisfait, e [ɛ̃satisfɛ, ɛt] ◇ *adj* **1.** [inassouvi - curiosité, besoin] unsatisfied, frustrated **2.** [mécontent - personne] unsatisfied, dissatisfied, displeased ■ **être ~ de** to be unhappy about.
◇ *nm, f* discontented person ■ **les ~s** the discontented ■ **c'est un perpétuel ~** he's never satisfied *ou* happy.

insaturé, e [ɛ̃satyre] *adj* unsaturated.

inscriptible [ɛ̃skriptibl] *adj* INFORM recordable.

inscription [ɛ̃skripsjɔ̃] *nf* **1.** [ensemble de caractères] inscription, writing *(U)* ■ **il y avait une ~ sur le mur** there was an inscription *ou* something written on the wall **2.** [action d'écrire] : **l'~ d'un slogan sur un mur** daubing *ou* writing a slogan on a wall **3.** [action d'inclure] : **une question dont l'~ à l'ordre du jour s'impose** a question which must go (down) *ou* be placed on the agenda ■ **l'~ des dépenses au budget** the listing of expenses in the budget **4.** [formalité] : **~ à** [cours, concours] registration for, enrolment in ; [club, parti] enrolment in, joining (of) ■ **~ à l'université** university registration *ou* enrolment, university matriculation *UK* ■ **~ sur les listes électorales** registration on the electoral roll *UK*, voter registration *US* ■ **dernière date pour les ~s** [à l'université] closing date for enrolment *ou* registration ; [dans un club] closing date for enrolment ● **dossier d'~** UNIV admission form, ≃ UCCA form *UK* ■ **droits d'~** UNIV registration fees ■ **service des ~s** UNIV admissions office **5.** [personne inscrite] : **il y a une trentaine d'~s au club/pour le rallye** about 30 people have joined the club/entered the rally **6.** DR : **~ de faux** challenge *(to the validity of a document)* ■ **~ hypothécaire** mortgage registration **7.** BOURSE quotation (privilege).

inscrire [99] [ɛ̃skrir] *vt* **1.** [écrire - chiffre, détail] to write *ou* to note (down) ■ **inscris ton nom au tableau/sur la feuille** write your name (up) on the board/(down) on the sheet ■ [graver] to engrave, to inscribe ■ **je ferai ~ son nom sur la tombe** I'll have his name engraved *ou* inscribed on the tombstone ■ **son visage reste inscrit dans ma mémoire** *fig* his face remains etched in my memory
2. [enregistrer - étudiant] to register, to enrol ; [- électeur, membre] to register ■ **(faire) ~ un enfant à l'école** to register *ou* to enrol a child for school, to put a child's name down for school ■ **les étudiants inscrits à l'examen** the students entered for the exam, the students sitting the exam *UK* ■ **les étudiants inscrits en droit** the students enrolled on *UK ou* in *US* the law course ■ **se faire ~ sur les listes électorales** to register as a voter, to put one's name on the electoral register ■ **être inscrit au registre du commerce** to be on the trade register ■ **être inscrit à un club** to be a member of a club ■ **~ qqn (pour un rendez-vous)** to put sb *ou* sb's name down for an appointment ■ **et la liste des passagers? – il n'y est pas inscrit non plus** the passenger list? – he's not listed there *ou* his name's not on it either
3. [inclure] to list, to include ■ **~ qqch au budget** to budget for sthg ■ **ces sommes sont inscrites au budget de la culture** these amounts are listed in the arts budget ■ **son style l'inscrit dans la tradition italienne** her style places *ou* situates her within the Italian tradition ■ **~ un prix littéraire/un disque d'or à son palmarès** to add a literary prize/a gold disc to one's list of achievements ■ **~ une question à l'ordre du jour** to put *ou* to place a question on the agenda ■ **parmi les sujets inscrits à l'ordre du jour** among the subjects on the agenda
4. SPORT [but, essai] to score
5. MATH to inscribe.
◆ **s'inscrire** ◇ *vp (emploi réfléchi)* : **s'~ à** [club, parti, bibliothèque] to join ; [université] to register *ou* to enrol at ; [concours, rallye] to enter *ou* to put one's name down for ■ **s'~ au chômage** to register as unemployed ■ **s'~ sur une liste électorale** to register to vote.
◇ *vpi* **1.** [apparaître] to appear, to come up ■ **le numéro de téléphone va s'~ sur vos écrans** the phone number will come up *ou* be displayed *ou* appear on your screens ■ **l'âge s'inscrit sur le visage** *fig* age leaves its mark on our faces
2. DR : **s'~ en faux contre** to lodge a challenge against ■ **s'~ en faux contre une politique/des allégations** *fig* to strongly denounce a policy/deny allegations
3. BOURSE : **s'~ en hausse/baisse** to be (marked) up/down ■ **les valeurs industrielles s'inscrivent en baisse de 13 points à la clôture** industrial shares closed 13 points down.
◆ **s'inscrire dans** *vp+prép sout* [suj: événement, attitude] to be consistent with, to be in keeping with, to be in line with ■ [suj: auteur] to belong to, to rank amongst ■ [suj: œuvre] to take its place in ■ **cette mesure s'inscrit dans le cadre de notre campagne** this measure comes *ou* lies within the framework of our campaign.

inscrit, e [ɛ̃skri, it] ◇ *adj* **1.** [étudiant, membre d'un club] enrolled, registered, matriculated *UK* ■ [chômeur] registered ■ POLIT [candidat, électeur] registered ■ [orateur] scheduled **2.** BANQUE & FIN registered ■ **créancier ~** ≃ member of the Finance Houses' Association *UK* **3.** MATH inscribed.
◇ *nm, f* [sur une liste] registered person ■ [à un club, à un parti] registered member ■ [étudiant] registered student ■ [candidat] registered candidate ■ [électeur] registered elector ■ **les ~s au prochain débat** POLIT the scheduled speakers for the next debate ● **~ maritime** NAUT registered seaman.

inscrivait *etc v* ▷ **inscrire**.

INSEAD [insead] (*abr de* **Institut européen d'administration**) *npr m European business school in Fontainebleau.*

insécable [ɛ̃sekabl] *adj* indivisible.

insecte [ɛ̃sɛkt] *nm* insect.

insecticide [ɛ̃sɛktisid] ◇ *adj* insecticide *(modif)*, insecticidal ■ **poudre ~** insecticide *ou* insect powder.
◇ *nm* insecticide.

insectivore [ɛ̃sɛktivɔr] ◇ *adj* insectivorous.
◇ *nm* insectivore ■ **les ~s** the Insectivora.

insécurité [ɛ̃sekyrite] *nf* **1.** [manque de sécurité] lack of safety ■ **l'~ qui règne dans les grandes villes** the collapse of law and order in big cities, the climate of fear reigning in big cities ■ **le gouvernement veut prendre des mesures contre l'~** the government wants to introduce measures to improve public safety **2.** [précarité - de l'emploi] insecurity, precariousness ; [- de l'avenir] uncertainty **3.** [angoisse] insecurity ■ **un sentiment d'~** a feeling of insecurity.

INSEE, Insee [inse] (*abr de* **Institut national de la statistique et des études économiques**) *npr m national institute of statistics and information about the economy.*

inséminateur, trice [ɛ̃seminatœr, tris] ◇ *adj* inseminating.
◇ *nm, f* inseminator.

insémination [ɛ̃seminasjɔ̃] *nf* insemination ■ **~ artificielle** artificial insemination ■ **~ artificielle entre conjoints/par donneur extérieur** artificial insemination by husband/by donor.

inséminer [3] [ɛ̃semine] *vt* to inseminate.

insensé, e [ɛ̃sɑ̃se] ◇ *adj* **1.** [déraisonnable - projet, initiative] foolish, insane ; [- espoir] unrealistic, mad ■ **il est complètement ~ de penser que...** it is utterly foolish *ou* absurd to think that... ■ **c'est ~!** this is absurd *ou* preposterous! **2.** [excessif] enormous, considerable ■ **une somme ~e** an excessive *ou* a ludicrous amount of money.
◇ *nm, f litt* madman (*f* madwoman).

insensibilisation [ɛ̃sɑ̃sibilizasjɔ̃] *nf* local anaesthesia.

insensibiliser [3] [ɛ̃sɑ̃sibilize] *vt* **1.** MÉD to anaesthetize **2.** [endurcir] to harden ■ **être insensibilisé aux souffrances d'autrui** to be hardened *ou* to have become immune to the sufferings of others.

insensibilité [ɛ̃sɑ̃sibilite] *nf* **1.** [absence de réceptivité] : **~ à** insensitiveness *ou* insensitivity to **2.** MÉD insensitivity, numbness.

insensible [ɛ̃sɑ̃sibl] *adj* **1.** [privé de sensation, de sentiment] : **~ à** insensitive to ■ **~ à la douleur** insensitive to pain ■ **elle demeura ~ à ses prières** she remained indifferent to *ou* unmoved by his pleas **2.** [imperceptible] imperceptible.

insensiblement [ɛ̃sɑ̃sibləmɑ̃] *adv* imperceptibly, gradually.

inséparable [ɛ̃separabl] *adj* inseparable ■ **le vice et le crime sont ~s** vice and crime are inseparable *ou* go hand in hand.
◆ **inséparables** *nmpl* ZOOL : **un couple d'~s** a pair of lovebirds.

inséparablement [ɛ̃separabləmɑ̃] *adv* inseparably.

insérable [ɛ̃serabl] *adj* insertable.

insérer [18] [ɛ̃sere] *vt* **1.** [ajouter - chapitre, feuille] to insert ■ **~ qqch dans/entre** to insert sthg into/between ■ **faire ~ une clause dans un contrat** to have a clause added to *ou* put in *ou* inserted into a contract **2.** [introduire - clé, lame] to insert ■ **~ qqch dans** to insert sthg into.
◆ **s'insérer dans** *vp+prép* **1.** [socialement] to become integrated into ■ **les jeunes ont souvent du mal à s'~ dans le monde du travail** young people often find it difficult to find their place in *ou* to fit into a work environment ■ **être bien/mal inséré dans la société** to be well/poorly integrated into society **2.** [s'inscrire dans] to be part of ■ **ces mesures s'insèrent dans le cadre d'une politique globale** these measures come within *ou* are part of an overall policy.

INSERM, Inserm [insɛrm] (*abr de* **Institut national de la santé et de la recherche médicale**) *npr m national institute for medical research.*

insert [ɛ̃sɛr] *nm* **1.** CINÉ & TV cut-in, insert **2.** TECHNOL moulding.

insertion [ɛ̃sɛrsjɔ̃] *nf* **1.** [introduction] insertion, introduction **2.** [intégration] integration ➲ **~ sociale** social integration **3.** PRESSE : **tarif des ~s** advertising rates ■ **frais d'~** advertising charge **4.** DR correction ■ **~ forcée** publication (of reply) by order of the court **5.** ANAT insertion.

insidieusement [ɛ̃sidjøzmɑ̃] *adv* insidiously.

insidieux, euse [ɛ̃sidjø, øz] *adj* **1.** [perfide - question] insidious, treacherous ; [- personne] *litt* insidious ■ **un raisonnement ~** a specious argument **2.** [sournois - odeur, poison] insidious **3.** MÉD insidious.

insigne [ɛ̃siɲ] ◇ *adj litt* [remarquable] remarkable, noteworthy ■ **faveur ~** signal favour ■ **mensonge/calomnie ~** unparalleled lie/slander.
◇ *nm* [marque distinctive - d'un groupe] badge, emblem, symbol ; [- d'une dignité] insignia ■ **les ~s de la royauté** royal insignia.

insignifiance [ɛ̃siɲifjɑ̃s] *nf* insignificance, unimportance.

insignifiant, e [ɛ̃siɲifjɑ̃, ɑ̃t] *adj* **1.** [sans intérêt] insignificant, trivial ■ **nous parlions de choses ~es** we were engaged in idle chatter ■ **des gens ~s** insignificant *ou* unimportant people **2.** [minime] insignificant, negligible ■ **erreur ~e** unimportant mistake ■ **somme ~e** trifling *ou* petty sum.

insinuant, e [ɛ̃sinɥɑ̃, ɑ̃t] *adj* [personne, ton] ingratiating ■ **il avait un odieux sourire ~** he had a horrible fawning smile.

insinuation [ɛ̃sinɥasjɔ̃] *nf* **1.** [allusion] insinuation, innuendo ■ **quelles sont ces ~s?** what are you hinting at *ou* insinuating *ou* trying to suggest? **2.** DR insinuation.

insinuer [7] [ɛ̃sinɥe] *vt* to insinuate ■ **que veut-elle ~?** what's she hinting at *ou* trying to insinuate? ■ **insinuez-vous que je mens?** are you insinuating *ou* implying that I'm lying?
◆ **s'insinuer** *vpi* : **s'~ dans** [suj: arôme, gaz] to creep in ; [suj: eau] to filter *ou* to seep in ; [suj: personne] to make one's way in, to infiltrate, to penetrate ■ **s'~ dans les bonnes grâces de qqn** to insinuate o.s. into sb's favour, to curry favour with sb ■ **le doute/une idée diabolique s'insinua en lui** doubt/an evil thought crept into his mind.

insipide [ɛ̃sipid] *adj* **1.** [sans goût] insipid, tasteless ■ **l'eau est ~** water has no taste *ou* doesn't taste of anything **2.** [sans relief - personne] insipid, bland, vapid ; [- conversation, livre] insipid, uninteresting, dull.

insipidité [ɛ̃sipidite] *nf sout* **1.** [absence de goût] insipidity, insipidness, tastelessness **2.** *fig* [ennui] insipidity, insipidness, tediousness.

insistance [ɛ̃sistɑ̃s] *nf* [obstination] insistence ■ **il lui demanda avec ~ de chanter** he insisted that she should sing ■ **regarder qqn avec ~** to stare at sb insistently.

insistant, e [ɛ̃sistɑ̃, ɑ̃t] *adj* **1.** [persévérant] insistent ■ **elle se faisait de plus en plus ~e** she was growing more and more insistent *ou* demanding **2.** [fort - parfum] pervasive, intrusive.

insister [3] [ɛ̃siste] *vi* **1.** [persévérer] to insist ■ **je ne vous dirai rien, inutile d'~!** I'm not telling you anything, so there's no point pressing me any further! ■ **ça ne répond pas – insistez!** there's no answer – keep trying *ou* try again! ■ **il était en colère, alors je n'ai pas insisté** he was angry, so I didn't push the matter (any further) *ou* I didn't insist **2.** [demander instamment] to insist ■ **j'insiste pour que vous m'écoutiez jusqu'au bout** I insist that you hear me out.
◆ **insister sur** *v+prép* **1.** [mettre l'accent sur - idée, problème] to stress, to emphasize, to underline ■ **on ne saurait trop ~ sur cette différence** this difference cannot be overemphasized ■ **si j'étais toi, je n'insisterais pas trop sur le salaire** if I were you, I wouldn't lay too much emphasis on the salary ■ **dans notre école, nous insistons beaucoup sur la discipline** in our school, we attach great importance to *ou* lay great stress on discipline **2.** [s'attarder sur - anecdote] to dwell on (*insép*) ; [- tache, défaut] to pay particular attention to ■ **mes années d'école, sur lesquelles je n'insisterai pas** my school years which I'd rather skate over *ou* I'd rather not dwell on.

in situ [insity] *adv* in situ.

insociable [ɛ̃sɔsjabl] *adj* [farouche] unsociable ■ [asocial] antisocial.

insolation [ɛ̃sɔlasjɔ̃] *nf* **1.** MÉD sunstroke, insolation *spéc* **2.** MÉTÉOR sunshine, insolation *spéc* ■ **avoir une faible ~** to get very little sunshine **3.** PHOTO exposure (to the light).

insolemment [ɛ̃sɔlamɑ̃] *adv* **1.** [avec arrogance] insolently, arrogantly **2.** [avec effronterie] unashamedly.

insolence [ɛ̃sɔlɑ̃s] *nf* **1.** [irrespect] insolence ■ **avec ~** insolently **2.** [remarque] insolent remark ■ [acte] insolent act **3.** [orgueil] arrogance.

insolent, e [ɛ̃sɔlɑ̃, ɑ̃t] ◇ *adj* **1.** [impoli] insolent **2.** [arrogant] arrogant **3.** [extraordinaire - luxe, succès] outrageous ■ **vous avez eu une chance ~e** you've been outrageously *ou* incredibly lucky.
◇ *nm, f* insolent person ■ **petit ~!** you impudent *ou* impertinent little boy!

insolite [ɛ̃sɔlit] ◇ *adj* unusual, strange.
◇ *nm* : **l'~** the unusual, the bizarre.

insolubilité [ɛ̃sɔlybilite] *nf* insolubility, insolubleness.

insoluble [ɛ̃sɔlybl] *adj* **1.** CHIM insoluble **2.** [problème] insoluble, insolvable *US* ■ **c'est une situation ~** there's no solution to this situation.

insolvabilité [ɛ̃sɔlvabilite] *nf* insolvency.

insolvable [ɛ̃sɔlvabl] *adj* & *nmf* insolvent.

insomniaque [ɛ̃sɔmnjak] *adj* & *nmf* insomniac.

insomnie [ɛ̃sɔmni] *nf* insomnia (*U*) ■ **des nuits d'~** sleepless nights.

insondable [ɛ̃sɔ̃dabl] *adj* **1.** [impénétrable - desseins, mystère] unfathomable, impenetrable ; [- regard, visage] inscrutable **2.** [très profond] unfathomable ■ **une crevasse ~** a seemingly bottomless crevasse **3.** [infini] abysmal ■ **il est d'une bêtise ~** he's abysmally stupid.

insonore [ɛ̃sɔnɔr] *adj* soundproof, sound-insulated *spéc.*

insonorisation [ɛ̃sɔnɔrizasjɔ̃] *nf* soundproofing, (sound) insulation.

insonoriser [3] [ɛ̃sɔnɔrize] *vt* to soundproof, to insulate ■ **studio d'enregistrement insonorisé** soundproof recording studio ■ **pièce mal insonorisée** inadequately soundproofed room.

insouciance [ɛ̃susjɑ̃s] *nf* lack of concern, carefree attitude, casualness ■ **avec ~** blithely, casually ■ **vivre dans l'~** to live a carefree *ou* untroubled existence ■ **son ~ à l'égard de ses études** his lack of concern for *ou* his happy-go-lucky attitude towards *ou* his easy-going attitude towards his studies ■ **l'~ de la jeunesse** the frivolity of youth.

insouciant, e [ɛ̃susjɑ̃, ɑ̃t] *adj* **1.** [nonchalant] carefree, unconcerned, casual **2.** [indifférent à] : **~ de** : **~ du danger** oblivious of *ou* to the danger ■ **~ de l'avenir** indifferent to *ou* unconcerned about the future.

insoumis, e [ɛ̃sumi, iz] *adj* **1.** [indiscipliné - jeunesse, partisan] rebellious ; [- enfant] unruly, refractory *sout* **2.** [révolté - tribu] rebel, rebellious ; [- pays] unsubdued, undefeated, rebellious **3.** MIL : **soldat ~** [réfractaire au service militaire] draft dodger ; [déserteur] soldier absent without leave.

◆ **insoumis** *nm* [réfractaire au service militaire] draft dodger ■ [déserteur] soldier absent without leave.

insoumission [ɛ̃sumisjɔ̃] *nf* **1.** [indiscipline] rebelliousness, insubordination **2.** [révolte] rebelliousness, rebellion ■ **un régiment était encore en état d'~** one regiment was still in open rebellion **3.** MIL [objection] draft-dodging ■ [désertion] absence without leave.

insoupçonnable [ɛ̃supsɔnabl] *adj* above suspicion.

insoupçonné, e [ɛ̃supsɔne] *adj* [vérité] unsuspected ■ [richesses] undreamt-of, unheard-of ■ **un trésor d'une valeur ~e** treasure which nobody expected to be so valuable.

insoutenable [ɛ̃sutnabl] *adj* **1.** [insupportable - douleur, scène, température] unbearable, unendurable ; [- lumière] blinding **2.** [impossible à soutenir - concurrence, lutte] unsustainable **3.** [indéfendable - opinion, thèse] untenable, unsustainable ; [- position] indefensible.

inspecter [4] [ɛ̃spɛkte] *vt* **1.** [contrôler - appartement, bagages, engin, travaux] to inspect, to examine ■ MIL [- troupes] to review, to inspect ; [- école, professeur] to inspect **2.** [scruter] to inspect ■ **~ qqn des pieds à la tête** to examine sb from head to foot.

inspecteur, trice [ɛ̃spɛktœr, tris] *nm, f* **1.** [contrôleur] inspector ■ **~ général** MIL inspector general ■ **~ (général) des Finances** ≃ general auditor *(of the Treasury with special responsibilities)* UK ■ ≃ Comptroller General US ■ **~ des impôts** FIN tax inspector ■ **~ des mines** inspector of mines ■ **~ du travail** factory inspector ■ **c'est un vrai ~ des travaux finis!** *fig & hum* he always turns up when the work's done! **2.** [policier] inspector, detective ■ **un ~ de la brigade criminelle** a detective from the crime squad ■ **~ de la police judiciaire** *inspector belonging to the criminal investigation department* ■ ≃ CID inspector UK ▶ **~ de police** detective sergeant UK, lieutenant US ■ **~ principal** ≃ detective inspector **3.** ÉDUC : **~ d'Académie** ≃ inspector of schools UK ■ ≃ Accreditation officer US ■ **~ de l'Éducation nationale** schools inspector *(mainly for the primary sector)* **4.** *(comme adj)* DR : **magistrat ~** visiting magistrate.

inspection [ɛ̃spɛksjɔ̃] *nf* **1.** [vérification] inspection ■ [surveillance] overseeing, supervising ■ **ils se livrèrent à une ~ détaillée du véhicule** they searched the vehicle thoroughly ■ **les douaniers soumirent la valise/le passager à une ~ en règle** the customs officers subjected the suitcase/the passenger to a thorough search ■ **après ~, le dossier se révéla être un faux** on inspection, the file turned out to be a forgery ■ **passer une ~** [l'organiser] to carry out an inspection, to inspect ; [la subir] to undergo an inspection, to be inspected ■ **passer l'~** [être en règle] to pass (the test) ■ **prêt pour l'~!** MIL ready for inspection! **2.** ADMIN inspectorate ■ **~ académique** ≃ Schools Inspectorate UK, ≃ Accreditation Agency US ■ **~ générale des Finances** *government department responsible for monitoring the financial affairs of state bodies* ■ **~ des impôts** ≃ Inland Revenue UK ■ ≃ Internal Revenue Service US ■ **~ du travail** ≃ Health and Safety Executive UK ■ ≃ Labor Board US **3.** [inspectorat] inspectorship.

inspirant, e [ɛ̃spirɑ̃, ɑ̃t] *adj fam* inspiring ■ **je ne trouve pas ça très ~** I don't find it particularly inspiring.

inspirateur, trice [ɛ̃spiratœr, tris] ◇ *adj* **1.** [inspirant] inspiring **2.** ANAT inspiratory.

◇ *nm, f* **1.** [guide] inspirer **2.** [instigateur] instigator ■ **l'~ d'un complot** the instigator of *ou* the person behind a plot.

◆ **inspiratrice** *nf* [égérie] muse, inspiration.

inspiration [ɛ̃spirasjɔ̃] *nf* **1.** [esprit créatif] inspiration ■ **tirer son ~ de, trouver son ~ dans** to draw (one's) inspiration from ■ **je n'ai pas d'~ ce matin** I don't feel inspired *ou* I don't have any inspiration this morning ■ **musique pleine d'~** inspired music **2.** [idée, envie] inspiration, (bright) idea ■ **agir selon l'~ du moment** to act on the spur of the moment **3.** [influence] influence, instigation ■ **c'est sous son ~ que le syndicat a été créé** the union was created at his instigation ■ **une architecture d'~ nordique** an architecture with a Scandinavian influence, a Scandinavian-inspired architecture **4.** PHYSIOL breathing in, inspiration *spéc* **5.** RELIG inspiration.

inspiratoire [ɛ̃spiratwar] *adj* inspiratory.

inspiré, e [ɛ̃spire] ◇ *adj* **1.** [artiste, air, livre] inspired **2.** [avisé] : **j'ai été bien ~ de lui résister** I was well-advised to resist him, I did the right thing in resisting him ■ **tu as été bien ~ de venir me voir aujourd'hui** you did well to come and see me today.

◇ *nm, f* **1.** [mystique] mystic, visionary **2.** *péj* [illuminé] crank.

inspirer [3] [ɛ̃spire] ◇ *vt* **1.** [provoquer - décision, sentiment] to inspire ; [- remarque] to inspire, to give rise to *(insép)* ; [- conduite] to prompt ; [- complot] to instigate ■ **~ confiance à qqn** to inspire confidence in sb, to inspire sb with confidence ■ **cette viande ne m'inspire pas confiance!** I don't much like the look of that meat! ■ **son état n'inspire pas d'inquiétude** his health gives no cause for concern ■ **sa fille lui a inspiré ses plus belles chansons** his daughter gave him the inspiration for his best songs **2.** [influencer - œuvre, personne] to inspire ■ **le sujet de dissertation ne m'inspire guère!** the subject of the essay doesn't really fire my imagination! **3.** [aspirer - air, gaz] to breathe in *(sép)*, to inspire *spéc* ■ **~ de l'air** to breathe air.

◇ *vi* to breathe in, to inspire *spéc.*

◆ **s'inspirer de** *vp+prép* to draw one's inspiration from, to be inspired by.

instabilité [ɛ̃stabilite] *nf* **1.** CHIM & PHYS instability **2.** [précarité] instability, precariousness ■ **l'~ du gouvernement** the instability of the government **3.** PSYCHOL instability.

instable [ɛ̃stabl] ◇ *adj* **1.** [branlant] unsteady, unstable ■ [glissant - terrain] unstable, shifting ■ **être en équilibre ~** to be balanced precariously **2.** [fluctuant - situation, régime politique, prix] unstable ; [- personnalité] unsteady, unreliable ; [- population] shifting, unsettled, unstable ; [- temps] unsettled **3.** CHIM, PHYS & PSYCHOL unstable.

◇ *nmf* unreliable *ou* unsteady person ■ PSYCHOL unstable person.

installateur, trice [ɛ̃stalatœr, tris] *nm, f* [d'appareils sanitaires] fitter ■ ÉLECTR, RADIO & TV installer.

installation [ɛ̃stalasjɔ̃] *nf* **1.** [dispositif, équipement] installation ■ [aménagement] set-up ■ **une ~ de fortune** a makeshift set-up ▶ **~ électrique** wiring ■ **~ informatique** computer facility ■ **~ téléphonique** telephone installation **2.** [d'un dentiste, d'un médecin] setting up (practice) ■ [d'un commerçant] opening, setting up (shop) ■ [d'un locataire] moving in **3.** [mise en service - de l'électricité, du gaz, du chauffage] installation, installing, putting in ; [- d'un appareil ménager] installation, installing ; [- d'une grue] setting up ; [- d'une antenne] installing ; [- d'une cuisine, d'un atelier, d'un laboratoire] fitting out ■ **qui a fait l'~ de la prise/du lave-linge?** who wired the socket/plumbed in the washing machine? ■ **refaire l'~ électrique (d'une maison)** to rewire (a house) **4.** [implantation - d'une usine] setting up.

◆ **installations** *nfpl* [dans une usine] machinery and equipment ▪ [complexe, bâtiment] installations ▪ **~s portuaires** port installations.

installé, e [ɛ̃stale] *adj* **1.** [aisé] well-off, established **2.** [aménagé] : **un laboratoire bien/mal ~** a well/badly equipped laboratory ▪ **ils sont mal ~s** they have a really uncomfortable house/flat *etc.*

installer [3] [ɛ̃stale] *vt* **1.** [mettre en service - chauffage, eau, gaz, électricité, téléphone] to install, to put in *(sép)* ; [- appareil ménager] to install ▪ **nous avons dû faire ~ l'eau/le gaz/l'électricité** we had to have the water laid on/the gas put in/the house wired
2. [mettre en place - meuble] to put in *(sép)* ; [- tente] to put up *(sép)*, to pitch ; [- barrière] to put up *(sép)*, to erect ; [- campement] to set up *(sép)* ; [- troupes] to position
3. [faire asseoir, allonger] to put, to place ▪ **installez-le sur la civière** lay him down on the stretcher ▪ **une fois qu'il est installé devant la télévision, il n'y a plus moyen de lui parler** once he's settled himself down *ou* planted himself *ou* installed (himself) in front of the TV, there's no talking to him
4. [pièce, logement - aménager] to fit out *(sép)* ; [- disposer] to lay out *(sép)* ▪ **nous avons installé la salle de jeu au grenier** we've turned the attic into a playroom
5. [loger - jeune couple] to set up *(sép)* ; [- visiteur] to put up *(sép)*, to install *sout* ▪ **les blessés furent installés dans la tour** the wounded were accommodated *ou* put in the tower
6. [implanter] : **~ une usine à la campagne** to set up a factory in the countryside
7. ADMIN to install ▪ **~ qqn dans ses fonctions** to install sb in his/her post
8. INFORM to install.
◆ **s'installer** *vpi* **1.** [s'asseoir, s'allonger] : **installez-vous comme il faut, je reviens tout de suite** make yourself comfortable *ou* at home, I'll be right back ▪ **s'~ au volant** to sit at the wheel ▪ **s'~ dans un canapé** to settle down on a couch
2. [s'implanter - cirque, marché] to (be) set up ; [- usine] to be set up ▪ **quand nous nous sommes installés** when we settled in ▪ **s'~ à la campagne** [emménager] to set up house *ou* to go and live *ou* to settle in the country ▪ **s'~ dans une maison** to move into a house ▪ **je m'installai dans un petit hôtel** I put up at a small hotel ▪ **s'~ dans de nouveaux bureaux** [entreprise] to move into new offices ; [employés] to move into one's new offices ▪ **si ça continue, elle va finir par s'~ chez moi!** if this goes on, she'll end up moving in (permanently)!
3. [pour exercer - médecin, dentiste] to set up a practice ; [- commerçant] to set up shop, to open ▪ **s'~ à son compte** to set up one's own business *ou* on one's own ▪ **quand je me suis installé, la clientèle était rare** when I started, there weren't many customers
4. [se fixer - statu quo] to become established ; [- maladie] to take a hold *ou* a grip ; [- doute, peur] to creep in ; [- silence] to take over ▪ **il s'est installé dans le mensonge** he's become an habitual liar, he's well used to lying ▪ **le pays s'installe peu à peu dans la crise** the country is gradually learning to live with the crisis.

instamment [ɛ̃stamɑ̃] *adv sout* insistently ▪ **demander ~ que** to insist that.

instance [ɛ̃stɑ̃s] *nf* **1.** [organisme] authority ▪ **les plus hautes ~s du parti** the leading bodies of the party ▪ **le dossier sera traité par une ~ supérieure** the file will be dealt with at a higher level *ou* by a higher authority **2.** DR (legal) proceedings ▪ **introduire une ~** to start *ou* to institute proceedings ▪ **en première ~** on first hearing ▪ **en seconde ~** on appeal **3.** PSYCHOL psychic apparatus.
◆ **instances** *nfpl sout* entreaties ▪ **sur** *ou* **devant les ~s de son père, il finit par accepter** in the face of his father's entreaties *ou* pleas, he eventually accepted.
◆ **en dernière instance** *loc adv* in the last analysis.
◆ **en instance** *loc adj* [dossier] pending, waiting to be dealt with ▪ DR [affaire] pending, sub judice *UK* ▪ [courrier] ready for posting.
◆ **en instance de** *loc prép* : **être en ~ de divorce** to be waiting for a divorce *ou* in the middle of divorce proceedings.

instant [ɛ̃stɑ̃] *nm* **1.** [courte durée] moment, instant ▪ **il s'arrêta un ~** he stopped for a moment ▪ **j'ai pensé, pendant un ~** *ou* **l'espace d'un ~, que...** for half a minute *ou* for a split second, I thought that... ▪ **il ne s'est pas demandé un ~ ce qui pouvait arriver** he never asked himself once what might happen ▪ **je n'en doute pas un seul ~** I don't doubt it at all, I've never doubted it for a minute ▪ **(attendez) un ~!** just a moment!, just a second! ▪ **je reviens dans un ~** I'll be right back, I'll be back in a minute ▪ **c'est l'affaire d'un ~** it won't take a minute ▪ **c'est prêt en un ~** it's ready in an instant *ou* in no time at all **2.** [moment précis] moment ▪ **l'~ suprême** the supreme moment.
◆ **à l'instant (même)** *loc adv* this instant, this minute ▪ **je suis rentré à l'~ (même)** I've just (this minute *ou* second) come in ▪ **je l'apprends à l'~ (même)** I've just this moment heard about it ▪ **nous devons partir à l'~ (même)** we must leave right now *ou* this instant *ou* this very minute *sout* ▪ **à l'~ (même) où je m'apprêtais à partir** just as I was about to leave.
◆ **à tout instant** *loc adv* [continuellement] all the time ▪ [d'une minute à l'autre] any time (now), any minute.
◆ **dans l'instant** *loc adv* at this moment, instantly.
◆ **de tous les instants** *loc adj* constant.
◆ **dès l'instant que** *loc conj* [si] if ▪ [puisque] since ▪ [aussitôt que] as soon as, from the moment ▪ **dès l'~ que tu me le promets** as long as you promise me.
◆ **par instants** *loc adv* at times, from time to time.
◆ **pour l'instant** *loc adv* for the moment, for the time being.

instantané, e [ɛ̃stɑ̃tane] *adj* **1.** [immédiat] instantaneous **2.** [soluble] : **café ~** instant coffee **3.** PHOTO : **cliché ~** snapshot.
◆ **instantané** *nm* snap, snapshot.

instantanément [ɛ̃stɑ̃tanemɑ̃] *adv* instantaneously, instantly ▪ **ce produit se dissout ~ dans l'eau** this product dissolves instantly in water.

instar [ɛ̃star] ◆ **à l'instar de** *loc prép sout* following (the example of) ▪ **à l'~ de ses parents, il sera enseignant** like his parents, he's going to be a teacher.

instaurateur, trice [ɛ̃stɔratœr, tris] *nm, f litt* founder, establisher, creator.

instauration [ɛ̃stɔrasjɔ̃] *nf* institution, foundation, establishing.

instaurer [3] [ɛ̃stɔre] *vt* to institute, to found, to establish ▪ **~ un régime** to set up a regime ▪ **~ une nouvelle mode** to introduce *ou* to start a new fashion ▪ **~ le couvre-feu dans une ville** to impose a curfew in a town.

instigateur, trice [ɛ̃stigatœr, tris] *nm, f* instigator.

instigation [ɛ̃stigasjɔ̃] *nf* instigation ▪ **à** *ou* **sur l'~ de qqn** at sb's instigation.

instillation [ɛ̃stilasjɔ̃] *nf* instillation.

instiller [3] [ɛ̃stile] *vt* **1.** MÉD to instil ▪ **~ un liquide dans l'œil** to drop *ou* to instil a liquid into the eye **2.** *litt* [insuffler] to instil ▪ **~ le doute dans l'esprit de qqn** to instil doubt into sb's mind.

instinct [ɛ̃stɛ̃] *nm* **1.** PSYCHOL & ZOOL instinct ▪ **~ de conservation** instinct of self-preservation ▪ **~ maternel** maternal instinct **2.** [intuition] instinct ▪ **il eut l'~ de parer le coup** he instinctively fended off the blow ▪ **se fier à son ~** to trust one's instincts *ou* intuition **3.** [don] instinct ▪ **elle a l'~ de la scène** she has a natural talent *ou* an instinct for the stage.
◆ **d'instinct** *loc adv* instinctively, by instinct.
◆ **par instinct** *loc adv* **1.** PSYCHOL & ZOOL instinctively, by instinct **2.** [intuitivement] instinctively.

instinctif, ive [ɛ̃stɛ̃ktif, iv] ◇ *adj* **1.** [irraisonné] instinctive **2.** [impulsif] instinctive, impulsive, spontaneous ▪ **c'est un être ~** he's a creature of instinct.
◇ *nm, f* instinctive person.

instinctivement [ɛ̃stɛ̃ktivmɑ̃] *adv* instinctively.

instit [ɛ̃stit] *nmf fam* primary school teacher.

instituer [7] [ɛ̃stitɥe] *vt* **1.** [instaurer, créer] to institute, to establish ▪ **le ministre a institué une commission d'enquête** the minister set up a commission of inquiry **2.** DR [désigner - héritier] to institute, to appoint.

◆ **s'instituer** *vpi* **1.** [se désigner] to set o.s. up ▪ **il s'est institué (comme) arbitre de leur querelle** he set himself up as the arbitrator of their quarrel **2.** [s'établir] to be *ou* to become established.

institut [ɛ̃stity] *nm* [établissement] institute ▪ **~ de recherches/scientifique** research/scientific institute ◗ **~ de beauté** beauty salon *ou* parlour ▪ **~ médico-légal** mortuary ▪ **l'Institut du Monde Arabe** *Arab cultural centre and library in Paris holding regular exhibitions of Arab art.*

◆ **Institut (de France)** *npr m* : **l'Institut de France** the Institut de France ▪ ≃ the Royal Society *UK* ▪ ≃ the National Science Foundation *US*.

L'INSTITUT DE FRANCE

L'Institut, as it is commonly known, is a learned society which includes the five *Académies* (the *Académie française* being one of them). Its headquarters are in the building of the same name on the banks of the Seine in Paris.

instituteur, trice [ɛ̃stitytœr, tris] *nm, f* [de maternelle] (nursery school) teacher ▪ [d'école primaire] (primary school) teacher ▪ **demande à ton institutrice** ask your teacher.

institution [ɛ̃stitysjɔ̃] *nf* **1.** [établissement privé] institution ◗ **~ religieuse** [catholique] Catholic school ; [autre] denominational school **2.** [coutume] institution **3.** [mise en place] institution, establishment ▪ [d'une loi] introduction ▪ [d'une règle] laying down **4.** DR : **~ d'un héritier** appointment *ou* institution of an heir ▪ **~ contractuelle** conventional designation *(of an heir)* **5.** RELIG : **~ d'un évêque** institution of a bishop.

◆ **institutions** *nfpl* institutions ▪ **les ~s politiques** political institutions.

institutionnaliser [3] [ɛ̃stitysjɔnalize] *vt* to institutionalize.

institutionnel, elle [ɛ̃stitysjɔnɛl] *adj* institutional.

institutrice [ɛ̃stitytris] *f* ⟹ **instituteur**.

instructeur, trice [ɛ̃stryktœr, tris] *nm, f* instructor.

◆ **instructeur** ◇ *nm* AÉRON (flying) instructor ▪ MIL instructor.

◇ *adj* : **sergent ~** drill sergeant.

instructif, ive [ɛ̃stryktif, iv] *adj* informative, instructive ▪ **c'est très ~ d'écouter aux portes!** *hum* you learn a lot listening at keyholes!

instruction [ɛ̃stryksjɔ̃] *nf* **1.** *vieilli* [culture] (general) education ▪ **manquer d'~** to be uneducated, to lack education **2.** [formation] education, teaching ▪ **l'~ que j'ai reçue à l'école** the teaching *ou* education I was given at school ◗ **~ militaire** MIL military training ▪ **~ religieuse** [gén] religious education ; ÉDUC religious instruction **3.** DR preliminary investigation *ou* inquiry *(of a case by an examining magistrate)* ▪ **qui est chargé de l'~?** who's setting up the inquiry? **4.** INFORM instruction, statement ▪ **jeu d'~s** instruction set **5.** [ordre] instruction ▪ **sur les ~s de ses supérieurs** following orders from his superiors **6.** ADMIN [circulaire] directive.

◆ **instructions** *nfpl* [d'un fabricant] instructions, directions ▪ **~s de montage** instructions *ou* directions for assembly.

instruire [98] [ɛ̃strɥir] ◇ *vt* **1.** [enseigner à] to teach, to instruct ▪ [former] to educate ▪ MIL [recrue] to train ▪ **une émission destinée à ~ en distrayant** a programme designed to be both entertaining and educational ▪ **instruit par l'expérience** taught by experience **2.** *sout* [aviser] : **~ qqn de qqch** to inform sb of sthg, to acquaint sb with sthg **3.** DR : **~ une affaire** *ou* **un dossier** to set up a preliminary inquiry.

◇ *vi* DR : **~ contre qqn** to set up a preliminary inquiry against sb.

◆ **s'instruire** ◇ *vp (emploi réfléchi)* [se cultiver] to educate o.s., to improve one's mind ▪ **il s'est instruit tout seul** he's a self-educated man.

◇ *vpi* [apprendre] to learn.

◆ **s'instruire de** *vp+prép* : **s'~ de qqch** to (try to) obtain information about sthg, to find out about sthg ▪ **s'~ de qqch auprès de qqn** to inquire of sb about sthg *sout*, to ask sb about sthg.

instruit, e [ɛ̃strɥi, it] *adj* well-educated, educated ▪ **un homme ~** an educated man.

instrument [ɛ̃strymɑ̃] *nm* **1.** [outil, matériel] instrument ▪ **~ tranchant** edged *ou* cutting tool ◗ **~s de bord** instruments ▪ **~ de mesure/d'observation** measuring/observation instrument ▪ **un ~de torture** an instrument of torture ▪ **~ de travail** tool ▪ **c'est un de mes ~s de travail** it's a tool of my trade **2.** MUS : **~ (de musique)** (musical) instrument ▪ **~ à cordes/à percussion/à vent** string/percussion/wind instrument **3.** *fig* [agent] instrument, tool ▪ **être l'~ de qqn** to be sb's instrument *ou* tool ▪ **il fut l'~ de leur ruine** he brought about their ruin ▪ **il fut l'un des ~s de leur ruine** he was instrumental in their ruin **4.** DR instrument.

instrumental, e, aux [ɛ̃strymɑ̃tal, o] *adj* instrumental.

◆ **instrumental** *nm* LING instrumental (case), *voir aussi* **pluriel**.

instrumentaliser [3] [ɛ̃strymɑ̃talize] *vt* to use, to manipulate.

instrumentation [ɛ̃strymɑ̃tasjɔ̃] *nf* **1.** MUS orchestration, instrumentation **2.** TECHNOL instrumentation.

instrumenter [3] [ɛ̃strymɑ̃te] ◇ *vi* to draw up an official document.

◇ *vt* **1.** MUS to orchestrate, to score (for instruments) **2.** TRAV PUB to instrument.

instrumentiste [ɛ̃strymɑ̃tist] *nmf* **1.** MUS instrumentalist **2.** MÉD theatre nurse.

insu [ɛ̃sy] ◆ **à l'insu de** *loc prép* **1.** [sans être vu de] without the knowledge of, unbeknown *ou* unbeknownst to ▪ **sortir à l'~ de ses parents** to go out without one's parents' knowing *ou* knowledge ▪ **à l'~ de tout le monde, il s'était glissé dans la cuisine** he'd slipped unnoticed into the kitchen **2.** [sans m'en/s'en apercevoir] : **à mon/son ~** unwittingly, without being aware of it.

insubmersible [ɛ̃sybmɛrsibl] *adj* [canot] insubmersible ▪ [jouet] unsinkable.

insubordination [ɛ̃sybɔrdinasjɔ̃] *nf* insubordination.

insubordonné, e [ɛ̃sybɔrdɔne] *adj* insubordinate.

insuccès [ɛ̃syksɛ] *nm* failure ▪ **son ~ aux élections l'a découragé** his poor performance at the polls has discouraged him.

insuffisamment [ɛ̃syfizamɑ̃] *adv* insufficiently, inadequately ▪ **~ nourri** underfed.

insuffisance [ɛ̃syfizɑ̃s] *nf* **1.** [manque] insufficiency, deficiency ▪ **~ de ressources** lack of *ou* insufficient resources ▪ **l'~ de la production industrielle** the inadequacy of industrial production **2.** [point faible] weakness, deficiency ▪ **ses ~s en matière de pathologie** his lack of knowledge of pathology **3.** MÉD : **elle est morte d'une ~ cardiaque** she died from heart failure ▪ **~ rénale** kidney failure *ou* insufficiency *spéc.*

insuffisant, e [ɛ̃syfizɑ̃, ɑ̃t] *adj* **1.** [en quantité] insufficient ▪ **nous avons des effectifs ~s** our numbers are too low, we're understaffed ▪ **c'est ~ pour ouvrir un compte** it's not enough to open an account **2.** [en qualité] inadequate ▪ **des résultats ~s en mathématiques** inadequate results in mathematics **3.** [inapte] incompetent ▪ **la plupart de nos élèves sont ~s en langues** most of our pupils are poor *ou* weak at languages.

insufflateur [ɛ̃syflatœr] *nm* **1.** MÉD insufflator **2.** TECHNOL blower.

insuffler [3] [ɛ̃syfle] *vt* **1.** MÉD & TECHNOL to insufflate ▪ **~ de l'air dans un corps** to blow *ou* to insufflate air into a body **2.** *sout* [inspirer] : **~ qqch à qqn** to instil sthg in sb, to infuse sb with sthg ▪ **la terreur lui insuffla du courage** terror inspired her to be brave.

insulaire [ɛ̃sylɛr] ◇ *adj* island *(modif)*, insular ▪ **la population ~** the population of the island, the island population.

◇ *nmf* islander.

insularité [ɛ̃sylarite] *nf* **1.** GÉOGR insularity ▪ **leur ~ en fait des gens à part** the fact that they live on an island sets them apart **2.** *péj* [étroitesse d'esprit] insularity.

insuline [ɛ̃sylin] *nf* insulin.

insulinodépendant, e [ɛ̃sylinɔdepɑ̃dɑ̃, ɑ̃t] *adj* insulin dependent.

insultant, e [ɛ̃syltɑ̃, ɑ̃t] *adj* insulting ▪ **c'est ~ pour moi** it's an insult to me, I'm insulted by it.

insulte [ɛ̃sylt] *nf* **1.** [parole blessante] insult ▪ **je n'ai pas relevé l'~** I didn't react ▪ **lancer des ~s à qqn** to throw abuse at sb **2.** *fig* & *sout* [atteinte, outrage] insult ▪ **une ~ au bon sens** an insult to common sense.

insulté, e [ɛ̃sylte] ◇ *adj* insulted ▪ **tu crois qu'elle s'est sentie ~e?** do you think she felt insulted *ou* offended?
◇ *nm, f* : **l'~** the injured party.

insulter [ɛ̃sylte] *vt* to insult ▪ **il m'a insulté** he insulted me ▪ **se faire ~** to be insulted ▪ **~ la mémoire de qqn** to insult sb's memory.

insupportable [ɛ̃sypɔrtabl] *adj* **1.** [insoutenable - démangeaison, vision] unbearable, unendurable ; [- bruit] unbearable, insufferable ; [- lumière] unbearably bright ; [- situation] intolerable ▪ **sans toi, la vie m'est ~** without you, life is more than I can bear *ou* is too hard to bear **2.** [turbulent - enfant, élève] impossible, insufferable, unbearable ▪ **tu es ~, si tu continues tu vas au lit!** you're being impossible, if you don't stop you're off to bed!

insupporter [3] [ɛ̃sypɔrte] *vt* : **il m'insupporte!** I can't stand him!

insurgé, e [ɛ̃syrʒe] *adj* insurgent *(avant n).*
◆ **insurgé** *nm* insurgent.

insurger [17] [ɛ̃syrʒe] ◆ **s'insurger** *vpi* : **s'~ contre qqn** to rise up *ou* to rebel against sb ▪ **s'~ contre qqch** to rebel against *ou* to strongly oppose sthg.

insurmontable [ɛ̃syrmɔ̃tabl] *adj* **1.** [infranchissable - obstacle] insurmountable, insuperable **2.** [invincible - aversion, angoisse] uncontrollable, unconquerable.

insurrection [ɛ̃syrɛksjɔ̃] *nf* **1.** [révolte] insurrection ▪ **le pays était en pleine ~** the country was in a state of open insurrection ▪ **~ armée** armed insurrection **2.** *litt* [indignation] revolt, rising up.

insurrectionnel, elle [ɛ̃syrɛksjɔnɛl] *adj* insurrectionary, insurrectional.

intact, e [ɛ̃takt] *adj* [réputation, économies] intact ▪ **le problème reste ~** the problem remains unsolved.

intangibilité [ɛ̃tɑ̃ʒibilite] *nf* intangibility ▪ **~ d'une loi** inviolability of a law.

intangible [ɛ̃tɑ̃ʒibl] *adj* **1.** [impalpable] intangible **2.** [inviolable] inviolable, sacred, sacrosanct.

intarissable [ɛ̃tarisabl] *adj* **1.** [inépuisable - source] inexhaustible, unlimited ; [- mine] inexhaustible ; [- imagination] inexhaustible, boundless, limitless **2.** [bavard] inexhaustible, unstoppable, tireless ▪ **sur le vin, il est ~** if you get him talking on wine, he'll go on for ever.

intarissablement [ɛ̃tarisabləmɑ̃] *adv* inexhaustibly ▪ **il discourait ~** he was going on and on (and on).

intégrable [ɛ̃tegrabl] *adj* [appareil] integrated.

intégral, e, aux [ɛ̃tegral, o] *adj* **1.** [complet] complete ▪ **édition ~e des poèmes de Donne** collected poems of Donne ▪ **remboursement ~ d'une dette** full *ou* complete repayment of a debt ▶ **texte ~** unabridged version ▪ **version ~e** [film] uncut version **2.** *hum* [en intensif] utter, complete.
◆ **intégrale** *nf* **1.** [œuvre] complete works ▪ **l'~e des quatuors à cordes de Chostakovitch** the complete set of Shostakovich string quartets **2.** MATH integral.

intégralement [ɛ̃tegralmɑ̃] *adv* in full, fully, completely ▪ **vous serez ~ remboursé** you'll get all your money back, you'll be fully reimbursed.

intégralité [ɛ̃tegralite] *nf* whole ▪ **l'~ de la dette** the entire debt, the debt in full ▪ **la presse dans son ~ protesta** the press protested as a body *ou* en bloc.

intégrant, e [ɛ̃tegrɑ̃, ɑ̃t] *adj* : **faire partie ~e de qqch** to be an integral part of sthg.

intégrateur [ɛ̃tegratœr] *nm* integrator.

intégration [ɛ̃tegrasjɔ̃] *nf* **1.** [insertion] integration ▪ **~ raciale** racial integration **2.** [entrée dans une école, une organisation] entry **3.** MATH, PHYS & PSYCHOL integration **4.** ÉCON integration.

intègre [ɛ̃tɛgr] *adj* **1.** [honnête] honest **2.** [équitable, impartial] upright, righteous, upstanding.

intégré, e [ɛ̃tegre] *adj* **1.** [appareil] built-in **2.** [entreprise] integrated **3.** NUCL integrated **4.** INFORM integrated ▪ **traitement ~ de l'information** integrated (data) processing ▪ **avec système ~** with in-house *ou* in-plant system.

intégrer [8] [ɛ̃tegre] ◇ *vt* **1.** [inclure] to integrate, to incorporate, to include ▪ **~ qqch à** *ou* **dans un ensemble** to integrate *ou* to incorporate sthg into a whole **2.** [assimiler - enseignement, notion] to assimilate, to internalize **3.** MATH to integrate **4.** [entrer à - école] to get into, to enter ; [- entreprise] to enter ; [- club] to join.
◇ *vi arg scol* to get into a Grande École.
◆ **s'intégrer** *vpi* **1.** [élément d'un kit] to fit ▪ **s'~ à** to fit into **2.** [personne] to become integrated *ou* assimilated ▪ **ils se sont mal intégrés à la vie du village** they never really fitted into village life.

intégrisme [ɛ̃tegrism] *nm* RELIG fundamentalism.

intégriste [ɛ̃tegrist] *adj* & *nmf* RELIG fundamentalist.

intégrité [ɛ̃tegrite] *nf* **1.** [totalité] integrity ▪ **dans son ~** as a whole, in its integrity ▶ **~ territoriale** *ou* **du territoire** territorial integrity **2.** [état originel] soundness, integrity *sout* **3.** [honnêteté] integrity, uprightness, honesty.

intellect [ɛ̃telɛkt] *nm* intellect, understanding.

intellectualiser [3] [ɛ̃telɛktɥalize] *vt* to intellectualize.

intellectualisme [ɛ̃telɛktɥalism] *nm* intellectualism.

intellectuel, elle [ɛ̃telɛktɥɛl] ◇ *adj* **1.** [mental - capacité] intellectual, mental ▪ **puissance ~le** brainpower **2.** [abstrait] intellectual, cerebral **3.** [non manuel - travail] nonmanual.
◇ *nm, f* intellectual.

intellectuellement [ɛ̃telɛktɥɛlmɑ̃] *adv* intellectually.

intelligemment [ɛ̃teliʒamɑ̃] *adv* intelligently, cleverly.

intelligence [ɛ̃teliʒɑ̃s] *nf* **1.** [intellect, discernement] intelligence ▪ **ils ont l'~ vive** they are sharp-witted *ou* quick, they have sharp minds ▪ **elle est d'une ~ supérieure** she's of superior *ou* above-average intelligence ▪ **avec ~** intelligently ▪ **il a eu l'~ de ne pas recommencer** he was bright *ou* intelligent enough not to try again ‖ [personne] : **c'est une grande ~** he's a great mind *ou* intellect **2.** *sout* [compréhension] : **pour l'~ de ce qui va suivre** in order to understand *ou* to grasp what follows ▪ **elle a l'~ des affaires** she has a good understanding *ou* grasp of what business is all about ▶ **avoir l'~ du cœur** to be highly intuitive **3.** [relation] : **vivre en bonne/mauvaise ~ avec qqn** to be on good/bad terms with sb **4.** INFORM : **~ artificielle** artificial intelligence.
◆ **intelligences** *nfpl* contacts.
◆ **d'intelligence** *loc adv* in collusion ▪ **être d'~ avec qqn** to be in collusion *ou* in league with sb ▪ **agir d'~ avec qqn** to act in (tacit) agreement with sb.

intelligent, e [ɛ̃teliʒɑ̃, ɑ̃t] *adj* **1.** [gén] intelligent, bright, clever ▪ **c'est ~!** *iron* brilliant!, that was clever! **2.** INFORM intelligent.

intelligentsia [ɛ̃teliʒɛnsja, ɛ̃teligɛnsja] *nf* : **l'~** the intelligentsia.

intelligibilité [ɛ̃teliʒibilite] *nf* intelligibility, intelligibleness *sout.*

intelligible [ɛ̃teliʒibl] *adj* **1.** [compréhensible - explication, raisonnement] intelligible, comprehensible ■ **je ne sais pas si mes propos sont ~s** I don't know if what I'm saying makes sense to you *ou* if you can make sense out of what I say **2.** [audible] intelligible, clear, audible ■ **parler à haute et ~ voix** to speak loudly and clearly.

intelligiblement [ɛ̃teliʒibləmɑ̃] *adv* **1.** [de façon compréhensible] intelligibly **2.** [de façon audible] intelligibly, clearly, audibly.

intello [ɛ̃telo] *fam péj* ◇ *adj* highbrow.
◇ *nmf* intellectual.

intempérance [ɛ̃tɑ̃perɑ̃s] *nf* **1.** *litt* [de comportement] immoderation, intemperance *litt*, excess ■ **ses ~s de langage** his immoderate *ou* excessive *ou* unrestrained language **2.** [dans la vie sexuelle] debauchery, intemperance *litt* ■ [dans le manger, le boire] intemperance *litt*, lack of moderation.

intempérant, e [ɛ̃tɑ̃perɑ̃, ɑ̃t] *adj* intemperate *litt*, excessive.

intempéries [ɛ̃tɑ̃peri] *nfpl* bad weather.

intempestif, ive [ɛ̃tɑ̃pɛstif, iv] *adj* untimely, ill-timed, inopportune ■ **sa remarque était intempestive** his comment was out of place.

intempestivement [ɛ̃tɑ̃pɛstivmɑ̃] *adv* at an untimely moment, inopportunely.

intemporalité [ɛ̃tɑ̃pɔralite] *nf* **1.** [immuabilité] timelessness **2.** [immatérialité] immateriality.

intemporel, elle [ɛ̃tɑ̃pɔrɛl] *adj* **1.** [immuable] timeless **2.** [immatériel] immaterial.

intenable [ɛ̃tənabl] *adj* **1.** [insupportable] unbearable, intolerable ■ **c'est devenu ~ au bureau** it's become unbearable *ou* intolerable at the office **2.** [indiscipliné] uncontrollable, unruly, badly-behaved **3.** [non défendable - thèse] untenable ; [- position] indefensible.

intendance [ɛ̃tɑ̃dɑ̃s] *nf* **1.** MIL [pour l'ensemble de l'armée de terre] Supply Corps ■ [dans un régiment] quartermaster stores **2.** ÉDUC [service, bureau] (domestic) bursar's office ■ [gestion] school management ■ **nous avons eu des problèmes d'~** we had supply problems.

intendant, e [ɛ̃tɑ̃dɑ̃, ɑ̃t] *nm, f* **1.** [administrateur] steward, bailiff **2.** UNIV bursar.
◆ **intendant** *nm* **1.** HIST intendant **2.** MIL ≃ Quartermaster General *UK*.

intense [ɛ̃tɑ̃s] *adj* **1.** [extrême - chaleur] intense, extreme ; [- froid] intense, extreme, severe ; [- bruit] loud, intense ; [- plaisir, désir, passion] intense, keen ; [- douleur] intense, severe, acute ; [- émotion] intense ■ **vivre de façon ~** to live intensely **2.** [très vif - couleur] intense, bright, strong **3.** [abondant, dense - circulation, bombardement] heavy.

intensément [ɛ̃tɑ̃semɑ̃] *adv* intensely.

intensif, ive [ɛ̃tɑ̃sif, iv] *adj* **1.** [soutenu] intensive ■ **cours ~s** crash *ou* intensive course **2.** LING [pronom, verbe] intensive ■ [préfixe] intensifying **3.** AGRIC & ÉCON intensive.
◆ **intensif** *nm* intensifier.

intensification [ɛ̃tɑ̃sifikasjɔ̃] *nf* intensification.

intensifier [9] [ɛ̃tɑ̃sifje] *vt* to intensify, to step up *(sép).*
◆ **s'intensifier** *vpi* [passion, recherche] to intensify, to become *ou* to grow more intense ■ [douleur] to become more intense, to worsen ■ [bombardements, circulation] to become heavier.

intensité [ɛ̃tɑ̃site] *nf* **1.** [de la chaleur, du froid] intensity ■ [d'une douleur] intensity, acuteness ■ [d'une couleur, d'une émotion] intensity, depth, strength ■ [de la circulation] density, heaviness ■ [des bombardements] severity **2.** OPT & PHYS intensity ■ [d'un son] loudness ■ **~ d'un tremblement de terre** GÉOL earthquake magnitude *ou* intensity ▶ **~ acoustique** intensity level ■ **~ de courant** ÉLECTR current ■ **~ lumineuse/de rayonnement** luminous/radiant intensity.

intensivement [ɛ̃tɑ̃sivmɑ̃] *adv* intensively.

intenter [3] [ɛ̃tɑ̃te] *vt* : **~ une action en justice à** *ou* **contre qqn** to bring an action against sb ■ **~ un procès à** *ou* **contre qqn** to institute (legal) proceedings against sb *sout*, to take sb to court.

intention [ɛ̃tɑ̃sjɔ̃] *nf* intention ■ **avoir de bonnes/mauvaises ~s** to be well-/ill- intentioned, to have good/bad intentions ■ **il est plein de bonnes ~s** he's full of good intentions ■ **c'est l'~ qui compte** it's the thought that counts ■ **avoir l'~ de faire qqch** to intend to do sthg, to have the intention of doing sthg ■ **elle a la ferme ~ de rester ici** she's determined to stay here, she's intent on staying here ■ **il n'est pas** *ou* **il n'entre pas dans mes ~s de l'acheter maintenant** I don't intend to buy it now, I have no intention of buying it now ■ **dans l'~ de** with the intention of, with a view to ■ **sans ~** without meaning to, unintentionally ▶ **~ d'achat** purchasing intention ■ **sans ~ de donner la mort** DR without intent to kill ■ **sans ~ de nuire** with no ill intent ■ **~ de vote** voting intention.
◆ **à cette intention** *loc adv* for that purpose, with this intention.
◆ **à l'intention de** *loc prép* for ■ **film à l'~ des enfants** film for *ou* aimed at children ■ **brochure à l'~ des consommateurs** brochure for (the information of) consumers ■ **collecte à l'~ des aveugles** fund-raising for *ou* in aid of the blind.

intentionnalité [ɛ̃tɑ̃sjɔnalite] *nf* PHILOS intentionality.

intentionné, e [ɛ̃tɑ̃sjɔne] *adj* : **bien/mal ~** well-/ill-intentioned.

intentionnel, elle [ɛ̃tɑ̃sjɔnɛl] *adj* intentional, deliberate.

intentionnellement [ɛ̃tɑ̃sjɔnɛlmɑ̃] *adv* intentionally, deliberately.

inter [ɛ̃tɛr] *nm* **1.** TÉLÉCOM & *vieilli* long-distance call, trunk call *UK vieilli* **2.** SPORT inside-forward.

inter- [ɛ̃tɛr] *préf* inter-.

interactif, ive [ɛ̃tɛraktif, iv] *adj* interactive.

interaction [ɛ̃tɛraksjɔ̃] *nf* **1.** [gén] interaction, interplay **2.** PHYS interaction.

interallié, e [ɛ̃tɛralje] *adj* Allied.

interarmées [ɛ̃tɛrarme] *adj inv* : **opération ~** interservice *ou* joint service operation.

interbancaire [ɛ̃tɛrbɑ̃kɛr] *adj* [relations] interbank ■ **le marché ~** the money markets.

intercalaire [ɛ̃tɛrkalɛr] ◇ *adj* **1.** [feuille] : **feuillet ~** inset, insert ■ **fiche ~** divider **2.** BOT intercalary.
◇ *nm* **1.** [feuillet] inset, insert **2.** [fiche] divider.

intercalation [ɛ̃tɛrkalasjɔ̃] *nf* **1.** [dans le calendrier] intercalation **2.** [de feuilles] insertion ■ [de termes] interpolation.

intercaler [3] [ɛ̃tɛrkale] *vt* **1.** IMPR to insert, to inset **2.** [inséré] to insert, to fit *ou* to put in *(sép)* ■ **des coupures de journaux intercalées dans un dossier** newspaper clippings inserted into a file **3.** [dans le calendrier] to intercalate.
◆ **s'intercaler** *vpi* : **s'~ entre** to come (in) *ou* to fit in between.

intercéder [8] [ɛ̃tɛrsede] *vi* : **~ (auprès de qqn) en faveur de qqn** to intercede (with sb) for *ou* on behalf of sb.

intercellulaire [ɛ̃tɛrselylɛr] *adj* intercellular.

intercepter [4] [ɛ̃tɛrsɛpte] *vt* **1.** [arrêter - véhicule] to stop ; [- lettre, message] intercept ■ **le store intercepte la lumière** the blind blocks out the light *ou* stops the light coming in **2.** MIL [avion] to intercept **3.** SPORT [ballon] to intercept.

intercepteur [ɛ̃tɛrsɛptœr] *nm* MIL interceptor.

interception [ɛ̃tɛrsɛpsjɔ̃] *nf* interception.

intercesseur [ɛ̃tɛrsesœr] *nm* RELIG & *litt* intercessor.

intercession [ɛ̃tɛrsesjɔ̃] *nf litt* intercession.

interchangeabilité [ɛ̃tɛrʃɑ̃ʒabilite] *nf* interchangeability.

interchangeable [ɛ̃tɛrʃɑ̃ʒabl] *adj* interchangeable.

interclasse [ɛ̃tɛrklas] *nm* ÉDUC break ■ **à l'~** at *ou* during the break.

interclubs [ɛ̃tɛrklœb] *adj* SPORT interclub.

intercommunal, e, aux [ɛ̃tɛrkɔmynal, o] *adj* intermunicipal ■ **projet ~** joint project *(between two or more French communes)* ■ **hôpital ~** ≃ County *ou* Regional Hospital.

intercommunautaire [ɛ̃tɛrkɔmynotɛr] *adj* intercommunity ■ **projet ~** joint project *(between two or more communities)* ■ **relations ~s** relations between EC countries.

interconnexion [ɛ̃tɛrkɔnɛksjɔ̃] *nf* interconnection.

intercontinental, e, aux [ɛ̃tɛrkɔ̃tinɑ̃tal, o] *adj* intercontinental ■ **sur les vols intercontinentaux** on intercontinental flights.

interculturel, elle [ɛ̃tɛrkyltyrɛl] *adj* cross-cultural.

interdépartemental, e, aux [ɛ̃tɛrdepartəmɑ̃tal, o] *adj* interdepartmental ■ **projet ~** joint project *(between two or more French départements)*.

interdépendance [ɛ̃tɛrdepɑ̃dɑ̃s] *nf* interdependence ■ **l'~ des salaires et des prix** the interdependence of prices and wages.

interdépendant, e [ɛ̃tɛrdepɑ̃dɑ̃, ɑ̃t] *adj* interdependent, mutually dependent.

interdiction [ɛ̃tɛrdiksjɔ̃] *nf* **1.** [prohibition] ban, banning ■ **passer outre à/lever une ~** to ignore/to lift a ban ■ **l'~ du livre en 1953 a assuré son succès** the banning of the book in 1953 guaranteed its success ■ **et maintenant, ~ d'utiliser la voiture!** and now you're banned from driving the car! ■ **~ m'avait été faite d'en parler** I'd been forbidden to talk about it ■ **'~ de faire demi-tour'** 'no U-turn' ■ **'~ de marcher sur les pelouses'** 'keep off the grass, do not walk on the grass' ■ **'~ de stationner'** 'no parking' ■ **'~ de déposer des ordures'** 'no dumping' ■ **'~ (formelle *ou* absolue) de fumer'** '(strictly) no smoking, smoking (strictly) prohibited' **2.** [suspension - d'un fonctionnaire] suspension (from duty) ; [- d'un aviateur] grounding ; [- d'un prêtre] interdict, interdiction ➊ **~ bancaire** stopping of payment on all cheques *UK ou* checks *US* ■ **vous risquez une ~ bancaire** you could have your chequebook *UK ou* checkbook *US* taken away ■ **~ d'écriture** INFORM write lockout ■ **~ de séjour** banning order.

Voir module d'usage

interdire [103] [ɛ̃tɛrdir] *vt* **1.** [défendre] to forbid ■ **~ l'alcool/le tabac à qqn** to forbid sb to drink/to smoke ■ **~ à qqn de faire qqch** [suj: personne] to forbid sb to do sthg ; [suj: règlement] to prohibit sb from doing sthg ■ **je lui ai interdit ma porte *ou* ma maison** I will not allow her into my *ou* I have banned her from my home ■ *(tournure impersonnelle)* **il m'est interdit d'en dire plus** I am not allowed *ou* at liberty to say any more ■ **il est interdit de fumer ici** smoking is forbidden *ou* isn't allowed here **2.** DR [prohiber - circulation, stationnement, arme à feu, médicament] to prohibit, to ban ; [- manifestation, revue] to ban **3.** [empêcher] to prevent, to preclude ■ **le mauvais temps interdit toute opération de sauvetage** bad weather is preventing any rescue operations **4.** [suspendre - magistrat] to suspend ; [- prêtre] to (lay under an) interdict.

◆ **s'interdire** *vpt* : **s'~ l'alcool/le tabac** to abstain from drinking/smoking ■ **elle s'interdit tout espoir de la revoir** she denies herself all hope of seeing her again.

interdisciplinaire [ɛ̃tɛrdisiplinɛr] *adj* interdisciplinary.

interdisez *etc v* ▷ **interdire.**

interdit, e [ɛ̃tɛrdi, it] ◇ *pp* ▷ **interdire.**

◇ *adj* **1.** [non autorisé] : **'décharge/baignade ~e'** 'no dumping/bathing' ■ **'affichage ~'** '(stick *ou* post) no bills' ■ **~ à : le pont est ~ aux voyageurs** the bridge is closed to passengers ■ **la zone piétonne est ~e aux véhicules** vehicles are not allowed in the pedestrian area ■ **'~ au public'** 'no admittance' ■ **'~ aux moins de 18 ans'** CINÉ adults only, '18' *UK*, 'NC-17' *US* ■ **'~ aux moins de 13 ans'** CINÉ 'PG' *UK*, 'PG-13' *US* **2.** [privé d'un droit] : **~ de séjour en France** DR banned *ou* prohibited from entering France ■ **être ~ de chéquier** to have (had) one's chequebook facilities *UK ou* checking privileges *US* withdrawn ■ **appareil/pilote ~ de vol** grounded aircraft/pilot **3.** [frappé d'interdiction - film, revue] banned **4.** [stupéfait] dumbfounded, flabbergasted ■ **laisser qqn ~** to take sb aback ■ **elle le dévisagea, ~e** she stared at him in bewilderment.

◇ *nm, f* DR : **~ de séjour en Suisse** person banned from *ou* not allowed to enter Switzerland.

◆ **interdit** *nm* **1.** [de la société] (social) constraint ■ [tabou] taboo ■ **lever un ~** to lift a restriction **2.** [condamnation] : **jeter l'~ sur *ou* contre qqn** to cast sb out, to exclude sb **3.** ANTHR prohibition **4.** RELIG interdict **5.** BANQUE : **~ bancaire** stopping of payment on all cheques *UK ou* checks *US*.

interentreprises [ɛ̃tɛrɑ̃trəpriz] *adj inv* intercompany.

intéressant, e [ɛ̃teresɑ̃, ɑ̃t] ◇ *adj* **1.** [conversation, œuvre, personne, visage *etc*] interesting ■ **elle cherche toujours à se rendre ~e** she's always trying to attract attention, she's an attention-seeker ➊ **être dans une situation ~e *ou* dans un état ~ *ou* dans une position ~e** *hum & vieilli* to be in the family way **2.** [avantageux] attractive, favourable ■ [lucratif] profitable, worthwhile ■ **c'est une affaire très ~e** it's a very good deal ■ **cette carte n'est ~e que si tu voyages beaucoup** this card is only worth having if you travel a lot ■ **pas ~** [offre, prix] not attractive, not worthwhile ; [activité] not worthwhile, unprofitable.

◇ *nm, f* : **faire l'~ *ou* son ~** *péj* to show off.

intéressé, e [ɛ̃terese] ◇ *adj* **1.** [personne] self-interested, self-seeking, calculating ■ [comportement] motivated by self-interest ■ **je ne suis pas du tout ~** I'm not doing it out of self-interest **2.** [concerné] concerned, involved ■ **les parties ~es** [gén] the people concerned *ou* involved ; DR the interested parties **3.** [financièrement] : **être ~ dans une affaire** to have a stake *ou* a financial interest in a business.

◇ *nm, f* : **l'~** the person concerned ■ **les premiers/principaux ~s** the persons most closely concerned *ou* most directly affected.

L'INTERDICTION

Smoking is not permitted in the office. Il est interdit de fumer dans les bureaux.

You're not meant to be in here at the weekend. Vous n'êtes pas censés être ici le week-end.

You're not allowed to run in the corridors. Il est interdit de courir dans les couloirs.

I'm afraid I'm not allowed to give out those details over the phone. Je regrette, mais je n'ai pas le droit de vous donner ces renseignements par téléphone.

Don't ever do that again! Ne t'avise plus jamais de recommencer !

I forbid you to talk to him. Je t'interdis de lui parler.

On no account must you tell anyone about this meeting. Vous ne devez surtout pas parler à qui que ce soit de cette réunion.

There's no way you're going out tonight! Il n'est pas question que tu sortes ce soir !

intéressement [ɛ̃terɛsmɑ̃] *nm* profit-sharing scheme.

intéresser [4] [ɛ̃terese] *vt* **1.** [passionner - suj: activité, œuvre, professeur *etc*] to interest ▪ **l'histoire l'intéresse beaucoup** he's very interested in history ▪ **notre offre peut peut-être vous ~** our offer might interest you *ou* might be of interest to you ▪ **le débat ne m'a pas du tout intéressé** I didn't find the debate at all interesting ▪ **continue, tu m'intéresses!** go on, you're starting to interest me! **2.** [concerner - suj: loi, réforme] to concern, to affect ▪ **ces mesures intéressent essentiellement les mères célibataires** these measures mainly affect single mothers ▪ **un problème qui intéresse la sécurité du pays** a problem which is relevant to *ou* concerns national security **3.** ÉCON & FIN : **notre personnel est intéressé aux bénéfices** our staff gets a share of our profits, we operate a profit-sharing scheme ▪ **être intéressé dans une entreprise** to have a stake *ou* a financial interest in a company.

◆ **s'intéresser à** *vp+prép* : **elle ne s'intéresse à rien** she is not interested *ou* she takes no interest in anything ▪ **à quoi vous intéressez-vous?** what are your interests (in life)? ▪ **je m'intéresse vivement à sa carrière** I take great *ou* a keen interest in her career ▪ **personne ne s'intéresse à moi!** nobody cares about me!, nobody's interested in me!

intérêt [ɛ̃terɛ] *nm* **1.** [attention, curiosité] interest ▪ **avoir** *ou* **éprouver de l'~ pour qqch** to be interested *ou* to take an interest in sthg ▪ **prendre ~ à qqch** to take an interest in sthg ▮ [bienveillance] interest, concern ▪ **porter de l'~ à qqn** to take an interest in sb ▪ **témoigner de l'~ à qqn** to show an interest in sb, to show concern for sb
2. [ce qui éveille l'attention] : **son essai offre peu d'~** her essay is of no great interest
3. [utilité] point, idea ▪ **l'~ d'un débat est que tout le monde participe** the point in *ou* the idea of having a debate is that everybody should join in ▪ **je ne vois pas l'~ de continuer cette discussion** I see no point in carrying on this discussion ▮ [importance] importance, significance ▪ **ses observations sont du plus haut** *ou* **grand ~** his comments are of the greatest interest *ou* importance
4. [avantage - d'une personne, d'une cause] interest ▪ **elle sait où se trouve son ~** she knows what's in her best interests ▪ **agir dans/contre son ~** to act in/against one's own interest ▪ **dans l'~ général** in the general interest ▪ **dans l'~ de son travail/sa santé** in the interest of her job/her health ▪ **d'~ public** of public interest ▪ **tu as ~ à te faire tout petit!** *fam* you'd be well-advised to *ou* you'd better keep your head down! ➲ **si elle va me rembourser? (il) y a ~!** *fam* will she pay me back? you bet (she will)!
5. [égoïsme] self-interest ▪ **il l'a fait par ~** he did it out of self-interest
6. ÉCON & FIN interest ▪ **à 5 % d'~** 5% interest (rate) ▪ **emprunter/prêter à ~** to borrow/to lend with interest ▪ **cela rapporte des ~s** it yields *ou* bears interest ➲ **~s dus/exigibles** interest due/payable ▪ **prêt sans ~** interest-free loan.

◆ **intérêts** *nmpl* [d'une personne, d'un pays] interests ▪ **servir les ~s de qqn/d'une société** to serve sb's/a company's interests ▪ **avoir des ~s dans une société** ÉCON & FIN to have a stake *ou* a financial interest in a company.

◆ **sans intérêt** <> *loc adj* [exposition, album] uninteresting, of no interest, devoid of interest ▪ **que disais-tu? – c'est sans ~** what were you saying? – it's not important *ou* it doesn't matter ▪ **c'est sans ~ pour la suite de l'enquête** it's of no importance for *ou* relevance to the rest of the inquiry.
<> *loc adv* uninterestedly, without interest ▪ **je fais mon travail sans ~** I take no interest in my work.

interface [ɛ̃tɛrfas] *nf* interface ▪ **~ de communication** communication interface ▪ **~ graphique** graphics interface ▪ **~ utilisateur** user interface.

interférence [ɛ̃tɛrferɑ̃s] *nf* **1.** MÉTÉOR, RADIO & PHYS interference *(U)* ▪ **il y a des ~s** there is interference **2.** [interaction] interaction.

interférer [18] [ɛ̃tɛrfere] *vi* **1.** PHYS to interfere **2.** [se mêler] to interact, to combine ▪ **les deux courants interfèrent** the two currents interact with each other **3.** [intervenir] : **~ dans la vie de qqn** to interfere *ou* to meddle in sb's life.

intergalactique [ɛ̃tɛrgalaktik] *adj* intergalactic.

intergouvernemental, e, aux [ɛ̃tɛrguvɛrnəmɑ̃tal, o] *adj* intergovernmental.

intérieur, e [ɛ̃terjœr] *adj* **1.** [du dedans] inside, inner ▪ **les peintures ~es de la maison** the interior decoration of the house
2. [sentiment, vie] inner ▪ **des voix ~es** inner voices
3. [national - ligne aérienne] domestic, internal ; [- politique, marché] domestic ➲ **la dette ~e** the national debt
4. [interne] internal ▪ **les problèmes ~s d'un parti** a party's internal problems
5. GÉOGR [désert, mer] inland
6. GÉOM interior.

◆ **intérieur** *nm* **1.** [d'un objet] inside, interior ▪ [d'un continent, d'un pays] : **l'~ (des terres)** the interior ▪ **l'~ de l'île** the interior of the island, the hinterland ▪ **les villages de l'~** inland villages
2. [foyer, décor] interior, home ▪ **tenir un ~** to housekeep, to keep house ➲ **homme d'~, femme d'~** homebody ▪ **scène d'~** interior
3. CINÉ interior (shot) ▪ **entièrement tourné en ~** with interior shots only
4. *fam* POLIT : **l'Intérieur** ≃ the Home Office *UK*, ≃ the Department of the Interior *US*
5. SPORT inside-forward ▪ **~ droit/gauche** inside right/left.

◆ **à l'intérieur** *loc adv* **1.** [dedans] inside
2. [dans la maison] inside, indoors.

◆ **à l'intérieur de** *loc prép* **1.** [lieu] in, inside ▪ **la pluie pénètre à l'~ du garage** the rain is coming into the garage ▪ **reste à l'~ de la voiture** stay in *ou* inside the car ▪ **à l'~ des frontières** within *ou* inside the frontiers ▪ **à l'~ des terres** inland
2. [groupe] within.

◆ **de l'intérieur** *loc adv* **1.** [d'un lieu] from (the) inside
2. [d'un groupe] from within.

intérieurement [ɛ̃terjœrmɑ̃] *adv* **1.** [à l'intérieur] inside, within **2.** [secrètement] inwardly.

intérim [ɛ̃terim] *nm* **1.** [période] interim (period) ▪ **dans l'~** meanwhile, in the meantime, in the interim **2.** [remplacement] : **j'assure l'~ de la secrétaire en chef** I'm deputizing *ou* covering for the chief secretary **3.** [emploi] temporary work ▪ **faire de l'~** to temp ➲ **agence d'~** temping agency.

◆ **par intérim** <> *loc adj* [président, trésorier] interim *(modif)*, acting *(modif)* ▪ **secrétaire par ~** acting secretary ▪ **gouvernement par ~** caretaker government.
<> *loc adv* in a temporary capacity, temporarily ▪ **gouverner par ~** to govern in the interim *ou* for an interim period.

intérimaire [ɛ̃terimɛr] <> *adj* **1.** [assurant l'intérim - directeur, trésorier, ministre] acting ; [- personnel, employé] temporary ; [- gouvernement, cabinet] caretaker ▪ **secrétaire ~** temporary secretary, temp **2.** [non durable - fonction] interim *(modif)* ; [- commission] provisional, temporary, stopgap.
<> *nmf* [cadre] deputy ▪ [secrétaire] temp ▪ **travailler comme ~** to temp, to do temping work.

intériorisation [ɛ̃terjɔrizasjɔ̃] *nf* internalization, interiorization.

intérioriser [3] [ɛ̃terjɔrize] *vt* **1.** PSYCHOL to internalize, to interiorize **2.** [garder pour soi] to internalize, to keep in *(sép)* ▪ **elle a intériorisé sa colère** she kept her anger in, she bottled up her anger.

intériorité [ɛ̃terjɔrite] *nf* inwardness, interiority *sout*.

interjection [ɛ̃tɛrʒɛksjɔ̃] *nf* [exclamation] interjection.

interjeter [27] [ɛ̃tɛrʒəte] *vt* : **~ appel** to lodge an appeal.

interlettrage [ɛ̃tɛrletraʒ] *nm* [typographie] leading.

interligne [ɛ̃tɛrliɲ] <> *nm* **1.** [blanc] space (between the lines) ▪ IMPR & INFORM line spacing ▪ **simple/double ~** single/double spacing **2.** [ajout] interlineation **3.** MUS space.
<> *nf* IMPR [lame] lead.

interlocuteur, trice [ɛ̃tɛrlɔkytœr, tris] *nm, f* **1.** [gén] *person speaking or being spoken to* ▪ LING speaker, interlocutor *sout* ▪ [dans un débat] speaker ▪ **mon ~ n'avait pas compris** the man I was talking to hadn't understood **2.** [dans une négociation] negotiating partner.

interlocutoire [ɛ̃tɛrlɔkytwar] <> *adj* interlocutory.
<> *nm* interlocutory judgement.

interlope [ɛ̃tɛrlɔp] *adj* **1.** [frauduleux] unlawful, illegal, illicit **2.** [louche] shady, dubious ■ **relations** *ou* **amitiés ~s** underworld connections.

interloquer [3] [ɛ̃tɛrlɔke] *vt* [décontenancer] to take aback *(sép)*, to disconcert ■ [stupéfier] to stun ■ **elle resta interloquée** she was dumbfounded *ou* flabbergasted *ou* stunned.

interlude [ɛ̃tɛrlyd] *nm* interlude.

intermède [ɛ̃tɛrmɛd] *nm* **1.** MUS interlude, intermedio, intermezzo *spéc* ■ THÉÂTRE interlude, interval piece ■ **un ~ comique** a comic interlude **2.** *fig* interlude, interval.

intermédiaire [ɛ̃tɛrmedjɛr] <> *adj* **1.** [moyen] intermediate, intermediary ■ **solution ~** compromise (solution) **2.** ÉDUC intermediate **3.** CINÉ, GÉOL & MÉTALL intermediate.
<> *nmf* **1.** [médiateur] intermediary, mediator, go-between ■ **servir d'~** to act as an intermediary *ou* as a go-between **2.** COMM intermediary, middleman **3.** BANQUE : **~ agréé** authorized intermediary.
◆ **par l'intermédiaire de** *loc prép* [personne] through, via ■ **il a appris l'anglais par l'~ de la radio** he learnt English from the radio.
◆ **sans intermédiaire** *loc adv* **1.** [directement] directly **2.** COMM direct, directly.

interminable [ɛ̃tɛrminabl] *adj* interminable, never-ending, endless ■ **la route lui paraissait ~** she thought the road would never end.

interminablement [ɛ̃tɛrminabləmɑ̃] *adv* interminably, endlessly, without end.

interministériel, elle [ɛ̃tɛrministerjɛl] *adj* POLIT interdepartmental, joint ministerial *UK*.

intermission [ɛ̃tɛrmisjɔ̃] *nf* MÉD (period of) remission, intermission.

intermittence [ɛ̃tɛrmitɑ̃s] *nf* **1.** [irrégularité] intermittence, irregularity ■ **l'~ d'un signal lumineux** the irregular flashing of a light **2.** MÉD intermission, remission.
◆ **par intermittence** *loc adv* intermittently ■ **travailler par ~** to work in fits and starts *ou* intermittently.

intermittent, e [ɛ̃tɛrmitɑ̃, ɑ̃t] *adj* **1.** [irrégulier - tir] intermittent, sporadic ; [- travail] casual, occasional ; [- pulsation] irregular, periodic ; [- éclairage] intermittent ; [- averses] occasional **2.** MÉD : **pouls ~** irregular pulse.
◆ **intermittent** *nm* : **les ~s du spectacle** *people working in the performing arts (and thus entitled to social security benefits designed for people without regular employment).*

internalisation [ɛ̃tɛrnalizasjɔ̃] *nf* ÉCON internalization ■ **~ du recrutement** recruiting in-house, in-house *ou* internal recruitment.

internat [ɛ̃tɛrna] *nm* **1.** ÉDUC [école] boarding school ■ **l'~** [régime] boarding **2.** MÉD [concours] *competitive examination leading to internship* ■ [stage] hospital training, time as a houseman *UK*, internship *US*.

international, e, aux [ɛ̃tɛrnasjɔnal, o] <> *adj* [gén] international.
<> *nm, f* international (player *ou* athlete).
◆ **internationaux** *nmpl* SPORT internationals ■ **les internationaux de France de tennis** the French Open.

Internationale [ɛ̃tɛrnasjɔnal] *npr f* **1.** [chant] : **l'~** the Internationale **2.** [groupement] : **l'~** the International.

internationalisation [ɛ̃tɛrnasjɔnalizasjɔ̃] *nf* internationalization.

internationaliser [3] [ɛ̃tɛrnasjɔnalize] *vt* to internationalize.
◆ **s'internationaliser** *vpi* to take on an international dimension ■ **le conflit s'est internationalisé** the conflict took on an international dimension.

internationalisme [ɛ̃tɛrnasjɔnalism] *nm* internationalism.

internaute [ɛ̃tɛrnot] *nmf* net surfer, Internet surfer.

interne [ɛ̃tɛrn] <> *adj* [intérieur - paroi] internal, inside ; [- face] internal ; [- raison, cause, logique] internal, inner ; [- conflit] internal ; [- personnel] in-house ■ [hémorragie, organe] internal ■ **il a fallu radiographier le côté ~ de la jambe/du pied** the inner part of the leg/foot had to be X-rayed ■ **le parti connaît des difficultés ~s** the party is having internal problems ■ **structure ~** internal structure ■ **médecine ~** internal medicine ■ **angle ~** interior angle.
<> *nmf* **1.** MÉD : **~ (des hôpitaux)** houseman *UK*, junior hospital doctor *UK*, intern *US* **2.** ÉDUC boarder ■ **c'est un ~** he's at boarding school.
◆ **en interne** *loc adv* [dans l'entreprise] in-house, on an in-house basis.

interné, e [ɛ̃tɛrne] <> *adj* **1.** MÉD committed, sectioned *UK spéc* **2.** [emprisonné] interned.
<> *nm, f* **1.** MÉD committed *ou* sectioned *UK spéc* patient **2.** [prisonnier] internee.

internement [ɛ̃tɛrnəmɑ̃] *nm* **1.** MÉD commitment, sectioning *UK spéc* **2.** [emprisonnement] internment ■ **~ abusif** illegal internment.

interner [3] [ɛ̃tɛrne] *vt* **1.** MÉD to commit, to section *UK spéc* **2.** POLIT to intern.

Internet [ɛ̃tɛrnɛt] *nm* : **(l') ~** (the) Internet.

interpellateur, trice [ɛ̃tɛrpelatœr, tris] *nm, f* POLIT [questionneur] questioner, interpellator *spéc*.

interpellation [ɛ̃tɛrpelasjɔ̃] *nf* **1.** [apostrophe] call, shout **2.** [par la police] (arrest for) questioning ■ **la police a procédé à plusieurs ~s** several people were detained *ou* taken in by police for questioning **3.** POLIT question, interpellation *spéc*.

interpeller [26] [ɛ̃tɛrpəle] *vt* **1.** [appeler] to call out, to hail **2.** [suj: police] to call in *ou* to stop for questioning **3.** [concerner] to call out *(insép)* to ■ **ça m'interpelle quelque part** *hum* it says something to me **4.** POLIT to put a question to, to interpellate *sout*.
◆ **s'interpeller** *vp (emploi réciproque)* [s'appeler] to call out to *ou* to hail one another.

interpénétration [ɛ̃tɛrpenetrasjɔ̃] *nf* interpenetration.

interpénétrer [18] [ɛ̃tɛrpenetre] ◆ **s'interpénétrer** *vp (emploi réciproque)* to interpenetrate, to penetrate mutually ■ **des cultures qui s'interpénètrent** intermingling cultures.

Interphone® [ɛ̃tɛrfɔn] *nm* [dans un bureau] intercom ■ [à l'entrée d'un immeuble] entry *ou* security phone.

interplanétaire [ɛ̃tɛrplanetɛr] *adj* interplanetary.

INTERPOL, Interpol [ɛ̃tɛrpɔl] *npr* Interpol.

interpolation [ɛ̃tɛrpɔlasjɔ̃] *nf* interpolation, insertion.

interpoler [3] [ɛ̃tɛrpɔle] *vt* **1.** [texte] to insert, to fit in *ou* into *(sép)*, to interpolate *spéc* ■ **~ une phrase dans un discours** to add a sentence to a speech **2.** MATH to interpolate.

interposer [3] [ɛ̃tɛrpoze] *vt* to place, to insert, to interpose *sout* ■ **ils ont pu se contacter par personne interposée** they were able to make contact through an intermediary.
◆ **s'interposer** *vpi* **1.** [faire écran] : **s'~ entre** to stand between **2.** [intervenir] to intervene, to step in *(insép)*, to interpose o.s. *sout* ■ **il s'est interposé pour l'empêcher de me frapper** he stepped in *ou* intervened to stop her hitting me.

interposition [ɛ̃tɛrpozisjɔ̃] *nf* **1.** [d'un objet, de texte] interposition, interposing **2.** [intervention] interposition, intervention.

interprétable [ɛ̃tɛrpretabl] *adj* interpretable ■ **c'est ~ de deux façons** this may be interpreted *ou* taken in two ways.

interprétariat [ɛ̃tɛrpretarja] *nm* interpreting ■ **faire de l'~** to work as an interpreter.

interprétatif, ive [ɛ̃tɛrpretatif, iv] *adj* **1.** [explicatif] expository, interpretative, interpretive **2.** INFORM interpretive **3.** PSYCHOL interpretative.

interprétation [ɛ̃tɛrpretasjɔ̃] *nf* **1.** [exécution - d'une œuvre musicale] interpretation, rendering, performance ; [- d'un rôle] interpretation ; [- d'un texte] reading **2.** [analyse] interpretation, analysis **3.** [interprétariat] interpreting **4.** PSYCHOL : **~ des rêves** interpretation of dreams **5.** INFORM interpretation.

interprète [ɛ̃tɛrprɛt] *nmf* **1.** [musicien, acteur] performer, player ▪ [chanteur] singer ▪ [danseur] dancer ▪ **les ~s** [d'un film, d'une pièce] the cast ▪ **l'~ de : il est devenu l'~ par excellence de Beckett** he became the foremost interpreter of Beckett's work ▪ **l'~ de Cyrano n'était pas à la hauteur** the actor playing Cyrano wasn't up to the part ▪ **les ~s de ce concerto sont...** the concerto will be played by... **2.** [traducteur] interpreter ▪ **servir d'~ à** to act as interpreter for ▪ **~ de conférence** conference interpreter **3.** [représentant] spokesperson, spokesman (*f* spokeswoman) ▪ **être l'~ de qqn auprès des autorités** to speak to the authorities on sb's behalf.

interpréter [18] [ɛ̃tɛrprete] *vt* **1.** [exécuter, jouer] to perform, to interpret *sout* ▪ **~ un rôle** to play a part ▪ **~ une sonate au piano** to play a sonata on the piano ▪ **~ un air** to perform *ou* to sing a tune **2.** [comprendre - texte] to interpret ▪ **mal ~ qqch** to misinterpret sthg ▪ **~ qqch en bien/mal** to take sthg well/ the wrong way **3.** [traduire] to interpret.
◆ **s'interpréter** *vp (emploi passif)* [être compris] to be interpreted.

interpréteur [ɛ̃tɛrpretœr] *nm* INFORM interpreter.

interprofessionnel, elle [ɛ̃tɛrprɔfɛsjɔnɛl] *adj* interprofessional.

interracial, e, aux [ɛ̃tɛrrasjal, o] *adj* interracial.

interrégional, e, aux [ɛ̃tɛrreʒjɔnal, o] *adj* interregional.

interrègne [ɛ̃tɛrrɛɲ] *nm* interregnum.

interrogateur, trice [ɛ̃terɔgatœr, tris] ◇ *adj* [geste, regard] questioning, inquiring, probing ▪ **sur un ton ~** questioningly, searchingly.
◇ *nm, f* ÉDUC (oral) examiner.

interrogatif, ive [ɛ̃terɔgatif, iv] *adj* **1.** [interrogateur] questioning, inquiring ▪ **d'un ton ~** questioningly **2.** LING interrogative.
◆ **interrogatif** *nm* interrogative (word) ▪ **l'~** the interrogative, *voir aussi* **pluriel**.
◆ **interrogative** *nf* interrogative *ou* question clause.

interrogation [ɛ̃terɔgasjɔ̃] *nf* **1.** [question] question, questioning ▪ [doute] questioning, questions, doubts **2.** ÉDUC test ▪ **~ écrite/orale** written/oral test **3.** LING : **~ directe/indirecte** direct/indirect question **4.** INFORM & TÉLÉCOM search.

interrogativement [ɛ̃terɔgativmɑ̃] *adv* **1.** LING interrogatively **2.** [en demandant] questioningly, inquiringly.

interrogatoire [ɛ̃terɔgatwar] *nm* **1.** [par la police - d'un prisonnier, d'un suspect] interrogation, questioning ▪ **faire subir à qqn un ~ serré** *fam* to grill sb ▪ **faire subir à qqn un ~ musclé** *fam* to work sb over *(to obtain information)* **2.** DR [dans un procès] examination, cross-examination, cross-questioning ▪ [par un juge d'instruction] hearing ▪ [procès-verbal] statement.

interrogeable [ɛ̃terɔʒabl] *adj fam* **répondeur ~ à distance** answering machine with remote-access facility.

interroger [17] [ɛ̃terɔʒe] *vt* **1.** [questionner - ami] to ask, to question ; [- guichetier] to ask, to inquire of ; [- suspect] to question, to interrogate, to interview ▪ **~ qqn pour savoir si** to ask sb whether, to inquire of sb whether *sout* ▪ **~ qqn sur qqch** to ask sb questions about sthg ▪ **~ qqn du regard** to look questioningly *ou* inquiringly at sb ▪ **~ sa mémoire/le ciel** to search one's memory/the sky **2.** SOCIOL to poll, to question ▪ **personne interrogée** respondent **3.** ÉDUC [avant l'examen] to test, to quiz ▪ [à l'examen] to examine ▪ **j'ai été interrogé sur la guerre de 14-18** I was asked questions on the 1914-18 war ▪ **être interrogé par écrit** to be given a written test *ou* exam **4.** INFORM & TÉLÉCOM to interrogate, to search (through) **5.** DR to examine, to cross-examine.
◆ **s'interroger** *vpi* : **s'~ sur qqch** to wonder about sthg ▪ **je ne sais pas si je vais l'acheter, je m'interroge encore** I don't know whether I'll buy it, I'm still wondering (about it) *ou* I haven't made up my mind yet.

interrompre [78] [ɛ̃terɔ̃pr] *vt* **1.** [perturber - conversation, études] to interrupt **2.** [faire une pause dans - débat] to stop, to suspend ; [- session] to interrupt, to break off ; [- voyage] to break ▪ **~ ses études pendant un an** to take a year off from one's studies **3.** [définitivement] to stop ▪ **~ sa lecture/son repas** to stop reading/eating ▪ **~ une grossesse** to terminate a pregnancy.
◆ **s'interrompre** *vpi* [dans une conversation] to break off, to stop ▪ [dans une activité] to break off.

interrupteur, trice [ɛ̃teryptœr, tris] *nm, f litt* [personne] interrupter.
◆ **interrupteur** *nm* [dispositif] switch ▪ **~ horaire/principal** time/master switch.

interruption [ɛ̃terypsjɔ̃] *nf* **1.** [arrêt définitif] breaking off ▪ **~ des relations diplomatiques** breaking off *ou* severance *sout* of diplomatic relations ▪ **sans ~** continuously, uninterruptedly, without stopping ▪ **'ouvert sans ~ de 9 h à 20 h'** 'open all day 9 a.m.-8 p.m' ➔ **~ volontaire de grossesse** MÉD voluntary termination of pregnancy **2.** [pause - dans un spectacle] break **3.** [perturbation] interruption ▪ **des ~s continuelles l'empêchaient de travailler** continual interruptions prevented him from working ▪ **veuillez excuser l'~ de nos programmes** we apologise for the break in transmission ➔ **~ de courant** ÉLECTR power cut.

interscolaire [ɛ̃tɛrskɔlɛr] *adj* interschools.

intersection [ɛ̃tɛrsɛksjɔ̃] *nf* **1.** [de routes] intersection, crossroads, junction ▪ **~ avec une route secondaire** intersection with a minor road ▪ **à l'~ des deux routes** where the two roads intersect *ou* meet ▪ **à l'~ de plusieurs courants politiques** where several different political tendencies meet *ou* come together **2.** MATH [de droites, de plans] intersection ▪ [d'ensembles] set ▪ LOGIQUE set.

intersession [ɛ̃tɛrsesjɔ̃] *nf* POLIT recess.

intersidéral, e, aux [ɛ̃tɛrsideral, o] *adj* intersideral ▪ **espace ~** deep space.

interspécifique [ɛ̃tɛrspesifik] *adj* interspecific.

interstice [ɛ̃tɛrstis] *nm* crack, chink, interstice *sout*.

interstitiel, elle [ɛ̃tɛrstisjɛl] *adj* interstitial.
◆ **interstitiel** *nm* PHYS interstitial.

intersyndical, e, aux [ɛ̃tɛrsɛ̃dikal, o] *adj* interunion, joint union.
◆ **intersyndicale** *nf* interunion committee.

intertitre [ɛ̃tɛrtitr] *nm* **1.** PRESSE subheading **2.** CINÉ subtitle.

interuniversitaire [ɛ̃tɛryniversitɛr] *adj* intercollegiate.

interurbain, e [ɛ̃tɛryrbɛ̃, ɛn] *adj* [gén] intercity, interurban ▪ TÉLÉCOM & *vieilli* long-distance *(avant n)*, trunk *UK (modif)*.
◆ **interurbain** *nm vieilli* long-distance telephone service, trunk call service *UK*.

intervalle [ɛ̃tɛrval] *nm* **1.** [durée] interval ▪ **un ~ de trois heures** a three-hour interval *ou* gap ▪ **ils se sont retrouvés à trois mois d'~** they met again after an interval of three months ▪ **par ~s** intermittently, at intervals, now and again ▪ **dans l'~, je ferai le nécessaire** meanwhile *ou* in the meantime I'll do what has to be done **2.** [distance] interval, space ▪ **plantés à ~s de trois mètres** *ou* **à trois mètres d'~** planted three metres apart **3.** [brèche] gap **4.** MATH, MIL & MUS interval.

intervenant, e [ɛ̃tɛrvənɑ̃, ɑ̃t] ◇ *adj* intervening.
◇ *nm, f* **1.** [dans un débat, un congrès] contributor, speaker **2.** DR intervening party.

intervenir [40] [ɛ̃tɛrvənir] *vi* **1.** [agir] to intervene, to step in ▪ **~ en faveur de qqn** to intercede *ou* to intervene on sb's behalf ▪ **~ auprès de qqn pour** to intercede with sb in order to ▪ **on a dû faire ~ la police** the police had to be brought in *ou* called in **2.** MÉD to operate **3.** [prendre la parole] to speak **4.** MIL to intervene **5.** [jouer un rôle - circonstance, facteur] : **~ dans** to influence, to affect **6.** [survenir - accord, décision] to be reached ; [- incident, changement] to take place ▪ **le changement/la mesure intervient au moment où...** the change/measure comes at a time when... **7.** DR to intervene.

intervention [ɛ̃tɛrvɑ̃sjɔ̃] *nf* **1.** [entrée en action] intervention ▪ **il a fallu l'~ des pompiers** the fire brigade had to be called in *ou* brought in ▪ **malgré l'~ rapide des secours** despite swift rescue action ▪ **~ en faveur de qqn** intervention in sb's favour **2.** MIL intervention ▪ **l'~ des forces armées** military intervention ➊ **~ aérienne** air strike ▪ **~ armée** armed intervention **3.** [ingérence] interference ▪ POLIT intervention **4.** [discours] : **j'ai fait deux ~s** I spoke twice **5.** MÉD : **~ (chirurgicale)** (surgical) operation, surgery *(U)* **6.** DR intervention.

interventionnisme [ɛ̃tɛrvɑ̃sjɔnism] *nm* interventionism.

interventionniste [ɛ̃tɛrvɑ̃sjɔnist] ◇ *adj* interventionist ▪ **non ~** non-interventionist.
◇ *nmf* interventionist.

intervenu, e [ɛ̃tɛrvəny] *pp* ▷ **intervenir**.

interversion [ɛ̃tɛrvɛrsjɔ̃] *nf* inversion ▪ **~ des rôles** role reversal.

intervertir [32] [ɛ̃tɛrvɛrtir] *vt* to invert (the order of) ▪ **~ les rôles** to reverse roles.

intervient *etc v* ▷ **intervenir**.

interview [ɛ̃tɛrvju] *nf ou nm* PRESSE interview ▪ **une ~ exclusive** an exclusive (interview).

interviewé, e [ɛ̃tɛrvjuve] ◇ *adj* PRESSE interviewed.
◇ *nm, f* PRESSE interviewee.

interviewer[1] [3] [ɛ̃tɛrvjuve] *vt* PRESSE to interview.

interviewer[2] [ɛ̃tɛrvjuvœr] *nm* PRESSE interviewer.

intervint *etc v* ▷ **intervenir**.

intervocalique [ɛ̃tɛrvɔkalik] *adj* intervocalic.

intestat [ɛ̃tɛsta] ◇ *adj inv* intestate ▪ **mourir ~** to die intestate.
◇ *nmf* intestate.

intestin[1] [ɛ̃tɛstɛ̃] *nm* ANAT intestine, bowel, gut ▪ **les ~s** the intestines, the bowels ➊ **~ grêle** small intestine ▪ **gros ~** large intestine.

intestin[2], e [ɛ̃tɛstɛ̃, in] *adj sout* [interne] internal ▪ **luttes ~es** internecine struggles.

intestinal, e, aux [ɛ̃tɛstinal, o] *adj* intestinal ▪ **douleurs ~es** stomach pains.

intimation [ɛ̃timasjɔ̃] *nf* **1.** [d'un ordre] notification **2.** DR [assignation] summons *(before a high court)* ▪ **signifier une ~** to issue *ou* to serve a summons.

intime [ɛ̃tim] ◇ *adj* **1.** [proche] close ▪ **un ami ~** a close friend, an intimate *sout* **2.** [privé - pensée, vie] intimate ▪ **conversation ~** private conversation, tête-à-tête ▪ **avoir des relations ~s avec qqn** to be on intimate terms with sb **3.** *euphém* [génital] : **hygiène ~** personal hygiene ▪ **parties ~s** private parts **4.** [discret] quiet, intimate ▪ **soirée ~** [entre deux personnes] quiet dinner ; [entre plusieurs] quiet get-together ▪ **restaurant ~** quiet little restaurant **5.** [profond] inner, intimate ▪ **il a une connaissance ~ de la langue** he has a thorough knowledge of the language, he knows the language inside out ▪ *(avant le n)* **j'ai l'~ conviction qu'il ment** I am privately convinced that he's lying.
◇ *nmf* [ami] close friend, intimate *sout* ▪ **moi, c'est Madeleine, Mado pour les ~s** I'm Madeleine, Mado to my friends *ou* my friends call me Mado.

intimé, e [ɛ̃time] ◇ *adj* : **partie ~e** respondent party.
◇ *nm, f* respondent.

intimement [ɛ̃timmɑ̃] *adv* [connaître] intimately ▪ **ces deux faits sont ~ liés** these two facts are closely connected ▪ **~ convaincu** *ou* **persuadé** profoundly convinced.

intimer [3] [ɛ̃time] *vt* **1.** [ordonner] to instruct, to order, to tell ▪ **~ à qqn l'ordre de se taire/de rester** to tell sb to be quiet/to stay **2.** DR [en appel] to summon ▪ [faire savoir] to notify.

intimidable [ɛ̃timidabl] *adj* easily intimidated.

intimidant, e [ɛ̃timidɑ̃, ɑ̃t] *adj* intimidating.

intimidation [ɛ̃timidasjɔ̃] *nf* intimidation ▪ **céder à des ~s** to give in to intimidation.

intimidé, e [ɛ̃timide] *adj* nervous.

intimider [3] [ɛ̃timide] *vt* **1.** [faire pression sur] to intimidate ▪ **vous croyez m'~?** do you think you scare me? **2.** [troubler] to intimidate, to overawe.

intimisme [ɛ̃timism] *nm* LITTÉR & ART intimism.

intimiste [ɛ̃timist] *adj* & *nmf* LITTÉR & ART intimist.

intimité [ɛ̃timite] *nf* **1.** [vie privée, caractère privé] privacy ▪ **l'~ du foyer** the privacy of one's own home ▪ **nous fêterons son succès dans l'~** we'll celebrate his success with just a few close friends ▪ **ils se sont mariés dans la plus stricte ~** they were married in the strictest privacy **2.** [familiarité] intimacy ▪ **l'~ conjugale** the intimacy of married life **3.** [confort] intimacy, cosiness, snugness **4.** *litt* [profondeur] intimacy ▪ **dans l'~ de la prière** in the privacy *ou* intimacy of prayer.

intitulé [ɛ̃tityle] *nm* **1.** [d'un livre] title ▪ [d'un chapitre] heading, title **2.** DR [d'un acte] premises ▪ [d'un titre] abstract (of title) ▪ [d'une loi] long title ▪ **~ de compte** account particulars.

intituler [3] [ɛ̃tityle] *vt* to call, to entitle ▪ **comment a-t-il intitulé le roman?** what did he call the novel?, what title did he give the novel?
◆ **s'intituler** ◇ *vp (emploi réfléchi)* [personne] to give o.s. the title of, to call o.s.
◇ *vpi* [œuvre] to be entitled *ou* called.

intolérable [ɛ̃tɔlerabl] *adj* **1.** [insupportable] intolerable, unbearable **2.** [inadmissible] intolerable, inadmissible, unacceptable ▪ **vos retards sont ~s** your lateness will not be tolerated.

intolérance [ɛ̃tɔlerɑ̃s] *nf* **1.** [sectarisme] intolerance **2.** MÉD intolerance ▪ **~ aux analgésiques** intolerance to painkillers ▪ **~ à l'alcool** lack of tolerance to alcohol ▪ **~ alimentaire** allergy (to food).

intolérant, e [ɛ̃tɔlerɑ̃, ɑ̃t] ◇ *adj* intolerant.
◇ *nm, f* intolerant person, bigot.

intonation [ɛ̃tɔnasjɔ̃] *nf* **1.** [inflexion de la voix] tone, intonation **2.** LING intonation.

intouchable [ɛ̃tuʃabl] ◇ *adj* [qui ne peut être - touché, sanctionné] untouchable ; [- critiqué] untouchable, beyond criticism, uncriticizable.
◇ *nmf* [paria] untouchable.

intox [ɛ̃tɔks] *nf fam* propaganda, brainwashing ▪ **tout ça, c'est de l'~** all that's just propaganda.

intoxicant, e [ɛ̃tɔksikɑ̃, ɑ̃t] *adj* poisonous, toxic.

intoxication [ɛ̃tɔksikasjɔ̃] *nf* **1.** MÉD poisoning ▪ **~ alimentaire** food poisoning **2.** *fig* propaganda, brainwashing.

intoxiqué, e [ɛ̃tɔksike] ◇ *adj* **1.** MÉD poisoned ▪ **~ par l'alcool** intoxicated, drunk ▪ **il fume beaucoup trop, il est complètement ~!** he smokes far too much, he's become addicted! **2.** [manipulé] indoctrinated, brainwashed.
◇ *nm, f* **1.** [drogué] (drug) addict **2.** [endoctriné] indoctrinated *ou* brainwashed person.

intoxiquer [3] [ɛ̃tɔksike] *vt* **1.** MÉD to poison **2.** *fig* to brainwash, to indoctrinate ▪ **une propagande qui intoxique les esprits** propaganda which poisons the mind.
◆ **s'intoxiquer** *vpi* to poison o.s. ▪ **s'~ avec de la viande/des fraises** to get food poisoning from (eating) meat/strawberries.

intracérébral, e, aux [ɛ̃traserebral, o] *adj* intracerebral.

intradermique [ɛ̃tradɛrmik] *adj* intradermal, intracutaneous.

intraduisible [ɛ̃tradɥizibl] *adj* **1.** [texte, mot] untranslatable ▪ **le mot est ~** there is no translation for the word **2.** [indicible] inexpressible, indescribable.

intraitable [ɛ̃trɛtabl] *adj* uncompromising, inflexible ▪ **il est resté ~ sur ce point** he remained adamant on this point.

intra-muros [ɛ̃tramyros] <> *loc adj inv* : **quartiers ~** districts within the city boundaries ▪ **Londres ~** inner London.
<> *loc adv* : **habiter ~** to live in the city itself.

intramusculaire [ɛ̃tramyskylɛr] *adj* intramuscular.

intranet [ɛ̃tranɛt] *nm* intranet.

intransigeance [ɛ̃trɑ̃ziʒɑ̃s] *nf* intransigence ▪ **faire preuve d'~** to be uncompromising *ou* intransigent *sout*.

intransigeant, e [ɛ̃trɑ̃ziʒɑ̃, ɑ̃t] <> *adj* uncompromising, intransigent *sout* ▪ **se montrer ~ envers** *ou* **vis-à-vis de qqn** to take a hard line *ou* to be uncompromising with sb ▪ **il est ~ sur la discipline** he's a stickler for discipline.
<> *nm, f* hardliner, uncompromising person.

intransitif, ive [ɛ̃trɑ̃zitif, iv] *adj* intransitive, *voir aussi* **pluriel.**
◆ **intransitif** *nm* intransitive (verb).

intransitivité [ɛ̃trɑ̃zitivite] *nf* intransitivity, intransitiveness.

intransmissibilité [ɛ̃trɑ̃smisibilite] *nf* **1.** BIOL intransmissibility **2.** DR untransferability, nontransferability, untransmissibility *spéc.*

intransmissible [ɛ̃trɑ̃smisibl] *adj* **1.** BIOL intransmissible **2.** DR untransferable, nontransferable, unassignable.

intransportable [ɛ̃trɑ̃spɔrtabl] *adj* **1.** [objet] untransportable ▪ **c'est ~** it can't be moved *ou* transported **2.** [blessé] : **il est ~** he shouldn't be moved, he's unfit to travel.

intrant [ɛ̃trɑ̃] *nm* ÉCON input.

intra-utérin, e [ɛ̃trayterɛ̃, in] (*mpl* **intra-utérins**, *fpl* **intra-utérines**) *adj* intrauterine ▪ **la vie ~e** life in the womb, life in utero *sout.*

intraveineux, euse [ɛ̃travɛnø, øz] *adj* intravenous.
◆ **intraveineuse** *nf* intravenous injection.

intrépide [ɛ̃trepid] <> *adj* **1.** [courageux] intrepid, bold, fearless **2.** *sout* [persévérant] unashamed, unrepentent ▪ **un buveur ~** a hardened drinker.
<> *nmf* intrepid *ou* brave person.

intrépidité [ɛ̃trepidite] *nf* **1.** [courage] intrepidness, intrepidity *sout*, boldness **2.** *sout* [persévérance] : **mentir avec ~** to lie shamelessly.

intrigant, e [ɛ̃trigɑ̃, ɑ̃t] <> *adj* scheming, conniving.
<> *nm, f* schemer, plotter, intriguer *sout.*

intrigue [ɛ̃trig] *nf* **1.** [scénario] plot **2.** [complot] intrigue, plot, scheme ▪ **déjouer une ~** to foil a plot ▪ **nouer une ~ contre qqn** to hatch a plot against sb ▪ **~s politiques** political intrigues **3.** *litt* [liaison amoureuse] (secret) love affair, intrigue *sout.*

intriguer [3] [ɛ̃trige] <> *vt* to intrigue, to puzzle ▪ **son appel m'a intrigué** his call puzzled me.
<> *vi* to scheme, to plot, to intrigue *sout.*

intrinsèque [ɛ̃trɛ̃sɛk] *adj* intrinsic.

intrinsèquement [ɛ̃trɛ̃sɛkmɑ̃] *adv* intrinsically.

intriqué, e [ɛ̃trike] *adj* intricate, entangled.

introducteur, trice [ɛ̃trɔdyktœr, tris] *nm, f* **1.** [auprès de qqn] : **il a été mon ~ auprès de Michel** he was the person who introduced me to Michel **2.** [d'une idée, d'une mode] initiator.

introductif, ive [ɛ̃trɔdyktif, iv] *adj* introductory ▪ **cours ~** foundation course ▪ **discours ~** opening remarks.

introduction [ɛ̃trɔdyksjɔ̃] *nf* **1.** [préambule] introduction ▪ **une ~ à la littérature** an introduction to literature ▪ **quelques mots d'~** a few introductory remarks **2.** [contact] introduction ▪ **après leur ~ auprès de l'attaché** after they were introduced to the attaché **3.** [importation] importing ▪ [adoption - d'un mot, d'un règlement] introduction ▪ **~ en France de techniques nouvelles/de drogues dures** introducing new techniques/smuggling hard drugs into France **4.** BOURSE : **~ en Bourse** listing on the stock market **5.** SPORT put-in.

introduire [98] [ɛ̃trɔdɥir] *vt* **1.** [insérer] to insert, to introduce ▪ **~ une clé dans une serrure** to put *ou* to insert a key into a lock ▪ **~ un sujet dans une conversation** to introduce a topic into a conversation **2.** [faire adopter - idée, mot] to introduce, to bring in *(sép)* ; [- règlement] to institute ; [- mode, produit] to introduce, to launch ▪ [illégalement] to smuggle in *(sép)*, to bring in *(sép)* ▪ **~ une instance** DR to institute an action at law, to institute legal proceedings ▪ **~ des valeurs en Bourse** BOURSE to list shares on the stock market ▪ **~ un produit sur le marché** ÉCON to bring out *(sép)* *ou* to launch a product onto the market **3.** [présenter] to introduce ▪ **~ qqn auprès de** to introduce sb to ▮ [faire entrer - visiteur] to show in *(sép)* **4.** SPORT : **~ le ballon** to put the ball in.
◆ **s'introduire dans** *vp+prép* **1.** [pénétrer dans - suj: clé, piston] to go *ou* to fit into ; [- suj: eau] to filter *ou* to seep into ; [- suj: cambrioleur] to break into ▪ *fig* [suj: date, erreur] to creep into **2.** [être accepté par - suj: idée] to penetrate (into), to spread throughout, to infiltrate *péj* ▪ **l'expression s'est introduite dans la langue** the expression entered the language **3.** [se faire admettre dans - suj: postulant] to gain admittance to ; [- suj: intrigant] to worm one's way into, to infiltrate.

introduit, e [ɛ̃trɔdɥi, it] *adj* : **il est très bien ~ dans ce milieu** he's well established in these circles.

introït [ɛ̃trɔit] *nm* introit.

introjection [ɛ̃trɔʒɛksjɔ̃] *nf* introjection.

intromission [ɛ̃trɔmisjɔ̃] *nf* intromission.

intronisation [ɛ̃trɔnizasjɔ̃] *nf* **1.** [d'un roi, d'un évêque] enthronement **2.** *fig* [mise en place] establishment ▪ **l'~ du nouveau gouvernement** POLIT the establishment of the new government.

introniser [3] [ɛ̃trɔnize] *vt* **1.** [roi, évêque] to enthrone ▪ **il s'est fait ~ à l'âge de 60 ans** [roi] he came to the throne when he was 60 ; [évêque] he was made bishop at the age of 60 **2.** *fig* [établir] to establish.

introspectif, ive [ɛ̃trɔspɛktif, iv] *adj* introspective.

introspection [ɛ̃trɔspɛksjɔ̃] *nf* introspection.

introuvable [ɛ̃truvabl] *adj* nowhere to be found ▪ **elle reste ~** she's still missing, her whereabouts are still unknown ▪ **ces pendules sont ~s aujourd'hui** you can't get hold of these clocks anywhere these days.

introversion [ɛ̃trɔvɛrsjɔ̃] *nf* introversion.

introverti, e [ɛ̃trɔvɛrti] <> *adj* introverted.
<> *nm, f* introvert.

intrus, e [ɛ̃try, yz] <> *adj* intruding, intrusive.
<> *nm, f* intruder ▪ **elle considère son gendre comme un ~** she treats her son-in-law like an outsider *ou* an unwelcome guest.

intrusion [ɛ̃tryzjɔ̃] *nf* **1.** [ingérence] intrusion ▪ **c'est une ~ dans ma vie privée** it's an intrusion into *ou* it's a violation of my privacy ▪ **~ dans les affaires d'un pays étranger** interference *ou* intervention in the affairs of a foreign country **2.** GÉOL intrusion.

intubation [ɛ̃tybasjɔ̃] *nf* intubation.

intuber [3] [ɛ̃tybe] *vt* to intubate.

intuitif, ive [ɛ̃tɥitif, iv] <> *adj* **1.** [perspicace] intuitive, instinctive **2.** PHILOS intuitive.
<> *nm, f* intuitive person.

intuition [ɛ̃tɥisjɔ̃] *nf* **1.** [faculté] intuition ▶ **l'~ féminine** feminine intuition **2.** [pressentiment] : **avoir l'~ d'un drame/de la mort** to sense tragedy/death ▪ **il en a eu l'~** he knew it intuitively, he intuited it *sout* ▪ **j'ai l'~ qu'il est rentré** I have a suspicion *ou* an inkling *ou* a hunch (that) he's home.

intuitivement [ɛ̃tɥitivmɑ̃] *adv* intuitively, instinctively.

inuit [inɥit] *adj inv* Inuit.

◆ **Inuit** *nmf* : **les Inuit** the Inuit *ou* Inuits.

inusable [inyzabl] *adj* which will never wear out, hard-wearing ■ **achetez-en une paire, c'est ~!** buy a pair, they'll last (you) forever!

inusité, e [inyzite] *adj* **1.** LING [mot] uncommon, not in use (any longer) ■ **le terme est ~ de nos jours** the word is no longer used **2.** *sout* [inhabituel] unusual, uncommon.

inusuel, elle [inyzɥɛl] *adj sout* unusual, inhabitual.

in utero [inyterɔ] *loc adj & loc adv* in utero.

inutile [inytil] <> *adj* **1.** [gadget] useless ■ [digression] pointless ■ [effort] useless, pointless, vain ■ **(il est) ~ de m'interroger** there's no point in questioning me ■ **~ de mentir!** it's no use lying!, lying is useless! ■ **j'ai écrit, téléphoné, tout s'est révélé ~** I wrote, I phoned, (but) all to no avail **2.** [superflu] needless, unnecessary ■ **quelques précisions ne seront pas ~s** a few explanations will come in useful ■ **une leçon de conduite supplémentaire ne serait pas ~ avant l'examen** an extra driving lesson wouldn't go amiss before the test ■ **~ de préciser qu'il faut arriver à l'heure** I hardly need to point out that *ou* needless to say you have to turn up on time ■ **~ de demander, sers-toi** just help yourself, there's no need to ask.
<> *nmf péj* useless person.

inutilement [inytilmɑ̃] *adv* needlessly, unnecessarily, to no purpose.

inutilisable [inytilizabl] *adj* unusable, useless ■ **après l'accident, la voiture était ~** the car was a write-off after the accident.

inutilisé, e [inytilize] *adj* unused ■ **des ressources ~es** untapped *ou* unused resources.

inutilité [inytilite] *nf* [d'un objet] uselessness ■ [d'un argument] pointlessness ■ [d'un effort, d'une tentative] uselessness, pointlessness ■ [d'un remède] uselessness, ineffectiveness.

invaincu, e [ɛ̃vɛ̃ky] *adj* [équipe] unbeaten, undefeated ■ [armée] unvanquished, undefeated ■ [maladie] unconquered.

invalidant, e [ɛ̃validɑ̃, ɑ̃t] *adj* incapacitating, disabling.

invalidation [ɛ̃validasjɔ̃] *nf* [d'une élection] invalidation, quashing ■ [d'une décision juridique] quashing ■ [d'un contrat] nullification ■ [d'un élu] removal from office.

invalide [ɛ̃valid] <> *adj* **1.** [infirme] disabled **2.** DR invalid, null and void.
<> *nmf* [infirme] disabled person ■ **~ du travail** *person disabled in an industrial accident.*
<> *nm* : **grand ~ civil** *officially recognized severely disabled person* ■ **(grand) ~ de guerre** *officially recognized war invalid.*

invalider [3] [ɛ̃valide] *vt* [élection] to invalidate, to make invalid, to nullify ■ [décision juridique] to quash ■ [élu] to remove from office.

invalidité [ɛ̃validite] *nf* disability, disablement.

invariable [ɛ̃varjabl] *adj* **1.** [constant] invariable, unchanging ■ **d'une ~ bonne humeur** invariably good-humoured **2.** GRAMM invariable.

invariablement [ɛ̃varjabləmɑ̃] *adv* invariably.

invasion [ɛ̃vazjɔ̃] *nf* **1.** MIL invasion ■ **armée/troupes d'~** invading army/troops **2.** [arrivée massive] invasion, influx ■ **une ~ de rats** an invasion of rats ■ **l'~ de produits étrangers sur le marché** the flooding of the market by foreign products.

invective [ɛ̃vɛktiv] *nf* invective *(U)*, insult ■ **il s'est répandu en ~s contre moi** he started hurling abuse at me.

invectiver [3] [ɛ̃vɛktive] *vt* to curse, to insult, to heap insults *ou* abuse upon.
◆ **invectiver contre** *v+prép* to curse.

invendable [ɛ̃vɑ̃dabl] *adj* unsaleable, unsellable ■ **vous m'apportez toujours des marchandises ~s** you always bring me goods that don't sell.

invendu, e [ɛ̃vɑ̃dy] *adj* unsold.
◆ **invendu** *nm* [gén] unsold article *ou* item ■ [journal] unsold copy ■ **les ~s** (the) unsold copies.

inventaire [ɛ̃vɑ̃tɛr] *nm* **1.** [liste] inventory ■ **les locataires doivent faire *ou* dresser un ~** (the) tenants must draw up an inventory ■ **faire l'~ des ressources d'un pays** to assess a country's resources **2.** COMM [procédure] stocktaking ■ [liste] stocklist, inventory *US* ■ **faire l'~ de la marchandise** to take stock of the goods ➲ **~ extracomptable** stocks, stock-in-trade *UK*, inventories *US* ■ **livre d'~** inventory *ou* stock book **3.** DR inventory **4.** NAUT inventory.

inventer [3] [ɛ̃vɑ̃te] *vt* **1.** [créer - machine] to invent ; [- mot] to coin ■ **il n'a pas inventé la poudre *ou* le fil à couper le beurre** he'll never set the world on fire **2.** [imaginer - jeu] to think *ou* to make up *(sép)*, to invent ; [- système] to think *ou* to dream up *(sép)*, to work out *(sép)*, to concoct *péj* ■ **je ne sais plus quoi ~ pour les amuser** I've run out of ideas trying to keep them amused ■ **ils ne savent plus quoi ~!** *fam* what will they think of next! ■ **qu'est-ce que tu vas ~ là?** whatever gave you that idea?, where on earth did you get that idea from? **3.** [forger] to think *ou* to make up *(sép)*, to invent ■ **je n'invente rien!** I'm not inventing a thing! ■ **une histoire inventée de toutes pièces** an entirely made-up story, a complete fabrication **4.** DR [trésor] to discover, to find.
◆ **s'inventer** *vp (emploi passif)* : **ça ne s'invente pas** nobody could make up a thing like that, you don't make that sort of thing up.

inventeur, trice [ɛ̃vɑ̃tœr, tris] *nm, f* **1.** [d'un appareil, d'un système] inventor **2.** DR [d'un trésor] finder, discoverer **3.** [de fausses nouvelles] fabricator.

inventif, ive [ɛ̃vɑ̃tif, iv] *adj* inventive, creative, resourceful ■ **les enfants sont très ~s** children have a lot of imagination.

invention [ɛ̃vɑ̃sjɔ̃] *nf* **1.** SC & TECHNOL invention ■ **grâce à l'~ du laser** thanks to the invention *ou* discovery of lasers **2.** [créativité] inventiveness, creativeness ■ **un modèle de mon ~** a pattern I designed myself, one of my own designs **3.** [idée] invention ■ **leur liaison est une ~ de l'auteur** their love affair was made up by the author *ou* is the author's own invention ❙ [mensonge] invention, fabrication ■ **c'est (de la) pure ~** it's all made up *ou* sheer invention *ou* pure fabrication **4.** DR [d'un trésor] finding, discovering **5.** MUS : **~s à deux voix** two-part inventions.

inventivité [ɛ̃vɑ̃tivite] *nf* inventiveness.

inventorier [9] [ɛ̃vɑ̃tɔrje] *vt* **1.** [gén] to list, to make a list of **2.** COMM to take stock of, to list (for stocktaking) **3.** DR to make an inventory of, to inventory *sout.*

invérifiable [ɛ̃verifjabl] *adj* unverifiable, uncheckable.

inverse [ɛ̃vɛrs] <> *adj* **1.** [opposé] opposite ■ **les voitures qui viennent en sens ~** cars coming the other way *ou* from the opposite direction ■ **dans l'ordre ~** in (the) reverse order, the other way round ■ **dans le sens ~ des aiguilles d'une montre** anticlockwise *UK*, counterclockwise *US* ■ **être en proportion *ou* raison ~ de** to be inversely proportional *ou* in inverse proportion to **2.** GÉOL reversed **3.** MATH inverse.
<> *nm* **1.** [contraire] : **l'~** the opposite, the reverse **2.** MATH inverse.
◆ **à l'inverse** *loc adv* conversely.
◆ **à l'inverse de** *loc prép* contrary to ■ **à l'~ de mon collègue/de ce que tu crois** contrary to my colleague/to what you think.

inversé, e [ɛ̃vɛrse] *adj* **1.** PHOTO reverse, reversed **2.** AÉRON & GÉOGR inverted.

inversement [ɛ̃vɛrsəmɑ̃] *adv* **1.** [gén] conversely ■ **vous pouvez l'aider, et ~ il peut vous renseigner** you can help him, and in return he can give you some information ■ **~, on pourrait conclure que...** conversely, you could conclude that... **2.** MATH inversely ■ **~ proportionnel à** inversely proportional to.

inverser [3] [ɛ̃vɛrse] *vt* **1.** [intervertir] to reverse, to invert ■ **~ les rôles** to swap parts *ou* roles ■ **les rôles ont été totalement inversés** there's been a complete role reversal **2.** ÉLECTR & PHOTO to reverse.

inverseur [ɛ̃vɛrsœr] *nm* ÉLECTR reversing switch ■ **~ de pôles** pole changing switch.

inversible [ɛ̃vɛrsibl] *adj* **1.** MATH invertible **2.** PHOTO reversible.

inversion [ɛ̃vɛrsjɔ̃] *nf* **1.** [changement] reversal, inversion ■ **~ des rôles** role reversal **2.** LING inversion **3.** ÉLECTR reversal **4.** PSYCHOL & *vieilli* inversion, homosexuality.

invertébré, e [ɛ̃vɛrtebre] *adj* invertebrate.
◆ **invertébré** *nm* invertebrate ■ **les ~s** the invertebrates *ou* Invertebrata *spéc.*

inverti, e [ɛ̃vɛrti] *adj* CHIM : **sucre ~** invert sugar.

investigateur, trice [ɛ̃vɛstigatœr, tris] ◇ *adj* **1.** [avide de savoir] inquiring, inquisitive ■ **un esprit fin et ~** a sharp, inquisitive mind **2.** [scrutateur - regard] searching, scrutinizing.
◇ *nm, f* investigator.

investigation [ɛ̃vɛstigasjɔ̃] *nf* investigation ■ **~s** [policières] inquiries, investigation ; [scientifiques] research, investigations.

investiguer [3] [ɛ̃vɛstige] *vi* to investigate, to research.

investir [32] [ɛ̃vɛstir] *vt* **1.** FIN to invest ■ *(en usage absolu)* **~ à court/long terme** to make a short-/long-term investment ■ **~ dans la pierre** to invest (money) in bricks and mortar *UK* *ou* in real estate *US* **2.** [engager - ressources, temps, efforts] to invest, to commit ■ **j'avais beaucoup investi dans notre amitié** I had put a lot into our friendship **3.** *sout* [d'un pouvoir, d'une fonction] : **~ qqn de : ~ qqn d'une dignité** to invest sb with a function ■ **~ qqn de sa confiance** to place one's trust in sb ■ **par l'autorité dont je suis investi** by the authority vested in *ou* conferred upon me ■ **elle se sentait investie d'une mission** she felt she'd been entrusted with a mission **4.** [encercler - suj: armée] to surround, to besiege ■ [suj: police] to block off *(sép)*, to surround.
◆ **s'investir dans** *vp+prép* : **s'~ dans son métier** to be involved *ou* absorbed in one's job ■ **une actrice qui s'investit entièrement dans ses rôles** an actress who throws herself heart and soul into every part she plays ■ **je me suis énormément investie dans le projet** the project really meant a lot to me.

investissement [ɛ̃vɛstismɑ̃] *nm* **1.** FIN investment ■ **ne te plains pas d'avoir appris l'arabe, c'est un ~ (pour l'avenir)** *fig* don't be sorry that you learnt Arabic, it'll stand you in good stead (in the future) **2.** [effort] investment, commitment ■ **un important ~ en temps** a big commitment in terms of time **3.** MIL [encerclement] surrounding, siege.
◆ **d'investissement** *loc adj* FIN [société, banque] investment *(modif)* ■ [dépenses] capital *(modif)*.

investisseur, euse [ɛ̃vɛstisœr, øz] *adj* investing.
◆ **investisseur** *nm* investor.

investiture [ɛ̃vɛstityr] *nf* **1.** POLIT [d'un candidat] nomination, selection ■ [d'un gouvernement] vote of confidence **2.** HIST & RELIG investiture.

invétéré, e [ɛ̃vetere] *adj* [habitude] ingrained, deep-rooted ■ [préjugé] deeply-held, deep-seated, confirmed ■ [buveur] inveterate, habitual ■ **un coureur ~** an inveterate *ou* incorrigible womanizer.

invincibilité [ɛ̃vɛ̃sibilite] *nf* invincibility, invincibleness.

invincible [ɛ̃vɛ̃sibl] *adj* **1.** [imbattable - héros, nation] invincible, unconquerable ■ **avec un courage ~** with invincible courage **2.** [insurmontable - dégoût] insuperable, insurmountable ; [- passion] irresistible **3.** [irréfutable - argument] invincible, unbeatable.

inviolabilité [ɛ̃vjɔlabilite] *nf* **1.** [gén] inviolability **2.** POLIT immunity ■ **l'~ parlementaire** Parliamentary privilege *UK*, congressional immunity *US* **3.** INFORM [de données] (data) protection.

inviolable [ɛ̃vjɔlabl] *adj* **1.** [droit, serment] inviolable **2.** [personne] untouchable, immune **3.** [imprenable] impregnable, inviolable *sout.*

inviolé, e [ɛ̃vjɔle] *adj sout* **1.** [non enfreint - loi] inviolate, unviolated **2.** [non forcé - lieu] unforced, inviolate ■ **le sommet ~ de la montagne** the unconquered summit of the mountain.

invisibilité [ɛ̃vizibilite] *nf* invisibility.

invisible [ɛ̃vizibl] *adj* **1.** [imperceptible] invisible ■ **~ à l'œil nu** invisible *ou* not visible to the naked eye **2.** [occulte] hidden, secret **3.** [non disponible] unavailable ■ **tu es devenu ~ dernièrement** you've been rather elusive recently.
◆ **invisibles** *nmpl* ÉCON : **les ~s** [échanges] invisible trade ; [exportations] invisible exports.

invitant, e [ɛ̃vitɑ̃, ɑ̃t] *adj* : **puissance ~e** host country.

invitation [ɛ̃vitasjɔ̃] *nf* **1.** [requête] invitation ■ **une ~ à un cocktail** an invitation to a cocktail party ■ **à** *ou* **sur l'~ de nos amis** at the invitation of *ou* invited by our friends ■ **'sur ~'** 'by invitation only' ➲ **lettre d'~** letter of *ou* written invitation **2.** [incitation] invitation, provocation ■ **ce film est une ~ au voyage** this film makes you want to travel.
Voir module d'usage

LES INVITATIONS

Would you and Alice like to come over for dinner one evening? Est-ce que vous aimeriez venir dîner un soir, Alice et toi ?

Thanks, we'd love to. I'll ask Alice and let you know. Avec plaisir, merci. Je vais en parler à Alice et je vous tiendrai au courant.

Are you free for a game of tennis any day next week? Est-ce que tu es libre un jour de la semaine prochaine pour faire une partie de tennis ?

I'm afraid not. How about the week after? Non, je regrette. La semaine d'après, ça irait ?

Why don't you come up next week, and we'll have a night out. Pourquoi tu ne viendrais pas la semaine prochaine ? On pourrait sortir.

That sounds like a great idea. Excellente idée.

Let's have lunch some time. Et si on déjeunait ensemble un de ces jours ?

Sorry, I'm a bit busy at the moment. Je regrette, je suis assez pris en ce moment.

What would you say to a holiday in Wales? Ça te dirait, des vacances au Pays de Galles ?

That'd be lovely. Oui, ça me plairait beaucoup.

How about going to see a play? Et si on allait au théâtre ?

Sure. When did you have in mind? D'accord. Quand ça ?

Do you feel like a drink? Tu as envie d'aller prendre un verre ?

Maybe some other time. Une autre fois, peut-être ?

Do you fancy going for a drive? *UK* Ça te dit d'aller faire un tour en voiture ?

Why not? Oui, pourquoi pas ?

invite [ɛ̃vit] *nf* **1.** *sout* [invitation] invitation, request ▪ **répondre aux ~s de qqn** to respond to sb's requests **2.** JEUX lead.

invité, e [ɛ̃vite] *nm, f* guest ▪ **~ de marque** distinguished guest ▪ **~ d'honneur** guest of honour.

inviter [3] [ɛ̃vite] <> *vt* **1.** [ami, convive] to invite ▪ **~ qqn à déjeuner** to invite *ou* to ask sb to lunch ▪ **~ qqn chez soi** to invite sb (over) to one's house ▪ **puis-je vous ~ à danser?** may I have this dance? ▪ *(en usage absolu)* [payer] : **allez, c'est moi qui invite!** *fam* it's on me! **2.** [exhorter] : **~ qqn à : je vous invite à observer une minute de silence** I invite you *ou* call upon you to observe a minute's silence ▪ **vous êtes invités à me suivre** would you be so kind as to follow me.
<> *vi* JEUX to lead.
◆ **s'inviter** *vp (emploi réfléchi)* to invite o.s.

in vitro [invitro] *loc adv* & *loc adj inv* in vitro.

invivable [ɛ̃vivabl] *adj* **1.** [personne] impossible, unbearable, insufferable **2.** [habitation] : **cette maison est devenue ~** this house has become impossible to live in.

in vivo [invivo] *loc adv* & *loc adj inv* in vivo.

invocation [ɛ̃vɔkasjɔ̃] *nf* invocation.

invocatoire [ɛ̃vɔkatwar] *adj* invocatory.

involontaire [ɛ̃vɔlɔ̃tɛr] *adj* **1.** [machinal] involuntary ▪ **j'eus un mouvement de recul ~** I recoiled involuntarily *ou* instinctively **2.** [non délibéré] unintentional ▪ **c'était ~** it was unintentional, I didn't do it on purpose ▪ **une erreur ~** an inadvertent error **3.** [non consentant] unwilling, reluctant **4.** DR involuntary.

involontairement [ɛ̃vɔlɔ̃tɛrmɑ̃] *adv* unintentionally, unwittingly, without meaning to ▪ **si je vous ai vexé, c'est tout à fait ~** if I've offended you, it really wasn't intentional *ou* I really didn't mean to.

involution [ɛ̃vɔlysjɔ̃] *nf* involution.

invoquer [3] [ɛ̃vɔke] *vt* **1.** [avoir recours à - argument, prétexte] to put forward *(sép)* ▪ **~ l'article 15 du Code pénal** to refer to *ou* to cite Article 15 of the Penal Code ▪ **~ son ignorance** to plead ignorance **2.** [en appeler à - personne] to invoke, to appeal to *(insép)* ; [- dieu] to invoke ; [- aide] to call upon *(insép)*.

invraisemblable [ɛ̃vrɛsɑ̃blabl] *adj* **1.** [improbable - hypothèse] unlikely, improbable, implausible **2.** [incroyable - histoire] incredible, unbelievable **3.** [bizarre - tenue] weird, incredible, extraordinary **4.** [en intensif] : **elle a un toupet ~!** she has an amazing cheek!

invraisemblance [ɛ̃vrɛsɑ̃blɑ̃s] *nf* **1.** [caractère improbable] unlikelihood, unlikeliness, improbability **2.** [fait] improbability ▪ **le scénario est truffé d'~s** the script is filled with implausible details.

invulnérabilité [ɛ̃vylnerabilite] *nf* invulnerability.

invulnérable [ɛ̃vylnerabl] *adj* **1.** [physiquement] invulnerable **2.** [moralement] invulnerable ▪ **le temps l'a rendue ~ aux critiques** with the passage of time she's become invulnerable *ou* immune *ou* impervious to criticism **3.** [socialement] invulnerable.

iode [jɔd] *nm* iodine.

iodé, e [jɔde] *adj* iodized, iodated.

ioder [3] [jɔde] *vt* to iodize, to iodate.

IOM (*abr de* **indice d'octane moteur**) *nm* MON.

ion [jɔ̃] *nm* ion.

ionien, enne [jɔnjɛ̃, ɛn] *adj* [de l'Ionie] Ionian, Ionic.

ionique [jɔnik] *adj* **1.** [de l'Ionie] Ionic **2.** ÉLECTR ionic, ion *(modif)* **3.** ASTRONAUT ion *(modif)*.

ionisant, e [jɔnizɑ̃, ɑ̃t] *adj* ionizing.

ionisation [jɔnizasjɔ̃] *nf* ionization.

ioniser [3] [jɔnize] *vt* to ionize.

iota [jɔta] *nm inv* iota ▪ **ne changez pas votre article d'un ~** *ou* **un ~ dans votre article** don't change a thing in your article *ou* your article one iota.

Iowa [ajɔwa] *npr m* : **l'~** Iowa.

IP (*abr de* **indice de protection**) *nm* SPF.

IPC (*abr de* **indice des prix à la consommation**) *nm* CPI.

Iphigénie [ifiʒeni] *npr* MYTHOL Iphigenia.

IPR (*abr de* **Inspecteur pédagogique régional**) *nm locally-based schools inspector*.

ipso facto [ipsofakto] *loc adv* ipso facto, by that very fact.

Ipsos [ipsos] *npr French market research institute*.

ira *etc v* ▻ **aller**.

IRA [ira] (*abr de* **Irish Republican Army**) *npr f* IRA.

Irak [irak] *npr m* : **(l')~** Iraq.

irakien, enne [irakjɛ̃, ɛn] *adj* Iraqi.
◆ **Irakien, enne** *nm, f* Iraqi.

Iran [irɑ̃] *npr m* : **(l')~** Iran.

iranien, enne [iranjɛ̃, ɛn] *adj* Iranian.
◆ **Iranien, enne** *nm, f* Iranian.
◆ **iranien** *nm* LING Iranian.

Iraq [irak] = **Irak**.

iraquien [irakjɛ̃] = **irakien**.

irascibilité [irasibilite] *nf sout* irascibility *sout*, irritability, testiness.

irascible [irasibl] *adj* irascible *sout*, short-tempered, testy.

ire [ir] *nf litt* ire, wrath.

iridium [iridjɔm] *nm* iridium.

iris [iris] *nm* **1.** ANAT iris **2.** BOT iris, flag **3.** PHOTO iris (diaphragm) **4.** *litt* [arc-en-ciel] iris *litt*, rainbow.

irisation [irizasjɔ̃] *nf* OPT iridescence, irization *spéc*.

irisé, e [irize] *adj* iridescent.

iriser [3] [irize] *vt* to make iridescent, to irizate *spéc*.
◆ **s'iriser** *vpi* to become iridescent.

irlandais, e [irlɑ̃dɛ, ɛz] *adj* Irish.
◆ **Irlandais, e** *nm, f* Irishman (*f* Irishwoman) ▪ **les Irlandais** the Irish.
◆ **irlandais** *nm* LING Irish (Gaelic).

Irlande [irlɑ̃d] *npr f* : **(l')~** Ireland ▪ **(l')~ du Nord/Sud** Northern/Southern Ireland ▪ **la mer d'~** the Irish Sea ▪ **la République d'~** the Irish Republic.

IRM (*abr de* **Imagerie par résonance magnétique**) [iɛrɛm] *nm* MÉD MRI.

ironie [irɔni] *nf* irony ▪ **l'~ du sort a voulu que je le rencontre** as fate would have it, I bumped into him.

ironique [irɔnik] *adj* ironic, ironical ▪ **regarder qqn d'un air ~** to look at sb quizzically.

ironiquement [irɔnikmɑ̃] *adv* ironically ▪ **répondre ~ à une question** to answer a question tongue-in-cheek *ou* ironically.

ironiser [3] [irɔnize] *vi* to be sarcastic ▪ **~ sur** to be sarcastic about.

iroquois, e [irɔkwa, az] *adj* Iroquois, Iroquoian.
◆ **Iroquois, e** *nm, f* Iroquois.
◆ **iroquoise** *nf* mohican (hairstyle) ▪ **coiffé à l'~e** with a mohican (hairstyle).

IRPP *nm* = **impôt sur le revenu des personnes physiques**.

irrachetable [iraʃtabl] *adj* unredeemable COMM unreturnable.

irradiation [iradjasjɔ̃] *nf* **1.** [rayonnement] radiation, irradiation **2.** [exposition - d'une personne, d'un tissu] irradiation, exposure to radiation ▪ **il y a des risques d'~** there is a risk of irradiation *ou* of being exposed to radiation **3.** MÉD [traitement] irradiation **4.** ANAT radiation **5.** PHOTO halation.

irradier [9] [iradje] <> *vi* **1.** PHYS to radiate **2.** [se propager] to spread ▪ **la douleur irradiait dans toute la jambe** the pain spread to the whole leg **3.** *litt* [se diffuser - bonheur] to radiate. <> *vt* **1.** [soumettre à un rayonnement] to irradiate **2.** *litt* [répandre - bonheur] to radiate.

irraisonné, e [irɛzɔne] *adj* unreasoned, irrational.

irrationalisme [irasjɔnalism] *nm* irrationalism.

irrationalité [irasjɔnalite] *nf* irrationality.

irrationnel, elle [irasjɔnɛl] *adj* [gén - MATH] irrational ▪ **de façon ~le** irrationally.
◆ **irrationnel** *nm* **1.** [gén] : **l'~** the irrational **2.** MATH irrational (number).

irrattrapable [iratrapabl] *adj* irretrievable, which cannot be put right *ou* made good.

irréalisable [irealizabl] *adj* [ambition] unrealizable, unachievable ▪ [idée] unworkable, impracticable ▪ **un projet de voyage ~** an unworkable travel plan.

irréalisé, e [irealize] *adj* *sout* unrealized, unachieved ▪ **un espoir ~** an unrealized hope.

irréalisme [irealism] *nm* lack of realism.

irréaliste [irealist] <> *adj* unrealistic.
<> *nmf* unrealistic person, (pipe) dreamer.

irréalité [irealite] *nf* unreality.

irrecevabilité [irəsəvabilite] *nf* **1.** *sout* [d'un argument] unacceptability **2.** DR inadmissibility.

irrecevable [irəsəvabl] *adj* **1.** [inacceptable] unacceptable **2.** DR inadmissible.

irréconciliable [irekɔ̃siljabl] *adj* [ennemis, adversaires] irreconcilable, unreconcilable ▪ **ils sont ~s** nothing can reconcile them.

irrécouvrable [irekuvrabl] *adj* irrecoverable.

irrécupérable [irekyperabl] *adj* [objet] beyong repair ▪ [personne] irremediable, beyond redemption.

irrécusable [irekyzabl] *adj* undeniable ▪ **des preuves ~s** indisputable evidence.

irréductibilité [iredyktibilite] *nf* **1.** [ténacité] insurmountability, intractability **2.** CHIM & MATH irreducibility.

irréductible [iredyktibl] <> *adj* **1.** [insurmontable - conflit, différence] insurmountable, intractable, insoluble **2.** [inflexible] invincible, implacable, uncompromising ▪ **il s'est fait quelques ennemis ~s** he's made himself a few implacable enemies **3.** MATH & CHIM irreducible.
<> *nmf* diehard, hardliner ▪ **les ~s de (la) gauche/droite** the left-wing/right-wing diehards.

irréductiblement [iredyktibləmɑ̃] *adv* implacably.

irréel, elle [ireɛl] *adj* unreal ▪ **des paysages ~s** unreal landscapes.
◆ **irréel** *nm* **1.** [gén - PHILOS] : **l'~** the unreal **2.** GRAMM : **~ du présent/passé** the hypothetical present/past.

irréfléchi, e [irefleʃi] *adj* [acte, parole] thoughtless, rash, reckless ▪ [personne] unthinking, rash, reckless.

irréflexion [irefleksjɔ̃] *nf* thoughtlessness, rashness, recklessness.

irréfutabilité [irefytabilite] *nf* irrefutability.

irréfutable [irefytabl] *adj* irrefutable.

irrégularité [iregylarite] *nf* **1.** [de forme, de rythme] irregularity, unevenness ▪ [en qualité] unevenness, patchiness ▪ **l'~ de votre travail ne permet pas le passage dans le groupe supérieur** (the quality of) your work is too uneven *ou* erratic for you to move up into the next group **2.** [surface irrégulière - bosse] bump ; [- creux] hole ▪ **les ~s du sol/relief** the unevenness of the ground/hilliness of the area **3.** [infraction] irregularity.

irrégulier, ère [iregylje, ɛr] *adj* **1.** [dessin, rythme, surface] irregular, uneven ▪ [traits] irregular ▪ **il avait une respiration irrégulière** his brathing was erratical *ou* irregular ▪ **je m'entraîne de façon irrégulière** I train intermittently *ou* sporadically ▪ **nous avons des horaires ~s** we don't work regular hours **2.** [qualité, travail] uneven ▪ **j'étais un étudiant ~** my work was erratic when I was a student **3.** [illégal] irregular ▪ **ils sont en situation irrégulière dans le pays** their residence papers are not in order ▪ **des retraits de fonds ~s** unauthorized withdrawals **4.** MIL irregular ▪ **les soldats des troupes irrégulières** the irregulars **5.** BOT, GÉOM & GRAMM irregular.
◆ **irrégulier** *nm* MIL irregular (soldier).

irrégulièrement [iregyljɛrmɑ̃] *adv* **1.** [de façon non uniforme] irregularly, unevenly **2.** [de façon illégale] irregularly, illegally **3.** [de façon inconstante] irregularly, erratically.

irréligieux, euse [ireliʒjø, øz] *adj* irreligious.

irrémédiable [iremedjabl] <> *adj* [rupture] irreparable, irretrievable ▪ [dégâts] irreparable, irreversible ▪ [maladie] incurable, fatal.
<> *nm* : **l'~ a été commis** irreversible harm has been done.

irrémédiablement [iremedjabləmɑ̃] *adv* irremediably, irretrievably ▪ **tout espoir de le retrouver est ~ perdu** we have definitely lost all hope of (ever) finding him.

irrémissible [iremisibl] *adj* *litt* **1.** [impardonnable] unpardonable, irremissible *sout* **2.** [inexorable] implacable, inexorable.

irrémissiblement [iremisibləmɑ̃] *adv* *litt* relentlessly, inexorably, irremissibly *sout*.

irremplaçable [irɑ̃plasabl] *adj* irreplaceable ▪ **personne n'est ~** no one is indispensable.

irréparable [ireparabl] <> *adj* **1.** [montre, voiture] unrepairable, beyond repair **2.** [erreur] irreparable.
<> *nm* : **l'~ est arrivé** irreparable harm has been done.

irréparablement [ireparabləmɑ̃] *adv* [définitivement] irreparably ▪ **sa réputation est ~ atteinte** his reputation has suffered an irreparable blow.

irrépréhensible [irepreɑ̃sibl] *adj* *litt* irreprehensible *sout*, irreproachable.

irrépressible [irepresibl] *adj* irrepressible.

irréprochable [ireprɔʃabl] *adj* **1.** [personne, conduite] irreproachable **2.** [tenue] impeccable ▪ **d'une propreté ~** immaculate ▪ **un travail ~** an impeccable *ou* a faultless piece of work.

irréprochablement [ireprɔʃabləmɑ̃] *adv* irreproachably, impeccably, faultlessly.

irrésistible [irezistibl] *adj* **1.** [séduisant] irresistible **2.** [irrépressible - besoin] compelling, pressing ; [- envie] irresistible, uncontrollable, compelling ▪ **elle fut prise d'une ~ envie de rire** she had an irresistible urge to laugh.

irrésistiblement [irezistibləmɑ̃] *adv* irresistibly ▪ **~ tenté par le gâteau** irresistibly tempted by the cake.

irrésolu, e [irezɔly] <> *adj* **1.** [personne] irresolute *sout*, indecisive, unresolved **2.** [problème] unsolved, unresolved.
<> *nm, f* irresolute person, ditherer *péj*.

irrésolution [irezɔlysjɔ̃] *nf* irresoluteness, indecisiveness.

irrespect [irɛspɛ] *nm* disrespect, lack of respect ▪ **son ~ envers l'autorité** his disrespect of authority.

irrespectueusement [irɛspɛktɥøzmɑ̃] *adv* disrespectfully.

irrespectueux, euse [irɛspɛktɥø, øz] *adj* disrespectful, lacking in (proper) respect ▪ **~ envers qqn** disrespectful to *ou* towards sb.

irrespirable [irɛspirabl] *adj* **1.** [qu'on ne peut respirer] : **à l'intérieur, l'air est ~** [trop chaud] it's close *ou* stifling *ou* stuffy inside ; [toxique] the air inside is unsafe *ou* not fit to breathe **2.** [oppressant - ambiance] unbearable, stifling.

irresponsabilité [irɛspɔ̃sabilite] *nf* **1.** [légèreté] irresponsibility ▪ **agir avec une totale ~** to behave totally irresponsibly

2. [du chef de l'État] irresponsibility *spéc*, royal prerogative *UK*, (head of State's) unimpeachability ■ **~ parlementaire** parliamentary privilege *UK*, congressional immunity *US*.

irresponsable [irɛspɔ̃sabl] <> *adj* **1.** [inconséquent] irresponsible ■ **de manière ~** irresponsibly **2.** DR (legally) incapable.
<> *nmf* irresponsible person.

irrétrécissable [iretresisabl] *adj* unshrinkable.

irrévérence [ireverɑ̃s] *nf* **1.** [irrespect] irreverence **2.** [remarque] irreverent remark ■ [acte] irreverent act.

irrévérencieusement [ireverɑ̃sjøzmɑ̃] *adv* irreverently.

irrévérencieux, euse [ireverɑ̃sjø, øz] *adj* irreverent.

irréversibilité [ireversibilite] *nf* irreversibility.

irréversible [ireversibl] *adj* **1.** [gén] irreversible ■ **le processus est ~** the process is irreversible **2.** CHIM & PHYS irreversible.

irrévocabilité [irevɔkabilite] *nf* irrevocability, finality.

irrévocable [irevɔkabl] *adj* irrevocable ■ **la décision est ~** the verdict is irrevocable *ou* final.

irrévocablement [irevɔkabləmɑ̃] *adv* irrevocably.

irrigable [irigabl] *adj* irrigable, suitable for irrigation.

irrigateur [irigatœr] *nm* AGRIC & MÉD irrigator.

irrigation [irigasjɔ̃] *nf* **1.** AGRIC & MÉD irrigation **2.** PHYSIOL : **l'~ des tissus par les vaisseaux sanguins** the supply of blood to the tissues by blood vessels.

irriguer [3] [irige] *vt* **1.** AGRIC to irrigate **2.** PHYSIOL to supply (blood to).

irritabilité [iritabilite] *nf* **1.** [irascibilité] irritability, quick temper **2.** MÉD irritability.

irritable [iritabl] *adj* **1.** [colérique] irritable, easily annoyed **2.** MÉD irritable.

irritant, e [iritɑ̃, ɑ̃t] *adj* **1.** [agaçant] irritating, annoying, aggravating **2.** MÉD irritant.
◆ **irritant** *nm* irritant.

irritation [iritasjɔ̃] *nf* **1.** [agacement] irritation, annoyance ■ **avec ~** irritably, petulantly **2.** MÉD irritation ■ **~ cutanée** skin irritation.

irrité, e [irite] *adj* **1.** [exaspéré] irritated, annoyed ■ **d'un ton ~** irritably, peevishly **2.** MÉD irritated.

irriter [3] [irite] *vt* **1.** [agacer] to irritate, to annoy ■ **ses petites manies m'irritent** her little quirks get on my nerves **2.** MÉD to irritate **3.** *litt* [exacerber - passion, désir] to inflame, to arouse.
◆ **s'irriter** *vpi* **1.** [s'énerver] to get annoyed *ou* irritated ■ **s'~ contre qqn** to get annoyed with *ou* at sb **2.** MÉD to become irritated.

irruption [irypsjɔ̃] *nf* **1.** [entrée] breaking *ou* bursting *ou* storming in ■ **ils n'ont pas pu empêcher l'~ des spectateurs sur le terrain** they were unable to stop spectators from storming *ou* invading the pitch *UK ou* field *US* ■ **faire ~ chez qqn** to burst in on sb ■ **faire ~ dans** to burst *ou* to barge into **2.** [émergence] upsurge, sudden development.

Isaac [izaak] *npr* Isaac.

isabelle [izabɛl] *adj inv* & *nm* [cheval] Isabel, Isabella.

Isaïe [izai] *npr* BIBLE Isaiah.

isard [izar] *nm* izard.

isba [izba] *nf* isba.

ISBN (*abr de* **International standard book number**) *nm* : **(numéro) ~** ISBN.

Iseut [izø] *npr* Isolde.

ISF *nm* = **impôt de solidarité sur la fortune**.

Isis [izis] *npr* Isis.

islam [islam] *nm* : **l'~** [religion] Islam.

Islam [islam] *nm* : **l'~** [civilisation] Islam.

islamique [islamik] *adj* Islamic.

islamisation [islamizasjɔ̃] *nf* Islamization.

islamisme [islamism] *nm* Islamism.

islamiste [islamist] <> *adj* Islamic.
<> *nmf* Islamic fundamentalist.

islandais, e [islɑ̃dɛ, ɛz] *adj* Icelandic.
◆ **Islandais, e** *nm, f* Icelander.

Islande [islɑ̃d] *npr f* : **(l')~** Iceland.

isobare [izɔbar] <> *adj* isobaric.
<> *nm* PHYS isobar.
<> *nf* MÉTÉOR isobar.

isocèle [izɔsɛl] *adj* isosceles ■ **triangle ~** isosceles triangle.

isolable [izɔlabl] *adj* isolable, isolatable ■ **un virus difficilement ~** a virus (which is) difficult to isolate.

isolant, e [izɔlɑ̃, ɑ̃t] *adj* **1.** CONSTR & ÉLECTR insulating ■ [insonorisant] soundproofing **2.** LING isolating.
◆ **isolant** *nm* insulator, insulating material ■ **~ thermique/électrique** thermal/electrical insulator.

isolateur, trice [izɔlatœr, tris] *adj* insulating.
◆ **isolateur** *nm* ÉLECTR & PHYS insulator.

isolation [izɔlasjɔ̃] *nf* **1.** CONSTR insulation ■ **~ thermique** heat *ou* thermal insulation ■ **~ phonique** *ou* **acoustique** soundproofing, sound insulation **2.** ÉLECTR insulation **3.** PSYCHOL isolation.

isolationnisme [izɔlasjɔnism] *nm* isolationism.

isolationniste [izɔlasjɔnist] *adj* & *nmf* isolationist.

isolé, e [izɔle] <> *adj* **1.** [unique - cas, exemple] isolated ■ **généraliser à partir d'un ou deux cas ~s** to generalize from one or two isolated examples **2.** [coupé du monde - personne] isolated ; [- hameau] isolated, cut-off, remote ; [- maison] isolated, secluded, remote ; [- forêt] remote, lonely **3.** [seul - activiste] maverick **4.** GÉOM & PHYS isolated.
<> *nm, f* **1.** [personne] isolated individual **2.** POLIT maverick, isolated activist.
◆ **isolé** *nm* MIL *soldier awaiting posting.*

isolement [izɔlmɑ̃] *nm* **1.** [éloignement - géographique] isolation, seclusion, remoteness ; [- affectif] isolation, loneliness ■ [sanction] solitary (confinement) ■ ÉCON & POLIT isolation **2.** BIOL & MÉD isolation ■ **l'~ du virus** isolating the virus **3.** ÉLECTR insulation **4.** CONSTR [contre le bruit] insulation, soundproofing ■ [contre le froid, la chaleur] insulation.

isolément [izɔlemɑ̃] *adv* separately, individually.

isoler [3] [izɔle] *vt* **1.** [séparer] to isolate, to separate off *ou* out *(sép)*, to keep separate ■ **~ une citation de son contexte** to lift a quotation out of context, to isolate a quotation from its context **2.** [couper du monde - personne] to isolate, to leave isolated ; [- endroit] to isolate, to cut off *(sép)* **3.** [distinguer] to isolate, to single *ou* to pick out *(sép)* ■ **on n'a pas pu ~ la cause de la déflagration** it was not possible to identify the cause of the explosion ■ **~ un cas parmi d'autres** to pick out an isolated case **4.** CONSTR [du froid, de la chaleur] to insulate ■ [du bruit] to insulate (against sound), to soundproof **5.** ÉLECTR to insulate **6.** MÉD [malade, virus] to isolate **7.** CHIM to isolate **8.** ADMIN [prisonnier] to put into *ou* to place in solitary confinement.
◆ **s'isoler** *vp (emploi réfléchi)* to isolate o.s., to cut o.s. off ■ **le jury s'isola pour délibérer** the jury withdrew to consider its verdict ■ **elles s'isolèrent** [pour voter] they went into separate booths ■ **pourrions-nous nous ~ un instant?** is there somewhere we could talk privately *ou* in private for a moment?

isoloir [izɔlwar] *nm* polling booth.

isomère [izɔmɛr] <> *adj* isomeric.
<> *nm* isomer.

isométrique [izɔmetrik] *adj* isometric.

isomorphe [izɔmɔrf] *adj* **1.** CHIM isomorphic, isomorphous **2.** LING & MATH isomorphic.

isomorphisme [izɔmɔrfism] *nm* isomorphism.

isoprène [izɔprɛn] *nm* isoprene.

isotherme [izɔtɛrm] ◇ *adj* isothermal.
◇ *nf* isotherm.

isotope [izɔtɔp] ◇ *adj* isotopic.
◇ *nm* isotope.

Ispahan [ispaɑ̃] *npr* Isfahan.

Israël [israɛl] *npr* Israel.

israélien, enne [israeljɛ̃, ɛn] *adj* Israeli.
◆ **Israélien, enne** *nm, f* Israeli.

israélite [israelit] *adj* **1.** [juif] Jewish **2.** BIBLE Israelite.
◆ **Israélite** *nmf* **1.** [juif] Jew (*f* Jewess) **2.** BIBLE Israelite.

issu, e [isy] *adj* : **être ~ de** [résulter de] to stem *ou* to derive *ou* to spring from ▪ **être ~ d'une famille pauvre/nombreuse** to be born into a poor/large family.

issue [isy] *nf* **1.** [sortie] exit ▪ [déversoir] outlet ▪ **~ de secours** emergency exit **2.** [solution] solution, way out ▪ **il n'y a pas d'autre ~ que de se rendre** there's no other solution *ou* we have no alternative but to surrender **3.** [fin] outcome ▪ **cet épisode a eu une ~ heureuse/tragique** the incident had a happy/tragic ending.
◆ **à l'issue de** *loc prép* at the end *ou* close of.
◆ **sans issue** *loc adj* **1.** [sans sortie] with no way out ▪ **ruelle sans ~** dead end ▪ **'sans ~'** 'no exit' **2.** [voué à l'échec] hopeless, doomed ▪ [discussions] deadlocked ▪ **une situation sans ~** a dead end *fig.*

Istanbul [istɑ̃bul] *npr* Istanbul.

isthme [ism] *nm* ANAT & GÉOGR isthmus ▪ **l'~ de Panama** the Isthmus of Panama ▪ **l'~ de Suez** the Isthmus of Suez.

isthmique [ismik] *adj* GÉOGR isthmian.

italianisant, e [italjanizɑ̃, ɑ̃t] ◇ *adj* [style] Italianate.
◇ *nm, f* **1.** UNIV Italianist, Italian scholar **2.** ART Italianizer.

italianiser [3] [italjanize] *vt* to Italianize.

italianisme [italjanism] *nm* Italianism.

Italie [itali] *npr f* : **(l')~** Italy.

italien, enne [italjɛ̃, ɛn] *adj* Italian.
◆ **Italien, enne** *nm, f* Italian.
◆ **italien** *nm* LING Italian.
◆ **à l'italienne** *loc adj* **1.** CULIN [sauce] à l'italienne *(cooked with mushrooms, ham and herbs)* ▪ [pâtes] al dente **2.** IMPR landscape.

italique [italik] ◇ *adj* **1.** IMPR italic **2.** LING Italic.
◇ *nm* **1.** IMPR italics ▪ **écrire un mot en ~** to write a word in italics, to italicize a word **2.** LING Italic.

item[1] [itɛm] *adv* COMM ditto.

item[2] [itɛm] *nm* LING & PSYCHOL item.

itératif, ive [iteratif, iv] *adj* **1.** [répété] repeated, reiterated, iterated *sout* **2.** INFORM & LING iterative.

itération [iterasjɔ̃] *nf* **1.** [répétition] iteration, repetition **2.** INFORM & LING iteration.

itérativement [iterativmɑ̃] *adv* iteratively, repeatedly.

itinéraire [itinerɛr] *nm* **1.** [trajet] itinerary, route ▪ **~ bis** diversion ▪ **~ de dégagement** alternative route **2.** [carrière] path ▪ **~ politique** political career.

itinérant, e [itinerɑ̃, ɑ̃t] *adj* [main-d'œuvre] itinerant, travelling ▪ [inspecteur] peripatetic ▪ [comédien, exposition] travelling.

itou [itu] *adv fam vieilli* likewise, ditto.

IUFM (*abr de* **institut universitaire de formation des maîtres**) *nm teacher-training college.*

IUT (*abr de* **institut universitaire de technologie**) *nm institute of technology offering two-year vocational courses leading to the DUT qualification.*

IVG *nf* = **interruption volontaire de grossesse**.

ivoire [ivwar] *nm* **1.** [matière] ivory *(U)* ▪ **statuette d'~** *ou* **en ~** ivory statuette **2.** [objet] (piece of) ivory.
◆ **d'ivoire** *loc adj litt* **1.** [blanc] ivory *(modif)*, ivory-coloured **2.** [ayant l'aspect de l'ivoire] ivory-like.

ivoirien, enne [ivwarjɛ̃, ɛn] *adj* Ivorian.
◆ **Ivoirien, enne** *nm, f* Ivorian.

ivoirier, ère [ivwarje, ɛr] *nm, f* ivory sculptor.

ivoirin, e [ivwarɛ̃, in] *adj litt* **1.** [blanc] ivory *(modif)*, ivory-coloured **2.** [ayant l'aspect de l'ivoire] ivory-like.

ivraie [ivrɛ] *nf* **1.** BOT : **~ commune** darnel **2.** *loc* **séparer le bon grain de l'~** *allus* & BIBLE to separate the wheat from the chaff.

ivre [ivr] *adj* **1.** [saoul] drunk, intoxicated ▪ **~ mort** blind drunk **2.** *fig* **être ~ de joie** to be deliriously happy ▪ **être ~ de colère/bonheur** to be beside o.s. with anger/happiness ▪ **~ de fatigue** dead tired ▪ **être ~ de sang** to be thirsting for blood.

ivresse [ivrɛs] *nf* **1.** [ébriété] drunkenness, intoxication ▪ **il était en état d'~** he was drunk *ou* intoxicated **2.** [excitation] ecstasy, euphoria, exhilaration ▪ **la vitesse procure un sentiment d'~** speed is exhilarating **3.** SPORT : **~ des profondeurs** (diver's) staggers.

ivrogne [ivrɔɲ] *nmf* drunk, drunkard.

ivrognerie [ivrɔɲri] *nf* drunkenness.

J

j, J [ʒi] *nm* [lettre] j, J, *voir aussi* **g**.

j' [ʒ] ▷ **je**.

J 1. (*abr écrite de* **joule**) J **2.** (*abr écrite de* **jour**) ▪ **le jour J** HIST D-day ; [le grand jour] the big day.

jabot [ʒabo] *nm* **1.** ZOOL crop **2.** [vêtement] ruffle, frill.

jacasse [ʒakas] *nf* magpie.

jacassement [ʒakasmɑ̃] *nm* **1.** ZOOL chatter **2.** *péj* [bavardage] chatter, prattle.

jacasser [3] [ʒakase] *vi* **1.** ZOOL to chatter **2.** *péj* [bavarder] to chatter, to prattle ▪ **~ comme une pie** to chatter like a magpie, to jabber away.

jacasseur, euse [ʒakasœr, øz] *péj* ◇ *adj* chattering, jabbering.
◇ *nm, f* chatterbox, jabberer.

jachère [ʒaʃɛr] *nf* **1.** [pratique] (practice of) fallowing land ▪ **mettre la terre en ~** to let the land lie fallow ▪ **laisser en ~** [talent] to leave undeveloped *ou* untapped **2.** [champ] fallow (land).

jacinthe [ʒasɛ̃t] *nf* hyacinth ▪ **~ sauvage** *ou* **des bois** bluebell, wild hyacinth.

jack [dʒak] *nm* **1.** TÉLÉCOM jack **2.** TEXT jack (lever).

jackpot [dʒakpɔt] *nm* **1.** [combinaison] jackpot ▪ **toucher le ~** *pr & fig* to hit the jackpot **2.** [machine] slot machine.

Jacob [ʒakɔb] *npr* Jacob.

jacobin, e [ʒakɔbɛ̃, in] *adj* **1.** HIST Jacobinic, Jacobinical, Jacobin *(modif)* **2.** POLIT radical, Jacobin.
◆ **Jacobin** *nm* HIST Jacobin.

jacobinisme [ʒakɔbinism] *nm* Jacobinism.

jacobite [ʒakɔbit] ◇ *adj* Jacobitic.
◇ *nmf* HIST & RELIG Jacobite.

jacquard [ʒakar] *nm* **1.** [vêtement] Jacquard *ou* Jacquard-style sweater **2.** TEXT [machine] Jacquard loom, jacquard ▪ [tissu] Jacquard weave.

jacquerie [ʒakri] *nf* peasants' revolt, jacquerie.

jactance [ʒaktɑ̃s] *nf* **1.** △ [baratin] chattering **2.** *litt* [infatuation] conceit, self-praise, vainglory *arch.*

jacter [3] △ [ʒakte] ◇ *vt* [parler - langue] to jabber away in ▪ **~ chinois** to jabber away in Chinese *péj.*
◇ *vi* [avouer] to squeal, to come clean.

Jacuzzi® [ʒakuzi] *nm* Jacuzzi®.

jade [ʒad] *nm* **1.** [matière] jade ▪ **bague de ~** jade ring **2.** [objet] jade (object) *ou* artefact.

jadis [ʒadis] ◇ *adv sout* formerly, long ago, in olden days ▪ **il y avait ~ un prince** there was once a prince, once upon a time there was a prince ▪ **la ville a conservé sa splendeur de ~** the town has kept its former splendour.
◇ *adj litt* : **au temps ~** in days of yore *ou* old, in bygone days.

jaguar [ʒagwar] *nm* jaguar.

jaillir [32] [ʒajir] *vi* **1.** [personne, animal] to spring *ou* to shoot *ou* to bolt out ▪ **il jaillit de derrière le mur** he sprang *ou* leapt out from behind the wall **2.** [liquide, sang, source] to spurt (out), to gush (forth), to spout ▪ [flamme] to leap *ou* to shoot *ou* to spring up ▪ [larmes] to gush, to start flowing ▪ [rire] to burst out *ou* forth ▪ **la lumière d'un projecteur jaillit dans l'obscurité** a spot-light suddenly shone out in the darkness **3.** [se manifester - doute] to spring up, to arise (suddenly) ▪ **une pensée jaillit dans son esprit** a thought suddenly came into his mind.

jaillissant, e [ʒajisɑ̃, ɑ̃t] *adj* spurting, gushing, spouting.

jaillissement [ʒajismɑ̃] *nm* [jet] spurting *(U)*, gushing *(U)* ▪ **un ~ d'idées** an outpouring of ideas.

jais [ʒɛ] *nm* MINÉR jet ▪ **des perles de ~** jet beads ▪ **des yeux de ~** *fig* jet black eyes.

Jakarta [dʒakarta] = **Djakarta**.

jalon [ʒalɔ̃] *nm* **1.** [piquet] ranging pole *ou* rod **2.** [référence] milestone, landmark ▪ **planter** *ou* **poser des ~s** *fig* to prepare the ground, to clear the way.

jalonnement [ʒalɔnmɑ̃] *nm* **1.** [de terrain] marking *ou* staking out **2.** MIL screening.

jalonner [3] [ʒalɔne] ◇ *vt* **1.** [terrain] to mark out *ou* off *(insép)* **2.** [longer] to line ▪ **une carrière jalonnée de succès** a career marked by a series of successes **3.** MIL to screen.
◇ *vi* [poser des jalons] to mark out *ou* off.

jalousement [ʒaluzmɑ̃] *adv* **1.** [avec jalousie] jealously **2.** [soigneusement] jealously ▪ **un secret ~ gardé** a closely *ou* jealously guarded secret.

jalouser [3] [ʒaluze] *vt* to be jealous of.

jalousie [ʒaluzi] *nf* **1.** [envie] jealousy, envy ▪ [possessivité] jealousy ▪ **tourmenté par la ~** tormented by jealousy **2.** [store] venetian blind, jalousie.

jaloux, ouse [ʒalu, uz] ◇ *adj* **1.** [possessif] jealous ▪ **rendre qqn ~** to make sb jealous ▪ **être ~ de qqn** to be jealous of sb ▶ **~ comme un tigre** horribly jealous **2.** [envieux] jealous, envious ▪ **~ de** jealous *ou* envious of **3.** *sout* **~ de** [attaché à] : **la France, jalouse de sa réputation en matière de vins** France, jealous of her reputation for good wine **4.** *sout* [extrême] : **garder qqch avec une attention jalouse** to keep a jealous watch over sthg ▪ **mettre un soin ~ à faire qqch** to do sthg with the utmost care.

<> *nm, f* jealous person ▪ **faire des ~** to make people jealous *ou* envious.

jamaïquain, e, jamaïcain, e [ʒamaikɛ̃, ɛn] *adj* Jamaican.
◆ **Jamaïquain, e, Jamaïcain, e** *nm, f* Jamaican.

Jamaïque [ʒamaik] *npr f* : **(la) ~** Jamaica ▪ **vivre à la ~** to live in Jamaica.

jamais [ʒamɛ] *adv* **1.** [sens négatif] never ▪ **il n'a ~ su à quoi s'en tenir** he never knew where he stood ▪ **il travaille sans ~ s'arrêter** he works without ever stopping ▪ **vous ne le verrez plus ~, plus ~ vous ne le verrez** you'll never (ever) see him again ▪ **~ (une) si grande émotion ne m'avait envahi** never before had I been so overcome with emotion ▪ **~ homme ne fut plus comblé** *litt* there was never a happier man ▪ **presque ~** hardly ever, almost never ▪ **c'est du ~ vu!** it's never happened before!, it's totally unheard of! ▪ **c'est le moment ou ~!** it's now or never! ▪ **c'est le moment ou ~ d'y aller** now it's the best time to go ▪ **on ne sait ~!** you never know!, who knows? ▪ *(en corrélation avec 'que')* **ce n'est ~ qu'à 20 minutes à pied** it's only 20 minutes' walk ▶ **~ deux sans trois** everything comes in threes, if it's happened twice, it'll happen a third time ▪ **~ de la vie!** not on your life! ▪ **~, au grand ~, je n'ai fait une telle promesse!** I never ever made such a promise!, I never made such a promise, never on your life! **2.** [sens positif] ever ▪ **a-t-on ~ vu pareille splendeur?** have you ever seen such splendour? ▪ **si ~ il reste des places, tu en veux?** if by any chance there are tickets left, do you want any? ▪ **plus/moins/pire que ~** more/less/worse than ever ▪ **le seul/le plus beau que j'aie ~ vu** the only one/the most beautiful I have ever seen.
◆ **à jamais** *loc adv sout* for good, forever ▪ **à tout ~** forever, for evermore *litt* ▪ **nous avons à tout ~ perdu l'espoir de le revoir** we have lost all hope of ever seeing him again.
◆ **pour jamais** *loc adv sout* forever.

jambage [ʒɑ̃baʒ] *nm* **1.** ARCHIT [pied-droit] jamb ▪ [pilier] jamb, post ▪ **~ de cheminée** fireplace cheek **2.** [trait d'une lettre - vers le bas] downstroke ; [- vers le haut] upstroke ; [- au-dessous de la ligne] tail, descender.

jambe [ʒɑ̃b] *nf* **1.** ANAT leg ▪ **avoir les ~s nues** to be bare-legged ▪ **elle est tout en ~s** she's all legs ▪ **il a (encore) des ~s de vingt ans** he's still very spry ▶ **~ artificielle/de bois** artificial/wooden leg ▪ **il a un bon jeu de ~s** SPORT his footwork is good ▪ **je n'ai plus de** *ou* **je ne sens plus mes ~s** I'm totally exhausted, my legs have gone ▪ **en avoir plein les ~s** *fam* to be worn out *ou* dead tired ▪ **il avait les ~s en coton** his legs were like jelly *ou* cotton wool ▪ **il est toujours dans mes ~s** [enfant] he's always under my feet *ou* in my way ▪ **ça me/lui fait une belle ~!** *fam* a fat lot of good that does me/him! ▪ **la peur lui donnait des ~s** fear drove her on ▪ **prendre ses ~s à son cou** to take to one's heels ▪ **détaler** *ou* **s'enfuir à toutes ~s** to make a bolt for it ▪ **tenir la ~ à qqn** *fam* to drone on (and on) at sb ▪ **tirer dans les ~s de qqn** *pr* to aim (a shot) at sb's legs ; *fig* to create (all sorts of) problems for sb ▪ **traiter qqn par-dessus la ~** to treat sb offhandedly ▪ **une partie de ~s en l'air**△ a bit of nooky **2.** [du cheval] leg **3.** [vêtement] (trouser) leg **4.** [d'un compas] leg **5.** CONSTR prop ▪ **~ de force** [d'une poutre] strut ; [d'un comble] joist stay **6.** AUTO radius rod ▪ **~ de force** *vieilli* torque rod.

jambière [ʒɑ̃bjɛr] *nf* **1.** [pour la danse] legwarmer **2.** [guêtre] legging, gaiter **3.** ÉQUIT pad, gaiter.

jambon [ʒɑ̃bɔ̃] *nm* **1.** [viande] ham ▪ **~ blanc** *ou* **de Paris** boiled *ou* cooked ham ▪ **~ cru** *ou* **de pays** raw ham ▪ **~ de Bayonne/Parme** Bayonne/Parma ham ▪ **~ salé/fumé** salted/smoked ham ▪ **~ à l'os** ham off the bone ▪ **~ d'York** boiled ham on the bone ▪ **un ~ beurre** *fam* a ham sandwich *(in buttered baguette)* ▪ **un ~ fromage** *fam* a ham and cheese sandwich *(in buttered baguette)* **2.** △ [cuisse] thigh.

jambonneau [ʒɑ̃bɔno] *nm* **1.** [petit jambon] knuckle of ham **2.** [mollusque] fan mussel.

jamboree [ʒɑ̃bɔri] *nm* jamboree.

jam-session [dʒamseʃœn] *(pl* **jam-sessions***) nf* jam session.

janissaire [ʒanisɛr] *nm* janissary.

jansénisme [ʒɑ̃senism] *nm* **1.** RELIG : **le ~** Jansenism **2.** *litt* [piété austère] puritanism *fig.*

janséniste [ʒɑ̃senist] <> *adj* **1.** RELIG Jansenist, Jansenistic **2.** *litt* [austère] puritanical *fig.*
<> *nmf* **1.** RELIG Jansenist **2.** *litt* [moraliste] puritan *fig.*

jante [ʒɑ̃t] *nf* (wheel) rim ▪ **~s en aluminium** AUTO (aluminium) alloy wheels.

janvier [ʒɑ̃vje] *nm* January, *voir aussi* **mars**.

japon [ʒapɔ̃] *nm* [papier] Japanese paper ▪ [porcelaine] Japanese porcelain.

Japon [ʒapɔ̃] *npr m* : **le ~** Japan ▪ **elle vit au ~** she lives in Japan.

japonais, e [ʒapɔnɛ, ɛz] *adj* Japanese.
◆ **Japonais, e** *nm, f* Japanese (person) ▪ **les Japonais** the Japanese.
◆ **japonais** *nm* LING Japanese.

japonisant, e [ʒapɔnizɑ̃, ɑ̃t] <> *adj* ART inspired by Japanese art.
<> *nm, f* specialist in Japanese studies.

jappement [ʒapmɑ̃] *nm* [d'un chien] yelp, yap ▪ [du chacal] bark.

japper [3] [ʒape] *vi* [chien] to yelp, to yap ▪ [chacal] to bark.

jaquette [ʒakɛt] *nf* **1.** [vêtement - d'homme] morning coat ; [- de femme] jacket **2.** [de livre] (dust) cover *ou* jacket, book jacket **3.** [couronne dentaire] crown **4.** TECHNOL jacket, casing.

jardin [ʒardɛ̃] *nm* **1.** [terrain clos - gén] garden ; [- d'une maison] garden, yard *US* ▪ **il est dans le** *ou* **au ~** he's in the garden ▪ **les ~s du château de Windsor** the grounds of Windsor Castle ▶ **~ botanique** botanical garden *ou* gardens ▪ **~ à la française/à l'anglaise** formal/landscape garden ▪ **~ zoologique** *ou* **d'acclimatation** zoological garden *ou* gardens, zoo ▪ **~ d'hiver** winter garden ▪ **~ maraîcher** market garden ▪ **~ ouvrier** allotment ▪ **~ paysager** landscaped garden ▪ **~ potager** vegetable *ou* kitchen garden ▪ **~ public** public garden *ou* gardens, park ▪ **c'est mon ~ secret** that's my little secret ▪ **mobilier de ~** garden furniture **2.** *litt* [région fertile] garden.
◆ **jardin d'enfants** *nm* kindergarten, playgroup *ou* preschool nursery *UK*.

jardinage [ʒardinaʒ] *nm* **1.** [d'un potager, de fleurs] gardening ▪ **faire un peu de ~** to potter *UK ou* to putter *US* around in the garden **2.** [de forêts] selective working.
◆ **de jardinage** *loc adj* [outil, magasin] gardening, garden *(modif).*

jardiner [3] [ʒardine] <> *vi* to garden ▪ **elle est dehors en train de ~** she's out doing some gardening.
<> *vt* to select, to cull.

Jardinerie® [ʒardinri] *nf* garden centre.

jardinet [ʒardinɛ] *nm* small garden.

jardinier, ère [ʒardinje, ɛr] <> *adj* **1.** HORT garden *(modif)* **2.** [de forêts] selective.
<> *nm, f* gardener.
◆ **jardinière** *nf* **1.** [sur un balcon] window box ▪ [pour fleurs coupées] jardiniere ▪ [meuble] plant holder **2.** CULIN : **jardinière (de légumes)** (diced) mixed vegetables, jardiniere.
◆ **jardinière d'enfants** *nf* nursery-school *ou* kindergarten teacher, playgroup assistant *UK*.

jargon [ʒargɔ̃] *nm* **1.** [langage incorrect] jargon ▪ [langage incompréhensible] jargon, mumbo jumbo **2.** [langue spécialisée] jargon, argot ▪ **~ administratif/des journalistes** officialese/journalese ▪ **le ~ judiciaire** lawyers' cant.

jargonner [3] [ʒargɔne] *vi* **1.** [s'exprimer - en jargon] to jargonize, to talk jargon ; [- de façon incompréhensible] to jabber away **2.** [jars] to honk.

jarre [ʒar] *nf* [vase] (earthenware) jar.

jarret [ʒarɛ] *nm* **1.** ANAT back of the knee, ham ▪ ZOOL hock ▪ **~ de veau** CULIN knuckle of veal, veal shank *US* ▪ **avoir des ~s d'acier** *ou* **du ~** *fam* to have a good (sturdy) pair of legs **2.** CONSTR [imperfection] break of outline ▪ [coude] knee joint (of pipe).

jarretelle [ʒartɛl] *nf* suspender *UK*, garter *US*.

jarretière [ʒartjɛr] *nf* [vêtement] garter ▪ **la ~ de la mariée** the bride's garter *(worn on the wedding day, removed by the best man and auctioned off to the guests)*.

jars [ʒar] *nm* gander.

jaser [3] [ʒaze] *vi* **1.** [médire] to gossip ▪ **ça va faire ~ dans le quartier** that'll set the neighbours' tongues wagging **2.** *fam* [avouer] to squeal, to blab **3.** [gazouiller - pie, geai] to chatter ; [- ruisseau, bébé] to babble ; [- personne] to chatter.

jaseur, euse [ʒazœr, øz] ◇ *nm, f* [bavard] chatterbox ▪ [mauvaise langue] gossip, scandal-monger.
◇ *adj* **1.** [oiseau] chattering **2.** [personne - qui bavarde] chattering ; [- qui médit] gossiping, gossipy.
◆ **jaseur** *nm* ORNITH waxwing.

jasmin [ʒasmɛ̃] *nm* jasmine ▪ **thé au ~** jasmine tea.

jaspe [ʒasp] *nm* **1.** MINÉR jasper ▪ **~ sanguin** bloodstone **2.** GÉOL jasperoid.

jatte [ʒat] *nf* [petite] bowl ▪ [grande] basin ▪ **une ~ de lait** a bowl of milk.

jauge [ʒoʒ] *nf* **1.** [pour calibrer] gauge **2.** [indicateur] gauge ▪ **~ d'essence** AUTO petrol gauge *UK*, gas gauge *US* ▪ **~ (de niveau) d'huile** AUTO dipstick **3.** [contenance d'un réservoir] capacity ▪ [tonnage d'un navire] tonnage, burden **4.** AGRIC trench **5.** MENUIS & PHYS gauge.

jauger [17] [ʒoʒe] ◇ *vt* **1.** [mesurer - fil] to gauge ; [- réservoir] to gauge (the capacity of) ; [- liquide] to gauge (the volume of) ; [- navire] to measure the tonnage *ou* burden of **2.** *litt* [juger - dégâts] to assess ▪ **~ qqn** to size sb up ▪ **~ la situation** to size *ou* to weigh up the situation.
◇ *vi* NAUT : **navire jaugeant 600 tonneaux** ship with a tonnage of *ou* measuring 600 tons.

jaunâtre [ʒonatr] *adj* [couleur] yellowish, yellowy ▪ [teint] yellowish, sallow, waxen.

jaune [ʒon] ◇ *adj* **1.** [couleur] yellow ▪ **avoir le teint ~** to look yellow *ou* sallow *ou* bilious ▶ **~ canari/citron** canary/lemon yellow ▪ **~ moutarde** mustard-coloured ▪ **~ d'or** golden yellow ▪ **~ paille** straw-coloured ▪ **~ comme un citron** *ou* **un coing** (as) yellow as a lemon **2.** *péj* & *vieilli* [d'Asie] yellow.
◇ *nmf* [non gréviste] strikebreaker.
◇ *nm* **1.** [couleur] yellow ▪ **elle aime s'habiller en ~** she likes to wear yellow **2.** CULIN : **~ (d'œuf)** (egg) yolk.
◆ **Jaune** *nmf péj* & *vieilli* Oriental.

jaunet, ette [ʒonɛ, ɛt] *adj litt* yellowish, yellowy.

jaunir [32] [ʒonir] ◇ *vt* **1.** [rendre jaune] to turn yellow ▪ **ses dents sont jaunies par le tabac** his teeth have been turned yellow by smoking **2.** [défraîchir] to yellow, to turn yellow ▪ **le soleil a jauni les pages** the sun has made the pages go *ou* turn yellow.
◇ *vi* **1.** [devenir jaune] to turn *ou* to become yellow, to yellow **2.** [se défraîchir] to fade.

jaunisse [ʒonis] *nf* MÉD jaundice ▶ **tu ne vas pas en faire une ~!** *fam* there's no need to get into a state *ou* to get worked up about it!

jaunissement [ʒonismɑ̃] *nm* yellowing.

java [ʒava] *nf* **1.** [danse] java **2.** *fam* [fête] knees-up *UK*, shindig *US* ▪ **faire la ~** to have a (good old) knees-up.

Java [ʒava] *npr* Java ▪ **à ~** in Java, *voir aussi* **île**.

javanais, e [ʒavanɛ, ɛz] *adj* Javanese.
◆ **Javanais, e** *nm, f* Javanese ▪ **les Javanais** the Javanese.
◆ **javanais** *nm* LING **1.** [langue indonésienne] Javanese **2.** [argot] *slang using -av- or -va- as an infix before each vowel sound* **3.** [langage incompréhensible] : **c'est du ~** *fam* that's gobbledegook.

Javel [ʒavɛl] *npr* : **eau de ~** bleach.

javelliser [3] [ʒavelize] *vt* to chlorinate.

javelot [ʒavlo] *nm* javelin.

jazz [dʒaz] *nm* jazz ▪ **musicien de ~** jazz musician.

jazz-band [dʒazbɑ̃d] (*pl* **jazz-bands**) *nm* jazz band.

jazzique [dʒazik], **jazzistique** [dʒazistik] *adj* jazz *(modif)*.

jazzman [dʒazman] (*pl* **jazzmans** *ou pl* **jazzmen** [dʒazmɛn]) *nm* jazzman, jazz player *ou* musician.

J.-C. (*abr écrite de* **Jésus-Christ**) J.C. ▪ **en (l'an) 180 avant/après ~** in (the year) 180 BC/AD.

je [ʒə] *(devant voyelle et 'h' muet* **j'** [ʒ]*)* ◇ *pron pers* I ▪ **puissé-je me tromper!** *sout* let us hope I am wrong!
◇ *nm inv* : **le je** LING the first person ; PHILOS the self.

jean [dʒin] *nm* **1.** [tissu] : **(toile de) ~** denim ▪ **un blouson en ~** a denim jacket **2.** [pantalon] (pair of) jeans.

Jean [ʒɑ̃] *npr* : **saint ~** Saint John.

Jean-Baptiste [ʒɑ̃batist] *npr* : **saint ~** Saint John the Baptist.

jean-foutre△ [ʒɑ̃futr] *nm inv* layabout, good-for-nothing.

Jeanne [ʒan] *npr* : **~ d'Arc** *ou* **la Pucelle** Joan of Arc ▪ **elle est coiffée à la ~ d'Arc** she wears her hair in a pageboy cut.

jeannette [ʒanɛt] *nf* **1.** [pour repasser] sleeve-board **2.** [croix] gold cross *(worn around the neck)* ▪ [chaîne] gold chain *(for wearing a cross)* **3.** [scout] Brownie (Guide) *UK*, Girl Scout *US*.

jeans [dʒins] = **jean** *(sens 2)*.

Jeep® [dʒip] *nf* Jeep®.

Jéhovah [ʒeɔva] *npr* Jehovah ▪ **les témoins de ~** the Jehovah's Witnesses.

je-m'en-foutisme [ʒmɑ̃futism] *nm fam* couldn't-give-a-damn approach *ou* attitude.

je-m'en-foutiste [ʒmɑ̃futist] *fam* ◇ *adj* couldn't give a damn *(avant n)*.
◇ *nmf* couldn't-give-a-damn sort of person.

je-ne-sais-quoi [ʒənsekwa] *nm inv* : **un ~** a certain je ne sais quoi, a certain something ▪ **un ~ de qqch** a hint of sthg.

jérémiades [ʒeremjad] *nfpl* [lamentations] wailing ▪ **assez de ~!** stop whining *ou* moaning *ou* complaining! ▪ **avec lui, ce ne sont que des ~** all you ever get from him is moaning.

Jérémie [ʒeremi] *npr* BIBLE Jeremiah.

jerk [dʒɛrk] *nm* DANSE jerk.

jerrican(e), jerrycan [ʒerikan] *nm* jerrycan.

jersey [ʒɛrzɛ] *nm* **1.** [vêtement] jersey, sweater **2.** TEXT jersey, jersey knit.

Jersey [ʒɛrzɛ] *npr* Jersey ▪ **à ~** in *ou* on Jersey, *voir aussi* **île**.

jersiais, e [ʒɛrzjɛ, ɛz] *adj* from Jersey ▪ **vache ~e** Jersey (cow).
◆ **Jersiais, e** *nmf sing inhabitant of or person from Jersey*.

Jérusalem [ʒeryzalɛm] *npr* Jerusalem ▪ **la nouvelle ~, la ~ céleste** the New Jerusalem.

jésuite [ʒezɥit] ◇ *adj* **1.** RELIG Jesuitic, Jesuitical **2.** *péj* [hypocrite] jesuitic, jesuitical, casuistic.
◇ *nmf péj* [hypocrite] jesuit, casuist.
◇ *nm* RELIG Jesuit ▪ **les ~s** the Jesuits.

jésuitique [ʒezɥitik] *adj* **1.** RELIG Jesuitic, Jesuitical **2.** *sout* & *péj* [hypocrite] jesuitic, jesuitical, casuistic.

jésuitisme [ʒezɥitism] *nm* **1.** [système moral] Jesuitism **2.** *sout* & *péj* [hypocrisie] casuistry, jesuitry.

jésus [ʒezy] *nm* **1.** [représentation] (figure of the) infant *ou* baby Jesus **2.** CULIN pork liver sausage *(from Franche-Comté and Switzerland)* ▪ **~ de Lyon** ≃ pork salami **3.** IMPR : **grand ~** ≃ imperial ▪ **petit ~** ≃ super royal **4.** *fam* [chérubin] cherub, angel.

Jésus [ʒezy] *npr* Jesus ▶ **(doux) ~!, ~ Marie!** sweet Jesus!, in the name of Jesus! ▪ **Compagnie** *ou* **Société de ~** Society of Jesus.

Jésus-Christ [ʒezykri] *npr* Jesus Christ ■ **en (l'an) 180 avant/après ~** in (the year) 180 BC/AD.

jet[1] [dʒɛt] *nm* AÉRON jet (plane).

jet[2] [ʒɛ] *nm* **1.** [embout] nozzle ■ [lance - de pompier] nozzle, fire (hose) ; [- de jardinier] (garden) hose ■ **laver** *ou* **passer qqch au ~** to hose sthg down **2.** [jaillissement - de flammes, de sang] spurt, jet ; [- d'eau, de vapeur] jet, gush ; [- de gaz] gush **3.** [lancer - de cailloux] throwing *(U)* ■ **des ~s de pierres** stone-throwing ▶ **à un ~ de pierre** a stone's throw away **4.** SPORT throw **5.** ASTRONAUT jet **6.** MÉTALL [veine libre] (pouring) stream ■ [arête] dead head.

◆ **d'un (seul) jet** *loc adv* in one go ■ **elle nous raconta tout d'un seul ~** she told us everything in one go *ou* breath.

◆ **jet d'eau** *nm* [filet d'eau] fountain, spray ■ [mécanisme] fountain ■ MENUIS weather strip ■ AUTO drip moulding.

jetable [ʒətabl] *adj* [couche, briquet, gobelet *etc*] disposable.

jeté [ʒəte] *nm* **1.** DANSE jeté ■ **petit ~** jeté ■ **grand ~** grand jeté **2.** SPORT jerk **3.** [maille] : **~ (simple), 1 ~** make 1 **4.** [couverture] : **~ de lit** bedspread ■ **~ de table** table runner.

jetée [ʒəte] *nf* **1.** [en bord de mer] pier, jetty **2.** [dans une aérogare] passageway.

jeter [27] [ʒəte] ◇ *vt* **1.** [lancer - balle, pierre] to throw ■ **elle m'a jeté la balle** she threw me the ball, she threw the ball to me ■ **~ qqch par terre** to throw sthg down (on the ground) ■ **ne jetez pas de papiers par terre** don't drop litter ■ **elle lui a jeté sa lettre à la figure** she threw the letter in his face ▶ **n'en jetez plus!** *fam* you're making me blush!, don't overdo it! ; *iron* give it a rest!
2. [avec un mouvement du corps] to throw ■ **l'enfant jeta ses bras autour de mon cou** the child threw *ou* flung his arms around my neck ■ **~ un (coup d')œil** to have a (quick) look at sthg, to glance at sthg ■ **jette un œil sur les enfants pendant mon absence** keep an eye on the children while I'm out
3. [émettre - étincelle] to throw *ou* to give out *(sép)* ; [- lumière] to cast, to shed ; [- ombre] to cast ; [- son] to let *ou* to give out *(sép)* ▶ **en ~** *fam* : **elle en jette, ta moto!** *fam* that's some *ou* a neat bike you've got there!
4. [dire brusquement] : **la petite phrase jetée par le ministre aux journalistes** the cryptic remark the minister threw at the press ■ **elle leur jeta à la figure qu'ils étaient des incapables** she told them straight (to their faces) that they were incompetent ■ **~ des injures à la tête de qqn** to hurl *ou* to fling insults at sb ▮ [écrire rapidement] to jot down *(sép)*, to scribble (down)
5. [mettre] to throw ■ **~ qqn dehors** *ou* **à la porte** to throw sb out ■ **~ qqn à terre** to throw sb down *ou* to the ground ■ **~ qqn en prison** to throw sb into jail *ou* prison ■ **~ qqn à l'eau** [à la piscine, sur la plage] to throw sb in *ou* into the water ; [d'un bateau] to throw sb overboard ■ **~ qqch par la fenêtre** to throw sthg out of the window ■ **~ un châle sur ses épaules** to throw on a shawl ■ **la statue du dictateur a été jetée bas** the dictator's statue was hurled to the ground ▶ **se faire ~** *fam* [expulser] to get kicked out ■ **ce n'est pas le moment de lui demander, tu vas te faire ~!** now is not the time to ask him, he'll just send you away (with a flea in your ear)!
6. [mettre au rebut - ordures, vêtements] to throw away *ou* out *(sép)* ■ **~ qqch à la poubelle** to throw sthg into the (dust)bin ■ **jette l'eau dans le caniveau** pour the water (out) into the gutter ■ **il ne faut jamais rien ~** waste not want not *prov* ■ **c'est bon à ~** it's fit for the (dust)bin UK *ou* trashcan US ▶ **~ le bébé avec l'eau du bain** to throw the baby out with the bathwater
7. [plonger - dans un état, dans une humeur] : **~ qqn dans l'embarras** to throw *ou* to plunge sb into confusion
8. [établir - fondations] to lay ; [- passerelle] to set up ; [- pont] to throw ■ **~ les fondements d'une loi/politique** to lay the foundations of a law/policy ■ [maille] to make
9. [répandre - doute] to cast ■ **~ le discrédit sur qqn/qqch** to cast discredit on sb/sthg, to discredit sb/sthg ■ **~ le trouble chez qqn** to disturb *ou* to trouble sb
10. *fam* [expulser] : **on a essayé d'aller en boîte mais on s'est fait ~ par un videur** we tried to get into a nightclub but got thrown out by a bouncer ■ **il s'est fait ~ par son père** [verbalement] his father sent him packing.
◇ *vi fam* [avoir de l'allure] : **ça jette!** it looks fantastic!
◆ **se jeter** ◇ *vp (emploi passif)* : **un rasoir qui se jette** a disposable razor.
◇ *vpi* **1.** [sauter] to throw *ou* to hurl o.s., to leap ■ **se ~ dans le vide** to throw o.s. *ou* to hurl o.s. into empty space ■ **se ~ par la fenêtre** to throw o.s. out of the window ■ **se ~ de côté** to leap aside, to take a sideways leap ▶ **se ~ à l'eau** *pr* to leap into the water ; *fig* to take the plunge
2. [se précipiter] to rush (headlong) ■ **se ~ sur qqn** to set about *ou* to pounce on sb ■ **les chiens se sont jetés sur la viande** the dogs fell on the meat ■ **les gens se sont jetés sur le buffet** the people fell on the food ■ **elle se jeta sur son lit** she threw herself on (to) her bed ■ **elle se jeta dans un taxi** she leapt into a taxi ■ **vous vous êtes tous jetés sur la question B** you all went for question B
3. [commencer] : **se ~ dans** : **se ~ à corps perdu dans une aventure** to fling o.s. body and soul into an adventure
4. [cours d'eau] to run *ou* to flow into ■ **là où la Marne se jette dans la Seine** where the river Marne flows *ou* runs into the Seine.
◇ *vpt*△ *loc* : **s'en ~ un (derrière la cravate)** to have a quick drink *ou* a quick one.

jeteur, euse [ʒətœr, øz] *nm, f* : **~ de sort** wizard (*f* witch).

jeton [ʒətɔ̃] *nm* **1.** [pièce] token ■ **~ de téléphone** token for the telephone **2.** JEUX counter ■ [à la roulette] chip, counter, jetton **3.** [dans une entreprise] : **~ (de présence)** director's fees ■ **il n'est là que pour toucher ses ~s** he's just a timeserver, all he does is draw his salary **4.** △ [coup de poing] whack.
◆ **jetons**△ *nmpl* : **avoir les ~s** to be scared stiff ■ **ficher les ~s à qqn** to put the wind up sb UK, to give sb the willies.

jet-set [dʒɛtsɛt], **jet-society** [dʒɛtsɔsajti] *nf* jet set ■ **membre de la ~** jet-setter.

jette *etc v* ⊳ **jeter**.

jeu, x [ʒø] *nm* **1.** LOISIRS game ■ **ce n'est qu'un ~!** it's only a game!, it's only for fun! ■ **c'est le ~!** it's fair (play)! ■ **ce n'est pas de** *ou* **du ~!** that's not fair! ■ **le ~** [activité] play ■ **par ~** for fun, in play ▶ **~ d'adresse/de hasard** game of skill/of chance ■ **~ électronique/vidéo** electronic/video game ■ **~ radiophonique/télévisé** radio/TV quiz (game) ■ **~ éducatif** educational game ■ **~ d'entreprise** management simulation (game) ■ **le Jeu des mille francs** *former famous radio quiz* ■ **~ de l'oie** ≃ snakes and ladders ■ **~ de plein air** outdoor game ■ **~ de rôle** role play ■ **~ de société** board game ■ **~ de stratégie** game of strategy ■ **c'est un ~ d'enfant!** this is child's play! ■ **se faire un ~ de** to make light work of
2. [cartes] hand ■ **avoir du ~** *ou* **un bon ~** to have a good hand ■ **étaler son ~** to lay down one's hand *ou* cards ▶ **elle nous a joué le grand ~** she pulled out all the stops for us ■ **avoir beau ~ (de faire qqch)** to have no trouble (doing sthg), to find it easy (to do sthg) ■ **il a bien caché son ~** he played his cards very close to his chest! *fig*
3. [ensemble de pièces] set ■ **~ de (32)/52 cartes** pack UK *ou* deck US of (32)/52 cards ■ **un ~ de dames/d'échecs/de quilles** a draughts/chess/skittles set ■ **un ~ de clés/tournevis** a set of keys/screwdrivers ▶ **~ de caractères** INFORM character set ■ **~ d'essai** INFORM sample data *ou* deck ■ **~ d'orgue** MUS organ stop
4. [manigances] game ■ **qu'est-ce que c'est que ce petit ~?** [ton irrité] what are you playing at?, what's your (little) game? ▶ **entrer dans le ~ de qqn** to play into sb's hands ■ **être pris à son propre ~** to be caught at one's own game ■ **se (laisser) prendre au ~** to get caught up *ou* involved in what's going on ■ **voir clair** *ou* **lire dans le ~ de qqn** to see through sb's little game, to see what sb is up to ■ **'le Jeu de l'amour et du hasard'** ***Marivaux*** 'The Game of Love and Chance'
5. SPORT [activité] game ■ **le ~ à XIII** Rugby League ▮ [action] play ■ **il y a eu du beau ~** there was some very good play ▮ [partie] game ■ **faire ~ égal** to be evenly matched ■ **il a fait ~ égal avec le champion** the champion met his match in him ▮ [au tennis] game ■ **~ Mériel!** game to Mériel! ■ **deux ~x partout** two games all ▶ **~ blanc** love game ■ **'~ jeux de ballon interdits'** 'no ball games'
6. [terrain] : **la balle est sortie du ~** the ball has gone out (of play) ▶ **~ de boules** [sur gazon] bowling green ; [de pétanque] ground *(for playing boules)* ■ **~ de quilles** skittle alley
7. [style d'un sportif] game, way of playing ■ **il a un ~ défensif/offensif** he plays a defensive/an attacking game ■ **avoir un**

bon ~ de jambes to move well ■ **il a un bon ~ de volée** he's a good volleyer, he volleys well ■ [interprétation - d'un acteur] acting ; [- d'un musicien] playing
8. [activité du parieur] : **le ~** gambling ■ **elle a tout perdu au ~** she gambled her entire fortune away, she lost her whole fortune (at) gambling
9. [effet] play ■ **~ d'eau** fountain ■ **~ de mots** play on words, pun ■ **des ~x de lumière** [naturels] play of light ; [artificiels] lighting effects
10. [espace] : **la vis a** *ou* **prend du ~** the screw is loose ■ **il y a du ~** there's a bit of play *ou* of a gap ■ **donner du ~ à qqch** to loosen sthg up
11. [action] play ■ **c'est un ~ de ton imagination/ta mémoire** it's a trick of your imagination/your memory ■ **laisser faire le ~ de la concurrence** to allow the free play of competition ■ **il n'a obtenu le siège que par le ~ des alliances électorales** he won the seat only through the interplay *ou* working of electoral alliances.
◆ **jeux** *nmpl* **1.** [mise] : **faites vos ~x(, rien ne va plus)** faites vos jeux (rien ne va plus) ■ **les ~x sont faits** *pr* les jeux sont faits ; *fig* the die is cast, there's no going back now
2. SPORT : **les ~x (Olympiques)** the (Olympic) Games ■ **les ~x (Olympiques) d'hiver** the Winter Olympics ■ **les ~x Olympiques pour handicapés** the Paralympic Games.
◆ **en jeu** ◇ *loc adj* **1.** [en question] at stake ■ **l'avenir de l'entreprise n'est pas en ~** the company's future is not at stake *ou* at risk *ou* in jeopardy
2. [en action] at play ■ **les forces en ~ sur le marché** the competing forces *ou* the forces at play *ou* the forces at work on the market
3. [parié] at stake ■ **la somme en ~** the money at stake *ou* which has been staked.
◇ *loc adv* **1.** SPORT : **mettre le ballon en ~** FOOTBALL to throw in the ball
2. [en marche] : **les disjoncteurs ont été mis en ~ par le programmateur** the circuit breakers were activated by the programmer
3. [en pariant] : **mettre une somme en ~** to place a bet ■ **mettre qqch en ~** [risquer qqch] to put sthg at stake ■ **entrer en ~** [intervenir] to come into play.
◆ **jeu de massacre** *nm* Aunt Sally ■ **le débat s'est transformé en ~ de massacre** *fig* the debate turned into a demolition session.

LE JEU DES MILLE EUROS

This radio programme formerly called *jeu des mille francs* was originally broadcast in the 1950s and has become a national institution. The quiz, whose top prize was originally one thousand francs, consists of a series of questions sent in by listeners.

jeudi [ʒødi] *nm* Thursday ■ **le Jeudi noir** Black Thursday *(day of the Wall Street Crash, 1929)* ■ **le ~ saint** Maundy Thursday, *voir aussi* **mardi**.

jeun [ʒœ̃] ◆ **à jeun** ◇ *loc adj* : **il est à ~** [il n'a rien mangé] he hasn't eaten anything ; [il n'a rien bu] he's sober.
◇ *loc adv* on an empty stomach ■ **venez à ~** don't eat anything before you come ■ **trois comprimés à ~** three tablets to be taken on an empty stomach.

jeune [ʒœn] ◇ *adj* **1.** [peu avancé en âge - personne, génération, population] young ■ **réussir ~** to succeed at a young age ■ **ma voiture n'est plus toute ~** *fam* my car's got quite a few miles on the clock now ■ **~ oiseau** fledgling, young bird ■ **~ chien** puppy, young dog ■ **un ~ homme** a young man, a youth ■ **une ~ femme** a (young) woman ■ **un ~ garçon** [enfant] a boy, a youngster ; [adolescent] a youth, a teenager ■ **une ~ fille** a girl, a young woman ■ **de ~s enfants** young *ou* small children ■ **~s gens** [garçons] young men ; [garçons et filles] youngsters, young people ■ **je suis plus ~ que lui de deux mois** I'm younger than him by two months, I'm two months younger than him ➲ **ils font ~** *ou* **~(s)** they look young
2. [débutant] : **on reparlera de ce ~ metteur en scène** we haven't heard the last of this young director ■ **'cherchons ~ ingénieur'** 'recently qualified engineer required' ■ **être ~ dans le métier** to be new to the trade *ou* business
3. [du début de la vie] young, early ■ **mes ~s années** my youth ■ **étant donné son ~ âge** given his youth *ou* how young he is
4. [qui a l'aspect de la jeunesse - personne] young, young-looking, youthful ; [- couleur, coiffure] young, youthful ■ **être ~ d'esprit** *ou* **de caractère** to be young at heart
5. [récent - discipline, entreprise, État] new, young
6. [vin] young, green ■ [fromage] young
7. [entreprise] : **~ pousse** start up (company)
8. *fam* [juste] : **ça fait** *ou* **c'est (un peu) ~!** [somme d'argent] that's a bit mean! ; [temps] that's cutting it a bit fine! ; [dimensions] that's a bit on the short *ou* small side! ; [poids] that's a bit on the light side!
◇ *adv* [comme les jeunes] : **s'habiller ~** to wear young-looking clothes.
◇ *nm* [garçon] young man, youngster ■ **petit ~** *fam* young man.
◇ *nf* [fille] (young) girl ■ **petite ~** *fam* young girl.
◆ **jeunes** *nmpl* : **les ~s d'aujourd'hui** today's young people, the young people of today, the young generation ■ **une bande de ~s** a bunch of kids.

jeûne [ʒøn] *nm* **1.** [période] fast ■ **le ~ du Ramadan** the fasting at Ramadan **2.** [pratique] fast, fasting *(U)* ■ **observer une semaine de ~** to fast for a week.

jeûner [3] [ʒøne] *vi* **1.** RELIG to fast **2.** [ne rien manger] to go without food.

jeunesse [ʒœnɛs] *nf* **1.** [juvénilité - d'une personne] youth, youthfulness ; [- d'une génération, d'une population] youthfulness, young age ; [- d'un arbre, d'un animal] young age ; [- des traits, d'un style] youthfulness ■ **elle m'a rendu ma ~** she made me feel young again ■ **tous furent impressionnés par la ~ de l'équipe gouvernementale** they were all impressed by how young the government ministers were ■ **j'apprécie la ~ d'esprit** *ou* **de caractère** I appreciate a youthful outlook *ou* frame of mind **2.** [enfance - d'une personne] youth ; [- d'une science] early period, infancy ■ **dans ma** *ou* **au temps de ma ~** in my youth, when I was young, in my early years ➲ **il faut que ~ se passe** *prov* youth will have its fling **3.** SOCIOL : **la ~** young people, the young ■ **la ~ ouvrière** young workers, working-class youth ■ **émissions pour la ~** TV programmes for younger viewers ; RADIO programmes for younger listeners ■ **alors, la ~, on se dépêche!** *fam* come on, you youngsters *ou* young folk, hurry up! ➲ **la ~ dorée** gilded youth *sout* ■ **si ~ savait, si vieillesse pouvait** *prov* if only youth could know and old age could **4.** *vieilli* [jeune fille] (young) girl ■ **ce n'est plus une ~** she's no longer young **5.** [d'un vin] youthfulness, greenness.
◆ **jeunesses** *nfpl* [groupe] youth ■ **les ~s hitlériennes** the Hitler Youth ■ **les ~s communistes/socialistes** Young Communists/Socialists.
◆ **de jeunesse** *loc adj* : **ses amours/œuvres/péchés de ~** the loves/works/sins of his youth.

jeunet, ette [ʒœnɛ, ɛt] *adj* youngish, rather young.

jeune-turc, jeune-turque [ʒœntyrk] *(mpl* **jeunes-turcs**, *fpl* **jeunes-turques**) *nm, f* HIST & POLIT Young Turk.

jeûneur, euse [ʒønœr, øz] *nm, f* faster.

jeunot, otte [ʒœno, ɔt] ◇ *adj* youngish, rather young ■ **il est un peu ~** he's a bit on the young side.
◇ *nm, f* youngster, young lad *(f* lass).

Jézabel [ʒezabɛl] *npr* Jezebel.

JF, jf **1.** = **jeune fille** **2.** = **jeune femme**.

JH = **jeune homme**.

jingle [dʒingœl] *nm* jingle.

jiu-jitsu [ʒjyʒitsy] *nm* ju-jitsu, jiu-jitsu.

Jivaro [ʒivaro] *nmf* Jivaro ■ **les ~s** the Jivaro.

JO ◇ *nm* = **Journal officiel**.
◇ *nmpl* = **jeux Olympiques**.

joaillerie [ʒɔajri] *nf* **1.** [art] : **la ~** jewelling ■ **la ~ du XVᵉ siècle** the art of the jeweller in the 15th century **2.** [commerce] : **la ~** the jewel trade, jewellery **3.** [magasin] jeweller's shop *UK*, jeweler's store *US* **4.** [articles] : **la ~** jewellery.

joaillier, ère [ʒɔaje, ɛr] ◇ *adj* jewel *(modif)*.
◇ *nm, f* jeweller.

job [dʒɔb] *nm* **fam** [travail - temporaire] (temporary) job ; [- permanent] job ■ **elle a un bon ~** she has a good job.

Job [ʒɔb] *npr* Job ■ **pauvre comme ~** as poor as Job, as poor as a church mouse.

jobard, e [ʒɔbar, ard] *fam* <> *adj* [très naïf] gullible, naive.
<> *nm, f* sucker, mug *UK*, patsy *US*.

Jocaste [ʒɔkast] *npr* Jocasta.

jockey [ʒɔkɛ] *nm* jockey.

Joconde [ʒɔkɔ̃d] *npr f*: **'la ~' *de Vinci*** 'The Mona Lisa'.

jodhpurs [ʒɔdpyr] *nmpl* jodhpurs.

jodler [3] [jɔdle] *vi* to yodel.

jogger[1] [dʒɔgœr] *nm ou nf* [chaussure] jogging shoe, trainer.

jogger[2] [3] [dʒɔge] *vi* to jog.

joggeur, euse [dʒɔgœr, øz] *nm, f* jogger.

jogging [dʒɔgiŋ] *nm* **1.** [activité] jogging ■ **faire son ~ matinal** to go for one's morning jog **2.** [vêtement] track suit *(for jogging)*.

Johannesburg [ʒɔanɛsbur] *npr* Johannesburg.

joie [ʒwa] *nf* **1.** [bonheur] joy, delight ■ **être fou de ~** to be wild with joy ■ **pousser un cri de ~** to shout *ou* to whoop for joy ■ **sauter** *ou* **bondir de ~** to jump *ou* to leap for joy ■ **travailler dans la ~ et la bonne humeur** to work cheerfully and good-humouredly ■ **pour la plus grande ~ de ses parents, elle a obtenu la bourse** much to the delight of her parents *ou* to her parent's great delight, she won the scholarship ➲ **~ de vivre** joie de vivre ■ **déborder de ~ de vivre** to be full of the joys of spring ■ **c'est pas la ~ à la maison** *fam* life at home isn't exactly a laugh-a-minute *ou* a bundle of laughs **2.** [plaisir] pleasure ■ **avec ~!** with great pleasure! ■ **il a accepté avec ~** he was delighted to accept ■ **nous avons la ~ de vous annoncer la naissance de Charles** we are happy to announce the birth of Charles ■ **je suis tout à la ~ de revoir mes amis** *sout* I'm overjoyed at the idea of *ou* I'm greatly looking forward to seeing my friends again ■ **des films qui ont fait la ~ de millions d'enfants** films which have given pleasure to *ou* delighted millions of children ■ **la petite Émilie fait la ~ de sa mère** little Emily is the apple of her mother's eye *ou* is her mother's pride and joy ■ **il se faisait une telle ~ de venir à ton mariage** he was so delighted at the idea of *ou* so looking forward to coming to your wedding ■ **je me ferai une ~ de lui dire ses quatre vérités** *hum* I shall be only too pleased to tell him a few home truths ➲ **fausse ~ : tu m'as fait une fausse ~** you got me all excited for nothing.
➡ **joies** *nfpl* [plaisirs] joys ■ **les ~s de la vie/retraite** the joys of life/retirement.

joignable [ʒwaɲabl] *adj*: **je suis ~ à ce numéro** I can be reached at this number.

joindre [82] [ʒwɛ̃dr] <> *vt* **1.** [attacher - ficelles, bâtons] to join (together), to put together ; [- câbler] to join, to connect ➲ **~ les deux bouts** to make ends meet
2. [rapprocher] to put *ou* to bring together ■ **~ les mains** [pour prier] to clasp one's hands, to put one's hands together
3. [points, lieux] to link
4. [ajouter] : **~ qqch à** to add sthg to ■ **~ un fichier à un message électronique** INFORM to attach a file to an email message ■ **je joins à ce pli un chèque de 300 euros** please find enclosed a cheque for 300 euros ■ **voulez-vous ~ une carte aux fleurs?** would you like to send a card with *ou* to attach a card to the flowers?
5. [associer] to combine, to link ■ **~ la technique à l'efficacité** to combine technical know-how and efficiency
6. [contacter] to contact, to get in touch with ■ **~ qqn par téléphone** to get through to sb on the phone, to contact sb by phone ■ **~ qqn par lettre** to contact sb in writing ■ **où pourrai-je vous ~?** how can I get in touch with you *ou* contact you?
<> *vi* [porte, planches, battants] : **des volets qui joignent bien/mal** shutters that close/don't close properly.
➡ **se joindre** *vp (emploi réciproque)* **1.** [se contacter - par téléphone] to get through to each other ; [- par lettre] to make contact
2. [se nouer] : **leurs mains se sont jointes** their hands came together *ou* joined.
➡ **se joindre à** *vp+prép* [s'associer à] to join ■ **tu veux te ~ à nous?** would you like to come with us? ■ **se ~ à une conversation/partie de rami** to join in a conversation/game of rummy ■ **puis-je me ~ à vous pour acheter le cadeau de Pierre?** may I join in to (help) buy Pierre's present? ■ **Lisa se joint à moi pour vous souhaiter la bonne année** Lisa and I wish you *ou* Lisa joins me in wishing you a Happy New Year.

joint, e [ʒwɛ̃, ɛ̃t] *adj* **1.** [rapproché] : **agenouillé, les mains ~es** kneeling with his hands (clasped) together **2.** [attaché] : **planches mal/solidement ~es** loose-/tight-fitting boards.
➡ **joint** *nm* **1.** CONSTR & MENUIS [garniture d'étanchéité] joint ■ [ligne d'assemblage] join ■ **les ~s d'un mur** the jointing *ou* pointing of a wall **2.** MÉCAN [ligne d'assemblage] joint ■ **~ de cardan** universal joint ■ **~ de culasse** AUTO (cylinder) head gasket ■ **~ (d'étanchéité)** gasket, seal **3.** RAIL (rail) joint **4.** [de robinet] washer **5.** GÉOL joint **6.** *fam* [moyen] : **il cherche un ~ pour payer moins d'impôts** he's trying to find a clever way of paying less tax **7.** *fam* [drogue] joint.

jointif, ive [ʒwɛ̃tif, iv] *adj* MENUIS butt-jointed.

jointoyer [13] [ʒwɛ̃twaje] *vt* CONSTR to point (up) *(sép)*.

jointure [ʒwɛ̃tyr] *nf* **1.** ANAT joint ■ **~s des doigts** knuckles ❙ [chez le cheval] pastern joint, fetlock **2.** [assemblage] joint ■ [point de jonction] join.

jojo [ʒoʒo] *fam* <> *adj inv* [joli] : **c'est pas ~ à regarder** it's not a pretty sight.
<> *nm* [enfant] : **ce gamin est un affreux ~** that child is a little horror.

jojoba [ʒɔʒɔba] *nm* jojoba.

joker [ʒɔkɛr] *nm* **1.** CARTES joker **2.** INFORM wild card.

joli, e [ʒɔli] <> *adj* **1.** [voix, robe, sourire] pretty, lovely, nice ■ [poème] pretty, lovely ■ [voyage, mariage] lovely, nice ■ [personne] attractive ■ **très ~** [enfant, vêtement] lovely ■ **il est ~ garçon** he's nice-looking *ou* attractive ■ **ce n'était pas ~ à voir, ce n'était pas ~, ~** *fam* it wasn't a pretty *ou* pleasant sight ➲ **être ~ comme un cœur** *ou* **~ à croquer** to be (as) pretty as a picture ■ **faire le ~ cœur** to flirt **2.** [considérable] : **une ~e (petite) somme, un ~ (petit) pécule** a nice *ou* tidy *ou* handsome (little) sum of money ■ **elle s'est taillé un ~ succès** she's been most *ou* very successful **3.** [usage ironique] : **elle est ~e, la politique!** what a fine *ou* nice thing politics is, isn't it? ■ **tu nous as mis dans un ~ pétrin** *fam* you got us into a fine mess *ou* pickle ➲ **tout ça c'est bien ~, mais...** that's all very well *ou* that's all well and good but...
<> *nm, f* lovely ■ **viens, ma ~e!** come here, honey *ou* darling *ou* lovely!
➡ **joli** <> *nm iron* **1.** [action blâmable] : **tu l'as cassé? c'est du ~!** you broke it? that's great! **2.** *loc* **faire du ~ : quand il va voir les dégâts, ça va faire du ~!** when he sees the damage, there'll be all hell to pay!
<> *adv* : **faire ~** to look nice *ou* pretty.

joliesse [ʒɔljɛs] *nf litt* prettiness, charm, grace.

joliment [ʒɔlimɑ̃] *adv* **1.** [élégamment] prettily, nicely ■ **~ dit** nicely *ou* neatly put **2.** *fam* [en intensif] pretty, jolly *UK* ■ **elle est ~ énervée!** she's jolly *UK ou* darn *US* annoyed! **3.** *iron* [très mal] : **on s'est fait ~ accueillir!** a fine *ou* nice welcome we got there!

Jonas [ʒɔnas] *npr* Jonah, Jonas.

jonc [ʒɔ̃] *nm* **1.** BOT rush ■ **~ à balais** broom **2.** [canne] (Malacca) cane, rattan **3.** JOAILL : **~ d'or** [bague] gold ring ; [bracelet] gold bangle *ou* bracelet.

joncher [3] [ʒɔ̃ʃe] *vt* [couvrir] to strew ■ **les corps jonchaient le sol** the bodies lay strewn on the ground ■ **jonché de détritus** littered with rubbish ■ **jonché de pétales** strewn with petals.

jonction [ʒɔ̃ksjɔ̃] *nf* **1.** [réunion] joining, junction ■ **opérer la ~ de deux câbles** to join up two cables ■ **opérer la ~ de deux armées** to combine two armies ■ **(point de) ~** meeting point *ou* junction ■ **à la ~** *ou* **au point de ~ des deux cortèges** where the two processions meet **2.** DR : **~ d'instance** joinder (of causes of action) **3.** ÉLECTRON, INFORM, RAIL & TÉLÉCOM junction.

jongler [3] [ʒɔ̃gle] *vi* **1.** [avec des balles] to juggle ■ **~ avec le ballon** FOOTBALL to juggle with the ball **2.** *fig* **~ avec** [manier avec aisance] to juggle with ■ **elle aime ~ avec les mots** she likes to juggle *ou* to play with words.

jonglerie [ʒɔ̃gləri] *nf* **1.** [action] juggling ■ [art] juggling, jugglery ■ [tour de passe-passe] juggling trick **2.** [ruse] juggling, trickery.

jongleur, euse [ʒɔ̃glœr, øz] *nm, f* juggler.
◆ **jongleur** *nm* HIST (wandering) minstrel, jongleur.

jonque [ʒɔ̃k] *nf* NAUT junk.

jonquille [ʒɔ̃kij] *nf* (wild) daffodil, jonquil.

Jordanie [ʒɔrdani] *npr f* : **(la) ~** Jordan.

jordanien, enne [ʒɔrdanjɛ̃, ɛn] *adj* Jordanian.
◆ **Jordanien, enne** *nm, f* Jordanian.

Joseph [ʒɔzef] *npr* : **saint ~** Saint Joseph.

Joséphine [ʒɔzefin] *npr* : **l'impératrice ~** the Empress Josephine.

Josué [ʒɔzɥe] *npr* Joshua.

jota [xɔta] *nf* [lettre, danse] jota.

jouable [ʒwabl] *adj* **1.** MUS & THÉÂTRE playable **2.** SPORT [coup] which can be played, feasible ■ **le coup n'est pas ~** it's not feasible, it's impossible.

joual [ʒwal] *nm* *Québec* joual.

joue [ʒu] *nf* **1.** ANAT cheek ■ **~ contre ~** cheek to cheek ■ **ce bébé a de bonnes ~s** this baby's got really chubby cheeks
2. CULIN : **~ de bœuf** ox cheek.
◆ **joues** *nfpl* NAUT bows.
◆ **en joue** *loc adv* : **coucher un fusil en ~** to take aim with *ou* to aim a rifle ■ **coucher *ou* mettre qqn/qqch en ~** to (take) aim at sb/sthg ■ **tenir qqn/qqch en ~** to hold sb/sthg in one's sights ■ **en ~!** take aim!

jouer [6] [ʒwe] ◇ *vi* **1.** [s'amuser] to play ■ **~ au ballon/au train électrique/à la poupée** to play with a ball/an electric train/a doll ■ **~ à la guerre** to play soldiers ■ **~ à la marchande/au docteur** to play (at) shops/doctors and nurses ■ **on ne joue pas avec un fusil!** a gun isn't a toy! ■ **il jouait avec sa gomme** he was playing *ou* fiddling with his eraser ■ **~ avec les sentiments de qqn** to play *ou* to trifle with sb's feelings ■ **tu joues avec ta santé/vie** you're gambling with your health/life ■ **il a passé sa soirée à faire ~ le chien avec la balle** he spent the evening throwing the ball around for the dog ▶ **je ne joue plus** *pr* I'm not playing anymore ; *fig* I don't want to have any part of this any more
2. LOISIRS & SPORT to play ■ **~ au golf/football/squash** to play golf/football/squash ■ **~ aux cartes/au billard** to play cards/billiards ■ **il joue à l'avant/à l'arrière** he plays up front/in defence ■ **(c'est) à toi de ~** [aux cartes] (it's) your turn ; [aux échecs] (it's) your move ; *fig* now it's your move ■ **ils ont bien joué en deuxième mi-temps** there was some good play in the second half ■ **~ contre qqn/une équipe** to play (against) sb/a team ▶ **à quel jeu joues-tu?** what do you think you're playing at? ■ **ne joue pas au plus fin avec moi!** don't try to be smart *ou* clever with me!
3. [parier - au casino] to gamble ; [- en Bourse] to play, to gamble ; [- aux courses] to bet ■ **~ à la roulette** to play roulette ■ **~ aux courses** to bet on horses ■ **~ au loto sportif** ≃ to do the pools *UK*, ≃ to play the pools *US* ■ **~ à la Bourse** to gamble on *ou* to speculate on *ou* to play the Stock Exchange
4. CINÉ & THÉÂTRE to act, to perform ■ **~ dans un film/une pièce** to be in a film/a play ■ **j'ai déjà joué avec lui** I've already worked with him ■ **nous jouons à l'Apollo en ce moment** at the moment, we are playing at *ou* our play is on at the Apollo ■ **elle joue vraiment bien** she's a really good actress
5. MUS to play, to perform ■ **bien/mal ~** [gén] to be a good/bad musician ; [dans un concert] to give a good/bad performance, to play well/badly ■ **tu joues d'un instrument?** do *ou* can you play an instrument? ■ **elle joue très bien du piano/de la clarinette** she's a very good pianist/a very good clarinet player
6. [intervenir - facteur] to be of consequence *ou* of importance ; [- clause] to apply ■ **les événements récents ont joué dans leur décision** recent events have been a factor in *ou* have affected *ou* have influenced their decision ■ **il a fait ~ la clause 3 pour obtenir des indemnités** he had recourse to *ou* made use of clause 3 to obtain compensation ■ **il a fait ~ ses relations pour obtenir le poste** he pulled some strings to get the job ■ **~ pour *ou* en faveur de qqn** to work in sb's favour ■ **~ contre *ou* en défaveur de qqn** to work against sb
7. [se déformer - bois] to warp ■ [avoir du jeu] to work loose
8. [fonctionner] : **faire ~ une clé (dans une serrure)** [pour ouvrir la porte] to turn a key (in a lock) ; [pour l'essayer] to try a key (in a lock) ■ **fais ~ le pêne** get the bolt to slide ■ **faire ~ un ressort** to trigger a spring
9. [faire des effets] : **une brise légère jouait dans *ou* avec ses cheveux** a gentle breeze was playing with her hair.
◇ *vt* **1.** LOISIRS & SPORT [match, carte] to play ■ [pièce d'échecs] to move, to play ■ **ils jouent la balle de match** it's match point ■ **ils ont joué le ballon à la main** they passed the ball ■ **j'ai joué cœur** I played hearts ‖ *fig* **il joue un drôle de jeu** he's playing a strange *ou* funny (little) game ▶ **bien joué!** CARTES & SPORT well played! ; JEUX good move! ; *fig* well done! ■ **~ le jeu** to play the game ■ **rien n'est encore joué** nothing has been decided yet
2. [au casino - somme] to stake, to wager ; [- numéro] to play (on) *(insép)* ■ [au turf - somme] to bet, to stake ; [- cheval] to bet on *(insép)*, to back ■ **je ne joue jamais d'argent** I never play for money ■ **il joue d'énormes sommes** he gambles vast sums, he plays for high stakes *ou* big money ■ **~ 50 euros sur un cheval** to bet 50 euros on a horse ■ **jouons les consommations!** the loser pays for the drinks! ▶ **~ gros jeu** *pr* & *fig* to play for high stakes *ou* big money
3. [risquer - avenir, réputation] to stake
4. [interpréter - personnage] to play (the part of), to act ; [- concerto] to play, to perform ■ **il a très bien joué Cyrano/la fugue** he gave an excellent performance as Cyrano/of the fugue ■ **l'intrigue est passionnante mais c'est mal joué** the plot is gripping but the acting is poor ■ **~ Brecht** [acteur] to play Brecht, to be in a Brecht play ; [troupe] to play Brecht, to put on (a) Brecht (play) ■ **~ du Chopin** to play (some) Chopin ■ **elle ne sait pas ~ la tragédie** she's not a good tragic actress ■ *fig* **ne joue pas les innocents!** don't play the innocent *ou* don't act innocent (with me)! ■ **~ la prudence** to play it safe ■ **~ l'étonnement/le remords** to pretend to be surprised/sorry ▶ **~ un rôle** *pr* & *fig* to play a part
5. [montrer - film, pièce] to put on *(sép)*, to show ■ **qu'est-ce qu'on joue en ce moment?** what's on at the moment? ■ **la pièce a toujours été jouée en anglais** the play has always been performed in English
6. *sout* [berner] to dupe, to deceive.
◆ **jouer de** *v+prép* **1.** [se servir de] to make use of, to use ■ **~ du couteau/marteau** to wield a knife/hammer ■ **elle joue de son infirmité** she plays on *ou* uses her handicap ▶ **~ des poings** to use one's fists
2. [être victime de] : **~ de malchance *ou* malheur** to be dogged by misfortune *ou* bad luck.
◆ **jouer sur** *v+prép* [crédulité, sentiment] to play on *(insép)* ■ **arrête de ~ sur les mots!** stop quibbling!
◆ **se jouer** ◇ *vp (emploi passif)* **1.** [film] to be on, to be shown ■ [pièce] to be on, to be performed ■ [morceau de musique] to be played *ou* performed ■ **ce passage se joue legato** this passage should be played legato ■ **bien des drames se sont joués derrière ces murs** *sout* these walls have witnessed many a scene
2. SPORT to be played
3. [être en jeu] to be at stake ■ **des sommes considérables se jouent chaque soir** huge amounts of money are played for every night.
◇ *vpi* **1.** [dépendre] : **mon sort va se ~ sur cette décision** my fate hangs on this decision ■ **l'avenir du pays se joue dans cette négociation** the fate of the country hinges *ou* depends on the outcome of these negotiations
2. *sout* [produire un effet] to play
3. *loc* **(comme) en se jouant** *sout* with the greatest of ease.
◆ **se jouer de** *vp+prép* **1.** [ignorer] to ignore
2. *litt* [duper] to deceive, to dupe, to fool.

jouet [ʒwɛ] *nm* **1.** [d'enfant] toy **2.** [victime] plaything ■ **j'ai été le ~ de leur machination** I was a pawn in their game ■ **tu as été le ~ d'une illusion** you've been the victim of an illusion **3.** ÉQUIT curb chain.

joueur, euse [ʒwœr, øz] ◇ *adj* **1.** [chaton, chiot] playful **2.** [parieur] : **être ~** to be fond of gambling.

<> *nm, f* **1.** MUS & SPORT player ▪ **~s de cartes/d'échecs** card/chess players ▪ **~ de tambour** drummer ▪ **~ de trompette** trumpeter **2.** [pour de l'argent] gambler ▪ **être beau/mauvais ~** to be a good/bad loser *ou* sport.

joufflu, e [ʒufly] *adj* [bébé] chubby-cheeked ▪ **un visage ~** a chubby *ou* moon *péj* face.

joug [ʒu] *nm* **1.** AGRIC yoke **2.** *litt* [assujettissement] yoke ▪ **secouer le ~** to throw off one's yoke **3.** [d'une balance] beam.

jouir [32] [ʒwir] *vi* **1.** △ [gén] : **ça me fait ~** I get a kick out of it **2.** △ [sexuellement] to come.

◆ **jouir de** *v+prép* **1.** [profiter de - vie, jeunesse] to enjoy, to get pleasure out of **2.** [se réjouir de - victoire] to enjoy, to delight in *(insép)* **3.** [avoir - panorama] to command ; [- ensoleillement, droit] to enjoy, to have ; [- privilège, réputation] to enjoy, to command ▪ **il ne jouit pas de toutes ses facultés** he isn't in full possession of his faculties.

jouissance [ʒwisɑ̃s] *nf* **1.** [plaisir] enjoyment, pleasure ▪ [orgasme] climax, orgasm **2.** DR [usage] use ▪ **avoir la ~ de qqch** to have the use of sthg ▪ **entrer en ~ de qqch** to enter *ou* to come into possession of sthg ▪ **avoir la (pleine) ~ de ses droits** to enjoy one's (full) rights ▶ **~ légale** legal enjoyment.

jouisseur, euse [ʒwisœr, øz] *nm, f* pleasure-seeker.

jouissif, ive [ʒwisif, iv] *adj fam* **ce film, c'était ~** that film was a treat!

joujou, x [ʒuʒu] *nm* [jouet] toy, plaything ▪ **faire ~ avec** *fam* to play with ▪ **va faire ~** *fam* go and play.

joujouthèque [ʒuʒutɛk] *nf Québec* games library.

joule [ʒul] *nm* joule ▪ **effet Joule** Joule effect.

jour [ʒur] *nm*

> **A.** DIVISION TEMPORELLE
> **B.** CLARTÉ
> **C.** OUVERTURE

A. DIVISION TEMPORELLE

1. [division du calendrier] day ▪ **un mois de trente ~s** a thirty-day month ▪ **un ~ de repos** a day of rest ▪ **un ~ de travail** a working day *UK*, a workday ▪ **il me reste des ~s à prendre avant la fin de l'année** I still have some (days) to take before the end of the year ▪ **dans deux/quelques ~s** in two/a few days' time ▪ **il est resté des ~s entiers sans sortir** he didn't go out for days on end ▪ **tous les ~s** every day ▶ **au ~ le ~** [sans s'occuper du lendemain] from day to day ; [précairement] from hand to mouth ▪ **de ~ en ~** [grandir] daily, day by day ; [varier] from day to day, from one day to the next ▪ **d'un ~ à l'autre** [incessamment] any day (now) ; [de façon imprévisible] from one day to the next ▪ **~ après ~** [constamment] day after day ; [graduellement] day by day ▪ **~ par ~** day by day ▪ **~ pour ~** to the day
2. [exprime la durée] : **un bébé d'un ~** a day-old baby ▪ **un ~ de : c'est à un ~ de marche/voiture** it's one day's walk/drive away ▪ **nous avons eu trois ~s de pluie** we had rain for three days *ou* three days of rain ▪ **j'en ai pour deux ~s de travail** it's going to take me two days' work ▪ **ça va prendre un ~ de lessivage et trois ~s de peinture** it'll take one day to wash down and three days to paint
3. [date précise] day ▪ **l'autre ~** the other day ▪ **le ~ où** the day *ou* time that ▪ **dès le premier ~** from the very first day ▪ **comme au premier ~** as it was in the beginning ▪ **ils sont amoureux comme au premier ~** they're as much in love as when they first met ▪ **le ~ est loin où j'étais heureux** it's a long time since I've been happy ▪ **le ~ viendra où** the day will come when ▪ **un ~** one day ▪ **un ~ que** one day when ▪ **le ~ de la rentrée** ÉDUC the first day (back) at school ▪ **le vendredi, c'est le ~ de Nora/du poisson** Friday is Nora's day/is the day we have fish ▶ **le ~ de l'an** New Year's Day ▪ **le ~ du Jugement dernier** doomsday, Judgment Day ▪ **le ~ des morts** All Souls' Day ▪ **le ~ des Rois** Twelfth Night ▪ **le ~ du Seigneur** the Lord's Day, the Sabbath ▪ **le grand ~ pour elle/lui** her/his big day ▪ **son manteau/son discours des grands ~s** the coat she wears/the speech she makes on important occasions ▪ **mes chaussures de tous les ~s** my everyday *ou* ordinary shoes, the shoes I wear everyday ▪ **ce n'est pas mon ~!** it's not my day! ▪ **ce n'est (vraiment) pas le ~!, tu choisis bien ton ~!** *iron* you really picked your day! ▪ **il est dans un mauvais ~** he's having one of his off days ▪ **un beau ~** one (fine) day ▪ **un de ces ~s, un ~ ou l'autre** one of these days ▪ **à un de ces ~s!** see you soon! ▪ **à ce ~** to this day, to date ▪ **au ~ d'aujourd'hui** *fam* in this day and age

B. CLARTÉ

1. [lumière] daylight ▪ **le ~ baisse** it's getting dark ▪ **il fait (encore) ~** it's still light ▪ **il faisait grand ~** it was broad daylight ▪ **le ~ se lève** the sun is rising ▪ **avant le ~** before dawn *ou* daybreak ▪ **au petit ~** at dawn *ou* daybreak ▪ **~ et nuit, nuit et ~** day and night, night and day ▪ **je dors le ~** I sleep during the day *ou* in the daytime ▪ **examine-le au *ou* en plein ~** look at it in the daylight ▶ **~ artificiel** artificial daylight
2. [aspect] : **sous un certain ~** in a certain light ▪ **le marché apparaît sous un ~ défavorable** the market does not look promising ▶ **enfin, il s'est montré sous son vrai ~!** he's shown his true colours at last! ▪ **voir qqch sous son vrai *ou* véritable ~** to see sthg in its true light ▪ **sous un faux ~** in a false light
3. *loc* **donner le ~ à** [enfant] to give birth to, to bring into the world ; [projet] to give birth to ; [mode, tendance] to start ▪ **jeter un ~ nouveau sur** to throw *ou* to cast new light on ▪ **mettre au ~** to bring to light ▪ **voir le ~** [bébé] to be born ; [journal] to come out ; [théorie, invention] to appear ; [projet] to see the light of day

C. OUVERTURE

1. [interstice - entre des planches] gap, chink ; [- dans un feuillage] gap
2. ARCHIT opening ▪ ART light
3. COUT opening *(made by drawing threads)* ▪ **des ~s** openwork, drawn work
4. *loc* **se faire ~** to emerge, to become clear ▪ **l'idée s'est fait ~ dans son esprit** the idea dawned on her.

◆ **jours** *nmpl* **1.** [vie] days, life ▪ **mettre fin à ses ~s** to put an end to one's life ▪ **ses ~s sont comptés** his days are numbered ▪ **ses ~s ne sont plus en danger** we no longer fear for her life **2.** [époque] : **de la Rome antique à nos ~s** from Ancient Rome to the present day ▪ **passer des ~s heureux** to have a good time ▶ **les mauvais ~s** [les moments difficiles] unhappy days, hard times ; [les jours où rien ne va] bad days ▪ **il a sa tête des mauvais ~s** it looks like he's in a bad mood ▪ **ce manteau a connu des ~s meilleurs** this coat has seen better days ▪ **ses vieux ~s** his old age ▪ **de nos ~s** these days, nowadays ▪ **les beaux ~s** [printemps] springtime ; [été] summertime ▪ **ah, c'étaient les beaux ~s!** [jeunesse] ah, those were the days!

◆ **à jour** <> *loc adj* [cahier, travail] kept up to date ▪ [rapport] up-to-date, up-to-the-minute ▪ **être à ~ de ses cotisations** to have paid one's subscription.
<> *loc adv* up to date ▪ **tenir/mettre qqch à ~** to keep/to bring sthg up to date ▪ **mettre sa correspondance à ~** to catch up on one's letter writing.

◆ **au grand jour** *loc adv* : **faire qqch au grand ~** *fig* to do sthg openly *ou* in broad daylight ▪ **l'affaire fut étalée au grand ~** the affair was brought out into the open.

◆ **de jour** <> *loc adj* [hôpital, unité] day, daytime *(modif).*
<> *loc adv* [travailler] during the day ▪ [conduire] in the daytime, during the day ▪ **être de ~** to be on day duty *ou* on days ▪ **de ~ comme de nuit** day and night.

◆ **du jour** *loc adj* [mode, tendance, préoccupation] current, contemporary ▪ [homme] of the moment ▪ **le journal du ~** the day's paper ▪ **un œuf du ~** a new-laid *ou* newly-laid *ou* freshly-laid egg ▪ **le poisson est-il du ~?** is the fish fresh (today)?

◆ **du jour au lendemain** *loc adv* overnight ▪ **il a changé d'avis du ~ au lendemain** he changed his mind overnight.

◆ **d'un jour** *loc adj* short-lived, ephemeral *sout*, transient *sout*.

◆ **par jour** *loc adv* a day, per day ▪ **trois fois par ~** three times a day.

Jourdain [ʒurdɛ̃] <> *npr m* : **le ~** the (River) Jordan.
<> *npr* : **Monsieur ~** *main character in Molière's 'le Bourgeois Gentilhomme' (1670), who takes lessons in his attempt to become a gentleman; best remembered for his amazed discovery that he has been speaking prose all his life.*

journal, aux [ʒurnal, o] *nm* **1.** [publication] paper, newspaper ▪ **~ du matin/soir/dimanche** morning/evening/Sunday paper *ou* newspaper ▪ **c'est dans *ou* sur le ~** it's in the paper

■ ~ grand format broadsheet ⊙ ~ à scandale ou à sensation scandal sheet ■ ~ interne in-house newspaper ■ le Journal officiel (de la République Française) *official publication in which public notices appear* ■ ≃ Hansard *UK*, ≃ Federal Register *US* **2.** [bureau] office, paper **3.** RADIO & TV [informations] : ~ parlé/télévisé radio/television news ■ ils l'ont dit au ~ *fam* they said so on the news **4.** [carnet] diary, journal ■ ~ (intime) private diary ■ tenir un ~ to keep a diary ■ ~ de bord NAUT log, logbook **5.** COMM account book.

LE JOURNAL OFFICIEL

This bulletin diffuses information about new laws, includes summaries of parliamentary debates, and informs the public of any important government business. New companies are obliged by law to publish an announcement in the *Journal officiel*.

journalier, ère [ʒurnalje, ɛr] *adj* daily.
◆ **journalier** *nm* AGRIC day labourer.

journalisme [ʒurnalism] *nm* journalism ■ **faire du ~** to be a journalist.

journaliste [ʒurnalist] *nmf* journalist ■ **assaillie par les ~s** mobbed by reporters ■ **les ~s de la rédaction** the editorial staff.

journalistique [ʒurnalistik] *adj* journalistic.

journée [ʒurne] *nf* **1.** [durée] day ■ **je n'ai rien fait de la ~** I haven't done a thing all day ■ **en début de ~** early in the morning *ou* day ■ **en fin de ~** at the end of the day, in the early evening ■ **bonne ~!** have a good *ou US* nice day! ■ **à une ~/deux ~s d'ici** one day's/two days' journey away **2.** ÉCON & INDUST : **la ~ de 8 heures** the 8-hour day ■ **faire des ~s de 12 heures** to work a 12-hour day *ou* 12 hours a day ■ **faire de longues ~s** to work long hours ■ **je commence/finis ma ~ à midi** I start/stop work at noon ■ **embauché/payé à la ~** employed/paid on a daily basis ■ **~ de travail** working day ■ **faire des ~s (chez)** [femme de ménage] to work as a daily *UK ou* a maid *US*(for) ⊙ **~ d'action** day of (industrial) action ■ **faire la ~ continue** [entreprise] to work a continuous shift ; [magasin] to stay open over the lunch hour **3.** [activité organisée] day ■ **les ~s du cancer** [séminaire] the cancer (research) conference ; [campagne] cancer research (campaign) week *UK* ■ **les ~s (parlementaires) du parti** POLIT ≃ the (Parliamentary) Party conference *UK*, ≃ the party convention *US* ⊙ **~ portes ouvertes** open day.

journellement [ʒurnɛlmɑ̃] *adv* **1.** [chaque jour] daily, every day **2.** [fréquemment] every day.

joute [ʒut] *nf* **1.** HIST joust, tilt **2.** *litt* [rivalité] joust ■ [dialogue] sparring match ■ **~ littéraire/oratoire** literary/verbal contest.

jouteur, euse [ʒutœr, øz] *nm, f* **1.** SPORT water jouster **2.** *fig & sout* adversary, opponent.

jouvence [ʒuvɑ̃s] *nf* ▷ **bain**, ▷ **eau**.

jouvenceau, x [ʒuvɑ̃so] *nm hum* youngster, stripling *hum* ■ **je ne suis plus un ~** I'm no spring chicken.

jouvencelle [ʒuvɑ̃sɛl] *nf hum* damsel, maiden ■ **ce n'est qu'une ~** she's a mere slip of a lass.

jouxter [3] [ʒukste] *vt* to be adjacent to, to adjoin.

jovial, e, als *ou* **aux** [ʒɔvjal, o] *adj* [visage] jovial, jolly ■ [rire] jovial, hearty ■ [caractère] jovial, cheerful.

jovialement [ʒɔvjalmɑ̃] *adv* jovially.

jovialité [ʒɔvjalite] *nf* joviality, cheerfulness ■ **sa ~ le rendait très populaire** his cheerful manner made him very popular.

joyau, x [ʒwajo] *nm* **1.** [bijou] gem, jewel ■ **les ~x de la couronne** the crown jewels **2.** *fig* [monument] gem ■ [œuvre d'art] jewel.

joyeusement [ʒwajøzmɑ̃] *adv* joyfully, gladly ■ **elle accepta ~** she gladly accepted.

joyeux, euse [ʒwajø, øz] *adj* joyful, joyous, merry ■ **une joyeuse nouvelle** glad tidings ■ **et elle vient avec lui? c'est ~!** *iron* so she's coming with him? that'll be nice for you! ⊙ **c'est un ~ drille** he's a jolly fellow.

JT *nm* = **journal télévisé.**

jubilaire [ʒybilɛr] ◇ *adj* jubilee *(modif)* ■ **année ~** jubilee year.
◇ *nmf Suisse* partygoer *(at a 'jubilé')*.

jubilant, e [ʒybilɑ̃, ɑ̃t] *adj fam* jubilant, exultant.

jubilation [ʒybilasjɔ̃] *nf* jubilation, exultation ■ **avec ~** jubilantly.

jubilé [ʒybile] *nm* **1.** [célébration de 50 ans d'existence] jubilee **2.** *Suisse celebration marking the anniversary of a club, the arrival of a member of staff in a company etc.*

jubiler [3] [ʒybile] *vi* to be jubilant, to rejoice, to exult.

jucher [3] [ʒyʃe] ◇ *vt* to perch ■ **juchée sur les épaules de son père** perched on her father's shoulders.
◇ *vi* **1.** [faisan, poule] to perch **2.** *fam* [personne] to live.
◆ **se jucher sur** *vp+prép* to perch (up) on.

Juda [ʒyda] *npr* Judah.

judaïcité [ʒydaisite] *nf* Jewishness.

judaïque [ʒydaik] *adj* Judaic, Judaical.

judaïser [3] [ʒydaize] *vt* to Judaize.

judaïsme [ʒydaism] *nm* Judaism.

judas [ʒyda] *nm* **1.** [ouverture] judas (hole) **2.** [traître] Judas.

Judas [ʒyda] *npr* : **~ (Iscariote)** Judas (Iscariot).

Judée [ʒyde] *npr f* : **(la) ~** Judaea, Judea.

judéo-allemand, e [ʒydeɔalmɑ̃, ɑ̃d] *(mpl* **judéo-allemands**, *fpl* **judéo-allemandes)** *adj* Judaeo-German.
◆ **judéo-allemand** *nm* LING Judaeo-German.

judéo-chrétien, enne [ʒydeɔkretjɛ̃, ɛn] *(mpl* **judéo-chrétiens**, *fpl* **judéo-chrétiennes)** *adj* Judaeo-Christian.
◆ **Judéo-Chrétien, enne** *nm, f* Judaeo-Christian.

judéo-christianisme [ʒydeɔkristjanism] *(pl* **judéo-christianismes)** *nm* Judaeo-Christianity.

judéo-espagnol, e [ʒydeɔɛspaɲɔl] *(mpl* **judéo-espagnols**, *fpl* **judéo-espagnoles)** *adj* Judaeo-Spanish.
◆ **judéo-espagnol** *nm* LING Judaeo-Spanish.

judiciaire [ʒydisjɛr] *adj* judicial, judiciary.

judiciairement [ʒydisjɛrmɑ̃] *adv* judicially.

judiciarisation [ʒydisjarizasjɔ̃] *nf* judicialization.

judiciariser [3] [ʒydisjarize] *vt* to settle (sthg) in court, to resort to legal action over (sthg) ■ *péj* to drag (sthg) through the courts.

judicieusement [ʒydisjøzmɑ̃] *adv* [décider] judiciously, shrewdly ■ [agencer, organiser] cleverly.

judicieux, euse [ʒydisjø, øz] *adj* [personne, esprit] judicious, shrewd ■ [manœuvre, proposition, décision] shrewd ■ [choix] judicious ■ [plan] well thought-out ■ **peu ~** ill-advised.

judo [ʒydo] *nm* judo ■ **au ~** in judo.

judoka [ʒydɔka] *nmf* judoka.

juge [ʒyʒ] *nmf* **1.** DR judge ■ **le ~ X** Judge X ■ **Madame/Monsieur le Juge X** ≃ Mrs/Mr Justice X *UK* ; ≃ Judge X *US* ■ **jamais, Monsieur le ~!** never, Your Honour! ■ **les ~s** ≃ the Bench ■ **être nommé ~** to be appointed judge, ≃ to be raised to the Bench *UK* ; ≃ to be appointed to the Bench *US* ■ **aller/se retrouver devant le ~** to appear/to end up in court ⊙ **~ aux affaires matrimoniales** divorce court judge ■ **~ de l'application des peines** *judge who follows up the way an individual sentence is carried out during probation and post-release periods* ■ **~ d'enfants** children's judge, juvenile magistrate *UK* ■ **~ d'instance, ~ de paix** *vieilli* Justice of the Peace ■ **~ d'instruction** ≃ examining magistrate *ou* justice *UK*, ≃ committing magistrate *US* **2.** [personne compétente] : **j'en suis seul ~** I am sole judge (of the matter) ■ **je te laisse ~ de la situation** I'll let you be the judge of the situation ■ **être bon/mauvais ~ en matière de** to be a good/bad judge of **3.** SPORT judge ■ **~ de filet/fond** net cord/foot fault judge ■ **~ d'arrivée** finishing judge ■ **~ de ligne**

linesman ■ ~ **de touche** FOOTBALL linesman ; RUGBY linesman, touch judge **4.** BIBLE : **le Livre des Juges, les Juges** the (Book of) Judges.

jugé [ʒyʒe] ◆ **au jugé** *loc adv* at a guess ■ **au ~, je dirais que...** at a guess, I would say that... ■ **tirer au ~** to fire blind.

jugeable [ʒyʒabl] *adj* DR judicable.

juge-arbitre [ʒyʒarbitr] (*pl* **juges-arbitres**) *nm* referee.

jugement [ʒyʒmɑ̃] *nm* **1.** DR [verdict] sentence, ruling, decision ■ **porter un ~ prématuré sur qqch** to judge sthg too hastily DR : **prononcer** *ou* **rendre un ~** to pass sentence, to give a ruling ■ **faire passer qqn en ~** to bring sb to (stand) trial ■ **passer en ~** to stand trial ➤ **~ déclaratoire** declaratory judgment ■ **~ par défaut** judgment in absentia *ou* default ■ **~ définitif** final judgment **2.** RELIG : **le ~ dernier** the Last Judgment, Day of Judgment ■ **le ~ de Dieu** HIST the Ordeal **3.** [discernement] judgment, flair ■ **erreur de ~** error of judgment ■ **faire preuve de ~** to show sound *ou* good judgment ■ **elle a du/n'a aucun ~ (en matière de...)** she's a good/no judge (of...) **4.** [évaluation] judgment ■ **~ préconçu** prejudgment, preconception ■ **formuler un ~ sur qqch/qqn** to express an opinion about sthg/sb ■ **porter un ~ sur qqch/qqn** to pass judgment on sthg/sb ■ **le ~ de l'histoire/la postérité** the verdict of history/posterity ➤ **~ de valeur** value judgment.

jugeote [ʒyʒɔt] *nf fam* commonsense.

juger [17] [ʒyʒe] *vt* **1.** DR [accusé] to try ■ [affaire] to judge, to try, to sit in judgment on ■ **être jugé pour vol** to be tried *ou* to stand trial for theft ■ **elle a été jugée coupable/non coupable** she was found guilty/not guilty ■ *(en usage absolu)* **l'histoire/la postérité jugera** history/posterity will judge
2. [trancher] to judge, to decide ■ **à toi de ~ (si/quand...)** it's up to you to decide *ou* to judge (whether/when...) ■ **~ un différend** to arbitrate in a dispute
3. [se faire une opinion de] to judge ■ **~ qqch/qqn à sa juste valeur** to form a correct opinion of sthg/sb ■ *(en usage absolu)* **moi, je ne juge pas** I'm not in a position to judge, I'm not making any judgment ■ **~ par soi-même** to judge for o.s. ■ **il ne faut pas ~ sur** *ou* **d'après les apparences** don't judge from *ou* go by appearances
4. [considérer] : **~ qqn capable/incompétent** to consider sb capable/incompetent ■ **son état est jugé très préoccupant** his condition is believed to be serious ■ **jugé bon pour le service** declared fit to join *ou* fit for the army ■ **mesures jugées insuffisantes** measures deemed inadequate ■ **~ qqn bien/mal** to have a good/poor opinion of sb ■ **vous me jugez mal** [à tort] you're misjudging me ■ **~ bon de faire qqch** to think fit to do sthg ■ **agissez comme vous jugerez bon** do as you think fit *ou* appropriate.
◆ **juger de** *v+prép* to judge ■ **à en ~ par son large sourire** if her broad smile is anything to go by ■ **si j'en juge par ce que j'ai lu** judging from *ou* by what I've read, if what I've read is anything to go by ■ **jugez-en vous-même** judge *ou* see for yourself ■ **jugez de mon indignation** imagine my indignation, imagine how indignant I felt.
◆ **se juger** ◇ *vp (emploi réfléchi)* : **elle se juge sévèrement** she has a harsh opinion of herself.
◇ *vp (emploi passif)* **1.** DR : **l'affaire se jugera mardi** the case will be heard on Tuesday
2. [se mesurer] to be judged
3. [se considérer] : **les commerçants se jugent lésés** shopkeepers consider *ou* think themselves hard done by.

jugulaire [ʒygylɛr] ◇ *adj* ANAT jugular ■ **glandes/veines ~s** jugular glands/veins.
◇ *nf* **1.** ANAT jugular (vein) **2.** [bride] chin strap.

juguler [3] [ʒygyle] *vt* **1.** [arrêter - hémorragie, maladie] to halt, to check ; [- sanglots] to suppress, to repress ; [- chômage] to curb ■ **~ l'inflation** to curb inflation **2.** [étouffer - révolte] to quell.

juif, ive [ʒɥif, iv] *adj* Jewish.
◆ **Juif, ive** *nm, f* Jew (*f* Jewess).
◆ **juif** *nm fam* **le petit ~** the funny bone.

juillet [ʒɥijɛ] *nm* July ■ **la fête du 14 ~** Bastille day celebrations, *voir aussi* **mars**.

LA FÊTE DU 14 JUILLET

The celebrations to mark the anniversary of the storming of the Bastille begin on July 13th with outdoor public dances *(les bals du 14 juillet)*, and continue on the 14th with a military parade in the morning and a firework display in the evening.

juilletiste [ʒɥijetist] *nmf person who goes on holiday in July.*

juin [ʒɥɛ̃] *nm* June, *voir aussi* **mars**.

juive [ʒɥiv] *f* ⊳ **juif**.

juke-box [dʒukbɔks] (*pl inv ou pl* **juke-boxes**) *nm* jukebox.

jules△ [ʒyl] *nm* [amant] boyfriend ■ [mari] old man.

Jules [ʒyl] *npr* [pape] Julius ■ **~ César** Julius Caesar.

julienne [ʒyljɛn] *nf* **1.** CULIN : **~ (de légumes)** (vegetable) julienne **2.** ZOOL ling **3.** BOT dame's violet.

jumbo-jet [dʒœmbodʒɛt] (*pl* **jumbo-jets**) *nm* jumbo (jet).

jumeau, elle, x [ʒymo, ɛl] ◇ *adj* **1.** BIOL twin *(modif)* **2.** [symétrique] twin *(modif)*, identical ■ **les flèches jumelles de la cathédrale** the twin spires of the cathedral.
◇ *nm, f* **1.** BIOL twin ■ **vrais/faux ~x** identical/fraternal twins **2.** [sosie] double.
◆ **jumeau, x** *nm* **1.** ANAT gemellus muscle **2.** CULIN neck of beef.

jumelage [ʒymlaʒ] *nm* **1.** [association] twinning **2.** RAIL paired running.

jumelé, e [ʒymle] *adj* **1.** [fenêtres] double ■ [colonne] twin ■ [villes] twin, twinned **2.** NAUT twin.
◆ **jumelé** *nm* first and second forecast.

jumeler [24] [ʒymle] *vt* **1.** [villes] to twin ■ **être jumelé à** to be twinned with **2.** [moteurs] to combine, to couple.

jumelle [ʒymɛl] *f* ⊳ **jumeau**.

jumellerai *etc v* ⊳ **jumeler**.

jumelles [ʒymɛl] ◇ *fpl* ⊳ **jumeau**.
◇ *nfpl* **1.** OPT binoculars ■ **~ de théâtre** *ou* **spectacle** opera glasses **2.** NAUT fishes, fish pieces.

jument [ʒymɑ̃] *nf* mare ■ **~ poulinière** brood mare.

jumping [dʒœmpiŋ] *nm* ÉQUIT showjumping.

jungle [ʒœ̃gl] *nf* **1.** GÉOGR jungle **2.** *fig* jungle ■ **la ~ des villes** the concrete jungle ■ **la ~ des affaires** the jungle of the business world.

junior [ʒynjɔr] ◇ *adj inv* **1.** [fils] junior ■ **Douglas Fairbanks ~** Douglas Fairbanks Junior **2.** [destiné aux adolescents] junior ■ **les nouveaux blousons ~** the new jackets for teenagers **3.** [débutant] junior.
◇ *adj* SPORT junior ■ **les équipes ~s** the junior teams.
◇ *nmf* SPORT junior.

junkie△ [dʒœnki, *(pl)* dʒœnkiz] *nmf* junkie△, junky△.

Junon [ʒynɔ̃] *npr* Juno.

junte [ʒœ̃t] *nf* junta.

jupe [ʒyp] *nf* **1.** [vêtement] skirt ■ **~ cloche/entravée/plissée** bell/hobble/pleated skirt ■ **~ à godets** *ou* **évasée** flared skirt ■ **~ portefeuille** wrapover *ou* wraparound (skirt) ■ **il est toujours dans les** *ou* **accroché aux ~s de sa mère** he's tied to his mother's apron strings **2.** TECHNOL [d'un aéroglisseur] skirt, apron ■ [d'un piston, d'un rouleau] skirt.

jupe-culotte [ʒypkylɔt] (*pl* **jupes-culottes**) *nf* (pair of) culottes.

jupette [ʒypɛt] *nf* short skirt.

Jupiter [ʒypitɛr] *npr* **1.** ASTRON Jupiter **2.** MYTHOL Jupiter, Jove.

jupon [ʒypɔ̃] *nm* [vêtement] petticoat, slip, underskirt.

Jura [ʒyra] *npr m* **1.** [en France] : **le ~** [chaîne montagneuse] the Jura (Mountains) ; [département] the Jura *(département in Franche-Comté; chef-lieu: Lons-le-Saunier, code: 39)* **2.** [en Suisse] : **le ~** the Jura (canton).

jurassien, enne [ʒyrasjɛ̃, ɛn] *adj* from the Jura.

jurassique [ʒyrasik] <> *adj* Jurassic.
<> *nm* : **le ~** the Jurassic period.

juré, e [ʒyre] <> *adj* [ennemi] sworn ▪ **je ne recommencerai plus – (c'est) ~?** I won't do it again – promise?
<> *nm, f* DR member of a jury, juror, juryman *(f* jurywoman) ▪ **les ~s ont délibéré** the jury has *ou* have reached a decision ▪ **elle a été convoquée comme ~** she's had to report for jury service *UK ou* jury duty *US.*

jurer [3] [ʒyre] <> *vt* **1.** [promettre] to swear ▪ **je ne l'ai jamais vue, je le jure!** I've never seen her, I swear it! ▪ **~ allégeance/fidélité/obéissance à qqn** to swear *ou* to pledge allegiance/loyalty/obedience to sb ▪ **il a juré ma perte** he has sworn *ou* vowed to bring about my downfall ▪ **je te jure que c'est vrai** I swear it's true ▪ **~ de faire qqch** to swear to do sthg ▪ **j'ai juré de garder le secret** I'm sworn to secrecy ▪ **elle m'a fait ~ de garder le secret** she swore me to secrecy *sout* **2.** DR [suj: témoin] to swear ▪ **jurez-vous de dire la vérité, toute la vérité, rien que la vérité?** do you swear to tell the truth, the whole truth and nothing but the truth? ▪ **dites je le jure – je le jure** do you so swear? – I swear *ou* I do ▪ *(en usage absolu)* **~ sur la Bible/devant Dieu** to swear on the Bible/to God ▪ **~ sur l'honneur** to swear on one's honour ▪ **~ sur la tête de qqn** to swear on one's mother's grave.
<> *vi* **1.** [blasphémer] to swear, to curse ▪ **~ après qqn/qqch** to curse *ou* to swear at sb/sthg ▶ **~ comme un charretier** to swear like a trooper **2.** [détonner - couleurs, architecture] to clash, to jar **3.** *fig* **ils ne jurent que par leur nouvel entraîneur** they swear by their new coach.
◆ **jurer de** *v+prép* **1.** [affirmer] : **~ de son innocence** to swear to one's innocence ▪ **~ de sa bonne foi** to swear that one is sincere ▶ **il ne faut ~ de rien** you never can tell **2.** [au conditionnel] : **j'en jurerais** I'd swear to it ▪ **c'est peut-être mon agresseur, mais je n'en jurerais pas** he might be the man who attacked me but I wouldn't swear to it.
◆ **se jurer** <> *vp (emploi réciproque)* : **se ~ fidélité** to swear *ou* to vow to be faithful to each other.
<> *vp (emploi réfléchi)* : **se ~ de faire** to promise o.s. *ou* to vow to do ▪ **se ~ que** to vow to o.s. that.

juridiction [ʒyridiksjɔ̃] *nf* **1.** [pouvoir] jurisdiction ▪ **exercer sa ~** to exercise one's power ▪ **tomber sous la ~ de** to come under the jurisdiction of **2.** [tribunal] court (of law) ▪ [tribunaux] courts (of law) ▪ **~ d'instruction/de jugement** examining/penal courts ▪ **~ d'exception** special court ▪ **~ militaire** ≃ military courts ▪ **~ de premier degré** ≃ Court of first instance *UK* ▪ **~ de second degré** ≃ Court of Appeal *UK;* ≃ Appellate Court *US.*

juridictionnel, elle [ʒyridiksjɔnɛl] *adj* jurisdictional.

juridique [ʒyridik] *adj* [vocabulaire] legal, juridical ▪ **il a une formation ~** he studied law ▪ **situation ~** legal situation.

juridiquement [ʒyridikmɑ̃] *adv* legally, juridically.

juridisme [ʒyridism] *nm* legalism.

jurisconsulte [ʒyriskɔ̃sylt] *nm* jurisconsult.

jurisprudence [ʒyrisprydɑ̃s] *nf* [source de droit] case law, jurisprudence ▪ **faire ~** to set *ou* to create a precedent.

juriste [ʒyrist] *nmf* jurist, law *ou* legal expert ▪ **~ d'entreprise** company lawyer.

juron [ʒyrɔ̃] *nm* swearword, oath ▪ **proférer des ~s** to swear, to curse.

jury [ʒyri] *nm* **1.** DR jury ▪ **membre du ~** juror, member of the jury ▪ **il fait partie du ~** he sits on the jury **2.** ÉDUC board of examiners, jury **3.** ART & SPORT panel *ou* jury *(of judges).*

jus [ʒy] *nm* **1.** [boisson] juice ▪ **ces oranges rendent *ou* donnent beaucoup de ~** these oranges are very juicy ▶ **~ de fruit *ou* fruits** fruit juice **2.** CULIN juice, gravy ▪ **~ (de viande)** juice (from the meat) ▪ **cuire *ou* mijoter dans son ~**△ to stew in one's (own) juice ▪ **c'est du ~ de chaussettes, leur café** *fam* their coffee tastes like dishwater **3.** *fam* [café] coffee **4.** *fam* [courant électrique] juice ▪ **attention, tu vas prendre le ~!** watch out, you'll get a shock! **5.** *fam* [eau] : **tout le monde au ~!** everybody in (the water)! **6.** ART glaze.

jusqu'au-boutisme [ʒyskobutism] *nm fam* [d'un individu] hard-line attitude ▪ POLIT hard-line policy.

jusqu'au-boutiste [ʒyskobutist] *(pl* **jusqu'au-boutistes**) *fam* <> *nmf* POLIT hard-liner ▪ **c'est un ~** he's a hard-liner.
<> *adj* hard-line.

jusque [ʒyskə] *(devant voyelle ou 'h' muet "jusqu'"* [ʒysk], *littéraire devant voyelle* "jusques" [ʒyskə]*) prep* **1.** [dans l'espace] *(suivi d'une prep)* **elle m'a suivi ~ chez moi** she followed me all the way home ▪ **les nuages s'étendront ~ vers la Bourgogne** the clouds will spread as far as Burgundy ▪ **je suis monté jusqu'en haut de la tour** I climbed (right) up to the top of the tower ▪ *(suivi d'un adverbe)* **jusqu'où?** how far? ▪ **jusqu'où peut aller la bêtise/cruauté!** (just) how stupid/cruel can people be! ▶ **jusques et y compris** up to and including
2. *(suivi d'une prep)* [dans le temps] : **j'attendrai ~ vers 11 h** I'll wait till *ou* until about 11 o'clock ▪ *(suivi d'un adverbe)* **jusqu'alors** (up) until *ou* till then
3. [même, y compris] even ▪ **il y avait du sable ~ dans les lits** there was even sand in the beds.
◆ **jusqu'à** *loc prép* **1.** [dans l'espace] : **jusqu'à Marseille** as far as Marseilles ▪ **il a rempli les verres jusqu'au bord** he filled the glasses (right up) to the brim ▪ **le sous-marin peut plonger jusqu'à 3 000 m de profondeur** the submarine can dive (down) to 3,000 m ▪ **elle avait de l'eau jusqu'aux genoux** she was up to her knees in water ▪ **il y a 300 m de chez nous jusqu'à la gare** it's 300 m from our house to the station
2. [dans le temps] until ▪ **la pièce dure jusqu'à quelle heure?** what time does the play finish? ▪ **jusqu'à quand peut-on s'inscrire?** when's the last (possible) date for registering? ▪ **tu vas attendre jusqu'à quand?** how long are you going to wait? ▪ **jusqu'à nouvel ordre** until further notice ▪ **jusqu'à preuve du contraire** as far as I know
3. [indiquant le degré] : **jusqu'à quel point peut-on lui faire confiance?** to what extent *ou* how far can we trust him? ▪ **sa désinvolture va jusqu'à l'insolence** he's relaxed to the point of insolence ▪ **j'irais jusqu'à dire que c'était délibéré** I would go as far as to say it was done on purpose ▪ **jusqu'à concurrence de 3 000 euros** up to 3,000 euros maximum, up to (a limit of) 3,000 euros ▶ **il nous aura embêtés jusqu'à la fin *ou* la gauche** *fam* ! he will have been a nuisance to us (right) to the bitter end!
4. [même, y compris] even ▪ **il a mangé tous les bonbons jusqu'au dernier** he's eaten all the sweets (down to the last one), he's eaten every last *ou* single sweet.
◆ **jusqu'à ce que** *loc conj* until ▪ **tout allait bien jusqu'à ce qu'il arrive** everything was going fine until he turned up.
◆ **jusqu'au moment où** *loc conj* until ▪ **je t'ai attendu jusqu'au moment où j'ai dû partir pour mon rendez-vous** I waited for you until I had to go to my meeting.
◆ **jusque-là** *loc adv* **1.** [dans le présent] up to now, (up) until *ou* till now ▪ [dans le passé] up to then, (up) until *ou* till then ▪ **~-là, tout va bien** so far so good
2. [dans l'espace] : **je ne suis pas allé ~-là pour rien** I didn't go all that way for nothing ▪ **ils sont arrivés ~-là et puis ils sont repartis** they got so far and then they left ▪ **on avait de l'eau ~-là** the water was up to here ▪ **je n'ai pas encore lu ~-là** I haven't got *ou* read that far yet ▶ **j'en ai ~-là de tes caprices!** *fam* I've had it up to here with your whims!, I'm sick and tired of your whims!
◆ **jusqu'ici** *loc adv* **1.** [dans l'espace] (up) to here, as far as here ▪ **je ne suis pas venu jusqu'ici pour rien!** I haven't come all this way *ou* as far as this for nothing!
2. [dans le temps] so far, until now, up to now.

justaucorps [ʒystokɔr] *nm* **1.** [de gymnaste, de danseur] leotard **2.** HIST jerkin.

juste [ʒyst] <> *adv* **1.** [avec justesse] : **chanter ~** to sing in tune ▪ **tomber ~** to guess right, to hit the nail on the head ▪ **tu as vu *ou* deviné ~!** you guessed correctly *ou* right!
2. [exactement] exactly, just ▪ **il est 9 h ~** it's exactly 9 o'clock ▪ **la balle est passée ~ à côté du poteau** the ball went just past the post ▪ **tu arrives ~ à temps** you've come just in time

■ **~ quand** *ou* **comme le téléphone sonnait** just as *ou* when the phone was ringing ■ **il s'est fait renvoyer? – tout ~!** so he was dismissed? – he was indeed!
3. [à peine, seulement] just ■ **il vient ~ d'arriver** he's just (this minute) arrived ■ **il est ~ 9 h, vous n'allez pas partir déjà** it's only 9 o'clock, you're not going to leave already ■ **tout ~ : j'ai tout ~ le temps de prendre un café** I've just about enough *ou* I've just got enough time to have a cup of coffee ■ **c'est tout ~ s'il ne m'a pas frappé** he very nearly *ou* all but hit me ■ **c'est tout ~ s'il dit bonjour** he hardly bothers to say hello, you're lucky if he says hello
4. [en quantité insuffisante] : **un gâteau pour 8, ça fait (un peu) ~** one cake for 8 people, that won't go very far ■ **tu as coupé le tissu un peu ~** you've cut the material a bit on the short side.
◇ *adj* **1.** [équitable - partage, décision, personne] fair ■ **être ~ envers** *ou* **avec qqn** to be fair to sb ■ **il ne serait que ~ qu'il soit remboursé** it would only be fair *ou* right for him to get his money back ■ **c'est pas ~!** *fam* it's not fair *ou* right! ■ *(avant le n)* [justifié - cause, récompense, punition] just ; [- requête] legitimate ; [- colère] just, legitimate
2. *(après le n)* [exact - calcul, compte, réponse] right ■ **as-tu l'heure ~?** have you got the right *ou* exact time? ■ [dans son fonctionnement - horloge] accurate, right ; [- balance] accurate, true
3. [précis - terme, expression] appropriate, right
4. [serré - habit] tight ; [- chaussures] tight, small ■ **la nappe est un peu ~ en longueur/largeur** the tablecloth is a bit on the short/narrow side ■ **une heure pour aller à l'aéroport, c'est trop ~** an hour to get to the airport, that's not enough ■ **ses notes sont trop ~s pour que vous le laissiez passer** his marks are too borderline for you to pass him ■ [de justesse] : **elle a réussi l'examen, mais c'était ~** she passed her exam, but it was a close thing
5. *(après le n)* [compétent] good ■ **avoir l'oreille/le coup d'œil ~** to have a good ear/eye ‖ [sensé, judicieux - raisonnement] sound ; [- objection, observation] relevant, apt ■ **ta remarque est tout à fait ~!** your comment is quite right! ■ **très ~!** quite right!, good point! ■ **j'ai moins d'expérience que lui – c'est ~** I'm less experienced than he is – that's true *ou* right ■ MUS [voix, instrument] true, in tune ■ [note] true, right ■ **le piano n'est pas ~** the piano is out of tune
6. *(avant le n)* [approprié] : **apprécier qqch à son ~ prix** to appreciate the true value *ou* worth of sthg ■ **apprécier qqn à sa ~ valeur** to appreciate the true worth *ou* value of sb.
◇ *nm* just man ■ **les ~s** the just.
◆ **au juste** *loc adv* exactly ■ **combien sont-ils au ~?** how many (of them) are there exactly?
◆ **au plus juste** *loc adv* : **calculer qqch au plus ~** to calculate sthg to the nearest penny.
◆ **comme de juste** *loc adv* of course, needless to say ■ **comme de ~, elle avait oublié** she'd forgotten, of course.
◆ **juste ciel, juste Dieu** *interj* good heavens, heavens (above).

justement [ʒystəmɑ̃] *adv* **1.** [à ce moment précis] : **voilà ~ Paul** talking of Paul, here he is ■ **j'ai ~ besoin d'une secrétaire** actually *ou* as it happens, I need a secretary ■ **j'allais ~ te téléphoner** I was just going to phone you **2.** [pour renforcer un énoncé] quite, just so ■ **il se met vite en colère – ~, ne le provoque pas!** he loses his temper very quickly – quite *ou* exactly *ou* that's right, so don't provoke him! **3.** [exactement] exactly, precisely ■ **j'ai ~ ce qu'il vous faut** I've got exactly *ou* just what you need **4.** [pertinemment] rightly, justly ■ **comme tu l'as dit si ~** as you (so) rightly said **5.** [avec justice] rightly, justly ■ **elle fut ~ récompensée/condamnée** she was justly rewarded/condemned.

justesse [ʒystɛs] *nf* **1.** [d'un raisonnement, d'un jugement] soundness ■ [d'une observation] appropriateness, aptness, relevance ■ [d'un terme, d'un ton] appropriateness, aptness ■ **elle raisonne avec ~** her reasoning is sound, she has sound reasoning **2.** MATH & MUS accuracy ■ [d'un mécanisme, d'une horloge, d'une balance] accuracy, precision.
◆ **de justesse** *loc adv* just, barely, narrowly ■ **il a gagné de ~** he won by a narrow margin *ou* by a hair's breadth ■ **j'ai eu mon permis de ~** I only just passed my driving test ■ **on a évité la collision de ~** we very nearly had a crash.

justice [ʒystis] *nf* **1.** [équité] justice, fairness ■ **il traite ses hommes avec ~** he treats his men fairly *ou* justly *ou* with fairness ■ **en bonne ~** in all fairness ■ **ce n'est que ~** it's only fair ▶ **~ sociale** social justice **2.** DR : **la ~** the law ■ **rendre la ~** to administer *ou* to dispense justice ■ **avoir la ~ pour soi** to have the law on one's side ■ **avoir des démêlés avec la ~** to fall foul of the law ■ **il a fait des aveux à la ~** he confessed to the law **3.** [réparation] justice ■ **demander ~** to ask for justice to be done ■ **obtenir ~** to obtain justice ■ **nous voulons que ~ soit faite!** we want justice to be done! ■ **faire ~** [venger une faute] to take the law into one's own hands ■ **faire ~ de qqch** [montrer que c'est nocif] to prove sthg to be bad ; [le réfuter] to prove sthg wrong, to give the lie to sthg ■ **se faire ~** [se venger] to take the law into one's own hands ; [se tuer] to take one's (own) life ■ **rendre ~ à qqn** to do sb justice ■ **la postérité rendra ~ à son courage** posterity will recognize his courage.
◆ **en justice** *loc adv* DR : **aller en ~** to go to court ■ **passer en ~** to stand trial, to appear in court.

justiciable [ʒystisjabl] ◇ *adj* **1.** [responsable] : **~ de** answerable for, responsible for **2.** [qui requiert] : **~ de** requiring ■ **maladie ~ d'hydrothérapie** illness requiring *ou* which calls for hydrotherapy **3.** DR : **il est ~ des tribunaux pour enfants** he is subject to *ou* comes under the jurisdiction of the juvenile courts.
◇ *nmf* person liable *ou* subject to trial ■ **les ~s** those due to be tried.

justicier, ère [ʒystisje, ɛr] ◇ *adj* **1.** [qui rend la justice] justiciary *(modif)* **2.** [qui fait justice lui-même] : **le jury a condamné le mari ~** the jury condemned the husband who took the law into his own hands.
◇ *nm, f* [redresseur de torts] righter of wrongs.
◆ **justicier** *nm* HIST justiciar.

justifiable [ʒystifjabl] *adj* justifiable ■ **tous vos arguments doivent être ~s** you must be able to justify *ou* to substantiate every one of your arguments ■ **sa négligence n'est pas ~** his negligence is unjustifiable *ou* cannot be justified.

justificatif, ive [ʒystifikatif, iv] *adj* [rapport] justificatory, supporting ■ [facture] justificatory ■ **document ~ d'identité** written proof of one's identity.
◆ **justificatif** *nm* **1.** ADMIN written proof *ou* evidence ■ [en comptabilité] receipt ■ **à adresser à la Comptabilité avec ~s** to be sent to the Accounts Department with all necessary receipts **2.** PRESSE press cutting *ou* clipping.

justification [ʒystifikasjɔ̃] *nf* **1.** [motivation - d'une attitude, d'une politique] justification **2.** [excuse] justification, reason ■ **vos ~s ne m'intéressent pas** I'm not interested in your reasons *ou* excuses *péj* **3.** ADMIN (written) proof *(of expenses incurred)* **4.** IMPR & INFORM justification.

justifier [9] [ʒystifje] *vt* **1.** [motiver - conduite, mesure, dépense] to justify, to vindicate ■ **rien ne saurait ~ de tels propos** there's no possible justification for speaking in such terms **2.** [confirmer - crainte, théorie] to justify, to confirm, to back up *(sép)* ■ **il a tout fait pour ~ ses dires** he did everything to try and back up his statements **3.** [prouver - affirmation] to prove, to justify ; [- versement] to give proof *ou* evidence of **4.** [innocenter] to vindicate **5.** IMPR & INFORM to justify ■ **le paragraphe est justifié à gauche/droite** the paragraph is left-/right-justified.
◆ **justifier de** *v+prép* : **~ de son identité** to prove one's identity.
◆ **se justifier** *vp (emploi réfléchi)* to justify o.s. ■ **se ~ d'une accusation** to clear o.s. of an accusation, to clear one's name.

jute [ʒyt] *nm* jute ■ **de** *ou* **en ~** jute *(modif)*.

juteux, euse [ʒytø, øz] *adj* **1.** [fruit, viande] juicy **2.** *fam* [transaction] juicy ■ **c'est une affaire bien juteuse!** that business is a real gold mine!
◆ **juteux**△ *nm arg mil* adjutant.

juvénile [ʒyvenil] *adj* **1.** [jeune - silhouette] young, youthful ; [- ardeur, enthousiasme] youthful ■ **il avait toujours gardé une passion ~ pour les motos** he'd always kept his youthful passion for motorbikes **2.** PHYSIOL juvenile **3.** GÉOL & MINÉR juvenile.

juxtaposé, e [ʒykstapoze] *adj* juxtaposed.

juxtaposer [3] [ʒykstapoze] *vt* to juxtapose, to place side by side ■ **~ un mot à un autre** to juxtapose two words.

juxtaposition [ʒykstapozisjɔ̃] *nf* juxtaposition.

K

k, K [ka] *nm* k, K, *voir aussi* **g**.

k (*abr écrite de* **kilo**) k.

K (*abr écrite de* **kilooctet**) K.

K7 (*abr de* **cassette**) *nf* cassette ■ **radio-~** radio cassette player.

kabbale [kabal] = **cabale** *(sens 2)*.

Kaboul [kabul] *npr* Kabul.

kabyle [kabil] *adj* Kabylian.
◆ **Kabyle** *nmf* Kabylian.
◆ **kabyle** *nm* LING Kabylian.

Kabylie [kabili] *npr f* : **(la)** ~ Kabylia.

kafkaïen, enne [kafkajɛ̃, ɛn] *adj* Kafkaesque.

Kaiser [kajzɛr] *npr m* : **le** ~ the Kaiser.

kakatoès [kakatɔɛs] = **cacatoès**.

kaki [kaki] ◇ *adj inv* [couleur] khaki.
◇ *nm* **1.** [couleur] khaki **2.** BOT [arbre] (Japanese) persimmon, kaki ■ [fruit] persimmon, sharon fruit.

kalachnikov [kalaʃnikɔf] *nm* kalashnikov.

Kalahari [kalaari] *npr m* : **le** ~ the Kalahari Desert.

kaléidoscope [kaleidɔskɔp] *nm* **1.** OPT kaleidoscope **2.** *fig* rapidly changing pattern.

kaléidoscopique [kaleidɔskɔpik] *adj* kaleidoscopic.

kamikaze [kamikaz] *nmf* kamikaze.

kamut [kamyt] *nm* kamut, Polish wheat.

kanak, e [kanak] = **canaque**.

Kandinsky [kɑ̃dinski] *npr* Kandinski.

kangourou [kɑ̃guru] *nm* ZOOL kangaroo, *voir aussi* **île**.

Kansas [kɑ̃sas] *npr m* : **le** ~ Kansas.

kantien, enne [kɑ̃sjɛ̃, ɛn] *adj* Kantian.

kantisme [kɑ̃tism] *nm* Kantianism.

kaolin [kaɔlɛ̃] *nm* kaolin.

kapok [kapɔk] *nm* kapok.

karaté [karate] *nm* karate.

karatéka [karateka] *nmf* : **c'est une** ~ she does karate.

karité [karite] *nm* [arbre] shea (tree) ■ [substance] : **beurre de** ~ shea butter.

karma [karma], **karman** [karman] *nm* karma.

karstique [karstik] *adj* karstic.

kart [kart] *nm* kart, go-kart ■ **faire du** ~ to go-kart, to go karting.

karting [kartiŋ] *nm* karting, go-karting ■ **faire du** ~ to go-kart, to go karting.

kasher [kaʃɛr] *adj inv* kosher.

kawa [kawa] *nm* **fam** [café] coffee.

kayak [kajak] *nm* kayak.

Kazakhstan [kazakstɑ̃] *npr m* : **le** ~ Kazakhstan ■ **au** ~ in Kazakhstan.

kelvin [kɛlvin] *nm* kelvin.

kendo [kɛndo] *nm* kendo.

Kentucky [kɛntyki] *npr m* : **le** ~ Kentucky.

Kenya [kenja] *npr m* : **le** ~ Kenya ■ **au** ~ in Kenya.

kenyan, e [kenjɑ̃, an] *adj* Kenyan.
◆ **Kenyan, e** *nm, f* Kenyan.

képi [kepi] *nm* kepi.

kératine [keratin] *nf* keratin.

kermesse [kɛrmɛs] *nf* [dans les Flandres] kermis, kirmess ■ [de charité] charity fête, bazaar ■ ~ **paroissiale** church fête.

kérosène [kerɔzɛn] *nm* kerosene, kerosine.

ketchup [kɛtʃœp] *nm* ketchup.

keynésien, enne [kenezjɛ̃, ɛn] *adj* Keynesian.

kg (*abr écrite de* **kilogramme**) kg.

KGB *npr m* KGB.

khâgne [kaɲ] *nf* **arg scol** *second year of a two-year Arts course preparing for entrance to the École normale supérieure.*

khâgneux, euse [kaɲø, øz] *nm, f* **arg scol** *student in "khâgne".*

khalife [kalif] = **calife**.

khan [kɑ̃] *nm* **1.** [titre] khan **2.** [abri] khan.

Khatchatourian [katʃaturjɑ̃] *npr* Khachaturian.

Khéops [keɔps] *npr* Cheops.

khmer, ère [kmɛr] *adj* Khmerian.
◆ **Khmer, ère** *nm, f* Khmer ■ **les Khmers** the Khmers.
◆ **khmer** *nm* LING Khmer.

khôl [kol] *nm* kohl.

Khrouchtchev [krutʃef] *npr* : **Nikita** ~ Nikita Khrushchev.

kibboutz [kibuts] (*pl inv* OU *pl* **kibboutzim** [-tsim]) *nm* kibbutz ■ **travailler dans un** ~ to work on a kibbutz.

kidnapper [3] [kidnape] *vt* [personne] to kidnap.

kidnappeur, euse [kidnapœr, øz] *nm, f* kidnapper.

kidnapping [kidnapiŋ] *nm* kidnapping.

kif [kif] *nm* [haschisch] kif, kef.

kif-kif [kifkif] *adj inv* **fam** **c'est** ~ **(bourricot)** it's all the same, it makes no odds *UK*, it's six of one and half a dozen of the other.

kiki [kiki] *nm fam* **1.** [cou] neck ■ [gorge] throat ■ **serrer le ~ à qqn** to throttle *ou* to strangle sb **2.** *loc* **c'est parti, mon ~!** here we go!

kil△ [kil] *nm* bottle (of wine) ■ **un ~ de rouge** a bottle of cheap red wine *ou* (red) plonk *UK*.

Kilimandjaro [kilimɑ̃dʒaro] *npr m* : **le (mont) ~** (Mount) Kilimanjaro.

kilo [kilo] (*abr de* **kilogramme**) *nm* kilo.

kilobar [kilɔbar] *nm* kilobar.

kilocalorie [kilɔkalɔri] *nf* kilocalorie.

kilogramme [kilɔgram] *nm* kilogramme.

kilohertz [kilɔɛrts] *nm* kilohertz.

kilojoule [kilɔʒul] *nm* kilojoule.

kilométrage [kilɔmetraʒ] *nm* **1.** [d'un véhicule] mileage **2.** [d'une voie] marking out *(in kilometres)*.

kilomètre [kilɔmɛtr] *nm* **1.** [distance] kilometre ■ **~ zéro** *point near Notre-Dame from which distances from Paris are measured* **2.** INFORM : **frappe** *ou* **saisie au ~** straight keying.

kilométrer [18] [kilɔmetre] *vt* to mark with kilometric reference points.

kilométrique [kilɔmetrik] *adj* : **au point ~ 21** at km 21 ➊ **distance ~** distance in kilometres.

kilooctet [kilɔɔktɛ] (*pl* **kilooctets**) *nm* kilobyte.

kilowatt [kilɔwat] *nm* kilowatt.

kilowattheure [kilɔwatœr] *nm* kilowatt-hour.

kilt [kilt] *nm* [d'Écossais, de femme] kilt.

kimono [kimɔno] ◇ *nm* [vêtement] kimono.
◇ *adj inv* : **manches ~** kimono *ou* loose sleeves.

kiné [kine] (*abr de* **kinésithérapeute**) *nmf fam* physio.

kinescope [kinɛskɔp] *nm* kinescope.

kinésithérapeute [kineziterapøt] *nmf* physiotherapist *UK*, physical therapist *US*.

kinésithérapie [kineziterapi] *nf* physiotherapy *UK*, physical therapy *US*.

kinesthésie [kinɛstezi] *nf* kinaesthesia.

kinesthésique [kinɛstezik] *adj* kinaesthetic.

kiosque [kjɔsk] *nm* **1.** [boutique] : **~ à journaux** newspaper kiosk *ou* stand, news-stand ■ **~ à fleurs** flower stall **2.** [édifice - dans un jardin] pavilion ■ **~ à musique** bandstand **3.** NAUT [d'un navire] wheelhouse ■ [d'un sous-marin] conning tower **4.** TÉLÉCOM : **Kiosque**® [d'un Minitel] ≃ (telephone) viewdata service.

kiosquier, ère [kjɔskje, ɛr] *nm, f* newspaper seller, newsvendor ■ **il est ~** he runs a newsstand.

kippa [kipa] *nf* kippa.

Kippour [kipur] *nm* : **le ~** the Kippur.

kir [kir] *nm* kir.

Kirghizistan [kirgizistɑ̃] *npr m* : **le ~** Kirgizia.

kirsch [kirʃ] *nm* kirsch.

kit [kit] *nm* **1.** [gén] kit ■ **meubles en ~** kit furniture ■ **vendu en ~** sold in kit form **2.** TÉLÉCOM : **~ de connexion** connection kit ■ **~ mains libres** hands-free kit.

kitchenette [kitʃənɛt] *nf* kitchenette.

kitsch [kitʃ] ◇ *adj inv* kitsch *(modif)*, kitschy.
◇ *nm inv* kitsch.

kiwi [kiwi] *nm* **1.** BOT [fruit] kiwi (fruit), Chinese gooseberry ■ [arbre] kiwi tree **2.** ZOOL kiwi.

Klaxon® [klaksɔn] *nm* horn ■ **donner un coup de ~** to hoot (one's horn) *UK*, to honk (one's horn) *US*.

klaxonner [3] [klaksɔne] ◇ *vi* to honk *ou* to hoot *UK* (one's horn).
◇ *vt* : **il m'a klaxonné** he tooted *ou* hooted *UK ou* honked at me.

Kleenex® [klinɛks] *nm* (paper) tissue, paper handkerchief, Kleenex®.

kleptomane [klɛptɔman] *nmf* kleptomaniac.

kleptomanie [klɛptɔmani] *nf* kleptomania.

km (*abr écrite de* **kilomètre**) km.

km/h (*abr écrite de* **kilomètre par heure**) kmph.

knickerbockers [nikœrbɔkœr], **knickers** [nikœr] *nmpl* knickerbockers *UK*, knickers *US*.

knock-down [nɔkdawn] *nm inv* SPORT knockdown.

knock-out [nɔkaut] ◇ *nm inv* knockout.
◇ *adj inv* knocked-out, out for the count ■ **il l'a mis ~** he knocked him out.

Ko (*abr écrite de* **kilooctet**) Kb.

K.-O. ◇ *nm inv* KO.
◇ *adj inv* **1.** SPORT KO'd ■ **mettre qqn ~** to knock sb out ■ **être ~** to be out for the count **2.** *fam* [épuisé] shattered *UK*, all in, dead beat.

koala [kɔala] *nm* koala (bear).

kola [kɔla] *nm* cola, Kola.

kolkhoz(e) [kɔlkoz] *nm* kolkhoz.

kolkhozien, enne [kɔlkozjɛ̃, ɛn] ◇ *adj* kolkhoz *(modif)*.
◇ *nm, f* kolkhoznik.

kommandantur [kɔmɑ̃dɑ̃tur] *nf* HIST German military command.

kopeck [kɔpɛk] *nm* kopeck.

kosovar, e [kɔsɔvar] *adj* Kosovan.
◆ **Kosovar, e** *nm, f* Kosovar.

Kosovo[1] [kɔsɔvo] *npr m* GÉOGR : **le ~** Kosovo.

kot [kɔt] *nm Belgique* **1.** [chambre d'étudiant] bedroom *(for student)* **2.** [débarras] storeroom.

kougelhof, kouglof [kuglɔf] *nm* kugelhopf *(cake)*.

Koweït [kɔwɛjt] *npr m* : **le ~** Kuwait, Koweit ■ **au ~** in Kuwait.

Koweït City [kɔwejtsiti] *npr* Kuwait, Koweit.

koweïtien, enne [kɔwɛjtjɛ̃, ɛn] *adj* Kuwaiti.
◆ **Koweïtien, enne** *nm, f* Kuwaiti.

krach [krak] *nm* : **~ (boursier)** crash.

kraft [kraft] ◇ *nm* kraft, (strong) brown wrapping paper.
◇ *adj inv* : **papier/pâte ~** kraft paper/pulp.

Kremlin [krɛmlɛ̃] *npr m* : **le ~** the Kremlin.

kriss [kris] *nm* kris.

krypton [kriptɔ̃] *nm* krypton.

Ku Klux Klan [kyklyksklɑ̃] *npr m* : **le ~** the Ku Klux Klan.

kumquat [kumkwat] *nm* kumquat, cumquat.

kung-fu [kuŋfu] *nm inv* kung fu.

kurde [kyrd] *adj* Kurd.
◆ **Kurde** *nmf* Kurd.
◆ **kurde** *nm* LING Kurdish.

Kurdistan [kyrdistɑ̃] *npr m* : **le ~** Kurdistan ■ **au ~** in Kurdistan.

K-way® [kawɛ] *nm inv* cagoule.

kWh (*abr écrite de* **kilowattheure**) kW/hr.

kyrielle [kirjɛl] *nf* : **une ~ de bambins** *fam* a whole bunch of kids ■ **une ~ d'insultes** a string of insults.

kyste [kist] *nm* cyst.

kystique [kistik] *adj* cystic.

L

l, L [ɛl] *nm* l, L.

l (*abr écrite de* **litre**) l.

l' [l] ▷ **le**.

L = **licence**.

la[1] [la] *f* ▷ **le**.

la[2] [la] *nm inv* **1.** MUS A ■ [chanté] lah **2.** *loc* **donner le la** to set the tone, *voir aussi* **fa**.

là [la] *adv* **1.** [dans l'espace - là-bas] there ; [- ici] here ■ **elle habite Paris maintenant, c'est là qu'elle a trouvé du travail** she lives in Paris now, that's where she found work ■ **à quelques kilomètres de là** a few kilometres away ■ **je ne peux rien faire, il est toujours là** I can't do anything, he's always around ■ **est-ce qu'il est là?** is he in? ■ **je ne suis là pour personne** if anybody asks I'm not in *ou* here ■ **je suis là pour vous répondre** it's my job to answer your questions
2. [dans le temps] : **c'est là que j'ai paniqué** that's when I panicked ■ **attendons demain et là nous déciderons** let's wait until tomorrow and then (we'll) decide ■ **à partir de là** from then on, from that moment on ■ **là, je n'ai pas le temps de lui en parler** I don't have time to tell him about it right now ■ **à quelque temps de là** some time after
3. [dans cette situation] : **c'est justement là où je ne vous suis plus** that's just where you've lost me ■ **nous n'en sommes pas encore là** we haven't reached that stage yet ■ **pour l'instant nous en sommes là** that's how things stand at the moment ■ **j'en étais là de mes réflexions quand le téléphone a sonné** I'd got that far with my thinking when the phone rang ■ **comment en es-tu arrivé là?** how did you manage to let things go so far? ■ **en rester** *ou* **en demeurer là** : **je n'ai pas l'intention d'en rester** *ou* **demeurer là** I don't intend leaving it at that
4. [dans cela] : **ne voyez là aucune malice de ma part** please don't take it the wrong way ■ **la santé, tout est là** (good) health is everything
5. [pour renforcer] : **c'est là mon intention** that's my intention *ou* what I intend to do ■ **c'est là le problème/la difficulté** that's where the problem/the difficulty lies
6. [emploi expressif] : **oui, j'ai refusé ce travail, là, tu es content?** yes I turned down that job, now are you satisfied? ■ **alors là, je ne sais pas!** well that I really don't know! ■ **alors là, tu exagères!** you've got a nerve! ■ **c'est une belle grippe que tu as là!** that's quite a bout of flu you've got there! ■ **que me chantes-tu là?** *fam* what are you on about? ■ **malheureux, qu'as-tu fait là!** what have you gone and done now? ■ **là, là, calme-toi!** now, now *ou* there, there, calm down!
◆ **de-ci de-là** *loc adv litt* here and there.
◆ **de là** *loc adv* **1.** [dans l'espace] : **de là je me suis dirigée vers l'église** from there I headed towards the church ■ **de là jusqu'à la poste il y a 500 m** it is 500 m from the post office ■ **de là à dire que c'est un criminel, il y a loin** *fig* there's a big difference between that and saying he's a criminal
2. [marquant la conséquence] : **de là son amertume** that's why he's bitter, that explains his bitterness, hence his bitterness ■ **on peut déduire de là que...** from that we can deduce that...
◆ **là contre** *loc adv sout* : **c'est votre droit, je n'ai rien à dire ~ contre** it's your right, I have nothing to say in opposition.
◆ **par là** *loc adv* **1.** [dans l'espace] : **c'est par là** it's over there ■ **vous devriez passer par là** you should go that way
2. *fig* **si tu vas par là** if you take that line, in that case ■ **qu'entendez-vous** *ou* **que voulez-vous dire par là?** what do you mean by that? ■ **il faut en passer par là!** there's no alternative!, it can't be helped!

-là [la] *adv* **1.** (*lié à un n introduit par un adj dém*) that, those (*pl*) ■ **cette femme~** that woman ■ **ce stylo~** that pen ■ **dans ces endroits~** in those places ■ **tu fréquentes ces gens~?** *péj* are those the kind of people you go around with? ■ **ne fais pas cette tête~!** you needn't look like that! **2.** (*lié à un pronom*) **quel livre voulez-vous? – celui~** which book do you want? – that one ■ **celui~, alors!** honestly, that one! **3.** [exprimant le passé] : **ce matin~** that morning ■ **en ce temps~** in those days, at that time.

là-bas [laba] *adv* **1.** [en bas] down *ou* under there **2.** [en un lieu éloigné] there ■ **une fois arrivés ~, nous nous arrangerons** we'll sort it out when we get there **3.** [à l'endroit que l'on indique] over there.

label [labɛl] *nm* [étiquette] label ■ **~ d'origine** label of origin ■ **~ de qualité/d'exportation** quality/export label.

labeur [labœr] *nm* **1.** *litt* [travail pénible] toil, labour ■ [effort] hard work ■ **une vie de ~** a life of toil **2.** IMPR bookwork.

labial, e, aux [labjal, o] *adj* **1.** ANAT lip (*modif*), labial **2.** PHON labial.
◆ **labiale** *nf* labial (consonant).

labialisation [labjalizasjɔ̃] *nf* [d'une voyelle] rounding ■ [d'une consonne] labialization.

labialiser [3] [labjalize] *vt* [voyelle] to round ■ [consonne] to labialize.

labié, e [labje] *adj* labiate.
◆ **labiée** *nf* labiate ■ **les ~es** the Labiatae.

labile [labil] *adj* **1.** CHIM & PSYCHOL labile **2.** *litt* [peu stable] unstable, temperamental.

labiodental, e, aux [labjɔdɑ̃tal, o] *adj* labiodental.
◆ **labiodentale** *nf* labiodental (consonant).

labo [labo] *nm fam* lab ■ **~ photo** darkroom.

laborantin, e [labɔrɑ̃tɛ̃, in] *nm, f* laboratory assistant, laboratory operator US.

laboratoire [labɔratwar] *nm* **1.** SC [lieu] laboratory ■ [équipe] (research) team ■ **~ d'analyses (médicales)** analytical laboratory ■ ~ **expérimental** testing laboratory ■ ~ **de recherche** research laboratory **2.** ÉDUC : ~ **de langue** *ou* **langues** language laboratory **3.** MÉTALL heating chamber **4.** PHOTO [salle] processing room ■ [usine] processing works.

◆ **en laboratoire** *loc adv* in the laboratory, under laboratory conditions ■ **embryon végétal obtenu en ~** plant embryo obtained in the laboratory *ou* under laboratory conditions.

laborieusement [labɔrjøzmɑ̃] *adv* [péniblement] laboriously, with great difficulty.

laborieux, euse [labɔrjø, øz] *adj* **1.** [long et difficile - procédure, tâche, manœuvre] laborious **2.** [lourd - style] heavy, laboured ■ **trois heures pour faire une lettre, ce fut ~!** three hours to write a letter, that's slow going! ■ **dans un anglais ~** in halting English ■ **lecture/récitation laborieuse** laboured reading/recitation **3.** [industrieux] hardworking, industrious ■ **la classe laborieuse** the working *ou* labouring class.

labour [labur] *nm* **1.** AGRIC tilling, ploughing ■ **les ~s** the ploughed fields ■ **commencer les ~s** to start ploughing **2.** HORT digging (over).

labourable [laburabl] *adj* ploughable ■ **des terres ~s** arable land.

labourage [laburaʒ] *nm* **1.** AGRIC tilling, ploughing **2.** HORT digging over.

labourer [3] [labure] *vt* **1.** AGRIC to plough ■ HORT to dig (over) **2.** [ravager] to furrow ■ **un terrain labouré par les obus** land churned up by artillery shells **3.** [lacérer] to dig into *(insép)*, to lacerate, to scratch.

laboureur [laburœr] *nm* **1.** *litt* ploughman **2.** HIST husbandman, ≃ yeoman.

labrador [labradɔr] *nm* **1.** MINÉR labradorite **2.** ZOOL Labrador retriever, labrador.

labyrinthe [labirɛ̃t] *nm* **1.** [dédale] labyrinth, maze ■ **la vieille ville est un ~ de ruelles étroites** the old (part of) town is a maze of narrow streets **2.** *fig* maze ■ **le ~ des lois** the intricacies of the law **3.** ANAT labyrinth.

labyrinthique [labirɛ̃tik] *adj* labyrinthine, mazelike.

lac [lak] *nm* [pièce d'eau] lake ■ ~ **artificiel/de barrage** artificial/barrier lake ■ **la région des Lacs** the Lakes, the Lake District ■ **c'est tombé dans le ~** *fam* it has fallen through.

LAC

le lac Baïkal Lake Baïkal ;
le lac Balaton Lake Balaton ;
le lac de Côme Lake Como ;
le lac de Constance Lake Constance ;
le lac Érié Lake Erie ;
le lac de Garde Lake Garda ;
le lac Huron Lake Huron ;
le lac Ladoga Lake Ladoga ;
le lac Léman Lake Geneva ;
le lac Majeur Lake Maggiore ;
le lac Malawi Lake Malawi ;
le lac Michigan Lake Michigan ;
le lac Mobutu Lake Mobutu ;
le lac Nasser Lake Nasser ;
le lac Ontario Lake Ontario ;
le lac Supérieur Lake Superior ;
le lac Tanganyika Lake Tanganyika ;
le lac Tchad Lake Chad ;
le lac de Tibériade the Sea of Galilee, Lake Tiberias ;
le lac Titicaca Lake Titicaca ;
le lac Victoria Lake Victoria ;
le lac Winnipeg Lake Winnipeg ;
le lac de Zoug Lake Zug ;
le lac de Zurich Lake Zürich.

lacer [16] [lase] *vt* [vêtement] to lace (up) *(sép)* ■ [chaussure] to lace up *(sép)*, to tie up *(sép)*.

◆ **se lacer** *vp (emploi passif)* to lace (up) ■ **comment cette botte se lace-t-elle?** how do you lace (up) this boot?

lacération [laserasjɔ̃] *nf* **1.** MÉD laceration, gash **2.** [fait de déchirer] ripping, tearing, slashing ■ **la ~ des affiches est monnaie courante en période électorale** during election time posters often get ripped *ou* slashed.

lacérer [18] [lasere] *vt* **1.** [affiche, rideau] to rip up *(sép)*, to tear (to shreds), to slash **2.** [blesser] to lacerate, to gash.

lacet [lasɛ] *nm* **1.** [de chaussure] (shoe)lace ■ [de botte] (boot)lace **2.** [piège] snare **3.** [d'une route] hairpin bend ■ **faire des ~s** [route] to twist and turn **4.** COUT tie.

◆ **à lacets** *loc adj* : **chaussures à ~s** lace-ups, lace-up shoes.

◆ **en lacets** ◇ *loc adj* [route] winding, twisting.

◇ *loc adv* : **la route monte en ~s** the road winds *ou* twists upwards.

lâchage [laʃaʒ] *nm fam* [abandon] : **c'est un ~ en règle de leur part** they've really let us down.

lâche [laʃ] ◇ *adj* **1.** [poltron] cowardly, spineless ■ **être ~** to be cowardly ■ **se montrer ~** to behave like a coward **2.** *(avant le n)* [méprisable] cowardly ■ **un ~ attentat** a cowardly *ou* despicable attack **3.** [non serré - nœud] loose, slack ; [- vêtement] loose, baggy **4.** [imprécis - dialogue, scénario] weak ; [- raisonnement] woolly, slipshod **5.** [sans rigueur - loi, règlement] lax, overlenient **6.** TEXT [étoffe] loose, loosely woven ■ [tricot] loose-knit.

◇ *nmf* coward.

lâché, e [laʃe] *adj* ART sloppy, careless.

lâchement [laʃmɑ̃] *adv* **1.** [sans courage] in a cowardly manner **2.** [sans tension] loosely, slackly.

lâcher¹ [laʃe] *nm* : **ils ont fait un ~ de colombes** they released a flock of doves ■ ~ **de ballons** balloon release.

lâcher² [3] [laʃe] ◇ *vt* **1.** [desserrer] to loosen, to slacken ■ ~ **la vapeur** to let off steam ● ~ **la bonde** *ou* **les bondes à** to give vent to ■ ~ **la bride à un cheval** *pr* to give a horse its head ■ ~ **la bride à qqn** *fig* to allow sb more freedom of movement

2. [cesser de tenir] to let go of *(insép)* ■ ~ **la pédale du frein** to take one's foot off the brake (pedal) ■ **elle a lâché la pile d'assiettes** she dropped the pile of plates ■ **il roule en lâchant le guidon** he rides with no hands ■ **lâche-moi!** let me go!, let go of me! ■ **elle ne la lâchait pas des yeux** *ou* **du regard** she didn't take her eyes off her for a moment ■ ~ **prise** to let go ■ **cette idée ne m'a pas lâché** I couldn't get this idea out of my mind ● **tu me lâches, oui?** *fam* get out of my sight, will you? ■ **lâche-moi les baskets!** *fam* leave me alone!, get off my back! ■ **il les lâche avec un élastique** *fam* he's a stingy *ou* tight-fisted old so-and-so ■ ~ **la proie pour l'ombre** to chase rainbows ■ ~ **pied** *pr & fig* to give way

3. AÉRON [bombe] to drop ■ [ballon] to launch

4. [libérer - oiseau] to let loose, to release, to let go ; [- chien] to let off, to unleash ; [- animal dangereux] to set loose ; [- meute, faucon] to slip ■ ~ **les chiens sur qqn** to set the dogs on sb ■ **le prof nous a lâchés plus tôt** *fam* the teacher let us out earlier

5. *fam* [abandonner - ami, amant] to drop ; [- emploi] to quit ■ ~ **ses études** to drop out of school ■ **le moteur nous a lâchés le deuxième jour** the engine broke down on us on the second day

6. [émettre] to let out, to come out with *(insép)* ■ ~ **un juron** to let out an oath ■ ~ **une sottise** to come out with a silly remark ■ ~ **un pet** *fam* to break wind

7. SPORT [distancer - concurrent] to get a lead on, to leave behind *(sép)* ■ ~ **le peloton** to leave the rest of the field behind, to (stage a) break from the pack.

◇ *vi* [se casser - câble] to snap, to break, to give (way) ; [- embrayage, frein] to fail.

lâcheté [laʃte] *nf* **1.** [manque de courage] cowardice **2.** [caractère vil] baseness, lowness ■ [procédé vil] low *ou* dirty trick ■ **commettre une ~** to do something despicable.

lâcheur, euse [laʃœr, øz] *nm, f fam* **quel ~, il n'est pas venu!** what an unreliable so-and-so, he didn't come!

lacis [lasi] *nm* **1.** [labyrinthe] maze, web ■ **un ~ de ruelles** a maze of little streets **2.** [entrelacement] lattice, network, tracery.

laconique [lakɔnik] *adj* [lettre, réplique] laconic *sout*, terse ■ [personne] laconic ■ **je n'ai obtenu qu'une réponse ~** all I got was a terse reply.

laconiquement [lakɔnikmɑ̃] *adv* laconically *sout*, tersely.

laconisme [lakɔnism] *nm* terseness, laconism *sout*.

lacrymal, e, aux [lakrimal, o] *adj* tear *(modif)*, lachrymal *spéc*, lacrimal *spéc*.

lacrymogène [lakrimɔʒɛn] *adj* [gaz] tear *(modif)*, lachrymatory *spéc*, lacrymogenic *spéc* ■ [grenade] tear-gas *(modif)* ■ [bombe] anti-mugger, tear-gas *(modif)*.

lacs [la] *nm* [piège] snare.

lactation [laktasjɔ̃] *nf* lactation.

lacté, e [lakte] *adj* **1.** [contenant du lait] milky, lacteal *spéc* ■ **farine ~e** milk-enriched cereal **2.** *litt* [pareil au lait] milky, lacteous *litt*.

lactifère [laktifɛr] *adj* lactiferous.

lactique [laktik] *adj* lactic.

lactose [laktoz] *nm* lactose.

lactosérum [laktɔserɔm] *nm* whey.

lacunaire [lakynɛr] *adj* **1.** [incomplet] incomplete, with gaps, lacunary *litt* ■ **il a des connaissances/des fichiers ~s** his knowledge is/his files are full of gaps **2.** ANAT & BOT [système] lacunar ■ [tissu] lacunal.

lacune [lakyn] *nf* **1.** [omission] gap ■ **il y a des ~s dans cette encyclopédie** there are some omissions in this encyclopedia ■ **j'ai des ~s en mathématiques** there are gaps in my knowledge of mathematics **2.** ANAT, BIOL & GÉOL lacuna.

lacustre [lakystr] *adj* **1.** BIOL & BOT lacustrian **2.** CONSTR : **cité ~** lakeside pile dwellings.

lad [lad] *nm* stable-boy, stable-lad *UK*.

là-dedans [laddɑ̃] *adv* **1.** [ici] in here ■ [là-bas] in there ■ **le tiroir est sens dessus dessous, je ne trouve rien ~** the drawer is in a mess, I can't find anything in here ■ **debout ~!** *fam* rise and shine! **2.** [dans ce texte] in here ■ [dans ce qui est dit] : **il y a ~ des choses qui m'échappent** there are things that escape me in what was said ■ **il y a du vrai ~** there's some truth in it **3.** *fam loc* **il y en a, ~!** *hum* now THAT'S a clever idea!

là-dessous [ladsu] *adv* **1.** [sous cet objet-ci] under here ■ [sous cet objet-là] under there **2.** [dans cette affaire] : **il y a quelque chose de bizarre ~** there's something strange *ou* odd about all this ■ **qu'est-ce qui se cache ~?** what's behind all this *ou* behind it all?

là-dessus [ladsy] *adv* **1.** [sur cet objet-ci] on here ■ [sur cet objet-là] on there ■ **ne t'appuie pas ~!** don't lean on it! **2.** [à ce sujet] about this *ou* it ■ **je n'en sais pas plus que toi ~** I don't know any more than you about it **3.** [sur ce] : **~ je vous dis bonsoir** at this point *ou* with that, I'll say good night ■ **~, elle se tut** at which point *ou* whereupon, she stopped talking.

ladite [ladit] *f* ▷ **ledit**.

ladre [ladr] <> *adj litt* [avare] miserly, measly.
<> *nmf litt* [avare] miser, skinflint.

ladrerie [ladrəri] *nf* **1.** *litt* [avarice] miserliness **2.** VÉTÉR measles.

lady [lɛdi] (*pl* **ladys** *ou pl* **ladies** [-di:z]) *nf* lady ■ **elle se prend pour une ~** she thinks she's really something.

lagon [lagɔ̃] *nm* (coral reef) lagoon.

Laguiole® [lajɔl] *nm distinctively-shaped knife*.

lagunaire [lagynɛr] *adj* lagoonal.

lagune [lagyn] *nf* lagoon.

là-haut [lao] *adv* **1.** [au-dessus] up there ■ **leur maison est ~ sur la colline** their house is up there on the hill ■ **mais que fait-elle ~?** [à l'étage] what's she doing upstairs? **2.** [aux cieux] up there, (up) in Heaven, on high *sout*.

lai, e [lɛ] *adj* RELIG : **frère ~** lay brother.
◆ **lai** *nm* LITTÉR lay.

◆ **laie** *nf* **1.** ZOOL wild sow **2.** AGRIC [trouée] (compartment) line ■ [sentier] forest path.

laïc, laïque [laik] <> *adj* lay.
<> *nm, f* layman (*f* laywoman) ■ **les ~s** the laity.
◆ **laïque** *adj* **1.** [non clérical] secular, lay, laic *litt* **2.** [indépendant du clergé] : **un État laïque** a secular state **3.** [empreint de laïcité] : **l'esprit laïque** secularism.

laïcisation [laisizasjɔ̃] *nf* secularization, laicization.

laïciser [3] [laisize] *vt* to secularize, to laicize.

laïcisme [laisism] *nm* secularism.

laïcité [laisite] *nf* secularism ■ **la défense de la ~** defence of secular education *(in France)*.

laid, e [lɛ, lɛd] *adj* **1.** [inesthétique - bâtisse] ugly, unsightly ; [- vêtement, tableau, décoration] ugly, unattractive, awful ; [- personne] unattractive, ugly ■ **il est/c'est très ~** he's/it's hideous ▶ **~ comme un pou** *ou* **un singe** *ou* **à faire fuir** (as) ugly as sin **2.** [impoli] rude, unseemly.

laidement [lɛdmɑ̃] *adv* **1.** [de façon laide] unattractively **2.** *sout* [ignoblement] basely *litt*, dirtily.

laideron [lɛdrɔ̃] *nm* ugly girl.

laideur [lɛdœr] *nf* **1.** [physique - d'une personne, d'une chose] ugliness ■ **d'une ~ repoussante** repulsively ugly **2.** [chose laide] monstrosity **3.** [morale - d'un crime] heinousness ; [- d'une accusation] meanness, baseness *litt* ■ **il a dépeint l'hypocrisie dans toute sa ~** he portrayed hypocrisy in all its ugliness.

lainage [lɛnaʒ] *nm* **1.** TEXT [tissu] woollen fabric *ou* material ■ [procédé] napping ■ **une robe de** *ou* **en ~** a woollen dress **2.** [pull] woollen jumper *UK*, woolen sweater *US* ■ [gilet] wool cardigan ■ **mets un ~** put on a sweater ■ **des ~s** woollens.

laine [lɛn] *nf* **1.** [poil - du mouton, de l'alpaga etc] wool ■ **~ vierge** new wool ■ **il se laisserait manger** *ou* **tondre la ~ sur le dos** *fam* he'd let you take the shirt off his back **2.** TEXT [tissu] wool ■ **en ~ peignée** worsted *(modif)* **3.** [vêtement] : **(petite) ~** *fam* woolly *UK*, sweater **4.** [isolant] : **~ de verre** glass wool.
◆ **de laine** *loc adj* wool *(modif)*, woollen ■ **bonnet/chaussettes de ~** woollen hat/socks.

lainer [4] [lɛne] *vt* TEXT [tissu] to nap.

laineux, euse [lɛnø, øz] *adj* **1.** TEXT [vêtement] woollen **2.** BOT woolly, piliferous *spéc*.

lainier, ère [lɛnje, ɛr] <> *adj* [production] wool *(modif)* ■ [usine] wool-producing.
<> *nm, f* **1.** [industriel] wool manufacturer **2.** [ouvrier] wool worker **3.** [commerçant] wool stapler.

laïque [laik] *f* ▷ **laïc**.

laisse [lɛs] *nf* **1.** [lien] leash, lead ■ **tirer sur la ~** to strain at the leash ■ **tenir un chien en ~** to keep a dog on the leash *ou* lead ■ **mener** *ou* **tenir qqn en ~** *fig* to keep a tight rein on sb, to have sb (well) under one's thumb *ou* in check **2.** GÉOGR [partie de plage] foreshore ■ [ligne] tide-mark, high-water mark.

laissé-pour-compte, laissée-pour-compte [lesepurkɔ̃t] (*mpl* **laissés-pour-compte**, *fpl* **laissées-pour-compte**) *nm, f* [personne] social reject *ou* outcast ■ **les laissés-pour-compte de l'industrialisation** the casualties *ou* victims of industrialization.
◆ **laissé-pour-compte** *nm* COMM reject, return.

laisser [4] [lese] *vt*

> **A.** ABANDONNER
> **B.** DONNER, CÉDER
> **C.** DANS UN ÉTAT, UNE SITUATION
> **D.** SUIVI D'UN INFINITIF

A. ABANDONNER

1. [ne pas prendre, renoncer à] to leave ■ **elle a laissé son dessert** she left her pudding (untouched), she didn't touch her pudding ■ **c'est à prendre ou à ~** (it's) take it or leave it ■ **il y a à prendre et à ~** [il y a du bon et du mauvais] you have to pick and

choose ; [il y a du vrai et du faux] you have to be selective ▶ **laissez toute espérance, vous qui entrez** *Dante allus* abandon hope all ye who enter here
2. [quitter momentanément - personne, chose] to leave ▪ **j'ai laissé mes enfants chez mon frère** I left my children at my brother's ▪ **j'ai laissé la voiture à la maison** I left the car at home ▪ **laisse-nous, nous avons à parler** leave us (alone), we have things to talk about ▪ **je vous laisse** [au téléphone] I must hang up *ou* go now ; [dans une lettre] that's all for now, I'll leave you now
3. [quitter définitivement] to leave, to abandon ▪ **il a laissé femme et enfants** he abandoned his wife and children, he walked out on his wife and children ‖ [après sa mort - famille] to leave ▪ **il laisse beaucoup de dettes** he has left considerable debts (behind him) ▪ **elle a laissé une œuvre considérable** she left (behind her) a vast body of work
4. [oublier] to leave, to forget ▪ **j'ai laissé mon sac à la maison** I left my bag at home
5. [perdre - membre, personne, bien matériel] to lose ▶ **y ~ la vie** *ou* **sa vie** to lose one's life ▪ **y ~ sa santé** to ruin one's health
6. [déposer - trace, marque] to leave ▪ **ce vin laisse un arrière-goût désagréable** this wine has an unpleasant aftertaste ▪ **il laisse un bon/un mauvais souvenir** we have good/bad memories of him ▪ **elle laisse le souvenir d'une femme énergique** she will be remembered as an energetic woman
7. [négliger] to leave ▪ **laisse ton livre et viens avec moi** put down *ou* leave your book and come with me ▪ **laissez la direction de Paris sur la gauche et tournez à droite** go past *ou* leave the road to Paris on your left and turn right ▪ **laisse tes soucis et viens avec nous** forget your worries and come with us
8. *litt* **ne pas ~ de** [ne pas manquer de] : **cette réponse ne laisse pas de m'étonner** I can't help but be surprised by this answer

B. DONNER, CÉDER
1. [accorder] to leave ▪ **~ qqch à qqn** to leave sthg for sb, to leave sb sthg ▪ **le juge lui a laissé les enfants** the judge gave her custody of the children ▪ **laissez la priorité à droite** give way to the right ▪ **laissez le passage à l'ambulance** let the ambulance through ▪ **~ sa place à qqn** [siège] to give up one's seat to sb ▪ **laisse-nous un peu de place!** let us have *ou* leave us some room! ▪ **laisse-lui le temps de le faire** leave *ou* give her time to do it
2. [confier] to leave ▪ **~ des consignes à qqn** to leave instructions with sb, to leave sb with instructions ▪ **laissez les clés chez le gardien** drop the keys off at the caretaker's, leave the keys with the caretaker ▪ **tu me laisses tout le travail!** you're leaving me with all the work! ▪ **~ qqch à faire à qqn** to leave sb to do sthg, to leave sthg for sb to do
3. [vendre] to let have ▪ **je vous le laisse pour 100 euros** I'll let you have it for 100 euros
4. [transmettre] : **après l'insurrection, il dut ~ le pouvoir à son fils** after the rebellion, he had to hand over power to his son ‖ [après sa mort] to leave, to bequeath *sout* ▪ **il a laissé d'immenses propriétés à sa famille** he left his family vast estates
5. [réserver] to leave ▪ **laissez une marge pour les corrections** leave a margin for corrections ▪ **~ qqch pour la fin** to leave sthg till last *ou* till the end
6. [suj: chose] : **~ à penser que** to make one think *ou* suppose that, to lead one to believe that ▪ **ta lettre laisse à penser que tu ne pourras pas venir** your letter implies that you won't be coming ▪ **je vous laisse à imaginer s'ils étaient surpris** I'll leave you to imagine how surprised they were ▪ *(en usage absolu)* **elle n'est pas là, cela laisse à penser** she's not here, it makes you wonder

C. DANS UN ÉTAT, UNE SITUATION
1. [faire demeurer] to leave, to keep ▪ **laisse la fenêtre fermée/ouverte** leave the window shut/open ▪ **~ un crime impuni** to let a crime go unpunished, to leave a crime unpunished ▪ **ceci me laisse sceptique** I remain sceptical (about it) ▪ **cela me laisse froid** *ou* **indifférent** it leaves me cold *ou* unmoved ▪ **~ qqn tranquille** *ou* **en repos** *ou* **en paix** to leave sb alone *ou* in peace ▪ **~ qqch tranquille** to leave sthg alone ▪ **~ qqn dans l'ignorance de qqch** to let sb remain ignorant of sthg, to leave sb in the dark about sthg ▪ **laissez le nom en blanc** leave the name blank, do not write the name in ▪ **les corps ont été laissés sans sépulture** the bodies remained *ou* were left unburied ▪ **~ derrière soi** *pr & fig* to leave behind ▶ **~ la bride sur le cou à un cheval** *pr* to give a horse its head ▪ **~ la bride sur le cou à qqn** *fig* to give sb free rein

2. *(en usage absolu)* [s'abstenir d'intervenir] : **laisse, je vais le faire** leave it, I'll do it myself ▪ **laisse, je vais me débrouiller, ça va aller** I'll be all right ▪ **laissez, je vous en prie** please don't bother (with that) ▪ **laisse, c'est moi qui paie** put your money away, I'll pay for this

D. SUIVI D'UN INFINITIF
1. [autoriser] to let, to allow, to permit ▪ **~ qqn faire qqch** to let sb do sthg, to allow sb to do sthg
2. [ne pas empêcher de] to let, to allow ▪ **~ qqn faire** to let sb do, to leave sb to do, to allow sb to do ▪ **laisse-le dormir** let him sleep, leave him to sleep ▪ **laisse-moi le lui dire** let me tell her/him (about it) ▪ **~ tomber qqch** to drop sthg ▪ **~ voir** [montrer] to show, to reveal ▪ **son décolleté laissait voir une peau satinée** her plunging neckline revealed skin like satin ▪ **~ voir son émotion** to show one's emotion ▪ **~ condamner un innocent** to allow an innocent man to be punished ▪ **~ échapper un cri de douleur** to let out a cry of pain ▪ **elle laissa échapper un soupir** she gave a sigh ▪ **~ sécher la colle** to leave *ou* to allow the glue to dry ▪ **laissez bouillir quelques secondes** let it boil for a few seconds ▪ **ceci laisse supposer que...** this implies that..., this makes one think that...
3. *loc* **~ dire : laissez dire et faites ce que vous avez à faire** let them talk and do what you have to do ▪ **~ faire : on n'y peut rien, il faut ~ faire** there's nothing we can do (about it), you just have to let things take their course ▪ **laisse faire, ça n'est pas grave!** don't worry, it doesn't matter! ▪ **tu t'imagines que je vais ~ faire ça?** do you think I'm just going to stand by and watch while this happens? ▪ **~ faire le temps** to let time take its course ▪ **~ tomber** *fam* : **~ tomber un ami** to drop a friend ▪ **tu devrais ~ tomber, ça ne marchera jamais** you should give up *ou* drop it *ou* forget it, it'll never work ▪ **je te dois encore dix euros – laisse tomber** I still owe you ten euros – forget it.

◆ **se laisser** ◇ *vp (emploi passif)* : **ça se laisse regarder** [à la télévision] it's watchable : **il se laisse boire, ton petit vin** your little wine goes down nicely *ou* is very drinkable ▪ **ça se laisse manger** it's rather tasty.
◇ *vpi* : **elle s'est laissé accuser injustement** she allowed herself to be *ou* she let herself be unjustly accused ▪ **il s'est laissé séduire** he let himself be seduced ▪ **il s'est laissé mourir** he let himself die, he just gave up living ▪ **ils se sont laissé surprendre par la nuit** they were caught out by nightfall ▪ **se ~ tomber sur une chaise/dans un fauteuil** to collapse onto a chair/into an armchair ▶ **se ~ aller** [se négliger] to let o.s. go ; [se détendre] to let o.s. go, to relax ▪ **se ~ aller à** to go as *ou* so far as ▪ **se ~ dire que** to have heard (it said) that ▪ **se ~ faire : ne te laisse pas faire!** stand up for yourself!, don't let yourself be taken advantage of! ▪ **la proposition est tentante, je crois que je vais me ~ faire** it's an attractive offer, I think I'll give in to temptation ▪ **laisse-toi faire, ça nous fait plaisir de te l'offrir** do take it *ou* come on, we'd love to give it to you ▪ **se ~ vivre** *fam* to live for the moment, to take life as it comes.

laisser-aller [lɛseale] *nm inv* : **il y a du ~ dans cette maison!** things are a bit too easy-going *ou* slack in this house! ▪ **il y a du ~ dans sa tenue** he dresses a bit too casually, he's a bit of a sloppy dresser.

laisser-faire [lɛsefɛr] *nm inv* laissez faire, non-interventionism.

laissez-passer [lɛsepase] *nm inv* **1.** [autorisation] pass **2.** COMM carnet **3.** NAUT transire.

lait [lɛ] *nm* **1.** [des mammifères] milk ▪ **avec ou sans ~?** black or white? *UK*, with or without milk? ▶ **~ caillé** curdled *ou* soured milk ▪ **~ concentré** *ou* **condensé non sucré** evaporated milk ▪ **~ concentré** *ou* **condensé sucré** (sweetened) condensed milk ▪ **~ demi-écrémé** semi-skimmed milk ▪ **~ écrémé** skimmed milk ▪ **~ entier** full-cream milk *UK*, whole milk ▪ **~ fraise** *milk with strawberry syrup* ▪ **~ homogénéisé** homogenized milk ▪ **~ longue conservation** long-life milk ▪ **~ maternel** mother's *ou* breast milk ▪ **~ maternisé** baby formula milk ▪ **~ en poudre** dried *ou* powdered milk ▪ **~ stérilisé** sterilized milk **2.** [de certains fruits] milk ▪ **~ d'amande** almond milk ▪ **~ de coco** coconut milk **3.** [boisson préparée] : **~ de poule** eggnog **4.** [pour la toilette] milk ▪ **~ démaquillant** cleansing milk **5.** CONSTR : **~ de chaux** slaked lime wash.
◆ **au lait** *loc adj* with milk.

◆ **de lait** *loc adj* **1.** [ayant la même nourrice] : **ce sont des frères de ~** they had the same wet-nurse **2.** [cochon, veau] suckling **3.** [semblable au lait] milky ■ **un teint de ~** a milk-white complexion.

laitage [lɛtaʒ] *nm* dairy product.

laitance [lɛtɑ̃s] *nf* ZOOL milt.

laiterie [lɛtri] *nf* **1.** [fabrique, ferme, magasin] dairy **2.** [secteur d'activité] dairy industry *ou* farming.

laiteux, euse [lɛtø, øz] *adj* **1.** [semblable au lait] milky ■ **un liquide ~** a milky *ou* cloudy liquid **2.** [de la couleur du lait] milk white, milky white ■ **un teint ~** a milky-white complexion.

laitier, ère [lɛtje, ɛr] ◇ *adj* **1.** [du lait] dairy *(modif)* ■ **des produits ~s** dairy produce **2.** [bête] milk *(modif)*.
◇ *nm, f* **1.** [livreur] milkman *(f* milkwoman) **2.** [éleveur] dairy farmer.
◆ **laitier** *nm* MÉTALL slag.
◆ **laitière** *nf* **1.** [ustensile] milk can *UK*, milk pail, milk bucket *US* **2.** [vache] milk *ou* milch *ou* dairy cow.

laiton [lɛtɔ̃] *nm* brass ■ **un fil de ~** a piece of brass wire.

laitue [lety] *nf* lettuce ■ **~ pommée** round lettuce.

laïus [lajys] *nm fam* long spiel, long-winded speech ■ **ne me fais pas tout un ~!** give me the short version!

lama [lama] *nm* **1.** RELIG lama ■ **le Grand ~** the Dalai Lama **2.** ZOOL llama.

lamaïsme [lamaism] *nm* Lamaism.

lamaserie [lamazri] *nf* lamasery.

lambda [lɑ̃bda] *nm inv* **1.** [lettre] lambda **2.** *fam (comme adj)* *fam* **un individu ~** your average bloke *UK ou* Joe *US*.

lambeau, x [lɑ̃bo] *nm* **1.** [morceau] scrap, strip, bit ■ **~x de chair** strips of flesh **2.** MÉD flap.
◆ **en lambeaux** ◇ *loc adj* [déchiré] in tatters, in shreds.
◇ *loc adv* : **les affiches partent** *ou* **tombent en ~x** the posters are getting really tattered.

lambin, e [lɑ̃bɛ̃, in] ◇ *adj* dawdling, slow.
◇ *nm, f* dawdler, slowcoach *UK*, slowpoke *US*.

lambiner [3] [lɑ̃bine] *vi fam* to dawdle ■ **pas le temps de ~** no time to dawdle *ou* to hang around.

lambourde [lɑ̃burd] *nf* **1.** BOT fruit-tree shoot **2.** CONSTR [pour solives] wall plate ■ [frise] (joist) backing strip.

lambrequin [lɑ̃brəkɛ̃] *nm* **1.** [motif décoratif] lambrequin **2.** CONSTR (eaves) cornice **3.** [d'un lit] valance ■ [d'une fenêtre] pelmet *UK*, lambrequin *US*.
◆ **lambrequins** *nmpl* HÉRALD mantle, mantling.

lambris [lɑ̃bri] *nm* **1.** [en bois] panelling, wainscoting ■ **~ de chêne** oak panelling ◐ **sous les ~ dorés du ministère** in the gilded halls of the ministry **2.** [en marbre, en stuc] casing.

lambrisser [3] [lɑ̃brise] *vt* to panel, to wainscot ■ **lambrissé de chêne** oak-panelled.

lambswool [lɑ̃bswul] *nm* lamb's wool.

lame [lam] *nf* **1.** [de couteau] blade ■ [de scie] web ■ [de tournevis] shaft ■ **~ de rasoir** razor blade ■ **il a le visage en ~ de couteau** he is hatchet-faced **2.** *litt* [épée] sword ■ **une bonne** *ou* **fine ~** [personne] a fine swordsman **3.** AUTO [de ressort] leaf **4.** CONSTR [de store] slat ■ [en bois] lath, strip ■ **~s de parquet** floorboards **5.** OPT slide **6.** TEXT [de lisses] leaf **7.** [vague] wave ■ **~ de fond** *pr* & *fig* ground swell.

lamé, e [lame] *adj* spangled, lamé.
◆ **lamé** *nm* lamé ■ **une robe en ~** a spangled *ou* lamé dress.

lamelle [lamɛl] *nf* **1.** BOT lamella, gill **2.** CULIN [de viande] thin strip ■ [de fromage, de pomme] thin slice, sliver **3.** MINÉR flake, lamella *spéc* **4.** OPT coverslip, cover glass.
◆ **en lamelles** *loc adj* CULIN sliced.

lamentable [lamɑ̃tabl] *adj* **1.** [désolant - accident] deplorable, frightful, lamentable ■ [pitoyable - plainte, vie] pathetic, pitiful ; [- état] awful, terrible **2.** [mauvais - performance, résultat] pathetic, appalling ■ **vous avez été ~s!** you were useless!

lamentablement [lamɑ̃tabləmɑ̃] *adv* miserably, dismally.

lamentation [lamɑ̃tasjɔ̃] *nf* **1.** [pleurs] wailing *(U)*, lamentation **2.** [récrimination] moaning *(U)*, complaining *(U)* ■ **se répandre en ~s** to burst into a torrent of complaints.
◆ **lamentations** *nfpl* RELIG : **les ~s** the Lamentations of Jeremiah ■ **le livre des Lamentations** the Book of Lamentations.

lamenter [3] [lamɑ̃te] ◆ **se lamenter** *vpi* [gémir] to moan, to whine ■ **se ~ sur qqch** to moan about sthg, to bemoan sthg *sout*.

lamento [lamɛnto] *nm* lament.

laminage [laminaʒ] *nm* **1.** [du plastique, du métal, du verre] rolling, laminating ■ [du caoutchouc, du papier] calendering **2.** *fig* [réduction] reduction.

laminer [3] [lamine] *vt* **1.** [plastique, métal, verre] to roll, to laminate ■ [caoutchouc, papier] to calender **2.** [réduire - revenus] to erode ; [- effectifs] to decimate **3.** *fam* [personne] to exhaust.

lamineur, euse [laminœr, øz] ◇ *adj* laminating.
◇ *nm, f* mill-hand *(in a roller-mill)*.
◆ **lamineuse** *nf* roller *(for glass)*.

laminoir [laminwar] *nm* **1.** MÉTALL rolling mill ◐ **passer au ~** to be put through the mill ■ **(faire) passer qqn au ~** *fig* to put sb through the mill **2.** [à papier] calender.

lampadaire [lɑ̃padɛr] *nm* **1.** [dans une maison] standard lamp *UK*, floor lamp *US* **2.** [dans la rue] street lamp, streetlight.

lampant, e [lɑ̃pɑ̃, ɑ̃t] *adj* lamp *(modif)*.

lamparo [lɑ̃paro] *nm* **1.** [lampe] (fishing) lamp **2.** [bateau] lamplight fishing boat.

lampe [lɑ̃p] *nf* **1.** [luminaire] lamp, light ■ **à la lumière de la ~** by lamplight ◐ **~ à arc** arc lamp *ou* light ■ **~ (d')architecte** *ou* **articulée** anglepoise lamp ■ **~ de bureau** desk lamp ■ **~ de chevet** bedside lamp ■ **~ à gaz** gaslight ■ **~ halogène** halogen lamp ■ **~ à huile** oil lamp ■ **~ à incandescence** incandescent lamp ■ **~ à pétrole** paraffin lamp *UK*, kerosene lamp *US* ■ **~ de poche** torch *UK*, flashlight *US* ■ **~ témoin** warning light ■ **~ tempête** storm lantern **2.** [appareil] : **~ à alcool** spirit lamp ■ **~ à bronzer** sunlamp ■ **~ à souder** blowlamp *UK*, blowtorch *US* **3.** RADIO valve (tube).

lampée [lɑ̃pe] *nf fam* swig, gulp.

lamper [3] [lɑ̃pe] *vt fam* to swig, to gulp down *(sép)*.

lampion [lɑ̃pjɔ̃] *nm* paper *ou* Chinese lantern ■ **scander des slogans sur l'air des ~s** to chant slogans.

lampiste [lɑ̃pist] *nm* **1.** HIST light maintenance man **2.** *fam* [subalterne] underling, menial, dogsbody *UK*.

lamproie [lɑ̃prwa] *nf* ZOOL lamprey ■ **~ de rivière** lampern.

lance [lɑ̃s] *nf* **1.** ARM spear **2.** [tuyau] : **~ à eau** hose, pipe ■ **~ d'incendie** fire hose **3.** MÉTALL : **~ à oxygène** oxygen lance.

lancé, e [lɑ̃se] *adj* [personne] : **le voilà ~!** he's made it!
◆ **lancée** *nf* [vitesse acquise] momentum.
◆ **sur ma lancée, sur sa lancée** *etc loc adv* : **il courait et sur sa ~e, il dribbla ses deux adversaires** he ran up the field, dribbling around two attackers as he went ■ **sur sa ~e, il s'en prit même à son père** he even took his father to task while he was at it ■ **continuer sur sa ~e** to keep going.

lance-amarre [lɑ̃samar] *nm inv* line-throwing gun.

lance-bombes [lɑ̃sbɔ̃b] *nm inv* bomb-dropping gear.

lancée [lɑ̃se] *f* ▻ **lancé**.

lance-flammes [lɑ̃sflam] *nm inv* flamethrower.

lance-fusées [lɑ̃sfyze] *nm inv* rocket launcher.

lance-grenades [lɑ̃sgrənad] *nm inv* grenade launcher ■ **~ sous-marines** depth-charge launcher.

lancement [lɑ̃smɑ̃] *nm* **1.** ASTRONAUT & NAUT launch, launching ▶ **créneau** *ou* **fenêtre de ~** firing *ou* launch window **2.** TRAV PUB : **le ~ d'un pont** the throwing of a bridge **3.** [en publicité - opération] launching ; [- cérémonie, réception] launch ■ **le ~ d'un produit** the launching of a product ▶ **prix de ~** launch price.

lance-missiles [lɑ̃smisil] *nm inv* missile launcher.

lance-pierres [lɑ̃spjɛr] *nm inv* **1.** [fronde] catapult **2.** *fam loc* **déjeuner/manger avec un ~** to gulp one's lunch/meal (down).

lancer¹ [lɑ̃se] *nm* **1.** PÊCHE casting ■ **~ léger/lourd** fixed/free reel casting **2.** SPORT throw ■ **le ~ du disque** the discus ■ **le ~ du javelot** the javelin ■ **le ~ du poids** the shot.

lancer² [16] [lɑ̃se] ◇ *vt*

> **A.** ENVOYER, ÉMETTRE
> **B.** METTRE EN MARCHE, FAIRE DÉBUTER

A. ENVOYER, ÉMETTRE

1. [jeter] to throw ■ **elle m'a lancé la balle** she threw me the ball, she threw the ball to me ■ **~ la jambe en l'air** to kick one's leg up ■ **~ le poids** to put the shot ■ **ils nous lançaient des regards curieux** they looked at us curiously ■ **ses yeux lançaient des éclairs** her eyes flashed ■ **~ qqch à la figure de qqn** to throw sthg in sb's face

2. [à l'aide d'un instrument] to fire, to shoot ■ [bombe] to drop ■ ASTRONAUT to launch ■ **~ un projectile téléguidé** to fire a remote-controlled missile

3. [émettre - cri] to let out *(insép)* ; [- remarque] to make ■ **~ un bon mot** to crack a joke ■ **~ des injures à qqn** to hurl insults at sb

4. [diffuser - décret, consigne] to send *ou* to put out *(sép)*, to issue ■ **~ des invitations** to send *ou* to give out invitations ■ **~ un SOS/un appel à la radio** to send out an SOS/an appeal on the radio ■ **~ un mandat d'amener/un ultimatum** to issue a summons/an ultimatum ■ **~ un emprunt** to float a loan ■ **~ une souscription** to start a fund

5. PÊCHE to cast

B. METTRE EN MARCHE, FAIRE DÉBUTER

1. [faire partir brusquement] : **ils lancèrent les chiens sur les rôdeurs** they set the dogs on the prowlers ■ **~ des troupes à l'attaque** to send troops into the attack ‖ [mettre en train - campagne] to launch ; [- affaire] to set up ; [- idée] to float ; [- mode] to start

2. [faire fonctionner - gén] to get going *ou* started, to start ■ INFORM [- programme] to start ■ **~ un balancier** to set a pendulum swinging ■ **~ un moteur** to rev up *ou* to start an engine ■ **une fois le moteur lancé** once the engine is running ■ **le train était lancé à 150 km/h quand...** the train was hurtling along at 150 km/h when...

3. [faire connaître - produit] to launch ■ **c'est ce roman/cette émission qui l'a lancé** this novel/programme made him famous

4. *fam* [orienter - discussion] to get going ■ **une fois qu'il est lancé sur ce sujet, on ne peut plus l'arrêter** once he gets going on the subject, there's no stopping him

5. [engager] to lead ■ **vous lancez le pays dans l'aventure** you're leading the country into the unknown

6. MIL to launch

7. NAUT to launch.

◇ *vi* [élancer - douleur] to stab ■ **ça me lance dans l'épaule, l'épaule me lance** I've got a sharp stabbing pain in my shoulder.

◆ **se lancer** ◇ *vp (emploi réciproque)* to throw at one another ■ **elles se lançaient des injures** they were hurling insults back and forth, they were exchanging insults.

◇ *vpi* **1.** [se précipiter] to throw o.s. ■ [courir] to rush (headlong), to dash ■ **se ~ à la poursuite de** to set off in pursuit of ■ **se ~ dans le vide** to jump *ou* to throw o.s. into empty space **2.** [se mettre à parler] : **se ~ sur un sujet** to get going on a topic **3.** [prendre l'initiative] : **allez, lance-toi et demande une augmentation** go on, take the plunge and ask for a rise ■ **le bébé s'est lancé et a traversé la pièce** the baby set off and crossed the room.

◆ **se lancer dans** *vp+prép* **1.** [s'aventurer dans - explication, aventure] to embark on ■ **ne te lance pas dans de grosses dépenses** don't go spending a lot of money **2.** [se mettre à pratiquer] to get involved in ■ **se ~ dans la politique** to take up politics.

lance-roquettes [lɑ̃srɔkɛt] *nm inv* (hand held) rocket launcher *ou* gun.

lance-torpilles [lɑ̃stɔrpij] *nm inv* torpedo (launching) tube.

lancette [lɑ̃sɛt] *nf* ARCHIT & MÉD lancet.

lanceur, euse [lɑ̃sœr, øz] *nm, f* **1.** [au baseball] pitcher ■ [au cricket] bowler ■ **~ de javelot** javelin thrower ■ **~ de poids** shot putter **2.** [promoteur] promoter, originator.

◆ **lanceur** *nm* ASTRONAUT launch vehicle, launcher.

lancier [lɑ̃sje] *nm* MIL lancer.

lancinant, e [lɑ̃sinɑ̃, ɑ̃t] *adj* **1.** [douleur] throbbing **2.** [obsédant - souvenir] haunting **3.** [répétitif] nerve-shattering ■ **une musique ~e** pounding music.

lancinement [lɑ̃sinmɑ̃] *nm* throbbing pain.

lanciner [3] [lɑ̃sine] ◇ *vt* [obséder] to obsess, to haunt, to plague ■ [tourmenter] to harass, to badger, to pester.

◇ *vi* to torment.

Land [lɑ̃d] (*pl* **Länder** [lɛndœr]) *nm* Land ■ **les Länder allemands** the German Länder.

landais, e [lɑ̃dɛ, ɛz] *adj* from the Landes.

landau, s [lɑ̃do] *nm* **1.** [pour bébés] pram, baby carriage US **2.** [attelage] landau.

lande [lɑ̃d] *nf* moor ■ **les ~s bretonnes** the Brittany moors.

Landes [lɑ̃d] *npr fpl* : **les ~** [région] the Landes ; [département] the Landes *(département in Aquitaine; chef-lieu: Mont-de-Marsan, code: 40).*

langage [lɑ̃gaʒ] *nm* **1.** LING & PSYCHOL language ■ **le ~ enfantin** baby talk ▶ **~ écrit/parlé** written/spoken language ■ **troubles du ~** speech *ou* language disorders

2. [code] language ■ **le ~ des animaux** animal language ■ **le ~ des fleurs** the language of flowers ■ **le ~ musical** the musical idiom ■ **le ~ de la peinture** the idiom of painting ▶ **le ~ des sourds-muets** deaf and dumb language, sign language

3. [jargon] language ■ **~ administratif/technique** administrative/technical language

4. [style] language ■ **~ familier/populaire** colloquial/popular language ■ **~ correct/incorrect** [d'après la bienséance] polite/impolite language ■ **~ argotique** slang ■ **~ imagé** colourful *ou* picturesque language ■ **~ poétique** poetic language ■ **qu'est-ce que c'est que ce ~?** what kind of language is that? ▶ **le beau ~** educated speech

5. [discours] language, talk ■ **tu tiens un drôle de ~ depuis quelque temps** you've been coming out with *ou* saying some very odd things recently ■ **tenir un tout autre ~** to change one's tune ■ **c'est le ~ de la raison** that's a sensible thing to say

6. INFORM & TÉLÉCOM language ■ **~ chiffré** cipher ■ **~ évolué** high-level language ■ **~ machine** internal *ou* machine language ■ **~ de programmation** programming language.

langagier, ère [lɑ̃gaʒje, ɛr] *adj* linguistic, language *(modif)*.

lange [lɑ̃ʒ] *nm* [pour bébé] baby blanket.

◆ **langes** *nmpl vieilli* swaddling clothes.

◆ **dans les langes** *loc adv* [à ses débuts] in infancy ■ **le cinéma était encore dans les ~s** *fig* the cinema was still in its infancy.

langer [17] [lɑ̃ʒe] *vt* to swaddle.

langoureusement [lɑ̃gurøzmɑ̃] *adv* languorously.

langoureux, euse [lɑ̃gurø, øz] *adj* [alangui] languishing ■ [mélancolique] languid, languorous ■ **un regard ~** a languid look.

langouste [lɑ̃gust] *nf* ZOOL crayfish ■ CULIN (spiny) lobster.

langoustier [lɑ̃gustje] *nm* **1.** [bateau] lobster (fishing) boat **2.** [filet] crayfish net.

langoustine [lɑ̃gustin] *nf* ≃ Dublin bay prawn.

langue [lɑ̃g] *nf*

A. ORGANE
B. LINGUISTIQUE
C. FORME

A. ORGANE

1. ANAT tongue ▪ **avoir la ~ blanche** *ou* **chargée** to have a coated *ou* furred tongue ▸ **une mauvaise ~, une ~ de vipère** a (malicious) gossip ▪ **les mauvaises ~s prétendent que...** some (ill-intentioned) gossips claim that... ▪ **c'est une ~ de vipère** she's got a venomous *ou* spiteful tongue ▪ **mauvaise ~!** that's a bit nasty of you!, that's a rather nasty thing to say! ▪ **les ~s vont bon train** tongues are wagging ▪ **tirer la ~ : tirez la ~ et dites ah** put *ou* stick your tongue out and say aah ▪ **tirer la ~ à qqn** to stick one's tongue out at sb ▪ **tirer la ~** *fam fig* [avoir soif] to be gasping (for a drink) ; [avoir du mal] to have a hard *ou* rough time ; [être fatigué] to be worn out ▪ **as-tu avalé** *ou* **perdu ta ~?** have you lost *ou* (has the) cat got your tongue? ▪ **avoir la ~ bien affilée** *ou* **bien pendue** *fam* to be a chatterbox, to have the gift of the gab ▪ **avoir la ~ fourchue** to speak with a forked tongue ▪ **avoir la ~ trop longue** to have a big mouth ▪ **coup de ~** lick ▪ **donner des coups de ~** to lick ▪ **le vin délie les ~s** wine always gets people chatting *ou* loosens people's tongues ▪ **elle n'a pas la ~ dans sa poche** *fam* she's never at a loss for something to say *ou* for words ▪ **donner sa ~ au chat** to give up (guessing) ▪ **tenir sa ~** to keep a secret ▪ **dans les réunions, il ne sait jamais tenir sa ~** he can never keep quiet in meetings ▪ **tourne sept fois ta ~ dans ta bouche avant de parler** *fam* think twice before you open your mouth

2. CULIN tongue ▪ **~ de bœuf** ox tongue

B. LINGUISTIQUE

1. [moyen de communication] language, tongue ▪ **~ commune** common language ▪ **décrire une ~** to describe a language ▪ **un professeur de ~s** a language teacher ▪ **les étudiants de ~ anglaise** English-speaking students ▸ **~ cible** *ou* **d'arrivée** target language ▪ **~ maternelle** mother tongue ▪ **~ nationale** national language ▪ **~ d'oc** langue d'oc *(language of southern France)* ▪ **~ d'oïl** langue d'oïl *(language of northern France)* ▪ **~ officielle** official language ▪ **dans la ~ parlée** colloquially, in the spoken language ▪ **~ source** *ou* **de départ** source language ▪ **~ de travail** working language ▪ **~ véhiculaire** lingua franca ▪ **la ~ vernaculaire** the vernacular ▪ **~s anciennes** *ou* **mortes** dead languages ▪ **~s étrangères** foreign languages ▪ **~s orientales** oriental languages ▪ **les ~s vivantes** ÉDUC modern languages ; [utilisées de nos jours] living languages

2. [jargon] language ▪ **dans la ~ du barreau** in legal parlance *sout*, in the language of the courts ▪ **la ~ populaire/littéraire** popular/literary language ▸ **~ de bois** hackneyed phrases ▪ **la ~ de bois des politiciens** the clichés politicians come out with ▪ **~ savante** LING & HIST [latin] language of learning ▪ **~ vulgaire** LING & HIST [langue du peuple] vernacular ▪ **la ~ verte** slang

3. [style - d'une époque, d'un écrivain] language ▪ **la ~ de la Renaissance** Renaissance language ▪ **dans la ~ de Molière/Shakespeare** in French/English

C. FORME

1. [gén] tongue ▪ **des ~s de feu léchaient le mur** tongues of fire were licking the wall

2. GÉOGR : **une ~ de terre** a strip of land, a narrow piece of land.

langue-de-bœuf [lɑ̃gdəbœf] (*pl* **langues-de-bœuf**) *nf* BOT beefsteak fungus.

langue-de-chat [lɑ̃gdəʃa] (*pl* **langues-de-chat**) *nf* langue de chat (biscuit).

Languedoc [lɑ̃gdɔk] *npr m* : **le ~** Languedoc.

languedocien, enne [lɑ̃gdɔsjɛ̃, ɛn] *adj* from Languedoc *ou* the Languedoc region.

Languedoc-Roussillon [lɑ̃gdɔkrusijɔ̃] *npr m* : **le ~** Languedoc-Roussillon.

LANGUEDOC-ROUSSILLON

This administrative region includes the *départements* of Aude, Gard, Hérault, Lozère and Pyrénées-Orientales (capital: Montpellier).

languette [lɑ̃gɛt] *nf* **1.** [petite bande] strip ▪ **les dossiers sont séparés par une ~ de papier** the files are separated by a strip of paper *ou* a paper marker **2.** [de chaussure] tab, stem **3.** [de balance] pointer **4.** MUS [d'orgue] languet ▪ [d'instrument à anche] reed.

langueur [lɑ̃gœr] *nf* **1.** [apathie] languidness **2.** [mélancolie] languor ▪ **un sourire plein de ~** a languid *ou* languorous smile.

languide [lɑ̃gid] *adj litt* languid, languishing.

languir [32] [lɑ̃gir] *vi* **1.** *litt* [personne, animal] to languish, to pine ▪ **~ (d'amour) pour qqn** to be consumed *ou* languishing with love for sb **2.** [plante] to wilt **3.** [conversation, situation] to flag ▪ **les affaires languissent** business is flagging *ou* slack **4.** [attendre] : **faire ~ qqn** to keep sb waiting.
◆ **languir après** *v+prép* to languish *ou* to pine for.
◆ **se languir** *vpi* [personne] to pine ▪ **il se languit de toi** he's pining for you ▪ **je me languis de la Provence** I'm longing to go back to Provence.

languissant, e [lɑ̃gisɑ̃, ɑ̃t] *adj* **1.** *litt* [qui dépérit] failing, dwindling **2.** *litt* [amoureux] languishing, lovelorn, lovesick **3.** [sans vigueur] languid, listless **4.** [morne] : **le commerce est ~** business is slack ▪ **conversation ~e** dull conversation.

lanière [lanjɛr] *nf* **1.** [sangle] strap **2.** [d'un fouet] lash.

lanoline [lanɔlin] *nf* lanolin.

lansquenet [lɑ̃skənɛ] *nm* HIST, MIL & JEUX lansquenet.

lanterne [lɑ̃tɛrn] *nf* **1.** [lampe] lantern ▪ **~ sourde/vénitienne** dark/Chinese lantern ▸ **les aristocrates à la ~!** HIST string the aristocrats up! **2.** CINÉ projector **3.** CONSTR lantern **4.** PHOTO : **~ magique** magic lantern.
◆ **lanternes** *nfpl* AUTO sidelights *UK*, parking lights *US*.
◆ **lanterne rouge** *nf* **1.** RAIL rear *ou* tail light **2.** *loc* **être la ~ rouge** [gén] to bring up the rear ; SPORT [dans une course] to come (in) last ; [équipe] to get the wooden spoon ; [à l'école] to be bottom of the class.

lanterneau, x [lɑ̃tɛrno] *nm* skylight, roof light.

lanterner [3] [lɑ̃tɛrne] *vi* **1.** [perdre son temps] to dawdle, to drag one's feet ▪ **il est toujours à ~** he is always dawdling **2.** [attendre] : **faire ~ qqn** to keep sb hanging about *ou* waiting.

lanternon [lɑ̃tɛrnɔ̃] *nm* lantern (tower) *ou* turret.

Laos [laos] *npr m* : **le ~** Laos ▪ **au ~** in Laos.

laotien, enne [laɔsjɛ̃, ɛn] *adj* Laotian.
◆ **Laotien, enne** *nm, f* Laotian.

La Palice [lapalis] *npr* : **une vérité de ~** a truism.

lapalissade [lapalisad] *nf* truism ▪ **c'est une ~** that's self-evident, that's stating the obvious.

La Paz [lapaz] *npr* La Paz.

lapement [lapmɑ̃] *nm* lapping, lap.

laper [3] [lape] *vt* to lap (up).

lapereau, x [lapro] *nm* young rabbit.

lapidaire [lapidɛr] ◇ *adj* **1.** [concis] terse, lapidary *sout* ▪ **un style ~** a pithy *ou* direct *ou* succinct style **2.** MINÉR lapidary.
◇ *nm* **1.** [artisan] lapidary **2.** [commerçant] gem merchant.

lapidation [lapidasjɔ̃] *nf* stoning, lapidation *sout*.

lapider [3] [lapide] *vt* **1.** [tuer] to stone to death, to lapidate *sout* **2.** *litt* [critiquer] to lambast.

lapié [lapje] *nm* lapiés.

lapin [lapɛ̃] *nm* **1.** ZOOL rabbit ▪ **~ mâle** buck (rabbit) ▸ **~ de garenne** wild rabbit ▪ **poser un ~ à qqn** *fam* to stand sb up **2.** CULIN rabbit **3.** [fourrure] rabbit (skin) *UK*, cony (skin) *US* **4.** *fam* [terme d'affection] poppet *UK*, honey *US*.

lapine [lapin] *nf* doe (rabbit).

lapiner [3] [lapine] *vi* to litter.

lapinière [lapinjɛr] *nf* rabbit hutches.

lapis(-lazuli) [lapis(lazyli)] *nm inv* lapis lazuli.

lapon, o(n)ne [lapɔ̃, ɔn] *adj* Lapp, Lappish.
◆ **Lapon, o(n)ne** *nm, f* Lapp, Laplander.

Laponie [lapɔni] *npr f* : **(la) ~** Lapland.

laponne [lapɔn] *f* ▷ **lapon.**

laps [laps] *nm* : **un ~ de temps** a lapse of time, a while.

lapsus [lapsys] *nm* **1.** [faute] : **~ linguae** slip (of the tongue), lapsus linguae *spéc* ■ **~ calami** slip of the pen **2.** PSYCHOL Freudian slip ■ **~ révélateur** *hum* Freudian slip.

laquage [lakaʒ] *nm* TECHNOL lacquering.

laquais [lakɛ] *nm* **1.** [valet] footman **2.** *litt* & *péj* [homme servile] lackey *péj.*

laque [lak] ◇ *nf* **1.** [vernis] lacquer **2.** [pour cheveux] hair spray, (hair) lacquer *UK.*
◇ *nm* [objet] piece of lacquerwork ■ **des ~s** lacquerware, lacquerwork.

laqué, e [lake] *adj* **1.** ART lacquered **2.** CONSTR gloss ■ **cuisine ~e (en) rouge** kitchen in red gloss **3.** CULIN ▷ **canard.**
◆ **laqué** *nm* [peinture] (high) gloss paint ■ [enduit] varnish *UK*, enamel *US.*

laquelle [lakɛl] *f* ▷ **lequel.**

laquer [3] [lake] *vt* **1.** [recouvrir de laque] to lacquer **2.** [vernir] to varnish.

larbin[△] [larbɛ̃] *nm* *pr* & *fig* flunkey.

larcin [larsɛ̃] *nm* *sout* **1.** [petit vol] petty theft ■ **commettre de menus ~s** to engage in petty theft **2.** [objet volé] : **le grenier était plein de ses ~s** the attic was filled with his booty *litt* OU spoils.

lard [lar] *nm* **1.** CULIN : **~ fumé** smoked bacon ■ **~ gras, gros ~** fat bacon ■ **~ maigre, petit ~, ~ de poitrine** streaky bacon ■ **~ salé** salt pork **2.** *loc* **faire du ~** *fam* to get fat ■ **avec eux, on se demande** OU **on ne sait pas si c'est du ~ ou du cochon** *fam* with that lot, you never know where you are ■ **rentrer dans le ~ à qqn** *fam* to hit out at sb ■ **un gros ~**[△] a fatso[△], a fat slob[△].

larder [3] [larde] *vt* **1.** CULIN to lard **2.** [poignarder] : **~ qqn de coups de couteau** to stab sb repeatedly **3.** [truffer] : **~ une lettre de citations** to pepper a letter with quotations.

lardon [lardɔ̃] *nm* **1.** CULIN piece of diced bacon ■ **achète des ~s pour le ragoût** buy some bacon pieces for the stew **2.** [△] [enfant] kid.

lare [lar] ◇ *adj* : **dieux ~s** lares.
◇ *nm* lar, household god.

largable [largabl] *adj* releasable ■ **réservoir ~** releasable tank.

largage [largaʒ] *nm* **1.** [par parachute] dropping ■ [de troupes, de matériel] dispatching, dropping ■ **point de ~** drop point **2.** [d'une bombe] dropping, releasing.

large [larʒ] ◇ *adj* **1.** [grand - gén] broad, wide ; [- plaine] big, wide ; [- rue] broad ; [- tache] large ■ **~ de 5 cm** 5 cm wide ■ **un chapeau à ~s bords** a wide-brimmed hat ■ **~ d'épaules** broad-shouldered ■ **un ~ mouvement du bras** a sweeping gesture with the arm ■ **un ~ sourire** a broad smile
2. [ample - vêtement] big, baggy ; [- chaussures] wide
3. [considérable] large ■ **elle a une ~ part de responsabilité** she must bear a large OU major share of the blame ■ **jouissant d'une ~ diffusion** widely distributed ■ **avoir un ~ vocabulaire** to have a wide OU wide-ranging vocabulary ■ **elle a fait de ~s concessions/un ~ tour d'horizon** she made generous concessions/an extensive survey of the situation ■ **les journaux ont publié de ~s extraits de son discours** the papers quoted extensively from his speech
4. [général] : **prendre un mot dans son sens ~** to take a word in its broadest sense
5. [généreux] generous
6. [ouvert] open ■ **leur père a l'esprit ~** their father is open-minded OU broad-minded
7. [excessif] : **ton estimation était un peu ~** your estimate was a bit wide of the mark.
◇ *nm* **1.** [dimension] width ■ **ici la rivière a 2 km de ~** here the river is 2 km wide
2. NAUT : **le ~** the open sea ■ **respirer l'air du ~** to breathe the sea air ■ **le vent du ~** offshore wind ■ **au ~** offshore, at sea ◗ **au ~ de Hong Kong** off Hong Kong ■ **se tenir au ~ de qqch** *fig* to stand clear of sthg ■ **gagner** OU **prendre le ~** *pr* to head for the open sea ■ **il est temps de prendre le ~** *fam fig* it's time we beat it.
◇ *adv* : **calculer** OU **prévoir ~** to allow a good margin for error ■ **voir ~** to think big.
◆ **en large** *loc adv* widthways.

largement [larʒəmɑ̃] *adv* **1.** [amplement] : **gagner ~ sa vie** to make a good living ■ **tu auras ~ le temps** you'll easily have enough time, you'll have more than enough time ■ **des pouvoirs ~ accrus** considerably increased powers ■ **une opinion ~ répandue** a widely held opinion **2.** [généreusement] generously **3.** [de beaucoup] greatly ■ **la demande excède ~ notre capacité** demand greatly exceeds our capacity **4.** [facilement] easily ■ **il vaut ~ son frère** he's easily as good as his brother.

largesse [larʒɛs] *nf* [magnanimité] generosity, largesse *sout* ■ **il fait toujours preuve de ~** he's always very generous.
◆ **largesses** *nfpl* [présents] gifts, liberalities *sout* ■ **il ne faisait pas de telles ~s avec tous** he didn't make such generous gifts to everybody.
◆ **avec largesse** *loc adv* : **traiter qqn avec ~** to be generous to sb.

largeur [larʒœr] *nf* **1.** [dimension] width ■ **quelle est la ~ de la pièce?** how wide is the room? ■ **la route a une ~ de 5 m** OU **5 m de ~** the road is 5 m wide ■ **une remorque barrait la route dans** OU **sur toute sa ~** there was a trailer blocking the entire width of the road ■ **déchiré dans** OU **sur toute la ~** torn all the way across ■ **~ hors tout** overall width **2.** *fig* broadness, breadth ■ **~ d'esprit** OU **de vues** broadness of mind, broad-mindedness **3.** COMM : **grande ~** double-width **4.** IMPR breadth, set, width ■ **~ de la colonne** width of column **5.** INFORM : **~ de la bande** bandwidth.
◆ **dans les grandes largeurs** *loc adv fam* **on a été roulés dans les grandes ~s!** we were well and truly taken for a ride!
◆ **en largeur** *loc adv* widthways, widthwise, crosswise ■ **la table fait 30 cm en ~** the table is 30 cm widthways OU across.

largue [larg] *nm* NAUT reaching.

largué, e [large] *adj fam* **être ~** to be out of one's depth.

larguer [3] [large] *vt* **1.** NAUT [voile] to slip, to let out *(sép)*, to unfurl ■ [amarre] to slip ■ *(en usage absolu)* **larguez!** let go! **2.** AÉRON [bombe, charge] to drop ■ [réservoir] to jettison ■ [fusée] to release **3.** [△] [abandonner - poste] to quit, to chuck(in) *(insép)*, to walk out on *(insép)* ; [- vieillerie, projet] to chuck, to bin *esp UK* ; [- amant] to dump, to jilt ; [- personne avec qui l'on vit] to walk out on ■ **se faire ~** to be dumped.

larme [larm] *nf* **1.** PHYSIOL tear ■ **verser des ~s** to shed tears ■ **retenir ses ~s** to hold back one's tears ■ **être en ~s** to be in tears ■ **ses yeux s'emplirent de ~s** his eyes filled with tears ■ **être au bord des ~s** to be on the verge of tears ■ **avec des ~s dans la voix** with OU in a tearful voice ■ **il y a de quoi vous arracher** OU **vous tirer des ~s** it's enough to make you burst into tears ■ **avoir les ~s aux yeux** to have tears in one's eyes ■ **il a toujours la ~ à l'œil, il a la ~ facile** he cries easily ■ **pleurer** OU **verser des ~s de joie** to cry for joy, to shed tears of joy ■ **il y est allé de sa (petite) ~** he shed a tear ◗ **~s de crocodile** crocodile tears ■ **~s de sang** *litt* tears of blood **2.** [petite quantité] : **une ~ (de)** a drop (of) **3.** [d'un cerf] tear.

larmoie *etc v* ▷ **larmoyer.**

larmoiement [larmwamɑ̃] *nm* PHYSIOL watering.
◆ **larmoiements** *nmpl litt* tears, snivelling *(U) péj.*

larmoyant, e [larmwajɑ̃, ɑ̃t] *adj* **1.** PHYSIOL watery **2.** *péj* [éploré] : **le récit ~ de ses malheurs** the sorry tale of her misfortunes ■ **d'une voix ~e, elle nous annonça...** she told us in a tearful voice...

larmoyer [13] [larmwaje] *vi* **1.** PHYSIOL [œil] to water **2.** *péj* [se lamenter] to weep, to snivel *péj*, to whimper *péj.*

larron [larɔ̃] *nm* **1.** *arch* [voleur] robber, thief **2.** BIBLE thief ▪ **le bon ~ et le mauvais ~** the penitent thief and the impenitent thief.

larsen [larsɛn] *nm* : **effet ~** feedback.

larvaire [larvɛr] *adj* **1.** ZOOL larval **2.** *fig* embryonic, unformed ▪ **le projet était encore à l'état ~** the plan was still in its early stage *ou* in embryo.

larve [larv] *nf* **1.** ZOOL larva ▪ [ver] maggot **2.** *fam* [fainéant] lazybones **3.** *sout* & *péj* **~ (humaine)** worm **4.** ANTIQ spectre.

larvé, e [larve] *adj* **1.** MÉD latent, larvate *spéc* **2.** [latent] latent, concealed ▪ **en 1964 il y avait déjà une révolte ~e** a rebellion was already brewing in 1964.

laryngé, e [larɛ̃ʒe] *adj* laryngeal.

laryngectomie [larɛ̃ʒɛktɔmi] *nf* laryngectomy.

laryngite [larɛ̃ʒit] *nf* laryngitis.

laryngologie [larɛ̃gɔlɔʒi] *nf* laryngology.

laryngologiste [larɛ̃gɔlɔʒist], **laryngologue** [larɛ̃gɔlɔg] *nmf* throat specialist, laryngologist *spéc.*

laryngoscope [larɛ̃gɔskɔp] *nm* laryngoscope.

laryngoscopie [larɛ̃gɔskɔpi] *nf* laryngoscopy.

laryngotomie [larɛ̃gɔtɔmi] *nf* laryngotomy.

larynx [larɛ̃ks] *nm* voice-box, larynx *spéc.*

las [las] *interj litt* alas.

las, lasse [la, las] *adj* **1.** *litt* [fatigué] weary **2.** [découragé, écœuré] weary ▪ **être ~ de qqch** to be weary of sthg.

lasagne [lazaɲ] (*pl inv ou pl* **lasagnes**) *nf* lasagna *(U)*.

lascar [laskar] *nm fam* **1.** [individu rusé] rogue ▪ **celui-là, c'est un drôle de ~!** he's a shady character! ▪ **tu vas le regretter, mon ~!** [homme] you'll be sorry, buster *ou* pal! ; [enfant] you'll be sorry, you little rascal! **2.** [individu quelconque] character, customer ▪ **un grand ~** a big chap.

lascif, ive [lasif, iv] *adj* **1.** [sensuel] lascivious, sensual **2.** [lubrique] lustful, lewd.

lascivement [lasivmɑ̃] *adv* lustfully.

lascivité [lasivite], **lasciveté** [lasivte] *nf* **1.** [sensualité] wantonness, lasciviousness **2.** [lubricité] lust, lewdness.

laser [lazɛr] *nm* laser ▪ **traitement au ~** laser treatment ▪ **enregistrement ~** [procédé] laser recording ; [disque] laser disc ▪ **faisceau ~** laser beam.

Lassa [lasa] *npr* : **fièvre de ~** Lassa fever.

lassant, e [lasɑ̃, ɑ̃t] *adj* tedious ▪ **tu es ~ à la fin!** you're beginning to irritate me!

lasse [las] *f* ▷ **las.**

lasser [3] [lase] *vt* **1.** *sout* [exténuer] to weary **2.** *sout* [importuner] to bore, to tire, to weary *sout* ▪ **tu me lasses avec tes problèmes** I'm tired of hearing about your problems **3.** [décourager] to tax, to exhaust, to fatigue *sout* ▪ **~ la patience de qqn** to try sb's patience ▪ *(en usage absolu)* **ses jérémiades finissent par ~** his moaning gets a bit trying after a while.

◆ **se lasser** *vpi* to get tired, to (grow) weary *sout* ▪ **se ~ de qqn/de faire qqch** to get tired of sb/of doing sthg ▪ **sans se ~** tirelessly.

lassitude [lasityd] *nf* **1.** [fatigue] tiredness, weariness, lassitude *litt* **2.** [découragement] weariness ▪ **être pris d'une immense ~** to be overcome by weariness.

lasso [laso] *nm* lasso, lariat *US* ▪ **attraper une bête au ~** to lasso an animal.

lasure [lazyr] *nf* wood stain, wood varnish.

lasurer [3] [lazyre] *vt* to stain, to varnish.

lat. (*abr écrite de* **latitude**) lat.

latence [latɑ̃s] *nf* latency ▪ **période de ~** latency period.

latent, e [latɑ̃, ɑ̃t] *adj* latent ▪ **à l'état ~** in the making.

latéral, e, aux [lateral, o] *adj* **1.** [sur le côté] lateral, side *(modif)* ▪ **porte/rue/sortie ~e** side door/street/exit **2.** [annexe] minor **3.** TÉLÉCOM : **bande ~e** sideband.

◆ **latérale** *nf* lateral.

latéralement [lateralmɑ̃] *adv* sideways, laterally ▪ **la lumière de la bougie l'éclairait ~** the light from the candle fell on him from the side.

latéralisation [lateralizasjɔ̃] *nf* lateralization.

latéralisé, e [lateralize] *adj* lateralized.

latex [latɛks] *nm* latex.

latin, e [latɛ̃, in] *adj* **1.** ANTIQ Latin **2.** LING [appartenant au latin] Latin ▪ [issu du latin] Romance *(modif)* ▪ **les langues ~es** the Romance *ou* Latin languages **3.** SOCIOL Latin ▪ **les peuples ~s** the Latin races ▪ **le tempérament ~** the Latin *ou* Mediterranean temperament **4.** RELIG Latin **5.** [à Paris] : **le Quartier Latin** the Latin Quarter *(area on the Left Bank of the Seine traditionally associated with students and artists)*.

◆ **Latin, e** *nm, f* Latin ▪ **les Latins** the Latin people, the Latins.

◆ **latin** *nm* LING Latin ▪ **bas ~** low Latin ▪ **~ de cuisine** dog Latin.

latinisant, e [latinizɑ̃, ɑ̃t] *adj* latinizing ▪ **pour ceux qui sont ~s** for those who know Latin, for the Latin scholars.

latinisation [latinizasjɔ̃] *nf* latinization.

latiniser [3] [latinize] *vt* to latinize.

latinisme [latinism] *nm* **1.** [idiotisme du latin] Latinism **2.** [emprunt au latin] Latin phrase.

latiniste [latinist] *nmf* Latin scholar, Latinist.

latinité [latinite] *nf* **1.** [caractère] Latinity **2.** [civilisation] Latin world.

latino-américain, e [latinoamerikɛ̃, ɛn] (*mpl* **latino-américains**, *fpl* **latino-américaines**) *adj* Latin American.

◆ **Latino-Américain, e** *nm, f* Latin American.

latitude [latityd] *nf* **1.** [liberté] latitude, scope ▪ **j'ai toute ~ pour mener mon enquête** I have full scope *ou* a free hand to conduct my enquiry **2.** ASTRON & GÉOGR latitude ▪ **cette ville est à 70° de ~ Nord** this city is situated at latitude 70° North ▪ **par 70° de ~ Nord** in latitude 70° North **3.** [région, climat] : **sous d'autres ~s** in other parts of the world.

latrines [latrin] *nfpl* latrine.

lattage [lataʒ] *nm* **1.** [action] lathing, battening **2.** [lattis] lathwork.

latte [lat] *nf* **1.** CONSTR lath ▪ [pour chevronnage] roof batten ▪ **~ de plancher** floorboard **2.** △ [pied] foot ▪ [chaussure] shoe ▪ **prendre un coup de ~** to get kicked.

latter [3] [late] *vt* CONSTR to lath, to batten.

lattis [lati] *nm* CONSTR lathwork *(U)*.

laudateur, trice [lodatœr, tris] *nm, f litt* laudator.

laudatif, ive [lodatif, iv] *adj* laudatory, laudative.

lauréat, e [lɔrea, at] ◇ *adj* prizewinning.

◇ *nm, f* prizewinner, laureate ▪ **~ du prix Nobel** Nobel prizewinner ▪ **~ du prix Goncourt** winner of the prix Goncourt.

laurier [lɔrje] *nm* **1.** BOT (bay) laurel, (sweet) bay **2.** CULIN : **mettre du ~ dans une sauce** to flavour a sauce with bay leaves ▶ **feuille de ~** bay leaf.

◆ **lauriers** *nmpl* [gloire] laurels ▪ **il est revenu couvert de ~s** he came home covered in glory.

laurier-cerise [lɔrjesəriz] (*pl* **lauriers-cerises**) *nm* cherry-laurel.

laurier-rose [lɔrjeroz] (*pl* **lauriers-roses**) *nm* rose bay, oleander.

laurier-sauce [lɔrjesos] (*pl* **lauriers-sauce**) *nm* bay tree.

Lausanne [lozan] *npr* Lausanne.

lavable [lavabl] *adj* washable ▪ **~ en machine** machine-washable.

lavabo [lavabo] *nm* **1.** [évier] washbasin *UK*, washbowl *US* **2.** RELIG lavabo.
◆ **lavabos** *nmpl* [toilettes] toilets, washroom *US*.

lavage [lavaʒ] *nm* **1.** [nettoyage - du linge] washing *(U)* ; [- d'une surface] scrubbing *(U)* ▪ **son jean a besoin d'un bon ~** his jeans need a good wash ▶ **'~ en machine'** 'machine wash' ▪ **'~ à la main'** 'hand wash (only)' ▪ **'instructions de ~'** 'washing instructions' **2.** MÉD lavage ▪ **~ d'estomac** pumping out (of) the stomach ▪ **faire un ~ d'estomac à qqn** to pump out sb's stomach **3.** MÉTALL & TEXT washing.
◆ **au lavage** *loc adv* in the wash ▪ **la tache est partie/n'est pas partie au ~** the stain came out/didn't come out in the wash.
◆ **lavage de cerveau** *nm* brainwashing ▪ **subir un ~ de cerveau** to be brainwashed.

lavallière [lavaljɛr] *nf necktie with a large bow.*

lavande [lavɑ̃d] *nf* BOT lavender.

lavandière [lavɑ̃djɛr] *nf* **1.** *litt* [blanchisseuse] washerwoman **2.** ORNITH (white) wagtail.

lavasse [lavas] *péj* ◇ *adj* [sans éclat] watery.
◇ *nf fam fam* [café, soupe] dishwater.

lave [lav] *nf* lava.

lavé, e [lave] *adj* **1.** [délayé - couleur] faded, washed out **2.** ART : **dessin ~** wash drawing.

lave-auto [lavɔto] *nm Québec* car wash.

lave-dos [lavdo] *nm inv* back-scrubber.

lave-glace [lavglas] (*pl* **lave-glaces**) *nm* windscreen washer *UK*, windshield washer *US*.

lave-linge [lavlɛ̃ʒ] *nm inv* washing machine, washer ▪ **~ à chargement frontal** front-loading washing machine.

lave-mains [lavmɛ̃] *nm inv* wash-hand basin *UK*, small washbowl *US*.

lavement [lavmɑ̃] *nm* MÉD enema.

laver [3] [lave] *vt* **1.** [vêtement, tissu] to wash ▪ [tache] to wash out *ou* off *(sép)* ▪ [surface] to wash down *(sép)* ▪ [vaisselle] to wash up *UK*, to do the washing up *UK*, to wash *US* ▪ [avec une brosse] to scrub ▪ **~ à grande eau** to swill out *ou* down *(sép)* ▪ **la voiture a besoin d'être lavée** the car needs washing *ou* a wash ▶ **il vaut mieux ~ son linge sale en famille** it's better not to wash one's dirty linen in public
2. [faire la toilette de] to wash ▪ **~ la tête** *ou* **les cheveux à qqn** to wash sb's hair ▪ **~ la tête à qqn** *fam fig* to give sb what for *ou* a good dressing down
3. [expier - péché] to wash away *(sép)* ▪ [dégager] to clear ▪ **~ qqn d'une accusation** to clear sb's name of an accusation ▪ **être lavé de tout soupçon** to be clear of all suspicion ▪ **~ un affront dans le sang** to avenge an insult (by fighting)
4. ART [dessin] to wash ▪ [couleur] to dilute, to wash
5. MÉD [plaie] to bathe, to cleanse ▪ [estomac] to wash *ou* to pump out *(sép)*
6. [minerai] to wash.
◆ **se laver** ◇ *vp (emploi réfléchi)* to (have a) wash ▪ **lave-toi tout seul, comme un grand** you're old enough to wash yourself ▪ **se ~ la figure/les mains** to wash one's face/hands ▪ **se ~ les dents** to clean *ou* to brush one's teeth ▶ **je m'en lave les mains** I wash my hands of the entire matter.
◇ *vp (emploi passif)* : **ça se lave très bien** it's very easy to wash, it washes very well.
◆ **se laver de** *vp+prép* : **se ~ d'un soupçon** to clear o.s. of suspicion ▪ **se ~ de ses péchés** to cleanse o.s. of one's sins.

laverie [lavri] *nf* **1.** [blanchisserie] : **~ (automatique)** self-service laundry, launderette *UK*, Laundromat® *US* **2.** MIN washing plant.

lave-tête [lavtɛt] *nm inv* shampoo basin.

lavette [lavɛt] *nf* **1.** [chiffon] dishcloth ▪ [brosse] washing-up brush *UK*, dish mop *US* **2.** *fam* [personne] drip **3.** *Belgique & Suisse* [gant de toilette] face flannel *UK*, washcloth *US* **4.** *Belgique* [éponge] cleaning cloth.

laveur, euse [lavœr, øz] *nm, f* [de vaisselle] washer, dishwasher ▪ [de linge] washerman (*f* washerwoman) ▪ [de voiture] car washer ▪ **~ de carreaux** *ou* **vitres** window cleaner.
◆ **laveur** *nm* **1.** AGRIC drum washer **2.** TECHNOL washer **3.** ZOOL ▷ **raton**.

lave-vaisselle [lavvesɛl] *nm inv* dishwasher.

lave-vitre [lavvitr] *nm* AUTO windscreen *UK or* windshield *US* washer.

lavis [lavi] *nm* **1.** [technique] washing *(U)* **2.** [dessin] wash drawing.

lavoir [lavwar] *nm* **1.** [lieu public] washhouse **2.** MIN washing plant.

Lawrence [lorɑ̃s] *npr* : **~ d'Arabie** Lawrence of Arabia.

laxatif, ive [laksatif, iv] *adj* laxative.
◆ **laxatif** *nm* laxative.

laxisme [laksism] *nm* **1.** [tolérance excessive] laxity, permissiveness **2.** RELIG laxism.

laxiste [laksist] ◇ *adj* **1.** [trop tolérant] soft, lax **2.** RELIG laxist.
◇ *nmf* **1.** [gén] over-lenient person **2.** RELIG laxist.

layette [lɛjɛt] *nf* baby clothes layette ▶ **bleu/rose ~** baby blue/pink.

Lazare [lazar] *npr* Lazarus.

lazulite [lazylit] *nf* lazulite.

lazzi [ladzi] (*pl inv ou pl* **lazzis**) *nm* jeer, gibe.

le [lə] *(devant voyelle ou 'h' muet l'* [l], *f* **la** [la], *pl* **les** [le]*)* ◇ *dét (art déf)* **1.** [avec un nom commun] the
2. [dans le temps] : **l'été dernier** last summer ▪ **l'été 1976** the summer of 1976 ▮ [devant une date] : **le premier juillet** the first of July ▪ **le 15 janvier 1991** 15 January, 1991 ▪ **il est passé nous voir le 15 août** he came to see us on the 15th of August *ou* on August the 15th ; [par écrit] he came to see us on August 15
3. [dans les fractions] a, an ▪ **le quart/tiers de** a quarter/third of ▪ **la moitié de** (a) half of
4. [avec un sens distributif] : **j'y vais le soir** I go there in the evening ▪ **elle vient deux fois la semaine** she comes twice a week ▪ **deux euros le kilo** two euros a *ou* per kilo ▪ **le docteur reçoit le lundi et le vendredi** *ou* **les lundis et vendredis** the doctor sees patients on Monday and Friday *ou* Mondays and Fridays
5. [avec valeur d'adjectif démonstratif] : **on sait que le problème est difficile** we know that it's a difficult problem
6. [avec une valeur expressive] what an *ou* a ▪ **la belle moto!** what a beautiful bike! ▪ **vise un peu la tenue!** *fam* look at that get-up! ▪ **alors, les amis, comment ça va?** well, folks, how are you?
7. [avec valeur d'adjectif possessif] : **le chapeau sur la tête** her/his *etc* hat on his/her *etc* head ▪ **il est parti le livre sous le bras** he went off with the book under his arm
8. [avec une valeur généralisante] : **les hommes et les femmes** men and women ▪ **la femme est l'égale de l'homme** woman is man's equal ▪ **le cheval, comme d'autres mammifères...** the horse *ou* horses, like other mammals... ▪ **l'important dans tout ça** the important thing (in all this) ▪ **ne fais pas l'idiot** don't be an idiot
9. [marquant l'approximation] : **vers les 4 h** about *ou* around 4 o'clock ▪ **il va sur la quarantaine** he's getting on for forty
10. [avec un nom propre] the ▪ **nous sommes invités chez les Durand** we are invited to the Durands' (house) ▪ **les Bourbons, les Stuarts** the Bourbons, the Stuarts ▪ **ce n'est plus la Sophie que nous avons connue** she's no longer the Sophie (that) we used to know ▪ **la Callas** Callas.
◇ *pron pers* **1.** [complément d'objet - homme] him ; [- femme, nation, bateau] her ; [- chose, animal] it ; [- bébé, animal domestique] him, her, it ▪ **ce bordeaux, je l'ai déjà goûté** I've already tasted this *ou* that Bordeaux ▪ **il l'a probablement oublié, ton livre** he's probably forgotten your book *ou* that book of yours
2. [représentant une proposition] : **elle est partie hier soir, du moins je l'ai entendu dire** she left last night, at least that's what I've heard ▪ **allez, dis-le-lui** go on, tell him (about it) ▪ **puisque je te le disais que ce n'était pas possible!** but I TOLD you it was impossible!
3. [comme attribut] : **êtes-vous satisfaite? – je le suis** are you satisfied? – I am ▪ **pour être timide, ça, il l'est!** boy, is he shy!, talk about shy!

lé [le] *nm* **1.** [d'un tissu, d'un papier peint] width **2.** [d'une jupe] gore.

LEA (*abr de* **langues étrangères appliquées**) *applied modern languages.*

leader [lidœr] *nm* **1.** [chef] leader **2.** COMM & ÉCON [entreprise] top *ou* leading firm ▪ *(comme adj)* **c'est le produit ~ de la gamme** it's the leading product in the range **3.** PRESSE leader, leading article **4.** SPORT : **le ~ du championnat de France** the team at the top of the French league.

leadership [lidœrʃip] *nm* [fonction de leader] leadership ▪ [position dominante] leading position.

leasing [liziŋ] *nm* leasing.
◆ **en leasing** *loc adv* on lease, as part of a leasing contract.

léchage [leʃaʒ] *nm* **1.** [gén] licking **2.** *fam* [fignolage] finishing touches.

lèche△ [lɛʃ] *nf* bootlicking ▪ **faire de la ~ à qqn** to suck up to sb.

léché, e [leʃe] *adj fam* **du travail ~** a highly polished piece of work ▪ **un roman policier bien ~** a neat little detective novel.

lèche-bottes [lɛʃbɔt] *nmf fam* bootlicker.

lèche-cul▲ [lɛʃky] *nmf* arse-licker△ *UK*, ass-kisser△ *US*.

lèchefrite [lɛʃfrit] *nf* dripping pan *UK*, broiler pan *US*.

lécher [18] [leʃe] *vt* **1.** [passer la langue sur] to lick ▶ **~ les bottes à qqn** *fam* to lick sb's boots ▪ **~ le cul à qqn**▲ to lick sb's arse△ *UK ou* ass△ *US* **2.** [confiture, miel] to lick up *(sép)* ▪ [lait, crème] to lap up *(sép)* ▪ **l'enfant lécha la cuillère** the child licked the spoon clean **3.** *fam* [perfectionner] to polish up *(sép)* **4.** [effleurer - suj: feu] to lick at.
◆ **se lécher** *vp (emploi réfléchi)* to lick o.s. ▪ **se ~ les doigts** to lick one's fingers ▶ **c'est à s'en ~ les doigts** *ou* **les babines!** it's scrumptious!, it's really yummy!

lécheur, euse [leʃœr, øz] *nm, f fam péj* bootlicker, groveller.
◆ **lécheur** *adj m* suctorial.

lèche-vitrines [lɛʃvitrin] *nm inv* window-shopping ▪ **faire du ~** to go window-shopping.

lécithine [lesitin] *nf* lecithin.

leçon [ləsɔ̃] *nf* **1.** ÉDUC [cours] lesson ▪ **donner/prendre des ~s de français** to give/to take French lessons ▪ **prenez la ~ sur la digestion à la page 50** turn to the lesson on digestion on page 50 ▪ **la couture en 15 ~s** needlework in 15 (easy) lessons ▶ **~ de choses** object lesson ▪ **~ de conduite** driving lesson ▪ **tu ne vas pas me faire une ~ de morale?** you're not going to start moralizing with me are you? ▪ **apprendre ses ~s** to do one's homework ▪ **sais-tu ta ~ pour demain?** have you learnt what you were set for tomorrow's lesson? ▪ [cours privé] lesson ▪ **prendre des ~s de danse/piano** to take dance/piano lessons ▶ **~ particulière** private lesson **2.** [conseil] advice ▪ **en matière de politesse, il pourrait te donner des ~s** as far as being polite is concerned, he could easily teach you a thing or two ▪ **je n'ai de ~s à recevoir de personne!** I don't need advice from you or anybody else!, nobody's going to tell ME what to do! ▪ **faire la ~ à qqn** to tell sb what to do **3.** [avertissement] lesson ▪ **ça lui donnera une (bonne) ~!, ça lui servira de ~!** that'll teach him (a lesson)! ▪ **que ceci vous serve de ~!** let that be a lesson to you! ▪ **donner une (bonne) ~ à qqn** to teach sb a lesson.

lecteur, trice [lɛktœr, tris] *nm, f* **1.** [personne qui lit] reader ▪ **c'est un grand ~ de BD** he reads a lot of comics SOCIOL : **nos ~s** our readers, our readership **2.** [récitant] reader **3.** [correcteur] reader **4.** ÉDUC foreign language assistant *(at university)* ▪ **~ de français** French foreign-language assistant **5.** IMPR proofreader **6.** RELIG lay reader.
◆ **lecteur** *nm* **1.** AUDIO player ▪ **~ de cassettes** cassette player ▪ **~ de disques compacts** *ou* **laser** CD player **2.** INFORM reader ▪ **~ biométrique** biometric reader ▪ **~ de code (à) barres** bar code reader ▪ **~ de disquette** disk drive ▪ **~ optique** optical reader *ou* scanner ▪ **~ de carte magnétique** card reader ▪ **~ de carte à puce** smart card reader.

lectorat [lɛktɔra] *nm* **1.** PRESSE readership ▪ SOCIOL readers **2.** ÉDUC foreign language assistantship.

lecture [lɛktyr] *nf* **1.** [déchiffrage - d'un texte, d'une carte] reading ▪ **la photocopie ne facilite pas la ~ du plan** the plan is more difficult to read because it has been photocopied ▪ **il est occupé à la ~ du scénario** he's busy reading the script ▪ **j'aime la ~** I like reading ▶ **~ rapide** speed reading
2. *(toujours sing)* [capacité] reading ▪ **l'apprentissage de la ~** learning to read
3. [à voix haute] reading ▪ **une ~ publique de qqch** a public reading of sthg ▪ **donner ~ de qqch** to read sthg out ▪ **faire la ~ à qqn** to read to sb
4. [interprétation] reading, interpretation
5. [ce qu'on lit] reading matter, something to read ▪ **il a de mauvaises ~s** he reads things he shouldn't
6. AUDIO reading
7. INFORM read-out ▪ **~ destructive** destructive read-out ▪ **~ optique** optical reading, optical character recognition
8. MUS reading ▪ **~ à vue** sight-reading
9. POLIT reading ▪ **le texte a été adopté en première ~** the bill was passed on its first reading
10. RELIG reading.

ledit [lədi] *(f ladite* [ladit], *mpl lesdits* [ledit], *fpl lesdites* [ledit]) *adj* DR the aforementioned, the aforesaid.

légal, e, aux [legal, o] *adj* DR [disposition] legal ▪ [héritier] lawful ▪ **employer des moyens légaux contre qqn** to take legal action against sb ▶ **adresse ~e** registered address.

légalement [legalmɑ̃] *adv* legally, lawfully.

légalisation [legalizasjɔ̃] *nf* **1.** [action de légaliser] legalization **2.** [authentification] certifying, ratification *sout*.

légaliser [3] [legalize] *vt* **1.** [rendre légal] to legalize **2.** [authentifier] to certify, to authenticate ▪ **une signature légalisée** a certified signature.

légalisme [legalism] *nm* legalism.

légaliste [legalist] ◇ *adj* legalistic, legalist.
◇ *nmf* legalist.

légalité [legalite] *nf* **1.** [caractère légal] legality **2.** [actes autorisés par la loi] : **la ~** the law ▪ **rester dans/sortir de la ~** to keep within/to break the law ▪ **en toute ~** quite legally.

légat [lega] *nm* **1.** ANTIQ legate **2.** [du pape] legate ▪ **~ a latere** legate a latere.

légataire [legatɛr] *nmf* legatee ▪ **~ universel** sole legatee.

légation [legasjɔ̃] *nf* **1.** [représentation diplomatique] legation **2.** [résidence] legation, legate's residence **3.** [charge] legateship.

légendaire [leʒɑ̃dɛr] *adj* **1.** [mythique] legendary ▪ **un passé/héros ~** a legendary past/hero **2.** [connu de tous] : **elle est d'une discrétion ~** she's well-known for her discretion.

légende [leʒɑ̃d] *nf* **1.** [récit mythique] legend, tale **2.** [renommée] : **la ~** legend ▪ **entrer dans la ~** to become a legend **3.** [commentaire - d'une photo] caption ; [- d'une carte] legend, key **4.** [d'une médaille] legend.
◆ **de légende** *loc adj* fairy-tale *(avant n)* ▪ **un chevalier de ~** a knight out of a fairy tale.

légender [3] [leʒɑ̃de] *vt* to caption ▪ **images copieusement légendées** pictures with a wealth of caption material.

léger, ère [leʒe, ɛr] *adj* **1.** [démarche] light, springy ▪ [métal, véhicule] light ▪ [ondée, vent] light, slight ▪ [brouillard] light ▪ **gaz plus ~ que l'air** lighter-than-air gas ▪ **je me sens plus ~** *fig* I feel (as though) a great weight's been lifted off my shoulders ▪ **d'un cœur ~** with a light heart ▶ **~ comme une plume** *ou* **bulle** (as) light as a feather **2.** [fin - couche] thin ; [- robe] light, flimsy **3.** [mobile - artillerie, industrie, matériel] light ▪ **escadre légère** flotilla **4.** [modéré - consommation] moderate ; [- bruit, odeur] faint, slight ; [- maquillage] light, discreet ▪ **une légère tristesse/ironie** a hint of sadness/irony ▪ **le beurre a un ~ goût**

de rance the butter tastes slightly rancid **5.** [sans gravité - blessure, perte] minor ; [- peine] light ; [- responsabilité] light, undemanding ; [- erreur] slight, minor, unimportant ; [- douleur, picotement] slight ; [- grippe] mild ▪ **il n'y a eu que des blessés ~s** there were only minor injuries **6.** [gracieux - architecture, forme] light, airy **7.** [digeste - café, thé] weak ; [- crème, vin] light ▪ **un repas ~** a snack, a light meal **8.** [irresponsable - personne, conduite] irresponsible, thoughtless, unthinking ; [- raison, justification] lightweight, flimsy ▪ [insuffisant - excuse, devoir] flimsy **9.** [immoral - femme, mœurs] loose ; [- plaisanterie] risqué ; [- ton] light-hearted **10.** MUS [opéra, ténor] light.
◆ **léger** *adv* : **manger ~** to avoid rich food.
◆ **à la légère** *loc adv* lightly ▪ **agir à la légère** to act thoughtlessly *ou* rashly ▪ **conclure à la légère** to jump to conclusions.

légèrement [leʒɛrmɑ̃] *adv* **1.** [un peu] slightly ▪ **loucher/boiter ~** to have a slight squint/limp ▪ **il est ~ paranoïaque** he's a bit paranoid ▪ **une boisson ~ alcoolisée** a slightly alcoholic drink ▪ **un gâteau ~ parfumé au citron** a cake with a hint of lemon flavouring **2.** [inconsidérément] lightly ▪ **agir ~** to act thoughtlessly *ou* without thinking **3.** [frugalement] : **déjeuner ~** to have a light lunch **4.** [avec des vêtements légers] : **s'habiller ~** to wear light clothes.

légèreté [leʒɛrte] *nf* **1.** [poids] lightness **2.** [agilité] lightness, nimbleness ▪ **marcher avec ~** to walk lightly **3.** [finesse - de la dentelle, d'une pâtisserie, d'un vin] lightness ; [- d'un parfum] discreetness, subtlety **4.** [désinvolture] casualness ▪ **il a fait preuve d'une certaine ~ dans ses propos** what he said was somewhat irresponsible ▪ **avec ~** casually **5.** [clémence - d'une punition] lightness.

légiférer [18] [leʒifere] *vi* to legislate.

légion [leʒjɔ̃] *nf* **1.** MIL : **la Légion (étrangère)** the (French) Foreign Legion **2.** [décoration] : **la Légion d'honneur** the Légion d'Honneur, the Legion of Honour **3.** ANTIQ legion **4.** [grand nombre] : **une ~ de cousins** an army of cousins ▪ **ses admirateurs sont ~** her admirers are legion.

légionnellose [leʒjɔnɛloz] *nf* MÉD Legionnaires' disease.

légionnaire [leʒjɔnɛr] ◇ *nm* **1.** [de la Légion étrangère] legionnaire **2.** ANTIQ legionary.
◇ *nmf* [membre de la Légion d'honneur] member of the Légion d'Honneur.

législateur, trice [leʒislatœr, tris] ◇ *adj* law-making.
◇ *nm, f* lawmaker, legislator.
◆ **législateur** *nm* : **le ~** the legislature.

législatif, ive [leʒislatif, iv] *adj* **1.** [qui fait les lois] legislative ▪ **les instances législatives** legislative bodies **2.** [de l'Assemblée] parliamentary *UK*.
◆ **législatif** *nm* : **le ~** the legislature.
◆ **législatives** *nfpl* ≃ general election *UK*, ≃ Congressional election *US*.

législation [leʒislasjɔ̃] *nf* legislation ▪ **la ~ viticole** the laws surrounding the wine trade ▶ **~ du travail** labour laws.

législatives [leʒislativ] *fpl* ▷ **législatif**.

législature [leʒislatyr] *nf* [durée du mandat] term (of office) ▪ **les crises qui ont agité la précédente ~** the crises in the previous administration.

légiste [leʒist] ◇ *adj* ▷ **médecin**.
◇ *nmf* legist.

légitimation [leʒitimasjɔ̃] *nf* **1.** DR [d'un enfant] legitimization **2.** [reconnaissance] recognition ▪ [justification] justification.

légitime [leʒitim] ◇ *adj* **1.** [légal - gén] lawful, legal ; [- mariage] lawful ; [- enfant] legitimate **2.** [justifié - revendication] legitimate ▪ **son refus ~ d'obéir** her rightful refusal to obey ▪ **une colère ~** a justifiable *ou* justified anger.
◇ *nf*[△] [épouse] missus.
◆ **légitime défense** *nf* self-defence.

légitimé, e [leʒitime] ◇ *adj* DR [enfant] legitimized.
◇ *nm, f* legitimized child.

légitimement [leʒitimmɑ̃] *adv* **1.** [justement] legitimately, justifiably ▪ **vous auriez ~ pu vous plaindre** you would have been justified in complaining ▪ **on peut ~ penser que...** we have good reason *ou* good cause to believe that... **2.** DR legitimately, lawfully.

légitimer [3] [leʒitime] *vt* **1.** DR [enfant] to legitimate ▪ [accord, union, titre] to (make) legitimate, to legitimize, to legitimatize **2.** [justifier] to justify, to legitimate.

légitimiste [leʒitimist] *adj* & *nmf* legitimist.

légitimité [leʒitimite] *nf* **1.** DR & POLIT legitimacy **2.** *sout* [bien-fondé] rightfulness ▪ **tu ne peux nier la ~ de ses réclamations** you cannot say that her complaints aren't justified *ou* well-founded.

Lego® [lego] *nm* (set of) Lego®.

Le Greco [ləgreko] *npr* El Greco.

legs [lɛg] *nm* **1.** DR legacy, bequest ▪ **faire un ~ à qqn** to leave a legacy to sb, to leave sb a legacy ▶ **~ à titre universel** residuary bequest *ou* legacy, residue of one's estate ▪ **~ à titre particulier** specific bequest *ou* legacy ▪ **~ universel** general legacy **2.** [héritage] legacy, heritage.

léguer [18] [lege] *vt* **1.** DR to bequeath ▪ **~ qqch à qqn** to bequeath *ou* to leave sthg to sb **2.** *fig* to hand down *(sép)*, to pass on *(sép)* ▪ **il lui a légué son goût pour la musique** he passed on his love of music to him.

légume [legym] *nm* **1.** BOT & CULIN vegetable ▶ **~s secs** dried vegetables ▪ **~s verts** green vegetables **2.** *fam* [personne] vegetable.

légumier, ère [legymje, ɛr] ◇ *adj* vegetable *(modif)*.
◇ *nm, f* *Belgique* greengrocer.
◆ **légumier** *nm* vegetable dish.

légumineuse [legyminøz] ◇ *nf* leguminous plant, legume.
◇ *adj f* leguminous.

leibnizien, enne [lɛbnitsjɛ̃, ɛn] *adj* Leibnizian.

leitmotiv [lajtmɔtif, lɛjtmɔtif] (*pl* **leitmotivs** *ou pl* **leitmotive**) *nm* **1.** LITTÉR & MUS leitmotiv, leitmotif **2.** *fig* hobbyhorse ▪ **elle dit qu'elle n'aime pas la capitale, c'est son ~** she's always harping on about not liking the capital.

Léman [lemɑ̃] *npr m* : **le lac ~** Lake Geneva.

lemming [lɛmiŋ] *nm* lemming.

lémurien [lemyrjɛ̃] *nm* lemur.

lendemain [lɑ̃dmɛ̃] *nm* **1.** [le jour suivant] : **le ~** the next *ou* the following day, the day after ▪ **le ~ matin** the next *ou* the following morning ▪ **le ~ de son arrestation** the day after he was arrested ▶ **les ~s de fête sont souvent difficiles** it's often hard to get through the morning after the night before *hum* ▪ **il ne faut pas remettre au ~ ce qu'on peut faire le jour même** *prov* never put off till tomorrow what you can do today *prov* **2.** [futur] : **le ~** tomorrow, the future ▪ **il dépense son argent sans penser au ~** he spends his money without thinking of the future.
◆ **lendemains** *nmpl* [avenir] future ▪ **des ~s difficiles** a bleak future ▶ **des ~s qui chantent** a brighter future.
◆ **au lendemain de** *loc prép* : **au ~ de la Révolution** immediately *ou* just after the Revolution ▪ **au ~ de son élection** in the days (immediately) following her election.
◆ **sans lendemain** *loc adj* short-lived.

lénifiant, e [lenifjɑ̃, ɑ̃t] *adj* **1.** MÉD calming **2.** *fig* & *sout* [images, paroles] soothing, lulling, assuaging *sout*.

lénifier [9] [lenifje] *vt* **1.** MÉD to calm **2.** *fig* & *sout* [calmer] to soothe, to lull, to assuage *sout*.

Lénine [lenin] *npr* Lenin.

léninisme [leninism] *nm* Leninism.

léniniste [leninist] *adj* & *nmf* Leninist.

lent, e [lɑ̃, lɑ̃t] *adj* **1.** [pas rapide - esprit, mouvement, film] slow ; [- circulation] slow, sluggish ; [- animal] slow-moving ▪ **à combustion ~e** slow-burning ▪ **~ à : il est ~ à comprendre** he's slow on the uptake ▪ **la fin est ~e à venir** the end is a long time coming **2.** [progressif - agonie] lingering ; [- effritement, évolution] slow, gradual ; [- poison] slow-acting.

lente [lɑ̃t] *nf* ENTOM nit.

lentement [lɑ̃tmɑ̃] *adv* slowly ▪ **~ mais sûrement** slowly but surely.

lenteur [lɑ̃tœr] *nf* slowness ▪ **avec ~** slowly ▪ **d'une ~ désespérante** appallingly slow ▪ **~s administratives** administrative delays ▪ **les ~s de la justice** the slowness of the courts, the slow course of justice.

lentigo [lɑ̃tigo] *mpl*, **lentigine** [lɑ̃tiʒin] *nf* mole, lentigo *spéc.*

lentille [lɑ̃tij] *nf* **1.** BOT & CULIN lentil ▪ **~ d'eau** duckweed *(U)* **2.** OPT & PHYS lens ▪ **~s cornéennes** *ou* **de contact** contact lenses ▪ **~s souples** soft (contact) lenses.

Léonard de Vinci [leɔnardəvɛ̃si] *npr* Leonardo da Vinci.

léonin, e [leɔnɛ̃, in] *adj* **1.** *sout* [commission, partage] unfair, one-sided ▪ [contrat] leonine **2.** [de lion] leonine **3.** [vers] Leonine.

léopard [leɔpar] *nm* **1.** ZOOL leopard ▪ [fourrure] leopard skin ▪ **veste en ~** leopard-skin jacket **2.** *(en apposition)* **tenue ~** MIL camouflage battle dress.

LEP, Lep [lɛp, ɛləpe] *nm* = **lycée d'enseignement professionnel.**

lépidoptère [lepidɔptɛr] *nm* lepidopteran ▪ **les ~s** the Lepidoptera.

lèpre [lɛpr] *nf* **1.** MÉD leprosy **2.** *litt* [moisissure] : **mur rongé par la ~** wall eaten away by damp **3.** *fig* [fléau] blight, scourge.

lépreux, euse [leprø, øz] ◇ *adj* **1.** MÉD leprous **2.** *litt* [mur] flaking, peeling ▪ **des baraquements ~** crumbling shacks.
◇ *nm, f* MÉD leper ▪ **traiter qqn comme un ~** to ostracize sb, to send sb to Coventry *UK.*

léproserie [leprozri] *nf* leper hospital, leprosy clinic.

lequel [ləkɛl] *(f* **laquelle** [lakɛl], *mpl* **lesquels** [lekɛl], *fpl* **lesquelles** [lekɛl]) *(avec 'à'* **auquel** [okɛl], **auxquels** [okɛl], *avec 'de'* **duquel** [dykɛl], **desquels** [dekɛl]*)* ◇ *pron rel* **1.** [sujet - personne] who ; [- chose] which **2.** [complément - personne] whom ; [- chose] which ▪ **un ami auprès duquel trouver un réconfort** a friend (who) one can find comfort with, a friend with whom one can find comfort *sout* ▪ **un ami avec ~ il sort souvent** a friend with whom he often goes out *sout*, a friend (who) he often goes out with ▪ **une réaction à laquelle je ne m'attendais pas** a reaction (which) *ou* that I wasn't expecting ▪ **la maison dans laquelle j'ai grandi** the house where *ou* in which I grew up, the house (that) I grew up in ▪ **un dispositif au moyen duquel on peut...** a device whereby *ou* by means of which it is possible to... ▪ **le livre à la rédaction duquel il se consacre** the book (which) he is engaged in editing.
◇ *dét (adj relatif) sout* : **il avait contacté un deuxième avocat, ~ avocat avait également refusé de le défendre** he contacted another lawyer who also refused to defend him ➊ **auquel cas** in which case.
◇ *pron interr* which (one) ▪ **~ d'entre vous a gagné?** which (one) of you won?

lérot [lero] *nm* garden dormouse.

les [le] *pl* ▷ **le.**

lès [lɛ *(devant voyelle* lɛz*)*] = **lez.**

lesbianisme [lɛsbjanism] *nm* lesbianism.

lesbien, enne [lɛsbjɛ̃, ɛn] *adj* lesbian.
◆ **lesbienne** *nf* lesbian.

lesdits [ledi] *mpl*, **lesdites** [ledit] *fpl* ▷ **ledit.**

lèse-majesté [lɛzmaʒɛste] *nf inv* lese-majesty, lèse-majesté.

léser [18] [leze] *vt* **1.** [désavantager] : **~ qqn** to wrong sb ▪ **~ les intérêts de qqn** to harm sb's interests ▪ **elle s'estime lésée par rapport aux autres** she feels badly done by *ou* unfavourably treated compared with the others **2.** DR : **partie lésée** injured party **3.** MÉD to injure.

lésiner [3] [lezine] ◆ **lésiner sur** *v+prép* to skimp on ▪ **tu n'as pas lésiné sur le sel!** you got a bit carried away with *ou* you were a bit too generous with the salt! ▪ **il n'a pas lésiné sur les critiques!** he didn't spare his criticism!

lésion [lezjɔ̃] *nf* **1.** MÉD injury, lesion *spéc* **2.** DR wrong.

lésionnel, elle [lezjɔnɛl] *adj* MÉD [résultant d'une lésion] due to a lesion ▪ [causant lésion] lesion-causing.

Lesotho [lezɔto] *npr m* : **le ~** Lesotho ▪ **au ~** in Lesotho.

lesquels [lekɛl] *mpl*, **lesquelles** *fpl* [lekɛl] ▷ **lequel.**

lessivable [lɛsivabl] *adj* washable.

lessivage [lɛsivaʒ] *nm* **1.** [d'un mur, d'un plancher] scrubbing, washing **2.** GÉOL leaching.

lessive [lɛsiv] *nf* **1.** [poudre] detergent, washing *ou* soap powder ▪ [liquide] (liquid) detergent **2.** [linge à laver] washing, laundry ▪ [contenu d'une machine] (washing-machine) load **3.** [lavage] wash ▪ **faire la ~** to do the washing *ou* the laundry ▪ **faites deux ~s séparées pour la laine et le coton** wash wool and cotton separately **4.** *fam* [épuration] clean-up (operation).

lessiver [3] [lesive] *vt* **1.** [laver - vêtement, tissu] to wash ; [- mur] to wash down *(sép)* **2.** *fam* [épuiser] to wear out *(sép)* ▪ **je suis lessivé** I'm whacked *UK ou* all in *US* **3.** CHIM & GÉOL to leach (out).

lessiveuse [lɛsivøz] *nf* boiler *(for clothes).*

lest [lɛst] *nm* AÉRON & NAUT ballast ▪ **navire sur ~** ship in ballast ➊ **lâcher du ~** *pr* to dump ballast ; *fig* to make concessions, to yield some ground.

lestage [lɛstaʒ] *nm* AÉRON & NAUT ballasting.

leste [lɛst] *adj* **1.** [souple et vif - personne] nimble ; [- animal] agile, nimble ▪ **il est encore ~ malgré son âge** he's still sprightly for his age **2.** [désinvolte - ton] offhand, disrespectful **3.** [libre - plaisanterie] risqué, crude.

lestement [lɛstəmɑ̃] *adv* **1.** [avec souplesse] nimbly **2.** [avec désinvolture] offhandedly, casually **3.** [hardiment] : **il plaisantait un peu ~** he was making rather risqué jokes.

lester [3] [lɛste] *vt* **1.** AÉRON & NAUT to ballast **2.** *fam* [charger] : **~ qqch de** to fill *ou* to cram sthg with.

let [lɛt] *adj inv* SPORT let ▪ **balle ~** let (ball).

létal, e, aux [letal, o] *adj* lethal.

léthargie [letarʒi] *nf* **1.** MÉD lethargy ▪ **tomber en ~** to fall into a lethargic state, to become lethargic **2.** *fig* [mollesse - physique] lethargy ; [- psychologique] apathy.

léthargique [letarʒik] *adj* MÉD & *fig* lethargic.

letton, one *ou* **onne** [lɛtɔ̃, ɔn] *adj* Latvian.
◆ **Letton, one** *ou* **onne** *nm, f* Latvian, Lett.

Lettonie [lɛtɔni] *npr f* : **(la) ~** Latvia.

lettre [lɛtr] *nf*

A. CARACTÈRE
B. ÉCRIT
C. SENS STRICT

A. CARACTÈRE

1. [d'un alphabet] letter ▪ **un mot de neuf ~s** a nine-letter word ➊ **~ majuscule** capital (letter), uppercase letter ▪ **~ minuscule** small *ou* lowercase letter ▪ **en ~s de feu/d'or/de sang : leur révolte est écrite en ~s de feu dans ma mémoire** their revolt is branded on my memory ▪ **leur abnégation est gravée en ~s d'or dans nos cœurs** their self-sacrifice is engraved indelibly in our hearts ▪ **cette page d'histoire est imprimée en ~s de sang dans notre mémoire** this page of history has left a bloody impression in our memory
2. IMPR [forme en plomb] character, letter

B. ÉCRIT

1. [correspondance] letter ▪ **pas de ~s pour moi?** no mail *ou* no letters for me? ▪ **mettre une ~ à la poste** to post a letter ➲ **~ d'amour/de menace** love/threatening letter ▪ **~ anonyme** anonymous letter ▪ **~ exprès** express letter ▪ **~ d'introduction** letter of introduction ▪ **~ de motivation** covering letter ▪ **~ de recommandation** letter of recommendation ▪ **~ recommandée** [avec accusé de réception] recorded delivery letter *UK*, letter sent by certified mail *US* ; [avec valeur déclarée] registered letter ▪ **~ de remerciements** letter of thanks, thank-you letter ▪ **elle lui a écrit une ~ de rupture** she wrote to tell him she was leaving him ▪ **passer comme une ~ à la poste** *fam* [boisson, aliment] to go down a treat ; [demande, mesure] to go off without a hitch, to go off smoothly

2. BANQUE : **~ de change** bill of exchange ▪ **~ de crédit** letter of credit

3. DR : **~ d'intention** letter of intent

4. HIST : **~s de noblesse** letters patent (of nobility) ▪ **conquérir** *ou* **recevoir des ~s de noblesse** *fig* to gain respectability

5. POLIT : **~s de créance** credentials

6. PRESSE : **~ ouverte** open letter

7. LITTÉR [titre] : **'les Lettres de mon moulin'** ***Daudet*** 'Letters from My Mill' ▪ **'Lettres persanes'** ***Montesquieu*** 'Persian Letters' ▪ **'Lettre à d'Alembert'** ***Rousseau*** 'Letter to d'Alembert'

C. SENS STRICT

letter ▪ **respecter la ~ de la loi** to respect *ou* observe the letter of the law ➲ **rester ~ morte** to go unheeded, to be disregarded.

◆ **lettres** *nfpl* **1.** ÉDUC : **les ~s** arts subjects, the arts, the humanities ▪ **étudiant en ~s** arts student ▪ **~s classiques** classics, Latin and Greek ▪ **~s modernes** modern literature ▪ **~s supérieures** preparatory class *(leading to the École Normale Supérieure and lasting two years)* **2.** LITTÉR : **les ~s** literature ▪ **le monde des ~s** the literary world ➲ **avoir des ~s** to be well-read ▪ **un homme/une femme de ~s** a man/a woman of letters.

◆ **à la lettre, au pied de la lettre** *loc adv* : **suivre des ordres au pied de la ~** to follow orders to the letter ▪ **ne prends pas ce qu'il dit au pied de la ~** don't take what he says at face value.

◆ **avant la lettre** *loc adv* : **c'était un surréaliste avant la ~** he was a surrealist before the term was ever invented.

◆ **en toutes lettres** *loc adv* **1.** [entièrement] in full ▪ **écrire qqch en toutes ~s** to write sthg (out) in full **2.** [très clairement] clearly, plainly ▪ **c'est écrit en toutes ~s dans le contrat** it's written in black and white *ou* it's spelt out plainly in the contract.

lettré, e [lɛtre] ◇ *adj* **1.** *sout* [cultivé] well-read **2.** *Belgique* [sachant lire et écrire] : **il est ~** he can read and write.
◇ *nm, f* : **c'est un fin ~** he's extremely well-read *ou* scholarly.

lettrine [lɛtrin] *nf* **1.** IMPR (initial) letter ▪ **~ abaissée/surélevée** dropped/raised initial **2.** [d'un dictionnaire] running initial.

lettrisme [lɛtrism] *nm* LITTÉR lettrism.

leu [lø] (*pl* **lei** [lɛ]) *nm* [monnaie] leu ▪ **quinze lei** fifteen lei.

leucémie [løsemi] *nf* leukaemia.

leucémique [løsemik] ◇ *adj* leukaemic.
◇ *nmf* leukaemia sufferer.

leucocyte [løkɔsit] *nm* leucocyte.

leur [lœr] ◇ *pron pers* them ▪ **je ~ ai donné la lettre** I gave them the letter, I gave the letter to them ▪ **il ~ est difficile de venir** it's difficult for them to come.
◇ *dét (adj poss)* their ▪ **c'est ~ tour** it's their turn ▪ **avec cette aisance qui a toujours été ~** *sout* with that characteristic ease of theirs ▪ **ils ont fait ~ la langue anglaise** *sout* they made the English language their own.

◆ **le leur** (*f* **la leur**, *pl* **les leurs**) *pron poss* theirs ▪ **ils ont pris une valise qui n'était pas la ~** they took a suitcase that wasn't theirs *ou* their own ➲ **je ne me suis jamais senti l'un des ~s** I never felt that I was one of them ▪ **serez-vous aussi des ~s dimanche?** will you be there on Sunday too? ▪ **ils ont été aidés, mais ils y ont mis beaucoup du ~** they were helped, but they put a lot of effort into it (themselves).

leurre [lœr] *nm* **1.** [illusion] delusion, illusion ▪ [tromperie] deception ▪ **son grand projet n'est qu'un ~** his great plan is just a trick **2.** CHASSE decoy, lure ▪ [en fauconnerie] lure **3.** PÊCHE lure ▪ [vivant] bait.

leurrer [5] [lœre] *vt* **1.** [tromper] to deceive, to delude ▪ **ne te laisse pas ~ par ses beaux discours** do not be deceived by his fine words **2.** [en fauconnerie] to lure.

◆ **se leurrer** *vp (emploi réfléchi)* [se laisser abuser] to deceive *ou* to delude o.s. ▪ **il ne faut pas se ~, on va perdre** let's not fool ourselves, we're going to lose.

levage [ləvaʒ] *nm* **1.** TECHNOL lifting ▪ **appareil de ~** lifting tackle *(U)* *ou* appliance **2.** CULIN raising, rising ▪ **après le deuxième ~** [du pain] after proving for the second time.

levain [ləvɛ̃] *nm* **1.** CULIN [substance, pâte] leaven, leavening ▪ **pain sans ~** unleavened bread **2.** *fig* & *litt* **le ~ de la révolte** the seeds of revolt.

levant [ləvɑ̃] *nm* *sout* **le ~** the east ▪ **baie exposée au ~** east-facing bay.

Levant [ləvɑ̃] *npr m* : **le ~** the Levant.

levantin, e [ləvɑ̃tɛ̃, in] *adj* Levantine.

levé [ləve] *nm* survey ▪ **faire le ~ d'un champ** to survey a field.

levée [ləve] *nf* **1.** [ramassage - du courrier, des impôts] collection **2.** [suppression - de sanctions] lifting ▪ **cela nécessiterait la ~ de son immunité parlementaire** this would involve withdrawing his parliamentary immunity **3.** DR : **~ d'écrou** release (from prison) ▪ **~ des scellés** removal of the seals **4.** GÉOL levee **5.** MIL [de troupes] levying ▪ [d'un siège] raising ▪ **~ en masse** levy en masse ▪ **~ de boucliers** *fig* outcry, uproar **6.** COMM : **~ d'option** taking up of the option **7.** [cérémonie] : **la ~ du corps** taking the body from the house *(for the funeral)*.

lève-glace [lɛvglas] (*pl* **lève-glaces**) *nm* window winder ▪ **~ électrique** electric window winder.

lever[1] [ləve] *nm* **1.** [apparition] : **le ~ du soleil** sunrise ▪ **le ~ du jour** daybreak, dawn **2.** [fait de quitter le lit] : **elle boit un grand verre d'eau au ~** she drinks a big glass of water as soon as she gets up *ou* first thing in the morning ▪ **le ~ du roi** the levee of the king **3.** THÉÂTRE : **au ~ de rideau** when the curtain goes up ▪ **un ~ de rideau** [pièce] a curtain raiser **4.** [d'un plan] survey.

lever[2] [19] [ləve] ◇ *vt*

A.

1. [faire monter] to raise, to lift ▪ [soulever] to lift ▪ [redresser] to lift up ▪ **lève la vitre** close the window ▪ **levons nos verres à sa réussite** let's raise our glasses to *ou* let's drink to his success ▪ **~ le rideau** THÉÂTRE to raise the curtain ➲ **~ l'ancre** to weigh anchor ▪ **~ l'étendard de la révolte** to rise up in revolt, to raise the banner (of rebellion)

2. [diriger vers le haut - partie du corps] to lift, to raise ▪ **~ la tête** to lift *ou* to raise one's head ▪ **~ le pied** [automobiliste] to drive slowly ▪ **~ les yeux** [de son livre *etc*] to look up ▪ **~ les yeux au ciel** to lift up *ou* to raise one's eyes to heaven ▪ **le chien lève la patte** the dog cocks its leg ▪ **~ les bras au ciel** to lift up *ou* to raise one's arms to heaven ➲ **~ le cœur à qqn** to turn sb's stomach

3. [sortir du lit] : **~ qqn** to get sb up, to get sb out of bed

B.

1. [ramasser - filets de pêche] to raise ; [- courrier, impôt] to collect

2. [dessiner - carte] to draw (up)

3. CULIN [viande] to carve ▪ **~ les filets d'un poisson** to fillet a fish

4. [faire cesser - blocus, interdiction] to lift ; [- séance, audience] to close ; [- scrupules, ambiguïté] to remove ; [- punition] to lift ; [- obstacle] to get rid of, to remove

5. BOURSE : **~ une valeur** to take up a security ▪ **~ des titres** to take delivery of stock ▪ **~ une option** to take up an option

6. JEUX to pick up *(sép)* ▪ **~ les cartes** to take *ou* to pick up a trick

C.

1. CHASSE to flush

2. △ [séduire] to pull△, to pick up△

3. MIL [mobiliser] to raise.

<> *vi* **1.** [pousser - blé] to come up *(insép)* **2.** CULIN to rise, to prove.

◆ **se lever** *vpi* **1.** [monter] to go up ■ **je vois une main qui se lève au fond de la classe** I see a hand going up at the back of the class ■ **tous les yeux** *OU* **regards se levèrent vers elle** all eyes turned towards her ■ **le rideau se lève sur un salon bourgeois** the curtain rises on a middle-class drawing room **2.** [se mettre debout] to stand up, to rise ■ **se ~ de sa chaise** to get up *OU* to rise from one's chair ■ **ne te lève pas de table!** don't leave the table! ■ **se ~ contre** *fig* to rise up against ■ **il est temps que les hommes de bonne volonté se lèvent** it is time for men of goodwill to stand up and be counted **3.** [sortir du lit - dormeur] to get up, to rise *litt* ; [- malade] to get up ■ **je ne peux pas me ~ le matin** I can't get up *OU* I can't get out of bed in the morning ➊ **se ~ avec le soleil** to be up with the lark ■ **pour la prendre en défaut il faut se ~ tôt** *OU* **de bonne heure!** *fig* you'd have to be on your toes to catch her out! ■ **pour trouver du bon pain ici, tu peux te ~ de bonne heure** you've got your work cut out finding *OU* you'll be a long time finding good bread round here ■ **ils m'ont encore fait ~ aux aurores aujourd'hui** they got me up at the crack of dawn today **4.** [apparaître - astre] to rise ; [- jour] to dawn, to break **5.** MÉTÉOR [vent] to get up ■ [brume] to lift, to clear ■ [orage] to break ■ **le temps se lève** [il fait meilleur] the sky's clearing (up) **6.** *litt* [surgir, naître] to rise (up) ■ **l'espoir commença à se ~ dans tous les cœurs** hope welled up in everyone's heart.

lève-tard [lɛvtar] *nmf* late riser.

lève-tôt [lɛvto] *nmf* early riser, early bird.

lève-vitre [lɛvvitr] (*pl* **lève-vitres**) = **lève-glace**.

levier [ləvje] *nm* **1.** MÉCAN lever ■ **faire ~ sur qqch** to lever sthg up *OU* off **2.** [manette] : **~ (de changement) de vitesse** gear lever *UK*, gearshift *US* ■ **~ de frein à main** handbrake lever ■ **~ de commande** control (lever) ■ **être aux ~s de commande** *pr* to be at the controls ; *fig* to be in command *OU* in the driver's seat *OU* at the controls **3.** *fig* [moyen de pression] means of pressure, lever **4.** ÉCON : **effet de ~** leverage, gearing.

lévitation [levitasjɔ̃] *nf* levitation.

lévite [levit] *nm* HIST Levite.

Lévitique [levitik] *npr m* : **le ~** Leviticus.

levraut [ləvro] *nm* leveret.

lèvre [lɛvr] *nf* **1.** [de la bouche] lip ■ **elle avait le sourire aux ~s** she had a smile on her lips ■ **lire sur les ~s** to lip-read ➊ **~ inférieure/supérieure** lower/upper lip ■ **être pendu** *OU* **suspendu aux ~s de qqn** to be hanging upon sb's every word **2.** [de la vulve] lip, labium ■ **les ~s** the labia ■ **grandes/petites ~s** labia majora/minora **3.** GÉOL edge, side, rim **4.** MÉD [d'une plaie] lip.

levrette [ləvrɛt] *nf* ZOOL greyhound bitch ■ **~ (d'Italie)** Italian greyhound.

lévrier [levrije] *nm* greyhound ■ **~ afghan** Afghan hound ■ **~ barzoï** borzoi, Russian wolfhound.

levure [ləvyr] *nf* yeast ■ **~ de bière** brewer's yeast, dried yeast ■ **~ (chimique)** baking powder.

lexème [lɛksɛm] *nm* lexeme.

lexical, e, aux [lɛksikal, o] *adj* lexical.

lexicaliser [3] [lɛksikalize] *vt* to lexicalize.

◆ **se lexicaliser** *vpi* to become lexicalized.

lexicographe [lɛksikɔgraf] *nmf* lexicographer.

lexicographie [lɛksikɔgrafi] *nf* lexicography.

lexicographique [lɛksikɔgrafik] *adj* lexicographical.

lexicologie [lɛksikɔlɔʒi] *nf* lexicology.

lexicologue [lɛksikɔlɔg] *nmf* lexicologist.

lexique [lɛksik] *nm* **1.** [ouvrage] glossary, lexicon **2.** [d'une langue] lexis, vocabulary ■ [d'un auteur] vocabulary.

lez [lɛ *(devant voyelle* lɛz*) prep* by, near.

lézard [lezar] *nm* **1.** ZOOL lizard ■ **faire le ~** to bask in the sun **2.** [peau] lizardskin ■ **ceinture en ~** lizardskin belt **3.** *fam* hitch.

lézarde [lezard] *nf* crack, crevice.

lézarder [3] [lezarde] <> *vi fam* [au soleil] to bask in the sun ■ [paresser] to laze about, to lounge (about).

<> *vt* [fissurer] to crack ■ **mur lézardé** cracked wall, wall full of cracks.

◆ **se lézarder** *vpi* to crack.

liage [ljaʒ] *nm* [action de lier] binding.

liaison [ljɛzɔ̃] *nf* **1.** [contact] : **le secrétaire assure la ~ entre les divers services** the secretary liaises between the various departments **2.** TÉLÉCOM contact ■ **la ~ téléphonique n'est pas très bonne** the line is not very good ■ **nous sommes en ~ directe avec notre correspondant** we have our correspondent on the line ➊ **~ radio** radio contact **3.** TRANSP link ■ **un train/car assure la ~ entre Édimbourg et Glasgow** there is a train/coach service operating between Edinburgh and Glasgow ➊ **~ aérienne/maritime/ferroviaire/fluviale/routière** air/sea/rail/river/road link **4.** [rapport] connection, link ■ **son départ est sans ~ avec la dispute d'hier** his departure is in no way linked to yesterday's argument **5.** *litt* [relation] relationship ■ **avoir une ~ (amoureuse) avec qqn** to have an affair with sb ■ **'les Liaisons dangereuses'** *Laclos* 'Dangerous Liaisons' **6.** CHIM bond **7.** INFORM link **8.** LING liaison **9.** MUS [pour tenir une note] tie ■ [pour lier plusieurs notes] phrase mark, slur.

◆ **de liaison** *loc adj* liaison *(modif)*.

◆ **en liaison** *loc adv* in touch, in contact ■ **être/rester en ~ (avec qqn)** to be/to remain in contact (with sb).

liane [ljan] *nf* [vigne, lierre] creeper ■ [en forêt équatoriale] liana.

liant, e [ljɑ̃, ɑ̃t] *adj* sociable ■ **il n'est pas très ~** he is not very sociable, he doesn't make friends easily.

◆ **liant** *nm* **1.** *litt* [affabilité] : **avoir du ~** to be sociable, to have a sociable nature **2.** CHIM & CONSTR binder.

liasse [ljas] *nf* [de billets] wad ■ [de documents] bundle ■ **des ~s de billets dépassaient de son portefeuille** wads of banknotes *OU* notes were sticking out of his wallet.

Liban [libɑ̃] *npr m* : **le ~** (the) Lebanon ■ **au ~** in (the) Lebanon.

libanais, e [libanɛ, ɛz] *adj* Lebanese.

◆ **Libanais, e** *nm, f* Lebanese (person) ■ **les Libanais** the Lebanese.

libation [libasjɔ̃] *nf* ANTIQ libation.

◆ **libations** *nfpl* : **faire de joyeuses ~s** to drink copious amounts (of alcohol).

Libé [libe] *fam* = **Libération**.

libelle [libɛl] *nm* lampoon ■ **écrire des ~s contre qqn** to lampoon sb.

libellé [libele] *nm* wording.

libeller [4] [libele] *vt* **1.** [lettre] to word **2.** ADMIN [texte juridique] to draw up *(sép)* **3.** [chèque] to make out *(sép)* ■ **libellez votre chèque au nom de...** make your cheque payable to...

libellule [libelyl] *nf* dragonfly.

libérable [liberabl] *adj* **1.** MIL [militaire, contingent] dischargeable ■ **permission ~** demob leave **2.** DR [prisonnier] eligible for release.

libéral, e, aux [liberal, o] <> *adj* **1.** [aux idées larges] liberal, liberal-minded, broad-minded **2.** ÉCON free-market, free-enterprise ■ **l'économie ~e** the free-market economy **3.** HIST liberal **4.** POLIT [en Grande-Bretagne, au Canada] Liberal ■ [en France] favouring the free-market economy.

<> *nm, f* **1.** POLIT [en Grande-Bretagne, au Canada] Liberal ■ [en France] free-marketeer **2.** [personne tolérante] broad-minded person.

libéralement [liberalmɑ̃] *adv* **1.** [généreusement] liberally, generously **2.** [librement] broad-mindedly.

libéralisation [liberalizasjɔ̃] *nf* **1.** POLIT liberalization **2.** ÉCON liberalization, easing (of restrictions) ▪ **la ~ complète de l'économie** the application of free-market principles throughout the economy.

libéraliser [3] [liberalize] *vt* **1.** [mœurs, régime] to liberalize **2.** ÉCON [commerce] to ease *ou* to lift restrictions on ▪ **~ l'économie** to reduce state intervention in the economy.
◆ **se libéraliser** *vpi* [régime] to become (more) liberal ▪ [mœurs] to become freer.

libéralisme [liberalism] *nm* **1.** POLIT liberalism **2.** ÉCON (doctrine of) free enterprise, liberalism **3.** [tolérance] broad-mindedness, liberal-mindedness.

libéralité [liberalite] *nf* [générosité] generosity, liberality *sout*.
◆ **libéralités** *nfpl sout* [dons] (cash) donations, liberalities ▪ **je ne tiens pas à vivre de vos ~s** I do not want to live off your generosity *ou* good favours.

libérateur, trice [liberatœr, tris] ◇ *adj* **1.** [rire, geste] liberating, cathartic *litt* **2.** POLIT liberating ▪ **l'armée libératrice** the liberating army, the army of liberation.
◇ *nm, f* liberator.

libération [liberasjɔ̃] *nf* **1.** [d'un pays] liberation ▪ [d'un soldat] discharge ▪ **la Libération** the Liberation (of France) ▪ **à la Libération** when France was liberated **2.** DR [d'un détenu] release ▪ **~ anticipée** early release ▪ **~ conditionnelle** (release on) parole **3.** [émancipation] : **éprouver un sentiment de ~** *fig* to feel liberated ⊙ **la ~ de la femme** women's liberation **4.** ÉCON : **la ~ des prix** the deregulation of prices, the removal of price controls ▪ **la ~ des loyers** the lifting of rent control **5.** PRESSE : **Libération** *French left-of-centre daily newspaper* **6.** CHIM, PHYS & PHYSIOL release.

libéré, e [libere] *adj* liberated.

libérer [18] [libere] *vt* **1.** [délivrer] to free ▪ **~ qqn de qqch** to free sb from sthg ▪ **quand les Alliés libérèrent Paris** when the Allies liberated Paris **2.** [remettre en liberté] to release, to (set) free **3.** [décharger] : **~ qqn d'une promesse** to free *ou* to release sb from a promise **4.** [soulager - conscience] to relieve **5.** [laisser partir - élèves, employés] to let go ▪ **on nous a libérés avant l'heure** we were allowed to leave *ou* they let us go early **6.** [rendre disponible - lieu] to vacate, to move out of ; [- étagère] to clear ▪ **libérez le passage** clear the way ▪ **je n'arrive même pas à ~ une heure pour jouer au tennis** I can't even find a free hour *ou* an hour to spare to play tennis ▪ **les postes libérés par les mises à la retraite anticipée** vacancies created by early retirement **7.** [débloquer - mécanisme, énergie, émotions] to release **8.** CHIM & PHYS to release **9.** ÉCON [prix, salaires] to free, to lift *ou* to remove restrictions on **10.** MIL [conscrit] to discharge ▪ **le candidat devra être libéré des obligations militaires** the applicant must be released from *ou* must have discharged his military service obligations.
◆ **se libérer** ◇ *vp (emploi réfléchi)* **1.** [se délivrer] to free o.s. ▪ **se ~ de ses chaînes** to free o.s. from one's chains **2.** [dans un emploi du temps] : **essaie de te ~ pour demain** try to be free *ou* to make some time tomorrow **3.** [s'émanciper - femmes] to become more liberated.
◇ *vp (emploi passif)* [emploi, appartement] to become vacant *ou* available ▪ **il y a une place qui s'est libérée au coin de la rue** somebody's just left a parking space at the corner of the street.

Liberia [liberja] *npr m* : **le ~** Liberia ▪ **au ~** in Liberia.

libertaire [libertɛr] *adj & nmf* libertarian, anarchist.

liberté [libɛrte] *nf* **1.** [gén, - DR] freedom ▪ **rendre la ~ à un otage** to release a hostage ▪ **rendre la ~ à un oiseau** to set a bird free ▪ **le pays de la ~** the land of the free *ou* of freedom ⊙ **~ conditionnelle** *ou* **sur parole** (release on) parole ▪ **~ individuelle** personal freedom ▪ **~ sous caution** release on bail ▪ **~ provisoire** bail ▪ **être mis en ~ provisoire** to be granted bail, to be released on bail ▪ **~ surveillée** probation ▪ **la statue de la Liberté** the Statue of Liberty
2. [droit] right, freedom ▪ **~ d'association/du travail** right of association/to work ▪ **~ du culte/d'opinion/de mouvement** freedom of worship/thought/movement ▪ **~ d'entreprise** free enterprise, right to set up a business ▪ **~ de la presse/d'expression** freedom of the press/of speech ▪ **Liberté, Égalité, Fraternité** Liberty, Equality, Fraternity *(motto of the French Revolution and, today, of France)*
3. [indépendance] freedom ▪ **~ de jugement/de pensée** freedom of judgment/thought ▪ **avoir toute ~ pour décider** to be totally free *ou* to have full freedom to decide ▪ **prendre la ~ de** to take the liberty to ▪ **reprendre sa ~** [sentimentale] to regain one's freedom
4. [temps libre] free time ▪ **tous mes moments de ~** all my free time ▪ **je n'ai pas un instant de ~** I haven't got a minute to myself
5. [désinvolture, irrévérence] : **il prend trop de ~ avec nous** he is a bit overfamiliar with us ▪ **il y a une trop grande ~ dans la traduction** the translation is not close enough to the original *ou* is too free ▪ **~ de langage** overfree use of language
6. ÉCON : **~ des prix** freedom from price controls ▪ **instaurer la ~ des prix** to end *ou* to abolish price controls.
◆ **libertés** *nfpl* **1.** [droits légaux] liberties, freedom ▪ **atteinte aux/défense des ~s** attack on/defence of civil liberties ▪ **les ~s publiques** civil liberties
2. [privautés] : **prendre** *ou* **se permettre des ~s avec qqn** to take liberties with sb ▪ **j'ai pris quelques ~s avec la recette** I took a few liberties with *ou* I didn't stick entirely to the recipe.
◆ **en liberté** *loc adj & loc adv* free ▪ **être en ~** [personne] to be free *ou* at large ; [animal] to be free *ou* in the wild ▪ **un parc national où les animaux vivent en ~** a national park where animals roam free ▪ **remettre qqn en ~** DR to release sb, to set sb free.
◆ **en toute liberté** *loc adv* freely ▪ **vous pouvez vous exprimer en toute ~** you can talk freely ▪ **agir en toute ~** to act quite freely.

libertin, e [libɛrtɛ̃, in] ◇ *adj* **1.** *litt* [personne] dissolute, dissipated, debauched ▪ [propos, publication] licentious **2.** HIST & RELIG libertine, freethinking.
◇ *nm, f* **1.** *litt* [personne dissolue] libertine **2.** HIST & RELIG libertine, freethinker.

libertinage [libɛrtinaʒ] *nm* **1.** *litt* [comportement] debauchery, dissipation, libertinism *sout* **2.** HIST & RELIG libertine philosophy, libertinism.

Liberty® [libɛrti] *nm inv* Liberty® print material.

libidinal, e, aux [libidinal, o] *adj* PSYCHOL libidinal.

libidineux, euse [libidinø, øz] *adj sout* [vieillard] lecherous ▪ [regard] libidinous *sout*, lustful.

libido [libido] *nf* libido.

libitum [libitɔm] ▷ **ad libitum**.

libraire [librɛr] *nmf* bookseller.

libraire-éditeur [librɛreditœr] (*pl* **libraires-éditeurs**) *nm* publisher and bookseller.

librairie [librɛri] *nf* **1.** [boutique] bookshop *UK*, bookstore *US* ▪ **un livre qu'on ne trouve plus en ~** a book which is no longer on sale ▪ **le rayon ~** the book department ⊙ **~ d'art/d'occasion** art/secondhand bookshop **2.** [commerce] : **la ~** bookselling ; [profession] the book trade.

librairie-papeterie [librɛripapɛtri] (*pl* **librairies-papeteries**) *nf* stationer's and bookseller's.

libre [libr] ◇ *adj* **1.** [gén - POLIT] free ▪ **à la suite du non-lieu, l'accusé s'est retrouvé ~** owing to lack of evidence, the accused found himself a free man again ▪ **~ de : il ne me laisse pas ~ d'inviter qui je veux** he doesn't leave me free to invite who *ou* whom *sout* I please ▪ **être ~ de ses mouvements** to be free to do what one likes ▪ **~ à toi/à elle de refuser** you're/she's free to say no ▪ **j'y vais? – alors là, ~ à toi!** shall I go? – well, that's entirely up to you *ou* you're (entirely) free to do as you wish! ⊙ **être ~ comme l'air** to be as free as (the) air **2.** [disponible - personne, salle] free, available ; [- poste, siège] vacant, free ; [- table] free ; [- toilettes] vacant ; [- passage] clear ▪ **la ligne n'est pas ~** [au téléphone] the line is engaged *UK ou* busy *US* ▪ **la voie est ~** the way is clear ▪ **'~'** [sur un taxi] 'for hire' ▪ **il faut que j'aie la tête** *ou* **l'esprit ~ pour prendre une décision** I have to have a clear head before I'm able to make a decision ▪ **tu as un moment de ~?** have you got a minute (to spare)? ▪ **êtes-vous ~ à déjeuner?** are you free for lunch? ▪ **j'ai**

deux après-midi (de) ~s par semaine I've got two afternoons off *ou* two free afternoons a week ▪ [sentimentalement] unattached ▪ **je ne suis pas ~** I'm already seeing somebody
3. [franc] free, open ▪ **je suis très ~ avec elle** I am quite free (and easy) *ou* open with her ▮ [désinvolte - personne] : **il se montre un peu trop ~ avec ses secrétaires** he is a bit overfamiliar *ou* too free with his secretaries ▪ [inconvenant - attitude] free, daring
4. [non réglementé - prix, marché] free, deregulated ▪ **l'entrée de l'exposition est ~** entrance to the exhibition is free ⊙ **la ~ entreprise** free enterprise ▪ **par le ~ jeu de la concurrence** through free competition
5. [privé - radio, télévision] independent ; [- école, enseignement] private *(in France, mostly Catholic)*
6. [non imposé - improvisation, style] free ▪ **je leur ai donné un sujet ~** I gave them a free choice of subject, I left it up to them to choose the subject ⊙ **escalade ~** free climbing ▪ **vers ~** free verse
7. [non entravé - mouvement, membre] free
8. [non fidèle - traduction, adaptation] free
9. CHIM & MATH free
10. MÉCAN & TECHNOL free, disengaged.
◇ *adv* : **ça sonne ~ ou occupé?** is it ringing or engaged *UK ou* busy *US*?

libre(-)arbitre [librarbitr] *nm* free will.

libre-échange [libreʃɑ̃ʒ] (*pl* **libres-échanges**) *nm* free trade.

libre-échangisme [libreʃɑ̃ʒism] (*pl* **libre-échangismes**) *nm* (doctrine of) free trade.

libre-échangiste [libreʃɑ̃ʒist] (*pl* **libre-échangistes**)
◇ *adj* [politique, économie] free-trade *(modif)* ▪ [idée, personne] in favour of free trade.
◇ *nmf* free trader.

librement [librəmɑ̃] *adv* freely.

libre-pensée [librəpɑ̃se] (*pl* **libres-pensées**) *nf* freethinking.

libre-penseur [librəpɑ̃sœr] (*pl* **libres-penseurs**) *nm* freethinker.

libre-service [librəsɛrvis] (*pl* **libres-services**) *nm* [magasin] self-service store ▪ [cantine] self-service canteen ▪ [restaurant] self-service restaurant ▪ [station-service] self-service petrol *UK ou* gas *US* station.
◆ **en libre-service** *loc adj* self-service.

librettiste [librɛtist] *nmf* librettist.

libretto [librɛto] *nm* libretto.

Libye [libi] *npr f* : **(la) ~** Libya ▪ **le désert de ~** the Libyan Desert.

libyen, enne [libjɛ̃, ɛn] *adj* Libyan.
◆ **Libyen, enne** *nm, f* Libyan.

lice [lis] *nf* **1.** SPORT [bordure de piste] line ▪ [en hippisme] rail **2.** HIST [palissade] lists ▪ [terrain] tilt-yard **3.** CHASSE bitch **4.** TEXT = lisse *(sens 2)*.
◆ **en lice** *loc adv* : **entrer en ~** to enter the lists.

licence [lisɑ̃s] *nf* **1.** *litt* [liberté excessive] licence ▪ [débauche] licentiousness ⊙ **avoir toute** *ou* **pleine ~ de faire qqch** to be at liberty *ou* quite free to do sthg **2.** UNIV (bachelor's) degree ▪ **~ d'économie** degree in economics ▪ **~ de russe/de droit** Russian/law degree ▪ **~ ès lettres** arts degree, ≃ BA ▪ **~ ès sciences** science degree, ≃ BSc **3.** DR licence **4.** SPORT membership card *(allowing entry into official competitions)*.
◆ **sous licence** ◇ *loc adj* licensed.
◇ *loc adv* : **fabriqué sous ~** produced under licence.

LICENCE

In French universities, students obtain the *licence* one year after the *DEUG*. It is the first year of the *Deuxième cycle* of university studies. During the subsequent year students prepare the *maîtrise*.

licencié, e [lisɑ̃sje] ◇ *adj* UNIV graduate.
◇ *nm, f* **1.** UNIV (university) graduate ▪ **~ ès lettres/ès sciences** arts/science graduate ▪ **~ en droit** law graduate ▪ **~ en anglais** English graduate, graduate in English **2.** SPORT registered member **3.** [chômeur - pour raisons économiques] laid off *ou* redundant *UK* employee ; [- pour faute professionnelle] dismissed employee ▪ **il y a eu 4 ~s** 4 employees were laid off *ou* made redundant *UK*, there were 4 layoffs *ou* redundancies *UK*.

licenciement [lisɑ̃simɑ̃] *nm* [pour faute professionnelle] dismissal ▪ **~ (économique)** lay-off *ou* redundancy *UK* ⊙ **avis de ~** [pour faute professionnelle] letter of dismissal, pink slip *US* ; [pour raison économique] redundancy notice *UK* ▪ **~ sec** enforced redundancy *(without any form of statutory compensation)*.

licencier [9] [lisɑ̃sje] *vt* [pour raison économique] to make redundant *UK*, to lay off *(sép)* ▪ [pour faute] to dismiss, to fire ▪ **se faire ~** to be made redundant *UK*, to be laid off.

licencieux, euse [lisɑ̃sjø, øz] *adj* licentious, lewd.

lichen [likɛn] *nm* BOT lichen ▪ **~ foliacé/fruticuleux** foliose/fruticose lichen.

lichette [liʃɛt] *nf fam* [petite quantité] : **une ~ de vin/lait** a (teeny) drop of wine/milk ▪ **une ~ de beurre** a smidgin *ou* a spot of butter ▪ **une ~ de gâteau** a sliver *ou* (tiny) bit of cake.

licite [lisit] *adj* licit, lawful.

liciter [3] [lisite] *vt* to auction *(an estate in co-ownership)*.

licol [likɔl] = **licou**.

licorne [likɔrn] *nf* MYTHOL unicorn.

licou [liku] *nm* halter ▪ **passer le ~ à un cheval** to put the halter on a horse.

lie [li] *nf* **1.** ŒNOL dregs, lees ▪ **~ de vin** wine dregs ▪ **il y a de la ~ au fond de la bouteille** there's some sediment at the bottom of the bottle ▪ **boire la coupe** *ou* **le calice jusqu'à la ~** to drink one's cup of sorrow to the dregs **2.** *sout* [rebut] dregs, rejects ▪ **la ~ de la société** the dregs of society.

lié, e [lje] *adj* **1.** MUS [notes différentes] slurred ▪ [note tenue] tied **2.** MATH bound.

Liechtenstein [liʃtɛnʃtajn] *npr m* : **le ~** Liechtenstein ▪ **au ~** in Liechtenstein.

lied [lid] (*pl* **lieds** *ou pl* **lieder** [lidər]) *nm* lied ▪ **un récital de ~s** *ou* **~er** a lieder recital.

lie-de-vin [lidvɛ̃] *adj inv* (red) wine-coloured.

liège [ljɛʒ] *nm* cork ▪ **de** *ou* **en ~** cork.

Liège [ljɛʒ] *npr* Liege.

liégé, e [ljeʒe] *adj* PÊCHE floated with cork, corked.

liégeois, e [ljeʒwa, az] *adj* **1.** [personne] from Liège **2.** CULIN : **café/chocolat ~** coffee/chocolate sundae *(topped with whipped cream)*.

lien [ljɛ̃] *nm* **1.** [entre des choses] link, connection ▪ **~ de cause à effet** causal relationship, relationship of cause and effect **2.** [entre des gens] link, connection ▪ **nouer des ~s d'amitié** to make friends, to become friends ▪ **les ~s conjugaux** *ou* **du mariage** marriage bonds *ou* ties ▪ **ils ont un vague ~ de parenté** there is some distant family connection between them, they're distantly related ▪ **les ~s du sang** blood ties **3.** [lanière] tie **4.** INFORM link, linkage.

lier [9] [lje] *vt* **1.** [attacher - cheveux, paquet, fagot] to tie up *(sép)* **2.** MÉD : **~ une veine** to ligate a vein **3.** [logiquement] to link, to connect ▪ **il faut ~ le nouveau paragraphe au reste du texte** the new paragraph must be linked to the rest of the text ▪ **tout est lié** everything's interconnected, it all fits together **4.** [enchaîner - gestes] to link together *(sép)* **5.** [par contrat] to bind **6.** [associer volontairement] : **~ son sort à qqn** to join forces with sb ▪ **~ son sort à qqch** to stick with sthg for better or worse **7.** [unir par des sentiments] to bind, to unite ▪ **l'amitié qui nous lie** the friendship which binds us ▪ **cette maison est liée à mon enfance** this house is linked to my childhood **8.** [commencer] : **~ amitié** to become friends ▪ **~ connaissance/conversation avec qqn** to strike up an acquaintance/a conversation with sb

9. CONSTR to bind **10.** CULIN [sauce] to thicken ▪ [farce] to bind **11.** LING to link words *(with liaisons)* **12.** MUS : **~ les notes** to slur the notes.

◆ **se lier** *vpi* : **se ~ (d'amitié)** to become friends ▪ **se ~ (d'amitié) avec qqn** to strike up a friendship with sb, to become friends with sb.

lierre [ljɛr] *nm* ivy.

liesse [ljɛs] *nf litt* jubilation, exhilaration ▪ **une foule en ~** a jubilant crowd.

lieu[1], s [ljø] *nm* ZOOL hake ▪ **~ jaune** pollack ▪ **~ noir** coalfish.

lieu[2], x [ljø] *nm* **1.** [endroit] place ▪ **leur ~ de promenade habituel** the place where they usually go for a walk ▪ **~ de rassemblement** place of assembly, assembly point ▪ **~ de rencontre** meeting place ▪ **fixons un ~ de rendez-vous** let's decide on somewhere to meet *OU* on a meeting place ⊙ **~ de culte** place of worship ▪ **~ de mémoire** memorial ; *fig* repository of culture ▪ **~ de naissance** birthplace, place of birth ▪ **~ de passage** port of call ▪ **~ de pèlerinage** place of *OU* centre for pilgrimage ▪ **~ de perdition** den of iniquity ▪ **~ public** public place ▪ **~ de résidence** (place of) residence ▪ **sur le ~ de travail** in the workplace ▪ **sur votre ~ de travail** at your place of work ▪ **le haut ~ de...** the Mecca of..., a Mecca for... **2.** GRAMM : **adverbe/complément (circonstanciel) de ~** adverb/complement of place **3.** *loc* **avoir ~** [entrevue, expérience, spectacle] to take place ; [accident] to happen ; [erreur] to occur ▪ **avoir ~ de** [avoir des raisons de] to have (good) reasons to ▪ **vous n'aurez pas ~ de vous plaindre** you won't find any cause *OU* any reason for complaint ▪ **tes craintes n'ont pas ~ d'être** your fears are groundless *OU* unfounded ▪ **il n'y a pas ~ de s'affoler** there's no need to panic ▪ **s'il y a ~** if necessary, should the need arise ▪ **il y a tout ~ de croire** there is every reason to believe ▪ **donner ~ à** [entraîner] : **donner ~ à des désagréments** to cause *OU* to give rise to trouble ▪ **sa mort a donné ~ à une enquête** his death prompted an investigation ▪ **tenir ~ de : ça tiendra ~ de champagne!** that will do instead of champagne! ▪ **le canapé tient ~ de lit** the settee is used as a bed.

◆ **lieux** *nmpl* **1.** [endroit précis] scene ▪ **la police est déjà sur les ~x (du crime)** the police are already at the scene of the crime ▪ **pour être efficace, il faut être sur les ~x 24 heures sur 24** if you want to do things properly, you have to be on the spot 24 hours a day ⊙ **les Lieux saints** the Holy Places **2.** [bâtiments] premises ▪ **les grévistes occupent les ~x** the strikers are occupying the premises ⊙ **les ~x d'aisances** *euphém* the smallest room *euphém*, the lavatory *UK*, the bathroom *US*.

◆ **au lieu de** *loc prép* instead of ▪ **elle aurait dû me remercier, au ~ de ça, elle m'en veut** she should have thanked me, instead of which she bears a grudge against me ▪ **au ~ de faire qqch** instead of doing sthg.

◆ **au lieu que** *loc conj* instead of ▪ **je préfère ranger moi-même mon bureau au ~ que tu viennes tout changer de place** I prefer to tidy my desk myself rather than having you changing everything around.

◆ **en dernier lieu** *loc adv* finally, lastly ▪ **n'ajoutez le sucre qu'en tout dernier ~** do not add the sugar until the last moment.

◆ **en haut lieu** *loc adv* in high places ▪ **ça se décidera en haut ~** the decision will be made at a high level.

◆ **en lieu et place de** *loc prép sout* in place of, on behalf of, in lieu of.

◆ **en lieu sûr** *loc adv* in a safe place ▪ **range-le en ~ sûr** put it away in a safe place, put it away somewhere safe.

◆ **en premier lieu** *loc adv* in the first place, firstly, first of all.

◆ **en tous lieux** *loc adv sout* everywhere.

◆ **lieu commun** *nm* commonplace, platitude.

lieu-dit [ljødi] *(pl* **lieux-dits***)* *nm* [avec maisons] hamlet ▪ [sans maisons] place ▪ **au ~ La Folie** at the place called La Folie.

lieue [ljø] *nf* **1.** [mesure] league ▪ **~ marine** league **2.** *loc* **être à cent** *OU* **mille ~s de** [être loin de] to be far from ▪ **nous étions à cent ~s de penser que...** it would never have occurred to us that..., we never dreamt that... ▪ **à cent ~s à la ronde** for miles (and miles) around.

Lieut. *(abr écrite de* **Lieutenant***)* Lieut.

Lieut.-col. *(abr écrite de* **Lieutenant-colonel***)* Lieut.-Col.

lieutenant, e [ljøtnɑ̃, ɑ̃t] *nm, f* **1.** MIL [de l'armée de terre, de la marine] lieutenant ▪ [de l'armée de l'air] flying officer *UK*, first lieutenant *US* **2.** [de la marine marchande] mate ▪ **~ de vaisseau** lieutenant commander **3.** *Suisse* second lieutenant ▪ **premier ~** lieutenant **4.** [assistant] lieutenant, second in command.

lieutenant-colonel, lieutenante-colonelle [ljøtnɑ̃kɔlɔnɛl] *(mpl* **lieutenants-colonels**, *fpl* **lieutenantes-colonelles***)* *nm, f* [de l'armée de terre] lieutenant colonel ▪ [de l'armée de l'air] wing commander *UK*, lieutenant colonel *US*.

lièvre [ljɛvr] *nm* **1.** ZOOL hare ▪ **lever un ~** *pr* to start a hare ; *fig* to raise a burning issue, to touch on a sore point **2.** [fourrure] hareskin **3.** SPORT pacemaker, pacesetter.

lift [lift] *nm* topspin.

lifté, e [lifte] *adj* : **une balle ~e** a ball with topspin ▪ **elle a un jeu très ~** she plays a heavy topspin game.

lifter [3] [lifte] ◇ *vi* to put topspin on the ball.
◇ *vt* to put topspin on.

liftier [liftje] *nm* lift attendant *UK*, elevator attendant *US*.

lifting [liftiŋ] *nm* **1.** [de la peau] face-lift **2.** *fam* [rénovation - d'une institution, d'un bâtiment] face-lift.

ligament [ligamɑ̃] *nm* ANAT ligament.

ligamentaire [ligamɑ̃tɛr], **ligamenteux, euse** [ligamɑ̃tø, øz] *adj* ligamentous, ligamentary.

ligature [ligatyr] *nf* **1.** MÉD [opération, fil] ligature ▪ **~ des trompes (de Fallope)** tubal ligation **2.** IMPR ligature, tied letter **3.** HORT [processus] tying up ▪ [attache] tie.

ligaturer [3] [ligatyre] *vt* **1.** [attacher] to tie on *(sép)* **2.** MÉD to ligate, to ligature ▪ **se faire ~ les trompes** to have one's (Fallopian) tubes tied.

lige [liʒ] *adj* liege.

light [lajt] *adj* [plat, préparation] low-fat ▪ [boisson] diet *(modif)*, slimline.

lignage [liɲaʒ] *nm* **1.** [ascendance] lineage ▪ **de haut ~** of noble lineage **2.** IMPR linage, lineage.

ligne [liɲ] *nf* **1.** [gén - GÉOM] line ▪ **tracer** *OU* **tirer une ~** to draw a line ▪ **les ~s de la main** the lines of the hand ⊙ **~ de cœur/de tête/de vie** heart/head/life line ▪ **une ~ droite** [route] a straight stretch of road ▪ **la route est en ~ droite sur 3 km** the road is straight for 3 km ▪ **une ~ de coke**△ a line of coke△
2. [texte] line ▪ **il est payé à la ~** he is paid by the *OU* per line ▪ **(allez) à la ~!** new paragraph!
3. [limite] line ▪ **~ blanche/jaune** white/yellow line *(on roads)* ▪ **~ de départ/d'arrivée** starting/finishing line ▪ **~ de fond/de service** TENNIS base/service line ▪ **tracer les ~s d'un court** to mark out a court ▪ **~ d'eau** *OU* **de flottaison** NAUT waterline ▪ **~ de mire** *OU* **de visée** line of sight ▪ **~ de ballon mort** RUGBY dead-ball line ▪ **~ de but** RUGBY goal line ▪ **~s de côté** TENNIS tramlines ▪ **~ de démarcation** [gén] boundary ; MIL demarcation line ▪ **~ d'eau** [en natation] (swimming) lane ▪ **passer la ~ (de l'équateur)** to cross the line ▪ **~ de faîte** watershed, crest line ▪ **~ d'horizon** skyline ▪ **~ de partage** dividing line ▪ **~ de partage des eaux** watershed ▪ **~ de touche** touchline
4. [silhouette - d'une personne] figure ▪ **avoir la ~** to be slim ▪ **je surveille ma ~** I look after *OU* watch my figure ▪ **garder la ~** to keep one's figure ▪ **la ~ de l'été sera très épurée** this summer's look will be very simple ▪ [forme - d'un objet] outline ▪ **l'avion a une très belle ~** the plane is beautifully designed
5. [rangée] line, row ▪ **hors ~** unrivalled, matchless ⊙ **la ~ d'avants/d'arrières** SPORT the forwards/backs ▪ **~ de défense** line of defence ▪ **les ~s ennemies** the enemy lines ▪ **être/monter en première ~** MIL & *fig* to be in/to go to the front line ▪ **un première/deuxième/troisième ~** RUGBY a front-row/second-row/back-row forward
6. [orientation] line ▪ **il suit la ~ du parti** he follows the party line ▪ **sa décision est dans la droite ~ de la politique gouvernementale** his decision is completely in line with government policy ⊙ **~ de conduite** line of conduct ▪ **~ directrice** main line ▪ **elle a décrit la situation dans ses grandes ~s** she gave a broad outline of the situation, she outlined the situation
7. [généalogique] line ▪ **~ directe/collatérale** direct/collateral line ▪ **descendre en ~ directe de** to be directly descended from

8. TRANSP line ■ **~ aérienne** [société] airline (company) ; [service] air service, air link ■ **~ d'autobus** [service] bus service ; [itinéraire] bus route ■ **~ de chemin de fer** railway line *UK*, railroad line *US* ■ **~ maritime** shipping line ■ **~ de métro** underground line *UK*, subway line *US* ■ **les ~s de banlieue** the suburban lines ■ **les grandes ~s** the main lines
9. ÉLECTR & TÉLÉCOM line ■ **la ~ est occupée** the line is engaged *UK ou* busy *US* ■ **il est en ~, vous patientez?** he's on another call just now, will you hold the line? ➊ **~ directe/intérieure/extérieure** TÉLÉCOM direct/internal/outside line ■ **~ à haute tension** ÉLECTR high voltage line
10. TV [d'une image] line
11. PÊCHE fishing line ■ **~ de fond** ground *ou* ledger line
12. FIN : **~ de crédit** *ou* **de découvert** line of credit, credit line
13. *Québec* [mesure] line
14. *loc* **entrer en ~ de compte** to come *ou* to be taken into consideration.
◆ **en ligne** *loc adv* **1.** [en rang] : **mettez-vous en ~!** line up!, get into line!
2. INFORM on line
3. MIL : **monter en ~** [aller à l'assaut] to advance (for the attack)
4. TÉLÉCOM : **restez en ~!** hold the line! ■ **parlez, vous êtes en ~** go ahead, you're through *ou* you're connected ■ **elle est en ~, vous patientez?** her line's engaged, will you hold?
◆ **sur toute la ligne** *loc adv* all down the line, from start to finish ■ **gagner sur toute la ~** to win hands down ■ **se tromper sur toute la ~** to be completely mistaken.

lignée [liɲe] *nf* **1.** [descendance] descendants ■ **le premier/dernier d'une longue ~** the first/last of a long line (of descent) **2.** [extraction, lignage] stock, lineage ■ **être de noble ~** to be of noble lineage **3.** [tradition] line, tradition ■ **elle s'inscrit dans la ~ des romancières féministes** she is in the tradition of feminist novelists **4.** BIOL line, stock.

ligner [3] [liɲe] *vt* to line.

ligneux, euse [liɲø, øz] *adj* ligneous, woody.

lignification [liɲifikasjɔ̃] *nf* lignification.

lignite [liɲit] *nm* MIN brown coal, lignite.

ligoter [3] [ligɔte] *vt* to bind, to tie up *(sép)* ■ **ligoté à sa chaise** tied to his chair.

ligue [lig] *nf* **1.** [groupe] league, pressure group ■ **~ antialcoolique** temperance league **2.** HIST & POLIT : **la Ligue** the League ■ **la Ligue Arabe** the Arab League.

liguer [3] [lige] *vt* : **être ligué contre** to be united against.
◆ **se liguer contre** *vp+prép* to join forces against.

Ligurie [ligyri] *npr f* : **(la) ~** Liguria.

ligurien, enne [ligyrjɛ̃, ɛn] *adj* Ligurian.

lilas [lila] ◇ *nm* [arbre] lilac (tree) ■ [fleur] lilac ➊ **~ simple/double** single/double bloom lilac.
◇ *adj inv* lilac *(modif)*, lilac-coloured.

liliacée [liljase] *nf* liliacea ■ **les ~s** the Liliaceae.

Lille [lil] *npr* Lille.

lilliputien, enne [lilipysjɛ̃, ɛn] *adj* Lilliputian, tiny.
◆ **Lilliputien, enne** *nm, f* Lilliputian.

lillois, e [lilwa, az] *adj* from Lille.
◆ **Lillois, e** *nm, f inhabitant of or person from Lille.*

limace [limas] *nf* **1.** ZOOL slug **2.** *fam péj* [personne] slowcoach *UK*, slowpoke *US* ■ **le bus se traîne comme une ~** the bus is crawling along.

limaçon [limasɔ̃] *nm* **1.** ZOOL snail **2.** ANAT cochlea.

limaille [limaj] *nf* filings ■ **~ de fer** iron filings.

limande [limɑ̃d] *nf* dab ■ **fausse ~** megrim, scald fish.

limbe [lɛ̃b] *nm* **1.** [d'un cadran] limb **2.** ASTRON limb **3.** BOT limb, lamina.

limbes [lɛ̃b] *nmpl* **1.** RELIG limbo ■ **dans les ~** in limbo **2.** [état vague, incertain] : **être dans les ~** to be in (a state of) limbo ■ **son projet est encore dans les ~** his project is still at the embryonic stage *ou* hasn't yet got off the ground.

lime [lim] *nf* **1.** [outil] file ■ **~ à ongles** nail file **2.** BOT & CULIN lime **3.** ZOOL lima.

limé, e [lime] *adj* [vêtement] worn, threadbare.

limer [3] [lime] *vt* [clé] to file ■ [rugosité] to file off *ou* away *(sép)* ■ [pièce de métal, de bois] to file down *(sép)* ■ [cadenas, barreau] to file through *(insép)* ■ **le cadenas a été limé** the padlock has been filed through.
◆ **se limer** *vpt* : **se ~ les ongles** to file one's nails.

limette [limɛt] *nf* BOT lime.

limier [limje] *nm* **1.** CHASSE bloodhound **2.** *fam* [policier] : **fin ~** sleuth.

liminaire [liminɛr] *adj* **1.** [discours] introductory, preliminary ■ **un discours ~** a keynote speech **2.** PSYCHOL liminal, threshold *(modif)*.

limitatif, ive [limitatif, iv] *adj* [liste] restrictive, limitative ■ [clause] restrictive.

limitation [limitasjɔ̃] *nf* limitation, restriction ■ **~ des naissances** birth control ■ **~ des prix** price restrictions *ou* controls ■ **~ de vitesse** speed limit *ou* restrictions.

limite [limit] ◇ *nf* **1.** [maximum ou minimum] limit ■ **~ de temps** time limit ■ **il veut mon article demain dernière ~** *fam* he wants my article by tomorrow at the (very) latest ■ **fixer une ~ à qqch** to set a limit to sthg, to limit sthg ■ **la ~ a été fixée à 30 participants** the number of participants has been limited *ou* restricted to 30 ■ **'entrée gratuite dans la ~ des places disponibles'** 'free admission subject to availability' ■ **dans les ~s du possible** as far as is humanly possible ■ **nos dépenses sont restées dans les ~s du raisonnable** our expenses stayed within reasonable bounds ■ **ma patience a des ~s!** there's a limit to my patience! ■ **sa haine ne connaît pas de ~s** his hatred knows no bounds ■ **son égoïsme est sans ~** his selfishness knows no bounds ➊ **~ d'âge** age limit **2.** [d'un bois] border, edge ■ [d'un pays] boundary, border ■ [d'un terrain de sport] : **essaie de jouer dans les ~s du court!** try to keep the ball inside the court! **3.** MATH limit **4.** [en boxe] : **avant la ~** inside *ou* within the distance ■ **tenir jusqu'à la ~** to go the (full) distance.
◇ *adj* **1.** [maximal] : **âge/vitesse ~** maximum age/speed **2.** *fam* [juste] : **j'ai réussi l'examen, mais c'était ~** I passed the exam, but it was a close *ou* near thing ■ **je suis un peu ~ côté fric** I'm a bit strapped for cash **3.** *fam* [grivois] : **des plaisanteries un peu ~** jokes bordering on the offensive ■ **ta remarque était un peu ~** your remark was a bit near the knuckle.
◆ **limites** *nfpl* [physiques, intellectuelles] limitations.
◆ **à la limite** *loc adv* : **à la ~, on peut toujours dormir dans la voiture** if the worst comes to the worst we can always sleep in the car ■ **à la ~ je préférerais rester ici** I'd almost prefer to stay here.
◆ **à la limite de** *loc prép* : **c'était à la ~ du mauvais goût/de l'insolence** it was verging on bad taste/on impertinence.

limité, e [limite] *adj* **1.** [influence, connaissances] limited ■ [nombre, choix, durée] limited, restricted ■ **d'une importance ~e** of limited *ou* minor importance **2.** *fam* [personne] : **être ~** to have limited abilities, to be of limited ability ■ **il est assez ~ en maths** he's rather weak *ou* poor at maths.

limiter [3] [limite] *vt* **1.** [réduire - dépenses, nombre] to limit, to restrict ; [- temps, influence] to limit ■ **la vitesse n'est pas limitée** there is no speed limit ■ **essayez de ~ les dégâts** *pr & fig* try and limit the damage ■ **~ qqch à** to limit *ou* to restrict sthg to **2.** [circonscrire] to mark the limit of, to delimit.
◆ **se limiter** *vp (emploi réfléchi)* : **il ne sait pas se ~** he's incapable of self-restraint ■ **plus de gâteaux, merci, il faut que je me limite** no more cakes, thanks, I've got to watch what I eat.
◆ **se limiter à** *vp+prép* **1.** [se résumer à] to be restricted to, to be confined to **2.** [se contenter de] : **il se limite à faire ce qu'on lui dit** he only does what he's told to do.

limiteur [limitœr] *nf* limiter ■ **~ de vitesse** governor.

limitrophe [limitrɔf] *adj* : **des comtés ~s** adjoining *ou* neighbouring counties ■ **nos villages sont ~s** our villages lie (just) next to each other ■ **les pays ~s de la Belgique** the countries bordering on Belgium.

limogeage [limɔʒaʒ] *nm* dismissal.

limoger [17] [limɔʒe] *vt* to dismiss ■ **il s'est fait ~** he was dismissed.

limon [limɔ̃] *nm* **1.** GÉOL silt, alluvium **2.** [d'attelage] shaft **3.** [d'escalier] stringboard.

limonade [limɔnad] *nf* (fizzy) lemonade.

limonaire [limɔnɛr] *nm* [petit] barrel organ, hurdy-gurdy ■ [grand] fairground organ.

limoneux, euse [limɔnø, øz] *adj* silty, silt-laden.

limousin, e [limuzɛ̃, in] *adj* from the Limousin.

Limousin [limuzɛ̃] *npr m* : **le ~** the Limousin.

LIMOUSIN

This administrative region includes the ***départements*** of Corrèze, Creuse and Haute-Vienne (capital: Limoges).

limousine [limuzin] *nf* [automobile] limousine.

Limoux [limu] *npr* ⊳ **blanquette.**

limpide [lɛ̃pid] *adj* **1.** [pur - lac, miroir, regard] limpid, clear ■ **pierre d'un bleu ~** limpid *ou* clear blue stone **2.** [intelligible - discours, style] clear, lucid ; [- affaire] clear.

limpidité [lɛ̃pidite] *nf* **1.** [d'une eau, d'un regard, d'un diamant] clearness, limpidity *litt* **2.** [d'un texte] lucidity ■ [d'une affaire] clarity, clearness.

lin [lɛ̃] *nm* **1.** BOT flax **2.** TEXT linen, flax ■ **en ~** linen *(modif).*

linceul [lɛ̃sœl] *nm* [suaire] shroud.

linéaire [lineɛr] ◇ *adj* **1.** BOT, ÉLECTRON, LING & MATH linear **2.** [simple - discours, exposé] reductionist, one-dimensional ■ **il a exposé le problème de façon ~** he gave a one-dimensional account of the problem.
◇ *nm* COMM shelf space.

linéaments [lineamɑ̃] *nmpl* *litt* [d'une sculpture] lineaments *sout* ■ [d'un visage] lineaments *sout*, features ■ [d'un ouvrage] lineaments *sout*, outline.

linéarité [linearite] *nf* linearity.

linge [lɛ̃ʒ] *nm* **1.** [pour l'habillement et la maison] linen ■ [lavé] washing ■ **étendre/repasser le ~** to hang out/to iron the washing ■ **pour un ~ plus blanc, employez X** for a whiter wash, use X ➲ **~ de corps** underwear, underclothes ■ **~ de maison** household linen ■ **~ de table** table linen ■ **du petit ~** small items (of laundry) ■ **du gros ~** big items (of laundry) ■ **il ne fréquente que du beau ~** *fam* he only mixes in high circles *ou* with the upper crust **2.** [chiffon] cloth.

lingère [lɛ̃ʒɛr] *nf* [d'une institution] laundry supervisor.

lingerie [lɛ̃ʒri] *nf* **1.** [sous-vêtements] lingerie, women's underwear ■ **~ fine** lingerie **2.** [lieu] linen room.

lingette [lɛ̃ʒɛt] *nf* [pour bébés] babywipe ■ **~ antibactérienne** anti-bacterial wipe ■ **~ antistatique** anti-static wipe ■ **~ démaquillante** facial *ou* cleansing wipe ■ **~ déodorante** deodorant wipe.

lingot [lɛ̃go] *nm* **1.** FIN ingot ■ **~ d'or** gold ingot *ou* bar ■ **or en ~** *ou* **en ~s** gold bullion **2.** IMPR space.

lingua franca [lingwafrɑ̃ka] *nf inv* lingua franca.

lingual, e, aux [lɛ̃gwal, o] *adj* lingual.

linguiste [lɛ̃gɥist] *nmf* linguist.

linguistique [lɛ̃gɥistik] ◇ *adj* linguistic.
◇ *nf* linguistics *(sing)* ■ **~ descriptive** descriptive linguistics.

linguistiquement [lɛ̃gɥistikmɑ̃] *adv* linguistically.

linier, ère [linje, ɛr] *adj* flax *(modif).*

liniment [linimɑ̃] *nm* liniment.

linkage [linkaʒ] *nm* linkage.

links [liŋks] *nmpl* SPORT links.

lino [lino] *nm fam* linoleum, lino *UK.*

linoléum [linɔleɔm] *nm* linoleum.

linotte [linɔt] *nf* linnet.

linteau, x [lɛ̃to] *nm* lintel.

lion [ljɔ̃] *nm* ZOOL lion ■ **~ de mer** sea lion ■ **tourner comme un ~ en cage** to pace up and down (like a caged lion).

Lion [ljɔ̃] *npr m* **1.** GÉOGR : **golfe du ~** Gulf of Lions **2.** ASTRON Leo **3.** ASTROL Leo ■ **je suis ~** I'm (a) Leo.

lionceau, x [ljɔ̃so] *nm* (lion) cub.

lionne [ljɔn] *nf* lioness.

lipémie [lipemi] *nf* lipaemia *UK*, lipemia *US.*

lipide [lipid] *nm* lipid.

lipidémie [lipidemi] = **lipémie.**

lipidique [lipidik] *adj* lipidic.

lipome [lipom] *nm* lipoma.

liposome [lipɔzom] *nm* liposome.

liposuccion [lipɔsy(k)sjɔ̃] *nf* liposuction.

lippe [lip] *nf* [lèvre inférieure] lower lip.

lippu, e [lipy] *adj* thick-lipped.

liquéfaction [likefaksjɔ̃] *nf* liquefaction.

liquéfiant, e [likefjɑ̃, ɑ̃t] *adj* **1.** CHIM & INDUST du pétrole liquefying **2.** *fam* [épuisant] exhausting.

liquéfier [9] [likefje] *vt* **1.** CHIM, MÉTALL & INDUST du pétrole to liquefy **2.** *fam* [épuiser - personne] to exhaust ■ **cette chaleur m'a liquéfié** this heat has knocked me out.
◆ **se liquéfier** *vpi* **1.** [plomb, gaz] to liquefy, to be liquefied **2.** *fam* [s'amollir] to collapse in a heap.

liquette [likɛt] *nf fam* [chemise] (granddad) shirt.

liqueur [likœr] *nf* **1.** [boisson] liqueur ■ **bonbon à la ~** liqueur-filled sweet *UK ou* candy *US* ■ **chocolat à la ~** liqueur (chocolate) **2.** PHARM solution.

liquidateur, trice [likidatœr, tris] *adj* liquidating.
◆ **liquidateur** *nm* liquidator ■ **~ judiciaire** official liquidator.

liquidatif, ive [likidatif, iv] *adj* of liquidation ■ **valeur liquidative** market *ou* breakup value.

liquidation [likidasjɔ̃] *nf* **1.** [règlement] settling **2.** *fam* [assassinat] elimination **3.** BOURSE settlement ■ **~ de fin de mois** monthly settlement **4.** [d'un commerce] closing down ■ [d'un stock] clearance ■ **~ de stock** stock clearance **5.** FIN & DR [d'une société] liquidation ■ [d'un impôt, d'une dette] settlement, payment ■ **~ de biens** selling (off) of assets.
◆ **en liquidation** *loc adv* DR : **être en ~** to have gone into liquidation ■ **l'entreprise a été mise en ~** the firm was put into liquidation.

liquide [likid] ◇ *adj* **1.** [qui coule] liquid ■ **des aliments ~s** liquid food *ou* foods **2.** [trop fluide] watery, thin ■ **soupe trop ~** watery soup ■ **ta sauce est trop ~** your sauce is too thin **3.** FIN [déterminé - créance] liquid **4.** [argent] : **argent ~** cash **5.** LING liquid.
◇ *nm* **1.** [substance fluide] liquid, fluid ➲ **~ de freins** brake fluid ■ **~ vaisselle** washing-up liquid, dish soap *US* **2.** [aliment] fluid **3.** PHYSIOL fluid ■ **~ amniotique** amniotic fluid ■ **~ céphalo-rachidien** spinal fluid **4.** [espèces] cash ■ **payer en ~** to pay cash.
◇ *nf* LING liquid (consonant).

liquider [3] [likide] *vt* **1.** FIN & DR [marchandises, société, biens] to liquidate ■ [succession, compte] to settle ■ [dette] to settle, to pay off *(sép)* **2.** COMM [volontairement - stock] to sell off *(sép)*, to clear ; [- commerce] to sell off *(sép)*, to wind up *(sép)* ■ **'on liquide'** 'closing down sale' **3.** [expédier - tâche] to finish off ; [- client] to deal with (quickly) ; [- affaire] to settle **4.** *fam* [tuer] to bump off, to liquidate ■ **il s'est fait ~** he was bumped off.

liquidité [likidite] *nf* CHIM & FIN liquidity.
◆ **liquidités** *nfpl* FIN liquid assets ■ **~s internationales** international liquidity.

liquoreux, euse [likɔrø, øz] *adj* syrupy.

liquoriste [likɔrist] *nmf* liqueur seller.

lire¹ [lir] *nf* [monnaie] lira.

lire² [106] [lir] *vt* **1.** [texte, thermomètre, carte] to read ▪ **j'ai lu tout Brecht** I've read everything Brecht wrote ▪ **~ un rapport en diagonale** to flick *ou* to skim through a report ▪ **il m'a lu ta lettre au téléphone** he read me your letter over the phone ▪ **je l'ai lu dans le magazine** I read (about) it in the magazine ▪ **vous êtes beaucoup lu** many people read your works ▪ **en espérant vous ~ bientôt** [dans la correspondance] hoping to hear from you soon ▪ **lu et approuvé** [sur un contrat] read and approved ▪ **allemand lu et parlé** [dans un curriculum] fluent German ▪ **il faut ~ 50 au lieu de 500** 500 should read 50 ▪ *(en usage absolu)* **apprendre à ~** to learn to read ▪ **elle lit bien maintenant** she can read well now ▪ **~ sur les lèvres** to lip-read ➋ **~ entre les lignes** to read between the lines **2.** [déceler] to read ▪ **on lisait la déception dans ses yeux** you could read *ou* see the disappointment in his eyes ▪ **~ les lignes de la main** to read sb's palm ▪ **~ l'avenir dans le marc de café** ≃ to read (the future in the) tea leaves **3.** [interpréter] to interpret ▪ **ils ne lisent pas Malraux de la même manière** their interpretations *ou* readings of Malraux differ **4.** INFORM [disquette] to read ▪ [signes] to sense ▪ [images] to scan.

◆ **lire dans** *v+prép* : **~ dans les pensées de qqn** to read sb's thoughts *ou* mind.

◆ **se lire** *vp (emploi passif)* **1.** [être déchiffré] to read ▪ **ça se lit facilement** it's easy to read ▪ **ça se lit comme un roman** it reads like a novel **2.** [apparaître] to show ▪ **l'inquiétude se lisait sur son visage** anxiety showed on *ou* was written all over his face.

lis [lis] *nm* lily ▪ **~ d'eau** water lily ▪ **un teint de ~** a lily-white complexion.

lisait *etc v* ⊳ **lire**.

Lisbonne [lizbɔn] *npr* Lisbon.

liseré [lizre], **liséré** [lizere] *nm* edging ribbon, piping.

liseron [lizrɔ̃] *nm* bindweed, convolvulus *spéc*.

liseur, euse [lizœr, øz] *nm, f* reader.

◆ **liseuse** *nf* [veste] bed jacket ▪ [lampe] reading light.

lisibilité [lizibilite] *nf* [d'une écriture] legibility ▪ [d'un texte] readability.

lisible [lizibl] *adj* **1.** [écriture, signe] legible **2.** [roman] readable.

lisiblement [liziblәmɑ̃] *adv* legibly.

lisier [lizje] *nm* slurry.

lisière [lizjɛr] *nf* **1.** [d'une forêt] edge **2.** TEXT selvage, selvedge.

lissage [lisaʒ] *nm* **1.** [d'un cuir] sleeking **2.** ÉCON & MATH smoothing (out) **3.** MÉD face-lift.

lisse [lis] ◇ *adj* [planche, peau, pâte] smooth ▪ [chevelure, fourrure] sleek ▪ [pneu].

◇ *nf* **1.** NAUT [membrures] ribband ▪ [garde-fou] handrail **2.** TEXT heddle.

lissé [lise] *nm* gloss stage *(in sugar boiling)*.

lisser [3] [lise] *vt* [barbe, mèche] to smooth (down) ▪ [papier, tissu] to smooth out *(sép)* ▪ [plumes] to preen ▪ [cuir] to sleek ▪ **le canard lissait sa queue** the duck was preening its tail.

lissier [lisje] *nm* TEXT loom setter.

listage [listaʒ] *nm* listing ▪ **faire le ~ des modèles en stock** to list the models in stock.

liste [list] *nf* **1.** [énumération - de noms, de chiffres] list ▪ **faire** *ou* **dresser une ~** to make (out) *ou* to draw up a list ▪ **tu as la ~ des courses (à faire)?** have you got the shopping list? ▪ **j'ai fait la ~ des avantages et des inconvénients** I have listed the *ou* made a list of the pros and cons ▪ **tu n'es pas sur la ~** you're not on the list, your name isn't listed ▪ **la ~ des invités** the guest list ➋ **~ d'attente** waiting list ▪ **~ de contrôle** checklist ▪ **~ de mariage** wedding list ▪ **~ noire** blacklist ▪ **elle est sur la ~ noire** she has been blacklisted ▪ **~ orange** telephone preference service *UK* ▪ **être sur la ~ rouge** TÉLÉCOM to be ex-directory *UK*, to have an unlisted number *US* **2.** POLIT : **~ électorale** electoral roll ▪ **la ~ d'opposition** the list of opposition candidates ▪ **~ commune** joint list (of candidates) **3.** INFORM list ▪ **~ déroulante** drop-down list ▪ **~ de diffusion** mailing list **4.** AÉRON : **~ de vérification** checklist **5.** [d'un cheval] star.

lister [3] [liste] *vt* **1.** [mettre en liste] to list **2.** INFORM to list (out).

listeriose, listériose [listerjoz] *nf* MÉD listeriosis.

listing [listiŋ] *nm* **1.** [gén] list **2.** INFORM printout, listing.

lit [li] *nm* **1.** [meuble] bed ▪ **~ en pin/en fer** pine/iron bed ▪ **garder le ~, rester au ~** to stay *ou* to be in bed ▪ **aller au ~** to go to bed ▪ **envoyer/mettre qqn au ~** to send/to put sb to bed ▪ **se mettre au ~** to get into bed ▪ **tu es encore au ~!** you are still in bed! ▪ **maintenant, au ~!** come on now, it's bedtime! ▪ **faire ~ à part** to sleep in separate beds ▪ **le ~ est/n'est pas défait** the bed has/hasn't been slept in ▪ **faire le ~ de qqn** to make sb's bed ▪ **c'est un hôpital de 150 ~s** it's a 150-bed hospital ➋ **~ à baldaquin** four-poster (bed) ▪ **~ de jour** *ou* **de repos** daybed ▪ **~ de camp** camp bed ▪ **~ d'enfant, petit ~** cot *UK*, crib *US* ▪ **~ à une personne** *ou* **place** single bed ▪ **~ à deux places** *ou* **pour deux personnes** double bed ▪ **grand ~** double bed ▪ **~ pliant** folding bed ▪ **~ en portefeuille** apple-pie bed *UK*, short-sheeted bed *US* ▪ **sur son ~ de mort** on his deathbed ▪ **sur son ~ de douleur** on her sickbed ▪ **~s gigognes** stowaway beds ▪ **~s jumeaux** twin beds ▪ **~s superposés** bunk bed, bunks ▪ **faire le ~ de qqch** to pave the way for sthg ▪ **comme on fait son ~ on se couche** *prov* as you make your bed, so you must lie in it *prov* **2.** DR [mariage] : **enfant d'un premier/deuxième ~** child of a first/second marriage **3.** [couche] bed, layer ▪ **~ de feuilles/mousse** bed of leaves/moss **4.** GÉOGR bed ▪ **la rivière est sortie de son ~** the river has burst *ou* overflowed its banks **5.** NAUT : **le ~ du courant** the tideway ▪ **le ~ du vent** the set of the wind, the wind's eye.

litanie [litani] *nf* [longue liste] : **une ~ de plaintes** a litany of complaints ▪ **(avec lui, c'est) toujours la même ~!** he never stops moaning!

◆ **litanies** *nfpl* RELIG litanies.

lit-cage [likaʒ] *(pl* **lits-cages***)* *nm* folding cot *UK ou* crib *US*.

litchi [litʃi] *nm* **1.** [arbre] litchi, lychee **2.** [fruit] litchi, lychee, lichee.

liteau, x [lito] *nm* **1.** [sur linge] coloured stripe **2.** [tasseau] bracket **3.** [bois débité] batten.

litée [lite] *nf* **1.** [groupe d'animaux - lions] pride ; [- loups] pack **2.** [portée d'une laie] wild sow's litter.

literie [litri] *nf* bedding.

lithiase [litjaz] *nf* lithiasis.

lithium [litjɔm] *nm* lithium.

litho [lito] *nf fam* litho.

lithographe [litɔgraf] *nm* lithographer.

lithographie [litɔgrafi] *nf* **1.** [procédé] lithography **2.** [estampe] lithograph.

lithographier [9] [litɔgrafje] *vt* to lithograph.

lithographique [litɔgrafik] *adj* lithographic.

lithologie [litɔlɔʒi] *nf* lithology.

lithosphère [litɔsfɛr] *nf* lithosphere.

litière [litjɛr] *nf* litter ▪ **~ pour chats** cat litter.

litige [litiʒ] *nm* **1.** [différend] dispute ▪ **question en ~** contentious *ou* controversial question ▪ **objet de ~** bone of contention **2.** DR dispute ▪ **être en ~** to be in dispute *ou* involved in litigation.

litigieux, euse [litiʒjø, øz] *adj* litigious *sout*, contentious.

litote [litɔt] *nf* litotes ▪ **c'est une ~** that's an understatement.

litre [litr] *nm* **1.** [unité] litre **2.** [bouteille] litre bottle.

litron△ [litrɔ̃] *nm* litre, bottle (of wine).

littéraire [literɛr] ◇ *adj* [style, œuvre, prix] literary ▪ **il fera des études ~s** he's going to study literature.

◇ *nmf* [étudiant] arts student ▪ [professeur] arts teacher ▪ [amateur de lettres] a literary *ou* literary-minded person.

littérairement [literɛrmɑ̃] *adv* in literary terms, literarily.

littéral, e, aux [literal, o] *adj* [transcription, traduction] literal, word-for-word ■ [sens] literal.

littéralement [literalmɑ̃] *adv* literally ■ **c'est ~ du chantage!** that's sheer blackmail!

littérarité [literarite] *nf* literariness.

littérateur [literatœr] *nm péj* hack (writer).

littérature [literatyr] *nf* **1.** [art, œuvres] : **la ~** literature ; [activité] writing ■ **les discours des politiciens c'est de la ~** *péj* the politicians' speeches are just (a lot of) fine words ▶ **~ de colportage** chapbooks **2.** [documentation] literature, material.

littoral, e, aux [litɔral, o] *adj* coastal, littoral *spéc.*
◆ **littoral, aux** *nm* coastline, littoral *spéc.*

Lituanie [litɥani] *npr f* : **(la) ~** Lithuania.

lituanien, enne [litɥanjɛ̃, ɛn] *adj* Lithuanian.
◆ **Lituanien, enne** *nm, f* Lithuanian.

liturgie [lityrʒi] *nf* liturgy.

liturgique [lityrʒik] *adj* liturgical.

livarot [livaro] *nm* livarot (cheese).

livide [livid] *adj* **1.** [pâle - visage, teint] pallid, sallow ; [- malade, blessé] whey-faced **2.** *litt* [d'une couleur plombée] livid.

lividité [lividite] *nf* lividness.

living [liviŋ], **living-room** [liviŋrum] (*pl* **living-rooms**) *nm* living room.

Livourne [livurn] *npr* Leghorn, Livorno.

livrable [livrabl] *adj* which can be delivered ■ **les marchandises ne sont pas ~s à domicile** 'no home deliveries', 'we do not deliver'.

livraison [livrɛzɔ̃] *nf* **1.** COMM delivery ■ **payer à la ~** to pay cash on delivery ■ **faire des ~s** to carry out *ou* to make deliveries ▶ **'~ à domicile'** 'we deliver' ■ **'~ gratuite'** 'free delivery' **2.** IMPR instalment.

livre [livr] ◇ *nm* **1.** [œuvre, partie d'une œuvre] book ■ **elle parlait comme un ~** she talked like a book *péj* ▶ **~ audio** audiobook ■ **~ cartonné** *ou* **relié** hardback (book) ■ **~ de grammaire/d'histoire** grammar/history book ■ **~ d'images/de prières** picture/prayer book ■ **~ de classe** schoolbook, textbook ■ **c'est mon ~ de chevet** it's a book I read and re-read ■ **~ de cuisine** cookery book UK, cookbook ■ **~s pour enfants** children's books ■ **~ d'heures** book of hours ■ **~ de messe** hymnbook, missal ■ **~ de poche** paperback (book) ■ **il est pour moi comme un ~ ouvert** I can read him like a book **2.** [l'édition] : **le ~** the book trade ■ **l'industrie du ~** the book industry ■ **les ouvriers du ~** the printworkers **3.** [registre] : **~ de bord** logbook ■ **~ de caisse** cash book ■ **~ de comptes** (account) books ■ **~ d'or** visitors' book ■ **~ de paie** payroll **4.** POLIT : **~ blanc** white paper.
◇ *nf* **1.** [unité de poids] half a kilo, ≃ pound ■ *Québec* pound **2.** FIN pound ▶ **~ égyptienne/chypriote** Egyptian/Cypriot pound ■ **~ irlandaise** Irish pound, punt ■ **~ sterling** pound (sterling) **3.** HIST livre.
◆ **à livre ouvert** *loc adv* at sight.

livre-cassette [livrəkasɛt] (*pl* **livres-cassettes**) *nm* spoken word cassette.

livrée [livre] *nf* **1.** [de domestique] livery ■ **chauffeur en ~** liveried chauffeur **2.** ZOOL coat.

livre-journal [livrəʒurnal] (*pl* **livres-journaux** [-no]) *nm* daybook.

livrer [3] [livre] *vt* **1.** [abandonner - personne, pays, ville] to hand over ■ **le pays est livré à la corruption** the country has been given over to *ou* has sunk into corruption ■ **son corps fut livré aux flammes** her body was committed to the flames ■ **être livré à soi-même** to be left to o.s. *ou* to one's own devices **2.** [dénoncer] to inform on *(insép)*, to denounce **3.** [révéler] : **~ un secret** to give away *ou* to betray a secret ■ **dans ses romans, elle livre peu d'elle-même** she doesn't reveal much about herself in her novels **4.** COMM [article, commande] to deliver ■ [client] to deliver to ■ **~ qqch à domicile** to deliver sthg *(to the customer's home)* **5.** *loc* **~ (une) bataille** *ou* **(un) combat** [se battre] to wage *ou* to do battle ■ **~ passage à** [laisser passer] to make way for.
◆ **se livrer** ◇ *vp (emploi réfléchi)* [se rendre] : **se ~ à la police** to give o.s. up to the police.
◇ *vpi* [faire des confidences] : **se ~ (à qqn)** to confide (in sb) ■ **elle ne se livre jamais** she never confides in anybody, she never opens up.
◆ **se livrer à** *vp+prép* **1.** [s'engager dans] : **se ~ à une enquête** to hold *ou* to conduct an investigation ■ **ils se livraient au chantage** they were engaged in blackmail ■ **se ~ à des suppositions** to make suppositions **2.** [s'abandonner à - débauche] to abandon o.s. to ; [- sentiment] to give o.s. up to.

livresque [livrɛsk] *adj* acquired from books ■ **son savoir n'est que ~** his knowledge comes straight out of books.

livret [livrɛ] *nm* **1.** [carnet] notebook **2.** BANQUE : **~ A** *savings account with a maximum holding* ■ **~ B** *savings account with no maximum holding* ■ **~ de caisse d'épargne** savings book ■ **compte sur ~** savings account **3.** DR : **~ de famille** *ou* **de mariage** family record book *(in which dates of births and deaths are registered)* **4.** ÉDUC : **~ scolaire** school report (book) **5.** MIL : **~ militaire** army *ou* military record **6.** MUS libretto **7.** *Suisse* multiplication table.

livreur, euse [livrœr, øz] *nm, f* delivery man (*f* woman).

LLD (*abr de* **location longue durée**) [ɛlɛlde] *nf* AUTO long-term rental *ou* leasing.

LOA (*abr de* **location avec option d'achat**) [ɛloa] *nf* leasing with an option to buy, lease-to-buy.

loader [lodœr] *nm* loader, loading machine.

lob [lɔb] *nm* lob ■ **~ lifté** spin lob.

lobby [lɔbi] (*pl* **lobbys** *ou pl* **lobbies**) *nm* lobby, pressure group.

lobe [lɔb] *nm* **1.** ANAT & BOT lobe ■ **~ de l'oreille** ear lobe **2.** ARCHIT foil.

lobé, e [lɔbe] *adj* **1.** BOT lobed **2.** ARCHIT foiled.

lober [3] [lɔbe] *vt & vi* to lob.

lobotomie [lɔbɔtɔmi] *nf* lobotomy.

lobotomiser [3] [lɔbɔtɔmize] *vt* : **il a été lobotomisé** he's had a lobotomy.

lobule [lɔbyl] *nm* lobule.

local, e, aux [lɔkal, o] *adj* [anesthésie, élu, radio] local ■ [averses] localized.
◆ **local, aux** *nm* **1.** [à usage déterminé] premises ■ **~ d'habitation** domestic premises ■ **locaux commerciaux** *ou* **professionnels** business premises **2.** [sans usage déterminé] place ■ **je cherche un ~ pour faire une fête** I'm looking for a place to hold a party.

localement [lɔkalmɑ̃] *adv* **1.** [à un endroit] locally **2.** [par endroits] in places ■ **demain, le ciel sera ~ nuageux** tomorrow there will be patchy cloud *ou* it will be cloudy in places.

localisable [lɔkalizabl] *adj* localizable.

localisation [lɔkalizasjɔ̃] *nf* **1.** [détection, emplacement] location **2.** ASTRONAUT location, tracking ■ [limitation] localization, confinement **3.** [adaptation] localization.

localisé, e [lɔkalize] *adj* **1.** [déterminé] located **2.** [limité] local, localized ■ **combats ~s** localized fighting.

localiser [3] [lɔkalize] *vt* **1.** [situer] to locate ■ **il a fallu ~ la fuite** we had to locate the leak **2.** [limiter] to confine, to localize **3.** [adaptater] to localize.

localité [lɔkalite] *nf* [petite] village ■ [moyenne] small town ■ **dans toute la ~** throughout the town, all over town.

locataire [lɔkatɛr] *nmf* [d'un appartement, d'une maison] tenant ■ [d'une chambre chez le propriétaire] lodger ■ **~ (à bail)** DR lessee.

locatif, ive [lɔkatif, iv] *adj* **1.** [concernant le locataire, la chose louée] : **valeur locative** rental value **2.** LING : **préposition locative** locative preposition.
◆ **locatif** *nm* locative (case), *voir aussi* **pluriel**.

location [lɔkasjɔ̃] *nf* **1.** [par le propriétaire - d'un logement] letting *esp UK*, renting (out) ; [- de matériel, d'appareils] renting (out), rental, hiring (out) *esp UK* ; [- de costumes, de skis] hire *esp UK*, rental ; [- d'un navire, d'un avion] leasing ▪ **~ de voitures** self-drive hire **2.** [par le locataire - d'un logement] renting ; [- d'une machine] hiring *esp UK*, renting ; [- d'un navire, d'un avion] leasing **3.** [logement] rented accommodation ▪ **désolé, nous n'avons pas de ~s** sorry, we have no accommodation for rent ▪ **~ meublée** furnished accommodation **4.** [réservation] : **la ~ est ouverte un mois à l'avance** booking starts a month in advance **5.** [période] lease ▪ **(contrat de) ~ de 2 ans** 2-year rental *ou* lease *ou* tenancy agreement **6.** [prix - d'un logement] rent ; [- d'un appareil] rental **7.** SOCIOL : **~ d'utérus** surrogate motherhood.
◆ **en location** ◇ *loc adj* : **être en ~** [locataire] to be renting *(a house)* ; [appartement] to be available for rent, to be up for rent ▪ **j'ai un appartement, mais il est en ~** [déjà loué] I've got a flat but it is rented out.
◇ *loc adv* : **donner** *ou* **mettre une maison en ~** to rent (out) *ou* to let a house.

location-accession [lɔkasjɔ̃aksɛsjɔ̃] (*pl* **locations-accessions**) *nf* mortgage.

location-gérance [lɔkasjɔ̃ʒerɑ̃s] (*pl* **locations-gérances**) *nf* COMM ≃ franchise.

location-vente [lɔkasjɔ̃vɑ̃t] (*pl* **locations-ventes**) *nf* **1.** [d'un véhicule, d'équipement] hire purchase *UK*, installment plan *US* ▪ **la voiture est en ~** the car is being bought in instalments *ou* on hire purchase **2.** [d'une maison] mortgage.

locative [lɔkativ] *f* ⊳ **locatif**.

loch [lɔk] *nm* **1.** GÉOGR loch **2.** NAUT log.

loche [lɔʃ] *nf* **1.** [poisson - de rivière] loach ; [- de mer] rockling **2.** [dialecte: limace] slug.

lock-out [lɔkaut] *nm inv* lockout.

lock-outer [3] [lɔkaute] *vt* to lock out *(sép)*.

locomoteur, trice [lɔkɔmɔtœr, tris] *adj* **1.** MÉCAN locomotive **2.** ANAT locomotive, locomotor *(modif)* ▪ **ataxie locomotrice** locomotor ataxia.
◆ **locomoteur** *nm* motor unit.

locomotion [lɔkɔmɔsjɔ̃] *nf* locomotion.

locomotive [lɔkɔmɔtiv] *nf* **1.** MÉCAN locomotive, (railway) engine **2.** *fam* [d'un parti, d'une économie] pacemaker, pacesetter **3.** SPORT pacesetter, pacer.

locomotrice [lɔkɔmɔtris] *f* ⊳ **locomoteur**.

locus [lɔkys] *nm inv* locus.

locuste [lɔkyst] *nf* locust.

locuteur, trice [lɔkytœr, tris] *nm, f* LING speaker ▪ **~ natif** native speaker.

locution [lɔkysjɔ̃] *nf* **1.** [expression] phrase, locution ▪ **une ~ figée** *ou* **toute faite** a set phrase, an idiom **2.** GRAMM phrase ▪ **~ adverbiale/nominale** adverbial/noun phrase.

loden [lɔdɛn] *nm* **1.** TEXT loden **2.** [manteau] loden coat.

lof [lɔf] *nm* windward side ▪ **aller au ~** to luff ▪ **virer ~ pour ~** to wear.

lofer [3] [lɔfe] *vi* to luff.

loft [lɔft] *nm* loft (conversion).

logarithme [lɔgaritm] *nm* logarithm ▪ **~ népérien** *ou* **naturel** natural logarithm.

logarithmique [lɔgaritmik] *adj* logarithmic.

loge [lɔʒ] *nf* **1.** [d'artiste] dressing room ▪ [de candidats] exam room **2.** [de concierge, de gardien] lodge **3.** [de francs-maçons] lodge ▪ **la Grande Loge** the Grand Lodge **4.** THÉÂTRE box ▪ **premières/secondes ~s** dress/upper circle boxes ▪ **être aux premières ~s** *fig* to have a ringside *ou* front seat ▪ **de notre fenêtre, on est aux premières ~s pour les défilés** we have a grandstand view of processions from our window **5.** ARCHIT loggia.

logeable [lɔʒabl] *adj* : **c'est ~ dans le placard** there's room for it in the cupboard.

logement [lɔʒmɑ̃] *nm* **1.** [habitation] accommodation *(U)* ▪ **un ~ de 3 pièces** a 3-room flat *UK ou* apartment *US* ▪ **ils ont construit des ~s pour leurs employés** they have built accommodation for their employees **2.** MIL [chez l'habitant] billet ▪ [sur une base] (married) quarters **3.** [hébergement] : **le ~** housing ▪ **la crise du ~** the housing shortage **4.** TECHNOL housing, casing.

loger [17] [lɔʒe] ◇ *vi* to live ▪ **pour l'instant je loge chez lui** I'm living *ou* staying at his place at the moment ▪ **les soldats logeaient chez l'habitant** the soldiers were billeted *ou* quartered with the local population ▪ **les touristes logeaient chez l'habitant** the tourists were staying in boarding houses *ou* in bed-and-breakfasts ▪ **je suis bien/mal logé** [chez moi] I'm comfortably/badly housed ; [en pension] I've got comfortable/poor lodgings ▪ **être logé, nourri et blanchi** to get board and lodging with laundry (service) included ▶ **on est tous logés à la même enseigne** everybody is in the same boat.
◇ *vt* **1.** [recevoir - ami, visiteur] to put up *(sép)* ; [- soldat] to billet **2.** [contenir - personnes] to accommodate ; [- choses] to put ▪ **le placard peut ~ trois grosses valises** the cupboard can take *ou* hold three big suitcases **3.** [mettre] : **~ une balle dans la tête de qqn** to lodge a bullet in sb's head ▪ **~ une idée dans la tête de qqn** to put an idea into sb's head.
◆ **se loger** ◇ *vpt* : **il s'est logé une balle dans la tête** he put a bullet through his head, he shot himself in the head.
◇ *vpi* **1.** [à long terme - couple, famille] to find somewhere to live **2.** [provisoirement - touriste, étudiant] to find accommodation **3.** [pénétrer] : **un éclat de verre s'était logé dans son œil droit** a splinter of glass had lodged itself in his right eye **4.** TECHNOL to fit, to be housed.

logeur, euse [lɔʒœr, øz] *nm, f* landlord (*f* landlady).

loggia [lɔdʒja] *nf* loggia.

logiciel, elle [lɔʒisjɛl] *adj* software *(modif)*.
◆ **logiciel** *nm* software ▪ **ils viennent de sortir un nouveau ~** they've just brought out a new piece of software ▶ **~ d'application** application *ou* software package ▪ **~ de base** systems teaching software ▪ **~ de bureautique** office software package ▪ **~ contributif** shareware ▪ **~ libre** freeware, open source (software) ▪ **~ de navigation** browser ▪ **~ public** freeware.

logicien, enne [lɔʒisjɛ̃, ɛn] *nm, f* logician.

logique [lɔʒik] ◇ *adj* **1.** PHILOS & SC logical **2.** [cohérent, clair] sensible, logical ▪ **ah oui, c'est ~, je n'y avais pas pensé!** ah, that makes sense, I hadn't thought of that! ▪ **sois ~ avec toi-même, tu veux qu'elle vienne ou pas?** you can't have it both ways, do you want her to come or not? **3.** [normal, compréhensible] logical, normal, natural ▪ **c'est dans la suite ~ des événements** it's part of the normal course of events ▪ **tu la brimes, elle t'en veut, c'est ~** if you pick on her she'll hold it against you, that's only normal *ou* natural *ou* logical **4.** INFORM logic.
◇ *nf* **1.** PHILOS & SC logic ▪ **~ formelle** *ou* **pure** formal logic **2.** [cohérence] logic ▪ **ton raisonnement manque de ~** your argument isn't very logical *ou* consistent ▪ **il n'y a aucune ~ là-dedans** none of this makes sense ▪ **c'est dans la ~ des choses** it's in the nature of things **3.** INFORM logic ▪ **~ binaire/booléenne** binary/Boolean logic ▪ **~ câblée** wired logic ▪ **~ programmable** field programmable logic array.

logiquement [lɔʒikmɑ̃] *adv* **1.** [avec cohérence] logically **2.** [normalement] : **~, il devrait bientôt être là** if all goes well *ou* unless something goes wrong, he should soon be here.

logis [lɔʒi] *nm litt* dwelling, abode ▪ **il n'y avait personne au ~** there was nobody (at) home.

logisticien, enne [lɔʒistisjɛ̃, ɛn] *nm, f* logistician.

logistique [lɔʒistik] ◇ *adj* **1.** MIL logistic **2.** [organisationnel] : **les élus locaux apportent un important soutien ~ au parti** local councillors make an important contribution to the running of the party.
◇ *nf* logistics *(sing)*.

logithèque [lɔʒitɛk] *nf* software library.

logo [logo] *nm* logo.

logomachie [lɔgɔmaʃi] *nf* **1.** [discussion] semantic argument **2.** [suite de mots creux] bombast, wordiness.

logorrhée [lɔgɔre] *nf* logorrhoea.

logotype [lɔgɔtip] *nm* logotype.

loi [lwa] *nf*

A.

1. [règles publiques] law ■ **selon la ~ en vigueur** according to the law as it stands

2. DR [décret] act, law ■ **la ~ Dupont a été votée la nuit dernière** the Dupont Act was passed last night ◐ **la ~ (de) 1901** *law concerning the setting up of non-profit making organizations* ■ **~ de 1948** *former law protecting tenants from unreasonable rent increases (rental on properties which still fall under this law is often extremely low)* ■ **~ anticasseurs** *law against violence and vandalism during demonstrations* ■ **~ d'exception** emergency legislation ■ **~ de finances** budget *ou* appropriation bill ■ **~ fondamentale** fundamental law ■ **la ~ Lang** *book price agreement introduced in 1982* ■ **~ d'orientation** *act laying down the basic principles for government action in a given field* ■ **la ~ Savary** *law of 1984 introducing selective entry to education courses* ■ **la ~ du talion** HIST lex talionis ■ **dans ce cas-là, c'est la ~ du talion** *fig* in that case, it's an eye for an eye (and a tooth for a tooth)

3. [légalité] : **la ~** the law ■ **ça devrait être interdit par la ~!** there ought to be a law against it! ■ **avoir la ~ pour soi** to have the law on one's side ■ **tomber sous le coup de la ~** to be an offence

B.

1. [devoir] rule ■ **les ~s de l'hospitalité/du savoir-vivre** the rules of hospitality/etiquette ■ **les ~s de l'honneur** the code of honour ■ **elle ne connaît d'autre ~ que son plaisir** she obeys only her desire for pleasure

2. RELIG law ■ **la ~ divine** divine law

C.

1. [domination] law, rule ■ **tenir qqn/un pays sous sa ~** to rule sb/a country ■ **dicter** *ou* **imposer sa ~, faire la ~** to lay down the law ■ **l'équipe de Bordeaux a dicté** *ou* **imposé sa ~ à celle de Marseille** Bordeaux dominated Marseilles

2. [règles d'un milieu] law, rule ■ **la ~ du milieu** the law of the underworld ■ **c'est la ~ de la nature** it's nature's way ◐ **la ~ de la jungle/du silence** the law of the jungle/of silence

D.

[principe] law ■ **la ~ de la gravitation universelle** *ou* **de la pesanteur** *ou* **de la chute des corps** the law of gravity ■ **les ~s de Mendel** Mendel's laws ■ **la ~ du moindre effort** *hum* the line of least resistance ■ **la ~ de l'offre et de la demande** the law of supply and demand.

loi-cadre [lwakadr] (*pl* **lois-cadres**) *nf* parent act.

loin [lwɛ̃] *adv* **1.** [dans l'espace] far (away) ■ **ils habitent ~** they live a long way away ■ **il n'y a pas ~ entre Paris et Versailles** it's not far from Paris to Versailles ■ **elle est ~ derrière nous** she is a long way behind us ■ **moins ~ (que)** not as *ou* so far (as) ■ **plus ~ (que)** further *ou* farther (than) ■ **voir plus ~ dans le texte** see below ■ **cette arme porte ~** this weapon has a long range **2.** [dans le temps] far (away) ■ **c'est ~ tout ça!** [dans le passé] that was a long time ago!, that seems a long way off now! ; [dans le futur] that's a long way off! **3.** *fig* far ■ **de là à lui faire confiance, il y a ~** there is a big difference between that and trusting him ■ **d'ici à l'accuser de mensonge, il n'y a pas ~** from here it's a short step to accusing him of lying ■ **aller un peu** *ou* **trop ~** to go (a bit) too far ■ **j'irai plus ~ et je dirai que...** I'd go even further and say that... ■ **la possession de stupéfiants, ça peut mener ~** possession of drugs can lead to serious trouble ■ **ils ont poussé les recherches très ~** they took the research as far as possible ■ **une analyse qui ne va pas très ~** an analysis lacking in depth ■ **avec 100 euros, on ne va pas ~** you can't get very far on 100 euros ■ **voir ~** to be far-sighted ◐ **elle ne voit pas plus ~ que le bout de son nez** she can't see further than the end of her nose ■ **il y a ~ de la coupe aux lèvres** *prov* there's many a slip 'twixt cup and lip *prov* **4.** *Suisse* [absent] : **il est ~** he's not here.

◆ **au loin** *loc adv* far away ■ **on voyait, au ~, une rangée de peupliers** a row of poplars could be seen in the far distance *ou* far off in the distance.

◆ **d'aussi loin que** *loc conj* : **il lui fit signe d'aussi ~ qu'il la vit** he signalled to her as soon as he saw her in the distance ■ **d'aussi ~ que je me souvienne** as far back as I can remember.

◆ **de loin** *loc adv* **1.** [depuis une grande distance] from a long way, from a distance ■ **je vois mal de ~** I can't see very well from a distance ■ **tu verras mieux d'un peu plus ~** you'll see better from a bit further away ■ **ils sont venus d'assez ~ à pied** they came a fair distance *ou* quite a long way on foot ◐ **je l'ai vu venir de ~** *fam* I saw him coming a mile off **2.** [assez peu] : **il ne s'intéresse que de ~ à la politique** he's only slightly interested in politics ■ **suivre les événements de ~** to follow events from a distance **3.** [de beaucoup] far and away, by far ■ **c'est de ~ le meilleur cognac** it's far and away *ou* it's by far the best brandy ■ **je le préfère à ses collègues, et de ~** I much prefer him to his colleagues.

◆ **de loin en loin** *loc adv sout* **1.** [dans l'espace] at intervals, here and there **2.** [dans le temps] from time to time, every now and then.

◆ **du plus loin que** *loc conj* : **il lui fit signe du plus ~ qu'il l'aperçut** he signalled to her as soon as he saw her in the distance ■ **du plus ~ qu'il se souvienne** as far back as he can remember.

◆ **loin de** *loc prép* **1.** [dans l'espace] a long way *ou* far (away) from ■ **non ~ de** not far from **2.** *fig* far from ■ **je ne suis pas ~ de leur dire le fond de ma pensée** it wouldn't take me much to tell them what I think, I have a good mind to tell them what I really think ■ **j'étais ~ de me douter que...** I never imagined... ■ **~ de moi l'idée de t'accuser** far be it from me to accuse you ■ **~ de moi cette idée!** nothing could be further from my mind! ◐ **~ des yeux, ~ du cœur** *prov* out of sight, out of mind *prov* ■ **~ de là** [endroit] far from there ; *fig* far from it **3.** [dans le temps] a long way (away) ■ **la Première Guerre mondiale est bien ~ de nous maintenant** the First World War is a long way away from us now ■ **nous ne sommes plus ~ de l'an 2000 maintenant** we're not far off the year 2000 now **4.** [au lieu de] : **~ de m'aider** far from helping me.

◆ **loin que** *loc conj litt* not that.

◆ **pas loin de** *loc adv* [presque] nearly, almost ■ **ça ne fait pas ~ de quatre ans qu'ils sont mariés** they've been married nearly four years.

lointain, e [lwɛ̃tɛ̃, ɛn] *adj* **1.** [dans l'espace] distant, far-off **2.** [dans le temps - passé] distant, far-off ; [- futur] distant ■ **dans un ~ avenir** in the distant *ou* remote future **3.** [indirect - parent, cousin] remote **4.** [absent - air, sourire] faraway ■ **je l'ai trouvée un peu ~e** [préoccupée] she seemed to have something on her mind ; [distraite] I found her rather vague **5.** [dans la pensée - lien, rapport] remote, distant ■ **il n'y a qu'un ~ rapport entre...** there's only the remotest connection between...

◆ **lointain** *nm* **1.** [fond] : **dans le** *ou* **au ~** [vers l'horizon] in the distance **2.** ART : **les ~s** the background ■ **~ vaporeux** sfumato background.

loi-programme [lwaprɔgram] (*pl* **lois-programmes**) *nf* (framework) legislation, ≃ Command Paper *UK*.

loir [lwar] *nm* dormouse.

Loire [lwar] *npr f* **1.** [fleuve] : **la ~** the (river) Loire **2.** [région] : **la ~** the Loire (area) *ou* valley.

loisible [lwazibl] *adj sout* **il vous est tout à fait ~ de partir** you are totally at liberty *ou* quite entitled to go.

loisir [lwazir] *nm* **1.** [temps libre] spare time ■ **comment occupez-vous vos heures de ~?** what do you do in your spare time? **2.** [possibilité] : **avoir (tout) le ~ de** to have the time *ou* the opportunity to ■ **on ne lui a pas donné** *ou* **laissé le ~ de s'expliquer** he was not allowed (the opportunity) to explain his actions.

◆ **loisirs** *nmpl* [activités] leisure *(U)*, spare-time activities ■ **nous vivons de plus en plus dans une société de ~s** we live in a society where leisure is taking on more and more importance.

◆ **(tout) à loisir** *loc adv* at leisure ■ **faites-le (tout) à ~** do it at (your) leisure.

lokoum [lɔkum] = **loukoum**.

lolo [lolo] *nm* **1.** *fam* [lait] milk **2.** △ [sein] boob△.

lombago [lɔ̃bago] = **lumbago**.

lombaire [lɔ̃bɛr] <> *adj* lumbar.
<> *nf* lumbar vertebra.

lombalgie [lɔ̃balʒi] *nf* lumbago.

lombard, e [lɔ̃bar, ard] *adj* Lombardic.
◆ **Lombard, e** *nm, f* Lombard.

Lombardie [lɔ̃bardi] *npr f* : **(la)** ~ Lombardy.

lombric [lɔ̃brik] *nm* earthworm, lumbricus *spéc.*

lompe [lɔ̃p] *nm* = **lump**.

londonien, enne [lɔ̃dɔnjɛ̃, ɛn] *adj* from London, London *(modif)* ▪ **les bus ~s** the London buses.
◆ **Londonien, enne** *nm, f* Londoner.

Londres [lɔ̃dr] *npr* London ▪ **le Grand ~** Greater London.

long, longue [lɔ̃ *(devant nm commençant par une voyelle ou 'h' muet* lɔ̃g*)*, lɔ̃g] *adj*

A. DANS L'ESPACE
B. DANS LE TEMPS

A. DANS L'ESPACE

1. [grand] long ▪ **une longue rangée d'arbres** a long row of trees ▪ **une fille aux longues jambes** a long-legged girl, a girl with long legs ▪ **~ de** [mesurant] : **tunnel ~ de deux kilomètres** two-kilometre long tunnel
2. BOT [feuille] elongated ▪ [tige] long
3. [vêtement] long ▪ **à manches longues** long-sleeved ● **une robe longue** a full-length *ou* long dress
4. CULIN thin
5. JEUX long

B. DANS LE TEMPS

1. [qui dure longtemps] long ▪ **je suis fatigué, la journée a été longue** I'm tired, it's been a long day ▪ **je suis restée de ~s mois sans nouvelles de lui** I had no word from him for months and months ▪ **obligé d'attendre un ~ quart d'heure** kept waiting for a good quarter of an hour ▪ **ne sois pas trop longue ou personne ne t'écoutera jusqu'à la fin** don't take too long *ou* don't speak for too long or nobody will listen to you all the way through ▪ **un congé de longue durée** a (period of) long leave ▪ **j'ai trouvé le temps ~** the time seemed to go (by) really slowly ▪ **~ de** [qui dure] : **une traversée longue de deux mois** a two-month (long) crossing
2. [qui tarde - personne] : **je ne serai pas ~** I won't be long ▪ **~ à** : **ne soyez pas trop ~ à me répondre** don't take too long answering me ▪ **je n'ai pas été longue à comprendre qu'elle mentait** it didn't take me long to see that she was lying ▪ **l'eau est longue à bouillir** the water is taking a long time to boil ▪ **il est ~ à venir, ce café!** that coffee's a long time coming!
3. [qui existe depuis longtemps] long, long-standing ▪ **sa longue expérience de journaliste** his many years spent *ou* his long experience as a journalist ▪ **une longue amitié** a long-standing friendship
4. [dans le futur] : **à longue échéance, à ~ terme** [prévision] long, long-term ▪ **ce sera rentable à ~ terme** it will be profitable in the long term ▪ **à plus ou moins longue échéance** sooner or later ▪ **emprunt à ~ terme** long-term loan
5. LING & LITTÉR long.

◆ **long** <> *adv* **1.** [vêtement] : **elle s'habille ~** she wears long skirts *ou* dresses **2.** [beaucoup] : **en dire ~** : **geste/regard qui en dit ~** eloquent gesture/look ▪ **une remarque qui en dit ~ sur ses intentions** a remark which says a lot about *ou* speaks volumes about his intentions ▪ **elle pourrait vous en dire ~ sur cette affaire** she could tell you a few things about this business ▪ **en connaître** *ou* **en savoir ~** : **demande-le-lui, il en sait ~** ask him, he knows all about it ▪ **elle en connaît déjà ~ sur la vie** she knows a thing or two about life.
<> *nm* [vêtement] : **le ~** long styles ▪ **la mode est au ~** long styles are in fashion.

◆ **longue** *nf* **1.** CARTES long suit **2.** LING & LITTÉR long syllable **3.** MUS long note.

◆ **à la longue** *loc adv* [avec le temps] in the long term *ou* run, eventually ▪ **à la longue, tout se sait** everything comes out in the end.

◆ **au long** *loc adv* in full, fully ▪ **elle a écrit le titre au ~** she wrote the title out in full.

◆ **au long de** *loc prép* **1.** [dans l'espace] along **2.** [dans le temps] during.

◆ **de long** *loc adv* long ▪ **le terrain a cent mètres de ~** the plot is one hundred metres long *ou* in length ● **faire une mine** *ou* **tête de dix pieds de ~** [par déconvenue] to pull a long face ; [par mauvaise humeur] to have *ou* to wear a long face.

◆ **de long en large** *loc adv* back and forth, up and down ▪ **j'ai arpenté le hall de la gare de ~ en large** I paced back and forth across *ou* I paced up and down the main hall of the station.

◆ **de tout son long** *loc adv* : **tomber de tout son ~** to fall flat ▪ **il était étendu de tout son ~** he was stretched out at full length.

◆ **en long** *loc adv* lengthwise, lengthways.

◆ **en long, en large et en travers** *loc adv* **1.** [examiner] from every (conceivable) angle **2.** [raconter] in the minutest detail, at some considerable length.

◆ **en long et en large** = **en long, en large et en travers**.

◆ **le long de** *loc prép* **1.** [horizontalement] along ▪ **en marchant le ~ de la rivière** walking along the river bank ▪ **les plaines qui s'étendent le ~ du fleuve** the plains which spread out from the river (banks) **2.** [verticalement - vers le haut] up ; [- vers le bas] down.

◆ **tout au long** *loc adv* [en détail] in detail.

◆ **tout au long de** *loc prép* **1.** [dans l'espace] all along ▪ **les policiers postés tout au ~ du parcours** policemen positioned all along the route **2.** [dans le temps] throughout, all through ▪ **tout au ~ de l'année** all year long, throughout the year.

◆ **tout du long** *loc adv* **1.** [dans l'espace] : **nous avons parcouru la rue tout du ~** we travelled the whole length of the street ▪ **ils ont descendu le fleuve tout du ~** they went all the way down the river, they descended the entire length of the river **2.** [dans le temps] all along.

◆ **tout le long de** *loc prép* all the way along ▪ **nous avons chanté tout le ~ du chemin** we sang all the way.

long. (*abr écrite de* **longitude**) long.

long-courrier [lɔ̃kurje] (*pl* **long-courriers**) <> *adj* **1.** AÉRON [vol] long-distance, long-haul ▪ [avion] long-haul **2.** NAUT ocean-going.
<> *nm* **1.** AÉRON long-haul aircraft ▪ **compagnie de ~** long-haul operator ▪ **transport par ~** long-haul (transport) **2.** NAUT [navire - marchand] ocean-going ship *ou* freighter ; [- avec passagers] ocean liner, oceaner ▪ [matelot] foreign-going seaman.

longe [lɔ̃ʒ] *nf* **1.** [demi-échine] loin ▪ **~ de porc** pork (rear) loin ▪ **~ de veau** loin of veal **2.** [lien - pour attacher] tether ; [- pour mener] lunge.

longer [17] [lɔ̃ʒe] *vt* **1.** [avancer le long de] to go along *(insép)*, to follow ▪ **ils ont longé la pinède à pied/en voiture/en canot/à bicyclette** they walked/drove/sailed/cycled along the edge of the pinewood **2.** [border] to run along, to border **3.** NAUT : **~ la côte** to sail along *ou* to hug the coast.

longeron [lɔ̃ʒrɔ̃] *nm* **1.** TRAV PUB (longitudinal) girder **2.** RAIL [d'un wagon] (side) frame (member), bar **3.** AÉRON [du fuselage] longeron, longitudinal ▪ [d'une aile] spar **4.** AUTO side member *ou* rail.

longévité [lɔ̃ʒevite] *nf* **1.** [d'une personne, d'une espèce] longevity **2.** SOCIOL life expectancy.

longiligne [lɔ̃ʒiliɲ] *adj* slender ▪ **elle est plutôt ~** she has quite a slender figure.

longitude [lɔ̃ʒityd] *nf* longitude ▪ **par 30° de ~ est/ouest** at longitude 30° east/west.

longitudinal, e, aux [lɔ̃ʒitydinal, o] *adj* **1.** [en longueur] lengthwise, lengthways, longitudinal *spéc* **2.** ÉLECTRON longitudinal ▪ **onde ~e** longitudinal wave.

long(-)métrage [lɔ̃metraʒ] (*pl* **longs(-)métrages**) *nm* feature (length) *ou* full-length film.

longtemps [lɔ̃tɑ̃] *adv* **1.** [exprimant une durée] for a long time ▪ **je n'ai pas attendu ~** I didn't wait long ▪ **on a ~ pensé que...** it was long thought that..., it was thought for a long time that... ▪ **il faut ~ pour...** it takes a long time *ou* a while to... ▪ **pas de ~** *ou* **d'ici ~** not for a (long) while *ou* long time ▪ **aussi**

~ que tu veux as long as you wish ▪ **moins ~ (que)** for a shorter time (than) ▪ **plus ~ (que)** longer (than) ▪ **mettre** *ou* **prendre ~** to take a while *ou* a long time ▪ **en avoir pour ~ : je n'en ai pas pour ~** I won't be long, it won't take me long ▪ **il n'en a plus pour ~** [pour finir] he won't be much longer ; [à vivre] he won't last much longer, he's not got much longer to live ▪ **d'ici à ce qu'il pleuve, il n'y en a pas pour ~!** *fam* it won't be long till the rain starts! ▪ **ça va durer (encore) ~, oui?** is this going to go on for much longer?, have you quite finished? ▪ **il a été absent pendant ~** he was away for a long time ▪ **avant ~** before long ▪ **je ne reviendrai pas avant ~** I won't be back for a long time ▪ **~ avant** long *ou* a long time before (that), much earlier ▪ **~ après** much later, long after (that), a long time after (that) **2.** [avec 'il y a', 'depuis'] : **il y a ~ (de ça)** ages *ou* a long time ago ▪ **il y a ~** *ou* **cela fait ~ que je l'ai lu** it's been a long time since I read it ▪ **il y a ~ que j'ai arrêté de fumer** I stopped smoking long *ou* ages ago ▪ **il y a** *ou* **cela fait ~ que je ne l'ai pas vu** it's a long time *ou* ages since I saw him ▪ **tiens, il y avait ~!** *fam* [qu'on ne t'avait pas vu] long time no see! ; [que tu n'avais pas parlé de ça] here we go again! ▪ **il travaille là depuis ~** he's been working there for ages *ou* a long time.

longue [lɔ̃g] *f* ▻ **long.**

longuement [lɔ̃gmɑ̃] *adv* **1.** [longtemps] for a long time, long ▪ **il faut ~ pétrir la pâte** the dough must be kneaded thoroughly **2.** [en détail - expliquer, commenter] in detail, in depth ; [- scruter] at length.

longuet, ette [lɔ̃gɛ, ɛt] *adj fam* a bit long, longish, a bit on the long side ▪ **il est ~, ce film!** it's dragging on a bit, this film!

longueur [lɔ̃gœr] *nf* **1.** [dimension] length ▪ **mesure de ~** linear measurement ▪ **unité de ~** unit of length ▪ **un ruban de 10 cm de ~** *ou* **d'une ~ de 10 cm** a ribbon 10 cm long *ou* in length ▪ **le jardin est tout en ~** the garden is long and narrow ▪ **quelle est la ~ de l'Amazone?** how long is the Amazon? ▪ **j'ai traversé l'île dans toute sa ~** [à pied] I walked the whole length of the island **2.** [unité de mesure] length ▪ **une ~ de fil** a length of cotton ▮ [dans une course, en natation] length ▪ **il l'a emporté d'une ~** he won by a length ▪ **elle a pris deux ~s d'avance** she's leading by two lengths **3.** SPORT : **saut en ~** long jump **4.** INFORM length, size ▪ **~ de bloc/de mot** block/word length ▪ **~ implicite** [d'un programme] sizing (estimate) **5.** RADIO : **~ d'onde** wave length **6.** [dans le temps] length ▪ **d'une ~ désespérante** sickeningly long.

◆ **longueurs** *nfpl* overlong passages ▪ **il y a des ~s dans le film** the film is a little tedious in parts ▪ **il y avait des ~s** some passages were a little boring.

◆ **à longueur de** *loc prép* : **à ~ de semaine/d'année** all week/year long ▪ **il se plaint à ~ de temps** he's forever complaining, he complains all the time.

longue-vue [lɔ̃gvy] (*pl* **longues-vues**) *nf* telescope, field-glass.

look [luk] *nm fam* **1.** [mode] look, fashion ▪ **le ~ des années 80** the 80s look **2.** [présentation] : **le magazine a changé de ~** the magazine has changed its image.

looping [lupiŋ] *nm* AÉRON loop ▪ **faire des ~s** to loop the loop.

lope△ [lɔp], **lopette**△ [lɔpɛt] *nf péj* **1.** [homme veule] wimp *fam* **2.** [homosexuel] fairy△, poofter△ *UK*, fag△ *US*.

lopin [lɔpɛ̃] *nm* **1.** [parcelle] : **~ (de terre)** patch *ou* plot (of land) **2.** MÉTALL [cylindre - grand] bloom ; [- petit] billet.

loquace [lɔkas] *adj* talkative, loquacious *sout* ▪ **tu n'es pas très ~, aujourd'hui!** you've not got much to say for yourself today!

loquacité [lɔkasite] *nf* talkativeness, loquacity *sout*.

loque [lɔk] *nf* **1.** [haillon] rag **2.** [personne] wreck ▪ **depuis sa faillite, c'est devenu une ~** since his bankruptcy, he's been a complete wreck **3.** *Belgique* [serpillière] mop.

◆ **en loques** *loc adj* & *loc adv* tattered, in tatters ▪ **ses vêtements tombaient en ~s** his clothes were all in rags *ou* tatters.

loquet [lɔkɛ] *nm* latch, catch bolt.

loqueteux, euse [lɔktø, øz] ◇ *adj* **1.** [personne] dressed in rags, in tatters **2.** [manteau] ragged, tattered.

◇ *nm, f* ragamuffin.

lord [lɔr(d)] *nm* lord.

lord-maire [lɔrdmɛr] (*pl* **lords-maires**) *nm* Lord Mayor.

lordose [lɔrdoz] *nf* lordosis.

lorgner [3] [lɔrɲe] *vt* to ogle, to eye ▪ **le type la lorgnait depuis un bon moment** the guy had been eyeing her up *ou* ogling her for some time ▪ **ils lorgnaient tous ses millions** *fam* they all had their (beady) eyes on her millions.

lorgnette [lɔrɲɛt] *nf* spyglass.

lorgnon [lɔrɲɔ̃] *nm* [à main] lorgnette, lorgnon ▪ [à ressort] pince-nez.

loriot [lɔrjo] *nm* oriole.

lorrain, e [lɔrɛ̃, ɛn] *adj* from Lorraine.

Lorraine [lɔrɛn] *npr f* : **(la) ~** Lorraine.

LORRAINE

This administrative region includes the *départements* of Meurthe-et-Moselle, Meuse, Moselle and Vosges (capital: Metz).

lorry [lɔri] (*pl* **lorries**) *nm* (platelayer's) trolley, lorry.

lors [lɔr] ◆ **lors de** *loc prép sout* [pendant] during ▪ [au moment de] at the time of ▪ **il la rencontra ~ d'un déjeuner d'affaires** he met her at a business lunch.

◆ **lors même que** *loc conj litt* even if, even though.

lorsque [lɔrskə] (*devant voyelle ou 'h' muet* **lorsqu'** [lɔrsk]) *conj* **1.** [au moment où] when ▪ **nous allions partir lorsqu'on a sonné** we were about to leave when the door bell rang **2.** [alors que] : **on a tort de parler lorsqu'il faudrait agir** we shouldn't be talking when we ought to be doing something.

losange [lɔzɑ̃ʒ] *nm* diamond, lozenge *spéc* ▪ **en forme de ~** diamond-shaped, rhomboid.

Los Angeles [lɔsɑ̃dʒəlɛs] *npr* Los Angeles, LA.

lot [lo] *nm* **1.** [prix] prize ▶ **~ de consolation** consolation prize ▪ **gagner le gros ~** *pr* & *fig* to win *ou* hit the jackpot **2.** [part - d'objets] share ; [- de terre] plot ▪ **à chacun son ~ d'infortunes** to each of us his share of misfortunes **3.** DR lot ▪ **en ~s** lot by lot **4.** [ensemble - de livres] collection ; [- de vaisselle, de linge] set ; [- de savons, d'éponges] (special offer) pack ▪ **dans le ~, il y aura bien quelque chose qui t'intéresse** out of all these things, you're bound to find something interesting ▪ **dans le ~, il y aura bien un fort en maths** there must be at least one person who's good at maths among them ▶ **~ de fabrication numéro 34** series *ou* batch number 34 ▪ **être au-dessus du ~** to be a cut above the rest **5.** INFORM batch ▪ **traitement par ~s** batch processing **6.** *litt* [destin] lot, fate ▪ **tel est notre ~ commun** such is our common fate.

lote [lɔt] = **lotte**.

loterie [lɔtri] *nf* **1.** JEUX lottery, draw ▶ **la Loterie nationale** the (French) national lottery *ou* sweepstake **2.** [hasard] lottery ▪ **le mariage est une ~** marriage is just a game of chance ▪ **c'est une vraie ~!** it's the luck of the draw!

loti, e [lɔti] *adj* : **être bien ~** to be well off *ou* well provided for ▪ **être mal ~** to be badly off *ou* poorly provided for.

lotion [losjɔ̃] *nf* lotion ▪ **~ après-rasage** after-shave lotion ▪ **~ capillaire** hair lotion.

lotionner [3] [losjɔne] *vt* [cuir chevelu] to rub lotion into ▪ [épiderme] to apply lotion to.

lotir [32] [lɔtir] *vt* **1.** [partager] to portion off (*sép*), to divide into plots ▪ [vendre] to sell by plots ▪ **'à ~'** to be divided up for sale **2.** *sout* [attribuer à] : **le sort l'avait loti d'une timidité maladive** he had the misfortune to be painfully shy.

lotissement [lɔtismɑ̃] *nm* **1.** [terrain - à construire] building plot, site (*for a housing development*) ; [- construit] (housing) estate *UK*, housing development **2.** [partage] division into lots, parcelling out.

loto [lɔto] *nm* **1.** JEUX de société lotto ■ [boîte] lotto set **2.** [jeux d'argent] : **le Loto** ≃ the (French state-run) lottery *(similar to the British National Lottery)* ■ **le Loto sportif** ≃ the football pools *UK* ■ ≃ the soccer sweepstakes *US*.

lotte [lɔt] *nf* [de rivière] burbot ■ [de mer] monkfish, angler fish.

lotus [lɔtys] *nm* lotus.

louable [lwabl] *adj* **1.** [comportement, décision] praiseworthy, commendable, laudable **2.** [appartement, maison] rentable, up for rent.

louage [lwaʒ] *nm* [cession] letting ■ [jouissance] renting ■ **~ de services** contract of employment, work contract.

louange [lwɑ̃ʒ] *nf* praise ■ **nous dirons à sa ~ que...** *litt* to his credit, it must be said that...

◆ **louanges** *nfpl* praise ■ **son interprétation fut saluée par un concert de ~s** his performance was praised to the skies ■ **chanter** *ou* **célébrer les ~s de qqn** to sing sb's praises ■ **couvrir qqn de ~s** to heap praise on sb.

loubard [lubar] *nm fam* yob *UK*, hood *US*.

louche¹ [luʃ] ◇ *adj* **1.** [douteux - personne] shifty, shady ; [- attitude] shady ; [- affaire] shady, sleazy ■ **un individu ~** a shady character ■ **n'y va pas, c'est ~** don't get involved, there's something fishy about it **2.** [endroit] sleazy **3.** [trouble - couleur, lumière] murky ; [- liquide] cloudy.

◇ *nm* : **il y a du ~ là-dessous!** there's something fishy going on!, I smell a rat!

louche² [luʃ] *nf* **1.** [ustensile] ladle ■ **à la ~** by the cartload ■ **en remettre une ~** to lay it on thick **2.** △ [main] mitt, paw.

loucher [3] [luʃe] *vi* **1.** MÉD to (have a) squint ■ **il louche** he has a squint, he's squint-eyed **2.** [volontairement] to go cross-eyed.

◆ **loucher sur** *v+prép fam* [convoiter - personne] to ogle ; [- biens] to have an eye on ■ **ils louchent tous sur les millions de leur oncle** they all have an eye *ou* their (beady) eyes on their uncle's millions.

louer [6] [lwe] *vt* **1.** [donner en location - logement] to let (out) *(sép)*, to rent ; [- appareil, véhicule] to rent *ou* to hire (out) *(sép)* ; [- usine] to lease (out) *(sép)* ; [- avion] to hire (out) *(sép)* ■ **~ qqch à qqn** to rent sthg to sb, to rent sb sthg ■ **le propriétaire me le loue pour 1 000 euros** the landlord rents it out to me for 1,000 euros ■ *(en usage absolu)* **elle ne loue pas cher** she doesn't ask for very much (by way of) rent

2. [prendre en location - logement] to rent ; [- appareil, véhicule] to hire *UK*, to rent *US* ; [- avion, usine] to lease ■ **on a loué le hall d'exposition à une grosse compagnie** we've leased the exhibition hall from a big firm ■ *(en usage absolu)* **l'été nous préférons ~** we prefer renting accommodation for our summer holidays ■ **vous êtes propriétaire? – non, je loue** do you own your house? – no, I rent *ou* I'm a tenant

3. [réserver] to book ■ **pour ce spectacle, il est conseillé de ~ les places à l'avance** advance booking is advisable for this show ■ *(en usage absolu)* **on peut ~ par téléphone** telephone bookings are accepted

4. [glorifier] to praise ■ **louons le Seigneur** praise the Lord ■ **Dieu soit loué** thank God ■ **~ qqn de** *ou* **pour qqch** to praise sb for sthg ■ **on ne peut que vous ~ d'avoir agi ainsi** you deserve nothing but praise for having acted in this way.

◆ **se louer** *vp (emploi passif)* **1.** [logement] to be rented *ou* let ■ **cette chambre se louerait aisément** you'd have no problem letting this room *ou* finding somebody to rent this room **2.** [appareil] to be hired *ou* rented ■ **le téléviseur se loue au mois** this TV set is rented on a monthly basis.

◆ **se louer de** *vp+prép* : **se ~ de qqch** to be pleased with sthg ■ **je peux me ~ d'avoir vu juste** I can congratulate myself for having got it right ■ **je n'ai qu'à me ~ de votre ponctualité/travail** I have nothing but praise for your punctuality/work.

◆ **à louer** *loc adj* to let ■ **chambres à ~ à la semaine** rooms to let *ou* to rent weekly ■ **'voitures à ~'** 'cars for hire *UK*, cars for rent *US*'.

loueur, euse [lwœr, øz] *nm, f* : **c'est un ~ de voitures** he rents out cars.

louf△ [luf] *adj* crazy, nuts ■ **il est complètement ~!** he's completely nuts *ou* off his rocker!

loufoque [lufɔk] ◇ *adj* **1.** [fou] crazy, daft *UK*, screwy *US* **2.** [invraisemblable - récit, histoire] weird, bizarre, freaky ■ **cette histoire est tout à fait ~!** that's a really weird story! **3.** [burlesque] : **un film ~** a zany comedy.

◇ *nmf* crank, nutter *UK*, screwball *US*.

louis [lwi] *nm* louis d'or.

Louis [lwi] *npr* **1.** : **saint ~** Saint Louis **2.** [roi de France] Louis **3.** [roi de Bavière] Ludwig.

Louisiane [lwizjan] *npr f* : **(la) ~** Louisiana.

Louis-Philippe [lwifilip] *npr* Louis Philippe.

loukoum [lukum] *nm* Turkish delight ■ **voulez-vous un ~?** would you care for a piece of Turkish delight?

loulou¹ [lulu] *nm* **1.** ZOOL spitz **2.** *fam* = **loubard**.

loulou², t(t)e [lulu, ut] *nm, f fam* **1.** [en appellatif] : **mon ~, ma louloutte** (my) darling **2.** [personne] : **c'est un drôle de ~!** he's a weird guy!

loup [lu] *nm* **1.** [mammifère] wolf ■ **faire entrer le ~ dans la bergerie** to set the fox to mind the geese **2.** [personne] : **jeune ~** [en politique] young Turk ; [en affaires] go-getter ■ **un vieux ~ de mer** an old sea-dog *ou* salt ■ **il est connu comme le ~ blanc** everybody knows him ■ **à pas de ~** stealthily ■ **l'homme est un ~ pour l'homme** *Plaute allus* brother will turn upon brother ■ **les ~s ne se mangent pas entre eux** *prov* there is honour among thieves *prov* ■ **quand on parle du ~ on en voit la queue** talk of the devil (and he appears) **3.** *fam* [en appellatif] : **mon (petit) ~** my (little) darling *ou* love *ou* sweetheart **4.** [masque] (eye) mask **5.** [poisson] (sea) bass.

loupage [lupaʒ] *nm fam* botch-up, messing up.

loupe [lup] *nf* **1.** OPT magnifying glass ■ **observer qqch à la ~** *pr* to look at sthg through a magnifying glass ; *fig* to put sthg under a microscope, to scrutinize sthg **2.** MÉD wen **3.** BOT knur ■ **~ d'érable** burr maple.

loupé, e [lupe] *adj fam* missed, failed ■ **~!** *fam* missed! ■ **mon gâteau est ~!** my cake's a failure!, I've made a mess of my cake! ■ **la soirée a été complètement ~e!** the party was a total flop *ou* wash-out!

◆ **loupé** *nm fam* boob *UK*, screw-up *US* ■ **il y a eu quelques ~s au début** we made a few boobs *ou* we screwed up a few times to start with.

louper [3] [lupe] *fam* ◇ *vt* **1.** [examen] to flunk ■ **il a complètement loupé son dessin** he's made a complete mess of his drawing ■ **~ son coup** to bungle it **2.** [train, personne] to miss ■ **je t'ai loupé de cinq minutes** I (just) missed you by five minutes ■ **dépêche-toi, tu vas me faire ~ mon bus!** hurry up! you're going to make me miss my bus! **3.** [bonne affaire] : **~ une occasion** to let an opportunity slip, to pass up an opportunity **4.** *loc* **ne pas ~ qqn** [le punir] to sort sb out, to give sb what for ■ **ne pas en ~ une** [faire des bêtises] : **il n'en loupe pas une!** he's always putting his foot in it!

◇ *vi* : **ça ne va pas ~** it's bound to happen, it (just) has to happen ■ **elle lui avait dit que ça ne marcherait pas et ça n'a pas loupé!** she told him it wouldn't work and sure enough it didn't!

◆ **se louper** *fam* ◇ *vp (emploi réciproque)* [ne pas se rencontrer] : **on s'est loupé de quelques secondes** we missed each other by (just) a few seconds.

◇ *vpi* [manquer son suicide] : **cette fois, il ne s'est pas loupé!** this time he hasn't bungled it!

loup-garou [lugaru] (*pl* **loups-garous**) *nm* **1.** MYTHOL werewolf **2.** [personnage effrayant] bogeyman.

loupiot, e [lupjo, ɔt] *nm, f fam* [enfant] kid, nipper *UK*.

loupiote [lupjɔt] *nf* (small) light.

lourd, e [lur, lurd] *adj* **1.** [pesant] heavy ■ **gaz plus ~ que l'air** heavier-than-air gas ■ **un regard ~** a hard stare ■ **j'ai la tête ~e/les jambes ~es** my head feels/my legs feel heavy ■ **les paupières ~es de sommeil** eyelids heavy with sleep

2. [complexe - artillerie, chirurgie, industrie] heavy

3. [indigeste] heavy, rich ■ **des repas trop ~s** excessively rich meals

4. [compact - sol, terre] heavy, thick ■ **terrain ~ aujourd'hui à Longchamp** the going is heavy today at Longchamp
5. [chargé] heavy, thick ■ **de ~es tapisseries** thick *ou* heavy wall-hangings ■ **de ~s nuages** thick *ou* dense clouds ■ **~ de** heavy with ■ **un ciel ~ de nuages** a heavily-clouded *ou* heavy sky ■ **son ton est ~ de menace** the tone of his voice is ominous *ou* menacing ■ **il régnait dans l'assistance un silence ~ d'angoisse** people sat there in anxious silence ■ **cette décision est ~e de conséquences** this decision will have far-reaching consequences
6. [accablant - atmosphère, temps] sultry, oppressive
7. [entêtant - odeur] heavy, strong
8. [sans grâce - bâtiment, façade] heavy, heavy-looking
9. [sans finesse - remarque, esprit] clumsy, heavy-handed ■ **des plaisanteries plutôt ~es** rather unsubtle jokes ■ **certains passages sont ~s** some passages are a bit laboured *ou* tedious ■ **tu ne comprends pas? ce que tu peux être ~!** don't you understand? how slow can you get!
10. [insistant] : **sans vouloir être ~, je te rappelle que ça doit être fini dans 15 minutes** I don't want to nag but don't forget that you have to finish in 15 minutes
11. [important - chiffres] high ; [- programme, horaire] heavy ■ **notre facture d'électricité a été ~e l'hiver dernier** we had a big electricity bill last winter ■ **les effectifs des classes sont trop ~s** class sizes are too big ■ **tu as là une ~e responsabilité** that is a heavy responsibility for you ■ [grave - perte] heavy, serious, severe ; [- dette] heavy, serious ; [- faute] serious, grave ■ **de ~es accusations pèsent sur le prévenu** the accused faces serious *ou* weighty charges ■ **elle a une ~e hérédité** she's got an unfortunate background.
◆ **lourd** *adv* **1.** [chaud] : **il fait très ~** it is very close *ou* sultry **2.** *fam loc* **pas ~ : tu n'en fais pas ~** you don't exactly kill yourself ■ **je ne gagne pas ~** I don't exactly make a fortune.

lourdaud, e [lurdo, od] ◇ *adj* oafish, clumsy.
◇ *nm, f* oaf.

lourde [lurd] ◇ *nf*△ [porte] door.
◇ *f* ▷ **lourd.**

lourdement [lurdəmɑ̃] *adv* **1.** [très] heavily **2.** [sans souplesse] heavily ■ **marcher ~** to tread heavily, to walk with a heavy step **3.** [beaucoup] greatly ■ **tu te trompes ~!** you are greatly mistaken!, you're making a big mistake! ■ **cet investissement grève ~ le budget** this investment puts a serious strain on the budget ■ **insister ~ sur qqch** to be most emphatic about sthg.

lourder [3] △ [lurde] *vt* to kick *ou* to throw out *(sép)*, to fire.

Lourdes [lurd] *npr* Lourdes *(the most famous place of pilgrimage in France since Bernadette Soubirous claimed to have had visions of the Virgin Mary there in 1858).*

lourdeur [lurdœr] *nf* **1.** [d'un fardeau, d'une valise] heaviness ■ **la ~ de la tâche m'effraie** *fig* the workload frightens me ■ **la ~ de l'appareil du parti** *fig* the unwieldiness of the party structure **2.** [d'un mouvement] heaviness, clumsiness **3.** [douleur] heavy feeling ■ **avoir des ~s d'estomac** to feel bloated **4.** [du temps] closeness, sultriness **5.** [d'une forme] heaviness **6.** [d'un propos, d'un comportement] bluntness, clumsiness ■ **~ d'esprit** dullness ■ **il est d'une telle ~ d'esprit!** he's such an oaf! **7.** [gravité] severity, gravity ■ **cette guerre égale la précédente par la ~ des pertes** this war must rank with the last one in terms of the heavy losses suffered.
◆ **lourdeurs** *nfpl* [maladresses] : **idées intéressantes mais trop de ~s** interesting ideas, but clumsily expressed.

lourdingue△ [lurdɛ̃g] *adj* **1.** [physiquement] clumsy, awkward **2.** [intellectuellement - personne] dim-witted, thick *UK* ; [- plaisanterie, réflexion] pathetic, stupid.

loustic [lustik] *nm fam* **1.** [individu louche] shady character ■ **c'est un drôle de ~** that guy's pretty fishy **2.** [farceur] joker, funny guy.

loutre [lutr] *nf* **1.** ZOOL otter ■ **~ de mer** sea-otter **2.** [fourrure] otter skin *ou* pelt.

Louvain [luvɛ̃] *npr* Leuven, Louvain.

louve [luv] *nf* ZOOL she-wolf.

louveteau, x [luvto] *nm* **1.** ZOOL wolf cub **2.** [scout] cub, cub-scout.

louvoie *etc v* ▷ **louvoyer.**

louvoiement [luvwamɑ̃] *nm* **1.** NAUT tacking **2.** *fig* [manœuvre] subterfuge.

louvoyer [13] [luvwaje] *vi* **1.** NAUT to tack (about) **2.** [biaiser] to hedge, to equivocate.

Louvre [luvr] *npr m* : **le (palais du) ~** the Louvre ■ **le Grand ~** the enlarged Musée du Louvre *(including all the new constructions and excavations)* ■ **l'école du ~** *art school in Paris.*

lover [3] [lɔve] *vt* NAUT to coil.
◆ **se lover** *vpi* to coil up.

loyal, e, aux [lwajal, o] *adj* **1.** [fidèle] loyal, faithful, trusty ■ **20 ans de bons et loyaux services** 20 years' unstinting devotion **2.** [honnête] loyal, honest, fair ■ **un adversaire ~** an honest opponent ■ **un procédé ~** honest behaviour, upright conduct ■ **un jeu ~** a fair game.

loyalement [lwajalmɑ̃] *adv* **1.** [fidèlement] loyally, faithfully ■ **très ~** with great loyalty, very loyally **2.** [honnêtement] loyally, honestly ■ **agir ~** to act honestly ■ **se battre ~** to fight cleanly.

loyalisme [lwajalism] *nm* **1.** [fidélité] loyalty **2.** POLIT loyalism, Loyalism.

loyaliste [lwajalist] ◇ *adj* **1.** [fidèle] loyal **2.** HIST & POLIT loyalist, Loyalist.
◇ *nmf* **1.** [fidèle] loyal supporter **2.** HIST & POLIT loyalist, Loyalist.

loyauté [lwajote] *nf* **1.** [fidélité] loyalty, faithfulness **2.** [honnêteté] honesty, fairness ■ **elle a répondu en toute ~** she answered completely fairly *ou* honestly.

loyer [lwaje] *nm* **1.** [d'un logement] rent ■ **une hausse des ~s** rent rise *ou* increase, rent hike *US* **2.** FIN : **le ~ de l'argent** the interest rate, the price of money.

lozérien, enne [lɔzerjɛ̃, ɛn] *adj* from the Lozère.

LP *nm* = **lycée professionnel.**

LSD (*abr de* **lysergic acid diethylamide**) *nm* LSD.

lu, e [ly] *pp* ▷ **lire.**

lubie [lybi] *nf* whim, craze ■ **sa dernière ~, c'est de faire le tour du monde en bateau!** his latest crazy *ou* madcap idea is to sail round the world!

lubricité [lybrisite] *nf* [d'une personne, d'un regard] lustfulness, lechery ■ [d'un propos, d'une conduite] lewdness.

lubrifiant, e [lybrifjɑ̃, ɑ̃t] *adj* lubricating.
◆ **lubrifiant** *nm* lubricant.

lubrificateur, trice [lybrifikatœr, tris] *adj* lubricating.
◆ **lubrificateur** *nm* lubricant.

lubrification [lybrifikasjɔ̃] *nf* lubrication.

lubrifier [9] [lybrifje] *vt* to lubricate.

lubrique [lybrik] *adj litt* [personne, regard] lustful, lecherous ■ [attitude, propos] lewd, libidinous.

lubriquement [lybrikmɑ̃] *adv* lecherously, lewdly.

lucarne [lykarn] *nf* **1.** [fenêtre] skylight ■ **~ faîtière** skylight ■ **~ pignon** dormer (window) **2.** FOOTBALL top corner (of the net).

lucide [lysid] *adj* **1.** [clairvoyant] lucid, clear-sighted, perceptive ■ **elle est très ~ sur elle-même** she's extremely perceptive about herself **2.** [conscient] conscious.

lucidement [lysidmɑ̃] *adv* clearly, lucidly.

lucidité [lysidite] *nf* **1.** [clairvoyance] lucidity, clear-sightedness ■ **une critique d'une grande ~** a very perceptive criticism **2.** [conscience] lucidity ■ **elle n'a plus toute sa ~** her mind's wandering a bit ■ **à ses moments de ~** in his lucid moments.

Lucifer [lysifɛr] *npr* Lucifer.

luciole [lysjɔl] *nf* firefly.

lucratif, ive [lykratif, iv] *adj* lucrative, profitable ▪ **un métier ~** a job that pays well, a well-paid job.

lucrativement [lykrativmɑ̃] *adv* lucratively.

lucre [lykr] *nm sout* lucre *sout*, profit ▪ **faire qqch par goût du ~** to do sthg out of love for money.

Lucrèce [lykrɛs] *npr* Lucretius ▪ **~ Borgia** Lucretia Borgia.

ludiciel [lydisjɛl] *nm* computer game *(software)*.

ludique [lydik] *adj* play *(modif)*, ludic *spéc* ▪ **le comportement ~ des enfants** children's behaviour in play.

ludothécaire [lydɔtekɛr] *nmf* librarian *(at a toy library)*.

ludothèque [lydɔtɛk] *nf* **1.** [lieu] toys and games library **2.** *Québec* [activité] ≃ playgroup.

luette [lɥɛt] *nf* uvula.

lueur [lɥœr] *nf* **1.** [lumière - de l'âtre, du couchant] glow ; [- de la lune, d'une lampe] light ; [- d'une lame] gleam ▪ **une faible ~** a glimmer ▪ **aux premières ~s de l'aube** in the first light of dawn ▪ **~ vacillante** flicker **2.** *fig* [éclat] glint, glimmer ▪ **une ~ de colère** a gleam *ou* glint of anger ▪ **une ~ d'intelligence/d'espoir/de joie** a glimmer of intelligence/of hope/of joy.

luge [lyʒ] *nf* toboggan, sledge *UK*, sled *US* ▪ **faire de la ~** to toboggan, to go sledging *UK ou* sledding *US*.

luger [17] [lyʒe] *vi* [descendre en luge] to toboggan, to sledge *UK*, to sled *US*.

lugubre [lygybr] *adj* **1.** [personne] lugubrious **2.** [endroit] gloomy **3.** [atmosphère] dismal ▪ **la soirée a été ~** it was a dismal party.

lugubrement [lygybrəmɑ̃] *adv* lugubriously, gloomily ▪ **les cris des pleureuses retentissaient ~** the cries of the mourners rang out lugubriously.

lui[1] [lɥi] *pp* ▷ **luire**.

lui[2] [lɥi] *pron pers*

> **A.** REPRÉSENTANT LE GENRE MASCULIN OU FÉMININ
> **B.** REPRÉSENTANT LE GENRE MASCULIN

A. REPRÉSENTANT LE GENRE MASCULIN OU FÉMININ

1. [complément - homme] him ; [- femme] her ; [- chose, animal] it ; [- animal domestique] him, her ▪ **je ~ ai parlé** I spoke to him/her ▪ **il a rencontré Hélène et (il) ~ a plu** he met Helen and she liked him ▪ **il entend qu'on ~ obéisse** he means to be obeyed ▪ **il le ~ a présenté** he introduced him to him/her ▪ **donne-le-~** give it to him/her ▪ **ça ne ~ rapporte rien** he/she isn't getting anything out of it ▪ **il ~ est difficile de venir** it's difficult for him/her to come

2. [se substituant à l'adjectif possessif] : **il ~ a serré la main** he shook his/her hand

B. REPRÉSENTANT LE GENRE MASCULIN

1. [sujet - personne] he ; [- chose, animal] it ; [- animal domestique] he ▪ **elle est charmante, mais ~ est impossible** she's charming but he's infuriating ▪ **~ ne voulait pas en entendre parler** HE didn't want to hear anything about it ▪ **si j'étais ~...** if I were him... ▪ **quant à ~, il n'était pas là** as for him, he wasn't there ▪ **qui ira avec elle? – ~** who'll go with her? – he will ▪ **~ aussi se pose des questions** he is wondering about it too

2. [avec un présentatif] : **c'est ~ qui vous le demande** HE's asking you ▪ **c'est encore ~?** is it him again? ▪ **c'est tout ~!** that's typical of him!, that's him all over!

3. [complément - personne] him ; [- chose, animal] it ; [- animal domestique] him ▪ **en ce moment on ne voit que ~** you see him everywhere at the moment ▪ **elle ne veut que ~ pour avocat** he's the only lawyer she will accept, she won't have any lawyer but him ▪ **elle ne ~ a pas plu, à ~** he didn't like her at all ▪ **je vais chez ~** I'm going to his house ▪ **cette valise n'est pas à ~?** isn't that his suitcase?, doesn't that suitcase belong to him? ▪ **une amie à ~** a friend of his ▪ **sans ~, tout était perdu** without him *ou* if it hadn't been for him, all would have been lost ▪ **il a réussi à le soulever à ~ (tout) seul** he managed to lift it on his own *ou* without any help

4. [en fonction de pronom réfléchi] himself ▪ **il ne pense qu'à ~** he only thinks of himself.

lui-même [lɥimɛm] *pron pers* [une personne] himself ▪ [une chose] itself ▪ **M. Dupont? – ~** Mr Dupont? – at your service ; [au téléphone] Mr Dupont? – speaking ▪ **~ paraissait surpris** he himself seemed surprised ▪ **de ~, il a parlé du prix** he mentioned the price without being prompted *ou* asked ▪ **il n'a qu'à venir voir par ~** all he has to do is come and see for himself ▪ **il pensait en ~ que...** he thought to himself that...

luire [97] [lɥir] *vi* **1.** [briller - métal, eau] to gleam ; [- surface mouillée] to glisten ; [- bougie, lumignon] to glimmer ; [- feu] to glow ; [- soleil] to shine ▪ **son uniforme luisait d'usure** his uniform was shiny with wear **2.** *fig* to shine, to glow ▪ **un faible espoir luit encore** there is still a glimmer of hope ▪ **cette phrase fit ~ un espoir dans son cœur** the words brought a glimmer of hope to his heart.

luisant, e [lɥizɑ̃, ɑ̃t] *adj* [métal] gleaming ▪ [soleil] shining ▪ [flamme] glowing ▪ [pavé, pelage] glistening.
◆ **luisant** *nm* [d'une étoffe] sheen ▪ [d'une fourrure] gloss.

luisent *etc v* ▷ **luire**.

lumbago [lœ̃bago, lɔ̃bago] *nm* lumbago.

lumière [lymjɛr] *nf* **1.** [naturelle - gén] light ; [- du soleil] sunlight ▪ **l'atelier reçoit la ~ du nord** the studio faces north ▶ **revoir la ~** [recouvrer la vue] to be able to see again ; [en sortant d'un lieu sombre] to see daylight again ; [retrouver la liberté] to be free again

2. [artificielle] light *(C)* ▪ **j'ai vu de la ~ et je suis entré** I saw a light (on) so I went in ▪ **allumer la ~** to turn *ou* to switch on the light ▪ **éteindre la ~** to turn *ou* to switch off the light ▪ **~s tamisées** soft lighting

3. [éclaircissement] light ▪ **apporter de la ~ sur qqch** to shed light on sthg ▪ **toute la ~ sera faite** we'll get to the bottom of this

4. [génie] genius, (shining) light ▪ **cet enfant n'est pas une ~!** that child is hardly a genius *ou* a shining light!

5. ASTRON & OPT light ▪ **~ noire** *ou* **de Wood** (ultraviolet) black light ▪ **~ cendrée** earthshine ▪ **~ froide** blue light ▪ **~ zodiacale** zodiacal light

6. ART light

7. RELIG : **la ~ éternelle** *ou* **de Dieu** divine light ▶ **cacher la ~ sous le boisseau** *allus* & BIBLE to hide one's light under a bushel

8. TECHNOL [orifice] opening.

◆ **lumières** *nfpl* **1.** [connaissances] insight *(U)*, knowledge *(U)* ▪ **elle a des ~s sur le problème** she has (some) insight into the problem ▪ **j'ai besoin de tes ~s** I need the benefit of your wisdom

2. AUTO lights

3. HIST : **le siècle des Lumières** the Enlightenment.

◆ **à la lumière de** *loc prép* in (the) light of ▪ **à la ~ de ce que tu me dis** in (the) light of what you're telling me.

◆ **en lumière** *loc adv* : **mettre qqch en ~** to bring sthg out, to shed light on sthg.

LE SIÈCLE DES LUMIÈRES

> The period beween the death of Louis XIV (1715) and the 1789 Revolution. The reformist, rationalist movement of the 18th century *philosophes* and *encyclopédistes* found its most comprehensive expression in the *Encyclopédie* edited by Diderot and, for a time, d'Alembert, between 1751 and 1765. The works of the *philosophes* were largely directed against the values of the *Ancien Régime*. They favoured the view that the purpose of government was the happiness of the people and laid the foundations for the democratic, egalitarian ideas of the following century.

lumignon [lymiɲɔ̃] *nm* **1.** [bougie] candle end **2.** [petite lumière] small light.

luminaire [lyminɛr] *nm* [lampe] light, lamp ▪ **magasin de ~s** lighting shop.

luminescence [luminɛsɑ̃s] *nf* luminescence.

luminescent, e [lyminɛsɑ̃, ɑ̃t] *adj* luminescent.

lumineusement [lyminøzmɑ̃] *adv* luminously, clearly ■ **il a très ~ exposé les faits** he gave a very lucid presentation of the facts.

lumineux, euse [lyminø, øz] *adj* **1.** [qui émet de la lumière] luminous **2.** [baigné de lumière] sunny **3.** [éclatant - couleur] bright, brilliant **4.** [radieux - teint, sourire] radiant **5.** [lucide - esprit] : **il a une intelligence lumineuse** he has great insight **6.** [clair - exposé] limpid, crystal clear.

luminosité [lyminozite] *nf* **1.** [éclat] brightness, radiance **2.** [clarté] luminosity ■ **le temps de pose dépend de la ~** shutter speed depends on the amount of light available **3.** ASTRON luminosity.

lump [lœp] *nm* lumpfish ■ **œufs de ~** lumpfish roe.

lumpenprolétariat [lœmpɛnprɔletarja] *nm* lumpenproletariat.

lunaire [lynɛr] *adj* **1.** ASTRON lunar ■ **mois ~** lunar month **2.** [qui évoque la lune - paysage] lunar.

lunaison [lynɛzɔ̃] *nf* lunar *ou* synodic *spéc* month, lunation *spéc.*

lunatique [lynatik] ◇ *adj* moody, temperamental.
◇ *nmf* temperamental *ou* capricious person.

lunch [lœʃ, lœntʃ] (*pl* **lunchs** *ou pl* **lunches**) *nm* cold buffet *(served at lunchtime for special occasions).*

lundi [lœdi] *nm* Monday ■ **le ~ de Pâques/Pentecôte** Easter/Whit Monday, *voir aussi* **mardi.**

lune [lyn] *nf* **1.** ASTRON moon ■ **la Lune** the Moon ■ **nuit sans ~** moonless night ➜ **pleine/nouvelle ~** full/new moon ■ **~ de miel** honeymoon ■ **~ rousse** April frost *(at night)* ■ **être dans la ~** to have one's head in the clouds ■ **pardon, j'étais dans la ~** sorry, I was miles away *ou* my mind was elsewhere ■ **promettre la ~ à qqn** to promise sb the moon *ou* the earth ■ **demander** *ou* **vouloir la ~** to ask for the moon ■ **il est con comme la ~**[△] he's as daft as a brush *UK ou* dead from the neck up *US* **2.** *fam* [fesses] behind.
◆ **lunes** *nfpl* [durée] moons.

luné, e [lyne] *adj fam* **bien/mal ~** in a good/bad mood ■ **toujours mal ~** always bad-tempered.

lunetier, ère [lyntje, ɛr] ◇ *adj* spectacle *(modif).*
◇ *nm, f* **1.** [fabricant] spectacle *UK ou* eyeglass *US* manufacturer **2.** [marchand] optician.

lunette [lynɛt] *nf* **1.** OPT telescope ■ **~ de tir/pointage** sights/sighting telescope ■ **~ d'approche** refracting telescope, spyglass *arch* ■ **~ astronomique** astronomical telescope **2.** [d'une montre] bezel **3.** [des toilettes] toilet-rim **4.** ARCHIT, ART & CONSTR lunette **5.** AUTO : **~ (arrière)** rear window.
◆ **lunettes** *nfpl* **1.** [verres correcteurs] glasses, spectacles ■ **une paire de ~s** a pair of glasses ■ **porter des ~s** to wear glasses ■ **mets des ~s!** [regarde mieux] buy yourself a pair of specs! ➜ **~s de vue** *ou* **correctrices** spectacles ■ **~s bifocales** bifocals ■ **~s noires** sunglasses, dark glasses ■ **~s de protection** goggles ■ **~s de soleil** sunglasses **2.** [verres protecteurs] goggles ■ **~s de ski** skiing goggles.

lunetterie [lynɛtri] *nf* **1.** [industrie] spectacle *UK ou* eyeglass *US* manufacture **2.** [commerce] spectacle *UK ou* eyeglass *US* trade.

lunule [lynyl] *nf* **1.** ANAT half-moon, lunule *spécialiste* **2.** GÉOM lune.

lupanar [lypanar] *nm litt* brothel, house of ill repute.

lupus [lypys] *nm* lupus ■ **~ vulgaire** lupus vulgaris.

lurette [lyrɛt] *nf* : **il y a belle ~** *fam* ages ago ■ **il y a belle ~ qu'elle est partie** [depuis des années] she left donkey's years ago ; [depuis des heures] she left hours ago *ou* ages ago.

luron, onne [lyrɔ̃, ɔn] *nm, f fam* **c'est un gai** *ou* **joyeux ~** he's a bit of a lad.

lusitanien, enne [lyzitanjɛ̃, ɛn] *adj* Lusitanian.

lusophone [lyzɔfɔn] ◇ *adj* Portuguese-speaking ■ **les populations ~s** Portuguese-speaking populations.
◇ *nmf* Portuguese speaker.

lustrage [lystraʒ] *nm* [d'une poterie] lustring ■ [d'un tissu, d'une peau] lustring, calendering ■ [d'une peinture] glazing ■ [d'une voiture] polishing.

lustral, e, aux [lystral, o] *adj* lustral.

lustre [lystr] *nm* **1.** [lampe - de Venise, en cristal] chandelier ; [- simple] (ceiling) light **2.** [reflet - mat] glow ; [- brillant] shine, polish **3.** TECHNOL [d'une poterie] lustre ■ [d'un tissu, d'une peau] lustre, calendering ■ [d'une peinture] glaze, gloss ■ [du papier] calendering ■ [d'un métal] polish **4.** *litt* [prestige] brilliance, glamour ■ **rendre** *ou* **redonner du ~ à** to improve the image of **5.** *litt* [cinq ans] lustrum.
◆ **lustres** *nmpl* : **il y a des ~s de ça!** it was ages ago!

lustré, e [lystre] *adj* **1.** TECHNOL [tissu, peau] lustred, calendered ■ [peinture] glazed, glossy ■ [poterie] lustred **2.** [brillant - pelage] sleek ; [- cheveux] glossy, shiny **3.** [usé] shiny (with wear).

lustrer [3] [lystre] *vt* **1.** TECHNOL [poterie] to lustre ■ [tissu, peau] to lustre, to calender ■ [peinture] to glaze **2.** [faire briller - voiture] to polish ■ **le chat lustre son pelage** the cat is cleaning its coat.

lustrerie [lystrəri] *nf* [lampes] chandeliers ■ [commerce] lighting.

lustrine [lystrin] *nf* **1.** [soie] lustring **2.** [percaline] lustre **3.** [coton] glazed cotton.

Lutèce [lytɛs] *npr* Lutetia.

luth [lyt] *nm* MUS lute.

luthéranisme [lyteranism] *nm* Lutheranism.

luthérien, enne [lyterjɛ̃, ɛn] *adj* Lutheran.
◆ **Luthérien, enne** *nm, f* Lutheran.

luthier, ère [lytje, ɛr] *nm, f* **1.** [fabricant] stringed-instrument maker **2.** [marchand] stringed-instrument dealer.

lutin, e [lytɛ̃, in] *adj litt* impish, mischievous.
◆ **lutin** *nm* **1.** [démon - gén] elf, goblin, imp ; [- en Irlande] leprechaun **2.** *arch* [enfant] (little) imp *ou* devil.

lutiner [3] [lytine] *vt litt* to fondle.

lutrin [lytrɛ̃] *nm* **1.** [pupitre] lectern **2.** [emplacement] schola cantorum.

lutte [lyt] *nf* **1.** [affrontement] struggle, fight, conflict ■ **des ~s intestines** infighting ■ **la ~ est inégale** they are unfairly matched ■ **se livrer à une ~ acharnée** to fight tooth and nail ■ **une ~ d'influence** a fight for domination
2. SOCIOL & POLIT struggle ■ **la ~ pour l'indépendance/pour la liberté** the struggle for independence/for freedom ➜ **~ armée** armed struggle ■ **la ~ des classes** the class struggle *ou* war
3. [efforts - contre un mal] fight ■ **la ~ contre le sida** the fight against AIDS
4. [résistance] struggle ■ **une ~ incessante contre elle-même** an incessant inner struggle ■ **la ~ d'un malade contre la mort** a sick person's struggle for life *ou* battle against death
5. [antagonisme] fight ■ **la ~ entre le bien et le mal** the fight between good and evil
6. AGRIC control ■ **~ biologique** biological (pest) control
7. BIOL : **la ~ pour la vie** the struggle for survival
8. SPORT wrestling ■ **~ libre/gréco-romaine** all-in/Graeco-Roman wrestling.
◆ **de haute lutte** *loc adv* after a hard fight ■ **conquérir** *ou* **emporter qqch de haute ~** to obtain sthg after a hard fight.
◆ **en lutte** *loc adj* : **les travailleurs en ~ ont défilé hier** the striking workers demonstrated yesterday ■ **nos camarades en ~** our struggling comrades ■ **être en ~ contre qqn** to be at loggerheads with sb.

lutter [3] [lyte] *vi* **1.** [se battre] : **~ contre** to fight (against) ■ **~ contre la mort** to struggle for one's life ■ **~ contre l'alcoolisme** to fight against *ou* to combat alcoholism ■ **~ contre le sommeil** to fight off sleep ■ **~ pour** to fight for ■ **~ de** *sout* : **ils ont lutté de vitesse** they had a race, they raced against each other **2.** SPORT to wrestle.

lutteur, euse [lytœr, øz] *nm, f* **1.** SPORT wrestler (*f* female wrestler) **2.** [battant] fighter ▪ **c'est une lutteuse, elle s'en remettra** she's a fighter, she'll get over it.

luxation [lyksasjɔ̃] *nf* dislocation, luxation *spéc.*

luxe [lyks] *nm* **1.** [faste] luxury, wealth ▪ **vivre dans le ~** to live in (the lap of) luxury ▪ **c'est le (grand) ~ ici!** it's the height of luxury *ou* it's luxurious in here! **2.** [plaisir] expensive treat, luxury, indulgence ▪ **elle ne peut pas s'offrir le ~ de dire ce qu'elle pense** *fig* she can't afford to speak her mind **3.** [chose déraisonnable] : **la viande, c'est devenu un ~** buying meat has become a luxury ▶ **ils ont nettoyé la moquette, ce n'était pas du ~!** *fam* they cleaned the carpet, (and) it was about time too! **4.** : **un ~ de** [beaucoup de] a host *ou* a wealth of ▪ **avec un ~ de détails** with a wealth of detail.
◆ **de luxe** *loc adj* **1.** [somptueux] luxury *(modif)* **2.** COMM de-luxe, luxury *(modif)*.

Luxembourg [lyksɑ̃bur] ◇ *npr* Luxembourg ▪ **à ~** in (the city of) Luxembourg.
◇ *npr m* **1.** [pays] : **le ~** Luxembourg ▪ **au ~** in Luxembourg **2.** [à Paris] : **le ~, les jardins du ~** the Luxembourg Gardens ▪ **le (palais du) ~** the (French) Senate.

luxembourgeois, e [lyksɑ̃burʒwa, az] *adj* from Luxembourg.
◆ **Luxembourgeois, e** *nm, f inhabitant of or person from Luxembourg.*

luxer [3] [lykse] *vt* to luxate *spéc*, to dislocate.
◆ **se luxer** *vpt* : **se ~ le genou** to dislocate one's knee.

luxueusement [lyksɥøzmɑ̃] *adv* luxuriously.

luxueux, euse [lyksɥø, øz] *adj* luxurious ▪ **vivre dans un cadre ~** to live in luxurious surroundings.

luxure [lyksyr] *nf litt* lechery, lust.

luxuriance [lyksyrjɑ̃s] *nf litt* luxuriance ▪ **une ~ de couleurs** a luxuriance of colours.

luxuriant, e [lyksyrjɑ̃, ɑ̃t] *adj litt* **1.** [végétation] luxuriant, lush ▪ [chevelure] thick **2.** [imagination] fertile.

luxurieux, euse [lyksyrjø, øz] *adj litt* lascivious, lustful.

luzerne [lyzɛrn] *nf* lucerne *UK*, alfalfa *US*.

lx (*abr écrite de* **lux**) lx.

lycée [lise] *nm* (upper) secondary school *UK*, high school *US* *(providing three years' teaching after the "collège", in preparation for the baccalauréat examination)* ▪ **~ d'enseignement général et technologique** technical (high) school ▪ **~ professionnel** vocational (high) school, technical college.

lycéen, enne [liseɛ̃, ɛn] ◇ *nm, f* ≃ secondary school pupil *UK*, ≃ high school student *US* ▪ **quand j'étais ~ne** when I was at school ▪ **un groupe de ~s** a group of school students ▪ **ce groupe attire surtout les ~s** this group is mainly a success with teenagers.
◇ *adj* school *(modif)* ▪ **le mouvement ~** the school students' movement.

lychee [litʃi] = **litchi**.

Lycra® [likra] *nm* Lycra®.

lymphatique [lɛ̃fatik] ◇ *adj* **1.** BIOL lymphatic **2.** [apathique] sluggish, lethargic.
◇ *nm* lymphatic vessel.

lymphe [lɛ̃f] *nf* lymph.

lymphocyte [lɛ̃fɔsit] *nm* lymphocyte.

lynchage [lɛ̃ʃaʒ] *nm* lynching.

lyncher [3] [lɛ̃ʃe] *vt* to lynch ▪ **se faire ~** to be *ou* get lynched.

lynx [lɛ̃ks] *nm* **1.** ZOOL lynx **2.** [fourrure] lynx fur, lucern.

Lyon [ljɔ̃] *npr* Lyons, Lyon.

lyonnais, e [ljɔnɛ, ɛz] *adj* from Lyons.
◆ **Lyonnais, e** *nm, f inhabitant of or person from Lyons.*
◆ **Lyonnais** *npr m* GÉOGR : **le Lyonnais, les monts du Lyonnais** the Lyonnais mountains.
◆ **lyonnais** *nm* LING Lyons variety.

lyophilisé, e [ljɔfilize] *adj* freeze-dried.

lyophiliser [3] [ljɔfilize] *vt* to freeze-dry, to lyophilize *spéc.*

lyre [lir] *nf* MUS lyre.

lyrique [lirik] *adj* **1.** LITTÉR [poésie] lyric ▪ [inspiration, passion] lyrical ▪ **quand il parle d'argent, il devient ~** *fig* he really gets carried away when he talks about money **2.** MUS & THÉÂTRE lyric ▪ **art/drame ~** lyric art/drama ▪ **artiste ~** opera singer.

lyrisme [lirism] *nm* lyricism ▪ **avec ~** lyrically.

lys [lis] = **lis**.

m, M [ɛm] *nm* [lettre de l'alphabet] m, M, *voir aussi* **g**.

m 1. (*abr écrite de* **mètre**) ▪ **60 m** 60 m **2.** (*abr écrite de* **milli**) m.

m^2 (*abr écrite de* **mètre carré**) sq m, m^2.

m^3 (*abr écrite de* **mètre cube**) cu m, m^3.

m' [m] *pron pers* ▷ **me**.

M 1. (*abr écrite de* **million**) M **2.** = **masculin 3.** (*abr écrite de* **méga**) M **4.** (*abr écrite de* **Major**) M **5.** (*abr écrite de* **mile (marin)**) nm.

M. (*abr écrite de* **Monsieur**) Mr.

M6 *npr private television channel broadcasting a high proportion of music and aimed at a younger audience.*

ma [ma] *f* ▷ **mon**.

MA *nm* = **maître auxiliaire**.

Maastricht [mastriʃt] *npr* Maastricht ▪ **les accords de ~** the Maastricht agreement ▪ **le traité de ~** the Maastricht treaty.

maboul, e [mabul] *fam* ◇ *adj* crazy, nuts.
◇ *nm, f* (raving) loony.

mac△ [mak] *nm arg crime* pimp.

macabre [makabr] *adj* [découverte] macabre, gruesome ▪ [spectacle] gruesome, macabre, grisly ▪ **un goût pour ce qui est ~** a taste for the macabre.

macadam [makadam] *nm* **1.** TRAV PUB [matériau, surface] macadam ▪ **~ goudronné** tarmacadam **2.** [route] road, roadway, macadam *spéc.*

macadamiser [3] [makadamize] *vt* to macadamize.

macaque [makak] ◇ *nm* ZOOL macaque.
◇ *nmf fam* [personne laide] : **un vieux ~** an old baboon.

macareux [makarø] *nm* : **~ (moine)** puffin.

macaron [makarɔ̃] *nm* **1.** CULIN macaroon **2.** [vignette - officielle] badge ; [- publicitaire] sticker **3.** *fam* [décoration honorifique] rosette, ribbon ▪ **il a eu son ~** he got his decoration **4.** [de cheveux] coil ▪ **porter des ~s** to wear (one's hair in) coils.

macaroni [makarɔni] ◇ *nm* CULIN macaroni ▪ **~s au gratin** macaroni cheese *UK*, macaroni and cheese *US*.
◇ *nmf*△ *offensive term used with reference to Italians*, ≃ wop△.

maccartisme, maccarthysme [makkartism] *nm* McCarthyism.

macchabée△ [makabe] *nm* [cadavre] stiff.

macédoine [masedwan] *nf* **1.** CULIN : **~ de fruits** macédoine, mixed fruit salad ▪ **~ de légumes** macédoine, (diced) mixed vegetables **2.** *fam* [mélange] mishmash.

Macédoine [masedwan] *npr f* : **(la) ~** Macedonia.

macédonien, enne [masedɔnjɛ̃, ɛn] *adj* Macedonian.
◆ **Macédonien, enne** *nm, f* Macedonian.

macération [maserasjɔ̃] *nf* **1.** CULIN maceration, steeping **2.** ŒNOL & PHARM maceration **3.** RELIG [punition] mortification of *ou* mortifying the flesh, maceration *sout.*

macérer [18] [masere] ◇ *vi* **1.** CULIN to macerate, to steep ▪ **faire ~ le poisson cru dans du jus de citron** macerate *ou* steep the raw fish in lemon juice **2.** PHARM to macerate **3.** *fig* **laisse-le ~ dans son jus** *fam* let him stew in his (own) juice.
◇ *vt* **1.** CULIN to macerate, to steep **2.** PHARM to macerate.

mâche [maʃ] *nf* corn salad, lamb's lettuce.

mâcher [3] [maʃe] *vt* **1.** [aliment, chewing-gum] to chew ▪ [brin d'herbe, tige de fleur] to chew *ou* to nibble (at) ▪ **ne fais pas tant de bruit quand tu mâches** don't munch so loudly ➤ **il ne mâche pas ses mots** he doesn't mince his words **2.** *fam* [tâche] : **faut-il que je te mâche tout le travail?** do I have to show *ou* tell you how to do everything? **3.** [déchiqueter - matériau, papier] to chew up *(sép)* **4.** *fig & litt* [ressasser] to chew *ou* to mull over.

machette [maʃɛt] *nf* machete.

machiavel [makjavɛl] *nm* : **c'est un ~** he's a Machiavellian character *ou* a Machiavelli.

Machiavel [makjavɛl] *npr* Machiavelli.

machiavélique [makjavelik] *adj* Machiavellian.

machiavélisme [makjavelism] *nm* Machiavellianism.

mâchicoulis [maʃikuli] *nm* machicolation.

machin [maʃɛ̃] *nm fam* **1.** [chose] whatsit, thing, thingummyjig ▪ **c'est quoi, ce ~?** what on earth's this? **2.** *péj* **vieux ~** old fogey *ou* fuddy-duddy.

Machin, e [maʃɛ̃, in] *nm, f fam* [en s'adressant à la personne] what's-your-name ▪ [en parlant de la personne] whatshisname (*f* whatshername) ▪ **~ chouette** [personne] whatshisname.

machinal, e, aux [maʃinal, o] *adj* [geste] involuntary, unconscious ▪ [parole] automatic ▪ **un travail ~** mechanical work ▪ **j'emprunte toujours ce chemin-là, c'est ~!** I always go that way, I do it without thinking!

machinalement [maʃinalmɑ̃] *adv* **1.** [involontairement] automatically, without thinking ▪ **excuse-moi, je l'ai fait ~** sorry, I did it automatically *ou* without thinking **2.** [mécaniquement] mechanically, without thinking.

machination [maʃinasjɔ̃] *nf* plot, conspiracy, machination ▪ **des ~s** plotting, machinations.

machine [maʃin] *nf* **1.** [appareil] machine, piece of machinery ▪ **l'âge des ~s** *ou* **de la ~** the machine age, the age of the machine ➤ **~ à coudre/à tricoter** sewing/knitting machine

■ ~ **à écrire** typewriter ■ ~ **à laver** washing machine ■ ~ **à laver la vaisselle** dishwasher ■ ~ **à repasser** steam press ■ ~ **à traitement de texte** word processor ■ ~ **à sous** JEUX one-armed bandit, fruit machine *UK* ■ ~ **à vapeur** steam engine
2. [véhicule - à deux roues, agricole] machine ■ **~s agricoles** agricultural machinery
3. NAUT [moteur] engine ■ **arrêtez** *ou* **stoppez les ~s!** stop all engines! ◐ **chambre** *ou* **salle des ~s** engine room ■ **faire ~ arrière** *pr* to go astern ; *fig* to backtrack
4. [organisation] machine, machinery ■ **les lourdeurs de la ~ judiciaire** the cumbersome machinery of the law
5. THÉÂTRE machine, piece of theatre machinery
6. *péj* [automate] machine ■ **je ne veux pas devenir une ~ à écrire des chansons** I don't want to become a song-writing machine.
◆ **à la machine** *loc adv* : **(fait) à la ~** machine-made ■ **coudre qqch à la ~** to sew sthg on the machine, to machine *ou* to machine-sew sthg ■ **laver qqch à la ~** to machine *ou* to machine-wash sthg, to wash sthg in the machine ■ **taper qqch à la ~** to type sthg ■ **tricoter qqch à la ~** to machine-knit sthg, to make sthg on the knitting machine.

machine-outil [maʃinuti] (*pl* **machines-outils**) *nf* machine tool ◐ ~ **à commande numérique** numerically controlled machine tool.

machiner [3] [maʃine] *vt* **1.** *fam* [fabriquer] to fiddle about **2.** [préparer - complot] to hatch ; [- affaire, histoire] to plot.

machinerie [maʃinri] *nf* **1.** [machines] machinery, equipment, plant ■ **c'est la ~ qui coûte le plus cher** most of the money goes on equipment **2.** NAUT engine room **3.** THÉÂTRE machinery.

machinisme [maʃinism] *nm* mechanization.

machiniste [maʃinist] *nmf* **1.** THÉÂTRE stagehand, scene shifter ■ **les ~s** stage staff ◐ ~ **de plateau** CINÉ & TV grip **2.** TRANSP driver.

machisme [matʃism] *nm* machismo, male chauvinism.

machiste [matʃist] *adj* & *nm* male chauvinist, macho.

macho [matʃo] *adj* & *nm* *fam* macho.

mâchoire [maʃwar] *nf* **1.** ANAT & ZOOL jaw ■ ~ **inférieure/supérieure** upper/lower jaw **2.** ENTOM mandible *spéc*, jaw **3.** [d'un outil] jaw, grip ■ ~ **de frein** brake shoe.

mâchonnement [maʃɔnmɑ̃] *nm* **1.** [fait de mâcher] chewing ■ **des ~s bruyants** munching, chomping **2.** MÉD bruxism.

mâchonner [3] [maʃɔne] *vt* **1.** [mâcher - aliment] to chew ; [- brin d'herbe, tige de fleur, crayon] to chew *ou* to nibble (at) ■ [suj: âne, cheval] to munch **2.** *fig* [marmonner] to mumble.

mâchouiller [3] [maʃuje] *vt fam* [aliment] to chew (away) at ■ [brin d'herbe, tige de fleur] to chew *ou* to nibble (away) at ■ **arrête de ~ des bonbons!** stop chewing sweets all the time!

mâchurer [3] [maʃyre] *vt* **1.** *vieilli* [noircir - vêtement, papier] to blacken, to stain, to daub ; [- peau, visage] to blacken **2.** IMPR to mackle, to blur **3.** [écraser] to crush, to squash, to mash.

maçon, onne [masɔ̃, ɔn] *adj* mason *(modif)*.
◆ **maçon** *nm* CONSTR [entrepreneur] builder ■ [ouvrier] bricklayer *UK*, mason *US* ■ *(comme adj)* **apprenti ~** builder's *ou* bricklayer's apprentice ■ **ouvrier ~** builder's mate *UK ou* helper *US*.

maçonnage [masɔnaʒ] *nm* **1.** [travail] building, bricklaying **2.** [ouvrage] masonry ■ **le ~ est solide** [les pierres] the stonework *ou* masonry is good ; [les briques] the brickwork *ou* bricklining is good **3.** [d'un animal] building.

maçonner [3] [masɔne] *vt* **1.** [construire] to build **2.** [réparer] to rebuild, to redo the brickwork for **3.** [revêtir - gén] to line ; [- avec des briques] to brickline, to line with bricks **4.** [boucher - gén] to block up *(sép)* ; [- avec des briques] to brick up *ou* over *(sép)* ■ **ça a été bien maçonné** [gén] the masonry's good ; [pierres] the stonework's good ; [briques] the brickwork's good.

maçonnerie [masɔnri] *nf* **1.** [ouvrage - en pierres, en moellons] stonework, masonry ; [- en briques] brickwork ■ ~ **à sec** *ou* **en pierres sèches** dry masonry **2.** [travaux] : **grosse/petite ~** major/minor building work **3.** = **franc-maçonnerie**.

maçonnique [masɔnik] *adj* Masonic.

macramé [makrame] *nm* macramé.

macreuse [makrøz] *nf* **1.** ZOOL scoter (duck) ■ ~ **noire** common scoter **2.** CULIN shoulder of beef.

macro [makro] *nf* INFORM macro.

macrobiotique [makrɔbjɔtik] ◇ *adj* macrobiotic. ◇ *nf* macrobiotics *(sing)*.

macrocosme [makrɔkɔsm] *nm* macrocosm.

macrocosmique [makrɔkɔsmik] *adj* macrocosmic.

macroéconomie [makrɔekɔnɔmi] *nf* macroeconomics *(U)*.

macroéconomique [makrɔekɔnɔmik] *adj* macroeconomic.

macro-instruction [makrɔɛ̃stryksjɔ̃] (*pl* **macro-instructions**) *nf* macroinstruction.

macromolécule [makrɔmɔlekyl] *nf* macromolecule.

macrophotographie [makrɔfɔtɔgrafi] *nf* macrophotography.

macroscopique [makrɔskɔpik] *adj* macroscopic.

macrosociologie [makrɔsɔsjɔlɔʒi] *nf* macrosociology.

macrostructure [makrɔstryktyr] *nf* macrostructure.

maculage [makylaʒ] *nm* **1.** IMPR mackle **2.** [fait de salir] dirtying, soiling ■ [salissures] stains, marks, dirt.

maculer [3] [makyle] *vt* **1.** IMPR to mackle **2.** *sout* to dirty, to spatter.

Madagascar [madagaskar] *npr* [île] Madagascar ■ **à ~** in Madagascar ■ **la République démocratique de ~** the Democratic Republic of Madagascar.

madame [madam] (*pl* **madames**) *nf* lady ■ **jouer à la ~** [femme] to put on airs ; [enfant] to play at being grown up.

Madame [madam] (*pl* **Mesdames** [medam]) *nf* **1.** [dans une lettre] : ~ Dear Madam *sout*, Dear Mrs Duval ■ **Mesdames** Ladies ■ **Chère ~** Dear Mrs Duval ■ ~ **le Maire** Madam *sout*, Dear Madam ‖ [sur l'enveloppe] : ~ **Duval** Mrs Duval ■ **Mesdames Duval** Mesdames Duval ■ **Mesdames Duval et Lamiel** Mrs Duval and Mrs Lamiel ■ ~ **la Présidente Duval** Mrs Duval
2. [terme d'adresse] : **bonjour ~ Duval!** good morning, Mrs Duval! ■ **bonjour Mesdames Duval!** good morning, ladies! ■ **bonjour ~ le Consul** good morning, Mrs Duval *ou* Madam ■ ~ **la Présidente, je proteste!** Madam Chairman, I must raise an objection! ■ **Mesdames les Députés, vous êtes priées de vous asseoir!** will the Honourable lady Members please sit down! *UK* ‖ [à une inconnue] : **bonjour ~** good morning(, Madam)! ■ **bonjour Mesdames** good morning(, ladies) ■ **Mesdames, Mesdemoiselles, Messieurs!** Ladies and Gentlemen! ■ **vous attendrez votre tour comme tout le monde, ~!** you'll have to wait your turn like everybody else, Madam! ■ ~ **désirerait voir les pantalons?** would Madam like to see some trousers? ‖ *sout* & *hum* ~ **est servie** [au dîner] dinner is served(, Madam) ; [pour le thé] tea is served(, Madam) ■ **le frère de ~ attend en bas** [à une roturière] your brother is waiting downstairs, Miss *ou* Madam *sout* ; [à une femme titrée] Your Ladyship's brother is waiting downstairs ■ **vous n'y pensez pas, chère ~!** you can't be serious, my dear lady *ou* Madam! ■ **peux-tu prêter un instant ton stylo à ~?** could you lend the lady your pen for a minute? ‖ [au téléphone] : **bonjour ~, je voudrais la comptabilité s'il vous plaît** hello, I'd like to speak to someone in the accounts department, please
3. [en se référant à une tierce personne] : **adressez-vous à ~ Duval** go and see Mrs Duval ■ ~ **veuve Duval** the wife of the late Mr Duval ■ ~ **votre mère** *sout* your (good) mother ■ **Monsieur le docteur Duval et ~** [pour annoncer] Doctor (Duval) and Mrs Duval ■ ~ **la Présidente regrette de ne pas pouvoir venir** Mrs Duval regrets she is unable to come

4. ÉDUC : **~, j'ai fini mon addition!** (please) Miss, I've finished my sums!
5. *fam* **et en plus, ~ exige des excuses!** and so Her Ladyship wants an apology as well, does she?
6. HIST Madame *(title given to some female members of the French royal family).*

madeleine [madlɛn] *nf* **1.** CULIN madeleine ■ **pour moi, ce fut (comme) la ~ de Proust** it triggered off (all) my old memories, it brought back (a flood of) old memories **2.** [cépage] madeleine *(vine ripening early, around St Mary Magdalene's Day, 22nd July).*

Mademoiselle [madmwazɛl] (*pl* **Mesdemoiselles** [medmwazɛl]) *nf* **1.** [dans une lettre] : **~** Dear Madam *sout*, Dear Miss Duval ■ **Chère ~** Dear Miss Duval ■ **Mesdemoiselles** Ladies ‖ [sur l'enveloppe] : **~ Duval** Miss Duval ■ **Mesdemoiselles Duval** the Misses Duval ■ **Mesdemoiselles Duval et Jonville** Miss Duval and Miss Jonville
2. [terme d'adresse - suivi du nom] : **bonjour ~ Duval!** good morning, Miss Duval! ■ **bonjour Mesdemoiselles Duval!** good morning, (young) ladies! ■ [à une inconnue] : **bonjour ~!** good morning(, miss)! ■ **~, vous attendrez votre tour comme tout le monde!** you'll have to wait your turn like everybody else, young lady! ■ **Mesdemoiselles, un peu de silence s'il vous plaît!** [à des fillettes] girls, please be quiet! ; [à des jeunes filles] ladies, would you please be quiet! ■ **~ désire-t-elle voir nos derniers modèles?** would Madam like to see our latest designs? ‖ *sout* & *hum* Miss, Madam ■ **~ est servie** [au dîner] dinner is served (, Miss) ; [pour le thé] tea is served(, Miss) ■ **vous n'y pensez pas, chère ~!** you can't be serious, dear *ou* young lady! ■ **peux-tu prêter un moment ton stylo à ~?** could you lend the young lady your pen for a minute?
3. [en s'adressant à une tierce personne] : **c'est ~ Duval qui s'en occupe** Miss Duval is dealing with it ■ **~ votre sœur** *sout* your good *ou* dear sister ■ **Monsieur le docteur Duval et ~** [pour annoncer] Doctor (Duval) and Miss Duval ■ **Mesdemoiselles, Messieurs!** Ladies and Gentlemen!
4. ÉDUC : **~, j'ai fini mon dessin!** (please) Miss (Duval), I've finished my drawing!
5. *fam* **et en plus, ~ se plaint!** *iron* so, Her Ladyship is complaining as well, is she?
6. HIST [titre royal] Mademoiselle *(title given to some female members of the French royal family)* ■ [pour une femme noble non titrée] Her Ladyship.

madère [madɛr] *nm* [vin] Madeira (wine).

Madère [madɛr] *npr* Madeira ■ **à ~** in Madeira.

madériser [3] [maderize] ◆ **se madériser** *vpi* to maderize.

madone [madɔn] *nf* **1.** ART Madonna ■ **un visage de ~** a Madonna-like face ▶ **une ~ à l'enfant** a Madonna and Child **2.** [statuette] Madonna, statue of the Virgin Mary **3.** RELIG : **la Madone** the Madonna, the Virgin Mary.

madras [madras] *nm* **1.** [étoffe] madras (cotton) **2.** [foulard] madras (scarf).

Madrid [madrid] *npr* Madrid.

madrier [madrije] *nm* CONSTR beam.

madrigal, aux [madrigal, o] *nm* **1.** MUS & LITTÉR madrigal **2.** *litt* [propos galant] compliment, gallant remark.

madrilène [madrilɛn] *adj* Madrilenian.
◆ **Madrilène** *nmf* Madrilenian.

maelström [maɛlstrɔm] *nm* **1.** GÉOGR maelstrom **2.** *fig* [agitation] maelstrom, whirlpool.

maestria [maɛstrija] *nf* (great) skill, mastery, brilliance.
◆ **avec maestria** *loc adv* masterfully, brilliantly.

maestro [maɛstro] *nm* MUS maestro ■ *fig* maestro, master.

maf(f)ia [mafja] *nf* **1.** [en Sicile, aux États-Unis] : **la Mafia** the Mafia **2.** [bande] gang **3.** *péj* [groupe fermé] clique ■ **le milieu du cinéma est une véritable ~** the cinema world is very cliquey.

maf(f)ieux, euse [mafjø, øz] *adj* : **le milieu ~** the Mafia ■ **des méthodes mafieuses** Mafia-like methods.

maf(f)ioso [mafjozo] (*pl* **mafiosi** *ou pl* **maffiosi** [-zi]) *nm* mafioso ■ **des mafiosi** mafiosi, mafiosos.

magasin [magazɛ̃] *nm* **1.** [boutique] shop *UK*, store *US* ■ **faire** *ou* **courir les ~s** to go round the shops, to go shopping ▶ **~ d'ameublement/de jouets** furniture/toy shop ■ **~ d'alimentation** food shop *UK*, grocery store *US* ■ **~ (d'articles) de sport** sports shop *UK*, sporting goods store *US* ■ **~ d'informatique** computer store ■ **~ à succursales (multiples)** chain *ou* multiple store ■ **~ d'usine** factory outlet ■ **~ de vêtements** clothes shop *UK*, clothing store *US* ■ **grand ~** department store **2.** [entrepôt - industriel] warehouse, store, storehouse ; [- d'une boutique] storeroom ; [- d'une unité militaire] quartermaster's store, magazine ■ **nous n'avons plus de tondeuses en ~** we're (right) out of lawnmowers, we haven't any more lawnmowers in stock ▶ **~ d'armes** MIL armoury ■ **~ d'explosifs** MIL explosives store *ou* magazine ■ **~ à grains** silo ■ **~s généraux** bonded warehouse **3.** THÉÂTRE : **~ des accessoires** prop room **4.** ARM & PHOTO magazine.

magasinage [magazinaʒ] *nm* **1.** COMM [mise en magasin] warehousing, storing ■ **frais de ~** storage (charges) **2.** *Québec* shopping.

magasiner [3] [magazine] *vi Québec* to shop ■ **aller ~** to go shopping.

magasinier [magazinje] *nm* [dans une usine] storekeeper, storeman ■ [dans un entrepôt] warehouseman.

magazine [magazin] *nm* magazine ▶ **~ littéraire** literary magazine *ou* review ■ **un ~ médical** a medical journal ■ **les ~s féminins** women's magazines.

mage [maʒ] *nm* **1.** ANTIQ & RELIG magus **2.** *fig* [magicien] magus.

Magellan [maʒɛlɑ̃] *npr* Magellan ■ **le détroit de ~** the Strait of Magellan.

magenta [maʒɛ̃ta] ◇ *adj inv* magenta *(modif).*
◇ *nm* magenta.

Maghreb [magrɛb] *npr m* : **le ~** the Maghreb.

maghrébin, e [magrebɛ̃, in] *adj* Maghrebi, North African.
◆ **Maghrébin, e** *nm, f* Maghrebi, North African.

MAGHRÉBIN

This term usually refers to people from Algeria, Morocco and Tunisia, although it can also refer to Libyans and Mauritanians. It has a particular resonance in contemporary France, where immigrants from these countries continue to suffer from racial prejudice.

magicien, enne [maʒisjɛ̃, ɛn] *nm, f* **1.** [illusionniste] magician **2.** [sorcier] magician, wizard **3.** *fig* [virtuose] magician ■ **un ~ de** a master of.

magie [maʒi] *nf* **1.** [sorcellerie] magic ■ **~ blanche/noire** white/black magic ■ **comme par ~** as if by magic ■ **alors, ce bracelet, il a disparu comme par ~?** *iron* so this bracelet just disappeared by magic, did it? **2.** [charme] magic ■ **la ~ du printemps** the magic of spring.

Maginot [maʒino] *npr* : **la ligne ~** the Maginot Line.

LA LIGNE MAGINOT

A magnificent but ultimately useless engineering achievement, these largely underground fortifications were built on the Franco-German border between 1927 and 1936, but not along the Belgian border, through which the German forces advanced in 1940.

magique [maʒik] *adj* **1.** [surnaturel] magical, magic ■ **dites le mot ~** say the magic word **2.** [féerique] magical, wonderful **3.** PHYS magical.

magiquement [maʒikmɑ̃] *adv* magically.

magistère [maʒistɛr] *nm* **1.** RELIG [dans un ordre] magister, master ■ [autorité] magisterium **2.** UNIV senior (professional) diploma **3.** PHARM magistery.

magistral, e, aux [maʒistral, o] *adj* **1.** [remarquable] brilliant, masterly ■ **une œuvre ~e** a masterpiece, a masterwork

| [en intensif] huge, exemplary ■ **elle lui a cloué le bec de façon ~e** she really shut him up in style **2.** [docte] authoritative, magisterial *sout*, masterful **3.** ÉDUC : **cours ~** lecture ■ **enseignement ~** lecturing **4.** PHARM specific, magistral *spéc.*

magistralement [maʒistralmɑ̃] *adv* brilliantly, magnificently *pr & hum.*

magistrat, e [maʒistra, ɑt] *nm, f* **1.** DR [qui rend la justice] judge ■ [qui applique la loi] public prosecutor *UK*, prosecuting attorney *US* ■ **~ du siège** judge ■ **~ à la cour** *ou* **du parquet** public prosecutor *UK*, prosecuting attorney *US* **2.** ADMIN & POLIT *any high-ranking civil servant with judicial authority* ■ **~ municipal** town councillor *UK* **3.** MIL : **~ militaire** judge advocate **4.** ANTIQ magistrate.

MAGISTRAT

The word *magistrat* can refer either to a judge or to any public servant who exercises judicatory or administrative power: mayors and the president of France are *magistrats*. The term *magistrat municipal* refers to a member of a local council.

magistrature [maʒistratyr] *nf* **1.** [personnes] : **la ~** the judicial authorities ➔ **la ~ assise** DR the Bench *ou* judges ■ **la ~ debout** DR the (body of) public prosecutors *UK*, the (body of) prosecuting attorneys *US* ■ **la ~ suprême** the presidency **2.** [fonction] office ■ **pendant sa ~** during her period in office.

magma [magma] *nm* **1.** CHIM & GÉOL magma **2.** *fig & péj* [mélange confus] jumble.

magnanime [maɲanim] *adj sout* magnanimous.

magnanimité [maɲanimite] *nf sout* magnanimity ■ **elle a fait preuve de ~ à leur égard** she displayed magnanimity *ou* she was magnanimous towards them.

magnat [maɲa] *nm* magnate, tycoon ■ **~ de la presse** press baron ■ **~ du pétrole** oil tycoon.

magner [3] △ [maɲe] ◆ **se magner** ◇ *vpi* to get a move on, to hurry up ■ **magnez-vous!** get your skates on! *UK*, get the lead out! *US*.
◇ *vpt* : **magne-toi le mou** *ou* **le popotin!** get a move on!, hurry up!

magnésium [maɲezjɔm] *nm* magnesium.

magnétique [maɲetik] *adj* **1.** INFORM & PHYS magnetic **2.** *fig* [regard, personnalité] magnetic.

magnétisant, e [maɲetizɑ̃, ɑt] *adj* magnetizing.

magnétisation [maɲetizasjɔ̃] *nf* **1.** PHYS magnetization **2.** [fascination] fascination, mesmeric effect.

magnétiser [3] [maɲetize] *vt* **1.** PHYS to magnetize **2.** [fasciner] to mesmerize, to fascinate, to hypnotize *fig* ■ **il sait ~ les foules** he hypnotizes audiences, he has a mesmerizing effect on audiences.

magnétiseur, euse [maɲetizœr, øz] *nm, f* magnetizer, hypnotist.

magnétisme [maɲetism] *nm* **1.** PHYS magnetism **2.** [fascination, charisme] magnetism, charisma.

magnéto [maɲeto] ◇ *nm fam* = **magnétophone**.
◇ *nf* ÉLECTR magneto.

magnétocassette [maɲetɔkasɛt] *nm* cassette deck *ou* recorder.

magnétophone [maɲetɔfɔn] *nm* tape recorder ■ **~ à cassette** cassette recorder ■ **je l'ai enregistré sur** *ou* **au ~** I've taped *ou* tape-recorded it.

magnétoscope [maɲetɔskɔp] *nm* videotape recorder, video, videorecorder.

magnétoscoper [3] [maɲetɔskɔpe] *vt* to videotape, to video.

magnificence [maɲifisɑ̃s] *nf* **1.** [faste] luxuriousness, magnificence, splendour **2.** *litt* [prodigalité] munificence, lavishness.

magnifier [9] [maɲifje] *vt* **1.** *sout* [célébrer] to magnify *sout*, to glorify ■ **~ le Seigneur** to magnify the Lord *arch* **2.** [élever] to exalt, to idealize.

magnifique [maɲifik] *adj* **1.** [très beau - vue, nuit, robe] magnificent, splendid, superb ■ **il faisait un temps ~** the weather was gorgeous *ou* glorious **2.** [de grande qualité] magnificent, excellent, wonderful ■ **elle a une situation ~ chez un agent de change** she has a fantastic *ou* marvellous job with a stockbroker **|** [remarquable - découverte, progrès] remarkable, wonderful **3.** [somptueux - appartement, repas] splendid, magnificent.

magnifiquement [maɲifikmɑ̃] *adv* **1.** [somptueusement] magnificently, lavishly, gorgeously ■ **~ illustré** lavishly illustrated **2.** [bien] superbly ■ **il se porte ~** he's in great shape ■ **la journée avait ~ commencé** the day had begun gloriously.

magnitude [maɲityd] *nf* GÉOL magnitude.

magnolia [maɲɔlja] *nm* magnolia (tree).

magnum [magnɔm] *nm* magnum *(bottle)*.

magot [mago] *nm* **1.** [singe] Barbary ape, magot **2.** [figurine orientale] magot **3.** *fam* [argent caché] stash ■ **où t'as mis le ~?** where've you stashed the loot? **4.** *fam* [argent] dough, loot, lolly *UK* ■ **il a amassé** *ou* **il s'est fait un ~ en Orient** he made a packet in the East.

magouillage [magujaʒ] *fam*, **magouille** *(nf)* [maguj] *nm fam* scheming, trickery, double-dealing ■ **des ~s électorales** electoral wheeler-dealing.

magouiller [3] [maguje] *vi fam* to scheme, to do a bit of wheeler-dealing, to wangle ■ **il l'a eu en magouillant** he got it by a wangle, he wangled it.

magouilleur, euse [magujœr, øz] *fam* ◇ *adj* scheming, wheeler-dealing, wangling.
◇ *nm, f* wheeler-dealer, schemer, wangler.

magret [magrɛ] *nm* : **~ (de canard)** magret of duck, fillet of duck breast.

magyar, e [magjar] *adj* Magyar.

maharadjah, maharaja [maaradʒa] *nm* maharajah, maharaja.

mahatma [maatma] *nm* mahatma.

Mahomet [maɔmɛ] *npr* Mahomet, Mohammed.

mahométan, e [maɔmetɑ̃, an] *adj* Mohammedan.

mai [mɛ] *nm* [mois] May ■ **en ~, fais ce qu'il te plaît** *prov* ≃ never cast a clout till May is out *prov* ■ **(les événements de) ~ 1968** May 1968, *voir aussi* **mars**.

MAI 68

The events of May 1968 came about when student protests, coupled with widespread industrial unrest, culminated in a general strike and rioting. De Gaulle's government survived the crisis, but the issues raised made the events a turning point in French social history.

maie [mɛ] *nf* **1.** [pour le pain - huche] bread chest *ou* box ; [- pétrin] dough *ou* kneading trough **2.** [d'un pressoir] squeezer base.

maïeutique [majøtik] *nf* maieutics *(U)*.

maigre [mɛgr] ◇ *adj* **1.** [très mince] thin ■ **tu deviens trop ~** you're getting too thin ➔ **~ comme un hareng saur** *ou* **un clou** *ou* **un coucou** as thin as a rake **2.** CULIN & RELIG : **du fromage/yaourt ~** low-fat cheese/yoghurt ■ **jambon/poisson ~** lean ham/fish ■ **régime ~** low-fat diet ■ **jour ~** RELIG day without meat **3.** AGRIC poor ■ **végétation ~** thin vegetation **4.** [insuffisant - gén] thin, poor ; [- ration, repas] small ■ **un ~ bouillon** a clear broth ■ **un ~ filet d'eau** a thin stream of water ■ **un ~ filet de voix** a thin voice ■ **les bénéfices sont ~s** the profits are low *ou* meagre *ou* paltry *péj* ■ **de ~s économies** (very) small savings ■ **de ~s ressources** meagre *ou* scant resources ■ **un ~ espoir** a slim *ou* slight hope ■ **quelques ~s idées** a few flimsy ideas **5.** *fam* [peu] : **30 euros après deux heures de collecte, c'est**

~! 30 euros after collecting for two hours, that's not much! ■ **c'est un peu ~ comme prétexte!** that's a pretty poor excuse! **6.** IMPR light, light-face.
<> *adv* : **manger ~** to be on a fat-free *OU* fatless diet.
<> *nmf* thin person ■ **c'est une fausse ~** she isn't as thin as she looks.
<> *nm* **1.** [d'une viande] lean part **2.** RELIG : **faire ~** to go without meat, to eat no meat **3.** IMPR light *OU* light-face type **4.** ZOOL meagre, maigre.

maigrelet, ette [mɛgrəlɛ, ɛt] *adj fam* (a bit) skinny *péj OU* thin.

maigrement [mɛgrəmɑ̃] *adv* meagrely, poorly ■ **il est ~ payé** he gets meagre wages.

Maigret [mɛgrɛ] *npr the subtle detective hero of many of the novels of the Belgian writer Georges Simenon (1903-1989).*

maigreur [mɛgrœr] *nf* **1.** [minceur excessive] thinness, leanness ■ **le malade était d'une ~ effrayante** the sick man was dreadfully thin **2.** [insuffisance] thinness, meagreness, scantiness ■ **la ~ de nos bénéfices/économies** the sparseness *OU* meagreness of our profits/savings.

maigrichon, onne [mɛgriʃɔ̃, ɔn] *fam* <> *adj* skinny ■ **il est tout ~** he's scrawny.
<> *nm, f* skinny person.

maigrir [32] [megrir] <> *vi* to get *OU* to grow thinner ■ **tu n'as pas besoin de ~** you don't need to lose (any) weight ■ **il faut que je maigrisse de trois kilos** I have to lose three kilos ■ **elle a beaucoup maigri du visage** her face has got a lot thinner ■ **produits pour ~** slimming *UK OU* diet aids ■ **faire ~ qqn** to make sb lose weight ■ **mes économies maigrissent à vue d'œil** *fig* my savings are just vanishing *OU* disappearing by the minute.
<> *vt* : **sa barbe/son costume le maigrit** his beard/his suit makes him look thinner.

mail[1] [maj] *nm* **1.** [allée] mall, promenade ■ **sur le ~** along the mall *OU* promenade **2.** HIST [jeu] mall, pall-mall ■ [maillet] mallet.

mail[2] [mel] *nm* INFORM email (message), mail.

mailing [mɛliŋ] *nm* **1.** [procédé] mailing, mail canvassing **2.** [envoi de prospectus] mailshot ■ **faire un ~** to do *OU* to send a mailshot.

maillage [majaʒ] *nm* **1.** PÊCHE mesh size **2.** ÉLECTR grid **3.** [d'un réseau] meshing, reticulation, meshwork.

maille [maj] *nf* **1.** [d'un filet] mesh ■ **filet à ~s fines/larges** close-/wide-meshed net ■ **passer à travers les ~s du filet** *pr & fig* to slip through the net **2.** COUT stitch ▶ **~ à l'endroit/à l'envers** plain/purl stitch ■ **tricoter une ~ à l'endroit, une ~ à l'envers** knit one, purl one **3.** [vêtements en maille] knitwear ■ **l'industrie de la ~** the knitwear industry **4.** ÉLECTR mesh **5.** NAUT frame space **6.** *loc* **avoir ~ à partir avec** to be at odds with ■ **il a eu ~ à partir avec la justice** he's been in trouble *OU* he's had a brush with the law.

maillé, e [maje] *adj* **1.** [réseau] grid *(modif)* **2.** [sanglier, perdreau] speckled **3.** [armure] (chain) mail *(modif)*.

maillet [majɛ] *nm* **1.** [marteau] mallet, maul **2.** SPORT [au croquet] mallet ■ [au polo] polo stick.

mailloche [majɔʃ] *nf* **1.** TECHNOL [maillet, outil chauffant] beetle ■ [de mouleur] rake **2.** MUS bass drumstick.

maillon [majɔ̃] *nm* **1.** [chaînon] link ■ **un ~ de la chaîne** a link in the chain **2.** NAUT shackle **3.** TEXT mail, eye.

maillot [majo] *nm* : **~ de bain** [de femme] swimming costume *UK*, bathing costume *UK OU* suit *US* ; [d'homme] (swimming *OU* bathing) trunks ■ **~ de corps** undershirt, vest *UK*, singlet *UK* ■ **~ de football** football jersey ■ **le ~ jaune** *(the yellow shirt worn by) the leading cyclist in the Tour de France.*

main [mɛ̃] <> *nf* **1.** ANAT hand ■ **donne-moi la ~** give me your hand, hold my hand ■ **les enfants, tenez-vous par *OU* donnez-vous la ~** hold hands, children ■ **ils peuvent se donner la ~!** *fig* they're as bad as each other! ■ **tenir la ~ de qqn** *fig* to hold sb's hand ■ **lève la ~** [à l'école] put your hand up, raise your hand ■ **levez la ~ droite et dites "je le jure"** raise your right hand and say "I swear to God" ■ **lever la ~ sur qqn** *fig* to raise one's hand to sb ■ **tu veux ma ~ sur la figure?** do you want a slap?, you're asking for a slap! ■ **les ~s en l'air!, haut les ~s!** hands up! ■ **la tasse lui a échappé des ~s** the cup slipped *OU* fell from her hands ▶ **en ~ propre, en ~s propres** [directement] personally **2.** [savoir-faire] : **avoir la ~** to have the knack ■ **garder *OU* s'entretenir la ~** to keep one's hand in ■ **se faire la ~** to practise ■ **perdre la ~** to lose one's touch ▌ [intervention] hand ■ **certains y voient la ~ des services secrets** some people believe that the secret service had a hand in it ■ **reconnaître la ~ de qqn** to recognize sb's touch
3. *vieilli* [permission d'épouser] : **demander/obtenir la ~ d'une jeune fille** to ask for/to win a young lady's hand (in marriage) ■ **elle m'a refusé sa ~** she refused my offer of marriage ■ **m'accorderez-vous votre ~?** will you give me your hand (in marriage)?
4. CARTES : **~ pleine** full house *(at poker)* ■ **avoir la ~** [faire la donne] to deal ; [jouer le premier] to lead ■ **céder *OU* passer la ~** to pass the deal ; *fig* to step *OU* to stand down
5. [gant de cuisine] (oven) glove
6. COUT : **petite ~** apprentice
7. COMM & IMPR [quantité] ≃ quire *(of 25 sheets)* ■ [tenue] : **papier qui a de la ~** paper which has bulk *OU* substance
8. FOOTBALL : **il y a ~!** handball!
9. CONSTR [poignée] handle ■ **~ courante** handrail
10. *loc* **à ~ levée** [voter] by a show of hands ; [dessiner] freehand ■ **~ libres** [téléphone, kit] hands-free ■ **à ~s nues** barehanded ■ **grand comme la ~** tiny ■ **~ de fer : mener *OU* régenter qqch d'une ~ de fer** to rule sthg with an iron hand ■ **une ~ de fer dans un gant de velours** an iron fist in a velvet glove ■ **la ~ sur le cœur** with one's hand on one's heart, in perfect good faith ■ **~ secourable : chercher une ~ secourable** to look for a helping hand *OU* for help ■ **aucune ~ secourable ne se présenta** nobody came forward to help ■ **de ~ de maître** masterfully, brilliantly ■ **la décision est entre les ~s du juge** the decision rests with *OU* is in the hands of the judge ■ **ton fils est en (de) bonnes ~s** your son is in good hands ■ **avoir/garder les ~s libres** *fig* to have/to keep a free hand ■ **j'ai les ~s liées** *fig* my hands are tied ■ **arriver/rentrer les ~s vides** to turn up/to go home empty-handed ■ **les ~s dans les poches** *fam fig* with not a care in the world, free and easy ■ **jeux de ~s, jeux de vilains** [à des enfants] no more horsing around or it'll end in tears ■ **gagner haut la ~** to win hands down ■ **avoir la haute ~ sur** to have total *OU* absolute control over ■ **avoir la ~ heureuse** to be lucky ■ **avoir la ~ légère** [être clément] to be lenient ; [en cuisine] to underseason ■ **avoir la ~ leste** to be quick with one's hands ■ **avoir la ~ lourde** [être sévère] to be harsh *OU* heavy-handed ; [en cuisine] to be heavy-handed (with the seasoning) ■ **avoir la ~ verte** to have green fingers *UK OU* a green thumb *US* ■ **avoir/garder qqch sous la ~** to have/to keep sthg at hand ■ **en venir aux ~s** to come to blows ■ **faire ~ basse sur** [palais] to raid, to ransack ; [marchandises, documents] to get one's hands on ■ **c'est toi qui as fait ~ basse sur les chocolats?** *hum* are you the one who's been at the chocolates? ■ **c'est lui, j'en mettrais ma ~ au feu** that's him, I'd stake my life on it ■ **il n'y est pas allé de ~ morte** he didn't pull his punches ■ **attention, la ~ me démange!** watch it or you'll get a slap! ■ **mettre la ~ à la poche** to put one's hand into one's pocket ■ **mettre la ~ à l'ouvrage *OU* à la pâte** to put one's shoulder to the wheel ■ **mettre *OU* prêter la ~ à** to have a hand *OU* to take part in ■ **mettre la ~ sur qqch** to lay *OU* to put one's hands on sthg ■ **je n'arrive pas à mettre la ~ dessus** I can't find it, I can't lay my hands on it ■ **c'est une photo à ne pas mettre entre toutes les ~s** this photo shouldn't be shown to just an ybody *OU* musn't fall into the wrong hands ■ **prendre qqn la ~ dans le sac** to catch sb red-handed ■ **ah, ah, je te prends la ~dans le sac!** *hum* ha! I've caught you at it! ■ **tu ne trouveras pas de travail si tu ne te prends pas par la ~** you won't find a job unless you get a grip on yourself *OU UK* you pull your socks up ■ **tendre la ~** [faire l'aumône] to hold out one's hand, to beg ■ **tendre la ~ à qqn** [lui pardonner] to hold out one's hand to sb (in forgiveness) ■ **tomber dans les *OU* aux ~s de** to fall into the hands *OU* clutches *péj* of ■ **la première chemise qui me tombe sous la ~** the first shirt that comes to hand.
<> *adv* [fabriqué, imprimé] by hand ■ **fait/tricoté/trié ~** hand-made/-knitted/-picked.
◆ **à la main** *loc adv* **1.** [artisanalement] : **fait à la ~** hand-made **2.** [dans les mains] : **avoir *OU* tenir qqch à la ~** to hold sthg in one's hand.

◆ **à main** *loc adj* [levier, outil] hand *(modif)*, manual.
◆ **à main droite** *loc adv* on the right-hand side.
◆ **à main gauche** *loc adv* on the left-hand side.
◆ **de la main** *loc adv* with one's hand ▪ **saluer qqn de la ~** [pour dire bonjour] to wave (hello) to sb ; [pour dire au revoir] to wave (goodbye) to sb, to wave sb goodbye ▪ **de la ~, elle me fit signe d'approcher** she waved me over.
◆ **de la main à la main** *loc adv* directly, without any middleman ▪ **j'ai payé le plombier de la ~ à la ~** I paid the plumber cash in hand.
◆ **de la main de** *loc prép* **1.** [fait par] by ▪ **la lettre est de la ~ même de Proust/de ma ~** the letter is in Proust's own hand/in my handwriting
2. [donné par] from (the hand of) ▪ **elle a reçu son prix de la ~ du président** she received her award from the President himself.
◆ **de main en main** *loc adv* from hand to hand, from one person to the next.
◆ **de première main** ◇ *loc adj* [information] first-hand ▪ [érudition, recherche] original.
◇ *loc adv* : **nous tenons de première ~ que...** we have it on the best authority that...
◆ **de seconde main** *loc adj* [information, voiture] second-hand.
◆ **d'une main** *loc adv* [ouvrir, faire] with one hand ▪ [prendre] with *ou* in one hand ➤ **donner qqch d'une ~ et le reprendre de l'autre** to give sthg with one hand and take it back with the other.
◆ **en main** ◇ *loc adj* : **l'affaire est en ~** the question is in hand *ou* is being dealt with ▪ **le livre est actuellement en ~** [il est consulté] the book is out on loan *ou* is being consulted at the moment.
◇ *loc adv* : **avoir qqch en ~** *pr* to be holding sthg ▪ **avoir** *ou* **tenir qqch (bien) en ~** *fig* to have sthg well in hand *ou* under control ▪ **quand tu auras la voiture bien en ~** when you've got the feel of the car ▪ **prendre qqch en ~** to take control of *ou* over sthg ▪ **prendre qqn en ~** to take sb in hand ▪ **la société a été reprise en ~** the company was taken over.
◆ **la main dans la main** *loc adv* [en se tenant par la main] hand in hand ▪ *fig* together ▪ *péj* hand in glove.

mainate [mɛnat] *nm* (hill) mynah (bird).

main-d'œuvre [mɛ̃dœvr] (*pl* **mains-d'œuvre**) *nf* **1.** [travail] labour ▪ **le prix de la ~** the cost of labour, labour costs **2.** [personnes] workforce, labour force ▪ **il y a une pénurie de ~ qualifiée** there is a shortage of skilled labour ▪ **les besoins en ~ ont augmenté** manpower requirements have increased ▪ **réserve** *ou* **réservoir de ~** labour pool *ou* reservoir.

Maine [mɛn] *npr m* **1.** HIST [en France] Maine **2.** [aux États-Unis] : **l'État du ~, le ~** Maine.

main-forte [mɛ̃fɔrt] *nf* : **prêter ~ à qqn** to give sb a (helping) hand.

mainlevée [mɛ̃ləve] *nf* DR withdrawal ▪ **~ d'une hypothèque** discharge *ou* withdrawal *ou* cancellation of a mortgage ▪ **~ de la saisie** replevin.

mainmise [mɛ̃miz] *nf* **1.** [physique] seizure ▪ **la ~ de Hitler sur les Balkans** Hitler's seizure *ou* takeover of the Balkans **2.** [psychologique] hold, grip, grasp ▪ **ses parents avaient la ~ sur sa vie** her parents had a strong hold *ou* tight grip on her life.

maint, e [mɛ̃, mɛ̃t] *dét litt* many a, a great many ▪ **~es et ~es fois, à ~es reprises** time and time again.

maintenance [mɛ̃tnɑ̃s] *nf* **1.** [de matériel, d'un bien] upkeep ▪ [d'un appareil, d'un véhicule] maintenance, servicing **2.** MIL [moyens] maintenance unit ▪ [processus] maintenance.

maintenant [mɛ̃tnɑ̃] *adv* **1.** [à présent] now ▪ **~ on peut y aller** we can go now ▪ **il y a ~ trois ans que cela dure** this has been going on for three years now ▪ **c'est ~ que tu arrives?** what time do you call this? ▪ **l'avion a sûrement décollé ~** the plane must have taken off (by) now ▪ **à partir de ~** from now on *ou* onwards ▪ **c'est ~ ou jamais** it's now or never ▪ **les jeunes de ~** today's youth, young people today **2.** [cela dit] now ▪ **je l'ai lu dans le journal, ~ si c'est vrai ou faux, je n'en sais rien** I read it in the paper, but *ou* now whether or not it's true, I don't know.
◆ **maintenant que** *loc conj* now (that) ▪ **~ que Durand est chef du département,...** with Durand now head of department,...

maintenir [40] [mɛ̃tnir] *vt* **1.** [tenir] to hold firm *ou* tight ▪ **le dispositif est maintenu par des rivets** the structure is held tight *ou* together by rivets ▪ **~ qqn assis/debout** to keep sb seated/standing ▪ **il a fallu trois hommes pour le ~ allongé** three men were needed to keep him down **2.** [garder] to keep ▪ **~ l'eau à ébullition** keep the water boiling ▪ **~ la température à -5°** keep the temperature at -5° ▪ **~ au frais** keep in a cool place ▪ **~ qqn en vie** to keep sb alive ▪ **~ les yeux fermés** to keep one's eyes shut **3.** [conserver - statu quo, tradition] to maintain, to uphold ; [- prix] to keep in check, to hold steady ; [- loi] to uphold ; [- paix] to maintain, to keep ▪ **des traditions qui maintiennent les clivages sociaux** traditions which sustain *ou* perpetuate divisions in society ▪ **~ l'ordre** to keep order ▪ **~ sa candidature** [pour un emploi] to maintain *ou* go through with one's application ; POLIT to continue to stand **4.** [continuer à dire] to maintain ▪ **je maintiens que c'est possible** I maintain that it's possible ▪ **~ une accusation** to stand by *ou* to maintain an accusation ▪ **l'accusée a maintenu sa version des faits** the defendant stuck to *ou* stood by *ou* maintained her story.
◆ **se maintenir** *vpi* to remain ▪ **la monarchie se maintient encore dans quelques pays** monarchy lives on *ou* survives in a few countries ▪ **le beau temps se maintiendra** the weather will stay *ou* remain fine, the good weather will hold ▪ **le taux du dollar se maintient** the dollar is holding *ou* remains steady ▪ **le niveau des commandes se maintient** orders are holding up *ou* steady ▪ **comment ça va? – on** *ou* **ça se maintient** *fam* how's everything going? – so-so *ou* not so bad *ou* bearing up ▪ **il se maintient au second tour** POLIT he's decided to stand again in the second round ▪ **pourra-t-elle se ~ dans les dix premiers?** will she be able to remain in the top ten? ▪ **se ~ à flot** [dans l'eau] to stay afloat ; [dans son travail] to keep one's head above water ▪ **se ~ en équilibre** to keep one's balance ▪ **se ~ en bonne santé** to stay in good health.

maintien [mɛ̃tjɛ̃] *nm* **1.** [conservation] maintenance, upholding ▪ **comment garantir le ~ du libre-échange?** how is it possible to uphold *ou* to preserve free trade? ➤ **~ dans les lieux** DR right of tenancy ▪ **le ~ de l'ordre** the maintenance of law and order ▪ **assurer le ~ de l'ordre** to maintain law and order ▪ **~ de la paix** peacekeeping **2.** [port] bearing, deportment ▪ **cours/professeur de ~** lesson in/teacher of deportment **3.** [soutien] support ▪ **ce soutien-gorge assure un bon ~** this bra gives good support.

maintient, maintint *etc v* ▷ **maintenir**.

maire [mɛr] *nmf* [d'une commune, d'un arrondissement] ≃ mayor (*f* mayoress) ▪ [d'une grande ville] ≃ (lord) mayor *UK*, ≃ mayor *US*.

MAIRE

> In France, the mayor has obligations not only to the community but also to national government. He or she is responsible for promulgating national law as well as supervising the local police and officiating at civic occasions. Mayors are elected by the *conseil municipal* (indirectly by the town's residents) for a six-year term.

mairesse [merɛs] *nf* **1.** [femme maire] (Lady) Mayor **2.** [épouse du maire] mayoress.

mairie [meri] *nf* **1.** [fonction] office of mayor, mayoralty *sout* ▪ **il brigue la ~ de Paris** he's running for the office of Mayor of Paris **2.** [administration - gén] town council ; [- d'une grande ville] city council ➤ **~ d'arrondissement** district council *(in Paris, Lyons or Marseilles)* **3.** [édifice] town *ou* city hall ▪ **demandez une attestation à la ~** you must apply to the town hall for a certificate ➤ **~ de quartier** local town hall *(in Paris, Lyons or Marseilles)* ▪ **~ du village** village *ou* town hall.

MAIRIE

> Also called the *hôtel de ville*, this is the centre of municipal government. The *mairie* serves as a vital information source for town residents. People go there to ask about taxes, to get married etc.

mais [mɛ] ◇ *conj* **1.** [servant à opposer deux termes] : **finalement je n'en veux pas un ~ deux** actually, I want two not one ▪ **ce n'est pas bleu, ~ vert** it's not blue, it's green
2. [introduisant une objection, une restriction, une précision] but ▪ **oui, ~...** yes, but... ▪ **ces chaussures sont jolies ~ trop chères** these shoes are nice, but they're too expensive ▪ **j'ai trouvé le même, ~ moins cher** I found the same thing, only *ou* but cheaper
3. [introduisant une transition] : **~ revenons à notre sujet** but let's get back to the point ▪ **~ Fred, tu l'as vu ou non?** (and) what about Fred, did you see him or not? ▪ **~ dis-moi, ton frère, il ne pourrait pas m'aider?** I was thinking, couldn't your brother help me? ▪ **~ alors, vous ne partez plus?** so you're not going any more?
4. [renforçant des adverbes] : **vous êtes d'accord? – ~ oui, tout à fait** do you agree? – yes, absolutely ▪ **tu pleures? – ~ non, ~ non...** are you crying? – no, no, it's alright... ▪ **tu as peur? – ~ non!** are you scared? – of course not! ▪ **vous venez aussi? – ~ bien sûr!** are you coming as well? – of course (we are)! ▪ **nous allons à Venise, ~ aussi à Florence et à Sienne** we're going to Venice, and to Florence and Siena too ▪ **...~ bon, il ne veut rien entendre**...but he just won't listen
5. [employé exclamativement - avec une valeur intensive] : **cet enfant est nerveux, ~ nerveux!** that child is highly-strung, and I mean highly-strung! ▪ **j'ai faim, ~ faim!** I'm so hungry! ▪ **il a pleuré, ~ pleuré!** he cried, how he cried! ▪ **c'était une fête, ~ une fête!** what a party that was!, that was a real party! ▪ [exprimant l'indignation, l'impatience] : **non ~ des fois!** (but) really! ▪ **non ~ ça ne va pas!** you're/he's *etc* mad! ▪ **~ dis donc, tu n'as pas honte?** well really, aren't you ashamed of yourself? ▪ **~ enfin, en voilà une manière de traiter les gens!** well *ou* I must say, that's a fine way to treat people! ▪ **non ~ tu plaisantes?** you can't be serious!, you must be joking! ▪ **~ puisque je te le dis!** it's true I tell you! ▪ **~ écoute-moi un peu!** will you just listen to me a minute! ▪ **~ tu vas te taire, bon sang!** *fam* for God's sake, will you shut up! ▪ **~ c'est pas un peu fini ce vacarme?** have you quite finished making all that racket? ▪ **~ ça suffit maintenant!** that's enough now! ▪ **~ je vais me fâcher, moi!** I'm not going to put up with this! ▮ [exprimant la surprise] : **~ tu saignes!** you're bleeding! ▪ **~ c'est Paul!** hey, it's Paul! ▪ **~ dis donc, tu es là, toi?** what (on earth) are you doing here?
◇ *adv* : **n'en pouvoir ~** *litt* to be helpless.
◇ *nm* but, buts ▪ **il n'y a pas de ~ (qui tienne), j'ai dit au lit!** no buts about it, I said bed!
◆ **non seulement... mais** *loc corrélative* : **non seulement tu arrives en retard, ~ (en plus) tu oublies ton livre** not only do you arrive late but on top of that you forget your book.

maïs [mais] *nm* BOT maize *UK*, corn *US* ▪ CULIN sweetcorn ▪ **~ en épi** corn on the cob.

maison [mɛzɔ̃] ◇ *nf*

A.

1. [bâtiment] house, dwelling *sout* ▪ **~s (d'habitation)** private dwellings *sout ou* houses ⊳ **~ bourgeoise** fine town house *ou* residence *sout* ▪ **~ de campagne** [gén] house *ou* home in the country ; [rustique] (country) cottage ▪ **~ individuelle** [non attenante] detached house ▪ **~ de maître** [en bien propre] owner-occupied house ; [cossue] fine large house ▪ **~ de poupée** doll's house ▪ **~ préfabriquée** prefabricated house ▪ **gros comme une ~** *fam* plain for all to see ▪ **il te drague, c'est gros comme une ~** *fam* he's flirting with you, it's as plain as the nose on your face
2. [foyer, intérieur] home, house ▪ **je l'ai cherché dans toute la ~** I've looked for it all over the house ▪ **il a quitté la ~ à 16 ans** he left home when he was 16 ▪ **tenir une ~** to look after a *ou* to keep house ▪ **les dépenses de la ~** household expenditure ▪ **à la ~** at home ▪ **cet après-midi, je suis à la ~** I'm (at) home this afternoon ▪ **rentre à la ~!** [locuteur à l'extérieur] go home! ; [locuteur à l'intérieur] come *ou* get back in! ▪ **'tout pour la ~'** 'household goods'

B.

1. [famille, groupe] family ▪ **visiblement, vous n'êtes pas de la ~** you obviously don't work here ▪ **toute la ~ est partie pour Noël** all the people in the house have *ou* the whole family has gone away for Christmas
2. [personnel] household ▪ **la ~ civile/militaire** the civil/military household
3. [dynastie] house ▪ **la ~ des Tudor** the House of Tudor ▪ **être le descendant d'une grande ~** to be of noble birth
4. [lieu de travail - d'un domestique] household *(where a person is employed as a domestic)* ▪ **j'ai fait les meilleures ~s** I've been in service with the best families ▪ **vous avez combien d'années de ~?** how long have you been in service?

C.

1. COMM firm, company ▪ **j'ai 20 ans de ~** I've been with the company for 20 years ▪ **un habitué de la ~** a regular (customer) ▪ **'la ~ ne fait pas crédit'** 'no credit given' ▪ **'la ~ n'accepte pas les chèques'** 'no cheques (accepted)' ⊳ **~ de détail/gros** retail/wholesale business ▪ **~ de commerce** (commercial) firm *ou* company ▪ **~ de couture** fashion house ▪ **~ d'édition** publishing house ▪ **~ d'import-export** import-export firm *ou* company *ou* business ▪ **la Maison de la presse** newsagent's ▪ **~ de titres** BANQUE ≃ clearing house *(for clearing stocks)*
2. RELIG : **la ~ de Dieu** *ou* **du Seigneur** the house of God, the Lord's house
3. [lieu spécialisé] : **~ close** *ou* **de tolérance** *vieilli* brothel ▪ **~ de correction** *ou* **de redressement** HIST reformatory *arch*, remand home *UK*, borstal *UK* ▪ **~ d'arrêt** remand centre ▪ **~ centrale (de force)** prison, State penitentiary *US* ▪ **~ de convalescence** convalescent home ▪ **~ de la culture** ≃ arts *ou* cultural centre ▪ **~ d'enfants** (residential) holiday centre for children, camp *US* ▪ **~ familiale** holiday home *UK*, vacation home *US (for low-income families)* ▪ **~ de fous** *péj* madhouse ▪ **~ de jeu** gambling *ou* gaming house ▪ **~ des jeunes et de la culture** ≃ youth and community centre ▪ **~ maternelle** family home ▪ **~ de passe** sleazy hotel *(used by prostitutes)* ▪ **~ du peuple** ≃ trade union and community centre ▪ **la Maison de la radio** *Parisian headquarters and studios of French public radio* ▪ ≃ Broadcasting House *UK* ▪ **~ de repos** rest *ou* convalescent home ▪ **~ de retraite** old people's home, retirement home ▪ **~ de santé** nursing home

D.

ASTROL house, mansion.
◇ *adj inv* **1.** [fabrication] home-made ▪ **spécialité ~** speciality of the house **2.** [employé] in-house ▪ **nous avons nos traducteurs ~** we have an in-house translation department ⊳ **syndicat ~** company union **3.** *fam* [en intensif] first-rate, top-notch ▪ **il s'est fait engueuler, quelque chose de ~!** he got one hell of a talking-to! ▪ **une engueulade ~**△ one hell of a dressing-down.
◆ **maison mère** *nf* **1.** COMM mother *UK ou* parent company **2.** RELIG mother house.

MAISON DE LA CULTURE

An ambitious project begun by André Malraux in the 1960s to establish cultural centres all over France. Designed to bring high culture to the provinces, these centres encountered much opposition and only eleven survived.

Maison-Blanche [mɛzɔ̃blɑ̃ʃ] *npr f* : **la ~** the White House.

maisonnée [mɛzɔne] *nf sout* household ▪ **son cri réveilla toute la ~** his scream woke up the whole household *ou* everyone in the house.

maisonnette [mɛzɔnɛt] *nf* small house.

maître, maîtresse [mɛtr, mɛtrɛs] ◇ *adj* **1.** *(après le n)* [essentiel] central, main, major ▪ **l'idée maîtresse du texte** the main theme *ou* central idea in the text ▪ **sa qualité maîtresse est le sang-froid** a cool head is his outstanding *ou* chief quality ▮ [le plus important] main ▪ **branche maîtresse** main branch ▪ **poutre maîtresse** main (supporting) beam ▪ *(avant le n)* **le ~ mot** the key word ▪ **maîtresse femme** powerful woman
2. [dans des noms de métiers] : **~ boulanger/forgeron** master baker/blacksmith ▪ **~ compagnon** ≃ master craftsman ▪ **~ coq** *ou* **queux** chef.
◇ *nm, f* **1.** [personne qui contrôle] master (*f* mistress) ▪ **ce chien n'obéit qu'à sa maîtresse** this dog only obeys his mistress ▪ **ils sont maintenant installés** *ou* **ils agissent en ~s dans le pays** they are now ruling the country, they have taken command of the country ▪ **il faut rester ~ de soi** you must keep your self-control ▪ **il est ~ de lui** he has a lot of self-control ▪ **être ~ d'une situation/de son véhicule** to be in control of a situation/of

one's vehicle ■ **les ~s du monde** the world's rulers ■ **se rendre ~ de** [d'un pays] to take *ou* seize control of ; [d'une personne] to bring under control ; [d'un incendie] to get under control ■ **à la maison, c'est lui le ~** he's (the) boss at home ■ **être son (propre) ~** to be one's own master *ou* boss ■ **il est son propre ~** he's his own man ■ **elle est son propre ~** she's her own woman ■ **être** *ou* **rester ~ de faire qqch** to be free to do sthg ▶ **le ~ de céans** the master of the house ■ **~ de maison** host ■ **maîtresse de maison** lady of the house *sout & hum*, hostess ■ **les bons ~s font les bons valets** *prov* a good master makes a good servant ■ **tel ~ tel valet** *prov* like master, like man *prov*
2. [professeur] : **~ (d'école), maîtresse (d'école)** teacher, schoolteacher ■ **elle fait très maîtresse d'école** she's very schoolmarmish ■ **Maîtresse, j'ai trouvé!** Miss UK *ou* teacher US, I know the answer! ■ **~/maîtresse de ballet** ballet master/mistress UK, ballet teacher ■ **~ de musique** music teacher.

◆ **maître** *nm* **1.** [dans des noms de fonctions] : **grand ~ (de l'ordre)** grand master ■ **~ d'armes** fencing master ■ **~ auxiliaire** supply UK *ou* substitute US teacher ■ **~ de chapelle** choirmaster ■ **~ de conférences** ≃ (senior) lecturer UK ■ ≃ assistant professor US ■ **~ d'ouvrage** [particulier] client *(of an architect)* ; [organisme public] contracting authority ■ **~ de recherches** research director ■ **~ de cérémonie** *ou* **des cérémonies** master of ceremonies
2. [expert] master ■ **elle est passée ~ dans l'art de tromper son monde** she is a past master in the art of misleading people
3. ART, LITTÉR & PHILOS master ■ **~ à penser** mentor, guru, intellectual model
4. RELIG : **le ~ de l'Univers** *ou* **du monde** the Master of the Universe ■ **se croire le ~ du monde** *fig* to feel invincible
5. CARTES : **être ~ à carreau** to hold the master *ou* top diamond
6. [titre] : **Maître Suzanne Thieu** Mrs. (*ou* Miss) Suzanne Thieu ■ **Maître Dulles, avocat à la cour** ≃ Mr. Dulles QC UK *ou* member of the Bar US ■ **cher Maître, à vous!** [à un musicien] Maestro, please!

◆ **maîtresse** *nf* [d'un homme] mistress ■ **devenir la maîtresse de qqn** to become sb's mistress.

◆ **de maître** *loc adj* **1.** [qui appartient à un riche particulier] : **chauffeur de ~** (personal) chauffeur ■ **voiture de ~** expensive car
2. [exécuté par un grand artiste] : **un tableau** *ou* **une toile de ~** an old master ■ **un coup de ~** *fig* a masterstroke ■ **pour un coup d'essai, c'est un coup de ~** for a first attempt, it was brilliant.

◆ **maître chanteur** *nm* **1.** [qui menace] blackmailer
2. MUS Meistersinger, mastersinger.

◆ **maître d'hôtel** ◇ *nm* [dans un restaurant] maître (d'hôtel), headwaiter ■ [chez un particulier] butler.
◇ *loc adj* : **beurre ~ d'hôtel** CULIN parsley butter, maître d'hôtel butter.

◆ **maître d'œuvre** *nm* **1.** CONSTR main contractor
2. *fig* **le Premier ministre est le ~ d'œuvre de l'accord signé hier** the Prime Minister was the architect of the agreement that was signed yesterday.

maître-assistant, maître-assistants [mɛtrasistɑ̃] *nm, f* ≃ lecturer UK, ≃ assistant professor US.

maître-autel [mɛtrotɛl] (*pl* **maîtres-autels**) *nm* high altar.

maître-chien [mɛtrəʃjɛ̃] (*pl* **maîtres-chiens**) *nm* dog trainer *ou* handler.

maître nageur [mɛtrənaʒœr] (*pl* **maîtres nageurs**) *nm* swimming teacher *ou* instructor ■ **~ sauveteur** lifeguard.

maîtresse [mɛtrɛs] *f* ▷ **maître**.

maîtrisable [metrizabl] *adj* **1.** [que l'on peut dominer - sentiment, douleur] controllable **2.** [que l'on peut apprendre] : **ces nouvelles techniques sont facilement ~s** these new techniques are easy to master.

maîtrise [metriz] *nf* **1.** [contrôle] mastery, control ■ **avoir la ~ des mers** to have complete mastery of the sea ■ **sa ~ du japonais est étonnante** she has an amazing command of Japanese ■ **avoir la ~ d'un art** to have mastered *ou* to master an art ■ **elle exécuta le morceau avec une grande ~** she performed the piece masterfully *ou* with great skill ▶ **~ de soi** self-control, self-possession **2.** [dans une entreprise] supervising staff **3.** UNIV ≃ master's degree ■ **elle a une ~ de géographie** she has a master's (degree) *ou* an MA in geography, she mastered in geography US **4.** RELIG [chœur] choir ■ [école] choir school.

MAÎTRISE

A degree obtained with one year's study after the *licence*. Students must attend seminars and prepare a long paper called a *mémoire*.

maîtriser [3] [metrize] *vt* **1.** [personne, animal] to overpower ■ [adversaire] to get the better of ■ **c'est un adversaire difficile, mais je le maîtriserai** he's a tough opponent, but I'll get the better of him **2.** [danger, situation] to bring under control ■ [sentiment] to master ■ **l'incendie a été rapidement maîtrisé** the fire was quickly brought under control ■ **ils maîtrisent maintenant la situation** they now have the situation (well) in hand *ou* under control ■ **je réussis à ~ ma colère** I managed to contain my anger **3.** [technique, savoir] to master.

◆ **se maîtriser** *vp (emploi réfléchi)* to control o.s. ■ **je sais que tu as du chagrin, mais il faut te ~** I know you're upset, but you must get a grip on yourself ■ **sous l'influence de l'alcool, on n'arrive plus à se ~** under the influence of alcohol, one loses (all) control.

Maïzena® [maizena] *nf* cornflour UK, cornstarch US.

majesté [maʒɛste] *nf* **1.** [grandeur] majesty, grandeur ▶ **~ divine/royale** divine/royal majesty **2.** [titre] : **Majesté** Majesty ■ **Sa Très Gracieuse Majesté, la reine Élisabeth** Her Most Gracious Majesty, Queen Elizabeth.

◆ **en majesté** *loc adj* ART [Christ, saint, Vierge] in majesty, enthroned.

majestueusement [maʒɛstɥøzmɑ̃] *adv* majestically.

majestueux, euse [maʒɛstɥø, øz] *adj* majestic, stately ■ **il avait en toute circonstance un port ~** his bearing was at all times majestic *ou* noble *ou* regal.

majeur, e [maʒœr] *adj* **1.** [le plus important] major, greatest ■ **le bonheur de son fils est son souci ~** his son's happiness is his major *ou* principal concern ■ **la ~e partie des gens** the majority of people, most people ■ **la raison ~e** the main *ou* chief reason **2.** [grave] major ■ **y a-t-il un obstacle ~ à sa venue?** is there any major reason why he shouldn't come? **3.** [adulte] : **être ~** to be of age ■ **tu auras une voiture quand tu seras ~** you'll have a car when you come of age *ou* when you reach your majority *sout* ■ **je n'ai pas besoin de tes conseils, je suis ~ (et vacciné)** *fam* I don't want any of your advice, I'm old enough to look after myself now **4.** MUS major ■ **concerto en la ~** concerto in A major ▶ **le mode ~** the major key *ou* mode **5.** RELIG : **causes ~es** causae majores.

◆ **majeur** *nm* **1.** [doigt] middle finger **2.** LOGIQUE major term **3.** MUS major key *ou* mode.

◆ **majeure** *nf* LOGIQUE major premise.

◆ **en majeure partie** *loc adv* for the most (part) ■ **son œuvre est en ~e partie hermétique** the major part *ou* the bulk of his work is abstruse.

Majeur [maʒœr] *npr* : **le lac ~** Lake Maggiore.

major [maʒɔr] ◇ *adj* [supérieur par le rang] chief *(modif)*, head *(modif)*.
◇ *nm* **1.** [dans la marine] ≃ master chief petty officer **2.** UNIV top student *(in the final examination at a grande école)* ■ **elle était le ~ de la promotion de 58** she came out first in her year in 1958 **3.** HIST & MIL [chef des services administratifs] adjutant ■ **(médecin) ~** medical officer ■ **~ général** ≃ major general **4.** *Suisse* commanding officer.
◇ *nf* major (company).

majorant [maʒɔrɑ̃] *nm* MATH upper bound.

majoration [maʒɔrasjɔ̃] *nf* **1.** [hausse] rise, increase ■ **procéder à une ~ des prix** to increase prices ■ **ils demandent une ~ de leurs salaires** they're asking for a wage increase ■ **~ d'impôts** surcharge on taxes **2.** [surestimation] overestimation.

majordome [maʒɔrdɔm] *nm* majordomo.

majorer [3] [maʒɔre] *vt* **1.** [augmenter] to increase, to raise ■ **tous les impôts impayés avant la fin du mois seront majorés de 5 %** there will be a 5% surcharge *ou* penalty charge on all taxes not paid by the end of the month **2.** [surestimer] to overestimate ▪ [donner trop d'importance à] *sout* to overstate, to play up *(sép)* **3.** MATH [suite] to majorize ▪ [sous-ensemble] to contain.

majorette [maʒɔrɛt] *nf* (drum) majorette.

majoritaire [maʒɔritɛr] ◇ *adj* **1.** [plus nombreux] majority *(modif)* ▪ **les femmes sont ~s dans l'enseignement** women outnumber men *ou* are in the majority in the teaching profession ▪ **quel est le parti ~ au Parlement?** which party has the majority *ou* which is the majority party in Parliament? ▪ **'coton ~'** 'high natural fibre content' **2.** ÉCON & FIN [actionnaire, participation] majority.
◇ *nmf* member of a majority group.

majorité [maʒɔrite] *nf* **1.** [le plus grand nombre] majority ▪ **la ~ de** the majority of, most ▪ **dans la ~ des cas** in most cases ▪ **la ~ silencieuse** the silent majority **2.** POLIT : **la ~** [parti] the majority, the party in power, the governing party ▪ **avoir la ~** to have the majority ▪ **ils ont gagné avec une faible/écrasante ~** they won by a narrow/overwhelming margin ▶ **~ absolue/simple** absolute/relative majority ▪ **être élu à la ~ absolue** to be elected with an absolute majority **3.** [âge légal] majority ▪ **atteindre sa ~** to reach one's majority *sout*, to come of age ▪ **à ta ~** [dans l'avenir] when you come of age ; [dans le passé] when you came of age ▪ **~ civile** (attainment of) voting age ▪ **~ pénale** legal majority.
◆ **en majorité** ◇ *loc adj* in the majority ▪ **nous sommes en ~** we are in the majority.
◇ *loc adv* : **les ouvriers sont en ~ mécontents** most workers *ou* the majority of workers are dissatisfied.

Majorque [maʒɔrk] *npr* Majorca ▪ **à ~** in Majorca.

majuscule [maʒyskyl] ◇ *adj* **1.** [gén] capital ▪ **B ~** capital B **2.** IMPR upper-case.
◇ *nf* **1.** [gén] capital, block letter ▪ **écrivez votre nom en ~s** write your name in capitals, print your name (in block letters) ▪ **mettez une ~ à Rome** write Rome with a capital, capitalize Rome *sout* **2.** IMPR upper case, upper-case letter.

mal [mal] (*pl* **maux** [mo]) ◇ *nm* **1.** [souffrance physique] pain ▪ **avoir ~ : où as-tu ~?** where does it hurt?, where is the pain? ▪ **j'ai ~ là** it hurts *ou* it's painful here ▪ **j'ai ~ aux dents** I've got toothache *UK ou* a toothache *US* ▪ **j'ai ~ aux oreilles** I've got earache *UK ou* an earache *US* ▪ **j'ai mal à la tête** I've got a headache ▪ **avoir ~ à la gorge** to have a sore throat ▪ **il a ~ au ventre** he has stomachache *UK ou* a stomachache ▪ **faire (du) ~ à** to hurt ▪ **ça vous fait encore ~?** does it still hurt?, is it still hurting you? ▪ **aïe, ça fait ~!** ouch, it *ou* that hurts! ▪ **se faire ~** to hurt o.s. ▪ **je me suis fait ~ à la main** I've hurt my hand ▶ **~ de dents** toothache ▪ **~ de dos** backache ▪ **~ de gorge** sore throat ▪ **~ de tête** headache ▪ **maux d'estomac** stomach pains ▪ **ça me ferait ~ au ventre** *fam* it would make me sick ▪ **ça me ferait ~ aux seins**△ it would really piss me off△ ▪ **ça va faire ~!** *fam fig* watch it, we're in for it now! ▪ **il n'y a pas de ~!** [après un heurt] no broken bones! ; [après une erreur] no harm done! ▪ **mettre qqn à ~** *ou* **à ~ qqn** *sout* to manhandle *ou* to maltreat sb
2. [maladie, malaise] illness, sickness, disease ▪ **tu vas attraper** *ou* **prendre du ~** *fam* watch you don't get a cold ▶ **~ de l'air** airsickness ▪ **~ blanc** whitlow ▪ **~ de mer** seasickness ▪ **avoir le ~ de mer** [habituellement] to suffer from seasickness ; [au cours d'un voyage] to be seasick
3. [dommage, tort] harm ▪ **le ~ est fait** the damage is done (now) ▪ **faire du ~ à qqch** to do harm to sthg, to harm *ou* to damage sthg ▪ **vouloir du ~ à qqn** to wish sb ill *ou* harm ▪ **il n'y a pas de ~ à demander** there's no harm in asking ▪ **et si j'en ai envie, où est le ~?** and if that's what I feel like doing, what harm is there in that? ▪ **dire du ~ de qqn** to gossip about sb, to speak ill of sb ▪ **penser du ~ de qqn** to think ill of sb ▶ **~ lui en a pris** he's had cause to regret it
4. [douleur morale] pain ▪ **faire (du) ~ à qqn** to hurt sb, to make sb suffer ▪ **quand j'y repense, ça me fait du** *ou* **ça fait ~** it hurts to think about it ▪ **n'essaie pas de la revoir, ça te ferait du ~** don't try to see her again, it'll only cause you pain *ou* upset you
5. [affliction, inconvénient] ill, evil ▪ **c'est un ~ nécessaire** it's a necessary evil ▶ **avoir le ~ de vivre** to be tired of life ▪ **entre deux maux, il faut choisir le moindre** *prov* always choose the lesser evil *ou* the lesser of two evils
6. [difficulté, tracas] trouble *(U)*, difficulty *(U)* ▪ **avoir du ~ à faire qqch** to have difficulty (in) *ou* trouble doing sthg ▪ **j'ai de plus en plus de ~ à me souvenir des noms** I'm finding it harder and harder to remember names ▪ **donner du ~ à qqn** to give sb trouble ▪ **se donner du ~ : il a réussi sans se donner de ~** he succeeded without much trouble ▪ **ne vous donnez pas tant de ~ pour moi** please don't go to all this trouble on my behalf
7. [par opposition au bien] : **le ~** evil ▪ **le bien et le ~** right and wrong, good and evil ▪ **faire le ~ pour le ~** to commit evil for evil's sake.
◇ *adv* **1.** [désagréablement] wrong ▪ **tout va ~** everything's going wrong ▪ **ça commence ~, c'est ~ parti** things are off to a bad start ▪ **ça va finir ~** *ou* **~ finir** [gén] it'll end in disaster ; [à des enfants turbulents] it'll all end in tears ▪ **il sera là aussi, ça tombe ~** he'll be there too, which is unfortunate ▪ **tu tombes ~** you've come at a bad time
2. [en mauvaise santé] : **aller ~, se porter ~** to be ill *ou* unwell, to be in poor health
3. [défavorablement] badly ▪ **elle a très ~ pris que je lui donne des conseils** she reacted badly *ou* she took exception to my giving her advice ▪ **ne le prends pas ~ mais...** I hope you won't be offended but..., don't take it the wrong way but... ▶ **être/se mettre ~ avec qqn** to be/to get on the wrong side of sb
4. [de façon incompétente ou imparfaite] badly, not properly ▪ **c'est du travail ~ fait** it's a shoddy piece of work ▪ **être ~ fait (de sa personne)** to be misshapen ▪ **cette veste lui va ~** that jacket doesn't suit him ▪ **ça lui va ~ de donner des conseils** he's hardly in a position to hand out advice ▪ **je le connais ~** I don't know him very well ▪ **s'ils croient que je vais me laisser faire, ils me connaissent ~!** if they think I'm going to take it lying down, they don't know me very well! ▪ **je dors ~** I have trouble sleeping ▪ **il mange ~** [salement] he's a messy eater ; [trop peu] he doesn't eat enough ; [mal équilibré] he doesn't eat properly ▪ **il parle ~** he can't talk properly ▪ **elle parle ~ l'allemand** her German isn't very good ▪ **tu te tiens ~** [tu es voûté] you've got poor posture ; [à table] you don't have any table manners ▪ **vivre ~ qqch** to have a bad time with sthg ▪ **je la vois ~ en bermuda** I can't quite see her in shorts ▪ **elle se voyait ~ le lui demander** *fam* she couldn't quite imagine *ou* she couldn't quite see herself asking him ▪ **s'y prendre ~ : je m'y prends ~** I'm not going about it the right way ▪ **elle s'y prend ~ avec les enfants** she's not very good with children ▪ **~ élevé** bad-mannered, impolite
5. [insuffisamment] badly, poorly ▪ **vivre ~** to have trouble making ends meet ▪ **être ~ nourri** [trop peu] to be underfed *ou* undernourished ; [avec de la mauvaise nourriture] to be fed bad *ou* poor food
6. [malhonnêtement - agir] badly ▪ **~ tourner** to turn out badly
7. [inconfortablement] uncomfortably ▪ **être ~ assis** to be uncomfortably seated *ou* uncomfortable ▪ **on dort ~ dans ton canapé-lit** your sofa bed isn't very comfortable
8. *loc* **ça la fiche** *fam ou* **fout**△ **~** it doesn't look good△ ▪ **si je n'y vais pas, ça la fiche ~** it won't look good if I don't go.
◇ *adj inv* **1.** [immoral] wrong ▪ **c'est ~ de tricher** it's wrong to cheat ▪ **je n'ai rien dit/fait de ~** I haven't said/done anything wrong
2. [malade] ill, unwell, not well ▪ **se trouver ~** [s'évanouir] to faint, to pass out, to swoon *sout*
3. [peu satisfaisant] : **ça n'était pas si ~** [film, repas, prestation] it wasn't that bad
4. *fam* [fou] mad, crazy.
◆ **au plus mal** *loc adj* **1.** [très malade] very sick, desperately ill, critical
2. [fâché] : **être au plus ~ avec qqn** to be at loggerheads with sb.
◆ **de mal en pis** *loc adv* from bad to worse.
◆ **en mal de** *loc prép* : **être en ~ d'affection** to be longing *ou* yearning for love ▪ **être en ~ d'inspiration** to be short of *ou* lacking inspiration.
◆ **mal à l'aise** *loc adj* uncomfortable, ill at ease ▪ **je suis ~ à l'aise devant elle** I feel ill at ease with her.
◆ **mal à propos** *loc adv* at the wrong time ▪ **faire une intervention ~ à propos** to speak out of turn.
◆ **mal portant, e** *loc adj* unwell, in poor health.

Mal = maréchal.

malabar [malabar] *nm fam* [colosse] muscle man, hulk.

Malacca [malaka] *npr* : **(la presqu'île de) ~** the Malay Peninsula.

malachite [malakit] *nf* malachite.

malade [malad] ◇ *adj* **1.** [souffrant] ill, sick, unwell ■ **une personne ~** a sick person ■ **un enfant toujours ~** a sickly child ■ **gravement ~** gravely *ou* seriously ill ■ **se sentir ~** to feel ill *ou* unwell ■ **tomber ~** to fall ill ■ **se faire porter ~** *fam* to call in *ou* to report sick ▶ **être ~ à crever**△ *ou* **comme un chien** *fam* [souffrir] to be incredibly ill *ou* at death's door *hum* ; [vomir] to be sick as a dog *ou* violently ill
2. [atteint d'une lésion] bad, diseased ■ **avoir le cœur ~** to have a heart condition *ou* heart trouble ■ **j'ai les intestins ~s, je suis ~ des intestins** I have troubles with my intestines ■ **une vigne ~** a diseased vine
3. [nauséeux] sick ■ **je suis ~ en bateau/voiture/avion** I suffer from seasickness/carsickness/airsickness ■ **rendre qqn ~** to make sb sick *ou* ill
4. [dément] (mentally) ill *ou* sick ■ **avoir l'esprit ~** to be mentally ill
5. [en mauvais état] decrepit, dilapidated ■ **nous avons une économie ~** our economy is sick *ou* shaky *ou* ailing ■ **la France ~ de l'inflation** *La Fontaine allus* France, sick *ou* crippled with inflation
6. [affecté moralement] ill, sick ■ **~ de jalousie** sick with jealousy, horribly jealous ■ **ça me rend ~ de la voir si démunie** it makes me ill to see her so penniless ■ **et pourtant c'est elle qui a eu le poste – tais-toi, ça me rend** *ou* **j'en suis ~!** all the same, she's the one who got the job – don't, it makes me sick *ou* vomit!
7. *fam* [déraisonnable] mad, crazy.
◇ *nmf* **1.** [patient - gén] sick person, sick man (*f* woman) ; [- d'un hôpital, d'un médecin] patient ■ [sujet atteint] sufferer ■ **c'est un ~ imaginaire** he's a hypochondriac ▶ **les grands ~s** the seriously ill ■ **'le Malade imaginaire'** *Molière* 'The Imaginary Invalid'
2. [dément] : **~ (mental)** mentally ill *ou* sick person DR ▶ **comme un ~** *fam* like a madman ■ **on a travaillé comme des ~s pour finir à temps** we worked like lunatics to finish on time
3. *fam* [passionné] : **un ~ de la vitesse** a speed fiend *ou* freak ■ **ce sont des ~s du golf** they're golf-crazy.

maladie [maladi] *nf* **1.** [mauvaise santé] illness, ill health, sickness **2.** [mal spécifique - MÉD & VÉTÉR] illness, disease ■ **une ~ grave** a serious illness ■ **il est mort des suites d'une longue ~** he died after a long illness ■ **'fermé pour cause de ~'** 'closed due to illness' ■ **être en congé ~** *ou* **en ~** *fam* to be on sick leave *ou* off sick ■ **je vais me mettre en ~** I'm going to take some sick leave *ou* time off sick ■ **être en longue ~** to be on indefinite sick leave ▶ **~ contagieuse/héréditaire** contagious/hereditary disease ■ **la ~ de Parkinson/d'Alzheimer** Parkinson's/Alzheimer's disease ■ **il avait la ~ bleue à la naissance** he was blue at birth ■ **~ de carence** deficiency disease ■ **~ du charbon** anthrax ■ **~ chronique** chronic illness *ou* condition ■ **~ infantile** childhood illness, infantile disorder ■ **~ infectieuse** infectious disease ■ **~ mentale** mental illness *ou* disorder ■ **~ mortelle** fatal disease *ou* illness ■ **~ orpheline** orphan disease *ou* illness ■ **~ professionnelle** occupational *ou* industrial disease ■ **~ sexuellement transmissible** sexually transmissible *ou* transmitted disease ■ **~ vénérienne** venereal disease, VD **3.** BOT disease ■ **les pruniers ont tous eu la ~** all the plum trees got diseased *ou* the disease **4.** [obsession] obsession ■ **elle a encore rangé tous mes journaux, c'est une ~ chez elle!** *hum* she's tidied up all my papers again, it's an obsession with her! ▶ **en faire une ~** *fam* to make a huge fuss ■ **il n'y a pas de quoi en faire une ~!** no need to make a song and dance about it *ou* to throw a fit!

maladif, ive [maladif, iv] *adj* **1.** [personne] puny, sickly ■ [teint] sickly-looking, unhealthy ■ [constitution] weak ■ **il a toujours un air ~** he always looks rather unhealthy *ou* ill **2.** [compulsif] obsessive, pathological *fig* ■ **d'une sensibilité maladive** acutely sensitive ■ **d'une jalousie maladive** pathologically *ou* obsessively jealous ■ **elle est d'une inquiétude maladive** she's a pathological *ou* an obsessive worrier ■ **il adore les jeux d'argent, c'est ~** he's a compulsive gambler *ou* he can't stop gambling, it's like a disease (with him).

maladivement [maladivmɑ̃] *adv* [à l'excès] pathologically, morbidly ■ **elle est ~ timide** she's excessively shy.

maladresse [maladrɛs] *nf* **1.** [manque de dextérité] clumsiness, awkwardness ■ **ne le laisse pas porter les verres, il est d'une telle ~!** don't let him carry the glasses, he's so clumsy! ■ [manque de tact] clumsiness, tactlessness ■ [manque d'assurance] awkwardness **2.** [remarque, acte] faux pas *sout*, blunder, gaffe ■ **ses ~s étaient devenues légendaires** [remarques] he'd become famous for his tactless remarks *ou* for (always) saying the wrong thing ; [actes] he'd become famous for his blunders **3.** ÉDUC : **bon devoir, mais des maladresses** good work if somewhat awkward in places.

maladroit, e [maladrwa, at] ◇ *adj* **1.** [manquant de dextérité] clumsy, awkward, heavy-handed **2.** [manquant - de savoir-faire] clumsy, inept ; [- d'assurance] clumsy, awkward, gauche ; [- de tact] clumsy, tactless, heavy-handed ■ **une initiative ~e** a clumsy *ou* bungling initiative.
◇ *nm, f* **1.** [de ses mains] clumsy person ■ **attention, ~, tu as failli lâcher la tasse!** look out, butterfingers, you nearly dropped the cup! **2.** [gaffeur] blunderer, blundering fool ■ [incompétent] blithering idiot.

maladroitement [maladrwatmɑ̃] *adv* **1.** [sans adresse] clumsily, awkwardly ■ **ils s'y sont pris ~** they set about it the wrong way **2.** [sans tact] clumsily, tactlessly, heavy-handedly.

malaga [malaga] *nm* **1.** [vin] Malaga (wine) **2.** [raisin] Malaga grape.

mal-aimé, e [maleme] (*mpl* **mal-aimés**, *fpl* **mal-aimées**) *nm, f* outcast ■ **c'est le ~ de la famille** he's the unpopular one in the family ■ **il a été le ~ de cette génération de réalisateurs** he was the forsaken member of that generation of (film) directors ■ **les ~s de la société** social outcasts.

malais, e [malɛ, ɛz] *adj* Malay, Malayan, Malaysian ■ **la presqu'île Malaise** the Malay Peninsula.
◆ **Malais, e** *nm, f* Malay, Malayan, Malaysian.

malaise [malɛz] *nm* **1.** [indisposition] (sudden) weakness, faintness, malaise *sout* ■ **ressentir un ~** to feel weak *ou* faint *ou* dizzy ■ [évanouissement] fainting fit, blackout ■ **j'ai eu un ~** I had a blackout **2.** [désarroi, angoisse] uneasiness *(U)*, anxiety *(U)*, disquiet *(U)* ■ **ce genre de film provoquait toujours chez elle un ~ profond** this sort of film always disturbed her deeply **3.** [mécontentement] discontent, anger ■ **il y a un ~ croissant chez les viticulteurs** there's mounting tension *ou* discontent among wine growers **4.** [gêne] unease, awkwardness ■ **la remarque a créé un ~** the remark caused a moment of unease *ou* embarrassment.

malaisé, e [maleze] *adj sout* difficult, hard, arduous ■ **il sera ~ de lui apprendre la vérité** telling him the truth will be no easy matter.

malaisément [malezemɑ̃] *adv sout* with difficulty.

Malaisie [malɛzi] *npr f* : **(la) ~** Malaya.

malandrin [malɑ̃drɛ̃] *nm* **1.** *litt* robber, thief ■ **une bande de ~s** a band of miscreants *litt* **2.** HIST highwayman.

malappris, e [malapri, iz] *vieilli* ◇ *nm, f* boor, lout ■ **eh bien, jeune ~, allez-vous me laisser passer!** well, you ill-bred young lout, are you going to let me past or not?
◇ *adj* boorish, loutish, ill-mannered.

malaria [malarja] *nf* malaria.

malaudition [malodisjɔ̃] *nf* MÉD hearing loss, hardness of hearing ■ **souffrir de ~** to be hearing-impaired *ou* hard of hearing.

malavisé, e [malavize] *adj sout* unwise, ill-advised ■ **tu as été ~ de ne pas venir** it was unwise of you *ou* you were ill-advised not to come.

Malawi [malawi] *npr m* **1.** [État] : **le ~** Malawi **2.** [lac] : **le lac ~** Lake Malawi.

malaxage [malaksaʒ] *nm* [d'une pâte] kneading ■ [d'un mélange] mixing.

malaxer [3] [malakse] *vt* **1.** [mélanger] to mix, to blend ■ [pétrir - pâte] to knead ■ **~ le beurre pour le ramollir** work the butter until soft **2.** [masser] to massage.

malaxeur [malaksœr] *nm* [gén] mixer, mixing machine ■ [de béton] cement mixer ■ [de sucre] mixer, agitator.

Malaysia [malɛzja] *npr f* : **(la) ~** Malaysia ■ **(la) ~ occidentale** Malaya.

malbouffe [malbuf] *nf* junk food, bad food.

malchance [malʃɑ̃s] *nf* **1.** [manque de chance] bad luck, misfortune ■ **il a eu la ~ de...** he was unlucky *ou* unfortunate enough to..., he had the misfortune to... ■ **jouer de ~** to be dogged by ill fortune **2.** [mésaventure] mishap, misfortune.
◆ **par malchance** *loc adv* unfortunately ■ **par ~ ils sont passés à Paris quand j'étais absent** unfortunately, they came to Paris when I was away.

malchanceux, euse [malʃɑ̃sø, øz] ◇ *adj* unlucky, luckless ■ **il a toujours été ~** he's never had any luck ■ **être ~ au jeu/en amour** to be unlucky at gambling/in love.
◇ *nm, f* unlucky person, unlucky man (*f* woman).

malcommode [malkɔmɔd] *adj* *sout* [appareil] impractical ■ [fauteuil, vêtement, position] uncomfortable ■ [horaire, système] inconvenient, awkward.

Maldives [maldiv] *npr fpl* : **les (îles) ~** the Maldive Islands, the Maldives, *voir aussi* **île**.

maldonne [maldɔn] *nf* **1.** JEUX misdeal ■ **tu as fait ~** you misdealt **2.** *fam fig* **il y a ~** there's been a misunderstanding.

mâle [mal] ◇ *adj* **1.** BIOL male ■ **le sexe ~** the male sex **2.** [viril] virile, masculine, manly ■ **son beau visage ~** his handsome, manly face ■ **avec une ~ assurance** with robust confidence **3.** TECHNOL male ■ **vis/connexion ~** male screw/connection ■ **prise ~** plug **4.** [avec des noms d'animaux] male ■ **chat ~** tom, tomcat ■ **éléphant ~** bull elephant ■ **hamster/hérisson ~** male hamster/hedgehog ■ **lapin ~** buck rabbit ■ **loup ~** male wolf, he-wolf.
◇ *nm* male ■ **est-ce un ~ ou une femelle?** it is a he or a she? ■ **le jars est le ~ de l'oie** a gander is a male goose ■ **la tigresse est à la recherche d'un ~** the tigress is looking for a mate ■ **quel ~!** *fam hum* what a man! ■ **hériter par les ~s** DR to inherit through the male line.

malédiction [malediksjɔ̃] ◇ *nf* **1.** [imprécation] curse, malediction *sout* ■ **donner sa ~ à qqn** to call down a curse upon sb, to curse sb **2.** [malheur] malediction *litt* ■ **encourir la ~ divine** to incur the wrath of God *ou* of the gods ■ **comme si le sort les poursuivait de sa ~** as if fate had cast her evil eye on them.
◇ *interj hum* curses, curse *ou* damn it.

maléfice [malefis] *nm* evil spell *ou* charm ■ **jeter un ~ sur qqn** to cast an evil spell on sb.

maléfique [malefik] *adj* [charme, signe, personne] evil, malevolent ■ [émanation, influence] evil, cursed ■ [étoile, planète] unlucky ■ **les puissances ~s** the forces of evil.

malencontreusement [malɑ̃kɔ̃trøzmɑ̃] *adv* ill-advisedly ■ **ayant ~ gardé ses lettres** having ill-advisedly kept *ou* having been ill-advised enough to have kept his letters.

malencontreux, euse [malɑ̃kɔ̃trø, øz] *adj* [fâcheux - retard, tentative, visite] ill-timed, inopportune ■ [mal choisi - parole] inopportune, ill-advised, unfortunate ■ **par un hasard ~** by a stroke of ill luck.

mal(-)en(-)point [malɑ̃pwɛ̃] *adj inv* [en mauvais état - de santé] in a bad way, poorly ; [- financier] badly off ■ **je l'ai trouvé ~** I found him very much out of sorts.

malentendant, e [malɑ̃tɑ̃dɑ̃, ɑ̃t] ◇ *adj* hard-of-hearing.
◇ *nm, f* person who is hard-of-hearing ■ **les ~s** the hard of hearing, the partially deaf.

malentendu [malɑ̃tɑ̃dy] *nm* misunderstanding, malentendu *sout* ■ **attends, je crois qu'il y a un ~ (entre nous)** wait, I think we're at cross purposes ■ **un ~ diplomatique** a diplomatic misunderstanding.

mal-être [malɛtr] *nm* discontent.

malfaçon [malfasɔ̃] *nf* defect ■ **la construction présente de nombreuses ~s** there are many defects in the building.

malfaisant, e [malfəzɑ̃, ɑ̃t] *adj* **1.** *sout* [qui cherche à nuire] evil, wicked **2.** [néfaste, pernicieux] evil, pernicious ■ **des idées ~es** pernicious ideas.

malfaiteur [malfɛtœr] *nm* criminal.

mal famé, e, malfamé, e [malfame] *adj* disreputable ■ **des lieux ~s** places of ill repute.

malformation [malfɔrmasjɔ̃] *nf* : **~ (congénitale)** (congenital) malformation.

malfrat [malfra] *nm* gangster, crook, hoodlum.

malgache [malgaʃ] *adj* Madagascan, Malagasy.
◆ **Malgache** *nmf* Madagascan, Malagasy.

malgré [malgre] *prep* in spite of, despite ■ **il a pénétré dans l'enceinte ~ les ordres** he entered the area against orders ■ **~ soi** [involontairement] unwillingly, in spite of oneself ; [à contrecœur] reluctantly, against one's better judgment ; [forcé] against one's will.
◆ **malgré que** *loc conj* [bien que] although, despite the fact that.
◆ **malgré tout** *loc adv* **1.** [en dépit des obstacles] in spite of *ou* despite everything **2.** [pourtant] all the same, even so ■ **il faut dire une chose ~ tout...** even so, one thing has to be said...

malhabile [malabil] *adj* [maladroit] clumsy ■ **elle est ~ de ses doigts** she's all fingers and thumbs.

malhabilement [malabilmɑ̃] *adv* *sout* clumsily, awkwardly.

malheur [malœr] ◇ *nm* **1.** [incident] misfortune ■ **un grand ~** a (great) tragedy *ou* catastrophe ■ **eh bien, tu en as des ~s!** *iron* oh dear, it's not your day, is it? ■ **si jamais il lui arrive (un) ~** if (ever) anything happens to him ▶ **faire un ~** *fam* : **ne le laissez pas rentrer ou je fais un ~** don't let him in or I can't answer for the consequences ■ **elle passait en première partie et c'est elle qui a fait un ~** she was the supporting act but it was she who brought the house down ■ **cette chanson a fait un ~ en son temps** that song was a huge success in its day ■ **pose cette tasse, un ~ est si vite arrivé!** put that cup down before there's an accident! ■ **parle pas de ~!** *fam* God forbid!, Lord save us! ■ **un ~ ne vient ou n'arrive jamais seul** *prov* it never rains but it pours *prov* **2.** [malchance] : **le ~** misfortune, bad luck ■ **le ~ a voulu que...** as bad luck would have it... ■ **avoir le ~ de** to be unfortunate enough to, to have the misfortune to ■ **j'ai eu le ~ de perdre mon père jeune** I had the *ou* it was my misfortune to lose my father when I was young ■ **j'ai eu le ~ de lui dire de se taire!** I was foolish enough to ask her *ou* I made the mistake of asking her to be quiet! ■ **une vie marquée par le ~** a life of misfortune *ou* sorrow ■ **être dans le ~** to suffer misfortunes *ou* hard times ■ **porter ~ à qqn** to bring sb bad luck ■ **arrête, ça porte ~!** stop, it brings bad luck! ■ **pour son/mon/ton ~ : je l'ai bien connu, pour mon ~** I knew him well, more's the pity ■ **pour son ~, il était l'aîné de six enfants** unfortunately for him, he was the oldest of six ▶ **je joue de ~ en ce moment** I'm dogged by *ou* I've got a run of bad luck at the moment ■ **c'est dans le ~ qu'on connaît ses vrais amis** *prov* a friend in need is a friend indeed *prov* **3.** [désespoir] : **faire le ~ de qqn** to cause sb unhappiness, to bring sorrow to sb ▶ **le ~ des uns fait le bonheur des autres** *prov* one man's joy is another man's sorrow *prov* **4.** [inconvénient] trouble, problem ■ **le ~ c'est que j'ai perdu l'adresse** unfortunately, *ou* the trouble is I've lost the address ■ **sans permis de travail, pas de possibilité d'emploi, c'est ça le ~** without a work permit you can't get a job, that's the snag *ou* the problem ■ **quel ~ que...** what a shame *ou* pity that...
◇ *interj* damn ■ **~ à** woe betide *litt hum* ▶ **~ aux vaincus!** *Brennus allus* vae victis!, woe to the vanquished!
◆ **de malheur** *loc adj* *fam hum* accursed, wretched ■ **je ne remonterai plus sur ce vélo de ~** I'll never ride that wretched *ou* accursed bike again.
◆ **par malheur** *loc adv* unfortunately ■ **par ~, son fils est né avec la même maladie** sadly, her son was born with the same disease.

malheureusement [malœrøzmɑ̃] *adv* unfortunately ▪ **je ne retrouve ~ pas mon agenda** unfortunately, *ou* I'm afraid I can't lay hands on my diary ▪ **~ pour toi, il ne reste plus de petites tailles** you're out of luck, there are no small sizes left.

malheureux, euse [malœrø, øz] ◇ *adj* **1.** [peiné] unhappy, miserable, wretched ▪ **je suis ~ de ne pouvoir l'aider** I feel sad *ou* wretched at not being able to help him ▪ **rendre qqn ~** to make sb miserable *ou* unhappy ▪ **n'y pense plus, tu ne fais que te rendre ~** don't think about it any more, you're only making yourself miserable ▪ **~ en ménage** unhappily married ▶ **être ~ comme une pierre** *ou* **les pierres** to be dreadfully unhappy
2. [tragique - enfance] unhappy ; [- destin] cruel
3. [malchanceux] unfortunate, unlucky ▪ **le candidat ~ verra ses frais de déplacement remboursés** the unsuccessful candidate will have his travel expenses paid ▪ **il est ~ au jeu/en amour** he has no luck with gambling/women ▪ *(avant le n)* **la malheureuse femme ne savait rien de la catastrophe** nobody had told the poor *ou* unfortunate *ou* wretched woman about the catastrophe
4. [infructueux - initiative, effort] thwarted ; [- amour] unrequited ▪ [malencontreux - tentative] unfortunate, ill-fated ; [- conséquences] unfortunate, unhappy ; [- incident] unfortunate ▪ **par un ~ hasard** by an unfortunate coincidence, as bad luck would have it
5. *(avant le nom)* [insignifiant] : **pleurer ainsi pour un ~ parapluie perdu/une malheureuse piqûre!** all these tears for a stupid lost umbrella/a tiny little injection! ▪ **ne nous battons pas pour quelques ~ centimes** let's not fight over a few measly cents
6. [dans des tournures impersonnelles] : **il est ~ que vous ne l'ayez pas rencontré** it's unfortunate *ou* a pity *ou* a shame you didn't meet him ▪ **ce serait ~ de ne pas en profiter** it would be a pity *ou* shame not to take advantage of it ▶ **c'est ~ à dire, mais c'est la vérité** it's an awful thing to say, but it's the truth ▪ **c'est ~ à dire, mais je m'ennuie** I hate to say so but I'm bored ▪ **si c'est pas ~ (de voir/d'entendre ça)!** *fam* it's a (crying) shame (to see/to hear that)!
◇ *nm, f* **1.** [indigent] poor *ou* needy man (*f* woman) ▪ **secourir les ~** to help the poor *ou* the needy *ou* those in need
2. [personne pitoyable] unfortunate *ou* wretched man (*f* woman) ▪ **il est bien seul maintenant, le pauvre ~** he's very much on his own now, the poor devil ▪ **vous allez faire des ~ avec votre nouvelle taxe** you'll make some people (very) unhappy with your new tax ▪ **attention, petit ~!** careful, you wretched boy *ou* little wretch! ▪ **qu'as-tu dit là, ~!** honestly, what a thing to say!

malhonnête [malɔnɛt] ◇ *adj* **1.** [sans scrupules] dishonest, crooked ▪ **c'est ~ de sa part** it's dishonest of him **2.** *vieilli* [impoli] rude, impolite, uncivil.
◇ *nmf* cheat, crook.

malhonnêtement [malɔnɛtmɑ̃] *adv* dishonestly.

malhonnêteté [malɔnɛtte] *nf* [manque de probité] dishonesty, crookedness ▪ **~ intellectuelle** intellectual dishonesty.

Mali [mali] *npr m* : **le ~** Mali ▪ **elle vit au ~** she lives in Mali.

malice [malis] *nf* mischievousness, impishness, prankishness ▪ **un regard plein** *ou* **pétillant de ~** an impish *ou* a mischievous look.
◆ **sans malice** ◇ *loc adj* guileless, innocent.
◇ *loc adv* : **je me suis moqué de lui, mais c'était sans ~** I made fun of him but it wasn't serious.

malicieusement [malisjøzmɑ̃] *adv* mischievously.

malicieux, euse [malisjø, øz] *adj* mischievous, impish ▪ **elle a la repartie malicieuse** she's never at a loss for a smart answer.

malien, enne [maljɛ̃, ɛn] *adj* Malian.
◆ **Malien, enne** *nm, f* Malian.

maligne [maliɲ] *f* ▷ **malin.**

malignité [maliɲite] *nf* **1.** [d'une action, d'une personne] malice, spitefulness, spite ▪ [du sort] cruelty ▪ **la ~ de cette remarque n'échappa à personne** the spitefulness of the remark wasn't lost on anyone **2.** MÉD malignancy.

malin, igne [malɛ̃, iɲ] ◇ *adj* **1.** [rusé] cunning, crafty, shrewd ▪ **elle avait un petit air ~** she had a wily *ou* cunning look about her ▶ **être ~ comme un singe** to be as cunning as a fox ▪ **jouer au plus ~ avec qqn** to try and outsmart *ou* outwit sb **2.** [intelligent] bright, clever, smart *esp US* ▪ **tu te crois ~ d'avoir copié sur les autres?** so you think cribbing from the others was a clever thing to do? ▪ **c'est ~!** *iron* very clever! **3.** MÉD [tumeur] malignant **4.** [malveillant] : **elle mettait une joie maligne à me poser les questions les plus difficiles** she would take a perverse pleasure in asking me the most difficult questions ▪ **éprouver un ~ plaisir à faire qqch** to experience (a) malicious pleasure in doing sthg ▶ **l'esprit ~** the Devil.
◇ *nm, f* clever person ▪ **c'est un ~, il trouvera bien une solution** he's a bright spark, he'll find a way ▶ **gros ~, va!** *fam iron* very clever! ▪ **alors, gros ~, montre-nous ce que tu sais faire** *fam iron* OK, wise guy, show us what you can do ▪ **la petite maligne avait tout prévu** the crafty little so-and-so had thought of everything ▪ **fais pas le ~ avec moi** don't (you) get smart with me ▪ **à ~, ~ et demi** *prov* there's always somebody smarter than you somewhere.
◆ **Malin** *nm* : **le Malin** the Devil, the Evil One.

malingre [malɛ̃gr] *adj* puny, sickly, frail ▪ **son corps ~** her puny *ou* frail body.

malintentionné, e [malɛ̃tɑ̃sjɔne] *adj* nasty, spiteful ▪ **des propos ~s** malicious *ou* spiteful remarks ▪ **être ~ à l'égard de** *ou* **envers qqn** to be ill-disposed towards sb.

malle [mal] *nf* **1.** [valise] trunk ▪ **faire sa ~** *ou* **ses ~ s** to pack one's bags ▶ **se faire la ~** *fam* : **allez, on se fait la ~!** come on, let's split! ▪ **quand je suis revenu, elle s'était fait la ~** when I got back she'd flown the coop **2.** AUTO & *vieilli* boot *UK*, trunk *US*.

malléabilité [maleabilite] *nf* **1.** [souplesse] flexibility, malleability, pliability **2.** MÉTALL malleability.

malléable [maleabl] *adj* **1.** [cire] soft ▪ [caractère, personnalité] easily influenced *ou* swayed *péj* **2.** MÉTALL malleable.

malle-poste [malpɔst] (*pl* **malles-poste**) *nf* mailcoach.

mallette [malɛt] *nf* [valise] suitcase ▪ [porte-documents] attaché case, briefcase ▪ [trousse à outils] tool box.

mal-logé, e [mallɔʒe] (*mpl* **mal-logés**, *fpl* **mal-logées**) *nm, f* person living in bad housing ▪ **les ~s** the badly housed, the poorly housed.

malmener [19] [malməne] *vt* **1.** [brutaliser] to manhandle, to handle roughly **2.** *fig* [traiter sévèrement] to bully, to push around ▪ **un metteur en scène réputé pour ~ ses acteurs** a director renowned for giving actors a rough *ou* hard time ▪ **malmené par la presse** mauled by the press ▪ **malmené par la critique** panned by the critics **3.** SPORT : **~ un adversaire** to give an opponent a hard time, to maul an opponent.

malnutrition [malnytrisjɔ̃] *nf* malnutrition.

malodorant, e [malɔdɔrɑ̃, ɑ̃t] *adj* malodorous *sout*, foul-smelling, smelly.

malotru, e [malɔtry] *nm, f sout* boor, lout, oaf.

malouin, e [malwɛ̃, in] *adj* from Saint-Malo.

Malouines [malwin] *npr fpl* : **les (îles) ~** the Falkland Islands, the Falklands, the Malvinas, *voir aussi* **île.**

mal pensant [malpɑ̃sɑ̃] (*pl* **mal pensants**) *nm* dissenter.

malpoli, e [malpɔli] ◇ *adj* rude, impolite, bad-mannered.
◇ *nm, f* lout, boor, rude man (*f* woman) ▪ **petit ~!** you rude (little) boy!

malpropre [malprɔpr] ◇ *adj* **1.** [crasseux] dirty, filthy, unclean **2.** [mal fait - ouvrage, tâche] shoddy, sloppily done **3.** [inconvenant, impudique] dirty, filthy, smutty **4.** [malhonnête] obnoxious, dishonest, unsavoury.
◇ *nmf* filthy swine ▪ **se faire chasser** *ou* **renvoyer comme un ~** to be sent packing.

malproprement [malprɔprəmɑ̃] *adv* [manger] messily ▪ [travailler] shoddily, sloppily ▪ [agir] vilely, sordidly.

malpropreté [malprɔprəte] *nf* **1.** [aspect sale] dirtiness, filthiness, uncleanliness **2.** [acte malhonnête] low *ou* dirty *ou* filthy trick **3.** [propos indécent] dirty *ou* smutty remark ▪ **dire des ~s** to talk smut.

malsain, e [malsɛ̃, ɛn] *adj* **1.** [nuisible à la santé] unhealthy **2.** [qui va mal - industrie] ailing **3.** [pervers - ambiance] unhealthy ▪ **c'est ~ de laisser les enfants voir de tels films** it's unhealthy *ou* dangerous to let children watch films like that **4.** *fam* [dangereux] : **c'est plutôt ~ par ici** it's a bit dodgy around here ▪ **un quartier ~** a rough *ou* tough area.

malséant, e [malseɑ̃, ɑ̃t] *adj litt* [contraire - aux conventions] unseemly, improper, indecorous ; [- à la décence] indecent, improper.

malsonnant, e [malsɔnɑ̃, ɑ̃t] *adj litt* [inconvenant] offensive.

malt [malt] *nm* malt.

maltage [maltaʒ] *nm* malting.

maltais, e [maltɛ, ɛz] *adj* Maltese.
◆ **Maltais, e** *nm, f* Maltese ▪ **les Maltais** the Maltese.
◆ **maltais** *nm* [chien] Maltese (dog).
◆ **maltaise** *nf* Maltese (blood orange).

Malte [malt] *npr* Malta ▪ **à ~** in Malta, *voir aussi* **île**.

malter [3] [malte] *vt* to malt.

malterie [maltəri] *nf* **1.** [usine] maltings **2.** [processus] malting.

malthusianisme [maltyzjanism] *nm* Malthusianism.

malthusien, enne [maltyzjɛ̃, ɛn] *adj* & *nm, f* Malthusian.

maltraitance [maltrɛtɑ̃s] *nf* (physical) abuse.

maltraiter [4] [maltrete] *vt* **1.** [brutaliser] to ill-treat, to mistreat, to maltreat ▪ **~ sa femme/ses enfants** to batter one's wife/one's children **2.** *fig* [malmener] to misuse ▪ **la pièce a été maltraitée par la critique** the play was mauled by the critics.

malus [malys] *nm* penalty *(claims premium)*.

malveillance [malvɛjɑ̃s] *nf* **1.** [méchanceté] malevolence, spite, malice ▪ **ne voyez là aucune ~ de ma part** please do not think there is any ill will on my part **2.** [intention criminelle] criminal intent, malice aforethought *(terme juridique)*.

malveillant, e [malvɛjɑ̃, ɑ̃t] ◇ *adj* [personne, propos] malicious, spiteful ▪ [sourire] malevolent, malicious ▪ **l'intention ~e a été prouvée** malicious intent has been proved.
◇ *nm, f* malicious *ou* hostile *ou* malevolent person.

malvenu, e [malvəny] *adj* **1.** *sout* [inopportun] untimely, inopportune **2.** [mal formé - arbre, enfant] underdeveloped, malformed.

malversation [malvɛrsasjɔ̃] *nf* embezzlement ▪ **il est coupable de ~s** he is guilty of embezzlement *ou* misappropriation (of funds).

malvoyant, e [malvwajɑ̃, ɑ̃t] ◇ *adj* partially-sighted.
◇ *nm, f* partially sighted person ▪ **les ~s** the partially sighted.

maman [mamɑ̃] *nf* **1.** [terme d'appellation] mum *UK*, mummy *UK*, mom *US* **2.** [mère] mother, mum.

mambo [mɑ̃mbo] *nm* mambo.

mamelle [mamɛl] *nf* **1.** [sein] breast ▪ **la pêche et l'élevage sont les deux ~s de notre économie** *Sully allus* fishing and farming are the lifeblood of our economy **2.** [pis] udder, dug *litt* **3.** [du sabot d'un cheval] side walls.

mamelon [mamlɔ̃] *nm* **1.** [d'une femme] nipple **2.** [colline] hillock, hummock, mamelon *spéc* **3.** [d'un gond] gudgeon.

mamelonné, e [mamlɔne] *adj* **1.** MÉD mamillated *UK*, mammillated *US* **2.** GÉOGR hummocky.

mamelouk [mamluk] *nm* Mameluke.

mamie [mami] *nf fam* granny, grannie.

mammaire [mamɛr] *adj* mammary.

mammectomie [mamɛktɔmi] *nf* mastectomy.

mammifère [mamifɛr] *nm* mammal ▪ **les grands ~s** the higher mammals.

mammographie [mamɔgrafi] *nf* mammography.

mammoplastie [mamɔplasti] *nf* mammoplasty, mammaplasty.

mammouth [mamut] *nm* mammoth.

mamours [mamur] *nmpl fam* cuddle ▪ **faire des ~ à qqn** to cuddle sb.

mam'selle [mamzɛl] *nf fam* Miss ▪ **alors, ma petite ~, ça va?** and how's my little Miss?

mamy [mami] *fam* = **mamie**.

mam'zelle [mamzɛl] *fam* = **mam'selle**.

Man [man] *npr* : **l'île de ~** the Isle of Man.

manade [manad] *nf herd of horses or bulls in the Camargue.*

management [manadʒmɛnt] *nm* COMM & SPORT management.

manager[1] [17] [manadʒe] *vt* COMM & SPORT to manage.

manager[2] [manadʒœr] *nm* COMM & SPORT manager.

managérial, e, aux [manadʒerjal, o] *adj* managerial.

manant [manɑ̃] *nm* **1.** HIST [villageois] villager ▪ [paysan] peasant HIST villein **2.** *litt* [mufle] churl, boor.

manche [mɑ̃ʃ] ◇ *nm* **1.** [d'un outil] handle ▪ **à ~ court** short-handled ▪ **à ~ long** longhandled ➤ **être** *ou* **se mettre du côté du ~** *fam* to side with the winner ▪ **il ne faut jamais jeter le ~ après la cognée** *prov* never say die *prov*, always have another go **2.** △ [personne maladroite] clumsy oaf ▪ **tu t'y prends comme un ~** you're making a right mess of it **3.** AÉRON : **~ à balai** *fam* joystick, control column **4.** MUS neck.
◇ *nf* **1.** [vêtement] sleeve ▪ **sans ~s** sleeveless ▪ **à ~s courtes/longues** short-/long-sleeved ▪ **être en ~s de chemise** to be in one's shirt-sleeves ➤ **~ bouffante/trois-quarts** puff/three-quarter sleeve ▪ **~ gigot/raglan** leg-of-mutton/raglan sleeve ▪ **~ ballon** puff sleeve ▪ **~ chauve-souris** batwing sleeve ▪ **avoir qqn dans sa ~** *fam fig* to have sb in one's pocket **2.** [conduit] : **~ à air** AÉRON wind-sock ; NAUT air shaft ▪ **~ à charbon** coal chute **3.** GÉOGR channel, straits *(sing)* **4.** JEUX [gén] round ▪ [au bridge] game ▪ SPORT [gén] leg ▪ TENNIS set ▪ **gagner la première ~** *fig* to win the first round **5.** *fam loc* **faire la ~** [mendiant] to beg ; [musicien, mime] to busk *UK*, to perform in the streets.

Manche [mɑ̃ʃ] *npr f* **1.** [mer] : **la ~** the (English) Channel **2.** [région d'Espagne] : **la ~** La Mancha **3.** [département] : **la ~** the Manche *(département in Basse-Normandie; chef-lieu: Saint-Lô, code: 50)*.

manchette [mɑ̃ʃɛt] *nf* **1.** [vêtement - décorative] cuff ; [- de protection] oversleeve **2.** PRESSE (front-page) headline ▪ **la nouvelle a fait la ~ de tous les journaux** the news made the headlines *ou* the story was headline news in all the papers **3.** IMPR [note] side note **4.** SPORT forearm smash ▪ ESCRIME slash on the sword wrist.

manchon [mɑ̃ʃɔ̃] *nm* **1.** [vêtement pour les mains] muff ▪ [guêtre] gaiter **2.** TECHNOL [de protection] sleeve, casing ▪ **~ à gaz** *ou* **à incandescence** incandescent mantle **3.** [papeterie, plomberie, verrerie] muff *spéc* **4.** CULIN : **~s de canard** duck drumsticks.

manchot, e [mɑ̃ʃo, ɔt] ◇ *adj* [d'un bras] one-armed ▪ [d'une main] one-handed ▪ **il n'est pas ~** *fam* [il est habile de ses mains] he's clever with his hands ; [il est efficace] he knows how to go about things.
◇ *nm, f* [d'un bras] one-armed person ▪ [d'une main] one-handed person.
◆ **manchot** *nm* ZOOL penguin ▪ **~ empereur** emperor penguin.

mandale△ [mɑ̃dal] *nf* slap (in the face), clout ▪ **tu veux une ~?** do you want a clip round the ear?

mandant, e [mɑ̃dɑ̃, ɑ̃t] *nm, f* **1.** DR principal **2.** POLIT [gén] voter ▪ [d'un député] constituent.

mandarin [mɑ̃darɛ̃] *nm* **1.** HIST mandarin **2.** [personnage influent] mandarin **3.** ZOOL mandarin duck **4.** LING Mandarin Chinese.

mandarine [mɑ̃darin] *nf* mandarin (orange).

mandarinier [mɑ̃darinje] *nm* mandarin tree.

mandat [mɑ̃da] *nm* **1.** DR proxy, power of attorney ■ **donner ~ à qqn pour faire qqch** to give sb power of attorney to do sthg ➤ **~ d'amener** ≃ subpoena *(to accused)* ■ **~ d'arrêt** (arrest) warrant ■ **un ~ d'arrêt à l'encontre de...** a warrant for the arrest of... ■ **~ de comparution** summons ■ **~ de dépôt** committal (order) ■ **~ de justice** (police) warrant ■ **~ de perquisition** search warrant **2.** POLIT [fonction] mandate ■ [durée] term of office ■ **solliciter le renouvellement de son ~** to seek reelection ■ **elle a rempli son ~** POLIT she's fulfilled her mandate ; [gén] she's done what she was asked to do **3.** FIN : **~ (de paiement)** order to pay ■ **~ poste** *ou* **postal** postal order *UK*, money order *US* ■ **~ international** *ou* **sur l'étranger** international money order **4.** HIST : **les pays sous ~ (international)** mandated countries, mandates.

mandataire [mɑ̃datɛr] *nmf* **1.** DR attorney, proxy ■ **constituer un ~** to appoint a proxy **2.** POLIT representative **3.** COMM : **~ aux Halles** sales agent *(at a wholesale market)*.

mandat-carte [mɑ̃dakart] (*pl* **mandats-cartes**) *nm* postal order *UK*, money order *US*.

mandater [3] [mɑ̃date] *vt* **1.** [députer] to appoint, to commission **2.** POLIT : **~ qqn** to elect sb, to give sb a mandate ■ **~ des délégués pour un congrès** to mandate delegates to a conference **3.** FIN to pay by postal order *UK ou* money order *US* **4.** DR [donner un mandatement] to make *ou* to issue an order to pay.

mandat-lettre [mɑ̃dalɛtr] (*pl* **mandats-lettres**) *nm* postal order *UK ou* money order *US (with space for a short message)*.

mandature [mɑ̃datyr] *nf* term of office.

mandchou, e [mɑ̃dʃu] *adj* Manchu, Manchurian.

Mandchourie [mɑ̃dʃuri] *npr f* : **(la) ~** Manchuria.

mander [3] [mɑ̃de] *vt litt & vieilli* to send for *(insép)*.

mandibule [mɑ̃dibyl] *nf* ANAT & ZOOL mandible.
◆ **mandibules** *nfpl fam* **jouer des ~s** to munch away.

mandoline [mɑ̃dɔlin] *nf* **1.** MUS mandolin, mandoline **2.** [hachoir] (vegetable) slicer, mandolin, mandoline.

mandragore [mɑ̃dragɔr] *nf* mandrake, mandragora.

mandrill [mɑ̃dril] *nm* mandrill.

mandrin [mɑ̃drɛ̃] *nm* **1.** [pour soutenir - sur un tour] mandril, mandrel ; [- sur une machine-outil] chuck ■ **~ à griffes/mâchoires** claw/jaw chuck **2.** [pour percer] punch ■ [pour agrandir des trous] drift **3.** MÉTALL swage, mandrel **4.** [papeterie] mandrel, core.

manège [manɛʒ] *nm* **1.** ÉQUIT [salle] manege ■ [école] riding school, manege ■ [exercices] riding exercises, manege work **2.** LOISIRS : **~ (de chevaux de bois)** merry-go-round, roundabout ■ **la foire a installé ses ~s** the fun fair has set up its attractions *ou* machines *ou* shows **3.** [comportement sournois] (little) game ■ **tu copies sur ton frère, j'ai bien vu ton (petit) ~** you've been cribbing from your brother's work, I've seen what you're up to *ou* I'm on to your little game ‖ [comportement mystérieux] : **j'observai quelques instants ce ~** I watched these goings-on for a few minutes ■ **je ne comprenais rien à leur ~** I couldn't figure out what they were up to **4.** DANSE manège **5.** [piste de cirque] ring.

mânes [man] *nmpl* **1.** ANTIQ manes **2.** *litt* spirits ■ **les ~ de nos ancêtres** the spirits of our ancestors.

manette [manɛt] *nf* (hand) lever, (operating) handle ■ **~ des gaz** AÉRON throttle (control *ou* lever) ■ **~ de jeux** INFORM joystick.

manga [mɑ̃ga] *nf* manga (comic).

manganate [mɑ̃ganat] *nm* manganate.

manganèse [mɑ̃ganɛz] *nm* manganese.

mangeable [mɑ̃ʒabl] *adj* [comestible] edible ■ [médiocre] (just about) edible *ou* eatable ■ **c'est bon? – c'est ~** is it good? – it's edible.

mangeaille [mɑ̃ʒaj] *nf* **1.** *vieilli* [pâtée d'animaux - gén] feed ; [- pour cochons] (pig) swill **2.** *péj* [nourriture] food.

mange-disque [mɑ̃ʒdisk] (*pl* **mange-disques**) *nm* slot-fed record player.

mangeoire [mɑ̃ʒwar] *nf* [pour le bétail] trough, manger ■ [pour les animaux de basse-cour] trough.

manger[1] [mɑ̃ʒe] *nm* food, meal ■ **je suis en train de lui faire son ~** *fam* I'm getting his food ready (for him).

manger[2] [17] [mɑ̃ʒe] ◇ *vt* **1.** [pour s'alimenter] to eat ■ **~ un sandwich** to eat a sandwich ; [au lieu d'un repas] to have a sandwich ■ **elle mange de tout** she'll eat anything, she's not a fussy eater ■ **elle a tout mangé** she's eaten it all up ■ **tu mangeras bien un morceau?** you'll have a bite to eat, won't you? ■ **qu'est-ce que vous avez mangé aujourd'hui à la cantine, les enfants?** what did you have (to eat) for dinner at school today, children? ■ **on en mangerait** it looks good enough to eat ■ **on s'est fait ~ par les moustiques** *fam fig* we were bitten to death by mosquitoes ➤ **~ de la vache enragée** *fam* to have a hard time of it ■ **il a mangé du lion aujourd'hui** *fam* he's full of beans today ■ **il ne mange pas de ce pain-là** he doesn't go in for that sort of thing, that's not his cup of tea ■ **il peut me ~ la soupe sur la tête** *fam* [il est beaucoup plus grand] he's a head taller than me ; [il est bien meilleur] he's miles better than me ■ **~ le morceau** *fam* to talk, to sing△ ■ **~ les pissenlits par la racine** *fam* to be pushing up (the) daisies
2. *fig* to eat ■ **elle ne va pas te ~!** she's not going to eat *ou* to bite you! ■ **elle le mangeait des yeux** [personne] she (just) couldn't take her eyes off him ; [objet] she gazed longingly at it ■ **~ qqn de baisers** to smother sb with kisses ■ **il est mignon, on le mangerait!** he's so cute I could eat him (all up)!
3. [ronger] : **~ ses ongles** to bite one's nails ■ **couvertures mangées aux mites** *ou* **par les mites** moth-eaten blankets ■ **une statue mangée par l'air marin** a statue eaten away by the sea air
4. [prendre toute la place dans] : **tes cheveux te mangent la figure** your hair is hiding your face ■ **elle avait de grands yeux qui lui mangeaient le visage** her eyes seemed to take up her whole face
5. [négliger] : **~ ses mots** *ou* **la moitié des mots** to swallow one's words, to mumble, to mutter
6. [dépenser] to get through *(insép)* ■ **~ son capital** to eat up one's capital ■ **la chaudière mange un stère de bois tous les cinq jours** the boiler gets through *ou* eats up *ou* consumes a cubic metre of wood every five days ➤ **~ son blé en herbe** to spend one's money even before one gets it ■ **on peut toujours essayer, ça ne mange pas de pain** *fam* we can always have a go, it won't cost us anything.
◇ *vi* **1.** [s'alimenter] to eat ■ **~ dans une assiette** to eat off a plate ■ **apprends-lui à ~ correctement à table** teach her some (proper) table manners ■ **il a bien mangé** [en quantité ou en qualité] he's eaten well ■ **il faut ~ léger** you should eat light meals ■ **~ à sa faim** to eat one's fill ■ **nous ne mangions pas tous les jours à notre faim** we didn't always have enough food *ou* enough to eat ■ **faire ~ qqn** to feed sb ➤ **~ comme un cochon** *fam* to eat like a pig ■ **~ comme quatre** *fam ou* **comme un ogre** *ou* **comme un chancre**△ to eat like a horse ■ **~ comme un moineau** to eat like a sparrow ■ **~ du bout des dents** to pick at one's food ■ **~ sur le pouce** to have a snack, to grab a bite to eat ■ **il faut ~ pour vivre et non pas vivre pour ~** *Molière allus* one must eat to live and not live to eat ■ **il mange à tous les râteliers** *péj* he's got a finger in every pie
2. [participer à un repas] to eat ■ **venez ~!** [à table!] come and get it! ■ **venez ~ demain soir** come to dinner tomorrow evening ■ **ils m'ont demandé de rester ~** they asked me to stay for a meal ■ **inviter qqn à ~** [chez soi] to ask sb round to eat ; [au restaurant] to ask sb out for a meal ■ **allez, je vous invite à ~** [au restaurant] come on, I'll buy you a meal ■ **on a eu les Michaud à ~** *fam* we had the Michauds round for a meal ■ **~ dehors** *ou* **au restaurant** to eat out ■ **c'est un restaurant simple mais on y mange bien** it's an unpretentious restaurant, but the food is good
3. [comme locution nominale] : **je veux à ~** I want something to eat ■ **as-tu eu assez à ~?** have you had enough to eat? ■ **donne**

à ~ **au chat** feed the cat ■ **faire à ~ à qqn** to make something to eat for sb ■ **que veux-tu que je fasse à ~ ce soir?** what would you like me to cook *ou* to make for dinner (tonight)?

◆ **se manger** ◇ *vp (emploi passif)* to be eaten ■ **ça se mange avec de la mayonnaise** you eat it *ou* it is served with mayonnaise ■ **cette partie ne se mange pas** you don't eat that part, that part shouldn't be eaten *ou* isn't edible.

◇ *vp (emploi réciproque) fam* [se disputer] to have a set-to ▶ **se ~ le nez** to quarrel.

mange-tout [mɑ̃ʒtu] *nm inv* BOT [haricot] (French) mange-tout bean ■ [petit pois] mangetout, sugar pea.

mangeur, euse [mɑ̃ʒœr, øz] *nm, f* eater ■ **c'est un gros ~** he's a big eater, he eats a lot ■ **~ de : les Asiatiques sont de gros ~s de riz** people from Asia eat a lot of rice *ou* are big rice-eaters ▶ **mangeuse d'hommes** *fam* man-eater.

mangouste [mɑ̃gust] *nf* mongoose.

mangrove [mɑ̃grɔv] *nf* mangrove swamp.

mangue [mɑ̃g] *nf* BOT mango.

manguier [mɑ̃gje] *nm* mango (tree).

maniabilité [manjabilite] *nf* **1.** [d'un outil] manageability, practicability ■ **une caméra d'une grande ~** a camera which is very easy to handle | [d'une voiture] handling ability, manoeuvrability **2.** [plasticité - de l'argile] plasticity ; [- du béton] workability.

maniable [manjabl] *adj* **1.** [facile à utiliser - outil] handy, practical, easy to use *ou* to handle ■ [facile à travailler - cuir] easy to work **2.** [manœuvrable - voiture] easy to drive *ou* to handle ; [- tondeuse] easy to handle *ou* to manoeuvre **3.** NAUT : **temps ~** fine weather ■ **vent ~** moderate wind **4.** [docile] tractable, malleable **5.** [matière plastique] plastic ■ [béton] workable ■ **l'argile est une matière ~** clay is an easily moulded material.

maniaco-dépressif, ive [manjakɔdepresif, iv] (*mpl* **maniaco-dépressifs**, *fpl* **maniaco-dépressives**) ◇ *adj* manic-depressive ■ **psychose maniaco-dépressive** manic depression.

◇ *nm, f* manic-depressive.

maniaque [manjak] ◇ *adj* **1.** [obsessionnel] fussy, fastidious ■ **il range ses livres avec un soin ~** he's obsessively *ou* fanatically tidy about his books | [exigeant] fussy **2.** PSYCHOL manic ■ **état ~** mania.

◇ *nmf* **1.** [personne - trop difficile] fussy person ; [- qui a une idée fixe] fanatic ■ **c'est une ~ de la propreté** she's always got a duster in her hand ■ **enfin, un logiciel pour les ~s de l'orthographe/des mots croisés!** at last, a software package for spelling/crossword buffs! **2.** [dément] maniac ■ **~ sexuel** sexual pervert, sex maniac.

maniaquerie [manjakri] *nf* fussiness, pernicketiness ■ **son exactitude frôle la ~** there's something almost obsessive about her punctuality.

manichéen, enne [manikeɛ̃, ɛn] ◇ *adj* **1.** RELIG Manichean, Manichaean **2.** *fig* **il est très ~** he sees everything in very black-and-white terms.

◇ *nm, f* Manichean, Manichaean.

manichéisme [manikeism] *nm* **1.** RELIG Manicheism, Manichaeism, Manichaeanism **2.** *fig* rigid *ou* uncompromising approach to things ■ **faire du ~** to see things in black and white.

manie [mani] *nf* **1.** [idée fixe] obsession, quirk ■ **avoir la ~ de la propreté** to be obsessively clean *ou* a stickler for cleanliness ■ **il a la ~ de fermer toutes les portes** he has a habit of always closing doors ■ **c'est une ~, chez toi!** it's an obsession with you! ■ **ça tourne à la ~** *fam* it's getting to be a fixation *ou* an obsession ■ **chacun a ses petites ~s** everyone has his own peculiar ways *ou* little quirks **2.** PSYCHOL mania.

maniement [manimɑ̃] *nm* **1.** [manipulation] handling, operating ■ **nous cherchons à simplifier le ~ de nos appareils** we're trying to make our equipment easier to handle *ou* to operate ■ **rompu au ~ des affaires/des foules** *fig* used to handling business/manipulating crowds ■ **à l'armée ils sont initiés au ~ des armes** in the army they learn how to use a gun ▶ **~ d'armes** MIL (arms) drill **2.** [des animaux de boucherie] points (in fatstock).

manier [9] [manje] *vt* **1.** [manipuler - objet, somme] to handle ■ **facile/difficile à ~** easy/difficult to handle **2.** [utiliser] to use, to operate ■ **une imprimante portative très facile à ~** an easy-to-use portable printer ■ **elle sait ~ la caméra** she's good with a cine camera ■ **il savait ~ la plume** he was a fine writer ■ **il sait ~ l'ironie** he knows how *ou* when to use irony **3.** [modeler - pâte] to knead ; [- argile] to handle, to fashion.

◆ **se manier** *vpi fam* to get a move on, to hurry up.

manière [manjɛr] *nf* **1.** [façon, méthode] way, manner ■ **d'une ~ bizarre** in a strange manner, strangely ■ **il y a différentes ~s d'accommoder le riz** there are many ways of preparing rice ■ **nous ne faisons pas les choses de la même ~** we don't do things (in) the same way ▶ **user de** *ou* **employer la ~ forte** to use strong-arm tactics ■ **il fallait bien que je lui dise la vérité – oui mais il y a ~ et ~** I had to tell him the truth – yes, but there are different ways of doing it

2. GRAMM manner ■ **adjectif/adverbe de ~** adjective/adverb of manner

3. [savoir-faire] : **avec les gosses, il a la ~** *fam* he's got a way *ou* he's good with kids ■ **il faut avoir la ~** you've got to have the knack ■ **refusez, mais mettez-y la ~** say no, but do it with tact

4. [style] way, style ■ **sa ~ de marcher/s'habiller** his way of walking/dressing, the way he walks/dresses ■ **il a une drôle de ~ de dire merci** he has a funny way of saying thank you people | ART & CINÉ manner, style ■ **un tableau dans la ~ de Watteau** a painting in the manner *ou* style of Watteau ■ **un Truffaut première/dernière ~** an early/late Truffaut

5. *sout* **une ~ de** [une sorte de] a *ou* some sort of, a *ou* some kind of ■ **c'est une ~ de poème épique** it's a sort of (an) epic *ou* an epic of sorts.

◆ **manières** *nfpl* [façons de se comporter] manners ■ **belles ~s** social graces ■ **bonnes ~s** (good) manners ■ **je vais t'apprendre les bonnes ~s, moi!** I'll teach you to be polite *ou* to behave yourself! ■ **mauvaises ~s** bad manners ■ **qu'est-ce que c'est que ces** *ou* **en voilà des ~s!** what a way to behave! | *péj* [minauderies] : **cesse de faire des ~s et prends un chocolat** stop pussyfooting around and have a chocolate ■ **sans ~s** without (a) fuss.

◆ **à la manière** *loc adv* : **à la ~ paysanne** in the peasant way *ou* manner.

◆ **à la manière de** *loc prép* **1.** [dans le style de] in the manner *ou* style of ■ **une chanson à la ~ de Cole Porter** a song in the style of Cole Porter

2. *(comme nom)* ART & LITTÉR : **un à la ~ de** a pastiche.

◆ **à ma manière, à sa manière** *etc loc adv* in my/his/her *etc* (own) way ■ **elle dit qu'elle l'aime à sa ~** she says she loves him in her own way.

◆ **de cette manière** *loc adv* (in) this *ou* that way.

◆ **de la belle manière, de la bonne manière** *loc adv iron* properly, well and truly.

◆ **de la manière que** *loc conj* as.

◆ **de la même manière** *loc adv* in the same way.

◆ **de manière à** *loc conj* so as to, so that, in order to.

◆ **de manière (à ce) que** *loc conj* [pour que] so (that) ■ **laisse la porte ouverte, de ~ que les gens puissent entrer** leave the door open so people can come in.

◆ **de telle manière que** *loc conj* in such a way that.

◆ **de toute manière, de toutes les manières** *loc adv* anyway, in any case *ou* event, at any rate ■ **de toute ~, tu as tort** in any case, you're wrong.

◆ **d'une certaine manière** *loc adv* in a way ■ **d'une certaine ~, je suis content que ce soit fini** in a way, I'm glad it's over.

◆ **d'une manière générale** *loc adv* **1.** [globalement] on the whole

2. [le plus souvent] generally, as a general rule.

◆ **d'une manière ou d'une autre** *loc adv* somehow (or other), one way or another.

◆ **en aucune manière** *loc adv* in no way, on no account, under no circumstances ■ **est-ce de sa faute? – en aucune ~** is it his fault? – no, not in the slightest *ou* least ■ **avez-vous eu connaissance des documents? – en aucune ~** did you get to see the documents? – no, not at all.

◆ **en manière de** *loc prép* by way of.

◆ **en quelque manière** *loc adv sout* in a way, as it were.

◆ **par manière de** = en manière de.

maniéré, e [manjere] *adj* **1.** [personne] affected ▪ **elle est tellement ~e dans sa façon de parler!** she has such an affected way of speaking! **2.** [style] mannered.

maniérisme [manjerism] *nm* **1.** [comportement] mannerism *sout*, affectation **2.** ART mannerism, Mannerism.

maniériste [manjerist] *adj & nmf* mannerist, Mannerist.

manieur, euse [manjœr, øz] *nm, f* : **~ d'argent** businessman ▪ **manieuse d'argent** businesswoman ▪ **c'est un ~ d'hommes** he's a leader of men *ou* a born leader.

manif [manif] *nf fam* demo ▪ **une ~ lycéenne/étudiante** a student protest.

manifestant, e [manifɛstɑ̃, ɑ̃t] *nm, f* demonstrator.

manifestation [manifɛstasjɔ̃] *nf* **1.** POLIT demonstration ▪ **une ~ contre le nucléaire** an anti-nuclear demonstration **2.** [marque] expression ▪ **des ~s de joie** expressions of joy **3.** [événement] event ▪ **~ artistique/sportive** artistic/sporting event ▪ **parmi les ~s musicales de l'été** among the summer's music events *ou* musical attractions **4.** MÉD sign, symptom **5.** RELIG manifestation.

manifeste [manifɛst] ◇ *adj sout* [évident] obvious, evident, manifest *sout* ▪ **n'est-ce pas une preuve ~ de son innocence?** isn't it clear proof of her innocence? ▪ **tel était son désir, rendu ~ dans son testament** such was her wish, as manifested in her will ▪ **erreur ~** obvious *ou* manifest error.
◇ *nm* **1.** LITTÉR & POLIT manifesto ▪ **'le Manifeste du parti communiste'** ***Marx, Engels*** 'The Communist Manifesto' **2.** AÉRON manifest ▪ NAUT (ship's) manifest.

manifestement [manifɛstəmɑ̃] *adv* evidently, obviously, plainly ▪ **~, elle nous a menti** she has plainly been lying to us.

manifester [3] [manifɛste] ◇ *vt* **1.** [exprimer] to express ▪ **~ son mécontentement à qqn** to indicate *ou* to express one's dissatisfaction to sb ▪ **~ son soutien à qqn** to assure sb of one's support ▪ **~ un désir** to express *ou* to indicate a wish ▪ **a-t-elle manifesté le désir d'être enterrée près de son mari?** was it her wish that she should be buried near her husband? **2.** [révéler] to show, to demonstrate ▪ **rien ne manifestait son désespoir intérieur** nothing indicated her inner despair ▪ **sans ~ la moindre irritation/admiration** without the slightest show of anger/admiration.
◇ *vi* to demonstrate ▪ **~ contre qqch** to demonstrate against sthg.
◆ **se manifester** *vpi* **1.** [personne] to come forward ▪ RELIG to become manifest ▪ **que le gagnant se manifeste, s'il vous plaît!** would the (lucky) winner step *ou* come forward please! ▪ **bon élève, mais devrait se ~ plus/moins souvent en classe** good student, but should contribute more/be quieter in class ▪ **le livreur ne s'est pas manifesté** the delivery man didn't show *ou* turn up **2.** [sentiment] to show ▪ [phénomène] to appear ▪ **sa joie de vivre se manifeste dans toutes ses toiles** her joie de vivre is expressed *ou* expresses itself in every one of her paintings.

manigance [manigɑ̃s] *nf (souvent au pl)* scheme, trick ▪ **à cause des ~s internes au conseil d'administration** on account of internal machinations at board level ▪ **victime de toutes sortes de ~s** victim of all kinds of scheming.

manigancer [16] [manigɑ̃se] *vt* to scheme, to plot ▪ **~ une évasion** to plot *ou* to engineer an escape ▪ **l'affaire a été manigancée pour déshonorer le ministre** the whole affair was set up to discredit the minister ▪ **je me demande ce que les enfants sont en train de ~** I wonder what the children are up to ▪ **toujours en train de ~ quelque chose** always up to some little game.

manille [manij] ◇ *nf* **1.** TECHNOL shackle, clevis ▪ NAUT shackle ▪ **~ d'assemblage** connecting shackle **2.** [jeu] manille *(French card game)* ▪ [carte] ten.
◇ *nm* **1.** [cigare] Manila (cigar) **2.** [chapeau] Manila hat.

Manille [manij] *npr* Manila.

manioc [manjɔk] *nm* manioc, cassava ▪ **farine de ~** cassava.

manip(e) [manip] *nf fam* **1.** [coup monté] frame-up **2.** ÉDUC practical, experiment **3.** [manipulation] manipulation.

manipulateur, trice [manipylatœr, tris] *nm, f* **1.** [opérateur] technician ▪ **~ de laboratoire** laboratory technician **2.** *péj* manipulator **3.** LOISIRS conjurer, conjuror.
◆ **manipulateur** *nm* **1.** MÉCAN : **~ à distance** remote-control manipulator **2.** TÉLÉCOM sending *ou* signalling key ▪ **~ automatique** automatic key.

manipulation [manipylasjɔ̃] *nf* **1.** [maniement] handling ▪ INFORM manipulation ▪ **s'exercer à la ~ des concepts mathématiques** *fig* to learn to handle *ou* to manipulate mathematical concepts **2.** ÉDUC & SC experiment, piece of practical work ▪ **~ génétique, ~s génétiques** genetic engineering **3.** MÉD manipulation ▪ **~ vertébrale** (vertebral) manipulation **4.** LOISIRS conjuring trick **5.** *péj* [intervention] interference, manipulation ▪ [coup monté] : **~s électorales** vote rigging.

manipuler [3] [manipyle] *vt* **1.** [manier - objet, somme] to handle ▪ INFORM to manipulate **2.** *péj* [influencer - opinion] to sway, to manipulate ; [- scrutin] to rig ; [- statistiques] to massage ; [- comptes] to fiddle ▪ **elle s'est fait complètement ~ par ce type** she allowed the guy to twist her around his little finger.

manitou [manitu] *nm* **1.** ANTHR manitu, manitou **2.** *fig* **(grand) ~** big shot *ou* chief ▪ **les grands ~s du pétrole** oil magnates *ou* tycoons ▪ **c'est un grand ~ de la finance** he's a big wheel in finance.

manivelle [manivɛl] *nf* **1.** MÉCAN crank ▪ **démarrer à la ~** to crank (up) the engine ▶ **bras/course de ~** crank arm/throw **2.** [de pédalier] pedal crank.

manne [man] *nf* **1.** BIBLE manna **2.** [aubaine] godsend, manna ▪ **la ~ céleste** manna from heaven **3.** ENTOM mayfly swarms **4.** BOT manna **5.** [panier] (large) wicker basket *ou* crate.

mannequin [mankɛ̃] *nm* **1.** [de vitrine] dummy, mannequin ▪ [de couture] dummy ▪ [de défilé] model ▪ **~ homme** male model ▪ **elle est ~ chez Zoot** she works as a model for Zoot **2.** *fig & péj* [fantoche] puppet **3.** ART lay figure **4.** [panier] small (two-handled) basket.

manœuvrabilité [manœvrabilite] *nf* manoeuvrability ▪ **à sa sortie, le véhicule a été acclamé pour sa ~** when it was launched, the vehicle was praised for its easy handling.

manœuvrable [manœvrabl] *adj* [maniable] easy to handle, manoeuvrable.

manœuvre [manœvr] ◇ *nf* **1.** [maniement] operation, handling ▪ **apprendre la ~ d'un fusil/d'un télescope** to learn how to handle a rifle/to operate a telescope **2.** [en voiture] manoeuvre **3.** [opération] : **fausse ~** *pr & fig* wrong move ▪ **une fausse ~ au clavier et tu risques d'effacer ton document** one simple keying error is enough to erase your document **4.** MIL [instruction] drill ▪ [simulation] exercise ▪ [mouvement] movement ▪ **les ~s, les grandes ~s** *vieilli* (army) manoeuvres ▪ **être en ~s** [à petite échelle] to be on exercise ; [à grande échelle] to be on manoeuvres ▪ **~ de repli** (movement of) withdrawal **5.** NAUT manoeuvre ▪ **le bateau a commencé sa ~ d'accostage** the ship has started docking ▶ **fausses ~s** preventer rigging *ou* stays **6.** *péj* [machination] manoeuvre ▪ **~s électorales** electioneering ▪ **la principale victime de ces ~s, c'est la démocratie** democracy is the first victim of this political manoeuvring **7.** MÉD manipulation ▪ **~ obstétricale** turning (of the baby) **8.** ASTRONAUT manoeuvre **9.** RAIL shunting *UK*, switching *US*.
◇ *nm* [ouvrier] unskilled worker ▪ CONSTR & TRAV PUB labourer ▪ **~ agricole** farm labourer *ou* hand ▪ **~ spécialisé** skilled worker.

manœuvrer [5] [manœvre] ◇ *vt* **1.** [faire fonctionner] to work, to operate ▪ **le monte-charge est manœuvré à la main** the hoist is hand-operated **2.** [faire avancer et reculer - véhicule] to manoeuvre ▪ *(en usage absolu)* **ne manœuvrez jamais sur une route à grande circulation** don't manoeuvre *ou* do any manoeuvring on a busy road **3.** [influencer] to manipulate **4.** PÊCHE to pull in.
◇ *vi* **1.** [agir] to manoeuvre ▪ **bien manœuvré!** clever *ou* good move! ▪ **ils manœuvrent tous pour devenir chef du parti** *péj* they're all jockeying for the position of party leader ▪ **~ dans l'ombre** to work behind the scenes **2.** MIL [s'exercer] to drill

■ **faites-les ~ dans la cour** drill them in the yard ‖ [simuler] to be on manoeuvres ■ **ils sont partis ~ sur la lande** they're off to the moors on manoeuvres.

manœuvrier, ère [manœvrije, ɛr] ◇ *adj* [tactique] skilful.
◇ *nm, f* [tacticien] tactician ■ [manipulateur] manoeuvrer ■ **un fin ~ de la politique** a clever political manoeuvrer.

manoir [manwar] *nm* manor (house), (country) mansion.

manomètre [manɔmɛtr] *nm* manometer.

manouche [manuʃ] *nmf* & *adj* Gypsy, Gipsy.

manquant, e [mɑ̃kɑ̃, ɑ̃t] ◇ *adj* missing ■ **désolé, ce titre est ~ pour le moment** sorry but we're temporarily out of this book *ou* this book's out of stock at the moment ■ **les soldats ~s à l'appel** the soldiers missing at roll-call.
◇ *nm, f* missing one ■ **les ~s** [élèves] the absent pupils.
◆ **manquant** *nm* COMM short fall.

manque[1] [mɑ̃k] *nm* **1.** [insuffisance] : **~ de** [imagination, place, sommeil] lack of ; [appartements, denrées] shortage of, scarcity of ; [personnel] lack of, shortage of ■ **~ de chance** *ou* **de bol** *fam* *ou* **de pot** *fam* hard *ou* tough luck ■ **être en ~ d'affection** to be in need of affection ■ **par ~ de** [originalité, audace] through lack of, for lack of, for want of ; [main-d'œuvre] through lack *ou* shortage of **2.** [absence - d'une personne] gap ■ **quand il sera parti, il y aura un ~** his departure will leave a gap **3.** [de drogue] : **être en (état de) ~** to have *ou* to feel withdrawal symptoms **4.** ÉCON & DR : **~ à gagner** loss of (expected) income *ou* earnings ■ **il y aura un ~ à gagner de 2 000 euros** there will be a shortfall of 2,000 euros **5.** JEUX manque **6.** COUT & TEXT slipped stitch.
◆ **manques** *nmpl* [insuffisances] failings, shortcomings ■ [lacunes] gaps ■ **elle n'a pas conscience de ses ~s** she's not conscious of her shortcomings.

manque[2] [mɑ̃k] ◆ **à la manque** *loc adj fam* pathetic.

manqué, e [mɑ̃ke] *adj* **1.** [non réussi - attentat] failed ; [- vie] wasted ; [- occasion] missed, lost ; [- tentative] failed, abortive, unsuccessful ; [- photo, sauce] spoilt ■ **je vais essayer de toucher la pomme – ~!** I'll try and hit the apple – missed! **2.** [personne] : **c'est un cuisinier/un médecin ~** he should've been a cook/a doctor.
◆ **manqué** *nm* CULIN ≃ sponge cake.

manquement [mɑ̃kmɑ̃] *nm* *sout* **~ à la discipline** breach of *ou* lapse in discipline ■ **~ à un devoir** dereliction of duty ■ **~ à une règle** breach *ou* violation of a rule.

manquer [3] [mɑ̃ke] ◇ *vt* **1.** [laisser échapper - balle] to miss, to fail to catch ; [- marche, autobus] to miss ■ **l'église est à droite, vous ne pouvez pas la ~** the church is on the right, you can't miss it ■ **~ le but** SPORT to miss the goal ■ **~ son but** *fig* to fail to reach one's goal ■ **~ la cible** MIL to miss the target ; *fig* to miss one's target, to fail to hit one's target, to shoot wide ■ **il l'a manqué de peu** he just missed it ■ **elle s'est moquée de moi mais je ne la manquerai pas!** *fig* she made a fool of me but I'll get even with her! ■ **je n'ai pas vu l'opéra – tu n'as rien manqué/tu as manqué quelque chose!** I didn't see the opera – you didn't miss anything/you really missed something there! ■ **c'est une émission à ne pas ~** this programme shouldn't be missed *ou* is a must ■ **~ une occasion** to miss (out on) an opportunity ■ **tu as manqué une bonne occasion de te taire** *hum* why couldn't you have just kept your mouth shut for once? ▶ **il n'en manque jamais une!** [il remarque tout] he never misses a trick! ; [il est gaffeur] (you can always) trust him to put his foot in it!
2. [ne pas rencontrer] to miss
3. [ne pas réussir - concours] to fail ; [- photo, sauce] to spoil, to make a mess of ■ **tu as manqué ta vocation** *pr* & *hum* you've missed your vocation ▶ **coup manqué** failure, botch-up ■ **moi qui croyais lui faire plaisir, c'est vraiment un coup manqué** *ou* **j'ai vraiment manqué mon coup!** and here's me thinking I would make him happy, (just) how wrong can you get!
4. [ne pas aller à] to miss.
◇ *vi* **1.** [être absent - fugueur, bouton, argenterie] to be missing ; [- employé, élève] to be away *ou* off *ou* absent ■ **~ à l'appel** MIL to be absent (at roll call) ; *fig* & *hum* to be missing ■ *(tournure impersonnelle)* *iron* **il ne manquait plus qu'elle/que ça!** she's/that's all we need *ou* needed! ■ **il ne manquerait plus qu'elle tombe enceinte!** it would be the last straw if she got pregnant!
2. [être insuffisant] to be lacking, to be in short supply ■ **quand le pain vint à ~, ils descendirent dans la rue** when the bread ran short, they took to the streets ■ **les occasions de te rendre utile ne manqueront pas** there will be no shortage of opportunities to make yourself useful ■ **la pluie/le travail, ce n'est pas ce qui manque!** there's no shortage of rain/work! ■ **~ à qqn : le pied m'a manqué** I lost my footing ■ **l'argent leur a toujours manqué** they've always been short of money *ou* lacked money ■ **la force/le courage lui manqua** (his) strength/courage failed him ■ **les mots me manquent** words fail me, I'm at a loss for words ■ **ce n'est pas l'envie qui m'en manque, mais...** not that I don't want to *ou* I'd love to, but... ■ *(tournure impersonnelle)* **il manque une bouteille/un bouton** there's a bottle/a button missing ■ **il nous manque trois joueurs** [ils sont absents] we have three players missing ; [pour jouer] we're three players short ■ **il ne manquait plus rien à son bonheur** his happiness was complete ■ **il ne manque pas de gens pour dire que...** there is no lack *ou* shortage of people who say that... ■ **il me manque un dollar** I'm one dollar short, I need one dollar ■ **il ne lui manque que la parole** [animal] the only thing it can't do is speak ; [machine] it does everything but talk
3. [être pauvre] to want ■ **elle a toujours peur de ~** she's always afraid of having to go without.
◆ **manquer à** *v+prép* **1.** [faillir à] : **~ à son devoir/son honneur** to fail in one's duty/one's honour ■ **~ à ses devoirs** to neglect one's duties ■ **~ à sa parole/promesse** to fail to keep one's word/promise, to break one's word/promise ■ **~ au règlement** to break the rules ■ **~ aux usages** to defy *ou* to flout convention
2. [être regretté par] : **ses enfants lui manquent** he misses his children
3. *litt* [offenser] to be disrespectful to *ou* towards, to behave disrespectfully towards.
◆ **manquer de** *v+prép* **1.** [ne pas avoir assez de] to lack, to be short of ■ **nous n'avons jamais manqué de rien** we never went short of anything ■ **ta soupe manque de sel** your soup lacks *ou* needs salt ■ **ça manque de musique!** *fam* we could do with some music! ■ **on manque d'air dans la chambrette du haut** there's no air in the little upstairs bedroom ■ **~ de personnel** to be short-staffed, to be short of staff ■ **je manque de sommeil** I'm not getting enough sleep ▶ **toi, tu ne manques pas d'air** *fam* *ou* **de culot**△ **!** you've (certainly) got some cheek *ou* nerve!
2. *sout* **ne pas ~ de dire/de faire** [ne pas oublier de] : **vous viendrez? – je n'y manquerai pas** will you come? – definitely *ou* without fail ■ **ne manquez pas de me le faire savoir** be sure to let me know, do let me know ■ **il n'a pas manqué de faire remarquer mon retard** he didn't fail to point out that I was late ‖ [par ellipse] : **ça ne manquera pas** it's sure *ou* bound to happen ■ **j'ai dit qu'elle reviendrait et ça n'a pas manqué!** I said she'd come back and sure enough(, she did)! ‖ [s'empêcher de] : **on ne peut ~ de constater/penser** one can't help but notice/think ■ **vous ne manquerez pas d'être frappé par cette coïncidence** you're bound to be struck by this coincidence
3. [faillir] : **elle a manqué (de) se noyer** she nearly *ou* almost drowned (herself).
◆ **se manquer** ◇ *vp (emploi réciproque)* : **nous nous sommes manqués à l'aéroport** we missed each other at the airport.
◇ *vp (emploi réfléchi)* to fail (in one's suicide attempt).

Mans [mɑ̃] *npr m* : **Le ~** Le Mans ■ **les 24 Heures du ~** the Le Mans 24-hour race.

mansarde [mɑ̃sard] *nf* [chambre] garret, attic (room).

mansardé, e [mɑ̃sarde] *adj* [chambre, étage] attic *(modif)* ■ [toit] mansard *(modif)* ■ **une pièce ~e** an attic room, a room with a sloping ceiling.

mansuétude [mɑ̃sɥetyd] *nf* *sout* indulgence, goodwill, mansuetude *sout*.

mante [mɑ̃t] *nf* **1.** ENTOM : **~ (religieuse** *ou* **prie-Dieu)** (praying) mantis **2.** ZOOL manta ray **3.** [vêtement] mantle.

manteau [mɑ̃to] *nm* **1.** [vêtement de ville] coat ■ [capote] greatcoat ■ **~ de fourrure** fur coat **2.** *fig* & *litt* [épaisse couche] layer, blanket, mantle *sout* ▪ **un lourd ~ de neige/silence** a heavy mantle of snow/silence **3.** ZOOL [d'un mollusque] mantle **4.** ARCHIT : **~ de cheminée** mantelpiece, mantel **5.** GÉOL mantle **6.** HÉRALD mantling, mantle **7.** ORNITH back, mantle **8.** *loc* **sous le ~** unofficially, on the sly ▪ **sous le ~ de** under cover of, under the cloak of.

mantelet [mɑ̃tlɛ] *nm* **1.** [cape - de femme] mantelet ; [- de prélat] mantelleta **2.** MIL mantelet **3.** NAUT deadlight.

mantille [mɑ̃tij] *nf* [vêtement] mantilla *(scarf)*.

mantisse [mɑ̃tis] *nf* mantissa.

Mantoue [mɑ̃tu] *npr* Mantua.

manucure [manykyr] <> *nmf* manicurist.
<> *nf* manicure.

manucurer [3] [manykyre] *vt* to manicure ▪ **se faire ~ les mains** to have a manicure.

manuel, elle [manɥɛl] <> *adj* **1.** [commande, métier, travailleur] manual ▪ [outil] hand-held **2.** AÉRON : **passer en ~** to switch (over) to manual.
<> *nm, f* **1.** [personne habile de ses mains] practical person ▪ **c'est une ~le** she's good with her hands **2.** SOCIOL manual worker.
◆ **manuel** *nm* [mode d'emploi, explications] manual, handbook ▪ **~ d'histoire/de géographie** history/geography book *ou* textbook ▪ **~ scolaire** ÉDUC (school) textbook ▪ **~ d'utilisation** instruction book *ou* manual ▪ **~ de vol** AÉRON flight manual.

manuellement [manɥɛlmɑ̃] *adv* manually, by hand ▪ **travailler ~** to work with one's hands ▪ **un dispositif qui fonctionne ~** a manually operated machine.

manufacturable [manyfaktyrabl] *adj* manufacturable ▪ **ces produits ne sont pas ~s dans nos usines** these products cannot be manufactured in our factories.

manufacture [manyfaktyr] *nf* **1.** [atelier] factory ▪ HIST manufactory ▪ **~ de soie/pipes** silk/pipe factory ▪ **la ~ des Gobelins** the Gobelins tapestry workshop **2.** [fabrication] manufacture, manufacturing.

manufacturer [3] [manyfaktyre] *vt* to manufacture.

manufacturier, ère [manyfaktyrje, ɛr] <> *adj* manufacturing.
<> *nm, f arch* industrialist, factory owner.

manu militari [manymilitari] *loc adv* **1.** [par la violence] by force ▪ **être expulsé ~** to be forcibly expelled, to be frogmarched out **2.** DR [par la gendarmerie] by the forces of law and order.

manuscrit, e [manyskri, it] *adj* [lettre] handwritten ▪ [page, texte] manuscript *(modif)*.
◆ **manuscrit** *nm* **1.** [à publier] manuscript ▪ **~ dactylographié** manuscript, typescript **2.** [texte ancien] : **~ (ancien)** ancient manuscript ; [sous forme de rouleau] scroll ▪ **les ~s de la mer Morte** the Dead Sea Scrolls.

manutention [manytɑ̃sjɔ̃] *nf* **1.** [manipulation] handling **2.** [entrepôt] warehouse, store house.

manutentionnaire [manytɑ̃sjɔnɛr] *nmf* warehouseman ▪ **il est ~ dans une fabrique de meubles** he's a packer in a furniture factory.

manutentionner [3] [manytɑ̃sjɔne] *vt* [déplacer] to handle ▪ [emballer] to pack.

maoïsme [maɔism] *nm* Maoism.

maoïste [maɔist] *adj* & *nmf* Maoist.

maori, e [maɔri] *adj* Maori.
◆ **Maori, e** *nm, f* Maori.

Mao Tsé-toung [maotsetuŋ], **Mao Zedong** [maodzedɔ̃g] *npr* Mao Tse-tung, Mao Zedong.

maous, ousse△ [maus] *adj* ginormous△, whopping (great).

mappemonde [mapmɔ̃d] *nf* [globe] globe ▪ [carte] map of the world *(showing both hemispheres)* ▪ **~ céleste** planisphere.

maquer [3] △ [make] ◆ **se maquer**△ *vp+prép* to shack with ▪ **elle est maquée?** [prostituée] has she got a pimp? ; [femme] has she got a man?

maquereau, x [makro] *nm* **1.** ZOOL mackerel **2.** △ [souteneur] pimp.

maquerelle△ [makrɛl] *nf* madam.

maquette [makɛt] *nf* **1.** [modèle réduit] (scale) model ▪ **~ d'avion/de village** model aircraft/village **2.** ART [d'une sculpture] model, maquette ▪ [d'un dessin] sketch **3.** IMPR [de pages] paste-up, layout ▪ [de livre] dummy **4.** INDUST mock-up, (full-scale) model.

maquettiste [makɛtist] *nmf* **1.** [modéliste] model maker **2.** IMPR graphic designer, layout artist.

maquignon [makiɲɔ̃] *nm* **1.** [marchand - de chevaux] horse trader ; [- de bestiaux] cattle trader **2.** *péj* [entremetteur] trickster.

maquignonnage [makiɲɔnaʒ] *nm* **1.** [vente - de chevaux] horse trading ; [- de bétail] cattle trading **2.** *péj* [manœuvre douteuse] sharp practice, shady dealing, wheeler-dealing.

maquignonner [3] [makiɲɔne] *vt* [bétail, cheval] to deal *ou* to trade *ou* to traffic in.

maquillage [makijaʒ] *nm* **1.** [cosmétiques] make-up ▪ [application] making-up **2.** [falsification - d'un passeport, d'un texte] doctoring, faking ; [- de preuves] doctoring ; [- d'un véhicule] disguising, respraying.

maquiller [3] [makije] *vt* **1.** [visage] to make up *(sép)* ▪ **être bien/mal/trop maquillé** to be nicely/badly/heavily made up ▪ **qui vous a maquillé?** who did your make-up? **2.** [falsifier - passeport, texte] to falsify, to fake ; [- preuves] to falsify ; [- comptes] to fiddle *esp* UK, to falsify ; [- véhicule] to disguise ▪ **~ un crime en suicide** to make a murder look like a suicide.
◆ **se maquiller** *vp (emploi réfléchi)* : **se ~ (le visage)** to make up (one's face), to put on one's make-up ▪ **se ~ les yeux** to put one's eye make-up on ▪ **tu te maquilles déjà à ton âge?** are you using make-up already at your age?

maquilleur, euse [makijœr, øz] *nm, f* make-up man *(f* girl), make-up artist ▪ **passer chez le ~** TV to have one's make-up put on.

maquis [maki] *nm* **1.** GÉOGR scrub, scrubland, maquis **2.** HIST : **le Maquis** the Maquis *(French Resistance movement)* ▪ **prendre le ~** HIST to take to the maquis ; *fig* to go underground.

maquisard [makizar] *nm* **1.** HIST maquis, French Resistance fighter **2.** [guérillero] guerrilla fighter.

marabout [marabu] *nm* **1.** [oiseau, plume] marabou, marabout **2.** [homme, tombeau] marabout.

marabouter [3] [marabute] *vt* [en Afrique] to put the evil eye on.

maraîchage [marɛʃaʒ] *nm* market gardening UK, truck farming *ou* gardening US.

maraîcher, ère [marɛʃe, ɛr] <> *nm, f* market gardener UK, truck farmer US.
<> *adj* vegetable *(modif)* ▪ **produits ~s** market garden produce UK, truck US.

marais [marɛ] *nm* **1.** [terrain recouvert d'eau] marsh, swamp ▪ **~ salant** salt marsh, salina **2.** [région] marsh, marshland, bog.

Marais [marɛ] *npr m* **1.** [quartier] : **le ~** the Marais *(historic district of Paris)* **2.** HIST : **le ~** the Marais *ou* the Swamp *(moderate party in the French Revolution)*.

LE MARAIS

One of the oldest areas in Paris, the Marais is known for its 17th century aristocratic residences (***hôtels particuliers***), art galleries, boutiques and smart cafés. It is home to Paris's oldest Jewish community, centered around the rue des Rosiers.

marasme [marasm] *nm* **1.** ÉCON slump, stagnation ▪ **nous sommes en plein ~** we're going through a slump, our economy's in the doldrums **2.** [apathie] listlessness, apathy, depression **3.** MÉD marasmus, cachexia.

marasquin [maraskɛ̃] *nm* maraschino ■ **cerises au ~** maraschino cherries.

marathon [maratɔ̃] *nm* **1.** SPORT marathon *(avant n)* ■ [épreuve d'endurance] : **~ de danse** dance marathon **2.** *fig* **~ diplomatique/électoral** diplomatic/electoral marathon **3.** *(comme adj inv; avec ou sans trait d'union)* marathon ■ **discussion/séance ~** marathon discussion/session.

marathonien, enne [maratɔnjɛ̃, ɛn] *nm, f* marathon runner.

marâtre [maratr] *nf* **1.** [méchante mère] unnatural *ou* wicked mother **2.** [belle-mère] stepmother.

maraud, e [maro, od] *nm, f* ***vieilli*** rascal, rapscallion.

maraudage [marodaʒ] *nm* pilfering *(of food)*.

maraude [marod] *nf* pilfering *(of food)* ■ **un taxi en ~** a cruising taxi.

marauder [3] [marode] *vi* **1.** [personne] to filch *ou* to pilfer (food) ■ [soldat] to maraud **2.** [taxi] to cruise.

maraudeur, euse [marodœr, øz] ◇ *nm, f* [gén] pilferer ■ [soldat] marauder.
◇ *adj* [renard] on the prowl ■ [oiseau] thieving ■ [taxi] cruising.

marbre [marbr] *nm* **1.** MINÉR marble ■ **~ veiné** streaked *ou* veined marble ■ **~ tacheté** mottled marble ■ **colonne/tombeau de ~** marble pillar/tomb ■ **mur en faux ~** marbleized wall **2.** ART marble (statue) ■ **les ~s romains** the Roman marbles ‖ [plaque] marble plate **3.** IMPR (forme) bed ■ **mettre sur le ~** [journal] to put to bed ; [livre] to put on the press ■ **rester sur le ~** to be excess copy **4.** MÉCAN surface plate **5.** [au baseball] home base, home plate.
◆ **de marbre** *loc adj* **1.** [insensible] insensitive ■ **la mort de sa mère l'a laissé de ~** his mother's death left him cold *ou* unmoved **2.** [impassible] impassive ■ **un visage de ~** a poker face.

marbré, e [marbre] *adj* **1.** [tacheté] marbled, mottled ■ [veiné] veined ■ **peau ~e** blotchy skin **2.** CONSTR marbleized.

marbrer [3] [marbre] *vt* **1.** [papier, tranche de livre] to marble **2.** [peau] to mottle, to blotch ■ **jambes/joues marbrées par le froid** legs/cheeks mottled with the cold.

marbrerie [marbrəri] *nf* **1.** [industrie] marble industry **2.** [atelier] marble (mason's) yard **3.** [métier, art] marble work ■ **~ funéraire** monumental (marble) masonry.

marbrier, ère [marbrije, ɛr] *adj* marble *(modif)*.
◆ **marbrier** *nm* marbler ■ **~ (funéraire)** monumental mason.

marbrure [marbryr] *nf* [aspect marbré] marbling ■ [imitation] marbleizing, marbling.
◆ **marbrures** *nfpl* blotches, streaks, veins.

marc [mar] *nm* **1.** [résidu de fruit] marc ■ **~ (de café)** coffee grounds *ou* dregs **2.** [eau-de-vie] marc (brandy) **3.** FIN mark.

Marc [mark] *npr* : **~ Antoine** Mark Antony ■ **~ Aurèle** Marcus Aurelius.

marcassin [markasɛ̃] *nm* young wild boar ■ **cuissot de ~** haunch of wild boar.

marchand, e [marʃɑ̃, ɑ̃d] ◇ *nm, f* [négociant] merchant, shopkeeper *UK*, storekeeper *US* ■ [sur un marché] stallholder ■ **~ ambulant** (street) pedlar ■ **~ de biens** ≃ estate agent *UK*, ≃ real estate agent *US* ■ **~ de canons** *péj* arms dealer ■ **~ de chaussures** shoe shop owner *UK*, shoe-store owner *US* ■ **~ de fleurs** florist ■ **~ de frites** ≃ chip shop man *UK* ■ ≃ hot-dog stand man *US* ■ **~ de fruits** fruit merchant, fruiterer ■ **~ d'illusions** *péj* illusionmonger ■ **~ de journaux** [en boutique] newsagent ; [en kiosque] newsstand man, newsvendor ■ **~ de légumes** greengrocer ■ **~ de marée** *ou* **de poisson** fishmonger ■ **~ des quatre-saisons** costermonger *UK*, fruit and vegetable seller *US* ■ **~ de tableaux/tapis** art/carpet dealer ■ **~ de vin** wine merchant, vintner ■ **le ~ de sable est passé** the sandman's on his way.
◇ *adj* **1.** [valeur, prix] market *(modif)* ■ [denrée] marketable ■ [qualité] standard **2.** [rue] shopping *(modif)* ■ [ville] market, commercial **3.** [marine] merchant.

marchandage [marʃɑ̃daʒ] *nm* **1.** [discussion d'un prix] haggling, bargaining ■ **faire du ~** to haggle **2.** *péj* [tractation] wheeler-dealing *péj* **3.** DR illegal subcontracting.

marchander [3] [marʃɑ̃de] ◇ *vt* **1.** [discuter le prix de] to bargain *ou* to haggle over *(insép)* **2.** *(au nég)* [lésiner sur] to spare ■ **ils n'ont pas marchandé leur effort** they spared no effort **3.** DR to subcontract (illegally).
◇ *vi* to haggle, to bargain.

marchandeur, euse [marʃɑ̃dœr, øz] *nm, f* haggler.
◆ **marchandeur** *nm* DR (illegal) subcontractor.

marchandise [marʃɑ̃diz] *nf* **1.** [produit] commodity, good ■ **~s** merchandise ■ **notre boucher a de la bonne ~** our butcher sells good quality meat ‖ [article interdit] : **la ~ est arrivée à bon port** the stuff got here all right **2.** [fret, stock] : **la ~** the goods, the merchandise ➤ **~ en gros/au détail** wholesale/retail goods ■ **wagon de ~s** goods wagon *UK*, freight car *US* **3.** *fam fig* **tromper** *ou* **voler qqn sur la ~** *pr* & *fig* to swindle sb ■ **il vend sa ~** *péj* he's plugging his own stuff.

marche [marʃ] *nf* **1.** [activité, sport] walking ■ **la ~ (à pied)** walking ■ **la ~ en montagne** hill walking ■ **elle fait de la ~** [comme sport] she goes walking ■ **la frontière n'est qu'à une heure de ~** the border is only an hour's walk away
2. [promenade] walk ■ **nous avons fait une ~ de 8 km** we did an 8 km walk
3. [défilé] march ■ **ouvrir la ~** to lead the way ■ **fermer la ~** to bring up the rear ➤ **~ nuptiale/funèbre/militaire** MUS wedding/funeral/military march ■ **~ silencieuse/de protestation** silent/protest march ■ **~ pour la paix** peace march
4. MIL march ■ **en avant, ~!** forward, march! ➤ **~ forcée** forced march
5. [allure] pace, step ■ **il régla sa ~ sur celle de l'enfant** he adjusted his pace to the child's ■ **ralentir sa ~** to slow (down) one's pace ‖ [démarche] walk, gait ■ **sa ~ gracieuse** her graceful gait
6. [déplacement - d'un train, d'une voiture] running ; [- d'une étoile] course ■ **dans le sens de la ~** facing the engine ■ **dans le sens contraire de la ~** (with one's) back to the engine ➤ **~ avant/arrière** AUTO forward/reverse gear ■ **entrer/sortir en ~ arrière** to reverse in/out, to back in/out ■ **faire ~ arrière** [conducteur] to reverse, to back up ; *fig* to backpedal, to backtrack ■ **en voyant le prix j'ai fait ~ arrière** when I saw the price I backed out of buying it
7. [fonctionnement - d'une machine] running, working ■ **~, arrêt** on, off ■ **en (bon) état de ~** in (good) working order ■ **ne pas ouvrir pendant la ~** do not open while the machine is running ■ [d'une entreprise, d'un service] running, working, functioning ■ **pour assurer la bonne ~ de notre coopérative** to ensure the smooth running of our co-op ➤ **~ à suivre** [instructions] directions (for use) ; [pour des formalités] procedure, form
8. [progression] : **la ~ du temps** the passing *ou* march ***sout*** of time ■ **la ~ des événements** the course *ou* march ***sout*** of events ■ **la révolution est en ~** revolution is on the march *ou* move
9. [degré - d'un escalier] step, stair ; [- d'un marchepied] step ■ **la première/dernière ~** the bottom/top step ■ **descendre/monter les ~s** to go down/up the stairs ■ **attention à la ~** mind the step
10. HIST & GÉOGR march.
◆ **en marche** *loc adv* : **monter/descendre d'un train en ~** to get on/off a moving train ■ **je suis descendue du bus en ~** I got off the bus while it was still moving ■ **mettre en ~** [moteur, véhicule] to start (up) ; [appareil] to switch *ou* to turn on *(sép)* ■ **le four se mettra automatiquement en ~ dans une heure** the oven will turn *ou* switch itself on automatically in an hour.

marché[1] [marʃe] *nm* **1.** [en ville] market ■ **aller au ~** to go to the market ■ **je l'ai acheté au ~** I bought it at the market ■ **faire les ~s** [commerçant] to go round *ou* to do the markets ➤ **~ aux poissons/bestiaux** fish/cattle market ■ **~ couvert** covered market ■ **~ en plein air** open-air market ■ **~ d'intérêt national** wholesale market for agricultural produce ■ **~ aux puces** flea market ■ [ce que l'on achète] : **faire son ~** to go (grocery) shopping

2. COMM & ÉCON market ▪ **~ du travail** labour market ▪ **~ extérieur/intérieur** foreign/home market, overseas/domestic market ▪ **mettre un produit sur le ~** to launch a product ▪ **le vaccin n'est pas encore sur le ~** the vaccine is not yet (available) on the market ▪ **il n'y a pas de ~ pour ce type d'habitation** there is no market for this type of housing ⊙ **le Marché commun** the Common Market ▪ **~ libre** free market ▪ **~ noir** black market ▪ **faire du ~ noir** to deal on the black market ▪ **le Marché unique (européen)** the Single (European) Market ▪ **le Grand Marché (européen)** the European Market ▪ **étude/économie de ~** market research/economy
3. BOURSE market ▪ **~ d'actions** stock market ▪ **~ des capitaux** capital market ▪ **~ des changes** foreign exchange market ▪ **~ au comptant** spot market ▪ **~ du crédit** credit market ▪ **~ financier** capital *ou* financial market ▪ **~ obligataire** bond market ▪ **~ secondaire** resale market ▪ **~ des titres** stock market
4. [accord] deal, transaction ▪ **conclure** *ou* **passer un ~ avec qqn** to make a deal with sb ▪ **~ conclu!** it's a deal!, that's settled! ⊙ **c'est un ~ de dupes** it's a con
5. *loc* **par-dessus le ~** *fam* into the bargain, what's more.
◆ **à bon marché** *loc adv* cheaply ▪ **fabriqué à bon ~** cheaply-made ▪ **je l'ai eu à bon ~** I got it cheap.
◆ **bon marché** ◇ *loc adj* cheap, inexpensive.
◇ *loc adv* : **il a fait bon ~ de mes conseils** he took no notice of my advice.
◆ **meilleur marché** *loc adj inv* cheaper ▪ **je l'ai eu meilleur ~ à Paris** I got it cheaper in Paris.

marché² [marʃe] *nm* SPORT travelling.

marchepied [marʃəpje] *nm* **1.** [d'un train] step, steps ▪ [d'un camion] footboard ▪ [d'une voiture] running board ▪ **~ amovible** retractable step **2.** *fig* [tremplin] stepping stone ▪ **ce petit rôle lui a servi de ~ pour devenir célèbre** this small role put him on the road to fame **3.** [estrade] dais ▪ [banc] footstool ▪ [escabeau] pair of steps **4.** [sur une berge] footpath.

marcher [3] [marʃe] *vi* **1.** [se déplacer à pied] to walk ▪ **j'ai marché longtemps/un peu** I took a long/short walk ▪ **~ sans but** to walk aimlessly ▪ **~ tranquillement** to amble along ▪ **descendre une avenue en marchant lentement/rapidement** to stroll/to hurry down an avenue ▪ **~ à grands pas** *ou* **à grandes enjambées** to stride (along) ▪ **~ à petits pas** to take small steps ▪ **~ à quatre pattes** to walk on all fours ▪ **~ à reculons** to walk backwards ▪ **~ de long en large (dans une salle)** to walk up and down (a room) ▪ **~ sur la pointe des pieds** to walk on tiptoe ▪ **~ sur les mains** to walk on one's hands ▪ **~ sur les traces de qqn** to follow in sb's footsteps ▪ **~ vers** *pr* to walk towards, to be headed for, to be on one's way to ; *fig* to be headed for ⊙ **~ droit** *pr* to walk straight *ou* in a straight line ; *fig* to toe the line ▪ **~ sur des œufs** to tread gingerly
2. MIL to march ▪ **~ au pas** to march in step ▪ **~ sur une ville/sur l'ennemi** to march on a city/against the enemy
3. [poser le pied] : **~ sur** to step *ou* to tread on ▪ **~ dans** [flaque, saleté] to step *ou* to tread in ▪ **ne marche pas sur les fleurs!** keep off the flowers!, don't walk on the flowers! ▪ **~ sur les pieds de qqn** to tread *ou* to stand *ou* to step on sb's feet ⊙ **il ne faut pas se laisser ~ sur les pieds** you shouldn't let people walk all over you
4. [fonctionner - machine] to work, to function ; [- moteur] to run ▪ **~ à l'électricité** to work *ou* to run on electricity ▪ **le jouet marche à piles** the toy is battery-operated ▪ **faire ~** [machine] to work, to operate ▪ **tu sais faire ~ la machine à laver?** do you know how to work the washing machine? ▪ **les trains ne marchent pas aujourd'hui** *fam* the trains aren't running today
5. [donner de bons résultats - manœuvre, ruse] to come off, to work ; [- projet, essai] to be working (out), to work ; [- activité, travail] to be going well ▪ **ses études marchent bien/mal** she's doing well/not doing very well at college ▪ **elle marche bien en chimie/au tennis** *fam* she's doing well in chemistry/at tennis ▪ **un jeune athlète qui marche très fort** *fam* an up-and-coming young athlete ▪ **les affaires marchent mal/très bien** business is slack/is going well ▪ **ça fait ~ les affaires** it's good for business *ou* for trade ▪ **rien ne marche** nothing's going right ▪ **ne t'inquiète pas, ça va ~** don't worry, it'll be OK ▪ **et le travail, ça marche?** how's work (going)? ▪ **si ça marche, je monterai une exposition** if it works out, I'll organize an exhibition ▪ **leur couple/commerce n'a pas marché** their relationship/business didn't work out ▪ **ça a l'air de bien ~ entre eux** they seem to be getting on fine together, things seem to be going well between them ▪ [en voiture] : **tu marches à combien, là?** *fam* what are you doing *ou* what speed are you doing at the moment?
6. [au restaurant] : **faites ~ deux œufs au plat!** two fried eggs! ▪ **ça marche!** coming up!
7. *fam* [s'engager] to go along with things ▪ **tu marches avec nous?** can we count you in? ▪ **je ne marche pas!** nothing doing!, count me out! ▪ **~ dans une affaire** to get mixed up *ou* involved in a scheme ▪ **elle ne marchera jamais** she'll never agree
8. *fam* [croire] to fall for it ⊙ **je lui ai dit que ma tante était malade et il n'a pas marché, il a couru** *hum* I told him that my aunt was ill and he bought the whole story *ou* and he swallowed it hook, line and sinker ▪ **faire ~ qqn** [le taquiner] to pull sb's leg, to have sb on *UK* ; [le berner] to take sb for a ride, to lead sb up the garden path.

marcheur, euse [marʃœr, øz] *nm, f* **1.** [gén - SPORT] walker ▪ **c'est un bon ~** he's a good walker **2.** [manifestant] marcher.

marcottage [markɔtaʒ] *nm* layering ▪ **~ aérien** air layering.

mardi [mardi] *nm* Tuesday ▪ **Nice, le ~ 10 août** Nice, Tuesday, August 10 *ou* 10 August *UK* ▪ **je suis né un ~ 18 avril** I was born on Tuesday the 18th of April ▪ **nous sommes ~ aujourd'hui** today's Tuesday ▪ **je reviendrai ~** I'll be back on Tuesday ▪ **~ dernier/prochain** last/next Tuesday ▪ **ce ~, ~ qui vient** this (coming) Tuesday, Tuesday next, next Tuesday ▪ **~ en huit** a week on Tuesday, Tuesday week *UK* ▪ **~ en quinze** a fortnight on Tuesday *UK*, two weeks from Tuesday *US* ▪ **il y aura huit jours ~** a week on Tuesday ▪ **tous les ~s** every Tuesday, on Tuesdays ▪ **l'autre ~** [dans le passé] (the) Tuesday before last ; [dans l'avenir] Tuesday after this ▪ **le premier/dernier ~ du mois** the first/last Tuesday of the month ▪ **un ~ sur deux** every other *ou* every second Tuesday ▪ **~ matin/après-midi** Tuesday morning/afternoon ▪ **~ midi** Tuesday lunchtime, Tuesday (at) noon ▪ **~ soir** Tuesday evening *ou* night ▪ **~ dans la nuit** Tuesday (during the) night ▪ **dans la nuit de ~ à mercredi** Tuesday night ▪ **la séance/le marché du ~** the Tuesday session/market ⊙ **Mardi gras** RELIG Shrove Tuesday ; [carnaval] Mardi Gras ▪ **ce n'est pas Mardi gras, aujourd'hui!** *fam* what do you think this is, a carnival or something?

mare [mar] *nf* **1.** [pièce d'eau] pond ▪ **~ aux canards** duck pond **2.** [de sang, d'essence] pool.

marécage [marekaʒ] *nm* [terrain bourbeux] marshland, swamp ▪ **les ~s** the swamp.

marécageux, euse [marekaʒø, øz] *adj* [région] marshy, swampy ▪ [champ] boggy ▪ [plante] marsh *(modif)*.

maréchal, aux [mareʃal, o] *nm* **1.** MIL [en France] marshal ▪ [en Grande-Bretagne] field marshal ▪ [aux États-Unis] five star general, general of the army ▪ **Maréchal de France** Marshal of France ▪ **~ des logis** sergeant **2.** HIST & MIL marshal *(in a royal household)*.

maréchale [mareʃal] *nf* **1.** MIL (field) marshal's wife **2.** MIN forge coal.

maréchalerie [mareʃalri] *nf* **1.** [métier] blacksmith's trade, farriery *UK spéc*, smithery *spéc* **2.** [atelier] blacksmith's (shop), smithy, farriery *UK spéc*.

maréchal-ferrant [mareʃalferɑ̃] (*pl* **maréchaux-ferrants**) *nm* blacksmith, farrier *UK*.

maréchaussée [mareʃose] *nf* **1.** HIST mounted constabulary *UK ou* police **2.** *fam hum* constabulary *UK*.

marée [mare] *nf* **1.** GÉOGR tide ▪ **(à) ~ haute/basse** (at) high/low tide ▪ **grande/faible ~** spring/neap tide ▪ **~ montante** flowing *ou* flood tide ▪ **~ descendante** ebb tide ▪ **lorsque la ~ monte/descend** when the tide is rising/ebbing, when the tide comes in/goes out ▪ **changement de ~** turn *ou* turning of the tide ▪ **une ~ humaine** *fig* a flood of people ⊙ **~ d'équinoxe** equinoctial tide ▪ **~ noire** ÉCOL oil slick **2.** [poissons] (fresh) fish, (fresh) seafood.

marégraphe [maregraf] *nm* tide gauge.

marelle [marɛl] *nf* hopscotch ■ **jouer à la ~** to play hopscotch.

marémoteur, trice [maremɔtœr, tris] *adj* tidal.

marengo [marɛ̃go] ◇ *adj inv* CULIN ⊳ **veau**.
◇ *nm* TEXT *black cloth flecked with white.*

mareyeur, euse [marɛjœr, øz] *nm, f* fish and seafood wholesaler.

margarine [margarin] *nf* margarine.

marge [marʒ] *nf* **1.** [espace blanc] margin ● **~ extérieure** IMPR outside margin ■ **~ intérieure** back *ou* inside *ou* inner margin ■ **~ de tête** head *ou* top margin ■ **~ de pied** tail **2.** *fig* extra time, leeway ■ **avoir de la ~** to have some leeway ■ **~ de manœuvre** room for manoeuvre ■ **prévoir une ~ d'erreur de 15 cm/de 100 euros** to allow for a margin of error of 15 cm/of 100 euros ■ **~ de sécurité** safety margin ■ **~ de tolérance** (range of) tolerance ■ **je vous donne 2 m de tissu/2 mois, comme ça, vous avez de la ~** I'll give you 2 m of cloth/2 months, that'll be more than enough **3.** COMM : **~ bénéficiaire** profit margin ■ **~ commerciale** gross profit *ou* margin ■ **~ de fluctuation** fluctuation band.
◆ **en marge** ◇ *loc adj* [original] fringe *(modif)* ■ **un artiste en ~** an unconventional *ou* a fringe artist ■ **annotations** *ou* **notes en ~** notes in the margin, marginalia *formal.*
◇ *loc adv* **1.** [d'une feuille de papier] in the margin **2.** [à l'écart] : **vivre en ~** to live on the fringe *ou* fringes (of society).
◆ **en marge de** *loc prép* : **vivre en ~ de la société** to live on the fringe *ou* margin *ou* edge of society ■ **les événements en ~ de l'histoire** footnotes to history, marginal events in history.

margelle [marʒɛl] *nf* edge *(of a well or fountain).*

marger [17] [marʒe] *vt* **1.** IMPR to feed in *(sép)*, to lay on *(sép)* **2.** [machine à écrire] to set the margins of.

margeur, euse [marʒœr, øz] *nm, f* [ouvrier] layer-on.
◆ **margeur** *nm* **1.** IMPR (paper) feed **2.** [sur une machine à écrire] margin setter.

marginal, e, aux [marʒinal, o] ◇ *adj* **1.** [secondaire - problème, rôle] marginal, minor, peripheral **2.** [à part] : **groupe ~** POLIT fringe group ; SOCIOL marginal group ■ **avec la crise, leur existence est de plus en plus ~e** the economic crisis is pushing them further and further out to the margins *ou* fringes of society **3.** ÉCON marginal **4.** [annotation] marginal.
◇ *nm, f* dropout ■ **ça a toujours été un ~** he's always been a bit of a dropout.

marginalement [marʒinalmɑ̃] *adv* : **vivre ~** to live on the fringe *ou* margin of society.

marginalisation [marʒinalizasjɔ̃] *nf* SOCIOL marginalization ■ **la pauvreté est un facteur de ~** poverty is one of the causes of marginalization.

marginaliser [3] [marʒinalize] *vt* to marginalize ■ **la toxicomanie a marginalisé une partie de la jeunesse** drug addiction has marginalized a large number of young people.
◆ **se marginaliser** ◇ *vp (emploi réfléchi)* to opt out ■ **elle a choisi de se ~** she has chosen to live outside the mainstream of society.
◇ *vpi* **1.** [personne] : **il se marginalise de plus en plus depuis son licenciement** he's been feeling increasingly isolated since he was made redundant **2.** [rôle, fonction] to become marginalized *ou* irrelevant ■ **le rôle du parti s'est marginalisé** the party no longer plays a central role.

marginalité [marʒinalite] *nf* **1.** [d'un problème, d'un rôle] minor importance, insignificance, marginality **2.** [d'une personne] nonconformism ■ **vivre** *ou* **être dans la ~** to live on the fringe *ou* fringes of society ■ **ils ont préféré vivre dans la ~** they preferred to opt out.

margoulette [margulɛt] *nf fam* **se casser la ~** to fall flat on one's face.

marguerite [margərit] *nf* **1.** BOT daisy ■ **grande ~** oxeye daisy **2.** IMPR daisy wheel.

mari [mari] *nm* husband ■ **comment va ton petit ~?** *fam* how's your hubby?

mariable [marjabl] *adj* marriageable.

mariage [marjaʒ] *nm* **1.** [union] marriage ■ **proposer le ~ à qqn** to propose (marriage) to sb ■ **il m'avait promis le ~** he had promised to marry me ■ **donner sa fille en ~** to give one's daughter in marriage ■ **je ne pense pas encore au ~** I'm not thinking about getting married yet ■ **faire un ~ d'amour** to marry for love, to make a love match ■ **faire un ~ d'argent** *ou* **d'intérêt** to marry for money ■ **~ arrangé** arranged marriage ■ **~ de convenance** *ou* **de raison** marriage of convenience ■ **enfants (nés) d'un premier ~** children from a first marriage ■ **enfants nés hors du ~** children born out of wedlock ‖ [vie commune] married life, matrimony *sout* ● **~ blanc** unconsummated marriage, marriage in name only ■ **~ mixte** mixed marriage ■ **'le Mariage de Figaro'** *Beaumarchais* 'The Marriage of Figaro' **2.** [cérémonie] wedding ■ [cortège] wedding procession ■ **de ~** wedding *(modif)* ■ **~ en blanc** white wedding ■ **~ civil/religieux** civil/church wedding **3.** [d'arômes] blend, mixture ■ [de couleurs] combination ■ [d'associations, d'organisations] merging **4.** JEUX [au bésigue] marriage.

MARIAGE

In France, a civil ceremony (which takes place at the *mairie*) is required of all couples wishing to marry, though some choose to have a church wedding as well. The traditional wedding involves a long and sumptuous meal at which the wedding cake, a pyramid of caramel-covered profiteroles (the *pièce montée*), is served.

marial, e, als *ou* **aux** [marjal, o] *adj* Marian.

Marianne [marjan] *npr* [figure] Marianne *(personification of the French Republic).*

MARIANNE

Marianne is the personification of the French Republic; there is a bust of her in every town hall in France, and her portrait appears on French stamps. Her face has changed over the years, but she can always be recognized by the ***bonnet phrygien*** she wears. Brigitte Bardot and Catherine Deneuve, and in more recent years Inès de la Fressange and Laetitia Casta, have been used as models for Marianne.

Marie [mari] *npr* **1.** RELIG Mary ■ **la Vierge ~** the Virgin Mary **2.** HIST : **~ Stuart** Mary Stuart.

marié, e [marje] *adj* married ■ **il est ~ avec Maud** he's married to Maud ■ **on n'est pas ~s, dis donc!** *fam* just a minute, you're not my mother!
◆ **marié** *nm* : **le (jeune) ~** the groom, the bridegroom ■ **futur ~** bridegroom-to-be.
◆ **mariée** *nf* : **la (jeune) ~e** the bride ■ **une robe de ~e** a wedding dress ● **future ~e** bride-to-be.
◆ **mariés** *nmpl* : **les ~s** [le jour de la cérémonie] the bride and groom ■ **les futurs ~s** the bride and groom-to-be ■ **les jeunes ~s** the newly-weds.

Marie-Antoinette [mariɑ̃twanɛt] *npr* Marie Antoinette.

marie-couche-toi-là△ [marikuʃtwala] *nf inv péj & vieilli* trollop, strumpet.

marie-jeanne△ [mariʒan] *nf inv arg crime* pot, Mary-Jane *US.*

marie-louise [marilwiz] (*pl* **maries-louises**) *nf* **1.** [passe-partout] inner frame **2.** [encadrement] harmonized border.

Marie-Madeleine [marimadlɛn] *npr* Mary Magdalene.

marier [9] [marje] *vt* **1.** [unir] to marry, to wed *litt* ■ **le maire/le prêtre les a mariés hier** the mayor/the priest married them yesterday **2.** [donner en mariage] to marry ■ **elle a encore un fils/une fille à ~** she still has a son/a daughter to marry off ■ **elle est bonne à ~** she's of marriageable age **3.** [parfums, couleurs] to blend, to combine, to marry *sout* ■ [styles, sons] to harmonize, to combine, to marry *sout.*
◆ **se marier** *vpi* **1.** [personnes] to get married, to marry, to wed *litt* ■ **se ~ à** *ou* **avec qqn** to marry sb, to get married to sb ■ **il veut se ~ à l'église** he wants to have a church wedding *ou*

to get married in church **2.** [couleurs, arômes, styles] to go together ■ **ça se marie bien avec le vert** it goes nicely with the green.

marie-salope [marisalɔp] (*pl* **maries-salopes**) *nf* **1.** [péniche] hopper (barge) ■ [drague] dredger **2.** △ [souillon] slut△.

marieur, euse [marjœr, øz] *nm, f* matchmaker.

Marignan [mariɲɑ̃] *npr*: **la bataille de ~** *famous victory of Francis I over the Swiss Holy League in 1515.*

marihuana [marirwana], **marijuana** [mariʒɥana] *nf* marijuana.

marin, e [marɛ̃, in] *adj* **1.** [air, courant, sel] sea *(modif)* ■ [animal, carte] marine, sea *(modif)* ■ [plante, vie] marine ■ **paysage ~** seascape **2.** INDUST du pétrole offshore.
◆ **marin** *nm* **1.** [gén] seaman, seafarer ■ **un peuple de ~s** a seafaring nation **2.** MIL & NAUT seaman, sailor ■ **costume/béret de ~** sailor suit/hat ⊃ **~s marchands** *ou* **du commerce** merchant seamen ■ **simple ~** able *ou* able-bodied seaman ■ **~ d'eau douce** *hum* Sunday sailor, landlubber.

marina [marina] *nf* marina.

marinade [marinad] *nf* marinade ■ **viande en ~** marinated *ou* marinaded meat.

marine [marin] ◇ *f* ▻ **marin**.
◇ *adj inv* navy (blue).
◇ *nf* **1.** NAUT navy ■ **~ marchande** merchant navy *ou* marine ■ **~ de plaisance** yachting **2.** MIL : **~ (de guerre)** navy **3.** ART seascape.
◇ *nm* **1.** [fusilier marin - britannique] Royal Marine ; [- des États-Unis] (US) Marine ■ **les Marines** the Royal Marines *UK*, the US Marine Corps *US*, the Marines *US* **2.** [couleur] navy (blue).

mariner [3] [marine] ◇ *vt* [dans une marinade] to marinate, to marinade ■ [dans une saumure] to pickle, to souse.
◇ *vi* **1.** CULIN to marinate ■ **laissez la viande ~** *ou* **faites ~ la viande pendant plusieurs heures** allow the meat to marinate for several hours **2.** *fam* [personne] to wait, to hang about ■ **il marine en prison** he's rotting in prison ■ **laisse-la ~!** let her stew for a while!

maringouin [marɛ̃gwɛ̃] *nm Québec* mosquito.

marinier, ère [marinje, ɛr] *nm, f* **1.** [batelier] bargee *UK*, bargeman (*f* bargewoman) *US* **2.** *arch* [marin] mariner.

marinière [marinjɛr] *nf* **1.** [blouse] sailor blouse ■ [maillot rayé] (white and navy blue) striped jersey **2.** CULIN : **sauce ~** white wine sauce.

mariol(le) [marjɔl] *fam* ◇ *adj* [astucieux] smart, clever.
◇ *nm* smart alec, clever dick *UK*, wise guy *US* ■ **faire le ~** to try to be smart *ou* clever.

marionnette [marjɔnɛt] *nf* **1.** [poupée] : **~ (à fils)** puppet, marionette ■ **on va aux ~s** we're going to the puppet show **2.** *péj* [personne] puppet.

marionnettiste [marjɔnɛtist] *nmf* puppeteer.

marital, e, aux [marital, o] *adj* DR **1.** [relatif au mari] marital ■ **l'autorisation ~e** the husband's authorization **2.** [relatif à l'union libre] : **au cours de leur vie ~e** while they lived together (as man and wife).

maritalement [maritalmɑ̃] *adv* : **vivre ~** to live as husband and wife.

maritime [maritim] *adj* **1.** [du bord de mer - village] coastal, seaside *(modif)*, seaboard *US (modif)* ■ **province ~** maritime *ou* coastal province ■ **région ~** ADMIN coastal area **2.** [naval - hôpital, entrepôt] naval ; [- commerce] seaborne, maritime ■ **puissance ~** maritime *ou* sea power **3.** DR [législation, droit] maritime, shipping *(modif)* ■ [agent] shipping *(modif)* ■ [assurance] marine.

Marius [marjys] *npr* THÉÂTRE *a play by Marcel Pagnol (1928), strongly evocative of the traditions of Marseilles.*

marivaudage [marivodaʒ] *nm sout* light-hearted banter.

marjolaine [marʒɔlɛn] *nf* marjoram.

mark [mark] *nm* FIN mark.

marketing [markətiŋ] *nm* marketing ■ **~ direct** direct marketing.

marmaille [marmaj] *nf fam péj* gang of kids *ou* brats *péj* ■ **elle est venue avec toute sa ~** she came with her whole brood.

marmelade [marməlad] *nf* CULIN : **~ de pommes** stewed apple *ou* apples, apple compote ; [pour viande] apple sauce ■ **~ d'oranges** (orange) marmalade.
◆ **en marmelade** *loc adj* **1.** CULIN stewed ■ [trop cuit, écrasé] mushy **2.** *fam* [en piteux état] : **j'ai les pieds en ~** my feet are all torn to shreds ■ **elle avait le visage en ~** her face was all smashed up.

marmite [marmit] *nf* CULIN [contenant] pot, cooking-pot ■ [contenu] pot.

marmiton [marmitɔ̃] *nm* young kitchen hand.

marmonnement [marmɔnmɑ̃] *nm* mumbling, muttering.

marmonner [3] [marmɔne] *vt & vi* to mumble, to mutter ■ **la vieille femme marmonnait dans son coin** the old woman was muttering (away) to herself.

marmoréen, enne [marmɔreɛ̃, ɛn] *adj* **1.** GÉOL marmoreal, marmorean **2.** *litt* marmoreal *litt*, marble *(modif)*.

marmot [marmo] *nm fam* (little) kid, nipper *UK*.

marmotte [marmɔt] *nf* **1.** ZOOL marmot ■ **tu es une vraie ~** you're a regular dormouse! **2.** [fourrure] marmot ■ **de** *ou* **en ~** marmot *(modif)* **3.** BOT (marmotte) cherry.

marmotter [3] [marmɔte] *vt & vi* to mutter, to mumble.

marne [marn] *nf* marl.

marner [3] [marne] ◇ *vt* AGRIC to marl.
◇ *vi* **1.** *fam* [personne] to slog *UK*, to plug away *US* ■ **il nous fait ~** he keeps us hard at it *ou* slaving away **2.** [mer] to rise.

Maroc [marɔk] *npr m* : **le ~** Morocco ■ **au ~** in Morocco.

marocain, e [marɔkɛ̃, ɛn] *adj* Moroccan.
◆ **Marocain, e** *nm, f* Moroccan.
◆ **marocain** *nm* LING Moroccan (Arabic).

maronite [marɔnit] *adj & nmf* Maronite.

maroquin [marɔkɛ̃] *nm* **1.** [peau] morocco **2.** *fam* [ministère] minister's portfolio.

maroquinerie [marɔkinri] *nf* **1.** [commerce] leather trade ■ [industrie] leather craft ■ [magasin] leather shop *UK ou* store *US* **2.** [articles] (small) leather goods **3.** [atelier] tannery ■ [tannage] tanning.

maroquinier, ère [marɔkinje, ɛr] ◇ *adj* : **ouvrier ~** leather worker.
◇ *nm, f* [ouvrier] tanner ■ [artisan] leather craftsman ■ [commerçant] : **je l'ai acheté chez un ~** I bought it from a leather (goods) shop *UK ou* store *US*.

marotte [marɔt] *nf fam* [passe-temps] pet hobby ■ **il a la ~ des mots croisés** crosswords are his pet hobby ■ **c'est devenu une ~** it's become an obsession.

maroufler [3] [marufle] *vt* **1.** [coller - sur un panneau] to mount **2.** ART to back ■ **toile marouflée** backed picture.

marquage [markaʒ] *nm* **1.** SPORT marking **2.** [de linge] marking ■ [d'animaux] marking, branding.

marquant, e [markɑ̃, ɑ̃t] *adj* **1.** [personne] prominent, outstanding ■ **les personnalités ~es de ce siècle** this century's most influential figures **2.** [détail, trait] striking ■ **un événement particulièrement ~** an event of particular *ou* outstanding importance.

marque [mark] *nf* **1.** [trace] mark ■ [cicatrice] mark, scar ■ **~s de coups** bruises *ou* marks of blows ■ **~s de doigts** [sales] fingermarks ; [empreintes] fingerprints ■ **il y avait encore la ~ de son corps dans l'herbe** the imprint of his body in the grass was still there ■ **les ~s de la vieillesse** marks *ou* traces of old age

2. [étiquette] label, tag, tab ■ [signet] marker, book mark ■ [trait] mark ■ **~ au crayon/à la craie** pencil/chalk mark
3. [preuve] mark ■ **comme ~ d'amitié/d'estime/de confiance** as a token of friendship/esteem/trust ■ **c'est là la ~ d'une grande générosité** that's the sign *ou* mark of real generosity
4. COMM [de produits manufacturés] make ■ [de produits alimentaires et chimiques] brand ■ **voiture de ~ française** French-made *ou* French-built car ➋ **produits de grande ~** top brand *ou* name products ■ **c'est une grande ~ de cigarettes/de voitures** [célèbre] it's a well-known brand of cigarette/make of car ; [de luxe] it's a brand of luxury cigarette/a make of luxury car ■ **~ déposée** registered trademark ■ **~ de fabrique** trademark, brand name
5. [identification - sur bijoux] hallmark ; [- sur meubles] stamp, mark ; [- sur animaux] brand ■ **il a dessiné ces jardins, il est facile de reconnaître sa ~** *fig* he designed these gardens, it's easy to recognize his style ■ **on reconnaît la ~ du génie** that's the hallmark *ou* stamp of genius
6. JEUX [jeton] chip ■ [décompte] score ■ **tenir la ~** to keep (the) score
7. SPORT [score] score
8. RUGBY : **~!** mark!
9. LING : **porter la ~ du féminin/pluriel** to be in the feminine/plural form.
◆ **marques** *nfpl* SPORT : **prendre ses ~s** [coureur] to take one's marks ; [sauteur] to pace out one's run up ■ **à vos ~s! prêts! partez!** on your marks! get set! go!, ready! steady! go!
◆ **de marque** *loc adj* [produit] upmarket, top-class ■ [hôte] distinguished ■ **articles de ~** branded goods ■ **personnage de ~** VIP.

marqué, e [marke] *adj* **1.** [évident - différence] marked, distinct ; [- préférence] marked, obvious ; [- accent] marked, broad, strong ; [- traits] pronounced ■ **il a le visage très ~** [par des blessures] his face is covered with scars ; [par la maladie] illness has left its mark on his face ■ **robe à la taille ~e** dress fitted at the waist **2.** [engagé] : **il est très ~ politiquement** politically he is very committed.

marque-page [markpaʒ] *nm inv* bookmark.

marquer [3] [marke] ◇ *vt* **1.** [montrer] to mark ■ **~ la limite de qqch** to mark sthg (off), to mark the limit of sthg ■ **l'horloge marque 3 h** the clock shows *ou* says 3 o'clock ■ **la balance marque 3 kg** the scales register *ou* read 3 kg ■ **le thermomètre marque 40°C** the thermometer shows *ou* registers 40°C ■ **les lignes bleues marquent les frontières** the blue lines show *ou* indicate where the border is
2. [signaler - passage d'un texte] to mark ; [- bétail] to brand, to mark ; [- arbre] to blaze ; [- linge] to label, to tag ■ **~ sa page** [avec un signet] to mark one's place (with a bookmark) ; [en cornant la page] to turn down the corner of one's page ■ **~ au fer rouge** to brand ➋ **ce jour est à ~ d'une pierre blanche** this will go down as a red-letter day
3. [témoigner de] to mark, to show ■ **pour ~ sa confiance** as a token *ou* mark of his trust
4. [événement, date] to mark ➋ **~ le coup** [fêter qqch] to mark the occasion ; [réagir] to react
5. [prendre en note] to write *ou* to take *ou* to note (down) *(sép)* ■ [tracer] to mark, to write ■ **tu l'as marqué?** have you made a note of it? ■ **marqué à l'encre/à la craie/au crayon sur le mur** marked in ink/chalk/pencil on the wall, inked/chalked/pencilled on the wall
6. [suj: difficulté, épreuve] to mark ■ **le chagrin a marqué son visage** his face is lined *ou* furrowed with sorrow
7. [impressionner] to mark, to affect, to make an impression on ■ **ça m'a beaucoup marqué** it made a big *ou* lasting impression on me
8. JEUX & SPORT : **~ (un point)** to score (a point) ■ **~ les points** to note *ou* to keep the score ■ **l'argument est judicieux, vous marquez un point** *fig* the argument is valid, that's one to you *ou* you've scored a point ■ **~ un joueur** to mark a player
9. [rythmer] : **il marquait la cadence du pied** he beat time with his foot ■ **~ la mesure** MUS to keep the beat ■ **~ un temps d'arrêt** to pause *(for a moment)* ➋ **~ le pas** to mark time
10. COUT : **les robes, cet été, marqueront la taille** this summer's dresses will emphasize the waist line.
◇ *vi* **1.** [personne, événement] to stand out ■ **les grands hommes qui ont marqué dans l'histoire** the great men who have left their mark on history ■ **sa mort a marqué dans ma vie** his death had a great effect *ou* impact on my life
2. [crayon, objet] : **attention, ça marque!** careful, it'll leave a mark!

marqueté, e [markəte] *adj* [meuble] inlaid.

marqueterie [markɛtri] *nf* **1.** [décoration] marquetry, inlay ■ **un panneau en ~** a marquetry panel **2.** [métier] marquetry.

marqueteur, euse [markətœr, øz] *nm, f* inlayer.

marqueur, euse [markœr, øz] *nm, f* [qui compte les points] scorekeeper, scorer ■ [qui gagne les points] scorer.
◆ **marqueur** *nm* **1.** [gros feutre] marker (pen) ■ [surligneur] highlighter ■ **la phrase indiquée au ~** the highlighted sentence **2.** BIOL, LING & MÉD marker **3.** NUCL tracer.
◆ **marqueuse** *nf* COMM marking *ou* stamping machine.

marquis [marki] *nm* marquess, marquis ■ **merci, Monsieur le Marquis** thank you, your Lordship.

marquisat [markiza] *nm* [rang, fief] marquessate.

marquise [markiz] *nf* **1.** [titre] marchioness, marquise ■ **merci, Madame la Marquise** thank you, your Ladyship **2.** [abri de toile] awning ■ [auvent vitré] (glass) canopy **3.** JOAILL marquise ring **4.** [chaise] marquise (chair).

Marquises [markiz] *npr fpl* : **les (îles) ~** the Marquesas Islands, *voir aussi* **île**.

marraine [marɛn] *nf* **1.** RELIG godmother **2.** [d'un bateau] : **elle fut choisie comme ~ du bateau** she was chosen to launch *ou* to name the ship ▮ [d'un nouveau membre] sponsor ■ **~ de guerre** soldier's wartime penfriend *ou* penpal.

Marrakech [marakɛʃ] *npr* Marrakech, Marrakesh.

marrant, e [marɑ̃, ɑ̃t] *fam* ◇ *adj* **1.** [drôle] funny ■ **il est (trop) ~!** he's a hoot *ou* scream! ■ **elle n'est pas ~e, sa femme** his wife is really bad news! ■ **je ne veux pas y aller -- tu n'es pas ~!** I don't want to go -- you're no fun! ■ **vous êtes ~s, je n'ai pas que ça à faire!** come on, I've got other things to do, you know! **2.** [bizarre] funny, odd, strange ■ **c'est ~ qu'elle ne soit pas encore là** funny (that) she hasn't arrived yet.
◇ *nm, f* joker, funny guy (*f* girl).

marre [mar] *adv* : **en avoir ~** *fam* : **il en a ~ de ses études** he's fed up with *ou* sick and tired of studying ■ **j'en ai ~!** I've had enough!

marrer [3] [mare] *vi fam* **faire ~ qqn** to make sb laugh.
◆ **se marrer** *vpi fam* to have a (good) laugh ■ **on s'est drôlement marrés hier soir** we really had a good laugh *ou* a great time last night.

marri, e [mari] *adj arch* [contrarié, fâché] : **être (fort) ~** to be (most) aggrieved.

marron[1] [marɔ̃] ◇ *nm* **1.** BOT chestnut ■ **~ d'Inde** horse chestnut, conker ■ **~s chauds** roast *ou* roasted chestnuts ■ **~s glacés** marrons glacés, crystallized *ou* candied chestnuts ■ **tirer les ~s du feu pour qqn** to be sb's cat's-paw, to do all the dirty work for sb **2.** [couleur] brown ■ **j'aime le ~** I like brown **3.** △ [coup] clout, bash, wallop.
◇ *adj inv* [brun] brown.
◇ *adj*△ : **être (fait) ~** [être dupé] to be taken in ■ **zut, voilà le contrôleur, on est ~s!** [on est coincés] oh, no, we've had it now, here comes the ticket collector!

marron[2]**, onne** [marɔ̃, ɔn] *adj* [malhonnête] crooked ■ **esclave ~** escaped slave ■ **médecin ~** quack.

marronnier [marɔnje] *nm* chestnut tree ■ **~ d'Inde** horse chestnut (tree).

mars [mars] *nm* [mois] March ■ **en ~** in March ■ **au mois de ~** in (the month of) March ■ **nous y allons tous les ans en ~** *ou* **au mois de ~** we go there every (year in) March ■ **au début du mois de ~, (au) début ~** at the beginning of March, in early March ■ **au milieu du mois de ~, à la mi-~** in the middle of March, in mid-March ■ **à la fin du mois de ~, (à la) fin ~** at the end of March, in late March ■ **en ~ dernier/prochain** last/next

March ■ **Nice, le 5 ~ 1989** Nice, March 5th 1989 *ou* 5th of March 1989 ■ **la commande vous a été livrée le 31 ~** your order was delivered on 31st March *ou* on March 31st *ou* on the 31st of March ■ **j'attendrai jusqu'au (lundi) 4 ~** I'll wait until (Monday) the 4th of March.

Mars [mars] *npr* ASTRON & MYTHOL Mars.

marseillais, e [marsɛjɛ, ɛz] *adj* from Marseilles ■ **histoire ~e** tall story.
◆ **Marseillais, e** *nm, f inhabitant of or person from Marseilles.*
◆ **Marseillaise** *nf* MUS : **la Marseillaise** the Marseillaise *(the French national anthem).*

LA MARSEILLAISE

The French national anthem, most likely written by Rouget de Lisle, was sung for the first time in 1792 by a group of revolutionaries as they arrived in Paris from Marseilles. It became the national song in 1795.

Marseille [marsɛj] *npr* Marseilles, Marseille.

marsouin [marswɛ̃] *nm* **1.** ZOOL common porpoise **2.** △ *arg mil* Marine.

marsupial, e, aux [marsypjal, o] *adj* marsupial.
◆ **marsupial, aux** *nm* marsupial.

marteau, x [marto] ◇ *nm* **1.** [maillet] hammer ■ **coup de ~** blow with a hammer ■ **enfoncer un clou à coups de ~** to hammer a nail home *ou* in ➤ **~ piqueur** *ou* **pneumatique** pneumatic drill ■ **~ perforateur** hammer drill **2.** [pièce - d'une horloge] striker, hammer ; [- d'une porte] knocker, hammer ; [- dans un piano] hammer **3.** ANAT hammer, malleus *spéc* **4.** SPORT hammer **5.** [poisson] hammerhead shark.
◇ *adj fam* bonkers *UK*, nuts.

marteau-pilon [martopilɔ̃] (*pl* **marteaux-pilons**) *nm* power *ou* drop hammer.

martel [martɛl] *nm* : **se mettre ~ en tête** to be worried sick ■ **ne te mets pas ~ en tête pour si peu** don't get worked *ou* wrought up about such a small thing.

martèlement [martɛlmɑ̃] *nm* [bruit - d'un marteau] hammering ; [- de pas, de bottes] pounding ■ **j'entends le ~ de la pluie sur le toit de zinc** I can hear the rain beating on the zinc roof.

marteler [25] [martəle] *vt* **1.** MÉTALL to hammer ■ **~ à froid** to cold-hammer **2.** [frapper] to hammer (at), to pound (at) ■ **il martelait la table de ses poings** he was hammering with *ou* banging his fists on the table **3.** [scander] to hammer out *(sép).*

martial, e, aux [marsjal, o] *adj* **1.** *litt* [guerrier] martial, warlike ■ **un discours ~** a warlike speech **2.** [résolu, décidé] resolute, determined ■ **une démarche/voix ~e** a firm tread/voice **3.** DR : **cour ~e** court martial ■ **loi ~e** martial law **4.** MÉD [relatif au fer] iron *(modif).*

martien, enne [marsjɛ̃, ɛn] *adj* Martian.
◆ **Martien, enne** *nm, f* Martian ■ **j'ai l'impression de parler à des Martiens** I might as well be talking to Martians.

martinet [martinɛ] *nm* **1.** [fouet] cat-o'-nine-tails **2.** MÉTALL (small) drop hammer **3.** ORNITH : **~ noir** swift.

martingale [martɛ̃gal] *nf* **1.** [vêtement] half belt **2.** ÉQUIT [sangle] martingale **3.** JEUX [façon de jouer] doubling-up, ≃ martingale ■ [combinaison] winning formula.

martini [martini] *nm* martini.
◆ **Martini®** *nm* Martini®.

martiniquais, e [martinikɛ, ɛz] *adj* Martinican.
◆ **Martiniquais, e** *nm, f* Martinican.

Martinique [martinik] *npr f* : **la ~** Martinique ■ **à la ~** in Martinique.

martin-pêcheur [martɛ̃pɛʃœr] (*pl* **martins-pêcheurs**) *nm* kingfisher.

martre [martr] *nf* **1.** ZOOL marten **2.** [fourrure] sable.

martyr, e [martir] ◇ *adj* martyred ■ **les enfants ~s** battered children.
◇ *nm, f* **1.** [personne qui se sacrifie] martyr ■ **les ~s chrétiens** the Christian martyrs ■ **les ~s de la Résistance** the martyrs of the Resistance **2.** *hum* martyr ■ **arrête de jouer les ~s** *ou* **de prendre des airs de ~** stop being a *ou* playing the martyr!
◆ **martyre** *nm* **1.** [supplice] martyrdom **2.** [épreuve] torture, martyrdom ■ [douleur] agony ■ **souffrir le ~** to be in agony ■ **cette visite a été un véritable ~!** that visit was sheer torture!

martyriser [3] [martirize] *vt* **1.** [supplicier - gén] to martyrize ■ RELIG to martyr **2.** [maltraiter - animal] to ill-treat, to torture ; [- enfant] to beat, to batter ; [- collègue, élève] to bully ■ **on n'imagine pas le nombre d'enfants qui se font ~ à l'école** you'd be amazed how many children are bullied at school.

marxisant, e [marksizɑ̃, ɑ̃t] *adj* Marxist-influenced.

marxisme [marksism] *nm* Marxism.

marxisme-léninisme [marksismleninism] *nm* Marxism-Leninism.

marxiste [marksist] *adj* & *nmf* Marxist.

marxiste-léniniste [marksistleninist] (*pl* **marxistes-léninistes**) *adj* & *nmf* Marxist-Leninist.

mas [ma] *nm type of house found in southeast France.*

mascara [maskara] *nm* mascara.

mascarade [maskarad] *nf* **1.** [bal] masked ball, masquerade ■ DANSE & HIST masquerade **2.** *péj* [accoutrement] : **qu'est-ce que c'est que cette ~?** what on earth is that outfit you're wearing? **3.** [simulacre] farce, mockery.

mascotte [maskɔt] *nf* mascot.

masculin, e [maskylɛ̃, in] *adj* **1.** [propre aux hommes] male ■ **le sexe ~** the male sex ■ **la mode ~e** men's fashion ■ **une voix ~e** [d'homme] a male *ou* man's voice ; [de femme] a masculine voice ■ **elle a une allure ~e** she looks quite masculine **2.** [composé d'hommes] : **une équipe ~e** a men's team ■ **main-d'œuvre ~e** male workers **3.** LING masculine.
◆ **masculin** *nm* LING masculine.

masculiniser [3] [maskylinize] *vt* **1.** [viriliser] to make masculine **2.** BIOL to produce male characteristics in, to masculinize.

masculinité [maskylinite] *nf* **1.** [comportement] masculinity, virility, manliness **2.** [dans des statistiques] : **taux de ~** sex ratio.

maso [mazo] *fam* ◇ *adj* masochistic ■ **t'es ~ ou quoi?** you're a real glutton for punishment ■ **je ne vais pas lui dire la vérité tout de suite, je ne suis pas ~** I won't tell her the truth right away, I'm not a masochist.
◇ *nmf* : **c'est un ~** he's a glutton for punishment *ou* a masochist.

masochisme [mazɔʃism] *nm* masochism.

masochiste [mazɔʃist] ◇ *nmf* masochist.
◇ *adj* masochist, masochistic.

masque [mask] *nm* **1.** [déguisement, protection] mask ➤ **~ de carnaval** *ou* **de Mardi gras** (carnival) mask ■ **~ funéraire** *ou* **mortuaire** death mask ■ **~ d'escrime/de plongée** fencing/diving mask ■ **~ d'anesthésie/à oxygène/stérile** anaesthetic/oxygen/sterile mask ■ **~ à gaz** gas mask **2.** [pour la peau] : **~ (de beauté)** face pack *ou* mask ■ **~ à l'argile** mudpack **3.** MÉD : **~ de grossesse** (pregnancy) chloasma **4.** [apparence] mask, front ■ **sous ce ~ jovial, elle cache son amertume** under that jovial facade *ou* appearance, she conceals her bitterness ■ **sa bonté n'est qu'un ~** his kindness is just a front *ou* is only skin-deep ➤ **lever** *ou* **tomber le ~, jeter (bas) son ~** to unmask o.s., to show one's true colours, to take off one's mask **5.** *litt* [personne masquée] mask **6.** MUS & THÉÂTRE mask, masque **7.** ACOUST : **effet de ~** (audio) masking **8.** ÉLECTRON, IMPR & PHOTO mask **9.** INFORM : **~ de saisie** template.

masqué, e [maske] *adj* **1.** [voleur] masked, wearing a mask ■ [acteur] wearing a mask, in a mask **2.** [virage] blind.

masquer [3] [maske] *vt* **1.** [dissimuler - obstacle, ouverture] to mask, to conceal ; [- lumière] to shade, to screen (off), to obscure ; [- difficulté, intentions, sentiments] to hide, to conceal, to disguise ; [- saveur, goût] to mask, to disguise, to hide ■ **le mur masque la vue** the wall blocks out *ou* masks the view ■ **la cuisine est masquée par** *ou* **avec un paravent** the kitchen is hidden behind a partition *ou* is partitioned off **2.** [déguiser - enfant] to put a mask on.

◆ **se masquer** ◇ *vp (emploi réfléchi)* [se déguiser] to put a mask on, to put on a mask.

◇ *vpt* [ignorer] : **se ~ qqch** to ignore sthg ■ **ne nous masquons pas les difficultés** let us not blind ourselves to *ou* ignore the difficulties.

Massachusetts [masaʃysɛts] *npr m* : **le ~** Massachusetts.

massacrant, e [masakrɑ̃, ɑ̃t] *adj fam* **être d'une humeur ~e** to be in a foul *ou* vile mood.

massacre [masakr] *nm* **1.** [tuerie] massacre, slaughter ■ **envoyer des troupes au ~** to send troops to the slaughter **2.** *fam* [d'un adversaire] massacre, slaughter ■ **5 à 0, c'est un ~!** 5 nil, it's a massacre! ■ **il a fait un ~ dans le tournoi** he massacred *ou* made mincemeat of all his opponents in the tournament **3.** *fam* [travail mal fait] : **c'est du** *ou* **un ~** [gâchis] it's a mess ; [bâclage] it's a botch-up *ou* botch *US* ■ **quel ~, son "Phèdre"!** she's managed to murder "Phèdre" ■ **regarde comment il m'a coupé les cheveux, c'est un vrai ~!** look at the mess he's made of my hair! ■ **attention en découpant le gâteau, quel ~!** watch how you cut the cake, you're making a pig's ear *ou* a real mess of it! **4.** *fam* [succès] : **faire un ~** to be a runaway success, to be a smash (hit) ■ **elle fait actuellement un ~ sur la scène de la Lanterne** she's currently bringing the house down at the Lantern theatre **5.** CHASSE [trophée] stag's antlers *ou* attire **6.** HÉRALD harts attired *ou* caboched.

massacrer [3] [masakre] *vt* **1.** [tuer - animal, personne] to slaughter, to massacre, to butcher **2.** *fam* [vaincre facilement - adversaire] to make mincemeat of, to massacre, to slaughter ■ **jouer aux échecs avec lui? tu vas te faire ~!** you're going to play chess with him? He'll wipe the floor with you! **3.** *fam* [critiquer] to slate *UK*, to pan ■ **la pièce s'est fait ~** the play got slated *UK ou* torn to pieces **4.** *fam* [gâcher - concerto, pièce de théâtre] to murder, to make a mess of ; [- langue] to murder ■ [bâcler - travail] to make a mess *ou* hash of, to botch (up) *(sép)*, to make a pig's ear (out) of.

massage [masaʒ] *nm* massage ■ **faire un ~ à qqn** to massage sb, to give sb a massage ■ **~ cardiaque** cardiac *ou* heart massage.

masse [mas] *nf* **1.** [bloc informe] mass ■ **~ de nuages** bank of clouds ■ **sculpté dans la ~** carved from the block ■ **s'abattre** *ou* **s'écrouler** *ou* **s'affaisser comme une ~** to collapse *ou* to slump heavily ■ **~ d'air** MÉTÉOR mass of air

2. *fam* [grande quantité] : **une ~ de** [objets] heaps *ou* masses of ; [gens] crowds *ou* masses of ▶ **pas des ~s** *fam* not that much, not that many ■ **des amis, il n'en a pas des ~s** he hasn't got that many friends ■ **vous vous êtes bien amusés? – pas des ~s!** did you have fun? – not that much!

3. COMM [grosse quantité] stock ■ [douze grosses] great gross

4. [groupe social] : **la ~** the masses ■ **communication/culture de ~** mass communication/culture ■ **les ~s (populaires)** the mass (of ordinary people) ■ **les ~s laborieuses** the toiling masses

5. [ensemble] body, bulk ■ [majorité] majority

6. ÉCON & FIN : **la ~ des créanciers/obligataires** the body of creditors/bondholders ▶ **~ active** assets ■ **~ critique** critical mass ■ **~ monétaire** money supply ■ **~ passive** liabilities ■ **~ salariale** wage bill

7. MIL [allocation] fund

8. ÉLECTR earth *UK*, ground *US* ■ **mettre à la ~** to earth *UK*, to ground *US*

9. CHIM & PHYS mass ■ **~ atomique/moléculaire** atomic/molecular mass ■ **~ volumique** relative density

10. JEUX stake

11. [outil] sledgehammer, beetle

12. ARM : **~ d'armes** mace

13. [de billard] butt (of cue).

◆ **à la masse**△ *loc adj* crazy.

◆ **en masse** ◇ *loc adj* [licenciements, production] mass *(modif)*.

◇ *loc adv* **1.** [en grande quantité] : **produire** *ou* **fabriquer en ~** to mass-produce ■ **la population a approuvé en ~ le projet de réforme** the reform bill gained massive support ■ **se déplacer en ~** to go in a body *ou* en masse

2. COMM [en bloc] in bulk.

massepain [maspɛ̃] *nm* marzipan.

masser [3] [mase] *vt* **1.** [membre, muscle] to massage ■ **~ qqn** to massage sb, to give sb a massage ■ **se faire ~** to be massaged, to have a massage ■ **masse-moi le bras** rub *ou* massage my arm **2.** [réunir - enfants] to gather *ou* to bring together ; [- soldats] to mass ; [- livres, pièces] to put together **3.** ART to group, to arrange into groups **4.** JEUX : **~ une bille** to play a massé shot.

◆ **se masser** ◇ *vpt* : **se ~ le genou/le bras** to massage one's knee/one's arm ■ **elle se masse les tempes quand elle a mal à la tête** she rubs her temples when she has a headache.

◇ *vpi* to gather, to assemble, to mass.

masseur, euse [masœr, øz] *nm, f* masseur (*f* masseuse).

masseur-kinésithérapeute [masœrkineziterapøt], **masseuse-kinésithérapeute** [masøzkineziterapøt] (*mpl* **masseurs-kinésithérapeutes**, *fpl* **masseuses-kinésithérapeutes**) *nm, f* physiotherapist *UK*, physical therapist *US*.

massicot [masiko] *nm* **1.** [d'imprimeur] guillotine ■ [pour papier peint] trimmer **2.** CHIM massicot.

massicoter [3] [masikɔte] *vt* [papier] to guillotine ■ [papier peint] to trim.

massif, ive [masif, iv] *adj* **1.** JOAILL & MENUIS solid ■ **argent ~** solid silver ■ **armoire en acajou ~** solid mahogany wardrobe **2.** [épais] massive, heavy-looking, bulky ■ **une bâtisse au fronton ~** a building with a massive pediment ■ **sa silhouette massive** his huge frame **3.** [en grand nombre] mass *(modif)*, massive ■ **des migrations massives vers le Nouveau Monde** mass migrations to the New World ■ [en grande quantité] massive, huge ■ **un apport ~ d'argent liquide** a massive cash injection ■ **une réponse massive de nos lecteurs** an overwhelming response from our readers.

◆ **massif** *nm* **1.** GÉOGR & GÉOL : **~ (montagneux)** mountainous mass, massif ■ **~ ancien** primary *ou* Caledonian massif ■ **le ~ du Hoggar** the Hoggar Mountains **2.** HORT : **~ (de fleurs)** flowerbed ■ **un ~ de roses** a rosebed, a bed of roses ■ **~ d'arbustes** clump of bushes ■ **les rhododendrons font de jolis ~s** rhododendrons look nice planted together in groups **3.** CONSTR underpin, foundation **4.** [panneaux publicitaires] composite site.

massification [masifikasjɔ̃] *nf* **1.** [uniformisation] uniformization, standardization **2.** [médiatisation] mass dissemination.

massique [masik] *adj* PHYS mass *(modif)*.

massive [masiv] *f* ▷ **massif**.

massivement [masivmɑ̃] *adv* [en grand nombre] massively, en masse ■ **ils ont voté ~ pour le nouveau candidat** they voted overwhelmingly for the new candidate ■ **les Français ont voté ~** the French turned out in large numbers to vote.

massivité [masivite] *nf* massiveness.

mass media [masmedja] *nmpl* mass media.

massue [masy] *nf* **1.** [gourdin] club, bludgeon ■ **coup de ~** [événement imprévu] staggering blow, bolt from the blue ; [prix excessif] *fam* rip-off **2.** *(comme adj)* **un argument ~** a sledgehammer argument.

mastectomie [mastɛktɔmi] = **mammectomie**.

mastic [mastik] ◇ *adj inv* putty, mastic, putty-coloured.

◇ *nm* **1.** BOT mastic **2.** CONSTR mastic ■ [pour vitrier] putty ■ [pour menuisier] filler **3.** IMPR transposition **4.** [d'arboriculteur] : **~ à greffer** grafting wax.

masticage [mastikaʒ] *nm* CONSTR [d'une vitre] puttying ■ [d'une cavité] filling, stopping.

masticateur, trice [mastikatœr, tris] *adj* masticatory.

mastication [mastikasjɔ̃] *nf* [d'aliments] chewing, mastication *spéc.*

masticatoire [mastikatwar] *adj* & *nm* masticatory.

mastiff [mastif] *nm* (bull) mastiff.

mastiquer [3] [mastike] *vt* **1.** [pain, viande] to chew, to masticate *spéc* **2.** [joindre - lézarde] to fill (in), to stop (up) ; [- vitre] to putty **3.** MÉD [dentisterie] to fill.

mastite [mastit] *nf* mastitis.

mastoc [mastɔk] *adj inv fam* [personne] hefty ▪ [objet] bulky.

mastodonte [mastɔdɔ̃t] *nm* **1.** ZOOL mastodon **2.** [personne] colossus, enormous man (*f* woman) ▪ **c'est un ~** he's built like a house **3.** [camion] juggernaut *UK*, tractor-trailer *US*.

mastoïde [mastɔid] *adj* mastoid.

masturbation [mastyrbasjɔ̃] *nf* masturbation.

masturber [3] [mastyrbe] *vt* to masturbate.
◆ **se masturber** ◇ *vp (emploi réfléchi)* to masturbate.
◇ *vp (emploi réciproque)* to masturbate each other.

m'as-tu-vu [matyvy] ◇ *adj inv* showy, flashy ▪ **leur maison est très ~** their house is very showy.
◇ *nmf* show-off ▪ **faire le** *ou* **son ~** to show off.

masure [mazyr] *nf* shack, hovel.

mat, e [mat] *adj* **1.** [couleur] dull, matt ▪ [surface] unpolished ▪ [peinture] matt ▪ PHOTO matt **2.** [teint] olive **3.** [son] : **un son ~** a thud, a dull sound.
◆ **mat** ◇ *adj inv* checkmated, mated ▪ **il m'a fait ~ en trois coups** he checkmated me in three moves ▪ **tu es ~** (you're) checkmate.
◇ *nm* **1.** JEUX checkmate, mate **2.** TEXT mat.

mât [ma] *nm* **1.** [poteau] pole, post ▪ [en camping] pole ▪ **~ de cocagne** greasy pole **2.** [hampe] flagpole **3.** TECHNOL : **~ de charge** cargo beam, derrick ▪ **~ de levage** lift mast ▪ **~ de forage** INDUST du pétrole drilling mast **4.** NAUT mast ▪ **~ d'artimon** mizzen, mizzenmast ▪ **~ de beaupré** bowsprit ▪ **~ de hune** topmast ▪ **~ de misaine** foremast ▪ **grand ~** main mast **5.** RAIL : **~ (de signal)** signal post.

matador [matadɔr] *nm* matador.

matamore [matamɔr] *nm sout* braggart ▪ **il joue les ~s** he's nothing but a braggart.

match [matʃ] (*pl* **matchs** *ou pl* **matches**) *nm* match, game *US* ▪ **~ de tennis** tennis match, game of tennis ▪ **~ aller/retour** first/second leg (match) ▪ **~ de sélection** trial ▪ **faire ~ nul** to draw, to tie *US*.

matelas [matla] *nm* **1.** [d'un lit] mattress ▪ **~ à ressorts/de laine** spring/wool mattress ▪ **~ de mousse** foam-rubber mattress ➲ **~ pneumatique** air mattress **2.** [couche - de feuilles mortes, de neige] layer, carpet ▪ **un ~ de billets de banque** *fam* [liasse] a wad *ou* roll of bank-notes ; [fortune] a pile (of money) **3.** CONSTR : **~ d'air** air space.

matelassé, e [matlase] *adj* **1.** [fauteuil] padded **2.** COUT lined **3.** TEXT matelassé.

matelasser [3] [matlase] *vt* **1.** [fauteuil] to pad **2.** [veste] to line ▪ [tissu] to quilt ▪ **matelassé de soie** silk-lined.

matelassure [matlasyr] *nf* padding, mattress filling.

matelot [matlo] *nm* **1.** [de la marine - marchande] sailor, seaman ; [- militaire] sailor ▪ **~ de pont** deck hand **2.** [bâtiment] ship, vessel.

matelotage [matlɔtaʒ] *nm* **1.** [solde] sailor's pay **2.** [travaux, connaissances] seamanship.

matelote [matlɔt] *nf* **1.** CULIN matelote, fish stew *(with wine, onion and mushroom sauce)* ▪ **~ d'anguilles** stewed eels *(in red wine sauce)* **2.** [danse] (sailor's) hornpipe.

mater [3] [mate] *vt* **1.** [aux échecs] to mate, to checkmate **2.** [dompter - personne, peuple] to bring to heel ; [- révolte] to quell, to curb, to put down *(insép)* ▪ **~ l'orgueil de qqn** to humble sb, to crush sb's pride ▪ **petit morveux, je vais te ~, moi!** *fam* you little swine, I'll show you who's boss! **3.** △ [vérifier] to check (out) *(sép)* ▪ **mate un peu si le prof arrive** keep your eyes peeled, see if the teacher's coming ▪ [avec convoitise] to ogle ▪ **t'as fini de le ~?** have you quite finished (staring at him)? **4.** [dépolir] to matt **5.** MÉTALL to caulk.

mâter [3] [mate] *vt* NAUT to mast.

matérialisation [materjalizasjɔ̃] *nf* **1.** [réalisation] materialization ▪ **c'est la ~ de tous mes rêves** it's a dream come true for me **2.** PHYS : **~ de l'énergie** mass-energy conversion **3.** [dans le spiritisme] materialization.

matérialiser [3] [materjalize] *vt* **1.** [concrétiser] to materialize ▪ **~ un projet** to carry out *ou* to execute a plan **2.** [indiquer] to mark out *(sép)*, to indicate ▪ **le poteau matérialise la frontière** the pole marks where the border is ▪ **'voie non matérialisée pendant 1 km'** 'no markings *ou* roadmarkings for 1 km' **3.** [symboliser] to symbolize, to embody.
◆ **se matérialiser** *vpi* to materialize.

matérialisme [materjalism] *nm* materialism ▪ **~ dialectique/historique** dialectical/historical materialism.

matérialiste [materjalist] ◇ *adj* **1.** PHILOS materialist **2.** [esprit, civilisation] materialistic.
◇ *nmf* materialist.

matériau, x [materjo] *nm* [substance] material.
◆ **matériaux** *nmpl* **1.** CONSTR material, materials **2.** [éléments] components, elements ▪ **rassembler des ~x pour une enquête** to assemble (some) material for a survey.

matériel, elle [materjɛl] *adj* **1.** [réel - preuve] material ▪ **je n'ai pas le temps ~ de faire l'aller et retour** I simply don't have the time to go there and back ▪ **il n'a pas le pouvoir ~ de le faire** he doesn't have the means to do it **2.** [pécuniaire, pratique - difficulté, aide etc] material ▪ **sur le plan ~, il n'a pas à se plaindre** from a material point of view, he has no grounds for complaint **3.** [physique] material ▪ **pour mon confort ~** for my material well-being **4.** [matérialiste - esprit, civilisation] material **5.** PHILOS [être, univers] physical, material **6.** MATH & MÉCAN [point] material, physical.
◆ **matériel** *nm* **1.** [équipement, machines] equipment ▪ **~ agricole/industriel** agricultural/industrial equipment ▪ **~ de bureau** office equipment ▪ **~ de camping** camping equipment *ou* gear ▪ **~ lourd** heavy equipment ▪ **~ de pêche** fishing tackle *ou* gear ▪ **~ pédagogique** teaching materials ▪ **~ roulant** RAIL rolling stock ▪ **~ scolaire** [papeterie] school materials ; [de laboratoire] school equipment **2.** MIL : **~ de guerre** materiel **3.** ÉCON : **le ~ humain** the workforce, human material **4.** BIOL & PSYCHOL material **5.** INFORM hardware **6.** ART material.
◆ **matérielle** *nf fam hum* wherewithal, (daily) sustenance ▪ **assurer la ~le** to make a living.

matériellement [materjɛlmɑ̃] *adv* **1.** [concrètement] materially ▪ **une tâche ~ impossible à effectuer** a physically impossible task **2.** [financièrement] materially, financially ▪ **des familles ~ défavorisées** families with financial difficulties.

maternage [matɛrnaʒ] *nm* mothering.

maternel, elle [matɛrnɛl] *adj* **1.** [propre à la mère - autorité, instinct, soins etc] maternal, motherly ▪ **il craignait la colère ~le** he feared his mother's anger **2.** [qui vient de la mère] maternal ▪ **du côté ~** on the mother's *ou* maternal side.
◆ **maternelle** *nf* nursery school, infant school *UK*, kindergarten.

maternellement [matɛrnɛlmɑ̃] *adv* maternally ▪ **elle s'occupait de lui ~** she cared for him like a mother *ou* in a motherly fashion.

materner [3] [matɛrne] *vt* to mother ▪ **tu ne vas pas ~ ton fils jusqu'à 30 ans, non?** you're not going to mollycoddle *ou* baby your son until he's 30, are you?

materniser [3] [matɛrnize] *vt* to make suitable for infants.

maternité [matɛrnite] *nf* **1.** [clinique] maternity hospital *ou* home ▪ [service] maternity ward **2.** [fait d'être mère] motherhood ▪ **ça te va bien, la ~!** being a mother suits you!

| [grossesse] : **des ~s successives** successive pregnancies **3.** DR maternity ■ **action en recherche de ~ naturelle** maternity suit **4.** ART mother and child.

math [mat] *nf* = **maths.**

mathématicien, enne [matematisjɛ̃, ɛn] *nm, f* mathematician.

mathématique [matematik] <> *adj* **1.** MATH mathematical **2.** [précis, exact] mathematical ■ **organisé avec une précision ~** organized with mathematical precision **3.** [inévitable] inevitable ■ **elle était sûre de perdre, c'était ~** she was sure to lose, it was a cert *UK ou* a surefire thing *US*.
<> *nf* mathematics *(U)*.

mathématiquement [matematikmɑ̃] *adv* **1.** MATH mathematically **2.** [objectivement] mathematically, absolutely ■ **c'est ~ impossible** it's mathematically *ou* utterly impossible **3.** [inévitablement] inevitably ■ **~, il devait perdre** he was bound to lose.

mathématiques [matematik] *nfpl* mathematics *(sing)* ■ **~ appliquées/pures** applied/pure mathematics ■ **Mathématiques supérieures/spéciales** *first/second year of a two-year science course preparing for entrance to the Grandes Écoles.*

matheux, euse [matø, øz] *nm, f fam* **1.** [gén] : **c'est un ~** he's a wizard at maths *UK ou* math *US* **2.** [étudiant] maths *UK ou* math *US* student.

maths [mat] *nfpl* maths *UK*, math *US* ■ **fort en ~** good at maths *UK ou* math *US* ➲ **~ sup/spé** *first/second year of a two-year science course preparing for entrance to the Grandes Écoles.*

mathusalem [matyzalɛm] *nm* ŒNOL Methuselah.

Mathusalem [matyzalɛm] *npr* Methuselah ■ **ça date de ~** it's out of the ark ■ **vieux comme ~** as old as Methuselah.

matière [matjɛr] *nf* **1.** [substance] matter, material ■ IMPR matter ■ **c'est en quelle ~?** what's it made of? ➲ **~ fissile/nucléaire** NUCL fissile/nuclear material ■ **~s (fécales)** faeces ■ **~ plastique, ~s plastiques** plastic, plastics ■ **~ première, ~s premières** raw material *ou* materials ■ **~ synthétique** synthetic material
2. BIOL & CHIM : **~ organique/inorganique** organic/inorganic matter ■ **la ~** PHILOS & PHYS matter ■ **~ inanimée/vivante** inanimate/living matter ➲ **~ grasse, ~s grasses** fat ■ **60 % de ~s grasses** 60% fat content ■ **sans ~s grasses** fat-free, non-fat
3. [contenu - d'un discours, d'un ouvrage] material, subject matter ■ **je n'avais pas assez de ~ pour en faire un livre** I didn't have enough material to write a book ■ **entrer en ~** to tackle a subject ■ **une entrée en ~** an introduction, a lead-in
4. [motif, prétexte] matter ■ **il n'y a pas là ~ à rire *ou* plaisanter** this is no laughing matter ■ **il y a ~ à discussion** there are a lot of things to be said about that ■ **y a-t-il là ~ à dispute/procès?** is this business worth fighting over/going to court for? ■ **~ d'une accusation** DR gravamen *spéc*, substance of a charge
5. [domaine] matter, subject ■ ÉDUC subject ■ **je suis incompétent en la ~** I'm ignorant on the subject ■ **il est mauvais/bon juge en la ~** he's a bad/good judge of this subject ■ **en ~ philosophique/historique** in the matter of philosophy/history, as regards philosophy/history ■ **le latin est ma ~ préférée** Latin is my favorite subject ■ **les ~s à l'écrit/à l'oral** the subjects for the written/oral examination
6. ART medium.
◆ **en matière de** *loc prép* as regards ■ **en ~ de cuisine** as far as cooking is concerned, as regards cooking.
◆ **matière grise** *nf fam* grey matter ■ **fais travailler ta ~ grise!** use your brains *ou* head! ■ **elle a de la ~ grise** she's brainy.

MATIF, Matif [matif] *npr m* **1.** (*abr de* **Marché à terme international de France**) *body regulating activities on the French stock exchange,* ≃ LIFFE *UK* **2.** (*abr de* **marché à terme des instruments financiers**) financial futures market.

Matignon [matiɲɔ̃] *npr* : **(l'hôtel) ~** *building in Paris which houses the offices of the Prime Minister.*

> ***MATIGNON***
> This eighteenth-century house located on Rue de Varennes is the official residence of the *Premier Ministre*. The name is often used to refer to the Prime Minister and his or her administrative staff: *Matignon ne semble pas être d'accord*.

matin [matɛ̃] <> *nm* **1.** [lever du jour] morning ■ **de bon *ou* grand ~** in the early morning, early in the morning ■ **partir au petit ~** to leave early in the morning ■ **rentrer au petit ~** to come home in the early *ou* small hours ■ **du ~ au soir** all day long, from morning till night ■ **l'étoile/la rosée du ~** the morning star/dew **2.** [matinée] morning ■ **par un ~ d'été/de juillet** one summer/July morning ■ **un beau ~** one fine day, one of these (fine) days ■ **le ~ du 8, le 8 au ~** on the morning of the 8th ■ **il est 3 h du ~** it's 3 a.m. *ou* 3 (o'clock) in the morning ■ **je suis du ~** [actif le matin] I'm an early riser ; [de service le matin] I'm on *ou* I do the morning shift, I'm on mornings ■ **à prendre ~, midi et soir** to be taken three times a day **3.** *litt* **au ~ de sa vie** in the morning of her life.
<> *adv* **1.** *litt* [de bonne heure] early in the morning, in the early hours (of the morning) **2.** [durant la matinée] : **demain/hier ~** tomorrow/yesterday morning ■ **tous les dimanches ~** every Sunday morning.

mâtin, e [matɛ̃, in] *nm, f fam vieilli* imp, monkey *hum* ■ **le ~, il a filé!** the little devil *ou* rascal has taken off!
◆ **mâtin** *nm* mastiff, guard dog.

matinal, e, aux [matinal, o] *adj* **1.** [du matin] morning *(modif)* ■ **promenade/brise ~e** morning walk/breeze | [du petit matin] : **heure ~e** early hour **2.** [personne] : **je suis assez ~** I'm quite an early riser ■ **vous êtes bien ~ aujourd'hui** you're up early today.

mâtiné, e [matine] *adj* crossbred.

matinée [matine] *nf* **1.** [matin] morning ■ **je vous verrai demain dans la ~** I'll see you sometime tomorrow morning ■ **en début/fin de ~** at the beginning/end of the morning ■ **par une belle ~ de printemps/de juillet** on a gorgeous spring/July morning **2.** THÉÂTRE matinee ■ **y a-t-il une séance en ~?** is there an afternoon *ou* matinee performance?

mâtiner [3] [matine] *vt* to cross ■ **un français mâtiné d'italien** *fig* French peppered with Italian words.

matines [matin] *nfpl* matins, mattins.

matir [32] [matir] *vt* to matt, to dull.

matois, e [matwa, az] <> *adj litt* sly, cunning, wily.
<> *nm, f* cunning person ■ **c'est un fin ~** he's a cunning old fox.

maton, onne△ [matɔ̃, ɔn] *nm, f arg crime* (prison) screw.

matos [matos] *nm fam* gear ■ **ils ont un sacré ~** they've got loads of gear.

matou [matu] *nm fam* tom, tomcat.

matraquage [matrakaʒ] *nm* **1.** [dans une bagarre] coshing *UK*, bludgeoning, clubbing ■ [dans une manifestation] truncheoning *UK*, clubbing *US* **2.** *fam* [propagande] : **~ publicitaire** plugging ■ **tu as vu le ~ qu'ils font pour le bouquin/le concert?** have you seen all the hype about the book/the concert?

matraque [matrak] *nf* **1.** [de police] truncheon *UK*, billy club *US*, night stick *US* ■ **il a reçu un coup de ~** he was hit with a truncheon *UK ou* billy club *US* ■ **500 euros, c'est le coup de ~!** *fam fig* 500 euros, that's a bit steep! **2.** [de voyou] cosh *UK*, bludgeon, club ■ **tué à coups de ~** bludgeoned *ou* clubbed *ou* coshed *UK* to death.

matraquer [3] [matrake] *vt* **1.** [frapper - suj: malfaiteur] to cosh *UK*, to bludgeon, to club ; [- suj: agent de police] to truncheon *UK*, to club *US* ■ **on se fait ~ dans ce restaurant!** *fam fig* they really soak you in this restaurant! **2.** *fam* [auditeur, consommateur] to bombard ■ [disque, chanson] to plug, to hype.

matraqueur, euse [matrakœr, øz] *nm, f* [agresseur] mugger.

matriarcal, e, aux [matrijarkal, o] *adj* matriarchal.

matriarcat [matrijarka] *nm* matriarchy.

matrice [matris] *nf* **1.** [moule - gén] mould, die, matrix *spéc* ; [- d'un caractère d'imprimerie] mat, matrix ▪ **~ d'un disque/d'une bande** matrix record/tape ▪ **coulé en ~** die-cast **2.** INFORM (core) matrix **3.** MATH matrix **4.** ADMIN : **~ du rôle des contributions** assessment roll ▪ **~ cadastrale** cadastre **5.** *vieilli* [utérus] womb **6.** MÉTALL [d'un alliage] matrix.

matricide [matrisid] ◇ *nmf* [personne] matricide.
◇ *nm litt* [crime] matricide.

matriciel, elle [matrisjɛl] *adj* **1.** ADMIN tax-assessment *(modif)* **2.** MATH : **calcul ~** matrix calculation ▪ **algèbre ~le** matrix algebra **3.** INFORM [écran] dot matrix *(modif)* ▪ [imprimante] matrix *(modif)*.

matricule [matrikyl] ◇ *adj* reference *(modif)*.
◇ *nm* **1.** ADMIN reference number **2.** MIL roll number ▪ **sois là à l'heure ou gare à ton ~!** *fam* be there on time or you'll be in for it!
◇ *nf* ADMIN register.

matrilinéaire [matrilineɛr] *adj* matrilinear.

matrimonial, e, aux [matrimɔnjal, o] *adj* matrimonial.

matrone [matrɔn] *nf* **1.** [femme - respectable] staid *ou* upright woman, matron ; [- corpulente] stout *ou* portly woman **2.** ANTIQ matron.

matronyme [matrɔnim] *nm* matronymic.

Matthieu [matjø] *npr* : **saint ~** Saint Matthew.

maturation [matyrasjɔ̃] *nf* **1.** BOT maturation ▪ **son talent est arrivé à ~** *fig* her talent has reached its peak **2.** [du fromage] ripening, maturing **3.** MÉD maturation **4.** MÉTALL age-hardening **5.** AGRIC maturation, ripening.

mature [matyr] *adj* **1.** ZOOL ripe **2.** [développé] mature.

mâture [matyr] *nf* NAUT [mâts] masts ▪ **dans la ~** aloft ▪ **pièces de ~** timber for masts ❚ [atelier] mast house.

maturité [matyrite] *nf* **1.** [d'un fruit] ripeness ▪ [de la pensée, d'un style] maturity ▪ **venir** *ou* **parvenir à ~** *pr* to become ripe, to ripen ; *fig* to become mature, to reach maturity ▪ **attendons qu'elle ait une plus grande ~ d'esprit** *ou* **de jugement** let's wait until she's more intellectually mature **2.** [âge] prime (of life) ▪ **l'artiste fut frappée en pleine ~** the artist was struck down at the height of her powers *ou* of her creative genius **3.** *Suisse* [baccalauréat] school-leaving diploma *(granting admission to university)*.

maudire [104] [modir] *vt* **1.** RELIG to damn **2.** [vouer à la calamité] to curse ▪ **~ le destin** to curse fate ▪ **maudit soit, maudite soit** a curse *ou* plague on.

maudit, e [modi, it] *adj* **1.** [mal considéré] accursed ▪ **c'est un livre ~** the book has been censured ▪ **poète ~** damned *ou* cursed poet **2.** *fam (avant le n) fam* [dans des exclamations] cursed, blasted, damned ▪ **~e bagnole!** blasted *ou* goddam *US* car!
◆ **maudit** *nm* RELIG : **le Maudit** Satan, the Fallen One ▪ **les ~s** the Damned.

maugréer [15] [mogree] *vi* to grumble ▪ **~ contre qqch** to grumble about sthg.

maure [mɔr] *adj* Moorish.
◆ **Maure** *nm* Moor ▪ **les Maures** the Moors.

mauresque [mɔrɛsk] *adj* Moorish.
◆ **mauresque** *nf* [motif] moresque, Moresque.
◆ **Mauresque** *nf* Moorish woman.

Maurice [moris] *npr* : **l'île ~** Mauritius, *voir aussi* **île**.

mauricien, enne [morisjɛ̃, ɛn] *adj* Mauritian.
◆ **Mauricien, enne** *nm, f* Mauritian.

Mauritanie [moritani] *npr f* : **(la) ~** Mauritania.

mauritanien, enne [moritanjɛ̃, ɛn] *adj* Mauritanian.
◆ **Mauritanien, enne** *nm, f* Mauritanian.

mausolée [mozɔle] *nm* mausoleum.

maussade [mosad] *adj* **1.** [de mauvaise humeur] glum, sullen ▪ **elle l'accueillit d'un air ~** she greeted him sullenly **2.** [triste - temps] gloomy, dismal.

maussaderie [mosadri] *nf sout* moroseness, glumness.

mauvais, e [movɛ, ɛz *(devant nm commençant par voyelle ou 'h' muet :* movɛz)] ◇ *adj*

> **A.** EN QUALITÉ
> **B.** DÉSAGRÉABLE
> **C.** NON CONFORME
> **D.** NÉFASTE

A. EN QUALITÉ

1. [médiocre] bad, poor ▪ **son deuxième roman est plus/moins ~ que le premier** her second novel is worse than her first/is not as bad as her first ▪ **en ~ état** in bad *ou* poor condition ▪ **un produit de ~e qualité** a poor quality product ▪ **la route est ~e** the road is bad *ou* in a bad state ▪ **j'ai une ~e vue** *ou* **de ~ yeux** I've got bad eyesight ▪ **après l'entracte, la pièce devient franchement ~e** after the interval, the play gets really bad ▪ **de ~ résultats** [dans une entreprise] poor results ; [à un examen] bad *ou* poor *ou* low grades ▪ **de ~ goût : c'est de ~ goût** it's in bad taste ▪ **il porte toujours des cravates de ~ goût** he always wears such tasteless ties ▪ **avoir ~ goût : elle a très ~ goût** she has very bad *ou* poor taste
2. [défectueux] bad, wrong, faulty ▪ **la ligne est ~e** [téléphone] the line is bad ▪ **la balle est ~e** SPORT the ball is out ▪ **le service est ~** SPORT it's a bad *ou* faulty serve
3. [incompétent] bad, poor ▪ **il a été ~ à la télévision hier** he was bad on TV yesterday ▪ **je suis ~e en économie** I'm bad *ou* poor at economics

B. DÉSAGRÉABLE

1. [odeur, goût] bad, unpleasant, nasty ▪ **prends ton sirop – c'est ~!** take your cough mixture – it's nasty! ▪ **je n'irai plus dans ce restaurant, c'était trop ~** I won't go to that restaurant again, it was too awful ▪ **il n'est pas si ~ que ça, ton café** your coffee isn't that bad ▪ **le poisson a une ~e odeur** the fish smells bad ▪ **elle a ~e haleine** she has bad breath ▪ **~ goût** [de la nourriture, d'un médicament] bad *ou* nasty *ou* unpleasant taste ▪ **jette ça, c'est ~** [pourri] throw that away, it's gone bad ▪ **enlève ce qui est ~** [dans un fruit] take off the bad bits ❚ [éprouvant] bad ▪ **passer un ~ hiver** to have a bad winter ▪ **le ~ temps** bad weather ➲ **la trouver** *ou* **l'avoir ~e** *fam* to be furious *ou* livid *ou* wild ▪ **tirer qqn d'un ~ pas** to get sb out of a fix
2. [défavorable] bad ▪ **~e nouvelle, elle ne vient plus** bad news, she's not coming anymore ▪ **tu as fait une ~e affaire** you've got a bad deal (there)

C. NON CONFORME

1. [erroné, inapproprié] wrong ▪ **prendre qqch dans le ~ sens** to take sthg the wrong way ▪ **faire un ~ calcul** *fig* to miscalculate
2. [inopportun] bad, inconvenient, wrong ▪ **j'ai téléphoné à un ~ moment** I called at a bad *ou* an inconvenient time ▪ **tu as choisi le ~ jour pour me parler d'argent** you've picked the wrong day to talk to me about money ▪ **il ne serait pas ~ de la prévenir** it wouldn't be a bad idea to warn her

D. NÉFASTE

1. [dangereux] bad, nasty ▪ **un ~ rhume** a bad *ou* nasty cold ▪ **c'est ~ pour les poumons/plantes** it's bad for your lungs/for the plants ▪ **ne bois pas l'eau, elle est ~e** don't drink the water, it's unsafe *ou* not safe ▪ **je trouve ~ que les enfants regardent trop la télévision** I think it's bad *ou* harmful for children to watch too much television
2. [malveillant] nasty, unpleasant ▪ **un rire/sourire ~** a nasty laugh/smile ▪ **~ coup** [de poing] nasty blow *ou* punch ; [de pied] nasty kick ▪ **faire un ~ coup** to get up to no good ▪ **faire un ~ coup à qqn** to play a dirty trick on sb ▪ **avoir l'air ~** to look nasty ▪ **en fait, ce n'est pas un ~ homme/une ~e femme** he/she means no harm(, really)
3. [immoral] bad ▪ **avoir de ~ instincts** to have bad *ou* base instincts
4. [funeste] bad ▪ **c'est (un) ~ signe** it's a bad sign ▪ **~ présage** bad *ou* ill omen.
◇ *nm, f* [personne méchante] bad person ▪ **oh, le ~/la ~e!** [à un enfant] you naughty boy/girl!

◆ **mauvais** ◇ *adv* **1.** MÉTÉOR : **faire ~ : il fait ~** the weather's bad *ou* nasty **2.** *(suivi d'un infin)* **il fait ~ être/avoir...** it's not a good idea to be/to have... ■ **à cette époque-là, il faisait ~ être juif** it was hard to be Jewish in those days.
◇ *nm* [ce qui est critiquable] : **le ~ : il n'y a pas que du ~ dans ce qu'il a fait** what he did wasn't all bad ■ **il y a du bon et du ~ dans leur proposition** there are some good points and some bad points in their proposal.

mauve [mov] ◇ *adj* & *nm* mauve.
◇ *nf* BOT mallow ■ **petite ~** least mallow.

mauviette [movjɛt] *nf* **1.** *fam* [gringalet] weakling ■ [lâche] sissy, softy ■ **t'es un homme ou t'es une ~?** are you a man or a mouse? **2.** ZOOL lark.

maux [mo] *pl* ▻ **mal**.

max (*abr écrite de* **maximum**) max.

max△ [maks] (*abr de* **maximum**) *nm* **1.** [peine] maximum sentence ■ **il a écopé du ~** he copped the full whack△ *UK*, he got the maximum sentence *ou* rap *US* **2.** *loc* **un ~** [beaucoup] : **ça va te coûter un ~** it's going to cost you a bomb *UK ou* a packet ■ **il débloque un ~** he's totally off his rocker ■ **il en a rajouté un ~** he went completely overboard ■ **un ~ de fric** loads of money.

maxi [maksi] ◇ *adj inv* **1.** [long] maxi ■ **un manteau ~** a maxi-coat **2.** *fam* [maximum] : **vitesse ~** top *ou* full speed.
◇ *nm* COUT maxi ■ **le ~ revient à la mode** maxis are back in fashion.
◇ *adv fam fam* [au maximum] : **7 degrés/deux heures ~** 7 degrees/two hours at the most.

maxillaire [maksilɛr] ◇ *adj* maxillary.
◇ *nm* jaw, jawbone, maxilla *spéc* ■ **les ~s** the maxillae ▶ **~ supérieur/inférieur** upper/lower jaw.

maxima *pl* ▻ **maximum**.

maximal, e, aux [maksimal, o] *adj* **1.** [le plus grand] maximal, maximum *(modif)* ■ **pour un confort ~** for maximum comfort ■ **à la vitesse ~e** at top speed ■ **température ~e** highest *ou* maximum temperature **2.** MATH maximal.

maximalisation [maksimalizasjɔ̃] *nf* maximation, maximization.

maximaliser [3] [maksimalize] *vt* to maximize.

maximaliste [maksimalist] *adj* & *nmf* maximalist.

maxime [maksim] *nf* maxim.

Maximilien [maksimiljɛ̃] *npr* Maximilian.

maximiser [maksimize] = **maximaliser**.

maximum [maksimɔm] (*pl* **maximums** *ou pl* **maxima** [maksima]) ◇ *adj* maximum ■ **pressions maxima** maximum pressures ■ **vitesse ~** maximum *ou* top speed.
◇ *nm* **1.** [le plus haut degré] maximum ■ **le ~ saisonnier** the maximum temperature for the season ■ **en rentrant, on a mis le chauffage au ~** when we got home, we turned the heating on full ■ **le thermostat est réglé sur le ~** the thermostat is on the highest setting ■ **nous ferons le ~ le premier jour** we'll do as much as we can on the first day **2.** *fam* [en intensif] : **un ~ de** an enormous amount of ■ **il y a eu un ~ de visiteurs le premier jour** we had an enormous number of visitors the first day ■ **pour ça il faut un ~ d'organisation** that sort of thing needs a huge amount of *ou* needs loads of organization ■ **on s'est amusés un ~** we had a really great time ■ **on en fera un ~ le premier jour** we'll do as much work as we can on the first day **3.** [peine] : **il a eu le ~** he got the maximum sentence.
◇ *adv* at the most *ou* maximum ■ **il fait 3°C ~** the temperature is 3°C at the most *ou* at the maximum.
◆ **au maximum** *loc adv* **1.** [au plus] at the most *ou* maximum ■ **au grand ~** at the very most **2.** [le plus possible] : **un espace utilisé au ~** an area used to full advantage ■ **je nettoie au ~ mais c'est quand même sale** I do as much cleaning as possible but it's still dirty.

maya[1] [maja] *adj* Maya, Mayan.
◆ **Maya** *nmf* Maya, Mayan ■ **les Mayas** the Maya *ou* Mayas.

maya[2] [maja] *nf* RELIG maya.

mayen [majɛ̃] *nm Suisse Alpine pasture in the Valais region for spring and autumn grazing.*

mayonnaise [majɔnɛz] *nf* CULIN mayonnaise ▶ **œufs ~** eggs mayonnaise.

Mayotte [majɔt] *npr* Mayotte Island.

mazagran [mazagrɑ̃] *nm glazed earthenware cup for drinking coffee.*

Mazarine [mazarin] *npr* : **la bibliothèque ~** *public library in Paris.*

mazette [mazɛt] *interj vieilli* & *hum* my (word).

mazot [mazo] *nm Suisse* farm building.

mazout [mazut] *nm* (fuel) oil ■ **chauffage central au ~** oil-fired central heating.

mazouter [3] [mazute] ◇ *vt* to pollute (with oil) ■ **plages mazoutées** oil-polluted beaches, beaches polluted with oil ■ **oiseaux mazoutés** oil-stricken birds.
◇ *vi* to refuel.

mazurka [mazyrka] *nf* mazurka.

MCJ (*abr de* **maladie de Creutsfeld-Jakob**) [ɛmseʒi] *nf* MÉD CJD.

MDR (*abr de* **mort de rire**) [ɛmdeɛr] *nf* LOL ■ [plus fort] ROFLMAO.

me [mə] *(devant voyelle ou 'h' muet m'* [m]*) pron pers (1ère pers sing)* **1.** [avec un verbe pronominal] : **je me suis fait mal** I've hurt myself ■ **je me suis évanoui** I fainted ■ **je ne m'en souviens plus** I don't remember anymore ■ **je me disais que...** I thought to myself... **2.** [complément] : **il me regarde sans me voir** he looks at me without seeing me, he looks right through me ■ **il me l'a donné** he gave it to me ■ **ton idée me plaît** I like your idea ■ **ton amitié m'est précieuse** your friendship is precious *ou* means a lot to me ■ **ça me soulève le cœur** it makes me sick ■ **il me court après depuis un certain temps** *fam* he's been chasing me for some time **3.** *fam* [emploi expressif] : **va me fermer cette porte** shut that door, will you? ■ **qu'est-ce qu'ils m'ont encore fait comme bêtises?** what kind of stupid tricks have they got up to now?

Me (*abr écrite de* **Maître**) *title for lawyers.*

mea culpa [meakylpa] ◇ *nm inv* **1.** RELIG mea culpa **2.** *fig* **ils ont fait leur ~** they acknowledged responsibility, they admitted it was their fault.
◇ *interj hum* my fault, mea culpa *sout* ■ **~! c'est moi le responsable** it's my fault!, I'm to blame!

méandre [meɑ̃dr] *nm* ARCHIT & GÉOGR meander ■ **le fleuve fait des ~s** the river meanders *ou* twists and turns ■ **l'affaire s'enlisait dans les ~s de la procédure** the case was getting bogged down in a morass *ou* maze of legalities ■ **les ~s de sa pensée** the twists and turns of his thoughts.

méat [mea] *nm* **1.** ANAT meatus ■ **~ urinaire** urinary meatus **2.** BOT lacuna.

mec△ [mɛk] *nm* **1.** [homme] guy, bloke *UK* ■ **hé, les ~s!** hey, you guys! ■ **un beau ~** a good-looking guy ■ **pauvre ~, va!** creep!△ ■ **écoute, petit ~!** look, (you little) punk! ■ **ça, c'est un vrai ~!** *hum* there's a real man for you! **2.** [petit ami] : **son ~** her bloke *UK ou* guy.

mécanicien, enne [mekanisjɛ̃, ɛn] *nm, f* **1.** [monteur, réparateur] mechanic ■ NAUT engineer ■ **~ (de bord)** AÉRON (flight) engineer **2.** [physicien] mechanical engineer **3.** RAIL engine driver *UK*, engineer *US*.
◆ **mécanicienne** *nf* COUT machinist.

mécanicien-dentiste [mekanisjɛ̃dɑ̃tist] (*pl* **mécaniciens-dentistes**) *nm* dental technician.

mécanique [mekanik] ◇ *adj* **1.** SC [loi] mechanical **2.** [non manuel - tapis, tissage] machine-made ; [- abattage, remblayage] mechanical, machine *(modif)* **3.** [non électrique, non électronique - commande] mechanical ; [- jouet] clockwork ; [- montre] wind-up **4.** [du moteur] engine *(modif)* ■ **nous avons eu un**

incident ~ ou des ennuis ~s en venant we had engine trouble on the way here **5.** [machinal] mechanical **6.** MIN & MINÉR mechanical.
◇ *nf* **1.** SC mechanics *(sing)* ▪ INDUST & TECHNOL mechanical engineering ▪ **~ quantique/relativiste** quantum/relativistic mechanics ▪ **~ ondulatoire** wave mechanics **2.** AUTO car mechanics *(sing)* **3.** [machine] piece of machinery ▪ [dispositif] mechanism ▪ **marcher ou tourner comme une ~ bien huilée** to work like a well-oiled machine ▪ **une belle ~** [moto, voiture] a fine piece of engineering.

mécanisation [mekanizasjɔ̃] *nf* mechanization ▪ **l'ère de la ~** the machine age.

mécaniser [3] [mekanize] *vt* to mechanize ▪ **ces tâches ont été mécanisées** these jobs have been mechanized *ou* are now done by machine.

mécanisme [mekanism] *nm* **1.** [processus] mechanism ▪ [dispositif] mechanism, device ▪ **le ~ de la violence** the mechanism of violence ▪ **le ~ du corps humain** the human mechanism ▪ **elle étudie le ~ ou les ~s de la finance** she's studying the workings of finance ▪ **~s de défense** PSYCHOL defence mechanisms **2.** TECHNOL [d'une serrure, d'une horloge] mechanism ▪ [d'un fusil] mechanism, workings **3.** PHILOS mechanism.

mécaniste [mekanist] ◇ *adj* PHILOS mechanistic.
◇ *nmf* mechanist.

mécano [mekano] *nm fam* **1.** AUTO mechanic **2.** RAIL engine driver *UK*, engineer *US*.

mécanographe [mekanɔgraf] *nmf* punch card (machine) operator.

mécénat [mesena] *nm* [par une personne] patronage, sponsorship ▪ [par une société] sponsorship ▪ **le ~ d'entreprise** corporate sponsorship.

mécène [mesɛn] *nm* [personne] patron, sponsor ▪ [société] sponsor.

méchamment [meʃamɑ̃] *adv* **1.** [avec cruauté] nastily, spitefully, wickedly ▪ **il ne l'a pas fait ~** he didn't do it nastily **2.** *fam* [en intensif] : **il est rentré ~ bronzé** he came back with a wicked tan.

méchanceté [meʃɑ̃ste] *nf* **1.** [volonté de nuire] spite, malice, nastiness ▪ **par pure ~** out of sheer spite ▪ **soit dit sans ~, elle n'est pas futée** without wishing to be unkind, she is not very bright **2.** [caractère méchant] maliciousness, nastiness, spitefulness ▪ **la ~ se lit dans son regard** you can see the malice in his eyes **3.** [propos, acte] : **dire des ~s à qqn** to say nasty *ou* horrible things to sb ▪ **faire des ~s à qqn** to be nasty *ou* horrible to sb.

méchant, e [meʃɑ̃, ɑ̃t] ◇ *adj* **1.** [cruel - animal] nasty, vicious ; [- personne] wicked ▪ [haineux] nasty, spiteful, wicked ▪ **il n'est pas ~** [pas malveillant] there's no harm in him, he's harmless ; [pas dangereux] he won't do you any harm ▪ **en fait, ce n'est pas une ~e femme** she means no harm *ou* she's not that bad, really **2.** [très désagréable] horrible, horrid, nasty ▪ **ne sois pas si ~ avec moi** don't be so nasty *ou* horrible to me ▪ *(avant le n)* **de fort ~e humeur** in a (really) foul mood ▮ [enfant] naughty, bad **3.** [grave] nasty, very bad ▪ **il a attrapé une ~e grippe** he caught a nasty dose of flu ▪ **ça n'était pas bien ~, finalement, cette piqûre/ce permis?** *fam* the injection/driving test wasn't that bad after all, was it? **4.** *fam (avant le n) fam* [formidable] tremendous, terrific, great ▪ **il y avait une ~e ambiance** there was a great atmosphere ▪ **ce tube a eu un ~ succès** that record was a huge hit **5.** *(avant le n)* [pitoyable] pathetic, wretched, miserable ▪ **elle essayait de vendre deux ou trois ~es salades** she was trying to sell a couple of pathetic-looking lettuces.
◇ *nm, f* **1.** *langage enfantin* naughty child ▪ **faire le ~** to turn nasty **2.** [dans un film, un livre] baddy *UK*, bad guy *US*.

mèche [mɛʃ] *nf* **1.** [de cheveux] lock ▪ **se faire faire des ~s** to have highlights *ou* (blond) streaks put in ▪ **~s folles** wispy curls ▪ **une ~ rebelle** a wayward strand of hair ▪ **une ~ dans les yeux** (a strand of) hair in his eyes **2.** [pour lampe, explosifs, feu d'artifice] wick ▪ [pour canon] match ▪ **~ lente ou de sûreté** safety fuse ▪ **découvrir ou éventer la ~** *fam* to uncover the plot **3.** MÉCAN bit **4.** MÉD [pour coaguler] pack ▪ [pour drainer] (gauze) wick **5.** *fam loc* **être de ~ avec qqn** to be in league *ou* in cahoots with sb ▪ **ils étaient de ~** they were in it together.

méchoui [meʃwi] *nm* [repas] barbecue *(of a whole sheep roasted on a spit)* ▪ [fête] barbecue (party).

mécompte [mekɔ̃t] *nm litt* disappointment.

méconduite [mekɔ̃dɥit] *nf Belgique* misbehaviour.

méconnais *etc v* ▷ **méconnaître**.

méconnaissable [mekɔnɛsabl] *adj* [à peine reconnaissable] hardly recognizable ▪ [non reconnaissable] unrecognizable ▪ **sans sa barbe il est ~** you wouldn't recognize him without his beard ▪ **dix ans après elle était ~** ten years later she had changed beyond recognition.

méconnaissait *etc v* ▷ **méconnaître**.

méconnaissance [mekɔnɛsɑ̃s] *nf* **1.** [ignorance] ignorance, lack of knowledge ▪ **il a fait preuve d'une totale ~ du sujet** he displayed a complete lack of knowledge of the subject **2.** [incompréhension] lack of comprehension *ou* understanding.

méconnaître [91] [mekɔnɛtr] *vt litt* **1.** [ignorer] to be unaware of **2.** [ne pas reconnaître] to fail to recognize ▪ **sans vouloir ~ ce qu'ils ont fait pour nous** while not wishing to minimize *ou* to underestimate what they have done for us ▪ **il était méconnu de ses contemporains** he went unrecognized by his contemporaries **3.** [mal comprendre] to fail to understand ▪ **c'est ~ le milieu universitaire!** you're/he's *etc* misjudging the academic world! ▮ [personne] to misunderstand, to misjudge.

méconnu, e [mekɔny] *adj* [incompris] unappreciated, unrecognized ▪ [peu connu] obscure ▪ **un coin ~ mais très joli de la Bretagne** a little-known but very pretty part of Brittany ▪ **rester ~** [non apprécié] to go unrecognized, to remain unappreciated ; [sans gloire] to remain unknown ▪ **malgré son grand talent il est mort pauvre et ~** in spite of his great talent he died penniless and in obscurity ▪ **mes mérites sont méconnus** my merits have never been acknowledged.

méconnut *etc v* ▷ **méconnaître**.

mécontent, e [mekɔ̃tɑ̃, ɑ̃t] ◇ *adj* **1.** [insatisfait] displeased, dissatisfied, discontented ▪ **elle est toujours ~e de quelque chose** she's always annoyed *ou* disgruntled about something ▪ **je ne suis pas ~e de mes résultats** I am not altogether dissatisfied *ou* unhappy with my results ▪ **nous ne sommes pas ~s que tout soit terminé** we are not sorry that it's all over **2.** [fâché] annoyed ▪ **il s'est montré très ~ de ma décision** he was very annoyed at my decision.
◇ *nm, f* **1.** [gén] complainer, grumbler, moaner **2.** POLIT : **les ~s** the discontented, the disgruntled ▪ **cette politique va faire des ~s** this measure is going to displease quite a few people.

mécontentement [mekɔ̃tɑ̃tmɑ̃] *nm* **1.** [agitation sociale] discontent, unrest, anger ▪ **cela risque de provoquer le ~ des agriculteurs** that might anger the farmers **2.** [agacement] annoyance ▪ **à mon grand ~** to my great annoyance.

mécontenter [3] [mekɔ̃tɑ̃te] *vt* [déplaire à] to fail to please, to displease ▪ [irriter] to annoy, to irritate ▪ **la réforme risque de ~ les milieux d'affaires** the reform might anger business circles.

Mecque [mɛk] *npr f* **1.** GÉOGR : **La ~** Mecca **2.** *fig* **la ~ de** the mecca of, a mecca for.

mécréant, e [mekreɑ̃, ɑ̃t] *nm, f litt* infidel, miscreant *arch.*

méd. = **médecin**.

médaille [medaj] *nf* **1.** [pour célébrer, récompenser] medal ▪ **~ d'or** gold medal ▶ **~ d'honneur** *medal for honourable service in a profession* ▪ **toute ~ a son revers** *prov* every rose has its thorn **2.** [pour identifier] (identity) disk *ou* tag **3.** [bijou] pendant.

médaillé, e [medaje] ◇ *adj* [soldat] decorated ▪ SPORT medal-holding *(modif)* ▪ **un camembert ~** an award-winning camembert.
◇ *nm, f* **1.** ADMIN & MIL medal-holder **2.** SPORT medallist ▪ **les ~s olympiques** the Olympic medallists.

médailler [3] [medaje] *vt* to award a medal to.

médaillier [medaje] *nm* **1.** [collection] medal collection **2.** [meuble] medal cabinet.

médaillon [medajɔ̃] *nm* **1.** [bijou] locket **2.** CULIN medallion **3.** [élément décoratif] medallion.

médecin [medsɛ̃] *nmf* [docteur] doctor, physician ▪ **une femme ~** a woman doctor ◗ **~ agréé** *doctor whose fees are partially reimbursed by the social security system* ▪ **~ des armées** army medical officer ▪ **~ de bord** ship's doctor ▪ **~ de campagne** country doctor ▪ **~ consultant** consultant ▪ **~ conventionné** *doctor who meets the French social security criteria* ▪ ≃ National Health doctor *UK* ▪ **~ de famille** family doctor ▪ **~ généraliste** general practitioner, GP ▪ **~ des hôpitaux** hospital doctor ▪ **~ légiste** forensic expert *ou* scientist, medical examiner *US* ▪ **~ spécialiste** specialist (physician) ▪ **~ traitant** attending physician ▪ **~ du travail** [dans le privé] company doctor ; [dans le secteur public] health (and safety) *ou* medical officer *UK* ▪ **Médecins du monde, Médecins sans frontières** *organizations providing medical aid to victims of war and disasters, especially in the Third World.*

médecin-chef [medsɛ̃ʃɛf] (*pl* **médecins-chefs**) *nmf* head doctor.

médecin-conseil [medsɛ̃kɔ̃sɛj] (*pl* **médecins-conseils**) *nmf* medical consultant *(who checks the validity of claims).*

médecine [medsin] *nf* **1.** SC medicine ▪ **exercer la ~** to practise medicine ▪ **ce n'est plus du ressort de la ~** it's no longer a medical matter ◗ **~ douce/hospitalière/légale** natural/hospital/forensic medicine ▪ **~ générale** general practice ▪ **~ interne** internal medicine ▪ **~ parallèle** alternative medicine ▪ **~ préventive** preventive *ou* preventative medicine ▪ **~ du travail** industrial *ou* occupational medicine **2.** ÉDUC medicine, medical studies ▪ **il fait (sa) ~, il est en ~** he's studying medicine, he's a medical student ▪ **elle est en troisième année de ~** she's in her third year at medical school, she's a third-year medical student ▪ **elle a fini sa ~ en 1980** she qualified (as a doctor) in 1980 **3.** *arch* [remède] medicine, remedy.

Médée [mede] *npr* Medea.

MEDEF (*abr de* **Mouvement des Entreprises de France**) [medɛf] *nf main employers' organization in France,* ≃ CBI *UK.*

média [medja] *nm* medium ▪ **les ~s** the (mass) media ▪ **une campagne dans tous les ~s** a media-wide campaign.

médian, e [medjɑ̃, an] *adj* **1.** GÉOM median **2.** LING medial.
◆ **médiane** *nf* median.

médiat, e [medja, at] *adj* mediate.

médiateur, trice [medjatœr, tris] ◇ *adj* mediating, mediatory ▪ **commission médiatrice** arbitration commission *ou* board.
◇ *nm, f* **1.** intermediary, go-between, mediator ▪ **servir de ~** to act as a go-between. **2.** INDUST arbitrator, mediator **3.** ADMIN & POLIT mediator, ombudsman ▪ **le Médiateur** ≃ the Parliamentary Commissioner *UK* ▪ ≃ the Ombudsman *UK.*
◆ **médiatrice** *nf* GÉOM midperpendicular.

médiathèque [medjatɛk] *nf* media library.

médiation [medjasjɔ̃] *nf* **1.** [entremise - POLIT] mediation ▪ INDUST arbitration ▪ **il a fallu la ~ de l'évêque** the bishop had to mediate ▪ **j'offre ma ~** I volunteer to act as a go-between *ou* as an intermediary **2.** PHYSIOL neurotransmission.

médiatique [medjatik] ◇ *adj* media *(modif)* ▪ **un événement ~** a media *ou* a media-staged *péj* event ▪ **c'est un sport très ~** it's a sport well suited to the media ▪ **il est très ~** [il passe bien à la télévision] he comes over well on television ; [il exploite les médias] he uses the media very successfully.
◇ *nf* communications, communication technology.

médiatisation [medjatizasjɔ̃] *nf* **1.** RADIO & TV popularization through the (mass) media ▪ **on assiste à une ~ croissante de la production littéraire** literary works are getting more and more media exposure ▪ **nous déplorons la ~ de la politique** it's a shame to see politics being turned into a media event **2.** POLIT mediatization.

médiatisé, e [medjatize] *adj* : **il est très ~** he's got a high media profile ▪ **un événement très ~** an event that was given a lot of media coverage, an event widely reported in the media.

médiatiser [3] [medjatize] *vt* **1.** RADIO & TV to popularize through the (mass) media ▪ **~ les élections/la guerre** to turn elections/the war into a media event **2.** POLIT to mediatize.

médiatrice [medjatris] *f* ▻ **médiateur**.

médical, e, aux [medikal, o] *adj* medical.

médicalement [medikalmɑ̃] *adv* medically ▪ **~, il est guéri** medically speaking, he's cured.

médicalisation [medikalizasjɔ̃] *nf* **1.** [d'une région] : **la ~ des pays pauvres** the provision of health care to poor countries **2.** [d'un état, d'une pathologie] : **la ~ croissante de la grossesse** the increasing reliance on medical technology during pregnancy.

médicaliser [3] [medikalize] *vt* **1.** [région, pays] to provide with health care **2.** [maternité, vieillesse] to increase medical intervention in.

médicament [medikamɑ̃] *nm* medicine, drug ▪ **prends tes ~s** take your medicine ▪ **~ de confort** *pharmaceutical product not considered to be essential and not fully reimbursed by the French social security system* ▪ **~ délivré sans ordonnance** medicine issued without a prescription, over-the-counter drug ▪ **~ en vente sur ordonnance** drug available on prescription, prescription drug *US.*

médicamenteux, euse [medikamɑ̃tø, øz] *adj* medicinal.

médication [medikasjɔ̃] *nf* medication.

médicinal, e, aux [medisinal, o] *adj* medicinal.

Médicis [medisis] *npr* **1.** HIST Medici ▪ **Catherine de ~** Catherine de' Medici ▪ **les ~** the Medicis **2.** LITTÉR : **le prix ~** *French literary prize.*

médico-légal, e, aux [medikɔlegal, o] *adj* forensic, medicolegal.

médico-pédagogique [medikɔpedagɔʒik] (*pl* **médico-pédagogiques**) *adj* : **institut ~** special school *(for children with special needs or learning disabilities who are under 14).*

médico-professionnel, elle [medikɔprɔfɛsjɔnɛl] (*mpl* **médico-professionnels**, *fpl* **médico-professionnelles**) *adj* : **institut ~** *social education workshop for young people with learning disabilities.*

médico-social, e, aux [medikɔsɔsjal, o] *adj* medico-social ▪ **services médico-sociaux** health and social services network.

médico-sportif, ive [medikɔspɔrtif, iv] (*mpl* **médico-sportifs**, *fpl* **médico-sportives**) *adj* : **institut ~** institute for sports medicine.

médiéval, e, aux [medjeval, o] *adj* medieval ▪ **l'époque ~e** the medieval period, the Middle Ages.

médiéviste [medjevist] *nmf* medievalist.

médina [medina] *nf* medina.

Médine [medin] *npr* Medina.

médiocre [medjɔkr] ◇ *adj* **1.** [rendement, efficacité, qualité etc] mediocre, poor ▪ **elle est ~ en mathématiques** she's pretty mediocre at mathematics ▪ **temps ~ sur toute la France** poor weather throughout France **2.** [quelconque] second-rate, mediocre ▪ **il a fait une carrière ~** his career has been unsuccessful ▪ **je refuse de mener une vie ~** I refuse to live a life of mediocrity **3.** *(avant le n) sout* [piètre] poor ▪ **un livre de ~ intérêt** a book of little interest.
◇ *nmf* [personne] nonentity.
◇ *nm* [médiocrité] mediocrity.

médiocrement [medjɔkrəmɑ̃] *adv* : **un enfant ~ doué pour les langues** a child with no great gift for languages ■ **~ satisfait, il décida de recommencer** not very satisfied, he decided to start again ■ **j'ai répondu assez ~ à l'examen oral** my answers in the oral exam were rather poor.

médiocrité [medjɔkrite] *nf* **1.** [en qualité] mediocrity, poor quality ■ [en quantité] inadequacy ■ **ce genre de spectacle ne souffre pas la ~** this type of show will not allow for *ou* admit mediocrity **2.** [personne] nonentity.

médire [103] [medir] ◆ **médire de** *v+prép* [critiquer] to speak ill of, to run down *(sép)* ■ [calomnier] to spread scandal about, to malign ■ *(en usage absolu)* **arrête de ~!** stop criticizing!

médisance [medizɑ̃s] *nf* **1.** [dénigrement] gossip, gossiping, scandalmongering ■ **c'est de la ~!** that's slander! **2.** [propos] gossip ■ **les ~s de ses collègues lui ont fait du tort** his colleagues' (malicious) gossip has damaged his good name.

médisant, e [medizɑ̃, ɑ̃t] ◇ *adj* slanderous ■ **sans vouloir être ~, je dois dire que je le trouve un peu naïf** no malice intended, but I have to say that I find him a bit naïve.
◇ *nm, f* [auteur - de ragots] gossip, gossipmonger, scandalmonger ; [- de diffamation] slanderer.

médisez *etc v* ▷ **médire.**

médit [medi] *pp* ▷ **médire.**

méditatif, ive [meditatif, iv] ◇ *adj* meditative, contemplative, thoughtful ■ **il avait un air ~** he appeared to be deep in thought.
◇ *nm, f* thinker.

méditation [meditasjɔ̃] *nf* **1.** PSYCHOL & RELIG meditation **2.** [réflexion] meditation, thought ■ **le fruit de mes ~s** the fruit of my meditation *ou* meditations.

méditer [3] [medite] ◇ *vt* **1.** [réfléchir à] to meditate on *ou* upon *(insép)*, to reflect on *ou* upon *(insép)*, to ponder (upon) *(insép)* ■ **elle veut encore ~ sa décision** she wants to think some more about her decision **2.** [projeter] to plan ■ **~ de faire qqch** to plan on doing sthg.
◇ *vi* to meditate ■ **~ sur** to meditate on *(insép)*, to think about *(insép)*.

Méditerranée [mediterane] *npr f* : **la (mer) ~** the Mediterranean (sea) ■ **en ~** in the Mediterranean ■ **une croisière sur la ~** a Mediterranean cruise, *voir aussi* **mer**.

méditerranéen, enne [mediteraneɛ̃, ɛn] *adj* Mediterranean.
◆ **Méditerranéen, enne** *nm, f* Mediterranean, Southern European *(from the Mediterranean area)*.

médium [medjɔm] ◇ *nmf* [spirite] medium.
◇ *nm* **1.** MUS middle register **2.** [liant] medium, vehicle.

médius [medjys] *nm* middle finger.

médoc [medɔk] *nm* Médoc (wine).

Médor [medɔr] *npr typical name for a dog,* ≃ Fido.

médullaire [medylɛr] *adj* medullary.

méduse [medyz] *nf* jellyfish, medusa *spéc.*

Méduse [medyz] *npr* Medusa.

médusé, e [medyze] *adj* stunned, dumbfounded, stupefied ■ **d'un air ~** in stupefaction ■ **j'en suis restée ~e** I was stunned *ou* dumbfounded by it.

méduser [3] [medyze] *vt* to astound, to stun, to stupefy ■ **sa réponse m'a médusé** his reply stunned me.

meeting [mitiŋ] *nm* (public) meeting ■ **~ aérien** air show ■ **~ d'athlétisme** athletics meeting *UK ou* meet *US*.

méfait [mefɛ] *nm* [mauvaise action] misdeed, wrong, wrongdoing ■ [délit] offence.
◆ **méfaits** *nmpl* [ravages] : **les ~s du temps/de la guerre** the ravages of time/war ■ **les ~s du laxisme parental** the damaging effects of a lack of parental discipline ■ **les ~s de la télévision** the harm done by television.

méfiance [mefjɑ̃s] *nf* distrust, mistrust, suspicion ■ **sa ~ envers les étrangers** her distrust *ou* suspicion of foreigners ■ **éveiller la ~ de qqn** to make sb suspicious ■ **il renifla le paquet avec ~** he warily sniffed the parcel ■ **elle est sans ~** she has a trusting nature ■ **~!** be careful!

méfiant, e [mefjɑ̃, ɑ̃t] *adj* distrustful, mistrustful, suspicious ■ **il n'est pas assez ~** he is too unsuspecting *ou* trusting ■ **~ envers qqch** dubious about sthg, sceptical of sthg ■ **on n'est jamais assez ~** you can never be too careful.

méfier [9] [mefje] ◆ **se méfier** *vpi* [faire attention] to be careful *ou* wary ■ **il ne se méfiait pas** he was not on his guard ■ **on ne se méfie jamais assez** you can't be too careful ■ **méfie-toi!** be careful!, watch out!, be on your guard!
◆ **se méfier de** *vp+prép* to be suspicious of, to distrust, to mistrust ■ **méfie-toi de lui/de son air doux** don't trust him/his mild manners ■ **méfiez-vous des contrefaçons** beware of forgeries ■ **il aurait dû se ~ davantage des derniers tournants** he should have been more careful on the last bends ■ **méfiez-vous qu'ils ne se sauvent pas** *fam* watch out *ou* mind they don't run away.

méforme [mefɔrm] *nf* unfitness, lack of fitness ■ **après quelques jours de ~** after a few days off form.

méga(-) [mega] *préf* **1.** SC mega, mega- **2.** *fam* [en intensif] huge, super ■ **ça a été la ~-discussion** there was a huge discussion ■ **une ~-entreprise** a huge firm.

mégahertz [megaɛrts] *nm* megahertz.

mégalithe [megalit] *nm* megalith.

mégalithique [megalitik] *adj* megalithic.

mégalo [megalo] *fam* ◇ *adj* megalomaniac, power-mad ■ **il est complètement ~** he thinks he's God ■ **tu n'es pas un peu ~?** don't you think you're aiming a bit high?
◇ *nmf* megalomaniac.

mégalomane [megalɔman] *adj* & *nmf* megalomaniac.

mégalomanie [megalɔmani] *nf* megalomania.

mégalopole [megalɔpɔl], **mégalopolis** [megalɔpɔlis] *nf* megalopolis.

méga-octet [megaɔktɛ] *nm* megabyte.

mégaphone [megafɔn] *nm* megaphone, loud-hailer *UK*, bullhorn *US*.

mégapole [megapɔl] *nf* megalopolis, huge city.

mégarde [megard] ◆ **par mégarde** *loc adv* [par inattention] inadvertently, by accident, accidentally ■ [par erreur] by mistake, inadvertently ■ [sans le vouloir] unintentionally, inadvertently, accidentally.

mégastore [megastɔr] *nm* megastore.

mégatonne [megatɔn] *nf* megaton.

mégawatt [megawat] *nm* megawatt.

mégère [meʒɛr] *nf sout* shrew *fig*, harridan *litt* ■ **'la Mégère apprivoisée'** ***Shakespeare*** 'The Taming of the Shrew'.

mégot [mego] *nm* [de cigarette] cigarette butt *ou* end ■ [de cigare] cigar butt.

mégoter [3] [megɔte] *vi fam* to skimp, to scrimp ■ **on ne va pas ~ pour quelques euros** let's not quibble about a few euros ■ **~ sur** to skimp *ou* to scrimp on.

méhari [meari] (*pl* **méharis** *ou pl* **méhara** [-ra]) *nm* racing camel *ou* dromedary, mehari.

meilleur, e [mɛjœr] ◇ *adj* **1.** *(comparatif)* better ■ **il n'y a rien de ~, il n'y a pas ~** there's nothing to beat it, there's nothing better ■ **il est ~ père que mari** he is a better father than he is a husband ■ **c'est ~ marché** it's cheaper **2.** *(superlatif)* **le ~** [de tous] the best ; [de deux] the better ■ **son ~ ami** his best friend ■ **c'est le ~ des maris** he's the best husband in the world ■ **avec la ~e volonté** with the best will in the world ■ **~s vœux** best wishes ■ **~s vœux de prompt rétablissement** get well soon ■ **~ souvenir de Cannes** (holiday *UK*) greetings from Cannes ;

[en fin de lettre] best wishes from Cannes ▪ **information prise aux ~es sources** information from the most reliable sources ▪ **il appartient au ~ monde** he moves in the best circles.
◇ *nm, f* best person ▪ **seuls les ~s participeront à la compétition** only the best (players) will take part in the competition ▪ **que le ~ gagne!** may the best man win!
◆ **meilleur** ◇ *nm* : **mange-le, c'est le ~** eat it, it's the best part ▪ **il a donné** *ou* **il y a mis le ~ de lui-même** he gave his all, he gave of his best ▪ **elle lui a consacré le ~ de sa vie** she gave him the best years of her life ▪ **et le ~ de l'histoire, c'est que c'est lui qui m'avait invité** and the best part of it is that he's the one who'd invited me ▪ **pour le ~ et pour le pire** for better or for worse.
◇ *adv* : **il fait ~ aujourd'hui** the weather's *ou* it's better today ▪ **il fait ~ dans la chambre** [plus chaud] it's warmer in the bedroom ; [plus frais] it's cooler in the bedroom.
◆ **meilleure** *nf fam* [histoire] : **tu ne connais pas la ~e** you haven't heard the best bit yet, wait until I tell you this one ▪ **ça alors, c'est la ~e!** that's the best (one) I've heard in a long time! ▪ **j'en passe, et des ~es** and I could go on.

méiose [mejoz] *nf* meiosis.

méjuger [17] [meʒyʒe] *vt litt* to misjudge.
◆ **se méjuger** *vp (emploi réfléchi)* to underestimate o.s.

Mékong [mekɔ̃g] *npr m* : **le ~** the Mekong.

mél [mel] *nm* INFORM email.

mélancolie [melɑ̃kɔli] *nf* **1.** [tristesse] melancholy ▪ **j'y pense avec ~** I feel melancholy when I think about it **2.** PSYCHOL & *arch* melancholia.

mélancolique [melɑ̃kɔlik] ◇ *adj* **1.** [triste, désenchanté] melancholy *(modif)* **2.** PSYCHOL melancholic.
◇ *nmf* melancholic.

Mélanésie [melanezi] *npr f* : **(la) ~** Melanesia.

mélanésien, enne [melanezjɛ̃, ɛn] *adj* Melanesian.
◆ **mélanésien** *nm* LING Melanesian.

mélange [melɑ̃ʒ] *nm* **1.** [processus] mixing, blending **2.** [résultat] mixture, blend ▪ **c'est un ~ de plusieurs thés/parfums** it's a blend of several teas/perfumes ▪ **attention aux ~s (d'alcools)** don't mix your drinks **3.** AUTO mixture ▪ **~ détonant/pauvre/riche** explosive/poor/rich mixture **4.** ACOUST mixing.
◆ **sans mélange** *loc adj* [joie] unalloyed ▪ [admiration] unmitigated.

mélangé, e [melɑ̃ʒe] *adj* [auditoire, population] mixed ▪ **c'est un coton ~** it's a cotton mixture.

mélanger [17] [melɑ̃ʒe] *vt* **1.** [remuer - cartes] to shuffle ; [- salade] to toss ▪ **ajoutez le lait et mélangez** add the milk and mix (well) **2.** [mettre ensemble] to mix, to blend ▪ **~ des couleurs** to blend colours ▪ **ils ne veulent pas ~ les filles et les garçons** they want to keep boys and girls separate ▪ **mélangez les œillets rouges avec les jaunes** mix the red carnations with the yellow ones **3.** [confondre] to mix up *(sép)* ▪ **ne mélange pas tout** don't get everything (all) mixed *ou* jumbled *ou* muddled up ◗ **il ne faut pas ~ les torchons et les serviettes** (don't get them mixed up,) they're in a different class.
◆ **se mélanger** *vpi* **1.** [se fondre] : **se ~ avec** to mix with **2.** [devenir indistinct] to get mixed up ▪ **mes souvenirs se mélangent après tant d'années** my memories are getting confused *ou* muddled after so many years ▪ **tout se mélange dans ma tête** I'm getting all mixed *ou* muddled up.

mélangeur [melɑ̃ʒœr] *nm* **1.** [robinet] mixer tap *UK*, mixing faucet *US* **2.** [de son] mixer.

mélanine [melanin] *nf* melanin.

mélanome [melanom] *nm* melanoma.

mélasse [melas] *nf* **1.** [sirop] molasses *(sing)*, (black) treacle *UK* **2.** *fam* [brouillard] pea-souper ▪ **être dans la ~** *fig* [avoir des ennuis] to be in a jam *ou* a fix *ou* a pickle ; [être sans argent] to be hard up.

mélatonine [melatɔnin] *nf* melatonin.

Melba [mɛlba] *adj inv* : **pêche/poire ~** peach/pear Melba.

Melchior [mɛlkjɔr] *npr* Melchior.

mêlé, e [mele] *adj* mixed ▪ **un chagrin ~ de pitié** sorrow mixed *ou* mingled with pity.

◆ **mêlée** *nf* **1.** [combat] melee, mêlée ▪ **être au-dessus de la ~e** to be on the sidelines ▪ **rester au-dessus de la ~e** to stay above the fray ▪ **entrer dans la ~e** to enter the fray **2.** [bousculade] scuffle, free-for-all ▪ [désordre] commotion, confusion **3.** SPORT scrum, scrummage ▪ **effondrer/tourner la ~e** to collapse/to wheel the scrum ◗ **~e ouverte** [gén] loose scrum ; [balle par terre] ruck ; [balle en main] maul.

mêler [4] [mele] *vt* **1.** [mélanger] to mix ▪ **des fleurs variées mêlaient leurs parfums** the scents of various flowers were mingling in the air **2.** [allier] to combine, to be a mixture *ou* combination of ▪ **elle mêle la rigueur à la fantaisie** she combines *ou* mixes seriousness with light-heartedness **3.** [embrouiller - documents, papiers] to mix *ou* to muddle *ou* to jumble up *(sép)* ; [- cartes, dominos] to shuffle **4.** [impliquer] : **~ qqn à** to involve sb in, to get sb involved in.
◆ **se mêler** *vpi* **1.** [se mélanger] to mix, to mingle ▪ **les styles se mêlent harmonieusement** the styles blend well together **2.** [s'unir] : **se ~ à** *ou* **avec** to mix *ou* to mingle with ▪ **ses cris se mêlèrent au bruit de la foule** his shouts mingled with the noise of the crowd **3.** [participer] : **se ~ à la conversation** to take part *ou* to join in the conversation.
◆ **se mêler de** *vp+prép* to interfere *ou* to meddle in, to get mixed up in ▪ **elle se mêle de ce qui ne la regarde pas** she is interfering in things that are no concern of hers ▪ **de quoi se mêle-t-il?** what business is it of his? ▪ **si le mauvais temps s'en mêle, la récolte est perdue** if the weather decides to turn nasty, the crop will be ruined ▪ **il se mêle de tout** he is very nosy ◗ **de quoi je me mêle?** *fam* mind your own business!

mélèze [melɛz] *nm* larch.

méli-mélo [melimelo] (*pl* **mélis-mélos**) *nm* [d'objets] mess, jumble ▪ [d'idées, de dates] hotchpotch *UK*, hodgepodge *US*, mishmash ▪ **ils ont fait un ~ incroyable avec les réservations** they made a real mix-up with the reservations.

mélisse [melis] *nf* (lemon) balm.

mélo [melo] *fam* ◇ *adj* melodramatic.
◇ *nm* melodrama ▪ **nous sommes en plein ~!** this is melodramatic *ou* blood-and-thunder stuff!

mélodie [melɔdi] *nf* **1.** [air de musique] melody, tune ▪ [en composition] melody, song **2.** *fig* **la ~ des vers de Lamartine** the melodic quality of Lamartine's verse.

mélodieux, euse [melɔdjø, øz] *adj* [son] melodious ▪ [air] tuneful ▪ [voix] melodious, musical ▪ **de sa voix mélodieuse** in her melodious *ou* musical voice.

mélodique [melɔdik] *adj* melodic.

mélodramatique [melɔdramatik] *adj* melodramatic.

mélodrame [melɔdram] *nm* melodrama ▪ **nous sommes en plein ~!** this is like (something out of) a melodrama!

mélomane [melɔman] ◇ *adj* music-loving ▪ **êtes-vous ~?** do you like music?, are you musical?
◇ *nmf* music lover.

melon [məlɔ̃] *nm* **1.** BOT melon ▪ [rond] cantaloup *ou* cantaloupe melon ▪ [ovale] honeydew melon ▪ **~ d'eau** watermelon **2.** [chapeau] bowler (hat) *UK*, derby *US*.

mélopée [melɔpe] *nf* **1.** [mélodie] dirge, lament **2.** ANTIQ melopoeia, threnody.

melting-pot [mɛltiŋpɔt] (*pl* **melting-pots**) *nm* melting pot.

membrane [mɑ̃bran] *nf* **1.** BIOL membrane ▪ **~ cellulaire** cell *ou* plasma membrane **2.** MUS membrane, skin **3.** TÉLÉCOM diaphragm **4.** TRAV PUB : **~ d'étanchéité** sealing membrane *ou* blanket.

membraneux, euse [mɑ̃branø, øz] *adj* membranous.

membre [mɑ̃br] *nm* **1.** ANAT limb ▪ **~ inférieur/supérieur** lower/upper limb ▪ **~ (viril)** (male) member **2.** ZOOL limb ▪ **~ antérieur** foreleg, fore limb ▪ **~ postérieur** back leg, rear limb **3.** [adhérent] member ▪ **être ~ d'un syndicat** to belong to *ou* to be a member of a union ▪ **devenir ~ d'une association** to join an association ▪ **ils le considèrent comme un ~ de la famille** they treat him as one of the family ▪ **tous les ~s de la famille** the whole family ▪ *(comme adj)* **les pays ~s** the member countries ◗ **~ bienfaiteur** supporter ▪ **~ honoraire** honorary member ▪ **~ fondateur** founder, founding member ▪ **~ perpétuel** life member **4.** MATH member ▪ **premier/second ~ d'une équation** left-hand/right-hand member of an equation **5.** GRAMM : **~ de phrase** member *ou* clause of a sentence **6.** ARCHIT & GÉOL member **7.** NAUT timber, rib.

membré, e [mɑ̃bre] *adj litt* **bien ~** strong-limbed ▪ **mal ~** weak-limbed.

membrure [mɑ̃bryr] *nf* **1.** [d'un corps humain] limbs **2.** CONSTR member ▪ MENUIS frame **3.** NAUT [en bois] rib ▪ [en métal] frame.

mémé [meme] *fam* ◇ *nf* **1.** [en appellatif] grandma, granny, gran *UK* **2.** [vieille dame] old dear **3.** *péj* old woman.
◇ *adj inv péj* dowdy, frumpy ▪ **elle fait très ~ avec cette coiffure** that hairstyle makes her look so dowdy.

même [mɛm] ◇ *dét (adj indéf)* **1.** *(avant le n)* [identique, semblable] same ▪ **mettre deux choses sur le ~ plan** to put two things on the same level ▪ *(en corrélation avec 'que')* **il a le ~ âge que moi** he's the same age as me **2.** *(après le n)* [servant à souligner] : **elle est la bonté ~** she is kindness itself ▪ **ce sont ses paroles ~s** those are his very words ▪ **ils sont repartis le soir ~** they left that very evening ▪ **c'est cela ~ que je cherchais** it's the very thing I was looking for.
◇ *pron indéf* : **le ~** the same ▪ **ce sont toujours les ~s qui gagnent** it's always the same ones who win ▪ **mes intérêts ne sont pas les ~s que les vôtres** my interests are not the same as yours ▸ **cela** *ou* **ça revient (strictement) au ~** it comes *ou* amounts to (exactly) the same thing.
◇ *adv* even ▪ **~ les savants** *ou* **les savants ~ peuvent se tromper** even scientists can make mistakes ▪ **elle ne va ~ plus au cinéma** she doesn't even go to the cinema any more.
◆ **à même** *loc prép* : **dormir à ~ le sol** to sleep on the floor ▪ **il boit à ~ la bouteille** he drinks straight from the bottle ▪ **je ne supporte pas la laine à ~ la peau** I can't stand wool next to my skin.
◆ **à même de** *loc prép* able to, in a position to.
◆ **de même** *loc adv* : **faire de ~** to do likewise *ou* the same ▪ **il est parti avant la fin, moi de ~** he left before the end, and so did I ▪ **il en va de ~ pour vous** the same is true for you.
◆ **de même que** *loc conj sout* just as.
◆ **même que** *loc conj fam* so much so that ▪ **elle roulait très vite, ~ que la voiture a failli déraper** she was driving so fast that the car nearly skidded.
◆ **même si** *loc conj* even if.

mêmement [mɛmmɑ̃] *adv vieilli* equally, likewise.

mémento [memɛ̃to] *nm* **1.** [agenda] diary **2.** ÉDUC summary ▪ **~ d'histoire** history handbook **3.** RELIG memento.

mémère [memɛr] *fam* ◇ *nf* **1.** [en appellatif] grandma, granny, gran *UK* **2.** *péj* old woman.
◇ *adj péj* dowdy, frumpy ▪ **si seulement elle portait des robes un peu moins ~ s** if only she wore slightly less old-fashioned dresses.

mémo [memo] *nm* **1.** [carnet] memo pad, note book, notepad **2.** [note de service] memo.

mémoire [memwar] ◇ *nf* **1.** [faculté] memory ▪ **avoir (une) mauvaise ~** to have a poor *ou* bad memory ▪ **avoir (une) bonne ~** to have a good memory ▪ **si j'ai bonne ~** if I remember correctly ▪ **avoir la ~ des noms** to have a good memory for names ▪ **je n'ai aucune ~!** I can never remember anything! ▪ **tu as la ~ courte!** you've got a short memory! ▪ **remettre qqch en ~ à qqn** to remind sb of sthg ▪ **ce détail est resté à jamais** *ou* **s'est gravé dans ma ~** this detail has stayed with me ever since *ou* has forever remained engraved in my memory ▸ **avoir une ~ d'éléphant** *fam* to have a memory like an elephant **2.** [souvenir] memory ▪ **honorer la ~ de qqn** to honour the memory of sb **3.** INFORM memory, storage ▪ **une ~ de 15 caractères** a 15-character memory ▸ **~ centrale** *ou* **principale** main memory *ou* storage ▪ **~ à accès direct** direct access storage ▪ **~ auxiliaire** auxiliary *ou* secondary storage ▪ **~ cache** INFORM cache (memory) ▪ **~ externe** external storage ▪ **~ de masse** mass storage ▪ **~ morte** read-only memory ▪ **~ tampon** buffer (storage) ▪ **~ vive** random-access memory ▪ **~ virtuelle** virtual storage ▪ **~ volatile** volatile memory.
◇ *nm* **1.** [rapport] report, paper **2.** UNIV thesis, dissertation paper ▪ **~ de maîtrise** ≃ MA thesis *ou* dissertation **3.** DR statement of case **4.** COMM & FIN bill, statement.
◆ **mémoires** *nmpl* memoirs ▪ **'Mémoires d'outre-tombe'** *Chateaubriand* 'Memoirs from Beyond the Tomb'.
◆ **à la mémoire de** *loc prép* in memory of, to the memory of ▪ **à la ~ du comique disparu** in memory of the late comedian.
◆ **de mémoire** *loc adv* from memory.
◆ **de mémoire de** *loc prép* : **de ~ de sportif** in all my/his *etc* years as a sportsman ▪ **de ~ d'homme** in living memory.
◆ **en mémoire de** = **à la mémoire de**.
◆ **pour mémoire** *loc adv* COMM & *fig* for the record.

mémorable [memɔrabl] *adj* memorable.

mémorandum [memɔrɑ̃dɔm] *nm* memorandum.

mémorial, aux [memɔrjal, o] *nm* **1.** [texte] memoir ▪ POLIT memorial **2.** [monument] memorial.

mémoriel, elle [memɔrjɛl] *adj* INFORM & PSYCHOL memory *(modif)*.

mémorisable [memɔrizabl] *adj* INFORM storable.

mémorisation [memɔrizasjɔ̃] *nf* **1.** [processus] memorization **2.** INFORM storage.

mémoriser [3] [memɔrize] *vt* **1.** [apprendre par cœur] to memorize ▪ **il a mémorisé les conjugaisons** he has learnt the verb tables by heart **2.** INFORM to store, to put into memory.

menaçant, e [mənasɑ̃, ɑ̃t] *adj* **1.** [comminatoire - personne, geste, ton] menacing, threatening ▪ **d'un ton ~** menacingly **2.** [inquiétant - signe, silence, nuage] menacing, threatening, ominous.

menace [mənas] *nf* **1.** [source de danger] menace, threat ▪ **une ~ pour l'ordre public** a danger *ou* menace *ou* threat to law and order **2.** [acte, parole] threat ▪ **des ~s en l'air** idle threats ▪ **mettre ses ~s à exécution** to carry out one's threats ▪ **la victime avait reçu des ~s de mort** the victim had been threatened with his life *ou* had received death threats ▪ **un geste de ~** a threatening *ou* menacing gesture ▪ **ton lourd** *ou* **plein de ~** tone heavy *ou* fraught with menace ▪ **un ciel lourd de ~** *litt* a sky heavy with foreboding ▪ **il a signé sous la ~** he signed under duress ▪ **sous la ~ de** under (the) threat of.
Voir module d'usage

LES MENACES

If you don't stop that noise, I'll call the police! Si vous n'arrêtez pas ce tapage, j'appelle la police !

Get out before I say something I'll regret! Sors d'ici, ou tu vas me faire dire des choses désagréables !

Leave her alone, or else! Laisse-la tranquille, sinon... !

You'll be sorry you said that! Je vais te faire regretter d'avoir dit ça !

I'm warning you, you'd better not say anything. Je te préviens, tu as intérêt à ne rien dire.

If you ever do that again,...! Si jamais tu recommences,... !

Don't say I didn't warn you! Je t'aurai prévenu !

Just you try it! Essaie un peu pour voir !

menacé, e [mənase] *adj* threatened, under threat, endangered ■ **ses jours sont ~s** his life is in danger.

menacer [16] [mənase] ◇ *vt* to threaten, to menace ■ **un danger mortel le menace** he's in mortal danger ■ **les fluctuations du dollar menacent notre système monétaire** fluctuations in the dollar are a threat to our monetary system ■ **~ qqn de** to threaten sb with ■ **~ qqn de mort** to threaten to kill sb.
◇ *vi* [crise] to threaten ■ **l'orage menace** there's a storm brewing *ou* on the way.
◆ **menacer de** *v+prép* : **~ de faire qqch** to threaten to do sthg ■ **le conflit menace de s'étendre** there is a (real) danger of the conflict spreading ■ **le mur menace de s'écrouler** the wall is in danger of collapsing ■ **l'orage menace d'éclater avant la fin de la soirée** the storm looks like it will break before the end of the evening.

ménage [menaʒ] *nm* **1.** [couple] couple ■ SOCIOL household ■ **leur ~ marche mal** their marriage isn't going very well ■ **faire bon/mauvais ~ avec qqn** to get on well/badly with sb ■ **ils se sont mis en ~** they've moved in together ■ **ils sont en ~** they live together ▶ **~ à trois** ménage à trois **2.** [économie domestique] housekeeping ■ **tenir le ~** to keep house ▮ [nettoyage] housework, cleaning ■ **faire le ~** to do the housework ■ **faire le ~ en grand** to clean the house from top to bottom ■ **le directeur a fait le ~ dans son service** *fig* the manager has shaken up *ou* spring-cleaned his department ■ **faire des ~s** to do housework (for people).
◆ **de ménage** *loc adj* **1.** [fabriqué à la maison] homemade **2.** [pour l'entretien] household, cleaning ■ **savon de ~** household soap.

ménagement [menaʒmɑ̃] *nm* thoughtfulness, consideration, solicitude *sout*.
◆ **avec ménagement** *loc adv* tactfully, gently ■ **traite ma voiture avec ~** treat my car with care, take (good) care of my car ■ **traiter qqn avec le plus grand ~** to treat sb with great consideration.
◆ **sans ménagement** *loc adv* [annoncer] bluntly ■ [éconduire, traiter] unceremoniously.

ménager[1] [17] [menaʒe] *vt* **1.** [économiser] to be sparing with ■ **sans ~ ses efforts** tirelessly ■ **elle ne ménage pas ses efforts** she spares no effort ■ **~ ses forces** to conserve one's strength **2.** [traiter avec soin] to treat *ou* to handle carefully ■ **je prends l'ascenseur pour ~ mes vieilles jambes** I take the lift to spare my old legs **3.** [respecter] to spare ■ **ménage sa susceptibilité** humour him ▶ **~ la chèvre et le chou** to sit on the fence, to run with the hare and hunt with the hounds **4.** [arranger - passage, escalier] to put in *(insép)* ; [- entretien, rencontre] to organize, to arrange ■ **j'ai ménagé un espace pour planter des légumes** I've left some space for growing vegetables.
◆ **se ménager** ◇ *vp (emploi réfléchi)* to spare o.s. ■ **elle ne se ménage pas assez** she drives herself too hard ■ **ménage-toi** take it easy, don't overdo it.
◇ *vpt* : **se ~ qqch** [se réserver qqch] to set sthg aside for o.s.

ménager[2]**, ère** [menaʒe, ɛr] *adj* [de la maison] domestic *(modif)*, household *(modif)* ■ **enseignement ~** domestic science ■ **équipement ~** domestic *ou* household appliances.
◆ **ménager** *nm* COMM : **le gros/petit ~** major/small household appliances.
◆ **ménagère** *nf* **1.** [femme] housewife **2.** [couverts] canteen (of cutlery) ■ **une ménagère en argent** a canteen of silver cutlery.

ménagerie [menaʒri] *nf* menagerie ■ **c'est une vraie ~ ici!** *fig* it's like a zoo in here!

menchevik [mɛnʃevik] *nmf* Menshevik.

Mendel [mɛndɛl] *npr* ▷ **loi**.

mendiant, e [mɑ̃djɑ̃, ɑ̃t] *nm, f* [clochard] beggar.
◆ **mendiant** ◇ *nm* CULIN *almond, fig, hazelnut and raisin biscuit*.
◇ *adj m* RELIG mendicant.

mendicité [mɑ̃disite] *nf* **1.** [action] begging ■ **vivre de ~** to beg for a living **2.** [état] beggary, mendicity *sout*, mendicancy *sout* ■ **être réduit à la ~** to be reduced to begging.

mendier [9] [mɑ̃dje] ◇ *vi* to beg.
◇ *vt* [argent, sourire] to beg for *(insép)* ■ **~ des votes** to canvass for votes.

meneau, x [məno] *nm* [horizontal] transom ■ [vertical] mullion ■ **fenêtre à ~x** mullioned window.

menée [məne] *nf* CHASSE (stag's) track.

menées [məne] *nfpl* [intrigues] intrigues, machinations ■ **des ~ subversives** subversive activities.

mener [9] [məne] ◇ *vt* **1.** [conduire - personne] to take, to lead ■ **elle mènera son club à la victoire** she'll lead her club to victory ▶ **~ qqn par le bout du nez** to lead sb by the nose ■ **~ qqn en bateau** to lead sb up the garden path
2. [suj: escalier, passage, route] to take, to lead ■ **le bus te mènera jusqu'à l'hôtel** the bus will take you (right) to the hotel ■ *(en usage absolu)* **cette porte mène à la cave** this door leads to the cellar ■ **la ligne n°1 mène à Neuilly** line No. 1 takes you *ou* goes to Neuilly ■ **la deuxième année mène au dessin industriel** after the second year, you go on to technical drawing ▶ **~ loin : un feu rouge grillé, ça va vous mener loin!** *fam* you went through the lights, that'll cost you!
3. [diriger - groupe, équipe] to lead ; [- combat, négociation] to carry on *(insép)* ; [- affaire, projet] to run, to manage ; [- enquête] to conduct, to lead ; [- débat] to lead, to chair ■ **il se laisse trop facilement ~** he's too easily led ■ **laissez-la ~ sa vie** let her live her life ▶ **~ le jeu** SPORT to be in the lead ; *fig* to have the upper hand, to call the tune ■ **~ joyeuse vie** to lead a merry life ■ **ne pas en ~ large : il n'en menait pas large avant la publication des résultats** his heart was in his boots before the results were released ■ **~ qqch à bien** *ou* **à terme** *ou* **à bonne fin** [finir] to see sthg through ; [réussir] to succeed in doing sthg
4. MATH to draw
5. MÉCAN to drive.
◇ *vi* to (be in the) lead ■ **l'équipe locale mène par 3 buts à 0** the local team is leading by 3 goals to 0 ■ **le skieur italien mène avec 15 secondes d'avance sur le Suisse** the Italian skier has a 15-second lead *ou* advantage over the Swiss ■ **de combien on mène?** what's our lead?

ménestrel [menɛstrɛl] *nm* minstrel.

ménétrier [menetrije] *nm* **1.** *arch* [violoneux] fiddler **2.** HIST musician.

meneur, euse [mənœr, øz] *nm, f* **1.** [dirigeant] leader ■ **c'est un ~ d'hommes** he's a born leader (of men) ▶ **meneuse de revue** chorus-line leader **2.** *péj* [agitateur - POLIT] ringleader, leader, agitator.

menhir [menir] *nm* menhir.

méninge [menɛ̃ʒ] *nf* ANAT meninx ■ **~s** meninges.
◆ **méninges** *nfpl fam* brains ■ **il ne se fatigue pas** *ou* **ne se creuse pas les ~s!** he's in no danger of wearing his brain *ou* grey matter out! ■ **fais travailler tes ~s** use your brains.

méningé, e [menɛ̃ʒe] *adj* meningeal.

méningite [menɛ̃ʒit] *nf* meningitis ■ **il ne risque pas la** *ou* **d'attraper une ~!** no danger of him wearing his brain out!

ménisque [menisk] *nm* ANAT, OPT & PHYS meniscus.

ménopause [menɔpoz] *nf* menopause.

ménopausée [menɔpoze] *adj f* : **une femme ~** a post-menopausal woman.

menotte [mənɔt] *nf* [main] tiny (little) hand.
◆ **menottes** *nfpl* handcuffs ■ **passer les ~s à qqn** to handcuff sb ■ **~s aux poignets** handcuffed, in handcuffs.

mens *etc v* ▷ **mentir**.

mensonge [mɑ̃sɔ̃ʒ] *nm* **1.** [action] : **le ~** lying, untruthfulness ■ **vivre dans le ~** to live a lie **2.** [propos] lie ■ **dire des ~s** to tell lies ■ **un ~ par omission** a lie of omission ▶ **c'est vrai, ce ~?** *fam* are you having me on?

mensonger, ère [mɑ̃sɔ̃ʒe, ɛr] *adj* untruthful, mendacious *sout* ■ **des déclarations mensongères** untruthful statements.

menstruation [mɑ̃stryasjɔ̃] *nf* menstruation, menstruating.

menstruel, elle [mɑ̃stryɛl] *adj* menstrual.

menstrues [mɑ̃stry] *nfpl vieilli* menses.

mensualisation [mɑ̃sɥalizasjɔ̃] *nf* [des salaires, du personnel] monthly payment ■ **pour vos règlements, pensez à la ~** don't forget that you can pay in monthly instalments.

mensualiser [3] [mɑ̃sɥalize] *vt* to pay on a monthly basis ■ **l'impôt est mensualisé** income tax is paid monthly.

mensualité [mɑ̃sɥalite] *nf* **1.** [somme perçue] monthly payment ■ [somme versée] monthly instalment **2.** [salaire] monthly salary.
◆ **par mensualités** *loc adv* monthly, on a monthly basis.

mensuel, elle [mɑ̃sɥɛl] ◇ *adj* monthly.
◇ *nm, f* worker paid by the month.
◆ **mensuel** *nm* PRESSE monthly (magazine).

mensuellement [mɑ̃sɥɛlmɑ̃] *adv* monthly, every month.

mensuration [mɑ̃syrasjɔ̃] *nf* mensuration.
◆ **mensurations** *nfpl* measurements ■ **des ~s à faire rêver** magnificent vital statistics.

mental, e, aux [mɑ̃tal, o] *adj* mental.
◆ **mental** *nm* : **le ~** the mind.

mentalement [mɑ̃talmɑ̃] *adv* mentally ■ **calcule-le ~** work it out *ou* calculate it in your head.

mentalité [mɑ̃talite] *nf* mentality ■ **faire changer les ~s** to change people's mentality *ou* the way people think ▶ **quelle sale ~!** what an unpleasant character! ■ **belle** *ou* **jolie ~!** *iron* that's a nice way of thinking!

menteur, euse [mɑ̃tœr, øz] ◇ *adj* untruthful ■ **enfant, il était très ~** he used to tell lies all the time when he was a child.
◇ *nm, f* liar.
◆ **menteur** *nm* JEUX : **jouer au ~** to play cheat.

menthe [mɑ̃t] *nf* **1.** BOT mint ■ **~ poivrée** peppermint ■ **~ verte** spearmint **2.** [tisane] mint tea *(U)* **3.** [sirop] : **~ à l'eau** mint cordial **4.** [essence] peppermint ■ **parfumé à la ~** mint-flavoured ■ **bonbons à la ~** mints, peppermints.

menthol [mɑ̃tɔl] *nm* menthol.

mentholé, e [mɑ̃tɔle] *adj* mentholated, menthol *(modif)*.

mention [mɑ̃sjɔ̃] *nf* **1.** [référence] mention ■ **faire ~ de qqch** to refer to *ou* to mention sthg **2.** [texte] note, comment ■ **l'enveloppe portait la ~ "urgent"** the word "urgent" appeared *ou* was written on the envelope **3.** ÉDUC & UNIV distinction ■ **être reçu sans ~** to get an ordinary pass ▶ **~ bien** ≃ upper second class Honours *UK*, ≃ pass with honors *US* ■ **~ très bien** ≃ first class Honours *UK*, ≃ pass with high honors *US* ■ **~ passable** *minimum pass grade* ■ **~ honorable** *first level of distinction for a PhD* ■ **~ très honorable** *second level of distinction for a PhD* ■ **~ très honorable avec les félicitations du jury** *highest level of distinction for a PhD*.

mentionner [3] [mɑ̃sjɔne] *vt* to mention ■ **le nom du traducteur n'est pas mentionné** the translator's name does not appear.

mentir [37] [mɑ̃tir] *vi* [gén] to lie ■ [une fois] to tell a lie ■ [plusieurs fois] to tell lies ■ **il m'a menti** he lied to me, he told me a lie ■ **tu mens (effrontément)!** you're lying (shamelessly)!, you're a (barefaced) liar! ■ **j'ai prédit que tu allais gagner, ne me fais pas ~** I said you'd win, don't prove me wrong *ou* don't make a liar out of me ■ **sans ~, elle me l'a dit quinze fois** without a word of a lie, she told me fifteen times ■ **~ par omission** to lie by omission ▶ **elle ment comme elle respire** *ou* **comme un arracheur de dents** she lies through her teeth ■ **faire ~ le proverbe** to give the lie to the proverb.
◆ **mentir à** *v+prép litt* [manquer à] to belie.
◆ **se mentir** ◇ *vp (emploi réfléchi)* : **se ~ à soi-même** to fool o.s.
◇ *vp (emploi réciproque)* to lie to each other, to tell each other lies.

menton [mɑ̃tɔ̃] *nm* chin ■ **~ en galoche/pointu/rond** protruding/pointed/round chin.

mentonnière [mɑ̃tɔnjɛr] *nf* **1.** [d'un chapeau] chin strap ■ [d'un casque] chin piece **2.** MÉD chin bandage **3.** MUS chin rest.

mentor [mɑ̃tɔr] *nm litt* mentor.

menu[1] [məny] *nm* **1.** [liste] menu ■ [carte] menu (card) ■ **qu'y a-t-il au ~ aujourd'hui?** *pr* what's on the menu? ; *fig* what's on the agenda for today? **2.** [repas] set meal ▶ **le ~ gastronomique** the gourmet menu, the special fare menu **3.** INFORM menu ■ **~ déroulant** drag-down menu.
◆ **par le menu** *loc adv* [raconter] in detail ■ [vérifier] thoroughly.

menu[2], **e** [məny] *adj* **1.** [attaches, silhouette] slim, slender ■ [voix] small, thin ■ [écriture] small, tiny ■ [enfant] tiny **2.** *(avant le n)* [petit] small, tiny **3.** *(avant le n)* [négligeable] : **il fait les ~s travaux** he does odd jobs ■ **~s frais** minor expenses ▶ **de la ~e monnaie** small change ■ **~ fretin** ZOOL fry ; *fig* small fry ■ **les ~s plaisirs** life's little pleasures ■ **les Menus Plaisirs** HIST the royal entertainment *(at the French Court)*.
◆ **menu** *adv* [couper, hacher] thoroughly, finely ■ **écrire ~** to write small.

menuet [mənɥɛ] *nm* minuet.

menuiserie [mənɥizri] *nf* **1.** [activité] joinery ■ **~ métallique** metal joinery **2.** [atelier] (joiner's) workshop **3.** [boiseries] woodwork.

menuisier, ère [mənɥizje, ɛr] *nm, f* joiner.

Méphistophélès [mefistɔfelɛs] *npr* Mephistopheles.

méplat, e [mepla, at] *adj* flat ■ **bois ~** (wood in) planks.
◆ **méplat** *nm* **1.** ART plane **2.** [partie du corps] : **un visage aux ~s accusés** a finely-chiselled face.

méprendre [79] [meprɑ̃dr] ◆ **se méprendre** *vpi sout* to make a mistake, to be mistaken ■ **je me suis mépris sur ses intentions réelles** I was mistaken about *ou* I misunderstood his real intentions ■ **se ~ sur qqn** to misjudge sb ■ **on dirait ta sœur, c'est à s'y ~** she looks just like your sister.

mépris [mepri] *nm* contempt, disdain, scorn ■ **avoir** *ou* **éprouver du ~ pour** to be filled with contempt for, to despise ■ **avec ~** scornfully, contemptuously ■ **le ~ de** [convenances, tradition] contempt for, lack of regard for.
◆ **au mépris de** *loc prép* with no regard for, regardless of ■ **au ~ du danger** regardless of the danger ■ **au ~ du règlement** in defiance of the rules ■ **au ~ des convenances** spurning convention.

méprisable [meprizabl] *adj* contemptible, despicable ■ **un être totalement ~** a creature beneath contempt.

méprisant, e [meprizɑ̃, ɑ̃t] *adj* contemptuous, disdainful, scornful ■ **se montrer très ~ envers qqn** to pour scorn on sb, to be very contemptuous towards sb.

méprise [mepriz] *nf* mistake, error ■ **victime d'une ~e** victim of a misunderstanding.
◆ **par méprise** *loc adv* by mistake.

mépriser [3] [meprize] *vt* **1.** [dédaigner] to look down on, to despise, to scorn ■ **je le méprise d'être si lâche** I despise him for being such a coward ■ **elle méprise l'argent** she thinks nothing of *ou* scorns money **2.** [braver - conventions, règlement] to disregard, to defy ; [- mort, danger] to defy, to scorn.

mer [mɛr] *nf* **1.** GÉOGR sea ■ **mettre un canot à la ~** [d'un navire] to lower *ou* to launch a boat ; [de la terre] to get out a boat ■ **jeter qqch à la ~** [d'un navire] to throw sthg overboard ; [de la terre] to throw sthg into the sea ■ **ils sont partis en ~** they've gone out to sea ■ **perdus en ~** lost at sea ■ **voyager par ~** to travel by sea ■ **prendre la ~** to put out to sea ■ **état de la ~** sea conditions ■ **~ calme/belle/peu agitée** calm/smooth/moderate sea ■ **~ agitée devenant forte** sea moderate becoming heavy ■ **la ~ est mauvaise** the sea is rough ■ **la ~ était d'huile** the sea was calm *ou* like a millpond ▶ **~ intérieure** inland sea ■ **ce n'est pas la ~ à boire** *fam* it's not that hard, there's nothing much to it ■ **la ~ Baltique/Caspienne/Égée/Morte/Rouge** the Baltic/Caspian/Aegean/Dead/Red Sea ■ **la ~ des Caraïbes** the Caribbean (Sea) ■ **la ~ du Nord** the North Sea ■ **la ~ des Sargasses** the Sargasso Sea ■ **la ~ de la Tranquillité** the

Sea of Tranquillity **2.** [marée] tide ■ **à quelle heure la ~ sera-t-elle haute/basse?** what time is high/low tide? **3.** [région côtière] seaside ■ **à la ~** at *ou* by the seaside **4.** [grande étendue] ▶ **~ de glace** glacier ■ **~ de sable** ocean of sand, sand sea **5.** ASTRON mare.

MER

la mer Adriatique the Adriatic Sea ;
la mer des Antilles the Caribbean Sea ;
la mer d'Aral the Aral Sea ;
la mer Baltique the Baltic Sea ;
la mer de Barents the Barents Sea ;
la mer de Béring the Bering Sea ;
la mer Blanche the White Sea ;
la mer Caraïbe ou des Caraïbes the Caribbean Sea ;
la mer Caspienne the Caspian Sea ;
la mer de Célèbes the Celebes Sea ;
la mer de Chine the China Sea ;
la mer de Corail the Coral Sea ;
la mer Égée the Aegean Sea ;
la mer de Galilée the Sea of Galilee ;
la mer Intérieure the Inland Sea ;
la mer Ionienne the Ionian Sea ;
la mer d'Irlande the Irish Sea ;
la mer Jaune the Yellow Sea ;
la mer Méditerranée the Mediterranean Sea ;
la mer Morte the Dead Sea ;
la mer Noire the Black Sea ;
la mer du Nord the North Sea ;
la mer d'Oman the Arabian Sea ;
la mer Rouge the Red Sea ;
la mer des Sargasses the Sargasso Sea ;
la mer de Tasman the Tasman Sea ;
la mer Tyrrhénienne the Tyrrhenian Sea ;
la mer des Wadden the Waddenzee.

mercantile [mɛrkɑ̃til] *adj* **1.** *péj* [intéressé] mercenary, self-seeking, venal *litt* **2.** [commercial] mercantile.

mercantilisme [mɛrkɑ̃tilism] *nm* **1.** *litt* [attitude] mercenary *ou* self-seeking attitude **2.** ÉCON [théorie] mercantilism ■ [système] mercantile system.

mercatique [mɛrkatik] *nf* marketing.

mercenaire [mɛrsənɛr] <> *adj litt* [troupe] mercenary ■ [travail] paid.
<> *nm* mercenary.

mercerie [mɛrsəri] *nf* **1.** [magasin] haberdasher's shop *UK*, notions store *US* **2.** [industrie, articles] haberdashery *UK*, notions *US* ■ **des articles de ~** sewing materials.

merchandising [mɛrʃɑ̃dajziŋ] *nm* merchandising, sales promotion.

merci [mɛrsi] <> *nm* thank-you ■ **dites-lui un grand ~ pour son aide** give him a big thank-you *ou* all our thanks for his help.
<> *interj* thank you ■ **as-tu dit ~ à la dame?** did you thank the lady *ou* say thank you to the lady? ■ **~ (beaucoup) d'être venu** thanks (a lot) for coming ■ **~ mille fois** thank you so *ou* very much ■ **voulez-vous du fromage? – (non) ~, je n'ai pas faim** would you like some cheese? – no thank you *ou* thanks, I'm not hungry ■ **~, très peu pour moi!** *fam* thanks but no thanks!
<> *nf litt* mercy.
◆ **à la merci de** *loc prép* at the mercy of ■ **tenir qqn à sa ~** to have sb at one's mercy *ou* in one's power.
◆ **sans merci** <> *loc adj* merciless, pitiless, ruthless ■ **une lutte sans ~** a merciless struggle.
<> *loc adv* mercilessly, pitilessly, ruthlessly.

mercier, ère [mɛrsje, ɛr] *nm, f* haberdasher *UK*, notions dealer *US*.

mercredi [mɛrkrədi] *nm* Wednesday ■ **~ des Cendres** Ash Wednesday, *voir aussi* **mardi**.

mercure [mɛrkyr] *nm* CHIM mercury.

Mercure [mɛrkyr] *npr* ASTRON & MYTHOL Mercury.

mercuriale [mɛrkyrjal] *nf* **1.** *litt* [accusation] remonstrance, admonition *sout* **2.** COMM market price list **3.** BOT mercury.

Mercurochrome® [mɛrkyrɔkrɔm] *nm* Mercurochrome®.

merde [mɛrd] <> *nf* **1.** ▲ [excrément] shit△, crap△ ■ **une ~ de chien** a dog turd△ ▶ **il ne se prend pas pour une** *ou* **pour de la ~** he thinks the sun shines out of his arse△ *UK*, he thinks he's God's gift to the world△ *US* ■ **ce temps de ~** this shitty weather△ **2.** △ [désordre] bloody△ *UK ou* godawful *US* mess ■ **foutre** *ou* **semer la ~** to make a bloody mess△ **3.** △ [ennuis] : **c'est la ~!** it's hell! ■ **être dans la ~ (jusqu'au cou)** to be (right) in the shit **4.** △ [mésaventure] shitty mess△ ■ **il m'arrive encore une ~** I've got another bloody problem△.
<> *interj*△ shit△ ■ **(je te dis) ~!** [ton agressif] to hell with you!△ ; [pour souhaiter bonne chance] fingers crossed!, break a leg! ■ **on y va, oui ou ~!** are we going or aren't we, for Christ's sake!△.

merder [3] △ [mɛrde] *vi* : **mon imprimante merde depuis trois jours** my printer's been on the blink for the last three days ■ **j'ai complètement merdé en littérature anglaise** I completely screwed up the English Lit paper△.

merdeux, euse△ [mɛrdø, øz] <> *adj* shitty△, crappy△.
<> *nm, f* [enfant] little shit△ ■ **un ~ de quatorze ans** a fourteen-year old brat△.

merdier△ [mɛrdje] *nm* **1.** [désordre] pigsty △ *fig* **2.** [situation confuse] : **on s'est retrouvé dans un beau ~ après son départ** we were in one hell of a mess after he left.

merdique△ [mɛrdik] *adj* shitty△, crappy△ ■ **sa voiture est complètement ~** her car's complete rubbish△.

merdoyer [3] △ [mɛrdwaje], **merdouiller** [3] △ [mɛrduje] *vi* : **j'ai complètement merdoyé à l'oral** I made a right cock-up *UK ou* a real screw-up *US* of the oral△.

mère [mɛr] <> *nf* **1.** [génitrice] mother ■ **elle est ~ de cinq enfants** she is a mother of five ■ **c'est une ~ pour lui** she's like a mother to him ■ **frères/sœurs par la ~** half-brothers/half-sisters on the mother's side ■ **veau élevé sous la ~** calf nourished on its mother's milk ▶ **~ adoptive** adoptive mother ■ **~ biologique** MÉD & BIOL biological *ou* natural mother ■ **~ célibataire** unmarried mother ■ **~ de famille** mother, housewife ■ **~ porteuse** surrogate mother
2. *fam* [madame] : **la ~ Vorel** old mother Vorel
3. RELIG Mother ▶ **la ~ supérieure** Mother Superior
4. *litt* [origine] mother ■ **~ patrie** mother country
5. CHIM : **~ de vinaigre** mother of vinegar
6. TECHNOL mould
7. *(comme adj)* **carte ~** INFORM motherboard ■ **disque ~** INFORM (positive) matrix ■ **maison ~** COMM headquarters, head office ■ **société ~** COMM parent company.
<> *adj f (avant le n)* **~ goutte** [huile] first pressing ; [vin] bottoms *(wine from the mother)*.

mère-grand [mɛrgrɑ̃] *nf vieilli* grandmother.

merguez [mɛrgɛz] *nf spicy North African mutton sausage.*

méridien, enne [meridjɛ̃, ɛn] *adj* **1.** *litt* [de midi] meridian *arch* **2.** ASTRON meridian.
◆ **méridien** *nm* **1.** ASTRON & MÉTÉOR meridian ■ **~ international** *ou* **origine** prime *ou* Greenwich meridian ■ **~ céleste/magnétique/terrestre** celestial/magnetic/terrestrial meridian **2.** MÉD meridian.
◆ **méridienne** *nf* **1.** MATH meridian (section) ■ GÉOGR meridian line ■ GÉOL triangulation line **2.** [sieste] siesta **3.** [lit] chaise longue.

méridional, e, aux [meridjɔnal, o] <> *adj* **1.** [du Sud] southern, meridional *sout* **2.** [du sud de la France] *from the South of France.*
<> *nm, f* **1.** [du Sud] Southerner **2.** [du sud de la France] *person from or inhabitant of the South of France.*

meringue [mərɛ̃g] *nf* meringue.

meringuer [3] [mərɛ̃ge] *vt* to cover with meringue ■ **tarte au citron meringuée** lemon meringue pie.

mérinos [merinos] *nm* **1.** ZOOL merino **2.** TEXT : **(laine) ~** merino wool.

merise [məriz] *nf* wild cherry, merise.

merisier [mərizje] *nm* **1.** [arbre] wild cherry (tree) **2.** [bois] cherry (wood).

méritant, e [meritɑ̃, ɑ̃t] *adj* worthy, deserving ▪ **les élèves les plus ~s ont été récompensés** the most deserving pupils were given a reward.

mérite [merit] *nm* **1.** [vertu] merit, worth ▪ **gens de ~** people of merit ▪ **avoir du ~** to be deserving of *ou* to deserve praise ▪ **tu as du ~ de t'occuper d'eux** it is greatly to your credit that you take such care of them **2.** [gloire] credit ▪ **s'attribuer le ~ de qqch** to take the credit for sthg ▪ **tout le ~ de l'affaire vous revient** all the credit for the deal is yours, you deserve all the credit for the deal **3.** [qualité] merit ▪ **sa déclaration a au moins le ~ d'être brève** her statement at least has the merit of being brief **4.** [décoration] : **Ordre du Mérite agricole** *award for service to farming.*

mériter [3] [merite] *vt* **1.** [suj: personne] to deserve, to merit *sout* ▪ **tu l'as bien mérité!** it serves you right!, you got what you deserve! ▪ **ils ne méritent pas qu'on s'intéresse à eux** they are not worth bothering with ▪ **un repos bien mérité** a well-deserved rest **2.** [suj: objet, idée] to merit *sout*, to be worth, to deserve ▪ **une exposition qui mérite d'être vue** an exhibition worth seeing *ou* which deserves to be seen ▪ **la proposition mérite réflexion** the proposal is worth thinking about.
◆ **mériter de** *v+prép* : **avoir bien mérité de la patrie** to have served one's country well.
◆ **se mériter** *vp (emploi passif)* : **un cadeau pareil, ça se mérite** you have to do something special to get a present like that.

méritocratie [meritɔkrasi] *nf* meritocracy.

méritoire [meritwar] *adj* commendable, praiseworthy.

merlan [mɛrlɑ̃] *nm* **1.** ZOOL whiting ▪ **il la regardait avec des yeux de ~ frit** *fam* he was gawking at her like an idiot **2.** CULIN topside *UK*, top round *US*.

merle [mɛrl] *nm* **1.** ORNITH : **~ (noir)** blackbird ▪ **~ migrateur** (American) robin **2.** [poisson] ballan wrasse.

merlin [mɛrlɛ̃] *nm* **1.** NAUT marline **2.** [pour fendre le bois] (clearing) axe ▪ [pour assommer le bétail] poleaxe.

Merlin [mɛrlɛ̃] *npr* : **~ l'Enchanteur** Merlin the Wizard.

merlon [mɛrlɔ̃] *nm* [d'une fortification] merlon ▪ [dans une poudrerie] earthwork.

merlu [mɛrly] *nm* hake.

mérou [meru] *nm* grouper ▪ **~ des Basques** stone bass *ou* basse, wreck fish.

mérovingien, enne [merɔvɛ̃ʒjɛ̃, ɛn] *adj* Merovingian.
◆ **Mérovingien, enne** *nm, f* Merovingian.

merveille [mɛrvɛj] *nf* **1.** [chose remarquable] marvel, wonder, treasure ▪ **cette liqueur est une ~** this liqueur is amazing ▪ **une ~ d'ingéniosité** a marvel of ingenuity ▪ **dire ~ de qqn** to heap praise upon sb ▪ **faire des ~s, faire ~** to work wonders **2.** CULIN ≃ doughnut.
◆ **à merveille** *loc adv* wonderfully, marvellously ▪ **ils s'entendent à ~** they get on marvellously (well) *ou* like a house on fire ▪ **se porter à ~** to be in perfect health ▪ **ce travail lui convient à ~** this job suits her down to the ground.

merveilleusement [mɛrvɛjøzmɑ̃] *adv* wonderfully, marvellously.

merveilleux, euse [mɛrvɛjø, øz] *adj* **1.** [formidable] wonderful, marvellous, amazing **2.** [qui surprend] marvellous, amazing ▪ **un travail ~ de délicatesse** a marvellously fine piece of work **3.** *(après le n)* [fantastique] magic ▪ **la lampe merveilleuse** the magic lamp.
◆ **merveilleux** *nm* **1.** [surnaturel] : **le ~** the supernatural *ou* marvellous **2.** [caractère extraordinaire] : **le ~ de l'histoire, c'est qu'il est vivant** the amazing thing about the whole story is that he's still alive.
◆ **merveilleuse** *nf* HIST merveilleuse, fine lady.

mes [me] *pl* ▻ **mon**.

mésalliance [mezaljɑ̃s] *nf* *sout* misalliance, mismatch ▪ **faire une ~** to marry beneath o.s. *ou* one's station.

mésange [mezɑ̃ʒ] *nf* tit, titmouse ▪ **~ bleue/noire** blue/coal tit.

mésaventure [mezavɑ̃tyr] *nf* misadventure, misfortune, mishap.

mesclun [mɛsklœ̃] *nm* mixed green salad.

Mesdames [medam] *pl* ▻ **Madame**.

Mesdemoiselles [medmwazɛl] *pl* ▻ **Mademoiselle**.

mésentente [mezɑ̃tɑ̃t] *nf* disagreement, difference of opinion ▪ **oublions notre ~ passée** let's forget our past disagreements.

mésestime [mezɛstim] *nf* *litt* lack of respect, low esteem *ou* regard ▪ **tenir qqn en ~** to hold sb in low esteem, to have little regard for sb.

mésestimer [3] [mezɛstime] *vt* [mépriser] to have a low opinion of ▪ [sous-estimer] to underestimate, to underrate.

mésinformer [3] [mezɛ̃fɔrme] *vt* to misinform.

mésintelligence [mezɛ̃teliʒɑ̃s] *nf* *litt* disagreement, lack of (mutual) understanding, discord *litt*.

mesmérisme [mɛsmerism] *nm* mesmerism.

méso-américain, e [mezɔamerikɛ̃, ɛn] *adj* Central American.

mésocarpe [mezɔkarp] *nm* mesocarp.

mésolithique [mezɔlitik] ◇ *adj* Mesolithic.
◇ *nm* : **le ~** the Mesolithic (age).

Mésopotamie [mezɔpɔtami] *npr f* : **(la) ~** Mesopotamia.

mésopotamien, enne [mezɔpɔtamjɛ̃, ɛn] *adj* Mesopotamian.
◆ **Mésopotamien, enne** *nm, f* Mesopotamian.

mésosphère [mezɔsfɛr] *nf* mesosphere.

mésothérapie [mezɔterapi] *nf* *treatment of cellulite, circulation problems, rheumatism etc involving the use of tiny needles.*

mésozoïque [mezɔzɔik] *adj* & *nm* Mesozoic.

mesquin, e [mɛskɛ̃, in] *adj* **1.** [médiocre] mean, petty **2.** [parcimonieux] mean, stingy, niggardly ▪ **des économies ~es** penny-pinching.

mesquinement [mɛskinmɑ̃] *adv* **1.** [selon des vues étroites] pettily, small-mindedly **2.** [avec parcimonie] meanly, stingily.

mesquinerie [mɛskinri] *nf* **1.** [étroitesse d'esprit] meanness, petty-mindedness, pettiness **2.** [parcimonie] meanness, stinginess ▪ **connu pour sa ~** renowned for his stinginess.

mess [mɛs] *nm* mess ▪ **le ~ des officiers** the officers' mess.

message [mesaʒ] *nm* **1.** [information] message ▪ **faire parvenir un ~ à qqn** to send a message to sb ➊ **~ chiffré** message in cipher ▪ **~ codé** coded message ▪ **~ électronique** E-mail (message) ▪ **~ d'erreur** INFORM error message ▪ **~ publicitaire** advertisement ▪ **~ téléphoné** TÉLÉCOM ≃ Telemessage® *UK*, ≃ telegram *US (delivered on the telephone)* **2.** [déclaration] speech ▪ **un ~ de bienvenue** a message of welcome **3.** [pensée] message ▪ **le ~ de l'Évangile** the message of the Gospel **4.** BIOL : **~ génétique** genetic information *ou* code ▪ **~ nerveux** nerve impulse *ou* message.
◆ **à message** *loc adj* with a message ▪ **un livre/une chanson à ~** a book/a song with a message.

message-guide [mesaʒgid] (*pl* **messages-guide**) *nm* INFORM prompt.

messager, ère [mesaʒe, ɛr] *nm, f* **1.** [personne qui transmet] messenger ▪ **je me ferai votre ~ auprès de lui** I'll speak to him on your behalf **2.** *litt* [annonciateur] : **~ de bonheur** harbinger of happiness.
◆ **messager** *nm* **1.** HIST messenger ▪ **Mercure, le ~ des dieux** MYTHOL Mercury, the messenger of the gods **2.** ORNITH carrier pigeon.

messagerie [mesaʒri] *nf* INFORM & TÉLÉCOM : **~ électronique** electronic mail service ▪ **les ~s télématiques** **vidéotex** messaging services ▪ **les ~s roses** *interactive Minitel services enabling individuals seeking companionship to make contact.*

◆ **messageries** *nfpl* parcels service ▪ **~s aériennes** air freight company ▪ **~s de presse** press delivery service ▪ **~s maritimes** shipping line.

messe [mɛs] *nf* **1.** RELIG Mass ▪ **aller à la ~** to go to Mass ▪ **faire dire une ~ pour qqn** to have a Mass said for sb ⊙ **~ basse** Low Mass ▪ **faire** *ou* **dire des ~s basses** *fig* to whisper ▪ **~ de minuit** midnight Mass ▪ **~ des morts** *ou* **de requiem** Mass for the dead, Requiem ▪ **~ noire** black mass **2.** MUS Mass ▪ **~ concertante** (oratorio-style) Mass ▪ **~ en si mineur** Mass in B minor.

Messeigneurs [mesɛɲœr] *pl* ▻ **Monseigneur**.

messeoir [67] [meswar] ◆ **messeoir à** *v+prép litt* to be unbecoming to, to ill befit ▪ **il ne messied pas parfois d'avoir un esprit critique** there are times when it behoves one to have a critical mind.

messianique [mesjanik] *adj* messianic.

messianisme [mesjanism] *nm* messianism.

messidor [mesidɔr] *nm tenth month of the French Revolutionary calendar (from June 19th or 20th to July 18th or 19th).*

messie [mesi] *nm* messiah ▪ **le Messie** the Messiah ⊙ **'le Messie'** ***Haendel*** 'The Messiah'.

messied *etc v* ▻ **messeoir**.

messieurs [mesjø] *pl* ▻ **monsieur**.

Messieurs [mesjø] *pl* ▻ **Monsieur**.

messire [mesir] *nm* HIST my lord ▪ **~ Thomas** my lord Thomas.

mesurable [məzyrabl] *adj* measurable.

mesurage [məzyraʒ] *nm* measurement, measuring.

mesure [məzyr] *nf* **1.** [évaluation d'une dimension] measuring *(U)*, measurement ▪ [résultat] measurement ▪ **prendre les ~s de qqch** to take the measurements of sthg
2. [valeur] measure, measurement ▪ **unité de ~** unit of measurement ▪ **~ de surface/longueur** a measure of surface area/of length
3. [récipient] measure ▪ **de vieilles ~s en étain** old pewter measures ⊙ **~ de capacité** [pour liquides] (liquid) measure ; [pour le grain, les haricots] (dry) measure ▪ **faire bonne ~** COMM to give good measure ▪ **et pour faire bonne ~, j'ai perdu ma clef** *hum* and to cap it all, I've lost my key ▪ **la ~ est (à son) comble** enough's enough
4. COUT measurement ▪ **prendre les ~s d'un client** to take a customer's measurements
5. [retenue] moderation ▪ **garder une juste ~** to keep a sense of moderation ▪ **tu passes** *ou* **dépasses la ~** you're going too far ▪ **leur cynisme passe la ~** they're excessively cynical ▪ **un homme plein de ~** a man with a sense of moderation ▪ **dépenser avec/sans ~** to spend with/without moderation
6. [qualité] measure ▪ **il ne donne (toute) sa ~ que dans la dernière scène** he only displays the full measure of his talent *ou* only shows what he's capable of in the last scene ▪ **prendre la ~ d'un adversaire** to size up an opponent
7. ADMIN, DR & POLIT measure, step ▪ **prendre des ~s pour enrayer une épidémie** to take steps to check an epidemic ⊙ **~ incitative** initiative ▪ **~ préventive** preventative measure *ou* step ▪ **~ de rétorsion** retaliatory measure, reprisal ▪ **~ de sécurité** safety measure ▪ **par ~ de : par ~ d'hygiène** in the interest of hygiene ▪ **par ~ de sécurité** as a safety precaution ▪ **~ d'urgence** emergency measure
8. [degré] extent ▪ **son attitude donne la ~ de son cynisme** his behaviour shows just how cynical he really is ▪ **prendre la (juste) ~ de qqch** to understand the full extent of sthg ▪ **dans la ~ de mes possibilités** insofar as I am able ▪ **dans la ~ du possible** as far as possible ▪ **dans la ~ où cela peut lui être agréable** insofar as *ou* inasmuch as he might enjoy it ▪ **dans une certaine ~** to some *ou* a certain extent ▪ **dans une large ~** to a large extent, in large measure *sout* ⊙ **être en ~ de** to be able *ou* in a position to
9. MUS [rythme] time, tempo ▪ **être en ~** to be in time ⊙ **~ composée/simple** compound/simple time ▪ **~ à quatre temps** four-four time *ou* measure, common time *ou* measure
10. LITTÉR metre
11. GÉOM measure
12. ÉQUIT gait
13. ESCRIME measure, reach.

◆ **à la mesure de** *loc prép* worthy of ▪ **elle a un adversaire à sa ~** she's got an opponent worthy of her *ou* who is a match for her.

◆ **à mesure que** *loc conj* as.

◆ **outre mesure** *loc adv* excessively, overmuch ▪ **ils ne s'aiment pas outre ~** they're not overkeen *ou* excessively keen on each other.

◆ **sur mesure** *loc adj* **1.** COUT made-to-measure ▪ **fabriquer des vêtements sur ~** to make clothes to measure ▪ **mousse sur ~** foam cut to size ▪ **fait sur ~** custom-made ▪ **j'ai trouvé un travail sur ~** I've found the ideal job (for me)
2. *(comme nom)* **c'est du sur ~** COUT it's made to measure ; *fig* it fits the bill.

mesuré, e [məzyre] *adj* **1.** [lent] measured ▪ **à pas ~s** at a measured pace **2.** [modéré] steady, moderate.

mesurer [3] [məzyre] ◇ *vt* **1.** [déterminer la dimension de] to measure ▪ **~ qqch en hauteur/largeur** to measure the height/width of sthg ▪ **je vais vous en ~ le double** [obj: coupon, liquide] I'll measure out twice as much for you **2.** [difficulté, qualité] to assess ▪ **il ne mesure pas sa force** *ou* **ses forces** he doesn't know his own strength ▪ **il n'a pas entièrement mesuré les risques** he didn't fully consider *ou* assess the risks ▪ **mesure-t-elle la portée de ses paroles?** is she aware of the consequences of what she's saying? ▪ **~ qqn du regard** to look sb up and down, to size sb up **3.** [limiter] to limit ▪ **on nous mesure les crédits** our funds are limited ▪ **il ne mesure pas sa peine** *sout* he doesn't spare his efforts ▪ **~ ses paroles** to be careful what one says, to weigh one's words ▪ **et pourtant, je mesure mes mots** and I'm choosing my words carefully **4.** [adapter] : **~ qqch à** to adapt sthg to.
◇ *vi* to measure ▪ **combien mesures-tu?** how tall are you? ▪ **le sapin mesure 2 mètres** the fir tree is 2 metres high ▪ **la cuisine mesure 2 mètres sur 3** the kitchen is *ou* measures 2 metres by 3.

◆ **se mesurer** *vp (emploi réciproque)* : **se ~ des yeux** *ou* **du regard** to size each other up, to look each other up and down.

◆ **se mesurer à** *vp+prép* to have a confrontation with, to pit o.s. against ▪ **je n'ai pas envie de me ~ à lui** I don't feel like tackling him.

mesureur [məzyrœr] ◇ *nm* **1.** [agent] measurer **2.** [instrument] gauge, measure.
◇ *adj m* : **verre ~** measuring cup *ou* jug.

mésuser [3] [mezyze] ◆ **mésuser de** *v+prép litt* to misuse.

met *etc v* ▻ **mettre**.

métabolique [metabɔlik] *adj* metabolic.

métabolisme [metabɔlism] *nm* metabolism.

métacarpe [metakarp] *nm* metacarpus.

métairie [meteri] *nf* sharecropping farm, metairie.

métal, aux [metal, o] *nm* **1.** MÉTALL metal ▪ **~ en barres/lingots** metal in bars/ingots ▪ **~ précieux** precious *ou* noble metal ▪ **le ~ jaune** gold ▪ **métaux lourds** heavy metals ▪ **métaux vils** base metals **2.** *litt* [caractère] metal **3.** FIN & HÉRALD metal.

métalangage [metalɑ̃gaʒ] *nm* metalanguage.

métalinguistique [metalɛ̃gɥistik] *adj* metalinguistic.

métallerie [metalri] *nf* structural metalwork.

métallifère [metalifɛr] *adj* metal-bearing, metalliferous.

métallique [metalik] *adj* **1.** [en métal] metal *(modif)* **2.** [semblable au métal] metallic, steel *(modif)*, steely ▪ **un bruit/une voix ~** a metallic noise/voice ⊙ **bleu ~** steel *ou* steely blue.

métallisé, e [metalize] *adj* [couleur, finition] metallic ▪ [papier] metallized.

métallo [metalo] *nm fam* [ouvrier] metalworker ▪ [dans une aciérie] steelworker.

métallurgie [metalyrʒi] *nf* metallurgy.

métallurgique [metalyrʒik] *adj* [procédé] metallurgical ▪ [atelier - gén] metalworking ; [- dans une aciérie] steelworking.

métallurgiste [metalyrʒist] *nm* **1.** [ouvrier] metalworker ▪ [dans une aciérie] steelworker **2.** [industriel, expert] metallurgist.

métamorphose [metamɔrfoz] *nf* **1.** BIOL & MYTHOL metamorphosis **2.** [transformation] metamorphosis, transformation **3.** LITTÉR : **'la Métamorphose' *Kafka*** 'Metamorphosis'.

métamorphoser [3] [metamɔrfoze] *vt* **1.** MYTHOL : **~ qqn en** to change *ou* to turn sb into **2.** [transformer] to transform, to change.
◆ **se métamorphoser** *vpi* **1.** MYTHOL : **se ~ en** to turn *ou* to be metamorphosed into **2.** [se transformer] to change, to transform ▪ **en 20 ans, la télévision s'est métamorphosée** television has undergone a transformation over the last 20 years.

métaphore [metafɔr] *nf* metaphor.

métaphorique [metafɔrik] *adj* metaphoric, metaphorical, figurative.

métaphoriquement [metafɔrikmɑ̃] *adv* metaphorically, figuratively.

métaphysicien, enne [metafizisjɛ̃, ɛn] *nm, f* metaphysician, metaphysicist.

métaphysique [metafizik] ◇ *adj* **1.** ART & PHILOS metaphysical **2.** [spéculatif] metaphysical, abstruse, abstract.
◇ *nf* **1.** PHILOS metaphysics *(sing)* ▪ [système de pensée] metaphysic ▪ **la ~ kantienne** the Kantian metaphysic **2.** [spéculations] abstractness, abstruseness ▪ **il ne s'embarrasse pas de ~ *fam*** he doesn't let anything get in his way.

métaphysiquement [metafizikmɑ̃] *adv* metaphysically.

métapsychique [metapsiʃik] *vieilli* ◇ *adj* psychic.
◇ *nf* parapsychology.

métapsychologie [metapsikɔlɔʒi] *nf* metapsychology.

métastase [metastaz] *nf* metastasis.

métatarse [metatars] *nm* metatarsus.

métayage [metɛjaʒ] *nm* sharecropping.

métayer, ère [meteje, ɛr] *nm, f* sharecropper, sharecropping tenant.

méteil [metɛi] *nm* AGRIC ≃ wheat mixture ▪ [récolte] mixed crop *(of wheat and rye)*.

métempsycose [metɑ̃psikoz] *nf* metempsychosis.

météo [meteo] ◇ *adj inv* (*abr de* **météorologique**) ▪ **bulletin ~** weather report ▪ **prévisions ~** (weather) forecast.
◇ *nf* (*abr de* **météorologie**) [service] Met Office *UK*, Weather Bureau *US* ▪ [temps prévu] weather forecast ▪ **la ~ a dit que...** the weatherman said...

météore [meteɔr] *nm* **1.** ASTRON meteor **2.** *fig* nine days' wonder ▪ **un ~ dans le monde de l'art** a flash in the pan in the art world.

météorique [meteɔrik] *adj* **1.** ASTRON meteoric **2.** [éphémère] meteoric, short-lived, fleeting.

météorite [meteɔrit] *nf* **1.** [météoroïde] meteoroid **2.** [aérolithe] meteorite.

météorologie [meteɔrɔlɔʒi] *nf* **1.** SC meteorology **2.** [organisme] Meteorological Office, Weather Centre *UK ou* Bureau *US*.

météorologique [meteɔrɔlɔʒik] *adj* meteorological, weather *(modif)*.

météorologiste [meteɔrɔlɔʒist], **météorologue** [meteɔrɔlɔg] *nmf* meteorologist.

métèque [metɛk] ◇ *nm* HIST metic.
◇ *nmf*▲ *offensive term used with reference to Mediterranean foreigners living in France.*

méthadone [metadɔn] *nf* methadone.

méthane [metan] *nm* methane (gas).

méthode [metɔd] *nf* **1.** [système] method ▪ SC & TECHNOL method, technique ▪ **c'est une bonne ~ pour apprendre l'anglais** it's a good way of learning English ▪ **j'ai ma ~ pour le convaincre** I have my own way of convincing him ▪ **~ de travail** working method, modus operandi *formal* ⊙ **~ globale** [d'apprentissage de la lecture] word recognition method **2.** [organisation] method ▪ **vous manquez de ~** you lack method, you aren't methodical enough ▪ **avec ~** methodically ▪ **sans ~** unmethodically **3.** *fam* [astuce] : **lui, il a la ~!** he's got the hang of it *ou* the knack! **4.** [manuel] : **~ de lecture** primer ▪ **~ de solfège** music handbook *ou* manual.

méthodique [metɔdik] *adj* methodical ▪ **de façon ~** methodically.

méthodiquement [metɔdikmɑ̃] *adv* methodically.

méthodisme [metɔdism] *nm* Methodism.

méthodiste [metɔdist] *adj* & *nmf* Methodist.

méthodologie [metɔdɔlɔʒi] *nf* methodology.

méthodologique [metɔdɔlɔʒik] *adj* methodological.

méthylène [metilɛn] *nm* CHIM methylene ▪ COMM methyl alcohol.

méticuleusement [metikyløzmɑ̃] *adv* meticulously.

méticuleux, euse [metikylø, øz] *adj* **1.** [minutieux - personne] meticulous ; [- enquête] probing, searsching ▪ **un élève ~** a meticulous pupil **2.** [scrupuleux] meticulous, scrupulous ▪ **d'une propreté méticuleuse** spotlessly *ou* scrupulously clean.

méticulosité [metikylɔzite] *nf litt* meticulousness.

métier [metje] *nm* **1.** [profession] trade ▪ **mon ~** my job *ou* occupation *ou* trade ▪ **les ~s manuels** the manual trades ▪ **les ~s d'art** (arts and) crafts ▪ **j'ai fait tous les ~s** I've done every sort of job there is ▪ **faire** *ou* **exercer le ~ de chimiste** to work as a chemist ▪ **la soudure ne tiendra pas, et je connais mon ~!** the welding won't hold, and I know what I'm talking about *ou* what I'm doing! ▪ **le ~ de mère** a mother's job ⊙ **le plus vieux ~ du monde *euphém*** the oldest profession in the world ▪ **il n'y a pas de sot ~(, il n'y a que de sottes gens)** there's no such thing as a worthless trade **2.** [expérience] skill, experience ▪ **avoir du ~** to have job experience ▪ **c'est le ~ qui rentre** it shows you're learning **3.** [machine] : **~ à filer/tricoter** spinning/knitting machine ▪ **~ à tapisserie** tapestry frame *ou* loom ▪ **~ à tisser** loom ▪ **avoir qqch sur le ~ *fig*** to have sthg lined up.
◆ **de métier** ◇ *loc adj* [homme, femme, armée] professional ▪ [argot] technical ▪ [technique] of the trade.
◇ *loc adv* : **avoir 15 ans de ~** to have been in the job *ou* business for 15 years.
◆ **de son métier** *loc adv* by trade ▪ **être boulanger/journaliste de son ~** to be a baker/journalist by trade.
◆ **du métier** *loc adj* of the trade ▪ **les gens du ~** people of the trade *ou* in the business ▪ **demande à quelqu'un du ~** ask a professional *ou* an expert.

métis, isse [metis] ◇ *adj* **1.** [personne] of mixed race ▪ **un enfant ~** a mixed-race child **2.** ZOOL crossbred, hybrid, cross ▪ BOT hybrid.
◇ *nm, f* **1.** [personne] person of mixed race **2.** ZOOL crossbreed, hybrid, cross ▪ BOT hybrid.
◆ **métis** *nm* TEXT (heavy) linen-cotton mixture.

métissage [metisaʒ] *nm* **1.** BIOL [de personnes] interbreeding ▪ [d'animaux] crossbreeding, hybridization ▪ [de plantes] hybridation **2.** SOCIOL intermarrying ▪ **~ culturel** cultural melting-pot, pick-and-mix culture, *péj* cross-cultural mish-mash ▪ **~ gastronomique/des habitudes culturelles** mixture of different cuisines/cultural traditions ▪ **le ~ de la salsa et du rock** the mixing of salsa with rock music.

métisser [3] [metise] *vt* ZOOL to cross, to crossbreed ▪ BOT to hybridize.

métonymie [metɔnimi] *nf* metonymy.

métonymique [metɔnimik] *adj* metonymic.

métrage [metraʒ] *nm* **1.** [prise de mesures] measurement **2.** [longueur] length ▪ COUT & COMM length, yardage ▪ **quel ~ faut-il pour un manteau?** how many yards are needed to make an overcoat? **3.** CINÉ footage, length.

mètre [mɛtr] *nm* **1.** [unité] metre ▪ **~ carré/cube** square/cubic metre ▪ **~ par seconde** metre per second ◐ **~ étalon** standard metre **2.** SPORT : **le 400 ~s** the 400 metres, the 400-metre race **3.** [instrument] (metre) rule ▪ **~ pliant** folding rule ▪ **~ à ruban** tape measure, measuring tape **4.** LITTÉR metre.

métré [metre] *nm* **1.** [mesure] quantity survey **2.** [devis] bill *ou* schedule of quantities.

métrer [8] [metre] *vt* **1.** [mesurer] to measure *(in metres)* **2.** CONSTR to survey, to do a quantity survey of.

métreur, euse [metrœr, øz] *nm, f* : **~ (vérificateur)** quantity surveyor.

métrique [metrik] <> *adj* GÉOM & LITTÉR metric.
<> *nf* **1.** LITTÉR metrics *(U)* **2.** MATH metric.

métro [metro] *nm* underground *UK*, subway *US* ▪ **prendre le ~** to take the underground *UK ou* subway *US* ▪ **premier ~** first *ou* milk train ▪ **le dernier ~** the last train ◐ **~ aérien** elevated *ou* overhead railway ▪ **elle a toujours un ~ de retard** she's slow to catch on ▪ **~, boulot, dodo** *fam* the daily grind *ou* routine.

métrologie [metrɔlɔʒi] *nf* metrology.

métrologique [metrɔlɔʒik] *adj* metrological.

métrologiste [metrɔlɔʒist] *nmf* metrologist.

métronome [metrɔnɔm] *nm* metronome ▪ **avec la régularité d'un ~** like clockwork, (as) regular as clockwork.

métropole [metrɔpɔl] *nf* **1.** [ville] metropolis **2.** ADMIN mother country ▪ **les Français de la ~** the metropolitan French **3.** RELIG metropolis, see.

métropolitain, e [metrɔpolitɛ̃, ɛn] *adj* ADMIN & RELIG metropolitan ▪ **troupes ~es** home troops.
◆ **métropolitain** *nm* **1.** *vieilli* [métro] underground (railway) *UK*, subway *US* **2.** RELIG metropolitan (primate).

métropolite [metrɔpɔlit] *nm* RELIG metropolitan.

mets [mɛ] *nm* [aliment] dish ▪ **des ~ de grande qualité** high-class fare.

mettable [metabl] *adj* wearable ▪ **la veste est encore ~** the jacket's still wearable ▪ **je n'ai plus rien de ~** I don't have anything decent left to wear.

metteur, euse [mɛtœr, øz] *nm, f* : **~ en scène** CINÉ director ; THÉÂTRE producer ▪ **~ au point** TECHNOL adjuster, setter.

mettre [84] [mɛtr] *vt* **1.** [placer] to put ▪ **~ sa confiance/tout son espoir en** to put one's trust/all one's hopes in ▪ **j'avais mis beaucoup de moi-même dans le projet** I'd put a lot into the project ▪ **elle a mis son talent au service des défavorisés** she used her talent to help the underprivileged ▪ **~ à : ~ une pièce à l'affiche** to bill a play ▪ **je n'ai pas pu la ~ à l'école du quartier** I couldn't get her into the local school ▪ **~ un enfant au lit** to put a child to bed ▪ **on m'a mis au standard** they put me on the switchboard ▪ **~ qqn dans : ~ qqn dans l'avion/le train** to put sb on the plane/the train ▪ **~ ses enfants dans le privé** to send one's children to private school ▪ **~ qqn en : ~ un enfant en pension** to put a child in a *ou* to send a child to boarding school ▪ **~ qqch sur : ~ 100 euros sur un cheval** to put *ou* to lay 100 euros on a horse ▪ **~ de l'argent sur son compte** to put *ou* to pay some money into one's account ◐ **~ qqn en boîte** *fam* to pull sb's leg
2. [poser horizontalement] to lay, to put ▪ **~ la main sur le bras de qqn** to lay *ou* to put one's hand on sb's arm ▪ **~ qqch à plat** to lay sthg down flat
3. [disposer] : **~ le loquet** to put the latch down
4. [ajuster] to set ▪ **~ qqch droit** to set sthg straight *pr* ▪ **~ une pendule à l'heure** to set a clock to the right time ▪ **mets la sonnerie à 20 h 30** set the alarm for 8:30 p.m
5. [établir - dans un état, une situation] : **~ qqch à : ~ un étang à sec** to drain a pond ▪ **mettez les verbes à l'infinitif** put the verbs into the infinitive ▪ **~ qqn à : ~ qqn à l'amende** to fine sb, to impose a fine on sb ▪ **~ qqn au travail** to set sb to work, to get sb working ▪ **~ qqn au désespoir** to cause sb to despair ▪ **~ qqn dans : ~ qqn dans la confidence** to let sb in on *ou* into the secret ▪ **~ qqn dans l'embarras** [perplexité] to put sb in a predicament ; [pauvreté] to put sb in financial difficulty ▪ **~ qqn dans l'obligation de faire qqch** to oblige sb to do sthg ▪ **~ en : ~ une maison en vente** to put a house up for sale ▪ **~ du vin en bouteilles** to put wine into bottles, to bottle wine ▪ **~ une plante en pot** to pot a plant ▪ **~ qqch en miettes** to smash sthg to bits ▪ **~ un poème en musique** to set a poem to music ▪ **~ qqch en vigueur** to bring sthg into force *ou* operation ▪ **~ qqch à : ~ qqch à cuire** to put sthg on to cook ▪ **~ qqch à réchauffer** to heat sthg up (again) ▪ **~ du linge à sécher** to put *ou* to hang clothes up to dry ▪ **~ qqch à tremper** to put sthg to soak, to soak sthg
6. [fixer] to put ▪ **~ une pièce à un pantalon** to put a patch on *ou* to patch a pair of trousers ▪ **~ un bouton à sa veste** to sew a button on one's jacket ‖ [ajouter] to put ▪ **il faut lui ~ des piles** you have to put batteries in it ▪ **j'ai fait ~ de nouveaux verres à mes lunettes** I had new lenses put in my glasses
7. [se vêtir, se coiffer, se chausser de] to put on *(sép)* ▪ [porter régulièrement] to wear ▪ **mets une barrette** put a (hair) slide in ▪ **je lui ai mis son manteau/ses gants** I put his coat/his gloves on (for him)
8. [faire fonctionner - appareil] to turn *ou* to put *ou* to switch on *(sép)* ▪ **mets de la musique** put some music on, play some music ▪ **mets les sports** *fam* **/la première chaîne** put on the sport channel/channel one
9. [installer] to put in *(sép)*, to install ▪ **faire ~ le chauffage central** to have central heating put in *ou* installed ▪ **~ du papier peint/de la moquette dans une pièce** to wallpaper/to carpet a room
10. [consacrer - temps] to take ▪ **elle a mis trois mois à me répondre** she took three months *ou* it took her three months to answer me ▪ **combien de temps met-on pour y aller?** how long does it take to get there? ▪ **nous y mettrons le temps/le prix qu'il faudra** we'll spend as much time/money as we have to ▪ **tu as mis le temps!** *fam* you took your time about it!, you took long enough! ▪ **tu en a mis du temps pour te décider!** you took some time to make up your mind! ▪ **~ de l'argent dans une voiture** to put money in *ou* into a car
11. [écrire] to put ▪ **on met un accent sur le "e"** "e" takes an accent ▪ **on met deux m à "pomme"** "pomme" has two m's ▪ **mets qu'il a refusé de signer** *fam* write *ou* put down that he refused to sign
12. [supposer] : **mettons** (let's) say ▪ **et mettons que tu gagnes?** suppose *ou* let's say you win? ▪ **il faut, mettons, 2 mètres de tissu** we need, (let's) say *ou* shall we say, 2 metres of material ▪ **mettons que j'ai mal compris!** [acceptation] let's just say I got it wrong!
13. [donner] to give ▪ **je vous mets un peu plus de la livre** I've put in a bit more than a pound ▪ **le prof m'a mis 18** ≃ the teacher gave me an A
14. *fam* [infliger] : **qu'est-ce qu'il m'a mis au ping-pong!** he really hammered me *ou* he didn't half thrash me at table tennis! ▪ **on leur a mis 5 buts en première mi-temps** we hammered in 5 goals against them in the first half ▪ **je lui ai mis une bonne claque** I gave *ou* landed him a good clout ▪ **qu'est-ce que son père va lui ~!** his father is really going to give it to him!
15. *loc* **on les met!**△ let's split!△ ▪ **va te faire ~!**▲ up yours!△.
◆ **se mettre** <> *vp (emploi passif)* **1.** [dans une position, un endroit - chose] to go ▪ **où se mettent les tasses?** where do the cups go? ▪ **les pieds, ça ne se met pas sur la table!** tables aren't made to put your feet on!
2. [aller - vêtement] to go ▪ **le noir se met avec tout** black goes with everything.
<> *vpi* **1.** [s'installer, s'établir - dans une position] : **se ~ debout** to stand up ▪ **se ~ sur le dos** to lie (down) on one's back ▪ **mets-toi près de la fenêtre** [debout] stand near the window ; [assis] sit near the window ▪ **mettez-vous en cercle** arrange yourselves into *ou* form a circle ▪ **je me mets dehors pour travailler** I go outside to work ▪ **mettez-vous dans la position du lotus** get into the lotus position
2. [entrer - dans un état, une situation] : **ne te mets pas dans un tel état!** don't get (yourself) into such a state! ▪ **se ~ en rage** to get into a rage ▪ **il s'est mis dans une position difficile** he's got *ou* put himself in a difficult situation
3. [s'habiller] : **se ~ en** to put on ▪ **se ~ en pantalon** to put on a pair of trousers ▪ **elle se met toujours en jupe** she always wears a skirt

4. [s'unir] : **se ~ avec qqn** [pour un jeu] to team up with sb ; [pour vivre] to move in with sb ; [dans une discussion] to side with sb ▪ **on s'est tous mis ensemble pour acheter le cadeau** we all clubbed together to buy the present ▪ **on s'est mis par équipes de 6** we split up into *ou* we formed teams of 6 (people) ▪ **ils ont dû s'y ~ à 4 pour porter le buffet** it took 4 of them to carry the dresser
5. *loc* **qu'est-ce qu'ils se mettent!**△ [dans un combat, un débat] they're really having a go at each other! ; [en mangeant] they're really getting stuck in!
◇ *vpt* to put on *(sép)* ▪ **se ~ une belle robe/du parfum** to put on a nice dress/some perfume.
◆ **se mettre à** *vp+prép* **1.** [passer à] : **quand le feu se met au rouge** when the lights turn *ou* go red ▮ MÉTÉOR : **le temps se met au beau** it's turning sunny ▪ **le temps se met au froid** it's getting *ou* turning cold
2. [commencer] : **se ~ au judo** to take up judo ▪ **se ~ à l'ouvrage** to set to work, to get down to work ▪ **voilà qu'il se met à pleuvoir!** now it's started to rain *ou* raining! ▪ **s'y ~** [au travail] to get down to it ; [à une activité nouvelle] to have a try ▪ **si tu t'y mets aussi, je renonce!** if you join in as well, I give up!

meublant, e [mœblɑ̃, ɑ̃t] *adj* ▷ **meuble nm**.

meuble[1] [mœbl] *adj* **1.** AGRIC & HORT loose, light **2.** GÉOL crumbly, friable ▪ **formation ~** crumb **3.** DR : **biens ~ s** movables, movable assets, personal estate.

meuble[2] [mœbl] *nm* **1.** [élément du mobilier] : **un ~** a piece of furniture ▪ **des ~s** furniture ▪ **êtes-vous dans vos ~s ici?** do you own the furniture here? ◗ **~ de rangement** cupboard ▪ **des ~s de salon** living room furniture ▪ **des ~s de style** period furniture ▪ **faire partie des ~s** *fam* to be part of the furniture **2.** DR movable ▪ **en fait de ~s, possession vaut titre** (as far as goods and chattels are concerned) possession amounts to title ◗ **les ~s meublants** (household) furniture, movables *(terme juridique)* **3.** HÉRALD charge.

meublé, e [mœble] *adj* furnished ▪ **une maison ~e/non ~ e** a furnished/an unfurnished house.
◆ **meublé** *nm* [une pièce] furnished room ▪ [plusieurs pièces] furnished flat *UK ou* apartment *US* ▪ **habiter** *ou* **vivre en ~** to live in furnished accommodation.

meubler [5] [mœble] *vt* **1.** [garnir de meubles] to furnish ▪ **ils ont meublé leur maison en Louis XIII** they furnished their home in the Louis XIII style ▪ **comment vas-tu ~ la cuisine?** what sort of furniture are you going to put in the kitchen? **2.** [remplir] to fill ▪ **~ le silence/sa solitude** to fill the silence/one's solitude ▪ **pour ~ la conversation** to stop the conversation from flagging, for the sake of conversation ▪ **~ ses soirées en lisant** to spend one's evenings reading.
◆ **se meubler** *vpi* to buy (some) furniture ▪ **meublez-vous chez Caudin** buy your furniture at Caudin's.

meuf△ [mœf] *nf* girl *("verlan" form of the word "femme")*.

meuglement [møgləmɑ̃] *nm* mooing.

meugler [5] [møgle] *vi* to moo.

meule [møl] *nf* **1.** AGRIC stack, rick ▪ **mettre en ~s** to stack, to rick ◗ **~ de foin** hayrick, haystack ▪ **~ de paille** stack of straw **2.** TECHNOL (grinding) wheel ▪ **~ à aiguiser** *ou* **affûter** grindstone ▪ **~ à polir/à rectifier** polishing/trueing wheel **3.** CULIN : **une ~ de fromage** a (whole) cheese **4.** [d'un moulin] millstone.

meunerie [mønri] *nf* **1.** [activité] (flour) milling **2.** [commerce] flour *ou* milling trade **3.** [usine] flour works *(sing)*.

meunier, ère [mønje, ɛr] *adj* milling *(modif)*.
◆ **meunier** *nm* **1.** [artisan] miller ▪ **échelle** *ou* **escalier de ~** narrow flight of steps **2.** [poisson] miller's thumb, bullhead **3.** ENTOM cockroach **4.** ORNITH [martin-pêcheur] kingfisher.
◆ **meunière** *nf* **1.** [épouse du meunier] miller's wife **2.** CULIN : **sole (à la) meunière** sole meunière.

meurt *etc v* ▷ **mourir**.

meurtre [mœrtr] *nm* murder ▪ **crier au ~** to scream blue murder ◗ **~ avec préméditation** premeditated murder.

meurtrier, ère [mœrtrije, ɛr] ◇ *adj* [qui tue - engin, lame] deadly, lethal, murderous ; [- avalanche] deadly, fatal ; [- route] lethal, murderous ; [- folie, passion] murderous ▪ **une chasse à l'homme meurtrière** a bloody *ou* murderous manhunt ▪ **humour ~** lethal *ou* devastating humour.
◇ *nm, f* murderer *(f* murderess).
◆ **meurtrière** *nf* ARCHIT (arrow) loophole.

meurtrir [32] [mœrtrir] *vt* **1.** [contusionner] to bruise ▪ **elle avait le visage tout meurtri** her face was all black and blue *ou* all bruised **2.** *fig & litt* to hurt, to wound **3.** [poire, fleur] to bruise.

meurtrissure [mœrtrisyr] *nf* **1.** [contusion] bruise **2.** *fig & litt* scar, wound **3.** [tache] bruise ▪ **des poires pleines de ~s** pears covered in bruises.

meut *etc v* ▷ **mouvoir**.

meute [møt] *nf* [de chiens] pack ▪ [de gens] mob, crowd ▪ **une ~ de paparazzi** a crowd of paparazzi.

meuvent *etc v* ▷ **mouvoir**.

mévente [mevɑ̃t] *nf* **1.** [baisse des ventes] slump **2.** [vente à perte] selling at a loss.

mexicain, e [mɛksikɛ̃, ɛn] *adj* Mexican.
◆ **Mexicain, e** *nm, f* Mexican.

Mexico [mɛksiko] *npr* Mexico City.

Mexique [mɛksik] *npr m* : **le ~** Mexico ▪ **au ~** in Mexico ▪ **le golfe du ~** the Gulf of Mexico.

mézigue△ [mezig] *pron pers* yours truly, muggins ▪ **et qui est-ce qui va casquer? c'est ~!** and who's going to pay? muggins here!

mezzanine [mɛdzanin] *nf* **1.** ARCHIT [entresol] mezzanine ▪ [fenêtre] mezzanine window **2.** THÉÂTRE [corbeille] mezzanine, lower balcony.

mezze [medze] *nmpl* CULIN meze.

mezzo-soprano [mɛdzosɔprano] *(pl* **mezzo-sopranos)**
◇ *nm* [voix] mezzo-soprano.
◇ *nf* [cantatrice] mezzo-soprano.

MF ◇ *nf (abr de* **modulation de fréquence)** FM.
◇ **= million de francs**.

Mgr. *(abr écrite de* **Monseigneur)** Mgr.

mi [mi] *nm inv* E ▪ [chanté] mi, me, *voir aussi* **fa**.

mi- [mi] *préf* **1.** [moitié] half- ▪ **~fil ~coton** half-linen half-cotton, 50% linen 50% cotton **2.** *loc* **~figue ~raisin** [accueil] somewhat mixed ; [réponse] ambiguous, enigmatic ; [sourire] quizzical, wry.

miam-miam [mjammjam] *interj fam* yum-yum ▪ **~, ça a l'air bon** that looks yummy.

miaou [mjau] *nm* miaow ▪ **faire ~** to miaow.

miasme [mjasm] *nm* miasma ▪ **des ~s** miasmas, miasmata.

miaulement [mjolmɑ̃] *nm* miaowing, mewing ▪ **on entendait de terribles ~s dans la cour** some cats were making a dreadful noise in the courtyard.

miauler [3] [mjole] *vi* to miaow, to mew.

mi-bas [miba] *nm inv* knee-high *ou* knee-length sock.

mica [mika] *nm* [roche] mica.

mi-carême [mikarɛm] *(pl* **mi-carêmes)** *nf* : **à la ~** on the third Thursday of Lent.

miche [miʃ] *nf* [pain] round loaf.
◆ **miches**△ *nfpl* [fesses] bum△ *UK*, fanny *US* ▪ [seins] knockers△, tits△.

Michel [miʃɛl] *npr* : **saint ~** Saint Michael.

Michel-Ange [mikɛlɑ̃ʒ] *npr* Michelangelo.

micheline [miʃlin] *nf* railcar.

mi-chemin [miʃmɛ̃] ◆ **à mi-chemin** *loc adv* halfway, midway.
◆ **à mi-chemin de** *loc prép* halfway to ▪ **à ~ de l'église et de l'école** halfway *ou* midway between the church and the school.

Michigan [miʃigɑ̃] *npr* : **le lac ~** Lake Michigan.

Mickey [mike] *npr* Mickey Mouse.

mi-clos, e [miklo, mikloz] *adj* half-closed.

micmac [mikmak] *nm fam* [affaire suspecte] funny *ou* fishy business, strange carry-on ▪ [complications] mix-up ▪ **ça a été tout un ~ pour pouvoir entrer** getting in was a real hassle.

mi-corps [mikɔr] ◆ **à mi-corps** *loc adv* [à partir - du bas] up to the waist ; [- du haut] down to the waist ▪ **l'eau nous arrivait à ~** the water came up to our waists.

mi-côte [mikot] ◆ **à mi-côte** *loc adv* [en partant - du bas] halfway up the hill ; [- du haut] halfway down the hill.

mi-course [mikurs] ◆ **à mi-course** *loc adv* halfway through the race.

micro [mikro] ◇ *nm* **1.** (*abr de* **microphone**) mike ▪ **parler dans le ~** to speak into the mike **2.** *fam* (*abr de* **micro-ordinateur**) PC.
◇ *nf fam* = **micro-informatique**.

microbe [mikrɔb] *nm* **1.** [germe] microbe, germ ▪ **attraper un ~** to catch a bug **2.** *fam* [personne] shrimp, (little) runt *ou* pipsqueak.

microbien, enne [mikrɔbjɛ̃, ɛn] *adj* [relatif aux microbes] microbial, microbic ▪ [causé par les microbes] bacterial.

microbiologie [mikrɔbjɔlɔʒi] *nf* microbiology.

micro-brasserie (*pl* - s) [mikrɔbrasri] *nf* microbrewery, small (independent) brewery.

microchimie [mikrɔʃimi] *nf* microchemistry.

microchirurgie [mikrɔʃiryrʒi] *nf* microsurgery.

microcircuit [mikrɔsirkɥi] *nm* microcircuit.

microclimat [mikrɔklima] *nm* microclimate.

microcosme [mikrɔkɔsm] *nm* microcosm.

micro-cravate [mikrɔkravat] (*pl* **micros-cravates**) *nm* lapel mike.

micro-crédit (*pl* - s) [mikrɔkredi] *nm* microcredit.

microéconomie [mikrɔekɔnɔmi] *nf* microeconomics (*sing*).

microéconomique [mikrɔekɔnɔmik] *adj* microeconomic.

microédition [mikrɔedisjɔ̃] *nf* desktop publishing.

microélectronique [mikrɔelɛktrɔnik] ◇ *adj* microelectronic.
◇ *nf* microelectronics (*U*).

micro-entreprise [mikroɑ̃trəpriz] *nf* microenterprise, microbusiness.

microfibre [mikrɔfibr] *nf* microfibre.

microfiche [mikrɔfiʃ] *nf* microfiche.

microfilm [mikrɔfilm] *nm* microfilm.

microflore [mikrɔflɔr] *nf* microflora.

micro-informatique [mikrɔɛ̃fɔrmatik] (*pl* **micro-informatiques**) *nf* computer science.

micromètre [mikrɔmɛtr] *nm* **1.** [instrument] micrometer **2.** [unité] micrometre.

micron [mikrɔ̃] *nm* micron.

Micronésie [mikrɔnezi] *npr f* : **(la) ~** Micronesia.

micro-ondable (*pl* - s) [mikrɔɔ̃dabl] *adj* [vaisselle] microwave-proof ▪ [produit alimentaire] microwavable.

micro-onde [mikrɔɔ̃d] (*pl* **micro-ondes**) *nf* microwave.

micro-ondes [mikrɔɔ̃d] *nm inv* microwave ▪ **faire cuire qqch au ~** to cook sthg in the microwave, to microwave sthg.

micro-ordinateur [mikrɔɔrdinatœr] (*pl* **micro-ordinateurs**) *nm* microcomputer.

micro-organisme [mikrɔɔrganism] (*pl* **micro-organismes**) *nm* microorganism.

microphone [mikrɔfɔn] *nm* microphone.

microphysique [mikrɔfizik] *nf* microphysics (*U*).

micropilule [mikrɔpilyl] *nf* minipill.

microprocesseur [mikrɔprɔsesœr] *nm* microprocessor.

microprogrammation [mikrɔprɔgramasjɔ̃] *nf* microprogramming.

microprogramme [mikrɔprɔgram] *nm* INFORM firmware.

microscope [mikrɔskɔp] *nm* microscope ▪ **étudier qqch au ~** *pr* to examine sthg under *ou* through a microscope ; *fig* to put sthg under the microscope ⊙ **~ électronique/optique** electron/optical microscope ▪ **~ électronique à balayage** scanning electron microscope.

microscopique [mikrɔskɔpik] *adj* SC microscopic ▪ [petit] microscopic, tiny, minute.

microsillon [mikrɔsijɔ̃] *nm* [sillon] microgroove ▪ **(disque) ~** microgroove record.

microsonde [mikrɔsɔ̃d] *nf* microprobe.

microstructure [mikrɔstryktyr] *nf* microstructure.

micro-trottoir (*pl* **micros-trottoirs**) [mikrotrɔtwar] *nm* voxpop.

miction [miksjɔ̃] *nf* urination, micturition *spéc*.

MIDEM, Midem [midɛm] (*abr de* **Marché international du disque et de l'édition musicale**) *npr m annual recorded music market in Cannes*.

midi [midi] *nm* **1.** [milieu du jour] midday, lunchtime, noon ▪ **je m'arrête à ~** I stop at lunchtime ; [pour déjeuner] I stop for lunch ▪ **tous les ~s** every day at lunchtime, every lunchtime ▪ **il mange des pâtes tous les ~s** he has pasta for lunch every day ⊙ **voir ~ à sa porte** to be wrapped up in oneself **2.** [heure] midday, twelve (o'clock), (twelve) noon ▪ **il est ~** it's midday, it's twelve (noon) ▪ **il est ~ passé** it's after twelve, it's past midday ▪ **~ et quart** a quarter past twelve ▪ **entre ~ et deux (heures)** between twelve and two, during lunch *ou* lunchtime ▪ **sur le coup de ~** on the stroke of twelve **3.** [sud] south ▪ **exposé au ~** south-facing, facing south.
◆ **Midi** *nm* [région du sud] South ▪ **le Midi (de la France)** the South of France ▪ **le climat du Midi** the Southern climate ▪ **l'accent du Midi** southern (French) accent.
◆ **de midi** *loc adj* [repas, informations] midday (*modif*) ▪ **la pause de ~** the lunch break.

midinette [midinɛt] *nf péj* [jeune fille] starry-eyed girl ▪ **des amours de ~** the loves of some starry-eyed young girl.

Midi-Pyrénées [midipirene] *npr m* Midi-Pyrénées.

MIDI-PYRÉNÉES

This administrative region includes the *départements* of Ariège, Aveyron, Gers, Haute-Garonne, Lot and Tarn-et-Garonne (capital: Toulouse).

mi-distance [midistɑ̃s] ◆ **à mi-distance** *loc adv* halfway, midway.
◆ **à mi-distance de** *loc prép* halfway *ou* midway between.

mie [mi] *nf* **1.** [de pain] white *ou* soft *ou* doughy part (of bread) **2.** *litt & arch* [femme] truelove, ladylove ▪ **venez, ma ~** come, fair damsel.

miel [mjɛl] ◇ *nm* **1.** [d'abeilles] honey ▪ **~ liquide/solide/rosat** clear/set/rose honey **2.** *loc* **il est (tout sucre) tout ~** he's a sweet talker.
◇ *interj fam euphém* **~!** sugar!
◆ **au miel** *loc adj* honey (*modif*), honey-flavoured.

miellé, e [mjele] *adj litt* **du thé ~** honey-sweetened tea ▪ **la couleur ~e de ses cheveux** the golden colour of her hair.

mielleusement [mjɛløzmɑ̃] *adv* smarmily.

mielleux, euse [mjɛlø, øz] *adj* **1.** [doucereux] sickly sweet ▪ **un sourire ~** a saccharine smile ▪ **d'un ton ~** in a syrupy voice **2.** [relatif au miel] honey (*modif*), honey-like.

mien [mjɛ̃] (*f* **mienne** [mjɛn], *mpl* **miens** [mjɛ̃], *fpl* **miennes** [mjɛn]) *adj poss sout* : **j'ai fait ~ ce mot d'ordre** I've adopted this slogan as my own ▪ **une mienne cousine** *litt* a cousin of mine.

◆ **le mien** (*f* **la mienne**, *mpl* **les miens**, *fpl* **les miennes**) *pron poss* mine ■ **je suis parti avec une valise qui n'était pas la mienne** I left with a suitcase that wasn't mine *ou* that didn't belong to me ■ **vos préoccupations sont aussi les miennes** I share your anxieties ■ **ton jour/ton prix sera le ~** name the day/your price ■ *(emploi nominal)* **les ~s** my family and friends ▶ **j'y mets du ~** [en faisant des efforts] I'm making an effort ; [en étant compréhensif] I'm trying to be understanding.

miette [mjɛt] *nf* **1.** [d'aliment] crumb ■ **des ~s de crabe** crab bits ■ **une ~ de pain** a crumb of bread ■ **des ~s de pain** breadcrumbs ■ **des ~s de thon** tuna flakes **2.** [petite quantité] : **pas une ~ de** not a shred of ■ **une ~ de** a little bit of.

◆ **miettes** *nfpl* [restes] leftovers, crumbs, scraps ■ [morceaux] piece, fragment, bit ■ **sa voiture est en ~s** her car's a wreck ■ **son rêve est en ~s** his dream is in shreds *ou* tatters.

mieux [mjø] ◇ *adv*

A. COMPARATIF DE 'BIEN'
B. SUPERLATIF DE 'BIEN'
C. EMPLOI NOMINAL

A. COMPARATIF DE 'BIEN'

1. [d'une manière plus satisfaisante] better ■ **elle va ~** she's better ■ **qui dit ~?** [aux enchères] any advance (on that)?, any more bids? ; *fig* who can top that? ■ **repassez demain, je ne peux pas vous dire ~** come again tomorrow, that's the best *ou* all I can tell you ■ **~ assis** [plus confortablement] sitting more comfortably ; [au spectacle] in a better seat ■ **moins je le vois, ~ je me porte!** the less I see of him, the better I feel! ■ **il ne lit pas ~ qu'il ne parle** he doesn't read any better than he speaks **2.** [conformément à la raison, à la morale] better ■ **son frère ne fait que des bêtises, et elle ce n'est pas ~** her brother is always misbehaving and she's no better ■ **il ferait ~ de travailler/de se taire** he'd do better to work/to keep quiet ■ **on ne peut pas ~ dire** you can't say better *ou* fairer than that

B. SUPERLATIF DE 'BIEN'

[par comparaison] : **le ~** [de deux] the better ; [de plusieurs] the best ■ **c'est le mannequin le ~ payé** [des deux] she's the better-paid model ; [de plusieurs] she's the best-paid model ■ **voilà ce qui me convient le ~** this is what suits me best ■ **le ~ qu'il peut** the best he can ■ **j'ai classé les dossiers le ~ possible** I filed everything as best I could ▶ **le ~ du monde** *sout* beautifully ■ **s'entendre le ~ du monde avec qqn** to be on the best of terms with sb

C. EMPLOI NOMINAL

better ■ **c'est pas mal, mais il y a ~** it's not bad, but there's better ■ **en attendant/espérant ~** while waiting/hoping for better (things) ■ **faute de ~, je m'en contenterai** since there's nothing better, I'll make do with it ■ **c'est sa mère en ~** she's like her mother, only better-looking ■ **changer en ~** to take a turn for *ou* to change for the better.

◇ *adj* **1.** [plus satisfaisant] better ■ **on ne se voit plus, c'est ~ ainsi** we don't see each other any more, it's better that way ■ **c'est ~ que rien** it's better than nothing **2.** [du point de vue de la santé, du bien-être] better ■ **on sent qu'il est ~ dans sa peau** you can feel he's more at ease with himself ■ **on est ~ dans ce fauteuil** this armchair is more comfortable **3.** [plus beau] better ■ **elle est ~ avec les cheveux courts** she looks better with short hair ■ **elle est ~ que sa sœur** she's better-looking than her sister.

◇ *nm* **1.** [amélioration] improvement ■ **il y a du ~** things have got better, there's some improvement **2.** [ce qui est préférable] : **le ~ est de ne pas y aller** it's best not to go ▶ **faire de son ~** to do one's (level) best ■ **le ~ est l'ennemi du bien** *prov* the best is the enemy of the good.

◆ **à qui mieux mieux** *loc adv* : **les enfants répondaient à qui ~~** the children were trying to outdo each other in answering.

◆ **au mieux** *loc adv* : **faire au ~** to do whatever's best, to act for the best ■ **ils sont au ~ (l'un avec l'autre)** they're on very good terms ■ **vous l'aurez lundi, en mettant les choses au ~** you'll get it on Monday at the very best ■ **au ~ de sa forme** on top form, in prime condition ■ **j'ai agi au ~ de vos intérêts** I acted in your best interest.

◆ **de mieux** *loc adj* **1.** [de plus satisfaisant] : **c'est ce que nous avons de ~** it's the best we have ■ **si tu n'as rien de ~ à faire, viens avec moi** if you've got nothing better to do, come with me **2.** [de plus] : **j'ai mis 300 euros de ~** I added an extra 300 euros.

◆ **de mieux en mieux** *loc adv* better and better ■ **et maintenant, de ~ en ~, j'ai perdu mes clefs!** *iron* and now, to cap it all, I've lost my keys!

◆ **des mieux** *loc adv* : **j'ai un ami qui est des ~ placé** *ou* **placés au ministère** I have a friend who's high up in the Ministry.

◆ **on ne peut mieux** *loc adv sout* extremely well ■ **le stage va on ne peut ~** the course couldn't be going better.

◆ **pour le mieux** *loc adv* for the best ■ **tout va pour le ~** everything is for the best.

◆ **qui mieux est** *loc adv* even better, better still.

mieux-disant [mjødizɑ̃] *nm inv* (bidder offering the) best value.

mieux-être [mjøzɛtr] *nm inv* better quality of life.

mièvre [mjɛvr] *adj péj* **1.** [fade] insipid, vapid, bland ■ [sentimental] mawkish, syrupy ■ **un roman ~** a mushy novel **2.** [maniéré] mawkish, precious **3.** [joli sans vrai talent - dessin] pretty-pretty, flowery.

mièvrerie [mjɛvrəri] *nf péj* **1.** [fadeur] insipidity, vapidity, blandness ■ [sentimentalité] mawkishness ■ [caractère maniéré] sickly affectation ■ [joliesse] floweriness, insipid prettiness **2.** [acte] mawkish behaviour *(U)* ■ [propos] mawkish *ou* twee UK remark.

mignard, e [miɲar, ard] *adj litt* [manières, geste] dainty, affected ■ [sourire] simpering, insincere ■ [style, décoration] over-pretty, overnice.

mignardise [miɲardiz] *nf* [manières] daintiness, affectation ■ [joliesse] preciousness, floweriness.

mignon, onne [miɲɔ̃, ɔn] ◇ *adj* **1.** [joli] sweet, pretty, cute ■ **c'est ~ tout plein à cet âge-là** *fam* children are so sweet at that age ■ **il est ~, ton appartement** you've got a lovely little flat **2.** *fam* [gentil] sweet, nice, lovely ■ **il m'a apporté des fleurs, c'était ~ comme tout** he brought me flowers, it was so sweet of him ■ **allez, sois ~ne, va te coucher** come on, be a darling *ou* sweetie *ou* dear and go to bed.

◇ *nm, f fam* [terme d'affection] darling, cutie, sweetie ■ **ma ~ne** darling, sweetheart.

◆ **mignon** *nm* HIST minion, favourite.

mignonnet, ette [miɲɔnɛ, ɛt] *adj* pretty-pretty.

◆ **mignonnette** *nf* **1.** BOT [réséda] mignonnette ■ [saxifrage] London pride ■ [œillet mignardise] (wild) pink **2.** [bouteille miniature] miniature (bottle).

migraine [migrɛn] *nf* MÉD migraine ■ [mal de tête] (bad) headache ■ **ces formulaires à remplir, c'est à vous donner la ~** filling in these forms is a real headache.

migraineux, euse [migrɛnø, øz] ◇ *adj* migrainous.

◇ *nm, f* migraine sufferer.

migrant, e [migrɑ̃, ɑ̃t] *adj* & *nm, f* migrant.

migrateur, trice [migratœr, tris] *adj* BIOL & ORNITH migratory.

◆ **migrateur** *nm* [oiseau] migrator, migrant.

migration [migrasjɔ̃] *nf* **1.** [des oiseaux, des travailleurs] migration ■ **les grandes ~s estivales vont commencer** *fig* the mass summer migrations are about to begin **2.** CHIM & GÉOL migration.

migratoire [migratwar] *adj* migratory.

migrer [3] [migre] *vi* to migrate.

mi-jambe [miʒɑ̃b] ◆ **à mi-jambe** *loc adv* [à partir - du bas] up to the knees ; [- du haut] down to the knees ■ **on était dans la neige à ~** we were knee-deep in snow.

mijaurée [miʒɔre] *nf* [pimbêche] (stuck-up) little madam ■ **faire la ~** to put on airs.

mijoter [3] [miʒɔte] <> *vt* **1.** CULIN to simmer, to slow-cook ▪ **~ des petits plats** to spend a lot of time cooking delicious meals **2.** *fam* [coup, plan] to plot, to cook up *(sép)* ▪ **qu'est-ce que tu mijotes?** what are you up to?
<> *vi* **1.** CULIN to simmer, to stew gently **2.** *fam fig* **laisse-la ~ dans son coin** leave her awhile to mull it over.
◆ **se mijoter** *vp (emploi passif) fam* [coup, plan] to be cooking *ou* brewing, to be afoot.

mi-journée [miʒurne] *nf* : **les informations de la ~** the lunchtime news.

mikado [mikado] *nm* **1.** [titre] mikado **2.** [jeu] mikado, spillikins *(sing)*.

mil[1] [mil] = **mille**.

mil[2] [mil] *nm* millet.

milan [milɑ̃] *nm* kite.

Milan [milɑ̃] *npr* Milan.

milanais, e [milanɛ, ɛz] *adj* Milanese.

mildiou [mildju] *nm* [gén] mildew.

mile [majl] *nm* (statute) mile.

milice [milis] *nf* **1.** HIST militia **2.** [organisation paramilitaire] militia ▪ **~ privée** private militia **3.** *Belgique* [service militaire] military service ▪ [armée] : **la ~** the army.

milicien, enne [milisjɛ̃, ɛn] *nm, f* militiaman (*f* militia woman).
◆ **milicien** *nm Belgique* conscript *UK*, draftee *US*.

milieu, x [miljø] *nm* **1.** [dans l'espace] middle, centre ▪ **sciez-la par le** *ou* **en son ~** saw it through *ou* down the middle ▪ **celui du ~** the one in the middle, the middle one **2.** [dans le temps] middle ▪ **l'incendie s'est déclaré vers le ~ de la nuit** the fire broke out in the middle of the night ▪ **en ~ de trimestre** in mid-term **3.** [moyen terme] middle way *ou* course ▶ **le juste ~** the happy medium ▪ **il faut trouver un juste ~** we have to find a happy medium **4.** [entourage] environment, milieu ▪ **~ socioculturel** (social) background ▪ **des gens de tous les ~x** people from all walks of life *ou* backgrounds ▪ **les ~x scientifiques** scientific circles ▪ **ne pas se sentir/se sentir dans son ~** to feel out of place/at home **5.** BIOL [environnement] environment, habitat ▶ **dans un ~ acide** in an acid medium ▪ **~ de culture** culture medium ▪ **~ naturel** natural habitat ▪ **en ~ stérile** in a sterile environment **6.** INDUST & SC : **en ~ réel** in the field **7.** [pègre] : **le ~** the underworld **8.** MATH midpoint, midrange.
◆ **au beau milieu de** *loc prép* right in the middle of.
◆ **au (beau) milieu** *loc adv* (right) in the middle, (right) in the centre.
◆ **au milieu de** *loc prép* **1.** [dans l'espace] in the middle of, in the centre of **2.** [dans le temps] in the middle of ▪ **elle est partie au ~ de mon cours** she left in the middle of *ou* halfway through my lesson ▪ **au ~ de l'hiver/l'été** in midwinter/midsummer ▪ **au ~ du mois de mars** in mid-March **3.** [parmi] amongst, in the midst of, surrounded by.
◆ **milieu de terrain** *nm* [zone] midfield (area) ▪ [joueur] midfield player.

militaire [militɛr] <> *adj* [gén] military ▪ [de l'armée de terre] army *(modif)*, service *(modif)* ▪ [de l'armée de l'air, de la marine] service *(modif)*.
<> *nm* [soldat - gén] soldier ; [- de l'armée de terre] soldier, serviceman ; [- de l'armée de l'air, de la marine] serviceman ▪ **c'est un ancien ~** he's an ex-serviceman ▶ **~ de carrière** professional soldier.

militairement [militɛrmɑ̃] *adv* : **il nous faut intervenir ~** we have to resort to military intervention.

militant, e [militɑ̃, ɑ̃t] <> *adj* militant.
<> *nm, f* militant ▪ **les ~s de base sont d'accord** the grassroots militants agree ▶ **~ syndical** trade union militant *ou* activist.

militantisme [militɑ̃tism] *nm* militancy, militantism.

militarisation [militarizasjɔ̃] *nf* militarization.

militariser [3] [militarize] *vt* to militarize.

militarisme [militarism] *nm* militarism.

militariste [militarist] <> *adj* militaristic.
<> *nmf* militarist.

militer [3] [milite] *vi* **1.** [agir en militant] to be a militant *ou* an activist ▪ **~ au** *ou* **dans le parti socialiste** to be a socialist party activist ▪ **~ pour/contre qqch** to fight for/against sthg **2.** [plaider] to militate ▪ **ces témoignages ne militent pas en votre faveur** this evidence goes *ou* militates against you.

milk-shake [milkʃɛk] (*pl* **milk-shakes**) *nm* milkshake.

millage [milaʒ] *nm Québec* mileage.

mille [mil] <> *dét* **1.** [dix fois cent] a *ou* one thousand ▪ **dix/cent ~** ten/a hundred thousand ▪ **en l'an ~ cinquante** *ou* **mil cinquante** in the year one thousand and fifty ▶ **'les Mille et Une Nuits'** 'The Arabian Nights', 'The Thousand and One Nights' **2.** [beaucoup de] : **c'est ~ fois trop grand** it's miles too big ▪ **~ baisers** lots *ou* tons of kisses ▪ **~ mercis, merci ~ fois** many thanks ▪ **~ excuses** *ou* **pardons si je t'ai blessé** I'm dreadfully sorry if I've hurt you ▪ **voilà un exemple entre ~** here's just one of the countless examples I could choose ▪ **en ~ morceaux** in pieces ▪ **il y a ~ et une manières de réussir sa vie** there are thousands of ways *ou* a thousand and one ways of being successful in life.
<> *nm inv* **1.** [nombre] a *ou* one thousand ▪ **vingt pour ~ des femmes** twenty women out of *ou* in every thousand ▪ **il y a une chance sur ~ que ça marche** there's a one-in-a-thousand chance that it'll work ▪ **acheter/vendre au ~** COMM to buy/to sell by the thousand ▶ **je te le donne en ~!** *fam* I bet you'll never guess! ▪ **des ~ et des cents** *fam* loads of money
2. [centre d'une cible] bull's eye ▪ **mettre** *ou* **taper (en plein) dans le ~** *fam pr* to hit the bull's-eye ; *fam fig* to score a bull's-eye, to be bang on target.
<> *nm* **1.** NAUT : **~ (marin)** nautical mile
2. *Québec* (statute) mile
3. HIST : **le ~ romain** the Roman mile.

mille-feuille [milfœj] (*pl* **mille-feuilles**) <> *nf* BOT milfoil, yarrow.
<> *nm* CULIN mille feuilles, napoleon *US*.

millénaire [milenɛr] <> *adj* thousand-year-old ▪ **un arbre ~** a thousand-year-old tree ▪ **des traditions (plusieurs fois) ~s** age-old *ou* time-honoured traditions.
<> *nm* **1.** [période] millennium **2.** [anniversaire] millennium, thousandth anniversary.

millénarisme [milenarism] *nm* millenarianism.

millénariste [milenarist] *adj* & *nmf* millenarian.

millenium [milenjɔm] *nm* RELIG millennium.

mille-pattes [milpat] *nm inv* millipede.

millésime [milezim] *nm* **1.** [date] date, year ▪ **une pièce au ~ de 1962** a coin dated 1962 **2.** ŒNOL [date de récolte] year, vintage ▪ **le ~ 1976 est l'un des meilleurs** the 1976 vintage is among the best.

millésimé, e [milezime] *adj* vintage *(modif)* ▪ **un bourgogne ~ 1970** a 1970 (vintage) Burgundy ▪ **une bouteille ~e 1880** a bottle dated 1880.

millésimer [3] [milezime] *vt* to date, to put a date on.

millet [mijɛ] *nm* millet.

milliampère [miliɑ̃pɛr] *nm* milliamp, milliampere.

milliard [miljar] *nm* thousand million *UK*, billion *US* ▪ **cela a coûté deux ~s (d'euros)** it cost two thousand million *ou* two billion (euros) ▪ **des ~s de globules rouges** billions of red corpuscles.

milliardaire [miljardɛr] <> *adj* : **sa famille est plusieurs fois ~** his family is worth billions.
<> *nmf* multimillionaire, billionaire *US*.

milliardième [miljardjɛm] *adj num, nmf* & *nm* thousand millionth, billionth.

millibar [milibar] *nm* millibar.

millième [miljɛm] <> *adj num* thousandth.
<> *nmf* thousandth.

<> *nm* thousandth ▪ **il ne fournit pas le ~ du travail nécessaire** he isn't doing a fraction of the work that has to be done.
<> *nf* THÉÂTRE thousandth performance.

millier [milje] *nm* thousand ▪ **un ~ de badges/livres ont été vendus** a thousand badges/books have been sold ▪ **des ~s de** thousands of.
◆ **par milliers** *loc adv* [arriver] in their thousands ▪ [envoyer, commander] by the thousand ▪ **des ballons ont été lâchés par ~s** thousands (upon thousands) of balloons have been released.

milligramme [miligram] *nm* milligram, milligramme.

millilitre [mililitr] *nm* millilitre.

millimètre [milimɛtr] *nm* millimetre.

millimétré, e [milimetre], **millimétrique** [milimetrik] *adj* millimetric ▪ **échelle ~e** millimetre scale.

million [miljɔ̃] *nm* **1.** [quantité] million ▪ **un ~ de personnes** a *ou* one million people ▪ **des ~s de** millions of **2.** [somme] : **il a joué et perdu dix ~s d'euros** he gambled away ten million euros ▪ **un ~ cinq** *fam* [de centimes] 15 000 de francs ▌[de francs français] 1.5 million francs.

millionième [miljɔnjɛm] *adj num, nmf* & *nm* millionth.

millionnaire [miljɔnɛr] <> *adj* millionaire, millionnaire ▪ **être/devenir ~** to be/to become a millionaire ▪ **elle est plusieurs fois ~ (en dollars)** she's a (dollar) millionaire *ou* millionairess several times over.
<> *nmf* millionaire (*f* millionairess).

millivolt [milivɔlt] *nm* millivolt.

mi-long, mi-longue [milɔ̃, milɔ̃g] (*mpl* **mi-longs**, *fpl* **mi-longues**) *adj* [jupe] half-length ▪ [cheveux] shoulder-length.

milord [milɔr] *nm* **1.** [en appellation] lord ▪ **après vous, ~** after you, my lord **2.** [véhicule] victoria.

mi-lourd [milur] (*pl* **mi-lourds**) *adj m* & *nm* light heavyweight.

mime [mim] <> *nmf* **1.** [artiste] mime (artist) **2.** [imitateur] mimic.
<> *nm* **1.** [art] mime ▪ **faire du ~** to be a mime (artist) ▪ **un spectacle de ~** a mime show **2.** [action de mimer] miming *(U)*.

mimer [3] [mime] *vt* **1.** THÉÂTRE to mime ▪ **le jeu consiste à ~ des titres de films** the idea of the game is to mime film titles **2.** [imiter] to mimic.

mimétique [mimetik] *adj* BIOL & THÉÂTRE mimetic.

mimétisme [mimetism] *nm* **1.** BIOL mimicry, mimesis **2.** [imitation] mimicry, mimicking ▪ **le nouveau-né sourit à sa mère par ~** a new-born baby mimics its mother's smile.

mimi [mimi] <> *adj inv fam* [mignon] lovely, sweet, cute.
<> *nm* **1.** *langage enfantin* [chat] pussy, pussycat **2.** *fam* [bisou] kiss ▪ [caresse] cuddle, hug **3.** *fam* [terme d'affection] (little) darling *ou* sweetie *ou* honey.

mimique [mimik] *nf* **1.** [gestuelle] gesture **2.** [grimace] facial expression.

mimolette [mimɔlɛt] *nf* Mimolette (cheese).

mi-mollet [mimɔlɛ] ◆ **à mi-mollet** *loc adv* [à partir - du bas] up to the calf ; [- du haut] down to the calf ▪ **robe à ~** midi dress.

mimosa [mimɔza] *nm* **1.** BOT mimosa **2.** CULIN : **œuf ~** egg mayonnaise *(topped with crumbled yolk)*.

mi-moyen [mimwajɛ̃] (*pl* **mi-moyens**) *adj m* & *nm* welterweight.

min (*abr écrite de* **minute**) min.

min. (*abr écrite de* **minimum**) min.

minable [minabl] *fam* <> *adj* **1.** [médiocre, laid - costume] shabby, tatty UK, tacky US ; [- chambre] dingy, shabby ; [- film] third-rate, rotten, lousy ; [- situation, salaire] pathetic **2.** [mesquin] petty, mean **3.** [sans envergure] small-time, third-rate ▪ **un escroc ~** a small-time crook.
<> *nmf fam* nonentity, no-hoper, loser ▪ **pauvre ~, va!** you pathetic little nobody!

minablement [minabləmɑ̃] *adv* **1.** [pauvrement] shabbily **2.** [lamentablement] pathetically, hopelessly ▪ **ils ont échoué ~** they failed miserably.

minage [minaʒ] *nm* MIN & TRAV PUB mining.

minaret [minarɛ] *nm* minaret.

minauder [3] [minode] *vi* to mince, to simper ▪ **elle répondait aux questions en minaudant** she answered the questions with a simper ▪ **arrête de ~!** don't be such a poser!

minauderie [minodri] *nf* **1.** [préciosité] (show of) affectation **2.** [acte, propos] affectation ▪ **~s** simpering.

minaudier, ère [minodje, ɛr] *adj* affected, simpering, mincing.

mince [mɛ̃s] <> *adj* **1.** [sans épaisseur] thin ▪ **un ~ filet d'eau** a tiny trickle of water ❶ **~ comme une feuille de papier à cigarette** paper-thin, wafer-thin **2.** [personne - svelte] slim, slender ❶ **~ comme un fil** as thin as a rake **3.** [négligeable] slim, slender ▪ **de ~s bénéfices** slender profits ▪ **les preuves sont bien ~s** the evidence is rather slim ▪ **ce n'est pas une ~ affaire** this is no trifling matter ▪ **ce n'est pas une ~ responsabilité** it's no small responsibility ▪ **un demi-chapitre sur la Révolution, c'est un peu ~** half a chapter on the French Revolution is a bit feeble ▪ **une livre de viande pour quatre, c'est un peu ~** a pound of meat for four, that's cutting it a bit fine.
<> *interj fam* damn.

minceur [mɛ̃sœr] *nf* **1.** [sveltesse] slimness, slenderness ▪ [finesse] slimness, thinness **2.** [insuffisance] weakness, feebleness ▪ **la ~ d'un argument** the weakness *ou* flimsiness of an argument.

mincir [32] [mɛ̃sir] <> *vi* [personne] to get slimmer *ou* thinner ▪ **elle essaie de ~** she's trying to lose weight.
<> *vt* [suj: vêtement, couleur] : **cette robe te mincit** that dress makes you look slimmer.

mine [min] *nf* **1.** [apparence] appearance, exterior ❶ **faire ~ de : elle fit ~ de raccrocher, puis se ravisa** she made as if to hang up, then changed her mind ▪ **ne fais pas ~ de ne pas comprendre** don't act as if *ou* pretend you don't understand ▪ **~ de rien** *fam* : **~ de rien, ça finit par coûter cher** it may not seem much but when you add it all up, it's expensive ▪ **~ de rien, elle était furieuse** although *ou* though she didn't show it, she was furious
2. [teint] : **avoir bonne ~** to look well ▪ **avoir mauvaise ~ : il a mauvaise ~** he doesn't look very well ▪ **tu as bonne ~, avec ta veste à l'envers!** *fig & iron* you look great with your jacket on inside out! ▪ **avoir une ~ superbe** to be the (very) picture of health ▪ **avoir une sale ~** *fam* to look dreadful *ou* awful ▪ **avoir une petite ~** *fam* to look peaky ▪ **avoir une ~ de papier mâché** *fam* to look like death warmed up ▪ **je lui trouve meilleure ~** I think she looks better *ou* in better health ▌[visage, contenance] look, countenance *litt* ▪ **avoir une ~ réjouie** to beam, to be beaming ▪ **faire grise** *ou* **triste** *ou* **piètre ~** to pull UK *ou* to make a long face ▪ **ne fais pas cette ~!** don't look so downhearted!
3. GÉOL deposit ▪ [installations - de surface] pithead ; [- en sous-sol] pit ▪ **mon fils n'ira pas à la ~** my son isn't going down the mine *ou* pit ❶ **~ de charbon** *ou* **de houille** coal mine ▪ **~ à ciel ouvert** opencast mine ▪ **une ~ d'or** *pr & fig* a gold mine
4. [source importante] : **une ~ de** a mine *ou* source of ▪ **une ~ d'informations** a mine of information
5. [d'un crayon] lead ▪ **crayon à ~ grasse/dure** soft/hard pencil ▪ **~ de plomb** graphite *ou* black lead
6. MIL [galerie] mine, gallery, sap ▪ [explosif] mine ▪ **~ aérienne/sous-marine/terrestre** aerial/submarine/land mine
7. [explosif] : **coup de ~** blast ▪ **ouvrir une roche à coups de ~** to blast a rock.
◆ **mines** *nfpl* **1.** [manières] : **il m'énerve à toujours faire des ~s** he irritates me, always simpering around
2. GÉOGR mining area, mines ▪ ÉCON mining industry ▪ **les Mines** ADMIN ≃ the Department of Transport UK ▪ ≃ the Department of the Interior US ; ÉDUC the (French) School of Mining Engineers.

miner [3] [mine] *vt* **1.** [poser des mines] to mine ■ **'danger! zone minée'** 'beware of mines' **2.** [ronger] to undermine, to erode, to eat away (at) *ou* into **3.** [affaiblir] to undermine, to sap ■ **~ les forces/la santé de qqn** to sap sb's strength/health ■ **miné par le chagrin** consumed with *ou* worn down by grief.

minerai [minrɛ] *nm* ore ■ **~ de fer/d'uranium** iron/uranium ore ■ **~ riche/pauvre** high-grade/low-grade ore ■ **~ brut** crude ore ■ **~ métallique** metalliferous *ou* metal-bearing ore.

minéral, e, aux [mineral, o] *adj* mineral.
◆ **minéral, aux** *nm* mineral.

minéralier [mineralje] *nm* ore carrier.

minéralisation [mineralizasjɔ̃] *nf* mineralization.

minéralisé, e [mineralize] *adj* mineralized ■ **eau faiblement ~e** water with a low mineral content.

minéraliser [3] [mineralize] *vt* [métal, eau] to mineralize.

minéralogie [mineralɔʒi] *nf* mineralogy.

minéralogique [mineralɔʒik] *adj* **1.** GÉOL mineralogical **2.** AUTO : **numéro ~** registration *UK ou* license *US* number.

minéralogiste [mineralɔʒist] *nmf* mineralogist.

minéralurgie [mineralyrʒi] *nf* ore processing.

minerval, s [minɛrval] *nm* *Belgique* school tuition fees.

minerve [minɛrv] *nf* MÉD neck brace, (surgical) collar.

Minerve [minɛrv] *npr* Minerva.

minet, ette [minɛ, ɛt] *nm, f fam* **1.** [jeune personne superficielle] (young) trendy **2.** [chat] puss, pussy, pussycat **3.** [terme d'affection] sweetie, sweetie-pie, honey.
◆ **minette** *nf* **1.** MIN minette **2.** BOT (black) medic *ou* medick.

mineur, e [minœr] ◇ *adj* **1.** [insignifiant] minor ■ **d'un intérêt ~** of minor interest **2.** DR below the age of criminal responsibility ■ **enfants ~s** under age children, minors ■ **être ~** to be under age *ou* a minor **3.** MUS minor ■ **concerto en sol ~** concerto in G minor ▶ **accord parfait ~** minor chord **4.** LOGIQUE minor.
◇ *nm, f* DR minor ■ **'interdit aux ~s'** 'adults only' ■ **délinquant ~** juvenile offender ▶ **détournement** *ou* **enlèvement de ~** abduction.
◆ **mineur** *nm* **1.** [ouvrier] miner, mineworker ■ **famille de ~s** mining family ▶ **~ de fond** underground worker ■ **~ de houille** coalminer, collier *UK* **2.** MIL sapper, miner **3.** MUS : **en ~** in the minor mode *ou* key **4.** LOGIQUE minor term.
◆ **mineure** *nf* LOGIQUE minor premise.

mini [mini] ◇ *adj inv* [vêtement] : **la mode ~** the mini-length *ou* thigh-length fashion.
◇ *nm* **1.** [vêtement] mini ■ **le ~ est de retour** minis *ou* miniskirts are back **2.** *fam* INFORM mini, minicomputer.

mini- [mini] *préf* mini-, small ■ **~bar** mini-bar ■ **~sondage** snap poll.

miniature [minjatyr] ◇ *adj* miniature ■ **un train ~** a model *ou* miniature train.
◇ *nf* **1.** [modèle réduit] small-scale replica *ou* model **2.** ART miniature.
◆ **en miniature** *loc adj* miniature *(avant n)* ■ **c'est un jardin en ~** it's a model *ou* miniature garden.

miniaturisation [minjatyrizasjɔ̃] *nf* miniaturization.

miniaturiser [3] [minjatyrize] *vt* to miniaturize.

miniaturiste [minjatyrist] ◇ *adj* : **un peintre ~** a miniaturist.
◇ *nmf* miniaturist.

minibar [minibar] *nm* minibar.

minibus [minibys], **minicar** [minikar] *nm* minibus.

Minicassette® [minikasɛt] ◇ *nf* (small) cassette.
◇ *nm* (small) cassette recorder.

minichaîne [miniʃɛn] *nf* mini (stereo) system.

Minidisc® [1] [minidisk] *nm* MiniDisc®.

minidisque [2] [minidisk] *nm* MiniDisc®.

minier, ère [minje, ɛr] *adj* mining.

minigolf [minigɔlf] *nm* crazy golf.

minijupe [miniʒyp] *nf* miniskirt.

minima [minima] *pl* ▷ **minimum.**

minimal, e, aux [minimal, o] *adj* **1.** [seuil, peine] minimum *(avant n)* ■ **température ~e** minimal *ou* minimum temperature **2.** MATH minimal.

minimalisation [minimalizasjɔ̃] *nf* minimalization.

minimaliser [3] [minimalize] *vt* to minimize.

minimalisme [minimalism] *nm* minimalism.

minimaliste [minimalist] *adj & nm* minimalist.

minime [minim] ◇ *adj* [faible] minimal, minor ■ **l'intrigue n'a qu'une importance ~** the plot is of only minor importance ■ **la différence est ~** the difference is negligible.
◇ *nmf* SPORT (school) Junior.
◇ *nm* RELIG Minim.

minimisation [minimizasjɔ̃] *nf* minimization, minimizing.

minimiser [3] [minimize] *vt* **1.** [rôle] to minimize, to play down *(sép)* ■ [risque] to minimize, to cut down *(sép)* ■ **sans vouloir ~ sa contribution** without wishing to minimize *ou* underrate her contribution **2.** MATH to minimize.

minimum [minimɔm] (*pl* **minimums** *ou pl* **minima** [minima])
◇ *adj* minimum ■ **poids/service ~** minimum weight/service ■ **charge ~** ÉLECTR base *ou* minimum load ■ **prix ~** minimum *ou* bottom price ; [aux enchères] reserve price.
◇ *nm* **1.** [le plus bas degré] minimum ■ **températures proches du ~ saisonnier** temperatures approaching the minimum *ou* the lowest recorded for the season ■ **mets le chauffage au ~** turn the heating down as low as it'll go ■ **j'ai réduit les matières grasses au ~** I've cut down on fat as much as possible, I've cut fat down to a minimum ▶ **avoir le ~ vital** [financier] to be on subsistence level, to earn the minimum living wage ■ **ils n'ont même pas le ~ vital** they don't even have the bare minimum **2.** DR [peine la plus faible] : **le ~** the minimum sentence **3.** [une petite quantité] : **un ~ (de)** a minimum (of) ■ **tu en as vraiment fait un ~!** you really have done just the bare minimum! ■ **s'il avait un ~ de bon sens/d'honnêteté** if he had a minimum of common sense/of decency **4.** ADMIN : **~ vieillesse** basic state pension.
◇ *adv* minimum ■ **il fait 3°C ~** the temperature is 3°C minimum.
◆ **au minimum** *loc adv* [au moins] at the least ■ **deux jours au ~** at least two days, a minimum of two days.

mini-ordinateur [miniɔrdinatœr] (*pl* **mini-ordinateurs**) *nm* minicomputer.

minipilule [minipilyl] *nf* low dose (contraceptive) pill, minipill.

mini-slip [minislip] (*pl* **mini-slips**) *nm* tanga.

ministère [ministɛr] *nm* **1.** POLIT [charge] ministry *UK*, administration *US* ■ **elle a refusé le ~ qu'on lui proposait** she turned down the government position she was offered ■ **sous le ~ de M. Thiers** under M. Thiers' ministry *UK ou* secretaryship *US*, when M. Thiers was (the) minister **2.** [cabinet] government, ministry **3.** [bâtiment] ministry *UK*, department (offices) *US* ■ [département] ministry *UK*, department *US* ■ **~ des Affaires étrangères** *ou* **des Relations extérieures** ≃ Ministry of Foreign Affairs, ≃ Foreign Office *UK*, ≃ State Department *US* ■ **~ de la Défense** ≃ Ministry of Defence *UK*, ≃ Department of Defense *US* ■ **~ de l'Économie et des Finances** ≃ Ministry of Finance, ≃ Treasury *UK*, ≃ Treasury Department *US* ■ **~ de l'Environnement** *ministry responsible for legislation relating to environmental issues* ■ **~ de l'Intérieur** ≃ Ministry of the Interior, ≃ Home Office *UK*, ≃ Department of the Interior *US* **4.** DR : **par ~ d'huissier** served by a bailiff ▶ **~ public** ≃ (office of the) Director of Public Prosecutions *UK* **5.** RELIG ministry ■ **exercer un ~** to serve as minister, to perform one's ministry.

ministériel, elle [ministerjɛl] *adj* **1.** [émanant d'un ministre] ministerial *UK*, departmental *US* **2.** [concernant le gouvernement] ministerial *UK*, cabinet *(modif)*.

ministrable [ministrabl] ◇ *adj* in line for a ministerial *UK* *OU* government position ■ **elle est ~** she's a likely candidate for a ministerial post *UK* *OU* a post in the administration *US*.
◇ *nmf* potential minister *UK*, potential secretary of state.

ministre [ministr] *nmf* **1.** POLIT minister *UK*, secretary *US* ■ **~ des Affaires étrangères** *OU* **des Relations extérieures** ≃ Minister of Foreign Affairs, ≃ Foreign Secretary *UK*, ≃ Secretary of State *US* ■ **~ de la Culture** ≃ Minister for the Arts *UK* ■ **~ de l'Économie et des Finances** ≃ Finance Minister, ≃ Chancellor of the Exchequer *UK*, ≃ Secretary of the Treasury *US* ■ **~ d'État** minister *UK*, Secretary of State ■ **~ de l'Intérieur** ≃ Minister of the Interior, ≃ Home Secretary *UK*, ≃ Secretary of the Interior *US* ■ **~ de la Justice** ≃ Minister of Justice, ≃ Lord (High) Chancellor *UK*, ≃ Attorney General *US* ■ **Premier ~** Prime Minister ‖ [ambassadeur] : **~ plénipotentiaire(auprès de)** minister plenipotentiary (to) **2.** RELIG [pasteur] : **~ du culte** minister.

Minitel® [minitɛl] *nm* viewdata service, ≃ Prestel® *UK*, ≃ Minitel® *US* ■ **sur ~** on viewdata, on Prestel® *UK*, on Minitel® *US* ▶ **~ rose** erotic viewdata service.

MINITEL

Before Internet, the domestic viewdata service run by *France Telecom* had become a familiar part of French life. The basic monitor and keyboard were given free of charge, and the subscriber was charged for the services used on his or her ordinary telephone bill. Some *Minitel* services were purely informative (the weather, road conditions, news etc); others were interactive (enabling users to carry out bank transactions, book tickets for travel or, on the *Minitel rose*, to look for companionship, for example). The *Minitel* also served as an electronic telephone directory.

minitéliste [minitelist] *nmf* Minitel® user.

minium [minjɔm] *nm* **1.** CHIM red lead, minium **2.** [peinture] red lead paint.

Minnesota [minezɔta] *npr m* : **le ~** Minnesota.

Minnie [mini] *npr* Minnie Mouse.

minois [minwa] *nm* (sweet little) face.

minoration [minɔrasjɔ̃] *nf* **1.** [baisse] reduction, cut ■ **une ~ de 5 % du tarif de base** a 5% cut in the basic rate ■ **procéder à une ~ des loyers** to reduce *OU* to lower rents **2.** [minimisation] minimizing.

minorer [3] [minɔre] *vt* **1.** [baisser] to reduce, to cut, to mark down ■ **~ les prix de 2 %** to cut prices by 2% **2.** [minimiser] to understate the importance of.

minoritaire [minɔritɛr] ◇ *adj* **1.** [moins nombreux] minority *(modif)* ■ **parti ~** minority party ■ **les femmes sont ~s dans cette profession** women are a minority in this profession **2.** [non reconnu] minority *(modif)*.
◇ *nmf* member of a minority (group) ■ **les ~s** the minority.

minorité [minɔrite] *nf* **1.** [le plus petit nombre] minority ■ **une ~ de** a minority of **2.** [groupe] minority (group) ■ **~ nationale** national minority **3.** [âge légal] minority ■ DR nonage **4.** ÉCON : **~ de blocage** blocking minority.
◆ **en minorité** ◇ *loc adj* in a *OU* the minority ■ **nous sommes en ~** we're in a minority.
◇ *loc adv* : **mettre le gouvernement en ~** to force the government into a minority.

Minorque [minɔrk] *npr* Minorca ■ **à ~** in Minorca.

Minotaure [minɔtɔr] *npr m* : **le ~** the Minotaur.

minoterie [minɔtri] *nf* **1.** [lieu] flourmill **2.** [activité] flour-milling.

minotier [minɔtje] *nm* miller, (flour) millowner.

minou [minu] *nm fam* **1.** [chat] pussy, pussycat ■ **~! ~! ~** puss! puss!, kitty! kitty! **2.** [chéri] (little) darling *OU* sweetie *OU* honey.

minuit [minɥi] *nm* **1.** [milieu de la nuit] midnight **2.** [heure] midnight, twelve midnight, twelve o'clock (at night) ■ **il est ~ passé** it's after *OU* past midnight ■ **~ et quart** a quarter past twelve *OU* past midnight ■ **à ~** at midnight, at twelve o'clock (at night) ■ **~, l'heure du crime!** midnight, the witching hour!
◆ **de minuit** *loc adj* midnight *(modif)*.

minus [minys] *nm fam* **1.** [nabot] midget, shortie, runt **2.** [incapable] no-hoper *esp UK*, nobody ■ **c'est un ~** he's a (born) loser.

minuscule [minyskyl] ◇ *adj* **1.** [très petit] minute, minuscule, tiny ■ **elle est ~ à côté de lui** she's minute *OU* tiny compared with him **2.** IMPR : **un b ~** a small b ▶ **lettre** *OU* **caractère ~** small *OU* lower-case letter.
◇ *nf* small letter ■ IMPR lower-case letter ■ **écrire en ~s** to write in small letters.

minus habens [minysabɛ̃s] *nmf sout* & *péj* halfwit.

minutage [minytaʒ] *nm* timing.

minute [minyt] ◇ *nf* **1.** [mesure - du temps] minute ■ **les ~s sont longues** time drags by ■ **une ~ de silence** a minute's silence, a minute of silence ■ **il n'y a pas une ~ à perdre** there's not a minute to lose ■ **à la ~ près** on the dot, right on time ■ **on n'est pas à la ~ près** *OU* **à la ~!** *fam* there's no hurry! ■ **à deux ~s (de voiture)/de marche de chez moi** two minutes' (drive)/walk away from my house **2.** [moment] minute, moment ■ **revenez dans une petite ~** come back in a minute *OU* moment (or two) ■ **il y a une ~** *OU* **il n'y a pas même une ~, tu disais tout le contraire** just a minute *OU* moment ago, you were saying the very opposite ■ **de ~ en ~** by the minute ■ **je n'ai pas une ~ à moi** I haven't got a minute *OU* moment to myself ■ **as-tu une ~? j'ai à te parler** do you have a minute? I have to talk to you ▶ **la ~ de vérité** the moment of truth **3.** *(comme adj inv)* [instantané] : **nettoyage ~** same-day cleaning ■ **talon ~** heel bar *UK*, on-the-spot shoe repair **4.** GÉOM minute **5.** DR original *(of a deed)* **6.** PRESSE : **Minute** *satirical weekly magazine of the Front national.*
◇ *interj fam* wait a minute *OU* moment ■ **~, je n'ai pas dit ça!** hang on *OU* wait a minute, I never said that! ▶ **~, papillon!** hold your horses!, not so fast!
◆ **à la minute** *loc adv* **1.** [il y a un instant] a moment ago ■ **elle est sortie à la ~** she's just this minute gone out **2.** [sans attendre] this minute *OU* instant ■ **je veux que ce soit fait à la ~** I want it done this instant **3.** [toutes les 60 secondes] per minute.
◆ **d'une minute à l'autre** *loc adv* any time ■ **il sera là d'une ~ à l'autre** he'll be arriving any minute, he won't be a minute.

minuter [3] [minyte] *vt* [spectacle, cuisson] to time ■ **sa journée de travail est soigneusement minutée** she works to a very tight *OU* strict schedule.

minuterie [minytri] *nf* **1.** ÉLECTR time switch ■ **il y a une ~ dans l'escalier** the stair light is on a time switch **2.** [d'une horloge] motion work ■ [d'un compteur] counter mechanism **3.** [minuteur] timer.

minuteur [minytœr] *nm* AUDIO & ÉLECTR timer.

minutie [minysi] *nf* meticulousness, thoroughness ■ **remarquez la ~ des broderies sur ce tissu** notice the intricacy of the embroidery on this material ■ **avec ~** [travailler] meticulously, carefully ; [examiner] in minute detail, thoroughly.

minutier [minytje] *nm* DR (lawyer's) minute book ■ **~ central** *archives for ancient records* ■ ≃ Public Records Office *UK*.

minutieusement [minysjøzmɑ̃] *adv* **1.** [avec précision] meticulously, carefully **2.** [en détail] in minute detail.

minutieux, euse [minysjø, øz] *adj* **1.** [personne] meticulous, thorough ■ **déjà enfant, il était très ~** even as a child, he used to do everything with great thoroughness **2.** [travail] meticulous, detailed, thorough ■ **enquête/recherche minutieuse** thorough investigation/research.

mioche [mjɔʃ] *nmf fam* kid, nipper *UK*.

mirabelle [mirabɛl] *nf* [fruit] mirabelle (plum) ■ [liqueur] mirabelle *(plum brandy)*.

miracle [mirakl] *nm* **1.** [intervention divine] miracle ■ **sa guérison tient du ~** his recovery is (nothing short of) a miracle **2.** [surprise] miracle, marvel ■ **le ~ de l'amour** the miracle *ou* wonder of love ■ **~ économique** economic miracle ■ **le deuxième mouvement est un ~ de délicatesse** the second movement is wonderfully delicate **3.** THÉÂTRE miracle play **4.** *(comme adj; avec ou sans trait d'union)* miracle *(modif)*, wonder *(modif)* ■ **médicament ~** miracle *ou* wonder drug ■ **la solution-~ à vos problèmes de rangement** the miracle solution to your storage problems.
◆ **par miracle** *loc adv* by a *ou* some miracle, miraculously ■ **comme par ~** as if by miracle.

miraculé, e [mirakyle] ◇ *adj* [d'une maladie] miraculously cured ■ [d'un accident] miraculously saved.
◇ *nm, f* **1.** RELIG : **c'est un ~ de Lourdes** he was miraculously cured at Lourdes **2.** [survivant] miraculous survivor ■ **une des rares ~es du tremblement de terre** one of the few (people) who miraculously survived the earthquake.

miraculeusement [mirakyløzmɑ̃] *adv* miraculously, (as if) by a *ou* some miracle.

miraculeux, euse [mirakylø, øz] *adj* **1.** [qui tient du miracle] miraculous, miracle *(modif)* ■ **cela n'a rien de ~!** there's nothing miraculous *ou* special about it! **2.** [très opportun] miraculous, wonderful **3.** [prodigieux] miraculous, miracle *(modif)* ■ **produit/sauvetage ~** miracle product/rescue.

mirador [miradɔr] *nm* **1.** ARCHIT mirador **2.** MIL watchtower, mirador.

mirage [miraʒ] *nm* **1.** [illusion optique] mirage **2.** *sout* [chimère] mirage, delusion ■ **je m'étais laissé prendre au ~ de l'amour** I had fallen for the illusion of perfect love.

mire [mir] *nf* **1.** ARM : **point de ~** *pr* aim, target ■ **pendant les Jeux, la ville sera le point de ~ du monde entier** *fig* the eyes of the world will be on the city during the Games **2.** [d'un téléviseur] TV test card, test pattern *spéc* **3.** TECHNOL [pour niveler] levelling rod *ou* staff.

mirer [3] [mire] *vt* [œuf] to candle.
◆ **se mirer** ◇ *vp (emploi réfléchi)* *litt* [se regarder] to gaze at o.s.
◇ *vpi* *litt* [se refléter] to be mirrored *ou* reflected ■ **les saules se miraient dans le lac** the willows were mirrored in the lake.

mirettes△ [mirɛt] *nfpl* eyes.

mirifique [mirifik] *adj* *hum* fabulous, amazing, staggering.

mirliton [mirlitɔ̃] *nm* **1.** MUS kazoo, mirliton ■ **une musique de ~** second-rate music **2.** MIL shako.

miro [miro] *fam* ◇ *adj* [myope] short-sighted ■ **sans mes lunettes, je suis complètement ~** I'm as blind as a bat without my glasses.
◇ *nmf* short-sighted (person).

mirobolant, e [mirɔbɔlɑ̃, ɑ̃t] *adj* *fam* [mirifique] fabulous, stupendous, amazing ■ **il touche un salaire ~** he earns an absolute fortune.

miroir [mirwar] *nm* **1.** [verre réflecteur] mirror ■ **~ déformant/grossissant** distorting/magnifying mirror ■ **~ à main/à barbe** hand/shaving mirror ■ **~ aux alouettes** CHASSE decoy ; *fig* trap for the unwary ■ **~ de courtoisie** AUTO vanity mirror **2.** *litt* [surface unie] mirror-like surface **3.** *litt* [image, reflet] mirror, reflection ■ **les yeux sont le ~ de l'âme** the eyes are the windows of the soul **4.** MÉD : **~ frontal** head mirror **5.** ENTOM [papillon] silver-spotted skipper moth.

miroitement [mirwatmɑ̃] *nm* **1.** [lueurs] glistening, gleaming **2.** [chatoiement] shimmering.

miroiter [3] [mirwate] *vi* **1.** *sout* [luire] to glisten, to gleam **2.** *fig* **faire ~ qqch à qqn** to (try and) lure sb with the prospect of sthg ■ **on lui a fait ~ une augmentation** they dangled the prospect of a rise before him.

miroiterie [mirwatri] *nf* **1.** [industrie] mirror industry **2.** [commerce] mirror trade **3.** [fabrique] mirror factory.

miroitier [mirwatje] *nm* **1.** [ouvrier] mirror cutter, silverer **2.** [fabricant] mirror manufacturer **3.** [vendeur] mirror dealer.

Mirza [mirza] *npr typical name for a small dog,* ≃ Fido.

mis, e [mi, miz] ◇ *pp* ▷ **mettre**.
◇ *adj* [vêtu] : **bien ~** well dressed, nicely turned out.

misandrie [mizɑ̃dri] *nf* misandry *sout*, hatred of men.

misanthrope [mizɑ̃trɔp] ◇ *adj* misanthropic.
◇ *nmf* misanthrope, misanthropist ■ **'le Misanthrope'** *Molière* 'The Misanthrope'.

misanthropie [mizɑ̃trɔpi] *nf* misanthropy.

misanthropique [mizɑ̃trɔpik] *adj* misanthropic.

mise [miz] ◇ *f* ▷ **mis**.
◇ *nf* **1.** JEUX stake ■ **augmenter la ~** to up the stakes ■ **doubler sa ~** to double one's stake **2.** *sout* [tenue] attire, dress ■ **soigner sa ~** to take care over one's appearance **3.** [dans des expressions] : **~ à** : **~ à l'abri** *fig* putting in a safe place ■ **~ à l'eau** NAUT launch ■ **~ à exécution** carrying out, implementation ■ **~ à jour** updating ; INFORM maintenance ■ **~ à mort** [gén] putting to death ; [en tauromachie] execution ; CHASSE kill, mort *spéc* ■ **~ à pied** [disciplinaire] suspension ; [économique] laying off ■ **~ à la retraite** pensioning off ■ **~ à sac** [d'une ville] sacking ; [d'un appartement] ransacking ■ **~ au** : **~ au monde** birth ■ **~ au pas** ÉQUIT reining in (to a walk) ; [d'une personne, de l'économie] bringing into line ■ **~ au propre** making a fair copy *ou* tidying up *(of a document)* ■ **~ au tombeau** entombment ■ **~ en** : **~ en accusation** indictment ■ **~ en application** implementation ■ **~ en attente** postponing, shelving ; INFORM & TÉLÉCOM hold ■ **~en bière** placing in the coffin ■ **~ en boîte** CINÉ & RADIO editing ■ **~ en cause** [d'une personne] implication ; [d'une idée] calling into question ■ **~ en circulation** FIN issue ■ **~ en condition** [du corps] getting fit ; [de l'esprit] conditioning ■ **~ en demeure** injunction, formal notification ■ **~ en disponibilité** leave of absence ■ **~ en doute** putting into doubt, questioning ■ **~ en état** DR preparation for hearing ; [d'un engin] getting into working order ; [d'un local] renovation ■ **~ en examen** DR indictment ■ **~ en forme** [d'un chapeau] shaping ; INFORM formatting ; IMPR imposition ; SPORT fitness training ■ **~ en garde** warning ■ **~ en jeu** FOOTBALL throw-in ; *fig* bringing into play ■ **~ en liberté** release ■ **~ en liberté provisoire** release on bail ■ **~ en marche** starting up ■ **~ en mémoire** INFORM storing (in the memory) ■ **~ en œuvre** implementation, bringing into play ■ **~ en ondes** RADIO production ■ **~ en orbite** putting into orbit ■ **~ en ordre** [d'un local] tidying up ; INFORM [d'un fichier] sequencing ; [d'un programme] housekeeping ; MATH ordering ■ **~ en place** setting up, organization ■ **~ en question** questioning, challenging ■ **~ en route** starting up ■ **~ en service** putting into service, bringing into operation ■ **~ en terre** burial ■ **~ en train** [d'un projet] starting up ; SPORT warming up ; [d'une soirée] breaking the ice ■ **~ en valeur** [d'un sol, d'une région] development ; [de biens] improvement ; [de qualités] setting off, enhancement ■ **~ en vente** (putting up for) sale ■ **~ en vigueur** bringing into force, enforcement ■ **~ hors** : **~ hors circuit** ÉLECTR disconnection ; TECHNOL disabling ■ **~ hors service** placing out of service ■ **~ sous** : **~ sous surveillance** putting under surveillance ■ **~ sous tension** supplying with electricity ■ **~ sur** : **~ sur écoutes** (phone) tapping ■ **~ sur pied** setting up.
◆ **de mise** *loc adj* appropriate ■ **ta colère n'est plus de ~** your anger is out of place now, there's no point in your being angry any more.
◆ **mise à feu** *nf* ARM firing ■ ASTRONAUT blast-off, launch.
◆ **mise à prix** *nf* reserve *UK ou* upset *US* price.
◆ **mise au point** *nf* **1.** OPT & PHOTO focusing, focussing **2.** TECHNOL tuning, adjustment **3.** INFORM trouble-shooting, debugging **4.** *fig* clarification, correction ■ **après cette petite ~ au point** now that the record has been set straight.
◆ **mise de fonds** *nf* capital outlay ■ **~ de fonds initiale** [pour un achat] initial outlay ; [pour monter une affaire] initial investment, seed money.
◆ **mise en page(s)** *nf* **1.** IMPR make-up, making up **2.** INFORM editing ■ **je n'aime pas la ~ en page de la revue** I don't like the layout of the review.
◆ **mise en plis** *nf* set.

◆ **mise en scène** *nf* CINÉ & THÉÂTRE production ■ **son remords n'était que de la ~ en scène** *fig* his remorse was only an act.

miser [3] [mize] ◇ *vt* [parier] to stake, to bet.
◇ *vi Suisse* [acheter] to buy *(at an auction sale)* ■ [vendre] to put up for auction.
◆ **miser sur** *v+prép* **1.** JEUX [cheval] to bet on, to back ■ **j'ai misé 50 euros sur le numéro 29** I've staked 50 euros on number 29 **2.** [compter sur - quelque chose] to bank *ou* to count on *(insép)* ; [- quelqu'un] to count on *(insép)* ■ **il vaut mieux ne pas ~ sur lui** we'd better not count on him.

misérabilisme [mizerabilism] *nm* miserabilism.

misérabiliste [mizerabilist] *adj & nmf* miserabilist.

misérable [mizerabl] ◇ *adj* **1.** *(placé après le nom)* [sans ressources] impoverished, poverty-stricken, poor ■ **tout le pays est ~** the whole country is wretchedly poor **2.** [pitoyable] pitiful, miserable, wretched **3.** [insignifiant] miserable, paltry ■ **elles se disputent pour un ~ vase** they're arguing over a stupid vase ■ **travailler pour un salaire ~** to work for a pittance.
◇ *nmf* **1.** *sout & hum* [malheureux] : **~, qu'as-tu fait là!** what have you done, you wretch! **2.** *litt* [miséreux] pauper, wretch ■ **'les Misérables'** *Hugo* 'les Miserables' **3.** *litt* [canaille] (vile) rascal *ou* scoundrel.

misérablement [mizerabləmɑ̃] *adv* **1.** [pauvrement] in poverty, wretchedly **2.** [lamentablement] pitifully, miserably, wretchedly.

misère [mizɛr] ◇ *nf* **1.** [indigence] poverty, destitution *sout* ■ **être dans la ~** to be destitute *ou* poverty-stricken ■ **être réduit à la ~** to be reduced to poverty ▶ **il se jeta sur la nourriture comme la ~ sur le monde** *hum* he went at the food like a starving man *ou* like a wolf on its prey **2.** *fig* poverty ■ **~ sexuelle** sexual deprevation **3.** [malheur] : **c'est une ~ de les voir se séparer** it's pitiful *ou* it's a shame to see them break up **4.** [somme dérisoire] pittance ■ **gagner une ~** to earn a pittance ■ **je l'ai eu pour une ~** I got *ou* bought it for next to nothing.
◇ *interj* : **~!** oh Lord! ■ **~ de moi!** *hum* woe is me!
◆ **misères** *nfpl fam* [broutilles, ennuis] : **faire des ~s à qqn** to give sb a hard time, to make sb's life a misery ■ **ne fais pas de ~s à ce chien!** stop tormenting that dog! ■ **raconte-moi tes ~s** tell me all your troubles *ou* woes ■ **il t'arrive des ~s?** what's the matter then? ■ **il te fait des ~s?** has he been horrible to you?
◆ **de misère** *loc adj* : **un salaire de ~** a starvation wage, a pittance.

miséreux, euse [mizerø, øz] *nm, f sout* poor person, pauper *vieilli* ■ **aider** *ou* **secourir les ~** to help the poor.

miséricorde [mizerikɔrd] *nf litt* **1.** [pitié] mercy, forgiveness ■ **implorer ~** to beg *ou* to cry for mercy ▶ **~!** *vieilli & hum* heaven help us!, mercy on us! **2.** [siège] misericord, misericorde.

miséricordieux, euse [mizerikɔrdjø, øz] *adj litt* merciful, forgiving ■ **être ~ envers qqn** to show mercy towards sb ■ **soyez ~** have mercy.

misogyne [mizɔʒin] ◇ *adj* misogynous, misogynistic.
◇ *nmf* misogynist, woman-hater.

misogynie [mizɔʒini] *nf* misogyny.

miss [mis] *(pl inv ou pl* **misses** [mis]) *nf* **1.** [gouvernante] governess **2.** *fam hum* **ça va, la ~?** how's things, beauty?
◆ **Miss** *nf inv* [reine de beauté] : **Miss Japon/Monde** Miss Japan/World.

missel [misɛl] *nm* missal.

missile [misil] *nm* missile ■ **~ antichar/antiaérien** antitank/antiaircraft missile ■ **~ intercontinental/stratégique/de croisière** intercontinental/strategic/cruise missile ■ **~ sol-sol/air-air** ground-to-ground/air-to-air missile ■ **~ Pershing** Pershing missile.

mission [misjɔ̃] *nf* **1.** [charge] mission, assignment ■ **au cours de votre ~ à Boston** while you were working in Boston **2.** [devoir] mission, task ■ **la ~ de notre organisation est de défendre les droits de l'homme** our organization's mission is to defend human rights ■ **la ~ du journaliste est d'informer** a journalist's task is to inform **3.** [groupe] mission ■ **~ diplomatique** diplomatic mission **4.** RELIG [organisation] mission ■ **~s étrangères** foreign missions ■ [lieu] mission (station).

missionnaire [misjɔnɛr] *adj & nmf* missionary.

Mississippi [misisipi] *npr m* **1.** [fleuve] : **le ~** the Mississippi (River) **2.** [État] : **le ~** Mississippi.

missive [misiv] ◇ *adj* missive.
◇ *nf sout* missive.

Missouri [misuri] *npr m* : **le ~** Missouri.

mistigri [mistigri] *nm* **1.** *fam* [chat] puss **2.** CARTES jack *ou UK* knave of clubs.

mistral [mistral] *nm* mistral.

mit *etc v* ▷ **mettre**.

mitaine [mitɛn] *nf* (fingerless) mitt ■ *Québec & Suisse* [moufle] mitten.

mitard△ [mitar] *nm arg crime* [cachot] can, clink ■ **être au ~** to be in solitary confinement *ou* in solitary.

mite [mit] *nf* [papillon] (clothes) moth ■ **rongé par les** *ou* **aux ~s** moth-eaten.

mité, e [mite] *adj* moth-eaten.

mi-temps [mitɑ̃] ◇ *nf inv* SPORT **1.** [moitié] half ■ **la première ~** the first half **2.** [pause] halftime ■ **le score est de 0 à 0 à la ~** the halftime score is nil nil ■ **siffler la ~** to blow the whistle for halftime.
◇ *nm inv* part-time job ■ **faire un ~** to work part-time.
◆ **à mi-temps** ◇ *loc adj* part-time ■ **travailleur à ~** part-timer, part-time worker.
◇ *loc adv* : **travailler à ~** to work part-time ■ **elle travaille à ~ comme serveuse** she's a part-time waitress.

miter [3] [mite] ◆ **se miter** *vpi* to become moth-eaten.

miteux, euse [mitø, øz] *fam* ◇ *adj* [costume] shabby, tatty *UK*, tacky *US* ■ [chambre] dingy, crummy ■ [situation, salaire] pathetic ■ [escroc] small-time.
◇ *nm, f* [incapable] nonentity, loser, no-hoper *UK* ■ [indigent] bum, dosser *UK*.

mitigation [mitigasjɔ̃] *nf* mitigation ■ **~ d'une peine** mitigation of a sentence.

mitigé, e [mitiʒe] *adj* **1.** [modéré] mixed ■ **des critiques ~es** mixed reviews ■ **manifester un enthousiasme ~** to be reserved in one's enthusiasm **2.** : **~ de** [mêlé de] mitigated *ou* qualified by.

mitiger [17] [mitiʒe] *vt vieilli* to mitigate ■ **~ qqch de** to mix *ou* to temper sthg with ■ **ayant mitigé ses critiques de quelques compliments** having tempered his criticism with a few words of praise.

mitigeur [mitiʒœr] *nm* mixer tap *UK ou* faucet *US* ■ **~ de douche** shower mixer.

mitonner [3] [mitɔne] ◇ *vt* **1.** CULIN to simmer, to slow-cook ■ **je vous ai mitonné une petite recette à moi** I've cooked you one of my tasty little recipes **2.** [coup, plan] to plot **3.** *litt* **~ qqn** to cosset *ou* to pamper sb.
◇ *vi* CULIN to simmer, to stew gently.

mitose [mitoz] *nf* mitosis.

mitoyen, enne [mitwajɛ̃, ɛn] *adj* **1.** [commun] common, shared ■ **puits ~ entre les deux maisons** well shared by *ou* common to the two houses **2.** [jouxtant] bordering, neighbouring ■ **les champs sont ~s** the fields are adjacent to each other ■ **le jardin ~ du nôtre** the garden (immediately) next to ours, the neighbouring garden (to ours) ■ **deux maisons ~nes** semi-detached houses ■ **une rue de maisons ~nes** a street of terrace(d) houses **3.** [en copropriété] commonly-owned, jointly-owned ■ **mur ~** party wall.

mitoyenneté [mitwajɛnte] *nf* **1.** [copropriété] common *ou* joint ownership **2.** [contiguïté] adjacency.

mitraillade [mitrajad] *nf* volley of shots.

mitraillage [mitrajaʒ] *nm* MIL machine-gunning.

mitraille [mitraj] *nf* **1.** MIL grapeshot ■ [décharge] volley of shots **2.** *fam* [monnaie] small *ou* loose change.

mitrailler [3] [mitraje] *vt* **1.** MIL to machine-gun **2.** *fam* [photographier] to snap (away) at **3.** *fig* [assaillir] : **~ qqn de questions** to fire questions at sb, to bombard sb with questions.

mitraillette [mitrajɛt] *nf* submachine gun.

mitrailleur [mitrajœr] *nm* machine gunner ■ **~ d'avion** air gunner.

mitrailleuse [mitrajøz] *nf* machine gun ■ **~ légère/lourde** light/heavy machine gun.

mitre [mitr] *nf* **1.** RELIG mitre ■ **recevoir la ~** to be mitred **2.** CONSTR (chimney) cowl.

mitré, e [mitre] *adj* mitred.

mitron [mitrɔ̃] *nm* [garçon pâtissier] pastry cook's apprentice *ou* boy ■ [garçon boulanger] baker's apprentice *ou* boy.

mi-voix [mivwa] ◆ **à mi-voix** *loc adv* in a low *ou* hushed voice, in hushed tones ■ **chanter à ~** to sing softly.

mixage [miksaʒ] *nm* AUDIO, RADIO, TV & MUS mixing.

mixer[1] [3] [mikse] *vt* **1.** CULIN [à la main] to mix ■ [au mixer] to blend, to liquidize **2.** MUS to mix.

mixer[2] [miksɛr], **mixeur** [miksœr] *nm* mixer, blender, liquidizer.

mixité [miksite] *nf* **1.** [gén] mixed nature **2.** ÉDUC coeducation, coeducational system.

mixte [mikst] ◇ *adj* **1.** [des deux sexes] mixed ■ **classe ~** ÉDUC mixed class ■ **école ~** mixed *ou* coeducational school ➊ **double ~** SPORT mixed doubles **2.** [de nature double] mixed **3.** [à double usage] : **cuisinière ~** combined gas and electric cooker *UK ou* stove *US*.
◇ *nm* SPORT mixed doubles match.

mixtion [miksjɔ̃] *nf* PHARM [action] blending, compounding ■ [médicament] mixture.

mixture [mikstyr] *nf* **1.** CHIM & PHARM mixture **2.** [boisson ou nourriture] mixture, concoction.

MJC *nf* = **maison des jeunes et de la culture.**

MJC

The *Maisons des jeunes et de la culture* or *MJC* are leisure clubs run in part by local authorities. They are funded by *communes*, the *conseil général* and also by the *Ministère de la jeunesse et des sports*. They offer all sorts of activities, some more specifically for youngsters (sports, music, art) and some for adults (keep fit, folk dancing, pottery, photography etc); their mission is to develop citizenship through education and culture.

MJD (*abr de* **Maison de la justice et du droit**) [ɛmʒide] *nf* law centre.

ml (*abr écrite de* **millilitre**) ml.

MLF (*abr de* **Mouvement de libération de la femme**) *npr m* *women's movement,* ≃ NOW *US*.

Mlle = **Mademoiselle** Miss.

mm (*abr écrite de* **millimètre**) mm.

MM. (*abr écrite de* **Messieurs**) Messrs.

Mme (*abr écrite de* **Madame**) [femme mariée] Mrs ■ [femme mariée ou célibataire] Ms.

MMS (*abr de* **multimedia message service**) *nm* TÉLÉCOM MMS.

mn (*abr écrite de* **minute**) min.

mnémonique [mnemɔnik] *adj* mnemonic ■ **procédé** *ou* **moyen ~** mnemonic.

mnémotechnie [mnemɔtɛkni] *nf* mnemonics *(sing)*.

mnémotechnique [mnemɔtɛknik] ◇ *adj* mnemonic ■ **formule ~** mnemonic.
◇ *nf* = **mnémotechnie.**

mnésique [mnezik] *adj* mnemonic.

Mo (*abr écrite de* **méga-octet**) Mb.

mobile [mɔbil] ◇ *adj* **1.** [qui se déplace - pont] moving ; [- main-d'œuvre] mobile ; [- panneau] sliding ■ [amovible] movable, removable ■ **carnet à feuilles ~s** loose-leaf notepad **2.** MIL [unité] mobile **3.** [changeant] mobile ■ **un visage ~** a lively *ou* animated face **4.** [à valeur non fixe] : **caractère ~** IMPR movable character.
◇ *nm* **1.** [de sculpteur, pour enfant] mobile **2.** [motif] motive ■ **le ~ d'un crime** the motive for a crime ■ **quel ~ l'a poussé à agir ainsi?** what motivated *ou* prompted him to act this way?

mobile home [mɔbilom] (*pl* **mobile homes**) *nm* mobile home.

mobilier, ère [mɔbilje, ɛr] *adj* DR [propriété] personal, movable ■ [titre] transferable ■ **biens ~s** movables ■ **effets ~s** chattels.
◆ **mobilier** *nm* **1.** [d'une habitation] furniture, furnishings ■ **du ~ Louis XIII/Renaissance** Louis XIII/Renaissance (style) furniture ➊ **Mobilier national** *state-owned furniture (in France)* **2.** [pour un usage particulier] : **~ de bureau/jardin** office/garden furniture ■ **~ scolaire** school furniture *ou* furnishings **3.** DR movable property, movables.
◆ **mobilier urbain** *nm* street fittings, street furniture.

mobilisable [mɔbilizabl] *adj* **1.** MIL liable to be called up, mobilizable **2.** [disponible] available **3.** FIN realizable, mobilizable.

mobilisateur, trice [mɔbilizatœr, tris] *adj* mobilizing ■ **c'est un thème très ~ en ce moment** it's an issue which is stirring a lot of people into action at the moment.

mobilisation [mɔbilizasjɔ̃] *nf* **1.** MIL [action] mobilization, mobilizing, calling up ■ [état] mobilization **2.** [d'une force politique] mobilization ■ [d'énergie, de volonté] summoning up ■ **il appelle à la ~ de tous les syndicats** he is calling on all the unions to mobilize **3.** FIN liquidation, realization ■ BANQUE mobilization **4.** MÉD & PHYSIOL mobilization.

mobiliser [3] [mɔbilize] *vt* **1.** MIL [population] to call up *(sép)*, to mobilize ■ [armée] to mobilize ■ **toute la famille fut mobilisée pour préparer la fête** the whole family was put to work to organize the party **2.** [syndicalistes, consommateurs, moyens techniques] to mobilize ■ [volontés] to mobilize, to summon up *(sép)* ■ **~ l'opinion en faveur des réfugiés politiques** to rally public opinion for the cause of the political refugees ■ **~ les forces vives d'une nation** to call upon the full resources of a nation **3.** BANQUE to mobilize **4.** MÉD [membre, articulation] to mobilize.
◆ **se mobiliser** *vpi* to mobilize ■ **tout le village s'est mobilisé contre le projet** the whole village rose up in arms against the plan *ou* mobilized to fight the plan.

mobilité [mɔbilite] *nf* **1.** [dans l'espace - d'une personne] mobility ■ [expression - d'un regard] expressiveness **2.** SOCIOL [dans une hiérarchie] mobility ■ **~ professionnelle** professional mobility ■ **~ sociale** social mobility.

Mobylette® [mɔbilɛt] *nf* Mobylette®, moped.

mocassin [mɔkasɛ̃] *nm* [chaussure] moccasin.

moche [mɔʃ] *adj fam* **1.** [laid - personne] ugly ; [- objet, vêtement] ugly, awful, horrible **2.** [détestable] lousy, rotten ■ **c'est ~, ce qu'elle lui a fait** it was rotten, what she did to him **3.** [pénible] : **tu ne peux pas prendre de congé? c'est ~, dis donc!** can't you take any time off? that's terrible! ■ **c'est ~ qu'il pleuve aujourd'hui!** it's a real drag *ou* pain that it had to rain today!

mocheté [mɔʃte] *nf fam* [personne] ugly thing, fright ■ [objet] eyesore ■ **c'est une vraie ~** she's as ugly as sin!

M-octet (*abr écrite de* **méga-octet**) Mb.

modal, e, aux [mɔdal, o] *adj* LING, LOGIQUE & MUS modal.
◆ **modal, aux** *nm* LING modal (auxiliary).

modalité [mɔdalite] *nf* **1.** [façon] mode ▪ **~s de paiement** conditions *ou* terms of payment ▪ **~s de remboursement** terms of repayment **2.** [circonstances] : **les ~s de l'accord** the terms of the agreement ▪ **~s d'intervention** procedure **3.** LING, MUS & PHILOS modality ▪ **adverbe de ~** modal adverb.

mode[1] [mɔd] <> *nf* **1.** [vêtement] : **la ~** fashion ▪ **la ~ (de) printemps/(d')hiver** the spring/winter fashion ▪ **la ~ courte/longue** (fashion for) high/low hemlines ▪ **c'est la dernière** *ou* **c'est la grande ~** it's the latest fashion ▪ **c'est la ~ des bas résille** fishnet stockings are in fashion *ou* in vogue ▪ **suivre la ~** to follow fashion ▪ **c'est passé de ~** it's out of fashion, it's no longer fashionable ▪ **lancer une ~** to set a fashion *ou* a trend ▪ **il a lancé la ~ de la fausse fourrure** he launched the fashion for imitation fur **2.** [activité] : **la ~** [gén] the fashion industry *ou* business ; [stylisme] fashion designing **3.** [goût du jour] fashion ▪ **c'était la ~ de faire du jogging** jogging was all the rage then ▪ **ce n'est plus la ~ de se marier** marriage is outdated *ou* has gone out of fashion ▪ **la ~ des années 80** the style of the eighties.
<> *adj inv* [coloris, coupe] fashion *(modif)*, fashionable.
◆ **à la mode** <> *loc adj* [vêtement] fashionable, in fashion ▪ [personne, sport] fashionable ▪ [chanson] (currently) popular ▪ **ce n'est plus à la ~** it's out of fashion.
<> *loc adv* : **se mettre à la ~** to follow the latest fashion ▪ **revenir à la ~** to come back into fashion.
◆ **à la mode de** *loc prép* **1.** [suivant l'usage de] in the fashion of ▪ **je les fais toujours à la ~ de chez nous** I always do them like we do at home **2.** *loc* **cousin à la ~ de Bretagne** distant cousin, first cousin once removed.

mode[2] [mɔd] *nm* **1.** [méthode] : **~ de** [méthode] mode *ou* method of ; [manière personnelle] way of ▪ **~ d'action** form *ou* mode of action ▪ **on ne connaît pas le ~ d'action de cette substance** we don't know how this substance works ▪ **~ d'emploi** directions *ou* instructions for use ▪ **~ d'existence** way of living ▪ **~ de paiement** mode *ou* method of payment ▪ **~ de production** mode of production ▪ **~ de scrutin** voting system ▪ **~ de vie** [gén] life style ; SOCIOL pattern of living **2.** LING mood, mode **3.** INFORM mode ▪ **~ multitâche** multitasking mode ▪ **~ autonome** *ou* **local** *ou* **hors ligne** off-line mode ▪ **~ connecté** *ou* **en ligne** on-line mode ▪ **~ d'accès** access mode ▪ **~ de transmission** data communication mode ▪ **~ utilisateur** user mode **4.** MATH, MUS & PHILOS mode.

modelage [mɔdlaʒ] *nm* **1.** [action] modelling ▪ MÉTALL moulding **2.** [objet] sculpture.

modelé [mɔdle] *nm* **1.** [sur tableau] relief ▪ [d'une sculpture, d'un buste] contours, curves **2.** GÉOGR (surface) relief.

modèle [mɔdɛl] <> *nm* **1.** [référence à reproduire - gén] model ; [- de tricot, de couture] pattern ▪ **prendre ~ sur qqch** to use sthg as a model ▪ **dessiner d'après un ~** ART to draw from life ▪ ÉDUC [corrigé] model answer
2. [bon exemple] model, example ▪ **elle est un ~ pour moi** she's my role model ▪ **prendre qqn pour ~** to model o.s. on sb ▪ **c'est le ~ du parfait employé** he's a model employee ▪ **c'est un ~ de discrétion** he's a model of discretion ▪ **c'est un ~ du genre** it's a perfect example of its type ▪ **un ~ de vertu** a paragon of virtue
3. COMM [prototype, version] model ▪ **grand/petit ~** large-scale/small-scale model ▪ **~ sport/deux portes** AUTO sports/two-door model ➲ **~ déposé** registered design
4. [vêtement] model, style, design ▪ **vous avez ce ~ en 38?** do you have this one in a 38?
5. [maquette] model ▪ **~ réduit** small-scale model ▪ **~ réduit d'avion** model aeroplane ▪ **un ~ au 1/10** a 1 to 10 (scale) model
6. ART model
7. INFORM model
8. LING pattern.
<> *adj* **1.** [parfait] model *(modif)* ▪ **il a eu un comportement ~** he was a model of good behaviour
2. [qui sert de référence] : **ferme/prison ~** model farm/prison.

modeler [25] [mɔdle] *vt* **1.** [argile] to model, to shape, to mould ▪ [figurine] to model, to mould, to fashion ▪ **les glaciers ont modelé le paysage** the glaciers moulded the landscape **2.** *fig* [idées, caractère, opinion publique] to shape, to mould ▪ **~ sa conduite sur (celle de) qqn** to model one's behaviour on sb *ou* sb's.
◆ **se modeler sur** *vp+prép* to model o.s. on.

modeleur, euse [mɔdlœr, øz] *nm, f* **1.** ART modeller **2.** MÉTALL pattern-maker.

modéliser [3] [mɔdelize] *vt* to model.

modélisme [mɔdelism] *nm* scale model making.

modéliste [mɔdelist] *nmf* **1.** [de maquettes] model maker **2.** COUT (dress) designer.

modem [mɔdɛm] *nm* modem ▪ **~ longue/courte distance** long-haul/limited distance modem.

modérateur, trice [mɔderatœr, tris] <> *adj* [élément, présence] moderating, restraining.
<> *nm, f* mediator, moderator ▪ INFORM moderator.
◆ **modérateur** *nm* **1.** TECHNOL regulator, moderator **2.** NUCL & RELIG moderator.

modération [mɔderasjɔ̃] *nf* **1.** [mesure] moderation, restraint ▪ **avec ~** [boire, manger, utiliser] in moderation ; [agir] moderately, with moderation ▪ **une réponse pleine de ~** a very restrained answer **2.** [réduction - de dépenses] reduction, reducing ▪ [atténuation - d'un sentiment] restraint, restraining **3.** NUCL moderation.

modéré, e [mɔdere] <> *adj* **1.** [prix] moderate, reasonable ▪ [vent, température] moderate ▪ [enthousiasme, intérêt, succès] moderate ▪ **mer ~e à belle** MÉTÉOR sea moderate to good **2.** [mesuré, raisonnable] moderate ▪ [plein de retenue] moderate, restrained **3.** POLIT moderate.
<> *nm, f* POLIT moderate ▪ **les ~s** the moderates.

modérément [mɔderemɑ̃] *adv* **1.** [sans excès] in moderation **2.** [relativement] moderately, relatively ▪ **je ne suis que ~ surpris** I'm only moderately surprised, I'm not really all that surprised.

modérer [18] [mɔdere] *vt* [ardeur, enthousiasme, impatience, dépenses] to moderate, to restrain, to curb ▪ [vitesse] to reduce ▪ [exigences] to moderate, to restrain ▪ **modérez vos propos!** please tone down *ou* moderate your language! ‖ INFORM [liste de diffusion] to moderate.
◆ **se modérer** *vp (emploi réfléchi)* **1.** [se contenir] to restrain o.s. **2.** [se calmer] to calm down ▪ **je t'en prie, modère-toi!** please calm down *ou* control yourself!

moderne [mɔdɛrn] <> *adj* **1.** [actuel, récent - mobilier, bâtiment, technique, théorie] modern ▪ **les temps ~s, l'époque ~** modern times ▪ **le mode de vie ~** modern living, today's way of life **2.** [progressiste - artiste, opinions, théoricien] modern, progressive ▪ **c'est une grand-mère très ~** she's a very modern *ou* up-to-date grandmother **3.** ART modern, contemporary **4.** ÉDUC [maths] modern, new ▪ [études, histoire] modern, contemporary **5.** LING [langue, sens] modern ▪ **grec ~** Modern Greek.
<> *nmf* ART modern artist ▪ LITTÉR modern writer, modern poet.
<> *nm* : **le ~** [genre] modern style ; [mobilier] modern furniture.

modernisateur, trice [mɔdɛrnizatœr, tris] <> *adj* [tendance, réforme] modernizing.
<> *nm, f* modernizer.

modernisation [mɔdɛrnizasjɔ̃] *nf* modernization, modernizing, updating.

moderniser [3] [mɔdɛrnize] *vt* to modernize, to bring up to date.
◆ **se moderniser** *vp (emploi réfléchi)* to modernize.

modernisme [mɔdɛrnism] *nm* modernism.

moderniste [mɔdɛrnist] *adj* & *nmf* modernist.

modernité [mɔdɛrnite] *nf* modernity.

modern style [mɔdɛrnstil] *nm inv* modern style, art nouveau ▪ *(comme adj inv)* **une glace ~** an art nouveau mirror.

modeste [mɔdɛst] <> *adj* **1.** [logement] modest ▪ [revenu] modest, small ▪ [goût, train de vie] modest, unpretentious

▪ [tenue] modest, simple ▪ **tu es trop ~ dans tes prétentions** you're not asking for enough money ▮ [milieu] modest, humble ▪ **être d'origine très ~** to come from a very modest *ou* humble background **2.** *(avant le n)* [modique] modest, humble, small ▪ **ce n'est qu'un ~ présent** it's only a very modest *ou* small gift, it's just a little something **3.** [sans vanité] modest ▪ **c'était facile – tu es trop ~** it was easy – you're (being) too modest **4.** *vieilli* [pudique - air, jeune fille] modest.
<> *nmf*: **allons, ne fais pas la** *ou* **ta ~!** come on, don't be (so) modest!

modestement [mɔdɛstəmɑ̃] *adv* **1.** [simplement] modestly, simply ▪ **ils vivent très ~** they live very modestly, they lead a very simple life **2.** [sans vanité] modestly **3.** *vieilli* [avec réserve] modestly, unassumingly ▪ [avec pudeur] modestly.

modestie [mɔdɛsti] *nf* **1.** [humilité] modesty ▪ **faire preuve de ~** to be modest ▪ **il a su garder une grande ~** he remained extremely modest ▪ **ce n'est pas la ~ qui l'étouffe!** you can't say she's overmodest! ▪ **en toute ~** in all modesty ◆ **fausse ~** false modesty ▪ **allons, pas de fausse ~!** come on, don't be so modest! *iron* **2.** *vieilli* [réserve] modesty, self-effacement ▪ [pudeur] modesty.

modicité [mɔdisite] *nf* lowness, smallness, paltriness ▪ **la ~ de leur salaire ne leur permet pas de partir en vacances** they can't go on holiday because of their low wages.

modifiable [mɔdifjabl] *adj* modifiable.

modificateur, trice [mɔdifikatœr, tris] *adj* modifying, modificatory.
◆ **modificateur** *nm* BIOL, GRAMM & INFORM modifier.

modification [mɔdifikasjɔ̃] *nf* **1.** [processus] modification, modifying, changing ▪ [altération] modification, alteration, change **2.** INFORM alteration, modification ▪ **~ d'adresse** address modification ▪ **~ de configuration binaire** bit handling.

modifier [9] [mɔdifje] *vt* **1.** [transformer - politique, texte] to modify, to change, to alter ; [- vêtement] to alter ; [- loi] to amend, to change **2.** GRAMM to modify **3.** INFORM to alter, to modify ▪ **~ la configuration de qqch** to reconfigure sthg.
◆ **se modifier** *vpi* to change, to alter, to be modified.

modique [mɔdik] *adj* [peu élevé - prix, rémunération] modest, small ▪ **et pour la ~ somme de 100 euros, mesdames, je vous donne deux couvertures!** and for the modest sum of 100 euros, ladies, I'll give you two blankets!

modiquement [mɔdikmɑ̃] *adv* [rétribuer] poorly, modestly, meagrely.

modiste [mɔdist] *nmf* milliner.

modulable [mɔdylabl] *adj* modular, flexible ▪ **bibliothèque composée d'éléments ~s** bookshelves made of versatile *ou* modular units.

modulateur, trice [mɔdylatœr, tris] *adj* modulatory ▪ **lampe modulatrice** modulator lamp.
◆ **modulateur** *nm* INFORM & TÉLÉCOM modulator ▪ **~ de fréquence** converter.

modulation [mɔdylasjɔ̃] *nf* **1.** [tonalité - de la voix] modulation ▪ ACOUST & MUS modulation **2.** ÉLECTRON, INFORM, RADIO & TÉLÉCOM modulation ▪ **~ d'amplitude/de fréquence** amplitude/ frequency modulation ▪ **poste à ~ de fréquence** frequency modulation *ou* FM (radio) set ▪ **rapidité/taux de ~** modulation rate/factor **3.** [nuance] modulation, variation **4.** ARCHIT building-block *ou* modular principle.

module [mɔdyl] *nm* **1.** [élément - gén] module, unit ▪ ARCHIT & CONSTR module **2.** MATH & PHYS modulus **3.** INFORM module ▪ **~ binaire** binary deck ▪ **~ chargeable** load module ▪ **~ exécutable** run module ▪ **~ maître** master module **4.** MÉCAN module.

moduler [3] [mɔdyle] <> *vt* **1.** TECHNOL to modulate **2.** [adapter] to adjust **3.** [nuancer] to vary.
<> *vi* MUS to modulate.

modus vivendi [mɔdysvivɛ̃di] *nm inv* modus vivendi ▪ **trouver un ~ avec** to come to a working arrangement with.

moelle [mwal] *nf* **1.** ANAT marrow, medulla *spéc* ▪ **~ épinière** spinal chord ▪ **jusqu'à la ~** to the core ▪ **être gelé** *ou* **transi jusqu'à la ~ des os** to be frozen to the marrow *ou* to the bone **2.** CULIN (bone) marrow **3.** BOT pith.

moelleusement [mwaløzmɑ̃] *adv sout* [s'installer] comfortably, snugly, luxuriously.

moelleux, euse [mwalø, øz] *adj* **1.** [au toucher] soft ▪ **des coussins ~** soft *ou* comfortable cushions ▮ [à la vue, à l'ouïe] mellow, warm ▪ **une voix moelleuse** a mellow voice ▮ [au palais - vin] mellow, well-rounded ; [- viande] tender ; [- gâteau] moist **2.** *litt* [gracieux] soft.
◆ **moelleux** *nm* softness, mellowness ▪ ŒNOL mellowness.

moellon [mwalɔ̃] *nm* CONSTR rubble, rubble-stone, moellon ◆ **~ d'appareil** ashlar.

mœurs [mœr(s)] *nfpl* **1.** [comportement social] customs, habits ▪ **les ~ politiques** political practice ▪ **c'est entré dans les ~** it's become part of everyday life ▪ **les ~ de notre temps** mores of our time the social **2.** [comportement personnel] manners, ways ▪ **elle a des ~ vraiment bizarres** she behaves in a really odd way ▪ **quelles drôles de ~!** what a strange way to behave! ▮ [style de vie] life-style **3.** [principes moraux] morals, moral standards ▪ **des ~ particulières** *euphém* particular tastes ▪ **une femme de ~ légères** a woman of easy virtue ◆ **c'est contraire aux bonnes ~** it goes against accepted standards of behaviour ▪ **la police/brigade des ~, les Mœurs** *fam* ≃ the vice squad **4.** ZOOL habits.
◆ **de mœurs** *loc adj* **1.** [sexuel] : **affaire de ~** sex case **2.** LITTÉR : **comédie/roman de ~** comedy/novel of manners.

Mogadiscio [mɔgadiʃjo] *npr* Mogadiscio, Mogadishu.

mogette [mɔʒɛt] *nf* white bean, haricot bean.

moghol, e [mɔgɔl] *adj* Mogul.
◆ **Moghol, e** *nm, f* Mogul.

mohair [mɔɛr] *nm* mohair.

Mohicans [mɔikɑ̃] *nmpl* Mohicans, Mohican.

moi [mwa] <> *pron pers* **1.** [sujet] : **qui est là? – ~** who's there? – me ▪ **je l'ai vue hier – ~ aussi** I saw her yesterday – so did I *ou* me too ▪ **je n'en sais rien – ~ non plus** I have no idea – neither do I *ou* me neither ▪ **et vous voulez que ~, j'y aille?** you want ME to go? ▪ **~ qui vous parle, je l'ai vu de mes propres yeux** I'm telling you, I saw him with my very own eyes ▪ **et ~ qui te faisais confiance!** and to think (that) I trusted you! ▪ **il faisait nuit, et ~ qui ne savais pas où aller!** it was dark, and there was me, not knowing where to go! ▪ **~ seul possède la clef** I'm the only one with the key
2. [avec un présentatif] : **c'est ~ qui lui ai dit de venir** I was the one who *ou* it was me who told him to come ▪ **salut, c'est ~!** hi, it's me! ▪ **c'est ~ qui te le dis!** I'm telling you! ▪ **je vous remercie – non, c'est ~** thank you – thank YOU
3. [complément] : **dites-~** tell me ▪ **donne-le-moi ~** give it to me ▪ **attendez-~!** wait (for me)! ▪ **il nous a invités, ma femme et ~** he invited both my wife and myself ▮ [avec une préposition] : **c'est à ~ qu'il l'a donné** he gave it to ME ▪ **une chambre à ~ tout seul** a room of my own ▪ **un ami à ~** *fam* a friend of mine ▪ **plus âgé que ~** older than me ▪ **tu as d'aussi bonnes raisons que ~** you have just as good reasons as me *ou* as I have ▪ **une lettre de ~** one of my letters ▪ **c'est de ~, cette lettre?** is this letter from me?, is this letter one of mine?, is this one of my letters? ◆ **à ~!** [au secours] help! ; [de jouer] it's my turn! ; [d'essayer] let me have a go!
4. [en fonction de pronom réfléchi] myself ▪ **je suis contente de ~** I'm pleased with myself
5. [emploi expressif] : **regardez-~ ça!** just look at that! ▪ **rangez-~ ça tout de suite!** put that away right now!
<> *nm* : **le ~** PHILOS the self ; PSYCHOL the ego.

moignon [mwaɲɔ̃] *nm* stump *(of a limb)*.

moi-même [mwamɛm] *pron pers* myself ▪ **j'ai ~ vérifié** I checked it myself ▪ **mon épouse et ~** my wife and I ▪ **je préfère vérifier par ~** I prefer to check for myself ▪ **j'y suis allé de ~** I went there on my own initiative.

moindre [mwɛ̃dr] *adj* **1.** *(comparatif)* [perte] lesser, smaller ▪ [qualité] lower, poorer ▪ [prix] lower ▪ **de ~ gravité** less serious ▪ **de ~ importance** less important, of lesser importance ▪ **c'est un ~ mal** it's the lesser evil **2.** *(superlatif)* **le ~, la ~** [de deux] the lesser ; [de trois ou plus] the least, the slightest ▪ **le ~ mouvement/danger** the slightest movement/danger ▪ **le ~ espoir** the slightest *ou* faintest hope ▪ **la ~ chance** the slightest *ou* remotest chance ▪ **je n'en ai pas la ~ idée** I haven't got the slightest *ou* faintest *ou* remotest idea ▪ **jusqu'au ~ détail** down to the last *ou* smallest detail ▪ **ce serait la ~ des politesses** it would be only common courtesy ▪ **c'est une pianiste, et non des ~s!** she's a pianist and a good one at that! ▪ **il n'a pas fait la ~ remarque** he didn't say a single word ➔ **c'est là son ~ défaut** *La Fontaine allus* that's the least of his faults ▪ **je vous en prie, c'est la ~ des choses!** don't mention it, it was the least I could do! ▪ **dis merci, c'est la ~ des choses!** you could at least say thank you!

moindrement [mwɛ̃drəmɑ̃] *adv litt* **il n'était pas le ~ gêné** he wasn't embarrassed in the least *ou* in the slightest.

moine [mwan] *nm* RELIG monk, friar ▪ **~ cistercien** Cistercian monk.

moineau, x [mwano] *nm* ORNITH sparrow ▪ **avoir une cervelle** *ou* **tête de ~** *fam* to be bird-brained *ou* scatterbrained.

moinillon [mwanijɔ̃] *nm* [jeune moine] young monk.

moins [mwɛ̃] ◇ *adv*

> **A.** COMPARATIF D'INFÉRIORITÉ
> **B.** SUPERLATIF D'INFÉRIORITÉ

A. COMPARATIF D'INFÉRIORITÉ

1. [avec un adjectif, un adverbe] less ▪ **cinq fois ~ cher** five times less expensive ▪ **deux fois ~ cher** half as expensive, twice as cheap ▪ **en ~ rapide** but not so *ou* as fast ▪ **c'est ~ bien que l'an dernier** it's not as good a last year ▪ **c'est le même appartement, en ~ bien/grand** it's the same flat only not as nice/not as big ▪ **beaucoup/un peu ~** a lot/a little less ▪ **il est ~ timide que réservé** he's not so much shy as reserved ▪ **il n'en est pas ~ vrai que...** it is nonetheless true that... ▪ **non ~ charmante que...** just as charming as..., no less charming than...
2. [avec un verbe] less, not... so *ou* as much ▪ **je souffre ~** I'm not in so much *ou* I'm in less pain ▪ **tu devrais demander ~** you shouldn't ask for so much ▪ **~ tu parles, mieux ça vaut** the less you speak, the better ▪ **j'y pense ~ que tu ne le crois** I think about it less than you think

B. SUPERLATIF D'INFÉRIORITÉ

1. [avec un adjectif, un adverbe] : **c'est lui le ~ riche des trois** he's the least wealthy of the three ▪ **c'est elle la ~ intelligente des deux** she's the less intelligent of the two ▪ **c'est le sommet le ~ élevé** it's the lowest peak ▪ **c'est le modèle le ~ cher qu'on puisse trouver** it's the least expensive (that) you can find ▪ **le ~ possible** as little as possible ▪ **c'est lui qui habite le ~ loin** he lives the least far away *ou* the nearest ➔ **je ne suis pas le ~ du monde surpris** I'm not at all *ou* not in the least bit surprised ▪ **je vous dérange? – mais non, pas le ~ du monde** am I disturbing you? – of course not *ou* not in the slightest
2. [avec un verbe] : **le ~** (the) least ➔ **le ~ qu'on puisse faire, c'est de les inviter** the least we could do is invite them ▪ **c'est le ~ qu'on puisse dire!** that's the least you can say!

◇ *prep* **1.** [en soustrayant] : **dix ~ huit font deux** ten minus *ou* less eight makes two ▪ **on est seize: ~ les enfants, ça fait douze** there are sixteen of us, twelve not counting the children **2.** [indiquant l'heure] : **il est ~ vingt** it's twenty to ▪ **il est 3 h ~ le quart** it's (a) quarter to 3 ➔ **il était ~ une** *ou* **cinq** *fam* that was a close call *ou* shave **3.** [introduisant un nombre négatif] : **~ 50 plus ~ 6 égalent ~ 56** minus 50 plus minus 6 is *ou* makes minus 56 ▪ **il fait ~ 25** it's 25 below *ou* minus 25 ▪ **plonger à ~ 300 m** to dive to a depth of 300 m.

◇ *nm* minus (sign).

◆ **à moins** *loc adv* : **j'étais terrifié – on le serait à ~!** I was terrified – and lesser things have frightened me!

◆ **à moins de** *loc prép* **1.** [excepté] : **à ~ d'un miracle** short of *ou* barring a miracle ▪ **nous n'arriverons pas à temps, à ~ de partir demain** we won't get there on time unless we leave tomorrow **2.** [pour moins de] for less than **3.** [dans le temps, l'espace] : **il habite à ~ de 10 minutes/500 mètres d'ici** he lives less than 10 minutes/500 metres from here.

◆ **à moins que** *loc conj* unless ▪ **à ~ que vous ne vouliez le faire vous-même...** unless you wanted to do it yourself...

◆ **au moins** *loc adv* **1.** [en tout cas] at least **2.** [au minimum] at least ▪ **ça fait au ~ un mois qu'on ne l'a pas vu** we haven't seen him for at least a month.

◆ **de moins** *loc adv* : **il y a 100 euros de ~ dans le tiroir** there are 100 euros missing from the drawer ▪ **je me sens 10 ans de ~** I feel 10 years younger ▪ *(en corrélation avec 'que')* **j'ai un an de ~ qu'elle** I'm a year younger than her ▪ **j'ai une tête de ~ qu'elle** I'm shorter than her by a head.

◆ **de moins en moins** *loc adv* less and less ▪ **de ~ en ~ souvent** less and less often.

◆ **de moins en moins de** *loc dét* [suivi d'un nom comptable] fewer and fewer ▪ [suivi d'un nom non comptable] less and less ▪ **il y a de ~ en ~ de demande pour ce produit** there is less and less demand for this product.

◆ **des moins** *loc adv* : **un accueil des ~ chaleureux** a less than warm welcome.

◆ **du moins** *loc adv* at least ▪ **ils devaient venir samedi, c'est du ~ ce qu'ils nous avaient dit** they were supposed to come on saturday, at least that's what they told us.

◆ **en moins** *loc adv* : **il y a une chaise en ~** there's one chair missing, we're one chair short.

◆ **en moins de** *loc prép* in less than ➔ **en ~ de temps qu'il n'en faut pour le dire** before you can say Jack Robinson ▪ **en ~ de rien** in no time at all ▪ **en ~ de deux** *fam* in a jiffy, in two ticks.

◆ **moins de** *loc dét* **1.** *(comparatif)* [avec un nom comptable] fewer ▪ [avec un nom non comptable] less ▪ **un peu ~ de bruit!** a little less noise! ▪ **il a ~ de 18 ans** he's under 18 ▪ **les ~ de 18 ans** the under 18's ▪ **il ne me faudra pas ~ de 3 heures pour tout faire** I'll need no less than *ou* at the very least 3 hours to do everything **2.** *(superlatif)* **le ~ de** [avec un nom comptable] the fewest ; [avec un nom non comptable] the least ▪ **c'est ce qui consomme le ~ d'énergie** it uses the least amount of energy.

◆ **moins... moins** *loc corrélative* the less... the less ▪ **~ il travaillera, ~ il aura de chances de réussir à son examen** the less he works, the less chance he'll have of passing his exam.

◆ **moins... plus** *loc corrélative* the less... the more.

◆ **moins que rien** ◇ *loc adv* next to nothing.
◇ *nmf* nobody ▪ **c'est un/une ~ que rien** he's/she's a nobody ▪ **des ~ que rien** a useless bunch (of individuals).

◆ **on ne peut moins** *loc adv* : **elle est on ne peut ~ honnête** she's as honest as they come ▪ **c'est on ne peut ~ compliqué!** it couldn't be less complicated!

◆ **pour le moins** *loc adv* at the very least, to say the least ▪ **il y a pour le ~ une heure d'attente** there's an hour's wait at the very least.

moins-disant [mwɛ̃dizɑ̃] *nm inv* [proposition] lowest bid *ou* tender ▪ [personne, société] lowest bidder *ou* tenderer.

moins-perçu [mwɛ̃pɛrsy] (*pl* **moins-perçus**) *nm* amount due.

moins-value [mwɛ̃valy] (*pl* **moins-values**) *nf* **1.** [dépréciation] depreciation, capital loss **2.** [déficit du fisc] (tax) deficit, shortfall.

moire [mwar] *nf* **1.** [tissu] moiré, watered fabric ▪ **~ de soie** watered *ou* shot silk **2.** *litt* [irisation] iridescence, irisation.

moiré, e [mware] *adj* **1.** TEXT moiré, watered **2.** [irisé] iridescent, irisated, moiré **3.** MENUIS moiré.
◆ **moiré** *nm* **1.** TEXT moiré, watered effect *ou* finish **2.** *litt* [irisation] iridescence, irisation.

moirer [3] [mware] *vt* **1.** [tissu] to moiré, to water **2.** [métal, papier] to moiré **3.** *litt* [iriser] to make iridescent, to irisate ▪ **un rayon de lune moirait la surface du lac** a ray of moonlight made the surface of the lake shimmer *ou* glimmer.

moirure [mwaryr] *nf litt* [irisation] iridescence, irisation.
◆ **moirures** *nfpl* TEXT moiré (effect), watered effect *ou* finish ▪ MÉTALL moiré (effect).

mois [mwa] *nm* **1.** [division du calendrier] month ▪ **le ~ de mai/décembre** the month of May/December ▪ **au début/à la fin du ~ d'avril** in early/late April ▪ **au milieu du ~ d'août** in mid-August *ou* the middle of August ▪ **le 15 de ce** *ou* **du ~** COMM the

15th inst *UK ou* instant *UK*, the 15th of this month ▶ **le ~ de Marie** RELIG the month of Mary *ou* May **2.** [durée] month ■ **tous les ~** every *ou* each month, monthly ■ **le comité se réunit tous les ~** the committee meets on a monthly basis ■ **dans un ~** in a month, in a month's time ■ **pendant mes ~ de grossesse/d'apprentissage** during the months when I was pregnant/serving my apprenticeship ■ **un ~ de préavis** a month's notice **3.** [salaire] monthly wage *ou* salary *ou* pay ■ [versement] monthly instalment ■ **je vous dois trois ~** [de salaire] I owe you three months' wages ; [de loyer] I owe you three months' rent ■ **toucher son ~** to get paid for the month ▶ **~ double, treizième ~** extra month's pay *(income bonus equal to an extra month's salary and paid annually).*

◆ **au mois** *loc adv* by the month, monthly, on a monthly basis ■ **les intérêts sont calculés au ~** interest is worked out on a monthly basis.

moïse [mɔiz] *nm* Moses basket.

Moïse [mɔiz] *npr* Moses.

moisi, e [mwazi] *adj* [papier, tissu] mildewy, mouldy ■ [fruit, pain] mouldy ■ [logement] mildewy, fusty.

◆ **moisi** *nm* [moisissure] mildew, mould ■ **ça sent le ~** *pr* it smells musty ■ *fam fig* I can smell trouble.

moisir [32] [mwazir] ◇ *vt* to make (go) mouldy.

◇ *vi* **1.** [pourrir] to go mouldy ■ **le pain a moisi** the bread's gone mouldy **2.** *fam* [s'éterniser] to rot ■ **je ne vais pas ~ ici jusqu'à la fin de mes jours!** I'm not going to stay and rot here forever! ■ **~ en prison** to rot in prison.

moisissure [mwazisyr] *nf* **1.** [champignon] mould, mildew ■ [tache] patch of mould **2.** *fig & litt* rottenness, rankness.

moisson [mwasɔ̃] *nf* **1.** AGRIC harvest ■ **faire la ~** to harvest (the crops) **2.** [grande quantité] **: une ~ de** an abundance *ou* a wealth of.

moissonner [3] [mwasɔne] *vt* **1.** AGRIC to harvest, to reap ■ **~ les blés** to harvest the corn **2.** *sout* [recueillir - informations, documents] to amass ■ [remporter - prix] to carry off **3.** *litt* [décimer] to decimate.

moissonneur, euse [mwasɔnœr, øz] *nm, f* harvester, reaper *litt.*

◆ **moissonneuse** *nf* **1.** [machine] harvester **2.** ENTOM harvesting ant.

moissonneuse-batteuse [mwasɔnøzbatøz] (*pl* **moissonneuses-batteuses**) *nf* combine (harvester).

moissonneuse-lieuse [mwasɔnøzljøz] (*pl* **moissonneuses-lieuses**) *nf* reaper, reaper-binder, self-binder.

moite [mwat] *adj* [air] muggy, clammy ■ [mains] sticky, sweaty ■ [front] damp, sweaty ■ **une journée ~ et oppressante** a muggy, stifling day.

moiteur [mwatœr] *nf* [sueur] stickiness, sweatiness ■ [humidité] dampness, moistness.

moitié [mwatje] *nf* **1.** [part] half ■ **une ~ de** *ou* **la ~ d'un poulet** half a chicken ■ **la ~ des élèves** half (of) the pupils ■ **quelle est la ~ de douze?** what's half of twelve? ■ **arrivé à la ~ du livre** halfway through the book ■ **nous ferons la ~ du trajet** *ou* **chemin ensemble** we'll do half the journey together ■ **partager qqch en deux ~s** to divide sthg in half *ou* into (two) halves, to halve sthg ■ *(comme modificateur)* half ■ **je suis ~ Français, ~ Canadien** I'm half French, half Canadian ■ **il mange ~ moins que moi** he eats half as much as me **2.** *fam hum* [épouse] **: sa/ma (tendre) ~** his/my better half.

◆ **à moitié** *loc adv* half ■ **je ne suis qu'à ~ surpris** I'm only half surprised ■ **faire les choses à ~** to do things by halves ■ **le travail n'est fait qu'à ~** only half the work's been done, the work's only half done ■ **vendre à ~ prix** to sell (at) half-price.

◆ **à moitié chemin** *loc adv* halfway.

◆ **de moitié** *loc adv* by half ■ **réduire qqch de ~** to reduce sthg by half, to halve sthg ■ **l'inflation a diminué de ~** inflation has been halved *ou* cut by half.

◆ **par la moitié** *loc adv* through *ou* down the middle.

◆ **par moitié** *loc adv* in two, in half.

◆ **pour moitié** *loc adv* partly ■ **tu es pour ~ dans son échec** you're half *ou* partly responsible for his failure.

moitié-moitié [mwatjemwatje] *adv* [à parts égales] half-and-half ■ **faire ~** [dans une affaire] to go halves *ou* fifty-fifty ; [au restaurant] to go halves, to split the bill.

moka [mɔka] *nm* **1.** [gâteau] mocha cake, coffee cream cake **2.** [café] mocha (coffee).

mol [mɔl] *m* ▷ **mou.**

molaire [mɔlɛr] ◇ *nf* [dent] molar.

◇ *adj* CHIM molar.

môlaire [molɛr] *adj* MÉD molar.

molasse [mɔlas] *nf* molasse.

moldave [mɔldav] *adj* Moldavian.

◆ **Moldave** *nmf* Moldavian.

Moldavie [mɔldavi] *npr f* **: (la) ~** Moldavia.

mole [mɔl] *nf* CHIM mole.

môle [mol] *nm* [jetée] mole, (stone) jetty *ou* breakwater.

moléculaire [mɔlekylɛr] *adj* molecular.

molécule [mɔlekyl] *nf* molecule.

moleskine [mɔlɛskin] *nf* **1.** TEXT moleskin **2.** [imitation cuir] imitation leather.

molester [3] [mɔlɛste] *vt* to maul, to manhandle, to molest ■ **la police a molesté les manifestants** the demonstrators were manhandled by the police.

molette [mɔlɛt] *nf* **1.** [pièce cylindrée] toothed wheel **2.** [dans un briquet] wheel **3.** [de verrier] cutting wheel.

Molière [mɔljɛr] *npr* Molière ■ **les ~s** *French theatre awards.*

mollah [mɔla] *nm* mullah, mollah.

mollard△ [mɔlar] *nm* gob, gob of spit.

mollasse [mɔlas] ◇ *adj* **1.** *fam* [apathique] wet *UK*, drippy, wimpish ■ **qu'il est ~!** he's such a drip! **2.** [flasque] flabby, flaccid, limp ■ **une poignée de main ~** a limp handshake.

◇ *nmf fam* wimp, drip.

mollasson, onne [mɔlasɔ̃, ɔn] *fam* ◇ *adj* wet *UK*, wimpy, soft.

◇ *nm, f* wimp.

molle [mɔl] *f* ▷ **mou.**

mollement [mɔlmɑ̃] *adv* **1.** [sans énergie] listlessly, limply ■ **il m'a serré ~ la main** he gave me a limp handshake ■ **~ allongé sur un divan** lying languidly *ou* limply on a sofa **2.** [sans conviction] feebly, weakly ■ **elle protesta ~** she protested feebly *ou* made a feeble protest.

mollesse [mɔlɛs] *nf* **1.** [d'une substance, d'un objet] softness ■ [des chairs] flabbiness ■ [d'une poignée de main] limpness **2.** [d'un relief] soft shape ■ [de contours] **: la ~ de ses traits** *péj* the flabbiness *ou* shapelessness of his features **3.** [apathie] feebleness, weakness ■ **c'est la ~ des parents/de l'opposition qui est en cause** parental laxness/the opposition's spinelessness is to blame.

mollet[1] [mɔlɛ] *nm* ANAT calf ■ **avoir des ~s de coq** *fam* to have legs like matchsticks *ou* spindly legs.

mollet[2]**, ette** [mɔlɛ, ɛt] *adj litt* [moelleux] soft.

molletière [mɔltjɛr] ◇ *nf* puttee.

◇ *adj f* ▷ **bande.**

molleton [mɔltɔ̃] *nm* [de coton] swansdown, swanskin, flannelette ■ [de laine] duffel, duffle ■ **~ de table** *felt underlay for a table.*

molletonné, e [mɔltɔne] *adj* [garni] covered with swansdown ■ [doublé] lined with swansdown.

molletonneux, euse [mɔltɔnø, øz] *adj* fleecy, fleece *(modif)* ■ **étoffe molletonneuse** napped cloth.

mollir [32] [mɔlir] ◇ *vi* **1.** [chanceler] **: j'ai senti mes jambes ~** I felt my legs give way (under me) **2.** [vent] to drop, to abate *sout* **3.** [volonté, résolution] **: sa détermination mollissait** her determination began to flag *ou* to wane.

◇ *vt* NAUT [cordage] to slacken ■ [barre] to ease.

mollo [mɔlo] *adv fam* easy ■ **vas-y ~ sur cette route!** take it easy on that road! ■ **~ avec le chocolat!** go easy on the chocolate!

mollusque [mɔlysk] *nm* **1.** ZOOL mollusc **2.** *fam* [personne] drip, wimp.

molosse [mɔlɔs] *nm* [chien] watchdog.

Molotov [mɔlɔtɔv] *npr* : **cocktail ~** Molotov cocktail.

Moluques [mɔlyk] *npr fpl* : **les ~** the Moluccas.

môme [mom] *fam* ◇ *nmf* [enfant] kid ■ **sale ~!** you little brat! ◇ *nf vieilli* [jeune femme] bird *UK*, chick *US*.

moment [mɔmɑ̃] *nm* **1.** [laps de temps] moment, while ■ **laisse-moi un ~ pour réfléchir** give me a moment *ou* minute to think it over ■ **il y a un (bon) ~ que j'attends** I've been waiting for (quite) a while ■ **pendant un bon ~** for quite some time, for quite a while ■ **j'en ai pour un petit ~** I'll be a (little) while **2.** [instant] moment, minute ■ **c'est l'affaire d'un ~** it'll only take a minute *ou* moment ■ **je n'en ai que pour un ~** I'll only be a moment ■ **dans un ~ de colère** in a moment of anger ■ **il eut un ~ d'hésitation** he hesitated for a moment ■ **un ~!** just a moment *ou* minute! ■ **attend un ~!** wait a minute!
3. [période] moment, time ■ **nous avons passé** *ou* **eu de bons ~s** we had some good times ■ **c'est un mauvais ~ à passer** it's just a bad patch *UK ou* a difficult spell ■ **les grands ~s de l'histoire** the great moments of history ■ **il l'a assistée jusqu'aux derniers ~s** he was by her side until the end ■ **elle a ses bons et ses mauvais ~s** she has her good days and her bad days ■ **à mes ~s perdus** in my spare time
4. [occasion] moment, opportunity ■ **à quel ~?** when? ■ **à quel ~ voulez-vous venir?** when *ou* (at) what time would you like to come? ■ **choisis un autre ~ pour lui parler** choose another time to speak to her ■ **c'est le ~ d'intervenir** now's the time to speak up ■ **c'est bien le ~!** *iron* what a time to pick! ■ **c'est le ~ ou jamais** it's now or never ■ **c'est le ~ ou jamais de lui demander** now's the time to ask him ■ **le ~ venu** when the time comes ■ **arriver au bon ~** to come at the right time ■ **il arrive toujours au bon ~, celui-là!** *iron* he really picks his moments! ■ **au mauvais ~** at the wrong time ■ **le ~ crucial du film/match** the crucial moment in the film/match
5. PHYS momentum.

◆ **à aucun moment** *loc adv* at no time ■ **à aucun ~ il ne s'est plaint** at no time *ou* point did he complain.

◆ **à ce moment-là** *loc adv* **1.** [dans le temps] at that time, then
2. [dans ce cas] in that case, if that's so ■ **à ce ~-là, tu aurais dû me le dire!** in that case *ou* if that was the case, you should have told me!

◆ **à tout moment** *loc adv* **1.** [n'importe quand] (at) any time *ou* moment ■ **il peut téléphoner à tout ~** we can expect a call from him any time *ou* moment now, he could call at any moment
2. [sans cesse] constantly, all the time ■ **elle s'interrompait à tout ~** she kept stopping, she was constantly stopping.

◆ **au moment de** *loc prép* : **au ~ de mon divorce** when I was getting divorced, at the time of my divorce ■ **il me l'a dit au ~ de mourir** he told me as he died.

◆ **au moment où** *loc conj* as, when ■ **juste au ~ où le téléphone a sonné** just when *ou* as the phone rang.

◆ **à un moment donné** *loc adv* at a certain point ■ **à un ~ donné, il a refusé** at one point he refused.

◆ **dès le moment où** *loc conj* **1.** [dans le temps] from the time *ou* moment that, as soon as
2. [dans un raisonnement] as soon as, once.

◆ **du moment** *loc adj* : **l'homme du ~** the man of the moment ■ **le succès/l'idole du ~** the current hit/idol ■ **un des sujets du ~** one of the issues of the day.

◆ **du moment que** *loc conj* [puisque] since ■ **du ~ que je te le dis!** *fam* you can take my word for it!

◆ **d'un moment à l'autre** *loc adv* [très prochainement] any moment *ou* minute *ou* time now ■ **il peut téléphoner d'un ~ à l'autre** he may phone any minute now.

◆ **en ce moment** *loc adv* at the moment, just now.

◆ **en un moment** *loc adv* in a moment.

◆ **par moments** *loc adv* at times, every now and then, every so often.

◆ **pour le moment** *loc adv* for the moment, for the time being.

◆ **sur le moment** *loc adv* at the time ■ **sur le ~, ça n'a pas fait mal** it didn't hurt at the time.

momentané, e [mɔmɑ̃tane] *adj* momentary, brief ■ **il y aura des pannes d'électricité ~es** there will be temporary *ou* brief power cuts ■ **sa passion n'a été que ~e** her passion was only short-lived.

momentanément [mɔmɑ̃tanemɑ̃] *adv* **1.** [en ce moment] for the time being, for the moment ■ **il est ~ absent** he's temporarily absent, he's absent for the moment **2.** [provisoirement] momentarily, for a short while ■ **les émissions sont ~ interrompues** we will be temporarily off the air.

momie [mɔmi] *nf* ARCHÉOL mummy.

momification [mɔmifikasjɔ̃] *nf* mummification.

momifier [9] [mɔmifje] *vt* to mummify.

mon [mɔ̃] *(devant nf ou adj f commençant par voyelle ou h muet* [mɔn]*)* *(f* **ma** [ma], *pl* **mes** [me]*)* *dét (adj poss)* **1.** [indiquant la possession] my ■ **~ père et ma mère** my father and mother ■ **mes frères et soeurs** my brothers and sisters ■ **un de mes amis** a friend of mine, one of my friends **2.** [dans des appellatifs] : **~ cher Pierre** my dear Pierre ■ **~ capitaine** Captain ■ **mes enfants, au travail!** time to work, children! ■ **alors là, ma grande, c'est ton problème!** *fam* well that, my dear, is your problem! ■ **mais ~ pauvre vieux, vous n'y arriverez jamais!** *fam* look, mate, you'll never manage it! **3.** [emploi expressif] : **j'ai ~ vendredi** *fam* I've got Friday off ■ **~ bonhomme n'était pas du tout content!** I don't mind telling you (that) the bloke wasn't at all pleased! ■ **ah ben ~ salaud**△ **!** *ou* **cochon**△ **!** lucky bastard!

monacal, e, aux [mɔnakal, o] *adj* monastic, monachal *sout*.

Monaco [mɔnako] *npr* : **(la principauté de) ~** (the principality of) Monaco.

monade [mɔnad] *nf* monad.

monarchie [mɔnarʃi] *nf* monarchy ■ **la ~ absolue/constitutionnelle/parlementaire** absolute/constitutional/parliamentary monarchy ■ **la ~ de droit divin** monarchy by divine right ■ **la monarchie de Juillet** the July Monarchy.

monarchique [mɔnarʃik] *adj* monarchic, monarchical.

monarchisme [mɔnarʃism] *nm* monarchism.

monarchiste [mɔnarʃist] ◇ *adj* monarchist, monarchistic.
◇ *nmf* monarchist.

monarque [mɔnark] *nm* monarch.

monastère [mɔnastɛr] *nm* monastery.

monastique [mɔnastik] *adj* monastic.

monceau, x [mɔ̃so] *nm* [amas] heap, pile ■ **des ~x d'erreurs** *fig* masses of mistakes.

mondain, e [mɔ̃dɛ̃, ɛn] ◇ *adj* **1.** [de la haute société] society *(modif)* ■ **avoir des relations ~es** to have friends in society *ou* high circles ■ **il mène une vie très ~e** he moves in society circles ➔ **carnet ~, rubrique ~e** society *ou* gossip column ■ **soirée ~e** society *ou* high-society evening **2.** [qui aime les mondanités] : **elle est très ~e** she likes moving in fashionable circles *ou* society, she's a great socialite **3.** RELIG worldly ■ PHILOS mundane **4.** DR : **brigade ~e** vice squad.
◇ *nm, f* socialite, society person.

◆ **mondaine** *nf fam* vice squad.

mondanité [mɔ̃danite] *nf* [style] society life.

◆ **mondanités** *nfpl* [réunions] fashionable gatherings ■ [politesses] social chitchat, polite conversation ■ **il aime les ~s** he likes society life.

monde [mɔ̃d] *nm* **1.** [univers] world ■ **dans le ~ entier** all over the world ■ **il est connu dans le ~ entier** he's known worldwide *ou* the world over ■ **venir au ~** to come into the world ■ **mettre un enfant au ~** to bring a child into the world ■ **il n'est plus de ce ~** he's no longer with us, he's gone to the next world ■ **en ce bas ~** here on earth, here below ■ **elle s'est créé un petit ~ à elle** she's created her own little world for herself ➔ **le ~**

est petit! it's a small world! ■ **depuis que le ~ est ~** since the beginning of time, since the world began ■ **c'est le ~ renversé** *ou* **à l'envers!** what's the world coming to?

2. [humanité] world ■ **le ~ entier attend cet événement** the whole world is awaiting this event ■ **tout le ~** everybody, everyone ■ **tout le ~ sait cela** everybody *ou* the whole world knows that ■ **tout le ~ ne peut pas le faire!** not everybody can do that! ▶ **il faut de tout pour faire un ~** it takes all sorts (to make a world)

3. [pour intensifier] : **le plus célèbre au** *ou* **du ~** the most famous in the world ■ **c'est la femme la plus charmante du ~** she's the most charming woman you could wish to meet ■ **le plus simplement/gentiment du ~** in the simplest/kindest possible way ■ **c'est ce que j'aime/je veux le plus au ~** it's what I love/want most in the world ■ **je vous dérange? – pas le moins du ~!** am I interrupting? – not in the least! ■ **ils s'entendent le mieux du ~** they get on famously ■ **tout s'est déroulé le mieux du ~** everything went off very smoothly ■ **rien au ~ ne pourrait me faire partir** nothing in the world would make me leave ■ **pour rien au ~** not for anything, not for the world ■ **nul** *ou* **personne au ~** nobody in the world ■ **on m'a dit tout le bien du ~ de ce nouveau shampooing** I've been told the most wonderful things about this new shampoo

4. [communauté] world ■ **le ~ des affaires** the business world ■ **le ~ de la finance** the world of finance, the financial world ■ **le ~ du spectacle** (the world of) show business ■ **le ~ capitaliste/communiste** the capitalist/communist world ■ **le ~ libre** the Free World ■ **le ~ animal/végétal** the animal/plant world

5. [gens] people *(pl)* ■ **il y a du ~?** [en entrant chez quelqu'un] is there anybody home *ou* there? ■ **il y a un ~ fou, c'est noir de ~** the place is swarming *ou* alive with people ■ **il n'y avait pas grand ~ au spectacle** there weren't many people at the show ■ **tu attends du ~?** are you expecting people *ou* company? ■ **il ne voit plus beaucoup de ~** he doesn't socialize very much any more ■ **j'ai du ~ à dîner** *fam* I've got people coming for dinner ■ **ne t'en fais pas, je connais mon ~!** don't worry, I know who I'm dealing with! ■ **grand-mère aime bien avoir tout son petit ~ autour d'elle** grandmother likes to have all her family *ou* brood *hum* around her ■ **c'est qu'il faut s'en occuper de tout ce petit ~!** [enfants] all that little lot takes some looking after! ▶ **il y a du ~ au balcon!** *fam hum* she's well-endowed! ■ **tu te moques** *ou* **fiches** *fam* *ou* **fous** *fam* **du ~!** you've got a nerve *ou* a bloody nerve!

6. [société] world ■ **se retirer du ~** to withdraw from society ■ **les plaisirs du ~** worldly pleasures ■ **le ~** RELIG the world ▮ [groupe social] circle, set ■ **ils ne sont pas du même ~** they don't move in the same circles ▮ [classes élevées] : **le (beau)** *ou* **grand ~** high society ■ **aller dans le ~** to mix in society ■ **fréquenter le beau** *ou* **grand ~** to mix with high society *ou* in society ▶ **femme du ~** socialite ■ **homme du ~** man-about-town ■ **gens du ~** socialites, society people

7. [domaine] world, realm ■ **le ~ de l'imaginaire** the realm of imagination ■ **le ~ du silence** *litt* the silent world (under the sea)

8. PRESSE : **Le Monde** *French daily newspaper*

9. *loc* **c'est un ~!** *fam* that beats everything!, well I never! ■ **pourquoi ne ranges-tu jamais tes affaires, c'est un ~ tout de même!** *fam* why in the world *ou* why oh why don't you ever put your things away? ■ **se faire (tout) un ~ de qqch** to get worked up about sthg ■ **ne te fais pas un ~ d'un rien** don't make a mountain out of a molehill.

monder [3] [mɔ̃de] *vt* **1.** [noisettes] to hull ■ [amandes] to blanch **2.** [arbres] to prune, to crop.

mondial, e, aux [mɔ̃djal, o] *adj* world *(modif)*, global ■ **production ~e de blé** world wheat production ■ **crise à l'échelle ~e** worldwide crisis, crisis on a world scale.

mondialement [mɔ̃djalmɑ̃] *adv* throughout *ou* all over the world ■ **~ renommé** famous all over the world, world-famous.

mondialisation [mɔ̃djalizasjɔ̃] *nf* globalization ■ **on assiste à la ~ de la reprise économique** a worldwide economic revival is taking place.

mondialiser [3] [mɔ̃djalize] *vt* to make worldwide in scope, to globalize.

◆ **se mondialiser** *vpi* to spread throughout the world ■ **la crise s'est rapidement mondialisée** the crisis has rapidly taken on an international dimension.

mondialiste [mɔ̃djalist] *adj* pro-globalization.

mondovision [mɔ̃dɔvizjɔ̃] *nf* worldwide satellite broadcasting ■ **en ~** broadcast all over the world by satellite.

monégasque [mɔnegask] *adj* Monegasque, Monacan.
◆ **Monégasque** *nmf* Monegasque, Monacan.

Moneo *nm french payment card.*

MONEO

Moneo is a payment card which is used like an electronic purse for small purchases under 30 euros. The electronic purse can be filled at a special terminal called *borne de rechargement* in post-offices and other public places. It can be used in shops that display the *Moneo* logo. When paying for your newspaper or your baguette, all you have to do is validate the amount that will be debited from your purse.

monétaire [mɔnetɛr] *adj* monetary ■ **marché/masse ~** money market/supply ■ **politique/système/unité ~** monetary policy/system/unit.

monétarisme [mɔnetarism] *nm* monetarism.

monétariste [mɔnetarist] *adj* & *nmf* monetarist.

Monétique® [mɔnetik] *nf* electronic banking (services).

monétiser [3] [mɔnetize] *vt* to monetize.

mongol, e [mɔ̃gɔl] *adj* Mongol, Mongolian.
◆ **Mongol, e** *nm, f* Mongol, Mongolian.

Mongolie [mɔ̃gɔli] *npr f* : **(la) ~** Mongolia.

mongolien, enne [mɔ̃gɔljɛ̃, ɛn] ◇ *adj* *vieilli* mongol *péj* & *vieilli*.
◇ *nm, f* *vieilli* mongol *péj* & *vieilli*.

mongolisme [mɔ̃gɔlism] *nm* *vieilli* mongolism.

moniteur, trice [mɔnitœr, tris] *nm, f* SPORT instructor (*f* instructress) ■ [de colonie de vacances] (group) supervisor *ou* leader, (camp) counsellor *US* ■ **~ d'auto-école** driving instructor.
◆ **moniteur** *nm* **1.** INFORM [écran] display unit ■ [dispositif matériel ou logiciel] monitor ■ **~ couleur** RGB *ou* colour monitor **2.** MÉD monitor.

monitorage [mɔnitɔraʒ] *nm* = **monitoring**.

monitorat [mɔnitɔra] *nm* [enseignement] instruction ■ [de colonie de vacances] group leading, camp counselling *US*.

monitoring [mɔnitɔriŋ] *nm* monitoring ■ **elle est sous ~** she's been placed on a monitor.

monnaie [mɔnɛ] ◇ *v* ▷ **monnayer**.
◇ *nf* **1.** ÉCON & FIN currency, money ■ **~ d'argent/de nickel/d'or** silver/nickel/gold coin ■ **les ~s étrangères** foreign currencies ■ **la ~ allemande** [gén] the German currency ; BOURSE the German mark ■ **le yen est la ~ du Japon** the yen is Japan's (unit of) currency *ou* monetary unit ▶ **~ décimale** decimal currency *ou* coinage ■ **~ d'échange** *fig* bargaining counter ■ **~ électronique** electronic *ou* plastic money ■ **~ flottante** floating currency ■ **~ légale** legal tender ■ **~ métallique** coin *(U)* ■ **~ de papier** paper money ■ **~ unique** single currency ■ **~ verte** green currency ■ **fausse ~** counterfeit *ou* false money ■ **c'est ~ courante** it's common practice, it's a common *ou* an everyday occurrence ■ **payer qqn en ~ de singe** to fob sb off **2.** [appoint] change ■ **faire de la ~** to get (some) change ■ **faire de la ~ à qqn** to give sb some change ■ **faire la ~ de 20 euros** to get change for 20 euros, to change a 20 euro note ■ **rendre la ~ à qqn** to give sb change ■ **il m'a rendu la ~ sur 10 euros** he gave me the change out of *ou* from 10 euros ▶ **~ d'appoint** right *ou* exact change ■ **menue/petite ~** small/loose change ■ **et par ici la ~!** *fam* let's be having your money! ■ **allez, envoyez la ~!** *fam* come on, get the pennies out *ou* cough up! ■ **je lui rendrai la ~ de sa pièce!** I'll give him a taste of his own medicine!

monnaie-du-pape [mɔnɛdypap] (*pl* **monnaies-du-pape**) *nf* HORT honesty.

monnayable [mɔnɛjabl] *adj* saleable ▪ **ton expérience est ~** you could make money out of your experience.

monnayer [11] [mɔnɛje] *vt* **1.** [convertir en monnaie] to mint **2.** [vendre] to sell, to make money out of ▪ **~ son expérience/savoir-faire** to cash in on one's experience/know-how **3.** [échanger] to exchange ▪ **il a monnayé ses services contre une lettre d'introduction** he asked for a letter of introduction in exchange for his services.
◆ **se monnayer** *vp (emploi passif)* : **tu devrais savoir que le talent se monnaye** you ought to know there's money to be made out of talent.

monnayeur [mɔnɛjœr] *nm* [pour faire la monnaie] change machine ▪ [pour payer] coin box.

mono [mɔno] ◇ *nf inv (abr de* **monophonie***)* mono.
◇ *nmf fam* **1.** SPORT *(abr de* **moniteur***)* instructor *(f* instructress) **2.** [de colonie de vacances] *(abr de* **moniteur***)* (group) supervisor *ou* leader, (camp) counsellor *US*.
◇ *nm (abr de* **monoski***)* monoski.

mono- [mɔno] *préf* mono-, single.

monobloc [mɔnɔblɔk] *adj* [fusil] cast en bloc, solid ▪ [cylindre, moteur, roue] monobloc.

monocamérisme [mɔnɔkamerism] *nm* unicameralism.

monochrome [mɔnɔkrom] *adj* monochrome, monochromic.

monochromie [mɔnɔkrɔmi] *nf* monochromaticity.

monocle [mɔnɔkl] *nm* (single) eyeglass, monocle.

monocoque [mɔnɔkɔk] ◇ *adj* AÉRON monocoque.
◇ *nm* NAUT monohull.
◇ *nf* AUTO monocoque.

monocorde [mɔnɔkɔrd] ◇ *adj* monotonous, droning.
◇ *nm* monochord.

monocotylédone [mɔnɔkɔtiledɔn] *nf* monocotyl, monocotyledon, monocot ▪ **les ~s** the Monocotyledoneae.

monocratie [mɔnɔkrasi] *nf* monocracy.

monoculture [mɔnɔkyltyr] *nf* monoculture ▪ **une région de ~** a monoculture area.

monocyclique [mɔnɔsiklik] *adj* CHIM & ZOOL monocyclic.

monocyte [mɔnɔsit] *nm* monocyte ▪ **angine à ~s** glandular fever.

monoentreprise [mɔnɔɑ̃trapriz] *nf* one-man, one-woman *f* business, sole trader.

monogame [mɔnɔgam] *adj* monogamous.

monogamie [mɔnɔgami] *nf* monogamy.

monogramme [mɔnɔgram] *nm* monogram.

monographie [mɔnɔgrafi] *nf* monograph.

monoï [mɔnɔj] *nm inv* Monoi.

monokini [mɔnɔkini] *nm* monokini, topless swimsuit ▪ **'~ interdit'** 'no topless bathing'.

monolingue [mɔnɔlɛ̃g] ◇ *adj* monolingual.
◇ *nmf* monolingual ▪ **les ~s** people who speak only one language, monolinguals.

monolinguisme [mɔnɔlɛ̃gɥism] *nm* monolingualism.

monolithe [mɔnɔlit] ◇ *adj* monolithic.
◇ *nm* monolith.

monolithique [mɔnɔlitik] *adj* GÉOL & *fig* monolithic.

monologue [mɔnɔlɔg] *nm* **1.** [discours] monologue ▪ THÉÂTRE monologue, soliloquy ▪ **il s'est lancé dans un long ~ sur le respect d'autrui** he launched into a long monologue on the need to respect others **2.** LITTÉR : **~ intérieur** stream of consciousness, interior monologue.

monologuer [3] [mɔnɔlɔge] *vi* to soliloquize ▪ **il monologue des heures durant** [en public] he can go on (talking) for hours ; [tout seul] he talks to himself for hours.

monôme [mɔnom] *nm* **1.** MATH monomial **2.** *arg scol* ≃ students' rag procession.

mononucléose [mɔnɔnykleoz] *nf* mononucleosis ▪ **~ infectieuse** glandular fever, infectious mononucleosis *spéc*.

monoparental, e, aux [mɔnɔparɑ̃tal, o] *adj* single-parent.

monoparentalité [mɔnɔparɑ̃talite] *nf* single *ou* lone parenthood.

monophasé, e [mɔnɔfaze] *adj* single-phase, monophase.

monophonique [mɔnɔfɔnik] *adj* MUS monophonic ▪ AUDIO monophonic, monaural.

monoplace [mɔnɔplas] ◇ *adj* one-seater *(avant n)*, single-seater *(avant n)*.
◇ *nm* one-seater *ou* single-seater (vehicle).
◇ *nf* single-seater racing car.

monoplan [mɔnɔplɑ̃] *nm* monoplane.

monoplégie [mɔnɔpleʒi] *nf* monoplegia.

monopole [mɔnɔpɔl] *nm* **1.** ÉCON monopoly ▪ **~ d'achat** buyer's monopoly ▪ **~ d'embauche** closed shop ▪ **~ d'État** state monopoly **2.** *fig* monopoly ▪ **vous pensez avoir le ~ de la vérité?** do you think you have a monopoly of the truth?

monopolisation [mɔnɔpɔlizasjɔ̃] *nf* monopolization.

monopoliser [3] [mɔnɔpɔlize] *vt* ÉCON & *fig* to monopolize ▪ **ne monopolisez pas notre jeune amie** don't keep our young friend to yourself.

Monopoly® [mɔnɔpɔli] *nm* Monopoly®.

monoposte [mɔnɔpɔst] *adj* INFORM single-computer.

monoprocesseur [mɔnɔprɔsesœr] ◇ *adj* INFORM single-unit *(avant n)*.
◇ *nm* single (central processing) unit.

monoprogrammation [mɔnɔprɔgramasjɔ̃] *nf* monoprogramming.

monorail [mɔnɔraj] *adj* & *nm* monorail.

monosémique [mɔnɔsemik] *adj* LING monosemous, monosemic.

monoski [mɔnɔski] *nm* monoski.

monosyllabique [mɔnɔsilabik] *adj* monosyllabic.

monothéisme [mɔnɔteism] *nm* monotheism.

monothéiste [mɔnɔteist] ◇ *adj* monotheistic, monotheistical.
◇ *nmf* monotheist.

monotone [mɔnɔtɔn] *adj* **1.** [voix, bruit] monotonous ▪ **le tic-tac ~ de la pendule** the monotonous ticking of the clock **2.** [discours, style] monotonous, dull **3.** [vie] monotonous, dreary, humdrum ▪ [paysage] monotonous, dreary.

monotonie [mɔnɔtɔni] *nf* monotony, dullness, dreariness.

monotype [mɔnɔtip] *nm* **1.** NAUT : **course de ~s** race between boats of the same class **2.** ART monotype.

monoxyde [mɔnɔksid] *nm* CHIM monoxide ▪ **~ de carbone** carbon monoxide.

Monseigneur [mɔ̃sɛɲœr] *(pl* **Messeigneurs** [mesɛɲœr]*) nm* **1.** [en s'adressant à un - archevêque] Your Grace ; [- évêque] My Lord (Bishop) ; [- cardinal] Your Eminence ; [- prince] Your Royal Highness ▪ [en parlant d'un - archevêque] His Grace ; [- évêque] His Lordship ; [- cardinal] His Eminence (Cardinal) ; [- prince] His Royal Highness **2.** HIST Monseigneur *(the heir to the throne of France)*.

monsieur [məsjø] *(pl* **messieurs** [mesjø]*) nm* man, gentleman ▪ **il se prend pour un ~** *péj* he thinks he's a gentleman ▪ **c'est un vilain ~** he's a wicked man.

Monsieur [məsjø] *(pl* **Messieurs** [mesjø]*) nm* **1.** [dans une lettre] : **~** Sir *sout*, Dear Sir ▪ **Cher ~ Duval** Dear Mr. Duval ▪ **Mes-**

sieurs Dear Sirs ■ **~ le Maire** Dear Sir ■ **~ le Vicomte** My Lord ‖ [sur l'enveloppe] : **~ Duval** Mr. Duval ■ **Messieurs Thon et Lamiel** Messrs Thon and Lamiel

2. [terme d'adresse - suivi du nom ou du titre] : **bonjour ~ Leroy!** good morning Mr. Leroy! ■ **bonjour Messieurs Duval!** good morning, gentlemen! ■ **bonjour ~ le Ministre!** good morning Sir! ■ **~ le Président, et l'inflation?** [au chef de l'État] Sir *ou* Mr. President *US*, what about inflation? ; [au directeur] Sir *ou* Mr. Chairman, what about inflation? ■ **Messieurs les députés, vous êtes priés de vous asseoir!** will the Honourable Members please be seated! *UK* ■ [à un inconnu] : **bonjour ~!** good morning! ■ **bonjour Messieurs** good morning(, gentlemen) ■ **bonjour Messieurs Dames** *fam* morning all *ou* everybody ■ **Mesdames, Mesdemoiselles, Messieurs!** Ladies and Gentlemen! ■ **Messieurs, un peu de silence s'il vous plaît!** [à des garçonnets] boys, please be quiet! ; [à des jeunes gens] gentlemen, would you please be quiet! ■ **~ désirerait voir les pantalons?** would you like to see the trousers, Sir? ‖ *sout* & *hum* **~ est servi** [au dîner] dinner is served(, Sir) ; [pour le thé] tea is served(, Sir) ■ **le frère de ~ attend en bas** [à un roturier] your brother is waiting downstairs, Sir ; [à un homme titré] Your Lordship's brother is waiting downstairs ■ **vous n'y pensez pas, cher** *ou* **mon bon** *ou* **mon pauvre ~!** my dear Sir, you can't be serious! ■ **peux-tu prêter un instant ton stylo à ~?** could you lend the gentleman your pen for a minute? ‖ [au téléphone] : **bonjour ~, je voudrais parler à quelqu'un de la comptabilité, s'il vous plaît** the President regrets he is unable to come [directeur] the Chairman *ou* Mr. X regrets he is unable to come

3. ÉDUC : **~, j'ai fini mon addition!** (please) Sir, I've done my addition!

4. *fam* [en appellatif] : **alors, ~ le frimeur, tu es satisfait?** so, are you pleased with yourself, Mr big shot? ■ **et en plus, ~ exige des excuses!** His Lordship wants an apology as well, does he?

5. HIST Monsieur *(title given to the King of France's younger brother)*

6. *loc* **il a été nommé ~ sécurité routière** he was made Mr. Road Safety ■ **~ Tout le Monde** the man in the street, Joe Public *UK hum*, Joe Blow *US*.

monstre [mɔ̃str] ◇ *nm* **1.** BIOL, MYTHOL & ZOOL monster ■ **le ~ du Loch Ness** the Loch Ness Monster ▶ **~ sacré** superstar **2.** [chose énorme] monster ■ **son camion est un vrai ~!** his lorry is an absolute monster! **3.** [personne laide] monster, monstrously ugly *ou* hideous person ■ [brute] monster, brute ■ **un ~ d'ingratitude/d'égoïsme** an ungrateful/a selfish brute **4.** *fam* [enfant insupportable] monster, little terror, perisher *UK* ■ **sortez d'ici, petits ~s!** out of here, you little monsters!

◇ *adj fam* [erreur, difficulté, déficit] monstrous, enormous, colossal ■ [rassemblement] monstrous, mammoth ■ [répercussions, succès, effet] tremendous, enormous ■ [soldes] gigantic, huge, colossal ■ **ça a eu un effet ~ sur le public** it had an enormous *ou* a tremendous effect on the audience ■ **il y a une queue ~ chez le boucher** there's a huge *ou* massive queue at the butcher's ■ **j'ai un boulot ~!** I've got loads *ou* tons *ou* piles of work to do! ■ **il a un culot ~** he's got a bloody cheek *UK ou* a damned nerve.

monstrueusement [mɔ̃stryøzmɑ̃] *adv* [laid] monstrously, hideously ■ [intelligent] prodigiously, stupendously.

monstrueux, euse [mɔ̃stryø, øz] *adj* **1.** [difforme] monstrous, deformed ■ **un être ~, une créature monstrueuse** a freak **2.** [laid] monstrous, hideous, ghastly **3.** [abject, cruel] monstrous, wicked, vile ■ **un crime ~** a heinous *ou* monstrous crime **4.** [très grave] monstrous, dreadful, ghastly ■ **une monstrueuse erreur** an awful *ou* a dreadful mistake.

monstruosité [mɔ̃stryozite] *nf* **1.** [difformité] deformity **2.** [acte, crime] monstrosity ■ **commettre/dire des ~s** to do/to say the most terrible things.

mont [mɔ̃] *nm* **1.** GÉOGR mountain ■ *litt* mount ■ **~ sous-marin** seamount ■ **aller par ~s et par vaux** to wander up hill and down dale ■ **il est toujours par ~s et par vaux** he's always on the move **2.** [de la main] mount **3.** ANAT : **le ~ de Vénus** mons veneris.

MONT

les monts Appalaches the Appalachian Mountains ;
le mont Ararat Mount Ararat ;
le mont Athos Mount Athos ;
le mont Aventin the Aventine Hill ;
le mont Blanc Mont Blanc ;
les monts Cantabriques the Cantabrian Mountains ;
le mont Capitolin the Capitoline Hill ;
le mont Cassin Monte Cassino ;
le mont Cervin the Matterhorn ;
le mont Etna Mount Etna ;
le mont Everest Mount Everest ;
le mont Fuji-Yama Mount Fuji ;
le mont des Oliviers the Mount of Olives ;
le mont Olympe Mount Olympus ;
le mont Palatin the Palatine Hill ;
le mont Parnasse Mount Parnassus ;
le mont Quirinal Quirinal ;
le mont Vésuve Mount Vesuvius ;
le mont Whitney Mount Whitney.

montage [mɔ̃taʒ] *nm* **1.** [assemblage - d'un meuble, d'un kit] assembly, assemblage ; [- d'une tente] pitching, putting up ; [- d'un vêtement] assembling, sewing together ; [- d'un col] setting in ■ IMPR (page) makeup, pasting up **2.** [installation - d'un appareil] installing, fixing ; [- d'une pierre précieuse] mounting, setting ; [- de pneus] fitting **3.** FIN : **~ de crédit** credit *ou* loan arrangement ■ **~ financier** financial arrangement **4.** AUDIO & CINÉ [processus] editing ■ [avec effets spéciaux] montage ■ [résultat] montage ■ **~ réalisé par X** [d'un film] film editing by X ; [du son] sound editing by X ▶ **~ audiovisuel** *ou* **sonorisé** sound slide show ■ **~ à la prise de vues** direct camera editing ■ **premier ~** rough cut **5.** PHOTO mounting ■ **faire du ~ de diapositives** to mount slides ▶ **~ de photos** photomontage **6.** ÉLECTR & ÉLECTRON wiring, connecting, connection ■ **~ en parallèle/série** connection in parallel/in series ■ **~ symétrique** push-pull circuit **7.** MIN overhand (stope).

montagnard, e [mɔ̃taɲar, ard] ◇ *adj* mountain *(modif)*, highland *(modif)*.
◇ *nm, f* mountain dweller ■ **les ~s** mountain people.
◆ **Montagnard** *nm* HIST : **les Montagnards** the Montagnards, the members of the Mountain.

montagne [mɔ̃taɲ] *nf* **1.** [mont] mountain ■ **les ~s d'Écosse** the Highlands of Scotland ■ **les ~s d'Europe** the European (mountain) ranges ▶ **~s russes** LOISIRS big dipper *UK*, roller coaster *US* ■ **moi, en ce moment, c'est les ~s russes** [moral, santé] I'm a bit up and down at the moment ■ **les Montagnes Rocheuses** the Rocky Mountains, the Rockies ■ **déplacer** *ou* **soulever des ~s** to move heaven and earth ■ **(se) faire une ~ de qqch** to make a great song and dance about sthg ■ **(se) faire une ~ de rien** *ou* **d'un rien** to make a mountain out of a molehill ■ **gros comme une ~** [mensonge] huge, colossal ; [canular] mammoth *(modif)* ■ **il n'y a que les ~s qui ne se rencontrent pas** *prov* there are none so distant that fate cannot bring together ■ **si la ~ ne va pas à Mahomet, Mahomet ira à la ~** *prov* if the mountain will not come to Mohammed, Mohammed must go to the mountain **2.** [région] : **la ~** the mountains ; [en Écosse] the highlands ■ **de ~** mountain *(modif)* ■ **faire de la ~** to go mountaineering ■ **de basse ~** low-mountain *(modif)* ■ **de haute ~** high-mountain *(modif)* ■ **en basse ~** in the foothills ■ **en haute ~** high in the mountains ▶ **ce n'est que de la ~ à vaches** it's only hills **3.** [grosse quantité] : **une ~ de** lots *ou* mountains *ou* a mountain of **4.** HIST : **la Montagne** the Mountain.

montagneux, euse [mɔ̃taɲø, øz] *adj* mountainous.

montant, e [mɔ̃tɑ̃, ɑ̃t] *adj* **1.** [qui grimpe - sentier] rising, uphill ■ **la génération ~e** the rising generation **2.** NAUT upstream *(modif)* ■ TRANSP up *(avant n)* **3.** [vêtement - col] high ; [- corsage] high-necked, high-neckline *(modif)* ■ **chaussures ~es** ankle boots, ankle-high shoes.
◆ **montant** *nm* **1.** [d'une échelle, d'un châssis] upright ■ [d'une tente] pole ■ [d'une porte, d'une fenêtre] stile ■ [d'un lit] post ■ **~ (de but)** SPORT (goal) post **2.** FIN amount, sum, total ■ **le ~ du découvert** the amount of the overdraft, the total overdraft ■ **chèque/facture d'un ~ de 500 euros** cheque/invoice for 500 euros ■ **le ~ total des réparations s'élève à..., les réparations s'élèvent à un ~ total de...** the total cost of the repairs adds up

to... ➋ **~s compensatoires (monétaires)** [dans l'Union européenne] (compensatory) subsidies, (monetary) compensatory amounts *spéc* ■ **'~ à régler'** 'amount due'.

mont-blanc [mɔ̃blɑ̃] (*pl* **monts-blancs**) *nm chestnut cream dessert.*

mont-de-piété [mɔ̃dpjete] (*pl* **monts-de-piété**) *nm* (state-owned) pawnshop ■ **mettre qqch au ~** to pawn sthg ■ **retirer** *ou* **dégager qqch du ~** to recover sthg from the pawnshop.

monte [mɔ̃t] *nf* **1.** ÉQUIT [technique] horsemanship ■ [participation à une course] mounting ■ **partants et ~s probables** probable runners and riders **2.** VÉTÉR covering ■ **mener une jument à la ~** to take a mare to be covered.

monté, e [mɔ̃te] *adj* **1.** [pourvu] provided, equipped ■ **être bien** *ou* **mal ~** to be well/badly equipped ■ **elle est bien ~e en vaisselle** she's got a lot of crockery ■ **tu es bien ~e avec un pareil mari!** *fam iron* you've married a right *UK ou* good one there! **2.** MIL mounted ■ **troupes ~es** mounted troops **3.** *fam* [irrité] : **être ~ contre qqn** to be angry with sb, to be dead set against sb **4.** [plante] seeded, gone to seed, bolted **5.** CULIN : **oeufs ~s en neige** whipped egg whites.

➡ **montée** *nf* **1.** [pente] climb, uphill *ou* upward slope ■ **méfiez-vous, la ~e est raide!** watch out, it's quite a steep climb! **2.** [ascension] climb ■ **la ~e jusqu'au chalet** the climb up *ou* the ascent *sout* to the chalet ■ **la ~e des escaliers lui fut très pénible** he climbed *ou* struggled up the stairs with great difficulty **3.** [élévation - d'une fusée, d'un dirigeable] ascent ; [- de la sève] rise ; [- des eaux] rise, rising **4.** [augmentation - de violence] rise ; [- de mécontentement] rise, increase, growth ■ **la ~e des prix/températures** the rise in prices/temperatures ■ **face à la ~e en flèche des prix du pétrole** faced with rocketing *ou* soaring oil prices ■ **devant la ~e de la violence/du racisme** faced with the rising tide of violence/racism **5.** [accession] rise, ascension *sout* ■ **sa ~e au pouvoir** her rise to power **6.** ARCHIT height **7.** PHYSIOL : **~e de lait** onset of lactation.

Monte-Carlo [mɔ̃tekarlo] *npr* Monte Carlo.

monte-charge [mɔ̃tʃarʒ] *nm inv* hoist, goods lift *UK*, freight elevator *US*.

montée [mɔ̃te] *f* ▷ **monté**.

monte-en-l'air [mɔ̃tɑ̃lɛr] *nm inv* cat burglar.

Monténégro [mɔ̃tenegro] *npr m* : **le ~** Montenegro.

monte-plats [mɔ̃tpla] *nm inv* service lift *UK*, dumbwaiter.

monter [3] [mɔ̃te] ◇ *vi (aux être ou avoir)* **1.** [personne, animal - vu d'en bas] to go up ; [- vu d'en haut] to come up ■ [avion, soleil] to rise, to climb (up) ■ [drapeau] to go up ■ [rideau de théâtre, air, fumée] to go up, to rise ■ [chemin] to go up, to rise, to climb ■ **monte par l'ascenseur** go up in *ou* use the lift ■ **monte sur une chaise pour que j'épingle ton ourlet** stand on a chair so I can pin up your hem ■ **le premier de cordée continuait à ~** the leader continued to climb *ou* continued the ascent ■ **es-tu déjà montée au dernier étage de la tour Eiffel?** have you ever been up to the top of the Eiffel Tower? ■ **~ en pente douce** to climb gently (upwards) ■ **~ en pente raide** to climb steeply *ou* sharply ■ **ça monte trop, passe en première** it's too steep, change down into first ■ **~ de** [suj: odeur, bruit] to rise (up) from, to come from

2. [dans un moyen de transport] : **~ dans** [avion, train] to get on *ou* onto, to board ; [bus] to get on, to board ; [voiture] to get into ■ **tu montes (avec moi)?** [dans ma voiture] are you coming with me (in my car)? ■ **elle monte à Versailles** [dans le train] she gets on at Versailles (station) ■ **~ sur un** *ou* **à bord d'un bateau** to board a ship ■ **~ sur un cheval** to get on *ou* to mount a horse ■ **~ sur une bicyclette** to get on a bicycle ■ **ça fait longtemps que je ne suis pas monté sur une bicyclette** it's a long time since I've been on a bicycle ■ **~ à** [pratiquer] : **~ à cheval/bicyclette** to ride (a horse)/a bicycle ‖ ÉQUIT to ride

3. [apparaître suite à une émotion] : **les larmes lui sont montées aux yeux** tears welled up in his eyes, his eyes filled with tears ■ **le rouge lui est monté aux joues** the colour rose to her cheeks ■ **le sang lui monta au visage** the blood rushed to his face

4. [s'élever - température] to rise, to go up ; [- fièvre] to rise ; [- prix, taux] to rise, to go up, to increase ; [- action] to rise ; [- rivière] to rise ; [- mer, marée] to come in ; [- anxiété, mécontentement] to grow, to increase ■ **faire ~** [tension, peur] to increase ■ **faire ~ les prix** [surenchère] to send *ou* to put prices up ; [marchand] to put up *ou* to increase prices ■ **empêcher les prix de ~** to keep prices down ■ **les loyers ont monté de 25 %** rents have gone up *ou* increased by 25% ■ **le thermomètre monte** *fam* MÉTÉOR it's *ou* the weather's getting warmer ■ **le lait monte** [il bout] the milk is boiling ; [chez une femme qui allaite] lactation has started ■ **prends de grosses aiguilles, ton pull montera plus vite** your sweater will knit up more quickly if you use big needles ■ **faire ~ des blancs en neige** CULIN to whisk up egg whites ■ **le soufflé a bien monté/n'a pas monté** the soufflé rose beautifully/didn't rise ■ **le ton montait** [de colère] voices were being raised, the discussion was becoming heated ; [d'animation] the noise level was rising

5. [atteindre un certain niveau] : **la cloison ne monte pas assez haut** the partition isn't high enough ■ **~ à** *ou* **jusqu'à** [eau, vêtement, chaussures] to come up to ■ **son plâtre monte jusqu'au genou** his leg is in a plaster cast up to the knee ■ **les pistes de ski montent jusqu'à 3 000 m** the ski runs go up to *ou* as high as 3,000 m ■ **je peux ~ jusqu'à 200 km/h** *fam* I can do up to 200 km/h ■ **l'hectare de vigne peut ~ jusqu'à 30 000 euros** one hectare of vineyard can cost up to *ou* fetch as much as 30,000 euros

6. MUS [voix] to go up, to rise ■ **il peut ~ jusqu'au "si"** he can go *ou* sing up to B

7. [pour attaquer] : **~ à l'abordage** NAUT to board ■ **~ à l'attaque** *ou* **à l'assaut** MIL to go into the attack ■ **~ à l'assaut de** to launch an attack on ■ **~ au filet** TENNIS [au volleyball] to go up to the net

8. [dans une hiérarchie] to rise ■ **~ en grade** to be promoted ■ **un chanteur qui monte** an up-and-coming singer ‖ [dans le temps] : **la génération qui monte** the rising *ou* new generation

9. [aller vers le nord] : **je monte à Paris demain** I'm going (up) to Paris tomorrow ■ **il a dû ~ à Lyon pour trouver du travail** he had to move (up) to Lyons in order to find work

10. JEUX : **~ sur le valet de trèfle** to play a club higher than the jack.

◇ *vt (aux avoir)* **1.** [gravir] to go up *(insép)* ■ **~ l'escalier** to go *ou* to climb up the stairs, to go upstairs ■ **la voiture a du mal à ~ la côte** the car has difficulty getting up the hill ■ **~ la gamme** MUS to go up *ou* to climb the scale

2. [porter en haut - bagages, colis] to take *ou* to carry up *(sép)* ; [- courrier] to take up *(sép)* ■ **monte-moi mes lunettes** bring my glasses up for me ■ **je lui ai monté son journal** I took the newspaper up to him ■ **peut-on se faire ~ le repas dans les chambres?** is it possible to have meals brought to the room?

3. [mettre plus haut] : **monte l'étagère d'un cran** put the shelf up a notch ■ **monte la vitre, j'ai froid** wind up the (car) window, I'm cold

4. [augmenter - son] to turn up *(sép)* ; [- prix] to put up *(sép)* ■ **monte la télé** *fam* turn the TV up ■ [mettre en colère] : **~ qqn contre** to set sb against

5. [assembler - kit] to assemble, to put together *(sép)* ; [- tente] to pitch, to put up *(sép)* ; [- abri] to rig up *(sép)* ■ **~ une page** IMPR to make up *ou* to paste up *ou* to lay out a page ■ **~ en parallèle/série** ÉLECTR to connect in parallel/series

6. [fixer - radiateur] to fit, to mount ; [- store] to put up *(sép)*, to mount ■ **~ une gravure** [sur une marie-louise] to mount an engraving ; [dans un cadre] to frame an engraving ■ **il a monté un moteur plus puissant sur sa voiture** he has put a more powerful engine into his car ■ JOAILL to mount, to set

7. [organiser - gén] to organize ; [- pièce, spectacle] to put on *(sép)*, to stage, to produce ; [- canular] to think up *(sép)* ; [- complot, machination] to set up *(sép)* ■ **~ un atelier de poterie** to set up a pottery workshop ■ **il avait monté tout un scénario dans sa tête** he'd thought up some weird and wonderful scheme

8. [pourvoir - bibliothèque, collection, cave] to set up *(sép)* ■ **~ son ménage** *ou* **sa maison** to set up house

9. ÉQUIT : **~ un cheval** to ride a horse

10. CINÉ [bobine] to mount ■ [film] to edit

11. COUT to fit (on) ■ **~ une manche** to sew on *ou* to attach a sleeve ■ **le pantalon est prêt à être monté** the trousers are ready to assemble *ou* to be made up ‖ [tricoter - maille] to cast on *(sép)*

12. CULIN : **~ des blancs en neige** to whisk up egg whites ■ **~ une mayonnaise** to make some mayonnaise

13. VÉTÉR & ZOOL to cover, to serve

14. NAUT to crew ■ **~ un gréement** to rig a ship ‖ PÊCHE to assemble.

➡ **se monter à** *vp+prép* [coût, dépenses] to come *ou* to amount *ou* to add up to.

◆ **se monter en** *vp+prép* to equip *ou* to provide o.s. with ■ **se ~ en vins** to stock (up) one's cellar.

monteur, euse [mɔ̃tœr, øz] *nm, f* **1.** INDUST & TECHNOL fitter **2.** AUDIO & CINÉ editor.

Montevideo [mɔ̃tevideo] *npr* Montevideo.

montgolfière [mɔ̃gɔlfjɛr] *nf* hot-air balloon, montgolfier (balloon).

monticule [mɔ̃tikyl] *nm* **1.** [colline] hillock, mound, monticule *sout* **2.** [tas] heap, mound ■ **un ~ de pierres** a heap *ou* pile of stones **3.** [au baseball] pitcher's mound.

montmartrois, e [mɔ̃martrwa, az] *adj* from Montmartre.
◆ **Montmartrois, e** *nm, f inhabitant of or person from Montmartre.*

montmorency [mɔ̃mɔrɑ̃si] *nf inv* morello cherry.

Montparnasse [mɔ̃parnas] *npr* Montparnasse.

MONTPARNASSE

This area of Paris was famous between the wars for its bohemian society, which included the "lost generation" of American writers; it is now well-known for its lively nightlife and the commercial centre surrounding the 200m high Tour Montparnasse.

montrable [mɔ̃trabl] *adj* [objet] exhibitable ■ [spectacle] fit to be seen ■ **est-ce ~ à des enfants?** is it fit to be seen by children?

montre [mɔ̃tr] *nf* **1.** [instrument] watch ■ **il est 11 heures à ma ~** it's 11 o'clock by my watch ▶ **~ antichoc** shockproof watch ■ **~ digitale** digital watch ■ **~ étanche** waterproof watch ■ **~ de gousset** fob *ou* pocket watch ■ **~ de plongée** diver's watch ■ **~ à quartz** quartz watch ■ **il a mis une heure ~ en main** it took him *ou* he took exactly one hour (by the clock) ■ **jouer la ~** FOOTBALL to play for time **2.** [preuve] : **faire ~ de prudence** to show caution, to behave cautiously ■ **faire ~ d'audace** to show *ou* to display one's boldness.

Montréal [mɔ̃real] *npr* Montreal, Montréal.

montréalais, e [mɔ̃realɛ, ɛz] *adj* from Montreal.
◆ **Montréalais, e** *nm, f* Montrealer.

montre-bracelet [mɔ̃trəbraslɛ] (*pl* **montres-bracelets**) *nf* wristwatch.

montrer [3] [mɔ̃tre] *vt* **1.** [gén] to show ■ [passeport, ticket] to show, to produce ■ [document secret] to show, to disclose ■ [spectacle, œuvre] to show, to exhibit ■ **~ qqch à qqn** to show sthg to sb, to show sb sthg ■ **il m'a montré son usine** he showed me (around) his factory ■ **j'ai montré Marie au docteur** *fam* I had the doctor have *ou* take a look at Marie ■ **les toiles ne sont pas encore prêtes à être montrées** the paintings aren't ready to go on show yet ■ **~ le poing à qqn** to shake one's fist at sb ▶ **~ patte blanche** to produce one's credentials *fig* ■ **~ ses cartes** *pr* & *fig* to show one's hand
2. [exhiber - partie du corps] to show ; [- bijou, richesse, talent] to show off (*sép*), to parade, to flaunt ■ **elle montrait ses charmes** she was displaying her charms *ou* leaving nothing to the imagination *euphém* ■ **tu n'as pas besoin de ~ ta science!** no need to show off your knowledge!
3. [faire preuve de - courage, impatience, détermination] to show, to display ■ [laisser apparaître - émotion] to show
4. [signaler] to point out (*sép*), to show ■ **~ la sortie** [de la tête] to nod towards the exit ; [du doigt] to point to the exit ; [de la main] to gesture towards the exit ■ **~ la porte à qqn** to show sb the door ▶ **~ le chemin à qqn** *pr* & *fig* to show sb the way ■ **~ l'exemple** to set an example, to give the lead ■ **~ la voie** *ou* **le chemin** to lead *ou* to show the way ■ **~ qqn du doigt** *pr* to point at sb ; *fig* to point the finger of shame at sb
5. [marquer - suj: aiguille, curseur, cadran] to show, to point to (*insép*) ; [- suj: écran] to show, to display
6. [prouver] to show, to prove ■ **comme le montrent ces statistiques** as these statistics show ■ **ça montre bien que** *fam*... it (just) goes to show that...
7. [évoquer] to show, to depict ■ **la vie des galériens, si bien montrée dans son roman** the lives of the galley slaves, so clearly depicted in her novel
8. [enseigner - technique, procédé] to show, to demonstrate ; [- recette, jeu] to show ■ **la brochure montre comment s'en servir** the booklet explains *ou* shows how to use it.
◆ **se montrer** *vpi* **1.** [se présenter] to show o.s., to appear (in public) ■ **je ne peux pas me ~ dans cet état!** I can't let people see me like this! ■ **le voilà, ne te montre pas!** here he is, stay out of sight! ■ **elle ne s'est même pas montrée au mariage de sa fille** she never even showed up *ou* showed her face *ou* turned up at her daughter's wedding ■ **se ~ à son avantage** to show o.s. in a good light *ou* to advantage
2. [s'afficher] to appear *ou* to be seen (in public) ■ **elle adore se ~** she loves to be seen (in public) ■ **il se montre partout à son bras** he parades everywhere with her on his arm
3. [se révéler] : **se ~ d'un grand égoïsme** to display great selfishness ■ **ce soir-là, il s'est montré odieux/charmant** he was obnoxious/charming that evening ■ **montre-toi un homme, mon fils!** show them you're a man, my son! ■ **finalement, elle s'est montrée digne/indigne de ma confiance** she eventually proved (to be) worthy/unworthy of my trust.

montreur, euse [mɔ̃trœr, øz] *nm, f* : **~ de marionnettes** puppeteer ■ **~ d'ours** bearkeeper.

monture [mɔ̃tyr] *nf* **1.** JOAILL setting ■ [de lunettes] frame ■ **des lunettes à ~ d'écaille/de plastique** horn-/plastic-rimmed glasses **2.** [d'un vase, d'un miroir] mounting **3.** ÉQUIT mount **4.** ARM [d'un fusil] stock ■ [d'une épée] guard **5.** PÊCHE tackle.

monument [mɔnymɑ̃] *nm* **1.** [stèle, statue] monument ■ **~ funéraire** (funerary) monument ■ **~ aux morts** war memorial **2.** ADMIN & LOISIRS monument, building ■ **~ historique** historic monument *ou* building ■ **~ public** civic building **3.** *litt* [travail admirable] monument, masterpiece **4.** *fam fig* **ce type est un ~ de naïveté/lâcheté** that guy is the ultimate dupe/coward.

monumental, e, aux [mɔnymɑ̃tal, o] *adj* **1.** LOISIRS : **plan ~ de la ville** city map showing buildings of interest **2.** [grandiose] monumental, incredible ■ **une oeuvre ~e** a monumental piece of work **3.** *fam* [canular, erreur] monumental, phenomenal, mammoth *(modif)* ■ **d'une stupidité ~e** monumentally *ou* astoundingly stupid **4.** ARCHIT monumental.

moque [mɔk] *nf* NAUT cringle.

moquer [3] [mɔke] *vt litt* to mock (at).
◆ **se moquer** *vpi litt* to jest ■ **vous vous moquez!** you jest! *hum.*
◆ **se moquer de** *vp+prép* **1.** [railler] to laugh at, to make fun of ■ **les gens vont se ~ d'elle** people will laugh at her *ou* make fun of her, she'll be a laughing stock **2.** [ignorer - danger, conseil] to disregard, to ignore **3.** [être indifférent à] : **je me/il se moque de tout ça** I/he couldn't care less (about all that) ■ **je me moque de travailler le dimanche** I don't mind having to work on Sundays ■ **je me moque que tu sois mécontent** I don't care if you're not pleased ■ **elle s'en moque pas mal** *fam* she couldn't care less **4.** [duper] to dupe, to deceive, to trick ■ **on s'est moqué de toi** you've been taken for a ride ■ **elle ne s'est pas moquée de toi!** *fam* [repas, réception] she did you proud (there)! ; [cadeau] she didn't skimp on your present! ■ **ce type se moque du monde!** *fam* that guy's got a real nerve!

moquerie [mɔkri] *nf* jeering, mocking ■ **il était en butte à des ~s continuelles** he was always being mocked *ou* made fun of.

moquette [mɔkɛt] *nf* wall-to-wall carpet, fitted carpet *UK* ■ **faire poser de la** *ou* **une ~** to have a (wall-to-wall) carpet laid.

moquetter [4] [mɔkete] *vt* to carpet... (wall-to-wall), to lay a (wall-to-wall) carpet in ■ **l'entrée est moquettée** the hall is (wall-to-wall) carpeted.

moqueur, euse [mɔkœr, øz] ◇ *adj* mocking ■ **d'un ton ~** mockingly, derisively ■ **d'un air ~** mockingly ■ **elle est très moqueuse** she likes to make fun of people.
◇ *nm, f* mocker ■ **les ~s** mocking *ou* jeering people.
◆ **moqueur** *nm* mockingbird.

moraine [mɔrɛn] *nf* moraine ■ **~ de fond** ground moraine.

moral, e, aux [mɔral, o] *adj* **1.** [éthique - conscience, jugement] moral ■ **il n'a aucun sens ~** he has no sense of morality ■ **se sentir dans l'obligation ~e de faire qqch** to feel morally obliged *ou* a moral obligation to do sthg ■ **prendre l'engagement ~ de**

faire qqch to be morally committed to do sthg ■ [édifiant - auteur, conte, réflexion] moral ■ **la fin de la pièce n'est pas très ~e!** the end of the play is rather immoral! **2.** [spirituel - douleur] mental ; [- soutien, victoire, résistance] moral.
◆ **moral** *nm* morale, spirits ■ **comment va le ~?** are you in good spirits? ■ **toutes ces épreuves n'ont pas affecté son ~** all these ordeals failed to shake her morale ■ **son ~ est bas** his spirits are low, he's in low spirits ➲ **avoir le ~, avoir bon ~** to be in good *ou* high spirits ■ **tu vas t'occuper de ses cinq enfants? dis-donc, tu as le ~!** *fam* so you're going to look after his five children? well, you're brave! ■ **il n'a pas le ~ en ce moment** he's a bit depressed *ou* low at the moment ■ **allez, il faut garder le ~!** come on, keep your chin *ou* spirits up! ■ **remonter le ~ de qqn** [consoler] to raise sb's spirits, to boost sb's morale ; [égayer] to cheer sb up ■ **retrouver le ~** to perk up ■ **avoir un ~ d'acier** to be a tower of strength ■ **j'ai le ~ à zéro** *fam* I feel down in the dumps *ou* really low.

morale [mɔral] *nf* **1.** [règles - de la société] moral code *ou* standards, morality ; [- d'une religion] moral code, ethic ; [- personnelles] morals, ethics ■ **ce n'est pas conforme à la ~** it's unethical ➲ **faire la ~ à qqn** to lecture sb, to preach at sb **2.** PHILOS moral philosophy, ethics *(U)* **3.** [d'une fable, d'une histoire] moral.

moralement [mɔralmɑ̃] *adv* **1.** [du point de vue de la morale] morally ■ **je me sens ~ obligé de...** I feel duty *ou* morally bound to... **2.** [sur le plan psychique] : **~, elle va mieux** she's in better spirits.

moralisateur, trice [mɔralizatœr, tris] ◇ *adj* **1.** [personne, propos] moralizing, moralistic ■ **parler à qqn sur un ton ~** to speak to sb sanctimoniously **2.** [histoire] edifying.
◇ *nm, f* moralizer.

moraliser [3] [mɔralize] ◇ *vt* **1.** [rendre conforme à la morale] to moralize *sout*, to improve the morals of **2.** [réprimander] to lecture.
◇ *vi* [prêcher] to moralize, to preach.

moralisme [mɔralism] *nm* moralism.

moraliste [mɔralist] ◇ *adj* moralistic.
◇ *nmf* moralist.

moralité [mɔralite] *nf* **1.** [éthique] morality, ethics *(sing)* ■ **d'une ~ douteuse** of questionable morals ■ **d'une haute ~** highly moral *ou* ethical **2.** [comportement] morals, moral standing *ou* standards **3.** [conclusion] : **~, il faut toujours...** and the moral (of the story) is, you must always... ■ **~, on ne l'a plus revu** *fam* and the result was, we never saw him again **4.** HIST & THÉÂTRE morality play.

moratoire [mɔratwar] ◇ *adj* moratory ■ **intérêts ~s** interest on overdue payments, moratorial interest.
◇ *nm* moratorium.

morave [mɔrav] *adj* Moravian.
◆ **Morave** *nmf* Moravian.

Moravie [mɔravi] *npr f* : **(la) ~** Moravia.

morbide [mɔrbid] *adj* **1.** [malsain] morbid, unhealthy **2.** MÉD morbid.

morbidité [mɔrbidite] *nf litt* **1.** [d'une obsession] morbidity, morbidness, unhealthiness **2.** MÉD & SOCIOL morbidity rate.

morbleu [mɔrblø] *interj arch* zounds, ye gods.

morceau, x [mɔrso] *nm* **1.** [de nourriture] piece, bit ■ **~ de sucre** lump of sugar, sugar lump ■ **sucre en ~x** lump sugar ■ **tu reprendras bien un petit ~!** come on, have another bit *ou* piece! ■ **si on allait manger un ~?** *fam* what about a snack?, how about a bite to eat? ▮ [de viande] cut, piece ➲ **~ de choix** titbit *UK*, tidbit *US*, choice morsel *sout* ■ **c'est un ~ de roi** *ou* **digne d'un roi** it's fit for a king ■ **cracher** *ou* **lâcher le ~** *fam* to spill the beans, to come clean **2.** [de bois, de métal - petit] piece, bit ; [- gros] lump, chunk ■ [de papier, de verre] piece ■ [d'étoffe, de câble - gén] piece ; [- mesuré] length ■ **assembler les ~x de qqch** to piece sthg together ■ **en ~x** in bits *ou* pieces ■ **mettre en ~x** [papier, étoffe] to tear up *(sép)* ; [jouet] to pull to pieces *ou* bits ■ **tomber en ~x** to fall apart, to fall to pieces **3.** [extrait] passage, extract, excerpt ■ **cette scène est un véritable ~ d'anthologie** it's a truly memorable scene ■ **~ de bravoure** purple passage ■ **(recueil de) ~x choisis** (collection of) selected passages *ou* extracts **4.** MUS [fragment] passage ■ [œuvre] piece **5.** *fam* [personne] : **un beau ~** a nice bit of stuff *UK*, a bit of all right ■ **c'est un sacré ~, leur fils!** [il est gros] their son is enormous! ; [il est musclé] their son is a real hunk! ; [il est insupportable] their son is a real pain!

morceler [24] [mɔrsəle] *vt* **1.** [partager] to parcel out *(sép)* ■ [démembrer] to divide (up), to break up *(sép)* **2.** MIL to split up *(sép)*.

morcellement [mɔrsɛlmɑ̃] *nm* **1.** [d'un terrain] dividing (up) ■ [d'un héritage] parcelling (out) **2.** MIL splitting (up).

morcellera *etc v* ▷ **morceler**.

mordant, e [mɔrdɑ̃, ɑ̃t] *adj* **1.** [caustique] biting, caustic, scathing **2.** [froid] biting, bitter.
◆ **mordant** *nm* **1.** [dynamisme - d'une personne] drive, spirit, punch ; [- d'un style, d'une publicité] punch, bite ■ **une campagne qui a du ~** a campaign which really packs a punch **2.** [d'une lame, d'une lime] bite **3.** [en gravure, teinture, dorure] mordant **4.** MUS mordent.

mordicus [mɔrdikys] *adv fam* stubbornly, doggedly ■ **il soutient ~ que c'est vrai** he absolutely insists that it's true.

mordillage [mɔrdijaʒ], **mordillement** [mɔrdijmɑ̃] *nm* nibbling.

mordiller [3] [mɔrdije] *vt* to nibble *ou* to chew (at).

mordoré, e [mɔrdɔre] *adj* golden brown, bronze *(modif)*.

mordre [76] [mɔrdr] ◇ *vt* **1.** [suj: animal, personne] to bite ■ **~ un fruit** to bite into a piece of fruit ■ **~ qqn jusqu'au sang** to bite sb and draw blood ■ **se faire ~** to get bitten ■ **il s'est fait ~ à la main** he was bitten on the hand ■ **prends la serpillière, elle ne mord pas** *ou* **elle ne te mordra pas!** *hum* take the mop, it won't bite (you)! ■ ➲ **~ la poussière** to bite the dust **2.** [suj: scie, vis] to bite into *(insép)* ■ [suj: acide] to eat into *(insép)* ■ [suj: pneus cloutés] to grip ■ [suj: ancre] to grip, to bite ■ [suj: froid] to bite **3.** [empiéter sur] : **~ la ligne** [saut en longueur] to cross the (take-off) board ; [sur la route] to cross the white line.
◇ *vi* **1.** PÊCHE to bite ■ **ça ne mord pas beaucoup par ici** the fish aren't biting *ou* rising much around here ➲ **~ (à l'appât)** *ou* **à l'hameçon** *pr* & *fig* to rise (to the bait), to bite ■ **il** *ou* **ça n'a pas mordu** *fam fig* he wasn't taken in, he didn't fall for it **2.** MÉCAN to mesh.
◆ **mordre à** *v+prép fam* **1.** [prendre goût à] to take to *(insép)*, to fall for *(insép)*, to be hooked by **2.** [être trompé par] to be taken in by, to fall for *(insép)*.
◆ **mordre dans** *v+prép* to bite into.
◆ **mordre sur** *v+prép* [ligne, marge] to go *ou* to cross over ■ [économies] to make a dent in, to eat into *(insép)* ■ [période] to overlap ■ **le stage mordra sur la deuxième semaine de mars** the course will go over into the second week in March.
◆ **se mordre** *vpt* : **se ~ la langue** to bite one's tongue *pr* ➲ **je m'en suis mordu les doigts** *fig* I could have kicked myself ■ **il va s'en ~ les doigts** he'll be sorry he did it, he'll live to regret it ■ **se ~ la queue** *pr* to chase one's tail ; *fig* to go round in circles.

mordu, e [mɔrdy] ◇ *adj* **1.** *fam* [passionné] : **il est ~ de jazz** he's mad *ou* crazy about jazz **2.** SPORT : **saut ~** no jump.
◇ *nm, f fam* [passionné] addict *hum*, fan ■ **un ~ de cinéma/d'opéra** a film/an opera buff ■ **les ~s du tennis/de Chaplin** tennis/Chaplin fans ■ **les ~s de la télé** TV addicts.

more [mɔr] = **maure**.

morène [mɔrɛn] *nf* hydrocharis, frogbit.

moresque [mɔrɛsk] = **mauresque** *(adj)*.

morfal, e, als△ [mɔrfal] *nm, f* gannet *UK*, greedy pig *ou* guts.

morfler [3] △ [mɔrfle] *vi* : **il a morflé!** he copped it! *UK*, he caught it! *US*.

morfondre [75] [mɔrfɔ̃dr] ◆ **se morfondre** *vpi* to mope.

morganatique [mɔrganatik] *adj* morganatic.

morgue [mɔrg] *nf* **1.** [établissement] morgue ■ [dans un hôpital] mortuary *UK*, morgue *US* **2.** *sout* [arrogance] arrogance, haughtiness, disdainfulness.

moribond, e [mɔribɔ̃, ɔ̃d] ◇ *adj* dying, moribund *sout*.

◇ nm, f dying person ■ **les ~s** the dying.

moricaud, e [mɔriko, od] *nm, f* **1.** *fam* [personne bronzée] dark-skinned *ou* dusky person **2.** ▲ *racist term used with reference to black people*, ≃ darkie *fam*.

morigéner [18] [mɔriʒene] *vt sout* to chide, to rebuke, to upbraid.

morille [mɔrij] *nf* morel.

mormon, e [mɔrmɔ̃, ɔn] *adj* Mormon.
◆ **Mormon, e** *nm, f* Mormon.

morne [mɔrn] ◇ *adj* **1.** [triste - personne] glum, gloomy **2.** [monotone - discussion] dull ; [- paysage] bleak, drab, dreary ■ **d'un ton ~** in a dreary voice **3.** [maussade - climat] dull, dreary, dismal **4.** [terne - couleur, style] dull.
◇ *nm* [aux Antilles] mound, hill.

morose [mɔroz] *adj* **1.** [individu, air, vie] glum, morose **2.** [économie] sluggish, slack ■ **la Bourse était ~ ce matin** trading on the Stock Exchange was sluggish this morning.

morosité [mɔrozite] *nf* **1.** [d'une personne] sullenness, moroseness **2.** [d'un marché] slackness, sluggishness.

Morphée [mɔrfe] *npr* Morpheus ■ **dans les bras de ~** *fig* in the arms of Morpheus *litt*.

morphème [mɔrfɛm] *nm* morpheme.

morphine [mɔrfin] *nf* morphine, morphia.

morphinomane [mɔrfinɔman] *nmf* morphinomaniac *spéc*, morphine addict.

morphisme [mɔrfism] *nm* homomorphism.

morphogenèse [mɔrfoʒənɛz] *nf* morphogenesis.

morphologie [mɔrfɔlɔʒi] *nf* morphology.

morphologique [mɔrfɔlɔʒik] *adj* morphological.

morpion [mɔrpjɔ̃] *nm* **1.** *fam péj* [enfant] brat, perisher *UK* **2.** *fam* [pou] crab **3.** JEUX : ≃ noughts and crosses *UK*, ≃ tic tac toe *US*.

mors [mɔr] *nm* **1.** [d'un cheval] bit ■ **~ de bride** curb bit ■ **prendre le ~ aux dents** *fig* to take the bit between one's teeth, to swing into action **2.** [d'un étau] jaw, chop ■ [d'une pince] jaw, pincer **3.** [d'un livre] joint, groove.

morse [mɔrs] *nm* **1.** ZOOL walrus **2.** [code] Morse (code).

morsure [mɔrsyr] *nf* **1.** [d'un animal] bite ■ **une ~ de serpent** a snakebite **2.** *fig* & *sout* pang ■ **les ~s du froid** biting cold.

mort, e [mɔr, mɔrt] ◇ *pp* ▷ **mourir**.
◇ *adj* **1.** [décédé - personne] dead ■ **elle est ~e depuis longtemps** she died a long time ago, she's been dead (for) a long time ■ **il était comme ~** he looked as if he were dead ■ **laisser qqn pour ~** to leave sb for dead ■ **~ et enterré, ~ et bien ~** *pr* & *fig* dead and buried, dead and gone, long dead ■ **~ sur le champ de bataille** *ou* **au champ d'honneur** killed in action ■ **~ ou vif** dead or alive ■ **être plus ~ que vif** to be more dead than alive ■ [arbre, cellule, dent] dead ▶ **~e la bête, ~ le venin** *prov* a dead enemy is no longer a threat
2. [en intensif] : **~ de : il était ~ de fatigue** he was dead tired ■ **on était ~s de froid** we were freezing cold ■ **j'étais ~e de rire** *fam* I nearly died laughing
3. [passé - amour, désir] dead ; [- espoir] dead, buried, long-gone
4. [inerte - regard] lifeless, dull ; [- quartier, bistrot] dead ; [- eau] stagnant
5. *fam* [hors d'usage - appareil, voiture] dead ■ **mon sac est ~** my bag's had it
6. *fam* [épuisé] : **je suis ~!** I'm dead! ■ **mes jambes sont ~es!** my legs are killing me!
7. GÉOGR : **la mer Morte** the Dead Sea.
◇ *nm, f* [personne] dead person ■ **les émeutes ont fait 300 ~s** 300 people died *ou* were killed in the rioting ■ **les ~s** the dead ▶ **c'est un ~ vivant** [mourant] he's at death's door ■ **les ~s vivants** the living dead ■ **jour** *ou* **fête des ~s** All Souls' Day ■ **messe/prière des ~s** mass/prayer for the dead ■ **faire le ~** *pr* to pretend to be dead, to play dead ■ **tu as intérêt à faire le ~** *fam fig* you'd better lie low.
◆ **mort** *nf* **1.** [décès] death ■ **la ~** death ■ **envoyer qqn à la ~** to send sb to his/her death ■ **frôler la ~** to have a brush with death ■ **il a vu la ~ de près** he saw death staring him in the face ■ **se donner la ~** *sout* to commit suicide, to take one's own life ■ **trouver la ~** to meet one's death, to die ■ **les émeutes ont entraîné la ~ de 30 personnes** the riots led to the death *ou* deaths of 30 people ■ **il y a eu ~ d'homme** [une victime] somebody was killed ; [plusieurs victimes] lives were lost ■ **il a eu une ~ douce** he died painlessly ■ **périr de ~ violente** to die a violent death ■ **~ aux traîtres!** death to the traitors! ▶ **~ cérébrale** *ou* **clinique** brain death ■ **~ accidentelle** [gén] accidental death ■ **~ naturelle** natural death ; DR death from natural causes ■ **~ subite du nourrisson** sudden infant death syndrome *spéc*, cot death ■ **la petite ~** *litt* (the moment of) climax ■ **avoir la ~ dans l'âme** to have a heavy heart ■ **je partis la ~ dans l'âme** I left with a heavy heart ■ **c'est pas la ~ (du petit cheval)!** *fam* it's not the end of the world! ■ **son cours, c'est vraiment la ~!** *fam* his class is deadly boring! ■ **la foule scandait à ~, à ~!** the crowd was chanting kill (him), kill (him)!
2. [économique] end, death.
◆ **à mort** ◇ *loc adj* [lutte, combat] to the death.
◇ *loc adv* **1.** *fam* [en intensif] : **j'ai freiné à ~** I braked like hell, I jammed on the brakes ■ **ils sont brouillés** *ou* **fâchés à ~** they're mortal enemies *ou* enemies for life ■ **je lui en veux à ~** I hate his guts
2. [mortellement] : **blesser qqn à ~** to mortally wound sb ■ **frapper qqn à ~** to strike sb dead ■ **mettre qqn à ~** to put sb to death ■ **mettre un animal à ~** to kill an animal.
◆ **de mort** *loc adj* [silence, pâleur] deathly, deathlike ■ **être en danger** *ou* **péril de ~** to be in mortal danger ▶ **menace/pulsion de ~** death threat/wish.
◆ **jusqu'à la mort** *loc adv pr* to the death ■ *fig* to the bitter end.
◆ **jusqu'à ce que mort s'ensuive** *loc adv* DR & *vieilli* until he/she be dead ■ *hum* to the bitter end.

mortadelle [mɔrtadɛl] *nf* mortadella.

mortaise [mɔrtɛz] *nf* **1.** MENUIS mortise, mortice **2.** [de clavette] keyway ■ [de serrure] mortice **3.** NAUT sheave slot, mortice.

mortalité [mɔrtalite] *nf* [gén] mortality ■ [dans des statistiques] death rate, mortality (rate).

mort-aux-rats [mɔrora] *nf inv* rat poison.

morte-eau [mɔrto] (*pl* **mortes-eaux** [mɔrtəzo]) *nf* neap tide, neaps.

mortel, elle [mɔrtɛl] ◇ *adj* **1.** [qui tue - accident] fatal ; [- dose, poison] deadly, lethal ; [- coup, blessure] fatal, lethal, mortal *sout* ; [- maladie] fatal ■ **c'est un coup ~ porté à notre petite communauté** *fig* this is a deathblow for our little community **2.** [dangereux] lethal, deadly ■ **tu as raté l'examen mais ça n'est pas ~!** *fam* you've failed the exam but it's not the end of the world! **3.** *fam* [ennuyeux] deadly *ou* excruciatingly boring **4.** [qui rappelle la mort - pâleur, silence] deathly **5.** [acharné - ennemi] mortal, deadly **6.** [qui n'est pas éternel] mortal.
◇ *nm, f* [être humain] mortal.

mortellement [mɔrtɛlmɑ̃] *adv* **1.** [à mort] : **être ~ blessé** to be fatally *ou* mortally *sout* wounded **2.** [en intensif] : **le film est ~ ennuyeux** the film is deadly boring ■ **tu l'as ~ offensé** you've mortally offended him.

morte-saison [mɔrtsɛzɔ̃] (*pl* **mortes-saisons**) *nf* slack *ou* off season ■ **à la ~** in the off season.

mortier [mɔrtje] *nm* **1.** ARM mortar **2.** CONSTR mortar ■ **~ bâtard/gras/maigre** gauged/fat/lean mortar **3.** [bonnet] judge's cap *(worn by certain judges in France)*.

mortifiant, e [mɔrtifjɑ̃, ɑ̃t] *adj* mortifying, humiliating.

mortification [mɔrtifikasjɔ̃] *nf* **1.** RELIG mortification **2.** [humiliation] mortification, humiliation.

mortifié, e [mɔrtifje] *adj* mortified.

mortifier [9] [mɔrtifje] *vt* **1.** RELIG to mortify **2.** [humilier] to mortify, to humiliate **3.** CULIN to (leave to) hang **4.** MÉD to mortify.

mort-né, e [mɔrne] (*mpl* **mort-nés**, *fpl* **mort-nées**) ◇ *adj pr* & *fig* stillborn.
◇ *nm, f* stillborn baby.

mortuaire [mɔrtɥɛr] ◇ *adj* **1.** [rituel] mortuary *(modif)*, funeral *(modif)* ▪ [cérémonie, chambre] funeral *(modif)* **2.** ADMIN : **acte ~** death certificate.
◇ *nf Belgique* house of the deceased.

morue [mɔry] *nf* **1.** CULIN & ZOOL cod ▪ **~ fraîche** fresh cod ▪ **~ (verte)** undried salt cod **2.** △ [prostituée] whore, hooker.

morutier, ère [mɔrytje, ɛr] *adj* cod-fishing *(modif)*.
◆ **morutier** *nm* **1.** [navire] cod-fishing boat **2.** [marin] cod-fisherman.

morve [mɔrv] *nf* **1.** [mucus] nasal mucus **2.** VÉTÉR glanders *(U)*.

morveux, euse [mɔrvø, øz] ◇ *adj* **1.** [sale] snotty-nosed ▪ **qui se sent ~, qu'il se mouche** *prov* if the cap fits, wear it **2.** VÉTÉR glandered.
◇ *nm, f fam* **1.** [enfant] (snotty-nosed) little kid **2.** [jeune prétentieux] (snotty) *ou* snotty-nosed little upstart.

mosaïque [mɔzaik] ◇ *nf* **1.** ART mosaic ▪ **sol en ~** mosaic floor **2.** [mélange - de couleurs] patchwork, mosaic ; [- de cultures] mixture, mosaic **3.** BOT mosaic (disease) **4.** BIOL & GÉOL mosaic.
◇ *adj* RELIG Mosaic.

Moscou [mɔsku] *npr* Moscow.

moscovite [mɔskɔvit] *adj* Muscovite.
◆ **Moscovite** *nmf* Muscovite.

mosellan, e [mɔzelɑ̃, an] *adj* from Moselle.

mosquée [mɔske] *nf* mosque.

mot [mo] *nm* **1.** LING word ▪ **un ~ à la mode** a buzzword ▪ **orgueilleux, c'est bien le ~** arrogant is the (right) word ▪ **riche n'est pas vraiment le ~** rich isn't exactly the word I would use ➊ **le ~ de Cambronne** *ou* **de cinq lettres** *euphém* the word "merde" ▪ **~ clé** key word ▪ **~ composé** compound (word) ▪ **~ d'emprunt** loanword ▪ **le ~ juste** the right *ou* appropriate word ▪ **~ de passe** password ▪ **gros ~** swearword
2. INFORM : **~ d'appel** call word ▪ **~ d'état** status word ▪ **~ machine** computer word ▪ **~ mémoire** storage *ou* memory word
3. [parole] word ▪ **il n'a pas dit un ~** he didn't say a word ▪ **dire un ~ à qqn** to have a word with sb ▪ **pourriez-vous nous dire un ~ sur ce problème?** could you say a word (or two) *ou* a few words about this problem for us? ▪ **tu n'as qu'un ~ à dire** (just) say the word ▪ **pas un ~!** don't say a word! ▪ **pas un ~ à qui que ce soit!** not a word to anybody! ▪ **les ~s me manquent** words fail me ▪ **les ~s me manquent pour vous remercier** I'm at a loss for words to express my gratitude ▪ **je ne trouve pas les ~s (pour le dire)** I cannot find the words (to say it) ▪ **chercher ses ~s** to try to find *ou* to search for the right words ▪ **à ces ~s** at these words ▪ **sur ces ~s** with these words ▪ **ce ne sont que des ~s!** it's just talk!, it's all hot air! ➊ **~ d'ordre** slogan ; MIL watchword ▪ **~ d'ordre de grève** call for strike action ▪ **dernier ~ : c'est mon dernier ~** it's my last *ou* final offer ▪ **avoir le dernier ~** to have the last word ▪ **grand ~ : voleur, c'est un bien grand ~** thief, that would be putting it a bit too strongly *ou* going a bit too far ▪ **avec toi, c'est tout de suite** *ou* **toujours les grands ~s** you're always exaggerating ▪ **~s doux** words of love, sweet nothings *hum* ▪ **avoir des ~s (avec qqn)** to have words (with sb) ▪ **avoir son ~ à dire** to have one's say ▪ **avoir toujours le ~ pour rire** to be a (great) laugh *ou* joker ▪ **dire un ~ de travers** to say something wrong, to put one's foot in it ▪ **il n'a jamais un ~ plus haut que l'autre** he never raises his voice ▪ **pas le premier** *ou* **un traître ~ de** not a single word of ▪ **prendre qqn au ~** to take sb at his word ▪ **se donner** *ou* **se passer le ~** to pass the word around ▪ **je vais lui en toucher** *ou* **je lui en toucherai un ~** I'll have a word with him about it ▪ **dire deux ~s à qqn** to give sb a piece of one's mind
4. [parole mémorable] saying ▪ **~ d'esprit, bon ~** witticism, witty remark ▪ **~ d'auteur** (author's) witty remark ▪ **~ d'enfant** child's remark ▪ **~ de la fin** concluding message, closing words
5. [message écrit] note, word ▪ **écrire un ~ à qqn** to write sb a note, to drop sb a line ➊ **~ d'absence** note *(explaining absence)* ▪ **~ d'excuse** word of apology ▪ **~ de remerciements** thank-you note.
◆ **à mots couverts** *loc adv* in veiled terms.
◆ **au bas mot** *loc adv* at (the very) least.
◆ **en d'autres mots** *loc adv* in other words.
◆ **en un mot** *loc adv* in a word ▪ **en un ~ comme en cent** *ou* **mille** [en bref] in a nutshell, to cut a long story short ; [sans détour] without beating about the bush.
◆ **mot à mot** *loc adv* [littéralement] word for word ▪ *(comme nom)* **faire du ~ à ~** to translate word for word.
◆ **mot pour mot** *loc adv* word for word ▪ **c'est ce qu'elle a dit, ~ pour ~** those were her very words, that's what she said, word for word.
◆ **sans mot dire** *loc adv* without (uttering) a word.

motard, e [mɔtar, ard] *nm, f fam* motorcyclist, biker.
◆ **motard** *nm* **1.** [policier] motorcycle policeman ▪ **voiture escortée de ~s** car with a motorcycle escort **2.** MIL ≃ dispatch rider.

motel [mɔtɛl] *nm* motel.

motet [mɔtɛ] *nm* motet.

moteur, trice [mɔtœr, tris] *adj* **1.** MÉCAN [force] driving, motive ▪ **voiture à quatre roues motrices** four-wheel drive car **2.** ANAT [nerf, neurone, muscle] motor *(modif)*.
◆ **moteur** *nm* **1.** MÉCAN engine ▪ **~ électrique** (electric) motor ▪ **~ à allumage commandé** *ou* **à explosion** internal combustion engine ▪ **~ à deux/quatre temps** two-/four-stroke engine ▪ **~ à essence/vapeur** petrol/steam engine ▪ **~ à combustion** combustion engine ▪ **~ Diesel** diesel engine ▪ **~ à injection** fuel injection engine ▪ **~ à réaction** jet engine **2.** [cause] mainspring, driving force ▪ **être le ~ de qqch** to be the driving force behind sthg **3.** CINÉ : **~!** action! **4.** INFORM : **~ de recherche** search engine.
◆ **motrice** *nf* locomotive (engine).
◆ **à moteur** *loc adj* power-driven, motor *(modif)*.

motif [mɔtif] *nm* **1.** [raison] reason ▪ **il a agi sans ~** he did it for no reason ▪ **peur/soupçons sans ~s** groundless fear/suspicions ▮ DR [jugement] grounds **2.** [intention] motive ▪ **est-ce pour le bon ~?** *hum & vieilli* [en vue du mariage] are his intentions honourable? **3.** [dessin] pattern, design ▪ **un ~ à petites fleurs** a small flower pattern *ou* design **4.** ART [élément] motif ▪ [sujet] subject **5.** MUS motif.

motion [mosjɔ̃] *nf* motion ▪ **voter une ~** to pass a motion ➊ **~ de censure** vote of no confidence.

motivant, e [mɔtivɑ̃, ɑ̃t] *adj* motivating.

motivation [mɔtivasjɔ̃] *nf* **1.** [justification] motivation, justification, explanation ▪ [raison] motivation, motive, reason **2.** LING *relationship between the signifier and the signified* **3.** ÉCON : **étude de ~** motivation *ou* motivational research **4.** PSYCHOL motivation.

motivé, e [mɔtive] *adj* **1.** [personne] motivated **2.** [justifié] well-founded, justified ▪ **sa peur n'est pas ~e** her fears are groundless ▪ **un refus ~** a justifiable refusal.

motiver [3] [mɔtive] *vt* **1.** [inciter à agir] to spur on *(sép)*, to motivate **2.** [causer] to be the reason for ▪ **qu'est-ce qui a motivé votre retard?** what's the reason for your being late? **3.** [justifier] to justify, to explain ▪ **~ un refus** to give grounds for a refusal.

moto [moto] *nf* motorbike, bike ▪ **~ tout terrain** *ou* **verte** trail bike.

motocross [mɔtɔkrɔs] *nm* (motorcycle) scramble *UK*, motocross.

motoculteur [mɔtɔkyltœr] *nm* (motor) cultivator.

motocyclette [mɔtɔsiklɛt] *nf vieilli* motorcycle.

motocyclisme [mɔtɔsiklism] *nm* motorcycle racing.

motocycliste [mɔtɔsiklist] *nmf* motorcyclist.

motonautique [mɔtɔnotik] *adj* : **réunion/sport ~** speedboat event/racing.

motonautisme [mɔtɔnotism] *nm* speedboat *ou* motorboat racing.

motoneige [mɔtɔnɛʒ] = **motoski**.

motoneigisme [mɔtɔneʒism] *nm Québec* snowbike riding.

motopompe [mɔtɔpɔ̃p] *nf* motorpump.

motorisation [mɔtɔrizasjɔ̃] *nf* **1.** [gén] motorization **2.** MÉCAN engine specification.

motorisé, e [mɔtɔrize] *adj* **1.** [agriculture, troupes] motorized **2.** *fam* [personne] : **être ~** to have transport *UK* *OU* transportation *US* ■ **tu es ~?** have you got a car?

motoriser [3] [mɔtɔrize] *vt* [mécaniser] to motorize, to mechanize ■ **~ l'agriculture** to mechanize agriculture ‖ [doter d'automobiles] to motorize.

motoriste [mɔtɔrist] *nmf* [industriel] engine manufacturer ■ [technicien] engine technician.

motoski [mɔtɔski] *nf* snowbike.

motrice [mɔtris] *f* ▷ **moteur**.

motricité [mɔtrisite] *nf* motor functions.

mots croisés [mokrwaze] *nmpl* crossword (puzzle) ■ **il aime faire des ~** he likes doing crosswords.

motte [mɔt] *nf* **1.** AGRIC : **~ (de terre)** clod *OU* clump (of earth) ■ **~ de gazon** sod **2.** HORT ball **3.** CULIN : **~ de beurre** slab of butter **4.** MÉTALL [moule] boxless *OU* flaskless mould.

motus [mɔtys] *interj fam* **~ (et bouche cousue)!** not a word (to anybody)!, mum's the word!

mot-valise [movaliz] (*pl* **mots-valises**) *nm* blend, portmanteau word.

mou [mu] *(devant nm commençant par voyelle ou h muet mol* [mɔl], *nf molle* [mɔl]*)* ◇ *adj* **1.** [souple - pâte, cire, terre, fruit] soft ; [- fauteuil, matelas] soft ■ **les biscuits sont tout ~s** the biscuits have gone all soft ■ [sans tenue - étoffe, vêtement] limp ; [- joues, chair] flabby **2.** [sans vigueur physique - mouvement] limp, lifeless, feeble ; [- poignée de main] limp ■ **mon revers est trop ~** my backhand is too weak *OU* lacks power ■ **j'ai les jambes toutes molles** *fam* my legs feel all weak *OU* feel like jelly ■ **je me sens tout ~** *fam* I feel washed out ■ **allez, rame plus vite, c'est ~ tout ça!** *fam* come on, pull on those oars, let's see some effort! ■ [estompé - contour] soft ■ **bruit ~** muffled noise **3.** [sans conviction - protestation, excuse, tentative] feeble, weak ; [- doigté, style] lifeless, dull ; [- élève] apathetic, lethargic ■ [sans force de caractère] spineless ■ **être ~ comme une chiffe** *fam* *OU* **chique** *fam* to be a real wimp ■ **je me sens ~ comme une chiffe** *OU* **chique** I feel like a wet rag **4.** [trop tolérant - parents, gouvernement] lax, soft **5.** LING soft.
◇ *nm, f fam* **1.** [moralement] spineless individual **2.** [physiquement] weak *OU* feeble individual.
◆ **mou** *nm* **1.** [jeu] slack, give, play ■ **avoir du ~** [cordage] to be slack ; [vis, charnière] to be loose, to have a bit of play ■ **donner du ~ à un câble** to give a cable some slack **2.** [abats] lights, lungs **3.** △ *loc* **rentrer dans le ~ à qqn** to lay into sb.

mouchard, e [muʃar, ard] *nm, f fam péj* **1.** [rapporteur] sneak **2.** [indic] informer, grass *UK*, stoolpigeon *US*.
◆ **mouchard** *nm* **1.** [enregistreur - d'un avion] black box, flight recorder ; [- d'un camion] tachograph **2.** AÉRON & MIL spy plane **3.** *fam* [sur une porte] judas (hole).

moucharder [3] [muʃarde] *fam péj* ◇ *vt* **1.** [suj: enfant] to sneak on *(insép)* *UK*, to tell tales about **2.** [suj: indic] to inform on *(insép)*, to grass on *(insép)* *UK*, to fink on *(insép)* *US*.
◇ *vi* **1.** [enfant] to sneak *UK*, to tell tales **2.** [indic] to inform, to grass *UK*, to fink *US*.

mouche [muʃ] *nf* **1.** ENTOM fly ■ **~ bleue** bluebottle ■ **~ à miel** honey bee ■ **~ tsé-tsé** tsetse fly ■ **~ à viande** blowfly ■ **~ à merde**△ *OU* **à ordure** dung fly ■ **quelle ~ te pique?** *fam* what's up *OU* wrong with you (all of a sudden)? ■ **tomber comme des ~s** *fam* to drop like flies ■ **il ne ferait pas de mal à une ~** he wouldn't hurt a fly ■ **prendre la ~ : elle prend facilement la ~** she's very touchy ■ **on ne prend** *OU* **n'attrape pas les ~s avec du vinaigre** *prov* gently does it **2.** PÊCHE : **~ (artificielle)** (artificial) fly ■ **pêche à la ~** fly-fishing **3.** [sur la peau] beauty spot ■ [poils] tuft of hair *(under the lower lip)* **4.** ESCRIME button ■ **faire ~** *pr* to hit the *OU* to score a bull's eye ; *fig* to hit the nail on the head.

moucher [3] [muʃe] *vt* **1.** [nettoyer] : **~ son nez** to blow one's nose ■ **~ qqn** to blow sb's nose **2.** *fam* [rabrouer] : **~ qqn** to put sb in his place, to teach sb a lesson **3.** [chandelle] to snuff (out).
◆ **se moucher** *vp (emploi réfléchi)* to blow one's nose ■ **elle ne se mouche pas du pied** *fam* *OU* **du coude** *fam* she thinks she's the cat's whiskers *OU* the bee's knees.

moucheron [muʃrɔ̃] *nm* **1.** ENTOM midge **2.** *fam* [gamin] kid.

moucheté, e [muʃte] *adj* **1.** [œuf, fourrure, laine etc] mottled, flecked ■ **rouge ~ de blanc** red flecked with white **2.** ESCRIME buttoned.

moucheter [27] [muʃte] *vt* **1.** [couvrir de taches] to speckle ■ [parsemer de taches] to fleck **2.** ESCRIME to button.

moucheture [muʃtyr] *nf* **1.** [d'un pelage, d'un plumage] speckling ■ [d'un tissu] flecks, flecking **2.** AGRIC leaf stripe **3.** HÉRALD : **~ d'hermine** ermine tail.

mouchoir [muʃwar] *nm* handkerchief ■ **~ en papier** (paper) tissue ■ **leur jardin est grand comme un ~ de poche** their garden is the size of a pocket handkerchief.

moudjahidin [mudʒaidin] *nmpl* mujaheddin.

moudre [85] [mudr] *vt* [café, poivre] to grind ■ [blé] to mill, to grind.

moue [mu] *nf* pout ■ **faire une ~ de dégoût** to screw one's face up in disgust ■ **faire une ~ de dépit** to pull a face ■ **faire la ~** to pout.

mouette [mwɛt] *nf* gull, seagull ■ **~ rieuse** blackheaded gull ■ **'la Mouette'** *Tchekhov* 'The Seagull'.

moufette [mufɛt] *nf* skunk.

moufle [mufl] ◇ *nf* **1.** [gant] mitt, mitten **2.** [poulie] pulley block.
◇ *nm* TECHNOL [four, récipient] muffle.

mouflet, ette△ [muflɛ, ɛt] *nm, f* kid, sprog *UK*.

mouflon [muflɔ̃] *nm* mouflon, moufflon ■ **~ d'Amérique** (American) bighorn.

moufter [3] △ [mufte] *vi* : **sans ~** without a peep.

mouillage [mujaʒ] *nm* **1.** NAUT [emplacement] anchorage, moorings, moorage ■ [manœuvre] mooring **2.** MIL : **~ de mines** mine laying.

mouillant, e [mujɑ̃, ɑ̃t] *adj* [gén - CHIM] wetting.

mouillé, e [muje] *adj* **1.** [surface, vêtement, cheveux] wet, damp ■ **je suis tout ~** I'm all wet *OU* drenched *OU* soaked **2.** [voix] tearful ■ [regard] tearful, watery **3.** LING palatalized.

mouiller [3] [muje] ◇ *vt* **1.** [accidentellement - vêtement, personne] to wet ■ **ne mouille pas tes chaussons!** don't get your slippers wet! ■ **il mouille encore son lit** *euphém* he still wets his *OU* the bed ■ **se faire ~** [par la pluie] to get wet **2.** [humecter - doigt, lèvres] to moisten ; [- linge] to dampen **3.** *fam* [compromettre] to drag in *(sép)* **4.** NAUT [ancre] to cast, to drop ■ MIL [mine] to lay ■ PÊCHE [ligne] to cast **5.** *(en usage absolu)* CULIN : **mouillez avec du vin/bouillon** moisten with wine/stock ‖ [lait, vin] to water down *(sép)* **6.** LING to palatalize.
◇ *vi* **1.** △ [avoir peur] to be scared stiff△ **2.** NAUT [jeter l'ancre] to cast *OU* to drop anchor ■ [stationner] to ride *OU* to lie *OU* to be at anchor.
◆ **se mouiller** *vp (emploi réfléchi)* **1.** [volontairement] : **se ~ les cheveux** to wet one's hair **2.** [accidentellement] to get wet **3.** *fam* [prendre un risque] to commit o.s.

mouillette [mujɛt] *nf* [de pain] finger of bread *(for dunking)*, soldier *UK*.

mouise [mwiz] *nf fam* [misère] : **être dans la ~** to be hard up, to be on one's uppers.

moujik [muʒik] *nm* muzhik, mujik, moujik.

moukère△ [mukɛr] *nf* female.

moulage [mulaʒ] *nm* **1.** ART [processus] casting ■ [reproduction] cast **2.** MÉTALL casting, moulding ■ **~ par compression/injection** compression/injection moulding **3.** [d'un fromage] moulding **4.** [du grain] grinding, milling.

moulait *etc v* ▷ **moudre**.

moulant, e [mulɑ̃, ɑ̃t] *adj* close-fitting, tight-fitting, clinging.

moule [mul] ◇ *nm* **1.** [récipient, matrice] mould ■ **~ à gaufre** *OU* **gaufres** waffle iron ■ **~ à gâteau** cake *OU* baking tin *UK*, cake *OU* baking pan *US* ■ **~ à manqué** sandwich tin *UK*, deep cake pan *US* ■ **~ à tarte** flan case *UK*, pie pan *US* **2.** [modèle imposé]

mould ▪ **elle rejette le ~ de l'école** she rejects the image the school demands of her ▶ **être coulé dans le même ~** *pr & fig* to be cast in the same mould.
◇ *nf* **1.** [mollusque] mussel ▪ **~s marinières** moules marinières, mussels in white wine ▪ **~s frites** mussels and chips *UK ou* French fries *(speciality of Belgium and the North of France)* **2.** *fam* [personne] drip.

moulé, e [mule] *adj* **1.** [pain] baked in a tin **2.** [écriture] neat, well-shaped ▪ [lettre] printed, copperplate **3.** MÉD [matières fécales] well-shaped, consistent.

mouler [3] [mule] *vt* **1.** [former - buste, statue] to cast ; [- brique, lingot, fromage] to mould **2.** [prendre copie de - visage, empreinte] to take *ou* to make a cast of ▪ **~ qqch en plâtre/cire** to take a plaster/wax cast of sthg **3.** [adapter] : **~ ses pensées/son mode de vie sur** to mould *ou* to model one's thoughts/lifestyle on **4.** [serrer - hanches, jambes] to hug, to fit closely (round) ▪ **cette jupe te moule trop** this skirt is too tight *ou* tight-fitting for you.

moulin [mulɛ̃] *nm* **1.** [machine, bâtiment] mill ▪ **~ à eau** water mill ▪ **~ à vent** windmill ▪ **on entre chez elle comme dans un ~** her door's always open **2.** [instrument] : **~ à café** coffee grinder ▪ **~ à légumes** vegetable mill ▪ **~ à poivre** peppermill ▪ **~ à prières** RELIG prayer wheel **3.** *fam* [moteur] engine **4.** TEXT [pour la soie] thrower ▪ [pour retordre] doubling frame, twister **5.** *Québec* **~ à viande** mincer ▪ **~ à bois** sawmill ▪ **~ à coudre** sewing machine.
◆ **moulin à paroles** *nm fam* windbag *péj*, chatterbox.

mouliner [3] [muline] ◇ *vt* **1.** [aliment] to mill **2.** PÊCHE to reel in *(sép)* **3.** TEXT [soie grège] to throw.
◇ *vi fam* [pédaler] to pedal.

moulinet [mulinɛ] *nm* **1.** PÊCHE reel **2.** MÉCAN winch **3.** [mouvement] : **faire des ~s avec un bâton** to twirl *ou* to whirl a stick around ▪ **il faisait des ~s avec ses bras** he was whirling *ou* waving his arms around **4.** [tourniquet] turnstile **5.** NAUT log reel.

Moulinette® [mulinɛt] *nf* **1.** CULIN (hand-held) vegetable mill, Moulinette® ▪ **passer de la viande à la ~** to put some meat through a food mill **2.** *fam fig* **passer qqch à la ~** to make mincemeat of sthg.

moult [mult] *adv hum & vieilli* **je suis venu ~ fois** I came many a time ▪ **avec ~ détails** with a profusion of details.

moulu, e [muly] ◇ *pp* ▷ **moudre**.
◇ *adj* **1.** [en poudre] ground ▪ **café fraîchement ~** freshly ground coffee **2.** *fam* [épuisé] : **~ (de fatigue)** dead beat, all in.

moulure [mulyr] *nf* moulding ▪ **~ creuse/lisse/ronde** concave/plain/convex moulding.

moulut *etc v* ▷ **moudre**.

moumoute [mumut] *nf fam* **1.** [perruque] wig, hairpiece **2.** [veste] sheepskin jacket *ou* coat.

mourant, e [murɑ̃, ɑ̃t] ◇ *adj* **1.** [personne, animal, plante] dying **2.** *sout* [lumière, son] dying, fading.
◇ *nm, f* dying man *(f* woman) ▪ **les ~s** the dying.

mourir [42] [murir] *vi* **1.** BIOL to die ▪ **~ d'une crise cardiaque/de vieillesse/d'un cancer** to die of a heart attack/of old age/of cancer ▪ **~ de mort naturelle** *ou* **de sa belle mort** to die a natural death ▪ **il mourut de ses blessures** he died from his wounds ▪ **~ sur le coup** to die instantly ▪ **~ en héros** to die a hero's death *ou* like a hero ▪ **je l'aime à en ~** I'm desperately in love with her ▪ **tu n'en mourras pas!** *fam* it won't kill you! ▶ **plus rapide/bête que lui, tu meurs!** *fam* you'd be hard put to be quicker/more stupid than him! **2.** *sout* [disparaître - culture] to die out ; [- flamme, bougie] to die out *ou* down ; [- bruit] to die away *ou* down **3.** [pour intensifier] : **~ d'envie de faire qqch** to be dying to do sthg ▪ **~ d'ennui, s'ennuyer à ~** to be bored to death *ou* to tears ▪ **la pièce est à ~ de rire** *fam* the play's hilarious *ou* a scream ▪ **elle me fait ~ de rire!** she really cracks me up! ▪ **~ de chaleur** to be boiling hot ▪ **~ de faim** to be starving *ou* famished ▪ **~ de froid** to be freezing cold ▪ **~ de soif** to be dying of thirst, to be parched ▪ **~ de peur** to be scared to death.
◆ **se mourir** *vpi litt* **1.** [personne] to be dying ▪ **se ~ d'amour pour qqn** *fig* to pine for sb **2.** [civilisation, coutume] to die out ▪ **une tradition qui se meurt** a dying tradition.

mouroir [murwar] *nm péj* (old people's) home.

mouron [murɔ̃] *nm* **1.** BOT : **faux ~, ~ rouge** scarlet pimpernel ▪ **~ blanc** *ou* **des oiseaux** common chickweed **2.** *fam loc* **se faire du ~** to worry o.s. sick ▪ **te fais pas de ~ pour lui!** don't (you) worry about him!

mourra, mourut *etc v* ▷ **mourir**.

mousquetaire [muskətɛr] *nm* musketeer.

mousqueton [muskətɔ̃] *nm* **1.** [anneau] snap hook *ou* clasp ▪ SPORT [alpinisme] karabiner **2.** ARM carbine.

moussaillon [musajɔ̃] *nm* (young) cabin boy.

moussaka [musaka] *nf* moussaka.

moussant, e [musɑ̃, ɑ̃t] *adj* [crème à raser] lathering ▪ [shampooing] foaming.

mousse [mus] ◇ *adj* **1.** TEXT : **collant ~** stretch tights **2.** CHIM : **caoutchouc ~** foam rubber.
◇ *adj inv* : **vert ~** mossgreen.
◇ *nm* cabin boy.
◇ *nf* **1.** [bulles - de shampooing, de crème à raser] lather, foam ; [- d'un bain] bubbles, foam ; [- de savon] suds, lather ; [- de champagne, de cidre] bubbles ; [- de bière] froth **2.** CULIN mousse ▪ **~ au chocolat** chocolate mousse ▪ **~ de saumon** salmon mousse **3.** *fam* [bière] (glass of) beer **4.** [dans les matériaux synthétiques] foam ▪ **~ de nylon** stretch nylon ▪ **balle en ~** rubber ball ▪ **~ de platine** platinum sponge **5.** BOT moss ▪ **couvert de ~** mossy.

mousseline [muslin] ◇ *nf* [de coton] muslin ▪ [de soie, de nylon, de laine] chiffon, mousseline ▪ **foulard en ~** muslin *ou* chiffon scarf.
◇ *adj inv* : **pommes ~** puréed potatoes.

mousser [3] [muse] *vi* **1.** [champagne, cidre] to bubble, to sparkle ▪ [bière] to froth ▪ [savon, crème à raser] to lather ▪ [détergent, shampooing] to foam, to lather **2.** *fam fig* **faire ~ qqn** [le mettre en colère] to wind sb up, to rile sb ; [le mettre en valeur] to sing sb's praises ▪ **se faire ~** to sell o.s.

mousseron [musrɔ̃] *nm* St George's mushroom.

mousseux, euse [musø, øz] *adj* **1.** [vin, cidre] sparkling ▪ [bière] frothy ▪ [eau] foamy ▪ [sauce, jaunes d'œufs] (light and) frothy ▪ **un chocolat ~** a cup of frothy hot chocolate **2.** BOT mossy.
◆ **mousseux** *nm* sparkling wine.

mousson [musɔ̃] *nf* monsoon.

moussu, e [musy] *adj* mossy.

moustache [mustaʃ] *nf* **1.** [d'un homme] moustache ▪ **porter la ~** *ou* **des ~s** to have a moustache ▪ **elle a de la ~** she's got a bit of a moustache ▶ **~ (à la) gauloise** walrus moustache ▪ **~ en brosse** toothbrush moustache **2.** ZOOL whiskers.

moustachu, e [mustaʃy] *adj* : **un homme ~** a man with a moustache ▪ **il est ~** he's got a moustache.
◆ **moustachu** *nm* man with a moustache.

moustiquaire [mustikɛr] *nf* [d'un lit] mosquito net ▪ [d'une ouverture] mosquito screen.

moustique [mustik] *nm* **1.** ENTOM mosquito **2.** *fam* [gamin] kid, mite ▪ [petite personne] (little) squirt.

moût [mu] *nm* [de raisin] must ▪ [de bière] wort.

moutard [mutar] *nm fam* kid.

moutarde [mutard] ◇ *nf* **1.** BOT mustard ▪ **graines de ~** mustard seeds **2.** CULIN mustard ▪ **~ à l'estragon** tarragon mustard ▪ **~ de Dijon** Dijon mustard **3.** *fam loc* **la ~ lui est montée au nez** he lost his temper, he saw red.
◇ *adj inv* mustard *(modif)*, mustard-coloured.

moutardier [mutardje] *nm* **1.** [récipient] mustard pot **2.** [fabricant] mustard maker *ou* manufacturer **3.** [marchand] mustard seller.

mouton [mutɔ̃] *nm* **1.** ZOOL sheep ▪ **~ à cinq pattes** rare bird *fig* ▪ **compter les ~s** to count sheep ▪ **revenons** *ou* **retournons à nos ~s** let's get back to the point **2.** [fourrure, cuir] sheepskin ▪ **veste en (peau de) ~** sheepskin jacket **3.** CULIN mutton ▪ **côte de ~** mutton chop **4.** *fam* [individu] sheep ▪ **c'est un vrai ~ de Panurge** he's easily led, he follows the herd.
◆ **moutons** *nmpl* [poussière] (bits of) fluff ▪ [nuages] fleecy *ou* fluffy clouds ▪ [écume sur la mer] white horses.

moutonner [3] [mutɔne] *vi* [mer] to break into white horses ▪ [ciel] to become covered with small fleecy clouds.

moutonneux, euse [mutɔnø, øz] *adj* [mer] flecked with white horses ▪ [ciel] spotted *ou* dotted with fleecy clouds.

moutonnier, ère [mutɔnje, ɛr] *adj* **1.** AGRIC ovine, sheep *(modif)* **2.** *sout* [trop docile] sheep-like, easily led.

mouture [mutyr] *nf* **1.** [version] version ▪ **ma première ~ était meilleure** my first draft was better **2.** *péj* [copie, reprise] rehash *péj* **3.** AGRIC & CULIN [des céréales] milling, grinding ▪ [du café] grinding ▪ **ayant obtenu une ~ fine** [farine, café] once it has been finely ground.

mouvance [muvɑ̃s] *nf* **1.** *sout* [domaine d'influence] circle of influence ▪ **ils se situent dans la ~ socialiste** they belong to the socialist camp **2.** *litt* [instabilité] unsettledness, instability **3.** HIST subtenure.

mouvant, e [muvɑ̃, ɑ̃t] *adj* **1.** [en mouvement - foule] moving, surging **2.** [instable - surface] unsteady, moving **3.** [changeant - situation] unstable, unsettled.

mouvement [muvmɑ̃] *nm* **1.** [geste] movement ▪ **un ~ de tête** [affirmatif] a nod ; [négatif] a shake of the head ▪ **un léger ~ de surprise** a start of surprise ▪ **avoir un ~ de recul** to start (back) ▪ **faire des ~s de gymnastique** to do some exercises ▪ **il y eut un ~ dans la foule à l'arrivée du président** a ripple ran through the crowd when the President arrived ➊ **faire un faux ~** to pull something
2. [impulsion] : **~ de colère** fit *ou* burst of anger ▪ **avoir un bon ~** to make a nice gesture ▪ **les ~s du cœur/de l'âme** *litt* the impulses of the heart/of the soul
3. [déplacement - d'un astre, d'un pendule] movement ; [- de personnes] movement ▪ PHYS motion ▪ **~s de capitaux** *ou* **de fonds** movement of capital ▪ **~ de personnel** ADMIN staff transfer *ou* changes ▪ **~ de repli** withdrawal ▪ **~s de marchandises** movement of goods ▪ **~s de troupes** troop movements ▪ **il y eut un ~ de foule** the crowd surged forward
4. [évolution - des prix, des taux] trend, movement ; [- du marché] fluctuation ▪ **~ en baisse/en hausse** downward/upward trend ▪ **le ~ des idées** the evolution of ideas ➊ **~ de la population** SOCIOL demographic changes
5. POLIT [action collective] movement ▪ **~ de contestation** protest movement ▪ **~ social** industrial action ➊ **~ de grève** strike (movement) ▪ **le ~ syndical** the trade-union *UK ou* labor-union *US* movement ▪ **Mouvement de libération de la femme** Women's Liberation Movement
6. [animation - d'un quartier] bustle, liveliness ; [- dans un aéroport, un port] movement ▪ **eh bien, il y a du ~ chez vous!** it's all go at your place!
7. GÉOGR : **~s sismiques** seismic movements ▪ **~ de terrain** undulation
8. [impression de vie - d'une peinture, d'une sculpture] movement ; [- d'un vers] flow, movement ; [- d'une robe] drape ; [- d'un paysage] undulations
9. MUS [rythme] tempo ▪ **~ perpétuel** moto perpetuo, perpetuum mobile ‖ [section d'un morceau] movement
10. [mécanisme] movement ▪ **~ d'horlogerie** movement, mechanism *(of a clock or watch)*.
◆ **en mouvement** ◇ *loc adj* [athlète] moving, in motion ▪ [population, troupes] on the move.
◇ *loc adv* : **mettre un mécanisme en ~** to set a mechanism going *ou* in motion ▪ **le balancier se mit en ~** the pendulum started moving ▪ **le cortège se mit en ~** the procession started *ou* set off.
◆ **sans mouvement** *loc adj* [personne] inert.

mouvementé, e [muvmɑ̃te] *adj* **1.** [débat] (very) lively, heated, stormy ▪ [voyage, vie] eventful ▪ [match] (very) lively, eventful ▪ **avec eux, c'est toujours ~** there's never a dull moment with them **2.** [paysage] rolling, undulating.

mouvoir [54] [muvwar] *vt sout* **1.** [bouger - membre, objet] to move ▪ **mécanisme mû par un ressort** spring-operated mechanism **2.** [activer - machine] to drive, to power **3.** *fig* [pousser] to move, to prompt ▪ **mû par l'intérêt/le désir/la jalousie** prompted by self-interest/desire/jealousy.
◆ **se mouvoir** *vpi sout* [se déplacer] to move.

moyen[1] [mwajɛ̃] *nm* **1.** [méthode] way ▪ **il n'y a pas d'autre ~** there's no other way *ou* solution ▪ **par quel ~ peut-on le contacter?** how can he be contacted? ▪ **nous avons les ~s de vous faire parler!** we have ways of making you talk! ▪ **je l'aurais empêché, si j'en avais eu les ~s** I would have stopped him, if I'd been able to ▪ **trouver (le) ~ de faire qqch** to manage to do sthg ▪ **et en plus, tu trouves le ~ d'être en retard!** not only that but you've managed to be late as well! ➊ **~ de défense/d'existence** means of defence/existence ▪ **~ de locomotion** *ou* **de transport** means of transport ▪ **il faudra faire avec les ~s du bord** we'll have to manage with what we've got ▪ **~ d'expression** means of expression ▪ **ils n'ont utilisé aucun ~ de pression** they didn't apply any pressure ▪ **~ de production** means of production ▪ **~ de subsistance** means of subsistance ▪ **employer** *ou* **utiliser les grands ~s** to take drastic steps ▪ **tous les ~s lui sont bons** he'll stop at nothing **2.** [pour intensifier] : **il n'y a pas ~ d'ouvrir la porte!** there's no way of opening the door!, the door won't open! ▪ **pas ~ de dormir ici!** *fam* it's impossible to get any sleep around here! ▪ **je voulais me reposer, mais non, pas ~!** *fam* I wanted to get some rest, but no such luck! ▪ **est-ce qu'il y a ~ d'avoir le silence?** can we please have some silence around here? **3.** GRAMM : **adverbe de ~** adverb of means.
◆ **moyens** *nmpl* [financiers] means ▪ **je n'ai pas les ~s de m'acheter un ordinateur** I haven't got the means to *ou* I can't afford to buy a computer ▪ **j'ai de tout petits ~s** I have a very small income ▪ **avoir de gros ~s** to be very well-off ▪ **je peux te payer une bière, c'est encore dans mes ~ s** I can buy you a beer, I can just about manage that ▪ **c'est au-dessus de mes ~s** it's beyond my means, I can't afford it ‖ [intellectuels, physiques] : **perdre (tous) ses ~s** to go to pieces ▪ **je suis venu par mes propres ~s** I made my own way here.
◆ **au moyen de** *loc prép* by means of, with.
◆ **par tous les moyens** *loc adv* by all possible means ▪ [même immoraux] by fair means or foul ▪ **j'ai essayé par tous les ~s** I've tried everything.

moyen[2], enne [mwajɛ̃, ɛn] *adj* **1.** [intermédiaire - selon des mesures] medium *(avant n)*, average ; [- selon une évaluation] medium ▪ **un arbre de taille ~ne** a medium-sized tree ▪ **à ~ne échéance** in the medium term ➊ **cadres ~s** middle-ranking executives ▪ **classes ~nes** middle classes ▪ **~ terme** PHILOS middle term ; [solution] compromise, middle course **2.** [prix, taille, consommation, distance] average ▪ [température] average, mean ▪ [aptitudes, niveau, service] average ▪ **ses notes sont trop ~nes** his marks are too poor ▪ **il est ~ en maths** he's average at maths **3.** [ordinaire] : **le spectateur/lecteur ~** the average spectator/reader ▪ **le Français ~** the average Frenchman **4.** LING [voyelle] middle.

Moyen Âge [mwajɛnaʒ] *nm* : **le ~** the Middle Ages.

moyenâgeux, euse [mwajɛnaʒø, øz] *adj* medieval ▪ **ils utilisent des techniques moyenâgeuses** *hum* they use methods out of the Dark Ages.

moyen-courrier [mwajɛ̃kurje] (*pl* **moyen-courriers**) *nm* medium-haul aeroplane.

moyen(-)métrage [mwajɛ̃metraʒ] (*pl* **moyens-métrages** *ou pl* **moyens métrages**) *nm* medium-length film.

moyennant [mwajɛnɑ̃] *prep* : **elle garde ma fille ~ 20 euros par jour** she looks after my daughter for twenty euros a day ▪ **~ finance** for a fee *ou* a consideration ▪ **~ quoi** in return for which.

moyenne [mwajɛn] ◇ *adj f* ▻ **moyen**.
◇ *nf* **1.** [gén] average ▪ **la ~ d'âge des candidats est de 21 ans** the average age of the applicants is 21 ▪ **calculer** *ou* **faire la ~ de** to work out the average of ‖ MATH mean, average ▪ **~ arithmétique/géométrique** arithmetic/geometric mean **2.** [vitesse moyenne] average speed ▪ **faire une ~ de 90 km/h** to average 90 km/h **3.** ÉDUC [absolue] pass mark *UK*, passing grade *US (of fifty per cent)* ▪ **notes au-dessus/au-dessous de la ~** marks above/under half ▪ **j'ai eu tout juste la ~** [à un examen] I just got a pass ‖ [relative] average (mark) ➊ **j'ai 13 de ~ générale** my average (mark) is 13 out of 20 **4.** [ensemble] : **la ~ des gens** most people, the vast majority of people ▪ **d'une intelligence au-dessus de la ~** of above-average intelligence.
◆ **en moyenne** *loc adv* on average.

moyennement [mwajɛnmɑ̃] *adv* moderately, fairly ▪ **il a ~ apprécié** he was not amused.

moyenner [3] [mwajɛne] *vt fam loc*: **pas moyen de ~** nothing doing.

Moyen-Orient [mwajɛnɔrjɑ̃] *npr m* : **le ~** the Middle East ■ **au ~** in the Middle East.

moyen-oriental, e, aux [mwajɛnɔrjɑ̃tal, o] *adj* Middle Eastern.

moyeu [mwajø] *nm* **1.** [d'une roue - de voiture] (wheel) hub ; [- de charrue] nave **2.** [d'une hélice] boss, hub.

mozambicain, e [mɔzɑ̃bikɛ̃, ɛn] *adj* Mozambican.

Mozambique [mɔzɑ̃bik] *npr m* : **le ~** Mozambique ■ **au ~** in Mozambique.

Mozart [mɔzar] *npr* Mozart.

mozzarelle [mɔdzarɛl], **mozarella** *nf* mozzarella.

MRAP [mrap] (*abr de* **Mouvement contre le racisme, l'antisémitisme et pour la paix**) *npr m pacifist anti-racist organization.*

MRG (*abr de* **Mouvement des radicaux de gauche**) *npr m left-wing political grouping of local councillors.*

MRP (*abr de* **Mouvement républicain populaire**) *npr m centre right political group influential under the fourth Republic.*

MSF *npr* = **Médecins sans frontières.**

MST *nf* **1.** (*abr de* **maladie sexuellement transmissible**) STD **2.** (*abr de* **maîtrise de sciences et techniques**) *master's degree in science and technology.*

MT (*abr écrite de* **moyenne tension**) MT.

mu [my] *nm* [lettre] mu.

mû, mue [my] *pp* ▻ **mouvoir.**

mucosité [mykozite] *nf* mucus.

mucoviscidose [mykovisidoz] *nf* cystic fibrosis.

mucus [mykys] *nm* mucus.

mue [my] *nf* **1.** ZOOL [transformation - d'un reptile] sloughing ; [- d'un volatile] moulting ; [- d'un mammifère à poils] shedding hair, moulting ; [- d'un mammifère sans poils] shedding *ou* casting (of skin) ; [- d'un cerf] shedding (of antlers) **2.** PHYSIOL [de la voix] breaking, changing **3.** [dépouille - d'un reptile] slough ; [- d'un volatile] moulted feathers ; [- d'un mammifère à poils] shed hair ; [- d'un mammifère sans poils] shed skin ; [- d'un cerf] shed antlers **4.** *fig* [métamorphose] change, transformation **5.** [cage] (hen) coop.

muer [7] [mɥe] ◇ *vi* **1.** ZOOL [reptile] to slough, to moult ■ [volatile] to moult ■ [mammifère à fourrure] to shed hair, to moult ■ [mammifère sans poils] to shed skin, to moult ■ [cerf] to shed (antlers) **2.** PHYSIOL [voix] to break, to change ■ **il mue** his voice is breaking.
◇ *vt litt* **~ qqch en** to change *ou* to turn sthg into.
◆ **se muer en** *vp+prép litt* to change *ou* to turn into.

muesli [mysli] *nm* muesli.

muet, ette [mɥɛ, ɛt] ◇ *adj* **1.** [qui ne parle pas] dumb ■ **~ de naissance** dumb from birth **2.** *fig* [silencieux] silent, mute, dumb ■ **~ d'admiration** in mute admiration ■ **~ de stupeur** dumbfounded ■ **il en resta ~ d'étonnement** he was struck dumb with astonishment ■ **alors, tu restes** *ou* **es ~?** well, have you nothing to say for yourself? ◗ **elle est restée ~te comme une carpe toute la soirée** she never opened her mouth all evening ■ **je serai ~ comme une tombe** my lips are sealed, I won't breathe a word **3.** *sout* [non exprimé - douleur, reproche] unspoken, mute, silent **4.** CINÉ [film, cinéma] silent ■ [rôle, acteur] non-speaking, walk-on **5.** LING mute, silent **6.** [sans indication - touche, carte] blank.
◇ *nm, f* [personne] mute, dumb person.
◆ **muet** *nm* CINÉ : **le ~** the silent cinema *UK ou* movies *US*.

muezzin [mɥɛdzin] *nm* muezzin.

mufle [myfl] *nm* **1.** ZOOL [d'un ruminant] muffle ■ [d'un félin] muzzle **2.** *fam péj* [malotru] boor, lout.

muflerie [myfləri] *nf* boorishness, loutishness, churlishness.

muflier [myflije] *nm* snapdragon, antirrhinum.

mufti [myfti] *nm* mufti.

mugir [32] [myʒir] *vi* **1.** [vache] to moo, to low *litt* **2.** *litt* [vent] to howl, to roar ■ [océan] to roar, to thunder.

mugissement [myʒismɑ̃] *nm* **1.** [d'une vache] mooing, lowing *litt* **2.** *litt* [du vent] howling, roaring ■ [des flots] roar, thundering.

muguet [mygɛ] *nm* **1.** BOT lily of the valley, May lily **2.** MÉD candidiasis *spéc*, thrush.

MUGUET

On May Day in France, bunches of lilies of the valley are sold in the streets and given as presents. The flowers are supposed to bring good luck.

mulâtre, mulâtresse [mylatr, mylatrɛs] *nm, f* mulatto.
◆ **mulâtre** *adj inv* mulatto.

mule [myl] *nf* **1.** ZOOL mule *(female)* **2.** *fam* [personne entêtée] mule **3.** [chausson] mule.

mulet [mylɛ] *nm* **1.** ZOOL mule *(male)* **2.** *fam* [voiture] back-up car **3.** [poisson] grey mullet.

muletier, ère [myltje, ɛr] ◇ *adj* : **chemin** *ou* **sentier ~** (mule) track.
◇ *nm, f* muleteer, mule driver.

Müller [mylɛr] *npr* : **canaux de ~** Müller canals.

mulot [mylo] *nm* field mouse.

multiaccès [myltiaksɛ] *adj* multiaccess.

multicanal [myltikanal] *adj* multichannel.

multicarte [myltikart] *adj* [voyageur de commerce] *representing several companies.*

multicolore [myltikɔlɔr] *adj* multicoloured, many-coloured.

multicoque [myltikɔk] ◇ *adj* : **(bateau) ~** multihull *ou* multihulled boat.
◇ *nm* multihull.

multiculturalisme [myltikyltyralism] *nm* multiculturalism.

multiculturel, elle [myltikyltyrɛl] *adj* multicultural.

multidirectionnel, elle [myltidirɛksjɔnɛl] *adj* multidirectional.

multifenêtre [myltifənɛtr] *adj* multiwindow.

multifonction [myltifɔ̃ksjɔ̃] *adj* multifunction.

multiforme [myltifɔrm] *adj* [aspect, créature] multiform ■ [question, personnalité] many-sided, multifaceted.

multilatéral, e, aux [myltilateral, o] *adj* multilateral.

multilingue [myltilɛ̃g] *adj* multilingual.

multimédia, multi-média [myltimedja] ◇ *adj* multimedia *(avant n).*
◇ *nm* : **le ~** multimedia.

multimédiatique [myltimedjatik] *adj* multimedia.

multimilliardaire [myltimiljardɛr] *adj* & *nmf* multimillionaire.

multimillionnaire [myltimiljɔnɛr] *adj* & *nmf* multimillionaire.

multinational, e, aux [myltinasjɔnal, o] *adj* multinational.
◆ **multinationale** *nf* multinational (company).

multipare [myltipar] ◇ *adj* multiparous.
◇ *nf* multipara.

multipartisme [myltipartism] *nm* multiparty system.

multipartite [myltipartit] *adj* multiparty *(modif).*

multiple [myltipl] ◇ *adj* **1.** [nombreux - exemples, incidents, qualités] many, numerous ; [- fractures] multiple ■ **à de ~s reprises** repeatedly, time and (time) again **2.** [divers - raisons, intérêts] many, multiple, manifold *sout* ■ **personnalité aux ~s facettes** many-sided *ou* multifaceted personality ■ **femme aux**

talents ~s multi-talented woman **3.** *sout* [complexe - problème, difficulté] many-sided, multifaceted, complex **4.** BOT [fleur, fruit] multiple **5.** MATH : **9 est ~ de 3** 9 is a multiple of 3.
◇ *nm* MATH multiple ➜ **le plus petit commun ~** the lowest common multiple.

multiplex [myltiplɛks] *adj* & *nm* multiplex.

multipliable [myltiplijabl] *adj* multipliable, multiplicable.

multiplicateur, trice [myltiplikatœr, tris] *adj* multiplying.
◆ **multiplicateur** *nm* MATH multiplier.

multiplication [myltiplikasjɔ̃] *nf* **1.** BIOL, MATH & NUCL multiplication ▪ **la ~ des accidents** *fig* the increase in the number of accidents **2.** RELIG : **la ~ des pains** the miracle of the loaves and fishes **3.** MÉCAN gear ratio.

multiplicité [myltiplisite] *nf* multiplicity ▪ **la ~ des choix qui nous sont offerts** the (very) many choices open to us.

multiplier [10] [myltiplije] *vt* **1.** [contrôles, expériences, efforts etc] to multiply, to increase **2.** MATH to multiply ▪ **2 multiplié par 3** 2 multiplied by 3 ▪ **la production a été multipliée par trois** *fig* output has tripled.
◆ **se multiplier** *vpi* **1.** [attentats, menaces] to multiply, to increase **2.** BIOL to multiply **3.** *fig* to be everywhere (at once) ▪ **je ne peux pas me ~** I can't be everywhere at once.

multiposte [myltipɔst] ◇ *adj* multiple-station.
◇ *nm* multiple-station computer.

multiprise [myltipriz] *nf* adapter.

multiprocesseur [myltiprɔsesœr] ◇ *adj m* multiprocessing.
◇ *nm* multiprocessor (system).

multiprogrammation [myltiprɔgramasjɔ̃] *nf* multiprogramming, multiple programming.

multipropriété [myltiprɔprijete] *nf* timeshare (system), time-sharing ▪ **investir dans la ~** to invest in a timeshare.

multiracial, e, aux [myltirasjal, o] *adj* multiracial.

multirisque [myltirisk] *adj* multiple risk *(modif)*.

multisalles [myltisal] *adj inv* : **complexe ~** multiplex (cinema) UK, movie theater complex US.

multistandard [myltistɑ̃dar] *adj* multistandard, multisystem.

multitâche [myltitaʃ] *adj* multitasking, multitask *(avant un nom)*.

multithérapie [myltiterapi] *nf* multitherapy.

multitude [myltityd] *nf* **1.** [grande quantité] : **une ~ de** a multitude of, a vast number of **2.** *litt* [foule] : **la ~** the multitude, the masses.

multiutilisateurs [myltiytilizatœr] *adj inv* INFORM multiuser.

multizone [myltizon] *adj* INFORM multi-region.

Munich [mynik] *npr* Munich.

munichois, e [mynikwa, az] *adj* from Munich.
◆ **Munichois, e** *nm, f* **1.** GÉOGR *inhabitant of or person from Munich* **2.** HIST : **les Munichois** the men of Munich.

municipal, e, aux [mynisipal, o] *adj* [élection, conseil] local, municipal ▪ [bibliothèque, parc, théâtre] public, municipal.
◆ **municipales** *nfpl* POLIT local *ou* council UK elections *(to elect the Conseil municipal)*.

MUNICIPALES

These elections, held every six years, are for the town councils (***conseils municipaux***). Electors vote for a list of council members headed by the ***tête de liste***, who will then become the mayor.

municipalité [mynisipalite] *nf* **1.** [communauté] town, municipality **2.** [représentants] ≃ (town) council ▪ **la ~ voulait faire un parking** the council wanted to build a car park.

munificence [mynifisɑ̃s] *nf litt* munificence.

munificent, e [mynifisɑ̃, ɑ̃t] *adj litt* munificent.

munir [32] [mynir] *vt* : **~ qqn de** to provide *ou* to supply sb with ▪ **munie d'un plan de la ville, elle se mit en route** equipped *ou* armed with a map of the town, she set off ▪ **~ qqch de** to equip *ou* to fit sthg with.
◆ **se munir de** *vp+prép* : **se ~ de vêtements chauds/d'un parapluie** to equip o.s. with warm clothes/an umbrella ▪ **munissez-vous de votre passeport** carry your passport *ou* take your passport with you.

munitions [mynisjɔ̃] *nfpl* ammunition *(U)*, munitions.

munster [mœ̃stɛr] *nm* Munster (cheese).

muphti [myfti] = **mufti**.

muqueux, euse [mykø, øz] *adj* mucous.
◆ **muqueuse** *nf* mucous membrane.

mur [myr] *nm* **1.** [construction] wall ▪ **il a passé la journée entière entre quatre ~s** he spent the day shut up inside ▪ **je serai dans mes ~s la semaine prochaine** I'll have moved in by next week ➜ **~ aveugle** blank *ou* windowless wall ▪ **~ d'appui** CONSTR parapet, leaning (height) wall ▪ **~ de clôture** enclosing wall ▪ **~ d'enceinte** outer *ou* surrounding wall ▪ **~ d'escalade** climbing wall ▪ **~ mitoyen** party wall ▪ **~ porteur** *ou* **portant** load-bearing wall ▪ **~ de séparation** dividing wall ▪ **~ de soutènement** retaining *ou* breast wall ▪ **le ~ d'Hadrien** Hadrian's Wall ▪ **le ~ des Lamentations** the Wailing Wall ▪ **faire le ~** *fam* [soldat, interne] to go *ou* to jump over the wall ▪ **c'est comme si tu parlais à un ~** it's (just) like talking to a brick wall ▪ **se heurter à un ~** to come up against a brick wall ▪ **les ~s ont des oreilles** walls have ears **2.** [escarpement] steep slope ➜ **~ artificiel** rock-climbing *ou* artificial wall **3.** GÉOL wall **4.** MIN footwall ▪ **faux ~** wall rock **5.** *fig* [de flammes, de brouillard, de pluie etc] wall, sheet ▪ [de silence] wall ▪ [de haine, d'incompréhension] wall, barrier **6.** AÉRON : **passer le ~ du son** to break the sound barrier **7.** SPORT wall.
◆ **murs** *nmpl* [remparts] (city) walls ▪ **l'ennemi est dans nos ~s** the enemy is within the gates ▪ **les ~s** [d'un commerce] the building.

mûr, e [myr] *adj* **1.** [fruit, graine, abcès etc] ripe ▪ **trop ~** overripe, too ripe ▪ **pas ~** unripe, not ripe **2.** [personne] mature ▪ **pas ~** immature **3.** [prêt - révolte, plan] ripe, ready ▪ **le pays est ~ pour la guerre civile** the country is ripe for civil war ▪ **après ~e réflexion** after careful thought *ou* consideration **4.** △ [saoul] smashed△ **5.** *fam* [tissu] worn.

muraille [myraj] *nf* **1.** [d'une ville, d'un château, de rocs] wall ▪ **la Grande Muraille (de Chine)** the Great Wall of China **2.** NAUT side, dead work (of hull).

mural, e, aux [myral, o] *adj* wall *(modif)*.
◆ **mural, als** *nm* [peinture] mural.

mûre [myr] ◇ *f* ▷ **mûr**.
◇ *nf* [fruit] mulberry ▪ **~ sauvage** blackberry, bramble.

mûrement [myrmɑ̃] *adv* : **après avoir ~ réfléchi** after careful thought *ou* consideration.

murène [myrɛn] *nf* moray (eel).

murer [3] [myre] *vt* **1.** [entourer de murs] to wall in *(sép)* **2.** [boucher - porte] to wall up *(sép)* ▪ **~ une fenêtre avec des briques** to brick up a window **3.** [enfermer - personne, chat] to wall in *ou* up *(sép)*.
◆ **se murer** *vpi* to shut o.s. away ▪ **se ~ dans le silence** *fig* & *sout* to retreat *ou* to withdraw into silence, to build a wall of silence around o.s.

muret [myrɛ], **te** [myrɛt], **muretin** [myrtɛ̃] *nm* low (dry stone) wall.

mûrier [myrje] *nm* mulberry tree *ou* bush ▪ **~ sauvage** bramble (bush), blackberry bush.

mûrir [32] [myrir] ◇ *vi* **1.** BOT to ripen ▪ **faire ~** to ripen **2.** ŒNOL to mature, to mellow **3.** [abcès] to come to a head **4.** [évoluer - pensée, projet] to mature, to ripen, to develop ; [- personne] to mature.
◇ *vt* **1.** [fruit] to ripen **2.** [pensée, projet, sentiment] to nurture, to nurse ▪ **une année à l'étranger l'a mûri** a year abroad has made him more mature ▪ **laisser ~ une idée** to give an idea time to gestate.

mûrissant, e [myrisɑ̃, ɑ̃t] *adj* **1.** BOT ripening **2.** [personne] of mature years.

mûrissement [myrismɑ̃] *nm* **1.** BOT ripening **2.** [d'une pensée, d'un plan] maturing, development.

murmure [myrmyr] *nm* **1.** [d'une personne] murmur ▪ *litt* [d'une source, de la brise] murmur, murmuring **2.** [commentaire] : **un ~ de protestation/d'admiration** a murmur of protest/admiration ▪ **il obtempéra sans un ~** he obeyed without a murmur **3.** MÉD murmur.
◆ **murmures** *nmpl* [plaintes] murmurs, murmurings.

murmurer [3] [myrmyre] ◇ *vi* **1.** [parler à voix basse] to murmur **2.** *litt* [source, brise] to murmur **3.** [se plaindre] : **~ (contre)** to mutter *ou* to grumble (about).
◇ *vt* to murmur ▪ **on murmure que...** there is a rumour (going about) that...

Mururoa [myryrɔa] *npr* Mururoa Atoll ▪ **à ~** on Mururoa Atoll.

mus [my] *v* ▻ **mouvoir.**

musaraigne [myzarɛɲ] *nf* shrew ▪ **~ commune** common shrew.

musarder [3] [myzarde] *vi sout* [flâner] to dawdle, to saunter ▪ [ne rien faire] to dillydally.

musc [mysk] *nm* musk.

muscade [myskad] *nf* BOT ▻ **noix.**

muscadet [myskadɛ] *nm* Muscadet (wine).

muscat [myska] *nm* [fruit] muscat grape ▪ [vin] Muscat, Muscatel (wine).

muscle [myskl] *nm* **1.** ANAT muscle ▪ **avoir des ~s** *ou* **du ~** *fam* to be muscular ▪ **être tout en ~** *fam* to be all muscle ◗ **~ cardiaque** cardiac *ou* heart muscle **2.** *sout* [vigueur] muscle, force, punch.

musclé, e [myskle] *adj* **1.** [corps, personne] muscular **2.** *fam* [énergique] powerful, forceful ▪ **mener une politique ~e contre qqch** to take a hard line *ou* a tough stance on sthg **3.** [vif - style] robust, vigorous, powerful ; [- discours] forceful, powerful.

muscler [3] [myskle] *vt* **1.** SPORT : **~ ses jambes/épaules** to develop one's leg/shoulder muscles **2.** *fig* [renforcer] to strengthen.
◆ **se muscler** *vp (emploi réfléchi)* to develop (one's) muscles ▪ **se ~ les bras** to develop one's arm muscles.

musculaire [myskylɛr] *adj* muscular, muscle *(modif).*

musculation [myskylasjɔ̃] *nf* bodybuilding (exercises).

musculature [myskylatyr] *nf* musculature, muscles.

musculeux, euse [myskylø, øz] *adj* [athlète] muscular, brawny ▪ [bras] muscular.

muse [myz] *nf* [inspiratrice] muse.
◆ **Muse** *nf* **1.** MYTHOL : **Muse** Muse ▪ **les (neuf) Muses** the (nine) Muses **2.** *fig* & *litt* **la Muse, les Muses** the Muse, the Muses ◗ **taquiner la Muse** to dabble in poetry, to court the Muse.

museau, x [myzo] *nm* **1.** ZOOL [d'un chien, d'un ours] muzzle ▪ [d'un porc] snout ▪ [d'une souris] nose **2.** *fam* [figure] face **3.** CULIN : **~ (de porc)** brawn *UK*, headcheese *US*.

musée [myze] *nm* **1.** [d'œuvres d'art] art gallery *UK*, museum *US* ▪ [des sciences, des techniques] museum ▪ **le ~ de l'homme** the Museum of Mankind ▪ **c'est le ~ des horreurs!** *hum* it's a dump! **2.** *(comme adj; avec ou sans trait d'union)* **une ville ~** a historical town.

museler [24] [myzle] *vt* **1.** [chien] to muzzle **2.** *sout* [presse, opposition] to muzzle, to gag, to silence.

muselière [myzəljɛr] *nf* muzzle ▪ **mettre une ~ à un chien** to muzzle a dog.

muselle *etc v* ▻ **museler.**

muséographie [myzeɔgrafi] *nf* museography.

muséologie [myzeɔlɔʒi] *nf* museology.

muser [3] [myze] *vi litt* [se promener] to dawdle, to saunter ▪ [ne rien faire] to dillydally.

musette [myzɛt] ◇ *adj inv* : **bal ~** dance (with accordion music) ▪ **valse ~** waltz (played on the accordion).
◇ *nm* (popular) accordion music.
◇ *nf* **1.** MUS [hautbois, gavotte] musette **2.** [d'un cheval] nosebag **3.** [d'un enfant] satchel ▪ [d'un soldat] haversack ▪ [d'un ouvrier] (canvas) haversack **4.** ZOOL common shrew.

muséum [myzeɔm] *nm* : **~ (d'histoire naturelle)** natural history museum.

musical, e, aux [myzikal, o] *adj* [voix, événement] musical ▪ **critique ~** music critic.

musicalité [myzikalite] *nf* musicality.

Musicassette® [myzikasɛt] *nf* prerecorded (audio) cassette.

music-hall [myzikol] (*pl* **music-halls**) *nm* [local] music hall ▪ [activité] : **le ~** variety, music hall ▪ **numéro de ~** variety act.

musicien, enne [myzisjɛ̃, ɛn] ◇ *adj* musical.
◇ *nm, f* musician.
◆ **musicien** *nm* MIL bandsman.

musicographe [myzikɔgraf] *nmf* musicographer.

musicographie [myzikɔgrafi] *nf* musicography.

musicologie [myzikɔlɔʒi] *nf* musicology.

musicologue [myzikɔlɔg] *nmf* musicologist.

musicothérapie [myzikɔterapi] *nf* musicotherapy.

musique [myzik] *nf* **1.** [art, notation ou science] music ▪ **ils dansaient sur une** *ou* **de la ~ rock** they were dancing to (the sound of) rock music ▪ **texte mis en ~** text set *ou* put to music ▪ **faire de la ~** [personne] to play (an instrument) ; [objet] to play a tune ▪ **lire la ~** to read music ▪ **étudier/dîner en ~** to study/to have dinner with music playing ◗ **~ d'ambiance** *ou* **de fond** background music ▪ **~ contemporaine/classique** contemporary/classical music ▪ **~ folklorique/militaire** folk/military music ▪ **~ sacrée/de chambre** sacred/chamber music ▪ **une ~ de film** a film *UK ou* movie *US* theme ▪ **la grande ~** *fam* classical music ▪ **connaître la ~** *fam* **: ça va, je connais la ~** I've heard it all before ▪ **c'est toujours la même ~ avec lui!** *fam* it's always the same old story with him! ▪ **la ~ adoucit les mœurs** music has charms to soothe a savage breast **2.** [musiciens] band ▪ **ils entrent dans le village, ~ en tête** they come into the village, led by the band.

musiquette [myzikɛt] *nf* : **on entendait une ~** we heard a simple little tune.

musqué, e [myske] *adj* [parfum, saveur] musky.

must [mœst] *nm fam* must ▪ **ce film est un ~** this film is compulsory viewing *ou* a must.

mustang [mystɑ̃g] *nm* mustang.

musulman, e [myzylmɑ̃, an] *adj* & *nm, f* Muslim.

mutabilité [mytabilite] *nf* mutability.

mutant, e [mytɑ̃, ɑ̃t] *adj* & *nm, f* mutant.

mutateur [mytatœr] *nm* [gén] mutator ▪ [changeur de fréquence] frequency changer.

mutation [mytasjɔ̃] *nf* **1.** [d'une entreprise, d'un marché] change, transformation ▪ **industrie en pleine ~** industry undergoing major change *ou* a radical transformation **2.** ADMIN & DR transfer **3.** BIOL mutation **4.** LING : **~ consonantique/vocalique** consonant/vowel shift.

muter [3] [myte] *vt* ADMIN to transfer, to move ▪ **il s'est fait ~ en province** he's been transferred to the provinces.

mutilateur, trice [mytilatœr, tris] ◇ *adj* mutilative, mutilatory.
◇ *nm, f litt* mutilator.

mutilation [mytilasjɔ̃] *nf* **1.** [du corps] mutilation **2.** *sout* [d'une œuvre] mutilation.

mutilé, e [mytile] *nm, f* disabled person ▪ **~s de guerre** disabled ex-servicemen ▪ **~ du travail** industrially disabled person.

mutiler [3] [mytile] *vt* **1.** [personne, animal] to mutilate, to maim **2.** *sout* [film, poème] to mutilate ■ [statue, bâtiment] to mutilate, to deface.
◆ **se mutiler** *vp (emploi réfléchi)* to mutilate o.s.

mutin, e [mytɛ̃, in] *adj litt* [enfant] impish, mischievous, cheeky ■ [air] mischievous.
◆ **mutin** *nm sout* rebel, mutineer.

mutiné, e [mytine] ◇ *adj* mutinous, rebellious.
◇ *nm, f* mutineer, rebel.

mutiner [3] [mytine] ◆ **se mutiner** *vpi* [marin, soldat] to mutiny, to rebel, to revolt ■ [employés, élèves, prisonniers] to rebel, to revolt.

mutinerie [mytinri] *nf* [de marins, de soldats] mutiny, revolt, rebellion ■ [d'employés, de prisonniers] rebellion, revolt.

mutisme [mytism] *nm* **1.** [silence] silence ■ **s'enfermer dans un ~ complet** to retreat into absolute silence **2.** MÉD muteness, dumbness ■ PSYCHOL mutism.

mutualiste [mytɥalist] ◇ *adj* mutualistic ■ **société** *ou* **groupement ~** mutual benefit insurance company, ≃ friendly society *UK*, ≃ benefit society *US*.
◇ *nmf* mutualist, member of a mutual benefit (insurance) company.

mutualité [mytɥalite] *nf* [système] mutual (benefit) insurance company ■ [ensemble des sociétés mutualistes] : **la ~ française** the French mutual (benefit) insurance system.

mutuel, elle [mytɥɛl] *adj* **1.** [partagé, réciproque] mutual ■ **responsabilité ~le** mutual responsibility **2.** [sans but lucratif] mutual ■ **assurance ~le** mutual insurance.
◆ **mutuelle** *nf* mutual (benefit) insurance company, ≃ friendly society *UK*, ≃ benefit society *US*.

MUTUELLE

An insurance company which provides complementary health cover and guarantees payment of all or part of the expenses not covered by the *Sécurité sociale*. These companies are often organized around professions. There is a *mutuelle* for students, one for teachers etc.

mutuellement [mytɥɛlmɑ̃] *adv* one another, each other.

Mycènes [misɛn] *npr* Mycenae.

mycénien, enne [misenjɛ̃, ɛn] *adj* Mycenaean, Mycenian.

mycologie [mikɔlɔʒi] *nf* mycology.

mycoplasme [mikɔplasm] *nm* mycoplasma.

mycose [mikoz] *nf* [gén] mycosis *(U) spéc*, thrush *(U)* ■ [aux orteils] athlete's foot.

myélome [mjelɔm] *nm* myeloma.

mygale [migal] *nf* mygale *spéc*, tarantula ■ **~ aviculaire/maçonne** bird/trapdoor spider.

myocarde [mjɔkard] *nm* myocardium.

myographie [mjɔgrafi] *nf* myography.

myopathe [mjɔpat] ◇ *adj* myopathic ■ **il est ~** he has muscular dystrophy.
◇ *nmf person with muscular dystrophy.*

myopathie [mjɔpati] *nf* [gén] myopathy ■ [dystrophie musculaire] muscular dystrophy.

myope [mjɔp] ◇ *adj* short-sighted *UK*, nearsighted *US*, myopic *spéc* ■ **~ comme une taupe** *fam* (as) blind as a bat.
◇ *nmf* short-sighted *UK ou* nearsighted *US* person, myope *spéc*.

myopie [mjɔpi] *nf* short-sightedness *UK*, nearsightedness *US*, myopia *spéc*.

myosotis [mjozɔtis] *nm* forget-me-not, myosotis *spéc*.

myriade [mirjad] *nf sout* myriad ■ **des ~s d'étoiles** myriads of stars.

myriapode [mirjapɔd] *nm* myriapod ■ **les ~s** the Myriapoda.

myrrhe [mir] *nf* myrrh.

myrte [mirt] *nm* myrtle.

myrtille [mirtij] *nf* bilberry *UK*, blueberry *US*.

mystère [mistɛr] *nm* **1.** [atmosphère] mystery ■ **entouré de ~** shrouded *ou* cloaked in mystery ⊙ **où est-elle? – ~ et boule de gomme!** *fam* where is she? – I haven't got a clue *ou* search me! **2.** [secret] mystery ■ **ne fais pas tant de ~s** don't be so mysterious ■ **si tu avais travaillé, tu aurais réussi l'examen, il n'y a pas de ~!** if you'd worked, you'd have passed your exam, it's as simple as that! ■ **ce n'est un ~ pour personne** it's no secret, it's an open secret ■ **je n'en fais pas (un) ~** I make no mystery *ou* secret of it **3.** RELIG mystery **4.** HIST & THÉÂTRE mystery (play) **5.** CULIN : **Mystère**® *ice-cream filled with meringue and coated with crushed almonds.*

mystérieusement [misterjøzmɑ̃] *adv* mysteriously.

mystérieux, euse [misterjø, øz] *adj* **1.** [inexplicable] mysterious, strange ■ **un crime ~** a mysterious crime **2.** [surnaturel] mysterious **3.** [confidentiel] secret **4.** [énigmatique] mysterious.

mysticisme [mistisism] *nm* mysticism.

mystificateur, trice [mistifikatœr, tris] ◇ *adj* : **une lettre mystificatrice** a hoax letter.
◇ *nm, f* hoaxer.

mystification [mistifikasjɔ̃] *nf* **1.** [canular] hoax, practical joke **2.** [tromperie] mystification, deception **3.** [imposture] myth.

mystifier [9] [mistifje] *vt* **1.** [duper, se jouer de] to fool, to take in *(sép)* **2.** [leurrer] to fool, to deceive ■ **mystifiés par la propagande** fooled by propaganda.

mystique [mistik] ◇ *adj* mystic, mystical.
◇ *nmf* mystic.
◇ *nf* RELIG : **la ~** mysticism ■ **la ~ de la démocratie/paix** *fig* the mystique of democracy/peace.

mythe [mit] *nm* myth ■ **elle fut un ~ vivant** she was a legend in her own lifetime, she was a living legend ⊙ **'le Mythe de Sisyphe'** *Camus* 'The Myth of Sisyphus'.

mythifier [9] [mitifje] *vt* to mythicize.

mythique [mitik] *adj* mythic, mythical.

mytho [mito] *(abr de* **mythomane**) *adj fam* **il est complètement ~** you can't believe anything he says.

mythologie [mitɔlɔʒi] *nf* mythology.

mythologique [mitɔlɔʒik] *adj* mythological.

mythomane [mitɔman] ◇ *adj* PSYCHOL mythomaniac ■ **il est un peu ~** he has a tendency to make things up (about himself).
◇ *nmf* PSYCHOL mythomaniac, compulsive liar.

mythomanie [mitɔmani] *nf* PSYCHOL mythomania.

mytiliculture [mitilikyltyr] *nf* mussel breeding.

myxomatose [miksɔmatoz] *nf* myxomatosis.

N

n, N [ɛn] *nm* n *m*, N *m* ▪ **à la puissance n** to the power (of) n, *voir aussi* **g**.

n = nano.

n (*abr écrite de* **numéro**) no.

n' [n] ⊳ **ne**.

N 1. (*abr écrite de* **newton**) N **2.** (*abr écrite de* **nord**) N.

na [na] *interj fam* so there, and that's that.

nabab [nabab] *nm* **1.** *fam* [homme riche] nabob **2.** HIST nabob.

Nabis [nabi] *npr pl* : **les ~** the Nabis *(group of 19th century painters including Bonnard and Vuillard who reacted against impressionism)*.

nabot, e [nabo, ɔt] *nm, f péj* dwarf, midget.

Nabuchodonosor [nabykɔdɔnɔzɔr] *npr* Nebuchadnezzar.

NAC [ɛnase] *ou* [nak] (*abr de* **nouveaux animaux de compagnie**) *nmpl* unusual pets.

nacelle [nasɛl] *nf* **1.** [d'un aérostat] basket, nacelle, gondola ▪ [d'un avion] nacelle, pod ▪ [d'un landau] carriage ▪ [pour un ouvrier] basket **2.** *litt* [bateau] (rowing) wherry **3.** CHIM boat.

nacre [nakr] *nf* : **la ~** mother-of-pearl, nacre *spéc* ▪ **de ~** mother-of-pearl *(modif)*.

nacré, e [nakre] *adj* pearly, nacreous *litt*.

nacrer [3] [nakre] *vt* **1.** [bijou] to give a pearly gloss to **2.** *litt* to cast a pearly shimmer over.

nadir [nadir] *nm* nadir.

nævus [nevys] (*pl* **nævi** [-vi]) *nm* naevus ▪ **~ pigmentaire** pigmented naevus *spéc*, mole.

Nagasaki [nagazaki] *npr* Nagasaki.

nage [naʒ] *nf* **1.** SPORT [activité] swimming ▪ [style] stroke ▪ **~ indienne** sidestroke ▪ **~ libre** freestyle **2.** NAUT rowing stroke.
◆ **à la nage** ◇ *loc adv* : **s'éloigner à la ~** to swim off *ou* away ▪ **traverser un lac à la ~** to swim across a lake ▪ **elle gagna la plage à la ~** she swam to the beach.
◇ *loc adj* CULIN à la nage *(cooked in a court-bouillon)*.
◆ **en nage** *loc adj* : **être en ~** to be dripping with sweat.

nageoire [naʒwar] *nf* **1.** ZOOL [de poisson] fin ▪ [d'otarie, de phoque etc] flipper ▪ **~ anale/dorsale** anal/dorsal fin ▪ **~ caudale** tail *ou* caudal fin **2.** AÉRON [flotteur] fin.

nager [17] [naʒe] ◇ *vi* **1.** SPORT to swim ▪ **il ne sait pas/sait ~** he can't/can swim ▪ **elle nage très bien** she's a very good swimmer ▶ **~ comme un poisson** to swim like a fish **2.** *fig* **la viande nageait dans la sauce** the meat was swimming in gravy ▪ **~ dans l'opulence** to be rolling in money ▪ **~ dans le bonheur** to be basking in bliss ▪ **on nageait dans le mystère** we were totally bewildered ▪ **tu nages dans ce pantalon!** those trousers are miles too big for you! **3.** [ne rien comprendre] to be completely lost *ou* out of one's depth.
◇ *vt* : **~ le crawl** to swim *ou* to do the crawl ▪ **~ la brasse** to swim *ou* to do (the) breast-stroke ▪ **~ le 200 mètres** to swim the 200 metres.

nageur, euse [naʒœr, øz] *nm, f* **1.** [personne] swimmer ▪ **~ de combat** naval frogman **2.** NAUT rower.

naguère [nagɛr] *adv litt* [autrefois] long ago, formerly ▪ [il y a peu de temps] not long ago.

naïade [najad] *nf* **1.** MYTHOL naiad ▪ *litt* nymph **2.** BOT & ENTOM naiad.

naïf, ïve [naif, iv] ◇ *adj* **1.** [candide - enfant, remarque] innocent, naïve, ingenuous **2.** [trop crédule] naïve, gullible ▪ **ne sois pas si ~, il ne te rendra pas l'argent** don't be so naïve, he won't give you your money back **3.** ART naïve, primitive.
◇ *nm, f* (gullible) *ou* naïve fool.
◆ **naïf** *nm* naïve *ou* primitive painter.

nain, naine [nɛ̃, nɛn] ◇ *adj* dwarf *(modif)*.
◇ *nm, f* dwarf.
◆ **nain** *nm* [jeu] : **~ jaune** Pope Joan *(card game)* ▪ [figurine] : **~ de jardin** garden gnome.

Nairobi [nɛrɔbi] *npr* Nairobi.

nais *etc v* ⊳ **naître**.

naissain [nɛsɛ̃] *nm* ZOOL spat.

naissait *etc v* ⊳ **naître**.

naissance [nɛsɑ̃s] *nf* **1.** BIOL birth ▪ **à ta ~** at your birth, when you were born ▪ **donner ~ à** to give birth to **2.** *sout* [début - d'un sentiment, d'une idée] birth ; [- d'un mouvement, d'une démocratie, d'une ère] birth, dawn ▪ **à la ~ du jour** at daybreak ▪ **donner ~ à qqch** to give birth *ou* rise to sthg ▪ **prendre ~** [mouvement] to arise, to originate ; [idée] to originate, to be born ; [sentiment] to arise, to be born **3.** *sout* [endroit] : **la ~ du cou** the base of the neck ▪ **la ~ d'un fleuve** the source of a river.
◆ **à la naissance** *loc adv* at birth.
◆ **de naissance** *loc adv* **1.** [congénitalement] congenitally, from birth ▪ **elle est aveugle de ~** she was born blind, she's been blind from birth ▪ **il est bête, c'est de ~!** *fam* he was born stupid! **2.** [d'extraction] : **italien de ~** Italian by birth ▪ **être de bonne** *ou* **haute ~** to be of noble birth.

naissant, e [nɛsɑ̃, ɑ̃t] *adj* **1.** *sout* [révolte] incipient ▪ [sentiment] growing, budding *litt* ▪ [beauté] budding *litt*, nascent *litt* ▪ [jour] dawning ▪ **il luttait contre cet amour ~** he fought against this growing *ou* burgeoning *litt* love **2.** CHIM : **à l'état ~** nascent **3.** HÉRALD naissant.

naître [92] [nɛtr] *vi (aux être)* **1.** BIOL to be born ▪ **quand tu es né** when you were born ▪ **mon bébé devrait ~ en mars** my baby is due in March ▪ **le bébé qui vient de ~** the newborn baby ▪ **il**

est né de parents inconnus he is of unknown parentage ▪ **enfant né d'un premier mariage** child born of a first marriage ▶ **je ne suis pas né d'hier** *ou* **de la dernière couvée** *ou* **de la dernière pluie** I wasn't born yesterday ▪ **il est né coiffé** *ou* **sous une bonne étoile** he was born under a lucky star
2. [être destiné à] : **être né pour** to be born *ou* destined *ou* meant to
3. *litt* ~ **à** [s'ouvrir à] to awaken to
4. [apparaître - sentiment, doute, espoir] to arise, to be born *sout* ; [- problème] to crop *ou* to come up ; [- projet] to be conceived ; [- communauté, entreprise] to spring up ; [- mouvement] to spring up, to arise ▪ **une idée naquit dans son esprit** an idea dawned on her ▪ **faire ~ des soupçons/la sympathie** to arouse suspicion/sympathy ▪ **~ de** [provenir de] to arise *ou* to spring from ▪ **de là sont nées toutes nos difficultés** that's the cause of all our difficulties ▪ **son intervention a fait ~ une polémique au sein du gouvernement** his intervention gave rise to *ou* caused much controversy in the government
5. *litt* [fleur] to spring *ou* to come up ▪ [jour] to break, to dawn
6. *(tournure impersonnelle)* **il naît un enfant toutes les secondes** a child is born every second ▪ **il ne naîtra rien de bon d'une telle alliance** *fig* nothing good can come of such a union.

naïve [naiv] *f* ▷ **naïf.**

naïvement [naivmɑ̃] *adv* **1.** [innocemment] innocently, naively, ingenuously **2.** [avec crédulité] naively, gullibly.

naïveté [naivte] *nf* **1.** [innocence] innocence, naivety **2.** [crédulité] naivety, gullibility ▪ **avec ~** naively ▪ **j'ai eu la ~ de lui faire confiance** I was naive enough to trust him.

naja [naʒa] *nm* cobra.

Namibie [namibi] *npr f* : **(la) ~** Namibia.

namibien, enne [namibjɛ̃, ɛn] *adj* Namibian.
◆ **Namibien, enne** *nm, f* Namibian.

nana [nana] *nf fam* girl ▪ **c'est sa ~** she's his girlfriend.

nanan [nanɑ̃] *nm fam vieilli* **c'est du ~!** [aisé] it's a piece of cake!, it's a walkover! ; [délicieux] yummy!

nanar [nanar] *nm fam péj* [objet] piece of junk ▪ [film] dreadful film.

nanisme [nanism] *nm* **1.** [d'une personne] dwarfism **2.** [d'une plante] nanism.

nano- [nanɔ] *préf* nano-.

nanoélectronique [nanoelɛktrɔnik] *nf* nanoelectronics *(sg)*.

nanomètre [nanɔmɛtr] *nm* nanometer.

nanoseconde [nanɔsəgɔ̃d] *nf* nanosecond.

nanotechnologie [nanɔtɛknɔlɔʒi] *nf* nanotechnology.

Nantes [nɑ̃t] *npr* Nantes ▪ **l'Édit de ~** the Edict of Nantes.

L'ÉDIT DE NANTES

Signed in 1598 by Henri IV, the Edict marked the end of the Wars of Religion and guaranteed a number of rights to the Protestant Huguenots, in particular freedom of conscience and the practice of their religion in certain prescribed areas. Its revocation in 1685 by Louis XIV resulted in a brutal repression which caused many Huguenots to emigrate to other European countries.

nanti, e [nɑ̃ti] ◇ *adj* [riche] affluent, well-to-do, well-off.
◇ *nm, f* affluent person ▪ **les ~s** the well-to-do.

nantir [32] [nɑ̃tir] *vt* **1.** [doter] : **~ qqn de** to provide sb with ▪ **les fées la nantirent de toutes les qualités** the fairies endowed her with all the qualities **2.** FIN & DR to secure.
◆ **se nantir de** *vp+prép* to equip o.s. with.

nantissement [nɑ̃tismɑ̃] *nm* **1.** [objet] security, pledge **2.** [contrat] security.

NAP [nap] (*abr écrite de* **Neuilly Auteuil Passy**) ◇ *adj* ≃ Sloaney **fam** *UK*, ≃ preppie **fam** *US*.
◇ *nmf* ≃ Sloane **fam** *UK*, ≃ preppie type **fam** *US*.

napalm [napalm] *nm* napalm.

naphta [nafta] *nm* naphtha.

naphtaline [naftalin] *nf* : **(boules de) ~** mothballs ▪ **ça sent la ~** it smells of mothballs.

naphte [naft] *nm* naphthene.

Naples [napl] *npr* Naples.

napoléon [napɔleɔ̃] *nm* napoleon (coin).

Napoléon [napɔleɔ̃] *npr* Napoleon ▪ **~ Bonaparte** Napoleon Bonaparte.

napoléonien, enne [napɔleɔnjɛ̃, ɛn] *adj* Napoleonic ▪ **les campagnes ~nes** the Napoleonic wars.

napolitain, e [napɔlitɛ̃, ɛn] *adj* Neapolitan.
◆ **Napolitain, e** *nm, f* Neapolitan.

nappage [napaʒ] *nm* topping.

nappe [nap] *nf* **1.** [linge] tablecloth **2.** [couche] : **~ de pétrole/gaz** layer of oil/gas ▪ **~ de brouillard** blanket of fog ▪ **~ d'eau** [en surface] stretch *ou* expanse *ou* sheet of water ; [souterraine] groundwater ▪ **~ de feu** sheet of flames ▪ **~ d'huile** patch of oil **3.** GÉOL : **~ phréatique** groundwater *ou* phreatic table **4.** GÉOM nappe **5.** TEXT lap (sheet).

napper [3] [nape] *vt* : **~ qqch de** to coat sthg with.

napperon [naprɔ̃] *nm* [sous un vase, un bougeoir] mat ▪ [sous un plat, un gâteau] doily ▪ **~ individuel** place mat.

naquit *etc v* ▷ **naître.**

narcisse [narsis] *nm* **1.** BOT narcissus **2.** *litt* narcissistic person, narcissist.

Narcisse [narsis] *npr* Narcissus.

narcissique [narsisik] *adj* narcissistic.

narcissisme [narsisism] *nm* narcissism.

narcodollars [narkɔdɔlar] *nmpl* narcodollars.

narcolepsie [narkɔlɛpsi] *nf* MÉD narcolepsy.

narcotique [narkɔtik] ◇ *adj* narcotic.
◇ *nm* narcotic.

narghilé [nargile] *nm* nargile, narghile.

narguer [3] [narge] *vt* **1.** [se moquer de, provoquer] to scoff at *(insép)* ▪ **il nous nargue avec sa nouvelle voiture** we're not good enough for him now he's got his new car **2.** *sout* [braver, mépriser] to scorn, to spurn, to deride.

narine [narin] *nf* nostril.

narquois, e [narkwa, az] *adj* mocking, derisive ▪ **sourire ~** mocking smile.

narrateur, trice [naratœr, tris] *nm, f* narrator.

narratif, ive [naratif, iv] *adj* narrative.

narration [narasjɔ̃] *nf* [exposé] narrative, narration ▪ [partie du discours] narration.

narrer [3] [nare] *vt litt* [conte] to narrate, to tell ▪ [événements] to narrate, to relate.

narval [narval] *nm* narwhal, narwal.

NASA, Nasa [naza] (*abr de* **National Aeronautics and Space Administration**) *npr f* NASA, Nasa.

nasal, e, aux [nazal, o] *adj* nasal.
◆ **nasale** *nf* LING nasal.

nasalisation [nazalizasjɔ̃] *nf* nasalization.

nase△ [naz] ◇ *adj* [inutilisable - appareil, meuble] kaput, bust ▪ [fou] cracked, screwy△ ▪ [fatigué, malade] knackered.
◇ *nm* [nez] conk.

naseau, x [nazo] *nm* ZOOL nostril.

nasillard, e [nazijar, ard] *adj* [ton] nasal ▪ [radio, haut-parleur] tinny ▪ **parler d'une voix ~e** to talk through one's nose *ou* with a (nasal) twang.

nasillement [nazijmɑ̃] *nm* **1.** [d'une voix] (nasal) twang ▪ [d'un haut-parleur] tinny sound **2.** [d'un canard] quacking.

nasiller [3] [nazije] *vi* **1.** [personne] to speak with a (nasal) twang ▪ [radio] to have a tinny sound **2.** [canard] to quack.

nasse [nas] *nf* **1.** PÊCHE (conical) lobster pot **2.** [pour oiseaux] hoop net **3.** ZOOL [mollusque] dog whelk.

natal, e, als [natal] *adj* [pays, ville] native ■ **sa maison ~e** the house where he was born.

nataliste [natalist] *adj* : **politique ~** policy to increase the birth rate.

natalité [natalite] *nf* birth rate, natality *US*.

natation [natasjɔ̃] *nf* swimming ■ **~ synchronisée** *ou* **artistique** synchronized swimming.

natif, ive [natif, iv] <> *adj* [originaire] native ■ **je suis ~ de Paris/Pologne** I was born in Paris/Poland.
<> *nm, f* native.

nation [nasjɔ̃] *nf* nation ■ **les Nations Unies** the United Nations.

national, e, aux [nasjɔnal, o] *adj* **1.** [de la nation] national ■ **l'économie ~e** the domestic economy ■ **funérailles** *ou* **obsèques ~es** state funeral ■ **la presse ~e en a parlé** the national newspapers *ou* the nationals carried stories about it **2.** [nationaliste - parti, politique] nationalist.
◆ **nationale** *nf* ≃ A road *UK*, ≃ interstate highway *US*.
◆ **nationaux** *nmpl* nationals.

nationalisation [nasjɔnalizasjɔ̃] *nf* nationalization.

nationalisé, e [nasjɔnalize] *adj* nationalized.

nationaliser [3] [nasjɔnalize] *vt* to nationalize.

nationalisme [nasjɔnalism] *nm* nationalism.

nationaliste [nasjɔnalist] <> *adj* nationalist, nationalistic.
<> *nmf* nationalist.

nationalité [nasjɔnalite] *nf* nationality ■ **être de ~ française/nigériane** to be French/Nigerian.

national-socialisme [nasjɔnalsɔsjalism] (*pl* **national-socialismes**) *nm* National Socialism.

national-socialiste [nasjɔnalsɔsjalist] (*pl* **nationaux-socialistes**) *adj* & *nmf* National Socialist.

native [nativ] *f* ▷ **natif**.

nativité [nativite] *nf* **1.** RELIG : **la Nativité** the Nativity **2.** ART Nativity scene ■ **une Nativité** a Nativity.

natte [nat] *nf* **1.** [tapis de paille] mat, (piece of) matting **2.** [de cheveux] pigtail, braid, plait.

natter [3] [nate] *vt* **1.** [cheveux] to braid, to plait **2.** [fils, osier] to plait, to weave, to interweave.

naturalisation [natyralizasjɔ̃] *nf* **1.** ADMIN, BOT & LING naturalization **2.** [empaillage] stuffing.

naturalisé, e [natyralize] <> *adj* naturalized ■ **il a été ~ américain** he was granted U.S. citizenship.
<> *nm, f* naturalized person.

naturaliser [3] [natyralize] *vt* **1.** ADMIN to naturalize ■ **il s'est fait ~ français** he was granted French citizenship **2.** BOT & LING to naturalize **3.** [empailler] to stuff.

naturalisme [natyralism] *nm* naturalism.

naturaliste [natyralist] <> *adj* naturalistic.
<> *nmf* **1.** BOT & ZOOL naturalist **2.** [empailleur] taxidermist.

nature [natyr] <> *nf* **1.** [univers naturel] : **la ~** nature ■ **la ~ fait bien les choses** nature works wonders ■ **laisser faire** *ou* **agir la ~** let nature take its course ⊃ **la ~ a horreur du vide** nature abhors a vacuum
2. [campagne] : **la ~** nature, the country, the countryside ■ **une maison perdue dans la ~** a house out in the wilds ■ **tomber en panne en pleine ~** to break down in the middle of nowhere ■ **disparaître** *ou* **s'évanouir dans la ~** to vanish into thin air
3. [caractère] nature ■ **ce n'est pas dans sa ~** it's not like him, it's not in his nature ■ **c'est dans la ~ des choses** it's in the nature of things, that's the way the world is ⊃ **la ~ humaine** human nature
4. [type de personne] type, sort ■ **une bonne ~** a good sort ■ **une heureuse ~** a happy person ■ **c'est une petite ~** he's the feeble type *ou* a weakling
5. [sorte] nature, type, sort ■ **les raisonnements de cette ~** this kind of argument, arguments of this kind ■ **quelle est la ~ de la fuite?** what kind of leak is it?
6. ART : **d'après ~** from life ⊃ **~ morte** still life.
<> *adj inv* **1.** [bœuf, choucroute] plain, with no trimmings ■ [salade, avocat] plain, with no dressing ■ ŒNOL still
2. *fam* [simple] natural.
◆ **contre nature** *loc adj* against nature, unnatural ■ **des sentiments/penchants contre ~** unnatural feelings/leanings ■ **c'est contre ~** it's not natural, it goes against nature.
◆ **de nature** *loc adj* by nature ■ **il est généreux de ~** he's generous by nature, it's (in) his nature to be generous ■ **elle est anxieuse de ~** she's the worrying kind *ou* anxious type.
◆ **de nature à** *loc conj* likely *ou* liable to ■ **je ne suis pas de ~ à me laisser faire** I'm not the kind *ou* type of person you can push around.
◆ **de toute nature** *loc adj* of all kinds *ou* types.
◆ **en nature** *loc adv* in kind ■ **payer en ~** *pr* & *fig* to pay in kind.
◆ **par nature** *loc adv* : **je suis conservateur par ~** I'm naturally conservative, I'm conservative by nature.

naturel, elle [natyrɛl] *adj* **1.** [du monde physique - phénomène, ressource, frontière] natural
2. [physiologique - fonction, processus] natural, bodily
3. [inné - disposition, talent] natural, inborn ; [- boucles, blondeur] natural ■ **ce n'est pas ma couleur ~le** it's not my natural *ou* real hair colour
4. [sans affectation] natural ■ **tu n'as pas l'air ~ sur cette photo** you don't look natural on this photograph ■ **être ~** to be oneself
5. [normal] natural ■ **c'est bien** *ou* **tout ~ que je t'aide** it's only natural that I should help you ■ **je vous remercie – je vous en prie, c'est tout ~!** thank you – please don't mention it, it's the least I could do! ■ **trouver ~ de faire qqch** to think nothing of doing sthg
6. [pur - fibre] pure ; [- nourriture] natural ■ **'soie ~le'** 'pure *ou* 100% silk' ■ COMM natural, organic
7. LING, MUS, PHILOS & RELIG natural
8. [illégitime] natural.
◆ **naturel** *nm* **1.** [tempérament] nature ■ **il est d'un ~ anxieux** he's the worrying kind, it's (in) his nature to worry ■ **être d'un bon ~** to be good-natured
2. [authenticité] naturalness ■ **manque de ~** affectation, artificiality ■ **ce que j'aime chez elle c'est son ~** what I like about her is she's so natural ■ **avec beaucoup de ~** with perfect ease, completely naturally ■ **elle est mieux au ~ qu'à la télévision** she's better in real life than on TV.
◆ **au naturel** *loc adj* CULIN plain.

naturellement [natyrɛlmɑ̃] *adv* **1.** [de façon innée] naturally **2.** [simplement] naturally, unaffectedly **3.** [bien sûr] naturally, of course.

naturisme [natyrism] *nm* **1.** [nudisme] naturism **2.** MÉD naturopathy **3.** PHILOS & RELIG naturalism.

naturiste [natyrist] <> *adj* **1.** [nudiste] naturist **2.** PHILOS naturalist, naturalistic.
<> *nmf* **1.** [nudiste] naturist, nudist **2.** PHILOS naturalist.

naturopathie [natyrɔpati], **naturothérapie** [natyrɔterapi] *nf* naturopathy.

naufrage [nofraʒ] *nm* **1.** [d'un navire] wreck, shipwreck ■ **faire ~** [personne] to be shipwrecked ; [navire] to be wrecked **2.** *fig* ruin, wreckage.

naufragé, e [nofraʒe] <> *adj* **1.** [personne - gén] shipwrecked ; [- sur une île] castaway (*modif*) **2.** [navire] wrecked.
<> *nm, f* [gén] shipwreck victim ■ [sur une île] castaway.

naufrageur, euse [nofraʒœr, øz] *nm, f* *pr* & *fig* wrecker.

nauséabond, e [nozeabɔ̃, ɔ̃d] *adj* **1.** [qui sent mauvais] putrid, foul, foul-smelling **2.** [répugnant] nauseating, sickening, repulsive.

nausée [noze] *nf* **1.** [envie de vomir] nausea ■ **avoir la ~** to feel sick ■ **avoir des ~s** to have bouts of sickness ■ **à vous donner la ~** [odeurs, images] nauseating **2.** *fig* [dégoût] : **une telle hypocrisie me donne la ~** such hypocrisy makes me sick.

nauséeux, euse [nozeø, øz] *adj* **1.** [odeur] nauseating, sickening, repulsive ■ [état] nauseous **2.** *litt* [révoltant] nauseating, sickening, repulsive.

nautique [notik] *adj* nautical ■ **carte/géographie ~** nautical map/geography ■ **le salon ~** ≃ the Boat Show.

nautisme [notism] *nm* water sports, aquatics *(sing).*

Navajos [navaro] *npr mpl* : **les ~** the Navajo.

naval, e, als [naval] *adj* naval ■ **construction ~e** shipbuilding (industry).

navarin [navarɛ̃] *nm* navarin *(mutton and vegetable stew).*

Navarre [navar] *npr f* : **(la) ~** Navarre.

navet [navɛ] *nm* **1.** BOT turnip **2.** *fam* [œuvre] : **c'est un ~** it's (a load of) tripe.

navette [navɛt] *nf* **1.** AÉRON & TRANSP shuttle ■ **faire la ~ (entre)** to shuttle back and forth *ou* to and fro (between) ■ **un bus fait la ~ entre la gare et l'aéroport** there is a shuttle bus (service) between the station and the airport ■ **il fait la ~ entre Paris et Marseille** he comes and goes *ou* goes to and fro between Paris and Marseilles ➡ **~ spatiale** space shuttle ■ **la ~ parlementaire** *successive readings of bills by the Assemblée nationale and Sénat* **2.** RELIG incense holder **3.** TEXT shuttle ■ [aiguille - pour filets] netting *ou* meshing needle **4.** BOT rape.

navigabilité [navigabilite] *nf* [d'un cours d'eau] navigability, navigableness ■ [d'un navire] seaworthiness ■ [d'un avion] airworthiness ■ **en état de ~** NAUT seaworthy ; AÉRON airworthy.

navigable [navigabl] *adj* navigable.

navigant, e [navigɑ̃, ɑ̃t] ◇ *adj* NAUT seafaring ■ **personnel ~** AÉRON flight personnel, aircrew, crew.
◇ *nm, f* : **les ~s** NAUT the crew ; AÉRON the aircrew, the crew.

navigateur, trice [navigatœr, tris] *nm, f* **1.** NAUT [voyageur] sailor, seafarer ■ **~ solitaire** single-handed yachtsman ■ [membre de l'équipage] navigator **2.** AÉRON & AUTO navigator, copilot *(in charge of navigation)* ■ INFORM browser.
◆ **navigateur** ◇ *nm* [appareil] navigator.
◇ *adj m* seafaring, seagoing.

navigation [navigasjɔ̃] *nf* **1.** NAUT navigation, sailing ■ **interdit à la ~** [des gros bateaux] closed to shipping ; [des petits bateaux] no sailing *ou* boating ■ **ouvert à la ~** [des gros bateaux] open to shipping ➡ **~ côtière** coastal navigation ■ **~ fluviale** *ou* **intérieure** inland navigation ■ **~ maritime** *ou* **extérieure** high seas navigation ■ **~ de plaisance** yachting, pleasure sailing **2.** AÉRON navigation, flying ■ **~ aérienne** aerial navigation ■ **~ spatiale** space flight *ou* travel ■ **~ à vue** contact flying **3.** INFORM browsing.
◆ **de navigation** *loc adj* [registre] navigational ■ [terme, école] nautical ■ [instrument] navigation *(modif)* ■ **compagnie de ~** NAUT shipping company ; AÉRON airline company.

naviguer [3] [navige] *vi* **1.** NAUT to sail ■ **depuis que je navigue** [plaisancier] since I first went sailing ; [marin] since I first went to sea ■ **~ au compas/à l'estime** to navigate by compass/by dead reckoning **2.** AÉRON to fly ■ **~ à vue** to use contact flight rules, to fly visually **3.** *fig* [se déplacer] to get about ■ **savoir ~** to know one's way around **4.** INFORM to browse.

navire [navir] *nm* ship, vessel *litt* ■ **~ marchand** *ou* **de commerce** merchant ship, merchantman ■ **~ de guerre** warship ■ **~ de haute mer** ocean-going ship.

navire-citerne [navirsitɛrn] (*pl* **navires-citernes**) *nm* (oil) tanker.

navire-école [navirekɔl] (*pl* **navires-écoles**) *nm* training ship.

navire(-)hôpital [navirɔpital] (*pl* **navires(-)hôpitaux** [-to]) *nm* hospital ship.

navire-usine [naviryzin] (*pl* **navires-usines**) *nm* factory ship.

navrant, e [navrɑ̃, ɑ̃t] *adj* **1.** [attristant - spectacle] distressing, upsetting, harrowing ■ **c'est ~ de les voir ainsi se quereller** it's distressing to see them quarrel like that ■ **tu es ~!** you're pathetic *ou* hopeless! ■ **sa bêtise est ~e** he's hopelessly stupid **2.** [regrettable] : **c'est ~, mais il n'y a rien à faire** it's a terrible shame, but there's nothing we can do.

navré, e [navre] *adj* sorry ■ **je suis ~ de vous l'entendre dire** I'm so sorry to hear you say that.

navrer [3] [navre] *vt* to upset, to distress, to sadden ■ **la vue d'une telle misère me navre** it distresses me to see such poverty.

nazaréen, enne [nazareɛ̃, ɛn] *adj* **1.** GÉOGR Nazarene **2.** ART : **l'école ~ne** the Nazarenes.
◆ **Nazaréen, enne** *nm, f* Nazarene ■ **le Nazaréen** the Nazarene.
◆ **nazaréen** *nm* ART Nazarene.

Nazareth [nazarɛt] *npr* Nazareth.

naze△ [naz] = **nase**.

nazi, e [nazi] *adj* & *nm, f* Nazi.

nazisme [nazism] *nm* Nazism.

NB (*abr écrite de* **Nota Bene**) NB.

NBC (*abr de* **nucléaire, bactériologique, chimique**) *adj* MIL NBC.

nbreuses = **nombreuses**.

nbrx = **nombreux**.

n.c. 1. (*abr écrite de* **non communiqué**) n.a **2.** (*abr écrite de* **non connu**) n.a.

n.d. 1. (*abr écrite de* **non daté**) n.d **2.** (*abr écrite de* **non disponible**) n.a.

N-D (*abr écrite de* **Notre-Dame**) OL.

NDA (*abr écrite de* **note de l'auteur**) *author's note.*

N'Djamena [ndʒamena] *npr* Ndjamena, N'Djamena.

NDLR (*abr écrite de* **note de la rédaction**) Ed.

NDT (*abr écrite de* **note du traducteur**) translator's note.

ne [nə] *(devant voyelle ou 'h' muet n'* [n]*) adv*

A. EN CORRÉLATION AVEC UN MOT NÉGATIF
B. EN CORRÉLATION AVEC 'QUE'
C. EMPLOYÉ SEUL

A. EN CORRÉLATION AVEC UN MOT NÉGATIF

[dans des négatives] : **je n'ai rien vu** I saw nothing, I didn't see anything ■ **ce n'est ni bleu ni vert** it's neither blue nor green ■ **je n'en parlerai ni à l'un ni à l'autre** I won't speak about it to either of them ■ **ne... jamais : il ne répond jamais au téléphone** he never answers the phone ■ **ne... plus : le téléphone ne marche plus** the telephone doesn't work any more ■ **ne... pas : ne le dérange pas!** don't disturb him!

B. EN CORRÉLATION AVEC 'QUE'

[dans une explication] : **je ne fais que d'arriver** *sout* I've only just arrived ■ **je n'ai pas que cette idée-là** that's not the only idea I have ■ **tu ne sais dire que des mensonges** all you ever do is tell lies ■ **je n'ai pas d'autre solution que celle-là** I have no other solution but that

C. EMPLOYÉ SEUL

1. *sout* [avec une valeur négative] : **il ne cesse de m'appeler** he won't stop calling me ■ **quel père n'aiderait son fils?** what father would refuse to help his son? ■ **il y a six jours qu'il n'est venu** he hasn't been for six days ■ **je lui demanderais, si ma timidité ne m'en empêchait** I would ask him if I were not so shy ■ **prenez garde qu'on ne vous voie** be careful (that) nobody sees you ■ **que ne le disais-tu plus tôt?** why didn't you say so earlier!, if only you had said so earlier! ■ **que ne ferais-je pour vous?** what wouldn't I do for you? ■ **n'était son grand âge, je l'aurais congédié** *litt* had it not been for his advanced age, I would have dismissed him
2. *sout* [avec une valeur explétive] : **je crains qu'il n'accepte** I'm afraid he might say yes ■ **sa seule crainte, c'était qu'on ne le renvoyât** all he was afraid of *ou* his only fear was of being dismissed ■ **évite qu'il ne te rencontre** try to avoid meeting him ■ **je ne doute pas qu'il ne soit sympathique** I don't doubt (that) he's nice ■ **à moins qu'il ne vous le dise** unless he tells you ■ **il se porte mieux que je ne croyais** he's better than I'd imagined.

N-E (*abr écrite de* **Nord-Est**) NE.

né, e [ne] ◇ *pp* ▷ **naître.**
◇ *adj* born ■ **Clara Brown, ~e Moore** Clara Brown, née *ou* nee Moore ■ **c'est une musicienne ~e** she's a born musician, she was born (to be) a musician ◐ **une personne bien ~e** a person of high birth.

néandertalien, enne [neɑ̃dɛrtaljɛ̃, ɛn] *adj* Neanderthal.
◆ **néandertalien** *nm* Neanderthal man.

néanmoins [neɑ̃mwɛ̃] *adv* nevertheless, nonetheless.

néant [neɑ̃] *nm* **1.** [non-être] nothingness ■ **une voix sortie du ~** a voice that seemed to come from nowhere **2.** [superficialité] vacuousness ■ **dans tous leurs discours, je ne trouve que le ~** I find all their speeches totally vacuous **3.** *sout* [manque de valeur] worthlessness, triviality **4.** ADMIN : **enfants: ~** children: none.

Nebraska [nebraska] *npr m* : **le ~** Nebraska ■ **au ~** in Nebraska.

nébuleux, euse [nebylø, øz] *adj* **1.** [nuageux] cloudy, clouded **2.** *fig* [obscur] obscure, nebulous.
◆ **nébuleuse** *nf* **1.** ASTRON nebula **2.** *fig* [amas confus] : **leur projet était encore à l'état de nébuleuse** their plan was still pretty vague, they still had only the bare outlines of a plan.

nébulosité [nebylozite] *nf* **1.** [nuage] haze, nebulosity **2.** MÉTÉOR cloud cover **3.** *litt* & *fig* [imprécision] haziness, nebulousness.

nécessaire [nesesɛr] ◇ *adj* **1.** [indispensable] necessary ■ **un mal ~** a necessary evil ■ **si (c'est) ~** if necessary, if need be ■ **est-il ~ de la mettre** *ou* **qu'elle soit au courant?** does she have *ou* need to know? ■ **leur séparation était devenue ~** it had become necessary for them to part ■ **~ à : l'eau est ~ aux plantes** plants need water ■ **cette introduction est ~ à la compréhension du texte** it is necessary to read this introduction to understand the text **2.** [requis - aptitude] necessary, requisite **3.** [logique, inévitable] necessary, unavoidable, inevitable.
◇ *nm* **1.** [choses indispensables] bare necessities ■ **n'emportez que le strict ~** just take the basic essentials *ou* what's absolutely necessary **2.** [démarche requise] : **faire le ~ : je ferai le ~ pour vos réservations** I'll see to your reservations ■ **ne vous inquiétez pas, j'ai fait le ~** don't worry, I've taken care of things *ou* I've done what had to be done **3.** [trousse, étui] : **~ à couture** needlework basket ■ **~ à ongles** manicure set ■ **~ à ouvrage** workbox ■ **~ de toilette** toilet case, sponge bag *UK* ■ **~ de voyage** grip, travel *ou* overnight bag *UK*.

nécessairement [nesesɛrmɑ̃] *adv* **1.** [inévitablement] necessarily, unavoidably, inevitably **2.** [obligatoirement] necessarily, of necessity *sout* ■ **pas ~** not necessarily ■ **ce n'est pas ~ vrai** it's not necessarily true ■ **il y a ~ une explication à tout cela** there must be an explanation for all this **3.** LOGIQUE necessarily.

nécessité [nesesite] *nf* **1.** [caractère nécessaire] necessity, need ■ **elle ne voit pas la ~ de se marier** she doesn't see any need to get married ■ **être dans la ~ de** to find it necessary to, to have no choice but to ‖ [chose indispensable] necessity ■ **c'est une ~ absolue de faire bouillir l'eau** it is absolutely necessary *ou* essential to boil the water ■ **de première ~** [dépenses, fournitures] basic ; [objets, denrées] essential ■ **vous devez de toute ~ réparer le toit** it's absolutely imperative *ou* essential that you repair the roof ◐ **faire de ~ vertu** to make a virtue out of necessity ■ **~ fait loi** *prov* necessity knows no law, what must be done must be done ■ **~ faisant loi, il dut vendre le parc** sheer necessity forced him to sell the park **2.** *vieilli* [indigence] destitution, poverty ■ **être dans la ~** to be in need **3.** PHILOS necessity **4.** DR : **état de ~** necessity.
◆ **nécessités** *nfpl* : **des ~s financières nous obligent à...** we are financially bound to...
◆ **par nécessité** *loc adv* of necessity, necessarily, unavoidably ■ **on dut par ~ vendre la moto** there was no choice but to sell the motorbike.

nécessiter [nesesite] *vt* to require, to demand ■ **ce travail nécessite beaucoup de patience** this job requires a lot of patience.

nécessiteux, euse [nesesitø, øz] *sout* ◇ *adj* needy, in need ■ **une famille nécessiteuse** a family in great need, a very needy family.
◇ *nm, f* needy person.

nec plus ultra [nɛkplyzyltra] *nm inv* last word, ultimate ■ **le ~ des cuisines intégrées** the last word in built-in kitchens.

nécrologie [nekrɔlɔʒi] *nf* **1.** [liste] necrology **2.** [notice biographique] obituary **3.** [rubrique] obituary column.

nécrologique [nekrɔlɔʒik] *adj* obituary *(modif)*.

nécromancie [nekrɔmɑ̃si] *nf* necromancy.

nécromancien, enne [nekrɔmɑ̃sjɛ̃, ɛn] *nm, f* necromancer.

nécrophage [nekrɔfaʒ] *adj* necrophagous.

nécrophilie [nekrɔfili] *nf* necrophilia, necrophilism.

nécropole [nekrɔpɔl] *nf* necropolis.

nécrose [nekroz] *nf* **1.** MÉD necrosis **2.** BOT canker, necrosis.

nécroser [3] [nekroze] *vt* **1.** MÉD to necrotize, to cause necrosis to **2.** BOT to canker.
◆ **se nécroser** *vpi* **1.** MÉD to necrotize, to undergo necrosis **2.** BOT to canker.

nectaire [nɛktɛr] *nm* nectary.

nectar [nɛktar] *nm* [gén] nectar.

nectarine [nɛktarin] *nf* nectarine.

néerlandais, e [neɛrlɑ̃dɛ, ɛz] *adj* Dutch.
◆ **Néerlandais, e** *nm, f* Dutchman (*f* Dutchwoman) ■ **les ~** the Dutch.
◆ **néerlandais** *nm* LING Dutch.

nef [nɛf] *nf* **1.** ARCHIT nave ■ **~ latérale** (side) aisle **2.** *arch* & *litt* [vaisseau] vessel, craft.

néfaste [nefast] *adj* **1.** [nuisible] harmful, noxious ■ **le gel a été ~ aux récoltes** the frost has been disastrous for the crops ■ **une influence ~** a bad influence **2.** *litt* [tragique] ill-fated.

nèfle [nɛfl] *nf* BOT medlar ■ **~ du Japon** loquat.

néflier [neflije] *nm* medlar (tree).

négateur, trice [negatœr, tris] *litt* ◇ *adj* negative.
◇ *nm, f* decrier, detractor.

négatif, ive [negatif, iv] *adj* **1.** [réponse, attitude] negative **2.** ÉLECTR, LING & MÉD negative, *voir aussi* **pluriel 3.** MATH : **un nombre ~** a negative *ou* minus number.
◆ **négatif** *nm* PHOTO negative.
◆ **négative** *nf* : **dans la négative** if not ■ **répondre par la négative** to give a negative answer, to answer in the negative.

négation [negasjɔ̃] *nf* **1.** [gén - PHILOS] negation **2.** GRAMM negative (form).

négativement [negativmɑ̃] *adv* negatively.

négativisme [negativism] *nm* negativism.

négativité [negativite] *nf* **1.** *sout* negativity, negativeness **2.** ÉLECTR negativity.

négligé, e [negliʒe] *adj* [tenue, personne] sloppy, scruffy, slovenly ■ [coiffure] unkempt, untidy.
◆ **négligé** *nm* **1.** [débraillé, laisser-aller] scruffiness, slovenly *ou* untidy appearance **2.** [robe d'intérieur] negligee, negligé.

négligeable [negliʒabl] *adj* [somme] trifling ■ [détail] unimportant, trifling ■ [différence] negligible, insignificant ■ **elle a une influence non ~ sur lui** she has a not inconsiderable influence over him.

négligemment [negliʒamɑ̃] *adv* **1.** [sans soin] negligently, carelessly **2.** [avec nonchalance] negligently, casually ■ **un foulard ~ noué autour du cou** a scarf casually tied around his neck.

négligence [negliʒɑ̃s] *nf* **1.** [manque de soin] negligence, carelessness ■ **habillé avec ~** sloppily *ou* carelessly dressed **2.** [manque d'attention] negligence, neglect ■ [oubli] oversight ■ **l'erreur est due à une ~ de ma secrétaire** the error is due to an oversight on the part of my secretary **3.** [nonchalance] negligence, casualness, nonchalance **4.** DR : **~ criminelle** criminal negligence.

négligent, e [negliʒɑ̃, ɑ̃t] *adj* **1.** [non consciencieux] negligent, careless, neglectful ■ **vous avez été très ~ dans l'exercice**

de vos fonctions you have been very negligent in your duty *ou* very neglectful of your duties **2.** [nonchalant] negligent, casual, nonchalant.

négliger [17] [neɡliʒe] *vt* **1.** [se désintéresser de - études, santé, ami] to neglect ■ **il néglige sa tenue ces derniers temps** he hasn't been taking care of his appearance lately ■ **ne négligez pas votre devoir de citoyen** don't be neglectful of your duty as a citizen **2.** [dédaigner] to disregard ■ **il ne faut pas ~ son offre** don't disregard her offer **3.** [omettre] to neglect ■ **les enquêteurs n'ont rien négligé pour retrouver l'assassin** the police left no stone unturned in their efforts to find the murderer.
◆ **se négliger** *vpi* **1.** [être mal habillé] to be careless about *ou* to neglect one's appearance **2.** [se désintéresser de sa santé] to be neglectful of *ou* to neglect one's health.

négoce [neɡɔs] *nm sout* **1.** [activité] business, trade, trading ■ **le ~ du vin** the wine trade **2.** [entreprise] business.

négociabilité [neɡɔsjabilite] *nf* negotiability.

négociable [neɡɔsjabl] *adj* negotiable ■ **non ~** non-negotiable.

négociant, e [neɡɔsjɑ̃, ɑ̃t] *nm, f* **1.** [commerçant] merchant, trader ■ **~ en vins** wine merchant **2.** [grossiste] wholesaler.

négociateur, trice [neɡɔsjatœr, tris] *nm, f* COMM & POLIT negotiator.

négociation [neɡɔsjasjɔ̃] *nf* negotiation ■ **~s salariales** wage bargaining ■ **les deux pays ont entamé des ~s** the two countries have started *ou* begun negotiations.

négocier [9] [neɡɔsje] ◇ *vt* **1.** COMM, FIN & POLIT to negotiate **2.** AUTO : **~ un virage** to negotiate a bend.
◇ *vi* to negotiate.
◆ **se négocier** *vp (emploi passif)* **l'ancien se négocie à plus de trois mille euros le mètre carré** old flats can go for over three thousand euros per square metre.

nègre, négresse [nɛɡr, neɡrɛs] *nm, f* Negro (*f* Negress) *(note: the terms "nègre" and "négresse", like their English equivalents, are considered racist)* ■ **~ blanc** [à peau claire] white Negro ■ **négresse blanche** white Negress ■ **~ marron** HIST maroon.
◆ **nègre** ◇ *nm* **1.** [écrivain] ghost (writer) **2.** CULIN : **~ en chemise** *chocolate coated with whipped cream.*
◇ *adj* ART & MUS Negro.

négrier, ère [neɡrije, ɛr] *adj* slave *(modif)* ■ **navire ~** slave ship, slaver.
◆ **négrier** *nm* **1.** [marchand d'esclaves] slave trader, slaver **2.** [bateau] slave ship, slaver **3.** *péj* [employeur] slave driver.

négrillon, onne▲ [neɡrijɔ̃, ɔn] *nm, f racist term used with reference to black children,* ≃ piccaninny.

négritude [neɡrityd] *nf* negritude.

négro▲ [neɡro] *nm racist term used with reference to black people,* ≃ nigger▲.

négroïde [neɡrɔid] *adj* & *nmf* Negroid.

negro spiritual [neɡrospiritɥɔl] (*pl* **negro spirituals**) *nm* Negro spiritual.

neige [nɛʒ] *nf* **1.** MÉTÉOR snow ■ **~ fondue** [pluie] sleet ; [boue] slush ■ **les ~s éternelles** permanent snow ■ **pneu~** snow tyre ■ **~ poudreuse** powdery snow ■ **~ tôlée** crusted snow **2.** CHIM : **~ carbonique** dry ice **3.** △ [cocaïne] snow△ **4.** CULIN : **battez les blancs en ~** whisk the whites until they form peaks.
◆ **à la neige** *loc adv fam* LOISIRS on a skiing holiday *UK ou* vacation *US*.
◆ **de neige** *loc adj* **1.** MÉTÉOR : **chute** *ou* **giboulée de ~** snowfall, fall of snow **2.** LOISIRS : **station de ~** winter sports *ou* ski resort **3.** *litt* [blanc] snow-white, snowy.

neiger [23] [neʒe] *v impers* : **il neige** it's snowing.

neigeux, euse [nɛʒø, øz] *adj* **1.** [cime] snowcapped, snow-clad **2.** [hiver, temps] snowy.

néné [nene] *nm fam* boob *(breast)*.

nénette [nenɛt] *nf fam* [femme] bird *UK*, broad *US*.

nénuphar [nenyfar] *nm* water lily ■ **~ jaune** *ou* **des étangs** yellow water *ou* pond lily.

néo- [neo] *préf* neo-.

néo-calédonien, enne [neɔkaledɔnjɛ̃, ɛn] (*mpl* **néo-calédoniens**, *fpl* **néo-calédoniennes**) *adj* New Caledonian.
◆ **Néo-Calédonien, enne** *nm, f* New Caledonian.

néocapitalisme [neɔkapitalism] *nm* neo-capitalism.

néocapitaliste [neɔkapitalist] *adj* & *nmf* neo-capitalist.

néoclassicisme [neɔklasisism] *nm* neoclassicism.

néoclassique [neɔklasik] *adj* neoclassic, neoclassical.

néocolonial, e [neɔkɔlɔnjal] *adj* neocolonial.

néocolonialisme [neɔkɔlɔnjalism] *nm* neocolonialism.

néocolonialiste [neɔkɔlɔnjalist] ◇ *adj* neocolonial, neocolonialist.
◇ *nmf* neocolonialist.

néodarwinisme [neɔdarwinism] *nm* neo-Darwinism.

néofascisme [neɔfaʃism] *nm* neofascism.

néofasciste [neɔfaʃist] *adj* & *nmf* neofascist.

néogothique [neɔɡɔtik] ◇ *adj* neogothic.
◇ *nm* neogothic (style).

néo-guinéen, enne [neɔɡineɛ̃, ɛn] (*mpl* **néo-guinéens**, *fpl* **néo-guinéennes**) *adj* New Guinean.
◆ **Néo-Guinéen, enne** *nm, f* New Guinean.

néo-impressionnisme [neɔɛ̃presjɔnism] (*pl* **néo-impressionnismes**) *nm* neo-impressionism.

néo-impressionniste [neɔɛ̃presjɔnist] (*pl* **néo-impressionnistes**) *adj* & *nmf* neo-impressionist.

néolibéralisme [neɔliberalism] *nm* neo-liberalism.

néolithique [neɔlitik] ◇ *adj* Neolithic.
◇ *nm* Neolithic (period).

néologie [neɔlɔʒi] *nf* neology.

néologique [neɔlɔʒik] *adj* neological.

néologisme [neɔlɔʒism] *nm* LING & PSYCHOL neologism.

néon [neɔ̃] *nm* **1.** [gaz] neon **2.** [éclairage] neon (lighting) ■ [lampe] neon (lamp).

néonatal, e, als [neɔnatal] *adj* neonatal.

néonazi, e [neɔnazi] *adj* & *nm, f* neo-Nazi.

néonazisme [neɔnazism] *nm* neo-Nazism, neo-Naziism.

néophyte [neɔfit] *nmf* **1.** [nouvel adepte] neophyte, novice **2.** RELIG neophyte, novice.

néoplasie [neɔplazi] *nf* neoplasm.

néoplatonicien, enne [neɔplatɔnisjɛ̃, ɛn] ◇ *adj* Neoplatonic.
◇ *nm, f* Neoplatonist.

néoplatonisme [neɔplatɔnism] *nm* Neoplatonism.

néopositivisme [neɔpozitivism] *nm* logical positivism.

néopositiviste [neɔpozitivist] *adj* & *nmf* logical positivist.

néo-québécois, e [neɔkebekwa, az] *adj* from New Quebec.
◆ **Néo-Québecois, e** *nm, f* New Quebecker.

néoréalisme [neɔrealism] *nm* neorealism.

néoréaliste [neɔrealist] *adj* & *nmf* neorealist.

néo-zélandais, e [neɔzelɑ̃dɛ, ɛz] (*mpl inv*, *fpl* **néo-zélandaises**) *adj* from New Zealand ■ **agneau ~** New Zealand lamb.
◆ **Néo-Zélandais, e** *nm, f* New Zealander.

Népal [nepal] *npr m* : **le ~** Nepal ■ **au ~** in Nepal.

népalais, e [nepalɛ, ɛz] *adj* Nepalese, Nepali.
◆ **Népalais, e** *nm, f* Nepalese (person), Nepali.
◆ **népalais** *nm* LING Nepali.

néphralgie [nefralʒi] *nf* nephralgia.

néphrétique [nefretik] *adj* nephritic.

néphrite [nefrit] *nf* **1.** MÉD nephritis **2.** MINÉR nephrite.

néphrologie [nefrɔlɔʒi] *nf* nephrology.

néphrologue [nefrɔlɔg] *nmf* nephrologist *spéc*, kidney specialist.

népotisme [nepɔtism] *nm* nepotism.

Neptune [nɛptyn] *npr* Neptune.

nerf [nɛr] *nm* **1.** ANAT nerve ▪ **~ moteur/sensitif/mixte** motor/sensor/mixed nerve ▪ **~ gustatif** gustatory nerve ▪ **avoir les ~s malades** *vieilli* to suffer from nerves ▪ **ses ~s ont fini par lâcher** she eventually cracked ▪ **avoir les ~s à cran** *fam* *ou* **en boule** *fam* *ou* **en pelote** to be wound up, to be on edge ▪ **avoir les ~s à fleur de peau** *ou* **à vif** to be a bundle of nerves ▪ **avoir les ~s solides** *ou* **des ~s d'acier** to have nerves of steel ▪ **être sur les ~s** to be worked up ▪ **on est tous sur les ~s depuis ce matin** we've all been on edge since this morning ▪ **il est toujours** *ou* **il vit sur les ~s** he's highly-strung, he lives on his nerves ▪ **ne passe pas tes ~s sur moi** *fam* don't take it out on me ▪ **porter** *fam* *ou* **taper** *fam* **sur les ~s à qqn** to get on sb's nerves **2.** *(toujours sing)* [énergie] : **elle manque de ~ pour diriger l'entreprise** she hasn't got what it takes to run the company ▪ **son style manque de ~** his style is a bit weak ▪ **ça, c'est une voiture qui a du ~!** now that's what I call a responsive car! ➲ **allez, du ~!** come on, put some effort into it! **3.** [tendon] piece of gristle **4.** IMPR rib **5.** MIN horse, rock vein.

◆ **nerf de bœuf** *nm* bludgeon.

Néron [nerɔ̃] *npr* Nero.

nerveusement [nɛrvøzmɑ̃] *adv* **1.** MÉD nervously ▪ **elle est fatiguée ~** she's suffering from nervous exhaustion ▪ **~, ça l'a beaucoup marqué** it really shook (up) his nerves **2.** [de façon agitée] nervously, restlessly ▪ [avec impatience] nervously, impatiently ▪ **rire ~** to laugh nervously.

nerveux, euse [nɛrvø, øz] ◇ *adj* **1.** ANAT & MÉD [système, dépression, maladie] nervous ▪ [centre, influx] nerve *(modif)* **2.** [énervé - de nature] nervous, highly-strung ; [- passagèrement] : **tu me rends ~** you're making me nervous ▪ **être ~ avant une entrevue** to be nervous *ou* on edge before an interview ▪ **tu ne manges pas? – c'est ~** aren't you eating? – it's my nerves **3.** [énergique - cheval] spirited, vigorous ; [- voiture] responsive ; [- style] energetic, forceful, vigorous **4.** [dur - viande] gristly, stringy.

◇ *nm, f* nervous *ou* highly-strung person.

nervosité [nɛrvozite] *nf* **1.** MÉD nervosity **2.** [excitation - passagère] nervousness, tension, agitation ; [- permanente] nervousness ▪ **la ~ du candidat** the candidate's uneasiness **3.** [irritabilité] irritability, touchiness **4.** [vigueur] responsiveness ▪ **un moteur d'une grande ~** a highly responsive engine.

nervure [nɛrvyr] *nf* **1.** BOT vein, nervure **2.** ZOOL vein **3.** AÉRON & MÉTALL rib ▪ AUTO stiffening rib **4.** IMPR rib **5.** TECHNOL flange **6.** COUT piping **7.** ARCHIT & CONSTR rib.

nervurer [3] [nɛrvyre] *vt* **1.** BOT & ZOOL to vein **2.** AÉRON & ARCHIT to rib **3.** IMPR to rib, to band **4.** TECHNOL to flange **5.** COUT to pipe.

Nescafé® [nɛskafe] *nm* Nescafé®, instant coffee.

n'est-ce pas [nɛspa] *loc adv* **1.** [sollicitant l'acquiescement] : **vous savez, ~, ce qu'il en est** you know what the situation is, don't you? ▪ **~ qu'ils sont mignons?** aren't they cute *ou* sweet? **2.** [emploi expressif] : **lui, ~, ne voyage qu'en première classe** *hum* he, of course, only ever travels first class.

net, nette [nɛt] *adj* **1.** [nettoyé] clean, neat ▪ **une chemise pas très nette** a grubby shirt ▮ [ordonné] (clean and) tidy, neat (and tidy)

2. [pur - peau, vin] clear ▪ **~ de** *litt* free from ▪ **être ~ de tout soupçon** to be above suspicion

3. [bien défini] clear ▪ **la cassure est nette** the break is clean ▪ **elle a une diction nette** she speaks *ou* articulates clearly ▪ **une réponse nette** a straight answer ▪ **sa position est nette** her position is clear-cut ▪ **un refus ~** a flat refusal ▪ **j'ai la nette impression que...** I have the distinct *ou* clear impression that... ▮ [évident] distinct, definite, striking ▪ **il y a une nette amélioration** there's a marked improvement ▪ **il veut t'épouser, c'est ~!** he wants to marry you, that's obvious!

4. PHOTO sharp ▪ **l'image n'est pas nette** the picture isn't very clear

5. COMM & FIN net ▪ **~ d'impôt** tax-free ▪ **~ de tout droit** exempt *ou* free from duty ➲ **bénéfice ~** net profit ▪ **revenu ~** net income

6. *fam loc* **pas ~** [équivoque] : **cette histoire n'est pas nette** there's something fishy *ou* not kosher about this business ▪ **ce mec n'est pas ~** [suspect] there's something shifty *ou* shady about that guy ; [fou] that guy's a bit funny *ou* weird

7. MIN washed, clean.

◆ **net** ◇ *adj inv* SPORT : **la balle est ~** (it's a) let.

◇ *adv* **1.** [brutalement] : **s'arrêter ~** to stop dead ▪ **être tué ~** to be killed outright ▪ **couper** *ou* **casser ~ avec qqn** to break with sb completely

2. [sans mentir] frankly, plainly ▪ [sans tergiverser] frankly, bluntly ▪ **je vous le dis tout ~** I'm telling you straight

3. COMM & FIN net ▪ **je gagne 200 euros ~ par semaine** *ou* **200 euros par semaine ~** I take home *ou* my take-home pay is 200 euros a week.

◆ **au net** *loc adv* : **mettre qqch au ~** to make a fair copy of sthg ▪ **après mise au ~ (du texte)** after tidying up (the text).

Net [nɛt] *nm* : **le ~** the Net.

netéconomie [nɛtekɔnɔmi] *nf* (inter)net economy.

netiquette [netikɛt] *nf* netiquette.

nettement [nɛtmɑ̃] *adv* **1.** [distinctement] clearly, distinctly **2.** [avec franchise] clearly, frankly, bluntly ▪ **je lui ai dit très ~ ce que je pensais de lui** I told him bluntly what I thought of him **3.** [beaucoup] definitely, markedly ▪ **il est ~ plus fort que Paul** he's much stronger than Paul ▪ **j'aurais ~ préféré ne pas y être** I would definitely have preferred not to be there.

netteté [nɛtte] *nf* **1.** [propreté] cleanness, cleanliness **2.** [clarté] clearness, clarity **3.** [précision - de l'écriture] neatness, clearness ; [- d'une image, d'un contour] sharpness, clearness ▪ **offensé par la ~ de son refus** offended by the flatness of her refusal.

nettoie *etc v* ▷ **nettoyer**.

nettoiement [netwamɑ̃] *nm* **1.** [des rues] cleaning **2.** AGRIC clearing.

nettoyage [netwajaʒ] *nm* **1.** [d'une maison, d'un vêtement] cleaning ▪ **porter sa robe au ~** *fam* to take one's dress to the cleaner's ➲ **~ de printemps** spring-cleaning ▪ **~ à sec** dry cleaning ; [sur une étiquette] 'dry clean only' ▪ **produits de ~** cleaning agents ▪ **faire le ~ par le vide** to make a clean sweep **2.** *fam fig* [d'un quartier, d'une ville] clean-up.

nettoyant [netwajɑ̃] *nm* [gén] cleaning product, cleanser ▪ [détachant] stain remover.

nettoyer [13] [nɛtwaje] *vt* **1.** [rendre propre - gén] to clean ; [- plaie] to clean, to cleanse ▪ **~ une maison à fond** to spring-clean a house ▪ **donner un vêtement à ~** to have a garment cleaned, to take a garment to the cleaner's ▪ **~ à sec** to dry-clean **2.** [enlever - tache] to remove **3.** *fam* [vider] to clean out *(sép)* ▪ **je me suis fait ~ au poker** I got cleaned out at poker ▪ **et l'héritage? – nettoyé!** what about the inheritance? – all gone! ▪ **en un instant, elle avait nettoyé son assiette** she emptied her plate in a flash **4.** *fam* [quartier] to clean up *ou* out *(sép)* **5.** *fam* [épuiser] to wear out *(sép)* **6.** △ [tuer] to wipe out *(sép)*, to bump off *(sép)*.

◆ **se nettoyer** *vpt* : **se ~ les mains** [gén] to clean one's hands ; [à l'eau] to wash one's hands.

neuf¹ [nœf] ◇ *dét* **1.** nine **2.** [dans des séries] : **Charles IX** Charles the Ninth, *voir aussi* **cinq**.

◇ *nm inv* nine, *voir aussi* **cinq**.

neuf², neuve [nœf *(devant an, heure et homme)*, [nœv] nœv] *adj* **1.** [n'ayant jamais servi] new ▪ **flambant** *ou* **tout ~** brand-new ▪ **mon appareil photo n'est plus tout ~** my camera is a bit old now **2.** [récemment créé - pays] new, young ▪ **une ville neuve** a new town **3.** [original - point de vue, idée] new, fresh, original ▪ **porter un regard ~ sur qqn/qqch** to take a fresh look at sb/sthg ▪ **connaissances toutes neuves** newly-acquired *ou* freshly-acquired knowledge ▪ **il est encore (un peu) ~ en matière de...** he's still (relatively) new *ou* a (relative) newcomer to...

◆ **neuf** *nm* **1.** [objets nouveaux] : **ici, on vend du ~ et de l'occasion** here we sell both new and second-hand items ▪ **vêtu de ~** (dressed) in new clothes **2.** [informations nouvelles] : **qu'est-ce** qu'il y a de *ou* quoi de ~? what's new? ■ rien de ~ depuis la dernière fois nothing new since last time ■ il y a eu du ~ dans l'affaire Peters there have been new developments in the Peters case.

◆ **à neuf** *loc adv* : un devis pour la remise à ~ du local/moteur an estimate for doing up the premises/overhauling the engine ■ j'ai remis *ou* refait la maison à ~ I did up the house like new.

◆ **coup de neuf** *nm* : donner un coup de ~ à qqch to spruce sthg up.

neurasthénie [nørasteni] *nf* MÉD & PSYCHOL neurasthenia ■ elle fait de la ~ *fam* [de la dépression] she's having a nervous breakdown.

neurasthénique [nørastenik] ◇ *adj* MÉD & PSYCHOL neurasthenic ■ *vieilli* [dépressif] depressed.
◇ *nmf* MÉD & PSYCHOL neurasthenic ■ *vieilli* [dépressif] depressed person.

neuro- [nørɔ] *préf* neuro-.

neurochirurgical, e, aux [nørɔʃiryrʒikal, o] *adj* neurosurgical.

neurochirurgie [nørɔʃiryrʒi] *nf* neurosurgery.

neurochirurgien, enne [nørɔʃiryrʒjɛ̃, ɛn] *nm, f* neurosurgeon.

neurodégénératif, ive [nørɔdeʒeneratif, iv] *adj* MÉD neurodegenerative.

neuroleptique [nørɔleptik] *adj* & *nm* neuroleptic.

neurolinguistique [nørɔlɛ̃gɥistik] *nf* neurolinguistics *(sing)*.

neurologie [nørɔlɔʒi] *nf* neurology.

neurologique [nørɔlɔʒik] *adj* neurologic, neurological.

neurologiste [nørɔlɔʒist], **neurologue** [nørɔlɔg] *nmf* neurologist.

neuromusculaire [nørɔmyskylɛr] *adj* neuromuscular.

neuronal, e, aux [nørɔnal, o] *adj* neuronal.

neurone [nørɔn] *nm* neuron, neurone.

neurophysiologie [nørɔfizjɔlɔʒi] *nf* neurophysiology.

neurophysiologique [nørɔfizjɔlɔʒik] *adj* neurophysiologic, neurophysiological.

neuropsychiatre [nørɔpsikjatr] *nmf* neuropsychiatrist.

neuropsychiatrie [nørɔpsikjatri] *nf* neuropsychiatry.

neuropsychologie [nørɔpsikɔlɔʒi] *nf* neuropsychology.

neuropsychologue [nørɔpsikɔlɔg] *nmf* neuropsychologist.

neurosciences [nørɔsjɑ̃s] *nfpl* neurosciences.

neurotransmetteur [nørɔtrɑ̃smɛtœr] *nm* neurotransmitter.

neurovasculaire [nørɔvaskylɛr] *adj* neurovascular.

neurovégétatif, ive [nørɔveʒetatif, iv] *adj* : système nerveux ~ autonomic nervous system.

neutralisant, e [nøtralizɑ̃, ɑ̃t] *adj* neutralizing.

neutralisation [nøtralizasjɔ̃] *nf* [gén] neutralization.

neutraliser [3] [nøtralize] *vt* **1.** [atténuer] to tone down *(sép)* **2.** [annuler] to neutralize, to cancel out *(sép)* **3.** [maîtriser] to overpower, to bring under control ■ les agents ont neutralisé le forcené the police overpowered the maniac **4.** [contrecarrer] to neutralize, to thwart ■ ~ un concurrent to thwart a competitor **5.** [bloquer] to close ■ la voie rapide est neutralisée dans le sens Paris-province the fast lane is closed to traffic leaving Paris **6.** POLIT [déclarer neutre] to neutralize **7.** CHIM, ÉLECTR, LING & MÉD to neutralize.

◆ **se neutraliser** *vp (emploi réciproque)* to neutralize ■ les deux forces se neutralisent the two forces cancel each other out.

neutraliste [nøtralist] ◇ *adj* neutralist, neutralistic.
◇ *nmf* neutralist.

neutralité [nøtralite] *nf* **1.** [d'une attitude] neutrality ■ observer la ~ to remain neutral **2.** CHIM & PHYS neutrality.

neutre [nøtr] ◇ *adj* **1.** [couleur, décor, attitude, pays] neutral ■ d'une voix ~ in a neutral *ou* an expressionless voice ■ rester ~ : je veux rester ~ I don't want to take sides ■ tu ne peux pas rester ~ you can't remain neutral **2.** CHIM, ÉLECTR & PHYS neutral **3.** LING & ZOOL neuter.
◇ *nmf* POLIT : les ~s the neutral countries.
◇ *nm* **1.** LING neuter **2.** ÉLECTR neutral (wire).

neutron [nøtrɔ̃] *nm* neutron.

neuvaine [nœvɛn] *nf* novena.

neuve [nœv] *f* ⊳ **neuf.**

neuvième [nœvjɛm] ◇ *adj num ord* ninth ■ le ~ art cartoons, *voir aussi* **cinquième.**
◇ *nmf* ninth ■ elle est la ~ de la classe she's ninth in the class.
◇ *nf* **1.** ÉDUC third form *UK ou* grade *US (in French primary school)* **2.** MUS ninth.
◇ *nm* ninth.

Nevada [nevada] *npr m* : le ~ Nevada.

névé [neve] *nm* **1.** [dans un glacier] névé **2.** [plaque] bank of snow.

neveu [nəvø] *nm* nephew ■ un peu, mon ~! *fam* you bet (your sweet life)!, and how!

névralgie [nevralʒi] *nf* neuralgia ■ avoir une ~ [un mal de tête] to have a headache.

névralgique [nevralʒik] *adj* **1.** MÉD neuralgic **2.** *fig* ⊳ **point.**

névrite [nevrit] *nf* neuritis.

névropathe [nevrɔpat] *nmf* neuropath.

névrose [nevroz] *nf* neurosis.

névrosé, e [nevroze] *adj* & *nm, f* neurotic.

névrotique [nevrɔtik] *adj* neurotic.

New Age [njuɛdʒ] *adj* New Age.

New Delhi [njudeli] *npr* New Delhi.

New Hampshire [njuɑ̃pʃœr] *npr m* : le ~ New Hampshire.

New Jersey [njuʒɛrzɛ] *npr m* : le ~ New Jersey.

new-look [njuluk] ◇ *nm inv* COUT New Look.
◇ *adj inv* **1.** COUT New Look *(modif)* **2.** [rénové] new look *(modif)*.

newton [njutɔn] *nm* newton.

newtonien, enne [njutɔnjɛ̃, ɛn] *adj* Newtonian.

New York [nujɔrk] *npr* **1.** [ville] New York (City) **2.** [état] New York State ■ dans l'État de ~ in New York State.

new-yorkais, e [nujɔrkɛ, ɛz] *(mpl inv, fpl* **new-yorkaises***)* *adj* from New York.

◆ **New-Yorkais, e** *nm, f* New Yorker.

nez [ne] *nm* **1.** ANAT nose ■ avoir le ~ bouché to have a stuffed up *ou* blocked nose ■ avoir le ~ qui coule to have a runny nose ■ avoir le ~ qui saigne, saigner du ~ to have a nosebleed ■ avoir un ~ grec to have a Grecian nose ■ ~ en trompette turned-up nose ■ parler du ~ to talk *ou* to speak through one's nose
2. [jugement] flair *(U)*, good judgment *(U)*, intuition *(U)* ■ avoir du ~ to have good judgment ■ il a du ~ pour acheter des antiquités he's got a flair for buying antiques ■ j'ai eu du ~ *ou* le ~ fin *ou* le ~ creux my intuition was good ■ tu vois, j'ai eu le ~ fin de partir avant minuit you see, I was right to trust my instinct and leave before midnight
3. [flair d'un chien] nose ■ avoir du ~ to have a good nose
4. [en parfumerie] *perfume tester*
5. AÉRON nose ■ sur le ~ tilting down
6. CONSTR (tile) nib
7. GÉOGR edge, overhang
8. NAUT bows
9. ŒNOL nose ■ un vin qui a du ~ a wine with a good nose
10. TECHNOL shank
11. *loc* le ~ en l'air *pr* looking upwards ; *fig* without a care in the world ■ il a toujours le ~ dans une BD he's always got his nose buried in a comic ■ sans lever le ~ de son travail without

looking up from his/her work ■ **montrer (le bout de) son ~** to show one's face, to put in an appearance ■ **le voisin/soleil n'a pas montré son ~ de la semaine** the man next door/sun hasn't come out all week ■ **fermer/claquer la porte au ~ à qqn** to shut/to slam the door in sb's face ■ **au ~ (et à la barbe)** *ou* **sous le ~ de qqn** under sb's nose ■ **tu as le ~ dessus!, il est sous ton ~!** it's right under your nose! ■ **le dernier billet m'est passé sous le ~** I just missed the last ticket ■ **se trouver ~ à ~ avec qqn** to find o.s. face to face with sb ■ **ce type, je l'ai dans le ~** *fam* that guy gets right up my nose *UK*, I can't stand that guy ■ **ça se voit comme le ~ au milieu de la figure** it's as plain as the nose on your face ■ **se manger** *ou* **se bouffer** *fam* **le ~** to be at each other's throats ■ **elle ne met jamais le ~ ici** she never shows her face in here ■ **je n'ai pas mis le ~ dehors depuis une semaine** I haven't put my nose outside the door for a week ■ **mettre** *ou* **fourrer son ~ dans les affaires de qqn** *fam* to poke *ou* to stick one's nose in sb's business ■ **je vais lui mettre le ~ dans son caca**△ *ou* **sa merde**▲**, moi!** I'm going to rub his nose right in it!

◆ **à plein nez** *loc adv* : **ça sent le fromage à plein ~** there's a strong smell of cheese.

NF (*abr de* **Norme française**) *nf label indicating compliance with official French standards*, ≃ BS *UK*, ≃ US standard *US*.

ni [ni] *conj* nor ■ **je ne peux ni ne veux venir** I can't come and I don't want to either, I can't come, nor do I want to ■ **il ne veut pas qu'on l'appelle, ni même qu'on lui écrive** he doesn't want anyone to phone him or even to write to him ■ **il est sorti sans pull ni écharpe** he went out without either his jumper or his scarf ■ **il ne manque pas de charme ni d'aisance** he lacks neither charm nor ease of manner.

◆ **ni... ni** *loc corrélative* neither... nor ■ **ni lui ni moi** neither of us ■ **ni l'un ni l'autre n'est tout à fait innocent** neither (one) of them is completely innocent ■ **je ne veux voir ni lui ni elle** I don't want to see either of them ■ **ni ici ni ailleurs** neither here nor elsewhere ■ **il n'a répondu ni oui ni non** he didn't say yes and he didn't say no ■ **il n'est ni plus sot, ni plus paresseux qu'un autre** he's no more silly or lazy than the next man ■ **c'était comment? – ni bien ni mal** how was it? – OK ➊ **ni vu ni connu** without anybody noticing.

niable [njabl] *adj* deniable ■ **les faits ne sont pas ~s** the facts cannot be denied.

Niagara [njagara] *npr m* : **les chutes du ~** the Niagara falls.

niais, e [njɛ, njɛz] ◇ *adj* [sot] simple, simple-minded, inane.

◇ *nm, f sout* simpleton, halfwit ■ **espèce de grand ~!** you great nincompoop!

niaisement [njɛzmɑ̃] *adv sout* inanely, stupidly, foolishly.

niaiser [njeze] *vi Québec* to dilly-dally.

niaiserie [njɛzri] *nf* **1.** [caractère] simpleness, inanity, foolishness **2.** [parole] stupid *ou* inane remark ■ **cesse de raconter des ~s** stop talking such silly nonsense.

niaiseux, euse [njezø, øz] *nm, f Québec* idiot.

Nicaragua [nikaragwa] *npr m* : **le ~** Nicaragua ■ **au ~** in Nicaragua.

nicaraguayen, enne [nikaragwɛjɛ̃, ɛn] *adj* Nicaraguan.

◆ **Nicaraguayen, enne** *nm, f* Nicaraguan.

niche [niʃ] *nf* **1.** [renfoncement] niche, (small) alcove **2.** GÉOGR niche, recess **3.** [pour chien] kennel **4.** ÉCON & ÉCOL niche **5.** MÉD niche (defect) **6.** *fam* [espièglerie] trick ■ **faire des ~s à qqn** to play pranks on sb.

nichée [niʃe] *nf* **1.** [d'oiseaux] nest, brood **2.** [de chiots, de chatons] litter **3.** *fam* [enfants] : **il est arrivé avec toute sa ~** he turned up with all his brood.

nicher [3] [niʃe] ◇ *vi* **1.** [faire son nid] to nest **2.** *fam* [habiter] to hang out, to doss *UK* **3.** [couver] to brood.

◇ *vt* to nestle ■ **elle nicha sa tête sur mon épaule** she nestled her head on *ou* against my shoulder.

◆ **se nicher** *vpi* **1.** [faire son nid] to nest **2.** [se blottir] to nestle ■ **je rêve d'un petit chalet niché dans la montagne** I dream of a little chalet nestling among the mountains **3.** [se cacher] : **où l'amour-propre va-t-il se ~?** pride is found in the strangest places!

nichoir [niʃwar] *nm* nesting box, nest box.

nichons△ [niʃɔ̃] *nmpl* tits, boobs.

nickel [nikɛl] ◇ *nm* nickel.

◇ *adj inv fam* : **c'est ~ chez toi!** your house is so spick-and-span *ou* spotless!

nickeler [24] [nikle] *vt* to plate with nickel, to nickel.

niçois, e [niswa, az] *adj* from Nice.

◆ **Niçois, e** *nm, f inhabitant of or person from Nice.*

◆ **à la niçoise** *loc adj* CULIN à la niçoise *(with tomatoes and garlic).*

Nicolas [nikɔla] *npr* : **saint ~** Saint Nicholas ■ **la Saint-~** Saint Nicholas' Day.

nicotine [nikɔtin] *nf* nicotine.

nid [ni] *nm* **1.** [d'oiseau, de guêpes etc] nest **2.** *fig* [habitation] (little) nest ■ **~ d'amour** love nest ■ **trouver le ~ vide** to find (that) the bird has flown ■ **faire son ~** to nest **3.** [repaire] : **~ de brigands** den of thieves ■ **un ~ d'espions** a spy hideout, a den of spies ■ **~ à poussière** dust trap ➊ **un ~ de vipères** a vipers' nest.

◆ **nid d'abeilles** *nm* = **nid-d'abeilles**.

◆ **nid d'aigle** *nm pr* eyrie, eagle's nest ■ *fig* eyrie.

◆ **nid d'ange** *nm* baby's sleeping bag *UK*, bunting bag *US*.

◆ **nid d'hirondelle** *nm* CULIN bird's nest.

nidation [nidasjɔ̃] *nf* nidation.

nid-d'abeilles [nidabɛj] (*pl* **nids-d'abeilles**) *nm* **1.** [tissu] honeycomb ■ [point de broderie] smocking ■ **une robe à ~** a smocked dress **2.** GÉOL honeycomb (weathering).

nid-de-pie [nidpi] (*pl* **nids-de-pie**) *nm* **1.** MIL breach stronghold **2.** NAUT crow's nest.

nid-de-poule [nidpul] (*pl* **nids-de-poule**) *nm* pothole.

nidification [nidifikasjɔ̃] *nf* nest building, nidification.

nidifier [9] [nidifje] *vi* to nest.

nièce [njɛs] *nf* niece.

nier [9] [nje] ◇ *vt* **1.** [démentir] to deny ■ **il nie l'avoir tuée** he denies that he killed her, he denies killing her ■ **je nierai tout en bloc** I'll deny it all outright ■ **cela, on ne peut le ~** that cannot be denied **2.** [rejeter, refuser] to deny.

◇ *vi* : **il continue de ~** he continues to deny it.

nigaud, e [nigo, od] ◇ *adj* simple, simple-minded, stupid.

◇ *nm, f* simpleton, halfwit ■ **quel ~!** what an idiot!

Niger [niʒɛr] *npr m* **1.** [fleuve] : **le ~** the River Niger **2.** [État] : **le ~** Niger ■ **au ~** in Niger.

Nigeria [niʒerja] *npr m* : **le ~** Nigeria ■ **au ~** in Nigeria.

nigérian, e [niʒerjɑ̃, an] *adj* Nigerian.

◆ **Nigérian, e** *nm, f* Nigerian.

nigérien, enne [niʒerjɛ̃, ɛn] *adj* Nigerien.

◆ **Nigérien, enne** *nm, f* Nigerien.

night-club [najtklœb] (*pl* **night-clubs**) *nm* nightclub.

nihilisme [niilism] *nm* nihilism.

nihiliste [niilist] ◇ *adj* nihilist, nihilistic.

◇ *nmf* nihilist.

Nil [nil] *npr m* : **le ~** the Nile.

nimbe [nɛ̃b] *nm* **1.** ART & RELIG nimbus, aureole *(round the head)* **2.** *litt* halo, nimbus *sout*.

nimber [3] [nɛ̃be] *vt* **1.** ART & RELIG to aureole, to halo **2.** *litt* **des nuages nimbés d'une lumière argentée** clouds wreathed in silvery light.

nimbo-stratus [nɛ̃bɔstratys] *nm inv* nimbostratus.

n'importe [nɛ̃pɔrt] *loc adv* **1.** [indique l'indétermination] : **quel pull mets-tu? - ~** which pullover are you going to wear? - any of them *ou* I don't mind **2.** [introduit une opposition] : **son roman est très discuté, ~, il a du succès** her novel is highly controversial, but all the same, it is successful.

◆ **n'importe comment** *loc adv* **1.** [sans soin] any old how **2.** [de toute façon] anyway, anyhow.

◆ **n'importe lequel, n'importe laquelle** *pron indéf* any ■ **~ lequel d'entre eux** any (one) of them ■ **tu veux le rouge ou le vert? – ~ lequel** do you want the red one or the green one? – either *ou* I don't mind.

◆ **n'importe où** *loc adv* anywhere ■ **ne laisse pas traîner tes affaires ~ où** don't leave your things just anywhere.

◆ **n'importe quand** *loc adv* anytime ■ **il peut arriver n'~ quand** he could come at any time *ou* moment.

◆ **n'importe quel, n'importe quelle** *adj indéf* any ■ **~ quel débutant sait ça** any beginner knows that.

◆ **n'importe qui** *pron indéf* anybody, anyone ■ **ce n'est pas ~ qui!** *fam* she's not just anybody! ■ **ne parle pas à ~ qui** don't talk to just anybody ■ **demande à ~ qui dans la rue** ask the first person you meet in the street.

◆ **n'importe quoi** *pron indéf* anything ■ **il ferait ~ quoi pour obtenir le rôle** he'd do anything *ou* he would go to any lengths to get the part ■ **tu dis vraiment ~ quoi!** you're talking absolute nonsense! ■ **c'est un bon investissement – ~ quoi!** *fam* that's a good investment – don't talk rubbish *esp UK ou* nonsense!

ninas [ninas] *nm inv* (French) cigar.

nippe [nip] *nf fam* [vêtement] : **je n'ai plus une ~ à me mettre** I've got nothing to wear.

◆ **nippes** *nfpl fam* [habits usagés] clobber *UK*, gear ■ **des (vieilles) ~s** old clothes.

nipper [3] [nipe] *vt fam* to rig out *(sép)*, to dress up *(sép)* ■ **elle est drôlement bien nippée ce soir!** she's dressed to the nines tonight!

◆ **se nipper** *vp fam (emploi réfléchi)* to rig o.s. out.

nippon, one *ou* **onne** [nipɔ̃, ɔn] *adj* Japanese.

◆ **Nippon, one** *ou* **onne** *nm, f* Japanese ■ **les Nippons** the Japanese.

nique [nik] *nf* : **faire la ~ à qqn** [faire un geste de bravade, de mépris à] to thumb one's nose at sb ; [se moquer de] to poke fun *ou* to gibe at sb ■ **ils se sont échappés en faisant la ~ aux gardiens** they got away making fun of the guards as they did it.

niquer [3] [nike] *vt* **1.** ▲ [sexuellement] to fuck▲, to screw△ **2.** △ [rouler] to con, to have **3.** *fam* [abîmer] to bugger△, to knacker△.

nirvana [nirvana] *nm* Nirvana.

nitrate [nitrat] *nm* nitrate ■ **~ de potassium** nitre.

nitrifier [9] [nitrifje] *vt* to nitrify.

◆ **se nitrifier** *vpi* to nitrify.

nitrique [nitrik] *adj* nitric.

nitroglycérine [nitrɔgliserin] *nf* nitroglycerin, nitroglycerine.

nival, e, aux [nival, o] *adj* GÉOGR nival.

niveau, x [nivo] *nm* **1.** [hauteur] level ■ **vérifie les ~x d'eau et d'huile** check the oil and water levels ■ **fixer les étagères au même ~ que la cheminée** put up the shelves level with *ou* on the same level as the mantelpiece
2. [étage] level, storey ■ **un parking à trois ~x** a car park on three levels
3. [degré] level ■ **la production atteint son plus haut ~** production is reaching its peak ■ **la natalité n'est jamais tombée à un ~ aussi bas** the birth rate is at an all-time low *ou* at its lowest level ever ■ **la décision a été prise au plus haut ~** the decision was made at the highest level ➤ **~ social** social level ■ **~ de langue** LING register
4. [étape] level, stage
5. [qualité] level, standard ■ **son ~ scolaire est-il bon?** is she doing well at school? ■ **j'ai un bon ~/un ~ moyen en russe** I'm good/average at Russian ■ **les élèves sont tous du même ~** the pupils are all on a par *ou* on the same level ■ **vous n'avez pas le ~ requis** you don't have the required standard ■ **la recherche de haut ~** high-level research ➤ **~ de vie** standard of living
6. GÉOGR level ■ **~ de la mer** sea level
7. MIN level, drift ■ [galerie] gallery, flat slope
8. INDUST **du pétrole** level
9. PHYS level ■ **~ (d'énergie)** energy level
10. TÉLÉCOM : **~ d'un signal** signal level
11. [instrument] level (tube) ■ **~ à bulle (d'air)** spirit level ■ **~ d'eau** water level.

◆ **au niveau** <> *loc adj* up to standard, of the required level ■ **dans deux mois, vous serez au ~** in two months' time you'll have caught up.
<> *loc adv* : **se mettre au ~** to catch up.

◆ **au niveau de** *loc prép* **1.** [dans l'espace] : **au ~ de la mer** at sea level ■ **l'eau lui arrivait au ~ du genou** the water came up to his knees ■ **je ressens une douleur au ~ de la hanche** I've got a pain in my hip ■ **au ~ du carrefour vous tournez à droite** when you come to the crossroads, turn right ■ **j'habite à peu près au ~ de l'église** I live by the church
2. [dans une hiérarchie] on a par with, at the level of ■ **ce problème sera traité au ~ du syndicat** this problem will be dealt with at union level.

◆ **de niveau** *loc adj* level ■ **les deux terrains ne sont pas de ~** the two plots of land are not level (with each other) ■ **la terrasse est de ~ avec le salon** the terrace is (on a) level with *ou* on the same level as the lounge.

nivelage [nivlaʒ] *nm* equalizing, levelling (out) ■ **~ par le bas** levelling down.

niveler [24] [nivle] *vt* **1.** [aplanir] to level (off) *(sép)* ■ **nivelé par l'érosion** worn (away) by erosion **2.** *fig* [égaliser] to level (off) *(sép)*, to even out *(sép)* ■ **~ par le bas** *ou* **au plus bas** to level down ■ **~ par le haut** *ou* **au plus haut** to level up **3.** TECHNOL to (measure with a spirit) level.

niveleur, euse [nivlœr, øz] *nm, f* leveller.

◆ **niveleuse** *nf* grader, motorgrader.

nivelle *etc v* ▷ **niveler**.

nivellement [nivɛlmɑ̃] *nm* **1.** [aplanissement] evening out, levelling (out) *ou* off **2.** GÉOGR (erosion) denudation **3.** *fig* [égalisation] equalizing, levelling ■ **le ~ des revenus** income redistribution **4.** GÉOL levelling.

nivôse [nivoz] *nm 4th month in the French Revolutionary calendar (from Dec 21 to Jan 20)*.

NN (*abr écrite de* **nouvelle norme**) *revised standard of hotel classification*.

N-O (*abr écrite de* **Nord-Ouest**) NW.

Nobel [nɔbel] *npr m* : **le ~ de la paix** the Nobel peace prizewinner.

nobiliaire [nɔbiljɛr] <> *adj* nobiliary.
<> *nm* peerage list.

noble [nɔbl] <> *adj* **1.** [de haute naissance] noble **2.** *fig* noble ■ **un geste ~** a noble deed **3.** ŒNOL noble, of noble vintage **4.** MÉTALL & PHYS noble.
<> *nmf* noble, nobleman (*f* noblewoman) ■ **les ~s** the nobility.
<> *nm* HIST noble (coin).

noblement [nɔbləmɑ̃] *adv* nobly.

noblesse [nɔblɛs] *nf* **1.** [condition sociale] nobleness, nobility ■ **~ de robe** *ou* **d'office** HIST *nobility acquired after having fulfilled specific judicatory duties* ■ **~ d'épée** old nobility ■ **~ terrienne** landed gentry ■ **la haute ~** the nobility ■ **la petite ~** the gentry ■ **~ oblige** (it's a case of) noblesse oblige **2.** [générosité] nobleness, nobility ■ **par ~ de cœur/d'esprit** through the nobleness of his heart/spirit **3.** [majesté] nobleness, majesty, grandness.

noce [nɔs] *nf* **1.** [fête] wedding ■ **être de la** *ou* **invité à la ~** to be invited to the wedding ■ **'~s et banquets'** 'weddings and all special occasions (catered for)' ➤ **elle n'avait jamais été à pareille ~** *fam* she had the time of her life ■ **il n'était pas à la ~** *fam* he felt far from comfortable ■ **faire la ~** *fam* to live it up **2.** [ensemble des invités] : **regarder passer la ~** to watch the wedding procession go by.

◆ **noces** *nfpl* wedding ■ **le jour des ~s** the wedding day ■ **elle l'a épousé en troisièmes ~s** he was her third husband ➤ **~s d'argent/de diamant/d'or** silver/diamond/golden wedding (anniversary) ■ **les ~s de Cana** BIBLE the marriage at Cana.

◆ **de noces** *loc adj* wedding *(modif)*.

noceur, euse [nɔsœr, øz] *nm, f fam* reveller, partyer *US*.

nocher [nɔʃe] *nm litt* pilot ■ **le ~ des Enfers** Charon the ferryman.

nocif, ive [nɔsif, iv] *adj* noxious, harmful.

nocivité [nɔsivite] *nf* noxiousness, harmfulness.

noctambule [nɔktɑ̃byl] *nmf* night owl.

noctambulisme [nɔktɑ̃bylism] *nm* night life.

nocturne [nɔktyrn] <> *adj* **1.** [gén] nocturnal, night *(modif)* **2.** BOT & ZOOL nocturnal **3.** OPT scotopic.
<> *nm* **1.** MUS nocturne **2.** RELIG nocturn.
<> *nf* **1.** SPORT evening fixture *UK ou* meet *US* **2.** COMM late-night closing ▪ **le magasin fait ~** *ou* **ouvre en ~ le jeudi** the shop stays open late on Thursdays ▪ **~ le mardi** late-night opening: Tuesday.

nodosité [nɔdozite] *nf* BOT & MÉD nodosity.

nodule [nɔdyl] *nm* **1.** MÉD nodule, node **2.** GÉOL nodule.

Noé [nɔe] *npr* Noah.

noël [nɔɛl] *nm* **1.** [chanson] (Christmas) carol **2.** *fam* [cadeau] : **(petit) ~** Christmas present.

Noël [nɔɛl] <> *nm* **1.** [fête] Christmas ▪ **joyeux ~!** Merry Christmas! ▪ **la veille de ~** Christmas Eve ▪ **le lendemain de ~** Boxing Day *UK*, the day after Christmas *US* **2.** [période] Christmas time ▪ **passer ~ en famille** to spend Christmas with the family ◗ **~ au balcon, Pâques au tison** *prov* a warm Christmas spells cold weather for Easter.
<> *nf* : **la ~** [fête] Christmas ; [période] Christmas time.

nœud [nø] *nm* **1.** [lien] knot ▪ **faire un ~** to tie *ou* to make a knot ▪ **faire un ~ à ses lacets** to do up *ou* to tie (up) one's shoelaces ▪ **fais un ~ à ton mouchoir** tie a knot in your handkerchief ▪ **faire un ~ de cravate** to knot *ou* to tie a tie ▪ **tu as des ~s dans les cheveux** your hair is (all) tangled ◗ **~ coulant** slipknot, running knot ▪ **faire un ~ coulant à une corde** to make a noose in a rope ▪ **~ plat** reef knot ▪ **couper** *ou* **trancher le ~ gordien** to cut the Gordian knot **2.** [étoffe nouée] bow ▪ **porter un ~ noir dans les cheveux** to wear a black bow *ou* ribbon in one's hair ◗ **~ papillon** *ou* **pap** *fam* bow tie **3.** NAUT [vitesse] knot **4.** [point crucial] crux ▪ **le ~ du problème** the crux *ou* heart of the problem **5.** ANAT node ▪ **~ vital** vital centre **6.** BOT [bifurcation] node ▪ [dans le bois] knot **7.** INFORM, LING, MATH & PHYS node **8.** TRAV PUB : **~ ferroviaire** rail junction ▪ **~ routier** interchange **9.** ▲ [verge] dick△.
◆ **nœud de vipères** *nm pr & fig* nest of vipers.

noie *etc v* ▷ **noyer.**

noir, e [nwar] *adj* **1.** [gén] black ◗ **~ comme de l'ébène** jet-black, ebony ▪ **~ comme un corbeau** *ou* **du charbon** (as) black as soot, pitch black ▪ **~ de jais** jet-black ▪ **~ de : ~ de suie** black with soot ▪ **~ de monde** *fig* teeming with people
2. [bronzée] : **elle est revenue ~e d'Italie** she was really brown when she came back from Italy
3. [sale] black, dirty, grimy
4. [obscur] black, dark ▪ **un ciel ~** a dark *ou* leaden sky ▪ **dans les rues ~es** in the pitch-black *ou* pitch-dark streets
5. [maléfique] black ▪ **il m'a regardé d'un œil ~** he gave me a black look ▪ **de ~s desseins** dark intentions
6. [pessimiste] black, gloomy, sombre
7. [extrême] : **saisi d'une colère ~e** livid with rage ▪ **être dans une misère ~e** to live in abject poverty
8. ANTHR black ▪ **le problème ~ aux États-Unis** the race problem in the United States
9. [illégal] : **travail ~** undeclared work ; [en plus de l'activité principale] moonlighting
10. △ [ivre] plastered△, blind-drunk
11. GÉOGR : **la mer Noire** the Black Sea.
◆ **Noir, e** *nm, f* Black, Black man (*f* woman) ▪ **les Noirs** (the) Blacks ▪ **Noir américain** African American.
◆ **noir** <> *nm* **1.** [couleur] black ▪ **se mettre du ~ aux yeux** to put on eyeliner ▪ **une photo/un film en ~ et blanc** a black and white photo/film ▪ **le ~ et blanc** PHOTO black and white photography ▪ **~ de carbone** *ou* **fumée** carbon black
2. [saleté] dirt, grime ▪ **tu as du ~ sur la joue** you've got a black mark on your face
3. [obscurité] darkness ▪ **dans le ~** in the dark, in darkness ▪ **avoir peur dans le ~** to be afraid *ou* scared of the dark ▪ **être dans le ~ le plus complet** *fig* to be totally in the dark
4. JEUX black
5. *fam* [café] (black) coffee.
<> *adv* dark ▪ **il fait ~ de bonne heure** it gets dark early ◗ **il fait ~ comme dans un four** *ou* **tunnel ici** it's pitch-dark *ou* pitch-black in here.
◆ **noire** *nf* MUS crotchet *UK*, quarter note *US*.
◆ **au noir** <> *loc adj* : **travail au ~** undeclared work ; [en plus de l'activité principale] moonlighting.
<> *loc adv* [illégalement] : **je l'ai eu au ~** I got it on the black market ▪ **travailler au ~** to do undeclared work ; [en plus de l'activité principale] to moonlight.
◆ **en noir** *loc adv* **1.** [colorié, teint] black ▪ **habillé en ~** dressed in black, wearing black
2. *fig* **voir tout en ~** to look on the dark side of things.

noirâtre [nwaratr] *adj* blackish.

noiraud, e [nwaro, od] <> *adj* dark, dark-skinned, swarthy.
<> *nm, f* dark *ou* swarthy person.

noirceur [nwarsœr] *nf* **1.** [couleur noire] blackness, darkness **2.** *litt* [d'un acte, d'un dessein] blackness, wickedness **3.** *litt* [acte] black *ou* evil *ou* wicked deed.

noircir [32] [nwarsir] <> *vt* **1.** [rendre noir] to blacken ▪ **noirci par le charbon** blackened with coal ◗ **~ du papier** *fam* to write pages and pages *ou* page after page **2.** [dramatiser] : **~ la situation** to make the situation out to be darker *ou* blacker than it is **3.** *sout* [dénigrer] : **~ la réputation de qqn** to blacken sb's reputation.
<> *vi* to go black, to darken ▪ **le ciel noircit à l'horizon** the sky is darkening on the horizon.
◆ **se noircir** <> *vp (emploi réfléchi) sout* [se dénigrer] to denigrate o.s.
<> *vpt* [se grimer] : **se ~ le visage** to blacken one's face.
<> *vpi* **1.** [s'assombrir] to darken ▪ **notre avenir se noircit** our future is looking blacker **2.** △ [s'enivrer] to get plastered△ *ou* blind drunk.

noircissement [nwarsismɑ̃] *nm* **1.** blackening, darkening **2.** MÉTALL facing, blacking.

noircissure [nwarsisyr] *nf* black mark *ou* smudge *ou* stain.

noise [nwaz] *nf* : **chercher ~** *ou* **des ~s à qqn** to try to pick a quarrel with sb.

noisetier [nwaztje] *nm* hazel, hazelnut tree.

noisette [nwazɛt] <> *nf* **1.** BOT hazelnut **2.** [petite portion] : **une ~ de pommade** a small dab of ointment ▪ **une ~ de beurre** a knob of butter ▮ [café] *small coffee with a drop of milk.*
<> *adj inv* hazel *(modif)*.

noix [nwa] *nf* **1.** BOT walnut ▪ **~ de cajou** cashew (nut) ▪ **~ de coco** coconut ▪ **~ (de) muscade** nutmeg **2.** CULIN : **~ de veau** cushion of veal, noix de veau **3.** [petite quantité] : **une ~ de beurre** a knob of butter **4.** *fam* [imbécile] nut ▪ **quelle ~, ce type!** he's such a nitwit! ▮ [camarade] : **salut, vieille ~!** hi, old chap *UK ou* buddy! **5.** MENUIS [rainure] half-round groove.
◆ **à la noix (de coco)** *loc adj fam* lousy, crummy ▪ **toi et tes idées à la ~ (de coco)!** you and your lousy ideas!

nom [nɔ̃] *nm* **1.** [patronyme] name ▪ [prénom] (Christian) *ou* first name ▪ **elle porte le ~ de sa mère** [prénom] she was named after her mother ; [patronyme] she has *ou* uses her mother's surname ▪ **Larousse, c'est un ~ que tout le monde connaît** Larousse is a household name ▪ **quelqu'un du ~ de** *ou* **qui a pour ~ Kregg vous demande** someone called Kregg *ou* someone by the name of Kregg is asking for you ▪ **je n'arrive pas à mettre un ~ sur son visage** I can't put a name to her (face) ▪ **je la connais de ~** I (only) know her by name ▪ **j'écris sous le ~ de Kim Lewis** I write under the name of Kim Lewis ▪ **en son/mon/ton ~** in his/my/your name, on his/my/your behalf ▪ **parle-lui en mon ~** speak to her on my behalf *ou* for me ◗ **~ à particule** *ou* **à rallonges** *fam ou* **à tiroirs** *fam ou* **à courants d'air** *fam* aristocratic surname, ≃ double-barrelled name ▪ **un ~ à coucher dehors** an unpronounceable name ▪ **~ de baptême, petit ~** *fam* Christian *ou* first name, given name *US* ▪ **~ de domaine** INFORM domain name ▪ **~ d'emprunt** assumed name ▪ **~ de famille** surname ▪ **~ de jeune fille** maiden name ▪ **~ de guerre** nom de guerre, alias ▪ **traiter** *ou* **appeler qqn de tous les ~s d'oiseaux** to call sb all the names under the sun ▪ **~ patronymique** patronymic (name) ▪ **~ de plume** nom de plume, pen name ▪ **~ de scène** stage name ▪ **sous un faux ~** under a false *ou* an assumed name ▪ **se faire un ~** to make a name for o.s. **2.** [appellation - d'une rue, d'un animal, d'un objet, d'une fonction] name ▪ **comme son ~ l'indique** as its name indicates ▪ **cet arbre porte le ~ de peuplier** this tree is called a poplar ▪ **il n'est roi que de ~** he is king in name only ▪ **d'empereur, il ne lui manquait que le ~** he was emperor in all but name ▪ **cruauté/douleur sans ~** unspeakable cruelty/pain ▪ **une censure qui ne dit pas son ~** hidden *ou* disguised censorship ▪ **c'est du racisme qui n'ose pas dire son ~** it's racism by any other name ◗ **~ scientifique/vulgaire d'une plante** scientific/common name of a plant ▪ **~ commercial** *ou* **de marque** trade name ▪ **~ déposé** trademark ▪ **appeler** *ou* **nommer les choses par leur ~** to call things by their names, to call a spade a spade **3.** GRAMM & LING noun ▪ **~ commun** common noun ▪ **~ composé** compound (noun) ▪ **~ propre** proper noun *ou* name **4.** *loc* **~ de Dieu, les voilà!**△ bloody hell△ *esp UK ou* goddam△ *US*, here they come! ▪ **je t'avais pourtant dit de ne pas y toucher, ~ de Dieu!**△ for Christ's sake, I did tell you not to touch it! ▪ **mais ~ de ~, qu'est-ce que tu as dans la tête!** *fam* for goodness' sake, birdbrain! ▪ **~ d'un chien** *ou* **d'une pipe** *ou* **de Zeus** *ou* **d'un petit bonhomme!** *fam* good heavens!

◆ **au nom de** *loc prép* in the name of ▪ **au ~ de la loi, je vous arrête** I arrest you in the name of the law ▪ **au ~ de notre longue amitié** for the sake of our long friendship ▪ **au ~ de toute l'équipe** on behalf of the whole team ▪ **au ~ du ciel!** in heaven's name!

nomade [nɔmad] ◇ *adj* **1.** [peuple] nomad, nomadic **2.** ZOOL migratory.
◇ *nmf* nomad.
◇ *nf* ENTOM Nomada.

nomadisme [nɔmadism] *nm* nomadism.

no man's land [nomanslɑ̃d] *nm inv* MIL & *fig* no-man's-land.

nombrable [nɔ̃brabl] *adj* countable, numerable.

nombre [nɔ̃br] *nm* **1.** MATH [gén] number ▪ [de 0 à 9] number, figure ▪ **un ~ de trois chiffres** a three-digit *ou* three-figure number ◗ **~ entier** whole number, integer ▪ **~ premier** prime (number) ▪ **~s naturels** natural numbers ▪ **~s parfaits** perfect numbers ▪ **~s rationnels** rational numbers ▪ **~s réels** real numbers
2. [quantité] number ▪ **inférieur/supérieur en ~** inferior/superior in number *ou* numbers ▪ **nous ne sommes pas en ~ suffisant** there aren't enough of us ▪ **les exemplaires sont en ~ limité** there's a limited number of copies ▪ **un ~ de** a number of ▪ **je te l'ai déjà dit (un) bon ~ de fois** I've already told you several times ▪ **un grand ~ de** a lot of, a great number of, a great many ▪ **le plus grand ~ d'entre eux a accepté** the majority of them accepted ▪ **un certain ~ de** a (certain) number of
3. [masse] numbers ▪ **vaincre par le ~** to win by sheer weight *ou* force of numbers ▪ **dans le ~, il y en aura bien un pour te raccompagner** there's bound to be one of them who will take you home ◗ **tu subiras la loi du ~** you'll be overwhelmed by sheer weight of numbers ▪ **tous ceux-là n'ont été invités que pour faire ~** those people over there have just been invited to make up the numbers
4. ASTRON & PHYS number ▪ **~ d'or** golden section *ou* mean
5. GRAMM number.

◆ **Nombres** *nmpl* BIBLE : **le livre des Nombres** (the Book of) Numbers.

◆ **au nombre de** *loc prép* : **les invités sont au ~ de cent** there are a hundred guests ▪ **tu peux me compter au ~ des participants** you can count me among the participants, you can count me in.

◆ **du nombre de** *loc prép* amongst ▪ **étiez-vous du ~ des invités?** were you amongst *ou* one of those invited?

◆ **sans nombre** *loc adj* countless, innumerable.

nombrer [3] [nɔ̃bre] *vt litt* to count (up) *(sép)*, to enumerate *sout*.

nombreux, euse [nɔ̃brø, øz] *adj* **1.** [comportant beaucoup d'éléments] : **une foule nombreuse** a large *ou* huge crowd ▪ **avoir une nombreuse descendance** to have many descendants **2.** [en grand nombre] many, numerous ▪ **ils sont trop ~** there are too many of them ▪ **avoir de ~ clients** to have a great number of *ou* many *ou* numerous customers ▪ **les étudiants sont plus ~ qu'avant** there are more students than before ▪ **les fumeurs sont de moins en moins ~** there are fewer and fewer smokers, the number of smokers is decreasing ▪ **nous espérons que vous viendrez ~** we hope that a large number of you will come.

nombril [nɔ̃bril] *nm* **1.** ANAT navel **2.** *fam loc* **il se prend pour le ~ du monde** he thinks he's the centre of the universe ▪ **il aime bien se contempler** *ou* **se regarder le ~** he's really self-centred.

nombrilisme [nɔ̃brilism] *nm* navel-gazing, self-centredness.

nomenclature [nɔmɑ̃klatyr] *nf* **1.** [ensemble de termes] nomenclature **2.** [liste - gén] list ; [- d'un dictionnaire] word list ; [- de soins] itemization of medical expenses *(with a view to obtaining reimbursement from the Health Service)*.

nomenklatura [nɔmɑ̃klatura] *nf* **1.** POLIT nomenklatura **2.** [élite] elite ▪ **faire partie de la ~** to be part of the Establishment.

nominal, e, aux [nɔminal, o] *adj* **1.** [sans vrai pouvoir] nominal ▪ **j'assume les fonctions purement ~es de recteur** I'm the rector in title only **2.** [par le nom] of names, nominal *sout* ▪ **appel ~** roll call ▪ **citation ~e** mention by name **3.** GRAMM nominal ▪ [en grammaire transformationnelle] noun *(modif)* **4.** BOURSE, ÉCON & FIN : **salaire ~** nominal wage *ou* salary ▪ **valeur ~e** face *ou* nominal value **5.** INDUST rated **6.** ASTRONAUT nominal.

nominalement [nɔminalmɑ̃] *adv* **1.** [sans vrai pouvoir] nominally, formally ▪ **il dirige ~ l'entreprise** he's the nominal head of the business *ou* the head of the business in name only **2.** [par le nom] : **être désigné ~** to be mentioned by name **3.** GRAMM : **un adverbe employé ~** the substantive *ou* nominal use of an adverb.

nominalisation [nɔminalizasjɔ̃] *nf* nominalization.

nominaliser [3] [nɔminalize] *vt* to nominalize.

nominatif, ive [nɔminatif, iv] *adj* **1.** [contenant les noms] : **liste nominative** nominative list of names **2.** BOURSE : **titre ~** inscribed stock **3.** [ticket, carte] non-transferable.

◆ **nominatif** *nm* GRAMM nominative (case), *voir aussi* **pluriel**.

nomination [nɔminasjɔ̃] *nf* **1.** [à un poste] appointment, nomination ▪ **elle a obtenu** *ou* **reçu sa ~ au poste de directrice** she was appointed (to the post of) manager **2.** [pour un prix, une récompense] nomination **3.** LING & PHILOS naming.

nominativement [nɔminativmɑ̃] *adv* by name.

nominer [3] [nɔmine] *vt* to nominate.

nommé, e [nɔme] ◇ *adj* [appelé] named.
◇ *nm, f* : **le ~ Georges Aland est accusé de...** Georges Aland is accused of... ▪ **elle fréquente un ~ Paul** she's going out with a man called Paul ▪ **Prudence, la bien ~e** the aptly named Prudence.

◆ **à point nommé** *loc adv* [au bon moment] (just) at the right moment *ou* time ▪ [au moment prévu] at the appointed time.

nommément [nɔmemɑ̃] *adv* **1.** [par le nom - citer, féliciter] by name ▪ **il est ~ mis en cause** he, in particular, is implicated ▪ **les trois candidats, ~ Francis, Anne et Robert** the three candidates, namely Francis, Anne and Robert **2.** [spécialement] especially, notably, in particular.

nommer [3] [nɔme] *vt* **1.** [citer] to name, to list ▪ **ceux qui sont responsables, pour ne pas les ~, devront payer** those who are responsible and who shall remain nameless, will have to pay ▪ **c'est la faute de Nina, pour ne pas la ~** *iron* without mentioning any names, it's Nina's fault **2.** [prénommer] to name, to call ▪ [dénommer] to name, to call, to term **3.** [désigner à une fonction] to appoint ▪ **~ qqn son héritier** to appoint sb as one's heir ▪ **être nommé à Paris** to be appointed to a post in Paris.

◆ **se nommer** ◇ *vp (emploi réfléchi)* [se présenter] to introduce o.s.
◇ *vpi* to be called *ou* named ▪ **comment se nomme-t-il?** what's his name?, what's he called?

non [nɔ̃] ◇ *adv* **1.** [en réponse négative] : **veux-tu venir? – ~** do you want to come? – no! ▪ **~ merci!** no, thank you! ▪ **mais ~!** no!, absolutely not! ▪ **mais ~, voyons!** no, of course not! ▪ **oh que ~!** definitely not!, certainly not! ▪ **ah ça ~!** definitely not! ▪ **ah ~ alors!** oh no! ▪ **~, ~ et ~!** no, no and no again!

2. [pour annoncer ou renforcer la négation] no ▪ **~, je ne veux pas y aller** no, I don't want to go there
3. [dans un tour elliptique] : **il part demain, moi ~** he's leaving tomorrow, I'm not ▪ **que tu le veuilles ou ~** whether you like it or not
4. [comme complément du verbe] : **il me semble que ~** I think not, I don't think so ▪ **il m'a demandé si c'était possible, je lui ai dit que ~** he asked me if it was possible, I told him it wasn't ▪ **il a fait signe que ~** [de la main] he made a gesture of refusal ; [de la tête] he shook his head ▪ **il paraît que ~** it would seem not, apparently not
5. [en corrélation avec 'pas'] : **~ pas** not ▪ **il l'a fait par gentillesse et ~ (pas) par intérêt** he did it out of kindness and not out of self-interest
6. [n'est-ce pas] : **il devait prendre une semaine de vacances, ~?** he was supposed to take a week's holiday, wasn't he? ▪ **c'est anormal, ~** that's not normal, is it? ▪ **j'ai le droit de dire ce que je pense, ~?** I am entitled to say what I think, am I not? *sout ou* aren't I?
7. [emploi expressif] : **~! pas possible!** no *ou* never! I don't believe it! ▪ **~ mais (des fois)!** honestly!, I ask you! ▪ **~ mais celui-là, pour qui il se prend?** who on earth does he think he is?
8. [devant un nom, un adjectif, un participe] : **la ~-observation du règlement** failure to comply with the regulations ▪ **un bagage ~ réclamé** an unclaimed piece of luggage ▪ **il a bénéficié d'une aide ~ négligeable** he received not insubstantial help.
◇ *nm inv* **1.** [réponse] no ▪ **les ~ de la majorité** the noes of the majority
2. INFORM & MATH not.
◆ **non (pas) que** *loc conj sout* not that ▪ **~ (pas) que je m'en méfie, mais...** it's not that I don't trust him, but...

non- *(devant consonne* [nɔ̃], *devant voyelle et 'h' muet* [nɔn]*)* *préf* non-.

non-activité [nɔnaktivite] *nf* MIL inactivity ▪ **être en ~** to be temporarily off duty.

non-affilié, e [nɔnafilje] *adj* nonaffiliated.

nonagénaire [nɔnaʒenɛr] *adj & nmf* nonagenarian, ninety-year-old.

non-agression [nɔnagrɛsjɔ̃] *nf* non-aggression.

non-aligné, e [nɔnaliɲe] ◇ *adj* nonaligned.
◇ *nm, f* nonaligned country.

non-alignement [nɔnaliɲmɑ̃] *nm* nonalignment.

nonantaine [nɔnɑ̃tɛn] *nf Belgique* about ninety ▪ **elle a la ~** she's about ninety.

nonante [nɔnɑ̃t] *dét* [dialecte] ninety.

nonantième [nɔnɑ̃tjɛm] *adj num & nmf* [dialecte] ninetieth.

non-assistance [nɔnasistɑ̃s] *nf* : **~ à personne en danger** failure to assist a person in danger.

non-belligérance [nɔ̃beliʒerɑ̃s] *nf* nonbelligerency.

non-belligérant, e [nɔ̃beliʒerɑ̃, ɑ̃t] *adj & nm, f* nonbelligerent.

nonce [nɔ̃s] *nm* nuncio ▪ **~ apostolique** papal nuncio.

nonchalamment [nɔ̃ʃalamɑ̃] *adv* nonchalantly, casually.

nonchalance [nɔ̃ʃalɑ̃s] *nf* [indifférence, insouciance] nonchalance ▪ [lenteur] listlessness ▪ **avec ~** nonchalantly.

nonchalant, e [nɔ̃ʃalɑ̃, ɑ̃t] *adj* [insouciant] nonchalant ▪ [lent] listless.

non-combattant, e [nɔ̃kɔ̃batɑ̃, ɑ̃t] *adj & nm, f* noncombatant.

non-comparution [nɔ̃kɔ̃parysjɔ̃] *nf* nonappearance, defaulting *(in court)*.

non-comptable [nɔ̃kɔ̃tabl] ◇ *adj* uncountable.
◇ *nm* mass noun.

non-concurrence [nɔ̃kɔ̃kyrɑ̃s] *nf* DR : **clause de ~** restraint of trade clause.

non-conformisme [nɔ̃kɔ̃fɔrmism] *nm* **1.** [originalité] nonconformism **2.** RELIG Nonconformism.

non-conformiste [nɔ̃kɔ̃fɔrmist] *adj & nmf* **1.** [original] nonconformist **2.** RELIG Nonconformist.

non-conformité [nɔ̃kɔ̃fɔrmite] *nf* nonconformity.

non-croyant, e [nɔ̃krwajɑ̃, ɑ̃t] ◇ *adj* unbelieving.
◇ *nm, f* unbeliever.

non-directif, ive [nɔ̃dirɛktif, iv] *adj* nondirective.

non-discrimination [nɔ̃diskriminasjɔ̃] *nf* nondiscrimination.

non-dit [nɔ̃di] *nm* : **le ~** the unsaid ▪ **il y avait trop de ~ dans notre famille** too much was left unsaid in our family.

non-engagé, e [nɔnɑ̃gaʒe] ◇ *adj* [personne] neutral ▪ [nation] nonaligned.
◇ *nm, f* [personne] neutral person ▪ [nation] nonaligned country.

non-engagement [nɔnɑ̃gaʒmɑ̃] *nm* [d'une personne] neutrality, noncommitment ▪ [d'une nation] nonalignment.

non-être [nɔnɛtr] *nm inv* nonbeing.

non-événement, non-évènement [nɔnevɛnmɑ̃] *nm* nonevent.

non-exécution [nɔnɛgzekysjɔ̃] *nf* nonfulfilment ▪ **~ d'un contrat** nonfulfilment of a contract.

non-existant, e [nɔnɛgzistɑ̃, ɑ̃t] *adj* nonexistent.

non-existence [nɔnɛgzistɑ̃s] *nf* nonexistence.

non-figuratif, ive [nɔ̃figyratif, iv] ◇ *adj* nonfigurative.
◇ *nm, f* nonfigurative artist, abstractionist.

non-fumeur, euse [nɔ̃fymœr, øz] *nm, f* nonsmoker ▪ **compartiment ~s** nonsmoking *ou* no smoking compartment.

non-ingérence [nɔnɛ̃ʒerɑ̃s] *nf* [par une personne] noninterference ▪ [par une nation] noninterference, nonintervention.

non-initié, e [nɔninisje] ◇ *adj* uninitiated ▪ **ce texte sera difficile pour le lecteur ~** this text will be difficult for the lay reader.
◇ *nm, f* : **pour les ~s** for the layman.

non-inscrit, e [nɔnɛ̃skri, it] ◇ *adj* independent, nonparty.
◇ *nm, f* independent member of Parliament.

non-intervention [nɔnɛ̃tɛrvɑ̃sjɔ̃] *nf* nonintervention ▪ **une politique de ~** a noninterventionist policy.

non-jouissance [nɔ̃ʒwisɑ̃s] *nf* DR nonenjoyment.

non-lieu [nɔ̃ljø] *(pl* **non-lieux***)* *nm* : **(ordonnance de) ~** no case to answer, no grounds for prosecution ▪ **il a bénéficié d'un ~** charges against him were dismissed.

nonne [nɔn] *nf vieilli* nun.

nonnette [nɔnɛt] *nf* **1.** ORNITH [mésange] titmouse **2.** CULIN iced gingerbread *(biscuit)*.

nonobstant [nɔnɔpstɑ̃] *prép* DR & *hum* notwithstanding, despite ▪ **ce ~** this notwithstanding.

non-paiement [nɔ̃pɛmɑ̃] *nm* nonpayment, failure to pay.

non-partant [nɔ̃partɑ̃] *nm* [cheval] nonstarter.

non-polluant, e [nɔ̃pɔlyɑ̃, ɑ̃t] *adj* nonpolluting.

non-prolifération [nɔ̃prɔliferasjɔ̃] *nf* nonproliferation.

non-recevoir [nɔ̃rəsəvwar] *nm inv* ▷ **fin**.

non-représentation [nɔ̃rəprezɑ̃tasjɔ̃] *nf* : **~ d'enfant** nonrestitution of a child (to its custodian), noncompliance with a custodianship order.

non-résident [nɔ̃rezidɑ̃] *nm* foreign national, nonresident.

non-respect [nɔ̃rɛspɛ] *nm* failure to respect ▪ **le ~ de la loi** failure to respect the law.

non-retour [nɔ̃rətur] *nm inv* : **point de ~** point of no return.

non-salarié, e [nɔ̃salarje] *nm, f* self-employed person.

non-sens [nɔ̃sɑ̃s] *nm inv* **1.** [absurdité] nonsense ▪ **cette situation est un ~** this situation is nonsensical *ou* a nonsense **2.** LING meaningless word or phrase *(in a translation)*.

non-spécialiste [nɔ̃spesjalist] ◇ *adj* nonspecialized.
◇ *nmf* nonspecialist.

non-stop [nɔnstɔp] ◇ *adj inv* nonstop.
◇ *nf inv* SPORT pre-race downhill run.

non-syndiqué, e [nɔ̃sɛ̃dike] ◇ *adj* nonunion, nonunionized.
◇ *nm, f* nonunion *ou* nonunionized worker.

non-titulaire [nɔ̃titylɛr] *nmf* nontenured member of staff.

non-valeur [nɔ̃valœr] *nf* **1.** *péj* [chose] valueless thing ▪ [personne] nonentity **2.** DR improductive asset **3.** FIN [créance] bad debt.

non-viable [nɔ̃vjabl] *adj* **1.** MÉD nonviable **2.** *fig* unfeasible ▪ **c'est un projet ~** the scheme isn't viable.

non-violence [nɔ̃vjɔlɑ̃s] *nf* nonviolence.

non-violent, e [nɔ̃vjɔlɑ̃, ɑ̃t] ◇ *adj* nonviolent.
◇ *nm, f* supporter of nonviolence.

non-voyant, e [nɔ̃vwajɑ̃, ɑ̃t] *nm, f* visually handicapped person.

nord [nɔr] ◇ *nm inv* **1.** [point cardinal] north ▪ **le vent vient du ~** it's a north *ou* northerly wind, the wind is coming from the north ▪ **nous allons vers le ~** we're heading north *ou* northwards ▪ **la cuisine est en plein ~ *ou* exposée au ~** the kitchen faces due north ▶ **~ géographique** true *ou* geographic north ▪ **~ magnétique** magnetic north **2.** [partie d'un pays, d'un continent] north ▪ **le ~ de l'Italie** northern Italy, the north of Italy ▪ **elle habite dans le ~** she lives in the north ▪ **les gens du ~** (the) Northerners.
◇ *adj inv* [septentrional] north *(modif)*, northern.
◆ **Nord** ◇ *adj inv* North.
◇ *npr m* GÉOGR : **le Nord** the North ▪ **le grand Nord** the Far North ▪ **la mer du Nord** the North Sea.
◆ **au nord de** *loc prép* (to the) north of.
◆ **du nord** *loc adj* north *(modif)*.

nord-africain, e [nɔrafrikɛ̃, ɛn] (*mpl* **nord-africains**, *fpl* **nord-africaines**) *adj* North African.
◆ **Nord-Africain, e** *nm, f* North African.

nord-américain, e [nɔramerikɛ̃, ɛn] (*mpl* **nord-américains**, *fpl* **nord-américaines**) *adj* North American.
◆ **Nord-Américain, e** *nm, f* North American.

nord-coréen, enne [nɔrkɔreɛ̃, ɛn] (*mpl* **nord-coréens**, *fpl* **nord-coréennes**) *adj* North Korean.
◆ **Nord-Coréen, enne** *nm, f* North Korean.

nord-est [nɔrɛst] *nm inv* & *adj inv* northeast.

nordique [nɔrdik] *adj* [pays, peuple] Nordic ▪ [langue] Nordic, Scandinavian.
◆ **Nordique** *nmf* Nordic.

nordiste [nɔrdist] *adj* **1.** [en France] from the Nord department **2.** [aux États-Unis - HIST] Northern, Yankee *(modif)*.
◆ **Nordiste** *nmf* **1.** [en France] *inhabitant of or person from the Nord department* **2.** [aux États-Unis - HIST] Northerner, Yankee.

nord-ouest [nɔrwɛst] *nm inv* & *adj inv* northwest.

Nord-Pas-de-Calais [nɔrpadkalɛ] *npr m* : **le ~** Nord-Pas-de-Calais.

NORD-PAS-DE-CALAIS

This administrative region includes the ***départements*** of Nord and Pas-de-Calais (capital: Lille).

nord-vietnamien, enne [nɔrvjɛtnamjɛ̃, ɛn] (*mpl* **nord-vietnamiens**, *fpl* **nord-vietnamiennes**) *adj* North Vietnamese.
◆ **Nord-Vietnamien, enne** *nm, f* North Vietnamese.

noria [nɔrja] *nf* **1.** [machine hydraulique] bucket elevator **2.** *fig* **une ~ de camions/d'ambulances** a fleet of lorries/of ambulances.

normal, e, aux [nɔrmal, o] *adj* **1.** [ordinaire - vie, personne] normal ; [- taille] normal, standard ; [- accouchement, procédure] normal, straightforward ▪ **la situation est redevenue ~e** the situation is back to normal ▪ **ce n'est pas ~ : la lampe ne s'allume pas, ce n'est pas ~** the light isn't coming on, there's something wrong (with it) ▪ **il n'est pas rentré, ce n'est pas ~** he's not back yet, something must have happened (to him) **2.** [habituel] normal, usual ▪ **elle n'était pas dans son état ~** she wasn't her normal self ▪ **ce n'était pas sa voix ~e** that wasn't his usual voice ▪ **en temps ~** in normal circumstances, normally
3. [compréhensible] normal, natural ▪ **mais c'est bien ~, voyons** it's only natural, don't worry about it
4. *fam* [mentalement] normal ▪ **elle n'est pas très ~e, celle-là!** she's not quite normal!
◆ **normale** *nf* **1.** [situation] normal (situation) ▪ **un retour à la ~e** a return to normal
2. GÉOM normal
3. MÉTÉOR normal ▪ **température au-dessous de la ~e (saisonnière)** temperature below the (seasonal) average
4. [moyenne] average ▪ **intelligence supérieure à la ~e** above average intelligence
5. ÉDUC : **Normale (Sup)** *fam grande école for training teachers.*

normalement [nɔrmalmɑ̃] *adv* **1.** [de façon ordinaire] normally ▪ **il est ~ constitué** he's of normal constitution ; *euphém* he's (a man of) flesh and blood **2.** [sauf changement] if all goes well ▪ **~, nous partirons en juin** if all goes well, we'll be leaving in June **3.** [habituellement] normally, usually, generally ▪ **~, elle rentre à 3 h** she normally *ou* generally comes home at 3 (o'clock).

normalien, enne [nɔrmaljɛ̃, ɛn] *nm, f* **1.** [de l'École normale] student at an École normale ▪ [ancien de l'École normale] graduate of an École normale **2.** [de l'École normale supérieure] student at the École Normale Supérieure ▪ [ancien de l'École normale supérieure] graduate of the École Normale Supérieure.

normalisateur, trice [nɔrmalizatœr, tris] ◇ *adj* standardizing.
◇ *nm, f* standardizer.

normalisation [nɔrmalizasjɔ̃] *nf* **1.** [d'un produit] standardization **2.** [d'une situation] normalization ▪ **jusqu'à la ~ de la situation** until the situation becomes normal.

normalisé, e [nɔrmalize] *adj* standardized.

normaliser [3] [nɔrmalize] *vt* **1.** [produit] to standardize **2.** [rapport, situation] to normalize.

normalité [nɔrmalite] *nf* normality, normalcy US.

normand, e [nɔrmɑ̃, ɑ̃d] *adj* **1.** [de Normandie] Normandy *(modif)* ▪ **je suis ~** I'm from Normandy **2.** HIST Norman **3.** LING Norman French **4.** [viking] Norse.
◆ **Normand, e** *nm, f* **1.** [en France] Norman **2.** [Viking] Norseman (*f* Norsewoman) ▪ **les Normands** the Norse.
◆ **normand** *nm* LING Norman French.
◆ **à la normande** *loc adj* CULIN à la Normande *(with cream and apples or cider)*.

Normandie [nɔrmɑ̃di] *npr f* : **(la) ~** Normandy.

normatif, ive [nɔrmatif, iv] *adj* normative.

norme [nɔrm] *nf* **1.** INDUST norm, standard ▪ **produit conforme aux ~s de fabrication** product conforming to manufacturing standards ▶ **~ française (homologuée)** French standard (of manufacturing), ≃ British Standard UK, ≃ US Standard US **2.** [règle] : **rester dans la ~** to keep within the norm **3.** LING : **la ~** the norm **4.** MATH norm.

normé, e [nɔrme] *adj* normed.

Norvège [nɔrvɛʒ] *npr f* : **(la) ~** Norway.

norvégien, enne [nɔrveʒjɛ̃, ɛn] *adj* Norwegian.
◆ **Norvégien, enne** *nm, f* Norwegian.
◆ **norvégienne** *nf* Norway yawl.

nos [no] *pl* ▻ **notre.**

nosocomial, e, aux [nɔzɔkɔmjal, o] *adj* nosocomial, contracted in hospital.

nostalgie [nɔstalʒi] *nf* **1.** [regret] nostalgia ▪ **avoir la ~ de** to feel nostalgic about **2.** [mal du pays] homesickness ▪ **j'ai la ~ du pays** I'm homesick.

nostalgique [nɔstalʒik] *adj* nostalgic ▪ **que ces chansons sont ~s!** these songs do take you back *ou* are full of nostalgia!

nota (bene) [nɔta(bene)] *nm inv* nota bene.

notable [nɔtabl] ◇ *adj* [fait] notable ▪ [différence] appreciable, noticeable.
◇ *nm* notable ▪ **tous les ~s de la ville** all the town notables.

notablement [nɔtabləmɑ̃] *adv* notably, considerably.

notaire [nɔtɛr] *nm* [qui reçoit actes et contrats] notary (public), lawyer ▪ [qui surveille les transactions immobilières] lawyer, solicitor UK.

notamment [nɔtamɑ̃] *adv* especially, in particular, notably ▪ **il y a certains avantages, ~ un abattement fiscal** there are some advantages, notably tax deductions.

notarial, e, aux [nɔtarjal, o] *adj* notarial, legal.

notariat [nɔtarja] *nm* : **le ~** [fonction] the profession of a lawyer ; [corporation] lawyers ▪ **son père la destinait au ~** her father wanted her to become a lawyer.

notarié, e [nɔtarje] *adj* legally drawn up, authentic.

notation [nɔtasjɔ̃] *nf* **1.** [remarque] note **2.** CHIM, DANSE, LING, MATH & MUS notation **3.** ÉDUC : **la ~ d'un devoir** marking *UK ou* grading *US ou* correcting homework.

note [nɔt] *nf* **1.** MUS [son] note ▪ [touche] key ⊙ **faire une fausse ~** MUS [pianiste] to hit a wrong note *ou* key ; [violoniste] to play a wrong note ; [chanteur] to sing a wrong note ▪ **la cérémonie s'est déroulée sans une fausse ~** the ceremony went (off) without a hitch ▪ **la ~ juste** the right note ▪ **donner la ~** MUS to give the keynote ; *fig* to give the lead ▪ **être dans la ~** to hit just the right note *fig*

2. [annotation] note ▪ **prendre des ~s** to take *ou* to make notes ▪ **voilà les ~s rapides que j'ai prises** here are the notes I jotted down ▪ **prendre qqch en ~** to make a note of sthg, to note sthg down ⊙ **~ de *ou* en bas de page** footnote ▪ **~ de l'auteur/de la rédaction/du traducteur** author's/editor's/translator's note ▪ **~ de l'éditeur** editor's note ▪ **~ marginale** marginal note ▪ **prendre bonne ~ de qqch** to take good note of sthg

3. [communication] : **~ diplomatique/officielle** diplomatic/official note ▪ **~ de service** memo, memorandum

4. ÉDUC mark *UK*, grade ▪ **avoir la meilleure ~** to get the best *ou* highest *ou* top mark

5. [nuance] note, touch, hint ▪ **avec une ~ de tristesse dans la voix** with a note *ou* hint of sadness in his voice ▪ **apporter une ~ personnelle à qqch** to give sthg a personal touch

6. [facture] bill, check *US* ▪ **~s de restaurant** restaurant bills ▪ **la ~, s'il vous plaît!** may I have the bill, please? ▪ **mettez-le sur ma ~** charge it to my account, put it on my bill ⊙ **~ de frais** [à remplir] expense *ou* expenses claim (form) ▪ **présenter sa ~ de frais** to put in for expenses ▪ **~ d'honoraires** invoice *(for work done by a self-employed person)*

7. [d'un parfum] note.

noter [3] [nɔte] *vt* **1.** [prendre en note] to note *ou* to write (down) ▪ **veuillez ~ notre nouvelle adresse** please note *ou* make a note of our new address ▪ **notez que chaque enfant doit apporter un vêtement chaud** please note that every child must bring something warm to wear **2.** [faire ressortir - gén] to mark ; [- en cochant] to tick ; [- en surlignant] to highlight **3.** [remarquer] to note, to notice ▪ **notez que je ne dis rien** please note that I'm making no comment ▪ **j'ai noté une erreur dans votre article** I noticed a mistake in your article ▪ **il est à ~ que...** it should be noted *ou* borne in mind that... ▪ **je ne veux pas que tu recommences, c'est noté?** *fam* I don't want you to do it again, do you understand *ou* have you got that *ou* is that clear? ▪ **notez bien, il a fait des progrès** mind you, he's improved **4.** [évaluer] to mark *UK*, to grade ▪ **j'étais bien/mal noté** I had a good/bad (professional) record ‖ ÉDUC [élève] to give a mark to *UK*, to grade ▪ [devoir, examen] to mark *UK*, to grade ▪ *(en usage absolu)* **~ sur 20** to mark *UK ou* grade *US* out of 20 ▪ **elle note généreusement/sévèrement** she gives high/low marks *UK ou* grades.

notice [nɔtis] *nf* **1.** [résumé] note ▪ **~ bibliographique** bibliographical details ▪ **~ biographique** biographical note ▪ **~ nécrologique** obituary (notice) ▪ **~ publicitaire** [brochure] advertising brochure ; [annonce] advertisement **2.** [instructions] : **~ explicative *ou* d'emploi** directions for use ▪ **~ de fonctionnement** instructions.

notificatif, ive [nɔtifikatif, iv] *adj* notifying.

notification [nɔtifikasjɔ̃] *nf* [avis] notification ▪ **donner à qqn ~ de qqch** to give sb notification of sthg, to notify sb of sthg.

notifier [9] [nɔtifje] *vt* to notify ▪ **on vient de lui ~ son renvoi** he's just received notice of his dismissal, he's just been notified of his dismissal ▪ **~ une assignation à qqn** to serve a writ on sb ▪ *(en usage absolu)* **veuillez ~ par courrier** please inform us in writing.

notion [nɔsjɔ̃] *nf* [idée] notion ▪ **perdre la ~ du temps** to lose all notion *ou* sense of time ▪ **je n'en ai pas la moindre ~** I haven't (got) the faintest *ou* slightest idea.

◆ **notions** *nfpl* [rudiments] : **~s de base** basics, basic knowledge ▪ **il a quelques ~s d'anglais** he has a smattering of English ▪ **'anglais: ~s'** [sur un CV] 'basic knowledge of English' ▪ **il a quelques ~s de physique** he has some knowledge of physics ‖ [comme titre d'ouvrage] primer ▪ **~s de géométrie** geometry primer.

notionnel, elle [nɔsjɔnɛl] *adj* notional.

notoire [nɔtwar] *adj* recognized ▪ **son sens politique est ~** her political acumen is acknowledged by all, she's famous for her political acumen ▪ **le fait est ~** it's an acknowledged *ou* accepted fact ▪ **un criminel ~** a notorious criminal.

notoirement [nɔtwarmɑ̃] *adv* : **ses ressources sont ~ insuffisantes** it's widely known that she has limited means.

notoriété [nɔtɔrjete] *nf* **1.** [renommée] fame, renown ▪ **sa thèse lui a valu une grande ~ *ou* a fait sa ~** his thesis made him famous ▪ **il est de ~ publique que...** it's public *ou* common knowledge that... **2.** [personne célèbre] celebrity, famous person **3.** DR : **acte de ~** attestation.

notre [nɔtr] (*pl* **nos** [no]) *dét (adj poss)* **1.** [indiquant la possession] our ▪ **un de nos amis** a friend of ours, one of our friends ▪ **~ fils et ~ fille** our son and daughter **2.** RELIG : **Notre Père** Our Father ▪ **le Notre Père** the Lord's Prayer **3.** [se rapportant au 'nous' de majesté ou de modestie] : **car tel est ~ bon plaisir** for such is our pleasure ▪ **dans ~ second chapitre** in the second chapter **4.** [emploi expressif] our ▪ **comment se porte ~ petit malade?** how's our little invalid, then?

nôtre [notr] *dét (adj poss) sout* ours ▪ **l'objectif que je considère comme ~** the aim which I consider to be ours.

◆ **le nôtre** (*f* **la nôtre**, *pl* **les nôtres**) *pron poss* ours ▪ **amenez vos enfants, les ~s ont le même âge** bring your children, ours are the same age ▪ *(emploi nominal)* **les ~s** our family and friends ▪ **c'est un des ~s** he's one of us ▪ **serez-vous des ~s demain soir?** will you be joining us tomorrow evening? ⊙ **il faut y mettre du ~** we must do our bit, we should make an effort ▪ **à la (bonne) ~!** cheers!

Notre-Dame [nɔtrədam] *nf* RELIG [titre] Our Lady ▪ [église] : **~ de Paris** [cathédrale] Notre Dame ▪ **'~ de Paris'** ***Hugo*** 'The Hunchback of Notre Dame'.

nouba [nuba] *nf fam* [fête] : **faire la ~** to live it up, to paint the town red.

noue [nu] *nf* valley (of roof) ▪ **pièce de ~** valley tile, ▻ **arêtier**.

nouer [6] [nwe] ◇ *vt* **1.** [attacher ensemble - lacets, cordes] to tie *ou* to knot (together) ▪ **elle noua ses bras autour de mon cou** she wrapped her arms round my neck **2.** [faire un nœud à] to tie (up), to knot ▪ **laisse-moi ~ ta cravate** let me knot your tie ▪ **j'ai noué le bouquet avec de la ficelle** I tied the bouquet together with string ▪ **il a noué le foulard autour de sa taille** he tied the scarf around his waist ▪ **elle noua ses cheveux avec un ruban** she tied her hair back *ou* up with a ribbon ▪ **la peur lui nouait la gorge/les entrailles** *fig* his throat/stomach tightened with fear **3.** [établir] : **~ des relations avec qqn** to enter into a relationship with sb ▪ **~ une intrigue** to hatch a plot **4.** TEXT to splice *ou* to knot (together).

◇ *vi* BOT to set.

◆ **se nouer** ◇ *vp (emploi passif)* [ceinture] to fasten, to do up.

◇ *vpi* **1.** [s'entrelacer] to intertwine ▪ **ses mains se nouèrent comme pour prier** his hands joined *ou* came together as if to pray **2.** [s'instaurer] to develop, to build up ▪ **c'est à cet âge que beaucoup d'amitiés se nouent** it's at that age that a lot of friendships are made ▪ **l'action ne se noue que dans le dernier chapitre** only in the last chapter does the plot come to a head *ou* climax.

noueux, euse [nwø, øz] *adj* **1.** [tronc, bois] knotty, gnarled **2.** [doigt] gnarled ▪ **un vieux paysan ~** a wizened old farmer.

nougat [nuga] *nm* CULIN nougat.

nougatine [nugatin] *nf* nougatine.

nouille [nuj] ◇ *adj inv* **1.** *fam* [niais] dumb, dopey ▪ **le premier acte est complètement ~** the first act is a load of tripe **2.** ART Art Nouveau *(modif)*.

◇ *nf* **1.** CULIN noodle **2.** *fam* [nigaud] nitwit, dumbo ■ [mollasson] drip, wimp.

◆ **nouilles** *nfpl* pasta *(U)*.

Nouméa [numea] *npr* Nouméa.

nounou [nunu] *nf fam* nanny ■ **jouer les ~s avec qqn** to molly-coddle *ou* to nursemaid sb.

nounours [nunurs] *nm fam* teddy (bear).

nourri, e [nuri] *adj* **1.** [dense - fusillade] sustained, heavy **2.** [ininterrompu - applaudissements] prolonged, sustained.

nourrice [nuris] *nf* **1.** [qui allaite] wet nurse **2.** [qui garde] childminder *UK*, nurse *US*, nursemaid *US* ■ **mettre un enfant en ~** to leave a child with a childminder **3.** AUTO [bidon] spare can ■ [réservoir] service tank **4.** ENTOM nurse (bee).

nourricier, ère [nurisje, ɛr] *adj* **1.** [qui nourrit] : **notre terre nourricière** mother Earth **2.** ANAT nutrient *(avant n)* **3.** BOT nutritive.

nourrir [32] [nurir] *vt* **1.** [alimenter] to feed, to nourish *sout* ■ **~ qqn (de qqch)** to feed sb (on sthg) ■ **~ un bébé au sein/au biberon/à la cuillère** to breast-feed/to bottle-feed/to spoon-feed a baby ■ **être bien nourri** to be well-fed ■ **être mal nourri** [sous-alimenté] to be undernourished **2.** *fig* **j'avais l'esprit nourri de Goethe** I was brought up on Goethe ■ **les lettres qu'elle lui envoyait nourrissaient sa passion** the letters she sent him sustained his passion **3.** [faire subsister] to feed ■ **j'ai trois enfants à ~** I've got three children to feed *ou* to provide for ▶ **la chanson/sculpture ne nourrit pas son homme** you can't live off singing/sculpture alone ■ **le métier est dangereux, mais il nourrit son homme** it's a dangerous job but it brings in the money *ou* it pays well **4.** *litt* [espoir] to nourish ■ [pensée] to entertain ■ [illusion, rancœur] to harbour, to nurse, to nourish *sout* ■ [haine] to feel, to harbour feelings of ■ **elle nourrissait déjà des projets ambitieux** she was already turning over some ambitious projects in her mind ■ **~ des doutes au sujet de** to entertain doubts *ou* to be doubtful about.

◆ **se nourrir** *vp (emploi réfléchi)* **1.** [s'alimenter] to feed (o.s.) ■ **il se nourrit mal** he doesn't feed himself *ou* eat properly ■ **elle ne se nourrit que de bananes** she eats only bananas **2.** *fig* **se ~ d'illusions** to revel in illusions ■ **se ~ de bandes dessinées** to read nothing but comics.

nourrissant, e [nurisɑ̃, ɑ̃t] *adj* nourishing, nutritious ■ **crème ~e** nourishing cream ■ **le dessert était un peu trop ~** the dessert was a bit too rich.

nourrisson [nurisɔ̃] *nm* **1.** [bébé] baby, infant ▶ **consultation de ~s** baby clinic **2.** *arch* [bébé au sein] nursling, suckling.

nourriture [nurityr] *nf* **1.** [alimentation] food ■ **donner à qqn une ~ saine** to provide sb with a healthy diet ■ **la ~** [aliments] food **2.** [aliment] food **3.** *litt* [de l'esprit, du cœur] nourishment.

nous [nu] ◇ *pron pers (1ère pers pl)* **1.** [sujet ou attribut d'un verbe] we ■ **toi et moi, ~ comprenons** you and I understand ■ **c'est ~ qui déciderons** we are the ones who'll decide ■ **~, nous restons** *ou* **on reste** *fam* **là** we are staying here ■ **~ deux, on s'aimera toujours** *fam* we two *ou* the two of us will always love each other ■ **~ autres médecins pensons que...** we doctors think that... ■ **coucou, c'est ~!** hullo, it's us! **2.** [complément d'un verbe ou d'une préposition] us ■ **à ~ six, on a fini la paella** between the six of us we finished the paella ■ **notre voilier à ~** our (own) yacht ■ **ces anoraks ne sont pas à ~** these anoraks aren't ours *ou* don't belong to us ■ **chez ~** [dans notre foyer] at home, in our house ; [dans notre pays] at *ou* back home ■ **entre ~** between us **3.** [sujet ou complément, représentant un seul locuteur] we ■ **dans notre thèse, ~ traitons le problème sous deux aspects** in our thesis we deal with the problem in two ways ■ **alors, comment allons-~ ce matin?** [à un malade, un enfant] and how are we this morning? ■ **alors, à ~, qu'est-ce qu'il ~ fallait?** [chez un commerçant] now, what can I do for you?

◇ *pron pers réfléchi* : **nous ~ amusons beaucoup** we're having a great time, we're really enjoying ourselves.

◇ *pron pers réciproque* each other ■ **nous ~ aimons** we love each other.

◇ *nm* : **le ~ de majesté** the royal we.

nous-mêmes [numɛm] *pron pers* ourselves ■ **nous y sommes allés de ~** we went there on our own initiative ■ **vérifions par ~** let's check for ourselves.

nouveau [nuvo] *(devant nm commençant par voyelle ou 'h' muet nouvel* [nuvɛl]*), f* **nouvelle** [nuvɛl], *mpl* **nouveaux** [nuvo], *fpl* **nouvelles** [nuvɛl]*) adj* **1.** [de fraîche date - appareil, modèle] new ; [- pays] new, young ■ **c'est tout ~, ça vient de sortir** it's new, it's just come out ; *fig* that's a new one on me ■ **mots ~x** new words ▶ **~x mariés** newlyweds, newly married couple ■ **les ~x pauvres** the new poor ■ **~ riche** nouveau riche ■ **~ venu** newcomer ■ **nouvelle venue** newcomer ■ **il est encore (un peu) ~ en politique** he's still (a bit of) a newcomer to politics **2.** [dernier en date] new, latest ■ **ce nouvel attentat a fait 52 morts** 52 people died in this latest bomb attack ■ **~x élus** [députés] new *ou* newly-elected deputies ▶ **carottes nouvelles** spring carrots ■ **pommes de terre nouvelles** new potatoes ■ **nouvel an, nouvelle année** New Year ■ **le Nouveau Monde** the New World ■ **le Nouveau Testament** the New Testament **3.** [autre] further, new ■ **le bail est reconduit pour une nouvelle période de trois ans** the lease is renewed for a further three years *ou* another three-year period **4.** [original - découverte, idée] new, novel, original ■ **un esprit/un son ~ est né** a new spirit/sound is born ■ **une conception nouvelle** a novel *ou* fresh approach ■ **porter un regard ~ sur qqn/qqch** to take a fresh look at sb/sthg ■ **elle est mécontente – ce n'est pas ~!** she's not happy – there's nothing new about that! **5.** [inhabituel] new ■ **ce dossier est ~ pour moi** this case is new to me, I'm new to this case **6.** [novateur] : **nouvelle critique** new criticism ■ **nouvelle cuisine** nouvelle cuisine ■ **les Nouveaux philosophes** *group of left-wing, post-Marxist thinkers including André Glucksmann and Bernard-Henri Lévy who came to prominence in the late 1970s* ■ **~ roman** nouveau roman *(term applied to the work, mainly in the 1950s and 1960s, of a number of novelists who rejected the assumptions of the traditional novel)*.

◆ **nouveau, elle** *nm, f* [élève] new boy (*f* girl) ■ [adulte] new man (*f* woman).

◆ **nouveau** *nm* : **rien de ~ depuis la dernière fois** nothing new *ou* special since last time ■ **il y a eu du ~ dans l'affaire Perron** there are new developments in the Perron case.

◆ **à nouveau** *loc adv* [encore] (once) again, once more ■ **je tiens à vous remercier à ~** I'd like to thank you once again ■ **recommence à ~** start again.

◆ **de nouveau** *loc adv* again, once again, once more ■ **tu as fait de ~ la même bêtise** you've made the same mistake again.

◆ **nouvelle vague** ◇ *nf* : **la nouvelle vague des ordinateurs** the new generation of computers.

◇ *loc adj inv* new-generation *(modif)* ■ **les imprimantes nouvelle vague** new-generation printers.

◆ **Nouvelle Vague** *nf* CINÉ New Wave, Nouvelle Vague.

LA NOUVELLE VAGUE

This expression refers to a group of French filmmakers, including François Truffaut and Jean-Luc Godard, who broke away from conventional style and methods in the late 1950s and produced some of the most influential films of the period using simple techniques and everyday settings.

Nouveau-Brunswick [nuvobrœsvik] *npr m* : **le ~** New Brunswick.

Nouveau-Mexique [nuvomɛksik] *npr m* : **le ~** New Mexico ■ **au ~** in New Mexico.

nouveau-né, e [nuvone] (*mpl* **nouveau-nés**, *fpl* **nouveau-nées**) ◇ *adj* newborn *(modif)* ■ **une fille ~e** a newborn baby girl.

◇ *nm, f* **1.** [bébé] newborn baby **2.** [appareil, technique] new arrival.

Nouveau-Québec [nuvokebɛk] *npr m* : **le ~** New Quebec ■ **au ~** in New Quebec.

nouveauté [nuvote] *nf* **1.** [chose nouvelle] novelty, new thing ■ **les ~s discographiques/littéraires** new releases/books ■ **le racisme a toujours existé, ce n'est pas une ~** racism has always existed, there's nothing new *ou* recent about it **2.** [originalité] novelty, newness ■ **l'exposition a l'attrait de la ~** the exhibition has novelty appeal **3.** COUT fashion ■ **~s de printemps** new spring fashions.

nouvel [nuvɛl] *m* ▷ **nouveau.**

nouvelle [nuvɛl] ◇ *f* ▷ **nouveau.**

◇ *nf* **1.** [information] (piece of) news *(U)* ■ **c'est une ~ intéressante** that's an interesting piece of news, that's interesting news ▪ **j'ai une bonne/mauvaise ~ pour toi** I have (some) good/bad news for you ▪ **voici une excellente ~!** this is good news! ▪ **tu ne connais pas la ~? elle est renvoyée** haven't you heard (the news)? she's been fired ▪ **fausse ~** false report ▪ **première ~!** that's news to me! **2.** LITTÉR short story, novella.

◆ **nouvelles** *nfpl* **1.** [renseignements] news *(U)* ▪ **je n'ai pas eu de ses ~s depuis** I haven't had any news from him *ou* heard from him since ▪ **donne vite de tes ~s** write soon ▪ **Paul m'a demandé de tes ~s** Paul was asking after you ▪ **prendre des ~s de qqn** to ask after sb ▪ **j'ai eu de tes ~s par ta sœur** your sister told me how you were getting on ▪ **aller aux ~s** to go and find out what's (been) happening ▪ **je venais aux ~s** I just wanted to find out what's been happening ▪ **on est sans ~s des trois alpinistes** there's been no news of the three climbers ▪ **les ~s vont vite** news travels fast ➲ **goûte-moi cette mousse, tu m'en diras des ~s** *fam* have a taste of this mousse, I think you'll like it ▪ **tu ferais mieux de signer, ou tu auras de mes ~s!** *fam* you'd better sign, or else! ▪ **pas de ~s, bonnes ~s** no news is good news **2.** RADIO & TV news *(U)* ▪ **à quelle heure sont les ~s?** when's the news on?

Nouvelle-Angleterre [nuvɛlɑ̃glətɛr] *npr f*: **(la) ~** New England.

Nouvelle-Calédonie [nuvɛlkaledɔni] *npr f*: **(la) ~** New Caledonia.

Nouvelle-Écosse [nuvɛlekɔs] *npr f*: **(la) ~** Nova Scotia.

Nouvelle-Galles du Sud [nuvɛlgaldysyd] *npr f*: **(la) ~** New South Wales.

Nouvelle-Guinée [nuvɛlgine] *npr f*: **(la) ~** New Guinea.

nouvellement [nuvɛlmɑ̃] *adv* newly, recently, freshly ▪ **~ élu/nommé** newly-elected/-appointed ▪ **~ arrivé dans cette ville, il ne savait où aller** being a newcomer to the city, he didn't know where to go.

Nouvelle-Orléans [nuvɛlɔrleɑ̃] *npr*: **La ~** New Orleans.

Nouvelles-Hébrides [nuvɛlzebrid] *npr fpl*: **(les) ~** the New Hebrides, Vanuatu.

Nouvelle-Zélande [nuvɛlzelɑ̃d] *npr f*: **(la) ~** New Zealand.

nouvelliste [nuvelist] *nmf* short story writer.

nova [nɔva] *nf* nova.

novateur, trice [nɔvatœr, tris] ◇ *adj* innovative, innovatory.
◇ *nm, f* innovator.

novation [nɔvasjɔ̃] *nf* **1.** *sout* [gén] innovation, innovating **2.** DR novation.

novatoire [nɔvatwar] *adj*: **acte ~** deed of novation.

novélisation [nɔvelizasjɔ̃] *nf* novelization.

novembre [nɔvɑ̃br] *nm* November, *voir aussi* **mars**.

novice [nɔvis] ◇ *adj* inexperienced, green ▪ **être ~ dans** *ou* **en qqch** to be inexperienced in *ou* a novice at sthg.
◇ *nmf* **1.** [débutant] novice, beginner **2.** RELIG novice.
◇ *nm* NAUT junior seaman.

noviciat [nɔvisja] *nm* **1.** RELIG [période, lieu] novitiate **2.** *litt* [apprentissage] probation, trial period.

noyade [nwajad] *nf* **1.** [fait de se noyer] drowning *(U)* **2.** [accident] drowning *(C)* ▪ **il y a eu beaucoup de ~s ici l'été dernier** many people (were) drowned here last summer.

noyau, x [nwajo] *nm* **1.** [de fruit] stone, pit *US* ▪ **~ de cerise/pêche** cherry/peach stone ▪ **enlever le ~ d'un fruit** to pit a fruit, to remove the stone from a fruit **2.** [centre] nucleus ▪ **~ familial** family nucleus **3.** [petit groupe] small group ➲ **le ~ dur** [d'un parti, de l'actionnariat] the hard core ▪ **~ de résistance** pocket *ou* centre of resistance **4.** ANAT, ASTRON, BIOL & PHYS nucleus **5.** ÉLECTR, GÉOL & NUCL core **6.** FIN : **~ dur** hard-core shareholders **7.** MÉTALL (mould) core.

noyautage [nwajotaʒ] *nm* **1.** POLIT infiltration **2.** MÉTALL core blowing.

noyauter [3] [nwajote] *vt* **1.** POLIT to infiltrate ▪ **le syndicat a été noyauté** the union has been infiltrated **2.** MÉTALL to blow *ou* to make cores.

noyé, e [nwaje] ◇ *pp* **1.** [personne] drowned ▪ **mourir ~** to drown **2.** [moteur] flooded **3.** *fig* **les yeux ~s de larmes** his eyes bathed with tears ▪ **être ~ dans la foule** to be lost in the crowd ▪ **l'essentiel est ~ dans les détails** the essentials have been buried *ou* lost in a mass of detail ▪ **~e dans la masse, sa voix pouvait passer pour puissante** blended in with the rest, his voice could be thought of as powerful.
◇ *nm, f* drowned person ▪ **trois disparus et deux ~s** three missing and two drowned.

noyer[1] [nwaje] *nm* **1.** [arbre] walnut (tree) **2.** [bois] walnut.

noyer[2] [13] [nwaje] *vt* **1.** [personne, animal] to drown ▪ [moteur, vallée] to flood ▪ **~ une sédition/mutinerie dans le sang** to bloodily suppress a revolt/mutiny ➲ **~ son chagrin (dans l'alcool)** to drown one's sorrows (in drink) ▪ **~ le poisson** PÊCHE to play the fish ▪ **ne cherche pas à ~ le poisson** *fam fig* don't try to confuse the issue ▪ **qui veut ~ son chien l'accuse de la rage** *prov* give a dog a bad name (and hang him) *prov* **2.** [faire disparaître] : **une épaisse brume noie la vallée** the valley is shrouded in fog ▪ **le piano est noyé par les violons** the violins are drowning out the piano.

◆ **se noyer** ◇ *vp (emploi réfléchi)* [se suicider] to drown o.s. ▪ **elle a essayé de se ~** she tried to drown herself.
◇ *vpi* [accidentellement] to drown.

◆ **se noyer dans** *vp+prép* **1.** [se plonger dans] to bury *ou* to absorb o.s. in **2.** [s'empêtrer dans] to get tangled up *ou* bogged down *ou* trapped in ▪ **vous vous noyez dans des considérations hors sujet** you're getting tangled up in *ou* lost in a series of side issues ➲ **se ~ dans un verre d'eau** to make a mountain out of a molehill.

NPI (*abr de* **nouveaux pays industrialisés**) *nmpl* NICs.

N/Réf (*abr écrite de* **Notre référence**) O/Ref.

NRF (*abr de* **Nouvelle Revue française**) *npr f* **1.** [revue] *literary review* **2.** [mouvement] *literary movement.*

NRJ *npr the largest and most successful of the independent French radio stations.*

NTIC (*abr de* **nouvelles technologies de l'information et de la communication**) *nfpl* (N)ICT.

nu, e [ny] *adj* **1.** [sans habits - personne] naked, nude ▪ **être ~** to be naked *ou* in the nude ▪ **ne te promène pas tout ~ devant la fenêtre** don't walk about in front of the window with nothing on ▪ **être à demi ~** *ou* **à moitié ~** to be half-naked ▪ **poser ~ pour un photographe** to pose in the nude for a photographer ▪ **se mettre (tout) ~** to take off all one's clothes, to strip naked ▪ **revue ~e** nude show ➲ **être ~ comme un ver** *ou* **la main** to be stark naked **2.** [découvert - partie du corps] : **avoir les bras ~s/fesses ~es** to be barearmed/bare-bottomed ▪ **se promener les jambes ~es** to walk about bare-legged *ou* with bare legs ▪ **être pieds ~s** to be barefoot *ou* barefooted ▪ **se baigner seins ~s** to go topless bathing ▪ **la tête ~e** bareheaded *ou* without a hat on ▪ **il travaillait torse ~** he was working without a shirt on ▪ **mettez-vous torse ~** strip to the waist ➲ **à l'œil ~ : ça ne se voit pas/ça se voit à l'œil ~** you can't/you can see it with the naked eye **3.** [dégarni - sabre] naked ; [- paysage] bare, empty ; [- mur] bare **4.** BOT [grain, graine] naked.

◆ **nu** *nm* ART nude ▪ **une photo de ~** a nude photo.

◆ **à nu** ◇ *loc adj* bare ▪ **le fil est à ~** [accidentellement] the wire is bare ; [exprès] the wire has been stripped ▪ **mon âme était à ~** my soul had been laid bare.
◇ *loc adv* : **mettre à ~** to expose ▪ **mettre un fil électrique à ~** to strip a wire ▪ **mettre son cœur à ~** to bare one's soul.

nuage [nɥaʒ] *nm* **1.** MÉTÉOR cloud ▪ **ciel chargé de ~s** cloudy *ou* overcast sky ▪ **~ de fumée/poussière** cloud of smoke/dust ▪ **~ toxique/radioactif** toxic/radioactive cloud **2.** [menace, inquiétude] cloud ▪ **il y avait de gros ~s à l'horizon économique de 1994** the economic outlook for 1994 was very gloomy *ou* bleak ▪ **un ~ passa dans ses yeux/sur son visage** his eyes/face clouded over ‖ [rêverie] : **être dans les ~s** to have one's head in the clouds, to be day-dreaming **3.** [masse légère] : **un ~ de tulle** a mass *ou* swathe of tulle ‖ [petite quantité] : **un ~ de lait** a drop of milk **4.** JOAILL cloud.

◆ **sans nuages** *loc adj* **1.** MÉTÉOR cloudless ▪ **sous un ciel sans ~s** under cloudless blue skies **2.** [amitié] untroubled, perfect ▪ [bonheur] unclouded, perfect.

nuageux, euse [nɥaʒø, øz] *adj* **1.** MÉTÉOR : **ciel ~** cloudy *ou* overcast sky ➲ **masse nuageuse** cloudbank **2.** [confus - esprit, idée] hazy, nebulous, obscure.

nuance [nɥɑ̃s] *nf* **1.** [différence - de couleur] shade, hue ; [- de son] nuance ■ des ~s de bleu shades of blue ■ ~ de sens shade of meaning, nuance ■ il y a une ~ entre indifférence et lâcheté there's a (slight) difference between indifference and cowardice ■ j'ai dit que je l'aimais bien et non que je l'aimais, ~! I said I liked him and not that I loved him, that's not the same thing! **2.** [subtilité] nuance, subtlety ■ toutes les ~s de sa pensée the many subtleties *ou* all the finer aspects of his thinking ■ personne/personnage tout en ~s very subtle person/character **3.** [trace légère] touch, tinge ■ il y avait une ~ d'amertume dans sa voix there was a touch *ou* hint of bitterness in his voice **4.** MÉTALL grade, type.

nuancer [16] [nɥɑ̃se] *vt* **1.** [couleur] to shade ■ [musique] to nuance **2.** [critique, jugement] to nuance, to qualify ■ cette opinion/déclaration demande à être nuancée this opinion/statement needs to be qualified **3.** TEXT to grade, to tone.

nuancier [nɥɑ̃sje] *nm* colour chart.

Nubie [nybi] *npr f* : (la) ~ Nubia.

nubile [nybil] *adj* nubile ■ l'âge ~ ≃ the age of consent.

nubilité [nybilite] *nf* nubility.

nucléaire [nykleɛr] ◇ *adj* BIOL, MIL & PHYS nuclear.
◇ *nm* [énergie] nuclear power *ou* energy ■ [industrie] nuclear industry.

nucléarisation [nyklearizasjɔ̃] *nf* INDUST *introduction of nuclear power to replace conventional energy sources* ■ MIL nuclearization.

nucléariser [3] [nyklearize] *vt* to supply with nuclear power ■ MIL to supply with nuclear weapons, to nuclearize.
◆ **se nucléariser** *vpi* to go nuclear.

nucléé, e [nyklee] *adj* nucleated.

nucléide [nykleid] = nuclide.

nucléique [nykleik] *adj* : acide ~ nucleic acid.

nucléon [nykleɔ̃] *nm* nucleon.

nucléoplasme [nykleɔplasm] *nm* nucleoplasm.

nuclide [nyklid] *nm* nuclide.

nudisme [nydism] *nm* nudism, naturism ■ pratiquer le ~ to practise nudism.

nudiste [nydist] ◇ *adj* nudist *(modif)*.
◇ *nmf* nudist ■ plage/village de ~s nudist beach/village.

nudité [nydite] *nf* **1.** [d'une personne] nakedness, nudity ■ *fig* ses crimes furent étalés dans toute leur ~ his crimes were exposed for all to see **2.** [d'un lieu] bareness **3.** ART nude.

nuée [nɥe] *nf* **1.** *litt* thick cloud ■ ~ d'orage storm cloud, thundercloud **2.** [multitude] horde, host ■ ~ de paparazzi/d'admirateurs a horde of paparazzi/admirers ■ ~ d'insectes horde *ou* swarm of insects ■ comme une ~ de sauterelles like a plague of locusts **3.** JOAILL cloud.

nue-propriété [nyprɔprijete] (*pl* **nues-propriétés**) *nf* bare ownership.

nues [ny] *nfpl* : les ~ *litt* & *arch* the skies ▶ porter qqn/qqch aux ~ to praise sb/sthg to the skies ■ tomber des ~ : nous sommes tombés des ~ we were flabbergasted *ou* dumbfounded.

nuire [97] [nɥir] ◆ **nuire à** *v+prép* [être néfaste pour] : ~ à qqn to harm *ou* to injure sb ■ ça ne peut que te ~ it can only do you harm ■ ils cherchent à nous ~ par une publicité mensongère they're trying to damage our reputation with misleading publicity ■ ~ à qqch to be harmful to *ou* to damage *ou* to harm sthg ■ le tabac nuit à la santé smoking is harmful to health ■ cela a nui à l'équilibre de leur couple their relationship suffered from it.
◆ **se nuire** *vp (emploi réfléchi)* to do o.s. harm ■ tu te nuis à toi-même en faisant cela you're only hurting yourself by doing that.

nuisance [nɥizɑ̃s] *nf* (environmental) nuisance ■ ~ sonore noise pollution.

nuisette [nɥizɛt] *nf* short *ou* babydoll nightgown.

nuisibilité [nɥizibilite] *nf* harmfulness.

nuisible [nɥizibl] *adj* harmful ■ gaz/fumées ~s noxious gases/fumes ■ des individus ~s à la société individuals harmful to society ▶ animaux ~s pests.
◆ **nuisibles** *nmpl* ZOOL vermin, pests.

nuisons *etc v* ⊳ nuire.

nuit [nɥi] *nf* **1.** [obscurité] night *(U)*, dark, darkness ■ il fait ~ it's dark ■ il fait ~ noire it's pitch-dark *ou* pitch-black ■ la ~ tombe it's getting dark, night is falling *sout* ■ rentrer avant la ~ to get back before nightfall *ou* dark ■ à la ~ tombante, à la tombée de la ~ at nightfall, at dusk ▶ la ~ des temps : remonter à/se perdre dans la ~ des temps to go back to the dawn of/to be lost in the mists of time ■ c'est le jour et la ~! it's like chalk and cheese! *UK*, it's like night and day! *US*
2. [intervalle entre le coucher et le lever du soleil] night, nighttime ■ je dors la ~ I sleep at *ou* during the night ■ une ~ étoilée a starry night ■ faire sa ~ to sleep through the night ■ bonne ~! goodnight! ■ passer une bonne ~ [malade] to have a comfortable night ■ une ~ de marche/repos/travail a night's walk/rest/work ■ une ~ d'extase/de désespoir a night of ecstasy/despair ■ une ~ d'insomnie a sleepless night ▶ la ~ de noces the wedding night ■ la ~ porte conseil *prov* I'd/you'd *etc* better sleep on it
3. [dans des expressions de temps] : cette ~ : que s'est-il passé cette ~? what happened last night? ■ nous partons cette ~ we're leaving tonight ■ des ~s entières nights on end ■ en pleine ~ in the middle of the night ■ en une ~ [pendant la nuit] in one night ; [vite] overnight ■ il y a deux ~s the night before last ■ il y a trois ~s three nights ago ■ la ~ : l'émission passe tard la ~ the programme is on late at night, it's a late-night programme ■ la ~ de mardi/vendredi Tuesday/Friday night ■ dans la ~ de mardi à mercredi during Tuesday night, during the night of Tuesday to Wednesday ■ la ~ où ils ont disparu the night (that) they disappeared ■ la ~ précédente *ou* d'avant the previous night, the night before ■ la ~ suivante *ou* d'après the next night, the night after ■ l'autre ~ the other night ■ ~ et jour, de ~ comme de jour night and day ■ stationnement interdit ~ et jour no parking day or night ■ toute la ~ all night (long), through the night ■ toutes les ~s nightly, every night ▶ la ~ tous les chats sont gris *prov* all cats are grey in the dark
4. [dans des noms de dates] : la ~ des longs couteaux the Night of the Long Knives ■ la ~ de Noël Christmas night ■ la ~ de la Saint-Sylvestre New Year's Eve night
5. [nuitée] : payer sa ~ to pay for the night ■ c'est combien la ~? how much is it for one night? ■ la chambre est à 130 euros la ~ rooms are 130 euros a night.
◆ **de nuit** ◇ *loc adj* **1.** ZOOL : animaux/oiseaux de ~ nocturnal animals/birds
2. [pharmacie] night *(modif)*, all-night *(avant n)*, twenty-four hour *(avant n)*
3. [qui a lieu la nuit] night *(modif)* ■ garde/vol de ~ night watch/flight ■ conduite de ~ night-driving, driving at night ■ aujourd'hui je suis de ~ à l'hôpital I'm on night-duty at the hospital tonight.
◇ *loc adv* : travailler de ~ to work nights *ou* the night shift *ou* at night ■ conduire de ~ to drive at *ou* by night.
◆ **nuit américaine** *nf* CINÉ day for night ■ tourné en ~ américaine shot in day for night.
◆ **nuit blanche** *nf* sleepless night.
◆ **nuit bleue** *nf* night of bomb attacks.

nuitamment [nɥitamɑ̃] *adv litt* at *ou* by night.

nuitée [nɥite] *nf* bed-night, person-night *spéc* ■ le gérant de l'hôtel nous a facturé deux ~s the hotel manager charged us for two nights.

nul, nulle [nyl] *sout* ◇ *dét (adj indéf: avant le n)* no, not any ■ tu ne peux faire confiance à ~ autre que lui you can trust nobody but him, he's the only one you can trust ■ ~ autre que lui n'aurait pu y parvenir nobody (else) but he could have done it ■ à ~ autre pareil peerless, unrivalled ■ sans ~ doute undoubtedly, without any doubt ■ ~ doute qu'il tiendra sa promesse there is no doubt that he will keep his promise.
◇ *pron indéf* no one, nobody ■ ~ mieux que lui n'aurait su analyser la situation no one could have analyzed the situation better than him ▶ ~ n'est parfait nobody's perfect ■ ~ n'est censé ignorer la loi ignorance of the law is no defence ■ ~ n'est prophète en son pays *prov* no man is a prophet in his own country.

◆ **nulle part** *loc adv* nowhere ▪ **on ne l'a trouvé nulle part** he was nowhere to be found ▪ **nulle part la nature n'est plus belle** nowhere is nature more beautiful ▪ **nulle part ailleurs** nowhere else.

nul, nulle [nyl] ◇ *adj* **1.** [inexistant] nil, nonexistent **2.** *fam* [très mauvais] useless, rubbish, hopeless ▪ **leur dernière chanson est nulle** their latest song is rubbish ▪ **être ~ en maths** to be hopeless *ou* useless at maths ▪ **c'est vraiment ~ de dire une chose pareille** what a pathetic thing to say ▪ **t'es ~!** [mauvais] you're useless! ; [méchant] you're pathetic! **3.** MATH null **4.** DR null ▪ **rendre ~** to nullify, to annul **5.** SPORT nil ▪ **le score est ~** the score is nil-nil.
◇ *nm, f fam* prat.

nullard, e [nylar, ard] *fam* ◇ *adj* thick UK, dumb US.
◇ *nm, f* numskull, dumbo, thicko UK.

nullement [nylmɑ̃] *adv litt* not at all, not in the least.

nullipare [nylipar] ◇ *adj* nulliparous.
◇ *nf* nullipara.

nullité [nylite] *nf* **1.** [manque de valeur] incompetence, uselessness ▪ **elle est d'une ~ totale** she's totally useless *ou* incompetent ▪ **ce film est d'une parfaite ~** this film is really terrible **2.** [personne] incompetent, nonentity ▪ **c'est une ~** he's useless **3.** DR nullity.

numéraire [nymerɛr] ◇ *adj* : **espèces ~s** legal tender *ou* currency ▪ **valeur ~** face value.
◇ *nm* cash.

numéral, e, aux [nymeral, o] *adj* numeral.
◆ **numéral, aux** *nm* numeral.

numérateur [nymeratœr] *nm* numerator.

numération [nymerasjɔ̃] *nf* **1.** [dénombrement] numeration, numbering *(U)* ▪ [signes] notation ▪ **~ décimale/binaire** decimal/binary notation **2.** MÉD : **~ globulaire** blood count.

numérique [nymerik] *adj* **1.** [gén] numerical ▪ **dans l'ordre ~** in numerical order **2.** MATH numerical **3.** INFORM digital.

numériquement [nymerikmɑ̃] *adv* **1.** [en nombre] numerically **2.** INFORM digitally.

numérisation [nymerizasjɔ̃] *nf* digitization.

numériser [3] [nymerize] *vt* to digitize.

numériseur [nymerizœr] *nm* digitizer.

numéro [nymero] *nm* **1.** [nombre] number ⊳ **~ atomique** PHYS atomic *ou* proton number ▪ **~ de commande** order number ▪ **~ de compte** account number ▪ **~ d'immatriculation** registration number UK, license number US ▪ **~ matricule** number ▪ **~ de vol** flight number ▪ **le ~ un/deux soviétique** the Soviet number one/two ▪ **le ~ un du tennis français** France's number one *ou* top tennis player ▪ **le ~ un du parti républicain** the leader of the Republicain party
2. TÉLÉCOM : **~ de fax** fax number ▪ **~ (de téléphone)** TÉLÉCOM (telephone) number ▪ **~ de poste** extension number ▪ **refais le ~** dial (the number) again ▪ **j'ai changé de ~** my number has changed ▪ **faire un faux ~** to dial a wrong number ▪ **'il n'y a pas d'abonné au ~ que vous avez demandé'** there's no subscriber at the number you've dialled ▪ **~ vert** ≃ Freefone number UK, ≃ 800 *ou* toll-free number US
3. [habitation, place] number ▪ **j'habite Rue Froment – à quel ~?** I live in rue Froment – what number?
4. [exemplaire] issue ▪ **il y a un article intéressant dans le ~ de ce mois-ci** there's an interesting article in this month's issue ▪ **il faudra chercher dans de vieux ~s** we'll have to look through some back issues *ou* numbers ▪ **deux ~s en un** double issue ⊳ **~ zéro** dummy issue
5. MUS number ▪ [dans un spectacle] act, turn ▪ **il fait le ~ le plus important du spectacle** he's top of the bill ▪ **elle a fait son ~ habituel** she went into her usual routine ▪ **il lui a fait un ~ de charme terrible** *fam* he really turned on the charm with her
6. JEUX [nombre] number ▪ **un ~ gagnant** a winning number ▪ **~ complémentaire** *bonus number* ▪ **tirer le bon/mauvais ~** to pick the right/wrong number ▪ **lui, il a tiré le bon ~!** *fig* he's really picked a winner!
7. [personne] : **quel ~!** *fam* [hurluberlu] what a character!
8. *(comme adj; après le n)* **le lot ~ 12** lot 12
9. OPT number.

numérologie [nymerɔlɔʒi] *nf* numerology.

numérologue [nymerɔlɔg] *nmf* numerologist.

numérotage [nymerɔtaʒ] *nm* **1.** [attribution d'un numéro] numbering **2.** TEXT (yarn) counting.

numérotation [nymerɔtasjɔ̃] *nf* **1.** [attribution d'un numéro] numbering ▪ **la ~ des pages** pagination, page numbering **2.** TÉLÉCOM dialling ▪ **~ abrégée** speed or memory dialling.

numéroter [3] [nymerɔte] *vt* to number ▪ **~ les pages d'un livre** to paginate a book, to number the pages of a book ⊳ **tu peux ~ tes abattis!** *fam hum* get ready, you're in for it!

numerus clausus [nymerysklozys] *nm inv* numerus clausus.

numide [nymid] *adj* Numidian.
◆ **Numide** *nmf* Numidian.

Numidie [nymidi] *npr f* : **(la) ~** Numidia.

numismate [nymismat] *nmf* numismatist, numismatologist.

numismatique [nymismatik] ◇ *nf* numismatics *(U)*, numismatology.
◇ *adj* numismatic.

nunuche [nynyʃ] *fam* ◇ *adj* simple, goofy, dumb.
◇ *nf* ninny, nincompoop.

nu-pieds [nypje] ◇ *loc adv* barefoot.
◇ *nmpl* sandals.

nuptial, e, aux [nypsjal, o] *adj* **1.** [de mariage] wedding *(modif)* ▪ **robe ~e** wedding dress, bridal gown **2.** ZOOL nuptial.

nuptialité [nypsjalite] *nf* marriage rate, nuptiality.

nuque [nyk] *nf* nape *(of the neck)* ▪ **une coiffure qui dégage la ~** a hairstyle that leaves the back of the neck *ou* the nape bare ▪ **saisir qqn par la ~** to grab sb by the scruff of the neck.

nurse [nœrs] *nf vieilli* nanny, governess.

nursery [nœrsəri] (*pl* **nurserys** *ou pl* **nurseries**) *nf* nursery.

nutriment [nytrimɑ̃] *nm* nutriment.

nutritif, ive [nytritif, iv] *adj* **1.** [nourrissant - aliment] nourishing, nutritious ▪ **substance nutritive** nutrient **2.** [relatif à la nutrition] nutritive, nutritional ▪ **valeur nutritive** food *ou* nutritional value.

nutrition [nytrisjɔ̃] *nf* **1.** PHYSIOL nutrition, feeding ▪ **maladies de la ~** nutritional diseases ▪ **spécialiste de la ~** dietary expert **2.** BOT nutrition.

nutritionnel, elle [nytrisjɔnɛl] *adj* nutritional, food *(modif)* ▪ **composition ~le du lait** food *ou* nutritional value of milk.

nutritionniste [nytrisjɔnist] *nmf* nutritionist, dietary expert.

nyctalope [niktalɔp] ◇ *adj* **1.** ZOOL : **la chouette est un oiseau ~** the owl has good nocturnal vision **2.** MÉD hemeralopic *spéc*, day-blind.
◇ *nmf* **1.** MÉD person suffering from day-blindess *ou* hemeralopia *spéc* **2.** ZOOL animal/bird with good nocturnal vision.

Nylon® [nilɔ̃] *nm* nylon ▪ **en** *ou* **de ~** nylon *(modif)*.

nymphe [nɛ̃f] *nf* **1.** MYTHOL nymph **2.** ENTOM nymph **3.** ANAT labia minora, nympha.

nymphéa [nɛ̃fea] *nm* white water lily ▪ **'les Nymphéas'** *Monet* 'Water Lilies'.

nymphette [nɛ̃fɛt] *nf* nymphet, nymphette.

nympho [nɛ̃fo] (*abr de* **nymphomane**) *fam* ◇ *adj* : **elle est ~** she's a nympho.
◇ *nf* nympho.

nymphomane [nɛ̃fɔman] *adj f* & *nf* nymphomaniac.

nymphomanie [nɛ̃fɔmani] *nf* nymphomania.

o, O [o] *nm inv* [lettre] o, O, *voir aussi* **g**.

ô [o] *interj litt* oh, O.

O (*abr écrite de* **Ouest**) W.

OAA (*abr de* **Organisation des Nations unies pour l'alimentation et l'agriculture**) *npr f* FAO.

OACI (*abr de* **Organisation de l'aviation civile internationale**) *npr f* IATA.

OAS (*abr de* **Organisation Armée Secrète**) *npr f* OAS (*French terrorist organization which opposed Algerian independence in the 1960s*).

oasis [ɔazis] *nf* oasis ■ **une ~ de paix** an oasis of peace.

obédience [ɔbedjɑ̃s] *nf* [adhésion] allegiance ■ **pays d'~ socialiste** socialist *ou* socialist-run countries ■ **musulman de stricte ~** devout Muslim ➲ **~ religieuse** religious persuasion.

obéir [32] [ɔbeir] ◆ **obéir à** *v+prép* **1.** [se soumettre à] : **~ à qqn/qqch** to obey sb/sthg ■ **il m'obéit au doigt et à l'œil** he's at my beck and call ■ **savoir se faire ~ de qqn** to command *ou* to compel obedience from sb ■ **~ à un ordre** to comply with *ou* to obey an order ■ *(en usage absolu)* **vas-tu ~?** will you do as you're told! **2.** [être régi par] : **~ à qqch** to submit to *ou* to obey sthg ■ **~ à une théorie/un principe** to obey *ou* to follow a theory/principle ■ **le marché obéit à la loi de l'offre et de la demande** the market is governed by *ou* follows the law of supply and demand ■ **~ à une impulsion** to follow an impulse ■ **obéissant à une soif de vengeance** moved *ou* prompted by a thirst for revenge **3.** [réagir à - suj: mécanisme] : **~ à qqch** to respond to sthg ■ *(en usage absolu)* **soudain les freins ont cessé d'~** all of a sudden, the brakes stopped responding.

obéissance [ɔbeisɑ̃s] *nf* **1.** [action d'obéir] obedience, submission ■ **~ à une règle** adherence to a rule **2.** [discipline] obedience ■ **les professeurs se plaignent du manque d' ~ des élèves** the teachers complain of the pupils' disobedience **3.** RELIG obedience.

obéissant, e [ɔbeisɑ̃, ɑ̃t] *adj* obedient ■ **être** *ou* **se montrer ~ envers qqn** to be obedient to *ou* towards sb.

obélisque [ɔbelisk] *nm* obelisk.

obèse [ɔbɛz] <> *adj* obese.
<> *nmf* obese person.

obésité [ɔbezite] *nf* obesity, obeseness.

objecter [4] [ɔbʒɛkte] *vt* **1.** [opposer - un argument] : **~ qqch à qqn** to put sthg forward as an argument against sb ■ **il n'a rien eu à ~ à ce que j'ai dit** he raised no objections to what I said ■ **on nous objectera le coût trop élevé de l'opération** they will object to the high cost of the operation **2.** [prétexter] : **il objecta son incompétence pour se débarrasser de la corvée** he pleaded incompetence to get out of doing the chore.

objecteur [ɔbʒɛktœr] *nm* : **~ de conscience** conscientious objector.

objectif, ive [ɔbʒɛktif, iv] *adj* **1.** [impartial] objective, unbiased **2.** [concret, observable] objective **3.** GRAMM & PHILOS objective.
◆ **objectif** *nm* **1.** [but à atteindre] objective, goal, aim ■ COMM [de croissance, de production] target ■ **se fixer/atteindre un ~** to set o.s./to reach an objective **2.** MIL [cible] target, objective **3.** OPT & PHOTO lens, objective ■ **braquer son ~ sur qqch** to train one's camera on sthg ■ **fixer l'~** to look into the camera.

objection [ɔbʒɛksjɔ̃] *nf* **1.** [gén] objection ■ **faire** *ou* **soulever une ~** to make *ou* to raise an objection ■ **tu as** *ou* **tu y vois une ~?** do you have any objection? ■ **je ne vois pas d'~ à continuer le débat/à ce que vous partiez** I have no objection to our continuing the debate/to your leaving **2.** DR : **~! objection!** ■ **~ accordée/refusée** objection sustained/overruled.
◆ **objection de conscience** *nf* conscientious objection.

objectivation [ɔbʒɛktivasjɔ̃] *nf* objectivization.

objectivement [ɔbʒɛktivmɑ̃] *adv* objectively ■ **vous n'avez pas rendu compte des faits ~** you didn't report the facts objectively, you didn't give an objective account of the facts.

objectiver [3] [ɔbʒɛktive] *vt* to objectify.

objectivisme [ɔbʒɛktivism] *nm* objectivism.

objectivité [ɔbʒɛktivite] *nf* objectivity ■ **manque d'~** lack of objectivity ■ **en toute ~** (quite) objectively.

objet [ɔbʒɛ] *nm* **1.** [chose] object, item ■ **traiter qqn comme un ~** to treat sb like an object *ou* a thing ➲ **~ d'art** objet d'art, art object ■ **~ de luxe** luxury item ■ **~ sexuel** sex object ■ **~ volant non identifié = OVNI** ■ **~s personnels** personal belongings *ou* effects ■ **~s de toilette** toiletries ■ **~s trouvés** lost property *(U)* ■ **c'est un homme-~** he's a sex object
2. [thème] subject ■ **l'~ de leurs discussions était toujours la politique** politics was always the subject of their discussions ➲ **~ mathématique** mathematical construct
3. [personne] object ■ [raison] cause ■ **~ de convoitise** object of envy ■ **l'~ de sa curiosité/passion** the object of her curiosity/passion
4. [but] object, purpose, aim ■ **exposer l'~ de sa visite** to explain the purpose of *ou* reason for one's visit ■ **le congrès a rempli son ~, qui était d'informer** the congress has achieved its aim *ou* purpose, which was to inform ■ **faire** *ou* **être l'~ de : faire** *ou* **être l'~ de soins particuliers** to receive *ou* to be given special care ■ **faire l'~ d'une fouille corporelle** to be subjected to a body search ■ **faire l'~ d'attaques répétées** to be the victim of repeated attacks ■ **l'ancien ministre fait actuellement l'~ d'une enquête** the former minister is currently being inves-

tigated ■ **faire l'~ de controverses** to be a controversial subject ■ **faire l'~ de vives critiques** to be the object *ou* target of sharp criticism
5. GRAMM object
6. DR matter ■ **l'~ du litige** the matter at issue ■ **l'~ de la plainte** the matter of the complaint ■ **l'~ désigné dans le contrat** the object of the contract.
◆ **sans objet** *loc adj* **1.** [sans but] aimless, pointless **2.** [non justifié] unjustified, groundless, unfounded ■ **ces arguments sont maintenant sans ~** these arguments no longer apply *ou* are no longer applicable.

objurgations [ɔbʒyrgasjɔ̃] *nfpl litt* **1.** [reproches] objurgations *litt*, castigations *sout* **2.** [prières] entreaties, pleas.

obligataire [ɔbligatɛr] ◇ *adj* bonded, debenture *(modif)* ■ **dette ~** bonded *ou* debenture debt ■ **emprunt/créancier ~** bonded loan/creditor.
◇ *nmf* debenture holder, bondholder.

obligation [ɔbligasjɔ̃] *nf* **1.** [contrainte] obligation ■ **~ de : je suis** *ou* **je me vois dans l'~ de vous expulser** I'm obliged *ou* forced to evict you ■ **faire ~ à qqn de** to oblige *ou* to require sb to ■ **la loi vous fait ~ de vous présenter en personne** the law requires you to appear in person ➊ **'sans ~ d'achat'** 'no purchase necessary' ■ **~ de réserve** duty of confidentiality
2. [devoir] obligation, duty, commitment ■ **mes ~s de président de la société** my duties as the chairman of the company ➊ **~s familiales** family obligations *ou* commitments ■ **~s militaires** military obligations *ou* duties ■ **l'~ scolaire** compulsory education
3. DR obligation ■ **~ alimentaire** alimony, maintenance (order) *UK* ■ **contracter une ~ envers qqn** to enter into an agreement with sb ■ **faire honneur à ses ~s** to fulfil one's obligations, to carry out one's duties
4. BOURSE & FIN bond, debenture ■ **~ portant un intérêt de 6 %** bond bearing interest at 6% ➊ **~ échue/négociable** matured/marketable bond ■ **~ remboursable** *ou* **amortissable** redeemable bond ■ **~ cautionnée** guaranteed bond ■ **~ d'entreprise** bond, debenture (stock) *UK* ■ **~ d'État** (government) bond ■ **~ hypothécaire** mortgage bond ■ **~ au porteur** bearer bond ■ **~ privilégiée** preference *ou* preferment bond
5. *litt* [gratitude] obligation.
Voir module d'usage

obligatoire [ɔbligatwar] *adj* **1.** [exigé, imposé] compulsory, obligatory ■ **(le port de) la ceinture de sécurité est ~** the wearing of seat belts is compulsory ■ **le vaccin est ~ pour entrer à la maternelle** children must be vaccinated before being admitted to infant school *UK ou* nursery school *US* ■ **'tenue de soirée ~'** formal dress required **2.** [inéluctable] : **un jour ou l'autre ils en viendront aux mains, c'est ~** one of these days they're bound to come to blows.

obligatoirement [ɔbligatwarmɑ̃] *adv* **1.** [par nécessité] : **il doit ~ avoir la licence pour s'inscrire** he must have a degree to enrol ■ **nous devons ~ fermer les portes à 20 h** we're obliged *ou* required to close the doors at 8 p.m **2.** *fam* [immanquablement] inevitably ■ **il va ~ tout aller lui répéter** he's bound to go and tell her everything.

obligé, e [ɔbliʒe] ◇ *adj* **1.** [inévitable] : **c'était ~!** *fam* it was bound to happen! **2.** [nécessaire - conséquence] necessary **3.** DR : **être ~ envers un créancier** to be under an obligation to a creditor **4.** *sout* [reconnaissant] : **je vous serais ~ de...** I would be much obliged if you would...
◇ *nm, f sout* obligor ■ **je suis votre ~ en cette affaire** I'm obliged to you in this matter.

obligeamment [ɔbliʒamɑ̃] *adv sout* obligingly ■ **elle distribuait les bonnes notes un peu trop ~** she was a little too free with high marks.

obligeance [ɔbliʒɑ̃s] *nf sout* **avoir l'~ de faire qqch : veuillez avoir l'~ de me répondre rapidement** please be so kind as to *ou* be kind enough to reply as quickly as possible ■ **un jeune homme d'une extrême ~** an extremely obliging young man.

obligeant, e [ɔbliʒɑ̃, ɑ̃t] *adj sout* kind ■ **des remarques peu ~es** rather unkind remarks.

obliger [17] [ɔbliʒe] *vt* **1.** [mettre dans la nécessité de] to oblige, to force ■ **~ qqn à faire qqch** to force sb to do sthg ■ **ne m'oblige pas à te punir** don't force me to *ou* don't make me punish you ■ **cela m'oblige à changer de train** it means I have to change trains ■ **être obligé de faire qqch** to be forced to do sthg, to have to do sthg ■ **je suis bien obligé de suivre** I have no option *ou* choice but to follow ■ **se croire obligé de** to feel obliged to ■ **ne te crois pas obligé de tout boire!** *iron* you don't have to drink it all! ■ *(en usage absolu)* **irez-vous? – bien obligé!** are you going? – I don't have any choice, do I? ■ **j'ai mis une cravate, réunion oblige** I had to wear a tie, what with the meeting and all **2.** [contraindre moralement ou juridiquement] : **la loi oblige les candidats à se soumettre à un test** applicants are legally required to take a test ■ **votre signature vous oblige** your signature is legally binding **3.** *sout* [faire plaisir à] to oblige ■ **vous m'obligeriez en venant** *ou* **si vous veniez** you would oblige me by coming, I would be obliged if you came ■ **nous vous sommes très obligés de votre soutien** we are very grateful to you for your support.
◆ **s'obliger à** *vp+prép* **1.** [se forcer à] to force o.s. to ■ **elle s'oblige à marcher un peu** *ou* **à un peu de marche chaque jour** she forces herself to *ou* she makes herself walk a little every day **2.** [s'engager à] to commit o.s. to ■ **par ce contrat, je m'oblige à évacuer les lieux avant le 21** in this contract I commit myself to leaving *ou* I undertake to leave the premises by the 21st.

oblique [ɔblik] ◇ *adj* **1.** [ligne] oblique ■ [pluie, rayon] slanting ■ [regard] sidelong **2.** LING oblique **3.** DR indirect.
◇ *nm* ANAT oblique (muscle).
◇ *nf* GÉOM oblique (line).
◆ **en oblique** *loc adv* diagonally.

L'OBLIGATION

Do I really have to go? Est-ce qu'il faut vraiment que j'y aille ?
Do you need to book first? Est-ce qu'il faut réserver ?
Am I expected to wear a tie? Dois-je porter une cravate ?
You all have to be there by 6 o'clock. Vous devez tous y être pour 6 heures.
It's vital *ou* **essential that you call us as soon as you arrive.** Il faut absolument que vous nous appeliez dès que vous arrivez.
You must do your homework before you go out. Il faut que tu fasses tes devoirs avant de sortir.
Education is compulsory up to the age of 16. La scolarité est obligatoire jusqu'à l'âge de seize ans.
You're under no obligation to buy. Vous n'avez pas l'obligation d'acheter.
You don't have to come if you don't want to. Tu n'es pas obligé de venir si tu n'as pas envie.
There's no need to ask. Ce n'est pas la peine de demander.
Please don't feel you have to leave. Ne vous sentez pas obligé de partir.

obliquement [ɔblikmɑ̃] *adv* **1.** [de biais] obliquely, diagonally, at an angle **2.** [hypocritement] obliquely, indirectly ▪ **il agit toujours ~** he never acts openly.

obliquer [3] [ɔblike] *vi* to turn *ou* to veer off *(insép)* ▪ **la voiture obliqua dans une ruelle étroite** the car swerved (off) into a narrow alley ▪ **la route oblique à gauche** the road veers left.

oblitérateur, trice [ɔbliteratœr, tris] *adj* cancelling *(avant n)*.
◆ **oblitérateur** *nm* cancelling machine.

oblitération [ɔbliterasjɔ̃] *nf* **1.** [apposition d'une marque] cancellation ▪ [marque - sur un timbre] postmark ; [- sur un ticket] stamp **2.** *litt* [altération] fading **3.** MÉD obturation.

oblitérer [18] [ɔblitere] *vt* **1.** [timbre] to postmark, to cancel ▪ **timbre oblitéré** used stamp **2.** *litt* [effacer] to obliterate *sout*, to erase, to efface **3.** MÉD to obturate.

oblong, ongue [ɔblɔ̃, ɔ̃g] *adj* **1.** GÉOM oblong **2.** [visage, pelouse] oblong, oval.

obnubiler [3] [ɔbnybile] *vt sout* **1.** [obséder] to obsess ▪ **être obnubilé par une idée** to be obsessed by an idea **2.** *fig* [obscurcir] to cloud, to obnubilate *litt.*

obole [ɔbɔl] *nf* **1.** [somme d'argent] (small) contribution *ou* donation ▪ **chacun verse son ~** each person is making a contribution **2.** HIST [monnaie - grecque] obol ; [- française] obole.

obscène [ɔpsɛn] *adj* [licencieux] obscene, lewd ▪ **langage ~** obscene *ou* filthy language.

obscénité [ɔpsenite] *nf* **1.** [caractère licencieux] obscenity, lewdness **2.** [parole, geste] obscenity ▪ **raconter** *ou* **dire des ~s** to utter obscenities.

obscur, e [ɔpskyr] *adj* **1.** [sombre] dark ▪ **une nuit ~e** a pitch-black night ▪ **des forces ~es dominaient leur planète** *fig* obscure forces *ou* forces of darkness ruled their planet **2.** [incompréhensible] obscure, abstruse **3.** [indéfini] obscure, vague, indefinite ▪ **un ~ pressentiment** a vague premonition **4.** [peu connu] obscure ▪ **une vie ~e** a modest existence.

obscurantisme [ɔpskyrɑ̃tism] *nm* obscurantism.

obscurantiste [ɔpskyrɑ̃tist] *adj* & *nmf* obscurantist.

obscurcir [32] [ɔpskyrsir] *vt* **1.** [priver de lumière] to darken, to make dark **2.** [rendre confus - discours, raisonnement] to make obscure ▪ **le jugement obscurci par l'alcool** his judgement clouded *ou* obscured *ou* confused by drink.
◆ **s'obscurcir** *vpi* **1.** [ciel] to darken ▪ **soudain, tout s'obscurcit et je m'évanouis** suddenly everything went dark *ou* black and I fainted ▪ **son visage s'obscurcit à ces mots** at these words, her face clouded (over) *ou* darkened **2.** [se compliquer] to become (more) obscure ▪ **le mystère s'obscurcit** the plot thickens.

obscurcissement [ɔpskyrsismɑ̃] *nm* **1.** [d'un lieu] darkening **2.** *sout* [de l'esprit] obscuring, clouding over ▪ **l'~ progressif de ses facultés** the gradual weakening *ou* loss of her faculties.

obscurément [ɔpskyremɑ̃] *adv* obscurely, vaguely, dimly ▪ **nous sentions ~ que...** we had a vague *ou* an obscure feeling that...

obscurité [ɔpskyrite] *nf* **1.** [manque d'éclairage] dark, darkness ▪ **dans l'~** in darkness, in the dark ▪ **soudain, l'~ se fit dans la chambre** it suddenly became *ou* went dark in the room **2.** [caractère complexe] obscurity, abstruseness *sout* **3.** [remarque, expression] obscure *ou* abstruse remark, obscurity **4.** *litt* [anonymat] : **vivre/tomber dans l'~** to live in/to fall into obscurity.

obsédant, e [ɔpsedɑ̃, ɑ̃t] *adj* [souvenir, musique] haunting, obsessive ▪ [besoin] obsessive.

obsédé, e [ɔpsede] ◇ *adj* [gén] obsessed ▪ [sexuel] (sexually) obsessed.
◇ *nm, f* **1.** [victime d'obsessions] obsessive ▪ **~ sexuel** sex maniac **2.** *fam* [fanatique] : **les ~s de la vitesse** speed merchants *UK*, speed fiends *US* ▪ **les ~s de l'hygiène** hygiene freaks.

obséder [18] [ɔpsede] *vt* **1.** [suj: image, souvenir, peur] to haunt, to obsess ▪ **obsédé par la pensée de la mort** obsessed *ou* gripped with the idea of death **2.** *litt* [suj: personne] to importune *sout*, to bother.

obsèques [ɔpsɛk] *nfpl* funeral.

obséquieux, euse [ɔpsekjø, øz] *adj* obsequious ▪ **être ~ avec qqn** to be obsequious to *ou* towards sb.

obséquiosité [ɔpsekjozite] *nf* obsequiousness.

observable [ɔpsɛrvabl] *adj* observable ▪ **le phénomène est ~ à l'œil nu** the phenomenon can be observed with the naked eye.

observance [ɔpsɛrvɑ̃s] *nf* [d'un rite, d'une loi] observance ▪ **franciscain de stricte ~** Franciscan of strict observance.

observateur, trice [ɔpsɛrvatœr, tris] ◇ *adj* [perspicace] observant ▪ **avoir un esprit très ~** to be very perceptive ▪ **rien n'échappe à l'œil ~ du peintre** nothing can escape the painter's perceptive eye.
◇ *nm, f* **1.** [témoin] observer **2.** POLIT observer ▪ **~ de l'ONU** UN observer **3.** MIL spotter **4.** PRESSE : **le Nouvel Observateur** *weekly news magazine.*

observation [ɔpsɛrvasjɔ̃] *nf* **1.** [remarque] observation, remark, comment ▪ **avez-vous des ~s à faire sur ce premier cours?** do you have any comments to make about this first class? ▪ **la réponse du ministre appelle plusieurs ~s** the minister's answer calls for some comment *ou* several observations **2.** [critique] (piece of) criticism, critical remark ▪ **je te prie de garder tes ~s pour toi** please keep your remarks to yourself ▪ **ma secrétaire est toujours en retard et je lui en ai fait l'~** my secretary's always late and I've had a word with her about it ▪ **j'ai horreur qu'on me fasse des ~s** I hate people criticizing me *ou* making remarks to me ▪ **à la première ~, vous sortez!** [à un élève] if I have to say one (more) word to you, you're out! **3.** SC [investigation, exposé] observation ▪ [exposé] observation ▪ [méthode d'étude] observation, observing ▪ **l'~ de la nature/d'une réaction chimique** observing nature/a chemical reaction ➋ **avoir l'esprit d'~** to be observant **4.** MIL observation **5.** [observance] observance, observing, keeping **6.** MÉD [description] notes ▪ [surveillance] observation ▪ **mettre un malade en ~** to put a patient under observation.
◆ **d'observation** *loc adj* **1.** AÉRON, ASTRON & MIL observation *(modif)* **2.** SC : **techniques/erreur d'~** observation techniques/error **3.** SPORT : **un round d'~** a sizing-up round.

observatoire [ɔpsɛrvatwar] *nm* **1.** ASTRON & MÉTÉOR observatory **2.** MIL & *fig* observation *ou* lookout post **3.** ÉCON : **~ du livre** *body in charge of monitoring book prices* ▪ **~ des prix** price-monitoring watchdog.

observer [3] [ɔpsɛrve] *vt* **1.** [examiner] to observe, to examine ▪ SC to observe ▪ **~ qqch à la loupe** to examine sthg under a magnifying glass **2.** [surveiller] to watch, to keep a watch *ou* an eye on ▪ **attention, on nous observe** careful, we're being watched ▪ **~ qqn avec attention/du coin de l'œil** to watch sb attentively/out of the corner of one's eye **3.** [respecter - trêve] to observe ; [- accord] to observe, to respect, to abide by ▪ **~ une minute de silence** to observe a minute's silence ▪ **~ le sabbat** to observe *ou* to keep the Sabbath ▪ **~ le code de la route** to observe *ou* to follow the highway code **4.** [conserver] : **~ une attitude digne** to maintain *ou* to keep a dignified attitude ▪ **~ la plus stricte neutralité** to observe *ou* to maintain the strictest neutrality **5.** [constater] to observe, to notice, to note ▪ **on observe un changement d'attitude chez les jeunes** there is a noticeable change in attitude amongst young people ▪ **on observe une tache noire dans le poumon droit** a dark patch can be seen in the right lung **6.** [dire] to observe, to remark ▪ **tu ne portes plus d'alliance, observa-t-il** you're not wearing a wedding ring any more, he observed *ou* remarked ▪ **je te ferai ~ que tu t'es trompé** let me point out to you that you were wrong.
◆ **s'observer** ◇ *vp (emploi réfléchi)* to keep a check on o.s.
◇ *vp (emploi réciproque)* to observe *ou* to watch each other.
◇ *vp (emploi passif)* to be seen *ou* observed ▪ **ce phénomène s'observe surtout par temps sec** this phenomenon is mainly seen *ou* encountered in dry weather.

obsession [ɔpsesjɔ̃] *nf* **1.** [hantise] obsession ▪ **beaucoup de femmes ont l'~ de grossir** many women are obsessed with the idea of putting on weight ▪ **il croit qu'on veut le tuer, c'est devenu une ~** he believes people want to kill him, it's become a real obsession (with him) **2.** [idée fixe] obsession.

obsessionnel, elle [ɔpsesjɔnɛl] ◇ *adj* **1.** [répétitif] obsessive, obsessional **2.** PSYCHOL [comportement] obsessive ▪ [névrose] obsessional ▪ **de manière ~le** obsessively.
◇ *nm, f* obsessive.

obsidienne [ɔpsidjɛn] *nf* obsidian.

obsolescent, e [ɔpsɔlɛsɑ̃, ɑ̃t] *adj* obsolescent.

obsolète [ɔpsɔlɛt] *adj* LING obsolete.

obstacle [ɔpstakl] *nm* **1.** [objet bloquant le passage] obstacle ▪ **l'immeuble d'en face fait ~ au soleil** the building opposite blocks (out) *ou* obstructs the sun **2.** SPORT hurdle ▪ ÉQUIT fence **3.** [difficulté] obstacle, difficulty, problem ▪ **il y a un gros ~** there's a big problem ▪ **buter sur un ~** to come up against an obstacle ▪ **être un** *ou* **faire ~ à** to be an obstacle to, to hinder, to impede ▪ **plus rien ne fait ~ à notre amour** nothing stands in the way of our love any longer ▪ **mettre un ~ aux ambitions de qqn** to put an obstacle in the way of sb's ambitions.

obstétricien, enne [ɔpstetrisjɛ̃, ɛn] *nm, f* obstetrician.

obstétrique [ɔpstetrik] *nf* obstetrics *(U)*.

obstination [ɔpstinasjɔ̃] *nf* **1.** [persévérance] persistence, perseverance ▪ **à force d'~ elle y est arrivée** she succeeded through strength of purpose **2.** [entêtement] obstinacy, obstinateness, stubbornness.

obstiné, e [ɔpstine] ◇ *adj* **1.** [entêté] obstinate, stubborn ▪ [persévérant] persevering, determined **2.** [assidu] obstinate ▪ **un travail ~** unyielding *ou* obstinate work.
◇ *nm, f*: **c'est un ~** [qui persévère] he's very determined ; [qui s'entête] he's very stubborn *ou* obstinate.

obstinément [ɔpstinemɑ̃] *adv* **1.** [avec entêtement] obstinately, stubbornly ▪ **l'enfant tenait ~ à rester avec sa mère** the child was obstinately *ou* doggedly determined to stay with his mother **2.** [avec persévérance] perseveringly, persistently.

obstiner [3] [ɔpstine] ◆ **s'obstiner** *vpi* to persist, to insist ▪ **ne t'obstine pas, abandonne le projet** don't be obstinate, give the project up ▪ **elle s'obstine à vouloir partir** she persists in wanting to leave *ou* insists on leaving ▪ **il s'obstinait à ne rien dire** he obstinately *ou* stubbornly refused to talk.

obstructif, ive [ɔpstryktif, iv] *adj* [tumeur] obstruent ▪ [maladie] obstructive.

obstruction [ɔpstryksjɔ̃] *nf* **1.** [obstacle] obstruction, blockage ▪ [blocage] obstruction, obstructing, blocking ▪ **faire ~ à** to block, to obstruct **2.** [action délibérée] : **faire de l'~** [gén] to be obstructive ; POLIT to obstruct (legislation) ; FOOTBALL to obstruct **3.** MÉD obstruction.

obstructionniste [ɔpstryksjɔnist] *adj* & *nmf* obstructionist.

obstructive [ɔpstryktiv] *f* ▷ **obstructif.**

obstruer [3] [ɔpstrye] *vt* **1.** [passage] to obstruct, to block ▪ **une tour obstrue maintenant la vue** now a tower blocks (out) the view **2.** MÉD to obstruct.
◆ **s'obstruer** *vpi* to become blocked *ou* obstructed.

obtempérer [18] [ɔptɑ̃pere] ◆ **obtempérer à** *v+prép* **1.** [se soumettre à] to comply with *(insép)* ▪ **~ à un ordre** to obey an order ▪ *(en usage absolu)* **le soldat s'empressa d'~** the soldier hurriedly obeyed **2.** DR to obey ▪ **~ à une sommation** to obey a summons.

obtenir [40] [ɔptənir] *vt* **1.** [acquérir - baccalauréat, licence, note, point] to obtain, to get ; [- prix, nomination] to receive, to win, to get ; [- consentement] to get, to win ; [- prêt] to secure, to obtain, to get ; [- accord] to reach, to obtain, to get ▪ **les résultats obtenus par l'équipe nationale** the national team's results ▪ **le numéro de trapèze obtient toujours un grand succès** the trapeze act is always a big success ▪ **~ la garde d'un enfant** to get *ou* to win custody of a child ▪ **~ le droit de vote** to win the right to vote, to get the vote ▪ **~ de qqn une permission** to obtain *ou* to get permission from sb ▪ **j'ai enfin obtenu qu'elle mette ses gants pour sortir** I eventually got her to wear her gloves to go out **2.** [procurer] : **~ qqch à qqn** to obtain *ou* to get *ou* to procure *sout* sthg for sb ▪ **elle lui a obtenu une augmentation** she got him a raise **3.** [arriver à - résultat] to get, to obtain ; [- effet, succès] to achieve ▪ **en divisant par deux on obtient 24** if you divide by two you get 24 **4.** TÉLÉCOM : **~ un numéro** to get *ou* obtain a number.
◆ **obtenir de** *v+prép* : **il a obtenu de repousser le rendez-vous** he managed to get the meeting postponed.
◆ **s'obtenir** *vp (emploi passif)* **le résultat demandé s'obtient en multipliant 3 par 5** to arrive at *ou* to reach the required result, multiply 3 by 5.

obtention [ɔptɑ̃sjɔ̃] *nf* **1.** [acquisition] obtaining, getting **2.** [production] creation, production ▪ **l'~ d'un nouveau vaccin** the production of a new vaccine.

obtenu, e [ɔptəny] *pp* ▷ **obtenir.**

obtient, obtint *etc v* ▷ **obtenir.**

obturateur, trice [ɔptyratœr, tris] *adj* **1.** TECHNOL obturating, shutting **2.** ANAT obturator *(modif)* ▪ **muscle ~** obturator muscle.
◆ **obturateur** *nm* **1.** PHOTO shutter ▪ **armer/déclencher l'~** to set/to release the shutter ▶ **~ d'objectif/à rideau** between-lens/roller-blind shutter **2.** ARM obturator, gas-check **3.** PÉTR (blow-out) preventor **4.** [en plomberie] shut-off.

obturation [ɔptyrasjɔ̃] *nf* **1.** TECHNOL sealing, stopping up **2.** MÉD : **l'~ d'une dent** the filling of a tooth **3.** ARM obturation.

obturer [3] [ɔptyre] *vt* **1.** TECHNOL [boucher] to seal, to stop up *(sép)* **2.** MÉD to fill.

obtus, e [ɔpty, yz] *adj* **1.** MATH obtuse **2.** [borné] obtuse, dull, slow-witted ▪ **ne sois pas ~** don't be obtuse.

obus [ɔby] *nm* **1.** ARM shell **2.** *(comme adj)* **homme ~, femme ~** human cannonball.

obvier [19] [ɔbvje] ◆ **obvier à** *v+prép litt* [parer à] to obviate *sout*, to ward off *(sép)* ▪ **~ à un danger/accident** to forestall a danger/an accident.

oc [ɔk] ▷ **langue.**

OC (*abr écrite de* **ondes courtes**) SW.

ocarina [ɔkarina] *nm* ocarina.

occase [ɔkaz] *nf fam* **1.** [affaire] bargain, snip *UK*, steal *US* **2.** [moment] : **à la première ~** asap, as soon as possible.
◆ **d'occase** *loc adv fam* secondhand ▪ **je l'ai acheté d'~** I bought it secondhand.
◆ **pour l'occasion** *loc adv* for the occasion.

occasion [ɔkazjɔ̃] *nf* **1.** [circonstance favorable] opportunity, chance ▪ **si l'~ se présente** if the opportunity arises ▪ **l'~ ne se représentera pas** there won't be another chance like that again ▪ **laisser passer l'~** to let the opportunity slip (by) ▪ **saisir l'~ au vol, sauter sur l'~** to seize the opportunity, to jump at the chance ▪ **je le lui dirai à la première ~** I'll tell him as soon as I get a chance ▪ **l'~ de : ça te donnera l'~ de la rencontrer** it'll give you the opportunity *ou* the chance to meet her ▪ **je n'ai jamais eu l'~ de me plaindre de lui** I've never had cause to complain about him ▪ **il a manqué** *ou* **perdu** *ou* **raté une belle ~ de se taire** *fam* he could have kept his mouth shut ▶ **l'~ fait le larron** *prov* opportunity makes a thief *prov* **2.** [moment] occasion ▪ **à deux ~s** twice ▪ **à trois/quatre ~s** three/four times ▪ **à toute ~** on every occasion ▪ **en plusieurs/maintes ~s** several/many times ▪ **à cette ~** at that point, on that occasion ▪ **dans les grandes ~s** on big *ou* important *ou* special occasions ▪ **être** *ou* **faire l'~ de : sa mort a été l'~ de changements importants** significant changes took place after his death ▪ **ces retrouvailles furent l'~ de grandes réjouissances** there were great festivities to celebrate this reunion **3.** [article non neuf] secondhand *ou* used item ▪ **le marché de l'~** the secondhand market ▮ [affaire] bargain ▪ **pour ce prix-là, c'est une ~!** it's a (real) bargain at that price!
◆ **à l'occasion** *loc adv* **1.** [un de ces jours] one of these days **2.** [éventuellement] should the opportunity arise ▪ **à l'~, passez nous voir** drop by some time *ou* if you get the chance.

◆ **à l'occasion de** *loc prép* on the occasion of, upon.
◆ **d'occasion** <> *loc adj* **1.** [non neuf] secondhand ■ **voiture d'~** secondhand *ou* used car **2.** [improvisé] : **des amours d'~** chance *ou* casual (love) affairs.
<> *loc adv* [acheter, vendre] secondhand *(adv)* ■ **j'ai fini par le trouver d'~** in the end I found a secondhand one.

occasionnel, elle [ɔkazjɔnɛl] *adj* **1.** [irrégulier] casual, occasional **2.** [fortuit] chance *(avant n)* ■ **rencontre ~le** chance meeting **3.** PHILOS : **cause ~le** occasional cause.

occasionnellement [ɔkazjɔnɛlmɑ̃] *adv* occasionally, every now and then, from time to time.

occasionner [3] [ɔkazjɔne] *vt* [causer] to cause, to bring about *(sép)*, to occasion *sout* ■ **~ des ennuis à qqn** to cause trouble for sb, to get sb into trouble.

occident [ɔksidɑ̃] *nm* **1.** GÉOGR west **2.** POLIT : **l'Occident** the West, the Occident *sout*.

occidental, e, aux [ɔksidɑ̃tal, o] *adj* **1.** GÉOGR west, western ■ **côte ~e** west coast ■ **Europe ~e** Western Europe **2.** POLIT Western, Occidental *sout* ■ **les pays occidentaux, le monde ~** Western countries, the West.
◆ **Occidental, e, aux** *nm, f* POLIT Westerner, Occidental *sout*.
◆ **à l'occidentale** *loc adv* : **vivre à l'~e** to live like a Westerner ■ **s'habiller à l'~e** to wear Western-style clothes.

occidentaliser [3] [ɔksidɑ̃talize] *vt* to westernize, to occidentalize *sout*.
◆ **s'occidentaliser** *vpi* to become westernized.

occipital, e, aux [ɔksipital, o] *adj* occipital.
◆ **occipital, aux** *nm* occipital (bone).

occiput [ɔksipyt] *nm* occiput.

occire [ɔksir] *vt arch* to slay.

occitan, e [ɔksitɑ̃, an] *adj* of Occitanie.
◆ **Occitan, e** *nm, f inhabitant of or person from Occitanie.*
◆ **occitan** *nm* LING langue d'oc *(language spoken in parts of Southern France)*.

Occitanie [ɔksitani] *npr f* : **(l')~** *area of Southern France in which langue d'oc is spoken.*

occlure [96] [ɔklyr] *vt* to occlude.

occlusif, ive [ɔklyzif, iv] *adj* occlusive.

occlusion [ɔklyzjɔ̃] *nf* CHIM, LING & MÉD occlusion ■ **~ intestinale** ileus *spéc*, intestinal obstruction.

occultation [ɔkyltasjɔ̃] *nf* **1.** ASTRON occultation **2.** RAIL occulting *(U)* **3.** *litt* [obscurcissement] obscuring, concealment, hiding.

occulte [ɔkylt] *adj* **1.** [surnaturel] occult **2.** [secret] occult, secret ■ **financements ~s** secret *ou* mystery funding ■ **fonds** *ou* **réserves ~s** slush funds.

occulter [3] [ɔkylte] *vt* **1.** ASTRON & RAIL to occult **2.** [ville, région] to black out *(sép)*, to black out TV programmes in **3.** [réalité, problème] to cover up *(sép)*, to hush up *(sép)*, to gloss over *(insép)* ■ [sentiment, émotion] to deny ■ **votre récit occulte un détail essentiel** your story glosses over *ou* overlooks an essential detail.

occultisme [ɔkyltism] *nm* occultism.

occupant, e [ɔkypɑ̃, ɑ̃t] <> *adj* occupying.
<> *nm, f* **1.** [d'un véhicule] occupant ■ [d'un lieu] occupant, occupier **2.** MIL occupier, occupying force ■ **collaborer avec l'~** to collaborate with the occupying forces.

occupation [ɔkypasjɔ̃] *nf* **1.** [professionnelle] occupation, job ■ [de loisirs] occupation **2.** [d'un endroit] : **l'~ de l'université par les étudiants** the student sit-in at the university ▶ **~ des lieux** occupancy **3.** ADMIN : **~ des sols** land use **4.** MIL occupation ■ **les troupes d'~** the occupying troops **5.** HIST : **l'Occupation** the (German) Occupation (of France) ■ **la vie sous l'Occupation** life in occupied France.

> ***L'OCCUPATION***
>
> The military occupation of part of France after the French-German armistice on 22nd June 1940, which spread throughout to the whole country in 1942. Under the terms of the armistice, France had to contribute financially to the upkeep of German troops in France and provide labour for German factories. Thousands of French Jews were deported during this period by the Vichy government.

occupationnel, elle [ɔkypasjɔnɛl] *adj* MÉD occupational.

occupé, e [ɔkype] *adj* **1.** [non disponible - ligne de téléphone] engaged *UK*, busy *US* ; [- toilettes] engaged *UK*, occupied *US* ■ **ça sonne ~** *fam* I'm getting the engaged tone *UK*, the line is busy *US* ■ **ces places sont ~es** these seats are taken ■ **maison vendue ~e** house sold with sitting tenant **2.** MIL & POLIT occupied **3.** [personne] busy ■ **j'ai des journées très ~es** my days are full.

occuper [3] [ɔkype] *vt* **1.** [donner une activité à] : **~ qqn** to keep sb busy *ou* occupied ■ **cela l'occupe beaucoup** it takes up a lot of his time ■ **la question qui nous occupe** the matter in hand ■ *(en usage absolu)* **ça occupe!** it keeps me busy
2. [envahir] to occupy, to take over *(sép)* ■ **les rebelles occupent tout le Nord** the rebels have occupied the north of the country ■ **les grévistes occupent les bureaux** the strikers have occupied the offices ▶ **~ le terrain** MIL & *fig* to have the field
3. [remplir - un espace, une durée] to take up *(insép)* ■ **le bar occupe le fond de la pièce/trop de place** the bar stands at the back of the room/takes up too much space ▶ **~ le devant de la scène** to be in the foreground
4. [consacrer] to spend ■ **j'occupe mes loisirs à lire** I spend my free time reading
5. [habiter] to occupy, to live (in)
6. [détenir - poste, place] to hold, to occupy ■ **il occupe un poste important** he holds an important position ■ **Liverpool occupe la seconde place du championnat** Liverpool are (lying) second in the league table.
◆ **s'occuper** *vp (emploi réfléchi)* to keep o.s. busy *ou* occupied, to occupy o.s. ■ **à quoi s'occupent les citadins au mois d'août?** how do city dwellers spend their time in August? ■ **il va falloir qu'elle s'occupe** she'll have to find something to keep her occupied ■ **tu n'as donc pas de quoi t'~?** haven't you got something to be getting on with? ■ **c'est juste histoire de m'~** *fam* it's just for something to do.
◆ **s'occuper de** *vp+prép* **1.** [avoir pour responsabilité ou tâche] to deal with, to be in charge of, to take care of ■ **qui s'occupe de votre dossier?** who's dealing with *ou* handling your file? ■ **je m'occupe de jeunes délinquants** I'm in charge of young offenders ■ **je m'en occuperai plus tard** I'll see to *ou* attend to it later ■ **je m'en occuperai dès demain matin** I'll see to *ou* attend to *ou* take care of it first thing in the morning ■ **t'es-tu occupé des réservations/de ton inscription?** did you see about the reservations/registering for your course? ▶ **occupe-toi de tes affaires** *ou* **oignons** *fam* mind your own business ■ **t'occupe!** *fam* none of your business!, don't be so nosy!
2. [entourer de soins] to look after, to care for ■ **s'~ d'un malade** to care for a patient ■ **s'~ d'un bébé** to look after a baby ■ **peux-tu t'~ des invités pendant que je me prépare?** would you look after *ou* see to the guests while I get ready? ■ **on s'occupe de vous, Madame?** are you being served, Madam? ■ **il ne s'occupe pas assez d'elle** he doesn't pay her enough attention.

occurrence [ɔkyrɑ̃s] *nf* **1.** *sout* [cas] case ■ **en pareille ~, il faut appeler la police** in such a case *ou* in such circumstances, the police must be called **2.** LING token, occurrence.
◆ **en l'occurrence** *loc adv* as it happens ■ **il voulait s'en prendre à quelqu'un, en l'~ ce fut moi** he wanted to take it out on somebody, and it happened to be me *ou* and as it happened, it was me.

OCDE *(abr de* **Organisation de coopération et de développement économiques**) *npr f* OECD.

océan [ɔseɑ̃] *nm* **1.** GÉOGR ocean ■ **l'~ Arctique/Atlantique/Antarctique/Indien/Pacifique** the Arctic/Atlantic/Antarctic/Indian/Pacific Ocean **2.** *fig* **un ~ de larmes** floods of tears.

océanaute [ɔseanot] *nmf* oceanaut.

océane [ɔsean] *adj f* CULIN [salade, sauce] seafood *(modif)*.

◆ **Océane** *npr f*: **l'Océane** [autoroute] *the Paris-Nantes motorway.*

Océanie [ɔseani] *npr f*: **(l')~** Oceania, the (Central and) South Pacific.

océanien, enne [ɔseanjɛ̃, ɛn] *adj* Oceanian, Oceanic.
◆ **Océanien, enne** *nm, f* Oceanian.

océanique [ɔseanik] *adj* oceanic.

océanographe [ɔseanɔgraf] *nmf* oceanographer.

océanographie [ɔseanɔgrafi] *nf* oceanography.

océanologie [ɔseanɔlɔʒi] *nf* oceanology.

océanologue [ɔseanɔlɔg] *nmf* oceanologist.

ocelot [ɔslo] *nm* **1.** [animal] ocelot **2.** [fourrure] ocelot (fur).

ocre [ɔkr] ◇ *nf* ochre ▪ **~ rouge** ruddle.
◇ *adj inv* & *nm* ochre.

octaèdre [ɔktaɛdr] ◇ *adj* octahedral.
◇ *nm* octahedron.

octane [ɔktan] *nm* octane.

octant [ɔktɑ̃] *nm* GÉOM & NAUT octant.

octante [ɔktɑ̃t] *dét* [dialecte] eighty.

octave [ɔktav] *nf* ESCRIME, MUS & RELIG octave ▪ **à l'~ inférieure/supérieure** one octave lower/higher.

octet [ɔktɛ] *nm* **1.** INFORM octet, (eight-bit) byte **2.** CHIM octet.

octobre [ɔktɔbr] *nm* October, *voir aussi* **mars**.

octogénaire [ɔktɔʒenɛr] *adj* & *nmf* octogenarian.

octogonal, e, aux [ɔktɔgɔnal, o] *adj* octagonal.

octogone [ɔktɔgɔn] ◇ *adj* octagonal.
◇ *nm* octagon.

octosyllabe [ɔktɔsilab] ◇ *adj* octosyllabic.
◇ *nm* octosyllable.

octroi [ɔktrwa] *nm* **1.** [don] granting, bestowing **2.** HIST [taxe, administration] : **l'~** the octroi.

octroyer [13] [ɔktrwaje] *vt* [accorder] to grant ▪ **~ qqch à** [faveur] to grant sthg to ; [permission, congé] to grant sthg to, to give to ▪ **le patron a octroyé un congé à tout le personnel** the boss granted *ou* gave a day off to the entire staff.
◆ **s'octroyer** *vpt*: **s'~ un congé** to take a day off *(without permission)* ▪ **s'~ le droit de faire qqch** to assume the right to do sthg.

octuor [ɔktɥɔr] *nm* octet.

oculaire [ɔkylɛr] ◇ *adj* ocular.
◇ *nm* **1.** OPT ocular, eyepiece **2.** PHOTO viewfinder.

oculiste [ɔkylist] *nmf* oculist.

odalisque [ɔdalisk] *nf* **1.** HIST odalisque **2.** *litt* [courtisane] courtesan, odalisque *litt.*

ode [ɔd] *nf* ode.

odeur [ɔdœr] *nf* **1.** [de nourriture] smell, odour ▪ [de fleur, de parfum] smell, fragrance, scent ▪ **une forte ~ de brûlé/chocolat venait de la cuisine** a strong smell of burning/chocolate was coming from the kitchen ▪ **chasser les mauvaises ~s** to get rid of (nasty *ou* unpleasant) smells ▪ **sans ~** odourless ▪ **ce médicament a une mauvaise ~** this medicine smells bad *ou* has a bad smell ▪ **ça n'a pas d'~** it has no smell, it doesn't smell **2.** RELIG : **en ~ de sainteté : mourir en ~ de sainteté** to die in the odour of sanctity ▪ **ne pas être en ~ de sainteté** *fig* to be out of favour.

odieusement [ɔdjøzmɑ̃] *adv* odiously, obnoxiously.

odieux, euse [ɔdjø, øz] *adj* **1.** [atroce - comportement] obnoxious ▪ **crime ~** heinous crime **2.** [désagréable - personne] hateful, obnoxious ▪ **l'examinateur a été ~ avec moi** the examiner was obnoxious *ou* vile to me ▪ **elle a deux enfants ~** she has two unbearable *ou* obnoxious children.

odontologie [ɔdɔ̃tɔlɔʒi] *nf* odontology.

odorant, e [ɔdɔrɑ̃, ɑ̃t] *adj* **1.** [qui a une odeur] odorous **2.** *sout* [parfumé] fragrant, sweet-smelling ▪ **leur jardin était lumineux et ~** their garden was bright and fragrant.

odorat [ɔdɔra] *nm* (sense of) smell ▪ **avoir l'~ développé** to have a keen sense of smell.

odoriférant, e [ɔdɔriferɑ̃, ɑ̃t] *adj litt* [parfumé] sweet-smelling, fragrant, odoriferous *litt.*

odoriser [3] [ɔdɔrize] *vt* [papier, emballage] to scent ▪ [gaz] to odorize ▪ [spectacle] to enhance with perfumes *ou* fragrances.

odyssée [ɔdise] *nf* odyssey ➤ **'l'Odyssée'** *Homère* 'The Odyssey'.

OEA (*abr de* **Organisation des États américains**) *npr f* OAS.

OECE (*abr de* **Organisation européenne de coopération économique**) *npr f* OEEC.

œcuménique [ekymenik] *adj* ecumenical.

œcuménisme [ekymenism] *nm* ecumenicalism, ecumenicism.

œcuméniste [ekymenist] ◇ *adj* ecumenic, ecumenical.
◇ *nm, f* ecumenist.

œdème [edɛm] *nm* oedema ▪ **~ aigu du poumon** pulmonary oedema.

œdipe [edip] *nm* Oedipus complex.

Œdipe [edip] *npr* Oedipus ▪ **'~ roi'** *Sophocle* 'Oedipus Rex'.

œdipien, enne [edipjɛ̃, ɛn] *adj* oedipal, oedipean.

œil [œj] (*pl* **yeux** [jø] *ou pl* **œils**) *nm* **1.** ANAT eye ▪ **j'ai le soleil dans les yeux** the sun's in *ou* I've got the sun in my eyes ▪ **avoir les yeux verts/marron** to have green/brown eyes ▪ **elle a des yeux de biche** she's got doe eyes ▪ **il ne voit plus que d'un ~** he can only see with one eye now ▪ **se faire les yeux** to make up one's eyes ▪ **je l'ai vu, de mes yeux vu, je l'ai vu de mes propres yeux** I saw it with my own eyes ▪ **faire** *ou* **ouvrir des yeux ronds** to stare wide-eyed ➤ **~ artificiel/de verre** artificial/glass eye ▪ **l'~ intérieur** *litt* the inner eye ▪ **mauvais ~** evil eye ▪ **jeter le mauvais ~ à qqn** to give sb the evil eye ▪ **généreux, mon ~!** generous, my foot! ▪ **attention les yeux!** *fam* get an eyeful of that! ▪ **avoir les yeux battus** to have (dark) rings *ou* bags under one's eyes ▪ **avoir de petits yeux** *pr* to have small eyes ; *fig* to look (all) puffy-eyed *ou* puffy round the eyes ▪ **faire qqch les yeux fermés** *pr* & *fig* to do sthg with one's eyes shut *ou* closed ▪ **avoir un ~ poché** *ou* **au beurre noir** *fam* to have a black eye *ou* a shiner *hum* ▪ **elle avait les yeux qui lui sortaient de la tête** her eyes were popping out of her head ▪ **avoir un ~ qui dit zut** *fam ou* **merde**△ **à l'autre** *hum*, **avoir les yeux qui se croisent les bras** *fam hum*, **avoir un ~ à Paris et l'autre à Pontoise** *fam hum* to have a squint, to be cross-eyed, to be boss-eyed *UK* ▪ **il faudrait avoir des yeux derrière la tête!** you'd need (to have) eyes in the back of your head! ▪ **faire les gros yeux à un enfant** to look sternly *ou* reprovingly at a child ▪ **faire qqch pour les beaux yeux de qqn** to do sthg for the love of sb ▪ **tu as les yeux plus grands que le ventre** *fam* [tu es trop gourmand] your eyes are bigger than your belly *ou* your stomach ▪ **tu as eu les yeux plus grands que le ventre** *fam* [tu as été trop ambitieux] you've bitten off more than you can chew ▪ **~ pour ~ (, dent pour dent)** *bible allus* an eye for an eye (and a tooth for a tooth) ▪ **ils ont des yeux et ils ne voient pas** *bible allus* eyes have they but they see not
2. [vision] sight, eyesight ▪ **avoir de bons yeux** to have good eyesight ▪ **avoir de mauvais yeux** to have bad *ou* poor eyesight ➤ **avoir des yeux de lynx** to be eagle-eyed ▪ **il a des yeux de chat** he can see like a cat in the dark
3. [regard] : **ne me fais pas ces yeux-là!** don't look *ou* stare at me like that! ▪ **les yeux dans les yeux** [tendrement] looking into each other's eyes ; [avec franchise] looking each other straight in the eye ▪ **chercher qqn des yeux** to look around for sb ▪ **jeter les yeux sur qqch** to cast a glance at sthg ▪ **jeter un ~ à** to have a quick look at ▪ **lever les yeux sur qqch/qqn** to look up at sthg/sb ▪ **sans lever les yeux de son livre** without looking up *ou* raising her eyes from her book ▪ **lever les yeux au ciel** [pour regarder] to look up at the sky ; [par exaspération] to raise one's eyes heavenwards ▪ **poser un ~ sur** to have a look at

■ **elle posait sur tout un ~ curieux** she was curious about everything ■ **devant les yeux de** before (the eyes of) ■ **les clefs sont devant tes yeux** the keys are right in front of you ■ **sous les yeux de, sous l'~ de** *litt* under the eye *ou* gaze of ■ **sous l'~ amusé/jaloux de son frère** under the amused/jealous gaze of her brother ■ **il l'a volé sous nos yeux** he stole it from under our very eyes ■ **j'ai votre dossier sous les yeux** I've got your file right here in front of me *ou* before me ■ **à l'abri des yeux indiscrets** away from prying eyes ▸ **il n'avait d'yeux que pour elle** he only had eyes for her
4. [expression, air] look ■ **elle est arrivée, l'~ méchant** *ou* **mauvais** she arrived, with a nasty look on her face *ou* looking like trouble ■ **il m'a regardé d'un ~ noir/furieux** he gave me a black/furious look ▸ **faire de l'~ à qqn** *fam* [pour aguicher] to give sb the eye, to make eyes at sb ; [en signe de connivence] to wink knowingly at sb ■ **faire les yeux doux** *ou* **des yeux de velours à qqn** to make sheep's eyes at sb
5. [vigilance] : **rien n'échappait à l'~ du professeur** nothing escaped the teacher's notice ▸ **avoir l'~** to be vigilant *ou* watchful ■ **aie l'~!** be on the lookout! ■ **il faut avoir l'~ à tout avec les enfants** you've got to keep an eye on everything when children are around ■ **il a l'~ du maître** [rien ne lui échappe] he doesn't miss a thing ■ **avoir l'~ sur qqn, avoir** *ou* **tenir qqn à l'~** to keep an eye *ou* a close watch on sb ■ **toi, je t'ai à l'~!** I've got my eye on you! ■ **ils étaient tout yeux et tout oreilles** they were all eyes and ears
6. [état d'esprit, avis] : **voir qqch d'un bon/mauvais ~** to look favourably/unfavourably upon sthg ■ **considérer** *ou* **voir qqch d'un ~ critique** to look critically at sthg ■ **voir les choses du même ~ que qqn** to see eye to eye with sb ■ **il voit avec les yeux de la foi/de l'amour** he sees things through the eyes of a believer/of love ■ **aux yeux de tous, il passait pour fou** he was regarded by everyone as being a madman ■ **ça n'a aucun intérêt à mes yeux** it's of no interest to me ■ **aux yeux de la loi** in the eyes of the law
7. [trou - dans une porte] Judas hole ; [- au théâtre] peep hole ; [- d'une aiguille, d'un marteau] eye ■ NAUT [d'un filin] grommet, eye ■ MÉTÉOR [d'un cyclone] eye, centre.
◆ **yeux** *nmpl* **1.** *fam hum* [lunettes] glasses, specs *UK*
2. CULIN : **les yeux du bouillon** the fat *(floating on the surface of the stock).*
◆ **à l'œil** *loc adv fam* (for) free, for nothing, gratis ■ **j'ai eu deux tickets à l'~** I got two tickets gratis *ou* (for) free *ou* on the house.

œil-de-bœuf [œjdəbœf] (*pl* **œils-de-bœuf**) *nm* [oculus] oculus ■ [lucarne] bull's eye.

œil-de-perdrix [œjdəpɛrdri] (*pl* **œils-de-perdrix**) *nm* **1.** ANAT (soft) corn **2.** [du bois] small knot **3.** ŒNOL œil-de-perdrix.

œil-de-tigre [œjdətigr] (*pl* **œils-de-tigre**) *nm* tigereye, tiger's eye.

œillade [œjad] *nf* wink, oeillade *litt* ■ **jeter** *ou* **lancer des ~s à qqn** to give sb the (glad) eye ■ **une ~ assassine** *hum* a provocative wink.

œillère [œjɛr] *nf* **1.** [de cheval] blinker *UK*, blinder *US* ■ **avoir des ~s** *fig* to be blinkered, to have a blinkered view of things **2.** [coupelle] eyebath.

œillet [œjɛ] *nm* **1.** BOT [plante] pink ■ [fleur] carnation ■ **~ des fleuristes** carnation ■ **~ d'Inde** African marigold ■ **~ mignardise** wild pink ■ **~ de poète** sweet william **2.** [perforation] eyelet hole **3.** [anneau - de papier gommé] (index) reinforcer ; [- de métal] eyelet, grommet.

œilleton [œjtɔ̃] *nm* **1.** BOT sucker **2.** OPT eyepiece shade **3.** [d'une porte] spyhole.

œnologie [ønɔlɔʒi] *nf* oenology ■ **un stage d'~** a wine-tasting course.

œnologue [ønlɔg] *nmf* oenologist.

œsophage [øzɔfaʒ] *nm* oesophagus.

œstrogène [østrɔʒɛn] *nm* oestrogen.

œuf [œf] (*pl* **œufs** [ø]) *nm* **1.** CULIN egg ■ **monter des ~s en neige** to beat egg whites until they form peaks ■ **~ du jour** new-laid egg ▸ **~ sur le plat** *ou* **au plat** *ou* **(au) miroir** fried egg ■ **~ en chocolat** chocolate egg ■ **~ (à la) coque** boiled egg ■ **~ dur** hard-boiled egg ■ **~ en gelée** egg in aspic ■ **~ mayonnaise** egg mayonnaise ■ **~ mollet** soft-boiled egg ■ **~ de Pâques** Easter egg ■ **~s brouillés/pochés** scrambled/poached eggs ■ **~s en neige** [mets] floating islands ; [préparation] beaten egg whites ■ **sortir de l'~** to be still wet behind the ears ■ **écraser** *ou* **étouffer** *ou* **tuer qqch dans l'~** to nip sthg in the bud ■ **c'est comme l'histoire de l'~ et de la poule** it's a chicken and egg situation ■ **c'est comme l' ~ de Christophe Colomb, il fallait y penser** it's easy when you know how ■ **il ne faut pas mettre tous ses ~s dans le même panier** *prov* never put all your eggs in one basket *prov* **2.** *fam* [imbécile] great ninny, oaf, blockhead ■ **tête d'~!** you nincompoop! **3.** BIOL (egg) cell, egg ■ ZOOL [d'insecte, de poisson] egg ■ [de homard] berry ■ **~s de lump** lumpfish eggs *ou* roe ■ **~s de poisson** ZOOL spawn ; CULIN fish roe **4.** COUT : **~ à repriser** darning egg **5.** [télécabine] cable car **6.** SPORT egg ■ **faire l'~** to (go into a) tuck.

œuvre[1] [œvr] *nm* **1.** ARCHIT & CONSTR : **mesure dans/hors ~** inside/outside measurement ▸ **gros ~** carcass, fabric ■ **le gros ~ est enfin terminé** the main building work is finished at last **2.** ART : **son ~ gravé et son ~ peint** his paintings and his etchings **3.** [en alchimie] : **le Grand Œuvre** the Great Work, the Magnum Opus.

œuvre[2] [œvr] *nf* **1.** [travail] work ■ **~ de longue haleine** long-term undertaking ■ **le troisième but a été l'~ de Bergova** FOOTBALL the third goal was the work of Bergova ■ **elle a fait ~ durable/utile** she's done a lasting/useful piece of work ■ **la vieillesse a fait son ~** old age has taken its toll *ou* done its work ■ **mettre qqch en ~** to bring sthg into play ■ **mettre tout en ~ pour que** to do everything in one's power to ensure that ■ **nous avons mis tous les moyens en ~ pour juguler l'incendie** we did everything we could to bring the fire under control ■ **elle a mis tout en ~ pour être sélectionnée** she pulled out all the stops in order to get selected ▸ **~ de chair** *litt* carnal knowledge ■ **~ maîtresse** magnum opus ■ **faire ~ de rénovateur** to act as a renovator **2.** [production artistique - unique] work ; [- ensemble de réalisations] works ■ **toute son ~** the whole of her works ■ **couronné pour l'ensemble de son ~** rewarded for his overall achievement ▸ **~ d'art** work of art ■ **~s choisies/complètes de Molière** selected/complete works of Molière ■ **~ de jeunesse** early work **3.** [charité] : **~ (de bienfaisance)** charity, charitable organization ■ **je fais la collecte pour une ~** I'm collecting for charity ■ **(bonnes) ~s** charity.
◆ **œuvres** *nfpl* ADMIN : **~s sociales** community service.
◆ **à l'œuvre** *loc adv* at work ■ **être à l'~** to be working *ou* at work ■ **se mettre à l'~** to get down to *ou* to start work ■ **voir qqn à l'~** to see sb at work.

œuvrer [5] [œvre] *vi sout* to work, to strive ■ **nous voulons la paix et nous allons ~ pour cela** we want peace and we will do our utmost to achieve it.

OFCE (*abr de* **Observatoire français des conjonctures économiques**) *npr m economic research institute.*

off [ɔf] *adj inv* **1.** CINÉ offscreen **2.** [théâtre, spectacle, festival] fringe *(modif).*

offensant, e [ɔfɑ̃sɑ̃, ɑ̃t] *adj* offensive.

offense [ɔfɑ̃s] *nf* **1.** [affront] insult ■ **faire ~ à** to offend, to give offence to ■ **soit dit sans ~, tu n'es plus tout jeune non plus** no offence meant, but you're not that young either ■ **il n'y a pas d'~** *fam* no offence taken **2.** RELIG trespass, transgression **3.** DR : **~ à la cour** contempt of Court.

offensé, e [ɔfɑ̃se] ◇ *adj* offended, insulted ■ **air ~** offended *ou* outraged look.
◇ *nm, f sout* offended *ou* injured party.

offenser [3] [ɔfɑ̃se] *vt* **1.** [blesser] to offend, to give offence to ■ **soit dit sans (vouloir) vous ~, votre fils n'est pas un ange** without wishing to offend you, your son is no angel ■ **~ la mémoire de qqn** *sout* to offend sb's memory **2.** [enfreindre] to violate ■ **~ un principe** to fly in the face of a principle ■ **~ Dieu** RELIG to offend God, to trespass against God.
◆ **s'offenser** *vpi sout* [se vexer] to take offence ■ **s'~ de la moindre critique** to take exception to the slightest criticism.

offenseur [ɔfɑ̃sœr] *nm sout* offender.

offensif, ive [ɔfɑ̃sif, iv] *adj* offensive ▪ **l'équipe a adopté un jeu très ~** the team has opted to play an attacking game ▶ **arme/guerre offensive** offensive weapon/war.
◆ **offensive** *nf* MIL & *fig* offensive ▪ **passer à/prendre l'offensive** to go on/to take the offensive ▪ **mener une offensive** to carry out *ou* to conduct an offensive ▪ **offensive de l'hiver** *fig* onslaught of winter ▶ **offensive de paix** POLIT peace offensive.

offert, e [ɔfɛr, ɛrt] *pp* ▷ **offrir**.

offertoire [ɔfɛrtwar] *nm* offertory.

office [ɔfis] ◇ *nm* **1.** [gén - HIST] office ▪ **dans son ~ de gouvernante** in her position as governess ▪ **le signal d'alarme n'a pas rempli son ~** the alarm didn't (fulfil its) function ▪ **faire ~ de : qu'est-ce qui peut faire ~ de pièce d'identité?** what could serve as proof of identity? ▪ **pendant le voyage, j'ai dû faire ~ de cuisinier** I had to act as cook during the trip ▶ **~ ministériel** ministerial office **2.** RELIG service ▪ **aller à/manquer l'~** to go to/to miss the church service ▶ **l'~ divin** the Divine Office ▪ **l'~ des morts** the office for the dead ▪ **~ du soir** evensong **3.** [agence] agency, bureau ▪ **~ du tourisme espagnol** Spanish tourist office *ou* bureau ▪ **l'Office national des forêts** the French Forestry commission **4.** COMM [dans l'édition] : **exemplaire d'~** copy sent on sale or return.
◇ *nm vieilli nf* [d'une cuisine] pantry ▪ [d'un hôtel, d'une grande maison] kitchen, kitchens.
◆ **offices** *nmpl* : **grâce aux bons ~s de M. Prat/du gouvernement allemand** thanks to Mr. Prat's good offices/to the good offices of the German government.
◆ **d'office** *loc adv* automatically ▶ **avocat commis d'~** (officially) appointed lawyer.

officialisation [ɔfisjalizasjɔ̃] *nf* officialization.

officialiser [3] [ɔfisjalize] *vt* to make official, to officialize.

officiant [ɔfisjɑ̃] ◇ *adj m* officiating.
◇ *nm* officiant.

officiel, elle [ɔfisjɛl] *adj* **1.** [public] official ▪ **langage** *ou* **jargon ~** officialese ▪ **rien de ce que je vous dis là n'est ~** everything I'm telling you is unofficial *ou* off the record ▪ **il a rendu ~le sa décision de démissionner** he made public *ou* he officially announced his decision to resign ▶ **congé ~** official holiday **2.** [réglementaire] formal ▪ **notre rencontre n'avait aucun caractère ~** our meeting took place on an informal *ou* unofficial basis.
◆ **officiel** *nm* **1.** [représentant] official ▪ **les ~s du Parti** the Party officials **2.** PRESSE : **l'Officiel des Spectacles** *weekly entertainments listings guide in Paris.*

officiellement [ɔfisjɛlmɑ̃] *adv* officially ▪ **je dépose plainte ~** I'm making an official complaint.

officier[1] [9] [ɔfisje] *vi* **1.** RELIG to officiate **2.** *fig* & *hum* to preside ▪ **qui officie aux fourneaux ce soir?** who's in charge *ou* presiding in the kitchen tonight?

officier[2] [ɔfisje] *nm* **1.** MIL officer ▪ **~ de marine/de l'armée de terre** naval/army officer ▪ **~ supérieur/général** field/general officer ▪ **~ de liaison** liaison officer ▪ **~ de paix** senior police officer ▪ **~ de service** duty officer ▪ **~ subalterne** junior *UK ou* company *US* officer **2.** [titulaire - d'une fonction, d'une distinction] : **~ de l'Armée du salut** Salvation Army Officer ▪ **~ de l'état civil** ≃ registrar ▪ **~ de police judiciaire** *police officer in the French Criminal Investigation Department* ▪ **~ de la Légion d'honneur** Officer of the Legion of Honour.

officieusement [ɔfisjøzmɑ̃] *adv* unofficially, informally.

officieux, euse [ɔfisjø, øz] *adj* unofficial, informal.

officinal, e, aux [ɔfisinal, o] *adj* [plante] medicinal ▪ [remède] officinal.

officine [ɔfisin] *nf* PHARM dispensary, pharmacy.

offrande [ɔfrɑ̃d] *nf* **1.** RELIG [don] offering ▪ [cérémonie] offertory **2.** [contribution] offering ▪ **verser une ~ à une œuvre** to give to a charity.

offrant [ɔfrɑ̃] *nm* bidder ▪ **vendre qqch au plus ~** to sell sthg to the highest bidder.

offre [ɔfr] *nf* **1.** [proposition] offer ▪ **ils lui ont fait une ~ avantageuse** they made him a worthwhile offer ▪ **faire une ~ à 1 000 euros** to make an offer of 1,000 euros ; [aux enchères] to bid 1,000 euros ▪ **'~ valable jusqu'au 31 mai'** 'offer closes May 31st' ▶ **'~s d'emploi'** 'situations vacant' ▪ **~s de service** offer to help **2.** ÉCON supply ▪ **~ de monnaie/devises** money/currency supply ▪ **l'~ et la demande** supply and demand **3.** FIN : **~ publique d'achat** takeover bid ▪ **~ publique d'échange** acquisition (by exchange of shares) ▪ **~ publique de vente** sales offer *(of shares at a fixed price)* **4.** DR : **~s réelles** payment into court.

offrir [34] [ɔfrir] *vt* **1.** [faire cadeau de] to give ▪ **~ qqch en cadeau à qqn** to give sb sthg as a present ▪ **on lui offrit une médaille** they presented him *ou* he was presented with a medal ▪ **je vous offre un café/un verre?** can I buy you coffee/a drink? ▪ **ils (nous) ont offert le champagne** they treated us to champagne ▪ *(en usage absolu)* **pourriez-vous me faire un paquet-cadeau, c'est pour ~** could you gift-wrap it for me, please, it's a present ▪ **c'est moi qui offre** I'll pay **2.** [donner - choix, explication, hospitalité] to give, to offer ▪ **~ son assistance** *ou* **son aide à qqn** to offer to help sb **3.** [proposer] : **~ son bras à qqn** to offer *ou* to lend sb one's arm ▪ **je lui ai montré mon autoradio, il m'en offre 20 euros** I showed him my car radio, he's offering me 20 euros for it ▪ **elle nous a offert sa maison pour l'été** she offered us her house for the summer **4.** [présenter - spectacle, vue] to offer, to present ▪ **la conversation n'offrait qu'un intérêt limité** the conversation was of only limited interest ▪ **cette solution offre l'avantage d'être équitable** this solution has *ou* presents the advantage of being fair.
◆ **s'offrir** ◇ *vp (emploi réfléchi)* **1.** [sexuellement] to offer *ou* to give o.s. **2.** [proposer ses services] to offer one's services ▪ **s'~ à payer les dégâts** to offer to pay for the damage.
◇ *vp (emploi réciproque)* to give *ou* to buy each other.
◇ *vpi* [se présenter - occasion] : **un seul moyen s'offrait à moi** there was only one course of action open to me ▪ **un panorama exceptionnel s'offre au regard** an amazing view meets your eyes.
◇ *vpt* [se faire cadeau de] to treat o.s. to.

offset [ɔfsɛt] ◇ *adj inv* offset.
◇ *nm inv* offset (process).
◇ *nf inv* offset (printing) machine.

off shore, offshore [ɔfʃɔr] ◇ *adj inv* BANQUE, PETR & SPORT offshore.
◇ *nm inv* INDUST **du pétrole** offshore technology ▪ SPORT [activité] powerboat racing ▪ [bateau] powerboat.

offusquer [3] [ɔfyske] *vt* to offend, to upset, to hurt.
◆ **s'offusquer** *vpi* : **s'~ de** to take offence at, to take umbrage at ▪ **s'~ d'un rien** to be easily offended, to be quick to take offence.

OFPRA (*abr de* **Office français de protection des réfugiés et des apatrides**) *nm government department dealing with refugees and stateless persons.*

ogival, e, aux [ɔʒival, o] *adj* [structure] ogive *(modif)*, ogival ▪ [art, style] gothic.

ogive [ɔʒiv] *nf* **1.** ARCHIT ogive, diagonal rib **2.** MIL & NUCL warhead **3.** GÉOM ogive.

OGM (*abr de* **organisme génétiquement modifié**) *nm inv* GMO.

ogre, ogresse [ɔgr, ɔgrɛs] *nm, f* **1.** [dans les contes] ogre (*f* ogress) **2.** *fam fig* ogre (*f* ogress), monster.

oh [o] ◇ *interj* **1.** [pour indiquer - la surprise, l'admiration, l'indignation] oh ▪ **~~, est-ce que j'aurais deviné juste?** oho, could I be right? **2.** [pour interpeller] hey.
◇ *nm inv* ooh, oh ▪ **pousser des ~ et des ah devant qqch** to ooh and aah at sthg.

ohé [ɔe] *interj* hey ▪ **~! vous, là-bas** hey, you over there!

Ohio [ɔajo] *npr m* : **l'~** Ohio.

ohm [om] *nm* ohm.

OHQ *nm* = **ouvrier hautement qualifié**.

oie [wa] *nf* **1.** ORNITH goose ■ **~ sauvage** wild goose **2.** JEUX : **jeu de l'~** ≃ snakes and ladders **3.** MIL : **pas de l'~** goosestep ■ **défiler** *OU* **marcher au pas de l'~** to goosestep **4.** *péj* [personne] silly goose ■ **c'est une ~ blanche** she's (wide-eyed and) innocent.

oignon [ɔɲɔ̃] *nm* **1.** CULIN onion ■ **~ blanc** spring onion ■ **petits ~s** pickling onions ■ **un week-end aux petits ~s** *fam* a great *OU* first-rate weekend ■ **soigner qqn aux petits ~s** to look after sb really well ■ **être soigné aux petits ~s** to get first-class attention ■ **ce ne sont pas tes ~s** *fam* that's none of your business ■ **mêle-toi** *OU* **occupe-toi de tes ~s** *fam* mind your own business **2.** HORT [bulbe] bulb **3.** MÉD bunion **4.** [montre] fob watch.

oïl [ɔjl] ▷ **langue.**

oindre [82] [wɛ̃dr] *vt* **1.** [enduire] to rub with oil **2.** RELIG to anoint.

oiseau, x [wazo] *nm* **1.** ZOOL bird ■ **~ migrateur** migratory bird ■ **~ de proie** bird of prey ■ **~ des îles** *pr* tropical bird ; *fig* exotic creature ■ **~ de mauvais augure** *OU* **de malheur** bird of ill omen ■ **~ de passage** bird of passage ■ **~ rare : il est parfait pour cet emploi, tu as vraiment déniché l'~ rare** he's perfect for this job, you've found a rare bird there ■ **être comme l'~ sur la branche** to be in a very precarious situation ■ **le petit ~ va sortir!** [photo] watch the birdie! ■ **petit à petit, l'~ fait son nid** *prov* every little helps ■ **'l'Oiseau de feu'** ***Stravinski*** 'The Firebird' **2.** *fam* [individu douteux] customer ■ **quand la police arriva, l'~ s'était envolé** by the time the police arrived the bird had flown **3.** CONSTR [auge de maçon] hod.

oiseau-lyre [wazolir] (*pl* **oiseaux-lyres**) *nm* lyrebird.

oiseau-mouche [wazomuʃ] (*pl* **oiseaux-mouches**) *nm* hummingbird.

oiseleur [wazlœr] *nm* bird catcher.

oiselier, ère [wazəlje, ɛr] *nm, f* bird-seller.

oisellerie [wazɛlri] *nf* **1.** [boutique] bird shop **2.** [commerce] birdselling.

oiseux, euse [wazø, øz] *adj* **1.** [futile] futile ■ **des rêveries oiseuses** daydreaming *(U)* **2.** [stérile] irrelevant, pointless.

oisif, ive [wazif, iv] ◇ *adj* **1.** [personne, vie] idle **2.** DR [biens] unproductive.
◇ *nm, f* idler ■ **les ~s** the idle.

oisillon [wazijɔ̃] *nm* fledgling.

oisive [waziv] *f* ▷ **oisif.**

oisivement [wazivmɑ̃] *adv* idly ■ **vivre ~** to live in idleness.

oisiveté [wazivte] *nf* idleness ■ **vivre dans l'~** to live in idleness ▶ **l'~ est la mère de tous les vices** *prov* the devil finds work for idle hands *prov.*

oison [wazɔ̃] *nm* ZOOL gosling.

OIT (*abr de* **Organisation internationale du travail**) *npr f* ILO.

OK [ɔke] *interj* OK, okay ■ **~! pour moi c'est bon!** okay! that's fine by me!

okapi [ɔkapi] *nm* okapi.

Oklahoma [ɔklaɔma] *npr m* : **l'~** Oklahoma.

ola [ɔla] *nf* Mexican wave *UK*, wave *US*.

oléagineux, euse [ɔleaʒinø, øz] *adj* oil-producing, oleaginous *spéc*.
◆ **oléagineux** *nm* oil-producing *OU* oleaginous *spéc* plant.

oléiculteur, trice [ɔleikyltœr, tris] *nm, f* **1.** [cultivateur] olive grower **2.** [fabricant d'huile - d'olive] olive oil manufacturer ; [- d'autres oléagineux] vegetable oil manufacturer.

oléiculture [ɔleikyltyr] *nf* [culture - des olives] olive growing ; [- des oléagineux] oil-crop growing.

oléifère [ɔleifɛr] *adj* oil-producing, oleiferous *spéc*.

oléoduc [ɔleɔdyk] *nm* (oil) pipeline.

olé olé [ɔleɔle] *adj inv fam* **être un peu ~** [de mœurs légères] to be a bit loose ; [peu respectueux] to be a bit too laid back ■ **cette blague est un peu ~** that joke is a bit risqué.

olfactif, ive [ɔlfaktif, iv] *adj* olfactory.

olfaction [ɔlfaksjɔ̃] *nf* olfaction.

olibrius [ɔlibrijys] *nm* oddball.

oligarchie [ɔligarʃi] *nf* oligarchy.

oligarchique [ɔligarʃik] *adj* oligarchic, oligarchical.

oligarque [ɔligark] *nm* oligarch.

oligo-élément [ɔligɔelemɑ̃] (*pl* **oligo-éléments**) *nm* trace element.

oligopole [ɔligɔpɔl] *nm* oligopoly.

oligothérapie [ɔligɔterapi] *nf alternative medicine using trace elements.*

olivaie [ɔlivɛ] *nf* olive grove.

olivâtre [ɔlivatr] *adj* olive-greenish.

olive [ɔliv] ◇ *nf* **1.** BOT olive ■ **~ noire/verte** black/green olive **2.** ÉLECTR switch **3.** ZOOL olive (shell) **4.** [bouton de vêtement] (olive-shaped) button.
◇ *adj inv* [couleur] : **(vert) ~** olive, olive-green.
◆ **olives** *nfpl* ARCHIT olive *OU* bead moulding.

oliveraie [ɔlivrɛ] = **olivaie.**

olivette [ɔlivɛt] *nf* **1.** [tomate] plum tomato **2.** [raisin] (olive-shaped) grape.

olivier [ɔlivje] *nm* **1.** BOT olive tree **2.** [bois] olive (wood).

olographe [ɔlɔgraf] *adj* holograph.

OLP (*abr de* **Organisation de libération de la Palestine**) *npr f* PLO.

olympe [ɔlɛ̃p] *nm litt* Olympus.

Olympe [ɔlɛ̃p] *npr m* GÉOGR & MYTHOL : **l'~** Olympus ■ **le mont ~** Mount Olympus.

olympiade [ɔlɛ̃pjad] *nf* **1.** [événement] Olympic Games ■ **à la dernière ~** during the last Olympics **2.** [quatre ans] olympiad.

Olympie [ɔlɛ̃pi] *npr* Olympia.

olympien, enne [ɔlɛ̃pjɛ̃, ɛn] *adj* MYTHOL & *hum* Olympian ■ **un calme ~** an Olympian calm.

olympique [ɔlɛ̃pik] *adj* Olympic ■ **les jeux Olympiques** the Olympic Games, the Olympics.

OM (*abr de* **Olympique de Marseille**) *npr m Marseilles football team.*

Oman [ɔman] *npr* Oman ■ **golfe d'~** Gulf of Oman ■ **le sultanat d'~** the Sultanate of Oman, *voir aussi* **mer.**

ombelle [ɔ̃bɛl] *nf* umbel ■ **en ~** umbellate.

ombellifère [ɔ̃belifɛr] *nf* umbellifer, member of the Umbelliferae.

ombilic [ɔ̃bilik] *nm* **1.** ANAT umbilicus *spéc*, navel **2.** BOT [renflement] hilum ■ [plante] navelwort **3.** MATH umbilical point **4.** ART boss, embossment.

ombilical, e, aux [ɔ̃bilikal, o] *adj* ANAT umbilical.

omble [ɔ̃bl] *nm* : **~ (chevalier)** char.

ombrage [ɔ̃braʒ] *nm* **1.** [ombre] shade **2.** [feuillage] canopy, foliage **3.** *litt* **prendre ~ de** to take offence *OU* umbrage at ■ **porter** *OU* **faire ~ à qqn** to cause offence to sb, to offend sb.

ombragé, e [ɔ̃braʒe] *adj* shady.

ombrager [17] [ɔ̃braʒe] *vt* to shade.

ombrageux, euse [ɔ̃braʒø, øz] *adj* **1.** *sout* [susceptible] touchy, easily offended **2.** [cheval] skittish, nervous, jumpy.

ombre[1] [ɔ̃br] *nm* ZOOL : **~ de rivière** grayling.

ombre[2] [ɔ̃br] *nf* **1.** [pénombre] shade ■ **dans l'~ des sous-bois** in the shadowy undergrowth ▶ **faire de l'~ : le gratte-ciel fait de l'~ à tout le quartier** the skyscraper casts a shadow over the whole area *OU* leaves the whole area in shadow ■ **faire de l'~ à qqn** *pr* to be in sb's light ; *fig* to be in sb's way ■ **pousse-toi, tu me fais de l'~** move, you're in my light ■ **sortir de l'~** *pr* to emerge from the dark *OU* darkness *OU* shadows ; *fig* [artiste] to emerge from obscurity, to come into the public eye **2.** [forme - d'une personne, d'un arbre, d'un mur] shadow ▶ **~ portée** OPT (projected) shadow ■ **il n'est plus que l'~ de lui-même** he's but a shadow of his former self **3.** [trace - de jalousie, de surprise] hint ; [- d'un sourire] hint, shadow ■ **pas l'~ d'un remords/d'une preuve** not a trace of remorse/shred of evidence ■ **cela ne fait pas** *ou* **il n'y a pas l'~ d'un doute** there's not a shadow of a doubt **4.** ART shade, shadow ■ **il y a une ~ au tableau** *fig* there's a fly in the ointment.

◆ **ombres** *nfpl* **1.** THÉÂTRE : **~s chinoises, théâtre d'~s** shadow theatre **2.** ANTIQ shadows, departed souls.

◆ **à l'ombre** *loc adv* **1.** [à l'abri du soleil] in the shade ■ **il fait 30°C à l'~** it's 30 °C in the shade **2.** *fam* [en prison] inside.

◆ **à l'ombre de** *loc prép pr* in the shade of ■ *litt* & *fig* under the protection of.

◆ **dans l'ombre** *loc adv* **1.** [dans la pénombre] in the shade **2.** [dans le secret] : **rester dans l'~** [raison] to remain obscure *ou* unclear ; [personne] to remain unknown ■ **l'enquête n'a rien laissé dans l'~** the enquiry left no stone unturned ■ **ceux qui œuvrent dans l'~ pour la paix** those who work behind the scenes to bring about peace ■ **vivre dans l'~ de qqn** to live in sb's shadow.

◆ **ombre à paupières** *nf* eye shadow.

ombrelle [ɔ̃brɛl] *nf* **1.** [parasol] parasol **2.** [d'une méduse] umbrella.

ombrer [3] [ɔ̃bre] *vt* **1.** ART to shade **2.** *litt* [faire de l'ombre à - suj: arbre, store] to shade ■ [assombrir - suj: couleur] to darken, to shade ■ **un maquillage violet ombrait ses paupières** she was wearing purple eyeshadow.

ombreux, euse [ɔ̃brø, øz] *adj litt* shady.

Ombrie [ɔ̃bri] *npr f* : **l'~** Umbria.

ombrien, enne [ɔ̃brijɛ̃, ɛn] *adj* Umbrian.

oméga [ɔmega] *nm* omega.

omelette [ɔmlɛt] *nf* omelette ■ **~ aux champignons/au fromage/au jambon** mushroom/cheese/ham omelette ■ **~ aux fines herbes** omelette with herbs, omelette (aux) fines herbes ■ **une ~ baveuse** a runny omelette ▶ **~ norvégienne** *ou* **surprise** baked Alaska ■ **on ne fait pas d'~ sans casser des œufs** *prov* you can't make an omelette without breaking eggs *prov.*

omettre [84] [ɔmɛtr] *vt* to omit, to leave out *(sép)* ■ **~ de** to fail *ou* to neglect *ou* to omit to.

OMI (*abr de* **Organisation maritime internationale**) *npr f* IMO.

omis, e [ɔmi, iz] *pp* ⊳ **omettre**.

omission [ɔmisjɔ̃] *nf* **1.** [oubli] omission ■ **l'~ d'un mot** leaving out *ou* omitting a word ■ **j'ai relevé plusieurs ~s dans la liste** I noticed that several things are missing *ou* have been omitted from the list **2.** RELIG omission.

omit *etc v* ⊳ **omettre**.

OMM (*abr de* **Organisation météorologique mondiale**) *npr f* WMO.

omnibus [ɔmnibys] ◇ *nm* **1.** RAIL slow *ou* stopping train *UK*, local (train) *US* **2.** [à chevaux] horse-drawn omnibus.
◇ *adj* : **le train est ~ entre Melun et Sens** the train calls at all stations between Melun and Sens.

omnicolore [ɔmnikɔlɔr] *adj* of all colours.

omnipotence [ɔmnipɔtɑ̃s] *nf* omnipotence ■ **l'~ de l'État** the omnipotence of the state.

omnipotent, e [ɔmnipɔtɑ̃, ɑ̃t] *adj* omnipotent.

omnipraticien, enne [ɔmnipratisjɛ̃, ɛn] ◇ *nm, f* general practitioner.
◇ *adj* : **médecin ~** general practitioner.

omniprésence [ɔmniprezɑ̃s] *nf* omnipresence.

omniprésent, e [ɔmniprezɑ̃, ɑ̃t] *adj* [souci, souvenir] omnipresent ■ [publicité, pollution] ubiquitous ■ **il est ~ dans l'usine** he's everywhere (at once) in the factory.

omniscience [ɔmnisjɑ̃s] *nf sout* omniscience.

omniscient, e [ɔmnisjɑ̃, ɑ̃t] *adj sout* omniscient.

omnisports [ɔmnispɔr] *adj inv* : **rencontre ~** all-round sports event ■ **salle ~** sports centre.

omnivore [ɔmnivɔr] ◇ *adj* omnivorous.
◇ *nm* omnivore.

omoplate [ɔmɔplat] *nf* shoulder blade, scapula *spéc* ■ **il lui avait pointé un fusil entre les ~s** he'd shoved a gun in his back.

OMS (*abr de* **Organisation mondiale de la santé**) *npr f* WHO.

on [ɔ̃] *pron pers (peut être précédé de l'article (l') dans un contexte soutenu)* **1.** [indéterminé] : **on lui a retiré son passeport** they took his passport away (from him), his passport was confiscated ■ **on vit de plus en plus vieux en Europe** people in Europe are living longer and longer
2. [avec une valeur généralisante] you, one *sout* ■ **souvent, on n'a pas le choix** often you don't have any choice, often there's no choice ■ **on n'arrive pas à dormir avec cette chaleur** it's impossible to sleep in this heat ■ **on ne sait jamais (ce qui peut arriver)** you never know *ou* one never knows *sout*(what could happen) ■ **on dirait qu'il va pleuvoir** it looks like rain ■ **on ne croirait pas qu'il est malade** you wouldn't think he was ill
3. [les gens] people, they ■ **on s'était rué sur les derniers billets** there'd been a rush for the last tickets ■ **on dit que la vie là-bas n'est pas chère** they say that the cost of living over there is cheap ■ **on rapporte que...** it is said that...
4. [désignant un nombre indéterminé de personnes] they ■ **en Espagne on dîne plus tard** in Spain they eat later ■ **on m'a dit que vous partiez bientôt** I've been told you're leaving soon ■ **qu'est-ce qu'on en dit chez toi?** what do your folks have to say about it?, what do they have to say about it at your place?
5. [quelqu'un] : **on vous a appelé ce matin** somebody called you *ou* there was a (phone) call for you this morning ■ **est-ce qu'on t'a vu?** did anyone see you? ■ **est-ce qu'on vous sert, Monsieur?** are you being served, Sir?
6. *fam* [nous] we ■ **on était très déçus** we were very disappointed
7. [se substituant à d'autres pronoms personnels] : **ça va, on a compris!** *fam* all right, I've got the message! ■ **dans ce premier chapitre, on a voulu montrer...** in this first chapter, the aim has been to show... ■ **on est bien habillé, aujourd'hui!** *fam* we are dressed-up today, aren't we? ■ **alors, on ne répond pas au téléphone?** *fam* aren't you going to answer the phone? ■ **alors les gars, on cherche la bagarre?** *fam* are you guys looking for a fight? ■ **on a tout ce qu'il faut et on passe son temps à se plaindre!** *fam* he/she has got everything and he/she still complains all the time!
8. [dans des annonces] : **'on cherche un vendeur'** 'salesman wanted *ou* required'.

onagre [ɔnagr] ◇ *nf* BOT evening primrose, oenothera.
◇ *nm* ARM & ZOOL onager.

onanisme [ɔnanism] *nm* onanism.

onc [ɔ̃k] = **oncques**.

once [ɔ̃s] *nf* **1.** [mesure] ounce ■ **il n'a pas une ~ de bon sens** he doesn't have an ounce of common sense **2.** ZOOL ounce, snow leopard.

oncle [ɔ̃kl] *nm* uncle ■ **~ d'Amérique** rich uncle ■ **l'Oncle Sam** Uncle Sam.

oncologiste [ɔ̃kɔlɔʒist], **oncologue** [ɔ̃kɔlɔg] *nmf* oncologist.

oncques [ɔ̃k] *adv arch* never.

onction [ɔ̃ksjɔ̃] *nf* **1.** MÉD unction **2.** *litt* [douceur - attendrissante] sweetness, gentleness ■ *péj* [- hypocrite] unctuousness, unctuosity **3.** RELIG unction.

onctueux, euse [ɔ̃ktɥø, øz] *adj* **1.** [huileux] smooth, unctuous *sout* **2.** CULIN creamy ■ **un fromage ~** a creamy cheese **3.** *litt* [personne] smooth, unctuous *sout.*

onctuosité [ɔ̃ktɥozite] *nf* **1.** [d'un dessert] creaminess ■ [d'une crème] smoothness **2.** TECHNOL lubricating quality, lubricity.

onde [ɔ̃d] *nf* **1.** PHYS wave ■ **~s courtes/moyennes** short/medium wave ■ **~ sonore/lumineuse/radioélectrique** sound/light/radio wave ■ **~ de choc** shock wave ■ **~s hertziennes** Hertzian waves ■ **~s longues, grandes ~s** long wave ■ **l'~ verte** *device which sets all traffic lights along a one-way system to green if drivers keep to the speed limit indicated* **2.** *fig* [vague] wave **3.** *litt* **l'~** [l'eau] the waters, the deep.
◆ **ondes** *nfpl* RADIO : **mettre en ~s** to produce ■ **sur les ~s** on the air.

ondée [ɔ̃de] *nf* shower (of rain).

ondin, e [ɔ̃dɛ̃, in] *nm, f* water sprite, undine *litt.*

on-dit [ɔ̃di] *nm inv* : **je ne me soucie guère des ~** I don't care about what people say ■ **fonder son opinion sur des ~** to base one's opinion on hearsay.

ondoie *etc v* ⊳ **ondoyer.**

ondoiement [ɔ̃dwamɑ̃] *nm* **1.** *litt* [du blé, des cheveux] undulation, swaying motion ■ [d'un ruisseau] undulation **2.** RELIG summary baptism.

ondoyant, e [ɔ̃dwajɑ̃, ɑ̃t] *adj litt* **1.** [blé] undulating, rippling ■ [flamme] dancing, wavering ■ [lumière, ruisseau] undulating **2.** [personne] changeable.

ondoyer [13] [ɔ̃dwaje] ◇ *vi* [champ de blé] to undulate, to ripple ■ [flamme] to dance, to waver ■ [lumière, ruisseau] to ripple.
◇ *vt* RELIG to baptize summarily.

ondulant, e [ɔ̃dylɑ̃, ɑ̃t] *adj* **1.** [terrain] undulating ■ [route, rivière] twisting (and turning), winding ■ [chevelure] flowing ■ [façon de marcher] swaying **2.** MÉD [pouls] irregular.

ondulation [ɔ̃dylasjɔ̃] *nf* **1.** *sout* [de l'eau, du terrain] undulation **2.** [du corps] undulation, swaying *(U)* ■ **les ~s de la danseuse** the undulations *ou* the swaying of the dancer **3.** [des cheveux] wave **4.** *litt* [d'une ligne, d'une mélodie] undulation **5.** ÉLECTRON ripple **6.** TRAV PUB corrugation.

ondulatoire [ɔ̃dylatwar] *adj* **1.** [forme] undulatory **2.** PHYS [mouvement] undulatory, wave *(modif).*

ondulé, e [ɔ̃dyle] *adj* [cheveux] wavy ■ [carton] corrugated.

onduler [3] [ɔ̃dyle] *vi* **1.** [eau, vagues, champs] to ripple, to undulate ■ **la foule ondulait sur la place** in the square, the crowd was swaying **2.** [cheveux] to be wavy **3.** [personne] to sway.

onduleur [ɔ̃dylœr] *nm* ÉLECTR inverter.

onduleux, euse [ɔ̃dylø, øz] *adj litt* **1.** [houleux - flots] swelling **2.** [souple] undulating ■ **elle avait une démarche onduleuse** her body swayed as she walked **3.** [paysage] undulating, rolling ■ [sentier, rivière] twisting, winding.

one-man-show [wanmanʃo] *nm inv* one-man show, solo act.

onéreux, euse [ɔnerø, øz] *adj* costly, expensive.

ONF *npr m* = **Office national des forêts.**

ONG (*abr de* **organisation non gouvernementale**) *nf* NGO.

ongle [ɔ̃gl] *nm* **1.** ANAT [des doigts de la main] nail, fingernail ■ [des orteils] toenail ■ **se faire les ~s** [les couper] to cut one's nails ; [les vernir] to do *ou* to paint one's nails ➊ **avoir les ~s crochus** to be mean ■ **avoir les ~s en deuil** to have dirty nails *ou* fingernails **2.** ZOOL claw ■ [de rapace] talon.
◆ **à ongles** *loc adj* [ciseaux, lime, vernis] nail *(modif).*

onglée [ɔ̃gle] *nf* : **j'avais l'~** the tips of my fingers were numb with cold.

onglet [ɔ̃glɛ] *nm* **1.** [entaille] thumb index ■ [d'un canif] thumbnail groove, nail nick **2.** CONSTR mitred angle ■ **tailler à** *ou* **en ~** to mitre **3.** IMPR [béquet] tab ■ [d'un livre] hinge **4.** BOT claw, unguis *spéc* **5.** MATH ungula **6.** MÉD pterygium **7.** CULIN top skirt *UK* ■ **~ à l'échalote** *long, narrow steak served fried with chopped shallots.*

onguent [ɔ̃gɑ̃] *nm* ointment, salve.

ongulé, e [ɔ̃gyle] *adj* hoofed, ungulate *spéc.*
◆ **ongulé** *nm* ungulate.

onirique [ɔnirik] *adj* **1.** PSYCHOL oneiric **2.** *fig & sout* **une vision ~** a dreamlike vision.

onirisme [ɔnirism] *nm* **1.** PSYCHOL hallucinations **2.** *fig & sout* **des dessins à l'~ troublant** drawings with a disturbing dreamlike quality.

ONISEP [ɔnisɛp] (*abr de* **Office national d'information sur les enseignements et les professions**) *nm national careers guidance service.*

onomastique [ɔnɔmastik] *nf* onomastics *(U).*

onomatopée [ɔnɔmatɔpe] *nf* onomatopoeia.

ont *v* ⊳ **avoir.**

Ontario [ɔ̃tarjo] ◇ *npr* : **le lac ~** Lake Ontario.
◇ *npr m* : **(l')~** Ontario.

ontogenèse [ɔ̃tɔʒənɛz] *nf* ontogenesis, ontogeny.

ontogénie [ɔ̃tɔʒeni] = **ontogenèse.**

ontologie [ɔ̃tɔlɔʒi] *nf* ontology.

ontologique [ɔ̃tɔlɔʒik] *adj* ontological.

ONU, Onu [ony] (*abr de* **Organisation des Nations unies**) *npr f* UN, UNO.

onusien, enne [ɔnyzjɛ̃, ɛn] *adj* : **projet/expert ~** UN project/expert.

onyx [ɔniks] *nm* onyx.

onze [ɔ̃z] ◇ *dét* **1.** eleven **2.** [dans des séries] : **le ~ novembre** Armistice *UK ou* Veterans' *US* Day ■ **Louis XI** Louis the Eleventh, *voir aussi* **cinq.**
◇ *nm inv* **1.** [onzième jour du mois] : **je te verrai le ~** I'll see you on the eleventh **2.** FOOTBALL : **le ~ tricolore** the French eleven *ou* team.

onzième [ɔ̃zjɛm] ◇ *adj num* eleventh ■ **elle est ~** she is in eleventh place ➊ **les ouvriers de la ~ heure** last-minute helpers, *voir aussi* **cinquième.**
◇ *nmf* eleventh.
◇ *nm* **1.** [fraction] eleventh **2.** MUS eleventh.
◇ *nf* ÉDUC first-year infants (class) *UK*, first-year nursery school (grade) *US.*

OP *nm* = **ouvrier professionnel.**

OPA *nf* = **offre publique d'achat.**

opacification [ɔpasifikasjɔ̃] *nf* opacifying.

opacifier [9] [ɔpasifje] *vt* to opacify, to make opaque.

opacité [ɔpasite] *nf* **1.** *litt* [ombre] shadow, darkness **2.** *litt* [inintelligibilité] opaqueness, opacity **3.** PHYS [d'un corps] opacity, opaqueness ■ [d'un liquide] cloudiness, turbidity *sout* **4.** MÉD : **~ radiologique** X-ray shadow.

opale [ɔpal] *nf* opal.

opalescence [ɔpalesɑ̃s] *nf* opalescence.

opalescent, e [ɔpalesɑ̃, ɑ̃t] *adj* opalescent.

opalin, e [ɔpalɛ̃, in] *adj* opaline.
◆ **opaline** *nf* opaline.

opaque [ɔpak] *adj* **1.** PHYS opaque **2.** [sombre] dark, impenetrable ■ **dans la nuit ~** in the pitch-dark *ou* jet-black night **3.** [incompréhensible] opaque, impenetrable.

op. cit. (*abr écrite de* **opere citato**) op. cit.

OPE *nf* = **offre publique d'échange.**

opéable [opeabl] *adj likely to be the target of a takeover bid.*

open [ɔpɛn] ◇ *adj inv* [billet, tournoi] open.
◇ *nm* SPORT open ■ **~ (de tennis)** open tennis championship *ou* tournament.

OPEP, Opep [ɔpɛp] (*abr de* **Organisation des pays exportateurs de pétrole**) *npr f* OPEC.

opéra [ɔpera] *nm* **1.** MUS [œuvre] opera ■ [genre] opera ➊ **~ rock** rock opera **2.** [bâtiment] opera (house).

opéra-ballet [ɔperabalɛ] (*pl* **opéras-ballets**) *nm* opéra ballet.

opérable [ɔperabl] *adj* operable ▪ **la malade n'est plus ~** the patient is no longer operable *ou* is beyond surgery.

opéra-bouffe [ɔperabuf] (*pl* **opéras-bouffes**) *nm* opera buffa, opéra bouffe.

opéra-comique [ɔperakɔmik] (*pl* **opéras-comiques**) *nm* light opera, opéra comique.

opérant, e [ɔperɑ̃, ɑ̃t] *adj* **1.** *sout* [effectif] effective ▪ **notre action a été ~e** our action proved to be effective **2.** RELIG operating.

opérateur, trice [ɔperatœr, tris] *nm, f* **1.** CINÉ : **~ (de prises de vues)** cameraman **2.** TÉLÉCOM [employé] (telephone) operator ▪ [exploitant] : **pour l'étranger, il faut passer par l'~** to phone abroad, you have to go through the operator ➊ **~ radio** radio operator **3.** IMPR operative, operator **4.** TECHNOL : **~ (sur machine)** (machine) operator **5.** INFORM operator **6.** BOURSE operator, dealer.
◆ **opérateur** *nm* LING & MATH operator.

opération [ɔperasjɔ̃] *nf* **1.** MÉD operation ▪ **pratiquer une ~** to carry out surgery *ou* an operation ▪ **subir une grave/petite ~** to undergo major/minor surgery, to have a major/minor operation ➊ **une ~ (chirurgicale)** surgery, a surgical operation ▪ **~ à chaud/froid** emergency/interval surgery ▪ **~ à cœur ouvert** open-heart surgery
2. MATH operation ▪ **poser une ~** to do a calculation
3. BANQUE & BOURSE operation, transaction ➊ **~ à la baisse/hausse** bull/bear transaction ▪ **~ boursière** *ou* **de Bourse** stock exchange transaction *ou* dealing ▪ **~ bancaire** *ou* **de banque** bank transaction ▪ **~ de change** exchange deal ▪ **~ au comptant** spot *ou* cash deal ▪ **~ à prime** option dealings *ou* bargains
4. [manœuvre] operation ▪ **nous faisons appel à lui pour des ~s ponctuelles** we call upon his services, when we need a specific job carried out ▪ **'~ prix cassés'** 'price-slashing drive' ➊ **~ de commando/sauvetage** commando/rescue operation ▪ **~ coup de poing : la police a effectué une ~ coup de poing dans le quartier** the police swooped on the area ▪ **'~ coup de poing sur les chaînes hi-fi'** 'hi-fi prices slashed' ▪ **une ~ escargot a perturbé la circulation hier** a go-slow UK *ou* slowdown US by drivers disrupted traffic yesterday ▪ **~ de police** police operation
5. [démarche] process
6. RELIG : **par l'~ du Saint-Esprit** through the workings of the Holy Spirit ▪ **crois-tu que tu y arriveras par l'~ du Saint-Esprit?** *hum* do you think you'll succeed just waiting for things to happen?
7. [ensemble de travaux] process, operation
8. INFORM operation.

opérationnel, elle [ɔperasjɔnɛl] *adj* **1.** [en activité] operational ▪ **les nouveaux ateliers ne seront ~s que l'année prochaine** the new workshops won't be operational until next year **2.** [fournissant le résultat optimal] efficient, operative **3.** MIL operational.

opératoire [ɔperatwar] *adj* **1.** MATH operative **2.** MÉD [chirurgical] operating, surgical ▪ [postopératoire] post-operative **3.** PHILOS [concept, modèle] working.

opercule [ɔpɛrkyl] *nm* **1.** BOT, ENTOM & ZOOL operculum **2.** [dans un emballage] lid.

opéré, e [ɔpere] *nm, f* patient (who has undergone surgery) ▪ **le chirurgien est passé voir son dernier ~** the surgeon came round to see the last person he operated on ➊ **les grands ~s** (post-operative) intensive care patients.

opérer [18] [ɔpere] ◇ *vt* **1.** MÉD [blessé, malade] to operate on ▪ **elle a été opérée de l'appendicite** she was operated on for appendicitis, she had her appendix removed ▪ **on va l'~ d'un kyste au poignet** they're going to remove a cyst from her wrist ▪ **se faire ~** to undergo *ou* to have surgery ▪ *(en usage absolu)* **le chirurgien a opéré toute la matinée** the surgeon was in the operating theatre all morning **2.** [procéder à - modification] to carry out *(sép)* ; [- miracle, retour en arrière] to bring about *(sép)* ; [- paiement] to make ▪ **tu dois ~ un choix** you have to choose *ou* to make a choice ▪ **le pays tente d'~ un redressement économique** the country is attempting to bring about an economic recovery **3.** MIL [retraite] to effect.
◇ *vi* **1.** [faire effet] to work **2.** [intervenir] to act, to operate.
◆ **s'opérer** ◇ *vp (emploi passif)* : **ce genre de lésion ne s'opère pas** this type of lesion can't be operated on.
◇ *vpi* to take place ▪ **une transformation s'opéra en elle** she underwent a transformation.

opérette [ɔperɛt] *nf* operetta.
◆ **d'opérette** *loc adj* : **le colonel n'est qu'un soldat d'~** the colonel is just a tin soldier ▪ **une armée d'~** a caricature of an army.

OPHLM (*abr de* **Office public d'habitations à loyer modéré**) *nm main office responsible for the allocation of council housing.*

ophtalmie [ɔftalmi] *nf* ophthalmia ▪ **~ des neiges** snow blindness.

L'OPINION

Pour exprimer son opinion

In my opinion,... À mon avis,...

As I see it,... Selon moi,...

As far as I'm concerned,... En ce qui me concerne,...

Personally, I think/feel/believe that... Personnellement, je pense/j'ai le sentiment/je crois que...

It seems to me that... Il me semble que...

If you ask me, it's all his fault. Si vous voulez mon avis, tout est de sa faute.

If you want to know what I think,... Si vous voulez savoir ce que j'en pense,...

Quite frankly, I'm not impressed. Franchement, je ne trouve pas ça terrible.

To be perfectly honest, I was disappointed. Pour être tout à fait franc, j'ai été déçu.

It strikes me that... Il me semble que...

I don't know about you, but I quite like it. Je ne sais pas ce que vous en pensez, mais moi j'aime bien.

Pour solliciter une opinion

What do you think about their proposal? Que pensez-vous de leur proposition ?

How do you feel about leaving France? Comment te sens-tu à l'idée de quitter la France ?

What about you? What do you think? Et toi ? Qu'est-ce que tu en penses ?

What's your take on the situation? *fam.* Qu'est-ce que tu dis de tout ça ?

Pour éviter de prendre position

It *ou* **That depends.** Ça dépend.

It all depends (on) what you mean by "expensive". Tout dépend de ce qu'on entend par « cher ».

It's difficult to say. C'est difficile à dire.

I wouldn't like to say. Je préférerais ne rien dire.

I haven't really thought about it. Je n'y ai pas vraiment réfléchi.

ophtalmique [ɔftalmik] *adj* ophthalmic.

ophtalmologie [ɔftalmɔlɔʒi] *nf* ophthalmology.

ophtalmologique [ɔftalmɔlɔʒik] *adj* ophthalmological.

ophtalmologiste [ɔftalmɔlɔʒist], **ophtalmologue** [ɔftalmɔlɔg] *nmf* ophthalmologist, eye specialist.

opiacé, e [ɔpjase] *adj* **1.** [qui contient de l'opium] opiate, opiated **2.** [qui sert d'opium] opiate, opium-scented.
◆ **opiacé** *nm* opiate.

Opinel® [ɔpinɛl] *nm folding knife used especially for outdoor activities, scouting etc.*

opiner [3] [ɔpine] *litt* ◇ *vi* : ~ **sur** to express an opinion about.
◇ *vt* : ~ **que** to be of the opinion that.
◆ **opiner à** *v+prép litt* to consent to.
◆ **opiner de** *v+prép* : ~ **de la tête** *ou* **du bonnet** *ou* **du chef** to nod one's assent *ou* agreement, to nod in agreement.

opiniâtre [ɔpinjatr] *adj* **1.** [personne] stubborn, obstinate **2.** [haine, opposition, lutte] unrelenting, relentless, obstinate ■ [détermination] dogged **3.** [toux] persistent.

opiniâtrement [ɔpinjatrəmɑ̃] *adv* **1.** [avec entêtement] stubbornly, obstinately **2.** [avec ténacité] relentlessly, persistently, doggedly.

opiniâtreté [ɔpinjatrəte] *nf litt* **1.** [entêtement] stubbornness, obstinacy **2.** [ténacité] relentlessness, doggedness.

opinion [ɔpinjɔ̃] *nf* **1.** [point de vue] opinion ■ **j'ai mon ~ sur lui** I have my own opinion about him ■ **se faire soi-même une ~** to make up one's own mind ■ **je ne partage pas votre ~** I don't agree with you, I don't share your views ■ **c'est une affaire d'~** it's a matter of opinion ■ **~s politiques/subversives** political/subversive views ▶ **l'~ (publique)** public opinion ■ **informer l'~** to inform the public ■ **les sans ~** the don't knows **2.** [jugement] opinion ■ **avoir une bonne/mauvaise/haute ~ de qqn** to have a good/bad/high opinion of sb ■ **je me moque de l'~ d'autrui** I don't care what others may think.
Voir module d'usage

opiomane [ɔpjɔman] *nmf* opium addict.

opiomanie [ɔpjɔmani] *nf* opium addiction, opiomania *spéc.*

opium [ɔpjɔm] *nm* opium.

OPJ *nm* = **officier de police judiciaire.**

opossum [ɔpɔsɔm] *nm* opossum.

opportun, e [ɔpɔrtœ̃, yn] *adj* opportune, timely ■ **je vous donnerai ma réponse en temps ~** I'll give you my answer in due course ■ **il lui est apparu ~ de partir avant elle** he found it appropriate *ou* advisable to leave before her.

opportunément [ɔpɔrtynemɑ̃] *adv* opportunely ■ **la police est arrivée ~** the police arrived just at the right time.

opportunisme [ɔpɔrtynism] *nm* opportunism.

opportuniste [ɔpɔrtynist] *adj & nmf* opportunist ■ **maladie ~** opportunistic infection.

opportunité [ɔpɔrtynite] *nf* **1.** [à-propos] timeliness, appropriateness **2.** [occasion] opportunity.

opposabilité [ɔpozabilite] *nf* DR opposability.

opposable [ɔpozabl] *adj* opposable ■ **tu ne trouveras pas d'argument ~ à ma décision** you won't be able to use any argument against my decision.

opposant, e [ɔpozɑ̃, ɑ̃t] ◇ *adj* **1.** [adverse] opposing **2.** DR opposing.
◇ *nm, f* [adversaire] opponent ■ **les ~s au régime** the opponents of the regime.

opposé, e [ɔpoze] *adj* **1.** [en vis-à-vis] opposite ■ **il est arrivé du côté ~** he came from the other *ou* opposite side ■ **sur le mur ~** on the opposite wall ; [par rapport au locuteur] on the wall facing us **2.** [contraire - sens, direction] opposite, other ; [- mouvement] opposing ; [- avis, goût] opposing, conflicting, different ■ **je suis d'une opinion ~e (à la vôtre)** I am of a different opinion **3.** [contrastant - couleur, ton] contrasting **4.** BOT [feuille, rameau] opposite **5.** GÉOM & MATH [côté, angle] opposite.
◆ **opposé** *nm* **1.** [direction] opposite ■ **vous cherchez l'église? vous allez à l'~** you want the church? you're going in the wrong direction **2.** [contraire] opposite, reverse ■ **chaque fois que je te dis quelque chose, tu soutiens l'~!** whenever I say anything, you say the opposite *ou* you contradict it! ■ **il est tout l'~ de sa sœur** he's the exact opposite of his sister **3.** MATH [nombre] opposite number.
◆ **à l'opposé de** *loc prép* unlike, contrary to ■ **à l'~ de sa mère, elle n'aimait pas la peinture** unlike her mother, she didn't like painting.

opposer [3] [ɔpoze] *vt* **1.** [objecter - argument] : **je n'ai rien à ~ à cette objection** I've nothing to say against that objection ■ **elle m'a opposé qu'elle n'avait pas le temps de s'en occuper** she objected that she didn't have time to take care of it
2. [mettre en confrontation] : **qui peut-on ~ au président sortant?** who can we put up against the outgoing president? ■ **le match de demain oppose Bordeaux à Lens** Bordeaux will play against Lens in tomorrow's match ■ **deux guerres ont opposé nos pays** two wars have brought our countries into conflict
3. PHYS : **~ une pression de sens contraire** to apply pressure from the opposite direction ■ **~ une résistance** *pr* to resist, to be resistant ; *fig* to put up a resistance
4. [disposer vis-à-vis] to set *ou* to place opposite each other.
◆ **s'opposer à** *vp+prép* **1.** [être contre] to object to, to oppose ■ **le règlement/ma religion s'y oppose** it goes against the rules/my religion ■ **les conditions météo s'opposent à toute navigation aérienne aujourd'hui** weather conditions are making flying inadvisable today ■ **je m'oppose à ce que tu reviennes** I'm against *ou* opposed to your coming back ▮ [être en désaccord avec] : **je m'oppose à lui sur la politique étrangère** I'm against him *ou* I oppose him on foreign policy
2. [affronter] to oppose, to be against ■ **il s'opposera ce soir au président dans un débat télévisé** he'll face the president tonight in a televised debate
3. [contraster avec - couleur, notion, mot] to be the opposite of.

opposition [ɔpozisjɔ̃] *nf* **1.** [désaccord] opposition ■ [contraste] contrast, difference ■ **~ de** *ou* **entre deux styles** clash of *ou* between two styles
2. [résistance] opposition ■ **le ministre a fait** *ou* **mis ~ au projet** the minister opposed the plan ■ **nous avons rencontré une forte ~** we encountered strong opposition ■ **la loi est passée sans ~** the bill went through unopposed ■ **il fait de l'~ systématique à tout ce qu'on lui propose** he's automatically against everything you suggest
3. POLIT : **l'~** the Opposition ■ **les dirigeants/partis de l'~** the leaders/parties of the Opposition
4. DR : **faire ~ à une décision** to appeal against a ruling ■ **faire ~ à un acte** to lodge an objection to a deed ■ **faire ~ à un chèque** to stop a cheque ■ **faire ~ à un mariage** to raise an objection to *ou* to enter a caveat to a marriage ▶ **valeurs frappées d'~** stopped *ou* countermanded bonds
5. ASTROL & ASTRON opposition
6. ÉLECTR & LING opposition.
◆ **en opposition avec** *loc prép* against, contrary to, in opposition to ■ **je me suis trouvée en ~ avec elle sur plusieurs points** I found myself at odds *ou* at variance with her on several points.
◆ **par opposition à** *loc prép* as opposed to, in contrast with.

oppositionnel, elle [ɔpozisjɔnɛl] ◇ *adj* POLIT oppositional, opposition *(modif)*.
◇ *nm, f* oppositionist.

oppressant, e [ɔpresɑ̃, ɑ̃t] *adj* oppressive.

oppressé, e [ɔprese] *adj* oppressed ■ **avoir la poitrine ~e** to have difficulty in breathing.

oppresser [4] [ɔprese] *vt* to oppress ■ **elle était oppressée par l'angoisse** she was gripped *ou* choked with anxiety.

oppresseur [ɔpresœr] *nm* oppressor.

oppressif, ive [ɔpresif, iv] *adj* oppressive.

oppression [ɔpresjɔ̃] *nf* **1.** [domination] oppression **2.** [suffocation] suffocation, oppression.

opprimant, e [ɔprimɑ̃, ɑ̃t] *adj* oppressive.

opprimé, e [ɔprime] <> *adj* oppressed.
<> *nm, f* oppressed person ▪ **elle prend toujours le parti des ~s** she always sides with the underdog.

opprimer [3] [ɔprime] *vt* **1.** [asservir] to oppress **2.** [censurer] to suppress, to stifle ▪ **~ la presse** to gag the press.

opprobre [ɔprɔbr] *nm litt* **1.** [honte] shame, opprobrium *sout* ▪ **jeter l'~ sur qqn** to heap shame *ou* opprobrium on sb ▪ **il est l'~ de sa famille** he's a disgrace to his family **2.** [avilissement] shame, infamy.

optatif, ive [ɔptatif, iv] *adj* optative.

opter [3] [ɔpte] ◆ **opter pour** *v+prép* to opt for *(insép)* ▪ **vous devez ~ pour une de ces deux possibilités** you'll have to choose between these two possibilities ▪ **le prix m'a fait ~ pour une plus petite voiture** the price finally made me come down in favour of a smaller car.

opticien, enne [ɔptisjɛ̃, ɛn] *nm, f* optician.

optimal, e, aux [ɔptimal, o] *adj* optimal, optimum *(avant n)* ▪ **pour un rendement ~** for optimal results.

optimalisation [ɔptimalizasjɔ̃] *nf* optimization.

optimaliser [3] [ɔptimalize] *vt* to optimize.

optimisation [ɔptimizasjɔ̃] = **optimalisation**.

optimiser [ɔptimize] = **optimaliser**.

optimisme [ɔptimism] *nm* optimism ▪ **avec ~** optimistically.

optimiste [ɔptimist] <> *adj* optimistic.
<> *nmf* optimist ▪ **c'est un éternel ~** he always looks on the bright side, he's an eternal optimist.

optimum [ɔptimɔm] *(pl* **optimums** *ou pl* **optima** [-ma]*)*
<> *adj* optimum *(avant n)*, optimal.
<> *nm* optimum ▪ **~ écologique** optimum ecological conditions.

option [ɔpsjɔ̃] *nf* **1.** [choix] option, choice ▪ **je n'ai pas d'autre ~** I have no other alternative *ou* choice **2.** ÉDUC : **(matière à) ~** optional subject **3.** FIN : **~ d'achat d'actions** stock option ▪ **~ d'achat** call option ▪ **~ de vente** put option **4.** COMM & DR option ▪ **prendre une ~ sur qqch** to take (out) an option on sthg ◉ **~ d'achat/de vente** option to buy/to sell **5.** [accessoire facultatif] optional extra ▪ **en ~** as an (optional) extra.

optionnel, elle [ɔpsjɔnɛl] *adj* optional.

optique [ɔptik] <> *adj* **1.** ANAT optic ▪ **nerf ~** optic nerve **2.** OPT optical **3.** PHYS optic **4.** INFORM optical.
<> *nf* **1.** SC optics *(U)* **2.** TECHNOL (set of) lenses **3.** [point de vue] point of view ▪ **dans cette ~** from this point of view.
◆ **d'optique** *loc adj* optical.

opulence [ɔpylɑ̃s] *nf* **1.** [richesse] opulence, affluence ▪ **vivre dans l'~** to live an opulent life *ou* a life of plenty **2.** *litt* [ampleur] fullness, ampleness.

opulent, e [ɔpylɑ̃, ɑ̃t] *adj* **1.** [riche] affluent, wealthy, opulent **2.** [physiquement - personne] corpulent ; [- forme] generous, full.

opus [ɔpys] *nm* opus.

opuscule [ɔpyskyl] *nm* [petit ouvrage] opuscule ▪ [brochure] brochure.

OQ *nm* = **ouvrier qualifié**.

or[1] [ɔr] *conj sout* : **il faut tenir les délais; or, ce n'est pas toujours possible** deadlines must be met; now this is not always possible ▪ **je devais y aller, or au dernier moment j'ai eu un empêchement** I was supposed to go, but then at the last moment something came up.

or[2] [ɔr] <> *nm* **1.** [métal] gold ▪ **le cours de l'~** the price of gold ◉ **~ monnayé/au titre/sans titre** coined/essayed/unessayed gold ▪ **~ en barre** gold bullion ▪ **ces actions, c'est de l'~ en barre** *fam* these shares are a rock-solid investment ▪ **l'~ blanc** [les sports d'hiver] the winter sports bonanza ▪ **~ brut** gold nuggets ▪ **~ jaune** yellow gold ▪ **~ massif** solid gold ▪ **la montre est en ~ massif** the watch is solid gold ▪ **l'~ noir** black gold ▪ **l'~ vert** agricultural earnings ▪ **l'étalon-~** the gold standard ▪ **la valeur ~** value in gold, gold exchange value ▪ **pour tout l'~ du monde** for all the tea in China *hum*, for all the money in the world ▪ **'l'Or du Rhin'** ***Wagner*** 'The Rhine Gold' **2.** [couleur] gold, golden colour.
<> *adj inv* gold *(modif)*, gold-coloured.
◆ **d'or** *loc adj* **1.** JOAILL & MINÉR gold *(modif)* **2.** [doré - cheveux] golden, gold *(modif)* ; [- cadre] gold *(modif)* **3.** *loc* **un cœur d'~** a heart of gold.
◆ **en or** *loc adj* **1.** JOAILL gold *(modif)* ▪ **une bague en ~** a gold ring **2.** [excellent] : **une mère en ~** a wonderful mother ▪ **une affaire en ~** [occasion] a real bargain ; [entreprise] a goldmine ▪ **c'est une occasion en ~** it's a golden opportunity.

oracle [ɔrakl] *nm* ANTIQ & *fig* oracle ▪ **rendre un ~** to pronounce an oracle ▪ **l'~ de Delphes** the Delphic oracle.

orage [ɔraʒ] *nm* **1.** MÉTÉOR storm, thunderstorm ▪ **le temps est à l'~** there's thunder in the air ▪ **un temps d'~** stormy *ou* thundery weather ▪ **il va y avoir un ~** there's a storm brewing, there's going to be a storm ◉ **~ magnétique/de chaleur** magnetic/heat storm ▪ **pluie d'~** rainstorm **2.** [dispute] row, argument ▪ **il y a de l'~ dans l'air** there's trouble brewing **3.** *litt* [déchirement, tourmente] upheaval, tumult.

orageusement [ɔraʒøzmɑ̃] *adv sout* stormily.

orageux, euse [ɔraʒø, øz] *adj* **1.** MÉTÉOR [ciel] stormy, thundery ▪ [chaleur, averse] thundery ▪ **le temps est ~** it's thundery *ou* stormy, the weather's thundery *ou* stormy **2.** [tumultueux - jeunesse, séance] stormy, turbulent.

oraison [ɔrɛzɔ̃] *nf* **1.** RELIG [prière] prayer ▪ **l'~ dominicale** the Lord's Prayer **2.** LITTÉR : **~ funèbre** funeral oration.

oral, e, aux [ɔral, o] *adj* **1.** [confession, déposition] verbal, oral ▪ [message, tradition] oral ▪ ÉDUC [épreuve] oral **2.** ANAT & LING oral.
◆ **oral, aux** *nm* **1.** [examen - gén] oral (examination) ; [- à l'université] viva (voce) *UK*, oral (examination) ▪ **notes d'~** oral marks *UK ou* grades *US* ▪ **j'ai raté l'~ de physique** I failed the physics oral **2.** ÉDUC & UNIV : **l'~** [l'expression orale] : **il n'est pas très bon à l'~** his oral work isn't very good.

oralement [ɔralmɑ̃] *adv* orally, verbally.

orange [ɔrɑ̃ʒ] <> *nf* orange ▪ **~ sanguine** blood orange ▪ **une ~ pressée** a glass of freshly squeezed orange juice.
<> *nm* orange (colour).
<> *adj inv* orange, orange-coloured.

orangé, e [ɔrɑ̃ʒe] *adj* orangey, orange-coloured.
◆ **orangé** *nm* orangey colour.

orangeade [ɔrɑ̃ʒad] *nf* orange drink.

oranger [ɔrɑ̃ʒe] *nm* orange tree ▪ **bois d'~** orange wood.

orangeraie [ɔrɑ̃ʒrɛ] *nf* orange grove.

orangerie [ɔrɑ̃ʒri] *nf* **1.** [serre] orangery **2.** [plantation] orange grove.

orangiste [ɔrɑ̃ʒist] <> *nmf* **1.** [en Irlande du Nord] Orangeman *(f* Orangewoman*)* **2.** HIST Orangist.
<> *adj* Orange *(modif)*.

orang-outan(g) [ɔrɑ̃utɑ̃] *(pl* **orangs-outans** *ou pl* **orangs-outangs***)* *nm* orangutang.

orateur, trice [ɔratœr, tris] *nm, f* **1.** [rhétoricien] orator **2.** [gén] speaker ▪ **c'est un excellent ~** he is an excellent speaker.

oratoire [ɔratwar] <> *adj* [style, talent] oratorical ▪ **passage ~** oration.
<> *nm* **1.** [chapelle] oratory **2.** RELIG : **l'Oratoire de France** the French Oratory ▪ **les pères de l'Oratoire** the Oratorian Fathers.

oratorio [ɔratɔrjo] *nm* oratorio.

orbital, e, aux [ɔrbital, o] *adj* orbital.

orbite [ɔrbit] *nf* **1.** ANAT (eye) socket, orbit *spéc* ■ **il était tellement en colère que les yeux lui sortaient des ~s** *fig* he was so angry that his eyes were popping out (of their sockets) **2.** ASTRON orbit ■ **être sur** *ou* **en ~** to be in orbit ■ **être en ~ autour de qqch** [suj: astre, engin] to be in orbit round sthg, to orbit sthg ■ **satellite en ~ autour de la Terre** Earth-orbiting satellite ■ **mettre en** *ou* **placer sur ~** to put into orbit **3.** PHYS orbital **4.** [d'une personne, d'un pays] sphere of influence, orbit.

orbiter [3] [ɔrbite] *vi* to orbit ■ **~ autour de** to orbit (round).

Orcades [ɔrkad] *npr fpl* : **les ~** the Orkney Islands, the Orkneys.

orchestral, e, aux [ɔrkɛstral, o] *adj* orchestral, orchestra *(modif)* ■ **la partition ~e** the orchestral *ou* orchestra score.

orchestrateur, trice [ɔrkɛstratœr, tris] *nm, f* orchestrator.

orchestration [ɔrkɛstrasjɔ̃] *nf* **1.** MUS orchestration **2.** [organisation] orchestration, organization.

orchestre [ɔrkɛstr] *nm* **1.** MUS [classique] orchestra ■ [de jazz] band, orchestra ■ **grand ~** full orchestra ■ **~ symphonique /de chambre** symphony/chamber orchestra ■ **~ de cuivres** brass band **2.** CINÉ & THÉÂTRE stalls *UK*, orchestra *US* **3.** ANTIQ orchestra.

orchestrer [3] [ɔrkɛstre] *vt* **1.** MUS [composer] to orchestrate ■ [adapter] to orchestrate, to score **2.** [préparer] to orchestrate, to organize.

orchidée [ɔrkide] *nf* orchid.

ordalie [ɔrdali] *nf arch* ordeal.

ordinaire [ɔrdinɛr] <> *adj* **1.** [habituel - journée] ordinary, normal ; [- procédure] usual, standard, normal ; [- comportement] ordinary, usual, customary ■ DR & POLIT [- session] ordinary ■ **en temps ~** usually, normally ■ **peu** *ou* **pas ~** [attitude, méthode, journée] unusual ; [volonté] unusual, extraordinary **2.** [de tous les jours - habits, vaisselle] ordinary, everyday *(avant n)* **3.** COMM [qualité, modèle] standard ■ [produit] ordinary **4.** [banal - cuisine, goûts] ordinary, plain ; [- gens] ordinary, common *péj* ; [- spectacle] ordinary, run-of-the-mill ; [- conversation] run-of-the-mill, commonplace ■ **c'est quelqu'un de très ~** he's a very ordinary person ■ **elle mène une existence très ~** she leads a very humdrum existence ■ **elle n'est pas ~, ton histoire!** your story is certainly an unusual one!
<> *nm* **1.** [norme] : **l'~** the ordinary ■ **sortir de l'~** to be out of the ordinary, to be unusual ■ **son mari sort vraiment de l'~!** her husband is one of a kind! **2.** [repas habituel] everyday *ou* ordinary fare **3.** [essence] : ≃ two-star petrol *UK*, ≃ regular *US* **4.** MUS & RELIG ordinary **5.** MIL (company) mess.
◆ **à l'ordinaire** *loc adv* : **plus intéressant qu'à l'~** more interesting than usual ■ **comme à l'~, il arriva en retard** as usual, he turned up late.
◆ **d'ordinaire** *loc adv* usually, ordinarily, normally ■ **plus tôt que d'~** earlier than usual.

ordinairement [ɔrdinɛrmɑ̃] *adv* usually, ordinarily, normally.

ordinal, e, aux [ɔrdinal, o] *adj* [adjectif, nombre] ordinal.
◆ **ordinal, aux** *nm* **1.** [nombre] ordinal (number) **2.** [adjectif] ordinal (adjective).

ordinateur [ɔrdinatœr] *nm* **1.** INFORM computer ■ **mettre qqch sur ~** to computerize sthg, to put sthg on computer ⊃ **~ portable/portatif** portable/laptop computer ■ **~ de bureau** desktop computer ■ **~ hôte** host computer ■ **~ individuel** *ou* **personnel** home *ou* personal computer, PC **2.** TECHNOL computer ■ **~ de bord** AUTO dashboard computer ; NAUT shipboard computer ■ **la vitesse a été calculée par ~** the speed was calculated by computer *ou* computer-calculated.

ordination [ɔrdinasjɔ̃] *nf* **1.** RELIG [d'un prêtre] ordination ■ [consécration] consecration **2.** MATH ordering.

ordinogramme [ɔrdinɔgram] *nm* (process) flowchart *ou* flow diagram.

ordonnance [ɔrdɔnɑ̃s] <> *nf* **1.** MÉD prescription ■ **un médicament vendu sans ~** a drug that can be bought over the counter ⊃ **'seulement sur ~'** 'on prescription only' **2.** DR [loi] ordinance, statutory instrument ■ [jugement] order, ruling ■ [de police] (police) regulation *ou* order ■ **~ de non-lieu** nonsuit **3.** [disposition] organization, order, arrangement ■ **l'~ des mots dans une phrase** the order of words in a sentence ■ **l'~ du dîner avait été décidée un mois auparavant** they had decided a month earlier what the order of the meal would be **4.** ARCHIT layout, disposition **5.** HIST ordinance (law), decree **6.** FIN : **~ de paiement** order to pay, authorization of payment **7.** MIL : **revolver d'~** service pistol ■ **officier d'~** aide-de-camp.
<> *nm ou nf arch* (military) orderly.

ordonnancement [ɔrdɔnɑ̃smɑ̃] *nm* **1.** INDUST [organisation des phases] sequencing ■ [prévision des délais] timing, scheduling **2.** FIN order to pay **3.** INFORM scheduling.

ordonnancer [16] [ɔrdɔnɑ̃se] *vt* **1.** *sout* [agencer] to arrange, to organize ■ **qui a ordonnancé la cérémonie?** who arranged the ceremony? **2.** FIN [déclarer bon à payer] to authorize **3.** INFORM to schedule.

ordonnateur, trice [ɔrdɔnatœr, tris] *nm, f* **1.** [organisateur] organizer ■ **le comité sera l'~ de la cérémonie** the committee will be in charge of *ou* will organize the ceremony ⊃ **~ des pompes funèbres** funeral director **2.** FIN *official in charge of overseeing public expenditure.*

ordonné, e [ɔrdɔne] *adj* **1.** [méthodique - personne] tidy, neat ; [- esprit] methodical, systematic **2.** [rangé - chambre] tidy, neat, orderly **3.** [régulier - existence, mode de vie] orderly, well-ordered **4.** MATH ordered.

ordonnée [ɔrdɔne] *nf* MATH ordinate.

ordonner [3] [ɔrdɔne] *vt* **1.** [commander - silence, attaque] to order ■ MÉD [traitement, repos] to prescribe ■ **ils ont ordonné le secret sur l'affaire** they've ordered that the matter (should) be kept secret ■ **~ à qqn de faire qqch** to order *ou* to command sb to do sthg ■ **~ à qqn d'entrer/de sortir** to order sb in/out **2.** [agencer - documents] to (put in) order ; [- arguments, idées] to (put into) order, to arrange ; [- chambre] to tidy (up) ■ MATH [nombres, suite] to arrange in order ■ **~ des nombres du plus petit au plus grand/du plus grand au plus petit** to list numbers in ascending/descending order **3.** RELIG to ordain.
◆ **s'ordonner** *vpi* [faits] to fall into order *ou* place ■ **les indices s'ordonnaient dans mon esprit** the clues began to fall into place in my mind.

ordre [ɔrdr] *nm*

A. INSTRUCTION
B. HIÉRARCHIE, AGENCEMENT
C. CLASSIFICATION, DOMAINE

A. INSTRUCTION

1. [directive, injonction] order ■ MIL order, command ■ **c'est un ~!** (and) that's an order! ■ **donner un ~** [parent] to give an order ; [officiel, policier, officier] to issue *ou* to give an order ■ **donner (l')~ de** to give the order to ■ **donner à qqn l'~ de faire qqch** to order sb to do sthg, to give sb the order to do sthg
2. BANQUE & BOURSE : **à l'~ de** payable to, to the order of ■ **chèque à mon ~** cheque made out *ou* payable to me ■ **c'est à quel ~?** who shall I make it payable to? ⊃ **~ d'achat/de vente** order to buy/to sell ■ **~ de paiement/virement** order to pay/to transfer

B. HIÉRARCHIE, AGENCEMENT

1. [succession] order, sequence ■ **l'~ des mots dans la phrase** the word order in the sentence ⊃ **par ~ d'arrivée/de grandeur/d'importance** in order of arrival/size/importance ■ **par ~ chronologique/croissant/décroissant** in chronological/ascending/descending order ■ **en ~ dispersé/serré** MIL in extended/close order ■ **noms classés par ~ alphabétique** names filed in alphabetical order ■ **par ~ d'apparition à l'écran** in order of appearance ■ **par ~ d'entrée en scène** in order of appearance ■ **~ de succession** DR intestate succession
2. [rangement] tidiness, orderliness, neatness ■ **la pièce était en ~** the room was tidy ■ **mettre qqch en ~** to put sthg in order

▪ **tenir une maison en ~** to keep a house tidy ▮ [sens du rangement] : **avoir de l'~** to be tidy ▪ **manquer** *OU* **ne pas avoir d'~** to be untidy
3. [organisation méthodique - de documents] order ▪ **mettre en ~, mettre de l'~ dans** [documents, comptabilité] to set in order, to tidy up *(sép)* ▪ **mettre de l'~ dans ses idées** to order one's ideas ▪ **il a laissé ses papiers/comptes en ~ avant de partir** he left his papers/accounts in order before leaving ➊ **mettre bon ~ à qqch** to sort sthg out
4. [discipline sociale] : **faire régner l'~** to keep *OU* maintain order ▪ **rappeler qqn à l'~** to call sb to order ▪ **se faire rappeler à l'~** [dans une assemblée] to be called to order ; [dans une classe] to get told off ▪ **la police est chargée du maintien de l'~** it's the police's job to keep law and order ➊ **l'~ établi** the established order ▪ **l'~ public** public order, law and order ▪ **rentrer dans l'~ : puis tout est rentré dans l'~** then order was restored, then everything went back to normal

C. CLASSIFICATION, DOMAINE
1. RELIG order ▪ **les ~s mineurs/majeurs** RELIG the minor/major orders ▪ **les ~s mendiants** the mendicant orders ▪ **les ~s monastiques** the monastic orders ▪ **entrer dans les ~s** RELIG to take (holy) orders
2. [nature, sorte] nature, order ▪ **des problèmes d'~ professionnel** problems of a professional nature ▪ **dans le même ~ d'idées** similarly ▪ **dans un autre ~ d'idées** in another connection ▪ **du même ~** [proposition, responsabilités] similar, of the same nature ▪ **de l'~ de** in the region *OU* order of ▪ **une augmentation de 5 %? – oui, de cet ~** a 5% rise? – yes, roughly *OU* in that region ➊ **donner un ~ de grandeur** to give a rough estimate ▪ **c'est dans l'~ des choses** it's in the order *OU* nature of things
3. ARCHIT & BIOL order ▪ **~ attique/dorique/ionique** Attic/Doric/Ionic order.
◆ **de dernier ordre** *loc adj* third-rate.
◆ **de premier ordre** *loc adj* first-rate.
◆ **de second ordre** *loc adj* [question] of secondary importance ▪ [artiste, personnalité] second-rate.
◆ **ordre du jour** *nm* **1.** [d'un comité] agenda ▪ **être à l'~ du jour** *pr* to be on the agenda ; *fig* to be in the news ▪ **mettre qqch à l'~ du jour** to put *OU* to place sthg on the agenda **2.** MIL general orders, order of the day ▪ **cité à l'~ du jour** mentioned in dispatches.
Voir module d'usage

ordré, e [ɔrdre] *adj Suisse* [ordonné] tidy, orderly, neat.

ordure [ɔrdyr] *nf* **1.** △ [personne abjecte] : ~! bastard!△ **2.** *litt* [fange] : **l'~** filth, mire *litt*.
◆ **ordures** *nfpl* **1.** [déchets] refuse *(U)*, rubbish *UK (U)*, garbage *US (U)* ▪ **ramasser les ~s** to collect the garbage *OU* rubbish ▪ **vider les ~s** to empty (out) the rubbish ▪ **jeter** *OU* **mettre qqch aux ~s** to throw sthg into the rubbish bin *UK OU* garbage can *US* ▪ **c'est bon à mettre aux ~s!** it's fit for the dustbin! ➊ **~s ménagères** household refuse **2.** [excréments] dirt *(U)*, filth *(U)* **3.** *fam* [obscénités] obscenities, filth *(U)* ▪ **dire/écrire des ~s sur qqn** to talk/to write filth about sb.

ordurier, ère [ɔrdyrje, ɛr] *adj* foul, filthy, obscene.

orée [ɔre] *nf* edge ▪ **à l'~ du bois** on the edge of the wood.

Oregon [ɔregɔ̃] *npr m* : **l'~** Oregon.

oreille [ɔrɛj] *nf* **1.** ANAT & ZOOL ear ▪ **j'ai mal aux ~s** I've got earache, my ears are hurting ▪ **avoir les ~s décollées** to have protruding *OU* sticking-out ears ▪ **avoir les ~s en feuille de chou** to have cauliflower ears ▪ **avoir les ~s qui bourdonnent** *OU* **des bourdonnements d'~** to have a buzzing in the ears ▪ **elle n'entend pas de l'~ gauche** she's deaf in the left ear ➊ **~ interne/moyenne** inner/middle ear ▪ **~ externe** outer *OU* external ear ▪ **les ~s ont dû lui siffler** *fig & hum* his ears must have been burning ▪ **elle est repartie l'~ basse** she left with her tail between her legs ▪ **frotter les ~s à qqn** to box sb's ears ▪ **montrer le bout de l'~** to show (o.s. in) one's true colours ▪ **tirer les ~s à qqn** *pr* to pull sb's ears ; [réprimander] to tell sb off ▪ **se faire tirer l'~** *fig* to need a lot of persuading **2.** [ouïe] (sense of) hearing ▪ **avoir l'~ fine** to have an acute sense of hearing ▪ **avoir de l'~** *OU* **l'~ musicale** to have a good ear for music
3. [pour écouter] ear ▪ **écouter une conversation d'une ~ distraite** to listen to a conversation with only half an ear ▪ **écouter de toutes ses ~s, être tout ~s** to be all ears ▪ **ouvrez bien vos ~s!** listen very carefully! ▪ **venir** *OU* **parvenir aux ~s de qqn** to come to *OU* to reach sb's ears ➊ **ça rentre par une ~ et ça sort par l'autre** *fam* it goes in one ear and out the other ▪ **ce n'est pas tombé dans l'~ d'un sourd!** it hasn't fallen on deaf ears!
4. TECHNOL [d'une cocotte] handle ▪ [d'un écrou] wing.

oreiller [ɔrɛje] *nm* pillow.

oreillette [ɔrɛjɛt] *nf* **1.** ANAT auricle **2.** [d'une casquette] earflap **3.** [d'un baladeur] earphone.

oreillon [ɔrɛjɔ̃] *nm* ARCHÉOL ear-piece, cheek-piece.
◆ **oreillons** *nmpl* MÉD mumps ▪ **avoir les ~s** to have (the) mumps.

ores [ɔr] ◆ **d'ores et déjà** *loc adv* already.

Oreste [ɔrɛst] *npr* Orestes.

orfèvre [ɔrfɛvr] *nm* **1.** [artisan qui travaille - l'or] goldsmith ; [- l'argent] silversmith **2.** *loc* **être ~ en la matière** to be an expert.

orfèvrerie [ɔrfɛvrəri] *nf* **1.** [métier - de l'or] goldsmithing, gold work ; [- de l'argent] silversmithing, silver work ▪ **l'~** [en or] gold plate ; [en argent] silver plate **2.** [boutique - d'objets d'or] goldsmith's shop *UK OU* store *US* ; [- d'objets d'argent] silversmith's shop *UK OU* store *US*.

orfraie [ɔrfrɛ] *nf* white-tailed eagle.

organdi [ɔrgɑ̃di] *nm* organdie ▪ **d'~, en ~** organdie *(modif)*.

organe [ɔrgan] *nm* **1.** ANAT organ ▪ **~s génitaux** *OU* **sexuels** genitals, genitalia ▪ **~s vocaux** *OU* **de la parole** speech *OU* vocal organs ▪ **~s des sens** sense organs **2.** *sout* [voix] voice **3.** TECHNOL part, component ▪ **~s de commande** controls ▪ **~s de transmission** transmission system **4.** [institution] organ ▪ **les ~s de l'État** the apparatus of the state ▪ **~ de presse** newspaper, publication ▪ **les ~s de presse** the press **5.** [porte-parole, publication] mouthpiece, organ **6.** [instrument] medium, vehicle.

organigramme [ɔrganigram] *nm* **1.** [structure] organization chart **2.** INFORM [de programmation] flow chart *OU* diagram.

organique [ɔrganik] *adj* organic.

organiquement [ɔrganikmɑ̃] *adv* organically.

DONNER DES ORDRES

Put the cases down here, please. Posez les valises là, s'il vous plaît.
Take the bags out to the car, will you? Portez les bagages à la voiture, voulez-vous ?
Quiet, please. Un peu de silence, s'il vous plaît.
Turn left at the traffic lights. Tournez à gauche au feu.
Don't walk on the grass - it's wet. Ne marche pas sur l'herbe, elle est mouillée.
Put that down! Pose ça !
Get out (of my house)! Sortez (d'ici) !
Just leave it alone, will you! Laisse-ça tranquille, tu m'entends !

organisateur, trice [ɔrganizatœr, tris] <> *adj* BIOL organizing *(avant n)*.
<> *nm, f* organizer.

organisateur-conseil [ɔrganizatœrkɔ̃sɛj] (*pl* **organisateurs-conseils**) *nm* management consultant.

organisation [ɔrganizasjɔ̃] *nf* **1.** [organisme] organization ▪ **~ internationale** international organization *ou* agency ▪ **~ non gouvernementale** nongovernmental organization ▪ **~ patronale** employers' organization *ou* association ▪ **~ syndicale** trade union ▪ **~ de travailleurs** workers' organization ▪ **l'Organisation mondiale de la santé** the World Health Organization **2.** [mise sur pied - d'une fête, d'une réunion, d'un service] organization ; [- d'une manifestation] organization, staging ; [- d'un attentat] organization, planning ▪ **l'~ du temps de travail** the organization of working hours **3.** [structure - d'un discours, d'une association, d'un système] organization, structure ; [- du travail] organization **4.** [méthode] organization ▪ **avoir de l'~** to be organized ▪ **ne pas avoir d'~** to be disorganized.

organisationnel, elle [ɔrganizasjɔnɛl] *adj* organizational.

organisé, e [ɔrganize] *adj* **1.** [regroupé - consommateurs, groupe] organized **2.** [aménagé] : **bien/mal ~** well-/badly-organized **3.** [méthodique - personne] organized, well-organized, methodical **4.** BIOL : **êtres ~s** organisms.

organiser [3] [ɔrganize] *vt* **1.** [mettre sur pied - gén] to organize ▪ MIL [attaque] to plan **2.** [agencer - association, journée, tâche] to organize ▪ **j'ai organisé mon emploi du temps de façon à pouvoir partir plus tôt** I've organized *ou* arranged my schedule so that I can leave earlier.

◆ **s'organiser** <> *vp (emploi passif)* [se préparer] to be planned.
<> *vpi* [personne] to get (o.s.) organized, to organize o.s. ▪ **il suffit de s'~** all you need is some organization ▪ **la société s'est vite organisée en classes sociales** society rapidly became organized into social classes.

organisme [ɔrganism] *nm* **1.** BIOL [animal, végétal] organism ▪ [humain] body, organism ▪ **les réactions de l'~** bodily reactions ▪ **c'est mauvais pour l'~** it's bad for your health *ou* for you ➊ **~ génétiquement modifié** genetically modified organism **2.** [institut] organism, body ▪ **~ de charité** charity (organization) ▪ **~ de crédit** credit institution.

organiseur [ɔrganizœr] *nm* **1.** [agenda] personnal organizer, Filofax® **2.** [agenda électronique] electronic organizer.

organiste [ɔrganist] *nmf* organist.

organza [ɔrgɑ̃za] *nm* organza.

orgasme [ɔrgasm] *nm* orgasm.

orge [ɔrʒ] <> *nf* barley.
<> *nm* barley.

orgeat [ɔrʒa] *nm* orgeat.

orgelet [ɔrʒəlɛ] *nm* sty, stye.

orgiaque [ɔrʒjak] *adj* orgiastic.

orgie [ɔrʒi] *nf* **1.** ANTIQ orgy **2.** *fig* **faire une ~ d'huîtres** to have a surfeit of oysters **3.** [débauche] orgy ▪ **faire une ~** to have an orgy **4.** *sout* [abondance] riot, profusion ▪ **une ~ de bleus et de rouges** a riot of blues and reds.

orgue [ɔrg] *nm* MUS organ ▪ **tenir l'~** to be at the organ ▪ **jouer de l'~** to play the organ ➊ **~ électrique/électronique/de chœur** electric/electronic/choir organ ▪ **~ de Barbarie** barrel organ ▪ **point d'~** pause.

◆ **orgues** *nfpl* **1.** MUS organ ▪ **les grandes ~s de la cathédrale** the great organ of the cathedral ▪ **faire donner les grandes ~s** *fig* to be pompous **2.** GÉOL columnar structure *ou* structures.

orgueil [ɔrgœj] *nm* **1.** [fierté] pride **2.** [amour-propre] pride ▪ **c'est de l'~ mal placé** it's just misplaced pride ▪ **gonflé** *ou* **bouffi d'~** puffed up *ou* bursting with pride **3.** [sujet de fierté] pride ▪ **j'étais l'~ de ma mère** I was my mother's pride and joy.

orgueilleusement [ɔrgœjøzmɑ̃] *adv* **1.** [avec arrogance] proudly, arrogantly **2.** [avec fierté] proudly.

orgueilleux, euse [ɔrgœjø, øz] <> *adj* **1.** [arrogant] conceited, arrogant **2.** [fier - personne] proud **3.** *litt* [majestueux - démarche, navire] proud.
<> *nm, f* **1.** [prétentieux] arrogant *ou* conceited person **2.** [fier] proud person.

orient [ɔrjɑ̃] *nm* **1.** [est] east, orient *litt* ▪ **parfum/tapis d'~** oriental scent/carpet **2.** GÉOGR : **l'Orient** the East *ou* Orient *litt* **3.** [d'une perle] orient **4.** [société maçonnique] : **le Grand Orient** the Grand Orient.

orientable [ɔrjɑ̃tabl] *adj* **1.** [antenne, rétroviseur] adjustable **2.** [lampe] rotating, swivel *(modif)*.

oriental, e, aux [ɔrjɑ̃tal, o] <> *adj* **1.** GÉOGR eastern, east *(modif)* ▪ **la plaine ~e** the eastern plain **2.** [de l'Orient - art, cuisine, civilisation] oriental, eastern.
<> *nm, f* Oriental, Easterner.

◆ **à l'orientale** *loc adv* in the oriental style.

orientalisme [ɔrjɑ̃talism] *nm* orientalism.

orientaliste [ɔrjɑ̃talist] *adj* & *nmf* orientalist.

orientation [ɔrjɑ̃tasjɔ̃] *nf* **1.** [direction - d'une enquête, de recherches] direction, orientation ; [- d'un mouvement] orientation ▪ **l'~ de notre entreprise doit changer** our firm must adopt a new outlook ▪ **~ politique** [d'un journal, d'une personne] political leanings *ou* tendencies ; [d'un parti] political direction **2.** [conseil - pour des études] academic counselling ▪ [vers un métier] careers guidance ▪ [direction - des études] course ; [- du métier] career **3.** [position - d'une antenne] direction ; [- d'un édifice] : **l'~ plein sud de l'appartement est ce qui le rend agréable** what makes the flat so pleasant to live in is the fact that it faces due south ▪ [positionnement - d'un faisceau, d'une lampe] directing ; [- d'un rétroviseur] adjustment **4.** [aptitude] : **avoir le sens de l'~** to have a good sense of direction **5.** ASTRONAUT attitude **6.** BIOL orientation **7.** NAUT set, trim.

orienté, e [ɔrjɑ̃te] *adj* **1.** [positionné] : **~ à l'ouest** [édifice] facing west, with a western aspect ; [radar] directed towards the west ▪ **local bien/mal ~** well-/badly-positioned premises **2.** [idéologiquement - discours, journal] biased, slanted ▪ **analyse ~e à droite** analysis with a right-wing bias **3.** ÉDUC : **élève bien/mal ~** pupil who has taken the right/wrong academic advice **4.** GÉOGR [carte] orientated.

orienter [3] [ɔrjɑ̃te] *vt* **1.** [antenne, haut-parleur, spot] to direct, to turn, to point ▪ [rétroviseur] to adjust, to position ▪ [plante] to position ▪ **orientez votre tente à l'est** pitch your tent so that it faces east ▪ **la chambre est orientée plein nord** the bedroom faces due north **2.** [mettre sur une voie] : **~ vers** [enquête, recherches] to direct *ou* to orientate towards ; [discussion] to turn round to ; [passant] to direct to ▪ **on l'a orienté vers un spécialiste** he was referred to a specialist ▪ **il m'a demandé où était la gare mais je l'ai mal orienté** he asked where the station was, but I misdirected him ▪ **elle a été orientée vers une école technique** she was advised to go to a technical school **3.** [rendre partial - discours] to give a bias *ou* slant to ▪ **ses cours sont politiquement orientés** her lectures are coloured by her political convictions **4.** [carte, plan] to orientate **5.** MATH to orient **6.** NAUT [voiles] to trim.

◆ **s'orienter** *vpi* [se repérer] to take one's bearings ▪ **j'ai toujours du mal à m'~** I've got no sense of direction.

◆ **s'orienter vers** *vp+prép* [suj: enquête, recherches] to be directed towards ▪ [suj: discussion] to turn round to ▪ [suj: parti, entreprise] to move towards ▪ [suj: étudiant] to turn to ▪ **il s'oriente vers une carrière commerciale** he's got his sights set on a career in sales.

orienteur, euse [ɔrjɑ̃tœr, øz] *nm, f* **1.** ÉDUC academic counsellor **2.** [conseiller professionnel] careers adviser, careers guidance officer.

orifice [ɔrifis] *nm* **1.** [ouverture] hole, opening **2.** ANAT orifice **3.** AUTO : **~ d'admission** intake port ▪ **~ de remplissage** filling hole.

oriflamme [ɔriflam] *nf* **1.** [bannière d'apparat] banner, standard **2.** HIST oriflamme.

origan [ɔrigɑ̃] *nm* oregano.

originaire [ɔriʒinɛr] *adj* **1.** [natif] : **être ~ de** to originate from ■ **ma mère est ~ de Paris** my mother was born in *ou* comes from Paris ■ **il est ~ de la Martinique** he's from Martinique ■ **animal/fruit/plante ~ des pays tropicaux** animal/fruit/plant native to tropical countries **2.** [originel] innate, inherent.

originairement [ɔriʒinɛrmɑ̃] *adv* originally, at first.

original, e, aux [ɔriʒinal, o] ◇ *adj* **1.** [nouveau - architecture, idée, système] original, novel ; [- cadeau, film, style, personne] original ■ **il n'y a rien d'~ dans son dernier roman** there's nothing original in his latest novel **2.** [excentrique - personne] odd, eccentric **3.** [d'origine - document, manuscrit] original.
◇ *nm, f* [excentrique] eccentric, character.
◆ **original, aux** *nm* **1.** [d'une œuvre] original ■ [d'un document] original *ou* master (copy) ■ [d'un texte] top copy, original ■ [d'un objet, d'un personnage] original **2.** [texte à traduire] original ■ **je préfère presque la traduction à l'~** I like the translation almost more than the original.

originalement [ɔriʒinalmɑ̃] *adv* [de façon nouvelle] originally, in an original *ou* novel way.

originalité [ɔriʒinalite] *nf* **1.** [caractère] originality, novelty ■ **cet artiste manque d'~** there is nothing new *ou* original in this artist's work ‖ [extravagance] eccentricity **2.** [nouveauté] original feature.

origine [ɔriʒin] *nf* **1.** [cause première - d'un feu, d'une maladie, d'une querelle] origin ■ **si nous remontons à l'~ du scandale** if we go back to the origin of the scandal ■ **avoir son ~ dans, tirer son ~ de** to have one's origins in, to originate in ■ **avoir qqch pour ~** to be caused by sthg ■ **être à l'~ d'un projet de loi** [personne] to be behind a bill ■ **ces erreurs judiciaires ont été à l'~ du projet de loi** these miscarriages of justice were the impetus for the bill ■ **être à l'~ d'une querelle** [personne] to be behind *ou* to be the cause of an argument ; [malentendu] to be at the origin *ou* root of an argument ■ **symptômes d'~ cardiaque** symptoms due to heart problems **2.** [début] origin, beginning ■ **les ~s de la civilisation** the origins of civilization ■ **les vêtements, des ~s à nos jours** [dans un livre, un musée] clothes, from their origins to the present day ■ **dès l'~** from the (very) beginning, from the outset **3.** [provenance - d'un terme] origin, root ; [- d'un produit manufacturé] origin ■ **la police connaît l'~ des appels** the police know who made the calls ■ **quelle est l'~ de ces pêches?** where are these peaches from? **4.** [d'une personne] origin ■ **il ne sait rien de ses ~s** he doesn't know anything about his origins *ou* where he comes from ■ **d'~ modeste** of humble origin *ou* birth ■ **d'~ espagnole** of Spanish origin **5.** DR : **~ de propriété** vendor's title **6.** GÉOM origin.
◆ **à l'origine** *loc adv* originally, initially, at the beginning.
◆ **d'origine** *loc adj* [pays] of origin ■ [couleur, emballage, nom, monnaie] original ■ **ma voiture a encore son moteur d'~** my car has still got its original engine.

originel, elle [ɔriʒinɛl] *adj* **1.** [primitif - innocence] original **2.** RELIG original **3.** [premier] original ■ **sens ~ d'un mot** original *ou* primary meaning of a word.

originellement [ɔriʒinɛlmɑ̃] *adv* [dès l'origine] from the (very) start *ou* beginning, from the outset ■ [à l'origine] originally, at first.

orignal, aux [ɔriɲal, o] *nm* moose.

Orion [ɔrjɔ̃] *npr* Orion.

oripeaux [ɔripo] *nmpl litt* [vêtements] tawdry rags.

ORL ◇ *nmf* (*abr de* **oto-rhino-laryngologiste**) ENT specialist.
◇ *nf* (*abr de* **oto-rhino-laryngologie**) ENT.

orme [ɔrm] *nm* elm (tree) ■ **~ blanc** wych elm.

Ormuz [ɔrmuz] *npr* ▷ **Hormuz**.

ornement [ɔrnəmɑ̃] *nm* **1.** [objet] ornament **2.** ART embellishment, adornment ■ **sans ~** plain, unadorned ■ **architecture surchargée d'~s** ornate architecture ■ **plafonds riches en ~s** ceilings rich in ornament *ou* ornamentation **3.** HÉRALD & MUS ornament **4.** RELIG : **~s sacerdotaux** vestments.
◆ **d'ornement** *loc adj* [plantes, poupée] ornamental.

ornemental, e, aux [ɔrnəmɑ̃tal, o] *adj* [motif] ornamental, decorative ■ [plante] ornamental.

ornementation [ɔrnəmɑ̃tasjɔ̃] *nf* ornamentation.

ornementer [3] [ɔrnəmɑ̃te] *vt sout* to ornament ■ **~ qqch de** *ou* **avec** to ornament *ou* to decorate sthg with.

orner [3] [ɔrne] *vt* **1.** [décorer - suj: personne] to decorate ■ [suj: dessin, plante, ruban] to adorn, to decorate, to embellish ■ **des bouquets ornaient la table** the table was decorated with bunches of flowers ■ **~ avec** *ou* **de** to decorate with ■ **~ une robe de dentelle** to trim a dress with lace ■ **sabre orné de joyaux** sword set with jewels **2.** [enjoliver - texte] to embellish ; [- vérité] to adorn, to embellish ■ **~ son esprit** *litt* to enrich one's mind.

ornière [ɔrnjɛr] *nf* **1.** [trou] rut ■ **une route pleine d'~s** a rutted road, a road full of potholes **2.** [routine] : **suivre l'~** to get into a rut ■ **sortir de l'~** to get out of a rut **3.** [impasse] : **tirer qqn de l'~** to help sb out of a difficulty ■ **sortir de l'~** to get o.s. out of trouble **4.** RAIL groove.

ornithologie [ɔrnitɔlɔʒi] *nf* ornithology.

ornithologique [ɔrnitɔlɔʒik] *adj* ornithological.

ornithologiste [ɔrnitɔlɔʒist], **ornithologue** [ɔrnitɔlɔg] *nmf* ornithologist.

ornithorynque [ɔrnitɔrɛ̃k] *nm* duck-billed platypus, ornithorynchus *spéc.*

orogenèse [ɔrɔʒənɛz], **orogénie** [ɔrɔʒeni] *nf* orogenesis, orogeny.

oronge [ɔrɔ̃ʒ] *nf* Caesar's mushroom ■ **fausse ~** fly agaric.

orpailleur [ɔrpajœr] *nm* gold washer.

Orphée [ɔrfe] *npr* Orpheus.

orphelin, e [ɔrfəlɛ̃, in] ◇ *adj* **1.** [enfant] orphan *(modif)* ■ **être ~ de père** to be fatherless, to have lost one's father ■ **les enfants ~s de mère** motherless children ■ **être ~ de père et de mère** to have lost both one's parents, to be an orphan **2.** [typographie] : **ligne ~e** orphan.
◇ *nm, f* orphan.

orphelinat [ɔrfəlina] *nm* [bâtiment] orphanage ■ [personnes] orphans.

orphéon [ɔrfeɔ̃] *nm* [chœur - d'hommes] male choir ; [- d'enfants] (mixed) children's choir.

orque [ɔrk] *nf* killer whale.

Orsay [ɔrsɛ] *npr* : **le musée d'~** *art museum in Paris.*

ORSEC, Orsec [ɔrsɛk] (*abr de* **Organisation des secours**) *adj* : **plan ~** *disaster contingency plan* ■ **plan ~-Rad** *disaster contingency plan in case of nuclear accident.*

LE PLAN ORSEC

This plan is set in motion whenever there is a major disaster in France, such as flooding or forest fires.

orteil [ɔrtɛj] *nm* toe ■ **gros ~** big toe.

ORTF (*abr de* **Office de radiodiffusion télévision française**) *npr m former French broadcasting corporation.*

orthodontie [ɔrtɔdɔ̃si] *nf* orthodontics *(U)*, dental orthopedics *(U)*.

orthodontiste [ɔrtɔdɔ̃tist] *nmf* orthodontist.

orthodoxe [ɔrtɔdɔks] ◇ *adj* **1.** RELIG Orthodox **2.** *fig* [méthode, pratique] orthodox ■ **pas très** *ou* **peu ~** rather unorthodox.
◇ *nmf* **1.** RELIG member of the Orthodox church ■ **les ~s** the Orthodox **2.** [disciple] : **les ~s de...** the orthodox followers of...

orthodoxie [ɔrtɔdɔksi] *nf* orthodoxy ■ **l'~ marxiste** marxist orthodoxy.

orthogenèse [ɔrtɔʒənɛz] *nf* BIOL orthogenesis.

orthogénie [ɔrtɔʒeni] *nf* birth control.

orthogonal, e, aux [ɔrtɔgɔnal, o] *adj* orthogonal.

orthographe [ɔrtɔgraf] *nf* [graphie] spelling ■ [règles] spelling system, orthography *spéc* ■ [matière] spelling, orthography *spéc* ■ **il y a deux ~s possibles** there are two ways of spelling it *ou* two possible spellings ■ **avoir une bonne/mauvaise ~** to be good/bad at spelling.

orthographier [9] [ɔrtɔgrafje] *vt* to spell ■ **mal/bien orthographié** wrongly/correctly spelt.
◆ **s'orthographier** *vp (emploi passif)* **comment s'orthographie votre nom?** how do you spell your name?

orthographique [ɔrtɔgrafik] *adj* spelling *(modif)*, orthographic.

orthopédique [ɔrtɔpedik] *adj* orthopedic.

orthopédiste [ɔrtɔpedist] *adj* & *nmf* orthopedist.

orthophonie [ɔrtɔfɔni] *nf* **1.** LING orthoepy **2.** MÉD speech therapy.

orthophoniste [ɔrtɔfɔnist] *nmf* speech therapist.

ortie [ɔrti] *nf* (stinging) nettle ■ **~ blanche/rouge** white/red dead-nettle.

ortolan [ɔrtɔlɑ̃] *nm* ortolan.

orvet [ɔrvɛ] *nm* slowworm.

os [ɔs *(pl* [o]*)*] *nm* **1.** ANAT & ZOOL bone ➊ **~ de seiche** cuttlebone ■ **être gelé/trempé jusqu'aux ~** to be frozen to the marrow/soaked to the skin ■ **il ne fera pas de vieux ~!** he's not long for this world! ■ **c'est un sac** *ou* **paquet** *ou* **tas d'~** she's a bag of bones, she's just skin and bones ■ **il l'a eu dans l'~!**△ [il n'a pas réussi] he got egg on his face! ; [il s'est fait escroquer] he's been had! **2.** CULIN bone ■ **viande avec ~** meat on the bone ■ **poulet sans ~** boneless chicken, boned chicken ➊ **~ à moelle** marrowbone ■ **acheter du jambon à l'~** to buy ham off the bone ■ **donner un ~ à ronger à qqn** to give sb sthg to keep him/her quiet **3.** *fam* [difficulté] : **il y a un ~** there's a snag *ou* hitch ■ **elle est tombée sur** *ou* **elle a trouvé un ~** she came across *ou* she hit a snag.

OS *nm* = **ouvrier spécialisé**.

oscar [ɔskar] *nm* **1.** CINÉ Oscar **2.** [récompense] : **l'~ de la meilleure publicité** the award for the best commercial.

oscariser [3] [ɔskarize] *vt* to award an oscar to.

oscillant, e [ɔsilɑ̃, ɑ̃t] *adj* **1.** [qui balance] oscillating **2.** [incertain] oscillating, fluctuating **3.** MÉD [fièvre] irregular **4.** ÉLECTR [décharge] oscillating **5.** PHYS : **circuit ~** oscillating circuit.

oscillateur [ɔsilatœr] *nm* oscillator ■ **maître ~, ~ pilote** RADIO master oscillator.

oscillation [ɔsilasjɔ̃] *nf* **1.** [balancement] swaying, rocking ■ **les ~s du téléphérique** the swaying *ou* swinging of the cable-car **2.** [variation] fluctuation, variation ■ **~s des prix** price variations **3.** ÉLECTR & PHYS oscillation **4.** MÉCAN vibration.

oscillatoire [ɔsilatwar] *adj* oscillatory.

osciller [3] [ɔsile] *vi* **1.** [bouger - pendule, objet suspendu] to oscillate, to swing, to sway ; [- branche, corde] to sway, to swing ; [- arbre, statue] to sway ; [- aiguille aimantée] to flicker ; [- personne, tête] to rock ■ **le courant d'air fit ~ la flamme** the flame was flickering in the draught **2.** [varier] : **~ entre** to vary *ou* to fluctuate between ■ **~ entre deux options** to waver *ou* to hesitate between two options.

oscillogramme [ɔsilɔgram] *nm* oscillogram.

oscillographe [ɔsilɔgraf] *nm* oscillograph.

oscilloscope [ɔsilɔskɔp] *nm* oscilloscope.

osé, e [oze] *adj* **1.** [audacieux - tentative] bold, daring **2.** [choquant - histoire] risqué, racy **3.** *sout* [téméraire - personne] bold, intrepid.

oseille [ozɛj] *nf* **1.** BOT & CULIN sorrel ■ **à l'~** with sorrel **2.** △ [argent] dough△, cash△.

oser [3] [oze] *vt* **1.** [avoir l'audace de] : **~ faire qqch** to dare (to) do sthg ■ **elle n'ose pas parler** she doesn't dare (to) speak, she daren't speak ■ *(en usage absolu)* **comment oses-tu!** how dare you! ■ **il faut ~ dans la vie!** one has to take risks in life! ‖ *sout* [suggestion, réponse] to risk ■ **ils furent trois à ~ l'ascension** three of them risked the climb *ou* were bold enough to climb **2.** [dans les tournures de politesse] : **j'ose croire/espérer que...** I trust/hope that... ■ **si j'ose dire** if I may say so ■ **si j'ose m'exprimer ainsi** if I may say so, if I may put it that way.

oseraie [ozrɛ] *nf* osier bed, osiery.

osier [ozje] *nm* BOT willow, osier ■ **~ rouge** purple willow.
◆ **d'osier, en osier** *loc adj* [fauteuil, panier] wicker, wickerwork *(modif)* ■ **chaise en ~** wicker *ou* wickerwork *ou* basketwork chair.

Osiris [ɔziris] *npr* Osiris.

Oslo [ɔslo] *npr* Oslo.

osmose [ɔsmoz] *nf* **1.** SC osmosis **2.** *fig* osmosis ■ **une ~ s'est produite entre les deux civilisations** the two civilizations have merged into one another.

ossature [ɔsatyr] *nf* **1.** ANAT [d'une personne] frame, skeleton ■ [du visage] bone structure **2.** CONSTR [d'un avion, d'un immeuble] frame, framework, skeleton ■ **pont à ~ métallique** bridge with a metal frame *ou* framework **3.** [d'un discours] framework, structure.

osselet [ɔslɛ] *nm* **1.** ANAT ossicle ■ ZOOL knucklebone **2.** JEUX jacks *(U)*, knucklebones *(U)* ■ **jouer aux ~s** to play jacks **3.** VÉTÉR osselet.

ossements [ɔsmɑ̃] *nmpl* remains, bones.

osseux, euse [ɔsø, øz] *adj* **1.** ANAT bone *(modif)*, osseous *spéc* **2.** MÉD : **greffe osseuse** bone graft ■ **maladie osseuse** bone disease **3.** [aux os apparents] bony.

ossification [ɔsifikasjɔ̃] *nf* ossification.

ossifier [9] [ɔsifje] ◆ **s'ossifier** *vpi* ANAT to ossify.

ossuaire [ɔsɥɛr] *nm* ossuary.

ostensible [ɔstɑ̃sibl] *adj sout* conspicuous, open, clear ■ **avec un mépris ~ pour les conventions** with open contempt for convention.

ostensiblement [ɔstɑ̃sibləmɑ̃] *adv* conspicuously, openly, clearly ■ **il manifesta ~ son ennui** he made it quite clear that he was bored.

ostensoir [ɔstɑ̃swar] *nm* monstrance, ostensory.

ostentation [ɔstɑ̃tasjɔ̃] *nf sout* [affectation, vanité] ostentation ■ **avec ~** with ostentation, ostentatiously ■ **sans ~** without ostentation, unostentatiously.

ostentatoire [ɔstɑ̃tatwar] *adj sout* ostentatious.

ostéologie [ɔsteɔlɔʒi] *nf* osteology.

ostéopathe [ɔsteɔpat] *nmf* osteopath.

ostéopathie [ɔsteɔpati] *nf* [traitement] osteopathy ■ [maladie] bone disease.

ostéoporose [ɔsteɔpɔroz] *nf* osteoporosis.

ostraciser [3] [ɔstrasize] *vt* to ostracize.

ostracisme [ɔstrasism] *nm* **1.** ANTIQ ostracism **2.** *sout* [exclusion] ostracism ■ **être victime d'~** to be ostracized ■ **frapper qqn d'~** to ostracize sb.

ostréicole [ɔstreikɔl] *adj* [région] oyster farming ■ [industrie] oyster *(modif)*.

ostréiculteur, trice [ɔstreikyltœr, tris] *nm, f* oyster farmer, oysterman (*f* oysterwoman).

ostréiculture [ɔstreikyltyr] *nf* oyster farming.

ostrogot(h), e [ɔstrogo, ɔt] *adj* Ostrogothic.
◆ **Ostrogot(h), e** *nm, f* Ostrogoth ■ **les Ostrogoths** the Ostrogoths.
◆ **ostrogot(h)** *nm fam* **un drôle d'~** a funny *ou* strange customer.

otage [ɔtaʒ] *nmf* hostage ■ **prendre qqn en ~** to take sb hostage.

OTAN, Otan [ɔtɑ̃] (*abr de* **Organisation du traité de l'Atlantique Nord**) *npr f* NATO.

otarie [ɔtari] *nf* eared seal.

OTASE [ɔtaz] (*abr de* **Organisation du traité de l'Asie du Sud-Est**) *npr f* SEATO.

ôter [3] [ote] *vt* **1.** [retirer] to take off *(sép)*, to remove (from) ■ **ôte tes pieds du fauteuil** take *ou* get your feet off the armchair ■ **ôtez votre veste** take your jacket off ■ **~ son masque** *pr* to take off *ou* to remove one's mask ; *fig* to unmask o.s. ■ **ôte-moi d'un doute, tu ne vas pas accepter!** wait a minute, you're not actually going to say yes! **2.** [mettre hors de portée] to take away ■ **personne n'a pensé à lui ~ son arme** nobody thought to take his weapon (away) from him **3.** [supprimer] to remove (from) ■ **~ la vie à qqn** to take sb's life ■ **cela m'ôte un poids** *fig* that's a weight off my mind ■ **son attitude m'a ôté mes dernières illusions** his attitude rid me of my last illusions ■ **on ne m'ôtera pas de l'idée que...** I can't help thinking that... **4.** MATH to take away *(sép)* ■ **20 ôté de 100 égale 80** 20 (taken away) from 100 leaves 80.
◆ **s'ôter** ◇ *vp (emploi passif)* [s'enlever] to come off, to be removed ■ **ces bottes s'ôtent facilement** these boots are easy to take off.
◇ *vpt* : **ôte-toi cette idée de la tête** get that idea out of your head.
◆ **s'ôter de** *vp+prép* : **ôte-toi de là (que je m'y mette)** budge up (for me) ■ **ôtez-vous de là, vous gênez le passage** move, you're in the way ▶ **ôte-toi de mon soleil** *Diogène allus* get out of my way.

otite [ɔtit] *nf* otitis *spéc* ■ **~ externe/moyenne** otitis externa/media ■ **~ interne** otitis interna.

oto-rhino [ɔtɔrino] (*pl* **oto-rhinos**) *nmf* ear, nose and throat specialist.

oto-rhino-laryngologie [ɔtɔrinɔlarɛ̃gɔlɔʒi] *nf* otorhinolaryngology.

oto-rhino-laryngologiste [ɔtɔrinɔlarɛ̃gɔlɔʒist] (*pl* **oto-rhino-laryngologistes**) *nmf* otorhinolaryngologist *spéc*, ear, nose and throat specialist.

otoscope [ɔtɔskɔp] *nm* otoscope, auriscope.

Ottawa [ɔtawa] *npr* Ottawa.

ottoman, e [ɔtɔmɑ̃, an] *adj* Ottoman.
◆ **Ottoman, e** *nm, f* Ottoman.
◆ **ottoman** *nm* TEXT ottoman *(rib)*.
◆ **ottomane** *nf* [siège] ottoman *(seat)*.

ou [u] *conj* **1.** [indiquant une alternative ou une équivalence] or ■ **tu peux venir aujourd'hui ou demain** you can come (either) today or tomorrow **2.** [indiquant une approximation] or ■ **ils étaient cinq ou six** there were five or six of them **3.** [indiquant la conséquence] or (else) ■ **rends-le moi, ou ça ira très mal** give it back, or (else) there'll be trouble.
◆ **ou (bien)... ou (bien)** *loc corrélative* either... or ■ **ou bien tu viens et tu es aimable, ou bien tu restes chez toi!** either you come along and be nice, or you stay at home! ■ **ou tu viens, ou tu restes, mais tu arrêtes de te plaindre** you (can) either come or stay, but stop complaining!

où [u] ◇ *pron rel* **1.** [dans l'espace] where ■ **pose-le là où tu l'as trouvé** put it back where you found it ■ **partout où vous irez** everywhere you go ■ **d'où j'étais, je voyais la cathédrale** from where I was, I could see the cathedral ■ **d'où viens-tu?** where have you come from? ■ **le pays d'où je viens** the country which *ou* where I come from ■ **d'où viens-tu en Angleterre?** whereabouts are you from in England? ■ **d'où que tu viennes** wherever you come from ■ **les villes par où nous passerons** the towns which we will go through
2. [dans le temps] : **le jour où je suis venu** the day (that) I came ■ **à l'époque où...** in the days when...
3. *fig* **là où je ne vous suis plus, c'est lorsque vous dites...** the bit where I lose track is when you say... ■ **c'est une spécialité où il excelle** it's a field in which he excels ■ **dans l'état où elle est** in her state, in the state she is ■ **au prix où c'est** at that price ■ **au point où nous en sommes** (at) the point we've reached.
◇ *adv rel* **1.** [dans l'espace] where ■ [avec 'que'] : **où que vous alliez** wherever you go ■ **par où que tu passes** whichever route you take, whichever way you go
2. *fig* **où je ne le comprends pas, c'est lorsque...** where I don't understand him is when...
◇ *adv interr* where ■ **par où voulez-vous passer?** which way do you want to go?, which route do you want to take? ■ **dites-moi vers où il est allé** tell me which direction he went in ■ **par où commencer?** where to begin?, where should I begin? ■ **où voulez-vous en venir?** what point are you trying to make?, what are you trying to say?
◆ **d'où** *loc conj* : **d'où on conclut que...** which leads us *ou* one to the conclusion that... ■ **d'où il suit que...** from which it follows that... ■ **je ne savais pas qu'il était déjà arrivé, d'où ma surprise** I didn't know that he'd already arrived, which is why I was so surprised.

OUA (*abr de* **Organisation de l'unité africaine**) *npr f* OAU.

ouah [wa] *onomat* : **ouah! ouah!** [chien] woof! woof!

ouailles [waj] *nfpl* *hum* flock.

ouais [wɛ] *interj* *fam* yeah.

ouananiche [wananiʃ] *nf* *Québec* Atlantic salmon.

ouaouaron [wawarɔ̃] *nm* *Québec* bullfrog.

ouate [wat] *nf* **1.** [coton] cotton wool ■ **~ de cellulose** cellulose fibre **2.** TEXT wadding, padding ■ **un manteau doublé d'~** a quilted coat.

ouaté, e [wate] *adj* **1.** [doublé] quilted **2.** [assourdi] muffled **3.** [douillet] cocooned.

ouater [3] [wate] *vt* **1.** [vêtement] to quilt ■ [couverture] to wad, to pad **2.** *litt* [estomper] to muffle.

ouatine [watin] *nf* quilting (material).

ouatiner [3] [watine] *vt* to quilt.

oubli [ubli] *nm* **1.** [fait de ne pas se rappeler] forgetting, neglecting ■ **l'~ d'un accent sur un mot coûte un point** forgetting *ou* neglecting to put an accent on a word will lose you one point **2.** [lacune] omission ■ **il y a beaucoup d'~s dans sa liste** she left a lot of items off her list, there are a lot of gaps in her list ■ [trou de mémoire] oversight, lapse of memory ■ **ce n'est qu'un ~** it's just an oversight **3.** *sout* [isolement] : **l'~** oblivion ■ **arracher qqch à** *ou* **tirer qqch de l'~** to snatch *ou* to rescue sthg from oblivion ■ **tomber dans l'~** to sink into oblivion **4.** [consolation] : **l'~ viendra avec le temps** time is a great healer **5.** *litt* [indifférence] : **l'~ de soi** selflessness, self-denial.

oublié, e [ublije] ◇ *adj* **1.** [pièce, roman, peintre] forgotten **2.** [abandonné] left, abandoned ■ **quelques jouets ~s** a few abandoned toys, toys that were left behind.
◇ *nm, f* abandoned *ou* neglected *ou* forgotten person.

oublier [10] [ublije] *vt* **1.** [ne pas se remémorer - nom, rue, date] to forget ■ **n'oublie pas le rendez-vous** don't forget (that) you have an appointment ■ **mon Dieu, le dentiste, je l'ai oublié!** God, the dentist, I'd forgotten all about him! ■ **~ son texte** to forget one's lines ■ **n'oublie pas que c'est son anniversaire** remember *ou* don't forget that it's her birthday ■ *(en usage absolu)* **qu'a-t-elle dit? j'ai oublié** what did she say? I've forgotten ■ [ne pas reconnaître - visage, mélodie] to forget
2. [ne plus penser à - héros, injure, souci] to forget (about) ■ **les preneurs de son sont souvent oubliés par les jurys de prix** sound technicians are often ignored by award juries ■ **j'ai oublié l'heure** I forgot the time ■ **oublions ce malentendu** let's forget (all) about this misunderstanding ■ **je veux bien ~ le passé** I'm ready to forget about the past *ou* to let bygones be bygones ■ **oublie-moi un peu, veux-tu?** *fam* just leave me alone, will you? ■ **se faire ~** to keep a low profile, to stay out of the limelight ■ *(en usage absolu)* to forget ■ **il boit pour ~** he drinks to forget
3. [omettre] to leave out *(sép)* ■ **je ferai en sorte de l'~ dans mon testament/sur le registre** I'll make sure she's left out of my will/left off the register
4. [négliger] to forget (about) ■ **depuis son mariage, il nous oublie** he's been neglecting us *ou* he's forgotten (about) us since he got married
5. [ne pas prendre] to forget, to leave (behind) ■ **~ son colis dans le train** to leave one's parcel on the train ■ **j'ai oublié la lettre à la maison** I left the letter at home
6. [ne pas mettre] to forget.
◆ **s'oublier** ◇ *vp (emploi passif)* : **une fois acquise, la technique ne s'oublie jamais** once you've learnt the technique, it stays with you forever *ou* you'll never forget it.

◇ *vp (emploi réfléchi)* [s'exclure] to forget o.s. ■ **tu ne t'es pas oublié, à ce que je vois!** *hum* I see you've not forgotten yourself!
◇ *vpi* **1.** [se relâcher] to forget o.s.
2. *euphém* [animal, enfant] to have an accident *euphém*.

oubliette [ublijɛt] *nf* [fosse] oubliette.
◆ **oubliettes** *nfpl* [cachot] dungeon, black hole ■ **le projet est tombé dans les** *ou* **aux ~s** *fig* the project has been shelved.

oublieux, euse [ublijø, øz] *adj litt* forgetful ■ **~ de ses devoirs** forgetful of one's duty.

oued [wɛd] *nm* wadi.

Ouessant [wɛsɑ̃] *npr* : **l'île d'~** the isle of Ushant, *voir aussi* **île**.

ouest [wɛst] ◇ *nm inv* **1.** [point cardinal] west ■ **nous allons vers l'~** we're heading west *ou* westwards ■ **aller droit vers l'~** to head due west ■ **la cuisine est plein ~** *ou* **exposée à l'~** the kitchen faces (due) west **2.** [partie d'un pays, d'un continent] west, western area *ou* region ■ **l'~ de l'Italie** Western Italy ■ **elle habite dans l'~** she lives in the west **3.** POLIT : **l'Ouest** Western countries, the West ■ **à l'Ouest, on croit que...** Westerners think that...
◇ *adj inv* west *(modif)*, western ■ **la façade ~ d'un immeuble** the west *ou* west-facing wall of a building.
◆ **à l'ouest de** *loc prép* (to the) west of.

ouest-allemand, e [wɛstalmɑ̃, ɑ̃d] (*mpl* **ouest-allemands**, *fpl* **ouest-allemandes**) *adj* West German.
◆ **Ouest-Allemand, e** *nm, f* West German.

Ouest-France [wɛstfrɑ̃s] *npr* PRESSE *daily newspaper for Western France having the widest circulation of all French newspapers.*

ouf [uf] *interj* phew ■ **je n'ai pas eu le temps de dire ~** I didn't even have time to catch my breath.

Ouganda [ugɑ̃da] *npr m* : **(l')~** Uganda.

ougandais, e [ugɑ̃dɛ, ɛz] *adj* Ugandan.
◆ **Ougandais, e** *nm, f* Ugandan.

oui [wi] ◇ *adv* **1.** [en réponse affirmative] yes ■ **tu en veux? – ~, s'il te plaît** do you want some? – (yes) please ■ **voulez-vous prendre X pour époux? – ~** do you take X to be your lawful wedded husband? – I do ■ **Michel! – ~, ~, voilà, j'arrive!** Michel! – yes *ou* all right, I'm coming! ■ **tu comprends? – ~ et non** do you understand? – yes and no *ou* I do and I don't ■ **alors c'est ~ ou c'est non?** so is it yes or no? ■ **mais ~** yes, of course ■ **~, bien sûr** yes, of course ■ **il est audacieux – certes ~** he's rather daring – he certainly is ■ **~ assurément** yes indeed ■ **c'est vraiment injuste! – ah ça ~!** that's really unfair! – you've said it! *ou* that's for sure! ■ **tu vas déposer une plainte? – ah ça ~!** *fam* are you going to lodge a complaint? – you bet I am! ■ **tu vas la laisser faire? – oh que ~!** *fam* are you going to let her go ahead? – you bet! ■ **~ mon capitaine!** MIL (yes) Sir! **2.** [en remplacement d'une proposition] : **il semblerait que oui** it would seem so ■ **tu vas voter? – je crois que ~** are you going to vote? – (yes) I think so *ou* I think I will ■ **elle n'a dit ni ~ ni non** she didn't say either yes or no, she was very noncommittal ■ **elle vient aussi? si ~, je reste** will she be there too? if so *ou* if she is I'll stay **3.** [emploi expressif] : **~, évidemment, elle a un peu raison** of course, she's right in a way ■ **eh bien ~, c'est moi qui le lui ai dit!** yes, I was the one who told her! ■ **je suis déçu, ~, vraiment déçu!** I'm disappointed, really disappointed! ■ **le nucléaire ~, mais pas à n'importe quel prix!** yes to nuclear energy, but not at any cost! ■ **tu viens, ~?** are you coming then? ■ **tu viens, ~ ou non?** are you coming or not? ■ **c'est bientôt fini de crier, ~?** will you stop shouting?, stop shouting, will you!
◇ *nm inv* : **je voudrais un ~ définitif** I'd like a definitive yes ■ **un ~ franc et massif** a solid yes vote ■ **les ~ et les non** the yesses *ou* ayes and the noes ■ **il y a eu 5 ~** [dans un vote] there were 5 votes for *ou* 5 ayes ▶ **ils se disputent pour un ~ pour un non** they quarrel over the slightest (little) thing ■ **il change d'avis pour un ~ pour un non** he changes his mind at the drop of a hat.

ouï-dire [widir] *nm inv* hearsay ■ **cette histoire n'est fondée que sur des ~** this story is just based on hearsay.
◆ **par ouï-dire** *loc adv* by hearsay, through the grapevine.

ouïe[1] [wi] *nf* **1.** ANAT (sense of) hearing ■ **avoir l'~ fine** to have a keen ear ▶ **continue, je suis tout ~** *hum* go on, I'm all ears **2.** ZOOL gill **3.** MUS sound hole **4.** AUTO louvre.

ouïe[2], **ouille** [uj] *interj* ouch.

Oui-Oui [wiwi] *npr* [personnage] Noddy.

ouïr [51] [wir] *vt* **1.** *litt ou hum* to hear (tell) ■ **j'ai ouï dire que tu avais déménagé** I heard tell that you had moved **2.** DR : **~ des témoins** to hear witnesses.

ouistiti [wistiti] *nm* **1.** ZOOL marmoset **2.** *fam* [personne] : **drôle de ~, celui-là!** funny customer *ou* bit of a weirdo, that one!

ouragan [uragɑ̃] *nm* **1.** MÉTÉOR hurricane ■ **il est entré comme un ~ et s'est mis à hurler** he burst in like a whirlwind and started yelling **2.** [tumulte] storm, uproar ■ **son discours provoqua un ~ de protestations** his speech caused a storm of protest *ou* an uproar.

Oural [ural] *npr m* [montagnes] : **l'~** the Urals, the Ural mountains ■ **dans l'~** in the Urals.

ouralien, enne [uraljɛ̃, ɛn] *adj* Uralic, Uralian.
◆ **ouralien** *nm* LING Uralic.

ourdir [32] [urdir] *vt* **1.** *litt* [complot] to hatch, to weave ■ [intrigue] to weave **2.** TECHNOL [tissage] to warp ■ [vannerie] to weave.

ourdou [urdu] = **urdu**.

ourler [3] [urle] *vt* **1.** COUT to hem **2.** *litt* [border] to fringe ■ **des paupières ourlées de longs cils** eyelids fringed with long eyelashes.

ourlet [urlɛ] *nm* **1.** COUT hem ■ **faire un ~ à une jupe** to hem a skirt ▶ **faux ~** false hem **2.** ANAT helix **3.** MÉTALL flange, rib.

ours [urs] *nm* **1.** ZOOL bear ■ **~ blanc** *ou* **polaire** polar bear ■ **~ brun** brown bear ■ **arrête de tourner en rond comme un ~ en cage!** stop pacing up and down like a caged animal! **2.** [personne] : **il est un peu ~** he's a bit grumpy ▶ **quel ~ mal léché!** grumpy old thing! **3.** [jouet] : **~ (en peluche)** teddy bear.

ourse [urs] *nf* ZOOL she-bear.

Ourse [urs] *npr f* ASTRON : **la Grande ~** Ursa Major, the Great Bear ■ **la Petite ~** Ursa Minor, the Little Bear.

oursin [ursɛ̃] *nm* sea urchin.

ourson [ursɔ̃] *nm* (bear) cub.

oust(e) [ust] *interj fam* out, scram ■ **allez, ~, tout le monde dehors!** come on, get a move on, everybody out!

out [awt] ◇ *adv* **1.** TENNIS out **2.** [en boxe] out, knocked out.
◇ *adj inv* out ■ **une balle ~** an out ball.

outarde [utard] *nf* bustard.

outil [uti] *nm* **1.** [pour travailler] tool ■ **cabane/boîte à ~s** tool shed/box ■ **~s de jardinage** garden implements *ou* tools ■ **savoir utiliser l'~ informatique** *fig* to know how to use computers **2.** ▲ [verge] tool△, cock△.

outillage [utijaʒ] *nm* **1.** [ensemble d'outils] (set of) tools ■ [pour un jardinier] (set of) tools *ou* implements **2.** [industrie] tool making *(U)* **3.** [dans une usine] (machine) tool workshop.

outillé, e [utije] *adj* : **être ~ pour faire qqch** to be properly equipped *ou* to have the proper tools to do sthg ■ **être bien ~ en qqch** to be well equipped with sthg.

outiller [3] [utije] *vt* [ouvrier] to supply with tools ■ [atelier, usine] to equip, to fit with tools.
◆ **s'outiller** *vp (emploi réfléchi)* to equip o.s. (with tools) ■ **vous auriez dû mieux vous ~** you should have made sure you were better equipped.

output [awtput] *nm* output.

outrage [utraʒ] *nm* **1.** [offense] insult ■ **subir les ~s de qqn** to be insulted by sb ■ **faire ~ à l'honneur de qqn** to insult sb's honour ■ **faire ~ à la raison** to be an insult to reason ■ **les ~s du**

temps the ravages of time **2.** DR : **~ à agent** insulting behaviour ▪ **~ aux bonnes mœurs** affront to public decency ▪ **~ à magistrat** (criminal) contempt of court ▪ **~ (public) à la pudeur** indecent exposure.

outrageant, e [utraʒɑ̃, ɑ̃t] *adj* offensive, insulting, abusive.

outrager [17] [utraʒe] *vt* **1.** [offenser] to offend, to insult, to abuse ▪ **~ une femme dans son honneur** to insult a woman's honour **2.** *litt* [porter atteinte à] : **~ le bon sens** *fig* to be an insult to *ou* to offend common sense.
◆ **s'outrager** *vpi sout* **parle franchement, personne ne s'outragera de tes propos** speak freely, your remarks will shock *ou* outrage no one.

outrageusement [utraʒøzmɑ̃] *adv* excessively, extravagantly, outrageously.

outrageux, euse [utraʒø, øz] *adj litt* insulting, offensive, outrageous.

outrance [utrɑ̃s] *nf* **1.** [exagération] excessiveness, extravagance, outrageousness ▪ **l'~ de sa remarque lui ôte toute crédibilité** her remark is so outrageous that it loses all credibility **2.** [acte] extravagance ▪ [parole] extravagant *ou* immoderate language.
◆ **à outrance** ◇ *loc adj* : **combat à ~** all-out fight.
◇ *loc adv* excessively, extravagantly, outrageously.

outrancier, ère [utrɑ̃sje, ɛr] *adj* excessive, extravagant, extreme ▪ **des propos ~s** extreme *ou* wild remarks.

outre[1] [utr] *nf* goatskin, wineskin.

outre[2] [utr] ◇ *prép* [en plus de] besides, as well as ▪ **~ le fait que...** besides the fact that...
◇ *adv* : **passer ~ à qqch** to disregard sthg ▪ **elle a passé ~ malgré l'interdiction** she carried on regardless of *ou* she disregarded the ban.
◆ **en outre** *loc adv* besides, furthermore, moreover.
◆ **outre mesure** *loc adv* overmuch ▪ **le voyage ne l'avait pas fatigué ~ mesure** he wasn't overly tired from the journey.
◆ **outre que** *loc conj* apart from ▪ **~ qu'il est très serviable, il est aussi très efficace** apart from being obliging he's also very efficient, not only is he obliging but he's also very efficient.

outré, e [utre] *adj* **1.** *litt* [exagéré] excessive, exaggerated, overdone **2.** [choqué] indignant, shocked, outraged.

outre-Atlantique [utratlɑ̃tik] *adv* across the Atlantic.

outrecuidance [utrəkɥidɑ̃s] *nf litt* **1.** [fatuité] overconfidence, self-importance **2.** [impertinence] impudence, impertinence.

outrecuidant, e [utrəkɥidɑ̃, ɑ̃t] *adj litt* **1.** [fat, prétentieux] overconfident, self-important **2.** [impertinent] arrogant, impudent, impertinent.

outre-Manche [utrəmɑ̃ʃ] *adv* across the Channel.

outremer [utrəmɛr] ◇ *nm* MINÉR lapis lazuli ▪ [teinte] ultramarine.
◇ *adj inv* ultramarine.

outre-mer [utrəmɛr] *adv* overseas ▪ **la France d'~** France's overseas territories and departments.

outrepasser [3] [utrəpase] *vt* [droit] to go beyond ▪ [ordre] to exceed ▪ **vous outrepassez vos droits** you're going beyond your rights.

outrer [3] [utre] *vt* **1.** *litt* [exagérer] to exaggerate, to magnify ▪ **~ la vérité** to exaggerate *ou* to overstate the truth **2.** [révolter] to outrage.

outre-Rhin [utrərɛ̃] *adv* across the Rhine.

outre-tombe [utrətɔ̃b] ◆ **d'outre-tombe** *loc adj inv* : **une voix d'~** a voice from beyond the grave.

outsider [awtsajdœr] *nm* outsider.

ouvala [uvala] *nf* uvala.

ouvert, e [uvɛr, ɛrt] ◇ *pp* ▷ **ouvrir**.
◇ *adj* **1.** [porte, tiroir] open ▪ **grand ~, grande ~e** wide open ▪ **'col de l'Iseran: ~'** 'Iseran Pass: open' ▪ **une voiture ~e est une tentation pour les voleurs** a car left unlocked *ou* open is an invitation to burglars ▪ **un robinet ~ peut causer une inondation** a tap that's been left on can cause flooding ▪ **il avait la chemise ~e** his shirt was open (to the waist) *ou* undone ▪ **n'achetez pas de tulipes ~es** don't buy tulips that are already open ▪ **elle s'avança la main ~e** she moved forward with her hand open **2.** [bouche, yeux] open ▪ **garder les yeux (grands) ~s** *pr* to keep one's eyes (wide) open ; *fig* to keep one's eyes peeled, to be on the lookout ‖ [coupé] cut, open ▪ **elle a eu la lèvre ~e** her lip was cut **3.** [magasin, bureau, restaurant] open ▪ **en ville, je n'ai rien trouvé d'~** none of the shops were open *ou* nothing was open in town ▪ **ils laissent toujours (tout) ~** they never lock the house ‖ CHASSE & PÊCHE open **4.** [réceptif] open ▪ **un visage ~** an open face ▪ **~ (d'esprit)** open-minded ▪ **avoir l'esprit ~** to be open-minded, to have an open mind ▪ **nous sommes ~s aux idées nouvelles** we are open to new ideas **5.** [non caché] open ▪ **c'est la lutte ~e entre eux** it's open warfare between them **6.** INFORM open ▪ [système] open-ended **7.** MATH open ▪ GÉOM wide **8.** SPORT [imprévisible] : **un match très ~** a wide open game ‖ [offensif] : **un jeu ~** an open game ▶ **tournoi ~** [au golf] open tournament, golf open **9.** LING [syllabe, voyelle] open **10.** ÉLECTR [circuit] open ▪ [machine] uninsulated **11.** FIN : **à capital ~** with an open *ou* a fluctuating capital.

ouvertement [uvɛrtəmɑ̃] *adv* openly.

ouverture [uvɛrtyr] *nf* **1.** [trou] opening ▪ **une ~ dans le mur** an opening *ou* a hole in the wall ▪ **l'événement représente une véritable ~ pour ces pays** *fig* this development will open up real opportunities for these countries
2. [action d'ouvrir] : **l'~ des grilles a lieu à midi** the gates are opened *ou* unlocked at noon ▪ **'~ des portes à 20 h'** 'doors open at eight' ▪ **nous attendons avec impatience l'~ du tunnel** we can hardly wait for the tunnel to open ▪ **l'~ du coffre se fera devant témoins** the safe will be opened *ou* unlocked in front of witnesses
3. [mise à disposition] : **pour faciliter l'~ d'un compte courant** to make it easier to open a current account ▪ **l'~ de vos droits ne date que de février dernier** you were not entitled to claim benefit before last February ▪ **~ de crédit** (bank) credit arrangement ‖ COMM : **les plus belles affaires se font à l'~** the best bargains are to be had when the shop opens ▶ **heures d'~** opening hours ▪ **jours d'~** opening days
4. [d'une session, d'un festival] opening ▪ **je tiens le rayon parfumerie depuis le jour de l'~** I've been in charge of the perfume department since the day we opened ▪ **à l'~** BOURSE at start of trading ▪ **depuis l'~** BOURSE since trading began *ou* opened ‖ CHASSE & PÊCHE opening ▪ **demain, on fait l'~ ensemble** tomorrow we're going out together on the first day of the open season
5. *fig* **l'~ vers la gauche/droite** POLIT broadening the base of government to the left/right ▶ **la politique d'~** consensus politics ▪ **~ d'esprit** open-mindedness
6. RUGBY opening up ▪ [en boxe] opening ▪ **contrôler l'~ des skis** to be in control of the angle of the skis ‖ CARTES & JEUX opening ▪ **avoir l'~** to have the opening move ▪ **avoir l'~ à trèfle** to lead clubs
7. MUS overture
8. PHOTO aperture ▪ **~ du diaphragme** f-stop
9. AUTO [des roues] toe-out
10. ÉLECTR opening, breaking
11. PRESSE front-page article.
◆ **ouvertures** *nfpl* overtures ▪ **faire des ~s de paix** to make peace overtures.

ouvrable [uvrabl] *adj* : **heures ~s** business hours, shop hours ▪ **pendant les heures ~s** COMM during opening hours ; ADMIN during office hours ▪ **jour ~** working day *UK*, workday.

ouvrage [uvraʒ] ◇ *nm* **1.** [travail] work ▪ **se mettre à l'~** to get down to work, to start work **2.** [œuvre] (piece of) work ▶ **~ d'art** ARCHIT & CONSTR construction works ▪ **~ (de dame)** COUT (piece of) needlework ▪ **~s de maçonnerie** masonry **3.** [livre] book **4.** MÉTALL hearth.
◇ *nf sout & hum* : **c'est de la belle ~!** that's a nice piece of work!

ouvragé, e [uvraʒe] *adj* [nappe] (finely *ou* elaborately) embroidered ▪ [construction] elaborate, ornate.

ouvrant, e [uvrɑ̃, ɑ̃t] *adj* opening, moving.

ouvré, e [uvre] *adj* **1.** [bois, fer] ornate, elaborate, elaborately decorated ▪ [nappe] (finely *ou* elaborately) embroidered, finely worked **2.** ADMIN & COMM : **jour ~** working day *UK*, workday.

ouvre-boîtes [uvrəbwat] *nm inv* tin opener *UK*, can opener.

ouvre-bouteilles [uvrəbutɛj] *nm inv* bottle opener.

ouvre-huîtres [uvrɥitr] *nm inv* oyster knife.

ouvrer [3] [uvre] *vt* **1.** [bois] to decorate (elaborately) ▪ [linge] to embroider, to work (finely) **2.** TEXT to open (silk).

ouvreur, euse [uvrœr, øz] *nm, f* **1.** JEUX opener **2.** CINÉ & THÉÂTRE usher, usherette *f* **3.** SPORT forerunner.

ouvrier, ère [uvrije, ɛr] <> *adj* [quartier, condition] working-class ▪ **agitation ouvrière** industrial unrest ➔ **la classe ouvrière** the working class.
<> *nm, f* (manual) worker ▪ **une ouvrière** a (female) worker ▪ **les ~ sur le chantier** the workmen on the site ➔ **~ qualifié/spécialisé** skilled/unskilled worker ▪ **~ agricole** agricultural worker, farm labourer ▪ **~ du bâtiment** builder ▪ **~ à domicile** home worker ▪ **~ à façon** outworker ▪ **~ hautement qualifié** highly-skilled worker ▪ **~ mécanicien** garage mechanic.
◆ **ouvrière** *nf* [abeille] worker (bee) ▪ [fourmi] worker (ant).

ouvriérisme [uvrijerism] *nm* workerism.

ouvriériste [uvrijerist] *adj* & *nmf* workerist.

ouvrir [34] [uvrir] <> *vt* **1.** [portail, tiroir, capot de voiture, fenêtre] to open ▪ [porte fermée à clé] to unlock, to open ▪ [porte verrouillée] to unbolt, to open ▪ **il ouvrit la porte d'un coup d'épaule** he shouldered the door open, he forced the door (open) with his shoulder ▪ **~ une porte par effraction** to force a door ▪ *(en usage absolu)* **je suis allé ~ chez les Loriot avant qu'ils rentrent de voyage** I went and opened up the Loriots' house before they came back from their trip ▪ **va ~** go and answer the door ▪ **on a sonné, je vais ~** there's someone at the door, I'll go ▪ **c'est moi, ouvre** it's me, open the door *ou* let me in
2. [bouteille, pot, porte-monnaie] to open ▪ [coquillage] to open (up) *(sép)* ▪ [paquet] to open, to unwrap ▪ [enveloppe] to open, to unseal
3. [déplier - éventail] to open ; [- carte routière] to open (up) *(sép)*, to unfold ; [- livre] to open (up) *(sép)*
4. [desserrer, écarter - compas, paupières] to open ; [- rideau] to open, to draw back *(sép)* ; [- aile, bras] to open (out) *(sép)*, to spread (out) *(sép)* ; [- mains] to open (out) *(sép)* ▪ [déboutonner - veste] to undo, to unfasten ▪ **~ les yeux** to open one's eyes ▪ **le matin, j'ai du mal à ~ les yeux** [à me réveiller] I find it difficult to wake up in the morning ▪ *(en usage absolu)* ➔ **~ l'œil** *pr* to open one's eye ; *fig* to keep one's eyes open ▪ **cette rencontre avec lui m'a ouvert les yeux** meeting him was a real eye-opener for me ▪ **~ de grands yeux** [être surpris] to be wide-eyed ▪ **ouvrez grands vos yeux** [soyez attentifs] keep your eyes peeled ▪ **~ l'esprit à qqn** to broaden sb's outlook ▪ **tu ferais mieux de ne pas l'~!** you'd better keep your mouth *ou* trap$^{\triangle}$ shut!
5. [commencer - hostilités] to open, to begin ; [- campagne, récit, enquête] to open, to start ; [- bal, festival, conférence, saison de chasse] to open ▪ **la scène qui ouvre la pièce** the opening scene of the play
6. [rendre accessible - chemin, voie] to open (up), to clear ; [- frontière, filière] to open ▪ **ils refusent d'~ leur marché aux produits européens** they refuse to open up their market to European products ▪ **pourquoi ne pas ~ cette formation à de jeunes chômeurs?** why not make this form of training available to young unemployed people? ▪ **le diplôme vous ouvre de nombreuses possibilités** the diploma opens up a whole range of possibilities for you
7. [créer - boutique, cinéma, infrastructure] to open ; [- entreprise] to open, to set up *(sép)*
8. [faire fonctionner - radiateur, robinet] to turn on *(sép)* ; [- circuit électrique] to open ▪ **ouvre la télé** *fam* turn *ou* switch the TV on ▪ **~ l'eau/l'électricité/le gaz** *fam* to turn on the water/the electricity/the gas
9. [être en tête de - défilé, procession] to lead ▪ **c'est son nom qui ouvre la liste** her name is (the) first on the list
10. [inciser - corps] to open (up), to cut open ; [- panaris] to lance, to cut open
11. SPORT : **~ le jeu** to open play ▪ **essayez d'~ un peu plus la partie** try to play a more open game ▪ **~ la marque** *ou* **le score** [gén] to open the scoring ; FOOTBALL to score the first goal
12. BANQUE [compte bancaire, portefeuille d'actions] to open ▪ [emprunt] to issue, to float ▪ **~ un crédit à qqn** to give sb credit facilities ▪ **~ un droit à qqn** [dans les assurances] to entitle sb to a claim
13. JEUX to open ▪ *(en usage absolu)* **~ à cœur** CARTES to open (the bidding) in hearts ; [commencer le jeu] to open *ou* to lead with a heart.
<> *vi* **1.** [boutique, restaurant, spectacle] to (be) open ▪ **la chasse au faisan/la conférence ouvrira en septembre** the pheasant season/the conference will open in September
2. [couvercle, fenêtre, porte] to open ▪ **le portail ouvre mal** the gate is difficult to open *ou* doesn't open properly.
◆ **ouvrir sur** *v+prép* **1.** [déboucher sur] to open onto ▪ **le vasistas ouvre sur le parking** the fanlight opens onto *ou* looks out over the car park
2. [commencer par] to open with
3. SPORT : **~ sur qqn** to pass (the ball) to sb ▪ **~ sur l'aile gauche** to release the ball on the blind side/to the left wing.
◆ **s'ouvrir** <> *vp (emploi passif)* **1.** [boîte, valise] to open ▪ [chemisier, fermeture] to come undone ▪ **ça s'ouvre en dévissant** the top unscrews ▪ **la fenêtre de ma chambre s'ouvre mal** the window in my room is difficult to open *ou* doesn't open properly
2. [être inauguré] to open.
<> *vpt* [se couper - personne] : **je me suis ouvert le pied sur un bout de verre** I've cut my foot (open) on a piece of glass ▪ **s'~ les veines** to slash *ou* to cut one's wrists.
<> *vpi* **1.** [se desserrer, se déplier - bras, fleur, huître, main] to open ; [- aile] to open (out), to spread, to unfold ; [- bouche, œil, paupière, livre, rideau] to open
2. [se fendre - foule, flots] to part ; [- sol] to open up ; [- melon] to open, to split (open) ▪ **la cicatrice s'est ouverte** the scar has opened up
3. [boîte, valise - accidentellement] to (come) open
4. [fenêtre, portail] to open ▪ **la fenêtre s'ouvrit brusquement** the window flew *ou* was flung *ou* was thrown open ▪ **la porte s'ouvre sur la pièce/dans le couloir** the door opens into the room/out into the corridor
5. [s'épancher] to open up ▪ **s'~ à qqn de qqch** to open one's heart to sb about sthg, to confide in sb about sthg ▪ **s'~ de qqch** to open up about sthg
6. [débuter - bal, conférence] : **s'~ par** to open *ou* to start with
7. [se présenter - carrière] to open up.
◆ **s'ouvrir à** *vp+prép* [des idées, des influences] : **s'~ à des cultures nouvelles** to become aware of new cultures ▪ **s'~ à la poésie** to become sensitive to poetry ▪ **leur pays s'ouvre peu à peu au commerce extérieur** their country is gradually opening up to foreign trade.

ouvroir [uvrwar] *nm* [dans un couvent] workroom ▪ [dans une paroisse] sewing room.

ouzbek [uzbɛk] *adj* Uzbek.
◆ **Ouzbek** *nmf* Uzbek.

Ouzbékistan [uzbekistɑ̃] *npr m* : **(l')~** Uzbekistan.

ovaire [ɔvɛr] *nm* ovary.

ovale [ɔval] <> *adj* [en surface] oval ▪ [en volume] egg-shaped, ovoid.
<> *nm* **1.** [forme] oval ▪ **son visage était d'un ~ parfait** her face was a perfect oval **2.** TEXT throwing mill.

ovarien, enne [ɔvarjɛ̃, ɛn] *adj* ovarian.

ovarite [ɔvarit] *nf* ovaritis, oophoritis.

ovation [ɔvasjɔ̃] *nf* ovation ▪ **le public lui a fait une véritable ~** the audience gave her a real ovation.

ovationner [3] [ɔvasjɔne] *vt* : **~ qqn** to give sb an ovation ▪ **le groupe s'est fait ~ pendant 10 minutes** the group were given a 10-minute standing ovation.

overdose [ɔvœrdoz] *nf* **1.** [surdose] overdose **2.** *fam fig* overdose, OD ▪ **j'ai eu une ~ de chocolat à Noël** I overdosed on chocolate at Christmas.

Ovide [ɔvid] *npr* Ovid.

ovin, e [ɔvɛ̃, in] *adj* ovine.
◆ **ovin** *nm* ovine, sheep.

oviné [ɔvine] *nm* [mouton] ovine ▪ [chèvre] caprid.

ovipare [ɔvipar] ◇ *adj* oviparous *spéc*, egg-laying.
◇ *nmf* egg-laying *ou* oviparous *spéc* animal.

OVNI, Ovni [ɔvni] (*abr de* **objet volant non identifié**) *nm* UFO.

ovocyte [ɔvɔsit] *nm* oocyte.

ovoïde [ɔvɔid], **ovoïdal, e, aux** [ɔvɔidal, o] *adj* egg-shaped, ovoid.

ovulation [ɔvylasjɔ̃] *nf* ovulation ▪ **pendant la période d'~** during ovulation.

ovule [ɔvyl] *nm* **1.** PHYSIOL ovum **2.** BOT & ZOOL ovule **3.** PHARM pessary.

ovuler [3] [ɔvyle] *vi* to ovulate.

oxford [ɔksfɔrd] *nm* Oxford (cloth).

oxydable [ɔksidabl] *adj* liable to rust, oxidizable ▪ **facilement ~** which rusts easily.

oxydant, e [ɔksidɑ̃, ɑ̃t] *adj* oxidizing.
◆ **oxydant** *nm* oxidant, oxidizer, oxidizing agent.

oxydation [ɔksidasjɔ̃] *nf* oxidation.

oxyde [ɔksid] *nm* oxide.

oxyder [3] [ɔkside] *vt* to oxidize.
◆ **s'oxyder** *vpi* to become oxidized.

oxygénation [ɔksiʒenasjɔ̃] *nf* oxygenation.

oxygène [ɔksiʒɛn] *nm* **1.** CHIM oxygen **2.** *fig* **j'ai besoin d'~** I need some fresh air.

oxygéné, e [ɔksiʒene] *adj* CHIM oxygenated.

oxygéner [18] [ɔksiʒene] *vt* **1.** CHIM to oxygenate **2.** [cheveux] to bleach, to peroxide.
◆ **s'oxygéner** *vpi* to get some fresh air.

oxymore [ɔksimɔr], **oxymoron** [ɔksimɔrɔ̃] *nm* oxymoron.

ozone [ozɔn] *nm* ozone.

ozoniser [3] [ozɔnize] *vt* to ozonize.

P

p, P [pe] *nm* p, P, *voir aussi* **g**.

p 1. (*abr écrite de* **pico**) p **2.** (*abr écrite de* **page**) p **3.** = **pièce**.

P. (*abr écrite de* **Père**) F.

Pa (*abr écrite de* **pascal**) Pa.

PA = **petites annonces**.

PAC, Pac [pak] (*abr de* **politique agricole commune**) *nf* CAP.

PACA, Paca [paka] (*abr de* **Provence-Alpes-Côte d'Azur**) *npr f southern French region.*

pacage [pakaʒ] *nm* **1.** [lieu] pasture, grazing-land **2.** [action] grazing.

pacane [pakan] *nf* pecan (nut).

pacemaker [pɛsmekœr] *nm* (cardiac) pacemaker.

pacha [paʃa] *nm* **1.** HIST pasha **2.** *fam fig* **mener une vie de ~** to live like a lord, to live a life of ease **3.** NAUT skipper.

pachyderme [paʃidɛrm] ◇ *adj* pachydermal, pachydermatous.
◇ *nm* **1.** ZOOL elephant, pachyderm *spéc* **2.** [personne] (great) elephant.

pacificateur, trice [pasifikatœr, tris] ◇ *adj* [réconciliateur] placatory, pacifying, pacificatory ■ POLIT peacemaking.
◇ *nm, f* pacifier, peacemaker ■ POLIT peacemaker.

pacification [pasifikasjɔ̃] *nf* [gén - POLIT] pacification.

pacifier [9] [pasifje] *vt* to pacify ■ **~ les esprits** to pacify people, to calm people down.

pacifique [pasifik] ◇ *adj* **1.** POLIT [pays, gouvernement] peace-loving **2.** [non militaire] peaceful, non-military ■ **exploitation ~ de l'atome** harnessing atomic power for peaceful purposes **3.** [débonnaire] peaceable **4.** [fait dans le calme] peaceful.
◇ *nmf* peace-loving person.

Pacifique [pasifik] *npr m* : **le ~** the Pacific (Ocean).

pacifiquement [pasifikmɑ̃] *adv* **1.** POLIT peacefully, pacifically ■ **le changement de régime s'est fait ~** the change of regime was achieved by peaceful means **2.** [sans colère] peaceably, peacefully.

pacifisme [pasifism] *nm* pacifism.

pacifiste [pasifist] *adj* & *nmf* pacifist.

pack [pak] *nm* **1.** SPORT pack **2.** GÉOGR pack ice **3.** COMM pack ■ **un ~ de bière** a pack of beer.

package [pakadʒ] *nm* package ■ **voyage en ~** package holiday.

packaging [pakadʒiŋ] *nm* packaging.

pacotille [pakɔtij] *nf* [camelote] cheap junk.
◆ **de pacotille** *loc adj* cheap ■ **des bijoux de ~** baubles *péj*, trinkets *péj*.

PACS [paks] (*abr de* **pacte civil de solidarité**) *nm* civil solidarity pact, *legally recognized cohabitation arrangement, between same-sex or opposite-sex couples.*

pacsé, e [pakse] *nm, f fam person who has signed a PACS agreement*, ≃ (life) partner.

pacser [3] [pakse] ◆ **se pacser** [pakse] *vpi* : **to sign a PACS agreement** to have one's relationship legally recognized.

pacson△ [paksɔ̃] *nm* **1.** [colis] parcel, package **2.** [somme d'argent] : **il a touché un sacré ~** he won a packet *UK ou* bundle *US*.

pacte [pakt] *nm* **1.** [gén] agreement ■ **faire un ~** to make an agreement **2.** POLIT pact, treaty, agreement ■ **~ de non-agression** non-aggression pact ■ **~ de stabilité (et de croissance)** stability (and growth) pact.

pactiser [3] [paktize] ◆ **pactiser avec** *v+prép* **1.** [conclure un accord avec] to make a deal *ou* pact with ■ **~ avec l'ennemi** to make a deal *ou* pact with the enemy **2.** [transiger avec] to collude with, to connive at ■ **~ avec sa conscience** to stifle one's conscience.

pactole [paktɔl] *nm* [profit] gold mine *fig* ■ **on peut se faire un joli ~ dans le pétrole** there are rich pickings to be had in the oil business ‖ [gros lot] jackpot.

paddock [padɔk] *nm* **1.** [enclos] paddock **2.** △ [lit] bed△ ■ **aller au ~** to hit the sack△ *ou* hay△.

Padoue [padu] *npr* Padua.

paella [paela] *nf* paella.

paf[1] [paf] *adj inv fam* sloshed, plastered.

paf[2] [paf] *onomat* bam, wham.

PAF [paf] ◇ *npr f* = **Police de l'air et des frontières**.
◇ *nm* = **paysage audiovisuel français**.

pagaie [pagɛ] ◇ *v* ▷ **pagayer**.
◇ *nf* [rame] paddle.

pagaille, pagaïe [pagaj] *nf fam* [désordre] mess, shambles ■ **pour mettre la ~, t'es champion** when it comes to making a mess, you're unbeatable ■ **arrête de mettre la ~ dans mes affaires** stop messing up my things.
◆ **en pagaille** *loc adv fam* **1.** [en désordre] : **mettre qqch en ~** to mess sthg up **2.** [en quantité] : **ils ont de l'argent en ~** they've got loads of money.

paganiser [3] [paganize] *vt* to paganize.

paganisme [paganism] *nm* paganism.

pagaye [pagaj] *nf* = **pagaille**.

pagayer [11] [pagɛje] *vi* to paddle.

pagayeur, euse [pagɛjœr, øz] *nm, f* paddler.

page¹ [paʒ] *nm* HIST page (boy).

page² [paʒ] *nf* **1.** [rectangle de papier] page ■ **~ blanche** blank page ■ **suite de l'article en ~ cinq** (article) continued on page five ■ **c'est en bas de ~** it's at the bottom of the page ■ **une lettre de huit ~s** an eight-page letter ■ **mettre en ~** IMPR to make up (into pages) ▸ **~ de garde** flyleaf ■ **les ~s jaunes** TÉLÉCOM Yellow Pages® ■ **tourner une ~** *pr* to turn (over) a page ; *fig* to turn over a new leaf ■ **une ~ politique vient d'être tournée avec la mort du sénateur** the death of the senator marks the end of a (political) era ■ **tourner la ~** to make a fresh start, to put something behind one **2.** [extrait] passage, excerpt ■ **une ~ de publicité** RADIO & TV a commercial break ▸ **~s choisies** selected (prose) passages **3.** [épisode] page, chapter ■ **quelques ~s de notre histoire** some pages *ou* chapters in our history **4.** INFORM page ■ **~ d'accueil** home page ■ **~ d'imprimante** printed page ■ **~ précédente** page up ■ **~ suivante** page down ■ **~Web** Web page.
◆ **à la page** *loc adj* up-to-the-minute, up-to-date ■ **tu n'es plus à la ~ du tout!** you're completely out of touch *ou* out of it!

page-écran [paʒekrɑ̃] (*pl* **pages-écrans**) *nf* INFORM screenful.

pager [pɛʒœr] *nm* INFORM pager.

pagination [paʒinasjɔ̃] *nf* **1.** IMPR pagination, page numbering ■ **il y a une erreur de ~** the pages have been numbered wrongly **2.** INFORM page numbering, paging.

paginer [3] [paʒine] *vt* to paginate, to number the pages of.

pagne [paɲ] *nm* [en tissu] loincloth, pagne ■ [en rafia] grass skirt.

pagode [pagɔd] *nf* ARCHIT pagoda.

paie [pɛ] ◇ *v* ▷ **payer**.
◇ *nf* **1.** [salaire] pay, wages ■ **toucher sa ~** to be paid ■ **c'est le jour de ~** it's payday **2.** *fam loc* **ça fait une (sacrée) ~** it's been ages.

paiement [pɛmɑ̃] *nm* payment ■ **faire** *ou* **effectuer un ~** to make a payment ■ **'les ~s par chèques ne sont plus acceptés'** 'cheques are no longer accepted' ▸ **~ comptant** cash payment ■ **~ mensuel** monthly payment ■ **à ~ différé** deferred.

païen, enne [pajɛ̃, ɛn] ◇ *adj* pagan, heathen.
◇ *nm, f* **1.** [polythéiste] pagan, heathen **2.** *sout* [athée] atheist, pagan ■ **jurer comme un ~** to swear like a trooper.

paillage [pajaʒ] *nm* **1.** HORT (straw) mulching **2.** [d'un siège] straw (bottom).

paillard, e [pajar, ard] ◇ *adj* [personne] bawdy, coarse ■ [chanson] dirty ■ [histoire] dirty, smutty.
◇ *nm, f* libertine.

paillardise [pajardiz] *nf* **1.** [caractère] bawdiness, coarseness **2.** [histoire] dirty *ou* smutty story.

paillasse¹ [pajas] *nf* **1.** [matelas grossier] straw *ou* straw-filled mattress ■ **crever la ~ à qqn**△ to do sb in **2.** [d'un évier] drainer, draining board.

paillasse² [pajas] *nm* clown.

paillasson [pajasɔ̃] *nm* **1.** [d'une entrée] doormat **2.** *fam* [personne] : **elle le traite comme un ~** she treats him like a doormat **3.** HORT (straw) mulch.

paille [paj] ◇ *nf* **1.** [chaume] straw ■ **~ de blé** wheat straw ■ **~ de riz** rice straw ■ **il est sur la ~** he's penniless ■ **mettre qqn sur la ~** to ruin sb ■ **une ~!** *fam* a mere bagatelle! **2.** [tige] piece of straw, straw ■ **voir la ~ dans l'œil du prochain et ne pas voir la poutre dans le sien** *allus* & BIBLE to see the mote in one's brother's eye but not the beam in one's own ■ **tirer à la courte ~** to draw straws **3.** [pour boire] (drinking) straw ■ **boire avec une ~** to drink through a straw **4.** MÉTALL flaw ■ **~ de fer** steel wool.
◇ *adj inv* straw-coloured.

paillé, e [paje] *adj* **1.** [siège] straw-bottomed **2.** MÉTALL flawed.

pailler¹ [paje] *nm* [grenier] straw loft ■ [cour] straw yard ■ [meule] straw stack.

pailler² [3] [paje] *vt* **1.** [siège] to straw-bottom **2.** HORT to (straw) mulch.

pailleté, e [pajte] *adj* [robe] sequined ■ [maquillage] glittery.

pailleter [27] [pajte] *vt* [vêtement] to spangle ■ [maquillage, coiffure] to put glitter on.

paillette [pajɛt] *nf* **1.** COUT sequin, spangle ■ **une robe à ~s** a sequined dress **2.** [parcelle - d'or] speck ; [- de quartz, de mica] flake ; [- de savon] flake.
◆ **paillettes** *nfpl* ARM chaff *(U) (metallic foil)*.

paillote [pajɔt] *nf* straw hut.

pain [pɛ̃] *nm* **1.** [baguette] French stick *UK*, French loaf ■ [boule] round loaf (of bread), cob ■ **~ de deux/quatre livres** long two-pound/four-pound loaf ▸ **~ azyme** unleavened bread ■ **~ bénit** consecrated bread ■ **c'est ~ bénit** *fig* that's a godsend ■ **~ biologique** organic wholemeal *UK ou* wholewheat *US* loaf ■ **~ bis** *ou Québec* **brun** brown loaf ■ **~ de blé entier** *Québec* wholemeal *UK ou* wholewheat *US* loaf ■ **~ brioché** brioche-like bread ■ **~ aux céréales** granary bread ■ **~ au chocolat** pain au chocolat *(chocolate-filled roll)* ■ **~ de campagne** farmhouse loaf ■ **~ complet** wholemeal *UK ou* wholewheat *US* loaf ■ **~ d'épices** ≃ gingerbread ■ **~ français** *Québec* French loaf, French stick *UK* ■ **~ de Gênes** ≃ Genoa cake ■ **~ au lait** finger roll *(made with milk)* ■ **~ de mie** sandwich bread ■ **~ parisien** thick French loaf ■ **~ de seigle** rye bread ■ **~ aux raisins** *circular pastry made with sweetened dough and raisins* ■ **~ viennois** Vienna loaf ■ **petits ~s** (bread) rolls
2. [substance] bread ■ **un peu de ~** a bit *ou* piece of bread ■ **un gros morceau de ~** a chunk of bread ■ **mettre qqn au ~ sec et à l'eau** to put sb on dry bread and water ▸ **~ grillé** toast ■ **~ perdu, ~ doré** French toast ■ **notre~ quotidien** our daily bread ■ **la maladie, les soucis d'argent, c'était son ~ quotidien** illness and money worries were her daily lot ■ **long comme un jour sans ~** interminable, endless ■ **avoir du ~ sur la planche** to have one's work cut out ■ **enlever** *ou* **retirer** *ou* **ôter le ~ de la bouche à qqn** to take the bread out of sb's mouth
3. [préparation] loaf ■ **~ de poisson** fish loaf
4. [bloc] : **~ de cire/savon** bar of wax/soap ■ **~ de glace** block of ice ■ **~ de sucre** CULIN sugarloaf ■ **le Pain de Sucre** GÉOGR Sugarloaf Mountain
5. △ [coup] smack ■ **je lui ai filé un de ces ~s!** I socked him one!
◆ **pain brûlé** *loc adj* [tissu, peinture] dark brown ■ [peau] brown as a berry.

pair¹ [pɛr] *nm* **1.** [noble] peer **2.** [égal] peer ■ **jugé par ses ~s** judged by one's peers **3.** BOURSE par (value) ■ **emprunt émis au-dessus du ~** loan issued above par ‖ FIN par (rate of exchange) ■ **~ d'une monnaie** par of a currency.
◆ **au pair** ◇ *loc adj* : **jeune fille au ~** au pair girl.
◇ *loc adv* : **travailler au ~** to work as an au pair.
◆ **de pair** *loc adv* together ■ **la méchanceté va souvent de ~ avec la bêtise** nastiness often goes together *ou* hand in hand with stupidity.
◆ **hors pair, hors de pair** *loc adj* outstanding ■ **c'est un cuisinier hors ~** he's an outstanding cook ■ **dans son domaine il est hors de ~** he is unequalled in his field.

pair², e [pɛr] *adj* even ■ **jouer un chiffre ~** to bet on an even number ■ **habiter du côté ~** to live on the even-numbered side of the street ■ **stationnement les jours ~s seulement** parking on even dates only.

paire [pɛr] *nf* [de ciseaux, chaussures] pair ■ [boeufs] yoke ■ **si tu continues, tu vas recevoir une ~ de gifles** if you go on like this, you'll get your face slapped ▸ **c'est une autre ~ de manches** that's a different kettle of fish ■ **se faire la ~** *fam* to beat it, to clear off.

pairesse [pɛrɛs] *nf* **1.** [en Grande-Bretagne] peeress **2.** [épouse d'un pair] wife of a peer.

paisible [pezibl] *adj* **1.** [doux] peaceful, quiet ■ **un homme ~** a quiet man **2.** [serein] quiet, calm, peaceful ■ **le bébé dort d'un sommeil ~** the baby is sleeping peacefully **3.** [silencieux] calm, quiet.

paisiblement [pezibləmɑ̃] *adv* **1.** [dormir] peacefully, quietly **2.** [parler, discuter] calmly.

paître [91] [pɛtr] <> *vi* [animaux] to graze ■ **faire ~ le bétail** to graze the cattle, to put the cattle out to graze.
<> *vt* [suj: animal] to feed on, to graze (on).

paix [pɛ] *nf* **1.** MIL & POLIT peace ■ **demander la ~** to sue for peace ■ **pourparlers/offres de ~** peace talks/proposals ■ **négocier la ~** to negotiate peace ■ **en temps de ~** in peacetime ■ **faire la ~** to make peace ■ **signer/ratifier un traité de ~** to sign/to ratify a peace treaty ➊ **~ séparée/armée** separate/armed peace ■ **la ~ des braves** an honourable peace ■ **~ romaine** Pax Romana ■ **si tu veux la ~, prépare la guerre** *prov* if you wish for peace, prepare for war
2. [ordre] peace ■ **favoriser la ~ sociale** to promote social peace
3. [entente] peace ■ **vivre en ~** to live in peace ■ **il a enfin fait la ~ avec sa soeur** he finally made his peace with *ou* made up with his sister ■ **je suis pour la ~ des ménages** I'm against stirring things up between couples
4. [repos] peace, quiet ■ **j'ai enfin la ~ depuis qu'il est parti** I've at last got some peace and quiet now that he's left ■ **laisse-moi en ~!** leave me alone! ■ **fiche-moi la ~!** *fam* buzz off!, clear off! ■ **la ~!** *fam* quiet!, shut up!
5. [sérénité] peace ■ **trouver la ~ de l'âme** to find inner peace ■ **avoir la conscience en ~** to have a clear conscience ➊ **qu'il repose en ~, ~ à son âme** may he *ou* his soul rest in peace
6. *sout* [harmonie] peace, peacefulness.

Pakistan [pakistɑ̃] *npr m* : **le ~** Pakistan ■ **au ~** in Pakistan.

pakistanais, e [pakistanɛ, ɛz] *adj* Pakistani.
◆ **Pakistanais, e** *nm, f* Pakistani.

pal [pal] *nm* stake, pale ■ **le supplice du ~** torture by impalement.

PAL, Pal [pal] (*abr de* **Phase Alternation Line**) *adj* PAL.

palabre [palabr] *nf* & *nm* HIST palaver.
◆ **palabres** *nfpl péj* [discussion oiseuse] endless talk ■ **à ces réunions, ce ne sont que des ~s** these meetings are just talking shops *péj*.

palabrer [3] [palabre] *vi* to talk endlessly ■ **vous ne faites que ~** all you ever do is talk.

palace [palas] *nm* luxury hotel.

paladin [paladɛ̃] *nm* **1.** HIST paladin **2.** *litt* [redresseur de torts] knight in shining armour, righter of wrongs.

palais [palɛ] *nm* **1.** [bâtiment] palace ■ **~ des expositions** exhibition hall ■ **~ des sports** sports stadium ▮ [monument] : **le ~ Garnier** *the (old) Paris opera house* ■ **le ~ des Papes** *the Papal Palace in Avignon* ■ **le Grand Palais, le Petit Palais** *galleries built for the Exposition universelle in 1900, now used for art exhibitions* **2.** ANAT palate **3.** [organe du goût] palate ■ **elle a le ~ fin** she has a refined palate.

PALAIS DES PAPES

This historic building, dating from the 13th and 14th centuries, is the prestigious venue for the most important events of the *Festival d'Avignon*.

Palais-Bourbon [palɛburbɔ̃] *npr m* the French National Assembly.

Palais-Royal [palɛrwajal] *npr m palace and gardens built for Cardinal Richelieu, which later became a popular place of leisure and now houses the Théâtre-Français, the Conseil d'État and the Ministry of Culture.*

palan [palɑ̃] *nm* hoist.

palanque [palɑ̃k] *nf* (timber) stockade.

palanquin [palɑ̃kɛ̃] *nm* **1.** [chaise] palanquin **2.** NAUT reef tackle.

palatal, e, aux [palatal, o] *adj* [voyelle] front ■ [consonne] palatal.

palatalisation [palatalizasjɔ̃] *nf* palatalization.

palatalisé, e [palatalize] *adj* palatalized.

palatin, e [palatɛ̃, in] *adj* **1.** [du palais] palace *(modif)* **2.** [du Palatinat] Palatine *(modif)* **3.** ANAT palatine, palatal.

Palatin [palatɛ̃] *npr m* : **le (mont) ~** the Palatine hill.

Palatinat [palatina] *npr m* : **le ~** the Palatinate.

pale [pal] *nf* **1.** [d'une hélice, d'une rame] blade ■ [d'un bateau à aube] paddle **2.** [vanne] shut-off **3.** RELIG pall.

pâle [pal] *adj* **1.** [clair] pale ■ [exsangue] pale, pallid ➊ **être ~ comme la mort** to be as pale as death ■ **être ~ comme un linge** to be as white as a sheet **2.** [couleur] pale ■ **une robe jaune ~** a pale yellow dress **3.** [insipide] pale, weak ■ **son spectacle n'est qu'une ~ imitation de l'œuvre** his show is nothing but a pale *ou* poor imitation of the book.

palefrenier, ère [palfrənje, ɛr] *nm, f* [homme] stableman, ostler ■ [femme] stable girl ■ [garçon] stable boy.

palefroi [palfrwa] *nm* palfrey.

paléo- [paleo] *préf* paleo-.

paléocène [paleɔsɛn] *adj* & *nm* Palaeocene.

paléochrétien, enne [paleɔkretjɛ̃, ɛn] *adj* ART early Christian.

paléographe [paleɔgraf] <> *adj* paleographic.
<> *nmf* paleographer.

paléographie [paleɔgrafi] *nf* paleography.

paléolithique [paleɔlitik] <> *adj* Paleolithic.
<> *nm* : **le ~** the Paleolithic period.

paléontologie [paleɔ̃tɔlɔʒi] *nf* paleontology.

paléontologiste [paleɔ̃tɔlɔʒist], **paléontologue** [paleɔ̃tɔlɔg] *nmf* paleontologist.

Palerme [palɛrm] *npr* Palermo.

Palestine [palɛstin] *npr f* : **(la) ~** Palestine.

palestinien, enne [palɛstinjɛ̃, ɛn] *adj* Palestinian.
◆ **Palestinien, enne** *nm, f* Palestinian.

palet [palɛ] *nm* **1.** SPORT puck **2.** JEUX [à la marelle] quoit.

paletot [palto] *nm* **1.** [vêtement] (short) jacket **2.** *fam loc* **il m'est tombé sur le ~** he laid into me.

palette [palɛt] *nf* **1.** ART palette ■ **proposer toute une ~ d'articles** to offer a wide choice *ou* range of articles **2.** INFORM : **~ flottante** floating toolbar **3.** CULIN shoulder **4.** NAUT paddle **5.** TECHNOL [instrument] pallet ■ [pour la manutention] pallet, stillage **6.** PÊCHE (hook) eye.

palettiser [3] [paletize] *vt* to palletize.

palétuvier [paletyvje] *nm* mangrove.

pâleur [palœr] *nf* [d'une couleur] paleness ■ [du teint] pallor ■ **je fus frappé par sa ~** I was surprised to see how pale she looked.

pâlichon, onne [paliʃɔ̃, ɔn] *adj fam* (a bit) pale *ou* peaky.

palier [palje] *nm* **1.** [plate-forme] landing ■ **~ de repos** half-landing **2.** [niveau] stage, level **3.** TRAV PUB level, flat **4.** AÉRON : **voler en ~** to fly level **5.** MÉCAN bearing.
◆ **par paliers** *loc adv* in stages, step by step ■ **la tension monte par ~s** tension is gradually mounting.

palière [paljɛr] *adj f* landing *(modif)*.

palimpseste [palɛ̃psɛst] *nm* palimpsest.

palindrome [palɛ̃drom] <> *adj* palindromic.
<> *nm* palindrome.

pâlir [32] [palir] *vi* **1.** [personne] to (turn *ou* go) pale ■ **~ de froid/peur** to turn pale with cold/fear ■ **~ de jalousie/d'envie** to go green with jealousy/envy **2.** [couleur, lumière] to grow dim *ou* pale, to fade **3.** [gloire] to fade (away), to grow faint *ou* fainter, to dim.

palissade [palisad] *nf* **1.** [clôture - de pieux] fence, paling, palisade ; [- de planches] hoarding ; [- d'arbres] hedgerow **2.** MIL palisade.

palissage [palisaʒ] *nm* [opération] training, trellising ▪ [support] trainer, trellis.

palissandre [palisɑ̃dr] *nm* rosewood, palissander.

pâlissant, e [palisɑ̃, ɑ̃t] *adj* [lumière] fading, growing *ou* becoming dim.

palladium [paladjɔm] *nm* palladium.

palliatif, ive [paljatif, iv] *adj* palliative.
◆ **palliatif** *nm* **1.** MÉD palliative **2.** [expédient] palliative, stopgap measure.

pallier [9] [palje] *vt* [remédier à] to alleviate, to mitigate, to make up for.
◆ **pallier à** *v+prép* to make up for, to offset.

palmarès [palmarɛs] *nm* [liste - de lauréats] prize list, list of prizewinners ; [- de sportifs] winners' list, list of winners ; [- de chansons] charts ▪ **être premier au ~** to top the charts, to be top of the pops ▪ **avoir de nombreuses victoires à son ~** to have numerous victories to one's credit.

palme [palm] *nf* **1.** BOT [feuille] palm leaf ▪ [palmier] palm tree ▪ **huile/vin de ~** palm oil/wine **2.** [distinction] palm ▪ **la ~ du martyre** the crown of martyrdom ▪ **la Palme d'Or** *trophy awarded for best film at the Cannes film festival* ▪ **remporter la ~** [être le meilleur] to be the best ; *iron* to win hands down **3.** LOISIRS & SPORT flipper.
◆ **palmes** *nfpl* : **~s académiques** *decoration for services to education, the arts or science.*

palmé, e [palme] *adj* **1.** BOT palmate ▪ ZOOL palmate *spéc*, webbed **2.** *fam loc* **les avoir ~es** to be workshy.

palmer[1] [palmɛr] *nm* [instrument] micrometer.

palmer[2] [palmœr] *nm* PÊCHE palmer.

palmeraie [palmərɛ] *nf* palm grove.

palmier [palmje] *nm* **1.** BOT palm (tree) ▪ **~ dattier** date palm **2.** [pâtisserie] palmier *(large sweet pastry).*

palmipède [palmipɛd] ◇ *adj* palmiped *spéc*, web-footed, web-toed.
◇ *nm* palmiped.

palombe [palɔ̃b] *nf* ringdove, woodpigeon.

palonnier [palɔnje] *nm* **1.** AÉRON rudder (bar) **2.** [d'un véhicule] rocking lever **3.** [en ski nautique] handle **4.** TECHNOL (lifting) beam *ou* leg.

pâlot, otte [palo, ɔt] *adj fam* (a bit) pale ▪ **bien ~, ton fils!** your boy's very pale *ou* pale-looking!

palourde [palurd] *nf* clam.

palpable [palpabl] *adj* **1.** [évident] palpable **2.** [que l'on peut toucher] palpable **3.** [concret] tangible ▪ **des avantages ~s** tangible benefits.

palper [3] [palpe] *vt* **1.** MÉD to palpate **2.** [tâter] to feel ▪ **~ un tissu** to finger a fabric **3.** *fam* [recevoir] : **elle a palpé une belle somme** she got a tidy sum.

palpeur [palpœr] *nm* sensor.

palpitant, e [palpitɑ̃, ɑ̃t] *adj* **1.** [passionnant] thrilling, exciting, exhilarating **2.** [frémissant] quivering, trembling.
◆ **palpitant** *nm fam* heart, ticker△.

palpitation [palpitasjɔ̃] *nf* **1.** [du cœur, des artères] pounding ▪ [des flancs] heaving ▪ [des paupières] fluttering **2.** *litt* [frémissement] quivering, trembling.
◆ **palpitations** *nfpl* palpitations ▪ **avoir des ~s** [une fois] to have (an attack of) palpitations ; [souvent] to suffer from palpitations.

palpiter [3] [palpite] *vi* [artère] to throb ▪ [paupière] to flutter ▪ [flancs] to quiver, to heave ▪ **son cœur palpitait violemment** PHYSIOL her heart was beating fast *ou* pounding ; [d'émotion] her heart was pounding *ou* throbbing.

paltoquet [paltɔkɛ] *nm fam* [personne insignifiante] pipsqueak.

palu [paly] *nm fam* malaria, paludism.

paluche [palyʃ] *nf fam* hand, paw, mitt.

paludéen, enne [palydeɛ̃, ɛn] *adj* **1.** MÉD malarial **2.** [des marais] marsh *(modif)*, paludal.

paludisme [palydism] *nm* malaria, paludism.

pâmer [3] [pame] ◆ **se pâmer** *vpi litt* to swoon ▪ **se ~ devant qqn** *hum* to swoon over sb.

pâmoison [pamwazɔ̃] *nf hum* swoon, fainting fit ▪ **tomber en ~** to swoon.

pampa [pɑ̃pa] *nf* pampas.

pamphlet [pɑ̃flɛ] *nm* lampoon, squib.

pamphlétaire [pɑ̃fletɛr] ◇ *adj* [ton, esprit] pamphleteering.
◇ *nmf* lampoonist, pamphleteer.

pamplemousse [pɑ̃pləmus] *nm* & *nf* grapefruit, pomelo *US*.

pamplemoussier [pɑ̃pləmusje] *nm* grapefruit (tree).

pampre [pɑ̃pr] *nm* **1.** BOT vine branch **2.** ART pampre.

pan[1] [pɑ̃] *interj* [gifle] wham, whack ▪ [coup de feu] bang.

pan[2] [pɑ̃] *nm* **1.** [d'un vêtement] tail ▪ [d'une nappe] fold **2.** CONSTR : **~ de bois/fer** wood/metal framing ▪ **~ coupé/de verre** canted/plate-glass wall ▪ **~ de mur** (face *ou* plain of a) wall **3.** [morceau] section, piece ▪ **un ~ de ciel bleu** a patch of blue sky ▪ **des ~s entiers de la société** whole sections *ou* strata of society **4.** TECHNOL side, face.

Pan [pɑ̃] *npr* Pan.

panacée [panase] *nf* panacea.

panachage [panaʃaʒ] *nm* **1.** [mélange] blend, blending, mixing **2.** POLIT *voting for candidates from different lists rather than for a list as a whole.*

panache [panaʃ] *nm* **1.** [plume] plume, panache ▪ **~ de fumée** *fig* plume of smoke **2.** [brio] panache, style, verve ▪ **avoir du ~** to have panache, to show great verve **3.** ARCHIT [ornement] panache, (ostrich) feather ▪ [surface] pendentive.

panaché, e [panaʃe] *adj* [sélection] mixed ▪ [fleurs] variegated ▪ [glace] mixed-flavour ▪ **un demi ~** a (lager) shandy.
◆ **panaché** *nm* (lager) shandy.

panacher [3] [panaʃe] *vt* **1.** [mélanger] to blend, to mix **2.** POLIT : **~ une liste électorale** *to vote for candidates from different lists rather than for a list as a whole.*

panade [panad] *nf* **1.** CULIN bread soup **2.** *fam loc* **être dans la ~** to be hard up.

panafricain, e [panafrikɛ̃, ɛn] *adj* Pan-African.

panafricanisme [panafrikanism] *nm* Pan-Africanism.

panama [panama] *nm* [chapeau] panama, Panama.

Panama [panama] ◇ *npr m* [pays] : **le ~** Panama ▪ **au ~** in Panama.
◇ *npr* [ville] Panama City.

Paname [panam] *npr fam* Paris.

panaméen, enne [panameɛ̃, ɛn] *adj* Panamanian.
◆ **Panaméen, enne** *nm, f* Panamanian.

panaméricain, e [panamerikɛ̃, ɛn] *adj* Pan-American.

panaméricanisme [panamerikanism] *nm* Pan-Americanism.

panamien, enne [panamjɛ̃, ɛn] = **panaméen.**

panarabe [panarab] *adj* Pan-Arab.

panarabisme [panarabism] *nm* Pan-Arabism.

panard, e [panar, ard] *adj* VÉTÉR cow-hocked, duck-footed.
◆ **panard**△ *nm* foot ▪ **t'as vu les ~s qu'il a?** have you seen the size of his feet?

panaris [panari] *nm* whitlow.

pan-bagnat [pɑ̃baɲa] (*pl* **pans-bagnats**) *nm* filled roll *(containing tomatoes, onions, green peppers, olives, tuna and anchovies and seasoned with olive oil)*.

pancarte [pɑ̃kart] *nf* [gén] sign, notice ▪ [dans une manifestation] placard ▪ **les manifestants ont levé leurs ~s** the demonstrators raised their placards.

pancréas [pɑ̃kreas] *nm* pancreas.

pancréatique [pɑ̃kreatik] *adj* pancreatic.

panda [pɑ̃da] *nm* panda.

pandémie [pɑ̃demi] *nf* pandemic.

Pandore [pɑ̃dɔr] *npr* Pandora ▪ **la boîte de ~** Pandora's box.

pané, e [pane] *adj* breaded.

panégyrique [paneʒirik] *nm* panegyric, eulogy ▪ **faire le ~ de qqn** to extol sb's virtues, to eulogize sb.

panel [panɛl] *nm* **1.** TV panel **2.** [échantillon] panel, sample group.

paner [3] [pane] *vt* to breadcrumb, to coat with breadcrumbs.

paneuropéen, enne [panørɔpeɛ̃, ɛn] *adj* Pan-European.

pangermanisme [pɑ̃ʒɛrmanism] *nm* Pan-Germanism.

pangermaniste [pɑ̃ʒɛrmanist] *adj & nmf* Pan-Germanist.

panhellénique [panelenik] *adj* Panhellenic.

panhellénisme [panelenism] *nm* Panhellenism.

panier [panje] *nm* **1.** [corbeille] basket ▪ PÊCHE lobster pot ▪ **~ à linge/pain** linen/bread basket ▪ **~ à bouteilles** bottle case *ou* carrier ▪ **~ à provisions** shopping basket ▪ **~ à salade** *pr* salad shaker ▪ *fam* [fourgon cellulaire] Black Maria ▪ **bon à mettre** *ou* **jeter au ~** fit for the bin *UK ou* trashcan *US* ▪ **ils sont tous à mettre dans le même ~** they're all much of a muchness ▪ **être un (véritable) ~ percé** to be a (real) spendthrift ▪ **mettre la main au ~ à qqn**△ to goose sb△ ▪ **c'est un (véritable) ~ de crabes** they're always at each other's throats **2.** [quantité] : **un (plein) ~ de** a basketful of **3.** SPORT basket ▪ **réussir un ~** to score a basket **4.** ÉCON : **~ de la ménagère** shopping basket ▪ **la hausse du beurre se répercute sur le ~ de la ménagère** the increase in the price of butter makes a difference to the housekeeping bill ▪ **~ de monnaies** basket of currencies.

panier-repas [panjerəpa] (*pl* **paniers-repas**) *nm* packed lunch.

panifier [9] [panifje] *vt* to make bread from.

panini [panini] *nm* panini.

paniquant, e [panikɑ̃, ɑ̃t] *adj* frightening, panic-inducing.

panique [panik] ◇ *nf* [terreur] panic ▪ **il s'est enfui, pris de ~** he ran away panic-stricken ▪ **c'était la ~!** *fam* it was panic stations! ▪ **pas de ~!** no need to *ou* there's no panic!
◇ *adj* panic ▪ **envahi par une peur ~** overcome by panic.

paniquer [3] [panike] ◇ *vt* [angoisser] to (throw into a) panic ▪ **l'approche des examens le panique** he's starting to panic as the exams get nearer ▪ **il est paniqué à l'idée de la rencontrer** he's panic-stricken at the thought of meeting her, the thought of meeting her fills him with panic.
◇ *vi* to panic ▪ **elle n'a pas paniqué** she didn't lose her head *ou* didn't panic ▪ **la nouvelle les a fait ~** the news panicked them.
◆ **se paniquer** *vpi* to panic ▪ **ne nous paniquons pas, nous avons tout le temps** let's not panic, we've got plenty of time.

panislamisme [panislamism] *nm* Pan-Islamism.

panjabi [pɑ̃dʒabi] *nm* LING Punjabi.

panne [pan] *nf* **1.** [de voiture] breakdown ▶ **~ d'électricité** *ou* **de courant** power cut *ou* failure ▪ **~ d'essence : avoir une ~ d'essence** to run out of petrol *UK ou* gas *US* ▪ **~ de secteur** local mains failure **2.** TEXT panne **3.** [d'un cochon] pig's fat *ou* lard **4.** [d'un marteau] peen ▪ [d'un bâtiment] purlin, purline **5.** THÉÂTRE bit part.
◆ **en panne** ◇ *loc adj* : **des automobilistes en ~** drivers whose cars have broken down ▪ **'en ~'** 'out of order' ▪ **la machine/voiture est en ~** the machine/car has broken down ▪ **je suis en ~ de poivre/d'idées** *fig* I've run out of *ou* I'm out of pepper/ideas.
◇ *loc adv* : **tomber en ~ : la machine est tombée en ~** the machine has broken down ▪ **je suis tombé en ~ d'essence** *ou* **sèche** *fam* I've run out of petrol.

panneau, x [pano] *nm* **1.** [pancarte] sign ▶ **~ d'affichage** notice board ▪ **~ électoral** election hoardings *UK ou* billboards *US* ▪ **~ indicateur** signpost ▪ **~ de signalisation** roadsign **2.** [plaque] panel ▪ **un ~ de contreplaqué** a piece *ou* panel of plywood ▪ **~ de particules** chipboard ▶ **~ solaire** solar panel **3.** ART panel **4.** COUT panel **5.** CHASSE (game) net ▪ **tomber** *ou* **donner dans le ~** to fall into the trap **6.** HORT (cold) frame **7.** NAUT hatch (cover).

panneau-réclame [panoreklam] (*pl* **panneaux-réclame**) *nm* hoarding *UK*, billboard *US*.

panneton [pantɔ̃] *nm* bit, web *(of a key)*.

panonceau, x [panɔ̃so] *nm* [plaque] plaque, sign ▪ [écriteau] sign ▪ **~ publicitaire** advert *UK*, advertisement.

panoplie [panɔpli] *nf* **1.** [ensemble d'instruments] (complete) set ▪ **la ~ du bricoleur** do-it-yourself equipment *ou* kit **2.** JEUX outfit ▪ **une ~ de Zorro/d'infirmière** a Zorro/nurse's outfit **3.** *fig* **une ~ de mesures contre les chauffards** a full array of measures against dangerous drivers **4.** HIST [armure complète] panoply.

panorama [panɔrama] *nm* **1.** [vue] panorama, view **2.** *fig* [vue d'ensemble] survey, overview ▪ **pour terminer ce ~ de l'actualité musicale** to end this roundup of current musical events **3.** ART panorama.

panoramique [panɔramik] ◇ *adj* panoramic ▪ **écran ~** panoramic screen.
◇ *nm* CINÉ panoramic shot.

panosse [panɔs] *nf Suisse* mop.

pansage [pɑ̃saʒ] *nm* grooming.

panse [pɑ̃s] *nf* **1.** ZOOL paunch, rumen **2.** *fam* [d'une personne] paunch, belly△ ▪ **s'en mettre plein** *ou* **se remplir la ~** to make a pig of o.s., to stuff one's face **3.** [d'un vase] belly.

pansement [pɑ̃smɑ̃] *nm* [action] dressing ▪ [objet] dressing, bandage ▪ **il lui a fait un ~ à la jambe** he bandaged her leg ▪ **couvert de ~s** bandaged up ▶ **~ adhésif** (sticking) plaster *UK*, Elastoplast® *UK*, Band Aid® *US*.

panser [3] [pɑ̃se] *vt* **1.** MÉD to dress (and bandage) ▪ **~ une blessure** to dress *ou* to put a dressing on a wound ▪ **~ un bras** to bandage an arm ▪ **~ les plaies de qqn** to tend sb's wounds **2.** [toiletter - animal] to groom.

panslave [pɑ̃slav] *adj* Pan-Slavic.

panslavisme [pɑ̃slavism] *nm* Pan-Slavism.

panslaviste [pɑ̃slavist] ◇ *adj* Pan-Slavic, Pan-Slav *(avant n)*.
◇ *nmf* Pan-Slavist.

pansu, e [pɑ̃sy] *adj* **1.** *fam* [ventripotent] paunchy, potbellied **2.** [renflé - cruche, bouteille] potbellied.

pantacourt [pɑ̃takur] *nm* capri pants, capris, clamdiggers.

Pantagruel [pɑ̃tagryɛl] *npr* LITTÉR *the eponymous giant son of Gargantua in Rabelais' novel (1534) and its three sequels (1546-1562)*.

pantagruélique [pɑ̃tagryelik] *adj* Pantagruelian ▪ **avoir un appétit ~** to have an enormous appetite ▪ **faire un repas ~** to have a gargantuan meal.

pantalon [pɑ̃talɔ̃] *nm* (pair of) trousers *UK ou* pants *US* ▪ **mon ~** my trousers ▪ **deux ~s** two pairs of trousers ▪ **~ de golf** (pair of) plus fours ▪ **~ de pyjama** pyjama trousers *ou* bottoms.

pantalonnade [pɑ̃talɔnad] *nf* **1.** [hypocrisie] hypocrisy *(U)*, cant *(U)*, pretence *(U)* **2.** THÉÂTRE (second-rate) farce.

pantelant, e [pɑ̃tlɑ̃, ɑ̃t] *adj* panting, gasping for breath ▪ **être ~ de terreur** *litt* to be panting *ou* gasping with terror.

panthéisme [pɑ̃teism] *nm* pantheism.

panthéiste [pɑ̃teist] ◇ *adj* pantheistic.
◇ *nmf* pantheist.

panthéon [pɑ̃teɔ̃] *nm* **1.** ANTIQ & RELIG pantheon ■ **le Panthéon** the Pantheon **2.** *fig* pantheon, hall of fame.

panthère [pɑ̃tɛr] *nf* **1.** ZOOL panther ■ **~ des neiges** snow leopard **2.** [fourrure] leopard (skin) **3.** POLIT : **les Panthères noires** the Black Panthers.

pantin [pɑ̃tɛ̃] *nm* **1.** [jouet] jumping jack **2.** *fig* puppet ■ **n'être qu'un ~ entre les mains de qqn** to be sb's puppet.

pantographe [pɑ̃tɔgraf] *nm* TECHNOL pantograph.

pantois, e [pɑ̃twa, az] *adj* speechless ■ **elle en est restée ~e** it left her speechless.

pantomime [pɑ̃tɔmim] *nf* **1.** [jeu de mime] mime ■ THÉÂTRE [pièce] mime show **2.** *péj* [mimique] scene, fuss.

pantouflage [pɑ̃tuflaʒ] *nm* *fam* *leaving a civil service post to work in the private sector.*

pantouflard, e [pɑ̃tuflar, ard] *nm, f* *fam* homebody, stay-at-home (type).

pantoufle [pɑ̃tufl] *nf* slipper ■ **~ de vair** [dans Cendrillon] glass slipper ■ **être en ~s** to be in one's *ou* to be wearing slippers.

pantoufler [3] [pɑ̃tufle] *vi* *fam* *to leave a civil service post and work for the private sector.*

panty [pɑ̃ti] (*pl* **panties** [pɑ̃tiz]) *nm* *vieilli* pantie girdle.

panure [panyr] *nf* ≃ breadcrumbs *(for coating).*

Panurge [panyrʒ] *npr* LITTÉR ▷ **mouton**.

panzer [pɑ̃dzɛr] *nm* panzer.

PAO (*abr de* **publication assistée par ordinateur**) *nf* DTP.

paon [pɑ̃] *nm* ORNITH peacock ■ **fier** *ou* **orgueilleux** *ou* **vaniteux comme un ~** (as) proud as a peacock ■ **faire le ~** to strut (like a peacock).

paonne [pan] *nf* peahen.

PAP (*abr de* **prêt d'accession à la propriété**) *nm* *loan for first-time homebuyers.*

papa [papa] *nm* **1.** [père] dad, daddy ■ **jouer au ~ et à la maman** to play mummies and daddies **2.** *fam* [homme d'un certain âge] : **alors, ~, tu traverses?** come on, grandad, get across!
◆ **à la papa** *loc adv* *fam* [tranquillement] in a leisurely way ■ **conduire à la ~** to drive at a snail's pace.
◆ **à papa** *loc adj* *fam* **c'est un fils/une fille à ~** he's/she's got a rich daddy.
◆ **de papa** *loc adj* *fam* old-fashioned.

papal, e, aux [papal, o] *adj* papal.

paparazzi [paparadzi] *nmpl* *péj* paparazzi.

papauté [papote] *nf* papacy.

papaye [papaj] *nf* papaya, pawpaw.

papayer [papaje] *nm* papaya (tree).

pape [pap] *nm* **1.** RELIG pope **2.** [chef de file] high priest, guru *fig.*

Papeete [papɛt] *npr* Papeete.

papelard [paplar] *nm* *fam* **1.** [bout de papier] scrap of paper **2.** PRESSE article, piece ■ **il a écrit un ~ sur la corruption** he wrote a piece on corruption.

paperasse [papras] *nf* *péj* papers, bumf *UK* ■ **je n'ai pas le temps de remplir toute cette ~** I don't have the time to fill up all these forms.

paperasserie [paprasri] *nf* *péj* **1.** [formulaires] paperwork ■ **toute cette ~ va sûrement retarder le projet** all this red tape is bound to delay the project **2.** [amoncellement] papers.

paperassier, ère [paprasje, ɛr] *péj* ◇ *adj* [personne] bureaucratic.
◇ *nm, f* bureaucrat, penpusher *péj.*

papesse [papɛs] *nf* female pope.

papet [papɛ] *nm* *Suisse* *Swiss dish made with potatoes, leeks and sausages.*

papeterie [papɛtri] *nf* **1.** [boutique] stationer's shop **2.** [matériel] stationery **3.** [usine] paper mill **4.** COMM stationery trade.

papetier, ère [paptje, ɛr] ◇ *adj* paper *(modif)*, stationery *(modif)*.
◇ *nm, f* **1.** COMM stationer **2.** INDUST paper-maker.

papi [papi] *fam* = **papy**.

papier [papje] *nm* **1.** [matériau] paper ■ **noircir du ~** *fig* to fill page after *ou* upon page ■ **sur le ~, le projet paraît réalisable** on paper, the project seems feasible ■ **jeter qqch sur le ~** to jot sthg down ▶ **~ alu** *ou* **d'aluminium** aluminium *UK* *ou* aluminum *US* foil ■ **~ d'Arménie** incense paper ■ **~ bible** bible paper, Oxford India paper ■ **~ brouillon** rough paper ■ **~ buvard** blotting paper ■ **~ cadeau** wrapping paper ■ **~ carbone** carbon (paper) ■ **~ à cigarette** cigarette paper ■ **~ collant** [adhésif] adhesive tape ; [gommé] gummed paper *ou* strip ■ **~ couché** art paper ■ **~ crépon** crêpe paper ■ **~ cul**△ bog paper ■ **~ d'emballage** brown (wrapping) paper ■ **~ émeri** emery paper ■ **~ à en-tête** headed paper *ou* notepaper ■ **~ glacé** glazed paper ■ **~ huilé** oil-paper ■ **~ hygiénique** toilet paper ■ **~ journal** newspaper, newsprint ■ **~ kraft** brown paper ■ **~ à lettres** writing paper ■ **sur ~ libre : le contrat a été rédigé sur ~ libre** the contract was drawn up on a sheet of plain paper ■ **envoyer une lettre sur ~ libre** apply in writing ■ **~ machine** typing paper ■ **~ millimétré** graph paper ■ **~ ministre** document *ou* official paper ■ **~ à musique** music paper ■ **~ peint** wallpaper ■ **~ pelure** onion skin (paper) ■ **~ photographique** photographic
paper ■ **~ quadrillé** squared paper ■ **~ en rouleau** web *ou* reel paper ■ **~ de soie** tissue paper ■ **~ sulfurisé** greaseproof *ou* *spéc* sulphurized paper ■ **~ timbré** stamped paper *(for official use)* ■ **~ de verre** sandpaper ■ **~ vélin** wove *UK* *ou* vellum paper **2.** [morceau] piece of paper ■ [page] sheet of paper, piece of paper ■ **as-tu un ~ et un crayon?** do you have a piece of paper and a pencil? ▶ **~ collé** ART papier collé ■ **être dans les petits ~s de qqn** to be in sb's good books
3. PRESSE article, piece ■ **faire un ~ sur** to do a piece *ou* an article on
4. ADMIN papers ■ **les ~s du véhicule, s'il vous plaît** may I see your logbook *UK* *ou* (vehicle) registration papers, please? ▶ **~s (d'identité)** (identity) papers ■ **faux ~s** false *ou* forged papers
5. BANQUE : **~ de commerce** commercial paper ■ **~ commercial** commercial bill ■ **~ financier** *ou* **de crédit** bank credit note.
◆ **de papier, en papier** *loc adj* paper *(modif)* ■ **lanterne en ~** paper lantern.
◆ **papiers gras** *nmpl* litter.

papier-calque [papjekalk] (*pl* **papiers-calque**) *nm* tracing paper.

papier-émeri [papjeemri] (*pl* **papiers-émeri**) *nm* emery paper.

papier-filtre [papjefiltr] (*pl* **papiers-filtres**) *nm* filter paper.

papier-monnaie [papjemɔnɛ] (*pl* **papiers-monnaies**) *nm* paper money.

papille [papij] *nf* papilla ■ **~s gustatives** taste buds ■ **~ optique** optic disk, blind spot.

papillon [papijɔ̃] *nm* **1.** ENTOM butterfly ■ **~ de nuit** moth **2.** *fam* [contravention] (parking) ticket **3.** *fam* [esprit volage] : **c'est un (vrai) ~** he's fickle **4.** TECHNOL [écrou] butterfly *ou* wing nut ■ [obturateur, clapet] butterfly valve **5.** SPORT butterfly (stroke).

papillonnage [papijɔnaʒ] = **papillonnement**.

papillonnant, e [papijɔnɑ̃, ɑ̃t] *adj* **1.** [versatile, instable - esprit] flighty, inattentive **2.** ZOOL fluttering.

papillonnement [papijɔnmɑ̃] *nm* **1.** [versatilité, inconstance] flightiness, inattentiveness **2.** [volettement] fluttering.

papillonner [3] [papijɔne] *vi* **1.** [voltiger] to flit *ou* to flutter about **2.** [être volage] to behave in a fickle manner **3.** [être inattentif] to be inattentive ■ **son esprit papillonne** he can't keep his mind on things.

papillotant, e [papijɔtɑ̃, ɑ̃t] *adj* **1.** [qui cligne - œil] blinking ; [- paupière] fluttering **2.** [scintillant - lumière, reflet] flickering, dancing, flashing.

papillote [papijɔt] *nf* **1.** [bigoudi] curlpaper **2.** CULIN [pour gigot] frill ■ **en ~s** en papillote *(cooked in foil or paper parcels)*.

papillotement [papijɔtmɑ̃] *nm* **1.** [clignement - des yeux] blinking ; [- des paupières] fluttering **2.** [scintillement - d'une lumière, d'un reflet] flickering, flashing, dancing **3.** CINÉ & TV flicker.

papilloter [3] [papijɔte] *vi* **1.** [œil] to blink ■ [paupière] to flicker, to flutter **2.** [lumière, reflet] to flicker, to flash, to dance.

papisme [papism] *nm* papism.

papiste [papist] ◇ *adj* papist.
◇ *nmf* papist.

papotage [papɔtaʒ] *nm* ***fam*** [action] chattering, nattering *UK* ■ [discussion] chatter, chit-chat, natter *UK*.

papoter [3] [papɔte] *vi* ***fam*** to chatter, to have a chinwag ■ **j'adore ~** I love a good old natter *UK ou* gab *US*.

papou, e [papu] *adj* Papuan.
◆ **Papou, e** *nm, f* Papuan.

Papouasie [papwazi] *npr f* : **(la) ~** Papua.

Papouasie-Nouvelle-Guinée [papwazinuvɛlgine] *npr f* : **(la) ~** Papua New Guinea.

papouille [papuj] *nf **fam*** tickle ■ **faire des ~s à un bébé** to give a baby a little tickle.

paprika [paprika] *nm* paprika.

papy [papi] *nm **fam*** grandad.

papy-boom [papibum] *nm* grey boom, ageing population ■ [en insistant sur les effets négatifs] demographic timebomb.

papyrus [papirys] *nm* ARCHÉOL & BOT papyrus.

Pâque [pak] *nf* : **la ~** Passover, Pesach.

paquebot [pakbo] *nm* liner.

pâquerette [pakrɛt] *nf* daisy.

Pâques [pak] *nm* Easter ■ **à ~ ou à la Trinité** never in a month of Sundays ■ **l'île de ~** Easter Island.
◆ **pâques** *nfpl* : **joyeuses pâques** Happy Easter ■ **faire ses pâques** to take communion (at Easter).

LES CLOCHES DE PÂQUES

In France, Easter is traditionally symbolized not only by eggs but also by bells; according to legend, church bells fly to Rome at Easter.

paquet [pakɛ] *nm* **1.** [colis, ballot] parcel, package ■ **faire un ~ de vieux journaux** to make up a bundle of old newspapers
2. COMM [marchandise emballée] : **un ~ de sucre/de farine** a bag of sugar/flour ■ **un ~ de cigarettes** a packet *UK ou* a pack *US* (of cigarettes) ▶ **je vous fais un ~-cadeau?** shall I gift-wrap it for you?
3. [valise] bag ■ **faire ses ~s** to pack one's bags
4. ***fam*** [quantité importante] : **il y a un ~ d'erreurs dans ce texte** this text is full of mistakes, there are loads of mistakes in this text ▶ **mettre le ~ : j'ai mis (tout) le ~** ***fig*** I gave it all I've got ■ **lâcher le ~** to get things off one's chest, to unburden o.s. ■ **toucher le ~** to make a packet *ou* mint *ou* pile
5. [masse] : **j'ai reçu un ~ de neige sur la tête** a lump of snow fell on my head ▶ **un ~ de mer** NAUT a big wave ■ **sa mère est un ~ de nerfs** her mother's a bundle *ou* bag of nerves
6. SPORT : **~ (d'avants)** pack
7. INFORM packet.

paquetage [paktaʒ] *nm* MIL kit, pack ■ **ils font leur ~** they're getting their kits ready.

paquet-poste [pakɛpɔst] (*pl* **paquets-poste**) *nm* mail parcel.

par[1] [par] *nm* [au golf] par.

par[2] [par] *prép* **1.** [indiquant la direction, le parcours] by ■ [en traversant un lieu] through ■ **il est arrivé ~ la route** he came by road ■ **il est arrivé ~ la gauche/~ la droite/~ le nord** he arrived from the left/the right/the north ■ **faut-il passer ~ Paris?** do we have to go through *ou* via Paris? ■ **il est passé ~ la maison avant de ressortir** he dropped in before going off again ‖ [indiquant la position] : **elle est assise ~ terre** she's sitting on the ground ■ **la neige avait fondu ~ endroits** the snow had melted in places ■ **~ 45 de latitude nord** NAUT lying at a latitude of 45 north ■ **~ 10 brasses d'eau** NAUT in 10 fathoms of water
2. [pendant] : **~ un beau jour d'été** on a fine summer's day ■ **~ grand froid/grosse chaleur** in extreme cold/intense heat ■ **~ le passé** in the past ■ **~ moments** at times, from time to time ■ **~ les temps qui courent** these days ■ **~ deux fois** twice
3. [indiquant le moyen, la manière] by ■ **les lettres sont classées ~ ordre d'arrivée** the letters are filed in order of arrival ■ **envoyer qqch ~ avion/télex** to send sthg by airmail/telex ■ **~ air/terre/mer** by air/land/sea ■ **voyager ~ avion** to travel by plane, to fly ■ **je l'ai appris ~ la radio** I heard it on the radio ■ **répondre ~ oui ou ~ non/~ la négative** to answer yes or no/in the negative ■ **obtenir qqch ~ la force/la douceur** to obtain sthg by force/through kindness ■ **je suis avec toi ~ la pensée** I'm thinking of you, my thoughts are with you
4. [indiquant la cause, l'origine] : **faire qqch ~ habitude/caprice/plaisir/paresse** to do sthg out of habit/on a whim/for the pleasure of it/out of laziness ■ **je l'ai rencontré ~ hasard** I met him by chance ■ **je le sais ~ expérience** I know it from experience ■ **nous sommes cousins ~ ma mère** we're cousins on my mother's side (of the family) ■ **une tante ~ alliance** an aunt by marriage
5. [introduisant le complément d'agent] by ■ **le logiciel est protégé ~ un code** the software is protected by *ou* with a code ■ **faire faire qqch ~ qqn** to have sthg done by sb ■ **je l'ai appris ~ elle** I heard it from her, I learned of it through her ■ **ils veulent le faire ~ eux-mêmes** they want to do it by *ou* for themselves ■ **elles se sont rencontrées ~ son intermédiaire** they met through him/her
6. [emploi distributif] : **une heure ~ jour** one hour a *ou* per day ■ **40 euros ~ personne** 40 euros per person ■ **une fois ~ an** once a year ■ **heure ~ heure** hour by hour ■ **mettez-vous deux ~ deux** line up in twos ■ **ils arrivaient ~ petits groupes/centaines** they arrived in small groups/in their hundreds
7. [avec les verbes 'commencer' et 'finir'] : **ça finira ~ arriver/~ ressembler à quelque chose** it will end up happening/looking like something ■ **commence ~ travailler** start (off) by working ■ **il a fini ~ avouer** he eventually owned up ■ **le concert débuta ~ une sonate de Mozart** the concert opened with a sonata by Mozart.
◆ **de par** *loc prép* **1.** [par l'ordre de] : **de ~ la loi** according to the law ■ **de ~ le roi** in the name of the king
2. *litt* [dans l'espace] throughout ■ **de ~ le monde** all over *ou* throughout the world
3. [du fait de] by virtue of.
◆ **par-ci par-là** *loc adv* **1.** [dans l'espace] here and there ■ **des livres traînaient ~-ci ~-là** books were lying around here and there
2. [dans le temps] now and then, from time to time, every now and then *ou* again
3. [marquant la répétition] : **avec lui, c'est mon yacht ~-ci, mon avion personnel ~-là** it's my yacht this, my plane that, all the time with him.

para [para] (*abr de* **parachutiste**) *nm **fam*** para.

para- [para] *préf* **1.** [en marge de] para- **2.** [qui protège] para-, anti- **3.** CHIM para-.

parabole [parabɔl] *nf* **1.** LITTÉR & RELIG parable **2.** MATH parabola **3.** TV (satellite) dish.

parabolique [parabɔlik] *adj* **1.** LITTÉR & RELIG parabolic, parabolical **2.** MATH parabolic.

paracentèse [parasɛ̃tɛz] *nf* paracentesis ***spéc***, tapping.

paracétamol [parasetamɔl] *nm* paracetamol.

parachèvement [paraʃɛvmɑ̃] *nm sout* [action] completion ■ [résultat] crowning.

parachever [19] [paraʃve] *vt sout* to complete ■ **~ un tableau** to put the finishing touches to a painting.

parachutage [paraʃytaʒ] *nm* **1.** MIL & SPORT parachuting **2.** *fam* POLIT *bringing in a candidate from outside the constituency.*

parachute [paraʃyt] *nm* parachute ■ **faire du ~** to go parachuting ■ **sans ~** *fig* without a parachute *ou* a safety-net ▶ **~ ascensionnel** parascending ■ **~ dorsal** back-pack parachute ■ **~ de freinage** parabrake ■ **~ ventral** lap-pack *ou* chest-pack parachute.

parachuter [3] [paraʃyte] *vt* **1.** MIL & SPORT to parachute **2.** *fam* POLIT to bring in from outside the constituency ■ **ils l'ont parachuté directeur dans une succursale** ADMIN he was unexpectedly given the job of branch manager.

parachutisme [paraʃytism] *nm* parachuting ■ **faire du ~** to go parachuting ▶ **~ ascensionnel** parascending ■ **~ en chute libre** free-fall parachuting.

parachutiste [paraʃytist] ◇ *nm* **1.** LOISIRS & SPORT parachutist **2.** MIL paratrooper.
◇ *adj* : **troupes ~s** paratroops.

parade [parad] *nf* **1.** [défilé] parade ■ **la grande ~ du cirque** the grand finale (at the circus) ■ **faire ~ de** [faire étalage de] : **faire ~ de ses connaissances** to show off *ou* to parade *ou* to display one's knowledge **2.** ZOOL (courtship) display **3.** [en boxe] parry ■ ESCRIME parade, parry ■ ÉQUIT checking ■ FOOTBALL save **4.** [riposte] retort, reply, riposte ■ **nous devons trouver la ~** we must find a way of counterattacking.
➡ **de parade** *loc adj litt* **1.** [ornemental] ceremonial **2.** [feint] : **une amabilité de ~** an outward show of friendliness.

parader [3] [parade] *vi* **1.** [troupes] to parade **2.** ÉQUIT to execute a dressage **3.** [personne] to show off, to pose, to strut about.

paradigmatique [paradigmatik] *adj* paradigmatic.

paradigme [paradigm] *nm* paradigm.

paradis [paradi] *nm* **1.** RELIG paradise, heaven ■ **aller au ~** to go to heaven ▶ **les ~ artificiels** drug-induced euphoria ■ **~ fiscal** tax haven ■ **le Paradis terrestre** *pr* the Garden of Eden *ou* Earthly Paradise ; *fig* heaven on earth **2.** THÉÂTRE : **le ~** the gods *UK*, the (top) gallery.

paradisiaque [paradizjak] *adj* heavenly, paradisal *sout*, paradisiacal *sout*.

paradisier [paradizje] *nm* bird of paradise.

paradoxal, e, aux [paradɔksal, o] *adj* **1.** [contradictoire] paradoxical **2.** [déconcertant] unexpected, paradoxical ■ **sa présence parmi eux était ~e** it was surprising to find her among them **3.** MÉD paradoxical.

paradoxalement [paradɔksalmɑ̃] *adv* paradoxically.

paradoxe [paradɔks] *nm* paradox.

parafe [paraf] = **paraphe**.

parafer [parafe] = **parapher**.

paraffine [parafin] *nf* paraffin *ou* paraffine (wax) ■ **mettre de la ~ sur des confitures** to seal jam jars with (paraffin) wax.

parafiscal, e, aux [parafiskal, o] *adj* parafiscal.

parafiscalité [parafiskalite] *nf* parafiscal measures.

parafoudre [parafudr] *nm* lightning conductor.

parages [paraʒ] *nmpl* **1.** [environs] area, surroundings ■ **il habite dans les ~** he lives around here somewhere **2.** NAUT waters.

paragraphe [paragraf] *nm* **1.** [passage] paragraph **2.** [signe typographique] paragraph (sign), par.

paragrêle [paragrɛl] ◇ *nm* anti-hail device.
◇ *adj* anti-hail.

Paraguay [paragɥɛj] *npr m* : **le ~** Paraguay ■ **au ~** in Paraguay.

paraguayen, enne [paragwejɛ̃, ɛn] *adj* Paraguayan.
➡ **Paraguayen, enne** *nm, f* Paraguayan.

paraître[1] [parɛtr] *nm sout* **le ~** appearance, appearances.

paraître[2] [91] [parɛtr] ◇ *vi* **1.** [se montrer - soleil] to appear, to come out ; [- émotion] to show ; [- personne attendue] to appear, to turn up ; [- dignitaire, prince] to appear, to make a public appearance ; [- acteur] to appear ■ **laisser ~ son émotion** to let one's emotion show **2.** [figurer] to appear **3.** [être publié - livre] to be published, to come out, to appear ■ **faire ~ une petite annonce dans un journal** to put an advertisement in a paper **4.** [sembler] to appear, to seem, to look ■ **il ne paraît pas très à l'aise dans son costume** he doesn't seem (to be) very comfortable in his suit ■ **~ plus jeune que l'on n'est** to seem *ou* to look *ou* to appear younger than one is ■ **il parut céder** he looked as though he was giving in ■ **paraît-il** apparently ■ **tu as retrouvé du travail, paraît-il** I hear you've got a new job **5.** [se donner en spectacle] to show off.
◇ *vt* : **75 ans? vous ne les paraissez pas** 75 years old? you don't look it.
◇ *v impers* : **ça ne paraît pas (mais...)** [ça ne se voit pas] it doesn't look like it (but...) ■ **il n'y paraît pas** it doesn't show ■ **dans une semaine il n'y paraîtra plus** in a week it won't show any more ■ **je tâche de l'aider sans qu'il y paraisse** I try to help him without letting it show ■ **il me paraît préférable de se décider maintenant** I think it's better *ou* it seems better to make up our minds now ■ **vous êtes renvoyé? – il paraît** have you been fired? – it looks like it *ou* so it seems ■ **il paraît que...** I've heard (that)..., it would seem (that)... ■ **il paraîtrait qu'il a trois enfants** it would seem *ou* appear (that) he's got three children ■ **paraît que tu vas te marier!** *fam* I hear you're getting married? ■ **à ce qu'il paraît** apparently.

paralittérature [paraliteratyr] *nf* literature with a small "l", minor literary works.

parallaxe [paralaks] *nf* ASTRON, GÉOM & PHOTO parallax.

parallèle [paralɛl] ◇ *adj* **1.** GÉOM, SPORT & INFORM parallel ■ **la droite AB est ~ à la droite CD** line AB is parallel to line CD **2.** [comparable - données, résultats] parallel, comparable, similar ■ **nous avons eu des carrières ~s** we had similar careers **3.** [non officiel - festival] unofficial, fringe *(modif)* ; [- marché, transaction] unofficial ; [- police] unofficial, secret ■ **mener une vie ~** to live a double life.
◇ *nm* **1.** ASTRON & GÉOGR parallel ■ **~ de latitude** parallel of latitude **2.** [comparaison] parallel ■ **établir un ~ entre deux phénomènes** to draw a parallel between two phenomena.
◇ *nf* GÉOM parallel (line).
➡ **en parallèle** *loc adv* **1.** [en balance] : **mettre deux faits en ~** to draw a parallel between *ou* to compare two facts **2.** INFORM (in) parallel **3.** ÉLECTR in parallel.

parallèlement [paralɛlmɑ̃] *adv* **1.** GÉOM in a parallel to **2.** SPORT : **skier ~** to do parallel turns **3.** [simultanément] : **~ à** at the same time as ■ **~ à mon cours de danse, je donne aussi un cours de musique** I teach music as well as dance.

parallélépipède [paralelepipɛd] *nm* parallelepiped.

parallélisme [paralelism] *nm* **1.** GÉOM parallelism **2.** AUTO wheel alignment **3.** SPORT parallel turning *ou* skiing **4.** [concordance] parallel, concordance ■ **établir un ~ entre deux faits** to draw a parallel between two facts.

parallélogramme [paralelɔgram] *nm* GÉOM parallelogram.

paralysant, e [paralizɑ̃, ɑ̃t] *adj pr* & *fig* paralysing.

paralysé, e [paralize] ◇ *adj* paralysed ■ **être ~ de peur** to be petrified.
◇ *nm, f* MÉD paralytic.

paralyser [3] [paralize] *vt* **1.** MÉD to paralyse **2.** [figer, inhiber] to paralyse ■ **paralysé par la peur** crippled with fear ■ **paralysé par le brouillard** fog-bound.

paralysie [paralizi] *nf* **1.** MÉD paralysis ■ **~ cérébrale** cerebral palsy **2.** [arrêt] paralysis.

paralytique [paralitik] *adj* & *nmf* MÉD paralytic.

paramécie [paramesi] *nf* paramecium.

paramédical, e, aux [paramedikal, o] *adj* paramedical.

paramètre [parametr] *nm* **1.** MATH parameter **2.** [élément variable] parameter, factor **3.** ANAT parametrium.

paramétrer [18] [parametre] *vt* INFORM to set, to program.

paramilitaire [paramilitɛr] *adj* paramilitary.

parangon [parɑ̃gɔ̃] *nm litt* paragon ■ **~ de vertu** paragon of virtue.

parano [parano] *fam* ◇ *adj* paranoid.
◇ *nmf* [personne] paranoiac ■ **c'est un/une ~** he's/she's paranoid.
◇ *nf* [maladie] paranoia.

paranoïa [paranɔja] *nf* paranoia.

paranoïaque [paranɔjak] ◇ *adj* paranoiac, paranoid.
◇ *nmf* paranoiac.

paranormal, e, aux [paranɔrmal, o] *adj* paranormal.

parapente [parapɑ̃t] *nm* paragliding.

parapet [parapɛ] *nm* CONSTR parapet.

parapharmacie [parafarmasi] *nf* (non-pharmaceutical) chemist's *UK ou* druggist's *US* merchandise.

paraphe [paraf] *nm* **1.** [pour authentifier] initials ■ [pour décorer] flourish, paraph **2.** DR & *litt* [signature] signature.

parapher [3] [parafe] *vt* **1.** [pour authentifier] to initial **2.** DR & *litt* [signer] to sign.

parapheur [parafœr] *nm portfolio for documents for signature.*

paraphrase [parafraz] *nf* [gén - LING] paraphrase.

paraphraser [3] [parafraze] *vt* to paraphrase.

paraplégie [parapleʒi] *nf* paraplegia.

paraplégique [parapleʒik] *adj* & *nmf* paraplegic.

parapluie [paraplɥi] *nm* **1.** [accessoire] umbrella **2.** POLIT : **~ nucléaire** nuclear umbrella **3.** *fam* [passe-partout] skeleton key *(for spring locks).*

parapsychologie [parapsikɔlɔʒi] *nf* parapsychology.

parapsychologue [parapsikɔlɔg] *nmf* parapsychologist.

parascolaire [paraskɔlɛr] *adj* extracurricular.

parasitaire [paraziter] *adj* BIOL & *fig* parasitic.

parasite [parazit] ◇ *adj* **1.** BIOL parasitical **2.** ÉLECTR & TÉLÉCOM : **bruit ~** interference.
◇ *nm* **1.** BIOL parasite **2.** [personne] scrounger.
◆ **parasites** *nmpl* RADIO & TV interference *(U)*, atmospherics *UK* ■ TÉLÉCOM noise, static ■ **il y a des ~s sur la ligne** the line's bad, there's static on the line.

parasiter [3] [parazite] *vt* **1.** BIOL to live as a parasite on, to be parasitical upon ■ **je me suis fait ~ par un ancien copain** *fam fig* an old friend came around to sponge off me **2.** RADIO, TÉLÉCOM & TV to interfere with, to cause interference on.

parasitisme [parazitism] *nm* **1.** BIOL parasitism **2.** *fig* scrounging.

parasitose [parazitoz] *nf* parasitosis.

parasol [parasɔl] *nm* **1.** [en ville, dans un jardin] parasol, sunshade ■ [pour la plage] beach umbrella, parasol **2.** AÉRON parasol (wing).

parasympathique [parasɛ̃patik] ◇ *adj* parasympathetic.
◇ *nm* parasympathetic nervous system.

paratonnerre [paratɔnɛr] *nm* lightning conductor.

paravalanche [paravalɑ̃ʃ] *nm* avalanche barrier.

paravent [paravɑ̃] *nm* **1.** [écran] (folding) screen *ou* partition **2.** *fig* (smoke) screen, cover ■ **il se sert de son nom comme d'un ~** he uses his name as a cover.

parbleu [parblø] *interj* certainly, of course ■ **je l'ai jeté dehors, ~!** I kicked him out, of course *ou* needless to say!

parc [park] *nm* **1.** [enclos - à bétail] pen, enclosure ; [- à moutons] fold ; [- pour bébé] pen, playpen ■ **~ à bestiaux** cattle pen ■ **~ de stationnement** car park *UK*, parking lot *US* **2.** PÊCHE bed ■ **~ à huîtres** oyster bed **3.** LOISIRS [jardin public] park ■ [domaine privé] park, grounds ■ **~ d'attractions** amusement park ■ **~ national** national park ■ **~ naturel** nature reserve ■ **le ~ des Princes** *large football stadium in Paris* **4.** COMM : **~ d'expositions** showground **5.** [unités d'équipement] stock ■ **le ~ automobile français** the total number of cars in France ■ **notre ~ ferroviaire** our (total) rolling stock **6.** INDUST [entrepôt] depot ■ **~ industriel** *Québec* industrial estate *UK ou* park *US* **7.** [énergie] **~ éolien** windfarm.

parcage [parkaʒ] *nm* **1.** AGRIC foldyard manuring **2.** AUTO parking **3.** PÊCHE bedding.

parcellaire [parselɛr] ◇ *adj* **1.** ADMIN & DR : **cadastre** *ou* **plan ~** cadastral survey **2.** [fractionné - connaissances, tâche] fragmented ■ **travail ~** INDUST division of labour.
◇ *nm* ADMIN & DR (detailed survey of) lots.

parcellariser [parselarize] = **parcelliser**.

parcelle [parsɛl] *nf* **1.** ADMIN parcel, plot ■ [lopin] plot (of land) **2.** [morceau - d'or] particle ■ **une ~ de liberté** *fig* a (tiny) bit of freedom ■ **pas une ~ de vérité** not a grain *ou* shred of truth.

parcellisation [parselizasjɔ̃] *nf* **1.** [gén] fragmentation, division **2.** INDUST : **~ des tâches** division of labour.

parcelliser [3] [parselize] *vt* to fragment, to divide, to subdivide.

parce que [parskə] *(devant voyelle ou h muet parce qu'* [parsk]*) loc conj* because ■ **pourquoi pleures-tu? – ~!** *fam* why are you crying? – because!

parchemin [parʃəmɛ̃] *nm* **1.** [pour écrire] (piece of) parchment **2.** *fam* [diplôme] diploma, degree.

parcheminé, e [parʃəmine] *adj* [peau] wrinkled ■ [visage] wizened.

parchet [parʃɛ] *nm Suisse* plot of land.

par-ci, par-là [parsiparla] *loc adv* ▷ **par**.

parcimonie[1] [parsimɔni] *nf sout* parsimony, parsimoniousness.
◆ **avec parcimonie** *loc adv* parsimoniously, sparingly ■ **il distribue les compliments avec ~** he's sparing with his praise.

parcimonie[2] [parsimɔni] *nm Suisse* plot of land.

parcimonieusement [parsimɔnjøzmɑ̃] *adv sout* parsimoniously, sparingly.

parcimonieux, euse [parsimɔnjø, øz] *adj sout* parsimonious, sparing.

parc(o)mètre [park(ɔ)mɛtr] *nm* (parking) meter.

parcotrain [parkɔtrɛ̃] *nm* train users' car park *UK ou* parking lot *US*.

parcourir [45] [parkurir] *vt* **1.** [distance - gén] to cover ; [- en courant] to run ; [- en marchant] to walk ; [- à cheval, à vélo] to ride ■ **chemin parcouru** distance covered ■ **le prix du kilomètre parcouru** RAIL ≃ unit cost per passenger-mile **2.** [pour visiter] to travel through *(insép)* ■ **ils ont parcouru toute l'Amérique** they've travelled the length and breadth of America ■ **~ les mers** [marin, bateau] to sail the seas ■ [dans une quête] to scour, to search (all over) ■ **je parcourais la ville à la recherche d'un emploi** I was searching all over town for a job **3.** [suj: douleur, frisson] to run through *(insép)* ■ **un murmure de protestation parcourut la salle** a murmur of protest ran through the audience **4.** [jeter un coup d'oeil à - journal, roman, notes de cours] to skim *ou* to leaf through *(insép)* ■ **je n'ai fait que ~ sa lettre** I've only glanced at her letter ■ **elle parcourut la liste des reçus** she scanned the list of successful students ■ **elle parcourut la scène du regard** her eyes scanned the scene.

parcours [parkur] *nm* **1.** [trajet - d'une personne] way, journey ▪ TRANSP route ▪ **il a effectué le ~ en deux heures** he did the trip *ou* journey in two hours **2.** *fig* career, record, path ▪ **son ~ scolaire a été irréprochable** she had a faultless school record **3.** MIL & *fig* **~ du combattant** assault course **4.** SPORT course.

parcouru, e [parkury] *pp* ▻ **parcourir**.

parc-relais, parcs-relais [parkralɛ] *nm car park for a park-and-ride scheme.*

par-dedans [pardədɑ̃] *adv* (on the) inside.

par-dehors [pardəɔr] *adv* (on the) outside.

par-delà [pardəla] *prép sout* beyond ▪ **~ les mers** over the seas ▪ **~ les siècles** across the centuries.

par-derrière [pardɛrjɛr] ◇ *prép* behind, round the back of ▪ **passe ~ la maison** go round the back of the house.
◇ *adv* **1.** [par l'arrière] from behind, at the rear **2.** [sournoisement] : **il me critique ~** he criticizes me behind my back ▪ **il fait ses coups ~** he operates behind people's backs.

par-dessous [pardəsu] ◇ *prép* under, underneath ▪ **passe ~ la barrière** go under the fence.
◇ *adv* underneath.

pardessus [pardəsy] *nm* overcoat.

par-dessus [pardəsy] ◇ *prép* **1.** [en franchissant] over, above ▪ **passe ~ la grille** go over the railings **2.** [sur] : **porter un manteau ~ sa veste** to wear an overcoat on top of one's jacket **3.** *fig* over ▪ **elle est passée ~ le directeur des ventes** she went over the head of the sales manager.
◇ *adv* [dans l'espace] : **saute ~!** jump over!
◆ **par-dessus tout** *loc adv* most of all, above all.

par-devant [pardəvɑ̃] ◇ *prép* ADMIN & DR : **~ notaire** in the presence of a solicitor *UK ou* lawyer *US*, with a solicitor *UK ou* lawyer *US* present ▪ **tout a été fait ~ notaire** everything was done in the proper legal way.
◇ *adv* [sur le devant] at *ou* round the front.

par-devers [pardəvɛr] *prép* **1.** DR [en présence de] before, in the presence of **2.** *sout* [en la possession de] : **garder qqch ~ soi** to keep sthg in one's possession *ou* to o.s.

pardi [pardi] *interj* of course ▪ **je l'ai jeté dehors, ~!** I kicked him out, of course *ou* needless to say!

pardieu [pardjø] *interj arch* by Jove.

pardon [pardɔ̃] *nm* **1.** [rémission] forgiveness, pardon *sout* ▪ **demander ~ à qqn** to apologize to sb, to ask for sb's forgiveness ▪ **pas de ~ pour** no mercy for ▪ **demander le ~ de ses fautes** to beg mercy for one's sins ▪ **demande ~ à la dame** say sorry to *ou* apologize to the lady ▪ **~?** [pour faire répéter] sorry?, (I beg your) pardon? ▪ **~, auriez-vous un crayon?** excuse me, do you have a pencil? ▪ **oh, ~!** [pour s'excuser] sorry!, excuse me! ; *iron* (so) sorry! ▪ **la mère est déjà désagréable, mais alors la fille, ~!** *fam* the mother's bad enough, but the daughter! **2.** [en Bretagne] religious festival **3.** RELIG : **Grand Pardon** Yom Kippur, Day of Atonement.

pardonnable [pardɔnabl] *adj* excusable, forgivable, pardonable ▪ **votre erreur n'est pas ~** your mistake is unforgivable *ou* inexcusable.

pardonner [3] [pardɔne] *vt* **1.** [oublier - offense] to forgive, to excuse ; [- péché] to forgive, to pardon ▪ **~ qqch à qqn** to forgive sb for sthg ▪ **allez, je te pardonne tout** all right, I'll let you off (everything) ▪ **~ ses péchés à qqn** to forgive sb (for) his sins ▪ **il ne me pardonne pas d'avoir eu raison** he won't forgive me for having been right ▪ **mais vous êtes tout pardonné!** but of course you're forgiven! ▪ **se faire ~** to be forgiven, to win forgiveness ▪ **pardonne-nous nos offenses** RELIG forgive us our trespasses ▪ *(en usage absolu)* to be forgiving ▪ **apprendre à ~** to learn forgiveness *ou* to forgive ▪ **une distraction au volant, ça ne pardonne pas!** one slip in concentration at the wheel is fatal! **2.** [dans des formules de politesse] to forgive, to excuse ▪ **pardonnez ma curiosité** *ou* **pardonnez-moi si je suis indiscret mais...** I'm sorry if I'm being *ou* excuse me for being nosy, but... ▪ **pardonnez-moi, mais vous oubliez un détail d'importance** excuse me, but you've forgotten an important point.
◆ **se pardonner** ◇ *vp (emploi réfléchi)* **je ne me le pardonnerai jamais** I'll never forgive myself.
◇ *vp (emploi passif)* to be excused *ou* forgiven ▪ **une traîtrise ne se pardonne pas** treachery cannot be forgiven.
◇ *vp (emploi réciproque)* to forgive one another.

PARE [par] (*abr de* **plan d'aide au retour à l'emploi**) *nm plan to help an unemployed person find work*, ≃ jobseeker's agreement *UK*.

pare-balles [parbal] ◇ *adj inv* bullet proof.
◇ *nm inv* bullet-shield.

pare-brise [parbriz] *nm inv* windscreen *UK*, windshield *US*.

pare-buffles [parbyfl] *nm inv* bull bar.

pare-chocs [parʃɔk] *nm inv* bumper ▪ **nous étions ~ contre ~** we were bumper to bumper.

pare-étincelles [paretɛ̃sɛl] *nm inv* **1.** [écran] sparkguard, fireguard **2.** RAIL spark arrester.

pare-feu [parfø] *nm inv* **1.** [en forêt] firebreak **2.** [d'une cheminée] fireguard **3.** [de pompier] (helmet) fire-shield **4.** INFORM firewall.

pare-fumée [parfyme] ◇ *adj inv* ▻ **écran**.
◇ *nm inv* smoke extractor.

pareil, eille [parɛj] ◇ *adj* **1.** [semblable, équivalent] the same, alike, similar ▪ **je n'ai jamais rien vu de ~** I've never seen anything like it ▪ **vous êtes (bien) tous ~s!** you're all alike *ou* the same! ▪ **comment vas-tu? - toujours ~!** how are you? - same as ever! ▪ **c'est toujours ~, personne n'ose se plaindre!** it's always the same, nobody ever dares complain! ▪ **leurs bagues sont presque ~les** their rings are almost identical *ou* the same ▪ **~ à** the same as, just like ▪ **~ que** *fam* (the) same as **2.** [de cette nature] such (a) ▪ **un talent ~** *ou* **un ~ talent est très rare** such talent is very rare ▪ **on n'avait jamais vu (un) ~ scandale!** there'd never been such a scandal! ▪ **qui peut bien téléphoner à une heure ~le?** who could be phoning at this hour *ou* time? ▪ **en ~ cas** in such a case ▪ **en ~les circonstances** in such circumstances.
◇ *nm, f* [semblable] : **son ~, sa ~le** [personne] another one like him/her ; [chose] another one like it ▪ **ne pas avoir son ~, ne pas avoir sa ~le** to be second to none ▪ **il n'a pas son ~ pour arriver au mauvais moment!** there's nobody quite like him for turning up at the wrong moment!
◆ **pareil** ◇ *nm* : **c'est du ~ au même** *fam* it's six of one and half a dozen of the other, it's the same difference.
◇ *adv fam* the same ▪ **on n'a pas dû comprendre ~** we can't have understood the same thing.
◆ **pareille** *nf* : **rendre la ~le à qqn** to repay sb in kind.
◆ **pareils** *nmpl* : **nos ~s** [semblables] our fellow men ; [égaux] our equals *ou* peers.
◆ **sans pareil, sans pareille** *loc adj* [éclat, beauté, courage] unrivalled, unequalled ▪ [talent, habileté] unparalleled, unequalled ▪ [artiste] peerless *sout*, unequalled ▪ **tu vas voir, la cuisine est sans ~le!** you'll see, the food is unique *ou* incomparable *ou* beyond compare!

pareillement [parɛjmɑ̃] *adv* **1.** [de la même manière] in the same way **2.** [aussi] equally, likewise ▪ **j'ai été ~ surprise** I was surprised too ▪ **bonne soirée! - et à vous ~!** have a nice evening! - you too!

parement [parmɑ̃] *nm* **1.** COUT facing ▪ [de manche] cuff **2.** CONSTR [surface] facing, face ▪ [revêtement] facing, dressing ▪ **~ brut** rough facing **3.** TRAV PUB kerbstone *UK*, curbstone *US* **4.** RELIG frontal.

parent, e [parɑ̃, ɑ̃t] ◇ *adj* **1.** [de la même famille] related ▪ **je suis ~e avec eux, nous sommes ~s** I'm related to them **2.** *sout* [analogue] : **ces deux interprétations sont ~es** the two interpretations are related **3.** BOT, GÉOL & ZOOL parent *(modif)* **4.** LING related, cognate *(modif)*.
◇ *nm, f* relative, relation ▪ **un proche ~** a close relative *ou* relation ▪ **un lointain ~, un ~ éloigné** a distant relative *ou* relation ▪ **un ~ du côté paternel/maternel** a relation on the father's/mother's side ▪ **nous sommes ~s par ma femme** we're

related through my wife ▪ **ce sont des ~s en ligne directe/par alliance** they're blood relations/related by marriage ▶ **~ pauvre** poor relation.

◆ **parent** *nm* parent.

◆ **parents** *nmpl* **1.** [père et mère] parents, father and mother ▪ **~s adoptifs** adoptive *ou* foster parents **2.** *litt* [aïeux] : **nos ~s** our forebears *litt ou* ancestors.

parental, e, aux [parɑ̃tal, o] *adj* parental ▪ **les responsabilités ~es** parental duties.

parentalité [parɑ̃talite] *nf* parenting.

parenté [parɑ̃te] *nf* **1.** [lien familial] relationship, kinship ▪ **il n'y a aucune ~ entre eux** they're not related in any way ▶ **~ par alliance** relationship by marriage ▪ **~ directe** blood relationship **2.** [ressemblance] relationship, connection **3.** [famille] family **4.** LING relatedness.

parenthèse [parɑ̃tɛz] *nf* **1.** [signe] parenthesis, bracket *UK* ▪ **ouvrir/fermer la ~** to open/to close the brackets *UK* **2.** [digression] digression, parenthesis ▪ **mais c'est une ~** but that's a digression *ou* an aside ▪ **je fais une (brève) ~ pour signaler que...** incidentally *ou* in parenthesis, we may briefly note that... ▪ **fermons la ~** anyway, enough of that **3.** GRAMM parenthesis, parenthetical clause.

◆ **entre parenthèses** ◇ *loc adj* [mot, phrase] in parenthesis, in *ou* between brackets *UK*.

◇ *loc adv* **1.** [mot, phrase] : **mettre qqch entre ~s** to put sthg in parenthesis, to put sthg in *ou* between brackets *UK* ▪ **il a dû mettre sa vie privée entre ~s** *fig* he had to put his private life to one side **2.** [à propos] incidentally, by the way.

◆ **par parenthèse** *loc adv* incidentally, by the way.

paréo [pareo] *nm* pareo.

parer [3] [pare] *vt* **1.** *litt* [embellir - pièce] to decorate, to deck out *(sép)*, to adorn ; [- personne] to deck out *(sép)*, to adorn ▪ **habit richement paré** richly ornamented *ou* decorated garment ▪ [vêtir] to dress ▪ **elle ne sort que parée de ses plus beaux atours** she only goes out attired in her best finery **2.** *sout* [attribuer à] : **~ qqn de toutes les vertus** to attribute many virtues to sb **3.** [préparer - ancre] to clear ▪ **paré à virer!** (get) ready to tack! **4.** CULIN [poisson, volaille] to dress ▪ [rôti] to trim **5.** TECHNOL [cuir] to dress ▪ [sur le bord] to pare **6.** MÉTALL to dress **7.** [éviter - coup, danger] to ward *ou* to fend *ou* to stave off *(sép)* ; [- attaque] to stave off *(sép)*, to parry ▪ [en boxe - ESCRIME] to parry **8.** [protéger] : **~ qqn contre qqch** to shield *ou* to protect sb against sthg.

◆ **parer à** *v+prép* **1.** [faire face à - incident] to cope *ou* to deal with *(insép)*, to handle ▪ **~ à toute éventualité** to prepare for *ou* to guard against any contingency ▪ **~ au plus pressé** [en voyageant, en emménageant] to deal with basic necessities (first) ▪ **parons au plus pressé et reconstruisons l'hôpital** first things first, we must rebuild the hospital **2.** [se défendre contre - tir, attaque] to ward off.

◆ **se parer** *vp (emploi réfléchi)* to put one's finery on ▪ **se ~ de** [bijoux, fourrures] to adorn o.s. with ; [titres, honneurs] to assume.

◆ **se parer contre** *vp+prép* to protect o.s. against ▪ **je me suis paré contre les rigueurs de l'hiver** I prepared for the rigours of winter.

pare-soleil [parsɔlɛj] *nm inv* sun visor, sunshade.

paresse [parɛs] *nf* **1.** [fainéantise] laziness, idleness ▪ **avoir la ~ de faire qqch** to be too lazy *ou* idle to do sthg **2.** [apathie] indolence, laziness **3.** RELIG [péché capital] sloth **4.** MÉD : **~ intestinale : souffrir de ~ intestinale** to be slow to digest (one's) food.

paresser [4] [parɛse] *vi* to laze (about *ou* around) ▪ **~ au soleil** to laze in the sun.

paresseusement [parɛsøzmɑ̃] *adv* **1.** [avec paresse] idly, lazily **2.** *sout* [avec lenteur] lazily, idly, sluggishly ▪ **les vagues viennent mourir ~ sur la plage** the waves break gently on the beach.

paresseux, euse [parɛsø, øz] ◇ *adj* **1.** [sans ardeur] lazy, idle ▶ **être ~ comme un loir** *ou* **une couleuvre** to be bone-idle *UK*, to be a goldbricker *US* **2.** *sout* [lent] lazy, slow, indolent **3.** MÉD [digestion] sluggish.

◇ *nm, f* lazy person ▪ **debout, grand ~!** get up, you lazy thing!

◆ **paresseux** *nm* ZOOL sloth.

parfaire [109] [parfɛr] *vt* **1.** [peaufiner] to perfect, to bring to perfection ▪ **~ une œuvre** to add the finishing touches to a work **2.** [compléter - opération] to round off *(sép)* ; [- somme] to make up.

parfait, e [parfɛ, ɛt] *adj* **1.** [sans défaut - beauté, crime, harmonie, conditions] perfect ; [- argumentation, diamant, maquillage] perfect, flawless ; [- scolarité, savoir-vivre, personne] perfect, faultless ▪ **son russe est ~** her Russian is perfect *ou* flawless, she speaks perfect Russian

2. BIOL mature ▪ ENTOM perfect ▪ MATH [cercle] perfect

3. [en intensif] perfect, utter ▪ **c'est le ~ homme du monde** he's a perfect gentleman ▪ **c'est un ~ goujat/idiot** he's an utter boor/fool ▪ **c'est le type même du ~ macho!** he's the epitome of the male chauvinist pig!

4. [complet, total - bonheur, calme, entente] perfect, complete, total ; [- ressemblance] perfect ; [- ignorance] utter, complete, total ▪ **elle s'est montrée d'une ~e délicatesse** she showed exquisite *ou* perfect tact ▪ **dans la plus ~e indifférence** in utter *ou* complete *ou* total indifference

5. [excellent] perfect, excellent ▪ **en ~ état/~e santé** in perfect condition/health ▪ **il a été ~** he was perfect *ou* marvellous ▪ **le rôle est ~ pour lui** the part is ideal *ou* made for him ▪ **10 heures, ça vous va? – c'est ~!** would 10 o'clock suit you? – that's perfect *ou* (just) fine!

◆ **parfait** *nm* **1.** CULIN parfait

2. LING perfect (tense), *voir aussi* **pluriel**.

parfaitement [parfɛtmɑ̃] *adv* **1.** [très bien] perfectly, impeccably, faultlessly ▪ **j'avais ~ entendu!** I heard all right! **2.** [absolument] perfectly, absolutely, thoroughly ▪ **tu as ~ le droit de refuser** you are perfectly entitled to refuse ▪ **cela lui est ~ indifférent** it's a matter of complete indifference to him **3.** [oui] (most) certainly, definitely ▪ **c'est vrai? – ~!** is that true? – it (most) certainly *ou* definitely is!

parfois [parfwa] *adv* **1.** [quelquefois] sometimes **2.** [dans certains cas] sometimes, at times, occasionally ▪ **ça m'amuse ~** there are times when *ou* occasionally I find it funny.

◆ **parfois... parfois** *loc corrélative* sometimes... sometimes.

parfum [parfœ̃] *nm* **1.** [odeur - d'une lotion, d'une fleur] perfume, scent, fragrance ; [- d'un mets] aroma ; [- d'un fruit] smell ▪ **le ~ frais des magnolias** the sweet scent *ou* fragrance of the magnolias ▪ **ce conte a un charmant ~ d'autrefois** *fig* this tale has a charming aura of times past ▪ **~ de scandale/d'hérésie** whiff of scandal/heresy **2.** [cosmétique] perfume, scent **3.** [goût] flavour ▪ **(tu veux une glace) à quel ~?** what flavour (ice cream) do you want? ▪ **yaourts sans ~ artificiel** yoghurts with no artificial flavouring.

◆ **au parfum** *loc adv fam* **être au ~** to be in the know ▪ **mettre qqn au ~** to put sb in the picture.

parfumé, e [parfyme] *adj* **1.** [personne] : **elle est ~e** she's wearing perfume **2.** [fruit] sweet-smelling.

parfumer [3] [parfyme] *vt* **1.** [embaumer] to perfume *sout* **2.** [mettre du parfum sur] to put *ou* to dab perfume on ▪ **être parfumé** [personne] to have perfume on, to be wearing perfume **3.** CULIN to flavour ▪ **parfumé à** flavoured with ▪ **yaourt parfumé à la mangue** mango-flavoured yoghurt.

◆ **se parfumer** *vp (emploi réfléchi)* to put on perfume ▪ **je ne me parfume jamais** I never wear *ou* use perfume.

parfumerie [parfymri] *nf* **1.** [magasin] perfumery (shop *UK* *ou* store *US*) **2.** [usine] perfume factory, perfumery **3.** [profession] perfumery, perfume trade *ou* industry **4.** [articles] perfumes (and cosmetics), perfumery.

parfumeur, euse [parfymœr, øz] *nm, f* perfumer.

pari [pari] *nm* **1.** [défi, enjeu] bet, wager ▪ **faire un ~** to lay a bet, to (have a) bet ▪ **je tiens le ~!** *pr & fig* I'll take you up on it! ▪ **perdre un ~** to lose a bet ▪ **cette politique est un ~ sur l'avenir** this policy is a gamble on the future **2.** JEUX [mise] bet, stake ▪ **il a gagné son ~** he won his bet ▪ **les ~s sont ouverts** *fig* it's anyone's guess ▶ **~ jumelé** double forecast ▪ **~ mutuel (urbain) = PMU 3.** PHILOS : **le ~ de Pascal** Pascal's wager.

paria [parja] *nm* **1.** [d'un groupe] outcast, pariah **2.** [en Inde] pariah, untouchable.

parier [9] [parje] <> *vt* **1.** [somme] to bet, to lay, to stake ▪ [repas, bouteille] to bet ▪ **j'ai parié gros sur le trois** I laid *ou* put a big bet on number three **2.** [exprimant la certitude] to bet ▪ **tu crois qu'il a terminé? – je parie que non** do you think he's finished? – I bet he hasn't ▪ **qu'est-ce que tu paries qu'il va refuser?** how much do you bet he'll say no? ▪ **je l'aurais parié!** I knew it! ▪ *(en usage absolu)* **tu paries?** *fam* want to bet? **3.** [exprimant la probabilité] : **il y a fort** *ou* **gros à ~ que...** the odds are *ou* it's odds on that...
<> *vi* **1.** [faire un pari] to (lay a) bet ▪ **~ sur un cheval** to bet on *ou* to back a horse **2.** [être parieur] to bet ▪ **~ aux courses** [de chevaux] to bet on the horses.

pariétal, e, aux [parjetal, o] *adj* **1.** ANAT parietal **2.** ART : **art ~** wall painting.
◆ **pariétal, aux** *nm* parietal bone.

parieur, euse [parjœr, øz] *nm, f* **1.** [qui fait un pari] better **2.** [qui aime parier] betting man (*f* woman).

parigot, e△ [parigo, ɔt] <> *adj* Parisian.
<> *nm, f* Parisian.

Paris [pari] *npr* Paris ▪ **dans les environs de ~** in the Paris area ▶ **~ vaut bien une messe** *Henri IV allus* Paris is worth a mass.

PARIS

1. The name *Paris* followed by a number or Roman numeral refers to a Paris university: *Paris-VII* (the science faculty at Jussieu), *Paris-IV* (the Sorbonne), *Paris-X* (Nanterre university) etc.
2. When *Paris* is followed by an ordinal number, this refers to an arrondissement: *Paris quinzième*, *Paris quatrième* etc.

paris-brest [paribrɛst] *nm inv* paris-brest *(choux pastry ring filled with praline cream).*

Pariscope [pariskɔp] *npr weekly entertainments listings magazine for Paris.*

Paris-Dakar [paridakar] *nm* : **le ~** *annual car and motorcycle race across the Sahara Desert.*

parisianisme [parizjanism] *nm* **1.** [attitude] Paris-centredness ▪ **le ~ des médias** the capital-city mentality of the Paris media **2.** [expression] Parisian (turn of) phrase **3.** [habitude] Parisian habit *ou* quirk *péj.*

parisien, enne [parizjɛ̃, ɛn] *adj* **1.** [relatif à Paris, sa région] Paris *(modif)* ▪ [natif de Paris, habitant à Paris] Parisian ▪ **la vie ~ne** life in Paris, Parisian life **2.** [typique de Paris] Parisian.
◆ **Parisien, enne** *nm, f* Parisian.

Paris-Match [parimatʃ] *npr* PRESSE *popular weekly magazine.*

parisyllabique [parisilabik] *adj* & *nm* parisyllabic.

paritaire [paritɛr] *adj* : **représentation ~** parity of representation, equal representation.

paritarisme [paritarism] *nm* INDUST (doctrine of) co-management.

parité [parite] *nf* **1.** [concordance - entre des rémunérations] parity, equality ; [- entre des monnaies, des prix] parity ; [- entre des concepts] comparability ▪ **la ~ des salaires** equal pay **2.** MATH parity **3.** INFORM parity check **4.** POLIT gender parity, equal numbers of men and women *(on electoral lists).*

parjure [parʒyr] <> *adj* disloyal, treacherous, underhand.
<> *nmf* [personne] disloyal person, traitor, betrayer.
<> *nm* [acte] disloyalty, treachery, betrayal ▪ **commettre un ~** to forswear.

parjurer [3] [parʒyre] ◆ **se parjurer** *vpi sout* [manquer à son serment] to break one's word *ou* promise.

parka [parka] *nm* & *nf* parka.

Parkérisation® [parkerizasjɔ̃] *nf* Parkerizing.

parking [parkiŋ] *nm* **1.** [parc de stationnement] car park *UK*, parking lot *US* ▪ **une place de ~** a parking space **2.** [action de se garer] : **le ~ est interdit** parking is prohibited here.

Parkinson [parkinsɔn] *npr* ▷ **maladie.**

parlant, e [parlɑ̃, ɑ̃t] *adj* **1.** CINÉ talking **2.** *fam* [bavard] : **il n'est pas très ~** he isn't very talkative *ou* hasn't got very much to say (for himself) **3.** [significatif - chiffre, exemple, schéma] which speaks for itself ▪ **leurs statistiques sont ~es** their figures speak volumes **4.** [bien observé - portrait] lifelike ; [- description] vivid, graphic.
◆ **parlant** *nm* CINÉ : **le ~** talking pictures.

parlé, e [parle] *adj* [anglais, langue] spoken.
◆ **parlé** *nm* [à l'opéra] spoken part, dialogue.

parlement [parləmɑ̃] *nm* **1.** POLIT : **le Parlement** [en France] (the French) Parliament ; [en Grande-Bretagne] (the Houses of) Parliament ▪ **au ~** in Parliament **2.** HIST [en France] parliament *ou* parlement *(under the Ancien Régime)* ▪ [en Grande-Bretagne] : **Parlement Court/Croupion/Long** Short/Rump/Long Parliament.

parlementaire [parləmɑ̃tɛr] <> *adj* **1.** [débat, habitude, régime] parliamentary ▪ **procédure ~** parliamentary procedure **2.** HIST [en Grande-Bretagne] Parliamentary.
<> *nmf* **1.** [député] member of Parliament ▪ [aux États-Unis] Congressman (*f* Congresswoman) **2.** HIST [en Grande-Bretagne] Parliamentarian **3.** [négociateur] mediator, negotiator.

parlementarisme [parləmɑ̃tarism] *nm* parliamentarianism, parliamentary government.

parlementer [3] [parləmɑ̃te] *vi* to negotiate ▪ **~ avec** POLIT to parley with ▪ **il a dû ~ avec l'agent pour qu'il le laisse passer** he had to talk the policeman into letting him through.

parler[1] [parle] *nm* **1.** [vocabulaire] speech, way of speaking ▪ **dans le ~ de tous les jours** in common parlance **2.** [langue d'une région] dialect, variety.

parler[2] [3] [parle] <> *vi*

A. FAIRE UN ÉNONCÉ
B. LOCUTIONS

A. FAIRE UN ÉNONCÉ

1. [articuler des paroles] to talk, to speak ▪ **~ du nez** to talk through one's nose ▪ **~ bas** *ou* **à voix basse** to speak softly *ou* in a low voice ▪ **~ haut** *ou* **à voix haute** to speak loudly *ou* in a loud voice ▪ **parle plus fort** speak louder *ou* up ▪ **parlez moins fort** keep your voice down, don't speak so loud ▪ **elle a une poupée qui parle** she's got a talking doll ▪ **~ par gestes** *ou* **signes** to use sign language ▪ **~ avec les mains** to talk with one's hands
2. [s'exprimer] to talk, to speak ▪ **parle donc!** speak up! ▪ **je n'ai pas l'habitude de ~ en public** I'm not used to speaking in public *ou* to public speaking ▪ **il parle mal** [improprement] he doesn't talk correctly ▪ **tu n'as qu'à ~ pour être servi** just say the word and you'll be served ▪ **mon père parlait peu** my father was a man of few words ▪ **tu parles en nouveaux francs?** are you talking in *ou* do you mean new francs? ▪ **il a fait ~ l'adolescent** he drew the adolescent out of himself, he got the adolescent to talk ▪ **les armes ont parlé** weapons were used ▪ **laisse ~ ton coeur** listen to your heart ▪ **~ pour** *ou* **à la place de qqn** to speak for sb *ou* on sb's behalf ▪ **parle pour toi!** speak for yourself! ▪ **~ contre/pour** to speak against/for ▪ **politiquement/artistiquement parlant** politically/artistically speaking ▪ **~ à qqn** [lui manifester ses sentiments] to talk to *ou* to speak to *ou* to have a word with sb ▪ **~ à qqn** [s'adresser à qqn] to talk *ou* to speak to sb ▪ **ne me parle pas sur ce ton!** don't talk to me like that! ▪ **je ne leur parle plus** I'm not on speaking terms with them any more, I don't speak to them any more ▪ **puis-je ~ à Virginie?** [au téléphone] may I speak to Virginie? ▪ **~ à qqn** [l'émouvoir, le toucher] to speak *ou* to appeal to sb ▶ **voilà ce qui s'appelle ~!, ça, c'est ~!** *fam* well said! ▪ **parlons peu mais parlons bien** let's be brief but to the point
3. [discuter] to talk ▪ **~ pour ne rien dire** to talk for the sake of talking ▪ **assez parlé, allons-y!** that's enough chat, let's go! ▪ **~ de qqch/qqn** to talk *ou* to speak about sthg/sb ▪ **je sais de quoi je parle** I know what I'm talking about ▪ **je ne sais pas de quoi**

tu veux ~ I don't know what you mean ▪ **~ de choses et d'autres** to talk about this and that ▪ **tiens, en parlant de vacances, Luc a une villa à louer** hey, talking of holidays, Luc has a villa to let ▪ **le professeur X va venir ~ de Proust** Professor X will give a talk on Proust ▪ **~ de qqn/qqch** [le mentionner] : **le livre parle de la guerre** the book is about *ou* deals with the war ▪ **tous les journaux en parlent ce matin** it's (mentioned) in all the newspapers this morning ▪ **ils en ont parlé aux informations** they talked about it on the news ▪ **~ (de) religion/(de) littérature** to talk religion/literature ▪ **~ de faire qqch** to talk about *ou* of doing sthg ▪ **qui parle de laisser tomber?** who said anything about giving up? ▪ **~ de qqch/qqn comme de : on parle d'elle comme d'une candidate possible** she's being talked about *ou* billed as a possible candidate ▪ **tu en parles comme d'une catastrophe** you make it sound like a catastrophe ▪ **on m'en avait parlé comme d'une femme austère** I'd been told she was *ou* she'd been described to me as a stern sort of woman ▪ **~ de qqn/qqch à qqn : n'en parle à personne!** don't mention it to anybody! ▪ **après ça, qu'on ne vienne plus me ~ de solidarité** after that, I don't want to hear any more about solidarity ▪ **elle nous a parlé de ses projets** she talked to us about her plans ▪ **parlez-moi un peu de vous/de ce que vous avez ressenti** tell me something about yourself/what you felt ▪ **je cherche un travail, alors, si vous pouviez lui ~ de moi** I'm looking for a job, so if you could have a word with her abou t me ▪ **on m'a beaucoup parlé de vous** I've heard a lot about you ▮ [jaser] to talk ▪ **tout le monde en parle** everybody's talking about it ▪ **on ne parle que de cela au village** it's the talk of the village ▪ **faire ~ de soi** to get o.s. talked about ; [dans la presse] to get one's name in the papers

4. [avouer] to talk ▪ **faire ~ qqn** to make sb talk, to get sb to talk

5. [être éloquent] to speak volumes ▪ **les chiffres/faits parlent d'eux-mêmes** the figures/facts speak for themselves

6. JEUX : **c'est à toi de ~** it's your bid

B. LOCUTIONS

(langage familier) **tu parles, vous parlez : tu parles comme je peux oublier ça!** as if I could ever forget it! ▪ **ça t'a plu? – tu parles!** [bien sûr] did you like it? – you bet! ; [pas du tout] did you like it? – you must be joking! ▪ **tu parles que je vais lui rendre!** [je vais lui rendre] you bet I'll give it back to him! ; [je ne vais pas lui rendre] there's no way I'm giving it back to him! ▪ **tu parles si c'est agréable/intelligent!** *iron* that's really nice/clever! ▪ **tu parles si ça m'aide!** much good that is to me! ▪ **tu parles de, vous parlez de : tu parles d'une déception!** talk about a letdown!, it was such a letdown! ▪ **tu parles d'une veine!** what a stroke of luck! ▪ **ne m'en parle pas, m'en parle pas : c'est difficile – ne m'en parle pas!** it's difficult – don't tell me *ou* you're telling me *ou* you don't say! ▪ **parlons-en : laisse faire la justice – ah, parlons-en, de leur justice!** let justice take its course – justice indeed *ou* some justice! ▪ **sa timidité? parlons-en!** her shyness? that's a good one *ou* you must be joking! ▪ **n'en parlons pas : l'échéance d'avril, n'en parlons pas** let's not even talk about *ou* mention the April deadline ▪ **n'en parlons plus** let's not mention it again, let's say no more about it.

◇ *vt* [langue] to speak ▪ **il parle bien (le) russe** he speaks good Russian ▪ **et pourtant je parle français, non?** *fig* don't you understand plain English? ▪ **nous ne parlons pas la même langue** *ou* **le même langage** *fig* we don't speak the same language ▪ **~ le langage de la raison** to talk sense ▪ **~ affaires/politique** to talk business/politics.

◆ **se parler** ◇ *vp (emploi réciproque)* to talk to one another *ou* each other ▪ **il faudrait qu'on se parle tous les deux** I think we two should have a talk ▪ **elles ne se parlent plus** they aren't on speaking terms any more.

◇ *vp (emploi réfléchi)* to talk to o.s.

◇ *vp (emploi passif)* to be spoken.

◆ **sans parler de** *loc prép* to say nothing of, not to mention, let alone ▪ **sans ~ du fait que...** to say nothing of..., without mentioning the fact that...

parleur, euse [parlœr, øz] *nm, f* talker ▪ **beau ~** *sout* fine talker.

parloir [parlwar] *nm* [d'une prison] visitors' room ▪ [d'un monastère] parlour.

parlot(t)e [parlɔt] *nf fam* chitchat, natter *UK* ▪ **faire la ~** to chat, to natter *UK*.

parme [parm] ◇ *adj inv* mauve.
◇ *nm* [couleur] mauve.

Parme [parm] *npr* Parma.

parmesan, e [parməzɑ̃, an] *adj* Parmesan.
◆ **parmesan** *nm* Parmesan (cheese) ▪ **spaghettis au ~** spaghetti with Parmesan.

parmi [parmi] *prép* among ▪ **elle erra ~ la foule** she wandered in *ou* among the crowd ▪ **nous souhaitons vous avoir bientôt ~ nous** we hope that you'll soon be with us ▪ **~ tout ce vacarme** in the midst of all this noise ▪ **c'est une solution ~ d'autres** that's one solution ▪ **je retiendrai cette solution ~ celles qui ont été proposées** I will choose this solution from those which have been suggested.

Parnasse [parnas] *npr m* **1.** GÉOGR : **le ~** (Mount) Parnassus **2.** LITTÉR & MYTHOL Parnassus.

parnassien, enne [parnasjɛ̃, ɛn] *adj* Parnassian.
◆ **Parnassien, enne** *nm, f* Parnassian *(member of the Parnassian school of French poets)*.

parodie [parɔdi] *nf* **1.** LITTÉR parody **2.** *fig* **une ~ de procès** a mockery of a trial.

parodier [9] [parɔdje] *vt* **1.** ART to parody **2.** [singer] to mimic, to parody ▪ **je le parodie un peu, mais c'est ce qu'il a dit** I'm parodying him a little, but that's what he said.

parodique [parɔdik] *adj* parodic.

parodiste [parɔdist] *nmf* parodist.

parodontologie [parɔdɔ̃tɔlɔʒi] *nf* periodontology.

paroi [parwa] *nf* **1.** [d'une chambre] partition (wall) ▪ [d'un ascenseur] wall ▪ [d'une citerne] inside **2.** ANAT & BOT wall **3.** [alpinisme - GÉOL] face, wall ▪ **~ rocheuse** rock face.

paroisse [parwas] *nf* parish.

paroissial, e, aux [parwasjal, o] *adj* [fête, église] parish *(modif)* ▪ [décision, don] parish *(modif)*, parochial.

paroissien, enne [parwasjɛ̃, ɛn] *nm, f* **1.** RELIG parishioner **2.** *fam* [type] : **c'est un drôle de ~** he's a strange customer.
◆ **paroissien** *nm* [gén] prayer book ▪ [catholique] missal.

parole [parɔl] *nf* **1.** [faculté de s'exprimer] : **la ~** speech ▪ **il ne lui manque que la ~, à ton chien** your dog does everything but talk ▪ **être doué de ~** to be endowed with speech ▪ **perdre l'usage de la ~** to lose one's power of speech ▶ **la ~ est d'argent, le silence est d'or** *prov* speech is silver, silence is golden *prov*

2. [fait de parler] : **demander la ~** to ask for the right to speak ; DR to request leave to speak ▪ **prendre la ~** [gén] to speak ; [au parlement, au tribunal] to take the floor ▪ **vous avez la ~** [à un avocat, un député] you have the floor ; [dans un débat] (it's) your turn to speak *ou* over to you ▪ **la ~ est à la défense** the defence may now speak ▪ **adresser la ~ à qqn** to talk *ou* to speak to sb ▪ **couper la ~ à qqn** to interrupt sb ▪ **passer la ~ à qqn** to hand over to sb ▶ **droit de ~** right to speak ▪ **temps de ~** speaking time ▪ **votre temps de ~ est révolu** your time is up

3. LING speech, parole

4. *(souvent pl)* [propos] word, remark ▪ **prononcer des ~s historiques** to utter historic words ▪ **ce sont ses (propres) ~s** those are his very (own) words ▪ **ce ne sont que des ~s en l'air** all that's just idle talk ▪ **il s'y connaît en belles ~s** he's full of fine words ▪ **en ~s, ça a l'air simple, mais...** it's easy enough to say it, but... ▪ **en ~s et en actes** in word and deed ▶ **répandre** *ou* **porter la bonne ~** to spread *ou* to carry the good word ▪ **la ~ de Dieu** the Word of God ▪ **c'est ~ d'Évangile** it's the gospel truth ▪ **les ~s s'envolent, les écrits restent** *prov* verba volant, scripta manent *prov*

5. [engagement] word ▪ **il n'a qu'une ~, il est de ~** his word is his bond *sout*, he's a man of his word ▪ **tu n'as aucune ~** you never keep your word ▪ **donner sa ~ (d'honneur) à qqn** to give sb one's word (of honour) ▪ **tenir ~** to keep one's word ▪ **reprendre** *ou* **retirer sa ~** to go back on one's word ▶ **c'est un homme de ~** he's a man of his word ▪ **~ d'honneur!** I give you my word (of honour)! ▪ **ma ~!** my word!

6. JEUX : **avoir la ~** to be the first to bid ■ **passer ~** to pass.
▸ **paroles** *nfpl* [d'une chanson] words, lyrics ■ [d'une illustration] words ■ **histoire sans ~s** wordless cartoon ■ **'sans ~s'** 'no caption'.
▸ **sur parole** *loc adv* on parole.

parolier, ère [parɔlje, ɛr] *nm, f* [d'une chanson] lyric writer, lyricist ■ [d'un opéra] librettist.

paronyme [parɔnim] ◇ *adj* paronymous.
◇ *nm* paronym.

paronymique [parɔnimik] *adj* paronymous.

paroxysme [parɔksism] *nm* **1.** [d'un état affectif] paroxysm, height ■ **le mécontentement a atteint son ~** discontent is at its height ■ **au ~ de la douleur** in paroxysms of pain ■ **les fans étaient au ~ du délire** the fans' enthusiasm had reached fever pitch **2.** MÉD paroxysm.

parpaing [parpɛ̃] *nm* **1.** [pierre de taille] perpend **2.** [aggloméré] breezeblock *UK*, cinderblock *US*.

Parque [park] *npr f* : **la ~** Fate ■ **les ~s** the Parcae, the Fates.

parquer [3] [parke] *vt* **1.** [mettre dans un parc - bétail] to pen in *ou* up *(sép)* ; [- moutons] to pen in *ou* up *(sép)*, to fold ■ **~ les huîtres** to lay down an oysterbed **2.** [enfermer - prisonniers] to shut in *ou* up *(sép)*, to confine ; [- foule, multitude] to pack *ou* to cram in *(sép)* **3.** [voiture] to park.
▸ **se parquer** *vpi* [en voiture] to park.

parquet [parkɛ] *nm* **1.** [revêtement de bois] (wooden) floor *ou* flooring ■ [à chevrons] parquet ■ **refaire le ~** to re-lay *ou* to replace the floorboards ▶ **~ à l'anglaise** strip flooring **2.** DR public prosecutor's department, ≃ Crown Prosecution Service *UK*, ≃ District Attorney's office *US* ■ **déposer une plainte auprès du ~** to lodge a complaint with the public prosecutor **3.** BOURSE : **le ~** [lieu] the (dealing) floor ; [personnes] the Stock Exchange **4.** ART wooden backing.

parqueter [27] [parkəte] *vt* to lay a wooden *ou* parquet floor in, to put a wooden *ou* parquet floor down in.

parrain [parɛ̃] *nm* **1.** RELIG godfather ■ **être le ~ d'un enfant** to be a child's godfather, to stand godfather to a child **2.** COMM sponsor **3.** [d'un projet] promoter ■ [d'une oeuvre charitable] patron ■ POLIT proposer, sponsor *US* **4.** [d'un navire] namer, christener ■ [d'une cloche] christener **5.** [de la mafia] godfather.

parrainage [parɛnaʒ] *nm* **1.** RELIG (act of) being a godparent **2.** COMM sponsorship, sponsoring **3.** [d'un projet] proposing, promoting ■ [d'une oeuvre charitable] patronage ■ POLIT proposing, sponsoring *US* **4.** [d'un navire] naming, christening ■ [d'une cloche] christening.

parrainer [4] [parene] *vt* **1.** [candidat, postulant] to propose, to sponsor *US* ■ [projet] to propose, to support ■ [oeuvre charitable] to patronize **2.** COMM to sponsor ■ **se faire ~** to be sponsored.

parricide [parisid] ◇ *adj* parricidal.
◇ *nmf* [assassin] parricide.
◇ *nm* [crime] parricide.

pars *etc v* ⊳ **partir**.

parsemer [19] [parsəme] *vt* **1.** [semer, saupoudrer] : **~ qqch de** to scatter sthg with **2.** *litt* [suj: fleurs, étoiles] : **le ciel était parsemé d'étoiles** the sky was studded *ou* scattered with stars.

parsi, e [parsi] *adj* Parsi, Parsee.
▸ **Parsi, e** *nm, f* Parsi, Parsee.
▸ **parsi** *nm* LING Parsee.

part [par] *nf* **1.** [dans un partage - de nourriture] piece, portion ; [- d'un butin, de profits, de travail etc] share ■ **une ~ de gâteau** a slice of cake ■ **à chacun sa ~** share and share alike ■ **elle a eu sa ~ de soucis** she's had her share of worries ■ **repose-toi, tu as fait ta ~** have a rest, you've done your bit ▶ **avoir ~ à** to have a share in, to share (in) ■ **avoir la ~ belle** to get a good deal ■ **faire la ~ belle à qqn** to give sb a good deal ■ **vouloir sa ~ de** *ou* **du gâteau** to want one's share of the cake ■ **se réserver** *ou* **se tailler la ~ du lion** to keep *ou* to take the lion's share **2.** DR [pour les impôts] *basic unit used for calculating personal income tax* ■ **un couple avec un enfant a deux ~s et demie** a couple with a child has a tax allowance worth two and a half *UK ou* has two and a half tax exemptions *US*
3. ÉCON & FIN : **~ de marché** market share ■ **~ sociale/d'intérêts** unquoted/partner's share
4. [fraction] part, portion ■ **en grande ~** for the most part, largely, to a large extent ■ **les sociétés, pour la plus grande ~, sont privatisées** firms, for the most part, are privatized ■ **il y a une grande ~ de peur dans son échec** her failure is due to a large extent to fear, fear goes a long way towards explaining her failure
5. [participation] : **prendre ~ à** [discussion, compétition, manifestation] to take part in ; [cérémonie, projet] to join in, to play a part in ; [attentat] to take part in, to play a part in ■ **prendre ~ à la joie/peine de qqn** to share (in) sb's joy/sorrow ▶ **il faut faire la ~ du hasard/de la malchance** you have to recognize the part played by chance/ill-luck, you have to make allowances for chance/ill-luck ■ **faire la ~ des choses** to take things into consideration ■ **faire la ~ du feu** to cut one's losses
6. THÉÂTRE [aparté] (artist's) cut
7. *loc* **de la ~ de** [au nom de] : **je viens de la ~ de Paula** Paula sent me ■ **donne-le lui de ma ~** give it to her from me ■ **dis-lui au revoir/merci de ma ~** say goodbye/thank you for me ■ **je vous appelle de la ~ de Jacques** I'm calling on behalf of Jacques ■ **de la ~ de** [provenant de] : **de ta ~, cela me surprend beaucoup** I'm surprised at you ■ **je ne m'attendais pas à une telle audace/mesquinerie de sa ~** I didn't expect such boldness/meanness from him ■ **c'est très généreux de ta ~** that's very generous of you ■ **cela demande un certain effort de votre ~** it requires a certain amount of effort on your part ■ **c'est de la ~ de qui?** [au téléphone, à un visiteur] who (shall I say) is calling? ■ **pour ma/sa ~** (as) for me/him ■ **faire ~ de qqch à qqn** to announce sthg to sb, to inform sb of sthg ■ **prendre qqch en bonne ~** to take sthg in good part ■ **prendre qqch en mauvaise ~** to take offence at sthg, to take sthg amiss ■ **ne le prenez pas en mauvaise ~, mais...** don't be offended, but..
▸ **à part** ◇ *loc adj* **1.** [séparé - comptes, logement] separate **2.** [original, marginal] odd ■ **ce sont des gens à ~** these people are rather special.
◇ *loc adv* **1.** [à l'écart] : **elle est restée à ~ toute la soirée** she kept herself to herself all evening ■ **mets les dossiers bleus à ~** put the blue files to one side ■ **mis à ~ deux ou trois détails, tout est prêt** except for *ou* apart from two or three details, everything is ready
2. [en aparté] : **prendre qqn à ~** to take sb aside *ou* to one side
3. [séparément] separately.
◇ *loc prép* **1.** [excepté] except for, apart *ou* aside from ■ **à ~ cela** apart from that, that aside
2. *sout* **elle se disait à ~ soi que...** she said to herself that...
▸ **à part entière** *loc adj* : **un membre à ~ entière de** a full *ou* fully paid up member of ■ **citoyen à ~ entière** person with full citizenship (status) ■ **elle est devenue une actrice à ~ entière** she's now a proper *ou* a fully-fledged actress.
▸ **à part que** *loc conj fam* except that, if it weren't *ou* except for the fact that ■ **c'est une jolie maison, à ~ qu'elle est un peu humide** it's a nice house, except that it's a bit damp.
▸ **de part en part** *loc adv* from end to end, throughout, right through ■ **la poutre est fendue de ~ en part** the beam is split from end to end.
▸ **de part et d'autre** *loc adv* **1.** [des deux côtés] on both sides, on either side
2. [partout] on all sides.
▸ **de part et d'autre de** *loc prép* on both sides of.
▸ **de toute(s) part(s)** *loc adv* (from) everywhere, from all sides *ou* quarters ■ **ils accouraient de toutes ~s vers le village** they were rushing towards the village from all directions.
▸ **d'une part... d'autre part** *loc corrélative* on the one hand... on the other hand.
▸ **pour une large part** *loc adv* to a great extent.

part. = **particulier**.

partage [partaʒ] *nm* **1.** [division - d'un domaine] division, dividing *ou* splitting up ; [- d'un rôti] carving ; [- d'un gâteau] slicing, cutting (up) ■ **faire le ~ de qqch** to divide sthg up **2.** [répartition - d'une fortune, des devoirs, des tâches] sharing out ; [- des torts, des fautes] sharing, apportioning ▪ **~ du pouvoir** power-sharing, the sharing of power **3.** DR [acte juridique] partition **4.** GÉOM division **5.** INFORM : **~ de temps** time-sharing.

◆ **en partage** *loc adv* : **donner qqch en ~ à qqn** to leave sb sthg (in one's will) ▪ **je n'ai reçu en ~ que la vieille horloge de mon père** all I got for my share was my father's old clock.

◆ **sans partage** *loc adj sout* [joie] unmitigated ▪ [affection] undivided ▪ [engagement, enthousiasme] thoroughgoing.

partagé, e [partaʒe] *adj* **1.** [opposé] split, divided ▪ **j'ai lu des critiques ~es** I've read mixed reviews ▪ **il était ~ entre la joie et la crainte** he was torn between joy and fear **2.** [mutuel - haine] mutual, reciprocal ; [- amour] mutual **3.** INFORM : **en temps ~** on a time-sharing basis.

partageable [partaʒabl] *adj* **1.** [bien, propriété] which can be shared out *ou* divided ▪ [nombre] divisible **2.** [point de vue] that can be shared ▪ **votre opinion est difficilement ~** your opinion is not one that can easily be shared **3.** DR partible.

partager [17] [partaʒe] *vt* **1.** [diviser - propriété] to divide up *(sép)*, to share out *(sép)* ▪ **~ qqch en deux/par moitié** to divide sthg in two/into two halves **2.** [diviser - pays, société] to divide ▪ **la question du désarmement partage le pays** the country is divided *ou* split over the question of disarmament ▪ **être partagé entre** to be split *ou* divided between ▪ **je suis partagée entre l'envie de finir mes études et celle de travailler** I can't make up my mind between finishing my course and starting work **3.** [répartir - bénéfices, provisions] to share out *(sép)* **4.** [avoir avec d'autres] to share ▪ **~ la joie/peine/surprise de qqn** to share (in) sb's joy/sorrow/surprise ▪ **le pouvoir est partagé entre les deux assemblées** power is shared *ou* split between the two Houses ▪ **voici une opinion partagée par beaucoup de gens** this is an opinion shared *ou* held by many (people) ▪ **j'ai été heureuse de pouvoir vous faire ~ ma joie** I was pleased to be able to share my joy with you ▪ *(en usage absolu)* **elle n'aime pas ~** she doesn't like to share.

◆ **se partager** ◇ *vpt* [biens, travail] to share (out) ▪ **se ~ la tâche** to share (out) the work ▪ **Lyon et Marseille se partagent la première place** SPORT Lyons and Marseilles share first place *ou* are equal first UK ▪ **se ~ les faveurs du public** to be joint favourites with the public.

◇ *vpi* **1.** [personne] : **elles se partagent entre leur carrière et leurs enfants** their time is divided between their professional lives and their families **2.** [se diviser] to fork, to divide ▪ **se ~ en** to be split *ou* divided into.

partageur, euse [partaʒœr, øz] *adj* sharing, willing to share ▪ **cet enfant n'est pas très ~** this child is not good at sharing.

partagiciel [partaʒisjɛl] *nm* shareware.

partance [partɑ̃s] ◆ **en partance** *loc adj* due to leave ▪ **le premier avion en ~** the first plane due to take off ▪ **le dernier bateau en ~** the last boat out *ou* due to sail ▪ **le dernier train en ~** the last train ▪ **les familles en ~ pour l'Amérique** families setting off *ou* bound for America.

partant¹ [partɑ̃] *conj litt* therefore, consequently, thus ▪ **et, ~, elle n'avait aucun droit sur la succession** and thus she had no claim on the estate.

partant², e [partɑ̃, ɑ̃t] ◇ *adj* : **être ~ pour (faire) qqch** to be willing *ou* ready to do sthg ▪ **aller danser? je suis ~e!** go dancing? I'd love to!

◇ *nm, f* SPORT [cheval] runner ▪ [cycliste, coureur] starter.

partenaire [partənɛr] *nmf* **1.** [gén] partner ▪ **les ~s sociaux** management and the workforce **2.** CINÉ & THÉÂTRE : **il était mon ~ dans la pièce** I played opposite him in the play.

partenariat [partənarja] *nm* partnership.

parterre [partɛr] *nm* **1.** HORT [en bordure] border ▪ [plus large] bed, flowerbed ▪ **un ~ de fleurs** a flowerbed **2.** THÉÂTRE [emplacement] stalls UK, orchestra US ▪ [spectateurs] (audience in the) stalls UK *ou* orchestra US ▪ **il y avait hier un ~ distingué** there was a distinguished *ou* select audience yesterday.

parthe [part] *adj* Parthian.

◆ **Parthe** *nmf* Parthian.

parthénogenèse [partenɔʒenɛz] *nf* parthenogenesis.

Parthénon [partenɔ̃] *npr m* : **le ~** the Parthenon.

parti¹ [parti] *nm* **1.** POLIT : **~ (politique)** (political) party ▪ **le ~ communiste/conservateur/démocrate/républicain/socialiste** the Communist/Conservative/Democratic/Republican/Socialist Party ▪ **les ~s de droite/gauche** the parties of the right/left, the right-wing/left-wing parties ▪ **le système du ~ unique** the one-party system **2.** *sout* [choix, décision] decision, course of action ▪ **prendre le ~ de : prendre le ~ de la modération** to opt for moderation ▪ **prendre le ~ de faire qqch** to make up one's mind to do sthg, to decide to do sthg ▪ **prendre ~** [prendre position] to take sides *ou* a stand ▪ **prendre ~ pour/contre qqch** to come out for/against sthg ▪ **prendre ~ pour qqn** to side *ou* to take sides with sb ▪ **prendre ~ contre qqn** to take sides against sb ▪ **prendre son ~ : son parti est pris** her mind is made up, she's made up her mind ◉ **en prendre son ~ : elle ne sera jamais musicienne, il faut que j'en prenne mon/qu'elle en prenne son ~** she'll never be a musician, I'll/she'll just have to accept it **3.** [avantage] : **tirer ~ de** [situation] to take advantage of ; [équipement] to put to good use ▪ **elle ne sait pas tirer ~ de ses qualifications** she doesn't know how to get the most out of her qualifications ▪ **elle tire ~ de tout** she can turn anything to her advantage **4.** *hum* [personne à marier] : **c'est un beau** *ou* **bon ~** he's/she's a good match.

◆ **parti pris** *nm* **1.** [prise de position] commitment ▪ **avoir un ~ pris de modernisme/clarté** to be committed to modernism/clear-thinking **2.** [préjugé] bias ▪ **je n'ai aucun ~ pris contre le tennis professionnel, mais...** I'm not biased against professional tennis, but... ▪ **être de ~ pris** to be biased ▪ **faire qqch de ~ pris** to do sthg deliberately *ou* on purpose ▪ **être sans ~ pris** to be unbiased *ou* objective ▪ **je dirais, sans ~ pris, qu'elle est la meilleure** without any bias on my part, I'd say that she's the best.

parti², e [parti] *adj fam* drunk, tight ▪ **tu étais bien ~ hier soir!** you were well away UK *ou* well gone last night!

partial, e, aux [parsjal, o] *adj* biased, partial.

partialement [parsjalmɑ̃] *adv* in a biased *ou* partial way.

partialité [parsjalite] *nf* [favorable] partiality ▪ [défavorable] bias ▪ **~ en faveur de qqn** partiality for sb, bias in favour of sb ▪ **~ contre qqn** bias against sb.

participant, e [partisipɑ̃, ɑ̃t] ◇ *adj* participant, participating.

◇ *nm, f* participant ▪ **les ~s au congrès** the participants in *ou* those taking part in the congress.

participatif, ive [partisipatif, iv] *adj* : **prêt ~** participating capital loan.

participation [partisipasjɔ̃] *nf* **1.** [engagement, contribution] participation, involvement ▪ **il nie sa ~ à** *ou* **dans l'enlèvement du prince** he denies having participated *ou* been involved in the prince's kidnapping ▪ **sa ~ aux jeux Olympiques semble compromise** there's a serious question mark hanging over his participation in the Olympic Games ▪ **apporter sa ~ à qqch** to contribute to sthg ▪ **la décision a été prise sans sa ~** the decision was made without her being involved *ou* having any part in it ▪ **notre foire du livre a dû se faire sans la ~ des éditeurs** our book fair had to be held in the absence of any *ou* without any publishers

2. [dans un spectacle] appearance ▪ **'avec la ~ des frères Jarry'** 'featuring the Jarry Brothers' ▪ **'avec la ~ spéciale de Robert Vann'** 'guest appearance by Robert Vann'

3. [contribution financière] contribution (to costs) ▪ **il y a 100 euros de ~ aux frais** you have to pay 100 euros towards costs ▪ **nous demandons à chacun une petite ~** we're asking every one of you to contribute a small amount *ou* to make a small contribution

4. POLIT : **~ (électorale)** (voter) turnout ▪ **un faible taux de** *ou* **une faible ~ aux élections** a poor *ou* low turnout at the polls

5. ÉCON & POLIT [détention de capital] interest, share ▪ **avoir une ~ majoritaire dans une société** to have a majority interest in a company ▪ **il détient une ~ de 6% dans l'entreprise** he holds a 6% share in the company ▪ **prendre des ~s dans une entreprise** to buy into a company ◉ **~ aux bénéfices** profit-sharing ▪ **~ ouvrière** worker participation

6. DR : **~ aux acquêts** *sharing of spouse's purchases after marriage subsequent to divorce* ▪ ≃ property adjustment UK.

◆ **en participation** *loc adj* profit-sharing *(modif).*

participe [partisip] *nm* participle (form) ▪ **~ passé/présent** past/present participle ▪ **proposition ~, ~ absolu** participial construction, *voir aussi* **pluriel**.

participer [3] [partisipe] ◆ **participer à** *v+prép* **1.** [prendre part à - concours, négociation, cérémonie] to take part in ; [- discussion] to contribute to ; [- projet] to be involved in ; [- aventure] to be involved in, to be part of ; [- épreuve sportive] to take part *ou* to be in ; [- attentat, vol] to be involved in, to take part in ; [- jeu] to join in ; [- émission] to take part in ▪ **j'aimerais te voir ~ plus souvent aux tâches ménagères!** I'd like to see you taking on a greater share of the household chores! ▪ *(en usage absolu)* [dans un jeu] to take part, to join in ▪ [à l'école] to contribute (during class) ▪ **l'idée principale du metteur en scène est de faire ~ le public** the director's basic idea is to get the public to participate in the show **2.** [partager] to share (in) ▪ **~ à la douleur/joie de qqn** to share in sb's pain/joy **3.** [financièrement - achat, dépenses] to share in, to contribute to ▪ **tous ses collègues ont participé au cadeau** all her colleagues contributed something towards the present ▪ ÉCON & FIN [profits, pertes] to share (in) ▪ **~ aux bénéfices** to share in the profits.
◆ **participer de** *v+prép sout* to pertain to ▪ **tout ce qui participe de la philosophie** everything pertaining *ou* relating to philosophy.

particularisation [partikylarizasjɔ̃] *nf* particularization.

particulariser [3] [partikylarize] *vt* **1.** [restreindre à un cas particulier] to particularize ▪ **~ une proposition générale** to particularize (from) a general statement **2.** [distinguer, singulariser] to distinguish, to characterize **3.** DR : **~ une affaire** to specify (the identity of) one of the accused (in a case).
◆ **se particulariser** *vpi* : **se ~ par** to be distinguished *ou* characterized by.

particularisme [partikylarism] *nm* particularism.

particularité [partikylarite] *nf* **1.** [trait distinctif - d'une personne, d'une culture, d'une langue etc] particularity, (specific) feature *ou* characteristic *ou* trait ; [- d'une région] distinctive feature ; [- d'une machine] special feature ▪ **les tortues de mer ont la ~ de pondre dans le sable** a distinctive feature of turtles is that they lay their eggs in the sand **2.** [élément] detail, particular.

particule [partikyl] *nf* **1.** GÉOL, GRAMM & PHYS particle ▪ **~ élémentaire** fundamental particle **2.** [dans un nom] particule *('de' in a surname, indicating aristocratic origin).*

particulier, ère [partikylje, ɛr] *adj* **1.** [précis - circonstance, exemple, point] particular, specific **2.** [caractéristique - odeur, humour, parler, style] particular, distinctive, characteristic ▪ **une odeur particulière au pois de senteur** a fragrance peculiar to sweetpeas ▪ **un trait bien ~** a highly distinctive feature **3.** [hors du commun] particular, special, unusual ▪ **porter une attention toute particulière à qqch** to pay particular *ou* special attention to sthg ▪ **ses photos n'offrent pas d'intérêt ~** his photographs are of *ou* hold no particular interest ▪ **il ne s'est rien passé de ~** nothing special *ou* particular happened **4.** [bizarre - comportement, goûts, mœurs] peculiar, odd **5.** [privé - avion, intérêts] private ▪ **j'ai une voiture particulière** I've got my own car *ou* a car of my own ➊ **cours ~, leçon particulière** private lesson.
◆ **particulier** *nm* **1.** ADMIN private individual ▪ **il loge chez des ~s** he's in private lodgings *UK*, he rooms with a family *US* **2.** [élément individuel] : **le ~** the particular.
◆ **en particulier** *loc adv* **1.** [essentiellement] in particular, particularly, especially **2.** [seul à seul] in private ▪ **puis-je vous parler en ~?** may I have a private word with you?

particulièrement [partikyljɛrmɑ̃] *adv* **1.** [surtout] particularly, specifically, in particular ▪ **nous nous attacherons plus ~ à cet aspect de l'oeuvre** we shall deal in particular *ou* more specifically with this aspect of the work ▪ **leurs enfants sont très beaux, ~ leur fille** their children are very good-looking, especially their daughter **2.** [exceptionnellement] particularly, specially, especially ▪ **il n'est pas ~ laid/doué** he's not particularly ugly/gifted ▪ **je n'aime pas ~ cela** I'm not particularly keen on it ▪ **tu aimes le whisky? – pas ~** do you like whisky? – not particularly.

partie [parti] <> *f* ▷ **parti** *(adj).*
<> *nf* **1.** [élément, composant] part ▪ **les ~s constituantes** the component parts ▪ **faire ~ de** [comité] to be a member of, to be on, to sit on ; [club, communauté] to be a member of, to belong to ; [équipe] to belong to, to be one of, to be in ; [licenciés] to be among, to be one of ; [métier, inconvénients, risques] to be part of ▪ **il fait presque ~ de la famille** he's almost one of the family ▪ **faire ~ intégrante de** to be an integral part of ➊ **~s communes/privatives** communal/private areas *(in a building or an estate)* ▪ **~s génitales** *ou* **sexuelles** genitals, private parts ▪ **ses ~s** *fam* his privates
2. [fraction, morceau] part ▪ **couper qqch en deux ~s** to cut sthg into two (parts) ▪ **la ~ visible de la Lune** the visible side of the Moon ▪ **une ~ du blé est contaminée** some *ou* part of the wheat is contaminated ▪ **une grande/petite ~ de l'électorat** a large/small part of the electorate, a large/small section of the electorate ▪ **il est absent une grande** *ou* **la plus grande ~ du temps** he's away much of *ou* most of the time ▪ **pendant la plus grande ~ du chemin** (for) most of the way
3. JEUX & SPORT game ▪ **faire une ~ de cartes** to have a game of cards ▪ **la ~ n'est pas égale** it's an uneven match, it's not a fair match ➊ **~ d'échecs/de billard/de tennis/de cartes** game of chess/billiards/tennis/cards ▪ **~ de golf** round of golf ▪ **abandonner** *ou* **quitter la ~** to give up the fight, to throw in the towel ▪ **avoir ~ gagnée** to be bound to succeed ▪ **la ~ est jouée/n'est pas jouée** the outcome is a foregone conclusion/is still wide open
4. [divertissement à plusieurs] : **~ de chasse/pêche** shooting/fishing party ▪ **~ de campagne** day *ou* outing in the country ▪ **~ carrée** wife-swapping party ▪ **~ fine** orgy ▪ **une ~ de jambes en l'air** *fam* a bit of nooky ▪ **ça n'est pas une ~ de plaisir!** *fam* it's no picnic *ou* fun! ▪ **être/se mettre de la ~ : on va lui faire une farce, qui veut être de la ~?** we're going to play a trick on him, who wants to join in? ▪ **s'il se met aussi de la ~, nous aurons les capitaux nécessaires** if he comes in on it too, we shall have the necessary capital ▪ **je ne peux pas partir avec toi cette fois, mais ce n'est que ~ remise** I can't go with you this time, but there'll be other opportunities
5. [domaine, spécialité] field, line ▪ **elle est de la ~** it's her line ▪ **moi qui suis de la ~, je peux te dire que ce ne sera pas facile** being in that line of business myself, I can tell you it won't be easy
6. MUS part
7. [participant - gén - DR] party ▪ **être ~ dans une négociation** to be a party to a negotiation ▪ **les ~s en présence** the parties ▪ **les deux ~s demandent le renvoi de l'affaire** both sides have requested an adjournment ➊ **~s contractantes/intéressées** contracting/interested parties ▪ **~ civile** private party *(acting jointly with the public prosecutor in criminal cases), plaintiff (for damages)* ▪ **se constituer** *ou* **se porter ~ civile** to act jointly with the public prosecutor ▪ **~ comparante** appearer ▪ **~ défaillante** party failing to appear (in court) ▪ **les ~s plaidantes** the litigants ▪ **~ prenante** payee, receiver ▪ **être ~ prenante dans qqch** *fig* to be directly involved *ou* concerned in sthg
8. GRAMM : **~ du discours** part of speech
9. MATH : **~ d'un ensemble** subset
10. CHIM : **~ par million** part per million
11. *loc* **avoir ~ liée avec qqn** to be hand in glove with sb.
◆ **à partie** *loc adv* : **prendre qqn à ~** [s'attaquer à lui] to set on sb ; [l'interpeller] to take sb to task.
◆ **en partie** *loc adv* in part, partly, partially ▪ **je ne l'ai cru qu'en ~** I only half believed him ▪ **c'est en ~ vrai** it's partly true ▪ **c'est en ~ de la fiction et en ~ de la réalité** it's part fiction and part truth ▪ **en grande** *ou* **majeure ~** for the most part, largely, mainly.
◆ **pour partie** *loc adv* partly, in part.

partiel, elle [parsjɛl] *adj* partial ▪ **contrôle** *ou* **examen ~** mid-year exam ▪ **(emploi à) temps ~** part-time job ▪ **elle ne le fait qu'à temps ~** she only does it part-time.
◆ **partiel** *nm* **1.** ÉDUC mid-year exam **2.** PHYS partial.

partiellement [parsjɛlmɑ̃] *adv* partially, partly ▪ **ce n'est que ~ vrai** it's only partly true.

partir [43] [partir] *vi* **1.** [s'en aller] to go, to leave ▪ **pars, tu vas rater ton train** (off you) go, or you'll miss your train ▪ **empêche-la de ~** stop her (going), don't let her go ▪ **je ne vous fais pas ~, j'espère** I hope I'm not chasing you away ▪ **laisser ~** [prisonnier, otage] to set free, to let go, to release ; [écolier] to let out ; [employé] to let go ▪ **laisse-moi ~** let me go ▪ **il est parti avec la caisse** he ran away *OU* off with the till ▪ **le climat les a fait ~** the climate drove them away ▪ **tout son argent part en disques** all his money goes on records ▪ **je ne peux pas ~ du bureau avant 17 h 30** I can't leave the office before 5:30 ‖ *euphém* [mourir] to pass on *OU* away
2. [se mettre en route] to set off *OU* out, to start off ▪ **pars devant, je te rattrape** go ahead, I'll catch up with you ▪ **regarde cette circulation, on n'est pas encore partis!** *fam* by the look of that traffic, we're not off yet! ▪ **le courrier n'est pas encore parti** the post hasn't gone yet ▪ **~ en avion** [personne] to fly (off) ; [courrier] to go air mail *OU* by air ▪ **~ en bateau** to go (off) by boat, to sail ▪ **~ en voiture** to go (off) by car, to drive off
3. [se rendre] to go, to leave ▪ **je pars à *OU* pour Toulon demain** I'm leaving for *OU* I'm off to Toulon tomorrow ▪ **~ à la campagne/montagne/mer** to go (off) to the countryside/mountains/seaside ▪ **~ vers le sud** to go south
4. [aller - pour se livrer à une activité] to go ▪ **elle est partie au tennis/à la danse** she's gone to play tennis/to her dance class ▪ **~ à la chasse/pêche** to go shooting/fishing ▪ **~ à la recherche de** to set off in search of, to go looking for ▪ **~ en week-end** to go off *OU* away for the weekend ▪ **nous partons en excursion/voyage demain** we're setting off on an excursion/a journey tomorrow ▪ **tu ne pars pas (en vacances) cet été?** aren't you going on holiday *UK OU* vacation *US* this summer? ▪ **~ skier/se promener** to go skiing/for a walk ▪ **sa tête est partie heurter le buffet** his head struck against the sideboard
5. [s'engager] : **~ dans : ~ dans un discours** to launch into a speech ▪ **~ dans une explication** to embark on an explanation ▪ **~ sur : ~ sur un sujet** to start off on a topic ▪ **quand elles sont parties sur leur boulot, c'est difficile de les arrêter** *fam* once they start on about their job, there's no stopping them ▪ **être parti à faire qqch** *fam* : **les voilà partis à refaire toute la maison** there they go doing up the entire house
6. [démarrer - machine, moteur, voiture] to start (up) ; [- avion] to take off, to leave ; [- train] to leave, to depart ; [- fusée] to go up ; [- pétard] to go off ; [- plante] to take ▪ **le coup (de feu) est parti tout seul** the gun went off on its own ▪ **il m'a insulté et la gifle est partie** he insulted me and I just slapped him ▪ **excuse-moi, le mot est parti (tout seul)** I'm sorry, the word just came out ▪ **faire ~** [moteur] to start (up) ; [pétard] to set *OU* to let off *(sép)* ; [fusil] to let off *(sép)* ; [plante] to get started
7. [se mettre en mouvement, débuter - coureur, match, concert] to start (off) ▪ **être parti pour : on est partis pour avoir des ennuis!** we're headed for trouble! ▪ **elle est partie pour nous faire la tête toute la soirée** she's all set to sulk the whole evening ▪ **le match est bien/mal parti pour notre équipe** the match has started well/badly for our team ▪ **le projet est bien parti** the project is off to a good start ▪ **je le vois mal parti pour récupérer son titre** the way he's going, I just can't see him winning back his title ▪ **elle a l'air bien partie pour remporter l'élection** she seems well set to win the election
8. [se vendre] to sell
9. [disparaître, s'effacer - inscription] to disappear, to be rubbed off *OU* out, to be worn off ; [- tache] to disappear, to go, to come out ; [- douleur] to go, to disappear ; [- boutons] to come off ; [- pellicules, odeur] to go ▪ **faire ~** [salissure] to get rid of, to remove ; [odeur] to get rid of, to clear ; [douleur] to ease ▪ **ça ne fera pas ~ ton mal de gorge** it won't get rid of your sore throat
10. [se défaire, se détacher - attache, bouton] to come off, to go ; [- maille] to run ; [- étiquette] to come off.
◆ **partir de** *v+prép* **1.** [dans l'espace] : **le ferry/marathon part de Brest** the ferry sails/the marathon starts from Brest ▪ **la rue part de la mairie** the street starts at the town hall ▪ **la cicatrice part du poignet et va jusqu'au coude** the scar goes *OU* stretches from the wrist to the elbow ▪ **c'est le quatrième en partant de la droite/du haut** it's the fourth (one) from the right/top
2. [dans le temps] : **nous allons faire ~ le contrat du 15 janvier** we'll make the contract effective (as) from January the 15th ▪ **votre congé part de la fin mai** your holidays begin at the end of May
3. [dans un raisonnement] : **~ du principe que** to start from the principle that, to start by assuming that ▪ **si l'on part de ce principe, il faudrait ne jamais contester** on that basis, one should never protest
4. [provenir de] : **tous les problèmes sont partis de là** all the problems stemmed from that ▪ **ça partait d'un bon sentiment** his intentions were good ▪ **sa remarque est partie du coeur** his comment came *OU* was (straight) from the heart, it was a heartfelt remark.
◆ **à partir de** *loc prép* **1.** [dans le temps] (as) from ▪ **à ~ de mardi** starting from Tuesday, from Tuesday onwards ▪ **à ~ de (ce moment-) là, il ne m'a plus adressé la parole** from that moment on *OU* from then on, he never spoke to me again
2. [dans l'espace] (starting) from ▪ **le deuxième à ~ de la droite** the second (one) from the right
3. [numériquement] : **imposé à ~ de 5 000 euros** taxable from 5,000 euros upwards
4. [avec, à base de] from ▪ **c'est fait à ~ d'huiles végétales** it's made from *OU* with vegetable oils ▪ **on ne peut pas tirer de conclusions à ~ de si peu de preuves** you can't reach any conclusion on the basis of so little evidence ▪ **j'ai fait un résumé à ~ de ses notes** I've made a summary based on his notes.

partisan, e [partizɑ̃, an] *adj* partisan ▪ **un choix ~** *péj* a biased choice ▪ **elle n'est pas ~e *OU* partisante** *fam* **de cette thèse** she doesn't favour this theory.
◆ **partisan** *nm* **1.** [adepte, défenseur] supporter ▪ **c'est un ~ de la censure** he's for *OU* in favour of censorship **2.** [dans une guerre] partisan.

partita [partita] *nf* partita.

partitif, ive [partitif, iv] *adj* partitive.
◆ **partitif** *nm* partitive (form), *voir aussi* **pluriel**.

partition [partisjɔ̃] *nf* **1.** MUS [symboles] score ▪ [livret] score, music **2.** HIST & POLIT partition, partitioning, splitting ▪ **lors de la ~ de l'Inde** when India was partitioned **3.** INFORM & MATH partition.

partouse△ [partuz] = **partouze**.

partout [partu] *adv* **1.** [dans l'espace] everywhere ▪ **je ne peux pas être ~ à la fois!** I can't be everywhere *OU* in two places at the same time! ▪ **il a voyagé un peu ~** he's been all over the place ▪ **j'ai mal ~** I ache all over ▪ **les gens accouraient de ~** people came rushing from all sides ▪ **~ où** everywhere (that), wherever **2.** SPORT : **15 ~** 15 all.

partouze△ [partuz] *nf* orgy.

parturition [partyrisjɔ̃] *nf* parturition.

paru, e [pary] *pp* ▻ **paraître**.

parure [paryr] *nf* **1.** [ensemble] set ▪ **~ de lit** set of bed linen **2.** JOAILL parure, set of jewels ▪ [colifichets] matching set of costume jewellery **3.** [vêtement] finery.
◆ **parures** *nfpl* CULIN scraps, trimmings.

parut *etc v* ▻ **paraître**.

parution [parysjɔ̃] *nf* publication ▪ **juste avant/après la ~ du livre** just before/after the book came out.

parvenir [40] [parvənir] ◆ **parvenir à** *v+prép (aux être)* **1.** [atteindre - suj: voyageur, véhicule, lettre, son] : **~ à *OU* jusqu'à** to get to, to reach ▪ **faire ~ un colis à qqn** to send sb a parcel ▪ **si cette carte vous parvient** if you get *OU* receive this card ▪ **l'histoire est parvenue aux oreilles de sa femme** the story reached his wife's ears **2.** [obtenir - célébrité, réussite] to achieve ▪ **étant parvenu au faîte de la gloire** having reached *OU* achieved the pinnacle of fame **3.** [réussir à] : **~ à faire qqch** to succeed in doing *OU* to manage to do sthg.

parvenu, e [parvəny] *adj* & *nm, f péj* parvenu, upstart, nouveau riche.

parvient, parvint *etc v* ▻ **parvenir**.

parvis [parvi] *nm* parvis *(in front of church)* ▪ **'stationnement interdit sur le ~ de la cathédrale'** 'no parking in front of the cathedral'.

pas[1] [pa] *nm* **1.** [déplacement] step ▪ **je vais faire quelques ~ dans le parc** I'm going for a short *OU* little walk in the park ▪ **le convalescent fit quelques ~ dehors** the convalescent took a few

steps outside ■ **revenir** *ou* **retourner sur ses ~** to retrace one's steps *ou* path, to turn back ■ **arriver sur les ~ de qqn** to follow close on sb's heels, to arrive just after sb ■ **avancer à** *ou* **faire de petits ~** to take short steps ■ **marcher à grands ~** to stride along ■ **faire un ~ sur le côté** to take a step to the *ou* to one side ■ **faire un ~ en avant** to step forward, to take a step *ou* pace forward ■ **faire un ~ en arrière** to step back ■ **faire ses premiers ~** *pr* to learn to walk ■ **il a fait ses premiers ~ de comédien dans un film de Hitchcock** *fig* he made his debut as an actor in a Hitchcock film ▶ **marcher à ~ de velours** to pad around
2. [progrès] : **avancer à petits ~** to make slow progress ■ **avancer à grands ~** [enquête] to make great progress ; [technique, science] to take big steps forward ; [échéance, événement] to be looming ■ **avancer à ~ comptés** *ou* **mesurés** [lentement] to make slow progress ; [prudemment] to tread carefully ; *fig* to proceed slowly but surely ■ **faire un grand ~ en avant** to take a great step *ou* leap forward ■ **faire un ~ en arrière** to take a step back *ou* backwards ■ **faire un ~ en avant et deux (~) en arrière** to take one step forward and two steps back *ou* backwards ■ **faire le premier ~** to make the first move ■ **il n'y a que le premier ~ qui coûte** the first step is the hardest ■ **marcher sur les ~ de qqn** to follow in sb's footsteps ; [étape] step ■ **c'est un ~ difficile pour lui que de te parler directement** talking to you directly is a difficult step for him to take ■ **c'est un grand ~ à faire** *ou* **franchir** it's a big step to take ▶ **franchir** *ou* **sauter le ~** to take the plunge ■ **le ~ est vite fait** *ou* **franchi** one thing very easily leads to the other
3. [empreinte] footprint ■ **des ~ sur le sable** footprints in the sand
4. [allure] pace ■ **allonger** *ou* **doubler le ~** to quicken one's step *ou* pace ■ **hâter** *ou* **presser le ~** to hurry on ■ **ralentir le ~** to slow one's pace, to slow down ■ **aller** *ou* **marcher d'un bon ~** to walk at a good *ou* brisk pace ■ **avancer** *ou* **marcher d'un ~ lent** to walk slowly
5. [démarche] gait, tread ■ **marcher d'un ~ alerte/léger/élastique** to walk with a sprightly/light/bouncy tread ■ **avancer d'un ~ lourd** *ou* **pesant** to tread heavily, to walk with a heavy tread ■ **elle entendait son ~ irrégulier/feutré sur la terrasse** she could hear his irregular/soft footfall on the terrace
6. MIL step ■ **~ accéléré** *marching step between quick march and double-quick* ■ **~ cadencé** quick march ■ **au ~ de charge** MIL at the charge ; *fig* charging along
7. DANSE pas, step ■ **esquisser un ~** to dance a few steps, to do a little dance ▶ **~ battu/tombé** pas battu/tombé
8. SPORT : **~ de patinage** *ou* **patineur** [en ski] skating ■ **~ de canard/de l'escalier** [en ski] herringbone/side stepping climb ■ **au ~ de course** at a run ; *fig* at a run, on the double ■ **au ~ de gymnastique** at a jog trot ■ **faire des ~ tournants** [en ski] to skate a turn
9. [mesure] pace ■ [espace approximatif] pace, step ■ **à quelques ~ de là** a few steps *ou* paces away ■ **à deux** *ou* **trois** *ou* **quelques ~ : l'église est à deux ~** the church is very close at hand *ou* is only a stone's throw from here ■ **le restaurant n'est qu'à deux ~ (de la gare)** the restaurant is (only) just round the corner (from the station) ■ **il se tenait à quelques ~ de moi** he was standing just a few yards from me ■ **il n'y a qu'un ~** *fig* : **entre la consommation de drogue et la vente, il n'y a qu'un ~** there's only a small *ou* short step from taking drugs to selling them ▶ **ne pas quitter qqn d'un ~** to follow sb's every footstep
10. [marche d'escalier] step ▶ **~ de porte** doorstep ■ **ne reste pas sur le ~ de la porte** don't stand at the door *ou* on the doorstep *ou* in the doorway
11. GÉOGR [en montagne] pass ■ [en mer] strait ■ **le ~ de Calais** the Strait of Dover
12. TECHNOL [d'une vis] thread ■ [d'une denture, d'un engrenage] pitch
13. AÉRON pitch
14. MATH pitch
15. *loc* **prendre le ~ (sur qqn/qqch)** to take precedence (over sb/sthg), to dominate (sb/sthg) ■ **céder le ~** to give way ■ **se tirer d'un mauvais ~** to get o.s. out of a fix.
◆ **à chaque pas** *loc adv* **1.** [partout] everywhere, at every step ■ **je la rencontre à chaque ~** I meet her everywhere (I go)
2. [constamment] at every turn *ou* step.
◆ **au pas** *loc adv* **1.** [en marchant] at a walking pace ■ **ne courez pas, allez au ~** don't run, walk
2. AUTO : **aller** *ou* **rouler au ~** [dans un embouteillage] to crawl along ; [consigne de sécurité] to go dead slow *UK*, to go slow
3. ÉQUIT walking, at a walk ■ **mettre son cheval au ~** to walk one's horse ▶ **mettre qqn/qqch au ~** to bring sb/sthg to heel.
◆ **de ce pas** *loc adv* straightaway, at once ■ **je vais de ce ~ lui dire ma façon de penser** I'm going to waste no time in telling him what I think.
◆ **pas à pas** *loc adv* **1.** [de très près] step by step ■ **il la suivait ~ à ~** he followed her step by step
2. [prudemment] step by step, one step at a time ■ **il faut refaire l'expérience ~ à ~** the experiment must be repeated step by step
3. INFORM step by step.

pas² [pa] *adv* **1.** [avec 'ne', pour exprimer la négation] : **elle ne viendra ~** she won't come ■ **ils ne sont ~ trop inquiets** they're not too worried ■ **ils n'ont ~ de problèmes/d'avenir** they have no problems/no future, they haven't got any problems/a future ■ **il a décidé de ne ~ accepter** he decided not to accept ■ **ce n'est ~ que je ne veuille ~, mais...** it's not that I don't want to, but... ‖ [avec omission du 'ne'] *fam* **elle sait ~** she doesn't know ■ **t'en fais ~!** don't (you) worry! ■ **c'est vraiment ~ drôle!** [pas comique] it's not in the least *ou* slightest bit funny ; [ennuyeux] it's no fun at all ■ **non, j'aime ~** no, I don't like it
2. [avec 'non', pour renforcer la négation] : **elle est non ~ belle mais jolie** she's not so much beautiful as pretty
3. [employé seul] : **sincère ou ~** sincere or not ■ **les garçons voulaient danser, les filles ~** the boys wanted to dance, the girls didn't ■ **pourquoi ~?** why not? ■ **~ la peine** *fam* (it's) not worth it ■ **~ assez** not enough ■ **des fraises ~ mûres** unripe strawberries
4. [dans des réponses négatives] : **~ de dessert pour moi, merci** no dessert for me, thank you ■ **qui l'a pris? – ~ moi, en tout cas!** who took it? – not me, that's for sure! ■ **~ du tout** not at all ■ **c'est toi qui as fini les chocolats? – ~ du tout!** was it you who finished the chocolates? – certainly not! ■ **~ le moins du monde** not in the least *ou* slightest, not at all ■ **absolument ~** not at all.
◆ **pas mal** *fam* ◇ *loc adj inv* not bad ■ **c'est ~ mal comme idée** that's not a bad idea.
◇ *loc adv* **1.** [bien] : **je ne m'en suis ~ mal tiré** I handled it quite well ■ **on ferait ~ mal de recommencer** we'd be better off starting again
2. [très] : **la voiture est ~ mal amochée** the car's pretty battered.
◆ **pas mal de** *loc dét fam* [suivi d'un nom comptable] quite a few, quite a lot of ■ [suivi d'un nom non comptable] quite a lot of ■ **~ mal d'argent** quite a lot of money ■ **quand? – il y a ~ mal de temps** when? – quite a while ago.
◆ **pas plus mal** *loc adv* : **il a maigri – c'est ~ plus mal** he's lost weight – good thing too *ou* that's not such a bad thing *ou* just as well ■ **il ne s'en est ~ trouvé plus mal** he ended up none the worse for it.
◆ **pas un, pas une** ◇ *loc dét* not a (single), not one ■ **~ un geste!** not one move!
◇ *loc pron* not (a single) one ■ **parmi elles, ~ une qui ne veuille y aller** every one of them wants to go there ■ **~ un n'a bronché** there wasn't a peep out of any of them ▶ **il s'y entend comme ~ un pour déranger les gens à 2 h du matin** he's a specialist at disturbing you at 2 in the morning ■ **il sait faire les crêpes comme ~ un** he makes pancakes like nobody else (on earth).

pas-à-pas [pazapa] ◇ *adj inv* INFORM step-by-step, single-step.
◇ *nm inv* **1.** MÉCAN step by step (mechanism) **2.** INFORM single-step operation.

pascal¹, s [paskal] *nm* PHYS pascal.

pascal², e, s *ou* **aux** [paskal, o] *adj* RELIG [de la fête - chrétienne] Easter *(modif)*, paschal *spéc* ; [- juive] paschal, Passover *(modif)*.

pas-d'âne [padɑn] *nm inv* BOT coltsfoot.

pas-de-porte [padpɔrt] *nm inv* **1.** COMM ≃ commercial lease **2.** DR key money.

pas-grand-chose [pagrɑ̃ʃoz] *nmf péj* good-for-nothing ■ **ces gens-là, c'est des ~** those people are nobodies.

pashmina [paʃmina] *nm* pashmina.

pasionaria [pasjɔnarja] *nf* pasionaria.

paso doble [pasodɔbl] *nm inv* paso doble.

passable [pasabl] *adj* **1.** [acceptable] passable, tolerable ▪ **leur vin est ~** their wine is drinkable **2.** ÉDUC [tout juste moyen] average **3.** *Québec* [praticable] negotiable, passable.

passablement [pasabləmɑ̃] *adv* **1.** [de façon satisfaisante] passably well, tolerably well **2.** [notablement] fairly, rather, somewhat ▪ **ils avaient ~ bu** they had drunk quite a lot.

passade [pasad] *nf* **1.** [amourette] fling, amourette *sout* ▪ **entre eux, ce ne fut qu'une ~** they just had a (little) fling **2.** [caprice] passing fancy, fad.

passage [pasaʒ] *nm*

> **A.** MOUVEMENT
> **B.** VOIE
> **C.** D'UN FILM, D'UN ROMAN

A. MOUVEMENT

1. [allées et venues] : **prochain ~ du car dans deux heures** the coach will be back *ou* will pass through again in two hours' time ▪ **chaque ~ du train faisait trembler les vitres** the windows shook every time a train went past ▪ **laisser le ~ à qqn/une ambulance** to let sb/an ambulance through, to make way for sb/an ambulance ▪ **ils attendaient le ~ des coureurs** they were waiting for the runners to go by ▪ **les gens se retournent sur son ~** heads turn when he walks by *ou* past ▪ **'~ de troupeaux'** 'cattle crossing'

2. [circulation] traffic

3. [arrivée, venue] : **elle attend le ~ de l'autobus** she's waiting for the bus

4. [visite] call, visit ▪ **c'est le seul souvenir qui me reste de mon ~ chez eux** that's the only thing I remember of my visit to them ▪ **lors de mon prochain ~ à Paris** next time I'm in Paris ▪ **'le relevé du compteur sera fait lors de notre prochain ~'** 'we will read your meter the next time we call'

5. [franchissement - d'une frontière, d'un fleuve] crossing ; [- d'un col] passing ; [- de la douane] passing (through) ▪ **après le ~ du sucre dans l'urine** after the sugar has gone *ou* passed into the urine ▪ **'~ interdit'** 'no entry' ▶ **~ à l'ennemi** MIL going over to the enemy

6. [changement, transition] change, transition ▪ **le ~ de l'hiver au printemps** the change *ou* passage from winter to spring ▪ **le ~ de l'autocratie à la démocratie** the changeover *ou* transition from autocracy to democracy

7. [dans une hiérarchie] move ▪ **~ d'un employé à l'échelon supérieur** promotion of an employee to a higher grade ▪ **le ~ dans la classe supérieure** ÉDUC going *ou* moving up to the next class *UK ou* grade *US*

8. [voyage sur mer, traversée] crossing ▪ **ils travaillaient durement pour payer leur ~** they worked hard to pay their passage *ou* to pay for their crossing

9. ASTRON transit

10. INFORM : **~ machine** run

11. PSYCHOL : **~ à l'acte** acting out

12. RADIO, THÉÂTRE & TV : **lors de son dernier ~ à la télévision** [personne] last time he was on TV ; [film] last time it was shown on TV ▪ **pour son premier ~ au Théâtre du Rocher** for her first appearance at the Théâtre du Rocher

B. VOIE

1. [chemin] passage, way ▪ **enlève ton sac du ~** move your bag out of the way ▪ **il y a des ~s dangereux dans la grotte** there are some dangerous passages in the cave ▪ **donner** *ou* **livrer ~ à qqn/qqch** to let sb/sthg in ▪ **essaye de trouver un ~ dans cette foule** try to find a way through the crowd ▶ **~ secret** secret passage

2. [ruelle] alley, passage ▪ [galerie commerçante] arcade ▪ **~ couvert** passageway

3. [tapis de couloir] runner

4. AUTO : **~ de roue** wheel housing

5. RAIL : **~ à niveau** level crossing *UK*, grade crossing *US*

6. TRAV PUB : **~ clouté** *ou* **(pour) piétons** pedestrian *ou* zebra crossing *UK*, crosswalk *US* ▪ **~ protégé** priority over secondary roads ▪ **~ souterrain** (pedestrian) subway *UK*, underpass

C. D'UN FILM, D'UN ROMAN

passage, section ▪ **elle m'a lu quelques ~s de la lettre de Paul** she read me a few passages from Paul's letter ▪ **tu te souviens du ~ où ils se rencontrent?** do you remember the bit where they meet?

◆ **au passage** *loc adv* [sur un trajet] on one's *ou* the way ▪ **les enfants doivent attraper la cocarde au ~** the children have to catch the ribbon as they go past ▮ *fig* in passing ▪ **j'ai noté au ~ que...** I noticed in passing that...

◆ **au passage de** *loc prép* : **au ~ du carrosse, la foule applaudissait** when the carriage went past *ou* through, the crowd clapped.

◆ **de passage** *loc adj* [client] casual ▪ **être de ~** [voyageur] to be passing through ▪ **je suis de ~ à Paris** I'm in Paris for a few days.

◆ **sur le passage de** *loc prép* : **la foule s'est massée sur le ~ du marathon** the crowd gathered on the marathon route.

◆ **passage à tabac** *nm* beating up.

◆ **passage à vide** *nm* : **avoir un ~ à vide** [syncope] to feel faint, to faint ; [moralement] to go through a bad patch ; [intellectuellement] to have a lapse in concentration ▪ **j'ai eu un petit ~ à vide juste avant midi** I was feeling a bit faint just before lunch.

passager, ère [pasaʒe, ɛr] ◇ *adj* **1.** [momentané] passing, temporary, transient ▪ **ne vous inquiétez pas, ces douleurs seront passagères** don't worry, the pain won't last **2.** [très fréquenté] busy.
◇ *nm, f* passenger ▶ **~ clandestin** stowaway.

passagèrement [pasaʒɛrmɑ̃] *adv* for a short while, temporarily, momentarily.

passant, e [pasɑ̃, ɑ̃t] ◇ *adj* [voie, route] busy.
◇ *nm, f* passer-by ▪ **les ~s s'arrêtaient pour regarder** passers-by would stop and stare.
◆ **passant** *nm* [vêtement] (belt) loop.

passation [pasasjɔ̃] *nf* **1.** DR : **la ~ d'un acte/d'un contrat** the drawing up (and signing) of an instrument/a contract **2.** POLIT : **~ des pouvoirs** transfer of power.

passe [pas] ◇ *nm* **1.** [passe-partout] master *ou* pass key **2.** [laissez-passer] pass.
◇ *nf* **1.** SPORT [aux jeux de ballon] pass ▪ **faire une ~** to pass (the ball), to make a pass ▮ [en tauromachie] pass ▶ **~ d'armes** sparring **2.** △ [d'une prostituée] trick△ ▪ **faire une ~** to turn a trick△ **3.** [situation] : **bonne/mauvaise ~** [commerce] : **être dans une bonne ~** to be thriving ▪ **leur couple traverse une mauvaise ~** their relationship is going through a rough *ou* bad period **4.** GÉOGR [col] pass ▪ [chenal] pass, channel **5.** [d'un prestidigitateur] pass **6.** *Québec* ZOOL : **~ migratoire** fish ladder **7.** IMPR overs, overplus **8.** FIN : **~ de caisse** allowance for cashier's errors **9.** INFORM pass **10.** JEUX [mise] stake ▪ [à la roulette] passe **11.** [sur un cours d'eau] passage **12.** [d'un chapeau] rim.
◆ **en passe de** *loc prép* about to, on the point of ▪ **ils sont en ~ de prendre le contrôle des médias** they're poised *ou* set to gain control of the media.

passé[1] [pase] *prép* after ▪ **~ minuit** after midnight.

passé[2], **e** [pase] *adj* **1.** [précédent - année, mois] last, past
2. [révolu] : **il est 3 h ~es** it's past *ou* gone *UK* 3 o'clock ▪ **elle a 30 ans ~s** she's over 30
3. [qui n'est plus] past, former ▪ **elle songeait au temps ~** she was thinking of times *ou* days gone by
4. [teinte, fleur] faded.
◆ **passé** *nm* **1.** [temps révolu] : **le ~** the past ▪ **oublions le ~** let bygones be bygones, let's forget the past ▪ **c'est du ~, tout ça** it's all in the past *ou* it's all behind us now
2. [d'une personne, d'une ville] past ▶ **il a un lourd ~** he's a man with a past
3. GRAMM past tense ▪ **verbe au ~** verb in the past tense ▶ **les temps du ~** past tenses ▪ **~ antérieur** past anterior ▪ **~ composé** (present) perfect ▪ **~ simple** *ou* **historique** simple past, past historic, *voir aussi* **pluriel**.
◆ **par le passé** *loc adv* in the past ▪ **il est beaucoup plus indulgent que par le ~** he's much more indulgent than before *ou* than he used to be ▪ **soyons amis, comme par le ~** let's be friends, like before.

passe-crassane [paskrasan] *nf inv* passe-crassane *(variety of winter pear).*

passe-droit [pasdrwa] *(pl* **passe-droits***)* *nm* privilege, special favour.

passée [pase] *f* ▻ **passé** *(adj).*

passéisme [paseism] *nm péj* attachment to the past, backward-looking attitude.

passéiste [paseist] *péj* <> *adj* backward-looking.
<> *nmf* backward-looking person.

passe-lacet [paslasɛ] *(pl* **passe-lacets***)* *nm* bodkin.

passement [pasmɑ̃] *nm* (piece of) braid *ou* braiding *ou* cord *(used as trimming).*

passementer [3] [pasmɑ̃te] *vt* to braid.

passementerie [pasmɑ̃tri] *nf* soft furnishings (and curtain fitments).

passe-montagne [pasmɔ̃taɲ] *(pl* **passe-montagnes***)* *nm* balaclava.

passe-partout [paspartu] <> *adj inv* **1.** [robe, instrument] versatile, all-purpose *(modif)* ▪ **un discours ~** a speech for all occasions **2.** RAIL UIC standard *(modif).*
<> *nm inv* **1.** [clef] master *ou* skeleton key **2.** ART & IMPR passe-partout **3.** [scie] two-handed saw.

passe-passe [paspas] *nm inv* : **tour de ~** [tour de magie] (magic) trick ; [tromperie] trick.

passe-plat [paspla] *(pl* **passe-plats***)* *nm* serving hatch.

passepoil [paspwal] *nm* piping *(U).*

passepoiler [3] [paspwale] *vt* to trim with piping, to pipe.

passeport [paspɔr] *nm* **1.** ADMIN passport ▪ **~ biométrique** biometric passport **2.** *fig* passport ▪ **ce diplôme est un ~ pour la vie professionnelle** this diploma is a passport to a job.

passer [3] [pase] <> *vi (aux être)*

> **A.** EXPRIME UN DÉPLACEMENT
> **B.** EXPRIME UNE ACTION
> **C.** EXPRIME UN CHANGEMENT D'ÉTAT
> **D.** EXPRIME UNE ÉVOLUTION DANS LE TEMPS

A. EXPRIME UN DÉPLACEMENT

1. [se déplacer - personne, véhicule] to pass (by), to go *ou* to come past ▪ **regarder ~ les coureurs** to watch the runners go past ▪ **~ à : ~ à droite/gauche** to go right/left ▪ **~ au-dessus de : l'avion est passé au-dessus de la maison** the plane flew over the house ▪ **~ dans : pour empêcher les poids lourds de ~ dans le village** to stop lorries from driving *ou* going through the village ▪ **~ devant qqch** to go past sthg ▪ **passe devant si tu ne vois pas** [devant moi] go in front of me if you can't see ; [devant tout le monde] go to the front if you can't see ▪ **~ sous : ~ sous une échelle** to go under a ladder ▪ **~ sous une voiture** [se faire écraser] to get run over (by a car) ▪ **~ sur : ~ sur un pont** to go over *ou* to cross a bridge ▪ **des péniches passaient sur le canal** barges were going past *ou* were sailing on the canal ▪ [fugitivement] : **j'ai vu un éclair de rage ~ dans son regard** I saw a flash of anger in his eyes ▪ **un sourire passa sur ses lèvres** a smile played about her lips, she smiled briefly ▪ **elle dit tout ce qui lui passe par la tête** she says the first thing that comes into her head ▪ **qu'est-ce qui a bien pu lui ~ par la tête?** whatever was he thinking of? ▸ **ne faire que ~ : le pouvoir n'a fait que ~ entre leurs mains** they held power only briefly

2. [s'écouler - fluide] to flow, to run ▪ **il y a de l'air qui passe sous la porte** there's a permanent draught coming under the door

3. [emprunter un certain itinéraire] : **si vous passez à Paris, venez me voir** come and see me if you're in Paris ▪ **~ par : le voleur est passé par la fenêtre** the burglar got in through the window ▪ **passe par l'escalier de service** use the service stairs ‖ [fleuve, route] to go, to run ▪ **le tunnel passera sous la montagne** the tunnel will go under the mountain ▪ **le pont passe au-dessus de l'avenue** the bridge crosses the avenue

4. MATH to pass ▪ **soit une droite passant par deux points A et B** given a straight line between two points A and B

5. [sur un parcours régulier - démarcheur, représentant] to call ; [- bateau, bus, train] to come *ou* to go past ▪ **le facteur n'est pas encore passé** the postman hasn't been yet ▪ **le facteur passe deux fois par jour** the postman delivers *ou* comes twice a day ▪ **le bus passe toutes les sept minutes** there's a bus every seven minutes ▪ **le bateau/train est déjà passé** the boat/train has already gone *ou* left ▪ **le prochain bateau passera dans deux jours** the next boat will call *ou* is due in two days

6. [faire une visite] to call ▪ **~ chez qqn** to call at sb's place ▪ **j'ai demandé au médecin de ~** I asked the doctor to call (in) *ou* to come *ou* to visit ▪ **j'essaierai de ~ dans la soirée** I'll try and call in the evening ▪ **je ne fais que ~** I'm not stopping ▪ *(suivi de l'infin)* **~ voir qqn** to call on sb ▪ **je passerai te chercher** I'll come and fetch you

7. [franchir une limite] to get through ▪ **ne laissez ~ personne** don't let anybody through ▪ **il est passé au rouge** he went through a red light ▸ **ça passe ou ça casse** it's make or break (time)

8. [s'infiltrer] to pass ▪ **~ dans le sang** to pass into *ou* to enter the bloodstream ▪ **la lumière passe à travers les rideaux** the light shines through the curtains ▪ **le café doit ~ lentement** [dans le filtre] the coffee must filter through slowly

9. [aller, se rendre] to go ▪ **où est-il passé?** where's he gone (to)? ▪ **où sont passées mes lunettes?** where have my glasses got *ou* disappeared to? ▪ **passons à table** let's eat ▪ **passons au salon** let's go through to the living room ▪ **~ de Suisse en France** to cross over *ou* to go from Switzerland to France ▪ **~ à l'ennemi** to go over to the enemy

10. CHASSE to pass, to go *ou* to come past

B. EXPRIME UNE ACTION

1. [se soumettre à] : **~ à** to go for ▪ **~ au scanner** to go for a scan ▪ **ce matin, je suis passé au tableau** I was asked to explain something at the blackboard this morning ▸ **y ~** *fam* : **je ne veux pas me faire opérer – il faudra bien que tu y passes, pourtant!** I don't want to have an operation – you're going to have to! ▪ **avec lui, toutes les femmes du service y sont passées** he's had all the women in his department ▪ **tout le monde a cru que tu allais y passer** everybody thought you were a goner

2. [être accepté] to pass ▪ **elle est passée à l'écrit mais pas à l'oral** she got through *ou* she passed the written exam but not the oral ▪ **j'ai mangé quelque chose qui ne passe pas** I've eaten something that won't go down ▪ **sa dernière remarque n'est pas passée** *fig* his last remark stuck in my throat ▪ **ton petit discours est bien passé** your little speech went down well *ou* was well received ▪ **la deuxième scène ne passe pas du tout** the second scene doesn't work at all ▪ **le film passe mal sur le petit écran/en noir et blanc** the film just isn't the same on TV/in black and white ▸ **passe (encore) : l'injurier, passe encore, mais le frapper!** it's one thing to insult him, but quite another to hit him!

3. [être transmis] to go ▪ **la ferme est passée de père en fils depuis cinq générations** the farm has been handed down from father to son for five generations ▪ **la carafe passa de main en main** the jug was passed around ▪ **la locution est passée du latin à l'anglais** the phrase came *ou* passed into English from Latin

4. [entrer] to pass ▪ **c'est passé dans le langage courant** it's passed into *ou* it's now part of everyday speech ▪ **c'est passé dans les moeurs** it's become standard *ou* normal practice

5. [être utilisé, absorbé] to go ▪ **tout son salaire passe dans la maison** all her salary goes on the house ▸ **y ~ : les deux bouteilles y sont passées** both bottles were drunk ▪ **toutes ses économies y passent** all her savings go towards *ou* into it

6. POLIT [être adopté - projet de loi, amendement] to pass, to be passed ▪ **la loi est passée** the law was passed ▪ [être élu - député] to be elected, to get in ▪ **si les socialistes passent** if the socialists get in *ou* are elected

7. CINÉ & THÉÂTRE to be on, to be showing ▪ **sa dernière pièce passe au Galatée** her latest play is on at the Galatée ‖ RADIO & TV : **les informations passent à 20 h** the news is on at 8 pm ▪ **~ à la radio** [émission, personne] to be on the radio *ou* the air ▪ **~ à la télévision** [personne] to be *ou* to appear on television ; [film] to be on television

8. DR [comparaître] : **~ devant le tribunal** to come up *ou* to go before the court ■ **~ en correctionnelle** ≃ to go before the magistrate's court ■ **l'affaire passera en justice le mois prochain** the case will be heard next month
9. JEUX to pass

C. EXPRIME UN CHANGEMENT D'ÉTAT

1. [accéder - à un niveau] : **~ dans la classe supérieure** to move up to the next form *UK ou* grade *US* ■ **~ en seconde** ÉDUC to move up to the fifth form *UK ou* to tenth grade *US* ■ **il est passé au grade supérieur** he's been promoted
2. [devenir] to become ■ **il est passé ailier** he plays on the wing now ■ **~ professionnel** to turn professional
3. [dans des locutions verbales] : **~ à** [aborder] : **passons à l'ordre du jour** let us turn to the business on the agenda ■ **~ à l'action** to take action ■ **~ de... à** [changer d'état] : **~ de l'état liquide à l'état gazeux** to pass *ou* to change from the liquid to the gaseous state ■ **quand on passe de l'adolescence à l'âge adulte** when you pass from adolescence to adulthood ■ **la production est passée de 20 à 30/de 30 à 20 tonnes** output has gone (up) from 20 to 30/(down) from 30 to 20 tonnes ■ **~ du français au russe** to switch from French to Russian ■ **comment êtes-vous passé du cinéma au théâtre?** how did you move *ou* make the transition from the cinema to the stage? ■ **il passe d'une idée à l'autre** he jumps *ou* flits from one idea to another
4. AUTO : **~ en troisième** to change *ou* go into third (gear) ■ **la seconde passe mal** second gear is stiff

D. EXPRIME UNE ÉVOLUTION DANS LE TEMPS

1. [s'écouler - temps] to pass, to go by ■ **la journée est passée agréablement** the day went off *ou* passed pleasantly ■ **comme le temps passe!** how time flies!
2. [s'estomper - douleur] to fade (away), to wear off ; [- malaise] to disappear ; [- mode, engouement] to die out ; [- enthousiasme] to wear off, to fade ; [- beauté] to fade, to wane ; [- chance, jeunesse] to pass ; [- mauvaise humeur] to pass, to vanish ; [- rage, tempête] to die down ; [- averse] to die down, to stop ■ **mon envie est passée** I don't feel like it anymore ■ **cette habitude lui passera avec l'âge** he'll grow out of the habit ■ **faire ~ : ce médicament fait ~ la douleur très rapidement** this medicine relieves pain very quickly
3. [s'altérer - fruit, denrées] to go off *UK*, to spoil, to go bad ■ [se faner - fleur] to wilt ■ [pâlir - teinte] : **le papier peint a passé au soleil** the sun has faded the wallpaper
4. *(aux avoir) vieilli* [mourir] : **il a passé cette nuit** he passed on *ou* away last night.

<> *vt (aux avoir)*

A. EXPRIME UN DÉPLACEMENT
B. EXPRIME UNE ACTION
C. EXPRIME UNE NOTION TEMPORELLE

A. EXPRIME UN DÉPLACEMENT

1. [traverser - pont, col de montagne] to go over *(insép)*, to cross ; [- écluse] to go through *(insép)* ■ **~ une rivière à la nage** to swim across a river ■ **~ un ruisseau à gué** to ford a stream
2. [franchir - frontière, ligne d'arrivée] to cross
3. [dépasser - point de repère] to pass, to go past *(insép)* ■ **~ l'arrêt de l'autobus** [le manquer] to miss one's bus stop ■ **~ le cap Horn** to (go) round Cape Horn, to round the Cape ■ **quand on passe les 1 000 mètres d'altitude** when you go over 1,000 metres high ■ **l'or a passé les 400 dollars l'once** gold has broken through the $ 400 an ounce mark
4. [transporter] to ferry *ou* to take across *(sép)*
5. [introduire] : **~ de la drogue/des cigarettes en fraude** to smuggle drugs/cigarettes
6. [engager - partie du corps] to put ■ **~ son bras autour de la taille de qqn** to put *ou* to slip one's arm round sb's waist ■ **je n'arrive pas à ~ ma tête dans l'encolure de cette robe** my head won't go through the neck of the dress ■ **il a passé la tête par l'entrebâillement de la porte** he poked his head round the door
7. [faire aller - instrument] to run ■ **~ un peigne dans ses cheveux** to run a comb through one's hair ■ **~ une éponge sur la table** to wipe the table ■ **~ un chiffon sur les meubles** to dust the furniture ■ **~ l'aspirateur** to vacuum, to hoover *UK* ■ **~ le balai** to sweep up ■ **passe le balai dans l'escalier** give the stairs a sweep, sweep the stairs
8. ÉQUIT [haie] to jump, to clear
9. SPORT [franchir - obstacle, haie] to jump (over) ■ **~ la barre à deux mètres** to clear the bar at two metres ■ **~ tous les obstacles** *fig* to overcome *ou* to surmount all the obstacles ■ [transmettre - ballon] to pass ■ [dépasser - coureurs] to overtake, to pass

B. EXPRIME UNE ACTION

1. [se soumettre à - permis de conduire] to take ; [- examen] to take, to sit *UK* ; [- entretien] to have ; [- scanner, visite médicale] to have, to go for *(insép)* ■ **la voiture doit ~ un contrôle technique** the car has to go for its MOT
2. *vieilli* [réussir - examen] to pass ; [- épreuve éliminatoire] to get through *(insép)* ■ **il a passé l'écrit, mais attendons l'oral** he's passed the written exam, but let's see what happens in the oral
3. [omettre] to miss *ou* to leave out *(sép)*, to omit ■ **je passe toutes les descriptions dans ses romans** I miss out *ou* I skip all the descriptions in her novels
4. [tolérer] : **elle lui passe tout** she lets him get away with anything ➊ **passez-moi l'expression/le mot** if you'll pardon the expression/excuse the term
5. [soumettre à l'action de] : **~ les parquets à l'encaustique** to polish the floors ■ **~ des légumes au mixeur** to put vegetables through the blender, to blend vegetables ■ **~ qqch sous l'eau** to rinse sthg *ou* to give sthg a rinse under the tap ■ **~ qqch au four** to put sthg in the oven ➊ **~ quelque chose à qqn** *fam* to give sb a good dressing-down, to tick sb off *UK* ■ **se faire ~ quelque chose** *fam* to get a good ticking off *UK*, to get a good chewing-out *US*
6. [donner, transmettre - gén] to pass, to hand, to give ; [- maladie] to give ; [- au téléphone] to put through *(sép)* ■ **passe(-moi) le couteau** give me the knife ■ **passe-moi le sel** pass me the salt ■ **fais ~ à ton voisin** pass it to your neighbour ■ **~ ses pouvoirs à son successeur** to hand over power to one's successor ■ **je te passe Fred** here's Fred, I'll hand you over to Fred ■ **passe-moi Annie** let me talk to Annie, put Annie on
7. [rendre public - annonce] : **~ une petite annonce** to place a small ad ■ **il a passé une annonce dans le journal de cette semaine** he put an ad in this week's paper
8. *fam* [prêter] to lend
9. [appliquer - substance] to apply, to put on *(sép)* ■ **~ de la cire sur qqch** to wax sthg ■ **~ une couche de peinture sur un mur** to paint a wall ■ **il faudra ~ une deuxième couche** it needs a second coat ■ **je vais te ~ de la crème dans le dos** I'm going to put *ou* to rub some cream on your back
10. [filtrer, tamiser - thé, potage] to strain ; [- farine] to sieve
11. [enfiler - vêtement] to slip *ou* to put on *(sép)* ■ **je passe une robe moins chaude et j'arrive** I'll put on a cooler dress and I'll be with you ■ **elle passa l'anneau à son doigt** she slipped the ring on her finger
12. AUTO : **~ la marche arrière** to go into reverse ■ **~ la troisième** to change *ou* to shift into third gear
13. CINÉ & TV [film] to show, to screen ■ [diapositive] to show ■ RADIO [émission] to broadcast ■ [cassette, disque] to play, to put on *(sép)* ■ **on passe un western au Rex** there's a western on at the Rex
14. COMM [conclure - entente] to conclude, to come to *(insép)*, to reach ; [- marché] to agree on *(insép)*, to strike, to reach ; [- commande] to place ■ **passez commande avant le 12** order before the 12th
15. [en comptabilité] to enter, to post ■ **~ un article en compte** to enter a sale into a ledger
16. DR [faire établir - acte juridique] to draw up *(sép)* ■ **un acte passé par-devant notaire** a deed drawn up in the presence of a notary

C. EXPRIME UNE NOTION TEMPORELLE

1. [employer - durée] to spend ■ **j'ai passé un an en Angleterre** I spent a year in England ■ **passez un bon week-end/une bonne soirée!** have a nice weekend/evening! ■ **~ ses vacances à lire** to spend one's holidays reading ■ **il va venir ~ quelques jours chez nous** he's coming to stay with us for a few days ■ **as-tu passé une bonne nuit?** did you sleep well last night?, did you have a good night? ■ **pour ~ le temps** to pass the time
2. [aller au-delà de - durée] to get through *(insép)*, to survive ■ **elle ne passera pas la nuit** she won't see the night out, she won't last the night
3. [assouvir - envie] to satisfy ■ **~ sa colère sur qqn** to take one's anger out on sb.

◆ **passer après** *v+prép* : **il faut le faire libérer, le reste passe après** we must get him released, everything else is secondary.

◆ **passer avant** *v+prép* to go *ou* to come before ■ **ses intérêts passent avant tout** his own interests come before anything else, he puts his own interests before everything else.

◆ **passer par** *v+prép* **1.** [dans une formation] to go through ■ **il est passé par une grande école** he studied at a Grande École ■ **elle est passée par tous les échelons** she rose through all the grades **2.** [dans une évolution] to go through, to undergo ■ **le pays est passé par toutes les formes de gouvernement** the country has experienced every form of government ■ **elle est passée par des moments difficiles** she's been through some difficult times **3.** [recourir à] to go through ■ **je passe par une agence pour avoir des billets** I get tickets through an agency ➤ **en ~ par : il va falloir en ~ par ses exigences** we'll just have to do what he says ■ **~ par là : je suis passé par là** it's happened to me too, I've been through that too ■ **pour comprendre, il faut être passé par là** you have to have experienced it to understand.

◆ **passer pour** *v+prép* **1.** [avec nom] to be thought of as ■ **dire qu'il passe pour un génie!** to think that he's considered a genius! ■ **je vais ~ pour un idiot** I'll be taken for *ou* people will take me for an idiot ■ **se faire ~ pour qqn** to pass o.s. off as sb ■ **il se fait ~ pour un professionnel** he claims to be a professional **2.** [avec adj] : **son livre passe pour sérieux** her book is considered to be serious ■ **il s'est fait ~ pour fou** he pretended to be mad **3.** [avec verbe] : **elle passe pour descendre d'une famille noble** she is said to be descended from an aristocratic family.

◆ **passer sur** *v+prép* [ne pas mentionner] to pass over, to skip ■ [excuser] to overlook ■ **passons sur les détails** let's pass over *ou* skip the details ■ **il l'aime et passe sur tout** he loves her and forgives everything ➤ **passons!** let's say no more about it!, let's drop it! ■ **tu me l'avais promis, mais passons!** you promised me, but never mind!

◆ **se passer** <> *vpi* **1.** [s'écouler - heures, semaines] to go by, to pass ■ **la soirée s'est passée tranquillement** the evening went by *ou* passed quietly ■ **si la journée de demain se passe sans incident** if everything goes off smoothly tomorrow **2.** [survenir - événement] to take place, to happen ■ **qu'est-ce qui se passe?** what's happening?, what's going on? ■ *(tournure impersonnelle)* **il se passe que ton frère vient d'être arrêté, (voilà ce qui se passe)!** your brother's just been arrested, that's what's! ■ **il ne se passe pas une semaine sans qu'il perde de l'argent aux courses** not a week goes by without him losing money on the horses **3.** [se dérouler - dans certaines conditions] to go (off) ■ **l'opération s'est bien/mal passée** the operation went (off) smoothly/badly ■ **si tout se passe bien, nous y serons demain** if all goes well, we'll be there tomorrow ■ **tout se passe comme prévu** everything's going according to plan *ou* going as planned ■ **ça ne se passera pas comme ça!** it won't be as easy as that!

<> *vpt* [s'appliquer, se mettre - produit] to apply, to put on *(sép)* ■ **il se passa un peigne/la main dans les cheveux** he ran a comb/his fingers through his hair ■ **elle se passait un mouchoir sur le front** she was wiping her forehead with a handkerchief.

◆ **se passer de** *vp+prép* **1.** [vivre sans] to do *ou* to go without ■ **si tu crois pouvoir te ~ de tout le monde!** if you think you can manage all by yourself! ■ **il ne peut pas se ~ de télévision** he can't live without the television **2.** [s'abstenir] : **je me passerais (volontiers) de ses réflexions!** I can do very well without her remarks! **3.** [ne pas avoir besoin de] : **sa déclaration se passe de tout commentaire** her statement needs no comment.

◆ **en passant** *loc adv* **1.** [dans la conversation] in passing ■ **faire une remarque en passant** to remark in passing, to make a casual remark ■ **soit dit en ~** it must be said **2.** [sur son chemin] : **il s'arrête de temps à autre en passant** he calls on his way by *ou* past from time to time.

◆ **en passant par** *loc prép* **1.** [dans l'espace] via ■ **l'avion va à Athènes en passant par Londres** the plane goes to Athens via London *ou* stops in London on its way to Athens **2.** [dans une énumération] (and) including ■ **toutes les romancières de Sand à Sarraute en passant par Colette** every woman novelist from Sand to Sarraute including Colette.

passereau, x [pasro] *nm* [oiseau] passerine.

passerelle [pasrɛl] *nf* **1.** [pour piétons] footbridge **2.** NAUT [plan incliné] gangway, gangplank ■ [escalier] gangway ■ **la ~ de commandement** the bridge **3.** AÉRON steps **4.** CINÉ catwalk **5.** ÉDUC [entre deux cycles] link ■ **établir une ~ entre deux cursus** to link two courses **6.** INFORM gateway.

passe-temps [pastɑ̃] *nm inv* pastime, hobby.

passe-thé [paste] *nm inv* tea strainer.

passeur, euse [pasœr, øz] *nm, f* **1.** [sur un bac, un bateau etc] ferryman *(nm)* **2.** [de contrebande] smuggler **3.** [d'immigrants clandestins] : **il trouva un ~ qui l'aida à gagner les États-Unis** he found someone to get him over the border into the United States **4.** SPORT passer.

passible [pasibl] *adj* : **~ de** liable to ■ **crime ~ de la prison** crime punishable by imprisonment ■ **~ de poursuites** actionable ■ **~ des tribunaux** liable to prosecution.

passif[1] [pasif] *nm* **1.** [dettes] liabilities **2.** *loc* **mettre qqch au ~ de qqn : cette décision est à mettre à son ~** this decision is a black mark against him.

passif[2], ive [pasif, iv] *adj* [gén - GRAMM] passive.

◆ **passif** *nm* GRAMM passive (form), *voir aussi* **pluriel**.

passing-shot [pasiŋʃɔt] *(pl* **passing-shots***)* *nm* passing shot.

passion [pasjɔ̃] *nf* **1.** [amour fou] passion, love **2.** [du jeu, des voyages etc] passion ■ **avoir la ~ de qqch** to have a passion for sthg, to be passionately interested in sthg **3.** [exaltation] passion, feeling ■ **débattre de qqch avec ~** to argue passionately about sthg **4.** RELIG : **la Passion (du Christ)** the Passion ■ **la Passion selon saint Jean** RELIG the Passion according to Saint John ; MUS the (Saint) John Passion.

◆ **passions** *nfpl* [sentiments] passions, emotions, feelings ■ **savoir dominer ses ~s** to be able to control one's emotions.

passionnant, e [pasjɔnɑ̃, ɑ̃t] *adj* [voyage, débat] fascinating, exciting ■ [personne] intriguing, fascinating ■ [récit] fascinating, enthralling, gripping ■ **nous avons eu une discussion ~e** we had a fascinating discussion.

passionné, e [pasjɔne] <> *adj* **1.** [aimant - amant, lettre] passionate **2.** [très vif - caractère, tempérament] passionate, emotional ; [- discours] passionate, impassioned ; [- intérêt, sentiment] passionate, keen **3.** [intéressé - spectateur, lecteur] keen, fervent, ardent.

<> *nm, f* **1.** [en amour] passionate person **2.** [fervent] enthusiast, devotee ■ **pour les ~s de flamenco** for flamenco lovers.

passionnel, elle [pasjɔnɛl] *adj* passionate ■ **drame ~ à Bordeaux** love drama in Bordeaux.

passionnément [pasjɔnemɑ̃] *adv* **1.** [avec passion] passionately, with passion **2.** [en intensif] keenly, fervently, ardently ■ **je désire ~ que tu réussisses** I very much hope that you will succeed.

passionner [3] [pasjɔne] *vt* **1.** [intéresser - suj: récit] to fascinate, to enthral, to grip ; [- suj: discussion, idée] to fascinate, to grip ■ **la politique la passionne** politics is her passion, she has a passion for politics **2.** [animer - débat] : **elle ne sait pas parler politique sans ~ le débat** every time she talks about politics it ends in a big argument.

◆ **se passionner pour** *vp+prép* [idée] to feel passionately about ■ [activité] to have a passion for ■ **je me passionne pour le reggae** I have a passion for reggae.

passive [pasiv] *f* ▷ **passif**.

passivement [pasivmɑ̃] *adv* passively.

passivité [pasivite] *nf* **1.** [attitude] passivity, passiveness **2.** MÉTALL passivity.

passoire [paswar] *nf* **1.** [à petits trous] sieve ■ [à gros trous] colander ➤ **~ à thé** tea strainer ■ **avoir la tête** *ou* **la mémoire comme une ~** *fam* to have a memory like a sieve **2.** *fam* [personne, institution négligente] : **leur service de contre-espionnage est une ~** their counter-espionage service is leaking like a sieve.

pastel [pastɛl] ◇ *nm* **1.** [crayon] pastel ▪ [dessin] pastel (drawing) ▪ **dessiner au ~** to draw in pastels **2.** [teinte douce] pastel (shade) **3.** BOT pastel woad **4.** [couleur bleue] pastel blue.
◇ *adj inv* pastel, pastel-hued.

pastèque [pastɛk] *nf* [plante] watermelon plant ▪ [fruit] watermelon.

pasteur [pastœr] *nm* **1.** RELIG [protestant] minister, pastor ▪ *arch* [prêtre] pastor ▪ **le Bon Pasteur** the Good Shepherd **2.** *litt* [berger] shepherd **3.** *fig* & *litt* [guide, gardien] shepherd **4.** ANTHR pastoralist *spéc*, shepherd ▪ **les Peuls sont un peuple de ~s** the Fulani are a pastoral people.

pasteurisation [pastœrizasjɔ̃] *nf* pasteurization, pasteurizing.

pasteuriser [3] [pastœrize] *vt* to pasteurize.

pastiche [pastiʃ] *nm* pastiche.

pasticher [3] [pastiʃe] *vt* to do a pastiche of.

pasticheur, euse [pastiʃœr, øz] *nm, f* **1.** [auteur de pastiches] writer of pastiches **2.** [plagiaire] plagiarist.

pastille [pastij] *nf* **1.** PHARM pastille, lozenge ▪ **~ pour la gorge** throat lozenge *ou* pastille **2.** CULIN : **~ de chocolat** chocolate drop ▪ **~ de menthe** mint **3.** [disque de papier, de tissu] disc.

pastis [pastis] *nm* **1.** [boisson] pastis **2.** *fam* [situation embrouillée] muddle, mess, fix.

pastoral, e, aux [pastɔral, o] *adj* LITTÉR, MUS & RELIG pastoral ▪ **'la Symphonie ~e'** *Beethoven* 'The Pastoral Symphony'.
◆ **pastorale** *nf* **1.** LITTÉR & MUS pastorale **2.** RELIG pastoral.

pastorat [pastɔra] *nm* pastorate.

pastoureau, elle, x [pasturo, ɛl] *nm, f litt* shepherd boy (*f* girl).
◆ **pastourelle** *nf* LITTÉR pastourelle.

pat [pat] ◇ *adj inv* : **le roi est ~** it's a stalemate.
◇ *nm* stalemate ▪ **éviter le ~** to avoid stalemate.

patachon [pataʃɔ̃] *nm fam* **mener une vie de ~** to lead a riotous existence.

patagon, one *ou* **onne** [patagɔ̃, ɔn] *adj* Patagonian.
◆ **Patagon, one** *ou* **onne** *nm, f* Patagonian.

Patagonie [patagɔni] *npr f* : **(la) ~** Patagonia.

pataphysique [patafizik] ◇ *adj* pataphysic.
◇ *nf* pataphysics *(U)*.

patapouf [patapuf] *fam* ◇ *nm* fatty, podge ▪ **un gros ~** a big fat lump.
◇ *interj* thump, thud.

pataquès [patakɛs] *nm* **1.** [faute de liaison] bad *ou* incorrect liaison **2.** [situation confuse] mess, muddle.

patata [patata] ⊳ **patati.**

patate [patat] *nf* **1.** BOT & CULIN : **~ (douce)** sweet potato **2.** *fam* [pomme de terre] spud **3.** *fam* [personne stupide] nitwit△, twerp **4.** *fam loc* **en avoir gros sur la ~** to be peeved **5.** *Québec fam* [cœur] ticker *UK*.

patati [patati] ◆ **et patati, et patata** *loc adv* and so on and so forth, etc. etc.

patatras [patatra] *interj* crash.

pataud, e [pato, od] ◇ *adj* [maladroit] clumsy ▪ [sans finesse] gauche.
◇ *nm, f* **1.** [chiot] (big-pawed) puppy **2.** *vieilli* [personne - maladroite] clumsy oaf ; [- à l'esprit lent] oaf.

Pataugas® [patogas] *nmpl canvas walking shoes.*

pataugeoire [patoʒwar] *nf* paddling pool.

patauger [17] [patoʒe] *vi* **1.** [dans une flaque, à la piscine] to splash *ou* to paddle about ▪ [dans la gadoue] to wade ▪ **les sauveteurs pataugeaient dans la boue** the members of the rescue party were wading about in the mud **2.** *fig* [s'empêtrer] to flounder ▪ **il patauge dans ses réponses** he's getting more and more bogged down trying to answer **3.** [ne pas progresser] : **l'enquête policière patauge** the police inquiry is getting bogged down.

pataugeur, euse [patoʒœr, øz] *nm, f* paddler.

patch [patʃ] *nm* MÉD nicotine patch.

patchouli [patʃuli] *nm* patchouli ▪ **huile de ~** patchouli oil.

patchwork [patʃwœrk] *nm* **1.** COUT [technique] patchwork ▪ [ouvrage] (piece of) patchwork **2.** [ensemble hétérogène] patchwork ▪ **le pays est un ~ de nationalités** the country is a patchwork of different nationalities.
◆ **en patchwork** *loc adj* patchwork *(modif)*.

pâte [pat] *nf* **1.** [à base de farine - à pain] dough ; [- à tarte] pastry *UK*, dough *US* ; [- à gâteau] mixture *UK*, batter *US* ; [- à frire] batter ▪ **~ brisée** short *ou* shortcrust pastry *UK*, pie dough *US* ▪ **~ à crêpes** pancake batter ▪ **~ à choux** choux pastry ▪ **~ feuilletée** flaky pastry, puff pastry *UK* ▪ **~ sablée** sweet biscuit *ou* sweet flan pastry *UK*, sweet *ou* sugar dough *US*
2. [pour fourrer, tartiner] paste ▪ **~ d'amandes** marzipan, almond paste ▪ **~ d'anchois** anchovy paste *ou* spread ▪ **~ de coing** quince jelly ▪ **une fraise en ~ de fruits** a jellied strawberry
3. [en fromagerie] : **(fromage à) ~ cuite** cheese made from scalded curds ▪ **(fromage à) ~ fermentée/molle** fermented/soft cheese
4. [tempérament] : **il est d'une ~ à vivre cent ans** he's the sort who'll live to be a hundred ⊙ **c'est une bonne ~, il est bonne ~** he's a good sort
5. [en céramique] paste
6. [en cosmétologie] paste ▪ **~ dentifrice** toothpaste
7. TECHNOL : **~ à papier** pulp ▪ **~ de verre** INDUST molten glass ; JOAILL paste ▪ **des bijoux en ~ de verre** paste (jewellery)
8. JEUX : **~ à modeler** Plasticine®, modelling clay.
◆ **pâtes** *nfpl* **1.** CULIN : **~s (alimentaires)** pasta *(U)* ▪ **les ~s sont trop cuites** the pasta's overcooked
2. PHARM : **~s pectorales** cough lozenges *ou* pastilles.

pâté [pate] *nm* **1.** CULIN pâté ▪ **~ en croûte** pâté en croûte, raised (crust) pie *UK* ▪ **~ de foie** liver pâté ▪ **~ impérial** spring roll **2.** *fam* [tache d'encre] (ink) blot ▪ **faire des ~s** [stylo] to smudge ; [élève] to make inkblots **3.** [tas] : **~ de sable** sand pie.
◆ **pâté de maisons** *nm* block.

pâtée [pate] *nf* **1.** [pour animaux] food, feed ▪ **~ pour chat/chien** cat/dog food **2.** [nourriture grossière] pap **3.** *fam* [correction, défaite écrasante] hiding, pasting.

patelin¹ [patlɛ̃] *nm fam* [village] little village.

patelin², e [patlɛ̃, in] *adj litt* fawning, unctuous *sout*.

patelle [patɛl] *nf* [coquillage] limpet.

patène [patɛn] *nf* paten.

patent, e [patɑ̃, ɑ̃t] *adj* **1.** [flagrant, incontestable] obvious, patent ▪ **c'est un fait ~** it's patently obvious **2.** HIST patent.

patente [patɑ̃t] *nf* **1.** [taxe] trading tax **2.** HIST (royal) patent.

patenté, e [patɑ̃te] *adj* **1.** *fam* [attesté] established ▪ **un raciste ~** an out-and-out racist **2.** [qui paie patente] trading under licence, licensed.

patenter [3] [patɑ̃te] *vt* to license.

pater [patɛr] *nm* **1.** *fam* [père] pater *UK hum*, father **2.** RELIG paternoster (bead).

Pater [patɛr] *nm inv* Paternoster, Our Father.

patère [patɛr] *nf* **1.** [à vêtements] coat peg **2.** [à rideaux] curtain hook **3.** ANTIQ & ARCHIT patera.

paterfamilias [patɛrfamiljas] *nm* **1.** ANTIQ paterfamilias **2.** *hum* domineering father.

paternalisme [patɛrnalism] *nm* paternalism.

paternaliste [patɛrnalist] *adj* paternalist, paternalistic.

paternel, elle [patɛrnɛl] *adj* **1.** [du père] paternal ▪ **cousins du côté ~** cousins on the father's *ou* paternal side **2.** [indulgent] fatherly.
◆ **paternel** *nm fam hum* [père] old man, pater *UK hum*.

paternellement [patɛrnɛlmɑ̃] *adv* paternally, in a fatherly way.

paternité [patɛrnite] *nf* **1.** [d'un enfant] paternity *sout*, fatherhood **2.** [d'une oeuvre] paternity *sout*, authorship ▪ [d'une théorie] paternity.

pâteux, euse [patø, øz] *adj* **1.** [peinture, soupe] pasty ▪ [gâteau] doughy ▪ **avoir la bouche** *ou* **langue pâteuse** to have a furred tongue ▪ **parler d'une voix pâteuse** to sound groggy **2.** [style] heavy, clumsy, lumbering.

pathétique [patetik] ◇ *adj* **1.** [émouvant] pathetic, moving, poignant ▪ **des descriptions ~s** descriptions full of pathos **2.** ANAT : **nerf ~** patheticus.
◇ *nm* **1.** [émotion] pathos **2.** ANAT patheticus.

pathétiquement [patetikmɑ̃] *adv* pathetically, movingly, poignantly.

pathogène [patɔʒɛn] *adj* pathogenic.

pathogénie [patɔʒeni] *nf* pathogenicity.

pathologie [patɔlɔʒi] *nf* pathology.

pathologique [patɔlɔʒik] *adj* **1.** MÉD pathologic, pathological **2.** *fam* [excessif, anormal] pathological.

pathologiquement [patɔlɔʒikmɑ̃] *adv* pathologically.

pathologiste [patɔlɔʒist] ◇ *adj* pathologistic.
◇ *nmf* pathologist.

pathos [patos] *nm* pathos.

patibulaire [patibylɛr] *adj* sinister ▪ **il avait une mine ~** he looked sinister.

patiemment [pasjamɑ̃] *adv* patiently.

patience [pasjɑ̃s] ◇ *nf* **1.** [calme] patience, forbearance *sout* ▪ **aie un peu de ~** be patient for a minute ▪ **ma ~ a des limites** there are limits to my patience ◆ **prendre son mal en ~** to put up with it ▪ **elle a une ~ d'ange** she has the patience of a saint *ou* of Job **2.** [persévérance] patience, painstaking care **3.** JEUX [cartes] patience ▪ **faire des ~s** to play patience ◆ **jeu de ~** *pr & fig* puzzle **4.** BOT dock.
◇ *interj* : **~!** hold on! ▪ **~, j'ai presque fini!** hold on *ou* just a minute, I've almost finished! ▪ **~, il va voir de quoi je suis capable!** just you wait (and see), I'll show him what I'm made of!

patient, e [pasjɑ̃, ɑ̃t] ◇ *adj* patient.
◇ *nm, f* [malade] patient.
◆ **patient** *nm* GRAMM [par opposition à agent] patient.

patienter [3] [pasjɑ̃te] *vi* [attendre] to wait ▪ **faites-la ~ un instant** ask her to wait for a minute ▪ **c'est occupé, vous voulez ~?** TÉLÉCOM it's engaged UK *ou* busy US, will you hold?

patin [patɛ̃] *nm* **1.** SPORT skate ▪ **~s à glace/roulettes** ice/roller skates ▪ **faire du ~ à glace/roulettes** to go ice-skating/roller-skating ▪ **~ de luge** sledge runner **2.** [pour marcher sur un parquet] felt pad *(used to move around on a polished floor)* **3.** △ [baiser] French kiss **4.** AÉRON landing pad **5.** AUTO : **~ de frein** brake shoe **6.** CONSTR [d'échafaudage] sole plate *ou* piece **7.** MÉCAN shoe, pad **8.** RAIL (rail) base **9.** [d'un blindé] (track) link.

patinage [patinaʒ] *nm* **1.** SPORT skating, ice-skating ▪ **~ artistique** figure skating ▪ **~ de vitesse** speed skating **2.** [d'une roue] spinning ▪ [de l'embrayage] slipping **3.** [patine artificielle] patination.

patine [patin] *nf* **1.** [d'un meuble] sheen **2.** ART & GÉOL patina.

patiné, e [patine] *adj* : **~ par le temps** that has acquired a patina of age.

patiner [3] [patine] ◇ *vi* **1.** SPORT to skate **2.** AUTO [roue] to spin ▪ [embrayage] to slip **3.** *Québec loc* **savoir ~** to know how to duck and weave *fig.*
◇ *vt* [un meuble] to patine, to patinize.
◆ **se patiner** *vpi* to patinate, to become patinated.

patinette [patinɛt] *nf* (child's) scooter.

patineur, euse [patinœr, øz] *nm, f* skater.

patinoire [patinwar] *nf* **1.** SPORT ice *ou* skating rink **2.** [surface trop glissante] : **ce trottoir est une véritable ~** this pavement is like an ice rink.

patio [patjo, pasjo] *nm* patio.

pâtir [32] [patir] ◆ **pâtir de** *v+prép* to suffer from, to suffer as a result of.

pâtisserie [patisri] *nf* **1.** [gâteau] cake, pastry ▪ **elle mange trop de ~s** she eats too many cakes **2.** [activité] cake-making ▪ **faire de la ~** to make *ou* to bake cakes **3.** [boutique] pâtisserie, cake shop UK *ou* store US ▪ **~-confiserie** confectioner's **4.** ARCHIT plaster moulding *ou* mouldings.

pâtissier, ère [patisje, ɛr] *nm, f* pastrycook, confectioner.

patois [patwa] *nm* patois, dialect ▪ **il parle encore le ~** he still speaks patois *ou* the dialect.

patoiser [3] [patwaze] *vi* to speak patois *ou* the dialect.

patouiller [3] [patuje] *fam* ◇ *vi* [patauger] to slosh *ou* to wallow about.
◇ *vt* [tripoter] to paw, to mess about with *(insép)*.

patraque [patrak] *adj fam* **1.** [souffrant] out of sorts, peaky UK, peaked US **2.** *vieilli* [détraqué - pendule] on the blink.

pâtre [patr] *nm litt* shepherd.

patres [patrɛs] ⊳ **ad patres.**

patriarcal, e, aux [patrijarkal, o] *adj* patriarchal.

patriarcat [patrijarka] *nm* **1.** RELIG [dignité, territoire] patriarchate **2.** SOCIOL patriarchy.

patriarche [patrijarʃ] *nm* [gén - RELIG] patriarch.

patricien, enne [patrisjɛ̃, ɛn] ◇ *adj* **1.** ANTIQ patrician **2.** *litt* [noble] : **une famille ~ne** an aristocratic family.
◇ *nm, f* ANTIQ patrician.

Patrick [patrik] *npr* : **la Saint-~** Saint Patrick's Day.

patrie [patri] *nf* **1.** [pays natal] homeland, fatherland ▪ **'morts pour la ~'** 'they gave their lives for their country' **2.** [communauté] home **3.** *fig* **la ~ de** the home *ou* cradle *sout* of ▪ **c'est la ~ du jazz** it's the home *ou* birthplace of jazz.

patrimoine [patrimwan] *nm* **1.** [possessions héritées] inheritance ▪ **~ immobilier** real estate assets **2.** [artistique, culturel] heritage **3.** BIOL : **~ génétique** gene pool.

patrimonial, e, aux [patrimɔnjal, o] *adj* patrimonial.

patriotard, e [patrijɔtar, ard] *fam péj* ◇ *adj* jingoistic.
◇ *nm, f* jingo, chauvinist.

patriote [patrijɔt] ◇ *adj* patriotic.
◇ *nmf* patriot.

patriotique [patrijɔtik] *adj* patriotic.

patriotisme [patrijɔtism] *nm* patriotism.

patron[1] [patrɔ̃] *nm* **1.** COUT pattern ▪ **~ de jupe** skirt pattern **2.** [vêtement] : **(taille) ~** medium size ▪ **demi-~** small size ▪ **grand ~** large size **3.** ART template **4.** IMPR [plaque] stencil (plate) ▪ **coloriage au ~** stencil-painting.

patron[2], **onne** [patrɔ̃, ɔn] *nm, f* **1.** [d'une entreprise - propriétaire] owner ; [- gérant] manager (*f* manageress) ; [- directeur] employer ; [- de café, d'auberge] owner, landlord (*f* landlady) ▪ **les grands ~s de la presse** the press barons **2.** *fam* [maître de maison] master (*f* mistress) **3.** UNIV : **~ de thèse** (doctoral) supervisor *ou* director **4.** [d'un service hospitalier] senior consultant **5.** *fam* [époux] old man (*f* old lady ou missus) **6.** RELIG (patron) saint.
◆ **patron** *nm* **1.** [d'une entreprise] boss **2.** ANTIQ & HIST patron **3.** NAUT skipper.

patronage [patrɔnaʒ] *nm* **1.** [soutien officiel] patronage ▪ **sous le haut ~ du président de la République** under the patronage of the President of the Republic **2.** [pour les jeunes] youth club **3.** [tutelle d'un saint] protection ▪ **placé sous le ~ de saint André** under the protection of Saint Andrew.
◆ **de patronage** *loc adj* moralistic ▪ **une mentalité de ~** a Sunday school mentality.

patronal, e, aux [patrɔnal, o] *adj* **1.** COMM & INDUST employer's, employers' **2.** RELIG patronal.

patronat [patrɔna] *nm* : **le ~** the employers.

patronne [patrɔn] *f* ▷ **patron.**

patronner [3] [patrɔne] *vt* **1.** [parrainer] to patronize, to support ■ **~ une entreprise auprès des banques** to secure a company with the banks **2.** COUT to make the pattern for.

patronnesse [patrɔnɛs] *adj f* ▷ **dame.**

patronyme [patrɔnim] *nm* patronymic.

patronymique [patrɔnimik] *adj* patronymic.

patrouille [patruj] *nf* **1.** MIL [groupe - d'hommes] patrol ; [- d'avions, de navires] squadron **2.** [mission] patrol ■ **faire une/être en ~** to go/to be on patrol.

patrouiller [3] [patruje] *vi* to patrol.

patrouilleur [patrujœr] *nm* **1.** MIL man on patrol ■ **les ~s** the patrol **2.** AÉRON [de chasse] (patrolling) fighter ■ [de détection] spotter plane **3.** NAUT patrol ship.

patte [pat] *nf* **1.** [d'un félin, d'un chien] paw ■ [d'un cheval, d'un bœuf] hoof ■ [d'un oiseau] foot ■ **donne la ~, Rex!** Rex, give a paw! ■ **être bas** *OU* **court sur ~s** [animal, personne] to be short-legged ➊ **~s de devant** [membres] forelegs ; [pieds] forefeet ■ **~s de derrière** [membres] hind legs ; [pieds] hind feet ■ **~s de mouche** [écriture] (spidery) scrawl ■ **pantalon (à) ~s d'éléphant** *OU* **d'éph** bell-bottoms, flares *UK* ■ **bas les ~s!** [à un chien] down! ■ **faire ~ de velours** [chat] to sheathe *OU* to draw in its claws ; [personne] to switch on the charm
2. *fam* [jambe] leg, pin *UK*, gam *US* ■ **il a une ~ folle** he's got a gammy leg *UK OU* gimpy leg *US* ■ **ils n'arrêtent pas de se tirer dans les ~s** *fig* they're always getting at each other
3. *fam* [main] hand, paw ➊ **un coup de ~** a swipe, a cutting remark ■ **eh, toi, bas les ~s!** [à une personne] hey, you, hands off *OU* (keep your) paws off! ■ **tomber dans** *OU* **entre les ~s de qqn** to fall into sb's clutches
4. [savoir-faire - d'un peintre] (fine) touch ; [- d'un écrivain] talent
5. CONSTR [pour fixer] (metal) tie, (heavy) fastener ■ [de couverture] saddle ■ **~ de scellement** expansion bolt *UK*, expansion anchor *US*
6. COUT strap ■ **~ de boutonnage** fly (front)
7. NAUT [d'une ancre] fluke, palm
8. TECHNOL [d'un grappin] claw ■ **~ d'attache** gusset plate
9. *Suisse* [torchon] cloth.
◆ **pattes** *nfpl* [favoris] sideburns, sidewhiskers.
◆ **à pattes** *loc adv fam* **allez, on y va à ~s!** come on, let's hoof it!

patte-de-loup [patdəlu] (*pl* **pattes-de-loup**) *nf* gipsywort.

patte-d'oie [patdwa] (*pl* **pattes-d'oie**) *nf* **1.** [rides] crow's-foot **2.** [carrefour] Y-shaped crossroads *OU* junction **3.** ANAT pes anserinus **4.** BOT silverweed **5.** CONSTR (crossbraced) truss **6.** TRAV PUB [d'un pont] starling ■ [balise] (marker) dolphin.

pattemouille [patmuj] *nf* damp cloth *(in ironing)*.

pâturage [patyraʒ] *nm* **1.** [prairie] pasture, pastureland **2.** [activité] grazing.

pâture [patyr] *nf* **1.** [nourriture] food, feed ■ **jeter** *OU* **donner qqn en ~ à qqn** to serve sb up to sb **2.** [lieu] pasture **3.** *sout* [pour l'esprit] food, diet ■ **la poésie est sa ~ favorite** poetry is his favourite reading matter.

pâturer [3] [patyre] *vt & vi* to graze.

Paul [pɔl] *npr* : **saint ~** Saint Paul.

paulinien, enne [polinjɛ̃, ɛn] *adj* Pauline.

paume [pom] *nf* **1.** ANAT palm **2.** MENUIS halving (lap joint) **3.** SPORT real tennis.

paumé, e [pome] *fam* ◇ *adj* **1.** [désemparé, indécis] confused ■ [marginal] out of it **2.** [isolé] remote, godforsaken ■ **un patelin complètement ~** a place in the middle of nowhere **3.** [perdu] lost.
◇ *nm, f* [marginal] dropout.

paumelle [pomɛl] *nf* **1.** CONSTR hinge **2.** [gant] sailmaker's palm **3.** [planchette] pommel (board) **4.** BOT two-rowed barley.

paumer [3] [pome] *fam* ◇ *vt* **1.** [égarer] to lose **2.** [attraper - délinquant, fautif] : **se faire ~** to get nicked *UK OU* busted *US*.
◇ *vi* [perdre] to lose ■ **celui qui paume paie à boire** the loser pays for the drinks.
◆ **se paumer** *vpi fam* to get lost, to lose one's way.

paupérisation [poperizasjɔ̃] *nf* pauperization.

paupériser [3] [poperize] *vt* to pauperize.
◆ **se paupériser** *vpi* to become pauperized.

paupérisme [poperism] *nm* pauperism.

paupière [popjɛr] *nf* eyelid.

paupiette [popjɛt] *nf* : **~ (de veau)** paupiette of veal, veal olive.

pause [poz] *nf* **1.** [moment de repos] break ■ **faire une ~** to have *OU* to take a break **2.** [temps d'arrêt - dans une conversation] pause ■ **marquer une ~** to pause **3.** [arrêt - d'un processus] halt ■ **il a annoncé une ~ dans les réformes** he declared a temporary halt to the reforms **4.** MUS pause **5.** SPORT half-time.

pause-café [pozkafe] (*pl* **pauses-café**) *nf* coffee break.

pauvre [povr] ◇ *adj* **1.** [sans richesse - personne, pays, quartier] poor **2.** *(avant le n)* [pitoyable - demeure, décor] humble, wretched ; [- personne] poor ■ **laisse donc ce ~ chien tranquille!** do leave that poor *OU* wretched dog alone! ■ **ah, ma ~ dame, si vous saviez!** but my dear lady, if only you knew! ■ **c'est la vie, mon ~ vieux!** that's life, my friend! ■ **~ crétin, va!** you idiot! ➊ **~ de moi!** woe is me! *arch hum* ■ **~ de nous!** (the) Lord protect us! **3.** [insuffisant] poor ■ **gaz/minerai ~** lean gas/ore ■ **un sous-sol ~** a poor subsoil ■ **une végétation ~** sparse vegetation ■ **elle a un vocabulaire très ~** her vocabulary is very poor ■ **~ en : la ville est ~ en espaces verts** the town is short of *OU* lacks parks ■ **alimentation ~ en sels minéraux** food lacking (in) minerals ■ **régime ~ en calories** low-calorie diet.
◇ *nmf* **1.** [par compassion] poor thing ■ **les ~s, comme ils ont dû souffrir!** poor things, they must have suffered so much! **2.** [en appellatif] : **mais mon ~/ma ~, il ne m'obéit jamais!** [pour susciter la pitié] but my dear fellow/my dear, he never does as I say! ■ **tu es vraiment trop bête, ma ~/mon ~!** [avec mépris] you're really too stupid for words, my dear girl/boy!
◇ *nm* poor man, pauper *litt* ■ **les ~s** the poor ■ **du ~ : c'est le champagne du ~** it's poor man's champagne.

pauvrement [povrəmɑ̃] *adv* **1.** [misérablement - décoré, habillé] poorly, shabbily ■ **vivre ~** to live in poverty **2.** [médiocrement] poorly ■ **il traduit ~** he's a poor translator.

pauvresse [povrɛs] *nf arch* poor woman, pauperess *arch* ■ **une pauvresse en haillons** a poor ragged woman.

pauvret, ette [povrɛ, ɛt] ◇ *adj* poor, poor-looking.
◇ *nm, f* : **le ~, la ~te** the poor (little) dear, the poor (little) thing.

pauvreté [povrəte] *nf* **1.** [manque d'argent] poverty ■ **il a fini ses jours dans la ~** he ended his days in poverty ➊ **~ n'est pas vice** *prov* poverty is not a crime **2.** [médiocrité] poverty ■ **avoir une imagination d'une extrême ~** to be extremely unimaginative **3.** [déficience] poverty ■ **la ~ du sol ne permet qu'un faible rendement** the poorness of the soil means that the yield is very low.

pavage [pavaʒ] *nm* **1.** [action] cobbling, paving ■ **le ~ des rues piétonnières est en cours** the pedestrian precinct is being paved **2.** [surface] cobbles, paving **3.** GÉOL pavement.

pavane [pavan] *nf* pavane.

pavaner [3] [pavane] ◆ **se pavaner** *vpi* to strut about.

pavé [pave] *nm* **1.** [surface - dallée] pavement *UK*, sidewalk *US* ; [- empierrée] cobbles ■ **tenir le haut du ~** to be on top ■ **être sur le ~** [sans domicile] to be on the streets ; [au chômage] to be jobless ■ **jeter** *OU* **mettre qqn sur le ~** [l'expulser de son domicile] to throw sb out on the streets ; [le licencier] to throw sb out of his/her job **2.** [pierre] paving stone, cobblestone ■ [dalle] flag, flagstone ■ **lui, quand il veut aider, c'est le ~ de l'ours** with friends like him, who needs enemies? ■ **un** *ou* **le ~ dans la mare** a bombshell *fig* ■ **son article a été le ~ dans la mare** his article caused a bit of a furore **3.** CULIN [viande] thick slab *ou* chunk ■ **~ de romsteck** thick rump steak ▌[gâteau] : **un ~ au chocolat** a (thick) chocolate cake **4.** PRESSE [encart] block (of text) ■ [publicité] (large) display advertisement **5.** INFORM pad, keypad ■ **~ numérique** numeric keypad **6.** *fam* [livre] huge *ou* massive tome ■ [article] huge article ■ [dissertation] huge essay.

pavement [pavmɑ̃] *nm* **1.** CONSTR flooring *ou* paving *(made of flags, tiles or mosaic)* **2.** GÉOGR sea floor.

paver [3] [pave] *vt* [avec des pavés] to cobble ■ [avec des dalles] to pave.

paveur, euse [pavœr, øz] *nm, f* TRAV PUB paver.

pavillon [pavijɔ̃] *nm* **1.** [maison particulière] detached house ■ **~ de banlieue** detached house *(in the suburbs)*
2. [belvédère, gloriette] lodge ➊ **~ de chasse** hunting lodge
3. [dans un hôpital] wing, wards ■ [dans une cité universitaire] house ■ [dans une exposition] pavilion ■ **il travaille au ~ de pédiatrie** he works on the pediatric ward *ou* in the pediatric wing
4. AUTO roof
5. JOAILL pavilion
6. ANAT [des trompes utérines] pavilion ■ **~ (auriculaire)** auricle, pinna
7. MUS [d'un instrument] bell ■ [d'un phonographe] horn
8. NAUT flag ■ **~ en berne** flag at half-mast ➊ **~ d'armateur** *ou* **de reconnaissance** house flag ■ **~ de complaisance** flag of convenience ■ **~ national** ensign ■ **~ de quarantaine** quarantine flag, yellow jack ■ **baisser ~** *pr* to lower *ou* to strike one's flag ; *fig* to back down.
◆ **en pavillon** *loc adj* ARCHIT [toit] pavilion *(modif)*.

pavillonnaire [pavijɔnɛr] *adj* : **un quartier ~** an area of low-rise housing ■ **un hôpital ~** a hospital (constructed) in wings, a multiwing hospital.

Pavlov [pavlɔf] *npr* : **ils réagissent comme les chiens de ~** they react like Pavlov's dogs.

pavois [pavwa] *nm* **1.** HIST shield ■ **élever** *ou* **hisser** *ou* **porter qqn sur le ~** to raise *ou* to carry sb on high **2.** NAUT [partie de la coque] bulwark ■ [pavillons] flags and bunting ■ **hisser le grand ~** to dress ship *ou* full ■ **hisser le petit ~** to dress (the ship) with masthead flags.

pavoiser [3] [pavwaze] ◇ *vt* **1.** [édifice] to deck with flags *ou* bunting **2.** NAUT to dress (with flags).
◇ *vi fam* [faire le fier] : **il n'y a pas de quoi ~** that's nothing to be proud of.

pavot [pavo] *nm* BOT poppy ■ **~ cornu** red-horned poppy.

payable [pɛjabl] *adj* payable ■ **chèque ~ à l'ordre de** cheque payable to ■ **facture ~ le 5 du mois** invoice payable *ou* due on the 5th of the month.

payant, e [pɛjɑ̃, ɑ̃t] *adj* **1.** [non gratuit] : **les consommations sont ~es** you have to pay for your drinks **2.** [qui paie] paying **3.** *fam* [qui produit - de l'argent] profitable ; [- un résultat] efficient ■ **ses efforts du premier trimestre ont été ~s** his efforts during the first term have borne fruit.

paye [pɛj] = **paie**.

payé, e [peje] *adj* : **bien/mal ~** well-/low-.

payement [pɛjmɑ̃] = **paiement**.

payer [11] [peje] ◇ *vt* **1.** [solder, régler] to pay ■ **~ sa dette à la société** to pay one's debt to society ■ *(en usage absolu)* **~ comptant/à crédit** to pay cash/by credit ■ **je paye par chèque/avec ma carte de crédit/en liquide** I'll pay by cheque/with my credit card/(in) cash ■ **~ d'avance** to pay in advance ■ **c'est moi qui paie** [l'addition] I'll pay, it's my treat ➊ **c'est le prix à ~ si tu veux réussir** that's the price you have to pay for success ■ **~ de ses deniers** *ou* **de sa poche** to pay out of one's own pocket ■ **~ rubis sur l'ongle** to pay (cash) on the nail
2. [rémunérer] to pay ■ *(en usage absolu)* **leur patron paie bien** their boss pays well ➊ **tu es pourtant payé pour le savoir!** you of all people should know that!
3. [acheter - repas, voyage] to pay for ■ **~ à boire à qqn** to buy sb a drink ■ **je lui ai payé un collier** I bought her a necklace ■ **combien as-tu payé ta maison?** how much did your house cost you?, how much did you pay for your house? ■ **je te paie le théâtre** I'll take you out to the theatre ■ **combien il t'a fait ~?** how much did he charge? ■ **il me l'a fait ~ trop cher** he overcharged me
4. [obtenir au prix d'un sacrifice] : **~ qqch de** to pay for sthg with ■ **~ sa réussite de sa santé** to succeed at the expense *ou* the cost of one's health ■ **elle me le paiera!** *fig* she'll pay for this! ➊ **c'est ~ cher la réussite** that's too high a price to pay for success
5. [subir les conséquences de] to pay for *(insép)* ■ *(en usage absolu)* **vous êtes coupable, vous devez ~** you're guilty, you're going to pay ■ **~ pour les autres** to be punished for others ➊ **~ les pots cassés** to foot the bill *fig*
6. [dédommager] to compensate, to repay ■ **ses félicitations me paient de mes efforts** his congratulations repay me my efforts ➊ **~ qqn de belles paroles** to fob sb off with smooth talk ■ **~ qqn d'ingratitude** to repay sb with ingratitude ■ **~ qqn de retour** to repay sb in kind
7. [acheter - criminel] to hire ; [- témoin] to buy (off) ■ **~ un tueur** to hire a gunman
8. [compenser] to pay ■ **la prime d'assurance ne paie pas complètement le remplacement de la voiture** the insurance premium does not cover you for full reimbursement of the car
9. [être soumis à - taxe] : **certaines marchandises paient un droit de douane** you have to pay duty on some goods, some goods are liable to duty.
◇ *vi* **1.** [être profitable] to pay ■ **l'ostréiculture ne paie plus** there's no money (to be made) in oyster farming nowadays ■ **c'est un travail qui paie mal** it's badly paid work, it's not a well paid job ➊ **l'honnêteté ne paie plus** it doesn't pay to be honest any more
2. *fam* [prêter à rire] to be *ou* to look a sight ■ **tu payes avec ces lunettes!** you do look a sight with those glasses on!
3. *loc* **~ d'audace** to risk one's all ■ **ne pas ~ de mine : la maison ne paie pas de mine, mais elle est confortable** the house isn't much to look at *ou* the house doesn't look much but it's very comfortable ■ **~ de sa personne** [s'exposer au danger] to put o.s. on the line ; [se donner du mal] to put in a lot of effort.
◆ **se payer** ◇ *vp (emploi réfléchi)* : **tenez, payez-vous** here, take what I owe you ➊ **se ~ de mots** to talk a lot of fine words.
◇ *vp (emploi passif)* to have to be paid for ■ **la qualité se paie** you have to pay for quality ■ **tout se paie** everything has its price.
◇ *vpt* **1.** *fam* [s'offrir] to treat o.s. to ■ **j'ai envie de me ~ une robe** I feel like treating myself to a dress *ou* like buying myself a dress ➊ **se ~ la tête de qqn** to make fun of sb ■ **s'en ~ (une tranche)** to have (o.s.) a great time
2. *fam* [être chargé de] to be landed *ou* saddled with ■ **je me paie tout le boulot** I end up doing all the work
3. *fam* [recevoir] to get, to land *UK* ■ **je me suis payé un 2 à l'oral** I got a 2 in the oral
4. *fam* [supporter] to put up with ■ **on s'est payé leurs gosses pendant tout le week-end** we had to put up with *ou* we were lumbered with their kids the whole weekend
5. *fam* [percuter] to run *ou* to bump into ■ **elle s'est payé le mur en reculant** she backed into the wall
6. *fam* [agresser] to go for ■ **celui-là, à la prochaine réunion, je me le paie** I'll have his guts for garters *UK ou* his head on a platter *US* at the next meeting
7. △ [avoir une relation sexuelle avec] to have△, to have it off with△ *UK*.

payeur, euse [pɛjœr, øz] ◇ *adj* [agent, fonctionnaire] payments *(modif)*.
◇ *nm, f* payer.
◆ **payeur** *nm* [débiteur] : **mauvais ~** bad debtor, defaulter.

pays [pei] *nm* **1.** [nation] country ■ **les nouveaux ~ industrialisés** the newly industrialized countries ■ **les ~ membres du pacte de Varsovie** the Warsaw Pact countries ■ **le ~ d'accueil** the host country ➊ **~ en (voie de) développement** developing country ■ **les vieux ~** *Québec* [pays d'Europe] the old countries ■ **ils se conduisent comme en ~ conquis** they're acting *ou* behaving as if they own the place ■ **voir du ~** to travel a lot ■ **au ~ des aveugles, les borgnes sont rois** in the land of the blind the one-eyed man is king

2. [zone, contrée] region, area ▪ **~ chaud/sec** hot/dry region ▶ **le Pays de la Loire** the Pays de la Loire (region) ▪ **en ~ de Loire** in the Loire area *ou* valley ▪ **au ~ des rêves** *ou* **des songes** in the land of dreams ▪ **en ~ de connaissance : vous serez en ~ de connaissance, Tom fait aussi du piano** you'll have something in common because Tom plays the piano too **3.** [agglomération] village, small town ▪ **un petit ~ de 2 000 âmes** a small town of 2,000 souls **4.** [peuple] people, country ▪ **tout le ~ se demande encore qui est l'assassin** the whole country's still wondering who the murderer might be **5.** [région d'origine] **: le ~** [nation] one's country ; [région] one's home (region) ; [ville] one's home (town) ▪ **c'est un enfant du ~** he's from these parts ▪ **on voit bien que tu n'es pas du ~!** it's obvious you're not from around here! ▶ **le mal du ~** homesickness ▪ **avoir le mal du ~** to be homesick **6.** *fig* [berceau, foyer] **: le ~ de : le ~ des tulipes** the country of the tulip ▪ **le ~ du bel canto** the cradle of bel canto.
◆ **de pays** *loc adj* [produits] local ▶ **saucisson de ~** traditional *ou* country-style sausage.

PAYS DE LA LOIRE
This administrative region includes the ***départements*** of Loire-Atlantique, Maine-et-Loire, Mayenne, Sarthe and Vendée (capital: Nantes).

paysage [peizaʒ] *nm* **1.** [étendue géographique] landscape ▪ **~ montagneux/vallonné** hilly/rolling landscape **2.** [panorama] view, scenery, landscape ▶ **faire bien dans le ~** *fam* to look good **3.** [aspect d'ensemble] landscape, scene ▪ **~ politique/social** political/social landscape ▶ **le ~ audiovisuel français** French broadcasting ▪ **~ urbain** townscape, urban landscape **4.** ART landscape (painting) ▪ **un ~ de Millet** a Millet landscape, a landscape by Millet **5.** INFORM landscape.

paysager, ère [peizaʒe, ɛr] *adj* landscape *(modif)* ▪ **parc ~** landscaped gardens.

paysagiste [peizaʒist] <> *adj* landscape *(modif)*.
<> *nmf* **1.** ART landscape painter, landscapist **2.** HORT landscape gardener.

paysan, anne [peizɑ̃, an] <> *adj* **1.** SOCIOL peasant *(modif)* ▪ [population] rural ▪ **le malaise ~** discontent amongst small farmers **2.** [rustique - décor] rustic ; [- style, vêtements] rustic, country *(modif)*.
<> *nm, f* **1.** [cultivateur] peasant, farmer ▪ **les ~s veulent des réformes** the farming community wants *ou* the farmers want reforms **2.** *péj* [rustre] peasant ▪ **~ du Danube** ***La Fontaine*** *allus* plain-speaking man.
◆ **à la paysanne** *loc adj* CULIN with small onions and diced bacon.

paysannat [peizana] *nm* **1.** [classe] peasantry ▪ [ensemble des agriculteurs] farming community **2.** [condition des paysans] peasant life.

paysannerie [peizanri] *nf* peasantry.

Pays-Bas [peiba] *npr mpl* **: les ~** the Netherlands ▪ **aux ~** in the Netherlands.

Pc = **pièce**.

PC *nm* **1.** (*abr de* **parti communiste**) Communist Party **2.** (*abr de* **personal computer**) PC, micro **3.** = **prêt conventionné** **4.** = **permis de construire** **5.** (*abr de* **poste de commandement**) HQ **6.** (*abr de* **Petite Ceinture**) [bus] *bus following the inner ring road in Paris*.

pcc (*abr écrite de* **pour copie conforme**) certified accurate.

pce = **pièce**.

PCF *npr m* = **Parti communiste français**.

PCV (*abr de* **à percevoir**) *nm* reverse-charge call *UK*, collect call *US* ▪ **appeler Paris en ~** to make a reverse-charge call to Paris *UK*, to call Paris collect *US*.

P-DG (*abr de* **président-directeur général**) *nmf inv* chairman and managing director *UK*, Chief Executive Officer *US* ▪ ≃ MD *UK*, ≃ CEO *US*.

PEA (*abr de* **plan d'épargne en actions**) *nm* ≃ investment trust.

péage [peaʒ] *nm* **1.** [sur une voie publique - taxe] toll ; [- lieu] toll (gate) ▪ **'~ à 5 km'** 'toll 5 km' **2.** TV **: chaîne à ~** pay channel.

péagiste [peaʒist] *nmf* toll collector.

peau, x [po] *nf* **1.** ANAT skin ▶ **avoir la ~ sèche/grasse** to have dry/greasy skin ▪ **~ mixte** combination skin ▪ **~x mortes** dead skin ▪ **n'avoir que la ~ et** *ou* **sur les os** to be all skin and bones ▪ **attraper qqn par la peau du cou** to grab sb by the scruff of the neck ▪ **prendre qqn par la ~ du dos** to grab sb by the scruff of the neck ▪ **être** *ou* **se sentir bien dans sa ~** *fam* to feel good about o.s., to be together ▪ **être mal dans sa ~** to feel bad about o.s., to be unhappy ▪ **entrer** *ou* **se mettre dans la ~ de qqn** to put o.s. in sb's shoes *ou* place ▪ **entrer dans la ~ du personnage** to get right into the part ▪ **avoir qqn dans la ~** to be crazy about sb, to have sb under one's skin ▪ **avoir qqch dans la ~** to have sthg in one's blood ▪ **changer de ~** to change one's look ▪ **faire ~ neuve** to get a facelift *fig* ▪ **l'université fait ~ neuve** the university system is being completely overhauled ▪ **avoir la ~ dure** to be thick-skinned ▪ **si tu tiens à ta ~** *fam* if you value your life *ou* hide ▪ **y laisser sa ~** *fam* to pay with one's life, to be killed ▪ **un jour, j'aurai ta ~!** *fam* I'll get you one of these days! ▪ **faire** *ou* **crever la ~ à qqn** *fam* to do sb in, to bump sb off ▪ **trouer la ~ à qqn**△ to fill *ou* to pump sb full of lead ▪ **coûter la ~ des fesses**△ *ou* **du cul**▲ to cost an arm and a leg **2.** ZOOL [gén] skin ▪ [fourrure] pelt ▪ [cuir - non tanné] hide ; [- tanné] leather, (tanned) hide ▪ **une valise en ~** a leather suitcase ▪ **le commerce des ~x** the fur and leather trade ▪ **sac en ~ de serpent** snakeskin bag ▶ **cuir pleine ~** full leather ▪ **une ~ d'âne** [diplôme] a diploma ▪ **~ de chagrin** shagreen ▪ **mes économies diminuent comme une ~ de chagrin** my savings are just melting away ▪ **~ de chamois** [chiffon] chamois leather ▪ **~ de tambour** (drum) skin ▪ **vieille ~**△ old bag△ ▪ **des révolutionnaires en ~ de lapin** *fam* Mickey Mouse *ou* tinpot revolutionaries **3.** [d'un fruit, d'un légume, du lait bouilli] skin ▪ [du fromage] rind ▪ **~ d'orange** orange peel ▪ **~ de banane** *pr & fig* banana skin **4.** *loc* **~ de balle (et balai de crin)**△, **~ de zébi**▲ [refus, mépris] no way *UK*, nothing doing *US*.
◆ **peau d'orange** *nf* MÉD orange-peel skin *(caused by cellulite)*.
◆ **peau de vache**△ *nf* [femme] cow *UK*, bitch ▪ [homme] bastard△.

peaucier [posje] <> *adj m* dermal.
<> *nm* **: ~ (du cou)** platysma.

peaufiner [3] [pofine] *vt* **1.** [à la peau de chamois] to shammy-leather **2.** *fig* to put the finishing touches to.

peau-rouge [poruʒ] (*pl* **peaux-rouges**) *adj* Red Indian *(modif)*, redskin *(modif)*.
◆ **Peau-Rouge** *nmf* Red Indian, Redskin.

peausserie [posri] *nf* **1.** [peaux] leatherwear **2.** [industrie] leather *ou* skin trade.

pébroque△ [pebrɔk] *nm* brolly *UK*, umbrella.

pécan [pekɑ̃] *nm* **: (noix de) ~** pecan.

pécari [pekari] *nm* **1.** ZOOL peccary **2.** [cuir] peccary (skin).

peccadille [pekadij] *nf* **1.** [péché] peccadillo ▪ **des ~s de jeunesse** youthful indiscretions **2.** [vétille] **: se disputer pour des ~s** to argue over trifles.

péché [peʃe] *nm* **1.** [faute] sin ▪ **~ de (la) chair** sin of the flesh ▪ **~ mortel/originel/véniel** mortal/original/venial sin ▪ **~ de jeunesse** youthful indiscretion ▪ **~ mignon** weakness ▪ **mon ~ mignon, c'est le chocolat** I just can't resist chocolate, chocolate is my little weakness ▪ **le ~ d'orgueil** the sin of pride ▪ **les sept ~s capitaux** the seven deadly sins ▪ **à tout ~ miséricorde** *prov* every sin can be forgiven **2.** [état] sin ▪ **vivre dans le ~** [gén] to lead a life of sin *ou* a sinful life ; [sans mariage religieux] to live in sin ▪ **retomber dans le ~** to relapse (into sin).

pêche[1] [pɛʃ] <> *nf* **1.** BOT peach ▪ **~ abricot/blanche** yellow/white peach ▪ **~ de vigne** red-fleshed peach *(grown amongst vines)* ▪ **elle a un teint de ~** she has a peaches and cream complexion **2.** *fam* [énergie] get-up-and-go ▪ **avoir la ~** to be full of get-up-and-go, to be on form.

◇ *adj inv* peach *(modif)*, peach-coloured.

pêche² [pɛʃ] *nf* **1.** [activité - en mer] fishing ; [- en eau douce] fishing, angling ▪ **aller à la ~** [en mer] to go fishing ; [en eau douce] to go angling ▪ **'~ interdite'** 'no fishing' ▪ **'~ réglementée'** 'fishing by permit only' ◆ **~ à la baleine** whaling, whale-hunting ▪ **~ à la cuiller** spinning ▪ **~ au gros** deep-sea fishing ▪ **~ au lamparo** fishing by lamplight ▪ **~ au lancer** cast fishing ▪ **~ à la ligne** angling ▪ **~ maritime** sea fishing ▪ **~ sous-marine** underwater fishing ▪ **aller à la ~ aux informations** to go in search of information **2.** [produit de la pêche] catch ▪ **la ~ a été bonne** *pr* there was a good catch ▪ **alors, la ~ a été bonne?** *fig* any luck? ◆ **~ miraculeuse** *allus* & BIBLE miraculous draught of fishes **3.** [lieu] fishery ▪ **~s maritimes** sea fisheries ▪ **~ côtière** coastal fishery ▪ **~ éloignée, grande ~, ~ hauturière** distant-water fishery.

pécher [18] [peʃe] *vi* **1.** RELIG to sin **2.** *sout* [commettre une erreur] : **~ par** : **~ par excès de minutie** to be overmeticulous ▪ **elle a péché par imprudence** she was too careless, she was over-careless ▪ **~ contre le bon goût** to go against the rules of good taste.

pêcher¹ [peʃe] *nm* **1.** BOT peach tree **2.** MENUIS peach wood.

pêcher² [4] [peʃe] ◇ *vt* **1.** PÊCHE [essayer de prendre] to fish for *(insép)* ▪ [prendre] to catch ▪ **~ la crevette** to shrimp, to go shrimping ▪ **~ le hareng au chalut** to trawl for herring **2.** [tirer de l'eau] to fish out *(sép)* **3.** *fam* [dénicher] to seek out *(sép)*, to hunt *ou* to track down *(sép)*, to unearth ▪ **où a-t-il été pêcher que j'avais démissionné?** where did he get the idea that I'd resigned?

◇ *vi* [aller à la pêche] to fish ▪ **il pêche tous les dimanches** he goes fishing every Sunday ◆ **~ en eau trouble** to fish in troubled waters.

pécheresse [peʃrɛs] *f* ▷ **pécheur.**

pêcherie [pɛʃri] *nf* fishery.

pécheur, eresse [peʃœr, peʃrɛs] *nm, f* sinner ▪ **~ endurci** unrepentant sinner.

pêcheur, euse [pɛʃœr, øz] *nm, f* [en mer] fisherman (*f* fisherwoman) ▪ [en eau douce] angler ▪ **~ de baleine** whaler ▪ **~ à la ligne** *pr* angler ; *fig* abstentionist ▪ **~ au chalut** trawlerman ▪ **~ de crevettes** shrimper ▪ **~ de perles** pearl diver.

pécloter [3] [peklote] *vi Suisse* to be in ill-health.

pecnot [pekno] = **péquenaud.**

pécore [pekɔr] *nf fam* **quelle ~, celle-là!** she's so stuck-up!

pectine [pɛktin] *nf* pectin.

pectique [pɛktik] *adj* pectic.

pectoral, e, aux [pɛktɔral, o] *adj* **1.** ANAT pectoral **2.** PHARM throat *(modif)*, cough *(modif)*.

◆ **pectoral, aux** *nm* **1.** ANAT pectoral muscle **2.** ANTIQ & RELIG pectoral.

pécule [pekyl] *nm* **1.** [petit capital] savings, nest egg ▪ **se constituer un (petit) ~** to put some money aside **2.** MIL (service) gratuity **3.** DR : **~ de libération** prison earnings *(paid on discharge)* **4.** HIST peculium.

pécuniaire [pekynjɛr] *adj* financial, pecuniary *sout* ▪ **des difficultés ~s** financial *ou* money problems.

pécuniairement [pekynjɛrmɑ̃] *adv* financially, pecuniarily *sout.*

pédagogie [pedagɔʒi] *nf* **1.** [méthodologie] educational methods **2.** [pratique] teaching skills ▪ **il manque de ~** he lacks teaching skills.

pédagogique [pedagɔʒik] *adj* [science, manière] educational, teaching *(modif)*, pedagogical *sout* ▪ **elle n'a aucune formation ~** she's not been trained to teach *ou* as a teacher ▪ **aides** *ou* **supports ~s** teaching materials.

pédagogiquement [pedagɔʒikmɑ̃] *adv* pedagogically, educationally.

pédagogue [pedagɔg] ◇ *adj* : **il n'est pas très ~** he's not very good at teaching ▪ **elle est très ~** she's a very good teacher.

◇ *nmf* **1.** [enseignant] teacher **2.** [éducateur] educationalist **3.** ANTIQ pedagogue.

pédale [pedal] *nf* **1.** [d'un véhicule] pedal **2.** [d'une poubelle] pedal ▪ [d'une machine à coudre] treadle **3.** AUTO pedal ▪ **~ d'embrayage** clutch ▪ **appuyer sur la ~ du frein** to step on *ou* to use the brake pedal **4.** MUS pedal ▪ **~ douce** soft pedal ▪ **~ forte** loud *ou* sustaining pedal ▪ **mettre la ~ douce** *pr* & *fig* to soft-pedal **5.** △ *péj* [homosexuel] queer△ *UK*, faggot△ *US*.

◆ **à pédales** *loc adj* pedal *(modif)* ▪ **auto à ~s** [jouet] pedal car.

pédaler [3] [pedale] *vi* **1.** [sur un vélo] to pedal ▪ **~ en danseuse** to pedal off the saddle **2.** *fam loc* **~ dans la choucroute** *ou* **la semoule** *ou* **le yaourt** to be all at sea.

pédalier [pedalje] *nm* **1.** [d'une bicyclette] (bicycle) drive **2.** MUS [d'un orgue] pedals, pedal board.

Pédalo® [pedalo] *nm* pedalo, pedal-boat.

pédant, e [pedɑ̃, ɑ̃t] ◇ *adj* [exposé, ton] pedantic.

◇ *nm, f* pedant.

pédanterie [pedɑ̃tri] *nf* pedantry.

pédantisme [pedɑ̃tism] *nm* = **pédanterie.**

pédé△ [pede] *nm péj* queer△ *UK*, fag△ *US*.

pédéraste [pederast] *nm* **1.** [avec des jeunes garçons] pederast **2.** [entre hommes] homosexual.

pédérastie [pederasti] *nf* **1.** [avec des jeunes garçons] pederasty **2.** [entre hommes] homosexuality.

pédérastique [pederastik] *adj* **1.** [avec des jeunes garçons] pederastic **2.** [entre hommes] homosexual.

pédestre [pedɛstr] *adj* ▷ **randonnée,** ▷ **statue.**

pédiatre [pedjatr] *nmf* paediatrician.

pédiatrie [pedjatri] *nf* paediatrics *(U)*.

pédiatrique [pedjatrik] *adj* paediatric.

pedibus [pedibys] *adv fam hum* on foot, on Shanks's pony *UK ou* mare *US*.

pédicule [pedikyl] *nm* **1.** ANAT peduncle **2.** ARCHIT stand, base **3.** BOT [pédicelle] pedicle ▪ [pédoncule] peduncle.

pédicure [pedikyr] *nmf* chiropodist.

pedigree [pedigre] *nm* pedigree ▪ **un chien avec ~** a pedigree dog.

pédiment [pedimɑ̃] *nm* GÉOL pediment.

pédologue [pedɔlɔg] *nmf* GÉOL pedologist.

pédoncule [pedɔ̃kyl] *nm* ANAT & BOT peduncle ▪ **~ cérébral** restiform body.

pédophile [pedɔfil] ◇ *adj* paedophiliac.

◇ *nmf* paedophile.

pédophilie [pedɔfili] *nf* paedophilia.

pédopsychiatre [pedɔpsikjatr] *nmf* child psychiatrist.

pedzouille△ [pedzuj] *nm péj* yokel, hick *US*.

PEE [peəə] (*abr de* **plan épargne entreprise**) *nm* employees' savings scheme *(with employer's contribution)*.

peeling [piliŋ] *nm* exfoliation (treatment) ▪ **se faire faire un ~** to be given a face (peeling) mask.

peep-show [pipʃo] *nm* peep-show.

pégase [pegaz] *nm* ZOOL pegasus.

Pégase [pegaz] *npr* ASTRON & MYTHOL Pegasus.

PEGC (*abr de* **professeur d'enseignement général de collège**) *nmf teacher qualified to teach one or two subjects to 11-to-15-year-olds in French secondary schools.*

pègre [pɛgr] *nf* (criminal) underworld.

peignait *etc v* **1.** ▷ **peindre 2.** ▷ **peigner.**

peigne [pɛɲ] *nm* **1.** [pour les cheveux] comb ◆ **passer une région/un document au ~ fin** to go over an area/a document with a fine-tooth comb **2.** TECHNOL [à fileter] comb **3.** TEXT [à lin, à laine] comb ▪ [à chanvre] hackle **4.** ZOOL [mollusque] scallop, pecten ▪ [chez l'oiseau] pecten ▪ [chez les scorpions] comb.

peigné [pepe] *nm* **1.** [fil] combed yarns **2.** [tissu] worsted (cloth).

peigne-cul△ [pɛpky] (*pl inv* OU *pl* **peigne-culs**) *nm péj* creep△, jerk△.

peignée [pepe] *nf* **1.** *fam* [volée de coups] beating, hiding **2.** TEXT cardful.

peigner [4] [pepe] *vt* **1.** [cheveux, personne] to comb ▪ **je suis vraiment mal peignée aujourd'hui** my hair is all over the place today ▶ **faire ça ou ~ la girafe** *fam* we might as well be whistling in the wind **2.** TEXT [lin, laine] to comb ▪ [chanvre] to hackle ▪ **coton peigné** brushed cotton.
◆ **se peigner** *vp (emploi réfléchi)* [se coiffer] to comb one's hair ▪ **se ~ la barbe** to comb one's beard.

peignoir [pɛpwar] *nm* **1.** [sortie de bain] : **~ (de bain)** bathrobe **2.** [robe de chambre] dressing gown, bathrobe *US* **3.** [chez le coiffeur] robe.

Pei-king [pejkiŋ] = **Pékin**.

peinard, e△ [pɛnar, ard] *adj* [vie, travail] cushy ▪ **rester** OU **se tenir ~** to keep one's nose clean ▪ **là-bas, on sera ~s** we'll have it easy there.

peinardement△ [pɛnardəmɑ̃] *adv* coolly.

peindre [81] [pɛ̃dr] ◇ *vt* **1.** [mur, tableau] to paint ▪ **j'ai peint la porte en bleu** I painted the door blue ▪ **~ à la bombe/au pistolet** to spray-paint ▪ **~ au pinceau/rouleau** to paint with a brush/roller ▪ **~ à l'huile/à l'eau** to paint in oils/in watercolours **2.** [décrire] to portray, to depict.
◇ *vi* to paint, to be a painter OU an artist ▪ **~ sur soie/verre** to paint on silk/glass.
◆ **se peindre** ◇ *vp (emploi passif)* to be painted on ▪ **c'est un revêtement qui se peint facilement** it's a covering which can easily be painted.
◇ *vp (emploi réfléchi)* **1.** [se représenter - en peinture] to paint one's (own) portrait ; [- dans un écrit] to portray o.s. **2.** [se grimer] : **se ~ le visage** to paint one's face.
◇ *vpi* to show ▪ **la stupéfaction se peignit sur son visage** amazement was written all over her face.

peine [pɛn] *nf*

A.
1. [châtiment] sentence, penalty ▪ **infliger une lourde ~ à qqn** to pass a harsh sentence on sb ▶ **~ correctionnelle** *imprisonment for between two months and five years, or a fine* ▪ **~ criminelle** *imprisonment for more than five years* ▪ **~ incompressible** sentence without remission ▪ **~ infamante** *penalty involving loss of civil rights* ▪ **la ~ de mort** capital punishment, the death penalty ▪ **~ de prison** prison sentence ▪ **~ de prison avec sursis** suspended (prison) sentence
2. RELIG [damnation] damnation, suffering

B.
1. [tourment, inquiétude] trouble ▪ **faire ~ à voir** to be a sorry sight ▶ **~s de cœur** heartache(s) ▪ **se mettre en ~ pour qqn** *sout* to be extremely worried about sb ▪ **'Peines d'amour perdues'** *Shakespeare* 'Love's Labours Lost'
2. [tristesse] sorrow, sadness, grief ▪ **il partageait sa ~** he shared her grief ▪ **avoir de la ~** to be sad OU upset ▪ **je ne voudrais pas lui faire de la ~ en lui disant** I wouldn't like to upset him by telling him ▪ **il me fait vraiment de la ~** I feel really sorry for him

C.
1. [effort] effort, trouble ▪ **ce n'est pas la ~** it's not worth it, it's pointless ▪ **ce n'est pas la ~ de tout récrire/que tu y ailles** there's no point writing it all out again/your going ▪ **c'était bien la ~ que je mette une cravate!** *iron* it was a real waste of time putting a OU my tie on! ▪ **il s'est donné beaucoup de ~ pour réussir** he went to a lot of trouble to succeed ▪ **prendre** OU **se donner la ~ de** to go to OU to take the trouble to ▪ **donnez-vous la ~ d'entrer** please do come in, (please) be so kind as to come in *sout* ▪ **il ne s'est même pas donné la ~ de répondre** he didn't even bother replying ▪ **valoir la ~** to be worth it ▪ **l'exposition vaut la ~ d'être vue** the exhibition is worth seeing ▶ **ne pas épargner** OU **ménager sa ~** to spare no effort ▪ **~ perdue : n'essaie pas de le convaincre, c'est ~ perdue** don't try to persuade him, it's a waste of time OU you'd be wasting your breath
2. [difficulté] : **avoir de la ~ à : avoir de la ~ à marcher** to have trouble OU difficulty walking ▪ **avoir ~ à** *sout* **: j'ai ~ à vous croire** I find it difficult OU hard to believe you ▶ **elle a eu toutes les ~s du monde à venir à la réunion** she had a terrible time OU the devil's own job getting to the meeting ▪ **être (bien) en ~ de : je serais bien en ~ de vous l'expliquer** I'd have a hard job explaining it to you, I wouldn't really know how to explain it to you ▪ **n'être pas en ~ pour** *sout* **: je ne suis pas en ~ pour y aller** it's no trouble for me to get there, I'll have no problem getting there.
◆ **à peine** *loc adv* **1.** [presque pas] hardly, barely, scarcely ▪ **j'arrive à ~ à soulever mon sac** I can hardly OU barely lift my bag ▪ **elle sait à ~ lire** she can hardly OU barely read ▪ **c'est à ~ si je l'ai entrevu** I only just caught a glimpse of him **2.** [tout juste] barely ▪ **il était à ~ dix heures** it was only just ten o'clock ▪ **il y a à ~ une semaine/deux heures** not quite a week/two hours ago, barely a week/two hours ago ▪ **elle gagne à ~ de quoi payer son loyer** she barely earns enough OU she only just earns enough to pay her rent **3.** [à l'instant] just **4.** [aussitôt] : **à ~ guérie, elle a repris le travail** no sooner had she recovered than she went back to work ▪ **à ~... que : à ~ était-elle couchée que le téléphone se mit à sonner** no sooner had she gone to bed than OU she'd only just gone to bed when the phone rang.
◆ **avec peine** *loc adv* **1.** [difficilement] with difficulty ▪ **il monte l'escalier avec ~** he has trouble climbing stairs **2.** *sout* [à regret] : **je vous quitte avec ~** it is with deep regret that I leave you *sout*.
◆ **sans peine** *loc adv* **1.** [aisément] without difficulty, easily ▪ **je suis arrivé à le faire en deux heures sans ~** I had no trouble doing it in two hours **2.** [sans regret] with no regrets, with a light heart.
◆ **sous peine de** *loc prép* : **'défense de fumer sous ~ d'amende'** 'smokers will be prosecuted' ▪ **sous ~ de mort** on pain of death.

PEINE DE MORT
The death penalty was abolished in France in 1981.

peiner [4] [pene] ◇ *vt* [attrister] to upset, to distress ▪ **je suis peiné par ton attitude** I'm unhappy about your attitude.
◇ *vi* **1.** [personne] to have trouble OU difficulty ▪ **j'ai peiné pour terminer dans les délais** I had to struggle to finish OU I had a lot of trouble finishing on time **2.** [machine] to strain, to labour ▪ **on entendait un moteur ~ dans la montée** you could hear a car engine toiling up the hill.

peint, e [pɛ̃, ɛ̃t] *pp* ▷ **peindre**.

peintre [pɛ̃tr] *nmf* **1.** [artiste] painter **2.** [artisan, ouvrier] painter ▪ **~ en bâtiment** house painter ▪ **~ de décors** specialist decorator ▪ **~ en lettres** signwriter **3.** *fig* [écrivain] portrayer ▪ **c'est un excellent ~ de la vie à la campagne** his depictions of country life are superb.

peintre-décorateur [pɛ̃trədekɔratœr] (*pl* **peintres-décorateurs**) *nm* painter and decorator.

peinture [pɛ̃tyr] *nf*

A. SENS GÉNÉRAL
B. COMME ART
C. DESCRIPTION

A. SENS GÉNÉRAL
1. [substance] paint ▪ **~ à l'eau** CONSTR water OU water-based paint ▪ **~ à l'huile** ART oil paint
2. [action] painting ▪ **faire de la ~ au rouleau** to paint with a roller
3. [couche de matière colorante] paintwork ▪ **donner un petit coup de ~ à qqch** to freshen sthg up, to give sthg a lick of paint ▪ **la ~ de la grille est écaillée** the paintwork on the gate is flaking off ▪ **'~ fraîche'** 'wet paint' ▪ **refaire la ~ d'une porte** to repaint a door ▪ **refaire la ~ d'une pièce** to redecorate a room

B. COMME ART

1. ART [art et technique] painting ▪ **~ au doigt** finger-painting ▪ **~ sur soie** silk painting, painting
2. [œuvre] painting, picture, canvas ➊ **une ~ murale** a mural ▪ **~s rupestres** cave paintings ▪ **je ne peux pas la voir en ~** *fam* I can't stand *OU* stick *UK* the sight of her
3. [ensemble d'œuvres peintes] painting ▪ **la ~ flamande** Flemish painting

C. DESCRIPTION

portrayal, picture ▪ **une ~ de la société médiévale** a picture of mediaeval society.

peinturlurer [3] [pẽtyrlyre] *vt fam* to daub with paint.
◆ **se peinturlurer** *vp (emploi réfléchi) fam* **elle s'était peinturluré le visage** she'd plastered make-up on her face.

péjoratif, ive [peʒɔratif, iv] *adj* pejorative, derogatory.
◆ **péjoratif** *nm* pejorative (term).

péjorativement [peʒɔrativmɑ̃] *adv* pejoratively, derogatorily.

Pékin [pekɛ̃] *npr* Peking.

pékinois, e [pekinwa, az] *adj* Pekinese, Pekingese.
◆ **Pékinois, e** *nm, f* Pekinese, Pekingese (person) ▪ **les Pékinois** the people of Peking.
◆ **pékinois** *nm* **1.** LING Pekinese, Mandarin (Chinese) **2.** ZOOL Pekinese, Pekingese.

PEL, Pel [pɛl, peœɛl] *nm* = **plan d'épargne logement**.

pelade [pəlad] *nf* MÉD alopecia areata, pelada.

pelage [pəlaʒ] *nm* coat, fur.

pélagique [pelaʒik] *adj* BIOL & GÉOL pelagic.

pelé, e [pəle] *adj* **1.** [chat, renard, fourrure] mangy **2.** [sans végétation] bare **3.** [fruit] peeled.
◆ **pelé** *nm fam* **1.** [chauve] bald *OU* bald-headed man **2.** *loc* **il y avait trois ~s et un tondu** there was one man and his dog *UK*, there was hardly anyone there.

Pelée [pəle] *npr* : **la montagne ~** Mount Pelée.

pêle-mêle [pɛlmɛl] ◇ *adv* in a jumble, every which way, pell-mell ▪ **les draps et les couvertures étaient ~ sur le lit** sheets and covers were all jumbled up *OU* in a heap on the bed ▪ **les spectateurs se sont engouffrés ~ dans la salle** the spectators piled pell-mell into the room.
◇ *nm inv* [cadre pour photos] multiple (photo) frame.

peler [25] [pəle] ◇ *vt* **1.** [fruit, légume] to peel **2.** ▲ *loc* **~ le jonc à qqn** to get on sb's wick△ *UK OU* nerves.
◇ *vi* **1.** [peau] to peel ▪ **j'ai le dos qui pèle** my back's peeling **2.** *fam loc* **~ de froid : on pèle (de froid) ici** it's dead cold *OU* freezing in here.
◆ **se peler** *vpi fam* : **qu'est-ce qu'on se pèle ici!** it's freezing in here!

pèlerin [pɛlrɛ̃] *nm* **1.** RELIG pilgrim **2.** ZOOL [requin] basking shark ▪ [faucon] peregrine falcon **3.** *fam* [individu] guy, bloke *UK*, character.

pèlerinage [pɛlrinaʒ] *nm* **1.** [voyage] pilgrimage ▪ **faire un *OU* aller en ~ à Lourdes** to go on a pilgrimage to Lourdes **2.** [endroit] place of pilgrimage.

pèlerine [pɛlrin] *nf* pelerine.

pélican [pelikɑ̃] *nm* pelican.

pelisse [pəlis] *nf* pelisse.

pellagre [pelagr] *nf* pellagra.

pellagreux, euse [pelagrø, øz] ◇ *adj* pellagrous.
◇ *nm, f* pellagra sufferer.

pelle [pɛl] *nf* **1.** [pour ramasser] shovel ▪ [pour creuser] spade ▪ **~ à charbon** coal shovel ▪ **~ à ordures** dustpan **2.** CULIN : **~ à poisson/tarte** fish/pie slice **3.** TRAV PUB : **~ mécanique** [sur roues] mechanical shovel ; [sur chenilles] excavator **4.** [extrémité d'un aviron] (oar) blade **5.** *fam loc* **(se) prendre *OU* (se) ramasser une ~** [tomber, échouer] to come a cropper *UK*, to take a spill *US* ▪ **rouler une ~ à qqn** to give sb a French kiss.
◆ **à la pelle** *loc adv* **1.** [avec une pelle] : **ramasser la neige à la ~** to shovel up the snow **2.** [en grande quantité] in huge numbers ▪ **gagner *OU* ramasser de l'argent à la ~** to earn huge amounts of money.

pelle-bêche [pɛlbɛʃ] (*pl* **pelles-bêches**) *nf* digging shovel.

pelle-pioche [pɛlpjɔʃ] (*pl* **pelles-pioches**) *nf combined pick and hoe.*

pelletée [pɛlte] *nf* **1.** [de terre - ramassée] shovelful ; [- creusée] spadeful **2.** *fam* [grande quantité] heap, pile.

pelleter [27] [pɛlte] *vt* to shovel (up).

pelleterie [pɛltri] *nf* **1.** [art] fur dressing **2.** [peaux] peltry, pelts **3.** [commerce] fur trade.

pelleteuse [pɛltøz] *nf* mechanical shovel *OU* digger ▪ **~ chargeuse** loading shovel, wheel loader.

pellicule [pelikyl] *nf* **1.** [peau] skin, film **2.** [mince croûte] film, thin layer ▪ **une ~ de glace sur la mare** a thin layer of ice over the pond **3.** [pour emballer] : **~ cellulosique** regenerated cellulose film *OU* foil **4.** PHOTO film ▪ **une ~** [bobine] a reel (of film) ; [chargeur] a (roll of) film.
◆ **pellicules** *nfpl* [dans les cheveux] dandruff *(U)* ▪ **avoir des ~s** to have dandruff.

Péloponnèse [pelɔpɔnɛz] *npr m* : **le ~** the Peloponnese.

pelotage [pəlɔtaʒ] *nm fam* (heavy) petting, necking.

pelotari [pəlɔtari] *nm* pelota player, pelotari.

pelote [pəlɔt] *nf* **1.** [de ficelle, de coton] ball ▪ **une ~ de laine** a ball of wool ▪ **faire sa ~** *fam* to make one's nest egg *OU* one's pile ▪ **mettre de la laine en ~** to ball wool **2.** *Québec* [boule] : **~ de neige** snowball **3.** COUT [coussinet] pincushion **4.** ENTOM (sticky) pad **5.** ORNITH : **~ de régurgitation** regurgitation pellet **6.** PÊCHE pellet **7.** SPORT pelota ▪ **jouer à la ~ basque** to play pelota.

peloter [3] [plɔte] *vt fam* to grope.
◆ **se peloter** *vp (emploi réciproque) fam* to neck ▪ **ils se sont pelotés pendant tout le trajet** they spent the whole journey necking.

peloteur, euse [plɔtœr, øz] *nm, f fam* : **quel ~!** what a groper!

peloton [pəlɔtɔ̃] *nm* **1.** MIL [division] platoon ▪ [unité] squad ▪ **~ d'exécution** firing squad ▪ **suivre *OU* faire le ~ (d'instruction)** to attend the training unit **2.** SPORT pack ▪ **être dans le ~ de tête** to be up with the leaders ; *fig* to be among the front runners **3.** [de coton, de laine] small ball.

pelotonner [3] [pəlɔtɔne] *vt* [laine] to wind up into a ball.
◆ **se pelotonner** *vpi* to curl up.

pelouse [pəluz] *nf* **1.** [terrain] lawn ▪ [herbe] grass ▪ **'~ interdite'** 'keep off the grass' **2.** SPORT field, ground ▪ [d'un champ de courses] paddock **3.** GÉOGR [prairie] short-grass prairie.

peluche [pəlyʃ] *nf* **1.** [jouet] cuddly toy ▪ **elle garde toutes ses ~s sur son lit** she keeps all her soft *OU* cuddly toys on her bed **2.** TEXT plush **3.** [poussière] (piece of) fluff *(U)*.
◆ **en peluche** *loc adj* : **chien/canard en ~** (cuddly) toy dog/duck.

peluché, e [pəlyʃe] *adj* **1.** [à poils longs] fluffy **2.** [usé] threadbare, shiny.

pelucher [3] [pəlyʃe] *vi* to pill.

pelucheux, euse [pəlyʃø, øz] *adj* **1.** [tissu] fluffy **2.** [fruit] downy.

pelure [pəlyr] *nf* **1.** [peau] peel *(U)* ▪ **~ d'oignon** onionskin (paper) **2.** *fam* [vêtement] coat.

pelvien, enne [pɛlvjɛ̃, ɛn] *adj* [cavité, organe] pelvic.

pelvis [pɛlvis] *nm* pelvis.

pénal, e, aux [penal, o] *adj* [droit] criminal ▪ [réforme] penal.

pénalement [penalmɑ̃] *adv* penally ▪ **être ~ responsable** to be liable in criminal law.

pénalisant, e [penalizɑ̃, ɑ̃t] *adj* disadvantageous, detrimental ▪ **une mesure ~e pour certaines catégories d'usagers** a measure which will penalize certain categories of users.

pénalisation [penalizasjɔ̃] *nf* **1.** SPORT penalty (for infringement) ▪ **points de ~** ÉQUIT faults, penalty points **2.** [désavantage] penalization.

pénaliser [3] [penalize] *vt* **1.** SPORT to penalize **2.** [désavantager] to penalize, to put *ou* to place at a disadvantage ▪ **ces enfants sont pénalisés dès leur entrée à l'école** these children are disadvantaged from the moment they start school.

pénaliste [penalist] *nmf* specialist in criminal law.

pénalité [penalite] *nf* **1.** FIN penalty ▪ **~ de retard** penalty for late *ou* overdue payment **2.** SPORT penalty ▪ **coup de pied de ~** penalty kick ▪ **jouer les ~s** to go into injury time.

penalty [penalti] (*pl* **penaltys** *ou* **penalties**) *nm* penalty (kick) ▪ **siffler/tirer un ~** to award/to take a penalty.

pénard [penar] = **peinard**.

pénates [penat] *nmpl* **1.** MYTHOL Penates **2.** *fam fig* **regagner ses ~** to go home.

penaud, e [pəno, od] *adj* sheepish, contrite ▪ **d'un air tout ~** sheepishly, with a hangdog look.

penchant [pɑ̃ʃɑ̃] *nm* **1.** [pour quelque chose] propensity, liking, penchant ▪ **un petit ~ pour le chocolat** a weakness for chocolate ▪ **de mauvais ~s** evil tendencies **2.** [pour quelqu'un] fondness, liking ▪ **éprouver un ~ pour qqn** to be fond of sb.

penché, e [pɑ̃ʃe] *adj* **1.** [tableau] crooked, askew ▪ [mur, écriture] sloping, slanting ▪ [objet] tilting **2.** [personne] : **il est toujours ~ sur ses livres** he's always got his head in a book.

pencher [3] [pɑ̃ʃe] ◇ *vi* **1.** *(aux être)* [être déséquilibré - entassement] to lean (over), to tilt ; [- bateau] to list ▪ **la tour/le mur penche vers la droite** the tower/the wall leans to the right ▪ **le miroir penche encore un peu, redresse-le** the mirror is still crooked, straighten it ▪ **faire ~ la balance en faveur de/contre qqn** *fig* to tip the scales in favour of/against sb **2.** *(aux être)* [être en pente] to slope (away) ▪ **le sol penche** the floor slopes *ou* is on an incline **3.** *(aux avoir)* **~ pour** [préférer] to be inclined to, to incline towards ▪ **je pencherais en sa faveur** I would tend to agree with him ▪ **la décision a l'air de ~ en ma faveur** the decision seems to weigh in my favour.
◇ *vt* to tilt, to tip up *(sép)* ▪ **il pencha la tête en arrière pour l'embrasser** he leaned backwards to kiss her ▪ **elle pencha la tête au-dessus du parapet** she leaned over the parapet.
◆ **se pencher** *vpi* [s'incliner] to lean, to bend ▪ **elle se pencha sur le berceau** she leaned over the cradle ▪ **'ne pas se ~ au-dehors'** 'do not lean out of the window'.
◆ **se pencher sur** *vp+prép* to look into.

pendable [pɑ̃dabl] *adj* : **ce n'est pas un cas ~** it's not a hanging matter ▪ **jouer un tour ~ à qqn** to play a rotten trick on sb.

pendaison [pɑ̃dɛzɔ̃] *nf* hanging ▪ **mort par ~** death by hanging.
◆ **pendaison de crémaillère** *nf* housewarming (party).

pendant[1] [pɑ̃dɑ̃] *prép* [au cours de] during ▪ [insistant sur la durée] for ▪ **quelqu'un a appelé ~ l'heure du déjeuner** somebody called while you were at lunch *ou* during your lunch break ▪ **~ ce temps-là** in the meantime, meanwhile ▪ **je suis là ~ tout l'été** I'm here during the *ou* for the whole (of the) summer ▪ **j'y ai habité ~ un an** I lived there for a year ▪ **nous avons roulé ~ 20 km** we drove for 20 km.
◆ **pendant que** *loc conj* **1.** [tandis que] while **2.** [tant que] while ▪ **~ que tu y es, pourras-tu passer à la banque?** while you're there *ou* at it, could you stop off at the bank? ▪ **traite-moi de menteur ~ que tu y es!** call me a liar while you're at it! ▪ **~ que j'y pense, voici l'argent que je te dois** while I think of it, here's the money I owe you **3.** [puisque] since, while ▪ **allons-y ~ que nous y sommes** let's go, since we're here.

pendant[2]**, e** [pɑ̃dɑ̃, ɑ̃t] *adj* **1.** [tombant] hanging ▪ **la langue ~e** [de chaleur, de fatigue] panting ; [de convoitise] drooling ▪ **chien aux oreilles ~es** dog with drooping *ou* droopy ears **2.** DR [en cours - d'instruction] pending ; [- de résolution] pending, being dealt with.
◆ **pendant** *nm* **1.** [bijou] pendant ▪ **~ (d'oreilles)** (pendant) earring **2.** [symétrique - d'une chose] : **faire ~ à qqch** to match sthg ▪ **se faire ~** to match, to be a matching pair ▪ [alter ego - d'une personne] counterpart, opposite number.

pendeloque [pɑ̃dlɔk] *nf* **1.** [de boucle d'oreille] pendant, eardrop **2.** [d'un lustre] pendant, drop **3.** [d'une chèvre] dewlap.

pendentif [pɑ̃dɑ̃tif] *nm* **1.** [bijou] pendant **2.** ARCHIT pendentive.

penderie [pɑ̃dri] *nf* [meuble] wardrobe ▪ [pièce] walk-in wardrobe *ou* closet ▪ **il n'y a pas de ~ dans la chambre** there's nowhere to hang (one's) clothes in the room.

pendiller [3] [pɑ̃dije] *vi* to hang (down), to dangle ▪ **des fanions pendillaient à la fenêtre** pennants hung from the window.

Pendjab [pɛndʒab] *npr m* : **(le) ~** Punjab.

pendouiller [3] [pɑ̃duje] *vi fam* to hang down, to dangle ▪ **ton ourlet pendouille** your hem is down.

pendre [73] [pɑ̃dr] ◇ *vt* **1.** [accrocher] to hang (up) ▪ **~ un tableau à un clou** to hang a picture from a nail ▪ **~ ses vêtements sur des cintres** to put one's clothes on hangers *ou* coathangers ▪ **~ son linge sur un fil** to hang up one's washing on a line ➋ **~ la crémaillère** to have a housewarming (party) **2.** [exécuter] to hang ▪ **il sera pendu à l'aube** he'll hang *ou* be hanged at dawn ▪ **pendez-les haut et court** hang them high ➋ **qu'il aille se faire ~ ailleurs** *fam* he can go to blazes *ou* go hang ▪ **je veux bien être pendu si j'y comprends quoi que ce soit** I'll be hanged if I understand any of it
3. *fig* **être pendu à : être pendu au cou de qqn** to cling to sb ▪ **être (toujours) pendu après qqn** *ou* **aux basques de qqn** to dog sb's every footstep, to hang around sb ▪ **être pendu au téléphone** to spend hours *ou* one's life on the phone.
◇ *vi* **1.** [être accroché] to hang ▪ **du linge pendait aux fenêtres** washing was hanging out of the windows ➋ **ça te pend au nez** *fam* you've got it coming to you
2. [retomber] to hang ▪ **sa natte pendait dans son dos** her plait was hanging down her back ▪ **des rideaux qui pendent jusqu'à terre** full-length curtains.
◆ **se pendre** ◇ *vp (emploi réfléchi)* [se suicider] to hang o.s.
◇ *vpi* [s'accrocher] to hang ▪ **les chauves-souris se pendent aux branches** the bats hang from the branches ▪ **se ~ au cou de qqn** to fling one's arms around sb's neck.

pendu, e [pɑ̃dy] hanged man (*f* woman) ▪ **le jeu du ~** (the game of) hangman.

pendulaire [pɑ̃dylɛr] ◇ *adj* oscillating, pendulous ▪ **migration ~** commuting.
◇ *nmf* commuter.

pendule [pɑ̃dyl] ◇ *nm* [instrument, balancier] pendulum.
◇ *nf* [horloge] clock ▪ **remettre les ~s à l'heure** *fig* to set the record straight ▪ **en faire une ~** *fam* to make a big fuss.

pendulette [pɑ̃dylɛt] *nf* small clock ▪ **~ de voyage** travel (alarm) clock.

pêne [pɛn] *nm* bolt (of lock) ▪ **~ demi-tour** latch.

Pénélope [penelɔp] *npr* Penelope ▪ **c'est un travail de ~** it's like repainting the Forth Bridge *UK*.

pénétrant, e [penetrɑ̃, ɑ̃t] *adj* **1.** [froid, pluie] : **une petite bruine ~e** the kind of drizzle that soaks one through ▪ **le froid était ~** it was bitterly cold **2.** [fort] strong, penetrating ▪ **un parfum ~** an overpowering perfume **3.** [clairvoyant] sharp, penetrating, acute ▪ **avoir un esprit ~** to be sharp ▪ **lancer à qqn un regard ~** to give sb a piercing look.

pénétration [penetrasjɔ̃] *nf* **1.** [par un solide] penetration ▪ [par un liquide] seepage, seeping ▪ [par un corps gras] absorption **2.** [acte sexuel] penetration **3.** [invasion] penetration, invasion ▪ **une tentative de ~** an attempted raid **4.** *fig* [perspicacité] perception ■ **un esprit plein de ~** a very perceptive *ou* sharp mind ■ **avec ~** perspicaciously **5.** COMM [d'un produit] (market) penetration.

pénétré, e [penetre] *adj* **1.** [rempli] : **~ de : être ~ de joie/honte** to be filled with joy/shame ■ **il se sentit ~ de la vérité de ces paroles** he felt convinced of the truth of these words ■ **~ de sa propre importance** *péj* self-important **2.** [convaincu] earnest, serious.

pénétrer [18] [penetre] ◇ *vi* **1.** [entrer] to go, to enter ■ **ils ont réussi à ~ en Suisse** they managed to cross into *ou* to enter Switzerland ■ **~ dans la maison de qqn** [avec sa permission] to enter sb's house ; [par effraction] to break into sb's house ■ **comment faire pour ~ dans le monde de la publicité?** how can one get into advertising? ■ **~ sur un marché** to break into a market, to make inroads into *ou* on a market ‖ [passer] to go, to penetrate ■ **la balle a pénétré dans la cuisse** the bullet entered the thigh ‖ [s'infiltrer] to seep, to penetrate ■ **l'eau a très vite pénétré dans la cale** water quickly flooded into the hold ■ **le vent pénètre par la cheminée** the wind comes in by the chimney ■ **faire ~ la crème en massant doucement** gently rub *ou* massage the cream in

2. *sout* **~ dans** [approfondir] to go (deeper) into ■ **~ dans les détails d'une théorie** to go into the details of a theory.

◇ *vt* **1.** [traverser] to penetrate, to go in *ou* into, to get in *ou* into ■ **un froid glacial me pénétra** I was chilled to the bone *ou* to the marrow

2. [imprégner] to spread into *ou* through ■ **ces idées ont pénétré toutes les couches de la société** these ideas have spread through all levels of society

3. [sexuellement] to penetrate

4. [deviner] to penetrate, to perceive ■ **~ un mystère** to get to the heart of a mystery ■ **~ le sens d'un texte** to grasp the meaning of a text ■ **~ les intentions de qqn** to guess sb's intentions.

◆ **se pénétrer de** *vp+prép* : **se ~ d'une vérité** to become convinced of a truth ■ **se ~ d'un principe** to internalize a principle ■ **il faut vous ~ de l'importance du facteur religieux** you must be aware of *ou* you must understand the importance of the religious element.

pénible [penibl] *adj* **1.** [épuisant] hard, tough, tiring ■ **un travail ~** a laborious job ■ **elle trouve de plus en plus ~ de monter les escaliers** it gets harder and harder for her to climb the stairs **2.** [attristant] distressing, painful ■ **en parler m'est très ~** I find it difficult to talk about (it) ■ **ma présence lui est ~** my being here bothers him **3.** [difficile à supporter] tiresome ■ **caractère ~** disagreeableness ■ **je trouve ça vraiment ~** I find it a real pain ■ **tu es ~, tu sais!** you're a real pain in the neck *ou* a nuisance!

péniblement [peniblәmɑ̃] *adv* **1.** [avec difficulté] laboriously, with difficulty **2.** [tout juste] just about ■ **j'arrive ~ à boucler les fins de mois** I barely manage to make ends meet at the end of the month.

péniche [peniʃ] *nf* [large] barge ■ [étroite] narrow boat ■ **~ de débarquement** MIL landing craft.

pénicilline [penisilin] *nf* penicillin.

péninsulaire [penɛ̃sylɛr] ◇ *adj* peninsular.
◇ *nmf* inhabitant of a peninsula.

péninsule [penɛ̃syl] *nf* peninsula ■ **la ~ Ibérique** the Iberian Peninsula.

pénis [penis] *nm* penis.

pénitence [penitɑ̃s] *nf* **1.** RELIG [repentir] penitence ■ [punition] penance ■ [sacrement] penance, sacrament of reconciliation ■ **faire ~** to repent **2.** [punition] punishment ■ **mettre qqn en ~** to punish sb.

pénitencier [penitɑ̃sje] *nm* **1.** [prison] prison, jail, penitentiary *US* **2.** RELIG penitentiary.

pénitent, e [penitɑ̃, ɑ̃t] ◇ *adj* penitent.
◇ *nm, f* penitent.

pénitentiaire [penitɑ̃sjɛr] *adj* prison *(modif)*.

pénitentiel, elle [penitɑ̃sjɛl] *adj* penitential, penitence *(modif)*.

penne [pɛn] *nf* **1.** ARM & ORNITH penna **2.** [d'une antenne] tip.

Pennsylvanie [pɛnsilvani] *npr f* : **(la) ~** Pennsylvania.

penny [peni] *nm* **1.** (*pl* pence [pɛns]) [somme] penny ■ **ça coûte 90 pence** it costs 90 pence *ou* 90 p **2.** (*pl* pennies [peniz]) [pièce] penny.

pénombre [penɔ̃br] *nf* **1.** [obscurité] half-light, dim light ■ **dans la ~** *pr* in the half-light ; *fig* in the background, out of the limelight **2.** ASTRON penumbra.

pensable [pɑ̃sabl] *adj* : **à cette époque-là, de telles vitesses n'étaient pas ~s** in those days, such speeds were unthinkable ■ **cette histoire n'est pas ~!** this story is incredible!

pensant, e [pɑ̃sɑ̃, ɑ̃t] *adj sout* thinking.

pense-bête [pɑ̃sbɛt] (*pl* **pense-bêtes**) *nm* reminder ■ **fais-toi un ~ pour ne pas oublier de téléphoner** make a note of it somewhere so that you don't forget to phone.

pensée [pɑ̃se] *nf* **1.** [idée] thought, idea ■ **la seule ~ d'une seringue me donne des sueurs froides** the very thought of a needle leaves me in a cold sweat ■ **tout à la ~ de son rendez-vous, il n'a pas vu arriver la voiture** deeply absorbed in *ou* by the thought of his meeting, he didn't see the car (coming) ■ **être tout à** *ou* **perdu dans ses ~s** to be lost in thought ■ **avoir une bonne ~ pour qqn** to spare a kind thought for sb ■ **avoir de mauvaises ~s** [méchantes] to have evil thoughts ; [sexuelles] to indulge in immoral *ou* bad thoughts ■ **avoir de sombres ~s** to have gloomy thoughts

2. [façon de raisonner] thought ■ **elle a une ~ rigoureuse** she's a rigorous thinker ■ **avoir une ~ claire** to be clear-thinking

3. [opinion] thought, (way of) thinking ■ **j'avais deviné ta ~** I'd guessed what you'd been thinking ■ **aller au bout** *ou* **au fond de sa ~ : pour aller jusqu'au bout** *ou* **fond de ma ~ je dirais que...** to be absolutely frank, I'd say that... ■ **allez donc jusqu'au bout de votre ~** come on, say what you really think *ou* what's really on your mind

4. [esprit] mind ■ **nous sommes avec vous par la** *ou* **en ~** our thoughts are with you ■ **je les vois en ~** I can see them in my mind *ou* in my mind's eye ■ **transportez-vous par la ~ dans une contrée exotique** let your thoughts take you to an exotic land

5. PHILOS thought ◗ **~ conceptuelle/logique/mathématique** conceptual/logical/mathematical thought ■ **'Pensées'** *Pascal* 'Pensées'

6. [idéologie] (way of) thinking ■ **la ~ chrétienne** Christian thinking, the Christian way of thinking

7. [dans les formules] : **avec nos affectueuses** *ou* **meilleures ~s** with (all) our love *ou* fondest regards

8. BOT pansy.

◆ **pensées** *nfpl* LITTÉR & PHILOS thoughts.

penser [3] [pɑ̃se] ◇ *vt* **1.** [croire] to think, to assume, to suppose ■ **qu'en penses-tu?** what do you think of it? ■ **je ne sais qu'en ~** I don't know what to think *ou* I can't make up my mind about it ■ **je pense que oui** (yes,) I think so ■ **je pense que non** (no,) I don't think so *ou* I think not ■ **je pense que tu devrais lui dire** I think you should tell him ■ **je n'en pense que du bien/mal** I have the highest/lowest opinion of it ■ **qu'est-ce qui te fait ~ qu'il ment?** what makes you think he's lying? ■ **quoi qu'on pense** whatever people (may) think ■ **quoi que tu puisses ~** whatever you (may) think ■ *(avec un adj attribut)* **je le pensais diplomate** I thought him tactful, I thought he was tactful ■ **je pensais la chose faisable, mais on me dit que non** I thought it was possible (to do), but I'm told it's not

2. [escompter] : **je pense partir demain** I'm thinking of *ou* planning on *ou* reckoning on leaving tomorrow ■ **je pense avoir réussi** [examen] I think I passed

3. [avoir à l'esprit] to think ■ **je ne sais jamais ce que tu penses** I can never tell what you're thinking *ou* what's on your mind ■ **dire tout haut ce que certains** *ou* **d'autres pensent tout bas** to say out loud what others are thinking in private ◗ **il a marché dans ce que je pense** he trod in some you-know-what ■ **tu vas prendre un coup de pied là où je pense!** you're going to get a kick up the backside! ■ **son contrat, il peut se le mettre (là) où je pense!**△ he can stuff his bloody contract!△

4. [comprendre] to think, to realize, to imagine ▪ **pense qu'elle a près de cent ans** you must realize that she's nearly a hundred
5. [se rappeler] to remember, to think ▪ **je n'ai plus pensé que c'était lundi** I forgot *ou* I never thought it was Monday
6. [pour exprimer la surprise, l'approbation, l'ironie] : **je n'aurais/on n'aurait jamais pensé que...** I'd never/nobody'd ever have thought that... ▪ **qui aurait pu ~ que...** who'd have thought *ou* guessed that... ▪ **quand je pense que...** to think that... ▪ **quand on pense qu'il n'y avait pas le téléphone à l'époque!** when you think that there was no such thing as the phone in those days! ➋ **lui, me dire merci? tu penses** *ou* **penses-tu** *ou* **pense donc!** *fam* him? thank me? I should be so lucky *ou* you must be joking! ▪ **tu penses bien que je lui ai tout raconté!** *fam* I told him everything, as you can well imagine ▪ **tu viendras à la fête? – je pense bien!** *fam* will you come to the party? – just (you) try and stop me! ▪ **il est content? – je pense** *ou* **tu penses bien!** *fam* is he pleased? – you bet! ▪ **tu penses bien que le voleur ne t'a pas attendu!** you can bet your life the thief didn't leave his name and address!
7. [concevoir] to think out *ou* through *(sép)* ▪ **une architecture bien pensée** a well-planned *ou* well-thought out architectural design
8. *litt* [être sur le point de] : **je pensai m'évanouir** I all but fainted ▪ **elle pensa devenir folle** she was very nearly driven to distraction.
<> *vi* **1.** [réfléchir] to think, to ponder ▪ **~ tout haut** to think aloud *ou* out loud ▪ **donner** *ou* **laisser à ~** to make one think, to start one thinking
2. [avoir une opinion] : **je n'ai jamais pensé comme toi** I never did agree with you *ou* share your views ▪ **je ne dis rien mais je n'en pense pas moins** I say nothing but that doesn't stop me thinking.
◆ **penser à** *v+prép* **1.** [envisager] to think about *ou* of *(insép)* ▪ **pense un peu à ce que tu dis!** just think for a moment (of) what you're saying! ▪ **vous éviteriez des ennuis, pensez-y** you'd save yourself a lot of trouble, think it over! ▪ **c'est simple mais il fallait y ~** it's a simple enough idea but somebody had to think of it (in the first place) ▪ **sans y ~** [par automatisme] without thinking ▪ **sans ~ à mal** without *ou* not meaning any harm (by it) ➋ **tu n'y penses pas** *fam* you can't be serious
2. [rêver à] to think about *ou* of *(insép)* ▪ **je pense à toi** [dans une lettre] I'm thinking of you
3. [se préoccuper de] to think of, to care about ▪ **elle ne pense qu'à elle** she only cares about herself ▪ **essaye de ~ un peu aux autres** try to think of others ➋ **il ne pense qu'à ça!** *fam euphém* he's got a one-track mind
4. [se remémorer] to think *ou* to remember to ▪ **et mon livre? – j'y pense, je te le rapporte demain** what about my book? – I haven't forgotten (it), I'll bring it back tomorrow ▪ **dis donc, j'y pense, qu'est devenu le vieux Georges?** by the way, whatever happened to old George? ▪ **tu ne penses à rien!** you've a head like a sieve! ▪ **n'y pense plus!** forget (all about) it! ▪ **faire ~ à : cela me fait ~ à mon frère** it reminds me of my brother ▪ **fais-moi ~ à l'appeler** remind me to call her.

penseur, euse [pɑ̃sœr, øz] *nm, f* thinker ▪ **'le Penseur'** *Rodin* 'The Thinker'.

pensif, ive [pɑ̃sif, iv] *adj* thoughtful, pensive, reflective ▪ **elle était toute pensive** she was lost in thought ▪ **d'un air ~** thoughtfully.

pension [pɑ̃sjɔ̃] *nf* **1.** [somme allouée] pension ▪ **toucher une ~** to draw a pension ➋ **~ alimentaire** maintenance *UK*, alimony *US* ▪ **~ de guerre** war pension ▪ **~ d'invalidité** disability pension ▪ **~ de retraite** (retirement *ou* old-age) pension ▪ **~ de réversion** survivor's pension **2.** [logement et nourriture] board and lodging ▪ **prendre ~ chez qqn** [client] to take board and lodgings with sb ; [ami] to be staying with sb ▪ **prendre qqn en ~** to take sb in as a lodger ➋ **être en ~ complète** to be on full board **3.** [hôtel] : **~ (de famille)** ≃ boarding house, ≃ guesthouse **4.** ÉDUC boarding school ▪ **être en ~** to be a boarder *ou* at boarding school ▪ **envoyer qqn en ~** to send sb to boarding school.

pensionnaire [pɑ̃sjɔnɛr] *nmf* **1.** [d'un hôtel] guest, resident ▪ [d'un particulier] (paying) guest, lodger **2.** ÉDUC boarder **3.** [à la Comédie-Française] *actor or actress on a fixed salary with no share in the profits (as opposed to a "sociétaire").*

pensionnat [pɑ̃sjɔna] *nm* **1.** [école] boarding school **2.** [pensionnaires] boarders.

pensionné, e [pɑ̃sjɔne] <> *adj* : **elle est ~e à 75 %** her pension represents 75% of her income.
<> *nm, f* pensioner.

pensionner [3] [pɑ̃sjɔne] *vt* : **~ qqn** to (grant sb a) pension.

pensive [pɑ̃siv] *f* ▻ **pensif**.

pensivement [pɑ̃sivmɑ̃] *adv* pensively, thoughtfully, reflectively.

pensum [pɛ̃sɔm] *nm* **1.** ÉDUC & *vieilli* extra work *(to be done at home or in school time as punishment)*, lines *UK* **2.** [corvée] chore ▪ **quel ~!** *fam* what a drag *ou* nuisance!

pentaèdre [pɛ̃taɛdr] <> *adj* pentahedral.
<> *nm* pentahedron.

pentagone [pɛ̃tagɔn] *nm* pentagon.

Pentagone [pɛ̃tagɔn] *npr m* : **le ~** the Pentagon.

pentamètre [pɛ̃tamɛtr] *nm* pentameter.

Pentateuque [pɛ̃tatøk] *npr m* : **le ~** the Pentateuch.

pentathlon [pɛ̃tatlɔ̃] *nm* pentathlon.

pente [pɑ̃t] *nf* **1.** [inclinaison] slope, incline ▪ **une forte ~** a steep incline *ou* slope ▮ [descente, montée] slope ▪ **gravir une ~** to climb a slope **2.** TRAV PUB slope ▪ **une ~ de 10 %** a 1 in 10 gradient **3.** [penchant] inclination, leaning **4.** GÉOGR : **~ continentale** continental slope **5.** *loc* **être sur une mauvaise ~** to be heading for trouble ▪ **remonter la ~ : il a bien remonté la ~** [en meilleure santé] he's back on his feet again ; [financièrement] he's solvent again ▪ **être sur une ~ glissante** *ou* **savonneuse** to be on a slippery slope.
◆ **en pente** <> *loc adj* sloping ▪ **la route est en ~** the road is on a slope *ou* an incline ▪ **en ~ douce** sloping gently ▪ **en ~ raide** on a steep incline.
<> *loc adv* : **descendre/monter en ~ douce** to slope gently down/up ▪ **descendre/monter en ~ raide** to slope sharply down/up.

Pentecôte [pɑ̃tkot] *nf* **1.** [fête chrétienne] Whitsun, Pentecost ▪ **la semaine de la ~** Whit Week, Whitsuntide ▪ **dimanche de ~** Whit Sunday **2.** [fête juive] Shabuoth.

pentecôtiste [pɑ̃tkotist] *nmf* Pentecostalist.

pentu, e [pɑ̃ty] *adj* [chemin] steep, sloping ▪ [toit] sloping, slanting, pointed ▪ [comble] sloping.

pénultième [penyltjɛm] <> *adj* penultimate.
<> *nf* penultimate (syllable).

pénurie [penyri] *nf* **1.** [pauvreté] destitution, penury **2.** [manque] : **~ d'argent** shortage of money, money shortage ▪ **il y a (une) ~ de viande** there is a meat shortage, meat is in short supply.

PEP, Pep [pɛp] (*abr de* **plan d'épargne populaire**) *nm personal pension plan.*

pépé [pepe] *nm fam* **1.** [grand-père] granddad, grandpa, gramps *US* **2.** *péj* [vieillard] old codger *ou* boy *UK*, old-timer *US*.

pépée△ [pepe] *nf vieilli* chick.

pépère [pepɛr] *fam* <> *adj* [tranquille] (nice and) easy ▪ **un petit boulot ~** a cushy number *ou* little job ▪ **une petite vie ~** a cosy little life.
<> *nm* **1.** [grand-père] grandpa, granddad *UK*, gramps *US* **2.** *péj* [vieillard] old boy *ou* codger *UK*, old-timer *US* **3.** *loc* **gros ~** [avec affection] tubby ; [avec mépris] fat slob.

pépie [pepi] *nf* **1.** ORNITH pip **2.** *fam loc* **avoir la ~** to be parched.

pépier [9] [pepje] *vi* to chirp, to tweet, to twitter.

pépin [pepɛ̃] *nm* **1.** [de fruit] pip ▪ **~s de pomme/poire** apple/pear pips ▪ **des mandarines sans ~s** seedless tangerines **2.** *fam* [problème] hitch, snag ▪ **il m'arrive un gros ~** I'm in big trouble ▪ **en cas de ~** if there's a snug *ou* hitch **3.** *fam* [parapluie] umbrella, brolly *UK*.

Pépin [pepɛ̃] *npr* : **~ le Bref** Pepin the Short.

pépinière [pepinjɛr] *nf* **1.** BOT (tree) nursery **2.** *fig* **une ~ de futurs Prix Nobel** a breeding-ground for future Nobel prize-winners.

pépiniériste [pepinjerist] ◇ *adj* nursery *(modif)*.
◇ *nmf* nurseryman (*f* nurserywoman).

pépite [pepit] *nf* nugget ▪ **~ d'or** gold nugget.

péplum [peplɔm] *nm* **1.** [vêtement] peplum **2.** [film] epic.

PEPS (*abr de* **premier entré, premier sorti**) FIFO.

pepsine [pɛpsin] *nf* pepsin.

péquenaud, e△ [pekno, od], **péquenot, otte**△ [pekno, ɔt] *nm, f* [rustre] yokel.

péquiste [pekist] *Québec* ◇ *nmf member of the Parti Québecois.*
◇ *adj of the Parti Québecois.*

PER, Per *nm* = **plan d'épargne retraite**.

perçage [pɛrsaʒ] *nm* **1.** [d'un trou] drilling, boring **2.** TEXT punching.

percale [pɛrkal] *nf* percale.

perçant, e [pɛrsɑ̃, ɑ̃t] *adj* **1.** [voix] piercing, shrill ▪ [regard] piercing, sharp ▪ **cris ~s** [d'une personne] earsplitting screams ; [d'un oiseau] shrill cries ▪ **pousser des cris ~s** to scream loudly ▪ **avoir une vue ~e** to have a sharp eye **2.** [froid] : **le froid était ~** it was bitterly cold **3.** [outil] piercing.

perce [pɛrs] *nf* **1.** [outil] punch, drill, bore **2.** MUS bore.
◆ **en perce** *loc adv* : **mettre un tonneau en ~** to broach a barrel.

percée [pɛrse] *nf* **1.** [ouverture - dans le mur] opening ; [- dans une forêt] clearing **2.** SPORT break ▪ MIL breakthrough ▪ **une ~ à travers les lignes ennemies** a breakthrough into enemy lines **3.** ÉCON & TECHNOL breakthrough ▪ **faire une ~ dans un marché** to break into a market **4.** AÉRON instrument letdown.

percement [pɛrsəmɑ̃] *nm* **1.** [d'une route, d'un passage] building ▪ [d'une porte, d'une fenêtre] opening **2.** TRAV PUB cutting through.

perce-muraille [pɛrsmyraj] (*pl* **perce-murailles**) *nf* wall pellitory.

perce-neige [pɛrsənɛʒ] *nf & nm inv* snowdrop.

perce-oreille [pɛrsɔrɛj] (*pl* **perce-oreilles**) *nm* earwig.

percepteur, trice [pɛrsɛptœr, tris] *nm, f* tax inspector, taxman.

perceptibilité [pɛrsɛptibilite] *nf* perceptibility.

perceptible [pɛrsɛptibl] *adj* **1.** [sensible] perceptible ▪ **à peine ~** almost imperceptible **2.** DR & FIN liable for collection *ou* to be levied.

perceptiblement [pɛrsɛptibləmɑ̃] *adv* perceptibly.

perceptif, ive [pɛrsɛptif, iv] *adj* perceptive.

perception [pɛrsɛpsjɔ̃] *nf* **1.** [notion] perception, notion ▪ **avoir une ~ claire des problèmes** to be clearly aware of the problems **2.** PSYCHOL perception **3.** FIN & DR [encaissement] collection, levying ▪ **~ d'un impôt** collection of a tax ▮ [lieu] tax office *UK*, internal revenue office *US* ▪ [recouvrement] tax collecting.

percer [16] [pɛrse] ◇ *vt* **1.** [trouer - gén] to pierce (through) ▪ **la malle d'osier était percée au fond** there was a hole in the bottom of the wickerwork trunk ▪ **se faire ~ les oreilles** to have one's ears pierced ▪ **il a eu le tympan percé dans l'accident** he suffered a burst *ou* perforated eardrum in the accident ▪ **~ un trou** to drill a hole
2. CONSTR & TRAV PUB to open, to build ▪ **~ une porte dans un mur** to put a door in *ou* into a wall ▪ **~ un tunnel dans la montagne** to drive *ou* to build a tunnel through the mountain
3. [pénétrer avec difficulté] to push through ▪ **le soleil perça enfin le brouillard** at last the sun pierced through the fog ▪ **ses yeux avaient du mal à ~ l'obscurité** she had trouble making things out in the dark ▪ **~ un mystère** to solve a mystery ▮ [déchirer] to pierce, to tear, to rend *litt* ▪ **un bruit à vous ~ les oreilles** *ou* **tympans** an ear-splitting noise ➊ **~ qqn/qqch à jour** to see right through sb/sthg
4. MÉD : **~ la poche des eaux** to break the waters ▪ **il faut ~ l'abcès** the abscess will have to be lanced
5. [suj: bébé] : **~ ses dents** to be teething ▪ **~ une dent** to cut a tooth *ou* have a tooth coming through.
◇ *vi* **1.** [poindre] to come through ▪ **le soleil perce enfin** the sun's finally broken through ▪ **ses dents ont commencé à ~** his teeth have begun to come through
2. [abcès] to burst
3. [filtrer] to filter through, to emerge ▪ **elle ne laisse rien ~ de ce qu'elle ressent** she keeps her feelings well hidden
4. [réussir] to become famous ▪ **commencer à ~** to be on the way up ▪ **un jeune chanteur en train de ~** an up-and-coming young singer ▪ **~ sur le marché des disques compacts** to emerge as leader of the compact disc industry.

perceur, euse [pɛrsœr, øz] *nm, f* [personne] driller ▪ **~ de coffre-fort** safebreaker, safecracker.
◆ **perceuse** *nf* [machine-outil] drill ▪ **perceuse électrique** power drill.

perceuse-visseuse [pɛrsœzvisœz] (*pl* **perceuses-visseuses**) *nf* electric drill/screwdriver.

percevable [pɛrsəvabl] *adj* FIN & DR liable to be levied *ou* for collection.

percevoir [52] [pɛrsəvwar] *vt* **1.** [vibration, sensation, chaleur] to feel ▪ **j'ai cru ~ une nuance de mépris dans sa voix** I thought I detected a note of contempt in his voice **2.** FIN [rente, intérêt] to receive, to be paid ▪ [impôt] to collect.

perche [pɛrʃ] *nf* **1.** [pièce de bois] pole ▪ [tuteur] beanpole, stake ▪ SPORT pole ▪ **jeter** *ou* **tendre la ~ à qqn** *fig* to throw sb a line, to help sb out of a tight corner ▪ **prendre** *ou* **saisir la ~** *fig* to take *ou* to rise to the bait **2.** CINÉ & TV boom **3.** *fam* [personne] : **grande ~** beanpole **4.** ZOOL perch ▪ **~ truitée** black bass.

perchée [pɛrʃe] *nf* roost.

percher [3] [pɛrʃe] ◇ *vi* **1.** [oiseau] to perch ▪ [poule] to roost **2.** *fam* [habiter] to live, to hang out.
◇ *vt* [placer] to put ▪ **une petite église perchée en haut de la colline** *fig* a little church perched on top of the hill.
◆ **se percher** *vpi* **1.** [oiseau] to perch ▪ [poule] to roost **2.** *fam* [monter] to perch ▪ **ils se sont perchés sur le balcon pour mieux voir** they perched on the balcony to get a better view.

percheron [pɛrʃərɔ̃] *nm* ZOOL Percheron.

perchiste [pɛrʃist] *nmf* **1.** SPORT polevaulter **2.** CINÉ & TV boom (operator), boom man.

perchman [pɛrʃman] *nm* boom (operator), boom man.

perchoir [pɛrʃwar] *nm* **1.** [pour les oiseaux] perch ▪ [pour la volaille] roost **2.** POLIT *raised platform for the seat of the President of the French National Assembly.*

perclus, e [pɛrkly, yz] *adj* crippled, paralysed ▪ **être ~ de rhumatismes** to be stiff *ou* crippled with rheumatism ▪ **être ~ de douleur** to be paralysed with pain.

perçoir [pɛrswar] *nm* drill, borer.

perçoit, perçoivent *etc v* ▷ **percevoir**.

percolateur [pɛrkɔlatœr] *nm* coffee (percolating) machine.

percolation [pɛrkɔlasjɔ̃] *nf* percolation.

perçu, e [pɛrsy] *pp* ▷ **percevoir**.

percussion [pɛrkysjɔ̃] *nf* MÉD, MUS & TECHNOL percussion.
◆ **percussions** *nfpl* percussion ensemble.

percussionniste [pɛrkysjɔnist] *nmf* percussionist.

perçut *etc v* ▷ **percevoir**.

percutané, e [pɛrkytane] *adj* percutaneous.

percutant, e [pɛrkytɑ̃, ɑ̃t] *adj* **1.** ARM percussion *(modif)* ▪ TECHNOL percussive **2.** [argument, formule] powerful, striking ▪ **titre ~** hard-hitting headlines ▪ **leur slogan est ~** their slogan hits you right between the eyes.

percuter [3] [pɛrkyte] ◇ *vt* **1.** [heurter] to crash *ou* to run into *(insép)* ▪ **la moto a percuté le mur** the motorbike crashed into the wall **2.** ARM & TECHNOL to strike **3.** MÉD to percuss.

◇ *vi* **1.** ARM to explode **2.** *fam* to twig, to get it.
◆ **percuter contre** *v+prép* : **aller** *OU* **venir ~ contre** to crash into.

percuteur [pɛrkytœr] *nm* **1.** ARM firing pin, hammer **2.** ARCHÉOL percussion tool.

perdant, e [pɛrdɑ̃, ɑ̃t] ◇ *adj* losing ■ **jouer un cheval ~** to bet on a losing horse ■ **être ~** [gén] to come off the loser ; [perdre de l'argent] to be out of pocket ■ **il est ~ dans cette affaire** he's losing out in this deal.
◇ *nm, f* loser ■ **bon ~** good loser ■ **mauvais ~** bad loser.
◆ **perdant** *nm* ebb (tide).

perdition [pɛrdisjɔ̃] *nf* RELIG perdition.
◆ **en perdition** *loc adj* **1.** NAUT in distress **2.** [en danger] lost ■ **des adolescents en ~** adolescents heading for trouble.

perdre [77] [pɛrdr] ◇ *vt* **1.** [égarer - clefs, lunettes] to lose, to mislay
2. [laisser tomber] : **~ de l'eau/de l'huile** to leak water/oil ■ **des sacs de sable qui perdaient leur contenu** sandbags spilling their contents ■ **la brosse perd ses poils** the brush is losing *OU* shedding its bristles ■ **il perd son pantalon** his trousers are falling down ■ **tu perds des papiers/un gant!** you've dropped some documents/a glove! ‖ [laisser échapper] to lose ■ **~ sa page** to lose one's page *OU* place ⊙ **~ la trace de qqn** *pr* & *fig* to lose track of sb ■ **~ qqn/qqch de vue** *pr* & *fig* to lose sight of sb/sthg, to lose track of sb/sthg ■ **ne pas ~ un mot/une miette de : je n'ai pas perdu un mot/une miette de leur entretien** I didn't miss a (single) word/scrap of their conversation ■ **~ les pédales** *fam* [ne plus comprendre] to be completely lost ; [céder à la panique] to lose one's head ■ **~ pied** *pr* & *fig* to get out of one's depth
3. [être privé de - bien, faculté] to lose ■ **~ son emploi** *OU* **sa situation** *OU* **sa place** to lose one's job ■ **n'avoir rien à ~** to have nothing to lose ■ **~ des/ses forces** to lose strength/one's strength ■ **~ la mémoire/l'appétit** to lose one's memory/appetite ■ **~ la parole** [la voix] to lose one's voice ; [dans une réunion] to lose the floor ■ **~ un œil/ses dents** to lose an eye/one's teeth ■ **~ du sang/poids** to lose blood/weight ■ **elle a perdu les eaux** MÉD her waters broke ■ **~ le contrôle de** to lose control of ■ **~ connaissance** to pass out, to faint ■ **~ le goût/sens de** to lose one's taste for/sense of ■ **~ espoir** to lose hope ■ **~ l'habitude de (faire)** to get out of the habit of (doing) ■ **~ patience** to run out of *OU* to lose patience ■ **~ (tous) ses moyens** to panic ⊙ **~ la tête** *OU* **le nord** *fam* *OU* **la boule** *fam* to go mad ■ **celui-là, il perd pas le nord!** *fam* he's certainly got his head screwed on! ■ **en ~ le boire et le manger : il en a perdu le boire et le manger** it worried him so much he lost his appetite ■ **j'y perds mon latin** I'm totally confused *OU* baffled
4. [avoir moins] : **~ de : la tapisserie n'a rien perdu de ses couleurs** the wallpaper has lost none of its colour ■ **les actions ont perdu de leur valeur** the shares have partially depreciated ■ **elle a beaucoup perdu de son anglais** she's forgotten a lot of her English
5. [être délaissé par] to lose ■ **il a perdu toute sa clientèle** he has lost all his customers ⊙ **un de perdu, dix de retrouvés** *fam* there's plenty more fish in the sea
6. [par décès] to lose
7. [contre quelqu'un] to lose ■ **~ l'avantage** to lose the *OU* one's advantage ■ **~ la partie** JEUX : **il a perdu la partie** he lost the game ■ **~ du terrain** to lose ground ‖ SPORT [set] to drop, to lose
8. [gâcher - temps, argent] to waste
9. *sout* [causer la ruine de] to ruin (the reputation of) ■ **c'est le jeu qui le perdra** gambling will be the ruin of him *OU* his downfall ■ **toi, c'est la curiosité qui te perdra** *hum* you're far too inquisitive for your own good!
10. *loc* **tu ne perds rien pour attendre!** just (you) wait and see!
◇ *vi* **1.** [dans un jeu, une compétition, une lutte etc] to lose ■ **~ à la loterie/aux élections** to lose at the lottery/polls ■ **je vous le vends 500 euros mais j'y perds** I'm selling it to you for 500 euros but I'm losing (money) on it ⊙ **~ au change** *pr* & *fig* to lose out ■ **je n'ai pas perdu au change** *pr* & *fig* I've come out of it quite well ■ **jouer à qui perd gagne** to play (a game of) loser takes all
2. [en qualité, psychologiquement] to lose (out) ■ **~ à : ces vins blancs perdent à être conservés trop longtemps** these white wines don't improve with age ■ **on perd toujours à agir sans réfléchir** you're bound to be worse off if you act without thinking ■ **~ en** [avoir moins de] : **le récit perd en précision ce qu'il gagne en puissance d'évocation** what the story loses in precision, it gains in narrative power.
◆ **se perdre** ◇ *vp (emploi réciproque)* : **se ~ de vue** to lose sight of each other.
◇ *vp (emploi passif)* [crayon, foulard, clef] to get lost, to disappear ⊙ **il y a des coups de pied au cul qui se perdent**△ somebody needs a good kick up the arse *UK* *OU* ass *US*△.
◇ *vpi* **1.** [s'égarer - personne] to get lost, to lose one's way ; [- avion, bateau] to get lost ■ *fig* **se ~ dans les détails** to get bogged down in too much detail ■ **se ~ dans ses calculs** to get one's calculations muddled up ■ **se ~ en conjectures** to be lost in conjecture
2. [disparaître] to disappear, to become lost, to fade ■ **ses appels se perdirent dans la foule** her calls were swallowed up by the crowd ⊙ **se ~ dans la nuit des temps** to be lost in the mists of time
3. [devenir désuet] to become lost, to die out ■ **la coutume s'est perdue** the custom is (now) lost
4. [nourriture, récolte - par pourrissement] to rot ; [- par surabondance] to go to waste.

perdreau, x [pɛrdro] *nm* young partridge.

perdrix [pɛrdri] *nf* : **~ (grise)** partridge ■ **~ des neiges** ptarmigan.

perdu, e [pɛrdy] ◇ *pp* ▷ **perdre**.
◇ *adj* **1.** [balle, coup] stray ■ [heure, moment] spare **2.** [inutilisable - emballage] disposable ; [- verre] non-returnable **3.** [condamné] lost ■ **sans votre intervention, j'étais un homme ~** if you hadn't intervened, I'd have been finished *OU* lost **4.** [désespéré] lost **5.** [gâché - vêtement, chapeau] ruined, spoiled ; [- nourriture] spoiled ■ **pleurant sa réputation ~e** crying for her lost *OU* tainted reputation **6.** [de mauvaise vie] : **femme ~e** loose woman **7.** [isolé - coin, village] lost, remote, godforsaken *hum.*
◇ *nm, f* *fam* : **comme un ~, comme une ~e** [courir] hell for leather ; [crier] like a mad thing.

perdurer [3] [pɛrdyre] *vi sout* to continue (on), to endure, to last.

père [pɛr] *nm* **1.** [géniteur] father ■ **tu es un ~ pour moi** you're like a father to me ■ **devenir ~** to become a father ■ **'~ inconnu'** 'father unknown' ■ **je suis né de ~ inconnu** it's not known who my father was ■ **le ~ Viot ne voulait pas que la propriété soit vendue** old Viot didn't want the estate to be sold ■ **John Smith ~** John Smith senior ■ **Alexandre Dumas ~** Alexandre Dumas père ⊙ **~ nourricier** foster father ■ **tel ~, tel fils** *prov* like father, like son *prov* ■ **à ~ avare, fils prodigue** *prov* a miser's son will be a spendthrift
2. [innovateur] father ■ **le ~ de la psychanalyse** the father of psychoanalysis ⊙ **~ fondateur** founding father
3. [chef] : **~ de famille : maintenant que je suis ~ de famille** now that I've got a family ■ **être bon ~ de famille** to be a (good) father *OU* family man ■ **conduire en ~ de famille** to drive carefully ■ **de ~ de famille : c'est un investissement de ~ de famille** it's a rock-solid *OU* copper-bottomed investment
4. [homme, enfant] : **gros ~** *fam* : **allez, mon gros ~, au lit!** come on now, little fellow, off to bed! ■ **petit ~** *fam* : **mon petit ~** (my) little one *OU* fellow ■ **il pleure, pauvre petit ~!** he's crying, poor little thing! ■ **moi, je conduis en ~ peinard** *fam* I like to drive nice and slowly ■ **le ~ Fouettard** the Bogeyman ■ **le ~ Noël** Santa Claus, Father Christmas ■ **le petit ~ des peuples** the little father of the people
5. RELIG father ■ **le ~ Lamotte** Father Lamotte ■ **merci, mon ~** thank you, Father ■ **il a fait ses études chez les ~s** he was educated at a religious institution ⊙ **le Père éternel** the Heavenly Father ■ **notre Père qui êtes aux cieux** our Father who art in Heaven
6. ZOOL sire.
◆ **pères** *nmpl litt* [aïeux] forefathers, fathers.
◆ **de père en fils** *loc adv* : **ils sont menuisiers de ~ en fils** they've been carpenters for generations ■ **cette tradition s'est transmise de ~ en fils** this tradition has been handed down from father to son.

pérégrination [peregrinasjɔ̃] *nf* peregrination ■ **au cours de ses ~s** on *OU* during his travels.

Père-Lachaise [pɛrlaʃɛz] *npr* : **le (cimetière du) ~** *the chief cemetery of Paris, where many famous people are buried.*

péremption [perɑ̃psjɔ̃] *nf* lapsing ■ **au bout de trois ans, il y a ~ et vous ne pouvez plus réclamer la dette** there is a strict time limit of three years on claims after which payment may not be demanded.

péremptoire [perɑ̃ptwar] *adj* [impérieux] peremptory ■ **de façon ~** peremptorily.

péremptoirement [perɑ̃ptwarmɑ̃] *adv* peremptorily.

pérenne [perɛn] *adj* perennial ■ **source ~** permanent spring.

pérenniser [3] [perenize] *vt sout* to perpetuate.

pérennité [perenite] *nf* perenniality, lasting quality.

péréquation [perekwasjɔ̃] *nf* **1.** [rajustement] adjustment **2.** [répartition] balancing out ■ ÉCON perequation.

perestroïka [perɛstrɔika] *nf* perestroika.

perfectible [pɛrfɛktibl] *adj* perfectible ■ **l'appareil n'est plus guère ~ maintenant** the machine can hardly be improved any further.

perfectif, ive [pɛrfɛktif, iv] *adj* perfective.
◆ **perfectif** *nm* perfective aspect, *voir aussi* **pluriel**.

perfection [pɛrfɛksjɔ̃] *nf* **1.** [qualité] perfection **2.** [trésor] gem, treasure.
◆ **à la perfection** *loc adv* perfectly (well) ■ **tout marche à la ~** things couldn't be better.

perfectionné, e [pɛrfɛksjɔne] sophisticated.

perfectionnement [pɛrfɛksjɔnmɑ̃] *nm* **1.** [d'un art, d'une technique] perfecting ■ **notre but est le ~ de nos techniques** our aim is to perfect our techniques **2.** [d'un objet matériel] improvement.
◆ **de perfectionnement** *loc adj* advanced.

perfectionner [3] [pɛrfɛksjɔne] *vt* **1.** [amener au plus haut niveau] to (make) perfect ■ **des techniques très perfectionnées** very sophisticated techniques **2.** [améliorer] to improve (upon).
◆ **se perfectionner** *vpi* to improve o.s. ■ **il s'est beaucoup perfectionné en français** his French has improved considerably.

perfectionnisme [pɛrfɛksjɔnism] *nm* perfectionism.

perfectionniste [pɛrfɛksjɔnist] *nmf* perfectionist.

Perfecto® [pɛrfɛkto] *nm* Perfecto® *(short leather jacket).*

perfide [pɛrfid] *litt* <> *adj* [personne, conseil] perfidious, treacherous, faithless ■ **la ~ Albion** *hum* perfidious Albion.
<> *nmf* traitor ■ **la ~ a volé mon cœur** *hum* the perfidious creature has stolen my heart.

perfidement [pɛrfidmɑ̃] *adv litt* perfidiously, treacherously.

perfidie [pɛrfidi] *nf sout* **1.** [caractère] perfidy, treacherousness **2.** [acte] piece of treachery, perfidy ■ [parole] perfidious *ou* treacherous remark.

perforant, e [pɛrfɔrɑ̃, ɑ̃t] *adj* **1.** [pointe, dispositif] perforating **2.** [balle, obus] armour-piercing **3.** ANAT [artère] perforating ■ [nerf] perforans.

perforateur, trice [pɛrfɔratœr, tris] <> *adj* perforating.
<> *nm, f* INFORM punch-card operator.
◆ **perforateur** *nm* **1.** MÉD perforator **2.** [pour documents] (hole) punch.
◆ **perforatrice** *nf* **1.** MIN rock drill **2.** INFORM card punch.

perforation [pɛrfɔrasjɔ̃] *nf* **1.** [action] piercing, perforating ■ INFORM punching **2.** [trou - dans du papier, du cuir] perforation ; [- dans une pellicule] sprocket hole ■ INFORM punch **3.** MÉD perforation.

perforer [3] [pɛrfɔre] *vt* **1.** [percer] to pierce **2.** INFORM to punch **3.** MÉD to perforate.

performance [pɛrfɔrmɑ̃s] *nf* **1.** SPORT [résultat] result, performance ■ **les ~s de l'année dernière sur le marché japonais** *fig* last year's results on the Japanese market **2.** [réussite] achievement **3.** LING & PSYCHOL performance.
◆ **performances** *nfpl* [d'ordinateur, de voiture etc] (overall) performance.

performant, e [pɛrfɔrmɑ̃, ɑ̃t] *adj* [machine, système] efficient ■ [produit, entreprise] successful ■ [employé] effective ■ [technicien] first-class ■ **une voiture ~e** a car that runs well.

performatif, ive [pɛrfɔrmatif, iv] *adj* performative.
◆ **performatif** *nm* performative (verb), *voir aussi* **pluriel**.

perfusion [pɛrfyzjɔ̃] *nf* drip, perfusion ■ **être sous ~** to be on a drip ■ **nourrir** *ou* **alimenter qqn par ~** to drip-feed sb.

pergola [pɛrgɔla] *nf* pergola.

périarthrite [periartrit] *nf* periarthritis.

péricarde [perikard] *nm* pericardium.

péricarpe [perikarp] *nm* pericarp.

péricliter [3] [periklite] *vi* to be on a downward slope, to be going downhill ■ **une industrie qui périclite** an industry with no future.

péridural, e, aux [peridyral, o] *adj* epidural.
◆ **péridurale** *nf* epidural (anaesthesia).

périgourdin, e [perigurdɛ̃, in] *adj* [de Périgueux] from Périgueux, of Périgueux ■ [du Périgord] from Périgord, of Périgord.

péri-informatique [periɛ̃fɔrmatik] *nf* computer environment.

péril [peril] *nm* **1.** *sout* [danger] danger ■ **au ~ de sa vie** at great risk to his (own) life ● **il n'y a pas ~ en la demeure** it's not a matter of life and death **2.** [menace] peril ■ **le ~ jaune** *péj* the yellow peril.
◆ **en péril** <> *loc adj* [monuments, animaux] endangered ■ **être en ~** to be in danger *ou* at risk.
<> *loc adv* : **mettre en ~** to endanger, to put at risk.

périlleux, euse [perijø, øz] *adj* perilous, hazardous, dangerous.

périmé, e [perime] *adj* **1.** [expiré] out-of-date ■ **mon passeport est ~** my passport is no longer valid *ou* has expired **2.** [démodé] outdated, outmoded.

périménopause [perimenɔpoz] *nf* perimenopause.

périmer [3] [perime] ◆ **se périmer** *vpi* **1.** [expirer] to expire ■ **laisser se ~ un billet** to let a ticket go out of date **2.** DR to lapse **3.** [disparaître] to become outdated *ou* outmoded.

périmètre [perimɛtr] *nm* **1.** [surface] perimeter ■ **des recherches ont été entreprises dans un vaste ~** searches were conducted over a vast area **2.** DR : **~ sensible** ≃ green belt *UK*.

périnatal, e, als *ou* **aux** [perinatal, o] *adj* perinatal.

périnatalité [perinatalite] *nf* perinatal period.

périnatalogie [perinatalɔʒi] *nf* perinatal paediatrics.

périnée [perine] *nm* perineum.

période [perjɔd] *nf* **1.** [époque] period, time ■ **traverser une ~ difficile** to go through a difficult period *ou* time ■ **pendant la ~ électorale** during election time ■ **pendant la ~ des fêtes** at Christmas time **2.** MIL : **~ (d'exercice)** training **3.** SC & MUS period ■ **~ radioactive** half-life **4.** TRANSP : **~ bleue/blanche/rouge** *period during which tickets are cheapest/medium-priced/most expensive.*
◆ **par périodes** *loc adv* from time to time, every now and then, every so often ■ **c'est par ~s** it comes and goes.

périodicité [perjɔdisite] *nf* frequency.

périodique [perjɔdik] <> *adj* **1.** CHIM, MATH, PHYS & PSYCHOL periodic **2.** [publication] periodical **3.** MÉD recurring.
<> *nm* periodical.

périodiquement [perjɔdikmɑ̃] *adv* **1.** CHIM, MATH & PHYS periodically **2.** [régulièrement] periodically, every so often ■ **les douleurs reviennent ~** the pain recurs periodically.

péripatéticien, enne [peripatetisjɛ̃, ɛn] <> *adj* ANTIQ Peripatetic.
<> *nm, f* ANTIQ Peripatetic, member of the Peripatetic school.
◆ **péripatéticienne** *nf litt & hum* streetwalker.

péripétie [peripesi] *nf* **1.** [événement] event, episode, adventure **2.** LITTÉR peripetia, peripeteia.

périph [perif] *nm fam* = **périphérique**.

périphérie [periferi] *nf* **1.** [bord] periphery ■ **sur la ~ de la plaie** on the edges of the wound **2.** [faubourg] outskirts ■ **à la ~ des grandes villes** on the outskirts of cities.

périphérique [periferik] <> *adj* **1.** [quartier] outlying **2.** PHYSIOL & INFORM peripheral.
<> *nm* **1.** [boulevard] ring road *UK*, beltway *US* ■ [à Paris] : **le ~** the Paris orbital *UK ou* beltway *US* **2.** INFORM peripheral device ■ **~ d'entrée/de sortie** input/output device.

périphrase [perifraz] *nf* periphrasis.

périphrastique [perifrastik] *adj* periphrastic.

périple [peripl] *nm* **1.** [voyage d'exploration] voyage, expedition **2.** [voyage touristique] tour, trip **3.** *litt* [durée de la vie] life, lifetime.

périr [32] [perir] *vi* **1.** *litt* [personne, souvenir] to perish *litt*, to die ■ **péri en mer** lost at sea **2.** *sout* [idéal] to be destroyed.

périscolaire [periskɔlɛr] *adj* extracurricular.

périscope [periskɔp] *nm* periscope.

périssable [perisabl] *adj* perishable.

péristyle [peristil] *nm* peristyle.

péritoine [peritwan] *nm* peritoneum.

péritonite [peritɔnit] *nf* peritonitis.

perle [pɛrl] <> *nf* **1.** [bijou] pearl ■ **~ fine/de culture** natural/cultured pearl ▶ **c'est la ~ de ma collection** it's the prize piece of my collection ■ **jeter des ~s aux pourceaux** to cast pearls before swine **2.** [bille] bead ■ **~s de verre** glass beads **3.** *litt* [goutte] drop ■ **des ~s de sueur** beads of sweat ■ **des ~s de rosée** dewdrops **4.** [personne] gem, treasure ■ **sa femme est une ~!** his wife is a real gem! **5.** *fam* [bêtise] howler **6.** ENTOM Perla (stonefly).
<> *adj inv* pearl, pearl-grey.

perlé, e [pɛrle] *adj* **1.** [nacré] pearly, pearl *(modif)* **2.** [orné de perles] beaded ■ **coton ~** [mercerisé] pearl *ou* perlé cotton **3.** [orge] pearl ■ [riz] polished **4.** [rire, son] rippling.

perler [3] [pɛrle] <> *vi* to bead ■ **la sueur perlait sur son visage** beads of sweat stood out on his face.
<> *vt vieilli* [travail] to execute perfectly.

perlier, ère [pɛrlje, ɛr] *adj* [barque] pearling ■ [industrie] pearl *(modif)*.

perlimpinpin [pɛrlɛ̃pɛ̃pɛ̃] *nm* ⊳ **poudre**.

perlingual, e, aux [pɛrlɛ̃gwal, o] *adj* perlingual ■ **'à prendre par voie ~e'** 'to be dissolved under the tongue'.

perlouse[△], **perlouze** [pɛrluz] *nf arg crime* pearl.

perm [pɛrm] *nf fam* **1.** MIL leave ■ **être en ~** to be on leave **2.** ÉDUC [tranche horaire] study period ■ [salle] study (period) room *UK ou* hall *US*.

permanence [pɛrmanɑ̃s] *nf* **1.** [persistance - gén] permanence, lasting quality ; [- d'une tradition] continuity **2.** [service de garde] duty (period) ■ **être de ~** to be on duty *ou* call ■ **une ~ est assurée à la mairie le mardi matin** council offices are open on Tuesday mornings ▶ **~ téléphonique** answering service **3.** [local, bureau - POLIT] committee room ■ ÉDUC study room *UK ou* hall *US*.
◆ **en permanence** *loc adv* permanently ■ **elle me harcèle en ~** she's forever harassing me.

permanent, e [pɛrmanɑ̃, ɑ̃t] <> *adj* **1.** [constant] permanent ■ **avec elle, ce sont des reproches ~s** she's forever nagging **2.** [fixe] permanent ■ **avoir un emploi ~** to have a permanent job ▶ **armée ~e** standing army **3.** CINÉ continuous, non-stop **4.** INFORM permanent.
<> *nm, f* [d'un parti] official ■ [d'une entreprise] salaried worker, worker on the payroll.
◆ **permanente** *nf* perm.

permanenté, e [pɛrmanɑ̃te] *adj* [cheveux] permed.

permanenter [pɛrmanɑ̃te] *vt* to perm ■ **se faire ~** to have one's hair permed, to get a perm.

permanganate [pɛrmɑ̃ganat] *nm* permanganate.

perme [pɛrm] *fam* = **perm**.

perméabilité [pɛrmeabilite] *nf* **1.** GÉOL & PHYS permeability **2.** [d'une personne] malleability.

perméable [pɛrmeabl] *adj* **1.** GÉOL & PHYS permeable **2.** [personne] malleable.

permettre [84] [pɛrmɛtr] *vt* **1.** [suj: personne] to allow ■ **~ à qqn de faire qqch, ~ que qqn fasse qqch** to allow sb to do sthg, to let sb do sthg ■ **je ne vous permets pas de me parler sur ce ton** I won't have you speak to me in that tone of voice ■ **il ne permettra pas qu'on insulte son frère** he won't allow his brother to be insulted ‖ [suj: chose] to allow, to permit, to enable ■ **le train à grande vitesse permettra d'y aller en moins de deux heures** the high-speed train will make it possible to get there in under two hours ■ **sa lettre permet toutes les craintes** her letter gives cause for concern ■ **ce document permet d'entrer dans le secteur turc** this document enables *ou* entitles you to enter the Turkish sector ■ **votre mission ne permet pas d'erreur** your mission leaves no room for error ■ **si le temps/sa santé le permet** weather/(his) health permitting
2. *(tournure impersonnelle)* **c'est permis?** is it allowed *ou* permitted? ■ **il n'est pas/il est permis de boire de l'alcool** drinking is not/is allowed *ou* permitted ■ **autant qu'il est permis d'en juger** as far as it is possible to judge ■ **est-il permis d'être aussi mal élevé?** how can anyone be so rude? ■ **elle est belle/insolente comme c'est pas permis** she's outrageously beautiful/cheeky ■ **un tel mauvais goût, ça devrait pas être** *ou* **c'est pas permis** there should be a law against such bad taste
3. [dans des formules de politesse] : **il reste un sandwich, vous permettez?** may I have the last sandwich? ■ **si vous me permettez l'expression** if I may be allowed to say so, if you don't mind my saying ■ **permettez-moi de ne pas partager votre avis** I beg to differ ■ **tu n'es pas sincère non plus, permets-moi de te le dire** and you're not being honest either, let me tell you ■ **non, mais tu permets que j'en place une?** *fam* I'd like to get a word in, if you don't mind ■ **ah permettez, j'étais là avant vous!** do you mind, I was there before you!
◆ **se permettre** *vpt* **1.** [s'accorder] to allow *ou* to permit o.s.
2. [oser] to dare ■ **il se permet de petites entorses au règlement** he's not averse to bending the rules now and then ■ **elle se permettait n'importe quoi** she thought she could get away with anything ■ **des critiques, oh mais je ne me permettrais pas!** *iron* criticize? I wouldn't dare! ■ **si je peux me ~, je ne pense pas que ce soit une bonne idée** if you don't mind my saying so, I don't think it's a very good idea
3. [pouvoir payer] to (be able to) afford.
◆ **se permettre de** *vp+prép* to take the liberty ■ **puis-je me ~ de vous rappeler mon nom/nos accords signés?** may I remind you of my name/our binding agreements? ■ **je me permets de vous écrire au sujet de mon fils** I'm writing to you about my son.

permis [pɛrmi] *nm* permit, licence ▶ **~ (de conduire)** driving licence *UK*, driver's license *US* ■ **rater/réussir le ~ (de conduire)** to fail/to pass one's (driving) test ■ **~ à points** *driving licence with a penalty points system, introduced in France in 1992* ■ **~ de construire** building permit *ou* licence, planning permission *UK* ■ **~ de chasse** [chasse à courre] hunting permit ; [chasse au fusil] shooting licence ■ **~ de séjour/travail** residence/work permit ■ **~ d'inhumer** burial certificate ■ **~ de port d'armes** firearms licence.

PERMIS DE CONDUIRE

To get one's driving licence in France one must be at least eighteen. The driving test has both a practical and a theoretical part, the latter taking the form of an exam paper at the test centre.

permissif, ive [pɛrmisif, iv] *adj* permissive.

permission [pɛrmisjɔ̃] *nf* **1.** [autorisation] permission, leave ▪ **demander/accorder la ~ de faire qqch** to ask/to grant permission to do sthg ▪ **les enfants n'ont la ~ de sortir qu'accompagnés** the children don't have permission *ou* aren't allowed to go out unaccompanied ▪ **avec votre ~, je vais aller me coucher** if you don't mind, I'll go to bed ▪ **sans demander la ~** without asking permission, without so much as a by-your-leave *hum* ▶ **j'ai la ~ de minuit** I'm allowed to stay out until midnight **2.** MIL leave, furlough ▪ **être en ~** to be on leave *ou* furlough ▪ **avoir une ~ de six jours** to have six days' leave.
Voir module d'usage

permissionnaire [pɛrmisjɔnɛr] *nm* soldier on leave *ou* furlough.

permissivité [pɛrmisivite] *nf* permissiveness.

permit *etc v* ▷ **permettre.**

permutabilité [pɛrmytabilite] *nf* permutability, interchangeability.

permutable [pɛrmytabl] *adj* **1.** [interchangeable] interchangeable **2.** MATH permutable.

permutation [pɛrmytasjɔ̃] *nf* **1.** [transposition] permutation, interchange ▪ **~ des roues** AUTO wheel interchange **2.** MATH permutation.

permuter [3] [pɛrmyte] ◇ *vt* **1.** [intervertir] to switch round *(sép)*, to permutate **2.** MATH to permute.
◇ *vi* [prendre la place de] : **les deux équipes permutent** the two teams swap shifts ▪ **~ avec** to swap with.

pernicieusement [pɛrnisjøzmɑ̃] *adv* perniciously.

pernicieux, euse [pɛrnisjø, øz] *adj* **1.** [néfaste] noxious, injurious, pernicious *sout* ▪ **des insinuations pernicieuses** *sout* insidious suggestions **2.** MÉD pernicious.

péroné [perɔne] *nm* fibula.

péronisme [perɔnism] *nm* Peronism.

péronnelle [perɔnɛl] *nf* scatterbrain.

péroraison [perɔrɛzɔ̃] *nf* [conclusion] peroration ▪ **après toute une ~ sur notre retard, elle en est venue au fait** [discours] after a long tirade about our being late, she came to the point.

pérorer [3] [perɔre] *vi* [discourir] to hold forth ▪ **il peut ~ devant un public pendant des heures** he can go on and on for hours in front of an audience.

Pérou [peru] *npr m* : **le ~** Peru ▪ **au ~** in Peru ▪ **ce n'est pas le ~** *fam* it's not exactly a fortune, it's not ideal.

Pérouse [peruz] *npr* Perugia.

peroxyde [pɛrɔksid] *nm* peroxide.

perpendiculaire [pɛrpɑ̃dikylɛr] ◇ *adj* **1.** [gén - MATH] perpendicular ▪ **la droite A est ~ à la droite B** line A is perpendicular *ou* at right angles to line B **2.** ARCHIT perpendicular.
◇ *nf* perpendicular.

perpendiculairement [pɛrpɑ̃dikylɛrmɑ̃] *adv* perpendicularly ▪ **~ à la rue** at right angles *ou* perpendicular to the street.

perpète[△] [pɛrpɛt] *nf arg crime* **il a eu ~** he got life.
◆ **à perpète** *loc adv fam* **1.** [loin] miles away, in the back of beyond **2.** [très longtemps] : **jusqu'à ~** till Doomsday, till the cows come home, forever and a day **3.** [à vie] : **être condamné à ~** to get life.

perpétration [pɛrpetrasjɔ̃] *nf* perpetration.

perpétrer [18] [pɛrpetre] *vt sout* to perpetrate *sout*, to commit.

perpette [pɛrpɛt] = **perpète.**

perpétuation [pɛrpetɥasjɔ̃] *nf* perpetuation.

perpétuel, elle [pɛrpetɥɛl] *adj* **1.** [éternel] perpetual, everlasting ▪ **être condamné à la prison ~le** to be sentenced to life imprisonment ▪ **un monde en ~ devenir** a perpetually *ou* an ever-changing world **2.** [constant] constant, continual, perpetual.

perpétuellement [pɛrpetɥɛlmɑ̃] *adv* forever, constantly, perpetually ▪ **j'avais ~ l'impression que...** I was constantly under the impression that...

perpétuer [7] [pɛrpetɥe] *vt* **1.** [tradition, préjugé] to carry on *(sép)* **2.** [souvenir] to perpetuate, to pass on *(sép)*.
◆ **se perpétuer** *vpi* **1.** [personne] to perpetuate one's name **2.** [tradition] to live on ▪ **certains rites se sont perpétués de père en fils** some rites have been handed down from father to son.

perpétuité [pɛrpetɥite] *nf litt* perpetuity ▪ **la ~ de l'espèce** the continuation of the species.
◆ **à perpétuité** ◇ *loc adj* **1.** [condamnation] life *(modif)* **2.** [concession] in perpetuity.
◇ *loc adv* : **être condamné à ~** to be sentenced to life imprisonment.

perplexe [pɛrplɛks] *adj* perplexed, puzzled ▪ **avoir l'air ~** to look puzzled ▪ **sa remarque m'a laissé ~** his remark perplexed *ou* puzzled me ▪ **je restai ~, ne sachant que faire** I was in a quandary about what to do.

perplexité [pɛrplɛksite] *nf* confusion, perplexity, puzzlement ▪ **être dans une profonde ~** to be in a state of great confusion ▪ **être plongé dans la ~** to be perplexed *ou* puzzled.

perquisition [pɛrkizisjɔ̃] *nf* search ▪ **procéder à** *ou* **faire une ~ chez qqn** to carry out *ou* to make a search of sb's home ▶ **~ domiciliaire** house search.

perquisitionner [3] [pɛrkizisjɔne] ◇ *vi* DR to (make a) search ▪ **~ chez qqn** to carry out *ou* to make *ou* to conduct a search of sb's home.
◇ *vt* DR to search.

LA PERMISSION

Can *ou* Could I use your mobile phone? Est-ce que je peux me servir de votre téléphone portable ?
Yes, of course you can. Go ahead. Bien sûr, allez-y.
I'm afraid you can't. It isn't working. Je regrette, mais il ne marche pas.
May I open the window? Puis-je ouvrir la fenêtre ?
Yes, of course you may. Oui, bien sûr.
I'd rather you didn't. It's a bit cold. J'aimerais mieux pas. Il fait un peu froid.
Do you mind if I smoke? Ça vous dérange si je fume ?
No, I don't mind. Non, ça ne me dérange pas.
I'm afraid smoking isn't allowed. Désolé, mais il est interdit de fumer ici.
Would it be all right if I left now? Ça pose un problème si je pars maintenant ?
Yes, I don't see why not. Non, je ne vois pas pourquoi.
Well, actually, I'd prefer you to stay. Eh bien, en fait, je préférerais que vous restiez.
I wonder if I might have a little more wine? Pourrais-je reprendre un peu de vin ?
Certainly, help yourself. Bien sûr, servez-vous.
Sorry, but there's none left. Désolé, mais il n'en reste plus.

perron [perɔ̃] *nm* steps *(outside a building)* ■ **sur le ~ de l'Élysée** on the (front) steps of the Élysée palace.

perroquet [perɔkɛ] *nm* **1.** ORNITH parrot ■ **apprendre/répéter qqch comme un ~** to learn/to repeat sthg parrot-fashion **2.** [boisson] pastis and mint cocktail.

perruche [peryʃ] *nf* **1.** [en cage] budgie ■ ORNITH : **~ (ondulée)** budgerigar ‖ [femelle du perroquet] parakeet **2.** *fam péj* [personne] chatterbox.

perruque [peryk] *nf* [postiche] wig ■ HIST periwig, peruke.

perruquier [perykje] *nm* wigmaker.

pers, e [pɛr, pɛrs] *adj litt* seagreen, perse *litt.*

persan, e [pɛrsɑ̃, an] *adj* Persian.
◆ **Persan, e** *nm, f* Persian.
◆ **persan** *nm* **1.** LING Persian **2.** ZOOL Persian cat.

perse [pɛrs] ◇ *adj* Persian ■ **l'Empire ~** the Persian Empire.
◇ *nm* LING Persian ■ **moyen/vieux ~** Middle/Old Persian.
◆ **Perse** *nmf* Persian.

Perse [pɛrs] *npr f* : **(la) ~** Persia.

persécuté, e [pɛrsekyte] ◇ *adj* persecuted.
◇ *nm, f* **1.** [opprimé] persecuted person ■ **les ~s** the downtrodden, the persecuted **2.** PSYCHOL persecution maniac.

persécuter [3] [pɛrsekyte] *vt* **1.** [opprimer] to persecute **2.** [harceler] to torment ■ **tu vas arrêter de ~ ta petite sœur?** will you stop bullying *ou* tormenting your little sister?

persécuteur, trice [pɛrsekytœr, tris] ◇ *adj* persecutory *sout*, tormenting.
◇ *nm, f* persecutor ■ **ses ~s** her tormentors.

persécution [pɛrsekysjɔ̃] *nf* **1.** [oppression] persecution **2.** [harcèlement] harassment, harassing, tormenting **3.** PSYCHOL : **délire** *ou* **manie de la ~** persecution mania.

Persée [pɛrse] *npr* Perseus.

Perséphone [pɛrsefɔn] *npr* Persephone.

persévérance [pɛrseverɑ̃s] *nf* perseverance, persistence, tenacity ■ **travailler avec ~** to persevere in one's work, to work steadily.

persévérant, e [pɛrseverɑ̃, ɑ̃t] *adj* persevering, persistent, tenacious ■ **être ~ (dans qqch)** to be persevering *ou* to persevere (in sthg).

persévérer [18] [pɛrsevere] *vi* to persevere, to persist ■ **~ dans qqch** to continue *ou* to carry on doing sthg ■ **~ dans l'effort** to sustain one's effort ■ **persévère!** don't give up!, persevere!

Pershing [pɛrʃiŋ] *npr* Pershing.

persienne [pɛrsjɛn] *nf* shutter, Persian blind.

persiflage [pɛrsiflaʒ] *nm* **1.** [attitude] scoffing, jeering, mocking **2.** [propos] taunts, scoffs, jeers.

persifler [3] [pɛrsifle] *vt* to scoff *ou* to jeer at, to deride *litt.*

persifleur, euse [pɛrsiflœr, øz] ◇ *adj litt* [moqueur] scoffing, jeering, mocking.
◇ *nm, f* scoffer, mocker, derider *litt.*

persil [pɛrsi] *nm* parsley.

persillade [pɛrsijad] *nf* chopped parsley (and garlic).

persillé, e [pɛrsije] *adj* **1.** [plat] sprinkled with parsley **2.** [viande] marbled **3.** [fromage] (green) *ou* blue veined.

persique [pɛrsik] *adj* [de l'ancienne Perse] (Ancient) Persian.

Persique [pɛrsik] *adj* : **le golfe ~** the Persian Gulf.

persistance [pɛrsistɑ̃s] *nf* **1.** [de quelque chose] persistence ■ **~ du mauvais temps sur tout le territoire demain** bad weather will continue in all areas tomorrow **2.** [de quelqu'un - dans le travail] persistence, perseverance, tenacity ; [- dans le refus] obdurateness *sout*, obstinacy, stubbornness ■ **je ne comprends pas sa ~ à vouloir partir ce soir** I don't understand why he persists in wanting to leave tonight.
◆ **avec persistance** *loc adv* [courageusement] persistently, tenaciously, indefatigably ■ [obstinément] obdurately *sout*, obstinately, stubbornly.

persistant, e [pɛrsistɑ̃, ɑ̃t] *adj* **1.** [tenace] persistent, lasting, enduring ■ **une odeur ~e** a persistent *ou* lingering smell **2.** BOT evergreen.

persister [3] [pɛrsiste] *vi* **1.** [durer] to last, to continue, to persist ■ **les doutes qui pouvaient encore ~** any lingering doubts **2.** [s'obstiner] : **~ à** : **je persiste à croire que tu avais tort** I still think you were wrong ■ **pourquoi persistes-tu à lui faire faire du grec?** why do you persist in making her learn Greek? ■ **~ dans** : **~ dans l'erreur** to persist in one's error ■ **~ dans une attitude** to continue with *ou* to maintain an attitude **3.** DR : **persiste et signe** I certify the truth of the above ■ **je persiste et signe!** *hum* I'm sticking to my guns!

perso [pɛrso] (*abr de* **personnel**) *adj fam* personal, private.

persona grata [pɛrsɔnagrata] *loc adj inv* persona grata ■ **je ne suis plus ~** I'm now persona non grata.

persona non grata [pɛrsɔnanɔ̃ngrata] *loc adj inv* persona non grata ■ **il est ~** he's persona non grata, his name is mud *hum.*

personnage [pɛrsɔnaʒ] *nm* **1.** [de fiction] character ■ **un ~ de roman/de théâtre** a character in a novel/in a play ■ **un ~ de bande dessinée** a cartoon character ■ **jouer un ~** CINÉ & THÉÂTRE to play *ou* to act a part ; *fig* to act a part, to put on an act ▶ **~ principal** main *ou* leading character ■ **~s secondaires** LITTÉR minor *ou* secondary characters ; CINÉ & THÉÂTRE & *fig* supporting roles **2.** [individu] character, individual ■ **sinistre ~** evil customer ■ **grossier ~** swine! **3.** [personnalité importante] person of note, important figure, big name ■ **grands ~s de l'État** state dignitaries ‖ [personne remarquable] character ■ **ce Frédéric, c'est un ~!** that Frederic's quite a character!

personnalisation [pɛrsɔnalizasjɔ̃] *nf* personalization ■ **~ d'un crédit** tailoring of a credit arrangement.

personnaliser [3] [pɛrsɔnalize] *vt* [papier à lettres] to personalize ■ [voiture] to customize ■ [plan, système] : **~ qqch** to tailor sthg to personal requirements ■ **comment ~ votre cuisine** how to give your kitchen a personal touch.

personnalité [pɛrsɔnalite] *nf* **1.** [caractère - d'une personne] personality, character ; [- d'une maison, d'une pièce etc] character ■ **un homme sans aucune ~** a man with no personality (whatsoever) **2.** [personne importante] personality **3.** DR : **~ civile** *ou* **juridique** *ou* **morale** legal personality.

personne[1] [pɛrsɔn] *nf* **1.** [individu] person ■ **plusieurs ~s** [sens courant] several people ; ADMIN several persons ■ **quelques ~s** a few people ■ **toute ~ intéressée peut** *ou* **les ~s intéressées peuvent s'adresser à Nora** all those interested *ou* all interested parties should contact Nora ■ **vingt euros par ~** twenty euros each *ou* per person *ou* a head ▶ **une ~ âgée** an elderly person ■ **les ~s âgées** the elderly ■ **grande ~** grown-up ■ **les grandes ~s** grown-ups
2. [être humain] : **s'en prendre aux biens et aux ~s** to attack property and people ■ **ce qui compte, c'est l'oeuvre/le rang et non la ~** it's the work/the rank that matters and not the individual ▶ **la ~ humaine** the individual
3. [femme] lady ■ **une jeune ~** a young lady ■ **une petite ~** a little woman
4. [corps] : **ma ~** myself ■ **ta ~** yourself ■ **sa ~** himself ■ **il s'occupe un peu trop de sa petite ~** *fam* he's a little too fond of number one ■ **la ~ de** : **ils s'en sont pris à la ~ (même) du diplomate** they attacked the diplomat physically ■ **un attentat sur la ~ du Président** an attempt on the President's life ■ **en la ~ de** in the person of ▶ **venir en ~** to come in person ■ **j'y veillerai en ~** I'll see to it personally ■ **il dînait avec Napoléon en ~** he was dining with Napoleon himself *ou* none other than Napoleon ■ **c'était lui? – en ~!** was it him? – none other! ■ **elle est la beauté en ~** she's the very embodiment of beauty, she's beauty personified ■ **être bien (fait) de sa ~** to have a good figure
5. GRAMM person ■ **à la première ~ du singulier** in the first person singular

6. DR : **~ juridique** juristic person ▪ **~ morale** legal entity ▪ **~ physique** natural person ▪ **~ à charge** dependant.

◆ **par personne interposée** *loc adv* through *ou* via a third party ▪ **dis-le-lui par ~ interposée** have a go-between tell her.

personne[2] [pɛrsɔn] *pron indéf* **1.** [avec un sens négatif] no one, nobody ▪ **que ~ ne sorte!** nobody *ou* no one leave (the room)! ▪ **~ d'autre que toi** nobody *ou* no one (else) but you ▪ **~ le sait** *fam* nobody knows ‖ [en fonction de complément] anyone, anybody ▪ **il n'y a ~** there's nobody *ou* no one there, there isn't anybody *ou* anyone there ▪ **il n'y a jamais ~ dans ce restaurant** there is never anyone *ou* anybody in this restaurant ▪ **je ne vois ~ que je connaisse** I can't see anybody *ou* anyone I know ▪ **je ne connais ~ d'aussi gentil qu'elle** I don't know anyone *ou* anybody as nice as her ▪ **elle ne parle à ~ d'autre** she doesn't speak to anyone *ou* anybody else ▪ **je n'y suis** *ou* **je ne suis là pour ~** if anyone calls, I'm not in ▪ **quand il faut se mettre au travail, il n'y a plus ~** *fam* when there's work to be done, (suddenly) everyone disappears **2.** [avec un sens positif] anyone, anybody ▪ **il est parti sans que ~ le remarque** he left without anybody *ou* anyone noticing him ▪ **sortez avant que ~ vous voie** leave before anyone *ou* anybody sees you ▪ **il est meilleur conseiller que ~** he's better at giving advice than anyone *ou* anybody (else) ▪ **y a-t-il ~ de plus rassurant que lui?** is there anyone *ou* anybody more reassuring than him? ▪ **c'est trop difficile pour laisser ~ d'autre que lui s'en charger** it is too difficult to let anyone *ou* anybody but him do it ▪ **~ de blessé?** nobody *ou* anybody injured? ▪ **tu le sais mieux que ~** you know it better than anybody *ou* anyone (else) ▪ **elle réussit les crêpes comme ~** there's no one *ou* nobody who makes pancakes quite like her.

personnel[1] [pɛrsɔnɛl] *nm* [d'une entreprise] staff, workforce ▪ [d'un service] staff, personnel ▪ MIL personnel ▪ **le ~ est en grève** the staff is *ou* are on strike ▪ **avoir trop/manquer de ~** to be overstaffed/understaffed *ou* short-staffed ▪ **le ~ est autorisé à...** (members of) staff are authorized to... ▪ **tout le ~ touchera une prime** everybody on the payroll will receive a bonus ➔ **~ au sol/navigant** AÉRON ground/flight crew *ou* staff ▪ **~ (de maison)** servants, (domestic) staff.

personnel[2]**, elle** [pɛrsɔnɛl] *adj* **1.** [privé] personal, individual ▪ **c'est un appel ~** [n'intéressant pas le travail] it's a private call ; [confidentiel] it's a rather personal call ▪ **avoir son hélicoptère ~** to have one's own *ou* a private helicopter ▪ **ce laissez-passer est ~** this pass is not transferable ▪ **le pouvoir ~** POLIT (absolute) personal power **2.** [original] : **très ~** highly personal *ou* idiosyncratic *sout* **3.** PHILOS individual **4.** RELIG personal **5.** GRAMM [pronom] personal ▪ **les formes ~les du verbe** finite verb forms.

personnellement [pɛrsɔnɛlmɑ̃] *adv* personally ▪ **~, je suis contre la peine de mort** I'm against the death penalty personally *ou* myself.

personne-ressource [pɛrsɔnrəsurs] *nf Québec* expert.

personnification [pɛrsɔnifikasjɔ̃] *nf* **1.** [symbole] personification **2.** [modèle] : **ma mère est la ~ de la patience** my mother is patience itself *ou* is the epitome of patience.

personnifié, e [pɛrsɔnifje] *adj* personified ▪ **Quasimodo est la laideur ~e** Quasimodo is the epitome of ugliness.

personnifier [9] [pɛrsɔnifje] *vt* **1.** [symboliser] to personify, to be the personification of ▪ **l'Oncle Sam personnifie les États-Unis** Uncle Sam personifies the United States **2.** [être le modèle de] to embody, to typify.

perspective [pɛrspɛktiv] *nf* **1.** ART perspective ▪ **~ aérienne** aerial perspective ▪ **~ cavalière/centrale** parallel/central perspective ▪ **manquer de ~** to lack depth **2.** [point de vue] angle, viewpoint, standpoint ▪ **dans une ~ sociologique** from a sociological standpoint **3.** [éventualité] idea, prospect, thought ▪ **la ~ de revoir mes parents** the prospect of seeing my parents again ➔ **~ d'avenir** outlook, prospects **4.** [avenir] (future) prospect, outlook ▪ **~s économiques** economic forecast *ou* outlook ▪ **ouvrir de nouvelles** *ou* **des ~s (pour)** to open up new horizons (for) **5.** [vue] view.

◆ **en perspective** *loc adv* **1.** ART in perspective **2.** [en vue] on the horizon, in sight ▪ **pas de reprise du travail en ~** no return to work in sight.

perspicace [pɛrspikas] *adj* perceptive, perspicacious *sout* ▪ **être très ~** to have a sharp *ou* clever mind.

perspicacité [pɛrspikasite] *nf* (clearness of) insight, perceptiveness, perspicacity ▪ **d'une grande ~** of acute perspicacity.

perspiration [pɛrspirasjɔ̃] *nf* perspiration.

persuader [3] [pɛrsɥade] *vt* to persuade, to convince ▪ **il ne se laissera pas ~** he won't be persuaded ▪ **~ qqn de qqch** to impress sthg on sb, to convince sb of sthg ▪ **~ qqn de faire qqch** to talk sb into doing sthg ▪ **rien n'aurait pu la ~ de repartir** nothing would have induced her to leave again ▪ **j'en suis persuadé** I'm convinced *ou* sure of it.

◆ **se persuader de** *vp+prép* to convince o.s. of, to become convinced of ▪ **elle s'est persuadée qu'elle est trop grosse** she's convinced herself that she's too fat.

persuasif, ive [pɛrsɥazif, iv] *adj* [personne] persuasive ▪ [argument] convincing, persuasive.

persuasion [pɛrsɥazjɔ̃] *nf* persuasion ▪ **force** *ou* **pouvoir de ~** persuasive force.
Voir module d'usage

perte [pɛrt] *nf* **1.** [décès] loss
2. [privation d'une faculté] : **~ de** : **~ de connaissance** fainting, blackout ▪ **~ d'appétit** loss of appetite ▪ **~ de mémoire** (memory) blank ▪ **~ de la vue** loss of eyesight
3. [disparition, destruction] loss ▪ **déclarer une ~** to declare the loss (of a thing) ▪ **ce n'est pas une grande** *ou* **grosse ~** it's no great loss ➔ **avec ~s et fracas** unceremoniously ▪ **~ sèche** dead loss
4. [gaspillage] waste ▪ **quelle ~ de temps!** what a waste of time!

LA PERSUASION

Persuader quelqu'un de faire quelque chose

Are you sure you won't come? Tu es sûr que tu ne veux pas venir ?

I really think you should tell her. Je pense vraiment que tu devrais le lui dire.

Oh, come on *ou* **go on - you know you'll enjoy it.** Allez, tu sais bien que ça va te plaire.

What have you got to lose? Qu'est-ce que tu as à perdre ?

But I'm telling you, you'll love the place! Mais je t'assure, tu vas adorer cet endroit !

Persuader quelqu'un de ne pas faire quelque chose

Are you sure you want to go through with this? Tu es sûr que c'est ce que tu veux faire ?

Don't go, you won't like it. N'y vas pas, ça ne va pas te plaire.

Do you really think you should go? Tu penses vraiment que tu devrais y aller ?

What good would it do? Ça t'avancera à quoi ?

I'd think twice about going if I were you. Si j'étais toi, je réfléchirais à deux fois avant d'y aller.

5. [réduction] loss ■ **~ de chaleur** heat loss ■ **~ de poids** weight loss ■ **~ de compression/de vitesse** loss of compression/of engine speed ■ **en ~ de vitesse** AUTO losing speed ; *fig* losing momentum
6. *litt* [ruine] ruin, ruination *sout* ■ **courir** *ou* **aller (droit) à sa ~** to be on the road to ruin ■ **ruminer** *ou* **jurer la ~ de qqn** to vow to ruin sb
7. FIN loss, deficit ■ **l'entreprise a enregistré une ~ de deux millions** the company has chalked up losses of two million ■ **~ sèche** dead loss *pr*
8. [défaite] loss ■ **très affecté par la ~ de son procès** very upset at having lost his case.
◆ **pertes** *nfpl* **1.** FIN losses, loss ■ **compte des ~s et profits** profit and loss account ■ **passer qqch aux** *ou* **par ~s et profits** *pr & fig* to write sthg off (as a total loss)
2. MIL losses
3. MÉD : **~s (blanches)** whites, (vaginal) discharge ■ **~s de sang** metrorrhagia.
◆ **à perte** *loc adv* at a loss.
◆ **à perte de vue** *loc adv* **1.** [loin] as far as the eye can see **2.** [longtemps] endlessly, interminably, on and on.
◆ **en pure perte** *loc adv* for nothing, to no avail ■ **il a couru en pure ~, il a quand même manqué son train** it was absolutely no use running, he missed the train all the same.

pertinemment [pɛrtinamɑ̃] *adv* **1.** [à propos] appropriately, pertinently, fittingly **2.** [parfaitement] : **je sais ~ que ce n'est pas vrai** I know perfectly well *ou* for a fact that it's not true.

pertinence [pɛrtinɑ̃s] *nf* **1.** [bien-fondé] pertinence, relevance, appositeness *sout* **2.** LING distinctiveness.

pertinent, e [pɛrtinɑ̃, ɑ̃t] *adj* [propos] pertinent, relevant, apt ■ **vos critiques ne sont pas ~es** your criticisms are irrelevant.

pertuis [pɛrtɥi] *nm* GÉOGR [détroit] straits, channel ■ [col] pass.

perturbant, e [pɛrtyrbɑ̃, ɑ̃t] *adj* disturbing.

perturbateur, trice [pɛrtyrbatœr, tris] ◇ *adj* [élève] disruptive ■ [agent, militant] subversive.
◇ *nm, f* [en classe] troublemaker, rowdy element ■ [agitateur] troublemaker, subversive element.

perturbation [pɛrtyrbasjɔ̃] *nf* **1.** [désordre] disturbance, disruption ■ **jeter** *ou* **semer la ~ dans qqch** to disrupt sthg **2.** ASTRON perturbation **3.** MÉTÉOR disturbance ■ **~ atmosphérique** (atmospheric) disturbance **4.** TÉLÉCOM & RADIO interference.

perturbé, e [pɛrtyrbe] *adj* **1.** [agité] upset, perturbed ■ [bouleversé] disturbed ■ [perplexe] troubled, confused, muddled ■ **des enfants ~s** children with behavioural problems ■ **j'ai un sommeil ~** I have difficulty sleeping **2.** [trafic, service] disrupted.

perturber [3] [pɛrtyrbe] *vt* **1.** [interrompre] to disrupt **2.** [rendre perplexe] to trouble, to perturb ■ **ça n'a pas l'air de te ~ outre mesure** you don't seem particularly bothered by it ‖ [troubler] to upset, to disconcert, to perturb ■ **il ne faut pas ~ l'enfant par des changements trop fréquents** don't disorient the child by changing his routine too often ■ **la mort de son frère l'a profondément perturbé** he was severely affected by his brother's death.

Pérugin [peryʒɛ̃] *npr* : **le ~** Il Perugino.

péruvien, enne [peryvjɛ̃, ɛn] *adj* Peruvian.
◆ **Péruvien, enne** *nm, f* Peruvian.

pervenche [pɛrvɑ̃ʃ] ◇ *nf* **1.** BOT periwinkle **2.** *fam* [contractuelle] (lady) traffic warden UK *ou* officer US *(in Paris)*.
◇ *nm* [couleur] periwinkle.
◇ *adj inv* periwinkle *(modif)* ■ **des yeux ~** periwinkle blue eyes.

pervers, e [pɛrvɛr, ɛrs] ◇ *adj* **1.** [obsédé] perverted ■ **avoir l'esprit ~, être ~** to have a perverted *ou* twisted mind **2.** *litt* [malfaisant] wicked **3.** [effet] perverse.
◇ *nm, f* : **~ (sexuel)** (sexual) pervert.

perversion [pɛrvɛrsjɔ̃] *nf* **1.** *litt* [corruption] perversion, corruption **2.** PSYCHOL : **~ (sexuelle)** (sexual) perversion.

perversité [pɛrvɛrsite] *nf* **1.** [caractère] perversity **2.** [acte] perverse act.

pervertir [32] [pɛrvɛrtir] *vt* **1.** *litt* [corrompre] to pervert, to corrupt **2.** [déformer] to pervert, to impair, to distort ■ **la consommation répétée de piment peut ~ le goût** eating chilli too often can impair one's sense of taste.
◆ **se pervertir** *vpi* to become perverted.

pervertissement [pɛrvɛrtismɑ̃] *nm litt* perversion, corruption, corrupting.

pesage [pəzaʒ] *nm* **1.** [action de peser] weighing **2.** SPORT [vérification] weigh-in ■ [lieu - pour les concurrents] weighing room ; [- pour les spectateurs] enclosure *(inside race courses)*.

pesamment [pəzamɑ̃] *adv* heavily ■ **marcher ~** to walk with a heavy step, to tread heavily.

pesant, e [pəsɑ̃, ɑ̃t] *adj* **1.** [lourd] heavy, weighty, unwieldy ■ **marcher à pas ~s** *ou* **d'une démarche ~e** to tread heavily **2.** [astreignant] hard, heavy, demanding **3.** [grave] heavy, weighty, burdensome *litt* **4.** [trop orné] heavy, cumbersome **5.** [insupportable] heavy.
◆ **pesant** *nm* : **valoir son ~ d'or** to be worth one's weight in gold ■ **valoir son ~ de nougat** *ou* **de cacahuètes** *fam hum* to be pretty good.

pesanteur [pəzɑ̃tœr] *nf* **1.** PHYS gravity **2.** [lourdeur - d'un objet] heaviness, weightiness ; [- d'une démarche] heaviness ; [- d'un style] ponderousness ; [- de l'esprit] slowness, sluggishness.

pèse-bébé [pɛzbebe] (*pl inv ou pl* **pèse-bébés**) *nm* (pair of) baby scales.

pèse-denrées [pɛzdɑ̃re] *nm inv small, high-precision kitchen scales.*

pesée [pəze] *nf* **1.** [avec une balance] weighing **2.** [pression] : **exercer une ~ sur qqch** to put one's whole weight on sthg **3.** MÉD weighing **4.** SPORT weigh-in.

pèse-lettre [pɛzlɛtr] (*pl inv ou pl* **pèse-lettres**) *nm* (pair of) letter scales.

pèse-personne [pɛzpɛrsɔn] (*pl inv ou pl* **pèse-personnes**) *nm* (pair of) bathroom scales.

peser [19] [pəze] ◇ *vt* **1.** [avec une balance] to weigh ■ **~ qqch dans sa main** to feel the weight of sthg **2.** *fam* [valoir] : **un mec qui pèse dix millions de dollars** a guy worth ten million bucks **3.** [évaluer, choisir] to weigh ■ **~ ses mots** to weigh *ou* to choose one's words ■ **et je pèse mes mots!** and I'm not saying this lightly! ■ **~ le pour et le contre** to weigh (up) the pros and cons ■ **~ les risques** to weigh up the risk, to evaluate the risks ■ **tout bien pesé** all things considered, all in all.
◇ *vi* **1.** [corps, objet] to weigh ■ **combien pèses-tu/pèse le paquet?** how much do you/does the parcel weigh? ■ **ce truc-là pèse une tonne!** *fam* that thing weighs a ton! **2.** *fig* [personne, opinion] to weigh ■ **~ lourd** to weigh a lot ■ **il ne pèse pas lourd face à lui** he's no match for him ■ **la question d'argent a pesé très lourd dans mon choix** the question of money was a determining *ou* major factor in my choice ➲ **mes raisons ne pèsent pas lourd dans la balance** my arguments don't carry much weight *ou* don't matter very much **3.** [faire pression sur] : **~ sur** to press (heavily) on ■ **~ sur un levier** to lean on a lever ■ **~ sur** [accabler] to weigh down, to be a strain on ■ **les responsabilités qui pèsent sur moi** the responsibilities I have to bear ■ **des présomptions pèsent sur elle** she's under suspicion ■ **ça me pèse sur l'estomac/la conscience** it's lying on my stomach/weighing on my conscience ■ **~ sur** [influer sur] to influence, to affect **4.** [être pénible pour] : **~ à** to weigh down *ou* heavy on ■ **ton absence me pèse** I find your absence difficult to bear ■ **la vie à deux commence à me ~** living with somebody else is beginning to weigh me down ■ **la solitude ne me pèse pas** being alone doesn't bother me.
◆ **se peser** ◇ *vp (emploi réfléchi)* to weigh o.s.
◇ *vp (emploi passif)* to be weighed ■ **les mangues ne se pèsent pas** [au magasin] mangoes are not sold by weight.

peseta [pezeta] *nf* peseta.

pesette [pəzɛt] *nf* (pair of) assay scales.

peseur, euse [pəzœr, øz] *nm, f* weigher.

pessimisme [pesimism] *nm* pessimism.

pessimiste [pesimist] ◇ *adj* pessimistic ■ **pourquoi es-tu toujours aussi ~?** why do you always look on the dark side?
◇ *nmf* pessimist.

peste [pɛst] *nf* **1.** MÉD plague ■ **~ bubonique** bubonic plague ■ **la Grande Peste, la Peste noire** HIST the Black Death ■ **~ bovine** VÉTÉR rinderpest, cattle plague ■ **~ porcine** VÉTÉR swine fever ■ **se méfier de qqn comme de la ~, fuir qqn comme la ~** to avoid sb like the plague **2.** *fam* [personne] (regular) pest, pain in the neck **3.** *litt* & *vieilli* **(la) ~ soit de toi!** a plague on you!

pester [3] [pɛste] *vi* : **~ contre qqn/qqch** to complain *ou* to moan about sb/sthg ■ **je l'entends qui peste dans sa barbe** I can hear him cursing under his breath.

pesticide [pɛstisid] ◇ *adj* pesticidal.
◇ *nm* pesticide.

pestiféré, e [pɛstifere] ◇ *adj* plague-stricken, plague-ridden.
◇ *nm, f* plague victim ■ **traiter qqn comme un ~** *fig* to treat sb like a pariah *ou* a leper.

pestilence [pɛstilɑ̃s] *nf* stench, foul smell.

pestilentiel, elle [pɛstilɑ̃sjɛl] *adj* foul, stinking, pestilential *sout*.

pet[1] [pɛ] *nm* [vent] fart ■ **lâcher un ~** to fart△, to break wind ➔ **ça ne vaut pas un ~ de lapin** it's not worth a damn *ou* a tinker's cuss ■ **elle a toujours un ~ de travers** there's always something wrong with her.

pet[2] [pɛt] *nm fam* **1.** [coup brutal] wallop, thump ■ [trace de choc] dent **2.** *Belgique* **j'ai eu un ~** I failed my exam **3.** *loc* **pas un ~ de : il n'y a pas un ~ de vent** there's not a breath of wind ■ **il n'a pas un ~ d'amour-propre** he doesn't have an ounce of self-respect.

pétainisme [petenism] *nm* Pétain's doctrine.

pétainiste [petenist] ◇ *adj* : **régime/propagande ~** Pétain's regime/propaganda.
◇ *nmf* Pétain supporter.

pétale [petal] *nm* petal ■ **~s de maïs** cornflakes.

pétanque [petɑ̃k] *nf* (game of) pétanque.

pétant, e [petɑ̃, ɑ̃t] *adj fam* **à 3 heures ~es** at 3 o'clock sharp *ou* on the dot.

pétaradant, e [petaradɑ̃, ɑ̃t] *adj fam* put-putting.

pétarade [petarad] *nf* [d'un moteur] put-putting ■ [d'un feu d'artifice] crackle, banging.

pétarader [3] [petarade] *vi* [feu d'artifice] to crackle, to bang ■ [moteur] to put-putt ■ **ils descendirent la rue en pétaradant** they went put-putting down the street.

pétard [petar] *nm* **1.** [explosif] firecracker, banger *UK* ■ **lancer** *ou* **tirer des ~s** to let off firecrackers ➔ **lancer un ~** to cause a sensation *ou* a stir **2.** △ [tapage] din, racket ■ **faire du ~** to kick up *ou* to make a racket **3.** △ [revolver] pistol, gat *US* **4.** *fam* [cigarette] joint **5.** △ [fesses] bum *UK*, ass△ *US* **6.** RAIL detonator *UK*, torpedo *US*.
◆ **en pétard** *loc adj fam* furious, livid, pissed *US*.

pétasse△ [petas] *nf vieilli* **1.** *péj* [prostituée] tart△ **2.** [frousse] : **avoir la ~** to be scared stiff△.

pétaudière [petodjɛr] *nf fam* [lieu] shambles *(sing)*, disaster area *fig* ■ [groupe] motley crew.

pet-de-nonne [pɛdnɔn] (*pl* **pets-de-nonne**) *nm* fritter.

pété, e△ [pete] *adj* **1.** [ivre] plastered, smashed△ ■ [drogué] stoned△, high (as a kite) **2.** [cassé] broken, bust.

péter [3] [pete] *fam* ◇ *vi* **1.** *fam* [faire un pet] to fart ■ **~ plus haut que son cul**△ to be full of oneself ■ **~ dans la soie**△ to be rolling in money **2.** [exploser] to blow up ■ [casser] : **la corde a pété** the rope snapped ■ **~ dans les mains de qqn** *fig* [projet, affaire] to fall through.
◇ *vt* **1.** [casser] to break, to bust ■ **~ la gueule à qqn** to smash sb's face in **2.** [être plein de] : **~ la santé** to be bursting with health ■ **~ le feu** to be a livewire ■ **~ les plombs** *ou* **un boulon** *fam* to lose it **3.** *Belgique* **il a été pété** he failed his exam **4.** *loc* **~ un câble** to go off the rails ■ **~ des flammes** to turn nasty.
◆ **se péter** *fam* ◇ *vpi* : **attention, ça va se ~!** watch out, it's going to break!
◇ *vpt* : **se ~ la jambe/mâchoire** to smash one's leg/jaw ➔ **se ~ la gueule** [s'enivrer] to get pissed△ *ou* plastered *UK* ; [en voiture] to get smashed up.

pète-sec [pɛtsɛk] ◇ *adj inv* overbearing, high-handed, bossy.
◇ *nmf* tyrant, dragon.

péteux, euse△ [petø, øz] *nm, f* **1.** [lâche] chicken ■ **tu n'es qu'un petit ~!** you're just chicken! **2.** [prétentieux] : **quel petit ~!** he's so full of himself!

pétillant, e [petijɑ̃, ɑ̃t] *adj* **1.** [effervescent - eau, vin] sparkling, fizzy **2.** [brillant] : **avoir le regard ~** to have a twinkle in one's eyes ■ **une réponse ~e d'humour** an answer sparkling with wit.
◆ **pétillant** *nm* sparkling wine.

pétillement [petijmɑ̃] *nm* **1.** [crépitement] crackling, crackle **2.** [effervescence] bubbling, sparkling **3.** [vivacité] sparkle ■ **le ~ de son regard** the sparkle in his eyes.

pétiller [3] [petije] *vi* **1.** [crépiter] to crackle **2.** [faire des bulles] to bubble, to fizz, to effervesce *sout* **3.** [briller] to sparkle ■ **son interprétation de Figaro pétille d'intelligence** his interpretation of Figaro shines *ou* sparkles with intelligence.

pétiole [pesjɔl] *nm* leafstalk, petiole *spéc*.

petiot, e [pətjo, ɔt] *fam* ◇ *adj* tiny, teenyweeny.
◇ *nm, f* (little) kiddy, tiny tot ■ **les ~s** the little toddlers *ou* tiny tots.

petit, e [p(ə)ti *(, devant nm commençant par voyelle ou h muet)*p(ə)tit, it] ◇ *adj* **1.** [en hauteur, en largeur] small, little ■ [en longueur] little, small, short ■ **une personne de ~e taille** a small *ou* short person ■ **un ~ gros** a tubby little man ■ **il y a un ~ mur entre les deux jardins** there's a low *ou* small wall between the two gardens ■ **une toute ~e bonne femme** *fam* [femme] a tiny little woman ; [fillette] a tiny little girl ■ **de ~es jambes grassouillettes** [de bébé] little fat legs ; [d'adulte] short fat legs ■ **à ~e distance on voyait une chaumière** a cottage could be seen a short way *ou* distance away ■ **elle a de ~s pieds** she's got small *ou* little feet ■ **un ~ "a"** a lower-case *ou* small "a" ■ **je voudrais ce tissu en ~e largeur** I'd like that material in a narrow width ■ **un ~ bout de papier** a scrap of paper ■ **une toute ~e maison** a tiny little house ■ **se faire tout ~** [passer inaperçu] to make o.s. inconspicuous, to keep a low profile ■ **se faire tout ~ devant qqn** [par respect ou timidité] to humble o.s. before sb ; [par poltronnerie] to cower *ou* to shrink before sb ■ [exprime l'approximation] : **ça vaut un ~ 12 sur 20** it's only worth 12 out of 20 ■ **on y sera dans une ~e heure** we'll be there in a bit less than *ou* in under an hour ■ **il y a un ~ kilomètre d'ici à la ferme** ≃ it's no more than *ou* just under three quarters of a mile from here to the farm
2. [faible] small ■ **expédition/émission à ~ budget** low-budget expedition/programme ■ **~ loyer** low *ou* moderate rent ■ **~e retraite/rente** small pension/annuity
3. [jeune - personne] small, little ; [- plante] young, baby *(modif)* ■ **quand j'étais ~** when I was little ■ **je ne suis plus une ~e fille!** I'm not a little girl any more! ■ **les ~s Français** French children ■ **une ~e Chinoise** a young *ou* little Chinese girl ■ **il est encore trop ~** he's still too small *ou* young ■ **un ~ chien** a puppy ■ **un ~ chat** a kitten ■ **un ~ lion/léopard** a lion/leopard cub ■ **un ~ éléphant** a baby elephant, an elephant calf ■ [plus jeune] little, younger
4. [bref, court] short, brief ■ **un ~ séjour** a short *ou* brief stay ■ **si on lui faisait une ~e visite?** shall we pop in to see her? ■ **donnez-moi un ~ délai** give me a little more time
5. [dans une hiérarchie] : **~e entreprise** small company ■ **les ~es et moyennes entreprises** small and medium-sized businesses ■ **le ~ commerce** (running of) small businesses ■ **les ~s commerçants** (owners of) small businesses ■ **les ~s agriculteurs/propriétaires** small farmers/landowners ■ **les ~s salaires** [sommes] low salaries, small wages ; [employés] low-paid workers

■ **il s'est trouvé un ~ emploi au service exportation** he found a minor post in the export department ■ **~ peintre/poète** minor painter/poet
6. [minime] small, slight, minor ■ **une ~e touche de peinture** a slight touch of paint ■ **ce n'est qu'un ~ détail** it's just a minor detail ■ **dans les plus ~s détails** down to the last detail ■ **une ~e intervention chirurgicale** minor surgery, a small *ou* minor operation ‖ [insignifiant] small, slight ■ **il y a un ~ défaut** there's a slight *ou* small *ou* minor defect ■ **j'ai un ~ ennui** I've got a bit of a problem ■ **j'ai eu un ~ rhume** I had a bit of a cold *ou* a slight cold
7. [léger] slight ■ **un ~ soupir** a little sigh ■ **elle a un ~ accent** she's got a slight accent ■ **dit-elle d'une ~e voix** she said in a faint voice ■ **~e montée** gentle slope ■ **~e brise** gentle breeze ■ **ça a un ~ goût** it tastes a bit strange ■ **ça a un ~ goût d'orange** it tastes slightly of orange
8. [avec une valeur affective] little ■ **j'ai trouvé une ~e couturière/un ~ garagiste** I've found a very good little seamstress/garage ■ **fais-moi une ~e place** make a little space for me, give me a (little) *ou* tiny bit of room ■ **il aimait faire son ~ poker le soir** he was fond of a game of poker in the evening ■ **tu mets ton ~ ensemble?** will you be wearing that nice little suit? ■ **un ~ vin sans prétention** an unpretentious little wine ■ **il y a un ~ vent frais pas désagréable** there's a nice little breeze ■ **ma ~e maman** Mummy *UK*, Mommy *US*, my Mum *UK ou* Mom *US* ■ **alors, mon ~ Paul, comment ça va?** [dit par une femme] how's life, Paul, dear? ; [dit par un homme plus âgé] how's life, young Paul? ‖ [pour encourager] : **tu mangeras bien une ~e glace!** come on, have an ice cream! ■ **je n'ai pas le temps de faire un match – juste un ~!** I've no time to play a match – come on, just a quick one! ‖ [avec une valeur admirative] : **c'est une ~e futée** she's a clever one ■ **~ débrouillard!** you're smart!, you don't miss a thing! ‖ *euphém* [notable] : **c'est une ~e surprise** it's quite a surprise ■ **c'est un ~ exploit!** it's quite an achievement! ‖ [avec une valeur dépréciative] : **~ imbécile!** you idiot! ■ **~ con!**△ you arsehole△ *UK ou* asshole△ *US*! ■ **j'en ai assez de ses ~s mystères/~es manigances!** I'm fed up with her little mysteries/intrigues!
9. *litt* [mesquin] mean, mean-spirited, petty.
◇ *nm, f* **1.** [fils, fille] little son *ou* boy (*f* daughter*f* girl) ■ **c'est le ~ de Monique** it's Monique's son ■ **c'est la ~e d'en face** *fam* it's the girl from across the street, it's the daughter of the people across the street, it's across the road's daughter *UK* ■ **elle va à la même école que le ~ (des) Verneuil** she goes to the same school as the Verneuil boy
2. [enfant] little *ou* small child, little *ou* small boy (*f* girl) ■ **quant aux ~s, nous les emmènerons au zoo** as for the younger children, we'll take them to the zoo ■ **la cour des ~es** the junior *UK ou* younger girls' playground ■ **c'est un livre qui fera les délices des ~s comme des grands** this book will delight young and old (alike)
3. *fam* [adolescent] (young) boy (*f* girl)
4. [avec une valeur affective - à un jeune] dear ; [- à un bébé] little one ■ **mon ~** [à un homme] dear ; [à une femme] dear, darling ■ **mon ~, je suis fier de toi** [à un garçon] young man, I'm proud of you ; [à une fille] young lady, I'm proud of you ■ **viens, mon tout ~** come here (my) little one ■ **ça, ma ~e, vous ne l'emporterez pas au paradis!** you'll never get away with it, my dear! ■ **la pauvre ~e, comment va-t-elle faire?** poor thing, however will she manage?
◆ **petit** ◇ *nm* **1.** [animal] baby ■ **ses ~s** [gén] her young ; [chatte] her kittens ; [chienne] her puppies ; [tigresse, louve] her cubs ▶ **faire des ~s** [chienne] to have pups ; [chatte] to have kittens ■ **mes économies ont fait des ~s** *fam* my savings have grown
2. [dans une hiérarchie] : **c'est toujours les ~s qui doivent payer** it's always the little man who's got to pay ■ **dans la course aux marchés, les ~s sont piétinés** in the race to gain markets, small firms *ou* businesses get trampled underfoot.
◇ *adv* **1.** COMM : **c'est un 38 mais ce modèle chausse/taille ~** it says 38 but this style is a small fitting *UK* runs small *US*
2. [juste] : **voir *ou* prévoir ~** to see *ou* to plan things on a small scale.
◆ **en petit** *loc adv* [en petits caractères] in small characters *ou* letters ■ [en miniature] in miniature ■ **un univers en tout ~** a miniature universe ■ **je voudrais cette jupe (mais) en plus ~** I'd like this skirt (but) in a smaller size.
◆ **petit à petit** *loc adv* little by little, gradually.

petit-beurre [p(ə)tibœr] (*pl* **petits-beurre**) *nm* petit beurre (biscuit *UK*) *ou* cookie *US*, ≃ rich tea biscuit *UK*.

petit-bois [p(ə)tibwa] (*pl* **petits-bois**) *nm* glazing *ou* window bar.

petit-bourgeois, petite-bourgeoise [p(ə)tiburʒwa, p(ə)titburʒwaz] (*mpl* **petits-bourgeois**, *fpl* **petites-bourgeoises**) ◇ *adj* lower middle-class, petit bourgeois. ◇ *nm, f* petit bourgeois.

petit-cousin, petite-cousine [p(ə)tikuzɛ̃, p(ə)titkuzin] (*mpl* **petits-cousins**, *fpl* **petites-cousines**) *nm, f* [au second degré] second cousin ■ [éloigné] distant cousin.

petit déjeuner [p(ə)tideʒœne] (*pl* **petits déjeuners**) *nm* breakfast.

petit-déjeuner [5] [p(ə)tideʒœne] *vi* to have breakfast.

petite-fille [p(ə)titfij] (*pl* **petites-filles**) *nf* granddaughter.

petitement [p(ə)titmɑ̃] *adv* **1.** [modestement] humbly ■ **vivre ~** to live in lowly *ou* humble circumstances ■ **être ~ logé** to live in cramped accommodation **2.** [mesquinement] pettily, meanly.

petite-nièce [p(ə)titnjɛs] (*pl* **petites-nièces**) *nf* great-niece.

petitesse [p(ə)titɛs] *nf* **1.** [taille] smallness, small size **2.** [caractère] pettiness, meanness ■ **~ d'esprit** narrow-mindedness **3.** [acte] piece of pettiness, petty act, mean-spirited action.

petit-fils [p(ə)tifis] (*pl* **petits-fils**) *nm* grandson.

petit-four [p(ə)tifur] (*pl* **petits-fours**) *nm* petit four.

petit-gris [p(ə)tigri] (*pl* **petits-gris**) *nm* **1.** [escargot] garden snail ■ CULIN petit-gris **2.** [écureuil] Siberian grey squirrel ■ [fourrure] squirrel fur.

pétition [petisjɔ̃] *nf* **1.** [texte] petition ■ **adresser une ~ à qqn** to petition sb ■ **faire une ~** to organize a petition **2.** PHILOS : **~ de principe** petitio principii.

pétitionnaire [petisjɔnɛr] *nmf* petitioner.

petit-lait [p(ə)tilɛ] (*pl* **petits-laits**) *nm* whey.

petit-nègre [p(ə)tinɛgr] *nm* pidgin ■ **ce n'est pas du français, c'est du ~** *péj* that isn't French, it's pidgin *ou* broken French.

petit-neveu [p(ə)tin(ə)vø] (*pl* **petits-neveux**) *nm* great-nephew.

petits-enfants [p(ə)tizɑ̃fɑ̃] *nmpl* grandchildren.

petit-suisse [p(ə)tisɥis] (*pl* **petits-suisses**) *nm thick fromage frais sold in small individual portions.*

pétoche△ [petɔʃ] *nf* [peur] : **avoir la ~** to have the jitters, to be in a blue funk *UK* ■ **filer *ou* flanquer la ~ à qqn** to scare the living daylights out of sb.

pétoire [petwar] *nf fam* [arme à feu] gun.

peton [pətɔ̃] *nm fam* tiny foot.

Pétrarque [petrark] *npr* Petrarch.

pétrarquisme [petrarkism] *nm* Petrarchism.

pétrifiant, e [petrifjɑ̃, ɑ̃t] *adj* **1.** *litt* [ahurissant] stunning, stupefying **2.** GÉOL petrifactive.

pétrification [petrifikasjɔ̃] *nf* petrification, petrifaction.

pétrifier [9] [petrifje] *vt* **1.** [abasourdir] to petrify, to transfix ■ **être pétrifié de terreur** to be rooted to the spot *ou* rigid with terror **2.** GÉOL to petrify.
◆ **se pétrifier** *vpi* **1.** [se figer] : **son visage se pétrifia** his face froze **2.** GÉOL to petrify, to become petrified.

pétrin [petrɛ̃] *nm* **1.** *fam* [embarras] jam, fix ■ **être dans le ~** to be in a jam *ou* pickle ■ **se fourrer dans un beau *ou* sacré ~** to get into a real jam ■ **mettre qqn dans un beau *ou* sacré ~** to land sb (right) in it *UK*, to land sb in a tough spot *US* **2.** [à pain] kneading trough ■ **~ mécanique** dough mixer, kneading machine.

pétrir [32] [petrir] *vt* **1.** [malaxer] to knead **2.** *litt* to shape, to mould **3.** *fig* **être pétri d'orgueil** to be filled with pride ■ **être pétri de préjugés** to be steeped in prejudice.

pétrochimie [petrɔʃimi] *nf* petrochemistry.

pétrochimique [petrɔʃimik] *adj* petrochemical.

pétrochimiste [petrɔʃimist] *nmf* petrochemist.

pétrodollar [petrɔdɔlar] *nm* petrodollar.

pétrole [petrɔl] ◇ *nm* oil, petroleum ■ **~ brut** crude (oil) ■ **~ vert** food (processing) industry ■ **en France, on n'a pas de ~, mais on a des idées** *slogan publicitaire allus* although we have no oil wells in France, we do have wells of imagination.
◇ *adj inv* [couleur] : **bleu ~** greyish blue.
◆ **à pétrole** *loc adj* [lampe, réchaud] oil *(modif)* UK, kerosene *(modif)* US.

pétrolette [petrɔlɛt] *nf fam* small (motor) bike, moped.

pétroleuse [petrɔløz] *nf* **1.** HIST female arsonist *(active during the Paris Commune)* **2.** *fam* [militante] militant female political activist.

pétrolier, ère [petrɔlje, ɛr] *adj* oil *(modif)*.
◆ **pétrolier** *nm* **1.** [navire] (oil) tanker **2.** [industriel] oil tycoon **3.** [technicien] petroleum *ou* oil engineer.

pétrolifère [petrɔlifɛr] *adj* oil-bearing.

pétrologie [petrɔlɔʒi] *nf* petrology.

Pétrone [petrɔn] *npr* Petronius.

pétulance [petylɑ̃s] *nf* exuberance, ebullience, high spirits.

pétulant, e [petylɑ̃, ɑ̃t] *adj* exuberant, ebullient.

pétunia [petynja] *nm* petunia.

peu [pø] *adv*

> **A.** EMPLOYÉ SEUL
> **B.** EMPLOI NOMINAL
> **C.** PRÉCÉDÉ DE 'UN'

A. EMPLOYÉ SEUL

1. [modifiant un verbe] little, not much ■ **il mange/parle ~** he doesn't eat/talk much ■ **je le connais ~** I don't know him well ■ **c'est ~ le connaître** it just shows how little you know him ■ **il vient très ~** he comes very rarely, he very seldom comes ■ **on s'est très ~ vu** we saw very little of each other ■ **j'ai trop ~ confiance en elle** I don't trust her enough
2. [modifiant un adjectif, un adverbe etc] not very ■ **une avenue ~ fréquentée** a quiet street ■ **il est assez ~ soigneux** he doesn't take much care ■ **l'alibi est fort ~ crédible** the alibi is highly implausible ■ **~ avant** shortly *ou* not long before ■ **~ après** soon after, shortly *ou* not long after ■ **je ne suis pas ~ fier du résultat** I'm more than a little proud of the result

B. EMPLOI NOMINAL

1. *(avec déterminant)* [indiquant la faible quantité] : **le ~ que tu gagnes** the little you earn ■ *(sans déterminant)* **il vit de ~** he lives off very little ■ **il est mon aîné de ~** he's only slightly older than me ■ **il a raté son examen de ~** *fam* he just failed his exam, he failed his exam by a hair's breadth ■ **c'est ~** it's not much ▶ **hommes/gens de ~** *litt* worthless men/people ■ **c'est ~ (que) de le dire, encore faut-il le faire!** that's easier said than done! ■ **c'est ~ dire** that's an understatement, that's putting it mildly ■ **ce n'est pas ~ dire!** and that's saying something! ■ **très ~ pour moi!** *fam* not on your life!
2. [dans le temps] : **ils sont partis il y a ~** they left a short while ago, they haven't long left ■ **d'ici ~** very soon, before long ■ **vous aurez de mes nouvelles avant ~** you'll hear from me before long ■ **je travaille ici depuis ~** I've only been working here for a while, I haven't been working here long
3. [quelques personnes] a few (people) ■ **nous étions ~ à le croire** only a few of us believed it

C. PRÉCÉDÉ DE 'UN'

1. [modifiant un verbe] : **un ~** a little, a bit ■ **je le connais un ~** I know him a little *ou* a bit ■ **reste un ~ avec moi** stay with me for a while ■ **veux-tu manger un ~?** do you want something to eat? ■ **pousse-toi un (tout) petit ~** move up a (little) bit ■ **viens un ~ par là** come here a minute ■ **pose-lui un ~ la question, et tu verras!** just ask him, and you'll see! ■ **fais voir un ~...** let me have a look... ▶ **tu l'as vu? – un ~!** *fam* did you see it? – you bet I did *ou* and how! ■ **un ~ que je vais lui dire ce que je pense!** *fam* I'll give him a piece of my mind, don't you worry (about that)!
2. [modifiant un adjectif, un adverbe etc] : **un ~** a little, a bit ■ **je suis un ~ pressée** I'm in a bit of a hurry ■ **il est un ~ poète** he's a bit of a poet ■ **un ~ partout** just about *ou* pretty much everywhere ■ **un ~ plus** a little *ou* bit more ■ **un ~ plus de** [suivi d'un nom comptable] a few more ; [suivi d'un nom non comptable] a little (bit) more ■ **un ~ moins** a little *ou* bit less ■ **roule un ~ moins vite** drive a little more slowly ■ **un ~ moins de** [suivi d'un nom comptable] slightly fewer, not so many ; [suivi d'un nom non comptable] a little (bit) less ■ **nous avons un ~ moins de difficultés** we're not having quite so many difficulties ■ **un ~ trop** a little *ou* bit too (much) ■ **il en fait vraiment un ~ trop!** he's really making too much of it! ■ **un ~ beaucoup** *fam* a bit much ■ **tu as bu un ~ beaucoup hier soir** *fam* you certainly had a few last night ■ **elle est jolie – un ~, oui!** *fam* she's pretty – just a bit! ▶ **un ~ plus et l'évier débordait!** another minute and the sink would have overflowed! ■ **un ~ plus et on se serait cru au bord de la mer** you could almost imagine that you were at the seaside ■ **un ~ plus, et je partais** I was just about to leave ■ **un ~ plus et je me faisais écraser!** I was within an inch of being run over!

◆ **peu à peu** *loc adv* little by little, bit by bit, gradually ■ **on s'habitue, ~ à ~** you get used to things, bit by bit *ou* gradually.

◆ **peu de** *loc dét* **1.** [suivi d'un nom non comptable] not much, little ■ [suivi d'un nom comptable] not many, few ■ **cela a ~ d'intérêt** it's of little interest ■ **~ de temps : je ne reste que ~ de temps** I'm only staying for a short while, I'm not staying long ■ **il n'a que ~ de temps à me consacrer** he can only give me a small amount of time ■ **~ de temps avant/après** not long before/after ■ **il y avait ~ de neige** there wasn't much snow ■ **j'ai ~ d'amis** I have few friends, I don't have many friends ■ **en ~ de mots** in a few words ▶ **on est ~ de chose** what an insignificant thing man is ■ **c'est ~ de chose** it's nothing **2.** [avec un déterminant] : **le ~ de** [suivi d'un nom comptable] the *ou* what few ; [suivi d'un nom non comptable] the *ou* what little ■ **le ~ de connaissances que j'ai** the *ou* what few acquaintances I have ■ **le ~ de fois où je l'ai vu** on the few *ou* rare occasions when I've seen him ■ **le ~ d'expérience que j'avais** what little experience I had ■ **son ~ d'enthousiasme** his lack of enthusiasm ■ **avec ce ~ de matériel/d'idées** with such limited material/ideas.

◆ **peu ou prou** *loc adv litt* more or less.

◆ **pour peu que** *loc conj* : **pour ~ qu'il le veuille, il réussira** if he wants to, he'll succeed.

◆ **pour un peu** *loc adv* : **pour un ~ il m'accuserait!** he's all but accusing me! ■ **pour un ~, j'oubliais mes clés** I nearly forgot my keys.

◆ **quelque peu** *loc adv sout* **1.** [modifiant un verbe] just a little **2.** [modifiant un adjectif] somewhat, rather ■ **il était quelque ~ éméché** he was somewhat *ou* rather tipsy.

◆ **quelque peu de** *loc dét sout* not a little.

◆ **si peu que** *loc conj* : **si ~ que j'y aille, j'apprécie toujours beaucoup l'opéra** although I don't go very often, I always like the opera very much.

◆ **si peu... que** *loc conj* : **si ~ réaliste qu'il soit** however unrealistic he may be.

◆ **sous peu** *loc adv* before long, in a short while ■ **vous recevrez sous ~ les résultats de vos analyses** you will receive the results of your tests in a short while.

◆ **un peu de** *loc dét* a little (bit) of ■ **prends un ~ de gâteau** have a little *ou* some cake ■ **un ~ de tout** a bit of everything ■ **avec un ~ de chance...** with a little luck... ■ **allons, un ~ de patience!** come on, let's be patient! ■ **avec un (tout) petit ~ de bonne volonté...** with (just) a little willingness... ■ **tu l'as quitté par dépit? – il y a un petit ~ de ça** so you left him in a fit of pique? – that was partly it *ou* that was part of the reason.

peuchère [pøʃɛr] *interj* [dialecte] heck, strewth UK.

peuh [pø] *interj* **1.** [avec indifférence] bah **2.** [avec dédain] humph.

peul, e [pøl] *adj* Fulani.
◆ **Peul, e** *nm, f* Fulani, Fula, Fulah.

peuplade [pœplad] *nf* (small) tribe, people.

peuple [pœpl] <> *nm* **1.** [communauté] people ■ **les ~s d'Asie** the people of Asia ■ **le ~ français a fait son choix** the French people have chosen ▶ **le ~ de Dieu** [dans l'Ancien Testament] the Hebrews ; [dans le Nouveau Testament] the Christians ■ **le ~ élu** RELIG the chosen people *ou* ones **2.** [prolétariat] : **le ~** the people ■ **parti du ~** people's party ■ **homme du ~** ordinary man ▶ **le bas** *ou* **petit ~** *vieilli* the lower classes *ou* orders *UK* **3.** *fam* [foule] crowd ■ **il va y avoir du ~** it's going to be a bit on the crowded side **4.** *fam loc* **il se fiche** *ou* **se moque du ~** he's got some nerve ■ **que demande le ~?** what more do you want?
<> *adj inv* working-class.

peuplé, e [pœple] *adj* populated ■ **région peu/très ~ e** sparsely/densely populated region.

peuplement [pœpləmɑ̃] *nm* **1.** SOCIOL populating, peopling ■ **au moment du ~ des États-Unis** while the United States was being populated *ou* peopled **2.** ÉCOL [d'une forêt] planting (with trees) ■ [d'une rivière] stocking (with fish) ■ [ensemble - des végétaux] stand *spéc*, plant population ; [- des arbres] tree population.

peupler [5] [pœple] *vt* **1.** [région, ville] to populate, to people ■ [forêt] to plant (with trees) ■ [rivière] to stock (with fish) **2.** [vivre dans] to live in *(insép)*, to inhabit ■ **les Indiens qui peuplent ces régions** the Indians who live in these areas **3.** *fig* & *litt* to fill.
◆ **se peupler** *vpi* to become populated, to acquire a population.

peupleraie [pøplərɛ] *nf* poplar grove.

peuplier [pøplije] *nm* poplar (tree) ■ **~ d'Italie** Lombardy poplar.

peur [pœr] *nf* **1.** [sentiment] fear, apprehension, alarm ■ **avoir ~** to be afraid *ou* frightened *ou* scared ■ **on a eu très ~** we were badly frightened ■ **je n'ai qu'une ~, c'est de les décevoir** my one fear is that I might disappoint them ■ **on a sonné tard, j'ai eu une de ces ~s!** *fam* someone rang the doorbell late at night and it gave me a terrible fright! ■ **avoir ~ pour qqn** to fear for sb ■ **avoir ~ d'un rien** to scare easily, to be easily frightened ■ **avoir horriblement ~ de qqch** to have a dread of sthg ■ **avoir grand-~** to be very much afraid *ou* frightened *ou* scared ■ **n'aie pas ~** [ne t'effraie pas] don't be afraid ; [ne t'inquiète pas] don't worry ■ **ça va, tu n'as pas besoin d'avoir ~!** don't you worry about that!, there's nothing to be afraid of! ■ **il double dans le virage, il n'a pas ~, lui au moins!** overtaking on the bend, he's certainly got some nerve! ■ **j'ai bien ~ qu'elle ne vienne pas** I'm really worried (that) she won't come ■ **j'en ai (bien) ~** I'm (very much) afraid so ■ **faire ~ : faire ~ à qqn** to frighten *ou* to scare sb ■ **le travail ne lui fait pas ~** he's not workshy *ou* afraid of hard work ■ **j'adore les films qui font ~** I love frightening films ■ **une tête à faire ~** a frightening face ■ **boiter/loucher à faire ~** to have a dreadful limp/squint ■ **prendre ~** to get frightened, to take fright ■ **être pris de ~** to be gripped by fear, to be overcome with fear, to take fright ▶ **~ bleue : avoir une ~ bleue de** to be scared stiff of ■ **faire une ~ bleue à qqn** to give sb a terrible fright ■ **la ~ du gendarme** the fear of authority ■ **avoir la ~ au ventre** to be gripped by fear ■ **être mort** *ou* **vert de ~** to be frightened out of one's wits ■ **elle était morte de ~ à cette idée** that idea scared her out of her wits ■ **plus de ~ que de mal : il y a eu plus de ~ que de mal** nobody was hurt, but it was frightening ■ **ça fait ~!** *fam iron* : **tu as l'air content, ça fait ~!** you don't exactly look beside yourself with joy! **2.** [phobie] fear ■ **avoir ~ de l'eau/du noir** to be afraid of water/of the dark ■ **il a ~ en avion** he's afraid of flying.
◆ **dans la peur de** *loc prép* : **vivre dans la ~ de qqch** to live in fear (and trembling *litt*) *ou* in dread of sthg.
◆ **de peur de** *loc prép* : **de ~ de faire** for fear of doing ■ **je ne disais rien de ~ de lui faire du mal** I said nothing for fear that I might *ou* in case I hurt her.
◆ **de peur que** *loc conj* for fear that.
◆ **par peur de** *loc prép* out of fear of ■ **il cèdera au chantage par ~ du scandale** the fear of a scandal will make him give in to blackmail.
◆ **sans peur** *loc adv* fearlessly, undaunted, gamely *litt*.

peureusement [pœrøzmɑ̃] *adv* fearfully, timorously, apprehensively.

peureux, euse [pœrø, øz] <> *adj* [craintif] timorous, fearful ■ **un enfant ~** a fearful child.
<> *nm, f* [poltron] fearful person.

peut *etc v* ▷ **pouvoir**.

peut-être [pøtɛtr] *adv* maybe, perhaps ■ **ils sont ~ sortis, ~ sont-ils sortis** maybe they've gone out, they may *ou* might have gone out ■ **elle est ~ efficace, mais guère rapide** she might be efficient, but she is not very quick ■ **~ pas** maybe *ou* perhaps not ■ **il est ~ bien déjà parti** he may well have already left ■ **~ bien, mais...** perhaps *ou* maybe so but... ▶ **j'y suis pour quelque chose, ~?** so you think it's my fault, do you! ■ **je suis ta bonne, ~?** what do you take me for? a maid?
◆ **peut-être que** *loc conj* perhaps, maybe ■ **~ qu'il est malade** perhaps *ou* maybe he is ill ■ **~ (bien) qu'il viendra** he may well come ▶ **~ bien que oui, ~ bien que non** maybe, maybe not (who knows?)

peuvent, peux *etc v* ▷ **pouvoir**.

pèze△ [pɛz] *nm arg crime* dough, bread, lolly *UK* ■ **ils sont pleins de ~** they're loaded *ou* stinking rich.

pff [pf], **pft** [pft], **pfut** [pfyt] *interj* pooh.

pgcd (*abr de* **plus grand commun diviseur**) *nm* HCF.

pH (*abr de* **potentiel hydrogène**) *nm* pH.

Phaéton [faetɔ̃] *npr* Phaëthon.

phagocyte [fagɔsit] *nm* phagocyte.

phagocyter [3] [fagɔsite] *vt* **1.** BIOL to phagocytose **2.** *fig* & *sout* [absorber] to engulf, to absorb.

phagocytose [fagɔsitoz] *nf* phagocytosis.

phalange [falɑ̃ʒ] *nf* **1.** ANAT phalanx **2.** [groupe] : **la Phalange (espagnole)** the Falange ■ **les Phalanges libanaises** the (Lebanese) Phalangist Party.

phalangiste [falɑ̃ʒist] *adj* & *nmf* [en Espagne] Falangist ■ [au Liban] Phalangist.

phalanstère [falɑ̃stɛr] *nm* **1.** [de Fourier] phalanstery **2.** *litt* [communauté] community, group.

phalène [falɛn] *nf* geometrid.

phallique [falik] *adj* phallic.

phallocentrique [falɔsɑ̃trik] *adj* phallocentric.

phallocentrisme [falɔsɑ̃trism] *nm* phallocentrism.

phallocrate [falɔkrat] <> *adj* male-chauvinist.
<> *nm* male chauvinist.

phallocratie [falɔkrasi] *nf* male chauvinism.

phallocratique [falɔkratik] *adj* male-chauvinist.

phallus [falys] *nm* ANAT phallus.

phantasme [fɑ̃tasm] = **fantasme**.

phantasmer [fɑ̃tasme] = **fantasmer**.

pharamineux, euse [faraminø, øz] *fam* = **faramineux**.

pharaon [faraɔ̃] *nm* **1.** HIST pharaoh **2.** JEUX faro.

pharaonien, enne [faraɔnjɛ̃, ɛn], **pharaonique** [faraɔnik] *adj* pharaonic.

phare [far] *nm* **1.** NAUT lighthouse ■ **~ à éclipses** *ou* **occultations** occulting light ■ **~ à feu fixe/tournant** fixed/revolving light **2.** AUTO headlight, headlamp *UK* ■ **allumer ses ~s** to switch one's headlights on ■ **mettre les ~s en code** to dip *UK ou* to dim *US* one's headlights ▶ **~ à iode** quartz-iodine lamp ■ **~ de recul** reversing *UK ou* back-up *US* light **3.** AÉRON light, beacon ■ **~s d'atterrissage** landing lights **4.** *litt* [guide] beacon, leading light **5.** *(comme adj; avec ou sans trait d'union)* [exemplaire] landmark *(modif)* ■ **industrie ~** flagship *ou* pioneering industry.

pharisaïsme [farizaism] *nm* HIST & RELIG Pharisaism, Phariseeism.

pharisien [farizjɛ̃] *nm* **1.** HIST & RELIG Pharisee ■ **les Pharisiens** the Pharisees **2.** *vieilli* [hypocrite] sanctimonious person, pharisee *litt*.

pharmaceutique [farmasøtik] *adj* pharmaceutic, pharmaceutical.

pharmacie [farmasi] *nf* **1.** [dans la rue] chemist's (shop) *UK*, pharmacy *US*, drugstore *US* ▪ [dans un hôpital] dispensary, pharmacy ▪ **~ de garde** duty chemist ▪ **aller à la ~** to go to the chemist *UK ou* chemist's *UK ou* pharmacy *US ou* drugstore *US* **2.** [meuble] medicine chest *ou* cabinet *ou* cupboard *UK* ▪ [boîte] first-aid box **3.** SC pharmacy, pharmaceutics *(U)* **4.** ÉDUC pharmacology.

pharmacien, enne [farmasjɛ̃, ɛn] *nm, f* **1.** [titulaire] pharmacist, chemist *UK* **2.** [vendeur] (dispensing) chemist *UK*, druggist *US*.

pharmacologie [farmakɔlɔʒi] *nf* pharmacology.

pharmacologique [farmakɔlɔʒik] *adj* pharmacological.

pharmacomanie [farmakɔmani] *nf* (pharmaceutical) drug-addiction, pharmacomania *spéc*.

pharmacopée [farmakɔpe] *nf* pharmacopeia, pharmacopoeia ▪ **la Pharmacopée internationale** the International Pharmacopoeia.

pharyngé, e [farɛ̃ʒe], **pharyngien, enne** [farɛ̃ʒjɛ̃, ɛn] *adj* ANAT pharyngal, pharyngeal.

pharyngite [farɛ̃ʒit] *nf* pharyngitis.

pharynx [farɛ̃ks] *nm* pharynx.

phase [faz] *nf* **1.** [moment] phase, stage ▪ **le projet en arrive à sa ~ d'exploitation** the project has moved into its first production run ◐ **~ critique** critical stage ; MÉD critical phase ▪ **~ terminale** final phase **2.** ÉLECTR & TECHNOL phase **3.** ASTRON phase **4.** CHIM phase.
◆ **en phase** *loc adj* ÉLECTR, PHYS & TECHNOL in phase ▪ **les mouvements ne sont plus en ~** the movements are now out of phase ▪ **être en ~** *fig* to see eye to eye ▪ **ils ne sont pas en ~** they don't see things the same way.

Phébus [febys] *npr* Phoebus.

Phèdre [fɛdr] *npr* Phaedra.

Phénicie [fenisi] *npr f* : **(la) ~** Phoenicia.

phénicien, enne [fenisjɛ̃, ɛn] *adj* Phoenician.
◆ **Phénicien, enne** *nm, f* Phoenician.
◆ **phénicien** *nm* LING Phoenician.

phénix [feniks] *nm* **1.** MYTHOL phoenix **2.** *litt* [prodige] paragon **3.** BOT palm tree.

phénol [fenɔl] *nm* phenol.

phénoménal, e, aux [fenɔmenal, o] *adj* **1.** [prodigieux] phenomenal, tremendous, amazing ▪ **il a un toupet ~** he's got (an) outrageous nerve, he's outrageously cheeky *UK* **2.** PHILOS phenomenal.

phénomène [fenɔmɛn] *nm* **1.** SC phenomenon ▪ **la grêle et autres ~s naturels** hail and other natural phenomena **2.** [manifestation] phenomenon ▪ **un ~ de société** a social phenomenon **3.** [prodige] prodigy, wonder **4.** *fam* [excentrique] character ▪ **un drôle de ~** an odd customer **5.** [monstre] : **~ (de foire)** freak **6.** PHILOS phenomenon.

phénoménologie [fenɔmenɔlɔʒi] *nf* phenomenology ▪ **'la Phénoménologie de l'esprit'** *Hegel* 'The Phenomenology of Mind'.

phénoménologique [fenɔmenɔlɔʒik] *adj* phenomenological.

phi [fi] *nm inv* phi.

Philadelphie [filadɛlfi] *npr* Philadelphia.

philanthrope [filɑ̃trɔp] *nmf* philanthrope, philanthropist.

philanthropie [filɑ̃trɔpi] *nf* philanthropy.

philanthropique [filɑ̃trɔpik] *adj* philanthropic.

philatélie [filateli] *nf* philately *spéc*, stamp-collecting.

philatélique [filatelik] *adj* philatelic.

philatéliste [filatelist] *nmf* philatelist *spéc*, stamp-collector.

philharmonie [filarmɔni] *nf* philharmonic *ou* musical society.

philharmonique [filarmɔnik] ◇ *adj* philharmonic.
◇ *nm* : **le ~ de Boston** the Boston Philharmonic (Orchestra).

Philippe [filip] *npr* : **~ le Bel** Philip the Fair.

philippin, e [filipɛ̃, in] *adj* Filipino.
◆ **Philippin, e** *nm, f* Filipino.

Philippines [filipin] *npr fpl* : **les ~** the Philippines, the Philippine Islands ▪ **aux ~** in the Philippines.

philippique [filipik] *nf litt* philippic.

philistin, e [filistɛ̃, in] *litt* ◇ *adj* philistine, uncultured.
◇ *nm, f* philistine.

Philistins [filistɛ̃] *npr mpl* : **les ~** the Philistines.

philo [filo] *nf fam* philosophy.

philodendron [filɔdɛ̃drɔ̃] *nm* philodendron.

philologie [filɔlɔʒi] *nf* philology.

philosophale [filɔzɔfal] *adj f* ⊳ **pierre**.

philosophe [filɔzɔf] ◇ *adj* philosophical.
◇ *nm, f* **1.** PHILOS philosopher **2.** [sage] : **il a pris la chose en ~** he took it philosophically *ou* calmly.

philosopher [3] [filɔzɔfe] *vi* to philosophize, to speculate ▪ **~ sur** to philosophize about *(inséр)*.

philosophie [filɔzɔfi] *nf* **1.** PHILOS philosophy **2.** ÉDUC philosophy ▪ **faire des études de ~** to study *ou* to read *UK* philosophy **3.** [conception] philosophy ▪ **quelle est votre ~ de la vie?** what's your philosophy of life? **4.** [sagesse] : **il est plein de ~** he is very wise.
◆ **avec philosophie** *loc adv* philosophically.

philosophique [filɔzɔfik] *adj* philosophical.

philosophiquement [filɔzɔfikmɑ̃] *adv* **1.** PHILOS philosophically **2.** [avec sagesse] philosophically.

philtre [filtr] *nm* love-potion, philtre.

phlébite [flebit] *nf* phlebitis.

phlébologie [flebɔlɔʒi] *nf* phlebology.

phlébologue [flebɔlɔg] *nmf* phlebologist.

phlegmon [flɛgmɔ̃] *nm* phlegmon.

pH-mètre [peaʃmɛtr] *(pl* **pH-mètres)** *nm* pH meter.

Phnom Penh [pnɔmpɛn] *npr* Phnom Penh.

phobie [fɔbi] *nf* **1.** PSYCHOL phobia **2.** [aversion] aversion ▪ **avoir la ~ de qqch** to have an aversion to sthg.

phobique [fɔbik] *adj* phobic.

phocéen, enne [fɔseɛ̃, ɛn] *adj* [de Marseille] from Marseilles ▪ **la cité ~ne** *the city of Marseilles.*
◆ **Phocéen, enne** *nm, f* **1.** ANTIQ Phocaean **2.** *vieilli inhabitant of or person from Marseilles.*

phoenix [feniks] = **phénix** *(sens 3)*.

phonatoire [fɔnatwar] *adj* phonatory ▪ **acte ~** phonatory act.

phone [fɔn] *nm* phon.

phonème [fɔnɛm] *nm* phoneme.

phonéticien, enne [fɔnetisjɛ̃, ɛn] *nm, f* phonetician.

phonétique [fɔnetik] ◇ *adj* phonetic.
◇ *nf* phonetics *(sing)*.

phonétiquement [fɔnetikmɑ̃] *adv* phonetically.

phoniatrie [fɔnjatri] *nf* speech therapy.

phonique [fɔnik] *adj* **1.** LING phonic **2.** [relatif aux sons] sound *(modif)*.

phono [fɔno] *nm* phonograph, gramophone.

phonogénique [fɔnɔʒenik] *adj* : **voix ~** RADIO good broadcasting voice ; AUDIO good recording voice.

phonographe [fɔnɔgraf] *nm* phonograph, gramophone.

phonologie [fɔnɔlɔʒi] *nf* phonology.

phonologique [fɔnɔlɔʒik] *adj* phonological.

phonothèque [fɔnɔtɛk] *nf* sound archives.

phoque [fɔk] *nm* **1.** ZOOL seal ▪ **~ à capuchon** hooded seal **2.** [fourrure] sealskin.

phosphate [fɔsfat] *nm* phosphate.

phosphaté, e [fɔsfate] *adj* AGRIC phosphatized ▪ **des engrais ~s** phosphates.

phosphater [3] [fɔsfate] *vt* **1.** AGRIC to phosphatize **2.** MÉTALL to phosphate, to phosphatize.

phosphore [fɔsfɔr] *nm* CHIM phosphorus.

phosphoré, e [fɔsfɔre] *adj* [naturellement] phosphorated ▪ [artificiellement] phosphoretted.

phosphorer [3] [fɔsfɔre] *vi fam* [réfléchir] to cogitate *hum*, to do a lot of hard thinking.

phosphorescence [fɔsfɔresɑ̃s] *nf* phosphorescence.

phosphorescent, e [fɔsfɔresɑ̃, ɑ̃t] *adj* **1.** PHYS phosphorescent **2.** [luisant] luminous, glowing.

phosphoreux, euse [fɔsfɔrø, øz] *adj* : **bronze ~** phosphor bronze.

photo [fɔto] *nf* **1.** [cliché] photo, shot ▪ **avez-vous fait des ~s?** did you take any pictures? ⊙ **~ de famille** family portrait ▪ **~ d'identité** passport photo ▪ **tu veux ma ~?** *fam* when you've quite finished gawping at me! ▪ **(entre les deux) (il n')y a pas ~** there's no comparison (between the two) **2.** [activité] photography ▪ **faire de la ~ en amateur/professionnel** to be an amateur/professional photographer.
◆ **en photo** ◇ *loc adj* on a photograph ▪ **des fleurs en ~** a photo of some flowers.
◇ *loc adv* : **prendre qqn en ~** to take sb's picture ▪ **prendre qqch en ~** to take a picture of sthg.

photochimie [fɔtɔʃimi] *nf* photochemistry.

photochimique [fɔtɔʃimik] *adj* photochemical.

photocomposer [3] [fɔtɔkɔ̃poze] *vt* to filmset, to photoset, to photocompose.

photocomposeuse [fɔtɔkɔ̃pozøz] *nf* photocomposer, photo *ou* phototype setter, filmsetter *UK*.

photocompositeur [fɔtɔkɔ̃pozitœr] *nm* photocomposer *ou* photosetter (technician), filmsetter *UK*.

photocomposition [fɔtɔkɔ̃pozisjɔ̃] *nf* photocomposition, photosetting, filmsetting *UK*.

photocopie [fɔtɔkɔpi] *nf* photocopy, Xerox®(copy).

photocopier [9] [fɔtɔkɔpje] *vt* to photocopy, to Xerox® ▪ **photocopiez-moi ce document en trois exemplaires, s'il vous plaît** please make three photocopies *ou* copies of this document for me.

photocopieuse [fɔtɔkɔpjøz] *nf*, **photocopieur** [fɔtɔkɔpjœr] *nm* photocopier, Xerox® machine.

photocopillage [fɔtɔkɔpijaʒ] *nm* *infringement of copyright through excessive use of photocopiers.*

photoélectrique [fɔtɔelɛktrik] *adj* photoelectric.

photo-finish [fɔtɔfiniʃ] (*pl* **photos-finish**) *nf* photo finish.

photogénique [fɔtɔʒenik] *adj* photogenic.

photographe [fɔtɔgraf] *nmf* **1.** [artiste] photographer ⊙ **~ de presse/mode** press/fashion photographer **2.** [commerçant] dealer in photographic equipment ▪ **je vais apporter ce film chez le ~** I'm taking this film to the developer's *ou* photo shop.

photographie [fɔtɔgrafi] *nf* **1.** [activité] photography ▪ **faire de la ~** [professionnel] to work as a photographer ; [amateur] to do amateur photography ⊙ **~ aérienne/en couleurs** aerial/colour photography **2.** [cliché - de professionnel] photograph, picture ; [- d'amateur] picture, snap, snapshot ▪ **prendre une ~ de qqn** to take a photograph *ou* a picture of sb ⊙ **~ d'identité** passport photograph **3.** [reproduction] : **ce sondage est une ~ de l'opinion** this survey is an accurate reflection of public opinion.

photographier [9] [fɔtɔgrafje] *vt* **1.** PHOTO to photograph, to take photographs *ou* pictures of ▪ **se faire ~** to have one's picture taken **2.** *fig* [mémoriser] to memorize (photographically).

photographique [fɔtɔgrafik] *adj* **1.** PHOTO photographic **2.** *fig* [fidèle à la réalité] : **il nous a fait une description presque ~ des lieux** he described the place in the minutest detail.

photograveur [fɔtɔgravœr] *nm* photoengraver.

photogravure [fɔtɔgravyr] *nf* photoengraving.

photo-journalisme [fɔtɔʒurnalism] *nm* photojournalism.

photolecture [fɔtɔlɛktyr] *nf* optical character recognition, OCR.

Photomaton® [fɔtɔmatɔ̃] *nm* photobooth.

photomontage [fɔtɔmɔ̃taʒ] *nm* photomontage.

photon [fɔtɔ̃] *nm* photon.

photophore [fɔtɔfɔr] *nm* photophore.

photoreportage [fɔtɔrəpɔrtaʒ] *nm* PRESSE report *(consisting mainly of photographs).*

photorésistant, e [fɔtɔrezistɑ̃, ɑ̃t] *adj* photoresistant.

photosensible [fɔtɔsɑ̃sibl] *adj* photosensitive.

photosynthèse [fɔtɔsɛ̃tɛz] *nf* photosynthesis.

photothèque [fɔtɔtɛk] *nf* picture *ou* photographic library.

phrase [fraz] *nf* **1.** LING sentence ▪ [en grammaire transformationnelle] phrase **2.** [énoncé] : **sa dernière ~** the last thing he said ▪ **laisse-moi finir ma ~** let me finish (what I have to say) ▪ **~ célèbre** famous saying *ou* remark ⊙ **~ toute faite** set phrase ▪ **petite ~** POLIT soundbite ▪ **faire de grandes ~s** *ou* **des ~s** to talk in flowery language **3.** MUS phrase.
◆ **sans phrases** *loc adv* straightforwardly.

phrasé [fraze] *nm* MUS phrasing.

phraséologie [frazeɔlɔʒi] *nf* phraseology.

phraser [3] [fraze] *vt* MUS to phrase.

phraseur, euse [frazœr, øz] *nm, f* speechifier *péj*, person of fine words *péj*.

phréatique [freatik] *adj* phreatic.

phrénique [frenik] *adj* phrenic.

phrénologie [frenɔlɔʒi] *nf* phrenology.

Phrygie [friʒi] *npr f* : **(la) ~** Phrygia.

phrygien, enne [friʒjɛ̃, ɛn] *adj* ANTIQ Phrygian.
◆ **Phrygien, enne** *nm, f* Phrygian.

phtisie [ftizi] *nf vieilli* consumption, phthisis *spéc* ▪ **~ galopante** galloping consumption.

phtisiologie [ftizjɔlɔʒi] *nf* phthisiology.

phtisiologue [ftizjɔlɔg] *nmf* phthisiologist.

phtisique [ftizik] *adj & nmf vieilli* consumptive, phthisic *spéc*.

phylactère [filaktɛr] *nm* **1.** RELIG phylactery, teffilah **2.** ART phylactery, scroll **3.** [dans une bande dessinée] bubble, balloon.

phylloxéra, phylloxera [filɔksera] *nm* phylloxera.

phylogenèse [filɔʒenɛz] *nf* phylogenesis, phylogeny.

physicien, enne [fizisjɛ̃, ɛn] *nm, f* physicist ▪ **~ nucléaire** nuclear physicist.

physiologie [fizjɔlɔʒi] *nf* physiology.

physiologique [fizjɔlɔʒik] *adj* physiological.

physiologiste [fizjɔlɔʒist] *nmf* physiologist.

physionomie [fizjɔnɔmi] *nf* **1.** [visage] features, facial appearance, physiognomy *litt* ■ **il y a quelque chose dans sa ~ qui attire la sympathie** there's something about his face that draws you to him **2.** [aspect] face, appearance ■ **la ~ des choses** the face of things ■ **ceci a modifié la ~ du marché** this has altered the appearance of the market.

physionomiste [fizjɔnɔmist] <> *adj* good at remembering faces, observant (of people's faces) ■ **je ne suis pas très ~** I'm not very good at (remembering) faces.
<> *nmf* physiognomist.

physiopathologique [fizjɔpatɔlɔʒik] *adj* physiopathologic, physiopathological.

physiothérapie [fizjɔterapi] *nf* natural medicine.

physique[1] [fizik] *nf* SC physics *(sing)* ■ **~ expérimentale/nucléaire** experimental/nuclear physics.

physique[2] [fizik] <> *adj* **1.** SC [propriété] physical **2.** [naturel - monde, univers] physical, natural **3.** [corporel - exercice, force, effort] physical, bodily ; [- symptôme] physical, somatic *spéc* ; [- souffrance] physical, bodily ■ **c'est ~** *fam* **: je ne le supporte pas, c'est ~** I can't stand him, it's a gut reaction **4.** [sexuel - plaisir, jouissance] physical, carnal.
<> *nm* **1.** [apparence] **: avoir un ~ ingrat** to be physically unattractive ■ **un ~ avantageux** good looks ➤ **avoir le ~ de l'emploi** THÉÂTRE & *fig* to look the part **2.** [constitution] physical condition ■ **au ~ comme au moral** physically as well as morally speaking.

physiquement [fizikmɑ̃] *adv* physically ■ **il n'est pas mal ~** he's quite good-looking.

phytophage [fitɔfaʒ] *adj* phytophagous.

phytoplancton [fitɔplɑ̃ktɔ̃] *nm* phytoplankton.

phytothérapeute [fitɔterapøt] *nmf* expert in herbal *ou* plant medicine.

phytothérapie [fitɔterapi] *nf* herbal medicine.

pi [pi] *nm inv* **1.** [lettre] pi **2.** MATH pi **3.** PHYS pion, pi meson.

piaf [pjaf] *nm fam* [moineau] sparrow ■ **cervelle** *ou* **crâne** *ou* **tête de ~!** *fig* birdbrain!

piaffement [pjafmɑ̃] *nm* pawing (the ground).

piaffer [3] [pjafe] *vi* **1.** [cheval] to paw the ground **2.** [personne] **: ~ d'impatience** to be champing at the bit, to be seething with impatience.

piaillement [pjajmɑ̃] *nm* squawking ■ **les ~s qui montaient de la basse-cour** the clucking noises coming from the farmyard.

piailler [3] [pjaje] *vi* **1.** [oiseau] to chirrup, to chirp, to tweet ■ [volaille] to squawk **2.** *fam* [enfant] to squawk, to screech.

piaillerie [pjajri] *nf* **1.** [cri - d'oiseau] chirping ; [- de volaille] squawking **2.** *fam (gén pl) fam* squawking, screeching.

piailleur, euse [pjajœr, øz] *nm, f fam* squawker.

pianissimo [pjanisimo] *adv* **1.** MUS pianissimo **2.** *fam* [doucement] nice and slowly.

pianiste [pjanist] *nmf* pianist, piano player.

pianistique [pjanistik] *adj* [aptitude, technique] piano *(modif)*, piano playing *(modif)* ■ **l'œuvre ~ de Mozart** Mozart's works for piano.

piano [pjano] <> *nm* [instrument] piano, pianoforte *sout* ■ **se mettre au ~** [s'asseoir] to sit at the piano ; [jouer] to go to the piano (and start playing) ; [apprendre] to take up the piano ➤ **~ droit/à queue** upright/grand piano ■ **~ à bretelles** *fam*, **~ du pauvre** accordion ■ **~ de concert** concert grand ■ **~ demi-queue** baby grand ■ **~ mécanique** Pianola®, player piano.
<> *adv* **1.** MUS piano *(adv)* **2.** *fam* [doucement] easy *(adv)*, gently.

piano-bar [pjanobar] *(pl* **pianos-bars***)* *nm bar with live piano music.*

pianoforte [pjanofɔrte] *nm* pianoforte.

pianotage [pjanɔtaʒ] *nm* **1.** [sur un piano] tinkling (on a piano) **2.** [sur un clavier] tapping away (at a keyboard).

pianoter [3] [pjanɔte] <> *vi* **1.** [jouer du piano] to tinkle away at the piano **2.** [tapoter sur un objet] to drum one's fingers **3.** *fam* [taper sur un clavier] to tap away ■ **~ sur un ordinateur** to tap away at a computer.
<> *vt* [sur un piano] to tinkle out on the piano.

piastre [pjastr] *nf* **1.** [au Proche-Orient] piastre **2.** *fam Québec fam* [dollar] one-dollar *ou* dollar bill **3.** HIST piastre, piece of eight.

piaule [pjol] *nf fam* **1.** [chambre] room **2.** [logement d'étudiant] place.

piauler [3] [pjole] *vi* **1.** [oiseau] to cheep **2.** [enfant] to whimper.

piazza [pjadza] *nf* piazza *UK*, gallery *US*.

PIB (*abr de* **produit intérieur brut**) *nm* GDP.

pic [pik] *nm* **1.** GÉOGR & TECHNOL peak **2.** [outil] pick, pickaxe ■ **~ à glace** ice-pick **3.** ORNITH woodpecker.
◆ **à pic** *loc adv* **1.** [verticalement] straight down ■ **couler à ~** to go straight down *ou* straight to the bottom **2.** *fam* [au bon moment] spot on *UK*, just at the right time ■ **tu tombes** *ou* **tu arrives à ~, j'allais t'appeler** you've come just at the right time *ou* right on cue, I was about to call you.

picador [pikadɔr] *nm* picador.

picard, e [pikar, ard] *adj* from Picardy.
◆ **picard** *nm* LING Picard *ou* Picardy dialect.

Picardie [pikardi] *npr f* **: (la) ~** Picardy.

PICARDIE

This administrative region includes the *départements* of Aisne, Oise and Somme (capital: Amiens).

picaresque [pikarɛsk] *adj* picaresque.

piccolo [pikɔlo] *nm* piccolo.

pichenette [piʃnɛt] *nf* flick ■ **d'une ~, elle envoya la miette par terre** she flicked the crumb onto the ground.

pichet [piʃɛ] *nm* jug, pitcher.

pickpocket [pikpɔkɛt] *nm* pickpocket.

pick-up [pikœp] *nm inv* **1.** [lecteur] pick-up (arm) ■ *vieilli* [tourne-disque] record player **2.** [camion] pick-up (truck).

pico- [piko] *préf* pico-.

picoler [3] [pikɔle] *vi fam* [boire] to booze ■ **qu'est-ce qu'on a picolé ce soir-là!** we didn't half knock it back *UK ou* we sure knocked it back *US* that night!

picoleur, euse [pikɔlœr, øz] *nm, f fam* [buveur] heavy drinker, boozer.

picorer [3] [pikɔre] *vt* **1.** [oiseau] to peck (at) **2.** [personne] to nibble (away) at *(insép)*, to pick at *(insép)* ■ *(en usage absolu)* **cette enfant ne fait que ~** that child doesn't eat enough (to keep a bird alive).

picot [piko] *nm* **1.** MÉCAN barb, point ■ **~ d'entraînement** feed pin **2.** [au crochet, en dentelle] picot.
◆ **à picots** *loc adj* [dispositif, entraînement] sprocket *(modif)*.

picotement [pikɔtmɑ̃] *nm* [dans les yeux] smarting *ou* stinging (sensation) ■ [dans la gorge] tickle ■ [sur la peau] tingle, prickle ■ **j'ai des ~s dans les doigts** my fingers are tingling.

picoter [3] [pikɔte] *vt* **1.** [piquer - yeux] to sting, to smart ; [- gorge] to irritate, to tickle ; [- peau, doigt] to sting ■ **j'ai les orteils qui me picotent** my toes are tingling **2.** [suj: oiseau] to peck at *(insép)*.

picotin [pikɔtɛ̃] *nm* **1.** [mesure] peck **2.** [ration] **: ~ (d'avoine)** peck of oats.

picrate [pikrat] *nm* **1.** CHIM picrate **2.** △ *péj* [vin] rotgut△, plonk *UK*.

picte [pikt] *adj* Pictish.
◆ **Picte** *nmf* Pict.

pictogramme [piktɔgram] *nm* pictogram, pictograph.

pictographique [piktɔgrafik] *adj* pictographic.

pictural, e, aux [piktyral, o] *adj* pictorial.

pic-vert [pivɛr] (*pl* **pics-verts**) = **pivert**.

pidgin [pidʒin] *nm* pidgin.

pie [pi] <> *adj* **1.** [couleur] pied ■ **cheval ~** piebald (horse) ■ **vache ~ noire** black and white cow **2.** *litt* [pieux] : **œuvre ~** pious work.
<> *nf* **1.** ORNITH magpie **2.** *fam* [personne] chatterbox.

Pie [pi] *npr* [pape] Pius.

pièce [pjɛs] <> *nf* **1.** [morceau] piece, bit ■ **une ~ de viande** [flanc] a side of meat ; [morceau découpé] a piece *ou* cut of meat ■ **une ~ de tissu** [coupée] a piece *ou* length of cloth ; [sur rouleau] a roll of cloth ■ **mettre qqch en ~s** [briser] to smash sthg to pieces ; [déchirer] to tear *ou* to pull sthg to pieces ; [critiquer] to tear sthg to pieces ■ **~ à ~** piecemeal, gradually ▶ **d'une seule ~, tout d'une ~** *pr* all of a piece ■ **il est tout d'une ~** *fig* he's very blunt *ou* straightforward ■ **monter qqch de toutes ~s : il n'a jamais travaillé pour nous, il a monté cela de toutes ~s** he never worked for us, he made up *ou* invented the whole thing ■ **c'est un mensonge monté de toutes ~s** it's an out-and-out lie *ou* a lie from start to finish ■ **fait de ~s et de morceaux** *pr* & *fig* made up of bits and pieces, cobbled together
2. [d'une collection] piece, item ■ [d'un mécanisme] part ■ [d'un jeu] piece ▶ **~ détachée** (spare) part ■ **en ~s détachées** in separate pieces *ou* parts ■ **~s et main-d'œuvre** parts and labour ■ **la ~ maîtresse de ma collection** the centrepiece of *ou* choicest piece in my collection ■ **la ~ maîtresse d'une argumentation** the main part *ou* the linchpin of an argument ■ **~ de musée** *pr* & *fig* museum piece ■ **~ de rechange** spare *ou* replacement part ■ **les ~s d'un puzzle** *pr* & *fig* the pieces of a puzzle
3. COUT patch ▶ **~ rapportée** *pr* patch ; *fig* [personne] odd person out
4. [salle] room ■ **un deux-~s** a one-bedroom flat *UK ou* apartment *US*
5. [document] paper, document ■ **~ comptable** (accounting) voucher ■ **~ à conviction** DR exhibit ■ **avez-vous une ~ d'identité?** do you have any proof of identity *ou* any ID? ■ **~s jointes** enclosures ■ **~s justificatives** supporting documents ■ **(avec) ~s à l'appui : je vous le démontrerai ~s à l'appui** I'll show you (actual) proof of it
6. LITTÉR & MUS piece ■ **~ de circonstance** situation piece ■ **~ (de théâtre)** play ■ **~ écrite pour la télévision** television play *UK*, play written for TV *US* ■ **monter une ~** to put on *ou* to stage a play
7. [argent] : **une ~ de 2 euros** a 2-euro coin *ou* piece ■ **je n'ai que quelques ~s dans ma poche** I've only got some loose change in my pocket
8. [champ] : **une ~ d'avoine** a field sown in oats
9. CULIN : **~ montée** [gâteau] ≃ tiered cake ; [pyramide] *pyramid of caramel-covered profiteroles often served at weddings and other special occasions* ■ **~ de résistance** *pr* main dish ; *fig* pièce de résistance
10. MIL : **~ (d'artillerie)** gun
11. *loc* **faire ~ à qqn** to set up in opposition to sb.
<> *adv* [chacun] each, apiece ■ **les roses sont à 20 euros ~** the roses are 20 euros each *ou* apiece.
◆ **à la pièce** *loc adv* [à l'unité] singly, separately ■ **ceux-ci sont vendus à la ~** these are sold separately *ou* individually.
◆ **à la pièce, aux pièces** *loc adv* : **travailler à la ~** to be on *ou* to do piecework ■ **être payé à la ~** to be paid a *ou* on piece rate ■ **le travail est payé à la ~** you get a piecework rate ▶ **on n'est pas aux ~s!** *fam* what's the big hurry?, where's the fire?
◆ **sur pièces** *loc adv* on evidence ■ **juger sur ~s** to judge for o.s.
◆ **pièce d'eau** *nf* **1.** [lac] (ornamental) lake
2. [bassin] (ornamental) pond.

PIÈCE

Flats in France are referred to in terms of the total number of rooms they have (excluding the kitchen and bathroom). *Un deux-pièces* is a flat with a living room and one bedroom; *un cinq-pièces* is a flat with five rooms.

piécette [pjesɛt] *nf* [monnaie] small coin.

pied [pje] *nm* **1.** ANAT & ZOOL foot ■ **~s nus** barefoot *(adv)* ■ **marcher/être ~s nus** to walk/to be barefoot ■ **avoir** *ou* **marcher les ~s en dedans** to be pigeon-toed, to walk with one's feet turned in ■ **avoir** *ou* **marcher les ~s en dehors** to be splay-footed *ou* duck-toed *US*, to walk with one's feet turned out ■ **sauter à ~s joints** to make a standing jump ■ **le ~ m'a manqué** my foot slipped, I lost my footing ■ **mettre le ~ (en plein) dans qqch** to step right in sthg ■ **je vais lui mettre mon ~ quelque part** *euphém* I'll kick him *ou* give him a kick up the backside ■ **mettre ~ à terre** [à cheval, à moto] to dismount ■ **lorsqu'ils mirent le ~ sur le sol de France** when they set foot on French soil ■ **je n'ai pas mis les ~s dehors/à l'église depuis longtemps** *fam* I haven't been out/to church for a long time ■ **je ne mettrai** *ou* **remettrai plus jamais les ~s là-bas** I'll never set foot there again ▶ **avoir les ~s plats** to have flat feet *pr*, to be flat-footed *pr* ■ **ni ~ ni patte** *fam* : **il ne remuait** *ou* **bougeait ni ~ ni patte** he stood stock-still *ou* didn't move a muscle ■ **aller** *ou* **avancer** *ou* **marcher d'un bon ~** to go apace ■ **aller** *ou* **marcher d'un ~ léger** to tread light-heartedly *ou* lightly ■ **avoir bon ~ bon œil** to be fit as a fiddle *ou* hale and hearty ■ **partir du bon/mauvais ~** to start off (in) the right/wrong way ■ **avoir le ~ marin** to be a good sailor ■ **je n'ai pas le ~ marin** to have one's feet (firmly) on the ground *ou* one's head screwed on (the right way) ■ **avoir ~** to touch bottom ■ **au secours, je n'ai plus ~!** help, I'm out of my depth *ou* I've lost my footing! ■ **avoir un ~ dans : j'ai déjà un ~ dans la place/l'entreprise** I've got a foot in the door/a foothold in the company already ■ **avoir un ~ dans la tombe** to have one foot in the grave ■ **elle n'a pas les deux ~s dans le même sabot** there are no flies on her ■ **bien fait pour tes/ses ~s** *fam*, **ça te/lui fera les ~s** *fam* serves you/him right! ■ **je suis ~s et poings liés** my hands are tied ■ **faire des ~s et des mains pour** to bend over backwards *ou* to pull out all the stops in order to ■ **faire du ~ à qqn** [flirter] to play footsie with sb ; [avertir] to kick sb (under the table) ■ **faire le ~ de grue** to cool *ou* to kick *UK* one's heels ■ **elle en est partie les ~s devant** she left there feet first *ou* in a box ■ **avoir le ~ au plancher** [accélérer] to have one's foot down ■ **lever le ~** [ralentir] to ease off (on the accelerator), to slow down ; [partir subrepticement] to slip off ■ **mettre le ~ à l'étrier** to get into the saddle ■ **il a fallu lui mettre le ~ à l'étrier** he had to be given a leg up *fig* ■ **mettre les ~s dans le plat** *fam* to put one's foot in it ■ **mettre qqch sur ~** to set sthg up ■ **il ne peut plus mettre un ~ devant l'autre** [ivre] he can't walk in a straight line any more ; [fatigué] his legs won't carry him any further ■ **reprendre ~** to get *ou* to find one's footing again ■ **retomber sur ses ~s** *pr* & *fig* to fall *ou* to land on one's feet ■ **ne pas savoir sur quel ~ danser** to be at a loss to know what to do ■ **se jeter** *ou* **se traîner aux ~s de qqn** to throw o.s. at sb's feet, to get down on one's knees to sb ■ **se lever du ~ gauche** to get out of the wrong side of the bed ■ **comme un ~** *fam* [très mal] : **je cuisine comme un ~** I'm a useless cook, I can't cook an egg ■ **on s'est débrouillés comme des ~s** we went about it the wrong *ou* in a cack-handed *UK* way ■ **prendre son ~** *fam* [s'amuser] to get one's kicks ■ **il prend son ~ en faisant du jazz!** he gets a real kick out of playing jazz! ■ **quel ~!** *fam* : **on a passé dix jours à Hawaï, quel ~!** we really had a ball *ou* we had the time of our lives during our ten days in Hawaï! ■ **ce n'est pas le ~!** *fam* : **les cours d'anglais, ce n'est pas le ~!** the English class isn't much fun!
2. [d'un mur, d'un lit] foot ■ [d'une table, d'une chaise] leg ■ [d'une lampe, d'une colonne] base ■ [d'un verre] stem ■ [d'un micro, d'un appareil photo] stand, tripod
3. IMPR [d'une lettre] bottom, foot
4. BOT plant ■ [de champignon] foot ■ **~ de laitue** lettuce plant ■ **~ mère** stool ■ **~ de vigne** vine (plant), vinestock
5. [mesure] foot ■ **le mur fait six ~s de haut** the wall is six-feet high ■ **un mur de six ~s de haut** a six-foot high wall
6. TECHNOL : **~ de bielle** AUTO end of connecting rod ■ **~ à coulisse** calliper rule ■ **~ de roi** *Québec* folding ruler
7. LITTÉR foot ■ **vers de 12 ~s** 12-foot verse *ou* line
8. CULIN : **~ de cochon** pig's trotter *UK ou* foot *US* ■ **~s paquets** stuffed mutton tripe dish *(from Marseilles)*
9. [d'un bas, d'une chaussette] foot
10. MUS foot.
◆ **à pied** *loc adv* **1.** [en marchant] on foot ■ **on ira au stade à ~** we'll walk to the stadium

2. [au chômage] : **mettre qqn à ~** [mesure disciplinaire] to suspend sb ; [mesure économique] to lay sb off, to make sb redundant *UK*.

◆ **à pied d'œuvre** *loc adj* : **être à ~ d'œuvre** to be ready to get down to the job.

◆ **à pied sec** *loc adv* on dry land, without getting one's feet wet.

◆ **au pied de** *loc prép* at the foot *ou* bottom of ■ **au ~ des Alpes** in the foothills of the Alps ▶ **au ~ du mur : être au ~ du mur** to be faced with no alternative ■ **mettre qqn au ~ du mur** to get sb with his/her back to the wall, to leave sb with no alternative.

◆ **au pied de la lettre** *loc adv* literally ■ **suivre des instructions au ~ de la lettre** to follow instructions to the letter.

◆ **au pied levé** *loc adv* at a moment's notice ■ **il faut que tu sois prêt à le faire au ~ levé** you must be ready to drop everything and do it.

◆ **de pied en cap** *loc adv* : **en vert de ~ en cap** dressed in green from top *ou* head to toe ■ **habillé de ~ en cap par un couturier japonais** wearing a complete outfit by a Japanese designer.

◆ **de pied ferme** *loc adv* resolutely ■ **je t'attends de ~ ferme** I'll definitely be waiting for you.

◆ **des pieds à la tête** *loc adv* from top to toe *ou* head to foot ■ **couvert de peinture des ~s à la tête** covered in paint from head to foot.

◆ **en pied** *loc adj* [photo, portrait] full-length ■ [statue] full-size standing.

◆ **pied à pied** *loc adv* inch by inch ■ **lutter** *ou* **se battre ~ à ~** to fight every inch of the way.

◆ **sur le pied de guerre** *loc adv* MIL on a war footing ■ *hum* ready (for action) ■ **dans la cuisine, tout le monde était sur le ~ de guerre** it was action stations in the kitchen.

◆ **sur pied** ◇ *loc adj* [récolte] uncut, standing ■ [bétail] on the hoof.
◇ *loc adv* : **être sur ~** [en bonne santé] to be up and about ■ **remettre qqn sur ~** to put sb on his/her feet again, to make sb better.

◆ **sur un pied d'égalité** *loc adv* on an equal footing ■ **être sur un ~ d'égalité avec** to stand on equal terms with.

pied-à-terre [pjetatɛr] *nm inv* pied-à-terre.

pied-bot [pjebo] (*pl* **pieds-bots**) *nm* club-footed person ■ **c'est un ~** he's got a *ou* he's a club-foot.

pied-de-biche [pjedbiʃ] (*pl* **pieds-de-biche**) *nm* **1.** [pince] nail puller *ou* extractor **2.** [levier] crowbar **3.** [pied de meuble] cabriole leg **4.** [d'une machine à coudre] foot.

pied-de-mouton [pjedmutɔ̃] (*pl* **pieds-de-mouton**) *nm* wood hedgehog (fungus).

pied(-)de(-)nez [pjedne] (*pl* **pieds-de-nez**) *nm* : **faire un ~ à qqn** to thumb one's nose at sb ■ **cette pièce est un ~ aux intellos** *fam* this play is a real slap in the face for intellectual types.

pied-de-poule [pjedpul] (*pl* **pieds-de-poule**) ◇ *nm* hound's-tooth (check), dogtooth (check).
◇ *adj inv* : **un tailleur ~** a hound's-tooth suit.

pied-de-roi [pjedərwa] *nm* *Québec* folding ruler.

pied-droit [pjedrwa] (*pl* **pieds-droits**) = **piédroit**.

piédestal, aux [pjedɛstal, o] *nm* pedestal ■ **mettre qqn sur un ~** to put *ou* to set *ou* to place sb on a pedestal.

piedmont [pjemɔ̃] = **piémont**.

pied-noir [pjenwar] (*pl* **pieds-noirs**) ◇ *adj* pied-noir.
◇ *nmf* pied-noir *(French settler in Algeria)*.

PIED-NOIR

This is the name given to former French settlers in Algeria who returned to France after Algeria regained its independence in 1962, many of them resettling in cities on the south coast.

piédroit [pjedrwa] *nm* **1.** ARCHIT [d'une voûte] pier ■ [d'une fenêtre] jamb **2.** TRAV PUB [jambage] piedroit.

piège [pjɛʒ] *nm* **1.** [dispositif] trap, snare ■ **prendre un animal au ~** to trap an animal ■ **poser** *ou* **tendre un ~** to set a trap ■ **attirer qqn dans un ~** to lure sb into a trap ■ **être pris à son propre ~** to fall into one's own trap, to be hoist by one's own petard *sout* ■ **se laisser prendre au ~ de l'amour** to be taken in by love ▶ **~ à cons**[△] : **c'est un vrai ~ à cons!** it's a real mug's game! *UK*, it's a con game *ou* gyp! *US* ■ **pris comme dans un ~ à rats** caught like a rat in a trap **2.** [difficulté] trap, snare, pitfall **3.** GÉOL trap.

piégé, e [pjeʒe] *adj* : **engin** *ou* **objet ~** booby trap ■ **colis ~** parcel bomb ■ **lettre/voiture ~e** letter/car bomb.

piéger [22] [pjeʒe] *vt* **1.** [animal] to trap, to ensnare ■ **la police les a piégés** the police trapped them ■ **je me suis fait ~ comme un débutant** *fig* I was taken in *ou* caught out like a complete beginner **2.** [voiture, paquet] to booby-trap.

piémont [pjemɔ̃] *nm* piedmont.

Piémont [pjemɔ̃] *npr m* : **le ~** Piedmont.

piémontais, e [pjemɔ̃tɛ, ɛz] *adj* Piedmontese.

pierraille [pjɛraj] *nf* loose stones, scree *(U)*.

pierre [pjɛr] *nf* **1.** [matière] stone ■ [caillou] stone, rock *US* ■ **tuer qqn à coups de ~** to stone sb to death ‖ ART : **sculpter la ~** to carve in stone ‖ [immobilier] : **la ~** the property *ou* real estate *US* business ■ **investir dans la ~** to invest in property *ou* in bricks and mortar ■ **les vieilles ~s** ruined buildings, ruins ▶ **~ d'achoppement** stumbling block ■ **~ levée** standing stone ■ **~ polie** neolith ■ **~ taillée** palaeolith, paleolith ■ **faire d'une ~ deux coups** to kill two birds (with one stone) ■ **jeter la ~ à qqn** to cast a stone at sb ■ **c'est une ~ dans ton jardin** that remark was (meant) for you ■ **se mettre une ~ autour du cou** to put an albatross round one's neck ■ **~ qui roule n'amasse pas mousse** *prov* a rolling stone gathers no moss
2. CONSTR : **~ de taille** *ou* **d'appareil** freestone ■ **~ angulaire** *pr* & *fig* keystone, cornerstone ■ **~ à bâtir** building stone ■ **mur en ~s sèches** drystone wall ■ **poser la première ~ (de)** *pr* to lay down the first stone (of) ; *fig* to lay the foundations (of)
3. JOAILL & MINÉR : **~ brute** rough *ou* uncut stone ■ **~ taillée** cut stone ▶ **~ fine** *ou* **semi-précieuse** semi-precious stone ■ **~ de lune** moonstone ■ **~ précieuse** gem, precious stone ■ **~ de touche** *pr* & *fig* touchstone
4. GÉOL : **~ calcaire** *ou* **à chaux** limestone ■ **~ meulière** *type of stone common in the Paris area once used for making millstones and as a building material* ■ **~ ponce** pumice stone
5. [instrument] : **~ à affûter** *ou* **aiguiser** whetstone ■ **~ à briquet** (lighter) flint ■ **~ à feu** *ou* **fusil** gun flint
6. [stèle] : **~ funéraire** *ou* **tombale** tombstone, gravestone
7. RELIG : **~ d'autel** altar stone ■ **~ noire** black stone
8. HIST & *fig* **~ philosophale** philosopher's stone
9. [dans un fruit] (piece of) grit
10. MÉD & *vieilli* (kidney) stone, calculus *spéc*.

◆ **de pierre** *loc adv* stony, of stone ■ **être/rester de ~** to be/to remain icy-cool ■ **son cœur/visage restait de ~** he remained stony-hearted/stony-faced.

◆ **pierre à pierre, pierre par pierre** *loc adv* *pr* stone by stone ■ *fig* painstakingly ■ **il a construit sa fortune ~ par ~** he built up his fortune from nothing.

◆ **pierre sur pierre** *loc adv* *litt* **après le tremblement de terre, il ne restait pas ~ sur ~** not a stone was left standing after the earthquake.

Pierre [pjɛr] *npr* : **saint ~** Saint Peter ■ **~ le Grand** Peter the Great.

pierreries [pjɛrri] *nfpl* precious stones, gems.

pierreux, euse [pjɛrø, øz] *adj* **1.** [terrain] stony, rocky ■ **un chemin ~** a stony path **2.** [fruit] gritty **3.** MÉD & *vieilli* calculous.

pierrot [pjɛro] *nm* **1.** THÉÂTRE Pierrot ■ [clown] pierrot, clown **2.** [moineau] sparrow.

pietà [pjeta] *nf* pietà.

piétaille [pjetaj] *nf* **1.** *fam hum* [fantassins] rank and file **2.** *péj* [subalternes] rank and file ■ **la direction nous considère comme de la ~** the management just thinks of us as skivvies *UK* *ou* flunkies *US*.

piété [pjete] *nf* **1.** RELIG piety **2.** [amour] devotion, reverence ■ **~ filiale** filial devotion.

piétinement [pjetinmɑ̃] *nm* **1.** [action] stamping ■ **le ~ des chevaux sur le pavé était assourdissant** the sound of the horses' hooves on the cobblestones was deafening **2.** *fig* [stagnation] : **le ~ de l'affaire arrange certaines personnes** the lack of progress in the case suits certain people.

piétiner [3] [pjetine] ◇ *vi* **1.** [s'agiter] to walk on the spot ■ **~ de rage** to stamp one's feet in rage ■ **~ d'impatience** *fig* to be fidgeting with impatience, to be champing at the bit **2.** *fig* [stagner] to fail to make (any) progress *ou* headway ■ **on piétine, il faut se décider!** we're not getting anywhere *ou* we're just marking time, let's make up our minds!
◇ *vt* **1.** [écraser] to trample *ou* to tread on **2.** *fig* [libertés, traditions] to trample underfoot, to ride roughshod over.

piétisme [pjetism] *nm* pietism.

piétiste [pjetist] ◇ *adj* pietistic, pietistical.
◇ *nmf* pietist.

piéton, onne [pjetɔ̃, ɔn] ◇ *adj* pedestrian *(modif)* ■ **rue** *ou* **zone ~ne** pedestrian precinct *UK ou* mall *US*.
◇ *nm, f* pedestrian.

piétonnier, ère [pjetɔnje, ɛr] *adj* pedestrian *(modif)* ■ **rue piétonnière** pedestrian area *ou* street.

piètre [pjɛtr] *adj (avant n)* very poor, mediocre ■ **faire ~ figure** to be a sorry sight ■ **de ~ qualité** very mediocre ■ **c'est une ~ consolation** that's small *ou* not much comfort.

piètrement [pjɛtrəmɑ̃] *adv* very mediocrely ■ **je suis bien ~ récompensée** this is (a) meagre recompense indeed for my effort.

pieu, x [pjø] *nm* **1.** [poteau - pour délimiter] post ; [- pour attacher] stake ■ **les jeunes arbres sont attachés à des ~x** the young trees are attached to stakes **2.** *fam* [lit] bed ■ **aller** *ou* **se mettre au ~** to turn in, to hit the hay *ou* the sack.

pieusement [pjøzmɑ̃] *adv* **1.** [dévotement] piously, devoutly **2.** [scrupuleusement] religiously, scrupulously.

pieuter [3] △ [pjøte] *vi* **1.** [passer la nuit] to crash (out) **2.** [coucher avec] : **~ avec qqn** to bunk down with sb.
◆ **se pieuter**△ *vpi* to turn in, to hit the hay *ou* the sack.

pieuvre [pjœvr] *nf* **1.** ZOOL octopus **2.** *fig* [personne] leech.

pieux, euse [pjø, øz] *adj* **1.** [dévot] pious, devout **2.** [charitable] : **~ mensonge** white lie.

pif [pif] ◇ *onomat* bang, splat.
◇ *nm* [nez] conk *UK*, hooter *UK*, shnoz *US*.
◆ **au pif** *loc adv fam* at random ■ **au ~, je dirais trois** I'd say three, at a rough guess *ou* off the top of my head ■ **j'ai pris celui-là au ~** I just took the first one that came to hand.

pif(f)er [3] △ [pife] *vt* [supporter] : **je ne peux pas le ~!** I can't stomach him!, I just can't stand him!

pifomètre [pifɔmɛtr] *nm fam* **au ~ : j'ai dit ça au ~** I was just guessing ■ **faire qqch au ~** to follow one's hunch in doing sthg.

Pigalle [pigal] *npr area of Paris famous for its nightclubs (including the Moulin Rouge) and as a red light district.*

pige [piʒ] *nf* **1.** [tige graduée] measuring stick **2.** TECHNOL gauge rod **3.** *fam* IMPR & PRESSE : **travailler à la ~, faire des ~s** to work freelance ■ **être payé à la ~** to be paid piece rate *ou* by the line **4.** △ [an] year ■ **pour quarante ~s, il est bien conservé** he still looks pretty good for a forty-year-old **5.** *fam loc* **faire la ~ à qqn** to go one better than sb.

pigeon [piʒɔ̃] *nm* **1.** ORNITH pigeon ■ **~ ramier** wood pigeon, ringdove ■ **~ voyageur** carrier *ou* homing pigeon **2.** JEUX : **~ vole** *children's game consisting of a yes or no answer to the question: does X fly?* **3.** CONSTR [plâtre] handful of plaster ■ [chaux] lump (in lime) **4.** SPORT : **~ d'argile** clay pigeon **5.** *fam* [dupe] mug *UK*, sucker *US* ■ **et c'est encore moi le ~!** and muggins here *UK ou* yours truly *US* ends up holding the baby as usual!

pigeonnant, e [piʒɔnɑ̃, ɑ̃t] *adj* : **soutien-gorge ~** uplift (bra) ■ **poitrine ~e** full bosom.

pigeonne [piʒɔn] *nf* hen pigeon.

pigeonneau, x [piʒɔno] *nm* ORNITH young pigeon, squab *spéc.*

pigeonner [3] [piʒɔne] *vt* **1.** CONSTR to plaster **2.** *fam* [duper] : **~ qqn** to take sb in *ou* for a ride, to hoodwink sb ■ **se faire ~** [tromper] to be led up the garden path, to be taken for a ride ; [pour de l'argent] to get ripped off.

pigeonnier [piʒɔnje] *nm* **1.** [pour pigeons] dovecote **2.** *fam* [mansarde] garret, attic.

piger [17] [piʒe] ◇ *vt* **1.** *fam* [comprendre] to get, to twig *UK* ■ **(t'as) pigé?** got it?, have you twigged? *UK*, have you got the picture? *US* ■ **elle pige rien** *ou* **que dalle à l'art** she hasn't got a clue about art ■ *(en usage absolu)* **il a fini par ~** the penny finally dropped *UK*, he finally got it *ou* got the picture *US* **2.** [mesurer] to rule (out).
◇ *vi fam* [travailler à la pige] to work freelance.

pigiste [piʒist] *nmf* **1.** IMPR piece-rate typographer **2.** PRESSE freelance journalist.

pigment [pigmɑ̃] *nm* pigment.

pigmentaire [pigmɑ̃tɛr] *adj* pigmentary.

pigmentation [pigmɑ̃tasjɔ̃] *nf* pigmentation.

pigmenter [3] [pigmɑ̃te] *vt* to pigment.

pigne [piɲ] *nf* **1.** [cône] pine cone **2.** [graine] pine kernel.

pignocher [3] [piɲɔʃe] *vi* **1.** *vieilli* [manger] to nibble *ou* to pick at food **2.** [peindre] *to paint with minutely fine strokes.*

pignon [piɲɔ̃] *nm* **1.** ARCHIT [de mur] gable ■ [de bâtiments] side wall ■ **avoir ~ sur rue** [personne] to be well-off (and respectable) ; [entreprise] to be well established **2.** TECHNOL [roue dentée] cogwheel, gear wheel ■ [petite roue] pinion ■ [d'une bicyclette] rear-wheel, sprocket **3.** BOT pine kernel *ou* nut.

pignouf△ [piɲuf] *nm* [rustre] slob.

pilaf [pilaf] *nm* pilaf, pilau.

pilage [pilaʒ] *nm* pounding, grinding.

pilaire [pilɛr] *adj* pilar, pilary.

pilastre [pilastr] *nm* ARCHIT pilaster ■ [d'escalier] newel (post) ■ [d'un balcon] pillar.

pile [pil] ◇ *nf* **1.** [tas - désordonné] pile, heap ; [- ordonné] stack **2.** INFORM stack **3.** CONSTR [pilier] pier **4.** TRAV PUB [appui] pier ■ [pieu] pile **5.** ÉLECTR battery ■ **une radio à ~s** a radio run on batteries, a battery radio ⊳ **~ atomique** pile reactor ■ **~ à combustible** fuel cell ■ **~ sèche** dry battery ■ **~ solaire** solar cell **6.** HÉRALD pile **7.** [côté d'une pièce] : **le côté ~** the reverse side ■ **~ ou face?** heads or tails? ■ **~, c'est moi** tails, I win ■ **jouer** *ou* **tirer à ~ ou face** to toss a coin ■ **tirons à ~ ou face** let's toss for it **8.** *fam* [coups] belting, thrashing **9.** *fam* [défaite] beating ■ **recevoir** *ou* **prendre une (bonne) ~** to get a beating *ou* hammering *UK ou* shellacking *US*.
◇ *adv fam* **1.** [net] dead ■ **s'arrêter ~** to stop dead ■ **ça commence à 8 h ~** it begins at 8 o'clock sharp *ou* on the dot **2.** [juste] right ■ **~ au milieu** right in the middle ■ **tomber ~ : tu es tombé ~ sur le bon chapitre** you just hit (on) the right chapter ■ **vous tombez ~, j'allais vous appeler** you're right on cue, I was about to call you.

piler [3] [pile] ◇ *vt* **1.** [broyer] to crush, to grind **2.** *fam* [vaincre] to make mincemeat of, to wipe the floor with ■ **il a pilé ses adversaires** he pulverized *ou* clobbered his opponents.
◇ *vi fam* [freiner] to slam (one's foot) on the brakes.

pileux, euse [pilø, øz] *adj* pilose, pilous.

pilier [pilje] *nm* **1.** ANAT, CONSTR & MIN pillar **2.** *fig* [défenseur] pillar ■ [bastion] bastion, bulwark ⊳ **c'est un ~ de bar** *ou* **bistrot** *fam péj* [habitué] he can always be found propping up the bar, he's a barfly **3.** [joueur de rugby] prop forward.

pili-pili [pilipili] *nm* bird pepper.

pillage [pijaʒ] *nm* **1.** [vol] pillage, looting, plundering ■ **le ~ de la ville par les soldats** the pillaging of the town by the soldiers ■ **mettre au ~** to pillage **2.** [plagiat] plagiarism, pirating **3.** [d'une ruche] robbing.

pillard, e [pijar, ard] <> *adj* pillaging, looting, plundering.
<> *nm, f* pillager, looter, plunderer.

piller [3] [pije] *vt* **1.** [dépouiller] to pillage, to loot, to plunder **2.** [détourner] to cream UK OU to siphon off *(sép)* ■ **~ les caisses de l'État** to siphon OU to cream UK off taxpayers' money **3.** [plagier] to plagiarize.

pilleur, euse [pijœr, øz] *nm, f* pillager, looter, plunderer ■ **~ d'épaves** wrecker.

pilon [pilɔ̃] *nm* **1.** [de mortier] pestle ■ TECHNOL pounder **2.** IMPR : **mettre un livre au ~** to pulp a book **3.** [jambe de bois] (straight) wooden leg **4.** [de volaille] drumstick.

pilonnage [pilɔnaʒ] *nm* **1.** [broyage] pounding, pestling **2.** IMPR pulping **3.** [bombardement] (heavy) bombardment, shelling ■ **~ publicitaire** *fig* barrage of publicity.

pilonner [3] [pilɔne] *vt* **1.** [broyer] to pound, to pestle **2.** IMPR to pulp **3.** [bombarder] to bombard, to shell.

pilori [pilɔri] *nm* **1.** HIST pillory **2.** *fig* **clouer** OU **mettre qqn au ~** to pillory sb.

pilosité [pilozite] *nf* pilosity.

pilotage [pilɔtaʒ] *nm* **1.** NAUT piloting **2.** AÉRON pilotage, piloting ■ **~ automatique** automatic piloting ■ **~ sans visibilité** blind flying **3.** *fig* [direction] : **le ~ d'une entreprise** running a business.

pilote [pilɔt] <> *nmf* **1.** AÉRON & NAUT pilot ■ **~ de chasse** fighter pilot ■ **~ d'essai** test pilot ■ **~ de ligne** airline pilot **2.** AUTO driver ■ **~ automobile** OU **de course** racing driver **3.** RAIL pilot, pilotman **4.** *(comme adj; avec ou sans trait d'union)* [expérimental] experimental ■ **école ~** experimental school ■ [promotionnel] promotional ■ **produit ~** promotional item, special offer.
<> *nm* **1.** AÉRON & NAUT ■ **~ automatique** auto pilot, automatic pilot **2.** *litt* [guide] guide **3.** ÉLECTR pilot **4.** ZOOL pilot fish **5.** INFORM driver.

piloter [3] [pilɔte] *vt* **1.** [conduire - avion] to pilot, to fly ; [- bateau] to sail ; [- voiture] to drive **2.** [guider - personne] to guide, to show around *(sép)* ; [- outil] to guide ■ **piloté par ordinateur** computer-driven **3.** TRAV PUB to drive piles into.

pilotis [pilɔti] *nm* : **des ~** piling ■ **maison sur ~** house built on piles OU stilts.

pilou [pilu] *nm* flannelette.

pilulaire [pilylɛr] <> *adj* pilular.
<> *nf* pillwort.

pilule [pilyl] *nf* **1.** [médicament] pill ■ **trouver la ~ amère** *fam* to find it a bitter pill to swallow ■ **faire passer la ~** *fam* to get sb to swallow the pill OU to take their medicine *fig* **2.** [contraceptif] : **~ contraceptive** contraceptive pill ■ **prendre la ~** to be on the pill ➡ **~ du lendemain** morning-after pill.

pilulier [pilylje] *nm* pillbox.

pimbêche [pɛ̃bɛʃ] <> *adj* stuck up ■ **ce qu'elle peut être ~!** she thinks she's Lady Muck UK OU the queen bee US!
<> *nf* : **c'est une ~** she's really stuck-up.

piment [pimɑ̃] *nm* **1.** BOT pepper, capsicum *spéc* ■ **~ doux** (sweet) pepper ■ **~ rouge** red pepper ■ **~ fort** hot pepper, pimento **2.** CULIN chilli, chili **3.** [charme] : **ça met un peu de ~ dans la vie!** it adds some spice to life! ■ **cette fille a du ~** she's certainly got character.

pimenté, e [pimɑ̃te] *adj* [sauce] hot, spicy.

pimenter [3] [pimɑ̃te] *vt* **1.** CULIN to season with chili, to spice up *(sép)* **2.** [corser] : **~ une histoire** to lace a story with spicy details ■ **~ la vie** to add spice to life.

pimpant, e [pɛ̃pɑ̃, ɑ̃t] *adj* [net] spruce, neat, smart ■ [frais] fresh, bright ■ **elle est arrivée toute ~e** she turned up all bright-eyed and bushy tailed.

pimprenelle [pɛ̃prənɛl] *nf* salad burnet.

pin [pɛ̃] *nm* **1.** BOT pine ■ **~ parasol** OU **pignon** stone pine ■ **~ maritime** maritime pine ■ **~ sylvestre** Scots OU Scotch pine **2.** MENUIS pine, pinewood.

pinacle [pinakl] *nm* **1.** ARCHIT pinnacle **2.** *fig* zenith, acme ■ **être au ~** to be at the top ■ **mettre** OU **porter qqn au ~** to praise sb to the skies, to put sb on a pedestal.

pinacothèque [pinakɔtɛk] *nf* art gallery.

pinaillage [pinajaʒ] *nm* *fam* nitpicking, hair-splitting.

pinailler [3] [pinaje] *vi* *fam* to quibble, to nitpick.

pinailleur, euse [pinajœr, øz] *fam* <> *adj* fussy, nitpicking, quibbling.
<> *nm, f* nitpicker.

pinard△ [pinar] *nm* vino, plonk UK, jug wine US.

pinardier [pinardje] *nm* **1.** [navire] wine tanker **2.** △ [marchand] wine merchant.

pinasse [pinas] *nf* (flat-bottomed) pinnace.

pinçage [pɛ̃saʒ] *nm* nipping off, pinching out.

pince [pɛ̃s] *nf* **1.** [outil] (pair of) pliers OU pincers ■ [pour un âtre] (fire) tongs ■ **~ à glaçons/sucre** ice/sugar tongs ■ **~ à cheveux** hair clip ■ **~ coupante** wire cutters ■ **~ à dessin** bulldog clip ■ **~ à épiler** (pair of) tweezers ■ **~ à linge** clothes peg OU pin US ■ **~ multiprise** multiple pliers ■ **~ à ongles** (nail) clippers ■ **~ universelle** universal OU all-purpose pliers ■ **~ à vélo** bicycle clip **2.** ZOOL claw, pincer ■ [d'un sabot de cheval] front part (of a horse's hoof) **3.** COUT dart, tuck ■ **ouvrir** OU **retirer des ~s** to take out tucks ➡ **~ de poitrine** dart **4.** *fam* [main] paw, mitt.
◆ **à pinces** <> *loc adj* COUT pleated ■ **pantalon à ~s** front-pleated trousers.
<> *loc adv* *fam* [à pied] on foot, on shanks's pony UK OU mare US ■ **j'irai à ~s** I'll hoof OU leg it.

pincé, e [pɛ̃se] *adj* **1.** [dédaigneux] : **un sourire ~** a thin-lipped smile ■ **il avait un air ~** he had a stiff OU starchy manner **2.** [serré] tight ■ **aux lèvres ~es** tight-lipped.

pinceau, x [pɛ̃so] *nm* **1.** [brosse - de peintre] paintbrush, brush ; [- de maquillage] brush **2.** [style] brushwork ■ **il a un bon coup de ~** he paints rather well **3.** OPT : **~ lumineux** light pencil **4.** *fam* [jambe] gam, pin.

pincée [pɛ̃se] <> *f* ▷ **pincé.**
<> *nf* pinch.

pincement [pɛ̃smɑ̃] *nm* **1.** [émotion] twinge, pang ■ **avoir un ~ au cœur** to have a lump in one's throat ■ **j'ai eu un ~ au cœur** it tugged at my heartstrings **2.** HORT nipping off, deadheading UK.

pince-monseigneur [pɛ̃smɔ̃sɛɲœr] (*pl* **pinces-monseigneur**) *nf* jemmy.

pince-nez [pɛ̃sne] *nm inv* pince-nez.

pincer [16] [pɛ̃se] *vt* **1.** [serrer] to pinch, to nip ■ **se faire ~ par un crabe** to get nipped by a crab ■ **pince-moi, je rêve!** pinch me, I must be dreaming! ■ **~ les lèvres** to go tight-lipped **2.** [suj: vent, froid] to nip at *(insép)* **3.** MUS to pluck **4.** HORT to pinch out *(sép)*, to nip off *(sép)*, to deadhead UK **5.** *fam* [arrêter] to nick UK, to pinch, to bust△ ■ **se faire ~ : un jour, tu vas te faire ~ par les flics** one day, you'll get nicked UK OU you'll be busted US **6.** *fam loc* **en ~ pour qqn** to be crazy about sb, to be gone on sb ■ *(en usage absolu)* **ça pince (dur), aujourd'hui!** it's bitterly OU freezing cold today!
◆ **se pincer** <> *vp (emploi réfléchi)* to pinch o.s. ■ **se ~ le nez** to hold OU to pinch one's nose.
<> *vpt* : **je me suis pincé le doigt dans le tiroir** I caught my finger in the drawer, my finger got caught in the drawer.

pince-sans-rire [pɛ̃ssɑ̃rir] *nmf* person with a deadpan OU dry sense of humour.

pincette [pɛ̃sɛt] *nf* [d'horloger] (pair of) tweezers.
◆ **pincettes** *nfpl* [pour attiser] (fireplace) tongs ■ **il n'est pas à prendre avec des ~s** [très énervé] he's like a bear with a sore head.

pinçon [pɛ̃sɔ̃] *nm* pinch mark.

Pindare [pɛ̃dar] *npr* Pindar.

pinède [pinɛd] *nf* pinewood, pine grove.

pingouin [pɛ̃gwɛ̃] *nm* [alcidé] auk ■ [manchot] penguin ■ **petit ~** razorbill.

ping-pong [piŋpɔ̃g] *nm* table tennis, ping-pong.

pingre [pɛ̃gr] *péj* ◇ *adj* [avare] stingy, mean, tight-fisted. ◇ *nmf* skinflint, penny-pincher.

pingrerie [pɛ̃grəri] *nf* [avarice] stinginess, meanness.

Pinocchio [pinɔkio] *npr* Pinocchio.

pinot [pino] *nm* pinot.

pin-pon [pɛ̃pɔ̃] *interj* **langage enfantin** *noise made by a fire engine's two-tone siren.*

pin's [pins] *nm inv* badge.

pinson [pɛ̃sɔ̃] *nm* chaffinch ■ **~ du Nord** brambling.

pintade [pɛ̃tad] *nf* guinea fowl.

pintadeau, x [pɛ̃tado] *nm* young guinea fowl.

pinte [pɛ̃t] *nf* **1.** [mesure - française] quart ; [- anglo-saxonne] pint ; [- canadienne] quart **2.** [verre] pint ■ **une ~ de bière** a pint of beer **3.** ***Suisse*** bar **4.** ***fam loc*** **s'offrir** *OU* **se faire** *OU* **se payer une ~ de bon sang** to have a good laugh.

pinté, e△ [pɛ̃te] *adj* [saoul] pie-eyed, blotto *UK*, pissed△ *UK*.

pinter [3] △ [pɛ̃te] ◆ **se pinter** *vpi* to booze.

pin-up [pinœp] *nf inv* pinup.

pioche [pjɔʃ] *nf* **1.** [outil] pick, pickaxe, mattock ■ **ils ont démoli le mur à coups de ~** they demolished the wall with a pick **2.** JEUX [aux dominos] stock ■ [aux cartes] talon, stock.

piocher [3] [pjɔʃe] ◇ *vt* **1.** [creuser] to dig (up) **2.** [tirer] to draw ■ **~ une carte/un domino** to draw a card/domino (from stock) **3.** ***fam*** [étudier] to cram, to swot at *UK (insép)*, to grind away at *US (insép)*.
◇ *vi* [puiser] to dig ■ **les cerises sont fameuses, vas-y, pioche (dans le tas)** the cherries are delicious, go ahead, dig in.

piocheur, euse [pjɔʃœr, øz] *nm, f* **1.** [ouvrier] digger **2.** ***fam*** [étudiant] swot *UK*, grind *US*.

piolet [pjɔlɛ] *nm* ice-axe.

pion[1] [pjɔ̃] *nm* **1.** JEUX [de dames] draughtsman, checker *US* ■ [d'échecs] pawn **2.** ***fig*** [personne] : **n'être qu'un ~ sur l'échiquier** to be just a cog in the machine *OU* a pawn in the game **3.** PHYS pion.

pion[2]**, pionne** [pjɔ̃, pjɔn] *nm, f* ***fam*** ÉDUC (paid) prefect *OU* monitor.

PION

In French *lycées*, the *pions* (officially called *surveillants*) are responsible for supervising pupils outside class hours; they are often university students who do the job to help finance their studies.

pioncer [16] [pjɔ̃se] *vi* ***fam*** to snooze, to (have a) kip *UK*.

pionnier, ère [pjɔnje, ɛr] *nm, f* **1.** [inventeur] pioneer **2.** [colon] pioneer ■ **les ~s de l'Ouest américain** the pioneers of the Wild West.
◆ **pionnier** *nm* MIL sapper.

pioupiou [pjupju] *nm* ***fam vieilli*** soldier, squaddie *UK*, GI (Joe) *US*.

pipe [pip] *nf* **1.** [à fumer - contenant] pipe ; [- contenu] pipe, pipeful ■ **une ~ de bruyère** a briar pipe **2.** TECHNOL pipe **3.** ŒNOL wine cask **4.** ▲ [fellation] blow-job▲ ■ **faire une ~ à qqn** to give sb a blow-job **5.** ***fam*** [cigarette] fag *UK*, butt *US*.

pipeau, x [pipo] *nm* **1.** MUS (reed) pipe ■ **c'est du ~** ***fig*** it's all fibs **2.** CHASSE bird call.
◆ **pipeaux** *nmpl* [pour les oiseaux] birdlimed *OU* limed twigs.

pipelet, ette [piplɛ, ɛt] *nm, f* ***fam vieilli*** concierge, doorman *US (nm)*.
◆ **pipelette** *nf* ***fam*** gossip (monger) ■ **mon oncle est une vraie ~te** my uncle loves a good chin-wag.

pipe-line (*pl* **pipe-lines**)**, pipeline** [pajplajn, piplin] *nm* pipeline.

piper [3] [pipe] *vt* **1.** [truquer - dés] to load ; [- cartes] to mark ■ **les dés sont pipés** ***fig*** the dice are loaded **2.** ***loc*** **ne pas ~ (mot)** to keep mum.

piperade [piperad] *nf* piperade *(cooked tomatoes, sweet peppers and ham mixed with scrambled eggs)*.

pipette [pipɛt] *nf* pipette.

pipi [pipi] *nm* ***fam*** [urine] (wee) wee, pee ■ **faire ~** to do a (wee) wee, to have a pee, to pee ■ **faire ~ au lit** to wet the bed ▶ **c'est du ~ de chat** [sans goût] it's tasteless, it's like dishwater ; [sans intérêt] it's a load of bilge *OU* tripe.

pipi-room [pipirum] (*pl* **pipi-rooms**) *nm* ***fam*** loo *UK*, bathroom *US*.

piquage [pikaʒ] *nm* **1.** COUT stitching **2.** TEXT punching.

piquant, e [pikɑ̃, ɑ̃t] *adj* **1.** [plante] thorny ■ **sa barbe est ~e** his beard's all prickly **2.** CULIN [moutarde, radis] hot **3.** ***sout*** [excitant - récit, détail] spicy, juicy **4.** ***fam*** [- eau] fizzy.
◆ **piquant** *nm* **1.** [de plante] thorn, prickle ■ [d'oursin, de hérisson] spine ■ [de barbelé] barb, spike ■ **couvert de ~s** prickly **2.** ***sout*** [intérêt] : **le ~ de l'histoire, c'est qu'elle n'est même pas venue!** the best part of it is that *OU* to crown it all she didn't even show up! ■ **des détails qui ne manquent pas de ~** juicy details.

pique [pik] ◇ *nf* **1.** [arme] pike ■ [de picador] pic **2.** [propos] barb, carping remark ■ **lancer des ~s à qqn** to make cutting remarks to sb.
◇ *nm* **1.** [carte] spade ■ **le roi de ~** the king of spades **2.** [couleur] spades.

piqué, e [pike] *adj* **1.** [abîmé - vin] sour ; [- miroir] mildewed ; [- bois] wormeater ; [- papier] foxed **2.** ***fam*** [fou] nutty, screwy, cracked **3.** MUS staccato ■ **note ~e** dotted note **4.** CULIN [de lard] larded, piqué ■ [d'ail] studded with garlic, piqué **5.** ***loc*** **pas ~ des hannetons** ***fam*** *OU* **vers** ***fam*** : **un alibi pas ~ des hannetons** the perfect alibi ■ **il est pas ~ des hannetons ton frangin!** your brother is really something else!
◆ **piqué** *nm* **1.** TEXT piqué **2.** AÉRON nose dive **3.** DANSE piqué.

pique-assiette [pikasjɛt] (*pl inv OU pl* **pique-assiettes**) *nmf* ***fam*** sponger, scrounger ■ **jouer les ~** to gatecrash.

pique-feu [pikfø] (*pl inv OU pl* **pique-feux**) *nm* poker.

pique-fleurs [pikflœr] *nm inv* flower holder *(vase)*.

pique-nique [piknik] (*pl* **pique-niques**) *nm* picnic ■ **faire un ~** to go on *OU* for a picnic.

pique-niquer [3] [piknike] *vi* to picnic, to go on *OU* for a picnic ■ **un bon endroit pour ~** a nice place to have *OU* for a picnic.

pique-niqueur, euse [piknikœr, øz] (*mpl* **pique-niqueurs**, *fpl* **pique-niqueuses**) *nm, f* picnicker.

piquer [3] [pike] ◇ *vt* **1.** MÉD [avec une seringue] : **~ qqn** to give sb an injection
2. VÉTÉR [tuer] : **~ un animal** to put an animal down, to put an animal to sleep ■ **faire ~ un chien** to have a dog put down
3. [avec une pointe] to prick ■ **~ un morceau de viande avec une fourchette/la pointe d'un couteau** to stick a fork/the tip of a knife into a piece of meat ■ **~ un bœuf avec un aiguillon** to goad an ox
4. [suj: animal, plante] to sting, to bite ■ **être piqué** *OU* **se faire ~ par une abeille** to get stung by a bee ■ **se faire ~ par un moustique** to get bitten by a mosquito
5. [enfoncer] to stick ■ **~ une fleur dans ses cheveux** to put a flower in *OU* to stick a flower in one's hair ■ **~ une broche sur un chemisier** to pin a brooch on *OU* onto a blouse
6. [brûler] to tickle, to tingle, to prickle ■ **ça pique la gorge** it gives you a tickle in your *OU* the throat ■ **le poivre pique la langue** pepper burns the tongue ■ **la fumée me pique les yeux** the smoke is making my eyes smart ■ **un tissu rêche qui pique la peau** a rough material which chafes the skin
7. [stimuler - curiosité, jalousie] to arouse, to awaken ; [- amour-propre] to pique ; [- intérêt] to stir (up)
8. ***fam*** [faire de manière soudaine] : **~ un cent mètres** *OU* **un sprint** ***pr*** to put on a sprint ; ***fig*** to take off in a flash ■ **~ une colère** to throw a fit (of anger) ■ **~ une crise (de nerfs)** to get hysterical

■ ~ **un somme** *ou* **un roupillon** *fam* to grab a nap *ou* some shut-eye ➊ ~ **un fard** to turn red *ou* crimson ■ ~ **une tête** to dive head first
9. *fam* [dérober] to steal, to pinch, to grab *US* ■ ~ **un porte-monnaie** to snatch a wallet ■ **il a piqué la femme de son copain** he ran off with his friend's wife ■ ~ **une phrase dans un livre/à un auteur** to lift a sentence from a book/an author
10. *fam* [arrêter] to nab, to collar, to nick *UK* ■ **se faire ~** [arrêter] to get nabbed *ou* nailed *US* ; [surprendre] to get caught
11. MUS : ~ **une note** to dot a note, to play a note staccato
12. COUT to sew ■ [cuir] to stitch
13. CULIN : ~ **un rôti d'ail** to stick garlic into a roast ■ ~ **une viande de lardons** to lard a piece of meat.
◇ *vi* **1.** [brûler - barbe] to prickle ; [- désinfectant, alcool] to sting ; [- yeux] to burn, to smart ■ **radis/moutarde qui pique** hot radish/mustard ■ **eau qui pique** *fam* fizzy water ■ **vin qui pique** sour wine ■ **gorge qui pique** sore throat
2. [descendre - avion] to (go into a) dive ; [- oiseau] to swoop down ; [- personne] to head straight towards ■ ~ **(droit) vers** to head (straight) for
3. *loc* ~ **du nez** [avion] to go into a nosedive ; [bateau] to tilt forward ; [fleur] to droop ; [personne] to (begin to) drop off.
◆ **se piquer** ◇ *vp (emploi réfléchi)* [avec une seringue - malade] to inject o.s. ; [- drogué] to take drugs *(intravenously)* ■ **il se pique à l'héroïne** he shoots *ou* does heroin.
◇ *vpi* **1.** [par accident] to prick o.s.
2. [s'abîmer - papier, linge] to turn mildewy, to go mouldy ; [- métal] to pit, to get pitted ; [- vin] to turn sour
3. *loc* **se ~ au jeu : elle s'est piquée au jeu** it grew on her.
◇ *vpt* : **se ~ le nez** *fam* to hit the bottle, to tipple.
◆ **se piquer de** *vp+prép* to pride o.s. on ■ **il se pique de connaissances médicales** he prides himself on his knowledge of medicine.

piquet [pikɛ] *nm* **1.** [pieu] post, stake, picket **2.** [groupe - de soldats, de grévistes] picket ■ ~ **d'incendie** fire fighting squad ■ ~ **de grève** picket **3.** [coin] : **mettre un enfant au ~** to send a child to stand in the corner **4.** JEUX piquet.

piquetage [piktaʒ] *nm* **1.** [marquage] staking (out) **2.** *Québec* picketing.

piqueter [27] [pikte] ◇ *vt* **1.** [route, chemin] to stake *ou* to peg (out) **2.** *litt* [parsemer] to stud, to dot ■ **un ciel piqueté d'étoiles** a sky studded with stars, a star-studded sky.
◇ *vi Québec* to picket.

piqueteur, euse [piktœr, øz] *nm, f Québec* picketer.

piquette [pikɛt] *nf* **1.** [vin] (cheap) wine, plonk **2.** *fam* [défaite] thrashing, beating ■ **prendre** *ou* **ramasser une ~** to get a good drubbing *ou* hammering *ou* shellacking *US* **3.** *fam loc* **c'est de la ~** it's a mere trifle.

piqûre [pikyr] *nf* **1.** [d'aiguille] prick ■ ~ **d'épingle** pinprick **2.** [d'insecte] sting, bite ■ ~ **de guêpe/d'abeille** wasp/bee sting ■ ~ **de moustique/puce** mosquito/flea bite **3.** [de plante] sting ■ **~s d'orties** nettle stings **4.** MÉD injection, shot ■ ~ **antitétanique** antitetanus *ou* tetanus shot ■ ~ **de rappel** booster (injection *ou* shot) ■ **faire une ~ à qqn** to give sb an injection **5.** COUT [point] stitch ■ [rangs, couture] stitching *(U)* **6.** [altération - du papier] foxing ; [- du métal] pitting ; [- du bois] wormhole ; [- du vin] souring **7.** [saleté] : **~s de mouches** fly specks.

piranha [pirana] *nm* piranha.

piratage [pirataʒ] *nm* pirating *(U)*, piracy ■ INFORM hacking.

pirate [pirat] *nm* **1.** [sur les mers] pirate ■ ~ **de l'air** hijacker **2.** [de logiciels, de cassettes] pirate ■ ~ **informatique** (computer) hacker **3.** *(comme adj; avec ou sans trait d'union)* pirate *(modif)*.

pirater [3] [pirate] ◇ *vt* **1.** *fam* [voler] to rip off *(sép)*, to rob ■ ~ **des idées** to pinch *ou* to steal ideas **2.** [copier illégalement] to pirate ■ ~ **un film/une cassette** to make a pirate copy of a film/a cassette.
◇ *vi litt* to pirate.

piraterie [piratri] *nf* **1.** [sur les mers] piracy ■ ~ **aérienne** air piracy, hijacking **2.** [plagiat] piracy, pirating ■ ~ **commerciale** industrial piracy.

pire [pir] ◇ *adj* **1.** *(compar)* worse ■ **si je dors, c'est ~ encore** if I sleep, it's even worse ■ **les conditions sont ~s que jamais** the conditions are worse than ever ■ **c'est de ~ en ~** it's getting worse and worse ➊ **il n'est ~ eau que l'eau qui dort** *prov* still waters run deep *prov* ■ **il n'est ~ sourd que celui qui ne veut pas entendre** *prov* there's none so deaf as he who will not hear **2.** *(superl)* worst ■ **mon ~ ennemi** my worst enemy ■ **se livrer aux ~s horreurs** to commit the worst *ou* foulest abominations.
◇ *nm* : **le ~** the worst ■ **je m'attends au ~** I expect the worst ■ **le ~ est qu'elle en aime un autre** the worst (part) of it is that she's in love with someone else ■ **dans le ~ des cas, (en mettant les choses) au ~** at worst.

Pirée [pire] *npr* : **Le ~** Piraeus ■ **prendre Le ~ pour un homme** *La Fontaine allus* to make a crude mistake.

pirogue [pirɔg] *nf* pirogue, dugout ■ ~ **à balancier** outrigger.

pirouette [pirwɛt] *nf* **1.** [tour sur soi-même] pirouette, body spin ■ **faire une ~** to pirouette, to spin (on one's heels) **2.** DANSE & ÉQUIT pirouette **3.** [changement d'opinion] about-face, about-turn **4.** [dérobade] : **répondre** *ou* **s'en tirer par une ~** to answer flippantly.

pirouetter [4] [pirwete] *vi* **1.** [pivoter] to pivot ■ ~ **sur ses talons** to turn on one's heels **2.** [faire une pirouette - danseur] to pirouette.

pis[1] [pi] *nm* [de vache] udder.

pis[2] [pi] *litt* ◇ *adj* worse.
◇ *nm* : **le ~** [le pire] the worst ➊ **dire ~ que pendre de qqn** to vilify sb *sout*, to drag sb's name through the mud.
◇ *adv* worse ■ **il a fait ~ encore** he's done worse things still.
◆ **au pis** *loc adv litt* if the worst comes to the worst.
◆ **qui pis est** *loc adv* what's *ou* what is worse.

pis-aller [pizale] *nm inv* [expédient] last resort ■ **disons lundi, mais ce serait un ~** let's say Monday, but that's if the worst comes to the worst.

piscicole [pisikɔl] *adj* fish-farming *(modif)*, piscicultural *spéc.*

pisciculture [pisikyltyr] *nf* fish-farming, pisciculture *spéc.*

pisciforme [pisifɔrm] *adj* fish-shaped, piscine *spéc.*

piscine [pisin] *nf* [de natation] (swimming) pool *ou* baths *UK* ■ ~ **couverte/découverte** indoor/outdoor (swimming) pool ■ ~ **municipale** public (swimming) pool *ou* baths.

piscivore [pisivɔr] ◇ *adj* fish-eating.
◇ *nmf* fish-eating animal.

Pise [piz] *npr* Pisa ■ **la tour de ~** the Leaning Tower of Pisa.

pisé [pize] *nm* pisé, rammed clay.

pisse△ [pis] *nf* piss△, pee.

pisse-froid [pisfrwa] *nm inv fam* wet blanket, killjoy.

pissenlit [pisɑ̃li] *nm* dandelion.

pisser [3]△ [pise] ◇ *vi* **1.** [uriner] to piss△, to (have a) pee ■ ~ **au lit** to wet the bed ➊ **c'est comme si on pissait dans un violon** it's a bloody waste of time△, it's like pissing into the wind△ ■ **laisse ~ (le mérinos)** forget it ■ **il ne se sent plus ~** he's too big for his boots **2.** [fuir] to leak.
◇ *vt* **1.** [uriner] to pass ■ ~ **du sang** to pass blood **2.** [laisser s'écouler] : **ça pissait le sang** there was blood gushing *ou* spurting everywhere ■ **mon nez pissait le sang** I had blood pouring from my nose ■ **le moteur commençait à ~ de l'huile** oil started to gush from the engine **3.** *loc* ~ **de la copie** to churn it out, to write reams.

pisseur, euse△ [pisœr, øz] *nm, f* pisser△ ■ ~ **de copie** hack *(who writes a lot)*.
◆ **pisseuse**△ *nf* little girl.

pisseux, euse [pisø, øz] *adj* **1.** [imprégné d'urine] urine-soaked **2.** [délavé] washed-out ■ **un vert ~** a washed-out shade of green **3.** [jauni] yellowing.

pisse-vinaigre [pisvinɛgr] *nm inv fam* **1.** [avare] skinflint, miser **2.** [rabat-joie] wet blanket.

pissoir△ [piswar] *nm* bog△ *UK*, john *US*.

pissotière [pisɔtjɛr] *nf fam* public urinal.

pistache [pistaʃ] <> *nf* pistachio (nut).
<> *adj inv* : **(vert)** ~ pistachio (green).

pistachier [pistaʃje] *nm* pistachio (tree).

pistage [pistaʒ] *nm* tracking, trailing, tailing.

piste [pist] *nf* **1.** [trace] track, trail ■ **être sur la ~ de qqn** to be on sb's track *ou* trail ■ **ils sont sur la bonne/une fausse ~** they're on the right/wrong track ➊ **jeu de ~** treasure hunt **2.** [indice] lead ■ **la police cherche une ~** the police are looking for leads **3.** SPORT [de course à pied] running track ■ [en hippisme - pour la course] track ; [- pour les chevaux] bridle path ■ [de patinage] rink ■ [de course cycliste] cycling track ■ [de course automobile] racing track ■ [d'athlétisme] lane ■ [d'escrime] piste ■ **~ de danse** dance floor ■ **~ de cirque** circus ring ■ **~ de ski** ski-run, run ■ **~ de ski artificielle** dry ski slope **4.** [chemin, sentier] trail, track ■ **~ cyclable** [sur la route] cycle lane ; [à côté] cycle track **5.** AÉRON runway ■ **en bout de ~** at the end of the runway ➊ **~ d'envol/d'atterrissage** take-off/landing runway **6.** AUDIO, CINÉ & INFORM track ■ **~ sonore** soundtrack **7.** CHASSE trail **8.** JEUX [de dés] dice run *ou* baize.
◆ **en piste** <> *interj* off you go.
<> *loc adv* : **entrer en ~** to come into play, to join in.

pister [3] [piste] *vt* [suivre - personne] to tail, to trail ; [- animal] to trail, to track.

pisteur [pistœr] *nm* [pour l'entretien en ski] ski slope maintenance man ■ [pour surveillance] ski patrolman.

pistil [pistil] *nm* pistil.

pistolet [pistɔlɛ] *nm* **1.** ARM pistol, gun ■ **~ à air comprimé** air pistol ■ **~ d'alarme** alarm pistol ■ **~ automatique** pistol ■ **~ mitrailleur** submachine-gun **2.** [instrument] : **~ agrafeur** staple gun ■ **~ à peinture** spray gun **3.** [jouet] : **~ à eau** water pistol **4.** *fam* MÉD bottle **5.** ART template **6.** *Belgique* [petit pain] bread roll.

pistolet-mitrailleur [pistɔlɛmitrajœr] (*pl* **pistolets-mitrailleurs**) *nm* submachine-gun.

piston [pistɔ̃] *nm* **1.** MÉCAN piston **2.** MUS valve **3.** *fam* [recommandation, protection] string-pulling, connections ■ **il est rentré par ~** he got in by knowing the right people ■ **elle a fait marcher le ~ pour se faire embaucher** she got somebody to pull a few strings for her to get the job **4.** *arg scol* [élève] *student of the École centrale des arts et manufactures* ■ **Piston** [l'ECAM] *nickname of the École centrale des arts et manufactures.*

pistonné, e [pistɔne] *nm, f* : **c'est un ~** someone pulled a few strings for him, he got where he is thanks to a bit of string-pulling.

pistonner [3] [pistɔne] *vt fam* to pull strings for ■ **elle s'est fait ~ pour entrer au ministère** she used her connections to get into the Ministry.

pistou [pistu] *nm Provençal vegetable soup (with garlic and basil).*

pita [pita] *nf* pitta bread.

pitance [pitɑ̃s] *nf litt* sustenance, daily bread.

pitbull [pitbul] *nm* pitbull (terrier).

pitchoun, e [pitʃun], **pitchounet, ette** [pitʃunɛ, ɛt] *nm, f* [dialecte] little one ■ **où il est, le ~?** where's the little one?

piteusement [pitøzmɑ̃] *adv* miserably, pathetically.

piteux, euse [pitø, øz] *adj* **1.** [pitoyable] pitiful, piteous ■ **être en ~ état** to be in a pitiful condition ■ **un manteau en ~ état** a shabby coat **2.** [mauvais, médiocre] poor, mediocre **3.** [triste] : **faire piteuse mine** to look sad **4.** [honteux] sheepish ■ **elle s'est excusée de façon piteuse** she apologized shamefacedly.

pithiviers [pitivje] *nm* puff-pastry cake *(filled with almond cream).*

pitié [pitje] <> *nf* **1.** [compassion] pity ■ **elle l'a fait par ~ pour lui** she did it out of pity for him ■ **avoir ~ de qqn** to feel pity for *ou* to pity sb ■ **faire ~ à qqn : elle me fait ~** I feel sorry for her ■ **vous me faites ~!** you look awful! ■ [avec mépris] you're pitiful! ■ **la pièce? c'était à faire ~** the play? it was a wretched *ou* pitiful performance ■ **prendre qqn en ~** to take pity on sb **2.** [désolation] pity ■ **quelle ~!, c'est une ~!** what a pity! **3.** [clémence] mercy, pity ■ **il a eu ~ de ses ennemis** he had mercy on his enemies.
<> *interj* : **(par) ~!** (have) mercy! ; [avec agacement] for pity's sake! ■ **~ pour ma pauvre carcasse!** *hum* have mercy on my poor old bones!
◆ **sans pitié** *loc adj* ruthless, merciless ■ **ils ont été sans ~** [jurés] they showed no mercy ; [terroristes] they were ruthless.

piton [pitɔ̃] *nm* **1.** [clou - gén] eye *ou* eye-headed nail ; [- d'alpiniste] piton **2.** GÉOGR [dans la mer] submarine mountain ■ [pic] piton, needle ■ **~ rocheux** rocky outcrop.

pitonner [3] [pitɔne] *vi* **1.** SPORT to hammer (in) pitons **2.** *Québec* to zap, to channel-hop.

pitoyable [pitwajabl] *adj* **1.** [triste - destin] pitiful ■ **c'est ~ à voir** it's a pitiful *ou* pathetic sight **2.** [mauvais - effort, résultat] pitiful, deplorable, dismal.

pitoyablement [pitwajabləmɑ̃] *adv* **1.** [tristement] pitifully **2.** [médiocrement] pitifully, deplorably.

pitre [pitr] *nm* **1.** [plaisantin] clown ■ **faire le ~** to clown *ou* to fool around **2.** *arch* [bouffon] clown.

pitrerie [pitrəri] *nf* piece of tomfoolery *ou* buffoonery.

pittoresque [pitɔrɛsk] <> *adj* picturesque, colourful.
<> *nm* picturesqueness.

pive [piv] *nf Suisse* pine cone.

pivert [pivɛr] *nm* (green) woodpecker.

pivoine [pivwan] *nf* peony.

pivot [pivo] *nm* **1.** [axe] pivot **2.** [centre] pivot, hub ■ **le ~ de toute son argumentation** the crux of his argument **3.** SPORT centre **4.** [système de parité du SME] : **cours ~** Euro value ■ **taux ~** designated (Euro) rate.

pivotant, e [pivɔtɑ̃, ɑ̃t] *adj* revolving, swivelling.

pivoter [3] [pivɔte] *vi* **1.** [autour d'un axe - porte] to revolve ; [- fauteuil] to swivel **2.** [personne] to turn ■ **~ sur ses talons** to spin round, to pivot on one's heels ■ **faire ~ qqch** to swing sthg (round) ■ [véhicule] to swing.

pixel [piksɛl] *nm* pixel.

pizza [pidza] *nf* pizza.

pizzeria [pidzerja] *nf* pizzeria.

PJ <> *npr f* (*abr de* **police judiciaire**) ≃ CID *UK*, ≃ FBI *US*.
<> (*abr écrite de* **pièces jointes**) encl.

Pl., pl. = **place**.

PL (*abr écrite de* **poids lourd**) HGV.

placage [plakaʒ] *nm* **1.** [revêtement - de bois] veneering ; [- de pierre, marbre] facing ; [- de métal] cladding, coating ■ **bois de ~** veneer **2.** SPORT tackle.

placard [plakar] *nm* **1.** [armoire] cupboard, closet *US* ■ **~ à balais** broom cupboard ■ **~ de cuisine** kitchen cupboard ■ **~ de salle de bains** bathroom cabinet ■ **~ à vêtements** wardrobe *UK*, closet *US* ■ **mettre qqn au ~** *fam* [l'écarter] to put sb on the sidelines, to sideline sb *US* ■ **mettre qqch au ~** *fam* [le retirer de la circulation] to put sthg in cold storage *ou* in mothballs **2.** IMPR galley (proof) ■ **~ publicitaire** [grand] large display advertisement ; [de pleine page] full-page advertisement **3.** NAUT patch **4.** △ [prison] nick *UK*, hoosegow *US* **5.** *fam* [couche de maquillage] dollop **6.** *vieilli* [avis écrit] proclamation.

placarder [3] [plakarde] *vt* **1.** [couvrir] : **~ qqch de** to cover sthg with **2.** [afficher] to plaster ■ **j'ai placardé des photos sur les murs** I plastered the walls with photos **3.** IMPR : **~ un ouvrage** to set a book in galleys.

placardisation [plakardizasjɔ̃] *nf transfer of highly placed but unwanted employees into harmless positions.*

place [plas] *nf* **1.** [espace disponible] space *(U)*, room *(U)* ■ **faire de la ~** to make room *ou* space ■ **faites-lui une petite ~** give her a bit of room ■ **il reste de la ~ pour quatre personnes** there's enough space *ou* room left for four people ■ **prendre de la ~** to take up a lot of space *ou* room ■ **ne prends pas toute la ~** [à table, au lit] don't take up so much room ; [sur la page] don't use up all the space ■ **laisser la** *ou* **faire ~ à** to make room *ou* way for ■ **la machine à écrire a fait ~ au traitement de texte** word-processors have taken over from *ou* superseded typewriters ■ **ce travail ne laisse aucune ~ à la créativité** there's no place *ou* room for creativity in this kind of work ■ **les anciens font ~ aux jeunes** older people give way to the young generation ■ **la musique tient une grande ~ dans ma vie** music is very important in *ou* is an important part of my life ▶ **~ au sol** [d'un ordinateur, d'une voiture] footprint ■ **faire ~ nette** *pr* to tidy up ; *fig* to clear up, to make a clean sweep
2. [endroit précis] place, spot ■ **changer les meubles/la cuisinière de ~** to move the furniture around/the stove ■ **mets/remets les clefs à leur ~** put the keys/put the keys back where they belong ■ **est-ce que tout est à sa ~?** is everything in order *ou* in its proper place? ❙ [d'une personne] : **savoir rester à sa ~** to know one's place ■ **je ne me sens pas à ma ~ parmi eux** I feel out of place among them ■ **ta ~ n'est pas ici** you're out of place here ■ **tu auras toujours une ~ dans mon cœur** there'll always be a place in my heart for you ■ **reprendre sa ~** [sa position] to go back to one's place ; [son rôle] to go back to where one belongs ■ **notre collègue ne pourra pas reprendre sa ~ parmi nous** our colleague is unable to resume his post with us ■ **pour rien au monde je ne donnerais ma ~** I wouldn't swop places for anything in the world ▶ **remettre qqn à sa ~** to put sb in his/her place ■ **se faire une ~ au soleil** to make a success of things, to find one's place in the sun
3. [siège] seat ■ [fauteuil au spectacle] seat ■ [billet] ticket ■ **avoir la ~ d'honneur** [sur l'estrade] to sit at the centre of the stage ; [à table] to sit at the top *ou* head of the table ■ **à la ~ du conducteur** in the driver's seat ■ **une voiture à deux ~s** a two-seater (car) ■ **une caravane à quatre ~s** a caravan that sleeps four ■ **une salle de 500 ~s** a room that can seat 500 people ■ **réserver une ~ d'avion/de train** to make a plane/train reservation ■ **payer ~ entière** to pay full price ■ **j'ai trois ~s de concert** I have three tickets for the concert ■ **ça vous ennuierait de changer de ~?** would you mind swapping *ou* changing places? ▶ **~ assise** seat ■ **il ne reste plus que des ~s debout** it's now standing room only ■ **à la ~ du mort** in the (front) passenger seat ■ **dans le monde du spectacle, les ~s sont chères** it's difficult to gain a foothold in show business ■ **la ~ est toute chaude** *pr* & *fig* the seat's still warm
4. [dans un parking] (parking) space ■ **un parking de 1 000 ~s** a car park with space for 1,000 cars
5. [espace urbain] square ■ **la ~ du village** the village square ▶ **sur la ~ de Paris : le plus cher sur la ~ de Paris** the most expensive in Paris ■ **sur la ~ publique** in public ■ **porter le débat sur la ~ publique** to make the debate public
6. [poste, emploi] position, post ■ **une bonne ~** a good job ■ **je cherche une ~ de secrétaire** I'm looking for a job as a secretary
7. [rang - dans une compétition] place, rank ■ **avoir la première ~** to come first *ou* top ■ **avoir la dernière ~** to come bottom UK *ou* last ■ **elle est en bonne ~ au dernier tour** she's well placed on the last lap ■ **être** *ou* **partir en bonne ~ pour gagner** to be (all) set to win
8. BOURSE : **~ financière** financial centre ■ **~ financière internationale** money market ■ **le dollar est à la hausse sur la ~ financière de New York** the dollar has risen on the New York exchange
9. MIL : **~ (forte)** fortress, stronghold ■ **nous voici dans la ~** *pr* [ville assiégée] here we are, inside the walls (of the city) ; [endroit quelconque] here we are ; *fig* we've now gained a foothold
10. *Belgique* [pièce d'habitation] room.

◆ **à la place** *loc adv* instead ■ **on ira en Espagne à la ~** we'll go to Spain instead ■ **j'ai rapporté la jupe et j'ai pris un pantalon à la ~** I returned the skirt and exchanged it for a pair of trousers.

◆ **à la place de** *loc prép* **1.** [au lieu de] instead of ■ **j'irai à sa ~** I'll go instead of him
2. [dans la situation de] : **à ma/sa ~** in my/his place ■ **à ta ~, j'irais** if I were you I'd go ■ **mettez-vous à ma ~** put yourself in my place *ou* shoes ■ **je ne voudrais pas être à sa ~** rather him than me, I wouldn't like to be in his shoes.

◆ **de place en place** *loc adv* here and there.

◆ **en place** ◇ *loc adj* [important] established ■ **un homme politique en ~** a well-established politician ■ **les gens en ~ disent que...** the powers that be say that...
◇ *loc adv* **1.** [là] in position ■ **les forces de police sont déjà en ~** the police have already taken up their position ■ **est-ce que tout est en ~?** is everything in order *ou* in its proper place?
2. *loc* **mettre en ~** [équipement] to set up *(sép)*, to install ; [plan] to set up *(sép)*, to put into action ; [réseau] to set up *(sép)* ■ **la méthode sera mise en ~ progressivement** the method will be phased in (gradually) ■ **ça va lui mettre/remettre les idées en ~** it'll give him a more realistic view of things/set him thinking straight again ■ **tenir en ~ : il ne tient pas en ~** [il est turbulent] he can't keep still ; [il est anxieux] he's nervous ; [il voyage beaucoup] he's always on the move.

◆ **par places** *loc adv* here and there.

◆ **sur place** *loc adv* there, on the spot ■ **je serai déjà sur ~** I'll already be there.

PLACE

la place Beauvau square in Paris (also refers to the Ministry of the Interior, whose offices are situated there);
la place de la Concorde square in Paris (one of the biggest and busiest squares in Paris, laid out in the reign of Louis XV);
la place du Colonel-Fabien square in Paris (also refers to the Communist party headquarters, which are situated there);
la place de Grève former name of the Place de l'Hôtel de Ville in Paris. (The place where the unemployed gathered to wait for work, it was the origin of the expression "se mettre en grève");
la place Rouge Red Square;
la place Saint-Marc Saint Mark's Square;
la place Tian'anmen Tiananmen Square;
la place Vendôme square in Paris (the name evokes opulence and luxury because of the Ritz hotel and the jewellery shops situated on the square);
la place des Vosges elegant and fashionable square in the Marais district of Paris, built under Henri IV.

placé, e [plase] *adj* **1.** [aux courses] : **cheval ~** placed horse ■ *(comme adv)* **arriver ~** to be placed **2.** [situé] : **bien ~** [magasin, appartement] well-situated ; [fermeture, bouton, couture] well-positioned ■ **mal ~** [magasin, appartement] badly-located ; [fermeture, bouton, couture] poorly-positioned ; [coup] below the belt ; [abcès] in an awkward spot ; *euphém* in an embarrassing place ; [orgueil] misplaced ■ **on était très bien/mal ~s** [au spectacle] we had really good/bad seats ■ **être bien/mal ~ pour** *fig* to be in a/no position to **3.** [socialement] : **haut ~** well up *ou* high up in the hierarchy ■ **des gens haut ~s** people in high places.

placebo [plasebo] *nm* placebo.

placement [plasmɑ̃] *nm* **1.** [investissement] investment ■ **un bon/mauvais ~** a sound/bad investment ■ **faire un ~** to make an investment, to invest **2.** [de chômeurs] placing **3.** [d'enfants] placing *(U)* ■ **je m'occupe du ~ des jeunes dans les familles** my job is finding homes for young people **4.** [installation] : **le ~ des invités autour de la table** the seating of the guests around the table **5.** [internement] : **~ d'office** hospitalization order **6.** [condamnation] : **~ sous surveillance électronique** electronic surveillance, electronic tagging.

placenta [plasɛ̃ta] *nm* placenta.

placentaire [plasɛ̃tɛr] *adj* placental.

placer [16] [plase] *vt* **1.** [mettre dans une position précise] to place ■ **~ un patron sur du tissu** to lay a pattern on *ou* over a piece of fabric ■ **~ ses doigts sur le clavier** to place one's fingers on the keyboard ■ **~ la balle** SPORT to place the ball ■ **~ sa voix** MUS to pitch one's voice
2. [faire asseoir] to seat ■ **l'ouvreuse va vous ~** the usherette will show you to your seats ■ **~ des convives à table** to seat guests around a table

3. [établir - dans une position, un état] to put, to place ▪ **~ qqn devant ses responsabilités** to force sb to face up to his/her responsibilities
4. [établir - dans une institution] to place ▪ **~ les jeunes chômeurs** to find jobs for unemployed young people ▪ **~ un enfant à l'Assistance publique** to place *ou* to put a child in care ▪ **~ qqn à l'hospice** to put sb in an old people's home
5. [classer] to put, to place ▪ **~ la loi au-dessus de tout** to set the law above everything else ▪ **moi, je le placerais parmi les grands écrivains** I would rate *ou* rank him among the great writers
6. [situer dans le temps] : **il a placé l'action du film en l'an 2000** he set the film in the year 2000
7. [situer dans l'espace] to locate
8. [mettre] to put ▪ **orchestre placé sous la direction de...** orchestra conducted by... ▪ **~ sa confiance en qqn** to put one's trust in sb ▪ **elle a placé tous ses espoirs dans ce projet** she's pinned all her hopes on this project
9. [dans la conversation] : **il essaie toujours de ~ quelques boutades** he always tries to slip in a few jokes ▪ **je n'ai pas pu ~ un mot** I couldn't get a word in edgeways ➋ **je peux en ~ une?** *fam* can I get a word in?
10. [vendre] to sell ▪ **j'essaie désespérément de ~ mon vieux canapé!** *hum* I'm desperately trying to find a home for my old sofa!
11. FIN to invest.
◆ **se placer** *vpi* **1.** [dans l'espace] : **place-toi près de la fenêtre** [debout] stand near the window ; [assis] sit near the window ▪ **placez-vous en cercle** get into a circle ▪ **venez vous ~ autour de la table** come and sit at the table ‖ [dans un jugement, une analyse] to look at *ou* to consider things ▪ **si l'on se place de son point de vue** if you look at things from his point of view
2. [occuper un rang] to rank, to finish ▪ **se ~ premier/troisième** to finish first/third
3. [trouver un emploi] : **elle s'est placée comme infirmière** she found *ou* got a job as a nurse
4. *fam* [se présenter avantageusement] : **se ~ auprès du patron** to butter up *ou* to sweet-talk the boss.

placeur, euse [plasœr, øz] *nm, f* **1.** [dans une salle de spectacle] usher (*f* usherette) **2.** [dans une agence pour l'emploi] employment agent.

placide [plasid] *adj* placid, calm.

placidité [plasidite] *nf* placidness, calmness.

placier [plasje] *nm* **1.** [forain] market pitch agent **2.** [représentant] travelling salesman, drummer *US*.

plafond [plafɔ̃] *nm* **1.** CONSTR ceiling ▪ **faux ~** false ceiling ▪ **bas de ~** *pr* : **la pièce est basse de ~** the room has got a low ceiling ▪ **il est un peu bas de ~** *fig* he's a bit slow on the uptake **2.** ART ceiling painting **3.** AÉRON ceiling **4.** MÉTÉOR : **~ (nuageux)** (cloud) ceiling **5.** [limite supérieure] : **~ de crédit** credit limit ▪ **le ~ des salaires** the wage ceiling, the ceiling on wages **6.** *(comme adj: avec ou sans trait d'union)* ceiling *(modif)* ▪ **vitesse ~** maximum speed **7.** [au bridge] ceiling.

plafonnage [plafɔnaʒ] *nm* ceiling installation.

plafonnement [plafɔnmɑ̃] *nm* : **~ des salaires** top-grading of wages.

plafonner [3] [plafɔne] ◇ *vt* **1.** [pièce, maison] to put a ceiling in *ou* into **2.** [impôts] to set a ceiling for.
◇ *vi* **1.** [avion] to reach maximum altitude *ou* absolute ceiling *spéc* ▪ [voiture] to reach maximum speed **2.** [ventes, salaires] to level off ▪ [taux d'intérêt, prix] to peak ▪ **je plafonne à 1 500 euros depuis un an** my monthly income hasn't exceeded 1,500 euros for over a year.

plafonnier [plafɔnje] *nm* **1.** [d'appartement] ceiling light **2.** AUTO (overhead) courtesy *ou* guide light.

plage [plaʒ] *nf* **1.** GÉOGR beach ▪ **~ de galets/de sable** pebble/sandy beach **2.** [espace de temps] : **~ horaire** (allotted) slot ▪ **~ musicale** musical intermission ▪ **~ publicitaire** commercial break **3.** [écart] range ▪ **~ de prix** price range **4.** *litt* [surface] zone, area ▪ **une ~ d'ombre** an area of shadow **5.** NAUT : **~ avant** foredeck ▪ **~ arrière** quarterdeck, after deck **6.** AUTO : **~ arrière** back shelf **7.** [d'un disque] track.
◆ **de plage** *loc adj* beach *(modif)* ▪ **vêtements de ~** beachwear.

plagiaire [plaʒjɛr] *nmf* plagiarizer, plagiarist.

plagiat [plaʒja] *nm* plagiary, plagiarism.

plagier [9] [plaʒje] *vt* [œuvre] to plagiarize ▪ **~ qqn** to plagiarize sb's work.

plagiste [plaʒist] *nmf* beach attendant.

plaid[1] [plɛ] *nm* HIST [assemblée] court ▪ [jugement] finding, judgement.

plaid[2] [plɛd] *nm* [pièce de tissu] plaid ▪ [couverture] car rug.

plaidant, e [plɛdɑ̃, ɑ̃t] *adj* ▷ **avocat.**

plaider [4] [plede] ◇ *vi* **1.** DR to plead ▪ **~ pour qqn** to defend sb ▪ **c'est lui qui plaide pour les Taylor** he's the Taylors' lawyer, he's counsel for the Taylors ▪ **~ contre qqn** to plead the case against sb *(in court)* **2.** [présenter des arguments] : **~ en faveur de qqn/qqch** *pr* & *fig* to speak in sb's/sthg's favour ▪ **~ contre qqn/qqch** *pr* & *fig* to speak against sb/sthg.
◇ *vt* to plead ▪ **~ une cause** DR to plead a case ; *fig* to speak (up) for *ou* to plead a cause ▪ **l'affaire sera plaidée en juin** the case will be heard in June ▪ **~ coupable/non coupable** to plead guilty/not guilty, to make a plea of guilty/not guilty ▪ **~ la légitime défense** to plead self-defence.

plaideur, euse [plɛdœr, øz] *nm, f* litigant.

plaidoirie [plɛdwari] *nf* **1.** [exposé] *pr* speech for the defence ▪ *fig* defence **2.** [action de plaider] pleading.

plaidoyer [plɛdwaje] *nm* **1.** DR speech for the defence **2.** [supplication] plea.

plaie [plɛ] *nf* **1.** [blessure] wound ▪ **~ profonde** deep wound ▪ **~ superficielle** surface wound ▪ **une ~ vive** *pr* an open wound ▪ **le départ de sa femme est resté pour lui une ~ vive** his wife's departure scarred him for life **2.** *litt* [tourment] wound *fig* ▪ **~ d'argent n'est pas mortelle** *prov* it's only money, money isn't

LES PLAINTES

I'd like to make a complaint. J'ai une réclamation à faire.

I have a complaint about the telephone you sold me. J'ai une réclamation au sujet du téléphone que vous m'avez vendu.

I'm not very happy/not at all happy with the service provided. Je ne suis pas très satisfait/pas du tout satisfait du service fourni.

I want my money back. Je veux être remboursé.

I think I'm (quite *ou* well) within my rights to ask for compensation. Je pense être (tout à fait) en droit de demander un dédommagement.

I'd like to see the manager, please. Je voudrais voir le directeur, s'il vous plaît.

This is just not good enough. Ça ne va pas du tout.

I know my rights! Je connais mes droits !

I expect something to be done about this. Je compte sur vous pour régler le problème.

everything **3.** BIBLE : **les sept~s d'Égypte** the seven plagues of Egypt **4.** *fam* [personne ou chose ennuyeuse] : **quelle ~!** what a pain!

plaignait *etc v* ▷ **plaindre.**

plaignant, e [plɛɲɑ̃, ɑ̃t] ◇ *adj* DR : **la partie ~e** the plaintiff.
◇ *nm, f* plaintiff.

plaindre [80] [plɛ̃dr] *vt* [avoir pitié de] to feel sorry for, to pity ■ **il adore se faire ~** he's always looking for sympathy ■ **elle est bien à ~ avec des enfants pareils!** with children like that, you can't help but feel sorry for her! ■ **avec tout l'argent qu'ils gagnent, ils ne sont vraiment pas à ~** with all the money they're making, they've got nothing to complain about.
◆ **se plaindre** *vpi* [protester] to complain, to moan ■ **plains-toi (donc)!** *iron* my heart bleeds for you! ■ **se ~ de** [symptôme] to complain of ; [personne, situation] to complain about ■ **ce n'est pas moi qui m'en plaindrai!** I'm not complaining!

plaine [plɛn] *nf* plain.

plain-pied [plɛ̃pje] ◆ **de plain-pied** *loc adv* **1.** [au même niveau] : **une maison construite de ~** [avec le sol extérieur] a bungalow *UK*, a ranch-house *US* ■ **la chambre et le salon sont de ~** the bedroom and the living room are on the same level **2.** [d'emblée] : **entrons de ~ dans le sujet** let's get straight down to the subject **3.** [sur un pied d'égalité] : **être de ~ avec qqn** to be on the same wavelength as sb.

plaint, e [plɛ̃, ɛ̃t] *pp* ▷ **plaindre.**
◆ **plainte** *nf* **1.** [gémissement] moan, groan **2.** [protestation] complaining, moaning **3.** DR complaint ■ **déposer une ~e** to lodge *ou* to file a complaint ■ **retirer une ~e** to withdraw a complaint ■ **porter ~e contre qqn** to bring an action against sb ➜ **~e contre X** action against person or persons unknown.
Voir module d'usage

plaintif, ive [plɛ̃tif, iv] *adj* **1.** [de douleur] plaintive, mournful ■ **d'un ton ~** querulously ■ **un cri ~** a plaintive cry **2.** *litt* plaintive.

plaintivement [plɛ̃tivmɑ̃] *adv* plaintively, mournfully.

plaire [110] [plɛr] ◆ **plaire à** *v+prép* **1.** [être apprécié par] : **cela me plaît** I like it ■ **ça vous plaît, le commerce?** how do you like business life? ■ **le nouveau professeur ne me plaît pas du tout** I really don't like *ou* care for the new teacher ■ **rien ne lui plaît** there's no pleasing him ■ **cette idée ne me plaît pas du tout** I'm not at all keen on this idea ■ *(en usage absolu)* **il a vraiment tout pour ~!** he's got everything going for him! ; *iron* he's so marvellous! ■ **offre du parfum, ça plaît toujours** give perfume, it's always appreciated **2.** [convenir à] : **si ça me plaît** if I feel like it ■ **quand ça me plaît** whenever I feel like it ■ **elle ne lit que ce qui lui plaît** she only reads what she feels like (reading) **3.** [séduire] to be appealing *ou* attractive ■ **il cherche à ~ aux femmes** he tries hard to make himself attractive to women ■ **c'est le genre de fille qui plaît aux hommes** she's the kind of girl that men find attractive ■ *(en usage absolu)* **aimer ~** to take pleasure in being attractive ■ **une robe doit ~ avant tout** a dress must above all be appealing.
◆ **il plaît** *v impers* **1.** *sout* [il convient] : **il lui plaît de croire que...** she likes to think that... ➜ **comme** *ou* **tant qu'il te plaira, comme** *ou* **tant qu' il vous plaira** [exprime l'indifférence] see if I care ■ **plaise à Dieu** *ou* **au ciel que...** [souhait] please God that... ■ **plût à Dieu** *ou* **au ciel que...** [regret] if only... **2.** *loc* **s'il te plaît, s'il vous plaît** please ■ **s'il vous plaît!** [dit par un client] excuse me! ; *Belgique* [dit par un serveur] here you are! ■ **sors d'ici, et plus vite que ça, s'il te plaît!** get out of here and please be quick about it! ■ **du caviar, s'il vous plaît, on ne se refuse rien!** *fam* caviar! my, my, we're splashing out a bit, aren't we? ■ **plaît-il?** I beg your pardon?
◆ **se plaire** ◇ *vp (emploi réciproque)* : **ces deux jeunes gens se plaisent, c'est évident** it's obvious that those two like each other.
◇ *vpi* [dans un endroit] : **je me plais (bien) dans ma nouvelle maison** I enjoy living in my new house, I like it in my new house ■ **mes plantes se plaisent ici** my plants are happy here.
◆ **se plaire à** *vp+prép sout* **il se plaît à la contredire** he loves contradicting her.

plaisamment [plɛzamɑ̃] *adv* **1.** [agréablement] pleasantly, agreeably **2.** [de façon amusante] amusingly.

plaisance [plɛzɑ̃s] *nf* (pleasure) boating.
◆ **de plaisance** *loc adj* pleasure *(modif)*.

plaisancier, ère [plɛzɑ̃sje, ɛr] *nm, f* amateur yachtsman (*f* yachtswoman).

plaisant, e [plɛzɑ̃, ɑ̃t] *adj* **1.** [agréable] pleasant, nice **2.** [drôle] funny, amusing **3.** [ridicule] ridiculous, laughable.
◆ **plaisant** *nm* **1.** *sout* [aspect] : **le ~ de l'histoire** the funny part of it ■ **le ~ de cette aventure** the funny thing about this adventure **2.** [personne] : **mauvais ~** joker.

plaisanter [3] [plɛzɑ̃te] ◇ *vi* **1.** [faire - de l'esprit] to joke ; [- une plaisanterie] to (crack a) joke ■ **assez plaisanté, au travail!** enough horsing around, back to work! ■ **elle n'était pas d'humeur à ~** she wasn't in a joking mood ■ **~ sur** to make fun of ■ **je l'ai dit pour ~** I meant it as a joke **2.** [parler à la légère] to joke ■ **tu plaisantes, ou quoi?** you can't be serious!, you've got to be joking! **3.** [prendre qqch très au sérieux] : **ne pas ~ avec qqch : on ne plaisante pas avec ces choses-là** you mustn't joke about such things ■ **le patron ne plaisante pas avec la discipline** the boss takes discipline very seriously *ou* is a stickler for discipline ■ **on ne plaisante pas avec la loi** you shouldn't fool around with the law.
◇ *vt* to make fun of, to tease.

plaisanterie [plɛzɑ̃tri] *nf* **1.** [parole amusante] joke ■ [acte amusant] joke, hoax ■ **lancer une ~** to make a joke ■ **faire une ~ à qqn** to play a joke on sb ■ **c'est une ~ j'espère?** I trust *ou* hope you're joking ■ **la ~ a assez duré** this has gone far enough ■ **une ~ de mauvais goût** a joke in bad *ou* poor taste **2.** [parole, action non sérieuse] joke ■ **~ à part** joking apart ■ **tourner qqch en ~** to make a joke of sthg ■ **c'est une** *ou* **ça a l'air d'une ~!** [ça ne peut être sérieux] it must be a joke! **3.** [raillerie] joke, jibe ■ **faire des ~s sur le nom/l'allure de qqn** to make fun of sb's name/appearance ■ **elle est en butte aux ~s de ses collègues** she's the laughing stock of her colleagues ➜ **mauvaise ~** cruel joke **4.** [chose facile] child's play *(U)*.

plaisantin [plɛzɑ̃tɛ̃] *nm* **1.** [farceur] joker, clown ■ **quel est le petit ~ qui m'a donné un faux numéro?** which joker gave me a wrong number? **2.** [fumiste] : **ce n'est qu'un ~** he's nothing but a fly-by-night.

plaisir [plezir] *nm* **1.** [joie] pleasure ■ **avoir (du) ~** *ou* **prendre (du) ~ à faire qqch** to take pleasure in doing sthg ■ **faire ~ à qqn** to please sb ■ **ça va lui faire ~** he'll be pleased *ou* delighted (with this) ➜ **le bon ~ de qqn** *sout* sb's wish *ou* desire **2.** [dans des formules de politesse] : **vous me feriez ~ en restant dîner** I'd be delighted if you stayed for dinner ■ **cela fait ~ de vous voir en bonne santé** it's a pleasure to see you in good health ■ **faites-moi le ~ d'accepter** won't you grant me the pleasure of accepting? ■ **fais-moi le ~ d'éteindre cette télévision** do me a favour, will you, and turn off the television ■ **je me ferai un ~ de vous renseigner** I'll be delighted *ou* happy to give you all the information ■ **cette chipie se fera un ~ de répandre la nouvelle** that little minx will take great pleasure in spreading the news ■ **aurai-je le ~ de vous avoir parmi nous?** will I have the pleasure of your company? ■ **j'ai le ~ de vous informer que...** I am pleased to inform you that... ■ **tout le ~ est pour moi** the pleasure is all mine, (it's) my pleasure ■ **au ~ (de vous revoir)** see you again *ou* soon **3.** [agrément] pleasure ■ **les ~s de la vie** life's pleasures ➜ **elle aime les ~s de la table** she loves good food **4.** [sexualité] pleasures ■ **les ~s de la chair** pleasures of the flesh ■ **les ~s défendus** forbidden pleasures ■ **~ solitaire** *euphém* self-abuse.
◆ **à plaisir** *loc adv* **1.** [sans motif sérieux] : **il se tourmente à ~** he's a natural worrier **2.** [sans retenue] unrestrainedly ■ **elle ment à ~** she lies through her teeth.
◆ **avec plaisir** *loc adv* with pleasure.
◆ **par plaisir, pour le plaisir** *loc adv* for its own sake, just for the fun of it ■ **il joue aux cartes par ~, non pas pour l'argent** he doesn't play cards for money, just for the fun of it.

plaisons *etc v* ▷ **plaire.**

plan¹ [plɑ̃] *nm*

A.

1. [surface plane] plane
2. CONSTR [surface] surface ■ **~ de travail** [d'une cuisine] worktop, working surface
3. ART & PHOTO plane

4. CINÉ shot ■ **gros ~, ~ serré** close-up ■ **~ américain** close-medium shot ■ **~ général/moyen/rapproché** long/medium/close shot
5. GÉOM plane ■ **~ horizontal/incliné/médian/tangent** level/inclined/median/tangent plane ■ **en ~ incliné** sloping

B.
1. [projet] plan, project ■ **ne vous inquiétez pas, j'ai un ~** *fam* don't worry, I've got a plan ■ **j'ai un bon ~ pour les vacances** I've got a great idea for the holidays ■ **un ~ foireux** *fam* a dead duck *fig* ▶ **un ~ d'action** a plan of action ■ **un ~ de bataille** a battle plan ■ **un ~ de carrière** a career strategy
2. [structure] plan, framework, outline ■ **je veux un ~ détaillé de votre thèse** I want a detailed outline *ou* a synopsis of your thesis
3. ADMIN plan, project ■ **~ d'aménagement rural** rural development plan *ou* scheme ■ **~ de sauvegarde** zoning plan ■ **~ d'urbanisme** town planning scheme
4. ÉCON plan ■ **~ comptable** FIN ≃ Statement of Standard Accounting Practices ■ **~ d'épargne** BANQUE savings plan ■ **~ d'épargne logement** *savings scheme offering low-interest mortgages* ■ **~ d'épargne retraite** *former personal pension plan* ■ **~ financier** financial plan ■ **~ de licenciement, ~ social** planned redundancy scheme ■ **~ d'occupation des sols** *document laying out local land development plans* ■ **~ quinquennal** five-year plan ■ **~ de restructuration** restructuring plan

C.
1. [carte] map, plan ▶ **~ de métro** underground UK *ou* subway US map ■ **~ de vol** flight plan
2. ARCHIT [dessin] plan, blueprint US ■ **lever un ~** to make a survey ▶ **~ d'ensemble** outline ■ **~ de masse** overall plan ■ **tirer des ~s sur la comète** to build castles in the air
3. TECHNOL plan, blueprint ■ **~ d'une machine/voiture** blueprint of a machine/car.

◆ **de second plan** *loc adj* [question] of secondary importance ■ [artiste, personnalité] second-rate.
◆ **en plan** *loc adv fam* in the lurch ■ **laisser qqn en ~** to leave sb in the lurch ■ **laisser qqch en ~** to drop sthg ■ **il m'a laissée en ~** he left me in the lurch ■ **rester en ~** [seul] : **je suis resté en ~** I was left stranded *ou* high and dry ■ **tous mes projets sont restés en ~** none of my plans came to anything.
◆ **sur le plan de** *loc prép* as regards, as far as... is concerned ■ **sur le ~ intellectuel** intellectually speaking ■ **sur le ~ personnel** at a personal level ■ **c'est le meilleur sur tous les ~s** he's the best whichever way you look at it.
◆ **plan d'eau** *nm* [naturel] stretch of water ■ [artificiel] reservoir ■ [ornemental] (ornamental) lake.
◆ **premier plan** *nm* **1.** CINÉ foreground ■ **au premier ~** in the foreground **2.** *fig* **au premier ~ de l'actualité** in the forefront of today's news ■ **de (tout) premier ~** [personnage] leading, prominent ■ **jouer un rôle de tout premier ~ dans** to play a leading *ou* major part in.

PLAN VIGIPIRATE

Plan VIGIPIRATE is a series of measures to fight against terrorist attacks. There are two levels: *simple* and *renforcé*. Vigipirate includes monitoring public buildings, public transportation system. Other measures such as no parking near school buildings can also be applied.

plan², e [plɑ̃, plan] *adj* **1.** [miroir] plane ■ [surface] flat **2.** MATH plane, planar ■ **surface ~e** plane.

planage [planaʒ] *nm* [d'une surface] planing ■ [d'un métal] planishing ■ [pour rendre la forme] straightening, flattening (out).

planaire [planɛr] *nf* planarian.

planant, e [planɑ̃, ɑ̃t] *adj fam* **leur musique est complètement ~e** their music really sends you.

planche [plɑ̃ʃ] *nf* **1.** [de bois] plank, board ■ **~ à découper** chopping board ■ **~ à dessin** drawing board ■ **~ à pain** *pr* breadboard ■ **c'est une ~ à pain** *fam* she's (as) flat as a board *ou* a pancake ■ **~ à pâtisserie** pastry board ■ **~ à repasser** ironing board ■ **~ de salut** last hope ■ **recourir à** *ou* **faire marcher la ~ à billets** *fam* to pump (more) money into the economy ■ **c'est une ~ pourrie** *fam* he can't be relied on **2.** *fam* [ski] ski **3.** IMPR plate **4.** HORT [de légumes] patch ■ [de plantes, fleurs] bed **5.** LOISIRS & SPORT : **faire la ~** to float on one's back.
◆ **planches** *nfpl* **1.** THÉÂTRE : **les ~s** the boards, the stage ■ **monter sur les ~s** to go on the stage **2.** [chemin] promenade UK, boardwalk US ■ **les ~s de Deauville** the promenade at Deauville.
◆ **planche à roulettes** *nf* skateboard.
◆ **planche à voile** *nf* sail board ■ **faire de la ~ à voile** to go windsurfing.

planchéier [4] [plɑ̃ʃeje] *vt* **1.** [parqueter] to floor **2.** [lambrisser] to board.

plancher¹ [plɑ̃ʃe] *nm* **1.** ARCHIT & CONSTR floor ■ **refaire le ~ d'une pièce** to refloor a room *(with floorboards)* ▶ **~ creux/plein** hollow/solid floor ■ **le ~ des vaches** *fam* dry land ■ **débarrasse le ~!** *fam* clear off!, get lost! **2.** AUTO floorboard **3.** *Québec* [étage] floor, story **4.** ANAT floor **5.** [limite inférieure] floor ▶ **~ des salaires** wage floor **6.** *(comme adj; avec ou sans trait d'union)* minimum ■ **prix ~** minimum *ou* bottom price.

plancher² [3] [plɑ̃ʃe] *vi arg scol* **demain on planche en maths** we've got a maths test tomorrow.
◆ **plancher sur** *v+prép fam* [travailler sur] to work on.

planchette [plɑ̃ʃɛt] *nf* **1.** [petite planche] small board **2.** [topographique] plane-table.

planchiste [plɑ̃ʃist] *nmf* windsurfer.

plancton [plɑ̃ktɔ̃] *nm* plankton.

planelle [planɛl] *nf Suisse* ceramic tile.

planer [3] [plane] ◇ *vi* **1.** [oiseau] to soar ■ [avion] to glide ■ [fumée, ballon] to float ■ **laisser son regard** *ou* **ses regards ~ sur** to gaze out over **2.** [danger, doute, mystère] to hover ■ **~ sur** to hover over, to hang over ■ **le doute plane encore sur cette affaire** this affair is still shrouded in mystery **3.** *fam* [être dans un état second] : **il plane complètement** [il est drogué] he's high ; [il n'est pas réaliste] he's got his head in the clouds ■ **cette musique me fait ~!** this music sends me wild!
◇ *vt* [surface] to make smooth ■ [métal] to planish.

planétaire [planetɛr] ◇ *adj* **1.** ASTRON planetary **2.** [mondial] worldwide, global ■ **à l'échelle ~** on a global scale.
◇ *nm* **1.** ASTRON orrery **2.** MÉCAN planetary gear *ou* gear-wheel, (axle drive) bevel wheel.

planétairement [planetɛrmɑ̃] *adv* worldwide.

planétarium [planetarjɔm] *nm* planetarium.

planète [planɛt] *nf* planet ■ **la ~** [la Terre] : **sur la ~ tout entière** all over the Earth *ou* world.

planétologie [planetɔlɔʒi] *nf* planetology.

planeur, euse [planœr, øz] *nm, f* [de métal] planisher ■ [d'orfèvrerie] chaser.
◆ **planeur** *nm* AÉRON glider.

planifiable [planifjabl] *adj* which can be planned.

planificateur, trice [planifikatœr, tris] ◇ *adj* planning *(modif)*, relating to (economic) planning.
◇ *nm, f* planner.

planification [planifikasjɔ̃] *nf* ÉCON (economic) planning.

planifier [9] [planifje] *vt* [gén - ÉCON] to plan.

planisphère [planisfɛr] *nm* planisphere.

plan-masse [plɑ̃mas] (*pl* **plans-masses**) *nm* overall plan.

planning [planiŋ] *nm* [programme] schedule ■ **faire un ~** to work out a schedule.
◆ **planning familial** *nm* [méthode] family planning ■ [organisme] family planning clinic.

planque [plɑ̃k] *nf fam* **1.** [cachette] hide-out, hideaway **2.** [travail - gén] cushy job ; [- en temps de guerre] safe job.

planqué, e [plɑ̃ke] *nm, f fam person who has landed himself a cushy job.*
◆ **planqué** *nm fam* MIL draft dodger.

planquer [3] [plɑ̃ke] *fam* ◇ *vt* [cacher] to hide ▪ **planque ton bouquin, voilà le prof** hide your book, the teacher's coming.
◇ *vi* [surveiller] to keep watch.
◆ **se planquer** *vpi fam* [se cacher] to hide out *ou* up.

plan-relief [plɑ̃rəljɛf] (*pl* **plans-reliefs**) *nm* street model.

plant [plɑ̃] *nm* **1.** [jeune végétal] seedling, young plant ▪ **~ de vigne** young vine ▪ **~ de tomate** tomato plant **2.** [ensemble - de légumes] patch ; [- de plantes, de fleurs] bed.

Plantagenêt [plɑ̃taʒnɛ] *npr* Plantagenet.

plantain [plɑ̃tɛ̃] *nm* [herbe, bananier] plantain.

plantaire [plɑ̃tɛr] *adj* plantar.

plantation [plɑ̃tasjɔ̃] *nf* **1.** [opération] planting **2.** [culture] plant, crop **3.** [exploitation agricole] plantation.

plante[1] [plɑ̃t] *nf* **1.** BOT plant ▪ **~ verte/à fleurs** green/flowering plant ▪ **~ textile/fourragère** fibre/fodder plant ▪ **~ grasse/vivace** succulent/perennial ▪ **~ d'appartement** *ou* **d'agrément** house *ou* pot plant ▪ **~ grimpante** creeper, climbing plant ▪ **~ d'intérieur** pot plant, indoor plant ▪ **~ médicinale** medicinal plant ▪ **se soigner par les ~s** to use herbal remedies **2.** *loc* **c'est une belle ~** *fam* she's a fine figure of a woman ▪ **~ de serre** *sout* delicate flower *fig*.

plante[2] [plɑ̃t] *nf* ANAT : **la ~ du pied** the sole of the foot.

planté, e [plɑ̃te] *adj* : **bien ~** *fam* [enfant] lusty, robust ▪ **bien ~** [dent] well-positioned, well-placed ▪ **avoir les dents mal ~es** to have uneven teeth ▪ **avoir les cheveux ~s bas/haut** to have a low/receding hairline.

planter [3] [plɑ̃te] ◇ *vt* **1.** AGRIC & HORT to plant ▪ **allée plantée d'acacias** avenue lined with acacia trees **2.** [enfoncer] to stick *ou* to drive in *(sép)* ▪ [avec un marteau] to hammer in *(sép)* **3.** [tente] to pitch, to put up *(sép)* ▪ **il a fini par ~ sa tente en Provence** *fig* he finally settled in Provence **4.** [poser résolument] : **~ un baiser sur les lèvres de qqn** to kiss sb full on the lips ▪ **il planta ses yeux dans les miens** he stared into my eyes **5.** [dépeindre - personnage] to sketch (in) ▪ **~ le décor** THÉÂTRE to set up the scenery ; LITTÉR to set the scene **6.** *fam* [abandonner - personne, voiture] to dump, to ditch ; [- travail, projet] to pack in *(sép)*.
◇ *vi fam* INFORM to crash, to go down ▪ **mon ordinateur a planté** my computer crashed.
◆ **se planter** *vpi* **1.** [s'enfoncer] to become stuck *ou* embedded, to embed o.s. ▪ **l'écharde s'est plantée dans la chair** the splinter embedded itself in the flesh **2.** *fam* [se tenir immobile] to stand ▪ **ne reste pas planté là comme une souche** don't just stand there like a lemon *UK ou* fool **3.** *fam* [se tromper] to get it wrong ▪ **on s'est complètement plantés, c'est infaisable** we've got it completely wrong, it can't be done **4.** *fam* [dans un accident] to (have a) crash ▪ **se ~ contre un arbre** to smash into a tree ▪ **je me suis planté en vélo** I came a cropper on my bike **5.** *fam* [échouer] to make a complete mess of things ▪ **je me suis complètement planté en biologie** I made a complete mess of the biology paper **6.** *fam* [ordinateur] to crash.

planteur, euse [plɑ̃tœr, øz] *nm, f* planter ▪ **des ~s de pommes de terre** potato planters.
◆ **planteur** *nm* **1.** AGRIC planter **2.** [cocktail] : **(punch) ~** planter's punch.
◆ **planteuse** *nf* planter, planting machine.

plantigrade [plɑ̃tigrad] *adj & nm* plantigrade.

plantoir [plɑ̃twar] *nm* dibble.

planton [plɑ̃tɔ̃] *nm* **1.** MIL orderly ▪ **faire le ~** *fam* to stand about *ou* around(waiting) **2.** *Belgique* [garçon de bureau] office boy.

plantureusement [plɑ̃tyrøzmɑ̃] *adv litt* copiously, lavishly.

plantureux, euse [plɑ̃tyrø, øz] *adj* **1.** [aux formes pleines - femme, beauté] buxom ; [- poitrine] full, generous **2.** [copieux - repas] sumptuous **3.** *litt* [fertile] fertile ▪ **la plantureuse province** the lush province.

plaquage [plakaʒ] *nm* **1.** [revêtement] cladding, coating **2.** SPORT tackling *(U)*, tackle.

plaque [plak] *nf* **1.** [surface - de métal] plate ; [- de marbre] slab ; [- de verre] plate, pane ▪ [revêtement] plate ▪ [pour commémorer] plaque ▪ **~ de cheminée** fire back ▪ **~ d'égout** manhole cover ▪ **~ minéralogique** *ou* **d'immatriculation** number plate *UK*, license plate *US* ▪ **~ de verglas** icy patch **2.** [inscription professionnelle] nameplate, plaque ▪ [insigne] badge **3.** JEUX [au casino] chip ▪ **une ~** *fam* [dix mille francs français] *ten thousand francs* **4.** ÉLECTR plate ▪ **~ d'accumulateur** accumulator plate ▮ ÉLECTRON plate, anode **5.** PHOTO plate **6.** CULIN [de four] baking tray ▪ *Suisse* [moule] cake tin ▪ **~ (de cuisson)** hot plate ▪ **~ à induction** induction hob ▪ **~ vitrocéramique** ceramic hob **7.** ANAT & MÉD [sur la peau] patch ▪ **des ~s rouges dues au froid** red blotches due to the cold ⊙ **~ dentaire** (dental) plaque ▪ **~s d'eczéma** eczema patches **8.** GÉOL : **~ (lithosphérique)** plate.
◆ **en plaques, par plaques** *loc adv* : **sa peau part par ~s** his skin is flaking.
◆ **plaque tournante** *nf* **1.** RAIL turntable **2.** *fig* nerve centre ▪ **la ~ tournante du trafic de drogue** the nerve centre of the drug-running industry.

plaqué, e [plake] *adj* JOAILL plated ▪ **~ d'or** *ou* **or** gold-plated ▪ **~ d'argent** *ou* **argent** silver-plated.
◆ **plaqué** *nm* **1.** JOAILL : **c'est du ~** [or] it's gold-plated ; [argent] it's silver-plated **2.** MENUIS veneer.

plaquer [3] [plake] *vt* **1.** MENUIS to veneer **2.** JOAILL to plate **3.** MÉTALL to clad **4.** [mettre à plat] to lay flat ▪ **les cheveux plaqués sur le front** hair plastered down on the forehead ▪ **je l'ai plaqué contre le mur/au sol** I pinned him to the wall/ground ▪ **le dos plaqué contre la porte** standing flat against the door ▪ **~ sa main sur la bouche de qqn** to put one's hand over sb's mouth **5.** [ajouter] : **la conclusion semble plaquée** the conclusion reads like an afterthought *ou* feels as though it's just been tacked on **6.** *fam* [abandonner - personne, travail, situation] to dump, to ditch ; [- amant, conjoint] to jilt ▪ **j'ai envie de tout ~** I feel like packing *ou* chucking it all in **7.** SPORT to tackle ▪ *fig* [personne en fuite] to rugby-tackle **8.** MUS [accord] to strike, to play ▪ **~ un accord** to strike a chord.
◆ **se plaquer** *vp (emploi réfléchi)* : **se ~ au sol** to throw o.s. flat on the ground ▪ **se ~ contre un mur** to flatten o.s. against a wall.

plaquette [plakɛt] *nf* **1.** [livre] booklet **2.** PHYSIOL blood-platelet, platelet, thrombocyte **3.** [petite plaque] : **~ commémorative** commemorative plaque **4.** COMM : **~ de beurre** pack of butter ▪ **~ de chocolat** bar of chocolate ▪ **~ de pilules** blister-pack of pills ▪ **~ insecticide** insecticide diffuser **5.** AUTO : **~ de frein** brake pad.

plasma [plasma] *nm* **1.** BIOL plasma ▪ **~ sanguin** blood plasma **2.** PHYS plasma.

plastic [plastik] *nm* plastic explosive.

plasticage [plastikaʒ] = **plastiquage**.

plasticien, enne [plastisjɛ̃, ɛn] *nm, f* **1.** ART (plastic) artist **2.** MÉD plastic surgeon **3.** TECHNOL plastics technician.

plasticité [plastisite] *nf* **1.** [d'un matériau] plasticity **2.** *sout* [du caractère] pliability, malleability **3.** ART plastic quality, plasticity.

plastifiant [plastifjɑ̃] *nm* **1.** CHIM plasticizer **2.** CONSTR (mortar) plasticizer.

plastification [plastifikasjɔ̃] *nf* **1.** [revêtement] plastic-coating **2.** [ajout d'un plastifiant] plasticization **3.** [d'un document] lamination.

plastifier [9] [plastifje] *vt* **1.** [recouvrir de plastique] to cover in *ou* with plastic ▪ **une couverture plastifiée** a plastic-coated cover **2.** [ajouter un plastifiant à] to plasticize.

plastiquage [plastikaʒ] *nm* bombing ▪ **après le ~ de l'ambassade** after the embassy was blown up, after the bombing of the embassy.

plastique [plastik] ◇ *adj* **1.** [malléable] plastic **2.** ART plastic.
◇ *nm* **1.** [matière] plastic **2.** [explosif] plastic explosive.
◇ *nf* **1.** ART (art of) modelling *ou* moulding ▪ **la ~ grecque** Greek sculpture **2.** [forme du corps] : **une belle ~** a beautiful figure.

◆ **en plastique** *loc adj* plastic.

plastiquer [3] [plastike] *vt* to blow up *(sép)*, to bomb ▪ **ils ont plastiqué l'ambassade cette nuit** they bombed the embassy last night.

plastiqueur, euse [plastikœr, øz] *nm, f* bomber.

plastron [plastrɔ̃] *nm* **1.** [vêtement - non amovible] shirtfront ; [- amovible] plastron, dickey ▪ **chemise à ~** dinner shirt **2.** ARM [de cuirasse] plastron, breastplate.

plastronner [3] [plastrɔne] *vi* **1.** [se rengorger] to throw out one's chest **2.** [parader] to swagger *ou* to strut around.

plat[1] [pla] *nm* **1.** [contenant] dish ▪ **~ ovale/à poisson** oval/fish dish ▪ **~ à gratin** baking dish ▪ **~ à tarte** flan dish **2.** [préparation culinaire] dish ◐ **~ cuisiné** precooked *ou* ready-cooked dish ▪ **~ garni** main dish served with vegetables ▪ **le ~ du jour** the dish of the day, today's special ▪ **un ~ en sauce** a dish cooked *ou* made with a sauce ▪ **elle aime les bons petits ~s** she enjoys good food ▪ **vendre qqch contre un ~ de lentilles** *allus* & BIBLE to sell something for very little **3.** [partie du menu] course ◐ **le ~ principal** *ou* **de résistance** the main course *ou* dish ▪ **mettre les petits ~s dans les grands** to put on a big spread ▪ **faire (tout) un ~ de qqch** *fam* to make a big deal out of *ou* a g reat fuss about sthg ▪ **il n'y a pas de quoi en faire tout un ~** it's not worth getting all worked up about.

plat[2]**, e** [pla, plat] *adj* **1.** [plan, horizontal - terrain] flat, level ; [- mer] still **2.** [non profond] flat, shallow **3.** [non saillant] flat ▪ **avoir la poitrine ~e** to be flat-chested ◐ **elle est ~e comme une planche à pain** *ou* **comme une limande** *fam* she's (as) flat as a board *ou* pancake **4.** [non épais - montre, calculatrice] slimline **5.** [sans hauteur - casquette] flat ▪ **ma coiffure est trop ~e** my hair lacks body ◐ **chaussures ~es** *ou* **à talons ~s** flat shoes **6.** [médiocre - style] flat, dull, unexciting ▪ [sans saveur - vin] insipid ▪ **une ~e imitation** a pallid imitation **7.** [obséquieux] cringing, fawning ▪ **je vous fais mes plus ~es excuses** please accept my most humble apologies **8.** [non gazeux] still, non-sparkling **9.** LITTÉR ▻ **rime 10.** GÉOM [angle] straight.

◆ **plat** *nm* **1.** [partie plate] flat (part) ▪ **le ~ de la main/d'une épée** the flat of the hand/a sword **2.** [lieu plan] : **sur le ~** on the flat *ou* level ‖ ÉQUIT [course] flat race **3.** *fam* [plongeon] belly-flop ▪ **faire un ~** to belly-flop **4.** *fam loc* **faire du ~ à qqn** [à une femme] to chat sb up *UK*, to give sb a line *US* ; [à son patron] to butter sb up *UK*, to sweet-talk sb **5.** [de bœuf] : **~ de côtes** best *UK ou* short *US* rib **6.** IMPR : **~s** boards **7.** MÉTALL (small) flat (bar).

◆ **plate** *nf* monkey-boat.

◆ **à plat** ◇ *loc adj* **1.** *fam* [fatigué] (all) washed out **2.** *fam* [déprimé] down ▪ **il est très à ~** he's feeling very low *ou* down **3.** [pneu, batterie, pile] flat.

◇ *loc adv* **1.** [horizontalement] flat ▪ **couché à ~** lying flat on his back ▪ **les mains à ~ sur la table** hands flat on the table ▪ **mettre qqch à ~** [robe] to unpick (and lay out the pieces) ; [projet, problème] to examine from all angles ▪ **tomber à ~** [plaisanterie] to fall flat **2.** [rouler] with a flat (tyre).

◆ **à plat ventre** *loc adv* face down *ou* downwards ▪ **se mettre à ~ ventre** [après avoir été allongé] to flop over onto one's stomach ; [après avoir été debout] to lie face downwards ▪ **tomber à ~ ventre** to fall flat on one's face ▪ **ils sont tous à ~ ventre devant elle** *fig* they all bow down to her.

platane [platan] *nm* plane tree ▪ **faux ~** sycamore.

plat-bord [plabɔr] *(pl* **plats-bords***)* *nm* gunwale, gunnel.

plateau, x [plato] *nm* **1.** [présentoir] tray ▪ **~ de viandes froides** selection of cold meats ◐ **~ à fromages** cheeseboard ▪ **~ de fruits de mer** seafood platter ▪ **il attend que tout lui soit apporté sur un ~ (d'argent)** *fig* he expects everything to be handed to him on a (silver) plate

2. THÉÂTRE stage ▪ CINÉ set ▪ TV panel ▪ **sur le ~** THÉÂTRE on stage ; CINÉ on set ▪ **nous avons un beau ~ ce soir** TV we have a wonderful line-up for you in the studio tonight

3. MÉCAN & TECHNOL [d'un électrophone] turntable ▪ [d'une balance] plate, pan ▪ [d'un véhicule] platform ▪ **~ de chargement** platform trolley ▪ **~ de frein** brake backing plate ▪ **~ d'embrayage** pressure plate ▪ **~ de pédalier** front chain wheel ▪ **mettre qqch sur les ~x de la balance** to weigh sthg up

4. [d'une courbe] plateau ▪ **faire un** *ou* **atteindre son ~** to reach a plateau, to level off

5. GÉOGR plateau, tableland ▪ **hauts ~x** high plateau ▪ **~ continental** continental shelf

6. ANTHR plate, labret

7. [d'une table] top

8. SPORT clay pigeon.

plateau-repas [platorəpa] *(pl* **plateaux-repas***)* *nm* [à la maison - TV] dinner ▪ [dans un avion] in-flight meal.

plate-bande [platbɑ̃d] *(pl* **plates-bandes***)* *nf* **1.** HORT [pour fleurs] flowerbed, bed ▪ [pour arbustes, herbes] bed **2.** *fam loc* **marcher sur** *ou* **piétiner les plates-bandes de qqn** to tread on sb's toes **3.** ARCHIT [linteau] platband ▪ [moulure] frieze.

platée [plate] *nf* [pleine assiette] plate, plateful ▪ [plein plat] dish, dishful ▪ *fam* [portion] big helping.

plate-forme [platfɔrm] *(pl* **plates-formes***)* *nf* **1.** TRANSP [d'un train, d'un bus] platform **2.** GÉOGR shelf ▪ **~ continentale** continental shelf **3.** INDUST du pétrole rig ▪ **~ de forage** drilling rig ▪ **~ de forage en mer** off-shore oil rig ▪ **~ pétrolière** oil rig **4.** POLIT platform ▪ **~ électorale** election platform **5.** ASTRONAUT & GÉOL platform **6.** ARM (gun) platform **7.** TRAV PUB road level (width) **8.** INDUST : **~ élévatrice** elevator platform **9.** CONSTR [terrassement] subgrade **10.** INFORM platform.

platement [platmɑ̃] *adv* **1.** [banalement] dully, stolidly, bluntly **2.** [servilement] cringingly, fawningly ▪ **s'excuser ~** to give a cringing apology.

platine [platin] ◇ *adj inv* ▻ **blond**, ▻ **blonde**.

◇ *nm* platinum.

◇ *nf* **1.** TECHNOL [d'une serrure, d'une horloge] plate ▪ [d'une machine à coudre] sinker **2.** ACOUST : **~ cassette** cassette deck ▪ **~ disque** *ou* **tourne-disque** record deck ▪ **~ double cassette** twin cassette deck ▪ **~ laser** CD player **3.** OPT stage **4.** IMPR platen **5.** ARM (gun) lock **6.** [dans une tuyauterie] (insert) washer.

platiné, e [platine] *adj* platinum *(modif)* ▪ **une blonde ~e** a platinum blonde.

platiner [3] [platine] *vt* [recouvrir de platine] to platinize.

platitude [platityd] *nf* **1.** [absence d'originalité] dullness, flatness, triteness **2.** [lieu commun] platitude, commonplace, trite remark **3.** [obséquiosité] obsequiousness, grovelling ▪ **elle ne reculera devant aucune ~ pour avoir ce poste** she'll stoop to anything to get this job.

Platon [platɔ̃] *npr* Plato.

platonicien, enne [platɔnisjɛ̃, ɛn] ◇ *adj* Platonic.

◇ *nm, f* Platonist.

platonique [platɔnik] *adj* **1.** *vieilli* & PHILOS Platonic **2.** [amour] platonic **3.** [de pure forme] token ▪ **la France a formulé une protestation ~** France has made a token protest.

platoniquement [platɔnikmɑ̃] *adv* **1.** [aimer, admirer] platonically **2.** [sans produire d'effet] futilely, to no effect.

platonisme [platɔnism] *nm* Platonism.

plâtrage [plɑtraʒ] *nm* CONSTR [action] plastering ▪ [ouvrage] plasterwork.

plâtras [plɑtra] *nm* **1.** [débris] (plaster) rubble *(U)* **2.** CONSTR rubblework *(U)*.

plâtre [plɑtr] *nm* **1.** CONSTR plaster ▪ **plafond en ~** plastered ceiling **2.** MÉD [matériau] plaster ▪ **être dans le ~** to be in plaster ‖ [appareil] plaster cast ▪ **il devra garder son ~** he'll have to keep his cast on ◐ **~ de marche** walking cast **3.** ART [matériau] plaster ▪ [objet] plaster cast *ou* model.

◆ **plâtres** *nmpl* : **les ~s** the plaster-work.

plâtrer [3] [plɑtre] *vt* **1.** MÉD [accidenté] to plaster (up) ▪ [membre] to put in plaster *UK ou* a cast ▪ **être plâtré de la taille jusqu'aux pieds** to be in a cast from the waist down ▪ **aura-t-il besoin d'être plâtré?** will he have to have a cast? **2.** CONSTR [couvrir] to plaster (over) ▪ [colmater] to plaster over *ou* up *(sép)*.

plâtreux, euse [plɑtrø, øz] *adj* **1.** [fromage] unripe, tasteless **2.** [mur] plastered, covered with plaster.

plâtrier [platrije] *nm* **1.** [maçon] plasterer **2.** [commerçant] builder's merchant **3.** [industriel] plaster manufacturer.

plâtrière [platrijɛr] *nf* **1.** [carrière] gypsum *ou* lime quarry **2.** [usine] plaster works.

plausibilité [plozibilite] *nf* plausibility.

plausible [plozibl] *adj* plausible, credible, believable ■ **pas très** *ou* **peu ~** implausible.

Plaute [plot] *npr* Plautus.

play-back [plɛbak] *nm inv* : **il chante en ~** he's miming (to a tape).

play-boy [plɛbɔj] (*pl* **play-boys**) *nm* playboy.

plèbe [plɛb] *nf* **1.** *litt* & *péj* **la ~** the hoi polloi **2.** ANTIQ : **la ~** the plebs.

plébéien, enne [plebejɛ̃, ɛn] ◇ *adj* **1.** *litt* & *péj* [du bas peuple] plebeian ■ **des manières ~nes** plebeian manners **2.** ANTIQ plebeian.
◇ *nm, f* **1.** *litt* & *péj* [personne vulgaire] plebeian **2.** ANTIQ plebeian.

plébiscitaire [plebisitɛr] *adj* plebiscitary.

plébiscite [plebisit] *nm* [scrutin] plebiscite.

plébisciter [3] [plebisite] *vt* **1.** [élire] to elect by (a) plebiscite **2.** [approuver] to approve (by a large majority) ■ **les spectateurs plébiscitent notre émission** viewers overwhelmingly support our programme.

pléiade [plejad] *nf* **1.** *sout* [grand nombre de] group, pleiad *litt* ■ **une ~ de vedettes** a glittering array of stars **2.** LITTÉR : **la Pléiade** [poètes] *group of seven French poets in the 16th century, including du Bellay and Ronsard* ; [édition] *prestigious edition of literary classics.*

Pléiades [plejad] *npr fpl* ASTRON & MYTHOL Pleiades.

plein, e [plɛ̃, plɛn] *adj* **1.** [rempli] full ■ **avoir l'estomac** *ou* **le ventre ~** to have a full stomach ■ **avoir les mains ~es** to have one's hands full ■ **verre à demi ~** half full glass ■ **~ à ras bord** full to the brim ■ **~ à ras bord de** brimming with ■ **~ de** full of ■ **une pièce ~e de livres** a room full of books ■ **un roman ~ d'intérêt** a very interesting novel ■ **être ~ d'enthousiasme/de bonne volonté** to show great enthusiasm/willingness ▸ **~ aux as** *fam* loaded, stinking rich ■ **~ à craquer** [valise] bulging, bursting, crammed full ; [salle] packed ■ **un gros ~ de soupe** *fam* a tub of lard, a fat slob ■ **être ~ comme un œuf** *fam* [valise, salle] to be chock-a-block ; [personne repue] to be stuffed ■ **être ~ (comme) une barrique** *ou* **une outre** *fam* to be (well) tanked up
2. [massif] solid ■ **une porte ~e** a solid door ■ **en bois ~** solid-wood
3. [complet] full ■ **année ~e** full (calendar) year ▸ **~ temps, temps ~** full-time ■ **être** *ou* **travailler à temps ~** to work full-time ■ **~e page** [gén] full page ; [en publicité, sur une page] full-page ad ; [en publicité, sur deux pages] spread ■ **avoir les ~s pouvoirs** to have full powers
4. [chargé] busy, full ■ **j'ai eu une journée ~e** I've had a busy day ■ **ma vie a été ~e** I've led a full life
5. [en intensif] : **une ~e carafe de** a jugful of ■ **une ~e valise de** a suitcase full of ■ **~ gré : de son ~ gré** of his own volition *sout ou* free will ■ **j'ai ~e conscience de ce qui m'attend** I know exactly what to expect ■ **être en ~e forme** to be on top form ■ **embrasser qqn à ~e bouche** to kiss sb full on the mouth ■ **rire à ~e gorge** to laugh one's head off ■ **chanter/crier à ~ gosier** to sing/to shout at the top of one's voice ■ **ramasser qqch à ~es mains** to pick up handfuls of sthg ■ **sentir qqch à ~ nez** to reek of sthg ■ **respirer à ~s poumons** to take deep breaths ▸ **~ tube** *fam*, **~s tubes** *fam* : **mettre la radio (à) ~s tubes** to put the radio on full blast ■ **foncer/rouler (à) ~ tube** to go/to drive flat out ■ **~e charge moteur** full throttle ■ **~s feux sur** spotlight on ■ **~s gaz** *fam*, **~s pots** *fam* full throttle ■ **~s phares** full beam *UK*, high beams *US*
6. [arrondi] full ■ **avoir des formes ~es** to have a well-rounded *ou* full figure ■ **avoir des joues ~es** to have chubby cheeks, to be chubby-cheeked
7. ZOOL [vache] in calf ■ [jument] in foal ■ [chatte] pregnant
8. *litt* [préoccupé] : **ses lettres sont ~es de vous** she talks about nothing but you in her letters ■ **être ~ de soi-même/son sujet** to be full of o.s./one's subject
9. JEUX [couleur] full
10. ASTRON & MÉTÉOR full ■ **la lune est ~e** the moon is full ▸ **la ~e mer** high tide.
◆ **plein** ◇ *nm* **1.** [de carburant] full tank ■ **avec un ~, tu iras jusqu'à Versailles** you'll get as far as Versailles on a full tank ■ **faire le ~** to fill up ■ **le ~, s'il vous plaît** fill her *ou* it up, please ■ **faire le ~ de vitamines/soleil** *fig* to stock up on vitamins/sunshine ‖ [de courses] : **on fait le ~ une fois par mois au supermarché** we stock up once a month at the supermarket
2. [maximum] : **donner son ~** [personne] to give one's best, to give one's all
3. [en calligraphie] downstroke ■ **les ~s et les déliés** the downstrokes and the upstrokes
4. CONSTR solid *ou* massive parts.
◇ *adv* **1.** *fam* **tout ~** [très] really ■ **il est mignon tout ~, ce bébé** what a cute little baby
2. [non creux] : **sonner ~** to sound solid.
◇ *prép* [partout dans] all over ■ **j'ai des plantes ~ ma maison** my house is full of plants, I have plants all over the house ■ **avoir de l'argent ~ les poches** *fig* to have loads of money ▸ **en avoir ~ les bottes de qqch** *fam* to be fed up with sthg ■ **j'en ai ~ les bottes** *ou* **pattes** *fam* my feet are killing me, I'm bushed ■ **j'en ai ~ le dos** *fam ou* **le cul**△ I've had it up to here ■ **s'en mettre ~ la lampe** *fam* to stuff one's face ■ **en mettre ~ la vue à qqn** *fam* to put on a show for sb ■ **en prendre ~ les dents** *ou* **les gencives** *fam ou* **la gueule**△ [se faire reprendre] to get a right rollocking *UK*, to get bawled out *US* ; [être éperdu d'admiration] to be bowled over.
◆ **à plein** *loc adv* : **les moteurs/usines tournent à ~** the engines/factories are working to full capacity ■ **utiliser des ressources à ~** to make full use of resources.
◆ **de plein droit** *loc adv* : **exiger** *ou* **réclamer qqch de ~ droit** to demand sthg as of right *ou* as one's right.
◆ **de plein fouet** ◇ *loc adj* head on.
◇ *loc adv* head on, full on ■ **les deux véhicules se sont heurtés de ~ fouet** the vehicles hit each other head on *ou* full on.
◆ **en plein** *loc adv* **1.** [en entier] in full, entirely ■ **le soleil éclaire la pièce en ~** the sun lights up the entire room
2. [complètement, exactement] : **en ~ dans/sur** right in the middle of/on top of ■ **tomber en ~ dans un piège** to fall right into a trap.
◆ **en plein, en pleine** *loc prép* [au milieu de, au plus fort de] : **en ~ air** in the open (air) ■ **en ~e campagne** right out in the country ■ **en ~ cœur de la ville** right in the heart of the city ■ **une industrie en ~ essor** a boom *ou* fast-growing industry ■ **en ~e figure** *ou fam* **poire** right in the face ■ **en ~ jour** in broad daylight ■ **en ~e mer** (out) in the open sea ■ **en ~e nuit** in the middle of the night ■ **en ~ soleil** in full sunlight ■ **en ~ vent** in the wind ■ **en ~ vol** in mid-flight.
◆ **plein de** *loc dét fam* lots of ■ **il y avait ~ de gens dans la rue** there were crowds *ou* masses of people in the street ■ **tu veux des bonbons/de l'argent? j'en ai ~** do you want some sweets/money? I've got loads *ou* lots.

plein-air [plɛnɛr] *nm inv* ÉDUC games.
◆ **de plein-air, en plein-air** *loc adj* open-air *(modif).*

pleinement [plɛnmɑ̃] *adv* wholly, fully, entirely ■ **vivre ~ sa passion** to live one's passion to the full ■ **je suis ~ convaincu** I'm fully convinced ■ **profiter ~ de qqch** to make the most of sthg.

plein(-)emploi [plɛnɑ̃plwa] *nm* full employment.

plein-temps [plɛ̃tɑ̃] (*pl* **pleins-temps**) ◇ *adj inv* full-time.
◇ *nm* full-time job ■ **faire un ~** to work full-time, to have a full-time job.
◆ **à plein-temps** *loc adv* : **travailler à ~** to work full-time.

plein-vent [plɛ̃vɑ̃] (*pl* **pleins-vents**) *nm* isolated *ou* exposed tree.

plénier, ère [plenje, ɛr] *adj* plenary.

plénipotentiaire [plenipɔtɑ̃sjɛr] *adj* & *nmf* plenipotentiary.

plénitude [plenityd] *nf* **1.** *litt* [des formes] fullness ■ **être dans la ~ de son talent** to be at the peak of one's talent **2.** [satisfaction totale] fulfilment.

plénum [plenɔm] *nm* POLIT plenum.

pléonasme [pleɔnasm] *nm* pleonasm.

pléonastique [pleɔnastik] *adj* pleonastic.

pléthore [pletɔr] *nf sout* excess, plethora *litt* ■ **il y a ~ de candidats à ce poste** far too many candidates have applied for the post.

pléthorique [pletɔrik] *adj* excessive, overabundant.

pleural, e, aux [plœral, o] *adj* pleural.

pleurant [plœrɑ̃] *nm* ART weeping figure, weeper.

pleurard, e [plœrar, ard] *fam* ◇ *adj* [sanglotant] whimpering ■ [plaintif] whining, whingeing *UK*.
◇ *nm, f* [qui sanglote] whimperer ■ [qui se plaint] whinger *UK*, whiner.

pleurer [5] [plœre] ◇ *vi* **1.** PHYSIOL to cry ■ **avoir un œil qui pleure** to have a weepy *ou* watery eye ■ [verser des larmes] to cry, to weep ■ **~ de joie/rage** to cry for joy/with rage ■ **j'en pleurais de rire!** I laughed so much that I cried! ■ **l'histoire est bête/triste à ~** the story is so stupid/sad you could weep ■ **faire ~ qqn** to make sb cry ■ **arrête, tu vas me faire ~!** *iron* my heart bleeds for you! ▶ **~ à chaudes larmes** *ou* **comme une Madeleine** *fam ou* **comme un veau** *fam ou* **comme une fontaine** to cry *ou* to bawl one's eyes out ■ **ne laisser à qqn que les yeux pour ~** to leave sb nothing but the clothes they stand up in ■ **il ne lui reste** *ou* **il n'a plus que les yeux pour ~** he has nothing left to his name ■ **aller ~ dans le gilet de qqn** *fam* to go crying to sb **2.** *fam* [réclamer] to beg ■ **il est allé ~ auprès du directeur pour avoir une promotion** he went cap in hand to the boss *ou* went and begged the boss for a promotion ■ **~ après** to beg for **3.** [se lamenter] : **~ sur** to lament, to bemoan, to bewail ■ **~ sur soi-même** *ou* **son sort** to bemoan one's fate **4.** *litt* [vent] to wail, to howl ■ [animal] to wail.
◇ *vt* **1.** [répandre] to cry, to shed, to weep ■ **~ des larmes de joie** to cry *ou* to shed tears of joy ▶ **~ toutes les larmes de son corps** to cry one's eyes out **2.** *sout* [être en deuil de] to mourn ■ **nous pleurons notre cher père** we're mourning (for) our dear father ■ [regretter] to lament, to bemoan ■ **~ une occasion perdue** to lament a lost opportunity **3.** *fam* [se plaindre de] to begrudge ■ **tu ne vas pas ~ les quelques euros que tu lui donnes par mois?** surely you don't begrudge her the few euros you give her a month? ■ **elle est allée ~ qu'on l'avait trompée** she went complaining that she'd been deceived **4.** *loc* **~ misère** to cry over *ou* to bemoan one's lot ■ **il est allé ~ misère chez ses parents** he went to his parents asking for money.

pleurésie [plœrezi] *nf* pleurisy.

pleurétique [plœretik] ◇ *adj* pleuritic.
◇ *nmf* pleurisy sufferer, pleuritic.

pleureur, euse [plœrœr, øz] *adj* : **enfant ~** child who cries a lot.
◆ **pleureuse** *nf* (professional) mourner.

pleurnichard, e [plœrniʃar, ard] = **pleurnicheur.**

pleurnicher [3] [plœrniʃe] *vi* [sangloter] to whimper ■ [se plaindre] to whine, to whinge *UK* ■ **~ auprès de qqn** to go crying to sb.

pleurnicherie [plœrniʃri] *nf* whining *(U)*, whingeing *(U) UK* ■ **lui, on l'aura toujours avec quelques ~s** you can always get round him if you whine a bit.

pleurnicheur, euse [plœrniʃœr, øz] ◇ *adj* [sanglotant] whimpering ■ [plaintif] whining, whingeing.
◇ *nm, f* [qui sanglote] whimperer ■ [qui se plaint] whiner, whinger *UK*.

pleurote [plœrɔt] *nm* oyster mushroom.

pleurs [plœr] *nmpl litt* tears ■ **répandre** *ou* **verser des ~** to shed tears, to weep ■ **en ~** in tears ■ **il y aura des ~ et des grincements de dents** there will be a great wailing and gnashing of teeth.

pleut *v* ▷ **pleuvoir.**

pleutre [pløtr] *litt* ◇ *adj* cowardly, faint-hearted, lily-livered ■ **il est trop ~ pour se battre** he's too lily-livered to put up a fight.
◇ *nm* coward.

pleutrerie [pløtrəri] *nf litt* **1.** [caractère lâche] cowardice, pusillanimity *litt* **2.** [acte] act of cowardice.

pleuviner [3] [pløvine] *v impers* to drizzle.

pleuvoir [68] [pløvwar] ◇ *v impers* to rain ■ **il pleut** it's raining ■ **on dirait qu'il va ~** it looks like rain ▶ **il pleut à seaux** *ou* **à verse** *ou fam* **des cordes** *ou fam* **des hallebardes** it's raining cats and dogs *ou* stair rods *UK* ■ **il pleut comme vache qui pisse** *fam* it's pouring ■ **qu'il pleuve ou qu'il vente** come rain come shine ■ **comme s'il en pleuvait : des récompenses comme s'il en pleuvait** rewards galore.
◇ *vi* [coup] to rain down, to fall like rain ■ [insulte] to shower down ■ **les punitions pleuvaient sur les élèves** punishments were showering down upon *ou* on the pupils ■ **faire ~ les malédictions sur qqn** to rain curses upon *ou* on sb's head.

pleuvoter [3] [pløvɔte] *v impers fam* to drizzle.

plèvre [plɛvr] *nf* pleura.

Plexiglas® [plɛksiglas] *nm* Plexiglas®.

plexus [plɛksys] *nm* plexus ■ **~ solaire** solar plexus.

Pleyel *npr* : **la salle ~** *large auditorium in Paris used for classical music concerts.*

pli [pli] *nm* **1.** [repli - d'un éventail, d'un rideau, du papier] fold ; [- d'un pantalon] crease ■ **le drap fait des ~s** the sheet is creased *ou* rumpled ■ **un tissu qui ne fait pas de ~s** a material that doesn't crease ▶ **~ d'aisance** inverted pleat ■ **~ plat** flat pleat ■ **faux ~** crease ■ **ça ne fait pas un ~** *fam* it goes without saying **2.** [habitude] habit ■ **c'est un ~ à prendre** you've (just) got to get into the habit **3.** [ride] wrinkle, line, crease ■ [bourrelet] fold ▶ **~ du bras** bend of the arm ■ **~ de l'aine** crease *ou* fold of the groin **4.** *sout* [enveloppe] envelope ■ [lettre] letter ■ **veuillez trouver sous ce ~ le document demandé** please find enclosed the required document ■ **sous ~ cacheté** in a sealed envelope **5.** JEUX trick ■ **faire un ~** to win *ou* to take a trick **6.** GÉOGR fold **7.** COUT pleat ■ **~ creux** box pleat **8.** MENUIS ply.
◆ **à plis** *loc adj* pleated.

pliable [plijabl] *adj* foldable ■ **difficilement ~** hard to fold.

pliage [plijaʒ] *nm* folding ■ **à ~ accordéon** fan-fold, Z-fold *US*.

pliant, e [plijɑ̃, ɑ̃t] *adj* folding, collapsible.
◆ **pliant** *nm* folding stool.

plie [pli] *nf* plaice.

plié [plije] *nm* plié.

plier [10] [plije] ◇ *vt* **1.** [journal, carte] to fold ■ **~ bagage** to pack up and go **2.** [tordre - fil de fer, doigt, genou] to bend ■ **la douleur le plia en deux** he was doubled up in pain ▶ **plié en deux** *fam ou* **en quatre** *fam* **(de rire)** doubled up (with laughter) **3.** [soumettre] : **je n'ai jamais pu la ~ à mes désirs/pu ~ sa volonté** I never managed to get her to submit to my desires/to bend her will.
◇ *vi* **1.** [se courber] to bend (over), to bow ■ **les branches pliaient sous le poids des fruits/de la neige** the branches were weighed down with fruit/snow ■ **~ sous le poids des responsabilités** to be weighed down by responsibility **2.** [se soumettre] to yield, to give in, to give way ■ **~ devant qqn** to submit *ou* to yield to sb.
◆ **se plier** *vpi* [meuble, appareil] to fold up *ou* away ■ [personne, corps] to bend, to stoop ■ **se ~ en deux** to bend double.
◆ **se plier à** *vp+prép* [se soumettre à] to submit to ■ [s'adapter à] to adapt to ■ **c'est une discipline à laquelle il faut se ~** you have to accept the discipline.

Pline [plin] *npr* : **~ l'Ancien/le Jeune** Pliny the Elder/Younger.

plinthe [plɛ̃t] *nf* **1.** CONSTR [en bois] skirting (board) *UK*, baseboard *US*, mopboard *US* ■ [en pierre] skirting ■ **~ chauffante** skirting fan convector **2.** ARCHIT plinth.

plissage [plisaʒ] *nm* pleating.

plissé, e [plise] *adj* **1.** [vêtement] pleated **2.** [ridé - front, visage] wrinkled, creased ■ **une petite figure toute ~e** a wrinkled little face **3.** GÉOL [terrain] folded.
◆ **plissé** *nm* [plis] pleats ■ **~ soleil** sunray pleat.

plissement [plismɑ̃] *nm* **1.** GÉOGR folding ■ **~ (de terrain)** fold ■ **montagnes formées par ~s** fold mountains **2.** [d'un front, d'un visage] wrinkling *(U)*.

plisser [3] [plise] ◇ *vt* **1.** [faire des plis à - volontairement] to fold ; [- involontairement] to crease **2.** [froncer - yeux] to screw up *(sép)* ; [- nez] to wrinkle ■ **la contrariété plissait son front** his brow was furrowed with worry **3.** GÉOGR to fold **4.** COUT to pleat.
◇ *vi* [faire des plis - pantalon, robe, nappe] to crease, to become creased ; [- collant] to wrinkle.
◆ **se plisser** *vpi* **1.** [se rider] to crease, to wrinkle ■ **son front se plissa** she frowned **2.** COUT to pleat.

pliure [plijyr] *nf* **1.** [marque] fold **2.** [pliage] folding.

ploc [plɔk] *onomat* plop ■ **on entendait le ~ des gouttes d'eau dans l'évier** we could hear the sound of water dripping into the sink.

ploie *etc v* ▷ **ployer**.

ploiement [plwamɑ̃] *nm litt* bending.

plomb [plɔ̃] *nm* **1.** MÉTALL lead ■ **ça te mettra un peu de ~ dans la tête** *ou* **cervelle** that will knock some sense into you ■ **avoir du ~ dans l'aile** [entreprise] to be in a sorry state *ou* bad way ; [personne] to be in bad shape *ou* on one's last legs **2.** ARM leadshot, shot ■ **un ~** a piece of shot ▶ **du gros ~** buckshot ■ **du petit ~** small shot **3.** ÉLECTR fuse ■ **faire sauter les ~s** to blow the fuses **4.** PÊCHE sinker **5.** COUT lead (weight) **6.** [de vitrail] lead, came **7.** [sceau] lead seal **8.** CONSTR plumb, bob, plummet **9.** IMPR type.
◆ **à plomb** *loc adv* : **mettre à ~** to plumb ■ **le mur n'est pas/est à ~** the wall is off plumb/is plumb.
◆ **de plomb** *loc adj* lead *(modif)* ■ **un ciel de ~** a leaden sky.

plombage [plɔ̃baʒ] *nm* **1.** [d'une dent] filling ■ **faire un ~ à qqn** to fill sb's tooth ■ **se faire faire un ~** to have a tooth filled *ou* a filling (put in) **2.** [d'un colis] sealing (with lead) **3.** PÊCHE leading.

plombe△ [plɔ̃b] *nf* hour.

plombé, e [plɔ̃be] *adj* **1.** [teint] leaden, pallid ■ [ciel] leaden, heavy **2.** [scellé - colis, wagon] sealed (with lead) **3.** PÊCHE weighted (with lead) *ou* with a sinker **4.** [dent] filled.

plomber [3] [plɔ̃be] *vt* **1.** [dent] to fill, to put a filling in **2.** [colis] to seal with lead **3.** PÊCHE to weight (with lead), to lead **4.** CONSTR to plumb **5.** [toit] to lead.
◆ **se plomber** *vpi sout* [ciel] to turn leaden *ou* the colour of lead.

plomberie [plɔ̃bri] *nf* **1.** [installation] plumbing ■ **toute la ~ est à refaire** all the plumbing in the house must be redone **2.** [profession] plumbing.

plombier [plɔ̃bje] *nm* [artisan] plumber.

plonge [plɔ̃ʒ] *nf* washing-up, washing the dishes ■ **faire la ~** to wash dishes *(in a restaurant)*.

plongeant, e [plɔ̃ʒɑ̃, ɑ̃t] *adj* plunging ■ **il y a une vue ~e jusqu'à la mer** the view plunges down to the sea.

plongée [plɔ̃ʒe] *nf* **1.** LOISIRS & SPORT (underwater) diving ■ **il fait de la ~ depuis deux ans** he has been diving for two years ■ **~ sous-marine** skin *ou* scuba diving **2.** CINÉ high angle shot **3.** [descente rapide] swoop, plunge, dive.

plongeoir [plɔ̃ʒwar] *nm* diving board.

plongeon [plɔ̃ʒɔ̃] *nm* **1.** [dans l'eau] dive ■ **faire un ~ en arrière** to do a back dive *ou* a back flip ▶ **faire le ~** *fam* to take a tumble, to come a cropper *UK fig* **2.** FOOTBALL dive ■ **faire un ~** to dive.

plonger [17] [plɔ̃ʒe] ◇ *vi* **1.** LOISIRS & SPORT to dive ■ [en profondeur] to dive, to go skin *ou* scuba diving ■ **il plongea du haut du rocher** he dived off the rock ‖ FOOTBALL to dive
2. [descendre - avion] to dive ; [- sous-marin] to dive ; [- oiseau] to dive, to swoop ; [- racine] to go down ■ **depuis le balcon, la vue plonge dans le jardin des voisins** there's a bird's-eye view of next door's garden from the balcony
3. [s'absorber dans] : **~ dans** to plunge into, to absorb o.s. in ■ **elle plongea dans la dépression** she plunged into depression
4. *sout* **cette tradition plonge dans la nuit des temps** this tradition goes back to the dawn of time
5. *fam* [échouer] to decline, to fall off ■ **beaucoup d'élèves plongent au deuxième trimestre** a lot of pupils' work deteriorates in the second term ‖ [faire faillite] to go bankrupt, to fold ■ **c'est ça qui a fait ~ la société** that's what sent the company to the wall ■ **c'est ce qui l'a fait ~** that's what caused his demise
6. △ [être arrêté] to get nabbed *ou* busted *ou* nicked *UK*.
◇ *vt* **1.** [enfoncer] to plunge, to thrust ■ **~ la main dans l'eau** to plunge one's hand into the water ■ **il plongea la main dans sa poche** he thrust his hand deep into his pocket
2. [mettre] to plunge ■ **la panne a plongé la pièce dans l'obscurité** the power failure plunged the room into darkness ■ **~ son regard** *ou* **ses regards dans** to look deep *ou* deeply into ■ **~ qqn dans l'embarras** to put sb in a difficult spot ■ **la remarque nous plongea tous dans la consternation** the remark appalled us all ■ **j'étais plongé dans mes pensées/comptes** I was deep in thought/in my accounts ■ **je suis plongé dans Proust pour l'instant** at the moment, I'm completely immersed in Proust ■ **il est plongé dans ses dossiers** he's engrossed in his files ■ **plongé dans un sommeil profond, il ne nous a pas entendus** as he was sound asleep, he didn't hear us.
◆ **se plonger dans** *vp+prép* [bain] to sink into ■ [études, travail] to throw o.s. into ■ [livre] to bury o.s. in.

plongeur, euse [plɔ̃ʒœr, øz] *nm, f* **1.** LOISIRS & SPORT diver ■ **~ sous-marin** skin *ou* scuba diver **2.** [dans un café] washer-up *UK*, dishwasher *US*.

plot [plo] *nm* **1.** ÉLECTR contact ■ [dans un commutateur] contact block **2.** [bille de bois] block **3.** SPORT block **4.** *Suisse* [billot] wooden block.

plouc [pluk] *nm fam péj* yokel, bumpkin, hick *US* ■ **ça fait ~** it's vulgar.

plouf [pluf] *interj* splash ■ **elle a fait ~ dans l'eau** *langage enfantin* she went splash into the water.

ploutocratie [plutɔkrasi] *nf* plutocracy.

ployer [13] [plwaje] ◇ *vt* **1.** *litt* [courber] to bend, to bow **2.** [fléchir] to bend, to flex ■ **~ les genoux** *pr* to bend one's knees ; *fig* to toe the line, to submit.
◇ *vi litt* **1.** [arbre] to bend ■ [étagère, poutre] to sag **2.** *fig* **~ sous le poids des ans** to be weighed down by age ■ **~ sous le joug** to bend beneath the yoke, to be subjugated *litt*.

plu [ply] *pp* **1.** ▷ **plaire 2.** ▷ **pleuvoir**.

pluches [plyʃ] *nfpl fam* **1.** [épluchage] peeling ■ **faire les ~** to peel the veg *UK ou* veggies *US* **2.** [épluchures] vegetable peelings.

pluie [plɥi] *nf* **1.** MÉTÉOR rain ■ **le temps est à la ~** it looks like rain ■ **~ battante** driving rain ■ **~ diluvienne** *ou* **torrentielle** pouring rain ■ **(petite) ~ fine** drizzle ▶ **~s acides** ÉCOL acid rain ■ **ennuyeux comme la ~** deadly boring ■ **faire la ~ et le beau temps** to be powerful ■ **il fait la ~ et le beau temps dans l'entreprise** he dictates what goes on in the company ■ **parler de la ~ et du beau temps** to talk of this and that ■ **après la ~, le beau temps** *prov* every cloud has a silver lining *prov* ■ **petite ~ abat grand vent** *prov* a soft answer turneth away wrath *prov* **2.** [retombée] shower ■ **une ~ d'étoiles filantes** a meteor-shower **3.** [série] shower, stream.
◆ **en pluie** *loc adv* : **verser la farine en ~ dans le lait** sprinkle the flour into the milk.

plumage [plymaʒ] *nm* plumage, feathers.

plumard△ [plymar] *nm* bed, sack ■ **aller au ~** to hit the hay *ou* sack.

plume[1] [plym] *nf* **1.** [d'oiseau] feather ■ **j'y ai laissé des ~s** *fam* I didn't come out of it unscathed **2.** [pour écrire] quill ■ [de stylo] nib ■ **dessiner à la ~** to draw in pen and ink ■ **je prends la ~ pour te dire que...** I take up my pen to tell you that... ■ **c'est**

un critique à la ~ acérée he's a scathing critic ◆ ~ d'oie goose quill ■ laisser aller ou courir sa ~ to write as the ideas come ■ avoir la ~ facile to have a gift for writing **3.** *sout* [écrivain] pen **4.** MÉD : ~ à vaccin vaccine point.

◆ **à plumes** *loc adj* ZOOL pennaceous.

◆ **en plumes** *loc adj* feather *(modif)*, feathered.

plume [2] △ [plym] = **plumard**.

plumeau, x [plymo] *nm* feather duster.

plumer [3] [plyme] *vt* **1.** [oiseau] to pluck **2.** *fam* [escroquer] to fleece.

plumet [plymɛ] *nm* plume.

plumetis [plymti] *nm* **1.** [broderie] raised satin stitch ■ collant (à) ~ dot *ou* dotted tights **2.** TEXT Swiss muslin.

plumier [plymje] *nm* pencil box *ou* case.

plupart [plypar] ◆ **la plupart** *nf* most ■ quelques-uns sont partis mais la ~ ont attendu some left but most (of them) waited.

◆ **la plupart de** *loc prép* most (of) ■ la ~ des enfants [du monde] the majority of *ou* most children ; [d'un groupe] the majority *ou* most of the children ■ la ~ du temps most of the time ■ dans la ~ des cas in the majority of *ou* in most cases.

◆ **pour la plupart** *loc adv* mostly, for the most part ■ les clients sont pour la ~ satisfaits the customers are mostly satisfied *ou* for the most part satisfied ■ ils te croient? – oui, pour la ~ do they believe you? – most of them do *ou* for the most part, yes.

plural, e, aux [plyral, o] *adj* plural ■ vote ~ plural vote.

pluralisme [plyralism] *nm* pluralism.

pluraliste [plyralist] ◇ *adj* pluralist, pluralistic.
◇ *nmf* pluralist.

pluralité [plyralite] *nf* plurality.

pluriannuel, elle [plyrianɥɛl] *adj* **1.** DR running over several years **2.** BOT perennial.

pluricellulaire [plyriselylɛr] *adj* multicellular.

pluridimensionnel, elle [plyridimɑ̃sjɔnɛl] *adj* multidimensional.

pluridisciplinaire [plyridisiplinɛr] *adj* multidisciplinary, joint *(modif)*.

pluridisciplinarité [plyridisiplinarite] *nf* : la ~ de notre formation the interdisciplinary nature of our training programme.

pluriel, elle [plyrjɛl] *adj* **1.** GRAMM plural **2.** [diversifié] diverse, multifarious ■ une société ~le a pluralist society.

◆ **pluriel** *nm* plural ■ la troisième personne du ~ the third person plural ■ au ~ in the plural ■ mettre au ~ to put in *ou* into the plural ■ quel est le ~ de « carnaval »? what's the plural of "carnaval"? ◆ le ~ de majesté the royal "we".

pluriethnique [plyriɛtnik] *adj* multiethnic.

pluripartisme [plyripartism] *nm* pluralist (party) *ou* multi-party system.

plus [ply(s)] ◇ *adv*

> **A.** COMPARATIF DE SUPÉRIORITÉ
> **B.** SUPERLATIF DE SUPÉRIORITÉ
> **C.** ADVERBE DE NÉGATION

A. COMPARATIF DE SUPÉRIORITÉ

1. [suivi d'un adverbe, d'un adjectif] : viens ~ souvent (do) come more often ■ ~ tôt earlier ■ ~ tard later ■ c'est ~ loin it's further *ou* farther ■ tu es ~ patient que moi you're more patient than I am *ou* than me ■ c'est ~ fatigant qu'on ne le croit it's more tiring than it seems ■ c'est ~ rouge qu'orange it's red rather than *ou* it's more red than orange ■ elle est ~ réservée que timide she's reserved rather than shy ■ c'est ~ que gênant it's embarrassing, to say the least ■ on a obtenu des résultats ~ qu'encourageants our results were more than encouraging ■ elle a eu le prix mais elle n'en est pas ~ fière pour ça she got the award, but it didn't make her any prouder for all that ■ je veux la même, en ~ large I want the same, only bigger ■ bien ~ gros much fatter ■ encore ~ beau more handsome still, even more handsome ■ cinq fois ~ cher five times dearer *ou* as dear *ou* more expensive ■ il l'a fait deux fois ~ vite (qu'elle) he did it twice as quickly (as she did)

2. [avec un verbe] more ■ j'apprécie ~ son frère I like his brother more *ou* better ■ je m'intéresse à la question ~ que tu ne penses I'm more interested in the question than you think ■ je ne peux vous en dire ~ I can't tell you any more

3. *(avec un n)* cela représente ~ qu'une simple victoire it means more than just a victory

B. SUPERLATIF DE SUPÉRIORITÉ

1. [suivi d'un adverbe, d'un adjectif] : le ~ loin the furthest *ou* farthest ■ la montagne la ~ haute the highest mountain ■ j'ai répondu le ~ gentiment que j'ai pu I answered as kindly as I could ■ j'y vais le ~ rarement possible I go there as seldom as possible ■ le ~ souvent most of the time ■ tu es le ~ gentil de tous you're the kindest of all ■ un de ses tableaux les ~ connus one of her best-known paintings ■ le ~ gros des deux the bigger of the two ■ le ~ gros des trois the biggest of the three ■ c'est ce qu'il y a de ~ original dans sa collection d'été it's the most original feature of his summer collection ■ choisis les fruits les ~ mûrs possible select the ripest possible fruit ■ faites au ~ vite do it as quickly as possible ■ aller au ~ pressé *ou* urgent to deal with the most urgent priority first

2. [précédé d'un verbe] most ■ c'est moi qui travaille le ~ I'm the one who works most *ou* the hardest ■ faites-en le ~ possible do as much as you can

C. ADVERBE DE NÉGATION

1. [avec 'ne'] : je n'y retournerai ~ I won't go back there any more ■ je ne les vois ~ I don't see them any more

2. [tour elliptique] : ~ de no more ■ ~ de glace pour moi, merci no more ice cream for me, thanks ■ ~ de tergiversations! let's not shilly-shally any longer! ■ ~ un mot! not another word!

◇ *adj* : B ~ ÉDUC B plus ■ H ~ CHIM H plus.

◇ *conj* **1.** MATH plus ■ 3 ~ 3 égale 6 3 plus 3 is *ou* makes 6 ■ il fait ~ 5° it's 5° above freezing, it's plus 5° **2.** [en sus de] plus ■ le transport, ~ le logement, ~ la nourriture, ça revient cher travel, plus *ou* and accommodation, plus *ou* then food, (all) work out quite expensive ■ ~ le fait que... plus *ou* together with the fact that...

◇ *nm* **1.** MATH plus (sign) **2.** [avantage, atout] plus, bonus, asset ■ la connaissance de l'anglais est toujours un ~ knowledge of English is always a plus.

◆ **au plus** *loc adv* [au maximum] at the most *ou* outside ■ ça coûtera au ~ 30 euros it'll cost a maximum of 30 euros *ou* 30 euros at most ■ il y a 15 km au ~ it's 15 km at the outside.

◆ **de plus** *loc adv* **1.** [en supplément] extra, another, more ■ mets deux couverts de ~ lay two extra *ou* more places ■ raison de ~ pour y aller all the more reason for going ■ je ne veux rien de ~ I don't want anything more ■ il est content, que te faut-il de ~? he's happy, what more do you want? ■ un mot/une minute de ~ et je m'en allais another word/minute and I would have left ■ 10 euros de ~ ou de moins, quelle différence? 10 euros either way, what difference does it make? **2.** [en trop] too many ■ en recomptant, je trouve trente points de ~ on adding it up again, I get thirty points too many **3.** [en outre] furthermore, what's more, moreover ■ de ~, il m'a menti what's more, he lied to me.

◆ **de plus en plus** *loc adv* **1.** [suivi d'un adjectif] more and more, increasingly ■ [suivi d'un adverbe] more and more ■ de ~ en ~ souvent more and more often ■ de ~ en ~ dangereux more and more *ou* increasingly dangerous ■ ça devient de ~ en ~ facile/compliqué it's getting easier and easier/more and more complicated ■ le ciel devenait de ~ en ~ sombre the sky was growing darker and darker **2.** [précédé d'un verbe] : les prix augmentent de ~ en ~ prices are increasing all the time.

◆ **de plus en plus de** *loc dét* [suivi d'un nom comptable] more and more, a growing number of ■ [suivi d'un nom non comptable] more and more ■ de ~ en ~ de gens more and more people, an increasing number of people ■ il y a de ~ en ~ de demande pour ce produit demand for this product is increasing, there is more and more demand for this product ■ elle a de ~ en ~ de fièvre her temperature is rising.

◆ **des plus** *loc adv* most ■ son attitude est des ~ compréhensibles her attitude is most *ou* quite understandable.

◆ **en plus** *loc adv* **1.** [en supplément] extra *(avant n)* ▪ **c'est le même appartement avec un balcon en ~** it's the same flat with a balcony as well ▪ **les boissons sont en ~** drinks are extra, you pay extra for the drinks ▪ **ça fait 45 minutes de transport en ~** it adds 45 minutes to the journey ▪ **10 euros en ~ ou en moins, quelle différence?** 10 euros either way, what difference does it make? ▮ [en trop] spare ▪ **tu n'as pas des tickets en ~?** do you have any spare tickets? ▪ **j'ai une carte en ~** [à la fin du jeu] I've got one card left over ; [en distribuant] I've got one card too many ▮ [en cadeau] as well, on top of that ▪ **et vous emportez une bouteille de champagne en ~!** and you get a bottle of Champagne as well *ou* on top of that *ou* into the bargain! **2.** [en outre] further, furthermore, what's more ▪ **elle a une excellente technique et en ~, elle a de la force** her technique's first-class and she's got strength too ▪ **mais c'est qu'elle est méchante en ~!** *fam* and she's nasty to cap it all *ou* to boot! ▪ **et elle m'avait menti, en ~!** not only that but she'd lied to me (as well)! **3.** [d'ailleurs] besides, what's more, moreover ▪ **je ne tiens pas à le faire et, en ~, je n'ai pas le temps** I'm not too keen on doing it, and besides *ou* what's more, I've no time.

◆ **en plus de** *loc prép* [en supplément de] besides, on top of, in addition to ▪ **en ~ du squash, elle fait du tennis** besides (playing) squash, she plays tennis.

◆ **et plus** *loc adv* over ▪ **45 kilos et ~** over 45 kilos, 45 odd kilos ▪ **les gens de 30 ans et ~** people aged 30 and over.

◆ **ni plus ni moins** *loc adv* no more no less, that's all ▪ **je te donne une livre, ni ~ ni moins** I'll give you one pound, no more no less ▪ **tu t'es trompé, ni ~ ni moins** you were mistaken, that's all.

◆ **non plus** *loc adv* : **moi non ~ je n'irai pas** I won't go either ▪ **je ne sais pas – moi non ~!** I don't know – neither do I *ou* nor do I *ou* me neither!

◆ **on ne peut plus** *loc adv* : **je suis on ne peut ~ désolé de vous voir partir** I'm ever so sorry you're leaving ▪ **c'est on ne peut ~ compliqué** it couldn't be more complicated.

◆ **plus de** *loc dét* **1.** [comparatif, suivi d'un nom] more ▪ **nous voulons ~ d'autonomie!** we want more autonomy! ▪ **je n'ai pas ~ de courage qu'elle** I'm no braver than she is *ou* her ▮ [suivi d'un nombre] more than, over ▪ **il y a ~ de 15 ans de cela** it's more than 15 years ago now ▪ **elle a bien ~ de 40 ans** she's well over 40 ▪ **elle roulait à ~ de 150 km/h** she was driving at more than 150 km/h *ou* doing over 150 km/h ▪ **il y en a ~ d'un qui s'est plaint** more than one person complained ▪ **il est ~ de 5 h** it's past 5 o'clock *ou* after 5 **2.** [superlatif, suivi d'un nom] : **le ~ de** (the) most ▪ **c'est ce qui m'a fait le ~ de peine** that's what hurt me (the) most ▪ **c'est notre équipe qui a le ~ de points** our team has (the) most points ▪ **celui qui a le ~ de chances de réussir** the one (who's the) most likely to succeed ▪ **le ~ possible de : le ~ possible de cerises** as many cherries as possible ▪ **le ~ d'argent possible** as much money as possible ▪ *(comme nom)* **les ~ de 20 ans** people over 20, the over-20s.

◆ **plus... moins** *loc corrélative* the more... the less ▪ **~ il vieillit, moins il a envie de sortir** the older he gets, the less he feels like going out ▪ **~ ça va, moins je la comprends** I understand her less and less (as time goes on).

◆ **plus... plus** *loc corrélative* the more... the more ▪ **~ je réfléchis, ~ je me dis que...** the more I think (about it), the more I'm convinced that... ▪ **~ ça va, ~ il est agressif** he's getting more and more aggressive (all the time) ▪ **~ ça va, ~ je me demande si...** the longer it goes on, the more I wonder if...

◆ **plus ou moins** *loc adv* more or less ▪ **c'est ~ ou moins cher, selon les endroits** prices vary according to where you are ▪ **je ne l'ai que ~ ou moins cru** I only half believed him.

◆ **qui plus est** *loc adv* what's *ou* what is more.

◆ **sans plus** *loc adv* nothing more ▪ **c'était bien, sans ~** it was nice, but nothing more.

◆ **tout au plus** *loc adv* at the most ▪ **c'est une mauvaise grippe, tout au ~** it's a bad case of flu, at the most.

plusieurs [plyzjœr] ◇ *dét (adj indéf pl)* several.
◇ *pron indéf pl* **1.** [désignant des personnes] several people ▪ **se mettre à ~ pour faire qqch** to do sthg as a group ▪ **vous venez à ~?** will there be several of you coming? ▪ **~ (d'entre eux) ont refusé** several of them refused **2.** [reprenant le substantif] several ▪ **n'utilisez pas une seule couleur, mais ~** don't use just one colour, but several.

plus-que-parfait [plyskəparfɛ] *nm* pluperfect, past perfect.

plus-value [plyvaly] *(pl* **plus-values***)* *nf* **1.** [augmentation de la valeur] increase (in value), appreciation **2.** [excédent d'impôts] (tax) budget surplus **3.** [surcoût] surplus value **4.** [somme ajoutée au salaire] bonus.

plut *etc v* **1.** ⊳ **plaire 2.** ⊳ **pleuvoir**.

Plutarque [plytark] *npr* Plutarch.

Pluton [plytɔ̃] *npr* ASTRON & MYTHOL Pluto.

plutonique [plytɔnik] *adj* plutonic.

plutonium [plytɔnjɔm] *nm* plutonium.

plutôt [plyto] *adv* **1.** [de préférence] rather ▪ [à la place] instead ▪ **~ mourir!** I'd rather die! ▪ **mets mon manteau ~, tu auras plus chaud** put my coat on instead, you'll be warmer ▪ **demande ~ à un spécialiste** you'd better ask a specialist ▪ **~ que** rather than, instead of ▪ **~ que de travailler, je vais aller faire des courses** I'm going to do some shopping instead of working ▪ **~ mourir que de céder!** I'd rather die than give in! **2.** [plus précisément] rather ▪ **la situation n'est pas désespérée, disons ~ qu'elle est délicate** the situation is not hopeless, let's say rather that it is delicate ▪ **ce n'était pas une maison de campagne, mais ~ un manoir** it wasn't a country house, it was more of a country manor ▪ **elle le méprise ~ qu'elle ne le hait** *sout* she doesn't so much hate as despise him **3.** [assez, passablement] rather, quite **4.** [en intensif] : **il est ~ collant, ce type!** *fam* that guy's a bit of a leech! ▪ **il est idiot, ce film! – ~, oui!** it's stupid, this film! – you can say that again *ou* you're telling me!

pluvial, e, aux [plyvjal, o] *adj* pluvial *spéc*, rainy.

pluvier [plyvje] *nm* plover ▪ **~ argenté/doré** grey/golden plover.

pluvieux, euse [plyvjø, øz] *adj* [temps, journée] rainy, wet ▪ [climat] wet, damp.

pluviomètre [plyvjɔmɛtr] *nm* pluviometer *spéc*, rain gauge.

pluviométrie [plyvjɔmetri] *nf* pluviometry.

pluviôse [plyvjoz] *nm fifth month of the French Revolutionary calendar (from January 20th, 21st or 22nd to February 18th, 19th or 20th).*

pluviosité [plyvjozite] *nf* (average) rainfall.

plv *(abr de* **publicité lieu de vente***)* *nf* POS.

PMA ◇ *nf (abr de* **procréation médicalement assistée***)* MAR.
◇ *nmpl (abr de* **pays les moins avancés***)* LDCs.

PME *(abr de* **petite et moyenne entreprise***)* *nf* small business ▪ **les ~** small and medium-sized firms.

PMI *nf* **1.** *(abr de* **petite et moyenne industrie***)* small industrial firm **2.** = **protection maternelle et infantile**.

PMR [peɛmɛr] *(abr de* **personne à mobilité réduite***)* *nf* PRM.

PMU *(abr de* **Pari mutuel urbain***)* *npr m French betting authority*, ≃ tote UK, ≃ pari-mutuel US.

PMU

These initials, often posted outside bars in France, indicate that there is a counter inside where bets on horse races can be placed.

PNB *(abr de* **produit national brut***)* *nm* GNP.

pneu [pnø] *nm* **1.** AUTO tyre ▪ **~ sans chambre à air** tubeless tyre ▪ **~ clouté** spiked tyre ▪ **~ neige** snow tyre **2.** *fam* [lettre] message *(sent through a compressed air tube system)*, pneumatic (dispatch).

pneumatique [pnømatik] ◇ *adj* **1.** [gonflable] inflatable, blow-up *(avant n)* **2.** PHYS & RELIG pneumatic.
◇ *nm* **1.** AUTO tyre **2.** [lettre] message *(sent through a compressed air tube system)*, pneumatic (dispatch).

pneumologie [pnømɔlɔʒi] *nf* pneumology.

pneumologue [pnømɔlɔg] *nmf* pneumologist.

pneumonie [pnømɔni] *nf* pneumonia.

pneumothorax [pnømɔtɔraks] *nm* pneumothorax.

PNUD, Pnud [pnyd] (*abr de* **Programme des Nations unies pour le développement**) *npr m* UNDP.

PO (*abr écrite de* **petites ondes**) MW.

pochade [pɔʃad] *nf* **1.** [peinture] (quick) sketch, thumbnail sketch **2.** [écrit] sketch.

pochard, e [pɔʃar, ard] *nm, f fam* drunk.

poche [pɔʃ] ◇ *nf* **1.** [vêtement] pocket ■ [d'un sac] pocket, pouch ■ **je n'ai même pas un euros en ~** I don't even have one euro on me ▶ **~ intérieure** inside (breast) pocket ■ **~ (de) poitrine** breast pocket ■ **~ à rabat** flapped pocket ■ **~ revolver** hip pocket ■ **avoir les ~s percées** to be a spendthrift ■ **s'en mettre plein les** *ou* **se remplir les ~s** *fam* to line one's pockets ■ **faire les ~s à qqn** to go through *ou* to rifle (through) sb's pockets ■ **j'en ai été de ma ~** I was out of pocket ■ **c'est dans la ~!** *fam* it's in the bag! ■ **il a mis tout le monde dans sa ~** he twisted everyone round his little finger, he took everyone in
2. [boursouflure] bag ■ **avoir des ~s sous les yeux** to have bags under one's eyes ■ **faire des ~s aux genoux/coudes** to go baggy at the knees/elbows
3. [amas] pocket ■ **~ d'air** air pocket ■ **~ d'eau/de gaz** pocket of water/gas ■ **~ de grisou** MIN pocket of firedamp
4. MÉD sac ■ **~ des eaux** (sac of) waters ■ **la ~ des eaux s'est rompue** her waters broke ■ **~ de pus** pus sac
5. ZOOL [d'un kangourou] pouch ■ [d'un poulpe] sac ■ [d'un oiseau] crop ■ **~ marsupiale** marsupium
6. MIL : **~ de résistance** pocket of resistance
7. [contenant] : **~ plastique** plastic bag ■ **~ à douille** CULIN piping bag
8. *Suisse* [louche] ladle.
◇ *nm* [livre] paperback (book).
◆ **de poche** *loc adj* [collection, édition] pocket *(modif)* ■ [cuirassé, théâtre] pocket *(modif)*, miniature *(avant n)*.
◆ **en poche** *loc adv* **1.** [avec soi - argent] on me/you *etc* ; [- diplôme] under one's belt ■ **elle est repartie, contrat en ~** she left with the contract signed and sealed
2. [livre] in paperback ■ **il est sorti en ~** he's come out in paperback.

poché, e [pɔʃe] *adj* **1.** [œuf] poached **2.** [meurtri] : **avoir un œil ~** to have a black eye.

pocher [3] [pɔʃe] ◇ *vt* CULIN [œuf, poisson] to poach.
◇ *vi* [vêtement] to go baggy.

pochette [pɔʃɛt] *nf* **1.** [vêtement] (breast) pocket handkerchief **2.** [sac - de femme] (small) handbag ; [- d'homme] clutch bag **3.** [sachet] wallet, envelope ■ **~ d'allumettes** book of matches **4.** [d'un disque] sleeve, cover.

pochette-surprise [pɔʃɛtsyrpriz] (*pl* **pochettes-surprises**) *nf* lucky bag *UK*, surprise pack *US* ■ **tu l'as trouvé dans une ~, ton permis de conduire?** *hum* find your driving licence in a Christmas cracker, did you?

pochoir [pɔʃwar] *nm* **1.** [plaque évidée] stencil ■ **décor au ~** stencilled ornamentation **2.** TEXT printing block.

podcaster [podkaste] *vt* [une émission] to podcast.

podium [pɔdjɔm] *nm* **1.** [plate-forme] podium ■ **monter sur le ~** SPORT to mount the podium ; [à la télévision, dans un jeu] to step onto the platform **2.** ARCHIT podium.

podologie [pɔdɔlɔʒi] *nf* chiropody.

podologue [pɔdɔlɔg] *nmf* chiropodist.

poêle [pwal] ◇ *nm* **1.** [chauffage] stove ■ [en céramique] furnace ■ **~ à accumulation** storage heater ■ **~ à mazout** oil *ou* oil-fired stove **2.** [drap] pall.
◇ *nf* [ustensile] : **~ (à frire)** frying pan.

poêlée [pwale] *nf* [contenu d'une poêle] : **une ~ de pommes de terre** a frying pan full of potatoes ‖ CULIN : **~ de champignons** panfried mushrooms.

poêler [3] [pwale] *vt* **1.** [frire] to fry **2.** [braiser] to braise *(in a shallow pan)*.

poêlon [pwalɔ̃] *nm* casserole.

poème [pɔɛm] *nm* **1.** LITTÉR poem ■ **un ~ en prose** a prose poem ■ **un ~ en vers** a poem **2.** *fam loc* **c'est (tout) un ~ : ça a été un ~, pour venir de l'aéroport jusqu'ici!** what a to-do *ou* business getting here from the airport! ■ **ta fille, c'est un ~!** your daughter's really something else! **3.** MUS : **~ symphonique** symphonic *ou* tone poem.

poésie [pɔezi] *nf* **1.** [genre] poetry ■ **écrire de la ~** to write poems *ou* poetry **2.** [poème] poem ■ **des ~s pour enfants** poems *ou* verse for children **3.** *litt* [charme] poetry.

poète [pɔɛt] ◇ *nm* [auteur] poet ■ **femme ~** (woman) poet.
◇ *adj* [allure, air] poetic, of a poet ■ **il est ~ à ses heures** he writes the occasional poem.

poétesse [pɔetɛs] *nf* poetess.

poétique [pɔetik] ◇ *adj* poetic, poetical.
◇ *nf* poetics *(U)*.

poétiquement [pɔetikmɑ̃] *adv* poetically.

poétiser [3] [pɔetize] *vt* to poetize, to poeticize.

pogne△ [pɔɲ] *nf* hand, mitt.

pognon [pɔɲɔ̃] *nm fam* readies *UK*, dough *US* ■ **ils ont plein de ~** they're rolling in it *UK ou* in dough *US*.

pogrom(e) [pɔgrɔm] *nm* pogrom.

poids [pwa] *nm* **1.** PHYS weight ■ **son ~ est de 52 kilos** she weighs 52 kilos ■ **prendre/perdre du ~** to gain/to lose weight ■ **reprendre du ~** to put weight back on *ou* on again ■ **je suis tombé de tout mon ~ sur le bras** I fell on my arm with all my weight ▶ **~ brut/net** gross/net weight ■ **~ en charge** (fully) loaded weight ■ **~ à vide** unladen weight, tare ■ **faire bon ~** COMM to give good weight ■ **faire le ~** COMM to make up the weight ; *fig* to hold one's own ■ **il ne fait pas le ~ face aux spécialistes** he's no match for *ou* not in the same league as the experts ■ **j'ai peur de ne pas faire le ~** I'm afraid of being out of my depth
2. [objet - gén, d'une horloge] weight ■ **avoir un ~ sur l'estomac** *fig* to feel bloated ▶ **les ~ et mesures** *fam* the weights and measures administration
3. SPORT : **~ et haltères** weightlifting ‖ [lancer] shotputting, shot ■ [instrument] shot ■ [catégorie en boxe] : **~ coq** bantamweight ■ **~ léger** lightweight ■ **~ lourd** heavyweight ■ **~ mi-lourd** light heavyweight ■ **~ mi-moyen** light middleweight ■ **~ mouche** flyweight ■ **~ moyen** middleweight ■ **~ plume** featherweight ■ **c'est un ~ plume, cette petite!** *fig* that little one weighs next to nothing! ‖ [aux courses] weight
4. [importance] influence, weight ■ **son avis a du ~ auprès du reste du groupe** her opinion carries weight with the rest of the group.
◆ **au poids** *loc adv* [vendre] by weight.
◆ **de poids** *loc adj* [alibi, argument] weighty ■ **un homme de ~** an influential man.
◆ **sous le poids de** *loc prép* **1.** [sous la masse de] under the weight of
2. *fig* under the burden of ■ **écrasé sous le ~ des responsabilités** weighed down by responsibilities.
◆ **poids lourd** *nm* **1.** TRANSP heavy (goods) vehicle *ou* lorry *UK ou* truck *US*
2. ▷ **poids** *(sens 3)*.
◆ **poids mort** *nm* MÉCAN & *fig* dead weight.

poignait *v* ▷ **poindre**.

poignant, e [pwaɲɑ̃, ɑ̃t] *adj* heartrending, poignant ■ **le souvenir ~ de leur dernière rencontre** the poignant memory of the last time they met.

poignard [pwaɲar] *nm* dagger ■ **coup de ~** stab ■ **recevoir un coup de ~** to get stabbed ■ **un coup de ~ dans le dos** *fig* a stab in the back.

poignarder [3] [pwaɲarde] *vt* to stab, to knife ■ **~ qqn dans le dos** *pr* & *fig* to stab sb in the back ■ **se faire ~** to be knifed *ou* stabbed.

poigne [pwaɲ] *nf* grip ■ **avoir de la ~** *pr* to have a strong grip ; *fig* to rule with a firm hand.
◆ **à poigne** *loc adj* firm, authoritarian, iron-handed.

poignée [pwaɲe] *nf* **1.** [contenu] handful, fistful **2.** [petit nombre] handful ■ **une ~ de manifestants** a handful of demonstrators **3.** [pour saisir - gén] handle ; [- un sabre] hilt ; [- une épée] handle.
◆ **à poignées** *loc adv* **1.** [en quantité] : **prendre des bonbons à ~s** to take handfuls of sweets **2.** [avec prodigalité] hand over fist.
◆ **par poignées** *loc adv* in handfuls ■ **je perds mes cheveux par ~s** my hair's coming out in handfuls.
◆ **poignée de main** *nf* handshake ■ **donner une ~ de main à qqn** to shake hands with sb, to shake sb's hand.

poignet [pwaɲɛ] *nm* **1.** ANAT wrist **2.** [vêtement] cuff ■ [bande de tissu] wristband.

poil [pwal] *nm* **1.** ANAT hair ■ **il n'a plus un ~ sur le caillou** *fam* he's bald as a coot *UK ou* an egg ▶ **~ pubien** pubic hair ■ **avoir un ~ dans la main** *fam* to be bone-idle ■ **être de bon/mauvais ~** *fam* to be in a good/foul mood ■ **reprendre du ~ de la bête** *fam* [guérir] to perk up again ; [reprendre des forces] to regain some strength for a fresh onslaught
2. *fam* [infime quantité] : **un ~ de** : **il n'a pas un ~ d'intégrité** he doesn't have one ounce *ou* a shred of integrity ■ **il n'y a pas un ~ de vrai dans ce qu'il dit** there's not an ounce of truth in what he says ▶ **manquer son train d'un ~** *ou* **à un ~ près** to miss one's train by a hair's breadth *ou* a whisker
3. [pelage - long] hair, coat ; [- court] coat ■ **chien à ~ ras/long** smooth-haired/long-haired dog ▶ **manteau en ~ de chameau** camel-hair coat ■ **en ~s de sanglier** made of bristle
4. [d'une brosse] bristle ■ [d'un pinceau] hair, bristle ■ [d'un tapis] pile ■ [d'un pull angora] down
5. BOT hair ■ **~ à gratter** itching powder.
◆ **à poil** *fam* ◇ *loc adj* stark naked, starkers.
◇ *loc adv* starkers *UK*, in the altogether ■ **se mettre à ~** to strip (off).
◆ **au poil** *fam* ◇ *loc adj* terrific, great ■ **tu peux venir samedi, au ~!** you can come on Saturday, great!
◇ *loc adv* terrifically.
◆ **au petit poil, au quart de poil** *loc adv fam* terrifically ■ **ça a marché au petit ~** it's all gone exactly according to plan.
◆ **de tout poil** *loc adj fam hum* of all kinds ■ **voleurs et escrocs de tout ~** all manner of thieves and crooks.

poilant, e [pwalɑ̃, ɑ̃t] *adj fam* hilarious, side-splitting.

poil de carotte [pwaldəkarɔt] *adj inv* [cheveux] red ■ [enfant] red-haired ■ **être ~** to be red-haired, to have carroty-red hair.
◆ **Poil de carotte** *npr* LITTÉR *the red-headed boy in Jules Renard's novel of the same name, which recounts an unhappy childhood.*

poiler [3] [pwale] ◆ **se poiler** *vpi fam* [rire] to laugh fit to burst ■ [s'amuser] to have a ball.

poilu, e [pwaly] *adj* hairy.
◆ **poilu** *nm* HIST poilu ■ **les ~s de 14** *ou* **de 1914** (French) soldiers in the 1914-18 war.

poinçon [pwɛ̃sɔ̃] *nm* **1.** JOAILL [marque] hallmark ■ **marquer une bague au ~** to hallmark a ring **2.** [de brodeuse, de couturière] bodkin ■ [de graveur] stylus ■ [de sculpteur] chisel **3.** IMPR (matrice) punch **4.** MÉTALL die, stamp.

poinçonnage [pwɛ̃sɔnaʒ], **poinçonnement** [pwɛ̃sɔnmɑ̃] *nm* **1.** [d'un ticket] punching **2.** JOAILL hallmarking **3.** MÉTALL stamping, diestamping **4.** IMPR drive, strike.

poinçonner [3] [pwɛ̃sɔne] *vt* **1.** [ticket] to punch **2.** JOAILL to hallmark **3.** MÉTALL to stamp.

poinçonneur, euse [pwɛ̃sɔnœr, øz] *nm, f* **1.** [employé] ticket puncher **2.** MÉTALL punching machine operator.
◆ **poinçonneuse** *nf* [machine] punching machine.

poindre [82] [pwɛ̃dr] *litt* ◇ *vi* **1.** [lumière] to break ■ **dès que le jour poindra** as soon as dawn breaks, at daybreak **2.** [mouvement, idée] : **une idée commençait à ~ dans son esprit** an idea was growing in his mind.
◇ *vt* **1.** [tourmenter] to stab *fig* ■ **ce souvenir le poignait parfois** the memory would stab him painfully from time to time **2.** [stimuler] to prick, to spur on *(sép).*

poing [pwɛ̃] *nm* fist ■ **lever le ~** to raise one's fist ■ **les ~s sur les hanches** with arms akimbo ■ **donner du ~ sur la table** to bang one's fist on *ou* to thump the table ■ **mettre son ~ dans la figure à qqn** *fam* to punch *ou* to smack sb in the face ▶ **ils sont entrés, revolvers/armes au ~** they came in, guns/arms at the ready ■ **gros comme le ~** (as) big as your fist.

point[1] [pwɛ̃] *v* ▷ **poindre.**

point[2] [pwɛ̃] *nm* **1.** [marque] point, dot, spot ■ [sur un dé, un domino] pip, spot ■ **un corsage à petits ~s bleus** a blouse with blue polka dots ■ **la voiture n'était plus qu'un ~ à l'horizon** the car was now no more than a speck on the horizon ▶ **~ lumineux** spot *ou* point of light ■ **~ de rouille** speck *ou* spot of rust
2. [petite quantité] spot, dab, blob ■ **un ~ de soudure** a spot *ou* blob of solder
3. [symbole graphique - en fin de phrase] full stop *UK*, period *US* ; [- sur un i ou un j] dot ; [- en morse, en musique] dot ■ MATH point ▶ **~ d'exclamation** exclamation mark *ou US* point ■ **~ d'interrogation** *pr & fig* question mark ■ **~s de suspension** ellipsis, suspension points *US* ■ **~ final** full stop *UK*, period *US (at the end of a piece of text)* ■ **j'ai dit non, ~ final** *ou* **un ~ c'est tout!** *fig* I said no and that's that *ou* that's final *ou* there's an end to it! ■ **mettre un ~ final à une discussion** to terminate a discussion, to bring a discussion to an end ■ **~, à la ligne!** *pr* new paragraph! ■ **il a fait une bêtise, ~ à la ligne!** *fig* he did something stupid, let's leave it at that!
4. AÉRON & NAUT [position] position ▶ **~ estimé/observé** estimated/observed position ■ **~ fixe** run-up ■ **faire le ~** NAUT to take a bearing, to plot one's position ; *fig* to take stock (of the situation) ■ **à 40 ans, on s'arrête et on fait le ~** when you reach 40, you stand back and take stock of your life ■ **et maintenant, le ~ sur la circulation** and now, the latest traffic news
5. GÉOM point ▶ **~ d'intersection/de tangence** intersection/tangential point
6. [endroit] point, spot, place ■ **en plusieurs ~s de la planète** in different places *ou* spots on the planet ▶ **~ de contrôle** checkpoint ■ **~ névralgique** MÉD nerve centre ; *fig* sensitive spot ■ **~ de rencontre** meeting point ■ **~ de vente** retail outlet
7. [douleur] twinge, sharp pain ■ MÉD pressure point ■ **j'ai un ~ au poumon** I can feel a twinge (of pain) in my chest ▶ **~ de côté** stitch
8. [moment, stade] point, stage ■ **à ce ~ de la discussion** at this point in the discussion ■ **les pourparlers en sont toujours au même ~** the negotiations haven't got any further
9. [degré] point ■ **porter qqch à son plus haut ~** to carry sthg to extremes ■ **si tu savais à quel ~ je te méprise!** if you only knew how much I despise you! ■ **il est radin, mais à un ~!** *fam* you wouldn't believe how tightfisted he is! ▶ **~ de saturation** *pr & fig* saturation point
10. [élément - d'un texte, d'une théorie] point ; [- d'un raisonnement] point, item ; [- d'une description] feature, trait ■ **le second ~ à l'ordre du jour** the second item on the agenda ■ **un programme social en trois ~s** a three-point social programme ■ **voici un ~ d'histoire que je souhaiterais éclaircir** I'd like to make clear what happened at that particular point in history ▶ **~ d'entente/de désaccord** point of agreement/of disagreement ■ **~ commun** common feature ■ **nous n'avons aucun ~ commun** we have nothing in common ■ **un ~ de droit** DR a point of law
11. [unité de valeur - dans un sondage, à la Bourse] point ; [- de retraite] unit ; [- du salaire de base] (grading) point ■ ÉDUC mark *UK*, point ■ JEUX & SPORT point ■ **sa cote de popularité a gagné/perdu trois ~s** his popularity rating has gone up/down by three points ■ **il me manquait 12 ~s pour avoir l'examen** I was 12 marks short of passing the exam ■ **battu aux ~s** [en boxe] beaten on points ■ **faire le ~** [le gagner] to win the point ▶ **bon ~** ÉDUC [image] *cardboard card or picture given to schoolchildren as a reward* ; [appréciation] mark *(for good behaviour)* ■ **un bon ~ pour toi!** *fig & hum* good on *UK ou* for you!, you get a brownie point! ■ **mauvais ~** ÉDUC black mark *(against sb's name)* ■ **un mauvais ~ pour toi!** *fig & hum* go to the back of the class! ■ **marquer un ~** *pr & fig* to score a point
12. COUT : **faire un ~ à** to put a stitch *ou* a few stitches in ■ **bâtir à grands ~s** to tack ▶ **~ de couture/crochet/tricot** sewing/crochet/knitting stitch ■ **~ de jersey** stocking stitch ■ **~ mousse** garter stitch ■ **~ de riz** moss stitch ■ **petit ~ : tapisserie au petit ~** petit point tapestry

13. INFORM [unité graphique] dot ■ [emplacement] : **~ d'accès/de retour** entry/reentry point
14. ART & JOAILL point.

◆ **à ce point, à un tel point** *loc adv* [tellement] so, that ■ **ton travail est dur à ce ~?** is your job so (very) *ou* that hard? ■ **j'en ai tellement assez que je vais démissionner – à ce ~?** I'm so fed up that I'm going to resign – that bad, is it?

◆ **à ce point que, à (un) tel point que** *loc conj* so much so that, to such a point that ■ **les choses en étaient arrivées à un tel ~ que...** things had reached such a pitch that... ■ **elle est déprimée, à ce ~ qu'elle ne veut plus voir personne** she's so depressed that she won't see anyone anymore.

◆ **à point** ◇ *loc adj* [steak] medium ■ [rôti] done to a turn ■ [fromage] ripe, just right ■ [poire] just *ou* nicely ripe ■ **ton bonhomme est à ~, tu n'as plus qu'à enregistrer ses aveux** *fam fig* your man's nice and ready now, all you've got to do is get the confession down on tape.
◇ *loc adv* **1.** CULIN : **le gâteau est cuit à ~** the cake is cooked (through)
2. [au bon moment] : **tomber à ~** [personne] to come (just) at the right time ; [arrivée, décision] to be very timely.

◆ **à point nommé** *loc adv* : **arriver à ~ nommé** to arrive (just) at the right moment *ou* when needed, to arrive in the nick of time.

◆ **au plus haut point** *loc adv* [énervé, généreux, irrespectueux] extremely, most ■ [méfiant] highly, extremely ■ **je le respecte au plus haut ~** I have the utmost respect for him ■ **je le déteste au plus haut ~** I can't tell you how much I hate him, I absolutely loathe him ■ **elle m'inquiète au plus haut ~** I'm really worried about her.

◆ **au point** ◇ *loc adj* PHOTO in focus ■ [moteur] tuned ■ [machine] in perfect running order ■ [technique] perfected ■ [discours, plaidoyer] finalized ■ [spectacle, artiste] ready ■ **ton revers n'est pas encore au ~** your backhand isn't good enough *ou* up to scratch yet ■ **le son/l'image n'est pas au ~** the sound/the image isn't right ■ **quand ma technique sera au ~** when I've perfected my technique ■ **mon texte n'est pas encore au ~** I haven't finished my text yet.
◇ *loc adv* : **mettre au ~** [texte à imprimer] to edit ; [discours, projet, rapport] to finalize, to put the finishing touches to ; [spectacle] to perfect ; [moteur] to tune ; [appareil photo] to (bring into) focus ; [affaire] to settle, to finalize ■ **mettre les choses au ~** to put *ou* set the record straight ■ **mettons les choses au ~: je refuse de travailler le dimanche** let's get this *ou* things straight: I refuse to work Sundays ■ **après cette discussion, j'ai tenu à mettre les choses au ~** following that discussion, I insisted on putting *ou* setting the record straight ■ **tu devrais mettre les choses au ~ avec lui** you should sort things out between you.

◆ **au point de** *loc prép* : **méticuleux au ~ d'en être agaçant** meticulous to the point of being exasperating ■ **il n'est pas stupide au ~ de le leur répéter** he's not so stupid as to tell them.

◆ **au point du jour** *loc adv litt* at dawn *ou* daybreak.

◆ **au point où** *loc conj* : **nous sommes arrivés au ~ où...** we've reached the point *ou* stage where... ■ **au ~ où j'en suis, autant que je continue** having got this far, I might as well carry on ■ **au ~ où en sont les choses** as things stand, the way things are (now).

◆ **au point que** *loc conj* so much that, so... that ■ **il était très effrayé, au ~ qu'il a essayé de se sauver** he was so frightened that he tried to run away.

◆ **point par point** *loc adv* point by point.

◆ **sur le point de** *loc prép* : **être sur le ~ de faire qqch** to be about to do *ou* on the point of doing *ou* on the verge of doing sthg ■ **j'étais sur le ~ de partir** I was about to *ou* going to leave ■ **sur le ~ de pleurer** on the verge of tears *ou* of crying.

◆ **point d'ancrage** *nm* **1.** AUTO seat-belt anchorage
2. *fig* cornerstone.

◆ **point d'appui** *nm* **1.** [d'un levier] fulcrum
2. MIL strongpoint
3. *fig* [soutien] support.

◆ **point de chute** *nm* **1.** ARM point of impact
2. *fig* **j'ai un ~ de chute à Milan** I have somewhere to stay in Milan.

◆ **point culminant** *nm* ASTRON zenith ■ GÉOGR peak, summit, highest point, *fig* acme, apex ■ **quel est le ~ culminant des Alpes?** what is the highest point *ou* peak in the Alps? ■ **les investissements sont à leur ~ culminant** investment has reached a peak.

◆ **point de départ** *nm* starting point ■ **nous voilà revenus au ~ de départ** *pr* & *fig* now we're back where we started.

◆ **point faible** *nm* weak spot ■ **son ~ faible, c'est sa susceptibilité** his touchiness is his weak spot *ou* point.

◆ **point fort** *nm* [d'une personne, d'une entreprise] strong point ■ [d'un joueur de tennis] best shot ■ **les maths n'ont jamais été mon ~ fort** I was never any good at maths, maths was never my strong point.

◆ **point mort** *nm* AUTO neutral ■ **au ~ mort** AUTO in neutral ; *fig* at a standstill.

◆ **point noir** *nm* **1.** MÉD blackhead
2. [difficulté] difficulty, headache *fig* ■ **un ~ noir de la circulation** [encombré] a heavily congested area ; [dangereux] an accident blackspot.

◆ **point sensible** *nm* **1.** [endroit douloureux] tender *ou* sore spot
2. MIL key *ou* strategic target
3. *fig* **toucher un ~ sensible** [chez qqn] to touch on a sore spot ; [dans un problème] to touch on a sensitive area.

point[3] [pwɛ̃] *adv litt* **1.** [en corrélation avec 'ne'] : **je ne l'ai ~ encore vu** I haven't seen him yet ■ **~ n'est besoin de** there's no need to **2.** [employé seul] : **du vin il y en avait, mais de champagne ~** there was wine, but no champagne *ou* not a drop of champagne ■ **il eut beau chercher, ~ de John** he searched in vain, John was nowhere to be found ■ **~ de démocratie sans liberté de critiquer** (there can be) no democracy without the freedom to criticize **3.** [en réponse négative] : **~ du tout!** not at all!, not in the least!

pointage [pwɛ̃taʒ] *nm* **1.** [d'une liste, d'un texte] ticking off *(U)*, checking *(U)*, marking *(U)* **2.** [des ouvriers - à l'arrivée] clocking in ; [- à la sortie] clocking out.

point-cadeau [pwɛ̃kado] (*pl* **points-cadeaux**) *nm* gift coupon.

point de vue [pwɛ̃dvy] (*pl* **points de vue**) *nm* **1.** [panorama] vista, view **2.** [opinion] point of view, standpoint ■ **quel est ton ~?** what is your opinion?, where do you stand on this? ■ **du ~ des prix, du ~ prix** pricewise, as far as prices are concerned ■ **de ce ~, il n'a pas tort** from that point of view *ou* viewed in this light, he's right ■ **adopter un ~ différent** to view things from a different angle.

pointe [pwɛ̃t] *nf* **1.** [extrémité - gén] point, pointed end, tip ; [- d'un cheveu] tip ■ **la ~ du sein** the nipple ■ **mets-toi sur la ~ des pieds** stand on tiptoe *ou* on the tips of your toes ■ **elle traversa la pièce/monta l'escalier sur la ~ des pieds** she tiptoed across the room/up the stairs ■ **allons jusqu'à la ~ de l'île** let's go to the farthest point of the island ➲ **~ d'asperge** asparagus tip ■ **~ feutre** fibre tip **2.** SPORT spike **3.** [vêtement] headscarf *(folded so as to form a triangle)* **4.** MIL [avancée] advanced party **5.** [accès] peak, burst ■ **~ (de vitesse)** burst of speed **6.** *sout* [moquerie] barb, taunt ■ [mot d'esprit] witticism ■ **lancer des ~s à qqn** to taunt sb **7.** [petite quantité - d'ail] hint ; [- d'ironie, de jalousie] trace, hint, note ■ **il a une ~ d'accent** he's got a slight accent ■ **il n'a pas une ~ d'accent** he hasn't got the slightest trace of an accent **8.** ACOUST : **~ de lecture** stylus **9.** ART : **~ sèche** dry point ■ **compas à ~s sèches** (pair of) dividers **10.** INDUST [d'un tour] (lathe) centre ■ [d'une machine-outil] cone **11.** [clou] nail, sprig, brad.

◆ **pointes** *nfpl* DANSE points ■ **faire des ~s** to dance on points.

◆ **à la pointe de** *loc prép* to the forefront of ■ **à la ~ du combat** *pr* & *fig* in the front line of battle ■ **à la ~ de l'actualité** right up to date.

◆ **à la pointe du jour** *loc adv litt* at daybreak *ou* dawn, at break of day *litt*.

◆ **de pointe** *loc adj* **1.** [puissance, période] peak *(avant n)* ■ **heure de ~** rush hour ■ **vitesse de ~** maximum *ou* top speed **2.** [secteur, industrie] key *(avant n)*, leading, growth *(modif)* ■ **technologie de ~** leading-edge technology.

◆ **en pointe** ◇ *loc adj* [menton] pointed ■ [décolleté] plunging.
◇ *loc adv* **1.** [en forme de pointe] to a point ■ **tailler en ~** [barbe] to shape to a point ; [diamant] to cut to a point **2.** [à grande vitesse] at top speed ■ **je fais plus de 200 en ~** *fam* I can do 200 plus top whack *UK*, I can do over 200.

pointé, e [pwɛ̃te] *adj* MUS dotted.

pointer[1] [pwɛ̃tœr] *nm* [chien] pointer.

pointer[2] [3] [pwɛ̃te] <> *vt* **1.** [dresser] : **l'animal pointa les oreilles** the animal pricked up its ears ‖ [montrer] : **~ son nez** *ou* **sa tête quelque part** *fig* to show one's face somewhere **2.** [diriger - arme] to aim ; [- doigt] to point ■ **~ son fusil vers le plafond** to aim one's rifle at the ceiling **3.** [à la pétanque] : **~ une boule** to make a draw shot **4.** [marquer - liste] to check (off), to tick off *(sép)* **5.** [contrôler - à l'arrivée] to check in *(sép)* ; [- à la sortie] to check out *(sép)*.
<> *vi* **1.** [faire saillie] to stick *ou* to jut out, to protrude **2.** [apparaître - aube, jour] to be dawning ; [- jalousie, remords] to be breaking *ou* seeping through ■ **j'ai vu une lueur d'effroi ~ dans son regard** I saw fear flashing in his eyes **3.** [à la pétanque] to draw (the jack) **4.** [ouvrier - arrivant] to clock in ; [- sortant] to clock out.
◆ **se pointer** *vpi fam* to show (up), to turn up ■ **alors, tu te pointes?** are you coming or aren't you?

pointeur, euse [pwɛ̃tœr, øz] *nm, f* [surveillant] timekeeper.
◆ **pointeur** *nm* INFORM & MIL pointer ■ **~ laser** laser pointer.
◆ **pointeuse** *nf* **1.** [machine-outil] jig borer **2.** [horloge] time clock.

pointillé [pwɛ̃tije] *nm* **1.** [trait] dotted line ■ **découper suivant le ~** cut along the dotted line **2.** [coloration] stipple, stippling.
◆ **en pointillé** <> *loc adj* : **les frontières sont en ~ sur la carte** the frontiers are drawn as dotted lines on the map.
<> *loc adv fig* in outline ■ **une solution lui apparaissait en ~** he was beginning to see the outline of a solution.

pointiller [3] [pwɛ̃tije] <> *vt* [surface] to stipple ■ [ligne] to dot, to mark with dots.
<> *vi* to draw in stipple.

pointilleux, euse [pwɛ̃tijø, øz] *adj* [personne] fussy, fastidious ■ [commentaire] nitpicking ■ **il est très ~ sur l'horaire** he's very particular about *ou* he's a stickler for time-keeping.

pointillisme [pwɛ̃tijism] *nm* [style] pointillism ■ [mouvement] Pointillism.

pointilliste [pwɛ̃tijist] *adj* & *nmf* pointillist.

pointu, e [pwɛ̃ty] *adj* **1.** [effilé] sharp, pointed **2.** [perspicace - esprit] sharp, astute ; [- étude] in-depth, astute ■ **une lecture ~e de l'œuvre** an astute *ou* in-depth interpretation of the work **3.** [revêche - air, caractère] querulous, petulant **4.** [aigu - voix, ton] shrill, sharp ■ **un accent ~** [parisien] a clipped Parisian accent **5.** [spécialisé - formation, marché] (very) narrowly-specialized, narrowly-targeted.
◆ **pointu** *adv* : **parler ~** to talk in a clipped (Parisian) way.

pointure [pwɛ̃tyr] *nf* **1.** [de chaussures] size ■ **quelle est ta ~?** what size do you take? **2.** *fam fig* **une grande ~ de la boxe** a big name in boxing.

point-virgule [pwɛ̃virgyl] (*pl* **points-virgules**) *nm* semicolon.

poire [pwar] <> *nf* **1.** [fruit] pear ■ **nous en avons parlé entre la ~ et le fromage** we talked idly about it at the end of the meal ➊ **~ conférence** conference pear **2.** [alcool] pear brandy **3.** [objet en forme de poire] : **~ électrique** (pear-shaped) switch ■ **~ à injections** douche ■ **~ à lavement** enema **4.** △ [visage] mug ■ **prendre qqch en pleine ~** to get smacked in the face *ou* between the eyes with sthg **5.** *fam* [imbécile] sucker, mug, dope.
<> *adj fam* : **ce que tu peux être ~!** you're such a sucker!
◆ **en poire** *loc adj* [sein, perle] pear-shaped.
◆ **poire d'angoisse** *nf* **1.** HIST (iron) gag **2.** *fig* & *litt* awful obligation to say nothing.

poiré [pware] *nm* perry.

poireau, x [pwaro] *nm* leek ■ **faire le ~** *fam* to be hanging around, to be kicking *ou* cooling one's heels.

poireauter [3] [pwarote] *vi fam* to be cooling *ou* kicking one's heels, to hang around ■ **faire ~ qqn** to keep sb hanging around.

poirier [pwarje] *nm* **1.** BOT pear tree **2.** MENUIS pear, pearwood **3.** SPORT : **faire le ~** to do a headstand.

pois [pwa] *nm* **1.** BOT & CULIN pea ■ **petits ~** (green) *ou* garden peas ; [extrafins] petit pois **2.** [motif] dot, spot ■ **un corsage à ~ blancs** a blouse with white polka dots.
◆ **pois chiche** *nm* chickpea.
◆ **pois de senteur** *nm* sweet pea.

poison [pwazɔ̃] <> *nm* **1.** [substance] poison ■ **ils avaient mis du ~ dans son café** they had poisoned his coffee **2.** *fam* [corvée] drag, hassle **3.** *litt* [vice] poison.
<> *nmf* [enfant, personne insupportable] pest.

poisse [pwas] *nf fam* bad *ou* rotten luck ■ **quelle ~!** what rotten luck! ■ **avoir la ~** to be really unlucky.

poisser [3] [pwase] *vt* **1.** [rendre poisseux] to make sticky **2.** △ [attraper] to nail, to nab **3.** [enduire de poix] to (cover with) pitch.

poisseux, euse [pwasø, øz] *adj* sticky.

poisson [pwasɔ̃] *nm* **1.** ZOOL fish ■ **attraper du ~** to catch fish ➊ **~ d'eau douce** freshwater fish ■ **les ~s plats** flatfish ■ **~ rouge** goldfish ■ **~ volant** flying fish ■ **être comme un ~ dans l'eau** to be in one's element ■ **être heureux comme un ~ dans l'eau** to be as happy as a sandboy *UK ou* as a clam *US ou* as a lark ■ **engueuler qqn comme du ~ pourri**△ to scream at sb ■ **petit ~ deviendra grand** *prov* tall oaks from little acorns grow *prov* **2.** CULIN fish.
◆ **poisson d'avril** *nm* **1.** [farce] April fool ■ **~ d'avril!** April fool! **2.** [papier découpé] *cut-out paper fish placed on someone's back as a prank on April 1st.*

poisson-chat [pwasɔ̃ʃa] (*pl* **poissons-chats**) *nm* catfish.

poisson-lune [pwasɔ̃lyn] (*pl* **poissons-lunes**) *nm* moonfish.

poissonnerie [pwasɔnri] *nf* **1.** [magasin] fishmonger's *UK ou* (fresh) fish shop ■ [au marché] fish stall **2.** [industrie] fish industry.

poissonneux, euse [pwasɔnø, øz] *adj* full of fish ■ **des eaux poissonneuses** waters rich in fish.

poissonnier, ère [pwasɔnje, ɛr] *nm, f* [personne] fishmonger *UK*, fish merchant *US*.
◆ **poissonnière** *nf* [ustensile] fish-kettle.

Poissons [pwasɔ̃] *npr mpl* **1.** ASTRON Pisces **2.** ASTROL Pisces ■ **elle est ~** she's Pisces.

poisson-scie [pwasɔ̃si] (*pl* **poissons-scies**) *nm* sawfish.

poitevin, e [pwatvɛ̃, in] *adj* [du Poitou] from Poitou.

Poitou-Charentes [pwatuʃarɑ̃t] *npr m* Poitou-Charentes.

POITOU-CHARENTES

This administrative region includes the *départements* of Charente, Charente-Maritime, Deux-Sèvres and Vienne (capital: Poitiers).

poitrail [pwatraj] *nm* **1.** ZOOL breast **2.** [partie de harnais] breastplate **3.** *hum* chest.

poitrinaire [pwatrinɛr] *adj* & *nmf vieilli* phtisic *vieilli*, consumptive.

poitrine [pwatrin] *nf* **1.** [thorax] chest ■ [seins] bust, chest ■ **avoir de la ~** to have a big bust ■ **elle n'a pas beaucoup de ~** she's flat-chested **2.** [poumons] chest, lungs ■ **être fragile de la ~** to have weak lungs *ou* a weak chest **3.** CULIN : **~ fumée** ≃ smoked bacon ■ **~ de porc** belly (of) pork ■ **~ salée** ≃ salt belly pork *UK* ■ ≃ salt pork *US*.

poivrade [pwavrad] *nf* [sauce] pepper sauce.
◆ **à la poivrade** *loc adj* CULIN with a peppery vinaigrette sauce.

poivre [pwavr] *nm* : **~ noir** *ou* **gris** (black) pepper ■ **~ blanc** white pepper ■ **~ de Cayenne** Cayenne (pepper) ■ **~ en grains** peppercorns, whole pepper ■ **~ moulu** ground pepper.
◆ **poivre et sel** *loc adj inv* pepper-and-salt ■ **cheveux/barbe ~ et sel** pepper-and-salt hair/beard.

poivré, e [pwavre] *adj* **1.** CULIN peppery **2.** [parfum] peppery, spicy **3.** [chanson, histoire] spicy, racy.

poivrer [3] [pwavre] *vt* CULIN to pepper ▪ **tu devrais ~ un peu plus ta sauce** you should put a little more pepper in your sauce.
◆ **se poivrer**△ *vpi* to get plastered△.

poivrier [pwavrije] *nm* **1.** BOT pepper plant **2.** [ustensile] pepper pot.

poivrière [pwavrijɛr] *nf* **1.** ARCHIT pepper box (fortification) **2.** [ustensile] pepper pot **3.** [plantation] pepper plantation.

poivron [pwavrɔ̃] *nm* sweet pepper, capsicum ▪ **~ vert/jaune/rouge** green/yellow/red pepper.

poivrot, e [pwavro, ɔt] *nm, f fam* drunkard.

poix [pwa] *nf* pitch.

poker [pɔkɛr] *nm* JEUX poker ▪ **jouer au ~** to play poker ▪ **faire un ~** *ou* **une partie de ~** to have a game of poker ➊ **~ d'as** [dés] poker dice ; [cartes] four aces.

polaire [pɔlɛr] <> *adj* MATH, SC & TECHNOL polar.
<> *nf* **1.** PHYS polar curve **2.** MATH polar axis **3.** [textile] (polar) fleece.

Polaire [pɔlɛr] *npr f* : **la ~** Polaris, the Pole Star, the North Star.

polar [pɔlar] *nm fam* [livre, film] thriller, whodunnit.

polard, e [pɔlar, ard] *fam* <> *adj* : **être complètement ~** to be a total swot *UK ou* grind *US*.
<> *nm, f* swot *UK*, grind *US*.

polarisation [pɔlarizasjɔ̃] *nf* **1.** SC polarization **2.** *sout* [de l'intérêt, des activités] focusing, concentrating.

polariser [3] [pɔlarize] *vt* **1.** SC to polarize **2.** [attention, énergie, ressources] to focus ▪ **il a polarisé l'attention de l'auditoire** he made the audience sit up and listen **3.** [faire se concentrer] : **~ qqn sur** to make sb concentrate (exclusively) on.
◆ **se polariser** *vpi* **1.** SC to polarize **2.** [se concentrer] : **se ~ sur qqch** to focus on sthg ▪ **il s'est trop polarisé sur sa carrière** he was too wrapped up in his career ▪ **être polarisé sur ses ennuis personnels/ses études** to be obsessed by one's personal problems/one's studies.

polarité [pɔlarite] *nf* polarity.

Polaroid® [pɔlarɔid] *nm* **1.** [appareil] Polaroid®(camera) **2.** [photo] Polaroid®(picture).

polder [pɔldɛr] *nm* polder.

pôle [pol] *nm* **1.** SC, GÉOGR & MATH pole ▪ **le ~ Nord/Sud** the North/South Pole ▪ **le ~ Nord/Sud magnétique** the magnetic North/South pole ▪ **Toulouse est devenue le ~ (d'attraction) économique de la région** Toulouse has become the focus *ou* hub of economic development in the region **2.** [extrême] pole ▪ **le gouvernement a réussi à concilier les deux ~s de l'opinion sur cette question** the government managed to reconcile the two poles of opinion on this subject **3.** ÉLECTR pole.

polémique [pɔlemik] <> *adj* **1.** [article] polemic, polemical, provocative ▪ [attitude] polemic, polemical, embattled **2.** [journaliste, écrivain] provocative.
<> *nf* polemic, controversy.

polémiquer [3] [pɔlemike] *vi* to be polemical ▪ **sans vouloir ~, je pense que...** I don't want to be controversial, but I think that...

polémiste [pɔlemist] *nmf* polemist, polemicist.

polémologie [pɔlemɔlɔʒi] *nf* polemology *spéc*, war studies.

polenta [pɔlɛnta] *nf* polenta.

pole position [polpozisjɔ̃] (*pl* **pole positions**) *nf* pole position.

poli, e [pɔli] *adj* **1.** [bien élevé] polite, courteous, well-bred ▪ **ce n'est pas ~ de répondre!** it's rude to answer back! ▪ **vous pourriez être ~!** keep a civil tongue in your head! ▪ **il est trop ~ pour être honnête** he's too sweet to be wholesome **2.** [pierre] smooth ▪ [métal] polished ▪ [marbre] glassed.
◆ **poli** *nm* [éclat] shine, sheen ▪ **la table a un beau ~** the table has a nice shiny finish *ou* a high polish *ou* a rich sheen.

police [pɔlis] *nf* **1.** [institution] police ▪ **entrer dans la ~** to join the police, to go into the police force ▪ **toutes les ~s d'Europe** police all over Europe ➊ **~ de l'air et des frontières** airport and border police ▪ **~ judiciaire** ≃ Criminal Investigation Department ▪ **~ mondaine** *ou* **des mœurs** Vice Squad ▪ **~ municipale** ≃ local police ▪ **la Police nationale** the police force *(excluding "gendarmes")* ▪ **~ secours** (police) emergency services ▪ **~ secrète** secret police ▪ **la ~ des ~s** *fam* ≃ police complaints committee **2.** [maintien de l'ordre] (enforcement of) law and order ▪ **faire la ~ dans les centres commerciaux** to maintain security in shopping centres ▪ **il n'a jamais voulu faire la ~ chez lui** he never tried to keep his family in order **3.** IMPR : **~ (de caractères)** bill (of fount) **4.** DR : **~ d'assurance** insurance policy.

POLICE NATIONALE

The *Police nationale* comes under the authority of the Ministry of the Interior, unlike the *Gendarmerie* which is an army corps. *Gendarmes* are usually to be found in rural areas.

policé, e [pɔlise] *adj litt* highly civilized, urbane.

polichinelle [pɔliʃinɛl] *nm* **1.** [pantin] (Punch) puppet **2.** *fam* [personne] puppet *péj*, clown, buffoon ▪ **arrête de faire le ~** stop clowning around ➊ **avoir un ~ dans le tiroir**△ to have a bun in the oven.

Polichinelle [pɔliʃinɛl] *npr* [aux marionnettes] Punchinello ▪ [à la commedia dell'arte] Pulcinella ▪ **aller voir ~** to go to a Punch-and-Judy show.

policier, ère [pɔlisje, ɛr] <> *adj* **1.** [de la police] police *(modif)* **2.** [roman, film] detective *(modif)*.
<> *nm, f* [agent] policeman (*f* policewoman), police officer ▪ **une femme ~** a policewoman, a woman police officer ▪ **~ en civil** detective.
◆ **policier** *m* [livre] detective story ▪ [film] detective thriller.

policlinique [pɔliklinik] *nf* outpatient clinic.

poliment [pɔlimɑ̃] *adv* politely ▪ **il s'effaça ~ pour la laisser passer** he politely stepped aside to let her pass.

polio [pɔljo] <> *nmf* polio victim.
<> *nf* polio ▪ **avoir la ~** to have polio.

poliomyélite [pɔljɔmjelit] *nf* poliomyelitis.

polir [32] [pɔlir] *vt* **1.** [métal] to polish (up), to burnish ▪ [meuble] to polish ▪ [chaussures] to polish, to clean, to shine ▪ [ongles] to buff **2.** *sout* [parfaire] to polish, to refine.

polissage [pɔlisaʒ] *nm* **1.** [d'un meuble] polishing ▪ [des ongles] buffing **2.** MÉTALL polishing, burnishing ▪ **~ électrolytique** electrolytic polishing, electropolishing.

polisseur, euse [pɔlisœr, øz] *nm, f* polisher.
◆ **polisseuse** *nf* **1.** [pour la pierre] glassing *ou* polishing machine **2.** MÉTALL polishing head *ou* stick.

polissoir [pɔliswar] *nm* [machine] polishing machine ▪ [outil] polishing stick ▪ **~ à ongles** (nail) buffer.

polisson, onne [pɔlisɔ̃, ɔn] <> *adj* **1.** [taquin] mischievous, cheeky **2.** [égrillard] saucy, naughty ▪ **une chanson ~ne** a racy *ou* saucy song.
<> *nm, f* [espiègle] little devil *ou* rogue *ou* scamp.

polissonnerie [pɔlisɔnri] *nf* **1.** [facétie] piece of mischief **2.** [parole grivoise] risqué *ou* saucy remark ▪ **dire des ~s** to make risqué remarks **3.** [acte grivois] : **des ~s** naughty goings-on.

politesse [pɔlitɛs] *nf* **1.** [bonne éducation] politeness, courteousness ▪ **faire/dire qqch par ~** to do/to say sthg out of politeness ▪ **brûler la ~ à qqn** to leave sb abruptly **2.** [propos] polite remark ▪ **échanger des ~s** *pr* to exchange polite small-talk ; *iron* to trade insults **3.** [acte] polite gesture ▪ **rendre la ~ à qqn** *pr* to pay sb back for a favour ; *iron* to give sb a taste of his/her own medicine.
◆ **de politesse** *loc adj* [lettre, visite] courtesy *(modif)*.

politicaillerie [pɔlitikajri] *nf fam péj* backroom politics.

politicard, e [pɔlitikar, ard] *fam péj* ◇ *adj* careerist.
◇ *nm, f* careerist politician.

politicien, enne [pɔlitisjɛ̃, ɛn] ◇ *adj* **1.** [d'habile politique] political ▪ **une manœuvre ~ne** a successful political move **2.** *péj* scheming.
◇ *nm, f* politician.

politique [pɔlitik] ◇ *adj* **1.** [du pouvoir de l'État - institution, carte] political
2. [de la vie publique] political ▪ **quelles sont ses opinions ~s?** what are his politics? ▪ **une carrière ~** a career in politics ▪ **dans les milieux ~s** in political circles ➤ **homme ~, femme ~** politician ▪ **les partis ~s** the political parties
3. [diplomate] diplomatic, politic *sout* ▪ **ce n'était pas très ~ de le licencier** it wasn't a very wise move to fire him.
◇ *nf* **1.** [activité] politics ▪ **faire de la ~** to be involved in politics ▪ **je ne fais pas de ~!** [je refuse de prendre parti] I don't want to bring politics into this!, no politics please! ▪ **elle se destine à la ~** she wants to go into politics ▪ **la ~ politicienne** *péj* party politics
2. [stratégie] policy ▪ **~ intérieure/extérieure** domestic/foreign policy ▪ **une ~ de gauche** a left-wing policy ▪ **une ~ des prix** a prices policy ▪ **c'est de bonne ~** POLIT it's good political practice ; *fig* it's good practice ➤ **la ~ agricole commune** the common agricultural policy ▪ **pratiquer la ~ de l'autruche** to bury one's head in the sand ▪ **la ~ du pire** *deliberately worsening the situation to further one's ends.*
◇ *nmf* **1.** [politicien] politician
2. [prisonnier] political prisoner.
◇ *nm* politics.

politique-fiction [pɔlitikfiksjɔ̃] (*pl* **politiques-fictions**) *nf* futuristic political fiction ▪ **un roman de ~** a futuristic political novel.

politiquement [pɔlitikmɑ̃] *adv* **1.** POLIT politically **2.** [adroitement] judiciously, diplomatically.

politisation [pɔlitizasjɔ̃] *nf* politicization ▪ **la ~ du sport** the politicization of sport, bringing politics into sport.

politiser [3] [pɔlitize] *vt* to politicize ▪ **ils sont moins/plus politisés** they are less/more interested in politics ▪ **~ une grève** to give a political dimension to a strike.
➡ **se politiser** *vpi* to become political.

politologie [pɔlitɔlɔʒi] *nf* political science.

politologue [pɔlitɔlɔg] *nmf* political scientist.

polka [pɔlka] *nf* polka.

pollen [pɔlɛn] *nm* pollen.

pollinisation [pɔlinizasjɔ̃] *nf* pollination ▪ **féconder par ~** to cross-pollinate.

polluant, e [pɔlɥɑ̃, ɑ̃t] *adj* polluting.

polluer [7] [pɔlɥe] *vt* **1.** ÉCOL to pollute **2.** *sout* [souiller] to pollute, to sully ▪ **la presse à scandale pollue toute la profession** the gutter press is a disgrace to the whole profession.

pollueur, euse [pɔlɥœr, øz] ◇ *adj* [industrie] polluting.
◇ *nm, f* polluter ▪ **les ~s devront payer les dégâts** the polluters will have to pay for the damage.

pollution [pɔlysjɔ̃] *nf* ÉCOL pollution.

polo [pɔlo] *nm* **1.** SPORT polo **2.** [vêtement] polo shirt.

polochon [pɔlɔʃɔ̃] *nm fam* bolster.

Pologne [pɔlɔɲ] *npr f*: **(la) ~** Poland.

polonais, e [pɔlɔnɛ, ɛz] *adj* Polish ▪ **notation ~e** INFORM Polish notation.
➡ **Polonais, e** *nm, f* Pole.
➡ **polonais** *nm* LING Polish.
➡ **polonaise** *nf* **1.** MUS [danse] polonaise **2.** CULIN polonaise *(brioche layered with candied fruit and covered with meringue)* **3.** [vêtement] polonaise.
➡ **à la polonaise** *loc adj* CULIN à la polonaise.

poltron, onne [pɔltrɔ̃, ɔn] ◇ *adj* cowardly, faint-hearted, lily-livered.
◇ *nm, f* coward, poltroon *litt.*

poltronnerie [pɔltrɔnri] *nf* cowardice, faint-heartedness.

polyamide [pɔliamid] *nm* polyamide.

polyandre [pɔljɑ̃dr] *adj* polyandrous.

polyandrie [pɔliɑ̃dri] *nf* polyandry.

polyarthrite [pɔliartrit] *nf* polyarthritis.

polychrome [pɔlikrom] *adj* polychrome.

polychromie [pɔlikrɔmi] *nf* polychromy.

polyclinique [pɔliklinik] *nf* polyclinic.

polycopie [pɔlikɔpi] *nf* duplication ▪ **envoyer un texte à la ~** to send a text to be duplicated.

polycopié [pɔlikɔpje] *nm* [gén] (duplicated) notes ▪ UNIV lecture handout.

polycopier [9] [pɔlikɔpje] *vt* to duplicate.

polyculture [pɔlikyltyr] *nf* polyculture, mixed farming.

polyèdre [pɔliɛdr] ◇ *adj* polyhedral.
◇ *nm* polyhedron.

polyester [pɔliɛstɛr] *nm* polyester.

polygame [pɔligam] ◇ *adj* polygamous.
◇ *nm* polygamist.

polygamie [pɔligami] *nf* polygamy.

polyglotte [pɔliglɔt] *adj* & *nmf* polyglot.

polygone [pɔligɔn] *nm* MATH polygon.

polyinsaturé, e [pɔliɛ̃satyre] *adj* polyunsaturated.

polymère [pɔlimɛr] ◇ *adj* polymeric.
◇ *nm* polymer.

polymérisation [pɔlimerizasjɔ̃] *nf* polymerization.

polymorphe [pɔlimɔrf] *adj* **1.** [gén - BIOL] polymorphous, polymorphic **2.** CHIM polymorphic.

Polynésie [pɔlinezi] *npr f*: **(la) ~** Polynesia ▪ **(la) ~ française** French Polynesia.

polynésien, enne [pɔlinezjɛ̃, ɛn] *adj* Polynesian.
➡ **Polynésien, enne** *nm, f* Polynesian.
➡ **polynésien** *nm* LING Polynesian.

polynévrite [pɔlinevrit] *nf* polyneuritis.

polynôme [pɔlinom] *nm* polynomial.

polype [pɔlip] *nm* **1.** MÉD polyp, polypus **2.** ZOOL polyp.

polyphasé, e [pɔlifaze] *adj* polyphase.

polyphonie [pɔlifɔni] *nf* polyphony.

polyphonique [pɔlifɔnik] *adj* polyphonic.

polypode [pɔlipɔd] *nm* BOT polypody.

polysémique [pɔlisemik] *adj* polysemous.

polystyrène [pɔlistirɛn] *nm* polystyrene ▪ **~ expansé** expanded polystyrene.

polysulfure [pɔlisylfyr] *nm* polysulphide.

polysyllabe [pɔlisilab], **polysyllabique** [pɔlisilabik] ◇ *adj* polysyllabic.
◇ *nm* polysyllable.

polytechnicien, enne [pɔlitɛknisjɛ̃, ɛn] *nm, f student or ex-student from the École Polytechnique.*

polytechnique [pɔlitɛknik] *adj* **1.** [polyvalent] polytechnic **2.** ÉDUC polytechnic ▪ **l'École Polytechnique** *grande école for engineers.*

ÉCOLE POLYTECHNIQUE

Founded in 1794, this prestigious engineering college has close connections with the Ministry of Defence. Formerly situated in the heart of the fifth arrondissement, the college moved to Palaiseau, near Paris, in the 1970s. It is popularly known as *l'X*. Students are effectively enlisted in the army and must repay their education through government service.

polythéisme [pɔliteism] *nm* polytheism.

polythéiste [pɔliteist] ◇ *adj* polytheistic.
◇ *nmf* polytheist.

polytransfusé, e [pɔlitrɑ̃sfyze] *nm, f person who has received multiple blood transfusions.*

polytraumatisme [pɔlitromatism] *nm* multiple trauma.

polyvalence [pɔlivalɑ̃s] *nf* [gén] versatility, adaptability ■ SC polyvalence.

polyvalent, e [pɔlivalɑ̃, ɑ̃t] ◇ *adj* [gén] versatile, adaptable ■ SC polyvalent.
◇ *nm, f* **1.** FIN & DR tax inspector **2.** [dans les services sociaux] social worker.
◆ **polyvalente** *nf Québec secondary school giving both general and vocational courses.*

polyvinyle [pɔlivinil] *nm* polyvinyl.

pomelo [pɔmelo] *nm* pomelo, pink grapefruit.

Poméranie [pɔmerani] *npr f* : **(la) ~** Pomerania.

pommade [pɔmad] *nf* **1.** MÉD [pour brûlures] ointment ■ [pour foulures] liniment ■ *vieilli* [cosmétique] cream ■ **~ pour les lèvres** lip salve ▶ **passer de la ~ à qqn** *fam* to butter sb up **2.** CULIN cream, paste *(made from pounding various ingredients together).*

pommader [3] [pɔmade] *vt* [cheveux] to put cream on, to pomade.

pomme [pɔm] *nf* **1.** [fruit] apple ■ **~ d'api** *variety of small, sweet apple* ■ **~ à cidre** cider apple ■ **~ de reinette** pippin ■ **la ~ de discorde** the bone of contention ■ **tomber dans les ~s** *fam fig* to pass out
2. [légume] potato ■ **~s dauphine/duchesse** dauphine/duchesse potatoes ■ **~s frites** chips *UK*, French fries *US* ■ **~s noisettes** deep-fried potato balls
3. [cœur - du chou, de la salade] heart
4. △ [figure] face, mug
5. △ [personne] : **ma ~** myself ■ **sa ~** himself, herself ■ **et les papiers à remplir, ce sera pour sa ~!** and he can damn well cope with the paperwork himself! ■ **être bonne ~** to be a mug *UK ou* a sucker
6. [objet rond] : **~ d'une canne** knob of a (walking) stick ▶ **~ d'arrosoir** rose *(of a watering can)* ■ **~ de douche** shower head.
◆ **aux pommes** *loc adj* **1.** CULIN apple *(modif)*, with apple **2.** △ [extraordinaire] terrific, great.
◆ **pomme d'Adam** *nf* Adam's apple.
◆ **pomme d'amour** *nf* **1.** [tomate] tomato **2.** [friandise] toffee apple.
◆ **pomme de pin** *nf* pine *ou* fir cone.

pommé, e [pɔme] *adj* [salade, chou] hearty, firm.

pommeau, x [pɔmo] *nm* [d'une canne] knob, pommel ■ [d'une selle, d'une épée] pommel ■ [d'un fût de pistolet] pommel, cascabel.

pomme de terre [pɔmdətɛr] (*pl* **pommes de terre**) *nf* potato ■ **des pommes de terre frites** chips *UK*, French fries *US*.

pommelé, e [pɔmle] *adj* **1.** [cheval] dappled **2.** [ciel] mackerel *(modif)*, dappled.

pommelle [pɔmɛl] *nf* drain grating *ou* cover.

pommer [3] [pɔme] *vi* [chou, laitue] to heart.

pommeraie [pɔmrɛ] *nf* apple orchard.

pommette [pɔmɛt] *nf* cheekbone.

pommier [pɔmje] *nm* **1.** BOT apple tree **2.** MENUIS apple wood.

pompage [pɔ̃paʒ] *nm* pumping (out).

pompe [pɔ̃p] *nf* **1.** [machine] pump ▶ **~ à air/chaleur** air/heat pump ■ **~ aspirante** suction pump ■ **~ à bicyclette** *ou* **à vélo** bicycle pump ■ **~ à essence** [distributeur] petrol pump *UK*, gas pump *US* ; [station] petrol *UK ou* gas *US* station ■ **les prix à la ~** pump prices ■ **~ foulante** force pump ■ **~ à incendie** water pump *(on a fire engine)* **2.** △ [chaussure] shoe ■ **être** *ou* **marcher à côté de ses ~s** to be in another world ■ **il est à côté de ses ~s aujourd'hui** he's not quite with it today **3.** [apparat] pomp ■ **en grande ~** with great pomp and ceremony.
◆ **pompes** *nfpl* SPORT press-ups *UK*, push-ups *US*.
◆ **à toute(s) pompe(s)** *loc adv fam* [courir] flat out ■ [s'enfuir] like a shot ■ **il est parti à toutes ~s** he was off like a shot!
◆ **pompes funèbres** *nfpl* : **(entreprise de) ~s funèbres** funeral parlour ■ **les ~s funèbres sont venues à 9 h** the undertakers came at 9 o'clock.

pompé, e [pɔ̃pe] *adj fam* fagged out *UK*, pooped *US* ■ **je suis ~!** I've had it!, I'm just about ready to drop!

Pompée [pɔ̃pe] *npr* Pompey.

Pompéi [pɔ̃pei] *npr* Pompeii.

pomper [3] [pɔ̃pe] ◇ *vt* **1.** [aspirer - pour évacuer] to pump (out) ; [- pour boire] to suck (up) ▶ **tu me pompes l'air** *fam* you're being a real pain in the neck **2.** [absorber - suj: éponge] to soak up *(sép)* ; [- suj: sol] to soak *ou* to drink up *(sép)* **3.** *fam* [utiliser - économies, réserves] to take up *(insép)*, to eat up *fig* ; [- prendre] : **il se fait ~ tout son argent par son ex-femme** his ex-wife spends all his money **4.** *fam* [fatiguer] to wear out *(sép)*, to do in *(sép)* **5.** △ [boire] to knock back *(sép)* **6.** *arg scol* [copier] to crib.
◇ *vi* **1.** [appuyer] to pump ■ **~ sur la pédale du frein** to pump the brake pedal **2.** *arg scol* [copier] to crib ■ **j'ai pompé sur Anne** I cribbed from Anne.

pompette [pɔ̃pɛt] *adj fam* tipsy, tiddly ■ **elle était complètement/un peu ~** she was far gone/a bit tipsy.

pompeux, euse [pɔ̃pø, øz] *adj* pompous, bombastic.

pompier, ère [pɔ̃pje, ɛr] *adj* ART pompier ■ *péj* [style, décor] pretentious, pompous ■ **art ~** *official paintings of the second half of the 19th century, today often considered grandiloquent and over- conventional (eg certain paintings by Gérôme and Meissonier).*
◆ **pompier** *nm* **1.** [sapeur] fireman ■ **les ~s** the fire brigade **2.** [style] pompier (style) **3.** [artiste] pompier.

pompiste [pɔ̃pist] *nm* petrol *ou* pump attendant *UK*, gas station attendant *US*.

pompon [pɔ̃pɔ̃] *nm* **1.** TEXT [vêtement] pompom **2.** *fam loc* **dans le genre désagréable, il tient le ~!** *fam* when it comes to unpleasantness, he certainly takes the biscuit *UK ou* cake *US*! ■ **ça, c'est le ~!** *fam* that's just about the limit!

pomponner [3] [pɔ̃pɔne] *vt* : **~ qqn** to do sb up nicely, to doll sb up *(sép)* ■ **se faire ~** to get dolled up.
◆ **se pomponner** *vp (emploi réfléchi)* to do o.s. up nicely, to doll o.s. up.

ponçage [pɔ̃saʒ] *nm* **1.** [à l'abrasif] sanding (down), sandpapering ■ [à la pierre ponce] pumicing **2.** ART pouncing.

ponce [pɔ̃s] *nf* ART pounce bag, pouncer.

Ponce Pilate [pɔ̃spilat] *npr* Pontius Pilate.

poncer [16] [pɔ̃se] *vt* **1.** [polir avec un abrasif - mur] to sandpaper, to sand (down) ; [- peinture] to rub down *(sép)* ■ [polir avec une machine] to sand (down) ■ [polir à la pierre ponce] to pumice (off) **2.** ART to pounce, to pounce in.

ponceur, euse [pɔ̃sœr, øz] *nm, f* **1.** [de murs] sander **2.** ART pouncer.
◆ **ponceuse** *nf* sander.

poncho [pɔ̃tʃo] *nm* **1.** [cape] poncho **2.** [chausson] Afghan-style sock.

poncif [pɔ̃sif] *nm* **1.** *péj* [cliché] cliché, commonplace, old chestnut **2.** ART pouncing pattern **3.** MÉTALL parting compound.

ponction [pɔ̃ksjɔ̃] *nf* **1.** MÉD puncture ■ **~ lombaire/du ventricule** lumbar/ventricular puncture **2.** [retrait] withdrawal ■ **faire une grosse ~ sur un compte** to withdraw a large sum from an account ■ **c'est une ~ importante sur mes revenus** it makes quite a big hole *ou* dent in my income.

ponctionner [3] [pɔ̃ksjɔne] *vt* **1.** MÉD [poumon] to tap ■ [région lombaire] to puncture **2.** [compte en banque] to withdraw money from ■ [économies] to make a hole *ou* dent in ■ **on nous ponctionne un tiers de notre salaire en impôts** a third of our salary goes in tax.

ponctualité [pɔ̃ktɥalite] *nf* [exactitude] punctuality, promptness ■ **avec ~** promptly, on time.

ponctuation [pɔ̃ktɥasjɔ̃] *nf* punctuation.

ponctuel, elle [pɔ̃ktɥɛl] *adj* **1.** [exact] punctual ■ **être ~** to be on time **2.** [action] one-off *UK*, one-shot *US* ■ [problèmes, difficultés] occasional ■ **l'État accorde une aide ~le aux entreprises en difficulté** the state gives backing to companies to see them through periods of financial difficulty ■ **nous avons une action ~le dans les entreprises** we visit companies on an irregular basis **3.** LING, MATH & PHYS punctual.

ponctuellement [pɔ̃ktɥɛlmɑ̃] *adv* **1.** [avec exactitude] punctually **2.** [de façon limitée] on an ad hoc basis ■ **agir ~** to take action as the need arises.

ponctuer [7] [pɔ̃ktɥe] *vt* **1.** GRAMM to punctuate **2.** *fig* to punctuate ■ **elle ponctuait les mots importants d'un hochement de tête** she emphasized *ou* stressed the important words with a nod **3.** MUS to phrase.

pondaison [pɔ̃dɛzɔ̃] *nf* laying season.

pondéral, e, aux [pɔ̃deral, o] *adj* weight *(modif)*.

pondérateur, trice [pɔ̃deratœr, tris] *adj* stabilizing.

pondération [pɔ̃derasjɔ̃] *nf* **1.** [sang-froid] level-headedness ■ **agir avec ~** to act with sound judgment **2.** BOURSE & ÉCON [de variables] weighting **3.** POLIT [de pouvoirs] balance, equilibrium.

pondéré, e [pɔ̃dere] *adj* **1.** [personne] level-headed, steady **2.** [indice, moyenne] weighted.

pondérer [18] [pɔ̃dere] *vt* **1.** [pouvoirs] to balance (out), to counterbalance **2.** BOURSE & ÉCON to weight.

pondéreux, euse [pɔ̃derø, øz] *adj* INDUST heavy.
◆ **pondéreux** *nm* heavy material ■ **les ~** heavy goods.

pondeuse [pɔ̃døz] *nf* [poule] laying hen, layer.

Pondichéry [pɔ̃diʃeri] *npr* Pondicherry.

pondre [75] [pɔ̃dr] ◇ *vt* **1.** [suj: oiseau] to lay **2.** *fam* [suj: femme] to produce **3.** [créer - gén] to come up with ; [- en série] to churn out *(sép)* ■ **je n'ai pondu que trois pages sur le sujet** I could only produce three pages on the subject.
◇ *vi* [poule] to lay (an egg) ■ [moustique, saumon etc] to lay its eggs.

poney [pɔnɛ] *nm* pony.

pongiste [pɔ̃ʒist] *nmf* table tennis player.

pont [pɔ̃] *nm* **1.** TRAV PUB bridge ■ **dormir** *ou* **vivre sous les ~s** to sleep under the arches *UK*, to be homeless ➤ **~ mobile/suspendu** movable/suspension bridge ■ **~ autoroutier** (motorway *UK*) *ou* freeway *US* flyover ■ **~ à bascule** *ou* **basculant** bascule *ou* balance bridge ■ **~ ferroviaire** railway bridge ■ **~ levant** lift bridge ■ **~ à péage** toll-bridge ■ **~ routier** road bridge ■ **~ tournant** [routier] swing bridge ; [ferroviaire] turntable ■ **faire/promettre un ~ d'or à qqn** to offer/to promise sb a fortune *(so that they'll take on a job)* ■ **jeter un ~** to build bridges *fig* ■ **se porter** *ou* **être solide comme le Pont-Neuf** to be as fit as a fiddle ■ **le ~ du Gard** *enormous Roman aqueduct at Nîmes* ■ **'le Pont de la rivière Kwaï'** ***Lean*** 'Bridge On The River Kwai' ■ **les Ponts** *nickname of the École des Ponts et Chaussées*
2. NAUT deck ■ **bateau à deux/trois ~s** two/three decker ➤ **~ inférieur/principal** lower/main deck ■ **~ arrière** aft *ou* after deck ■ **~ avant** foredeck ■ **~ promenade** promenade deck ■ **~ supérieur** upper *ou* top deck ■ **tout le monde sur le ~!** [levez-vous] everybody up! ; [mettez-vous au travail] let's get down to business!
3. [week-end] long weekend ■ [jour] *day off between a national holiday and a weekend* ■ **faire le ~** [employé] *to take the intervening working day or days off* ■ **le 11 novembre tombe un jeudi, je vais faire le ~** the 11th of November is on Thursday, I'll take Friday off (and have a long weekend)
4. [structure de manutention] : **~ élévateur** *ou* **de graissage** garage ramp, car lift, elevator platform ■ **~ de chargement** loading platform ■ **~ roulant** gantry *ou* travelling crane
5. AUTO : **~ arrière** rear axle (and drive)
6. AÉRON : **~ aérien** airlift
7. GÉOM : **~ aux ânes** *pr* pons asinorum ; *fig* old chestnut
8. MIL : **~ de bateaux** pontoon bridge.
◆ **Ponts et Chaussées** *nmpl* : **les Ponts et Chaussées** ADMIN Department of Civil Engineering ; ÉDUC College of Civil Engineering.

pontage [pɔ̃taʒ] *nm* **1.** MÉD bypass (operation) **2.** TRAV PUB (gantry) bridging **3.** CHIM bridging.

pont-bascule [pɔ̃baskyl] (*pl* **ponts-bascules**) *nm* weighbridge.

ponte[1] [pɔ̃t] *nm* **1.** *fam* [autorité] : **un (grand) ~** a bigshot, a bigwig ■ **ce sont tous de grands ~s de l'université/de la médecine** they're all top-flight academics/high up in the medical profession **2.** JEUX punter.

ponte[2] [pɔ̃t] *nf* **1.** ZOOL [action] laying (of eggs) ■ [œufs - d'un oiseau] clutch, eggs ; [- d'un insecte, d'un poisson] eggs **2.** PHYSIOL : **~ ovulaire** ovulation.

ponter [3] [pɔ̃te] ◇ *vi* JEUX to punt.
◇ *vt* **1.** [miser] to bet **2.** NAUT to deck.

Pont-Euxin [pɔ̃tøksɛ̃] *npr m* : **le ~** the Euxine Sea.

pontife [pɔ̃tif] *nm* **1.** *fam* [autorité] pundit, bigwig, big shot **2.** ANTIQ pontifex, pontiff **3.** RELIG pontiff.

pontifiant, e [pɔ̃tifjɑ̃, ɑ̃t] *adj* pontificating.

pontifical, e, aux [pɔ̃tifikal, o] *adj* **1.** RELIG [insignes, cérémonie] pontifical ■ [États, trône] papal **2.** ANTIQ pontifical.

pontificat [pɔ̃tifika] *nm* pontificate.

pontifier [9] [pɔ̃tifje] *vi* to pontificate ■ **arrête de ~** stop pontificating.

pont-levis [pɔ̃ləvi] (*pl* **ponts-levis**) *nm* drawbridge.

ponton [pɔ̃tɔ̃] *nm* **1.** [d'un port de commerce] pontoon, floating dock ■ [d'un port de plaisance] landing stage, jetty ■ [pour nageurs] (floating) platform **2.** [chaland] hulk, lighter ■ [vieux vaisseau] hulk.

pontonnier [pɔ̃tɔnje] *nm* pontonier.

pont-rail [pɔ̃raj] (*pl* **ponts-rails**) *nm* railway *UK ou* railroad *US* bridge.

pont-route [pɔ̃rut] (*pl* **ponts-routes**) *nm* road bridge.

pool [pul] *nm* ÉCON pool ■ **~ de dactylos** typing pool.

pop [pɔp] ◇ *adj inv* [art, chanteur, mouvement] pop ■ **musique ~** pop (music).
◇ *nm* & *nf* pop (music).

pop-corn [pɔpkɔrn] *nm inv* popcorn.

pope [pɔp] *nm* (Eastern Orthodox Church) priest.

popeline [pɔplin] *nf* poplin ■ **en** *ou* **de ~** poplin *(modif)*.

pop music [pɔpmyzik, pɔpmjuzik] (*pl* **pop musics**) *nf* = **pop** *(nm ou nf)*.

popote [pɔpɔt] *fam* ◇ *nf* [repas] : **faire la ~** to do the cooking.
◇ *adj inv* : **elle est très ~** she's very much the stay-at-home type.

popotin [pɔpɔtɛ̃] *nm fam* bottom.

popu [pɔpy] (*abr de* **populaire**) *adj fam* working-class.

populace [pɔpylas] *nf fam péj* rabble, hoi polloi, plebs.

populacier, ère [pɔpylasje, ɛr] *adj* vulgar, common.

populaire [pɔpylɛr] *adj* **1.** SOCIOL [du peuple] working-class **2.** [tradition, croyance] popular ■ **bon sens ~** popular wisdom **3.** POLIT [gouvernement] popular ■ [démocratie, tribunal] people's ■ [soulèvement] mass *(modif)* ■ **la volonté ~** the will of the people **4.** [qui a du succès - chanteur, mesures] popular **5.** LING [étymologie] popular ■ [niveau de langue] colloquial.

populairement [pɔpylɛrmɑ̃] *adv* LING colloquially ■ **comme on dit ~** as the popular phrase goes.

populariser [3] [pɔpylarize] *vt* : **~ qqch** to popularize sthg, to make sthg available to all.

popularité [pɔpylarite] *nf* popularity ■ **elle jouit d'une grande ~ parmi les étudiants** she's very popular with the students.

population [pɔpylasjɔ̃] *nf* **1.** SOCIOL population ■ **~ mondiale** world population ■ **~ active/civile** working/civilian population **2.** [peuple] people ■ **la ~ locale** the local people, the locals **3.** ASTRON & PHYS population.

populationniste [pɔpylasjɔnist] ◇ *adj* encouraging population growth.
◇ *nmf supporter of measures encouraging population growth.*

populeux, euse [pɔpylø, øz] *adj* [quartier] heavily *ou* densely populated, populous *litt* ■ [place, rue] crowded, very busy.

populisme [pɔpylism] *nm* **1.** HIST Populism **2.** LITTÉR Naturalism.

populiste [pɔpylist] ◇ *adj* **1.** HIST Populist **2.** LITTÉR Naturalist.
◇ *nmf* **1.** HIST Populist **2.** LITTÉR Naturalist (writer).

populo [pɔpylo] *nm fam* **1.** [foule] crowd **2.** [peuple] : **le ~** the plebs *ou* hoi polloi.

porc [pɔr] *nm* **1.** ZOOL pig *UK*, hog *US* **2.** CULIN pork **3.** [peau] pigskin **4.** *fam* [personne] pig, swine.
◆ **de porc** *loc adj* **1.** CULIN pork *(modif)* **2.** [en peau] pigskin *(modif)*.

porcelaine [pɔrsəlɛn] *nf* **1.** [produit] china, porcelain **2.** [pièce] piece of china *ou* porcelain **3.** [ensemble] : **la ~** china, chinaware, porcelain ⊙ **~ de Limoges** Limoges porcelain ■ **~ de Saxe** Dresden china ■ **~ de Sèvres** Sèvres china.
◆ **de porcelaine** *loc adj* **1.** [tasse, objet] china *(modif)*, porcelain *(modif)* **2.** [teint] peaches-and-cream *(avant n)*.

porcelainier, ère [pɔrsəlenje, ɛr] ◇ *adj* china *(modif)*, porcelain *(modif)*.
◇ *nm, f* porcelain *ou* china manufacturer.

porcelet [pɔrsəlɛ] *nm* piglet.

porc-épic [pɔrkepik] (*pl* **porcs-épics**) *nm* **1.** ZOOL porcupine **2.** [personne revêche] prickly person.

porche [pɔrʃ] *nm* porch.

porcherie [pɔrʃəri] *nf pr* & *fig* pigsty.

porcin, e [pɔrsɛ̃, in] *adj* **1.** [industrie, production] pig *(modif)* **2.** [yeux, figure] pig-like, piggy.
◆ **porcin** *nm* pig.

pore [pɔr] *nm* pore ■ **elle sue la suffisance par tous les ~s** *fig* she exudes *ou* oozes self-importance.

poreux, euse [pɔrø, øz] *adj* porous.

porno [pɔrno] *fam* ◇ *adj* [film, magazine, scène] porn, porno ■ **des photos ~s** dirty pictures.
◇ *nm* **1.** activité : **le ~** [genre] porn ; [industrie] the porn industry **2.** [film] porno film *UK*, blue movie.

pornographe [pɔrnɔgraf] *nmf* pornographer.

pornographie [pɔrnɔgrafi] *nf* pornography.

pornographique [pɔrnɔgrafik] *adj* pornographic.

porosité [pɔrozite] *nf* porosity.

porridge [pɔridʒ] *nm* porridge.

port[1] [pɔr] *nm* **1.** [infrastructure] port *UK*, harbour ■ [ville] port ■ **dans le ~ de Dunkerque** in Dunkirk harbour ■ **sur le ~** on the quayside ⊙ **~ maritime** *ou* **de mer** sea port ■ **~ d'attache** NAUT port of registry, home port ; *fig* home base ■ **~ de commerce** commercial port ■ **~ d'embarquement** [de marchandises] port of shipment ; [de personnes] port of embarkation ■ **~ fluvial** river port ■ **~ franc** free port ■ **~ de pêche** fishing port ■ **~ de plaisance** marina **2.** *litt* [havre, refuge] haven **3.** INFORM port ■ **~ USB/parralèle** USB/parallel port.
◆ **à bon port** *loc adv* safely, safe and sound ■ **les verres sont arrivés à bon ~** the glasses got there in one piece *ou* without mishap.

port[2] [pɔr] *nm* **1.** [d'une lettre, d'un colis] postage ■ **frais de ~** (cost of) postage ■ **(en) ~ dû/payé** postage due/paid **2.** TRANSP [de marchandises] carriage ■ **franco de ~** carriage paid *ou* included **3.** [possession - d'une arme] carrying ; [- d'un uniforme, d'un casque] wearing ■ **~ d'armes prohibé** illegal carrying of weapons ■ **le ~ du casque est obligatoire** a crash helmet must be worn **4.** *sout* [maintien] bearing, deportment ■ **elle a un ~ de tête très gracieux** she holds her head very gracefully ⊙ **avoir un ~ de reine** to have a queenly bearing **5.** MUS : **~ de voix** port de voix, appogiatura.

port[3] [pɔr] *nm* [dialecte] pass *(in the Pyrenees)*.

portable [pɔrtabl] ◇ *adj* **1.** [téléphone] mobile **2.** [téléviseur, machine à écrire, ordinateur] portable **3.** [vêtement] wearable **4.** FIN to be paid in person.
◇ *nm* **1.** [téléphone] mobile **2.** [ordinateur] laptop.

portage [pɔrtaʒ] *nm* **1.** [d'équipement] porterage **2.** NAUT portage **3.** COMM : **~ salarial** system whereby self-employed people can have their earnings converted into a regular salary.

portail [pɔrtaj] *nm* **1.** [d'une église] portal ■ [d'un jardin, d'une école] gate **2.** INFORM portal.

portance [pɔrtɑ̃s] *nf* **1.** AÉRON lift **2.** TRAV PUB bearing capacity.

portant, e [pɔrtɑ̃, ɑ̃t] *adj* **1.** NAUT : **vent ~** fair wind **2.** *loc* **bien/mal ~** in good/poor health.
◆ **portant** *nm* **1.** NAUT outrigger **2.** THÉÂTRE upright, support *(for flats)* **3.** [pour vêtements] rail.

portatif, ive [pɔrtatif, iv] *adj* [ordinateur] portable.

Port-au-Prince [pɔroprɛ̃s] *npr* Port-au-Prince.

porte [pɔrt] ◇ *nf* **1.** [d'une maison, d'un véhicule, d'un meuble] door ■ [d'un passe-plat] hatch ■ **le piano est resté coincé dans la ~** the piano got stuck in the door *ou* doorway ■ **fermer** *ou* **interdire** *ou* **refuser sa ~ à qqn** to bar sb from one's house ■ **fermer ses ~s** [magasin] to close down ■ **ouvrir sa ~ à qqn** to welcome sb ■ **ouvrir ses ~s** [magasin, musée] to open ■ **un père magistrat, ça ouvre pas mal de ~s** a father who happens to be a magistrate can open quite a few doors ⊙ **~ arrière** AUTO rear passenger door ■ **~ avant** AUTO [côté conducteur] driver door ; [côté passager] front passenger door ■ **~ de derrière/devant** back/front door ■ **~ coupe-feu** firedoor ■ **~ d'entrée** front door ■ **~ de service** trademen's entrance ■ **~ de sortie** *pr* way out, exit ; *fig* way out ■ **à ma/sa ~** *pr* & *fig* at my/his door, on my/his doorstep ■ **l'hiver est à nos ~s** winter is at the door ■ **Lyon, ce n'est pas la ~ à côté** it's a fair way to Lyons ■ **il n'habite pas la ~ à côté** he doesn't exactly live round the corner ■ **entrer par la grande/petite ~ : elle est entrée dans l'entreprise par la grande ~** she went straight in at the top of the company ■ **entrer dans une profession par la petite ~** to get into a profession by the back door ■ **l'équipe quitte le tournoi par la grande ~** the team is leaving the tournament in style ■ **cette décision ouvre toute grande la ~ à l'injustice** this decision throws the door wide open to injustice ■ **prendre la ~** to leave ■ **il lui a dit de prendre la ~** he showed him the door ■ **trouver ~ close : j'y suis allé mais j'ai trouvé ~ close** I went round but nobody was in *ou* at home ■ **il a essayé tous les éditeurs, mais partout il a trouvé ~ close** he tri ed a ll the publishers, but without success ■ **c'est la ~ ouverte à tous les abus** it leaves the door wide open to all kinds of abuses ■ **il faut qu'une ~ soit ouverte ou fermée** *prov* it's either yes or no, one can't sit on the fence forever
2. [passage dans une enceinte] gate ■ **les ~s de Paris** *the old city gates around Paris* ⊙ **~ d'embarquement** (departure) gate ■ **les ~s de l'enfer** the gates of hell ■ **les ~s du paradis** heaven's gates, the pearly gates ■ **la ~ de Versailles** *site of a large exhibition complex in Paris where major trade fairs take place*

3. [panneau] door (panel) ■ **~ basculante/battante** up-and-over/swing door ■ **~ coulissante** *ou* **roulante** sliding door ■ **~ à deux battants** double door ■ **~ palière** landing door ■ **~ tournante** revolving door ■ **~ vitrée** glass door
4. SPORT gate
5. INFORM gate.
<> *adj* PHYSIOL portal.
◆ **à la porte** *loc adv* out ■ **à la ~!** out of here! ■ **ne reste pas à la ~** don't stay on the doorstep ■ **je suis à la ~ de chez moi** [sans clefs] I'm locked out ; [chassé] I've been thrown out (of my home) ■ **mettre qqn à la ~** [importun] to throw sb out ; [élève] to expel sb ; [employé] to fire *ou* to dismiss sb.
◆ **de porte à porte** *loc adv* door-to-door ■ **je mets 40 minutes de ~ à ~** it takes me 40 minutes door-to-door.
◆ **de porte en porte** *loc adv* from door to door.

porté [pɔrte] *nm* porté.

porte-à-faux [pɔrtafo] *nm inv* overhang.
◆ **en porte(-)à(-)faux** *loc adv* : **être en ~** [mur] to be out of plumb, to be out of true ; [roche] to be in a precarious position ; *fig* to be in an awkward position ■ **mettre qqn en ~** to put sb in an awkward position.

porte-affiches [pɔrtafiʃ] *nm inv* noticeboard.

porte-aiguilles [pɔrtegɥij] *nm inv* COUT needle case.

porte-à-porte [pɔrtapɔrt] *nm inv* : **faire du ~** to sell from door-to-door, to be a door-to-door salesman (*f* saleswoman).

porte-autos [pɔrtoto] *adj inv* car-carrying, transporter *(modif)*.

porte-avions [pɔrtavjɔ̃] *nm inv* aircraft carrier.

porte-bagages [pɔrtbagaʒ] *nm inv* [d'un vélo] rack ■ [d'une voiture, d'un train] (luggage) rack.

porte-bébé [pɔrtbebe] (*pl inv ou pl* **porte-bébés**) *nm* **1.** [nacelle] carry-cot **2.** [harnais] baby sling.

porte-billets [pɔrtbijɛ] *nm inv* wallet *UK*, billfold *US*.

porte-bonheur [pɔrtbɔnœr] *nm inv* lucky charm ■ **une patte de lapin ~** a lucky rabbit's foot.

porte-bouteilles [pɔrtbutɛj] *nm inv* **1.** [châssis] wine rack **2.** [panier] bottle-carrier **3.** [d'un réfrigérateur] bottle rack.

porte-cartes [pɔrtəkart] *nm inv* **1.** [portefeuille] cardholder, wallet *UK*, billfold *US* *(with spaces for cards, photos etc)* **2.** [de cartes géographiques] map holder.

porte-cigares [pɔrtsigar] *nm inv* cigar case.

porte-cigarettes [pɔrtsigarɛt] *nm inv* cigarette case.

porte-clefs, porte-clés [pɔrtəkle] *nm inv* **1.** [anneau] key ring **2.** [étui] key case.

porte-couteau [pɔrtkuto] (*pl inv ou pl* **porte-couteaux**) *nm* knife rest.

porte-crayon [pɔrtkrɛjɔ̃] (*pl inv ou pl* **porte-crayons**) *nm* pencil holder.

porte-documents [pɔrtdɔkymɑ̃] *nm inv* document case.

porte-drapeau [pɔrtdrapo] (*pl inv ou pl* **porte-drapeaux**) *nm pr & fig* standard bearer.

portée [pɔrte] *nf* **1.** MIL & OPT range ■ **à** *ou* **de faible ~** short-range ■ **à** *ou* **de longue ~** long-range ■ **à** *ou* **de moyenne ~** medium-range **2.** [champ d'action - d'une mesure, d'une loi] scope ■ [impact - d'une décision] impact, significance ; [- d'un événement] consequences, repercussions ■ **l'incident a eu une ~ considérable** the incident had far-reaching consequences **3.** ZOOL litter **4.** MUS staff, stave **5.** CONSTR & TRAV PUB [dimension] span ■ [charge] load.
◆ **à la portée de** *loc prép* **1.** [près de] close *ou* near to ■ **'ne pas laisser à la ~ des enfants'** 'keep out of the reach of children' **2.** [pouvant être compris par] : **son livre est à la ~ de tous** her book is easily accessible to the ordinary reader ■ **un jeu à la ~ des 10-12 ans** a game suitable for 10-12 year olds **3.** *loc* **à la ~ de toutes les bourses** easily affordable, to suit all pockets ■ **ce n'est pas à la ~ de toutes les bourses** not everyone can afford it.
◆ **à portée de** *loc prép* within reach of ■ **à ~ de (la) main** within (easy) reach ■ **avoir** *ou* **garder qqch à ~ de (la) main** to keep sthg handy *ou* close at hand *ou* within (easy) reach ■ **à ~ de voix** within earshot.

portefaix [pɔrtəfɛ] *nm inv* [porteur] porter.

porte-fenêtre [pɔrtfənɛtr] (*pl* **portes-fenêtres**) *nf* French window.

portefeuille [pɔrtəfœj] *nm* **1.** [étui] wallet *UK*, billfold *US* ■ **avoir le ~ rembourré** *fam* to be comfortably off **2.** BOURSE portfolio ■ **~ de titres** portfolio of securities **3.** POLIT portfolio ■ **on lui a confié le ~ des Affaires étrangères** he has been given *ou* he holds the foreign affairs portfolio.

porte-hélicoptères [pɔrtelikɔptɛr] *nm inv* helicopter carrier *ou* ship.

porte-jarretelles [pɔrtʒartɛl] *nm inv* suspender belt *UK*, garter belt *US*.

porte-malheur [pɔrtmalœr] *nm inv* **1.** [personne] jinx, Jonah *litt* **2.** [objet] jinx.

portemanteau, x [pɔrtmɑ̃to] *nm* **1.** [sur pied] hat stand ■ [mural] coat rack **2.** [cintre] coathanger.

porte-menu [pɔrtməny] (*pl inv ou pl* **porte-menus**) *nm* menu holder.

portemine [pɔrtəmin] *nm* propelling pencil.

porte-missile [pɔrtmisil] (*pl inv ou pl* **porte-missiles**) *nm* missile carrier.

porte-monnaie [pɔrtmɔnɛ] *nm inv* purse *UK*, change purse *US* ■ **avoir le ~ bien garni** to be well off.

porte-outil [pɔrtuti] (*pl inv ou pl* **porte-outils**) *nm* [gén] tool holder ■ [d'une perceuse] chuck ■ [d'une raboteuse] stock ■ [d'un tour] slide rest.

porte-papier [pɔrtpapje] *nm inv* toilet roll holder.

porte-parapluies [pɔrtparaplɥi] *nm inv* umbrella stand.

porte-parole [pɔrtparɔl] <> *nmf inv* [personne] spokesperson, spokesman (*f* spokeswoman) ■ **se faire le ~ de qqn** to speak on sb's behalf.
<> *nm* [périodique] mouthpiece, organ.

porte-plume [pɔrtəplym] (*pl inv ou pl* **porte-plumes**) *nm* pen holder.

porter[1] [pɔrte] = **porté**.

porter[2] [pɔrtɛr] *nm* [bière] porter.

porter[3] [3] [pɔrte] <> *vt*

A. TENIR, SUPPORTER
B. METTRE, AMENER
C. AVOIR SUR SOI, EN SOI

A. TENIR, SUPPORTER

1. [soutenir - colis, fardeau, meuble] to carry ; [- bannière, pancarte, cercueil] to carry, to bear ■ **deux piliers portent le toit** two pillars take the weight of *ou* support the roof ■ **la glace n'est pas assez épaisse pour nous ~** the ice is too thin to bear our weight ■ **~ qqn sur son dos/dans ses bras** to carry sb on one's back/in one's arms ■ **ses jambes ne la portaient plus** her legs couldn't carry her anymore ■ **se laisser ~ par le courant** to let o.s. be carried (away) by the current ■ *(en usage absolu)* **l'eau de mer porte plus que l'eau douce** sea water is more buoyant than fresh water ‖ *fig* **elle porte bien son âge** she looks young for her age ■ **~ la responsabilité de** to bear (the) responsibility for **2.** [soutenir moralement - suj: foi, religion] to give strength to, to support ■ **c'est l'espoir de le retrouver qui la porte** the hope of finding him again keeps her going

B. METTRE, AMENER

1. [amener] to take, to bring ■ **~ qqch à qqn** to take sthg to sb ■ **~ des fleurs sur la tombe de qqn** to take flowers to sb's grave ■ **se faire ~ un repas** to have a meal brought (to one) ‖ [mettre] : **~ une œuvre à l'écran/à la scène** to adapt a work for the

screen/the stage ■ **~ le débat sur la place publique** to make the debate public ■ **~ une affaire devant les tribunaux** to take *ou* to bring a matter before the courts ■ **~ qqn/qqch à : ~ qqn au pouvoir** to bring sb to power ■ **~ son art à la perfection** to perfect one's art ■ **cela porte le total à 506 euros** that brings the total (up) to 506 euros ■ **les frais d'inscription ont été portés à 25 euros** the registration fees have been increased *ou* raised to 25 euros ■ **~ qqch à ébullition** CULIN to bring sthg to the boil ■ **~ qqch au rouge** MÉTALL to heat sthg to red-heat
2. [diriger] : **~ sa** *ou* **la main à sa tête** to raise one's hand to one's head ■ **il porta la main à sa poche** he put his hand to his pocket ■ **il porta la main à son revolver** he reached for his gun ■ **~ son regard vers** *ou* **sur** to look towards *ou* in the direction of ■ **~ ses pas vers** to make one's way towards, to head for
3. [enregistrer - donnée] to write *ou* to put down *(sép)* ■ **~ sa signature sur un registre** to sign a register ■ **porte ce point sur le graphique** plot that point onto the graph ■ **se faire ~ absent/malade** to go absent/sick ■ **~ qqn disparu** to report sb missing ■ **~ 200 euros au crédit de qqn** to credit sb's account with 200 euros, to credit 200 euros to sb's account ■ **~ 200 euros au débit de qqn** to debit 200 euros from sb's account
4. [appliquer - effort, énergie] to direct, to bring, to bear ■ **~ son attention sur** to focus one's attention on, to turn one's attention to ■ **~ son choix sur** to choose ■ **~ une accusation contre qqn** to bring a charge against sb ■ **il a fait ~ tout son effort** *ou* **ses efforts sur la réussite du projet** he did his utmost to make the project successful ▶ **~ ses vues sur qqn** [pour accomplir une tâche] to have sb in mind *(for a job)* ; [pour l'épouser] to have one's eye on sb
5. [inciter] : **~ qqn à qqch : mon intervention l'a portée à plus de clémence** my intervention made her inclined *ou* prompted her to be more lenient ■ **l'alcool peut ~ les gens à des excès/à la violence** alcohol can drive people to excesses/induce people to be violent ■ **tout porte à croire que...** everything leads one to believe that... ■ **tous les indices portent à penser que c'est lui le coupable** all the evidence suggests he is the guilty one ■ **être porté à faire** to be inclined to do ■ **être porté sur : il est porté sur la boisson** *ou* *fam* **bouteille** he likes a drink ■ **être porté sur la chose** *fam euphém* to have a one-track mind
6. [éprouver] : **~ de l'intérêt à qqn/qqch** to be interested in sb/sthg ■ **~ de l'admiration à qqn** to admire sb ■ **je lui porte beaucoup d'amitié** I hold him very dear ■ **l'amour qu'il lui portait** the love he felt for her ■ **la haine qu'il lui portait** the hatred he felt towards her *ou* bore her

C. AVOIR SUR SOI, EN SOI

1. [bijou, chaussures, lunettes, vêtement] to wear, to have on *(sép)* ■ [badge, décoration] to wear ■ [barbe, couettes, moustache, perruque] to have ■ [cicatrice] to bear, to have, to carry ■ [pistolet, stylo] to carry ■ **son cheval porte le numéro 5** his horse is number 5 ■ **elle porte toujours du noir** she always dresses in *ou* wears black ■ **~ les cheveux longs/courts/relevés** to wear one's hair long/short/up
2. [laisser voir - trace] to show, to bear ; [- date, inscription] to bear ■ **l'étui portait ses initiales gravées** the case was engraved with his initials ■ **le couteau ne porte aucune empreinte** there are no fingerprints on the knife ■ **la signature que porte le tableau** the signature (which) appears *ou* is on the painting ■ **elle portait la résignation sur son visage** resignation was written all over *ou* on her face
3. [nom, prénom, patronyme] to have ■ **il porte le nom de Legrand** he's called Legrand ■ **elle porte le nom de son mari** she has taken her husband's name ■ **c'est un nom difficile à ~** it's not an easy name to be called by
4. [en soi] to carry, to bear ■ **l'espoir/la rancune que je portais en moi** the hope/resentment I bore within me
5. MÉD [virus] to carry ■ **tous ceux qui portent le virus** all carriers of the virus
6. [enfant, petit, portée] to carry
7. AGRIC & HORT [fruits] to bear ■ **la tige porte trois feuilles** there are three leaves on the stem ■ **lorsque l'arbre porte ses fleurs** when the tree's in bloom ■ **~ ses fruits** *fig* to bear fruit.

◇ *vi* **1.** [son, voix] to carry ■ **sa voix ne porte pas assez** his voice doesn't carry well ■ **aussi loin que porte la vue** as far as the eye can see ‖ [canon, fusil] : **~ à** to have a range of ■ **le coup de feu a porté à plus de 2 km** the shot carried more than 2 km **2.** [faire mouche - critique, mot, plaisanterie] to hit *ou* to strike home ; [- observation] to be heard *ou* heeded ; [- coup] to hit home, to tell **3.** [cogner] : **c'est le crâne qui a porté** the skull took the impact *ou* the full force ■ **~ sur** *ou* **contre** to hit **4.** [dans l'habillement masculin] : **~ à droite/gauche** to dress on the right/left.

◆ **porter sur** *v+prép* **1.** [concerner - suj: discussion, discours, chapitre, recherches] to be about, to be concerned with ; [- suj: critiques] to be aimed at ; [- suj: loi, mesures] to concern ; [- suj: dossier, reportage] to be about *ou* on ■ **le détournement porte sur plusieurs millions d'euros** the embezzlement concerns several million euros **2.** [reposer sur - suj: charpente] to rest on ■ **l'accent porte sur la deuxième syllabe** LING the accent falls on the second syllable, the second syllable is stressed.

◆ **se porter** ◇ *vp (emploi passif)* [bijou, chaussures, vêtement] to be worn ■ **les manteaux se porteront longs cet hiver** coats will be (worn) long this winter.
◇ *vpi* **1.** [personne] : **comment vous portez-vous?** how do you feel?, how are you (feeling)? ■ **à bientôt, portez-vous bien!** see you soon, look after yourself! ▶ **il va bientôt s'en aller, je ne m'en porterai que mieux** he's going to leave soon and I'll feel all the better for it ■ **nos parents ne prenaient pas de congés et ne s'en portaient pas plus mal** our parents never took time off and they were none the worse for it **2.** [se proposer comme] : **se ~ acquéreur de qqch** to offer to buy sthg ■ **se ~ candidat** to put o.s. up *ou* to stand *UK* *ou* to run *US* as a candidate ■ **se ~ caution** to stand security ■ **se ~ volontaire pour faire** to volunteer to do **3.** [aller] : **se ~ au-devant de qqn** to go to meet sb ■ **se ~ en tête d'une procession/course** to take the lead in a procession/race ■ **il s'est porté à l'avant du peloton** he went to the head of the pack ■ **tout son sang s'est porté à sa tête** the blood rushed to his head.

◆ **se porter à** *vp+prép sout* [se livrer à] to give o.s. over to, to indulge in ■ **comment a-t-il pu se ~ à de telles extrémités?** how could he go to such extremes?

◆ **se porter sur** *vp+prép* [choix, soupçon] to fall on ■ [conversation] to turn to ■ **tous les regards se portèrent sur elle** all eyes turned towards her.

porte-revues [pɔrtrəvy] *nm inv* magazine rack.

porte-savon [pɔrtsavɔ̃] *(pl inv ou pl* **porte-savons***)* *nm* soap dish.

porte-serviettes [pɔrtsɛrvjɛt] *nm inv* towel rail.

porteur, euse [pɔrtœr, øz] ◇ *adj* **1.** [plein d'avenir] flourishing ■ **un marché ~** a buoyant market ■ **l'informatique est un secteur ~** computing is a flourishing *ou* booming industry ■ **une idée porteuse** an idea with great potential **2.** [chargé] : **~ de : un vaccin ~ d'espoir** a vaccine which brings new hope **3.** TECHNOL [essieu] loadbearing ■ [roue] carrying **4.** PHYS : **onde/fréquence porteuse** carrier wave/frequency **5.** ASTRONAUT [fusée] booster *(modif)*.
◇ *nm, f* **1.** MÉD carrier ■ **~ sain** (unaffected) carrier **2.** [de bagages] porter ■ [d'un cercueil, d'un brancard, d'un étendard] bearer ■ [d'eau] carrier ■ [de nouvelles, d'une lettre] bearer.

◆ **porteur** *nm* BANQUE & BOURSE bearer ■ **chèque/obligations au ~** bearer cheque/bonds ■ **payable au ~** payable to bearer.

porte-vélos [pɔrtəvelo] *nm inv* bicycle rack.

porte-voix [pɔrtəvwa] *nm inv* [simple] megaphone ■ [électrique] loud-hailer *UK*, bullhorn *US* ■ **parler dans un ~** to talk through a megaphone.

portier, ère [pɔrtje, ɛr] *nm, f* doorman *(f* doorwoman*)* ■ **~ de nuit** night porter.

◆ **portière** *nf* **1.** [d'un véhicule] door **2.** [tenture] portière, door curtain.

portillon [pɔrtijɔ̃] *nm* [d'une porte cochère] wicket ■ [dans le métro] : **~ automatique** ticket barrier.

portion [pɔrsjɔ̃] *nf* **1.** [part - de nourriture] portion, helping ; [- d'argent] share, cut ■ **~ congrue** (income providing) a meagre living **2.** [segment - de ligne, d'autoroute] stretch.

◆ **en portions** *loc adj* in individual helpings.

portique [pɔrtik] *nm* **1.** ARCHIT portico **2.** SPORT crossbeam **3.** [dispositif de sécurité] security gate **4.** INDUST gantry crane.

porto [pɔrto] *nm* port (wine).

Porto [pɔrto] *npr* Porto.

portoricain, e [pɔrtɔrikɛ̃, ɛn] *adj* Puerto Rican.

◆ **Portoricain, e** *nm, f* Puerto Rican.

Porto Rico [pɔrtoriko] *npr* Puerto Rico.

portrait [pɔrtrɛ] *nm* **1.** [dessin, peinture, photo] portrait ▪ **le ~ n'est pas très ressemblant** it is not a very good likeness ▪ **faire le ~ de qqn** [dessinateur] to draw sb's portrait ; [peintre] to paint sb's portrait ▪ **'votre ~ en 5 minutes'** [photo] 'your photo in 5 minutes' ◐ **~ de famille** family portrait ▪ **être tout le ~** *ou* **le ~ vivant de qqn** to be the spitting image of sb **2.** ART : **l'art du ~, le ~** portraiture **3.** *fam* [figure] : **il lui a abîmé le ~** he rearranged his face (for him) *hum* **4.** [description] portrayal, description, portrait ▪ **faire** *ou* **tracer le ~ de qqn** to portray sb **5.** INFORM portrait.

portrait-interview [pɔrtrɛɛ̃tɛrvju] (*pl* **portraits-interviews**) *nm* close-up *(interview)*.

portraitiste [pɔrtretist] *nmf* portraitist.

portrait-robot [pɔrtrɛrɔbo] (*pl* **portraits-robots**) *nm* **1.** [d'un criminel] Photofit® *ou* Identikit® picture **2.** [caractéristiques] typical profile.

portraiturer [3] [pɔrtretyre] *vt litt* to portray, to depict.

Port-Saïd [pɔrsaid] *npr* Port Said.

portuaire [pɔrtɥɛr] *adj* port *(modif)*, harbour *(modif)*.

portugais, e [pɔrtygɛ, ɛz] *adj* Portuguese.

◆ **Portugais, e** *nm, f* Portuguese ▪ **les Portugais** the Portuguese.

◆ **portugais** *nm* LING Portuguese.

◆ **portugaise** *nf* [huître] Portuguese oyster.

◆ **portugaises**△ *nfpl arg crime* lugholes *UK*, ears ▪ **avoir les ~es ensablées** to be deaf as a post.

Portugal [pɔrtygal] *npr m* : **le ~** Portugal ▪ **au ~** in Portugal.

POS, Pos [pɔs] *nm* = **plan d'occupation des sols.**

pose [poz] *nf* **1.** [mise en place] putting in, installing ▪ **la ~ de la fenêtre vous coûtera 250 euros** it will cost you 250 euros to have the window put in ▪ **la ~ d'un carrelage** laying tiles ▪ **la ~ d'une moquette** fitting *ou* laying (wall-to-wall) carpet **2.** [attitude] position, posture ▪ **prendre une ~ avantageuse** to strike a flattering pose ▮ [pour un artiste] pose ▪ **prendre la ~** to start posing, to take up a pose ▪ **garder** *ou* **tenir la ~** to hold the pose **3.** PHOTO [cliché, durée] exposure ▪ **24/36 ~s** 24/36 exposures **4.** *sout* [affectation] affectation.

posé, e [poze] *adj* **1.** [mesuré - personne] self-possessed, collected, composed ; [- manières, ton] calm, cool, tranquil **2.** MUS : **voix bien/mal ~e** steady/unsteady voice.

posément [pozemɑ̃] *adv* calmly, coolly.

poser¹ [poze] *nm* MIL landing *(of a helicopter)*.

poser² [3] [poze] ◇ *vt* **1.** [mettre] to put, to lay, to place ▪ **~ ses coudes sur la table** to rest *ou* to put one's elbows on the table ▪ **~ un sac par terre** to put a bag (down) on the floor ▪ **j'ai tellement mal que je ne peux plus ~ le pied par terre** my foot hurts so much, I can't put my weight on it any longer ▪ **il posa un baiser sur ses paupières** he kissed her on the eyelids ▪ **je ne sais pas où ~ mes fesses** *fam hum* I don't know where to sit ▪ *(en usage absolu)* **à toi de ~!** [aux dominos] your turn! ▮ [cesser d'utiliser] to put away *ou* down *(sép)* ▪ **pose ton ballon et viens dîner** put away your ball and come and have dinner ▪ **posez vos stylos et écoutez-moi** put your pens down and listen to me

2. [installer - papier peint, cadre, tentures, affiche] to put up *(sép)* ; [- antenne] to put up *(sép)*, to install ; [- radiateur, alarme] to put in *(sép)*, to install ; [- verrou] to fit ; [- cadenas] to put on *(sép)* ; [- moquette] to fit, to lay ; [- carrelage, câble, mine, rail, tuyau] to lay ; [- vitre] to put in ; [- placard] to put in, to install ; [- prothèse] to fit, to put in ; [- enduit] to put on ▪ **faire ~ un double vitrage** to have double-glazing put in *ou* fitted ▪ **se faire ~ une couronne** to have a crown fitted

3. [énoncer - question] to ask ; [- devinette] to ask, to set ▪ **~ une question à qqn** to ask sb a question, to put a question to sb ▪ **~ un problème** [causer des difficultés] to raise *ou* to pose a problem ; [l'énoncer] to set a problem ▪ **de la façon dont il m'avait posé le problème...** the way he'd put *ou* outlined the problem to me... ▪ **elle me pose de gros problèmes** she's a great problem *ou* source of anxiety to me ▪ **si ça ne pose pas de problème, je viendrai avec mon chien** if it's not a problem (for you) I'll bring my dog

4. [établir - condition] to state, to lay down ; [- principe, règle] to lay *ou* to set down *(sép)*, to state ▪ **une fois posées les bases du projet** once the foundations of the project have been laid down ▪ **~ qqch comme condition/principe** to lay sthg down as a condition/principle ▪ **si l'on pose comme hypothèse que...** if we take as a hypothesis that...

5. *fam* [mettre en valeur] to establish the reputation of, to give standing to ▪ **une voiture comme ça, ça vous pose** that kind of car gives you a certain status

6. MATH to put down *(sép)* ▪ **je pose 2 et je retiens 1** put down 2, carry 1 ▪ **~ une opération** to set out a sum

7. MUS : **~ sa voix** to pitch one's voice

8. SPORT to place

9. AÉRON [avion, hélicoptère] to land, to set down *(sép)*.

◇ *vi* **1.** [pour un peintre, un photographe] to pose, to sit ▪ **~ pour une photo/un magazine** to pose for a photo/magazine ▪ **et maintenant, tout le monde va ~ pour la photo souvenir** let's have everyone together now for the souvenir photograph

2. [fanfaronner] to put on airs, to show off, to pose ▪ [faire semblant] to put on airs, to strike a pose *ou* an attitude ▪ **elle n'est pas vraiment malheureuse, elle pose** she's not really unhappy, it's just a façade *ou* it's all show ▪ **~ à** [se faire passer pour] to pretend to be, to act, to play.

◆ **se poser** ◇ *vp (emploi passif)* : **se ~ facilement** [chaudière] to be easy to install ; [moquette] to be easy to lay.

◇ *vpt* [faire surgir] : **se ~ la question** *ou* **le problème de savoir si...** to ask o.s. *ou* to wonder whether... ▪ **il va finir par se ~ des questions** he's going to start having doubts.

◇ *vpi* **1.** [descendre - avion, hélicoptère] to land, to touch down ; [- papillon] to land, to alight ; [- oiseau] to land, to perch ▪ **se ~ en catastrophe** to make an emergency landing ▪ **se ~ en douceur** to make a smooth landing ▪ **une plume est venue se ~ sur sa tête** a feather floated down onto his head ▪ **tous les regards se posèrent sur elle** all eyes turned to her ▪ **il sentit leurs yeux se ~ sur lui** he could feel their eyes on him ▪ **sa main se posa sur la mienne** she put her hand on mine

2. *fam* [s'asseoir] : **pose-toi là** sit (yourself) down here

3. [surgir - question, problème] to arise, to come up ▪ **la question ne se pose plus maintenant** the question is irrelevant now ▪ **la question qui se pose maintenant est la suivante** the question which must now be asked is the following ▪ **le problème qui se pose à moi** the problem I've got to face *ou* to solve ▪ **le problème se pose de savoir si l'on doit négocier** there's the problem of whether or not we should negotiate ▪ **le problème ne se pose pas exactement en ces termes** that's not exactly where the problem lies

4. [se faire passer pour] : **se ~ en** *ou* **comme** to pass o.s. off as ▪ **je ne me suis jamais posé en expert** I never set myself up to be *ou* I never pretended I was an expert

5. *fam loc* **se ~ là** [il est brillant] : **pour l'intelligence, son frère se pose là!** her brother's got quite a brain! ▪ **elle se pose là, leur bagnole!** [avec admiration] their car's an impressive bit of machinery! ▪ **comme plombier, tu te poses là!** call yourself a plumber, do you? ▪ **comme gaffe, ça se pose là!** that's what you might call a blunder!

poseur, euse [pozœr, øz] ◇ *adj* [prétentieux] affected, pretentious, mannered.

◇ *nm, f* **1.** [m'as-tu-vu] poseur, show-off **2.** [installateur] : **~ de : ~ de parquet/carrelage** floor/tile layer ▪ **~ de mines** mine layer ▪ **~ de rails** tracklayer ▪ **les ~s de bombes se sont enfuis** those responsible for planting the bombs *ou* the bombers ran away.

posidonie [pozidɔni] *nf* posidonia.

positif, ive [pozitif, iv] *adj* **1.** [constructif - mesures, suggestion, attitude] positive, constructive ; [- réaction, échos, critique] favourable *UK*, favorable *US* **2.** [réaliste] pragmatic, practical-minded **3.** [affirmatif - réponse] positive ▪ **si sa réponse est positive** if he says yes **4.** MATH, MÉD, PHOTO & PHYS positive.

◆ **positif** *nm* **1.** [quelque chose de constructif] : **il nous faut du ~** we need something positive **2.** LING, MATH & PHOTO positive **3.** MUS [orgue] positive organ ▪ [clavier secondaire] choir *ou* positive organ.

position [pozisjɔ̃] *nf* **1.** MIL [lieu d'où l'on mène une action] position ■ **une ~ dominante** a commanding position ◗ **~ avancée/défensive** advanced/defensive position ■ **~ clef** key position ■ **être en ~ de combat** to be ready to attack ■ **des ~s fortifiées** a fortified position ■ **~ de repli** MIL & *fig* fall-back position
2. [lieu où l'on se trouve] position ■ **déterminer sa ~** to find one's bearings ■ **déterminer la ~ de qqch** to locate sthg
3. [dans un sondage, une course] position, place ■ **nous sommes en dernière/première ~ dans le championnat** we're bottom of the league/in the lead in the championship ■ **arriver en première/dernière ~** [coureur] to come first/last ; [candidat] to come top/be last ■ **ils ont rétrogradé en quatrième ~ au hit-parade** they went down to number four in the charts
4. [posture] posture, position ■ **tu as une mauvaise ~** you've got bad posture ◗ **dans la** *ou* **en ~ verticale** when standing up ■ **dans la** *ou* **en ~ allongée** when lying down ■ **dans la** *ou* **en ~ assise** when sitting, in a sitting position
5. [angle, orientation] position, setting ■ **mettez le siège en ~ inclinée** tilt the seat back
6. [opinion] position, stance, standpoint ■ **prendre ~ (sur qqch)** to take a stand *ou* to take up a position (on sthg) ■ **prendre ~ pour** *ou* **en faveur de qqch** to come down in favour of sthg ■ **prendre ~ contre qqch** to come out against sthg ■ **rester sur ses ~s** *pr* & *fig* to stand one's ground, to stick to one's guns ■ **quelle est la ~ de la France dans ce conflit?** what's France's position on this conflict? ■ **~ commune** POLIT common stance
7. [situation] position, situation ■ **en ~ de : en ~ de force** in a strong position *ou* a position of strength ■ **être en ~ de faire qqch** to be in a position to do sthg ▮ [dans une entreprise] position, post ■ **dans sa ~, elle devrait se sentir responsable** a woman in her position should feel responsible ◗ **~ sociale** social standing
8. BANQUE balance (of account) ◗ **~ de place** BOURSE market position ■ **feuille de ~** interim statement
9. LING [d'un terme, d'une syllabe, d'une voyelle] position ■ **phonème en ~ forte/faible** stressed/unstressed phoneme
10. DANSE position
11. MUS [accord, doigté] position
12. GÉOM & PSYCHOL position
13. DR status.
◆ **de position** *loc adj* [balise] position *(modif)*.

positionnement [pozisjɔnmɑ̃] *nm* **1.** COMM positioning **2.** MÉCAN positioning.

positionner [3] [pozisjɔne] *vt* **1.** COMM [produit] to position **2.** MÉCAN to position **3.** [localiser] to locate, to determine the position of.
◆ **se positionner** *vp (emploi réfléchi)* to position o.s., to get into position.

positionneur [pozisjɔnœr] *nm* positioner.

positive [pozitiv] *f* ▻ **positif**.

positivement [pozitivmɑ̃] *adv* positively.

positivisme [pozitivism] *nm* positivism ■ **~ logique** logical positivism.

positiviste [pozitivist] *adj* & *nmf* positivist.

positivité [pozitivite] *nf* positivity.

posologie [pozɔlɔʒi] *nf* **1.** [instructions] dosage ■ **respectez la ~** use as directed **2.** [science] posology.

possédant, e [pɔsedɑ̃, ɑ̃t] *adj* propertied, property-owning.
◆ **possédants** *nmpl* : **les ~s** people with property, property owners.

possédé, e [pɔsede] *nm, f* : **comme un ~** like a man possessed.

posséder [18] [pɔsede] *vt* **1.** [détenir - demeure, collection, fortune, terres] to own, to possess, to have ; [- colonies] to have ; [- preuve, document, titre, ticket] to hold, to have ; [- arme, armée] to possess **2.** [être doté de - talent, mémoire] to possess, to have **3.** [maîtriser - art, langue] to have mastered ■ **(bien) ~ son sujet** to be master *ou* on top of one's subject ■ **être possédé par** to be possessed by *ou* with ■ **le démon qui le possède** the devil within him **4.** *fam* [tromper - suj: escroc] to con, to have ■ **je me suis fait ~** I've been conned *ou* had **5.** *litt* [sexuellement] to possess, to have carnal knowledge of.
◆ **se posséder** *vpi* [se dominer] : **je ne me possédais plus** I was not myself any more, I was no longer master of myself.

possesseur [pɔsesœr] *nm* **1.** [propriétaire - d'une maison, d'une collection, d'une fortune] owner, possessor ; [- d'un hôtel, d'une ferme] owner, proprietor ; [- d'une charge, d'un ticket] holder ; [- d'un titre] incumbent, holder ; [- de documents] possessor, holder ■ **être le ~ d'une propriété** to own *ou* to possess a property **2.** [détenteur - d'une preuve] possessor.

possessif, ive [pɔsesif, iv] *adj* LING & PSYCHOL possessive.
◆ **possessif** *nm* GRAMM possessive (form), *voir aussi* **pluriel**.

possession [pɔsesjɔ̃] *nf* **1.** [détention - d'une maison, d'un hôtel, d'une collection, d'une fortune] ownership, possession ; [- d'informations] possession ; [- d'actions, d'un diplôme] holding ; [- d'une charge, d'un titre] possession, holding ; [- d'un poste] tenure ■ **avoir qqch en sa ~** to have sthg in one's possession ■ **être en ~ de** to be in possession of ■ **prendre ~ de** [maison] to take possession of ; [fonctions] to take up ■ **entrer en ~ de** to come into possession of, to come by **2.** DR possession ■ **~ utile** quiet possession **3.** [territoire] possession, dominion **4.** [contrôle] control ■ **une force étrange a pris ~ de lui** a strange force has gained possession of him **5.** PSYCHOL & RELIG possession.

possessivité [pɔsesivite] *nf* possessiveness.

possibilité [pɔsibilite] *nf* **1.** [chose envisageable ou faisable] possibility **2.** [moyen] possibility ■ [occasion] opportunity ■ **il n'a pas vraiment la ~ de refuser** he can't really refuse **3.** [éventualité] possibility ■ **le syndicat n'a pas nié la ~ d'une reprise des négociations** the trade union has not ruled out the possible re-opening of negotiations.
◆ **possibilités** *nfpl* [financières] means ■ **100 euros, c'est dans mes ~s** 100 euros, that's within my means ■ **la maison était au-dessus de nos ~s** we couldn't afford the house ▮ [intellectuelles, physiques] possibilities, potential ■ **écrire une thèse serait au-dessus de mes ~s** I couldn't cope with writing a thesis ▮ [techniques] facilities ■ **machine qui offre de multiples ~s d'utilisation** machine with many features.

possible [pɔsibl] ◇ *adj* **1.** [réalisable - gén] possible ; [- construction] feasible ■ **rendre qqch ~** to make sthg possible ■ **il est ~ de dire/de faire** it is possible to say/to do ■ **il est toujours ~ d'annuler la réunion** the meeting can always be cancelled ■ **il ne m'est financièrement pas ~ de partir pour l'étranger** I cannot afford to go abroad ■ **j'ai fait tout ce qu'il m'était techniquement ~ de faire** I did everything that was technically possible ■ [par exagération] : **ce n'est pas ~ d'être aussi maladroit!** how can anyone be so clumsy! ■ **il faut qu'on divorce, ce n'est pas ~ autrement** we've got to get a divorce, it's the only solution ■ **on a dû le pousser, ce n'est pas ~ autrement!** somebody MUST have pushed him! ■ **il est pas ~, ce mec!** *fam* this guy's just too much!
2. [probable] possible ■ **il est ~ que je vous rejoigne plus tard** I may *ou* might join you later ■ **serait-il ~ qu'il m'ait menti?** could he (possibly) have lied to me? ■ **il t'aime – c'est bien ~, mais moi pas!** he loves you – quite possibly *ou* that's as may be, but I don't love him!
3. [pour exprimer l'étonnement] : **elle est morte hier – c'est pas ~!** *fam* she died yesterday – I can't believe it! ■ **pas ~! c'est ta fille?** *fam* is this your daughter? well, I never! ■ **Noël c'est le 25 – pas ~!** *iron* Christmas is on the 25th – you don't say!
4. [envisageable - interprétation, explication, option] possible
5. [potentiel] possible ■ **je l'ai cherché dans tous les endroits ~s** I looked for it everywhere imaginable *ou* in every possible place ■ **il a eu tous les problèmes ~s et imaginables pour récupérer son argent** he had all kinds of problems getting his money back ■ **bougez le moins ~** move as little as possible ■ **je veux un rapport aussi détaillé que ~** I want as detailed a report as possible ■ **j'ai acheté les moins chers ~** I bought the cheapest I could find ■ **il mange le plus/le moins de gâteaux ~** *ou* **~s** he eats as many/as few cakes as possible.
◇ *nm* : **le ~** the possible ■ **c'est dans le domaine du ~** it's within the bounds of possibility, it's quite possible ◗ **faire (tout) son ~** to do one's best *ou* all one (possibly) can *ou* one's utmost.

◆ **au possible** *loc adv* in the extreme ■ **ennuyeux au ~** extremely boring ■ **elle a été désagréable/serviable au ~** she couldn't have been more unpleasant/helpful.

postal, e, aux [pɔstal, o] *adj* [colis] (sent) by post *UK OU* mail ■ [frais, service, tarif] postal.

postchèque [pɔstʃɛk] *nm* Post Office traveller's cheque.

postcure [pɔstkyr] *nf* rehabilitation ■ **foyer de ~** rehabilitation centre.

postdater [3] [pɔstdate] *vt* to postdate.

poste[1] [pɔst] *nm* **1.** RADIO & TV : **~ (de) radio/télévision** (radio)/television set ■ **~ émetteur/récepteur** transmitting/receiving set
2. TÉLÉCOM [appareil] telephone ■ [d'un standard] extension ■ **passez-moi le ~ 1421** give me extension 1421
3. [métier] post, job, position ■ **un ~ à pourvoir** a post to be filled, a vacancy ■ **elle a un ~ très élevé au ministère** she has a very senior position *OU* post in the ministry
4. [local, installation] : **~ d'aiguillage** signal box ■ **~ de douane** customs post ■ **~ d'essence** petrol *UK OU* gas *US OU* filling station ■ **~ d'incendie** fire point ■ **~ de police** police station ■ **~ de ravitaillement** service station ■ **~ de secours** first-aid post
5. MIL : **être/rester à son ~** *pr* & *fig* to be/to stay at one's post ⊙ **~ de combat** action *OU* battle station ■ **~ de commandement** command post ■ **~ de garde** guardroom ■ **~ de contrôle** checkpoint ■ **~ d'observation/d'écoute/de surveillance** *pr* & *fig* observation/listening/look-out post
6. FIN [d'un compte] item, entry ■ [d'un budget] item
7. INDUST [division du temps] shift ⊙ **~ de nuit** nightshift ■ **~ de travail** [emplacement] workplace ; [emploi] job
8. CHASSE hide.

poste[2] [pɔst] *nf* **1.** [établissement] post office ■ **~ restante** poste restante **2.** [moyen d'acheminement] post *UK*, mail *US* ■ **envoyer qqch par la ~** to send sthg by post *UK*, to mail sthg *US* ■ **mettre une lettre à la ~** to post *UK OU* to mail *US* a letter ■ **~ aérienne** air-mail **3.** ADMIN : **la ~** ≃ the Post Office ■ **travailler à la ~** ≃ to work for the Post Office ⊙ **les Postes et Télécommunications** *the French postal and telecommunications service*
4. HIST [relais] post.

LA POSTE

The French post office is responsible for the collection and delivery of mail. It also offers financial services. Many people choose to bank at the post office.

posté, e [pɔste] *adj* INDUST shift *(modif)*.

poste-frontière [pɔst(ə)frɔ̃tjɛr] (*pl* **postes-frontières**) *nm* customs post.

poster[1] [pɔstɛr] *nm* poster.

poster[2] [3] [pɔste] *vt* **1.** [envoyer - colis, courrier] to post *UK*, to mail *US* **2.** [placer - garde, complice] to post, to station ■ **l'inspecteur fit ~ un homme à chaque issue** the inspector gave orders for a man to be stationed at each exit.
◆ **se poster** *vpi* [sentinelle] to station *OU* to post *OU* to position o.s. ■ **se ~ sur le parcours d'une course/d'un cortège** to go and stand on the route of a race/procession.

postérieur, e [pɔsterjœr] *adj* **1.** [ultérieur - date, époque] later ; [- fait, invention] subsequent, later ■ **le tableau est ~ à 1930** the picture was painted after 1930 **2.** [de derrière - pattes] hind, rear, back *(modif)* ; [- partie] back, posterior *sout* **3.** PHON [voyelle, articulation] back *(modif)*.
◆ **postérieur** *nm fam* behind, bottom, posterior.

postérieurement [pɔsterjœrmɑ̃] *adv* later, subsequently, at a later date ■ **~ à** later than, after.

posteriori [pɔsterjɔri] **a posteriori**.

postériorité [pɔsterjɔrite] *nf sout* posteriority.

postérité [pɔsterite] *nf* **1.** *litt* [lignée] posterity, descendants **2.** [générations futures] posterity ■ **passer à la ~** [artiste] to become famous, to go down in history ; [mot, œuvre] to be handed down to posterity *OU* to future generations.

postface [pɔstfas] *nf* postscript, afterword.

posthume [pɔstym] *adj* [enfant, ouvrage] posthumous ■ **médaille décernée à titre ~** posthumously awarded medal.

postiche [pɔstiʃ] <> *adj* **1.** [cheveux, barbe, chignon] false **2.** *sout* [fictif] sham, spurious.
<> *nm* hairpiece.

postier, ère [pɔstje, ɛr] *nm, f* postal worker.

postillon [pɔstijɔ̃] *nm* **1.** [de salive] : **~s** spluttering **2.** [cocher] postilion **3.** PÊCHE slide float.

postillonner [3] [pɔstijɔne] *vi* to splutter.

postimpressionnisme [pɔstɛ̃presjɔnism] *nm* Postimpressionism.

postindustriel, elle [pɔstɛ̃dystrijɛl] *adj* postindustrial.

postmoderne [pɔstmɔdɛrn] *adj* postmodern.

postmodernisme [pɔstmɔdɛrnism] *nm* postmodernism.

postmoderniste [pɔstmɔdɛrnist] *adj* & *nmf* postmodernist.

postnatal, e, als *OU* **aux** [pɔstnatal, o] *adj* postnatal.

postopératoire [pɔstɔperatwar] *adj* postoperative.

postposer [3] [pɔstpoze] *vt* to place after ■ **un adjectif postposé** a postpositive adjective, an adjective that comes after the noun.

postposition [pɔstpozisjɔ̃] *nf* [particule] postposition.

post-scriptum [pɔstskriptɔm] *nm inv* postscript.

postsynchronisation [pɔstsɛ̃krɔnizasjɔ̃] *nf* postsynchronization.

postsynchroniser [3] [pɔstsɛ̃krɔnize] *vt* to post-synchronize.

postulant, e [pɔstylɑ̃, ɑ̃t] *nm, f* **1.** [à un emploi] applicant, candidate **2.** RELIG postulant.

postulat [pɔstyla] *nm* **1.** LOGIQUE & MATH postulate ■ **nous partons du ~ que...** we take it as axiomatic that... **2.** [principe de base] postulate **3.** RELIG postulancy.

postuler [3] [pɔstyle] <> *vt* **1.** [poste] to apply for **2.** LOGIQUE & MATH to postulate, to assume.
<> *vi* DR to represent.
◆ **postuler à** *v+prép* to apply for.

post(-)universitaire [pɔstynivɛrsitɛr] *adj* postgraduate.

postural, e, aux [pɔstyral, o] *adj* PHYSIOL postural.

posture [pɔstyr] *nf* **1.** [position du corps] posture, position ■ **prendre une ~ comique** to strike a comic pose ■ **dans une ~ inconfortable** in an uncomfortable position **2.** [situation] position ■ **être en bonne/en mauvaise ~** to be in a good/in an awkward position.

pot [po] *nm* **1.** [contenant] pot ■ **~ en étain/verre/terre** tin/glass/earthenware pot ■ **mettre en ~** [plantes] to pot ; [fruits, confitures] to put into jars ⊙ **~ à eau/lait** water/milk jug ■ **~ à** *OU* **de yaourt** yoghurt pot ■ **~ de chambre** (chamber) pot ; [pour enfant] pot, potty ■ **~ à confiture** *OU* **à confitures** jam jar ■ **~ de fleurs** [vide] flowerpot, plant pot ; [planté] flowers in a pot, potted flowers ■ **tourner autour du ~** to beat around the bush ■ **c'est le ~ de terre contre le ~ de fer** *La Fontaine allus* that's the danger of confronting someone more powerful than oneself ■ **c'est dans les vieux ~s qu'on fait les bonnes** *OU* **les meilleures soupes** *prov* experience always wins the day *prov*
2. [contenu] pot, potful ■ **~ de confiture/miel** jar of jam/honey ■ **~ de peinture** pot *OU* can of paint ■ **petit ~ (pour bébé)** (jar of) baby food
3. *fam* [boisson] drink, jar *UK*, snort *US* ■ [fête] : **ils font un ~ pour son départ à la retraite** they're having a little get-together for his retirement ■ **je suis invité à un ~ ce soir** I've been invited out for drinks tonight
4. *fam* [chance] luck ■ **avoir du ~** [souvent] to be lucky ; [à un certain moment] to be in luck ■ **il n'a pas de ~** [jamais] he's unlucky ; [en ce moment] he's out of luck ■ **pas de ~ !** hard *OU* tough luck! ■ **coup de ~** stroke of luck
5. *fam* [derrière] backside, bottom, bum *UK*

6. CARTES [talon] stock ■ [enjeux] pot
7. AUTO : ~ **d'échappement** exhaust (pipe) *UK*, tail pipe *US* ■ ~ **catalytique** catalytic converter.
◆ **en pot** *loc adj* [plante] pot *(modif)*, potted ■ [confiture, miel] in a jar.
◆ **pot de colle** *nm fig fam* nuisance ■ *(comme adj)* **elle est ~ de colle** she sticks to you like glue, you just can't get rid of her.

potable [pɔtabl] *adj* **1.** [buvable] : **eau ~** drinking water ■ **eau non ~** water unsuitable for drinking **2.** *fam* [acceptable - travail] passable, reasonable ; [- vêtement] wearable.

potache [pɔtaʃ] *nm fam* schoolkid ■ **blague de ~** schoolboy joke.

potage [pɔtaʒ] *nm* CULIN soup.

potager, ère [pɔtaʒe, ɛr] *adj* [culture] vegetable *(modif)* ■ [plante] grown for food, food *(modif)*.
◆ **potager** *nm* kitchen garden, vegetable plot.

potasse [pɔtas] *nf* **1.** [hydroxyde] potassium hydroxide, (caustic) potash **2.** [carbonate] (impure) potassium carbonate, potash.

potasser [3] [pɔtase] *vt fam* [discipline, leçon] to swot up *UK*, to bone up on *US* ■ [examen] to cram for.

potassium [pɔtasjɔm] *nm* potassium.

pot-au-feu [pɔtofø] *nm inv* CULIN pot-au-feu, beef and vegetable stew.

pot-de-vin [podvɛ̃] (*pl* **pots-de-vin**) *nm* bribe ■ **verser des pots-de-vin à qqn** to grease sb's palm, to bribe sb.

pote [pɔt] *nm fam* pal, mate *UK*, buddy *US*.

poteau, x [pɔto] *nm* **1.** [mât] post, pole ■ **~ indicateur** signpost ■ **~ télégraphique** telegraph pole *ou* post ■ **~ (d'exécution)** (execution) stake ■ **le proviseur, au ~!** *fam* down with the headmaster! **2.** SPORT [support de but] post, goal-post ■ **entre les ~x** between the goal posts *ou* the uprights ‖ [dans une course] : **~ d'arrivée** winning post ■ **~ de départ** starting post ■ **rester au ~** [cheval] to be left at the starting post ■ **se faire coiffer au** *ou* **battre sur le ~ (d'arrivée)** *pr* to be beaten at the (finishing) post ; *fig* to be pipped at the post *UK*, to be beaten by a nose *US* **3.** *fam vieilli* [ami] mate *UK*, buddy *US*.

potée [pɔte] *nf* **1.** pork hotpot *(with cabbage and root vegetables)* **2.** TECHNOL [d'étain] putty powder ■ [de fer] crocus, jeweller's rouge.

potelé, e [pɔtle] *adj* plump, chubby ■ **une petite bonne femme ~e** a dumpy little woman.

potelet [pɔtlɛ] *nm* bollard.

potence [pɔtɑ̃s] *nf* **1.** [supplice, instrument] gallows **2.** CONSTR [d'une charpente] post and braces ■ [pour une lanterne, une enseigne] support **3.** [d'une grue] crane jib.

potentat [pɔtɑ̃ta] *nm* **1.** *sout* [monarque] potentate **2.** [despote] despot ■ **il se comporte en vrai ~ avec ses employés** he's a real despot as far as his employees are concerned.

potentialiser [pɔtɑ̃sjalize] *vt* to potentiate.

potentialité [pɔtɑ̃sjalite] *nf* potentiality.

potentiel, elle [pɔtɑ̃sjɛl] *adj* potential ■ **un client ~** a prospective client.
◆ **potentiel** *nm* **1.** ÉLECTR, MATH, PHYS & PHYSIOL potential **2.** [possibilités] potential, potentiality ■ **avoir un certain ~** [personne] to have potential ▶ **~ de croissance** growth potential **3.** LING potential (mood).

potentiellement [pɔtɑ̃sjɛlmɑ̃] *adv* potentially.

poterie [pɔtri] *nf* **1.** [art] pottery **2.** [article] piece of pottery ■ **des ~s grecques** Greek pottery.

poterne [pɔtɛrn] *nf* [porte] postern.

potiche [pɔtiʃ] *nf* **1.** [vase] rounded vase **2.** *fam* [personne] figurehead *fig*, puppet *fig*.

potier, ère [pɔtje, ɛr] *nm, f* potter.

potin [pɔtɛ̃] *nm fam* [bruit] racket, rumpus ■ **faire du ~** [machine, personne] to make a racket ; [scandale, affaire] to cause a furore.
◆ **potins** *nmpl fam* [ragots] gossip, idle rumours ■ **(rubrique des) ~s mondains** society gossip (column).

potiner [3] [pɔtine] *vi fam* to gossip, to spread rumours.

potion [posjɔ̃] *nf* potion, draft ■ **~ magique** magic potion.

potiron [pɔtirɔ̃] *nm* pumpkin.

pot-pourri [popuri] (*pl* **pots-pourris**) *nm* **1.** MUS potpourri, medley **2.** LITTÉR potpourri **3.** [fleurs] potpourri.

pou, x [pu] *nm* **1.** [parasite de l'homme] louse ■ **des ~x** lice ■ **~ de tête/du corps** head/body louse **2.** *loc* **être laid** *ou* **moche** *fam* **comme un ~** to be as ugly as sin ■ **être fier** *ou* **orgueilleux comme un ~** to be as proud as a peacock.

pouah [pwa] *interj* ugh, yuck.

poubelle [pubɛl] *nf* **1.** [récipient à déchets] dustbin *UK*, trash *ou* garbage can *US* ■ **mettre** *ou* **jeter qqch à la ~** to put *ou* to throw sthg in the dustbin ■ **je vais mettre ces vieilles chaussures à la ~** I'm going to throw these old shoes out ■ **faire les ~s** to go scavenging (from the dustbins) **2.** [dépotoir] dumping-ground, rubbish *UK ou* garbage *US* dump **3.** INFORM recycle bin.

pouce [pus] *nm* **1.** ANAT [doigt] thumb ■ [orteil] big toe ■ **se tourner les ~s** *fam* to twiddle one's thumbs **2.** [dans un jeu] : **~!** pax! *UK*, time out! *US* **3.** [mesure] inch ■ **on n'avançait pas d'un ~ sur la route** the traffic was solid ■ **je ne changerai pas d'un ~ les dispositions de mon testament** I won't change one jot *ou* iota of my will **4.** *Québec loc* **faire du ~, voyager sur le ~** to hitchhike.

pouding [pudiŋ] = **pudding**.

poudrage [pudraʒ] *nm* **1.** [gén] (light) powdering *ou* sprinkling **2.** AGRIC dusting, crop-dusting.

poudre [pudr] *nf* **1.** [aliment, médicament] powder ■ [de craie, d'os, de diamant, d'or] dust, powder ■ **mettre** *ou* **réduire qqch en ~** to reduce sthg to powder, to pulverize *ou* to powder sthg ▶ **~ à éternuer** sneezing powder ■ **~ à laver** washing *UK ou* soap powder ■ **~ à récurer** scouring powder **2.** ARM powder, gunpowder ■ **~ à canon** gunpowder ■ **faire parler la ~** to settle the argument with guns **3.** [cosmétique - pour le visage] (face) powder ; [- pour une perruque] powder ■ **~ de riz** face powder ■ **~ compacte/libre** pressed/loose powder ■ **se mettre de la ~** to powder one's face *ou* nose **4.** *loc* **prendre la ~ d'escampette** to decamp ■ **jeter de la ~ aux yeux à qqn** to try to dazzle *ou* to impress sb ■ **tout ça c'est de la ~ aux yeux** all that's just for show ■ **~ de perlimpinpin** [faux remède] quack remedy **5.** △ *arg crime* [héroïne] smack△.
◆ **en poudre** *loc adj* [amandes, lait] powdered ■ **chocolat en ~** drinking chocolate ■ **noix de muscade en ~** ground nutmeg.

poudrer [3] [pudre] *vt* **1.** [maquiller] to powder **2.** *litt* [saupoudrer] : **la neige poudrait les arbres** the trees had a light powdering *ou* sprinkling of snow.
◆ **se poudrer** *vp (emploi réfléchi)* to powder one's nose *ou* face.

poudrerie [pudrəri] *nf* **1.** ARM gun-powder factory **2.** *Québec* [neige] flurry of snow.

poudreux, euse [pudrø, øz] *adj* [terre] dusty ■ [substance] powdery.
◆ **poudreuse** *nf* **1.** [neige] powdery snow, powder **2.** AGRIC sprinkler, powder-sprinkler.

poudrier [pudrije] *nm* (powder) compact.

poudrière [pudrijɛr] *nf* ARM (gun) powder store ■ **la maison était une vraie ~** the house was packed with explosives ‖ *fig* power keg.

poudroie *etc v* ▷ **poudroyer**.

poudroiement [pudrwamɑ̃] *nm litt* [de la neige] sparkle ■ [de la poussière] fine cloud.

poudroyer [13] [pudrwaje] *vi litt* [sable, neige] to rise in clouds ▪ [soleil, lumière] to shine hazily ▪ **au loin, la route poudroyait** in the distance, fine clouds of dust could be seen rising up from the road.

pouf[1] [puf] *nm* pouf, pouffe.

pouf[2] [puf] *onomat* [dans une chute] thump, bump ▪ **faire ~** to go thump ▪ **et ~, par terre!** whoops-a-daisy!

pouffer [3] [pufe] *vi* : **~ (de rire)** to titter.

pouf(f)iasse△ [pufjas] *nf péj* **1.** [femme vulgaire] cow **2.** *vieilli* [prostituée] tart△.

pouilleux, euse [pujø, øz] <> *adj* **1.** [couvert de poux] covered in lice, lousy, verminous **2.** [pauvre et sale - individu] grubby, filthy ; [- restaurant, quartier] shabby, seedy.
<> *nm, f péj* grubby person ▪ **sur ce, arrive une espèce de ~** in comes a scruffy wretch.

poujadisme [puʒadism] *nm* POLIT & *fig* **le ~** Poujadism.

poulailler [pulaje] *nm* **1.** [hangar] hen house ▪ [cour] henrun **2.** *fam* THÉÂTRE : **le ~** the gods *UK*, the peanut gallery *US*.

poulain [pulɛ̃] *nm* **1.** ZOOL colt **2.** [protégé] (young) protégé ▪ **il avait plusieurs ~s** he had several young people under his patronage.

poulaine [pulɛn] *nf* **1.** [chaussure] poulaine **2.** NAUT head.

poularde [pulard] *nf* fattened hen, poulard, poularde.

poulbot [pulbo] *nm* (Montmartre) urchin.

poule [pul] *nf* **1.** ZOOL hen ▪ **~ d'eau** moorhen ▪ **la ~ aux œufs d'or** the goose that laid the golden eggs ▪ **se coucher avec les ~s** to go to bed very early ▪ **se lever avec les ~s** to be an early riser ▪ **~ mouillée** drip ▪ **quand les ~s auront des dents : ton argent, tu le reverras quand les ~s auront des dents** you can kiss your money good-bye ▪ **tu crois qu'on va avoir une augmentation? – c'est ça, quand les ~s auront des dents!** do you think we're going to have a pay rise? – and pigs might fly! ▪ **une ~ n'y retrouverait pas ses poussins** it's an awful mess ▪ **la ~ ne doit pas chanter devant le coq** *prov* it's the man who should wear the trousers **2.** CULIN (boiling) fowl ▪ **~ au riz** boiled chicken with rice ▪ **~ au pot** *casseroled chicken with vegetables* **3.** *fam* [maîtresse] mistress ▪ *vieilli* [prostituée] whore, tart△ **4.** *fam* [terme d'affection] : **ma ~** (my) pet, (my) love **5.** *(comme adj)* **c'est une mère ~** she's a real mother hen ▪ **c'est un papa ~** he's a real mother hen *hum* **6.** SPORT pool *(in a round robin)* ▪ **en ~ A, Metz bat Béziers** in group *OU* pool A Metz beat Béziers ▮ ÉQUIT : **~ d'essai** 1,600 m maiden race.

poulet [pulɛ] *nm* **1.** CULIN & ZOOL chicken ▪ **~ de grain** corn-fed chicken **2.** △ [policier] cop, copper *UK* **3.** *fam* [terme d'affection] : **mon ~** my pet, (my) love **4.** *fam* [lettre galante] love letter.

poulette [pulɛt] *nf* **1.** ZOOL pullet **2.** *fam* [terme d'affection] : **ma ~** (my) pet, (my) love **3.** *fam* [femme] bird *UK*, chick *US*.
◆ **à la poulette** *loc adj* CULIN with a poulette sauce *(made from butter, cream and egg yolks)*.

pouliche [puliʃ] *nf* filly.

poulie [puli] *nf* [roue] pulley ▪ [avec enveloppe] block ▪ **~ folle** idler.

pouliner [3] [puline] *vi* to foal.

poulinière [pulinjɛr] <> *nf* brood mare.
<> *adj f* ▻ **jument**.

poulpe [pulp] *nm* octopus.

pouls [pu] *nm* MÉD pulse ▪ **prendre le ~ de** [malade] to feel *OU* to take the pulse of ▪ **prendre** *OU* **tâter le ~ de** [électorat] to feel the pulse of, to sound out ; [entreprise, secteur] to feel the pulse of.

poumon [pumɔ̃] *nm* lung ▪ **~ artificiel** *OU* **d'acier** artificial *OU* iron lung.

poupard [pupar] *nm* [bébé] chubby-cheeked baby.

poupe [pup] *nf* stern.

poupée [pupe] *nf* **1.** [figurine] doll ▪ **jouer à la ~** to play with dolls ● **~ de chiffon/cire/porcelaine** rag/wax/china doll ▪ **~ qui parle/marche** talking/walking doll ▪ **~ Barbie®** Barbie® doll ▪ **~ de son** stuffed doll ▪ **~ gonflable** blow-up doll ▪ **des ~s gigognes** *OU* **russes** a set of Russian dolls **2.** *fam* [jolie femme] doll, looker **3.** *fam* [bandage] (large) finger bandage **4.** MÉCAN [gén] headstock ▪ [d'un tour] poppet.
◆ **de poupée** *loc adj* : **une chambre de ~** a doll's bedroom ▪ **un visage de ~** a doll-like face.

poupin, e [pupɛ̃, in] *adj* [visage] chubby.

poupon [pupɔ̃] *nm* **1.** [bébé] little baby **2.** [jouet] baby doll.

pouponner [3] [pupɔne] *vi fam* to look after babies *OU* a baby.

pouponnière [pupɔnjɛr] *nf* nursery *(for babies and toddlers who can neither stay with their parents nor be fostered)*.

pour [pur] <> *prép* **1.** [indiquant le lieu où l'on va] for ▪ **partir ~ l'Italie** to leave for Italy ▪ **un billet ~ Paris** a ticket for *OU* to Paris ▪ **je m'envole ~ Rome** I'm flying to Rome
2. [dans le temps - indiquant le moment] for ▪ **pourriez-vous avoir fini ~ lundi/demain?** could you have it finished for Monday/tomorrow? ▪ **~ dans une semaine** for a week's time ▪ **j'ai repeint la chambre ~ quand tu viendras** I've redecorated the room for when you visit ▪ [indiquant la durée] for ▪ **partir ~ 10 jours** to go away for 10 days ▪ **il n'en a plus ~ longtemps** he won't be long now ; [à vivre] he hasn't got long to live ▪ **j'en ai bien ~ cinq heures** it'll take me at least five hours
3. [exprimant la cause] : **je l'ai remercié ~ son amabilité** I thanked him for his kindness ▪ **ils se querellent ~ des broutilles** they quarrel over trifles ▪ **désolé ~ dimanche** sorry about Sunday ▪ **il est tombé malade ~ avoir mangé trop d'huîtres** he fell ill after eating *OU* because he ate too many oysters ▪ **condamné ~ vol** found guilty of theft ● **sa bonne constitution y est ~ quelque chose** his strong constitution had something to do with *OU* played a part in it ▪ **elle est ~ beaucoup dans le succès de la pièce** the success of the play is to a large extent due to her, she has had a great deal to do with the success of the play ▪ **ne me remerciez pas, je n'y suis ~ rien** don't thank me, I didn't have anything to do with it
4. [exprimant la conséquence] to ▪ **~ la plus grande joie des enfants** to the children's great delight ▪ **il a erré trois heures en forêt ~ se retrouver à son point de départ** he wandered for three hours in the forest, only to find he was back where he'd started from ▪ **ses paroles n'étaient pas ~ me rassurer** his words were far from reassuring to me ▪ **ce n'est pas ~ me déplaire** I can't say I'm displeased with it
5. [capable de] : **je me suis trompé et il ne s'est trouvé personne ~ me le dire** I made a mistake and nobody was capable of telling me
6. [par rapport à] for ▪ **il est en avance ~ son âge** he's advanced for his age ▪ **c'est cher ~ ce que c'est** it's expensive for what it is
7. [avec une valeur emphatique] : **mot ~ mot** word for word ▪ **~ un champion, c'est un champion!** that's what I call a (real) champion! ▪ **perdre ~ perdre, autant que ce soit en beauté** if we are going to lose, we might as well do it in style ▪ **~ être en colère, je l'étais!** I was so angry!
8. [indiquant une proportion, un pourcentage] per ▪ **cinq ~ cent** five per cent ▪ **il faut 200 g de farine ~ une demi-livre de beurre** take 200 g of flour to *OU* for half a pound of butter
9. [moyennant] : **~ la somme de** for the sum of ▪ **il y en a bien ~ 80 euros de réparation** the repairs will cost at least 80 euros
10. [à la place de] for ▪ **prendre un mot ~ un autre** to mistake a word for another
11. [au nom de] for, on behalf of ▪ **~ le directeur** [dans la correspondance] pp Director
12. [en guise de, en qualité de] : **prendre qqn ~ époux/épouse** to take sb to be one's husband/wife ▪ **avoir qqn ~ ami/professeur** to have sb as a friend/teacher ▪ **j'ai son fils ~ élève** his son is one of my pupils ▪ **~ tout remerciement voilà ce que j'ai eu** that's all the thanks I got ▪ **avoir ~ conséquence** to have as a consequence ▪ **j'ai ~ principe que...** I believe on principle that... ▪ **il se fait passer ~ un antiquaire** he claims to be an antique dealer ▪ **le livre a ~ titre...** the book's title is..., the book is entitled...
13. [indiquant l'attribution, la destination, le but] for ▪ **mes sentiments ~ elle** my feelings towards *OU* for her ▪ **tant pis ~ lui!** that's too bad (for him)! ▪ **c'est ~ quoi faire, ce truc?** what's that thing for? ▪ **sirop ~ la toux** cough mixture ▪ **voyager ~ son plai-**

sir to travel for pleasure ■ **l'art ~ l'art** art for art's sake ■ **~ 4 personnes** [recette] serves 4 ; [couchage] sleeps 4 ➋ **c'est fait ~** that's what it's (there) for

14. *(suivi de l'infin)* [afin de] (in order) to ■ **je suis venu ~ vous voir** I'm here *ou* I've come to see you ■ *(elliptiquement)* **si tu veux réussir, il faut tout faire ~** if you want to succeed you have to do everything possible

15. [en faveur de] for, in favour of ■ **voter ~ qqn** to vote for *ou* in favour of sb ■ **il a ~ lui de nombreuses qualités** he has a number of qualities in his favour ➋ **être ~** to be in favour ■ **je suis ~ qu'on s'y mette tout de suite** I'm in favour of getting down to it immediately

16. [du point de vue de] : **ça compte peu ~ toi, mais ~ moi c'est tellement important** it matters little to you but to *ou* for me it's so important ■ **~ moi, il a dû se réconcilier avec elle** if you ask me, he must have made it up with her

17. [en ce qui concerne] : **et ~ le salaire?** and what about the salary? ■ **ne t'en fais pas ~ moi** don't worry about me ■ **~ certains de nos collègues, la situation est inchangée** as far as some of our colleagues are concerned, the situation has not changed ■ **~ ce qui est de l'avancement, voyez avec le responsable du personnel** as far as promotion is concerned, see the personnel officer

18. *sout* [exprimant la concession] : **~ être jeune, elle n'en est pas moins compétente** young though she is she's very able ‖ [en corrélation avec 'que'] : **~ patient qu'il soit, il ne supportera pas cette situation** for all his patience, he won't put up with this situation

19. *(suivi de l'infin) litt* [sur le point de] about to, on the point of ■ **il était ~ partir** he was about to leave *ou* on the point of leaving.

◇ *nm inv* : **peser le ~ et le contre** to weigh up the pros and cons ■ **les ~ l'emportent** POLIT & *hum* the argument in favour is overwhelming, the ayes have it.

◆ **pour que** *loc conj* **1.** [exprimant le but] so that, in order that *formal* ■ **j'ai pris des places non-fumeurs ~ que vous ne soyez pas incommodés par la fumée** I've got non-smoking seats so that you won't be bothered by the smoke

2. [exprimant la conséquence] : **il est assez malin ~ qu'on ne l'arrête pas** he is cunning enough to avoid being caught ■ **mon appartement est trop petit ~ qu'on puisse tous y dormir** my flat is too small for us all to be able to sleep there.

pourboire [purbwar] *nm* tip ■ **donner un ~ à qqn** to give a tip to sb, to tip sb ■ **j'ai laissé trois euros de ~** I left a 3 euros tip.

pourceau, x [purso] *nm litt* **1.** [porc] pig, hog *US* **2.** [homme - sale] pig ; [- vicieux] animal.

pour-cent [pursɑ̃] *nm inv* FIN percentage.

pourcentage [pursɑ̃taʒ] *nm* **1.** FIN & MATH percentage ■ **ça fait combien, en ~?** what's the percentage figure? **2.** COMM percentage, commission ■ **travailler au ~** to work on commission *ou* on a percentage basis ■ **être payé au ~** to be paid by commission.

pourchasser [3] [purʃase] *vt* **1.** [criminel] to chase, to pursue ■ **pourchassé par ses créanciers** pursued *ou* hounded by his creditors **2.** *sout* [erreur, abus] to track down *(sép)* ■ **nous pourchasserons les injustices** we'll root out injustice wherever we find it.

pourfendeur, euse [purfɑ̃dœr, øz] *nm, f litt* **~ d'idées reçues/de l'hypocrisie** declared *ou* sworn enemy of received ideas/of hypocrisy.

pourfendre [73] [purfɑ̃dr] *vt litt* **1.** [avec une épée - ennemi] to kill (by the sword) **2.** [hypocrisie, préjugés] to combat.

pourlécher [18] [purleʃe] ◆ **se pourlécher** ◇ *vpi* to lick one's lips.
◇ *vpt* : **je m'en pourlèche les babines à l'avance** *hum* my mouth is watering already.

pourparlers [purparle] *nmpl* negotiations, talks ■ **être/entrer en ~ avec qqn** to have/to enter into talks *ou* negotiations with sb.

pourpoint [purpwɛ̃] *nm* doublet, pourpoint ■ **des personnages en ~** characters wearing doublet and hose.

pourpre [purpr] ◇ *adj* crimson ■ **son visage devint ~** he went *ou* turned crimson.
◇ *nm* **1.** [couleur] crimson **2.** [mollusque] murex, purple fish.
◇ *nf* **1.** [teinte] purple (dye) **2.** RELIG : **la ~** [robe] the purple ■ **revêtir la ~ cardinalice** to don the red hat.

pourpré, e [purpre] *adj litt* crimson.

pourquoi [purkwa] ◇ *adv* why ■ **~ m'avoir menti?** why did you lie to me? ■ **~ cet air triste?** why are you looking so sad? ■ **~ chercher des difficultés?** why make things more complicated? ■ **~ pas?** why not? ■ **elle a bien réussi l'examen, ~ pas moi?** she passed the exam, why shouldn't I? ■ **~ ça?** why? ■ **et ~ donc?** but why? ■ **je ne sais pas ~ tu dis ça** I don't know why you're saying that ■ **voilà ~ je démissionne** that's (the reason) why I am resigning, that's the reason for my resignation ■ **il boude, va savoir** *ou* **comprendre ~!** he's sulking, don't ask me why!
◇ *nm inv* : **nous ne saurons jamais le ~ de cette affaire** we'll never get to the bottom of this affair ■ **il s'interroge toujours sur le ~ et le comment des choses** he's always bothered about the whys and wherefores of everything ■ **dans sa lettre, il explique le ~ de son suicide** in his letter, he explains the reason *ou* reasons for his suicide.

pourra *etc v* ⊳ **pouvoir**.

pourri, e [puri] ◇ *adj* **1.** [nourriture] rotten, bad ■ [planche, arbre, plante] rotten ■ [dent] rotten, decayed ■ [chairs] decomposed, putrefied ■ **complètement ~** rotten to the core **2.** *fam* [mauvais - climat, saison] rotten ; [- individu, système] stinking, rotten ■ **elle est complètement ~e ta voiture!** your car is a wreck *ou* is nothing but a pile of rust! ■ **vous pouvez le garder, votre boulot ~!** *fam* you can keep your stinking job! **3.** [trop gâté - enfant] spoilt **4.** *fam* **~ de** [plein de] : **il est ~ de fric** he's stinking rich *ou* loaded ■ **être ~ d'orgueil/d'ambition** to be eaten up with pride/ambition.
◇ *nm, f fam* [terme d'injure] swine ■ **tas de ~s!** you rotten swine!
◆ **pourri** *nm* [partie pourrie] rotten *ou* bad part.

pourrir [32] [purir] ◇ *vi* **1.** [se gâter - fruit, légume, viande, œuf] to go rotten, to go bad *ou* *UK* off ; [- planche, arbre] to rot ; [- végétation, dent] to decay, to rot ; [- chairs] to decay, to putrefy ■ **~ sur pied** to rot on the stalk ■ **la pluie a fait ~ toute la récolte** the rain rotted the entire harvest **2.** *fig* **laisser ~ une situation** to let a situation deteriorate **3.** *fam* [croupir - personne] to rot ■ **~ en prison** to rot in prison.
◇ *vt* **1.** [putréfier - nourriture] to rot, to putrefy ; [- végétation, dent] to decay **2.** [gâter - enfant] to spoil **3.** [pervertir - individu] to corrupt, to spoil ; [- société] to corrupt.

pourrissant, e [purisɑ̃, ɑ̃t] *adj* [chairs] putrescent, putrefying, decaying ■ **des fruits ~s** rotting fruit.

pourrissement [purismɑ̃] *nm* **1.** [de fruits, du bois, de la viande] rotting ■ [de chairs] putrefaction ■ [d'une dent, de la végétation] decay, rotting, decaying **2.** [d'une situation] deterioration.

pourriture [purityr] *nf* **1.** [partie pourrie] rotten part *ou* bit **2.** [état] rottenness **3.** [corruption] rottenness, corruption **4.** *fam* [personne] rotten swine.

pour-soi [purswa] *nm inv* pour-soi.

poursuit *etc v* ⊳ **poursuivre**.

poursuite [pursɥit] *nf* **1.** [pour rattraper - animal, fugitif] chase ■ **~ en voiture** car chase ■ **les voilà partis dans une ~ effrénée** off they go in hot pursuit ■ **ils sont à la ~ des voleurs** [ils courent] they're chasing the thieves ; [ils enquêtent] they're on the trail of the thieves ■ **se mettre** *ou* **se lancer à la ~ de qqn** to set off in pursuit of sb, to give chase to sb **2.** [prolongation - de pourparlers, d'études, de recherches] continuation ■ **ils ont décidé la ~ de la grève** they've decided to carry on *ou* to continue with the strike **3.** [recherche - du bonheur, d'un rêve] pursuit **4.** ASTRONAUT tracking **5.** SPORT pursuit.
◆ **poursuites** *nfpl* DR : **~s (judiciaires)** [en droit civil] legal proceedings ; [en droit pénal] prosecution ■ **entamer** *ou* **engager des ~s contre qqn** [en droit civil] to institute legal proceedings *ou* to take legal action against sb ; [en droit pénal] to prosecute sb ■ **vous pouvez faire l'objet de ~s** you're liable to prosecution.

poursuivant, e [pursɥivɑ̃, ɑ̃t] <> *adj* DR : **la partie ~e** the plaintiff.
<> *nm, f* **1.** [dans une course] pursuer **2.** DR plaintiff.

poursuivre [89] [pursɥivr] *vt* **1.** [courir après - animal, voleur, voiture] to chase (after), to pursue *sout* ▪ **il sentait leurs regards qui le poursuivaient** he could feel their eyes following *ou* on him **2.** [s'acharner contre - suj: créancier, rival] to hound, to harry, to pursue ; [- suj: image, passé, remords] to haunt, to hound, to pursue ▪ **~ qqn de ses assiduités** to pester sb with one's attentions ▪ **il est poursuivi par la malchance** he is dogged *ou* pursued by misfortune **3.** [continuer - interrogatoire, récit, recherche, voyage] to go *ou* to carry on with *(insép)*, to continue ; [- lutte] to continue, to pursue ▪ **~ son chemin** to press on ▪ **elle poursuivit sa lecture** she carried on reading, she read on ▪ **ils poursuivirent la discussion jusqu'à une heure tardive** they went on talking into the night ▪ **"quelques années plus tard", poursuivit-il** "a few years later", he went on ▪ *(en usage absolu)* **veuillez ~, Monsieur** please proceed, sir ▪ **bien, poursuivons** right, let's go on *ou* continue **4.** [aspirer à - objectif] to pursue, to strive towards *(insép)* ; [- rêve] to pursue ; [- plaisirs] to pursue, to seek **5.** DR : **~ qqn (en justice)** [en droit civil] to institute (legal) proceedings against *ou* to sue sb ; [en droit pénal] to prosecute sb ▪ **être poursuivi pour détournement de fonds** to be prosecuted for embezzlement.
◆ **se poursuivre** <> *vp (emploi réciproque)* [se courir après] to chase one another *ou* each other.
<> *vpi* [se prolonger - pourparlers, recherches] to go on, to continue ; [- opération] to go on.

pourtant [purtɑ̃] *adv* **1.** [malgré tout] yet, even so, all the same ▪ **elle est ~ bien gentille** and yet she's very nice ▪ **il faut ~ bien que quelqu'un le fasse** somebody has to do it all the same ▪ **et ~** and yet **2.** [emploi expressif] : **c'est ~ simple!** but it's quite simple! ▪ **il n'est pas bête, ~!** he's not exactly stupid! ▪ **je t'avais ~ prévenu...!** I did warn you...!

pourtour [purtur] *nm* **1.** [délimitation - d'un terrain] perimeter ; [- d'un globe] circumference **2.** [bordure - d'un plat] edge, rim ; [- d'une feuille] edge ; [- d'une baignoire] surround.

pourvoi [purvwa] *nm* DR appeal ▪ **il a présenté un ~ en cassation** he has taken his case to the Appeal Court ▪ **~ en révision** review.

pourvoir [64] [purvwar] *vt* **1.** [équiper] : **~ qqn de** *ou* **en** [outils] to equip *ou* to provide sb with ; [vivres, documents] to provide sb with ▪ **~ qqch de** to equip *ou* to fit sthg with **2.** [doter] : **la nature l'a pourvue d'une remarquable intelligence** nature has endowed *ou* graced her with extraordinary intelligence ▪ **ses parents l'ont pourvu d'une solide éducation** his parents provided him with a sound education ▪ **la cigogne est pourvue d'un long bec** storks have *ou* possess long beaks **3.** [remplir - emploi] to fill ▪ **le poste est toujours à ~** the post is still vacant *ou* is still to be filled.
◆ **pourvoir à** *v+prép* [besoin] to provide *ou* to cater for ▪ [dépense] to pay for ▪ **nous pourvoirons au transport des médicaments** we will provide for *ou* deal with the transport of medicine.
◆ **se pourvoir** *vpi* DR to appeal ▪ **se ~ en cassation** to take one's case to the Supreme Court of Appeal.
◆ **se pourvoir de** *vp+prép* [se munir de] : **se ~ d'outils** to equip o.s. with tools ▪ **se ~ de vivres** to provide o.s. with food.

pourvoyeur, euse [purvwajœr, øz] *nm, f* [d'armes, de marchandises] supplier ▪ [de drogue] dealer.
◆ **pourvoyeur** *nm* MIL ammunition server.

pourvoyons *etc v* ▻ **pourvoir**.

pourvu, e [purvy] <> *pp* ▻ **pourvoir**.
<> *adj* : **bien ~** well-off, well-provided for.

pourvu que [purvykə] *(devant voyelle ou h muet pourvu qu'* [purvyk]*) loc conj* **1.** [exprimant un souhait] : **pourvu qu'il vienne!** I hope *ou* let's hope he's coming! **2.** [exprimant une condition] provided (that), so *ou* as long as ▪ **tout ira bien ~ vous soyez à l'heure** everything will be fine so long as you're on time.

pourvut *etc v* ▻ **pourvoir**.

pousse [pus] *nf* **1.** ANAT growth **2.** BOT [bourgeon] (young) shoot, sprout ▪ [début de croissance] sprouting ▪ [développement] growth ▪ **ma plante fait des ~s** my plant is sprouting new leaves ▶ **~s de bambou** bamboo shoots ▪ **~s de soja** beansprouts **3.** [de la pâte à pain] proving.

poussé, e [puse] *adj* **1.** [fouillé - interrogatoire] thorough, probing, searching ; [- recherche, technique] advanced ; [- description] thorough, exhaustive ▪ **d'une efficacité très ~e** highly efficient ▪ **je n'ai pas fait d'études ~es** I didn't stay in education very long **2.** [exagéré] excessive ▪ **35 euros pour une coupe, c'est un peu ~!** 35 euros for a haircut is a bit steep! **3.** AUTO [moteur] customized.

pousse-café [puskafe] *nm inv fam* liqueur, pousse-café ▪ **voulez-vous un ~?** would you like a liqueur with your coffee?

poussée [puse] *nf* **1.** CONSTR, GÉOL & PHYS thrust ▪ **~ d'Archimède** upthrust buoyancy **2.** [pression] push, shove, thrust ▪ **la barrière a cédé sous la ~ des manifestants** the barrier gave way under the pressure of the demonstrators **3.** MÉD eruption, outbreak ▪ **le bébé fait une petite ~ de boutons rouges** the baby has a red rash ▪ **faire une ~ de fièvre** to have a sudden rise in temperature ▪ **une ~ d'adrénaline** a surge of adrenalin **4.** [progression] upsurge, rise ▪ **une ~ de racisme** an upsurge of racism ▪ **une ~ de l'inflation** a rise in inflation **5.** [attaque] thrust ▪ **la ~ des troupes hitlériennes contre la Pologne** the thrust *ou* offensive of Hitler's troops against Poland **6.** AÉRON & ASTRONAUT thrust.

pousse-pousse [puspus] *nm inv* **1.** [en Extrême-Orient] rickshaw **2.** *Suisse* [poussette] pushchair *UK*, baby buggy® *UK*, stroller *US*.

pousser [3] [puse] <> *vt* **1.** [faire avancer - caddie, fauteuil roulant, landau] to push, to wheel (along) ; [- moto en panne] to push, to walk ; [- caisse] to push (along) *ou* forward ; [- pion] to move forward ▪ **on va ~ la voiture** [sur une distance] we'll push the car (along) ; [pour la faire démarrer] we'll push-start the car, we'll give the car a push (to start it) ▪ **ils essayaient de ~ les manifestants vers la place** they were trying to drive *ou* to push the demonstrators towards the square ▪ **je me sentais irrésistiblement poussé vers elle** I was irresistibly attracted to her
2. [enclencher, appuyer sur - bouton, interrupteur] to push (in) *(sép)*, to press on *(insép)* ▪ **~ un levier vers le haut/bas** to push a lever up/down ▪ **~ un verrou** [pour ouvrir] to slide a bolt out ; [pour fermer] to slide a bolt in *ou* home ▪ **~ une porte** [doucement, pour l'ouvrir] to push a door open ; [doucement, pour la fermer] to push a door to *ou* shut
3. [bousculer] to push, to shove ▪ **~ qqn du coude** [pour l'alerter, accidentellement] to nudge sb with one's elbow
4. [enlever] to push (away), to push *ou* to shove aside *(sép)* ▪ **pousse ton derrière de là!** *fam* shift up! *UK*, shove over!
5. [inciter, entraîner - personne] to spur on *(sép)*, to drive ▪ **c'est l'orgueil qui le pousse** he is spurred on *ou* driven by pride ▪ **on n'a pas eu à le ~ beaucoup pour qu'il accepte** he didn't need much pressing *ou* persuasion to accept ▪ **~ qqn à qqch : ~ qqn à la consommation** to encourage sb to buy *ou* to consume ▪ **~ qqn au désespoir/suicide** to drive sb to despair/suicide ▪ **sa curiosité l'a poussé à l'indiscrétion** his curiosity made him indiscreet ▪ **~ qqn à faire qqch** [suj: curiosité, jalousie] to drive sb to do sthg ; [suj: pitié soudaine] to prompt sb to do sthg ; [suj: personne] to incite sb to do *ou* to push sb into doing *ou* to prompt sb to do sthg ▪ **~ qqn à boire** to drive sb to drink ▪ **elle le pousse à divorcer** [elle l'en persuade] she's talking him into getting a divorce
6. [poursuivre - recherches] to press on *ou* to carry on with *(insép)* ; [- discussion, études, analyse] to continue, to carry on (with) ; [- argumentation] to carry on (with) *(insép)*, to push further ; [- comparaison, interrogatoire] to take further ; [- avantage] to press home *(insép)* ▪ **en poussant plus loin l'examen de leur comptabilité** by probing deeper into their accounts ▪ **~ la plaisanterie un peu loin** to take *ou* to carry the joke a bit too far ▪ **elle a poussé l'audace jusqu'à...** she was bold enough to... ▪ [aux enchères] : **~ un tableau** to push up the price of a painting
7. [forcer - moteur] to push ; [- voiture] to drive hard *ou* fast ; [- chauffage] to turn up *(sép)* ; [- son] to turn up *(sép)* ▪ [exiger

un effort de - étudiant, employé] to push ; [- cheval] to urge *ou* to spur on *(sép)* ■ [encourager - candidat, jeune artiste] to push ■ **si tu la pousses un peu sur le sujet, tu verras qu'elle ne sait pas grand-chose** if you push her a bit on the subject, you'll see that she doesn't know much about it
8. [émettre] : **~ un cri** [personne] to cry, to utter *ou* to let out a cry ; [oiseau] to call ■ **~ un soupir** to sigh, to heave a sigh ■ **~ des cris/hurlements de douleur** to scream/to yell with pain ▶ **~ la chansonnette** *fam* *ou* **la romance** *fam*, **en ~ une** *fam* to sing a song
9. AGRIC & BOT [plante, animal] to force.
◇ *vi* **1.** [grandir - arbre, poil, ongle] to grow ; [- dent] to come through ■ **les plants de tomates poussent bien** the tomato plants are doing well ■ **ses dents commencent à ~** he's cutting his teeth, he's teething ■ **et les enfants, ça pousse?** *fam* how're the kids (then), growing *ou* shooting up? ■ **des tours poussent partout dans mon quartier** there are high-rise blocks springing up all over the place where I live ■ **et si tu laissais ~ ta barbe?** what about growing *ou* why don't you grow a beard? ■ **elle a laissé ~ ses cheveux** she's let her hair grow
2. [avancer] to push on ■ **poussons un peu plus loin** let's go *ou* push on a bit further
3. *fam* [exagérer] : **deux heures de retard, tu pousses!** you're two hours late, that's a bit much! ■ **je veux 25 % d'augmentation – tu ne trouves pas que tu pousses un peu?** I want a 25% pay rise – don't you think that's pushing it a bit? ■ **faut pas ~!** enough's enough!
4. [bousculer] to push, to shove ■ **ne poussez pas, il y en aura pour tout le monde!** stop shoving *ou* pushing, there's plenty for everyone!
5. [appuyer] to push ■ **~ sur** : **~ sur un bouton** to push a button ■ **~ sur ses pieds/jambes** to push with one's feet/legs ■ **'poussez'** 'push'
6. PHYSIOL [à la selle] to strain ■ [dans l'enfantement] to push.
◆ **se pousser** ◇ *vp (emploi passif)* to be pushed ■ **la manette se pousse d'un seul doigt** the lever can be pushed with a single finger.
◇ *vp (emploi réciproque)* : **les gens se poussaient pour voir arriver le Président** people were pushing and shoving to get a look at the President.
◇ *vpi* **1.** [se déplacer] to move ■ **tu peux te ~ un peu?** [dans une rangée de chaises] could you move along a bit *ou* a few places? ; [sur un canapé, dans un lit] could you move over slightly? ■ **pousse-toi de là, tu vois bien que tu gênes!** *fam* move over *ou* shove over, can't you see you're in the way? ■ **pousse-toi de devant la télé!** *fam* stop blocking the TV!
2. *fam* [hiérarchiquement] : **se ~ dans une entreprise** to make one's way up (the ladder) in a firm.

poussette [pusɛt] *nf* [pour enfant] pushchair *UK*, stroller *US* ■ [à provisions] shopping trolley *UK ou* cart *US*.

poussette-canne [pusɛtkan] (*pl* **poussettes-cannes**) *nf* folding pushchair *UK ou* stroller *US*.

poussier [pusje] *nm* coal dust.

poussière [pusjɛr] *nf* **1.** [terre sèche, salissures] dust ■ **la voiture souleva un nuage de ~** the car raised a cloud of dust ■ **tu en fais de la ~ en balayant!** you're making *ou* raising a lot of dust with your broom! ■ **prendre la ~** to collect dust ■ **faire la ~** to dust, to do the dusting ■ **mettre** *ou* **réduire qqch en ~** to smash sthg to smithereens ■ **tomber en ~** to crumble into dust **2.** [dans l'œil] mote *litt*, piece of grit **3.** [particules - de roche, de charbon, d'or] dust ■ **~ cosmique/interstellaire** cosmic/interstellar dust ■ **~ radioactive** radioactive particles *ou* dust.
◆ **poussières** *nfpl fam* **50 euros et des ~s** just over 50 euros.

poussiéreux, euse [pusjerø, øz] *adj* **1.** [couvert de poussière] dusty, dust-covered ■ **vitres poussiéreuses** grimy windows **2.** *sout* [dépassé - législation, théorie] outmoded, outdated.

poussif, ive [pusif, iv] *adj* **1.** [essoufflé - cheval] broken-winded ; [- vieillard] short-winded, wheezy ; [- locomotive] puffing, wheezing **2.** [laborieux - prose] dull, flat, laboured ; [- campagne électorale, émission] sluggish, dull.

poussin [pusɛ̃] *nm* **1.** ZOOL chick ■ COMM poussin **2.** *fam* [terme d'affection] : **mon ~** my pet *ou* darling ■ **pauvre petit ~!** poor little thing! **3.** SPORT under-eleven *(member of junior team or club)* **4.** *arg mil first-year student in the French Air Force training school.*

poussive [pusiv] *f* ▷ **poussif.**

poussivement [pusivmɑ̃] *adv* : **monter ~** to puff *ou* to wheeze (one's way) up ■ **le train avançait ~** the train was wheezing *ou* puffing along.

poussoir [puswar] *nm* **1.** [d'une montre] button **2.** MÉCAN tappet.

poutre [putr] *nf* **1.** CONSTR [en bois] beam ■ [en fer] girder ■ **~ apparente** exposed beam **2.** SPORT beam ■ **exercices à la ~** beam exercises.

poutrelle [putrɛl] *nf* **1.** CONSTR [en bois] small beam ■ [en fer] small girder **2.** MÉTALL I-beam.

poutser [3] [putse] *vt Suisse fam* to clean.

pouvoir¹ [puvwar] *nm* **1.** [aptitude, possibilité] power ■ **avoir un grand ~ de concentration/de persuasion** to have great powers of concentration/persuasion ■ **je n'ai pas le ~ de lire l'avenir!** I cannot predict the future! ■ **il n'est plus en notre ~ de décider de la question** we're no longer in a position to decide on this matter ■ **je ferai tout ce qui est en mon ~ pour t'aider** I'll do everything *ou* all in my power to help you ▶ **~ d'achat** ÉCON purchasing power
2. ADMIN & DR [d'un président, d'un tuteur] power ■ **avoir ~ de décision** to have the authority to decide ▶ **~ disciplinaire** disciplinary powers
3. POLIT : **le ~** [exercice] power ; [gouvernants] government ■ **elle est trop proche du ~ pour comprendre** she's too close to the seat of power to understand ■ **arriver au ~** to come to power ■ **être au ~** [parti élu] to be in power *ou* office ; [junte] to be in power ■ **les gens au ~ ne connaissent pas nos problèmes** those in power *ou* the powers that be don't understand our difficulties ■ **prendre le ~** [élus] to take office ; [dictateur] to seize power ■ **exercer le ~** to exercise power, to govern, to rule ▶ **le ~ central** central government ■ **le ~ exécutif** executive power, the executive ■ **le ~ judiciaire** judicial power, the judiciary ■ **le ~ législatif** legislative power, the legislature ■ **le ~ local** local government, the local authorities
4. [influence] power, influence ■ **avoir du ~ sur qqn** to have power *ou* influence over sb ■ **avoir qqn en son ~** to have sb in one's power
5. PHYS & TECHNOL power, quality ■ **~ calorifique (inférieur)/supérieur** (net)/gross calorific value ■ **~ couvrant (d'une peinture)** opacity (of a paint) ■ **~ isolant** insulating capacity.
◆ **pouvoirs** *nmpl* **1.** [fonctions] powers, authority ■ **outrepasser ses ~s** to overstep *ou* to exceed one's authority ■ **avoir tous ~s pour faire qqch** [administrateur] to have full powers to do sthg ; [architecte, animateur] to have carte blanche to do sthg ▶ **~s exceptionnels** POLIT special powers *(available to the President of the French Republic in an emergency)*
2. [gouvernants] : **les ~s constitués** the legally constituted government ■ **les ~s publics** the authorities
3. [surnaturels] powers.

pouvoir² [58] [puvwar] ◇ *v aux* **1.** [avoir la possibilité, la capacité de] : **je peux revenir en France** I'm able to *ou* I can return to France ■ **je peux vous aider?** [gén, dans un magasin] can I help you? ■ **on peut toujours s'arranger** some sort of an arrangement can always be worked out ■ **comment as-tu pu lui mentir!** how could you lie to him! ■ **quand il pourra de nouveau marcher** when he's able to walk again ■ **je ne peux pas dormir** I'm unable to *ou* I can't sleep ■ **tout le monde ne peut pas le faire/en dire autant!** not everybody can do it/say that! ■ **le projet ne pourra pas se faire sans sa collaboration** the project can't be carried out without her collaboration ■ **tu ne peux pas ne pas l'aider** you MUST help her, you can't refuse to help her ▶ **il ne peut pas la voir (en peinture)** *fam* he can't stand (the sight of) her
2. [parvenir à] to manage *ou* to be able to ■ **avez-vous pu entrer en contact avec lui?** did you succeed in contacting *ou* manage to contact him? ■ **c'est construit de telle manière que l'on ne puisse pas s'échapper** it's built in such a way that it's impossible to escape *ou* as to make escape impossible
3. [avoir la permission de] : **vous pouvez disposer** you may *ou* can go now ■ **si je peux** *ou sout* **si je puis m'exprimer ainsi** if I may

use the phrase ■ **si on ne peut plus plaisanter, maintenant!** it's a pretty sad thing if you can't have a laugh anymore! ■ [avoir des raisons de] : **on ne peut que s'en féliciter** one can't but feel happy about it ■ **je suis désolé – ça, tu peux (l'être)!** *fam* I'm so sorry – so you should be *ou* and with good reason *ou* and I should think so too!
4. [exprime une éventualité, un doute, un risque] : **la maladie peut revenir** the disease can *ou* may recur ■ **attention, tu pourrais glisser** careful, you might *ou* could slip ■ **ce ne peut être déjà les invités!** (surely) it can't be the guests already! ■ **j'aurais pu l'attendre longtemps, elle n'arrive que demain!** I could have waited a long time, she's not coming until tomorrow! ■ **après tout, il pourrait bien ne pas avoir menti** he may well have been telling the truth after all ■ **c'est plus facile qu'on ne pourrait le croire** it's easier than you might think ■ **je peux toujours m'être trompé** it's possible I might have got it wrong ■ **ça aurait pu être pire** it could have been worse ■ *(tournure impersonnelle)* **il pourrait s'agir d'un suicide** it could *ou* may *ou* might be a suicide ■ **il peut arriver que...** it may (so) *ou* can happen that...
5. [exprime une approximation] : **elle pouvait avoir entre 50 et 60 ans** she could have been between 50 and 60 (years of age)
6. [exprime une suggestion, une hypothèse] : **tu peux toujours essayer de lui téléphoner** you could always try phoning him ■ **tu pourrais au moins t'excuser!** you could at least apologize!, the least you could do is (to) apologize! ■ **il aurait pu me prévenir!** he could've *ou* might've warned me! ■ **on peut s'attendre à tout avec elle** anything's possible with her
7. [en intensif] : **où ai-je bien pu laisser mes lunettes?** what on earth can I have done with my glasses? ■ **qu'a-t-elle (bien) pu leur dire pour les mettre dans cet état?** what can she possibly have said for them to be in such a state!
8. *litt* [exprime le souhait] : **puisse-t-il vous entendre!** let us hope he can hear you! ■ **puissé-je ne jamais revivre des moments pareils!** may I never have to live through that again!
◇ *vt* [être capable de faire] : **qu'y puis-je?** what can I do about it? ■ **vous seul y pouvez quelque chose** only you can do anything about it ■ **on n'y peut rien** it can't be helped, nothing can be done about it ■ **que puis-je pour vous?** what can I do for you? ■ **j'ai fait tout ce que j'ai pu** I did my level best *ou* all I could ◗ **je n'en peux plus** [physiquement] I'm exhausted ; [moralement] I can't take anymore *ou* stand it any longer ; [je suis rassasié] I'm full (up) ■ **ma voiture n'en peut plus** *fam* my car's had it ■ **je n'en peux plus de l'entendre se plaindre sans cesse** I just can't take his continual moaning any more ■ **regarde-le danser avec elle, il n'en peut plus!** *fam hum* just look at him dancing with her, he's in seventh heaven!
◆ **se pouvoir** *v impers* : **ça se peut** it may *ou* could be ■ **ça se peut, mais...** that's as may be, but... ■ **il va pleuvoir – ça se pourrait bien!** it's going to rain – that's quite possible! ■ **sois calme, et s'il se peut, diplomate** keep calm and, if (at all) possible, be tactful ■ **il** *ou* **ça se peut que : il se peut qu'il soit malade** he might be ill, maybe he's ill ■ **il se pourrait bien qu'il n'y ait plus de places** it might *ou* could well be fully booked.

pp 1. (*abr écrite de* **pages**) pp **2.** (*abr écrite de* **par procuration**) pp.

PP (*abr de* **préventive de la pellagre**) *adj* : **vitamine ~** niacin.

ppcm (*abr de* **plus petit commun multiple**) *nm* LCM.

PQ[△] *nm* (*abr de* **papier-cul**) bog paper.

Pr (*abr écrite de* **professeur**) Prof.

PR ◇ *npr m* (*abr de* **parti républicain**) *right-wing French political party.*
◇ (*abr écrite de* **poste restante**) PR.

praesidium [prezidjɔm] *nm* praesidium, presidium.

pragmatique [pragmatik] ◇ *adj* [politique] pragmatic ■ [personne, attitude] pragmatic, practical.
◇ *nf* pragmatics *(U)*.

pragmatisme [pragmatism] *nm* pragmatism.

Prague [prag] *npr* Prague.

praguois, e [pragwa, az] *adj* from Prague.
◆ **Praguois, e** *nm, f inhabitant of or person from Prague.*

praire [prɛr] *nf* clam.

prairie [preri] *nf* **1.** [terrain] meadow **2.** [formation végétale] grassland **3.** [aux États-Unis et au sud du Canada] : **la Prairie, les Prairies** the Prairie, the Prairies.

pralin [pralɛ̃] *nm* CULIN praline *(toasted almonds in caramelized sugar).*

praline [pralin] *nf* **1.** CULIN [amande] praline, sugared almond ■ ***Belgique*** [chocolat] (filled) chocolate **2.** [△] [balle d'arme à feu] slug[△].

praliné, e [praline] *adj* [glace, entremets] almond-flavoured ■ [amande] sugared ■ [chocolat] with (toasted) sugared almonds.
◆ **praliné** *nm* chocolate with (toasted) sugared almonds.

praticable [pratikabl] ◇ *adj* **1.** [sentier] passable, practicable **2.** [réalisable - suggestion, solution] practicable, feasible.
◇ *nm* **1.** CINÉ (tray) dolly **2.** THÉÂTRE platform **3.** INDUST cradle **4.** SPORT (floor) mat.

praticien, enne [pratisjɛ̃, ɛn] *nm, f* practitioner.

pratiquant, e [pratikɑ̃, ɑ̃t] ◇ *adj* practising ■ **je ne suis pas ~** I don't attend church regularly, I'm not a (regular) churchgoer ■ **non ~** nonpractising.
◇ *nm, f* RELIG churchgoer.

pratique[1] [pratik] *adj* **1.** [utile - gadget, outil, voiture, dictionnaire] practical, handy ; [- vêtement] practical ■ **peu ~** not very practical ■ **quand on a des invités, c'est bien ~ un lave-vaisselle!** when you've got guests, a dishwasher comes in handy! **2.** [facile] : **il faut changer de bus trois fois, ce n'est pas ~!** you have to change buses three times, it's very inconvenient! **3.** [concret - application, connaissance, conseil, formation] practical ■ **régler les détails ~s d'une excursion** to sort out the practical details of an excursion **4.** [pragmatique] practical ■ **avoir le sens** *ou* **l'esprit ~** to have a practical turn of mind, to be practical.

pratique[2] [pratik] *nf* **1.** [application - d'une philosophie, d'une politique] practice ; [- de l'autocritique, d'une vertu] exercise ; [- d'une technique, de la censure] application ■ **mettre en ~** [conseils, préceptes] to put into practice ; [vertu] to exercise ■ **en** *ou* **dans la ~** in (actual) practice **2.** [d'une activité] practice ■ **la ~ régulière du tennis/vélo** playing tennis/cycling on a regular basis ■ **~ illégale de la médecine** illegal practice of medicine **3.** [expérience] practical experience ■ **on voit que tu as de la ~** you've obviously done this before **4.** [usage] practice ■ **des ~s religieuses** religious practices ■ **le marchandage est une ~ courante là-bas** over there, it's common practice to barter.

pratiquement [pratikmɑ̃] *adv* **1.** [presque] practically, virtually ■ **il n'y avait ~ personne** there was hardly anybody *ou* practically nobody **2.** [en fait] in practice *ou* (actual) fact.

pratiquer [3] [pratike] ◇ *vt* **1.** [faire - entaille] to make, to cut ; [- ouverture] to make ; [- passage] to open up ; [- intervention chirurgicale] to carry out *(sép)*, to perform ■ **~ un trou** [à la vrille] to bore *ou* to drill a hole ; [aux ciseaux] to cut (out) a hole **2.** [appliquer - préceptes, politique] to practise ; [- autocritique, vertu] to practise, to exercise ; [- technique] to use, to apply ; [- censure] to apply ; [- sélection] to make ■ **la vivisection est encore pratiquée dans certains laboratoires** vivisection is still carried out *ou* practised in some laboratories **3.** [s'adonner à - jeu de ballon] to play ; [- art martial, athlétisme] to do ; [- art, médecine, religion] to practise ; [- langue] to speak ; [- humour, ironie] to use ■ **~ un sport** to do *ou* practise a sport ■ **~ la natation** to swim ■ **~ la boxe** to box **4.** [fréquenter] : **~ un auteur** to read an author's works regularly **5.** COMM [rabais] to make, to give ■ **ce sont les prix pratiqués dans tous nos supermarchés** these are the current prices in all our supermarkets.
◇ *vi* RELIG to attend church (regularly), to be a (regular) churchgoer ■ **il est catholique, mais il ne pratique pas** he is not a practising Catholic.
◆ **se pratiquer** *vp (emploi passif)* **cette coutume se pratique encore dans certains pays** this custom still exists in certain countries ■ **les prix qui se pratiquent à Paris** current Paris prices ■ **cela se pratique couramment dans leur pays** it is common practice in their country.

Pravda [pravda] *npr f* : **la ~** Pravda.

praxis [praksis] *nf* PHILOS praxis.

pré [pre] *nm* AGRIC meadow.

préadolescence [preadɔlesɑ̃s] *nf* preadolescence, preteen years.

préadolescent, e [preadɔlesɑ̃, ɑ̃t] *nm, f* preadolescent, preteen, pre-teenager.

préalable [prealabl] ◇ *adj* [discussion, entrevue, sélection] preliminary ■ [travail, formation] preparatory ■ [accord, avertissement] prior ■ **faites un essai ~ sur un bout de tissu** test first *ou* beforehand on a piece of cloth ■ **sans avertissement ~** without prior notice.
◇ *nm* prerequisite, precondition.
◆ **au préalable** *loc adv* first, beforehand.

préalablement [prealabləmɑ̃] *adv* first, beforehand ■ **appliquer sur la plaie ~ nettoyée** apply after cleansing the wound.
◆ **préalablement à** *loc prép* prior to, before.

préallumage [prealymaʒ] *nm* AUTO pre-ignition.

Préalpes [prealp] *npr fpl* : **les ~** the Pre-Alps, the Lower Alps.

préalpin, e [prealpɛ̃, in] *adj* of the Pre-Alps.

préambule [preɑ̃byl] *nm* **1.** [d'une constitution, d'une conférence] preamble ■ **épargnez-nous les ~s!** spare us the preliminaries!, get straight to the point! **2.** [prémices] : **cet incident a été le ~ d'une crise grave** this incident was the prelude to a serious crisis.
◆ **sans préambule** *loc adv* without warning.

préapprentissage [preaprɑ̃tisaʒ] *nm* ≃ sandwich course.

préau, x [preo] *nm* [d'une école] covered part of the playground ■ [d'un pénitencier] yard ■ [d'un cloître] inner courtyard.

préavis [preavi] *nm* (advance) notice ■ **mon propriétaire m'a donné un mois de ~** my landlord gave me a month's notice (to move out) ➊ **déposer un ~ de grève** to give strike notice ■ **~ (de licenciement)** notice (of dismissal).
◆ **sans préavis** *loc adv* ADMIN without prior notice *ou* notification.

précâblé, e [prekable] *adj* prewired.

précaire [prekɛr] *adj* [équilibre] fragile, precarious ■ [vie, situation] precarious ■ [santé] delicate, frail ■ **il a un emploi ~** he's got no job security.

précairement [prekɛrmɑ̃] *adv* precariously.

précarisation [prekarizasjɔ̃] *nf* loss of security *ou* stability ■ **la ~ du travail** reduced job security.

précariser [prekarize] *vt* to make (sthg) less secure *ou* stable ■ **~ l'emploi** to threaten job security ■ **la crise a précarisé leur situation** the recession has made them more vulnerable.

précarité [prekarite] *nf* precariousness ■ **la ~ de l'emploi** the lack of job security.

précaution [prekosjɔ̃] *nf* **1.** [disposition préventive] precaution ■ **prendre la ~ de faire qqch** to take the precaution of doing *ou* to be especially careful to do sthg ■ **prendre des** *ou* **ses ~s** *pr & euphém* to take precautions ■ **avec beaucoup de ~s oratoires** in carefully chosen phrases ➊ **~s d'emploi** caution (before use) **2.** [prudence] caution, care.
◆ **avec précaution** *loc adv* cautiously, warily.
◆ **par (mesure de) précaution** *loc adv* as a precaution *ou* precautionary measure.
◆ **pour plus de précaution** *loc adv* to be on the safe side, to make absolutely certain.
◆ **sans précaution** *loc adv* carelessly, rashly ■ **elle manipule les produits toxiques sans la moindre ~** she handles toxic substances without taking the slightest precaution.

précautionneusement [prekosjɔnøzmɑ̃] *adv* **1.** [avec circonspection] cautiously, warily **2.** [avec soin] carefully, with care.

précautionneux, euse [prekosjɔnø, øz] *adj* **1.** [circonspect] cautious, wary **2.** [soigneux] careful.

précédemment [presedamɑ̃] *adv* before (that), previously ■ **comme je l'ai dit ~** as I have said *ou* mentioned before.

précédent, e [presedɑ̃, ɑ̃t] *adj* previous ■ **la semaine ~e** the week before, the previous week.
◆ **précédent** *nm* precedent.
◆ **sans précédent** *loc adj* without precedent, unprecedented.

précéder [18] [presede] ◇ *vt* **1.** [marcher devant] to precede ■ **le groupe, précédé par le guide** the group, led *ou* preceded by the guide **2.** [être placé avant] to precede, to be in front of **3.** [avoir lieu avant] to precede ■ **le film sera précédé par un** *ou* **d'un documentaire** the film will be preceded by *ou* will follow a documentary ■ **le jour qui précéda son arrestation** the day before *ou* prior to his arrest ■ **celui qui vous a précédé à ce poste** the person who held the post before you, your predecessor **4.** [arriver en avance sur] to precede, to arrive ahead of *ou* before ■ **il précède le favori de trois secondes** he has a three second lead over the favourite ■ **il avait été précédé de sa mauvaise réputation** his bad reputation had preceded him.
◇ *vi* to precede ■ **as-tu lu ce qui précède?** have you read what comes before? *sout* ■ **les semaines qui précédèrent** the preceding weeks.

précepte [presɛpt] *nm* precept.

précepteur [presɛptœr] *nm* private *ou* home tutor.

préceptrice [presɛptris] *nf* governess.

préchauffer [3] [preʃofe] *vt* to preheat.

prêche [prɛʃ] *nm* sermon.

prêcher [4] [preʃe] ◇ *vt* **1.** RELIG [Évangile, religion] to preach ■ [carême, retraite] to preach for *(insép)* ■ [personne] to preach to *(insép)* ■ **vous prêchez un converti** you're preaching to the converted **2.** [recommander - doctrine, bonté, vengeance] to preach ■ **~ le faux pour savoir le vrai** to make false statements in order to discover the truth.
◇ *vi* [prêtre] to preach ■ [moralisateur] to preach ■ **~ d'exemple** *ou* **par l'exemple** to practise what one preaches ■ **~ dans le désert** *allus* & BIBLE to preach in the wilderness ■ **~ pour son saint** *ou* **son clocher** *ou* **sa paroisse** to look after one's own interests.

prêcheur, euse [prɛʃœr, øz] ◇ *adj fam péj* [ennuyeux] moralizing, preachy.
◇ *nm, f* **1.** *fam péj* [sermonneur] moralizer **2.** RELIG preacher.

prêchi-prêcha [preʃipreʃa] *nm inv fam péj* sermonizing, lecturing.

précieusement [presjøzmɑ̃] *adv* **1.** [soigneusement] preciously ■ **conserver qqch ~** to keep sthg safe, to look after sthg **2.** [avec affectation] : **c'est écrit un peu ~** the style is a little bit precious.

précieux, euse [presjø, øz] *adj* **1.** [de valeur - temps, santé] precious ; [- pierre, métal] precious ; [- ami, amitié] precious, valued ; [- objet, trésor, bijou] precious, priceless **2.** [très utile] invaluable ■ **elle fut d'une aide précieuse** her help was invaluable ■ **elle m'a été d'un ~ secours** her help was invaluable to me **3.** [maniéré] mannered, affected, precious **4.** ART & LITTÉR precious.
◆ **précieuse** *nf* précieuse.

préciosité [presjozite] *nf* **1.** [maniérisme] affectedness, mannered style **2.** ART & LITTÉR preciosity.

précipice [presipis] *nm* **1.** [gouffre] precipice **2.** [catastrophe] : **être au bord du ~** to be on the brink of disaster.

précipitamment [presipitamɑ̃] *adv* [annuler, changer] hastily, hurriedly ■ **monter/traverser ~** to dash up/across.

précipitation [presipitasjɔ̃] *nf* **1.** [hâte] haste ■ **les ouvriers ont quitté l'usine avec ~** the workers rushed *ou* hurried out of the factory ■ **dans ma ~, j'ai oublié l'adresse** in the rush, I forgot the address ■ **tout s'est fait dans la plus grande ~** everything was done in a great hurry **2.** [irréflexion] rashness ■ **agir avec ~** to act rashly **3.** CHIM precipitation.

◆ **précipitations** *nfpl* MÉTÉOR precipitation ■ **fortes ~s sur l'ouest du pays demain** tomorrow, it will rain heavily in the west.

précipité, e [presipite] *adj* **1.** [pressé - pas] hurried ; [- fuite] headlong **2.** [rapide - respiration] rapid ■ **tout cela a été si ~** it all happened so fast **3.** [hâtif - retour] hurried, hasty ; [- décision] hasty, rash.
◆ **précipité** *nm* precipitate.

précipiter [3] [presipite] ◇ *vt* **1.** [faire tomber] to throw *ou* to hurl (down) **2.** *fig* [plonger] to plunge ■ **~ un pays dans la guerre/crise** to plunge a country into war/a crisis **3.** [faire à la hâte] : **il ne faut rien ~** we mustn't rush (into) things *ou* be hasty ■ **nous avons dû ~ notre départ/mariage** we had to leave/ get married sooner than planned **4.** [accélérer - pas, cadence] to quicken, to speed up *(sép)* ; [- mouvement, mort] to hasten **5.** CHIM to precipitate (out).
◇ *vi* CHIM to precipitate (out).
◆ **se précipiter** *vpi* **1.** [d'en haut] to hurl o.s. ■ **se ~ dans le vide** to hurl o.s. into space **2.** [se ruer] to rush ■ **il s'est précipité dans l'escalier pour la rattraper** [vers le bas] he rushed downstairs after her ; [vers le haut] he rushed upstairs after her ■ **se ~ vers** *ou* **au-devant de qqn** to rush to meet sb ■ **se ~ sur qqn** to rush at sb **3.** [s'accélérer - pouls, cadence] to speed up, to quicken ■ **depuis peu, les événements se précipitent** things have been moving really fast recently **4.** [se dépêcher] to rush, to hurry ■ **on a tout notre temps, pourquoi se ~?** we've got plenty of time, what's the rush? ■ **ne te précipite pas pour répondre** take your time before answering.

précis, e [presi, iz] *adj* **1.** [exact - horloge, tir, instrument] precise, exact ; [- description] precise, accurate ■ **la balance n'est pas très ~e** the scales aren't very accurate ■ **à 20 h ~es** at precisely 8 p.m., at 8 p.m. sharp ■ **à cet instant ~** at that precise *ou* very moment ■ **il arriva à l'instant ~ où je partais** he arrived just as I was leaving **2.** [clair, net] precise, specific ■ **je voudrais une réponse ~e** I'd like a clear answer ■ **je n'ai aucun souvenir ~ de cette année-là** I don't remember that year clearly at all **3.** [particulier] particular, specific ■ **sans raison ~e** for no particular reason ■ **sans but ~** with no specific aim in mind ■ **tu penses à quelqu'un de ~?** do you have a specific person in mind?
◆ **précis** *nm* **1.** [manuel] handbook **2.** [résumé] précis, summary.

précisément [presizemɑ̃] *adv* **1.** [exactement] precisely ■ **il nous reste très ~ 52 euros** we've got precisely *ou* exactly 52 euros left **2.** [justement, par coïncidence] precisely, exactly ■ **c'est ~ le problème** that's exactly *ou* precisely what the problem is **3.** [oui] that's right.

préciser [3] [presize] *vt* **1.** [clarifier - intentions, pensée] to make clear ■ **cette fois-ci, je me suis bien fait ~ les conditions d'admission** this time I made sure they explained the conditions of entry clearly to me **2.** [spécifier] : **l'invitation ne précise pas si l'on peut venir accompagné** the invitation (card) doesn't specify *ou* say whether you can bring somebody with you ■ **j'ai oublié de leur ~ le lieu du rendez-vous** I forgot to tell them where the meeting is taking place ■ **la Maison-Blanche précise que la rencontre n'est pas officielle** the White House has made it clear that this is not an official meeting ■ **"cela s'est fait sans mon accord", précisa-t-il** "this was done without my agreement," he pointed out ■ *(en usage absolu)* **vous dites avoir vu quelqu'un, pourriez-vous ~?** you said you saw somebody, could you be more specific?
◆ **se préciser** *vpi* [idée, projet] to take shape ■ [situation, menace] to become clearer.

précision [presizjɔ̃] *nf* **1.** [exactitude] preciseness, precision ■ **avec une ~ mathématique** with mathematical precision **2.** [netteté] precision, distinctness ■ **les visages sont peints avec une extraordinaire ~** the faces are painted with extraordinary precision *ou* attention to detail **3.** [explication] point ■ **apporter une ~ à qqch** to add a point to sthg ■ **nous y reviendrons dès que nous aurons plus de ~s** we'll come back to that as soon as we have further information *ou* details **4.** ARM accuracy.
◆ **de précision** *loc adj* precision *(modif)* ■ **horlogerie de haute ~** high-precision watchmaking.

précité, e [presite] *adj* [oralement] aforesaid, aforementioned ■ [par écrit] above-mentioned, aforesaid ■ **les auteurs ~s** the authors quoted above.

précoce [prekɔs] *adj* **1.** [prématuré - surdité, mariage] premature **2.** [en avance - intellectuellement] precocious, mature (beyond one's years) ; [- sexuellement] precocious ■ **j'étais un garçon ~ pour mon âge** I was advanced for a boy of my age **3.** BOT & MÉTÉOR early.

précocité [prekɔsite] *nf* **1.** [d'un enfant] precociousness, precocity ■ [d'une faculté, d'un talent] early manifestation, precociousness **2.** BOT & MÉTÉOR early arrival, earliness.

précolombien, enne [prekɔlɔ̃bjɛ̃, ɛn] *adj* pre-Columbian.

précombustion [prekɔ̃bystjɔ̃] *nf* precombustion.

précompte [prekɔ̃t] *nm* **1.** [retenue] tax deduction (from one's salary) *UK*, withholding tax *US* ■ **~ mobilier** (withholding) tax on company income **2.** [estimation] (deduction) schedule.

précompter [3] [prekɔ̃te] *vt* **1.** [déduire] to deduct ■ **vos cotisations sont précomptées sur votre salaire** your contribution is deducted automatically from your salary **2.** [estimer] to schedule, to estimate.

préconçu, e [prekɔ̃sy] *adj* set, preconceived ■ **idée ~e** preconceived idea.

préconiser [3] [prekɔnize] *vt* **1.** [recommander - solution, méthode] to advocate ; [- remède] to recommend ■ **il préconise d'augmenter les tarifs douaniers** he advocates *ou* is an advocate of higher trade tariffs **2.** RELIG to preconize.

préconscient, e [prekɔ̃sjɑ̃, ɑ̃t] *adj* preconscious.
◆ **préconscient** *nm* preconscious.

précuit, e [prekɥi, it] *adj* precooked, ready-cooked.

précurseur [prekyrsœr] ◇ *adj m* warning.
◇ *nm* forerunner, precursor ■ **faire figure** *ou* **œuvre de ~** to break new ground.

prédateur, trice [predatœr, tris] *adj* BOT & ZOOL predatory.
◆ **prédateur** *nm* BOT & ZOOL predator.

prédécesseur [predesesœr] *nm* predecessor.
◆ **prédécesseurs** *nmpl* [ancêtres] forebears.

prédécoupé, e [predekupe] *adj* precut, ready-cut.

prédéfini, e [predefini] *adj* predefined.

prédélinquant, e [predelɛ̃kɑ̃, ɑ̃t] *nm, f* predelinquent.

prédestination [predɛstinasjɔ̃] *nf* predestination.

prédestiné, e [predɛstine] ◇ *adj* [voué à tel sort] fated.
◇ *nm, f* RELIG chosen *ou* predestined one.

prédestiner [3] [predɛstine] *vt* **1.** [vouer] to prepare, to predestine ■ **rien ne me prédestinait à devenir acteur** nothing marked me out to become an actor *ou* for an acting career **2.** RELIG to predestine, to predestinate.

prédétermination [predetɛrminasjɔ̃] *nf* predetermination.

prédéterminer [3] [predetɛrmine] *vt* to predetermine.

prédicat [predika] *nm* **1.** LING [verbe] predicator ■ [adjectif] predicate **2.** LOGIQUE predicate.

prédicateur, trice [predikatœr, tris] *nm, f* preacher.

prédicatif, ive [predikatif, iv] *adj* **1.** LING & LOGIQUE predicative **2.** RELIG predicatory, predicant.

prédiction [prediksjɔ̃] *nf* [prophétie] prediction ■ **tes ~s se sont accomplies** *ou* **réalisées** what you predicted came true.

prédigéré, e [prediʒere] *adj* predigested.

prédilection [predilɛksjɔ̃] *nf* predilection, partiality ■ **avoir une ~ pour qqch** to be partial to sthg, to have a predilection for sthg.
◆ **de prédilection** *loc adj* favourite.

prédire [103] [predir] *vt* to predict, to foretell ▪ **~ l'avenir** [par hasard ou estimation] to predict the future ; [voyant] to tell fortunes ▪ **je lui prédis des jours difficiles** I can see difficult times ahead for her.

prédisposer [3] [predispoze] *vt* **1.** [préparer] to predispose ▪ **sa taille la prédisposait à devenir mannequin** her height made modelling an obvious choice for her **2.** [incliner] : **être prédisposé en faveur de qqn** to be favourably disposed to sb ▪ *(en usage absolu)* **cette époque-là ne prédisposait pas à la frivolité** that period was not conducive to frivolity.

prédisposition [predispozisjɔ̃] *nf* **1.** [tendance] predisposition ▪ **avoir une ~ au diabète** to have a predisposition to diabetes **2.** [talent] gift, talent.

prédit, e [predi, it] *pp* ▷ **prédire.**

prédominance [predɔminɑ̃s] *nf* predominance.

prédominant, e [predɔminɑ̃, ɑ̃t] *adj* [principal - couleur, trait] predominant, main ; [- opinion, tendance] prevailing ; [- souci] chief, major.

prédominer [3] [predɔmine] *vi* [couleur, trait] to predominate ▪ [sentiment, tendance] to prevail ▪ **le soleil va ~ sur presque tout le pays** the weather will be sunny in most parts of the country ▪ **c'est ce qui prédomine dans tous ses romans** that's the predominant feature of all his novels.

préélectoral, e, aux [preelɛktɔral, o] *adj* pre-electoral.

préemballé, e [preɑ̃bale] *adj* prepacked.

prééminence [preeminɑ̃s] *nf* pre-eminence, dominance ▪ **donner la ~ à qqch** to put sthg first.

prééminent, e [preeminɑ̃, ɑ̃t] *adj* pre-eminent ▪ **occuper un rang ~** to hold a prominent position.

préemption [preɑ̃psjɔ̃] *nf* pre-emption.

préencollé, e [preɑ̃kɔle] *adj* prepasted.

préenregistré, e [preɑ̃rəʒistre] *adj* prerecorded.

préenregistrer [preɑ̃rəʒistre] *vt* to prerecord.

préétabli, e [preetabli] *adj* pre-established.

préétablir [32] [preetablir] *vt* to pre-establish.

préexistant, e [preɛgzistɑ̃, ɑ̃t] *adj* existing ▪ **les immeubles ~s seront détruits** existing buildings will be torn down.

préexister [3] [preɛgziste] ◆ **préexister à** *v+prép* to go before, to preexist ▪ **toutes les civilisations qui ont préexisté à la nôtre** all the civilizations that came before ours.

préfabriqué, e [prefabrike] *adj* prefabricated.
◆ **préfabriqué** *nm* **1.** [construction] prefab **2.** [matériau] prefabricated material ▪ **en ~** prefabricated.

préface [prefas] *nf* preface.

préfacer [16] [prefase] *vt* [livre, texte] to preface ▪ **~ un ouvrage** to write a preface to *ou* to preface a book.

préfacier [prefasje] *nm* prefacer, preface writer.

préfectoral, e, aux [prefɛktɔral, o] *adj* prefectorial, prefectural ▪ **par arrêté ~, par mesure ~e** by order.

préfecture [prefɛktyr] *nf* **1.** ADMIN [chef-lieu] prefecture ▪ [édifice] prefecture building ▪ [services] prefectural office ▪ [emploi] post of préfet ➊ **~ maritime** port prefecture ▪ **~ de police** (Paris) police headquarters **2.** ANTIQ prefecture.

PRÉFECTURE

The main administrative office of each *département*. The word has also come to refer to the town where the office is located. One goes to the *préfecture* to get a driving licence or a *carte de séjour*, for example.

préférable [preferabl] *adj* preferable ▪ **ne va pas trop loin, c'est ~** it'd be better if you didn't go too far away ▪ **~ à** preferable to, better than.

préférablement [preferabləmɑ̃] *adv litt* **~ à** [de préférence à] in preference to.

préféré, e [prefere] ◇ *adj* favourite ▪ **quel est ton passe-temps ~?** what is your favourite hobby?
◇ *nm, f* favourite.

préférence [preferɑ̃s] *nf* **1.** [prédilection] preference ▪ **donner la ~ à** to give preference to ▪ **avoir une ~ pour** to have a preference for ▪ **ça m'est égal, je n'ai pas de ~** it doesn't matter to me, I've no particular preference ▪ **avoir la ~ sur qqn** to have preference over sb **2.** DR : **droit de ~** right to preferential treatment **3.** ÉCON : **~ douanière** preferential duties.
◆ **de préférence** *loc adv* preferably ▪ **'à consommer de ~ avant fin 2006'** 'best before end 2006'.
◆ **de préférence à** *loc prép* in preference to, rather than.
Voir module d'usage

préférentiel, elle [preferɑ̃sjɛl] *adj* **1.** [traitement, tarif, vote] preferential **2.** BOURSE : **actions ~les** preference shares *UK*, preferred stock *US*.

préférer [18] [prefere] *vt* to prefer ▪ **préférez-vous du vin ou de la bière?** would you rather have wine or beer? ▪ **je me préfère avec un chignon** I think I look better with my hair in a bun ▪ **il préférait mourir plutôt que (de) partir** he would rather die than leave ▪ **je préfère que tu n'en dises rien à personne** I'd prefer it if *ou* I'd rather you didn't tell anybody ▪ *(en usage absolu)* **si tu préfères, nous allons rentrer** if you'd rather, we'll go home.

préfet [prefɛ] *nm* **1.** ADMIN préfet, prefect ➊ **le ~ de Paris** the prefect of Paris ▪ **~ de police** [en France] prefect *ou* chief of police ; [en Grande-Bretagne] ≃ chief constable ≃ head of the constabulary ▪ **~ de région** regional prefect *ou* préfet **2.** RELIG prefect ▪ **~ des études** master of studies *(in a religious school)* **3.** NAUT : **~ maritime** *port admiral overseeing the defence of certain maritime departments* **4.** *Belgique* head teacher *UK ou* principal *US (of a secondary school)* **5.** ANTIQ prefect.

PRÉFET

One of a body of civil servants which was created by Napoleon in 1800. The *préfet*, who is appointed by a *décret* of the *Président de la République* is the government representative of a *département*.

LA PRÉFÉRENCE

I (much) prefer cricket to baseball. Je préfère (de loin) le cricket au base-ball.

I like baseball better *ou* more than cricket. J'aime mieux le base-ball que le cricket.

I prefer reading to watching television. Je préfère lire plutôt que de regarder la télévision.

She prefers making her own clothes rather than buying ready-to-wear. Elle préfère confectionner ses vêtements plutôt que d'acheter du prêt-à-porter.

I would prefer to walk rather than take *ou* taking the bus. Je préfère y aller à pied plutôt que de prendre le bus.

I'd rather walk than take the bus. Je préfère y aller à pied plutôt que de prendre le bus.

I'd rather you went (instead of me). Je préférerais que tu y ailles (à ma place).

I'd prefer you not to smoke. J'aimerais mieux que tu ne fumes pas.

préfète [prefɛt] *nf* **1.** [épouse] prefect's *ou* préfet's wife **2.** [titulaire] préfète, woman prefect.

préfiguration [prefigyrasjɔ̃] *nf sout* prefiguration, foreshadowing ■ **ce rêve était-il la ~ de mon avenir?** was this dream a premonition?

préfigurer [3] [prefigyre] *vt sout* [annoncer] to prefigure ■ **cette nouvelle ne préfigure rien de bon** this news bodes ill for the future.

préfinancement [prefinɑ̃smɑ̃] *nm* bridging loan.

préfixe [prefiks] *nm* prefix.

préfixer [3] [prefikse] *vt* to prefix.

prégénital, e, aux [preʒenital, o] *adj* pregenital.

préglaciaire [preglasjɛr] *adj* preglacial.

préhensile [preɑ̃sil] *adj* prehensile.

préhension [preɑ̃sjɔ̃] *nf* prehension ■ **doué de ~** able to grip.

préhistoire [preistwar] *nf* prehistory.

préhistorique [preistɔrik] *adj* **1.** [ère, temps] prehistoric, prehistorical **2.** *fam* [dépassé] ancient, prehistoric ■ **elle est ~, sa bagnole!** his car's virtually an antique!

préindustriel, elle [preɛ̃dystrijɛl] *adj* preindustrial.

préinscription [preɛ̃skripsjɔ̃] *nf* preregistration.

préjudice [preʒydis] *nm* harm *(U)*, wrong *(U)* ■ **subir un ~ matériel/financier** to sustain damage/financial loss ■ **subir un ~ moral** to suffer mental distress ■ **causer un** *ou* **porter ~ à qqn** to harm sb, to do sb harm ■ **les magnétoscopes ont-ils porté ~ au cinéma?** have videorecorders been detrimental to the cinema?
◆ **au préjudice de** *loc prép* to the detriment *ou* at the expense of.
◆ **sans préjudice de** *loc prép* without prejudice to.

préjudiciable [preʒydisjabl] *adj sout* prejudicial, detrimental ■ **de telles déclarations seraient ~s à votre candidature** such statements would be harmful *ou* injurious to your candidature.

préjugé [preʒyʒe] *nm* prejudice ■ **avoir un ~ contre qqn** to be prejudiced *ou* biased against sb ■ **avoir un ~ favorable pour qqn** to be prejudiced in sb's favour, to be biased towards sb ■ **n'avoir aucun ~** to be totally unprejudiced *ou* unbiased.

préjuger [17] [preʒyʒe] *vt litt* to prejudge ■ **autant qu'on puisse ~** as far as one can judge beforehand.
◆ **préjuger de** *v+prép litt* **~ de qqch** to judge sthg in advance, to prejudge sthg ■ **son attitude ne laisse rien ~ de sa décision** his attitude gives us no indication of what he is going to decide ■ **je crains d'avoir préjugé de mes forces** I'm afraid I've overestimated my strength.

prélasser [3] [prelase] ◆ **se prélasser** *vpi* to be stretched out, to lounge (around), to laze around.

prélat [prela] *nm* prelate.

prélavage [prelavaʒ] *nm* prewash.

prêle, prèle [prɛl] *nf* horsetail.

prélèvement [prelɛvmɑ̃] *nm* **1.** MÉD [échantillon - de sang] sample ; [- sur les tissus] swab ■ **il faut faire un ~ dans la partie infectée** we have to take a swab of the infected area **2.** BANQUE [retrait] : **~ automatique** *ou* **bancaire** direct debit ■ **~ en espèces** cash withdrawal **3.** FIN [retenue - sur le salaire] deduction ; [- sur les biens] levy ■ **~ sur le capital** capital levy ■ **les cotisations sont payées par ~ à la source** contributions are deducted at source ■ **~s fiscaux** tax deductions ■ **~s obligatoires** tax and social security contributions ■ **~s sociaux** social security contributions.

prélever [19] [prelәve] *vt* **1.** MÉD [échantillon] to take ■ **~ du sang** to take a blood sample **2.** FIN [somme - au distributeur] to withdraw ; [- sur un salaire] to deduct, to withdraw ■ **la somme sera prélevée sur votre compte tous les mois** the sum will be deducted *ou* debited from your account every month.

préliminaire [preliminɛr] *adj* preliminary ■ **remarque ~** preliminary *ou* prefatory remark.
◆ **préliminaires** *nmpl* [préparatifs] preliminaries ■ [discussions] preliminary talks.

prélude [prelyd] *nm* **1.** MUS prelude **2.** *sout* [préliminaire] prelude ■ **cette première rencontre fut le ~ de bien d'autres** this was the first of many meetings.

préluder [3] [prelyde] *vi* MUS to warm up, to prelude ■ **~ par des vocalises** to warm up by doing vocal exercises.
◆ **préluder à** *v+prép* to be a prelude to.

prématuré, e [prematyre] ◇ *adj* **1.** [naissance, bébé] premature **2.** [décision] premature ■ [décès] untimely ■ **il est ~ de dresser un bilan de la situation** it is too early to assess the situation.
◇ *nm, f* premature baby *ou* infant.

prématurément [prematyremɑ̃] *adv* prematurely ■ **il nous a quittés ~** his was an untimely death.

prémédication [premedikasjɔ̃] *nf* premedication.

préméditation [premeditasjɔ̃] *nf* premeditation ■ **avec ~** with malice aforethought ■ **meurtre avec ~** premeditated murder ■ **si on ne peut pas prouver la ~** if proof of intent cannot be shown.

prémédité, e [premedite] *adj* **1.** DR [crime] premeditated, wilful **2.** [insulte, réponse] deliberate.

préméditer [3] [premedite] *vt* [crime, vol] to premeditate ■ **~ de faire qqch** to plan to do sthg ■ **ils avaient bien prémédité leur coup** they'd thought the whole thing out really well.

prémenstruel, elle [premɑ̃stryɛl] *adj* premenstrual.

prémices [premis] *nfpl* **1.** *litt* [début] beginnings ■ **les ~ d'un grand talent** the first *ou* early stirrings of a great talent **2.** ANTIQ [récolte] premices, primices, first fruits ■ [animaux] premices, primices.

premier, ère [prәmje, ɛr] ◇ *adj num* **1.** *(souvent avant le n)* [initial] early ■ **les ~s hommes** early man ■ **ses premières œuvres** her early works ■ **les ~s temps** at the beginning, early on ■ **il n'est plus de la première jeunesse** he's not as young as he used to be ■ **un Matisse de la première période** an early Matisse
2. [proche] nearest ■ **au ~ rang** CINÉ & THÉÂTRE in the first *ou* front row ; ÉDUC in the first row
3. [à venir] next, first ■ **ce n'est pas le ~ venu** he's not just anybody ■ **le ~ imbécile venu pourrait le faire** any idiot could do it ■ **on s'est arrêtés dans le ~ hôtel venu** we stopped at the first hotel we came to *ou* happened to come to
4. [dans une série] first ■ **chapitre ~** Chapter One ■ **à la première heure** first thing, at first light ■ **à première vue** at first (sight) ■ **au ~ abord** at first ■ **dans un ~ temps** (at) first, to start with, to begin with ■ **de la première à la dernière ligne** from beginning to end ■ **le ~ nom d'une liste** the top name on a list ■ **du ~ coup** *fam* first off, at the first attempt ■ **faire ses premières armes** to make one's debut ■ **il a fait ses premières armes à la "Gazette du Nord"** he cut his teeth at the "Gazette du Nord" ■ **j'ai fait mes premières armes dans le métier comme apprenti cuisinier** I started in the trade as a cook's apprentice ■ **~ amour** first love ■ **le ~ arrivé** the first person to arrive ■ **première prise** CINÉ first take *ou* shot ■ **~ jet** (first) *ou* rough *ou* initial draft ■ **~s secours** [personnes et matériel] emergency services ; [soins] first aid ■ **première fois : c'est la première fois que...** it's the first time that... ■ **il y a toujours une première fois** there's always a first time ■ **première page** PRESSE front page ■ **faire la première page des journaux** to be headline news ■ **première partie** [gén] first part ; [au spectacle] opening act ■ **qui va (lui) jeter** *ou* **lancer la première pierre?** *allus* & BIBLE who will cast the first stone?
5. [principal] main ■ **de (toute) première nécessité/urgence** (absolutely) essential/urgent ■ **c'est vous le ~ intéressé** you're the main person concerned *ou* the one who's got most at stake ■ **le ~ pays producteur de vin au monde** the world's leading wine-producing country
6. [haut placé - clerc, commis] chief ; [- danseur] leading ■ **le ~ personnage de l'État** the country's Head of State ■ **sortir ~ d'une**

Grande école to be first on the pass list *(in the final exam of a Grande école)* ▶ **~ secrétaire (du parti)** first secretary (of the party)
7. *(après le n)* [originel] first, original, initial ■ **l'idée première était de...** the original idea was to...
8. [spontané] first ■ **son ~ mouvement** his first *ou* spontaneous impulse
9. *(après le n)* [fondamental] first ■ MATH [nombre] prime ■ [polynôme] irreducible ■ **cause première** first cause ■ **principe ~** first *ou* basic principle
10. [moindre] : **et ta récitation, tu n'en connais pas le ~ mot!** you haven't a clue about your recitation, have you? ■ **la robe coûte 400 euros et je n'en ai pas le ~ sou** the dress costs 400 euros and I haven't a penny UK *ou* cent US to my name
11. GRAMM : **première personne du singulier/pluriel** first person singular/plural, *voir aussi* **pluriel**
12. CULIN : **côte/côtelette première** prime rib/cutlet.
◇ *nm, f* **1.** [personne] : **le ~** the first ■ **entre la première** go in first ■ **elle a fini dans les cinq premières** she finished amongst the top five ■ **elle est la première de sa classe/au hit-parade** she's top of her class/the charts ▶ **jeune ~** CINÉ & THÉÂTRE juvenile lead ■ **jeune première** young female lead ■ **le Premier (britannique)** POLIT the (British) Prime Minister *ou* Premier ■ **les ~s seront les derniers** *allus* & BIBLE the first shall be last
2. [chose] : **le ~** the first (one)
3. [celui-là] : **le ~** the former ■ **plantez des roses ou des tulipes, mais les premières durent plus longtemps** plant roses or tulips, but the former last longer, *voir aussi* **cinquième**.
◆ **premier** *nm* **1.** [dans une charade] : **mon ~ sent mauvais** my first has a nasty smell
2. [étage] first floor UK, second floor US ■ **la dame du ~** the lady on the first floor
3. [dans des dates] : **le ~ du mois** the first of the month ■ **Aix, le ~ juin** Aix, June 1st ■ **le ~ avril** April Fool's *ou* All Fools Day ■ **le Premier Mai** May Day ■ **le ~ janvier** *ou* **de l'an** New Year's Day.
◆ **première** *nf* **1.** CINÉ & THÉÂTRE first night, opening night ■ **première mondiale** world première
2. [exploit] : **c'est une (grande) première chirurgicale** it's a first for surgery ■ **la première des Grandes Jorasses** the first ascent of the Grandes Jorasses
3. ÉDUC lower sixth (form) UK, eleventh grade US ■ **première supérieure** *class leading to the entrance exam for the École normale supérieure*
4. AUTO first (gear) ■ **être/passer en première** to be in/to go into first
5. TRANSP first class ■ **voyager en première** to travel first class ■ **billet/wagon de première** first-class ticket/carriage
6. COUT head seamstress
7. DANSE first (position)
8. IMPR [épreuve] first proof ■ [édition - d'un livre] first edition ; [- d'un journal] early edition
9. [d'une chaussure] insole.
◆ **de première** *loc adj fam* first-rate ■ **un imbécile de première** *iron* a prize idiot.
◆ **en premier** *loc adv* first, in the first place, first of all ■ **je dois m'occuper en ~ de mon visa** the first thing I must do is to see about my visa.
◆ **premier de cordée** *nm* leader *(of a roped climbing team)*.
◆ **premier degré** *nm* **1.** ÉDUC primary UK *ou* elementary US education
2. [phase initiale] first step ■ **brûlure au ~ degré** first-degree burn
3. *fig* **des gags à ne pas prendre au ~ degré** jokes which mustn't be taken at face value.
◆ **premier prix** *nm* **1.** COMM lowest *ou* cheapest price ■ **dans les ~s prix** at the cheaper *ou* lower end of the scale
2. [récompense] first prize ■ **elle a eu le ~ prix d'interprétation** she's won the award for best actress.

premièrement [prəmjɛrmɑ̃] *adv* **1.** [dans une énumération] in the first place, first **2.** [pour objecter] firstly, in the first place, to start with ■ **~, ça ne te regarde pas!** to begin *ou* to start with, it's none of your business!

premier-né, première-née [prəmjene, prəmjɛrne] *(mpl* **premiers-nés**, *fpl* **premières-nées**) *adj* & *nm, f* first-born.

prémisse [premis] *nf* premise.

prémolaire [premɔlɛr] *nf* premolar.

prémonition [premɔnisjɔ̃] *nf* premonition.

prémonitoire [premɔnitwar] *adj* premonitory ■ **j'ai fait un rêve ~** I had a premonition in my dream.

prémunir [32] [premynir] *vt sout* **~ qqn contre** to protect sb against.
◆ **se prémunir contre** *vp+prép* to protect o.s. *ou* to guard against sthg.

prenait *etc v* ▷ **prendre**.

prenant, e [prənɑ̃, ɑ̃t] *adj* **1.** [captivant] engrossing, gripping **2.** [qui prend du temps] time-consuming **3.** [préhensile] prehensile.

prénatal, e, als *ou* **aux** [prenatal, o] *adj* prenatal, antenatal.

prendre [79] [prɑ̃dr] ◇ *vt*

> **A.** SAISIR, ACQUÉRIR
> **B.** AVOIR RECOURS À, SE SERVIR DE
> **C.** PRENDRE POSSESSION DE, CONTRÔLER
> **D.** ADMETTRE, RECEVOIR
> **E.** CONSIDÉRER DE TELLE MANIÈRE
> **F.** ENREGISTRER
> **G.** DÉCIDER DE, ADOPTER

A. SAISIR, ACQUÉRIR
1. [saisir] to take ■ **la chatte prend ses chatons par la peau du cou** the cat picks up her kittens by the scruff of the neck ■ **prends la casserole par le manche** pick the pan up by the handle ■ **il prit son manteau à la patère** he took his coat off the hook ■ **prends le livre qui se trouve sur la table** take the book on the table ■ **~ qqch des mains de qqn** to take sthg off sb ‖ [saisir et garder] to take (hold of), to hold ■ **~ sa tête entre ses mains** to hold one's head in one's hands ■ **prenez cette médaille qui vous est offerte par tous vos collègues** accept this medal as a gift from all your colleagues ■ **~ un siège** to take a seat, to sit down
2. [emporter - lunettes, document, en-cas] to take ■ **tu as pris tes papiers (avec toi)?** have you got your papers (with you)? ■ **inutile de ~ un parapluie** there's no need to take *ou* no need for an umbrella ■ **quand prendrez-vous le colis?** when will you collect the parcel? ■ [emmener] to take (along) ■ **(passer) ~ qqn : je suis passé la ~ chez elle à midi** I picked her up at *ou* collected her from her home at midday ■ **~ qqn en voiture** to give sb a lift
3. [trouver] to get ■ **où as-tu pris ce couteau?** where did you get that knife (from)? ■ **où as-tu pris cette idée/cette citation/ces manières?** where did you get that idea/this quotation/those manners?
4. [se procurer] : **~ des renseignements** to get some information
5. [acheter - nourriture, billet de loterie] to get, to buy ; [- abonnement, assurance] to take out *(sép)* ■ [réserver - chambre d'hôtel, place de spectacle] to book ■ **j'ai pris des artichauts pour ce soir** I've got *ou* bought some artichokes for tonight ■ **je vais vous ~ un petit poulet aujourd'hui** I'll have *ou* take a small chicken today
6. [demander - argent] to charge ■ **je prends une commission de 3 %** I take a 3% commission ■ **mon coiffeur ne prend pas cher** *fam* my hairdresser isn't too expensive *ou* doesn't charge too much ■ **je prends 30 euros de l'heure** I charge 30 euros per hour ■ **elle l'a réparé sans rien nous ~** she fixed it free of charge *ou* without charging us (anything) for it
7. [retirer] : **les impôts sont pris à la source** tax is deducted at source ■ **~ de l'argent sur son compte** to withdraw money from one's account, to take money out of one's account

B. AVOIR RECOURS À, SE SERVIR DE
1. [utiliser - outil] to use ■ **prends un marteau, ce sera plus facile** use a hammer, you'll find it's easier ■ [emprunter] to take, to borrow ■ **je peux ~ ta voiture?** can I take *ou* borrow your car?
2. [consommer - nourriture] to eat ; [- boisson] to drink, to have ; [- médicament] to take ; [- sucre] to take ■ **je ne prends jamais de somnifères** I never take sleeping pills ■ **nous en discuterons en prenant le café** we'll discuss it over a cup of coffee ■ **qu'est-ce**

que tu prends? what would you like to drink, what will it be? ▪ **je prendrais bien une bière** I could do with a beer ▪ **si on allait ~ un verre?** how about (going for) a drink? ▪ **à ~ matin, midi et soir** to be taken three times a day ▪ **tu lui as fait ~ ses médicaments?** did you make sure he took his medicine? ▪ [comme ingrédient] to take ▪ **~ 50 g de beurre et 200 g de farine** take 50 g of butter and 200 g of flour
3. [se déplacer en] to take, to go *ou* to travel by *(insép)* ▪ **~ l'avion** to take the plane, to fly ▪ **~ le bateau** to take the boat, to sail, to go by boat ▪ **~ le bus/le train** to take the bus/train, to go by bus/train ▪ **~ un taxi** to take a taxi ▪ **je ne prends jamais la voiture** I never use the car
4. [monter dans - bus, train] to catch, to get on *(insép)*
5. [louer] : **on a pris une chambre dans un petit hôtel** we took a room in a small hotel ▪ **j'ai pris un petit studio** I rented a little studio flat
6. [suivre - voie] to take ▪ **prends la première à droite** take the first (on the) right ▪ **prenez la direction de Lille** follow the signs for Lille ▪ **j'ai pris un sens interdit** I drove *ou* went down a one-way street

C. PRENDRE POSSESSION DE, CONTRÔLER
1. [retenir par la force - fugitif] to capture ; [- prisonnier] to take ; [- animal] to catch ▪ MIL [ville, position] to take ▪ **~ qqn en otage** to take sb hostage
2. [voler] to take ▪ **il a tout pris dans la maison** he took everything in the house ▪ **~ une citation dans un livre** [sans permission] to lift *ou* to poach a quotation from a book ▪ **~ qqch à qqn : combien vous a-t-on pris?** how much was taken *ou* stolen from you? ▪ **elle m'a pris mon tour** she took my turn ▪ **elle m'a pris mon idée/petit ami** she stole my idea/boyfriend
3. [occuper - temps] to take (up), to require *sout* ; [- place] to take (up) ▪ **pousse-toi, tu prends toute la place** move up, you're taking up all the space ▪ **ça (m')a pris deux heures** it took (me) two hours ▪ **ça prend du temps de chercher un appartement** it takes time to find a flat, flat-hunting is time-consuming
4. [envahir - suj: malaise, rage] to come over *(insép)* ; [- suj: peur] to seize, to take hold of ▪ **quand ses quintes de toux le prennent** when he has a bout of coughing ▪ **l'envie le** *ou* **lui prit d'aller nager** he felt like going for a swim ▪ **qu'est-ce qui te prend?** what's wrong with *ou* what's the matter with *ou* what's come over you? ▪ **qu'est-ce qui le** *ou* **lui prend de ne pas répondre?** why on earth isn't he answering? ▪ **ça te prend souvent?** *fam hum* are you often like this? ▪ **quand ça le** *ou* **lui prend, il casse tout** *fam* when he gets into this state, he just smashes everything in sight ▪ *(tournure impersonnelle)* **il me prend parfois le désir de tout abandonner** I sometimes feel like giving it all up ➊ **il est rentré chez lui et bien/mal lui en a pris** he went home and it was just as well he did/, but he'd have done better to stay where he was ▪ **~ la tête à qqn**△ **: ça me prend la tête** it's a real hassle ▪ **arrête de me ~ la tête** stop being such a pain
5. [surprendre - voleur, tricheur] to catch ▪ **si tu veux le voir, il faut le ~ au saut du lit** if you want to see him, you must catch him as he gets up ▪ **~ qqn à faire qqch** to catch sb doing sthg ▪ **je t'y prends, petit galopin!** caught *ou* got you, you little rascal!
6. JEUX [pion, dame] to take ▪ **demain, je te prends aux échecs** *fam* tomorrow I'll take you on at *ou* play you at chess ▪ *(en usage absolu)* CARTES : **je prends** I'll try it ▪ **j'ai pris à cœur** I went hearts
7. SPORT : **~ le service de qqn** to break sb's service ▪ **il est venu ~ la deuxième place** [pendant la course] he moved into second place ; [à l'arrivée] he came in second

D. ADMETTRE, RECEVOIR
1. [recevoir] : **le docteur ne pourra pas vous ~ avant demain** the doctor won't be able to see you before tomorrow ▪ **après 22 heures, nous ne prenons plus de clients** after 10 pm, we don't let anymore customers in
2. [cours] to take
3. [accueillir - pensionnaire] to take in *(sép)* ; [- passager] to take ▪ [admettre par règlement] to take, to allow ▪ [engager - employé, candidat] to take on *(sép)* ▪ **nous ne prenons pas les cartes de crédit/les bagages en cabine** we don't take credit cards/cabin baggage ▪ **~ un comptable** to take on *ou* to hire an accountant ▪ **~ qqn comme stagiaire** to take sb on as a trainee
4. [acquérir, gagner] : **~ de l'avance/du retard** to be earlier/later than scheduled ▪ **j'ai pris trois centimètres de tour de taille** I've put on three centimetres round the waist ▪ **quand le gâteau commence à ~ une jolie couleur dorée** when the cake starts to take on a nice golden colour ▪ **le projet commence à ~ forme** *ou* **tournure** the project's starting to take shape ▮ [terminaison] to take ▪ **le a prend un accent circonflexe** there's a circumflex on the a
5. [subir] to get ▪ **~ un coup de soleil** to get sunburnt ▪ **~ froid** *ou vieilli* **du mal** to catch *ou* to get a cold ▪ **j'ai pris la tuile en plein sur la tête** the tile hit me right on the head ▪ **c'est elle qui a tout pris** *fam* [coups, reproches] she got the worst *ou* took the brunt of it ; [éclaboussures] she got most *ou* the worst of it ▪ **qu'est-ce qu'on a pris!** *fam*, **on a pris quelque chose!** *fam* [averse] we got soaked *ou* drenched! ; [réprimande] we got a real dressing down! ; [critique] we got panned! ; [défaite] we got thrashed! ▪ *(en usage absolu)* **c'est toujours les mêmes qui prennent!** *fam* they always pick on the same ones, it's always the same ones who get it in the neck! ➊ **il en a pris pour 15 ans** *fam* he got 15 years, he got put away for 15 years

E. CONSIDÉRER DE TELLE MANIÈRE
1. [accepter] to take ▪ **il a essayé de le ~ avec le sourire** *ou* **en souriant** he tried to pass it off with a smile ▪ **bien/mal ~ qqch** to take sthg well/badly ▮ [interpréter] : **ne prends pas ça pour toi** [ne te sens pas visé] don't take it personally ▪ **~ qqch en bien/en mal** to take sthg as a compliment/badly ▪ **elle a pris mon silence pour de la désapprobation** she took my silence as a criticism
2. [considérer] to take, to consider ▪ **prenons un exemple** let's take *ou* consider an example ▪ **~ qqn/qqch en : ~ qqn en amitié** to grow fond of sb ▪ **~ qqn en pitié** to take pity on sb ▪ **~ qqch/qqn pour** [par méprise] to mistake sthg/sb for ; [volontairement] to take sthg/sb for, to consider sthg/sb to be ▪ **on me prend souvent pour ma sœur** I'm often mistaken for my sister ▪ **pour qui me prenez-vous?** what do you take me for?, who do you think I am? ▪ **elle va me ~ pour un idiot** she'll think I'm a fool ▪ **~ qqch/qqn comme** to take sthg/sb as ➊ **à tout ~** all in all, by and large, all things considered
3. [traiter - qqn] to handle, to deal with *(insép)* ▪ **~ qqn par la douceur** to use gentle persuasion on sb ▪ **~ l'ennemi de front/à revers** MIL & *fig* to tackle the enemy head on/from the rear

F. ENREGISTRER
1. [consigner - notes] to take *ou* to write down *(sép)* ; [- empreintes, mesures, température, tension] to take
2. PHOTO : **~ qqch/qqn (en photo)** to take a picture *ou* photo *ou* photograph of sthg/sb

G. DÉCIDER DE, ADOPTER
1. [s'octroyer - vacances] to take, to have ; [- bain, douche] to have, to take ▪ **~ un jour de congé** to take *ou* to have the day off ▪ **~ le temps de faire qqch** to take the time to do sthg ▪ **~ son temps** to take one's time ▪ **~ un amant** to take a lover ▪ **tu n'as pas le droit! – je le prends!** you've no right! – that's what you think!
2. [s'engager dans - mesure, risque] to take ▪ **~ une décision** [gén] to make a decision ; [après avoir hésité] to make up one's mind, to come to a decision ▪ **~ la décision de** to make up one's mind to, to decide to ▪ **~ l'initiative de qqch** to initiate sthg ▪ **~ l'initiative de faire qqch** to take the initiative in doing sthg, to take it upon o.s. to do sthg ▪ **~ de bonnes résolutions pour l'avenir** to resolve to do better in the future ▪ **~ la résolution de** to resolve to
3. [choisir - sujet d'examen, cadeau] to take, to choose, to have ▪ **j'ai pris le docteur Valiet comme médecin** I chose Dr Valiet to be *ou* as my GP ▪ **qu'est-ce qu'on lui prend comme glace?** which ice cream shall we get him? ▪ **ils n'ont pris que les 20 premiers** they only took *ou* selected the top 20 ➊ **c'est à ~ ou à laisser** (you can) take it or leave it ▪ **il y a à ~ et à laisser dans son livre** his book is a bit of a curate's egg *UK ou* is good in parts
4. [se charger de - poste] to take, to accept ▪ **~ ses fonctions** to start work ▪ **j'ai un appel pour toi, tu le prends?** I've got a call for you, will you take it?
5. [adopter - air] to put on *(sép)*, to assume ; [- ton] to assume.
◇ *vi* **1.** [se fixer durablement - végétal] to take (root) ; [- bouture, greffe, vaccin] to take ; [- mode, slogan] to catch on ▪ **la peinture ne prend pas sur le plastique** the plastic won't take the paint ➊ **ça ne prendra pas avec elle** [mensonge] it won't work with her, she won't be taken in **2.** [durcir - crème, ciment, colle] to set ; [- lac, étang] to freeze (over) ; [- mayonnaise] to thicken **3.** [passer] : **prends à gauche** [tourne à gauche] turn left ▪ **tu peux ~ par Le Mans** you can go via Le Mans ▪ **~ à travers bois/champs** to cut through the woods/fields **4.** [commencer] to start, to get going ▪ **je n'arrive pas à faire ~ le feu/les brindilles** I can't get

the fire going/the twigs to catch **5.** MUS & THÉÂTRE : **prenons avant la sixième mesure/à la scène 2** let's take it from just before bar six/from scene 2.

◆ **prendre sur** *v+prép* **1.** [entamer] to use (some of) ■ **je ne prendrai pas sur mon week-end pour finir le travail!** I'm not going to give up *ou* to sacrifice part of my weekend to finish the job! **2.** *loc* **~ sur soi** to grin and bear it ■ **~ sur soi de faire qqch** to take (it) upon o.s. to do sthg.

◆ **se prendre** ◇ *vp (emploi passif)* : **ces cachets se prennent avant les repas** the tablets should be taken before meals.

◇ *vp (emploi réciproque)* : **ils se sont pris pour époux** they were united in matrimony.

◇ *vpi* to get caught *ou* trapped ■ **le foulard s'est pris dans la portière** the scarf got caught *ou* shut in the door.

◇ *vpt* **1.** [se coincer] : **attention, tu vas te ~ les doigts dans la charnière!** careful, you'll trap your fingers *ou* get your fingers caught in the hinge! ■ **se ~ les pieds dans qqch** to trip over sthg **2.** *fam* [choisir] : **prends-toi un gâteau** get yourself a cake.

◆ **se prendre à** *vp+prép* **1.** [se laisser aller à] : **se ~ à faire qqch** to find o.s. starting to do sthg ■ **se ~ à rêver** to find o.s. dreaming **2.** *loc* **s'y ~ : comment pourrions-nous nous y ~?** how could we go about it? ■ **tu t'y prends un peu tard pour t'inscrire!** you've left it a bit late to enrol! ■ **il faut s'y ~ deux mois à l'avance pour avoir des places** you have to book two months in advance to be sure of getting seats ■ **elle s'y est prise à trois fois pour faire démarrer la tondeuse** she made three attempts before the lawn mower would start ■ **s'y ~ bien/mal : s'y ~ bien/mal avec qqn** to handle sb the right/wrong way ■ **elle s'y prend bien** *ou* **sait s'y ~ avec les enfants** she's good with children ■ **je n'arrive pas à repasser le col – c'est parce que tu t'y prends mal** I can't iron the collar properly – that's because you're going about it the wrong way *ou* doing it wrong.

◆ **se prendre de** *vp+prép* : **se ~ d'amitié pour qqn** to grow fond of sb, to feel a growing affection for sb.

◆ **se prendre pour** *vp+prép* : **il ne se prend pas pour rien** *ou* **pour n'importe qui** he thinks he's God's gift to humanity ■ **tu te prends pour qui pour me parler sur ce ton?** who do you think you are, talking to me like that?

◆ **s'en prendre à** *vp+prép* : **s'en ~ à qqn/qqch** [l'attaquer] to attack sb/sthg ; [le rendre responsable] to put the blame on sb/sthg ■ **pourquoi faut-il toujours que tu t'en prennes à moi?** why do you always take it out on me? ■ **ne t'en prends qu'à toi-même** you've only (got) yourself to blame.

preneur, euse [prənœr, øz] *nm, f* **1.** [acheteur] buyer ■ **trouver ~ pour qqch** to find someone (willing) to buy sthg, to find a buyer for sthg ■ **si vous me le laissez à 100 euros, je suis ~** I'll buy it if you'll take 100 euros for it **2.** [locataire] potential tenant **3.** [ravisseur] : **~ d'otages** hostage-taker.

◆ **preneur de son, preneuse de son** *nm, f* sound engineer.

prenne *etc v* ▷ **prendre.**

prénom [prenɔ̃] *nm* first *ou* Christian UK *ou* given US name.

prénommé, e [prenɔme] ◇ *adj* : **un garçon ~ Julien** a boy called Julien ■ **la ~e Maria** the said Maria *hum.*

◇ *nm, f* DR above-named (person).

prénommer [3] [prenɔme] *vt* to call ■ **si c'est une fille, nous la prénommerons Léa** if it's a girl, we'll call her Léa.

◆ **se prénommer** *vpi* : **comment se prénomme-t-il?** what's his first name?

prénuptial, e, aux [prenypsjal, o] *adj* premarital, antenuptial ■ **la visite ~e obligatoire** the compulsory pre-marriage medical check *(in French law).*

préoccupant, e [preɔkypɑ̃, ɑ̃t] *adj* worrying ■ **la situation est ~e** the situation gives cause for concern *ou* is worrying.

préoccupation [preɔkypasjɔ̃] *nf* **1.** [souci] concern, worry ■ **le chômage reste notre ~ première** unemployment remains our major cause for concern ■ **ceux pour qui l'argent n'est pas une ~** those who don't have to worry about money *ou* who don't have money worries ■ **j'ai été un sujet de ~ pour mes parents** I was a worry to my parents ■ **~s d'ordre moral/esthétique** moral/aesthetic considerations **2.** [priorité] concern, preoccupation ■ **depuis qu'elle est partie, il n'a plus qu'une ~, la retrouver** since she left his one thought is to find her again.

préoccupé, e [preɔkype] *adj* [inquiet] worried, preoccupied, concerned ■ **elle avait l'air ~** she looked worried, there was a look of concern on her face.

préoccuper [3] [preɔkype] *vt* **1.** [tracasser - suj: avenir, question] to worry **2.** [obséder] to preoccupy, to concern, to be of concern to ■ **il est trop préoccupé de sa petite personne** he's too wrapped up in himself.

◆ **se préoccuper de** *vp+prép* to be concerned with, to care about ■ **se ~ de ses enfants** to worry about one's children ■ **ne te préoccupe donc pas de ça!** don't you worry *ou* bother about that!

préopératoire [preɔperatwar] *adj* preoperative, presurgical.

prépa [prepa] (*abr de* **classe préparatoire**) *nf fam class preparing for the competitive entrance exam to a Grande école.*

préparateur, trice [preparatœr, tris] *nm, f* **1.** ÉDUC *assistant to a professor of science* **2.** PHARM : **~ en pharmacie** assistant to a dispensing chemist UK *ou* pharmacist US.

préparatifs [preparatif] *nmpl* preparations ■ **~ de départ/guerre** preparations for leaving/war ■ **commencer les ~ du voyage** to start preparing for the trip.

préparation [preparasjɔ̃] *nf* **1.** [réalisation - d'un plat, d'un médicament] preparation ■ **les moules ne demandent pas une longue ~** mussels don't take long to prepare ■ [apprêt - d'une peau, de la laine] dressing **2.** [organisation - d'un voyage, d'une fête, d'un attentat] preparation ■ **la randonnée avait fait l'objet d'une soigneuse ~** the ramble had been carefully thought out *ou* prepared **3.** [entraînement - pour un examen] preparation ; [- pour une épreuve sportive] training, preparation ■ **la ~ d'un examen** preparing *ou* working for an exam ■ **manquer de ~** to be insufficiently prepared ➤ **~ militaire** pre-call-up training **4.** [chose préparée] preparation ■ **~ culinaire** dish ■ **~ (pharmaceutique)** (pharmaceutical) preparation **5.** ÉDUC : **faire une ~ à une Grande école** to attend preparatory classes for the entrance to a Grande école.

◆ **en préparation** *loc adv* being prepared, in hand ■ **avoir un livre/disque en ~** to have a book/record in the pipeline.

◆ **sans préparation** *loc adv* [courir] without preparation, cold *(adv)* ■ [parler] extempore, ad lib.

préparatoire [preparatwar] *adj* : **travail ~** groundwork ■ **~ à** preparatory to, in preparation for.

préparer [3] [prepare] *vt* **1.** [réaliser - plat] to prepare, to make ; [- sandwich] to prepare, to make ; [- médicament, cataplasme] to prepare ■ **qu'est-ce que tu nous as préparé de bon?** what delicious dish have you cooked for us? **2.** [rendre prêt - valise] to pack ; [- repas, chambre, champ] to prepare, to get ready ; [- peaux, laine] to dress ; [- document] to prepare, to draw up *(sép)* ■ **préparez la monnaie, s'il vous plaît** please have change ready ■ **plats tout préparés** precooked *ou* ready-cooked meals ■ **poulet tout préparé** oven-ready *ou* dressed chicken ■ **on dirait qu'il nous prépare une rougeole** *fam* (it) looks like he's getting the measles ➤ **~ le terrain (pour)** *pr* to prepare the ground *ou* to lay the ground (for) ; *fig* to pave the way (for) **3.** [organiser - attentat, conférence] to prepare, to organize ; [- complot] to prepare, to hatch ■ **elle avait préparé sa réponse** she'd got her *ou* an answer ready ■ **~ une surprise à qqn** to have a surprise in store for sb **4.** [travailler à - œuvre] to be preparing, to be working on ; [- examen] to be preparing for ; [- épreuve sportive] to be in training for ■ **il prépare une grande école** he's studying for the entrance exam to a 'Grande École' **5.** [former - élève] to prepare ; [- athlète] to train ■ **~ qqn à qqch** to prepare sb for sthg ■ **on les prépare intensivement à l'examen** they're being coached for the exam **6.** [habituer] to accustom.

◆ **se préparer** ◇ *vp (emploi réfléchi)* **1.** [s'apprêter] to get ready ■ **le temps qu'elle se prépare, on aura raté la séance** by the time she's ready, we'll have missed the show **2.** [s'entraîner] to train ■ **se ~ pour Roland-Garros** to train *ou* to prepare for the French Open tennis tournament.

◇ *vpi* : **un orage se prépare** there's a storm brewing ■ *(tournure impersonnelle)* **je sens qu'il se prépare quelque chose** I can feel there's something afoot *ou* in the air.

◇ *vpt* : **se ~ des déceptions** to prepare o.s. for disappointment.

se préparer à *vp+prép* **1.** [être disposé à] to be ready *ou* prepared for ▪ **je ne m'étais pas préparé à un tel accueil** I wasn't prepared for such a welcome **2.** [être sur le point de] to be about to.

prépondérance [prepɔ̃derɑ̃s] *nf* predominance, preponderance, primacy.

prépondérant, e [prepɔ̃derɑ̃, ɑ̃t] *adj* prominent ▪ **jouer un rôle ~** to play a prominent part *ou* role.

préposé, e [prepoze] *nm, f* **1.** [employé] : **~ des douanes** customs official *ou* officer ▪ **~ au vestiaire** cloakroom attendant **2.** ADMIN : **~ (aux postes)** postman *UK*, mailman *US* **3.** DR agent.

préposer [3] [prepoze] *vt* [affecter] : **~ qqn à** to place *ou* to put sb in charge of.

préposition [prepozisjɔ̃] *nf* preposition.

prépositionnel, elle [prepozisjɔnɛl] *adj* prepositional.

prépubère [prepybɛr] *adj* prepubescent.

prépuce [prepys] *nm* foreskin, prepuce *spéc.*

préraphaélisme [prerafaelism] *nm* Pre-Raphaelism.

préraphaélite [prerafaelit] *adj & nmf* Pre-Raphaelite.

préréglage [prereglaʒ] *nm* TECHNOL preselection, presetting.

prérégler [18] [preregle] *vt* TECHNOL to preselect, to preset.

prérentrée [prerɑ̃tre] *nf* ÉDUC *start of the new school year for teachers (a few days before the pupils).*

prérequis [prerəki] *nm* prerequisite.

préretraite [prerətrɛt] *nf* **1.** [allocation] early retirement allowance **2.** [période] : **partir en ~** to take early retirement ▪ **être mis en ~** to be retired early.

préretraité, e [prerətrete] *nm, f person who takes or has been given early retirement.*

prérévolutionnaire [prerevɔlysjɔnɛr] *adj* prerevolutionary.

prérogative [prerɔgativ] *nf* prerogative, privilege.

préromantique [prerɔmɑ̃tik] ◇ *adj* pre-Romantic.
◇ *nmf* pre-Romantic *(poet or artist).*

près [prɛ] ◇ *adv* **1.** [dans l'espace] near, close ▪ **cent mètres plus ~** one hundred metres nearer *ou* closer ▪ **le bureau est tout ~** the office is very near *ou* just around the corner **2.** [dans le temps] near, close, soon ▪ **jeudi c'est trop ~, disons plutôt samedi** Thursday is too soon, let's say Saturday.
◇ *prép sout* : **ambassadeur ~ le Saint-Siège** ambassador to the Holy See.

à ... près *loc corrélative* : **c'est parfait, à un détail ~** it's perfect but for *ou* except for one thing ▪ **j'ai raté mon train à quelques secondes ~** I missed my train by a few seconds ▪ **vous n'en êtes plus à un procès ~** what's one more trial to you? ▪ **on n'est pas à 50 euros ~** we can spare 50 euros ▪ **tu n'es plus à cinq minutes ~** another five minutes won't make much difference.

à cela près que *loc conj* except that.

à peu de choses près *loc adv* more or less ▪ **à peu de choses ~, il y en a cinquante** there are fifty of them, more or less *ou* give or take a few.

à peu près *loc adv* **1.** [environ] about, around ▪ **on était à peu ~ cinquante** there were about *ou* around fifty of us **2.** [plus ou moins] more or less ▪ **il sait à peu ~ comment y aller** he knows more or less *ou* roughly how to get there.

de près *loc adv* at close range *ou* quarters ▪ **il est rasé de ~** he's clean-shaven ▪ **surveiller qqn de ~** to keep a close watch *ou* eye on sb ▪ **frôler qqch de ~** to come within an inch of sthg ▪ **les explosions se sont suivies de très ~** the explosions took place within seconds of each other ▪ **ses enfants se suivent de ~** her children are close together in age ▪ **regarder qqch de (très) ~** *pr* to look at sthg very closely ; *fig* to look (very) closely at sthg, to look carefully into sthg ▪ **étudions la question de plus ~** let's take a closer look at the problem ▪ **cela ressemble, de ~ ou de loin, à une habile escroquerie** however *ou* whichever way you look at it, it's a skilful piece of fraud ▪ **tout ce qui touche, de ~ ou de loin à** everything (which is) even remotely connected with.

près de *loc prép* **1.** [dans l'espace] near ▪ **assieds-toi ~ de lui** sit near him *ou* next to him ▪ **vêtements ~ du corps** close-fitting *ou* tight-fitting clothes ‖ [affectivement, qualitativement] close to ▪ **les premiers candidats sont très ~ les uns des autres** there's very little difference between the first few candidates ➤ **être ~ de ses sous** *ou* **de son argent** to be tightfisted **2.** [dans le temps] : **on est ~ des vacances** it's nearly the holidays ▪ **il doit être ~ de la retraite** he must be about to retire ▪ **nous étions ~ de partir** we were about to leave ▪ **vous êtes ~ d'avoir deviné** you've nearly guessed ▪ **je ne suis pas ~ d'oublier ça** I'm not about to *ou* it'll be a long time before I forget that **3.** [environ, presque] nearly, almost ▪ **on était ~ de cinquante** there were almost *ou* nearly fifty of us.

présage [prezaʒ] *nm* **1.** [signe] omen, portent *litt*, presage *litt* ▪ **heureux/mauvais ~** good/bad omen ▪ **j'y ai vu le ~ d'un avenir meilleur** I viewed it as a sign of better days to come **2.** [prédiction] prediction ▪ **tirer un ~ de qqch** to make a prediction on the basis of sthg.

présager [17] [prezaʒe] *vt* **1.** [être le signe de] to be a sign of, to portend *litt* ▪ **cela ne présage rien de bon** that's an ominous sign, nothing good will come of it **2.** [prévoir] to predict ▪ **laisser ~ qqch** to be a sign of sthg.

présalaire [presalɛr] *nm allowance paid to students.*

pré-salé [presale] (*pl* **prés-salés**) *nm* [mouton] salt-meadow sheep ▪ [viande] salt-meadow *ou* pré-salé lamb ▪ **un gigot de ~** a salt-meadow leg of lamb.

presbyte [prɛsbit] ◇ *adj* longsighted *UK*, farsighted *US*, presbyopic *spéc.*
◇ *nmf* longsighted *UK ou* farsighted *US* person, presbyope *spéc.*

presbytère [prɛsbitɛr] *nm* presbytery.

presbytérien, enne [prɛsbiterjɛ̃, ɛn] *adj & nm, f* Presbyterian.

presbytie [prɛsbisi] *nf* longsightedness *UK*, farsightedness *US*, presbyopia *spéc.*

prescience [presjɑ̃s] *nf* **1.** [pressentiment] prescience *litt*, foreknowledge, foresight **2.** RELIG prescience.

préscientifique [presjɑ̃tifik] *adj* prescientific.

préscolaire [preskɔlɛr] *adj* preschool.

prescripteur, trice [prɛskriptœr, tris] *nm, f* prescriber.

prescriptible [prɛskriptibl] *adj* DR prescriptible.

prescription [prɛskripsjɔ̃] *nf* **1.** DR prescription ▪ **~ de la peine** lapse *ou* lapsing of the sentence ▪ **y a-t-il ~ pour les crimes de guerre?** is there a statutory limitation relating to war crimes? **2.** [instruction] : **se conformer aux ~s** to conform to instructions *ou* regulations ▪ **les ~s de la morale** moral dictates **3.** MÉD [gén] orders, instructions ▪ [ordonnance] prescription.

prescrire [99] [prɛskrir] *vt* **1.** [recommander] to prescribe ▪ **~ qqch à qqn** to prescribe sthg for sb ▪ **on lui a prescrit du repos** she was ordered to rest ▪ **~ à qqn de faire qqch** to order sb to do sthg **2.** [stipuler] to prescribe, to stipulate ▪ **accomplir les formalités que prescrit le règlement** to go through the procedures stipulated in the regulations **3.** DR [propriété] to obtain by prescription ▪ *(en usage absolu)* **on ne prescrit pas contre les mineurs** one cannot obtain property from minors by prescription ‖ [sanction, peine] to lapse.

se prescrire *vp (emploi passif)* DR [s'acquérir] to be obtained by prescription ▪ [se périmer] to lapse ▪ **la peine se prescrit par cinq ans** the penalty lapses after five years.

prescrit, e [prɛskri, it] *adj* **1.** [conseillé - dose] prescribed, recommended **2.** [fixé] : **au jour ~** on the set day ▪ **à l'heure ~e** at the agreed hour ▪ **dans le délai ~** within the agreed time.

prescrivait *etc v* ▷ **prescrire**.

préséance [preseɑ̃s] *nf* **1.** [priorité] precedence, priority ■ **avoir la ~ sur qqn** to have precedence over sb **2.** *sout* [étiquette] : **la ~ veut qu'on le serve avant vous** according to (the rules of) etiquette, he should be served before you.

présélecteur [preselɛktœr] *nm* preselector.

présélection [preselɛksjɔ̃] *nf* **1.** [choix] preselection, short-listing **2.** AUTO : **boîte de vitesses à ~** preselector gearbox **3.** RADIO : **poste avec/sans ~** radio with/without preset.

présélectionné, e [preselɛksjɔne] *nm, f* short-listed candidate.

présélectionner [3] [preselɛksjɔne] *vt* **1.** [candidat] to preselect, to short-list **2.** [heure, programme] to preset.

présence [prezɑ̃s] *nf* **1.** [fait d'être là] presence ■ **faire acte de ~** to put in an appearance ■ **réunion à 9 h, ~ obligatoire** meeting at 9 o'clock, attendance compulsory ■ **~ assidue aux cours** regular attendance in class **2.** THÉÂTRE [personnalité] presence ■ **il n'a aucune ~ sur scène** he has no stage presence whatsoever **3.** [influence] presence ■ **la ~ française en Afrique** the French presence in Africa.

◆ **en présence** <> *loc adj* **1.** [en opposition] : **les armées/équipes en ~** the opposing armies/teams **2.** DR : **les parties en ~** the opposing parties, the litigants *spéc.*

<> *loc adv* : **mettre deux personnes en ~** to bring two people together *ou* face-to-face.

◆ **en présence de** *loc prép* : **je ne parlerai qu'en ~ de mon avocat** I refuse to talk unless my lawyer is present ■ **en ma ~** in my presence.

◆ **présence d'esprit** *nf* presence of mind ■ **mon voisin a eu la ~ d'esprit de me prévenir** my neighbour had the presence of mind to warn me.

présent, e [prezɑ̃, ɑ̃t] <> *adj* **1.** [dans le lieu dont on parle] present ■ **les personnes ici ~es** the people here present ■ **le racisme est ~ à tous les niveaux** racism can be found at all levels ■ **être ~ à une conférence** to be present at *ou* to attend a conference ■ **être ~ à l'appel** MIL to be present at roll call ■ **Duval? – ~!** Duval? – here *ou* present! ■ **avoir qqch ~ à l'esprit** to bear *ou* to keep sthg in mind ■ **des images que nous garderons longtemps ~es à l'esprit** images which will linger in our minds ⊃ **répondre ~** ÉDUC to answer to one's name, to be present at roll call ; *fig* to rise to the challenge ■ **des centaines de jeunes ont répondu ~ à l'appel du pape** hundreds of young people answered the Pope's call **2.** [actif] : **les Français ne sont pas du tout ~s dans le jeu** the French team is making no impact on the game at all ‖ THÉÂTRE : **on a rarement vu un chanteur aussi ~ sur scène** seldom has one seen a singer with such stage presence **3.** *(après le n)* [en cours] : **dans le cas ~** in the present case ■ *(avant le n)* **la ~e convention** *sout* this agreement.

<> *nm, f* : **il y avait 20 ~s à la réunion** 20 people were present at *ou* attended the meeting.

◆ **présent** *nm* **1.** [moment] present ■ **vivre dans le ~** to live in the present ■ **pour le ~** for the time being, for the moment **2.** GRAMM present (tense) ■ **au ~** in the present ■ **~ de l'indicatif/du subjonctif** present indicative/subjunctive ■ **~ historique** historic present ■ **~ progressif** present progressive ■ **~ simple** simple present, *voir aussi* **pluriel 3.** *litt* [cadeau] gift, present ■ **faire ~ de qqch à qqn** to present sb with sthg.

◆ **présente** *nf* ADMIN [lettre] the present (letter), this letter ■ **je vous informe par la ~e que...** I hereby inform you that... ■ **je joins à la ~e un chèque à votre nom** I herewith enclose a cheque payable to you.

◆ **à présent** *loc adv* now ■ **je travaille à ~ dans une laiterie** I'm working in a dairy at present.

◆ **à présent que** *loc conj* now that.

◆ **d'à présent** *loc adj* modern-day, present-day ■ **les hommes politiques d'à ~** today's *ou* present-day politicians, the politicians of today.

présentable [prezɑ̃tabl] *adj* presentable ■ **ta tenue n'est pas ~** you're not fit to be seen in that outfit ■ **griffonnés comme ça, les documents ne sont pas ~s** these hastily scribbled documents are not fit to be seen.

présentateur, trice [prezɑ̃tatœr, tris] *nm, f* RADIO & TV [des programmes] announcer, presenter ■ [du journal] newscaster, anchorman (*f* anchorwoman) *US* ■ [de variétés] host.

présentation [prezɑ̃tasjɔ̃] *nf* **1.** [dans un groupe] introduction ■ **Robert, faites donc les ~s** [entre plusieurs personnes] Robert, could you introduce everybody? ■ **venez par ici, vous deux, je vais faire les ~s** come over here, you two, I want to introduce you **2.** RADIO & TV [des informations] presentation, reading ■ [des variétés, d'un jeu] hosting, compering *UK* **3.** COUT fashion show ■ **aller à une ~ de collection** *ou* **couture** *ou* **mode** to attend a fashion show **4.** [exposition] presenting, showing ■ **la ~ des modèles a d'abord provoqué une vive controverse** there was fierce controversy when the models were first presented *ou* unveiled ‖ COMM [à un client potentiel] presentation **5.** [aspect formel - d'un texte] presentation ■ **l'idée de départ est bonne mais la ~ des arguments n'est pas convaincante** the original idea is good but the arguments are not presented in a convincing manner ■ COMM presentation, packaging **6.** [allure] : **il a une mauvaise/bonne ~** he doesn't look/he looks very presentable **7.** [d'un document, d'un laissez-passer] showing ■ [d'un compte, d'une facture] presentation ■ **la ~ de la facture a lieu un mois après** the bill is presented a month later **8.** MÉD : **~ du sommet/siège** head/breech presentation.

◆ **sur présentation de** *loc prép* on presentation of ■ **vous n'entrerez que sur ~ d'une invitation/de ce coupon** you'll only be admitted on presentation of an invitation/this coupon.

Voir module d'usage

LES PRÉSENTATIONS

Se présenter

I don't think we've met *ou* **been introduced.** Je ne crois pas que nous nous connaissons.

Allow me to introduce myself, I'm Lily. Je me présente, je m'appelle Lily.

Hello, my name's Robert. Bonjour, je m'appelle Robert.

Hi, I'm Tom. Salut, moi c'est Tom.

Présenter quelqu'un

Do you know everybody? Tu connais tout le monde ?

Have you two met/been introduced? Est-ce que vous avez été présentés ?

Shall I do the introductions? Je vais faire les présentations : ...

Fred, I'd like to introduce you to some friends of mine. Fred, j'aimerais te présenter des amis.

John, I'd like you to meet Emma. John, je te présente Emma.

David, (this is) Vicki. Vicki, (this is) David. David, (voici) Vicki. Vicki, (voici) David.

Paul, do you know Katie? Paul, tu connais Katie ?

Une fois que les présentations sont faites

Pleased to meet you. Ravi de faire votre connaissance.

How do you do. Enchanté.

I've heard so much about you. J'ai beaucoup entendu parler de vous.

I'm sorry, I didn't (quite) catch your name. Excusez-moi, je n'ai pas (bien) saisi votre nom.

présentement [prezɑ̃tmɑ̃] *adv* at present, presently *US*.

présenter [3] [prezɑ̃te] <> *vt* **1.** [faire connaître] to introduce ▪ **je te présente ma sœur Blanche** this is *ou* let me introduce my sister Blanche ▪ **on ne vous présente plus** [personne célèbre] you need no introduction from me ▪ **~ qqn à la Cour/au Roi** to present sb at Court/to the King
2. [décrire] to describe, to portray ▪ **on me l'a présenté comme un homme de parole** he was described to me as a man of his word
3. [remettre - ticket, papiers] to present, to show ; [- facture, devis] to present
4. [montrer publiquement] to present ▪ **les Ballets de la Lune (vous) présentent...** the Moon Ballet Company presents...
5. COMM to present, to package ▪ **bouteille/vitrine joliment présentée** attractively packaged bottle/dressed window
6. RADIO & TV [informations] to present, to read ▪ [variétés, jeu] to host, to compere *UK*
7. [soumettre - démission] to present, to submit, to hand in *(sép)* ; [- pétition] to put in *(sép)*, to submit ; [- projet de loi] to present, to introduce ▪ **~ sa candidature à un poste** to apply for a position ▪ [dans un festival] to present ▪ [dans un concours] to enter ▪ **pourquoi présentez-vous votre film hors festival?** why aren't you showing your film as part of the festival? ▪ **~ l'anglais à l'oral** ÉDUC & UNIV to take English at the oral exam ▪ **il a présenté un de ses élèves au Conservatoire** he has entered one of his pupils for the Conservatoire entrance exam ▪ **~ un candidat** [à un concours] to enter a candidate ; POLIT to put up a candidate
8. [expliquer - dossier] to present, to explain ; [- rapport] to present, to bring in *(sép)* ▪ **vous avez présenté votre cas de manière fort convaincante** you have set out *ou* stated your case most convincingly ▪ **présentez-leur la chose gentiment** put it to them nicely ▪ **présentez vos objections** state your objections
9. [dans des formules de politesse] to offer ▪ **je vous présente mes condoléances** please accept *ou* I'd like to offer my condolences ▪ **~ ses hommages à qqn** to pay one's respects to sb ▪ **~ ses excuses** to offer (one's) apologies ▪ **~ ses félicitations à qqn** to congratulate sb
10. [comporter - anomalie, particularité] to present *sout*, to have ; [- symptômes, traces, signes] to show ; [- difficulté, risque] to involve ▪ **~ l'avantage de** to have the advantage of ▪ **cette œuvre présente un intérêt particulier** this work is of particular interest ▪ **les deux systèmes présentent peu de différences** the two systems present *sout ou* display very few differences
11. [offrir] : **~ son bras à une dame** to offer one's arm to a lady ▪ **~ sa main à qqn** to hold out one's hand to sb ▪ **~ des petits fours** to offer *ou* to pass round petit fours
12. MIL [armes] to present.
<> *vi fam* **il présente bien, ton ami** your friend looks good.
◆ **se présenter** <> *vp (emploi réfléchi)* [décliner son identité] to introduce o.s.
<> *vp (emploi passif)* : **ça se présente sous forme de poudre ou de liquide** it comes as a powder or a liquid.
<> *vpi* **1.** [se manifester] to appear ▪ **aucun témoin ne s'est encore présenté** no witness has come forward as yet ▪ **vous devez vous ~ au tribunal à 14 h** you are required to be in court at 2 pm ▪ **elle s'est présentée à son entretien avec une heure de retard** she arrived one hour late for the interview ▪ **se ~ chez qqn** to call on sb, to go to sb's house ▪ **après cette soirée, il n'a pas osé se ~ chez elle** after the party, he didn't dare show his face at her place ▪ *(tournure impersonnelle)* **il ne s'est présenté aucun acheteur/volontaire** no buyer/volunteer has come forward
2. [avoir telle tournure] : **les choses se présentent plutôt mal** things aren't looking too good ▪ **tout cela se présente fort bien** it all looks very promising ▪ **l'affaire se présente sous un jour nouveau** the matter can be seen *ou* appears in a new light
3. [être candidat] : **se ~ aux présidentielles** to run for president ▪ **se ~ à un examen** to take an exam ▪ **se ~ à un concours de beauté** to go in for *ou* to enter a beauty contest ▪ **se ~ pour un poste** to apply for a job
4. [survenir] to arise ▪ **si une difficulté se présente** if any difficulty should arise ▪ **elle a épousé le premier qui s'est présenté** she married the first man that came along ▪ **j'attends que quelque chose d'intéressant se présente** I'm waiting for something interesting to turn up *ou* to come my way
5. MÉD to present ▪ **le bébé se présente par le siège** the baby is in a breech position, it's a breech baby ▪ **le bébé se présente par la tête** the baby's presentation is normal, the baby's in a head position.

présentoir [prezɑ̃twar] *nm* [étagère] (display) shelf ▪ [support] (display) stand, display unit.

préservatif, ive [prezɛrvatif, iv] *adj litt* preventive, protective.
◆ **préservatif** *nm* condom, sheath ▪ **~ féminin** female condom ; [diaphragme] diaphragm.

préservation [prezɛrvasjɔ̃] *nf* preservation, protection ▪ **la ~ de l'emploi** safeguarding jobs.

préserver [3] [prezɛrve] *vt* **1.** [maintenir] to preserve, to keep ▪ **pour ~ l'intégrité de notre territoire** in order to retain our territorial integrity **2.** [protéger] : **~ de** to protect *ou* to preserve from ▪ **'à ~ de l'humidité/la chaleur'** 'to be kept in a dry/cool place' ▪ **Dieu** *ou* **le ciel me préserve de tomber jamais aussi bas!** God *ou* Heaven forbid that I should ever fall so low!
◆ **se préserver de** *vp+prép* to guard against ▪ **tu apprendras à te ~ des dangers** you'll learn to guard against *ou* to keep yourself safe from danger.

présidence [prezidɑ̃s] *nf* **1.** [fonction - POLIT] presidency ▪ UNIV principalship, vice-chancellorship *UK*, presidency *US* ▪ COMM [d'un homme] chairmanship, directorship ▪ ADMIN chairmanship ▪ **la ~ du jury** UNIV the chief examinership ▪ **une femme a été nommée à la ~** POLIT a woman was made President ; ADMIN a woman was appointed to the chair *ou* made chairperson **2.** [durée - prévue] term of office ; [- effectuée] period in office ▪ **sa ~ aura duré un an** she'll have been in office for a year **3.** [lieu] presidential residence *ou* palace **4.** [services] presidential office ▪ **à la ~, on ne dit rien** presidential aides are keeping silent.

président [prezidɑ̃] *nm* **1.** POLIT president ▪ **le ~ de la République française** the French President **2.** ADMIN chairman (*f* chairwoman), chairperson **3.** COMM chairman (*f* chairwoman) ▪ **~-directeur général** chairman and managing director *UK*, president and chief executive officer *US* ▪ **~ du conseil d'administration** Chairman of the Board **4.** DR : **~ d'audience** presiding magistrate *ou* judge ▪ **~ du tribunal** vice-chancellor *UK* **5.** UNIV principal, vice-chancellor *UK*, president *US* ▪ **~ du jury (d'examen)** chief examiner **6.** SPORT : **~ d'un club de football** president of a football club ▪ **le ~ du comité olympique** the chairman of the Olympic Committee ➲ **~ du jury** chairman of the panel of judges.

présidente [prezidɑ̃t] *nf* **1.** POLIT [titulaire] (woman) president ▪ *vieilli* [épouse du président] president's wife **2.** COMM [titulaire] chairwoman ▪ *vieilli* [épouse du président] chairman's wife **3.** DR presiding judge.

présidentiable [prezidɑ̃sjabl] *nmf* would-be presidential candidate.

présidentialisme [prezidɑ̃sjalism] *nm* presidential (government) system.

présidentiel, elle [prezidɑ̃sjɛl] *adj* **1.** [du président] presidential, president's ▪ **dans l'entourage ~** among the president's close associates **2.** [centralisé - régime] presidential.
◆ **présidentielles** *nfpl* presidential election *ou* elections.

LES PRÉSIDENTIELLES

Under France's Fifth Republic, the president is elected directly for a renewable five-year term (*le quinquennat*). Candidates are usually nominated by the main political parties, but anyone who collects the requisite number of sponsors can run. If no candidate wins the absolute majority in the first round of voting, a runoff between the two frontrunners is held two weeks later.

présider [3] [prezide] *vt* [diriger - séance] to preside at *ou* over *(insép)* ; [- œuvre de bienfaisance, commission] to preside over, to be the president of ▪ [table] to be at the head of.

◆ **présider à** *v+prép sout* ~ **aux destinées d'un pays** to rule over a country, to steer the ship of state *sout* ■ **un réel esprit de coopération a présidé à nos entretiens** a genuine spirit of co-operation prevailed during our talks.

présidium [prezidjɔm] = **praesidium.**

présomptif, ive [prezɔ̃ptif, iv] *adj* presumptive.

présomption [prezɔ̃psjɔ̃] *nf* **1.** [prétention] presumption, presumptuousness **2.** [supposition] presumption, assumption ■ **il s'agit là d'une simple ~ de votre part** you're only assuming this (to be the case) **3.** DR presumption ■ **~ d'innocence** presumption of innocence ■ **~ légale** presumption of law ■ **~ de paternité** presumption of legitimacy.

présomptueux, euse [prezɔ̃ptɥø, øz] *adj* presumptuous.

présonorisation [presɔnɔrizasjɔ̃] *nf* playback.

presque [prɛsk] *adv* **1.** [dans des phrases affirmatives] almost, nearly ■ **l'espèce a ~ entièrement disparu** the species is virtually *ou* all but extinct ■ **l'ambulance est arrivée ~ aussitôt** the ambulance arrived almost immediately *ou* at once **2.** [dans des phrases négatives] : **ils ne se sont ~ pas parlé** they hardly spoke to each other ■ **je n'avais ~ pas mangé de la journée** I'd eaten next to *ou* almost *ou* virtually nothing all day ■ **tu fumes beaucoup en ce moment? – non, ~ pas** do you smoke much at the moment? – no, hardly at all ■ **est-ce qu'il reste des gâteaux? – non, ~ pas** are there any cakes left? – hardly any ■ **il n'y a ~ plus de café** there's hardly any coffee left **3.** *sout* [quasi] : **avoir la ~ certitude de qqch** to be almost *ou* practically certain of sthg.

◆ **ou presque** *loc adv* : **des écrivains ignorés ou ~** writers who are unknown or almost unknown ■ **c'est sûr, ou ~** it's almost *ou* practically certain.

presqu'île [prɛskil] *nf* peninsula.

pressage [presaʒ] *nm* **1.** [d'un disque] pressing **2.** [du fromage] draining *ou* pressing of curds.

pressant, e [prɛsɑ̃, ɑ̃t] *adj* **1.** [urgent] urgent ■ **un travail ~** an urgent piece of work **2.** [insistant - question, invitation] pressing, insistent ■ **elle se faisait de plus en plus ~e** she was becoming more and more insistent.

press-book [prɛsbuk] (*pl* **press-books**) *nm* portfolio.

presse [prɛs] *nf* **1.** [journaux, magazines etc] : **la ~ (écrite)** the press, the papers ▶ **~ féminine/financière/sportive** women's/ financial/sports magazines ■ **~ à sensation** *ou* **à scandale** popular press, gutter press ■ ≃ tabloids ■ **la ~ d'opinion** the quality newspapers ■ **~ quotidienne régionale** local daily press ■ **avoir bonne/mauvaise ~** *pr* to have a good/bad press ; *fig* to be well/badly thought of
2. IMPR press ■ **être mis sous ~** to go to press ■ **au moment où nous mettons sous ~** at the time of going to press ■ **sortir de ~** to come out ▶ **~ rotative** rotary press
3. AGRIC, MÉCAN & TEXT press ■ MENUIS bench vice ■ **~ à forger** forging machine ■ **~ hydraulique/mécanique** hydraulic/ power press ■ **~ monétaire** coining press
4. ŒNOL winepress
5. *litt* [foule, bousculade] press, throng.

◆ **de presse** *loc adj* **1.** [campagne, coupure, attaché] press (*modif*)
2. *sout* [moment, période] peak *(avant n)* ■ **nous avons des moments de ~** we get very busy at times.

PRESSE

The main newspapers in France are:
l'Équipe: a popular daily sports newspaper;
le Figaro: a quality broadsheet newspaper (it has a predominantly conservative readership);
France-Dimanche: a popular weekend broadsheet with a tendency to sensationalism;
France-Soir: a conservative broadsheet newspaper;
l'Humanité ("l'Huma"): a quality daily broadsheet (it is the organ of the French Communist Party);
Libération ("Libé"): a quality daily tabloid (with a predominantly left-of-centre readership);
le Monde: a quality broadsheet newspaper which appears in the evening (its readership is predominantly left-of-centre).

pressé, e [prese] *adj* **1.** [personne] : **être ~** to be pressed for time, to be in a hurry *ou* rush ■ **tu n'as pas l'air ~ de la revoir** you seem in no hurry *ou* you don't seem eager to see her again ■ **je suis ~ d'en finir** I'm anxious to get the whole thing over with **2.** [précipité - démarche, geste] hurried **3.** [urgent - réparation, achat] urgent ■ **il n'a rien trouvé de plus ~ que d'aller tout raconter à sa femme** he wasted no time in telling his wife the whole story ■ **le plus ~, c'est de prévenir son mari** the first thing to do is to tell her husband ■ [agrume] freshly squeezed ■ **~ à froid** cold-pressed **4.** TECHNOL pressed.

presse-agrumes [prɛsagrym] *nm inv* electric (orange or lemon) squeezer.

presse-ail [prɛsaj] *nm inv* garlic press.

presse-bouton [prɛsbutɔ̃] *adj inv* ▷ **guerre.**

presse-citron [prɛssitrɔ̃] (*pl inv ou pl* **presse-citrons**) *nm* lemon squeezer.

pressens *etc v* ▷ **pressentir.**

pressentiment [presɑ̃timɑ̃] *nm* premonition, feeling, hunch ■ **avoir le ~ de/que** to have a feeling of/that ■ **j'ai eu le curieux ~ que je reviendrais ici un jour** I had the odd feeling *ou* a hunch that I'd be back again some day.

pressentir [37] [presɑ̃tir] *vt* **1.** [prévoir] to sense (in advance), to have a premonition of ■ **~ un danger/des difficultés** to sense danger/trouble ■ **rien ne laissait ~ qu'elle allait démissionner** nothing suggested that she would resign **2.** [contacter] to approach, to contact ■ **toutes les personnes pressenties** all the people who were contacted.

presse-papiers [prɛspapje] *nm inv* paperweight.

presse-purée [prɛspyre] *nm inv* potato masher.

presser [4] [prese] ◇ *vt* **1.** [extraire le jus de] to squeeze ■ **~ le raisin** to press grapes ▶ **~ le citron à qqn** *fam*, **~qqn comme un citron** *fam* to exploit sb to the full, to squeeze sb dry ■ **on presse l'orange et on jette l'écorce** *Frédéric II allus* you use people and then cast them aside
2. [faire se hâter] to rush ■ **j'ai horreur qu'on me presse** I hate being rushed ■ **qu'est-ce qui te presse?** what's the hurry?, what's (all) the rush for? ■ **~ le pas** to speed up
3. [serrer] to squeeze ■ **elle pressait sa poupée dans ses bras** she was hugging her doll ■ **il pressait sur son cœur la photo de sa fille** he was clasping a picture of his daughter to his heart
4. [inciter à faire] : **~ qqn de faire qqch** to urge sb to do sthg
5. [accabler] : **~ qqn de questions** to ply *ou* to bombard sb with questions ■ **être pressé par le temps/l'argent** to be pressed for time/money
6. TECHNOL [disque, pli] to press.
◇ *vi* : **le temps presse** time is short ■ **l'affaire presse** it's an urgent matter ■ **rien ne presse, ça ne presse pas** there's no (need to) rush *ou* hurry.

◆ **se presser** ◇ *vpi* **1.** [se dépêcher] to hurry ■ **il n'est que 2 h, il n'y a pas de raison de se ~** it's only 2 o'clock, there's no point in rushing *ou* no need to hurry ■ **allons les enfants, pressons-nous un peu** come on children, get a move on ■ **se ~ de faire qqch** to be in a hurry to do sthg ■ **je ne me pressai pas de répondre** I was in no hurry to reply
2. [se serrer] : **il se pressait contre moi tant il avait peur** he was pressing up against me from fright ■ **les gens se pressaient au guichet** there was a crush at the box office ■ **on se pressait pour entrer** people were pushing to get in.
◇ *vpt* : **se ~ le citron** *fam* to rack one's brains.

presse-raquette [prɛsrakɛt] (*pl inv ou pl* **presse-raquettes**) *nm* racket press.

presse-viande [prɛsvjɑ̃d] *nm inv* juice extractor *(for meat)*.

pressing [presiŋ] *nm* **1.** [repassage] pressing ■ **~ à la vapeur** steam-pressing **2.** [boutique] dry cleaner's **3.** *fam* SPORT : **faire le ~** to put *ou* to pile on the pressure.

pression [presjɔ̃] *nf* **1.** [action] pressure ■ **une simple ~ de la main suffit** you just have to press lightly
2. PHYS pressure ■ **la ~ de l'eau** water pressure ■ **mettre sous ~** to pressurize ■ **récipient sous ~** pressurized container ■ **à**

haute/basse ~ high-/low-pressure ▶ **~ artérielle** MÉD blood pressure ■ **~ atmosphérique** MÉTÉOR atmospheric pressure ■ **être sous ~** to be stressed *ou* under pressure
3. [contrainte morale] pressure ■ **céder à la ~ populaire/familiale** to give in to popular/family pressure ■ **faire ~ sur qqn** to put pressure on sb ■ **il faut exercer une ~ sur la classe politique** we must put pressure on *ou* bring pressure to bear on the political community ■ **il y a une forte ~ sur le dollar/l'équipe belge** the dollar/the Belgian team is under heavy pressure ▶ **~ fiscale** tax burden
4. [vêtement] press stud UK, snap (fastener) US
5. [bière] draught UK *ou* draft US (beer)
6. ÉCON : **~ fiscale** tax burden.
◆ **à la pression** *loc adj* [bière] draught UK, draft US.

pressoir [prɛswar] *nm* **1.** [appareil] : **~ (à vin)** winepress ■ **~ à cidre/huile** cider/oil press **2.** [lieu] presshouse.

pressurage [presyraʒ] *nm* ŒNOL pressing.

pressurer [3] [presyre] *vt* **1.** [raisin] to press ■ [citron] to squeeze **2.** *fig* [exploiter] to squeeze, to extort, to exploit.

pressurisation [presyrizasjɔ̃] *nf* pressurization.

pressuriser [3] [presyrize] *vt* to pressurize.

prestance [prɛstɑ̃s] *nf* : **un jeune homme de belle/noble ~** a handsome/noble-looking young man ■ **il a de la ~** he is a fine figure of a man.

prestataire [prɛstatɛr] *nmf* **1.** [bénéficiaire] recipient *(of an allowance)* ■ **depuis la majorité de mes enfants, je ne suis plus ~ des allocations familiales** since my children came of age, I have not been able to claim child benefit **2.** [fournisseur] : **~ de service** service provider.

prestation [prɛstasjɔ̃] *nf* **1.** [allocation] allowance, benefit ▶ **~s familiales** family benefits *(such as child benefit, rent allowance etc)* ■ **~ d'invalidité** (industrial) disablement benefit ■ **~s sociales** social security benefits **2.** COMM : **~ de service** provision *ou* delivery of a service **3.** [d'un artiste, d'un sportif etc] performance ■ **faire une bonne/mauvaise ~** to play well/ badly ■ **faire une bonne ~ scénique/télévisuelle** to put on a good stage/television performance **4.** DR & ADMIN : **~s locatives** service charge *(paid by the tenant to the landlord)*.

preste [prɛst] *adj* swift, nimble ■ **avoir la main ~** [être adroit] to have a light touch.

prestement [prɛstəmɑ̃] *adv* [se faufiler] swiftly, nimbly ■ [travailler] swiftly, quickly.

prestidigitateur, trice [prɛstidiʒitatœr, tris] *nm, f* conjuror, magician.

prestidigitation [prɛstidiʒitasjɔ̃] *nf* conjuring, prestidigitation *sout* ■ **faire de la ~** [en amateur] to do conjuring (tricks) ; [en professionnel] to be a conjuror.

prestige [prɛstiʒ] *nm* prestige ■ **jouir d'un grand ~** to enjoy great prestige ■ **redonner du ~ à une institution** to restore prestige to an institution ■ **le ~ de l'uniforme** the glamour of the uniform.
◆ **de prestige** *loc adj* [politique] prestige *(modif)* ■ [résidence] luxury *(modif)*.
◆ **pour le prestige** *loc adv* for the sake of prestige ■ **collectionner les œuvres d'art pour le ~** to collect works of art for their prestige value.

prestigieux, euse [prɛstiʒjø, øz] *adj* **1.** [magnifique] prestigious, glamorous ■ **notre prestigieuse collection "Histoire"** our magnificent History collection **2.** [renommé - produit] renowned, famous, world-famous.

presto [presto] *adv* **1.** MUS presto **2.** *fam* [vite] at *ou* on the double, double-quick ■ **il faudra que tu me rembourses ~** you'll have to repay me double-quick.

présumable [prezymabl] *adj sout* presumable ■ **il est ~ que...** it is to be presumed that...

présumé, e [prezyme] *adj* **1.** [considéré comme] presumed ■ **tout accusé, en l'absence de preuves, est ~ innocent** in the absence of proof, all defendants are presumed innocent **2.** [supposé] presumed, putative ■ **Max Dalbon est l'auteur ~ du pamphlet** Max Dalbon is presumed to be the author of this pamphlet.

présumer [3] [prezyme] *vt* [supposer] to presume, to assume ■ **je présume que vous êtes sa sœur** I take it *ou* presume you're his sister.
◆ **présumer de** *v+prép* [surestimer] : **j'ai un peu présumé de mes forces** I overdid things somewhat ■ **~ de qqn** to rely on sb too much.

présupposé [presypoze] *nm* presupposition.

présupposer [3] [presypoze] *vt* to presuppose ■ **la question présuppose une grande culture historique** the question calls for *ou* presupposes a thorough grasp of history.

présupposition [presypozisjɔ̃] *nf* presupposition.

présure [prezyr] *nf* rennet.

présurer [3] [prezyre] *vt* to curdle with rennet.

prêt[1] [prɛ] *nm* **1.** [action] lending, loaning ■ [chose prêtée] loan ■ **c'est seulement un ~** it's only a loan ■ **le ~ de livres est réservé aux étudiants** the lending of books is restricted to students ■ **conditions de ~** lending conditions **2.** [bancaire] loan ■ **solliciter un ~** to apply for a loan ■ **obtenir un ~ d'une banque** to secure a bank loan ■ **~ bancaire** bank loan ■ **~ à la construction** building loan ■ **~ conventionné** fixed-rate mortgage ■ **~ hypothécaire** mortgage, home loan ■ **~ immobilier** mortgage, home loan, ≃ mortgage ■ **~ à intérêt** loan at *ou* with interest ■ **~ relais** bridging loan **3.** [dans une bibliothèque - document] loan, issue, book issued.

prêt[2], e [prɛ, prɛt] *adj* **1.** [préparé] ready ■ **je suis ~, on peut partir** I'm ready, we can go now ■ **mes valises sont ~es** my bags are packed ■ **~ à : ~ à emporter** take-away *(avant un nom)* ■ **poulet ~ à cuire** *ou* **rôtir** ovenready *ou* dressed chicken ■ **être (fin) ~ au départ** to be all set to go ■ **l'armée se tient ~e à intervenir** the army is ready to step in *ou* to intervene ■ **~ pour : vous n'êtes pas encore ~ pour la compétition** you're not ready for competition yet ■ **tout est (fin) ~ pour la cérémonie** everything is ready for the ceremony ■ **j'ai toujours une cassette de ~e** *fam* I always have a tape ready **2.** [disposé] : **~ à** ready *ou* willing to ■ **être ~ à tout** to be game for anything ■ **pour l'argent il est ~ à tout (faire)** he'd do anything *ou* stop at nothing for money.

prêt-à-coudre [prɛtakudr] (*pl* **prêts-à-coudre**) *nm* ready-to-sew garment, garment in kit form.

prêt-à-manger [prɛtamɑ̃ʒe] (*pl* **prêts-à-manger**) *nm* **1.** [nourriture] fast food **2.** [restaurant] fast-food restaurant.

prêt-à-monter [prɛtamɔ̃te] (*pl* **prêts-à-monter**) *nm* kit.

prêt-à-porter [prɛtapɔrte] (*pl* **prêts-à-porter**) *nm* (ready-to-wear) fashion ■ **elle n'achète que du ~** she only buys ready-to-wear *ou* UK off-the-peg clothes.

prêté [prete] *nm* *loc* **c'est un ~ pour un rendu** it's tit for tat.

prétendant, e [pretɑ̃dɑ̃, ɑ̃t] *nm, f* : **~ au trône** pretender to the throne.
◆ **prétendant** *nm hum* [soupirant] suitor, wooer *vieilli*.

prétendre [73] [pretɑ̃dr] *vt* **1.** [se vanter de] to claim **2.** [affirmer] to claim, to say, to maintain ■ **~ que : je ne prétends pas que ce soit** *ou* **que c'est de ta faute** I'm not saying *ou* I don't say it's your fault ■ **on la prétend folle** she's said *ou* alleged to be mad ■ **à ce qu'elle prétend, son mari est ambassadeur** according to her, her husband is an ambassador ■ **ce n'est pas le chef-d'œuvre qu'on prétend** it's not the masterpiece it's made out to be **3.** [avoir l'intention de] to intend, to mean.
◆ **prétendre à** *v+prép* **1.** [revendiquer] to claim ■ **vous pouvez ~ à une indemnisation** you can claim compensation **2.** *litt* [aspirer à] to aspire to ■ **il prétend au titre de champion** he is aiming for the championship.
◆ **se prétendre** *vpi* [se dire] to claim to be ■ **il se prétend avocat** he claims to be a lawyer.

prétendu, e [pretɑ̃dy] ◇ *adj* [par soi-même] so-called, self-styled ■ [par autrui] so-called, alleged ■ **le ~ professeur était en fait un espion** the so-called professor was in fact a spy.
◇ *nm, f* [dialecte: fiancé, fiancée] betrothed, intended.

prétendument [pretɑ̃dymɑ̃] *adv* [par soi-même] supposedly ■ [par autrui] supposedly, allegedly.

prête-nom [prɛtnɔ̃] (*pl* **prête-noms**) *nm* figurehead, man of straw ■ **servir de ~ à qqch** to act as a figurehead for sthg.

prétentieusement [pretɑ̃sjøzmɑ̃] *adv* pretentiously, self-importantly.

prétentieux, euse [pretɑ̃sjø, øz] ◇ *adj* [personne] pretentious ■ [style, remarque] pretentious ■ **mauvaise langue, et en plus prétentieuse!** she's a scandalmonger and pretentious into the bargain!
◇ *nm, f* conceited *ou* self-important person, poseur.

prétention [pretɑ̃sjɔ̃] *nf* **1.** [orgueil] pretentiousness, conceit, self-conceit ■ **il est plein de ~** he's so conceited **2.** [ambition] pretension, pretence ■ **avoir la ~ de faire qqch : tu n'as tout de même pas la ~ de te représenter?** do you really have the nerve to run again? ■ **je n'ai pas la ~ d'avoir été complet sur ce sujet** I don't claim to have fully covered the subject ■ **l'article a des ~s littéraires** the article has literary pretensions.
◆ **prétentions** *nfpl* **1.** [exigences] claims ■ **avoir des ~s sur un héritage/une propriété** to lay claim to an inheritance/a property **2.** [financières] : **vos ~s sont trop élevées** you're asking for too high a salary ■ **envoyez une lettre spécifiant vos ~s** send a letter specifying your salary expectations.
◆ **sans prétention** *loc adj* unpretentious ■ **un écrivain sans ~** an unassuming writer.

prêter [4] [prete] ◇ *vt* **1.** [argent, bien] to lend ■ **peux-tu me ~ ta voiture?** can you lend me *ou* can I borrow your car? ■ *(en usage absolu)* **la banque prête à 9 %** the bank lends at 9% ■ **~ sur gages** to lend (money) against security ▶ **on ne prête qu'aux riches** *prov* to those who have shall be given **2.** [attribuer] to attribute, to accord ■ **~ de l'importance à qqch** to attach importance to sthg ■ **on lui a parfois prêté des pouvoirs magiques** he was sometimes alleged *ou* claimed to have magical powers ■ **on me prête des talents que je n'ai malheureusement pas** I am credited with skills that I unfortunately do not possess ■ **ce sont les propos prêtés au sénateur** these are the words attributed to the senator **3.** [offrir] : **~ asile à qqn** to give *ou* to offer sb shelter ■ **~ assistance** *ou* **secours à qqn** to give *ou* to lend assistance to sb ■ **~ attention à** to pay attention to ■ **ne pas ~ attention à** to ignore ■ **~ l'oreille** to listen ■ **~ une oreille attentive à qqn** to listen attentively to sb ■ **~ une oreille distraite à qqn** to listen to sb with only half an ear ■ **~ serment** to take the oath ; POLIT to be sworn in ■ **faire ~ serment à qqn** to put sb under oath ■ **~ son nom à une cause** to lend one's name to a cause ▶ **~ le flanc à : ~ le flanc à la critique** to lay o.s. open to *ou* to invite criticism ■ **~ le flanc à l'adversaire** to give the adversary an opening.
◇ *vi* [tissu, cuir] to give, to stretch.
◆ **prêter à** *v+prép* [donner lieu à] to give rise to, to invite ■ **le texte prête à confusion** the text is open to misinterpretation ■ **la déclaration prête à équivoque** the statement is ambiguous ■ **il est d'une naïveté qui prête à rire** he is ridiculously naive.
◆ **se prêter à** *vp+prép* **1.** [consentir à] to lend o.s. to ■ **se ~ à une fraude** to countenance a fraud ■ **se ~ au jeu** to enter into the spirit of the game **2.** [être adapté à] to be suitable for ■ **si le temps s'y prête** weather permitting ■ **les circonstances ne se prêtaient guère aux confidences** it was no time for confidences.

prétérit [preterit] *nm* preterite, *voir aussi* **pluriel**.

prétériter [3] [preterite] *vt Suisse* [personne] to wrong.

prêteur, euse [prɛtœr, øz] ◇ *adj* : **elle n'est pas prêteuse** she doesn't like lending, she's very possessive about her belongings.
◇ *nm, f* lender, moneylender ■ **~ sur gages** pawnbroker ■ **~ sur hypothèque** mortgagee.

prétexte [pretɛkst] ◇ *adj f* ANTIQ [toge] praetexta.
◇ *nm* **1.** [excuse] pretext, excuse ■ **trouver un bon ~** to come up with a good excuse ■ **un mauvais ~** a lame *ou* feeble excuse ■ **servir de ~ à qqn** to provide sb with a pretext ■ **prendre ~ de qqch** to use sthg as an excuse ■ **pour toi, tous les ~s sont bons pour ne pas travailler** any excuse is good for avoiding work as far as you are concerned **2.** [occasion] : **pour toi, tout est ~ à rire/au sarcasme** you find cause for laughter/sarcasm in everything.
◆ **sous aucun prétexte** *loc adv* on no account ■ **vous ne quitterez cette pièce sous aucun ~** on no account *ou* under no circumstances will you leave this room, you will not leave this room on any account.
◆ **sous prétexte de, sous prétexte que** *loc conj* : **il est sorti sous ~ d'aller acheter du pain** he went out on the pretext of buying some bread ■ **sous ~ qu'elle a été malade, on lui passe tout** just because she's been ill, she can get away with anything.

prétexter [4] [pretɛkste] *vt* to give as a pretext, to use as an excuse ■ **~ que** to pretend (that).

prétimbré, e [pretɛ̃bre] *adj* prepaid.

prétoire [pretwar] *nm* **1.** DR court **2.** ANTIQ [tente, palais] praetorium.

Pretoria [pretɔrja] *npr* Pretoria.

prétorien, enne [pretɔrjɛ̃, ɛn] *adj* ANTIQ [d'un magistrat] pretorian, praetorian ■ [d'un garde] Praetorian.
◆ **prétorien** *nm* Praetorian Guard.

prétraitement [pretrɛtmɑ̃] *nm* **1.** INFORM preprocessing **2.** TECHNOL pretreatment.

prêtre [prɛtr] *nm* RELIG priest ■ **les ~s** the clergy ▶ **grand ~** *pr & fig* high priest.

prêtre-ouvrier [prɛtruvrije] (*pl* **prêtres-ouvriers**) *nm* worker-priest.

prêtresse [prɛtrɛs] *nf* RELIG priestess ■ **grande ~** *pr & fig* high priestess.

prêtrise [pretriz] *nf* priesthood ■ **recevoir la ~** to be ordained a priest.

preuve [prœv] *nf* **1.** [indice] proof, (piece of) evidence ■ **avoir la ~ que** to have proof that ■ **avez-vous des ~s de ce que vous avancez?** can you produce evidence of *ou* can you prove what you're saying? ■ **c'est à nous de fournir la ~** it's up to us to show proof, the onus of proof is on us ■ **~ d'amour** token of love ▶ **~ littérale** *ou* **par écrit** written evidence ■ **~ recevable** admissible evidence ■ **~ tangible** hard evidence **2.** [démonstration] proof ■ **mon avocat fera la ~ de mon innocence** my lawyer will prove that I'm innocent, my lawyer will prove my innocence ■ **la ~ de son inexpérience, c'est qu'il n'a pas demandé de reçu** his not asking for a receipt goes to show *ou* proves that he lacks experience ■ **il n'est pas fiable, la ~, il est déjà en retard** *fam* you can never rely on him, look, he's already late ■ **faire ~ d'un grand sang-froid** to show *ou* to display great presence of mind ▶ **faire ses ~s : c'est un produit qui a fait ses ~s** it's a tried and tested product ■ **il avait fait ses ~s dans le maquis** he'd won his spurs *ou* proved himself in the Maquis **3.** TECHNOL *test measuring the alcohol content of a liquid* **4.** MATH : **~ par neuf** casting out nines ■ **faire une ~ par neuf** to cast out nines.
◆ **à preuve** *loc adv fam* **tout le monde peut devenir célèbre, à ~ moi-même** anybody can become famous, take me for instance *ou* just look at me.
◆ **à preuve que** *loc conj fam* which goes to show that ■ **il m'a trahi, à ~ qu'on ne peut se fier à personne** he betrayed me, which (just) goes to show that you can't trust anybody.
◆ **preuves en main** *loc adv* with cast-iron proof available ■ **affirmer qqch ~s en main** to back up a statement with cast-iron evidence *ou* proof.

preux [prø] *arch* ◇ *adj m* valiant, gallant.
◇ *nm* valiant knight.

prévalence [prevalɑ̃s] *nf* prevalence.

prévaloir [61] [prevalwar] *vi* [prédominer] to prevail ■ **nous lutterons pour faire ~ nos droits légitimes** we will fight for our legitimate rights ■ **~ sur** to prevail over *ou* against ■ **~ contre** to prevail against, to overcome.
◆ **se prévaloir de** *vp+prép* **1.** [profiter de] : **elle se prévalait de son ancienneté pour imposer ses goûts** she took advantage

of her seniority to impose her preferences **2.** [se vanter de] : **il se prévalait de ses origines aristocratiques** he boasted of *ou* about his aristocratic background.

prévaricateur, trice [prevarikatœr, tris] DR ◇ *adj* corrupt.
◇ *nm, f* corrupt official.

prévarication [prevarikasjɔ̃] *nf* DR [corruption] breach of trust, corrupt practice.

prévaudrai, prévaux *etc v* ▷ **prévaloir**.

prévenance [prevnɑ̃s] *nf* kindness, consideration, thoughtfulness ■ **être plein de ~ à l'égard de qqn** to show consideration for *ou* to be considerate towards sb ■ **entourer qqn de ~s** to do *ou* to show sb many kindnesses.

prévenant, e [prevnɑ̃, ɑ̃t] *adj* kindly, considerate, thoughtful ■ **des manières ~es** attentive manners ■ **être ~ à l'égard de qqn** to be considerate *ou* thoughtful towards sb.

prévenir [40] [prevnir] *vt* **1.** [informer] : **~ qqn** to inform sb, to let sb know ■ **préviens-moi s'il y a du nouveau** let me know if anything new comes up ■ **en cas d'accident, qui dois-je ~?** who should I inform *ou* notify in case of an accident? ■ **~ la police** to call *ou* to notify the police **2.** [mettre en garde] to warn, to tell ■ **je te préviens, si tu recommences, c'est la fessée!** I'm warning you, if you do that again I'll spank you! ■ *(en usage absolu)* **partir sans ~** to leave without warning *ou* notice **3.** [empêcher] to prevent, to avert ■ **~ une rechute** to prevent a relapse ■ **~ un danger** to ward *ou* to stave off a danger **4.** [anticiper - désir, besoin] to anticipate ; [- accusation, critique] to forestall **5.** *sout* [influencer] : **~ qqn en faveur de/contre** to predispose sb towards, to prejudice sb against.

préventif, ive [prevɑ̃tif, iv] *adj* preventive, preventative ■ **prendre des mesures préventives** to take preventive *ou* precautionary measures ■ **prenez ce médicament à titre ~** take this medicine as a precaution.
◆ **préventive** *nf* custody *(pending trial)* ■ **faire de la préventive** to be remanded in custody ■ **ils ont fait trois mois de préventive** they were imprisoned without trial for three months.

prévention [prevɑ̃sjɔ̃] *nf* **1.** [ensemble de mesures] prevention ■ **nous nous attachons à la ~ des accidents** we endeavour to prevent accidents ➊ **la ~ routière** the road safety administration, ≃ Royal Society for the Prevention of Accidents *UK* **2.** *sout* [parti pris] prejudice, bias ■ **avoir des ~s à l'égard de** *ou* **contre qqn** to be prejudiced *ou* biased against sb **3.** DR custody ■ **il a fait un an de ~ avant d'être jugé** he was remanded in custody for one year before being tried.

prévenu, e [prevny] ◇ *pp* ▷ **prévenir**.
◇ *adj* **1.** *sout* [partial] biased ■ **~ en faveur de** *ou* **pour qqn** biased in favour of sb ■ **~ contre qqn** biased against sb **2.** DR [poursuivi judiciairement] charged ■ **il est ~ de meurtre avec préméditation** he is charged with premeditated murder.
◇ *nm, f* [à un procès] defendant ■ [en prison] prisoner ■ **le ~ nie toute participation aux faits** the defendant denies being involved.

prévient [prevjɛ̃], **prévint** *etc v* ▷ **prévenir**.

prévisibilité [previzibilite] *nf* foreseeability.

prévisible [previzibl] *adj* foreseeable, predictable ■ **ses réactions ne sont pas toujours ~s** his reactions are sometimes unexpected *ou* unpredictable ■ **son échec était ~** it was to be expected that he'd fail.

prévision [previzjɔ̃] *nf* **1.** *(gén pl)* [calcul] expectation ■ **le coût de la maison a dépassé nos ~s** the house cost more than we expected **2.** ÉCON [processus] forecasting ■ **~ budgétaire** budget forecast *ou* projections ■ **~ économique** economic forecasting **3.** MÉTÉOR [technique] (weather) forecasting ■ **~s météorologiques** [bulletin] weather forecast.
◆ **en prévision de** *loc prép* in anticipation of ■ **isoler une maison en ~ du froid** to insulate a house in anticipation of cold weather.

prévisionnel, elle [previzjɔnɛl] *adj* [analyse, étude] forward-looking ■ [coût] estimated ■ [budget] projected.

prévisionniste [previzjɔnist] *nmf* forecaster.

prévoir [63] [prevwar] *vt* **1.** [prédire] to foresee, to expect, to anticipate ■ MÉTÉOR to forecast ■ **on ne peut pas toujours tout ~** you can't always think of everything in advance ■ **alors ça, ça n'était pas prévu au programme** *fam* we weren't expecting that to happen ■ **rien ne laissait ~ pareil accident** nothing indicated that such an accident could happen ■ **rien ne laissait ~ qu'il nous quitterait si rapidement** we never expected him to pass away so soon **2.** [projeter] to plan ■ **tout s'est passé comme prévu** everything went according to plan *ou* smoothly ■ **on a dîné plus tôt que prévu** we had dinner earlier than planned ■ **tout est prévu pour les invités** everything has been laid on *ou* arranged for the guests ■ **l'ouverture du centre commercial est prévue pour le mois prochain** the opening of the shopping centre is scheduled for next month **3.** [préparer] to allow, to provide ■ **prévoyez des vêtements chauds** make sure you bring some warm clothes **4.** DR to provide for ■ **dans tous les cas prévus par la loi** in all cases provided for by law.

prévôt [prevo] *nm* **1.** HIST provost **2.** MIL provost marshal.

prévoyait *etc v* ▷ **prévoir**.

prévoyance [prevwajɑ̃s] *nf* foresight, foresightedness, forethought ■ **faire preuve de ~** to be provident.

prévoyant, e [prevwajɑ̃, ɑ̃t] *adj* provident, prudent.

prévu, e [prevy] *pp* ▷ **prévoir**.

priant [prijɑ̃] *nm* kneeling statue.

priapisme [prijapism] *nm* priapism.

prie-Dieu [pridjø] *nm inv* prie-dieu, prayer stool.

prier [10] [prije] ◇ *vt* **1.** [ciel, Dieu] to pray to ■ **je prie Dieu et tous ses saints que...** I pray (to) God and all his saints that...
2. [supplier] to beg, to beseech *litt* ■ **je vous en prie, emmenez-moi** I beg you to take me with you ■ **je te prie de me pardonner** please forgive me ■ **se faire ~ : il adore se faire ~** he loves to be coaxed ■ **elle ne s'est pas fait ~ pour venir** she didn't need any persuasion to come along ■ **j'ai accepté sans me faire ~** I said yes without any hesitation ■ **je vous prie de croire qu'il m'a écouté cette fois!** believe (you) me, he listened to me this time!
3. [enjoindre] to request ■ **vous êtes priés d'arriver à l'heure** you're requested to arrive on time
4. [dans des formules de politesse orales] : **merci - je vous en prie** thank you - (please) don't mention it ■ **puis-je entrer? - je vous en prie** may I come in? - please do ■ **pourriez-vous m'indiquer où est le commissariat, je vous prie?** could you please tell me *ou* would you be kind enough to tell me where the police station is? ❙ [par écrit] : **M. et Mme Lemet vous prient de bien vouloir assister au mariage de leur fille** Mr and Mrs Lemet request the pleasure of your company at their daughter's wedding ■ **je vous prie de croire à mes sentiments distingués** *ou* **les meilleurs** yours sincerely
5. *litt* [inviter] : **~ qqn à** to ask *ou* to invite sb for, to request sb to *litt*.
◇ *vi* to pray ■ **~ pour qqn** to pray for sb ■ **prions pour la paix** let us pray for peace.

prière [prijɛr] *nf* **1.** RELIG prayer ■ **dire** *ou* **faire** *ou* **réciter ses ~s** to pray, to say one's prayers ■ **être en ~** to be praying ■ **je l'ai trouvé en ~** I found him at prayer ■ **tu peux faire tes ~s** [menace] say your prayers **2.** [requête] request, plea, entreaty ■ **elle a fini par céder aux ~s de ses enfants** she finally gave in to her children's pleas ■ **'~ de ne pas fumer'** 'no smoking (please)'.
◆ **prière d'insérer** *nm & nf* insert *(publisher's blurb for press release)*.

prieur, e [prijœr] *nm, f* : **(père) ~** prior ■ **(mère) ~e** prioress.

prieuré [prijœre] *nm* [communauté] priory ■ [église] priory (church).

prima donna [primadɔna] (*pl* **prime donne** [primedɔne]) *nf* prima donna.

primaire [primɛr] ◇ *adj* **1.** [premier - d'une série] primary ■ **école/enseignement ~** primary school/education ■ **ère ~** GÉOL

Palaeozoic (age) **2.** [couleur] primary **3.** [de base] : **connaissances ~s** basic knowledge **4.** [borné - personne] simpleminded ; [- attitude] simplistic, unsophisticated ■ **faire de l'anticommunisme ~** to be a dyed-in-the-wool anticommunist.
◇ *nmf* [personne bornée] simpleton.
◇ *nm* : **le ~** ÉDUC primary education ; GÉOL the Palaeozoic age ; ÉCON the primary sector.
◇ *nf* POLIT primary (election) ■ **les ~s** the primaries.

primal, e, aux [primal, o] *adj* primal ■ **cri ~** primal scream.

primarité [primarite] *nf* simplemindedness.

primat [prima] *nm* **1.** RELIG primate ■ **le ~ des Gaules** the Archbishop of Lyons **2.** *litt* [supériorité] sway, primacy.

primate [primat] *nm* **1.** ZOOL primate ■ **les ~s** the Primates **2.** *fam* [homme grossier] ape, brute.

primauté [primote] *nf* **1.** [supériorité] primacy ■ **donner la ~ à la théorie sur la pratique** to accord more importance to theory than to practice **2.** RELIG primacy.

prime [prim] ◇ *adj* **1.** MATH prime
2. *litt* [premier] : **dès sa ~ enfance** *ou* **jeunesse** from her earliest childhood ■ **elle n'est plus vraiment dans la ~ jeunesse** she's not that young anymore.
◇ *nf* **1.** [gratification] bonus ■ [indemnité - par un organisme] allowance ; [- par l'État] subsidy ■ **~ d'ancienneté** seniority bonus ■ **~ d'objectif** incentive bonus ■ **~ de rendement** *ou* **de résultat** productivity bonus ■ **~ de transport/déménagement** travel/relocation allowance ■ **~ d'intéressement** incentive bonus ■ **~ de licenciement** redundancy payment, severance pay ■ **~ de précarité** *bonus paid to compensate for lack of job security* ■ **~ de risque** danger money
2. [incitation] subsidy ■ **cette mesure est une ~ à la délation** *fig* this measure will only encourage people to denounce others ▶ **~ à l'exportation** export subsidy ■ **~ au retour** repatriation allowance
3. [assurances - FIN] [cotisation] premium ■ **~ d'assurance** insurance premium ■ **ils ne toucheront pas la ~** [bonus] they will not qualify for the no-claims bonus
4. BOURSE [taux] option rate ■ [somme] option money ▶ **~ d'émission** premium on option to buy shares
5. *loc* **faire ~** to be at a premium.
◆ **de prime abord** *loc adv* at first sight *ou* glance.
◆ **en prime** *loc adv* as a bonus ■ **en ~, vous gagnez trois tasses à café** as a bonus, you get a free gift of three coffee cups ■ **non seulement il fait rien mais en ~ il se plaint!** not only does he do nothing, but he complains as well!

primé, e [prime] *adj* [film, vin, fromage] award-winning ■ [animal] prizewinning.

primer [3] [prime] ◇ *vt* **1.** [récompenser - animal, invention] to award a prize to ■ **elle a été primée au concours du plus beau bébé** she won *ou* was awarded a prize in the beautiful baby contest ■ **un film primé à Cannes l'année dernière** a film which won an award at Cannes last year **2.** *sout* [prédominer sur] to take precedence over.
◇ *vi* [avoir l'avantage] to be dominant ■ **~ sur** to take precedence over ■ **son dernier argument a primé sur tous les autres** her final argument won out over all the others.

primerose [primroz] *nf* hollyhock, rose mallow.

primesautier, ère [primsotje, ɛr] *adj sout* **1.** [spontané] impulsive, spontaneous **2.** [vif] jaunty.

primeur [primœr] *nf sout* [exclusivité] : **notre chaîne a eu la ~ de l'information** our channel was first with the news ■ **je vous réserve la ~ de mon reportage** you'll be the first one to have *ou* you'll have first refusal of my article.
◆ **primeurs** *nfpl* early fruit and vegetables.

primevère [primvɛr] *nf* [sauvage] primrose ■ [cultivée] primula ■ **~ officinale** cowslip.

primipare [primipar] ◇ *adj* primiparous.
◇ *nf* primipara.

primitif, ive [primitif, iv] ◇ *adj* **1.** [initial] primitive, original ■ **voici notre projet dans sa forme primitive** here is our project in its original form ▶ **l'Église primitive** the early *ou* primitive Church ■ **l'homme ~** primitive *ou* early man ■ **langage ~** primitive language **2.** [non industrialisé - société] primitive **3.** [fruste - personne] primitive, unsophisticated **4.** ART primitive **5.** OPT : **couleurs primitives** major colours.
◇ *nm, f* **1.** ANTHR (member of a) primitive (society) **2.** ART primitive (painter).
◆ **primitive** *nf* INFORM & MATH primitive.

primitivement [primitivmɑ̃] *adv* originally, in the first place ■ **~, mon intention était de rester une semaine** I originally intended to stay for one week.

primitivisme [primitivism] *nm* ART primitivism.

primo [primo] *adv* first (of all), firstly ■ **~, je n'en ai pas envie, (et) secundo je n'ai pas le temps** first of all, I don't feel like it, (and) second, I haven't got (the) time.

primo-accédant, e [primoaksedɑ̃t] (*mpl* **primo-accédants***fpl* **primo-accédantes**) *nm, f* first-time buyer.

primo-arrivant, e [primoarivɑ̃t] (*mpl* **primo-arrivants,** *fpl* **primo-arrivantes**) *nm, f child from an immigrant family, often with poor language skills.*

primo-délinquant, e [primodelɛ̃kɑ̃t] (*mpl* **primo-délinquants,** *fpl* **primo-délinquantes**) *nm, f* first offender.

primordial, e, aux [primɔrdjal, o] *adj* **1.** [essentiel] fundamental, essential ■ **elle a eu un rôle ~ dans les négociations** she played a crucial role in the negotiations ■ **il est ~ que tu sois présent** it's essential for you to be there **2.** *sout* [originel - élément, molécule] primordial, primeval ■ **les instincts primordiaux de l'homme** man's primal instincts.

prince [prɛ̃s] *nm* **1.** [souverain, fils de roi] prince ■ **le ~ consort** the prince consort ■ **le ~ héritier** the crown prince ■ **le ~ de Galles** the Prince of Wales ■ **le ~ régent** the Prince Regent ■ **les ~s qui nous gouvernent** ***Debré*** *allus* the powers that be ■ **le Prince Charmant** Prince Charming ■ **être** *ou* **se montrer bon ~** to behave generously ■ **tu as été bon ~** that was generous of you ■ **il a agi en ~** he behaved royally ■ **cet enfant est traité/vêtu comme un ~** that child is treated/dressed like a prince ■ **'le Petit Prince'** ***Saint-Exupéry*** 'The Little Prince' **2.** [personnage important] prince ▶ **le ~ des enfers** *ou* **des ténèbres** Satan, the prince of darkness ■ **le ~ des Apôtres** [saint Pierre] the prince of the Apostles **3.** *sout* [sommité] prince **4.** *fam* [homme généreux] real gent *UK ou* gem ■ **merci, mon ~!** thanks, squire *UK ou* buddy *US*!

prince-de-galles [prɛ̃sdəgal] ◇ *adj inv* Prince-of-Wales check *(modif)*.
◇ *nm inv* (Prince-of-Wales) check material.

princesse [prɛ̃sɛs] *nf* [souveraine, fille de roi] princess ■ **arrête de faire la ~, tu veux!** stop giving yourself airs!

princier, ère [prɛ̃sje, ɛr] *adj* **1.** [du prince] prince's, royal ■ **dans la loge princière** in the royal box **2.** [luxueux - don] princely.

princièrement [prɛ̃sjɛrmɑ̃] *adv* princely ■ **nous avons été accueillis ~** we were given a (right) royal welcome.

principal, e, aux [prɛ̃sipal, o] *adj* **1.** [essentiel] main ■ **les principaux intéressés** the main parties involved ■ **la porte/l'entrée ~e** the main gate/entrance ▶ **c'est lui l'acteur ~** he's the leading man **2.** GRAMM [verbe, proposition] main **3.** [supérieur] principal, chief.
◆ **principal, aux** ◇ *nm* FIN [capital] principal.
◇ *nmf* ÉDUC (school) principal.
◆ **principal** *nm* : **le ~** the most important thing ■ **le ~, c'est que tu ne sois pas blessé** what is most important is that you're not hurt ■ **c'est fini, c'est le ~** it's over, that's the main thing.
◆ **principale** *nf* LING main clause.

principalement [prɛ̃sipalmɑ̃] *adv* chiefly, mostly, principally ■ **nous avons besoin ~ d'un nouveau directeur** what we need most is a new manager.

principauté [prɛ̃sipote] *nf* principality.

principe [prɛ̃sip] *nm* **1.** [règle morale] principle, rule of conduct ■ **j'ai des ~s** I've got principles ■ **j'ai toujours eu pour ~ d'agir honnêtement** I have always made it a principle to act

with honesty ▪ **vivre selon ses ~s** to live in accordance with one's principles ▪ **manquer à tous ses ~s** to fail to live up to one's principles
2. [axiome] principle, law, axiom ▪ **les ~s de la philosophie** the principles of philosophy ▪ **je pars du ~ que...** I start from the principle *ou* I assume that... ▪ **posons comme ~ que nous avons les crédits nécessaires** let us assume that we get the necessary credits ⊙ **le ~ d'Archimède** Archimedes' principle ▪ **c'est le ~ des vases communicants** *pr* it's the principle of communicating vessels ; *fig* it's a knock-on effect
3. [notion - d'une science] principle
4. [fonctionnement] principle ▪ **le ~ de la vente par correspondance, c'est...** the (basic) principle of mail-order selling is...
5. [fondement] principle, constituent ▪ **votre déclaration contredit le ~ même de notre Constitution** your statement goes against the very principle *ou* basis of our Constitution
6. [origine] origin ▪ **le ~ de la vie** the origin of life ▪ **remonter au ~ des choses** to go back to first principles
7. CHIM [extrait] principle
8. ÉCON [produit] : **~ de précaution** precautionary principle.
◆ **de principe** *loc adj* [accord, approbation] provisional.
◆ **en principe** *loc adv* [en théorie] in principle, in theory, theoretically ▪ [d'habitude] : **en ~, nous descendons à l'hôtel** we usually stop at a hotel.
◆ **par principe** *loc adv* on principle ▪ **il refuse de l'écouter par ~** he refuses to listen to her on principle.
◆ **pour le principe** *loc adv* on principle ▪ **tu refuses de signer pour le ~ ou pour des raisons personnelles?** are you refusing to sign for reasons of principle or for personal reasons?

printanier, ère [prɛ̃tanje, ɛr] *adj* **1.** [du printemps] spring ▪ **il fait un temps ~** the weather feels like spring, spring is in the air ▪ **une température printanière** springlike weather **2.** [gai et jeune - tenue, couleur] springlike **3.** CULIN [potage, salade] printanier *(garnished with early mixed vegetables, diced).*

printemps [prɛ̃tɑ̃] *nm* **1.** [saison] spring ▪ **au ~** in (the) springtime ▪ **~ précoce/tardif** early/late spring ▪ **le Printemps de Bourges** *annual music festival in Bourges* **2.** *litt* [année] summer *litt*, year ▪ **une jeune fille de vingt ~** a young girl of twenty summers *ou* years **3.** *litt* [commencement] spring.

prion [prijɔ̃] *nm* BIOL & MÉD prion.

priorat [prijɔra] *nm* priorate.

priori [prijɔri] ▻ **a priori**.

prioritaire [prijɔritɛr] ◇ *adj* **1.** TRANSP priority *(modif)*, having priority ▪ **ce véhicule est ~ lorsqu'il quitte son arrêt** this vehicle has (the) right of way when leaving a stop **2.** [usager, industrie] priority *(modif)* ▪ **notre projet est ~ sur tous les autres** our project has priority over all the others ▪ **mon souci ~, c'est de trouver un logement** my main *ou* first problem is to find somewhere to live.
◇ *nmf* person with priority ▪ **cette place est réservée aux ~s titulaires d'une carte** this seat is reserved for priority cardholders.

prioritairement [prijɔritɛrmɑ̃] *adv* as a priority, as a matter of urgency.

priorité [prijɔrite] *nf* **1.** [sur route] right of way ▪ **avoir la ~** to have the right of way ▪ **tu as la ~** it's your right of way ▪ **'~ à droite'** 'give way *UK*', 'yield to right *US* *(in France, road law that gives right of way to vehicles coming from the right)*'
2. [en vertu d'un règlement] priority ▪ **les handicapés ont la ~ pour monter à bord** disabled people are entitled to board first
3. [antériorité] priority, precedence **4.** [primauté] priority ▪ **la ~ sera donnée à la lutte contre le cancer** top priority will be given to the fight against cancer **5.** BOURSE : **action de ~** preference share *UK*, preferred stock *US*.
◆ **en priorité, par priorité** *loc adv* as a priority, as a matter of urgency ▪ **nous discuterons en ~ des droits de l'homme** we'll discuss human rights as a priority.

pris, e [pri, iz] ◇ *pp* ▻ **prendre**.
◇ *adj* **1.** [occupé - personne] busy ▪ **aide-moi, tu vois bien que j'ai les mains ~es** help me, can't you see my hands are full?
2. MÉD [gorge] sore ▪ [nez] blocked
3. [envahi] : **~ de** : **~ de pitié/peur** stricken by pity/fear ▪ **~ de panique** panic-stricken ▪ **~ d'une violente douleur** seized with a terrible pain ▪ **~ de boisson** *sout* under the influence of alcohol.
◆ **prise** *nf* **1.** [point de saisie] grip, hold ▪ **trouve une ~e et dis-moi quand tu es prêt à soulever (le piano)** get a grip (on the piano) and tell me when you're ready to lift it ⊙ **avoir ~e sur qqn** to have a hold over sb ▪ **je n'ai aucune ~e sur mes filles** I can't control my daughters at all ▪ **donner ~e à la critique** [personne] to lay o.s. open to attack ; [idée, réalisation] to be open to attack ▪ **lâcher ~e** *pr* & *fig* to let go
2. [absorption - d'un médicament] taking ▪ **la ~e d'insuline doit se faire aux heures prescrites** insulin must be injected at the prescribed times
3. [dose - de tabac] pinch ; [- de cocaïne] snort△
4. [capture - de contrebande, de drogue] seizure, catch ▪ JEUX capture ▪ PÊCHE catch ▪ MIL : **la ~e de la Bastille** the storming of the Bastille ▪ **~es de guerre** spoils of war
5. ÉLECTR : **~e (de courant)** *ou* **électrique** [mâle] plug ; [femelle] socket ▪ **~e multiple** adaptor ▪ **~e de terre** earth *UK*, ground *US* ▪ **l'appareil n'a pas de ~e de terre** the appliance is not earthed *UK ou* grounded *US*
6. TECHNOL : **~e d'air** [ouverture] air inlet ; [introduction d'air] ventilation ▪ **~e d'eau** water point ▪ **~e directe** AUTO direct drive
7. [durcissement - du ciment, de la colle] setting ; [- d'un fromage] hardening ▪ **à ~e rapide** [ciment, colle] quick-setting
8. [dans des expressions] : **~e de conscience** realization ▪ **ma première ~e de conscience de la souffrance humaine** the first time I became aware of human suffering ▪ **~e en considération** taking into account ▪ **~e de contact** meeting ▪ **~e de contrôle** ÉCON takeover ▪ **~e d'habit** [action] taking the habit ; [cérémonie] profession ▪ **~e d'otages** hostage-taking ▪ **~e de parole : encore trois ~es de parole avant la fin de la session** three more speeches to go before the end of the session ▪ **~e de participation** ÉCON acquisition of holdings ▪ **~e de position** opinion, stand ▪ **~e de possession** [d'un héritage] acquisition ; [d'un territoire] taking possession ▪ **~e de pouvoir** [légale] (political) takeover ; [illégale] seizure of power ▪ **~e de tête**△ hassle ▪ **~e de voile** taking the veil.
◆ **aux prises avec** *loc prép* fighting *ou* battling against, grappling with ▪ **je l'ai laissé aux ~es avec un problème de géométrie** I left him grappling *ou* wrestling with a geometry problem.
◆ **en prise** ◇ *loc adv* AUTO in gear ▪ **mets-toi en ~e** put the car in *ou* into gear.
◇ *loc adj* : **être en ~e (directe) avec la réalité** *fig* to have a good hold on *ou* to have a firm grip on reality.
◆ **prise de bec** *nf* row, squabble.
◆ **prise de sang** *nf* blood test.
◆ **prise de son** *nf* sound (recording) ▪ **la ~e de son est de Raoul Fleck** sound (engineer), Raoul Fleck.
◆ **prise de vues** *nf* CINÉ & TV [technique] shooting ▪ [image] (camera) shot ▪ **~e de vues: Marie Vilmet** camera: Marie Vilmet.
◆ **prise en charge** *nf* **1.** [par la Sécurité sociale] refunding *(of medical expenses through the social security system)*
2. [par un taxi] minimum (pick-up) charge.

prisé, e [prize] *adj* valued ▪ **des qualités très ~es** highly valued qualities.

priser [3] [prize] ◇ *vt* **1.** *litt* [estimer] to prize, to value highly ▪ **je ne prise guère sa compagnie** I don't particularly relish his company **2.** [tabac] to take ▪ [cocaïne] to snort.
◇ *vi* to take snuff.

priseur, euse [prizœr, øz] *nm, f* [de tabac] snuff-taker.

prisme [prism] *nm* **1.** SC prism **2.** *fig* **tu vois toujours la réalité à travers un ~** you always distort reality.

prison [prizɔ̃] *nf* **1.** [lieu] prison, jail ▪ **envoyer/mettre qqn en ~** to send sb to/to put sb in jail ▪ **sortir de ~** to get out (of jail)
2. [peine] imprisonment ▪ **faire de la ~** to be in prison *ou* jail, to serve time ▪ **il a été condamné à cinq ans de ~** he was sentenced to five years in jail ⊙ **~ à vie** life sentence ▪ **~ ferme** imprisonment.

prisonnier, ère [prizɔnje, ɛr] ◇ *adj* **1.** [séquestré] captive ▪ **plusieurs mineurs sont encore ~s au fond de la mine** several

miners are still trapped at the bottom of the shaft ▪ **il gardait ma main prisonnière** he wouldn't let go of my hand **2.** *fig* **on est ~ de son éducation** we're prisoners of our upbringing.
◇ *nm, f* prisoner ▪ **il a été fait ~** he was taken prisoner ▪ **se constituer ~** to give o.s. up, to turn o.s. in ▪ **les ~s sont montés sur le toit pour protester** the inmates staged a rooftop protest ▶ **les ~s de droit commun et les ~s politiques** common criminals and political prisoners ▪ **~ de guerre** prisoner of war, POW.
◆ **prisonnier** *nm* **1.** [tige filetée] stud (bolt) **2.** [pièce sertie] insert.

prit *etc v* ▷ **prendre**.

privatif, ive [privatif, iv] *adj* **1.** [privé] private ▪ **avec jardin ~** with a private garden **2.** [réservé à une personne] exclusive **3.** DR : **peine privative de liberté** detention **4.** LING [élément, préfixe] privative.

privation [privasjɔ̃] *nf* [perte] loss, deprivation ▶ **~ des droits civiques** loss *ou* deprivation of civil rights.
◆ **privations** *nfpl* [sacrifices] hardship, hardships ▪ **à force de ~s** through constant sacrifice, by constantly doing without ▪ **affaibli par les ~s** weakened by deprivation.

privatique [privatik] *nf* stand-alone system.

privatisation [privatizasjɔ̃] *nf* privatization, privatizing.

privatiser [3] [privatize] *vt* to privatize.

privatiste [privatist] *nmf* private law specialist.

privative [privativ] *f* ▷ **privatif**.

privauté [privote] *nf* [familiarité] : **~ de langage** crude *ou* coarse language.
◆ **privautés** *nfpl* [libertés déplacées] liberties ▪ **avoir** *ou* **se permettre des ~s avec qqn** to take liberties with sb.

privé, e [prive] *adj* **1.** [personnel] private ▪ **ma vie ~e** my private life **2.** [non public] private ▪ **une audience ~e** a private audience **3.** [officieux] unofficial ▪ **nous avons appris sa démission de source ~e** we've learned unofficially that he has resigned **4.** [non géré par l'État] private.
◆ **privé** *nm* **1.** INDUST private sector ▪ **travailler dans le ~** to work for the private sector *ou* a private company ▪ **elle est médecin à l'hôpital mais elle fait aussi du ~** *fam* she works as a doctor in a hospital but she also has *ou* takes private patients **2.** [intimité] private life ▪ **dans le ~, c'est un homme très agréable** in private life, he's very pleasant **3.** *fam* [détective] sleuth, private detective.
◆ **en privé** *loc adv* in private ▪ **pourrais-je vous parler en ~?** could I talk to you privately *ou* in private?

priver [3] [prive] *vt* **1.** [démunir] to deprive ▪ **ça la prive beaucoup de ne plus fumer** she misses smoking a lot ▪ **être privé de** to be deprived of, to have no ▪ **nous sommes privés de voiture depuis une semaine** we've been without a car for a week ▪ **privé d'eau/d'air/de sommeil** deprived of water/air/sleep ▪ **privé de connaissance** *litt* unconscious, bereft of consciousness *litt* **2.** [comme sanction] to deprive ▪ **~ qqn de qqch** to make sb go *ou* do without sthg ▪ **tu seras privé de dessert/télévision** no dessert/television for you ▪ **il a été privé de ses droits de citoyen** he was deprived *ou* stripped of his civil rights.
◆ **se priver de** *vp+prép* **1.** [renoncer à] to deprive o.s. of, to do without ▪ **il se prive d'alcool** he cuts out drink, he goes without drink ▪ *(en usage absolu)* **elle s'est privée pour leur payer des études** she made great sacrifices to pay for their education ▪ **il n'aime pas se ~** he hates denying himself anything ▪ **un jour de congé supplémentaire, il ne se prive pas!** another day off, he certainly looks after himself! **2.** [se gêner pour] : **il ne s'est pas privé de se moquer de toi** he didn't hesitate to make fun of you ▪ **je ne vais pas me ~ de le lui dire!** I'll make no bones about telling him!

privilège [privilɛʒ] *nm* **1.** [avantage] privilege ▪ **le ~ de l'âge** the prerogative of old age ▪ **j'ai eu le ~ de la voir sur scène** I was privileged (enough) to see her perform ▪ **j'ai le triste ~ de vous annoncer...** it is my sad duty to inform you... ▪ **j'ai eu le triste ~ de connaître cet individu** it was once my misfortune to be acquainted with this individual **2.** [exclusivité] : **l'homme a le ~ de la parole** man is unique in being endowed with the power of speech **3.** [faveur] privilege, favour ▪ **accorder des ~s à qqn** to grant sb favours **4.** HIST : **les ~s** privileges **5.** BANQUE : **~ d'émission** right to issue (banknotes).

privilégié, e [privileʒje] ◇ *adj* **1.** [avantagé] privileged ▪ **l'île jouit d'un climat ~** the island enjoys an excellent climate ▪ **appartenir aux classes ~es** to belong to the privileged classes **2.** [choisi - client, partenaire] favoured **3.** DR : **créancier ~** preferential creditor.
◇ *nm, f* privileged person ▪ **quelques ~s ont assisté à la représentation** a privileged few attended the performance.

privilégier [9] [privileʒje] *vt* **1.** [préférer] to privilege ▪ **nous avons privilégié cette méthode pour l'enseignement de la langue** we've singled out this method for language teaching **2.** [avantager] to favour ▪ **les basketteurs adverses sont privilégiés par leur haute taille** the basketball players in the opposing team are helped by the fact that they're taller ▪ **cette augmentation privilégie les hauts salaires** this increase works in favour of high salaries.

prix [pri] *nm* **1.** [tarif fixe] price, cost ▪ **'~ écrasés/sacrifiés!'** 'prices slashed!' ▪ **~ et conditions de transport d'un produit** freight rates and conditions for a product ▪ **le ~ de l'essence à la pompe** the cost of petrol UK *ou* gas US to the motorist ▪ **ça coûte un ~ fou** it costs a fortune *ou* the earth ▪ **mes bottes, dis un ~ pour voir!** how much do you think my boots cost? ▪ **laissez-moi au moins régler le ~ des places** let me at least pay for the tickets ▪ **à bas** *ou* *sout* **vil ~** very cheaply ▪ **à ce ~-là** at that price ▪ **dans mes ~** within my (price) range ▪ **ce n'est déjà plus tout à fait dans ses prix** that's already a little more than he wanted to spend ▪ **le ~ fort** [maximal] top *ou* maximum price ; [excessif] high price ▪ **j'ai payé le ~ fort pour ma promotion** I was promoted but I paid a high price for it *ou* it cost me dear ▪ **un bon ~ : je l'ai acheté un bon ~** I bought it for a very reasonable price ▪ **je l'ai vendu un bon ~** I got a good price for it ▶ **~ imposé/libre** fixed/deregulated price ▪ **~ d'achat** purchase price ▪ **~ d'appel** loss leader ▪ **~ courant** going *ou* market price ▪ **~ comptant** cash price ▪ **~ conseillé** recommended retail price ▪ **~ coûtant** cost price ▪ **~ de détail** retail price ▪ **~ de gros** wholesale price ▪ **~ hors taxes** price before tax *ou* duties ▪ **~ au kilo** price per kilo ▪ **~ net** net price ▪ **~ public** retail price ▪ **~ de revient** cost price ▪ **~ à l'unité** unit price ▪ **~ de vente** selling price ▪ **oui, mais à quel ~!** *fig* yes, but at what cost! ▪ **à ~ d'or : on achète aujourd'hui ses esquisses à ~ d'or** his sketches are now worth their weight in gold *ou* now cost the earth ▪ **je l'ai acheté à ~ d'or** I paid a small fortune for it ▪ **au ~ où sont les choses** *ou* **où est le beurre** *fam* seeing how expensive everything is ▪ **y mettre le ~ : j'ai fini par trouver le cuir que je voulais mais j'ai dû y mettre le ~** I finally found the type of leather I was looking for, but I had to pay top price for it ▪ **elle a été reçue à son examen, mais il a fallu qu'elle y mette le ~** *fig* she pa ssed her exam, but she really had to work hard for it
2. [étiquette] price (tag) *ou* label ▪ **il n'y avait pas de ~ dessus** it wasn't priced, there was no price tag on it
3. [barème convenu] price ▪ **votre ~ sera le mien** name your price ▪ **faire un ~ (d'ami) à qqn** to do a special deal for sb ▪ **c'était la fin du marché, elle m'a fait un ~ pour les deux cageots** the market was nearly over, so she let me have both boxes cheap ▪ **mettre qqch à ~** [aux enchères] to set a reserve UK *ou* an upset US price on sthg ▪ **sa tête a été mise à ~** *fig* there's a price on his head *ou* a reward for his capture
4. [valeur] price, value ▪ **le ~ de la vie/liberté** the price of life/freedom ▪ **donner du ~ à qqch** to make sthg worthwhile ▪ **il donne** *ou* **attache plus de ~ à sa famille depuis sa maladie** his family is more important to him since his illness ▪ **on attache plus de ~ à la vie quand on a failli la perdre** life is more precious to you when you have nearly lost it ▪ **ça n'a pas de ~** you can't put a price on it
5. [dans un concours commercial, un jeu] prize ▪ [dans un concours artistique, un festival] prize, award ▪ **premier/deuxième ~** first/second prize ▪ **~ littéraire** literary prize ▪ **elle a eu le ~ de la meilleure interprétation** she got the award for best actress ▶ **le Grand Prix (automobile)** SPORT the Grand Prix ▪ **le film qui a gagné le Grand Prix d'Avoriaz** the film which won the Grand Prix at the Avoriaz festival ▪ **le ~ Femina** *annual literary prize whose winner is chosen by a jury of women* ▪ **le ~ Goncourt** *the most prestigious French annual literary prize* ▪ **le**

~ **Louis-Delluc** the Louis Delluc film *UK* *OU* movie *US* award *(annual prize for a French film)* ■ **le ~ Nobel** the Nobel prize ■ **le ~ Pulitzer** the Pulitzer prize
6. [œuvre primée - livre] award-winning book *OU* title ; [- disque] award-winning record ; [- film] award-winning film *UK* *OU* movie *US*
7. [lauréat] prizewinner ■ **il a été Prix de Rome** he won the Prix de Rome
8. ÉDUC [distinction] : **jour de la distribution des ~** prize *OU* prize-giving day ◆ **~ de consolation** consolation prize ■ **~ d'excellence** first prize ■ **~ d'honneur** second prize.
◆ **à aucun prix** *loc adv* not at any price, not for all the world, on no account ■ **je ne quitterais le pays à aucun ~!** nothing would induce me to leave the country!
◆ **à n'importe quel prix** *loc adv* at any price, no matter what (the cost) ■ **il veut se faire un nom à n'importe quel ~** he'll stop at nothing to make a name for himself.
◆ **à tout prix** *loc adv* **1.** [obligatoirement] at all costs ■ **tu dois à tout ~ être rentré à minuit** you must be back by midnight at all costs
2. [coûte que coûte] at any cost, no matter what (the cost) ■ **nous voulons un enfant à tout ~** we want a child no matter what (the cost).
◆ **au prix de** *loc prép* at the cost of ■ **ma mère m'a élevé au ~ de grands sacrifices** my mother made great sacrifices to bring me up.
◆ **de prix** *loc adj* [bijou, objet] valuable.
◆ **sans prix** *loc adj* invaluable, priceless ■ **l'estime de mes amis est sans ~** I value the esteem of my friends above all else.

pro [pro] (*abr de* **professionnel**) *fam* ◇ *adj* SPORT professional.
◇ *nmf* pro ■ **c'est une vraie ~** she's a real pro ■ **passer ~** to turn pro ■ **ils ont fait un vrai travail de ~** they did a really professional job.

proactif, ive [prɔaktif,iv] *adj* proactive.

probabilisme [prɔbabilism] *nm* probabilism.

probabiliste [prɔbabilist] ◇ *adj* probabilist, probabilistic.
◇ *nmf* probabilist.

probabilité [prɔbabilite] *nf* **1.** [vraisemblance] probability, likelihood ■ **selon toute ~** in all probability *OU* likelihood **2.** [supposition] probability ■ **je ne dis pas qu'il l'a volé, c'est une ~** I'm not saying he stole it, but it's probable ■ **la ~ qu'il gagne est plutôt faible** there's little chance of him winning **3.** MATH & PHYS probability.

probable [prɔbabl] *adj* **1.** [vraisemblable] likely, probable ■ **il est peu ~ qu'elle soit sa sœur** it's not very likely that she's his sister **2.** [possible] probable ■ **est-il à Paris? - c'est ~** is he in Paris? - quite probably (he is) ■ **je parie qu'elle va refuser - ~!** *fam* I bet she'll say no - more than likely!

probablement [prɔbabləmɑ̃] *adv* probably ■ **tu viendras demain? - très ~** will you come tomorrow? - very probably *OU* quite likely.

probant, e [prɔbɑ̃, ɑ̃t] *adj* **1.** [convaincant - argument, fait, expérience] convincing **2.** DR [pièce] probative.

probation [prɔbasjɔ̃] *nf* DR & RELIG probation ■ **être en ~** to be on probation.

probatoire [prɔbatwar] *adj* probationary ■ **période ~** trial period.

probe [prɔb] *adj* *litt* upright, endowed with integrity.

probité [prɔbite] *nf* probity, integrity, uprightness.

problématique [prɔblematik] ◇ *adj* problematic, problematical.
◇ *nf* set of problems *OU* issues.

problème [prɔblɛm] *nm* **1.** MATH problem ■ **~ de géométrie** geometry problem ■ **~s de robinet** *mathematical problems for schoolchildren, typically about the volume of water in a container* **2.** [difficulté] problem, difficulty ■ **ne t'inquiète pas, tu n'auras aucun ~** don't worry, you'll be all right ■ **pas de ~, viens quand tu veux** no problem, you can come whenever you want ■ **nous avons un gros ~** we have a major problem, we're in big trouble here ■ **un ~ personnel** a personal matter ■ **il a toujours eu des ~s d'argent** he always had money troubles *OU* problems **3.** [question] problem, issue, question ■ **soulever un ~** to raise a question *OU* an issue ■ **la clé du ~** the key to the problem ■ **faux ~** red herring *fig* ■ **nous discutons d'un faux ~** we're going around in circles **4.** JEUX problem.
◆ **à problèmes** *loc adj* problem *(modif)* ■ **ma cousine, c'est une femme à ~s** *fam* my cousin's always got problems.

procédé [prɔsede] *nm* **1.** *sout* [comportement] conduct, behaviour ■ **je n'ai pas du tout apprécié son ~** I wasn't very impressed with what he did **2.** [technique] process ■ **mettre un ~ au point** to perfect a process ■ **~ de fabrication** manufacturing process **3.** *péj* [artifice] : **toute la pièce sent le ~** the whole play seems contrived **4.** JEUX [billard] tip.

procéder [18] [prɔsede] *vi* **1.** [progresser] to proceed ■ **procédons par ordre** let's do one thing at a time **2.** [se conduire] to behave ■ **j'apprécie sa manière de ~ avec nous** I like the way he deals with us.
◆ **procéder à** *v+prép* **1.** [effectuer] to conduct ■ **~ à une étude** to conduct a study ■ **~ à un examen approfondi de la situation** to examine the situation thoroughly ■ **~ à l'élection du bureau national du parti** to elect the national executive of the party **2.** DR : **~ à l'arrestation d'un criminel** to arrest a criminal ■ **~ à l'ouverture d'un testament** to open a will.
◆ **procéder de** *v+prép* **1.** *litt* [provenir de] to proceed from, to originate in ■ **tous ses problèmes procèdent d'une mauvaise administration** all his problems spring *OU* derive from poor management **2.** RELIG to proceed from.

procédural, e [prɔsedyral] *adj* procedural.

procédure [prɔsedyr] *nf* **1.** [démarche] procedure, way to proceed ■ **voici la ~ à suivre** this is the way to proceed **2.** DR [ensemble des règles] procedure, practice ■ **Code de ~ civile/pénale** civil law/criminal law procedure ‖ [action] proceedings ■ **entamer une ~ contre qqn** to start proceedings against sb ◆ **~ de divorce** divorce proceedings **3.** INFORM subroutine, procedure.

procédurier, ère [prɔsedyrje, ɛr] ◇ *adj* **1.** *péj* [personne] pettifogging, quibbling ■ **être ~** to be a pettifogger *OU* a nitpicker **2.** [action, démarche] litigious ■ **formalités procédurières** procedural formalities, red tape.
◇ *nm, f* pettifogger, quibbler.

procès [prɔsɛ] *nm* **1.** DR [pénal] trial ■ [civil] lawsuit, legal proceedings ■ **faire** *OU* **intenter un ~ à qqn** to institute legal proceedings against sb ■ **entreprendre** *OU* **engager un ~ contre qqn** to take sb to court ■ **instruire un ~** to prepare a lawsuit ■ **il a gagné/perdu son ~ contre nous** he won/lost his case against us ■ **un ~ pour meurtre** a murder trial ◆ **sans autre forme de ~** without further ado **2.** [critique] : **faire le ~ de qqn/qqch** to put sb/sthg on trial ◆ **~ d'intention : vous me faites un ~ d'intention** you're assuming too much about my intentions ■ **pas de ~ d'intention, s'il vous plaît!** don't put words in my mouth, please! ■ **faire un mauvais ~ à qqn** to make groundless accusations against sb ■ **tu lui fais un mauvais ~** you're being unfair to him **3.** ANAT process **4.** LING process.

processeur [prɔsesœr] *nm* INFORM **1.** [organe] (hardware) processor ■ [unité centrale] central processing unit **2.** [ensemble de programmes] (language) processor ■ **~ entrée/sortie** input/output processor, I/O processor ■ **~ RISC** RISC processor.

processif, ive [prɔsesif, iv] *adj* *litt* litigious.

procession [prɔsesjɔ̃] *nf* **1.** RELIG procession ■ **~ rituelle** religious procession **2.** [cortège] procession ■ **une ~ de voitures** a motorcade.

processionnaire [prɔsesjɔnɛr] ◇ *adj* ENTOM processionary.
◇ *nf* processionary caterpillar.

processionnel, elle [prɔsesjɔnɛl] *adj* processional.

processive [prɔsesiv] *f* ▷ **processif.**

processus [prɔsesys] *nm* **1.** process ▪ **le ~ d'acquisition de la lecture** learning how to read ▪ **~ de fabrication** manufacturing process ▪ **~ industriel** industrial processing **2.** ANAT process.

procès-verbal, aux [prɔsɛvɛrbal, o] *nm* **1.** DR [acte - d'un magistrat] (official) report, record ; [- d'un agent de police] (police) report **2.** [pour une contravention] parking ticket **3.** [résumé] minutes, proceedings ▪ **le ~ de la dernière réunion** the minutes of the last meeting.

prochain, e [prɔʃɛ̃, ɛn] *adj* **1.** [dans le temps] next ▪ **je te verrai la semaine ~e** I'll see you next week ▪ **à samedi ~!** see you next Saturday! ▪ **le mois ~** next month, this coming month ▪ **ça sera pour une ~e fois** we'll do it some other time ▪ **la ~e fois, fais attention** next time, be careful **2.** [dans l'espace] next ▪ **je descends au ~ arrêt** I'm getting off at the next stop **3.** [imminent] imminent, near ▪ **on se reverra dans un avenir ~** we will see each other again in the near future **4.** *sout* [immédiat - cause, pouvoir] immediate.
◆ **prochain** *nm* : **son ~** one's fellow man ▪ **aime ton ~ comme toi-même** love your neighbour as yourself.
◆ **prochaine** *nf fam* **1.** [arrêt] next stop ▪ **je descends à la ~e** I'm getting off at the next stop **2.** *loc* **à la ~e!** see you (soon)!, be seeing you!, so long! US.

prochainement [prɔʃɛnmɑ̃] *adv* shortly, soon ▪ **il revient ~** he'll be back soon ▪ **'~ sur vos écrans'** 'coming soon'.

proche [prɔʃ] ◇ *adj* **1.** [avoisinant] nearby ▪ **le bureau est tout ~** the office is close at hand *ou* very near ▪ **le village le plus ~ est Pigny** Pigny's the nearest village **2.** [dans l'avenir] near, imminent ▪ [dans le passé] in the recent past ▪ **dans un avenir ~** in the near future ▪ **le dénouement est ~** the end is in sight ▪ **Noël est ~** we're getting close to Christmas ▪ **la fin du monde est ~** the end of the world is nigh **3.** [cousin, parent] close ▪ **adresse de votre plus ~ parent** address of your next of kin **4.** [intime] close ▪ **l'un des ~s conseillers du président** one of the president's trusted *ou* close advisors **5.** [semblable] similar.
◇ *nm* close relative *ou* relation ▪ **ses ~s** his friends and relatives.
◆ **de proche en proche** *loc adv* [petit à petit] gradually, step by step ▪ **de ~ en ~, j'ai fini par reconstituer les événements** step by step, I finally reconstructed the events.
◆ **proche de** *loc prép* **1.** [dans l'espace] near (to), close to, not far from ▪ **plus ~ de chez lui** closer to his home **2.** [dans le temps] close ▪ **la guerre est encore ~ de nous** the war is still close to us **3.** [en contact avec] close to ▪ **il est resté ~ de son père** he remained close to his father ▪ **être ~ de la nature** to be close to *ou* in touch with nature ▪ **d'après des sources ~s de la Maison-Blanche** according to sources close to the White House **4.** [semblable à - langage, espèce animale] closely related to ; [- style, solution] similar to ▪ **la haine est ~ de l'amour** hatred is akin to love ▪ **portrait ~ de la réalité** accurate *ou* lifelike portrait ▪ **une obsession ~ de la névrose** an obsession verging on the neurotic ▪ **ils sont ~s de nous par la religion et la culture** religiously and culturally they have a lot in common with us **5.** [sans différence de rang, d'âge avec] close to ▪ **mes frères et moi sommes ~s les uns des autres** my brothers and I are close together (in age).

Proche-Orient [prɔʃɔrjɑ̃] *npr m* : **le ~** the Near East.

proclamation [prɔklamasjɔ̃] *nf* **1.** [annonce] (official) announcement *ou* statement ▪ **~ du résultat des élections à 20 h** the results of the election will be announced at 8 p.m **2.** [texte] proclamation.

proclamer [3] [prɔklame] *vt* **1.** [déclarer - innocence, vérité] to proclaim, to declare ▪ **~ que** to declare that **2.** [annoncer publiquement] to publicly announce *ou* state, to proclaim ▪ **~ le résultat des élections** to announce the outcome of the election ▪ **~ qqn empereur** to proclaim sb emperor.

proconsul [prɔkɔ̃syl] *nm* proconsul.

procréateur, trice [prɔkreatœr, tris] *litt* ◇ *adj* procreant, procreative.
◇ *nm, f* procreator.

procréation [prɔkreasjɔ̃] *nf* procreation ▪ **~ artificielle** artificial reproduction ▪ **~ médicalement assitée** medically assisted conception *ou* procreation *ou* reproduction.

procréer [15] [prɔkree] *vt litt* to procreate.

procuration [prɔkyrasjɔ̃] *nf* **1.** DR [pouvoir - gén] power *ou* letter of attorney ; [- pour une élection] proxy (form) ▪ **donner ~ à qqn** to authorize *ou* to empower sb **2.** BANQUE mandate ▪ **il a une ~ sur mon compte** he has a mandate to operate my account.
◆ **par procuration** *loc adv* **1.** [voter] by proxy **2.** *fig* vicariously ▪ **vivre/voyager par ~** to live/to travel vicariously.

procurer [3] [prɔkyre] *vt* **1.** [fournir] to provide ▪ **~ de l'argent à qqn** to provide sb with money, to obtain money for sb ▪ **je lui ai procuré un emploi** I found her a job **2.** [occasionner] to bring ▪ **la lecture me procure beaucoup de plaisir** reading brings me great pleasure, I get a lot of pleasure out of reading.
◆ **se procurer** *vpt* to get, to obtain ▪ **essaye de te ~ son dernier livre** try to get his latest book.

procureur, euse [prɔkyrœr, øz] *nm, f* **1.** DR prosecutor ▪ **~ général** *public prosecutor at the 'Parquet'*, ≃ Director of Public Prosecutions UK, ≃ district attorney US ▪ **~ de la République** *public prosecutor at a 'tribunal de grande instance'*, ≃ Attorney General **2.** HIST [syndic] procurer **3.** RELIG procurator *arch.*

prodigalité [prɔdigalite] *nf* **1.** [générosité] prodigality *sout*, profligacy *sout*, extravagance **2.** [dépenses] prodigality *sout*, extravagance ▪ **connu pour ses ~s** well-known for his extravagance *ou* for his extravagant spending habits **3.** *litt* [surabondance] (lavish) abundance, prodigality *sout.*

prodige [prɔdiʒ] ◇ *nm* **1.** [miracle] marvel, wonder ▪ **faire des ~s** to work wonders, to achieve miracles ▪ **tenir du ~** to be nothing short of miraculous *ou* a miracle ▪ **un ~ de** a wonder of ▪ **il nous a fallu déployer des ~s d'ingéniosité pour tout ranger** we had to use boundless ingenuity to find space for everything **2.** [personne] prodigy.
◇ *adj* : **musicien ~** musical prodigy.

prodigieusement [prɔdiʒjøzmɑ̃] *adv* **1.** [beaucoup] enormously, tremendously ▪ **il m'agace ~** he really gets on my nerves **2.** [magnifiquement] fantastically, magnificently ▪ **elle dessine ~ bien** she draws fantastically well.

prodigieux, euse [prɔdiʒjø, øz] *adj* **1.** [extrême] huge, tremendous ▪ **être d'une force prodigieuse** to be tremendously strong ▪ **une quantité prodigieuse** a huge amount **2.** [peu commun] prodigious, astounding, amazing **3.** *litt* [miraculeux] prodigious, miraculous.

prodigue [prɔdig] ◇ *adj* **1.** [dépensier] extravagant, profligate *sout* **2.** *fig* **~ de** generous *ou* overgenerous with ▪ **elle n'est guère ~ de détails** she doesn't go in much for detail ▪ **~ de compliments** lavish with compliments ▪ **tu es toujours ~ de bons conseils** you're always full of good advice.
◇ *nmf* spender, spendthrift.

prodiguer [3] [prɔdige] *vt* [faire don de] to be lavish with ▪ **la nature nous prodigue ses bienfaits** nature is profuse *ou* lavish in its bounty ▪ **elle a prodigué des soins incessants à son fils** she lavished endless care on her son ▪ **prodiguant des sourires à tous** smiling bountifully on everybody *péj.*

producteur, trice [prɔdyktœr, tris] ◇ *adj* producing ▪ **les pays ~s de pétrole** oil-producing countries ▪ **zone productrice de betteraves** beetroot-producing *ou* beetroot-growing area.
◇ *nm, f* CINÉ, RADIO, THÉÂTRE & TV [personne] producer ▪ [société] production company.
◆ **producteur** *nm* AGRIC & ÉCON producer ▪ **les ~s sont mécontents** AGRIC the farmers are up in arms ▪ **les ~s de melons** melon growers *ou* producers.

productible [prɔdyktibl] *adj* [marchandise] producible.

productif, ive [prɔdyktif, iv] *adj* **1.** [travailleur] productive ▪ [auteur] prolific ▪ **de manière productive** productively **2.** FIN : **capital ~** interest-bearing *ou* interest-yielding capital **3.** AGRIC & MIN productive ▪ **le sol est peu ~** the yield from the soil is poor.

production [prɔdyksjɔ̃] *nf* **1.** [activité économique] : **la ~** production ▪ **la ~ ne suit plus la consommation** supply is failing to keep up with demand **2.** [rendement - INDUST] output ▪ AGRIC yield ▪ **la ~ a augmenté/diminué** INDUST output has risen/dropped ; AGRIC the yield is higher/lower ▪ **l'usine a une ~ de 10 000 voitures par an** the factory turns out *ou* produces 10,000 cars a year **3.** [produits - AGRIC] produce *(U)*, production *(U)* ▪ INDUST products, production ▪ **le pays veut écouler sa ~ de maïs** the country wants to sell off its maize crop *ou* the maize it has produced **4.** [fabrication] production, manufacturing ▪ **~ textile** textile manufacturing **5.** [d'une œuvre d'art] production, creation ▪ **une importante ~ littéraire** a large literary output ▮ CINÉ, THÉÂTRE & TV production ▪ **assurer la ~ de** to produce ➔ **assistant/directeur de ~** production assistant/manager **6.** [œuvres] : **la ~ contemporaine** contemporary works ▪ **la ~ dramatique/romanesque du XVIIIe siècle** 18th-century plays/novels ▮ CINÉ production, film *UK*, movie *esp US* ▪ RADIO production, programme ▪ THÉÂTRE production, play **7.** [présentation] presentation ▪ **sur ~ d'un acte de naissance** on presentation of a birth certificate **8.** [fait d'occasionner] production, producing, making ▪ **la ~ d'un son** making a sound **9.** TECHNOL : **~ combinée** heat and power (generation).

productique [prɔdyktik] *nf* computer-aided *ou* computer-integrated manufacturing.

productivité [prɔdyktivite] *nf* **1.** [fertilité - d'un sol, d'une région] productivity, productiveness **2.** [rentabilité] productivity ▪ **~ de l'impôt** FIN (net) tax revenue **3.** ÉCOL productivity, production.

produire [98] [prɔdɥir] *vt* **1.** [fabriquer - bien de consommation] to produce, to manufacture ; [- énergie, électricité] to produce, to generate ▪ AGRIC [faire pousser] to produce, to grow **2.** [fournir - suj: usine] to produce ; [- suj: sol] to produce, to yield ▪ *(en usage absolu)* **tes arbres ne produiront jamais** your trees will never bear fruit ▮ FIN [bénéfice] to yield, to return **3.** [causer - bruit, vapeur] to produce, to make, to cause ; [- douleur, démangeaison] to produce, to cause ; [- changement] to effect, to bring about *(sép)* ; [- résultat] to produce ▪ **la lumière produit une illusion spectaculaire** the light creates a spectacular illusion ▪ **l'effet produit par son discours a été catastrophique** the effect of her speech was disastrous **4.** [créer - suj: artiste] to produce ▪ **il a produit quelques bons romans** he has written *ou* produced a few good novels ▪ *(en usage absolu)* **il produit beaucoup** [écrivain] he writes a lot ; [musicien] he writes *ou* composes a lot ; [cinéaste] he makes a lot of films **5.** CINÉ, RADIO, THÉÂTRE & TV to produce, to be the producer of **6.** [engendrer] to produce ▪ **combien le XIXe siècle/Mexique a-t-il produit de romancières?** how many women novelists did 19th century produce/has Mexico produced? **7.** [présenter - passeport] to produce, to show ; [- preuve] to adduce *sout*, to produce ; [- témoin] to produce.

◆ **se produire** *vpi* **1.** [événement] to happen, to occur ▪ **il s'est produit un très grave accident près d'ici** there was a very serious accident near here ▪ **une transformation majeure s'est produite** a major change has taken place **2.** [personne] to appear, to give a performance ▪ **se ~ sur scène** to appear on stage ▪ **se ~ en public** to give a public performance.

produit [prɔdɥi] *nm* **1.** INDUST product ▪ AGRIC produce ▪ **~ brut/fini** raw/finished product ▪ **~s de grande consommation** *ou* **de consommation courante** consumer goods ▪ **~s alimentaires** food, foodstuffs ▪ **~ de beauté** beauty product ▪ **les ~s de beauté** cosmetics, beauty products ▪ **~s chimiques** chemicals ▪ **garanti sans ~s chimiques** guaranteed no (chemical) additives ▪ **~ colorant** colouring agent ▪ **~ dérivé** by-product ▪ **~ d'entretien** (household) cleaning product ▪ **~s de luxe** luxury goods *ou* articles ▪ **~ manufacturé** manufactured product ▪ **~s manufacturés** manufactured goods ▪ **~s pharmaceutiques** drugs, pharmaceuticals, pharmaceutical products ▪ **~ de substitution** substitute ▪ **~ de synthèse** synthetic product
2. [résultat] product, outcome ▪ **le ~ d'une matinée de travail** the result *ou* product of a morning's work ▪ **c'est un pur ~ de ton imagination** it's a complete figment of your imagination
3. [bénéfice] profit ▪ **le ~ de la vente** the profit made on the sale ▪ **il vit du ~ de ses terres** he lives off his land ➔ **~ de l'impôt** tax revenue
4. FIN : **~s financiers** financial services
5. ÉCON : **~ intérieur brut** gross (domestic) product ▪ **~ intérieur net** net domestic product ▪ **~ national brut** gross national product
6. CHIM & MATH product ▪ **~ cartésien** Cartesian product ▪ **~ vectoriel** vector product

7. ZOOL offspring.

proéminence [prɔeminɑ̃s] *nf* **1.** *litt* [caractère] prominence, conspicuousness **2.** [saillie] protuberance ▪ **la montagne présente une ~ à gauche du pic** the mountain juts out *ou* protrudes left of the peak.

proéminent, e [prɔeminɑ̃, ɑ̃t] *adj* prominent.

prof [prɔf] *nmf fam* **1.** ÉDUC teacher ▪ **ma ~ de maths** my maths teacher **2.** UNIV [sans chaire] lecturer *UK*, instructor *US* ▪ [titulaire de chaire] prof ▪ **elle est ~ de fac** she's a lecturer **3.** [hors d'un établissement scolaire] teacher, tutor.

profanateur, trice [prɔfanatœr, tris] *litt* <> *adj* blasphemous, sacrilegious.
<> *nm, f* profaner.

profanation [prɔfanasjɔ̃] *nf* **1.** [sacrilège] blasphemy, sacrilege, profanation ▪ **~ de sépultures** desecration of graves **2.** *sout* [avilissement] defilement, debasement ▪ **une ~ de la justice** a travesty of justice.

profane [prɔfan] <> *adj* **1.** [ignorant] uninitiated ▪ **je suis ~ en la matière** I know nothing about the subject **2.** [non religieux] non-religious, secular, profane *litt.*
<> *nmf* **1.** [ignorant] lay person, layman (*f* laywoman) ▪ **pour le ~** to the layman *ou* uninitiated **2.** [non religieux] lay person, non-initiate.
<> *nm* : **le ~** the secular, the profane *litt.*

profaner [3] [prɔfane] *vt* **1.** RELIG [tombe, église, hostie] to desecrate, to violate the sanctity of, to profane *sout* **2.** [dégrader - justice, talent] to debase, to defile, to profane *sout.*

proférer [18] [prɔfere] *vt* [insultes, menaces] to utter ▪ **~ des injures contre qqn** to heap insults on sb.

professer [4] [prɔfese] *vt* **1.** *litt* [déclarer] to affirm, to claim, to profess ▪ **~ des opinions révolutionnaires** to profess revolutionary opinions **2.** *vieilli* [enseigner] to teach.

professeur [prɔfɛsœr] *nmf* **1.** [du primaire, du secondaire] teacher, schoolteacher ▪ **mon ~ d'anglais** my English teacher ▪ **~ certifié** qualified schoolteacher *(who has passed the CAPES)* ▪ **~ des écoles** primary school teacher *(formerly called an 'instituteur')* ▪ **~ principal** ≃ form tutor *UK*, ≃ homeroom teacher *US* **2.** [de l'enseignement supérieur - assistant] ≃ lecturer ; [- au grade supérieur] professor ▪ **elle est ~ à l'université de Lyon** she teaches at Lyons University ➔ **~ agrégé** ÉDUC qualified teacher *(who has passed the agrégation)* ; MÉD *professor qualified to teach medicine* **3.** *Québec* **~ adjoint** assistant professor ▪ **~ agrégé** associate professor ▪ **~ titulaire** ÉDUC staff teacher, member of (teaching) staff ; UNIV full professor **4.** [hors d'un établissement scolaire] teacher, tutor.

profession [prɔfɛsjɔ̃] *nf* **1.** [métier] occupation, job, profession ▪ [d'un commerçant, d'un artisan] trade ▪ [d'un artiste, d'un industriel] profession ▪ **quelle est votre ~?** what is your occupation?, what do you do (for a living)? ▪ **je suis mécanicien de ~** I'm a mechanic by trade ▪ **rebelle de ~** *hum* professional rebel ➔ **les ~s libérales** the professions **2.** [corporation - de commerçants, d'artisans] trade ; [- d'artistes, d'industriels] profession **3.** [déclaration] : **faire ~ de** to profess, to declare ▪ **faire ~ de libéralisme/socialisme** to declare o.s. a liberal/socialist **4.** RELIG : **~ religieuse** profession ▪ **~ de foi** profession of faith.

◆ **sans profession** *loc adj* ADMIN unemployed.

professionnalisation [prɔfɛsjɔnalizasjɔ̃] *nf* professionalization.

professionnalisme [prɔfɛsjɔnalism] *nm* professionalism.

professionnel, elle [prɔfɛsjɔnɛl] <> *adj* **1.** [lié à une profession - maladie, risque] occupational ; [- enseignement] vocational ▪ **avoir des soucis ~s** to have work problems ▪ **une vie ~le satisfaisante** a rewarding job ➔ **école ~le** ≃ technical college **2.** [qualifié - musicien, sportif] professional **3.** [compétent] professional, accomplished ▪ **elle a réagi d'une manière très ~le** she reacted in a very professional way ▪ **le jeu des jeunes acteurs était très ~** the young actors performed like real professionals.

◇ *nm, f* **1.** SPORT professional ▪ **les ~s de la boxe** professional boxers ▪ **passer ~** to turn professional **2.** [personne expérimentée] professional ▪ **c'est l'œuvre d'un ~** this is the work of a professional.

◆ **professionnelle** *nf fam* [prostituée] pro *(prostitute)*.

professionnellement [prɔfɛsjɔnɛlmɑ̃] *adv* professionally ▪ **~, il a plutôt réussi** he did rather well in his professional life ▪ **je n'ai affaire à elle que ~** I only have a professional relationship with her, my relations with her are strictly business.

professoral, e, aux [prɔfɛsɔral, o] *adj* **1.** [de professeur] professorial **2.** [pédant] patronizing, lecturing.

professorat [prɔfɛsɔra] *nm* teaching ▪ **il a choisi le ~** he chose teaching as a *ou* his profession.

profil [prɔfil] *nm* **1.** [côté du visage] profile ▪ **mon meilleur ~** my best profile ▪ **avoir un ~ de médaille** to have very regular features **2.** [silhouette] profile, outline ▪ **on devinait le ~ du volcan dans la brume** the volcano was silhouetted in the mist ⊃ **conserver** *ou* **maintenir un ~ bas** to keep a low profile **3.** [aptitude] profile ▪ **elle a le ~ de l'emploi** she seems right for the job ▪ **il a le ~ parfait pour être président** he's ideal presidential material ⊃ **son ~ de carrière** her career profile ▪ **~ psychologique** PSYCHOL psychological profile **4.** GÉOGR profile **5.** COMM : **le ~ des ventes montre une augmentation** the sales outline *ou* profile shows a definite increase **6.** ARCHIT (perpendicular) section **7.** INFORM : **~ (utilisateur)** (user) profil.

◆ **de profil** *loc adv* in profile ▪ **mettez-vous de ~ par rapport à la caméra** show your profile *ou* stand side-on to the camera.

profilage [prɔfilaʒ] *nm* streamlining.

profilé, e [prɔfile] *adj* AUTO streamlined.

◆ **profilé** *nm* MÉTALL section.

profiler [3] [prɔfile] *vt* **1.** MENUIS to profile, to mould ▪ MÉTALL to form **2.** *litt* [laisser voir] : **les montagnes au loin profilaient leur silhouette** the mountains were silhouetted in the distance.

◆ **se profiler** *vpi* **1.** [se découper] to stand out, to be silhouetted **2.** *sout* [apparaître] to emerge ▪ **des nuages noirs se profilent à l'horizon** black clouds are coming up on the horizon ▪ **des périodes difficiles/des ennuis se profilent à l'horizon** a difficult time/trouble is looming on the horizon.

profileur, euse [prɔfilœr, øz] *nm, f* profiler.

profit [prɔfi] *nm* **1.** [avantage] profit, advantage ▪ **tirer ~ de ses lectures** to benefit from one's reading ▪ **tirer ~ de l'expérience des autres** to profit from other people's experience ▪ **j'ai lu ton livre avec ~** reading your book taught me a lot ▪ **mettre qqch à ~** to take advantage of *ou* to make the most of sthg ▪ **il y a trouvé son ~, sinon il ne l'aurait pas fait** he got something out of it otherwise he wouldn't have done it **2.** COMM & FIN [bénéfice] profit ▪ **faire** *ou* **réaliser des ~s** to make profits *ou* a profit ▪ **le ~ réalisé sur la vente de la propriété** the return on *ou* the revenue from the sale of the property ⊃ **~ brut/net** gross/net profit ▪ **~ minimal** minimum trading profit.

◆ **au profit de** *loc prép* in aid of ▪ **à son/mon seul ~** for his/my sole benefit.

profitabilité [prɔfitabilite] *nf* profitability.

profitable [prɔfitabl] *adj* profitable ▪ **ce séjour en Italie lui a été ~** the time she spent in Italy did her a lot of good.

profiter [3] [prɔfite] *vi fam* to thrive, to do well ▪ **cet enfant profite (bien)** this child is thriving.

◆ **profiter à** *v+prép* to benefit, to be beneficial to ▪ **cet argent ne profite à personne** this money's not benefitting anyone ▪ **les études ne t'ont guère profité** studying didn't do you much good.

◆ **profiter de** *v+prép* **1.** [financièrement] to profit from ▪ **tous n'ont pas profité de l'expansion** not everybody gained by the expansion **2.** [jouir de] to enjoy **3.** [tirer parti de] to take advantage of ▪ **~ du soleil** to make the most of the sun ▪ **il profite de ce qu'elle est absente** he's taking advantage of the fact that she's away ▪ **~ de la situation** to take advantage of the situation ▪ **comme j'avais un deuxième billet, j'en ai fait ~ ma copine** since I had a second ticket, I took my girlfriend along **4.** [exploiter] to take advantage of, to use.

profiteroles [prɔfitrɔl] *nfpl* : **~ (au chocolat)** (chocolate) profiterole.

profiteur, euse [prɔfitœr, øz] *nm, f* profiteer.

profond, e [prɔfɔ̃, ɔ̃d] *adj* **1.** [enfoncé - lac, racine, blessure] deep ▪ **peu ~** shallow ▪ **un puits ~ de 10 mètres** a well 10 metres deep ▪ **la haine de l'ennemi est ~e** hatred of the enemy runs deep **2.** [plongeant - révérence, salut] deep, low ; [- regard] penetrating ; [- décolleté] plunging **3.** [intense - respiration] deep ; [- soupir, sommeil] deep, heavy ; [- silence] profound, utter ; [- changement] profound ▪ **absorbé dans de ~es pensées** deep in thought **4.** [grave - voix] deep **5.** [obscur] deep, dark ▪ **dans la nuit ~e** at dead of night **6.** [foncé - couleur] dark ▪ **bleu ~** deep blue **7.** [sagace] deep, profound ▪ **avoir un esprit ~** to have profound insight **8.** [véritable - cause] deep, underlying, primary ▪ **la raison ~e de son acte** his basic *ou* primary *ou* underlying motivation **9.** LING deep.

◆ **profond** ◇ *adv* [aller, creuser] deep.

◇ *nm* : **au plus ~ de la terre** in the depths *ou* bowels of the earth ▪ **au plus ~ de mon cœur** deep in my heart.

profondément [prɔfɔ̃demɑ̃] *adv* **1.** [creuser, enfouir] deep ▪ **il salua ~ la foule** he greeted the crowd with a deep bow **2.** [respirer] deeply ▪ [soupirer] heavily, deeply ▪ **dormir ~** to be sound asleep ▪ **d'habitude, je dors très ~** I usually sleep very heavily, I'm usually a sound sleeper **3.** [en intensif] profoundly, deeply ▪ **je suis ~ choqué** I'm deeply shocked ▪ **elle est ~ convaincue de son bon droit** she's utterly convinced she's right ▪ **je regrette ~!** I'm deeply sorry!

profondeur [prɔfɔ̃dœr] *nf* **1.** [dimension] depth ▪ **quelle est la ~ du puits?** how deep is the well? ▪ **un trou de trois mètres de ~** a hole three metres deep ▪ **on s'est arrêtés à huit mètres de ~** we stopped eight metres down ▪ **la faible ~ de l'étang** the shallowness of the lake **2.** [intensité - d'un sentiment] depth, profundity *sout* **3.** [perspicacité] profoundness, profundity ▪ **sa ~ d'esprit** her insight **4.** OPT & PHOTO : **~ de champ** depth of field **5.** AÉRON [d'une aile] chord (length).

◆ **profondeurs** *nfpl litt* depths.

◆ **en profondeur** ◇ *loc adj* [étude] in-depth, thorough ▪ **il nous faut des changements en ~** we need fundamental changes.

◇ *loc adv* [creuser] deep ▪ **notre crème antirides agit en ~** our anti-wrinkle cream works deep into the skin ▪ **il faut agir en ~** we need to make fundamental changes.

profusion [prɔfyzjɔ̃] *nf* **1.** *sout* [abondance] profusion, abundance **2.** [excès] excess ▪ **avec une ~ de détails** with too much detail.

◆ **à profusion** *loc adv* galore, plenty ▪ **il y avait à boire et à manger à ~** there was food and drink galore, there was plenty to eat and drink.

progéniture [prɔʒenityr] *nf* offspring, progeny *sout*, issue *sout* ▪ **que fais-tu de ta nombreuse ~ le dimanche?** *hum* what do you do with all your offspring on Sundays?

progestatif, ive [prɔʒɛstatif, iv] *adj* progestational.

progestérone [prɔʒɛsterɔn] *nf* progesterone.

progiciel [prɔʒisjɛl] *nm* INFORM package.

prognathe [prɔgnat] *adj* prognathous, prognathic.

programmable [prɔgramabl] *adj* programmable.

programmateur, trice [prɔgramatœr, tris] *nm, f* RADIO & TV programme planner.

◆ **programmateur** *nm* [d'une cuisinière] programmer, autotimer ▪ [d'une machine à laver] programme selector.

programmation [prɔgramasjɔ̃] *nf* **1.** RADIO & TV programme planning **2.** INFORM programming ▪ **~ absolue/dynamique/linéaire** absolute/dynamic/linear programming ▪ **~ orientée objet** object-oriented programming **3.** ÉCON programming.

programme [prɔgram] *nm* **1.** [contenu - d'une cérémonie, d'un spectacle] programme ▪ **qu'est-ce qu'il y a au ~ ce soir à l'Opéra?** what's on tonight at the Opera? ▪ **~s d'été** TV summer

schedule *ou* programmes ▶ ~ **minimum** RADIO & TV minimum programme schedule *(provided during strike actions by journalists and technicians)*
2. [brochure - d'un concert, d'une soirée] programme ; [- de cinéma, de télévision] listings, guide ▪ **il y a un bon ~ ce soir à la télé** it's a good night on TV tonight
3. [emploi du temps] schedule ▪ **qu'avons-nous au ~ aujourd'hui?** what's on (our schedule) today? ▪ **inscrire qqch au ~** to schedule sthg
4. ÉDUC [d'une année] curriculum ▪ [dans une matière] syllabus ▪ **une question hors ~** a question not covered by the syllabus ▪ **Shakespeare figure au ~ cette année** Shakespeare is on this year's syllabus
5. POLIT [plate-forme] manifesto *UK*, platform *US* ▪ **~ commun** common *ou* joint manifesto ▪ **~ de gouvernement** government manifesto
6. [projet] programme ▪ **lancer un ~ de réformes** to launch a package *ou* programme of reforms ▪ **le ~nucléaire/spatial français** the French nuclear/space programme ▶ **ton voyage, c'est tout un ~!** *fam* this trip sounds like it's quite something! ▪ **je voudrais l'intéresser à l'actualité – tout un ~!** *hum* I'd like to get him interested in current affairs – that's a tall order!
7. INFORM program ▪ **~ d'assemblage** assembler ▪ **~ de chargement** loader ▪ **~ de diagnostic** malfunction routine.

programmé, e [prɔgrame] *adj* computerized.

programmer [3] [prɔgrame] ◇ *vt* **1.** CINÉ, RADIO, THÉÂTRE & TV to bill, to programme **2.** [planifier] to plan ▪ **j'ai programmé tout le week-end** I planned the entire weekend **3.** ÉLECTRON to set, to programme **4.** INFORM to program.
◇ *vi* INFORM to (write a) program.

programmeur, euse [prɔgramœr, øz] *nm, f* INFORM programmer.

progrès [prɔgrɛ] *nm* **1.** [amélioration] progress ▪ **faire des ~** to make progress ▪ **être en ~** to (make) progress, to improve ▪ **il y a du ~, continuez** that's better, keep it up **2.** [avancée] breakthrough, advance ▪ **le XXᵉ siècle a connu de grands ~ scientifiques** the 20th century has witnessed some great scientific breakthroughs ▪ **le ~** progress ▪ **tu vois, c'est ça le ~!** that's progress for you! *iron* **3.** [développement] : **les ~ de** [incendie] the progress of ; [criminalité] the upsurge *ou* increase in ; [maladie] the progress *ou* progression of **4.** MIL advance.

progresser [4] [prɔgrese] *vi* **1.** [s'améliorer] to improve, to (make) progress **2.** [gagner du terrain - ennemi] to advance, to gain ground ▪ **je progresse lentement dans ma lecture** I'm getting on *ou* progressing slowly in my reading ; [- maladie] to progress ; [- inflation] to creep up, to rise ▪ **nos bénéfices ont progressé de 2% l'année dernière** our profits rose by 2% last year ▪ **la recherche scientifique progresse de jour en jour/à grands pas** scientific research is making progress every day/is advancing by leaps and bounds.

progressif, ive [prɔgresif, iv] *adj* **1.** [graduel] gradual, progressive ▪ **exercices ~s** graded exercises **2.** LING progressive.

progression [prɔgresjɔ̃] *nf* **1.** [avancée] progress, advance ▪ **l'ennemi a poursuivi sa ~ vers l'intérieur des terres** the enemy advanced *ou* progressed inland **2.** [développement - d'une maladie] progression, progress ; [- du racisme] development ▪ **notre chiffre d'affaires est en constante ~** our turnover is constantly increasing *ou* improving **3.** MATH & MUS progression.

progressisme [prɔgresism] *nm* belief in the possibility of (social) progress, progressivism.

progressiste [prɔgresist] ◇ *adj* [politique, parti] progressive.
◇ *nmf* progressive.

progressivement [prɔgresivmɑ̃] *adv* progressively, gradually.

progressivité [prɔgresivite] *nf* progressiveness.

prohibé, e [prɔibe] *adj* [interdit] prohibited, banned, illegal.

prohiber [3] [prɔibe] *vt* to prohibit, to ban.

prohibitif, ive [prɔibitif, iv] *adj* [prix, tarif] prohibitive ▪ **pareil prix, c'est ~ en ce qui me concerne** it's just too expensive for me.

prohibition [prɔibisjɔ̃] *nf* **1.** [interdiction] prohibition, ban, banning **2.** HIST : **la Prohibition** Prohibition.

prohibitionniste [prɔibisjɔnist] *adj* & *nmf* prohibitionist.

proie [prwa] *nf* **1.** [animal] prey **2.** [victime] prey ▪ **vu son grand âge, il est une ~ facile pour les cambrioleurs** being so old makes him an easy prey for burglars ▪ **la ville devint rapidement la ~ des flammes** the city rapidly became engulfed in flames.
◆ **en proie à** *loc prép* in the grip of ▪ **en ~ au doute** racked with *ou* beset by doubt ▪ **être en ~ à des hallucinations** to suffer from hallucinations.

projecteur [prɔʒɛktœr] *nm* **1.** [pour illuminer - un spectacle] spotlight ; [- un édifice] floodlight ▪ [pour surveiller] searchlight ▪ **sous les ~s de l'actualité** *fig* in the spotlight **2.** [d'images] projector ▪ **~ (de diapositives)** slide projector **3.** AUTO headlight.

projectif, ive [prɔʒɛktif, iv] *adj* GÉOM & PSYCHOL projective.

projectile [prɔʒɛktil] *nm* **1.** ARM projectile **2.** [objet lancé] projectile, missile.

projection [prɔʒɛksjɔ̃] *nf* **1.** CINÉ & PHOTO projection, showing ▪ **une ~ de diapos** a slide show ▶ **~ privée** private showing **2.** [jet] splash, spatter ▪ **sali par des ~s de boue** spattered with mud ▪ **quand vous cuisinez, attention aux ~s d'huile** when cooking, be careful of the hot oil splashing ▶ **~ de cendres** GÉOL ash fall ▪ **~s volcaniques** ejecta, volcanic debris **3.** PSYCHOL projection **4.** MATH projection ▪ **~ orthogonale** orthogonal projection **5.** GÉOM : **~ (cartographique)** (map) projection ▪ **~ de Mercator** Mercator *ou* Mercator's projection.

projectionniste [prɔʒɛksjɔnist] *nmf* projectionist.

projet [prɔʒɛ] *nm* **1.** [intention] plan ▪ **faire** *ou* **former le ~ de** to plan to ▪ **faire des ~s** to make plans ▪ **quels sont tes ~s de spectacle?** what are your plans for new shows? **2.** [esquisse] plan, outline ▪ **ma pièce n'est encore qu'à l'état de ~** my play is still only a draft *ou* at the planning stage ▶ **~ d'accord/de contrat** DR draft agreement/contract **3.** ARCHIT & TECHNOL plan ▪ **~ de construction** building project.
◆ **en projet** *loc adv* : **qu'avez-vous en ~ pour le printemps?** what are your plans for the spring? ▪ **nous avons un nouveau modèle d'avion en ~** we're working on (the plans for) a new design of aircraft.
◆ **projet de loi** *nm* bill.

projeter [27] [prɔʃte] *vt* **1.** [prévoir] to plan, to arrange ▪ **j'ai projeté un voyage pour cet été** I've planned a trip for this summer ▪ **nous avons projeté de monter une affaire ensemble** we're planning on setting up a business together **2.** [lancer] to throw, to hurl ▪ **être projeté au sol** to be hurled to the ground ▪ **le volcan projette des cendres** the volcano throws up ashes **3.** [faire apparaître - ombre, lumière] to project, to cast, to throw **4.** CINÉ & PHOTO to show, to project **5.** PSYCHOL to project ▪ **~ ses fantasmes sur qqn** to project one's fantasies onto sb **6.** MATH to project ▪ **~ un cercle/une droite sur un plan** to project a circle/a straight line onto a plane **7.** [voix] to project.
◆ **se projeter** *vpi* [ombre] to be outlined *ou* silhouetted ▪ **son ombre se projetait sur l'écran** he was silhouetted against the screen.

projeteur [prɔʃtœr] *nm* **1.** [technicien] design engineer **2.** [dessinateur] industrial (design) draughtsman.

projette *etc v* ▷ **projeter**.

prolapsus [prɔlapsys] *nm* prolapse ▪ **~ de l'utérus** prolapse of the womb.

prolégomènes [prɔlegɔmɛn] *nmpl* prolegomena.

prolétaire [prɔletɛr] ◇ *adj* **1.** *vieilli* [masse, parti] proletarian **2.** [quartier] working-class.
◇ *nmf* proletarian, member of the proletariat.

prolétariat [prɔletarja] *nm* proletariat.

prolétarien, enne [prɔletarjɛ̃, ɛn] *adj* proletarian ▪ **solidarité ~ne** solidarity of the working class.

prolétarisation [prɔletarizasjɔ̃] *nf* proletarianization.

prolétariser [3] [prɔletarize] *vt* to proletarianize.

prolifération [prɔliferasjɔ̃] *nf* **1.** [gén] proliferation, multiplication ■ **la ~ des industries** the mushrooming of industry **2.** BIOL & NUCL proliferation.

prolifère [prɔlifɛr] *adj* BOT proliferous.

proliférer [18] [prɔlifere] *vi* to proliferate ■ **les clichés prolifèrent dans ses derniers poèmes** *fig* his later poems abound in clichés.

prolifique [prɔlifik] *adj* **1.** [fécond] prolific **2.** *fig* [auteur, peintre] prolific, productive.

prolixe [prɔliks] *adj* **1.** [description, style] wordy, verbose, prolix *sout* **2.** [écrivain] verbose, prolix *sout* ■ **il n'est pas ~** [pas bavard] he's a man of few words.

prolixité [prɔliksite] *nf sout* **1.** [d'un discours] wordiness, verbosity **2.** [d'un auteur] verbosity, prolixity.

prolo [prɔlo] *fam* ◇ *adj* working-class.
◇ *nmf* : **les ~s** the working class.

PROLOG, prolog [prɔlɔg] *nm* INFORM PROLOG, prolog.

prologue [prɔlɔg] *nm* **1.** LITTÉR, MUS & THÉÂTRE prologue **2.** [début] prologue, prelude, preamble ■ **en ~ à la réunion** as a prologue *ou* prelude *ou* preamble to the meeting.

prolongateur [prɔlɔ̃gatœr] *nm* ÉLECTR extension.

prolongation [prɔlɔ̃gasjɔ̃] *nf* **1.** [allongement] extension **2.** SPORT extra time *UK*, overtime *US* ■ **jouer les ~s** *pr* to play *ou* to go into extra time.

prolongé, e [prɔlɔ̃ʒe] *adj* **1.** [long - applaudissements, séjour] lengthy, prolonged **2.** [trop long] protracted, prolonged ■ **le séjour ~ au soleil abîme la peau** prolonged exposure to the sun is harmful to the skin ■ **en cas d'arrêt ~ entre deux stations** in the event of unduly long halts between stations.

prolongement [prɔlɔ̃ʒmɑ̃] *nm* [extension - d'une route] continuation ; [- d'un mur, d'une période] extension.
◆ **prolongements** *nmpl* [conséquences] effects, consequences, repercussions ■ **cette affaire aura des ~s** this matter will have significant repercussions.
◆ **dans le prolongement de** *loc prép* : **les deux rues sont dans le ~ l'une de l'autre** the two streets are a continuation of each other ■ **c'est tout à fait dans le ~ de mes préoccupations actuelles** that's along exactly the same lines as what I'm concerned with at the moment.

prolonger [17] [prɔlɔ̃ʒe] *vt* **1.** [dans le temps] to extend, to prolong **2.** [dans l'espace] to extend, to continue ■ **la route sera prolongée de deux kilomètres** the road will be made 2 km longer *ou* will be extended by 2 km ■ **la ligne de métro n° 7 a été prolongée jusqu'en banlieue** the no. 7 underground line was extended to the suburbs **3.** MUS [note] to hold.
◆ **se prolonger** *vpi* **1.** [dans le temps] to persist, to go on ■ **notre discussion s'est prolongée tard** our conversation went on until late **2.** [dans l'espace] to go on, to continue.

promenade [prɔmnad] *nf* **1.** [à pied] walk, stroll ■ [à bicyclette, à cheval] ride ■ [en voiture] ride, drive ■ **aller faire une ~** [à pied] to go for a walk *ou* stroll ; [à bicyclette, à cheval] to go for a ride ■ **et si on faisait une ~ en mer?** shall we go for a sail? ■ **je lui ai fait faire une ~** I took her out for a walk ▶ **ça a été une vraie ~** *fam* [victoire facile] it was a real walkover ■ **la Promenade des Anglais** *fashionable street running along the seafront in Nice* **2.** [allée] walk **3.** DANSE promenade.
◆ **en promenade** *loc adv* out walking, out for a walk.

promener [19] [prɔmne] *vt* **1.** [sortir - à pied] to take (out) for a walk *ou* stroll ; [- en voiture] to take (out) for a drive ■ **j'ai passé le week-end à ~ un ami étranger dans Paris** I spent the weekend showing a foreign friend around Paris ■ **~ le chien** to walk the dog, to take the dog for a walk **2.** *fig* [emmener - personne] : **j'en ai assez d'être promené de poste en poste** I've had enough of being sent from job to job ■ [mentir à] : **il m'a promené pendant trois semaines** he kept me hanging on for three weeks **3.** [déplacer] : **elle promène son regard sur la foule** her eyes scan the crowd ■ **~ ses doigts sur le piano** [en jouant] to run one's fingers over the keys ; [pour le toucher] to finger the piano **4.** *sout* [traîner] : **~ son ennui/désespoir** to go around looking bored/disconsolate **5.** [transporter] to take around ■ **ses récits de voyage nous ont promenés dans le monde entier** her travel stories have taken us all around the world.
◆ **se promener** *vpi* **1.** [à pied] to go for a walk *ou* stroll ■ [en voiture] to go for a drive ■ [à bicyclette, à cheval] to go for a ride ■ [en bateau] to go for a sail ■ **viens te ~ avec moi** come for *ou* on a walk with me **2.** [mains, regard] : **ses doigts se promenaient sur le clavier** her fingers wandered over the keyboard **3.** *fam* [traîner] : **j'en ai assez que tes affaires se promènent dans toute la maison!** I've had enough of your things lying about all over the house!

promeneur, euse [prɔmnœr, øz] *nm, f* walker, stroller.

promenoir [prɔmnwar] *nm* **1.** THÉÂTRE promenade **2.** CONSTR gallery, arcade, walkway.

promesse [prɔmɛs] *nf* **1.** [engagement] promise, assurance ■ **faire une ~** to (make a) promise ■ **faire des ~s** to make promises ■ **manquer à/tenir sa ~** to break/to keep one's promise ■ **il m'a fait la ~ de revenir** he promised me he would come back ▶ **encore une ~ en l'air** *ou* **d'ivrogne** *ou* **de Gascon!** promises, promises! **2.** FIN commitment ■ **~ (unilatérale) d'achat/de vente** (unilateral) commitment *ou* undertaking to buy/to sell **3.** *litt* [espoir] promise ■ **la ~ d'une journée magnifique/d'un avenir meilleur** the promise of a beautiful day/a better future.
◆ **promesses** *nfpl* [avenir] promise ■ **un jeune joueur plein de ~s** a young player showing great promise, a very promising young player.

promet *etc v* ▷ **promettre**.

Prométhée [prɔmete] *npr* Prometheus.

prométhéen, enne [prɔmeteɛ̃, ɛn] *adj* Promethean.

prometteur, euse [prɔmɛtœr, øz] *adj* **1.** [début, situation] promising, encouraging ■ **voilà qui est ~!** that's a good sign! *iron* **2.** [musicien, acteur] promising, of promise.

promettre [84] [prɔmɛtr] ◇ *vt* **1.** [jurer] to promise ■ **je ne peux rien vous ~** I can't promise anything ■ **je te promets de ne pas lui en parler** I promise I won't say a word to him about it ■ **je te promets que je ne dirai rien** I promise (you) I won't say anything ■ **on nous a promis de l'aide** we were promised help ▶ **~ la lune, ~ monts et merveilles** to promise the earth, to promise the moon and stars ■ **~ et tenir sont deux** *prov* it's easier to make a promise than to keep one
2. [annoncer] to promise ■ **la météo nous promet du beau temps pour toute la semaine** the weather forecast promises nice weather for the whole week ■ **tout cela ne promet rien de bon** it doesn't look *ou* sound too good ■ **voilà une émission qui promet d'être intéressante** this programme should be interesting, it sounds like an interesting programme
3. [destiner] to destine ■ **ses récents succès le promettent à une brillante carrière** considering his recent successes, he has a brilliant career ahead of him
4. *fam* [affirmer] to assure ■ **je te promets qu'il s'en souviendra, de ce dîner!** I can assure you *ou* you can take my word for it that he'll remember that dinner!
◇ *vi* **1.** [faire naître des espérances] to promise ■ **un jeune auteur qui promet** a promising young author
2. *fam* [laisser présager des difficultés] : **ce gamin promet!** that kid's got a great future ahead of him! ■ **eh bien, ça promet!** *iron* that's a good start!
◆ **se promettre** ◇ *vp (emploi réciproque)* : **ils se sont promis de se revoir** they promised (each other) that they would meet again.
◇ *vpt* **1.** [espérer] : **je m'étais promis beaucoup de joie de cette rencontre** I'd been looking forward to the meeting ■ **se ~ du bon temps** to look forward to enjoying o.s.
2. [se jurer à soi-même] to swear, to promise (to) o.s. ■ **je me suis bien promis de ne jamais recommencer** I swore never to do it again, I promised myself I would never do it again.
◆ **se promettre à** *vp+prép vieilli* **se ~ à qqn** to plight one's troth to sb *arch*.

promeut, promeuvent *etc v* ▷ **promouvoir**.

promis, e [prɔmi, iz] ◇ *adj* promised ■ **voici le document ~** here is the promised document.

<> *nm, f vieilli* [dialecte] betrothed.

promiscuité [prɔmiskɥite] *nf* promiscuity ■ **vivre dans la ~** to have no privacy ■ **la ~ des plages en été/de l'hôpital** the overcrowding of beaches in summer/lack of privacy in hospital.

promit *etc v* ▷ **promettre**.

promo [prɔmo] *nf fam* **1.** MIL, ÉDUC & UNIV year *UK*, class *US* ■ **la ~ 94** the class of 94 **2.** TV promotional video.

promontoire [prɔmɔ̃twar] *nm* **1.** GÉOGR headland, promontory **2.** ANAT promontory.

promoteur, trice [prɔmɔtœr, tris] *nm, f* **1.** *litt* [créateur] promoter, instigator ■ **le ~ de la réforme** the instigator of the reform **2.** CONSTR developer.
◆ **promoteur** *nm* CHIM promoter.

promotion [prɔmɔsjɔ̃] *nf* **1.** [avancement] promotion ■ **j'ai eu une ~** I've been promoted ■ **~ au mérite/à l'ancienneté** promotion on merit/by seniority ➊ **~ sociale** upward mobility **2.** COMM promotion ■ **'la ~ du jour'** 'today's special offer' ➊ **~ des ventes** sales promotion **3.** MIL, ÉDUC & UNIV year *UK*, class *US* ■ **ils étaient camarades de ~** they were in the same class *ou* year **4.** CONSTR : **~ immobilière** property development **5.** JEUX queening.
◆ **en promotion** *loc adj* COMM on special offer.

promotionnel, elle [prɔmɔsjɔnɛl] *adj* promotional ■ **tarifs ~s sur ce voyage en Israël!** special offer on this trip to Israel!

promouvoir [56] [prɔmuvwar] *vt* **1.** [faire monter en grade] to promote ■ **il a été promu capitaine** he was promoted (to the rank of) captain **2.** [encourager - réforme] to advocate, to push for.

prompt, e [prɔ̃, prɔ̃t] *adj* prompt, quick, swift ■ **~ à répondre** quick with an answer ■ **~ à la colère** easily moved to anger.

promptement [prɔ̃tmɑ̃] *adv* quickly, swiftly ■ **exécuter ~ des ordres** to waste no time in carrying out orders.

prompteur [prɔ̃ptœr] *nm* autocue, teleprompt.

promptitude [prɔ̃tityd] *nf* quickness, swiftness.

promu, e [prɔmy] <> *pp* ▷ **promouvoir**.
<> *nm, f* promoted person.

promulgation [prɔmylgasjɔ̃] *nf* promulgation.

promulguer [3] [prɔmylge] *vt* to promulgate.

prôner [3] [prone] *vt sout* to advocate, to extol.

pronom [prɔnɔ̃] *nm* pronoun ■ **~ indéfini/interrogatif/personnel/relatif** indefinite/interrogative/personal/relative pronoun.

pronominal, e, aux [prɔnɔminal, o] *adj* [adjectif, adverbe] pronominal ■ [verbe] reflexive, *voir aussi* **pluriel**.
◆ **pronominal, aux** *nm* reflexive verb.

prononçable [prɔnɔ̃sabl] *adj* pronounceable ■ **un nom qui n'est pas ~** an unpronounceable name.

prononcé, e [prɔnɔ̃se] *adj* pronounced, strongly marked.
◆ **prononcé** *nm* DR (announcement of) decision.

prononcer [16] [prɔnɔ̃se] <> *vt* **1.** [dire - parole] to utter ; [- discours] to make, to deliver ■ **sans ~ un mot** without a word **2.** [proclamer - jugement] to pronounce ■ **~ un divorce** to issue a divorce decree, to pronounce a couple divorced **3.** RELIG : **~ ses vœux** to take one's vows **4.** [articuler - mot, langue] to pronounce ; [- phonème] to articulate ■ **c'est un mot que je prononce toujours de travers** I always mispronounce that word ■ *(en usage absolu)* **il prononce mal** his pronunciation is poor.
<> *vi* **1.** DR to deliver *ou* to give a verdict **2.** *litt* & *vieilli* [choisir] to pronounce ■ **~ en faveur de/contre** to pronounce in favour of/against.
◆ **se prononcer** <> *vp (emploi passif)* [mot] to be pronounced ■ **le deuxième « i » ne se prononce pas** the second "i" isn't sounded *ou* is silent ■ **ça s'écrit comme ça se prononce** it's spelled as it sounds.
<> *vpi* [personne] to come to a decision, to decide ■ **je ne peux pas encore me ~** I can't decide yet ■ **ils se sont prononcés pour/contre la peine de mort** they pronounced *ou* declared themselves in favour of/against the death penalty ■ **'ne se prononcent pas'** 'don't know'.

prononciation [prɔnɔ̃sjasjɔ̃] *nf* **1.** [d'un mot] pronunciation ■ **la ~ du "th" anglais est difficile pour un Français** pronouncing the English "th" is difficult for a French person **2.** [d'une personne] pronunciation ■ **elle a une bonne/mauvaise ~ en allemand** her German pronunciation is good/bad **3.** [d'un jugement] pronouncing ■ **j'attends la ~ du divorce** I'm waiting for the divorce to be made final *ou* to come through.

pronostic [prɔnɔstik] *nm* **1.** SPORT forecast ■ [pour les courses] forecast, (racing) tip ■ **vos ~s sur le match Bordeaux-Marseille?** what is your prediction for the Bordeaux-Marseilles match? **2.** [conjecture] forecast ■ **les ~s économiques** economic forecasts **3.** MÉD prognosis.

pronostique [prɔnɔstik] *adj* [gén - MÉD] prognostic.

pronostiquer [3] [prɔnɔstike] *vt* **1.** [prévoir] to forecast, to prognosticate *sout* **2.** *sout* [être signe de] to be a sign *ou* forerunner of ■ **le vent d'ouest pronostique la pluie** westerly winds are a sign *ou* harbinger of rain.

pronostiqueur, euse [prɔnɔstikœr, øz] *nm, f* **1.** ÉCON forecaster **2.** SPORT tipster.

propagande [prɔpagɑ̃d] *nf* **1.** [politique] propaganda ■ **~ électorale** electioneering **2.** [publicité] publicity, plugging ■ **faire de la ~ pour qqn/qqch** to advertise sb/sthg ■ **tu me fais de la ~!** you're a good advert for my cause!
◆ **de propagande** *loc adj* [film, journal] propaganda *(modif)*.

propagandiste [prɔpagɑ̃dist] *adj* & *nmf* propagandist.

propagateur, trice [prɔpagatœr, tris] *nm, f* propagator *(person)*.

propagation [prɔpagasjɔ̃] *nf* **1.** *litt* [reproduction] propagation, spreading **2.** [diffusion - d'un incendie, d'une doctrine etc] spreading ■ **la ~ des idées révolutionnaires** the spreading of revolutionary ideas.

propager [17] [prɔpaʒe] *vt* **1.** [répandre - foi, idées] to propagate, to disseminate, to spread ; [- épidémie, feu, rumeur] to spread **2.** BOT & ZOOL to propagate.
◆ **se propager** *vpi* **1.** [s'étendre - nouvelle, épidémie etc] to spread **2.** PHYS [onde, son] to be propagated.

propane [prɔpan] *nm* propane.

propension [prɔpɑ̃sjɔ̃] *nf* **1.** [tendance] proclivity, propensity ■ **avoir une forte ~ à faire qqch** to have a strong tendency to do sthg **2.** ÉCON propensity ■ **~ à consommer/épargner** propensity to spend/to save.

propergol [prɔpɛrgɔl] *nm* propellant ■ **~ liquide/solide** liquid/solid propellant.

prophète [prɔfɛt] *nm* prophet ■ **grands/petits ~s** major/minor prophets ■ **le Prophète** the Prophet ➊ **~ de malheur** prophet of doom.

prophétesse [prɔfetɛs] *nf* prophetess.

prophétie [prɔfesi] *nf* prophecy ■ **faire une ~** to prophesy.

prophétique [prɔfetik] *adj* **1.** RELIG prophetic **2.** *fig* & *sout* prophetic, premonitory *sout*.

prophétiser [3] [prɔfetize] <> *vt* **1.** RELIG to prophesy **2.** *fig* & *sout* to foretell, to predict, to prophesy.
<> *vi sout* [prédire] to make pompous predictions.

prophylaxie [prɔfilaksi] *nf* prophylaxis.

propice [prɔpis] *adj* **1.** *sout* [temps, période, vent] favourable ■ **les cieux n'ont pas l'air bien ~s** the sky looks rather menacing ■ **l'automne est ~ à la méditation** autumn is conducive to *ou* is an appropriate time for meditation **2.** [opportun] suitable ■ **peu ~** inauspicious ■ **au moment ~** at the right moment.

propitiatoire [prɔpisjatwar] <> *adj* RELIG propitiatory ■ **offrande/sacrifice ~** propitiatory gift/sacrifice.

◇ *nm* BIBLE : **le ~** the mercy seat.

proportion [prɔpɔrsjɔ̃] *nf* **1.** [rapport] proportion, ratio ■ **dans la ~ de 15%** in the ratio of 15% ■ **dans la même ~** in equal proportions ■ **dans une juste ~** in the correct proportion ■ **tu n'as pas respecté les ~s dans le dessin** your drawing isn't in proportion **2.** CHIM : **loi des ~s définies** law of constant *OU* definite proportions ■ **loi des ~s multiples** law of multiple proportions.

◆ **proportions** *nfpl* **1.** [importance] (great) importance ■ **prendre des ~s énormes** to grow out of all proportions ■ **pourquoi un incident aussi minime a-t-il pris de telles ~s?** why was such a trivial incident blown out of all proportion? **2.** [dimensions] dimensions, size ■ **tout dépendra des ~s de l'armoire** it will all depend on the size of the wardrobe ▶ **c'est la même chose, toutes ~s gardées** it's the same thing but on a different scale.

◆ **à proportion de** *loc prép* in proportion to.

◆ **en proportion** ◇ *loc adj* in proportion ■ **il a de gros frais, mais son salaire est en ~** he has a lot of expenses, but he has a correspondingly high salary.

◇ *loc adv* proportionately, at the same rate ■ **vous serez récompensé en ~** you'll be rewarded accordingly.

◆ **en proportion de** *loc prép* : **son succès est en ~ de son talent** his success is proportional *OU* in proportion to his talent ■ **il est payé en ~ des risques qu'il court** he is payed in proportion to the risks he takes.

proportionnalité [prɔpɔrsjɔnalite] *nf* **1.** MATH proportionality **2.** [rapport] balance, (good) proportions **3.** [répartition] equal distribution.

proportionné, e [prɔpɔrsjɔne] *adj* **1.** [harmonieux] : **bien ~** well-proportioned ■ **mal ~** out of proportion **2.** [adapté] : **~ à** commensurate with, in proportion to, proportional to.

proportionnel, elle [prɔpɔrsjɔnɛl] *adj* **1.** [en rapport avec] : **~ à** proportional to, in proportion with, commensurate with ■ **directement/inversement ~ (à)** directly/inversely proportional (to) **2.** COMM & ÉCON [droits, impôt] ad valorem **3.** MATH & POLIT proportional.

◆ **proportionnelle** *nf* POLIT : **la ~le** [processus] proportional system ; [résultat] proportional representation ■ **être élu à la ~le** to be elected by proportional representation.

proportionnellement [prɔpɔrsjɔnɛlmɑ̃] *adv* [gén] proportionately ■ MATH & ÉCON proportionally, in direct ratio ■ **~ à une valeur donnée** proportionally to *OU* in ratio to a given value.

proportionner [3] [prɔpɔrsjɔne] *vt* to match ■ **il faudrait ~ la note à l'effort fourni par l'élève** the mark should reflect *OU* match the amount of effort put in by the pupil.

propos [prɔpo] ◇ *nm* **1.** [sujet] subject, topic ■ **à ce ~** in this respect *OU* connection ■ **c'est à quel ~?** what's it about? ■ **à quel ~ a-t-elle téléphoné?** what was the reason for her telephone call? **2.** [but] intention, aim ■ **mon ~ n'est pas de vous convaincre** my aim is not to convince you ■ **là n'est pas le/mon ~** that is not the/my point.

◇ *nmpl* [paroles] words, talk ■ **tenir des ~ injurieux** to make offensive remarks.

◆ **à propos** ◇ *loc adj* appropriate ■ **elle n'a pas trouvé à ~ de nous le dire** she didn't think it appropriate to tell us.

◇ *loc adv* **1.** [opportunément] at the right moment ■ **arriver** *OU* **tomber à ~** to occur at the right time ■ **répondre à ~** [pertinemment] to answer appropriately ; [au bon moment] to answer at the right moment ■ **mal à ~** at the wrong moment **2.** [au fait] by the way, incidentally ■ **à ~, as-tu reçu ma carte?** by the way *OU* incidentally, did you get my postcard?

◆ **à propos de** *loc prép* about, concerning, regarding ■ **j'ai quelques remarques à faire à ~ de votre devoir** I have a few things to say to you about your homework ■ **dis donc, à ~ d'argent** hey, (talking) about money *OU* on the subject of money ■ **elle se met en colère à ~ de tout et de rien** *OU* **à ~ d'un rien** she gets angry for no reason at all.

◆ **à tout propos** *loc adv* constantly, at the slightest provocation.

◆ **de propos délibéré** *loc adv* deliberately, on purpose.

proposer [3] [prɔpoze] *vt* **1.** [suggérer] to suggest ■ **je propose qu'on aille au cinéma** I suggest going to the cinema ■ **je vous propose de rester dîner** I suggest (that) you stay for dinner ■ **l'agence nous a proposé un projet original** the agency submitted an original project to us ■ **proposez vos idées** put forward your ideas ■ **le chef vous propose sa quiche au saumon** the chef's suggestion *OU* recommendation is the salmon quiche ■ [dire] : **asseyons-nous, proposa-t-elle** let's sit down, she said **2.** [offrir] to offer ■ **il a proposé sa place à la vieille dame** he offered the old lady his seat ■ **on m'en propose un bon prix** I've been offered a good price for it **3.** [personne] to recommend, to put forward *(sép)* **4.** ÉDUC [sujet] to set *UK*, to assign *US* **5.** ADMIN & POLIT : **~ une loi** to introduce a bill ■ **~ un ordre du jour** to move an agenda ■ **~ la suspension de la séance** to move that the session be suspended.

◆ **se proposer** *vpi* [être volontaire] to offer one's services ■ **je me propose pour coller les enveloppes** I'm volunteering to stick the envelopes.

◆ **se proposer de** *vp+prép* [avoir l'intention de] to intend to ■ **ils se proposaient de passer ensemble une semaine tranquille** they intended to spend a quiet week together.

proposition [prɔpozisjɔ̃] *nf* **1.** [suggestion] suggestion ■ **quelqu'un a-t-il une autre ~ à faire?** has anyone any other suggestion *OU* anything else to suggest? ■ **faire une ~ à qqn** to make sb a proposition
2. [offre] offer ■ **refuser une ~** to turn down an offer ■ **j'ai déjà eu quelques ~s de tournage** I've already had one or two film offers ▶ **faire des ~s à qqn** *euphém* to proposition sb
3. LOGIQUE & PHILOS proposition ■ **calcul des ~s** propositional calculus
4. [recommandation] recommendation ■ **sur ~ du comité** on the committee's recommendation

LES PROPOSITIONS

Would you like me to call him for you? Tu veux que je l'appelle ?

If you don't mind *OU* **If it's no trouble.** Je veux bien, si ça ne vous dérange pas.

Thanks, but I'd rather do it myself. Merci, mais je préfère le faire moi-même.

Is there anything I can do to help? Est-ce que je peux faire quelque chose ?

That's very kind of you. Oui, merci, c'est très gentil.

No thanks, I'm fine/I can manage. Non, merci, ça va aller/je vais y arriver.

Why don't you let us look after him while you're away? Vous ne voulez pas qu'on s'occupe de lui pendant votre absence ?

Are you sure you don't mind? Vous êtes sûrs que ça ne vous dérange pas ?

No, really, I'll be fine. Non, ça va aller, je vous assure.

What if I tell him? Et si je le lui disais ?

Would you mind? Ça ne te dérange pas ?

Thanks for offering, but I'd better do it myself. C'est gentil, mais il vaut mieux que je le fasse moi-même.

You can stay at my flat for a few days, if you like. Vous pouvez loger chez moi pendant quelques jours, si vous voulez.

Thanks, it's very generous of you to offer. Merci, c'est très gentil de ta part.

Thanks, but we've already got somewhere to stay. Merci, mais nous avons déjà trouvé un endroit.

5. POLIT : **~s et contre-propositions** proposals and counterproposals ▪ **la ~ est votée** the motion is passed ▪ **~ de loi** private member's bill *UK*, private bill *US*
6. GRAMM clause ▪ **~ consécutive** *ou* **de conséquence** consecutive *ou* result clause.
Voir module d'usage

propositionnel, elle [prɔpozisjɔnɛl] *adj* propositional ▪ **calcul ~** propositional calculus.

propre [prɔpr] <> *adj*

A.
1. [nettoyé, lavé] clean ▪ [rangé] neat, tidy ▪ **chez eux c'est bien ~** their house is neat and tidy ▪ **gardez votre ville ~** don't drop litter! *UK*, don't litter! *US* ▶ **~ sur lui** *hum* neat and proper ▪ **nous voilà ~s!** *iron* now we're in a fine mess! ▪ **~ comme un sou neuf** spick and span, clean as a new pin
2. *euphém* [éduqué - bébé] toilet-trained, potty-trained ; [- chiot] house-trained *UK*, house-broken *US*
3. [honnête] honest ▪ **une affaire pas très ~** a shady business
4. [bien exécuté - travail] neat, well done
5. ÉCOL clean, non-polluting, non-pollutant ▪ NUCL clean

B.
1. *(avant le nom)* [en intensif] own ▪ **de mes ~s yeux** with my own eyes ▪ **de son ~ chef** on his own initiative *ou* authority ▪ **les ~s paroles du Prophète** the Prophet's very *ou* own words ▪ [privé] own, private ▪ **son ~ hélicoptère** his own helicopter, a helicopter of his own, his private helicopter
2. [caractéristique] : **~ à** specific *ou* peculiar to ▪ **sa méthode de travail lui est ~** he has his own particular way of working
3. [adapté] proper ▪ **le mot ~** the proper *ou* correct term ▪ **~ à** suited to, fit for, appropriate to ▪ **~ à la consommation humaine** fit for human consumption ▪ **mesures ~s à stimuler la production** appropriate measures for boosting production
4. LING [nom] proper ▪ [sens] literal
5. ASTRON : **mouvement ~** proper motion
6. PHYS : **oscillation ~** natural oscillation
7. INFORM : **erreur ~** inherent error
8. MATH [nombre, valeur] characteristic ▪ [partie] proper
9. FIN : **capitaux** *ou* **fonds ~s** capital stock.
<> *nm* **1.** [propreté] cleanliness, tidiness ▪ **sentir le ~** to smell clean ▪ **c'est du ~!** *fam iron* [gâchis] what a mess! ; [action scandaleuse] shame on you! **2.** [caractéristique] peculiarity, distinctive feature ▪ **la raison est le ~ de l'homme** reason is unique to man **3.** RELIG proper.
◆ **propres** *nmpl* DR separate property (of each spouse).
◆ **au propre** *loc adv* **1.** [en version définitive] : **mettre qqch au ~** to copy sthg out neatly, to make a fair copy of sthg **2.** LING literally ▪ **le mot peut s'employer au ~ et au figuré** the word can be used both literally and figuratively.
◆ **en propre** *loc adv* by rights ▪ **avoir en ~** to possess (by rights) ▪ **la fortune qu'il a en ~** his own fortune, the fortune that's his by rights.

propre-à-rien [prɔprarjɛ̃] (*pl* **propres-à-rien**) *nmf* good-for-nothing ▪ **ce sera toujours un ~** he'll never amount to anything.

proprement [prɔprəmɑ̃] *adv* **1.** [avec propreté] cleanly ▪ [avec netteté] tidily, neatly ▪ **écrire ~** to write neatly ▪ **l'hôtel est très ~ tenu** the hotel is spotlessly clean ▪ **mange ~!** eat properly!
2. *litt* [convenablement] decently, properly, honourably
3. [absolument] truly, totally, absolutely ▪ **elle est ~ insupportable!** she's absolutely unbearable! ▪ **il s'est fait ~ éjecter** *fam* he was thrown out unceremoniously *ou* well and truly thrown out
4. [spécifiquement] specifically, strictly ▪ **l'aspect ~ éducatif du projet leur a échappé** they missed the specifically educational significance of the project.
◆ **à proprement parler** *loc adv* strictly speaking.
◆ **proprement dit, proprement dite** *loc adj* actual ▪ **la maison ~ dite** the house proper, the actual house, the house itself.

propret, ette [prɔprɛ, ɛt] *adj* neat and tidy ▪ **un petit jardin bien ~** a neat little garden.

propreté [prɔprəte] *nf* **1.** [absence de saleté] cleanness, cleanliness ▪ [fait d'être rangé] tidiness ▪ [hygiène] hygiene **2.** ÉCOL cleanness, absence of pollution **3.** *euphém* **l'apprentissage de la ~** [chez l'enfant] toilet-training, potty-training.

propriétaire [prɔprijetɛr] *nmf* **1.** [celui qui possède] owner ▪ **ils ont voulu être ~s** they wanted to own their (own) place ▪ **tous les ~s seront soumis à la taxe** all householders *ou* homeowners will be liable to tax ▪ **qui est le ~ de cette valise?** to whom does this case belong? ▪ **vous êtes maintenant l'heureux ~ d'une machine à laver** you are now the proud owner *ou* possessor of a washing machine ▶ **~ foncier** property owner ▪ **~ terrien** landowner **2.** [celui qui loue] landlord (*f* landlady).

propriétaire-éleveur [prɔprijetɛrelvœr] (*pl* **propriétaires-éleveurs**) *nm* AGRIC & SPORT owner-breeder.

propriétaire-récoltant [prɔprijetɛrrekɔltɑ̃] (*pl* **propriétaires-récoltants**) *nm* wine grower.

propriété [prɔprijete] *nf* **1.** [biens] estate, property ▪ **une très belle/une grande/une petite ~** an excellent/a large/a small property ▪ **~ foncière/immobilière** landed/real estate ▪ **~ de l'État** government *ou* state property ▪ **~ mobilière** DR personal property, movables ▪ **~ privée** private (property) ▪ **'~ privée, défense d'entrer'** 'private property, keep out'
2. [fait de posséder] ownership
3. DR ownership ▪ **posséder en toute ~** to hold in fee simple ▶ **~ collective des moyens de production** collective ownership of the means of production ▪ **~ commerciale** leasehold ownership *(covenant to extend lease)* ▪ **~ individuelle** personal *ou* private property ▪ **~ indivise** joint ownership ▪ **~ industrielle** patent rights ▪ **~ littéraire et artistique** copyright
4. [propriétaires] property owners ▪ **la grande/petite ~** the big/small landowners
5. [qualité] property, characteristic, feature ▪ **la codéine a des ~s antitussives** codeine suppresses coughing
6. [exactitude - d'un terme] aptness, appropriateness.

proprio [prɔprijo] *nmf fam* landlord (*f* landlady).

propulser [3] [prɔpylse] *vt* **1.** AUTO to drive ▪ ASTRONAUT to propel ▪ MÉCAN to propel, to drive **2.** [pousser] to push, to fling ▪ **il s'est trouvé propulsé sur le devant de la scène** he was pushed towards the front of the stage ▪ **elle s'est trouvée propulsée à la tête de l'entreprise** *fig* she suddenly found herself in charge of the business.

propulseur [prɔpylsœr] *nm* **1.** MÉCAN & NAUT [hélice] (screw) propeller ▪ [moteur] power unit ▪ [carburant] propellant ▪ **~ d'étrave** bow propeller **2.** ASTRONAUT rocket engine ▪ **~ auxiliaire** booster.

propulsif, ive [prɔpylsif, iv] *adj* propellant, propelling, propulsive ▪ **roue propulsive** driving wheel.

propulsion [prɔpylsjɔ̃] *nf* **1.** AÉRON, MÉCAN & NAUT [phénomène] propulsion, propelling force ▪ [résultat] propulsion, propulsive motion, drive ▪ **fusée à ~ atomique/nucléaire** atomic-powered/nuclear-powered rocket **2.** ÉLECTR : **~ électrique** electric drive ▪ **~ turbo-électrique** turbo-electric propulsion.

prorata [prɔrata] *nm inv* proportion ▪ **en respectant le ~** in due ratio.
◆ **au prorata** *loc adv* proportionally, pro rata.
◆ **au prorata de** *loc prép* in proportion to ▪ **bénéfices au ~ du nombre d'actions** profits shared out pro rata to (the number of) shares held.

prorogatif, ive [prɔrɔgatif, iv] *adj* DR prorogating.

prorogation [prɔrɔgasjɔ̃] *nf* **1.** ADMIN & DR [d'un délai] extension ▪ [d'un visa] renewal ▪ **~ de compétence** *ou* **de juridiction** extension of jurisdiction **2.** POLIT adjournment, prorogation *spéc.*

proroger [17] [prɔrɔʒe] *vt* **1.** ADMIN & DR [délai, compétence] to extend ▪ [traité] to renew ▪ [échéance] to defer **2.** POLIT [suspendre - assemblée] to prorogue *spéc*, to adjourn.

prosaïque [prozaik] *adj* mundane, pedestrian, prosaic.

prosaïsme [prozaism] *nm sout* ordinariness, prosaicness ▪ **quel ~!** how romantic! *iron.*

prosateur, trice [prozatœr, tris] *nm, f* prose writer.

proscription [prɔskripsjɔ̃] *nf* **1.** HIST [exil] exiling, banishment ▪ ANTIQ proscription **2.** [interdiction] prohibition, banning, proscription *sout*.

proscrire [99] [prɔskrir] *vt* **1.** [exiler] to banish, to proscribe *sout* **2.** [interdire - gén] to forbid ; [- par la loi] to outlaw ▪ [déconseiller] to advise against ▪ **cet usage est à ~** this expression is to be avoided.

proscrit, e [prɔskri, it] ◇ *adj sout* **1.** [exilé] proscribed *sout* **2.** [interdit] forbidden ▪ **c'est un usage ~** [déconseillé] the expression is to be avoided ; [tabou] the expression is taboo.
◇ *nm, f* outlaw.

proscrivait *etc v* ⊳ **proscrire.**

prose [proz] *nf* **1.** LITTÉR prose **2.** *fam* [style] (writing) style **3.** *fam hum* [écrit] work, masterpiece *iron.*
◆ **en prose** ◇ *loc adj* prose ▪ **texte en ~** prose text.
◇ *loc adv* : **écrire en ~** to write (in) prose.

prosélyte [prɔzelit] *nmf* **1.** *sout* [adepte] proselyte ▪ **l'idée a fait de nombreux ~s** there were many converts to the idea, many people espoused the idea **2.** HIST & RELIG convert, proselyte.

prosélytisme [prɔzelitism] *nm* **1.** RELIG proselytism **2.** *sout* [propagande] proselytism, missionary zeal ▪ **faire du ~** to proselytize *UK*, to proselyte *US*.

prosodie [prɔzɔdi] *nf* **1.** LITTÉR prosody **2.** MUS rules of musical arrangement.

prospect[1] [prɔspɛ] *nm* COMM prospect, potential customer *ou* client.

prospect[2] [prɔspɛkt] *nm* CONSTR & DR minimum distance between buildings.

prospecter [4] [prɔspɛkte] ◇ *vt* **1.** COMM & ÉCON [région] to comb ▪ [clientèle] to canvass ▪ [marché] to explore, to investigate **2.** MIN to prospect ▪ **on prospecte la région pour trouver du pétrole** they're looking for oil in the area.
◇ *vi* to comb an area.

prospecteur, trice [prɔspɛktœr, tris] ◇ *adj* prospecting, investigating.
◇ *nm, f* **1.** COMM canvasser **2.** MIN prospector.

prospectif, ive [prɔspɛktif, iv] *adj* prospective.
◆ **prospective** *nf* **1.** ÉCON (long-term) forecasting **2.** [science] futurology.

prospection [prɔspɛksjɔ̃] *nf* **1.** MIN prospecting ▪ **~ minière/pétrolière** mining/oil exploration **2.** COMM [de la clientèle] canvassing ▪ [des tendances] exploring ▪ **~ du marché** surveying *ou* exploring the market.

prospectus [prɔspɛktys] *nm* **1.** COMM [feuillet publicitaire] leaflet, handout ▪ **il n'y a rien que des ~ dans la boîte aux lettres** there's nothing but advertising leaflets in the letter box ▪ **nous avons envoyé des ~ à tous nos clients** we have sent a mailshot to *ou* we have circularized all our customers **2.** DR : **~ d'émission** (pathfinder) prospectus.

prospère [prɔspɛr] *adj* **1.** [fructueux] flourishing, thriving ▪ **les affaires sont ~s** business is booming **2.** [riche] prosperous.

prospérer [18] [prɔspere] *vi* [entreprise] to flourish, to thrive ▪ [personne] to fare well, to thrive ▪ [plante] to thrive ▪ **le tourisme a fait ~ toute la région** tourism brought wealth to the whole area.

prospérité [prɔsperite] *nf* prosperity, success ▪ **une période de (grande) ~** a boom.

prostate [prɔstat] *nf* prostate (gland) ▪ **se faire opérer de la ~** to have a prostate operation.

prosternation [prɔstɛrnasjɔ̃] *nf,* **prosternement** [prɔstɛrnəmɑ̃] *nm* **1.** RELIG bowing-down, prosternation *sout* **2.** *fig* & *litt* toadying.

prosterner [3] [prɔstɛrne] ◆ **se prosterner** *vpi* RELIG to bow down ▪ **se ~ devant qqn** *fig* to grovel to sb.

prostitué, e [prɔstitɥe] *nm, f* [femme] prostitute ▪ [homme] male prostitute.

prostituer [7] [prɔstitɥe] *vt* **1.** [personne] to make a prostitute of, to prostitute **2.** *fig* & *sout* **~ ses talents** to sell *ou* to prostitute one's talent.
◆ **se prostituer** *vp (emploi réfléchi) pr* & *fig* to prostitute o.s.

prostitution [prɔstitysjɔ̃] *nf pr* & *fig* prostitution.

prostration [prɔstrasjɔ̃] *nf* **1.** MÉD & RELIG prostration **2.** ÉCON collapse, crash.

prostré, e [prɔstre] *adj* **1.** [accablé] prostrate, despondent **2.** MÉD prostrate.

protagoniste [prɔtagɔnist] *nmf* **1.** [principal participant] protagonist ▪ **les ~s du conflit vont entamer des pourparlers** the protagonists in the conflict are to start negotiations **2.** CINÉ & LITTÉR (chief) protagonist, main character **3.** ANTIQ protagonist.

protecteur, trice [prɔtɛktœr, tris] ◇ *adj* **1.** [qui protège] protective ▪ **crème protectrice** barrier cream **2.** [condescendant] patronizing **3.** ÉCON protectionist.
◇ *nm, f* **1.** [gardien] custodian, guardian, guarantor **2.** [mécène] patron.
◆ **protecteur** *nm* [d'une prostituée] procurer.

protection [prɔtɛksjɔ̃] *nf* **1.** [défense] protection ▪ **assurer la ~ de qqn** to protect sb ▪ **prendre qqn sous sa ~** to take sb under one's wing ➲ **~ aérienne** MIL aerial protection ▪ **~ civile** [en temps de guerre] civil defence ; [en temps de paix] disaster management ▪ **~ contre les rayonnements** NUCL radiological protection ▪ **~ diplomatique** diplomatic protection ▪ **~ de l'emploi** personal security, job protection ▪ **~ de l'enfance** child welfare ▪ **~ des espèces menacées** protection of endangered species ▪ **~ judiciaire** (court) supervision (of a minor), wardship ▪ **~ maternelle et infantile** mother and child care *(including antenatal and postnatal clinics and family planning)* ▪ **~ de la nature** nature conservation *ou* conservancy ▪ **~ rapprochée** [d'une personne] police protection **2.** [prévention] protection, preservation, conservation ▪ **c'est une bonne ~ contre la rouille/les fraudes** it's a good protection against rust/fraud **3.** [soutien] : **solliciter la ~ de qqn** to ask for sb's support, to ask sb to use their influence on one's behalf **4.** ART & SPORT patronage **5.** [serviette hygiénique] : **~ (féminine)** sanitary towel *UK*, sanitary napkin *US* **6.** INFORM security ▪ **~ de fichier** protected file access ▪ **~ mémoire** protected location **7.** MÉTALL coating ▪ **~ cathodique** cathodic protection.
◆ **de protection** *loc adj* protective, safety *(modif)* ▪ **gaine de ~** protective cover ▪ **couche/vernis de ~** protective coating/varnish.

protectionnisme [prɔtɛksjɔnism] *nm* protectionism.

protectionniste [prɔtɛksjɔnist] *adj* & *nmf* protectionist.

protectorat [prɔtɛktɔra] *nm* protectorate.

protégé, e [prɔteʒe] ◇ *adj* **1.** AÉRON : **espace aérien ~** protected airspace **2.** ÉCOL [espèce, zone] protected **3.** ÉLECTRON protected **4.** INFORM [disquette] write-protected **5.** [relations sexuelles] protected ▪ **rapports non ~s** unprotected sex.
◇ *nm, f* protégé.

protège-cahier [prɔtɛʒkaje] (*pl* **protège-cahiers**) *nm* exercise-book cover.

protège-dents [prɔtɛʒdɑ̃] *nm inv* gum-shield.

protège-matelas [prɔtɛʒmatla] *nm inv* mattress cover.

protège-poignets [prɔtɛʒpwanjɛ] *nm inv* wrist guard, wrist protector.

protéger [22] [prɔteʒe] *vt* **1.** [assurer - la sécurité de] to protect, to defend ; [- la santé, la survie de] to protect, to look after *(insép)*, to shield against ▪ **~ qqch contre le** *ou* **du froid** to protect *ou* to insulate sthg against the cold ▪ **~ qqch contre les radiations** to shield sthg from radiation **2.** COMM & ÉCON to protect

■ ~ **par un brevet** DR to patent **3.** [favoriser] to encourage, to protect **4.** [faire du racket] to protect **5.** *euphém* [prostituée] to act as a procurer (*f* procuress) for.
◆ **se protéger** *vp (emploi réfléchi)* to protect o.s. ■ **protégez-vous contre la grippe** protect yourself against the flu ■ **se ~ contre le** *ou* **du soleil** to shield o.s. from the sun ■ **les jeunes sont encouragés à se ~ lors de leurs relations sexuelles** young people are encouraged to protect themselves (by using a condom).

protège-slip [prɔtɛʒslip] (*pl* **protège-slips**) *nm* panty liner.

protège-tibia [prɔtɛʒtibja] (*pl* **protège-tibias**) *nm* shin pad.

protéine [prɔtein] *nf* protein ■ **~s animales/végétales** animal/vegetable proteins.

protestant, e [prɔtɛstɑ̃, ɑ̃t] *adj & nm, f* Protestant.

protestantisme [prɔtɛstɑ̃tism] *nm* Protestantism.

protestataire [prɔtɛstatɛr] ◇ *adj* [délégué] protesting ■ [mesure] protest *(modif)*.
◇ *nmf* protester, protestor.

protestation [prɔtɛstasjɔ̃] *nf* **1.** [mécontentement] protest, discontent ■ **grand mouvement/grande manifestation de ~ demain à 14 h** a big protest rally/demonstration will be held tomorrow at 2 p.m **2.** [opposition] protest ■ **sans ~** without protest ■ **en signe de ~** as a protest ■ **sans une ~** without a murmur **3.** DR protesting, protestation.
◆ **protestations** *nfpl litt* [déclarations] : **~s d'amitié** protestations *ou* assurances of friendship ■ **faire à qqn des ~s d'amour/de loyauté** to profess one's love/loyalty to sb.

protester [3] [prɔtɛste] ◇ *vi* [dire non] to protest ■ **je proteste!** I protest!, I object! ■ **~ contre** to protest against *ou* about.
◇ *vt* **1.** DR to protest **2.** *vieilli* [affirmer] to protest, to declare.
◆ **protester de** *v+prép litt* **~ de son innocence** to protest one's innocence.

prothèse [prɔtɛz] *nf* **1.** [technique] prosthetics *(U)* ■ **~ dentaire** prosthodontics *(U)* **2.** [dispositif] prosthesis ■ **~ dentaire totale** (set of) dentures ■ **une ~ dentaire fixe** a bridge, a fixed dental prosthesis *spéc.*

prothésiste [prɔtezist] *nmf* prosthetist ■ **~ dentaire** prosthodontist, dental prosthetist.

protide [prɔtid] *nm* protein.

proto- [prɔto] *préf* proto, proto-.

protocolaire [prɔtɔkɔlɛr] *adj* [respectueux des usages] formal ■ [conforme à l'étiquette] mindful of *ou* conforming to etiquette ■ **le prince dans une attitude peu ~** the Prince in a relaxed pose.

protocole [prɔtɔkɔl] *nm* **1.** DR & POLIT protocol ■ **~ d'accord** draft agreement **2.** INFORM protocol ■ **~ multivoie/univoie** multi-channel/single-channel protocol **3.** IMPR style sheet **4.** [cérémonial] : **le ~** protocole, etiquette **5.** SC : **~ d'une expérience** experimental procedure **6.** MÉD : **~ opératoire** protocol.

protohistoire [prɔtɔistwar] *nf* protohistory.

proton [prɔtɔ̃] *nm* proton.

prototype [prɔtɔtip] *nm* **1.** INDUST prototype **2.** [archétype] standard ■ **c'est le ~ du vieil imprimeur** he's the archetypal old printer **3.** *(comme adj; avec ou sans trait d'union)* prototype *(modif)*.

protozoaire [prɔtɔzɔɛr] *nm* protozoan, protozoon ■ **les ~s** the Protozoa.

protubérance [prɔtyberɑ̃s] *nf* **1.** [bosse] bump ■ [enflure] bulge, protuberance *spéc* **2.** ANAT protuberance ■ **~ cérébrale** mesencephalon **3.** ASTRON : **~ solaire** solar prominence.

protubérant, e [prɔtyberɑ̃, ɑ̃t] *adj* [muscle] bulging ■ [menton, front] prominent ■ [œil, ventre] protruding, bulging.

prou [pru] *adv* ▷ **peu.**

proue [pru] *nf* NAUT bow, bows, prow.

prouesse [pruɛs] *nf* exploit, feat ■ **le convaincre était une ~** *fig* convincing him was quite a feat ■ **faire des ~s** [briller] to perform outstandingly ; [faire des efforts] to do one's utmost ■ **j'ai fait des ~s pour finir dans les délais** I did my utmost to finish on time.

prouver [3] [pruve] *vt* **1.** [faire la preuve de] to prove ■ **cela n'est pas encore prouvé** it remains to be proved ■ **il n'est pas prouvé que...** there's no proof that... ■ **les faits ont prouvé qu'elle était bel et bien absente** the facts proved her to have indeed been absent ■ **prouve-moi le contraire!** give me proof of *ou* to the contrary! ■ **il t'a menti – prouve-le-moi!** he lied to you – prove it! ■ **~ le bien-fondé d'une accusation** DR to substantiate a charge ⊙ **il m'a prouvé par A + B que j'avais tort** he demonstrated that I was wrong in a very logical way **2.** [mettre en évidence] to show ■ **cela prouve bien que j'avais raison** it shows that I was right ■ **son désintéressement n'est plus à ~** her impartiality is no longer open to question **3.** [témoigner] to demonstrate ■ **~ à qqn son amitié/sa reconnaissance** to demonstrate one's friendship/gratitude to sb, to give sb proof of one's friendship/gratitude.
◆ **se prouver** *vpt* : **se ~ qqch (à soi-même)** to prove sthg (to o.s.)

provenance [prɔvnɑ̃s] *nf* [d'un mot] origin ■ [d'une rumeur] source ■ **des marchandises de ~ étrangère** imported goods ■ **quelle est la ~ de ces légumes?** where do these vegetables come from?
◆ **en provenance de** *loc prép* (coming) from ■ **le train en ~ de Genève** the train from Geneva, the Geneva train.

provençal, e, aux [prɔvɑ̃sal, o] *adj* Provençal.
◆ **provençal** *nm* LING Provençal.
◆ **à la provençale** *loc adj* CULIN à la provençale.

Provence [prɔvɑ̃s] *npr f* : **(la) ~** Provence ■ **herbes de ~** ≃ mixed herbs.

Provence-Alpes-Côte d'Azur [prɔvɑ̃salpkotdazyr] *npr* Provence-Alpes-Côte d'Azur.

PROVENCE-ALPES-CÔTE D'AZUR

This administrative region, also known as *PACA*, includes the *départements* of Alpes-de-Haute-Provence, Alpes-Maritimes, Bouches-du-Rhône, Hautes-Alpes, Var and Vaucluse (capital: Marseille).

provenir [40] [prɔvnir] ◆ **provenir de** *v+prép* **1.** [lieu] to come from *(insép)* ■ **d'où provient cette statuette?** where does this statuette come from? **2.** [résulter de] to arise *ou* to result from, to arise out of.

proverbe [prɔvɛrb] *nm* proverb, adage ■ **comme dit le ~** as the proverb goes.

proverbial, e, aux [prɔvɛrbjal, o] *adj* **1.** [de proverbe] proverbial **2.** [connu] well-known, proverbial ■ **au lycée, son talent d'imitateur est ~** he's become well-known throughout the school for his impersonations.

providence [prɔvidɑ̃s] *nf* **1.** RELIG Providence ■ **les voies de la Providence** the ways of Providence **2.** [aubaine] salvation, piece of luck **3.** [personne] : **vous rentrez à Nice en voiture? vous êtes ma ~!** you're driving back to Nice? you've saved my life!

providentiel, elle [prɔvidɑ̃sjɛl] *adj* providential, miraculous ■ **c'est l'homme ~!** he's the man we need! ■ **sans cette grève ~le, nous n'aurions jamais fait connaissance** if that strike hadn't happened at just the right time, we'd never have met.

provient *etc v* ▷ **provenir.**

province [prɔvɛ̃s] *nf* **1.** [régions en dehors de la capitale] : **la ~** [en France] provincial France ; [dans d'autres pays] the provinces ■ **il doit bientôt partir en ~** he'll soon be leaving town ■ **un week-end en ~** a weekend out of town ■ **arriver** *ou* **débarquer tout droit de sa ~** to be fresh from the country *ou* the provinces ■ **une petite ville de ~** a small country town ■ **Bordeaux est une grande ville de ~** Bordeaux is a major provincial town **2.** HIST province ⊙ **la Belle Province** *Québec* Quebec

3. *(comme adj inv)* **notre quartier est encore très ~** there's still a small-town feeling to our area ■ **sa famille est restée un peu ~** her family's kept up a rather provincial way of life.

Provinces Maritimes [prɔvɛ̃smaritim] *npr fpl* [au Canada] : **les ~** the Maritime Provinces, the Maritimes.

provincial, e, aux [prɔvɛ̃sjal, o] ◇ *adj* **1.** [en dehors de Paris] provincial ■ **sa tournée ~e** her tour of the provinces **2.** *péj* [personne, comportement] provincial, parochial.
◇ *nm, f* provincial.
◆ **provincial, aux** *nm* **1.** RELIG provincial **2.** *Québec* **le Provincial** the Provincial Government.

provincialisme [prɔvɛ̃sjalism] *nm* **1.** LING provincialism **2.** *péj* [étroitesse d'esprit] small-town *ou* village-pump mentality, parochialism.

provint *etc v* ▷ **provenir.**

proviseur [prɔvizœr] *nmf* **1.** [directeur] head teacher *UK*, headmaster (*f* headmistress) *UK*, principal *US* **2.** *Belgique* [adjoint] deputy head *(with overall responsibility for discipline within the school)*.

provision [prɔvizjɔ̃] *nf* **1.** [réserve] stock, store, supply ■ **avoir une bonne ~ de chocolat/patience** to have a good supply of chocolate/plenty of patience ■ **faire ~ de sucre/d'enveloppes** to stock up with sugar/envelopes ■ **faire des ~s** to stock up on food, to lay in stocks of food **2.** [acompte] advance *ou* down payment ■ BANQUE (sufficient) funds **3.** [d'un bilan comptable] provision ■ [couverture] cover **4.** [honoraires] retainer **5.** DR interim payment, interlocutory relief ■ **par ~** [décision, acte] provisional, interim.
◆ **provisions** *nfpl* [courses] : **~s (de bouche)** shopping *(U)*, groceries.
◆ **à provisions** *loc adj* [filet, sac] shopping *(modif)* ■ **armoire à ~s** store cupboard ■ **c'est mon étagère à ~s** it's the shelf where I keep my food.

provisionnel, elle [prɔvizjɔnɛl] *adj* provisional.

provisionner [3] [prɔvizjɔne] *vt* BANQUE [compte] to deposit funds into ■ **son compte n'a pas été provisionné depuis plusieurs mois** there has been no money paid into his account for several months.

provisoire [prɔvizwar] ◇ *adj* **1.** [momentané] temporary, provisional ■ **c'est une solution ~** it's a temporary solution *ou* a stopgap **2.** [précaire] makeshift ■ **une réparation ~** a makeshift repair **3.** [intérimaire - gouvernement] provisional ; [- directeur] acting **4.** DR [jugement] provisional, interlocutory *sout* ■ [mise en liberté] conditional.
◇ *nm* : **le ~** that which is temporary.

provisoirement [prɔvizwarmɑ̃] *adv* temporarily, provisionally ■ **~, je fais des ménages** for the time being, I do cleaning for people.

provo [prɔvo] *nm* **1.** △ *arg scol* [proviseur] head *(of a school)* **2.** [aux Pays-Bas] provo.

provoc [prɔvɔk] *nf fam* provocation ■ **tu fais de la ~ ou quoi?** are you trying to wind me up *UK ou* tick me off *US*?

provocant, e [prɔvɔkɑ̃, ɑ̃t] *adj* **1.** [agressif] aggressive, provoking ■ **une remarque ~e** an aggressive remark ■ **sur un ton ~** provocatively **2.** [osé] blatant ■ **un modernisme ~** blatant modernism **3.** [excitant] exciting, provocative, teasing.

provocateur, trice [prɔvɔkatœr, tris] ◇ *adj* [discours, propagande] inflammatory ■ [argument, propos] provocative ■ **geste ~** offensive gesture.
◇ *nm, f* POLIT provocateur.

provocation [prɔvɔkasjɔ̃] *nf* **1.** [stratégie] provocation, incitement ■ [acte] provocation ■ **c'est de la ~!** it's an act of provocation! ■ **faire qqch par ~** to do sthg as an act of provocation **2.** *litt* [séduction] teasing, provocativeness.

provoquer [3] [prɔvɔke] *vt* **1.** [défier] to provoke, to push (to breaking point) ■ **arrête de me ~!** *fam* don't push me! ■ **c'est lui qui m'a provoqué!** he started it! ■ **~ le destin** to tempt fate ■ **~ qqn en duel** to challenge sb to a duel **2.** [sexuellement] to tease **3.** [occasionner - maladie, sommeil] to cause, to induce ■ **pouvant ~ la mort** potentially fatal ■ [sentiment] to arouse, to stir up *(sép)*, to give rise to ■ **il ne se doutait pas qu'il allait ~ sa jalousie** he didn't realize that he would make her jealous ■ **ses dénégations ne provoquèrent aucune réaction chez le juge** his denials brought no reaction from the judge ■ **l'explosion provoqua la panique générale** the explosion caused general panic ‖ [événement] to cause, to be the cause of, to bring about *(sép)* ■ **elle fit cette déclaration pour ~ une nouvelle enquête** she made that statement so that there would be a new enquiry **4.** MÉD : **~ l'accouchement** to induce labour.

prox. (*abr écrite de* **proximité**) ■ **'~ commerces'** 'near shops'.

proxénète [prɔksenɛt] *nmf* procurer (*f* procuress).

proxénétisme [prɔksenetism] *nm* procuring.

proximité [prɔksimite] *nf* **1.** [dans l'espace] closeness, nearness, proximity ■ **la ~ de la gare est un des avantages de cet appartement** one of the advantages of this apartment is having the station so close **2.** [dans le temps] closeness, imminence ■ **la ~ du départ les rend fébriles** the approaching departure is making them excited **3.** *vieilli* [parenté] kinship ■ **~ du sang** blood kinship.
◆ **à proximité** *loc adv* nearby, close at hand.
◆ **à proximité de** *loc prép* near, close to, not far from.
◆ **de proximité** *loc adj* **1.** TECHNOL proximity *(modif)* **2.** [de quartier] : **commerces de ~** local shops ■ **police de ~** community policing ■ **élu de ~** local councillor, local representative [faisant valoir ses liens avec la communauté] local man *ou* woman ■ **stratégie de ~** strategy of decentralization ■ **média de ~** local (communications) medium ■ **médias de ~** locals *ou* community media **3.** COMM : **stratégie de ~** getting close to the customer.

pruche [pryʃ] *nf Québec* hemlock spruce.

prude [pryd] ◇ *adj* prudish, prim and proper ■ **et pourtant, je ne suis pas ~** and yet I'm not afraid to call a spade a spade.
◇ *nf* prude, puritan.

prudemment [prydamɑ̃] *adv* **1.** [avec précaution] carefully, cautiously, prudently **2.** [avec sagesse] wisely, prudently ■ **il préféra ~ battre en retraite** he was wise enough to retreat.

prudence [prydɑ̃s] *nf* **1.** [précaution] caution, carefulness ■ **elle conduit avec la plus grande ~** she's a very careful driver ▶ **~ est mère de sûreté** *prov* look before you leap *prov* **2.** [méfiance] wariness, caginess ■ [ruse] cunning ■ **avoir la ~ du serpent** to be a sly fox **3.** *vieilli* [sagesse] wisdom, good judgment, prudence.
◆ **avec prudence** *loc adv* [avec attention] cautiously, carefully.
◆ **par prudence** *loc adv* as a precaution ■ **prends ton parapluie par ~** take your umbrella just in case.

prudent, e [prydɑ̃, ɑ̃t] *adj* **1.** [attentif] careful, prudent ■ **sois ~!** be careful! **2.** [mesuré] discreet, circumspect, cautious ■ **une réponse ~e** a diplomatic *ou* circumspect answer **3.** [prévoyant] judicious, wise ■ **un homme de loi ~** a wise lawyer **4.** [préférable] advisable, better ■ **il est ~ de réserver ses places** advance booking is advisable.

pruderie [prydri] *nf* prudishness, prudery.

prud'homal, e, aux [prydɔmal, o] *adj* : **conseiller ~** *member of an elected industrial tribunal* ■ **élections ~es** industrial tribunal election.

prud'homme [prydɔm] *nm* **1.** [conseiller] *member of an elected industrial tribunal* **2.** *(comme adj)* **conseiller ~** *member of an elected industrial tribunal.*
◆ **prud'hommes** *nmpl* [tribunal] : **les ~s, le conseil de ~s** the elected industrial tribunal.

prune [pryn] ◇ *nf* **1.** BOT plum **2.** *fam loc* **des ~ s!** no way!, nothing doing! ■ **pour des ~s** for nothing **3.** [alcool] plum brandy.
◇ *adj inv* plum-coloured.

pruneau, x [pryno] *nm* **1.** [fruit sec] prune **2.** *Suisse* [prune] red plum **3.** △ *arg crime* [balle] bullet, slug ■ **il s'est pris un ~ dans le buffet** someone filled his belly with lead△.

prunelle [prynɛl] *nf* **1.** BOT sloe **2.** [alcool] sloe gin **3.** ANAT pupil ▪ **je tiens à ce livre comme à la ~ de mes yeux** I wouldn't give this book up *ou* away for the world **4.** [regard] eye ▪ **jouer de la ~** *fam* to make eyes at sb.

prunellier [prynelje] *nm* sloe, blackthorn.

prunier [prynje] *nm* plumtree ▪ **~ du Japon** Japanese cherry.

prurigineux, euse [pryriʒinø, øz] *adj* pruritic.

prurit [pryrit] *nm* pruritus.

Prusse [prys] *npr f* : **(la) ~** Prussia.

prussien, enne [prysjɛ̃, ɛn] *adj* Prussian.
◆ **Prussien, enne** *nm, f* Prussian.

prytanée [pritane] *nm* **1.** ANTIQ prytaneum **2.** [école] : **le Prytanée militaire de La Flèche** the La Flèche military academy *(free school for sons of members of the armed forces)*.

PS ◇ *npr m* (*abr de* **parti socialiste**) *French socialist party*.
◇ *nm* (*abr de* **post-scriptum**) PS, ps.

psalmodie [psalmɔdi] *nf* **1.** RELIG psalmody, intoning **2.** *fig & litt* drone.

psalmodier [9] [psalmɔdje] ◇ *vi* **1.** RELIG to chant **2.** *fig & litt* to drone (on).
◇ *vt* **1.** RELIG to chant **2.** *fig* to intone, to drone (out).

psaume [psom] *nm* psalm ▪ **le livre des Psaumes** Psalms.

psautier [psotje] *nm* psalter.

PSE [peɛsø] (*abr de* **placement sous surveillance électronique**) *nm* electronic tagging.

pseudo- [psødo] *préf* pseudo-, false ▪ **méfie-toi de leur ~contrat** beware of their so-called contract ▪ **le ~démarcheur attaquait les vieilles dames** the bogus salesman preyed on old ladies ▪ **c'est du ~style anglais** it's in pseudo-English style.

pseudonyme [psødɔnim] *nm* [nom d'emprunt - gén] assumed name ; [- d'un écrivain] pen name, pseudonym ; [- d'acteur] stage name ; [- de criminel] alias.

PS-G (*abr de* **Paris St-Germain**) *npr m Paris football team*.

psi [psi] *nm* **1.** [lettre grecque] psi **2.** NUCL psi (particle), J.

psoriasis [psɔrjazis] *nm* psoriasis.

PSU (*abr de* **parti socialiste unifié**) *npr m former French socialist party*.

psy [psi] *fam* ◇ *nmf* [psychanalyste] psychoanalyst, shrink.
◇ *nf* [psychanalyse] : **il est très branché ~** he's really into psychoanalysis.

psychanalyse [psikanaliz] *nf* analysis, psychoanalysis ▪ **il fait une ~** he's undergoing psychoanalysis.

psychanalyser [3] [psikanalize] *vt* to psychoanalyse, to analyse ▪ **elle se fait ~** she's undergoing psychoanalysis, she's in therapy.

psychanalyste [psikanalist] *nmf* analyst, psychoanalyst.

psychanalytique [psikanalitik] *adj* analytical, psychoanalytical.

psyché [psiʃe] *nf* **1.** PSYCHOL psyche **2.** [miroir] cheval glass.

psychédélique [psikedelik] *adj* psychedelic.

psychédélisme [psikedelism] *nm* psychedelic state.

psychiatre [psikjatr] *nmf* psychiatrist.

psychiatrie [psikjatri] *nf* psychiatry ▪ **~ infantile** child psychiatry.

psychiatrique [psikjatrik] *adj* psychiatric.

psychique [psiʃik] ◇ *adj* **1.** MÉD [blocage] mental ▪ [troubles] mental, psychic *spéc* **2.** *fam* [psychologique] psychological ▪ **je ne peux pas voir une souris sans défaillir, c'est ~** I feel faint whenever I see a mouse, I know it's all in the mind but I can't help it.
◇ *nm fam* mind, psychological side ▪ **chez lui, c'est le ~ qui va mal** he's got a psychological problem.

psychisme [psiʃism] *nm* psyche, mind ▪ **son ~ est perturbé** the balance of her mind is disturbed.

psycho [psiko] *nf fam* [psychologie] : **il a fait des études de ~** he studied psychology.

psychodrame [psikɔdram] *nm* **1.** [thérapie] role-play techniques, psychodrama **2.** [séance] (psychotherapeutic) role-play session.

psychogenèse [psikɔʒənɛz] *nf* psychogenesis.

psycholinguistique [psikɔlɛ̃gɥistik] ◇ *adj* psycholinguistic.
◇ *nf* psycholinguistics *(U)*.

psychologie [psikɔlɔʒi] *nf* **1.** [étude] psychology ▪ **~ appliquée/comparative** applied/comparative psychology ▪ **~ expérimentale/sociale** experimental/social psychology ▪ **~ du travail** occupational psychology **2.** [intuition] perception ▪ **tu manques de ~** you're not very perceptive **3.** [mentalité] psychology ◐ **~ des foules** crowd psychology **4.** [dimension psychologique] psychology, mind ▪ **étudiez la ~ des personnages** study the psychological make-up of the characters.

psychologique [psikɔlɔʒik] *adj* **1.** [méthode, théorie] psychological **2.** MÉD [état, troubles] psychological, mental ▪ **il suffit qu'elle aille parler à son médecin pour aller mieux, c'est ~** she only has to talk to her doctor to feel better, it's all in her mind **3.** [dimension] psychological ▪ **la vérité ~ de ces personnages** his/her true-to-life characters **4.** [propice] : **le moment** *ou* **l'instant ~** the right *ou* appropriate moment.

psychologiquement [psikɔlɔʒikmɑ̃] *adv* psychologically.

psychologue [psikɔlɔg] ◇ *adj* insightful, perceptive.
◇ *nmf* psychologist ▪ **~ scolaire** educational psychologist ▪ **~ du travail** occupational psychologist.

psychomoteur, trice [psikɔmɔtœr, tris] *adj* psychomotor.

psychopathe [psikɔpat] *nmf* psychopath.

psychopathologie [psikɔpatɔlɔʒi] *nf* psychopathology.

psychopathologique [psikɔpatɔlɔʒik] *adj* psychopathological.

psychopédagogie [psikɔpedagɔʒi] *nf* educational psychology.

psychophysiologie [psikɔfizjɔlɔʒi] *nf* psychophysiology.

psychose [psikoz] *nf* **1.** PSYCHOL psychosis **2.** [angoisse - individuelle] (obsessive) fear ; [- collective] fear ▪ **il règne ici une véritable ~ de guerre** people here are in the grip of war hysteria.

psychosensoriel, elle [psikɔsɑ̃sɔrjɛl] *adj* psychosensory.

psychosocial, e [psikɔsɔsjal, o] *adj* psychosocial.

psychosociologie [psikɔsɔsjɔlɔʒi] *nf* psychosociology.

psychosociologue [psikɔsɔsjɔlɔg] *nmf* psychosociologist.

psychosomatique [psikɔsɔmatik] ◇ *adj* [médecine, trouble] psychosomatic.
◇ *nf* psychosomatics *(U)*.

psychothérapeute [psikɔterapøt] *nmf* psychotherapist.

psychothérapie [psikɔterapi] *nf* psychotherapy ▪ **faire une ~** to be in therapy ▪ **~ non directive** nondirective therapy.

psychotique [psikɔtik] *adj* & *nmf* psychotic.

psychotrope [psikɔtrɔp] ◇ *adj* psychotropic, psychoactive.
◇ *nm* psychotropic (drug).

Pte = **porte**.

ptérodactyle [pterodaktil] *nm* pterodactyl.

Ptolémée [ptɔleme] *npr* Ptolemy.

PTT (*abr de* **Postes, télécommunications et télédiffusion**) *nfpl* *former French post office and telecommunications network.*

pu [py] *pp* ▷ **pouvoir**.

puant, e [pɥɑ̃, ɑ̃t] *adj* **1.** [nauséabond] stinking, foul-smelling **2.** *fam* [prétentieux] insufferably conceited ▪ **tu es vraiment ~!** you really think you're something special!

puanteur [pɥɑ̃tœr] *nf* foul smell, stench.

pub [1] [pyb] *nf fam* **1.** [publicité] advertising ▪ **il travaille dans la ~** he's in advertising ▪ **faire de la ~ pour un produit** to plug *ou* to push a product ⊳ **un coup de ~** a plug ▪ **ils ont fait un gros coup de ~ autour de ce livre** they really hyped the book **2.** [annonce - gén] ad, advertisement ▪ RADIO & TV commercial.

pub [2] [pœb] *nm* [bar] bar *(in the style of an English pub).*

pubère [pybɛr] *adj* pubescent ▪ **il est ~** he's reached (the age of) puberty.

pubertaire [pybɛrtɛr] *adj* pubertal.

puberté [pybɛrte] *nf* puberty.

pubien, enne [pybjɛ̃, ɛn] *adj* pubic.

pubis [pybis] *nm* [os] pubis ▪ [bas-ventre] pubis, pubes *spéc.*

publiable [pyblijabl] *adj* publishable ▪ **ce n'est guère ~** it's hardly fit for publication *ou* to be printed.

public, ique [pyblik] *adj* **1.** [ouvert à tous] public ▪ **la séance est publique** it's an open session **2.** [connu] public, well-known ▪ **sa nomination a été rendue publique ce matin** his nomination was officially announced *ou* was made public this morning ▪ **l'homme ~** the man the public sees **3.** [de l'État] public, state *(modif).*
◆ **public** *nm* **1.** [population] public ▪ **le grand ~** the general public, the public at large **2.** [audience - d'un spectacle] public, audience ; [- d'un écrivain] readership, readers ; [- d'un match] spectators ▪ **~ féminin/familial** female/family audience ▪ **s'adresser à un vaste ~/à un ~ restreint** to address a vast/limited audience ▪ **c'est un excellent livre, mais qui n'a pas encore trouvé son ~** although the book is excellent, it hasn't yet found the readership it deserves ⊳ **être bon ~** to be easy to please **3.** [secteur] : **le ~** the public sector.
◆ **en public** *loc adv* publicly, in public ▪ **faire honte à qqn en ~** to show sb up in public.
◆ **grand public** *loc adj* : **produits grand ~** consumer goods ▪ **émission grand ~** programme designed to appeal to a wide audience ▪ **film grand ~** blockbuster ▪ **l'électronique grand ~** consumer electronics.

publication [pyblikasjɔ̃] *nf* **1.** [d'un livre, d'un journal] publication, publishing ▪ **le journal a dû cesser sa ~** the paper had to cease publication *ou* to fold ▪ **interdire la ~ de qqch** to stop sthg coming out *ou* being published ⊳ **~ assistée par ordinateur = PAO 2.** DR [d'un arrêté, d'une loi] promulgation, publication ▪ **la ~ des bans** announcement of *ou* publishing the banns **3.** [document] publication, magazine ▪ **~ scientifique** scientific publication *ou* journal ▪ **~ spécialisée** specialist review.

publiciste [pyblisist] *nmf* **1.** DR specialist in public law **2.** [publicitaire] advertiser, advertising man *(nm).*

publicitaire [pyblisitɛr] ◇ *adj* advertising, promotional. ◇ *nmf* : **c'est un ~** he's an advertising man, he's in advertising ▪ **c'est une ~** she's in advertising.

publicité [pyblisite] *nf* **1.** [action commerciale, profession] advertising ⊳ **~ audiovisuelle/par affichage** audiovisual/poster advertising ▪ **~ aérienne** sky writing ▪ **~ clandestine** underhand advertising ▪ **~ comparative** comparative advertising ▪ **~ rédactionnelle** promotional article, advertorial *US* ▪ **~ subliminale** subliminal advertising ▪ **~ sur le lieu de vente** point-of-sale advertising **2.** [annonce commerciale] advertisement ▪ RADIO & TV commercial ▪ [pour une association] publicity ▪ **passer une ~ à la télévision** to advertise on TV ▪ **faire sa propre ~** to sell o.s. ▪ **faire de la ~ pour** to publicize ⊳ **~ mensongère** misleading advertising **3.** [caractère public] public nature **4.** DR [en droit civil] public announcement.

publier [10] [pyblije] *vt* **1.** [éditer - auteur, texte] to publish ▪ **dans un article qui n'a jamais été publié** in an unpublished article **2.** [rendre public - communiqué] to make public, to release ; [- brochure] to publish, to issue, to release ; [- bans] to publish, to announce ; [- décret, loi] to promulgate, to publish.

Publiphone® [pyblifɔn] *nm* cardphone.

publipostage [pyblipɔstaʒ] *nm* mailing ▪ **~ d'essai** test *ou* cold mailing ▪ **~ massif** blanket mailing.

publique [pyblik] *f* ▷ **public**.

publiquement [pyblikmɑ̃] *adv* publicly, in public ▪ **il s'est confessé ~** he admitted his fault in public ▪ **sa mère lui a fait honte ~** her mother showed her up in front of everybody.

publireportage [pyblirəpɔrtaʒ] *nm* special advertising section, advertorial *US*.

puce [pys] ◇ *nf* **1.** ZOOL flea ▪ **ce nom m'a mis la ~ à l'oreille** the name gave me a clue *ou* set me thinking ▪ **il est excité comme une ~** *fam* he's so excited he can't sit still **2.** *fam* [par affection] : **ma ~** sweetie ▪ **où elle est, la petite ~?** where's my little girl then? **3.** ÉLECTRON chip ▪ **~ mémoire** memory chip.
◇ *adj inv* [couleur] puce.
◆ **puces** *nfpl* **1.** JEUX : **jeu de ~s** tiddlywinks **2.** [marché] flea market ▪ **elle s'habille aux ~s** she wears secondhand clothes.

puceau, elle [pyso, ɛl] *adj fam* **il est ~** he's a virgin.
◆ **puceau** *nm* virgin.
◆ **pucelle** *nf* virgin, maid *litt.*

pucelage [pyslaʒ] *nm fam* [d'un homme] virginity ▪ [d'une femme] maidenhead *arch litt*, virginity ▪ **perdre son ~** to lose one's virginity.

pucelle [pysɛl] *f* ▷ **puceau**.

Pucelle [pysɛl] *npr f* : **la ~ d'Orléans, Jeanne la ~** the Maid of Orléans, Joan of Arc.

puceron [pysrɔ̃] *nm* greenfly, aphid, plant louse.

pucier△ [pysje] *nm* bed.

pudding [pudiŋ] *nm bread pudding.*

pudeur [pydœr] *nf* **1.** [décence] modesty, decency, propriety ▪ **avec ~** modestly ▪ **manquer de ~** to have no sense of decency ▪ **fausse ~** false modesty **2.** [délicatesse] tact, sense of propriety ▪ **il aurait pu avoir la ~ de se taire** he could have been tactful enough to keep quiet.

pudibond, e [pydibɔ̃, ɔ̃d] ◇ *adj* prudish, prim.
◇ *nm, f* prude.

pudibonderie [pydibɔ̃dri] *nf* prudishness.

pudique [pydik] *adj* **1.** [chaste] chaste, modest ▪ **une jeune fille très ~** a very demure young lady **2.** [discret] discreet.

pudiquement [pydikmɑ̃] *adv* **1.** [avec pudeur] modestly ▪ **elle tira ~ sa jupe sur ses genoux** she modestly drew her skirt over her knees **2.** [avec tact] discreetly.

puer [7] [pɥe] ◇ *vi* to stink ▪ **ça pue ici!** what a stink *ou* stench!
◇ *vt* **1.** [répandre - odeur] to stink of ▪ **il pue l'ail à quinze pas!** he *ou* his breath reeks of garlic! ▪ **tu pues des pieds** your feet stink **2.** [laisser paraître - défaut] : **~ la méchanceté/l'hypocrisie** to be oozing spitefulness/hypocrisy ▪ **il pue l'arriviste** you can smell the social climber (in him) a mile off.

puéricultrice [pɥerikyltris] *nf* **1.** [dans une crèche] nursery nurse **2.** [à l'hôpital] pediatric nurse.

puériculture [pɥerikyltyr] *nf* **1.** [gén] child care *ou* welfare **2.** ÉDUC nursery nursing **3.** [à l'hôpital] pediatric nursing.

puéril, e [pɥeril] *adj* **1.** [enfantin] childlike ▪ **un enthousiasme ~** a childish excitement **2.** [immature, naïf] childish, infantile, puerile.

puérilement [pɥerilmɑ̃] *adv* childishly.

puérilité [pɥerilite] *nf* [non-maturité] childishness, puerility.
◆ **puérilités** *nfpl* childish *ou* petty trifles.

puerpéral, e, aux [pɥɛrperal, o] *adj* puerperal.

pugilat [pyʒila] *nm* **1.** [bagarre] brawl, scuffle, (bout of) fisticuffs *hum* **2.** ANTIQ boxing.

pugiliste [pyʒilist] *nm* **1.** *litt* [boxeur] boxer, pugilist *sout* **2.** ANTIQ boxer.

pugnace [pygnas] *adj litt* **1.** [combatif] combative, belligerent *litt* **2.** [dans la discussion] argumentative, pugnacious *litt*.

pugnacité [pygnasite] *nf litt* **1.** [combativité] combativeness, belligerence *litt* **2.** [dans la discussion] argumentativeness, pugnacity *litt*.

puîné, e [pɥine] *vieilli* ◇ *adj* [de deux enfants] younger ■ [de plusieurs enfants] youngest.
◇ *nm, f any child born after the eldest* ■ **les ~s n'avaient pas droit à l'héritage paternel** the younger children had no right to their father's inheritance.

puis[1] [pɥi] *v* ⊳ **pouvoir**.

puis[2] [pɥi] *adv* **1.** [indiquant la succession] then ■ **il sortit ~ se mit à courir** he went out and (then) started to run **2.** [dans une énumération] then.
◆ **et puis** *loc adv* **1.** [indiquant la succession] : **il a dîné rapidement et ~ il s'est couché** he ate quickly and then he went to bed ■ **en tête du cortège, le ministre et ~ les conseillers** at the head of the procession the minister followed by the counsellors ⊙ **et ~ après?** [pour solliciter la suite] what then?, what happened next? ■ *fam* [pour couper court] it's none of your business! ■ *fam* [exprimant l'indifférence] so what! **2.** [dans une énumération] : **il y avait ses parents, ses frères et ~ aussi ses cousins** there were his parents, his brothers and also his cousins **3.** [d'ailleurs] : **je n'ai pas envie de sortir, et ~ il fait trop froid** I don't feel like going out, and anyway *ou* and what's more it's too cold.

puisage [pɥizaʒ] *nm* drawing (of water).

puisard [pɥizar] *nm* **1.** [pour l'évacuation] sump ■ **~ de rue** catch pit **2.** [pour l'épuration] cesspool, drainage well **3.** NAUT bilge well **4.** MIN sump.

puiser [3] [pɥize] ◇ *vt* **1.** [eau] to draw ■ **~ l'eau d'un puits/d'une citerne** to draw water from a well/a tank **2.** *sout* [extraire] to get, to take, to derive ■ **~ son inspiration dans** to take *ou* to draw one's inspiration from **3.** [prélever] to draw, to take ■ **tu peux ~ de l'argent sur mon compte si tu en as besoin** you can draw some money from my account if you need any.
◇ *vi* [avoir recours à] to draw ■ **~ dans ses économies** to draw on *ou* upon one's savings ■ **est-ce que je peux ~ dans ta réserve de crayons?** can I dip into *ou* help myself from your stock of pencils? ■ **~ dans son expérience** to draw on one's experience.

puisque [pɥiskə] *(devant voyelle ou 'h' muet puisqu'* [pɥisk]*)* *conj* **1.** [parce que] since, because ■ **tu ne peux pas acheter de voiture, ~ tu n'as pas d'argent** you can't buy a car because *ou* since you don't have any money **2.** [étant donné que] since ■ **je viendrai dîner, ~ vous insistez** I will come to dinner, since you insist ■ **bon, ~ tu le dis/y tiens** alright, if that's what you say/want ■ **~ c'est comme ça, je m'en vais!** if that's how it is, I'm leaving! **3.** [emploi exclamatif] : **mais ~ je te dis que je ne veux pas!** but I'm telling you that I don't want to! ■ **tu vas vraiment y aller? – ~ je te le dis!** so are you really going? – isn't that what I said?

puissamment [pɥisamɑ̃] *adv* **1.** [avec efficacité] greatly ■ **ils ont ~ contribué à la victoire** their part in the victory was decisive ■ **~ raisonné!** *iron* brilliant thinking! **2.** [avec force] powerfully, mightily *sout*.

puissance [pɥisɑ̃s] *nf* **1.** [force physique] power, force, strength **2.** [pouvoir, autorité] power ■ **un État au sommet de sa ~** a state at the height of its power **3.** [capacité] power, capacity ■ **une grande ~ de travail** a great capacity for work ■ **une grande ~ de séduction** great powers of seduction **4.** [d'un appareil] power, capacity, capability ■ [d'une arme nucléaire] yield ■ **augmenter/diminuer la ~** AUDIO to turn the volume up/down ⊙ **~ d'entrée/de sortie** ÉLECTR input/output (power) ■ **~ de feu** ARM fire power ■ **~ fiscale** AUTO engine rating ■ **~ nominale/au frein** AUTO nominal/brake horsepower **5.** COMM power ■ **~ commerciale** sales power **6.** MATH : **six ~ cinq** six to the power (of) five ■ **c'est comme une étincelle, mais à la ~ mille** *fig* it's like a spark, but a thousand times bigger **7.** DR authority ■ **~ paternelle** paternal authority ■ **~ maritale** authority of a husband over a wife ■ **être en ~ de mari** to be under a husband's authority *ou* control **8.** ADMIN : **la ~ publique** the authorities **9.** [pays puissant] power ■ **~ économique** economic power ■ **~ mondiale** world power **10.** OPT (optical) power **11.** ÉQUIT puissance **12.** GÉOL thickness, depth.
◆ **puissances** *nfpl* powers ■ **les ~s de l'argent** the moneyed classes ■ **les ~s des ténèbres** the powers of darkness ⊙ **les grandes ~s** POLIT the great powers.
◆ **en puissance** *loc adj* [virtuel] potential, prospective ■ **un client en ~** a prospective customer ■ **c'est un fasciste en ~** he's got latent fascist tendencies.

puissant, e [pɥisɑ̃, ɑ̃t] *adj* **1.** [efficace - remède] powerful, potent, efficacious *sout* ; [- antidote, armée, ordinateur] powerful ; [- membre, mouvement] strong, powerful, mighty *litt* **2.** [intense - odeur, voix] strong, powerful **3.** [influent] powerful, mighty *litt* **4.** [profond] powerful ■ **un ~ instinct de conservation** a powerful instinct of self-preservation **5.** GÉOL thick.
◆ **puissants** *nmpl* : **les ~s** the powerful.

puisse *etc v* ⊳ **pouvoir**.

puits [pɥi] *nm* **1.** [pour l'eau] well ■ **~ à ciel ouvert** open well ■ **~ perdu** cesspool ■ **~ artésien** artesian well **2.** INDUST **du pétrole : ~ de pétrole** oil well ■ **~ d'exploration** exploration *ou* wild cat well ■ **~ d'intervention** relief *ou* killer well ■ **~ sec** *ou* **improductif** duster **3.** MIN shaft, pit ■ **~ d'aérage** ventilation *ou* ventilating shaft ■ **~ d'extraction** extraction shaft **4.** *fig* **un ~ de science** a walking encyclopedia, a fount of knowledge, a mine of information **5.** GÉOGR pothole.
◆ **puits d'amour** *nm* CULIN cream puff.

pull [pyl] = **pull-over**.

pullman [pulman] *nm* **1.** RAIL Pullman®(car) **2.** [autocar] luxury coach *UK*, luxury touring bus.

pull-over [pylɔvɛr] (*pl* **pull-overs**) *nm* sweater, pullover, jumper *UK*.

pullulement [pylylmɑ̃] *nm* **1.** [processus] proliferation ■ **empêcher le ~ des bactéries** to stop bacteria from proliferating **2.** *sout* [grand nombre] : **un ~ d'insectes** swarms of insects.

pulluler [3] [pylyle] *vi* **1.** [abonder] to congregate, to swarm ■ **égouts où les rats pullulent** sewers overrun by rats **2.** [se multiplier] to multiply, to proliferate ■ **les mauvaises herbes pullulaient dans le jardin abandonné** weeds were taking over the abandoned garden **3.** [fourmiller de] : **~ de** to swarm *ou* to be alive with ■ **ce texte pullule de fautes de frappe** your text is riddled with typing errors.

pulmonaire [pylmɔnɛr] ◇ *adj* **1.** ANAT pulmonary **2.** MÉD pulmonary, lung *(modif)*.
◇ *nf* BOT lungwort.

pulpe [pylp] *nf* **1.** [de fruit] pulp ■ **yaourt/boisson à la ~ de fruit** yoghurt/drink with real fruit **2.** ANAT pulp ■ [des doigts] pad, digital pulp *spéc* ■ **~ dentaire** tooth *ou* dental pulp.

pulpeux, euse [pylpø, øz] *adj* **1.** ANAT & BOT pulpy **2.** [charnu - lèvres, formes] fleshy, voluptuous ■ **une blonde pulpeuse** a curvaceous blonde.

pulsar [pylsar] *nm* pulsar.

pulsation [pylsasjɔ̃] *nf* **1.** ANAT : **~s cardiaques** heartbeats **2.** ASTRON pulsation **3.** ÉLECTR pulsatance, angular frequency **4.** PHYS (mechanical) pulsation **5.** MUS beat.

pulser [3] [pylse] ◇ *vt* [air] to extract, to pump out *(sép)*.
◇ *vi* **1.** MÉD & MUS to throb **2.** ASTRON to pulsate.

pulsion [pylsjɔ̃] *nf* **1.** [motivation] impulse, unconscious motive **2.** PSYCHOL drive, urge ■ **~s sexuelles** sexual desire, sexual urge.

pulvérisateur [pylverizatœr] *nm* **1.** [vaporisateur] spray **2.** AGRIC sprayer ■ **~ rotatif/va-et-vient** rotary/travelling sprayer.

pulvérisation [pylverizasjɔ̃] *nf* **1.** [action] spraying **2.** [médicament] spray ▪ **prendre un médicament en ~** to take a medicine in the form of a spray.

pulvériser [3] [pylverize] *vt* **1.** [broyer] to pulverise, to turn into powder **2.** *fig* [détruire] to demolish, to smash to pieces ▪ **~ un record** to smash a record ▪ **je vais le ~, ce type!** *fam* I'm going to flatten *ou* make mincemeat out of this guy! **3.** [vaporiser] to spray.

pulvériseur [pylverizœr] *nm* disc harrow.

pulvérulence [pylverylɑ̃s] *nf* powderiness, dustiness.

pulvérulent, e [pylverylɑ̃, ɑ̃t] *adj* powdery, dusty.

puma [pyma] *nm* puma, cougar, mountain lion.

punaise [pynɛz] ◇ *nf* **1.** ZOOL bug **2.** [clou] tack, drawing pin *UK*, thumbtack *US* ▪ **~ d'architecte** three-pointed tack **3.** *fam* [personne] vixen **4.** *fam péj* **~ de sacristie** sanctimonious person.
◇ *interj fam* : **~!** blimey! *UK*, gee whizz! *US*.

punaiser [4] [pyneze] *vt* to pin up *(sép)*, to put up *(sép)* with drawing pins.

punch[1] [pɔ̃ʃ] *nm* [boisson] punch.

punch[2] [pœnʃ] *nm inv* **1.** *fam* [dynamisme] pep, get-up-and-go ▪ **avoir du ~** to be full of get-up-and-go ▪ **une politique qui a du ~** a hard-hitting policy **2.** SPORT [d'un boxeur] : **il a le ~** he's got a knock-out *ou* devastating punch.

puncheur [pœnʃœr] *nm* SPORT powerful boxer.

punching-ball [pœnʃiŋbol] *(pl* **punching-balls***) nm* punch *ou* speed ball.

puni, e [pyni] *nm, f* punished pupil ▪ **les ~s resteront dans la classe pendant la récréation** those who have been punished will stay in during break.

punique [pynik] ◇ *adj* [civilisation] Carthaginian, Punic ▪ [guerre] Punic.
◇ *nm* LING Punic.

punir [32] [pynir] *vt* **1.** [élève, enfant] to punish **2.** DR to punish, to penalize ▪ **être puni par la loi** to be punished by law, to be prosecuted ▪ **être puni de prison** to be sentenced to prison ▪ **'tout abus sera puni'** 'penalty for improper use' ▪ **~ qqn de qqch** to punish sb for sthg ▪ **elle est bien punie de sa méchanceté** she's paying the price for her spitefulness ⊙ **c'est le ciel** *ou* **le bon Dieu qui t'a puni** *fam* it serves you right.

punissable [pynisabl] *adj* punishable, deserving (of) punishment ▪ **~ de trois mois de prison** [délit] carrying a penalty of three months imprisonment ; [criminel] liable to three months in jail.

punitif, ive [pynitif, iv] *adj* punitive ▪ **en agissant ainsi, je n'ai pas d'intentions punitives** I do not intend this as punishment.

punition [pynisjɔ̃] *nf* **1.** [sanction] punishment ▪ **en guise de ~** as (a) punishment ▪ **il est en ~** he is being kept in detention ⊙ **~ corporelle** corporal punishment ▪ **~ de Dieu** *ou* **du ciel** divine retribution **2.** *fam* [défaite] thrashing ▪ **les Bordelais ont infligé une rude ~ aux Parisiens** the Bordeaux team wiped the floor with *ou* thrashed the Paris club **3.** [conséquence] punishment, penalty ▪ **la ~ est lourde** it's a heavy price to pay.
◆ **en punition de** *loc prép* as a punishment for.

punk [pœnk] *adj inv* & *nmf* punk.

pupillaire [pypilɛr] *adj* **1.** DR pupillary **2.** ANAT pupillary.

pupille [pypij] ◇ *nmf* **1.** [en tutelle] ward (of court) **2.** [orphelin] orphan ▪ **~ de l'État** child in care ▪ **~s de la Nation** war orphans.
◇ *nf* ANAT pupil.

pupitre [pypitr] *nm* **1.** AÉRON, AUDIO & INFORM console ▪ [clavier] keyboard ▪ **~ de commande** control console *ou* desk ▪ **~ de mélange** mixing-desk, mixing console, audio-mixer **2.** MUS [support - sur pied] music stand ; [- sur un instrument] music rest ▪ [groupe] section ▪ **le ~ des violons** the violin section, the violins ⊙ **~ d'orchestre** orchestra stand **3.** [tablette de lecture] (table) lectern **4.** *vieilli* [bureau d'écolier] desk.

pupitreur, euse [pypitrœr, øz] *nm, f* console operator ▪ [claviste] keyboarder.

pur, e [pyr] ◇ *adj* **1.** [non pollué - eau] pure, clear, uncontaminated ; [- air] clean, pure
2. [sans mélange - liquide] undiluted ; [- race] pure ; [- bonheur, joie] unalloyed, pure ; [- note, voyelle, couleur] pure ▪ **il parle un anglais très ~** he speaks very refined *ou* polished English ▪ **le cognac se boit ~** cognac should be taken straight *ou* neat ▪ **~e laine (vierge)** pure (new) wool ▪ **biscuits ~ beurre** (100 %) butter biscuits ▪ **c'est un ~ produit de la bourgeoisie** he's a genuine middle-class product ▪ **à l'état ~** pure, unalloyed, unadulterated ⊙ **~ et dur** [fidèle] strict ; [intransigeant] hard-line ▪ **les amateurs de café ~s et durs** *hum* serious *ou* dedicated coffee drinkers ▪ **c'est un socialiste ~ jus** he's a socialist through and through
3. [sans défaut] faultless, perfect ▪ **des lignes ~es** neat *ou* perfect lines ▪ **un style ~** an unaffected style
4. [innocent] pure, clean ▪ **être ~** to be pure at heart ▪ **le regard ~ d'un enfant** a child's innocent gaze
5. [théorique] pure, theoretical ▪ **sciences ~es** pure science
6. [en intensif] sheer, utter, pure ▪ **c'est de la folie ~e!** it's sheer lunacy! ▪ **par ~e méchanceté** out of sheer malice ▪ **c'était un ~ hasard de le trouver là** I found him there purely by chance ⊙ **c'est de la lâcheté ~e et simple** it's sheer cowardice, it's cowardice pure and simple
7. AUDIO, CHIM & OPT pure
8. MINÉR flawless.
◇ *nm, f* **1.** POLIT [fidèle] dedicated follower ▪ [intransigeant] hardliner
2. RELIG true believer.

purée [pyre] ◇ *nf* **1.** CULIN [de légumes] purée ▪ **~ de tomates/carottes** tomato/carrot purée ▪ **~ (de pommes de terre)** mashed potatoes ▪ **~ en flocons** instant mashed potato ▪ **~Mousseline®** instant mashed potato ▪ **réduire qqch en ~** CULIN to purée sthg ; *fig* to smash sthg to a pulp **2.** △ [misère] : **être dans la ~** to be broke.
◇ *interj fam* crumbs, crikey.
◆ **purée de pois** *nf fam* [brouillard] peasouper.

purement [pyrmɑ̃] *adv* **1.** [uniquement] purely, only, solely ▪ **ses connaissances sont ~ techniques** his knowledge is purely technical **2.** [entièrement] purely, wholly ⊙ **~ et simplement** purely and simply.

pureté [pyrte] *nf* **1.** [propreté] cleanness, purity **2.** AUDIO, CHIM & OPT purity ▪ MINÉR purity, flawlessness ▪ **une émeraude d'une grande ~** a perfect *ou* flawless emerald **3.** [harmonie - d'un contour] neatness, purity ; [- d'une langue, d'un style] purity, refinement ▪ **la ~ de ses traits** the perfection in her face *ou* of her features **4.** [innocence] purity, chastity ▪ **je doute de la ~ de ses intentions** I doubt whether his intentions are honourable.

purgatif, ive [pyrgatif, iv] *adj* purgative.
◆ **purgatif** *nm* purgative.

purgatoire [pyrgatwar] *nm* RELIG & *fig* purgatory ▪ **au ~** in purgatory.

purge [pyrʒ] *nf* **1.** TECHNOL [processus] draining, bleeding ▪ [d'un radiateur] bleeding ▪ [dispositif] bleed key **2.** MÉD purge, purgative **3.** *fig* [au sein d'un groupe] purge **4.** TEXT cleaning.

purger [17] [pyrʒe] *vt* **1.** TECHNOL [radiateur] to bleed ▪ [réservoir] to drain ▪ [tuyau à gaz] to allow to blow off, to blow off *(sép)* **2.** CHIM [métal] to refine ▪ [substance] to purify **3.** DR [peine] to serve, to purge *sout* **4.** [dette] to pay off *(sép)* ▪ [hypothèque] to redeem **5.** MÉD to purge, to give a laxative to **6.** [débarrasser] to rid of *(sép)* ▪ **le parti a été purgé de ses contestataires** the party has been purged of disloyal elements **7.** *sout* [nettoyer, purifier] : **ils ont purgé le texte de toute allusion politique** they removed all political references from the text.
◆ **se purger** *vp (emploi réfléchi)* to take a purgative.

purgeur [pyrʒœr] *nm* [vidange] draincock ▪ [trop-plein] bleed tap ▪ **~ de vapeur** pet cock.

purifiant, e [pyrifjɑ̃, ɑ̃t] *adj* **1.** [crème, lotion] cleansing, purifying **2.** [air] healthy.

purificateur, trice [pyrifikatœr, tris] *adj* purifying.

◆ **purificateur** *nm* : ~ **(d'air)** (air) purifier.

purification [pyrifikasjɔ̃] *nf* **1.** CHIM purifying ■ ~ **de l'air/l'eau** air/water purifying ‖ *fig* cleansing ■ ~ **ethnique** ethnic cleansing **2.** RELIG purification ■ **la Purification** Candlemas, the Purification.

purificatoire [pyrifikatwar] ◇ *adj* purificatory.
◇ *nm* RELIG purificator (napkin).

purifier [9] [pyrifje] *vt* **1.** [rendre pur - air] to purify, to clear ■ **la pluie a purifié l'atmosphère** the rain has cleared the air **2.** [âme] to cleanse **3.** [corriger] to purify **4.** CHIM [filtrer] to purify, to decontaminate **5.** MÉTALL to refine.
◆ **se purifier** *vpi sout* **1.** [devenir propre] to become clean *ou* pure **2.** RELIG to be cleansed *ou* purified.

purin [pyrɛ̃] *nm* liquid manure.

purisme [pyrism] *nm* **1.** [gén - LING] purism **2.** ART Purism.

puriste [pyrist] *adj* & *nmf* **1.** [gén - LING] purist **2.** ART Purist.

puritain, e [pyritɛ̃, ɛn] ◇ *adj* **1.** [strict] puritan, puritanical **2.** HIST Puritan.
◇ *nm, f* **1.** [personne stricte] puritan **2.** HIST : **les ~s** the Puritans.

puritanisme [pyritanism] *nm* **1.** [austérité] puritanism, austerity **2.** HIST Puritanism.

pur-sang [pyrsɑ̃] *nm inv* ZOOL thoroughbred.

purulence [pyrylɑ̃s] *nf* purulence, purulency.

purulent, e [pyrylɑ̃, ɑ̃t] *adj* MÉD [plaie] suppurating ■ [sinusite] purulent.

pus [py] *nm* pus.

pusillanime [pyzilanim] *adj sout* pusillanimous *sout*, spineless.

pusillanimité [pyzilanimite] *nf sout* pusillanimity *sout*, spinelessness.

pustule [pystyl] *nf* **1.** MÉD pustule *spéc*, pimple ■ ~ **maligne** malignant pustule *spéc* **2.** BOT & ZOOL pustule.

put *etc v* ▷ **pouvoir**.

putain△ [pytɛ̃] ◇ *nf* [prostituée] whore△ ■ **faire la ~** [être prostituée] to be on the game *UK*, to hustle *US* ; [renoncer à ses principes] to sell out.
◇ *adj* : **il est très ~** he's a real bootlicker.
◇ *interj* shit△ ■ ~ **de voiture!** that bloody△ *UK ou* goddam *US* car!

putassier, ère▲ [pytasje, ɛr] *adj péj* **1.** [qui concerne la prostitution] whorish△ **2.** [servile, obséquieux] ingratiating.

putatif, ive [pytatif, iv] *adj* **1.** DR putative **2.** [supposé] assumed, supposed.

pute▲ [pyt] *nf* whore△ ■ **fils de ~!** you son of a bitch!△.

putois [pytwa] *nm* **1.** ZOOL polecat **2.** [fourrure] fitch.

putréfaction [pytrefaksjɔ̃] *nf* putrefaction, decomposition.

putréfié, e [pytrefje] *adj* putrefied, putrid, rotten.

putréfier [9] [pytrefje] ◆ **se putréfier** *vpi* to putrify, to become putrid.

putrescible [pytresibl] *adj* putrescible, putrefiable.

putride [pytrid] *adj* **1.** *sout* [pourri - viande, cadavre] decomposed, putrid ; [- eau] putrid, contaminated **2.** [nauséabond] foul, putrid ■ **odeur ~** putrid smell, foul stench **3.** *sout* [immoral - lettre, pièce] depraved, offensive.

putsch [putʃ] *nm* military coup, putsch.

putschiste [putʃist] *nmf* putschist, author of a military coup.

putt [pœt] *nm* putt.

puy [pɥi] *nm* puy, mountain *(in the Auvergne)*.

puzzle [pœzl] *nm* **1.** JEUX (jigsaw) puzzle **2.** [énigme] puzzle, puzzling question, riddle ■ **je commence à rassembler les morceaux du ~** I'm beginning to fit the pieces of the puzzle together.

P-V (*abr de* **procès-verbal**) *nm fam* (parking) ticket ■ **mettre un ~ à qqn** to give sb a ticket.

PVC (*abr de* **polyvinyl chloride**) *nm* PVC.

PVD = **pays en voie de développement**.

px (*abr écrite de* **prix**) : ~ **à déb.** offers.

pygmée [pigme] ◇ *adj* Pygmy.
◇ *nmf* **1.** *arch* & *péj* [nain] pygmy, dwarf **2.** *litt* & *péj* [personne insignifiante] nobody, pygmy *litt*.
◆ **Pygmée** *nmf* ANTHR & MYTHOL Pygmy.

pyjama [piʒama] *nm* : **un ~** (a pair of) pyjamas.

pylône [pilon] *nm* **1.** ÉLECTR & TÉLÉCOM pylon **2.** ARCHIT monumental column, pylon **3.** ANTIQ pylon **4.** TRAV PUB tower.

pylore [pilɔr] *nm* pylorus.

pyramidal, e, aux [piramidal, o] *adj* **1.** ARCHIT, ÉCON, GÉOM & MÉD pyramidal **2.** [forme] pyramid-shaped **3.** ANAT : **voie ~e** pyramidal tract.

pyramide [piramid] *nf* **1.** ARCHIT & GÉOM pyramid ■ **la ~ de Kheops** the (Great) Pyramid of Cheops ■ **la Pyramide du Louvre** *glass pyramid in the courtyard of the Louvre which serves as its main entrance* **2.** [empilement] : **une ~ de fruits** a pyramid of fruit ➲ ~ **humaine** human pyramid **3.** SOCIOL : ~ **des âges** population pyramid **4.** ÉCOL : ~ **alimentaire** food pyramid **5.** ANAT pyramid ■ ~ **de Malpighi** pyramid of Malpighi.

pyranne [piran] *nm* pyran.

pyrénéen, enne [pireneɛ̃, ɛn] *adj* Pyrenean.

Pyrénées [pirene] *npr fpl* : **les ~** the Pyrenees.

Pyrex® [pirɛks] *nm* Pyrex® ■ **en ~** Pyrex.

pyrite [pirit] *nf* pyrite ■ ~ **blanche** marcasite.

pyrograver [3] [pirɔgrave] *vt* : ~ **qqch** to work sthg with a heated stylus, to pyrograph sthg *spéc*.

pyrogravure [pirɔgravyr] *nf* pokerwork, pyrography *spéc*.

pyrolyse [pirɔliz] *nf* pyrolysis.

pyromane [pirɔman] *nmf* arsonist, pyromaniac.

pyromanie [pirɔmani] *nf* pyromania.

pyrotechnie [pirɔtɛkni] *nf* pyrotechnics *(U)*, pyrotechny, fireworks.

pyrotechnique [pirɔtɛknik] *adj* pyrotechnic, pyrotechnical ■ **un spectacle ~** a firework display.

Pythagore [pitagɔr] *npr* Pythagoras.

pythagoricien, enne [pitagɔrisjɛ̃, ɛn] *adj* & *nm, f* Pythagorean ■ **la gamme ~ne** the Pythagorean scale.

pythagorique [pitagɔrik] *adj* : **nombres ~s** Pythagorean numbers.

pythie [piti] *nf* **1.** ANTIQ : **la ~** Pythia **2.** *litt* [prophétesse] pythoness.

python [pitɔ̃] *nm* ZOOL python.

q, Q [ky] *nm* q, Q ■ **fièvre Q** Q fever, *voir aussi* **g**.

q = **quintal**.

Qatar [katar] *npr m* : **le ~** Qatar, Katar.

QCM (*abr de* **questionnaire à choix multiple**) *nm* multiple-choice questionnaire.

QG (*abr de* **quartier général**) *nm* HQ.

QHS *nm* = **quartier de haute sécurité**.

QI (*abr de* **quotient intellectuel**) *nm* IQ.

quad [kwad] *nm* [moto] four-wheel motorbike, quad bike ■ [rollers] roller skate.

quadra[1] [k(w)adra] *nm* POLIT fortysomething, babyboomer.

quadra[2] [k(w)adra] *nmf* fortysomething.

quadragénaire [k(w)adraʒenɛr] ◇ *adj* : **être ~** [avoir de 40 à 50 ans] to be in one's forties ; [avoir 40 ans] to be forty.
◇ *nmf* [de 40 à 50 ans] person in his/her forties ■ [de 40 ans] forty-year-old man (*f* woman), quadragenarian ■ **un sémillant ~** a dashing forty-year old.

quadrangulaire [kwadrɑ̃gylɛr] *adj* quadrangular, four-angled ■ **une tour ~** a four-sided tower.

quadrant [kwadrɑ̃] *nm* ANAT & GÉOM quadrant.

quadrature [kwadratyr] *nf* **1.** GÉOM quadrature, squaring ■ **~ du cercle** squaring the circle ■ **c'est la ~ du cercle** it's like trying to square a circle *ou* to get a quart into a pint pot **2.** ASTRON quadrature **3.** MATH integration.

quadriceps [kwadrisɛps] *nm* quadriceps.

quadrichromie [kwadrikrɔmi] *nf* four-colour processing *ou* printing.

quadriennal, e, aux [kwadrijenal, o] *adj* quadrennial, four-year *(avant n)*.

quadrilatéral, e, aux [k(w)adrilateral, o] *adj* four-sided.

quadrilatère [k(w)adrilatɛr] ◇ *adj* quadrilateral.
◇ *nm* GÉOM & MIL quadrilateral.

quadrillage [kadrijaʒ] *nm* **1.** [réseau] grid ■ **~ des rues** grid arrangement *ou* layout of streets **2.** [tracé] grid *ou* criss-cross pattern ■ **pour dessiner, tu peux utiliser le ~ de ton cahier** you can use the squares on your exercise book to make your drawing **3.** [division] division ■ **~ administratif** division into administrative areas ■ **~ hospitalier** hospital area division **4.** [contrôle] surveillance **5.** [sur une carte] grid, graticule.

quadrille [kadrij] *nm* quadrille ■ **le ~ des lanciers** the lancers.

quadrillé, e [kadrije] *adj* squared, cross-ruled.

quadriller [3] [kadrije] *vt* **1.** [papier] to criss-cross, to mark into squares **2.** [surveiller] to surround ■ **la police quadrille le quartier** police presence is heavy in the district **3.** [être réparti sur] to be scattered about *ou* dotted over.

quadrimoteur [k(w)adrimɔtœr] ◇ *adj m* four-engined.
◇ *nm* four-engined plane.

quadripartite [kwadripartit] *adj* **1.** BOT quadripartite **2.** [conférence, commission] quadripartite ■ **réunion ~** [de groupements] quadripartite meeting ; [de pays] meeting between four countries ; [de partis] four-party meeting.

quadriphonie [kwadrifɔni] *nf* quadraphony, quadraphonics *(sing)*.

quadripôle [kwadripol] *nm* quadripole.

quadriréacteur [k(w)adrireaktœr] ◇ *adj m* four-engined.
◇ *nm* four-engined plane *ou* jet.

quadrisyllabe [kwadrisilab] *nm* quadrisyllable, tetrasyllable.

quadrupède [k(w)adrypɛd] ◇ *adj* quadruped, four-footed.
◇ *nm* quadruped.

quadruple [k(w)adrypl] ◇ *adj* quadruple.
◇ *nm* quadruple ■ **j'ai gagné 100 euros et le vendeur le ~** I earned 100 euros and the seller four times that.

quadrupler [3] [k(w)adryple] ◇ *vi* to quadruple, to increase fourfold ■ **la peur du conflit a fait ~ les ventes de boîtes de conserve** fears of war pushed sales of tinned food up by 400%.
◇ *vt* to increase fourfold, to quadruple.

quadruplés, ées [k(w)adryple] *nm, f pl* quadruplets, quads.

quai [kɛ] *nm* **1.** [d'une gare] platform ■ **le train est à ~** the train is in ■ **arrivée du train ~ numéro cinq** train arriving on platform five **2.** NAUT quay, wharf ■ **le navire est à ~** the ship has berthed **3.** [berge] bank, embankment ■ **sur les ~s de la Seine** on the banks of the Seine **4.** [rue bordant un fleuve] street ■ **prendre les ~s** to drive along the river *(in a town)* ■ **le Quai** [le Quai d'Orsay] the (French) Foreign Ministry ; [le Quai des Orfèvres] Police Headquarters *(in Paris)* **5.** TECHNOL platform.

QUAI

The names *Quai d'Orsay* and *Quai des Orfèvres* are often used to refer to the government departments situated on the streets of the same name (the foreign office and the police department respectively). *Le quai de Conti* is sometimes used to refer to the *Académie française*.

quaker, eresse [kwɛkœr, kwɛkrɛs] *nm, f* Quaker (*f* Quakeress) ■ **les ~s** the Quakers, the Society of Friends.

qualifiable [kalifjabl] *adj* **1.** SPORT [athlète, concurrent] liable to qualify **2.** [descriptible] : **son attitude n'est pas ~** his attitude can't be justified.

qualificatif, ive [kalifikatif, iv] *adj* qualifying.
➡ **qualificatif** *nm* **1.** [mot] term, word ■ **ce ~ suave ne lui convient guère!** she hardly deserves to be described in such a pleasant way! **2.** LING qualifier, modifier.

qualification [kalifikasjɔ̃] *nf* **1.** [formation] qualification, skill ■ **sans ~** unskilled ➊ **~ professionnelle** professional qualifications **2.** SPORT preliminary, qualifying ■ **obtenir sa ~** to qualify ➊ **épreuves/match de ~** qualifying heats/match **3.** [appellation] name ■ **la ~ de faussaire paraît exagérée** the term forger seems a bit extreme **4.** DR legal definition.

qualifié, e [kalifje] *adj* **1.** [compétent] skilled, qualified ■ **non ~ pour** ineligible for **2.** SPORT [choisi] qualifying **3.** DR aggravated.

qualifier [9] [kalifje] *vt* **1.** [appeler] : **~ qqn/qqch de...** to describe sb/sthg as... ■ **il qualifie tout le monde de snob** he calls *ou* dubs everybody a snob **2.** [apprécier] to consider ■ **je ne sais comment ~ son attitude** I don't know what to think of his attitude **3.** [professionnellement] to qualify **4.** SPORT to qualify **5.** LING to qualify, to modify.
➡ **se qualifier** ◇ *vp (emploi réfléchi)* : **se ~ de** [se dire] to call o.s.
◇ *vpi* [être choisi] to qualify ■ **se ~ pour une finale** to qualify for *ou* to get through to a final.

qualitatif, ive [kalitatif, iv] *adj* qualitative ■ **d'un point de vue ~** from a qualitative point of view.

qualitativement [kalitativmɑ̃] *adv* qualitatively.

qualité [kalite] *nf* **1.** [côté positif - d'une personne] quality, virtue ; [- d'une chose] good point, positive feature ■ **~s morales/intellectuelles** moral/intellectual qualities ■ **avoir des ~s de cœur** to have a good heart **2.** [propriété] quality, property ■ **cette plante a des ~s laxatives** this plant has laxative properties **3.** [niveau] quality, grade ■ **~ ordinaire** standard *ou* regular grade ■ **de ~ inférieure** low-quality, shoddy ■ **la ~ de l'impression est insuffisante/bonne** the quality of the printing is inadequate/good ➊ **~ de vie** quality of life ■ **~ totale** COMM total quality management **4.** [statut] position ■ DR quality, capacity ■ **nom, prénom, âge et ~** name, first name, age and occupation ■ **avoir ~ pour faire qqch** [être habilité] to be entitled to do sthg ; [être capable] to be qualified to do sthg **5.** [supériorité qualitative] quality ■ **la ~ se paie** you get what you pay for **6.** PHILOS quality.
➡ **qualités** *nfpl* [mérites] skills, qualifications ■ **pensez-vous avoir les ~s requises?** do you think you've got the required skills?
➡ **de qualité** *loc adj* **1.** [de luxe] quality *(modif)*, high-standard ■ **vêtements de ~** quality clothes **2.** *vieilli* [noble] noble.
➡ **en qualité de** *loc prép* : **en ~ de tuteur, je peux intervenir** (in my capacity) as guardian, I can intervene.
➡ **ès qualités** *loc adv* ADMIN & DR in one's official capacity.

quand [kɑ̃] ◇ *conj* **1.** [lorsque] when ■ **réveille-moi ~ tu partiras** wake me when you leave ■ **~ je te disais qu'il serait en retard!** I TOLD you he'd be late! ■ **~ je pense à l'argent que j'ai dépensé!** when I think *ou* to think of the money I spent! ➊ **~ le vin est tiré, il faut le boire** *prov* you've made your bed and must lie in it **2.** [alors que] when ■ **pourquoi rester enfermé ~ il fait si beau dehors?** why stay cooped up when it's so lovely outside? **3.** [introduisant une hypothèse] even if ■ **et ~ ce serait, j'ai bien le droit de rêver** even if that is the case, I'm allowed to dream, aren't I?
◇ *adv* when ■ **~ viendras-tu nous voir?** when will you come and visit us? ■ **depuis ~ es-tu là?** how long have you been here? ■ **à ~ le mariage?** when's the wedding? ■ **c'est pour ~, ce mariage?** when is this wedding going to happen? ■ **~ est-ce que tu y vas?** *fam* when are you going there?
➡ **quand bien même** *loc conj* even if.
➡ **quand même** ◇ *loc conj sout* even though, even if.
◇ *loc adv* **1.** [malgré tout] all the same, even so ■ **c'était ~ même bien** it was still good, it was good all the same ■ **je pense qu'il ne viendra pas, mais je l'inviterai ~ même** I don't think he'll come but I'll invite him all the same **2.** [en intensif] : **tu pourrais faire attention ~ même!** you really should be more careful!

quant [kɑ̃] ➡ **quant à** *loc prép* as for *ou* to ■ **je partage votre opinion ~ à ses capacités** I share your opinion about his ability ■ **~ à lui** as for him.

quanta [kwɑ̃ta] *pl* ⊳ **quantum**.

quant-à-soi [kɑ̃taswa] *nm inv* : **rester** *ou* **se tenir sur son ~** to remain distant *ou* aloof.

quantième [kɑ̃tjɛm] *nm* day (and date) of the month ■ **dû le jour ayant le même ~** DR due on the same day and date.

quantifiable [kɑ̃tifjabl] *adj* quantifiable.

quantificateur [kɑ̃tifikatœr] *nm* quantifier.

quantification [kɑ̃tifikasjɔ̃] *nf* **1.** PHILOS quantification **2.** PHYS quantization.

quantifier [9] [kɑ̃tifje] *vt* **1.** PHILOS to quantify **2.** PHYS to quantize.

quantique [kwɑ̃tik, kɑ̃tik] ◇ *adj* quantic ■ **nombre ~** quantic number.
◇ *nf* quantum mechanics.

quantitatif, ive [kɑ̃titatif, iv] *adj* **1.** [concernant la quantité] quantitative ■ **évaluation quantitative des résultats des tests** quantitative analysis of test results **2.** LING quantitative ■ **terme ~** quantifier.

quantitativement [kɑ̃titativmɑ̃] *adv* quantitatively.

quantité [kɑ̃tite] *nf* **1.** [mesure] amount, quantity ■ **quelle ~ de lessive faut-il mettre?** how much detergent do you have to put in? ■ **une ~ de** lots of, a lot of, a great many ■ **une ~ industrielle de** *fam* masses and masses of, heaps and heaps of **2.** SC [grandeur] quantity ■ **~ constante/variable** constant/variable quantity ■ **~ de mouvement** linear momentum **3.** *loc* **~ négligeable** : **tenir qqn/qqch pour ~ négligeable** to disregard sb/sthg ■ **traiter qqn/qqch comme une ~ négligeable** to treat sb/sthg as unworthy of consideration **4.** PHILOS & LING quantity.
➡ **en quantité** *loc adv* in abundance, in great amounts ■ **du vin/des prix en ~** lots of wine/prizes.
➡ **quantité de** *loc dét sout* a great many, lots of ■ **elle trouve ~ de raisons pour ne pas le faire** she finds any amount *ou* lots of reasons not to do it.

quantum [kwɑ̃tɔm] (*pl* **quanta** [kwɑ̃ta]) *nm* **1.** MATH & PHYS quantum ■ **théorie des quanta** quantum theory **2.** [montant] amount ■ **~ des dommages et intérêts** sum of damages **3.** [proportion] proportion, ratio.

quarantaine [karɑ̃tɛn] *nf* **1.** [nombre] about forty ■ **une ~ de chevaux** about forty *ou* forty or so horses **2.** [âge] : **avoir la ~** to be in one's forties ■ **elle frise la ~** she's pushing forty **3.** [isolement] quarantine **4.** BOT annual *ou* hairy stock.
➡ **en quarantaine** ◇ *loc adj* **1.** MÉD & VÉTÉR in quarantine **2.** *fig* excluded, ostracized.
◇ *loc adv* : **mettre en ~** MÉD & VÉTÉR to quarantine ; *fig* to ostracize, to exclude.

quarante [karɑ̃t] ◇ *dét* forty ■ **elle a ~ de fièvre** her temperature is 40° C ■ **en ~** [en 1940] in 1940.
◇ *nm inv* **1.** [numéro] forty ■ **les Quarante** the French Academy **2.** TENNIS forty ■ **~ partout** deuce.

quarante-cinq-tours [karɑ̃tsɛ̃tur] *nm inv* 45 (rpm), single.

quarantenaire [karɑ̃tnɛr] ◇ *adj* [qui dure quarante ans] forty-year *(avant n)*.
◇ *nm* [lieu] quarantine.
◇ *nf* [maladie] notifiable *UK ou* quarantinable *US* disease.
◇ *nmf* [personne de quarante ans] forty-year-old.

quarantième [karɑ̃tjɛm] ◇ *adj num* & *nmf* fortieth, *voir aussi* **cinquième**.

◇ *nm* **1.** [fraction] fortieth **2.** NAUT : **les ~s rugissants** the roaring forties.

quark [kwark] *nm* quark.

quart¹ [kar] *nm* **1.** [quatrième partie] quarter ▪ **5 est le ~ de 20** 5 is a quarter of 20 ▪ **un ~ de beurre** a quarter (of a pound) of butter ▪ **un ~ de la tarte** one quarter of the tart ▶ **un ~ de cercle** [gén] a quarter (of a) circle ; GÉOM a quadrant ▪ **~ de finale** quarter final ▪ **un ~ de tour** a quarter turn ▪ **démarrer** *ou* **partir au ~ de tour** *pr* to start first go ▪ **il a réagi au ~ de tour** he reacted straight away ▪ **au ~ de poil** *fam* perfectly ▪ **le frigo rentre au ~ de poil** the fridge just fits **2.** MUS : **~ de soupir** semiquaver *UK ou* sixteenth *US* rest ▪ **~ de ton** quarter tone **3.** [période de quinze minutes] quarter of an hour, quarter hour *US* ▪ **c'est le ~ qui sonne** that's the bell for quarter past ▪ **une heure et ~** a quarter past one ▪ **une heure moins le ~** a quarter to one ▪ **j'étais là à moins le ~** *fam* I was there at a quarter to **4.** [petite quantité] fraction ▪ **il dit cela mais il n'en pense pas le ~** that's what he says but he doesn't really mean it **5.** NAUT [garde] watch ▪ [aire de vent] rhumb ▪ **être de ~** to be on watch *ou* duty **6.** [bouteille ou pichet] quarter litre **7.** [gobelet] (quarter litre) mug *ou* beaker.

quart², e [kar, kart] *adj vieilli* fourth.

quart-de-finaliste [kardəfinalist] (*pl* **quart-de-finalistes**) *nmf* quarterfinalist.

quart d'heure [kardœr] (*pl* **quarts d'heure**) *nm* **1.** [quinze minutes] quarter of an hour **2.** *loc* **le ~ américain** *the time when the girls can invite the boys to dance (at a party)* ▪ **passer un mauvais ~** *fam* to have a bad time of it ▪ **faire passer un mauvais ~ à qqn** *fam* to give sb hell.

quarte [kart] ◇ *f* ▷ **quart.**
◇ *nf* **1.** TÉLÉCOM quad ▪ **câble à ~s** quad cable **2.** MUS fourth **3.** ESCRIME quarte **4.** CARTES quart.

quarté [karte] *nm* forecast *(of the first four horses).*

quarteron, onne [kartərɔ̃, ɔn] *nm, f* [métis] quadroon.
◆ **quarteron** *nm péj* [petit nombre] bunch, gang ▪ **un ~ de politiciens véreux** a bunch of shady politicians.

quartet [kwartɛ] *nm* INFORM fourbit byte.

quartette [kwartɛt] *nm* MUS quartet, quartette.

quartier [kartje] *nm* **1.** [division d'une ville] district, area ▪ **le ~ des affaires** the business district ▪ **le ~ juif** the Jewish quarter *ou* area ▪ **le ~ chinois** Chinatown ▪ **le ~** the neighbourhood ▪ **je ne suis pas du ~** I'm not from around here ▪ **c'est un garçon du ~** he's a local boy ▶ **les beaux ~s** fashionable districts ▪ **les bas ~s** the less salubrious parts of town ▪ **les vieux ~s** the old town *ou* quarter (of town) ▪ **le Quartier latin** the Latin Quarter *(area on the Left Bank of the Seine traditionally associated with students and artists)*
2. MIL quarters ▶ **~ général** *pr & fig* headquarters ▪ **grand ~ général** General Headquarters ▪ **~s d'hiver** winter quarters ▪ **prendre ses ~s d'hiver à** to winter at ▪ **avoir ~ libre** MIL to be off duty ; *fig* to be free
3. [partie d'une prison] wing ▪ **~ de haute sécurité** *ou* **de sécurité renforcée** high- *ou* top-security wing
4. [quart] quarter ▪ **un ~ de pomme** a quarter of an apple ▮ [morceau] portion, section ▪ **un ~ d'orange** an orange segment ▪ **un ~ de bœuf** a quarter of beef
5. ASTRON quarter ▪ **la Lune est dans son premier/dernier ~** the Moon is in its first/last quarter
6. HÉRALD quarter
7. [degré de descendance noble] : **un prince à seize ~s** *a prince of noble descent through all of his great-great-grandparents* ▶ **~s de noblesse** degree of noble descent ▪ **avoir ses ~s de noblesse** *fig* to be well established
8. [pitié] mercy, quarter ▪ **l'armée victorieuse n'a pas fait de ~** the victorious army gave no quarter
9. [d'une chaussure] quarter ▪ [d'une selle] (half) panel
10. ZOOL [partie du sabot] quarter
11. MIN (overseers) district.
◆ **de quartier** *loc adj* [médecin, cinéma] local.

quartier-maître [kartjemɛtr] (*pl* **quartiers-maîtres**) *nm* NAUT leading seaman.

quart(-)monde [karmɔ̃d] (*pl* **quarts(-)mondes**) *nm* : **le ~** [ensemble de pays] the least developed countries, the Fourth World ; [dans un pays] the poor.

quarto [kwarto] *adv* fourthly.

quartz [kwarts] *nm* quartz.
◆ **à quartz** *loc adj* quartz *(modif).*

quasar [kazar] *nm* quasar.

quasi [kazi] ◇ *adv* = **quasiment.**
◇ *nm* chump end.

quasi- [kazi] *préf* quasi-, near, almost ▪ **j'en ai la ~certitude** I'm virtually certain ▪ **la ~totalité de...** almost the whole...

quasi-délit [kazideli] (*pl* **quasi-délits**) *nm* criminal negligence.

quasiment [kazimɑ̃] *adv fam* almost, practically ▪ **c'est ~ la même chose** it's more or less the same.

Quasimodo [kazimɔdo] ◇ *nf* RELIG Quasimodo, Low Sunday.
◇ *npr* LITTÉR Quasimodo, the hunchback of Notre-Dame.

quaternaire [kwatɛrnɛr] ◇ *adj* **1.** GÉOL Quaternary ▪ **ère ~** Quaternary era **2.** CHIM & MATH quaternary.
◇ *nm* GÉOL Quaternary (period).

quatorze [katɔrz] ◇ *dét* **1.** fourteen **2.** [dans des séries] fourteenth ▪ **à ~ heures** at 2 pm ▪ **en ~** during World War I ▶ **le 14 Juillet** Bastille Day, the fourteenth of July ▪ **la guerre de ~** World War I, the First World War ▪ **c'est parti comme en ~!** *fam hum* off we go, lads! ▪ **c'est reparti comme en ~!** *hum* once more into the breach!, *voir aussi* **cinq.**
◇ *nm inv* fourteen.

quatorzième [katɔrzjɛm] *adj num, nmf & nm* fourteenth, *voir aussi* **cinquième.**

quatrain [katrɛ̃] *nm* quatrain.

quatre [katr] ◇ *dét* **1.** four ▪ **les ~ vertus cardinales** the cardinal virtues, *voir aussi* **cinq 2.** AUTO : **4 x 4 = quatre-quatre 3.** *loc* **il lui fallait se tenir à ~ pour ne pas rire/parler** he had to bite his lip not to laugh/to bite his tongue not to speak ▪ **faire les ~ cents coups : il a fait les ~ cents coups dans sa jeunesse** he sowed his wild oats when he was young ▪ **cet enfant fait les ~ cents coups** that child's a bit of a handful ▪ **il n'y est pas allé par ~ chemins** he came straight to the point *ou* didn't beat about the bush ▪ **ils viennent des ~ coins du monde** they come from the four corners of the world ▪ **jouer aux ~ coins** JEUX *to run from one corner of a room to another trying to reach a corner before the player standing in the middle* ▪ **être tiré à ~ épingles** to be immaculately dressed *ou* dressed to the nines ▪ **les ~ fers en l'air** *fam* flat on one's back ▪ **un de ces ~ matins** one of these days ▪ **être enfermé entre ~ murs** to be shut away indoors ▪ **~ sous** *fam* : **il a eu vite dépensé ses ~ sous** he soon spent the little money he had ▪ **bague de ~ sous** cheap ring ▪ **dire ses ~ vérités à qqn** to tell sb few home truths ▪ **faire les ~ volontés de qqn** to pander to sb's every whim ▪ **se mettre en ~ pour qqn** to go to no end of trouble *ou* to bend over backwards for sb ▪ **se mettre en ~ pour faire qqch** to go out of one's way to do sthg.
◇ *nm inv* **1.** [nombre] four **2.** NAUT four.
◆ **à quatre mains** MUS ◇ *loc adj* : **morceau à ~ mains** piece for four hands.
◇ *loc adv* : **jouer à ~ mains** to play a duet.
◆ **à quatre pattes** *loc adv* on all fours ▪ **se mettre à ~ pattes** to go down on all fours.
◆ **comme quatre** *loc adv* : **boire/manger/parler comme ~** to eat/to drink/to talk a lot ▪ **avoir de l'esprit comme ~** to be a bit of a wit.

quatre-cent-vingt-et-un [kat(rə)sɑ̃vɛ̃teœ̃] *nm inv simple dice game usually played in cafés: the loser pays for a round of drinks.*

quatre-mâts [katrəma] *nm inv* four-master.

quatre-quarts [katkar] *nm inv* ≃ pound cake *(without fruit).*

quatre-quatre [katkatr] ◇ *adj inv* four-wheel drive.

◇ *nm inv* & *nf inv* four-wheel drive (vehicle).

quatre-saisons [kat(rə)sɛzɔ̃] *nf inv* [légume] second-crop *ou* second-cropping vegetable ▪ [fruit] second-crop *ou* second-cropping fruit.

quatre-vingt-dix [katrəvɛ̃dis] ◇ *dét* ninety, *voir aussi* **cinquante**.
◇ *nm inv* **1.** [nombre] ninety **2.** *fam* [sur une voiture] *sticker showing the maximum speed at which a new licence holder can drive a car.*

quatre-vingt-dixième [katrəvɛ̃dizjɛm] *adj num, nmf* & *nm* ninetieth, *voir aussi* **cinquième**.

quatre-vingtième [katrəvɛ̃tjɛm] *adj num, nmf* & *nm* eightieth, *voir aussi* **cinquième**.

quatre-vingts [katrəvɛ̃] ◇ *dét* eighty ▪ **~ personnes** eighty people, *voir aussi* **cinquante**.
◇ *nm* eighty.

quatrième [katrijɛm] ◇ *adj num* & *nmf* fourth, *voir aussi* **cinquième**.
◇ *nf* **1.** ÉDUC ≃ third form *UK*, ≃ ninth grade *US* **2.** DANSE fourth position.
◆ **en quatrième vitesse** *loc adv fam* in a hurry, at breakneck speed ▪ **rapporte ce livre à la bibliothèque, et en ~ vitesse!** take this book back to the library and be quick about it!

quatrièmement [katrijɛmmɑ̃] *adv* fourthly, in (the) fourth place, *voir aussi* **cinquièmement**.

quatuor [kwatɥɔr] *nm* **1.** MUS quartet ▪ **~ à cordes/vent** string/wind quartet **2.** *fam Québec* [groupe] foursome.

que [kə] *(devant voyelle ou 'h' muet qu'* [k]*)* ◇ *adv* **1.** [combien] : **~ tu es naïf!** you're so naive!, aren't you naive! ▪ **~ de bruit ici!** it's so noisy here!, what a lot of noise there is in here! ▪ **~ de choses à faire dans une maison!** there are so many things to do in a house! ▪ **qu'il a un grand nez!** he's got such a big nose! ▪ **qu'est-ce ~ tu es bête!** *fam* you're (ever) so stupid! ▪ **qu'est-ce qu'il m'a déçu!** *fam* he really disappointed me!
2. [exprimant l'indignation] : **~ m'importent ses états d'âme!** what do I care about what he feels! ▮ *sout* [pourquoi] why ▪ **~ ne l'as-tu (pas) dit plus tôt!** why didn't you say so earlier?, I wish you had said so *ou* that earlier!
◇ *pron rel* **1.** [représente une personne] whom *sout*, who, that ▪ **la fille qu'il a épousée** the girl (whom) he married ▪ **sa sœur, ~ je n'avais pas vue depuis 10 ans, était là aussi** her sister, whom *ou* who I hadn't seen for 10 years, was there too ▪ **la femme qu'elle était devenue** the woman (that) she'd become
2. [représente un animal] which, that
3. [représente une chose, une idée] which, that ▪ **le contrat ~ j'ai signé** the contract (which) *ou* that I signed ➊ **je ne suis pas la seule, ~ je sache** I'm not the only one as far as I know
4. [pour souligner une caractéristique] : **malheureux ~ vous êtes!** you unfortunate man! ▪ **fatiguée qu'elle était, elle continuait à l'aider** tired though *ou* as she was, she carried on helping him ▪ **de timide qu'il était, il est devenu expansif** once a shy man, he's now an extrovert ▪ **toute jaune qu'elle était, l'eau!** *fam* the water was all yellow, really it was! ▪ **en bon père/électricien qu'il était** being the good father/electrician he was ▪ **bel exploit ~ le sien!** what he's done is quite a feat! ▪ **une chance, ~ cette panne!** very lucky, this breakdown!
5. [dans des expressions de temps, de durée] : **ça fait deux heures ~ j'attends** I've been waiting for two hours ▪ **un soir qu'il faisait très chaud** one very hot evening, one evening when the weather was very hot ▪ **le temps ~ tu te prépares, il sera trop tard** by the time you're ready it'll be too late ▪ **il n'y a pas longtemps qu'elle l'a vendu** it wasn't long ago that she sold it ▪ **il y a bien longtemps ~ je le sais** I've known for a long time ▪ **chaque fois ~ je m'absente, il téléphone** every time I'm out he phones.
◇ *pron interr* **1.** [dans le discours direct] what ▪ **qu'y a-t-il?** what's the matter? ▪ **~ devient-elle?** what's become of her? ▪ **qu'est-ce que je vois/j'entends?** [ton menaçant ou hum] what is this I see/hear? ▪ **qu'est-ce qui t'arrive?** what's the matter with you? ▪ **qu'est-ce que la liberté?** what is freedom?
2. [dans le discours indirect] what.
◇ *conj* **1.** [après des verbes déclaratifs ou des verbes d'évaluation] that ▪ **je sais ~ je peux le faire** I know (that) I can do it ▪ **il est possible ~ je revienne** I may come back ▪ **exigez qu'on vous indemnise** demand compensation *ou* to be compensated ▪ **elle murmura qu'elle devait s'en aller** she whispered that she had to go ▮ [en début de proposition] : **~ leur fils ait fugué, cela ne devrait pas nous surprendre** the fact that their son ran away shouldn't come as a surprise to us ▪ **~ tu pleures ne changera rien** your *ou* you crying won't change anything
2. *(à valeur circonstancielle)* [et déjà] than ▪ **il n'a pas fini de lire un roman qu'il en commence un autre** no sooner has he finished one novel than he starts reading another ▮ [afin que] so that ▪ **approche-toi, ~ je te voie mieux** come closer so that I can see you better ▮ [à tel point que] : **elle tousse ~ ça réveille tout le monde** *fam* she coughs so much (that) she wakes everybody up ▪ **il est têtu ~ ça en devient un vrai problème** *fam* he's so *ou* that stubborn (that) it's a real problem ▮ [dialecte: parce que] : **ne viens pas, ~ si je te vois je te tue!** don't come, 'cos if I see you I'll kill you!
3. *(suivi du subj)* [pour formuler un ordre, un souhait, une éventualité] : **qu'elle parle!** [faites-la parler] make her talk! ; [laissez-la parler] let her speak! ▪ **~ l'on apporte à boire!** bring some drinks! ▪ **eh bien, qu'il s'en aille s'il n'est pas content!** he can leave if he doesn't like it! ▪ **~ Dieu nous pardonne** may God forgive us ▪ **qu'il m'attaque et je dis tout** just let him (try and) attack me, and I'll reveal everything
4. *sout* [dans une double hypothèse] : **il me l'interdirait ~ je le ferais quand même** I would do it even if he forbade me to
5. [répète la conjonction précédente] : **quand je serai grande et ~ j'aurai un métier** when I'm grown up and (I) have a job
6. [formule de présentation et d'insistance] : **je croyais l'affaire faite et voilà qu'elle n'est pas d'accord** I thought the deal was clinched and now I find she disagrees ▪ **si je n'ai rien dit, c'est ~ je craignais de te vexer** if I said nothing, it was because I was afraid of upsetting you ▪ **~ oui!** oh yes indeed! ▪ **~ non!** certainly not! ▪ **tu n'iras pas – ~ si!** you won't go – oh yes I will *ou* I will too! ▪ **~ tu crois/dis!** *fam* that's what YOU think/say!
7. [dans une formule interrogative] : **est-ce ~ tu viendras?** will you come? ▪ **comment qu'il a fait?** *fam* how did he manage?
◆ **que... ne** *loc conj* without ▪ **aucune décision n'est prise ~ je ne sois préalablement consulté** no decision is made without my being consulted first.
◆ **que... ou non** *loc conj* whether... or not ▪ **~ tu me croies ou non** whether you believe me or not.
◆ **que... (ou) que** *loc conj* whether... or ▪ **qu'il fasse beau, qu'il pleuve, je sors me promener** come rain or come shine, I go out for a walk.

Québec [kebɛk] *npr m* **1.** [province] : **le ~** Quebec ▪ **au ~** in Quebec ▪ **la province de** *ou* **du ~** Quebec State **2.** [ville] Quebec ▪ **à ~** in (the city of) Quebec.

LE QUÉBEC

Founded by Champlain in 1608, this Canadian province remained predominantly French-speaking after Canada became a British possession in 1763. Today, with French as its official language, it is the centre of French-Canadian culture.

québécisme [kebesism] *nm* Quebec French (turn of) phrase.

québécois, e [kebekwa, az] *adj* from Quebec.
◆ **Québécois, e** *nm, f* Québecois, Quebecker.
◆ **québécois** *nm* LING Canadian French.

Queensland [kwinslɑ̃d] *npr m* : **le ~** Queensland.

quel [kɛl] *(f* **quelle**, *mpl* **quels**, *fpl* **quelles***)* ◇ *dét (adj interr)* [personne] which ▪ [animal, chose] which, what ▪ **de ~ côté es-tu?** which *ou* whose side are you on? ▪ **je ne sais ~s sont ses projets** I don't know what his plans are ▪ **~le heure est-il?** what's the time?, what time is it?
◇ *dét (adj excl)* what ▪ **~ idiot!** what a fool! ▪ **~ sale temps!** what terrible weather! ▪ **il s'est exprimé en japonais, et avec ~le aisance!** he spoke in Japanese, and so fluently too! ▪ **~le ne fut pas ma surprise (quand je le vis entrer)!** *sout* imagine my surprise (when I saw him come in)!
◇ *dét (adj relatif)* [en corrélation avec 'que' - personne] whoever ; [- animal] whichever ; [- chose] whichever, whatever ▪ **il a refusé de recevoir les nouveaux arrivants, ~s qu'ils fussent** he refused to see the new arrivals, whoever they were ▪ **les mam-**

mifères ~s qu'ils soient all mammals ▪ **~le que soit l'assurance que vous choisissiez...** whichever the insurance policy you choose... ▪ **il se baigne ~ que soit le temps** he goes swimming whatever the weather.
◇ *pron interr* which (one) ▪ **de tous vos matches, ~ fut le plus difficile?** of all the matches you've played, which (one) was the most difficult *ou* which was the most difficult one?

quelconque [kɛlkɔ̃k] ◇ *dét (adj indéf)* **1.** [quel qu'il soit] any, some or other ▪ **si, pour une raison ~, tu ne pouvais pas venir** if, for some reason or other *ou* if, for any reason, you can't come ▪ **une ~ de ses connaissances** some acquaintance of his ▪ **as-tu une ~ idée du prix?** have you got any idea of the price? **2.** MATH & SC any.
◇ *adj* [insignifiant, banal - nourriture, visage] ordinary, plain ; [- personne] average, ordinary ; [- comédien, film, spectacle] run-of-the-mill, second-rate, (pretty) average ; [- exécution, réalisation] mediocre, lacklustre ▪ **moi, je le trouve très ~** I don't think there's anything special about him.

quelle [kɛl] *f* ▷ **quel**.

quelles [kɛl] *fpl* ▷ **quel**.

quelque [kɛlk(ə)] ◇ *dét (adj indéf)* **1.** [un peu de] some ▪ **elle est bizarre depuis ~ temps** she's been acting strangely for a *ou* some time now
2. *sout* [n'importe quel] some ▪ **il trouvera bien une ~ autre excuse** he's bound to find some new excuse or other
3. [en corrélation avec 'que'] : **dans ~ pays que tu sois** whichever *ou* whatever country you may be in ▪ **à ~ heure que ce soit** whatever the time, at whatever time.
◇ *adv sout* **1.** [approximativement] around, about ▪ **il y a ~ 40 ans de cela** that was about 40 years ago, that was 40 or so years ago
2. [en corrélation avec 'que'] : **nous y arriverons, ~ difficile que ce soit** we will manage, however difficult it may be.
◆ **quelques** *dét (adj indéf pl)* **1.** *(sans déterminant)* a few, some ▪ **amène ~s amis** bring some *ou* a few friends along ▪ **~s dizaines de journalistes** a few dozen journalists ➲ **et ~s** *fam* : **ça pèse deux kilos et ~s** it's a little *ou* a bit over two kilos ▪ **il était cinq heures et ~s** it was just after five o'clock
2. *(avec déterminant)* few ▪ **les ~s millions de téléspectateurs qui nous regardent** the few million viewers watching us.
◆ **en quelque sorte** *loc adv* **1.** [en un sens] as it were, so to speak, in a manner of speaking ▪ **c'est en ~ sorte un cheval avec un buste d'homme** it is, as it were *ou* so to speak, a horse with the head and shoulders of a man
2. [en résumé] in a nutshell, in fact.
◆ **quelque chose** *pron indéf* **1.** [dans une affirmation] something ▪ **elle a ~ chose aux poumons** she's got something wrong with her lungs ▪ **ça m'a fait ~ chose de le revoir 20 ans plus tard** it was really weird to see him 20 years later ▪ **quand il est parti, ça m'a vraiment fait ~ chose** when he left, it really affected me
2. [dans une question, une négation, une hypothèse] anything, something ▪ **s'il m'arrivait ~ chose, contactez mon notaire** if anything *ou* something should happen to me, contact my solicitor ▪ **ça te ferait vraiment ~ chose si je partais?** would it really matter to you *ou* would you feel anything if I left?
3. *fam* [dans une approximation] : **elle a ~ chose comme 80 ans** she's about 80 *ou* 80 or so ▪ **c'était une Renault 5 ou ~ chose comme ça** it was a Renault 5 or something (of the kind) *ou* like that ▪ **Anne ~ chose a téléphoné** *fam* Anne something phoned
4. *fam* [emploi expressif] : **tu vas recevoir ~ chose!** you're asking for it! ▪ **je vais te corriger, ~ chose de bien!** I'm going to give you a good *ou* proper hiding! ▪ **c'est ~ chose!** [ton exaspéré] that's a bit much! ; [ton admiratif] that's quite something!
◆ **quelque part** *loc adv* **1.** [dans un lieu] somewhere ▪ **tu vas ~ part à Noël?** are you going anywhere (special) for Christmas?
2. *fam euphém* [aux toilettes] : **elle est allée ~ part** she went to wash her hands *euphém*
3. *fam euphém* [au derrière] : **c'est mon pied ~ part que tu veux?** do you want a kick up the backside?
◆ **quelque part que** *loc conj litt* : **~ part qu'elle regardât** wherever she looked.

quelquefois [kɛlkəfwa] *adv* sometimes, from time to time ▪ **je vais ~ au concert** sometimes *ou* from time to time I go to the concerts.

quelques-uns, quelques-unes [kɛlkəzœ̃, yn] *pron indéf pl* **1.** [certains] some ▪ **~ de ses collaborateurs étaient au courant** some of his colleagues knew about it **2.** [un petit nombre] a few ▪ **tu connais ses pièces? – seulement quelques-unes** do you know his plays? – only a few of them.

quelqu'un, e [kɛlkœ̃, yn] *pron indéf litt* **~e de ces demoiselles va vous conduire** one of these young ladies will show you the way.
◆ **quelqu'un** *pron indéf m* **1.** [dans une affirmation] someone, somebody ▪ **~ te demande au téléphone** there's someone *ou* somebody on the phone for you ▪ **~ de très grand est venu** somebody very tall called ▪ **c'est ~ de bien** he's a nice person ▪ **il faut ~ de plus** one more (person) is needed ▪ **c'est ~!** [ton admiratif] she's quite somebody! ▪ **ce garçon, c'est ~!** *péj* that boy's a little horror! ▪ **elle veut devenir ~ (dans le monde de l'art)** she wants to become someone famous (in the world of art) ▪ **il se prend pour** *ou* **se croit ~** *péj* he thinks he's really something, he thinks he's it **2.** [dans une question, une négation, une hypothèse] anybody, anyone ▪ **il y a ~?** is (there) anybody in? ▪ **~ parmi vous le connaît-il?** do any of you know him?

quels [kɛl] *mpl* ▷ **quel**.

quémander [3] [kemɑ̃de] *vt* [aide, argent, nourriture] to beg for *(insép)* ▪ [compliment] to fish *ou* to angle for *(insép)* ▪ **ton chien est toujours à ~ des caresses** your dog is always wanting to be stroked.

quémandeur, euse [kemɑ̃dœr, øz] *nm, f litt* [mendiant] beggar.

qu'en-dira-t-on [kɑ̃diratɔ̃] *nm inv* gossip ▪ **elle a peur du ~** she's afraid of what people will say.

quenelle [kənɛl] *nf* : **~ (de poisson)** (fish) quenelle.

quenotte [kənɔt] *nf fam* toothy (peg).

quenouille [kənuj] *nf* **1.** TEXT distaff ▪ **tomber en ~** HIST to fall to the distaff ; [échouer] to go to rack and ruin **2.** [d'un lit] bedpost **3.** MÉTALL stopper **4.** BOT [tige] bulrush.

quéquette△ [kekɛt] *nf* willy *UK*, peter *US*.

querelle [kərɛl] *nf* quarrel ▪ [verbale] quarrel, argument ▪ **une vieille ~** a long-standing quarrel ▪ **ce n'est qu'une ~ d'amoureux** it's only a lovers' tiff ▪ **~ de famille** [brouille] family squabble ; [sérieuse] family feud ▪ **la ~ déclenchée au sein du gouvernement** the row sparked off within the cabinet ➲ **~ de personnes** ad personam quarrel.

quereller [4] [kərele] *vt sout* to reprimand.
◆ **se quereller** *vp (emploi réciproque)* to quarrel (with one another) ▪ **elles se querellent pour des riens** they quarrel *ou* squabble over nothing.
◆ **se quereller avec** *vp+prép* to have an argument *ou* to quarrel with.

querelleur, euse [kərɛlœr, øz] ◇ *adj* quarrelsome, belligerent ▪ **il est très ~** he's always picking fights *ou* looking for arguments.
◇ *nm, f* quarrelsome person.

quérir [kerir] *vt (infinitif seulement) litt* **envoyer** *ou* **faire ~ qqn** to summon sb ▪ **venir/aller ~ qqn** to come/to go and fetch sb.

qu'est-ce que [kɛskə], **qu'est-ce qui** [kɛski] = **que** *(pron interr)*.

questeur [kɛstœr] *nm* **1.** ANTIQ quaestor **2.** POLIT parliamentary administrator.

question [kɛstjɔ̃] *nf* **1.** [interrogation] question ▪ **je ferme la porte à clé? – bien sûr, quelle** *ou* **cette ~!** shall I lock the door? – of course, what a question! ▪ **peut-on lui faire confiance, toute la ~ est là** *ou* **voilà la ~!** can she be trusted, that's the question! ▪ **poser une ~ à qqn** to ask sb a question ▪ **c'est moi qui pose les ~s!** I'm (the one) asking the questions!, I do the asking! ▪ **poser une ~** POLIT to table a question ▪ **je commence à me poser des ~s sur sa compétence** I'm beginning to have (my) doubts about *ou* to wonder how competent he is ▪ **se poser la ~ de savoir si** to ask o.s. whether ➲ **~ écrite/orale** POLIT written/oral question ▪ **poser la ~ de confiance** POLIT to ask for a

vote of confidence ▪ ~ **piège** JEUX trick question ; [dans un interrogatoire] loaded *ou* leading question ▪ ~ **subsidiaire** JEUX tiebreaker
2. [sujet] question, topic ▶ **être ~ de : de quoi est-il ~ dans ce paragraphe?** what is this paragraph about? ▪ **dans notre prochaine émission, il sera ~ de l'architecture romane** in our next programme, we will examine Roman architecture ▪ **il n'est jamais ~ de la répression dans son livre** repression is never mentioned in his book ▪ **prête-moi 1 000 euros – pas ~!** *fam* lend me 1,000 euros – no way *ou* nothing doing! ▪ **il n'en est pas ~!, c'est hors de ~!** it's out of the question! ▪ **avec mon salaire, une voiture c'est hors de ~** with my salary, a car is out of the question ▪ **je veux sortir ce soir – c'est hors de ~!** I want to go out tonight – you can forget it *ou* it's out of the question! ▪ **il n'est pas ~ *ou* il est hors de ~ que je le voie!** there's no way I'll see him!, there's no question of my seeing him! ▪ ~ **salaire, je ne me plains pas** *fam* as far as the salary is concerned *ou* salary-wise, I'm not complaining
3. [affaire, difficulté] question, matter, point (at issue) ▪ **la ~ du nucléaire** the nuclear energy question *ou* issue ▪ **là n'est pas la ~** that's not the point (at issue) *ou* the issue ▪ **ce n'est plus qu'une ~ de temps** it's only a question *ou* matter of time ▪ **c'est une ~ de vie ou de mort** it's a matter of life and death ▪ **ils se sont disputés pour des ~s d'argent** they had an argument over *ou* about money ▪ **je ne lis pas les critiques, ~ de principe!** I don't read reviews on principle! ▪ **ça c'est une autre ~!** that's another problem *ou* story!
4. *sout* **faire ~** [être douteux] : **son talent ne fait pas (de) ~** her talent is beyond (all) question *ou* (any) doubt
5. HIST question ▪ **mettre *ou* soumettre qqn à la ~** to put sb to the question.
➡ **en question** ◇ *loc adj* in question, concerned.
◇ *loc adv* : **mettez-vous mon honnêteté en ~?** are you questioning my honesty? ▪ **remettre en ~** [mettre en doute] to (call into) question, to challenge ; [compromettre] to call into question ▪ **la moindre querelle et leur couple est remis en ~** the slightest argument and their relationship is put in jeopardy ▪ **se remettre en ~** to do some soul searching.

questionnaire [kɛstjɔnɛr] *nm* questionnaire ▪ ~ **à choix multiple = QCM.**

questionner [3] [kɛstjɔne] *vt* [interroger] : ~ **qqn** to question sb, to ask sb questions.

questionneur, euse [kɛstjɔnœr, øz] *nm, f litt* questioner ▪ **les enfants sont souvent des ~s** children often ask a lot of questions.

questure [kɛstyr] *nf* **1.** ANTIQ quaestorship **2.** POLIT treasury and administrative department of the French Parliament.

quête [kɛt] *nf* **1.** [d'argent] collection ▪ **faire une ~** to collect money, to make a collection ▪ **faire la ~** [à l'église] to take (the) collection ; [dans la rue] to go round with the hat, to pass the hat round **2.** *litt* [recherche] quest ▪ **la ~ du Graal** the Quest for the Holy Grail **3.** CHASSE search **4.** NAUT rake.
➡ **en quête de** *loc prép sout* in search *ou* pursuit of, searching for, questing for *litt* ▪ **se mettre en ~ de** to go in search of ▪ **elle est en ~ d'un travail** she's job-hunting.

quêter [4] [kete] ◇ *vi* [à l'église] to take (the) collection ▪ [parmi un groupe] to collect money, to make a collection ▪ [dans la rue] to pass the hat round, to go round with the hat ▪ ~ **pour les pauvres/handicapés** to collect money for the poor/handicapped.
◇ *vt litt* [pitié, regard approbateur] to beg for *(insép)*.

quêteur, euse [kɛtœr, øz] *nm, f* collector.

quetsche [kwɛtʃ] *nf* **1.** BOT quetsch (plum) **2.** [eau-de-vie] quetsch brandy.

queue [kø] *nf* **1.** ZOOL tail ▪ **faire une ~ de poisson à qqn** AUTO to cut in in front of sb ▪ **il est parti la ~ basse** *fam ou* **entre les jambes** *fam* he left with his tail between his legs **2.** BOT [d'une cerise, d'une feuille] stalk ▪ [d'une fleur] stalk, stem **3.** [extrémité - d'une poêle] handle ; [- d'un avion, d'une comète, d'un cerf-volant] tail ; [- d'une étoile filante] trail ; [- d'un cortège] back, tail (end) ; [- d'un orage, d'un tourbillon] tail (end) ; [- d'une procession, d'un train] rear ▪ **je monte toujours en ~** I always get on at the rear (of the train) ▪ **il est en ~ de peloton** SPORT he is at the back *ou* rear of the bunch ▪ **pas la ~ d'un** *fam ou* **d'une** *fam* : **on pourrait prendre un taxi – je n'en ai pas encore vu la ~ d'un** *fam familier* we could get a taxi – I haven't seen hide nor hair of one yet ▶ **n'avoir ni ~ ni tête : ce que tu dis n'a ni ~ ni tête** you make no sense at all, you're talking nonsense ▪ **la pièce n'avait ni ~ ni tête** you couldn't make head or *ou* nor tail of the play ▪ **une histoire sans ~ ni tête** a shaggy-dog story **4.** [dans un classement] bottom ▪ **être à la ~ de la classe/du championnat** to be at the bottom of the class/league **5.** [file d'attente] queue *UK*, line *US* ▪ **faire la ~** to queue (up) *(insép) UK*, to stand in line *US* **6.** ▲ [pénis] cock▲, prick▲ **7.** JEUX : ~ **(de billard)** (billiard) cue **8.** CONSTR [d'une marche] tail ▪ [d'une pierre] (inner) tail ▪ ~ **d'aronde** dovetail **9.** INDUST du pétrole tails, bottoms **10.** IMPR [d'une lettre] stem, tail, descender *spéc* ▪ [d'une note de musique] stem ▪ [d'une page] tail, foot.
➡ **à la queue leu leu** *loc adv* in single *ou* Indian file.

queue-de-cheval [køtʃəval] (*pl* **queues-de-cheval**) *nf* **1.** [cheveux] ponytail **2.** ANAT cauda equina.

queue-de-pie [kødpi] (*pl* **queues-de-pie**) *nf* tail coat.

queue-de-renard [kødrənar] (*pl* **queues-de-renard**) *nf* BOT [amarante] love lies bleeding ▪ [mélampyre] cow-wheat ▪ [vulpin] foxtail fescue.

qui [ki] ◇ *pron rel* **1.** [représente une personne] who, that ▪ **il y a des gens ~ aiment ça** there are people who like that ▪ **toi ~ connais le problème, tu pourras m'aider** you who *ou* as you are acquainted with the problem, you can help me out ▪ *(après une prép)* whom, who ▪ **la personne à ~ je l'ai prêté** the person to whom I lent it *sout*, the person I lent it to ▪ **il ne peut résister à ~ lui fait des compliments** he can't resist anyone who pays him compliments ▪ **c'est à ~ aura le dernier mot** each tries *ou* they all try to have the last word ▪ **les personnes au nom de ~ ils ont agi** the people in whose name they acted ▪ **l'amie par ~ j'ai eu cette adresse** the friend from whom I got this address *sout*, the friend I got this address from ▪ **c'est rebutant pour ~ n'est pas habitué** it's disconcerting for somebody who isn't *ou* for whoever isn't used to it ‖ [sans antécédent] whoever, anyone (who) ▪ ~ **tu sais, ~ vous savez** you know who ▪ **il est allé chez ~ tu sais hier soir** he went to you know who's last night
2. [représente un animal] which, that
3. [représente une chose, une idée] which, that ▪ **le festival, ~ débutera en mai** the festival, which will start in May ▪ **donne-moi le magazine ~ est sur la table** give me the magazine (that) *ou* which is on the table
4. [après des verbes de perception] : **je l'ai entendu ~ se plaignait** I heard him moaning
5. [formule de présentation] : **le voilà ~ pleure, maintenant!** now he's crying!
6. [en corrélation avec 'que'] : ~ **que tu sois, ~ que vous soyez** whoever you are *ou* you may be *sout* ▪ ~ **que ce soit qui téléphone, répondez que je suis absent** whoever phones, tell them I'm not here
7. *loc* : ~ **aime bien châtie bien** spare the rod and spoil the child ▪ ~ **ne dit mot consent** silence is consent ▪ ~ **vole un œuf vole un bœuf** he that will steal a penny will steal a pound.
◇ *pron interr* **1.** [sujet ou attribut dans le discours direct] who ▪ ~ **donc t'a frappé?** who hit you? ▪ ~ **est-ce qui en veut?** who wants some? ▪ **c'est ~ qui** *fam*, ~ **c'est qui** *fam* who ‖ [objet dans le discours direct] who, whom *sout* ▪ ~ **cherchez-vous?** who are you looking for? ▪ **c'est à ~?** whose is it, to whom does it belong? *sout* ▪ **à ~ le tour?** whose turn (is it)? ▪ **de ~ parles-tu?** who *ou* whom *sout* are you talking about? ▪ ~ **est-ce que** who, whom *sout* ▪ ~ **est-ce que tu connais ici?** who do you know around here? ▪ **à ~ est-ce que je dois de l'argent?** who do I owe money to?, to whom do I owe money? *sout*
2. [sujet dans le discours indirect] who ▪ **je ne vois pas ~ pourrait t'aider** I can't see who could *ou* I can't think of anyone who could help you ‖ [objet dans le discours indirect] who, whom *sout* ▪ **sais-tu ~ j'ai rencontré ce matin?** do you know who I met this morning? ▪ **je ne me souviens pas à ~ je l'ai donné** I can't remember who I gave it to.
➡ **qui... qui** *loc corrélative sout* : **ils étaient déguisés, ~ en Pierrot, ~ en bergère** they were in fancy dress, some as Pierrots, others as shepherdesses.

quia [kɥija] ◆ **à quia** *loc adv* ***sout*** **être à ~** to be at a loss for an answer ■ **mettre** *ou* **réduire qqn à ~** to confound sb.

quiche [kiʃ] *nf* quiche ■ **~ lorraine** quiche lorraine.

quiconque [kikɔ̃k] ◇ *pron rel* whoever ■ **~ frappera par l'épée périra par l'épée** BIBLE he who lives by the sword shall die by the sword.
◇ *pron indéf* anyone *ou* anybody (else) ■ **il connaît les volcans mieux que ~** he knows volcanoes better than anybody else *ou* than anyone alive.

quid [kwid] *pron interr* ***sout*** & ***hum*** **: ~ de...?** what about...?

Quid® [kwid] *npr m annually updated one-volume encyclopedia of facts and figures.*

quidam [kidam] *nm* ***hum*** & ***sout*** fellow, individual.

qui est-ce que [kiɛskø], **qui est-ce qui** [kiɛski] = **qui** *(pron interr).*

quiet, ète [kjɛ, ɛt] *adj* ***litt*** calm, tranquil ***litt.***

quiétisme [kjetism] *nm* quietism.

quiétude [kjetyd] *nf* ***litt*** **1.** [d'une demeure] quiet, tranquillity, quietude ***litt*** **2.** [d'esprit] peace of mind ■ **elle attendait les résultats en toute ~** she was calmly waiting for the results.

quignon [kiɲɔ̃] *nm* **: ~ (de pain)** [morceau] (crusty) chunk of bread ; [extrémité] heel (of the loaf).

quille [kij] *nf* **1.** JEUX skittle ■ **jouer aux ~s** to play ninepins *ou* skittles **2.** ***fam*** [jambe] pin ***esp UK***, leg **3.** △ ***arg mil*** [fin du service] demob *UK*, discharge **4.** NAUT keel.

quilleur, euse [kijœr, øz] *nm, f* ***Québec*** skittle player.

quincaillerie [kɛ̃kajri] *nf* **1.** [articles, commerce] hardware **2.** [boutique] ironmonger's *UK*, hardware store *US* **3.** ***fam*** [bijoux, décorations] (cheap) baubles ***péj*** ■ [armes] guns ■ **il ne sort jamais sans toute sa ~** he's always armed to the teeth when he goes out **4.** ***fam*** INFORM hardware.

quincaillier, ère [kɛ̃kaje, ɛr] *nm, f* hardware dealer, ironmonger *UK.*

quinconce [kɛ̃kɔ̃s] *nm* HORT quincunx ■ **en ~** quincuncial, arranged in a quincunx.

quinine [kinin] *nf* quinine.

quinqua [kɛ̃ka] *nmf* fiftysomething.

quinquagénaire [kɛ̃kaʒenɛr] ◇ *adj* **: être ~** [avoir de 50 à 60 ans] to be in one's fifties ; [avoir 50 ans] to be fifty.
◇ *nmf* [de 50 à 60 ans] person in his/her fifties ■ [de 50 ans] 50-year-old man (*f* woman).

quinquennal, e, aux [kɛ̃kenal, o] *adj* [plan] five-year *(avant n)* ■ [élection, foire] five-yearly, quinquennial.

quinquennat [kɛ̃kena] *nm* five-year period, quinquennium, lustrum.

quinquina [kɛ̃kina] *nm* **1.** BOT & PHARM cinchona **2.** [boisson] quinine tonic wine.

quintal, aux [kɛ̃tal, o] *nm* (metric) quintal.

quinte [kɛ̃t] *nf* **1.** MÉD **: ~ (de toux)** coughing fit, fit of coughing **2.** MUS fifth **3.** JEUX quint **4.** ESCRIME quinte.

quintessence [kɛ̃tesɑ̃s] *nf* ***litt*** quintessence ■ **la ~ du romantisme** the epitome *ou* quintessence *ou* very essence of Romanticism.

quintet [kɛ̃tɛt] *nm* jazz quintet.

quintette [kɛ̃tɛt] *nm* quintet, quintette ■ **~ à cordes/vent** string/wind quintet.

quintuple [kɛ̃typl] ◇ *adj* [somme, quantité] quintuple, fivefold.
◇ *nm* quintuple ■ **le ~ de sa valeur** five times its value.

quintupler [3] [kɛ̃typle] ◇ *vt* to quintuple, to increase fivefold.
◇ *vi* **: la paix a fait ~ le nombre des naissances** peace has increased the number of births by five.

quintuplés, ées [kɛ̃typle] *nm, f pl* quintuplets, quins.

quinzaine [kɛ̃zɛn] *nf* **1.** [durée] **: une ~ de jours** a fortnight, two weeks ■ **venez me voir dans une ~** come and see me in a couple of weeks *ou* in two weeks *ou* in a fortnight's time **2.** [quantité] **: une ~ de** about fifteen ■ **une ~ de crayons** about fifteen pencils, fifteen pencils or so **3.** COMM **: ~ commerciale** two-week sale ■ **la grande ~ des prix littéraires** the literary prize season *(two-week period in November and December when all the major French literary prizes are awarded)* **4.** [salaire] fortnight's pay, two-week's pay *ou* wages.

quinze [kɛ̃z] ◇ *dét* fifteen ■ **~ jours** two weeks, a fortnight, *voir aussi* **cinq.**
◇ *nm inv* **1.** [nombre] fifteen ■ **lundi en ~** a fortnight on *UK ou* two weeks from Monday **2.** SPORT **: le ~ de France** the French Fifteen.

quinzième [kɛ̃zjɛm] *adj num, nmf* & *nm* fifteenth, *voir aussi* **cinquième.**

quiproquo [kiprɔko] *nm* [sur l'identité d'une personne] mistake ■ **l'intrigue est fondée sur un ~** the plot revolves round a case of mistaken identity ‖ [sur le sujet d'une conversation] misunderstanding ■ **il y a ~, nous ne parlons pas du même étudiant** there is a misunderstanding, we're not talking about the same student.

quittance [kitɑ̃s] *nf* **: ~ de gaz/d'électricité** gas/electricity bill ■ **~ de loyer** rent receipt.

quitte [kit] *adj* **1.** [libéré - d'une dette, d'une obligation] **: être ~ envers qqn** to be even *ou* quits *ou* (all) square with sb ■ **être ~ d'une dette** to be rid *ou* clear of a debt ■ **donne-moi seulement 500 euros, tu es ~ du reste** just give me 500 euros, let's not worry about the rest *ou* I'll let you off the rest ■ **être ~ envers la société** [après une peine de prison] to have paid one's debt to society ■ **je ne te tiens pas ~ de ta promesse!** I don't consider that you have fulfilled your promise! **2.** [au même niveau] **: être ~s** to be quits *ou* all square **3.** [s'en tirer avec qqch] **: en être ~ pour qqch** to get away with sthg ■ **il en a été ~ pour quelques égratignures/la peur** he got away with a few scratches/a bit of a fright **4.** [devoir faire] **: en être ~ pour faire : j'ai oublié mes papiers à la banque, j'en suis ~ pour y retourner** I've left my papers at the bank, so I have to go back there now **5.** JEUX **: ~ ou double** double or quits *UK ou* nothing ■ **c'est jouer à ~ ou double** ***fig*** it's a big gamble *ou* risk.
◆ **quitte à** *loc prép* **1.** [au risque de] **: je lui dirai, ~ à me faire renvoyer** I'll tell him, even if it means being fired **2.** [puisqu'il faut] since it is necessary to ■ **~ à les inviter, autant le faire dans les règles** since we have to invite them, we may as well do things properly.

quitter [3] [kite] *vt* **1.** [lieu] to leave ■ [ami, époux] to leave, to split up with *(insép)* ■ [emploi] to leave, to quit, to give up *(sép)* ■ [habitude] to drop, to get rid of *(insép)* ■ **je quitte (le bureau) à 5 h** I leave the office *ou* I finish at 5 o'clock ■ **la voiture a quitté la route** the car came off *ou* ran off *ou* left the road ■ **il faut que je te quitte** I must be going, I must go ■ **il ne la quitta pas des yeux** *ou* **du regard** he never took his eyes off her, he watched her every move ■ **il nous a quittés hier** ***euphém*** he passed away yesterday ■ **elle a quitté ce monde** ***euphém*** she has departed this world *ou* this life **2.** ***sout*** [abandonner - suj: courage, force] to leave, to forsake ***sout***, to desert ■ **son optimisme ne l'a jamais quitté** he remained optimistic throughout ■ **son bon sens semblait l'avoir quitté** he seemed to have taken leave of his senses **3.** [retirer - habit] to take off *(sép)* ■ **~ le deuil** to come out of mourning **4.** [au téléphone] **: ne quittez pas** hold on, hold the line **5.** INFORM to exit.
◆ **se quitter** *vp (emploi réciproque)* [amis] to part ■ [époux] to part, to break *ou* to split up ■ **quittons-nous bons amis** let's part on good terms ■ **depuis qu'ils se sont rencontrés, ils ne se quittent plus** ever since they met they have been inseparable.

quitus [kitys] *nm* DR (full) discharge, quietus ■ **donner ~ à qqn** to discharge sb.

qui-vive [kiviv] *nm inv* : **être sur le ~** [soldat] to be on the alert *ou* the qui vive ; [animal] to be on the alert ▪ **je la sentais sur le ~** I felt she was on edge, I felt she was waiting for something to happen.

qui vive [kiviv] *interj* : **~?** who goes there?

quoi [kwa] ◇ *pron rel* what, which ▪ **c'est ce à ~ je voulais en venir** that's what I was getting at ▪ **il a refusé, ce en ~ il a eu raison** he refused, which was quite right of him ▪ **on est allés au jardin, après ~ il a fallu rentrer** we went to the garden, and then we had to come back in ▪ **prends de ~ boire/écrire/payer** get something to drink/to write/to pay with ▪ **il y a de ~ nourrir au moins 10 personnes** there's enough to feed at least 10 people ▪ **il n'y a pas de ~ se faire du souci** there's nothing to worry about ▪ **je suis en colère – il y a de ~!** *fam* I'm angry – it's no wonder *ou* with good reason! ▪ **sur ~ il se lève et sort** whereupon he got up and left ➊ **merci! – il n'y a pas de ~** thank you! – not at all *ou* you're welcome *ou* don't mention it.
◇ *adv interr* **1.** [quelle chose] what ▪ **c'est ~?** what's that? ▪ **tu fais ~ ce soir?** *fam* what are you doing this evening? ▪ **elle est à ~ ta glace?** *fam* what flavour is your ice cream? ▪ **en ~ puis-je vous être utile?** how can I help you? ▪ **par ~ se sent-il concerné?** what does he feel concerned about? ▪ **je voudrais parler au directeur – c'est pour ~?** I'd like to talk to the manager – what (is it) about? ▪ **sur ~ va-t-elle travailler?** what is she going to work on? ▪ **salut, alors ~ de neuf?** *fam* hi, what have you been up to *ou* what's new? ▪ **~ de plus naturel?** what could be more natural? ▪ **à ~ bon?** what's the use? ▪ **à ~ bon l'attendre?** what's the use of waiting for him? ▪ **~ encore?** what else? ; [ton irrité] what is it now? **2.** *fam* [pour faire répéter] : **~?** what? **3.** [emplois expressifs] : **eh bien ~, qu'est-ce que tu as?** well, what's the matter with you? ▪ **enfin ~,** *ou* **eh bien ~, tu pourrais regarder où tu vas!** come on now, watch where you're going! ▪ **de ~? tu n'es pas d'accord?** what's that, you don't agree? ▪ **tu viens (oui) ou ~?** are you coming or not? ▪ **décide-toi, ~!** well make up your mind! ▪ **si je comprends bien, tu es fauché, ~!** if I've understood you, you're broke, aren't you? ▪ **je vais lui acheter ce livre, pour lui faire un petit cadeau, ~** I'm going to buy her this book... you know, just as a little present.
◆ **quoi que** *loc conj* : **~ qu'il arrive** whatever happens ▪ **~ qu'il en soit** be that as it may, however that may be ▪ **je te défends de lui dire ~ que ce soit!** I forbid you to tell her/him anything (whatsoever)! ▪ **si je peux t'aider en ~ que ce soit** if I can help you in any way ➊ **~ qu'il en ait** *sout* whatever he feels about it.

quoique [kwakə] *(devant voyelle ou 'h' muet* **quoiqu'** [kwak]*)* *conj* **1.** [bien que] though, although ▪ **quoiqu'il fût déjà minuit** though *ou* although it was already midnight **2.** [introduisant une restriction] : **il a l'air compétent... ~...** he seems competent... mind you...

quolibet [kɔlibɛ] *nm* *sout* gibe, jeer, taunt ▪ **les enfants le poursuivaient de leurs ~s** the children jeered at him *ou* taunted him relentlessly.

quorum [k(w)ɔrɔm] *nm* *sout* quorum ▪ **nous avons atteint le ~** we're quorate *sout*, we have a quorum.

quota [k(w)ɔta] *nm* quota ▪ **~ à l'exportation** export quota ▪ **~ laitier** milk quota.

quote-part [kɔtpar] (*pl* **quotes-parts**) *nf* share.

quotidien, enne [kɔtidjɛ̃, ɛn] *adj* **1.** [de chaque jour - entraînement, promenade, repas] daily ; [- préoccupations] everyday ▪ **leurs disputes étaient devenues presque ~nes** they'd got to the stage where they were arguing almost every day **2.** [routinier - tâche] run-of-the-mill, humdrum.
◆ **quotidien** *nm* daily (paper) ▪ **un grand ~** a (major) national daily.
◆ **au quotidien** *loc adv fam* on a day-to-day basis ▪ **vivre sa vie au ~** to live from day to day.

quotidiennement [kɔtidjɛnmɑ̃] *adv* daily, every day.

quotidienneté [kɔtidjɛnte] *nf* everyday nature ▪ **la ~ de leur existence** the routine of their everyday life.

quotient [kɔsjɑ̃] *nm* **1.** MATH quotient **2.** PSYCHOL : **~ intellectuel** intelligence quotient **3.** DR : **~ électoral** electoral quota ▪ **~ familial** tax code.

quotité [kɔtite] *nf* **1.** FIN quota **2.** DR : **~ disponible** disposable portion (of estate).

QWERTY [kwɛrti] *adj inv* : **clavier ~** QWERTY keyboard.

R

r, R [ɛr] *nm* r, R, *voir aussi* **g**.

r = **rue**.

R 1. = **röntgen 2.** (*abr écrite de* **rand**) R.

Râ [ra] = **Rê**.

rab [rab] *nm* *fam* **qui veut du ~?** [à table] anyone for seconds? ■ **alors, on fait du ~?** [au travail] doing some overtime, are we?
◆ **en rab** *loc adj* *fam* **il y a des patates en ~** there are some spuds left (over) ■ **un ticket en ~** a spare ticket.

rabâchage [rabaʃaʒ] *nm* *fam* **son cours, c'est vraiment du ~** he's always going over the same old things in class.

rabâcher [3] [rabaʃe] *fam* ◇ *vt* **1.** [conseils] to keep (on) repeating ■ [malheurs] to keep harping on about ■ **tu n'arrêtes pas de ~ la même chose** you're like a record that's got stuck, you do go on **2.** [leçon] to go over (and over) *(insép)*.
◇ *vi* to keep repeating o.s., to keep harping on.

rabâcheur, euse [rabaʃœr, øz] *nm, f* *fam* drone, bore.

rabais [rabɛ] *nm* reduction, discount ■ **avec un ~ de 15 %, avec 15 % de ~** with a 15% discount *ou* reduction ■ **faire un ~ de 10 % sur le prix** to knock 10% off the price.
◆ **au rabais** ◇ *loc adj* [vente] cut-price ■ *péj* [formation] second-rate ■ [travail] underpaid.
◇ *loc adv* : **vendre au ~** to sell at a reduced price *ou* discount ■ **elle travaille au ~** she works for a pittance.

rabaissant, e [rabɛsɑ̃, ɑ̃t] *adj* degrading, debasing.

rabaisser [4] [rabese] *vt* **1.** [diminuer - prétentions] to moderate, to reduce ; [- niveau] to lower ; [- orgueil] to humble ; [- prix] to reduce, to lower **2.** [dévaloriser - mérites, personne] to devalue, to belittle ■ **de tels actes rabaissent l'homme au niveau des animaux** such actions reduce man to the level of an animal.
◆ **se rabaisser** *vp (emploi réfléchi)* **1.** [se dévaloriser] to belittle o.s., to sell o.s. short **2.** [s'avilir] to degrade o.s.

rabat [raba] ◇ *v* ▷ **rabattre**.
◇ *nm* [d'un sac, d'une poche] flap ■ [de toge] bands.

Rabat [raba] *npr* Rabat.

rabat-joie [rabaʒwa] ◇ *nmf* killjoy, spoilsport.
◇ *adj inv* : **ce qu'ils sont ~!** what a bunch of killjoys they are!

rabattable [rabatabl] *adj* [siège] folding.

rabattage [rabataʒ] *nm* CHASSE beating.

rabattement [rabatmɑ̃] *nm* GÉOM rabatment.

rabatteur, euse [rabatœr, øz] *nm, f* **1.** CHASSE beater **2.** COMM tout **3.** POLIT canvasser.
◆ **rabatteur** *nm* AGRIC reel.

rabattre [83] [rabatr] *vt* **1.** [toit ouvrant, strapontin - pour baisser] to pull down *(sép)* ; [- pour lever] to pull up *(sép)* ■ [couvercle] to shut down *(sép)*, to close ■ [chapeau] to pull down *(sép)* ■ [col, visière] to turn down *(sép)* ■ **rabats le drap sur la couverture** fold the sheet back over the blanket ■ **les cheveux rabattus sur le front** hair brushed forward *ou* down over the forehead ■ **rabats le capot de la voiture** close the bonnet of the car ■ **une bourrasque rabattit le volet contre le mur** a gust of wind blew the shutter back against the wall ■ **de la fumée rabattue par le vent** smoke blown back by the wind ■ **le vent rabattait la pluie contre son visage** the wind was driving the rain against his face
2. CHASSE to drive ■ **la police rabattait les manifestants vers** *ou* **sur la place** the police were driving the demonstrators (back) towards the square ▌[racoler] : **~ des clients** *fam* to tout for customers
3. [déduire] to take off *(sép)*, to deduct ■ **il a rabattu 5 % sur le prix affiché** he took *ou* knocked 5 % off the marked price
4. [diminuer] : **~ l'orgueil de qqn** to humble sb ➊ **en ~** *sout* [modérer ses exigences] to climb down *(insép)*, to lower one's sights
5. COUT to stitch down *(sép)* ■ **~ une couture** to fell a seam ▌[en tricot] : **~ deux mailles** to decrease two stitches ■ **~ toutes les mailles** to cast off
6. TEXT to tone down *(sép)*.
◆ **se rabattre** *vpi* **1.** [véhicule - graduellement] to move back into position ; [- brusquement] to cut in ■ **le car s'est rabattu juste devant moi** the bus cut in just in front of me
2. [se fermer - volet] to slam shut ; [- table] to fold away.
◆ **se rabattre sur** *vp+prép* [se contenter de] to fall back on, to make do with ■ **il a dû se ~ sur un emploi de veilleur de nuit** he had to make do with a night watchman's job.

rabbin [rabɛ̃] *nm* rabbi ■ **grand ~** Chief Rabbi.

rabelaisien, enne [rablɛzjɛ̃, ɛn] *adj* Rabelaisian.

rabibocher [3] [rabibɔʃe] *vt* *fam* **1.** [réconcilier] to patch things up between, to bring together again **2.** *vieilli* [réparer] to fix *ou* to patch up.
◆ **se rabibocher** *vpi* to make up ■ **se ~ avec qqn** to patch things up with sb.

rabioter [3] [rabjɔte] *vt* *fam* **1.** [obtenir en supplément] to wangle **2.** [s'octroyer] : **il m'a rabioté 2 euros sur la monnaie** he pocketed 2 euros when he gave me my change.

rabique [rabik] *adj* rabies *(modif)*, rabic.

râble [rabl] *nm* **1.** ZOOL back ■ **~ de lièvre** CULIN saddle of hare ■ **tomber** *ou* **sauter sur le ~ de qqn** *fam* [attaquer] to lay into sb, to go for sb ; [critiquer] to go for sb **2.** MÉTALL rabble, rake ■ TECHNOL rake.

râblé, e [rable] *adj* **1.** [animal] broad-backed **2.** [personne] stocky.

râbler [3] [rable] *vt* MÉTALL to rabble ■ TECHNOL to rake (out).

rabot [rabo] *nm* MENUIS plane ■ **dent ~** straight tooth *(in raker set)*.

rabotage [rabɔtaʒ], **rabotement** [rabɔtmɑ̃] *nm* planing (down).

raboter [3] [rabɔte] *vt* to plane (down).
◆ **se raboter** *vpt*: **je me suis raboté le genou contre le mur** I scraped my knee on the wall.

raboteur [rabɔtœr] *nm* [ouvrier] planer.

raboteux, euse [rabɔtø, øz] *adj* **1.** [sentier] bumpy, rugged ▪ [plancher] uneven, rough **2.** *litt* [style] rugged, unpolished, rough.
◆ **raboteuse** *nf* [outil] planing machine, planer.

rabougri, e [rabugri] *adj* **1.** [étiolé] scraggy ▪ [desséché] shrivelled **2.** *fam* [chétif] stunted ▪ [ratatiné] shrivelled, wizened.

rabougrir [32] [rabugrir] *vt* [dessécher] to shrivel (up) ▪ [entraver la croissance de] to stunt (the growth of).
◆ **se rabougrir** *vpi* **1.** [plante] to shrivel (up) **2.** *fam* [personne] to become wizened, to become shrivelled (with age).

rabouter [3] [rabute] *vt* [tuyaux] to join, to put end to end ▪ [cordes] to tie together *(sép)*, to put end to end ▪ **ce n'est pas une anthologie, seulement quelques textes raboutés** *fig* it's not an anthology, only a few bits of prose thrown *ou* stuck together.

rabrouer [3] [rabrue] *vt* to send packing ▪ **se faire ~ par qqn** to feel the sharp end of sb's tongue.

racaille [rakaj] *nf péj* rabble, riff-raff.

raccard [rakar] *nm Suisse grain store typical of the Valais region.*

raccommodable [rakɔmɔdabl] *adj* mendable, repairable.

raccommodage [rakɔmɔdaʒ] *nm* [de linge, d'un filet] mending, repairing ▪ [d'une chaussette] darning, mending ▪ **j'ai du ~ à faire** I've got some mending to do.

raccommodement [rakɔmɔdmɑ̃] *nm fam* reconciliation.

raccommoder [3] [rakɔmɔde] *vt* **1.** [réparer - linge, filet] to repair, to mend ; [- chaussette] to darn, to mend **2.** *fam* [réconcilier] to bring together (again) ▪ **je suis raccommodé avec elle** I've made it up with her, I'm back with her again.
◆ **se raccommoder** *vpi fam* [se réconcilier] to be reconciled, to get together (again) ▪ **ils finiront bien par se ~** they're bound to get back together again.

raccommodeur, euse [rakɔmɔdœr, øz] *nm, f* mender.

raccompagner [3] [rakɔ̃paɲe] *vt* **1.** [reconduire à la porte] : **~ qqn** to show *ou* to see sb out **2.** [accompagner] : **je vais te ~ chez toi** [à pied] I'll walk *ou* take you back home ; [en voiture] I'll give you a lift home, I'll drive *ou* run you home ▪ **~ qqn à la gare/à l'aéroport** to see sb off at the station/airport ▪ **je me suis fait ~ en voiture après la soirée** I asked someone to give me a lift home after the party.

raccord [rakɔr] *nm* **1.** [en décoration] join ▪ **papier avec ~** wallpaper with pattern match ▪ **tissu sans ~** random match material **2.** CINÉ [liaison de scènes] continuity ▪ [plan] link shot ▪ **scène de ~** link scene ▮ LITTÉR link **3.** [retouche] touch-up ▪ **la peinture de la cuisine a besoin de quelques ~s** the kitchen paintwork needs some touching up ▪ **elle s'est fait un petit ~ devant la glace** *fam* she touched up her make-up in front of the mirror **4.** TECHNOL [pour tuyaux différents] adaptor ▪ [joint] connector ▪ **~ en T** T-union.

raccordement [rakɔrdəmɑ̃] *nm* **1.** [opération de connexion - RAIL] linking, joining ▪ TRAV PUB connecting, linking, joining ▪ ÉLECTR joining, connecting ▪ **faire le ~ (au réseau)** TÉLÉCOM to connect the phone **2.** [voie ferrée] junction.

raccorder [3] [rakɔrde] *vt* **1.** [route, chemin de fer] to link *ou* to join up *(sép)* **2.** [morceaux cassés, papier peint] to align, to join (up) ▪ [bandes magnétiques] to splice ▪ **les motifs ne sont pas raccordés** the pattern doesn't line up **3.** ÉLECTR [au secteur] to couple ▪ [à un circuit] to join **4.** TÉLÉCOM : **~ qqn au réseau** to connect (up) sb's phone **5.** *fig* [indices, faits] to link up *(sép)*, to connect **6.** CINÉ [scènes] to link up *(sép)*.
◆ **se raccorder à** *vp+prép* **1.** [route, voie ferrée] to join up with **2.** [être lié à] to tie in with ▪ **le dernier paragraphe ne se raccorde pas au reste** the last paragraph doesn't tie in with the rest.

raccourci [rakursi] *nm* **1.** [trajet] shortcut **2.** INFORM : **~ clavier** keyboard shortcut **3.** [énoncé] : **un ~ saisissant** a pithy turn of phrase **4.** ART foreshortening *(U)*.
◆ **en raccourci** *loc adv* [en résumé] in brief, in a nutshell ▪ [en miniature] on a small scale, in miniature.

raccourcir [32] [rakursir] <> *vt* [vêtement, rideau] to shorten, to take up *(sép)* ▪ [cheveux, barbe] to trim ▪ [discours] to shorten ▪ [film] to shorten ▪ **tu as trop raccourci les manches** you've made the sleeves too short ▮ [trajet] to shorten ▪ **le sentier raccourcit le trajet de deux kilomètres** the path shortens the trip by two kilometres ▮ [séjour] to cut short ▪ **elle a dû ~ ses vacances d'une semaine** she had to come back from her holidays a week early.
<> *vi* **1.** [durée] : **les jours raccourcissent** the days are growing shorter *ou* drawing in **2.** [mode] : **les manteaux vont ~ à l'automne prochain** coats will be shorter next autumn **3.** [distance] : **ça raccourcit** it's shorter.
◆ **se raccourcir** *vpi* [diminuer] : **les délais de livraison se sont considérablement raccourcis** delivery times have been considerably shortened *ou* reduced.

raccourcissement [rakursismɑ̃] *nm* [des jours] shortening, drawing in ▪ [des robes] shortening ▪ [des délais] shortening, reducing.

raccroc [rakro] ◆ **par raccroc** *loc adv* by a stroke of good luck.

raccrocher [3] [rakrɔʃe] <> *vt* **1.** [remettre en place - habit, rideau] to hang back up ; [- tableau] to put back on the hook, to hang *ou* to put back up ; [- téléphone] to put down, to hang up ▪ **~ les gants** *fam* [boxeur] to hang up one's gloves, to retire **2.** [relier - wagons] to couple, to hitch together **3.** [rattraper - affaire] to save at the last minute **4.** *fam* [obtenir par chance - commande] to pull *ou* to bring off *(sép)*.
<> *vi* **1.** [au téléphone] to hang up, to put the receiver down ▪ **elle m'a raccroché au nez** *fam* she hung up *ou* put the phone down on me **2.** *fam* [prendre sa retraite - boxeur] to hang up one's gloves.
◆ **se raccrocher à** *vp+prép* **1.** [se rattraper à] to grab *ou* to catch hold of ▪ **il n'a personne à qui se ~** *fig* he has nobody to turn to ▪ **il se raccrochait à cet espoir** he hung on to that hope **2.** [être relié à] to be linked *ou* related to.

raccrocheur, euse [rakrɔʃœr, øz] *adj* [publicité] eye-catching.

race [ras] *nf* **1.** ANTHR race ▪ **la ~ blanche/noire** the white/black race ▪ **de ~ blanche** white ▪ **de ~ noire** black ▪ **il est de ~ asiatique** he's of Asian origin **2.** [catégorie] : **la ~ des honnêtes gens est en voie de disparition** decent people are a dying breed **3.** ZOOL breed ▪ **la ~ canine/féline/bovine/porcine** dogs/cats/cattle/pigs **4.** *litt* [lignée] line ▪ **être de ~ noble** to be of noble stock *ou* blood **5.** [distinction] : **avoir de la ~** to have breeding.
◆ **de race** *loc adj* [chien, chat] purebred, pedigree *(modif)* ▪ [cheval] thoroughbred.

racé, e [rase] *adj* **1.** ZOOL [chien] purebred, pedigree *(modif)* ▪ [cheval] thoroughbred **2.** [personne] wellbred **3.** [voilier, voiture] handsome.

racer [rɛsœr] *nm* racer *(car, boat)*.

rachat [raʃa] *nm* **1.** [de ce qu'on avait vendu] repurchase, buying back **2.** [achat] : **'nous vous proposons le ~ de votre ancienne voiture!'** COMM 'we offer to take your old car in part-exchange *UK ou* as a trade-in *US*!' **3.** FIN [d'actions, d'obligations] buying up *ou* in ▪ [d'une affaire] take over ▪ **~ de l'entreprise par ses salariés** management buyout ▮ [d'une franchise, d'une rente] redemption **4.** *sout* [des péchés] redemption.

rachetable [raʃtabl] *adj* **1.** *fam* [remplaçable] : **un vase, c'est ~** you can always buy another vase **2.** *litt* [dette, rente, péché] redeemable.

racheter [28] [raʃte] *vt* **1.** [en plus] to buy some more (of) ▪ **~ des actions** [en supplément] to buy some more shares ; [pour remplacer celles qu'on a vendues] to buy back *ou* to repurchase shares ■ **je vais ~ un service à café** I'm going to buy another *ou* a new coffee set **2.** [acheter] to buy ■ **'on vous rachète vos anciens meubles'** COMM your old furniture taken in part-exchange *UK ou* as a trade-in *US* ■ **j'ai racheté sa part/son affaire** FIN I've bought him out (of the business)/bought him up ■ **~ une entreprise** to take over a company **3.** [rente, cotisations] to redeem **4.** [erreur, défaut] to make up for *(insép)*, to compensate for *(insép)* ■ [péché] to atone for *(insép)*, to expiate *sout* ■ [vie dissolue] to make amends for, to make up for *(insép)* ■ [pécheur] to redeem ■ **il n'y en a pas un pour ~ l'autre** one's as bad as the other **5.** CONSTR to modify, to compensate **6.** HIST [soldat] to buy out *(sép)* ■ [prisonnier, esclave] to ransom, to buy the freedom of **7.** ÉDUC : **~ un candidat** to pass a candidate *(in spite of insufficient marks)* ■ **~ une (mauvaise) note** to make up for a (poor) grade.

◆ **se racheter** *vp (emploi réfléchi)* [gén] to make amends, to redeem o.s. ■ [pécheur] to redeem o.s.

rachidien, enne [raʃidjɛ̃, ɛn] *adj* rachidian, rachidial.

rachitique [raʃitik] ◇ *adj* **1.** MÉD suffering from rickets, rachitic *spéc* **2.** [chétif - plante] stunted ; [- chien, personne] puny, scrawny.
◇ *nmf* person suffering from rickets.

rachitisme [raʃitism] *nm* rickets *(U)*, rachitis *spéc.*

Rachmaninov [rakmaninɔf] *npr* Rachmaninoff.

racial, e, aux [rasjal, o] *adj* racial, race *(modif)* ■ **émeute ~e** race riot.

racine [rasin] *nf* **1.** BOT root ■ **~s alimentaires** root crops ■ **~s (comestibles)** root vegetables ■ **~ de gingembre** root ginger ■ **il prend ~** *fam* [il s'installe] he's getting a bit too comfortably settled ■ **tu vas prendre racine!** *fam* [l'attente est longue] you'll take root! **2.** ANAT [d'un cheveu, d'un poil, d'une dent] root ■ [du nez] base **3.** LING & MATH root ■ **~ carrée/cubique/énième** square/cube/nth root **4.** INFORM root.

◆ **racines** *nfpl* [origines] roots ■ **retrouver ses ~s** to go back to one's roots ■ **cette croyance a ses ~s dans le folklore breton** this belief is rooted in Breton folklore.

racisme [rasism] *nm* racism, racial prejudice ■ **c'est du ~ anti-vieux** that's ageism ■ **c'est du ~ anti-jeunes** that's prejudice against young people.

raciste [rasist] ◇ *adj* racist, prejudiced.
◇ *nmf* racist.

racket [rakɛt] *nm* (protection) racket ■ **la lutte contre le ~** the fight against racketeering.

racketter [4] [rakɛte] *vt* to racketeer, to run a (protection) racket ■ **il est inadmissible que les enfants se fassent ~ dans les écoles** it is unacceptable for children to be subject to racketeering in schools.

racketteur, euse [rakɛtœr, øz] *nm, f* racketeer.

raclage [raklaʒ] *nm* scraping.

raclée [rakle] *nf fam* **1.** [coups] thrashing, hiding ■ **donner une ~ à qqn** to give sb a good thrashing *ou* hiding **2.** [défaite] thrashing, hammering ■ **il a pris sa ~ en finale** he got thrashed *ou* hammered in the final.

raclement [rakləmɑ̃] *nm* scraping (noise) ■ **on entendit quelques ~s de gorge** some people could be heard clearing their throats.

racler [3] [rakle] *vt* **1.** [frotter] to scrape ■ **un petit vin blanc qui racle le gosier** a white wine that is rough on *ou* that burns your throat ➊ **~ les fonds de tiroir** *fam* to scrape some money together **2.** *péj* [instrument] : **~ du violon** to scrape away at the fiddle.

◆ **se racler** *vpt* : **se ~ la gorge** to clear one's throat.

raclette [raklɛt] *nf* **1.** CULIN [plat] *Swiss speciality consisting of melted cheese prepared at the table using a special heater or grill, served with potatoes and cold meats* ■ [fromage] raclette *(cheese)* **2.** [grattoir] scraper **3.** [pour vitres] squeegee.

racloir [raklwar] *nm* **1.** MIN scraper **2.** MENUIS scraper plane **3.** MÉTALL strickle **4.** ARCHÉOL racloir, side scraper.

raclure [raklyr] *nf* **1.** [résidu] scraping **2.** △ [personne] : **c'est une ~** he's the lowest of the low.

racolage [rakɔlaʒ] *nm* [par une prostituée] soliciting ■ [par un vendeur] touting (for customers) ■ [par un militant] canvassing ■ **faire du ~** [prostituée] to solicit ; [commerçant] to tout (for customers) ; [militant] to canvass (support).

racoler [3] [rakɔle] *vt* **1.** [clients - suj: prostituée] to accost ; [- suj: vendeur] to tout for ■ [électeurs] to canvass **2.** HIST [soldat] to press-gang.

racoleur, euse [rakɔlœr, øz] *adj* [sourire] enticing ■ [affiche] eye-catching ■ [titre, journal] sensationalist ■ [campagne électorale] vote-catching.

◆ **racoleur** *nm* tout.

◆ **racoleuse** *nf* streetwalker.

racontable [rakɔ̃tabl] *adj* : **ce n'est pas ~ devant des enfants** I can't say it in front of children.

racontar [rakɔ̃tar] *nm fam* piece of gossip ■ **n'écoute pas les ~s** don't listen to gossip.

raconter [3] [rakɔ̃te] *vt* **1.** [conte, histoire] to tell ■ **il a raconté l'histoire à son voisin** he told his neighbour the story, he told the story to his neighbour **2.** [événement, voyage] to tell, to relate ■ **~ ses malheurs à qqn** to tell sb all one's troubles, to pour one's heart out to sb ➊ **~ sa vie** *fam* to tell one's (whole) life story ■ **nous raconte pas ta vie!** *fam* we don't want to hear your life history! **3.** [dire] to tell ■ **on raconte beaucoup de choses sur lui** you hear all sorts of stories about him ■ **on raconte qu'il a été marié plusieurs fois** people say he's been married several times ■ **à ce qu'on raconte, elle était la maîtresse du docteur** she was the doctor's mistress, at least that's what people say ■ **mais enfin qu'est-ce que tu racontes?** what (on earth) are you on about? ■ **ne raconte pas de bêtises** don't be silly ■ *(en usage absolu)* **vite, raconte!** go on!, quick, tell me! ➊ **qu'est-ce que tu racontes (de beau)?** so, what's new?

◆ **se raconter** ◇ *vp (emploi passif)* [événement] : **des choses pareilles ne se racontent pas** such things are best left unsaid ■ **il faut l'avoir vécu, ça ne se raconte pas** I couldn't describe what it was like.
◇ *vpi* [personne] to talk about o.s.

raconteur, euse [rakɔ̃tœr, øz] *nm, f* storyteller ■ **c'est un bon ~** he tells a good story.

racorni, e [rakɔrni] *adj* **1.** [vieillard] wizened, shrivelled ■ [mains] gnarled ■ [plante] shrivelled ■ [parchemin] dried-up **2.** *sout* [esprit] hardened.

racornir [32] [rakɔrnir] *vt* **1.** [peau, mains] to toughen ■ [cœur] to harden **2.** [plante] to shrivel up *(sép)*.

◆ **se racornir** *vpi* **1.** [plante] to shrivel up *(insép)*, to become shrivelled up **2.** *sout* [personne] to become hardened *ou* hardhearted.

radar [radar] *nm* radar ■ **~ de veille** military surveillance radar ■ **écran/système ~** radar screen/system ■ **contrôle-~** [sur la route] radar (speed) trap *(on a road)* ■ **aujourd'hui je suis** *ou* **je marche au ~** *fam* I'm on automatic pilot today.

rade [rad] ◇ *nf* **1.** [bassin] harbour, roads *spéc* ■ **en ~ de San Francisco** in San Francisco harbour **2.** *fam loc* **laisser qqn en ~** [l'abandonner] to leave sb in the lurch ■ **on est restés en ~** we were left stranded.
◇ *nm*△ *arg crime* [bar] joint.

radeau, x [rado] *nm* raft ■ **~ de sauvetage** life raft ■ **~ pneumatique** inflatable raft ■ **'le Radeau de la Méduse'** *'Géricault* 'The Raft of the Medusa'.

radial, e, aux [radjal, o] *adj* MATH & ANAT radial.

◆ **radiale** *nf* [autoroute urbaine] urban expressway *(leading out from the city centre)*.

radian [radjɑ̃] *nm* radian.

radiant, e [radjɑ̃, ɑ̃t] *adj* radiant.

radiateur [radjatœr] *nm* [à eau, d'un véhicule] radiator ■ : **~ à gaz** gas heater ■ **~ électrique** electric radiator *ou* heater ■ **~ soufflant** fan heater.

radiatif, ive [radjatif, iv] *adj* radiative.

radiation [radjasjɔ̃] *nf* **1.** BIOL & PHYS radiation **2.** [élimination] removal, striking off ■ **ils ont demandé sa ~ de l'ordre des médecins/du barreau** they asked that he should be struck off the register/that he should be struck off.

radical, e, aux [radikal, o] ◇ *adj* **1.** [complet] radical, drastic ■ **une réorganisation ~e** a thoroughgoing *ou* root and branch reorganization **2.** [efficace] : **l'eucalyptus c'est ~ contre le rhume** eucalyptus is just the thing for colds ■ **il s'endort quand je mets la radio, c'est ~** *fam* he goes to sleep as soon as I put the radio on, it works like a dream **3.** BOT radical, root *(modif)* **4.** LING root *(modif)*.
◇ *nm, f* POLIT Radical.
◆ **radical** *nm* **1.** LING radical, stem **2.** CHIM radical **3.** MATH radical (sign).

radicalement [radikalmɑ̃] *adv* radically, completely ■ **il a ~ changé** he's completely different, he's a different person.

radicalisation [radikalizasjɔ̃] *nf* radicalization ■ **la ~ du conflit** the heightening of the conflict.

radicaliser [3] [radikalize] *vt* to radicalize, to make more radical.
◆ **se radicaliser** *vpi* : **le mouvement étudiant s'est radicalisé** the student movement has become more radical.

radicalisme [radikalism] *nm* radicalism.

radical-socialisme [radikalsɔsjalism] *nm* radical-socialism.

radical-socialiste [radikalsɔsjalist] (*pl* **radicaux-socialistes** [radikosɔsjalist]) *adj* & *nmf* radical-socialist.

radicelle [radisɛl] *nf* radicel *spéc*, rootlet.

radicule [radikyl] *nf* radicle.

radié, e [radje] *adj* **1.** [cadran] marked in rays, radiate *spéc* **2.** BOT radiate, rayed.

radier[1] [radje] *nm* **1.** CONSTR [dalle] concrete slab ■ [revêtement] apron **2.** MIN sill.

radier[2] [9] [radje] *vt* to strike off *(sép)* ■ **elle a été radiée de l'ordre des médecins/du barreau** she was struck off the register/struck off.

radiesthésie [radjɛstezi] *nf* divination, divining.

radiesthésiste [radjɛstezist] *nmf* diviner.

radieux, euse [radjø, øz] *adj* [matinée, temps] glorious ■ [soleil, beauté] brilliant, radiant ■ [visage, personne] radiant, glowing (with happiness) ■ : **un sourire ~** a beaming smile.

radin, e [radɛ̃, in] *fam* ◇ *adj* tightfisted, stingy.
◇ *nm, f* skinflint.

radiner [3] △ [radine] *vi* [arriver] to turn *ou* to show up *(insép)*.
◆ **se radiner**△ *vpi* : **allez, vite, radine-toi!** come on, get a move on!

radinerie [radinri] *nf fam* stinginess, tightfistedness.

radio [radjo] ◇ *nf* **1.** [récepteur] radio **2.** [diffusion] : **la ~** radio (broadcasting) ■ **à la ~** on the radio ■ **passer à la ~** [personne] to be on the radio ; [chanson] to be played on the radio ; [jeu, concert] to be broadcast (on the radio), to be radiocast US **3.** [station] radio station ■ **sur toutes les ~s** on all stations ➊ **Radio France** *state-owned radio broadcasting company* ■ **Radio France Internationale** ≃ BBC World Service ■ **~ locale privée** *ou* **libre** independent local radio station ■ **~ périphérique** *radio station broadcasting from outside national territory* ■ **~ pirate** pirate radio station ■ **~ privée** independent *ou* commercial radio station **4.** *(comme adj inv)* MIL : **message ~** radio message **5.** MÉD X-ray (photograph) ■ **passer une ~** *ou* **à la ~** *fam* to have an X-ray (done), to be X-rayed.
◇ *nm* radio operator.

radioactif, ive [radjɔaktif, iv] *adj* radioactive.

radioactivité [radjɔaktivite] *nf* radioactivity.

radioamateur [radjɔamatœr] *nm* radio ham.

radiobalise [radjɔbaliz] *nf* radio beacon.

radiobaliser [3] [radjɔbalize] *vt* to equip with a radio beacon signalling system.

radiocarbone [radjɔkarbɔn] *nm* radiocarbon.

radiocassette [radjɔkasɛt] *nf* radio cassette player.

radiocommande [radjɔkɔmɑ̃d] *nf* radio control.

radiocommunication [radjɔkɔmynikasjɔ̃] *nf* radiocommunication.

radiodétection [radjɔdetɛksjɔ̃] *nf* radiodetection.

radiodiffusé, e [radjɔdifyze] *adj* RADIO radio *(modif)*.

radiodiffuser [3] [radjɔdifyze] *vt* to broadcast (on radio), to radiocast US.

radiodiffusion [radjɔdifyzjɔ̃] *nf* radio broadcasting.

radioélectricien, enne [radjɔelɛktrisjɛ̃, ɛn] *nm, f* radio engineer.

radioélectrique [radjɔelɛktrik] *adj* ÉLECTR radio *(modif)*.

radiofréquence [radjɔfrekɑ̃s] *nf* radio frequency.

radiogénique [radjɔʒenik] *adj* : **voix ~** good broadcasting voice.

radiographie [radjɔgrafi] *nf* [technique] radiography ■ [image] X-ray, radiograph.

radiographier [9] [radjɔgrafje] *vt* to X-ray.

radiographique [radjɔgrafik] *adj* [technique] radiographic ■ [examen] X-ray *(modif)*.

radioguidage [radjɔgidaʒ] *nm* **1.** AÉRON radio direction finding, radio guidance **2.** AUTO traffic news.

radioguidé, e [radjɔgide] *adj* [avion] radio-controlled ■ [projectile, missile] guided.

radiologie [radjɔlɔʒi] *nf* radiology.

radiologique [radjɔlɔʒik] *adj* radiological ■ **examen ~** X-ray examination.

radiologiste [radjɔlɔʒist], **radiologue** [radjɔlɔg] *nmf* radiologist.

radioluminescence [radjɔlyminɛsɑ̃s] *nf* radio-luminescence.

radionavigation [radjɔnavigasjɔ̃] *nf* radio navigation ■ **techniques de ~** radio navigational techniques.

radiophare [radjɔfar] *nm* radio beacon.

radiophonie [radjɔfɔni] *nf* broadcasting.

radiophonique [radjɔfɔnik] *adj* [émission, feuilleton] radio *(modif)* ■ [studio] broadcasting *(modif)*.

radioreportage [radjɔrəpɔrtaʒ] *nm* [émission] (radio) report ■ [commentaire] (radio) commentary.

radioreporter [radjɔrəpɔrtɛr] *nm* (radio) reporter *ou* correspondent.

radioréveil [radjɔrevɛj] *nm* radio alarm (clock).

radioscopie [radjɔskɔpi] *nf* **1.** MÉD radioscopy **2.** [étude] indepth analysis.

radioscopique [radjɔskɔpik] *adj* X-ray *(modif)*.

radiosondage [radjɔsɔ̃daʒ] *nm* radiosondage, radiosonde sounding.

radiosonde [radjɔsɔ̃d] *nf* MÉTÉOR radiosonde, radiometeorograph.

radio-taxi [radjɔtaksi] (*pl* **radio-taxis**) *nm* radio cab, radiotaxi.

radiotechnique [radjɔtɛknik] ◇ *adj* radiotechnical.
◇ *nf* radiotechnics (U), radio technology.

radiotélégramme [radjɔtelegram] *nm* radiotelegram.

radiotéléphone [radjɔtelefɔn] *nm* radiotelephone.

radiotélescope [radjɔteleskɔp] *nm* radio telescope.

radiotélévisé, e [radjɔtelevize] *adj* broadcast simultaneously on radio and TV, simulcast.

radiotélévision [radjɔtelevizjɔ̃] *nf* radio and television.

radiothérapie [radjɔterapi] *nf* radiotherapy.

radis [radi] *nm* **1.** BOT radish ▪ **~ noir** black radish **2.** △ *loc* **je n'ai plus un ~** I haven't got a bean *esp* UK *ou* a red cent US.

radium [radjɔm] *nm* radium.

radius [radjys] *nm* radius.

radjah [radʒa] = **raja(h)**.

radôme [radom] *nm* radome.

radotage [radɔtaʒ] *nm* drivel.

radoter [3] [radɔte] *fam* ◇ *vi* to witter on ▪ **excuse-moi si je radote, mais...** sorry to go on and on about it, but... ▪ **là, il radote!** he's going soft in the head!
◇ *vt* **1.** [raconter] : **qu'est-ce que tu radotes?** what are you wittering UK *ou* drivelling on about? **2.** [répéter] : **il radote cent fois les mêmes histoires** he's always going on about the same old things.

radoteur, euse [radɔtœr, øz] *nm, f* drivelling fool.

radoub [radu] *nm* **1.** [réparation] repair, refitting ▪ **le voilier est en ~** the yacht is being refitted **2.** [cale] dry dock.

radouber [3] [radube] *vt* **1.** [bateau] to repair, to refit **2.** [filet] to mend.

radoucir [32] [radusir] *vt* **1.** [caractère] to soften ▪ [personne] to calm down *(sép)*, to mollify *sout* **2.** MÉTÉOR to make milder ▪ **les chutes de neige ont radouci le temps** there's been a slight rise in temperature due to the snowfall.
◆ **se radoucir** *vpi* **1.** [voix] to soften, to become gentler ▪ [personne] to yield, to soften **2.** [température] to get milder ▪ **le temps s'est radouci** the weather's milder.

radoucissement [radusismɑ̃] *nm* **1.** MÉTÉOR (slight) rise in temperature ▪ **net ~ des températures ce matin** a marked rise in temperature this morning **2.** [d'une personne] softening.

rafale [rafal] *nf* **1.** MÉTÉOR blast, gust ▪ **le vent souffle en ~s** it's blustery **2.** ARM burst ▪ **une ~ de mitraillette** a burst of machine-gun fire **3.** *fig* burst ▪ **par** *ou* **en ~s** intermittently.

raffermir [32] [rafɛrmir] *vt* **1.** [muscle, peau] to tone *ou* to firm up *(sép)* **2.** [consolider] to strengthen, to reinforce ▪ **~ sa position** to consolidate one's position ▪ **~ le courage de qqn** to bolster up sb's courage.
◆ **se raffermir** *vpi* **1.** [muscle, peau] to tone *ou* to firm up **2.** [se consolider] to get stronger ▪ **se ~ dans ses intentions** to stiffen one's resolve **3.** FIN [monnaie, prix] to strengthen.

raffermissement [rafɛrmismɑ̃] *nm* [de la peau] firming up ▪ [de la voix] steadying ▪ [d'une autorité] strengthening, consolidation ▪ **~ des tendances à la Bourse** strengthening of trends on the Stock Exchange.

raffinage [rafinaʒ] *nm* refining.

raffiné, e [rafine] ◇ *adj* **1.** INDUST refined ▪ **pétrole ~** refined oil **2.** [élégant] refined, sophisticated **3.** [subtil - raisonnement] subtle ; [- politesse] extreme, exquisite ; [- goût] refined, discriminating.
◇ *nm, f* person of taste.

raffinement [rafinmɑ̃] *nm* **1.** [élégance] refinement, sophistication **2.** [détail élégant] subtlety, refinement **3.** [surenchère] : **avec un ~ de cruauté** with exquisite *ou* refined cruelty.

raffiner [3] [rafine] *vt* **1.** INDUST to refine **2.** [rendre plus délicat] to polish, to refine.
◆ **raffiner sur** *v+prép* to be overparticular about ▪ **je n'ai pas eu le temps de ~ sur les détails** I didn't have time to pay that much attention to the details.

raffinerie [rafinri] *nf* refinery.

raffoler [3] [rafɔle] ◆ **raffoler de** *v+prép* to be crazy *ou* mad about ▪ **chic, des glaces, j'en raffole!** ooh, ice cream, I love ice cream!

raffut [rafy] *nm fam* **1.** [bruit] racket ▪ **pourquoi tout ce ~?** [voix] what's all this shouting about? **2.** [esclandre] to-do.

rafiot [rafjo] *nm fam* [bateau] : **vieux ~** old tub.

rafistolage [rafistɔlaʒ] *nm fam* patching up ▪ **c'est le roi du ~** he's always making do.

rafistoler [3] [rafistɔle] *vt fam* to patch up *(sép)*, to fix temporarily.

rafle [rafl] *nf* **1.** [arrestation] raid ▪ **une ~ de police** a police raid ▶ **la ~ du Vel' d'Hiv** HIST *the rounding up of Jews in the Paris Vélodrome d'Hiver in 1942* **2.** BOT stalk ▪ [du maïs] cob.

rafler [3] [rafle] *vt fam* **1.** [voler] to nick UK, to swipe **2.** [saisir] to grab ▪ COMM to buy up *(sép)* ▪ **les clients ont tout raflé en moins de deux heures** the customers cleared the shelves in less than two hours **3.** [remporter - prix] to walk off with ▪ **le film a raflé toutes les récompenses** the film made a clean sweep of the awards.

rafraîchir [32] [rafrɛʃir] ◇ *vt* **1.** [refroidir] to cool (down) ▪ **ces averses ont rafraîchi le temps** the weather's a bit cooler because of the showers **2.** [remettre en état - vêtement] to smarten *ou* to brighten up *(sép)* ; [- barbe, coupe de cheveux] to trim ; [- peintures] to freshen up *(sép)* ▪ **la cuisine a besoin d'être rafraîchie** the kitchen needs a lick of paint **3.** *fam fig* [raviver] : **~ la mémoire à qqn** to refresh *ou* to jog sb's memory **4.** INFORM to refresh ▪ [navigateur] to reload.
◇ *vi* **1.** MÉTÉOR to get cooler *ou* colder **2.** CULIN to chill.
◆ **se rafraîchir** *vpi* **1.** [se refroidir] to get colder **2.** [faire sa toilette] to freshen up **3.** [boire] to have a cool drink.

rafraîchissant, e [rafrɛʃisɑ̃, ɑ̃t] *adj* **1.** [froid] cool, refreshing ▪ [tonique] refreshing, invigorating ▪ **une boisson ~e** a refreshing drink **2.** [charmant] refreshing.

rafraîchissement [rafrɛʃismɑ̃] *nm* **1.** [refroidissement] cooling ▪ **net ~ des températures sur tout le pays** temperatures are noticeably cooler throughout the country **2.** [boisson] cool *ou* cold drink **3.** INFORM refreshing *(U)*, refresh.

raft(ing) [raft(iŋ)] *nm* white water rafting.

ragaillardir [32] [ragajardir] *vt* to buck *ou* to perk up *(sép)* ▪ **ragaillardi par une nuit de sommeil** refreshed after a good night's sleep.

rage [raʒ] *nf* **1.** MÉD & VÉTÉR : **la ~** rabies ▶ **~ de dents** (severe) toothache **2.** [colère - d'adulte] rage, fury ; [- d'enfant] tantrum ▪ **être fou de ~** to be absolutely furious ▪ **elle est repartie la ~ au cœur** she went off boiling *ou* seething with rage **3.** [passion] passion, mania ▪ **avoir la ~ de vivre** to have an insatiable lust for life **4.** *loc* **faire ~** [feu, ouragan] to rage ; [mode] to be all the rage.

rageant, e [raʒɑ̃, ɑ̃t] *adj* infuriating, exasperating ▪ **c'est ~!** it makes you mad!

rager [17] [raʒe] *vi* : **je rage de la voir se pavaner** it makes me mad *ou* it infuriates me to see her strutting about ▪ **je rageais!** I was fuming *ou* furious!

rageur, euse [raʒœr, øz] *adj* **1.** [irrité - ton] angry, enraged ; [- geste, réponse] bad-tempered, angry **2.** [coléreux] hot-tempered.

rageusement [raʒøzmɑ̃] *adv* angrily, furiously ▪ **il claqua la porte** he slammed the door angrily.

raglan [raglɑ̃] ◇ *adj inv* raglan.
◇ *nm* raglan coat.

ragot [rago] *nm* piece of gossip ▪ **des ~s** gossip.

ragoût [ragu] *nm* stew, ragout.
◆ **en ragoût** *loc adj* stewed.

ragoûtant, e [ragutɑ̃, ɑ̃t] *adj* : **peu ~** [mets] unappetizing ; [personne] unsavoury ; [lieu] insalubrious.

rahat-loukoum [raatlukum] *(pl* **rahat-loukoums***)*, **rahat-lokoum** [raatlɔkum] *(pl* **rahat-lokoums***)* *nm* Turkish delight *(U)*.

rai [rɛ] *nm* **1.** *litt* [rayon] : **un ~ de lumière** a shaft of light **2.** [d'une roue] spoke.

raï [raj] *nm* MUS rai *(mixture of North African and Western music)*.

raid [rɛd] *nm* **1.** MIL raid, surprise attack ▪ **~ aérien** air raid **2.** SPORT [avec des véhicules] long-distance rally ▪ [à pied] trek **3.** BOURSE raid.

raide [rɛd] ◇ *adj* **1.** [rigide - baguette, matériau] stiff, rigid ▪ [tendu - fil, ficelle] taut, tight ▪ [droit] straight ▪ **avoir une jambe ~** to have a stiff leg ▶ **avoir les cheveux ~s (comme des baguettes de tambour)** to have straight hair ▪ **se tenir ~ comme un piquet** to stand as stiff as a pole *ou* a poker **2.** [guindé - personne] stiff, starchy ; [- style, jeu de scène] wooden ▪ [inébranlable - personne, comportement] rigid, inflexible ▪ **être ~ comme la justice** *litt* to be totally unbending *ou* inflexible **3.** [abrupt] steep ▪ **la côte est (en pente) ~** the hill climbs steeply **4.** *fam* [fort - café] strong ; [- alcool] rough **5.** *fam* [osé - détail, récit] risqué ; [- scène] explicit, daring ▪ **le vieux canapé a dû en voir de ~s** the old sofa has seen a thing or two **6.** *fam* [surprenant] : **elle est ~, celle-là!** that's a bit far-fetched *ou* hard to believe ▪ **je vais t'en raconter une ~** I'll tell you an amazing story **7.** △ [désargenté] broke, skint *UK*.
◇ *adv* **1.** [à pic] steeply **2.** [en intensif] : **tomber ~** to drop dead ▪ **~ mort** stone dead *UK*, dead as a doornail.

raider [rɛdœr] *nm* raider.

raideur [rɛdœr] *nf* **1.** [d'une étoffe, d'une attitude] stiffness ▪ [d'une baguette] stiffness, rigidity ▪ [d'une corde] tautness ▪ [des cheveux] straightness ▪ [d'un sentier] steepness ▪ [d'un style, d'un jeu de scène] woodenness **2.** [d'un muscle] stiffness ▪ **avoir une ~ dans l'épaule** to have a stiff shoulder.

raidillon [rɛdijɔ̃] *nm* steep path *ou* climb ▪ **juste avant le ~** just before the road starts climbing.

raidir [32] [rɛdir] *vt* **1.** [tendre] to stiffen **2.** [faire perdre sa souplesse à] to stiffen ▪ **l'eau calcaire raidit le tissu** hard water stiffens fabric.
◆ **se raidir** *vpi* **1.** [perdre sa souplesse] to stiffen, to go stiff, to become stiffer **2.** [se tendre - muscle, corps] to tense (up), to stiffen ; [- cordage] to tighten, to grow taut **3.** [rassembler sa volonté] to steel *ou* to brace o.s. ▪ **se ~ contre l'adversité** to stand firm in the face of adversity.

raidissement [rɛdismɑ̃] *nm* **1.** [physique] tensing, stiffening **2.** [moral] : **face au ~ des patrons** faced with the tougher line taken by the employers.

raie [rɛ] ◇ *v* ▷ **rayer**.
◇ *nf* **1.** [trait] line ▪ [rayure] stripe ▪ [griffure] scratch, mark ▪ **une ~ de lumière** a ray of light **2.** [dans les cheveux] parting *UK*, part *US* ▪ **une ~ sur le côté** a side parting ▪ **se coiffer avec la ~ à gauche/droite** to part one's hair on the left/right **3.** ANAT slit ▪ **~ des fesses** cleft of the buttocks **4.** AGRIC furrow **5.** OPT & PHYS line **6.** ZOOL ray, skate ▪ CULIN skate ▪ **~ électrique/venimeuse** electric/sting ray.

raifort [rɛfɔr] *nm* horseradish.

rail [raj] *nm* **1.** [barre d'acier] rail ▪ **les ~s** [la voie] the tracks, the rails ▪ **poser des ~s** to lay track ▶ **~ conducteur** live rail ▪ **~ fixe** main rail ▪ **~ mobile** switch (rail) ▪ **sortir des ~s** to leave the rails, to go *ou* to come off the rails ▪ **remettre qqch/qqn sur les ~s** *fig* to put sthg/sb back on the rails **2.** [moyen de transport] : **le ~** rail ▪ **une grève du ~** a rail strike ▪ **transport par ~** rail transport **3.** [glissière] track ▶ **~ d'éclairage** lighting track ▪ **~ de travelling** dolly (tracks) **4.** NAUT shipping lane.

railler [3] [raje] *litt* ◇ *vt* to mock, to laugh *ou* to scoff at *(inséρ)* ▪ **il en a eu assez de se faire ~ par tout le monde** he was fed up with everyone making fun of him.
◇ *vi* to jest.
◆ **se railler de** *vp+prép litt* : **se ~ de qqn/qqch** to scoff at sb/sthg.

raillerie [rajri] *nf* **1.** [attitude] mocking, raillery *litt* **2.** [remarque] jibe, jest *arch & hum.*

railleur, euse [rajœr, øz] ◇ *adj* mocking, scoffing.
◇ *nm, f* mocker, scoffer ▪ **faire taire les ~s** to silence the scoffers.

rail-route [rajrut] *adj inv* road-rail *(modif)*.

rainette [renɛt] *nf* tree frog.

rainurage [rɛnyraʒ] *nm* [sur route] : **'rainurage'** 'grooved surface'.

rainure [rɛnyr] *nf* **1.** [sillon] groove ▪ [guide] channel, slot ▪ **les ~s du parquet** the gaps between the floorboards **2.** ANAT groove.

raisin [rɛzɛ̃] *nm* **1.** [en grappes] grapes ▶ **~ blanc/noir** white/black grapes ▪ **~ de cuve/table** wine/eating grapes ▪ **'les Raisins de la colère'** *Steinbeck* 'The Grapes of Wrath' **2.** CULIN : **~s de Corinthe** currants ▪ **~s secs** raisins ▪ **~s de Smyrne** sultanas.

raisiné [rɛzine] *nm* **1.** [confiture] grape jelly **2.** △ *arg crime* [sang] blood.

raisinet [rezinɛ] *nm Suisse* redcurrant.

raison [rɛzɔ̃] *nf* **1.** [motif] reason ▪ **il n'y a aucune ~ pour que vous partiez** there's no reason for you to leave ▪ **y a-t-il une ~ de s'inquiéter?** is there any reason to worry? ▪ **quelle est la ~ de...?** what's the reason for...? ▪ **quelle est la ~ de son départ?** why is she leaving? ▪ **la ~ pour laquelle je vous écris** the reason (why) *ou* that I'm writing to you ▪ **pour quelle ~?** why? ▪ **avoir de bonnes ~s** *ou* **des ~s (de faire qqch)** to have good reasons (for doing sthg) ▪ **avoir ses ~s** to have one's reasons ▪ **je n'ai pas de ~s à te donner!** I don't have to tell you why! ▪ **avec ~** with good reason ▪ **sans ~** for no reason (at all) ▪ **pour une ~ ou pour une autre** for one reason or another ▪ **pour la (bonne et) simple ~ que** for the simple reason that ▪ **ce n'est pas une ~!, c'est pas une ~!** that's no excuse! ▪ **ce n'est pas une ~ pour vous fâcher** there's no need for you to get angry ▶ **~ de vivre** reason to live ▪ **cet enfant c'est sa ~ de vivre** he lives for that child ▪ **à plus forte ~** all the more so ▪ **~ de plus : mais je suis malade! – ~ de plus!** but I'm not feeling well! – all the more reason! ▪ **~ de plus pour le faire** that's one more reason for doing so ▪ **qu'elle se débrouille toute seule, y a pas de ~!** *fam* there's no reason why she shouldn't sort it out for herself! ▪ **le cœur a ses ~s que la ~ ne connaît point** *Pascal allus* the heart has its reasons that reason ignores ▪ **se rendre aux ~s de qqn** to yield to sb's arguments
2. [lucidité] : **il n'a pas/plus toute sa ~** he's not/he's no longer in his right mind ▪ **perdre la ~** to lose one's mind ▪ **recouvrer la ~** to recover one's faculties ▪ **troubler la ~ de qqn** to affect sb's mind
3. [bon sens] reason ▪ **agir contre toute ~** to behave quite unreasonably ▪ **faire entendre ~ à qqn, ramener qqn à la ~** to make

DONNER RAISON À QUELQU'UN

You're probably right. Vous avez probablement raison.

I suppose so. Peut-être bien.

That's one way of looking at it, I suppose. C'est une façon de voir les choses, effectivement.

If you say so... Si tu le dis...

I see what you mean. Je vois ce que tu veux dire.

Point taken. D'accord.

You've got a point there. C'est juste.

sb see reason ■ **rappeler qqn à la ~** to bring sb to his/her senses ■ **revenir à la ~** to come to one's senses ⊙ **plus que de ~** to excess, more than is reasonable
4. [faculté de penser] reason ■ **l'homme est un être doué de ~** man is a thinking being
5. MATH proportion ■ **en ~ inverse/directe (de)** in inverse/direct proportion (to)
6. *loc* **avoir ~** to be right ■ **donner ~ à qqn** [personne] to agree that sb is right ; [événement] to prove sb right ■ **se faire une ~** to resign o.s. ■ **fais-toi une ~, c'est trop tard** you'll just have to put up with *ou* to accept the fact that it's too late ■ **avoir ~ de qqn/qqch** *sout* to get the better of sb/sthg, to overcome sb/sthg ■ **rendre ~ de qqch à qqn** to justify sthg to sb ■ **la ~ du plus fort est toujours la meilleure** *prov* might is right *prov*.
◆ **à raison de** *loc prép* at the rate of.
◆ **comme de raison** *loc adv* and rightly so.
◆ **en raison de** *loc prép* **1.** [à cause de] on account of, because of ■ **le vol est annulé en ~ du mauvais temps** the flight has been cancelled because of bad weather
2. [en proportion de] according to.
◆ **raison d'État** *nf* : **le gouvernement a invoqué la ~ d'État pour justifier cette mesure** the government said that it had done this for reasons of State.
◆ **raison d'être** *nf* raison d'être ■ **sa présence n'a plus aucune ~ d'être** there's no longer any reason for him to be here.
◆ **raison sociale** *nf* corporate *ou* company name.
Voir module d'usage

raisonnable [rɛzɔnabl] *adj* **1.** [sensé - personne, solution, décision] sensible ■ **sois ~!** be reasonable! ■ **tu n'es (vraiment) pas ~ de boire autant** it's not sensible to drink so much ■ **à cet âge ils sont ~s** when they get to that age they know how to behave sensibly ■ **il devrait être plus ~** he should know better ■ **c'est ~** it makes sense ■ **est-ce bien ~?** *hum* is that wise? **2.** [normal, naturel] reasonable ■ **il est ~ de penser que...** it's reasonable to think that... **3.** [acceptable - prix, taux, heure] reasonable ; [- salaire] decent ■ **un appartement de taille ~** a reasonably *ou* fairly large flat ■ **leurs exigences restent très raisonnables** they're very moderate in their demands **4.** [doué de raison] rational.

raisonnablement [rɛzɔnabləmɑ̃] *adv* **1.** [de manière sensée] sensibly, properly **2.** [normalement] reasonably **3.** [modérément] in moderation ■ **vous pouvez boire, mais ~** you may drink, but in moderation.

raisonné, e [rɛzɔne] *adj* **1.** [analyse, projet, décision] reasoned **2.** [grammaire, méthode] structured.

raisonnement [rɛzɔnmɑ̃] *nm* **1.** [faculté, réflexion] : **le ~** reasoning ⊙ **~ par l'absurde** reductio ad absurdum ■ **~ par analogie** analogical reasoning ■ **~ déductif/inductif** deductive/inductive reasoning **2.** [argumentation] reasoning ■ **la conclusion de mon ~ est la suivante** after careful thought, I have come to the following conclusion ■ **je ne suis pas bien votre ~** I don't follow your line of argument *ou* thought ■ **son ~ est assez convaincant** her arguments are quite convincing ■ **il ne faudra pas tenir ce ~ avec lui** we mustn't use that argument with him.

raisonner [3] [rɛzɔne] ◇ *vi* **1.** [penser] to think ⊙ **~ comme un tambour** *ou* **une pantoufle** to talk nonsense, to talk through one's hat **2.** [enchaîner des arguments] : **~ par analogie** to use analogy as the basis of one's argument ■ **~ par induction/déduction** to use inductive/deductive reasoning **3.** [discuter] : **~ sur** to argue about ■ **~ avec qqn** to reason with sb.
◇ *vt* **1.** [faire appel à la raison de] to reason with *(insép)* **2.** *sout* [examiner] to think out *ou* through *(sép)*.
◆ **se raisonner** ◇ *vp (emploi réfléchi)* : **raisonne-toi, essaie de manger moins** be reasonable and try not to eat so much.
◇ *vp (emploi passif)* : **la passion ne se raisonne pas** there's no reasoning with passion, passion knows no reason.

raja(h) [raʒa] *nm* rajah.

rajeunir [32] [raʒœnir] ◇ *vi* **1.** [redevenir jeune] to grow young again ■ **elle voudrait ~** she'd like to be younger **2.** [paraître plus jeune] to look *ou* to seem younger ■ **elle rajeunit de jour en jour, on dirait!** she seems to get younger every day! **3.** [retrouver de l'éclat - façade] to look like new.
◇ *vt* **1.** [rendre jeune] : **~ qqn** *pr* to rejuvenate sb, to make sb younger ; *fig* to make sb look younger ■ **~ le personnel d'une société** to bring new blood into a company **2.** [attribuer un âge moins avancé à] : **très aimable à vous, mais vous me rajeunissez!** that's very kind of you but you're making me younger than I am! ■ **vous me rajeunissez de cinq ans** I'm five years older than you said **3.** [faire se sentir plus jeune] : **ça me rajeunit!** it makes me feel younger! ■ **ça ne nous rajeunit pas!** it makes you realize how old we are!, it makes you feel your age! **4.** [moderniser - mobilier, équipement] to modernize.
◆ **se rajeunir** *vp (emploi réfléchi)* **1.** [se faire paraître plus jeune] to make o.s. look younger **2.** [se dire plus jeune] to lie about one's age ■ **elle se rajeunit de cinq ans/d'au moins cinq ans** she claims to be five years younger/at least five years younger than she really is.

rajeunissant, e [raʒœnisɑ̃, ɑ̃t] *adj* rejuvenating.

rajeunissement [raʒœnismɑ̃] *nm* **1.** BIOL & PHYSIOL rejuvenation **2.** [modernisation - d'un équipement, d'une entreprise] modernization **3.** [abaissement de l'âge] : **le ~ de la population** the decreasing average age of the population.

rajout [raʒu] *nm* addition ■ **faire des ~s à qqch** to make additions to sthg, to add things to sthg.

rajouter [3] [raʒute] *vt* **1.** [ajouter] : **~ qqch (à)** to add sthg (to) **2.** [dire en plus] : **~ qqch (à)** to add sthg (to) ■ **je n'ai rien à ~** I have nothing to add, I have nothing more to say ■ **~ que** to add that **3.** *fam loc* **en ~** to lay it on a bit thick ■ **je t'en prie, n'en rajoute pas!** oh, for God's sake, give it a rest!

rajustement [raʒystəmɑ̃] *nm* adjustment ■ **un ~ des salaires** a wage adjustment.

rajuster [3] [raʒyste] *vt* **1.** [prix, salaires, vêtements] to adjust **2.** [rectifier] : **~ le tir** to adjust *ou* to correct one's aim.
◆ **se rajuster** *vpi* to tidy o.s. up ■ **il avait oublié de se ~** he'd forgotten to do up his fly *ou* to adjust his dress *hum*.

râlant, e [ralɑ̃, ɑ̃t] *adj fam* infuriating, exasperating ■ **c'est ~!** it's enough to drive you mad!

râle [ral] *nm* **1.** [d'un agonisant] : **~ (d'agonie)** death rattle **2.** MÉD rale **3.** [oiseau] rail ■ **~ d'eau** water rail ■ **~ des genêts** corncrake.

ralenti, e [ralɑ̃ti] *adj* : **mener une vie ~e** to live quietly.
◆ **ralenti** *nm* **1.** CINÉ slow motion **2.** AUTO & MÉCAN idling speed ■ **régler le ~** to adjust the idling speed.
◆ **au ralenti** *loc adv* **1.** CINÉ : **passer une scène au ~** to show a scene in slow motion **2.** [à vitesse réduite] : **tourner au ~** [moteur] to idle ■ **l'usine tourne au ~** the factory is running under capacity ■ **depuis qu'il est à la retraite, il vit au ~** now that he's retired, he doesn't do as much as he used to ■ **ils travaillent au ~** [pour protester] they're on a go-slow *UK ou* a slowdown *US* ; [par nécessité] they're working at a slower pace.

ralentir [32] [ralɑ̃tir] ◇ *vi* to slow down ■ **'attention, ~'** 'reduce speed now' ■ **'~, travaux'** 'slow, roadworks ahead'.
◇ *vt* **1.** [mouvement, effort] to slow down ■ **~ sa course** *ou* **l'allure** to reduce speed, to slow down ■ **~ le pas** to slow down **2.** [processus] to slow down *(sép)*.
◆ **se ralentir** *vpi* to slow down.

ralentissement [ralɑ̃tismɑ̃] *nm* **1.** [décélération] decrease in speed ■ **un ~ de 10 km sur la N10** slow-moving traffic for 6 miles on the N10 **2.** [diminution] reduction ■ **un ~ des ventes** a falloff in sales ■ **un ~ de l'économie** economic turndown.

ralentisseur [ralɑ̃tisœr] *nm* **1.** [sur une route] speed bump, sleeping policeman *UK* **2.** AUTO & MÉCAN idler, speed reducer **3.** PHYS moderator ■ **~ de particules/neutrons** particle/neutron moderator.

râler [3] [rale] *vi* **1.** [agonisant] to give a death rattle **2.** *fam* [se plaindre] to grumble, to moan ■ **ça me fait ~!** it makes me so mad *ou* furious! ■ **juste pour la faire ~** just to make her angry **3.** [tigre] to growl.

râleur, euse [ralœr, øz] *fam* ◇ *adj* bad-tempered, grumpy.
◇ *nm, f* grouch, moaner ■ **quel ~!** he never stops moaning!

ralliement [ralimɑ̃] *nm* **1.** [adhésion] : **lors de son ~ à notre parti/notre cause** when he came over to our party/cause **2.** [rassemblement] rally, gathering ▪ **signe/cri de ~** rallying sign/cry ▪ **point de ~** rallying point.

rallier [9] [ralje] *vt* **1.** [rejoindre - groupe, poste] to go back to **2.** [adhérer à] to join **3.** [rassembler - autour de soi, d'un projet] to win over *(sép)* ; [- des troupes] to gather together, to rally ▪ **~ tous les suffrages** to meet with general approval **4.** NAUT : **~ la terre** to haul in for the coast.
◆ **se rallier à** *vp+prép* **1.** [se joindre à] : **se ~ à qqn** to join forces with sb ▪ **se ~ à un parti** to join a party **2.** [se montrer favorable à] : **se ~ à un avis/un point de vue** to come round to an opinion/a point of view ▪ **se ~ à l'avis général** to come round to *ou* to rally to the opinion of the majority.

rallonge [ralɔ̃ʒ] *nf* **1.** [électrique] extension (cable) **2.** [planche] extension **3.** [tuyau] extension tube *(of a vacuum cleaner)* **4.** *fam* [délai] extra time *(U)* ▪ **une ~ de quelques jours** a few extra days **5.** *fam* [supplément] extra money *(U)* ▪ **il nous a donné une ~ de quinze euros** he gave us an extra fifteen euros.
◆ **à rallonge(s)** *loc adj* **1.** [objet] : **table à ~** *ou* **~s** extending table **2.** [week-end] long ▪ [histoire] never-ending ▪ [nom] double-barrelled.

rallonger [17] [ralɔ̃ʒe] ◇ *vt* **1.** [gén] to extend ▪ [durée, liste] to lengthen, to make longer, to extend **2.** [vêtement - en défaisant l'ourlet] to let down *(sép)* ; [- en ajoutant du tissu] to make longer **3.** *fam* [suj: trajet, itinéraire] : **ça nous rallonge** it's taking us out of our way ▪ **en passant par Lille, ça te rallonge d'une heure** if you go via Lille, it'll add an hour to your journey time ▪ *(en usage absolu)* **ça rallonge de passer par Lille** it takes longer if you go via Lille.
◇ *vi* : **les jours rallongent** the days are getting longer ▪ **la mode rallonge** hemlines are coming down again.

rallumer [3] [ralyme] *vt* **1.** [feu] to rekindle, to light again ▪ [lampe, télévision] to put back on, to switch on again ▪ [électricité] to turn on again ▪ **~ une cigarette** [éteinte] to relight a cigarette ; [une autre] to light up another cigarette ▪ *(en usage absolu)* **rallume!** put the light back on! **2.** *sout* [faire renaître - haine, passion] to rekindle.
◆ **se rallumer** ◇ *vpi* **1.** [feu, incendie] to flare up again ▪ [lampe] to come back on **2.** *sout* [espoir] to be revived ▪ [conflit] to break out again ▪ [passion] to flare up.
◇ *vpt* : **elle se ralluma une énième cigarette** she lit yet another cigarette.

rallye [rali] *nm* **1.** [course] : **~ (automobile)** rally, car-rally **2.** [soirée] *exclusive upper-class ball for young people.*

RAM, Ram [ram] *(abr de* **Random Access Memory***) nf* Ram, ram.

ramadan [ramadɑ̃] *nm* Ramadan, Ramadhan ▪ **faire** *ou* **observer le ~** to observe Ramadan.

ramage [ramaʒ] *nm litt* [d'un oiseau] song.
◆ **ramages** *nmpl* floral pattern ▪ **un tissu à grands ~s** material with a bold floral pattern.

ramassage [ramasaʒ] *nm* **1.** [cueillette - du bois, des fruits] gathering ; [- des pommes de terre] picking, digging up ; [- des champignons] picking, gathering **2.** [collecte] : **~ des ordures** rubbish *UK ou* garbage *US* collection **3.** [transport] picking up ▪ **ils se chargent du ~ des ouvriers** they pick up the workers ⊃ **point/zone de ~** pick-up point/area ▪ **~ scolaire** school bus service.

ramassé, e [ramase] *adj* **1.** [homme, corps] stocky, squat ▪ [bâtisse, forme] squat **2.** [style] terse.

ramasse-miettes [ramasmjɛt] *nm inv* brush and pan *(for sweeping crumbs off a table).*

ramasser [3] [ramase] *vt* **1.** [objet à terre] to pick up *(sép)* ▪ **~ qqch à la pelle** *fam* : **ils ramassent des fraises à la pelle dans leur jardin** they get loads of strawberries from their garden ▪ **des mauvaises notes, il en a ramassé à la pelle cette année** he's been getting bad marks by the dozen this year ▪ **~ qqn dans le ruisseau** to pick sb up out of the gutter ▪ **il était à ~ à la petite cuillère** *fam* [épuisé] he was all washed out ; [blessé] you could have scraped him off the ground ▪ **encore un pas et je serai bon à ~ à la petite cuillère!** one more step and I'll fall to bits! **2.** [cueillir - champignons] to pick, to gather ; [- pommes de terre] to dig ; [- marrons] to gather
3. [rassembler - copies] to collect, to take in *(sép)* ; [- cartes à jouer] to gather up *(sép)* ; [- feuilles mortes] to sweep up *(sép)* ▪ **~ du bois** to gather wood ▪ **il a ramassé pas mal d'argent** *fam* he's picked up *ou* made quite a bit of money ⊃ **~ ses forces** to gather one's strength ▪ **~ la monnaie** to pick up the change ▪ **~ le paquet** *fam* to hit the jackpot
4. [élèves, ouvriers] to collect
5. [résumer] to condense ▪ **ramassez vos idées en quelques lignes** condense your ideas into just a few lines
6. *fam* [trouver] to pick up, to dig up
7. *fam* [arrêter] to collar, to nab ▪ **se faire ~** to get nabbed, to be collared
8. *fam* [recevoir - mauvais coup, gifle] to get ▪ **qu'est-ce que tu vas ~!** you're in for it!
9. *fam* [attraper - maladie] to catch
10. *arg scol* **se faire ~** to fail.
◆ **se ramasser** ◇ *vp (emploi passif)* to be picked (up) ⊃ **les truffes se ramassent à la pelle dans cette région** *fam* there are loads of truffles around here.
◇ *vp (emploi réfléchi) fam fam* [se relever] to pick o.s. up.
◇ *vpi* **1.** [avant de bondir] to crouch
2. *fam* [tomber] to come a cropper *UK*, to fall flat on one's face ▪ [échouer] to fail.

ramassette [ramasɛt] *nf Belgique* dustpan.

ramasseur, euse [ramasœr, øz] *nm, f* gatherer ▪ **~/ramasseuse de balles** [au tennis] ball boy/girl.
◆ **ramasseur** *nm* [machine - AGRIC] pick-up.

ramassis [ramasi] *nm péj* [d'objets] jumble ▪ [de personnes] bunch ▪ **un ~ de mensonges** a tissue of lies.

ramassoire [ramaswar] *nf Suisse* dustpan.

rambarde [rɑ̃bard] *nf* rail, guardrail.

ramdam [ramdam] *nm fam* racket ▪ **faire du ~** to make a racket.

rame [ram] *nf* **1.** [aviron] oar **2.** [de papier] ream **3.** [train] train ▪ **~ (de métro)** (underground *UK*) *ou* subway *US* train **4.** [branche] prop, stake **5.** *fam loc* **il n'en a pas fichu une ~** he hasn't done a stroke (of work).

rameau, x [ramo] *nm* **1.** [branche] (small) branch ▪ **~ d'olivier** olive branch **2.** *fig* [division] branch, subdivision **3.** ANAT ramification.
◆ **Rameaux** *nmpl* : **les Rameaux, le dimanche des Rameaux** Palm Sunday.

ramée [rame] *nf litt* [feuillage] foliage ▪ **sous la ~** under the leafy boughs.

ramener [19] [ramne] *vt* **1.** [personne, véhicule - au point de départ] to take back *(sép)* ; [- à soi] to bring back *(sép)* ▪ **je vous ramène?** [chez vous] shall I give you a lift home? ; [à votre point de départ] shall I give you a lift back? ▪ **son chauffeur le ramène tous les soirs** his chauffeur drives him back every evening ▪ **~ à** [un endroit] to take back to
2. [rapporter] : **ramène-moi un journal** bring me back a newspaper ▪ **il faut que je ramène les clefs à l'agence** I've got to take the keys back to the estate agent
3. [rétablir] to bring back *(sép)*, to restore ▪ **~ la paix** to restore peace
4. [placer] : **elle ramena le châle sur ses épaules** she pulled the shawl around her shoulders ▪ **~ ses cheveux en arrière** to draw one's hair back ▪ **~ ses genoux sous son menton** to pull one's knees up under one's chin
5. [faire revenir] : **l'été a ramené les visiteurs** the summer has brought back the tourists ▪ **le film m'a ramené dix ans en arrière** the film took me back ten years ▪ **~ à : ~ le débat au sujet principal** to lead *ou* to steer the discussion back to the main subject ▪ **ce qui nous ramène au problème de...** which brings us back to the problem of... ▪ **~ la conversation à** *ou* **sur qqch** to bring the conversation back (round) to sthg ▪ **~ qqn à la vie** to bring sb back to life, to revive sb ▪ **~ un malade à lui** to bring a patient round

6. [réduire] : **cela ramène le problème à sa dimension financière** it reduces the problem to its purely financial aspects ■ **~ tout à soi** to bring everything back to *ou* to relate everything to o.s.
7. *loc* **la ~, ~ sa fraise** *fam* [vouloir s'imposer] to stick one's oar in ; [faire l'important] to show off.
◆ **se ramener** *vpi fam* [arriver] to turn *ou* to show up ■ **ramène-toi en vitesse!** come on, hurry up!
◆ **se ramener à** *vp+prép* [se réduire à] to boil down to ■ **toute l'affaire se ramenait finalement à une querelle de famille** in the end the whole business boiled down to *ou* was nothing more than a family quarrel.

ramequin [ramkɛ̃] *nm* **1.** [récipient] ramekin (mould) **2.** [tartelette] (small) cheese tart.

ramer [3] [rame] ◇ *vi* **1.** [pagayer] to row ■ **~ en couple** to scull **2.** *fam* [peiner] : **j'ai ramé trop longtemps, maintenant je veux un vrai boulot** I've been slaving away for too long, now I want a decent job ■ **qu'est-ce qu'on a ramé pour trouver cet appartement!** it was such a hassle finding this flat!
◇ *vt* HORT to stick, to stake.

ramette [ramɛt] *nf* ream *(of 125 sheets)*, five quires.

rameur, euse [ramœr, øz] ◇ *nm, f* rower, oarsman (*f* oarswoman) ■ **~ en couple** sculler.
◇ *nm* SPORT rowing machine.

rameuter [3] [ramøte] *vt* **1.** [regrouper - foule] to draw **2.** [mobiliser - militants, partisans] to rouse ■ **~ les populations** to stir people into action **3.** [chiens] to round up *(sép)*.

rami [rami] *nm* rummy ■ **faire ~** to go rummy.

ramier [ramje] *adj m* & *nm* : **(pigeon) ~** ringdove, wood pigeon.

ramification [ramifikasjɔ̃] *nf* **1.** BOT ramification *spéc*, offshoot **2.** ANAT ramification ■ **~s nerveuses** nerve plexus **3.** [d'un fleuve] ramification, distributary ■ [d'une voie ferrée] branch line ■ [d'un réseau, d'une organisation] branch.

ramifier [9] [ramifje] ◆ **se ramifier** *vpi* **1.** ANAT & BOT to ramify, to divide **2.** [se subdiviser - réseau] to split ■ **la famille s'est ramifiée en trois branches** the family split into three branches.

ramille [ramij] *nf* twig, branchlet.

ramolli, e [ramɔli] ◇ *adj* **1.** [mou] soft **2.** *fam* [gâteux] soft ■ **il est un peu ~ du cerveau** he's gone a bit soft (in the head) *ou* soft-headed **3.** *fam* [sans énergie] : **se sentir tout ~** to feel washed out.
◇ *nm, f fam* **un vieux ~** an old dodderer.

ramollir [32] [ramɔlir] ◇ *vt* **1.** *fam* [rendre mou] to soften **2.** [affaiblir] to weaken **3.** *fam* [rendre gâteux] : **l'âge l'a ramolli** he's gone soft in the head with age.
◇ *vi* to go soft.
◆ **se ramollir** *vpi* **1.** [devenir mou] to go soft **2.** *fam* [perdre son tonus] : **depuis que j'ai arrêté le sport, je me suis ramolli** I've been out of condition since I stopped doing sport **3.** *fam* [devenir gâteux] : **j'ai l'impression que je me ramollis** I feel like I'm going senile.

ramollissement [ramɔlismɑ̃] *nm* [du beurre, de la cire] softening ■ **~ cérébral** softening of the brain.

ramollo [ramɔlo] *adj fam* **1.** [mou] sluggish ■ **se sentir tout ~** to feel like a wet rag **2.** [gâteux] doddery.

ramonage [ramɔnaʒ] *nm* **1.** [d'une cheminée] chimney-sweeping ■ [d'une machine] cleaning **2.** SPORT [en alpinisme] chimneying.

ramoner [3] [ramɔne] *vt* **1.** [cheminée] to sweep ■ [machine] to clean ■ [pipe] to clean (out) **2.** SPORT [en alpinisme] to climb *(using chimneying method)*.

ramoneur [ramɔnœr] *nm* chimney sweep.

rampant, e [rɑ̃pɑ̃, ɑ̃t] *adj* **1.** [animal] creeping, crawling ■ **insecte ~** flightless insect **2.** BOT creeping ■ **plante ~e** creeper **3.** [évoluant lentement] : **inflation ~e** creeping inflation **4.** HÉRALD rampant **5.** ARCHIT [arc] rampant ■ [pièce] raked.
◆ **rampant** *nm* **1.** *fam* AÉRON member of the ground staff ■ **les ~s** the ground staff **2.** ARCHIT pitch.

rampe [rɑ̃p] *nf* **1.** [main courante] handrail, banister ■ **~ (d'escalier)** banister ■ **lâcher la ~** *fam euphém* to kick the bucket **2.** [plan incliné] slope, incline ■ **~ d'un échangeur** sloping approach to an interchange ▶ **~ d'accès** approach ramp **3.** THÉÂTRE footlights ■ **passer la ~** to get across to the audience ■ **il passe mal la ~** he doesn't come across well **4.** AÉRON : **~ (de balisage)** marker *ou* runway lights **5.** TECHNOL : **~ de chargement** loading ramp ■ **~ de graissage** lubricating rack ■ **~ de lancement** ASTRONAUT launchpad, launching pad ; *fig* launchpad.

ramper [3] [rɑ̃pe] *vi* **1.** [lierre] to creep ■ [personne] to crawl ■ [serpent] to slither, to crawl ■ [doute, inquiétude] to lurk **2.** *fig* [s'abaisser] to grovel ■ **~ devant qqn** to grovel before sb.

rampon [rɑ̃pɔ̃] *nm Suisse* lamb's lettuce.

ramure [ramyr] *nf* **1.** BOT : **la ~** the branches, the tree tops **2.** ZOOL : **la ~** the antlers.

rancard△ [rɑ̃kar] *nm* **1.** [rendez-vous - gén] meeting ; [- amoureux] date ■ **j'ai ~ avec lui à 15 h** I'm meeting him at 3 ■ **filer (un) ~ à qqn** to arrange to meet sb **2.** △ *arg crime* [renseignement] info *(U)*, gen *(U) UK* ■ [tuyau] tip, tip-off.

rancarder [3] [rɑ̃karde] *vt* **1.** *arg crime* [renseigner] to fill in *(sép)*, to clue up *(sép)* ■ **qui t'a rancardé?** who tipped you off? **2.** △ [donner un rendez-vous à] : **~ qqn** to arrange to meet sb.
◆ **se rancarder**△ *vp (emploi réfléchi) arg crime* to get information.

rancart [rɑ̃kar] *nm* **1.** △ **= rancard 2.** *fam loc* **mettre qqch au ~** to chuck sthg out, to bin sthg *UK* ■ **on a mis le projet au ~** we scrapped the project.

rance [rɑ̃s] ◇ *adj* [beurre, huile] rancid ■ [noix] stale.
◇ *nm* : **odeur/goût de ~** rancid smell/taste.

ranch [rɑ̃tʃ] (*pl* **ranchs** *ou pl* **ranches**) *nm* ranch.

ranci [rɑ̃si] *nm* : **sentir le ~** to have a rancid smell.

rancir [32] [rɑ̃sir] *vi* **1.** [beurre, huile] to go rancid ■ [noix] to go stale **2.** *fig* & *litt* to become stale.

rancœur [rɑ̃kœr] *nf sout* resentment, rancour ■ **avoir de la ~ envers qqn** to feel resentful towards sb.

rançon [rɑ̃sɔ̃] *nf* **1.** [somme d'argent] ransom **2.** [contrepartie] : **c'est la ~ de la gloire/du succès** that's the price you have to pay for being famous/successful.

rançonner [3] [rɑ̃sɔne] *vt* **1.** [exiger une rançon de] to hold to ransom **2.** *fam* [exploiter] to fleece, to swindle.

rancune [rɑ̃kyn] *nf* grudge ■ **garder ~ à qqn** to bear *ou* to harbour a grudge against sb ■ **sans ~?** no hard feelings? ■ **sans ~!** let's shake hands and forget it!

rancunier, ère [rɑ̃kynje, ɛr] ◇ *adj* spiteful ■ **être ~** to bear grudges.
◇ *nm, f* spiteful person.

randomisation [rɑ̃dɔmizasjɔ̃] *nf* randomization.

randonnée [rɑ̃dɔne] *nf* : **faire une ~** [à pied] to go for a hike ■ **faire une ~ à bicyclette** to go for a (long) bike ride ■ **faire une ~ à skis** to go cross-country skiing ■ **la ~ (pédestre)** walking, hiking ■ **grande ~** long-distance hiking.

randonneur, euse [rɑ̃dɔnœr, øz] *nm, f* hiker.

rang [rɑ̃] *nm* **1.** [rangée - de personnes] row, line ; [- de fauteuils] row ; [- de crochet, de tricot] row (of stitches) ■ **on était au premier ~** we were in the front row
2. [dans une hiérarchie] rank ■ **ce problème devrait être au premier ~ de nos préoccupations** this problem should be at the top of our list of priorities ■ **venir au deuxième/troisième ~** to rank second/third ■ **par ~ d'âge** according to age ■ **par ~ d'ancienneté** in order of seniority ■ **il a pris ~ parmi les meilleurs** he ranks among the best ■ **avoir ~ d'ambassadeur** to hold the office of ambassador ▶ **de premier ~** high ranking, first-class, top-class ■ **de second ~** second-rate

3. [condition sociale] (social) standing ■ **le respect qui est dû à son ~** the respect which his position commands ■ **elle a épousé quelqu'un d'un ~ plus élevé** she married above her station ◆ **tenir son ~** to maintain one's position in society
4. MIL : **le ~** the ranks ■ **les militaires du ~** the rank and file ◆ **sortir du ~** *pr* to come up through the ranks ; *fig* to stand out ■ **rentrer dans le ~** *pr* to return to the ranks ; *fig* to give in, to submit
5. *Québec* long strip of farmland *(at right angles to a road or a river)*.
◆ **rangs** *nmpl* ranks ■ **en ~s serrés** MIL in close order ◆ **être** *ou* **se mettre sur les ~s** to line up ■ **servir dans les ~s d'un parti/syndicat** to be a member *ou* to serve in the ranks of a party/union.
◆ **au rang de** *loc prép* **1.** [dans la catégorie de] : **une habitude élevée** *ou* **passée au ~ de rite sacré** a habit which has been raised to the status of a sacred rite
2. [au nombre de] : **mettre qqn au ~ de ses amis** to count sb among one's friends
3. [à la fonction de] : **élever qqn au ~ de ministre** to raise *ou* to promote sb to the rank of minister.
◆ **de rang** *loc adv* : **trois heures de ~** three hours in a row.
◆ **en rang** *loc adv* in a line *ou* row ■ **entrez/sortez en ~** go in/out in single file ■ **se mettre en ~** to line up, to form a line ◆ **en ~ d'oignons** in a line *ou* row.

rangé, e [rɑ̃ʒe] *adj* **1.** [en ordre - chambre, vêtements] tidy **2.** [raisonnable - personne] steady, level-headed ; [- vie] settled ■ **une jeune personne ~e** a very sober *ou* well-behaved young person **3.** *fam* [assagi] settled ■ **être ~ des voitures** to have settled down.

rangée [rɑ̃ʒe] *nf* row.

rangement [rɑ̃ʒmɑ̃] *nm* **1.** [mise en ordre - d'une pièce] tidying (up) ■ **faire du ~** to tidy up **2.** [d'objets, de vêtements] putting away **3.** [agencement] arrangement, classification **4.** [meuble] storage unit ■ [cagibi] storage room ■ [espace] storage space ■ **quelques solutions de ~** a few storage ideas.

ranger[1] [rɑ̃dʒœr] *nm* MIL ranger.
◆ **rangers** *nmpl* combat boots.

ranger[2] [17] [rɑ̃ʒe] *vt* **1.** [mettre en ordre - pièce] to tidy (up) **2.** [mettre à sa place - vêtement, objets] to put away *(sép)* ; [- document] to file away *(sép)* ■ **j'ai rangé la voiture au garage** I've put the car in the garage ■ **je ne sais pas, je l'ai rangé là** I don't know, I put it there **3.** [classer] to sort (out) ■ **~ des dossiers par année** to file documents according to year ‖ *fig* **~ qqn parmi** to rank sb amongst.
◆ **se ranger** <> *vp (emploi passif)* : **où se rangent les serviettes?** where do the towels go?, where are the towels kept?
<> *vpi* **1.** [s'écarter - piéton] to stand aside ; [- véhicule] to pull over **2.** [se mettre en rang - élèves, coureurs] to line up **3.** [se placer] : **se ~ du côté de qqn** to side with sb ■ **se ~ contre** to pull up next to ■ **la voiture se rangea le long du trottoir** the car pulled up beside the kerb **4.** [s'assagir] to settle down.
◆ **se ranger à** *vp+prép* [adhérer à] : **se ~ à l'avis/au choix de qqn** to go along with sb's opinion/decision.

ranimer [3] [ranime] *vt* **1.** [feu] to rekindle, to relight **2.** [conversation] to bring back to life ■ [haine, passion] to rekindle, to revive ■ [douleur] to bring back ■ **~ le moral des troupes** to restore the morale of the troops ■ **~ le débat** to revive the controversy **3.** [malade] to revive, to bring round *(sép)* ■ *fig* [passé] to bring back.
◆ **se ranimer** *vpi* [conversation] to pick up again ■ [personne] to come round ■ [haine, passion] to flare up again, to be rekindled ■ **leurs espoirs se ranimèrent** their hopes were revived.

raout [raut] *nm arch* (social) gathering.

rap [rap] *nm* MUS rap.

rapace [rapas] <> *adj* **1.** ORNITH predatory **2.** *litt* [avare] grasping, avaricious.
<> *nm* ORNITH bird of prey.

rapatriable [rapatrijabl] *adj* : **est-il ~ dans l'état où il est?** can he be repatriated in his present state?

rapatrié, e [rapatrije] *nm, f* repatriate ■ **les ~s d'Algérie** *French settlers in Algeria who were repatriated as a result of Algerian independence in 1962.*

rapatriement [rapatrimɑ̃] *nm* repatriation ■ **le ~ des bénéfices** repatriation of profits.

rapatrier [10] [rapatrije] *vt* [personnes, capitaux] to repatriate ■ [objets] to send *ou* to bring home ■ **se faire ~** to be sent back to one's home country.

râpe [rap] *nf* **1.** [de cuisine] grater ■ **~ à fromage/muscade** cheese/nutmeg grater **2.** TECHNOL [en distillerie] rotary peeler ■ [en outillage] rasp *ou* rough file **3.** BOT rape.

râpé, e [rape] *adj* **1.** [carotte, fromage etc] grated **2.** [vêtement] worn out, threadbare **3.** *fam loc* **c'est ~!** that's the end of that! ■ **avec cette pluie, c'est ~ pour la promenade** with all this rain, we might as well forget about going for a walk.
◆ **râpé** *nm* **1.** [fromage] grated cheese **2.** [tabac] scraped tobacco.

râper [3] [rape] *vt* **1.** [carotte, fromage etc] to grate **2.** TECHNOL to file down *(sép)* **3.** *fig* **un vin qui râpe la gorge** a rough wine.

rapetissement [raptismɑ̃] *nm* **1.** [réduction] : **il observa le ~ de l'image sur l'écran** he watched the picture get smaller and smaller on the screen **2.** *fig & sout* belittling.

rapetisser [3] [raptise] <> *vt* **1.** [rendre plus petit] to make smaller **2.** [faire paraître plus petit] : **~ qqn/qqch** to make sb/sthg seem smaller **3.** [dévaloriser] to belittle.
<> *vi* to get smaller ■ **la piste rapetissait à vue d'œil** the runway looked smaller and smaller by the minute.
◆ **se rapetisser** *vp (emploi réfléchi)* [se dévaloriser] : **se ~ aux yeux de qqn** to belittle o.s. in front of sb.

râpeux, euse [rapø, øz] *adj* rough ■ **vin ~** rough wine.

Raphaël [rafaɛl] *npr* Raphael.

raphia [rafja] *nm* **1.** BOT raffia *ou* raphia palm **2.** TEXT raffia, raphia.

rapiat, e△ [rapja, at] *nm, f* skinflint, meany *UK*.
◆ **rapiat**△ *adj* [avare] tightfisted, stingy.

rapide [rapid] <> *adj* **1.** [véhicule, sportif] fast ■ [cheval] fast ■ [courant] fast flowing ■ **approche ~** AÉRON fast approach ■ **décélération/descente ~** AÉRON rapid deceleration/descent ◆ **~ comme l'éclair** quick as lightning
2. [esprit, intelligence, travail] quick ■ [progrès, réaction] rapid ■ **c'est l'homme des décisions ~s** he's good at reaching quick decisions ■ **une réponse ~** a quick *ou* speedy reply ■ **il n'a pas l'esprit très ~** he's a bit slow on the uptake ◆ **être ~ à la détente** to be quick off the mark
3. [rythme] quick, fast ■ **marcher d'un pas ~** to walk at a brisk *ou* quick pace ■ **battements de cœur ~s** MÉD rapid heartbeat
4. [court, sommaire] quick ■ **le chemin le plus ~** the shortest *ou* quickest way ■ **un examen ~ des dossiers** a quick *ou* cursory glance through the documents ■ **jeter un coup d'œil ~ sur qqch** to have a quick glance at sthg
5. [hâtif - jugement, décision] hurried, hasty
6. [facile - recette] quick.
<> *nmf fam* [personne qui comprend vite] : **c'est un ~** he's really quick on the uptake ■ **ce n'est pas un ~** he's a bit slow on the uptake.
<> *nm* **1.** [cours d'eau] rapid
2. [train] express (train), fast train.

rapidement [rapidmɑ̃] *adv* **1.** [vite] quickly, rapidly ■ **aussi ~ que possible** as quickly as possible **2.** [superficiellement] briefly ■ **j'ai lu ~ les journaux de ce matin** I had a quick look at *ou* I briefly glanced at the papers this morning.

rapidité [rapidite] *nf* **1.** [vitesse - d'une course, d'une attaque] speed ; [- d'une réponse] quickness ■ **avec ~** quickly, speedily, rapidly ■ **la ~ de son geste m'étonna** I was surprised at how quickly his hand moved ◆ **avec la ~ de l'éclair** in a flash, with lightning speed **2.** [du pouls] rapidity.

rapido [rapido] *adv fam* pronto.

rapiéçage [rapjesaʒ] = **rapiècement**.

rapiècement [rapjɛsmɑ̃] *nm* **1.** [raccommodage] patching (up) **2.** [pièce de tissu, de cuir] patch.

rapiécer [20] [rapjese] *vt* to patch up *(sép)*.

rapière [rapjɛr] *nf* rapier.

rapine [rapin] *nf litt* **1.** [pillage] pillage, plunder **2.** [butin] plunder.

raplapla [raplapla] *adj inv fam* **1.** [fatigué] whacked *UK*, bushed *US* **2.** [plat] flat ■ **il est ~, ton ballon!** your ball's as flat as a pancake!

raplatir [32] [raplatir] *vt* to make flatter, to flatten.

rappareiller [4] [rapareje] *vt* to match up *(sép)* again.

rappel [rapɛl] *nm* **1.** [remise en mémoire] reminder ■ **le ~ de ces événements tragiques la bouleversait** being reminded of those tragic events upset her deeply ■ **~ des titres de l'actualité** a summary of today's news ▶ **~ d'échéance** reminder of due date ■ **~ à l'ordre** [gén] call to order ; POLIT ≃ naming *UK* ■ **il a fallu trois ~s à l'ordre pour qu'il se taise** he had to be called to order three times before he stopped talking
2. [d'un ambassadeur] recalling ■ [de produits défectueux] recalling ■ [de réservistes] : **~ sous les drapeaux** (reservists) call-up *ou* recall
3. THÉÂTRE curtain call
4. [répétition - dans un tableau, une toilette] : **~ de couleur** colour repeat
5. MÉD booster ■ **ne pas oublier le ~ l'an prochain** don't forget to renew the vaccination next year
6. [arriéré] : **~ de salaire** back pay ■ **~ de cotisation** payment of contribution arrears
7. TÉLÉCOM : **~ automatique** recall
8. MÉCAN [retour] return ■ **ressort/vis de ~** return spring/screw
9. SPORT [en voile] : **faire du ~** to sit *ou* to lean out ‖ [en alpinisme] abseiling ■ **descendre en ~** to rope *ou* to abseil down ■ **faire un ~** to abseil.

rappelé, e [raple] ◇ *adj* recalled.
◇ *nm, f* MIL reservist *(who has been recalled)*.

rappeler [24] [raple] *vt* **1.** [remettre en mémoire] : **~ qqch à qqn** to remind sb of sthg ■ **rappelez-moi votre nom** what was your name again, please? ■ **rappelle-moi de lui écrire** remind me to write to him ■ **il faut ~ que...** it should be borne in mind *ou* remembered that... ■ **le premier mouvement n'est pas sans ~ Brahms** the first movement is somewhat reminiscent of Brahms ■ **ça me rappelle quelque chose** that rings a bell ■ **'numéro à ~ dans toute correspondance'** 'please quote this number in all correspondence'
2. [faire revenir] to recall, to call back *(sép)* ■ **rappelez donc votre chien!** call your dog off! ■ **~ un ambassadeur** to recall an ambassador ■ **~ des réservistes** MIL to recall reservists ■ **l'acteur a été rappelé plusieurs fois** the actor had several curtain calls ■ **la mort de sa mère l'a rappelé à Aix** the death of his mother took him back to Aix
3. [au téléphone] to call back *(sép)*, to ring *UK ou* to phone back *(sép)*
4. [faire écho à] : **son collier de turquoise rappelle la couleur de ses yeux** her turquoise necklace echoes the colour of her eyes
5. INFORM to call up *(sép)*
6. SPORT [en alpinisme] to fly back *(sép)*
7. *loc* **~ qqn à la raison** to bring sb back to his/her ■ **~ qqn à la vie** to bring sb back to life ■ **~ qqn à l'ordre** to call sb to order ■ **se faire ~ à l'ordre** [dans une assemblée] to be called to order ; [dans une classe] to get told off.
◆ **se rappeler** ◇ *vp (emploi réciproque)* **on se rappelle demain?** shall we talk again tomorrow?
◇ *vp (emploi réfléchi)* : **se ~ au bon souvenir de qqn** *sout* to send sb one's best regards.
◇ *vpt* [se souvenir de] to remember ■ **rappelle-toi que je t'attends!** remember *ou* don't forget (that) I'm waiting for you! ■ **elle se rappelle avoir reçu une lettre** she remembers receiving a letter.

rapper [rape] *vi* to rap.

rappeur, euse [rapœr, øz] *nm, f* rapper.

rappliquer [3] △ [raplike] *vi* to show *ou* to turn up (again).

rapport [rapɔr] *nm* **1.** [compte rendu - gén] report ■ MIL briefing ■ **faire un ~ sur les conditions de travail** to report on working conditions ■ **~ détaillé** item-by-item report, full rundown ▶ **~ annuel** annual report ■ **~ d'expert** audit report ■ **~ financier** annual (financial) report *ou* statement ■ **~ de police** police report ■ **~ quotidien** MIL (daily) briefing ■ **~ de recherche** research paper ■ **au ~!** *pr* read! ; *fig & hum* let's hear it then!
2. [profit] profit ■ **il vit du ~ de son capital** he lives on the income from his investments ■ **d'un bon ~** profitable ■ **cette terre est d'un bon ~** this land gives a good yield
3. [ratio] ratio ■ **dans le ~ de 1 à 5** in a ratio of 1 to 5 ▶ **~ du changement de vitesse** AUTO gear ratio ■ **~ profit-ventes** profit-volume *ou* profit-to-volume ratio ■ **~ qualité-prix** [gén] value for money ; COMM quality-price ratio ■ **c'est d'un bon ~ qualité-prix** it's good value for money ■ **~ signal-bruit** signal-to-noise ratio
4. [relation] connection, link ■ **n'avoir aucun ~ avec qqch** to have no connection with *ou* to bear no relation to sthg ■ **son dernier album n'a aucun ~ avec les précédents** her latest record is nothing like her earlier ones ■ **c'est sans ~ avec le sujet** that's beside the point, that's irrelevant ■ **je ne vois pas le ~** I don't see the connection ■ **où est le ~?** what's that got to do with it? ■ **mais ça n'a aucun ~!** but that's got nothing to do with it! ■ **cette décision n'est pas sans ~ avec les récents événements** this decision isn't totally unconnected with recent events ▶ **~ de forces : le ~ de forces entre les deux pays** the balance of power between the two countries ■ **il y a un ~ de forces entre eux** they are always trying to see who can get the upper hand
5. DR : **~ à succession** hotchpot.
◆ **rapports** *nmpl* [relations] relationship, relations ■ **nous n'avons plus de ~s avec cette société** we no longer deal with that company ■ **entretenir de bons ~s avec qqn** to be on good terms with sb ▶ **~s sexuels** (sexual) intercourse ■ **avoir des ~s (avec qqn)** to have sex (with sb).
◆ **de rapport** *loc adj* ▷ **immeuble.**
◆ **en rapport avec** *loc prép* **1.** [qui correspond à] in keeping with
2. [en relation avec] : **mettre qqn en ~ avec qqn** to put sb in touch with sb ■ **mettre qqch en ~ avec** to link sthg to ■ **se mettre en ~ avec qqn** to get in touch *ou* contact with sb.
◆ **par rapport à** *loc prép* **1.** [en ce qui concerne] regarding
2. [comparativement à] compared with, in comparison to ■ **on constate un retrait de l'euro par ~ aux autres monnaies européennes** the euro has dropped sharply against other European currencies.
◆ **sous le rapport de** *loc prép* as regards ■ **sous ce ~** in this respect.
◆ **sous tous (les) rapports** *loc adv* in every respect ■ **'jeune homme bien sous tous ~s'** 'respectable young man'.

rapporté, e [rapɔrte] *adj* added on ▶ **poche ~e** patch *ou* sewn-on pocket ■ **terre ~e** made ground.

rapporter [3] [rapɔrte] ◇ *vt* **1.** [remettre à sa place] to bring *ou* to put back ■ **tu rapporteras la clé** bring back the key
2. [apporter avec soi] to bring ■ **as-tu rapporté le journal?** did you get *ou* buy the paper? ■ **le chien rapporte la balle** the dog brings back the ball ■ **je rapporte une impression favorable de cet entretien** I came away with a favourable impression of that meeting ‖ [apporter de nouveau ou en plus] : **rapporte-nous un peu plus de vin** bring us a little more wine ‖ CHASSE to retrieve
3. [rendre] to take back *(sép)*, to return ■ **quelqu'un a rapporté le sac que tu avais oublié** somebody has brought back *ou* returned the bag you left behind
4. [ajouter] to add ■ COUT to sew on *(sép)* ■ **~ un angle** MATH to plot an angle
5. [produire] to produce, to yield ■ **~ des bénéfices** to yield a profit ■ **~ des intérêts** to yield interest ■ **le compte d'épargne vous rapporte 3,5 %** the savings account has a yield of 3.5% *ou* carries 3.5% interest ■ **sa boutique lui rapporte beaucoup d'argent** her shop brings in a lot of money ■ **et qu'est-ce que ça t'a rapporté en fin de compte?** what did you get out of it in the end? ■ **ça peut ~ gros!** *slogan du Loto allus* it could make you a lot of money!
6. [répéter - propos] to tell, to say
7. [faire le compte rendu de] to report (on) ■ **~ les décisions d'une commission** POLIT to report on the decisions of a committee

8. ADMIN & DR [annuler] to cancel, to revoke ■ **~ un projet de loi** to throw out a bill
9. [rattacher qqch à] : **~ qqch à** to relate sthg to ■ **elle rapporte tout à elle** she always brings everything back to herself.
◇ *vi* **1.** [être rentable] to yield a profit ■ **ça rapporte** *fam* it pays
2. CHASSE to retrieve ■ **rapporte, mon chien!** fetch, boy!
3. *fam* [enfant] to tell tales, to sneak.
◆ **se rapporter à** *vp+prép* **1.** [avoir un lien avec] to refer *ou* to relate to
2. GRAMM to relate to
3. *sout* **s'en ~ à** [s'en remettre à] to rely on.

rapporteur, euse [rapɔrtœr, øz] ◇ *adj* telltale, sneaky *UK*.
◇ *nm, f* **1.** telltale, sneak *UK*, tattletale *US*. **2.** ADMIN & POLIT [porte-parole] rapporteur, reporter ■ **~ officiel** official recorder ■ **~ de la commission** *committee member who acts as spokesman*.
◆ **rapporteur** *nm* GÉOM protractor.

rapproché, e [raprɔʃe] *adj* close.

rapprochement [raprɔʃmɑ̃] *nm* **1.** [réconciliation - entre groupes, personnes] rapprochement, reconciliation **2.** [comparaison] link, connection ■ **elle fait un ~ saisissant entre Mao et Jung** she draws a striking parallel between Mao and Jung ■ **le ~ de ces deux textes établit le plagiat** comparing the two texts provides proof of plagiarism **3.** [convergence] coming together ■ **on assiste à un ~ des thèses des deux parties** the arguments of the two parties are coming closer together.

rapprocher [3] [raprɔʃe] *vt* **1.** [approcher] to bring closer *ou* nearer ■ **~ les morceaux bord à bord** COUT to put the two pieces edge to edge ■ **'à ~'** IMPR 'close up' **2.** [dans le temps] : **chaque minute le rapprochait du moment fatidique** every minute brought the fateful moment closer ■ **l'émission/la fête a été rapprochée à cause des événements** the programme/party has been brought forward because of what's happened ■ **je vais ~ mes rendez-vous** I'm going to group my appointments together **3.** [faire paraître proche] to bring closer ■ **le dessin japonais rapproche les différents plans** Japanese drawing techniques foreshorten perspective ■ *(en usage absolu)* **mon nouveau zoom rapproche quinze fois** my new zoom lens magnifies fifteen times **4.** [de sa destination] : **~ qqn** to take *ou* to bring sb closer ■ **je te dépose à Concorde, ça te rapprochera** I'll drop you off at Concorde, that'll get you a bit closer to where you're going **5.** [affectivement] to bring (closer) together ■ **ça m'a rapproché de mon père** it's brought me closer to my father, it's brought my father and me closer together ■ **qu'est-ce qui vous rapproche?** what do you have in common? **6.** [comparer] to compare.
◆ **se rapprocher** ◇ *vp (emploi réciproque)* : **les deux pays cherchent à se ~** the two countries are seeking a rapprochement.
◇ *vpi* [venir près] to come close *ou* closer ■ **rapprochez-vous de l'estrade** move closer to the stage.
◆ **se rapprocher de** *vp+prép* **1.** [se réconcilier avec] : **j'ai essayé sans succès de me ~ d'elle avant sa mort** I tried in vain to get closer to her before she died **2.** [être comparable à] to be similar to.

rapsodie [rapsɔdi] = **rhapsodie**.

rapt [rapt] *nm* [kidnapping] abduction, kidnapping ■ **~ d'enfant** abduction of a child.

raquer [3] △ [rake] ◇ *vt* to cough up *(insép)*.
◇ *vi* to foot the bill.

raquette [rakɛt] *nf* **1.** TENNIS racket ■ [au ping pong] bat ■ **c'est une bonne ~** *fam* he's a good tennis player **2.** [pour la neige] snowshoe **3.** BOT prickly pear.

raquetteur, euse [rakɛtœr, øz] *nm, f* *Québec* snowshoer.

rare [rar] *adj* **1.** [difficile à trouver] rare, uncommon ■ **ce qui est ~ est cher** anything that is in short supply is expensive ■ **un musicien d'un ~ talent** an exceptionally talented musician ■ **plantes/timbres ~s** rare plants/stamps
2. [peu fréquent] rare ■ **on le voyait chez nous à de ~s intervalles** once in a (very long) while, he'd turn up at our house ■ **tes visites sont trop ~s** you don't visit us nearly often enough ■ **il est ~ qu'elle veuille bien venir avec moi** she rarely *ou* seldom agrees to come with me ■ **il n'est pas ~ de le voir ici** it's not uncommon *ou* unusual to see him here ■ **tu te fais ~ ces derniers temps** *fam* you've become quite a stranger lately, where have you been hiding lately? ■ **c'est un mot ~** that's a rare word
3. [peu nombreux] few ■ **les ~s électeurs qui ont voté pour lui** the few who voted for him ■ **~s sont ceux qui l'apprécient** not many people like him ■ **à de ~s exceptions près** with only *ou* apart from a few exceptions ■ **elle est une des ~s personnes que je connaisse à aimer le jazz** she's one of the very few people I know who enjoys jazz ■ **les visiteurs se font ~s** there are fewer and fewer visitors ‖ [peu abondant] scarce ■ **la nourriture était ~ pendant la guerre** food was scarce during the war
4. [clairsemé] thin, sparse ■ **il a le cheveu ~** his hair is thinning
5. PHYS [raréfié] rare.

raréfaction [rarefaksjɔ̃] *nf* **1.** PHYS [de l'air] rarefaction **2.** [des denrées, de l'argent] increasing scarcity.

raréfier [9] [rarefje] *vt* **1.** PHYS [air, oxygène] to rarefy, to rarify **2.** [denrées] to make scarce.
◆ **se raréfier** *vpi* **1.** PHYS [air] to rarefy, to rarify **2.** [argent, denrées] to become scarce ■ [visites] to become less frequent.

rarement [rarmɑ̃] *adv* rarely, seldom ■ **elle téléphone ~, pour ne pas dire jamais** she seldom, if ever, calls.

rareté [rarte] *nf* **1.** [d'un fait, d'un phénomène] rarity ■ [d'une denrée] scarcity ■ **une poterie d'une très grande ~** an extremely rare piece of pottery **2.** [objet - rare] rarity, rare object ; [- bizarre] curio.

rarissime [rarisim] *adj* extremely rare, most unusual.

ras[1] [ra] *nm* [radeau] raft.

ras[2] [ra] *nm* [titre éthiopien] ras.

ras[3]**, e** [ra, raz] *adj* **1.** [cheveux] close-cropped, very short ■ [barbe] very short **2.** [végétation] short ■ [pelouse] closely-mown **3.** [plein] : **mesure ~e** full measure **4.** TEXT short-piled **5.** *loc* **en ~e campagne** in the open countryside ■ **la voiture est tombée en panne en ~e campagne** the car broke down in the middle of nowhere.
◆ **ras** *adv* **1.** [très court] short ■ **avoir les ongles coupés ~** to keep one's nails cut short ■ **une haie taillée ~** a closely-clipped hedge **2.** *loc* **en avoir ~ le bol** *fam ou* **~ le cul**▲ **de qqch** to be fed up to the (back) teeth with sthg, to have had it up to here with sthg ■ **~ le bol!** *fam* enough is enough!
◆ **à ras** *loc adv* : **coupé à ~** cut short.
◆ **à ras bord(s)** *loc adv* to the brim *ou* top.
◆ **à ras de** *loc prép* level with.
◆ **au ras de** *loc prép* : **au ~ de l'eau** just above water level, level with the water ▶ **ses remarques étaient au ~ des pâquerettes** *fam* he came out with some very uninspired comments ■ **le débat est au ~ des pâquerettes** *fam* the discussion isn't exactly highbrow.

RAS = **rien à signaler**.

rasade [razad] *nf* glassful.

rasage [razaʒ] *nm* **1.** [de la barbe] shaving **2.** TEXT shearing **3.** MÉTALL (machine) shaving.

rasant, e [razɑ̃, ɑ̃t] *adj* **1.** [bas] : **vue ~e** panoramic view ■ **un soleil ~** a low sun **2.** MIL : **tir ~** grazing fire **3.** *fam* [assommant] boring ■ **il est vraiment ~!** he's so boring!, he's such a bore!

rascasse [raskas] *nf* scorpion fish.

ras(-)du(-)cou [radyku] ◇ *adj inv* round neck *(modif)* ■ **un pull ~** a round neck sweater.
◇ *nm inv* round neck sweater.

rase-mottes [razmɔt] *nm inv* AÉRON hedgehopping ■ **voler en** *ou* **faire du ~** to hedgehop.

raser [3] [raze] *vt* **1.** [cheveux, poils] to shave off *(sép)* ■ [crâne] to shave ■ **~ qqn** to give sb a shave, to shave sb ■ **mal rasé** ill-shaven ■ **être rasé de près** to be close-shaven **2.** [détruire] to raze ■ **la vieille église a été rasée** the old church was razed to the ground **3.** [frôler] : **l'hirondelle rase le sol** the swallow is skimming the ground ■ **la balle lui rasa l'épaule** the bullet grazed his shoulder ▶ **~ les murs** to hug the walls **4.** *fam* [lasser] to bore **5.** TEXT to shear.

◆ **se raser** ◇ *vp (emploi réfléchi)* to shave ■ **se ~ les jambes** to shave one's legs ■ **se ~ la barbe** to shave off one's beard.
◇ *vpi fam* [s'ennuyer] to get bored ■ **on se rase ici, allons-nous-en** it's deadly boring here, let's go.
◆ **à raser** *loc adj* shaving *(modif)* ■ **mousse à ~** shaving foam.

raseur, euse [razœr, øz] *nm, f fam* **c'est un ~** he's a real drag *ou* pain.

rasibus [razibys] *adv fam* very close.

ras-le-bol [ralbɔl] *nm inv fam* **il y a un ~ général dans la population** people in general are sick and tired of *ou* fed up with the way things are going.

rasoir [razwar] ◇ *nm* razor ■ **~ électrique** (electric) shaver ■ **~ mécanique** *ou* **de sûreté** safety razor ■ **demander une coupe au ~** to ask for a razor cut.
◇ *adj fam* boring.

rassasier [9] [rasazje] *vt* **1.** [faim] to satisfy ■ **je suis rassasié** I'm full **2.** *fig* **alors, vous êtes rassasiés de plein air?** so, have you had your fill of fresh air?
◆ **se rassasier** *vpi* **1.** [apaiser sa faim] to eat one's fill **2.** [assouvir son désir] : **se ~ de qqch** to get one's fill of sthg.

rassemblement [rasɑ̃bləmɑ̃] *nm* **1.** [réunion sur la voie publique] gathering, group ■ **disperser un ~** to break up *ou* to disperse a gathering ‖ [en politique] rally ■ **~ pour la paix** peace rally **2.** [dans un nom de parti] party, union, alliance ■ **votez pour le Rassemblement écologiste** vote for the Green party **3.** [fait de se rassembler] gathering ■ **tous les ~s sont strictement interdits** all rallies *ou* gatherings are strictly forbidden ■ **vous devez empêcher le ~ des élèves dans le hall** you must prevent the pupils from gathering in the hall **4.** MIL : **sonner le ~** to sound the assembly ■ **~!** fall in!

rassembler [3] [rasɑ̃ble] *vt* **1.** [objets, idées, preuves] to collect, to gather ■ [documents] to collect, to assemble ■ **j'eus à peine le temps de ~ quelques affaires** I hardly had enough time to gather *ou* to put a few things together ■ **~ ses forces** to gather *ou* to muster one's strength ■ **~ ses esprits** to gather *ou* to collect one's wits ■ **~ son courage** to summon up one's courage **2.** [personnes] to gather together *(sép)* ■ [animaux] to round up *(sép)* ■ **leur manifestation a rassemblé des milliers de personnes** their demonstration drew *ou* attracted thousands of people **3.** ÉQUIT to collect.
◆ **se rassembler** *vpi* to gather together, to assemble ■ **ils se sont rassemblés devant chez moi** they gathered together *ou* assembled outside my home.

rassembleur, euse [rasɑ̃blœr, øz] *nm, f sout* **ce fut un grand ~** he was a great unifier of people.

rasseoir [65] [raswar] *vt* **1.** [asseoir de nouveau] : **~ qqn** to sit sb down (again) ■ **veuillez ~ le malade** [dans son lit] please sit the patient up again ■ **je vous en prie, faites ~ tout le monde** please, have everybody sit down again **2.** [replacer] to put back *(sép)* ■ **~ une statue sur son socle** to put a statue back on its plinth.
◆ **se rasseoir** *vpi* to sit down again ■ **allez vous ~** go back to your seat, go and sit down again.

rasséréner [18] [raserene] *vt litt* to make calm ■ **ses déclarations m'ont complètement rasséréné** what he said put my mind completely at rest.
◆ **se rasséréner** *vpi litt* to become calm *ou* serene again.

rasseyait, rassied *etc v* ▷ **rasseoir**.

rassir [32] [rasir] *vi* [gâteau, pain] to go stale ■ [viande] : **laisser ~ un morceau de bœuf** to let a piece of beef hang.
◆ **se rassir** *vpi* to go stale.

rassis¹, e [rasi, iz] *pp* ▷ **rasseoir**.

rassis², e [rasi, iz] *adj* **1.** [gâteau, pain] stale ■ [viande] properly hung **2.** *litt* [calme] calm, composed ■ [pondéré] balanced.

rassoit *etc v* ▷ **rasseoir**.

rassortiment [rasɔrtimɑ̃] = **réassortiment**.

rassortir [rasɔrtir] = **réassortir**.

rassoyait *etc v* ▷ **rasseoir**.

rassurant, e [rasyrɑ̃, ɑ̃t] *adj* **1.** [personne] reassuring ■ **le président n'a pas été très ~ dans ses dernières déclarations** the president's most recent statements were not very reassuring **2.** [nouvelle, déclaration, ton, voix] reassuring, comforting.

rassurer [3] [rasyre] *vt* to reassure ■ **va vite ~ ta mère** go and tell your mother she has nothing to worry about, go and set your mother's mind at ease ■ **je n'étais pas très rassuré** I felt rather worried.
◆ **se rassurer** ◇ *vp (emploi réfléchi)* to reassure o.s. ■ **j'essaie de me ~ en me disant que tout n'est pas fini** I try to reassure myself by saying it's not all over.
◇ *vpi* : **elle a mis longtemps à se ~** it took her a while to calm down ■ **rassure-toi** don't worry.

rasta [rasta] ◇ *adj inv* Rasta *(inv)*.
◇ *nmf* Rasta.
◇ *nm*▲ = **rastaquouère**.

rastaquouère▲ [rastakwɛr] *nm dated and racist term used with reference to wealthy foreigners.*

Rastignac [rastiɲak] *npr* LITTÉR *character from Balzac's 'la Comédie humaine', the typical young man from the provinces trying to make good in the capital.*

rat [ra] ◇ *nm* **1.** ZOOL rat ■ **faire la chasse aux ~s** to go ratting ▶ **~ des champs** field mouse ■ **~ d'eau** water vole *ou* rat ■ **~ d'égout** sewer rat **2.** *fig* **~ de bibliothèque** bookworm ■ **~ d'hôtel** hotel thief ■ **être fait comme un ~**△ *fam* to have no escape, to be cornered **3.** DANSE : **petit ~ de l'Opéra** ballet student *(at the Opéra de Paris)* **4.** *fam péj* [avare] miser, skinflint **5.** [par affection] : **mon (petit) ~** my darling.
◇ *adj m fam péj* [avare] stingy, tightfisted.

ratafia [ratafja] *nm* ratafia (liqueur).

ratage [rataʒ] *nm* failure ■ **après un ou deux ~s, il a réussi son soufflé à la perfection** after one or two disastrous attempts, he got the soufflé just right.

rataplan [rataplɑ̃] *onomat* rat-a-tat.

ratatiné, e [ratatine] *adj* **1.** [fruit] shrivelled (up) **2.** [visage] wrinkled, wizened **3.** *fam* [voiture, vélo] smashed up ■ [soufflé] flat.

ratatiner [3] [ratatine] *vt* **1.** *fam* [démolir] : **le bâtiment a été ratatiné en quelques secondes** the building was reduced to a pile of rubble within seconds ■ **la voiture a été complètement ratatinée** the car was completely smashed up **2.** [flétrir] : **l'âge l'a complètement ratatiné** he has become wizened with age **3.** *fam* [battre] : **je me suis fait ~ au tennis/aux échecs** I got thrashed at tennis/chess ‖ [assassiner] : **il s'est fait ~** he got done in.
◆ **se ratatiner** *vpi* **1.** [se dessécher] to shrivel **2.** *fam* [rapetisser] to shrink ■ **elle se ratatine en vieillissant** she's shrinking with age **3.** *fam* [s'écraser] to crash ■ **la voiture s'est ratatinée contre un mur** the car crashed *ou* smashed into a wall.

ratatouille [ratatuj] *nf* CULIN : **~ (niçoise)** ratatouille.

rate [rat] *nf* **1.** ZOOL she-rat, female rat **2.** ANAT spleen.

raté, e [rate] ◇ *adj* **1.** [photo, sauce] spoilt ■ [coupe de cheveux] disastrous ■ **il est complètement ~, ce gâteau** this cake is a complete disaster **2.** [attentat] failed ■ [vie] wasted ■ [occasion] missed ■ [tentative] failed, abortive, unsuccessful ■ **un musicien ~** a failed musician.
◇ *nm, f* failure, loser.
◆ **raté** *nm* **1.** [bruit] misfiring *(U)* ■ **le moteur a des ~s** the engine is misfiring **2.** [défaut] hitch **3.** ARM misfire.

râteau, x [rato] *nm* rake ■ **~ faneur** tedder.

râtelier [ratəlje] *nm* **1.** [support] rack ■ **~ à fusils/outils/pipes** gun/tool/pipe rack **2.** [mangeoire] rack **3.** *fam* [dentier] dentures, (set of) false teeth.

rater [3] [rate] ◇ *vi* **1.** *fam* [échouer] to fail ■ **je t'avais dit qu'elle serait en retard, et ça n'a pas raté!** I told you she'd be late, and sure enough she was! ■ **ça ne rate jamais** it never fails ■ **tais-toi, tu vas tout faire ~!** shut up or you'll ruin everything! **2.** ARM : **le coup a raté** the gun failed to go off.
◇ *vt* **1.** [but] to miss ■ **elle a raté la marche** she missed the step ▶ **j'ai raté mon coup** *fam* I made a mess of it ■ **s'il**

recommence, je te jure que je ne le raterai pas! *fam* if he does it again, I swear I'll get him! **2.** [avion, rendez-vous, visiteur, occasion] to miss ■ **je n'ai pas vu le concert – tu n'as rien raté/tu as raté quelque chose!** I didn't see the concert – you didn't miss anything/you really missed something! ■ **c'est une émission à ne pas ~** this programme is a must ➲ **tu n'en rates pas une!** *fam* you're always putting your foot in it! **3.** [ne pas réussir] : **il a complètement raté son oral** he made a complete mess of his oral ■ **il a raté son effet** he didn't achieve the desired effect ■ **il rate toujours les mayonnaises** his mayonnaise always goes wrong ■ **~ sa vie** to make a mess of one's life.

◆ **se rater** *vp (emploi réfléchi) fam* : **il s'est coupé les cheveux lui-même, il s'est complètement raté!** he cut his hair himself and made a complete mess of it! ■ **elle est tombée de vélo, elle ne s'est pas ratée!** she didn't half hurt herself when she fell off her bike! ■ **elle s'est ratée pour la troisième fois** that's her third (unsuccessful) suicide attempt.

ratiboiser [3] [ratibwaze] *vt fam* **1.** [voler] to pinch, to nick *esp UK* **2.** [ruiner] to clean out *(sép)* **3.** [tuer] to bump off *(sép)*, to do in *(sép)* **4.** [cheveux] : **je suis ressorti ratiboisé de chez le coiffeur** I got scalped at the hairdresser's.

raticide [ratisid] *nm* rat poison.

ratification [ratifikasjɔ̃] *nf* ratification.

ratifier [9] [ratifje] *vt* **1.** DR to ratify ■ **ils ont fait ~ le traité par le gouvernement** they put the treaty before Parliament for ratification **2.** *litt* [confirmer] to confirm.

ratio [rasjo] *nm* ÉCON & FIN ratio.

ratiocination [rasjɔsinasjɔ̃] *nf sout* quibble ■ **ce sont des ~s!** you're just splitting hairs!

ratiociner [3] [rasjɔsine] *vi sout* to quibble, to split hairs.

ration [rasjɔ̃] *nf* **1.** [portion] ration ■ **~s de guerre** war rations ■ **sa ~ de problèmes** *fig* his share of problems ■ **non merci, j'ai eu ma ~!** *hum* no thanks, I've had my fill (of it)! **2.** [quantité nécessaire] daily intake ■ **~ alimentaire** food (intake) **3.** MIL rations.

rationaliser [3] [rasjɔnalize] *vt* to rationalize.

rationalisme [rasjɔnalism] *nm* rationalism.

rationaliste [rasjɔnalist] *adj & nmf* rationalist.

rationalité [rasjɔnalite] *nf* rationality.

rationnel, elle [rasjɔnɛl] *adj* **1.** MATH & PHILOS rational **2.** [sensé] rational ■ **il n'a pas une attitude très ~le** his attitude is not very rational.

rationnellement [rasjɔnɛlmɑ̃] *adv* **1.** MATH & PHILOS rationally **2.** [avec bon sens] rationally, sensibly, logically.

rationnement [rasjɔnmɑ̃] *nm* rationing.

rationner [3] [rasjɔne] *vt* **1.** [quelque chose] to ration **2.** [quelqu'un] to put on rations, to ration ■ **il va bientôt falloir le ~!** *hum* we'll have to put him on (short) rations soon!

◆ **se rationner** *vp (emploi réfléchi)* to ration o.s.

ratisser [3] [ratise] ◇ *vt* **1.** [gravier, allée] to rake ■ [feuilles, herbe coupée] to rake up *(sép)* **2.** *fam* [voler] to pinch, to nick *esp UK* ■ [ruiner] to clean out *(sép)* ■ **il s'est fait ~ au poker** he got cleaned out playing poker **3.** [fouiller] to comb **4.** SPORT to heel.

◇ *vi* : **~ large** *fam* to cast one's net wide *fig*.

raton [ratɔ̃] *nm* **1.** ZOOL young rat ■ **~ laveur** raccoon **2.** [par affection] : **mon ~!** my darling! **3.** ▲ *racist term used with reference to North African Arabs.*

ratonnade [ratɔnad] *nf violent racist attack on North African Arab immigrants.*

RATP (*abr de* **Régie autonome des transports parisiens**) *npr f Paris transport authority.*

rattachement [rataʃmɑ̃] *nm* : **opérer le ~ de territoires à la métropole** to bring territories under the jurisdiction of the home country ■ **demander son ~ à un service** to ask to be attached to a department.

rattacher [3] [rataʃe] *vt* **1.** [paquet] to tie up *(sép)* again, to do up *(sép)* again ■ [ceinture, lacet] to do up *(sép)* again ■ [chien] to tie up *(sép)* again ■ [plante grimpante] to tie back *(sép)* **2.** ADMIN & POLIT : **~ plusieurs services à une même direction** to bring several departments under the same management ■ **~ un territoire à un pays** to bring a territory under the jurisdiction of a country **3.** [établir un lien] : **~ qqch à** to connect *ou* to link sthg with, to relate sthg to.

◆ **se rattacher à** *vp+prép* **1.** [découler de] to derive from **2.** [avoir un lien avec] to be connected *ou* linked with, to be related to ■ **laissez de côté tout ce qui ne se rattache pas au problème central** put everything that isn't (directly) related to the key issue to one side.

ratte [rat] *nf* BOT & CULIN fingerling potato, (La) Ratte potato.

rattrapable [ratrapabl] *adj* : **une telle erreur ne serait pas ~** a mistake like that couldn't be put right.

rattrapage [ratrapaʒ] *nm* **1.** [d'un étudiant] passing, letting through ■ [remise à niveau] : **~ scolaire** ≃ remedial teaching ■ **cours de ~** *extra class for pupils who need to catch up* ■ **je dois passer l'oral de ~** I've got to resit the oral ■ **session de ~** resit **2.** [d'une maille] picking up **3.** ÉCON : **~ des salaires** wage adjustment.

rattraper [3] [ratrape] *vt* **1.** [animal, prisonnier] to recapture, to catch again **2.** [objet qui tombe] to catch (hold of) ■ **~ la balle au vol/bond** to catch the ball in the air/on the bounce **3.** [quelqu'un parti plus tôt] to catch up with **4.** [compenser] : **~ le temps perdu** *ou* **son retard** to make up for lost time ■ **il a rattrapé les cours manqués** he has caught up on the lessons he missed ■ **~ du sommeil** to catch up on one's sleep ■ **pour ~ nos pertes** to make good our losses **5.** [erreur, maladresse] to put right **6.** [étudiant] to let through **7.** [maille] to pick up *(sép)*.

◆ **se rattraper** ◇ *vp (emploi passif)* : **le temps perdu ne se rattrape jamais** *prov* you can never make up for lost time.

◇ *vpi* **1.** [éviter la chute] to catch o.s. (in time) ■ **se ~ à qqn/qqch** to grab *ou* to catch hold of sb/sthg to stop o.s. falling **2.** [compenser] : **j'ai l'intention de me ~!** I'm going to make up for it! ■ **la limonade est en promotion, mais ils se rattrapent sur le café** lemonade is on special offer, but they've put up the price of coffee to make up for it **3.** [élève] to catch up.

rature [ratyr] *nf* crossing out, deletion ■ **tu as fait trop de ~s** you've crossed too many things out ■ **'sans ~s ni surcharges'** 'without deletions or alterations'.

raturer [3] [ratyre] *vt* to cross out *(sép)*, to delete.

rauque [rok] *adj* **1.** [voix] husky **2.** [cri] raucous.

ravage [ravaʒ] *nm* [destruction] devastation ■ **les ~s de la maladie/du temps** the ravages of disease/of time ■ **faire des ~s** *pr* to wreak havoc ■ **l'alcoolisme faisait des ~s** *fig* alcoholism was rife ■ **notre cousin fait des ~s (dans les cœurs)!** our cousin is a heartbreaker!

ravagé, e [ravaʒe] *adj* **1.** [par la fatigue, le désespoir] haggard ■ [par la maladie, la douleur] ravaged **2.** *fam* [fou] loopy, barmy *esp UK*, nuts ■ **c'est un mec complètement ~!** he's completely loopy!

ravager [17] [ravaʒe] *vt* [région, ville] to ravage, to lay waste *(insép)*, to devastate ■ **la guerre a ravagé leur vie** the war wreaked havoc upon their lives.

ravageur, euse [ravaʒœr, øz] ◇ *adj* **1.** [destructeur] destructive ■ **des insectes ~s** insect pests **2.** [séducteur - sourire] devastating.

◇ *nm, f* ravager.

ravalement [ravalmɑ̃] *nm* [d'une façade] cleaning.

ravaler [3] [ravale] *vt* **1.** CONSTR to clean ■ **ils ont ravalé la façade de la mairie** they've given the front of the town hall a clean ➲ **se faire ~ la façade**△ *ou* **le portrait**△ to have a facelift **2.** [salive] to swallow ■ [larmes] to hold *ou* to choke back ■ [colère] to stifle, to choke back ■ [fierté] to swallow ■ **faire ~ ses paroles à qqn** *fam* to make sb eat his words **3.** [abaisser] to lower **4.** MIN to deepen.

◆ **se ravaler** ◇ *vp (emploi réfléchi)* [s'abaisser] to debase *ou* to lower o.s. ■ **se ~ aux pires bassesses** to stoop to the meanest acts.

◇ *vpt*△ : **se ~ la façade** [se maquiller] to slap some make-up on, to put on one's warpaint.

ravaudage [ravodaʒ] *nm* ***vieilli*** [de chaussettes] darning ■ [de vêtements] mending, repairing.

ravauder [3] [ravode] *vt* ***vieilli*** [chaussettes] to darn ■ [vêtements] to sew up *(sép)*, to mend.

rave[1] [rav] *nf* BOT rape.

rave[2] [rɛv] *nm* [soirée] rave.

Ravenne [ravɛn] *npr* Ravenna.

ravi, e [ravi] *adj* delighted ■ **il n'a pas eu l'air ~** he didn't look too pleased ■ **être ~ de qqch** to be delighted with sthg ■ **~ (de faire votre connaissance)** (I'm) delighted *ou* very pleased to meet you.

ravier [ravje] *nm* hors-d'œuvres dish.

ravigotant, e [ravigɔtɑ̃, ɑ̃t] *adj* ***fam*** [vent] invigorating, bracing ■ [soupe, vin] warming.

ravigote [ravigɔt] *nf* ravigote sauce *(vinaigrette with herbs and hard-boiled eggs)*.

◆ **à la ravigote** *loc adj* with a ravigote sauce.

ravigoter [3] [ravigɔte] *vt* ***fam*** to buck up *(sép)* ■ **ravigoté par une nuit de repos** refreshed *ou* restored by a night's sleep.

ravin [ravɛ̃] *nm* gully, ravine.

ravine [ravin] *nf* gully.

ravinement [ravinmɑ̃] *nm* [action] gullying.

raviner [3] [ravine] *vt* **1.** GÉOGR to gully **2.** ***fig*** & ***sout*** to furrow ■ **un visage raviné** a deeply lined face.

ravioli [ravjɔli] *(pl inv ou pl* **raviolis***)* *nm* ravioli *(U)*.

ravir [32] [ravir] *vt* **1.** [enchanter] to delight ■ **cette naissance les a ravis** they were thrilled with the new baby **2.** ***litt*** [enlever] : **~ qqch à qqn** to rob sb of sthg ■ **prématurément ravi à l'affection des siens** taken too early from (the bosom of) family and friends.

◆ **à ravir** *loc adv* [merveilleusement] : **la robe lui va à ~** the dress looks lovely on her.

raviser [3] [ravize] ◆ **se raviser** *vpi* to change one's mind ■ **il s'est ravisé** he changed his mind, he thought better of it, he had second thoughts.

ravissant, e [ravisɑ̃, ɑ̃t] *adj* [vêtement] gorgeous, beautiful ■ [endroit, maison] delightful, beautiful ■ [femme] strikingly *ou* ravishingly beautiful.

ravissement [ravismɑ̃] *nm* **1.** [enchantement] : **c'est un véritable ~ (pour les yeux)** it is an enchanting sight ■ **avec ~** delightedly ■ **mettre *ou* plonger qqn dans le ~** to send sb into raptures **2.** ***litt*** [enlèvement] abduction **3.** RELIG rapture.

ravisseur, euse [ravisœr, øz] *nm, f* abductor ***sout***, kidnapper.

ravitaillement [ravitajmɑ̃] *nm* **1.** MIL & NAUT supplying ■ **assurer le ~ de qqn en munitions/carburant/vivres** to supply sb with ammunition/fuel/food ▶ **bateau/véhicule de ~** supply ship/vehicle **2.** AÉRON refuelling ■ **~ en vol** in-flight *ou* mid-air refuelling **3.** [denrées] food supplies ■ **je vais au ~** ***fam*** I'm off to buy some food, I'm going for fresh supplies.

ravitailler [3] [ravitaje] *vt* **1.** MIL to supply ■ **~ un régiment en vivres** to supply a regiment with food, to supply food to a regiment **2.** AÉRON to refuel **3.** [famille, campement] : **~ qqn en** to supply sb with, to give sb fresh supplies of.

◆ **se ravitailler** *vp (emploi réfléchi)* **1.** [en nourriture] to get (fresh) supplies **2.** [en carburant] to refuel.

ravitailleur, euse [ravitajœr, øz] ◇ *adj* : **avion ~** supply plane, (air) tanker ■ **véhicule/navire ~** supply vehicle/ship.
◇ *nm, f* MIL quartermaster ■ NAUT supply officer.

◆ **ravitailleur** *nm* **1.** AÉRON [avion] tanker aircraft ■ **~ d'avions** [camion-citerne] (airport) supply tanker **2.** MIL supply vehicle **3.** NAUT [d'escadre, de sous-marin] supply ship ■ [pour travaux en mer] refurbishment ship.

raviver [3] [ravive] *vt* **1.** [feu] to rekindle, to revive ■ [couleur] to brighten up *(sép)* **2.** [sensation, sentiment] to rekindle, to revive ■ **le procès va ~ l'horreur/les souffrances de la guerre** the trial will bring back the horrors/sufferings of the war **3.** MÉTALL [gén] to clean ■ [à l'abrasif] to scour ■ [à l'acide] to pickle ■ [au chalumeau] to burn off *(sép)*.

◆ **se raviver** *vpi* [sentiment] to return ■ **sa haine se ravivait dès qu'il le voyait** every time he saw him, his hatred flared up again.

ravoir [ravwar] *vt (à l'infinitif seulement)* **1.** [récupérer] to get back **2.** ***fam*** [vêtement] : **~ une chemise** to get a shirt clean **3.** [maladie] : **je ne veux pas ~ la grippe** I don't want to get flu again.

rayé, e [rɛje] *adj* **1.** [à raies - papier] lined, ruled ; [- vêtement] striped ■ **tissu ~ bleu et rouge** blue and red striped fabric, fabric with blue and red stripes **2.** [éraflé - verre, disque] scratched **3.** ARM rifled.

rayer [11] [rɛje] *vt* **1.** [abîmer] to scratch **2.** [éliminer - faute, coquille] to cross *ou* to score out *(sép)* ; [- clause, codicille] to cancel ; [- avocat, médecin] to strike off *(sép)* ■ **'~ la mention inutile'** 'delete where inapplicable' ■ **j'ai rayé son souvenir de ma mémoire** I've erased his memory from my mind ▶ **rayé de la carte** wiped off the face of the earth **3.** ARM to rifle.

rayon [rɛjɔ̃] *nm*

A.

1. OPT & PHYS ray ■ **~ cathodique** cathode ray ■ **~ laser** laser beam ■ **~ lumineux** (light) ray ■ **~ vert** green flash
2. [de lumière] beam, shaft ■ [du soleil] ray ■ **un ~ de lune** a moonbeam ■ **un ~ de soleil** a ray of sunshine, a sunbeam ; MÉTÉOR a brief sunny spell ; ***fig*** a ray of sunshine
3. MATH [vecteur] radius vector ■ [d'un cercle] radius
4. [de roue] spoke
5. [distance] radius ■ **dans un ~ de vingt kilomètres** within (a radius of) twenty kilometres
6. AUTO : **~ de braquage** turning circle
7. MIL : **~ d'action** range ■ **à grand ~ d'action** long-range ■ **étendre son ~ d'action** ***fig*** to increase *ou* to widen the scope of one's activities

B.

1. [étagère - gén] shelf ; [- à livres] shelf, bookshelf
2. COMM department ■ **nous n'en avons plus en ~** we're out of stock
3. ***fam*** [domaine] : **demande à ton père, c'est son ~** ask your father, that's his department ■ **il en connaît un ~ en électricité** he really knows a thing or two about electricity
4. ZOOL comb ■ [d'abeilles] honeycomb
5. HORT small furrow, drill.

◆ **rayons** *nmpl* **1.** MÉD X-ray treatment *(U) (for cancer)* ■ **on lui fait des ~s** ***fam*** he's having radiotherapy *ou* radiation treatment **2.** PHYS : **~s bêta/gamma** beta/gamma rays ■ **~s infrarouges/ultraviolets** infrared/ultraviolet light ■ **~s X** X-rays ■ **passer qqch aux ~s X** to X-ray sthg.

rayonnage [rɛjɔnaʒ] *nm* [étagères] shelving *(U)*, shelves ■ **sur les ~s** on the shelves.

rayonnant, e [rɛjɔnɑ̃, ɑ̃t] *adj* **1.** [radieux] radiant ■ **~ de joie** radiant with joy ■ **~ de santé** glowing *ou* blooming with health **2.** ARCHIT & ART radiating ▶ **gothique ~** High Gothic **3.** PHYS : **chaleur/énergie ~e** radiant heat/energy **4.** MÉD : **douleur ~e** radiating pain.

rayonne [rɛjɔn] *nf* rayon.

rayonnement [rɛjɔnmɑ̃] *nm* **1.** [influence] influence ■ **le ~ de la France au siècle des Lumières** the influence of France during the Enlightenment **2.** ***litt*** [éclat] radiance **3.** [lumière - d'une étoile, du feu] radiance **4.** SC radiation ■ **~ électromagnétique/optique/visible** electromagnetic/optical/visible radiation ■ **chauffage par ~** radiant heating ■ **énergie de ~** radiant energy.

rayonner [3] [rɛjɔne] ◇ *vi* **1.** [personne, physionomie] to be radiant ■ **~ de joie** to be radiant with joy ■ **~ de santé** to be blooming with health **2.** ***litt*** [soleil] to shine **3.** [circuler - influence] to spread ; [- touriste] to tour around ; [- chaleur] to

radiate ■ **nos cars rayonnent dans toute la région** our coaches cover every corner of the region **4.** [être disposé en rayons] to radiate **5.** OPT & PHYS to radiate **6.** MÉD : **douleur qui rayonne** radiating pain.
◇ *vt* HORT to furrow.

rayure [rɛjyr] *nf* **1.** [ligne] line, stripe ■ [du pelage] stripe ■ **papier à ~s** lined *ou* ruled paper ■ **tissu à ~s** striped fabric ■ **une chemise à ~s bleues** a blue-striped shirt **2.** [éraflure] score, scratch **3.** ARM groove, rifling.

raz [ra] *nm* **1.** [détroit] strait *(run by fast tidal races, in Brittany)* **2.** [courant] race.

raz(-)de(-)marée [radmare] *nm inv* **1.** GÉOGR tidal wave, tsunami *spéc* **2.** *fig* tidal wave ■ **~ électoral** landslide victory.

razzia [razja] *nf* **1.** MIL foray, raid **2.** *fam fig* raid ■ **faire une ~ sur qqch** to raid sthg.

RBE *nm* = **revenu brut d'exploitation.**

R-C = **rez-de-chaussée.**

R-D (*abr de* **recherche-développement**) *nf* R & D.

RDA (*abr de* **République démocratique allemande**) *npr f* GDR ■ **en ~** in the GDR.

RDB *nm* = **revenu disponible brut.**

RdC = **rez-de-chaussée.**

ré [re] *nm inv* D ■ [chanté] re, ray, *voir aussi* **fa.**

Rê [rɛ] *npr* Râ.

réa [rea] *nm* pulley (wheel).

réabonnement [reabɔnmɑ̃] *nm* [à un cinéma, théâtre *etc*] renewal of one's season ticket ■ [à une revue] subscription renewal ■ [à un club] membership renewal.

réabonner [3] [reabɔne] *vt* : **~ qqn à une revue** to renew sb's subscription to a magazine.
◆ **se réabonner** *vp (emploi réfléchi)* [à un cinéma, théâtre *etc*] to renew one's season ticket ■ [à une revue] to renew one's subscription.

réac [reak] *adj* & *nmf fam péj* reactionary.

réaccoutumer [3] [reakutyme] *vt sout* to reaccustom ■ **~ qqn à qqch** to reaccustom sb to sthg, to get sb used to sthg again.
◆ **se réaccoutumer à** *vp+prép* to reaccustom o.s. to, to become reaccustomed to.

réacheminer [3] [reaʃmine] *vt* to forward.

réactance [reaktɑ̃s] *nf* reactance ■ **bobine de ~** reaction coil.

réacteur [reaktœr] *nm* **1.** AÉRON jet (engine) **2.** CHIM, NUCL & PHYS reactor ■ **~ nucléaire** nuclear reactor.

réactif, ive [reaktif, iv] *adj* CHIM & PHYS reactive ■ **papier ~** reagent paper ■ **substance réactive** reactant.
◆ **réactif** *nm* **1.** CHIM reactant **2.** PSYCHOL reactive.

réaction [reaksjɔ̃] *nf* **1.** [réponse] reaction, response ■ **la nouvelle l'a laissée sans ~** she showed no reaction to the news ■ **il a eu une ~ très violente** he reacted very violently ⊙ **temps de ~** MÉD reaction time ; PSYCHOL latent period *ou* time **2.** [riposte] reaction ■ **en ~ contre** as a reaction against **3.** POLIT reaction ■ **gouvernement/vote de ~** reactionary government/vote **4.** AÉRON, ASTRONAUT, CHIM & PHYS reaction ■ **propulsion par ~ atomique** atomic-powered propulsion ■ **~ en chaîne** *pr* chain reaction ; *fig* chain reaction, domino effect **5.** ÉLECTRON : **~ négative** negative feedback.

réactionnaire [reaksjɔnɛr] *adj* & *nmf* reactionary.

réactionnel, elle [reaksjɔnɛl] *adj* **1.** CHIM & PHYSIOL reactional ■ **formation ~le** reaction formation **2.** PSYCHOL reactive.

réactive [reaktiv] *f* ▷ **réactif.**

réactiver [3] [reaktive] *vt* **1.** [feu] to rekindle ■ [circulation sanguine] to restore ■ [système] to reactivate ■ [négociations] to revive **2.** CHIM to reactivate.

réactivité [reaktivite] *nf* **1.** CHIM reactivity **2.** BIOL reactivity, excitability.

réactualisation [reaktɥalizasjɔ̃] *nf* **1.** [ajustement] adapting, readjustment **2.** [modernisation] updating, bringing up to date.

réactualiser [3] [reaktɥalize] *vt* **1.** [adapter - système] to adapt, to readjust **2.** [moderniser - dictionnaire] to update, to bring up to date.

réadaptation [readaptasjɔ̃] *nf* **1.** [rééducation] reeducation **2.** BIOL readaptation.

réadapter [3] [readapte] *vt* [handicapé] to reeducate, to rehabilitate ■ [muscle] to reeducate.
◆ **se réadapter** *vpi* [handicapé, exilé] to readjust ■ **se ~ à qqch** to readjust to sthg.

réaffecter [4] [reafɛkte] *vt* **1.** [personne - à une fonction] to reappoint, to renominate ; [- à une région, un pays] to post back *(sép)* **2.** [crédits] to reallocate.

réaffirmer [3] [reafirme] *vt* to reaffirm, to reassert.

réagir [32] [reaʒir] *vi* **1.** CHIM, PHOTO & PHYS to react **2.** [répondre] to react ■ **il a bien/mal réagi à son départ** he reacted well/badly to her leaving ■ **il faut absolument ~** we really have to do something **3.** MÉD to respond.

réajuster [reaʒyste] = **rajuster.**

réalisable [realizabl] *adj* **1.** [projet] feasible, workable ■ [rêve] attainable ■ **tu sais bien que ce n'est pas ~!** you know it can't *ou* it won't work! **2.** FIN realizable.

réalisateur, trice [realizatœr, tris] *nm, f* **1.** CINÉ director, film-maker ■ RADIO & TV producer **2.** [maître d'œuvre] : **il a été le ~ du projet** he was the one who brought the project to fruition.

réalisation [realizasjɔ̃] *nf* **1.** [d'un projet] carrying out, execution ■ [d'un rêve] fulfilment ■ [d'un exploit] achievement **2.** [chose réalisée] achievement ■ **être en cours de ~** to be under way **3.** DR [d'un contrat] fulfilment ■ COMM [d'une vente] clinching, closing ■ FIN [liquidation] realization **4.** CINÉ & TV [mise en scène] directing, filmmaking ■ [film] production, film *UK*, movie *US* ■ **'~ (de) George Cukor'** 'directed by George Cukor' ■ **la ~ de ce film coûterait trop cher** making this film would cost too much **5.** RADIO [émission] production ■ [enregistrement] recording ■ **à la ~, Fred X** sound engineer, Fred X **6.** MUS realization.

réaliser [3] [realize] *vt* **1.** [rendre réel - projet] to carry out *(sép)* ; [- rêve] to fulfil, to realize ; [- espoir] to realize **2.** [accomplir - œuvre] to complete, to carry out *(sép)* ; [- exploit] to achieve, to perform ■ **les efforts réalisés** the efforts that have been made **3.** COMM [vente] to make ■ FIN [capital, valeurs] to realize ■ [bénéfice] to make **4.** CINÉ, RADIO & TV to direct **5.** MUS to realize **6.** [comprendre] to realize ■ *(en usage absolu)* **je ne réalise pas encore** it hasn't sunk in yet ■ **elle est encore sous le choc, mais quand elle va ~!** she's still in a state of shock, but wait till it hits her!
◆ **se réaliser** *vpi* **1.** [s'accomplir - projet] to be carried out ; [- rêve, vœu] to come true, to be fulfilled ; [- prédiction] to come true **2.** [personne] to fulfil o.s.

réalisme [realism] *nm* **1.** [gén] realism ■ **faire preuve de ~** to be realistic **2.** ART & LITTÉR realism.

réaliste [realist] ◇ *adj* **1.** [gén] realistic **2.** ART & LITTÉR realist.
◇ *nmf* realist.

réalité [realite] *nf* **1.** [existence] reality ■ **douter de la ~ d'un fait** to doubt the reality of a fact **2.** [univers réel] : **la ~** reality ■ **regarder la ~ en face** to face up to reality ■ **dans la ~** in real life ■ **quand la ~ dépasse la fiction** when fact is stranger than fiction **3.** [fait] fact ■ **prendre conscience des ~s (de la vie)** to face facts **4.** INFORM : **~ virtuelle** virtual reality, VR.
◆ **en réalité** *loc adv* **1.** [en fait] in (actual) fact **2.** [vraiment] in real life ■ **à la scène, elle paraît plus jeune qu'elle n'est en ~** on stage, she looks younger than she does in real life.

réaménagement [reamenaʒmɑ̃] *nm* **1.** [modification - d'un bâtiment] refitting *(U)* ; [- d'un projet] reorganization, replanning *(U)* ■ **~ urbain** urban redevelopment **2.** FIN readjustment.

réaménager [17] [reamenaʒe] *vt* **1.** [espace, salle] to refit, to refurbish **2.** [horaire] to replan, to readjust ■ [politique] to reshape **3.** FIN [dette] to reschedule.

réamorcer [16] [reamɔrse] *vt* **1.** [pompe] to prime again ■ **~ la pompe** *fig* to get things rolling again **2.** [discussion] to begin *ou* to start again, to reinitiate **3.** INFORM to reboot.

réanimation [reanimasjɔ̃] *nf* [action] resuscitation ■ **service de ~ (intensive)** intensive care unit ■ **admis en ~** [service] put in intensive care.

réanimer [3] [reanime] *vt* **1.** [malade] to resuscitate, to revive **2.** [conversation, intérêt] to revive.

réapparaître [91] [reaparɛtr] *vi (aux être ou avoir)* to come back, to reappear, to appear again ■ **tous ces facteurs ont contribué à faire ~ les conflits entre les ethnies** all of these factors have contributed to the resurgence of ethnic conflicts.

réapparition [reaparisjɔ̃] *nf* **1.** [du soleil] reappearance **2.** [d'une vedette] comeback.

réapparu, e [reapary] *pp* ▻ **réapparaître**.

réapprendre [79] [reaprɑ̃dr] *vt* to learn again.

réapprovisionnement [reaprɔvizjɔnmɑ̃] *nm* COMM [d'un magasin] restocking ■ [d'un commerçant] re-supplying.

réapprovisionner [3] [reaprɔvizjɔne] *vt* COMM [magasin] to restock ■ [commerçant] to resupply.

réarmement [rearməmɑ̃] *nm* **1.** MIL rearmament, rearming ■ POLIT rearmament **2.** NAUT refitting **3.** ARM cocking.

réarmer [3] [rearme] ◇ *vt* **1.** MIL & POLIT to rearm **2.** NAUT to refit **3.** ARM to cock.
◇ *vi* [pays] to rearm.

réassort [reasɔr] *nm* new stock.

réassortiment [reasɔrtimɑ̃] *nm* **1.** COMM [d'un magasin] restocking ■ [d'un stock] renewing ■ [de marchandises] new stock, fresh supplies **2.** [de pièces d'un service] matching (up) ■ [d'une soucoupe] replacing.

réassortir [32] [reasɔrtir] *vt* COMM [magasin] to restock ■ [stock] to renew.

réassurance [reasyrɑ̃s] *nf* reinsurance.

rebaisser [4] [rəbese] ◇ *vi* to go down again, to drop *ou* to fall again.
◇ *vt* [prix] to bring down *(sép)* again, to lower again ■ [chauffage, feu, son] to turn down *(sép)* again, to turn down low again.

rebaptiser [3] [rəbatize] *vt* to rename.

rébarbatif, ive [rebarbatif, iv] *adj* **1.** [personne] cantankerous, surly **2.** [idée] off-putting *esp UK*, daunting.

rebat *etc v* ▻ **rebattre**.

rebâtir [32] [rəbatir] *vt* to rebuild.

rebattre [83] [rəbatr] *vt* **1.** [cartes] to reshuffle **2.** *loc* **elle m'a rebattu les oreilles de son divorce** she went on and on *ou* she kept harping on about her divorce.

rebattu, e [rəbaty] *adj* [éculé] hackneyed, worn out.

rebelle [rəbɛl] ◇ *adj* **1.** POLIT rebel *(modif)* **2.** [indomptable - cheval] rebellious ; [- cœur, esprit] rebellious, intractable ; [- enfant] rebellious, wilful ; [- mèche] unruly, wild **3.** [réfractaire à] : **~ à** impervious to ■ **~ à tout conseil** unwilling to heed advice, impervious to advice **4.** [acné, fièvre] stubborn, refractory *spéc.*
◇ *nmf* rebel.

rebeller [4] [rəbele] ◆ **se rebeller** *vpi* to rebel ■ **la jeune génération de cinéastes qui se rebellent contre les conventions** the younger generation of filmmakers who flout established conventions.

rébellion [rebɛljɔ̃] *nf* **1.** [révolte] rebellion **2.** [les rebelles] : **la ~** the rebels.

rebelote [rəbəlɔt] *nf* **1.** JEUX rebelote *(said when playing the second card of a pair of king and queen of trumps while playing belote)* **2.** *fam loc* **~!** here we go again!

rebiffer [3] [rəbife] ◆ **se rebiffer** *vpi fam* **quand je lui fais une remarque, il se rebiffe** when I say anything to him he reacts really badly ■ **se ~ contre qqch** to kick out against sthg.

rebiquer [3] [rəbike] *vi fam* to stick up.

reblochon [rəblɔʃɔ̃] *nm* Reblochon (cheese).

reboisement [rəbwazmɑ̃] *nm* reafforestation.

reboiser [3] [rəbwaze] *vt* to reafforest.

rebond [rəbɔ̃] *nm* bounce, rebound ■ **je l'ai attrapé au ~** I caught it on the rebound.

rebondi, e [rəbɔ̃di] *adj* [joue, face] chubby, plump ■ [formes] well-rounded ■ **à la poitrine ~e** buxom.

rebondir [32] [rəbɔ̃dir] *vi* **1.** [balle, ballon] to bounce **2.** [conversation] to get going again ■ [intérêt] to be revived *ou* renewed ■ [procès, scandale] to get new impetus ■ **faire ~ qqch** to give sthg a fresh start *ou* a new lease of life **3.** [intrigue] to take off again.

rebondissement [rəbɔ̃dismɑ̃] *nm* **1.** [d'une balle] bouncing **2.** [d'une affaire] (new) development.

rebord [rəbɔr] *nm* [d'un fossé, d'une étagère] edge ■ [d'une assiette, d'un verre] rim ■ [d'une cheminée] mantelpiece ■ [d'une fenêtre] (window) ledge *ou* sill ■ **le savon est sur le ~ de la baignoire** the soap is on the side *ou* edge of the bath.

reboucher [3] [rəbuʃe] *vt* **1.** [bouteille de vin] to recork ■ [flacon, carafe] to restopper ■ **'~ après usage'** 'replace lid after use' **2.** CONSTR [trou] to fill, to plug ■ [fissure] to fill, to stop.
◆ **se reboucher** *vpi* [évier] to get blocked again.

rebours [rəbur] ◆ **à rebours** *loc adv* **1.** [à l'envers - compter, lire] backwards ■ [dans le mauvais sens] the wrong way ■ **tu prends tout à ~!** you're always getting the wrong idea!, you're always getting the wrong end of the stick! *UK* **2.** TEXT against the nap *ou* the pile.
◆ **à rebours de** *loc prép* : **aller à ~ de tout le monde** to go *ou* to run counter to the general trend.

rebouteur, euse [rəbutœr, øz], **rebouteux, euse** [rəbutø, øz] *nm, f* bonesetter.

reboutonner [3] [rəbutɔne] *vt* to button up *(sép)* again, to rebutton.
◆ **se reboutonner** *vp (emploi réfléchi)* to do o.s. up again.

rebrousse-poil [rəbruspwal] ◆ **à rebrousse-poil** *loc adv* **1.** TEXT against the nap *ou* the pile **2.** [maladroitement] the wrong way ■ **mieux vaut ne pas prendre le patron à ~** better not rub the boss up the wrong way.

rebrousser [3] [rəbruse] *vt* **1.** [cheveux] to ruffle **2.** [poil] to brush the wrong way ■ **~ le poil à qqn** *fam* to rub sb up the wrong way **3.** TEXT [drap] to brush against the nap **4.** *loc* **~ chemin** to turn back, to retrace one's steps.

rebuffade [rəbyfad] *nf* rebuff ■ **essuyer une ~** to suffer a rebuff.

rébus [rebys] *nm* rebus ■ **ce texte est un ~ pour moi** *fig* this text is a real puzzle for me.

rebut [rəby] *nm* **1.** [article défectueux] second, reject **2.** [poubelle, casse] : **mettre** *ou* **jeter au ~** to throw away, to discard ■ **bon à mettre au ~** [vêtement] only fit to be thrown out ; [véhicule] ready for the scrapheap **3.** [envoi postal] dead letter.
◆ **de rebut** *loc adj* **1.** [sans valeur] : **meubles de ~** unwanted furniture ■ **vêtements de ~** cast-offs **2.** [défectueux] : **marchandises de ~** seconds, rejects.

rebutant, e [rəbytɑ̃, ɑ̃t] *adj* **1.** [repoussant] repulsive **2.** [décourageant] off-putting *esp UK*, disheartening ■ **mon travail est ~** my work is very disheartening.

rebuter [3] [rəbyte] *vt* **1.** [décourager] to discourage, to put off *(sép)* **2.** [dégoûter] to put off *(sép)* **3.** [choquer] : **ses manières me rebutent** I find his behaviour quite shocking.
◆ **se rebuter** *vpi* [se lasser] : **il était plein d'ardeur mais il s'est vite rebuté** he used to be very keen but he soon lost heart *ou* his enthusiasm.

récalcitrant, e [rekalsitrɑ̃, ɑ̃t] <> *adj* [animal] stubborn ▪ [personne] recalcitrant, rebellious.
<> *nm, f* recalcitrant.

recalculer [3] [rəkalkyle] *vt* to work out *(sép)* again, to recalculate.

recalé, e [rəkale] *fam* <> *adj* : **~e en juin, j'ai réussi en septembre** I failed in June but passed in September.
<> *nm, f* failed candidate.

recaler [3] [rəkale] *vt* *fam* [candidat] to fail ▪ **il s'est fait ~ à l'examen pour la deuxième fois** he failed the exam for the second time.

récapitulatif, ive [rekapitylatif, iv] *adj* **1.** [note] summarizing ▪ [tableau] summary *(modif)* **2.** BANQUE : **tableau ~ (d'un compte)** (summary) statement.
◆ **récapitulatif** *nm* summary, recapitulation, résumé.

récapitulation [rekapitylasjɔ̃] *nf* **1.** [résumé] recapitulation, summary, résumé ▪ [liste] recapitulation, summary **2.** BANQUE (summary) statement.

récapituler [3] [rekapityle] *vt* **1.** [résumer] to summarize, to recapitulate **2.** [énumérer] to go *ou* to run over *(insép)*.

recaser [3] [rəkaze] *vt* *fam* [personne] to find a new job for.
◆ **se recaser** *vp (emploi réfléchi)* *fam* [retrouver un emploi] to get fixed up with a new job ▪ [se remarier] to get hitched again.

recel [rəsɛl] *nm* DR **1.** [d'objets] possession of stolen goods ▪ **faire du ~** to deal in stolen goods **2.** [de personnes] : **~ de déserteur/malfaiteur** harbouring a deserter/a (known) criminal.

receler [25] [rəsəle] *vt* **1.** [bijoux, trésor] to receive ▪ [personne] to harbour **2.** [mystère, ressources] to hold ▪ **la maison recèle un secret** the house holds a secret.

receleur, euse [rəsəlœr, øz] *nm, f* receiver (of stolen goods).

récemment [resamɑ̃] *adv* **1.** [dernièrement] recently, not (very) long ago ▪ **un journaliste ~ rentré d'Afrique** a journalist just back from Africa ▪ **l'as-tu rencontrée ~?** have you met her lately? **2.** [nouvellement] recently, newly ▪ **membres ~ inscrits** newly registered members.

recensement [rəsɑ̃smɑ̃] *nm* **1.** [de population] census ▪ **faire le ~ de la population** to take a census of the population **2.** POLIT : **~ des votes** registering *ou* counting of the votes **3.** MIL [des futurs conscrits] *registering men for military service* ▪ [des équipements] inventorying.

recenser [3] [rəsɑ̃se] *vt* **1.** [population] to take *ou* to make a census of ▪ [votes] to count, to register **2.** [biens] to inventory, to make an inventory of ▪ [marchandises] to check, to take stock of **3.** MIL [futurs conscrits] to register ▪ [équipements] to inventory ▪ **se faire ~** to register for military service.

récent, e [resɑ̃, ɑ̃t] *adj* **1.** [événement] recent ▪ **leur mariage est tout ~** they've just *ou* recently got married ▪ **jusqu'à une date ~e** until recently **2.** [bourgeois, immigré] new.

recentrage [rəsɑ̃traʒ] *nm* **1.** AUTO recentring ▪ MÉCAN realigning **2.** ÉCON streamlining, rationalization **3.** POLIT adoption of a moderate stance.

recentrer [3] [rəsɑ̃tre] *vt* **1.** AUTO to recentre ▪ MÉCAN to realign **2.** ÉCON to streamline **3.** POLIT to revise, to realign **4.** SPORT to centre again.
◆ **se recentrer** *vpi* to become refocussed.

récépissé [resepise] *nm* (acknowledgment of) receipt.

réceptacle [resɛptakl] *nm* **1.** [réservoir] container, vessel, receptacle **2.** *fig & litt* [lieu de rendez-vous] meeting place **3.** BOT receptacle.

récepteur, trice [resɛptœr, tris] *adj* RADIO, TÉLÉCOM & TV receiving, receiver *(modif)*.
◆ **récepteur** *nm* **1.** ÉLECTRON receiver **2.** RADIO & TV (receiving) set, receiver ▪ **~ de contrôle** TV monitor **3.** [téléphonique] receiver **4.** MÉD receptor ▪ [en neurologie] receptor (molecule) **5.** LING receiver.

réceptif, ive [resɛptif, iv] *adj* **1.** [ouvert] receptive ▪ **~ à** open *ou* receptive to **2.** MÉD susceptible (to infection).

réception [resɛpsjɔ̃] *nf* **1.** [du courrier] receipt ▪ **acquitter *ou* payer à la ~** to pay on receipt *ou* delivery **2.** RADIO & TV reception **3.** [accueil] welcome, reception **4.** [fête, dîner] party, reception ▪ **~ mondaine** society event **5.** [d'un hôtel, d'une société - lieu] reception area *ou* desk ; [- personnel] reception staff **6.** [cérémonie d'admission] admission **7.** CONSTR : **~ des travaux** acceptance (of work done) **8.** SPORT [d'un sauteur] landing ▪ [du ballon - avec la main] catch ; [- avec le pied] : **bonne ~ de Pareta qui passe à Loval** Pareta traps the ball well and passes to Loval.

réceptionnaire [resɛpsjɔnɛr] *nmf* **1.** [dans un hôtel] head of reception **2.** COMM [de marchandises] receiving clerk **3.** NAUT receiving agent, receiver, consignee.

réceptionner [3] [resɛpsjɔne] *vt* **1.** [article] to check and sign for **2.** SPORT [balle - avec la main] to catch ; [- avec le pied] to trap **3.** [recevoir] to receive.
◆ **se réceptionner** *vpi* to land ▪ **il s'est bien/mal réceptionné** he made a good/poor landing.

réceptionniste [resɛpsjɔnist] *nmf* receptionist.

réceptive [resɛptiv] *f* ▷ **réceptif**.

réceptivité [resɛptivite] *nf* **1.** [sensibilité] receptiveness, responsiveness **2.** MÉD susceptibility (to infection) **3.** PSYCHOL receptiveness.

récessif, ive [resesif, iv] *adj* **1.** BIOL [gène] recessive **2.** ÉCON recessionary.

récession [resesjɔ̃] *nf* **1.** [crise économique] recession **2.** ASTRON & GÉOGR receding.

recette [rəsɛt] *nf* **1.** COMM takings *UK*, take *US* ▪ **on a fait une bonne/mauvaise ~** the takings were good/poor ⊙ **faire ~** [idée] to catch on ; [mode] to be all the rage ; [personne] to be a great success, to be a hit **2.** DR & FIN tax (collector's) office ▪ **~ fiscale** [administration] revenue service, Inland Revenue *UK* ▪ **~ municipale** local tax office ▪ **~ principale** [de la poste] main post office ; [des impôts] main tax office **3.** CULIN : **~ (de cuisine)** recipe ▪ **elle m'a donné la ~ des crêpes** she gave me the recipe for pancakes ⊙ **livre de ~s** cookbook, cookery book *UK* **4.** *fig* [méthode] : **elle a une ~ pour enlever les taches** she's got a formula for getting rid of stains.
◆ **recettes** *nfpl* [sommes touchées] income *(U)*, receipts, incomings ▪ **~s et dépenses** [gén] income and expenses, incomings and outgoings ; [en comptabilité] credit and debit ⊙ **~s publiques** public revenue *ou* income.

recevabilité [rəsəvabilite] *nf* DR admissibility.

recevable [rəsəvabl] *adj* **1.** [offre, excuse] acceptable **2.** DR [témoignage] admissible ▪ [demande] allowable ▪ **témoignage non ~** inadmissible evidence ▌ [personne] entitled.

receveur, euse [rəsəvœr, øz] *nm, f* **1.** TRANSP : **~ (d'autobus)** (bus) conductor **2.** ADMIN : **~ (des postes)** postmaster (*f* postmistress) ▪ **~ (des impôts)** tax collector *ou* officer ▪ **~ des contributions** income tax collector **3.** MÉD recipient ▪ **~ universel** universal recipient.

recevoir [52] [rəsəvwar] <> *vt* **1.** [courrier, coup de téléphone, compliments] to receive, to get ▪ [salaire, somme] to receive, to get, to be paid ▪ [cadeau] to get, to receive, to be given ▪ [prix, titre] to receive, to get, to be awarded ▪ [déposition, réclamation, ordre] to receive ▪ **voilà longtemps que je n'ai pas reçu de ses nouvelles** it's a long time since I last heard from him ▪ **nous avons bien reçu votre courrier du 12 mai** we acknowledge receipt *ou* confirm receipt of your letter dated May 12th ▪ **la**

rose a reçu le nom de la cantatrice the rose took its name from *ou* was named after the singer ■ **cette hypothèse n'a pas encore reçu de confirmation** that hypothesis has yet to receive confirmation *ou* to be confirmed ■ **je n'ai de conseils à ~ de personne!** I don't have to take advice from anybody! ■ **veuillez ~, Madame, l'expression de mes sentiments les meilleurs** *ou* **mes salutations distinguées** yours sincerely
2. [attention] to receive, to get ■ [affection, soins] to receive
3. [subir - coups] to get, to receive ■ **~ un coup sur la tête** to receive a blow to *ou* to get hit on the head ■ **la bouteille est tombée et c'est lui qui a tout reçu** the bottle fell over and it went all over him
4. [chez soi - accueillir] to greet, to welcome ; [- inviter] to entertain ; [- héberger] to take in *(sép)*, to put up *(sép)* ■ **je reçois quelques amis lundi, serez-vous des nôtres?** I'm having a few friends round on Monday, will you join us? ■ **~ qqn à dîner** [avec simplicité] to have sb round for dinner, to invite sb to dinner ; [solennellement] to entertain sb to dinner ■ **j'ai été très bien reçu** I was made (to feel) most welcome ■ **j'ai été mal reçu** I was made to feel unwelcome ■ **ils ont reçu la visite de la police** they received a visit from the police ➤ **se faire ~** *fam* to get told off
5. [à son lieu de travail - client, représentant] to see ■ **ils furent reçus par le Pape** they had an audience with *ou* were received by the Pope
6. [dans un club, une société - nouveau membre] to admit
7. [abriter] : **le chalet peut ~ six personnes** the chalet sleeps six (people) ■ **le stade peut ~ jusqu'à 75 000 personnes** the stadium can hold up to 75,000 people *ou* has a capacity of 75,000
8. [eaux de pluie] to collect ■ [lumière] to receive
9. *(surtout au passif)* [candidat] to pass ■ **elle a été reçue à l'épreuve de français** she passed her French exam ■ **je ne suis pas reçu** I didn't pass
10. RADIO & TV to receive, to get
11. RELIG [sacrement, vœux] to receive ■ [confession] to hear.
◇ *vi* **1.** [donner une réception] to entertain ■ **elle sait merveilleusement ~** she's marvellous at entertaining, she's a marvellous hostess ‖ [tenir salon] : **la comtesse recevait le mardi** the countess used to be at home (to visitors) on Tuesdays
2. [avocat, conseiller, médecin] to be available (to see clients) ■ **le médecin reçoit/ne reçoit pas aujourd'hui** the doctor is/isn't seeing patients today.
◆ **se recevoir** ◇ *vp (emploi réciproque)* [s'inviter] to visit each other.
◇ *vpi* SPORT to land.

rechange [rəʃɑ̃ʒ] ◆ **de rechange** *loc adj* **1.** [de secours] spare ■ [pour se changer] extra ■ **elle n'avait même pas de linge de ~** she didn't even have a change of clothes ■ **apporte un maillot de ~** bring an extra *ou* a spare swimming costume **2.** [de remplacement - solution] alternative.

rechanger [17] [rəʃɑ̃ʒe] *vt* to change (again), to exchange (again).

rechanter [3] [rəʃɑ̃te] *vt* to sing again.

rechaper [3] [rəʃape] *vt* AUTO to retread ■ **pneus rechapés** retreads.

réchapper [3] [reʃape] ◆ **réchapper à, réchapper de** *v+prép* to come *ou* to pull through ■ **en ~** [rester en vie] to come through, to escape alive.

recharge [rəʃarʒ] *nf* **1.** [d'arme] reload ■ [de stylo, briquet, parfum] refill **2.** [action - ARM] reloading ■ ÉLECTR recharging.

rechargeable [rəʃarʒabl] *adj* [briquet, stylo] refillable ■ [batterie] rechargeable.

recharger [17] [rəʃarʒe] *vt* **1.** [réapprovisionner - arme, appareil photo] to reload ; [- briquet, stylo] to refill ; [- poêle à bois, à mazout, à charbon] to refill ; [- batterie] to recharge ■ **~ ses accus** *fam fig* to recharge one's batteries **2.** [voiture, camion] to load again **3.** TRAV PUB to remetal ■ RAIL to reballast, to relay **4.** INDUST to strengthen, to consolidate **5.** INFORM to reload.

réchaud [reʃo] *nm* **1.** [de cuisson] (portable) stove ■ **~ de camping** [à gaz] camping stove ; [à pétrole] Primus®(stove) ■ **~ à gaz** (portable) gas stove **2.** [chauffe-plats] plate warmer, chafing dish.

réchauffage [reʃofaʒ] *nm* reheating.

réchauffé, e [reʃofe] *adj* **1.** [nourriture] reheated, warmed-up, heated-up **2.** *fig* [plaisanterie] stale.
◆ **réchauffé** *nm* reheated *ou* warmed-up food ➤ **c'est du ~** *fig* & *péj* that's old hat.

réchauffement [reʃofmɑ̃] *nm* warming up *(U)* ■ **~ de l'atmosphère** global warming ■ **on annonce un léger ~ pour le week-end** temperatures will rise slightly this weekend.

réchauffer [3] [reʃofe] *vt* **1.** [nourriture] to heat *ou* to warm up *(sép)*(again) **2.** [personne, salle] to warm up *(sép)* ■ **tu as l'air** *ou* **tu es bien réchauffé!** don't you feel the cold? **3.** *fig* [ambiance] to warm up *(sép)* ■ [ardeur] to rekindle ■ **ça vous réchauffe le cœur de les voir** it warms (the cockles of) your heart to see them.
◆ **se réchauffer** ◇ *vp (emploi passif)* : **un soufflé ne se réchauffe pas** you can't reheat a soufflé.
◇ *vpi* **1.** [personne] to warm up ■ **je n'arrive pas à me ~ aujourd'hui** I just can't get warm today ■ **alors, tu te réchauffes?** well now, are you warming up a bit? **2.** [pièce, sol, temps] to warm up, to get warmer.
◇ *vpt* : **se ~ les pieds/mains** to warm one's feet/hands (up).

réchauffeur [reʃofœr] *nm* heater ■ **~ à mélange** (liquid) mixture preheater.

rechausser [3] [rəʃose] *vt* **1.** [personne] : **~ qqn** to put sb's shoes back on for him/her **2.** AGRIC & HORT to earth *ou* to bank up *(sép)* **3.** CONSTR to consolidate (the base of).
◆ **se rechausser** *vp (emploi réfléchi)* to put one's shoes back on.

rêche [rɛʃ] *adj* **1.** [matière, vin] rough ■ [fruit] bitter **2.** *fig* [voix, ton] harsh, rough.

recherche [rəʃɛrʃ] *nf* **1.** [d'un objet, d'une personne, d'un emploi *etc*] search ■ [du bonheur, de la gloire, du plaisir] pursuit ■ [d'informations] research ➤ **~ documentaire** documentary research **2.** INFORM search, searching *(U)* **3.** DR search ■ **~ de paternité** paternity proceedings *ou* suit *US* **4.** [prospection] : **~ minière** mining ■ **~ pétrolière** oil prospecting **5.** SC & UNIV : **la ~** research ■ **bourse/travaux de ~** research grant/work ■ **faire de la ~** to do research ■ **elle fait de la ~ en chimie** [spécialiste] she's a research chemist ; [étudiante] she's a chemistry research student ➤ **~ fondamentale** fundamental research ■ **~ opérationnelle** operational *UK ou* operations *US* research ■ **~ scientifique** scientific research **6.** [raffinement] sophistication, refinement ■ **vêtu avec ~** elegantly dressed ■ **sans ~** simple, plain ‖ [affectation] affectation, ostentatiousness.
◆ **recherches** *nfpl* [enquête] search ■ **faire faire des ~s pour retrouver un parent disparu** to have a search carried out for a missing relative ‖ [travaux - gén] work, research ; [- de médecine] research ■ **une équipe d'archéologues mène déjà des ~s sur le site** a team of archeologists is already working on *ou* researching the site.
◆ **à la recherche de** *loc prép* in search of, looking *ou* searching for ■ **être/partir/se mettre à la ~ de** to be/to set off/to go in search of ■ **depuis combien de temps êtes-vous à la ~ d'un emploi?** how long have you been looking for a job? ■ **'À la ~ du temps perdu'** ***Proust*** 'In Search of Lost Time'.

recherché, e [rəʃɛrʃe] *adj* **1.** [prisé - mets] choice *(modif)* ; [- comédien] in demand, much sought-after ; [- objet rare] much sought-after **2.** [raffiné - langage] studied ; [- tenue] elegant ; [- style] ornate ■ **dans sa toilette la plus ~e** in her best finery.

rechercher [3] [rəʃɛrʃe] *vt* **1.** [document, objet] to look *ou* to search for *(insép)* ■ [disparu] to search for *(insép)* ■ [assassin] to look for *(insép)* ■ **nous recherchons votre correspondant** TÉLÉCOM we're trying to connect you ■ **il est recherché par la police** the police are looking for him ■ **'on recherche pour meurtre homme brun, 32 ans'** 'wanted for murder brown-haired, 32-year-old man' **2.** [dans une annonce] : **(on) recherche jeunes gens pour travail bien rémunéré** young people wanted for well-paid job **3.** [cause] to look into *(insép)*, to investigate ■ **on recherche toujours la cause du sinistre** the cause of the fire is still being investigated **4.** [compliment, pouvoir, gloire] to seek (out) ■ [sécurité] to look for *(insép)* ■ [fortune, plaisirs] to be in search of ■ [beauté, pureté] to strive for *(insép)*, to aim at *(inséр)* **5.** [récupérer - une personne] to collect, to fetch back (again) ▪ **je viendrai te ~** I'll come and fetch you **6.** [chercher à nouveau] to search *ou* to look for *(insép)* again ▪ [prendre à nouveau] : **va me ~ du pain chez le boulanger/à la cuisine** go and get me some more bread from the baker's/kitchen **7.** INFORM to search.

rechigner [3] [rəʃiɲe] *vi* **1.** [montrer sa mauvaise humeur] to grimace, to frown **2.** [protester] to grumble ▪ **fais-le sans ~** do it without making a fuss.
◆ **rechigner à** *v+prép* : **elle rechigne à faire cette vérification** she's reluctant to carry out this check.

rechute [rəʃyt] *nf* **1.** MÉD relapse ▪ **avoir** *ou* **faire une ~** to (have a) relapse **2.** [d'une mauvaise habitude] relapse **3.** ÉCON : **on craint une ~ de l'activité économique** there are fears of a further slump in economic activity.

rechuter [3] [rəʃyte] *vi* **1.** MÉD to (have a) relapse **2.** [dans une mauvaise habitude] to relapse.

récidive [residiv] *nf* **1.** DR [après première condamnation] second offence ▪ [après deuxième condamnation] subsequent offence ▪ **en cas de ~** in the event of a subsequent offence **2.** MÉD recurrence.

récidiver [3] [residive] *vi* **1.** DR [après première condamnation] to commit a second offence ▪ [après deuxième condamnation] to commit a subsequent offence **2.** [recommencer] : **il récidive dans ses plaintes** he's bringing up the same complaints again **3.** MÉD to recur, to be recurrent.

récidiviste [residivist] <> *adj* recidivist.
<> *nmf* [pour la première fois] second offender, recidivist *spéc* ▪ [de longue date] habitual offender, recidivist *spéc.*

récif [resif] *nm* reef ▪ **~ corallien** *ou* **de corail** coral reef ▪ **~ frangeant** fringing reef.

récipiendaire [resipjɑ̃dɛr] *nmf* **1.** [nouveau venu] member elect **2.** [d'une médaille, d'un diplôme] recipient.

récipient [resipjɑ̃] *nm* container, receptacle *sout*, vessel *litt.*

réciprocité [resiprosite] *nf* reciprocity ▪ **mais à titre de ~, laissez-moi vous inviter à déjeuner** but allow me to repay you by inviting you to lunch.

réciproque [resiprɔk] <> *adj* **1.** [mutuel] mutual ▪ **je vous hais! - c'est ~!** I hate you! - I hate you too *ou* the feeling's mutual! **2.** [bilatéral - accord] reciprocal **3.** LOGIQUE converse ▪ **proposition ~** converse (proposition) **4.** GRAMM & MATH reciprocal.
<> *nf* **1.** [l'inverse] : **la ~** the reverse, the opposite ▪ **pourtant la ~ n'est pas vraie** though the reverse isn't true, but not vice versa ▪ **je ne l'aime pas, et la ~ est vraie** I don't like him and he doesn't like me **2.** [la même chose] : **la ~** the same ▪ **ils vous ont invités, à vous de leur rendre la ~** they invited you, now it's up to you to do the same *ou* to invite them in return **3.** MATH reciprocal function.

réciproquement [resiprɔkmɑ̃] *adv* **1.** [mutuellement] : **ils ont le devoir de se protéger ~** it is their duty to protect each other *ou* one another, they must provide each other with mutual protection **2.** [inversement] vice versa.

récit [resi] *nm* **1.** [histoire racontée] story, tale, narration *sout* ▪ **faire le ~ de qqch** to narrate sthg **2.** [exposé] account ▪ **un ~ circonstancié** a blow-by-blow account **3.** LITTÉR & THÉÂTRE narrative ▪ **~ de voyage** [livre] travel book **4.** MUS [dans un opéra] recitative ▪ [solo] solo ▪ [clavier d'orgue] third manual, choir (organ).

récital, als [resital] *nm* recital ▪ **~ de piano** piano recital.

récitant, e [resitɑ̃, ɑ̃t] <> *adj* MUS solo.
<> *nm, f* CINÉ & THÉÂTRE narrator.

récitatif [resitatif] *nm* recitative.

récitation [resitasjɔ̃] *nf* **1.** [d'un texte] recitation **2.** ÉDUC [poème] recitation piece ▪ **on leur a fait apprendre une belle ~** they were given a beautiful poem to learn (by heart).

réciter [3] [resite] *vt* **1.** [dire par cœur - leçon] to repeat, to recite ; [- discours] to give ; [- poème, prière] to say, to recite ; [- formule] to recite **2.** [dire sans sincérité] : **elle avait l'air de ~ un texte** she sounded as if she was reading from a book ▪ **le témoin a récité sa déposition** the witness reeled off his statement.

réclamation [reklamasjɔ̃] *nf* **1.** ADMIN [plainte] complaint ▪ **pour toute ~, s'adresser au guichet 16** all complaints should be addressed *ou* referred to desk 16 ▪ **faire une ~** to lodge a complaint ➔ **service/bureau des ~s** complaints department/office **2.** DR [demande] claim, demand ▪ **faire une ~** to lodge a claim ▪ **faire droit à une ~** to allow *ou* to satisfy a claim **3.** [récrimination] complaining *(U).*
◆ **réclamations** *nfpl* TÉLÉCOM [service] : **appeler les ~s** to call the (telephone) engineer.

réclame [reklam] *nf vieilli* **1.** [la publicité] : **la ~** advertising *(U)* ▪ **faire de la ~ pour qqch** to advertize sthg **2.** [annonce] advertisement.
◆ **en réclame** <> *loc adj* on (special) offer ▪ **le café est en ~ cette semaine** there's a special offer on coffee *ou* coffee's on special offer this week.
<> *loc adv* at a discount.

réclamer [3] [reklame] <> *vt* **1.** [argent, augmentation] to demand ▪ [attention, silence] to call for *(insép)*, to demand ▪ [personne] to ask *ou* to clamour for *(insép)* ▪ **je réclame le silence!** silence, please! ▪ **elle me doit encore de l'argent mais je n'ose pas le lui ~** she still owes me money but I daren't ask for it back ▪ **~ le secours de qqn** to ask sb for assistance ▪ *(en usage absolu)* **le chien est toujours à ~** *fam* the dog's always begging **2.** [revendiquer - droit] to claim ; [- somme due] to put in for *(insép)*, to claim **3.** [nécessiter - précautions] to call for *(insép)* ; [- soins] to require ; [- explication] to require, to demand.
<> *vi* **1.** [se plaindre] : **~ auprès de qqn** to complain to sb **2.** [protester] : **~ contre qqch** to cry out against sthg.
◆ **se réclamer de** *vp+prép* : **se ~ de qqn** [utiliser son nom] to use sb's name ; [se prévaloir de lui] to invoke sb's name ▪ **elle ne se réclame d'aucun mouvement politique** she doesn't identify with any political movement ▪ **les organisations se réclamant du marxisme** organizations calling *ou* labelling themselves Marxist.

reclasser [3] [rəklase] *vt* **1.** [par ordre alphabétique] to reorder ▪ [par ordre numérique] to reorder, to resequence **2.** [ranger] to put back, to refile ▪ [réorganiser] to reclassify, to reorganize ▪ **~ les dossiers par ordre chronologique** to reclassify the files in chronological order **3.** ADMIN [salaires] to restructure ▪ [fonctionnaire] to regrade **4.** [chômeur] to place ▪ [handicapé, ex-détenu] to rehabilitate.

reclus, e [rəkly, yz] <> *adj* solitary, secluded.
<> *nm, f* recluse ▪ **vivre en ~** to live like a hermit *ou* recluse.

réclusion [reklyzjɔ̃] *nf* **1.** *litt* reclusion, seclusion **2.** DR imprisonment ▪ **~ criminelle** imprisonment with labour ▪ **condamné à la ~ criminelle à perpétuité** sentenced to life (imprisonment), given a life sentence.

réclusionnaire [reklyzjɔnɛr] *nmf* prisoner.

recoiffer [3] [rəkwafe] *vt* : **~ ses cheveux** to do *ou* to redo one's hair ▪ **~ qqn** to do sb's hair (again).
◆ **se recoiffer** *vp (emploi réfléchi)* **1.** [se peigner] to do *ou* to redo one's hair **2.** [remettre son chapeau] to put one's hat on again *ou* back on.

recoin [rəkwɛ̃] *nm* **1.** [coin] corner, nook ▪ **chercher dans le moindre ~** *ou* **dans tous les (coins et) ~s** to search every nook and cranny **2.** *fig* [partie secrète] recess.

reçoit, reçoivent *etc v* ⊳ **recevoir.**

recollage [rəkɔlaʒ] *nm* resticking.

récollection [rekɔlɛksjɔ̃] *nf* RELIG recollection.

recoller [3] [rəkɔle] *vt* **1.** [objet brisé] to stick *ou* to glue back together ▪ [timbre] to stick back on ▪ [enveloppe] to stick back down, to restick ▪ [semelle] to stick *ou* to glue back on ➔ **~ les morceaux** [avec de la colle] to stick *ou* to glue the pieces back together (again) ; [avec de l'adhésif] to tape the pieces back together (again) ; *fig* to patch things up **2.** *fam* [redonner] : **on m'a recollé une amende** I've been landed with another fine ▪ **on nous a recollé un prof nul** we've been landed with another useless teacher **3.** *fam* [remettre] to stick *ou* to shove back ▪ **ils l'ont recollé à l'hôpital** they stuck him back in hospital.

◆ **se recoller** ◇ *vp (emploi passif)* : **ça se recolle très facilement** it can easily be stuck back together.

◇ *vpi* **1.** [se ressouder - os] to knit (together), to mend ; [- objet] to stick (together) **2.** *fam fig* **se ~ avec qqn** [se réinstaller avec qqn] to move back in with sb.

récoltant, e [rekɔltɑ̃, ɑ̃t] *nm, f* grower.

récolte [rekɔlt] *nf* **1.** [des céréales] harvest *(U)* ▪ [des fruits, des choux] picking *(U)* ▪ [des pommes de terre] lifting *(U)* ▪ [du miel] gathering, collecting *(U)* ▪ **ils ont déjà commencé à faire la ~** they've already started harvesting **2.** [quantité récoltée] harvest ▪ [denrées récoltées] crop **3.** [de documents, d'information] gathering, collecting.

récolter [3] [rekɔlte] *vt* **1.** [céréales] to harvest, to gather ▪ [légumes, fruits] to pick ▪ [miel] to collect, to gather ▪ [tubercules] to lift, to pick **2.** [informations, argent] to collect, to gather ▪ **~ des voix** to get sb's votes *(in a transferable vote system)* **3.** *fam* [ennuis, maladie *etc*] to get.

recombiner [rəkɔ̃bine] *vt* BIOL & CHIM to recombine.

recommandable [rəkɔmɑ̃dabl] *adj* commendable ▪ **un individu peu ~** a rather disreputable character ▪ **le procédé est peu ~** that isn't a very commendable thing to do.

recommandation [rəkɔmɑ̃dasjɔ̃] *nf* **1.** [conseil] advice, recommendation ▪ **faire qqch sur la ~ de qqn** to do sthg on sb's recommendation ▪ **je lui ai fait mes dernières ~s** I gave him some last-minute advice **2.** [appui] recommendation, reference ▪ **je me suis procuré des ~s** I've got some people to give me a reference **3.** [d'un courrier - sans avis de réception] registering *UK*, certifying *US* ; [- avec avis de réception] recording **4.** POLIT : **~ de l'ONU** UN recommendation.

recommandé, e [rəkɔmɑ̃de] *adj* **1.** [conseillé] advisable ▪ **il est ~ de...** it is advisable to... ▪ **il est ~ aux visiteurs de se munir de leurs passeports** visitors are advised to take their passports ▪ **la réservation est fortement ~e** you are strongly advised to book in advance **2.** [courrier - avec avis de réception] recorded *UK*, certified *US* ; [- à valeur assurée] registered.

◆ **recommandé** *nm* [courrier - avec avis de réception] recorded *UK ou* certified *US* delivery item ; [- à valeur assurée] registered item ▪ **en ~** [avec avis de réception] by recorded delivery *UK ou* certified mail *US* ; [à valeur assurée] by registered post *UK ou* mail *US*.

recommander [3] [rəkɔmɑ̃de] *vt* **1.** [conseiller - produit, personne] to recommend ▪ **je te recommande vivement mon médecin** I (can) heartily recommend my doctor to you ▪ **un homme que ses états de service recommandent** a man with a very commendable service record *ou* whose service record commends him **2.** [exhorter à] to recommend, to advise ▪ **je vous recommande la prudence** I recommend *ou* I advise you to be cautious, I advise caution ▪ **je ne saurais trop vous ~ d'être vigilant** I cannot advise you too strongly to be watchful **3.** [confier] : **~ qqn à qqn** to place sb in sb's care ▪ **~ son âme à Dieu** RELIG to commend one's soul *ou* o.s. to God **4.** [courrier - pour attester sa réception] to record ; [- pour l'assurer] to register.

◆ **se recommander à** *vp+prép* [s'en remettre à] to commend o.s. to.

◆ **se recommander de** *vp+prép* : **se ~ de qqn** [postulant] to give sb's name as a reference ▪ **tu peux te ~ de moi** [chez un marchand] you can say I sent you ; [à un postulant] you can quote me as a referee.

recommencement [rəkɔmɑ̃smɑ̃] *nm* renewal, resumption ▪ **la vie est un éternel ~** every day is a new beginning.

recommencer [16] [rəkɔmɑ̃se] ◇ *vt* **1.** [refaire - dessin, lettre, travail *etc*] to start *ou* to begin again ; [- attaque] to renew, to start again ; [- expérience] to repeat ; [- erreur] to repeat, to make again ▪ **ne recommence pas tes bêtises** don't start being silly again ▪ **recommençons la scène 4** let's do scene 4 again ▪ **si seulement on pouvait ~ sa vie!** if only one could start one's life afresh *ou* begin one's life all over again! ▪ **tout est à ~, il faut tout ~** we have to start *ou* to begin all over again ▪ *(en usage absolu)* **ne recommence pas!** don't do that again! **2.** [reprendre - histoire, conversation] to resume, to carry on *(insép)* with ; [- lecture, travail] to resume, to go back *(insép)* to ; [- campagne, lutte] to resume, to take up *(sép)* again.

◇ *vi* **1.** [depuis le début] to start *ou* to begin again ▪ [après interruption] to resume ▪ **pour moi, la vie va ~** my life is about to begin anew, a new life is beginning for me ▪ **ça y est, ça recommence!** here we go again! **2.** [se remettre] : **~ à faire qqch** to start doing *ou* to do sthg again ▪ *(tournure impersonnelle)* **il a recommencé à neiger dans la nuit** it started snowing again during the night ▪ **il recommence à faire froid** it's beginning *ou* starting to get cold again.

recomparaître [91] [rəkɔ̃parɛtr] *vi* DR to appear again.

récompense [rekɔ̃pɑ̃s] *nf* **1.** [d'un acte] reward, recompense *sout* ▪ **en ~ de** as a reward *ou* in return for ▪ **il a trimé toute sa vie, et voilà sa ~!** *fam iron* he's slaved away all his life and that's all the thanks *ou* the reward he gets! ▪ **qu'il soit heureux, ce serait là ma plus belle ~** as long as he is happy, that will be ample recompense *ou* reward for me ▪ **'forte ~'** 'generous reward' **2.** [prix] award, prize **3.** DR financial provision **4.** MIL award.

récompenser [3] [rekɔ̃pɑ̃se] *vt* **1.** [pour un acte] to reward, to recompense *sout* ▪ **voilà comment je suis récompensé de ma peine!** *iron* that's all the reward I get for my troubles! **2.** [primer] to give an award *ou* a prize to, to reward ▪ **le scénario a été récompensé à Cannes** the script won an award at Cannes.

recomposer [3] [rəkɔ̃poze] *vt* **1.** [reconstituer] to piece *ou* to put together *(sép)*(again), to reconstruct ▪ **son esprit recomposait peu à peu la scène** he gradually reconstructed the scene in his mind **2.** IMPR [page] to reset ▪ [texte] to rekey **3.** [réarranger - chanson] to rewrite ; [- photo] to compose again **4.** CHIM to recompose **5.** TÉLÉCOM : **~ un numéro** to dial a number again.

recompter [3] [rəkɔ̃te] *vt* to count again.

réconciliation [rekɔ̃siljasjɔ̃] *nf* **1.** [entente] reconciliation ▪ **leur ~ a été de courte durée** their reconciliation didn't last long **2.** DR & RELIG reconciliation.

réconcilier [9] [rekɔ̃silje] *vt* **1.** [deux personnes] to reconcile **2.** *fig* **~ qqn avec qqch** to reconcile sb to *ou* with sthg ▪ **~ qqch avec qqch** to reconcile sthg with sthg **3.** RELIG to reconcile.

◆ **se réconcilier** *vpi* [personnes] to make up ▪ [pays] to make peace ▪ **se ~ sur l'oreiller** *hum* to make up in bed ▪ **se ~ avec soi-même** to come to terms with oneself.

reconductible [rəkɔ̃dyktibl] *adj* DR renewable.

reconduction [rəkɔ̃dyksjɔ̃] *nf* [d'un contrat, d'un budget] renewal ▪ [d'un bail] renewal, extension.

reconduire [98] [rəkɔ̃dɥir] *vt* **1.** [accompagner] : **~ qqn** to see sb home ▪ **~ qqn à pied/en voiture** to walk/to drive sb home ▪ [vers la sortie] to show to the door ▪ **inutile de me ~, je connais le chemin** please don't trouble yourself, I know the way **2.** [expulser] to escort ▪ **les terroristes ont été reconduits à la frontière sous bonne escorte** the terrorists were escorted (back) to the border by the police *ou* were taken (back) to the border under police escort **3.** [renouveler - contrat, budget, mandat] to renew ; [- bail] to renew, to extend.

réconfort [rekɔ̃fɔr] *nm* comfort ▪ **tu m'es d'un grand ~** you're a great comfort to me.

réconfortant, e [rekɔ̃fɔrtɑ̃, ɑ̃t] *adj* **1.** [rassurant] comforting, reassuring **2.** [revigorant] fortifying, invigorating, stimulating.

réconforter [3] [rekɔ̃fɔrte] *vt* **1.** [consoler] to comfort, to reassure **2.** [revigorer] : **bois ça, ça va te ~** drink this, it'll make you feel better.

reconnais *etc v* ▷ **reconnaître**.

reconnaissable [rəkɔnɛsabl] *adj* recognizable ▪ **après trois mois de prison, il était à peine ~** after three months in prison he was hardly recognizable *ou* you could hardly recognize him ▪ **~ à** identifiable by.

reconnaissait *etc v* ▷ **reconnaître**.

reconnaissance [rəkɔnɛsɑ̃s] *nf* **1.** [gratitude] gratitude ▪ **avoir/éprouver de la ~ envers qqn** to be/to feel grateful to *ou* towards sb ▪ **je lui en ai une vive ~** I am most grateful to her ▪ **témoigner de la ~ à qqn** to show gratitude to sb ▪ **avec ~** gratefully, with gratitude ▪ **en ~ de votre dévouement** as a token of my/our *etc* gratitude for *ou* in recognition of your devotion ◗ **il n'a même pas la ~ du ventre!** *fam* he'd bite the hand that fed him!
2. [exploration] reconnaissance ▪ **envoyer des hommes en ~** to send men out on reconnaissance ▪ **faire une ~** to go on reconnaissance ▪ **elle est partie en ~** *ou* **est allée faire une ~ des lieux** *fig* she went to check the place out ◗ **patrouille de ~** reconnaissance patrol ▪ **vol de ~** reconnaissance flight
3. [identification] recognition
4. [aveu] admission ▪ **la ~ de ses torts lui a valu l'indulgence du jury** his admission of his wrongs won him the leniency of the jury
5. POLIT [d'un gouvernement] recognition ▪ **~ d'un État** recognition (of statehood)
6. DR [d'un droit] recognition, acknowledgment ◗ **~ de dette** acknowledgment of a debt ▪ **~ d'enfant** legal recognition of a child
7. [reçu] : **acte de ~ (du mont-de-piété)** pawn ticket
8. INFORM recognition ▪ **~ de la parole/de formes** speech/pattern recognition ▪ **~ optique de caractères** optical character recognition, OCR
9. PSYCHOL recognition.

reconnaissant, e [rəkɔnɛsɑ̃, ɑ̃t] *adj* grateful ▪ **se montrer ~** to show gratitude ▪ **je te suis ~ de ta patience** I'm most grateful to you for your patience ▪ **je vous serais ~ de me fournir ces renseignements dans les meilleurs délais** I would be (most) obliged *ou* grateful if you would provide me with this information as soon as possible.

reconnaître [91] [rəkɔnɛtr] *vt* **1.** [air, personne, pas] to recognize ▪ **je t'ai reconnu à ta démarche** I recognized you *ou* I could tell it was you by your walk ▪ **je ne l'aurais pas reconnue, elle a vieilli de dix ans!** I wouldn't have known (it was) her, she looks ten years older! ▪ **je te reconnais bien (là)!** that's just like you!, that's you all over! ▪ **tu veux fonder une famille? je ne te reconnais plus!** you want to start a family? that's not like you at all *ou* you've changed your tune! ▪ **je reconnais bien là ta mauvaise foi!** that's just typical of your bad faith!
2. [admettre - torts] to recognize, to acknowledge, to admit ; [- aptitude, talent, vérité] to acknowledge, to recognize ▪ **il faut au moins lui ~ cette qualité** you have to say this for him ▪ **l'accusé reconnaît-il les faits?** does the accused acknowledge the facts? ▪ **sa prestation fut décevante, il faut bien le ~** it has to be admitted that his performance was disappointing ▪ **je reconnais que j'ai eu tort** I admit I was wrong ▪ **il n'a jamais reconnu avoir falsifié les documents** he never admitted to having falsified the documents
3. DR & POLIT [État, chef de file] to recognize ▪ [enfant] to recognize legally ▪ [dette, document, signature] to authenticate ▪ **tous le reconnaissent comme leur maître** they all acknowledge him as their master ▪ **être reconnu coupable** to be found guilty ▪ **organisme reconnu d'utilité publique** officially approved organization ▪ **~ un droit à qqn** to recognize *ou* to acknowledge sb's right ▪ **je ne reconnais à personne le droit de me juger** nobody has the right to judge me
4. [explorer] to reconnoitre ▪ **il envoya dix hommes ~ le terrain** he ordered ten men to go and reconnoitre the ground ▪ **l'équipe de tournage est allée ~ les lieux** the film crew went to have a look round (the place).
◆ **se reconnaître** ◇ *vp (emploi réfléchi)* [physiquement, moralement] to see o.s. ▪ **je me reconnais dans la réaction de ma sœur** I can see myself reacting in the same way as my sister ▪ **je ne me reconnais pas dans votre description** I don't see myself as fitting your description.
◇ *vp (emploi réciproque)* to recognize each other.
◇ *vp (emploi passif)* to be recognizable ▪ **un poisson frais se reconnaît à l'odeur** you can tell a fresh fish by the smell.
◇ *vpi* **1.** [se retrouver] : **je ne me reconnais plus dans ma propre ville** I can't even find my way about *ou* around my own home town any more ▪ **mets des étiquettes sur tes dossiers, sinon comment veux-tu qu'on s'y reconnaisse?** label your files, otherwise we'll get completely confused
2. [s'avouer] : **se ~ coupable** to admit *ou* to confess to being guilty.

reconnecter [rəkɔnɛkte] *vt* to reconnect.
◆ **se reconnecter** *vpi* INFORM to reconnect o.s., to get back on line.

reconnu, e [rəkɔny] ◇ *pp* ▷ **reconnaître.**
◇ *adj* **1.** [admis] recognized, accepted ▪ **ce diplôme n'est pas ~ dans tous les pays** this diploma is not recognized in all countries **2.** [célébré] famous, well-known.

reconquérir [39] [rəkɔ̃kerir] *vt* **1.** [territoire, peuple] to reconquer, to recapture **2.** [honneur, avantage] to win back *(sép)*, to recover **3.** [personne] to win back *(sép)*.

reconquête [rəkɔ̃kɛt] *nf* **1.** [d'un territoire, d'un peuple] reconquest, recapture **2.** [de l'honneur, d'un avantage] winning back *(U)*, recovery.

reconquiert *etc v* ▷ **reconquérir.**

reconquis, e [rəkɔ̃ki, iz] *pp* ▷ **reconquérir.**

reconsidérer [18] [rəkɔ̃sidere] *vt* to reconsider.

reconstituant, e [rəkɔ̃stitɥɑ̃, ɑ̃t] *adj* [aliment, boisson] fortifying ▪ [traitement] restorative.
◆ **reconstituant** *nm* restorative.

reconstituer [7] [rəkɔ̃stitɥe] *vt* **1.** [reformer - groupe] to bring together *(sép)* again, to reconstitute ; [- capital] to rebuild, to build up *(sép)* again ; [- fichier] to recreate ; [- histoire, meurtre] to reconstruct ▪ **ils ont reconstitué un décor d'époque** they created a period setting ◗ **lait reconstitué** reconstituted milk **2.** [réparer] to piece together *(sép)*(again).

reconstitution [rəkɔ̃stitysjɔ̃] *nf* **1.** [d'un groupe] reconstituting *(U)*, bringing together *(sép)* again *(U)* ▪ [d'un capital] rebuilding, building up *(sép)* again ▪ [d'un fichier] recreating *(U)* ▪ [d'une histoire, d'un meurtre] reconstruction **2.** [réparation] piecing together (again).

reconstruction [rəkɔ̃stryksjɔ̃] *nf* **1.** [gén] reconstruction, rebuilding ▪ **en ~** being rebuilt **2.** LING reconstruction.

reconstruire [98] [rəkɔ̃strɥir] *vt* **1.** [bâtiment] to reconstruct, to rebuild ▪ [fortune, réputation] to rebuild, to build up *(sép)* again **2.** LING to reconstruct.

reconversion [rəkɔ̃vɛrsjɔ̃] *nf* [d'une usine] reconversion ▪ [d'un individu] retraining.

reconvertir [32] [rəkɔ̃vɛrtir] *vt* **1.** [usine] to reconvert **2.** [armes] to convert.
◆ **se reconvertir** *vpi* to retrain ▪ **il s'est reconverti dans l'informatique** he retrained and went into computing.

recopier [9] [rəkɔpje] *vt* **1.** [mettre au propre] to write up *(sép)*, to make *ou* to take a fair copy of **2.** [copier à nouveau] to copy again, to make another copy of.

record [rəkɔr] *nm* **1.** SPORT & *fig* record ▪ **battre un ~ de vitesse** to break a speed record ▪ **tu bats tous les ~s d'idiotie!** *fam* they don't come any more stupid than you! ▪ **ça bat tous les ~s** *fam* that beats everything *ou* the lot **2.** *(comme adj, avec ou sans trait d'union)* record *(modif)* ▪ **l'inflation a atteint le chiffre-~ de 200 %** inflation has risen to a record *ou* record-breaking 200% ▪ **en un temps-~** in record time.

recorder [3] [rəkɔrde] *vt* [raquette] to restring.

recordman [rəkɔrdman] (*pl* **recordmans** *ou pl* **recordmen** [-mɛn]) *nm* (men's) record holder ▪ **le ~ du 5 000 m** the record holder for the (men's) 5,000 m.

recordwoman [rəkɔrdwuman] (*pl* **recordwomans** *ou pl* **recordwomen** [-mɛn]) *nf* (women's) record holder ▪ **la ~ du saut en hauteur** the record holder for the women's high jump.

recoudre [86] [rəkudr] *vt* **1.** [bouton, badge *etc*] to sew on *(sép)* again ▪ [accroc, ourlet *etc*] to sew up *(sép)* again **2.** MÉD to sew *ou* to stitch up *(sép)* (again).

recoupement [rəkupmɑ̃] *nm* **1.** [vérification] crosschecking ▪ **procéder par ~s** to carry out a crosscheck **2.** CONSTR [action] stepping ▪ [résultat] retreat **3.** GÉOM resection.

recouper [3] [rəkupe] ◇ *vt* **1.** [couper à nouveau] : ~ **de la viande** to cut *ou* to carve some more meat **2.** COUT to cut again, to alter the cut of **3.** [concorder avec] to tally with *(insép)*, to match up with *(insép)*.
◇ *vi* JEUX to cut again.
◆ **se recouper** *vp (emploi réciproque)* **1.** [ensembles, routes] to intersect **2.** [statistiques, témoignages] to tally, to confirm one another ■ **les deux versions ne se recoupent pas** the two stories don't tally.

recourbé, e [rəkurbe] *adj* [cils] curved ■ [nez] hooked.

recourber [3] [rəkurbe] *vt* to bend, to curve.

recourir [45] [rəkurir] ◇ *vt* to run again.
◇ *vi* SPORT to run *ou* to race again.
◆ **recourir à** *v+prép* **1.** [personne] : ~ **à qqn** to appeal *ou* to turn to sb ■ **en cas de désaccord, il faudra ~ à un expert** in case of disagreement you will have to turn to *ou* to seek the help of an expert **2.** [objet, méthode *etc*] : ~ **à qqch** to resort to sthg.

recours [rəkur] *nm* **1.** [ressource] recourse, resort ■ **c'est sans ~** there's nothing we can do about it ■ **avoir ~ à** [moyen] to resort to ; [personne] to turn to **2.** DR appeal ■ **~ en cassation** appeal (to the appellate court) ■ **~ en grâce** [pour une remise de peine] petition for pardon ; [pour une commutation de peine] petition for clemency *ou* remission.
◆ **en dernier recours** *loc adv* as a last resort.

recouru, e [rəkury] *pp* ▻ **recourir**.

recousait *etc v* ▻ **recoudre**.

recouvert, e [rəkuvɛr, ɛrt] *pp* ▻ **recouvrir**.

recouvrage [rəkuvraʒ] *nm* recovering, re-upholstering.

recouvrement [rəkuvrəmɑ̃] *nm* **1.** [récupération - d'une somme] collecting, collection ; [- de la santé] recovering, recovery **2.** FIN [perception] collection ■ [d'une créance] recovery ▶ **date de mise en ~** date due, due date ■ **modalités de ~** methods of payment **3.** [d'une surface] covering (over) **4.** CONSTR & MENUIS lap **5.** INFORM & MATH overlap **6.** GÉOL overlap, overthrust.

recouvrer [3] [rəkuvre] *vt* **1.** [récupérer] to recover ■ **laissez-lui le temps de ~ ses esprits** give her time to recover her wits *ou* to get her wits back ■ **~ la liberté** to regain one's freedom **2.** FIN [percevoir] to collect, to recover.

recouvrir [34] [rəkuvrir] *vt* **1.** [couvrir] to cover ■ **~ un gâteau de chocolat** to coat a cake with chocolate **2.** [couvrir à nouveau - personne] to cover (up) *(sép)* again ; [- siège] to re-cover, to reupholster ; [- livre] to re-cover.
◆ **se recouvrir** *vpi* **1.** MÉTÉOR to get cloudy again **2.** [surface] : **la glace s'est recouverte de buée** the mirror steamed up.

recracher [3] [rəkraʃe] ◇ *vt* **1.** [cracher] to spit out *(sép)* (again) ■ **le distributeur de billets a recraché ma carte** *fam* the cash dispenser rejected my card **2.** *fam* [cours, leçon] to regurgitate.
◇ *vi* to spit again.

récré [rekre] *nf fam* [dans le primaire] playtime *UK*, recess *US* ■ [dans le secondaire] break.

récréatif, ive [rekreatif, iv] *adj sout* recreational ■ **une journée récréative** a day of recreation *ou* relaxation.

récréation [rekreasjɔ̃] *nf* **1.** ÉDUC [dans le primaire] playtime *esp UK*, recess *US* ■ [dans le secondaire] break **2.** [délassement] recreation, leisure activity.

recréer [15] [rəkree] *vt* **1.** [suivant un modèle] to recreate **2.** [créer] to create ■ **il recrée un décor à son goût** he is creating a decor more to his liking.

récréer [15] [rekree] *vt litt* to entertain, to amuse, to divert.
◆ **se récréer** *vpi* to entertain *ou* to amuse *ou* to divert o.s.

récrier [10] [rekrije] ◆ **se récrier** *vpi* **1.** [protester] : **se ~ contre qqch** to cry out *ou* to protest against sthg **2.** *litt* [s'exclamer] : **se ~ de surprise/joie** to cry out *ou* to exclaim in surprise/joy.

récriminateur, trice [rekriminatœr, tris] ◇ *adj* recriminative, recriminatory.
◇ *nm, f* recriminator.

récrimination [rekriminasjɔ̃] *nf* recrimination, protest.

récriminer [3] [rekrimine] *vi* [critiquer] : **~ (contre qqn)** to recriminate (against sb).

récrire [rekrir] = **réécrire**.

recroquevillé, e [rəkrɔkvije] *adj* **1.** [confortablement] curled up ■ [dans l'inconfort] hunched *ou* huddled up **2.** [feuille, pétale] curled *ou* shrivelled up.

recroqueviller [3] [rəkrɔkvije] ◆ **se recroqueviller** *vpi* **1.** [confortablement] to curl up ■ [dans l'inconfort] to hunch *ou* to huddle up **2.** [feuille, pétale] to shrivel *ou* to curl (up).

recru, e [rəkry] *adj litt* : **être ~ de fatigue** to be exhausted.

recrudescence [rəkrydɛsɑ̃s] *nf* [aggravation - d'une maladie] aggravation, worsening ; [- de la fièvre] new bout ; [- d'une épidémie] fresh *ou* new outbreak ; [- du froid] new spell ■ **la ~ du terrorisme** the new wave *ou* outbreak of terrorism.

recrudescent, e [rəkrydɛsɑ̃, ɑ̃t] *adj litt* increasing, mounting, recrudescent *sout*.

recrue [rəkry] *nf* **1.** MIL recruit **2.** *fig* recruit, new member.

recrutement [rəkrytmɑ̃] *nm* recruiting, recruitment *(U)* ■ **le ~ du personnel s'effectue par concours** staff are recruited by competitive examination.

recruter [3] [rəkryte] *vt* **1.** [engager] to recruit ■ **nous recrutons des bonnes volontés pour déménager** *hum* do we have any volunteers to help with the move? **2.** MIL & POLIT to recruit, to enlist.
◆ **se recruter** *vp (emploi passif)* **1.** [être engagé] to be recruited ■ **les ingénieurs se recrutent sur diplôme** engineers are recruited on the basis of their qualifications **2.** [provenir de] to come from.

recruteur, euse [rəkrytœr, øz] *nm, f* recruiter ■ *(comme adj; avec ou sans trait d'union)* recruiting ■ **sergent ~** recruiting officer.

recta [rɛkta] *adv fam* **payer ~** to pay on the nail.

rectal, e, aux [rɛktal, o] *adj* rectal.

rectangle [rɛktɑ̃gl] ◇ *nm* **1.** [forme] rectangle, oblong **2.** GÉOM rectangle.
◇ *adj* : **triangle ~** right-angled triangle.

rectangulaire [rɛktɑ̃gylɛr] *adj* **1.** [forme] rectangular, oblong **2.** GÉOM rectangular.

recteur, trice [rɛktœr, tris] *nm, f* ÉDUC [d'académie] *chief administrative officer of an education authority*, ≃ (Chief) Education Officer *UK* ■ [d'une université catholique] ≃ rector ■ [chez les jésuites] : **père ~** rector.
◆ **recteur** *nm* RELIG [d'un sanctuaire] ≃ rector ■ [en Bretagne] priest, rector.

rectifiable [rɛktifjabl] *adj* **1.** [réparable] rectifiable ■ **les erreurs ne sont pas ~s après coup** mistakes cannot be rectified afterwards **2.** CHIM rectifiable.

rectificatif, ive [rɛktifikatif, iv] *adj* correcting ■ **mention rectificative** correction.
◆ **rectificatif** *nm* correction, rectification.

rectification [rɛktifikasjɔ̃] *nf* **1.** [action] rectification, correction **2.** [rectificatif] correction ■ **apporter une ~ à une déclaration** to correct a statement ▶ **droit de ~** PRESSE ≃ right of reply **3.** CHIM & MATH rectification **4.** MÉCAN precision grinding.

rectifier [9] [rɛktifje] *vt* **1.** [rajuster] to adjust, to rectify **2.** [corriger] to correct, to rectify **3.** CHIM & MATH to rectify **4.** MÉCAN to precision grind.

rectiligne [rɛktiliɲ] ◇ *adj* rectilinear.
◇ *nm* MATH rectilinear angle.

rectitude [rɛktityd] *nf* [justesse] (moral) rectitude, uprightness.

recto [rɛkto] *nm* first side *ou* front of a page, recto *sout* ■ **n'écrivez qu'au ~** write on this side only.

◆ **recto verso** *loc adv* on both sides.

rectoral, e, aux [rɛktɔral, o] *adj* ≃ of the (Chief) Education Officer *UK* ■ **décision ~e** ≃ decision by *ou* emanating from the Education Office *UK*.

rectorat [rɛktɔra] *nm* ÉDUC [d'une académie - administration] ≃ Education Office *UK* ; [- bâtiment] ≃ Education offices *UK* ■ [chez les jésuites] rectorship.

rectrice [rɛktris] *nf* ORNITH rectrix.

rectum [rɛktɔm] *nm* rectum.

reçu, e [rəsy] ◇ *pp* ▷ **recevoir**.
◇ *nm, f* [candidat] pass ■ **les ~s** the successful candidates, the passes.
◆ **reçu** *nm* [quittance] receipt.

recueil [rəkœj] *nm* collection ■ **un ~ de poèmes** a collection *ou* a selection *ou* an anthology of poems.

recueillement [rəkœjmɑ̃] *nm* contemplation, meditation ■ **écouter qqch avec ~** to listen reverently to sthg.

recueillera *etc v* ▷ **recueillir**.

recueilli, e [rəkœji] *adj* contemplative, meditative ■ **un public très ~** a very attentive audience ■ **un visage ~** a composed expression.

recueillir [41] [rəkœjir] *vt* **1.** [récolter] to gather, to pick ■ **les abeilles recueillent le pollen** bees collect *ou* gather pollen ■ **~ le fruit de son travail** to reap the fruit of one's labour ■ **elle espère ~ plus de la moitié des suffrages** she hopes to win more than half the votes **2.** [renseignements] to collect, to obtain ■ [argent] to collect ■ **j'ai recueilli ses dernières paroles** *litt* I received his last words **3.** [personne] to take in *(sép)* ■ **~ un oiseau tombé du nid** to take care of a bird which has fallen from its nest.
◆ **se recueillir** *vpi* [penser] to spend some moments in silence ■ [prier] to pray ■ **aller se ~ sur la tombe de qqn** to spend some moments in silence at sb's graveside.

recuire [98] [rəkɥir] ◇ *vt* **1.** CULIN [à l'eau] to cook longer ■ [au four] to cook longer in the oven **2.** MÉTALL to anneal ■ [lingot] to soak.
◇ *vi* : **faire ~ un rôti** to recook a joint.

recuit [rəkɥi] *nm* MÉTALL annealing.

recul [rəkyl] *nm* **1.** [mouvement] moving back, backward movement ■ ARM recoil, kick ■ **il eut un mouvement de ~** he stepped back **2.** [distance] : **as-tu assez de ~ pour juger du tableau/prendre la photo?** are you far enough away to judge the painting/to take the photograph? **3.** [réflexion] : **avec le ~** retrospectively, with (the benefit of) hindsight ■ **prendre du ~ par rapport à un événement** to stand back (in order) to assess an event ■ **nous n'avons pas assez de ~ pour juger des effets à long terme** it's too early *ou* there's not been enough time to assess what long-term effects there might be **4.** [baisse] fall, drop ■ **le ~ de l'industrie textile** the decline of the textile industry ■ **le ~ du yen par rapport au dollar** the fall of the yen against the dollar.

reculade [rəkylad] *nf* [d'une armée] retreat ■ [politique] climbdown, back-tracking *(U)*.

reculé, e [rəkyle] *adj* **1.** [dans l'espace] remote, far-off ■ **ils habitent dans un coin ~** they live in an out-of-the-way place **2.** [dans le temps] remote, far-off, distant.
◆ **reculée** *nf* GÉOGR blind valley.

reculer [3] [rəkyle] ◇ *vt* **1.** [dans l'espace] to push *ou* to move back *(sép)* **2.** [dans le temps - rendez-vous] to delay, to postpone, to defer ; [- date] to postpone, to put back *(sép)* ; [- décision] to defer, to postpone, to put off *(sép)*.
◇ *vi* **1.** [aller en arrière - à pied] to step *ou* to go *ou* to move back ; [- en voiture] to reverse, to move back ■ **recule d'un pas!** take one step backwards! ■ **mets le frein à main, la voiture recule!** put the handbrake on, the car is rolling backwards! ■ **il a heurté le mur en reculant** he backed *ou* reversed into the wall **2.** [céder du terrain - falaise, forêt] to recede **3.** [renoncer] to retreat, to shrink (back), to draw back ■ **~ devant l'ennemi** to retreat in the face of the enemy ■ **le prix m'a fait ~** I backed down when I saw the price ⊃ **c'est ~ pour mieux sauter** that's just putting off the inevitable **4.** [faiblir - cours, valeur] to fall, to weaken ; [- épidémie, criminalité, mortalité] to recede, to subside ■ **le yen recule par rapport au dollar** the yen is losing ground *ou* falling against the dollar **5.** ARM to recoil.
◆ **se reculer** *vpi fam* : **recule-toi!** get back!

reculons [rəkylɔ̃] ◆ **à reculons** *loc adv* **1.** [en marche arrière] backwards ■ **sortir à ~** to back out ⊃ **avancer à ~** *hum* to be getting nowhere **2.** [avec réticence] reluctantly, under protest ■ **je le fais à ~** I'm reluctant to do it ■ **on sent bien qu'il a accepté à ~** you can tell he wasn't happy about accepting *ou* he was reluctant to accept.

récupérable [rekyperabl] *adj* **1.** [objet] salvageable, worth rescuing ■ **vêtements ~s** (still) serviceable clothes **2.** [personne] redeemable **3.** [temps] recoverable ■ **ces heures supplémentaires sont ~s** time off will be given in lieu of overtime worked.

récupérateur, trice [rekyperatœr, tris] ◇ *adj* **1.** [qui recycle] : **industrie récupératrice** *industry based on reclaimed or recycled materials* **2.** [qui repose] : **sommeil ~** refreshing *ou* restorative *sout* sleep.
◇ *nm, f industrialist or builder working with reclaimed materials.*
◆ **récupérateur** *nm* ARM & TECHNOL recuperator.

récupération [rekyperasjɔ̃] *nf* **1.** [après séparation, perte] recovery **2.** ÉCOL recycling, reclaiming ■ **matériau de ~** scrap *(U)* **3.** POLIT takeover ■ **il y a eu ~ du mouvement par les extrémistes** the extremists have taken over and manipulated the movement **4.** [au travail] making up ■ **quand je fais des heures supplémentaires, j'ai des jours de ~** when I work overtime, I get time off in exchange *ou* in lieu **5.** ASTRON recovery **6.** INFORM : **~ de données** data recovery.

récupérer [18] [rekypere] ◇ *vt* **1.** [retrouver] to get back *(sép)* ■ **il doit ~ son chien au chenil** he's got to pick up *ou* to collect his dog from the kennels ■ **je passe te ~ en voiture** I'll come and pick you up ■ **veux-tu ~ ton anorak?** do you want your anorak back? ■ **j'ai récupéré l'usage de ma main gauche** I recovered the use of my left hand ■ **il a récupéré toutes ses forces** [il s'est reposé] he has recuperated, he's back to normal ■ **tout a brûlé, ils n'ont rien pu ~** everything was destroyed by the fire, they didn't manage to salvage anything ■ **~ sa mise** to recoup one's outlay **2.** [pour utiliser - chiffons, papier, verre, ferraille] to salvage ; [- chaleur, énergie] to save ■ **j'ai récupéré des chaises dont personne ne voulait** I've rescued some chairs no one wanted ■ **regarde si tu peux ~ quelques pommes** see if you can save a few apples **3.** [jour de congé] to make up for, to compensate for ■ **on récupère ce jour férié samedi prochain** we are making up for this public holiday by working next Saturday ❙ [jour de travail] : **les jours fériés travaillés seront récupérés** employees will be allowed time off in lieu of public holidays worked **4.** POLIT to take over *(sép)* ■ **le mouvement a été récupéré par le gouvernement** the movement has been taken over by the government for its own ends **5.** INFORM : **~ des données** to recover data.
◇ *vi* [se remettre] to recover, to recuperate.

récurage [rekyraʒ] *nm* [nettoyage] scouring ■ [avec une brosse] scrubbing.

récurant, e [rekyrɑ̃, ɑ̃t] *adj* scouring.
◆ **récurant** *nm* scouring cream *ou* agent, cleaning cream.

récurer [3] [rekyre] *vt* [casserole, évier] to scour, to scrub.

récurrence [rekyrɑ̃s] *nf* **1.** [gén - MÉD] recurrence **2.** MATH [d'une décimale] recurrence ■ [induction] induction.

récurrent, e [rekyrɑ̃, ɑ̃t] *adj* **1.** [à répétition] recurrent, recurring **2.** MÉD [fièvre] recurrent, relapsing **3.** INFORM & MATH : **suite** *ou* **série ~e** recursion series **4.** ÉCON : **chômage ~** periodic *ou* recurrent unemployment.

récursif, ive [rekyrsif, iv] *adj* recursive.

récusable [rekyzabl] *adj* impugnable *sout*, challengeable.

récusation [rekyzasjɔ̃] *nf* challenge DR recusal ■ **droit de ~** right to challenge.

récuser [3] [rekyze] *vt* **1.** DR [juge, juré, expert] to challenge **2.** [décision, témoignage] to challenge, to impugn *sout.*
◆ **se récuser** *vpi* **1.** [lors d'un procès] to declare o.s. incompetent **2.** [lors d'une entrevue, d'un débat] to refuse to give an opinion, to decline to (make any) comment.

reçut *etc v* ▷ **recevoir.**

recyclable [rәsiklabl] *adj* recyclable.

recyclage [rәsiklaʒ] *nm* **1.** INDUST recycling **2.** ÉDUC [perfectionnement] refresher course ▪ [reconversion] retraining **3.** [stage - pour employés] retraining course ; [- pour chômeurs] retraining course, restart (course) *UK.*

recycler [3] [rәsikle] *vt* **1.** INDUST to recycle ▪ **papier recyclé** recycled paper **2.** [perfectionner] to send on a refresher course ▪ [reconvertir] to retrain.
◆ **se recycler** *vpi* [pour se perfectionner] to go on a refresher course ▪ [pour se reconvertir] to retrain ▪ **le vocabulaire des jeunes change, j'ai dû me ~** *hum* young people speak differently nowadays, I've had to bring myself up to date.

rédacteur, trice [redaktœr, tris] *nm, f* **1.** [auteur - d'un livre] writer ; [- d'un guide] compiler ▪ **les ~s de l'encyclopédie** the contributors to the encyclopedia **2.** PRESSE writer, contributor ▪ **~ en chef** [d'une revue] (chief) editor ; [du journal télévisé] television news editor.

rédaction [redaksjɔ̃] *nf* **1.** [écriture] writing ▪ **équipe chargée de la ~ d'un guide/dictionnaire** team responsible for compiling a guide/dictionary ▪ **la ~ d'un projet de loi/d'un contrat d'assurance** the drafting of a bill/of an insurance contract **2.** PRESSE [lieu] editorial office ▪ TV newsdesk, newsroom ▪ [équipe] editorial staff **3.** ÉDUC [composition] ≃ essay, ≃ composition.

rédactionnel, elle [redaksjɔnɛl] *adj* editorial.

reddition [redisjɔ̃] *nf* **1.** MIL surrender **2.** FIN & DR rendering ▪ **~ de compte** presentation of account.

redécoupage [rәdekupaʒ] *nm* POLIT : **~ électoral** redrawing of electoral *ou* constituency boundaries.

redécouverte [rәdekuvɛrt] *nf* rediscovery.

redécouvrir [34] [rәdekuvrir] *vt* to rediscover.

redéfinir [32] [rәdefinir] *vt* to redefine ▪ **~ la politique du logement** to lay down new housing policy guidelines.

redéfinition [rәdefinisjɔ̃] *nf* redefinition.

redemander [3] [rәdәmɑ̃de] *vt* **1.** [demander à nouveau] to ask again **2.** [demander davantage] to ask for more ▪ **sa correction ne lui a pas suffi, il en redemande** one spank obviously wasn't enough because he's asking for another one **3.** [après un prêt] to ask for *(insép).*

redémarrage [rәdemaraʒ] *nm* **1.** [d'une machine] starting up again *(U)* **2.** [économique] resurgence.

redémarrer [3] [rәdemare] ◇ *vi* **1.** [moteur] to start up *(sép)* again **2.** [processus] to get going *ou* to take off again ▪ **l'économie redémarre** the economy is looking up again ▪ **les cours redémarrent fin octobre** classes start again at the end of October.
◇ *vt* INFORM to reboot, to restart.

rédempteur, trice [redɑ̃ptœr, tris] ◇ *adj* redeeming, redemptive *sout.*
◇ *nm, f* redeemer.

rédemption [redɑ̃psjɔ̃] *nf* RELIG : **la Rédemption** Redemption.

redéploiement [rәdeplwamɑ̃] *nm* **1.** MIL redeployment **2.** ÉCON reorganization, restructuring.

redescendre [73] [rәdesɑ̃dr] ◇ *vt* **1.** [colline, montagne *etc* - en voiture] to drive (back) down ; [- à pied] to walk (back) down ▪ [suj: alpiniste] to climb back down *(insép)* **2.** [passager, fret] to take *ou* to drive (back) down *(sép)* ▪ **je redescendrai les cartons plus tard** [je suis en haut] I'll take the cardboard boxes back down later ; [je suis en bas] I'll bring the cardboard boxes back down later.
◇ *vi (aux être)* **1.** [descendre] to go *ou* to come *ou* to get (back) down ▪ **la température/le niveau de l'eau redescend** the temperature/the water level is falling (again) ▪ **je suis redescendu en chasse-neige** I snowploughed (back) down **2.** [descendre à nouveau] to go down again.

redevable [rәdәvabl] *adj* **1.** FIN : **être ~ d'une somme d'argent à qqn** to owe sb a sum of money ▪ **vous êtes ~ d'un acompte provisionnel** you are liable for an interim payment **2.** *fig* **être ~ de qqch à qqn** to be indebted to sb for sthg ▪ **je lui suis ~ de ma promotion** I owe him my promotion, I owe it to him that I was promoted.

redevance [rәdәvɑ̃s] *nf* **1.** TV licence fee *UK* ▪ TÉLÉCOM rental charge **2.** COMM & FIN [pour un service] dues, fees ▪ [royalties] royalties **3.** HIST tax.

redevenir [40] [rәdәvnir] *vi (aux être)* to become again ▪ **le ciel redevient nuageux** the sky is clouding over again ▪ **~ amis** to become friends again.

rédhibitoire [redibitwar] *adj* **1.** DR : **vice ~** latent (principal) defect **2.** *fig* **une mauvaise note à l'écrit, c'est ~** a bad mark in the written exam is enough to fail the candidate.

rediffuser [3] [rәdifyze] *vt* to rebroadcast, to repeat ▪ **nous rediffuserons ces images** we'll be showing these scenes again, we'll be rebroadcasting these scenes.

rediffusion [rәdifyzjɔ̃] *nf* repeat, rerun, rebroadcast.

rédiger [17] [rediʒe] *vt* [manifeste, contrat] to write, to draw up *(sép)* ▪ [thèse, rapport] to write up *(sép)* ▪ [lettre] to write, to compose ▪ [guide, manuel] to write, to compile ▪ *(en usage absolu)* **il rédige bien** he writes well.

redimensionner [3] [rәdimɑ̃sjɔne] *vt* INFORM to resize.

redingote [rәdɛ̃gɔt] *nf* **1.** [de femme] tailored *ou* fitted coat **2.** [d'homme] frock coat.

redire [102] [rәdir] *vt* **1.** [répéter] to say *ou* to tell again, to repeat ▪ [rabâcher] to keep saying, to repeat ▪ **on lui a dit et redit** he's been told again and again **2.** [rapporter] to (go and) tell, to repeat ▪ **surtout, n'allez pas le lui ~** whatever you do, don't go and tell him **3.** *loc* **il n'y avait rien à ~ à cela** there was nothing wrong with *ou* nothing to object to in that ▪ **trouver à ~ (à)** to find fault (with).

redisons *etc v* ▷ **redire.**

redistribuer [7] [rәdistribɥe] *vt* [cartes] to deal again ▪ [fortune] to redistribute ▪ [emplois] to reallocate ▪ **~ les rôles** *pr* to recast the show ; *fig* to reallocate the tasks.

redit, e [rәdi, it] *pp* ▷ **redire.**
◆ **redite** *nf* superfluous *ou* needless repetition ▪ **son texte est plein de ~es** his text is very repetitive.

redites *v* ▷ **redire.**

redondance [rәdɔ̃dɑ̃s] *nf* **1.** [répétition] redundancy **2.** INFORM, LING & TÉLÉCOM redundancy ▪ **vérification par ~** redundancy check.

redondant, e [rәdɔ̃dɑ̃, ɑ̃t] *adj* **1.** [mot] redundant, superfluous ▪ [style] redundant, verbose, wordy **2.** INFORM, LING & TÉLÉCOM redundant.

redonner [3] [rәdɔne] *vt* **1.** [donner de nouveau] to give again ▪ **j'ai redonné les chaussures au cordonnier** I took the shoes back *ou* returned the shoes to the cobbler's **2.** [rendre] to give back *(sép)* ▪ **ça m'a redonné confiance** it restored my confidence in myself ▪ **la lessive qui redonne l'éclat du neuf à tout votre linge** the powder that puts the brightness back into your washing **3.** THÉÂTRE to stage again ▪ **~ "Hamlet" au théâtre** to stage "Hamlet" again.
◆ **redonner dans** *v+prép sout* to lapse *ou* to fall back into.

redorer [3] [rәdɔre] *vt* TECHNOL to regild.

redoublant, e [rәdublɑ̃, ɑ̃t] *nm, f* pupil repeating a year *UK ou* grade *US* ▪ **combien y a-t-il de ~s?** how many pupils are repeating their year?

redoublement [rәdublәmɑ̃] *nm* **1.** ÉDUC repeating a year *UK ou* grade *US* ▪ **son ~ l'a fait progresser** she's doing much better at school since she was held back a year **2.** LING reduplication **3.** [accroissement] increase, intensification ▪ **seul un ~ d'efforts lui permettra de réussir** he will only succeed if he works much harder.

redoubler [3] [rəduble] <> *vt* **1.** [rendre double] : ~ **une consonne** to double a consonant ▪ **frapper à coups redoublés** [plus fort] to knock even harder *ou* with renewed vigour ; [plus vite] to knock even more urgently **2.** ÉDUC : ~ **une classe** to repeat a year *UK ou* grade *US* ▪ *(en usage absolu)* **ils l'ont fait ~** they made him do the year again.
<> *vi* [froid, tempête] to increase, to intensify, to become more intense.
◆ **redoubler de** *v+prép* to increase in ▪ ~ **d'efforts** to strive doubly hard, to redouble one's efforts ▪ ~ **de patience** to be doubly *ou* extra patient ▪ ~ **de ruse** to be doubly *ou* extra cunning.

redoutable [rədutabl] *adj* **1.** [dangereux] formidable ▪ **un ennemi ~** a fearsome *ou* formidable enemy ▪ **une maladie ~** a dreadful illness ▪ **la compagnie d'assurances a des enquêteurs ~s** the insurance company has very able investigators ▪ **elle a un revers ~** she has a lethal backhand **2.** [effrayant - aspect, réputation] awesome, fearsome, awe-inspiring.

redoute [rədut] *nf* [fortification] redoubt.

Redoute [rədut] *npr f* : **la ~** *French mail order firm.*

redouter [3] [rədute] *vt* to dread ▪ **il redoute de te rencontrer** he dreads meeting you.

redoux [rədu] *nm* mild spell *(during winter).*

redressement [rədrɛsmɑ̃] *nm* **1.** [du corps, d'une barre] straightening up **2.** [d'un véhicule] : **son pneu a explosé juste après un ~ dans un virage** his tyre burst just after he straightened up coming out of a bend **3.** COMM & ÉCON recovery ▪ **plan de ~** recovery programme **4.** FIN : ~ **fiscal** payment of back taxes **5.** ÉLECTRON rectification.

redresser [4] [rədrɛse] *vt* **1.** [arbre, poteau] to straighten (up), to set upright ▪ [véhicule, volant] to straighten (up) ▪ [bateau] to right ▪ ~ **la tête** [la lever] to lift up one's head ; [avec fierté] to hold one's head up high **2.** *(en usage absolu)* AUTO to straighten up, to recover ▪ **il n'a pas redressé assez vite à la sortie du virage** he didn't straighten up quickly enough after the bend **3.** [corriger - courbure] to put right, to straighten out *(sép)* ; [- anomalie] to rectify, to put right ; [- situation] to sort out *(sép)*, to put right, to put back on an even keel **4.** ÉLECTRON to rectify.
◆ **se redresser** *vpi* **1.** [personne assise] to sit up straight ▪ [personne allongée] to sit up ▪ [personne voûtée ou penchée] to straighten up ▪ **redresse-toi!** [personne assise] sit up straight! ; [personne debout] stand up straight! **2.** *fig* [remonter] to recover ▪ **la situation se redresse un peu** the situation is on the mend.

redresseur, euse [rədrɛsœr, øz] *adj* **1.** ÉLECTR rectifying **2.** OPT erecting.
◆ **redresseur** *nm* ÉLECTR rectifier.
◆ **redresseur de torts** *nm* HIST & *hum* righter of wrongs.

réducteur, trice [redyktœr, tris] *adj* **1.** [limitatif] simplistic ▪ **une analyse réductrice** an over-simplistic analysis **2.** MÉCAN reduction *(modif)* **3.** CHIM reducing.
◆ **réducteur** *nm* **1.** MÉCAN reduction gear **2.** CHIM reducer, reductant, reducing agent **3.** ANTHR : ~ **de têtes** headshrinker.

réductibilité [redyktibilite] *nf* reducibility.

réductible [redyktibl] *adj* **1.** [dépenses, dimensions] which can be reduced ▪ [théorie] which can be reduced *ou* simplified **2.** CHIM, MATH & MÉD reducible.

réduction [redyksjɔ̃] *nf* **1.** [remise] discount, rebate ▪ **accorder** *ou* **faire une ~ de 50 euros sur le prix total** to give a 50-euro discount on the overall cost ▪ **carte de ~** discount card **2.** [baisse] cut, drop ▪ **ils nous ont imposé une ~ des dépenses/salaires** they've cut our expenditure/wages ▪ **ils ont promis une ~ des impôts** they promised to reduce *ou* to lower taxes **3.** [copie plus petite - d'une œuvre] (scale) model **4.** BIOL, CHIM & MÉTALL reduction **5.** MÉD setting, reducing **6.** MATH, MUS & PHILOS reduction **7.** DR : ~ **de peine** mitigation (of sentence) ▪ **il a eu une ~ de peine** he got his sentence cut *ou* reduced.
◆ **en réduction** *loc adj* scaled-down.

réductionnisme [redyksjɔnism] *nm* reductionism.

réductionniste [redyksjɔnist] *adj & nmf* reductionist.

réduire [98] [redɥir] <> *vt* **1.** [restreindre - consommation] to reduce, to cut down on ; [- inflation] to reduce, to bring down *(sép)*, to lower ; [- dépenses, effectifs] to reduce, to cut back on ; [- distance] to reduce, to decrease ; [- chauffage] to lower, to turn down *(sép)* ▪ **il a réduit le prix de 10 %** he cut *ou* reduced the price by 10% ▪ ~ **qqch de moitié** to cut sthg by half, to halve sthg
2. [refaire en petit - photo] to reduce ; [- schéma] to scale down *(sép)*
3. [changer] : ~ **qqch à néant : il a réussi à ~ à néant le travail de dix années** he managed to reduce ten years' work to nothing ▪ ~ **qqch en miettes** to smash sthg to bits *ou* pieces ▪ ~ **qqch en cendres** to reduce sthg to ashes ▪ ~ **qqch à sa plus simple expression** to reduce sthg to its simplest expression
4. [forcer] : ~ **qqn à** to reduce sb to ▪ ~ **la presse/l'opposition au silence** to silence the press/the opposition ▪ **ils en sont réduits aux dernières extrémités** they are in dire straits ▪ ~ **qqn à faire** to force *ou* to compel *ou* to drive sb to do
5. [vaincre] to quell, to subdue, to crush ▪ ~ **les poches de résistance** to crush the last pockets of resistance
6. INFORM to minimize
7. CHIM & CULIN to reduce
8. MÉD to set, to reduce
9. MATH & MUS to reduce
10. *Suisse* [ranger] to put away *(sép)*.
<> *vi* CULIN : **faire ~** to reduce.
◆ **se réduire** *vpi* [économiser] to cut down.
◆ **se réduire à** *vp+prép* [consister en] to amount to.

réduit, e [redɥi, it] *adj* **1.** [échelle, format *etc*] scaled-down, small-scale **2.** [taille] small ▪ [tarif] reduced, cut ▪ **à vitesse ~e** at reduced *ou* low speed ▪ **à prix ~** cut price ▪ **la fréquentation est ~e l'hiver** attendance is lower in the winter **3.** [peu nombreux - débouchés] limited, restricted.
◆ **réduit** *nm* **1.** *péj* [logement] cubbyhole **2.** [recoin] recess ▪ [placard] cupboard **3.** [fortification] reduit.

rééchelonnement [reeʃlɔnmɑ̃] *nm* rescheduling.

réécouter [3] [reekute] *vt* : ~ **qqch** to listen to sthg again ▪ **fais-moi ~ ce passage** let me listen to that bit again.

réécrire [99] [reekrir] *vt* to rewrite ▪ ~ **l'histoire** to rewrite history.

réécriture [reekrityr] *nf* rewriting.

réécrivait *etc v* ⊳ **réécrire**.

rééditer [3] [reedite] *vt* **1.** IMPR to republish ▪ **son livre a été réédité chez Leroux** his book has been republished by Leroux *ou* brought out again by Leroux **2.** *fam* [refaire] to repeat.

réédition [reedisjɔ̃] *nf* **1.** IMPR [nouvelle édition] new edition ▪ [action de rééditer] republishing, republication **2.** [répétition] repeat, repetition.

rééducation [reedykasjɔ̃] *nf* **1.** MÉD [d'un membre] reeducation ▪ [d'un malade] rehabilitation, reeducation ▪ **faire de la ~** to undergo physiotherapy *esp UK ou* physical therapy *US* ➊ ~ **motrice** motor reeducation **2.** [morale] reeducation ▪ DR [d'un délinquant] rehabilitation.

rééduquer [3] [reedyke] *vt* **1.** MÉD [malade] to give physiotherapy *esp UK ou* physical therapy *US* to, to reeducate ▪ [membre] to reeducate **2.** [délinquant] to rehabilitate.

réel, elle [reɛl] *adj* **1.** [concret] real ▪ **besoins ~s** genuine needs ▮ [prix, profit, salaire] real ▪ [date] effective ▪ **résultats ~s** actual results **2.** *(avant le n)* [appréciable] genuine, real ▪ **elle a fait preuve d'un ~ talent** she's shown true *ou* genuine talent.
◆ **réel** *nm* : **le ~** reality, the real.

réélection [reelɛksjɔ̃] *nf* reelection.

réélire [106] [reelir] *vt* to reelect ▪ **elle compte bien se faire ~** she's pretty sure she'll be reelected.

réellement [reɛlmɑ̃] *adv* really ▪ **ces faits ont ~ eu lieu** these events really did take place.

réélu, e [reely] *pp* ▻ **réélire.**

réenregistrable [reɑ̃rəʒistrabl] *adj* rerecordable.

rééquilibrage [reekilibraʒ] *nm* readjustment, rebalancing ▪ **le ~ des forces européennes** the restabilizing of power in Europe ▪ **~ du budget** balancing the budget again.

rééquilibre [reekilibr] *nm* restoration of balance.

rééquilibrer [3] [reekilibre] *vt* **1.** [budget] to balance again ▪ [situation] to restabilize **2.** [personne] : **son séjour à l'étranger l'a rééquilibré** his stay abroad has helped him (to) find his feet again.

réessayer [11] [reesɛje] *vt* [voiture, produit, méthode] to try again ▪ [vêtement] to try on *(sép)* again.

réévaluer [7] [reevalɥe] *vt* **1.** FIN [devise, monnaie] to revalue ▪ [salaire, taux] to reappraise ▪ [à la hausse] to upgrade ▪ [à la baisse] to downgrade **2.** [qualité, travail] to reassess, to reevaluate.

réexaminer [3] [reegzamine] *vt* to reexamine, to reassess.

réexpédier [9] [reɛkspedje] *vt* **1.** [courrier - à l'expéditeur] to return (to sender), to send back *(sép)* ; [- au destinataire] to forward **2.** *fam* [personne] to throw out *(sép)* ▪ **je l'ai réexpédié vite fait** I got rid of him in no time.

réexpédition [reɛkspedisjɔ̃] *nf* [pour renvoyer] sending back, returning (to sender) ▪ [pour faire suivre] forwarding, redirecting ▪ **service de ~ du courrier** mail forwarding *ou* redirecting service.

réf. (*abr écrite de* **référence**) ref.

réfaction [refaksjɔ̃] *nf* **1.** COMM reimbursement, allowance **2.** FIN adjustment.

refaire [109] [rəfɛr] *vt* **1.** [à nouveau] to redo, to do again ▪ **~ une addition** to add a sum up again ▪ **~ une opération pour la vérifier** to do a calculation again to check it ▪ **~ une piqûre** to give another injection ▪ **j'ai dû ~ le trajet** I had to make the same journey again ▪ **quand pourras-tu ~ du sport?** when will you be able to do some sport again? ▪ **je vais ~ quelques longueurs de bassin** I'm going to swim a few more lengths ‖ *fig* **vous ne la referez pas** you won't change her ▪ **~ sa vie** to start a new life, to make a fresh start (in life) ▪ **si c'était à ~? – je suis prête à recommencer** and if you had to do it all again? – I would do the same thing **2.** [réparer] to redo ▪ **ils refont la route** they are resurfacing the road ▪ **le moteur a été complètement refait à neuf** the engine has had a complete overhaul **3.** *fam* [berner] to take in *(sép)* ▪ **il m'a refait de cent euros** he did me out of a hundred euros.

◆ **se refaire** ◇ *vp (emploi réfléchi)* [se changer] : **on ne se refait pas** you can't change the way you are.

◇ *vpi fam* [financièrement] to recoup one's losses ▪ **j'ai besoin de me ~** I need to get hold of some more cash.

◇ *vpt* : **se ~ une tasse de thé** to make o.s. another cup of tea ➊ **se ~ une beauté** to powder one's nose ▪ **se ~ une santé** to recuperate.

◆ **se refaire à** *vp+prép* : **se ~ à qqch** to get used to sthg again.

réfection [refɛksjɔ̃] *nf* [gén] redoing ▪ [d'une pièce] redecorating ▪ [d'une maison] redoing, doing up ▪ [d'une route] repairs ▪ **pendant les travaux de ~** [d'une maison] while the house is being done up ; [d'une route] during repairs to the road, while there are roadworks.

réfectoire [refɛktwar] *nm* [dans une communauté] refectory ▪ ÉDUC dining hall, canteen ▪ UNIV (dining) hall.

refera *etc v* ▻ **refaire.**

référé [refere] *nm* [procédure] special hearing ▪ [arrêt] temporary ruling ▪ [ordonnance] temporary injunction ▪ **introduire un ~** to issue a temporary injunction.

référence [referɑ̃s] *nf* **1.** [renvoi] reference **2.** ADMIN & COMM reference number ▪ **'~ à rappeler dans toute correspondance'** 'reference number to be quoted when replying *ou* in all correspondence' **3.** [base d'évaluation] reference ▪ **un prix littéraire, c'est une ~** a literary prize is a good recommendation for a book ▪ **ton ami n'est pas une ~** your friend is nothing to go by ▪ **faire ~ à** to refer to, to make (a) reference to **4.** LING reference.

◆ **références** *nfpl* [pour un emploi - témoignages] references, credentials *fig* ; [- document] reference letter, testimonial ▪ **'sérieuses ~s exigées'** 'good references required'.

◆ **de référence** *loc adj* reference *(modif)* ▪ **année de ~** FIN base year ▪ **prix de ~** reference price.

référencement [referɑ̃smɑ̃] *nm* **1.** COMM listing **2.** INFORM (website) referencing.

référencer [16] [referɑ̃se] *vt* to reference ▪ **un site bien référencé** a well-referenced website.

référendaire [referɑ̃dɛr] *adj* referendum *(modif)* ▪ **conseiller ~** ≃ public auditor.

référendum [referɛ̃dɔm] *nm* referendum.

référent [referɑ̃] *nm* referent.

référentiel, elle [referɑ̃sjɛl] *adj* referential.

◆ **référentiel** *nm* frame of reference.

référer [18] [refere] ◆ **en référer à** *v+prép* to refer back to ▪ **il ne peut rien décider sans en ~ à son supérieur** he can't decide anything without referring back to his boss.

◆ **se référer à** *vp+prép* to refer to ▪ **nous nous référons à la définition ci-dessus** the reader is referred to the above definition.

refermer [3] [rəfɛrme] *vt* to close *ou* to shut (again) ▪ **~ ses mâchoires sur qqch** to clamp one's jaws on sthg.

◆ **se refermer** *vpi* [porte] to close *ou* to shut (again) ▪ [blessure] to close *ou* to heal up ▪ [piège] to snap shut ▪ **la porte s'est refermée sur mes doigts** the door closed on my fingers.

refiler [3] [rəfile] *vt fam* **1.** [donner] to give **2.** *loc* **~ le bébé à qqn** to unload a problem onto sb.

refinancement [rəfinɑ̃smɑ̃] *nm* refinancing.

refit *etc v* ▻ **refaire.**

réfléchi, e [refleʃi] *adj* **1.** [caractère, personne] reflective, thoughtful ▪ **une analyse ~e** a thoughtful *ou* well thought-out analysis ▪ **un enfant très ~ pour son âge** a child who thinks very seriously for his age **2.** LING reflexive.

réfléchir [32] [refleʃir] ◇ *vt* PHOTO & PHYS to reflect.

◇ *vi* to think ▪ **as-tu bien réfléchi?** have you thought about it carefully? ▪ **je n'ai pas eu le temps de ~** I haven't had time to think ▪ **il fallait ~ avant de parler!** you should have thought before you spoke! ▪ **j'ai longuement réfléchi** I gave it a lot of thought ▪ **quand on voit comment ça se passe, ça fait ~** when you see what's happening, it makes you think ▪ **tout bien réfléchi** all things considered, after careful consideration ▪ **c'est tout réfléchi, je refuse!** my mind's made up, the answer is no!

◆ **se réfléchir** *vpi* [lumière, son] to be reflected.

réfléchissant, e [refleʃisɑ̃, ɑ̃t] *adj* PHYS reflecting.

réflecteur, trice [reflɛktœr, tris] *adj* reflecting.

◆ **réflecteur** *nm* **1.** ASTRON reflector, reflecting telescope **2.** PHYS reflector.

réflectif, ive [reflɛktif, iv] *adj* PHYSIOL reflexive.

reflet [rəflɛ] *nm* **1.** [lumière] reflection, glint, light **2.** [couleur] tinge, glint, highlight ▪ **des cheveux châtains avec des ~s dorés** brown hair with tints of gold ▪ **se faire faire des ~s** to have highlights put in **3.** [image] reflection ▪ **ses lettres sont le ~ de son caractère** her letters reflect *ou* mirror her character.

refléter [18] [rəflete] *vt* **1.** [renvoyer - lumière] to reflect ; [- image] to reflect, to mirror **2.** [représenter] to reflect, to mirror ▪ **son air perplexe reflétait son trouble intérieur** his puzzled look indicated *ou* betrayed his inner turmoil ▪ **ce qu'il dit ne reflète pas ce qu'il pense/mon opinion** his words are not a fair reflection of what he thinks/of my opinion.

◆ **se refléter** *vpi* **1.** [lumière, rayon] to be reflected **2.** [se manifester] to be reflected ▪ **le bonheur se reflète sur son visage** happiness shines in his face.

refleurir [32] [rəflœrir] *vi* **1.** [plante] to flower again, to blossom again **2.** *fig* & *litt* to blossom *ou* to flourish again.

réflexe [reflɛks] <> *nm* **1.** BIOL & PHYSIOL reflex ▶ **~ inné/conditionné** instinctive/conditioned reflex **2.** [réaction] reaction ▪ **il a eu/n'a pas eu le ~ de tirer le signal d'alarme** he instinctively pulled/he didn't think to pull the alarm.
<> *adj* reflex *(modif)*.

réflexible [reflɛksibl] *adj* reflexible.

réflexif, ive [reflɛksif, iv] *adj* MATH & PHILOS reflexive.

réflexion [reflɛksjɔ̃] *nf* **1.** [méditation] thought ▪ **après mûre ~** after careful consideration, after much thought ▪ **leur proposition demande ~** their offer will need thinking over ▪ **s'absorber dans ses ~s** to be deep *ou* lost in thought ▶ **~ faite, à la ~** on reflection **2.** [discernement] : **agir sans ~** to act without thinking, to act thoughtlessly ▪ **son rapport manque de ~** his report hasn't been properly thought out *ou* through **3.** [remarque] remark, comment, reflection *sout* ▪ **faire des ~s à qqn** to make remarks to sb ▪ **sa ~ ne m'a pas plu** I didn't like his remark *ou* what he said ▪ **elle a eu des ~s de la direction** the management have had a word with her *euphém* **4.** TECHNOL [de la lumière] reflection ▪ **angle de ~** angle of reflection.

réflexivité [reflɛksivite] *nf* reflexivity.

réflexologie [reflɛksɔlɔʒi] *nf* reflexology.

refluer [3] [rəflye] *vi* **1.** [liquide] to flow back ▪ [marée] to ebb ▪ [foule, public] to surge back ▪ **faire ~ les manifestants** to push back the demonstrators **2.** *fig & litt* [pensée, souvenir] to come flooding *ou* rushing back.

reflux [rəfly] *nm* **1.** [de la marée] ebb **2.** [d'une foule] backward surge **3.** MÉD reflux.

refondre [75] [rəfɔ̃dr] *vt* **1.** [métal] to remelt, to melt down *(sép)* again ▪ [cloche] to recast **2.** *fig* [remanier] to recast, to reshape, to refashion ▪ **~ un projet de loi** to redraft *ou* to recast a bill ▪ **la 3e édition a été entièrement refondue** the third edition has been entirely revised.

refont *v* ▷ **refaire.**

refonte [rəfɔ̃t] *nf* **1.** MÉTALL [nouvelle fonte] remelting ▪ [nouvelle coulée] recasting **2.** *fig* [remaniement] recasting, reshaping, refashioning ▪ **il y a eu ~ de l'ouvrage** the work has been completely *ou* entirely revised.

reforestation [rəfɔrɛstasjɔ̃] *nf* reforestation.

réformable [refɔrmabl] *adj* **1.** MIL *liable for exemption from military service* **2.** [modifiable] reformable, capable of being modified.

reformage [rəfɔrmaʒ] *nm* reforming ▪ **~ catalytique/à la vapeur** catalytic/steam reforming.

réformateur, trice [refɔrmatœr, tris] <> *adj* reforming ▪ **idées réformatrices** ideas of reform.
<> *nm, f* reformer.

réformation [refɔrmasjɔ̃] *nf* **1.** *litt* [action] reform, reformation **2.** RELIG & *vieilli* **la Réformation** the Reformation **3.** DR reversal.

réforme [refɔrm] *nf* **1.** [modification] reform ▪ **nous choisirons la voie des ~s** we shall opt for reformism *ou* a policy of reform *ou* reforms ▶ **~ fiscale** tax reform **2.** MIL [de matériel] scrapping ▪ [d'un soldat] discharge ▪ [d'un appelé] declaration of unfitness for service **3.** RELIG : **la Réforme** the Reformation.

réformé, e [refɔrme] <> *adj* [religion] Reformed, Protestant.
<> *nm, f* [calviniste] Protestant ▪ [moine] member of a Reformed Order.
◆ **réformé** *nm* MIL [recrue] *conscript declared unfit for service* ▪ [soldat] discharged soldier.

reformer [3] [rəfɔrme] *vt* **1.** [à nouveau] to re-form, to form again ▪ **~ un groupe** to bring a group back together ▪ **reformez les groupes!** get back into your groups! **2.** INDUST du pétrole to reform.
◆ **se reformer** *vpi* to re-form, to form again ▪ **l'association va se ~ autour d'une nouvelle équipe** the association will be set up again *ou* re-formed around a new team.

réformer [3] [refɔrme] *vt* **1.** [modifier] to reform **2.** *litt* [supprimer] to put an end to **3.** [mettre au rebut] to scrap, to discard **4.** MIL [recrue] to declare unfit for service ▪ [soldat] to discharge ▪ [tank, arme] to scrap ▪ **se faire ~** to be exempted from military service **5.** RAIL to overhaul.

réformiste [refɔrmist] *adj* & *nmf* reformist.

reformulation [rəfɔrmylasjɔ̃] *nf* rewording.

reformuler [3] [rəfɔrmyle] *vt* to rephrase, to reword ▪ **je ne comprends pas votre question, pouvez-vous la ~?** I don't understand your question, could you rephrase it?

refoulant, e [rəfulɑ̃, ɑ̃t] *adj* pumping *(avant n)* ▪ **pompe ~e** force pump.

refoulé, e [rəfule] <> *adj* [instinct, sentiment] repressed ▪ [ambition] frustrated ▪ [personne] inhibited.
<> *nm, f* inhibited person.
◆ **refoulé** *nm* PSYCHOL : **le ~** repressed content.

refoulement [rəfulmɑ̃] *nm* **1.** [d'assaillants] pushing *ou* forcing back ▪ [d'immigrants] turning back *ou* away **2.** PSYCHOL repression **3.** RAIL backing.

refouler [3] [rəfule] <> *vt* **1.** [assaillants] to drive *ou* to push back *(sép)*, to repulse ▪ [immigrants] to turn back *ou* away *(sép)* ▪ **ils se sont fait ~ à la frontière** they were driven back at the border **2.** [liquide] to force to flow back ▪ [courant] to stem ▪ [air] to pump out *(sép)* **3.** [retenir] : **~ ses larmes** to hold *ou* to choke back one's tears ▪ **~ sa colère** to keep one's anger in check **4.** PSYCHOL to repress **5.** RAIL to back.
<> *vi* **1.** [pieu, cheville] to balk **2.** [mal fonctionner] : **l'égout refoule** a stench is coming up from the sewer ▪ **la cheminée refoule** the fire is blowing back.

réfractaire [refraktɛr] <> *adj* **1.** [matériau] refractory, heat-resistant **2.** [personne] : **~ à** resistant *ou* unamenable to ▪ **je suis ~ aux mathématiques** I'm incapable of understanding mathematics, mathematics is a closed book to me ▪ **~ aux charmes de la nature** impervious to nature's charms **3.** MÉD resistant **4.** PHYSIOL : **période ~** refractory period *ou* phase.
<> *nm* **1.** TECHNOL refractory (material) **2.** HIST *French citizen refusing to work in Germany during World War II.*

réfracter [3] [refrakte] *vt* to refract.
◆ **se réfracter** *vpi* to be refracted.

réfracteur, trice [refraktœr, tris] *adj* refracting.
◆ **réfracteur** *nm* refracting telescope, refractor.

réfraction [refraksjɔ̃] *nf* refraction ▪ **indice de ~** refractive index.

refrain [rəfrɛ̃] *nm* **1.** [d'une chanson] chorus, refrain ▪ [chanson] tune, song **2.** *péj* [sujet] : **change de ~** can't you talk about something else? ▪ **avec toi c'est toujours le même ~** it's always the same old story with you.

refréner [rəfrene], **réfréner** [18] [refrene] *vt* to hold back *(sép)*, to hold in check ▪ **~ sa colère** to stifle one's anger.

réfrigérant, e [refriʒerɑ̃, ɑ̃t] *adj* **1.** [liquide] cooling, refrigerant *spéc* ▪ **mélange ~** refrigerant **2.** *fig* [comportement, individu] frosty, icy.
◆ **réfrigérant** *nm* INDUST & SC cooler.

réfrigérateur [refriʒeratœr] *nm* refrigerator *sout*, fridge, icebox *US*.

réfrigérateur-congélateur [refriʒeratœrkɔ̃ʒelatœr] (*pl* **réfrigérateurs-congélateurs**) *nm* fridge-freezer.

réfrigération [refriʒerasjɔ̃] *nf* refrigeration.

réfrigéré, e [refriʒere] *adj* **1.** *fam* [personne] frozen **2.** [véhicule] refrigerated.

réfrigérer [18] [refriʒere] *vt* [denrée] to cool, to refrigerate.

réfringent, e [refrɛ̃ʒɑ̃, ɑ̃t] *adj* refringent.

refroidir [32] [rəfrwadir] <> *vt* **1.** TECHNOL to cool **2.** *fig* [personne] to cool (down) ▪ [sentiment] to dampen, to put a damper on **3.** △ [assassiner] to bump off.

◇ *vi* **1.** [devenir froid] to cool (down), to get cold *ou* colder ■ **faites ~ pendant deux heures dans le réfrigérateur** cool *ou* leave to cool in the refrigerator for two hours **2.** ***fam fig*** **laisser ~ qqch** to leave *ou* to keep *ou* to put sthg on ice.

◆ **se refroidir** *vpi* [devenir froid] to get cold *ou* colder, to cool down ■ **le temps va se ~** [légèrement] it'll get cooler ; [sensiblement] it'll get cold *ou* colder.

refroidissement [rəfrwadismɑ̃] *nm* **1.** TECHNOL cooling ■ **à ~ par ventilation** air-cooled **2.** [rhume] chill ■ **elle a pris un ~** she caught a chill **3.** ***fig*** [dans une relation] cooling (off).

refroidisseur [rəfrwadisœr] *nm* TECHNOL cooler.

refuge [rəfyʒ] *nm* **1.** [abri] refuge ■ **servir de ~ à qqn** to offer refuge to sb, to provide a roof for sb ■ **chercher/trouver ~ dans une grange** to seek/to find shelter in a barn ■ **donner ~ à** to give shelter to, to shelter ❙ [en montagne] (mountain) refuge **2.** ***sout*** [réconfort] haven ■ **chercher ~ dans les livres** to seek refuge in books **3.** [dans une rue] refuge, (traffic) island **4.** *(comme adj)* ▭> **valeur**.

réfugié, e [refyʒje] *nm, f* refugee.

réfugier [9] [refyʒje] ◆ **se réfugier** *vpi* **1.** [s'abriter] to take refuge *ou* shelter ■ **ils se sont réfugiés dans une grotte** they took refuge in a cave ■ **ils se sont réfugiés sous un arbre** they sheltered under a tree **2.** ***fig*** **elle se réfugie dans ses livres** she takes refuge in her books.

refus [rəfy] *nm* **1.** [réponse négative] refusal, rebuff ■ **s'exposer à un ~** to run the risk of a refusal *ou* of being turned down ■ **opposer un ~ catégorique à qqn** to give an outright refusal to sb ■ **~ de vente/de priorité/d'obéissance** refusal to sell/to give way/to comply ➊ **ce n'est pas de ~!** ***fam*** I wouldn't say no!, I don't mind if I do! **2.** ÉQUIT refusal.

Voir module d'usage

refusable [rəfyzabl] *adj* [gén] refusable ■ [offre] which can be rejected.

refusé, e [rəfyze] *nm, f* ÉDUC failed candidate.

refuser [3] [rəfyze] *vt* **1.** [don, livraison] to refuse to accept, to reject ■ **il a refusé tous les cadeaux** he's refused to accept any present, he's turned down every gift ❙ [offre, proposition] to turn down, to refuse ■ **~ une invitation** to turn down *ou* to decline an invitation ■ **le restaurant refuse du monde tous les soirs** the restaurant turns people away every evening **2.** [autorisation] to refuse, to turn down ■ [service] to refuse, to deny ■ **il refuse de sortir de sa chambre** he refuses to leave his room ■ **il ne peut rien lui ~** he can refuse him nothing ■ **on leur a refusé l'entrée du château** they weren't allowed in the castle **3.** ÉQUIT to refuse **4.** [maladie, responsabilité] to refuse, to reject ■ **je refusais tout à fait cette idée** I wouldn't accept that idea at all ■ **~ le combat** to refuse battle *ou* to fight ■ **~ les responsabilités** to shun responsibilities, to refuse to take on responsibilities.

◆ **se refuser** ◇ *vp (emploi passif, à la forme négative)* **une telle offre ne se refuse pas** such an offer is not to be refused *ou* can't be turned down ■ **un séjour au bord de la mer, ça ne se refuse pas** a stay at the seaside, you can't say no to that.

◇ *vpt* to deny o.s. ■ **des vacances au Brésil, on ne se refuse rien!** ***fam hum*** a holiday in Brazil, no less!

◆ **se refuser à** *vp+prép* : **je me refuse à croire de pareilles sornettes!** I refuse to believe such twaddle! ■ **l'avocat se refuse à tout commentaire** the lawyer is refusing to make any comment *ou* is declining to comment.

réfutable [refytabl] *adj* refutable ■ **arguments qui ne sont pas ~s** arguments which cannot be refuted.

réfutation [refytasjɔ̃] *nf* refutation.

réfuter [3] [refyte] *vt* **1.** [en prouvant] to refute, to disprove **2.** [contredire] to contradict.

reg [rɛg] *nm* GÉOGR reg.

regagner [3] [rəgaɲe] *vt* **1.** [gagner - à nouveau] to win back *(sép)*, to regain ; [- après perte] to win back ■ **le dollar regagne quelques centimes sur le marché des changes** the dollar has regained a few cents on the foreign exchange market ■ **~ du terrain** to recover lost ground **2.** [retourner à] to go back *ou* to return to ■ **il a regagné la côte à la nage** he swam (back) to the shore ■ **~ sa place** to get back to one's seat *ou* place.

regain [rəgɛ̃] *nm* **1.** [retour, accroissement] renewal, revival ■ **un ~ de vie** a new lease of life ■ **avec un ~ de bonne humeur** with renewed cheerfulness ■ **un ~ d'énergie** fresh energy **2.** AGRIC aftermath.

régal, als [regal] *nm* **1.** [délice] delight, treat ■ **ce repas est un vrai ~** this meal is a real treat **2.** [plaisir] delight ■ **la mousse au chocolat est son ~** chocolate mousse is his favourite ■ **c'est un ~ pour les yeux** it's a sight for sore eyes.

régalade [regalad] *nf* : **boire à la ~** *to drink without letting the bottle touch one's lips.*

régale [regal] *adj f* CHIM : **eau ~** aqua regia.

régaler [3] [regale] *vt* **1.** [offrir à manger, à boire] to treat ■ **aujourd'hui, c'est moi qui régale** ***fam*** today it's on me *ou* I'm treating you *ou* it's my treat **2.** ***fig*** to regale ■ **elle régalait ses collègues d'anecdotes croustillantes** she regaled her colleagues with *ou* treated her colleagues to spicy anecdotes **3.** [terrain] to level **4.** FIN to apportion (a tax).

◆ **se régaler** *vpi* **1.** [en mangeant] : **je me suis régalé** it was a real treat, I really enjoyed it **2.** ***fig*** **je me régale à l'écouter** it's a real treat for me to listen to her.

régalien, enne [regaljɛ̃, ɛn] *adj* kingly, royal ■ **droit ~** royal prerogative.

regard [rəgar] *nm* **1.** [expression] look, expression ■ **son ~ était haineux** he had a look of hatred in his eye *ou* eyes, his eyes were full of hatred ■ **un ~ concupiscent** a leer ■ **un ~ méfiant** a suspicious look **2.** [coup d'œil] look, glance, gaze ■ **mon ~ s'arrêta sur une fleur** my eyes fell on a flower ■ **attirer les ~s** to be the centre of attention ■ **nos ~s se croisèrent** our eyes met ■ **il a détourné le ~** he averted his gaze, he looked away ■ **ils échangèrent un ~ de connivence** they exchanged knowing looks ■ **chercher du ~** to look (around) for ■ **interroger qqn du ~** to give sb a questioning look ■ **il est parti sans même un ~** he left without even a backward glance ■ **lancer un ~ à qqn** to look at sb, to glance at sb ■ **il lançait aux visiteurs des ~s mauvais** he glared at the visitors *ou* gave the visitors nasty looks ■ **caché aux ~s du public** out of the public eye ■ **loin des ~s curieux** far from prying eyes ■ **porter un ~ nouveau sur qqn/qqch**

LE REFUS

I'm afraid I can't possibly do that. Je regrette, mais je ne peux vraiment pas.

I'm sorry, but it's not up to me. Désolé, ça ne dépend pas de moi.

I'd like to help you, but there's really nothing I can do. J'aimerais vous aider, mais je ne peux vraiment rien faire.

It's out of the question. Il n'en est pas question.

No, I (most certainly) will not! Non (certainement pas) !

I won't do it! Je refuse de le faire !

Certainly not! Certainement pas !

You must be joking! Tu veux rire !

No way! Pas question !

Forget it! Alors là, tu peux toujours courir !

fig to look at sb/sthg in a new light ■ **couver qqch/qqn du ~** to stare at sthg/sb with greedy eyes ◆ **suivez mon ~** *hum* mentioning no names **3.** [d'égout] manhole ■ [de four] peephole.

◆ **au regard de** *loc prép* **1.** [aux termes de] in the eyes of ■ **mes papiers sont en règle au ~ de la loi** my papers are in order from a legal point of view **2.** [en comparaison avec] in comparison with, compared to.

◆ **en regard** *loc adv* : **un texte latin avec la traduction en ~** a Latin text with a translation on the opposite page.

◆ **en regard de** *loc prép* **1.** [face à] : **en ~ de la colonne des chiffres** facing *ou* opposite the column of figures **2.** [en comparaison avec] compared with.

regardant, e [rəgardɑ̃, ɑ̃t] *adj* **1.** [avare] careful with money *euphém*, sparing, grudging **2.** [pointilleux] demanding ■ **elle n'est pas très ~e sur la propreté** she's not very particular when it comes to cleanliness.

regarder [3] [rəgarde] ◇ *vt* **1.** [voir] to look at *(insép)*, to see ■ [observer] to watch, to see ■ **regarde s'il arrive** see if he's coming ■ **si tu veux t'instruire, regarde-le faire** if you want to learn something, watch how he does it ■ **as-tu regardé le match?** did you watch *ou* see the match? ■ **regarde voir dans la chambre** *fam* go and look *ou* have a look in the bedroom ■ **regarde-moi ça!** *fam* just look at that! ■ **regarde-moi ce travail!** *fam* just look at this mess! ◆ **tu ne m'as pas regardé!** *fam* what do you take me for?, who do you think I am?
2. [examiner - moteur, blessure] to look at *(insép)*, to check ; [- notes, travail] to look over *ou* through *(sép)* ; [- causes] to examine, to consider, to look into *(insép)* ■ **as-tu eu le temps de ~ le dossier?** did you have time to look at *ou* to examine the file?
3. [vérifier] to look up *(sép)* ■ **tu regardes constamment la pendule!** you're always looking at *ou* watching the clock! ■ **je vais ~ quelle heure il est** *ou* **l'heure** I'm going to see *ou* to check what time it is ■ *(en usage absolu)* **regarde à la lettre D** look through the D's, look at the letter D
4. [concerner] to concern ■ **ceci ne regarde que toi et moi** this is (just) between you and me ■ **ça ne te regarde pas!** that's *ou* it's none of your business! ■ **cette affaire ne me regarde plus** this affair is no longer any concern *ou* business of mine ■ **cela ne les regarde en rien** it's absolutely no business of theirs ■ **en quoi est-ce que ça me regarde?** what's that got to do with me?
5. [considérer - sujet, situation] to look at *(insép)*, to view ■ **il regarde avec envie la réussite de son frère** he casts an envious eye upon his brother's success, he looks upon his brother's success with envy ■ **ne ~ que** [ne penser qu'à] to be concerned only with, to think only about ■ **~ qqn comme** to consider sb as, to regard sb as, to look upon sb as ■ **~ qqch comme** to regard sthg as, to look upon sthg as, to think of sthg as.

◇ *vi* **1.** [personne] to look ■ **nous avons regardé partout** we looked *ou* searched everywhere ■ **tu ne sais pas ~** you should learn to use your eyes ■ **ne reste pas là à ~, fais quelque chose!** don't just stand there (staring), do something!
2. [bâtiment, pièce] : **~ à l'ouest** to face West.

◆ **regarder à** *v+prép* [morale, principes] to think of *ou* about, to take into account ■ [apparence, détail] to pay attention to ■ **je regarde avant tout à la qualité** I'm particularly *ou* primarily concerned with quality ■ **regarde à ne pas faire d'erreur** watch you don't make a mistake ■ **~ à la dépense** to be careful with one's money ◆ **y ~ à deux** *ou* **à plusieurs fois avant de faire qqch** to think twice before doing sthg ■ **à y bien ~, à y ~ de plus près** when you think it over, on thinking it over ■ **il ne faut pas y ~ de trop près** *pr* don't look too closely ; *fig* don't be too fussy.

◆ **se regarder** ◇ *vp (emploi réfléchi)* *pr* & *fig* to look at oneself ◆ **tu ne t'es pas regardé!** *fam* you should take a (good) look at yourself!

◇ *vp (emploi réciproque)* [personnes] to look at each other *ou* at one another ■ [bâtiments] to be opposite one another, to face each other.

◇ *vp (emploi passif)* [spectacle] : **cette émission se regarde en famille** this is a family show, this show is family viewing ■ **ça se regarde volontiers** it's quite pleasant to watch.

regarnir [32] [rəgarnir] *vt* [rayons] to refill, to restock, to stock up *(sép)* again ■ [maison] to refurnish.

régate [regat] *nf* NAUT regatta ■ **faire une ~** to sail in a regatta.

régater [3] [regate] *vi* to race *ou* to sail in a regatta ■ **~ avec qqn** to race sb in a regatta.

régence [reʒɑ̃s] *nf* regency.

◆ **Régence** ◇ *nf* : **la Régence** the Regency of Philippe II *(in France)*.

◇ *adj inv* (French) Regency ■ **un fauteuil Régence** a Regency armchair.

régénérateur, trice [reʒeneratœr, tris] *adj* regenerative.

◆ **régénérateur** *nm* regenerator.

régénérer [18] [reʒenere] *vt* **1.** BIOL & CHIM to regenerate ■ **caoutchouc régénéré** regenerated rubber (fibres) **2.** *litt* [rénover] to regenerate, to restore.

régent, e [reʒɑ̃, ɑ̃t] *nm, f* regent.

régenter [3] [reʒɑ̃te] *vt* to rule over *(insép)*, to run ■ **il veut ~ tout le monde** he wants everybody to be at his beck and call.

reggae [rege] *nm* reggae.

régicide [reʒisid] *adj, nmf* & *nm* regicide.

régie [reʒi] *nf* **1.** [d'une entreprise publique] : **(société) en ~** [par l'État] state-controlled (corporation) ; [par le département] local authority controlled (company) ; [par la commune] ≃ local district controlled (company) ■ **il travaille à la ~ municipale des eaux** he works for the local water board **2.** [pièce - dans un studio de télévision ou de radio] control room ; [- dans un théâtre] lighting box **3.** CINÉ, THÉÂTRE & TV [équipe] production team **4.** ÉCON : **travaux en ~** (net) timework **5.** FIN excise.

regimber [3] [rəʒɛ̃be] *vi* **1.** [cheval] to rear up, to jib **2.** [personne] to rebel, to grumble ■ **faire qqch sans ~** to do sthg without complaining.

régime [reʒim] *nm* **1.** POLIT [système] regime, (system of) government ■ **~ militaire/parlementaire/totalitaire** military/parliamentary/totalitarian regime ■ [gouvernement] regime
2. ADMIN & DR [système] system, scheme ■ [règlement] rules, regulations ■ **le ~ des visites à l'hôpital** hospital visiting hours and conditions ■ **~ de Sécurité sociale** *subdivision of the French social security system applying to certain professional groups* ◆ **être marié sous le ~ de la communauté** to opt for a marriage based on joint ownership of property ■ **~ complémentaire** additional retirement cover ■ **le ~ général de la Sécurité sociale** the social security system ■ **~ matrimonial** marriage settlement ■ **~ pénitentiaire** prison system ■ **~ de retraite** retirement scheme
3. ÉCON : **~ préférentiel** special arrangements
4. MÉD : **faire un ~** to go on a diet ■ **être au ~** to be on a diet, to be dieting ◆ **~ (alimentaire)** diet ■ **~ amaigrissant** slimming UK *ou* reducing US diet ■ **je suis au ~ sec** *fam hum* I'm on an alcohol-free diet ■ **~ sans sel** salt-free diet ■ **se mettre au ~ jockey** to go on a starvation diet
5. INDUST & MÉCAN engine speed ■ **fonctionner à plein ~** [usine] to work to full capacity ■ **travailler à plein ~** [personne] to work flat out ■ **à ce ~ vous ne tiendrez pas longtemps** at this rate you won't last long ◆ **~ de croisière** economic *ou* cruising speed ■ **~ de production** production rate
6. GÉOGR : **~ d'un fleuve** rate of flow, regimen of a river ■ **~ glaciaire/nivo-glaciaire/nivo-pluvial** glacial/snow and ice/snow and rain regime ■ **~ des pluies** rainfall pattern ■ **le ~ des vents** the prevailing winds *ou* wind system
7. LING : **~ direct/indirect** direct/indirect object
8. PHYS regimen, flow rate ■ **~ laminaire** laminary flow
9. BOT : **un ~ de bananes** a hand *ou* stem *ou* bunch of bananas ■ **un ~ de dattes** a bunch *ou* cluster of dates.

RÉGIME DE SÉCURITÉ SOCIALE

The French *Sécurité sociale* system is divided into the following types of *régimes*: 1. *Le régime général des salariés*, which provides social security cover for people in paid employment.
2. *Les régimes spéciaux*, which provide tailor-made cover for certain socioprofessional groups (civil servants, miners, students, etc).
3. *Les régimes particuliers*, designed for the self-employed.
4. *Les régimes complémentaires*, which provide additional retirement cover for wage-earners.

régiment [reʒimɑ̃] *nm* **1.** MIL [unité] regiment ▶ **~ d'infanterie** infantry regiment **2.** *fam vieilli* [service militaire] : **un de mes camarades de ~** a friend from my military service days **3.** *fam* [grande quantité] : **il a tout un ~ de cousins** he's got a whole army of cousins.

régimentaire [reʒimɑ̃tɛr] *adj* MIL regimental.

région [reʒjɔ̃] *nf* **1.** GÉOGR region ▪ **~ industrielle/agricole** industrial/agricultural region ▪ **les ~s tempérées/polaires** the temperate/polar regions ▪ **les habitants de Paris et sa ~** the inhabitants of Paris and the surrounding region *ou* area ▪ **le nouveau médecin n'est pas de la ~** the new doctor isn't from the area *ou* from around here ▶ **la ~ parisienne** the Paris area, the area around Paris **2.** ANAT : **~ cervicale/lombaire** cervical/lumbar region.

◆ **Région** *nf* ADMIN region *(French administrative area made up of several departments)*.

RÉGION

One of the three main administrative divisions in France, the *région* was created in 1982. There are twenty-six in all, four of which are overseas. Each *région* groups together several ***départements*** and is administered by a ***conseil régional***, headed by the ***président du conseil régional***.

régional, e, aux [reʒjɔnal, o] *adj* **1.** [de la région] regional ▪ [de la localité] local **2.** [sur le plan international] local, regional ▪ **un conflit ~** a regional conflict.

régionalisation [reʒjɔnalizasjɔ̃] *nf* regionalization.

régionaliser [3] [reʒjɔnalize] *vt* to regionalize.

régionalisme [reʒjɔnalism] *nm* regionalism.

régionaliste [reʒjɔnalist] *adj* & *nmf* regionalist.

régir [32] [reʒir] *vt* to govern.

régisseur, euse [reʒisœr, øz] *nm, f* **1.** [d'un domaine] steward **2.** CINÉ & TV assistant director ▪ THÉÂTRE stage manager ▪ **~ de plateau** floor manager **3.** ÉCON comptroller.

registraire [reʒistrɛr] *nmf Québec* ÉDUC registrar.

registre [rəʒistr] *nm* **1.** ADMIN & DR register ▶ **~ d'audience** DR record ▪ **s'inscrire au ~ du commerce** to register one's company ▪ **~ de l'état civil** ≃ register of births, marriages and deaths **2.** IMPR & INFORM register **3.** MUS [d'un orgue] stop ▪ [d'une voix] range, register ▪ **un ~ aigu/grave** a high/low pitch **4.** LING register, level of language **5.** TECHNOL damper.

réglable [reglabl] *adj* **1.** [adaptable] adjustable ▪ **le dossier est ~ en hauteur** the height of the seat is adjustable **2.** [payable] payable ▪ **~ par mensualités** payable in monthly instalments.

réglage [reglaʒ] *nm* **1.** [mise au point] adjustment, regulation ▪ **procéder au ~ des phares** to adjust the headlights ▪ **~ d'un thermostat** thermostat setting **2.** AUTO, RADIO & TV tuning ▪ **le ~ de l'appareil est automatique** PHOTO the camera is fully automatic **3.** MIL : **~ du tir** range finding *ou* adjustment **4.** [du papier] ruling.

règle [rɛgl] *nf* **1.** [instrument] ruler ▪ **~ à calcul** slide rule **2.** [principe, code] rule ▪ **les ~s de l'honneur** the rules *ou* code of honour ▪ **enfreindre la ~** to break the rule *ou* rules ▪ **il est de ~ de porter une cravate ici** it's usual to wear a tie here ▪ **les ~s de base en grammaire** the basic rules of grammar ▶ **la ~ du jeu** the rules of the game ▪ **respecter la ~ du jeu** to play by the rules ▪ **~ d'or** golden rule ▪ **~ de trois** rule of three ▪ **dans les ~s (de l'art)** according to the (rule) book.

◆ **règles** *nfpl* PHYSIOL [en général] periods ▪ [d'un cycle] period ▪ **avoir ses ~s** to be menstruating, to be having one's period ▪ **avoir des ~s douloureuses** to suffer from period *ou* pains *UK*, to suffer from menstrual cramps *US*, to have painful periods.

◆ **en règle** *loc adj* : **être en ~** [document] to be in order ; [personne] to have one's papers in order, to be in possession of valid papers ▪ **se mettre en ~** to sort out one's situation ▪ **recevoir un avertissement en ~** to be given an official warning.

◆ **en règle générale** *loc adv* generally, as a (general) rule.

réglé, e [regle] *adj* **1.** [organisé] regular, well-ordered ▪ **une vie bien ~e** a well-ordered existence **2.** [rayé ou quadrillé] : **papier ~** ruled *ou* lined paper.

◆ **réglée** *adj f* : **être ~e** [avoir ses règles] : **depuis combien de temps êtes-vous ~e?** how long have you been having your periods? ▪ **est-elle ~e?** has she started to menstruate (yet)?

règlement [rɛgləmɑ̃] *nm* **1.** ADMIN regulation, rules ▪ **observer le ~** to abide by the rules ▪ **d'après le ~, il est interdit de...** it's against the regulations to... ▶ **~ administratif** ≃ statutory policy ▪ **~ intérieur** house rules ▪ **~ de police municipale** *ou* **municipal** ≃ by-law ▪ **~ sanitaire** health regulations **2.** [paiement] payment, settlement ▪ **~ par carte de crédit** payment by credit card **3.** [résolution] settlement, settling ▪ **~ de compte** *ou* **comptes** settling of scores ▪ **il y a eu des ~s de comptes** some old scores were settled ▪ **~ judiciaire** DR compulsory liquidation, winding-up *UK*.

réglementaire [rɛgləmɑ̃tɛr] *adj* **1.** [conforme] regulation *(modif)* ▪ **modèle de chaudière ~** approved *ou* standard type of boiler ▪ **il a passé l'âge ~** he's above the statutory age limit **2.** ADMIN [décision] statutory.

réglementairement [rɛgləmɑ̃tɛrmɑ̃] *adv* according to regulations, statutorily.

réglementation [rɛgləmɑ̃tasjɔ̃] *nf* **1.** [mesures] regulations **2.** [limitation] control, regulation ▪ **la ~ des prix** price controls.

réglementer [3] [rɛgləmɑ̃te] *vt* to regulate, to control ▪ **la vente des boissons alcoolisées est très réglementée** the sale of alcoholic drinks is under strict control *ou* is strictly controlled.

régler [18] [regle] *vt* **1.** [résoudre - litige] to settle, to resolve ; [- problème] to solve, to iron out *(sép)*, to sort out *(sép)* ▪ **alors c'est réglé, nous irons au bord de la mer** it's settled then, we'll go to the seaside ▪ **c'est une affaire réglée** it is (all) settled now **2.** [payer - achat] to pay (for) ; [- facture, mensualité] to settle ; [- créancier] to settle up *(insép)* with ▪ **mon salaire ne m'a pas été réglé** my salary hasn't been paid (in) ▪ **~ l'addition** to pay *ou* settle the bill ▪ **~ qqch en espèces** to pay cash for sthg ▪ **~ qqch par chèque/par carte de crédit** to pay for sthg by cheque/by credit card ▶ **~ ses comptes (avec qqn)** *pr* to settle up *(insép)* (with sb) ; *fig* to settle (one's) scores (with sb) ▪ **j'ai un compte à ~ avec toi** I've got a bone to pick with you ▪ **~ son compte à qqn** *fam* [se venger de lui] to get even with sb ; [le tuer] to take care of sb *euphém*
3. [volume, allumage, phare *etc*] to adjust ▪ [vitesse, thermostat] to set ▪ [température] to regulate ▪ [circulation] to control ▪ [moteur] to tune ▪ **j'ai réglé mon réveil sur 7 h/le four à 200°** I've set my alarm for seven o'clock/the oven at 200 degrees ▪ **comment ~ la radio sur France-Musique?** how do you tune in to France-Musique? ▪ **~ qqch sur** [accorder par rapport à] to set sthg by ▪ **~ son rythme sur celui du soleil** to model one's rhythm of life on the movement of the sun
4. [déterminer] to decide (on), to settle ▪ **quelques détails à ~** a few details to be settled
5. [papier] to rule.

◆ **se régler** *vp (emploi passif)* [mécanisme] to be set *ou* regulated ▪ [luminosité, phare] to be adjusted ▪ [récepteur] to be tuned.

◆ **se régler sur** *vp+prép* [imiter] to model o.s. on, to follow (the example of) ▪ **elle a tendance à se ~ sur (l'exemple de) sa mère** she has a tendency to model herself on her mother.

réglette [reglɛt] *nf* **1.** [petite règle] short ruler, straight-edge **2.** IMPR lead, reglet **3.** [au Scrabble] rack.

régleur, euse [reglœr, øz] <> *adj* adjusting.
<> *nm, f* setter.

◆ **régleur** *nm* **1.** [dans l'industrie du froid] regulator *(of freezing mixture)* **2.** [dans les assurances] : **(inspecteur) ~** loss adjuster.

◆ **régleuse** *nf* INDUST ruling machine.

réglisse [reglis] *nf* liquorice ▪ **bâton de ~** stick of liquorice.

réglo△ [reglo] *adj inv* regular, OK, on the level ■ **un type ~** an OK *fam* *ou* a regular guy *fam* ■ **il trempe toujours dans des affaires pas très ~** he's always mixed up in some kind of shady business.

régnant, e [reɲɑ̃, ɑ̃t] *adj* **1.** [qui règne] reigning **2.** *sout* [qui prédomine] prevailing, reigning, dominant.

règne [rɛɲ] *nm* **1.** [gouvernement] reign ■ **sous le ~ de Catherine II** in the reign of Catherine II **2.** [domination - de la bêtise, de la justice] rule, reign **3.** BIOL : **~ animal/végétal** animal/plant kingdom.

régner [8] [reɲe] *vi* **1.** [gouverner] to reign, to rule **2.** [dominer - idée] to predominate, to prevail ; [- ordre, silence] to reign, to prevail ■ **le chaos règne** chaos reigns *ou* prevails ■ **~ sur** to rule over ■ **~ en maître (sur)** to rule supreme (over) ■ **faire ~ la paix** to keep the peace ■ **faire ~ le silence** to keep everybody quiet ■ **faire ~ l'ordre** to keep things under control ■ **la confiance règne!** *iron* there's trust *ou* confidence for you! ■ *(tournure impersonnelle)* **il règne enfin une paix profonde** a great peace reigns at last.

regonfler [3] [rəgɔ̃fle] <> *vt* **1.** [gonfler de nouveau - ballon, bouée] to blow up *(sép)*(again), to reinflate ; [- matelas pneumatique] to pump up *(sép)*(again), to reinflate ■ **son séjour à la mer l'a regonflée à bloc** *fam fig* her stay at the seaside has bucked her up (no end) **2.** [gonfler davantage - pneus] to put more air in *ou* into ■ **faites le plein et regonflez les pneus avant** fill her up and put some air in the front tyres.
<> *vi* [gén - MÉD] to swell (up) again.

regorger [17] [rəgɔrʒe] *vi litt* [liquide] to overflow.
◆ **regorger de** *v+prép* to overflow with *(insép)*, to abound in *(insép)* ■ **la terre regorge d'eau** the ground is waterlogged ■ **les vitrines regorgent de marchandises** the shop windows are packed with goods.

regreffer [4] [rəgrefe] *vt* to regraft.

régresser [4] [regrese] *vi* **1.** [baisser - chiffre, population] to drop ■ **le chiffre d'affaires a régressé** there has been a drop in turnover ■ [civilisation] to regress **2.** [s'atténuer] : **la maladie a régressé** the patient's condition has improved **3.** PSYCHOL to regress.

régressif, ive [regresif, iv] *adj* regressive ■ **impôt ~** degressive tax.

régression [regresjɔ̃] *nf* **1.** [recul] decline, decrease, regression **2.** PSYCHOL & SC regression.

regret [rəgrɛ] *nm* **1.** [remords] regret ■ **sans un ~** without a single regret ■ **'~s éternels'** 'deeply regretted', 'greatly lamented' **2.** [tristesse] regret ■ **je vous quitte avec beaucoup de ~** I leave you with great regret, I'm sorry I have to leave you ■ **nous sommes au** *ou* **nous avons le ~ de vous annoncer que...** we are sorry *ou* we regret to have to inform you that...
◆ **à regret** *loc adv* [partir, sévir] regretfully, with regret ■ **il s'éloigna comme à ~** he walked away with apparent reluctance.
Voir module d'usage

regrettable [rəgrɛtabl] *adj* regrettable, unfortunate ■ **il est ~ que tu n'aies pas été informée à temps** it is unfortunate *ou* a pity (that) you were not informed in time.

regretter [4] [rəgrete] *vt* **1.** [éprouver de la nostalgie pour - personne, pays] to miss ; [- jeunesse, passé] to be nostalgic for ■ **son regretté mari** her late lamented husband **2.** [se repentir de] to be sorry about, to regret ■ **tu n'as rien à ~** you've got nothing to feel sorry about *ou* to regret ■ **je ne regrette pas le temps passé là-dessus/l'argent que ça m'a coûté** I'm not sorry I spent time/money on it ■ **je ne regrette rien** I've no regrets ■ **vous regretterez vos paroles!** you'll be sorry that you said that!, you'll regret those words!
◆ **regretter de** *v+prép* **1.** [se reprocher de] : **tu ne regretteras pas de m'avoir écoutée** you won't be sorry you listened to me **2.** [dans des expressions de politesse] : **nous regrettons de ne pouvoir donner suite à votre appel** we regret *ou* we are sorry we are unable to connect you ■ *(en usage absolu)* **pouvez-vous venir? – non, je regrette!** will you be able to come? – no, I'm afraid not *ou* – sorry, no! ■ **ah non! je regrette! j'étais là avant toi!** I'm sorry but I was here first!

regrossir [32] [rəgrosir] *vi* to put on weight again.

regroupement [rəgrupmɑ̃] *nm* : **~ de troupes** gathering *ou* grouping together of troops ■ **le ~ des différentes tendances politiques** the rallying (together) of various shades of political opinion.

regrouper [3] [rəgrupe] *vt* **1.** [rassembler] to bring together *(sép)*, to group *ou* to gather together *(sép)* **2.** [contenir] to contain ■ **le centre culturel regroupe sous un même toit un cinéma et un théâtre** the arts centre accommodates *ou* has a cinema and a theatre (under the same roof).
◆ **se regrouper** *vpi* **1.** [institutions] to group together ■ [foule] to gather ■ **les sociétés se sont regroupées pour mieux faire face à la concurrence** the companies have joined forces to deal more effectively with the competition **2.** MIL to regroup.

régularisation [regylarizasjɔ̃] *nf* **1.** [d'une situation] straightening out, regularization **2.** FIN : **paiement de dix mensualités avec ~ annuelle** ten monthly payments with end-of-year adjustments **3.** GÉOGR grading.

régulariser [3] [regylarize] *vt* **1.** [rendre légal] to regularize ■ **il a fait ~ son permis de séjour** he got his residence permit sorted out *ou* put in order **2.** [rendre régulier] to regulate.

régularité [regylarite] *nf* **1.** [dans le temps] regularity, steadiness ■ **un emploi du temps d'une parfaite ~** a schedule that is (as) regular as clockwork ■ **les factures tombent avec ~** there's a steady flow of bills to pay **2.** [dans l'espace - de la dentition] evenness ; [- d'une surface] smoothness ; [- de plantations] straightness **3.** [en valeur, en intensité] consistency ■ **élève d'une grande ~** very consistent pupil ■ **travailler avec ~** to work steadily *ou* consistently **4.** [légalité] lawfulness, legality.

régulateur, trice [regylatœr, tris] *adj* regulating, control *(modif)*.
◆ **régulateur** *nm* **1.** [dispositif, horloge] regulator **2.** BIOL [gène] regulator *ou* regulatory gene **3.** ÉLECTRON controller.

régulation [regylasjɔ̃] *nf* **1.** [contrôle] control, regulation ■ [réglage] regulation, correction ■ **~ de la circulation** traffic control **2.** BIOL regulation ■ **~ thermique** (body) temperature control **3.** ÉLECTRON regulation **4.** RAIL control.

réguler [3] [regyle] *vt* to control.

EXPRIMER DES REGRETS

Unfortunately, we didn't get there on time. Malheureusement, nous ne sommes pas arrivés à temps.

If there's one thing I regret, it's not learning to drive. S'il y a une chose que je regrette, c'est de ne pas avoir passé mon permis.

I'm sorry I ever mentioned it now! J'aurais mieux fait de ne pas en parler !

I (only) wish I'd told him earlier. Je regrette de ne pas le lui avoir dit plus tôt.

If only I hadn't left them alone together. Si seulement je ne les avais pas laissés seuls tous les deux.

What a pity you didn't say something before! Quel dommage que tu n'aies rien dit !

It's a real shame I won't get to meet her. Dire que je n'aurai pas l'occasion de la rencontrer.

régulier, ère [regylje, ɛr] *adj* **1.** [fixe] regular ■ **des revenus ~s** a regular *ou* steady income ■ **manger à heures régulières** to eat regularly *ou* at regular intervals ‖ [permanent] regular ■ **les vols ~s** scheduled flights ➲ **armée régulière** regular *ou* standing army **2.** [dans l'espace - gén] regular, even ; [- plantations] evenly distributed ■ **une écriture régulière** regular *ou* neat handwriting **3.** [montée, déclin] steady ■ [distribution] even **4.** [harmonieux - traits] regular **5.** [conforme à la règle - transaction] legitimate ; [- procédure] correct, fair ■ [conforme à la loi] legal ■ **c'est un procédé pas très ~** that's not quite above board ■ **être en situation régulière** to be in line with the law **6.** *fam* [honnête] on the level, straight **7.** BOT, GÉOM, LING & ZOOL regular.
◆ **régulier** *nm* MIL & RELIG regular.
◆ **régulière** *nf fam hum* **ma régulière** [épouse] my missus, my old lady ; [maîtresse] my girlfriend.

régulièrement [regyljɛrmɑ̃] *adv* **1.** [dans l'espace - disposer] evenly, regularly, uniformly **2.** [dans le temps - progresser] steadily ■ **~ révisé** updated regularly *ou* at regular intervals ■ **donne de tes nouvelles ~** write often *ou* regularly *ou* on a regular basis ■ **elle avait ~ de bonnes notes** she got consistently good marks ■ **je la vois assez ~** I see her quite regularly *ou* quite frequently **3.** [selon la règle] lawfully ■ **assemblée élue ~** lawfully *ou* properly elected assembly.

régurgitation [regyrʒitasjɔ̃] *nf* regurgitation.

régurgiter [3] [regyrʒite] *vt* to regurgitate.

réhabilitation [reabilitasjɔ̃] *nf* **1.** DR rehabilitation ■ **~ judiciaire** judicial discharge **2.** [d'une personne] rehabilitation, clearing the name of **3.** [d'un quartier] rehabilitation.

réhabiliter [3] [reabilite] *vt* **1.** DR [condamné] to rehabilitate ■ [failli] to discharge ■ **~ la mémoire de qqn** to clear sb's name ■ **~ qqn dans ses fonctions** to reinstate sb **2.** [revaloriser - profession] to rehabilitate, to restore to favour ; [- quartier] to rehabilitate.

réhabituer [7] [reabitɥe] *vt* : **~ qqn à qqch** to get sb used to sthg again.
◆ **se réhabituer à** *vp+prép* to get used to again ■ **se ~ à faire qqch** to get back into the habit of doing sthg.

rehaussement [rəosmɑ̃] *nm* **1.** CONSTR [d'un mur] raising, building up *ou* higher ■ [d'un plafond] raising **2.** FIN upward adjustment, increment.

rehausser [3] [rəose] *vt* **1.** [surélever - plafond] to raise ; [- mur] to make higher **2.** [faire ressortir - goût] to bring out ; [- beauté, couleur] to emphasize, to enhance ■ **du velours noir rehaussé de broderies** black velvet set off by embroidery **3.** [revaloriser] to enhance, to increase.

réhydratation [reidratasjɔ̃] *nf* moisturizing, rehydration *spéc* ■ **pour une meilleure ~ de votre peau** to ensure that your skin retains its moisture.

réhydrater [3] [reidrate] *vt* [peau] to moisturize, to rehydrate *spéc*.

réification [reifikasjɔ̃] *nf* reification.

réimplantation [reɛ̃plɑ̃tasjɔ̃] *nf* **1.** MÉD reimplantation **2.** [d'une entreprise] reestablishment ■ [d'une tribu] resettling.

réimplanter [3] [reɛ̃plɑ̃te] *vt* **1.** MÉD to reimplant **2.** [industrie, usine] to set up *(sép)* again, to reestablish ■ [tribu] to resettle.

réimporter [3] [reɛ̃pɔrte] *vt* to reimport.

réimpression [reɛ̃prɛsjɔ̃] *nf* [processus] reprinting ■ [résultat] reprint ■ **ce livre est en cours de ~** this book is being reprinted.

Reims [rɛ̃s] *npr* Reims, Rheims.

rein [rɛ̃] *nm* **1.** ANAT kidney ■ **~ artificiel** artificial kidney, kidney machine ■ **coup de ~** heave ■ **il donna un violent coup de ~ pour soulever l'armoire** he heaved the wardrobe up **2.** CONSTR springer.
◆ **reins** *nmpl* [dos] back, loin *sout* ■ *litt* [taille] waist ■ **avoir mal aux ~s** to have (a) backache ■ **avoir mal dans le bas des** *ou* **au creux des ~s** to have a pain in the small of one's back ➲ **avoir les ~s solides** to have good financial backing ■ **je lui briserai** *ou* **casserai les ~s** I'll break him.

réincarcération [reɛ̃karserasjɔ̃] *nf* reimprisonment ■ **après sa ~** after he was sent back to jail.

réincarnation [reɛ̃karnasjɔ̃] *nf* RELIG reincarnation.

réincarner [3] [reɛ̃karne] ◆ **se réincarner** *vpi* to be reincarnated ■ **il voulait se ~ en oiseau** he wanted to be reincarnated as a bird.

reine [rɛn] *nf* **1.** [femme du roi] queen (consort) ■ [souveraine] queen ■ **la ~ de Suède/des Pays-Bas** the Queen of Sweden/of the Netherlands ■ **la ~ de Saba** the Queen of Sheba ➲ **la ~ mère** the Queen Mother **2.** JEUX queen ■ **la ~ de cœur/pique** the queen of hearts/spades **3.** *fig* queen ■ **la ~ de la soirée** the belle of the ball, the star of the party ■ **tu es vraiment la ~ des imbéciles** you're the most stupid woman I've ever come across ➲ **~ de beauté** beauty queen ■ **la petite ~** *vieilli* the bicycle **4.** ZOOL queen ■ **la ~ des abeilles/termites** the queen bee/termite **5.** HORT : **~ des reinettes** rennet.

reine-claude [rɛnklod] (*pl* **reines-claudes**) *nf* (Reine Claude) greengage.

reine-marguerite [rɛnmargərit] (*pl* **reines-marguerites**) *nf* (China *ou* annual) aster.

reinette [rɛnɛt] *nf* ≃ pippin ■ **~ grise** russet *(apple)*.

réinfecter [4] [reɛ̃fɛkte] *vt* to reinfect.
◆ **se réinfecter** *vpi* to become reinfected.

réinscriptible [reɛ̃skriptibl] *adj* INFORM (re-)recordable ■ [cédérom] rewritable.

réinscription [reɛ̃skripsjɔ̃] *nf* reregistration.

réinscrire [99] [reɛ̃skrir] *vt* [étudiant] to reregister, to reenrol ■ [électeur] to reregister ■ [sur un agenda] to put down *(sép)* again.
◆ **se réinscrire** *vp (emploi réfléchi)* to reregister, to reenrol ■ **je me suis réinscrit pour la poterie** I put my name down for *ou* I joined the pottery class again.

réinsérer [18] [reɛ̃sere] *vt* **1.** [paragraphe] to reinsert **2.** [détenu, drogué] to rehabilitate, to reintegrate.
◆ **se réinsérer** *vp (emploi réfléchi)* to rehabilitate o.s., to become rehabilitated.

réinsertion [reɛ̃sɛrsjɔ̃] *nf* **1.** [d'un paragraphe] reinsertion **2.** [d'un détenu] rehabilitation ■ **la ~ sociale** social rehabilitation, reintegration into society.

réinstaller [3] [reɛ̃stale] *vt* [chauffage, électricité, téléphone] to reinstall, to put back *(sép)* ■ **j'ai réinstallé mon bureau au premier étage** I've moved my office back to the first floor ‖ INFORM ro reinstall.
◆ **se réinstaller** *vpi* **1.** [retourner] to go back, to settle again ■ **il s'est réinstallé dans son ancien bureau** he's gone *ou* moved back to his old office **2.** [se rasseoir] to settle (back) down in one's seat.

réintégration [reɛ̃tegrasjɔ̃] *nf* **1.** [d'un fonctionnaire] reinstatement **2.** [d'un évadé] reimprisonment **3.** [recouvrement d'un droit] reintegration.

réintégrer [18] [reɛ̃tegre] *vt* **1.** [employer à nouveau] to reinstate ■ **il a été réintégré dans l'Administration** he was reinstated in the Civil Service **2.** [regagner] to go back *ou* to return to ■ **~ le domicile conjugal** to return to the marital home.

réintroduire [98] [reɛ̃trɔdɥir] *vt* [dans un texte] : **~ qqch** to reintroduce sthg, to put sthg back in ‖ [projet de loi] to put up *(sép)* again, to reintroduce.

réinventer [3] [reɛ̃vɑ̃te] *vt* to reinvent ■ **il a su ~ la mise en scène** he has a totally new approach to production.

réinviter [3] [reɛ̃vite] *vt* to reinvite ■ **il faudra les ~** we'll have to ask *ou* invite them (round) again.

réitérer [18] [reitere] *vt sout* [interdiction, demande] to reiterate, to repeat.

rejaillir [32] [rəʒajir] *vi* **1.** [gicler - gén] to splash (back) ; [- violemment] to spurt (up) **2.** *sout* [se répercuter] : **~ sur** to reflect on *ou* upon ■ **sa notoriété a rejailli sur nous tous** his fame reflected on *ou* was shared by all of us ■ **la honte rejaillit sur lui** he was covered in shame.

rejet [rəʒɛ] *nm* **1.** [physique] throwing back *ou* up, driving back ■ **interdire le ~ de substances polluantes** to prohibit the discharge of pollutants **2.** [refus] rejection ■ **elle a été très déçue par le ~ de son manuscrit/de son offre** she was very disappointed when her manuscript/her offer was turned down ■ **il y a eu ~ de toutes les accusations par le juge** the judge dismissed all charges ▶ **les enfants handicapés sont parfois victimes d'un phénomène de ~ à l'école** handicapped children are sometimes rejected by other children at school **3.** LITTÉR [enjambement] run-on ■ **il y a ~ du verbe à la fin de la proposition subordonnée** GRAMM the verb is put *ou* goes at the end of the subordinate clause **4.** MÉD rejection ■ **~ d'une greffe** rejection of a transplant **5.** GÉOL throw **6.** BOT shoot **7.** INFORM ignore (character) **8.** ZOOL cast (swarm).

rejeter [27] [rəʒte] ◇ *vt* **1.** [relancer] to throw back *(sép)* ■ [violemment] to hurl back *(sép)* ■ *fig* **elle rejeta ses cheveux en arrière** she tossed her hair back ■ **~ la tête en arrière** to throw one's head back ■ **~ les épaules en arrière** to put one's shoulders back ■ **~ un verbe en fin de phrase** to put a verb at the end of a sentence **2.** [repousser - ennemi] to drive *ou* to push back *(sép)* ■ **~ une armée au-delà des frontières** to drive an army back over the border ■ [bannir] to reject, to cast out *(sép)*, to expel ■ **la société les rejette** society rejects them *ou* casts them out **3.** [rendre - nourriture] to spew out *(sép)*, to throw up *(sép)*, to reject ; [- déchets] to throw out *(sép)*, to expel ■ **son estomac rejette tout ce qu'elle absorbe** she can't keep anything down ■ **la mer a rejeté plusieurs épaves** several wrecks were washed up *ou* cast up by the sea **4.** [refuser] to reject, to turn down *(sép)* ■ **~ un projet de loi** to throw out a bill **5.** [déplacer] : **~ la faute/la responsabilité sur qqn** to shift the blame/responsibility on to sb **6.** INFORM to reject.

◇ *vi* BOT to shoot.

◆ **se rejeter** ◇ *vpi* : **se ~ en arrière** to jump backwards.

◇ *vpt* [se renvoyer] : **ils se rejettent mutuellement la responsabilité de l'accident** they blame each other for the accident.

rejeton [rəʒtɔ̃] *nm* **1.** *péj & hum* [enfant] kid ■ **que fais-tu de tes ~s cet été?** what will you do with your offspring *ou* kids this summer? **2.** BOT offshoot, shoot.

rejette *etc v* ▷ **rejeter**.

rejoindre [82] [rəʒwɛ̃dr] *vt* **1.** [retrouver] to meet (up with) *(insép)*, to join ■ [avec effort] to catch up with ■ **il est parti ~ sa femme** he went to meet up with *ou* join *ou* rejoin his wife ■ **il a rejoint le gros du peloton** he's caught up with the pack **2.** [retourner à] to get back *ou* to return to ■ **il a reçu l'ordre de ~ son régiment** he was ordered to rejoin his regiment **3.** [aboutir à] to join *ou* to meet (up with) ■ **le chemin rejoint la route à la hauteur de la borne** the path meets *ou* joins (up with) the road at the milestone **4.** [être d'accord avec] to agree with ■ **mon point de vue rejoint entièrement le vôtre** my point of view is much the same as *ou* very similar to yours ■ **je ne peux vous ~ sur ce point** I cannot agree *ou* see eye to eye with you (on this matter) ‖ POLIT [adhérer à] to join ■ **elle a fini par ~ l'opposition** she ended up joining the opposition.

◆ **se rejoindre** *vp (emploi réciproque)* **1.** [se réunir] to meet again *ou* up ■ **nous nous rejoindrons à Marseille** we'll meet up in Marseilles **2.** [concorder] : **nos opinions se rejoignent entièrement** our views concur perfectly, we are in total agreement.

rejouer [6] [rəʒwe] ◇ *vt* **1.** [refaire - jeu] to play again ; [- match] to replay, to play again ■ **~ le même cheval** to bet on the same horse again ■ **elle a rejoué toute sa fortune sur le 7** she gambled her whole fortune on the 7 again ■ **tu devrais ~ atout** you should lead trumps again **2.** [pièce de théâtre] to perform again ■ [morceau] to play again.

◇ *vi* JEUX to start gambling again ■ SPORT to play again.

réjoui, e [reʒwi] *adj* joyful, happy, pleased ■ **avoir** *ou* **prendre un air ~** to look cheerful.

réjouir [32] [reʒwir] *vt* to delight ■ **la nouvelle a réjoui tout le monde** everyone was delighted at the news ■ **ça ne me réjouit guère d'y aller** I'm not particularly keen on *ou* thrilled at going.

◆ **se réjouir** *vpi* to be delighted ■ **se ~ du malheur des autres** to gloat over other people's misfortunes ■ **je me réjouis de votre succès** I'm glad to hear of your success ■ **je me réjouis à la pensée de les retrouver** I'm thrilled at the idea of meeting them again.

réjouissance [reʒwisɑ̃s] *nf* [gaieté] rejoicing ■ **les occasions de ~ manquent** opportunities for rejoicing are scarce.

◆ **réjouissances** *nfpl* [fête] festivities ■ **quel est le programme des ~s?** *hum* what exciting things lie in store for us today?

réjouissant, e [reʒwisɑ̃, ɑ̃t] *adj* joyful, cheerful ■ **peu ~** rather grim ■ **c'est ~!** *iron* that's just great! ■ **je ne vois pas ce que tu trouves de si ~ à cette histoire** I don't see what you find so funny *ou* amusing about this story.

relâche [rəlaʃ] *nf* **1.** *sout* [pause] respite, rest **2.** CINÉ & THÉÂTRE [fermeture] : **nous ferons ~ en août** no performances in August ■ **'~ le mardi'** 'no performance on Tuesdays' **3.** NAUT : **le navire a fait ~ à Nice** the boat called in at Nice ▶ **(port de) ~** port of call.

◆ **sans relâche** *loc adv* without respite ■ **il écrit sans ~ jusqu'à l'aube** he writes without letting up *ou* without any break till dawn.

relâché, e [rəlaʃe] *adj* **1.** [négligé - discipline, effort] lax, loose ; [- style] flowing, loose *péj* ■ **la surveillance était plutôt ~e** surveillance was a bit lax **2.** [détendu - muscle, corde] lax, relaxed.

relâchement [rəlaʃmɑ̃] *nm* **1.** [laisser-aller] laxity, loosening ■ **il y a du ~ dans votre travail** you're letting your work slide ■ **le ~ des mœurs** the laxity of *ou* decline in moral standards **2.** MÉD [de l'intestin] loosening ■ [d'un muscle] relaxation **3.** [d'une corde, d'un lien] loosening, slackening.

relâcher [3] [rəlaʃe] ◇ *vt* **1.** [libérer - animal] to free ; [- prisonnier] to release, to set free *(sép)* **2.** [diminuer] to relax, to slacken ■ **~ son attention** to let one's attention wander **3.** [détendre - câble] to loosen, to slacken ; [- muscle] to relax ■ **elle a relâché son étreinte** she relaxed *ou* loosened her grip **4.** MÉD [intestin] to loosen.

◇ *vi* NAUT to put into port.

◆ **se relâcher** *vpi* **1.** [muscle] to relax, to loosen ■ [câble] to loosen, to slacken **2.** [devenir moins rigoureux] to become lax *ou* laxer ■ **se ~ dans son travail** to become lax about one's work ■ **son attention se relâche** his attention is flagging.

relaie *etc v* ▷ **relayer**.

relais [rəlɛ] *nm* **1.** [succession] shift ■ **travail par ~** shift work ■ **prendre le ~ (de qqn)** to take over (from sb) ■ **j'ai commencé le travail, tu n'as plus qu'à prendre le ~** I started the job, just carry on *ou* take over **2.** SPORT relay **3.** HIST [lieu] coaching inn ■ [chevaux] relay **4.** [auberge] inn ■ **~ autoroutier** motorway café *UK*, truck stop *US* ■ **ce restaurant est donné comme ~ gastronomique dans le guide** this restaurant is recommended in the guide as an excellent place to eat **5.** *(comme adj; avec ou sans trait d'union)* ÉLECTR [appareil, station] relay *(modif)* ■ [processus] relaying **6.** TÉLÉCOM : **~ hertzien** radio relay **7.** BANQUE : **(crédit) ~** bridging loan.

relance [rəlɑ̃s] *nf* **1.** [nouvelle impulsion] revival, boost **2.** ÉCON : **il y a une ~ de la production sidérurgique** steel production is being boosted *ou* increased ■ **politique de ~** reflationary policy ▶ **~ économique** reflation **3.** ADMIN & COMM : **des ~s téléphoniques** follow-up calls ■ **lettre de ~** follow-up letter **4.** JEUX raise ■ **faire une ~** to raise (the stakes).

relancer [16] [rəlɑ̃se] ◇ *vt* **1.** [donner un nouvel essor à] to relaunch, to revive ■ **~ l'économie d'un pays** to give a boost to *ou* to boost *ou* to reflate a country's economy **2.** [solliciter] to chase up *UK*, to chase after *fig* ■ **arrête de me ~!** stop badgering me! **3.** [jeter à nouveau] to throw again **4.** CHASSE to start again **5.** INFORM to restart.

◇ *vi* JEUX : **~ (de)** : **je relance de 1 000 euros** I raise (the bid) by 1,000 euros.

relaps, e [rəlaps] ◇ *adj* relapsed.

◇ *nm, f* relapsed person, backslider RELIG.

relater [3] [rəlate] *vt* **1.** *sout* [raconter] to relate, to recount ▪ **les faits ont été relatés dans la presse** the facts were reported *ou* detailed in the papers **2.** DR [consigner] to record.

relatif, ive [rəlatif, iv] *adj* **1.** [gén - GRAMM] & MATH relative ▪ **tout est ~** it's all relative **2.** [concernant] : **~ à** relating to, concerning **3.** [approximatif] : **un confort très ~** very limited comfort ▪ **nous avons goûté un repos tout ~** we enjoyed a rest of sorts ▪ **un isolement ~** relative *ou* comparative isolation **4.** MUS relative.
◆ **relatif** *nm* GRAMM relative pronoun.
◆ **relative** *nf* relative clause.

relation [rəlasjɔ̃] *nf* **1.** [corrélation] relationship, connection ▪ **~ de cause à effet** relation *ou* relationship of cause and effect ▪ **mettre deux questions en ~ l'une avec l'autre, faire la ~ entre deux questions** to make the connection between *ou* to connect two questions ▪ **c'est sans ~ avec..., il n'y a aucune ~ avec...** there's no connection with..., it's nothing to do with... **2.** [rapport] relationship ▪ **nouer des ~s professionnelles** to form professional contacts ▪ **les ~s sino-japonaises** relations between China and Japan, Sino-Japanese relations ▪ **en ~** *ou* **~s : nous sommes en ~ d'affaires depuis des années** we've had business dealings *ou* a business relationship for years ▪ **en excellentes/mauvaises ~s avec ses collègues** on excellent/bad terms with one's colleagues ▪ **entrer en ~ avec qqn** [le contacter] to get in touch *ou* to make contact with sb ▪ **mettre qqn en ~ avec un ami/une organisation** to put sb in touch with a friend/an organization ➲ **~s diplomatiques** diplomatic relations *ou* links ▪ **~s humaines** [gén] dealings between people ; SOCIOL human relations ▪ **~s internationales** international relations ▪ **~s publiques** public relations ▪ **~s sexuelles** sexual relations
3. [connaissance] acquaintance ▪ **avoir de nombreuses ~s** to know a lot of people ▪ **utilise tes ~s** use your connections ▪ **heureusement que j'ai des ~s!** it's a good thing I'm well connected *ou* I know the right people! ▪ **j'ai trouvé à me loger par ~s** I found a place to live through knowing the right people *ou* through the grapevine
4. MATH relation
5. *sout* [compte rendu] relation, narration
6. DR account.

relationnel, elle [rəlasjɔnɛl] *adj* **1.** PSYCHOL relationship *(modif)* ▪ **avoir des difficultés ~les** to have trouble relating to people **2.** LING relational, relation *(modif)*.

relationniste [rəlasjɔnist] *nmf* *Québec* public relations officer.

relative [rəlativ] *f* ▷ **relatif**.

relativement [rəlativmɑ̃] *adv* **1.** [passablement] relatively, comparatively, reasonably **2.** *sout* [de façon relative] relatively, contingently *sout*.
◆ **relativement à** *loc prép* **1.** [par rapport à] compared to, in relation to **2.** [concernant] concerning ▪ **entendre un témoin ~ à une affaire** to hear a witness in relation to a case.

relativisation [rəlativizasjɔ̃] *nf* relativization.

relativiser [3] [rəlativize] *vt* : **~ qqch** to consider sthg in context, to relativize sthg *spéc* ▪ **il faut ~ tout ceci, ça pourrait être pire** you've got to keep things in perspective, it could be worse.

relativiste [rəlativist] ◇ *adj* **1.** PHYS relativistic **2.** PHILOS relativist, relativistic.
◇ *nmf* PHILOS relativist.

relativité [rəlativite] *nf* **1.** [gén] relativity **2.** PHYS relativity ▪ **(théorie de) la ~ générale/restreinte** general/special (theory of) relativity.

relaver [3] [rəlave] *vt* [laver de nouveau] to wash again, to rewash.

relax [rəlaks] *adj inv fam* [personne, ambiance] easy-going, laid back ▪ [activité, vacances] relaxing ➲ **fauteuil ~** reclining chair.

relaxant, e [rəlaksɑ̃, ɑ̃t] *adj* relaxing, soothing.

relaxation [rəlaksasjɔ̃] *nf* **1.** [détente] relaxation, relaxing ▪ **faire de la ~** to do relaxation exercises **2.** PHYS & PSYCHOL relaxation.

relaxe [rəlaks] ◇ *adj fam* = **relax**.
◇ *nf* DR discharge, release.

relaxer [3] [rəlakse] *vt* **1.** [relâcher - muscle] to relax **2.** DR [prisonnier] to discharge, to release.
◆ **se relaxer** *vpi* to relax.

relayer [11] [rəlɛje] *vt* **1.** [suppléer] to relieve, to take over from ▪ **il l'a relayée au chevet du malade** he took over from her at the patient's bedside **2.** RADIO & TV to relay **3.** SPORT to take over, to take the baton.
◆ **se relayer** *vp (emploi réciproque)* to take turns ▪ **se ~ auprès d'un malade** to take turns at a sick person's bedside.

relayeur, euse [rəlɛjœr, øz] *nm, f* SPORT relay runner.

relecture [rəlɛktyr] *nf* : **à la ~, j'ai trouvé que...** on reading it again *ou* when I reread it, I found that... ➲ **~ d'épreuves** IMPR proofreading.

relégation [rəlegasjɔ̃] *nf* **1.** SPORT relegation **2.** HIST & DR banishment, relegation.

reléguer [18] [rəlege] *vt* **1.** [cantonner] to relegate ▪ **~ qqn au second plan** to put sb in the background ▪ **leur équipe a été reléguée en deuxième division cette année** SPORT their team went down into the second division this year **2.** HIST & DR to banish, to relegate.

relent [rəlɑ̃] *nm* **1.** *(gén pl)* [mauvaise odeur] stink *(U)*, stench *(U)* ▪ **des ~s de tabac froid** a stench of stale tobacco **2.** *sout* [trace] residue, hint, trace.

relevable [rələvabl] *adj* (vertically) adjustable ▪ **siège à dossier ~** reclinable seat.

relevé, e [rəlve] *adj* **1.** [redressé - col, nez] turned-up ▪ **ses manches étaient ~es jusqu'au coude** his sleeves were rolled up to the elbows **2.** CULIN [assaisonné] seasoned, well-seasoned ▪ [pimenté] spicy, hot **3.** *sout* [distingué] elevated, refined.
◆ **relevé** *nm* **1.** [de recettes, de dépenses] summary, statement ▪ [de gaz, d'électricité] reading ▪ [de noms] list ▪ **~ mensuel** BANQUE monthly statement ➲ **~ d'identité bancaire** ≃ bank and account number, particulars of one's bank account ▪ **~ de notes** ÉDUC examination results **2.** GÉOGR survey **3.** ARCHIT layout **4.** DANSE relevé.

RELEVÉ D'IDENTITÉ BANCAIRE

A *RIB* is a small slip of paper comprising all of a person's bank details. Employers, utility companies and other financial institutions may ask for one to effect standing orders.

relève [rəlɛv] *nf* **1.** [manœuvre] relieving, changing ▪ **prendre la ~ (de qqn)** to take over (from sb) ➲ **la ~ de la garde** the changing of the guard **2.** [groupe] replacement, stand-in ▪ **la ~** [au travail] the relief team ; MIL the relief troops ; [garde] the relief guard.

relèvement [rəlɛvmɑ̃] *nm* **1.** [rétablissement] recovery, restoring **2.** [fait d'augmenter] raising ▪ [résultat] increase, rise ▪ **le ~ des impôts/des salaires** tax/salary increase **3.** [reconstruction] reerecting, rebuilding **4.** [rehaussement] raising, increase **5.** DR release **6.** NAUT bearing *(U)* ▪ **faire un ~ (de sa position)** to plot *ou* to chart one's position **7.** RADIO (radio) direction finding.

relever [19] [rəlve] ◇ *vt* **1.** [redresser - lampe, statue] to stand up *(sép)* again ; [- chaise] to pick up *(sép)* ; [- tête] to lift up *(sép)* again ▪ **ils m'ont relevé** [debout] they helped me (back) to my feet ; [assis] they sat me up *ou* helped me to sit up
2. [remonter - store] to raise ; [- cheveux] to put up *(sép)* ; [- col, visière] to turn up *(sép)* ; [- pantalon, manches] to roll up *(sép)* ; [- rideaux] to tie back *(sép)* ; [- strapontin] to lift up *(sép)* ▪ **le virage est trop relevé** the banking on the bend has been made too steep
3. [augmenter - prix, salaires] to increase, to raise, to put up *(sép)* ; [- notes] to put up, to raise

4. [ramasser, recueillir] to pick up *(sép)* ▪ **~ les copies ÉDUC** to collect the papers
5. [remettre en état - mur] to rebuild, to re-erect ; [- pylône] to re-erect, to put up *(sép)* again ▪ **~ des ruines** [ville] to reconstruct *ou* to rebuild a ruined city ; [maison] to rebuild a ruined house ▪ **c'est lui qui a relevé la nation** ***fig*** he's the one who put the country back on its feet (again) *ou* got the country going again ▪ **~ l'économie** to rebuild the economy ▪ **~ le moral des troupes** to boost the troops' morale
6. [mettre en valeur] to enhance
7. CULIN to season, to spice up *(sép)* ▪ **relevez l'assaisonnement** make the seasoning more spicy
8. [remarquer] to notice ▪ **elle n'a pas relevé l'allusion** [elle n'a pas réagi] she didn't pick up the hint ; [elle l'a sciemment ignorée] she pretended not to notice the hint ▪ *(en usage absolu)* **je ne relèverai pas!** I'll ignore that!
9. [enregistrer - empreinte digitale] to record ; [- cote, mesure] to take down *(sép)*, to plot ; [- informations] to take *ou* to note down ; [- plan] to sketch ▪ **on a relevé des traces de boue sur ses chaussures** traces of mud were found *ou* discovered on his shoes ▪ **~ l'eau** ***fam*** *ou* **le compteur d'eau** to read the water-meter ▪ **~ le gaz** ***fam*** *ou* **le compteur de gaz** to read the gas meter ▪ **températures relevées à 16 h** MÉTÉOR temperatures recorded at 4 p.m. ▪ **~ sa position** to plot *ou* to chart one's position ▪ **~ un point** to take a bearing
10. [relayer - garde] to relieve ; [- coéquipier] to take over *(insép)* from ▪ **~ qqn de : ~ qqn de ses vœux** to release sb from his/her vows ▪ **~ qqn de ses fonctions** to relieve sb of his/her duties
11. DR [prisonnier] to release
12. JEUX to pick up (one's cards).
◇ *vi* [remonter - vêtement] to ride up.
◆ **relever de** *v+prép* **1.** [être de la compétence de - juridiction] to fall *ou* to come under ; [- spécialiste] to be a matter for ; [- magistrat] to come under the jurisdiction of ▪ **cela relève des tribunaux/de la psychiatrie** it's a matter for the courts/the psychiatrists
2. [tenir de] : **cela relève du miracle** it's truly miraculous
3. ***sout*** [se rétablir de] : **~ de couches** to come out of confinement ***sout*** ▪ **elle relève d'une grippe** she is recovering from flu.
◆ **se relever** ◇ *vp (emploi passif)* [être inclinable] to lift up.
◇ *vpi* **1.** [se remettre - debout] to get *ou* to stand up again ; [- assis] to sit up again ▪ **il l'aida à se ~** he helped her to her feet again
2. [remonter] : **les commissures de ses lèvres se relevèrent** the corners of his mouth curled up.
◆ **se relever de** *vp+prép* to recover from, to get over ▪ **le parti se relève de ses cendres** *ou* **ruines** the party is rising from the ashes ▪ **je ne m'en relèverai/ils ne s'en relèveront pas** I'll/they'll never get over it.

relief [rəljɛf] *nm* **1.** ART, GÉOGR & OPT relief ▪ **la région a un ~ accidenté** the area is hilly ▪ **pays sans (aucun) ~** flat country ▪ **un ~ calcaire** limestone relief **2.** [contraste] relief, highlight ▪ **donner du ~ à qqch** to highlight sthg ▪ **son discours manquait de ~** his speech was a rather lacklustre affair **3.** ACOUST : **~ acoustique** spatial effect (of a sound).
◆ **reliefs** *nmpl* ***litt*** **les ~s** [d'un repas] the remnants *ou* leftovers.
◆ **en relief** ◇ *loc adj* ART & IMPR relief *(modif)*, raised ▪ **impression en ~** relief printing ▪ **lettres en ~** embossed letters ▪ **motif en ~** raised design, design in relief.
◇ *loc adv* [en valeur] : **mettre qqch en ~** to bring sthg out.

relier [9] [rəlje] *vt* **1.** [faire communiquer] to link up *(sép)*, to link (together), to connect ▪ **la route qui relie Bruxelles à Ostende** the road running from *ou* linking Brussels to Ostend **2.** [mettre en rapport] to connect, to link (together), to relate **3.** [livre] to bind ▪ **relié en cuir** leather-bound ▪ **relié toile** cloth-bound **4.** [tonneau] to hoop.

relieur, euse [rəljœr, øz] *nm, f* bookbinder.

religieusement [rəliʒjøzmɑ̃] *adv* **1.** [pieusement] religiously ▪ **se marier ~** to get married in church **2.** [soigneusement] religiously, rigorously, scrupulously ▪ [avec vénération] reverently, devoutly.

religieux, euse [rəliʒjø, øz] *adj* **1.** [cérémonie, éducation, ordre, art] religious ▪ **un mariage ~** a church wedding **2.** [personne] religious **3.** [empreint de gravité] religious ▪ **un silence ~ se fit dans la salle** a reverent silence fell on the room.
◆ **religieux** *nm* member of a religious order.
◆ **religieuse** *nf* **1.** RELIG nun **2.** CULIN cream puff ▪ **religieuse au chocolat/au café** chocolate/coffee cream puff.

religion [rəliʒjɔ̃] *nf* **1.** [croyance] religion ▪ **la ~ juive** the Jewish religion *ou* faith ▪ **être sans** *ou* **n'avoir pas de ~** to have no religion, to be of no religious faith ▪ **se convertir à la ~ catholique/musulmane** to be converted to Catholicism/Islam ➊ **entrer en ~** to join a religious order ▪ **la ~ est l'opium du peuple** ***Marx allus*** religion is the opium of the people **2.** [piété] religious faith.

religiosité [rəliʒjozite] *nf* religiosity, religiousness.

reliquaire [rəlikɛr] *nm* reliquary.

reliquat [rəlika] *nm* remainder, balance ▪ **un ~ de vacances** outstanding leave ▪ **~ d'impôts** outstanding taxes ▪ **après apurement des comptes, il n'y a plus aucun ~** after balancing the accounts, there is nothing left over *ou* there is no surplus.

relique [rəlik] *nf* RELIG relic ▪ **conserver qqch comme une ~** to treasure sthg.

relire [106] [rəlir] *vt* to read again, to reread.
◆ **se relire** *vp (emploi réfléchi)* to read (over) what one has written ▪ **j'ai du mal à me ~** I have difficulty reading my own writing.

reliure [rəljyr] *nf* **1.** [technique] binding, bookbinding **2.** [couverture] binding ▪ **~ pleine** full binding ▪ **~ sans couture** perfect binding.

relocalisation [rəlokalizasjɔ̃] *nf* relocation.

relocaliser [rəlokalize] *vt* to relocate.

relogement [rəlɔʒmɑ̃] *nm* rehousing.

reloger [17] [rəlɔʒe] *vt* to rehouse.

relu, e [rəly] *pp* ▷ **relire.**

reluire [97] [rəlɥir] *vi* [casque, casserole] to gleam, to shine ▪ [pavé mouillé] to glisten ▪ **faire ~ ses cuivres** to do *ou* to polish the brasses.

reluisant, e [rəlɥizɑ̃, ɑ̃t] *adj* **1.** ***fam (gén nég)*** **peu** *ou* **pas ~** [médiocre] shabby ▪ **un individu peu ~** an unsavoury character ▪ **notre avenir n'apparaît guère ~** our future hardly looks bright **2.** [brillant] shining, shiny, gleaming.

reluisent *etc v* ▷ **reluire.**

reluquer [3] [rəlyke] *vt* ***fam*** [personne] to ogle, to eye up ▪ [objet] to have one's eye on, to covet ▪ **se faire ~** to be *ou* get stared at.

relut *etc v* ▷ **relire.**

rem [rɛm] *nm* rem.

remâcher [3] [rəmaʃe] *vt* **1.** [mâcher de nouveau] to chew again ▪ [suj: ruminant] to ruminate **2.** [ressasser] to brood over *(insép)*.

remailler [3] [rəmaje] *vt* [filet] to mend ▪ [bas, chaussette] to darn.

remake [rimɛk] *nm* CINÉ remake ▪ **à quand le ~?** when are you doing the remake?

rémanence [remanɑ̃s] *nf* **1.** PHYS remanence, retentivity **2.** PHYSIOL [durabilité] persistence.

rémanent, e [remanɑ̃, ɑ̃t] *adj* **1.** PHYS [aimantation] remanent, retentive ▪ [magnétisme] residual **2.** [gén - CHIM] persistent ▪ **image ~e** after-image.

remanger [17] [rəmɑ̃ʒe] ◇ *vt* to have *ou* to eat again ▪ **je n'ai plus jamais remangé d'huîtres depuis** I've never eaten oysters since.
◇ *vi* to eat again.

remaniable [rəmanjabl] *adj* [discours, projet, texte] revisable, amendable ■ **son plan sera difficilement ~** his plan is going to be hard to revise *ou* to rework.

remaniement [rəmanimɑ̃] *nm* **1.** [d'un projet de loi] redrafting, altering, amending ■ [d'un discours] revision, altering ■ [d'un programme] modification **2.** [d'un gouvernement, d'un ministère] reshuffle ■ **~ ministériel** cabinet reshuffle.

remanier [9] [rəmanje] *vt* **1.** [texte, discours] to revise ■ [projet de loi] to draft again, to redraft **2.** [gouvernement, ministère] to reshuffle.

remaquiller [3] [rəmakije] *vt* to make up *(sép)* again.
◆ **se remaquiller** *vp (emploi réfléchi)* [entièrement] to reapply one's make-up ■ [partiellement] to touch up one's make-up.

remarcher [3] [rəmarʃe] *vi* **1.** [accidenté, handicapé] to walk again **2.** [mécanisme] to work again.

remariage [rəmarjaʒ] *nm* remarriage ■ **son ~ avec...** his remarriage to...

remarier [9] [rəmarje] *vt* to remarry ■ **finalement, il a réussi à ~ son fils** he eventually managed to marry off his son again.
◆ **se remarier** *vpi* to get married *ou* to marry again, to remarry.

remarquable [rəmarkabl] *adj* **1.** [marquant] striking, notable, noteworthy ■ **un événement ~** a noteworthy event **2.** [émérite - personne] remarkable, outstanding, exceptional ■ **un travail ~** a remarkable *ou* an outstanding piece of work **3.** [particulier] conspicuous, prominent ■ **la girafe est ~ par la longueur de son cou** the giraffe is notable for its long neck.

remarquablement [rəmarkabləmɑ̃] *adv* remarkably, strikingly, outstandingly ■ **elle joue ~ du violon** she plays the violin outstandingly well.

remarque [rəmark] *nf* **1.** [opinion exprimée] remark, comment ■ [critique] (critical) remark ■ **je l'ai trouvée insolente et je lui en ai fait la ~** I thought she was insolent and (I) told her so ■ **j'en ai assez de tes ~s** I've had enough of your criticisms ■ **faire une ~ à qqn sur qqch** to pass a remark to sb about sthg **2.** [commentaire écrit] note.

remarqué, e [rəmarke] *adj* conspicuous, noticeable, striking ■ **il a fait une intervention très ~e** the speech he made attracted a great deal of attention ■ **une entrée ~e** a conspicuous entrance.

remarquer [3] [rəmarke] *vt* **1.** [constater] to notice ■ **faire ~ qqch à qqn** to point sthg out to sb ■ **on m'a fait ~ que...** it's been pointed out to me *ou* it's been drawn to my attention that... ■ **remarque, je m'en moque éperdument** mind you, I really couldn't care less ▮ [distinguer] to notice ■ **se faire ~** to draw attention to o.s. ■ **elle partit sans se faire ~** she left unnoticed *ou* without drawing attention to herself **2.** [dire] to remark ■ **"il ne viendra pas", remarqua-t-il** "he won't come," he remarked **3.** [marquer de nouveau - date, adresse] to write *ou* to note down *(sép)* again ; [- linge] to tag *ou* to mark again.
◆ **se remarquer** *vp (emploi passif)* [être visible] to be noticed, to show ■ **le défaut du tissu se remarque à peine** the flaw in the material is scarcely noticeable *ou* hardly shows ■ **si elle continue à bouder, ça va se ~** if she keeps (on) sulking, people are going to notice.

remballer [3] [rɑ̃bale] *vt* **1.** [marchandise] to pack up *(sép)* again **2.** *fam fig* **tu peux ~ tes compliments** you can keep your compliments to yourself.

rembarquement [rɑ̃barkəmɑ̃] *nm* [de passagers] re-embarkation ■ [de produits] reloading.

rembarquer [3] [rɑ̃barke] ◇ *vt* [produits] to reload.
◇ *vi* [passagers] to re-embark.
◆ **se rembarquer** *vpi* **1.** [passagers] to re-embark **2.** *fig* **se ~ dans qqch** to get involved in sthg again ■ **tu ne vas pas te ~ dans une histoire pareille** you're not going to get mixed up in a mess like that again.

rembarrer [3] [rɑ̃bare] *vt fam* **~ qqn** to put sb in his place, to tell sb where to get off.

remblai [rɑ̃blɛ] *nm* **1.** RAIL & TRAV PUB embankment ■ [terre rapportée] ballast ■ **terre de ~** backfill **2.** MIN packing, backfill.

remblaie *etc v* ⊳ **remblayer.**

remblaiement [rɑ̃blɛmɑ̃] *nm* GÉOL depositing.

remblayer [11] [rɑ̃bleje] *vt* **1.** TRAV PUB to bank up *(sép)* ■ **~ un fossé** to fill up a ditch **2.** MIN to backfill, to pack.

rembobiner [3] [rɑ̃bɔbine] *vt* [film, bande magnétique] to rewind, to spool back *(sép)*.

rembourrage [rɑ̃buraʒ] *nm* [d'un vêtement] padding ■ [d'un siège] stuffing.

rembourrer [3] [rɑ̃bure] *vt* [coussin, manteau] to pad ■ [siège] to stuff ■ **il est plutôt bien rembourré** *fam hum* he's a bit podgy *ou* a bit on the plump side.

remboursable [rɑ̃bursabl] *adj* [billet] refundable ■ [prêt] repayable ■ **~ en 20 mensualités** repayable in 20 monthly instalments ■ **non ~** non-redeemable.

remboursement [rɑ̃bursəmɑ̃] *nm* [d'un billet, d'un achat] refund ■ [d'un prêt] repayment, settlement ■ [d'une dépense] reimbursement ■ FIN [d'une obligation] redemption ➊ **envoi** *ou* **expédition contre ~** cash on delivery.

rembourser [3] [rɑ̃burse] *vt* [argent] to pay back *ou* off *(sép)*, to repay ■ [dépense, achat] to reimburse, to refund ■ [personne] to pay back, to reimburse ■ FIN [obligation] to redeem ■ **frais de port remboursés** postage refunded ■ **est-ce que tu peux me ~?** can you pay me back? ■ **se faire ~** to get a refund ■ **tu t'es fait ~ pour ton trajet en taxi?** did they reimburse you for your taxi journey? ■ **ce médicament n'est remboursé qu'à 40 % (par la Sécurité sociale)** only 40% of the price of this drug is refunded (by the Health Service).

Rembrandt [rɑ̃brɑ̃] *npr* Rembrandt.

rembrunir [32] [rɑ̃brynir] ◆ **se rembrunir** *vpi* **1.** *litt* [s'assombrir] to darken, to cloud (over) **2.** [se renfrogner] to darken ■ **son visage s'est rembruni à l'annonce de la nouvelle** his face darkened when he heard the news.

remède [rəmɛd] *nm* **1.** [solution] remedy, cure ■ **trouver un ~ au désespoir/à l'inflation** to find a cure for despair/for inflation ■ **porter ~ à qqch** to cure *ou* to find a cure for sthg **2.** [thérapeutique] cure, remedy ■ **un ~ contre le cancer/le SIDA** a cure for cancer/for AIDS ■ **le ~ est pire que le mal** *fig* the remedy is worse than the disease ■ **c'est un (vrai) ~ contre l'amour** *fam* he's/she's a real turn-off **3.** *vieilli* [médicament] remedy ■ **un ~ de bonne femme** a traditional *ou* an old-fashioned remedy ■ **un ~ de cheval** a drastic remedy ■ **aux grands maux les grands ~s** *prov* desperate situations call for desperate remedies.

remédiable [rəmedjabl] *adj* curable, remediable *litt.*

remédier [9] [rəmedje] ◆ **remédier à** *v+prép* **1.** [maladie] to cure ■ [douleur] to alleviate, to relieve **2.** *sout* [problème] to remedy, to find a remedy *ou* solution for ■ **nous ne savons pas comment ~ à la situation** we don't know how to remedy the situation ■ **~ à une erreur** to put right a mistake.

remembrement [rəmɑ̃brəmɑ̃] *nm* land consolidation *ou* reallotment.

remembrer [3] [rəmɑ̃bre] *vt* to redistribute *ou* to reallot.

remémorer [3] [rəmemɔre] *vt sout* **~ qqch à qqn** to remind sb of sthg, to bring sthg to sb's mind.
◆ **se remémorer** *vpt sout* to recollect, to remember.

remerciement [rəmɛrsimɑ̃] *nm* **1.** [action] thanks, thanking ■ **une lettre de ~** a letter of thanks, a thank-you letter ■ **un geste/un mot de ~** a gesture/a word of thanks **2.** [parole] thanks ■ **(je vous adresse) tous mes ~s pour ce que vous avez fait** (I) thank you for what you did ■ **il a balbutié quelques ~s et s'est**

enfui he mumbled a few words of thanks and ran off ■ **avec mes ~s** with (many) thanks.
Voir module d'usage

remercier [9] [rəmɛrsje] *vt* **1.** [témoigner sa gratitude à] to thank ■ **je te remercie** thank you ■ **elle nous a remerciés par un superbe bouquet de fleurs** she thanked us with a beautiful bunch of flowers ■ **je te remercie de m'avoir aidé** thank you for helping me *ou* for your help ■ **et c'est comme ça que tu me remercies!** and that's all the thanks I get! **2.** [pour décliner une offre] : **encore un peu de thé? – je vous remercie** would you like some more tea? – no, thank you ■ **je te remercie du conseil** *iron* thanks for the advice **3.** *euphém* [licencier] to dismiss, to let go ■ **ils ont décidé de la ~** they decided to dispense with her services.

remettre [84] [rəmɛtr] *vt* **1.** [replacer - gén] to put back *(sép)* ; [- horizontalement] to lay, to put ■ **remets le livre où tu l'as trouvé** put the book back where you found it ■ **~ qqch à plat** to lay sthg flat again *ou* back (down) flat ■ [personne] : **~ qqn debout** to stand sb up again *ou* sb back up ■ **je l'ai remis en pension** I sent him back to boarding school ■ **~ qqn sur la voie** to put sb back on the right track ■ **~ qqn sur le droit chemin** to set sb on the straight and narrow again ■ **~ qqch à cuire** to put sthg back on to cook ǁ [pour remplacer] : **il faut simplement lui ~ des piles** you just have to put new batteries in (it)
2. [rétablir dans un état] : **~ qqch en marche** to get sthg going again ■ **~ qqch en état** to repair sthg ■ **~ qqch à neuf** to restore sthg ■ **ces mots me remirent en confiance** those words restored my faith ■ **elle a remis la pagaille dans toute la maison** *fam* she plunged the whole household into chaos again
3. [rajouter] to add ➊ **il est assez puni comme ça, n'en remets pas** *fam* he's been punished enough already, no need to rub it in
4. [vêtements, chaussures] to put on *(sép)* again, to put back on *(sép)*
5. [recommencer] : **la balle est à ~** TENNIS play a let ➊ **~ ça** *fam* : **voilà qu'elle remet ça!** there she goes again!, she's at it again! ■ **les voilà qui remettent ça avec leur grève!** here they go striking again! ■ **je n'ai pas envie de ~ ça!** I don't want to go through that again! ■ **allez, on remet ça!** [au café] come on, let's have another round *ou* another one!
6. [donner - colis, lettre, message] to deliver, to hand over *(sép)* ; [- objet, dossier à régler, rançon] to hand over *(sép)*, to give ; [- dossier d'inscription, dissertation] to hand *ou* to give in *(sép)* ; [- pétition, rapport] to present, to hand in ; [- démission] to hand in, to tender ■ *sout* [- médaille, récompense] to present, to give ■ **on nous a remis 100 euros à chacun** we were each given 100 euros ■ **~ qqn aux autorités** to hand *ou* to turn sb over to the authorities ■ **on lui a remis le prix Nobel** he was presented with *ou* awarded the Nobel prize
7. [confier] to place ■ **~ son âme à Dieu** to commit one's soul to God, to place one's soul in God's keeping
8. [rendre - copies] to hand *ou* to give back *(sép)* ; [- clés] to hand back *(sép)*, to return ■ **l'enfant a été remis à sa famille** the child was returned to his family
9. [ajourner - entrevue] to put off *(sép)*, to postpone, to put back *(sép)* UK ; [- décision] to put off *(sép)*, to defer ■ **~ qqch à huitaine** to postpone sthg *ou* to put sthg off for a week ■ **la réunion a été remise à lundi** the meeting has been put off *ou* postponed until Monday ■ **~ qqch à plus tard** to put sthg off until later
10. MÉD [replacer - articulation, os] to put back *(sép)* in place ■ **sa cheville n'est pas vraiment encore remise** her ankle isn't reset yet
11. [reconnaître - personne] to remember
12. [faire grâce de - peine de prison] to remit ■ **~ une dette à qqn** to let sb off a debt ■ [pardonner - péché] to forgive, to remit *sout* ; [- offense] to forgive, to pardon
13. *Belgique* [vomir] to vomit.
◆ **se remettre** ◇ *vp (emploi réfléchi)* [se livrer] : **se ~ à la police** to give o.s. up to the police ■ **se ~ entre les mains de qqn** to put *ou* to place o.s. in sb's hands.
◇ *vpi* **1.** [se replacer - dans une position, un état] : **se ~ au lit** to go back to bed ■ **se ~ debout** to stand up again, to get back up ■ **se ~ en route** to get started *ou* going again ■ **tu ne vas pas te ~ en colère!** don't go getting angry again! ■ **se ~ avec qqn** [se réconcilier] to make it up with sb ; [se réinstaller] to go *ou* to be back with sb again
2. [guérir] to recover, to get better ■ **se ~ de qqch** to get over sthg ■ **se ~ d'un accident** to recover from *ou* to get over an accident ■ **allons, remets-toi!** come on, pull yourself together *ou* get a grip on yourself! ■ **je ne m'en remets pas** I can't get over it.
◆ **se remettre à** *vp+prép* **1.** [recommencer à] : **se ~ à (faire) qqch** to start (doing) sthg again, to take up (doing) sthg again ■ **il s'est remis à fumer** he started smoking again ■ **je me suis remis à l'espagnol** I've taken up Spanish again
2. MÉTÉOR : **la pluie se remet à tomber, il se remet à pleuvoir** the rain's starting again, it's started raining again ■ **le temps se remet au beau** it's brightening up.
◆ **s'en remettre à** *vp+prép* [se fier à] to rely on, to leave it (up) to ■ **s'en ~ à la décision de qqn** to leave it (up) to sb to decide.

remeubler [5] [rəmøble] *vt* [de nouveau] to refurnish ■ [avec de nouveaux meubles] to put new furniture into.

rémige [remiʒ] *nf* remex ■ **les ~s** remiges.

remilitarisation [rəmilitarizasjɔ̃] *nf* remilitarization.

remilitariser [3] [rəmilitarize] *vt* to remilitarize.

reminéraliser [rəmineralize] *vt* [eau, organisme] to remineralize.

réminiscence [reminisɑ̃s] *nf* **1.** [souvenir] reminiscence, recollection ■ **quelques ~s de ce qu'elle avait appris à l'école** a few vague memories of what she'd learned at school **2.** [influence] overtone ■ **il y a des ~s de Mahler dans ce morceau** there are some echoes of Mahler in this piece, this piece is reminiscent of Mahler **3.** PHILOS & PSYCHOL reminiscence.

remis, e [rəmi, iz] ◇ *pp* ▷ **remettre**.

LES REMERCIEMENTS

Remercier quelqu'un

Thank you (very much)! Merci (beaucoup) !

Thanks (a lot)! Merci (beaucoup) !

Many thanks! Merci infiniment !

Thank you for your help. Je vous remercie de votre aide.

Thank you very much for offering to help. Merci beaucoup d'avoir proposé de nous aider.

I can't thank you enough (for looking after Toby). Je ne sais pas comment vous remercier (d'avoir gardé Toby).

I really appreciate this. Je vous suis vraiment reconnaissant.

I'm very grateful for your support. Je vous suis très reconnaissant de votre soutien.

Réponses

Not at all. Je vous en prie.

It was nothing. Ce n'est rien.

Don't mention it. Il n'y a pas de quoi.

You're welcome. De rien.

My pleasure. Je vous en prie.

Any time! N'hésite pas !

No problem! De rien !

◇ *adj* : **être ~** to be well again ■ **une semaine de repos et me voilà ~e** a week's rest and I'm back on my feet (again) ■ **être ~ de** to have recovered from, to have got over ■ **il n'est pas encore ~ de sa frayeur/son cauchemar** he hasn't yet got over his fright/nightmare.

◆ **remise** *nf* **1.** [dans un état antérieur] : **la ~e en place des meubles/en ordre des documents nous a pris du temps** putting all the furniture back into place/sorting out the papers again took us some time ■ **la ~e en marche du moteur** restarting the engine ▶ **~e en cause** *OU* **question** calling into question ■ **~e en jeu** *OU* **en touche** [au hockey] push-in ; RUGBY line-out ; FOOTBALL throw-in ■ **~e à neuf** restoration ■ **il a besoin d'une ~e à niveau** he needs to be brought up to scratch ■ **~e à zéro** INFORM [effacement] core flush ; [réinitialisation] resetting ■ **la ~e à zéro du compteur kilométrique a été faite récemment** AUTO the mileometer has recently been put back to zero
2. [livraison] delivery ■ **~e d'une lettre/d'un paquet en mains propres** personal delivery of a letter/package ■ **la ~e des clés sera faite par l'agence** the agency will be responsible for handing over the keys ■ **la ~e de la rançon aura lieu derrière le garage** the ransom will be handed over *ou* paid behind the garage ▶ **~e des prix** ÉDUC prize-giving
3. COMM [réduction] discount, reduction, remittance *spéc* ■ **une ~e de 15 %** a 15% discount ■ **faire une ~e à qqn** to give sb a discount *ou* a reduction
4. [d'effet, de chèque, de banque] remittance ■ **faire une ~e de fonds à qqn** to send sb a remittance, to remit funds to sb ■ **faire une ~e de chèque** to pay in a cheque
5. FIN [d'un impôt] allowance
6. DR remission ■ **faire ~e d'une dette** to discharge a debt ■ **faire ~e d'une amende** to remit *ou* to reduce a fine ▶ **~e de peine** reduction of (the) sentence
7. *sout* [ajournement] putting off, postponement ■ **la ~e à huitaine de l'ouverture du procès** the postponement *ou* deferment *sout* of the opening of the trial for a week
8. [resserre] shed
9. CHASSE covert.

remisage [rəmizaʒ] *nm* [gén] putting away, storing (away).

remise [rəmiz] *f* ▷ **remis.**

remiser [3] [rəmize] ◇ *vt* **1.** [ranger] to store away *(sép)*, to put away *(sép)* **2.** *fam vieilli* [rabrouer] : **~ qqn** to send sb packing.
◇ *vi* JEUX to place another bet.

rémission [remisjɔ̃] *nf* **1.** RELIG remission, forgiveness ■ **la ~ des péchés** the remission of sins **2.** DR remission **3.** MÉD remission ■ **la ~ fut de courte durée** the remission didn't last.

◆ **sans rémission** *sout* ◇ *loc adj* [implacable] merciless, pitiless.
◇ *loc adv* **1.** [sans pardon possible] mercilessly, without mercy **2.** [sans relâche] unremittingly, relentlessly ■ **travailler sans ~** to work unremittingly *ou* relentlessly.

remit *etc v* ▷ **remettre.**

remmener [19] [rɑ̃mne] *vt* [au point de départ] to take back ■ [à soi] to bring back *(sép)* ■ **je te remmènerai chez toi en voiture** I'll drive you back home.

remodeler [25] [rəmɔdle] *vt* **1.** [silhouette, traits] to remodel **2.** [quartier] to replan **3.** [institution] to reorganize ■ [projet] to redesign, to revise.

remontage [rəmɔ̃taʒ] *nm* **1.** [d'une pendule] winding up, rewinding **2.** [d'une étagère] reassembly, reassembling.

remontant, e [rəmɔ̃tɑ̃, ɑ̃t] *adj* **1.** BOT [fraisier] double-cropping, remontant *spéc* ■ [rosier] remontant **2.** [fortifiant] invigorating.

◆ **remontant** *nm* tonic.

remonté, e [rəmɔ̃te] *adj fam* **1.** [plein d'énergie] full of beans **2.** [irrité] : **~ contre qqn/qqch** up in arms about sb/sthg.

◆ **remontée** *nf* **1.** [d'une côte] ascent, climb ■ **la ~e du fleuve** the trip upriver *ou* upstream ■ **la ~e des mineurs a lieu à 4 h** the miners are brought back up at 4 o'clock **2.** [rattrapage] catching up ■ **le coureur colombien a fait une belle ~e face à ses adversaires** the Colombian competitor is catching up with his opponents ■ **on constate une brusque ~e de la cote du président** the popularity of the President has shot up **3.** GÉOGR upwelling.

◆ **remontée mécanique** *nf* ski lift.

remonte-pente [rəmɔ̃tpɑ̃t] *(pl* **remonte-pentes***)* *nm* ski tow.

remonter [3] [rəmɔ̃te] ◇ *vt* **1.** [côte, étage] to go *ou* to climb back up
2. [porter à nouveau] to take back up
3. [parcourir - en voiture, en bateau *etc*] to go up *(insép)* ■ **~ le Nil** to sail up the Nile ■ **les saumons remontent le fleuve** the salmon are swimming upstream ■ **nous avons remonté la Seine en voiture jusqu'à Rouen** we drove along the Seine (upriver) to Rouen ■ **~ le défilé** [aller en tête] to work one's way to the front of the procession ■ **~ la rue** to go *ou* to walk back up the street ■ **en remontant le cours des siècles** *OU* **du temps** going back several centuries
4. [relever - chaussette] to pull up *(sép)* ; [- manche] to roll up *(sép)* ; [- col, visière] to raise, to turn up *(sép)* ; [- robe] to raise, to lift ; [- store] to pull up, to raise ■ **~ qqch** to put sthg higher up, to raise sthg ■ **remonte ton pantalon** pull your trousers *UK* *ou* pants *US* up ■ **elle a remonté la vitre** she wound the window up ■ [augmenter - salaire, notation] to increase, to raise, to put up *(sép)* ■ **tous les résultats des examens ont été remontés de 2 points** all exam results have been put up *ou* raised by 2 marks
5. [assembler à nouveau - moteur, kit] to reassemble, to put back *(sép)* together (again) ; [- étagère] to put back *(sép)* up ■ CINÉ [film] to reedit
6. COMM [rouvrir] to set up *(sép)* again ■ **à sa sortie de prison, il a remonté une petite affaire de plomberie** when he came out of prison he started up another small plumbing business ■ [faire prospérer à nouveau] : **il a su ~ l'entreprise** he managed to set *ou* to put the business back on its feet
7. [renouveler] to restock, to stock up again ■ **~ son stock (de cassettes vidéo)** to stock up again (on video cassettes)
8. [mécanisme, montre] to wind (up)
9. [ragaillardir - physiquement] to pick up *(sép)* ; [- moralement] to cheer up *(sép)* ■ **prends un whisky, ça te remontera** *fam* have a whisky, it'll make you feel better ■ **~ le moral à qqn** to cheer sb up
10. SPORT [concurrent] to catch up (with)
11. THÉÂTRE to stage again, to put on (the stage) again.
◇ *vi (surtout aux être)* **1.** [monter de nouveau] to go back up, to go up again ■ **l'enfant remonta dans la brouette/sur l'escabeau** the child got back into the wheelbarrow/up onto the stool ■ **remonte dans ta chambre** go back up to your room ■ **~ à Paris** to go back to Paris
2. TRANSP : **~ dans** [bateau, bus, train] to get back onto ; [voiture] to get back into ■ **~ à cheval** [se remettre en selle] to remount ; [refaire de l'équitation] to take up riding again
3. [s'élever - route] to go back up, to go up again ■ **le sentier remonte jusqu'à la villa** the path goes up to the villa ■ [avoir un niveau supérieur] : **la mer remonte** the tide's coming in (again) ■ **le baromètre remonte** the barometer is rising ■ **le prix du sucre a remonté** [après une baisse] the price of sugar has gone back up again ■ **sa fièvre remonte de plus belle** his temperature is going up even higher ■ **tu remontes dans mon estime** you've gone up in my esteem ■ **sa cote remonte** *fig* he's becoming more popular ■ **ses actions remontent** *fig* things are looking up *ou* picking up for him
4. [jupe] to ride *ou* to go up
5. [faire surface - mauvaise odeur] to come back up ■ **~ à la surface** [noyé] to float back (up) to the surface ; [plongeur] to resurface ; [scandale] to reemerge, to resurface
6. [retourner vers l'origine] : **~ dans le temps** to go back in time ■ **~ à** [se reporter à] to go back to, to return to ■ **le renseignement qui nous a permis de ~ jusqu'à vous** the piece of information which enabled us to trace you ■ **~ de l'effet à la cause** to trace the effect back to the cause ■ **~ à** [dater de] to go *ou* to date back to ■ **on fait généralement ~ la crise à 1910** the crisis is generally believed to have started in 1910
7. NAUT [navire] to sail north ■ [vent] to come round the north ■ **~ au vent** to tack into the wind.

◆ **se remonter** ◇ *vp (emploi passif)* : **ces nouvelles montres ne se remontent pas** these new watches don't have to be wound up.

◇ *vp (emploi réfléchi)* [physiquement] to recover one's strength ▪ [moralement] to cheer o.s. up ▪ **elle dit qu'elle boit pour se ~** she says she drinks to cheer herself up *ou* to make herself feel better ▪ **se ~ le moral** to cheer o.s. up.
◆ **se remonter en** *vp+prép fam* [se réapprovisionner en] to replenish one's stock of.

remontoir [rəmɔ̃twar] *nm* [d'une montre] winder.

remontrance [rəmɔ̃trɑ̃s] *nf* **1.** *sout (gén pl)* [reproche] remonstrance, reproof ▪ **faire des ~s à qqn** to reprimand *ou* to admonish sb **2.** HIST remonstrance.

remontrer [3] [rəmɔ̃tre] *vt* **1.** [montrer de nouveau] to show again ▪ **j'aimerais que tu me remontres comment tu as fait** I'd like you to show me again *ou* once more how you did it **2.** *litt* [faute, tort] to point out *(sép)* **3.** *loc* **en ~ à qqn : crois-tu vraiment pouvoir m'en ~?** do you really think you have anything to teach me? ▪ **il veut toujours en ~ à tout le monde** he's always trying to show off to people.
◆ **se remontrer** *vpi* to show up again ▪ **et ne t'avise pas de te ~ ici!** and don't ever show your face (around) here again!

remords [rəmɔr] *nm* [repentir] remorse ▪ **avoir des ~** to be full of remorse ▪ **être bourrelé de** *ou* **torturé par le ~** to be stricken with remorse ▪ **elle est rongée par le ~** she is consumed with remorse ▪ **il a été pris de ~** his conscience got the better of him ▪ **sans aucun ~** without a qualm, without any compunction, without (the slightest) remorse.

remorquage [rəmɔrkaʒ] *nm* towing.

remorque [rəmɔrk] *nf* **1.** [traction - d'une voiture] towing ; [- d'un navire] tugging, towing ▪ **câble de ~** towline, towrope ▪ **prendre une voiture en ~** to tow a car ▪ **être en ~** to be on tow *UK ou* in tow *US* ▪ **'véhicule accidenté en ~'** 'on tow' **2.** [voiture] trailer **3.** *fig* **être à la ~ de qqn** to tag (along) behind sb ▪ **il est toujours à la ~** he always lags behind.

remorquer [3] [rəmɔrke] *vt* **1.** [voiture] to tow ▪ [navire] to tug, to tow ▪ [masse] to haul ▪ **se faire ~ jusqu'au garage** to get a tow to the garage **2.** *fam* [traîner - enfant, famille] to drag along *(sép)*.

remorqueur, euse [rəmɔrkœr, øz] *adj* [avion, bateau, train] towing.
◆ **remorqueur** *nm* **1.** NAUT towboat, tug **2.** ASTRONAUT space tug.

rémoulade [remulad] *nf* rémoulade (sauce).

remoulage [rəmulaʒ] *nm* **1.** [du café] regrinding **2.** [en meunerie - action] remilling ; [- résultat] middlings.

rémouleur [remulœr] *nm* (itinerant) knife grinder.

remous [rəmu] *nm* **1.** [tourbillon] swirl, eddy ▪ [derrière un bateau] wash, backwash **2.** [mouvement] ripple, stir ▪ **un ~ parcourut la foule** a ripple *ou* stir went through the crowd **3.** *sout* [réaction] stir, flurry ▪ **l'article va sûrement provoquer quelques ~ dans la classe politique** the article will doubtless cause a stir *ou* raise a few eyebrows in the political world.

rempaillage [rɑ̃pajaʒ] *nm* [d'une chaise] reseating (with rushes), rushing.

rempailler [3] [rɑ̃paje] *vt* [chaise] to reseat (with rushes).

rempailleur, euse [rɑ̃pajœr, øz] *nm, f* chair-rusher.

rempart [rɑ̃par] *nm* **1.** [enceinte] rampart, bulwark ▪ **les ~s** [d'une ville] ramparts, city walls **2.** *fig & litt* bulwark, bastion ▪ **elle lui fit un ~ de son corps** she shielded him with her body.

rempiler [3] [rɑ̃pile] ◇ *vt* to pile (up) again.
◇ *vi*△ *arg mil* to re-enlist, to sign up again.

remplaçable [rɑ̃plasabl] *adj* replaceable ▪ **difficilement ~** hard to replace.

remplaçant, e [rɑ̃plasɑ̃, ɑ̃t] *nm, f* **1.** [gén] replacement, stand-in ▪ UNIV supply *UK ou* substitute *US* teacher ▪ [d'un médecin] replacement, locum *UK* **2.** SPORT reserve ▪ [au cours du match] substitute **3.** MUS, THÉÂTRE & TV understudy.

remplacement [rɑ̃plasmɑ̃] *nm* **1.** [substitution] replacement ▪ **il y a eu quelques ~s dans le personnel** some members of staff have been replaced **2.** [suppléance] : **je ne trouve que des ~s** I can only find work standing in *ou* covering for other people ▪ **faire un ~** to stand in *(insép)*, to fill in *(insép)* ▪ **faire des ~s** [gén] to do temporary replacement work ; [comme secrétaire] to do temporary secretarial work ; [comme enseignant] to work as a supply *UK ou* substitute *US* teacher.
◆ **de remplacement** *loc adj* : **produit de ~** substitute product ▪ **solution de ~** alternative *ou* fallback (solution).

remplacer [16] [rɑ̃plase] *vt* **1.** [renouveler - pièce usagée] to replace, to change **2.** [mettre à la place de] to replace **3.** [prendre la place de] to replace, to take the place of ▪ **dans de nombreuses tâches, la machine remplace maintenant l'homme** in a lot of tasks, machines are now taking over from men ▪ **le pétrole a remplacé le charbon** oil has taken the place of coal **4.** [suppléer] to stand in *ou* to substitute for ▪ **tu dois absolument trouver quelqu'un pour le ~** you must find someone to replace him ▪ **rien ne peut ~ une mère** there is no substitute for a mother ▪ **personne ne peut la ~** she's irreplaceable ▪ **si vous ne pouvez pas venir, faites-vous ~** if you can't come, get someone to stand in for you ▪ **on l'a remplacé pendant la seconde mi-temps** he was taken off *ou* substituted during the second half ▪ **tu as l'air épuisé, je vais te ~** you look exhausted, I'll take over from you.
◆ **se remplacer** *vp (emploi passif)* to be replaced ▪ **une sœur, ça ne se remplace pas** there's no substitute for a sister ▪ **une secrétaire comme ça, ça ne se remplace pas** you won't find another secretary like her.

rempli, e [rɑ̃pli] *adj* : **j'ai eu une journée bien ~e** I've had a very full *ou* busy day ▪ **un emploi du temps très** *ou* **bien ~** a very busy schedule ▪ **j'ai le ventre bien ~, ça va mieux!** *fam* I feel a lot better for that meal!

remplir [32] [rɑ̃plir] *vt* **1.** [emplir] to fill ▪ **le vase est rempli à ras bord** the vase is full to the brim ▪ **on ne remplit plus les salles avec des comédies** comedy doesn't pull audiences *ou* fill the house anymore ▪ **la cave est remplie de bons vins** the cellar is filled *ou* stocked with good wines ▪ **l'accident a rempli les premières pages des journaux** the front pages of the newspapers were full of news about the accident **2.** [compléter - questionnaire, dossier] to fill in *ou* out *(sép)* ; [- chèque] to fill *ou* to make out *(sép)* ▪ **elle a rempli des pages et des pages** she wrote pages and pages **3.** [combler - trou] to fill in *(sép)* **4.** [accomplir - engagement] to fulfil ; [- fonction, mission] to carry out *(sép)* **5.** [satisfaire - condition] to fulfil, to satisfy, to meet ; [- besoin] to meet, to satisfy **6.** [d'émotion] : **~ qqn de joie/d'espoir** to fill sb with joy/with hope ▪ **être rempli de soi-même/de son importance** to be full of o.s./of one's own importance.
◆ **se remplir** ◇ *vpi* to fill (up) ▪ **le ciel s'est rapidement rempli de nuages noirs** the sky quickly filled with dark clouds.
◇ *vpt* : **se ~ l'estomac** *fam ou* **la panse** *fam* to stuff o.s. *ou* one's face△.

remplissage [rɑ̃plisaʒ] *nm* **1.** [d'une fosse, d'un récipient] filling (up) **2.** *fig* [d'un texte] padding ▪ **faire du ~** to pad **3.** CONSTR studwork ▪ **~ en briques** nogging **4.** MUS filling-in.

remploi [rɑ̃plwa] *nm* **1.** [d'un travailleur] re-employment **2.** [d'une machine, de matériaux] reuse **3.** FIN reinvestment.

remployer [13] [rɑ̃plwaje] *vt* **1.** [travailleur] to take on *(sép)* again, to re-employ **2.** [machine] to reuse, to use again **3.** FIN to reinvest.

remplumer [3] [rɑ̃plyme] ◆ **se remplumer** *vpi fam* **1.** [physiquement] to fill out again, to put weight back on **2.** [financièrement] to improve one's cash flow, to straighten out one's cash situation ▪ **il a réussi à se ~ en vendant ses tableaux** he managed to improve his cash flow situation by selling his paintings.

rempocher [3] [rɑ̃pɔʃe] *vt* to pocket again, to put back in one's pocket.

remporter [3] [rɑ̃pɔrte] *vt* **1.** [reprendre] to take back *(sép)* **2.** [obtenir] to win, to get ▪ **~ un prix** to carry off *ou* to win a prize ▪ **~ un succès** to be successful **3.** SPORT to win.

rempoter [3] [rɑ̃pɔte] *vt* to repot.

remprunter [3] [rɑ̃prœ̃te] *vt* **1.** [emprunter - de nouveau] to borrow again ; [- en supplément] to borrow more **2.** [route] : **~ le même chemin** to take the same road again.

remuant, e [rəmɥɑ̃, ɑ̃t] *adj* **1.** [agité] restless, fidgety ■ **que cet enfant est ~!** that child never sits still! **2.** [entreprenant] energetic, active, lively ■ **son parti trouve qu'il est un peu trop ~** his party finds him somewhat over-enthusiastic *euphém.*

remue-ménage [rəmymenaʒ] *nm inv* **1.** [d'objets] jumble, disorder ■ **il a fallu tout déménager, tu aurais vu le ~ dans le bureau hier** we had to move out all the furniture, you should've seen the mess *ou* shambles in the office yesterday **2.** [agitation bruyante] commotion, hurly-burly, rumpus.

remue-méninges [rəmymenɛ̃ʒ] *nm inv* brainstorming.

remuement [rəmymɑ̃] *nm litt* movement, moving, stirring.

remuer [7] [rəmɥe] <> *vt* **1.** [agiter] to move, to shift ■ **~ les lèvres** to move one's lips ■ **~ les bras** to wave one's arms (about) ■ **la brise remue les branches/les herbes** the breeze is stirring the branches/the grass ■ **le chien remuait la queue** the dog was wagging its tail **2.** [déplacer - objet] to move, to shift **3.** [retourner - cendres] to poke ; [- terre, compost] to turn over *(sép)* ; [- salade] to toss ; [- boisson, préparation] to stir ■ **~ des fortunes** *ou* **de grosses sommes** to handle huge amounts of money ◐ **~ ciel et terre** to move heaven and earth, to leave no stone unturned **4.** *sout* [ressasser] to stir up *(sép)*, to brood over *(sép)* ■ **~ des souvenirs** to turn *ou* to go over memories **5.** [troubler] to move ■ **être (tout)/profondément remué** to be (very)/deeply moved.
<> *vi* **1.** [s'agiter - nez, oreille] to twitch ■ **la queue du chien/du chat/du cheval remuait** the dog was wagging/the cat was wagging/the horse was flicking its tail **2.** [branler - dent, manche] to be loose **3.** [bouger] to move ■ [gigoter] to fidget ■ **les gosses, ça remue tout le temps** *fam* kids can't stop fidgeting *ou* never keep still ■ **qu'est-ce qui remue dans le panier?** what's that moving about in the basket? **4.** *fig* to get restless ■ **les mineurs commencent à ~** the miners are getting restless.
◆ **se remuer** *vpi* **1.** [bouger] to move ■ **j'ai besoin de me ~ un peu** *pr* I need to move around *ou* to walk around a bit ; *fig* I need to wake myself up a bit **2.** [se démener] to put o.s. out ■ **il a fallu que je me remue pour t'inscrire** I had to go to a lot of trouble to get you on the course.

remugle [rəmygl] *nm litt* mustiness, fustiness.

rémunérateur, trice [remyneratœr, tris] *adj* [investissement] remunerative ■ [emploi] lucrative, well-paid.

rémunération [remynerasjɔ̃] *nf* remuneration, payment ■ **sa ~** his income *ou* earnings.

rémunérer [18] [remynere] *vt* to remunerate, to pay ■ **travail bien/mal rémunéré** well-paid/badly-paid work ■ **vous êtes-vous fait ~ pour ce travail?** did you get paid for this job?

renâcler [3] [rənakle] *vi* **1.** [cheval] to snort **2.** [personne] to grumble, to moan ■ **il a accepté en renâclant** he reluctantly accepted ■ **~ à faire qqch** to be (very) loath *ou* reluctant to do sthg ■ **~ à une tâche** to recoil from a task.

renais, renaissait *etc v* ⊳ **renaître.**

renaissance [rənɛsɑ̃s] *nf* **1.** [réincarnation] rebirth **2.** [renouveau] revival, rebirth.

Renaissance [rənɛsɑ̃s] <> *nf* : **la ~** the Renaissance (period).
<> *adj inv* ARCHIT & ART Renaissance *(modif)*.

renaissant, e [rənɛsɑ̃, ɑ̃t] *adj* **1.** [intérêt, enthousiasme] renewed ■ [douleur] recurring ■ [économie] reviving ■ **leur amour ~** their new-found love ■ **sans cesse ~** [espoir] ever renewed ; [problème] ever recurring **2.** ARCHIT & ART Renaissance *(modif)*.

renaître [92] [rənɛtr] *vi (inusité aux temps composés)* **1.** [naître de nouveau - gén] to come back to life, to come to life again ; [- végétation] to spring up again ■ **se sentir ~** to feel like a new person ■ **~ à** *litt* : **~ à la vie** to come alive again ■ **~ à l'espoir/l'amour** to find new hope/a new love ◐ **~ de ses cendres** to rise from the ashes **2.** [revenir - jour] to dawn ; [- courage, économie] to revive, to recover ; [- bonheur, espoir] to return ■ **faire ~ le passé/un antagonisme** to revive the past/an antagonism ■ **l'espoir renaît dans l'équipe/le village** the team/the village has found fresh hope ■ **l'espoir** *ou* **l'espérance renaît toujours** hope springs eternal.

rénal, e, aux [renal, o] *adj* kidney *(modif)*, renal *spéc.*

renaquit *etc v* ⊳ **renaître.**

renard [rənar] *nm* **1.** ZOOL fox ■ **~ argenté/bleu** silver/blue fox **2.** [fourrure] fox fur ■ **un manteau en ~ argenté** a silver fox fur coat **3.** *fig* **vieux ~** (sly) old fox, cunning old devil.

renarde [rənard] *nf* ZOOL vixen.

renardeau, x [rənardo] *nm* fox cub.

renardière [rənardjɛr] *nf* **1.** [tanière] fox's earth *ou* den **2.** *Québec* [élevage] fox farm.

Renaudot [rənodo] *npr* : **le prix ~** *annual literary prize for a work of fiction.*

rencaisser [4] [rɑ̃kese] *vt* **1.** HORT to plant in a tub **2.** FIN [toucher] to cash again ■ [remettre en caisse] to put back in the till.

rencard△ [rɑ̃kar] = **rancard.**

renchérir [32] [rɑ̃ʃerir] *vi* **1.** [devenir plus cher] to become more expensive, to go up **2.** [faire une surenchère] to make a higher bid, to bid higher.
◆ **renchérir sur** *v+prép* [obj: personne] to outbid ■ [obj: enchère] to bid higher than ■ [en actes ou en paroles] to go further than, to outdo ■ **il renchérit toujours sur ce que dit sa femme** he always goes further *ou* one better than his wife.

renchérissement [rɑ̃ʃerismɑ̃] *nm* increase, rise ■ **un ~ des produits laitiers** an increase *ou* a rise in the price of dairy products.

rencontre [rɑ̃kɔ̃tr] *nf* **1.** [entrevue] meeting, encounter ■ **faire la ~ de qqn** to meet sb ■ **faire beaucoup de ~s** to meet a lot of people ■ **faire une ~** to meet someone ■ **faire une mauvaise ~** to have an unpleasant encounter ■ **faire des mauvaises ~s** to meet the wrong kind of people ■ **aller** *ou* **marcher à la ~ de qqn** to go to meet sb **2.** [conférence] meeting, conference ◐ **~ au sommet** summit meeting **3.** SPORT match, game, fixture *UK* ■ **une ~ d'athlétisme** an athletics meeting **4.** [combat] engagement, encounter ■ HIST duel **5.** [jonction - de deux fleuves] confluence ; [- de deux routes] junction.
◆ **de rencontre** *loc adj* [liaison] passing, casual ■ [amitié] chance *(modif)*.

rencontrer [3] [rɑ̃kɔ̃tre] *vt* **1.** [croiser] to meet, to encounter *sout* ■ [faire la connaissance de] to meet ■ **je l'ai rencontré (par hasard) au marché** I met him (by chance) *ou* ran into him at the market ■ **je lui ai fait ~ quelqu'un qui peut l'aider professionnellement** I've put him in touch with somebody who can offer him professional help **2.** [donner audience à] to meet, to have a meeting with **3.** [affronter] to meet ■ SPORT to play against *(insép)*, to meet **4.** [heurter] to strike, to hit **5.** [trouver] to meet with, to come across ■ **sans ~ la moindre résistance** without meeting with *ou* experiencing the least resistance ■ **~ l'amour/Dieu** to find love/God.
◆ **se rencontrer** <> *vp (emploi réciproque)* **1.** [se trouver en présence] to meet ■ **c'est elle qui les a fait se ~** she arranged for them to meet ◐ **comme on se rencontre!** it's a small world! **2.** SPORT to play (against), to meet **3.** [se rejoindre - fleuves] to meet, to join ; [- routes] to meet, to merge ■ **leurs yeux** *ou* **regards se sont rencontrés** their eyes met.
<> *vp (emploi passif)* : **un homme intègre, ça ne se rencontre pas souvent** it's not often you come across *ou* meet an honest man ■ *(tournure impersonnelle)* **il se rencontrera toujours des gens pour nier la vérité** you will always find people who deny the truth.

rendement [rɑ̃dmɑ̃] *nm* **1.** [production] output **2.** [rentabilité] productivity ■ **le ~ de cette machine est supérieur** this machine is more productive **3.** [efficacité] efficiency ■ **mon ~ s'en est trouvé affecté** I'm not as efficient because of it **4.** AGRIC yield ■ **le ~ de ces champs est faible** those fields give a low yield ■ **une terre sans aucun ~** a land that yields no return **5.** FIN yield, return ■ **à haut/bas ~** high-/low-yield **6.** CHIM yield **7.** ÉLECTR & PHYS efficiency.

rendez-vous [rɑ̃devu] *nm inv* **1.** [rencontre] appointment ■ **prendre ~** to make an appointment ■ **j'ai ~ chez le médecin** I have an appointment with the doctor ■ **donner ~ à qqn** to make an appointment with sb ■ **se donner ~** to arrange to meet ■ **avez-vous ~?** do you have an appointment? ■ **~ chez**

mes parents à 10 h let's meet at 10 o'clock at my parents' (house) ■ **un ~ manqué** a missed meeting ■ **c'était un ~ manqué** we/they didn't meet up ■ **son premier ~** [amoureux] her first date ◆ **~ spatial** ASTRONAUT docking in space **2.** [endroit] meeting place ■ **j'étais le premier au ~** I was the first one to turn up *ou* to arrive ■ **ici, c'est le ~ des étudiants** this is where all the students meet.

Voir module d'usage

rendormir [36] [rɑ̃dɔrmir] *vt* to put *ou* to send back to sleep.
◆ **se rendormir** *vpi* to go back to sleep, to fall asleep again ■ **je n'arrive pas à me ~** I can't get back to sleep.

rendre [73] [rɑ̃dr] ◇ *vt* **1.** [restituer - objet prêté ou donné] to give back *(sép)*, to return ; [- objet volé] to give back *(sép)*, to return ; [- objet défectueux] to take back *(sép)*, to return ; [- somme] to pay back *(sép)* ; [- réponse] to give ■ **il est venu ~ la chaise** he brought the chair back ■ **donne-moi trente euros, je te les rendrai demain** give me thirty euros, I'll pay you back *ou* I'll give it back to you tomorrow ■ **~ un devoir** [élève] to hand *ou* to give in a piece of work ; [professeur] to hand *ou* to give back a piece of work ■ **~ un otage** to return *ou* to hand over a hostage
2. [donner en retour] to return ■ **~ un baiser à qqn** to kiss sb back ■ **~ le bien pour le mal/coup pour coup** to return good for evil/ blow for blow ■ **elle m'a rendu cinq euros de trop** she gave me five euros (change) too much ■ **~ la monnaie (sur)** to give change (out of *ou* from) ■ **elle me méprise, mais je le lui rends bien** she despises me, but the feeling's mutual
3. *(suivi d'un adj)* [faire devenir] to make ■ **~ qqch public** to make sthg public ■ **~ qqn aveugle** *pr* to make sb (go) blind, to blind sb ; *fig* to blind sb ■ **~ qqn fou** to drive *ou* to make sb mad
4. [faire recouvrer] : **~ l'ouïe/la santé/la vue à qqn** to restore sb's hearing/health/sight, to give sb back his hearing/health/ sight ■ **l'opération ne lui a pas rendu l'usage de la parole/de son bras** the operation did not give him back the power of speech/the use of his arm ■ **tu m'as rendu l'espoir** you've given me new hope ■ **~ son honneur à qqn** to restore sb's honour ■ **~ sa forme à un chapeau** to pull a hat back into shape
5. [exprimer - personnalité] to portray, to capture ; [- nuances, pensée] to convey, to render *sout*, to express ■ **voyons comment il a rendu cette scène à l'écran** [metteur en scène] let's see how he transferred this scene to the screen ■ **l'enregistrement ne rend pas la qualité de sa voix** the recording doesn't do justice to the quality of her voice
6. [produire] : **ici le mur rend un son creux** the wall sounds hollow here ■ **ça ne rend rien** *ou* **pas grand-chose** [décor, couleurs] it doesn't look much ■ **les photos n'ont pas rendu grand-chose** the pictures didn't come out very well ■ **mes recherches n'ont encore rien rendu** my research hasn't come up with anything yet *ou* hasn't produced any results yet
7. CULIN to give out *(sép)*
8. [vomir - repas] to vomit, to bring up *(sép)*
9. [prononcer - jugement, arrêt] to pronounce ; [- verdict] to deliver, to return ■ **~ une sentence** to pass *ou* to pronounce sentence ■ **~ un oracle** to prophesy
10. AGRIC & HORT [produire] to yield, to have a yield of.
◇ *vi* **1.** AGRIC & HORT to be productive ■ **les vignes ont bien rendu** the vineyards have given a good yield *ou* have produced well ■ **cette terre ne rend pas** this land is unproductive *ou* yields no return
2. [ressortir] to be effective ■ **ce tapis rend très bien/ne rend pas très bien avec les rideaux** this carpet looks really good/ doesn't look much with the curtains
3. [vomir] to vomit, to be sick.
◆ **se rendre** *vpi* **1.** [criminel] to give o.s. up, to surrender ■ [ville] to surrender ■ **se ~ à la police** to give o.s. up to the police ■ **rendez-vous!** give yourself up!, surrender! ■ **il a fini par se ~** *fig* he finally gave in
2. *(suivi d'un adj)* [devenir] to make o.s. ■ **rends-toi utile!** make yourself useful! ■ **ne te rends pas malade pour ça!** it's not worth making yourself ill about *ou* over it!
3. [aller] to go ■ **je me rends à l'école à pied/à vélo/en voiture** I walk/ride (my bike)/drive to school, I go to school on foot/by bike/by car ■ **il s'y rend en train** he goes *ou* gets *ou* travels there by train ■ **les pompiers se sont rendus sur les lieux** the fire brigade went to *ou* arrived on the scene.
◆ **se rendre à** *vp+prép* [accepter] to yield to ■ **se ~ à l'avis de ses supérieurs** to bow to the opinion of one's superiors ■ **se ~ à la raison** to give in to reason ■ **se ~ à l'évidence** [être lucide] to face facts ; [reconnaître les faits] to acknowledge *ou* to recognize the facts.

rendu, e [rɑ̃dy] *adj* **1.** [arrivé] : **nous/vous voilà ~s** here we/ you are **2.** [harassé] exhausted, worn *ou* tired out.
◆ **rendu** *nm* **1.** COMM return **2.** ART rendering.

rêne [rɛn] *nf* [courroie] rein ■ *fig* **lâcher les ~s** to slacken the reins ■ **prendre les ~** to take over the reins ■ **c'est lui qui tient les ~s (à la direction)** he's the one who's really in charge (up in management).

renégat, e [rənega, at] *nm, f sout* renegade.

renégocier [9] [rənegɔsje] *vt* [contrat] to renegotiate ■ [dette] to reschedule.

renfermé, e [rɑ̃fɛrme] *adj* uncommunicative, withdrawn, silent ■ **elle est du genre ~** she's the uncommunicative type.
◆ **renfermé** *nm* : **une odeur de ~** a stale *ou* musty smell ■ **ça sent le ~ ici** it smells musty in here.

renfermer [3] [rɑ̃fɛrme] *vt* to hold, to contain ■ **son histoire renferme une part de vérité** there's some truth in what he says.
◆ **se renfermer** *vpi* to withdraw (into o.s.)

renfiler [3] [rɑ̃file] *vt* [aiguille] to rethread, to thread again ■ [perles] to restring ■ [vêtement] to slip back into.

renflé, e [rɑ̃fle] *adj* [colonne, forme] bulging, bulbous.

renflement [rɑ̃fləmɑ̃] *nm* [d'une colonne, d'un vase] bulge ■ **la poche forme un ~ à hauteur de la hanche** the pocket bulges (out) at the hip.

LES RENDEZ-VOUS

Can I see you tonight? Est-ce qu'on peut se voir ce soir ?

Why don't we go for a drink sometime? On pourrait aller prendre un verre un de ces jours ?

How about meeting up next week? Et si on se voyait la semaine prochaine ?

Let's get together soon. On se revoit bientôt, d'accord ?

Are you free any time next week? Tu es libre la semaine prochaine ?

How about Friday? Vendredi, ça te va ?

Would Monday at 10.30 be OK? Lundi 10 h 30, ça irait ?

Can you make Tuesday lunchtime? Tu es libre mardi midi ?

When's a good time for you? Quand est-ce que ça t'arrange ?

When is the best time for you? *ou* **When would suit you best?** Quand est-ce que ça t'irait le mieux ?

Let's say tomorrow outside the cinema at 7.30. Disons demain devant le cinéma à 19 h 30.

See you on Friday then! À vendredi, alors !

I look forward to it! Ce sera sympa !

It's a date, then! C'est d'accord !

renfler [3] [rɑ̃fle] *vt* : **le pigeon renfla ses plumes** the pigeon fluffed up its feathers.

renflouage [rɑ̃fluaʒ], **renflouement** [rɑ̃flumɑ̃] *nm* **1.** NAUT refloating **2.** ÉCON bailing out, refloating.

renflouer [3] [rɑ̃flue] *vt* **1.** NAUT to refloat **2.** [entreprise, projet] to bail out *(sép)* ▪ **ça va ~ nos finances** that will bail us out.

renfoncement [rɑ̃fɔ̃smɑ̃] *nm* **1.** [dans un mur] recess, hollow **2.** IMPR indentation.

renfoncer [rɑ̃fɔ̃se] *vt* [bouchon] to push further in ▪ [clou] to knock further in ▪ [chapeau] to pull down.

renforcement [rɑ̃fɔrsəmɑ̃] *nm* **1.** [augmentation] reinforcement ▪ **le ~ des pouvoirs du président** the strengthening of the President's powers **2.** PHOTO intensification **3.** PSYCHOL reinforcement.

renforcer [16] [rɑ̃fɔrse] *vt* **1.** CONSTR & COUT to reinforce **2.** [grossir - effectif, service d'ordre] to reinforce, to strengthen ▪ **le candidat choisi viendra ~ notre équipe de chercheurs** the ideal candidate will join our team of researchers **3.** [affermir - conviction] to reinforce, to strengthen, to intensify ▪ **il m'a renforcé dans mon opinion** he confirmed me in my belief **4.** [mettre en relief] to set off *(sép)*, to enhance **5.** PSYCHOL to reinforce.
◆ **se renforcer** *vpi* [devenir plus fort] to become stronger, to be consolidated ▪ **sa popularité s'est beaucoup renforcée** his popularity has greatly increased *ou* has grown considerably ▪ **notre équipe se renforce maintenant de plusieurs jeunes ingénieurs** our team has now been strengthened by the arrival of several young engineers.

renfort [rɑ̃fɔr] *nm* **1.** [aide] reinforcement ▪ **il amène toujours sa sœur en ~** he always brings his sister along to back him up **2.** [pièce de tissu] lining ▪ **collant avec ~s aux talons/à l'entrejambe** tights with reinforced heels/gusset **3.** TECHNOL reinforcement.
◆ **renforts** *nmpl* MIL [soldats] reinforcements ▪ [matériel] (fresh) supplies.
◆ **à grand renfort de** *loc prép* with a lot of, with much ▪ **il s'expliquait à grand ~ de gestes** he expressed himself with the help of a great many gestures.
◆ **de renfort** *loc adj* reinforcement *(modif)*.

renfrogné, e [rɑ̃frɔɲe] *adj* [air, visage] sullen, dour ▪ [personne] sulky, dour ▪ **il est toujours ~** he's always sulking.

renfrogner [3] [rɑ̃frɔɲe] ◆ **se renfrogner** *vpi* to scowl, to frown ▪ **elle se renfrognait quand on parlait de lui** she became sullen whenever his name was mentioned.

rengager [17] [rɑ̃gaʒe] *vt* [combat] to re-engage ▪ [conversation] to start again, to take up *(sép)* again ▪ [employé] to re-engage, to take on *(sép)* again ▪ [argent] to reinvest, to plough back *(sép)*.
◆ **se rengager** *vpi* MIL to re-enlist, to join up again.

rengaine [rɑ̃gɛn] *nf* **1.** [refrain] (old) tune, (old) song **2.** *fig* **avec eux, c'est toujours la même ~** they never change their tune, with them it's always the same (old) story.

rengainer [4] [rɑ̃gɛne] *vt* **1.** [arme] : **~ un revolver** to put a revolver back in its holster ▪ **~ une épée** to put a sword back in its sheath **2.** *fig* to hold back *(sép)*, to contain ▪ **tu peux ~ tes compliments** you can keep your compliments to yourself.

rengorger [17] [rɑ̃gɔrʒe] ◆ **se rengorger** *vpi* **1.** [volatile] to puff out its throat **2.** [personne] to puff o.s. up ▪ **il se rengorge quand on lui parle de sa pièce** he puffs up with pride when you talk to him about his play.

reniement [rənimɑ̃] *nm* [d'une promesse] breaking ▪ [de sa famille] disowning, repudiation *sout* ▪ [d'un principe] renouncing, abandonment, giving up.

renier [9] [rənje] *vt* [promesse] to break ▪ [famille, patrie] to disown, to repudiate *sout* ▪ [religion] to renounce ▪ **Pierre a renié Jésus par trois fois** Peter denied Christ three times.
◆ **se renier** *vpi* to retract.

reniflement [rənifləmɑ̃] *nm* [action - en pleurant] sniffing, sniffling ; [- à cause d'un rhume] snuffling ▪ [bruit] sniff, sniffle, snuffle ▪ **~s** snivelling.

renifler [3] [rənifle] <> *vt* **1.** [humer] to sniff at *(insép)* ▪ **~ le bouquet d'un vin** to smell a wine's bouquet **2.** [aspirer par le nez] : **~ de la cocaïne** to sniff cocaine **3.** *fam fig* to sniff out *(sép)* ▪ **~ une histoire louche** to smell a rat.
<> *vi* [en pleurant] to sniffle ▪ [à cause d'un rhume] to snuffle, to sniff.

renifleur, euse [rənifløer, øz] *fam* <> *adj* sniffing, sniffling, snuffling.
<> *nm, f* sniffer, sniffler, snuffler.

renne [rɛn] *nm* reindeer.

renom [rənɔ̃] *nm* **1.** [notoriété] fame, renown ▪ **il doit son ~ à son invention** he became famous thanks to his invention **2.** *litt* [réputation] reputation.
◆ **de renom, en renom** *loc adj* famous, renowned ▪ **un musicien de (grand) ~** a musician of high renown *ou* repute.

renommé, e [rənɔme] *adj* [célèbre] famous, renowned, celebrated ▪ **~ pour : elle est ~e pour ses omelettes** she's famous for her omelettes.
◆ **renommée** *nf* **1.** [notoriété] fame, repute ▪ **un musicien de ~e internationale** a world-famous musician, a musician of international repute ▪ **ce vin est digne de sa ~e** this wine is worthy of its reputation ▪ **de bonne/fâcheuse ~e** of good/ill repute **2.** *litt* [rumeur publique] public opinion.

renommer [3] [rənɔme] *vt* **1.** [à un poste] to reappoint, to renominate **2.** INFORM to rename.

renonce [rənɔ̃s] *nf* JEUX : **je fais une ~** I can't follow suit.

renoncement [rənɔ̃smɑ̃] *nm* renunciation ▪ **vivre dans le ~** to live a life of renunciation *ou* abnegation.

renoncer [16] [rənɔ̃se] *vi* JEUX to give up *ou* in.
◆ **renoncer à** *v+prép* [gén] to renounce, to give up ▪ [projet, métier] to give up, to abandon ▪ [habitude] to give up ▪ **elle ne veut à aucun prix ~ à son indépendance** nothing would make her give up her independence ▪ **~ au monde** RELIG to renounce the world ▪ *(en usage absolu)* **je ne renoncerai jamais** I'll never give up.

renonciation [rənɔ̃sjasjɔ̃] *nf* **1.** *sout* [renoncement] renunciation **2.** DR release.

renoncule [rənɔ̃kyl] *nf* buttercup, ranunculus *spéc.*

renouer [6] [rənwe] <> *vt* **1.** [rattacher - ruban, cravate] to retie, to tie again, to reknot **2.** [reprendre - discussion] to resume, to renew ▪ **~ une liaison** to rekindle *ou* to revive an old affair.
<> *vi* to get back together again ▪ **~ avec : j'ai renoué avec mes vieux amis** I've taken up with my old friends again ▪ **~ avec la tradition/l'usage** to revive traditions/customs.

renouveau, x [rənuvo] *nm* **1.** [renaissance] revival ▪ **connaître un ~** to undergo a revival **2.** [recrudescence] : **un ~ de succès** renewed success **3.** *litt* [retour du printemps] springtime, springtide.

renouvelable [rənuvlabl] *adj* **1.** [offre] repeatable ▪ [permis, bail, abonnement] renewable ▪ **l'expérience est facilement ~** the experience is easy to repeat ▪ **énergie ~** renewable energy ▪ **non ~** nonrenewable **2.** ADMIN & POLIT : **le comité est ~ tous les ans** the committee must stand *UK ou* run *US* for office each year ▪ **mon mandat est ~** I am eligible to stand *UK ou* run *US* (for office) again **3.** ÉCOL & DR renewable.

renouveler [24] [rənuvle] *vt* **1.** [prolonger] to renew ▪ **~ un abonnement/un permis de séjour** to renew a subscription/a residence permit ▪ **le crédit a été renouvelé pour six mois** the credit arrangement was extended for a further six months ▪ **ordonnance à ~** repeat prescription, prescription to be renewed **2.** [répéter] to renew, to repeat ▪ **~ un exploit/une tentative** to repeat a feat/an attempt ▪ **il faudra ~ votre candidature** you'll have to apply again *ou* to reapply ▪ **avec une ardeur renouvelée** with renewed vigour ▪ **j'ai préféré ne pas ~ l'expérience** I chose not to repeat the experience **3.** [changer] to renew, to change ▪ **~ l'eau d'un l'aquarium** to change the water in an aquarium ▪ **~ l'air d'une pièce** to let some fresh

air into a room ■ ~ **sa garde-robe** to get *ou* to buy some new clothes ■ **elle a renouvelé le genre policier** she gave the detective story new life **4.** [réélire - groupe, assemblée] to re-elect.
◆ **se renouveler** *vpi* **1.** [se reproduire] to recur, to occur again and again ■ **je te promets que cela ne se renouvellera pas** I promise you it won't happen again **2.** [changer de style] to change one's style ■ **c'est un bon acteur mais il ne se renouvelle pas assez** he's a good actor but he doesn't vary his roles enough **3.** [groupe, assemblée] to be re-elected *ou* replaced.

renouvellement [rənuvɛlmɑ̃] *nm* **1.** [reconduction] renewal ■ **solliciter le ~ d'un mandat** to stand *UK ou* to run *US* for re-election **2.** [répétition] repetition, recurrence **3.** [changement] : **procéder au ~ d'une équipe** to change the line-up of a team ■ **la marée assure le ~ de l'eau dans les viviers** the water in the tanks is changed by the action of the tide ■ **dans la mode actuelle, il n'y a aucun ~** there are no new ideas in (the world of) fashion today ▶ ~ **de stock** restocking.

renouvellerai *etc v* ▷ **renouveler**.

rénovateur, trice [renɔvatœr, tris] ◇ *adj* reformist, reforming.
◇ *nm, f* reformer ■ **les grands ~s de la science** the people who revolutionized *ou* radically transformed science.
◆ **rénovateur** *nm* [pour nettoyer] restorer.

rénovation [renɔvasjɔ̃] *nf* **1.** [d'un meuble, d'un immeuble] renovation ■ [d'un quartier] redevelopment, renovation ■ **la maison est en ~** the house is being done up *ou* is having a complete facelift ▶ ~ **urbaine** urban renewal **2.** *fig* [rajeunissement] updating.

rénover [3] [renɔve] *vt* **1.** [remettre à neuf - meuble] to restore, to renovate ; [- immeuble] to renovate, to do up *(sép)* ; [- quartier] to redevelop, to renovate ; [- salle de bains] to modernize ■ **toute la façade ouest a été rénovée** the whole of the west front has been done up *ou* has been given a facelift **2.** [transformer en améliorant] : ~ **des méthodes pédagogiques** to update teaching methods ■ ~ **les institutions politiques** to reform political institutions.

renseignement [rɑ̃sɛɲəmɑ̃] *nm* **1.** [information] piece of information, information *(U)* ■ **de précieux ~s** (some) invaluable information ■ **pour avoir de plus amples ~s, s'adresser à...** for further information *ou* details, apply to... ■ **demander un ~** *ou* **des ~s à qqn** to ask sb for information ■ **prendre des ~s sur** to make enquiries about ■ **~s pris, elle était la seule héritière** after making some enquiries it turned out (that) she was the sole heir ■ **tu n'obtiendras aucun ~** you won't get any information ■ **merci pour le ~** thanks for letting me know *pr & iron* ■ **aller aux ~s** to go and (see what one can) find out **2.** *fam* [surveillance] : **être/travailler dans le ~** to be/to work in intelligence.
◆ **renseignements** *nmpl* **1.** ADMIN [service] enquiries (department) ■ [réception] information *ou* enquiries (desk) ■ **appeler les ~s** TÉLÉCOM to phone directory enquiries *UK ou* information *US* **2.** [espionnage] : **agent/services de ~s** intelligence agent/services ■ **les Renseignements généraux** ≃ Special Branch *UK* ■ ≃ the FBI *US*.

LES RENSEIGNEMENTS GÉNÉRAUX

Created under Vichy, this agency is the intelligence arm of the Ministry of the Interior. It keeps tabs on political parties, lobby groups, and various individuals.

renseigner [4] [rɑ̃seɲe] *vt* **1.** [mettre au courant - étranger, journaliste] to give information to, to inform ; [- automobiliste] to give directions to ■ **elle vous renseignera sur les prix** she'll tell you the prices, she'll give you more information about the prices ■ **pardon, Monsieur, pouvez-vous me ~?** excuse me, sir, could you help me, please? ■ ~ **qqn sur** to tell sb about ■ **bien renseigné** well-informed ■ **mal renseigné** misinformed ■ **je suis mal renseigné sur l'horaire des marées** I don't have much information about the times of the tides **2.** [donner des indices à] : **seule sa biographie peut nous ~ sur son passé militaire** only his biography can tell us something of *ou* about his military career ■ **nous voilà bien renseignés!** *iron* that doesn't get us very far!, that doesn't give us much to go on!
◆ **se renseigner** *vpi* to make enquiries ■ **se ~ sur qqn/qqch** to find out about sb/sthg ■ **il aurait fallu se ~ sur son compte** you should have made (some) enquiries about him ■ **renseignez-vous auprès de votre agence de voyages** ask your travel agent for further information.

rentabilisation [rɑ̃tabilizasjɔ̃] *nf* : **la ~ de l'affaire prendra peu de temps** it will not be long before the business becomes profitable *ou* starts to make a profit.

rentabiliser [3] [rɑ̃tabilize] *vt* to make profitable.

rentabilité [rɑ̃tabilite] *nf* profitability ■ **taux de ~** rate of profit.

rentable [rɑ̃tabl] *adj* profitable ■ **si je les vends moins cher, ce n'est plus ~** if I sell them any cheaper, I no longer make a profit *ou* any money ■ **c'est plus ~ d'acheter que de louer en ce moment** you're better off buying than renting at the moment.

rente [rɑ̃t] *nf* **1.** [revenu] private income ■ **avoir des ~s** to have a private income, to have independent means ■ **vivre de ses ~s** to live on *ou* off one's private income **2.** [pension] pension, annuity, rente *spéc* ■ **servir une ~ à qqn** to pay sb an allowance ▶ ~ **viagère** life annuity **3.** ÉCON rent ■ ~ **foncière** ground rent **4.** BOURSE (government) bond ■ **~s amortissables** redeemable securities *ou* bonds ■ **~s consolidées** BANQUE consols ■ **~s perpétuelles** undated *ou* irredeemable securities.

rentier, ère [rɑ̃tje, ɛr] *nm, f* person of private means ■ **mener une vie de ~** to live a life of ease ▶ ~ **viager** life annuitant.

rentrant, e [rɑ̃trɑ̃, ɑ̃t] *adj* AÉRON : **train d'atterrissage ~** retractable undercarriage.

rentré, e [rɑ̃tre] *adj* **1.** [refoulé] suppressed ■ **colère/jalousie ~e** suppressed anger/jealousy **2.** [creux] : **des joues ~es** hollow *ou* sunken cheeks.

rentrée [rɑ̃tre] *nf* **1.** ÉDUC : ~ **(scolaire** *ou* **des classes)** start of the (new) academic year ■ **depuis la ~ de Noël/Pâques** since the spring/summer term began, since the Christmas/Easter break ■ **la ~ est fixée au 6 septembre** school starts again *ou* schools reopen on September 6th ■ **j'irai le mardi de la ~** I'll go on the first Tuesday of the (new) term ■ **c'est quand, la ~, chez vous?** when do you go back? *(to school, college etc)* ■ **les vitrines de la ~** back-to-school window displays **2.** [au Parlement] reopening (of Parliament), new (parliamentary) session ▶ **faire sa ~ politique** [après les vacances] to start the new political season *(after the summer)* ; [après une absence] to make one's (political) comeback
3. [saison artistique] : **la ~ musicale/théâtrale** the new musical/theatrical season *(after the summer break)* ■ **le disque sortira à la ~** the record will be released in the autumn *UK ou* fall *US* ■ **pour votre ~ parisienne** [après les vacances] for the start of your autumn *UK ou* fall *US* season in Paris ; [après une absence] for your Paris comeback
4. [retour - des vacances d'été] (beginning of the) autumn *UK ou* fall *US* ; [- de congé ou de week-end] return to work ■ **la ~ a été dure** it was hard to get back to work after the summer holidays *UK ou* vacation *US* ■ TRANSP city-bound traffic
5. JEUX pick-up
6. [des foins] bringing *ou* taking in.
◆ **rentrées** *nfpl* FIN income, money coming in ■ **avoir des ~s (d'argent) régulières** to have a regular income *ou* money coming in regularly ▶ **~s de caisse** cash receipts ■ **~s fiscales** tax receipts *ou* revenue.

LA RENTRÉE

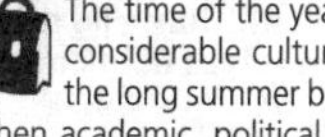

The time of the year when children go back to school has considerable cultural significance in France; coming after the long summer break or *grandes vacances*, it is the time when academic, political, social and commercial activity begins again in earnest.

rentrer [3] [rɑ̃tre] ◇ *vi (aux être)* **1.** [personne - vue de l'intérieur] to come in ; [- vue de l'extérieur] to go in ■ [chose] to go in ■ **tu es rentré dans Lyon par quelle route?** which way did you come to Lyons?, which road did you take into Lyons? ■ **impossible de faire ~ ce clou dans le mur** I can't get this nail to go into the wall ■ **la clé ne rentre pas dans la serrure** the key won't go in ■ **tu n'arriveras pas à tout faire ~ dans cette valise** you'll

never fit everything in this case ■ **c'est par là que l'eau rentre** that's where the water is coming *ou* getting in ■ [s'emboîter] to go *ou* to fit in ■ **~ dans** [poteau] to crash into ; [véhicule] to collide with ➜ **~ dedans : je lui suis rentré dedans** [en voiture] I drove straight *ou* right into him ; *fam* [verbalement] I laid into him ■ **rentre-lui dedans!** *fam* [frappe-le] smack him one!△
2. [faire partie de] to be part of, to be included in ■ **cela ne rentre pas dans mes attributions** that is not part of my duties
3. [pour travailler] : **~ dans les affaires/la police** to go into business/join the police ■ **il est rentré dans la société grâce à son oncle** he got a job with the company thanks to his uncle
4. [retourner - gén] to return, to come *ou* to get back ■ [revenir chez soi] to come *ou* to get (back) home ■ [aller chez soi] to go (back) *ou* to return home ■ **je rentre tout de suite!** I'm on my way home!, I'm coming home straightaway! ■ **les enfants, rentrez!** children, get *ou* come back in! ■ **je ne rentrerai pas dîner** I won't be home for dinner ■ **je rentre chez moi pour déjeuner** [tous les jours] I have lunch at home ■ **je vous laisse, il faut que je rentre** I'll leave you now, I must go home *ou* get (back) home ■ **en rentrant de l'école** on the way home *ou* back from school ■ **~ dans son pays** to go back *ou* to return home (to one's country)
5. [reprendre ses occupations - lycéen] to go back to school, to start school again ; [- étudiant] to go back, to start the new term ; [- école] to start again, to go back ; [- parlementaire] to start the new session, to return to take one's seat ; [- parlement] to reopen, to reassemble ; [- cinéaste] to start the season
6. [être perçu - argent] to come in ■ **faire ~ l'argent/les devises** to bring in money/foreign currency ■ **faire ~ l'impôt/les cotisations** to collect taxes/dues
7. *fam* [explication, idée, connaissances] to sink in ■ **ça rentre, l'informatique?** are you getting the hang of computing? ■ **le russe, ça rentre tout seul avec Sophie!** [elle apprend bien] Sophie is having no trouble picking up Russian! ; [elle enseigne bien] Sophie makes learning Russian easy ■ **je le lui ai expliqué dix fois, mais ça n'est toujours pas rentré** I've told him ten times but it hasn't gone *ou* sunk in yet ■ **faire ~ qqch dans la tête de qqn** to get sthg into sb's head, to drum sthg into sb
8. JEUX & SPORT : **~ dans la mêlée** RUGBY to scrum down.
◇ *vt (aux avoir)* **1.** [mettre à l'abri - linge, moisson] to bring *ou* to get in *(sép)* ; [- bétail] to bring *ou* to take in *(sép)* ; [- véhicule] to put away *(sép)* ; [- chaise] to carry *ou* to take in *(sép)*
2. [mettre - gén] to put in *(sép)* ■ [faire disparaître - antenne] to put down *(sép)* ; [- train d'atterrissage] to raise, to retract ; [- griffes] to draw in *(sép)*, to retract ■ **~ une clé dans une serrure** to put a key in a lock ■ **~ son chemisier dans sa jupe** to tuck one's blouse into one's skirt ■ **rentre ton ventre/tes fesses!** pull your stomach/bottom in! ■ **~ la tête dans les épaules** to hunch (up) one's shoulders
3. [réprimer - colère] to hold back *(sép)*, to suppress ■ **~ ses larmes/son humiliation** to swallow one's tears/humiliation
4. INFORM to input, to key in *(sép)*
5. IMPR : **~ une ligne** to indent a line.

➜ **rentrer dans** *v+prép* [recouvrer] to recover ■ **~ dans son argent/ses dépenses** to recover one's money/expenses, to get one's money/expenses back ■ **~ dans ses fonds** to recoup (one's) costs ■ **~ dans ses droits** to recover one's rights ■ **~ dans la légalité** [criminel] to reform ; [opération, manœuvre] to become legal.

➜ **rentrer en** *v+prép* : **~ en grâce auprès de qqn** to get back into sb's good graces *ou* good books ■ **~ en possession de** to regain possession of.

➜ **se rentrer** *vp (emploi passif)* : **les foins ne se rentrent pas avant juillet** the hay isn't brought in until July ■ **les rallonges se rentrent sous la table** the extension leaves fit in under the table.

➜ **se rentrer dedans** *vp (emploi réciproque) fam* **ils se sont rentrés dedans** [heurtés] they smashed *ou* banged into one another ; [disputés] they laid into one another.

renuméroter [3] [rənymerɔte] *vt* to renumber TECHNOL.

renversant, e [rɑ̃vɛrsɑ̃, ɑ̃t] *adj* [nouvelle] astounding, amazing, staggering ■ [personne] amazing, incredible.

renverse [rɑ̃vɛrs] *nf* NAUT [du vent] change ■ [du courant] turn (of tide).

➜ **à la renverse** *loc adv* : **tomber à la ~** [sur le dos] to fall flat on one's back ■ **j'ai failli tomber à la ~** I almost fell over backwards ■ **il y a de quoi tomber à la ~** *fig* it's amazing *ou* staggering.

renversé, e [rɑ̃vɛrse] *adj* **1.** [image] reverse *(modif)*, reversed, inverted ■ [objet] upside down, overturned **2.** [penché] : **le corps ~ en arrière** with the body leaning *ou* tilted back **3.** [stupéfait] : **être ~** to be staggered.

renversement [rɑ̃vɛrsəmɑ̃] *nm* **1.** [inversion] reversal ■ **~ d'une image** inversion of an image **2.** [changement] : **~ des alliances** reversal *ou* switch of alliances ➜ **~ des rôles** role reversal ■ **~ de situation** reversal of the situation ■ **~ de tendance** shift *ou* swing (in the opposite direction) **3.** [chute - d'un régime] overthrow **4.** [inclinaison - du buste, de la tête] tipping *ou* tilting back **5.** MUS inversion.

renverser [3] [rɑ̃vɛrse] *vt* **1.** [répandre - liquide] to spill ■ [faire tomber - bouteille, casserole] to spill, to knock over *(sép)*, to upset ; [- table, voiture] to overturn ■ [retourner exprès] to turn upside down **2.** [faire tomber - personne] to knock down *(sép)* ■ **être renversé par qqn** to be knocked down *ou* run over by sb ■ **se faire ~ par une voiture** to get *ou* be knocked over by a car **3.** [inverser] to reverse ■ **le Suédois renversa la situation au cours du troisième set** the Swedish player managed to turn the situation round during the third set ➜ **~ les rôles** to reverse the roles ■ **~ la vapeur** *pr* to reverse engines ; *fig* to change direction **4.** [détruire - obstacle] to overcome ; [- valeurs] to overthrow ; [- régime] to overthrow, to topple ■ **le président a été renversé** the President was thrown out of *ou* removed from office ■ **~ un gouvernement** [par la force] to overthrow *ou* to topple a government ; [par un vote] to bring down *ou* to topple a government **5.** [incliner en arrière] to tilt *ou* to tip back *(sép)* **6.** [stupéfier] to amaze, to astound.

➜ **se renverser** *vpi* **1.** [bouteille] to fall over ■ [liquide] to spill ■ [véhicule] to overturn ■ [bateau] to overturn, to capsize ■ [marée] to turn **2.** [personne] to lean over backwards ■ **se ~ sur sa chaise** to tilt back on one's chair ■ **se ~ dans un fauteuil** to lie back in an armchair.

renvoi [rɑ̃vwa] *nm* **1.** [d'un colis - gén] return, sending back ; [- par avion] flying back ; [- par bateau] shipping back ■ **'~ à l'expéditeur'** 'return to sender' **2.** TÉLÉCOM : **~ automatique** call forwarding **3.** SPORT : **~ (de la balle)** return ■ **~ en touche** touch kick, kick for touch **4.** [congédiement - d'un employé] dismissal, sacking *UK* ; [- d'un élève] expulsion **5.** [ajournement] postponement ■ **le tribunal décida le ~ du procès à huitaine** the court decided to put off *ou* to adjourn the trial for a week **6.** [transfert] transfer ■ **ordonnance de ~ aux assises** order of transfer to the assizes ■ **après le ~ du texte en commission** after the text was sent to a committee **7.** [indication] cross-reference ■ [note au bas du texte] footnote ■ **faire un ~ à** to make a cross-reference to, to cross-refer to **8.** [éructation] belch, burp ■ **ça me donne des ~s** it makes me belch *ou* burp, it repeats on me **9.** DR amendment ■ **~ des fins de poursuite** discharge of case ■ **demande de ~** application for removal of action **10.** MUS repeat mark.

renvoyer [30] [rɑ̃vwaje] *vt* **1.** [colis, formulaire] to send back *(sép)* ■ [cadeau] to return, to give back *(sép)* ■ [importun] to send away *(sép)* ■ [soldat, troupes] to discharge ■ **on les a renvoyés chez eux** they were sent (back) home *ou* discharged ■ **je le renvoie chez sa mère demain** I'm sending him back *ou* off to his mother's tomorrow **2.** [lancer de nouveau - ballon] to send back *(sép)*, to return ■ **j'étais renvoyé de vendeur en vendeur** I was being passed *ou* shunted around from one salesman to the next ➜ **~ la balle à qqn** FOOTBALL to kick *ou* to pass the ball back to sb ; RUGBY to throw *ou* to pass the ball back to sb ; TENNIS to return to sb ; *fig* to answer sb tit for tat ■ **~ l'ascenseur à qqn** *pr* to send the lift back to sb ; *fig* to return sb's favour **3.** [congédier] to dismiss ■ **tu vas te faire ~** [de ton travail] you're going to lose your job ; [de ton lycée] you're going to get yourself expelled **4.** [différer] to postpone, to put off *(sép)* ■ **la réunion est renvoyée à mardi prochain** the meeting has been put off until *ou* put back to next Tuesday **5.** [transférer] to refer ■ **l'affaire a été renvoyée en cour d'assises** the matter has been referred to the assize court **6.** [faire se reporter] to refer ■ **les numéros renvoient aux notes de fin de chapitre** the numbers refer to notes at the end of each chapter **7.** [refléter] to reflect ▪ **la glace lui renvoyait son image** she saw her reflection in the mirror ▪ [répercuter] : **la falaise nous renvoyait nos cris** the cliff echoed our cries.

◆ **se renvoyer** *vp (emploi réciproque) loc* **se ~ la balle : on peut se ~ la balle comme ça longtemps!** we could go on forever blaming each other like this! ▪ **dans cette affaire d'évasion, Français et Suisses se renvoient la balle** in this escape business, the French and Swiss authorities are trying to make each other carry the can.

réoccuper [3] [reɔkype] *vt* [usine, lieu public] to reoccupy ▪ [habitation] to move back into ▪ [emploi] to take up *(sép)* again.

réopérer [18] [reɔpere] *vt* to operate again on ▪ **il va falloir vous ~** you're going to require further surgery *sout*, you'll have to have another operation.

réorganisation [reɔrganizasjɔ̃] *nf* reorganization.

réorganiser [3] [reɔrganize] *vt* to reorganize.

◆ **se réorganiser** *vpi* to reorganize o.s., to get reorganized.

réorientation [reɔrjɑ̃tasjɔ̃] *nf* **1.** POLIT redirecting **2.** ÉDUC changing to a different course.

réorienter [3] [reɔrjɑ̃te] *vt* **1.** POLIT to reorientate, to redirect **2.** ÉDUC to put onto a different course.

réouverture [reuvɛrtyr] *nf* **1.** [d'un magasin, d'un guichet, d'un musée, d'une route, d'un col] reopening **2.** [reprise - d'un débat] resumption ▪ **à la ~ des marchés ce matin** BOURSE when trading resumed this morning.

repaie *etc v* ▻ **repayer.**

repaire [rəpɛr] *nm* **1.** [d'animaux] den, lair **2.** [d'individus] den, haunt ▪ **un ~ d'espions/de malfaiteurs** a den of spies/of criminals.

repaître [91] [rəpɛtr] *vt litt* [nourrir] to feed ▪ **~ son esprit de connaissances nouvelles** to feast one's mind on knowledge.

◆ **se repaître de** *vp+prép* **1.** *litt* [manger] to feed on *(insép)* **2.** *fig* [savourer] : **se ~ de bandes dessinées** to feast on comic strips.

répandre [74] [repɑ̃dr] *vt* **1.** [renverser - liquide] to spill ▪ [verser - sable, sciure] to spread, to sprinkle, to scatter ▪ **~ des larmes** to shed tears ▪ **~ le sang** to spill *ou* to shed blood **2.** [propager - rumeur, terreur, usage] to spread **3.** [dégager - odeur] to give off *(insép)* ; [- lumière] to shed, to give out *(insép)* ; [- chaleur, fumée] to give out *ou* off *(insép)* **4.** [dispenser - bienfaits] to pour out *(sép)*, to spread (around).

◆ **se répandre** *vpi* **1.** [eau, vin] to spill ▪ [se disperser] : **les supporters se sont répandus sur le terrain** the fans spilled (out) *ou* poured onto the field **2.** [se propager - nouvelle, mode, coutume] to spread, to become widespread ➊ **se ~ comme une traînée de poudre** to spread like wildfire **3.** [se dégager - odeur] to spread, to be given off ▪ *(tournure impersonnelle)* **il se répandit une odeur de brûlé** the smell of burning filled the air.

◆ **se répandre en** *vp+prép sout* **se ~ en compliments/en propos blessants** to be full of compliments/hurtful remarks ▪ **inutile de se ~ en commentaires là-dessus** no need to keep on (making comments) about it.

répandu, e [repɑ̃dy] *adj* widespread ▪ **un préjugé (très) ~** a very widespread *ou* widely held prejudice ▪ **une vue (très) ~e** a commonly held *ou* widely found view ▪ **la technique n'est pas encore très ~e ici** the technique isn't widely used here yet.

réparable [reparabl] *adj* **1.** [appareil] repairable ▪ **j'espère que c'est ~** I hope it can be mended *ou* repaired, I hope it's not beyond repair ▪ **la voiture n'est pas ~** [après un accident] the car is a write-off ; [à cause de sa vétusté] the car isn't worth repairing **2.** [erreur, perte] reparable ▪ **une maladresse difficilement ~** a blunder which will be hard to correct *ou* to put right.

reparaître [91] [rəparɛtr] *vi* **1.** [journal, revue] to be out again, to be published again **2.** = **réapparaître.**

réparateur, trice [reparatœr, tris] ◇ *adj* : **un sommeil ~** restorative *ou* refreshing sleep.

◇ *nm, f* repairer, repairman (*f* repairwoman) ▪ **~ d'antiquités** antiques restorer.

réparation [reparasjɔ̃] *nf* **1.** [processus] repairing, fixing, mending ▪ [résultat] repair ▪ **pendant les ~s** during (the) repairs ➊ **atelier/service de ~** repair shop/department **2.** [compensation] redress, compensation ▪ **en ~ des dégâts occasionnés** in compensation for *ou* to make up for the damage caused ▪ **demander/obtenir ~** *litt* to demand/to obtain redress **3.** DR damages, compensation ▪ **les ~s** HIST (war) reparations **4.** [correction - d'une négligence] correction ; [- d'une omission] rectification *sout.*

◆ **de réparation** *loc adj* SPORT penalty *(modif)* ▪ **surface de ~** penalty area.

◆ **en réparation** *loc adj* under repair, being repaired.

réparer [3] [repare] *vt* **1.** [appareil, chaussure] to repair, to mend ▪ [défaut de construction] to repair, to make good ▪ [meuble, porcelaine] to restore ▪ **faire ~ qqch** to get sthg repaired *ou* put right ▪ *(en usage absolu)* **aujourd'hui, les gens ne réparent plus, ils jettent** people today don't mend things, they just throw them away **2.** [compenser] to make up for *(insép)*, to compensate for *(insép)* ▪ **il est encore temps de ~ le mal qui a été fait** there's still time to make up for *ou* to undo the harm that's been done ➊ **~ les dégâts** *pr* to repair the damage ; *fig* to pick up the pieces **3.** [corriger - omission] to rectify, to repair *sout* ; [- négligence, erreur] to correct, to rectify **4.** *sout* [santé, forces] to restore.

◆ **se réparer** *vp (emploi passif)* to mend ▪ **ça ne se répare pas** it can't be mended.

reparler [3] [rəparle] ◇ *vt* [langue] : **ce voyage m'a donné l'occasion de ~ arabe** this trip gave me the opportunity to speak Arabic again.

◇ *vi* to speak again ▪ **~ de : il a reparlé de son roman** he talked about his novel again ▪ **retenez bien son nom, c'est un chanteur dont on reparlera** remember this singer's name, you'll be hearing more of him ▪ **je laisse là les Incas, nous allons en ~** I won't say any more about the Incas now, we'll come back to them later ▪ **il n'en a plus reparlé** he never mentioned it again ▪ **~ à qqn (de qqch)** to speak to sb (about sthg) again.

◆ **se reparler** *vp (emploi réciproque)* to get back on speaking terms.

repars *etc v* ▻ **repartir.**

repartie [rəparti] *nf* [réplique] retort, repartee ▪ **avoir de la ~** to have a good sense of repartee.

repartir[1] [43] [rəpartir] *vt (aux avoir) litt* [répliquer] to retort, to reply, to rejoin ▪ **on me repartit que le maître serait bientôt de retour** I received the reply that the master would soon be back.

repartir[2] [43] [rəpartir] *vi (aux être)* **1.** [se remettre en route] to start *ou* to set off again ▪ **quand repars-tu?** when are you off *ou* leaving again? ▪ **l'économie est bien repartie** the economy has picked up again ▪ **c'est reparti, encore une hausse de l'électricité!** here we go again, another rise in the price of electricity! ➊ **~ à l'assaut** *ou* **à l'attaque** *pr* to mount a fresh assault ; *fig* to try again ▪ **~ à zéro** to start again from scratch, to go back to square one ▪ **~ du bon pied** to make a fresh start **2.** HORT to start growing *ou* to sprout again.

répartir [32] [repartir] *vt* **1.** [distribuer - encouragements, sanctions] to give ; [- héritage, travail] to share out *(sép)*, to divide up *(sép)* ; [- soldats, policiers] to deploy, to spread out *(sép)* ; [- chaleur, ventilation] to distribute ▪ **répartissez les enfants en trois groupes** get *ou* split up the children into three groups **2.** [étaler - confiture, cirage] to spread **3.** [dans le temps] : **~ des remboursements** to pay back in instalments ▪ **~ des paiements** to spread out the payments **4.** INFORM : **être réparti** to be distributed *(over a network).*

◆ **se répartir** ◇ *vpi* [se diviser] to split, to divide (up) ▪ **répartissez-vous en deux équipes** get yourselves *ou* split into two teams ▪ **les dépenses se répartissent en trois catégories** expenditure falls under three headings.

◇ *vpt* [partager] : **se ~ le travail/les responsabilités** to share out the work/the responsibility.

répartition [repartisjɔ̃] *nf* **1.** [partage - de l'impôt, des bénéfices] distribution ; [- d'un butin] sharing out, dividing up ;

[- d'allocations, de prestations] allotment, sharing out ■ **comment se fera la ~ des tâches?** how will the tasks be shared out *ou* allocated? **2.** [agencement - dans un appartement] layout ■ **la ~ des pièces est la suivante** the layout of the rooms is as follows, the rooms are laid out as follows **3.** [étalement - dans l'espace] distribution ■ **la ~ géographique des gisements** the geographical distribution of the deposits **4.** ÉCON assessment.

reparu, e [rəpary] *pp* ▷ **reparaître.**

reparution [rəparysjɔ̃] *nf* [d'un journal] republishing, reappearance ■ **le jour de sa ~, le quotidien s'est vendu à un million d'exemplaires** on the day the paper was back on the newsstands *ou* resumed publication, it sold a million copies.

repas [rəpa] *nm* **1.** [gén] meal ■ [d'un nourrisson, d'un animal] feed *UK*, feeding *US* ■ **faire un bon ~** to have a square *ou* good meal ■ **prendre ses ~ à la cantine** [de l'école] to have school lunches *ou* dinners *UK* ; [de l'usine] to eat in the (works) canteen ■ **à l'heure des ~** at mealtimes ◗ **~ à la carte** à la carte meal ■ **~ livrés à domicile** meals on wheels ■ **~ de midi** lunch, midday *UK ou* noon *US* meal ■ **~ de noces** wedding meal ■ **~ du soir** dinner, evening meal **2.** *(comme adj; avec ou sans trait d'union)* **plateau-~** lunch *ou* dinner tray ■ **ticket-~** luncheon voucher *UK*, meal ticket *US*.

repassage [rəpasaʒ] *nm* [du linge] ironing ■ **'~ superflu'** 'wash and wear', 'non-iron'.

repasser [3] [rəpase] ◇ *vi* **1.** [passer à nouveau dans un lieu] to go (back) again ■ **elle repassera** she'll drop by again ■ **je suis repassé la voir à l'hôpital** I went to see her in the hospital again ■ **si tu repasses à Berlin, fais-moi signe** if you're in *ou* passing through Berlin again, let me know ■ **~ par le même chemin** to go back the way one came ■ **il passait et repassait sous l'horloge de la gare** he kept walking up and down under the station clock ■ *fig* **~ sur un dessin** to go over a drawing again, to go back over a drawing ■ **j'ai horreur qu'on repasse derrière moi** I hate to have people go over what I've done ■ **le dollar est repassé au-dessous de un euro** the dollar has fallen *ou* dropped below one euro again ◗ **s'il veut être payé, il peut toujours ~** *fam* if he wants to be paid, he's got another think coming!
2. CINÉ & TV to be on *ou* to be shown again.
◇ *vt* **1.** [défriper] to iron
2. [aiguiser - gén] to sharpen ; [- avec une pierre] to whet
3. [réviser] : **~ ses leçons/le programme de physique** ÉDUC to go over one's homework/the physics course ■ **~ des comptes** to reexamine a set of accounts
4. *fam* [donner] : **elle m'a repassé sa tunique** she let me have her smock
5. [traverser à nouveau] : **~ un fleuve** to go back across a river, to cross a river again
6. [subir à nouveau] : **~ un examen** to resit an exam *UK*, to take an exam again ■ **je dois ~ l'allemand/le permis demain** I have to retake German/my driving test tomorrow ■ **~ une échographie** to go for another ultrasound scan
7. [à nouveau] to pass again ■ **voulez-vous ~ la salade?** would you hand *ou* pass the salad round again? ■ **repasse-moi mon mouchoir** hand me back my handkerchief
8. [remettre] : **~ une couche de vernis** to put on another coat of varnish ■ **~ un manteau** [le réessayer] to try a coat on again ■ **~ un poisson sur le gril** to put a fish back on the grill, to give a fish a bit more time on the grill ■ **repasse-moi la face A du disque** play me the A-side of the record again
9. [au téléphone] : **je te repasse Paul** I'll put Paul on again, I'll hand you back to Paul ■ **repassez-moi le standard** put me through to the switchboard again.
◆ **se repasser** *vp (emploi passif)* to iron ■ **le voile ne se repasse pas** [ne doit pas être repassé] the veil mustn't be ironed ; [n'a pas besoin de repassage] the veil doesn't need ironing.

repasseur, euse [rəpasœr, øz] *nm, f* **1.** [de linge] ironer **2.** [rémouleur] knife-grinder, knife-sharpener.
◆ **repasseuse** *nf* [machine] ironing machine.

repayer [11] [rəpeje] *vt* [payer à nouveau] to pay again ■ [payer en plus] to pay more for ■ **si l'on veut visiter la maison des reptiles, il faut ~** if you wish to visit the reptile house, you have to pay extra.

repêchage [rəpeʃaʒ] *nm* **1.** [d'un objet] fishing out ■ [d'un corps] recovery **2.** ÉDUC letting through **3.** SPORT repechage.

repêcher [4] [rəpeʃe] *vt* **1.** [noyé] to fish out *(sép)*, to recover **2.** ÉDUC to let through *(sép)* ■ **j'ai été repêché à l'oral** I passed on my oral **3.** SPORT to let through on the repechage.

repeindre [81] [rəpɛ̃dr] *vt* to repaint, to paint again.

repens *etc v* ▷ **repentir.**

repenser [3] [rəpɑ̃se] *vt* to reconsider, to rethink ■ **l'entrepôt a été entièrement repensé** the layout of the warehouse has been completely redesigned.
◆ **repenser à** *v+prép* to think about again ■ **en y repensant** thinking back on it all ■ **ah mais oui, j'y repense, elle t'a appelé ce matin** oh yes, now I come to think of it, she phoned you this morning.

repentant, e [rəpɑ̃tɑ̃, ɑ̃t] *adj* repentant, penitent ■ **pécheur ~** repentant sinner.

repenti, e [rəpɑ̃ti] ◇ *adj* repentant, penitent ■ **alcoolique/fumeur ~** reformed alcoholic/smoker.
◇ *nm, f* penitent ■ **les ~s du terrorisme** repentant terrorists.

repentir[1] [rəpɑ̃tir] *nm* **1.** [remords] remorse ■ **verser des larmes de ~** to shed tears of remorse *ou* regret **2.** RELIG repentance ■ **mener une vie de ~** to live a life of repentance *ou* penance **3.** [correction] alteration **4.** ART reworking, retouching.

repentir[2] [37] [rəpɑ̃tir] ◆ **se repentir** *vpi* to repent *sout.*
◆ **se repentir de** *vp+prép* to regret, to be sorry for ■ **j'ai refusé son offre et je m'en suis amèrement repenti** I turned down his offer and I've lived to rue the day *ou* I bitterly regret it ■ **se ~ d'une faute/d'avoir péché** to repent of a fault/of having sinned.

repérable [rəperabl] *adj* [maison] easily found ■ [changement, signe] easily spotted ■ **le bar est facilement ~** the bar is easy to find ■ **les oiseaux de cette espèce sont ~s à leur bec coloré** birds of this species are recognizable *ou* identifiable by their coloured beaks.

repérage [rəperaʒ] *nm* **1.** [gén] spotting, pinpointing **2.** MIL location **3.** CINÉ : **être en ~** to be looking for locations *ou* choosing settings **4.** IMPR registry, laying.

répercussion [reperkysjɔ̃] *nf* **1.** [conséquence] repercussion, consequence, side-effect **2.** [renvoi - d'un son] repercussion, echo **3.** FIN : **le coût final est aggravé par la ~ de l'impôt** the final cost is increased because taxes levied are passed on (to the buyer).

répercuter [3] [reperkyte] *vt* **1.** [renvoyer - son] to echo, to reflect ■ **un coup de feu répercuté par l'écho** the sound of an echoing shot **2.** FIN : **~ l'impôt sur le prix de revient** to pass a tax on in the selling price **3.** [transmettre] to pass on *ou* along *(sép)*.
◆ **se répercuter** *vpi* [bruit] to echo.
◆ **se répercuter sur** *vp+prép* to have an effect on *ou* upon, to affect ■ **les problèmes familiaux se répercutent sur le travail scolaire** family problems have repercussions on *ou* affect children's performance at school.

reperdre [77] [rəpɛrdr] *vt* to lose again ■ **j'ai reperdu 2 kilos** my weight's gone back down by 2 kilos.

repère [rəpɛr] *nm* **1.** [gén] line, mark ■ [indice - matériel] landmark ; [- qui permet de juger] benchmark, reference mark ◗ **point de ~** landmark **2.** TECHNOL (index) mark ■ **~ de montage** assembly *ou* match mark **3.** [référence] reference point, landmark ■ **servir de ~ à qqn** to serve as a (guiding) light to sb ■ **j'ai l'impression de n'avoir plus aucun (point de) ~** I've lost my bearings **4.** *(comme adj; avec ou sans trait d'union)* reference *(modif)* ■ **date/point ~** reference date/point.

repérer [18] [rəpere] *vt* **1.** [indiquer par un repère] to mark ■ TECHNOL to mark out *ou* off *(sép)* **2.** [localiser] to locate, to pinpoint **3.** [remarquer] to spot, to pick out *(sép)*, to notice ■ **je l'avais repéré au premier rang** I'd noticed *ou* spotted him in the first row ■ **tu vas nous faire ~ avec tes éternuements** you'll get us caught *ou* spotted with your sneezing ■ **les ravisseurs se sont fait ~ près de l'hôpital** the kidnappers were spotted near the hospital **4.** [dénicher] to discover.

◆ **se repérer** *vpi* **1.** [déterminer sa position] to find *ou* to get one's bearings ■ **on n'arrive jamais à se ~ dans un aéroport** you can never find your way about *ou* around in an airport **2.** *fig* **je n'arrive plus à me ~ dans ses mensonges** I don't know where I am any more with all those lies she tells.

répertoire [repɛrtwar] *nm* **1.** [liste] index, list ■ **~ alphabétique/thématique** alphabetical/thematic index **2.** [livre] notebook, book ⊃ **~ d'adresses** address book ■ **~ des rues** street index **3.** DANSE & MUS repertoire ■ THÉÂTRE repertoire, repertory ■ **jouer une pièce du ~** [acteur] to be in rep ; [théâtre] to put on a play from the repertoire *ou* a stock play ■ **tu devrais ajouter ça à ton ~** *fig* that could be another string to your bow **4.** DR : **~ civil** civil register ■ **~ général** record of cases **5.** INFORM directory.

répertorier [9] [repɛrtɔrje] *vt* **1.** [inventorier] to index, to list ■ **~ les erreurs** to list *ou* to pick out the mistakes **2.** [inscrire dans une liste] to list ■ **répertorié par adresses/professions** listed under addresses/professions.

répéter [18] [repete] *vt* **1.** [dire encore] to repeat ■ **je n'arrête pas de vous le ~** that's what I've been trying to tell you ■ **elle ne se l'est pas fait ~ (deux fois)** she didn't need telling twice ■ *(en usage absolu)* **répétez après moi** repeat after me ■ **répète un peu pour voir?** let's hear you repeat that (if you dare)!
2. [révéler par indiscrétion - fait] to repeat ; [- histoire] to retell, to relate ■ **ne lui répète pas** don't tell her, don't repeat this to her ■ **ne va pas le ~ (à tout le monde)** don't go telling everybody
3. [recommencer] to repeat, to do again
4. [mémoriser - leçon] to go over *(insép)*, to practise ; [- morceau de musique] to practise ; [- pièce, film] to rehearse ■ *(en usage absolu)* **on ne répète pas demain** there's no rehearsal tomorrow
5. [reproduire - motif] to repeat, to duplicate ; [- refrain] to repeat
6. DR to obtain recovery of.

◆ **se répéter** *vpi* **1.** [redire la même chose] to repeat o.s. ■ **au risque de me ~** at the risk of repeating myself ■ **depuis son premier roman, elle se répète** since her first novel, she's just been rewriting the same thing
2. [se reproduire] to recur, to reoccur, to be repeated ■ **et que ça ne se répète plus!** don't let it happen again! ■ **la disposition des locaux se répète à tous les étages** the layout of the rooms is the same on every floor ■ **l'histoire se répète** history repeats itself.

répétiteur, trice [repetitœr, tris] *nm, f* *vieilli* coach *(at home or in school)*.

répétitif, ive [repetitif, iv] *adj* repetitive, repetitious.

répétition [repetisjɔ̃] *nf* **1.** [d'un mot, d'un geste] repetition **2.** [séance de travail] rehearsal ■ **être en ~** to be rehearsing ⊃ **~ générale** dress rehearsal.

◆ **à répétition** *loc adj* **1.** [en armurerie, en horlogerie] repeater *(modif)* **2.** *fam* [renouvelé] : **il fait des bêtises à ~** he keeps doing stupid things.

repeuplement [rəpœpləmɑ̃] *nm* [par des hommes] repopulation ■ [par des animaux] restocking ■ [par des plantes] replantation, replanting *(U)* ■ [par des arbres] reafforestation *UK*, reforestation *US*.

repeupler [5] [rəpœple] *vt* [secteur] ro repopulate ■ [étang] to restock ■ [forêt] to reafforest *UK*, to reforest *US*.

◆ **se repeupler** *vpi* : **cette région commence à se ~** people are starting to move back to the area ■ **la rivière se repeuple** life is coming back to the river.

repiquage [rəpikaʒ] *nm* **1.** AGRIC planting *ou* bedding out **2.** AUDIO [sur bande] rerecording, taping ■ [sur disque] transfer.

repiquer [3] [rəpike] ◇ *vt* **1.** [planter - riz, salades] to plant *ou* to pick *ou* to bed out **2.** △ [attraper de nouveau] to catch *ou* to nab again **3.** [enregistrer - sur cassette] to rerecord, to tape ; [- sur disque] to transfer **4.** COUT to restitch **5.** △ *arg scol* [classe] to repeat **6.** [repaver] to repave **7.** PHOTO to touch up.

◇ *vi fam* [recommencer] to start again ■ **~ à un plat** to have a second helping.

répit [repi] *nm* respite, rest ■ **un moment de ~** a breathing space ■ **s'accorder quelques minutes de ~** to give o.s. a few minutes' rest.

◆ **sans répit** *loc adv* [lutter] tirelessly ■ [poursuivre, interroger] relentlessly, without respite.

replacer [16] [rəplase] *vt* **1.** [remettre] to replace, to put back *(sép)* ■ **~ les événements dans leur contexte** to put events into their context **2.** *fam* [réutiliser] to put in *(sép)* again ■ **elle est bonne, celle-là, je la replacerai!** that's a good one, I must remember it *ou* use it myself sometime! **3.** [trouver un nouvel emploi pour - domestique] to find a new position for ; [- employé] to reassign.

◆ **se replacer** *vpi* **1.** [se remettre en place] to take up one's position again **2.** [domestique] to find (o.s.) a new job **3.** [dans une situation déterminée] to imagine o.s., to visualize o.s.

replanter [3] [rəplɑ̃te] *vt* to replant ■ **après le phylloxéra, ils ont replanté en blé** after the phylloxera epidemic they planted the area with wheat.

replat [rəpla] *nm* GÉOGR sloping ledge, shoulder.

replâtrer [3] [rəplatre] *vt* **1.** CONSTR to replaster **2.** *fam fig* to patch up *(sép)*.

replet, ète [rəplɛ, ɛt] *adj* [personne] plump, podgy, portly ■ [visage] plump, chubby ■ [ventre] full, rounded.

repli [rəpli] *nm* **1.** [pli - du terrain] fold ■ [courbe - d'une rivière] bend, meander **2.** MIL withdrawal, falling back *(U)* ■ **solution** *ou* **stratégie de ~** fallback option **3.** *fig* & *litt* [recoin] recess ■ **les sombres ~s de l'âme** the dark recesses *ou* reaches of the soul **4.** [baisse] fall, drop ■ **on note un léger ~ de la livre sterling** sterling has fallen slightly *ou* has eased (back) **5.** [introversion] : **un ~ sur soi** a turning in on o.s.

repliement [rəplimɑ̃] *nm* *sout* [introversion] withdrawal ■ **~ sur soi-même** withdrawal (into o.s.), turning in on o.s., self-absorption.

replier [10] [rəplije] *vt* **1.** [plier - journal] to fold up *(sép)* again ; [- couteau] to close again ■ **replie le bas de ton pantalon** turn up the bottom of your trousers **2.** [ramener - ailes] to fold ; [- jambes] to tuck under *(sép)* **3.** MIL : **~ des unités derrière le fleuve** to withdraw units back to the other side of the river ■ **~ les populations civiles** to move the civilian population back.

◆ **se replier** ◇ *vp (emploi passif)* to fold back.
◇ *vpi* MIL to withdraw, to fall back.

◆ **se replier sur** *vp+prép* : **se ~ sur soi-même** to withdraw into o.s., to turn in on o.s. ■ **il est trop replié sur lui-même** he's too much of an introvert.

réplique [replik] *nf* **1.** [réponse] reply, retort, rejoinder *sout* ■ **ce gamin a la ~ facile** this kid is always ready with *ou* is never short of an answer ■ **argument sans ~** irrefutable *ou* unanswerable argument ■ **c'est sans ~** what can you say to that!, there's no answer to that! **2.** [dans une pièce, un film] line, cue ■ **manquer une ~** to miss a cue ■ **oublier sa ~** to forget one's lines ■ **donner la ~ à un acteur** [en répétition] to give an actor his cues ; [dans une distribution] to play opposite an actor **3.** [reproduction] replica, studio copy ■ **il est la ~ vivante de son père** he's the spitting image of *ou* a dead ringer for his father **4.** GÉOL aftershock.

répliquer [3] [replike] *vt* [répondre] to reply, to retort ■ **il n'y a rien à ~ à un tel argument** there's no answer to an argument like that ■ **que ~ à ça?** how can you reply to that? ■ **il n'en est pas question, répliqua-t-il** it's out of the question, he replied *ou* retorted.

◆ **répliquer à** *v+prép* **1.** [répondre à] to reply to ■ **~ à une critique** to reply to *ou* to answer criticism ■ *(en usage absolu)* **monte te coucher et ne réplique pas!** go upstairs to bed and no argument! **2.** [contre-attaquer] to respond to ■ *(en usage absolu)* **le pays a été attaqué et a répliqué immédiatement** the country was attacked and immediately retaliated.

replonger [17] [rəplɔ̃ʒe] ◇ *vt* **1.** [plonger à nouveau] to dip back *(sép)* **2.** *fig* [faire sombrer à nouveau] to plunge back *(sép)*, to push back ▪ **le choc la replongea dans la démence** the shock pushed *ou* tipped her back into madness.
◇ *vi* **1.** [plonger à nouveau] to dive again **2.** *fig* **~ dans l'alcool/la délinquance** to relapse into drinking/delinquency ▪ **~ dans la dépression** to sink back *ou* to relapse into depression **3.** △ *arg crime* [retourner en prison] to go back inside.
◆ **se replonger dans** *vp+prép* to go back to ▪ **se ~ dans son travail** to immerse o.s. in work again, to go back to one's work ▪ **se ~ dans ses recherches** to get involved in one's research again.

répondant, e [repɔ̃dɑ̃, ɑ̃t] *nm, f* [garant] guarantor, surety ▪ **être le ~ de qqn** [financièrement] to stand surety for sb, to be sb's guarantor ; [moralement] to answer *ou* to vouch for sb.
◆ **répondant** *nm* **1.** RELIG & *vieilli* server **2.** *loc* **avoir du ~** to have money.

répondeur, euse [repɔ̃dœr, øz] *adj* [insolent] who answers back ▪ **il est déjà ~ à son âge** he's got a lot of cheek *UK ou* he's very sassy *US* for his age.
◆ **répondeur** *nm* : **~ (téléphonique)** (telephone) answering machine ▪ **~ enregistreur** Ansafone® *UK*, answering machine ▪ **~ interrogeable à distance** remote-control (telephone) answering machine.

répondre [75] [repɔ̃dr] ◇ *vi* **1.** [répliquer] to answer, to reply ▪ **bien répondu!** well said *ou* spoken! ▪ **répondez par oui ou par non** answer *ou* say yes or no ▪ **elle répondit en riant** she answered *ou* replied with a laugh ▪ **~ par un clin d'œil/hochement de tête** to wink/to nod in reply ▪ **seul l'écho lui répondit** the only reply was an echo ▪ **~ à qqn** to answer sb ▪ **~ à qqch** to answer sthg
2. [être insolent] to answer back ▪ **~ à ses parents/professeurs** to answer one's parents/teachers back
3. [à une lettre] to answer, to reply, to write back ▪ **~ à une note** to answer *ou* to reply to a note ▪ **répondez au questionnaire suivant** answer the following questions, fill in the following questionnaire ▪ **je suis ravie que vous ayez pu ~ à mon invitation** [que vous soyez venu] I'm delighted that you were able to accept my invitation ▪ **vous devez ~ à la convocation** [dire que vous l'avez reçue] you must acknowledge receipt of the notification
4. [à la porte, au téléphone] to answer ▪ **je vais ~** [à la porte] I'll go ; [au téléphone] I'll answer it, I'll get it ▪ **ça ne répond pas** nobody's answering, there's no answer
5. [réagir - véhicule, personne, cheval] to respond ▪ **le public répond mal** there is a low level of public response ▪ **les freins répondent bien** the brakes respond well ▪ **~ à** to respond to ▪ **son organisme ne répond plus au traitement** her body isn't responding to treatment any more ▪ **~ à un coup** *ou* **à une attaque** to fight back, to retaliate ▪ **~ à une accusation/critique** to counter an accusation/a criticism ▪ **~ à la force par la force** to meet *ou* to answer force with force.
◇ *vt* **1.** [gén] to answer, to reply ▪ [après une attaque] to retort ▪ **~ (que) oui/non** to say yes/no in reply, to answer yes/no ▪ **qu'as-tu répondu?** what did you say?, what was your answer? ▪ **je n'ai rien trouvé à ~** I could find no answer *ou* reply ▪ **ils m'ont répondu des bêtises** they answered me with a lot of nonsense ▪ **elle m'a répondu de le faire moi-même** she told me to do it myself
2. [par lettre] to answer *ou* to reply (in writing *ou* by letter) ▪ **~ que...** to write (back) that...
3. RELIG : **~ la messe** to give the responses (at Mass).
◆ **répondre à** *v+prép* **1.** [satisfaire - besoin, demande] to answer, to meet ; [- attente, espoir] to come *ou* to live up to, to fulfil ▪ [correspondre à - norme] to meet ; [- condition] to fulfil ; [- description, signalement] to answer, to fit ▪ **les dédommagements ne répondent pas à l'attente des sinistrés** the amount offered in compensation falls short of the victims' expectations
2. [s'harmoniser avec] to match ▪ **au bleu du ciel répond le bleu de la mer** the blue of the sky matches the blue of the sea
3. [s'appeler] : **~ au nom de** to answer to the name (of).
◆ **répondre de** *v+prép* **1.** [cautionner - filleul, protégé] to answer for ▪ **~ de l'exactitude de qqch/de l'intégrité de qqn** to vouch for the accuracy of sthg/sb's integrity ▪ **je réponds de lui comme de moi-même** I can fully vouch for him ▪ **je ne réponds plus de rien** I am no longer responsible for anything ▪ **elle répond des dettes de son mari jusqu'au divorce** she's responsible *ou* answerable for her husband's debts until the divorce
2. *sout* [assurer] : **elle cédera, je vous en réponds!** she'll give in, you can take it from me *ou* take my word for it! ▪ **je vous réponds que cela ne se renouvellera pas!** I guarantee (you) it won't happen again!
3. [expliquer] to answer *ou* to account for, to be accountable for ▪ **les ministres répondent de leurs actes devant le Parlement** ministers are accountable for their actions before Parliament ▪ **il lui faudra ~ de plusieurs tentatives de viol** he'll have to answer several charges of attempted rape.
◆ **se répondre** *vp (emploi réciproque)* [instruments de musique] to answer each other ▪ [sculptures, tableaux] to match each other ▪ [couleurs, formes, sons] to harmonize.

répons [repɔ̃] *nm* RELIG response.

réponse [repɔ̃s] *nf* **1.** [réplique] answer, reply ▪ **avoir (toujours) ~ à tout : elle a toujours ~ à tout** [elle sait tout] she has an answer for everything ; [elle a de la repartie] she's never at a loss for *ou* she's always ready with an answer ▪ **pour toute ~, elle me claqua la porte au nez** her only answer was to slam the door in my face ⊳ **une ~ de Normand** an evasive answer ▪ **c'est la ~ du berger à la bergère** it's tit for tat **2.** [à un courrier] reply, answer, response ▪ **en ~ à votre courrier du 2 mai** in reply *ou* response to your letter of May 2nd ▪ **leur lettre est restée sans ~** their letter remained *ou* was left unanswered ▪ **leur demande est restée sans ~** there was no reply *ou* response to their request ▪ **~ par retour du courrier** reply by return of post ▪ **je lui ai donné une ~ positive** [à son offre] I accepted his offer ; [à sa candidature] I told him his application had been successful ▪ **je lui ai donné une ~ négative** I turned him down ⊳ **~ payée** TÉLÉCOM reply paid ▪ **bulletin-~** reply slip ▪ **coupon-~** reply coupon **3.** [réaction] response ▪ **la ~ du gouvernement fut d'imposer le couvre-feu** the government's response was to impose a curfew **4.** ÉDUC & UNIV [solution] answer ▪ **la ~ à la question nº 5 est fausse** the answer to number 5 is wrong **5.** TECHNOL response ▪ **temps de ~ d'un appareil** response time of a device **6.** MUS answer **7.** PSYCHOL response, reaction.

repopulation [rəpɔpylasjɔ̃] *nf* repopulation.

report [rəpɔr] *nm* **1.** [renvoi à plus tard] postponement, deferment ▪ **~ du jugement sine die** deferment of the verdict to an unspecified date ⊳ **~ d'échéance** FIN extension of due date **2.** [en comptabilité] carrying forward *ou* over ▪ **faire le ~ d'une somme** to carry forward *ou* over an amount ⊳ **~ d'écritures** posting ▪ **~ à nouveau** balance (carried forward) ; [en haut de colonne] brought forward ; [en bas de colonne] carried forward **3.** [au turf] rebetting **4.** [transfert] : **~ des voix** transfer of votes **5.** BOURSE contango, carry over **6.** PHOTO transfer **7.** IMPR : **papier à ~** transfer paper.

reportage [rəpɔrtaʒ] *nm* **1.** [récit, émission] report ▪ **~ télévisé/photo** television/photo report ▪ **faire un ~ sur qqch** to do a report on sthg **2.** [métier] (news) reporting, reportage ▪ **faire du ~** to be a news reporter ▪ **être en ~** to be on an assignment ⊳ **faire du grand ~** to do international reporting, to cover stories from all over the world.

reporter[1] [rəpɔrtɛr] *nmf* (news) reporter ▪ **grand ~** international reporter ▪ **~ sportif** sports commentator.

reporter[2] [3] [rəpɔrte] *vt* **1.** [rapporter] to take back *(sép)* **2.** [transcrire - note, insertion] to transfer, to copy out ▪ [en comptabilité] to carry forward *(sép)* ▪ **~ à nouveau** to carry forward (to new account) ▪ **~ le montant des exportations dans le livre des comptes** to post exports (to the ledger) **3.** [retarder - conférence, rendez-vous] to postpone, to put off *(sép)* ; [- annonce, verdict] to put off, to defer ; [- date] to defer, to put back *esp UK* ▪ **~ qqch à une prochaine fois** to put sthg off until another time ▪ [en arrière dans le temps] to take back *(sép)* **4.** [transférer] to shift, to transfer ▪ **les votes ont été reportés sur le candidat communiste** the votes were transferred to the Communist candidate **5.** [miser] to put, to place, to transfer ▪ **~ tous ses gains sur le 8** to put *ou* to place all one's winnings on the 8 **6.** BOURSE to carry over *(sép)* ▪ **faire ~ des titres** to give on *ou* to lend stock.

◆ **se reporter à** *vp+prép* [se référer à] to turn *ou* to refer to, to see ■ **reportez-vous à notre dernier numéro** see our last issue.
◆ **se reporter sur** *vp+prép* [se transférer sur] to be transferred to ■ **tout son amour s'est reporté sur sa fille** all his love was switched to his daughter.

reporter-cameraman [rəpɔrtɛrkameraman] (*pl* **reporters-cameramans** *ou pl* **reporters-cameramen** [-mɛn]) *nm* television news reporter.

reporter-photographe [rəpɔrtɛrfɔtɔgraf] (*pl* **reporters-photographes**) *nmf* news photographer, photojournalist.

reporteur [rəpɔrtœr] *nm* **1.** BOURSE taker (of stock) **2.** IMPR transfer printer (person) **3.** PRESSE : ~ **d'images** television news reporter.

repos [rəpo] *nm* **1.** [détente] rest ■ **prendre quelques jours de ~** to take *ou* to have a few days' rest ■ **un moment de ~** a short rest **2.** [période d'inactivité] rest (period), time off ■ **trois jours de ~, un ~ de trois jours** three days off ▶ **~ compensateur** ≃ time off in lieu ■ **~ dominical** Sunday rest ■ **~ hebdomadaire** weekly time off **3.** *litt* [tranquillité - de la nature] peace and quiet ; [- intérieure] peace of mind ■ **je n'aurai pas de ~ tant que...** I won't rest as long as... **4.** *litt* [sommeil] sleep, rest ■ **respecte le ~ des autres** let other people sleep (in peace) ■ **~ éternel** eternal rest **5.** MUS cadence ■ LITTÉR break **6.** MIL : ~ at ease! **7.** SPORT break.
◆ **au repos** ◇ *loc adj* [moteur, animal] at rest ■ [volcan] dormant, inactive ■ [muscle, corps] relaxed.
◇ *loc adv* **1.** AGRIC : **laisser un champ au ~** to let a field lie fallow **2.** MIL : **mettre la troupe au ~** to order the troops to stand at ease.
◆ **de tout repos** *loc adj* : **le voyage n'était pas de tout ~** it wasn't exactly a restful journey ■ **des placements de tout ~** gilt-edged investments.
◆ **en repos** *loc adj* **1.** [inactif] : **l'imagination de l'artiste ne reste jamais en ~** an artist's imagination never rests *ou* is never at rest **2.** [serein] : **elle a la conscience en ~** she has an easy *ou* a clear conscience.

reposant, e [rəpozɑ̃, ɑ̃t] *adj* [vacances] relaxing ■ [ambiance, lumière, musique] soothing.

reposé, e [rəpoze] *adj* fresh, rested ■ **on repartira quand tu seras bien ~** we'll set off again once you've had a good rest ■ **tu as l'air ~** you look rested.

repose-pieds [rəpozpje] *nm inv* footrest.

repose-poignets [rəpozpwanjɛ] *nm inv* INFORM wrist rest, wrist pillow, wrist pad.

reposer [3] [rəpoze] ◇ *vt* **1.** [question] to ask again, to repeat ■ [problème] to raise again, to bring up *(sép)* again **2.** [objet] to put down (again) *ou* back down ■ **on a dû faire ~ de la moquette** we had to have the carpet relaid ■ **~ une serrure** to refit a lock **3.** [personne, corps, esprit] to rest ■ **~ ses jambes** to rest one's legs **4.** MIL : **reposez armes!** order arms!
◇ *vi* **1.** [être placé] to rest, to lie ■ **sa tête reposait sur l'oreiller** her head rested *ou* lay on the pillow **2.** *litt* [dormir] to sleep ■ [être allongé] to rest, to be lying down ■ **~ sur son lit de mort** to be lying on one's deathbed ▌[être enterré] : **elle repose non loin de son village natal** she rests *ou* she's buried not far from her native village ■ **ici reposent les victimes de la guerre** here lie the victims of the war **3.** [être posé] to rest, to lie, to stand ■ **l'épave reposait par cent mètres de fond** the wreck lay one hundred metres down **4.** [liquide, mélange] : **laissez le vin ~** leave the wine to settle, let the wine stand ■ **laissez ~ la pâte/colle** leave the dough to stand/glue to set **5.** AGRIC : **laisser la terre ~** to let the land lie fallow.
◆ **reposer sur** *v+prép* **1.** [être posé sur] to rest on, to lie on, to stand on ■ CONSTR to be built *ou* to rest on **2.** [être fondé sur - suj: témoignage, conception] to rest on ■ **sur quelles preuves repose votre affirmation?** what evidence do you have to support your assertion?, on what evidence do you base your assertion?
◆ **se reposer** *vpi* [se détendre] to rest ■ **va te ~ une heure** go and rest *ou* go take a rest for an hour ▶ **se ~ sur ses lauriers** to rest on one's laurels.
◆ **se reposer sur** *vp+prép* [s'en remettre à] to rely on ■ **le Président se repose trop sur ses conseillers** the President relies *ou* depends too much on his advisers.

repose-tête [rəpoztɛt] *nm inv* headrest.

repositionnable [rapɔzisjɔnabl] *adj* repositionable, removable.

repositionner [3] [rəpozisjɔne] *vt* **1.** [remettre en position] to reposition **2.** COMM : **~ un produit** to reposition a product.
◆ **se repositionner** *vpi* : **se ~ sur le marché** to reposition o.s. in the market.

reposoir [rəpozwar] *nm* [dans une église] repository ■ [dans une maison] (temporary) altar.

repoussant, e [rəpusɑ̃, ɑ̃t] *adj* repulsive, repellent ■ **être d'une laideur ~e** to be repulsively *ou* horribly ugly.

repousse [rəpus] *nf* new growth ■ **des pilules qui facilitent la ~ des cheveux** hair-restoring pills.

repoussé [rəpuse] ◇ *adj m* repoussé *(modif).*
◇ *nm* [technique - gén] repoussé (work) ; [- au marteau] chasing ■ [relief] repoussé.

repousse-peaux [rəpuspo] *nm inv* cuticle remover.

repousser [3] [rəpuse] ◇ *vt* **1.** [faire reculer - manifestants] to push *ou* to drive back *(sép)* ■ **~ une attaque** to drive back *ou* to repel an attack ■ **~ les frontières de l'imaginaire/l'horreur** to push back the frontiers of imagination/horror **2.** [écarter] to push aside *ou* away *(sép)* ■ **elle repoussa violemment l'assiette** she pushed the plate away violently ■ **~ qqn d'un geste brusque** to push *ou* to shove sb out of the way roughly ■ **il repoussa du pied la bouteille vide** [violemment] he kicked the empty bottle away ; [doucement] he nudged *ou* edged the empty bottle out of the way with his foot **3.** [refuser - offre, mesure, demande en mariage] to turn down *(sép)*, to reject ; [- solution, thèse] to reject, to dismiss, to rule out *(sép)* ; [- tentation, idées noires] to resist, to reject, to drive away *(sép)* ■ **~ les avances de qqn** to reject sb's advances **4.** [mendiant] to turn away *(sép)* ■ [prétendant] to reject **5.** [dégoûter] to repel, to put off *(sép)* **6.** [retarder - conférence, travail] to postpone, to put off *(sép)* ; [- date] to defer, to put back *(sép)* UK ; [- décision, jugement] to defer ■ **repoussé au 26 juin** postponed until the 26th of June **7.** TECHNOL [cuir] to emboss ■ [métal] to chase, to work in repoussé.
◇ *vi* [barbe, plante] to grow again *ou* back.
◆ **se repousser** *vp (emploi réciproque)* [particules] to repel each other.

repoussoir [rəpuswar] *nm* **1.** [faire-valoir] foil ■ **servir de ~ à (la beauté de) qqn** to act as a foil to sb's beauty **2.** ART repoussoir **3.** CONSTR [ciseau] drift (chisel) **4.** [spatule de manucure] orange stick.

répréhensible [repreɑ̃sibl] *adj* reprehensible, blameworthy ■ **un acte ~** a reprehensible *ou* an objectionable deed ■ **je ne vois pas ce que ma conduite a de ~** I don't see what's reproachable about my behaviour.

reprendre [79] [rəprɑ̃dr] ◇ *vt* **1.** [saisir à nouveau - objet] to pick up *(sép)* again, to take again ▶ **~ les rênes** *pr* to take in the reins ; *fig* to resume control
2. [s'emparer à nouveau de - position, ville] to retake, to recapture ; [- prisonnier] to recapture, to catch again
3. [suj: maladie, doutes] to take hold of again ■ **quand la douleur me reprend** when the pain comes back ■ **l'angoisse me reprit** anxiety took hold of me again ■ **ça y est, ça le reprend!** there he goes again!
4. [aller rechercher - personne] to pick up *(sép)* ; [- objet] to get back *(sép)*, to collect ■ [remporter] to take back *(sép)* ■ **je (te) reprendrai mon écharpe demain** I'll get my scarf back (from you) tomorrow ■ **ils reprennent aux uns ce qu'ils donnent aux autres** they take away from some in order to give to others ■ **tu peux ~ ton parapluie, je n'en ai plus besoin** I don't need your umbrella anymore, you can take it back ■ **je te reprendrai à la sortie de l'école** I'll pick you up *ou* I'll collect you *ou* I'll come and fetch you after school ■ **vous pouvez (passer) ~ votre montre demain** you can come (by) and collect *ou* pick up your watch tomorrow

5. [réengager - employé] to take *ou* to have back *(sép)* ■ [réadmettre - élève] to take *ou* to have back ■ **nous ne pouvons ~ votre enfant en septembre** we can't take *ou* have your child back in September
6. [retrouver - un état antérieur] to go back to ■ **elle a repris son nom de jeune fille** she went back to her maiden name ■ **il a repris sa bonhomie coutumière** he has recovered his usual good spirits ■ **je n'arrivais plus à ~ ma respiration** I couldn't get my breath back ■ **~ son sang-froid** to calm down ■ **~ courage** to regain *ou* to recover courage ■ **si tu le fais sécher à plat, il reprendra sa forme** if you dry it flat, it'll regain its shape *ou* it'll get its shape back
7. [à table] : **reprends un biscuit** have another biscuit ■ **reprends un comprimé dans deux heures** take another tablet in two hours' time ‖ [chez un commerçant] to have *ou* to take more (of)
8. [recommencer, se remettre à - recherche, combat] to resume ; [- projet] to take up again ; [- enquête] to restart, to reopen ; [- lecture] to go back to, to resume ; [- hostilités] to resume, to reopen ; [- discussion, voyage] to resume, to carry on (with), to continue ■ **~ ses études** to take up one's studies again, to resume one's studies ■ **je reprends l'école le 15 septembre** I start school again *ou* I go back to school on September 15th ■ **~ le travail** [après des vacances] to go back to work, to start work again ; [après une pause] to get back to work, to start work again ; [après une grève] to go back to work ■ **~ contact avec qqn** to get in touch with sb again ■ **~ la plume/la caméra/le pinceau** to take up one's pen/movie camera/brush once more ■ **~ la route** *ou* **son chemin** to set off again, to resume one's journey ■ **elle a repris le volant après quelques heures** she took the wheel again after a few hours ■ **~ la mer** [marin] to go back to sea ; [navire] to (set) sail again ■ **~ une instance** DR to resume a hearing
9. [répéter - texte] to read again ; [- argument, passage musical] to repeat ; [- refrain] to take up *(sép)* ■ **on reprend tout depuis le** *ou* **au début** [on recommence] let's start (all over) again from the beginning ■ **un sujet repris par tous vos hebdomadaires** an issue taken up by all your weeklies ■ TV to repeat ■ CINÉ to rerun ■ THÉÂTRE to revive, to put on again, to put back on the stage ■ **quand j'ai repris le rôle de Tosca** [que j'avais déjà chanté] when I took on the part of Tosca again ; [que je n'avais jamais chanté] when I took on *ou* over the part of Tosca ‖ [récapituler - faits] to go over *(insép)* again
10. [dire] to go *ou* to carry on ■ **"et lui?", reprit-elle** "what about him?" she went on
11. COMM [article refusé] to take back *(sép)* ■ **les vêtements ne sont ni repris ni échangés** clothes cannot be returned or exchanged ■ **nous vous reprenons votre vieux salon pour tout achat de plus de 2000 euros** your old lounge suite accepted in part exchange for any purchase over 2,000 euros ■ **ils m'ont repris ma voiture pour 1000 euros** I traded my car in for 1,000 euros ‖ [prendre à son compte - cabinet, boutique] to take over *(sép)*
12. [adopter - idée, programme politique] to take up *(sép)*
13. [modifier - texte] to rework, to go over *(insép)* again ; [- peinture] to touch up *(sép)* ■ **il a fallu tout ~** it all had to be gone over *ou* done again ■ **c'était parfait, je n'ai rien eu à ~** it was perfect, I didn't have to make a single correction *ou* alteration ■ COUT [gén] to alter ■ [rétrécir] to take in ■ [en tricot] : **~ une maille** to pick up a stitch ‖ CONSTR to repair ■ **~ un mur en sous-œuvre** to underpin a wall ‖ MÉCAN [pièce] to rework, to machine
14. [réprimander] to pull up, to reprimand *sout*, to tell off *(sép)* ■ [corriger] to correct, to pull up *(sép)* ■ **j'ai été obligée de la ~ en public** I had to put her straight in front of everybody
15. [surprendre] : **que je ne t'y reprenne plus!** don't let me catch you at it again! ■ **on ne m'y reprendra plus!** that's the last time you'll catch me doing that!
16. SPORT to return.
◇ *vi* **1.** [s'améliorer - affaires] to improve, to recover, to pick *ou* to look up ■ [repousser - plante] to pick up, to recover
2. [recommencer - lutte] to start (up) again, to resume ; [- pluie, vacarme] to start (up) again ; [- cours, école] to start again, to resume ; [- feu] to rekindle ; [- fièvre, douleur] to return, to start again ■ **je n'arrive pas à faire ~ le feu** I can't get the fire going again ■ **la tempête reprit de plus belle** the storm started again with renewed ferocity ■ **le froid a repris** the cold weather has set in again *ou* has returned
3. [retourner au travail - employé] to start again.
◆ **se reprendre** *vpi* **1.** [recouvrer ses esprits] to get a grip on o.s., to pull o.s. together ■ [retrouver son calme] to settle down ■ **ils ne nous laissent pas le temps de nous ~ entre deux questions** they don't give us time to take a breather between questions
2. SPORT [au cours d'un match] to make a recovery, to rally ■ **après un mauvais début de saison, il s'est très bien repris** he started the season badly but has come back strongly *ou* has staged a good comeback
3. [se ressaisir - après une erreur] to correct o.s. ■ **se ~ à temps** [avant une bévue] to stop o.s. in time.
◆ **se reprendre à** *vp+prép* : **elle se reprit à divaguer** she started rambling again ■ **je me repris à l'aimer** I started to fall in love with her again ◆ **s'y ~** [recommencer] : **je m'y suis reprise à trois fois** I had to start again three times *ou* to make three attempts.

repreneur, euse [rəprənœr, øz] *nm, f* ÉCON buyer ■ **les ~s de la chaîne** the people who bought up *ou* acquired the channel.

reprennent, reprenons *etc v* ▷ **reprendre.**

représailles [rəprezaj] *nfpl* reprisals, retaliation *(U)* ■ **user de ~ contre un pays** to take retaliatory measures *ou* to retaliate against a country ■ **exercer des ~ contre** *ou* **envers qqn** to take reprisals against sb ■ **en (guise de) ~ contre** in retaliation for, as a reprisal for.

représentant, e [rəprezɑ̃tɑ̃, ɑ̃t] *nm, f* **1.** POLIT (elected) representative **2.** [porte-parole] representative **3.** [délégué] delegate, representative ■ **le ~ de la France à l'ONU** France's *ou* the French representative at the UN ◆ **~ du personnel** staff delegate *ou* representative ■ **~ syndical** shop steward *esp UK*, union representative **4.** COMM : **~ (de commerce)** (sales) representative, commercial traveller, travelling salesman ■ **je suis ~ en électroménager** I'm a sales representative for an electrical appliances firm.

représentatif, ive [rəprezɑ̃tatif, iv] *adj* representative ■ **être ~ de qqn/qqch** to be representative of sb/sthg ■ **c'est assez ~ de la mentalité des jeunes** it's fairly typical of the way young people think.

représentation [rəprezɑ̃tasjɔ̃] *nf* **1.** [image] representation, illustration ■ **c'est une ~ très fidèle des lieux** it's a very accurate description of the place **2.** THÉÂTRE performance **3.** [évocation] description, portrayal **4.** [matérialisation par un signe] representing *(U)* **5.** ADMIN & POLIT representation ■ **assurer la ~ d'un pays** to represent a country, to act as a country's representative ◆ **~ proportionnelle** proportional representation **6.** DR : **~ en justice** legal representation **7.** COMM sales representation, agency ■ **avoir la ~ exclusive de X** to be sole agents for X ■ **faire de la ~** to be a sales representative **8.** PSYCHOL representation **9.** ART representation **10.** GÉOGR : **~ plane** projection.
◆ **en représentation** *loc adj* **1.** [personne] : **il est toujours en ~** he's always trying to project a certain image of himself **2.** [pièce de théâtre] in performance.

représentativité [rəprezɑ̃tativite] *nf* representativeness ■ **quelle est la ~ de cet exemple?** how representative *ou* typical is this example?

représenter [3] [rəprezɑ̃te] *vt* **1.** [montrer] to depict, to show, to represent ■ **~ qqch par un graphique** to show sthg with a diagram ■ **la scène représente un intérieur bourgeois** the scene is *ou* represents a middle-class interior **2.** [incarner] to represent ■ **elle représentait pour lui l'idéal féminin** she represented *ou* symbolized *ou* embodied the feminine ideal for him ■ **tu ne représentes plus rien pour moi** you don't mean anything to me anymore ‖ [symboliser] to represent, to stand for *(insép)* **3.** [constituer] to represent, to account for *(insép)* ■ **les produits de luxe représentent 60 % de nos exportations** luxury items account for *ou* make up 60% of our exports ■ **le loyer représente un tiers de mon salaire** the rent amounts *ou* comes to one third of my salary **4.** THÉÂTRE [faire jouer] to stage, to put on *(sép)* ■ [jouer] to play, to perform **5.** [être le représentant de] to represent ■ **le maire s'est fait ~ par son adjoint** the mayor was represented by his deputy, the mayor sent his deputy to represent him ■ **si vous n'êtes pas disponible, faites-vous ~** if you are not available, have someone stand in for you *ou* delegate someone **6.** COMM to be a representative of *ou* for **7.** *litt* [faire remarquer] to explain, to outline ▪ [mettre en garde quant à] to point out *(sép)* ▪ **elle me représenta les avantages fiscaux de son plan** she pointed out to me the tax benefits of her plan **8.** [traite] to present for payment again.

se représenter <> *vpi* **1.** [à une élection] to stand *UK ou* to run *US* (for election) again ▪ [à un examen] to sit *UK ou* to take an examination again **2.** [se manifester à nouveau - problème] to crop *ou* to come up again ▪ **une occasion qui ne se représentera sans doute jamais** an opportunity which doubtless will never again present itself ▪ **la même pensée se représenta à mon esprit** the same thought crossed my mind once more.

<> *vpt* [imaginer] to imagine, to picture ▪ **représentez-vous le scandale que c'était à l'époque!** just imagine *ou* think how scandalous it was in those days!

répressif, ive [represif, iv] *adj* repressive ▪ **par des moyens ~s** through coercion.

répression [represjɔ̃] *nf* **1.** [punition] : **ils exigent une ~ plus sévère des actes terroristes** they are demanding a crackdown on terrorist activities **2.** [étouffement - d'une révolte] suppression, repression ▪ **la ~ ne mène à rien** coercive methods are no use **3.** PSYCHOL repression.

réprimande [reprimɑ̃d] *nf* [semonce - amicale] scolding, rebuke ; [- par un supérieur hiérarchique] reprimand ▪ **faire** *ou* **adresser une ~ à qqn** to rebuke *ou* to reprimand sb ▪ **face aux ~s de toute la famille** reprimanded by the whole family.

réprimander [3] [reprimɑ̃de] *vt* [gronder] to reprimand, to rebuke ▪ **il s'est fait ~** [par son père] he was told off ; [par son patron] he was given a reprimand.

réprimer [3] [reprime] *vt* **1.** [étouffer - rébellion] to suppress, to quell, to put down *(sép)* **2.** [punir - délit, vandalisme] to punish ▪ **~ le banditisme/terrorisme** to crack down on crime/terrorism **3.** [sourire, colère] to suppress ▪ [larmes] to hold *ou* to choke back *(sép)* ▪ [bâillement] to stifle ▪ **des rires réprimés** repressed *ou* stifled laughter.

repris, e [rəpri, iz] *pp* ⊳ **reprendre**.

repris *nm* : **~ de justice** ex-convict.

reprise *nf* **1.** [d'une activité, d'un dialogue] resumption ▪ **~e des hostilités hier sur le front oriental** hostilities resumed on the eastern front yesterday ▪ **la ~e du travail a été votée à la majorité** the majority voted in favour of going back *ou* returning to work ▪ **à la ~e des cotations** when trading resumed ▪ **une ~e des affaires** an upturn *ou* a recovery in business activity ◐ **~e (économique)** (economic) recovery **2.** RADIO & TV repeat, rerun ▪ CINÉ rerun, reshowing ▪ THÉÂTRE revival, reprise ▪ MUS [d'un passage] repeat, reprise ▪ **une ~e d'une chanson des Beatles** a cover (version) of a Beatles' song **3.** [rachat] : **deux hommes sont candidats à la ~e de la chaîne** two men have put in an offer to take over *ou* to buy out the channel **4.** COMM [action - de reprendre] taking back ; [- d'échanger] trade-in, part exchange *UK* ▪ **nous ne faisons pas de ~e** goods cannot be returned *ou* exchanged ▪ **il m'offre une ~e de 2 000 euros pour ma vieille voiture** he'll give me 2,000 euros as a trade-in *ou* in part exchange *UK* for my old car **5.** [entre locataires] *payment made to an outgoing tenant (when renting property)* ▪ **la ~e comprend l'équipement de la cuisine** the sum due to the former tenant includes the kitchen equipment ▪ **ils demandent une ~e de 1 500 euros** they're asking 1,500 euros for furniture and fittings *UK ou* for the furnishings **6.** AUTO speeding up, acceleration ▪ **une voiture qui a de bonnes ~es** a car with good acceleration **7.** SPORT [à la boxe] round ▪ ÉQUIT [leçon] riding lesson ▪ [cavaliers] riding team ▪ **~e de volée** TENNIS return volley ▪ **à la ~e, la Corée menait 2 à 0** FOOTBALL Korea was leading 2-0 when the game resumed after halftime *ou* at the start of the second half **8.** COUT [dans la maille] darn ▪ [dans le tissu] mend **9.** DR : **droit de ~e** right of repossession *ou* reentry ▪ **~e des propres** recovery of personal property **10.** INDUST overhauling, repairing ▪ **~e d'usinage** remachining.

reprises *nfpl* : **à maintes ~es** on several *ou* many occasions ▪ **à trois ou quatre ~es** three or four times, on three or four occasions.

reprisage [rəprizaʒ] *nm* darning, mending.

reprise [rəpriz] *f* ⊳ **repris**.

repriser [3] [rəprize] *vt* [raccommoder - bas, moufle] to darn, to mend ; [- pantalon] to mend.

reprit *etc v* ⊳ **reprendre**.

réprobateur, trice [reprɔbatœr, tris] *adj* reproving, reproachful ▪ **jeter un regard ~ à qqn** to give sb a reproving look, to look at sb reprovingly *ou* reproachfully.

réprobation [reprɔbasjɔ̃] *nf* **1.** [blâme] reprobation *sout*, disapproval ▪ **soulever la ~ générale** to give rise to general reprobation, to be unanimously reproved ▪ **encourir la ~ générale** to meet with general disapproval **2.** RELIG reprobation.

reproche [rəprɔʃ] *nm* **1.** [blâme] reproach ▪ **accabler qqn de ~s** to heap reproaches on sb ▪ **faire un ~ à qqn** to reproach sb ▪ **les ~s qu'on lui fait sont injustifiés** the reproaches levelled *ou* directed at him are unjustified ▪ **il y avait un léger ~ dans sa voix/remarque** there was a hint of reproach in her voice/remark ▪ **faire ~ à qqn de qqch** *sout* to upbraid sb for sthg ▪ **je ne vous fais pas ~ de vous être trompé, mais d'avoir menti** what I hold against you is not the fact that you made a mistake, but the fact that you lied **2.** [critique] : **le seul ~ que je ferais à la pièce, c'est sa longueur** the only thing I'd say against the play *ou* my only criticism of the play is that it's too long.

sans reproche <> *loc adj* [parfait] above *ou* beyond reproach, irreproachable ▪ [qui n'a pas commis d'erreur] blameless.

<> *loc adv* : **soit dit sans ~, tu n'aurais pas dû y aller** I don't mean to blame *ou* to reproach you, but you shouldn't have gone.

reprocher [3] [rəprɔʃe] *vt* **1.** [erreur, faute] : **~ qqch à qqn** to blame *ou* to reproach sb for sthg ▪ **je lui reproche son manque de ponctualité** what I don't like about her is her lack of punctuality ▪ **on ne peut pas ~ au gouvernement son laxisme** you can't criticize the government for being too soft ▪ **~ à qqn de faire qqch** to blame sb for doing sthg **2.** [défaut] : **~ qqch à qqch** to criticize sthg for sthg ▪ **ce que je reproche à ce beaujolais, c'est sa verdeur** the criticism I would make of this Beaujolais is that it's too young ▪ **je n'ai rien à ~ à son interprétation** in my view her interpretation is faultless, I can't find fault with her interpretation ▪ **~ à qqch d'être...** to criticize sthg for being...

se reprocher *vpt* : **n'avoir rien à se ~** to have nothing to feel guilty about ▪ **tu n'as pas à te ~ son départ** you shouldn't blame yourself for her departure.

reproducteur, trice [rəprɔdyktœr, tris] <> *adj* [organe, cellule] reproductive ▪ **cheval ~** stud-horse, stallion ▪ **poule reproductrice** breeder hen.

<> *nm, f* [poule] breeder ▪ [cheval] stud.

reproductible [rəprɔdyktibl] *adj* reproducible, repeatable.

reproductif, ive [rəprɔdyktif, iv] *adj* reproductive.

reproduction [rəprɔdyksjɔ̃] *nf* **1.** BIOL & BOT reproduction ▪ AGRIC breeding ▪ **cycle/organes de la ~** reproductive cycle/organs ◐ **~ sexuée/asexuée** sexual/asexual reproduction **2.** [restitution] reproduction, reproducing ▪ **techniques de ~ des sons** sound reproduction techniques **3.** IMPR [nouvelle publication] reprinting, reissuing ▪ [technique] reproduction, duplication ▪ **'~ interdite'** 'all rights reserved' **4.** [réplique] reproduction, copy ▪ **une ~ du Baiser de Rodin/de Guernica** a copy of Rodin's Kiss/of Guernica ▪ **une ~ en couleur** a colour print ▪ **une ~ en plâtre** a plaster cast ▪ **une ~ en résine** a resin replica **5.** [département] reprographic department.

reproduire [98] [rəprɔdɥir] *vt* **1.** [faire un autre exemplaire de] to copy ▪ **~ une clé** to cut a key **2.** [renouveler] to repeat **3.** [imiter] to reproduce, to copy **4.** [représenter] to show, to depict, to portray **5.** [restituer - son] to reproduce **6.** IMPR [republier - texte] to reissue ; [- livre] to reprint ▪ [photocopier] to photocopy ▪ [reprographier] to duplicate, to reproduce ▪ [polycopier] to duplicate **7.** HORT to reproduce, to breed ▪ **plantes reproduites en serre** plants propagated in a greenhouse.

se reproduire *vpi* **1.** BIOL & BOT to reproduce, to breed **2.** [se renouveler] to recur ▪ **ces tendances se reproduisent de gé-**

nération en génération these trends recur *ou* are repeated with each successive generation ■ **que cela ne se reproduise plus!** don't let it happen again!

reprogrammer [3] [rəprɔgrame] *vt* **1.** CINÉ & TV to reschedule **2.** INFORM to reprogramme.

reprographie [rəprɔgrafi] *nf* reprography, repro.

réprouvé, e [repruve] <> *adj* RELIG reprobate.
<> *nm, f* **1.** RELIG reprobate **2.** *sout* [personne rejetée] : **vivre en ~** to live as an outcast.

réprouver [3] [repruve] *vt* **1.** [attitude, pratique] to condemn, to disapprove of ■ **des pratiques/tendances que la morale réprouve** morally unacceptable practices/tendencies **2.** RELIG to reprobate, to damn.

reps [rɛps] *nm* rep, repp.

reptation [rɛptasjɔ̃] *nf* crawling, reptation *spéc.*

reptile [rɛptil] *nm* reptile.

reptilien, enne [rɛptiljɛ̃, ɛn] *adj* reptilian.

repu, e [rəpy] <> *pp* ▷ **repaître.**
<> *adj* [rassasié] sated *sout*, satiated *sout* ■ **être ~** to be full (up), to have eaten one's fill ■ **je suis ~ de films policiers** I've had my fill of detective films.

républicain, e [repyblikɛ̃, ɛn] <> *adj* [esprit, système] republican.
<> *nm, f* [gén] republican ■ [aux États-Unis, en Irlande] Republican.

républicanisme [repyblikanism] *nm* republicanism.

république [repyblik] *nf* **1.** [régime politique] republic ■ **vivre en ~** to live in a republic ■ **je fais ce que je veux; on est en ~, non?** *fam* I'll do as I like, it's a free country, isn't it? ➊ **'la République'** *Platon* 'The Republic' **2.** [État] Republic ■ **la République française** the French Republic ■ **la République arabe unie** the United Arab Republic ■ **la République d'Irlande** the Irish Republic, the Republic of Ireland ■ **la République démocratique allemande** HIST the German Democratic Republic ■ **la République fédérale d'Allemagne** the Federal Republic of Germany ■ **la République islamique d'Iran** the Islamic Republic of Iran ■ **la République populaire de Chine** the People's Republic of China ■ **~ bananière** *péj* banana republic **3.** [confrérie] : **dans la ~ des lettres** in the literary world, in the world of letters.

répudiation [repydjasjɔ̃] *nf* **1.** [d'une épouse] repudiation, disowning **2.** [d'un principe, d'un devoir] renunciation, renouncement.

répudier [9] [repydje] *vt* **1.** [renvoyer - épouse] to repudiate, to disown ■ **se faire ~** to be rejected **2.** [renoncer à - nationalité, héritage] to renounce, to relinquish ; [- foi] to renounce ■ **~ ses convictions** to go back on *ou* to renounce one's beliefs.

répugnance [repyɲɑ̃s] *nf* **1.** [dégoût] repugnance, disgust, loathing ■ **avoir de la ~ pour qqch/qqn** to loathe sthg/sb **2.** [mauvaise volonté] reluctance ■ **éprouver une certaine ~ à faire qqch** to be somewhat reluctant *ou* loath to do sthg ■ **je m'attelai à la tâche avec ~** I set about the task reluctantly *ou* unwillingly.

répugnant, e [repyɲɑ̃, ɑ̃t] *adj* **1.** [physiquement] repugnant, loathsome, disgusting ■ **avoir un physique ~** to be repulsive ■ **odeur ~e** disgusting smell ■ **tâche ~e** revolting task ■ **une chambre d'une saleté ~e** a revoltingly *ou* disgustingly filthy room **2.** [moralement - individu, crime] repugnant ; [- livre, image] disgusting, revolting.

répugner [3] [repyɲe] ◆ **répugner à** *v+prép* **1.** [être peu disposé à] : **~ à faire qqch** to be reluctant *ou* loath to do sthg ■ **il ne répugnait pas à faire ce voyage** he didn't hesitate to make this trip **2.** [dégoûter] : **~ à qqn** to repel sb, to be repugnant to sb ■ **tout ce qui est tâche domestique me répugne** I can't bear anything to do with housework ■ **ça ne te répugne pas, l'idée de manger du serpent?** doesn't the idea of eating snake disgust you *ou* put you off? ■ **tout en cet homme me répugne** everything about that man is repulsive (to me) ■ *(tournure impersonnelle) sout* **il me répugne de travailler avec lui** I hate *ou* loathe working with him.

répulsion [repylsjɔ̃] *nf* **1.** [dégoût] repulsion, repugnance ■ **éprouver de la ~ pour qqch** to feel repulsion for sthg, to find sthg repugnant ■ **leurs méthodes m'inspirent une grande ~** I find their methods repugnant **2.** PHYS repulsion.

réputation [repytasjɔ̃] *nf* **1.** [renommée] reputation, repute ■ **jouir d'une bonne ~** to have *ou* to enjoy a good reputation ■ **se faire une ~** to make a reputation *ou* name for o.s. ■ **un hôtel de bonne/mauvaise ~** a hotel of good/ill repute ■ **il n'a pas volé sa ~ de frimeur** *fam* they don't call him a show-off for nothing ■ **elle a la ~ de noter sévèrement** she has a reputation *ou* she's well-known for being a tough marker ■ **marque de ~ mondiale** *ou* **internationale** world-famous brand, brand of international repute ■ **tu me fais une sale ~** *fam* you're giving me a bad name ■ **leur ~ n'est plus à faire** their reputation is well-established ■ **connaître qqn de ~** to know sb by repute *ou* reputation **2.** [honorabilité] reputation, good name ■ **je suis prêt à mettre ma ~ en jeu** I'm willing to stake my reputation on it ■ **porter atteinte à la ~ de qqn** to damage *ou* to blacken sb's good name.

réputé, e [repyte] *adj* **1.** [illustre - orchestre, restaurant] famous, renowned ■ **l'un des musiciens les plus ~s de son temps** one of the most famous musicians of his day ■ **des vins très ~s** wines of great repute ■ **elle est ~e pour ses colères** she's famous *ou* renowned for her fits of rage ■ **il est ~ pour être un avocat efficace** he has the reputation of being *ou* he's reputed to be a good lawyer **2.** [considéré comme] reputed ■ **elle est ~e intelligente** she has a reputation for intelligence, she's reputed to be intelligent.

requérant, e [rəkerɑ̃, ɑ̃t] <> *adj* DR claiming ■ **la partie ~e** the claimant, the petitioner.
<> *nm, f* DR claimant, petitioner.

requérir [39] [rəkerir] *vt* **1.** [faire appel à] to call for, to require ■ **ce travail requiert beaucoup d'attention** the work requires *ou* demands great concentration ■ **~ la force publique** to ask the police to intervene ■ **~ de l'aide** to request help **2.** DR to call for, to demand ■ **le juge a requis une peine de deux ans de prison** the judge recommended a two-year prison sentence ■ *(en usage absolu)* **pendant qu'il requérait** during his summing up **3.** *sout* [sommer] : **~ qqn de faire qqch** to request that sb do sthg.

requête [rəkɛt] *nf* **1.** [demande] request, petition ■ **soumettre une ~ à un service** to put in *ou* to submit a request to a department ■ **à la** *ou* **sur la ~ de qqn** *sout* at sb's request *ou* behest **2.** DR petition ■ **adresser une ~ au tribunal** to petition the court, to apply for legal remedy ➊ **~ en cassation** application for appeal.

requiem [rekɥijɛm] *nm inv* requiem.

requiert *etc v* ▷ **requérir.**

requin [rəkɛ̃] *nm* **1.** ZOOL shark ■ **~ bleu** blue shark **2.** [personne] shark ■ **les ~s du show-business** the sharks of the show business world.

requinquer [3] [rəkɛ̃ke] *vt fam* [redonner des forces à] to pep *ou* to buck up *(sép)*.
◆ **se requinquer** *vpi* to recover, to perk up ■ **il a eu du mal à se ~** it took him a while to recover *ou* to get back to his old self again.

requis, e [rəki, iz] <> *pp* ▷ **requérir.**
<> *adj* **1.** [prescrit] required, requisite ■ **remplir les conditions ~es** to meet the required *ou* prescribed conditions ■ **avoir l'âge ~** to meet the age requirements ■ **avoir les qualifications ~es** to have the requisite *ou* necessary qualifications **2.** [réquisitionné] commandeered, requisitioned.
◆ **requis** *nm* commandeered civilian ■ **les ~ du travail (obligatoire)** labour conscripts.

réquisition [rekizisjɔ̃] *nf* **1.** MIL & *fig* requisition, requisitioning, commandeering ■ **il y a eu ~ de tous les véhicules par l'armée** the army has requisitioned *ou* commandeered all vehicles **2.** DR : **~ d'audience** petition to the court **3.** FIN : **~ de paiement** demand for payment.
◆ **réquisitions** *nfpl* DR [conclusions] closing speech (for the prosecution) ■ [réquisitoire] charge.

réquisitionner [3] [rekizisjɔne] *vt* **1.** [matériel, troupe, employé] to requisition, to commandeer **2.** [faire appel à] : **~ qqn pour faire qqch** to rope sb into doing sthg.

réquisitoire [rekizitwar] *nm* **1.** DR [dans un procès] prosecutor's arraignment *ou* speech *ou* charge **2.** *fig* **ces résultats constituent un véritable ~ contre la politique du gouvernement** these results are an indictment of the government's policy.

requit *etc v* ▷ **requérir**.

RER (*abr de* **Réseau express régional**) *nm Paris metropolitan and regional rail system*.

RES (*abr de* **rachat de l'entreprise par ses salariés**) *nm* MBO.

resaler [3] [rəsale] *vt* to put more salt in, to add more salt to.

resalir [32] [rəsalir] *vt* : **j'ai resali le tailleur que je viens de faire nettoyer** I've just got my suit back from the cleaners and I've got it dirty again ■ **évitez de ~ des assiettes** try not to dirty any more plates.
◆ **se resalir** *vp (emploi réfléchi)* to get o.s. dirty again.

rescapé, e [rɛskape] ◇ *adj* surviving.
◇ *nm, f* **1.** [d'un accident] survivor ■ **les ~s de la catastrophe** the survivors of the catastrophe **2.** *fig* **les quelques ~s du Tour de France** the few remaining participants in the Tour de France.

rescousse [rɛskus] ◆ **à la rescousse** *loc adv* : **aller/venir à la ~ de qqn** to go/to come to sb's rescue *fig* ■ **nous avons appelé quelques amis à la ~** we called on a few friends for help ■ **tout le monde à la ~!** rally round, everybody!

réseau, x [rezo] *nm* **1.** TRANSP network ■ **~ aérien/ferroviaire/routier** air/rail/road network ■ **~ urbain** city bus network ➲ **Réseau express régional = RER**
2. TÉLÉCOM & TV network ■ **~ téléphonique** telephone network ■ **~ de télévision** television network
3. [organisation] network ■ **développer un ~ commercial** to develop *ou* to expand a sales network ■ **~ de distribution** distribution network ■ **~ d'espionnage** spy ring, network of spies ■ **~ de résistance** HIST resistance network *ou* group
4. ARCHIT tracery
5. ÉLECTR grid ■ **~ bouclé** ring main
6. GÉOGR : **~ fluvial** river system
7. INFORM network ■ **~ étoilé/maillé** star/mesh network ■ **~ à commutation par paquets** packet-switching network ■ **en ~** networked
8. OPT (diffraction) grating.

réséda [rezeda] *nm* reseda.

réservataire [rezɛrvatɛr] ◇ *adj* DR : **elle est ~ pour un tiers** a third of the legacy devolves to her by law ➲ **héritier ~** heir who cannot be totally disinherited.
◇ *nmf* heir who cannot be totally disinherited.

réservation [rezɛrvasjɔ̃] *nf* **1.** [d'un billet, d'une chambre, d'une table] reservation, booking ■ **faire une ~** [à l'hôtel] to make a reservation ; [au restaurant] to reserve a table **2.** DR reservation.

réserve [rezɛrv] *nf* **1.** [stock] reserve, stock ■ **nous ne disposons pas d'une ~ suffisante d'eau potable** we do not have sufficient reserves of drinking water ■ **une ~ d'argent** some money put by ■ **faire des ~s de** to lay in supplies *ou* provisions of ■ **il a des ~s!** *fam hum* he's got plenty of fat in reserve! ➲ **~ légale** ÉCON reserve assets
2. [réticence] reservation ■ **faire** *ou* **émettre des ~s** to express reservations
3. [modestie, retenue] reserve ■ **elle est** *ou* **demeure** *ou* **se tient sur la ~** she's being *ou* remaining reserved (about it) ■ **il a accueilli mon frère avec une grande ~** he welcomed my brother with great restraint
4. ANTHR reservation ■ ÉCOL reserve ■ **~ de chasse/pêche** hunting/fishing preserve ■ **~ naturelle** nature reserve ■ **~ ornithologique** *ou* **d'oiseaux** bird sanctuary
5. [resserre - dans un magasin] storeroom ■ [collections réservées - dans un musée, une bibliothèque] reserve collection
6. DR [clause] reservation ■ **~ (héréditaire)** *that part of a legacy legally apportioned to a rightful heir*
7. MIL : **la ~** the reserve
8. NAUT : **~ de flottabilité** reserves buoyancy
9. PHYSIOL : **~ alcaline (du sang)** concentration of alkaline substance (in the blood).
◆ **réserves** *nfpl* FIN reserves ■ **~s de change** monetary reserves ■ **~s monétaires/de devises** monetary/currency reserves ■ **les ~s de charbon d'un pays** MIN [gisements] a country's coal reserves ; [stocks] a country's coal stocks ➲ **~s obligatoires** FIN statutory reserves.
◆ **de réserve** *loc adj* **1.** [conservé pour plus tard] reserve *(modif)* ■ **nous avons un stock de ~** we have a reserve supply
2. FIN : **monnaie de ~** reserve currency
3. MIL : **officier de ~** officer of the reserve ■ **régiment de ~** reserve regiment.
◆ **en réserve** *loc adv* **1.** [de côté] in reserve ■ **avoir de la nourriture en ~** to have food put by, to have food in reserve ■ **je tiens en ~ quelques bouteilles pour notre anniversaire** I've put a few bottles aside *ou* to one side for our anniversary
2. COMM in stock ■ **avoir qqch en ~** to have sthg in stock.
◆ **sans réserve** ◇ *loc adj* [admiration] unreserved ■ [dévotion] unreserved, unstinting ■ [approbation] unreserved, unqualified.
◇ *loc adv* without reservation, unreservedly.
◆ **sous réserve de** *loc prép* subject to ■ **sous ~ de vérification** subject to verification, pending checks.
◆ **sous toute réserve** *loc adv* with all proper reserves ■ **attention, c'est sous toute ~!** there's no guarantee as to the accuracy of this! ■ **la nouvelle a été publiée sous toute ~** the news was published with no guarantee as to its accuracy.

réservé, e [rezɛrve] *adj* **1.** [non public] : **'chasse ~e'** private hunting ■ **cuvée ~e** reserved vintage, vintage cuvée ➲ **quartier ~** *euphém* red-light district **2.** [retenu] reserved, booked *UK* ■ **'réservé'** 'reserved' **3.** [distant] reserved ■ **une jeune fille très ~e** a very reserved *ou* demure young girl **4.** DR reserved.

réserver [3] [rezɛrve] *vt* **1.** [retenir à l'avance] to reserve, to book ■ **Mesdames, bonsoir, avez-vous réservé?** good evening, ladies, have you booked *UK ou* do you have a reservation?
2. [garder - pour un usage particulier] to save, to keep, to set *ou* to put aside ■ **j'avais réservé des fonds pour l'achat d'une maison** I had put *ou* set some money aside to buy a house ■ **~ qqn pour une mission spéciale** to keep sb for a special mission ■ **les nouvelles installations seront réservées aux superpétroliers** the new installations will be reserved for the use of supertankers ■ [conserver] to reserve, to keep ■ **~ le meilleur pour la fin** to keep *ou* to save the best till last ■ **~ sa réponse** to delay one's answer ■ **~ son opinion** to reserve one's opinion ■ **être réservé à qqn** to be reserved for sb ■ **un privilège/sport réservé aux gens riches** a privilege/sport enjoyed solely by rich people ■ **toilettes réservées aux handicapés** toilets (reserved) for the disabled ■ **emplacements réservés aux médecins** parking (reserved) for doctors only
3. [destiner] to reserve, to have in store ■ **~ une surprise à qqn** to have a surprise (in store) for sb ■ **~ un accueil glacial/chaleureux à qqn** to reserve an icy/a warm welcome for sb ■ **que nous réserve l'avenir?** what does the future have in store for us?
◆ **se réserver** ◇ *vpi* **1.** [par prudence] to hold back ■ **je me réserve pour le fromage** I'm keeping some room *ou* saving myself for the cheese
2. SPORT & *fig* to save one's strength.
◇ *vpt* : **se ~ qqch** to reserve *ou* to keep sthg (for o.s.) ■ **se ~ un droit de regard sur** to retain the right to inspect sthg ■ **se ~ le droit de faire qqch** to reserve the right to do sthg.

réserviste [rezɛrvist] *nm* reservist.

réservoir [rezɛrvwar] *nm* **1.** [d'essence, de mazout] tank ■ AUTO (petrol *UK ou* fuel) tank ■ [d'eau] (water) tank ■ [des W-C] cistern ■ **~ d'eau chaude** hot water tank **2.** BIOL reservoir.

résidant, e [rezidɑ̃, ɑ̃t] *adj* & *nm, f* resident.

résidence [rezidɑ̃s] *nf* **1.** [domicile] residence ■ **établir sa ~ à Nice** to take up residence in Nice ■ **~ d'été** summer quarters ➲ **~ principale/secondaire** main/second home ■ **~ officielle** official residence **2.** [bâtiment] block of (luxury) flats *UK*, (luxury) apartment block *US* ■ **~ universitaire** UNIV hall of residence *UK*, dormitory *US* **3.** [maison] residential property **4.** DR residence ■ **assigner qqn à ~** to put sb under house arrest ■ **être en ~ surveillée** to be under house arrest.

résident, e [rezidɑ̃, ɑ̃t] <> *nm, f* resident, (foreign) national ■ **tous les ~s français de Londres** all French nationals living in London.
<> *adj* INFORM resident.

résidentiel, elle [rezidɑ̃sjɛl] *adj* residential.

résider [3] [rezide] *vi* **1.** [habiter] : **~ à** to reside *sout* OU to live in ■ **~ à l'étranger/à Genève** to live abroad/in Geneva **2.** *fig* **~ dans** to lie in ■ **c'est là que réside tout l'intérêt du film** that is where the strength of the film lies.

résidu [rezidy] *nm* **1.** [portion restante] residue ■ **~s de raffinage** waste oil **2.** [détritus] residue, remnants.

résiduel, elle [rezidɥɛl] *adj* **1.** [qui constitue un résidu - huile, matière] residual **2.** [persistant - chômage] residual ■ **fatigue ~le** constant tiredness.

résignation [reziɲasjɔ̃] *nf* **1.** [acceptation] resignation, resignedness ■ **accepter son destin avec ~** to accept one's fate resignedly *ou* with resignation **2.** DR abandonment (of a right).

résigné, e [reziɲe] *adj* resigned ■ **prendre un air ~** to look resigned ■ **parler d'un ton ~** to speak in a resigned *ou* philosophical tone of voice.

résigner [3] [reziɲe] *vt sout* [se démettre de] to resign, to relinquish.
◆ **se résigner à** *vp+prép* to resign o.s. to ■ **il s'est résigné à vivre dans la pauvreté** he has resigned himself to living in poverty ■ **se ~ à une perte** to resign o.s. to a loss ■ *(en usage absolu)* **il n'a jamais voulu se ~** he would never give up *ou* in, he would never submit ■ **il faut se ~** you must resign yourself to it *ou* accept it.

résiliable [reziljabl] *adj* [bail, contrat, marché] cancellable, terminable DR voidable ■ **non ~** indefeasible.

résiliation [reziljasjɔ̃] *nf* [d'un bail, d'un contrat, d'un marché - en cours] cancellation DR avoidance ; [- arrivant à expiration] termination.

résilience [reziljɑ̃s] *nf* PSYCHOL resilience.

résilier [9] [rezilje] *vt* [bail, contrat, marché - en cours] to cancel ; [- arrivant à expiration] to terminate.

résille [rezij] *nf* [à cheveux] hairnet.

résine [rezin] *nf* BOT & TECHNOL resin ■ **~ époxyde** *ou* **epoxy** epoxy resin.

résiné, e [rezine] *adj* resinated.
◆ **résiné** *nm* resinated wine.

résineux, euse [rezinø, øz] *adj* **1.** [essence, odeur] resinous **2.** [arbre, bois] resiniferous.
◆ **résineux** *nm* resiniferous tree.

résistance [rezistɑ̃s] *nf* **1.** [combativité] resistance ■ **elle a opposé une ~ farouche à ses agresseurs** she put up a fierce resistance to her attackers ■ **il s'est laissé emmener sans ~** he let himself be taken away quietly *ou* without resistance **2.** [rébellion] resistance ■ **~ active/passive** active/passive resistance ■ **la Résistance** HIST the (French) Resistance **3.** [obstacle] resistance ■ **en fermant le tiroir j'ai senti une ~** when I shut the drawer I felt some resistance **4.** [robustesse] resistance, stamina ■ **elle a survécu grâce à sa ~ exceptionnelle** she survived thanks to her great powers of resistance ■ **~ à la fatigue/au froid** resistance to tiredness/cold ■ **les limites de la ~ humaine** the limits of human resistance *ou* endurance **5.** TECHNOL resistance, strength ■ **~ aux chocs** resilience ■ **~ des matériaux** strength of materials **6.** ÉLECTR resistance ■ [dispositif chauffant] element ■ **quelle est l'unité de ~ en électricité?** what's the unit of electrical resistance? **7.** PSYCHOL resistance.

LA RÉSISTANCE

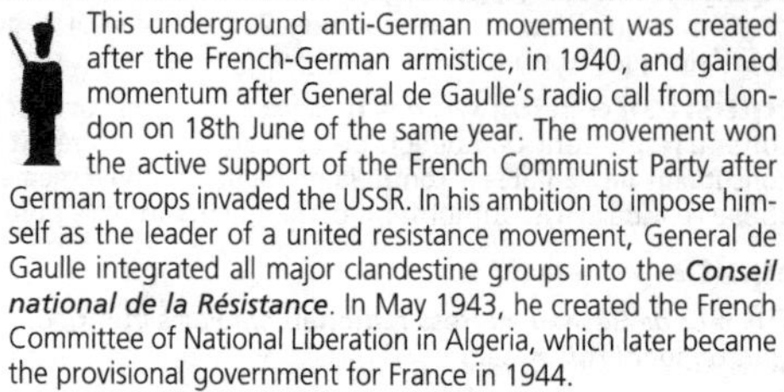

This underground anti-German movement was created after the French-German armistice, in 1940, and gained momentum after General de Gaulle's radio call from London on 18th June of the same year. The movement won the active support of the French Communist Party after German troops invaded the USSR. In his ambition to impose himself as the leader of a united resistance movement, General de Gaulle integrated all major clandestine groups into the *Conseil national de la Résistance*. In May 1943, he created the French Committee of National Liberation in Algeria, which later became the provisional government for France in 1944.

résistant, e [rezistɑ̃, ɑ̃t] <> *adj* **1.** [personne] resistant, tough ■ [emballage] resistant, strong, solid ■ [couleur] fast ■ **c'est une enfant peu ~e** she's not a very strong child **2.** ÉLECTR & PHYS resistant ■ **~ au froid/gel** cold/frost resistant ■ **~ aux chocs** shockproof ■ **~ à la chaleur** heatproof, heat-resistant.
<> *nm, f* HIST (French) Resistance fighter.

résister [3] [reziste] ◆ **résister à** *v+prép* **1.** [agresseur, attaquant] to resist, to hold out against ■ [autorité] to resist, to stand up to ■ [gendarme, huissier] to put up resistance to ■ **j'ai toujours résisté à ses caprices** I've always stood up to *ou* opposed his whims ■ **je ne peux pas lui ~, il est si gentil** I can't resist him, he's so nice **2.** [fatigue, faim] to withstand, to put up with ■ [solitude, douleur] to stand, to withstand ■ **~ à la tentation** to resist temptation ■ **~ à ses désirs/penchants** to fight against one's desires/inclinations **3.** [à l'usure, à l'action des éléments] to withstand, to resist, to be proof against ■ **qui résiste au feu** fireproof ■ **qui résiste à la chaleur** heatproof ■ **qui résiste aux chocs** shockproof ■ **~ au temps** to stand the test of time ■ **couleurs qui résistent au lavage** fast colours ■ **la porte a résisté à ma poussée** the door wouldn't open when I pushed it ■ *(en usage absolu)* **la serrure résiste** the lock is sticking ■ **la toiture/théière n'a pas résisté** the roof/teapot didn't stand up to the shock **4.** [suj: livre, projet] to stand up ■ **~ à l'analyse/l'examen** to stand up to analysis/investigation.

résistivité [rezistivite] *nf* resistivity, specific resistance.

résolu, e [rezɔly] <> *pp* ▷ **résoudre.**
<> *adj* **1.** [personne] resolute, determined ■ **il m'a paru plutôt ~** he looked quite determined to me ■ **je suis ~ à ne pas céder** I'm determined not to give in **2.** [attitude] : **une foi ~e en l'avenir** an unshakeable faith in the future.

résoluble [rezɔlybl] *adj* **1.** [question, situation] soluble, solvable ■ **le problème est aisément ~** the problem is easy to solve *ou* can be solved easily **2.** DR [bail, contrat] annullable, cancellable.

résolument [rezɔlymɑ̃] *adv* **1.** [fermement] resolutely, firmly, determinedly ■ **je m'oppose ~ à cette décision** I'm strongly *ou* firmly opposed to this decision **2.** [vaillamment] resolutely, steadfastly, unwaveringly.

résolut *v* ▷ **résoudre.**

résolution [rezɔlysjɔ̃] *nf* **1.** [décision] resolution ■ **prendre une ~** to make a resolution ■ **prendre la ~ de faire qqch** to make up one's mind *ou* to resolve to do sthg ■ **sa ~ est prise** her mind is made up ■ **bonnes ~s** [gén] good intentions ; [du nouvel an] New Year resolutions **2.** [solution] solution, resolution ■ **la ~ d'une énigme/d'un problème** the solution to an enigma/a problem **3.** POLIT resolution **4.** DR annulment, cancellation **5.** [d'un écran] resolution ■ **mauvaise/bonne ~** poor/high resolution **6.** MÉD resolution ■ **~ des membres** muscular relaxation **7.** OPT : **pouvoir de ~** resolving power.

résolutoire [rezɔlytwar] *adj* DR resolutive.

résolvait *etc v* ▷ **résoudre.**

résonance [rezɔnɑ̃s] *nf* **1.** PHYS & TÉLÉCOM resonance ■ **entrer en ~** to start resonating ■ **sa déclaration a eu quelque ~ dans la classe politique** his statement found an echo *ou* had a certain effect amongst politicians ▶ **~ magnétique** magnetic resonance **2.** *litt* [écho] connotation, colouring *(U)* ■ **un poème de Donne aux ~s très modernes** a poem by Donne with very modern overtones.

résonant, e [rezɔnɑ̃, ɑ̃t] = **résonnant**.

résonnant, e [rezɔnɑ̃, ɑ̃t] *adj* resonant.

résonner [3] [rezɔne] *vi* **1.** [sonner] to resonate, to resound ▪ **la cloche résonne faiblement** the bell rings feebly **2.** [renvoyer le son] to resound, to be resonant ▪ **la pièce résonne** sound reverberates *ou* echoes in the room ▪ **la halle résonnait des cris des vendeurs** the hall resounded with the cries of the traders.

résorber [3] [rezɔrbe] *vt* **1.** [éliminer - chômage, déficit] to reduce, to bring down *(sép)*, to curb **2.** MÉD to resorb.
◆ **se résorber** *vpi* **1.** [chômage, inflation] to be reduced ▪ **la crise ne va pas se ~ toute seule** the crisis isn't going to just disappear **2.** MÉD to be resorbed.

résorption [rezɔrpsjɔ̃] *nf* **1.** [de l'inflation, du chômage] curbing, reduction ▪ **la ~ des dépenses** bringing down *ou* curbing spending ▪ **la ~ des excédents prendra plusieurs années** it will take several years for the surplus to be absorbed **2.** MÉD resorption.

résoudre [88] [rezudr] *vt* **1.** [querelle] to settle, to resolve ▪ [énigme, mystère] to solve ▪ [difficulté] to resolve, to sort out *(sép)* ▪ [problème] to solve, to resolve ▪ **non résolu** unresolved **2.** MATH to resolve ▪ **~ une équation** to solve an equation ▪ **~ une parenthèse** to remove the brackets **3.** *sout* [décider] to decide (on) ▪ **ils ont résolu sa perte** they decided on his ruin ▪ **je résolus finalement de rentrer chez moi** in the end I decided to go back home **4.** *sout* [entraîner] : **~ qqn à faire qqch** to induce *ou* to move sb to do sthg **5.** CHIM, MÉD & MUS to resolve **6.** DR [bail, contrat] to annul, to avoid.
◆ **se résoudre** *vpi* MÉD to resolve ▪ **la tumeur s'est résolue lentement** the tumor slowly resolved itself.
◆ **se résoudre à** *vp+prép* **1.** [accepter de] to reconcile o.s. to ▪ **je ne peux m'y ~** I can't reconcile myself to doing it **2.** [consister en] to amount to, to result in.

respect [rɛspɛ] *nm* [estime] respect ▪ **avec ~** with respect, respectfully ▪ **~ de soi** self-respect ▪ **elle m'inspire beaucoup de ~** I have a great deal of respect for her ▪ **élevé dans le ~ des traditions** brought up to respect traditions ▪ **manquer de ~ à qqn** to be disrespectful to sb ▪ **avec (tout)** *ou* **sauf le ~ que je vous dois** with all due respect ▪ **sauf votre ~** with respect ▪ **tenir qqn en ~** to keep sb at bay *ou* at a (respectful) distance.
◆ **respects** *nmpl* respects, regards ▪ **présenter ses ~s à qqn** to present one's respects to sb ▪ **mes ~s à madame votre mère** please give my respects to your mother.

respectabilité [rɛspɛktabilite] *nf* respectability.

respectable [rɛspɛktabl] *adj* **1.** [estimable] respectable, deserving of respect ▪ *hum* respectable ▪ **c'est une dame fort ~!** *hum* she's a real pillar of society! **2.** [important] respectable ▪ **avec une avance ~** SPORT with an impressive lead.

respecter [4] [rɛspɛkte] *vt* **1.** [honorer] to respect, to have *ou* to show respect for ▪ **il a un nom respecté dans notre ville** his name is held in respect in our city ▪ **elle sait se faire ~** she commands respect ▪ **il n'a pas su se faire ~** he was unable to gain respect **2.** [se conformer à] to respect, to keep to *(insép)* ▪ **~ les dernières volontés de qqn** to abide by sb's last wishes ▪ **~ l'ordre alphabétique** to keep to alphabetical order ▪ **~ la parole donnée** to keep one's word ▪ **~ les lois** to respect *ou* to obey the law **3.** [ne pas porter atteinte à] to show respect for ▪ **~ la tranquillité/le repos de qqn** to respect sb's need for peace and quiet/rest.
◆ **se respecter** *vp (emploi réfléchi)* to respect o.s. ▪ **elle ne se respecte plus** she's lost all her self-respect ▪ **une chanteuse qui se respecte ne prend pas de micro** no self-respecting singer would use a microphone.

respectif, ive [rɛspɛktif, iv] *adj* respective ▪ **nous sommes rentrés dans nos foyers ~s** we went back to our respective homes.

respectivement [rɛspɛktivmɑ̃] *adv* respectively ▪ **Paul et Jean sont âgés ~ de trois et cinq ans** Paul and John are three and five years old respectively.

respectueusement [rɛspɛktɥøzmɑ̃] *adv* respectfully, with respect ▪ **puis-je vous faire ~ remarquer que vous vous êtes trompé?** may I respectfully point out that you have made a mistake?

respectueux, euse [rɛspɛktɥø, øz] *adj* **1.** [personne] respectful ▪ **se montrer ~ envers qqn** to be respectful to sb ▪ **~ de** respectful of ▪ **~ des lois** law-abiding **2.** [lettre, salut] respectful **3.** [dans des formules de politesse] : **je vous prie d'agréer mes respectueuses salutations** yours faithfully.

respirable [rɛspirabl] *adj* **1.** [qu'on peut respirer] breathable ▪ **l'air est difficilement ~ ici** it's hard to breathe in here **2.** *fig* [supportable] : **l'ambiance du bureau est à peine ~** the atmosphere at the office is almost unbearable.

respirateur [rɛspiratœr] *nm* **1.** [masque] gas mask, respirator **2.** MÉD [poumon d'acier] iron lung ▪ [à insufflation] positive-pressure respirator.

respiration [rɛspirasjɔ̃] *nf* **1.** PHYSIOL [action] breathing, respiration *spéc* ▪ [résultat] breath ▪ **reprendre sa ~** to get one's breath back ▪ **retenir sa ~** to hold one's breath ▪ **j'en ai eu la ~ coupée** it took my breath away ➲ **~ artificielle** artificial respiration **2.** MUS phrasing.

respiratoire [rɛspiratwar] *adj* breathing, respiratory *spéc.*

respirer [3] [rɛspire] ◇ *vi* **1.** PHYSIOL to breathe ▪ **~ par la bouche/le nez** to breathe through one's mouth/nose ▪ **respirez à fond, expirez!** breathe in, and (breathe) out! **2.** [être rassuré] to breathe again ▪ **ouf, je respire!** phew, thank goodness for that! **3.** [marquer un temps d'arrêt] : **du calme, laissez-moi ~!** give me a break! ▪ **on n'a jamais cinq minutes pour ~** you can't even take a breather for five minutes.
◇ *vt* **1.** PHYSIOL to breathe (in), to inhale *spéc* ▪ [sentir] to smell **2.** [exprimer] to radiate, to exude ▪ **elle respire la santé** she radiates good health ▪ **il respire le bonheur** he's the very picture of happiness ▪ **la maison respire la douceur de vivre** the whole house is bathed in *ou* alive with the joy of living.

resplendir [32] [rɛsplɑ̃dir] *vi litt* **1.** [étinceler - casque, chaussure] to gleam, to shine ▪ **~ de propreté** to be spotlessly clean **2.** [s'épanouir] : **son visage resplendit de bonheur** her face is shining *ou* radiant with happiness.

resplendissant, e [rɛsplɑ̃disɑ̃, ɑ̃t] *adj* **1.** [éclatant - meuble, parquet] shining ; [- casserole, émail] gleaming ; [- soleil, temps] glorious **2.** [radieux] radiant, shining, resplendent *litt* ▪ **tu as une mine ~e** you look radiant ▪ **~ de santé** radiant *ou* blooming with health.

resplendissement [rɛsplɑ̃dismɑ̃] *nm litt* resplendence *litt*, radiance, brilliance.

responsabilisation [rɛspɔ̃sabilizasjɔ̃] *nf* : **développer la ~ des jeunes** to make young people aware of their responsibilities.

responsabiliser [3] [rɛspɔ̃sabilize] *vt* **1.** [donner des responsabilités à] : **tu ne le responsabilises pas assez** you don't give him enough responsibility **2.** [rendre conscient de ses responsabilités] : **~ qqn** to make sb aware of their responsibilities.

responsabilité [rɛspɔ̃sabilite] *nf* **1.** [obligation morale] responsibility ▪ **nous déclinons toute ~ en cas de vol** we take no responsibility in the event of theft ▪ **c'est une grosse ~!** it's a big responsibility! ▪ **prends tes ~s!** face up to your responsibilities! ▪ **faire porter la ~ de qqch à qqn** to hold sb responsible for sthg ▪ **assumer entièrement la ~ de qqch** to take on *ou* to shoulder the entire responsibility for sthg **2.** [charge administrative] function, position ▪ **des ~s gouvernementales/ministérielles** a post in the government/cabinet ▪ **démis de ses ~s** relieved of his responsibilities *ou* position ▪ **elle a la ~ du département publicité** she's in charge of the advertising department **3.** DR liability, responsibility ▪ [acte moral] responsibility ▪ **~ civile** [d'un individu] civil liability, strict liability ; [d'une société] business liability ▪ **~ contractuelle/délictuelle** contractual/negligence liability ▪ **~ du fait d'autrui** ≃ parental liability ▪ **~ collective** collective responsibility ▪ **~ pénale** legal responsibility **4.** [rapport causal] : **la ~ du tabac dans les affections respiratoires a été démontrée** it has been proved that tobacco is the main contributing factor in respiratory diseases.

responsable [rɛspɔ̃sabl] ◇ *adj* **1.** [garant de] : **~ de** responsible (for) ▪ **j'en suis ~** I'm responsible for it ▪ **il n'est pas ~ de ses actes** DR he cannot be held responsible for his (own)

actions **2.** [chargé de] : ~ **de** in charge of, responsible for ■ **il est ~ du service après-vente** he's in charge of the after-sales department **3.** : ~ **de** [à l'origine de] : **l'abus des graisses animales est largement ~ des affections cardiaques** the main contributing factor to heart disease is over-consumption of animal fats **4.** DR liable ■ ~ **civilement** liable in civil law **5.** [réfléchi] responsible ■ **ce n'est pas très ~ de sa part** that isn't very responsible of him ■ **elle s'est toujours comportée en personne ~** she has always acted responsibly.
◇ *nmf* **1.** [coupable] : **le ~, la ~** the person responsible *ou* to blame ■ **qui est le ~ de l'accident?** who's responsible for the accident? ■ **nous retrouverons les ~s** we will find the people *ou* those responsible **2.** [dirigeant - politique] leader ; [- administratif] person in charge ■ **parler avec les ~s politiques** to speak with the political leaders ■ **réunion avec les ~s syndicaux** meeting with the union representatives.

resquillage [rɛskijaʒ] *nm*, **resquille** [rɛskij] *nf fam* [sans payer] sneaking in ■ TRANSP fare-dodging ■ [sans attendre son tour] queue-jumping *UK*, line-jumping *US*.

resquiller [3] [rɛskije] *fam* ◇ *vi* [ne pas payer] to sneak in ■ TRANSP to dodge the fare *UK* ■ [ne pas attendre son tour] to push in, to jump the queue *UK*, to cut in the line *US*.
◇ *vt* : ~ **une place pour le concert** to fiddle *ou* to wangle o.s. a seat for the concert.

resquilleur, euse [rɛskijœr, øz] *nm, f fam* [qui ne paie pas] person who sneaks in without paying ■ TRANSP fare-dodger *UK* ■ [qui n'attend pas son tour] queue-jumper *UK*, line-jumper *US*.

ressac [rəsak] *nm* backwash *(of a wave)*.

ressaisir [32] [rəsezir] *vt* **1.** [agripper de nouveau] to catch *ou* to grab again, to seize again ■ **le chien ressaisit sa proie** the dog got hold of *ou* caught his prey again **2.** *fig* [occasion] to seize again **3.** INFORM to rekey.
◆ **se ressaisir** *vpi* [se calmer] to pull o.s. together ■ **ressaisis-toi!** pull yourself together!, get a hold of *ou* a grip on yourself! ■ **il s'est ressaisi et a finalement gagné le deuxième set** he recovered *ou* rallied and finally won the second set.

ressasser [3] [rəsase] *vt* **1.** [répéter] to go *ou* harp on about ■ **les mêmes histoires ressassées l'amusent toujours** he's still amused by the same worn-out old stories **2.** [repenser à] to turn over in one's mind.

ressemblance [rəsɑ̃blɑ̃s] *nf* **1.** [entre êtres humains] likeness, resemblance ■ **'toute ~ avec des personnages réels ne peut être que fortuite'** 'any resemblance to persons living or dead is purely accidental' **2.** [entre choses] similarity.

ressemblant, e [rəsɑ̃blɑ̃, ɑ̃t] *adj* [photo, portrait] true to life, lifelike ■ **ta photo n'est pas très ~e** your photo doesn't look like you.

ressembler [3] [rəsɑ̃ble] ◆ **ressembler à** *v+prép* **1.** [avoir la même apparence que] to resemble, to look like ■ **elle me ressemble un peu** she looks a bit like me **2.** [avoir la même nature que] to resemble, to be like ■ **il a toujours cherché à ~ à son père** he always tried to be like his father **3.** *loc* **son tableau ne ressemble à rien** *fam* her painting looks like nothing on earth ■ **ça ne ressemble à rien de ne pas vouloir venir** *fam* there's no sense in not wanting to come ■ **à quoi ça ressemble de quitter la réunion sans même s'excuser?** *fam* what's the idea *ou* meaning of leaving the meeting without even apologizing? ■ **cela ne me/te/leur ressemble pas** that's not like me/you/them ■ **ça lui ressemble bien d'oublier mon anniversaire** it's just like him to forget my birthday.
◆ **se ressembler** ◇ *vp (emploi réciproque)* to look alike, to resemble each other ▶ **se ~ comme deux gouttes d'eau** to be as like as two peas (in a pod) ■ **qui se ressemble s'assemble** *prov* birds of a feather flock together *prov*.
◇ *vpi sout* **depuis sa maladie, il ne se ressemble plus** he's not been himself since his illness.

ressemelage [rəsəmlaʒ] *nm* [action] soling, resoling ■ [nouvelle semelle] new sole.

ressemeler [24] [rəsəmle] *vt* to sole, to resole.

ressens *etc v* ▷ **ressentir**.

ressentiment [rəsɑ̃timɑ̃] *nm sout* resentment, ill will ■ **éprouver du ~ à l'égard de qqn** to feel resentment against sb, to feel resentful towards sb ■ **je n'ai aucun ~ à ton égard** I don't bear you any resentment *ou* ill will.

ressentir [37] [rəsɑ̃tir] *vt* **1.** [éprouver - bienfait, douleur, haine] to feel **2.** [être affecté par] to feel, to be affected by ■ **il a ressenti très vivement la perte de son père** he was deeply affected by his father's death ■ **j'ai ressenti ses propos comme une véritable insulte** I felt *ou* was extremely insulted by his remarks.
◆ **se ressentir de** *vp+prép* to feel the effect of ■ **la production a été accélérée et la qualité s'en ressent** they've speeded up production at the expense of quality ■ **elle est inquiète et son travail s'en ressent** she's worried and it shows in her work.

resserre [rəsɛr] *nf* [à outils] shed, outhouse ■ [à produits] storeroom ■ [à provisions] store cupboard, larder.

resserré, e [rəsere] *adj* [étroit] narrow.

resserrement [rəsɛrmɑ̃] *nm* **1.** [passage étroit] narrow part **2.** [limitation] tightening ■ **le ~ du crédit** the credit squeeze, the tightening of credit controls **3.** [consolidation - d'un lien affectif] strengthening **4.** [des pores] closing.

resserrer [4] [rəsere] *vt* **1.** [boulon, nœud - serrer de nouveau] to retighten, to tighten again ; [- serrer davantage] to tighten up *(sép)* **2.** [renforcer - amitié] to strengthen **3.** [fermer] to close (up) ■ **pour ~ les pores** to close the pores **4.** [diminuer - texte, exposé] to condense, to compress.
◆ **se resserrer** *vpi* **1.** [devenir plus étroit] to narrow **2.** [se refermer] to tighten ■ **les mailles du filet se resserrent** *fig* the police are closing in **3.** [devenir plus fort] : **nos relations se sont resserrées depuis l'année dernière** we have become closer (to each other) *ou* our relationship has grown stronger since last year.

resservir [38] [rəsɛrvir] ◇ *vt* **1.** [de nouveau] to serve again **2.** [davantage] to serve (out) some more *ou* another helping ■ **donne-moi ton assiette, je vais te ~** give me your plate, I'll give you another helping **3.** *fam* [répéter] : **il nous ressert la même excuse tous les ans** he comes out with *ou* he trots out the same (old) excuse every year.
◇ *vi* **1.** [être utile] : **j'ai une vieille robe longue qui pourra bien ~ pour l'occasion** I have an old full-length dress which would do for this occasion ■ **garde-le, ça pourra toujours ~** keep it, it might come in handy *ou* useful again (one day) **2.** MIL & TENNIS to serve again.
◆ **se resservir** *vp (emploi réfléchi)* [reprendre à manger] to help o.s. to some more *ou* to a second helping ■ **ressers-toi** help yourself to (some) more.
◆ **se resservir de** *vp+prép* [réutiliser] to use again.

ressors *etc v* ▷ **ressortir**.

ressort [rəsɔr] *nm* **1.** [mécanisme] spring ■ **faire ~** to act as a spring ▶ **~ hélicoïdal/spiral** helical/spiral spring ■ **~ de montre** watch spring, hairspring ■ **~ de sommier** bedsprings **2.** [force morale] spirit, drive ■ **manquer de ~** to lack drive **3.** [mobile] motivation ■ **les ~s de l'âme humaine** the deepest motivations of the human soul *ou* spirit **4.** PHYS [propriété] springiness, elasticity *spéc* **5.** [compétence] : **les problèmes qui sont de mon ~** problems I am qualified to deal with ■ **ce n'est pas de mon/son ~** it is not my/his responsibility **6.** DR jurisdiction ■ **juger en premier ~** to judge (a case) in the first instance.
◆ **à ressort(s)** *loc adj* spring-loaded ■ **matelas à ~s** spring mattress.
◆ **en dernier ressort** *loc adv* as a last resort.

ressortir[1] [43] [rəsɔrtir] ◇ *vt (aux avoir)* **1.** [vêtement, ustensile] to take out *(sép)* again **2.** [film] to rerelease, to bring out *(sép)* again ■ [pièce de théâtre] to rerun **3.** *fam* [répéter] to trot out *(sép)* again ■ **tu ne vas pas ~ cette vieille histoire?** you're not going to come out with that old story again, are you?
◇ *vi (aux être)* **1.** [sortir de nouveau] to go out *ou* to leave again ■ [sortir] to go out, to leave ■ **il n'est pas encore ressorti de chez le médecin** he hasn't left the doctor's yet **2.** [se détacher] to stand out ■ **le foulard qu'elle porte fait ~ ses yeux bleus** the scarf she's wearing brings out the blue of her eyes ■ **faire ~ les avantages d'une solution** to stress *ou* to highlight the advantages of a solution **3.** [réapparaître] : **la pointe est ressortie de**

l'autre côté du mur the tip came through the other side of the wall **4.** [film] to show again, to be re-released **5.** JEUX [chiffre, carte] to come up *(insép)* again.

◆ **ressortir de** *v+prép* to emerge *ou* to flow from ▪ **il ressort de votre analyse que les affaires vont bien** according to your analysis, business is good ▪ **il ressort de tout cela qu'il a menti** the upshot of all this is that he's been lying.

ressortir[2] [32] [rəsɔrtir] ◆ **ressortir à** *v+prép* **1.** DR : ~ **à la juridiction de** to come under the jurisdiction of **2.** *litt* [relever de] to pertain to ▪ **pareil sujet ressortit au roman plutôt qu'à l'essai** such a subject pertains to the novel rather than to the essay (genre).

ressortissant, e [rəsɔrtisɑ̃, ɑ̃t] *nm, f* national ▪ ~ **d'un État membre de la CE** EC national.

ressouder [3] [rəsude] *vt* **1.** [tuyau] to resolder, to reweld, to weld together *(sép)* again **2.** *fig* [alliance, couple] to bring *ou* to get together *(sép)* again, to reunite.

ressource [rəsurs] *nf* **1.** [secours] recourse, resort ▪ **tu es mon unique** ~ you're the only person who can help me *ou* my only hope ▪ **elle n'a eu d'autre ~ que de le lui demander** there was no other course (of action) open *ou* left to her but to ask him ▪ **en dernière** ~ as a last resort **2.** [endurance, courage] : **avoir de la** ~ to have strength in reserve.

◆ **ressources** *nfpl* **1.** [fonds] funds, resources, income ▪ **25 ans et sans ~s** 25 years old and no visible means of support ➲ **~s personnelles** private means **2.** [réserves] resources ▪ **~s naturelles/minières d'un pays** natural/mineral resources of a country ▪ **~s humaines** human resources, personnel ▪ **des ~s en hommes** manpower resources **3.** [moyens] resources, possibilities ▪ **nous mobilisons toutes nos ~s pour retrouver les marins disparus** we're mobilizing all our resources *ou* all the means at our disposal to find the missing sailors ▪ **toutes les ~s de notre langue** all the possibilities *ou* resources of our language.

ressourcer [16] [rəsurse] ◆ **se ressourcer** *vpi* **1.** [retourner aux sources] to go back to one's roots **2.** [reprendre des forces] to recharge one's batteries.

ressouvenir [40] [rəsuvnir] ◆ **se ressouvenir de** *vp+prép litt* to remember, to recall ▪ **à chaque retour dans son village natal, il se ressouvenait de son enfance** each time he returned to his home village, he would recall his childhood.

ressurgir [32] [rəsyrʒir] *vi* **1.** [source] to reappear **2.** [problème] to arise again, to reoccur ▪ **faire ~ de vieux souvenirs** to bring back old memories.

ressuscité, e [resysite] *nm, f* RELIG resurrected person ▪ **les ~s** those who have risen again, the risen.

ressusciter [3] [resysite] <> *vt (aux avoir)* **1.** RELIG to resurrect, to raise from the dead ▪ **le Christ ressuscitera les morts** Christ will raise the dead to life **2.** [ranimer] to resuscitate ▪ MÉD to bring back to life, to revive **3.** *litt* [faire resurgir] to revive, to resurrect ▪ ~ **le passé** to summon up *ou* to revive the past.

<> *vi* **1.** *(aux être)* RELIG to rise again *ou* from the dead ▪ **le Christ est ressuscité** Christ has risen (from the dead) **2.** *(aux avoir)* [revivre - sentiment, nature] to come back to life, to revive.

restant, e [rɛstɑ̃, ɑ̃t] *adj* remaining ▪ **ils se sont partagé les chocolats ~s** they shared the chocolates that were left.

◆ **restant** *nm* [reste] rest, remainder ▪ **dépenser le ~ de son argent** to spend the rest of one's money *ou* one's remaining money ▪ **pour le ~ de mes/ses jours** until my/his dying day.

restau [rɛsto] *nm fam* restaurant.

restaurant [rɛstɔrɑ̃] *nm* restaurant ▪ **manger au** ~ to eat out ➲ ~ **d'entreprise** (staff) canteen ▪ ~ **universitaire** ≃ university cafeteria *ou* refectory.

restaurateur, trice [rɛstɔratœr, tris] *nm, f* **1.** [d'œuvres d'art] restorer **2.** [qui tient un restaurant] restaurant owner, restaurateur *sout.*

restauration [rɛstɔrasjɔ̃] *nf* **1.** [d'œuvres d'art] restoration **2.** [rétablissement] restoration ▪ **la Restauration** HIST the Restoration **3.** [hôtellerie] catering ▪ **dans la** ~ in the restaurant trade *ou* the catering business ➲ **la ~ rapide** the fast-food business.

restaurer [3] [rɛstɔre] *vt* **1.** [édifice, œuvre d'art] to restore **2.** *litt* [rétablir] to restore, to reestablish ▪ ~ **la paix** to restore peace **3.** *litt* [nourrir] to feed.

◆ **se restaurer** *vp (emploi réfléchi)* to have something to eat ▪ **on s'arrêtera vers midi pour se ~ un peu** we'll stop around noon to have a bite to eat.

reste [rɛst] *nm* **1.** [suite, fin] rest ▪ **si vous êtes sages, je vous raconterai le ~ demain** if you're good, I'll tell you the rest of the story tomorrow ▪ **et (tout) le ~!** and so on (and so forth)! ▪ **tout le ~ n'est que littérature/qu'illusion** everything else is just insignificant/an illusion ➲ **sans attendre** *ou* **demander son** ~ without (any) further ado ▪ **être** *ou* **demeurer en** ~ to be outdone, to be at a loss **2.** [résidu - de nourriture] food left over, leftovers (of food) ; [- de boisson] drink left over ; [- de tissu, de papier] remnant, scrap ▪ CINÉ out-takes ▪ **un ~ de jour** *ou* **de lumière** a glimmer of daylight ▪ **un ~ de sa gloire passée** a vestige *ou* remnant of his past glory **3.** MATH remainder.

◆ **restes** *nmpl* **1.** [d'un repas] leftovers ▪ **on mangera les ~s ce soir** we'll have the leftovers tonight **2.** [vestiges] remains **3.** [ossements] (last) remains **4.** *fam loc* **elle a de beaux ~s** she's still beautiful despite her age.

◆ **au reste** = **du reste.**

◆ **de reste** *loc adj* surplus *(modif)*, spare ▪ **passez me voir demain, j'aurai du temps de ~** come and see me tomorrow, I'll have some spare time ▪ **il a de la patience de ~** he has patience to spare.

◆ **du reste** *loc adv* besides, furthermore, moreover ▪ **inutile de discuter, du ~, ça ne dépend pas de moi** there's no point in arguing and, besides, it's not up to me to decide.

reste-à-vivre [rɛstavivr] *nm inv* subsistence allowance *(for person paying off debts).*

rester [3] [rɛste] *vi* **1.** [dans un lieu, une situation] to stay, to remain ▪ **c'est mieux si la voiture reste au garage** it's better if the car stays in the garage ▪ **ceci doit ~ entre nous** this is strictly between me and you, this is for our ears only ▪ **restez donc à déjeuner/dîner** do stay for lunch/dinner ▪ **je ne reste pas** I'm not staying *ou* stopping ▪ **savoir ~ à sa place** *fig* to know one's place ▪ ~ **debout/assis** to remain standing/seated ▪ **elle est restée debout toute la nuit** she stayed up all night ▪ ~ **paralysé** to be left paralysed ▪ ~ **fidèle à qqn** to be *ou* to stay faithful to sb ▪ ~ **en fonction** to remain in office ▪ ~ **dans l'ignorance** to remain in ignorance ▪ ~ **célibataire** to remain single ▪ **elle ne reste pas en place** she never keeps still ▪ **tu veux bien ~ tranquille!** will you keep still! ▪ ~ **en contact avec qqn** to keep *ou* to stay in touch with sb ▪ **je reste sur une impression désagréable** I'm left with an unpleasant impression ▪ **je n'aime pas ~ sur un échec** I don't like to stop at failure ▪ ~ **dans les mémoires** *ou* **les annales** to go down in history ▪ **en ~ à : nous en sommes restés à la page 160** we left off at *ou* got as far as page 160 ▪ **nous en resterons à cet accord** we will limit ourselves to *ou* go no further than this agreement ▪ **restons-en là!** let's leave it at that! ➲ ~ **en rade** *fam ou* **en plan** *fam ou* **en chemin** *fam ou* **en carafe** *fam* to be left high and dry *ou* stranded ▪ **ça m'est resté sur le cœur** it still rankles with *ou* galls me ▪ **j'y suis, j'y reste!** here I am and here I stay!

2. [subsister] to be left ▪ **c'est tout ce qui me reste** that's all I have left ▪ **cette mauvaise habitude lui est restée** he still has that bad habit ▪ **restent les deux dernières questions à traiter** the last two questions still have to be dealt with ▪ **reste à savoir qui ira** there still remains the problem of deciding who is to go ▪ *(tournure impersonnelle)* **il nous reste un peu de pain et de fromage** we have a little bit of bread and cheese left ▪ **il me reste la moitié à payer** I (still) have half of it to pay ▪ **il nous reste de quoi vivre** we have enough left to live on ▪ **lisez beaucoup, il en restera toujours quelque chose** do a lot of reading, there will always be something to show for it *ou* there's always something to be got out of it ▪ **cinq ôté de quinze, il reste dix** five (taken away) from fifteen leaves ten ▪ **il reste un doute** a doubt still remains ▪ **il ne reste plus rien à faire** there's nothing left to be done ▪ **il reste à faire l'ourlet** the hem is all that remains *ou* that's left to be done ▪ **il reste encore 12 km à faire** there's still 12 km to go ▪ **il reste que, il n'en reste pas moins que : il reste que le problème de succession n'est pas réglé**

the fact remains that the problem of the inheritance hasn't been solved ■ **il n'en reste pas moins que vous avez tort** you are nevertheless wrong ▶ **et s'il n'en reste qu'un, je serai celui-là** *Victor Hugo allus* and if anyone will be there at the finish, it will be me
3. *euphém* [mourir] to meet one's end ■ **il est resté sur le champ de bataille** he died on the battlefield ▶ **y ~** *fam* to kick the bucket
4. [durer] to live on *(insép)*, to endure.

restituer [7] [rɛstitɥe] *vt* **1.** [rendre - bien] to return, to restore ; [- argent] to refund, to return ■ **~ qqch à qqn** to return sthg to sb **2.** [reconstituer - œuvre endommagée] to restore, to reconstruct ; [- ambiance] to reconstitute, to render ■ **~ fidèlement les sons** to reproduce sounds faithfully **3.** [vomir] to bring up *(sép)*.

restitution [rɛstitysjɔ̃] *nf* **1.** [d'un bien] return, restitution ■ [d'argent] refund **2.** [d'un son, d'une couleur] reproduction.

resto [rɛsto] *nm fam* restaurant ■ **les ~s du cœur** *charity food distribution centres.*

LES RESTOS DU CŒUR

Set up by the comedian Coluche, the *restos du cœur* (full name, *les Restaurants du Cœur*) are run by volunteers who distribute free meals to the poor and homeless, during the winter months.

Restoroute® [rɛstorut] *nm* [sur autoroute] ≃ motorway *UK ou* freeway *US* restaurant ■ [sur route] roadside restaurant.

resto-U [rɛstoy] *nm fam* = **restaurant universitaire**.

restreindre [81] [rɛstrɛ̃dr] *vt* [ambition, dépense] to restrict, to limit, to curb ■ [consommation] to cut down *(sép)* ■ **~ les libertés** to restrict liberties ■ **elle a dû ~ ses recherches à un domaine précis** she had to limit her research to a precise field.
◆ **se restreindre** *vpi* **1.** [se rationner] to cut down ■ **tu ne sais pas te ~** you don't know when to stop **2.** [diminuer] : **le champ d'activités de l'entreprise s'est restreint** the company's activities have become more limited ■ **son cercle d'amis s'est restreint** his circle of friends has got smaller.

restreint, e [rɛstrɛ̃, ɛ̃t] *adj* **1.** [réduit] limited ■ **l'espace est ~** there's not much room ▶ **édition à tirage ~** limited edition **2.** [limité] restricted ■ **la distribution de ces produits est ~e à Paris et à sa région** these products are sold exclusively in Paris and in the Paris area.

restrictif, ive [rɛstriktif, iv] *adj* restrictive.

restriction [rɛstriksjɔ̃] *nf* **1.** [réserve] reservation **2.** [limitation] restriction, limitation ■ **~ de crédit** restriction on credit, credit squeeze.
◆ **restrictions** *nfpl* restrictions ■ **les ~s en temps de guerre** wartime restrictions *ou* austerity.
◆ **sans restriction** *loc adv* [entièrement] : **je vous approuve sans ~** you have my unreserved approval.

restructuration [rəstryktyrasjɔ̃] *nf* **1.** [d'un quartier, d'une ville] redevelopment **2.** [d'une société, d'un service] restructuring, reorganization.

restructurer [3] [rəstryktyre] *vt* [société, organisation] to restructure, to reorganize.

resucée [rəsyse] *nf fam* **1.** [de boisson] : **une ~ de** another swig *ou* slug of **2.** [répétition] rehash ■ **ils ne montrent que des ~s à la télévision** all they ever show on TV is (old) repeats.

résultant, e [rezyltɑ̃, ɑ̃t] *adj* resulting.
◆ **résultante** *nf* **1.** [résultat] result, outcome **2.** PHYS resultant.

résultat [rezylta] *nm* **1.** [réalisation positive] result ■ **sans ~** [action] fruitless ■ **ne donner aucun ~** to have no effect **2.** [aboutissement] result, outcome ■ **le ~ final** the end result ■ **son attitude a eu pour ~ de rapprocher le frère et la sœur** her attitude led to *ou* resulted in closer ties between brother and sister **3.** *fam* [introduisant une conclusion] : **il a voulu trop en faire, ~, il est malade** he tried to do too much and sure enough he fell ill ■ **~, je n'ai toujours pas compris** so I'm still none the wiser **4.** MATH result **5.** POLIT & SPORT result ■ **~ partiel pour la Corse et les Alpes-Maritimes** by-election result for Corsica and the Alpes-Maritimes ▶ **le ~ des courses** SPORT the racing results ; *fig* the outcome (of the situation) **6.** [en comptabilité] profit ■ **~ net** net profit ■ **dégager un ~** to make a profit.
◆ **résultats** *nmpl* FIN, POLIT & SPORT results ■ ÉDUC results, marks ■ **les ~s du Loto** the winning lottery numbers.

résulter [3] [rezylte] ◆ **résulter de** *v+prép* to result *ou* to ensue from ■ **il est difficile de dire ce qui en résultera** at the moment it's difficult to say what the result *ou* outcome will be ■ **le travail/souci qui en résulte** the ensuing work/worry ■ *(tournure impersonnelle)* **il résulte de l'enquête que...** the result of the investigation shows that... ■ **il en a résulté que...** the result *ou* the outcome was that...

résumé [rezyme] *nm* **1.** [sommaire] summary, résumé ■ **faites un ~ du passage suivant** write a summary *ou* a précis of the following passage ■ **~ des épisodes précédents** the story so far **2.** [bref exposé] summary ■ **faites-nous le ~ de la situation** sum up *ou* summarize the situation for us **3.** [ouvrage] summary, précis.
◆ **en résumé** *loc adv* [en conclusion] to sum up ■ [en bref] in short, in brief, briefly ■ **en ~, nous ne sommes d'accord sur aucun des points soulevés** in short, we do not agree on any of the points raised.

résumer [3] [rezyme] *vt* **1.** [récapituler] to summarize, to sum up *(sép)* **2.** [symboliser] to typify, to symbolize ■ **ce cas résume tous les autres du même genre** this case sums up all others of the same type.
◆ **se résumer** *vpi* [récapituler] to sum up ■ **pour me ~, je dirai que nous devons être vigilants** to sum up, I would say that we must be vigilant.
◆ **se résumer à** *vp+prép* to come down to ■ **cela se résume à peu de chose** it doesn't amount to much.
Voir module d'usage

résurgence [rezyrʒɑ̃s] *nf* **1.** GÉOGR resurgence **2.** *sout* [réapparition] resurgence, revival.

resurgir [rəsyrʒir] = **ressurgir**.

RÉSUMER SES IDÉES

All in all, it was a very enjoyable day. Tout compte fait, c'était une journée très agréable.

When all is said and done, she's still my sister. Après tout, c'est quand même ma sœur.

All things considered, it wasn't a bad start. Tout bien considéré, ça n'a pas trop mal commencé.

Anyway, to cut a long story short, she's decided to come next week instead. Bref, elle a décidé de venir plutôt la semaine prochaine.

All of which goes to show that you were wrong about him. Ce qui prouve que tu t'étais trompé sur son compte.

In a nutshell, we can't go. Bref, nous ne pouvons pas y aller.

résurrection [rezyrɛksjɔ̃] *nf* **1.** RELIG resurrection ■ **la Résurrection (du Christ)** the Resurrection (of Christ) **2.** [renaissance] revival.

retable [rətabl] *nm* [sur l'autel] retable ■ [derrière l'autel] reredos.

rétablir [32] [retablir] *vt* **1.** [établir de nouveau] to restore ■ **~ l'équilibre** to redress the balance ■ **nous prendrons les mesures nécessaires pour ~ la situation** we'll take the measures required to restore the situation to normal ■ **~ qqn dans son emploi** to reinstate sb ■ **elle a été rétablie dans tous ses droits** all her rights were restored **2.** INFORM to redo **3.** [guérir] : **~ qqn** to restore sb to health ■ **son séjour l'a complètement rétabli** his holiday brought about his complete recovery **4.** [rectifier] to reestablish ■ **rétablissons les faits** let's reestablish the facts, let's get down to what really happened.
◆ **se rétablir** *vpi* **1.** [guérir] to recover ■ **elle est partie se ~ à la campagne** she went to the country to recuperate *ou* to recover **2.** [revenir - ordre, calme] to be restored **3.** [reprendre son équilibre] to get one's balance back.

rétablissement [retablismɑ̃] *nm* **1.** [action] restoration ■ [résultat] restoration, reestablishment **2.** [guérison] recovery ■ **nous vous souhaitons un prompt ~** we wish you a speedy recovery **3.** SPORT : **faire un ~ à la barre fixe** to do a pull-up on the horizontal bar.

retailler [3] [rətaje] *vt* [rosier, vigne] to reprune ■ [diamant, vêtement] to recut ■ [crayon] to resharpen ■ [haie] to retrim ■ [cartes à jouer] to shuffle and cut again.

rétamé, e [retame] *adj* **1.** [étamé de nouveau] retinned **2.** △ [épuisé] worn out, knackered△ *UK* ■ [ivre] pissed△ *UK*, wrecked△ ■ [démoli] wrecked, smashed up.

rétamer [3] [retame] *vt* **1.** [étamer de nouveau] to retin **2.** △ [enivrer] to knock out *(sép)* **3.** △ [battre au jeu] to clean out ■ **je me suis fait ~ au casino** I got cleaned out at the casino **4.** △ [fatiguer] to wreck△ **5.** △ [démolir] to wreck **6.** △ [refuser - candidat] to fail ■ **ils ont rétamé la moitié des candidats** they failed half the candidates.
◆ **se rétamer** *vpi* **1.** *fam* [tomber] to come a cropper *UK*, to take a tumble **2.** [échouer] to flunk ■ **je me suis rétamée à l'oral** I messed up *ou* flunked my oral exam.

retape△ [rətap] *nf* **1.** [racolage] : **faire (de) la ~** to be on the game△ *UK*, to hustle△ *US* **2.** [publicité] loud advertising, hyping (up), plugging.

retaper [3] [rətape] *vt* **1.** [lit] to straighten, to make **2.** *fam* [maison] to do up *(sép)* ■ [voiture] to fix *ou* to do up *(sép)* **3.** *fam* [malade] to buck up *(sép)* ■ **mon séjour à la montagne m'a retapé** my stay in the mountains set me back on my feet again **4.** [lettre] to retype, to type again.
◆ **se retaper** *fam* ◇ *vp (emploi réfléchi)* **1.** [physiquement] to get back on one's feet again ■ **elle a grand besoin de se ~** she badly needs to recharge her batteries **2.** [financièrement] to sort out one's finances, to get straightened out (financially).
◇ *vpt* : **j'ai dû me ~ la lecture du rapport** I had to read through the blasted report again.

retard [rətar] ◇ *nm* **1.** [manque de ponctualité] lateness ■ **il ne s'est même pas excusé pour son ~** he didn't even apologize for being late ■ **avoir du ~** to be late ■ **j'avais plus d'une heure de ~** I was over *ou* more than an hour late ■ **l'avion Londres-Paris est annoncé avec deux heures de ~** a two-hour delay is expected on the London to Paris flight ■ **rapportez vos livres sans ~** return your books without delay ■ **tout ~ dans le paiement des intérêts sera sanctionné** all late payments of interest *ou* any delay in paying interest will incur a penalty
2. [intervalle de temps, distance] : **le peloton est arrivé avec cinq minutes de ~ sur le vainqueur** the pack arrived five minutes after *ou* behind the winner
3. [d'une horloge] : **ma montre a plusieurs minutes de ~** my watch is several minutes slow
4. [d'un élève] backwardness *péj* ■ **il a du ~ en allemand** he's behind in German ■ **il doit combler son ~ en physique** he's got to catch up in physics ▶ **~ scolaire** learning difficulties
5. [handicap] : **nous avons comblé notre ~ industriel en quelques années** we caught up on *ou* we closed the gap in our industrial development in a few years ■ **nous avons des années de ~ (sur eux)** we're years behind (them) ▶ **~ mental** backwardness
6. MÉCAN : **~ à l'allumage** retarded ignition.
◇ *adj inv* delayed(-action), retarded ■ **insuline/pénicilline ~** slow-release insulin/penicillin.
◆ **en retard** ◇ *loc adj* : **être en ~** to be late ■ **elle est très en ~ pour son âge** PSYCHOL she's rather immature *ou* slow for her age ; ÉDUC she's rather behind for her age ▶ **paiement en ~** [qui n'est pas fait] arrears, overdue payment ; [qui est fait] late payment ■ **il est en ~ dans ses paiements** he's behind *ou* in arrears with (his) payments ■ **être en ~ sur son époque** *ou* **son temps** to be behind the times.
◇ *loc adv* : **arriver en ~** to arrive late ■ **elle s'est mise en ~** she made herself late ■ **nous avons rendu nos épreuves en ~** we were late handing in our tests.

retardataire [rətardatɛr] ◇ *adj* **1.** [qui n'est pas à l'heure] late ■ [qui a été retardé] delayed **2.** [désuet] obsolete, old-fashioned ■ **vous avez vraiment des méthodes ~s** your methods are completely obsolete *ou* outdated.
◇ *nmf* latecomer.

retardateur, trice [rətardatœr, tris] *adj* retarding ■ **action retardatrice** MIL delaying tactics.

retardé, e [rətarde] ◇ *adj fam* [arriéré] retarded, backward, slow.
◇ *nm, f* : **~ (mental)** (mentally) retarded person.

retardement [rətardəmɑ̃] ◆ **à retardement**
◇ *loc adj* [mécanisme] delayed-action *(modif)*.
◇ *loc adv* : **comprendre à ~** to understand after the event.

retarder [3] [rətarde] ◇ *vt* **1.** [ralentir - visiteur, passager] to delay, to make late ■ [entraver - enquête, progrès, travaux] to delay, to hamper, to slow down *(sép)* ■ **les problèmes financiers l'ont retardé dans ses études** financial problems slowed him down *ou* hampered him in his studies **2.** [ajourner] to postpone, to put back *(sép)* **3.** [montre] to put back *(sép)*.
◇ *vi* **1.** [montre] to be slow ■ **je retarde de quelques minutes** *fam* I'm *ou* my watch is a few minutes slow **2.** *fam* [personne] to be out of touch ■ **~ sur son temps** *ou* **son siècle** to be behind the times ■ **il retarde de vingt ans sur notre époque** *ou* **temps** he's twenty years behind the times ▶ **~ (d'un métro)** to be out of touch.
◆ **se retarder** *vpi* to make o.s. late ■ **ne te retarde pas pour ça** don't let this hold you up *ou* delay you.

retâter [3] [rətate] *vt* [étoffe] to feel again.
◆ **retâter de** *v+prép fam* **il n'a pas envie de ~ de la prison** he doesn't want to sample the delights of prison life again.

retendre [73] [rətɑ̃dr] *vt* [corde, câble] to retighten, to tauten (again) ■ [ressort] to reset ■ [muscle] to brace *ou* to tense again ■ [corde de raquette] to tauten (again).

retenir [40] [rətənir] *vt* **1.** [immobiliser] to hold, to keep ■ **retiens le chien, il va sauter!** hold the dog back, it's going to jump! ■ **~ le regard de qqn** to arrest sb's gaze ■ **~ l'attention de qqn** to hold sb's attention ■ **votre CV a retenu toute mon attention** I studied your CV with great interest ■ **~ qqn prisonnier** to hold sb prisoner ■ **~ qqn à dîner** to invite sb for dinner ■ **je ne vous retiens pas, je sais que vous êtes pressé** I won't keep you, I know you're in a hurry
2. [empêcher d'agir] to hold back *(sép)* ■ **je ne sais pas ce qui me retient de l'envoyer promener** *fam* I don't know what's stopping *ou* keeping me from telling him to go to hell ■ **retiens-moi ou je fais un malheur** *fam* hold me back or I'll do something desperate
3. [refouler - émotion] to curb, to hold in check, to hold back *(sép)* ; [- larmes, sourire] to hold back ; [- cri] to stifle ■ **~ un geste d'impatience** to hold back *ou* to check a gesture of impatience ■ **~ son souffle** *ou* **sa respiration** to hold one's breath
4. [réserver] to book, to reserve ■ **retiens la date du 20 juin pour notre réunion** keep June the 20th free for our meeting
5. [se rappeler] to remember ■ **~ qqch** to remember *ou* to recall sthg ■ **et surtout, retiens bien ce qu'on t'a dit** and above all, remember *ou* don't forget what you've been told ▶ **je te retiens, toi et tes soi-disant bonnes idées!** *fam* I'll remember you and your so-called good ideas!

6. [candidature, suggestion] to retain, to accept ■ **~ une accusation contre qqn** to uphold a charge against sb
7. [décompter] to deduct, to keep back *(sép)* ■ **j'ai retenu 300 euros sur votre salaire** I've deducted 300 euros from your salary ■ **sommes retenues à la base** *ou* **source** sums deducted at source
8. [conserver - chaleur] to keep in *(sép)*, to retain, to conserve ; [- eau] to retain ; [- lumière] to reflect
9. MATH to carry ■ **je pose 5 et je retiens 4** I put down 5 and carry 4.
◆ **se retenir** ◇ *vp (emploi réfléchi)* **1.** [se contrôler] to restrain o.s. ■ **se ~ de pleurer** to stop o.s. crying
2. *fam euphém* to hold on.
◇ *vpi* [s'agripper] to hold on.

retenter [rətɑ̃te] *vt* : **~ sa chance** to try one's luck again.

rétention [retɑ̃sjɔ̃] *nf* **1.** MÉD retention ■ **faire de la ~ d'urines/d'eau** to suffer from urine/water retention **2.** DR reservation **3.** PSYCHOL retention.

retentir [32] [rətɑ̃tir] *vi* **1.** [résonner] to resound, to ring ■ **de bruyants applaudissements retentirent dans la salle** loud applause burst forth in the hall ■ **la voix des enfants retentissait dans l'escalier** the children's voices were ringing out in the stairway ■ **la maison retentit du bruit des ouvriers** the house is filled with the noise of the workers **2.** [avoir des répercussions] : **~ sur** to have an effect on.

retentissant, e [rətɑ̃tisɑ̃, ɑ̃t] *adj* **1.** [éclatant - cri, bruit, gifle] resounding, ringing ; [- voix] ringing ; [- sonnerie] loud **2.** [remarquable] tremendous ■ **un succès ~** resounding success ■ **un bide ~** *fam* a resounding flop.

retentissement [rətɑ̃tismɑ̃] *nm* **1.** [contrecoup] repercussion **2.** [impact] effect, impact ■ **le ~ dans l'opinion publique a été considérable/nul** there was considerable/no effect on public opinion ■ **cette déclaration devrait avoir un certain ~** this statement should create quite a stir **3.** *litt* [bruit] ringing, resounding.

retenu, e [rətəny] ◇ *pp* ▷ **retenir.**
◇ *adj* [discret] subdued.
◆ **retenue** *nf* **1.** [déduction] deduction ■ **opérer une ~e de 9 % sur les salaires** to deduct *ou* to stop 9% from salaries ➤ **~e à la source** payment (of income tax) at source, ≃ PAYE *UK* **2.** [réserve] reserve, self-control, restraint ■ **se confier à qqn sans ~e** to confide in sb unreservedly *ou* freely ■ **c'est une jeune femme pleine de ~e** she's a very reserved young woman ■ **un peu de ~e!** show some restraint!, keep a hold of yourself! **3.** ÉDUC [punition] detention ■ **mettre qqn en ~e** to keep sb in after school, to put sb in detention **4.** MATH : **reporter la ~e** to carry over **5.** CONSTR [d'une poutre] pinning **6.** NAUT [entre écluses] reach **7.** TRAV PUB damming up *(U)* ■ **~e d'eau** volume of water *(in dam)*.

réticence [retisɑ̃s] *nf* reluctance, reticence ■ **avoir des ~s (sur qqch)** to feel reticent *ou* to have reservations (about sthg) ■ **j'ai remarqué un peu de ~ dans son accord** I noticed she agreed somewhat reluctantly ■ **parler avec ~** to speak reticently ■ **parlez sans ~** don't be reticent, feel free to speak quite openly.

réticent, e [retisɑ̃, ɑ̃t] *adj* **1.** [hésitant] reticent, reluctant, reserved ■ **se montrer ~** to seem rather doubtful **2.** *litt* [discret] reticent.

réticule [retikyl] *nm* **1.** [sac] reticule **2.** OPT reticle.

réticulum [retikylɔm] *nm* reticulum.

retient *etc v* ▷ **retenir.**

rétif, ive [retif, iv] *adj* **1.** [cheval] stubborn **2.** [enfant] restive, fractious, recalcitrant *sout.*

rétine [retin] *nf* retina.

retint *etc v* ▷ **retenir.**

retirage [rətiraʒ] *nm* reprint ■ **je voudrais faire un ~ de ces photos** I'd like prints of these photos.

retiré, e [rətire] *adj* **1.** [isolé] remote, secluded, out-of-the-way ■ **ils cherchent une maison ~e** they're looking for a secluded house **2.** [solitaire] secluded ■ **vivre ~ du monde** to live in seclusion **3.** [à la retraite] retired.

retirer [3] [rətire] ◇ *vt* **1.** [ôter] to take off *ou* away *(sép)*, to remove ■ **il aida l'enfant à ~ son manteau** he helped the child off with his coat
2. [ramener à soi] : **retire ta main** take your hand away ■ **retire tes jambes** move your legs back
3. [faire sortir] to take out *(sép)*, to remove ■ **elle a été obligée de ~ son fils de l'école** she had to remove her son from the school
4. [annuler - droit] to take away *(sép)* ; [- plainte, offre] to withdraw ; [- accusation] to take back *(sép)* ■ **~ sa candidature** to withdraw one's candidature, to stand down ■ **~ un magazine de la circulation** to withdraw a magazine (from circulation) ■ **la pièce a été retirée de l'affiche après une semaine** the play came off *ou* closed after a week
5. [confisquer] : **~ qqch à qqn** to take sthg away from sb ■ **on lui a retiré la garde des enfants** he lost custody of the children ■ **on lui a retiré son permis de conduire** he's been banned from driving ■ **~ sa confiance à qqn** to no longer trust sb
6. [récupérer - argent] to withdraw, to take out *(sép)*, to draw ; [- bagage, ticket] to pick up *(sép)*, to collect ■ **j'ai retiré un peu d'argent de mon compte** I drew *ou* withdrew some money from my bank account
7. [obtenir] to gain, to get ■ **~ un bénéfice important d'une affaire** to make a large profit out of a deal ■ **je n'ai retiré que des désagréments de cet emploi** I got nothing but trouble from that job
8. [coup de feu] to fire again
9. IMPR to reprint ■ **~ une photo** to make a new *ou* fresh print (from a photo).
◇ *vi* **1.** ARM to fire again
2. SPORT to shoot again.
◆ **se retirer** *vpi* **1.** [s'éloigner] to withdraw ■ **il est tard, je vais me ~** *sout* it's late, I'm going to retire *ou* to withdraw ■ **se ~ de** to withdraw from ■ **se ~ de la vie active** to retire ➤ **se ~ dans ses appartements** *hum* to retire *ou* to withdraw to one's room
2. [s'établir] to retire ■ **il s'est retiré dans le Midi** he retired to the South of France ‖ [se cloîtrer] to retire, to withdraw ■ **se ~ du monde** to cut o.s. off from the world
3. [mer] to recede, to ebb.

rétive [retiv] *f* ▷ **rétif.**

retombant, e [rətɔ̃bɑ̃, ɑ̃t] *adj* hanging, trailing, drooping *péj.*

retombée [rətɔ̃be] *nf* **1.** *litt* [déclin] : **la ~ de l'enthousiasme populaire** the decline in popular enthusiasm **2.** ARCHIT & CONSTR springing.
◆ **retombées** *nfpl* NUCL fallout ■ *fig* [répercussions] repercussions, effects ■ **les ~s d'une campagne publicitaire** the results of an advertising campaign.

retomber [3] [rətɔ̃be] *vi (aux être)* **1.** [bouteille, balai] to fall over again ■ [mur, livres empilés] to fall down again *ou* back down ■ [ivrogne, bambin] to fall over *ou* down again ■ **se laisser ~ sur son lit** to flop *ou* to fall back onto one's bed
2. [atterrir - chat, sauteur, parachutiste, missile] to land ; [- balle] to come (back) down ■ [redescendre - couvercle, rideau de fer, clapet] to close ; [- soufflé, mousse] to collapse ■ **laissez ~ votre main droite** let your right hand come down *ou* drop down
3. [devenir moins fort - fièvre, prix] to drop ; [- agitation] to fall, to tail off, to die away ; [- enthousiasme] to fall, to wane ■ **le dollar est retombé** the dollar has fallen *ou* dropped again
4. [dans un état, une habitude] to fall back, to lapse *sout* ■ **~ dans les mêmes erreurs** to make the same mistakes again ■ **~ en enfance** to go into one's second childhood
5. MÉTÉOR [vent] to fall (again), to drop, to die down ■ [brume] to disappear, to be dispelled ■ **: il retombe de la pluie/neige/grêle** it's raining/snowing/hailing again
6. [pendre - drapé, guirlande, ourlet] to hang ■ **les fleurs retombent en lourdes grappes** the flowers are hanging in heavy clusters
7. [redevenir] : **~ amoureux** to fall in love again.
◆ **retomber sur** *v+prép* **1.** [rejaillir] : **la responsabilité retombe sur moi** the blame for it falls on me ■ **tous les torts sont**

retombés sur elle she had to bear the brunt of all the blame ▶ **un de ces jours ça va te ~ sur le nez!** *fam* one of these days you'll get your come-uppance *ou* what's coming to you!
2. *fam* [rencontrer à nouveau] : **~ sur qqn** to bump into *ou* to come across sb again ■ **~ sur qqch** to come across sthg again ■ **je suis retombé sur le même prof/sujet à l'oral** *fam* I got the same examiner/question for the oral exam ■ **en tournant à droite, vous retombez sur l'avenue** if you turn right you're back on the avenue again.

retordre [76] [rətɔrdr] *vt* **1.** TEXT to twist **2.** [linge] to wring out *(sép)* again.

rétorquer [3] [retɔrke] *vt* to retort ■ **certainement pas!, rétorqua-t-elle vivement** certainly not! she snapped back.

retors, e [rətɔr, ɔrs] *adj* [machiavélique] crafty, tricky ■ **méfie-toi, il est ~** be careful, he's a wily customer *ou* he knows all the tricks of the trade.

rétorsion [retɔrsjɔ̃] *nf* **1.** [représailles] retaliation ■ **par ~** in retaliation ■ **user de ~ envers** to retaliate against **2.** DR retortion.

retouche [rətuʃ] *nf* **1.** [correction] alteration ■ **sans ~s** unaltered **2.** ART retouching *(U)* **3.** COUT alteration ■ **faire des ~s à un vêtement** to make alterations to a garment **4.** PHOTO touching up *(U)*.

retoucher [3] [rətuʃe] *vt* [modifier - texte, vêtement] to alter ; [- œuvre] to retouch ; [- photo] to retouch, to touch up *(sép)* ■ **j'ai seulement retouché les ombres** I just touched up the shadows.
◆ **retoucher à** *v+prép* [se remettre à] to go back to ■ **et depuis, tu n'as plus jamais retouché à une cigarette?** and since then you haven't touched a *ou* another cigarette? ■ **il n'a plus jamais retouché à son piano** he never touched *ou* played his piano again.

retoucheur, euse [rətuʃœr, øz] *nm, f* **1.** COUT alterer **2.** PHOTO retoucher.

retour [rətur] ◇ *nm* **1.** [chez soi, au point de départ] return ■ **à ton ~** when you return home *ou* get back ■ **nous comptons sur ton ~ pour Noël** we expect you back (home) for Christmas ■ **après dix années d'exil, c'est le ~ au pays** after a ten-year exile he's coming home ■ **~ à un stade antérieur** reverting *ou* returning to an earlier stage ■ **sur le chemin** *ou* **la route du ~** on the way back ▶ **~ à la normale** return to normal ■ **~ aux sources** return to one's roots ■ **~ à la terre** return to the land ■ **être sur le ~** *pr* to be about to return, to be on the point of returning ; *fig* to be past one's prime ■ **ils doivent être sur le ~ à présent** they must be on their way back now ■ **un don Juan sur le ~** an ageing Don Juan ■ **une beauté sur le ~** a waning beauty
2. [nouvelle apparition - d'une célébrité] return, reappearance ■ [récurrence - d'une mode, d'un thème] return, recurrence ■ **on note un ~ des jupes longues** long skirts are back (in fashion)
3. [mouvement inverse] : **faire un ~ sur soi-même** to review one's past life ▶ **~ arrière** IMPR backspace ■ **~ de bâton** kickback ■ **~ (de) chariot** carriage return ■ **~ de flamme** TECHNOL & *fig* backfire ■ **~ rapide** [cassette] rewind ■ **~ à la case départ** JEUX back to the start ; *fig* back to square one *ou* to the drawing board ■ **par un juste ~ des choses il a été licencié** he was sacked, which seemed fair enough under the circumstances
4. [réexpédition] return ■ **~ à l'envoyeur** *ou* **à l'expéditeur** return to sender ■ **par ~ du courrier** by return of post
5. TRANSP [trajet] return (journey), journey back ■ **combien coûte le ~** how much is the return fare?
6. DR reversion ■ **faire ~ à** to revert to
7. TENNIS return ■ **~ de service** return of serve, service return
8. INFORM : **~ (d'information)** (information) feedback
9. ARCHIT return, (corner) angle
10. FIN : **~ sur investissements** return on investments
11. COMM return ■ **avec possibilité de ~** on a sale or return basis
12. [meuble] : **bureau avec ~** desk with a right-angled extension unit.
◇ *adj inv* SPORT : **match ~** return match.
◆ **retours** *nmpl* [de vacances] return traffic *(from weekends etc)* ■ **il y a beaucoup de ~s ce soir** many people are driving back to the city tonight.
◆ **de retour** *loc adv* back ■ **je serai de ~ demain** I'll be back tomorrow ■ **de ~ chez lui, il réfléchit** (once he was) back home, he thought it over.
◆ **de retour de** *loc prép* back from ■ **de ~ de Rio, je tentai de la voir** on my return from Rio, I tried to see her.
◆ **en retour** *loc adv* in return.
◆ **sans retour** *loc adv* *litt* [pour toujours] forever, irrevocably.
◆ **retour d'âge** *nm* change of life.
◆ **retour de manivelle** *nm* **1.** MÉCAN kickback **2.** [choc en retour] backlash ■ [conséquence néfaste] backlash, repercussion.
◆ **retour en arrière** *nm* **1.** CINÉ & LITTÉR flashback **2.** [régression] step backwards *fig.*

retournement [rəturnəmɑ̃] *nm* **1.** [revirement] : **un ~ de situation** a turnaround *ou* a reversal (of the situation) **2.** GÉOM turning (over).

retourner [3] [rəturne] ◇ *vt (aux avoir)* **1.** [orienter dans le sens contraire] to turn round *ou* around *(sép)* ■ **~ une arme contre** *ou* **sur qqn** to turn a weapon on sb ‖ [renverser - situation] to reverse, to turn inside out *ou* back to front ■ **je lui ai retourné son** *ou* **le compliment** I returned the compliment
2. [renvoyer - colis, lettre] to send back *(sép)*
3. [mettre à l'envers - literie] to turn round *ou* around ; [- carte à jouer] to turn up *(sép)* ; [- champ, paille] to turn over *(sép)* ; [- verre] to turn upside down ; [- grillade] to turn over *(sép)* ; [- gant, poche] to turn inside out ■ **il a retourné la photo contre le mur** he turned the photo against the wall ▶ **~ sa veste** to sell out ■ **il te retournera comme une crêpe** *ou* **un gant** he'll twist you round his little finger
4. [mélanger - salade] to toss
5. [fouiller - maison, pièce] to turn upside down
6. [examiner - pensée] : **tourner et ~ une idée dans sa tête** to mull over an idea (in one's head)
7. *fam* [émouvoir] : **j'en suis encore tout retourné!** I'm still reeling from the shock!
◇ *vi (aux être)* **1.** [aller à nouveau] to return, to go again *ou* back ■ **je n'y étais pas retourné depuis des années** I had not been back there for years ■ **si tu étais à ma place, tu retournerais le voir?** if you were me, would you (ever) go and see him again? ■ **je retournai la voir une dernière fois** I paid her one *ou* my last visit
2. [revenir] to go back, to return ■ **~ chez soi** to go (back) home ■ **~ à sa place** [sur son siège] to go back to one's seat.
◇ *v impers* : **peut-on savoir de quoi il retourne?** what is it all about?, what exactly is going on?
◆ **retourner à** *v+prép* [reprendre, retrouver] to return to, to go back to ■ **~ à un stade antérieur** to revert to an earlier stage.
◆ **se retourner** ◇ *vpi* **1.** [tourner la tête] to turn round ■ **partir sans se ~** to leave without looking back ■ **tout le monde se retournait sur eux** everybody turned round to look at them
2. [se mettre sur l'autre face] to turn over ■ **se ~ sur le dos/ventre** to turn over on one's back/stomach ■ **je me suis retourné dans mon lit toute la nuit** I tossed and turned all night ▶ **elle doit se ~ dans sa tombe** she must be turning in her grave
3. [se renverser - auto, tracteur] to overturn, to turn over
4. [réagir] to sort things out ■ **ils ne me laissent pas le temps de me ~** [de décider] they won't give me time to make a decision ; [de me reprendre] they won't give me time to sort things out
5. [situation] to be reversed, to change completely ■ **le lendemain, la situation s'était retournée** the following day, the situation had changed beyond recognition
6. [déplacement] : **s'en ~** [partir] to depart, to leave ; [rentrer] to make one's way back.
◇ *vpt* : **se ~ un ongle/doigt** to twist a nail/finger.
◆ **se retourner contre** *vp+prép* **1.** [agir contre] : **se ~ contre qqn** to turn against sb ■ **tout cela finira par se ~ contre toi** all this will eventually backfire on you
2. DR to take (legal) action against.

retracer [16] [rətrase] *vt* **1.** [relater] to relate, to recount *sout*, to tell of *(insép)* *sout* ■ **retraçons les faits** let's go back over the facts **2.** [dessiner à nouveau] to draw again, to redraw.

rétractable [retraktabl] *adj* **1.** DR retractable, revocable **2.** [emballage] : **film ~** shrink wrap *ou* film.

rétracter [3] [retrakte] *vt* **1.** ZOOL [griffes] to retract, to draw back *(sép)* ■ [cornes] to retract, to draw in *(sép)* **2.** *sout* [aveux, témoignage] to retract, to withdraw.
◆ **se rétracter** *vpi* **1.** [griffes] to draw back, to retract *spéc* **2.** [témoin] to recant *sout*, to retract ■ **il lui a fallu se ~** he had to withdraw his statement.

rétractile [retraktil] *adj* retractile.

rétraction [retraksjɔ̃] *nf* **1.** MÉD retraction **2.** TECHNOL shrink-wrapping.

retraduction [rətradyksjɔ̃] *nf* **1.** [d'un texte traduit d'une autre langue] retranslation **2.** [nouvelle traduction] new translation.

retraduire [98] [rətradɥir] *vt* **1.** [texte traduit d'une autre langue] to retranslate **2.** [à nouveau] to make a new translation of.

retrait [rətrɛ] *nm* **1.** [annulation - d'une licence] cancelling ; [- d'un mot d'ordre] calling off ■ **~ de candidature** [par un prestataire] withdrawal of application ; [par un député] standing down, withdrawal ■ **~ de permis (de conduire)** DR revocation of driving licence **2.** BANQUE withdrawal ■ **faire un ~** to withdraw money ■ **je veux faire un ~ de 3 000 euros** I want to take out *ou* to withdraw 3,000 euros ■ **~ d'espèces** cash withdrawal **3.** [récupération] : **le ~ des billets/bagages se fera dès 11 h** tickets/luggage may be collected from 11 o'clock onwards **4.** [départ - d'un joueur, du contingent] withdrawal **5.** [recul - des eaux d'inondation] subsiding, receding ; [- de la marée] ebbing ; [- des glaces] retreat **6.** DR [d'un acte administratif] revocation ■ [d'un acte de vente] redemption **7.** TECHNOL shrinkage.
◆ **en retrait** *loc adv* set back ■ **en ~ par rapport au mur** [clôture] set back from the wall ; [étagère] recessed ■ **rester en ~** *pr* to stand back ; *fig* to remain in the background ■ **vivre en ~** to lead a quiet life.
◆ **en retrait de** *loc prép* below, beneath ■ **son offre est en ~ de ce qu'il avait laissé entendre** his offer doesn't come up to what he'd led us to expect.

retraite [rətrɛt] *nf* **1.** [pension] pension, superannuation ADMIN : **~ des fonctionnaires/des non-salariés** public service/ self-employed pension ■ **toucher** *ou* **percevoir sa ~** to get *ou* to draw one's pension ➤ **~ complémentaire** supplementary pension ■ **~ par répartition** contributory pension scheme ■ **~ par capitalisation** self-funded pension scheme **2.** [cessation d'activité] retirement ■ **il est à la** *ou* **en ~** he has retired ■ **prendre sa ~** to retire ■ **être mis à la ~** to be retired ➤ **~ anticipée** early retirement **3.** MIL & RELIG retreat ■ **suivre** *ou* **faire une ~** RELIG to go on a retreat **4.** *litt* [cachette] hiding place, refuge, shelter.

RETRAITE

The normal retirement age for men and women in France is 60.

retraité, e [rətrɛte] ◇ *adj* [qui est à la retraite] retired.
◇ *nm, f* ADMIN pensioner ■ [personne ne travaillant plus] retired person.

retraitement [rətrɛtmɑ̃] *nm* reprocessing ■ **centre** *ou* **usine de ~ (des déchets nucléaires)** (nuclear) reprocessing plant.

retraiter [4] [rətrete] *vt* INDUST & NUCL to reprocess.

retranchement [rətrɑ̃ʃmɑ̃] *nm* MIL retrenchment, entrenchment ■ *fig* **pousser qqn dans ses derniers ~s** to force sb to the wall.

retrancher [3] [rətrɑ̃ʃe] *vt* **1.** MATH to subtract ■ **~ 10 de 20** to take 10 away from 20, to subtract 10 from 20 **2.** *sout* [enlever] to remove, to excise **3.** [déduire - pour des raisons administratives] to deduct ; [- par sanction] to deduct, to dock.
◆ **se retrancher** *vpi* **1.** [se protéger] : **se ~ derrière** [se cacher] to hide behind ; [se réfugier] to take refuge behind ■ **se ~ sur ses positions** to remain entrenched in one's position **2.** MIL to entrench o.s.

retranscription [rətrɑ̃skripsjɔ̃] *nf* **1.** [processus] retranscription **2.** [résultat] new transcript.

retranscrire [99] [rətrɑ̃skrir] *vt* to retranscribe.

retransmettre [84] [rətrɑ̃smɛtr] *vt* RADIO to broadcast ■ TV to broadcast, to screen, to show ■ **concert retransmis en direct** live concert ■ **~ une émission en direct/différé** to broadcast a programme live/a recorded programme.

retransmission [rətrɑ̃smisjɔ̃] *nf* RADIO broadcast ■ TV broadcast, screening, showing ■ **~ en direct/différé** live/ recorded broadcast.

retransmit *etc v* ▷ **retransmettre.**

retravailler [3] [rətravaje] ◇ *vt* to work on *(insép)* again.
◇ *vi* to (start) work again.

retraverser [3] [rətravɛrse] *vt* **1.** [à nouveau] to cross again, to recross **2.** [en sens inverse] to go *ou* to cross back over ■ **elle a retraversé l'estuaire à la nage** she swam back across the estuary.

rétrécir [32] [retresir] ◇ *vt* TEXT [vêtement] to shrink ■ **~ une jupe** COUT to take in a skirt.
◇ *vi* TEXT [vêtement] to shrink ■ **~ au lavage** to shrink in the wash.
◆ **se rétrécir** *vpi* [allée, goulot] to narrow, to get narrower ■ [cercle, diaphragme] to contract, to get smaller ■ [budget] to shrink, to dwindle.

rétrécissement [retresismɑ̃] *nm* **1.** [d'un couloir, d'un diaphragme] narrowing *(U)* **2.** MÉD stricture **3.** TEXT [vêtement] shrinkage.

retremper [3] [rətrɑ̃pe] *vt* **1.** MÉTALL to requench **2.** [doigt] to dip again ■ [linge] to soak again **3.** *sout* & *fig* **cette épreuve lui a retrempé le caractère** this experience gave him new strength.
◆ **se retremper** *vpi* : **se ~ dans** *pr* to have another dip into ; *fig* to go back into ■ **se ~ aux sources** *litt* to go back to basics.

rétribuer [7] [retribɥe] *vt* [employé] to pay, to remunerate ■ [travail, service rendu] to pay for *(insép)*.

rétribution [retribysjɔ̃] *nf* **1.** [salaire] remuneration, salary **2.** *sout* [récompense] recompense, reward.

rétro [retro] ◇ *adj inv* retro ■ **mode ~** retro fashion.
◇ *nm* **1.** *fam* = **rétroviseur 2.** [mode] : **le ~** retro style.

rétroactif, ive [retrɔaktif, iv] *adj* retroactive ■ **avec effet ~ au 1er janvier** backdated to January 1st ■ **la loi a été votée, avec effet ~ à dater de mars** the bill was passed, retroactive *ou* retrospective to March.

rétroactivement [retrɔaktivmɑ̃] *adv* retrospectively, with retrospective *ou* retroactive effect.

rétroactivité [retrɔaktivite] *nf* retroactivity ■ DR retrospectiveness.

rétrocéder [18] [retrɔsede] *vt* to cede back *(sép)*, to retrocede.

rétrocession [retrɔsɛsjɔ̃] *nf* retrocedence, retrocession.

rétrograde [retrɔgrad] *adj* **1.** [passéiste - esprit] reactionary, backward ; [- mesure, politique] reactionary, backward-looking, retrograde *sout* **2.** [de recul - mouvement] backward, retrograde *sout* **3.** ASTRON, GÉOL, MÉD & MUS retrograde **4.** [au billard] : **effet ~** screw.

rétrograder [3] [retrɔgrade] ◇ *vt* [fonctionnaire] to downgrade, to demote ■ [officier] to demote ■ **il a été rétrogradé** he was demoted.
◇ *vi* **1.** AUTO to change down *UK*, to shift down *US* **2.** [dans une hiérarchie] to move down **3.** ASTRON to retrograde.

rétropédalage [retrɔpedalaʒ] *nm* backpedalling *pr.*

rétroprojecteur [retrɔprɔʒɛktœr] *nm* overhead projector.

rétrospectif, ive [retrɔspɛktif, iv] *adj* [étude] retrospective ■ **examen ~** retrospective study.
◆ **rétrospective** *nf* ART retrospective ■ CINÉ season ■ **une rétrospective Richard Burton** a Richard Burton season.

rétrospectivement [retrɔspɛktivmɑ̃] *adv* in retrospect, retrospectively, looking back.

retroussé, e [rətruse] *adj* **1.** [jupe] bunched *ou* pulled up ▪ [manches, pantalon] rolled *ou* turned up **2.** [nez] turned up **3.** [babines] curled up ▪ [moustache] curled *ou* twisted up.

retrousser [3] [rətruse] *vt* **1.** [jupe] to bunch *ou* to pull up *(sép)* ▪ [pantalon] to roll *ou* to turn up *(sép)* ▪ [manches] to roll up *(sép)* ▪ **il va falloir ~ nos manches** *pr & fig* we'll have to roll our sleeves up **2.** [babines] to curl up *(sép)* ▪ [moustache] to curl *ou* to twist up *(sép)*.
◆ **se retrousser** ◇ *vp (emploi réfléchi)* to pull *ou* to hitch up one's skirt/trousers *etc* ▪ **j'ai dû me ~ jusqu'aux genoux pour ne pas mouiller ma robe** I had to pull my dress up around my knees to stop it getting wet.
◇ *vpi* [bords, feuille] to curl up.

retrouvailles [rətruvaj] *nfpl* **1.** [après une querelle] getting back on friendly terms again ▪ [après une absence] reunion, getting together again **2.** [retour - dans un lieu] rediscovery, return ; [- à un travail] return ▪ **mes ~ avec le train-train quotidien** getting back into my daily routine.

retrouver [3] [rətruve] *vt* **1.** [clés, lunettes] to find (again) ▪ **je ne le retrouve plus** I can't find it ▪ **a-t-elle retrouvé sa clef?** [elle-même] did she find her key? ; [grâce à autrui] did she get her key back? ▪ **~ un poste** to find a (new) job ▪ **~ son (ancien) poste** to get one's (old) job back ▪ **~ son chemin** to find one's way (again) ▪ **là vous retrouvez la Nationale** that's where you join up with the main road ‖ [après un changement] to find ▪ **~ tout propre/sens dessus dessous** to find everything clean/upside down ▪ **~ qqn affaibli/changé** to find sb weaker/a different person
2. [ami, parent] to be reunited with, to meet up with *(insép)* (again) ▪ [voleur] to catch up with *(insép)* (again), to find ▪ **et que je ne vous retrouve pas ici!** don't let me catch you (around) here again! ▪ **celle-là, je la retrouverai** I'll get even with her (one day) ‖ [revoir par hasard] to come across *(insép)* (again), to run into *(insép)* again ▪ [rejoindre] to meet up with again ▪ **retrouve-moi en bas** meet me downstairs
3. [se rappeler] to remember, to recall *sout* ▪ **ça y est, j'ai retrouvé le mot!** that's it, the word's come back to me now!
4. [redécouvrir - secret, parchemin, formule] to uncover
5. [jouir à nouveau de] to enjoy again ▪ **à partir de la semaine prochaine nous allons ~ nos émissions littéraires** our book programmes will be back on as from next week ▪ **nous avons retrouvé notre petite plage/maison** here we are back on our little beach/in our little house ▪ **~ son calme** to regain one's composure ▪ **~ l'appétit/ses forces/sa santé** to get one's appetite/strength/health back ▪ **~ la forme** to get fit again, to be back on form ▪ **~ la foi** to find (one's) faith again ▪ **~ la mémoire** to get one's memory back again ▪ **~ le sommeil** to go back to sleep ▪ **il a retrouvé le sourire** he's smiling again now, he's found his smile again ▪ **j'avais retrouvé mes vingt ans** I felt twenty years old again ▪ **le bonheur/l'amour retrouvé** new-found happiness/love
6. [reconnaître] to recognize, to trace ▪ **on retrouve les mêmes propriétés dans les polymères** the same properties are to be found in polymers ▪ **enfin, je te retrouve!** I'm glad to see you're back to your old self again!
◆ **se retrouver** ◇ *vp (emploi réciproque)* **1.** [avoir rendez-vous] to meet (one another)
2. [se réunir] to get together
3. [se rencontrer à nouveau] to meet again ▪ **on se retrouvera, mon bonhomme!** *fam* I'll get even with you, chum! ◐ **comme on se retrouve!** fancy meeting you here!, well, well, well, look who's here!
◇ *vpi* **1.** [être de nouveau] to find o.s. back (again) ▪ **se ~ dans la même situation (qu'avant)** to find o.s. back in the same situation (as before)
2. [par hasard] to end up ▪ **à quarante ans, il s'est retrouvé veuf** he (suddenly) found himself a widower at forty ▪ **tu vas te ~ à l'hôpital** you'll end up in hospital
3. [se repérer] to find one's way ▪ **je ne m'y retrouve plus dans tous ces formulaires à remplir** I can't make head or tail of all these forms to fill in ◐ **s'y ~** [résoudre un problème] to sort things out ; [faire un bénéfice] to make a profit
4. [se ressourcer] to find o.s. again, to go back to one's roots.

rétrovirus [retrɔvirys] *nm* retrovirus.

rétroviseur [retrɔvizœr] *nm* : **~ central** (rearview) mirror ▪ **~ extérieur** wing mirror ▪ **~ latéral** wing mirror *UK*, side-view mirror *US*.

rets [rɛ] *nm* **1.** *(gén pl) litt* [piège] snare ▪ **attraper** *ou* **prendre qqn dans ses ~** to ensnare sb ▪ **tomber dans les ~ de qqn** to be caught in sb's trap **2.** [filet - de chasse] net, snare ; [- de pêche] (fishing) net.

réunification [reynifikasjɔ̃] *nf* reunification.

réunifier [9] [reynifje] *vt* to reunify, to reunite.

réunion [reynjɔ̃] *nf* **1.** [rassemblement] gathering, get-together ▪ **~ de famille** family reunion *ou* gathering
2. [fête] gathering, party
3. [retrouvailles] reunion ▪ **~ d'anciens élèves** reunion of former pupils
4. [congrès] meeting ▪ **~ publique** public *ou* open meeting ▪ **dites que je suis en ~** say that I'm at *ou* in a meeting ‖ [séance] session, sitting ▪ **~ de la Cour** court session ▪ **~ du Parlement** Parliamentary session *UK*
5. [regroupement - de faits, de preuves] bringing together, assembling, gathering ; [- de sociétés] merging ; [- d'États] union
6. SPORT meeting ▪ **~ (sportive)** sports meeting, sporting event ▪ **~ d'athlétisme** athletics meeting ▪ **~ hippique** horse show
7. MATH union.

Réunion [reynjɔ̃] *npr f* : **(l')île de la ~** Réunion ▪ **à la ~** in Réunion, *voir aussi* **île**.

réunionnais, e [reynjɔnɛ, ɛz] *adj* from Réunion.
◆ **Réunionnais, e** *nm, f inhabitant of Réunion.*

réunir [32] [reynir] *vt* **1.** [relier - pôles, tuyaux] to join (together) ; [- brins, câbles] to tie together **2.** [mettre ensemble - objets] to collect together *(sép)* ; [- bétail] to round up *(sép)* ▪ **le spectacle réunit ses meilleures chansons** the show is a collection of her best hits ▪ [province] : **~ à** to join to ▪ **propriétés réunies au domaine royal en 1823** land acquired by the crown in 1823 **3.** [combiner - goûts, couleurs] to combine **4.** [recueillir - statistiques, propositions] to put *ou* to collect together ; [- preuves] to put together ; [- fonds] to raise **5.** [rassembler - personnes] to bring together, to reunite ▪ **nous sommes enfin réunis** [après rendez-vous manqué] at last we are together ; [après querelle] we are reunited at last ▪ **réunissez les élèves par groupes de dix** gather *ou* put the pupils into groups of ten.
◆ **se réunir** *vpi* **1.** [se retrouver ensemble] to meet, to get together **2.** [fusionner] to unite, to join (together).

réunis, ies [reyni] *adj pl* **1.** [rassemblés] combined **2.** [dans un titre commercial] : **les Cavistes/Mareyeurs Réunis** United Vintners/Fisheries.

réussi, e [reysi] *adj* successful ▪ **ton tricot/soufflé est très ~** your sweater/soufflé is a real success ▪ **comme fête, c'était ~!** *iron* call that a party!

réussir [32] [reysir] ◇ *vt* [manœuvre, œuvre, recette] to make a success of, to carry off *(sép)* ▪ [exercice] to succeed in doing ▪ [examen] to pass ▪ **il a réussi son saut périlleux/sa nature morte** his somersault/still life was a success ▪ **j'ai bien réussi mon coup** *fam* it worked out (well) for me, I managed to pull it off ▪ **~ sa vie** to make a success of one's life ▪ **~ son effet** to achieve the desired effect ▪ **avec ce concert, il réussit un tour de force** his concert is a great achievement.
◇ *vi* **1.** [dans la vie, à l'école] to do well, to be successful ▪ **je veux ~** I want to succeed *ou* to be a success *ou* to be successful ▪ **il a réussi dans la vie** he's done well in life, he's a successful man ▪ **~ à un examen** to pass an exam ▪ **nous sommes ravis d'apprendre que vous avez réussi** we're delighted to hear of your success
2. [affaire, entreprise] to succeed, to be a success ▪ **l'opération n'a pas vraiment réussi** the operation wasn't really a success
3. [parvenir] : **~ à faire qqch** to manage to do sthg, to succeed in doing sthg ▪ **j'ai réussi à le réparer/à me couper** I managed to mend it/to cut myself
4. [convenir] : **~ à qqn** [climat, nourriture] to agree with sb, to do sb good ▪ **le café lui réussit/ne lui réussit pas** coffee agrees/doesn't agree with him ▪ **on dirait que ça te réussit, le mariage!** being married seems to make you thrive *ou* to suit you! ▪ **il**

a essayé de les rouler, mais ça ne lui a pas réussi he tried to swindle them but it didn't do him any good *ou* it didn't get him very far ■ **rien ne lui réussit** he can't do anything right **5.** AGRIC & HORT to thrive, to do well.

réussite [reysit] *nf* **1.** [affaire, entreprise] success ■ **c'est une ~!** it's a (real) success! ■ **~ à un examen** exam pass **2.** JEUX patience ■ **faire une ~** to have a game of patience.

réutilisable [reytilizabl] *adj* reusable ■ **non ~** disposable, throwaway.

réutilisation [reytilizasjɔ̃] *nf* reuse TECHNOL reutilization.

réutiliser [3] [reytilize] *vt* to reuse, to use again.

revacciner [3] [rəvaksine] *vt* to revaccinate.

revaloir [60] [rəvalwar] *vt* : **je te revaudrai ça** [en remerciant] I'll repay you some day ; [en menaçant] I'll get even with you for that, I'll pay you back for that.

revalorisation [rəvalɔrizasjɔ̃] *nf* **1.** [d'une monnaie] revaluation **2.** [des salaires] raising, revaluation, increment **3.** [d'une théorie, d'une fonction] upgrading, reassertion ■ **on assiste à une ~ du rôle des pères** the role of the father is becoming more important.

revaloriser [3] [rəvalɔrize] *vt* **1.** [monnaie] to revaluate **2.** [salaires] to raise, to revalue **3.** [théorie, fonction] to improve the status *ou* prestige *ou* standing of, to upgrade.

revanchard, e [rəvɑ̃ʃar, ard] *péj* <> *adj* [attitude, politique] of revenge, revengeful, revanchard *spéc* ■ [personne] revengeful, set on revenge, revanchist *spéc*.
<> *nm, f* revanchist.

revanche [rəvɑ̃ʃ] *nf* **1.** [sur un ennemi] revenge ■ **prendre sa ~ (sur qqn)** to take *ou* to get one's revenge (on sb) **2.** JEUX & SPORT return game ■ **donner sa ~ à qqn** to give sb his revenge.
◆ **en revanche** *loc adv* on the other hand.

revanchisme [rəvɑ̃ʃism] *nm* revanchism, spirit of revenge.

rêvasser [3] [rɛvase] *vi* to daydream, to dream away, to muse ■ **arrête de ~** stop daydreaming!

rêvasserie [rɛvasri] *nf* daydream ■ **des ~s sans fin** endless musing *ou* daydreaming.

revaudra *etc v* ▻ **revaloir**.

rêve [rɛv] *nm* **1.** [d'un dormeur] dream ■ **faire un ~** to have a dream ■ **je l'ai vu en ~** I saw him in my *ou* in a dream ■ **comme dans un ~** as if in a dream ■ **bonne nuit, fais de beaux ~s!** good night, sweet dreams! ■ **le ~** PSYCHOL dreams, dreaming **2.** [d'un utopiste] dream, fantasy, pipe dream ■ **mon ~, ce serait d'aller au Japon** my dream is to go to Japan, I dream of going to Japan **3.** *fam* **le ~** [l'idéal] the ideal thing ■ **c'est/ce n'est pas le ~** it's/it isn't ideal.
◆ **de mes rêves, de ses rêves** *etc loc adj* of my/his *etc* dreams ■ **j'ai le métier de mes ~s** I've got the job I always dreamed of having.
◆ **de rêve** *loc adj* ideal ■ **une vie de ~** a sublime *ou* an ideal existence ■ **il fait un temps de ~** the weather is perfect.

rêvé, e [rɛve] *adj* perfect, ideal ■ **c'est l'endroit ~ pour camper** this is the ideal place *ou* just the place to camp.

revêche [rəvɛʃ] *adj* [personne] surly, cantankerous, tetchy ■ [voix, air] surly, grumpy.

revécu, e [rəveky] *pp* ▻ **revivre**.

réveil [revɛj] *nm* **1.** [après le sommeil] waking (up), awakening *litt* ■ **j'attendrai ton ~ pour partir** I'll wait until you have woken up *ou* until you are awake before I leave ■ **j'ai des ~s difficiles** *ou* **le ~ difficile** I find it hard to wake up ■ **à mon ~ il était là** when I woke up he was there **2.** [prise de conscience] awakening **3.** MIL reveille ■ **j'ai eu droit à un ~ en fanfare, ce matin!** *fig* I was treated to a very noisy awakening this morning! **4.** [de la mémoire, de la nature] reawakening ■ [d'une douleur] return, new onset ■ [d'un volcan] (new) stirring, fresh eruption **5.** [pendule] alarm (clock) ■ **j'ai mis le ~ (à 7 h)** I've set the alarm (for 7 o'clock) ➊ **~ téléphonique** wake-up service ■ **~ de voyage** travel alarm (clock).

réveille-matin [revɛjmatɛ̃] *nm inv vieilli* alarm (clock).

réveiller [4] [reveje] *vt* **1.** [tirer - du sommeil, de l'évanouissement] to wake (up) *(sép)* ; [- d'une réflexion, d'une rêverie] to rouse, to stir ■ **il faut que l'on se fasse ~ à 7 heures si on ne veut pas rater l'avion** we need to make sure somebody wakes us up at 7 a.m. if we don't want to miss the plane ■ **un bruit/une explosion à ~ les morts** a noise/an explosion loud enough to wake the dead **2.** [faire renaître - enthousiasme, rancœur, envie] to reawaken, to revive.
◆ **se réveiller** *vpi* **1.** [sortir - du sommeil, de l'évanouissement] to wake (up), to awake *litt*, to awaken *litt* ; [- d'une réflexion, de la torpeur] to wake up, to stir *ou* to rouse o.s. ■ **se ~ en sursaut** to wake up with a start ■ **il faut vous ~!** you'd better pull yourself together! **2.** [se ranimer - passion, souvenir] to revive, to be stirred up *ou* aroused (again) ; [- volcan] to stir *ou* to erupt again ; [- maladie, douleur] to start up again, to return.

réveillon [revɛjɔ̃] *nm family meal eaten on Christmas Eve or New Year's Eve* ■ **~ (de Noël)** [fête] Christmas Eve party ; [repas] Christmas Eve supper ■ **~ de la Saint-Sylvestre** *ou* **du Jour de l'An** [fête] New Year's Eve party ; [repas] New Year's Eve supper.

réveillonner [3] [revɛjɔne] *vi* [faire une fête - à Noël] to have a Christmas Eve party ; [- pour la Saint-Sylvestre] to have a New Year's Eve party ■ [faire un repas - à Noël] to have a Christmas Eve supper ; [- pour la Saint-Sylvestre] to have a New Year's Eve supper ■ **nous avons trop bien réveillonné** we had too much to eat and drink *(on Christmas Eve or New Year's Eve)*.

révélateur, trice [revelatœr, tris] <> *adj* [détail] revealing, indicative, significant ■ [lapsus, sourire] revealing, telltale ■ **les chiffres sont ~s** the figures speak volumes ■ **ce sondage est très ~ de la tendance actuelle** this poll tells us *ou* reveals a lot about the current trend ■ **c'est tout à fait ~ de notre époque** it says a lot about our times ■ **un décolleté ~** a plunging neckline.
<> *nm, f* revealer.
◆ **révélateur** *nm* **1.** *sout* [indice] telltale sign **2.** PHOTO developer.

révélation [revelasjɔ̃] *nf* **1.** [information] revelation, disclosure ■ **faire des ~s à la presse/police** to give the press a scoop/the police important information **2.** [personne] revelation ■ **il pourrait bien être la ~ musicale de l'année** he could well turn out to be this year's musical revelation *ou* discovery **3.** [prise de conscience] revelation ■ **avoir une ~** to have a brainwave **4.** [divulgation] disclosure, revealing ■ **la ~ d'un complot** the revealing *ou* uncovering of a plot **5.** RELIG revelation.

révélé, e [revele] *adj* [religion] revealed.

révéler [18] [revele] *vt* **1.** [secret, information, intention] to reveal ■ [état de fait] to reveal, to bring to light ■ [vérité] to reveal, to tell ■ **j'ai des choses importantes à ~ à la police** I have important information to give to the police ■ **elle a révélé mon secret** [intentionnellement] she revealed my secret ; [involontairement] she gave away my secret ■ **il refuse de ~ son identité** he's refusing to disclose his identity *ou* to say who he is **2.** [montrer - don, qualité, anomalie] to reveal, to show ■ **la mauvaise gestion révélée par ces chiffres** the bad management brought to light *ou* evidenced by these results ■ **une grosseur que les radios n'avaient pas révélée** a growth which hadn't shown up on the X-rays **3.** [faire connaître] : **~ qqn** to make sb famous ■ **révélé par un important metteur en scène** discovered by an important director **4.** PHOTO to develop.
◆ **se révéler** *vpi* **1.** [s'avérer] : **se ~ coûteux/utile** to prove (to be) expensive/useful ■ **elle se révéla piètre vendeuse** she turned out *ou* proved to be a poor salesgirl **2.** [se faire connaître] to be revealed *ou* discovered, to come to light ■ **tu t'es révélé sous ton vrai jour** you've showed yourself in your true colours ■ **elle s'est révélée (au grand public) dans Carmen** she had her first big success in Carmen.

revenant, e [rəvnɑ̃, ɑ̃t] *nm, f fam hum* **tiens, un ~!** hello, stranger!, long time no see! *hum*.
◆ **revenant** *nm* [fantôme] ghost, spirit.

revendeur, euse [rəvɑ̃dœr, øz] *nm, f* **1.** [détaillant] retailer, dealer **2.** [de billets, de tickets] tout *UK*, scalper *US* ■ [d'articles d'occasion] (second-hand) dealer ■ **~ de drogue** drug dealer ■ **~ de voitures** second-hand car dealer.

revendicateur, trice [rəvɑ̃dikatœr, tris] *adj* : **des discours ~s** speeches setting out demands *ou* claims.

revendicatif, ive [rəvɑ̃dikatif, iv] *adj* protest *(modif)* ■ **un mouvement ~** a protest movement.

revendication [rəvɑ̃dikasjɔ̃] *nf* [réclamation] demand ■ **journée de ~** day of action *ou* of protest ■ **~s salariales** wage demands *ou* claims.

revendiquer [3] [rəvɑ̃dike] *vt* **1.** [réclamer - dû, droit, part d'héritage] to claim ; [- hausse de salaire] to demand ■ *(en usage absolu)* **le personnel revendique** the staff are making demands *ou* have put in a claim **2.** [assumer] to lay claim to, to claim ■ **~ la responsabilité de qqch** to claim responsibility for sthg ■ **l'attentat n'a pas été revendiqué** nobody has claimed responsibility for the attack ■ **il n'a jamais revendiqué cette paternité** he never claimed this child as his **3.** DR to lay claim to, to claim.

revendre [73] [rəvɑ̃dr] *vt* **1.** [vendre - gén] to sell ■ [suj: détaillant] to retail ■ **revends ta voiture, si tu as besoin d'argent** if you need money sell your car **2.** *fam loc* **elle a du talent/de l'ambition à ~** she's got masses of talent/ambition.

◆ **se revendre** *vp (emploi passif)* : **ce genre d'appareil ne se revend pas facilement** this sort of equipment isn't easy to resell.

revenez-y [rəvnezi] *nm inv* **1.** *litt* [retour vers le passé] reversion, throwback **2.** *fam loc* **un goût de ~ : ce vin a un petit goût de ~!** this wine is rather moreish!

revenir [40] [rəvnir] *vi* **1.** [venir à nouveau - gén] to come back ; [- chez soi] to come back, to come (back) home, to return home ; [- au point de départ] to return, to come *ou* to get back ■ **pouvez-vous ~ plus tard?** could you come back later? ■ **passe me voir en revenant du bureau** call in to see me on your way back *ou* home from the office ■ **je reviens (tout de suite)** I'll be (right) back ■ **je suis revenue déçue de la visite** I came back disappointed after the visit ■ **la lettre m'est revenue** the letter was returned to me ■ **enfin tu me reviens!** at last, you've come back to me! ■ **d'où nous revenez-vous?** and where have you been? ■ **~ en arrière** [dans le temps] to go back (in time) ; [dans l'espace] to retrace one's steps, to go back ➤ **~ au point de départ** to go back to the starting point ; *fig* to be back to square one ■ **elle revient de loin!** [elle a failli mourir] it was touch and go (for her)! *euphém* ; [elle a eu de graves ennuis] she's had a close shave!
2. [se manifester à nouveau - doute, inquiétude] to return, to come back ; [- calme, paix] to return, to be restored ; [- symptôme] to recur, to return, to reappear ; [- problème] to crop up *ou* to arise again ; [- occasion] to crop up again ; [- thème, rime] to recur, to reappear ; [- célébration] to come round again ; [- saison] to return, to come back ; [- soleil] to come out again, to reappear ■ **le temps des fêtes est revenu** the festive season is with us again *ou* has come round again ■ **ses crises reviennent de plus en plus souvent** her fits are becoming more and more frequent
3. SPORT [dans une course] to come back, to catch up ■ **le peloton est en train de ~ sur les échappés** the pack is catching up with *ou* gaining on the breakaway group
4. [coûter] : **~ cher** to be expensive ■ **~ à** to cost, to amount to, to come to
5. CULIN : **faire ~** to brown
6. *fam* [retrouver son état normal - tissu] : **les draps sont bien revenus au lavage** the sheets came up like new in the wash.

◆ **revenir à** *v+prép* **1.** [équivaloir à] to come down to, to amount to ■ **ce qui revient à dire que...** which amounts to saying that... ■ **ça revient au même!** (it) amounts to *ou* comes to the same thing!
2. [reprendre - mode, procédé, thème] to go back to, to revert to, to return to ■ **on revient aux *ou* à la mode des cheveux courts** short hair is coming back *ou* on its way back ■ **~ à une plus juste vision des choses** to come round to a more balanced view of things ■ **(en) ~ à : mais revenons *ou* revenons-en à cette affaire** but let's get *ou* come back to this matter ■ **bon, pour (en) ~ à notre histoire...** right, to get back to *ou* to go on with our story... ■ **j'en *ou* je reviens à ma question, où étiez-vous hier?** I'm asking you again, where were you yesterday? ■ **et si nous (en) revenions à vous, M. Lebrun?** now what about you, Mr Lebrun? ➤ **y ~ : voilà dix euros, et n'y reviens plus!** here's ten euros, and don't ask me again! ■ **il n'y a pas *ou* plus à y ~!** and that's final *ou* that's that! ■ **~ à soi** to come to, to come round
3. [suj: part, récompense] to go *ou* to fall to, to devolve on *ou* upon *sout* ■ [suj: droit, tâche] to fall to ■ **à chacun ce qui lui revient** to each his due ■ **avec les honneurs qui lui reviennent** with the honours (which are) due to her ■ **ses terrains sont revenus à l'État** his lands passed *ou* went to the State ■ **il devrait encore me ~ 200 euros** I should still get 200 euros ■ **ce titre lui revient de droit** this title is his by right ■ **tout le mérite t'en revient** the credit is all yours, you get all the credit for it ■ **la décision nous revient, il nous revient de décider** it's for us *ou* up to us to decide
4. [suj: faculté, souvenir] to come back to ■ **l'appétit lui revient** she's recovering her appetite *ou* getting her appetite back ■ **la mémoire lui revient** her memory is coming back ■ **son nom ne me revient pas (à la mémoire)** his name escapes me *ou* has slipped my mind ■ **ça me revient seulement maintenant, ils ont divorcé** I've just remembered, they got divorced ■ *(tournure impersonnelle)* **il me revient que tu étais riche à l'époque** *sout* as I recall, you were rich at the time ■ **~ à qqn *ou* aux oreilles de qqn** to get back to sb, to reach sb's ears ■ **il m'est revenu que...** word has got back to me *ou* has reached me that...
5. *fam* [plaire à] : **elle a une tête qui ne me revient pas** I don't really like the look of her.

◆ **revenir de** *v+prép* **1.** [émotion, étonnement, maladie] to get over, to recover from ■ [évanouissement] to come round from, to come to after ■ **en ~** [guérir] to come *ou* to pull through it, to recover ; [échapper à un danger] to come through (it) ➤ **je n'en reviens pas!** I can't get over it! ■ **je n'en reviens pas qu'il ait dit ça!** it's amazing he should say that!, I can't get over him saying that! ■ **quand je vais te le raconter, tu n'en reviendras pas** when I tell you the story you won't believe your ears
2. [idée, préjugé] to put *ou* to cast aside *(sép)*, to throw over *(sép)* ■ [illusion] to shake off *(sép)* ■ [principe] to give up *(sép)*, to leave behind ■ **~ de ses erreurs** to realize *ou* to recognize one's mistakes ■ **moi, l'homéopathie, j'en suis revenu!** *fam* as far as I'm concerned, I've done *ou* I'm through with homeopathy! ■ **il est revenu de tout** he's seen it all (before).

◆ **revenir sur** *v+prép* **1.** [question] to go back over, to hark back to ■ **elle ne peut s'empêcher de ~ sur cette triste affaire** she can't help going *ou* mulling over that sad business
2. [décision, déclaration, promesse] to go back on ■ **ma décision est prise, je ne reviendrai pas dessus** my mind is made up and I'm not going to change it ■ **~ sur sa parole *ou* sur la parole donnée** to go back on one's word, to break one's promise.

◆ **s'en revenir** *vpi sout* to be on one's way back ■ **nous nous en revenions tranquillement lorsque...** we were slowly making our way home when...

revente [rəvɑ̃t] *nf* resale ■ **la ~ d'un tableau** the resale of a painting.

revenu¹ [rəvəny] *nm* **1.** [rétribution - d'une personne] income *(U)* ■ **elle a de gros/petits ~s** she has a large/small income ■ **sans ~s** without any income ➤ **~ disponible** disposable income ■ **~ foncier** income from real estate ■ **~ par habitant *ou* par tête** per capita income ■ **~ imposable** taxable income ■ **~ minimum d'insertion** minimum guaranteed income *(for people with no other source of income)* **2.** [recettes - de l'État] revenue ■ **~ national** gross national product ■ **~s publics *ou* de l'État** public revenue **3.** [intérêt] income, return ■ **un investissement produisant un ~ de 7 %** an investment with a 7% rate of return ‖ [dividende] yield ■ **le ~ d'une action** the yield on a share **4.** [bénéfice] : **~ brut d'exploitation** gross profit.

revenu², e [rəvəny] *pp* ⊳ **revenir**.

rêver [4] [reve] ◇ *vi* **1.** [en dormant] to dream ■ **elle rêve (tout) éveillée** she's a daydreamer, she's lost in a dream *ou* daydream ■ **c'est ce qu'il m'a dit, je n'ai pas rêvé!** that's what he said, I didn't dream it up *ou* imagine it! ■ **toi ici? (dites-moi que) je rêve!** you here? I must be dreaming! ■ **~ de** to dream of ➤ **on croit ~!** [ton irrité] is this a joke? ■ **elle en rêve la nuit** *pr* she has dreams about it at night ; *fig* she's obsessed by it **2.** [divaguer] to be imagining things, to be in cloud-cuckooland

■ **toi, gagner ta vie tout seul, non mais tu rêves!** you, earn your own living? you must be joking! ■ **ça fait ~!** that's the stuff that dreams are made of! ■ **des plages/salaires à faire ~** dream beaches/wages ■ **(quand on voit) des paysages comme ça, ça fait ~** scenery like that is just out of this world ■ **on peut toujours ~** there's no harm in dreaming!, there's no harm in a little fantasizing! ▶ **faut pas ~!** let's not get carried away! ■ **la semaine de 25 heures? faut pas ~!** the 25 hour week? that'll be the day! **3.** [songer] to dream, to daydream ■ **~ à** to dream of *(insép)*, to muse over *(insép)* ***sout***.
◇ *vt* **1.** [suj: dormeur] to dream ■ **~ que...** to dream that... **2.** [souhaiter] to dream of *(insép)* ■ **on ne saurait ~ (une) occasion plus propice** you couldn't wish for a more appropriate occasion ■ **je n'ai jamais rêvé mariage/fortune!** I've never dreamed of marriage/being wealthy! ■ [inventer de toutes pièces] to dream up *(sép)*.
◆ **rêver de** *v+prép* [espérer] to dream of ■ **j'avais tellement rêvé de ton retour** I so longed for your return ■ **l'homme dont toutes les femmes rêvent** the man every woman dreams about *ou* desires ■ **je n'avais jamais osé ~ d'un bonheur pareil!** I'd never have dared dream of such happiness! ■ **~ de faire qqch** to be longing to do sthg.

réverbérant, e [revɛrberɑ̃, ɑ̃t] *adj* reverberant.

réverbération [revɛrberasjɔ̃] *nf* [du son] reverberation ■ [de la chaleur, de la lumière] reflection ■ **à cause de la ~ du soleil sur la neige** because of the glare of the sun on the snow.

réverbère [revɛrbɛr] *nm* **1.** [lampe] street lamp, streetlight **2.** [réflecteur] reflector.

réverbérer [18] [revɛrbere] *vt* [chaleur, lumière] to reflect ■ [son] to reverberate, to send back *(sép)*.

reverdir [32] [rəvɛrdir] *vi* to grow *ou* to turn green again.

révérence [reverɑ̃s] *nf* **1.** *litt* [déférence] reverence ■ **traiter qqn avec ~** to treat sb with reverence *ou* reverently **2.** [salut] bow, curtsy, curtsey ■ **elle fit une ~ à Son Altesse** she curtseyed to Her Highness ▶ **tirer sa ~ à qqn** to walk out on sb ■ **tirer sa ~ à qqch** to bow out of sthg **3.** RELIG : **Votre Révérence** Your Reverence.

révérencieux, euse [reverɑ̃sjø, øz] *adj litt* reverent ***sout***, respectful.

révérend, e [reverɑ̃, ɑ̃d] *adj* reverend ■ **le Révérend Père Thomas** (the) Reverend Father Thomas.
◆ **révérend** *nm* reverend.

révérendissime [reverɑ̃disim] *adj* [archevêque] Most Reverend.

révérer [18] [revere] *vt* ***sout*** to revere, to reverence ***sout*** ■ **il révère son frère** he's devoted to *ou* he reveres his brother.

rêverie [rɛvri] *nf* **1.** [réflexion] daydreaming *(U)*, reverie ■ **plongé dans ses ~s** *ou* **sa ~** deep in thought **2.** [chimère] dream, daydream, delusion.

revérifier [9] [rəverifje] *vt* to check again, to double-check.

reverra *etc v* ▷ **revoir.**

revers [rəvɛr] *nm* **1.** [d'une blouse, d'un veston] lapel ■ [d'un pantalon] turn-up *UK*, cuff *US* ■ [d'une manche] (turned-back) cuff ■ [d'un uniforme] facing ■ **col/bottes à ~** turned-down collar/boots **2.** [d'une feuille, d'un tissu, d'un tableau, de la main] back ■ [d'une médaille, d'une pièce] reverse (side) ■ **c'est le ~ de la médaille** that's the other side of the coin, there's the rub **3.** [échec, défaite] setback ■ **essuyer un ~** to suffer a setback ■ **~ économiques** economic setbacks ▶ **~ de fortune** reverse of fortune, setback (in one's fortunes) **4.** TENNIS backhand (shot) ■ **faire un ~** to play a backhand shot.
◆ **à revers** *loc adv* MIL from *ou* in the rear.

reverser [3] [rəvɛrse] *vt* **1.** [verser - de nouveau] to pour again, to pour (out) more (of) ; [- dans le récipient d'origine] to pour back *(sép)* **2.** FIN [reporter] to transfer ■ **~ des intérêts sur un compte** to pay interest on an account ■ **la prime d'assurance vous sera intégralement reversée au bout d'un an** the total premium will be paid back to you after one year.

réversibilité [revɛrsibilite] *nf* DR revertibility.

réversible [revɛrsibl] *adj* **1.** [vêtement] reversible **2.** DR [bien, pension] revertible ■ **annuité ~** reversionary annuity **3.** CHIM & PHYS reversible.

revêtement [rəvɛtmɑ̃] *nm* **1.** CONSTR [intérieur - peinture] covering ; [- enduit] coating ■ [extérieur - gén] facing ; [- crépi] rendering ■ **~ de sol** flooring *(U)* **2.** TRAV PUB : **refaire le ~ d'une route** to resurface a road **3.** TECHNOL [d'un câble électrique] housing, sheathing ■ [d'un pneu] casing ■ [d'un conduit] lining **4.** AÉRON skin **5.** ARCHIT revetment **6.** MIN lining.

revêtir [44] [rəvɛtir] *vt* **1.** ***sout*** [endosser] to don ***sout***, to array o.s. in ***sout***, to put on ■ **~ ses plus beaux atours** to array o.s. in *ou* to don one's finest attire **2.** ***sout*** [habiller] : **~ qqn de** to dress *ou* to array sb in, to clothe sb in *ou* with **3.** ***sout*** [importance, signification] to take on *(insép)*, to assume ■ [forme] to appear in, to take on, to assume **4.** ARCHIT, CONSTR & TRAV PUB [rue - asphalter] to surface ; [- paver] to pave ■ **~ une surface de** to cover a surface with **5.** TECHNOL [chaudière] to line, to lag ■ [puits de mine] to line **6.** DR : **~ un contrat de signatures** to append signatures to a contract ■ **laissez-passer revêtu du tampon obligatoire** authorization bearing the regulation stamp.

rêveur, euse [rɛvœr, øz] ◇ *adj* **1.** [distrait] dreamy ■ **avoir un caractère ~** to be a daydreamer ■ **d'un air ~** dreamily **2.** [perplexe] : **cette dernière phrase me laissa ~** these last words puzzled *ou* baffled me ■ **ça laisse ~!** it makes you wonder!
◇ *nm, f* dreamer, daydreamer.

rêveusement [rɛvøzmɑ̃] *adv* dreamily ■ **regarder ~ par la fenêtre** to gaze absentmindedly out of the window.

revient[1] [rəvjɛ̃] *v* ▷ **revenir.**

revient[2] [rəvjɛ̃] *nm* ▷ **prix.**

revigorant, e [rəvigɔrɑ̃, ɑ̃t] *adj* invigorating.

revigorer [3] [rəvigɔre] *vt* **1.** [stimuler - personne] to invigorate, to liven up *(sép)* ■ **une petite promenade pour vous ~?** how about a bracing little walk? **2.** [relancer - économie] to boost, to give a boost to.

revint *etc v* ▷ **revenir.**

revirement [rəvirmɑ̃] *nm* [changement - d'avis] about-face, change of mind ; [- de situation] turnaround, about-face, sudden turn ■ **un ~ dans l'opinion publique** a complete swing *ou* turnaround in public opinion ■ **un ~ de la tendance sur le marché des valeurs** a sudden reversal of stock market trends.

révisable [revizabl] *adj* **1.** [gén] revisable **2.** DR reviewable.

réviser [3] [revize] *vt* **1.** ÉDUC & UNIV to revise, to go over *(insép)* (again) **2.** [réévaluer - jugement, situation] to review, to reexamine, to reappraise ■ **~ à la baisse/hausse** to downgrade/upgrade, to scale down/up **3.** DR : **~ un procès** to reopen a trial ■ **~ le procès de qqn** to retry sb ■ **~ un jugement** to review a judgment **4.** [voiture] to service ■ [machine] to overhaul ■ **faire ~ une voiture** to have a car serviced ■ **faire ~ les freins** to have the brakes checked **5.** [clause] to revise ■ [liste électorale] to update, to revise ■ [manuscrit] to check, to go over *(insép)* ■ [épreuves] to revise, to line edit ***spéc.***

réviseur, euse [revizœr, øz] *nm, f* **1.** ÉCON : **~ comptable** auditor **2.** IMPR reviser, checker.

révision [revizjɔ̃] *nf* **1.** ÉDUC & UNIV revision *(U)*, revising *(U)* **2.** [d'une clause] revision ■ [d'une liste électorale] updating, revision ■ [d'un manuscrit] checking ■ [d'épreuves] checking, revising **3.** [d'une voiture] service ■ [d'une machine] overhaul, overhauling **4.** [fait de réestimer] reevaluation, reappraisal ■ **la ~ à la baisse/hausse des prévisions** the downgrading/upgrading of the forecast figures **5.** DR [d'un procès] rehearing ■ [d'un jugement] reviewing.

révisionnel, elle [revizjɔnɛl] *adj* revisionary, review *(modif)*.

révisionnisme [revizjɔnism] *nm* revisionism.

révisionniste [revizjɔnist] *adj & nmf* revisionist.

revisser [3] [rəvise] *vt* to screw back again.

revit *v* **1.** ▷ **revivre 2.** ▷ **revoir.**

revitalisant, e [rəvitalizɑ̃, ɑ̃t] *adj* revitalizing.

revitalisation [rəvitalizasjɔ̃] *nf* revitalization.

revitaliser [3] [rəvitalize] *vt* **1.** [ranimer - économie] to revitalize ▪ **ce nouveau plan économique est destiné à ~ la région** this new economic programme is designed to revitalize *ou* bring new life to the area **2.** [régénérer - peau] to revitalize.

revivifiant, e [rəvivifjɑ̃, ɑ̃t] *adj* bracing, revivifying.

revivifier [9] [rəvivifje] *vt* **1.** [personne] to revivify, to revitalize **2.** *litt* [souvenir] to bring back to life, to revive.

reviviscence [rəvivisɑ̃s] *nf* **1.** BIOL anabiosis, reviviscence *sout* **2.** *litt* revival, reappearance.

reviviscent, e [rəvivisɑ̃, ɑ̃t] *adj* BIOL anabiotic, reviviscent *sout.*

revivre [90] [rəvivr] ◇ *vi* **1.** [renaître] to come alive (again) ▪ **les examens sont terminés, je revis!** the exams are over, I can breathe again *ou* what a weight off my mind! ▪ **quel calme, je me sens ~!** how quiet it is around here, I feel like a new person! **2.** [nature, campagne] to come alive again **3.** [personne ou animal mort] to come back to life **4.** [redevenir actuel] : **faire ~ qqch: faire ~ la tradition** to restore *ou* to revive tradition ▪ **faire ~ les années de guerre** to bring back the war years.
◇ *vt* **1.** [se souvenir de] to relive, to live *ou* to go through *(insép)* (again) **2.** [vivre à nouveau] to relive.

révocabilité [revɔkabilite] *nf* **1.** ADMIN [d'un fonctionnaire] dismissibility **2.** DR [d'un acte juridique] revocability **3.** POLIT [d'un élu] recallability.

révocable [revɔkabl] *adj* **1.** ADMIN [fonctionnaire] dismissible **2.** DR [acte juridique] revocable, subject to repeal **3.** POLIT [élu] recallable, subject to recall.

révocation [revɔkasjɔ̃] *nf* **1.** ADMIN [d'un fonctionnaire] dismissal ▪ [d'un dirigeant] removal **2.** DR [d'un acte juridique] repeal, revocation ▪ [d'un testament] revocation ▪ [d'un ordre] rescinding ▪ **la ~ de l'édit de Nantes** the Revocation of the Edict of Nantes **3.** POLIT [d'un élu] removal, recall.

révocatoire [revɔkatwar] *adj* revocatory.

revoici [rəvwasi] *prép* : **me ~!** here I am again!, it's me again!

revoilà [rəvwala] *prép* : **~ le printemps!** it looks like spring's here again! ▪ **enfin, te ~!** you're back at last! ▪ **les ~!** there they are again! ⊃ **nous y ~, je m'y attendais!** here we go again! I just knew it.

revoir[1] [rəvwar] ◆ **au revoir** ◇ *interj* goodbye.
◇ *nm* : **ce n'est qu'un au ~** we'll meet again.
Voir module d'usage

revoir[2] [62] [rəvwar] *vt* **1.** [rencontrer à nouveau] to see *ou* to meet again ▪ **et que je ne te revoie plus ici, compris?** and don't let me see *ou* catch you around here again, is that clear? ▪ [retourner à] to see again, to go back to **2.** [examiner à nouveau - images] to see again, to have another look at ; [- exposition, spectacle] to see again ; [- dossier] to reexamine, to look at *(insép)* again ; [- vidéocassette] to watch again **3.** [assister de nouveau à - incident] to see *ou* to witness again **4.** [par l'imagination] : **je nous revois encore, autour du feu de camp** I can still see *ou* picture us around the campfire **5.** [vérifier - installation, mécanisme, moteur] to check, to look at *(insép)* again **6.** [modifier - texte] to reexamine, to revise ; [- opinion] to modify, to revise ▪ **'édition revue et corrigée'** 'revised edition' ▪ **~ à la hausse/baisse** to revise upwards/downwards **7.** ÉDUC [cours] to go over *(insép)* (again), to revise *UK*, to review *US* ▪ **tu ferais bien de ~ ta physique!** [réviser] you'd better revise your physics! ; [réapprendre] you'd better study *ou* learn your physics again!
◆ **se revoir** ◇ *vp (emploi réciproque)* to meet again.
◇ *vp (emploi réfléchi)* to see *ou* to picture o.s. again ▪ **je me revois enfant, chez ma grand-mère** I can still see myself as a child at my grandmother's.

révoltant, e [revɔltɑ̃, ɑ̃t] *adj* [violence, lâcheté] appalling, shocking ▪ [grossièreté] revolting, outrageous, scandalous.

révolte [revɔlt] *nf* **1.** [sédition] revolt, rebellion **2.** [insoumission] rebellion, revolt ▪ **être en ~ contre qqn** to be in revolt against sb ▪ **elle est en ~ contre ses parents** she's rebelling *ou* revolting against her parents **3.** [réprobation] outrage.

révolté, e [revɔlte] ◇ *adj* **1.** [rebelle] rebellious, rebel *(avant n)* **2.** [indigné] outraged **3.** MIL mutinous.
◇ *nm, f* **1.** [gén] rebel **2.** MIL rebel, mutineer.

révolter [3] [revɔlte] *vt* [scandaliser] to appal, to revolt, to shock ▪ **ça ne te révolte pas, toi?** don't you think that's disgusting *ou* revolting *ou* shocking? ▪ **révolté par la misère/tant de violence** outraged by poverty/at so much violence.
◆ **se révolter** *vpi* **1.** [gén] to revolt ▪ **adolescent, il s'est révolté contre ses parents** he rebelled against his parents when he was a teenager **2.** [marin, soldat] to mutiny.

révolu, e [revɔly] *adj* **1.** *litt* [d'autrefois] : **aux jours ~s de ma jeunesse** in the bygone days of my youth ▪ **en des temps ~s** in days gone by **2.** [fini] past ▪ **l'époque des hippies est ~e** the hippie era is over **3.** ADMIN : **âgé de 18 ans ~s** over 18 (years of age) ▪ **au bout de trois années ~es** after three full years.

révolution [revɔlysjɔ̃] *nf* **1.** POLIT revolution ▪ **la ~ industrielle** the Industrial Revolution ▪ **une ~ de palais** a palace coup *ou* revolution ▪ **la Révolution culturelle** the Cultural Revolution ▪ **la Révolution (française)** the French Revolution ▪ **la ~ d'octobre** the October Revolution **2.** [changement] revolution ▪ **faire** *ou* **causer une ~ dans qqch** to revolutionize sthg **3.** [agitation] turmoil ▪ **tous ces cambriolages ont mis la ville en ~** the town is up in arms *ou* in uproar because of all these burglaries **4.** ASTRON & MATH revolution.

LA RÉVOLUTION FRANÇAISE

One of the most important events in the history of modern France, from which it emerged as a Republic with an egalitarian constitution. Precipitated by the social and financial abuses of the *Ancien Régime*, it was a turbulent period lasting from the Fall of the Bastille in 1789 until the end of the century. It was marked by the Declaration of Human Rights, the execution of Louis XVI, the Reign of Terror (1793-94) and war against the other European powers.

révolutionnaire [revɔlysjɔnɛr] ◇ *adj* **1.** POLIT revolutionary **2.** HIST revolutionary **3.** *fig* revolutionary ▪ **une découverte ~** a revolutionary discovery.
◇ *nmf* **1.** POLIT revolutionary, revolutionist *US* **2.** HIST : **un ~** a revolutionary **3.** *fig* innovator.

DIRE AU REVOIR

Goodbye Mrs Jones! It was nice meeting you. Au revoir, madame ! Enchanté d'avoir fait votre connaissance.

See you soon *ou* **around.** À bientôt.

See you again some time. À un de ces jours.

See you in July, then! On se revoit en juillet, alors !

Right, then. See you tomorrow/later. Bon, à demain/à tout à l'heure.

Good night! Give my love to Anne. Bonsoir ! Mes amitiés à Anne.

Take care! À bientôt !

All the best! Bonne continuation !

See you! À plus !

Bye! Salut !

Night! Bonne nuit !

Speak to you soon *ou* **later.** *(au téléphone)* À bientôt.

révolutionner [3] [revɔlysjɔne] *vt* [système, domaine] to revolutionize ■ [vie] to change radically.

revolver [revɔlvɛr] *nm* **1.** ARM revolver ■ **un coup de ~** a gunshot **2.** TECHNOL capstan, turret.

revolving [revɔlviŋ] *adj inv* BANQUE revolving ■ **crédit ~** revolving credit.

révoquer [3] [revɔke] *vt* **1.** ADMIN [fonctionnaire] to dismiss ■ [dirigeant] to remove (from office) **2.** DR [acte juridique] to revoke, to repeal ■ [testament] to revoke ■ [ordre] to revoke, to rescind **3.** POLIT [élu] to recall.

revoyait *etc v* ▷ **revoir.**

revoyure△ [rəvwajyr] *nf* : **à la ~!** see you (around)!, so long!, toodle-oo!

revu, e [rəvy] *pp* ▷ **revoir.**

revue [rəvy] *nf* **1.** [publication - gén] magazine ■ **~ économique** economic journal *ou* review ■ **~ financière** financial review ■ **~ de mode** fashion magazine ■ **~ porno** *fam* porno *ou* porn magazine ■ **~ scientifique** science journal ■ **~ spécialisée** trade paper, journal, review **2.** [de music-hall] variety show ■ [de chansonniers] revue ■ **~ à grand spectacle** spectacular **3.** MIL [inspection] inspection, review ■ [défilé] review, march-past ■ **la ~ du 14 juillet** the 14th of July (military) parade ➜ **passer en ~** [troupes] to hold a review of, to review ; [uniformes] to inspect **4.** [inventaire] : **faire la ~ de, passer en ~** [vêtements, documents] to go *ou* to look through ; [solutions] to go over in one's mind, to review.

◆ **revue de presse** *nf* review of the press *ou* of what the papers say.

révulsé, e [revylse] *adj* [traits, visage] contorted ■ **~ de douleur** [visage] contorted with pain ■ **les yeux ~s** with his eyes rolled upwards.

révulser [3] [revylse] *vt* **1.** [dégoûter] to revolt, to fill with loathing, to disgust **2.** [crisper] to contort.

◆ **se révulser** *vpi* [traits, visage] to contort, to become contorted ■ [yeux] to roll upwards.

révulsif, ive [revylsif, iv] *adj* revulsant.

◆ **révulsif** *nm* revulsant, revulsive.

révulsion [revylsjɔ̃] *nf* **1.** MÉD revulsion **2.** [dégoût] revulsion, loathing.

rewriter[1] [rirajtœr] *nm* rewriter.

rewriter[2] [3] [rirajte] *vt* to rewrite.

rewriting [rirajtiŋ] *nm* rewriting.

rez-de-chaussée [redʃose] *nm inv* ground floor *UK*, first floor *US* ■ **au ~** on the ground floor ■ **habiter un ~** to live in a ground-floor flat *UK ou* first-floor apartment *US*.

rez-de-jardin [redʒardɛ̃] *nm inv* ground *ou* garden level ■ **pièces en ~** ground-level rooms.

RF = **République française.**

RFA (*abr de* **République fédérale d'Allemagne**) *npr f* FRG, West Germany.

RFI (*abr de* **Radio France Internationale**) *npr French World Service radio station.*

RFO (*abr de* **Radio-télévision française d'outre-mer**) *npr French overseas broadcasting service.*

r.g. = **rive gauche.**

RG *npr mpl* = **Renseignements généraux.**

Rh (*abr écrite de* **Rhésus**) Rh.

rhabiller [3] [rabije] *vt* **1.** [habiller à nouveau] to dress again ■ **rhabille-le** put his clothes back on (for him) **2.** ARCHIT to revamp, to refurbish ■ **on a rhabillé tout le foyer du théâtre** the entire foyer of the theatre has been refurbished **3.** TECHNOL [montre] to overhaul ■ [meule] to dress.

◆ **se rhabiller** *vp (emploi réfléchi)* **1.** [s'habiller à nouveau] to put one's clothes back on, to dress *ou* to get dressed again **2.** *fam loc* **tu peux aller te/il peut aller se ~!** you've/he's got another think coming!

rhapsodie [rapsɔdi] *nf* MUS rhapsody.

rhénan, e [renɑ̃, an] *adj* **1.** [du Rhin] of the Rhine, Rhenish ■ **le pays ~** the Rhineland **2.** [de la Rhénanie] of the Rhineland.

Rhénanie [renani] *npr f* : **(la) ~** the Rhineland.

rhéostat [reɔsta] *nm* rheostat ■ **~ de glissement** slip regulator.

Rhésus [rezys] *nm* [système sanguin] : **facteur ~** Rhesus *ou* Rh factor ■ **~ positif/négatif** Rhesus positive/negative.

rhéteur [retœr] *nm* **1.** ANTIQ rhetor **2.** *litt* rhetorician.

rhétoricien, enne [retɔrisjɛ̃, ɛn] ◇ *adj* rhetorical.
◇ *nm, f* [spécialiste] rhetorician.

rhétorique [retɔrik] ◇ *adj* rhetoric, rhetorical.
◇ *nf* **1.** [art] rhetoric **2.** *Belgique* ÉDUC ≃ lower sixth form *UK*, ≃ sixth grade *US*.

Rhin [rɛ̃] *npr m* : **le ~** the Rhine.

rhinite [rinit] *nf* rhinitis.

rhinocéros [rinɔserɔs] *nm* **1.** ZOOL rhinoceros, rhino **2.** ENTOM rhinoceros beetle.

rhino-pharyngite [rinofarɛ̃ʒit] (*pl* **rhino-pharyngites**) *nf* rhinopharyngitis.

rhizome [rizom] *nm* rhizome.

rhodanien, enne [rɔdanjɛ̃, ɛn] *adj* [du Rhône] from the Rhone ■ **le couloir ~** the Rhone corridor.

Rhode Island [rɔdajlɑ̃d] *npr m* : **le ~** Rhode Island.

Rhodes [rɔd] *npr* Rhodes, *voir aussi* **île.**

rhododendron [rɔdɔdɛ̃drɔ̃] *nm* rhododendron.

Rhône [ron] *npr m* [fleuve] : **le ~** the (River) Rhône.

Rhône-Alpes [ronalp] *npr* Rhône-Alpes.

RHÔNE-ALPES

This administrative region includes the *départements* of Ain, Ardèche, Drôme, Haute-Savoie, Isère, Loire, Rhône and Savoie (capital: Lyon).

Rhovyl® [rɔvil] *nm man-made fibre used in warm clothing.*

rhubarbe [rybarb] *nf* rhubarb.

rhum [rɔm] *nm* rum ■ **au ~** [dessert] rum-flavoured ; [boisson] rum-based.

rhumatisant, e [rymatizɑ̃, ɑ̃t] *adj & nm, f* rheumatic.

rhumatismal, e, aux [rymatismal, o] *adj* rheumatic.

rhumatisme [rymatism] *nm* rheumatism *(U)* ■ **avoir un ~** *ou* **des ~s au genou** to have rheumatism in one's knee ➜ **~ articulaire aigu** rheumatic fever ■ **~ déformant** polyarthritis.

rhumatologie [rymatɔlɔʒi] *nf* rheumatology.

rhumatologue [rymatɔlɔg] *nmf* rheumatologist.

rhume [rym] *nm* cold ■ **tu vas attraper un ~** you're going to catch (a) cold ➜ **~ de cerveau** head cold ■ **~ des foins** hay fever.

rhumerie [rɔmri] *nf* rum distillery.

ri [ri] *pp* ▷ **rire.**

ria [rija] *nf* ria.

riant, e [rijɑ̃, ɑ̃t] *adj* **1.** [visage, yeux] smiling **2.** [nature, paysage] pleasant ■ **une ~e vallée** a pleasant valley **3.** *litt* [heureux] happy.

RIB, Rib [rib] *nm* = **relevé d'identité bancaire.**

ribambelle [ribɑ̃bɛl] *nf* **1.** [quantité] flock, swarm ■ **suivie d'une ~ de gamins** *fam* followed by a long flock of *ou* a swarm of kids **2.** [papier découpé] paper dolls.

◆ **en ribambelle** *loc adv* : **les enfants sortent de l'école en ~** the children stream out of the school.

ribaud, e [ribo, od] *arch* ◇ *adj* ribald.
◇ *nm, f* : **un ~** a ribald fellow ■ **une ~e** a brazen wench.

ribonucléique [ribonykleik] *adj* ribonucleic.

ricain, e△ [rikɛ̃, ɛn] *nm, f pejorative or humorous term used with reference to Americans,* ≃ Yank *fam.*

ricanement [rikanmɑ̃] *nm* [rire - méchant] sniggering *(U)*, snigger ; [- nerveux] nervous *ou* jittery laugh ; [- bête] giggle, giggling *(U)* ▪ **~s** sniggering.

ricaner [3] [rikane] *vi* [rire - méchamment] to snigger ; [- nerveusement] to laugh nervously ; [- bêtement] to giggle.

Ricard® [rikar] *nm brand of pastis.*

RICE, Rice (*abr de* **relevé d'identité de caisse d'épargne**) *nm savings account identification slip.*

richard, e [riʃar, ard] *nm, f fam péj* rich person ▪ **un gros ~** a fat cat.

Richard [riʃar] *npr* : **~ Cœur de Lion** Richard the Lion-Heart, Richard Cœur de Lion.

riche [riʃ] <> *adj* **1.** [fortuné - famille, personne] rich, wealthy, well-off ; [- nation] rich, wealthy ▪ **elle a fait un ~ mariage** she's married into a rich family *ou* into money ▪ **on n'est pas bien ~ chez nous** we're not very well-off ▪ **je suis plus ~ de 5 000 euros maintenant** I'm 5,000 euros better off now ➊ **être ~ comme Crésus** *ou* **à millions** to be as rich as Croesus *ou* Midas ▪ **elle est ~ à millions** she's extremely wealthy
2. *(avant le n)* [demeure, décor] lavish, sumptuous, luxurious ▪ [étoffe, enluminure] magnificent, splendid ▪ **un ~ cadre doré** a heavy gilt frame
3. [végétation] lush, luxuriant, profuse ▪ [terre] fertile, rich ▪ [aliment] rich ▪ [vie] rich ▪ **c'est une ~ nature** *fam* he is a hearty *ou* an exuberant person ▪ **vous y trouverez une documentation très ~ sur Proust** you'll find a wide range of documents on Proust there ▪ **c'est une ~ idée que tu as eue là** *fam iron* that's a wonderful *ou* great idea you've just had
4. [complexe] rich ▪ **elle a un vocabulaire/une langue ~** she has a rich vocabulary/a tremendous command of the language ▪ **une imagination ~** a fertile imagination
5. : **~ en** [vitamines, minerais] rich in ; [événements] full of ▪ **~ en lipides** with a high lipid content ▪ **régime ~ en calcium** calcium-rich diet ▪ **la journée fut ~ en émotions** the day was packed full of excitement ▪ **leur bibliothèque n'est pas ~ en livres d'art** they don't have a very large collection *ou* choice of art books ▪ **je ne suis pas ~ en papier/farine!** *fam* I'm not very well-off for paper/flour!
6. : **~ de** [qualités, possibilités] : **un livre ~ d'enseignements** a very informative book ▪ **un magazine féminin ~ d'idées** a women's magazine packed full of ▪ **son premier roman est ~ de promesses** his first novel is full of promise *ou* shows great promise.
<> *nmf* rich person ▪ **les ~s** the rich, the wealthy ▪ **voiture de ~** rich man's car.
<> *adv fam* : **ça fait ~** it looks posh.

richelieu [riʃəljø] (*pl inv ou pl* **richelieus**) *nm* lace-up shoe.

richement [riʃmɑ̃] *adv* **1.** [luxueusement] richly, handsomely **2.** [abondamment] lavishly, sumptuously, richly ▪ **~ illustré** lavishly illustrated **3.** [de manière à rendre riche] : **il a ~ marié sa fille** *ou* **marié sa fille ~** he married his daughter into a wealthy family.

richesse [riʃɛs] *nf* **1.** [fortune - d'une personne] wealth ; [- d'une région, d'une nation] wealth, affluence, prosperity ▪ **ses livres sont sa seule ~** his books are all he has **2.** [d'un décor] luxuriousness, lavishness, sumptuousness ▪ [d'un tissu] beauty, splendour **3.** [luxuriance - de la végétation] richness, lushness, profuseness, luxuriance ▪ **la ~ du sous-sol** the wealth of (underground) mineral deposits ▪ **~ en : la ~ en fer d'un légume** the high iron content of a vegetable ▪ **pour préserver notre ~ en forêts** in order to protect our many forests **4.** [complexité - du vocabulaire, de la langue] richness ; [- de l'imagination] creativeness, inventiveness ▪ **la ~ culturelle de notre capitale** the cultural wealth of our capital city **5.** *sout* [réconfort] blessing ▪ **avoir un ami fidèle est une grande ~** to have a faithful friend is to be rich indeed.
◆ **richesses** *nfpl* [biens, capital] riches, wealth *(U)* ▪ [articles de valeur] treasures, wealth ▪ [ressources] resources ▪ **~s minières/naturelles** mining/natural resources.

richissime [riʃisim] *adj* fantastically wealthy.

Richter [riʃtɛr] *npr* : **échelle de ~** Richter scale.

ricin [risɛ̃] *nm* castor-oil plant.

ricocher [3] [rikɔʃe] *vi* **1.** [caillou] to ricochet, to bounce, to glance ▪ **les enfants font ~ des pierres sur l'eau** the children are skimming stones across the water *ou* are playing ducks and drakes **2.** [balle] to ricochet ▪ **la balle a ricoché sur le mur** the bullet ricochetted *ou* glanced off the wall.

ricochet [rikɔʃɛ] *nm* **1.** [d'un caillou] bounce, rebound ▪ **j'ai fait trois ~s!** I made the pebble bounce three times! ▪ **faire des ~s** to skim pebbles, to play ducks and drakes ▪ **par ~** *fig* indirectly ▪ **les épargnants ont perdu de l'argent par ~** savers lost money as an indirect consequence ▪ **ces mesures feront ~** *fig* these measures will have a knock-on effect **2.** [d'une balle] ricochet.

ric-rac [rikrak] *adv fam* **1.** [très exactement] : **il nous a payés ~** he paid us right down to the last penny **2.** [de justesse] : **avec mon petit salaire, à la fin du mois c'est ~** on my salary, money gets a bit tight at the end of the month.

rictus [riktys] *nm* grimace, rictus *sout* ▪ **un affreux ~ déformait son visage** his face was twisted into a hideous grimace ▪ **un ~ de colère** an angry scowl *ou* grimace.

ride [rid] *nf* **1.** [d'un visage] line, wrinkle ▪ **creusé de ~s** furrowed with wrinkles ▪ **le documentaire n'a pas pris une ~** *fig* the documentary hasn't dated in the slightest **2.** [sur l'eau, sur le sable] ripple, ridge.

ridé, e [ride] *adj* **1.** [visage] wrinkled, lined ▪ [pomme] wrinkled ▪ **un front ~** a deeply lined forehead ➊ **~ comme une vieille pomme** wrinkled like a prune **2.** [eau, sable] ridged, rippled.

rideau, x [rido] *nm* **1.** [en décoration intérieure] curtain, drape *US* ▪ **fermé par un ~** curtained off ▪ **mettre des ~x aux fenêtres** to put curtains up ▪ **tirer** *ou* **ouvrir les ~x** to draw *ou* to open the curtains ▪ **tirer** *ou* **fermer les ~x** to draw *ou* to close the curtains ➊ **~ de douche** shower curtain ▪ **doubles ~x** thick curtains ▪ **~x bonne femme** tieback curtains ▪ **tirer le ~ sur qqch** to draw a veil over sthg ▪ **ça risque de le faire grimper aux ~x** *fam* he'll hit the roof **2.** THÉÂTRE curtain ▪ **le ~ se lève sur un jardin japonais** the curtain rises on a Japanese garden ➊ **~!** curtain! ▪ **ça suffit, ~!** *fam* (that's) enough!, lay off! **3.** [écran] screen, curtain ▪ **~ de bambou** bamboo curtain ▪ **~ de cyprès** screen of cypress trees ▪ **~ de fumée** smokescreen ▪ **~ de pluie** sheet of rain.
◆ **rideau de fer** *nm* **1.** [d'un magasin] (metal) shutter **2.** HIST & POLIT Iron Curtain.

ridelle [ridɛl] *nf* [d'un camion] side panel.

rider [3] [ride] *vt* **1.** [peau] to wrinkle, to line, to furrow *litt* **2.** [eau, sable] to ripple, to ruffle the surface of.
◆ **se rider** *vpi* **1.** [fruit] to shrivel, to go wrinkly ▪ [visage] to become wrinkled **2.** [eau] to ripple, to become rippled.

ridicule [ridikyl] <> *adj* **1.** [risible - personne] ridiculous, laughable ; [- tenue] ridiculous, ludicrous **2.** [absurde] ridiculous, ludicrous, preposterous ▪ **c'est ~ d'avoir peur de l'avion** it's ridiculous to be afraid of flying **3.** [dérisoire] ridiculous, laughable, derisory ▪ **un salaire ~** [trop bas] a ridiculously low salary.
<> *nm* ridicule ▪ **se couvrir de ~** to make o.s. a laughing stock, to make a complete fool of o.s. ▪ **couvrir qqn de ~** to heap ridicule on sb ▪ **tourner qqn/qqch en ~** to ridicule sb/sthg, to hold sb/sthg up to ridicule ▪ **c'est d'un ~ (achevé** *ou* **fini)!** it's utterly ridiculous!, it's a farce! ▪ **s'exposer au ~** to lay o.s. open to ridicule ▪ **tomber** *ou* **donner dans le ~** to become ridiculous ➊ **le ~ ne tue pas** ridicule never did anyone any real harm.

ridiculement [ridikylmɑ̃] *adv* **1.** [dérisoirement] ridiculously, ludicrously ▪ **~ petit/bas/grand** ridiculously small/low/big **2.** [risiblement] ridiculously, laughably.

ridiculiser [3] [ridikylize] *vt* to ridicule.
◆ **se ridiculiser** *vp (emploi réfléchi)* to make o.s. (look) ridiculous, to make a fool of o.s.

ridule [ridyl] *nf* small wrinkle.

rien [rjɛ̃] <> *pron indéf* **1.** [nulle chose] nothing ■ **créer qqch à partir de ~** to create something out of nothing ■ **~ de tel qu'un bon (roman) policier** there's nothing like a good detective story ■ **~ de cassé/grave, j'espère?** nothing broken/serious, I hope? ■ **~ d'autre** nothing else ■ **~ de nouveau** no new developments ■ **~ de plus** nothing else *ou* more ■ **~ de moins** nothing less ‖ [en réponse négative à une question] : **à quoi tu penses? – à ~!** what are you thinking about? – nothing! ■ **qu'est-ce que tu lui laisses? – ~ de ~!** what are you leaving him – not a thing! ■ **~ du tout** nothing at all ◆ **je vous remercie – de ~!** thanks – you're welcome *ou* not at all *ou* don't mention it ■ **une affaire de ~ du tout** a trifling *ou* trivial matter ■ **une égratignure de ~ du tout** a little scratch ■ **c'est ça ou ~** take it or leave it ■ **c'est tout ou ~** it's all or nothing ■ **~ à dire, c'est parfait!** what can I say, it's perfect! ■ **~ à faire, la voiture ne veut pas démarrer** it's no good, the car (just) won't start ■ **~ à déclarer** nothing to declare ■ **j'en ai ~ à faire** *fam ou* **àcirer**△ I don't give a damn *ou* a toss△ ■ **faire semblant de ~** to pretend that nothing happened

2. [en corrélation avec 'ne'] : **~ n'est plus beau que...** there's nothing more beautiful than... ■ **plus ~ n'a d'importance** nothing matters any more ■ **~ de grave n'est arrivé** nothing serious happened ■ **~ n'y a fait, elle a refusé** (there was) nothing doing, she said no ■ **ce n'est ~, ça va guérir** it's nothing, it'll get better ■ **ce n'est pas ~** it's no small thing *ou* matter ■ **je croyais avoir perdu, il n'en est ~** I thought I'd lost, but not at all *ou* quite the contrary ■ **ils se disaient mariés, en fait il n'en est ~** they claimed they were married but they're nothing of the sort ■ **je ne suis ~ sans mes livres** I'm lost without my books ■ **il n'est (plus) ~ pour moi** he's *ou* he means nothing to me (anymore) ■ **et moi alors, je ne suis ~ (dans tout ça)?** and what about me (in all this), don't I count for anything *ou* don't I matter? ■ **je ne me souviens de ~** I remember nothing, I don't remember anything ■ **on ne voit ~ avec cette fumée** you can't see anything *ou* a thing with all this smoke ■ **il n'y a ~ entre nous** there is nothing between us ■ **cela** *ou* **ça ne fait ~** it doesn't matter ■ **ça ne (te) fait ~ si je te dépose en dernier?** would you mind if I dropped you off last?, is it OK with you if I drop you off last? ■ **cela ne fait ~ à l'affaire** that makes no difference (to the matter in hand) ■ **dis-lui – je n'en ferai ~** tell him – I shall do nothing of the sort ■ **ça n'a ~ à voir avec toi** it's got nothing to do with you, it doesn't concern you ■ **Paul et Fred n'ont ~ à voir l'un avec l'autre** there's no connection between Paul and Fred ■ **je n'ai ~ contre lui** I have nothing against him, I don't have anything against him ■ **ne t'inquiète pas, tu n'y es pour ~** don't worry, it's not your fault ■ **ça n'a ~ d'un chef-d'œuvre** it's far from being a masterpiece ■ **il n'a ~ du séducteur** there's nothing of the lady-killer about him ■ **il n'y a ~ de moins sûr** nothing could be less certain ■ **~ de moins que** nothing less than ■ **~ tant que** nothing so much as ■ **pour ne ~ vous cacher...** to be completely open with you... ■ **elle n'avait jamais ~ vu de semblable** she had never seen such a thing *ou* anything like it ■ **je ne sais ~ de ~** I don't know a thing ◆ **~ ne sert de courir (il faut partir à point)** *La Fontaine allus* slow and steady wins the race *prov*

3. [quelque chose] anything ■ **y a-t-il ~ d'autre?** is there anything else? ■ **y a-t-il ~ que je puisse faire?** is there nothing I can do? ■ **j'ai compris sans qu'il dise ~** I understood without him having to say anything

4. JEUX : **~ ne va plus** rien ne va plus

5. [au tennis] love ■ **~ partout** love all ■ **40 à ~** 40 love

6. *loc* **~ moins que** [bel et bien] : **elle est ~ moins que décidée à le poursuivre en justice** she's well and truly determined to take him to court ■ **elle est ~ moins que sotte** [nullement] she is far from stupid.

<> *adv* △ really ■ **ils sont ~ riches** they really are rolling in it△ *UK*, they sure as hell are rich *US*.

<> *nm* **1.** [néant] : **le ~** nothingness

2. [chose sans importance] : **un ~** the merest trifle *ou* slightest thing ■ **un ~ l'habille** she looks good in anything ■ **il se fâche pour un ~** he loses his temper over the slightest little thing ■ **il a passé son examen comme un ~** he took the exam in his stride ■ **perdre son temps à des ~s** to waste one's time over trivia *ou* trifles ■ **les petits ~s dont la vie est faite** the little things in life

3. : **un ~ de** [très peu de] a touch of ■ **un ~ de frivolité** a touch *ou* tinge *ou* hint of frivolity ◆ **en un ~ de temps** in (next to) no time.

◆ **en rien** *loc adv* : **il ne ressemble en ~ à son père** he looks nothing like his father ■ **ça n'a en ~ affecté ma décision** it hasn't influenced my decision at all *ou* in the least *ou* in any way.

◆ **pour rien** *loc adv* : **ne le dérange pas pour ~** don't disturb him for no reason ■ **il est venu pour ~** he came for nothing ■ **ça compte pour ~** that doesn't mean anything ■ **j'ai acheté ça pour ~ chez un brocanteur** I bought it for next to nothing in a second-hand shop ◆ **pour deux/trois fois ~** for next to nothing.

◆ **rien du tout** *nmf* : **un/une ~ du tout** a nobody.

◆ **rien que** *loc adv* : **~ que cette fois** just this once ■ **~ qu'une fois** just *ou* only once ■ **viens, ~ qu'un jour** do come, (even) if only for a day ■ **~ que le billet coûte une fortune** the ticket alone costs a fortune ■ **~ que d'y penser, j'ai des frissons** the mere thought of it *ou* just thinking about it makes me shiver ■ **la vérité, ~ que la vérité** the truth and nothing but the truth ■ **~ que ça?** *iron* is that all?

◆ **un rien** *loc adv* a touch, a shade, a tiny bit ■ **sa robe est un ~ trop étroite** her dress is a touch *ou* a shade *ou* a tiny bit too tight ■ **elle est un ~ farce!** *fam vieilli* she's a bit of a clown!

rieur, euse [rijœr, øz] <> *adj* [enfant] cheery, cheerful ■ [visage, regard] laughing.

<> *nm, f* laugher ■ **les ~s** those who laugh ◆ **avoir les ~s de son côté** to have the last laugh.

◆ **rieuse** *nf* ORNITH black-headed gull.

Rif [rif] *npr m* : **le ~** Er Rif.

rififi△ [rififi] *nm arg crime* [bagarre] aggro△ *UK*.

rifle [rifl] *nm* rifle ■ **carabine (de) .22 long ~** .22 calibre (rifle).

rift [rift] *nm* rift valley.

rigide [riʒid] *adj* **1.** [solide] rigid **2.** [intransigeant] rigid, inflexible, unbending **3.** [austère] rigid, strict ■ **une éducation ~** a strict upbringing.

rigidement [riʒidmɑ̃] *adv* rigidly, inflexibly, strictly.

rigidifier [9] [riʒidifje] *vt* to rigidify, to stiffen.

rigidité [riʒidite] *nf* **1.** [raideur] rigidity, stiffness ■ **~ cadavérique** rigor mortis **2.** [austérité] strictness, inflexibility.

rigolade [rigɔlad] *nf fam* **1.** [amusement] fun ■ **il n'y a pas que la ~ dans la vie** there's more to life than just having fun *ou* a good laugh ■ **prendre qqch à la ~** to make a joke of sthg ■ **chez eux, l'ambiance n'est pas/est franchement à la ~** it isn't exactly/ it's a laugh a minute round their place ■ **élever quatre enfants, ce n'est pas une (partie de) ~** raising four children is no laughing matter ■ **c'est de la ~!** [ce n'est pas sérieux] it's a joke! ; [c'est sans importance] it's nothing! ; [c'est très facile] it's a piece of cake! **2.** [fou rire] fit of laughter ■ **t'aurais vu la ~!** it was a right *UK ou* good laugh!

rigolard, e [rigɔlar, ard] *fam adj* joking, laughing.

rigole [rigɔl] *nf* **1.** [fossé] rivulet, rill **2.** CONSTR [d'un mur] ditch ■ [d'une fenêtre] drainage groove **3.** HORT [sillon] furrow ■ [conduit] trench, channel.

rigoler [3] [rigɔle] *vi fam* **1.** [rire] to laugh ■ **tu me fais ~ avec tes remords** you, sorry? don't make me laugh! **2.** [plaisanter] to joke ■ **il a dit ça pour ~** he said that in jest, he meant it as a joke ■ **tu rigoles!** you're joking *ou* kidding! **3.** [s'amuser] to have fun ■ **on a bien rigolé cette année-là** we had some good laughs *ou* great fun that year ■ **avec lui comme prof, tu ne vas pas ~ tous les jours** it won't be much fun for you having him as a teacher.

rigolo, ote [rigɔlo, ɔt] *fam* <> *adj* **1.** [amusant] funny ■ **ce serait ~ que tu aies des jumeaux** wouldn't it be funny if you had twins ■ **c'est pas ~ de bosser avec lui** working with him is no joke **2.** [étrange] funny, odd.

<> *nm, f* **1.** [rieur] laugh, scream ■ **c'est une ~te** she's a hoot **2.** [incompétent] joker, clown, comedian *péj* ■ **c'est un (petit) ~** he's a real comedian.

rigorisme [rigɔrism] *nm* rigorism.

rigoriste [rigɔrist] <> *adj* rigid, rigoristic.

<> *nmf* rigorist.

rigoureusement [rigurøzmɑ̃] *adv* **1.** [scrupuleusement] rigorously **2.** [complètement] : **~ interdit** strictly forbidden ▪ **les deux portraits sont ~ identiques** the two portraits are exactly the same *OU* absolutely identical ▪ **c'est ~ vrai** it's perfectly true.

rigoureux, euse [rigurø, øz] *adj* **1.** [sévère - personne] severe, rigorous ; [- sanction] harsh, severe ; [- principe] strict **2.** [scrupuleux - analyse, définition, raisonnement] rigorous ; [- contrôle] strict ; [- description] minute, precise ; [- discipline] strict ▪ **observer une rigoureuse neutralité** to remain strictly neutral ▪ **soyez plus ~ dans votre travail** be more thorough in your work **3.** [rude - climat] harsh.

rigueur [rigœr] *nf* **1.** [sévérité] harshness, severity, rigour ▪ **tenir ~ à qqn de qqch** to hold sthg against sb **2.** [austérité - d'une gestion] austerity, stringency ; [- d'une morale] rigour, strictness, sternness ▪ **politique de ~** austerity (measures) **3.** [âpreté - d'un climat, d'une existence] rigour, harshness, toughness ▪ **l'hiver a été d'une ~ exceptionnelle** the winter has been exceptionally harsh **4.** [précision - d'un calcul] exactness, precision ; [- d'une logique, d'un esprit] rigour ▪ **~ professionnelle** professionalism.
➡ **rigueurs** *nfpl litt* rigours ▪ **les ~s de l'hiver/de la vie carcérale** the rigours of winter/of prison life.
➡ **à la rigueur** *loc adv* **1.** [peut-être] : **il a bu deux verres à la ~, mais pas plus** he may possibly have had two drinks but no more **2.** [s'il le faut] at a pinch, if need be.
➡ **de rigueur** *loc adj* : **la ponctualité est de ~** punctuality is insisted upon, it's de rigueur to be on time *sout* ▪ **'tenue de soirée de ~'** 'dress formal'.

rikiki [rikiki] *fam* = **riquiqui**.

rillettes [rijɛt] *nfpl* rillettes *(potted meat)*.

rimailler [3] [rimaje] *vi fam vieilli & péj* to write poetry of a sort, to dabble in writing poetry.

rimailleur, euse [rimajœr, øz] *nm, f fam vieilli & péj* rhymester, versifier, poetaster.

rime [rim] *nf* **1.** LITTÉR rhyme ➔ **~ masculine/féminine** masculine/feminine rhyme ▪ **~ pauvre** poor rhyme ▪ **~ riche** rich *OU* perfect rhyme ▪ **~s croisées** *OU* **alternées** alternate rhymes ▪ **~s embrassées** abba rhyme scheme ▪ **~s plates** rhyming couplets **2.** *loc* **il me tenait des propos sans ~ ni raison** what he was telling me had neither rhyme nor reason to it, there was neither rhyme nor reason in what he was telling me.

rimer [3] [rime] ◇ *vt* to versify, to put into verse.
◇ *vi* **1.** *litt* [faire de la poésie] to write poetry *OU* verse **2.** [finir par le même son] to rhyme **3.** *sout* **~ avec** [équivaloir à] : **amour ne rime pas toujours avec fidélité** love and fidelity don't aways go together *OU* hand in hand.
➡ **rimer à** *v+prép* : **à quoi rime cette scène de jalousie?** what's the meaning of this jealous outburst? ▪ **tout cela ne rime à rien** none of this makes any sense, there's no sense in any of this.

rimeur, euse [rimœr, øz] *nm, f péj* versifier, rhymester, poetaster.

Rimmel® [rimɛl] *nm* mascara.

rinçage [rɛ̃saʒ] *nm* **1.** [au cours d'une lessive] rinse, rinsing ▪ **les draps ont besoin d'un ~** the sheets need rinsing (out) *OU* a rinse **2.** [pour les cheveux] (colour) rinse.

rince-bouteilles [rɛ̃sbutɛj] *nm inv* **1.** [brosse] bottlebrush **2.** [machine] bottle-washing machine.

rince-doigts [rɛ̃sdwa] *nm inv* finger bowl.

rincée [rɛ̃se] *nf fam* **1.** *vieilli* [défaite] licking, hammering, thrashing **2.** [averse] downpour ▪ **prendre une ~** to get caught in a downpour.

rincer [16] [rɛ̃se] *vt* **1.** [passer à l'eau] to rinse ▪ **~ qqch abondamment** to rinse sthg thoroughly, to give sthg a thorough rinse **2.** *fam* [mouiller] : **se faire ~** to get soaked *OU* drenched.
➡ **se rincer** *vpt* : **se ~ la bouche/les mains** to rinse one's mouth (out)/one's hands ➔ **se ~ le bec** *fam OU* **la dalle** *fam OU* **le gosier** *fam* [boire] to wet one's whistle ▪ **se ~ l'œil** *fam* [regarder] to get an eyeful.

rincette [rɛ̃sɛt] *nf fam* [eau-de-vie] nip of brandy, brandy chaser *(after coffee)*.

rinçure [rɛ̃syr] *nf* [eau de vaisselle] dishwater.

ring [riŋ] *nm* **1.** [estrade] (boxing) ring ▪ **monter sur le ~** [au début d'un combat] to get into the ring ▪ **quand il est monté sur le ~** [quand il a débuté] when he took up boxing **2.** [boxe] : **le ~** the ring ▪ **une légende du ~** a boxing legend, a legend of the ring.

ringard, e [rɛ̃gar, ard] ◇ *adj péj* [démodé - gén] corny, naff *UK* ; [- chanson] corny ; [- décor] naff *UK*, tacky *US* ▪ **elle est ~e** she's such a fuddy-duddy.
◇ *nm, f* [individu démodé] has-been.

Rio de Janeiro [rijodədʒanɛro] *npr* Rio de Janeiro.

ripaille [ripaj] *nf fam arch* **faire ~** to have a feast.

ripailler [3] [ripaje] *vi fam arch* to have a feast.

ripailleur, euse [ripajœr, øz] *fam arch* ◇ *nm, f* reveller.
◇ *adj* revelling, feasting.

riper [3] [ripe] ◇ *vt* **1.** CONSTR to scrape **2.** NAUT : **~ un cordage** to let a rope out *OU* slip **3.** RAIL : **~ une voie** to shift a track.
◇ *vi* **1.** [glisser] to slip **2.** △ [s'en aller] to clear off.

Ripolin® [ripɔlɛ̃] *nm* enamel paint, Ripolin®.

ripoliner [3] [ripɔline] *vt* to paint *(with enamel paint)* ▪ **murs ripolinés** walls painted with enamel paint *OU* with Ripolin®.

riposte [ripɔst] *nf* **1.** [réplique] retort, riposte ▪ **elle a été prompte à la ~** she was quick to retort, she was ready with an answer **2.** [réaction] reaction **3.** MIL [contre-attaque] counterattack, reprisal **4.** ESCRIME riposte.

riposter [3] [ripɔste] ◇ *vi* **1.** [rétorquer] to answer back **2.** [réagir] to respond ▪ **il a riposté à son insulte par une gifle** he countered his insult with a slap **3.** [contre-attaquer] to counterattack ▪ **~ à une agression** to counter an aggression **4.** ESCRIME to riposte.
◇ *vt* : **elle riposta que ça ne le regardait pas** she retorted that it was none of his business.

ripou [ripu] (*pl* **ripoux** *OU pl* **ripous**) *fam* ◇ *adj* rotten.
◇ *nm* : **ce flic est un ~** he's a bent copper *UK OU* a crooked cop *US*.

riquiqui [rikiki] *adj inv fam* **1.** [minuscule] tiny ▪ **une portion ~** a minute *OU* minuscule helping **2.** [étriqué - mobilier] shabby, grotty ; [- vêtement] skimpy.

rire[1] [rir] *nm* laugh, laughter *(U)* ▪ **j'adore son ~** I love her laugh *OU* the way she laughs ▪ **j'entends des ~s** I hear laughter *OU* people laughing ▪ **gros ~** guffaw ▪ **~ gras** coarse laugh, cackle ▪ **un petit ~ sot** a silly giggle ▪ **un petit ~ méchant** a wicked little laugh ➔ **~s préenregistrés** *OU* **en boîte** *fam* RADIO & TV prerecorded *OU* canned laughter.

rire[2] [95] [rir] *vi* **1.** [de joie] to laugh ▪ **ta lettre nous a beaucoup fait ~** your letter made us all laugh a lot ▪ **ça ne me fait pas ~** that's not funny ▪ **c'est vrai, dit-il en riant** that's true, he said with a laugh ▪ **~ de bon cœur** to laugh heartily ▪ **~ bruyamment** to guffaw ▪ **~ de** to laugh *OU* to scoff at ▪ **il n'y a pas de quoi ~** this is no joke *OU* no laughing matter ▪ **un jour nous rirons de tout cela** we'll have a good laugh over all this some day ▪ **j'étais morte de ~** *fam* I nearly died laughing, I was doubled up with laughter ▪ **c'est à mourir** *OU* **crever** *fam* **de ~** it's a hoot *OU* a scream ➔ **il vaut mieux en ~ qu'en pleurer** you have to laugh or else you cry ▪ **~ aux éclats** *OU* **à gorge déployée** to howl with laughter ▪ **il m'a fait ~ aux larmes avec ses histoires** his jokes made me laugh until I cried ▪ **~ du bout des dents** *OU* **des lèvres** to force a laugh ▪ **~ dans sa barbe** *OU* **sous cape** to laugh up one's sleeve, to laugh to o.s. ▪ **~ au nez** *OU* **à la barbe de qqn** to laugh in sb's face ▪ **~ comme un bossu** *fam OU* **une baleine** *fam* to laugh like a drain *UK*, to laugh o.s. silly ▪ **se tenir les côtes** *OU* **se tordre de ~** to split one's sides (with laughter), to be in stitches ▪ **~ jaune** to give a hollow laugh ▪ **tu me fais ~, laisse-moi ~, fais-moi ~!** *iron* don't make me laugh! ▪ **rira bien qui rira le dernier** *prov* he who laughs last laughs longest *UK OU* best *US prov* **2.** [plaisanter] : **j'ai dit ça pour ~** *OU* **pour de ~** *fam* I (only) said it in jest, I was only joking ▪ **elle a pris ça en riant** it just made her laugh ➔ **tu veux ~!** you must be joking!, you've got to be kidding! ▪ **sans ~, tu comptes y aller?** joking apart *ou* aside, do you intend to go? **3.** [se distraire] to have fun **4.** *litt* [yeux] to shine *ou* to sparkle (with laughter) ■ [visage] to beam (with happiness).

◆ **se rire de** *vp+prép* **1.** [conseil, doute] to laugh off *(sép)*, to make fun of *(insép)* ■ [danger, maladie, difficultés] to make light of *(insép)* **2.** *litt* [se moquer de] to laugh *ou* to scoff at.

ris [ri] *nm* **1.** CULIN sweetbread ■ **~ de veau** calf sweetbreads **2.** NAUT reef.

risée [rize] *nf* **1.** [moquerie] : **être un objet de ~** to be a laughing stock ■ **devenir la ~ du village/de la presse** to become the laughing stock of the village/the butt of the press's jokes **2.** [brise] flurry (of wind).

risette [rizɛt] *nf fam* **1.** [sourire d'enfant] : **allez, fais ~ à mamie** come on, give grandma a nice little smile **2.** [flagornerie] : **faire ~** *ou* **des ~s à qqn** to smarm up *UK ou* to play up *US* to sb.

risible [rizibl] *adj* **1.** [amusant] funny, comical **2.** [ridicule] ridiculous, laughable.

risotto [rizɔto] *nm* risotto.

risque [risk] *nm* **1.** [danger] risk, hazard, danger ■ **il y a un ~ de contagion/d'explosion** there's a risk of contamination/of an explosion ■ **au ~ de te décevoir/de le faire souffrir** at the risk of disappointing you/of hurting him ➲ **~ professionnel** occupational hazard ■ **zone/population à haut ~** high-risk area/population ■ **à mes/tes ~s et périls** at my/your own risk ■ **ce sont les ~s du métier** it's an occupational hazard **2.** [initiative hasardeuse] risk, chance ■ **il y a une part de ~** there's an element of risk ■ **courir** *ou* **prendre un ~** to run a risk, to take a chance ■ **courir le ~ de se faire prendre** to run the risk of getting caught ■ **avoir le goût du ~, aimer le ~** to enjoy taking chances ➲ **~ calculé** calculated risk **3.** [préjudice] risk ■ **~ d'incendie** fire hazard *ou* risk ■ **~ de cambriolage** risk of burglary ➲ **capitaux à ~s** FIN risk *ou* venture capital.

risqué, e [riske] *adj* **1.** [dangereux] risky, dangerous ■ **c'est une entreprise ~e** it's a risky business **2.** [osé] risqué, racy.

risquer [3] [riske] *vt* **1.** [engager - fortune, crédibilité] to risk ■ **~ sa peau** *fam ou* **sa vie** to risk one's neck *ou* life ■ **~ le paquet** *fam* to chance one's arm, to stake one's all ■ **on risque le coup** *ou* **la partie?** shall we have a shot at it?, shall we chance it? ■ **qui ne risque rien n'a rien** *prov* nothing ventured nothing gained *prov* **2.** [s'exposer à] to risk ■ **elle risque la mort/la paralysie** she runs the risk of dying/of being left paralysed ■ **on ne risque rien à essayer** we can always try ■ **tu peux laisser ça dehors, ça ne risque rien** you can leave it outside, it'll be safe ■ **ne t'en fais pas, ces gants ne risquent rien** don't worry, I'm not bothered about those gloves ■ **qu'est-ce qu'on risque?** what are the dangers? **3.** [oser] to venture ■ **~ une comparaison** to venture a comparison ■ **risquerai-je la question?** shall I be bold enough to put *ou* shall I risk putting the question? ■ **~ un regard** *ou* **un œil** *fam* to venture a look *ou* a peep ■ **~ le nez dehors** *fam* to poke one's nose outside.

◆ **risquer de** *v+prép* to risk ■ **ton idée risque de ne pas marcher** there's a chance your idea mightn't work ■ **il risque de se faire mal** he might hurt himself ■ **ils risquent d'être renvoyés** they run the risk of being sacked ■ **ne m'attends pas, je risque d'être en retard** don't wait for me, I'm likely to be late *ou* the chances are I'll be late ■ **je ne risque pas de me remarier!** *hum* (there's) no danger of my getting married again! ■ **ça ne risque pas de se faire!** there's no chance of that happening! ■ **ça risque d'être long** this might take a long time ■ **ça ne risque pas!** no chance!

◆ **se risquer** *vpi* : **se ~ dehors** to venture outside ■ **se ~ à faire qqch** to venture *ou* to dare to do sthg ■ **je ne m'y risquerais pas si j'étais toi** I wouldn't take a chance on it if I were you.

risque-tout [riskətu] *nmf* daredevil.

rissole [risɔl] *nf* CULIN rissole.

rissoler [3] [risɔle] ◇ *vt* to brown ■ **pommes rissolées** sauté *ou* sautéed potatoes.
◇ *vi* : **faire ~** to brown.

ristourne [risturn] *nf* **1.** [réduction] discount, reduction ■ **j'ai eu une ~ de 20 % sur la moto** I got a 20% discount on the motorbike **2.** [remboursement] refund, reimbursement **3.** COMM [versement] bonus.

ristourner [3] [risturne] *vt* **1.** [réduire] to give a discount on **2.** [rembourser] to refund, to give a refund of.

ristrette [ristrɛt], **ristretto** [ristrɛto] *nm Suisse* very strong black coffee *(served in a small cup)*.

rital, als▲ [rital] *nm péj offensive term used with reference to Italians,* ≃ Eyetie△ *UK,* ≃ Macaroni *fam US.*

rite [rit] *nm* **1.** ANTHR & RELIG rite ■ **~ de passage** rite of passage **2.** [coutume] ritual.

ritournelle [riturnɛl] *nf* **1.** *fam* [histoire] : **avec lui c'est toujours la même ~** he's always giving us the same old story **2.** MUS ritornello.

ritualiser [3] [ritɥalize] *vt* to ritualize.

ritualisme [ritɥalism] *nm* ritualism.

ritualiste [ritɥalist] ◇ *adj* ritualistic.
◇ *nmf* ritualist.

rituel, elle [ritɥɛl] *adj* **1.** [réglé par un rite] ritual **2.** [habituel] ritual, usual, customary.

◆ **rituel** *nm* **1.** [ensemble de règles] ritual, rite **2.** RELIG [livre] ceremonial.

rituellement [ritɥɛlmɑ̃] *adv* **1.** [selon un rite] ritually **2.** [invariablement] invariably.

rivage [rivaʒ] *nm* **1.** [littoral] shore **2.** [plage] : **~ de sable/de galets** sand/pebble beach.

rival, e, aux [rival, o] ◇ *adj* [antagonique] rival *(avant n)*.
◇ *nm, f* **1.** [adversaire] rival, opponent ■ **~ politique** political rival *ou* opponent **2.** [concurrent] rival ■ **elle n'a pas eu de ~e en son temps** she was unrivalled in her day.

◆ **sans rival, e** *loc adj* unrivalled.

rivaliser [3] [rivalize] *vi* : **~ avec** to compete with, to vie with, to rival ■ **nos vins peuvent ~ avec les meilleurs crus français** our wines can compare with *ou* hold their own against *ou* rival French vintages ■ **elles rivalisent d'élégance** they are trying to outdo each other in elegance.

rivalité [rivalite] *nf* [gén] rivalry ■ [en affaires] competition ■ **des ~s d'intérêts** conflicting interests.

rive [riv] *nf* [bord - d'un lac, d'une mer] shore ; [- d'une rivière] bank ■ **~ droite/gauche** [gén] right/left bank ■ **mode/intellectuels ~ gauche** [à Paris] Left Bank fashion/intellectuals *(in Paris)*.

RIVE DROITE, RIVE GAUCHE

The Right (north) Bank of the Seine is traditionally associated with business and trade, and has a reputation for being more conservative than the Left Bank. The Left (south) Bank includes districts traditionally favoured by artists, students and intellectuals, and has a reputation for being bohemian and unconventional.

river [3] [rive] *vt* **1.** [joindre - plaques] to rivet ; [- clou] to clinch ■ **~ son clou à qqn** *fam* to shut sb up **2.** *fig* [fixer] to rivet ■ **il avait les yeux rivés sur elle/les diamants** he couldn't take his eyes off her/the diamonds ■ **être rivé à la télévision/à son travail** to be glued to the television/chained to one's work ■ **rester rivé sur place** to be riveted *ou* rooted to the spot ■ **ils étaient rivés au sol par une force invisible** an invisible force held *ou* pinned them to the ground.

riverain, e [rivrɛ̃, ɛn] ◇ *adj* [d'un lac] lakeside, waterside ■ [d'une rivière] riverside, waterside, riparian *sout* ■ **les restaurants ~s de la Seine** the restaurants along the banks of the Seine ■ **les maisons ~es de la grande route** the houses stretching along *ou* bordering the main road.
◇ *nm, f* [qui vit au bord - d'un lac] lakeside resident ; [- d'une rivière] riverside resident ■ **'interdit sauf aux ~s'** 'residents only', 'no entry except for access'.

rivet [rivɛ] *nm* rivet ■ **~ bifurqué/fendu** slotted/split rivet.

riveter [27] [rivte] *vt* to rivet.

riveteuse [rivtøz] *nf* riveting machine, rivet gun.

Riviera [rivjera] *npr f* : **la ~** the (Italian) Riviera.

rivière [rivjɛr] *nf* **1.** GÉOGR river ▪ **remonter/descendre une ~** to go up/down a river ▪ **une ~ de feu coule du Vésuve** *fig* a river of fire is flowing from Vesuvius **2.** JOAILL : **~ de diamants** (diamond) rivière **3.** ÉQUIT water jump.

rixe [riks] *nf* brawl, scuffle.

Riyad [rijad] *npr* Riyadh.

riz [ri] *nm* rice ▪ **~ court/long** short-grain/long-grain rice ▪ **~ pilaf/cantonnais/créole** pilaff/Cantonese/Creole rice ▪ **~ complet** brown rice ▪ **~ au lait** rice pudding ▪ **~ rond** pudding rice.

rizerie [rizri] *nf* rice-processing plant.

rizicole [rizikɔl] *adj* [région] rice-producing, rice-growing ▪ [production] rice *(modif)*.

riziculture [rizikyltyr] *nf* [processus] rice-growing ▪ [secteur] rice production.

rizière [rizjɛr] *nf* rice field, paddyfield.

RMC (*abr de* **Radio Monte-Carlo**) *npr independent radio station.*

RMI *nm* = **revenu minimum d'insertion**.

RMiste [ɛrɛmist] *nmf person receiving the 'RMI'.*

RMN (*abr de* **résonance magnétique nucléaire**) *nf* NMR.

RN (*abr de* **route nationale**) *nf* ≃ A-road *UK*, ≃ state highway *US*.

RNIS (*abr de* **réseau numérique à intégration de services**) *nm* ISDN.

robe [rɔb] *nf* **1.** [vêtement] dress ◐ **~ de bal** ballgown ▪ **~ de baptême** christening robe ▪ **~ de chambre** dressing gown, bathrobe *US* ▪ **pomme de terre en ~ de chambre** jacket potato ▪ **~-chasuble** pinafore dress ▪ **~-chemisier** shirtwaister *UK*, shirtwaist *US* ▪ **~ de grossesse** maternity dress ▪ **~ d'intérieur** housecoat ▪ **~ de mariée** wedding dress, bridal gown ▪ **~ de plage** sundress ▪ **~-sac** sack-dress ▪ **~ du soir** evening dress **2.** [tenue - d'un professeur] gown ; [- d'un cardinal, d'un magistrat] robe ▪ **la ~** *sout* the legal profession **3.** [pelage] coat **4.** [enveloppe - d'un fruit] skin ; [- d'une plante] husk **5.** [feuille de tabac] wrapper leaf **6.** ŒNOL colour *(general aspect of wine in terms of colour and clarity)*.

roberts△ [rɔbɛr] *nmpl* tits△, boobs△.

Robin des Bois [rɔbɛ̃debwa] *npr* Robin Hood.

robinet [rɔbinɛ] *nm* **1.** [à eau, à gaz] tap *UK*, faucet *US* ▪ [de tonneau] spigot ▪ **~ d'eau chaude/froide** hot/cold water tap ▪ **~ d'arrivée d'eau** stopcock ▪ **~ mélangeur/mitigeur** mixer tap **2.** *fam* [sexe masculin] willy *UK*, peter *US*.

robinetterie [rɔbinɛtri] *nf* **1.** [dispositif] plumbing **2.** [usine] tap *UK ou* faucet *US* factory ▪ [commerce] tap *UK ou* faucet *US* trade.

roboratif, ive [rɔbɔratif, iv] *adj litt* [activité] invigorating ▪ [mets] hearty ▪ [climat] bracing.

robot [rɔbo] *nm* robot ▪ **comme un ~** robot-like, like an automaton ◐ **~ ménager** *ou* **de cuisine, Robot Marie**® food processor.

robotique [rɔbɔtik] *nf* robotics *(U)*.

robotisation [rɔbɔtizasjɔ̃] *nf* robotizing.

robotiser [3] [rɔbɔtize] *vt* **1.** [atelier, usine, travail] to automate, to robotize **2.** [personne] to robotize.

robusta [rɔbysta] *nm* robusta (coffee).

robuste [rɔbyst] *adj* **1.** [personne] robust, sturdy, strong **2.** [santé] sound ▪ **doté d'une ~ constitution** blessed with a robust *ou* sound constitution **3.** [arbre, plante] hardy **4.** [meuble] sturdy ▪ [voiture, moteur] rugged, heavy-duty **5.** *sout* [conviction] firm, strong.

robustesse [rɔbystɛs] *nf* [d'une personne] robustness ▪ [d'un meuble] sturdiness ▪ [d'un arbre] hardiness.

roc [rɔk] *nm* **1.** [pierre] rock ▪ **dur** *ou* **ferme comme un ~** solid *ou* firm as a rock **2.** JEUX [pièce] rook, castle ▪ [action] castling.

rocade [rɔkad] *nf* **1.** TRAV PUB bypass **2.** MIL communications line.

rocaille [rɔkaj] *nf* **1.** [pierraille] loose stones ▪ [terrain] stony ground **2.** [jardin] rock garden, rockery **3.** ARCHIT rocaille ▪ **grotte/fontaine en ~** rocaille grotto/fountain.

rocailleux, euse [rɔkajø, øz] *adj* **1.** [terrain] rocky, stony **2.** [voix] gravelly **3.** *sout* [style] rough, rugged.

rocambole [rɔkɑ̃bɔl] *nf* rocambole, sand leek.

rocambolesque [rɔkɑ̃bɔlɛsk] *adj* [aventures] fantastic ▪ [histoire] incredible ▪ **le scénario est ~** the script is all thrills and spills.

roche [rɔʃ] *nf* **1.** GÉOL rock ▪ **~ mère** parent rock **2.** [pierre] rock, boulder ▪ **sculpté à même la ~** *ou* **dans la ~** [bas-relief] carved in the rock ; [statue] carved out of the rock ◐ **la ~ Tarpéienne** ANTIQ the Tarpeian Rock.

rocher [rɔʃe] *nm* **1.** GÉOL rock ▪ **grimper/pousser à flanc de ~** to climb up/to grow on the rock face ▪ **côte hérissée de ~s** rocky coast ◐ **le Rocher** *the town of Monaco* ▪ **le ~ de Gibraltar** the Rock of Gibraltar **2.** ANAT petrous bone **3.** [en chocolat] rocher *(rock-shaped chocolate)*.

Rocheuses [rɔʃøz] *npr fpl* : **les (montagnes) ~** the (Great) Rocky Mountains, the Rockies.

rocheux, euse [rɔʃø, øz] *adj* rocky.

Roch ha-Shana [rɔʃaʃana] *nm* Rosh Hashana *ou* Hashanah.

rock [rɔk] ◇ *adj inv* MUS rock.
◇ *nm* MUS rock.

rock and roll [rɔkɛnrɔl] *nm inv* rock and roll, rock'n'roll ▪ **danser le ~** to jive, to rock (and roll).

rocker [rɔkœr] *nm* **1.** [artiste] rock singer *ou* musician **2.** *fam* [fan] rocker.

rocket [rɔkɛt] = **roquette** *(sens 1)*.

rockeur, euse [rɔkœr, øz] *nm, f* **1.** [artiste] rock singer *ou* musician ▪ **les plus grands ~s** the greatest rock stars **2.** *fam* [fan] rocker.

rocking-chair [rɔkiŋtʃɛr] (*pl* **rocking-chairs**) *nm* rocking chair.

rococo [rɔkɔko] ◇ *adj inv* **1.** ART rococo **2.** *péj* [tarabiscoté] over-ornate, rococo ▪ [démodé] antiquated, rococo.
◇ *nm* ART rococo.

rodage [rɔdaʒ] *nm* **1.** [d'un moteur, d'une voiture] running in *UK*, breaking in *US* ▪ **tant que la voiture est en ~** while the car is being run in *UK ou* broken in *US* **2.** *fig* [mise au point] : **le ~ de ce service va prendre plusieurs mois** it'll take several months to get this new service running smoothly **3.** TECHNOL grinding.

rodéo [rɔdeo] *nm* **1.** [à cheval] rodeo **2.** *fam* [en voiture] : **les policiers et les gangsters ont fait un ~ dans le quartier** the police and the gangsters had a high-speed car chase through the streets.

roder [3] [rɔde] *vt* **1.** [moteur, voiture] to run in *UK (sép)*, to break in *US (sép)* **2.** *fig* [mettre au point] : **~ un service/une équipe** to get a department/a team up and running ▪ **il est rodé maintenant** he knows the ropes now **3.** TECHNOL [surface] to grind.

rôder [3] [rode] *vi* [traîner - sans but] to hang around, to roam *ou* to loiter about ; [- avec une mauvaise intention] to lurk *ou* to skulk around ▪ **l'animal rôde toujours** the animal is still on the prowl *ou* prowling about ▪ **arrêtez de ~ autour de ma fille** stop hanging round my daughter.

rôdeur, euse [rodœr, øz] *nm, f* prowler.

rodomontade [rɔdɔmɔ̃tad] *nf litt* bragging *(U)*, swaggering *(U)* ■ **faire des ~s** to brag, to bluster.

Rodrigue [rɔdrig] *npr character from Corneille's play 'le Cid', a dashing hero torn between passion for Chimène and duty towards his family and country.*

rogations [rɔgasjɔ̃] *nfpl* rogations.

rogatoire [rɔgatwar] *adj* rogatory.

rogaton [rɔgatɔ̃] *nm arch* [objet de rebut] rubbish *(U)*.
◆ **rogatons** *nmpl fam* [restes de nourriture] scraps (of food), leftovers.

rogne [rɔɲ] *nf fam* anger ■ **être/se mettre en ~ (contre qqn)** to be/to get hopping mad(with sb) ■ **mettre qqn en ~** to make sb hopping mad.

rogner [3] [rɔɲe] ◇ *vt* **1.** [couper - métal] to pare, to clip ; [- cuir] to pare, to trim ; [- papier] to trim ; [- livre] to guillotine, to trim **2.** [réduire - budget, salaire] to cut (back) ■ **~ sur** to cut back *ou* down on ■ **~ sur la nourriture** to cut back *ou* to skimp on food.
◇ *vi fam* [être en colère] to be hopping mad.

rognon [rɔɲɔ̃] *nm* **1.** CULIN kidney **2.** GÉOL nodule.

rognures [rɔɲyr] *nfpl* [de métal, de carton, d'étoffe] clippings, trimmings ■ [d'ongles] clippings, parings ■ [de viande] scraps, offcuts.

rogue [rɔg] ◇ *adj sout* [arrogant] arrogant, haughty.
◇ *nf* ZOOL roe.

roi [rwa] *nm* **1.** [monarque] king ■ **le Roi Très Chrétien** the King of France ■ **les ~s fainéants** *the last Merovingian kings, in the seventh century* ■ **les Rois mages** the Magi, the Three Wise Men ■ **les Rois** [Épiphanie] Twelfth Night ■ **tirer les Rois** to eat "galette des rois" ■ **digne d'un ~** fit for a king ■ **être heureux comme un ~** to be as happy as a sandboy *UK ou* a king ■ **vivre comme un ~** to live like a king *ou* a lord ■ **le ~ n'est pas son cousin** he's terribly stuck-up ■ **le ~ est mort, vive le ~** the King is dead, long live the King! ■ **le ~ est nu** the emperor has no clothes **2.** *fig* **le ~ des animaux** the king of beasts ■ **les ~s du pétrole** the oil tycoons *ou* magnates ■ **le ~ du surgelé** *hum* the leading name in frozen food, the frozen food king ■ **tu es vraiment le ~ de la gaffe!** you're an expert at putting your foot in it! ■ **c'est vraiment le ~ des imbéciles** he's a prize idiot **3.** JEUX king ■ **~ de carreau/pique** king of diamonds/spades.

roiller [3] [rɔje] *vi Suisse fam* to pour with rain.

Roi-Soleil [rwasɔlɛj] *npr m* : **le ~** the Sun King *(Louis XIV)*.

Roissy [rwasi] *npr* [aéroport] *commonly-used name for Charles-de-Gaulle airport.*

roitelet [rwatlɛ] *nm* **1.** *péj* [roi] kinglet **2.** [oiseau] wren *UK*, winter wren *US* ■ **~ huppé** goldcrest.

Roland [rɔlɑ̃] *npr* : **'la Chanson de ~'** 'The Chanson de Roland'.

Roland-Garros [rɔlɑ̃garos] *npr* : **(le stade) ~** *stadium in Paris where international tennis championships are held.*

rôle [rol] *nm* **1.** CINÉ, THÉÂTRE & TV role, part ■ **apprendre son ~** to learn one's part *ou* lines ■ **il joue le ~ d'un espion** he plays (the part of) a spy ■ **distribuer les ~s** to do the casting, to cast ■ **avec Jean Dumay dans le ~ du Grand Inquisiteur** starring Jean Dumay as the Inquisitor General ◘ **~ de composition** character part *ou* role ■ **petit ~** walk-on part ■ **premier ~** [acteur] leading actor (*f* actress) ; [personnage] lead ■ **avoir le premier ~** *ou* **le ~ principal** *pr* to have the starring role, to play the leading role ; *fig* to be the star of the show ■ **second ~** secondary *ou* supporting role ■ **jouer les seconds ~s (auprès de qqn)** to play second fiddle (to sb) ■ **meilleur second ~ masculin/féminin** best supporting actor/actress ■ **jeu de ~** role play ■ **avoir le beau ~** to have it *ou* things easy **2.** [fonction] role ■ **jouer un ~ important dans qqch** to play an important part in sthg ■ **il prend très à cœur son ~ de père** he takes his role as father *ou* his paternal duties very seriously ■ **ce n'est pas mon ~ de m'occuper de ça** it's not my job *ou* it's not up to me to do it **3.** [liste] roll **4.** DR : **mettre une affaire au** *ou* **sur le ~** to put a case on the cause list ◘ **~ nominatif** FIN income tax (units) list **5.** SOCIOL role.

rôle-titre [roltitr] (*pl* **rôles-titres**) *nm* title role.

rollers [rɔlœr(s)] *nmpl* rollerskates.

rollmops [rɔlmɔps] *nm* rollmop (herring).

ROM, Rom [rɔm] (*abr de* **read only memory**) *nf* ROM, Rom.

romain, e [rɔmɛ̃, ɛn] *adj* Roman.
◆ **Romain, e** *nm, f* Roman.
◆ **romaine** *nf* **1.** [salade] cos lettuce *UK*, ≃ romaine *US* **2.** *fam loc* **être bon comme la ~e** to be too kind-hearted for one's own good.

roman[1] [rɔmɑ̃] *nm* **1.** LITTÉR novel ■ **il n'écrit que des ~s** he only writes novels *ou* fiction ■ **on dirait un mauvais ~** it sounds like something out of a cheap novel ■ **sa vie est un vrai ~** you could write a book about his life ■ **tout ça c'est du ~** it's all fantasy *ou* make-believe ◘ **~ d'aventures/d'amour** adventure/love story ■ **~ d'anticipation** science-fiction novel ■ **~ de cape et d'épée** swashbuckling tale ■ **~ de chevalerie** tale of chivalry ■ **~ à clef** roman à clef ■ **~ d'épouvante** horror novel ■ **~ d'espionnage** spy story ■ **~ de gare** *péj* airport *ou US* dime novel ■ **~ historique** historical novel ■ **~ noir** Gothic novel ■ **~ policier** detective story *ou* novel ■ **~ psychologique** psychological novel ■ **~ de science-fiction** science-fiction *ou* sci-fi novel **2.** [genre médiéval] romance ■ **'le Roman de la Rose'** 'The Romance of the Rose'.

roman[2]**, e** [rɔmɑ̃, an] *adj* **1.** LING Romance *(modif)* **2.** ARCHIT Romanesque.
◆ **roman** *nm* **1.** LING Romance **2.** ARCHIT : **le ~** the Romanesque.

romance [rɔmɑ̃s] *nf* [poème, musique] romance ■ [chanson sentimentale] sentimental lovesong *ou* ballad.

romancer [16] [rɔmɑ̃se] ◇ *vt* [histoire] to novelize ■ **~ une biographie** to write a biography in the form of a novel.
◇ *vi fig* **tu as tendance à ~** you have a tendency to embroider the facts.

romancero [rɔmɑ̃sero] *nm* : **le ~ du Cid** the romances of El Cid.

romanche [rɔmɑ̃ʃ] *adj* & *nm* Romansh.

romancier, ère [rɔmɑ̃sje, ɛr] *nm, f* novelist, novel *ou* fiction writer.

romand, e [rɔmɑ̃, ɑ̃d] *adj* of French-speaking Switzerland.
◆ **Romand, e** *nm, f* French-speaking Swiss ■ **les Romands** the French-speaking Swiss.

romanesque [rɔmanɛsk] ◇ *adj* **1.** LITTÉR [héros] fiction *(modif)*, fictional ■ [technique, style] novelistic **2.** *fig* [aventure] fabulous, fantastic ■ [imagination, amour] romantic.
◇ *nm* LITTÉR : **les règles du ~** the rules of fiction writing.

roman-feuilleton [rɔmɑ̃fœjtɔ̃] (*pl* **romans-feuilletons**) *nm* serialized novel, serial ■ **sa vie est un vrai ~** his life is a real adventure story.

roman-fleuve [rɔmɑ̃flœv] (*pl* **romans-fleuves**) *nm* roman-fleuve, saga ■ **il m'a écrit un ~** the letter he sent me was one long *ou* endless saga.

romanichel, elle [rɔmaniʃɛl] *nm, f péj* **1.** [Tsigane] Romany, Gipsy **2.** [nomade] Gipsy.

romanisation [rɔmanizasjɔ̃] *nf* romanization.

romaniste [rɔmanist] *nmf* **1.** DR & LING Romanist **2.** ART romanist.

roman-photo [rɔmɑ̃fɔto] (*pl* **romans-photos**) *nm* photo novel, photo romance.

romantique [rɔmɑ̃tik] ◇ *adj* **1.** ART & LITTÉR Romantic **2.** [sentimental] romantic.
◇ *nmf* **1.** ART & LITTÉR Romantic ■ **les ~s** the Romantics **2.** [personne] romantic.

romantisme [rɔmɑ̃tism] *nm* **1.** ART & LITTÉR Romanticism **2.** [sentimentalisme] romanticism.

romarin [rɔmarɛ̃] *nm* rosemary.

rombière [rɔ̃bjɛr] *nf fam* **une vieille ~** a stuck-up old bat.

Rome [rɔm] *npr* Rome ■ **la ~ antique** Ancient Rome.

Roméo [rɔmeo] *npr* : **'~ et Juliette'** ***Shakespeare*** 'Romeo and Juliet'.

rompre [78] [rɔ̃pr] ◇ *vt* **1.** [mettre fin à - jeûne, silence, contrat] to break ; [- fiançailles, relations] to break off *(sép)* ; [- marché] to call off *(sép)* ; [- équilibre] to upset ■ **~ le charme** to break the spell **2.** [briser] to break ■ **le fleuve a rompu ses digues** the river has burst its banks ■ **~ ses chaînes** *ou* **fers** *litt* to break one's chains ■ **~ les amarres** NAUT to break (free from) the moorings ▶ **~ le pain** to break bread ■ **~ des lances contre qqn** to cross swords with sb **3.** *sout* [accoutumer] to break in *(sép)* ■ **~ qqn à qqch** to break sb in to sthg ■ **~ qqn à une discipline** to initiate sb into *ou* to train sb in a discipline **4.** MIL to break ■ **~ les rangs** to break ranks ■ **rompez (les rangs)!** dismiss!, fall out!
◇ *vi* **1.** [se séparer] to break up ■ **~ avec** to break with **2.** *sout* [se briser - corde] to break, to snap ; [- digue] to break, to burst **3.** SPORT [reculer] to break.
◆ **se rompre** ◇ *vpi* [se briser - branche] to break *ou* to snap (off) ; [- digue] to burst, to break.
◇ *vpt* : **se ~ les os** to break one's neck.

rompu, e [rɔ̃py] *adj* **1.** [épuisé] : **~ (de fatigue)** tired out, worn out, exhausted ■ **j'ai les jambes ~es** my legs are giving way under me **2.** *sout* [habitué] : **~ à** : **~ aux affaires/à la diplomatie** experienced in business/in diplomacy ■ **il est ~ à ce genre d'exercice** he's accustomed *ou* used to this kind of exercise.
◆ **rompu** *nm* BOURSE fraction.

romsteck [rɔmstɛk] *nm* [partie du bœuf] rumpsteak ■ [morceau coupé] slice of rumpsteak.

Romulus [rɔmylys] *npr* : **~ et Rémus** Romulus and Remus.

ronce [rɔ̃s] *nf* **1.** BOT blackberry bush ■ **les ~s** [buissons] the brambles ▶ **~ artificielle** barbed wire **2.** [nœud dans le bois] burr, swirl *spéc.*

Roncevaux [rɔ̃svo] *npr* Roncesvalles.

ronchon, onne [rɔ̃ʃɔ̃, ɔn] *fam* ◇ *adj* crotchety, grumpy, grouchy.
◇ *nm, f* grumbler, grouse, grouch US.

ronchonnement [rɔ̃ʃɔnmɑ̃] *nm fam* grousing *(U)*, grouching *(U)*, griping *(U)*.

ronchonner [3] [rɔ̃ʃɔne] *vi fam* **~ (après qqn)** to grouse *ou* to gripe *ou* to grouch(at sb).

ronchonneur, euse [rɔ̃ʃɔnœr, øz] *fam* = **ronchon.**

roncier [rɔ̃sje] *nm*, **roncière** [rɔ̃sjɛr] *nf* bramble (bush).

rond, e [rɔ̃, rɔ̃d] *adj* **1.** [circulaire] round, circular ■ **faire** *ou* **ouvrir des yeux ~s** to stare in disbelief **2.** [bien en chair] round, full, plump ■ **un petit bébé tout ~** a chubby little baby ■ **de jolies épaules bien ~es** well-rounded *ou* well-turned shoulders ■ **des seins ~s** full breasts ■ **un visage tout ~** a round face, a moon face *péj* **3.** *fam* [ivre] tight, well-oiled ■ **~ comme une queue de pelle** three sheets to the wind **4.** [franc] straightforward, straight **5.** [chiffre, somme] round.
◆ **rond** ◇ *nm* **1.** [cercle] circle, ring ■ **faire des ~s de fumée** to blow *ou* to make smoke rings ▶ **faire des ~s dans l'eau** *pr* to make rings in the water ; *fig* to fritter away one's time **2.** [anneau] ring ■ **~ de serviette** napkin ring ■ **~ central** FOOTBALL centre circle **3.** *fam* [sou] : **je n'ai plus un ~** I'm flat broke, I'm skint UK ■ **ils ont des ~s** they're rolling in it, they're loaded **4.** DANSE : **~ de jambe** rond de jambe ■ **faire des ~s de jambe** *fig* to bow and scrape.
◇ *adv fam loc* **tourner ~** to go well, to run smoothly ■ **qu'est-ce qui ne tourne pas ~?** what's the matter?, what's the problem? ■ **ça ne tourne pas ~** things aren't going (very) well ■ **il ne tourne pas ~** he's got a screw loose ■ **tout ~** [exactement] exactly.
◆ **en rond** *loc adv* [se placer, s'asseoir] in a circle ■ [danser] in a ring ■ **tourner en ~** *pr* & *fig* to go round (and round) in circles.

rond-de-cuir [rɔ̃dkɥir] (*pl* **ronds-de-cuir**) *nm péj* pen-pusher.

ronde [rɔ̃d] *nf* **1.** [inspection - d'un vigile] round, rounds, patrol ; [- d'un soldat] patrol ; [- d'un policier] beat, round, rounds ■ **faire sa ~** [veilleur] to make one's round *ou* rounds ; [policier] to be on patrol *ou* on the beat ■ **croiser une ~ de police** to come across a police patrol **2.** [mouvement circulaire] circling, turning **3.** MUS semibreve UK, whole note US **4.** [danse] round (dance), ronde ■ **faire la ~** to dance round in a circle *ou* ring **5.** [écriture] round hand.
◆ **à la ronde** *loc adv* : **il n'y a pas une seule maison à 20 km à la ~** there's no house within 20 km, there's no house within *ou* in a 20-km radius ■ **boire à la ~** to pass the bottle round ■ **répétez-le à la ~** go round and tell everybody.

rondeau, x [rɔ̃do] *nm* **1.** LITTÉR rondeau **2.** MUS rondo.

ronde-bosse [rɔ̃dbɔs] (*pl* **rondes-bosses**) *nf* sculpture in the round.

rondelet, ette [rɔ̃dlɛ, ɛt] *adj fam* **1.** [potelé] chubby, plump, plumpish **2.** [important] : **une somme ~te** a tidy *ou* nice little sum.

rondelle [rɔ̃dɛl] *nf* **1.** [de salami, de citron] slice ■ **couper qqch en ~s** to slice sthg, to cut sthg into slices **2.** TECHNOL disc ■ [d'un écrou] washer ■ [d'une canette] ring **3.** [au hockey].

rondement [rɔ̃dmɑ̃] *adv* **1.** [promptement] briskly, promptly, quickly and efficiently ■ **des négociations ~ menées** competently conducted negotiations **2.** [franchement] frankly, outspokenly ■ **il me l'a dit ~** he told me straight out.

rondeur [rɔ̃dœr] *nf* **1.** [forme - d'un visage, d'un bras] roundness, plumpness, chubbiness ; [- d'un sein] fullness ; [- d'une épaule] roundness **2.** [franchise] straightforwardness, directness.
◆ **rondeurs** *nfpl euphém* curves ■ **~s disgracieuses** unsightly bulges.

rondin [rɔ̃dɛ̃] *nm* [bois] round billet, log.

rondo [rɔ̃do] *nm* rondo.

rondouillard, e [rɔ̃dujar, ard] *adj fam* tubby, podgy UK, pudgy US.

rond-point [rɔ̃pwɛ̃] (*pl* **ronds-points**) *nm* roundabout UK, traffic circle US.

Ronéo® [rɔneo] *nf* Roneo®.

ronéoter [rɔneɔte], **ronéotyper** [3] [rɔneɔtipe] *vt* to Roneo®, to duplicate.

ronflant, e [rɔ̃flɑ̃, ɑ̃t] *adj* **1.** [moteur] purring, throbbing ■ [feu] roaring **2.** *péj* [discours] bombastic, high-flown ■ [promesses] grand ■ **titre ~** grand-sounding title.

ronflement [rɔ̃fləmɑ̃] *nm* **1.** [d'un dormeur] snore, snoring *(U)* **2.** [bruit - sourd] humming *(U)*, droning *(U)* ; [- fort] roar, roaring *(U)*, throbbing *(U)*.

ronfler [3] [rɔ̃fle] *vi* **1.** [en dormant] to snore ■ **~ comme un soufflet de forge** to snore like anything **2.** *fam* [dormir] to snooze, to snore away **3.** [vrombir] to roar, to throb ■ **faire ~ le moteur** to rev up the engine.

ronfleur, euse [rɔ̃flœr, øz] *nm, f* snorer.
◆ **ronfleur** *nm* ÉLECTR & TÉLÉCOM buzzer.

ronger [17] [rɔ̃ʒe] *vt* **1.** [mordiller] to gnaw (away) at *(insép)*, to eat into *(insép)* ■ **~ un os** to gnaw at a bone ■ **rongé par les vers/mites** worm-/moth-eaten ▶ **~ son frein** *pr* & *fig* to champ at the bit **2.** [corroder - suj: mer] to wear away *(sép)* ; [- suj: acide, rouille] to eat into *(insép)* ■ **rongé par la rouille** eaten away with rust, rusted away ■ **être rongé par la maladie** to be wasted by disease ■ **le mal qui ronge la société** the evil that eats away at society ■ **être rongé par les soucis** to be careworn.
◆ **se ronger** *vpt* : **se ~ les ongles** to bite one's nails.

rongeur, euse [rɔ̃ʒœr, øz] *adj* gnawing.
◆ **rongeur** *nm* rodent.

ronron [rɔ̃rɔ̃] *nm* **1.** [d'un chat] purr, purring *(U)* **2.** [routine] routine ■ **le ~ de la vie quotidienne** the daily routine.

ronronnement [rɔ̃rɔnmɑ̃] *nm* **1.** [d'un chat] **2.** *fam* [d'une machine] drone, whirr, droning *(U)*, whirring *(U)*.

röntgen [rœntgɛn] *nm* roentgen, rontgen, röntgen.

ronronner [3] [rɔ̃rɔne] *vi* [chat] to purr ▪ [machine] to drone, to hum.

roque [rɔk] *nm* JEUX castling ▪ **petit/grand ~** king's/queen's side castling.

roquefort [rɔkfɔr] *nm* Roquefort (cheese).

roquer [3] [rɔke] *vi* JEUX to castle.

roquet [rɔkɛ] *nm* **1.** [chien] yappy *ou* noisy dog **2.** *fam péj* [personne] pest ▪ **espèce de petit ~** you little runt!

roquette [rɔkɛt] *nf* **1.** [projectile] rocket **2.** BOT rocket.

ROR [ɛroɛr] *ou* [rɔr] (*abr de* **rougeole oreillons rubéole**) *nm* MMR (vaccine).

rosace [rozas] *nf* ARCHIT [moulure] (ceiling) rose ▪ [vitrail] rose window, rosace ▪ [figure] rosette.

rosacée [rozase] *nf* **1.** BOT rosaceous plant, rosacean ▪ **les ~s** the Rosaceae **2.** MÉD rosacea.

rosaire [rozɛr] *nm* **1.** [chapelet] rosary ▪ **égrener un ~** to count *ou* to tell one's beads **2.** [prières] : **dire** *ou* **réciter le ~** to recite the rosary.

rosâtre [rozatr] *adj* pinkish, roseate *litt.*

rosbif [rɔzbif] *nm* **1.** [cru] roasting beef *(U)*, joint *ou* piece of beef *(for roasting)* ▪ [cuit] roast beef *(U)*, joint of roast beef **2.** *fam* [Anglais] *pejorative or humorous term used with reference to British people.*

rose [roz] <> *adj* **1.** [gén] pink ▪ [teint, joue] rosy ▪ **~ bonbon/saumon** candy/salmon pink ▪ **~ fluo** *fam* fluorescent *ou* dayglo pink ▪ **~ thé** tea rose ▪ **vieux ~** old rose **2.** [agréable] : **ce n'est pas (tout) ~** it isn't exactly a bed of roses **3.** [érotique] erotic, soft-porn *(modif)* **4.** POLIT left-wing.
<> *nf* **1.** BOT rose ▪ **~ blanche/rouge** white/red rose ➊ **~ de Jéricho** rose of Jericho, resurrection plant ▪ **~ de Noël** Christmas rose ▪ **~ pompon** fairy rose ▪ **~ sauvage** wild rose ▪ **~ trémière** hollyhock *UK*, rose mallow ▪ **ça ne sent pas la ~ ici** *euphém* it's a bit smelly in here ▪ **il n'y a pas de ~ sans épines** *prov* there's no rose without a thorn *prov* **2.** ARCHIT rose window, rosace.
<> *nm* **1.** [couleur] pink ▪ **~ nacré** oyster pink **2.** *loc* **voir la vie** *ou* **les choses en ~** to see things through rose-tinted spectacles *UK ou* glasses *US*.
◆ **rose des sables, rose du désert** *nf* gypsum flower.
◆ **rose des vents** *nf* wind rose.

ROSE

The rose is the symbol of the French socialists, and this word is sometimes used to suggest socialist leanings.
The word *rose* can also suggest soft pornography (*le Minitel rose* used to refer to erotic call lines available on Minitel).
Les villes roses (Albi, Montauban and Toulouse) are so called because they are largely built of pink stone.
Le carnet rose is the list of births and marriages in a newspaper.

rosé, e [roze] *adj* **1.** [teinte] pinkish, rosy **2.** [vin] rosé.
◆ **rosé** *nm* rosé (wine).

roseau, x [rozo] *nm* reed ▪ **le ~ plie mais ne rompt pas** *La Fontaine allus* the reed bends but does not break ▪ **l'homme est un ~ pensant** *Pascal allus* man is a thinking reed.

rose-croix [rozkrwa] *nm inv* Rosicrucian.

rosé-des-prés [rozedepre] (*pl* **rosés-des-prés**) *nm* [champêtre] field mushroom ▪ [des jachères] horse mushroom.

rosée [roze] *nf* dew.

roseraie [rozrɛ] *nf* rose garden, rosery.

rosette [rozɛt] *nf* **1.** [nœud] bow **2.** [cocarde] rose, rosette ▪ **avoir/recevoir la ~** to be/to be made an officer *(of an order of knighthood or merit)* **3.** CULIN : **~ (de Lyon)** *broad type of salami* **4.** BOT rosette.

Rosette [rozɛt] *npr* : **la pierre de ~** the Rosetta stone.

rosicrucien, enne [rozikrysjɛ̃, ɛn] *adj* Rosicrucian.

rosier [rozje] *nm* rosebush, rose tree ▪ **~ grimpant/nain** climbing/dwarf rose.

rosière [rozjɛr] *nf young girl traditionally awarded a crown of roses and a prize for virgin purity.*

rosiériste [rozjerist] *nmf* rose grower, rosarian.

rosir [32] [rozir] <> *vt* to give a pink hue to ▪ **l'air de la montagne avait rosi ses joues** the mountain air had tinged *ou* suffused her cheeks with pink.
<> *vi* to turn pink.

rosse [rɔs] *fam* <> *adj* [chanson, portrait] nasty, vicious ▪ [conduite] rotten, lousy, horrid ▪ [personne] nasty, horrid, catty ▪ **être ~ envers** *ou* **avec qqn** to be horrid *ou* nasty to sb ▪ **un professeur ~** a hard *ou* tough teacher.
<> *nf* **1.** [personne] rotter *UK*, rotten beast **2.** *vieilli* [cheval] nag, jade.

rossée [rɔse] *nf fam* thrashing ▪ **flanquer une ~ à qqn** to give sb a good hiding *ou* thrashing.

rosser [3] [rɔse] *vt* **1.** [frapper] to thrash **2.** [vaincre] to thrash, to hammer ▪ **se faire ~** to get thrashed, to get hammered.

rossignol [rɔsiɲɔl] *nm* **1.** [oiseau] nightingale ▪ **~ des murailles** redstart **2.** [clef] picklock, skeleton key **3.** *fam* [objet démodé] piece of junk.

rossinante [rɔsinɑ̃t] *nf litt* scrag, nag.

rostre [rɔstr] *nm* ANTIQ & ZOOL rostrum.
◆ **rostres** *nmpl* [tribune] rostrum.

rot[1] [rɔt] *nm* BOT rot.

rot[2] [ro] *nm* [renvoi] belch, burp ▪ **faire** *ou* **lâcher un ~** to (let out a) belch *ou* burp ▪ **il a fait son ~?** [bébé] has he burped? ▪ **faire faire son ~ à un bébé** to burp a baby.

rôt [ro] *nm arch* roast.

rotary [rɔtari] *nm* **1.** INDUST du pétrole rotary drill **2.** TÉLÉCOM uniselector system **3.** : **Rotary-Club** Rotary Club.

rotateur [rɔtatœr] *nm* rotator.

rotatif, ive [rɔtatif, iv] *adj* rotary, rotating ▪ **mouvement ~** rotary *ou* rotating motion.
◆ **rotative** *nf* IMPR (rotary) press ▪ **faire tourner** *ou* **marcher les rotatives** *fig* to give the newspapers something to write about.

rotation [rɔtasjɔ̃] *nf* **1.** [mouvement] rotation ▪ [sur un axe] spinning ▪ **angle/sens/vitesse de ~** angle/direction/speed of rotation ▪ **mouvement de ~** rotational *spéc ou* rotary motion ▪ SPORT turn, turning *(U)* **2.** [renouvellement] turnover ▪ **~ des stocks/du personnel** inventory/staff turnover ▪ **~ des postes** job rotation **3.** FIN turnover **4.** TRANSP turnround *UK*, turnaround *US* **5.** AGRIC : **la ~ des cultures** crop rotation.

roter [3] [rote] *vi* to belch, to burp.

rôti [roti] *nm* [viande - crue] joint *(of meat for roasting)* ; [- cuite] joint, roast ▪ **~ de porc** [cru] joint *ou* piece of pork for roasting ; [cuit] piece of roast pork.

rôtie [roti] *nf* [pain grillé] slice of toast ▪ [pain frit] slice of fried bread.

rotin [rɔtɛ̃] *nm* rattan ▪ **chaise en ~** rattan chair.

rôtir [32] [rotir] <> *vt* **1.** [cuire] to roast ▪ **faire ~ une viande** to roast a piece of meat **2.** *fam* [dessécher] to parch.
<> *vi* [cuire] to roast ▪ **baisse le thermostat, on va ~** *fam* lower the thermostat or we'll roast.
◆ **se rôtir** *vp (emploi réfléchi) fam* **se ~ au soleil** to bask *ou* to fry in the sun.

rôtisserie [rotisri] *nf* [magasin] rotisserie.

rôtisseur, euse [rotisœr, øz] *nm, f* [vendeur] seller of roast meat.

rôtissoire [rotiswar] *nf* [appareil] roaster ▪ [broche] (roasting) spit, rotisserie.

rotonde [rɔtɔ̃d] *nf* **1.** ARCHIT rotunda ▪ **disposition en ~** circular layout **2.** [dans les autobus] semicircular bench seat *(at rear)*.

rotor [rɔtɔr] *nm* AÉRON & ÉLECTR rotor.

rotule [rɔtyl] *nf* **1.** ANAT kneecap, patella *spéc* ▪ **être sur les ~s** *fam* to be on one's last legs **2.** TECHNOL ball-and-socket joint.

roture [rɔtyr] *nf litt* commonalty *sout* ▪ **elle a épousé quelqu'un de la ~** she married a commoner.

roturier, ère [rɔtyrje, ɛr] ◇ *adj* **1.** HIST [non noble] common ▪ **être d'origine roturière** to be of common birth *ou* stock **2.** *sout* [vulgaire] low, common, vulgar ▪ **des façons roturières** plebeian manners.
◇ *nm, f* HIST commoner, plebeian.

rouage [rwaʒ] *nm* **1.** TECHNOL moving part, movement ▪ [engrenage] cogwheel ▪ **les ~s d'une horloge** the works *ou* movement of a clock **2.** *fig* cog ▪ **les ~s de la Justice** the wheels of Justice.

roublard, e [rublar, ard] *fam* ◇ *adj* [rusé] sly, wily, crafty.
◇ *nm, f* dodger ▪ **c'est un fin ~** he's a sly (old) fox *ou* devil, he's an artful dodger.

roublardise [rublardiz] *nf fam* **1.** [habileté] slyness, craftiness, wiliness **2.** [manœuvre] clever *ou* crafty trick, dodge.

rouble [rubl] *nm* rouble.

roucoulade [rukulad] *nf* **1.** [d'un pigeon] (billing and) cooing *(U)* **2.** *fam* [d'un amoureux] cooing, sweet nothings.

roucoulement [rukulmɑ̃] *nm* **1.** [cri du pigeon] (billing and) cooing *(U)* **2.** *fam* [propos tendres] cooing, sweet nothings **3.** *péj* [d'un chanteur] crooning *(U)*.

roucouler [3] [rukule] ◇ *vi* **1.** [pigeon] to (bill and) coo **2.** *fam* [amoureux] to coo, to whisper sweet nothings **3.** *péj* [chanteur] to croon.
◇ *vt* **1.** [suj: amoureux] to coo **2.** *péj* [suj: chanteur] to croon.

roudoudou [rududu] *nm fam* hard sweet UK, candy US *(licked out of a small round box or shell)*.

roue [ru] *nf* **1.** TRANSP wheel ▪ **véhicule à deux/trois ~s** two-wheeled/three-wheeled vehicle ▪ **j'étais dans sa ~** I was right behind him ▶ **~ directrice** guiding *ou* leading wheel ▪ **~ motrice** drive *ou* driving wheel ▪ **~ de secours** spare (wheel) ▪ **pousser à la ~** to give a helping hand **2.** MÉCAN (cog *ou* gear) wheel ▪ **~ d'angle** bevel gear wheel ▪ **~ crantée** toothed wheel ▪ **~ dentée** cogwheel ▪ **~ hydraulique** waterwheel ▪ **~ libre** freewheel ▪ **j'ai descendu la côte en ~ libre** I freewheeled down the hill **3.** [objet circulaire] wheel ▪ **une ~ de gruyère** a large round Gruyère cheese ▶ **la grande ~** the big wheel UK, the Ferris wheel US ▪ **la ~ de la Fortune** the wheel of Fortune ▪ **la ~ tourne** the wheel of Fortune is turning ▪ **faire la ~** [paon] to spread *ou* to fan its tail ; [gymnaste] to do a cartwheel ; [séducteur] to strut about *péj* **4.** HIST : **(le supplice de) la ~** the wheel **5.** IMPR : **~ à caractères** *ou* **d'impression** print *ou* type wheel **6.** NAUT : **~ à aubes** *ou* **à palettes** paddle wheel ▪ **~ du gouvernail** helm.

roué, e [rwe] ◇ *adj* sly, tricky, wily.
◇ *nm, f* **1.** [fripon] sly dog, tricky customer ▪ [friponne] sly *ou* tricky customer **2.** HIST [homme] roué, rake ▪ [femme] hussy, trollop, jezebel.

rouf [ruf] *nm* deckhouse.

rouelle [rwɛl] *nf* **1.** CULIN : **~ (de veau)** thick round of veal **2.** [rondelle] (round) slice.

rouer [6] [rwe] *vt* **1.** *loc* **~ qqn de coups** [le frapper] to pummel sb **2.** HIST : **~ qqn** to break sb on the wheel.

rouerie [ruri] *nf litt* **1.** [caractère] cunning, foxiness, wiliness **2.** *sout* [manœuvre] sly *ou* cunning trick.

rouet [ruɛ] *nm* [pour filer] spinning wheel.

rouflaquette [ruflakɛt] *nf fam* [accroche-cœur] kiss UK *ou* spit US curl.
◆ **rouflaquettes** *nfpl fam* [favoris] sideburns, sidewhiskers, sideboards UK.

rouge [ruʒ] ◇ *adj* **1.** [gén] red ▪ **être ~** [après un effort] to be flushed, to be red in the face ; [de honte] to be red in the face (with shame), to be red-faced ; [de plaisir, de colère] to be flushed ▶ **~ brique** brick-red ▪ **~ sang** bloodred ▪ **~ vermillon** vermilion ▪ **être ~ comme un coq** *ou* **un coquelicot** *ou* **une écrevisse** *ou* **un homard** *ou* **une pivoine** *ou* **une tomate** to be as red as a beetroot UK *ou* a lobster ▪ **la mer Rouge** the Red Sea ▪ **la place Rouge** Red Square ▪ **'le Rouge et le noir'** ***Stendhal*** 'Scarlet and Black' **2.** [pelage, cheveux] red, ginger, carroty *péj* **3.** MÉTALL red-hot **4.** *péj* [communiste] red.
◇ *nmf péj* [communiste] Red.
◇ *nm* **1.** [couleur] red ▪ **le ~ lui monta au visage** he went red in the face, his face went red **2.** TRANSP : **le feu est passé au ~** the lights turned to *ou* went red ▪ **la voiture est passée au ~** the car went through a red light **3.** *fam* [vin] red wine ▪ **du gros ~** rough red wine **4.** [cosmétique] : **~ (à joues)** blusher, rouge **5.** MÉTALL : **porté au ~** red-hot **6.** JEUX red ▪ **le ~ est mis** *fam* the die is cast **7.** BANQUE red ▪ **je suis dans le ~** I'm in the red *ou* overdrawn.
◇ *nf* [au billard] red (ball).
◇ *adv* **1.** *loc* **voir ~** to see red **2.** POLIT : **voter ~** *péj* to vote communist.
◆ **rouge à lèvres** *nm* lipstick.

rougeâtre [ruʒatr] *adj* reddish, reddy.

rougeaud, e [ruʒo, od] ◇ *adj* red-faced, ruddy, ruddy-cheeked.
◇ *nm, f* red-faced *ou* ruddy *ou* ruddy-faced person.

rouge-gorge [ruʒgɔrʒ] (*pl* **rouges-gorges**) *nm* (robin) redbreast, robin.

rougeoie *etc v* ▷ **rougeoyer**.

rougeoiement [ruʒwamɑ̃] *nm* reddish glow.

rougeole [ruʒɔl] *nf* MÉD measles *(sing)* ▪ **avoir la ~** to have (the) measles.

rougeoyant, e [ruʒwajɑ̃, ɑ̃t] *adj* glowing (red) ▪ **lueur ~e** flush of red, red glow.

rougeoyer [13] [ruʒwaje] *vi* to turn red, to redden, to take on a reddish hue.

rouget [ruʒɛ] *nm* ZOOL : **~ de roche** surmullet.

rougeur [ruʒœr] *nf* **1.** [couleur - du ciel] redness, glow ; [- des joues] redness, ruddiness **2.** [rougissement] flush, blush **3.** MÉD red patch *ou* blotch ▪ **être sujet aux ~s** to be prone to developing red patches *(on one's skin)*.

rougir [32] [ruʒir] ◇ *vt* **1.** [colorer en rouge] : **un dernier rayon de soleil rougissait le firmament** one last ray of sun spread a red glow across the skies ▪ **~ son eau** to put a drop of (red) wine in one's water ▪ **des yeux rougis par les larmes/la poussière** eyes red with weeping/with the dust **2.** MÉTALL to heat to red heat *ou* until red-hot **3.** *fig & litt* **mes mains sont rougies de (son) sang** my hands are stained with (his) blood.
◇ *vi* **1.** [chose, personne - gén] to go *ou* to turn red ▪ [personne - de gêne] to blush ▪ **~ de plaisir** to flush with pleasure ▪ **~ de honte** to blush with shame ▪ **je vous aime, dit-il en rougissant** I love you, he said, blushing *ou* with a blush ▪ **je me sentais ~** I could feel myself going red (in the face) ▪ **faire ~ qqn** to make sb blush ▪ **arrête, tu vas me faire ~** *hum* spare my blushes, please ▶ **~ jusqu'au blanc des yeux** *ou* **jusqu'aux oreilles** to blush to the roots of one's hair **2.** *fig* **~ de** [avoir honte de] to be ashamed of ▪ **tu n'as pas/il n'y a pas à en ~** there's nothing for you/nothing to be ashamed of ▪ **ne ~ de rien** to be shameless **3.** MÉTALL to become red-hot.

rougissant, e [ruʒisɑ̃, ɑ̃t] *adj* **1.** [de honte] blushing ▪ [d'excitation] flushing **2.** [horizon, forêt] reddening.

rougissement [ruʒismɑ̃] *nm sout* [gén] reddening ▪ [de honte] blushing ▪ [d'excitation] flushing.

rouille [ruj] ◇ *nf* **1.** [corrosion d'un métal] rust ▪ **traiter une surface contre la ~** to rustproof a surface **2.** BOT : **~ blanche** white rust ▪ **~ du blé** wheat rust **3.** CULIN rouille sauce *(served with fish soup and bouillabaisse)*.
◇ *adj inv* rust, rust-coloured.

rouillé, e [ruje] *adj* **1.** [grille, clef] rusty, rusted ■ **la serrure est complètement ~e** the lock is rusted up **2.** *fig* [muscles] stiff ■ **être ~** [physiquement] to feel stiff ; [intellectuellement] to feel a bit rusty ■ **mes réflexes au volant sont un peu ~s** my driving reflexes are a bit rusty **3.** BOT [blé] affected by rust, rusted ■ [feuille] mouldy.

rouiller [3] [ruje] ◇ *vt* **1.** [métal] to rust **2.** [intellect, mémoire] to make rusty.
◇ *vi* to rust, to go rusty.
◆ **se rouiller** *vpi* **1.** [machine] to rust up, to get rusty **2.** [esprit] to become *ou* to get rusty **3.** [muscle] to grow *ou* to get stiff ■ [athlète] to get rusty.

roulade [rulad] *nf* **1.** MUS roulade, run **2.** [d'un oiseau] trill **3.** CULIN rolled meat, roulade **4.** [culbute] roll ■ **~ avant/arrière** forward/backward roll.

roulage [rulaʒ] *nm* **1.** AGRIC & MÉTALL rolling **2.** MIN haulage, hauling **3.** NAUT : **manutention par ~** roll-on roll-off.

roulant, e [rulɑ̃, ɑ̃t] *adj* **1.** [surface] moving ■ [meuble] on wheels **2.** RAIL : **matériel ~** rolling stock ■ **personnel ~** train crews.
◆ **roulant** *nm fam* TRANSP crewman.
◆ **roulante** *nf* field *ou* mobile kitchen.

roulé, e [rule] *adj* **1.** COUT rolled **2.** LING : **r ~** rolled *ou* trilled R **3.** CULIN [gâteau, viande] rolled **4.** *fam loc* **elle est bien ~e** she's got curves in all the right places.
◆ **roulé** *nm* **1.** CULIN [gâteau] Swiss roll ■ [viande] rolled meat **2.** CONSTR rolled pebbles.

rouleau, x [rulo] *nm* **1.** [de papier, de tissu *etc*] roll ■ **~ de parchemin** roll *ou* scroll of parchment ■ **~ de papier hygiénique** toilet roll *UK*, roll of toilet paper ■ **~ de pièces** roll of coins **2.** [outil - de peintre, de jardinier, de relieur] roller ■ **~ imprimeur** *ou* **encreur** (press) cylinder ■ **~ à pâtisserie** rolling pin **3.** [bigoudi] roller, curler **4.** CULIN : **~ de printemps** spring roll **5.** SPORT : **~ costal** western roll ■ **~ ventral** straddle **6.** [vague] roller **7.** ART [vase] rouleau **8.** CONSTR arch moulding **9.** TRAV PUB roller ■ **~ compresseur** *pr* [à gazole] roadroller ; [à vapeur] steamroller ; *fig* steamroller.

roulé-boulé [rulebule] (*pl* **roulés-boulés**) *nm* [culbute] roll ■ **faire des roulés-boulés** to roll.

roulement [rulmɑ̃] *nm* **1.** [mouvement] : **un ~ d'yeux** a roll of the eyes ■ **un ~ de hanches** a swing of the hips **2.** [grondement] rumble, rumbling *(U)* ■ **le ~ du tonnerre** the rumble *ou* roll *ou* peal of thunder ■ **~ de tambour** drum roll **3.** [rotation] rotation ■ **établir un ~** to set up a rota *UK ou* a rotation system *US* **4.** MÉCAN [déplacement] rolling ■ **~ à billes/à rouleaux/à aiguilles** ball/roller/needle bearings **5.** TRANSP rolling motion **6.** ARM [d'un char] bogie and tread, tracking.

rouler [3] [rule] ◇ *vt* **1.** [faire tourner] to roll ■ **~ les yeux** to roll one's eyes ■ **~ de sombres pensées** to turn dark thoughts over in one's mind ▶ **~ un patin**△ *ou* **une pelle**△ **à qqn** to snog *UK ou* to neck *US* sb ■ **~ qqn dans la farine** to pull the wool over sb's eyes
2. [poster, tapis, bas de pantalon] to roll up *(sép)* ■ [corde, câble] to roll up, to wind up *(sép)* ■ [cigarette] to roll ■ **~ du fil sur une bobine** to spool *ou* to wind thread around a reel ■ **~ un blessé dans une couverture** to wrap an injured person in a blanket
3. [déplacer - Caddie] to push (along) ; [- balle, tronc, fût] to roll (along) ▶ **j'ai roulé ma bosse** I've been around, I've seen it all
4. *fam* [escroquer - lors d'un paiement] to diddle ; [- dans une affaire] to swindle ■ **elle m'a roulé de 30 euros** she diddled *ou* did me out of 30 euros ■ **se faire ~** to be conned *ou* had ■ **ce n'est pas du cuir, je me suis fait ~** it's not genuine leather, I've been done *ou* had
5. [balancer] : **~ des** *ou* **les épaules** to sway one's shoulders ■ **~ des** *ou* **les hanches** to swing one's hips ▶ **~ des mécaniques** *fam* to sway one's shoulders ; *fig* to come *ou* to play the hard guy
6. [aplatir - gazon, court de tennis] to roll ■ CULIN [pâte] to roll out *(sép)*
7. LING : **~ les r** to roll one's r's
8. MÉTALL to roll.
◇ *vi* **1.** [véhicule] to go, to run ■ [conducteur] to drive ■ **une voiture qui a peu/beaucoup roulé** a car with a low/high mileage ■ **à quelle vitesse rouliez-vous?** what speed were you travelling at?, what speed were you doing?, how fast were you going? ■ **j'ai beaucoup roulé quand j'étais jeune** I did a lot of driving when I was young ■ **seulement deux heures? tu as bien roulé!** only two hours? you've made good time! ■ **~ au pas** to go at a walking pace, to crawl along ■ **'roulez au pas'** 'dead slow' ■ **roule moins vite** slow down, drive more slowly ■ **elle roule en Jaguar** she drives (around in) a Jaguar ■ **~ à moto/à bicyclette** to ride a motorbike/a bicycle ■ **ça roule mal/bien dans Anvers** there's a lot of traffic/there's no traffic through Antwerp ▶ **ça roule!** *fam* everything's going alright! ■ **salut! ça roule?** hi, how's life?
2. [balle, dé, rocher] to roll ■ **faire ~** [balle] to roll ; [chariot] to wheel (along) ; [roue] to roll along ■ **il a roulé jusqu'en bas du champ** he rolled *ou* tumbled down to the bottom of the field ▶ **~ sous la table** to end up (dead drunk) under the table
3. NAUT to roll
4. [gronder - tonnerre] to roll, to rumble ; [- tambour] to roll
5. [se succéder] to take turns ■ **nous ferons ~ les équipes dès janvier** as from January, we'll start the teams off on a rota system *UK ou* rotation *US*
6. [argent] to circulate
7. : **~ sur** [conversation] to be centred upon
8. *fam loc* **~ pour qqn** to be for sb, to back sb ■ **~ sur l'or** to be rolling in money *ou* in it.
◆ **se rouler** *vpi* [se vautrer] : **se ~ par terre** [de colère] to have a fit ; [de douleur] to be doubled up with pain ; [de rire] to be doubled up with laughter ■ **c'était à se ~ par terre** [de rire] it was hysterically funny ; [de douleur] it was so painful.

roulette [rulɛt] *nf* **1.** [roue - libre] wheel ; [- sur pivot] caster ■ **à ~s** on wheels ▶ **marcher** *ou* **aller comme sur des ~s** *fam* [opération] to go off without a hitch ; [organisation, projet] to proceed smoothly, to go like clockwork **2.** [ustensile - de relieur] fillet (wheel) ; [- de graveur] roulette ■ COUT tracing wheel ■ **~ de dentiste** dentist's drill **3.** JEUX [jeu] roulette ■ [roue] roulette wheel ■ **~ russe** Russian roulette ■ **jouer à la ~ russe** *pr* & *fig* to play Russian roulette.

roulier [rulje] *nm* **1.** HIST cart driver **2.** NAUT roll-on roll-off ship.

roulis [ruli] *nm* AÉRON & NAUT roll, rolling ■ **il y a du ~** the ship is rolling ▶ **coup de ~** strong roll.

roulotte [rulɔt] *nf* **1.** [tirée par des chevaux] horse-drawn caravan **2.** [caravane] caravan, mobile home.

roulure△ [rulyr] *nf péj* slut△, slag△ *UK*.

roumain, e [rumɛ̃, ɛn] *adj* Rumanian, Ro(u)manian.
◆ **Roumain, e** *nm, f* Rumanian, Ro(u)manian.
◆ **roumain** *nm* LING Romanian.

Roumanie [rumani] *npr f* : **(la) ~** Rumania, Ro(u)mania.

roupettes△ [rupɛt] *nfpl*△ nuts, balls.

roupie [rupi] *nf* **1.** [monnaie] rupee **2.** *loc* **c'est de la ~ de sansonnet** that's (worthless) rubbish.

roupiller [3] [rupije] *vi fam* to have a kip△ *UK*, to get some shut-eye△ *US* ■ **c'est pas le moment de ~!** this is no time for lying down on the job!

roupillon [rupijɔ̃] *nm fam* **faire** *ou* **piquer un ~** to have a snooze *ou* a nap *ou* a kip *UK*.

rouquette [rukɛt] = **roquette** *(sens 2)*.

rouquin, e [rukɛ̃, in] *fam* ◇ *adj* [personne] red-haired ■ [chevelure] red, ginger *(modif)*, carroty *péj* ■ **elle est ~e** she has red *ou* ginger *ou* carroty hair.
◇ *nm, f fam* redhead.
◆ **rouquin**△ *nm* [vin] (red) plonk *UK*, cheap red wine.

rouspétance [ruspetɑ̃s] *nf fam* grumbling, moaning (and groaning).

rouspéter [18] [ruspete] *vi fam* to grumble, to complain, to make a fuss.

rouspéteur, euse [ruspetœr, øz] *nm, f fam* grumbler, moaner, groucher ■ **il n'y a que les ~s qui obtiennent satisfaction** you only get what you want if you complain.

roussâtre [rusatr] *adj* [eau] reddish ■ [feuilles] reddish-brown, russet *sout.*

rousse [rus] ◇ *f* ▷ **roux.**
◇ *nf*△ *arg crime & vieilli* **la ~** the fuzz△.

roussette [rusɛt] *nf* **1.** [requin] large spotted dogfish CULIN rock salmon **2.** [chauve-souris] flying fox.

rousseur [rusœr] *nf sout* [teinte] redness, gingery colour.
◆ **rousseurs** *nfpl* [pigmentation] freckles.

roussi [rusi] *nm* **: ça sent le ~** *pr* something's burning ■ *fam fig* there's trouble ahead *ou* brewing.

roussir [32] [rusir] ◇ *vt* **1.** [rendre roux] **: ~ qqch** to turn sthg brown **2.** [brûler] to scorch, to singe ■ **la gelée a roussi l'herbe** the grass has turned brown with the frost.
◇ *vi* **1.** [feuillage, arbre] to turn brown *ou* russet *sout* **2.** CULIN **: faire ~** to brown.

rouste△ [rust] *nf* thrashing, walloping ■ **flanquer une ~ à qqn** to give sb a good hiding.

routage [rutaʒ] *nm* **1.** IMPR sorting and mailing **2.** NAUT steering.

routard, e [rutar, ard] *nm, f fam* [auto-stoppeur] hitchhiker ■ [marcheur] trekker ■ [touriste avec sac à dos] backpacker.

route [rut] *nf* **1.** [voie de circulation] road ■ **c'est la ~ de Genève** it's the road to Geneva ■ **sur ~, la voiture consomme moins** when cruising *ou* on the open road, the car's fuel consumption is lower ■ **il va y avoir du monde sur la ~** *ou* **les ~s** there'll be a lot of cars *ou* traffic on the roads ■ **tenir la ~** [voiture] to hold the road ■ **cette politique ne tient pas la ~** *fig* there's no mileage in that policy ➤ **~ départementale** secondary road ■ **~ nationale** major road, trunk road *UK* ■ **~ de montagne** mountain road
2. [moyen de transport] **: par la ~** by road ■ **les transports sur ~** road transport ■ **les accidents de la ~** road accidents ■ **les victimes de la ~** road casualties
3. [itinéraire] way ■ **c'est sur ma ~** it's on my way ■ **faire ~ vers** [bateau] to be headed for, to be en route for, to steer a course for ; [voiture, avion] to head for *ou* towards ; [personne] to be on one's way to, to head for ■ **en ~ pour** *ou* **vers** bound for ■ **faisant ~ vers** [bateau, avion] bound for, heading for, on its way to ; [personne] on one's way to, heading for ■ **prendre la ~ des vacances/du soleil** to set off on holiday/to the south ➤ **~ aérienne** air route ■ **~ maritime** shipping *ou* sea route ■ **la ~ des épices** the spice trail *ou* route ■ **la ~ des Indes** the road to India ■ **la ~ de la soie** the silk road ■ **la Route des Vins** *tourist trail passing through wine country* ■ **faire fausse ~** [conducteur] to go the wrong way, to take the wrong road ; [dans un raisonnement] to be on the wrong track
4. [trajet] journey ■ **j'ai fait la ~ à pied** I did the journey on foot ■ **il y a six heures de ~** [en voiture] it's a six-hour drive *ou* ride *ou* journey ; [à bicyclette] it's a six-hour ride *ou* journey ■ **il y a une bonne heure de ~** it takes at least an hour to get there ■ **(faites) bonne ~!** have a good *ou* safe journey! ■ **faire ~ avec qqn** to travel with sb ■ **faire de la ~** to do a lot of driving *ou* mileage ■ **en ~** on the way ■ **prendre la** *ou* **se mettre en ~** to set off, to get going ■ **reprendre la ~, se remettre en ~** to set off again, to resume one's journey ■ **allez, en ~!** come on, let's go! ➤ **en ~, mauvaise troupe!** *fam hum* come on you lot, we're off!
5. *fig* [voie] road, way, path ■ **la ~ du succès** the road to success ■ **la ~ est toute tracée pour lui** the path is all laid out for him
6. : en ~ [en marche] **: mettre en ~** [appareil, véhicule] to start (up) *(sép)* ; [projet] to set in motion, to get started *ou* under way ■ **se mettre en ~** [machine] to start (up) ■ **j'ai du mal à me mettre en ~ le matin** *fam* I find it hard to get started *ou* going in the morning.

routier, ère [rutje, ɛr] ◇ *adj* road *(modif).*
◇ *nm, f* **1.** [chauffeur] (long-distance) lorry *UK ou* truck *US* driver ■ **c'est un vieux ~ du journalisme** *fig* he's a veteran journalist **2.** *fam* [restaurant] transport café *UK*, truck-stop *US* **3.** SPORT [cycliste] road racer *ou* rider.
◆ **routière** *nf* AUTO touring car ■ **c'est une excellente routière** it's an ideal car for long-distance trips, it's an excellent touring car.

routine [rutin] *nf* **1.** [habitude] routine ■ **se laisser enfermer dans la ~** to get into a rut **2.** INFORM routine.
◆ **de routine** *loc adj* [contrôle, visite] routine *(avant n)* ■ **une vérification de ~** a routine check.

routinier, ère [rutinje, ɛr] ◇ *adj* [tâche, corvée] routine *(avant n)*, humdrum *péj* ■ [vérification, méthode] routine *(avant n)* ■ [personne] routine-minded, conventional ■ **de façon routinière** routinely.
◇ *nm, f* **: c'est un ~** he's a creature of habit, he's tied to his routine.

rouvrir [34] [ruvrir] ◇ *vt* **1.** [livre, hôtel, débat, dossier] to re-open **2.** *fig* [raviver] **: ~ une blessure** *ou* **plaie** to open an old wound.
◇ *vi* [magasin] to reopen, to open again.
◆ **se rouvrir** *vpi* [porte, fenêtre] to reopen ■ [blessure] to re-open, to open up again.

roux, rousse [ru, rus] ◇ *adj* [feuillage, fourrure] reddish-brown, russet ■ [chevelure, moustache] red, ginger.
◇ *nm, f* redhead.
◆ **roux** *nm* **1.** [teinte - d'un feuillage] reddish-brown (colour), russet ; [- d'une chevelure, d'une moustache] reddish *ou* gingery colour **2.** CULIN roux.

royal, e, aux [rwajal, o] *adj* **1.** HIST & POLIT [puissance] royal, regal ■ [bijoux, insignes, appartements, palais, académie] royal ■ **la famille ~e** [en Grande-Bretagne] the Royal Family ; [ailleurs] the royal family ■ **prince ~** crown prince, heir apparent **2.** [somptueux - cadeau] magnificent, princely ; [- pourboire] lavish ; [- salaire] princely ; [- accueil] royal ■ **un train de vie ~** a sumptuous lifestyle **3.** [extrême - mépris] total ■ **il m'a fichu une paix ~e** *fam* he left me in total peace.
◆ **royale** *nf fam* [marine] **: la Royale** *the French Navy.*

royalement [rwajalmɑ̃] *adv* **1.** [avec magnificence] royally, regally ■ **ils nous ont reçus ~** they treated us like royalty ■ **il l'a ~ payé** he paid him a princely sum **2.** *fam* [complètement] totally ■ **je m'en fiche** *ou* **moque ~!** I really couldn't care less!, I don't give a damn!

royalisme [rwajalism] *nm* royalism.

royaliste [rwajalist] ◇ *adj* royalist ■ **il ne faut pas être plus ~ que le roi** one mustn't try to out-Herod Herod *ou* to be more Catholic than the Pope.
◇ *nmf* royalist.

royalties [rwajalti] *nfpl* royalties *(for landowner or owner of patent).*

royaume [rwajom] *nm* **1.** HIST & POLIT kingdom **2.** RELIG **: le ~ céleste** *ou* **des cieux** the kingdom of Heaven ■ **le ~ des morts** *litt* the kingdom of the dead **3.** *fig* [domaine] realm ■ **mon atelier, c'est mon ~** my workshop is my private world *ou* domain **4.** *loc* **je ne le ferais pas/je n'en voudrais pas pour un ~** I wouldn't do it/have it for all the tea in China.

Royaume-Uni [rwajomyni] *npr m* **: le ~ (de Grande-Bretagne et d'Irlande du Nord)** the United Kingdom (of Great Britain and Northern Ireland), the UK.

royauté [rwajote] *nf* **1.** [monarchie] monarchy **2.** [rang] royalty, kingship ■ **il aspirait à la ~** he had designs on the throne.

RP ◇ *nfpl* (*abr de* **relations publiques**) PR.
◇ *nf* **1. = recette principale 2. = région parisienne**.
◇ (*abr écrite de* **Révérend Père**) Rev.

RPR (*abr de* **Rassemblement pour la République**) *npr m right-wing French political party.*

RSVP (*abr de* **répondez s'il vous plaît**) RSVP.

RTB (*abr de* **Radio-télévision belge**) *npr f Belgian broadcasting company.*

rte = route.

RTL *npr* (*abr de* **Radio-télévision Luxembourg**) *Luxembourg broadcasting company.*

RTT (*abr de* **réduction du temps de travail**) [ɛrtete] ◇ *nf* (statutory) reduction in working hours.

◇ *nm* (extra) day off *(as a result of shorter working hours)* ■ **poser/prendre un ~** to book *ou* claim a day's holiday ■ **prendre un ~** ro take a day off.

RTT

Initially planned as a measure to reduce unemployment, the law on a 35-hour working week known as *les trente-cinq heures* has not entirely succeeded but it has generated more leisure time for people in paid employment. They now have *journées RTT*.

RTTiste [ɛrtetist] *nmf person taking a day off as a result of the reduction in working hours.*

ru [ry] *nm litt* [dialecte] rill *litt*, brook.

RU [ry] *nm* = **restaurant universitaire**.

ruade [ryad] *nf* kick ■ **lancer** *ou* **décocher une ~ à** to kick *ou* to lash out at.

Ruanda [rwɑ̃da] *npr m* : **le ~** Rwanda ■ **au ~** in Rwanda.

ruandais, e [rwɑ̃dɛ, ɛz] *adj* Rwandan.
◆ **Ruandais, e** *nm, f* Rwandan.

ruban [rybɑ̃] *nm* **1.** [ornement] ribbon ■ [liseré] ribbon, tape ■ [bolduc] tape ■ [sur chapeau] band ■ **le ~ rouge** the ribbon of the Légion d'honneur **2.** *litt* **la rivière déroule son long ~** the river winds before us like a long ribbon **3.** [de cassette] tape ■ [de machine à écrire] ribbon ■ **~ adhésif** adhesive tape ■ **~ isolant** insulating tape ■ **~ perforé** INFORM perforated tape.

rubéole [rybeɔl] *nf* German measles *(U)*, rubella *spéc*.

Rubicon [rybikɔ̃] *npr m* Rubicon ■ **franchir** *ou* **passer le ~** to cross the Rubicon.

rubicond, e [rybikɔ̃, ɔ̃d] *adj litt* rubicund *litt*, ruddy.

rubis [rybi] *nm* **1.** JOAILL ruby **2.** [couleur] ruby (colour) **3.** [d'une montre] jewel, ruby.

rubrique [rybrik] *nf* **1.** [dans la presse] column ■ **la ~ scientifique** the science column ■ **la ~ littéraire** the book page ■ **la ~ nécrologique** the obituaries **2.** [catégorie] heading **3.** [d'un livre liturgique] rubric ■ [d'un dictionnaire] field label.

ruche [ryʃ] *nf* **1.** ENTOM [abri - en bois] beehive ; [- en paille] beehive, skep *spéc* ■ [colonie d'abeilles] hive **2.** *fig* hive of activity.

rucher [ryʃe] *nm* apiary.

rude [ryd] *adj* **1.** [rugueux - surface, vin] rough ; [- toile] rough, coarse ; [- peau] rough, coarse ; [- son] rough, harsh ; [- voix] gruff ; [- manières, personne] uncouth, unrefined ; [- traits] rugged **2.** [difficile - climat, hiver] harsh, severe ; [- conditions, concurrent] tough ; [- concurrence] severe, tough ; [- vie, tâche] hard, tough ; [- côte] hard, stiff ■ **être mis à ~ épreuve** [personne] to be severely tested, to be put through the mill ; [vêtement, matériel] to get a lot of wear and tear ■ **ma patience a été mise à ~ épreuve** it was a severe strain on my patience **3.** [sévère - ton, voix] rough, harsh, hard ; [- personne] harsh, hard, severe **4.** *fam* [important, remarquable] : **avoir un ~ appétit** to have a hearty appetite ■ **un ~ gaillard** a hearty fellow ■ **ça a été un ~ coup pour lui** it was a hard blow for him.

rudement [rydmɑ̃] *adv* **1.** *fam* [diablement] : **c'est ~ bon** it's really good ■ **c'est ~ cher** it's incredibly *ou* awfully expensive ■ **elle est ~ culottée!** she's got some cheek *UK ou* gall! ■ **ils étaient ~ nombreux** there were a heck of a lot of them **2.** [sans ménagement] roughly, harshly **3.** [brutalement] hard.

rudesse [rydɛs] *nf* **1.** [rugosité - d'une surface, de la peau] roughness ; [- d'une toile] roughness, coarseness ; [- d'une voix, d'un son] roughness, harshness **2.** [rusticité - des manières] roughness, uncouthness ; [- des traits] ruggedness **3.** [sévérité - d'un ton, d'une voix] roughness, harshness, hardness ; [- d'un maître] severity, harshness **4.** [dureté - d'un climat, d'un hiver] hardness, harshness, severity ; [- d'une concurrence, d'une tâche] toughness.

rudiment [rydimɑ̃] *nm* **1.** *litt* [début, ébauche] rudiment ■ **il en est encore au ~** he's still learning the basics **2.** BIOL rudiment.
◆ **rudiments** *nmpl* [d'un art, d'une science] basics, rudiments *sout* ■ **apprendre les ~s de la grammaire** to learn some basic grammar, to get a basic (working) knowledge of grammar ■ **je n'ai que des ~s d'informatique** I have only a rudimentary knowledge of computing.

rudimentaire [rydimɑ̃tɛr] *adj* **1.** [élémentaire] rudimentary, basic **2.** [commençant] rudimentary, undeveloped **3.** [succinct] basic ■ **des informations trop ~s** inadequate information **4.** BIOL rudimentary.

rudoie *etc v* ⊳ **rudoyer**.

rudoiement [rydwamɑ̃] *nm litt* harsh treatment.

rudoyer [13] [rydwaje] *vt* to treat harshly ■ **il les a un peu rudoyés** he was a bit harsh with them.

rue [ry] *nf* [voie] street ■ **de la ~, des ~s** street *(modif)* ■ **c'est la ~ qui dicte sa loi aujourd'hui** *fig* it's mob rule these days ■ **~ pavée** paved street *(with small, flat paving stones)* ▶ **~ piétonnière** pedestrian street ■ **~ à sens unique** one-way street ■ **la grande ~** the high *UK ou* main street ■ **les petites ~s** the side streets ■ **être à la ~** to be on the streets ■ **mettre** *ou* **jeter qqn à la ~** to turn *ou* to put sb out into the street.

RUE

The names of some Paris streets are used to refer to the establishments situated there: *la rue de Grenelle* the Ministry of Education; *la rue de Valois* the Ministry of Culture; *la rue d'Ulm* the *École Normale Supérieure*.

ruée [rɥe] *nf* rush ■ **il y a eu une ~ vers le buffet** everybody made a mad dash for the buffet ▶ **la ~ vers l'or** HIST the gold rush.

ruelle [rɥɛl] *nf* **1.** [voie] lane, narrow street, alley **2.** [de lit] space between bed and wall, ruelle *arch*.

ruer [7] [rɥe] *vi* **1.** [animal] to kick (out) **2.** *fam loc* **~ dans les brancards** [verbalement] to kick up a fuss ; [par ses actions] to kick *ou* to lash out.
◆ **se ruer** *vpi* : **se ~ sur qqn** [gén] to rush at sb ; [agressivement] to hurl *ou* to throw o.s. at sb ■ **se ~ vers la sortie** to dash *ou* to rush towards the exit ■ **ils se sont tous rués sur le buffet** they made a mad dash for the buffet ■ **dès qu'une chambre se libère, tout le monde se rue dessus** as soon as a room becomes vacant, everybody pounces on it ■ **se ~ à l'attaque** SPORT to rush into the attack.

ruf(f)ian [ryfjɑ̃] *nm* **1.** *arch* [souteneur] whoremonger **2.** [aventurier] adventurer.

rugby [rygbi] *nm* rugby (football) ■ **~ à quinze** Rugby Union ■ **~ à treize** Rugby League.

rugbyman [rygbiman] (*pl* **rugbymans** *ou pl* **rugbymen** [mɛn]) *nm* rugby player.

rugir [32] [ryʒir] ◇ *vi* **1.** [fauve] to roar **2.** [personne] to bellow.
◇ *vt* [insultes, menaces] to bellow *ou* to roar out *(sép)*.

rugissant, e [ryʒisɑ̃, ɑ̃t] *adj* **1.** [fauve, moteur] roaring **2.** *litt* [flots] roaring ■ [vent, tempête] roaring, howling.

rugissement [ryʒismɑ̃] *nm* **1.** [d'un lion, d'un moteur] roar, roaring **2.** *litt* [des flots] roar, roaring ■ [du vent, de la tempête] roar, roaring, howling **3.** [d'une personne] roar ■ **~ de douleur** howl of pain.

rugosité [rygozite] *nf* [d'une écorce, d'un plancher, de la peau] roughness ■ [d'une toile] roughness, coarseness.
◆ **rugosités** *nfpl* bumps, rough patches.

rugueux, euse [rygø, øz] *adj* [écorce, planche, peau] rough ■ [toile] rough, coarse.

Ruhr [rur] *npr f* : **la ~** the Ruhr.

ruine [rɥin] *nf* **1.** [faillite financière] ruin ■ **courir à la ~** to head for ruin **2.** *fam* [dépense exorbitante] ruinous expense ■ **100 euros, ce n'est pas la ~!** 100 euros won't break *ou* ruin you! **3.** [bâtiment délabré] ruin **4.** [personne usée] wreck **5.** [destruction - d'une institution] downfall, ruin ■ *fig* ruin ■ **ce fut la ~ de notre mariage** it wrecked *ou* ruined our marriage ■ **il veut ma ~** he wants to ruin *ou* finish me.
◆ **ruines** *nfpl* ruins.

◆ **en ruine** <> *loc adj* ruined ▪ **il y a beaucoup de moulins en ~ dans la région** there're a lot of ruined windmills in the area.
<> *loc adv* in ruins ▪ **tomber en ~** to go to ruin.

ruiner [3] [rɥine] *vt* **1.** [financièrement] to ruin, to cause the ruin of, to bring ruin upon *sout* ▪ **ça ne va pas te ~!** it won't break *ou* ruin you! **2.** *litt* [endommager - architecture, cultures] to ruin, to destroy ; [- espérances] to ruin, to dash ; [- carrière, santé] to ruin, to wreck ▪ **cet échec ruine tous ses espoirs** this failure wrecks all his hopes.
◆ **se ruiner** <> *vpi* [perdre sa fortune] to ruin *ou* to bankrupt o.s. ▪ [dépenser beaucoup] to spend a fortune ▪ **elle se ruine en vêtements/disques** she spends a fortune on clothes/records.
<> *vpt* : **se ~ la santé** to ruin one's health ▪ **se ~ la vue** to destroy one's eyesight.

ruineux, euse [rɥinø, øz] *adj* extravagantly expensive, ruinous ▪ **10 euros, ce n'est pas ~** 10 euros is hardly extravagant.

ruisseau, x [rɥiso] *nm* **1.** [ru] brook, stream **2.** [lit du cours d'eau] bed of a stream ▪ **un ~ à sec** a dried-up stream **3.** *litt* [torrent] stream ▪ **~x de larmes** floods of tears ➊ **les petits ~x font les grandes rivières** *prov* tall oaks from little acorns grow *prov* **4.** [rigole] gutter **5.** *péj* gutter ▪ **tirer qqn du ~** to pull *ou* to drag sb out of the gutter.

ruisselant, e [rɥislɑ̃, ɑ̃t] *adj* **1.** [inondé] : **~ (d'eau)** [imperméable, personne] dripping (wet) ; [paroi] streaming *ou* running with water ▪ **le visage ~ de sueur** her face streaming *ou* dripping with sweat ▪ **les joues ~es de larmes** his cheeks streaming with tears ▪ **une pièce ~e de lumière** a room bathed in *ou* flooded with light **2.** [qui ne cesse de couler] : **eaux ~es** running waters.

ruisseler [24] [rɥisle] *vi* [couler - eau, sang, sueur] to stream, to drip ▪ **la sueur ruisselait sur son front** his brow was streaming *ou* dripping with sweat ▪ **la lumière ruisselait par la fenêtre** *fig* light flooded in through the window ▪ **~ sur** *litt* [suj: chevelure] to flow over ; [suj: air, lumière] to stream.
◆ **ruisseler de** *vp+prép* [être inondé de] : **~ de sang/sueur** to stream with blood/sweat ▪ **les murs ruisselaient d'humidité** the walls were streaming *ou* oozing with damp ▪ **le palais ruisselait de lumière** *fig* the palace was bathed in *ou* flooded with *ou* awash with light.

ruisselet [rɥislɛ] *nm* little stream, brook.

ruisselle *etc v* ▷ **ruisseler**.

ruissellement [rɥisɛlmɑ̃] *nm* **1.** [écoulement] : **le ~ de la pluie sur les vitres** the rain streaming *ou* running down the window panes ▪ **~ de lumière** *litt* stream of light **2.** GÉOL : **~ pluvial, eaux de ~** (immediate) runoff.

rumba [rumba] *nf* rumba.

rumeur [rymœr] *nf* **1.** [information] rumour ▪ **il y a des ~s de guerre** there's talk of war ▪ **selon certaines ~s, le réacteur fuirait toujours** rumour has it *ou* it's rumoured that the reactor is still leaking **2.** *sout* [bruit - d'un stade, d'une classe] hubbub, hum ; [- de l'océan] murmur ; [- de la circulation] rumbling, hum **3.** [manifestation] : **~ de mécontentement** rumblings of discontent **4.** [opinion] : **la ~ publique : la ~ publique le tient pour coupable** rumour has it that he is guilty.

ruminant [ryminɑ̃] *nm* ruminant.

ruminer [3] [rymine] <> *vi* ZOOL to ruminate *spéc*, to chew the cud.
<> *vt* **1.** [ressasser - idée] to ponder, to chew over *(sép)* ; [- malheurs] to brood over *(insép)* ; [- vengeance] to ponder **2.** ZOOL to ruminate.

rumsteck [rɔmstɛk] = **romsteck**.

rune [ryn] *nf* rune.

runique [rynik] *adj* runic.

rupestre [rypɛstr] *adj* **1.** ARCHÉOL & ART [dessin] rock *(modif)* ▪ [peinture] cave *(modif)* **2.** BOT rock *(modif)*.

rupin, e△ [rypɛ̃, in] <> *adj* [quartier] posh ▪ [intérieur] ritzy, posh ▪ [famille] well-heeled, posh.
<> *nm, f* : **c'est des ~s** they're rolling in money *ou* rolling in it ▪ **les ~s** the rich.

rupture [ryptyr] *nf* **1.** MÉD [dans une membrane] breaking, tearing, splitting ▪ [dans un vaisseau] bursting ➊ **~ d'anévrysme** aneurysmal rupture **2.** TECHNOL : **~ de circuit** circuit break **3.** [cessation - de négociations, de fiançailles] breaking off ▪ **une ~ avec le passé** a break with the past **4.** [dans un couple] break-up **5.** [changement] break ▪ **~ de cadence** sudden break in rhythm ▪ **~ de ton** sudden change in *ou* of tone **6.** COMM : **~ de stock : être en ~ de stock** to be out of stock **7.** DR : **~ de ban** illegal return (from banishment) ▪ **être en ~ de ban avec son milieu/sa famille** *fig* to be at odds with one's environment/one's family ▪ **~ de contrat** breach of contract **8.** POLIT : **~ des relations diplomatiques** breaking off of diplomatic relations **9.** INDUST : **~ de charge** break of load **10.** MIL breakthrough.

rural, e, aux [ryral, o] <> *adj* [droit, population] rural ▪ [vie, paysage] country *(modif)*, rural ▪ **en milieu ~** in rural areas.
<> *nm, f* country person ▪ **les ruraux** country people, countryfolk.
<> *nm Suisse* farm building.

ruse [ryz] *nf* **1.** [trait de caractère] cunning, craftiness, slyness ▪ **s'approprier qqch par ~** to obtain sthg through *ou* by trickery **2.** [procédé] trick, ruse, wile ▪ **~ de guerre** *pr* tactics, stratagem ; *fig* good trick ▪ **~s de Sioux** *fam* crafty tactics, fox's cunning.

rusé, e [ryze] <> *adj* [personne] crafty, sly, wily ▪ [air, regard] sly ▪ **il est ~ comme un renard** he's as sly *ou* cunning *ou* wily as a fox.
<> *nm, f* : **tu es une petite ~e!** you're a crafty one *ou* a sly one, my girl!

ruser [3] [ryze] *vi* to use cunning *ou* trickery *ou* guile *sout* ▪ **il va falloir ~** we'll have to be clever! ▪ **~ avec qqn** to outsmart sb ▪ **~ avec qqch** to get round sthg by using cunning.

rush [rœʃ] (*pl* **rushs** *ou pl* **rushes**) *nm* **1.** [ruée] rush, stampede **2.** SPORT [effort soudain] spurt.

rushes [rœʃ] *nmpl* CINÉ rushes.

russe [rys] *adj* Russian.
◆ **Russe** *nmf* Russian.
◆ **russe** *nm* LING Russian.

Russie [rysi] *npr f* : **(la) ~** Russia.

russifier [9] [rysifje] *vt* to Russianize, to Russify.

russkof △ [ryskɔf] *nmf offensive term used with reference to Russian people,* ≃ Russky.

russophile [rysɔfil] *adj* & *nmf* Russophile.

russophone [rysɔfɔn] <> *adj* Russian-speaking.
<> *nmf* Russian speaker.

rustaud, e [rysto, od] *péj* <> *adj* yokelish.
<> *nm, f* yokel, (country) bumpkin ▪ **les ~s du coin** *fam* the locals.

rusticité [rystisite] *nf* **1.** [d'un comportement, d'une personne] uncouthness, boorishness **2.** [d'un mobilier] rusticity **3.** AGRIC hardiness.

Rustine® [rystin] *nf (bicycle tyre) rubber repair patch.*

rustique [rystik] <> *adj* **1.** *sout* [de la campagne - vie] rustic, rural **2.** [meubles] rustic ▪ [poterie] rusticated **3.** *litt* [fruste - manières, personne] country *(epith)*, rustic **4.** AGRIC hardy.
<> *nm* : **le ~** [style] rustic style ; [mobilier] rustic furniture.

rustre [rystr] <> *adj* boorish, uncouth.
<> *nmf* boor, lout.

rut [ryt] *nm* rut ▪ **au moment du ~** during the rutting season ▪ **être en ~** to (be in) rut.

rutabaga [rytabaga] *nm* swede, rutabaga *US*.

rutilant, e [rytilɑ̃, ɑ̃t] *adj* **1.** [propre - carrosserie, armure] sparkling, gleaming **2.** *litt* [rouge - cuivre] rutilant *litt* ; [- visage] ruddy.

rutile [rytil] *nm* rutile.

rutiler [3] [rytile] *vi sout* [étinceler] to gleam, to shine.

R-V = **rendez-vous**.

Rwanda [rwɑ̃da] = **Ruanda**.

rythme [ritm] *nm* **1.** MUS rhythm ■ **avoir du ~** [musique] to have a good (strong) beat *ou* rhythm ■ **avoir le sens du ~** [personne] to have rhythm ■ **marquer le ~** to mark time ■ **suivre le ~** to keep up **2.** CINÉ, THÉÂTRE & LITTÉR rhythm ■ **le ~ du film est trop lent** the film is too slow-moving **3.** [allure - d'une production] rate ; [- des battements du cœur] rate, speed ; [- de vie] tempo, pace ■ **travailler à un ~ soutenu** to work at a sustained pace ■ **à ce ~-là** at that rate ■ **suivre le ~** to keep up the pace **4.** [succession - de marées, de saisons] rhythm **5.** ANAT & BIOL : **~ biologique** biorhythm ■ **~ cardiaque** heartbeat, cardiac rhythm *spéc* ■ **~ respiratoire** breathing rate.

◆ **au rythme de** *loc prép* **1.** [au son de] to the rhythm of **2.** [à la cadence de] at the rate of.

rythmé, e [ritme] *adj* [musique] rhythmic, rhythmical ■ [prose] rhythmical ■ **musique très ~e** music with a good rhythm *ou* beat.

rythmer [3] [ritme] *vt* **1.** [mouvements de danse, texte] to put rhythm into, to give rhythm to **2.** *sout* [ponctuer] : **ces événements ont rythmé sa vie** these events gave a certain rhythm to *ou* punctuated his life.

rythmique [ritmik] ◇ *adj* rhythmic, rhythmical.
◇ *nf* **1.** LITTÉR rhythmics *(U)* **2.** [gymnastique] rhythmic gymnastics *(U)*.

S

s, S [ɛs] *nm inv* **1.** [lettre] s, S, *voir aussi* **g** **2.** [forme] S-shape ▪ **faire des S** [voiture] to zigzag ; [sentier] to twist and turn ▪ **à cet endroit, la route fait un S** at this point, there's a double *ou* an S bend in the road.
◆ **en S** *loc adj* [crochet] S-shaped ▪ [voie] winding, zigzagging ▪ [rivière] meandering.

s (*abr écrite de* **seconde**) s.

s' [s] ▷ **se, si conj.**

s/ = **sur.**

S (*abr écrite de* **Sud**) S.

sa [sa] *f* ▷ **son.**

SA (*abr de* **société anonyme**) *nf* ≃ plc *UK*, ≃ Inc *US* ▪ **une SA** a limited company.

S.A. (*abr écrite de* **Son Altesse**) HH.

sabayon [sabajɔ̃] *nm* [entremets] zabaglione ▪ [sauce] sabayon sauce.

sabbat [saba] *nm* **1.** RELIG Sabbath ▪ **que faites-vous le jour du ~?** what do you do on the Sabbath? **2.** [de sorcières] witches' sabbath.

sabbatique [sabatik] *adj* **1.** RELIG sabbatical **2.** UNIV sabbatical ▪ **demander une année ~** to ask for a sabbatical (year).

Sabin, e [sabɛ̃, in] *nm, f* Sabine ▪ **l'enlèvement des ~es** the rape of the Sabine women.

sabir [sabir] *nm* **1.** LING lingua franca **2.** *fam* [jargon] gobbledygook, mumbo-jumbo.

sablage [sablaʒ] *nm* **1.** TRAV PUB gritting **2.** CONSTR sandblasting.

sable [sabl] ◇ *nm* **1.** GÉOL sand ▪ **~ fin** fine sand ◉ **~ de construction** coarse sand ▪ **être sur le ~** *fam fig* [sans argent] to be skint *UK ou* broke *ou* strapped ; [sans emploi] to be out of a job ▪ **mettre qqn sur le ~** [le ruiner] : **ils m'ont mis sur le ~** they've ruined *ou* bankrupted me **2.** MÉTALL (moulding) sand **3.** HÉRALD sable.
◇ *adj inv* sand-coloured, sandy.
◆ **sables** *nmpl* : **~s mouvants** quicksand *(U)*.
◆ **de sable** *loc adj* [château] sand *(modif)* ▪ [dune] sand *(modif)*, sandy ▪ [fond] sandy.

sablé, e [sable] *adj* [allée] sandy.
◆ **sablé** *nm* (shortbread-type) biscuit *UK ou* cookie *US*.

sabler [3] [sable] *vt* **1.** TRAV PUB to grit **2.** CONSTR to sandblast **3.** *loc* **~ le champagne** to crack a bottle of champagne.

sableux, euse [sablø, øz] *adj* **1.** [mêlé de sable - eau, terrain] sandy ; [- champignons, moules] gritty ▪ **alluvions sableuses** sandy alluvium **2.** [rugueux - pâte] grainy.

◆ **sableuse** *nf* **1.** TRAV PUB sander, sandspreader **2.** CONSTR sandblaster.

sablier, ère [sablije, ɛr] *adj* [industrie, commerce] sand *(modif)*.
◆ **sablier** *nm* **1.** [gén] hourglass, sand glass ▪ [de cuisine] egg timer **2.** [pour sécher l'encre] sandbox **3.** BOT sandbox tree.
◆ **sablière** *nf* **1.** [lieu] sand quarry, sandpit **2.** CONSTR [de toiture] inferior purlin ▪ [dans un mur] wall plate ▪ **sablière haute** head rail.

sablonneux, euse [sablɔnø, øz] *adj* sandy.

sablonnière [sablɔnjɛr] *nf* sand quarry, sandpit.

sabord [sabɔr] *nm* port *(square opening in ship's side)*.

sabordage [sabɔrdaʒ], **sabordement** [sabɔrdəmɑ̃] *nm* NAUT & *fig* scuttling.

saborder [3] [sabɔrde] *vt* **1.** NAUT to scuttle, to sink **2.** [stopper - entreprise, journal] to scuttle, to sink, to wind up *(sép)* **3.** [faire échouer - plans, recherche] to scuttle, to put paid to *UK*, to scupper *UK*.
◆ **se saborder** *vp (emploi réfléchi)* **1.** [navire] to go down *(by the deliberate actions of the crew)* **2.** [entreprise] to fold, to close down ▪ [parti] to wind (o.s.) up.

sabot [sabo] *nm* **1.** [soulier] clog, sabot ▪ **je te vois venir avec tes gros ~s** *fam* I know what you're after, I can see you coming a mile off ▪ **comme un ~** *fam* : **elle danse comme un ~** she's got two left feet ▪ **je chante comme un ~** I can't sing to save my life **2.** ZOOL hoof **3.** *fam péj* [instrument, machine] pile of junk **4.** JEUX shoe *(for cards)* **5.** MÉCAN : **~ de frein** brake shoe ▪ **~ de Denver** wheel clamp *UK*, Denver boot *US* **6.** [jouet] whipping top **7.** TRAV PUB [d'un pilot] shoe.

sabotage [sabɔtaʒ] *nm* **1.** [destruction - de matériel] sabotage ▪ **c'est du ~!** *fig* this is sheer sabotage! **2.** [acte organisé] : **un ~** an act *ou* a piece of sabotage **3.** [travail bâclé] botched job **4.** RAIL chairing **5.** TRAV PUB shoeing.

saboter [3] [sabɔte] *vt* **1.** [détruire volontairement] to sabotage ▪ **des manifestants sont venus ~ l'émission** demonstrators came to sabotage *ou* to disrupt the programme **2.** [bâcler] to bungle **3.** RAIL to chair **4.** TRAV PUB to shoe.

saboteur, euse [sabɔtœr, øz] *nm, f* **1.** [destructeur] saboteur **2.** [mauvais travailleur] bungler.

sabotier, ère [sabɔtje, ɛr] *nm, f* **1.** [fabricant] clog-maker **2.** [vendeur] clog seller.

sabre [sabr] *nm* ARM & SPORT sabre ▪ **tirer son ~** to draw one's sword ◉ **aller/charger ~ au clair** to go/to charge with drawn sword ▪ **le ~ et le goupillon** the Army and the Church.

sabrer [3] [sabre] *vt* **1.** [texte] to make drastic cuts in ▪ [paragraphe, phrases] to cut, to axe ▪ **~ tout un passage dans un**

chapitre to slash *ou* to hack a whole section out of a chapter **2.** *fam* [critiquer - étudiant, copie] to savage, to lay into *(insép)* ; [- projet] to lay into **3.** *fam* [renvoyer - employé] to fire, to sack *UK*, to can *US* ■ **se faire ~** to get the chop *ou* sack *UK ou* boot **4.** [marquer vigoureusement] to slash ■ **la toile avait été sabrée à coups de crayon** *fig* great pencil slashes marked the canvas **5.** [bâcler] to botch, to bungle **6.** [ouvrir] : **~ le champagne** to break open a bottle of champagne *(originally, using a sabre)*.

sabreur, euse [sabrœr, øz] *nm, f* **1.** ESCRIME fencer (specializing in the sabre) **2.** MIL swordsman (*f* swordswoman) *(using a sabre)*.

sac [sak] *nm* **1.** [contenant - petit, léger] bag ; [- grand, solide] sack ● **~ de billes** bag of marbles ■ **~ de classe** *ou* **d'école** *vieilli* satchel, school bag ■ **~ de couchage** sleeping bag ■ **~ à dos** rucksack, knapsack ■ **~ à main** [à poignée] handbag *UK*, purse *US* ; [à bandoulière] shoulder bag ■ **~ à pain** bread bag *(made of cloth)* ■ **~ en papier** paper bag ■ **~ de plage** beach bag ■ **~ (en) plastique** [petit] plastic bag ; [solide et grand] plastic carrier (bag) *UK*, large plastic bag *US* ■ **~ poubelle** bin liner *UK*, garbage can liner *US* ; [noir] black bag ■ **~ à provisions** shopping bag ■ **~ de voyage** overnight *ou* travelling bag
2. [contenu - petit, moyen] bag, bagful ; [- grand] sack, sackful
3. △ [argent] : **dix ~s** a hundred francs
4. ANAT & BOT sac
5. [pillage] sack, pillage ■ **mettre qqch à ~** to ransack *ou* to plunder *ou* to pillage sthg
6. *fam loc* **méfie-toi, c'est un ~ de nœuds, leur affaire** be careful, that business of theirs is a real hornets' nest ■ **~ à malices** bag of tricks ■ **c'est un ~ d'os** he's all skin and bones *ou* a bag of bones ■ **~ à puces** [chien] fleabag ■ **~ à vin** drunk, lush ■ **être fagoté** *ou* **ficelé comme un ~** to look like a feather bed tied in the middle ■ **ça y est, l'affaire est** *ou* **c'est dans le ~!** it's as good as done!, it's in the bag! ■ **dans le même ~ : ils sont tous à mettre dans le même ~** they're all as bad as each other ■ **attention, ne mettons pas le racisme et le sexisme dans le même ~!** let's not lump racism and sexism together!

saccade [sakad] *nf* jerk, jolt, (sudden) start ■ **après quelques ~s, le moteur s'arrêta** the engine jolted to a halt.
◆ **par saccades** *loc adv* jerkingly, joltingly, in fits and starts ■ **la voiture avançait par ~s** the car was lurching *ou* jerking forward ■ **elle parlait par ~s** she spoke haltingly *ou* in a disjointed manner.

saccadé, e [sakade] *adj* [pas] jerky ■ [mouvement] disjointed ■ [voix] halting.

saccage [sakaʒ] *nm* (wanton) destruction ■ **quel ~!** what a mess!

saccager [17] [sakaʒe] *vt* [maison, parc] to wreck, to wreak havoc in, to devastate ■ [matériel, livres] to wreck, to ruin ■ [cultures] to lay waste, to devastate ■ [ville] to lay waste, to sack ■ **le village a été saccagé par l'inondation/le tourbillon** the village was devastated by the flood/hurricane.

saccageur, euse [sakaʒœr, øz] *nm, f sout* vandal.

saccharin, e [sakarɛ̃, in] *adj* sugar *(modif)*.
◆ **saccharine** *nf* saccharin.

saccharose [sakaroz] *nm* saccharose.

sacco [sakɔ] *nm* beanbag.

SACEM, Sacem [sasɛm] (*abr de* **Société des auteurs, compositeurs et éditeurs de musique**) *npr f body responsible for collecting and distributing royalties*, ≃ Performing Rights Society *UK*, ≃ Copyright Royalty Tribunal *US*.

sacerdoce [sasɛrdɔs] *nm* **1.** RELIG priesthood **2.** [vie de dévouement] vocation *ou* calling *(requiring the utmost dedication)* ■ **la vie d'un militant est un ~** being a militant calls for great dedication.

sacerdotal, e, aux [sasɛrdɔtal, o] *adj* priestly, sacerdotal.

sachant *p prés* ▷ **savoir**.

sachet [saʃɛ] *nm* **1.** [petit sac] (small) bag **2.** [dose - de soupe, d'entremets] packet, sachet ; [- d'herbes aromatiques] sachet ■ **un ~ d'aspirine** a dose of aspirin ■ **un ~ de thé** a teabag ■ **du thé en ~s** teabags.

sachet-cuisson [saʃɛkyisɔ̃] (*pl* **sachets-cuissons**) *nm* : **en ~** boil-in-the-bag.

sacoche [sakɔʃ] *nf* **1.** [de facteur] bag, post bag *UK*, mail bag **2.** [de vélo] pannier **3.** [d'encaisseur] money bag **4.** *Belgique* handbag, purse *US*.

sac-poubelle [sakpubɛl] (*pl* **sacs-poubelle**) *nm* dustbin *UK ou* garbage can *US* liner, binbag.

sacquer [3] △ [sake] *vt* **1.** [employé] : **~ qqn** to give sb the sack *UK ou* ax *US*, to sack *UK ou* to can *US* sb ■ **se faire ~** to get the sack *UK ou* axe *US* **2.** [étudiant] to fail, to flunk ■ **elle va se faire ~ à l'examen** she'll get slaughtered in the exam **3.** *loc* **il ne peut pas te ~** he can't stand (the sight of) you.

sacral, e, aux [sakral, o] *adj* sacred.

sacralisation [sakralizasjɔ̃] *nf* **1.** [d'une chose profane] : **notre époque voit la ~ de la liberté individuelle** today, individual freedom is considered to be sacred **2.** MÉD sacralization.

sacraliser [3] [sakralize] *vt* to regard as sacred.

sacramentel, elle [sakramɑ̃tɛl] *adj* **1.** RELIG sacramental **2.** *fig & litt* [moment, paroles] ritual, sacramental *sout*.

sacre [sakr] *nm* **1.** [d'un empereur] coronation and anointment ■ [d'un évêque] consecration **2.** MUS : **'le Sacre du printemps'** *Stravinski* 'The Rite of Spring' **3.** ORNITH saker **4.** *Québec* [juron] expletive *(usually the name of a religious object)*.

sacré, e [sakre] *adj* **1.** RELIG [édifice] sacred, holy ■ [art, textes, musique] sacred, religious ■ [animal] sacred ■ **dans l'enceinte ~e** within the place of worship **2.** [devoir, promesse] sacred, sacrosanct ■ [droit] sacred, hallowed ■ **sa voiture, c'est ~!** her car is sacred! ■ **rien de plus ~ que sa promenade après le repas** his after-dinner walk is sacrosanct **3.** *fam (avant le n) fam* [en intensif] : **j'ai un ~ mal de dents!** I've got (an) awful toothache! ■ **j'ai un ~ boulot en ce moment!** I've got a hell of a lot of work on at the moment! ■ **c'est un ~ cuisinier, ton mari!** your husband is a damn good cook *ou* a terrific cook! ■ **~ Marcel, toujours le mot pour rire!** good old Marcel, never a dull moment with him! *pr & iron* ■ **~ farceur!** you old devil! ■ **t'as eu une ~e veine!** you were damn lucky! **4.**△ *(avant le n)* [satané] damned, blasted ■ **~ nom de nom!** damn and blast it! **5.** ANAT sacral.
◆ **sacré** *nm* : **le ~** the sacred.

sacrebleu [sakrəblø] *interj arch* zounds *arch*, hell's bells *hum*.

Sacré-Cœur [sakrekœr] *npr m* **1.** [édifice] : **le ~, la basilique du ~** Sacré-Cœur *(one of the landmarks of Paris, the church situated on the butte Montmartre)* **2.** [fête] : **le ~, la fête du ~** the (Feast of the) Sacred Heart.

sacredieu [sakrədjø] *arch* = **sacrebleu**.

sacrement [sakrəmɑ̃] *nm* sacrament ■ **les derniers ~s** the last rites.

sacrément [sakremɑ̃] *adv fam vieilli* **c'est ~ bon!** it's jolly *UK ou* damn good! ■ **il était ~ furieux!** he was awfully angry.

sacrer [3] [sakre] ◇ *vt* **1.** [empereur] to crown and anoint, to sacre *arch* ■ [évêque] to consecrate **2.** [nommer, instituer] to consecrate ■ **on l'a sacré meilleur acteur du siècle** he was acclaimed *ou* hailed as the greatest actor of the century.
◇ *vi vieilli* to swear, to curse.

sacrificateur, trice [sakrifikatœr, tris] *nm, f* ANTIQ sacrificer.

sacrifice [sakrifis] *nm* **1.** RELIG sacrifice, offering ■ **offrir qqch en ~ à Dieu** to offer sthg as a sacrifice to God, to sacrifice sthg to God ● **le ~ de la Croix** the Sacrifice of the Cross **2.** [effort, compromis] sacrifice ■ **faire des ~s/un ~** to make sacrifices/a sacrifice ■ **faire le ~ de sa vie pour qqn** to lay down *ou* to sacrifice one's life for sb.

◆ **au sacrifice de** *loc prép* at the cost of ■ **au ~ de mon bien-être personnel** to the detriment of *ou* at the cost of my personal well-being.

sacrifié, e [sakrifje] ◇ *adj* sacrificed, lost ■ **la génération ~e** the lost generation.
◇ *nm, f* (sacrificial) victim.

sacrifier [9] [sakrifje] *vt* **1.** RELIG to sacrifice **2.** [renoncer à - carrière, santé] to sacrifice ; [- loisirs] to give up *(sép)* ■ **~ sa vie** to make the ultimate sacrifice ■ **il a sacrifié sa vie pour sa patrie** he sacrificed *ou* laid down his life for his country ■ **~ ses amis à sa carrière** to sacrifice one's friends to one's career **3.** COMM [articles] to sell at rockbottom prices.
◆ **sacrifier à** *v+prép* **1.** RELIG to sacrifice to **2.** *sout* [se conformer à] to conform to ■ **~ à la mode** to conform to *ou* to go along with (the dictates of) fashion.
◆ **se sacrifier** *vpi* to sacrifice o.s. ■ **se ~ pour son pays/ses enfants** to sacrifice o.s. for one's country/children ■ **il reste des frites - allez, je me sacrifie!** *fam hum* there are some chips left over - oh well, I suppose I'll have to eat them myself!

sacrilège [sakrilɛʒ] ◇ *adj* sacrilegious.
◇ *nmf* profaner.
◇ *nm* **1.** RELIG sacrilege, profanation **2.** *fig* [crime] sacrilege, crime *fig* ■ **ce serait un ~ de retoucher la photo** it would be criminal *ou* a sacrilege to touch up the photograph.

sacripant [sakripɑ̃] *nm vieilli* scoundrel, rogue, scallywag.

sacristain [sakristɛ̃] *nm* **1.** RELIG [catholique] sacristan ■ [protestant] sexton **2.** CULIN *small puff pastry cake in the shape of a paper twist.*

sacristi [sakristi] *vieilli* = **sapristi.**

sacristie [sakristi] *nf* [d'une église - catholique] sacristy ; [- protestante] vestry.

sacro-iliaque [sakrɔiljak] (*pl* **sacro-iliaques**) *adj* sacroiliac.

sacro-saint, e [sakrɔsɛ̃, ɛ̃t] (*mpl* **sacro-saints**, *fpl* **sacro-saintes**) *adj* **1.** *vieilli* sacrosanct **2.** *fam* [intouchable] sacred, sacrosanct.

sacrum [sakrɔm] *nm* sacrum.

sadique [sadik] ◇ *adj* sadistic.
◇ *nmf* sadist.

sadiquement [sadikmɑ̃] *adv* sadistically.

sadisme [sadism] *nm* sadism.

sado [sado] *fam* ◇ *adj* sadistic ■ **il est un peu ~** he's a bit of a sadist.
◇ *nmf* sadist.

sadomaso [sadɔmazo] *fam* ◇ *adj* sadomasochistic.
◇ *nmf* sadomasochist.

sadomasochisme [sadɔmazɔʃism] *nm* sadomasochism.

sadomasochiste [sadɔmazɔʃist] ◇ *adj* sadomasochistic.
◇ *nmf* sadomasochist.

safari [safari] *nm* safari ■ **faire un ~** to go on (a) safari.

safari-photo [safarifɔto] (*pl* **safaris-photos**) *nm* photographic *ou* camera safari.

SAFER, Safer [safɛr] (*abr de* **Société d'aménagement foncier et d'établissement rural**) *npr f agency entitled to buy land and earmark it for agricultural use.*

safran [safrɑ̃] ◇ *nm* **1.** BOT & CULIN saffron **2.** NAUT rudder blade.
◇ *adj inv* saffron *(modif)*, saffron-yellow.

safrané, e [safrane] *adj* **1.** [teinte] saffron *(modif)*, saffron-yellow **2.** CULIN saffron-flavoured.

saga [saga] *nf* saga.

sagace [sagas] *adj* sharp, acute, sagacious *sout.*

sagacité [sagasite] *nf* sagacity *sout*, judiciousness, wisdom ■ **avec ~** shrewdly, judiciously.

sagaie [sagɛ] *nf* assagai, assegai.

sage [saʒ] ◇ *adj* **1.** [tranquille, obéissant] good, well-behaved ■ **sois ~, Paul!** [recommandation] be a good boy, Paul ; [remontrance] behave yourself, Paul ▶ **être ~ comme une image** to be as good as gold **2.** [sensé, raisonnable - personne] wise, sensible ; [- avis, conduite, décision] wise, sensible, reasonable ■ **le plus ~ serait de...** the most sensible thing (to do) would be... ■ **il serait plus ~ que tu prennes une assurance** it would be wiser for you to take out insurance **3.** [sobre - tenue] modest, sober ; [- vie sentimentale] quiet ; [- film, livre] restrained, understated ; [- goûts] tame, unadventurous *péj* **4.** *euphém* & *vieilli* [chaste] : **elle est ~** she's a good girl.
◇ *nmf* **1.** [personne] wise person **2.** POLIT : **une commission de ~s** an advisory committee.
◇ *nm* ANTIQ sage.

sage-femme [saʒfam] (*pl* **sages-femmes**) *nf* midwife ■ **homme ~** male midwife.

sagement [saʒmɑ̃] *adv* **1.** [tranquillement] quietly, nicely ■ **attends-moi ~ ici, Marie** wait for me here like a good girl, Marie **2.** [raisonnablement] wisely, sensibly **3.** [pudiquement] : **elle baissa ~ les yeux** she modestly lowered her eyes.

sagesse [saʒɛs] *nf* **1.** [discernement - d'une personne] good sense, insight, wisdom ; [- d'une décision, d'une suggestion] good sense, wisdom ■ **elle n'a pas eu la ~ d'attendre** she wasn't sensible enough *ou* didn't have the good sense to wait ■ **agir avec ~** to act wisely *ou* sensibly ▶ **la ~ des nations** popular wisdom **2.** [obéissance] good behaviour ■ **elle n'a pas été d'une grande ~ aujourd'hui!** she wasn't particularly well behaved today! **3.** [sobriété - d'une toilette, d'un livre] soberness, tameness ; [- d'une vie sentimentale] quietness **4.** *euphém* [chasteté] proper behaviour.

Sagittaire [saʒitɛr] *npr m* **1.** ASTRON Sagittarius **2.** ASTROL Sagittarius ■ **elle est ~** she's Sagittarius *ou* a Sagittarian.

sagouin, e [sagwɛ̃, in] *nm, f fam* [personne - malpropre] filthy pig ; [- incompétente] slob ■ **faire qqch comme un ~** to make a complete mess of sthg.
◆ **sagouin** *nm* ZOOL sagoin, marmoset.

Sahara [saara] *npr m* : **le (désert du) ~** the Sahara (desert) ■ **au ~** in the Sahara ■ **le ~ occidental** the Western Sahara.

saharien, enne [saarjɛ̃, ɛn] *adj* Saharan.
◆ **Saharien, enne** *nm, f* Saharan.
◆ **saharienne** *nf* [vêtement] safari jacket.

Sahel [saɛl] *npr m* : **le ~** the Sahel.

sahélien, enne [saeljɛ̃, ɛn] *adj* Sahelian.
◆ **Sahélien, enne** *nmf* Sahelian.

saignant, e [sɛɲɑ̃, ɑ̃t] *adj* **1.** CULIN [steak] rare **2.** [blessure] bleeding.

saignée [seɲe] *nf* **1.** MÉD bleeding *(U)*, bloodletting *(U)* ■ **faire une ~ à qqn** to bleed sb, to let sb's blood **2.** *sout* [pertes humaines] : **la terrible ~ de la Première Guerre mondiale** the terrible slaughter of the First World War **3.** ANAT : **à la ~ du bras** at the crook of the arm **4.** [dépenses] drain ■ **des ~s dans le budget** drains on the budget **5.** [entaille] notch **6.** TRAV PUB (surface) drainage channel.

saignement [sɛɲmɑ̃] *nm* bleeding ■ **~ de nez** nosebleed.

saigner [4] [seɲe] ◇ *vi* [plaie, blessé] to bleed ■ **je saigne du nez** my nose is bleeding, I've got a nosebleed ▶ **~ comme un bœuf** to bleed profusely.
◇ *vt* **1.** [malade, animal] to bleed **2.** [faire payer - contribuable] to bleed, to fleece ■ [épuiser - pays] to drain the resources of, to drain *ou* to suck the lifeblood from ▶ **~ qqn à blanc** to bleed sb dry, to clean sb out.
◆ **se saigner** *vp (emploi réfléchi)* ▶ **se ~ aux quatre veines pour qqn** to bleed o.s. dry for sb.

saillant, e [sajɑ̃, ɑ̃t] *adj* **1.** [en relief - veines] prominent ; [- os, tendon, menton] protruding ; [- muscle, yeux] bulging, protruding ; [- rocher] protruding ; [- corniche] projecting ■ **avoir les pommettes ~es** to have prominent *ou* high cheekbones **2.** [remarquable - trait, fait] salient, outstanding.
◆ **saillant** *nm* **1.** [de fortification] salient **2.** [angle] salient angle.

saillie [saji] *nf* **1.** [d'un mur, d'une montagne] ledge ▪ [d'un os] protuberance ▪ **faire ~, être en ~** [balcon, roche] to jut out, to project **2.** CONSTR projection **3.** *litt* [trait d'esprit] sally, witticism, flash of wit **4.** ZOOL covering, serving.

saillir[1] [32] [sajir] *vt* ZOOL to cover, to serve.

saillir[2] [50] [sajir] *vi* [rocher, poutre] to project, to jut out ▪ [menton] to protrude ▪ [os] to protrude, to stick out ▪ [yeux] to bulge, to protrude ▪ [muscle, veine] to stand out, to bulge ▪ **l'effort faisait ~ les veines de son cou** the veins on his neck were swelling *ou* bulging with the strain.

sain, e [sɛ̃, sɛn] *adj* **1.** [robuste - enfant] healthy, robust ; [- cheveux, peau] healthy ; [- dent] sound, healthy ▪ **être ~ d'esprit** to be sane ▪ **~ de corps et d'esprit** sound in mind and body **2.** [en bon état - charpente, fondations, structure] sound ; [- situation financière, entreprise, gestion] sound, healthy ; [- viande] good **3.** [salutaire - alimentation, mode de vie] wholesome, healthy ; [- air, climat] healthy, invigorating ▪ **tu ne devrais pas rester enfermé toute la journée, ce n'est pas ~** you shouldn't stay in all day long, it's not good for you *ou* it's unhealthy **4.** [irréprochable - opinion] sane, sound ; [- lectures] wholesome ▪ **son rapport avec sa fille n'a jamais été très ~** her relationship with her daughter was never very healthy **5.** NAUT safe.

◆ **sain et sauf, saine et sauve** *loc adj* safe and sound, unhurt, unharmed ▪ **j'en suis sorti ~ et sauf** I escaped unharmed *ou* without a scratch.

saindoux [sɛ̃du] *nm* lard.

sainement [sɛnmɑ̃] *adv* **1.** [hygiéniquement] healthily ▪ **se nourrir ~** to eat wholesome *ou* healthy food **2.** [sagement] soundly.

saint, e [sɛ̃, sɛ̃t] <> *adj* **1.** *(après le n)* [sacré - lieu, livre, image, guerre] holy ▪ **la semaine ~e** Holy Week ▪ *(avant le n)* **la Sainte Famille** the Holy Family ▪ **les Saintes Écritures** the Scriptures ▪ **leur ~ patron** their patron saint ▪ **le ~ sacrement** the sacrament of Holy Communion, the Eucharist ▪ **le ~ suaire (de Turin)** the Turin Shroud **2.** [canonisé] Saint ▪ **~ Pierre/Paul** Saint Peter/Paul **3.** *(avant le n)* [exemplaire] holy ▪ **le curé est un ~ homme** the priest is a holy man ▪ **sa mère était une ~e femme** his mother was a real saint **4.** [en intensif] : **toute la ~e journée** the whole blessed day ▪ **j'ai une ~e horreur des araignées** I have a real horror of spiders.
<> *nm, f* **1.** RELIG saint ▪ **le ~ du jour** the Saint of the day ➊ **les ~s de glace** *the three Saints (Mamert, Gervase and Pancras) on whose name days (11th, 12th and 13th May) late frosts often occur according to tradition* ▪ **les ~s du dernier jour** the Latter-Day Saints, the Mormons ▪ **il lasserait la patience d'un ~** he'd try the patience of a saint ▪ **je ne sais (plus) à quel ~ me vouer** I don't know which way to turn (any more) ▪ **comme on connaît ses ~s on les honore** *prov* treat each person according to *ou* on his merits **2.** ART *(statue or effigy of a) saint* **3.** *fig* saint.

◆ **saint** *nm* : **le ~ des ~s** RELIG the Holy of Holies ; *fig* the inner sanctum.

◆ **Saint, e** *adj* **1.** RELIG : **la Sainte Vierge** the Blessed Virgin, the Virgin Mary **2.** *(avec trait d'union)* [dans des noms de lieux, de fêtes] : **c'est la Saint-Marc aujourd'hui** it's Saint Mark's day today, it's the feast of Saint Mark today.

Saint-Barthélemy [sɛ̃bartelemi] <> *npr f* : **(le massacre de) la ~** the Saint Bartholomew's Day Massacre.
<> *npr* GÉOGR Saint Bart's.

saint-bernard [sɛ̃bɛrnar] *nm inv* **1.** ZOOL Saint Bernard (dog) **2.** *hum* [personne généreuse] : **c'est un vrai ~** he's a good Samaritan.

saint-cyrien, enne [sɛ̃sirjɛ̃, ɛn] (*mpl* **saint-cyriens**, *fpl* **saint-cyriennes**) *nm, f* [élève] *cadet training at the Saint-Cyr military academy.*

Saint-Domingue [sɛ̃dɔmɛ̃g] *npr* Santo Domingo.

Sainte-Catherine [sɛ̃tkatrin] *npr* : **coiffer ~** *to be 25 and still unmarried on Saint Catherine's Day (25th November).*

Sainte-Chapelle [sɛ̃tʃapɛl] *npr f* : **la ~** *thirteenth-century church within the Palais de Justice on the île de la Cité.*

Sainte-Hélène [sɛ̃telɛn] *npr* St Helena.

saintement [sɛ̃tmɑ̃] *adv* : **vivre ~** to lead a saintly life.

Sainte-Mère-Église [sɛ̃tmɛregliz] *npr the first place to experience the Normandy landings when American parachute troops landed there on the night of 5-6 June, 1944.*

saint-émilion [sɛ̃temiljɔ̃] *nm inv* Saint Emilion (wine).

sainte-nitouche [sɛ̃tnituʃ] (*pl* **saintes-nitouches**) *nf péj* hypocrite ▪ **avec ses airs de ~** looking as if butter wouldn't melt in her mouth.

Saintes [sɛ̃t] *npr fpl* : **les (îles des) ~** the Îles des Saintes, *voir aussi* **île**.

Saint-Esprit [sɛ̃tɛspri] *npr m* : **le ~** the Holy Spirit *ou* Ghost.

sainteté [sɛ̃tte] *nf* **1.** [d'une personne] saintliness, godliness ▪ [d'une action, d'une vie] saintliness ▪ [d'un édifice, des Écritures, de la Vierge] holiness, sanctity ▪ [du mariage] sanctity **2.** [titre] : **Sa/Votre Sainteté** His/Your Holiness.

Sainte-Trinité [sɛttrinite] *npr f* RELIG : **la ~** the Holy Trinity.

saint-frusquin [sɛ̃fryskɛ̃] *nm inv* *fam* **elle a débarqué hier avec tout son ~** she turned up yesterday with all her worldly goods ▪ **j'ai jeté la vaisselle, les meubles et tout le ~** I've thrown away the plates, the furniture, the whole lot *ou* caboodle.

Saint-Germain-des-Prés [sɛ̃ʒɛrmɛ̃depre] *npr* Saint-Germain-des-Prés *(area of Paris).*

SAINT-GERMAIN-DES-PRÉS

This is the literary centre of Paris near the oldest church in the city. Situated on the left bank of the Seine, it is famous for its bookshops, publishing houses, literary cafés and nightclubs. Its heyday was in the years following the Second World War, when Sartre and other existentialist intellectuals met regularly in its cafés.

saint-glinglin [sɛ̃glɛ̃glɛ̃] ◆ **à la saint-glinglin** *loc adv fam* : **je t'écrirai – c'est ça, à la ~!** I'll write to you – and pigs might fly! ▪ **elle te remboursera à la ~** she'll never pay you back in a month of Sundays ▪ **je ne vais pas attendre jusqu'à la ~!** I'm not hanging around all day!

Saint-Graal [sɛ̃gral] = **Graal**.

Saint-Guy [sɛ̃gi] *npr* : **danse de ~** Saint Vitus's dance.

saint-honoré [sɛ̃tɔnɔre] *nm inv* Saint Honoré gateau.

Saint-Jacques [sɛ̃ʒak] *npr* : **coquille ~** scallop.

Saint-Jacques-de-Compostelle [sɛ̃ʒakdəkɔ̃pɔstɛl] *npr* Santiago de Compostela.

Saint-Jean [sɛ̃ʒɑ̃] *npr f* : **la ~** Midsummer's Day.

Saint-Laurent [sɛ̃lɔrɑ̃] *npr m* : **le ~** [fleuve] the St Lawrence (River) ▪ **le (golfe du) ~** the St Lawrence Seaway.

saint-marcellin [sɛ̃marsəlɛ̃] *nm inv small round cheese produced in the Lyon area.*

Saint-Marin [sɛ̃marɛ̃] *npr* San Marino.

saint-nectaire [sɛ̃nɛktɛr] *nm inv* Saint Nectaire cheese.

Saint-Nicolas [sɛ̃nikɔla] *npr f* : **la ~** Saint Nicholas' Day *(December 6th, celebrated especially in Belgium and the north of France).*

saintpaulia [sɛ̃polja] *nm* African violet, saintpaulia.

Saint-Père [sɛ̃pɛr] *nm* Holy Father.

Saint-Pétersbourg [sɛ̃petɛrsbur] *npr* St Petersburg.

saint-pierre [sɛ̃pjɛr] *nm inv* John Dory, dory.

Saint-Pierre [sɛ̃pjɛr] *npr* : **la basilique ~** Saint Peter's Basilica.

Saint-Pierre-et-Miquelon [sɛ̃pjɛremiklɔ̃] *npr* St Pierre and Miquelon.

Saint-Siège [sɛ̃sjɛʒ] *npr m* : **le ~** the Holy See.

saint-simonien, enne [sɛ̃simɔnjɛ̃, ɛn] (*mpl* **saint-simoniens**, *fpl* **saint-simoniennes**) *nm, f* & *adj* Saint-Simonian.

Saint-Sylvestre [sɛ̃silvɛstr] *npr f* : **la ~** *New Year's Eve* ■ **le réveillon de la ~** *traditional French New Year's Eve celebration.*

Saint-Valentin [sɛ̃valɑ̃tɛ̃] *npr f* : **la ~** Saint Valentine's Day.

saisi, e [sezi] *nm, f* distrainee.
◆ **saisie** *nf* **1.** INFORM : **~e de données** keyboarding of data **2.** IMPR [clavetage] keyboarding **3.** DR [d'une propriété, d'un bien mobilier] seizure, distraint, distress ■ [de produits d'une infraction] seizure, confiscation ■ [d'un bien pour non-paiement des traites] repossession ■ **~e immobilière** seizure of property ■ **~e mobilière** seizure *ou* distraint of goods ■ **faire** *ou* **opérer une ~e** to levy a distress.

saisie-arrêt [seziarɛ] (*pl* **saisies-arrêts**) *nf* garnishment.

saisie-exécution [seziɛgzekysjɔ̃] (*pl* **saisies-exécutions**) *nf* distraint (for an auction).

saisine [sezin] *nf* **1.** DR [d'un héritier] seisin ■ **~ d'un tribunal** referral (of a case) to a court **2.** NAUT lashing.

saisir [32] [sezir] *vt* **1.** [avec brusquerie] to grab (hold of), to seize, to grasp ■ [pour porter, déplacer] to catch (hold of), to take hold of, to grip ■ [pour s'approprier] to snatch ■ **~ qqch au vol** to catch sthg in mid-air ■ **~ qqn aux épaules** to grab *ou* to grip sb by the shoulders ■ **il m'a saisi par la manche** he grabbed me by the sleeve ■ **elle saisit ma main** she gripped my hand **2.** [mettre à profit] to seize, to grab ■ **~ l'occasion de faire qqch** to seize *ou* to grasp the opportunity to do sthg ■ **je n'ai pas su ~ ma chance** I missed (out on) my chance, I didn't seize the opportunity **3.** [envahir - suj: colère, terreur, dégoût] to take hold of, to seize, to grip ■ **elle a été saisie d'un malaise, un malaise l'a saisie** she suddenly felt faint ■ **le froid me saisit** the cold hit me **4.** [impressionner] to strike, to stun **5.** [percevoir - bribes de conversation, mot] to catch, to get **6.** [comprendre - explications, sens d'une phrase] to understand, to get, to grasp **7.** DR [débiteur, biens] to seize, to levy distress (upon) ■ [articles prohibés] to seize, to confiscate ■ [tribunal] to submit *ou* to refer a case to ■ **la justice, saisie de l'affaire, annonce que...** the judicial authorities, apprised of the case, have indicated that... ■ **la juridiction compétente a été saisie** the case was referred to the appropriate jurisdiction **8.** INFORM to capture ■ **~ des données (sur clavier)** to keyboard data **9.** CULIN to seal, to sear.
◆ **se saisir de** *vp+prép* **1.** [prendre] to grab (hold of), to grip, to seize **2.** *sout* [étudier] to examine ■ **le conseil doit se ~ du dossier** the council will put the file on its agenda.

saisissable [sezisabl] *adj* **1.** DR distrainable **2.** *sout* [perceptible] perceptible.

saisissant, e [sezisɑ̃, ɑ̃t] *adj* **1.** [vif - froid] biting, piercing **2.** [surprenant - ressemblance] striking, startling ; [- récit, spectacle] gripping ; [- contraste] startling **3.** DR [qui opère ou fait opérer une saisie] seizing.

saisissement [sezismɑ̃] *nm* **1.** [surprise] astonishment, amazement ■ **je suis resté muet de ~ devant tant de beauté** I was dumbfounded by so much beauty **2.** [sensation de froid] sudden chill.

saison [sɛzɔ̃] *nf* **1.** [période de l'année] season ■ **en cette ~** at this time of (the) year ■ **en toutes ~s** all year round ▶ **la belle ~** [printemps] the spring months ; [été] the summer months ■ **la mauvaise ~, la ~ froide** the winter months ■ **à la belle/mauvaise ~** when the weather turns warm/cold ■ **la ~ sèche** the dry season ■ **la ~ des pluies** the rainy season, the rains **2.** [époque pour certains travaux, certains produits] : **ce n'est pas encore la ~ des aubergines** aubergines aren't in season yet ■ **la ~ des cerises** the cherry season ■ **la ~ des vendanges** grape-harvesting time ▶ **la ~ des amours** the mating season ■ **la ~ de la chasse** [à courre] the hunting season ; [à tir] the shooting season **3.** [temps d'activité périodique] season ■ **la ~ théâtrale** the theatre season ■ **la ~ touristique** the tourist season ■ **une ~ sportive** a season ▮ COMM season ▶ **en basse** *ou* **morte ~** off season ■ **en haute ~** during the high season ■ **la pleine ~** the busy season ■ **en pleine ~** at the height of the season **4.** [cure] season *sout* **5.** *litt* [âge de la vie] age, time of life.
◆ **de saison** *loc adj* **1.** [adapté à la saison] seasonal ■ **ce n'est pas un temps de ~** this weather's unusual for the time of the year ■ **être de ~** [fruit] to be in season ; [vêtement] to be seasonable **2.** *sout* [opportun] timely ■ **tes critiques ne sont pas de ~** your criticism is out of place.

saisonnier, ère [sɛzɔnje, ɛr] *adj* seasonal, seasonable ■ **nous avons un temps bien ~** this is just the (right) sort of weather for the time of year.
◆ **saisonnier** *nm* [employé] seasonal worker ■ **les ~s** seasonal staff.

sait *etc v* ▷ **savoir**.

saké [sake] *nm* sake.

salace [salas] *adj* [histoire, allusion] salacious *sout*, lewd, lascivious *sout* ■ [individu] salacious, lecherous, lewd.

salacité [salasite] *nf litt* salaciousness *sout*, lewdness.

salade [salad] *nf* **1.** BOT lettuce **2.** CULIN salad ■ **~ de concombre/haricots** cucumber/bean salad ■ **champignons en ~** mushroom salad ▶ **~ composée** mixed salad ■ **~ de fruits** fruit salad ■ **~ niçoise** salade niçoise, niçoise salad **3.** *fam* [embrouillamini] muddle, tangle.
◆ **salades** *nfpl fam* [mensonges] tall stories, fibs ■ **dis-moi tout, et ne me raconte pas de ~s!** tell me everything and spare me the fairy tales!

saladier [saladje] *nm* [récipient] (salad) bowl.

salage [salaʒ] *nm* CULIN & TRAV PUB salting.

salaire [salɛr] *nm* **1.** ÉCON [gén] pay ■ [d'un ouvrier] wages, pay ■ [d'un cadre] salary ■ **un ~ de famine** starvation wages ▶ **~ à la tâche** *ou* **aux pièces** pay for piece work, piece rate ■ **~ de base** basic salary *ou* pay ■ **~ brut** gross pay ■ **~ d'embauche** starting salary ■ **~ horaire** hourly wage ■ **~ mensuel** monthly pay ■ **~ minimum interprofessionnel de croissance = SMIC** ■ **~ net** take-home pay, net salary ■ **à ~ unique** single-income ■ **je n'ai pas droit au ~ unique** I'm not entitled to supplementary benefit *UK ou* the welfare benefit *US* for single-income families **2.** *fig* [dédommagement] reward ■ [punition] retribution ■ **et pour tout ~ il reçut quelques coups** his only reward was a beating.

salaison [salɛzɔ̃] *nf* [opération] salting.
◆ **salaisons** *nfpl* [gén] salted foods ■ [viande, charcuterie] salt *ou* salted meat.

salamalecs [salamalɛk] *nmpl fam* **faire des ~ à qqn** to kowtow to sb, to bow and scrape before sb ■ **épargnez-moi tous ces ~** spare me the soft soap.

salamandre [salamɑ̃dr] *nf* ZOOL salamander.

salami [salami] *nm* salami.

salant [salɑ̃] ◇ *adj m* salt *(modif)* ■ **puits ~** brine well.
◇ *nm* salt marsh.

salarial, e, aux [salarjal, o] *adj* [politique, revendications] pay *(modif)*, wage *(modif)*, salary *(modif)* ■ **revenus salariaux** income from salaries.

salariat [salarja] *nm* **1.** [personnes] wage earners **2.** [mode de rémunération - à la semaine] (weekly) wages ; [- au mois] (monthly) salary **3.** [état] : **le ~ ne lui convient pas** being an employee doesn't suit her.

salarié, e [salarje] ◇ *adj* **1.** [au mois] salaried ■ [à la semaine] wage-earning ■ **êtes-vous ~?** [non chômeur] are you in paid employment? ; [non libéral] are you paid a salary? **2.** [travail] paid ■ [emploi, poste] salaried.
◇ *nm, f* [au mois] salaried employee ■ [à la semaine] wage-earner ■ **les ~s** the employees.

salarier [9] [salarje] *vt* to put on one's salaried staff ■ **je voudrais me faire ~** I'd like to get a permanent (salaried) job.

salaud △ [salo] ◇ *nm* bastard△, swine ■ **je pars à Tahiti – ben mon ~!** I'm off to Tahiti – you lucky sod△ *UK ou* bastard!
◇ *adj m* : **il est ~** he's a bastard△ *ou* a swine.

sale [sal] ◇ *adj* **1.** [malpropre - visage] dirty, filthy ; [- eau] dirty, murky ; [- mur] dirty, grimy ■ **blanc ~** dirty white ■ **oh que tu es ~!** [à un enfant] you mucky pup! ▶ **il est ~ comme un cochon** *ou* **peigne** *ou* **porc** he's filthy dirty **2.** [salissant] dirty **3.** [obscène] filthy, dirty **4.** *fam (avant le n) fam* [mauvais,

désagréable] nasty ■ **c'est une ~ affaire** it's a nasty business ■ **elle a un ~ caractère** she has a filthy *ou* rotten temper ■ **quel ~ temps!** what rotten *ou* foul weather! ■ **il m'a joué un ~ tour** he played a dirty trick on me ➲ **~ bête** [insecte] nasty creature, creepy crawly *hum* ; [personne] nasty character *ou* piece of work *UK* ■ **avoir une ~ tête** *ou* **gueule**△ [à faire peur] to look evil, to be nasty-looking ■ **il a une ~ tête ce matin** [malade] he looks under the weather *ou UK* off-colour this morning ; [renfrogné] he's got a face like a thundercloud this morning ■ **quand je vais lui dire, il va faire une ~ tête** he's not going to be very pleased when I tell him.
◇ *nmf* [personne] dirty person.
◇ *nm* : **ton pantalon est au ~** your trousers are with the dirty washing.

salé, e [sale] *adj* **1.** CULIN [beurre, cacahuètes, gâteaux secs] salted ■ [non sucré - mets] savoury ; [- goût] salty ■ [conservé dans le sel - morue, porc] salt *(modif)*, salted **2.** [lac] salt *(modif)* ■ **eau ~e** salt water **3.** *fam* [exagéré - condamnation] stiff, heavy ; [- addition] steep, stiff **4.** *fam* [osé - histoire, plaisanterie] spicy, risqué.
◆ **salé** ◇ *nm* **1.** [non sucré] : **le ~** savoury food ; [avec adjonction de sel] salt *ou* salty food **2.** CULIN salt pork ■ **petit ~** salted (flank end of) belly pork.
◇ *adv* : **je ne mange pas ~** I don't like too much salt in my food ■ **je mange ~** I like my food well salted.

salement [salmɑ̃] *adv* **1.** [malproprement] dirtily ■ **qu'il mange ~!** he's such a messy eater! **2.** △ [en intensif] : **je suis ~ embêté** I'm in a hell of a mess ■ **ça m'a fait ~ mal** it hurt like hell, it was damn *ou UK* bloody △ painful.

saler [3] [sale] *vt* **1.** CULIN [assaisonner] to salt, to add salt to ■ [en saumure] to pickle, to salt (down) ■ *(en usage absolu)* **je ne sale presque pas** I hardly use any salt **2.** TRAV PUB [chaussée] to salt **3.** *fam* [inculpé] to throw the book at **4.** *fam* [facture] to inflate ■ **c'était bon, mais ils ont salé l'addition!** it was good but the bill was a bit steep!

saleté [salte] *nf* **1.** [manque de propreté] dirtiness ■ **les rues sont d'une ~ incroyable** the streets are incredibly dirty *ou* filthy
2. [tache, crasse] speck *ou* piece of dirt ■ **tu as une ~ sur ta veste** you've got some dirt on your jacket ■ **il y a des ~s qui bloquent le tuyau** the pipe is blocked up with muck ■ **faire des ~s** to make a mess ■ **ne rentre pas avec tes bottes, tu vas faire des ~s** don't come in with your boots on, you'll get dirt everywhere
3. *fam* [chose de mauvaise qualité] rubbish *UK*, trash *US* ■ **c'est de la ~** it's rubbish ■ **à la récréation, ils ne mangent que des ~s** all they eat at break is junk food
4. [chose nuisible] foul thing, nuisance ■ **j'ai attrapé cette ~ à la piscine** I caught this blasted thing at the swimming pool ■ **je dois prendre cette ~ avant chaque repas!** I have to take this foul stuff before every meal!
5.△ [en injure] : **~!** [à un homme] swine!, bastard!△ ; [à une femme] bitch!△, cow!△ *UK* ■ **~ de chien!** damned dog! ■ **quelle ~ de temps!** what foul *ou* lousy weather!
6. [calomnie] (piece of) dirt ■ **tu as encore raconté des ~s sur mon compte** you've been spreading filthy rumours about me again
7. [acte] dirty *ou* filthy trick ■ **il m'a fait une ~** he played a dirty trick on me.
◆ **saletés** *nfpl* [grossièretés] dirt, filth, smut ■ **raconter des ~s** to say dirty things ‖ *euphém* **les chiens font leurs ~s dans les jardins publics** dogs do their business in the parks.

saleur, euse [salœr, øz] *nm, f* CULIN salter.
◆ **saleuse** *nf* TRAV PUB salt spreader.

salicylique [salisilik] *adj* salicylic.

salière [saljɛr] *nf* **1.** [petit bol] saltcellar ■ [avec trous] salt cellar, salt shaker *US* ■ [à couvercle] salt box, salt pot **2.** *fam* [d'une personne maigre] saltcellar.

salifère [salifɛr] *adj* saliferous.

salification [salifikasjɔ̃] *nf* salification.

salifier [9] [salifje] *vt* to salify, to form into a salt.

saligaud, e△ [saligo, od] *nm, f* **1.** [homme méprisable] swine ■ [femme méprisable] cow△ *UK*, bitch△ *US* **2.** *vieilli* [homme sale] filthy pig△ ■ [femme sale] slut.

salin, e [salɛ̃, in] *adj* saline.
◆ **salin** *nm* **1.** GÉOGR salt marsh **2.** CHIM saline.
◆ **saline** *nf* **1.** [établissement] saltworks, saltpan **2.** [marais] salt marsh.

salinier, ère [salinje, ɛr] ◇ *adj* salt *(modif)*, salt-producing.
◇ *nm, f* salt producer.

salinité [salinite] *nf* **1.** [degré] (degree of) salinity **2.** [fait d'être salé] salinity.

salique [salik] *adj* salic.

salir [32] [salir] *vt* **1.** [eau, surface] to (make) dirty ■ [vêtements] to (make) dirty, to mess up *(sép)*, to soil **2.** [honneur, amitié] to besmirch *litt* ■ [réputation] to smear, to besmirch, to sully *litt*.
◆ **se salir** ◇ *vp (emploi réfléchi)* to get dirty, to dirty o.s. ■ *fig* to lose one's reputation ■ **se ~ les mains** *pr* & *fig* to get one's hands dirty.
◇ *vpi* to get soiled *ou* dirty ■ **ne prends pas un manteau beige, ça se salit vite** don't buy a beige coat, it shows the dirt *ou* it gets dirty very quickly.

salissant, e [salisɑ̃, ɑ̃t] *adj* **1.** [qui se salit] : **c'est une teinte ~e** this shade shows the dirt ■ **c'est très ~** [couleur, vêtement] it marks easily **2.** [qui salit - travail] dirty, messy.

salissure [salisyr] *nf* [restée en surface] speck of dirt, piece of grime ■ [ayant pénétré le tissu] dirty mark, stain.

salivaire [salivɛr] *adj* salivary.

salivation [salivasjɔ̃] *nf* salivation.

salive [saliv] *nf* **1.** PHYSIOL saliva, spit **2.** *fam loc* **n'usez pas** *ou* **ne gaspillez pas** *ou* **épargnez votre ~** save *ou* don't waste your breath ■ **avaler** *ou* **ravaler sa ~** [se taire] to keep quiet.

saliver [3] [salive] *vi* **1.** PHYSIOL to salivate **2.** [avoir l'eau à la bouche] : **le menu me fait ~** the menu makes my mouth water ■ **le chien salivait devant sa pâtée** the dog was drooling *ou* dribbling at the sight of his food **3.** *fam* [d'envie] to drool ■ **il salivait devant les voitures de sport** he was drooling over the sports cars ■ **il me fait ~ en me parlant de ses vacances aux Caraïbes** he makes me green with envy talking about his holidays in the Caribbean.

salle [sal] *nf* **1.** [dans une habitation privée] room ■ **~ de bains** [lieu] bathroom ; [mobilier] bathroom suite ■ **~ d'eau** shower room ■ **~ de jeu** [d'une maison] playroom *UK*, rumpus room *US* ; [d'un casino] gaming room ■ **~ à manger** [lieu] dining room ; [mobilier] dining room suite ■ **~ de séjour** living room **2.** [dans un édifice public] hall, room ■ [dans un café] room ■ [dans un musée] room, gallery ■ **~ d'armes** MIL arms room ; ESCRIME fencing hall ■ **~ d'attente** waiting room ■ **~ d'audience** courtroom ■ **~ de bal** ballroom ■ **~ des banquets** banqueting hall ■ **~ de classe** classroom ■ **~ des coffres** strongroom ■ **~ de concert** concert hall, auditorium ■ **~ de conférences** UNIV lecture theatre *UK ou* hall *US* ; [pour colloques] conference room ■ **~ d'embarquement** departure lounge ■ **~ d'études** prep room *UK*, study hall *US* ■ **~ des fêtes** village hall ■ **~ de garde** (hospital) staffroom ■ **~ d'hôpital, ~ commune** *vieilli* hospital ward ■ **~ d'opération** [à l'hôpital] operating theatre *UK ou* room *US* ; MIL operations room ■ **~ paroissiale** church hall ■ **~ des pas perdus** RAIL (station) concourse ; [au tribunal] waiting room *ou* hall ■ **~ des professeurs** ÉDUC (school) staffroom ; UNIV senior common room *UK*, professors' lounge *US* ■ **~ de projection** projection room ■ **~ de réanimation** resuscitation unit ■ **~ de rédaction** [d'un journal] newsroom ■ **~ de restaurant** (restaurant) dining room ■ **~ de réception** [dans un hôtel] function room ; [dans un palais] stateroom ■ **~ de réunion** assembly room ■ **~ de spectacle** auditorium ■ **~ de travail** labour ward ■ **~ du trône** stateroom, throne room ■ **~ des tortures** torture chamber ■ **~ des ventes** auction room *UK*, auction gallery *US* **3.** CINÉ & THÉÂTRE [lieu] theatre, auditorium ■ [spectateurs] audience ■ **faire ~ comble** to pack the house ■ **le cinéma a cinq ~s** it's a five-screen cinema *UK ou* movie theater *US* ■ **sa dernière production sort en ~ en septembre** her latest production will be released *ou* out in September ■ **dans les ~s d'art et d'essai** *ou* **les petites ~s** in art cinemas *UK ou* movie theaters *US* ➲ **dans les ~s obscures** in the cinemas *UK ou* movie theaters *US* **4.** SPORT : **athlétisme en ~** indoor athletics ■ **jouer en ~** to play indoors.

salmigondis [salmigɔ̃di] *nm* **1.** *sout* [embrouillamini] mishmash, hotchpotch *UK*, hodgepodge *US* **2.** *arch* & CULIN hotchpotch *UK*, hodgepodge *US*.

salmis [salmi] *nm* salmi, salmis ■ **~ de pintade, pintades en ~** salmi of guinea fowl.

salmonelle [salmɔnɛl] *nf* salmonella.

salmonellose [salmɔneloz] *nf* salmonellosis.

saloir [salwar] *nm* **1.** [récipient] salting *ou* brine tub **2.** [pièce] salting room.

Salomé [salɔme] *npr* Salome.

Salomon [salɔmɔ̃] ◇ *npr* BIBLE (King) Solomon.
◇ *npr fpl* GÉOGR : **les (îles) ~** the Solomon Islands, *voir aussi* **île**.

salon [salɔ̃] *nm* **1.** [chez un particulier - pièce] living *ou* sitting room, lounge *UK* ; [- meubles] living room suite ■ **~ en cuir** leather suite ◗ **~ de jardin** garden set ■ **~ de réception** reception room **2.** [dans un hôtel] lounge ■ [pour réceptions, fêtes] function room ■ [d'un paquebot] saloon, lounge **3.** [boutique] : **~ de beauté** beauty parlour *ou* salon ■ **~ de coiffure** hairdressing salon ■ **~ de thé** tearoom ■ **~ d'essayage** fitting room, changing room **4.** COMM [exposition] : **Salon des arts ménagers** ≃ Ideal Home Exhibition *UK* ■ ≃ home crafts exhibition *ou* show *US* ■ **Salon de l'automobile** Motor *UK ou* Car *ou* Automobile *US* Show ■ **Salon du livre** *annual book fair in Paris* ■ **Salon nautique** *ou* **de la navigation** Boat Show **5.** ART salon **6.** LITTÉR salon ■ **tenir ~** to hold a salon ■ **alors, mesdemoiselles, on fait** *ou* **tient ~?** *fig* busy discussing important matters, are we, young ladies? ■ **conversation de ~** idle chatter.

saloon [salun] *nm* saloon *(bar in the Wild West)*.

salopard△ [salɔpar] *nm* bastard△, swine△, sod△ *UK*.

salope▲ [salɔp] ◇ *nf* **1.** [femme de mauvaise vie] slut, slag △ *UK* **2.** [femme méprisable] bitch△, cow△ *UK*.
◇ *adj f* : **tu as été ~ avec moi** you were a bitch△ to me.

saloper [3] △ [salɔpe] *vt* **1.** [réparation, travail] to make a mess *ou* hash of, to cock up△ *UK (sép)* **2.** [souiller - vêtements, mur] to mess up *(sép)*.

saloperie△ [salɔpri] *nf* **1.** [camelote] rubbish *UK*, trash *US* ■ **c'est de la ~, ces ouvre-boîtes** these can-openers are absolute rubbish *ou* trash△ ■ **toutes ces ~s vous détraquent l'estomac** all this rubbish *ou* junk food upsets your stomach **2.** [chose désagréable, nuisible] : **c'est de la ~ à poser, ce papier peint** this wallpaper's a real pain to put on ■ **quelles ~s, ces taupes!** these moles are a damn nuisance! ■ **le chien a avalé une ~** the dog has eaten something nasty ■ **depuis que j'ai cette ~ au poumon...** since I've had this blasted thing on my lung... ■ **~ de voiture, elle ne veut pas démarrer!** the damn *ou* bloody △ *UK ou* blasted car won't start! **3.** [chose sale] : **tu as une ~ sur ta manche** you've got something dirty on your sleeve **4.** [calomnie] nasty *ou* catty remark ■ [action méprisable] nasty *ou* dirty trick ■ **faire une ~ à qqn** to play a dirty *ou* nasty trick on sb.
◆ **saloperies** *nfpl* [grossièretés] filthy language *(U)*.

salopette [salɔpɛt] *nf* [de ville] dungarees, salopette, salopettes ■ [de ski] salopette ■ [d'un plombier] overalls.

salpêtre [salpɛtr] *nm* saltpetre.

salpingite [salpɛ̃ʒit] *nf* salpingitis.

salsa [salsa] *nf* salsa.

salsepareille [salsəparɛj] *nf* sarsaparilla.

salsifis [salsifi] *nm* salsify.

saltimbanque [saltɛ̃bɑ̃k] *nmf* **1.** [acrobate] acrobat **2.** [forain] fairground *ou* travelling entertainer **3.** [professionnel du spectacle] entertainer.

salubre [salybr] *adj* **1.** [climat] salubrious, hygienic, wholesome ■ [logement] salubrious **2.** *fig* & *sout* [mesures] salubrious, hygienic.

salubrité [salybrite] *nf* **1.** [d'un local] salubrity ■ [d'un climat] salubriousness, salubrity, healthiness **2.** DR : **~ publique** public health.

saluer [7] [salɥe] ◇ *vt* **1.** [dire bonjour] to say hello to ■ **~ qqn** [de la main] to wave to sb ; [de la tête] to nod to sb ; [en arrivant] to greet sb ; [en partant] to take one's leave of sb ■ **l'acteur salue le public** the actor bows to the audience *ou* takes his bow ■ **il m'a demandé de vous ~** he asked me to give you his regards ■ **Messieurs, je vous salue (bien)!** good day (to you), gentlemen! **2.** MIL to salute **3.** RELIG : **je vous salue Marie** Hail Mary **4.** [accueillir] to greet ■ **son film a été unanimement salué par la presse** her film was unanimously acclaimed by *ou* met with unanimous acclaim from the press **5.** [rendre hommage à - courage, génie] to salute, to pay homage *ou* tribute to ■ [reconnaître en tant que] to hail ■ **on a salué en elle le chef de file du mouvement** she was hailed as the leader of the movement ■ **~ la mémoire** *ou* **le souvenir de qqn** to salute sb's memory.
◇ *vi* NAUT : **~ du pavillon** *ou* **des pavillons** to dip a flag (in salute).

salut [saly] ◇ *nm* **1.** [marque de politesse] : **faire un ~ de la main à qqn** to wave (one's hand) to sb ■ **faire un ~ de la tête à qqn** to nod to sb ■ **il lui retourna son ~** [en paroles] he returned her greeting ; [de la main] he waved back at her ■ **répondre au ~ de qqn** to return sb's greeting ■ **en guise** *ou* **signe de ~** as a greeting **2.** MIL salute ■ **faire le ~** to (give the military) salute ◗ **~ au drapeau** saluting the colours **3.** [survie - d'une personne, d'un pays] salvation, safety ; [- d'une entreprise, d'une institution] salvation ■ **chercher/trouver le ~ dans la fuite** to seek/to find safety in flight **4.** *litt* [sauveur] saviour **5.** RELIG salvation ■ **faire son ~ (sur la terre)** to earn one's salvation on earth.
◇ *interj fam* [en arrivant] hi *ou* hello *ou* hullo (there) ■ [en partant] bye, see you, so long *US* ■ **~ la compagnie!** [en partant] bye everybody!

salutaire [salytɛr] *adj* **1.** [physiquement - air] healthy ; [- remède] beneficial ; [- exercice, repos] salutary, beneficial ■ **cette semaine dans les Alpes m'a été ~** that week in the Alps did my health a power of good **2.** [moralement - conseil, épreuve] salutary ; [- lecture, effet] beneficial.

salutations [salytasjɔ̃] *nfpl* greetings, salutation ■ **elle t'envoie ses ~** she sends you her regards, she sends her regards to you ■ **je vous prie d'agréer mes ~ distinguées** yours sincerely *ou* faithfully *UK*, sincerely *ou* truly yours *US*.

salutiste [salytist] *adj* & *nmf* Salvationist.

Salvador [salvadɔr] *npr m* : **le ~** El Salvador ■ **au ~** in El Salvador.

salvadorien, enne [salvadɔrjɛ̃, ɛn] *adj* Salvadorian, Salvadorean.

salvateur, trice [salvatœr, tris] *adj litt* saving *(avant un nom)* ■ **mesures salvatrices** safeguards.

salve [salv] *nf* **1.** MIL salvo, volley **2.** *fig* **~ d'applaudissements** round *ou* burst of applause.

Salzbourg [salzbur] *npr* Salzburg.

Sam [sam] *npr* : **Oncle ~** [citoyen, gouvernement des USA] Uncle Sam.

samaritain, e [samaritɛ̃, ɛn] *adj* Samaritan.
◆ **samaritain** *nm Suisse* [secouriste] *person qualified to give first aid.*
◆ **Samaritain, e** *nm, f* Samaritan ■ **le bon ~** the good Samaritan ■ **les Samaritains** the Samaritans.
◆ **Samaritaine** *nf* RELIG : **la Samaritaine** the Samaritan woman.

samba [sɑ̃ba] *nf* samba.

samedi [samdi] *nm* Saturday ■ **Samedi saint** Holy *ou* Easter Saturday, *voir aussi* **mardi**.

Samoa [samɔa] *npr fpl* Samoa.

Samothrace [samɔtras] *npr* Samothrace ■ **la Victoire de ~** the Victory of Samothrace.

samouraï [samuraj] *nm* samurai.

samovar [samɔvar] *nm* samovar.

SAMU, Samu [samy] *(abr de* **Service d'aide médicale d'urgence***) npr m French ambulance and emergency service,* ≃ ambulance service *UK,* ≃ Paramedics *US.*

SAMU

The *SAMU* coordinates medical emergency calls within a department and decides how best to deal with a situation. The *SAMU social* deals with the homeless and assists persons in need. Its volunteers help those with nowhere to live find emergency housing and help.

samurai [samuraj] *nm inv* = **samouraï.**

sana [sana] *fam* = **sanatorium.**

sanatorium [sanatɔrjɔm] *nm* sanatorium *UK,* sanatarium *US.*

sancerre [sɑ̃sɛr] *nm* Sancerre (wine).

sanctification [sɑ̃ktifikasjɔ̃] *nf* sanctification.

sanctifier [9] [sɑ̃ktifje] *vt* **1.** RELIG [rendre sacré] to sanctify ▪ [célébrer] to hallow **2.** *fig* [patrie, valeurs] to hold sacred.

sanction [sɑ̃ksjɔ̃] *nf* **1.** [mesure répressive] sanction ▪ **imposer des ~s à** to apply sanctions against, to impose sanctions on ▪ **lever des ~s (prises) contre** to raise (the) sanctions against ▪ **prendre des ~s contre** to take sanctions against ▶ **~s diplomatiques/économiques** diplomatic/economic sanctions **2.** ÉDUC & SPORT punishment, disciplinary action *(U) sout* ▪ **prendre des ~s contre un élève** to punish a pupil ▪ **prendre des ~s contre un sportif** to take disciplinary action against an athlete **3.** DR sanction, penalty ▪ **~ pénale** penal sanction **4.** [approbation] sanction, ratification **5.** *sout* [conséquence] result, outcome.

sanctionner [3] [sɑ̃ksjɔne] *vt* **1.** [punir - délit, élève] to punish ; [- sportif, haut fonctionnaire] to take disciplinary action against ; [- pays] to impose sanctions on ▪ **il s'est fait ~ pour sa grossièreté envers l'arbitre** he was penalized for being rude to the umpire **2.** [ratifier - loi] to sanction, to ratify ; [- décision] to sanction, to agree with *(insép).*

sanctuaire [sɑ̃ktɥɛr] *nm* **1.** RELIG sanctuary **2.** *sout* [asile] sanctuary ▪ **l'île est un ~ pour les oiseaux** the island is a favorite haunt for birds **3.** [foyer, centre vital] hub, centre **4.** POLIT territory under the nuclear umbrella.

sanctus [sɑ̃ktus] *nm* Sanctus.

sandale [sɑ̃dal] *nf* sandal.

sandalette [sɑ̃dalɛt] *nf* (light) sandal.

sandiniste [sɑ̃dinist] *adj* & *nmf* Sandinista.

Sandow® [sɑ̃do] *nm* **1.** [tendeur] elastic luggage strap **2.** AÉRON catapult.

sandre [sɑ̃dr] *nm* zander, pike perch.

sandwich [sɑ̃dwitʃ] *(pl* **sandwichs** *ou pl* **sandwiches***) nm* sandwich ▪ **~ au fromage** cheese sandwich ▶ **j'étais pris en ~ entre eux** *fam* I was sandwiched between them.

sandwicherie [sɑ̃dwitʃ(a)ri] *nf* sandwich shop ▪ [avec possibilité de manger sur place] sandwich bar.

sang [sɑ̃] *nm* **1.** BIOL blood ▪ **à ~ froid/chaud** cold-/warm-blooded ▶ **~ artériel/veineux** arterial/venous blood ▪ **avoir du ~ sur les mains** to have blood on one's hands ▪ **répandre** *ou* **verser** *ou* **faire couler le ~** *sout* to shed *ou* to spill blood ▪ **le ~ a coulé** *ou* **a été répandu** blood was shed ▪ **noyer une révolte dans le ~** to put down a revolt ruthlessly ▪ **en ~ : être en ~, nager** *ou* **baigner dans son ~** to be covered in blood ▪ **se mordre les lèvres jusqu'au ~** to bite one's lips until one draws blood ▪ **avoir du ~ dans les veines** to have courage *ou* guts ▪ **ne pas avoir de ~ dans les veines, avoir du ~ de poulet** *fam,* **avoir du ~ de navet** *fam* to have no guts, to be a complete wimp ▪ **avoir le ~ chaud** [colérique] to be *ou* to have a short fuse ; [impétueux] to be hot-headed ; [sensuel] to be hot-blooded ▪ **il a ça dans le ~** it's in his blood ▪ **mon ~ s'est glacé** *ou* **figé dans mes veines** my blood ran cold *ou* turned to ice in my veins ▪ **le ~ lui est monté au visage** *ou* **à la tête** the blood rushed to her cheeks ▪ **mon ~ n'a fait qu'un tour** [d'effroi] my heart missed *ou* skipped a beat ; [de rage] I saw red ▪ **se faire du mauvais ~** *ou* **un ~ d'encre, se manger** *ou* **se ronger les ~s** to worry o.s. sick, to be worried stiff, to fret ▪ **ça m'a tourné le ~** *ou* **les ~s** it gave me quite a turn **2.** *litt* [vie] (life) blood ▪ **payer de son ~** to pay with one's life ▶ **du ~ frais** *ou* **nouveau** *ou* **neuf** [personnes] new blood ; [argent] new *ou* fresh money **3.** *sout* [race, extraction] blood ▪ **épouser qqn de son ~** to marry sb of the same blood *ou* a blood relative ▪ **de ~ royal** of royal blood ▪ **avoir du ~ noble** to be of noble blood ▶ **~ bleu** blue blood ▪ **lorsque l'on a du ~ bleu dans les veines...** when one is blue-blooded... ▪ **bon ~ ne saurait mentir** *prov* blood is thicker than water *prov* **4.** *fam loc* **bon ~ (de bonsoir)!** damn and blast it!

◆ **au sang** *loc adj* CULIN [canard] *served with a sauce incorporating its own blood.*

sang-froid [sɑ̃frwa] *nm inv* composure, calm, sang-froid ▪ **garder** *ou* **conserver son ~** to stay calm, to keep one's cool ▪ **perdre son ~** to lose one's self-control *ou* cool.

◆ **de sang-froid** *loc adv* **: tuer qqn de ~** to kill sb in cold blood *ou* cold-bloodedly ▪ **commis de ~** cold-blooded.

sanglant, e [sɑ̃glɑ̃, ɑ̃t] *adj* **1.** [blessure, bataille, règne] bloody ▪ [bras, mains] covered in blood, bloody ▪ [linge] bloody, blood-soaked ▪ [spectacle] gory **2.** [blessant - critiques] scathing ; [- affront] cruel **3.** *litt* [couleur de sang] blood-red.

sangle [sɑ̃gl] *nf* **1.** [lanière - gén] strap ; [- d'un lit, d'une chaise] webbing ; [- d'un cheval] girth ; [- d'un parachute] **: ~ d'ouverture automatique** static line **2.** ANAT : **~ abdominale** abdominal muscles.

sangler [3] [sɑ̃gle] *vt* **1.** [cheval] to girth **2.** [paquet, valise] to strap up *(sép)* **3.** *fig* [serrer] **: sanglée dans son corset** tightly corseted.

sanglier [sɑ̃glije] *nm* ZOOL (wild) boar.

sanglot [sɑ̃glo] *nm* **1.** [hoquet, pleurs] sob ▪ **non, dit-il dans un ~** no, he sobbed ▪ **avec des ~s dans la voix** with a sob in one's voice **2.** *litt* [bruit plaintif] lamentation.

sangloter [3] [sɑ̃glɔte] *vi* **1.** [pleurer] to sob ▪ **elle s'endormit en sanglotant** she cried herself to sleep **2.** *litt* [océan, vent] to sob, to sigh ▪ [accordéon] to sigh.

sang-mêlé [sɑ̃mele] *nmf vieilli* half-caste.

sangria [sɑ̃grija] *nf* sangria.

sangsue [sɑ̃sy] *nf* **1.** ZOOL leech **2.** *sout* & *vieilli* [profiteur] bloodsucker **3.** *fam* [importun] leech ▪ **son frère est une véritable ~!** her brother sticks *ou* clings to you like a leech!

sanguin, e [sɑ̃gɛ̃, in] ◇ *adj* **1.** [groupe, plasma, transfusion, vaisseau] blood *(modif)* ▪ [système] circulatory **2.** [rouge] blood-red **3.** [humeur, tempérament] sanguine.

◇ *nm, f* fiery person.

◆ **sanguine** *nf* **1.** ART [crayon] red chalk, sanguine ▪ [dessin] red chalk drawing, sanguine **2.** GÉOL haematite **3.** BOT blood orange.

sanguinaire [sɑ̃ginɛr] ◇ *adj* **1.** [assoiffé de sang] bloodthirsty ▪ **une foule ~ réclamait la mort de l'accusé** a bloodthirsty crowd was screaming for the death of the accused **2.** *litt* [féroce - bataille, conquête] bloody, sanguinary *sout.*

◇ *nf* bloodroot, sanguinaria *spéc.*

sanguinolent, e [sɑ̃ginɔlɑ̃, ɑ̃t] *adj* **1.** [sécrétion] spotted *ou* streaked with blood, sanguinolent *litt* ▪ [linge, pansement] soiled *ou* tinged with blood, sanguinolent ▪ [personne] covered in blood, blood-streaked **2.** *litt* [rouge - lèvres] blood-red.

Sanibroyeur® [sanibrwajœr] *nm* Saniflo® *(toilet with macerator unit).*

Sanisette® [sanizɛt] *nf* superloo.

sanitaire [sanitɛr] ◇ *adj* **1.** ADMIN & MÉD [conditions] sanitary, health *(modif)* ▪ [règlement] health **2.** CONSTR sanitary, plumbing *(U)* ▪ **l' équipement ~** the plumbing.

◇ *nm* **1.** [installations] plumbing (for bathroom and toilet) **2.** [profession] sanitary ware (dealing).

◆ **sanitaires** *nmpl* (bathroom and) toilet ▪ **les ~s du camp sont tout à fait insuffisants** the sanitary arrangements in the camp are totally inadequate.

sans [sɑ̃] ◇ *prép* **1.** [indiquant l'absence, la privation, l'exclusion] without ■ **avec ou ~ sucre?** with or without sugar? ■ **j'ai trouvé ~ problème** I found it without any difficulty *ou* with no difficulty ■ **son comportement est ~ reproche** his behaviour is beyond reproach ■ **être ~ scrupules** to have no scruples, to be unscrupulous ■ **tu as oublié le rendez-vous? tu es ~ excuse!** you forgot the appointment? that's unforgivable! ■ **homme ~ cœur/pitié** heartless/pitiless man ■ **couple ~ enfants** childless couple ■ **~ additif** additive-free ■ **essence ~ plomb** unleaded *ou* lead-free petrol ■ **marcher ~ but** to walk aimlessly ■ **~ commentaire!** no comment! ■ **la chambre fait 40 euros, ~ le petit déjeuner** the room costs 40 euros, breakfast not included *ou* exclusive of breakfast ▶ **être ~ un**^△ to be skint *ou* broke **2.** [exprimant la condition] but for ■ **~ toi, je ne l'aurais jamais fait** if it hadn't been for you *ou* but for you, I would never have done it **3.** [avec un infinitif] without ■ **~ être vu** without being seen ■ **partons ~ plus attendre** come on, let's not wait any more ■ **~ plus attendre, je passe la parole à M. Blais** without further ado, I'll hand you over to Mr Blais ■ **cette découverte n'est pas ~ l'inquiéter** she's somewhat worried by this discovery ■ **tu n'es pas ~ savoir qu'il est amoureux d'elle** you must be aware that he's in love with her ■ **je comprends ~ comprendre** I understand, but only up to a point.
◇ *adv* without ■ **il faudra faire ~!** we'll have to go without! ■ **passe-moi mon manteau, je ne peux pas sortir ~** hand me my coat, I can't go out without it ▶ **c'est un jour ~!** [tout va mal] it's one of those days!
◆ **non sans** *loc prép* not without ■ **il l'a persuadé, mais non ~ mal** he persuaded her, but not without difficulty, he had quite a job persuading her ■ **je suis parti non ~ leur dire ma façon de penser** I didn't leave without telling them what I thought.
◆ **sans cela, sans ça** *loc conj fam* otherwise.
◆ **sans que** *loc conj* : **ils ont réglé le problème ~ que nous ayons à intervenir** they dealt with the problem without us having to intervene ■ **le projet était passé ~ que personne (ne) s'y opposât** the bill was passed without any opposition.
◆ **sans quoi** *loc conj* : **soyez ponctuels, ~ quoi vous ne pourrez pas vous inscrire** be sure to be on time, otherwise you won't be able to register.

sans-abri [sɑ̃zabri] *nmf* homeless person ■ **les ~** the homeless.

sans-cœur [sɑ̃kœr] ◇ *adj inv* heartless ■ **ne sois pas ~!** have a heart!
◇ *nmf* heartless person ■ **donne-le-lui, espèce de ~!** give it to her, you heartless monster!

sanscrit, e [sɑ̃skri, it] = **sanskrit.**

sans-culotte [sɑ̃kylɔt] (*pl* **sans-culottes**) *nm* sans-culotte ■ **les ~s** HIST the sans-culottes.

LES SANS-CULOTTES

The name given to the Republican revolutionaries during the Convention (1792-1795) because, instead of the short breeches (*culotte*) worn by the upper classes, they adopted the trousers of the ordinary people.

sans-emploi [sɑ̃zɑ̃plwa] *nmf* unemployed *ou* jobless person ■ **les ~** the unemployed.

sans-faute [sɑ̃fot] *nm inv* : **faire un ~** ÉQUIT to do *ou* to have a clear round ; ÉDUC to get a series of answers right ■ **pour l'instant c'est un ~!** [dans un jeu] so far so good!

sans-fil [sɑ̃fil] *nm inv* cordless telephone.

sans-gêne [sɑ̃ʒɛn] ◇ *nm inv* lack of consideration, casualness.
◇ *nmf* ill-mannered person ■ **en voilà une ~!** well, she's a cool customer!

sanskrit, e [sɑ̃skri, it] *adj* Sanskrit.
◆ **sanskrit** *nm* LING Sanskrit.

sans-le-sou [sɑ̃lsu] *nmf fam* pauper, penniless person ■ **les ~** the have-nots.

sans-logis [sɑ̃lɔʒi] *nmf* homeless person ■ **les ~** the homeless.

sansonnet [sɑ̃sɔnɛ] *nm* starling, ▷ **roupie.**

sans-papiers [sɑ̃papje] *nmf* illegal immigrant worker.

sans-souci [sɑ̃susi] *nmf litt* happy-go-lucky person.

Santa Fé [sɑ̃tafe] *npr* Santa Fe.

santal, als [sɑ̃tal] *nm* BOT sandal ■ **bois de ~** sandalwood.

santé [sɑ̃te] *nf* **1.** [de l'esprit, d'une économie, d'une entreprise] health, soundness ■ [d'une personne, d'une plante] health ■ **comment va la ~?** *fam* how are you keeping? ■ **c'est mauvais pour la ~** it's bad for your health *ou* for you ■ **en bonne ~** [personne] healthy, in good health ; [plante] healthy ; [économie] healthy, sound ; [monnaie] strong ■ **vous êtes en parfaite ~** you're perfectly healthy *ou* there's nothing wrong with you ■ **en mauvaise ~** [animal, personne] in bad *ou* poor health ; [plante] unhealthy ; [économie, monnaie] weak ▶ **état de ~** health ■ **~ mentale** mental health ■ **avoir la ~** *fam* [être infatigable] to be a bundle of energy ■ **avoir une ~ de fer** to have an iron constitution, to be (as) strong as a horse ■ **avoir une petite ~** to be very delicate **2.** ADMIN : **la ~ publique** public health ■ **services de ~** health services **3.** MIL : **service de ~ des armées** medical corps.
◆ **Santé** *npr f* : **la Santé** [prison] *men's prison in Paris.*
◆ **à la santé de** *loc prép* [en portant un toast] : **à votre ~!, à ta ~!** cheers!, your (good) health! ■ **à la ~ de ma femme!** (here's) to my wife!

santiag [sɑ̃tjag] *nf* cowboy boot.

Santiago [sɑ̃tjago] *npr* : **~ (du Chili)** Santiago.

santon [sɑ̃tɔ̃] *nm* crib *ou* manger figurine *(in Provence).*

saoudien, enne [saudjɛ̃, ɛn] *adj* Saudi (Arabian).
◆ **Saoudien, enne** *nm, f* Saudi (Arabian).

saoudite [saudit] *adj* Saudi (Arabian).

saoul, e [su, sul] = **soûl.**

saouler [sule] = **soûler.**

sapajou [sapaʒu] *nm* ZOOL sapajou.

sape [sap] *nf* **1.** MIL & TRAV PUB [travaux] sapping ■ [tranchée] sap **2.** *fig* **travail de ~** (insidious) undermining ■ **par un patient travail de ~, ils ont fini par avoir raison de lui** they chipped away at him until he gave in **3.** *fam (gén pl) fam* [vêtement] rig-out *UK*, gear.

saper [3] [sape] *vt* **1.** [miner] to sap, to undermine ■ **~ le moral à qqn** to get sb down **2.** *fam* [habiller] to dress ■ **il est toujours bien sapé** he's always really smartly turned out *ou* dressed.
◆ **se saper** *fam* ◇ *vp (emploi réfléchi)* to do *ou* to tog o.s. up, to rig o.s. out *UK*.
◇ *vpi* : **où est-ce que tu te sapes?** where do you buy your togs *ou* gear?

saperlipopette [sapɛrlipɔpɛt] *interj fam vieilli* zounds *arch*, struth *arch & hum.*

sapeur [sapœr] *nm* sapper.

sapeur-pompier [sapœrpɔ̃pje] (*pl* **sapeurs-pompiers**) *nm* fireman ■ **les sapeurs-pompiers** the fire brigade *UK*, the fire department *US*.

saphique [safik] *adj* Sapphic ■ **vers ~** Sapphic metre.

saphir [safir] ◇ *adj inv litt* sapphire *(modif).*
◇ *nm* **1.** JOAILL sapphire **2.** [d'un tourne-disque] needle, stylus **3.** *litt* [bleu] sapphire.

saphisme [safism] *nm litt* sapphism, lesbianism.

Sapho [safo] = **Sappho.**

sapide [sapid] *adj* sapid.

sapidité [sapidite] *nf* sapidity.

sapin [sapɛ̃] *nm* **1.** BOT fir (tree) **2.** MENUIS fir, deal ■ **en ~** fir *(modif)*, deal *(modif)* ▶ **~ blanc** *ou* **pectiné** (common) silver fir.
◆ **sapin de Noël** *nm* Christmas tree ■ **faire un ~ de Noël** [chez soi] to have a Christmas tree ; [dans une collectivité] to have a Christmas party for the staff's children *(with presents).*

sapinette [sapinɛt] *nf Québec* [boisson] spruce beer.

sapinière [sapinjɛr] *nf* **1.** [plantation] fir plantation **2.** [forêt] fir forest.

saponaire [sapɔnɛr] *nf* soapwort.

Sappho [safo] *npr* Sappho.

sapristi [sapristi] *interj vieilli* ~! [étonnement] Heavens! ; [colère] Great Scott! *vieilli*.

saquer △ [sake] = **sacquer**.

sarabande [sarabɑ̃d] *nf* **1.** DANSE & MUS saraband **2.** *fam* [tapage] racket, row *UK* ▪ **les enfants font la ~ dans la salle de jeux** the children are making a racket in the playroom **3.** *sout* [ribambelle] string, succession.

Sarajevo [sarajevo] *npr* Sarajevo.

sarbacane [sarbakan] *nf* blowpipe.

sarcasme [sarkasm] *nm* **1.** [ironie] sarcasm ▪ **tu n'arriveras à rien par le ~** being sarcastic won't get you anywhere **2.** [remarque] sarcastic remark.

sarcastique [sarkastik] *adj* sarcastic ▪ **d'un ton ~** sarcastically.

sarcastiquement [sarkastikmɑ̃] *adv* sarcastically.

Sarcelles [sarsɛl] *npr town in the Paris suburbs often associated with the social problems prevalent in highly developed suburban areas.*

sarclage [sarklaʒ] *nm* weeding.

sarcler [3] [sarkle] *vt* **1.** [mauvaises herbes - à la main] to pull up *(sép)*, to weed out *(sép)* ; [- avec une houe] to hoe ; [- avec une bêche] to spud **2.** [betteraves, champ - à la main] to weed ; [- avec une houe] to hoe.

sarcloir [sarklwar] *nm* (Dutch) hoe, spud.

sarcome [sarkom] *nm* sarcoma.

sarcophage [sarkɔfaʒ] *nm* **1.** [cercueil] sarcophagus **2.** ENTOM fleshfly.

Sardaigne [sardɛɲ] *npr f* : **(la) ~** Sardinia.

sarde [sard] *adj* Sardinian.
◆ **Sarde** *nmf* Sardinian.

sardine [sardin] *nf* **1.** [poisson] sardine ▪ **~s à l'huile** sardines in oil **2.** △ *arg mil* stripe.

sardinerie [sardinri] *nf* sardine cannery.

sardinier, ère [sardinje, ɛr] *nm, f* **1.** [pêcheur] sardine fisher **2.** [ouvrier] sardine canner.
◆ **sardinier** *nm* **1.** [bateau] sardine boat *ou* fisher **2.** [filet] sardine net.

sardonique [sardɔnik] *adj* sardonic.

Sargasses [sargas] *npr fpl* ▷ **mer**.

sari [sari] *nm* sari, saree.

sarigue [sarig] *nf* possum, opossum.

SARL, Sarl (*abr de* **société à responsabilité limitée**) *nf* limited liability company [cotée en Bourse] public limited company ▪ **Balacor, ~** ≃ Balacor Ltd *UK* ▪ ≃ Balacor plc *UK* ▪ ≃ Balacor Inc. *US*.

sarment [sarmɑ̃] *nm* [tige] twining *ou* climbing stem, bine ▪ **~ de vigne** vine shoot.

saroual [sarwal] *nm wide-legged canvas trousers (worn generally in North Africa).*

sarrasin[1] [sarazɛ̃] *nm* BOT buckwheat.

sarrasin[2]**, e** [sarazɛ̃, in] *adj* Saracen.
◆ **Sarrasin, e** *nm, f* Saracen.

sarrau, s [saro] *nm* **1.** [d'artiste] smock **2.** [de paysan] smock frock **3.** [d'écolier] overalls.

Sarre [sar] *npr f* **1.** [région] : **la ~** Saarland, the Saar **2.** [rivière] : **la ~** the (River) Saar.

Sarrebruck [sarbryk] *npr* Saarbrücken.

sarriette [sarjɛt] *nf* savory ▪ **~ commune** wild basil.

sas [sas] *nm* **1.** [crible] sieve, screen **2.** AÉRON airlock **3.** NAUT [d'écluse] lock (chamber) ▪ [passage] airlock **4.** [d'une banque] security (double) door.

Satan [satɑ̃] *npr* Satan.

satané, e [satane] *adj (avant le n) fam* **1.** [détestable] : **faites donc taire ce ~ gosse!** shut that blasted kid up! ▪ **~ temps!** what dreadful weather! **2.** [en intensif] : **c'est un ~ menteur** he's a downright liar.

satanique [satanik] *adj* **1.** [de Satan] satanic **2.** [démoniaque, pervers] fiendish, diabolical, satanic ▪ **avoir l'œil ~** to have an evil glint in one's eye.

satanisme [satanism] *nm* **1.** [culte] satanism **2.** [méchanceté] fiendishness, evil.

satellisation [satelizasjɔ̃] *nf* **1.** ASTRONAUT [d'une fusée] putting *ou* launching into orbit **2.** *fig* [d'une nation, d'une ville, d'une organisation] satellization.

satelliser [3] [satelize] *vt* **1.** ASTRONAUT : **~ qqch** to put *ou* to launch sthg into orbit, to orbit sthg ▪ **fusée satellisée** orbiting rocket **2.** *fig* [pays, ville] to satellize.

satellite [satelit] ◇ *nm* **1.** ASTRON, ASTRONAUT & TÉLÉCOM satellite ▪ **en direct par ~** live via satellite ➊ **~ artificiel/météorologique/de télécommunications** artificial/meteorological/communications satellite ▪ **~ antisatellite** MIL killer satellite ▪ **~ lunaire/terrestre** moon-orbiting/earth-orbiting satellite ▪ **~ d'observation** observation satellite ▪ **transmission par ~** satellite transmission **2.** POLIT [personne, pays, ville] satellite ▪ **les ~s du bloc socialiste** the satellite countries of the socialist bloc **3.** [d'une aérogare] satellite **4.** MÉCAN bevel (wheel) ▪ **engrenage à ~** planetary gear.
◇ *adj* [ville, pays] satellite *(modif)* ▪ **ordinateur ~** satellite computer.

satello-opérateur (*pl* **satello-opérateurs**) [satelɔɔperatœr] *nm* satellite TV company, satellite broadcaster.

satiété [sasjete] *nf* satiety ▪ **à ~, jusqu'à ~ : manger à ~** to eat one's fill ▪ **redire jusqu'à ~** to repeat ad nauseam.

satin [satɛ̃] *nm* **1.** TEXT satin ▪ **~ de coton** satin cotton, sateen ▪ **de ~** satin *(modif)* ▪ **une peau de ~** *fig* a satin-smooth skin **2.** [douceur - gén] softness, silkiness ; [- de la peau] silky softness.

satiné, e [satine] *adj* [étoffe, reflets] satiny, satin *(modif)* ▪ [papier] calendered ▪ [peau] satin *(modif)*, satin-smooth ▪ **un fini ~** a satin finish ➊ **peinture ~e** silk finish emulsion.
◆ **satiné** *nm* [d'une peinture] silk finish ▪ [d'un papier, d'un tissu] satin finish ▪ **la lumière mettait en valeur le ~ de sa peau** the light showed off her satin-like complexion.

satiner [3] [satine] *vt* [tissu] to give a satin finish to, to put a satin finish on ▪ [papier] to surface, to glaze ▪ [peau] to make smooth.

satinette [satinɛt] *nf* [en coton] sateen ▪ [en soie et coton] (silk and cotton) satinet.

satire [satir] *nf* **1.** LITTÉR satire **2.** [critique] satire, spoof ▪ **sa ~ du Premier ministre est excellente** he's good at taking off the Prime Minister.

satirique [satirik] ◇ *adj* satirical.
◇ *nmf* satirist.

satiriste [satirist] *nmf* satirist.

satisfaction [satisfaksjɔ̃] *nf* **1.** [plaisir] satisfaction, gratification ▪ **éprouver de la ~/une grande ~ à faire qqch** to feel satisfaction/great satisfaction in doing sthg ▪ **il a la ~ d'être utile** he has the satisfaction of being useful, he can rest assured that he's being useful ▪ **donner (entière** *ou* **toute) ~ à qqn** [personne] to give sb (complete) satisfaction ; [travail] to fulfil *UK ou* to fulfill *US* sb completely, to give sb a lot of (job) satisfaction ▪ **mon travail me donne peu de ~** my work is not very satisfying *ou* fulfilling *ou* gratifying ▪ **à ma grande ~** to my great satisfaction, to my gratification ▪ **le problème fut résolu à la ~**

générale the problem was solved to everybody's satisfaction ▪ **je constate/vois avec ~ que...** I am pleased to note/to see that.
2. [sujet de contentement] source *ou* cause for satisfaction ▪ **mon travail m'apporte de nombreuses ~s** my job gives me great satisfaction ▪ **mon fils m'apporte de nombreuses ~s** my son is a great satisfaction to me ▪ **avoir des ~s professionnelles/financières** to be rewarded professionally/financially
3. [assouvissement - d'un désir] satisfaction, gratification, fulfilment ; [- d'ambitions, d'un besoin] satisfying, fulfilment ; [- de la faim] appeasement, satisfying ; [- de la soif] quenching, slaking ▪ **c'est pour elle une ~ d'amour-propre** it flatters her self-esteem
4. [gain de cause] satisfaction ▪ **accorder** *ou* **donner ~ à qqn** to give sb satisfaction ▪ **obtenir ~** to obtain satisfaction
5. [réparation] satisfaction ▪ **exiger/obtenir ~ (de qqch)** *sout* to demand/to obtain satisfaction (for sthg).

satisfaire [109] [satisfɛr] *vt* **1.** [contenter - suj: résultat, travail] to satisfy, to give satisfaction to ; [- suj: explication] to satisfy ▪ **elle est difficile à ~** she's hard to please ▪ **votre rapport ne me satisfait pas du tout** I'm not satisfied at all with your report, I don't find your report at all satisfactory ▪ **ce que j'ai me satisfait pleinement** I'm quite content with what I've got ▪ **j'espère que cet arrangement vous satisfera** I hope (that) you'll find this arrangement satisfactory *ou* to your satisfaction ▪ [sexuellement] to satisfy **2.** [répondre à - attente] to come *ou* to live up to ; [- désir] to satisfy, to fulfil ; [- besoin] to satisfy, to answer ; [- curiosité] to satisfy ; [- demande] to meet, to satisfy, to cope with *(insép)*, to keep up with *(insép)* ; [- faim] to satisfy, to appease ; [- soif] to satisfy, to quench, to slake ▪ **il reste des revendications non satisfaites** there are still a few demands which haven't been met ▪ **~ un besoin naturel** *euphém* to relieve o.s.
◆ **satisfaire à** *v+prép* [conditions] to fulfil *UK*, to fulfill *US*, to meet, to satisfy ▪ [besoin, exigences] to meet, to fulfil ▪ [désir] to satisfy, to gratify ▪ [attente] to live *ou* to come up to ▪ [promesse] to fulfil, to keep ▪ [goût] to satisfy ▪ [norme] to comply with *(insép)*, to satisfy ▪ **avoir satisfait à ses obligations militaires** to have fulfilled one's national service commitments.
◆ **se satisfaire** ◇ *vp (emploi réfléchi)* [sexuellement] to have one's pleasure.
◇ *vpi* : **se ~** [uriner] to relieve o.s.
◆ **se satisfaire de** *vp+prép* to be satisfied *ou* content with ▪ **tu te satisfais de peu!** you're content with very little!, it doesn't take much to make you happy!

satisfaisant, e [satisfəzɑ̃, ɑ̃t] *adj* [réponse, travail, devoir scolaire] satisfactory ▪ **en quantité ~e** in sufficient quantities ▪ **ce n'est pas une excuse/raison ~e** it's not a good enough excuse/reason ▪ **peu ~** [résultat, travail] unsatisfactory ; ÉDUC poor ▪ **cette solution n'était ~e pour personne** this solution pleased nobody.

satisfaisons *etc v* ▷ **satisfaire**.

satisfait, e [satisfɛ, ɛt] ◇ *pp* ▷ **satisfaire**.
◇ *adj* [air, personne, regard] satisfied, happy ▪ **être ~ de qqn** to be satisfied *ou* happy with sb ▪ **être ~ de soi** *ou* **de soi-même** to be satisfied with o.s., to be self-satisfied ▪ **être ~ de** [arrangement, résultat] to be satisfied with, to be happy with *ou* about ; [voiture, service] to be satisfied with ▪ **elle est partie maintenant, tu es ~?** now she's gone, are you satisfied?

satisfecit [satisfesit] *nm inv* **1.** ÉDUC star, credit **2.** *sout* full credit ▪ **décerner un ~ à qqn pour qqch** to congratulate sb for (having done) sthg.

satisfera *etc v* ▷ **satisfaire**.

satisfont *v* ▷ **satisfaire**.

satrape [satrap] *nm* **1.** HIST satrap **2.** *litt* [tyran] satrap, despot ▪ [homme riche] nabob.

saturable [satyrabl] *adj* saturable.

saturant, e [satyrɑ̃, ɑ̃t] *adj* saturating, saturant.

saturateur [satyratœr] *nm* **1.** CHIM saturator, saturater **2.** [pour radiateur] humidifier.

saturation [satyrasjɔ̃] *nf* **1.** SC saturation **2.** [d'une autoroute, d'un aéroport] saturation, paralysis, gridlocking ▪ [d'un circuit] saturation, overloading ▪ [d'un marché] saturation (point) ▪ **arriver** *ou* **parvenir à ~** [marché, aéroport] to reach saturation point ; [marcheur, travailleur] to reach saturation point, to be unable to take anymore.

saturé, e [satyre] *adj* **1.** [imprégné - gén] impregnated ; [- d'un liquide] saturated ▪ **sol ~ de sel** very salty soil **2.** [encombré - marché] saturated, glutted **3.** [rassasié, écœuré] : **~ de** sated with ▪ **des enfants ~s de télévision** children who have had too much television **4.** [engorgé - autoroute] saturated, blocked, gridlocked ; [- circuit de communication] saturated **5.** SC & TECHNOL saturated.

saturer [3] [satyre] ◇ *vt* **1.** CHIM to saturate ▪ **~ qqch de** to saturate sthg with **2.** [surcharger, remplir en excès] to saturate, to glut ▪ **être saturé de travail** to be up to one's eyes in work, to be swamped with work ▪ **le jardin est saturé d'eau** the garden is waterlogged *ou* saturated with water.
◇ *vi fam* [marché] to become saturated ▪ [lignes téléphoniques] to overload ▪ [sonorisation] : **ça sature** we're getting distortion ▪ [personne] : **deux heures d'informatique et je sature** after two hours of computer science, I can't take anything in any more.

saturnales [satyrnal] *nfpl* **1.** *litt* [débauche] saturnalia *(pl)*, (wild) orgies **2.** ANTIQ saturnalia *(pl)*.

saturne [satyrn] *nm* Saturn *(in alchemy)*.

Saturne [satyrn] *npr* ASTRON & MYTHOL Saturn.

saturnien, enne [satyrnjɛ̃, ɛn] *adj* **1.** ASTRON Saturnian **2.** *litt* [morose] saturnine, gloomy, glum, taciturn.

saturnisme [satyrnism] *nm* (chronic) lead poisoning, saturnism *spéc.*

satyre [satir] *nm* **1.** MYTHOL & ENTOM satyr **2.** [homme lubrique] lecher.

satyrique [satirik] *adj* satyric, satyrical.

sauce [sos] *nf* **1.** CULIN sauce ▪ [de salade] salad dressing ▪ [vinaigrette] French dressing ▪ [jus de viande] gravy ▪ **~/à la moutarde/aux câpres** mustard/caper sauce ➊ **~ béarnaise/hollandaise** béarnaise/hollandaise sauce ▪ **~ madère/piquante** Madeira/hot sauce ▪ **~ béchamel** béchamel *ou* white sauce ▪ **pâtes à la ~ tomate** pasta with tomato sauce ▪ **mettre** *ou* **servir qqch à toute les ~s** to make sthg fit every occasion ▪ **une expression qui a été mise à toutes les ~s** a hackneyed phrase ▪ **je me demande à quelle ~ nous allons être mangés** I wonder what lies in store for us *ou* what they're going to do to us ▪ **la ~ fait passer le poisson** *prov* a spoonful of sugar helps the medicine go down ▪ **allonger** *ou* **rallonger la ~** *fam* to pad sthg out **2.** *fam* [pluie] : **prendre** *ou* **recevoir la ~** to get soaked *ou* drenched **3.** *fam* [courant électrique] juice **4.** ART soft black crayon.
◆ **en sauce** *loc adj* with a sauce ▪ **viande/poisson en ~** meat/fish served in a sauce.

saucée [sose] *nf fam* downpour ▪ **prendre** *ou* **recevoir la ~** to get drenched *ou* soaked (to the skin) ▪ **il va y avoir une ~** it's going to bucket down.

saucer [16] [sose] *vt* **1.** [essuyer] : **~ son assiette (avec un morceau de pain)** to wipe (off) one's plate (with a piece of bread) **2.** *fam loc* **se faire ~** to get soaked (to the skin) *ou* drenched.

saucier [sosje] *nm* **1.** [employé] sauce cook *ou* chef **2.** [appareil] sauce-maker.

saucière [sosjɛr] *nf* [pour sauce] sauce boat ▪ [pour jus] gravy boat.

sauciflard △ [sosiflar] *nm* sausage.

saucisse [sosis] *nf* **1.** CULIN sausage ▪ **~ de Francfort** frankfurter ▪ **~ de Strasbourg** Strasbourg (pork) sausage, knackwurst **2.** △ *arg mil* [ballon captif] sausage **3.** *fam* [imbécile] : **espèce de grande ~** you great lump!, you numbskull!

saucisson [sosisɔ̃] *nm* **1.** CULIN : **~ (sec)** (dry) sausage ▪ **~ à l'ail** garlic sausage **2.** [pain] sausage-shaped loaf.

saucissonner [3] [sosisɔne] *fam* ◇ *vi* to picnic, to have a snack.

◇ *vt* **1.** [attacher - personne] to tie up *(sép)* ▪ **ils ont saucissonné le gardien sur la chaise** they trussed up the caretaker and tied him to a chair **2.** [diviser] **: le film a été saucissonné** the film was divided up into episodes.

sauf[1] [sof] *prép* **1.** [à part] except, apart from, save *sout* ▪ **il a pensé à tout, ~ à ça** he thought of everything, except that ▪ **il sait tout faire ~ cuisiner** he can do everything except *ou* but cook ▪ **il s'arrête toujours ici ~ s'il n'a pas le temps** he always stops here except if *ou* unless he's in a hurry **2.** [à moins de] unless ▪ **~ avis contraire** unless otherwise instructed ▪ **~ indications contraires** unless otherwise stated ▪ **~ erreur ou omission** errors and omissions excepted.
◆ **sauf à** *loc prép sout* **: il a pris cette décision, ~ à changer plus tard** he took this decision, but reserved the right to change it later.
◆ **sauf que** *loc conj* except (for the fact) that, apart from the fact that ▪ **il n'a pas changé, ~ que ses cheveux ont blanchi** he hasn't changed, except (for the fact) that he has gone grey.

sauf[2], **sauve** [sof, sov] *adj* **1.** [indemne - personne] safe ▪ **elle est sauve** she's safe, she escaped unhurt *ou* unharmed **2.** *fig* [intact] **: au moins, les apparences sont sauves** at least appearances have been kept up *ou* saved.

sauf-conduit [sofkɔ̃dɥi] *(pl* **sauf-conduits***)* *nm* safe-conduct.

sauge [soʒ] *nf* **1.** BOT salvia ▪ **~ officinale** sage **2.** CULIN sage.

saugrenu, e [sogrəny] *adj* peculiar, weird ▪ **en voilà une idée ~e!** what a cranky *ou* daft idea!

saulaie [solɛ] *nf* willow plantation.

saule [sol] *nm* willow ▪ **~ pleureur/blanc** weeping/white willow.

saumâtre [somatr] *adj* **1.** [salé] brackish, briny **2.** *fam* [désagréable] bitter, nasty ▪ **il l'a trouvée ~!** he wasn't amused!, he was unimpressed! *euphém.*

saumon [somɔ̃] ◇ *nm* **1.** ZOOL salmon ▪ **~ fumé** CULIN smoked salmon *UK*, lox *US* **2.** [couleur] salmon-pink **3.** MÉTALL pig.
◇ *adj inv* salmon *(modif)*, salmon-pink.

saumoné, e [somɔne] *adj* [rose] salmon, salmon-pink.

Saumur [somyr] *npr town in western France with a military academy famous as a centre for cavalry training.*

saumure [somyr] *nf* brine ▪ **conserver du poisson/des cornichons dans la ~** to pickle fish/gherkins (in brine).

sauna [sona] *nm* [cabine] sauna (bath) ▪ [établissement] sauna.

saupoudrage [sopudraʒ] *nm* **1.** CULIN sprinkling, dusting **2.** FIN & POLIT [de crédits] *allocation of small amounts of finance to numerous posts.*

saupoudrer [3] [sopudre] *vt* **1.** CULIN to dust, to sprinkle ▪ **~ un gâteau de sucre** to sprinkle *ou* to dust sugar over a cake **2.** FIN & POLIT **: ~ des crédits** to allocate small amounts of finance to numerous posts **3.** *fig & litt* [parsemer] to scatter, to sprinkle ▪ **~ un discours de citations** to pepper a speech with quotations.
◆ **se saupoudrer** *vpt* **: se ~ les mains de talc** to dust one's hands with talcum powder.

saupoudreuse [sopudrøz] *nf* sprinkler.

saur [sɔr] *adj m* smoked, cured.

saura *etc v* ▷ **savoir.**

saurien [sɔrjɛ̃] *nm* saurian ▪ **les ~s** the saurians, the Sauria *spéc.*

saut [so] *nm* **1.** SPORT jump ▪ **le ~** jumping ▪ **championnat/épreuves de ~** jumping championship/events ▸ **~ en hauteur/longueur** high/long jump ▪ **~ de l'ange** swallow *UK ou* swan *US* dive ▪ **~ de carpe** jack-knife dive ▪ **~ en chute libre** free fall jump ▪ **~ en ciseaux** scissors jump ▪ **~ à la corde** skipping ▪ **~ à l'élastique** bungee jumping ▪ **~ groupé** tuck ▪ **~ de haies** hurdling ▪ **~ de la mort** death jump ▪ **~ d'obstacles** show jumping ▪ **~ en parachute** [discipline] parachuting, skydiving ; [épreuve] parachute jump ▪ **~ à la perche** [discipline] pole vaulting ; [épreuve] pole vault ▪ **~ périlleux** somersault ▪ **~ à skis** [discipline] skijumping ; [épreuve] (ski) jump
2. [bond] leap ▪ **se lever d'un ~** to leap *ou* to jump to one's feet ▸ **~ de puce** step ▪ **au ~ du lit** [en se levant] on *ou* upon getting up ; [tôt] first thing in the morning
3. [chute] drop ▪ **elle a fait un ~ de cinq mètres dans le vide** she fell *ou* plunged five metres into the void
4. [brève visite] flying visit ▪ **elle a fait un ~ chez nous hier** she dropped by (our house) yesterday ▪ **je ne fais qu'un ~** [quelques instants] I'm only passing, I'm not staying ; [quelques heures] I'm only on a flying visit ▪ **fais un ~ chez le boucher** pop over *ou* along *ou* across to the butcher's
5. *fig* leap ▪ **faire un ~ dans l'inconnu** to take a leap in the dark ▪ **faire un ~ dans le passé** to go back into the past ▪ **faire un ~ d'un siècle** to jump a century ▸ **le grand ~** [la mort] the big sleep ▪ **faire le ~** to take the plunge
6. GÉOGR falls, waterfall ▪ **le ~ du Doubs** the Doubs falls
7. INFORM & MATH jump
8. INFORM **: ~ de colonne** (insert) column break ▪ **~ de page** (insert) page break.

saut-de-lit [sodli] *(pl* **sauts-de-lit***)* *nm* dressing-gown, light robe.

saut-de-mouton [sodmutɔ̃] *(pl* **sauts-de-mouton***)* *nm* flyover *UK*, overpass *US*.

saute [sot] *nf* **1.** MÉTÉOR **: ~ de vent** shift (of the wind) ▪ **~ de température** sudden change in temperature **2.** *fig* **~ d'humeur** mood swing ▪ **sujet à de fréquentes ~s d'humeur** prone to frequent changes of mood.

sauté [sote] *nm* sauté ▪ **~ de veau** sauté of veal.

saute-mouton [sotmutɔ̃] *nm inv* leapfrog ▪ **jouer à ~** to play leapfrog.

sauter [3] [sote] ◇ *vi* **1.** [bondir - personne] to jump, to spring up ; [- chat] to jump, to leap ; [- oiseau, insecte] to hop ; [- grenouille, saumon] to leap ; [- balle, curseur] to bounce, to jump ▪ **~ dans une tranchée/dans un puits** to jump into a trench/down a well ▪ **~ d'une branche/falaise** to leap off a branch/cliff ▪ **~ par-dessus une corde/un ruisseau** to leap over a rope/across a stream ▪ **il faut ~ pour atteindre l'étagère** you've got to jump up to reach the shelf ▪ **~ par la fenêtre** to jump out of the window ▪ *fig* **~ de joie** to jump for joy ▸ **~ au plafond** *fam*, **~ en l'air** *fam* [de colère] to hit the roof ; [de joie] to be thrilled to bits ▪ **~ comme un cabri** to frolic
2. JEUX & SPORT **: ~ à cloche-pied** to hop ▪ **~ à la corde** to skip (with a rope) *UK*, to skip *ou* to jump rope *US* ▪ **~ en parachute** to (parachute) jump, to parachute ▪ **~ en hauteur/longueur** to do the high/long jump ▪ **~ à la perche** to pole-vault ▪ **~ en ciseaux** to do a scissors jump
3. [se ruer] to jump, to pounce ▪ **~ (à bas) du lit** to jump *ou* to spring out of bed ▪ **~ dans un taxi** to jump *ou* to leap into a taxi ‖ *fig* **je lui sauterai dessus dès qu'il reviendra** *fam* I'll grab him as soon as he gets back ▪ **~ sur l'occasion** *fam* to jump at the chance ▪ **c'est une excellente occasion, je saute dessus** it's a great opportunity, I'll grab it ▸ **~ à la gorge** *ou* **au collet de qqn** to jump down sb's throat ▪ **va te laver les mains, et que ça saute!** *fam* go and wash your hands and get a move on *ou* get your skates on *UK* ▪ **ça saute aux yeux** it's plain for all to see *ou* as the nose on your face
4. [exploser] to blow up, to explode, to go off ▪ **faire ~ un pont/char** to blow up a bridge/tank ▪ **faire ~ une mine** to explode a mine ▪ **les plombs ont sauté** ÉLECTR the fuses have blown ▪ **faire ~ les plombs** to blow the fuses ▪ **la lampe/le circuit a sauté** the lamp/circuit has fused *UK*, the lamp fuse/the circuit has blown *US* ‖ [être projeté] **: les boutons ont sauté** the buttons flew off *ou* popped off ▪ **faire ~ le bouchon d'une bouteille** to pop a cork ▸ **se faire ~ la cervelle** *fam* *ou* **le caisson** *fam* to blow one's brains out ▪ **faire ~ la banque** *pr & fig* to break the bank
5. [changer sans transition] to jump
6. [cesser de fonctionner - chaîne, courroie] to come off ; [- image de télévision] to flicker ; [- serrure] to snap
7. *fam* [être renvoyé] to fall ▪ **le gouvernement a sauté** the government has fallen ▪ **le ministre a sauté** the minister got fired *ou UK* got the sack ▪ **faire ~ un directeur** to kick out *ou* to fire a manager

8. CULIN : **faire ~ des pommes de terre** to sauté potatoes ▪ **faire ~ des crêpes** to toss pancakes.
◇ *vt* **1.** [obstacle] to jump *ou* to leap over *(insép)* ▪ **~ le pas** *fig* to take the plunge
2. [omettre] to skip, to leave out *(sép)*
3. △ *loc* **la ~** to be starving
4. ▲ [sexuellement] : **~ qqn** to lay sb△.

sauterelle [sotrɛl] *nf* **1.** ENTOM grasshopper ▪ [criquet] locust **2.** *fam* [femme osseuse] : **grande ~** beanpole **3.** [en manutention] travelling belt, conveyor (belt).

sauterie [sotri] *nf hum* party ▪ **donner une petite ~** to throw a party.

sauternes [sotɛrn] *nm* Sauternes *UK ou* Sauterne *US* (wine).

sauteur, euse [sotœr, øz] ◇ *adj* jumping, hopping.
◇ *nm, f* SPORT jumper ▪ **~ en hauteur/longueur** high/long jumper ▪ **~ à la perche** polevaulter.
◆ **sauteuse** *nf* **1.** CULIN high-sided frying pan **2.** MENUIS jigsaw, scroll saw.

sautillant, e [sotijɑ̃, ɑ̃t] *adj* **1.** [démarche, oiseau] hopping, skipping ▪ **d'un pas ~** with a dancing step **2.** *fig* [style] light ▪ [refrain] gay, bouncy.

sautillement [sotijmɑ̃] *nm* [petit saut] hop, skip, skipping *(U)*.

sautiller [3] [sotije] *vt* [faire de petits sauts] to hop, to skip ▪ **marcher en sautillant** to skip along ▪ **~ sur un pied** to hop.

sautoir [sotwar] *nm* **1.** JOAILL chain ▪ **en ~** on a chain ▶ **~ de perles** string of pearls **2.** SPORT jumping pit **3.** CULIN high-sided frying pan **4.** HÉRALD saltire.

sauvage [sovaʒ] ◇ *adj* **1.** ZOOL [non domestique] wild ▪ [non apprivoisé] untamed ▪ **il est redevenu ~** [chat] he's gone feral *ou* wild ; [jeune fauve] he's gone back to the wild **2.** [non cultivé] wild ▪ **le jardin est redevenu ~ depuis leur départ** since they left the garden has become overgrown **3.** [peu fréquenté - lieu] wild, remote ▪ **les régions ~s du nord de l'Écosse** the wilds *ou* the remote regions of northern Scotland **4.** [réservé, timide] shy **5.** *vieilli* & ANTHR savage, uncivilized **6.** [incontrôlé - geste, violence] savage, vicious, brutal **7.** [illégal - camping, vente] unauthorized ; [- urbanisme] unplanned.
◇ *nmf* **1.** *vieilli* & ANTHR savage ▪ **le bon ~** the noble savage **2.** [personne fruste, grossière] boor, brute ▪ **il se conduit comme un ~** he's a real brute **3.** [personne farouche] unsociable person, recluse.

sauvagement [sovaʒmɑ̃] *adv* savagely, viciously ▪ **~ assassiné** savagely *ou* brutally murdered.

sauvageon, onne [sovaʒɔ̃, ɔn] *nm, f* wild child.
◆ **sauvageon** *nm* [arbre] wildling.

sauvagerie [sovaʒri] *nf* **1.** [méchanceté] viciousness, brutality **2.** [misanthropie] unsociableness.

sauvagine [sovaʒin] *nf* CHASSE wildfowl *(U)*.

sauve [sov] *f* ▷ **sauf.**

sauvegarde [sovgard] *nf* **1.** [protection] safeguard, safeguarding *(U)* ▪ **~ des ressources naturelles** conservation of natural resources ▪ **sous la ~ de la justice** DR under the protection of the Court **2.** [sécurité] safety **3.** INFORM backup *(U)* ▪ **faire une ~** to make a backup **4.** NAUT safety rope.

sauvegarder [3] [sovgarde] *vt* **1.** [protéger - bien] to safeguard, to watch over *(insép)* ; [- honneur, réputation] to protect **2.** INFORM to save.

sauve-qui-peut [sovkipø] *nm inv* panic ▪ **ce fut un ~ général** there was a general stampede.

sauver [3] [sove] *vt* **1.** [personne - gén] to save, to rescue ; [- dans un accident, une catastrophe] to rescue ▪ **~ la vie à qqn** to save sb's life ▪ **être sauvé** [sain et sauf] to be safe ; [par quelqu'un] to have been saved *ou* rescued ▪ **ils ont atteint la côte, ils sont sauvés!** they've reached the shore, they're safe! ▪ *fig* **il y a une banque ouverte, je suis sauvé!** there's a bank open, saved again! ▶ **~ sa peau** *fam* to save one's skin *ou* hide **2.** [protéger] : **~ les apparences** to keep up appearances ▪ **pour ~ l'honneur** so that honour may be saved ▪ **~ la situation** to save *ou* to retrieve the situation ▪ **la musique sauve le film** the music saves the film ▶ **je lui ai sauvé la mise** *fam* I've got him out of trouble, I've bailed him out **3.** [préserver] to salvage, to save ▪ **~ qqch de l'oubli** to rescue sthg from oblivion ▶ **~ les meubles** *fam* to salvage something from the situation **4.** RELIG to save.
◆ **se sauver** ◇ *vp (emploi réfléchi)* RELIG to be saved.
◇ *vpi* **1.** [animal] to escape ▪ [pensionnaire] to run away ▪ [prisonnier] to escape, to break out *(insép)* ▪ [matelot] to jump ship ▪ **se ~ à toutes jambes** to take to one's heels (and run) **2.** *fam* [lait] to boil over **3.** *fam* [s'en aller] to leave, to split *US* ▪ **sauve-toi!** run along now! ▪ **bon, je me sauve!** right, I'm off *ou* on my way!
◆ **sauve qui peut** *interj* run for your life, every man for himself.

sauvetage [sovtaʒ] *nm* **1.** [d'un accidenté] rescue ▪ **opérer** *ou* **effectuer le ~ d'un équipage** to rescue a crew ▪ **~ d'une entreprise** *fig* financial rescue of a company ▶ **~ aérien/en montagne** air/mountain rescue **2.** NAUT [de l'équipage] life saving, sea rescue ▪ [de la cargaison] salvage.
◆ **de sauvetage** *loc adj* life *(modif)*.

sauveteur [sovtœr] *nm* rescuer.

sauvette [sovɛt] ◆ **à la sauvette** ◇ *loc adj* : **marchand** *ou* **vendeur à la ~** (illicit) street peddler *ou* hawker ▪ **vente à la ~** (illicit) street peddling *ou* hawking.
◇ *loc adv* **1.** [illégalement] : **vendre qqch à la ~** to hawk *ou* to peddle sthg (without authorization) **2.** [discrètement] : **faire qqch à la ~** to do sthg stealthily ▪ **il m'a glissé un mot à la ~** he slipped me a note.

sauveur [sovœr] ◇ *nm* **1.** [bienfaiteur] saviour **2.** RELIG : **le Sauveur** Our Saviour.
◇ *adj m* saving *(avant n)*.

SAV *nm* = **service après-vente.**

savamment [savamɑ̃] *adv* **1.** [avec érudition] learnedly **2.** [habilement] cleverly, cunningly ▪ **des tresses ~ enroulées** cleverly arranged tresses.

savane [savan] *nf* **1.** [dans les pays chauds] bush, savanna, savannah **2.** *Québec* [marécage] swamp.

savant, e [savɑ̃, ɑ̃t] ◇ *adj* **1.** [érudit - livre, moine, société] learned ; [- traduction, conversation] scholarly ▪ **c'est trop ~ pour lui!** that's (totally) beyond his grasp! **2.** [habile] skilful, clever ▪ **un ~ édifice de paquets de lessive** a cleverly constructed tower of soap powder packs **3.** [dressé - chien, puce] performing.
◇ *nm, f* [lettré] scholar.
◆ **savant** *nm* [scientifique] scientist ▪ **Marie Curie fut un grand ~** Marie Curie was a great scientist.

savarin [savarɛ̃] *nm* savarin (cake).

savate [savat] *nf* **1.** [chaussure] worn-out (old) shoe ▪ [pantoufle] old slipper ▪ **il est en ~s toute la journée** he pads around in his old slippers all day long ▶ **comme une ~** appallingly badly **2.** SPORT : **la ~** French boxing.

saveur [savœr] *nf* **1.** [goût] savour, flavour ▪ **une poire pleine de ~** a tasty pear ▪ **quelle ~!** very tasty! **2.** [trait particulier] fragrance, savour ▪ **il y a toute la ~ de l'Italie dans son accent** there is all the flavour of Italy in his accent **3.** [attrait] : **la ~ du péché** the sweet taste of sin.

Savoie [savwa] *npr f* : **(la) ~** Savoy, Savoie *(département in Rhône-Alpes; chef-lieu: Chambéry, code: 73)*.

savoir[1] [savwar] *nm* knowledge.

savoir[2] [59] [savwar] ◇ *vt* **1.** [connaître - donnée, réponse, situation] to know ▪ **que savez-vous de lui?** what do you know about *ou* of him? ▪ **tu sais la nouvelle?** have you heard the news? ▪ **on le savait malade** we knew *ou* we were aware (that) he was ill ▪ **je ne te savais pas si susceptible** I didn't know *ou* I didn't realize *ou* I never thought you were so touchy
2. [être informé de] : **que va-t-il arriver à Tintin? pour le ~, lisez notre prochain numéro!** what's in store for Tintin? find out in our next issue! ▪ **c'est toujours bon à ~** it's (always) worth knowing ▪ **je sais des choses...** *fam* [sur un ton taquin] I know a thing or two, I know what I know! ▪ **c'est sa maîtresse – tu en**

sais des choses! she's his mistress – you seem well informed! ■ **pour en ~ plus, composez le 34 15** for more information *ou* (if you want) to know more, phone 34 15 ■ **ce n'est pas elle qui l'a dénoncé – qu'en savez-vous?** she wasn't the one who turned him in – what do you know about it *ou* how do you know? ■ **je n'en sais rien du tout** I don't know anything about it, I haven't got a clue ■ **après tout, tu n'en sais rien!** after all, what do YOU know about it! ■ **il est venu ici, mais personne n'en a rien su** he came here, but nobody found out about it ■ **en ~ long sur qqn/qqch** to know a great deal about sb/sthg ■ **oh oui ça fait mal, j'en sais quelque chose!** yes, it's very painful, I can tell you! ■ **il n'aime pas les cafardeurs – tu dois en ~ quelque chose!** he doesn't like sneaks – you'd know all about that! ■ **pour ce que j'en sais** for all I know ■ **je sais à quoi m'en tenir sur lui** I know what kind of (a) person he is ■ **je crois ~ qu'ils ont annulé la conférence** I have reason *ou* I'm led to believe that they called off the conference ■ **tout le monde sait que...** it's a well-known fact *ou* everybody knows that... ■ **je ne sais combien, on ne sait combien** [d'argent] who knows how much ■ **il y a je ne sais combien de temps** a very long time ago ■ **il a fallu je ne sais combien de soldats** God knows how many soldiers were needed ■ **je ne sais comment, on ne sait comment** God knows how ■ **je ne sais où, on ne sait où** God knows where ■ **il est je ne sais où** God knows where he is ■ **je ne sais quel/quelle** some... or other ■ **sans trop ~ quoi faire** [attendre, marcher] aimlessly ■ **je ne sais qui, on ne sait qui** somebody or other ■ **il y a je ne sais quoi de bizarre chez lui** there's something a bit weird about him ■ **il vendait des tapis, des bracelets et que sais-je encore** he was selling carpets, bracelets and goodness/God knows what else ■ **sachant que x = y, démontrez que...** MATH if x = y, show that... ■ *(en usage absolu)* **oui, oui, je sais!** yes, yes, I'm aware of that *ou* I know *ou* I realize! ■ **où est-elle? – est-ce que je sais, moi?** *fam* where is she? – search me *ou* don't ask me *ou* how should I know? ■ **si j'avais su, je ne t'aurais rien dit** if I'd known, I wouldn't have said a word (to you) ■ *(au subjonctif)* **je ne sache pas qu'on ait modifié le calendrier** *sout & hum*, **on n'a pas modifié le calendrier, que je sache** the calendar hasn't been altered that I know of *ou* as far as I know ▸ **va ~ ce qui lui a pris!** who knows what possessed her?

3. [être convaincu de] to know, to be certain *ou* sure ■ **je savais bien que ça ne marcherait pas!** I knew it wouldn't work! ■ **je n'en sais trop rien** I'm not too sure, I don't really know ■ *(en usage absolu)* **comment ~?** how can you tell *ou* know? ■ **qui sait?** who knows? ■ **on ne sait jamais, sait-on jamais** you never know

4. [apprendre] : **je l'ai su par son frère** I heard it from her brother ■ **on a fini par ~ qu'un des ministres était compromis** it finally leaked out that one of the ministers was compromised ■ **faire ~ qqch à qqn** to inform sb *ou* to let sb know of sthg ■ **si elle arrive, faites-le moi ~** if she comes, let me know

5. [se rappeler] to know, to remember ■ **je ne sais plus la fin de l'histoire** I can't remember the end of the story ■ **est-ce que tu sais ton rôle?** THÉÂTRE do you know your lines? ; *fig* do you know what you are supposed to do?

6. [pouvoir] to know how to, to be able to ■ **~ faire qqch** to know how to *ou* to be able to do sthg ■ **tu sais plonger/conduire?** can you dive/drive? ■ **elle ne sait ni lire ni écrire** she can't read or write ■ **il ne sait pas/sait bien faire la cuisine** he's a bad/good cook ■ **si je sais bien compter/lire** if I count/read right ■ **il sait parler/vendre** he's a good talker/salesman ■ **quand on lui a demandé qui était président à l'époque, il n'a pas su répondre** when asked who was President at the time, he didn't know (what the answer was) ■ **je ne sais pas mentir** I can't (tell a) lie ■ **il sait se contenter de peu** he can make do with very little ■ **je n'ai pas su la réconforter** I wasn't able to comfort her ■ **elle ne sait pas se reposer** [elle travaille trop] she doesn't know when to stop ■ **il a su rester jeune/modeste** he's managed to remain young/modest ■ **~ s'y prendre : ~ s'y prendre avec les enfants** to know how to handle children, to be good with children ■ **je n'ai jamais su m'y prendre avec les filles** I've never known how to behave with girls! ■ **~ y faire : laisse-moi découper le poulet, tu ne sais pas y faire** let me carve the chicken, you don't know how to do it ■ **~ y faire avec qqn** to know how to handle sb ■ **il sait y faire avec les filles!** he knows how to get his (own) way with girls! ■ **on ne saurait tout prévoir** you can't think of everything ■ **on ne saurait être plus aimable/déplaisant** you couldn't be nicer/more unpleasant

7. [être conscient de] to know, to be aware of ■ **sachez-le bien** make no *ou* let there be no mistake about this ■ **il faut ~ que le parti n'a pas toujours suivi Staline** you've got to remember that the Party didn't always toe the Stalinist line ■ **sache qu'en fait, c'était son idée** you should know that in fact, it was his idea ■ **sachez que je le fais bénévolement** for your information, I do it for nothing ■ **elle ne sait plus ce qu'elle fait ni ce qu'elle dit** [à cause d'un choc, de la vieillesse] she's become confused ; [sous l'effet de la colère] she's beside herself (with anger) ■ **il est tellement soûl qu'il ne sait plus ce qu'il dit** he's so drunk he doesn't know what he's saying ■ **je sais ce que je dis** I know what I'm saying ■ **tu ne sais pas ce que tu veux/dis** you don't know what you want/what you're talking about ■ **il faudrait ~ ce que tu dis!** make up your mind! ■ *(en usage absolu)* **faudrait ~!** make up your mind!

8. [imaginer] : **ne (plus) ~ que** *ou* **quoi faire** to be at a loss as to what to do, not to know what to do ■ **je ne sais (plus) que faire avec ma fille** I just don't know what to do with my daughter ■ **il ne sait plus quoi faire pour se rendre intéressant** he'd stop at nothing *ou* there's nothing he wouldn't do to attract attention to himself ■ **je ne savais plus où me mettre** *ou* **me fourrer** *fam* [de honte] I didn't know where to put myself

9. *Belgique* **il ne sait pas venir demain** [il ne peut pas venir demain] he can't make it tomorrow ■ **ses résultats ne sont pas brillants, savez-vous?** [n'est-ce pas] his results aren't very good, are they *ou* am I right?

10. [pour prendre l'interlocuteur à témoin] : **ce n'est pas toujours facile, tu sais!** it's not always easy, you know! ■ **tu sais, je ne crois pas à ses promesses** to tell you the truth, I don't believe in her promises ■ **tu sais que tu commences à m'énerver?** *fam* you're getting on my nerves, you know that *ou* d'you know that?

<> *adv* namely, specifically, i.e.

◆ **se savoir** <> *vp (emploi passif)* [nouvelle] to become known ■ **tout se sait dans le village** news travels fast in the village ■ **ça finira par se ~** people are bound to find out ■ **je ne veux pas que ça se sache** I don't want it to be publicized *ou* to get around ▸ **cela** *ou* **ça** *fam* **se saurait : ça se saurait s'il était si doué que ça** *fam* if he was that good, you'd know about it.

<> *vpi* [personne] : **il se sait malade** he knows he's ill.

◆ **à savoir** *loc adv* namely, that is, i.e ■ **son principal prédateur, à ~ le renard** its most important predator, namely the fox.

◆ **à savoir que** *loc conj* meaning *ou* to the effect that *sout* ■ **il nous a donné sa réponse, à ~ qu'il accepte** he's given us his answer, that is, he accepts *ou* to the effect that he accepts.

◆ **savoir si** *loc conj fam* but who knows whether.

savoir-faire [savwarfɛr] *nm inv* know-how ■ **elle a du ~** she's got the know-how.

savoir-vivre [savwarvivr] *nm inv* good manners, savoir vivre *sout*, breeding ■ **avoir du ~** to have (good) manners ■ **manquer de ~** to have no manners ■ **manque de ~** bad manners, ill-breeding.

savon [savɔ̃] *nm* soap ■ **un (morceau de) ~** a bar of soap ▸ **~ en paillettes/poudre** soap flakes/powder ■ **~ à barbe** shaving soap ■ **~ de Marseille** ≃ household soap ■ **~ noir** soft soap ■ **passer un (bon) ~ à qqn** *fam* to give sb a (good) telling-off ■ **tu vas encore recevoir** *ou* **te faire passer un ~!** you'll get it in the neck again!

SAVON DE MARSEILLE

The soap industry has existed in Marseilles since the 16th century, and soap from Marseilles, usually sold in large square bricks, is renowned for its purity.

savonnage [savɔnaʒ] *nm* [de linge] washing (with soap).

savonner [3] [savɔne] *vt* **1.** [linge, surface] to soap **2.** [barbe] to lather.

◆ **se savonner** *vp (emploi réfléchi)* to soap o.s. (down) ■ **se ~ le visage/les mains** to soap (up) one's face/one's hands.

savonnerie [savɔnri] *nf* **1.** [usine] soap factory **2.** [tapis] Savonnerie (carpet).

savonnette [savɔnɛt] *nf* [savon] (small) bar of soap, bar of toilet soap.

savonneux, euse [savɔnø, øz] *adj* soapy.

savourer [3] [savure] *vt* **1.** [vin, mets, repas] to enjoy, to savour **2.** *fig* [moment, repos *etc*] to relish, to savour ■ **elle savoure sa vengeance** she savours her vengeance.

savoureux, euse [savurø, øz] *adj* **1.** [succulent] tasty, flavoursome, full of flavour **2.** *fig* [anecdote, plaisanterie] good, delightful ■ **je vais te raconter une histoire savoureuse** let me tell you a really lovely story.

savoyard, e [savwajar, ard] *adj* from Savoie.

saxe [saks] *nm* **1.** [matière] Dresden china *(U)*, Meissen porcelain **2.** [objet] piece of Dresden china *ou* of Meissen porcelain.

Saxe [saks] *npr f* : **(la) ~** Saxony ■ **(la) Basse-~** Lower Saxony.

saxifrage [saksifraʒ] *nf* saxifrage.

saxo [sakso] *nm fam* **1.** [instrument] sax **2.** [musicien] sax (player).

saxon, onne [saksɔ̃, ɔn] *adj* Saxon.
◆ **Saxon, onne** *nm, f* Saxon.

saxophone [saksɔfɔn] *nm* saxophone.

saxophoniste [saksɔfɔnist] *nmf* saxophone player, saxophonist.

saynète [sɛnɛt] *nf* playlet, sketch.

sbire [sbir] *nm* henchman.

sc. (*abr écrite de* **scène**) sc.

scabreux, euse [skabrø, øz] *adj* **1.** [indécent] obscene **2.** *litt* [dangereux] risky, tricky.

scalaire [skalɛr] ◇ *adj* MATH scalar.
◇ *nm* **1.** MATH scalar **2.** ZOOL angel fish, scalare *spéc.*

scalène [skalɛn] ◇ *adj* **1.** ANAT scalenus *(modif)* **2.** MATH scalene.
◇ *nm* ANAT scalenus (muscle).

scalp [skalp] *nm* **1.** [chevelure] scalp **2.** [action] scalping *(U)*.

scalpel [skalpɛl] *nm* scalpel.

scalper [3] [skalpe] *vt* to scalp ■ **se faire ~** to get scalped.

scampi [skɑ̃pi] *nmpl* scampi.

scandale [skɑ̃dal] *nm* **1.** [indignation] scandal ■ **au grand ~ de...** to the indignation of... ■ **faire ~ : son discours a fait ~** his speech caused a scandal **2.** [scène] scene, fuss ■ **il va encore faire un ~** he's going to make a fuss again **3.** [honte] : **c'est un ~!** (it's) outrageous!, it's an outrage! **4.** DR : **pour ~ sur la voie publique** for causing a public disturbance, for disturbing the peace.
◆ **à scandale** *loc adj* [journal, presse] sensationalist.

scandaleusement [skɑ̃daløzmɑ̃] *adv* scandalously, outrageously ■ **~ riche** outrageously rich.

scandaleux, euse [skɑ̃dalø, øz] *adj* [attitude, mensonge] disgraceful, outrageous, shocking ■ [article, photo] sensational, scandalous ■ **vie scandaleuse** life of scandal, scandalous life ‖ [prix] outrageous, shocking ■ **les loyers ont atteint des prix ~** rents have reached outrageously high levels.

scandaliser [3] [skɑ̃dalize] *vt* to shock, to outrage ■ **son cynisme a scandalisé la classe politique** his cynicism scandalized the politicians.
◆ **se scandaliser** *vpi* : **se ~ de qqch** to be shocked *ou* scandalized by sthg.

scander [3] [skɑ̃de] *vt* **1.** LITTÉR to scan **2.** [slogan] to chant ■ [mots, phrases] to stress.

scandinave [skɑ̃dinav] *adj* Scandinavian.
◆ **Scandinave** *nmf* [personne] Scandinavian.
◆ **scandinave** *nm* LING Scandinavian, Northern Germanic.

Scandinavie [skɑ̃dinavi] *npr f* : **(la) ~** Scandinavia.

Scanie [skani] *npr f* : **(la) ~** Scandia.

scanner[1] [skanɛr] *nm* **1.** IMPR scanner **2.** MÉD scanner ■ **passer au ~** to have a scan (done).

scanner[2] [3] [skane] *vt* to scan.

scanographe [skanɔgraf] = **scanner nm sens 2**.

scanographie [skanɔgrafi] *nf* **1.** [technique] scanning *(U)*, computerized (axial) tomography *spéc* **2.** [image] scan, scanner image, tomogram *spéc.*

scansion [skɑ̃sjɔ̃] *nf* scanning *(U)*, scansion.

scaphandre [skafɑ̃dr] *nm* **1.** NAUT diving gear, frogman suit ■ **~ autonome** aqualung **2.** ASTRONAUT spacesuit.

scaphandrier [skafɑ̃drije] *nm* NAUT (deep-sea) diver.

scapulaire [skapylɛr] *adj* & *nm* scapular.

scarabée [skarabe] *nm* **1.** ENTOM beetle, scarabaeid *spéc* **2.** ARCHÉOL scarab, scarabaeus.

scarification [skarifikasjɔ̃] *nf* **1.** MÉD scarring *(U)*, scarification *spéc* **2.** [d'un arbre] scarifying.

scarifier [9] [skarifje] *vt* to scarify.

scarlatine [skarlatin] *nf* scarlet fever, scarlatina *spéc.*

scarole [skarɔl] *nf* endive *(broad-leaved variety)*.

scato [skato] *fam* = **scatologique**.

scatologie [skatɔlɔʒi] *nf* scatology.

scatologique [skatɔlɔʒik] *adj* [goûts, écrit] scatological ■ [humour] lavatorial.

sceau, x [so] *nm* **1.** [cachet] seal ■ **apposer** *ou* **mettre son ~ sur un document** to affix one's seal on *ou* to a document ◐ **sous le ~ du secret** under the seal of secrecy **2.** *litt* [empreinte] mark ■ **le ~ du génie** the mark *ou* stamp of genius.

scélérat, e [selera, at] *litt* ◇ *adj* heinous, villainous.
◇ *nm, f* villain, scoundrel, rogue.

scélératesse [selerates] *nf litt* **1.** [caractère] villainy *litt*, wickedness **2.** [action] villainy *litt*, evil *ou* wicked deed, heinous crime.

scellement [sɛlmɑ̃] *nm* embedding, sealing.

sceller [4] [sele] *vt* **1.** [officialiser] to seal ■ **le mariage scella leur alliance** *fig* the marriage set the seal on their alliance **2.** [fermer] to put seals on, to seal up *(sép)* **3.** [fixer] to fix, to set, to embed ■ **~ une couronne sur une dent** to crown a tooth.

scellés [sele] *nmpl* seals ■ **mettre les ~ sur qqch** to seal sthg off.
◆ **sous scellés** *loc adv* under seal.

scénarimage [senarimaʒ] *nm* story-board.

scénario [senarjo] (*pl* **scénarios** *ou pl* **scenarii** [-rii]) *nm* **1.** CINÉ [histoire, trame] screenplay, scenario ■ [texte] (shooting) script, scenario ■ **tout s'est déroulé selon le ~ prévu** *fig* everything went as scheduled *ou* according to plan **2.** THÉÂTRE scenario **3.** [d'une bande dessinée] story, storyboard, scenario **4.** ÉCON [cas de figure] case, scenario.

scénariste [senarist] *nmf* scriptwriter.

scène [sɛn] *nf* **1.** [plateau d'un théâtre, d'un cabaret *etc*] stage ■ **(tout le monde) en ~, s'il vous plaît!** the whole cast on stage, please! ■ **monter sur ~** to go on the stage ■ **remonter sur ~** to go back on the stage ■ **sortir de ~** to come off stage, to exit ◐ **~ tournante** revolving stage ■ **entrer en ~** THÉÂTRE to come on stage ; *fig* to come *ou* to step in ■ **le Duc entre en ~** enter the Duke
2. [art dramatique] : **la ~** the stage ■ **adapter un livre pour la ~** to adapt a book for the stage *ou* theatre ■ **mettre "Phèdre" en ~** [monter la pièce] to stage "Phèdre" ; [diriger les acteurs] to direct "Phèdre" ■ **la façon dont il met Polonius en ~** the way he presents Polonius
3. CINÉ & THÉÂTRE [séquence] scene ■ **la première ~** the first *ou* opening scene ■ **la ~ finale** the last *ou* closing scene ■ **dans la ~ d'amour/du balcon** in the love/balcony scene ■ **~ de violence** scene of violence ■ **la ~ se passe à Montréal** the action takes place in *ou* the scene is set in Montreal

4. [décor] scene ■ **la ~ représente une clairière** the scene represents a clearing
5. [moment, événement] scene ■ **une ~ de la vie quotidienne** a scene of everyday life
6. [dispute] scene ■ **faire une ~ (à qqn)** to make a scene ➋ **~ de ménage** row ■ **~ de rupture** break-up scene
7. ART scene ■ **~ de genre** genre painting
8. *fig* **la ~ internationale/politique** the international/political scene
9. PSYCHOL : **~ primitive** *ou* **originaire** primal scene.

scénique [senik] *adj* theatrical.

scénographe [senɔgraf] *nmf* **1.** [peintre] scenographer **2.** THÉÂTRE theatre designer.

scénographie [senɔgrafi] *nf* **1.** [peinture] scenography **2.** THÉÂTRE theatre designing.

scepticisme [sɛptisism] *nm* scepticism ■ **avec ~** sceptically.

sceptique [sɛptik] <> *adj* [incrédule] sceptical.
<> *nmf* [personne qui doute] sceptic ■ PHILOS Sceptic.

sceptre [sɛptr] *nm* **1.** [d'un roi] sceptre **2.** *litt* [autorité] authority, royalty ■ **disputer son ~ à qqn** to try to usurp sb's authority.

schéma [ʃema] *nm* **1.** TECHNOL diagram ■ [dessin] sketch ■ **faire un ~** to make *ou* to draw a diagram ➋ **~ de câblage/montage** wiring/set-up diagram **2.** ADMIN & DR : **~ directeur** urban development plan **3.** [aperçu] (broad) outline **4.** [système] pattern **5.** LING schema.

schématique [ʃematik] *adj* **1.** TECHNOL diagrammatical, schematic **2.** [simplificateur] schematic, simplified ■ **présenter un projet de façon ~** to present a project in a simplified form ■ **un peu trop ~** oversimplified, simplistic.

schématiquement [ʃematikmɑ̃] *adv* **1.** TECHNOL diagrammatically, schematically **2.** [en simplifiant] : **décrire un projet/une opération ~** to give the basic outline of a project/an operation ■ **~, voici comment nous allons nous y prendre** in broad outline, this is how we're planning to handle it.

schématisation [ʃematizasjɔ̃] *nf* **1.** TECHNOL schematization, presenting as a diagram **2.** [simplification] simplification, simplifying *(U)*, oversimplification *péj.*

schématiser [3] [ʃematize] *vt* **1.** TECHNOL to schematize, to present in diagram form **2.** [simplifier] to simplify ■ *(en usage absolu)* **il schématise à l'extrême** he's being much too oversimplistic.

schématisme [ʃematism] *nm* **1.** PHILOS schema **2.** [simplification] simplification.

schismatique [ʃismatik] *adj* & *nmf* schismatic.

schisme [ʃism] *nm* **1.** RELIG schism ■ **le grand ~ d'Occident** the Great (Western) Schism **2.** *fig* schism, split.

schiste [ʃist] *nm* **1.** MINÉR schist ■ **~ bitumineux** oil shale **2.** MIN [déchets] deads.

schisteux, euse [ʃistø, øz] *adj* schistose, schistous.

schizo [skizo] (*abr de* **schizophrène**) *adj fam* schizo.

schizoïde [skizɔid] *adj* PSYCHOL schizoid.

schizophrène [skizɔfrɛn] *adj* & *nmf* schizophrenic.

schizophrénie [skizɔfreni] *nf* schizophrenia.

schlague [ʃlag] *nf fam* [autorité brutale] : **elle mène son monde à la ~** she rules everybody with a rod of iron.

schlass△ [ʃlas] *adj* [ivre] pissed ■ [fatigué] knackered *UK*, beat *US*.

schlinguer [ʃlɛ̃ge] = **chlinguer**.

schmilblik [ʃmilblik] *nm fam* **ça ne fait pas avancer le ~** it doesn't get us any further.

schnaps [ʃnaps] *nm* schnapps.

schnock△ [ʃnɔk] <> *adj inv* [cinglé] nuts.
<> *nm* [imbécile] blockhead ■ **espèce de vieux ~!** you old fogey *ou* duffer! ■ **alors, tu viens, du ~?** are you coming, dumbo?

schnouf△ [ʃnuf] *nf arg crime* & *vieilli* dope.

Schtroumpf [ʃtrumf] *npr* Smurf ■ **les ~s** the Smurfs.

Schubert [ʃubɛr] *npr* Schubert.

schuss [ʃus] <> *nm* schuss.
<> *adv* : **descendre (tout) ~** to schuss down.

sciage [sjaʒ] *nm* sawing.

sciant, e [sjɑ̃, ɑ̃t] *adj fam* [étonnant] staggering ■ [drôle] hilarious.

sciatique [sjatik] <> *adj* sciatic ■ **nerf petit/grand ~** small/great sciatic nerve.
<> *nf* sciatica.

scie [si] *nf* **1.** TECHNOL saw ■ **~ à bois** wood saw ■ **~ à chaîne** chainsaw ■ **~ circulaire** circular saw ■ **~ électrique** power saw ■ **~ à métaux** hacksaw ■ **~ à ruban** bandsaw, ribbon saw ■ **~ sabre** *ou* **sauteuse** jigsaw, scroll saw **2.** MUS : **~ musicale** musical saw **3.** ZOOL sawfish **4.** *fam* [chanson] song played ad nauseam ■ [message] message repeated again and again **5.** *fam péj* [personne ou chose ennuyeuse] bore, drag.

sciemment [sjamɑ̃] *adv* **1.** [consciemment] knowingly **2.** [délibérément] deliberately, on purpose.

science [sjɑ̃s] *nf* **1.** [connaissances] : **la ~** science ■ **dans l'état actuel de la ~** in the current state of (our) knowledge
2. *(gén pl)* [domaine spécifique] science ■ **les ~s appliquées/physiques** the applied/physical sciences ■ **les ~s économiques** economics ■ **les ~s exactes** exact sciences ■ **les ~s humaines** [gén] human sciences, the social sciences ; UNIV ≃ Arts ■ **les ~s mathématiques, la ~ mathématique** *sout* mathematics, the mathematical sciences ■ **les ~s naturelles** [gén] the natural sciences ; ÉDUC biology ■ **~ occulte, ~s occultes** the occult (sciences) ■ **les ~s politiques** politics, political sciences ■ **les ~s sociales** UNIV social studies
3. [technique] science, art ■ [habileté] skill
4. [érudition] knowledge ■ **il croit qu'il a la ~ infuse** he thinks he's a fount of knowledge *ou* he's omniscient ■ **je n'ai pas la ~ infuse!** I don't know everything! ■ **il faut toujours qu'il étale sa ~** he's always trying to impress everybody with what he knows
5. RELIG : **Science chrétienne** Christian Science.
◆ **sciences** *nfpl* UNIV [par opposition aux lettres] science, sciences.

science-fiction [sjɑ̃sfiksjɔ̃] (*pl* **sciences-fictions**) *nf* science fiction ■ **livre/film de ~** science fiction book/film.

Sciences-Po [sjɑ̃spo] *npr grande école for political sciences.*

scientificité [sjɑ̃tifisite] *nf* scientificity, scientific quality.

scientifique [sjɑ̃tifik] <> *adj* scientific ■ **de manière ~** scientifically.
<> *nmf* scientist.

scientifiquement [sjɑ̃tifikmɑ̃] *adv* scientifically.

scientisme [sjɑ̃tism] *nm* **1.** PHILOS scientism **2.** RELIG Christian Science.

scientiste [sjɑ̃tist] <> *adj* PHILOS & RELIG scientistic.
<> *nmf* **1.** PHILOS proponent of scientism **2.** RELIG (Christian) Scientist.

scientologie [sjɑ̃tɔlɔʒi] *nf* Scientology®.

scier [9] [sje] *vt* **1.** [couper] to saw ■ **~ une planche en deux** to saw through a plank, to saw a plank in two ■ **~ la branche d'un arbre** to saw a branch off a tree ■ **~ un tronc en rondins** to saw up a tree trunk (into logs) **2.** [blesser] to cut into *(insép)* ■ **la ficelle du paquet me scie les doigts** the string around the parcel is cutting into my fingers **3.** *fam* [surprendre] : **sa réponse m'a scié** I couldn't believe my ears when I heard his answer.

scierie [siri] *nf* sawmill.

scieur [sjœr] *nm* **1.** [ouvrier] sawyer ■ **~ de long** pit sawyer **2.** [patron] sawmill owner.

scinder [3] [sɛ̃de] *vt* to divide, to split (up) ■ **~ qqch en deux** to divide *ou* to split sthg (up) into two.
◆ **se scinder** *vpi* to split ■ **le parti s'est scindé en deux tendances** the party split into two.

scintigraphie [sɛ̃tigrafi] *nf* scintigraphy.

scintillant, e [sɛ̃tijɑ̃, ɑ̃t] *adj* [yeux] sparkling, twinkling ■ [bijoux, reflet] glittering, sparkling ■ [étoile] twinkling.

scintillation [sɛ̃tijasjɔ̃] *nf* [éclat lumineux] scintillation.

scintillement [sɛ̃tijmɑ̃] *nm* **1.** [des yeux] sparkling, twinkling ■ [de bijoux, d'un reflet] glittering, scintillating ■ [d'une étoile] twinkling **2.** TV : **écran sans ~** flicker-free screen.

scintiller [3] [sɛ̃tije] *vi* [lumière, bijoux, eau, reflet] to sparkle, to glitter ■ [yeux] to sparkle, to twinkle ■ [étoile] to twinkle ■ **le ciel tout entier scintillait** the whole of the sky was aglitter *litt*.

scion [sjɔ̃] *nm* **1.** BOT [pousse] (year's) shoot ■ [à greffer] scion **2.** PÊCHE tip (of rod).

Scipion [sipjɔ̃] *npr* Scipio ■ **~ l'Africain** Scipio Africanus.

scission [sisjɔ̃] *nf* **1.** POLIT & RELIG scission, split, rent ■ **faire ~** to split off *(insép)*, to secede **2.** BIOL & PHYS fission, splitting.

scissure [sisyr] *nf* [du cerveau] fissure, sulcus ■ [du foie] scissura, scissure.

sciure [sjyr] *nf* sawdust.

scléreux, euse [sklerø, øz] *adj* sclerotic.

sclérosant, e [sklerozɑ̃, ɑ̃t] *adj* **1.** MÉD sclerosing, sclerosis-causing **2.** *fig* ossification.

sclérose [skleroz] *nf* **1.** MÉD sclerosis ■ **~ artérielle** arteriosclerosis ■ **~ en plaques** multiple sclerosis **2.** *fig* ossification.

sclérosé, e [skleroze] ◇ *adj* **1.** MÉD sclerotic **2.** *fig* antiquated, ossified, creaky (with age) ■ **avoir l'esprit ~** to have become set in one's ways.
◇ *nm, f* sclerosis sufferer.

scléroser [3] [skleroze] *vt* **1.** MÉD to cause sclerosis of ■ **molécule qui sclérose les tissus** tissue-sclerosing molecule **2.** *fig* [système] to ossify, to paralyze ■ [esprit] to make rigid ■ **le parti a été sclérosé par des années d'inactivité** years of inertia have brought the party to a political standstill.
◆ **se scléroser** *vpi* **1.** MÉD to sclerose **2.** *fig* [se figer] to ossify, to become paralyzed ■ **se ~ dans ses habitudes** to become set in one's ways.

sclérothérapie [skleroterapi] *nf* MÉD sclerotherapy.

sclérotique [sklerɔtik] *nf* sclerotic, sclera.

scolaire [skɔlɛr] ◇ *adj* **1.** [de l'école] school *(modif)* ■ [du cursus] school, academic ■ **le milieu ~** the school environment ■ **niveau/succès ~** academic standard/achievement ■ **livre** *ou* **manuel ~** (school) textbook **2.** *péj* [écriture, raisonnement] dry, unimaginative ■ **il a un style très ~** his style is very unoriginal.
◇ *nmf* [enfant] schoolchild.

scolarisable [skɔlarizabl] *adj* : **population ~** school-age population.

scolarisation [skɔlarizasjɔ̃] *nf* **1.** [éducation] schooling, (formal) education **2.** ADMIN & DR school attendance, schooling ■ **la ~ est obligatoire à partir de six ans** (attendance at) school *ou* schooling is compulsory from the age of six **3.** [d'une région, d'un pays] school-building programme.

scolariser [3] [skɔlarize] *vt* **1.** [enfant] to send to school, to provide with formal education ■ **l'enfant est-il déjà scolarisé?** is the child already at school? **2.** [région, pays] to equip with schools.

scolarité [skɔlarite] *nf* **1.** ADMIN & DR school attendance, schooling **2.** [études] school career ■ [période] schooldays ■ **j'ai eu une ~ difficile** I had a difficult time at school.

scolastique [skɔlastik] ◇ *adj* **1.** HIST scholastic **2.** *sout* [formaliste] scholastic, pedantic *péj*.
◇ *nf* PHILOS & RELIG scholasticism.
◇ *nm* **1.** HIST Scholastic, Schoolman **2.** RELIG theology student.

scoliose [skɔljoz] *nf* scoliosis.

scolopendre [skɔlɔpɑ̃dr] *nf* **1.** BOT hart's-tongue, scolopendrium *spéc* **2.** ZOOL centipede, scolopendra *spéc*.

sconse [skɔ̃s] *nm* **1.** ZOOL skunk **2.** [fourrure] skunk (fur).

scoop [skup] *nm* scoop ■ **faire un ~** to get a scoop.

scooter [skutœr] *nm* (motor) scooter.

scorbut [skɔrbyt] *nm* scurvy.

scorbutique [skɔrbytik] ◇ *adj* scorbutic.
◇ *nmf* scurvy sufferer.

score [skɔr] *nm* **1.** SPORT score ■ **où en est** *ou* **quel est le ~?** what's the score? **2.** [résultat] : **faire un bon ~ aux élections** to get a good result in the election.

scorie [skɔri] *nf* **1.** MÉTALL slag ■ [laitier] cinders ■ [de fer] (iron) clinker *ou* dross **2.** *litt* [déchet] : **toutes les ~s d'une vie** the waste *ou* dregs of a lifetime.

scorpion [skɔrpjɔ̃] *nm* **1.** ZOOL scorpion ■ **~ de mer** scorpion fish **2.** ARM scorpion.

Scorpion [skɔrpjɔ̃] *npr m* **1.** ASTRON Scorpio **2.** ASTROL Scorpio ■ **être ~** to be Scorpio *ou* a Scorpian.

scotch [skɔtʃ] (*pl* **scotchs** *ou pl* **scotches**) *nm* Scotch (whisky).

Scotch® [skɔtʃ] *nm* adhesive tape, Sellotape® *UK*, Scotchtape® *US*.

scotché, e [skɔtʃe] *adj* : **être ~ devant la télévision** to be glued to the television.

scotcher [3] [skɔtʃe] *vt* to sellotape *UK*, to scotchtape *US*.

scottish-terrier [skɔtiʃterje] (*pl* **scottish-terriers**) *nm* Scottish terrier, Scottie.

scoumoune△ [ʃkumun] *nf* rotten luck ■ **avoir la ~** to be jinxed.

scout, e [skut] ◇ *adj* **1.** [relatif au scoutisme] scout *(modif)* ■ **camp/mouvement ~** scout camp/movement **2.** *fig* boy scout *(modif)* ■ **il a un petit côté ~** he's a boy scout at heart.
◇ *nm, f* [personne] (Boy) Scout (*f* (Girl) Guide) ■ **~, toujours prêt!** [devise des scouts] be prepared! ; *hum* always at your service!

scoutisme [skutism] *nm* **1.** [activité] scouting **2.** [association - pour garçons] Boy Scout movement ; [- pour filles] Girl Guide movement.

Scrabble® [skrabl] *nm* Scrabble®.

scrabbleur, euse [skrablœr, øz] *nm, f* Scrabble® player.

scratcher [3] [skratʃe] *vt* SPORT to scratch, to withdraw.

scribe [skrib] *nm* **1.** ANTIQ & RELIG scribe **2.** *péj* & *vieilli* [gratte-papier] pen pusher *péj*.

scribouillard, e [skribujar, ard] *nm, f fam péj* pen pusher.

script [skript] *nm* **1.** [écriture] script *(modif)* ■ **écrire en ~** to write in block letters, to print (in block letters) **2.** CINÉ & RADIO script **3.** BOURSE scrip.

scripte [skript] *nmf* continuity man (*f* continuity *ou* script girl).

scripteur [skriptœr] *nm* **1.** RELIG composer of Papal Bulls **2.** LING writer.

script-girl [skriptgœrl] (*pl* **script-girls**) *nf* continuity *ou* script girl.

scriptural, e, aux [skriptyral, o] *adj* scriptural.

scrotal, e, aux [skrɔtal, o] *adj* scrotal.

scrotum [skrɔtɔm] *nm* scrotum.

scrupule [skrypyl] *nm* **1.** [cas de conscience] scruple, qualm (of conscience) ■ **n'aie pas de ~s** don't have any qualms ■ **elle n'a aucun ~** she has no scruples ■ **ce ne sont pas les ~s qui l'étouffent** *fam* he's completely unscrupulous ■ **avoir ~ à faire**

qqch *sout* to have scruples *ou* qualms about doing sthg ■ **n'ayez aucun ~ à faire appel à moi** don't hesitate to ask for my help **2.** [minutie] punctiliousness ■ **exact jusqu'au ~** scrupulously *ou* punctiliously exact.
◆ **sans scrupules** *loc adj* [individu] unscrupulous, unprincipled, without scruples.

scrupuleusement [skrypyløzmɑ̃] *adv* scrupulously, punctiliously.

scrupuleux, euse [skrypylø, øz] *adj* **1.** [honnête] scrupulous ■ **peu ~** unscrupulous ■ **d'une honnêteté scrupuleuse** scrupulously honest **2.** [minutieux] scrupulous, meticulous.

scrutateur, trice [skrytatœr, tris] ◇ *adj* searching *(avant n)* ■ **d'un air ~** searchingly.
◇ *nm, f* ADMIN scrutineer *UK*, teller *US*.

scruter [3] [skryte] *vt* **1.** [pour comprendre] to scrutinize, to examine ■ **~ qqn du regard** to give sb a searching look ■ **il scruta son visage** he searched her face **2.** [en parcourant des yeux] to scan, to search ■ **elles scrutaient l'horizon** they scanned *ou* searched the horizon.

scrutin [skrytɛ̃] *nm* **1.** [façon d'élire] vote, voting *(U)*, ballot ■ **procéder au ~** to take a ballot ■ **dépouiller le ~** to count the votes ▶ **~ plurinominal** *ou* **de liste** voting for a list *ou* ticket ■ **~ d'arrondissement** district election system ■ **~ majoritaire** first past the post election *UK*, election on a majority basis ■ **~ proportionnel** *ou* **à la proportionnelle** (voting using the system of) proportional representation ■ **~ secret** secret ballot ■ **voter au ~ secret** to have a secret ballot ■ **~ uninominal** voting for a single candidate **2.** [fait de voter] ballot ■ **par (voie de) ~** by ballot ▶ **~ de ballottage** second ballot, run-off election *US* **3.** [consultation électorale] election.

sculpter [3] [skylte] *vt* **1.** ART to sculpt ■ [orner de sculptures] to sculpture ■ **~ qqch dans le marbre** to sculpt sthg out of marble **2.** [bois] to carve ■ [bâton] to scrimshaw **3.** *sout* [façonner] to sculpt, to carve, to fashion ■ **la mer a sculpté la falaise** the cliff has been sculpted by the sea.

sculpteur [skyltœr] *nm* sculptor.

sculptural, e, aux [skyltyral, o] *adj* **1.** ART sculptural **2.** [beauté, formes] statuesque.

sculpture [skyltyr] *nf* **1.** ART sculpture *(U)*, sculpting *(U)* ■ **faire de la ~** to sculpt ■ **il fait de la ~** he's a sculptor ■ **~ sur bois** woodcarving **2.** [œuvre] sculpture, piece of sculpture.
◆ **sculptures** *nfpl* AUTO [d'un pneu] tread pattern.

sdb = salle de bains.

SDF *(abr de* **sans domicile fixe***)* *nmf* homeless person ■ **les ~** the homeless.

SDN *npr f* = **Société des Nations**.

se [sə] *(devant voyelle ou 'h' muet s'* [s]*) pron pers réfléchi (3e pers sing et pl, m et f)* **1.** [avec un verbe pronominal réfléchi] : **se salir** to get dirty ■ **s'exprimer** to express o.s. ■ **elle se coiffe** she's doing her hair ■ **elles s'en sont persuadées** they've convinced themselves of it ■ **il s'écoute parler** he listens to his own voice ▮ [se substituant à l'adjectif possessif] : **il s'est fracturé deux côtes** he broke two ribs ■ **se mordre la langue** to bite one's tongue
2. [avec un verbe pronominal réciproque] : **pour s'aider, ils partagent le travail** to help each other *ou* one another, they share the work
3. [avec un verbe pronominal passif] : **cette décision s'est prise sans moi** this decision has been taken without me ■ **ce modèle se vend bien** this model sells well ■ **ça se mange?** can you eat it?
4. [avec un verbe pronominal intransitif] : **ils s'en vont** they're leaving ■ **il se laisse convaincre trop facilement** he is too easily persuaded ■ **il s'est fait avoir!** *fam* he's been had! ■ **il se croyait lundi** he thought it was Monday today ■ **elle se croyait en sécurité** she thought she was safe ■ **il se dit médecin** he claims to be a doctor
5. [dans des tournures impersonnelles] : **il se fait tard** it's getting late ■ **il se peut qu'ils arrivent plus tôt** it's possible that they'll arrive earlier, they might arrive earlier
6. *fam* [emploi expressif] : **il se fait 7 000 euros par mois** he's got 7,000 euros coming in per month ■ **elle se l'est écouté au moins trente fois, ce disque** she listened to this record at least thirty times.

SE *(abr écrite de* **Son Excellence***)* HE.

S-E *(abr écrite de* **Sud-Est***)* SE.

séance [seɑ̃s] *nf* **1.** [réunion] session ■ **être en ~** [comité, Parlement] to be sitting *ou* in session ; [tribunal] to be in session ■ **lever la ~** [groupe de travail] to close the meeting ; [comité] to end *ou* to close the session ; [Parlement] to adjourn ■ **la ~ est levée!** [au tribunal] the court will adjourn! ■ **suspendre la ~** [au Parlement, au tribunal] to adjourn ■ **la ~ est ouverte!** [au tribunal] this court is now in session! ■ **en ~ publique** [au tribunal] in open court
2. BOURSE : **ce fut une bonne/mauvaise ~ aujourd'hui à la Bourse** it was a good/bad day today on the Stock Exchange ■ **en début/fin de ~, les actions Roman étaient à 80 euros** the Roman shares opened/closed at 80 euros
3. [période - d'entraînement, de traitement] session ■ **~ de pose** sitting ■ **~ de projection** slide show ■ **~ de rééducation** (session of) physiotherapy ■ **~ de spiritisme** seance ■ **~ de travail** working session ■ **~ d'information** briefing session
4. CINÉ showing ■ **~ à 19 h 10, film à 19 h 30** program 7.10, film starts 7.30 ■ **la dernière ~** the last showing
5. *fam* [crise] scene, fuss, tantrum.
◆ **séance tenante** *loc adv* forthwith, right away, without further ado ■ **il l'épousa ~ tenante** he married her without further ado.

séant, e [seɑ̃, ɑ̃t] *adj litt* [convenable] becoming, seemly.
◆ **séant** *nm* [postérieur] : **se mettre sur son ~** to sit up ■ **tomber sur son ~** to fall on one's behind.

seau, x [so] *nm* **1.** [récipient] bucket, pail ■ **~ à champagne** Champagne bucket ■ **~ à glace** ice-bucket *UK*, ice-pail *US* ■ **~ hygiénique** slop pail **2.** [contenu] bucketful ■ **un ~ de lait** a bucket of milk.
◆ **à seaux** *loc adv fam* **il pleut à ~x, la pluie tombe à ~x** it's pouring *ou* bucketing *UK* down.

sébacé, e [sebase] *adj* sebaceous.

sébile [sebil] *nf litt* begging bowl.

séborrhée [sebɔre] *nf* seborrhoea.

sébum [sebɔm] *nm* sebum.

sec, sèche [sɛk, sɛʃ] *adj* **1.** [air, bois, endroit, vêtement *etc*] dry ■ **il fait un froid ~** it's cold and dry, there's a crisp cold air ■ **avoir l'œil ~** *ou* **les yeux ~s** MÉD to have dry eyes ; *fig* to be dry-eyed **2.** [légume, fruit] dried ■ [alcool] neat ■ **shampooing ~** dry shampoo **3.** [non gras - cheveux, peau, mine de crayon] dry ■ [maigre - personne] lean ■ **être ~ comme un coup de trique** *fam* to be all skin and bone *ou* as thin as a rake **4.** [désagréable - ton, voix] harsh, curt, terse ; [- explication, refus, remarque] curt, terse ; [- rire] dry ■ **avoir le cœur ~** to be hard-hearted *ou* cold-hearted ■ **un bruit ~** a snap *ou* crack ■ **ouvrir/fermer qqch avec un bruit ~** to snap sthg open/shut ■ **d'un coup ~** smartly, sharply ■ **retire le sparadrap d'un coup ~** pull the sticking plaster off smartly **5.** ART [graphisme, style] dry **6.** ŒNOL [champagne, vin] dry **7.** CARTES : **atout/roi ~** singleton trumps/king.
◆ **sec** ◇ *adv* **1.** MÉTÉOR : **il fera ~ toute la semaine** the weather will be dry for the whole week **2.** [brusquement] hard ■ **démarrer ~** [conducteur] to shoot off at top speed ; [course] to get a flying start ■ **il a pris son virage assez ~** he took the bend rather sharply.
◇ *nm* AGRIC dry feed.
◆ **à sec** ◇ *loc adj* **1.** [cours d'eau, source *etc*] dry, dried-up ■ [réservoir] empty **2.** *fam* [sans argent - personne] hard up, broke, cleaned out ; [- caisse] empty.
◇ *loc adv* **1.** [sans eau] : **on met la piscine à ~ chaque hiver** the pool's drained (off) every winter ■ **le soleil a mis le marais à ~** the sun has dried up the marsh **2.** *fam* [financièrement] : **mettre une entreprise à ~** to ruin a firm.
◆ **au sec** *loc adv* : **garder** *ou* **tenir qqch au ~** to keep sthg in a dry place, to keep sthg dry ■ **rester au ~** to stay dry.

sécable [sekabl] *adj* **1.** PHARM breakable **2.** GÉOM divisible.

SECAM, Secam [sekam] *(abr de* **séquentiel couleur à mémoire***)* *nm* SECAM.

sécant, e [sekɑ̃, ɑ̃t] *adj* intersecting, secant.
◆ **sécante** *nf* secant.

sécateur [sekatœr] *nm* : un ~ [pour les fleurs] (a pair of) secateurs ; [pour les haies] pruning shears.

sécession [sesesjɔ̃] *nf* secession ▪ **faire ~** to secede.

sécessionniste [sesesjɔnist] *adj & nmf* secessionist.

séchage [seʃaʒ] *nm* **1.** [du linge, des cheveux, du foin] drying **2.** [du bois] seasoning.

sèche [sɛʃ] ◇ *f* ▷ **sec**.
◇ *nf fam* cig, fag *UK*.

sèche-cheveux [sɛʃʃəvø] *nm inv* hair dryer.

sèche-linge [sɛʃlɛ̃ʒ] *nm inv* [à tambour] tumble-drier ▪ [placard] airing cupboard.

sèche-mains [sɛʃmɛ̃] *nm inv* hand-dryer.

sèchement [sɛʃmɑ̃] *adv* **1.** [durement] dryly, curtly, tersely ▪ **ne comptez pas sur moi, répondit-elle ~** don't count on me, she snapped back **2.** [brusquement] sharply ▪ **prendre un virage un peu ~** to take a bend rather sharply **3.** [sans fioritures] dryly ▪ **il expose toujours ses arguments un peu ~** he always sets out his arguments rather unimaginatively.

sécher [18] [seʃe] ◇ *vt* **1.** [gén] to dry ▪ [avec un torchon, une éponge] to wipe dry ▪ **sèche tes larmes** *ou* **tes yeux** dry your tears *ou* your eyes ▪ **~ les larmes** *ou* **les pleurs de qqn** *sout* to console sb **2.** [vêtement] to dry ▪ **'~ en machine'** 'to tumble dry' **3.** [suj: chaleur, soleil - terrain, plante] to dry up *(sép)* ▪ [déshydrater - fruits] to dry (up) ▪ **figues séchées au soleil** sun-dried figs **4.** *arg scol* [manquer] : **~ les cours** ÉDUC to play truant *UK ou* hooky *US* ; UNIV to cut lectures *UK ou* class *US* **5.** *fam* [boire] : **il a séché trois cognacs** he knocked back three brandies.
◇ *vi* **1.** [surface] to dry (off) ▪ [linge] to dry ▪ [éponge] to dry (out) ▪ [sol, puits] to dry up ▪ [cours d'eau] to dry up, to run dry **2.** [vêtement] : **faire ~ du linge** to leave clothes to dry, to let linen dry ▪ **mettre le linge à ~** to put the washing out to dry ▪ **'faire ~ sans essorer'** 'do not spin dry', 'dry flat' ▪ **'faire ~ à plat'** 'dry flat' **3.** [plante] to dry up *ou* out ▪ [bois] to dry out ▪ [fruits, viande] to dry ▪ **faire ~ du bois** to season wood ▪ **~ sur pied** [plante] to wilt, to wither **4.** *fam loc* **j'ai séché en physique/sur la deuxième question** I drew a blank in the physics exam/on the second question.
◆ **se sécher** *vp (emploi réfléchi)* to dry o.s. ▪ **se ~ les mains/cheveux** to dry one's hands/hair.

sécheresse [sɛʃrɛs] *nf* **1.** [d'un climat, d'un terrain, d'un style] dryness ▪ [d'un trait] dryness, harshness ▪ [d'une réplique, d'un ton] abruptness ▪ **répondre avec ~** to answer curtly *ou* abruptly *ou* tersely ▪ **la ~ de sa remarque** the curtness *ou* terseness of his remark ▪ **montrer une grande ~ de cœur** to show great heartlessness **2.** MÉTÉOR drought ▪ **pendant la** *ou* **les mois de ~** during the dry months.

sécheur [seʃœr] *nm* [à tabac] dryer.

sécheuse [seʃøz] *nf* [de linge] tumble-drier.

séchoir [seʃwar] *nm* **1.** AGRIC & TECHNOL [salle] drying room ▪ [hangar] drying shed ▪ [râtelier] drying rack **2.** [à usage domestique] dryer ▪ **~ à cheveux** hair dryer ▪ **~ à linge** [à tambour] tumble-drier ; [pliant] clotheshorse ; [suspendu] ceiling airer.

second, e [səgɔ̃, ɔ̃d] ◇ *adj* **1.** [dans l'espace, le temps] second ▪ **pour la ~e fois** for the second time ▪ **en ~ lieu** secondly, in the second place ⊙ **le Second Empire** HIST the French Second Empire **2.** [dans une hiérarchie] second ▪ [éclairagiste, maquilleur] assistant *(modif)* ▪ **la ~e ville de France** France's second city ⊙ **~e classe** TRANSP second class ▪ **le ~ marché** BOURSE the unlisted securities market **3.** [autre - chance, jeunesse, vie] second ▪ **c'est une ~e nature chez lui** it's second nature to him ▪ **elle a été une ~e mère pour moi** she was like a mother to me ⊙ **~e vue** clairvoyance, second sight ▪ **être doué de ~e vue** to be clairvoyant **4.** MATH : **a ~e** a double point, a''.
◇ *nm, f* **1.** [dans l'espace, le temps] second ▪ **je lis le premier paragraphe, et toi le ~** I read the first paragraph, and you the second one *ou* the next one **2.** [dans une hiérarchie] second ▪ **arriver le ~** [dans une course, une élection] to come second.
◆ **second** *nm* **1.** [assistant - d'un directeur] right arm ; [- dans un duel] second ▪ NAUT first mate ▪ MIL second in command **2.** [dans une charade] : **mon ~ est...** my second is... **3.** [étage] second floor *UK*, third floor *US*.
◆ **seconde** *nf* **1.** AUTO second gear ▪ **passe en ~e** change into *ou* to second gear **2.** TRANSP [classe] second class ▪ [billet] second-class ticket ▪ **les ~es, les wagons de ~e** second-class carriages ▪ **voyager en ~e** to travel second class **3.** ÉDUC ≃ fifth form *UK*, ≃ tenth grade *US* **4.** ESCRIME seconde **5.** DANSE second position **6.** MUS second.
◆ **secondes** *nfpl* IMPR second proofs.
◆ **en second** ◇ *loc adj* : **capitaine en ~** first mate.
◇ *loc adv* second, secondly ▪ **passer en ~** to be second.

secondaire [səgɔ̃dɛr] ◇ *adj* **1.** [question, personnage, route] secondary ▪ **c'est ~** it's of secondary importance *ou* of minor interest **2.** ÉDUC & SC secondary ▪ **ère ~** GÉOL Mesozoic era.
◇ *nm* **1.** GÉOL : **le ~** the Mesozoic **2.** ÉDUC secondary *UK ou* high *US* school *(U)* **3.** ÉCON : **le ~** secondary production.

secondairement [səgɔ̃dɛrmɑ̃] *adv* secondarily.

seconde [səgɔ̃d] *nf* **1.** [division horaire] second **2.** [court instant] : **(attendez) une ~!** just a second! ▪ **je reviens dans une ~** I'll be back in a second, I'll be right back ▪ **une ~ d'inattention** a momentary lapse in concentration ▪ **à une ~ près, je ratais le train** I was within a second of missing the train ▪ **à la ~** instantly, there and then.

secondement [səgɔ̃dmɑ̃] *adv* second, secondly.

seconder [3] [səgɔ̃de] *vt* **1.** [assister] to assist, to back up *(sép)* **2.** *sout* [action, dessein] to second.

secouer [6] [səkwe] *vt* **1.** [arbre, bouteille, personne] to shake ▪ [tapis] to shake (out) ▪ **~ la tête** [acquiescer] to nod one's head ; [refuser] to shake one's head ⊙ **~ qqn comme un prunier** *fam* to shake sb like a rag doll ▪ **~ le cocotier** to get rid of the dead wood *fig* **2.** [poussière, sable, miettes] to shake off *(sép)* ▪ *fig* [paresse, torpeur *etc*] to shake off ▪ **~ les puces** *fam* **à qqn** [le gronder] to tell sb off, to give sb a good ticking-off *UK ou* chewing out *US* **3.** *fam* [houspiller - personne] to shake up *(sép)* **4.** [bouleverser - personne] to shake up *(sép)*, to give a jolt *ou* shock to.
◆ **se secouer** *vp (emploi réfléchi) fam* to shake o.s. up, to snap out of it ▪ **il serait grand temps de te ~!** it's high time you pulled yourself together!

secourable [səkurabl] *adj* helpful ▪ **un automobiliste ~** a helpful driver.

secourir [45] [səkurir] *vt* **1.** [blessé] to help ▪ [personne en danger] to rescue ▪ **les skieurs avaient perdu tout espoir d'être secourus** the skiing party had lost all hope of being rescued *ou* of a rescue **2.** *sout* [pauvre, affligé] to aid, to help **3.** *litt* [misères] to relieve, to ease.

secourisme [səkurism] *nm* first aid.

secouriste [səkurist] *nmf* **1.** [d'une organisation] first-aid worker **2.** [personne qualifiée] *person who is qualified in first aid.*

secourra *etc v* ▷ **secourir**.

secours [səkur] *nm* **1.** [assistance] help, assistance, aid ▪ **appeler** *ou* **crier au ~** to call out for help ▪ **au ~!** help! ▪ **appeler qqn à son ~** [blessé, entreprise] to call upon sb for help, to call sb to the rescue ▪ **porter ~ à qqn** to give sb assistance ▪ **porter ~ à un blessé** to give first aid to an injured person ▪ **venir au ~ de qqn** to come to sb's aid ▪ **venir au ~ d'une entreprise** to rescue a company ⊙ **le Secours catholique, le Secours populaire (français)** *charity organizations giving help to the poor* **2.** [sauvetage] aid, assistance ▪ **le** *ou* **les ~ aux brûlés** aid *ou* assistance for burn victims ▪ **envoyer des ~ à qqn** to send relief to sb ▪ **les** *ou* **les ~ ne sont pas encore arrivés** aid *ou* help hasn't arrived yet ⊙ **le ~ en montagne/en mer** sea/mountain rescue ▪ **le** *ou* **les ~ d'urgence** emergency aid **3.** [appui] help ▪ **être d'un grand ~ à qqn** to be of great help to sb ▪ **la calculette ne m'a pas été d'un grand ~** the calculator was of (very) little help *ou* use to me **4.** DR emergency payment *ou* allowance.
◆ **de secours** *loc adj* [équipement, porte, sortie] emergency *(modif)* ▪ [équipe, poste] rescue *(modif)*.

secouru, e [səkury] *pp* ▷ **secourir.**

secousse [səkus] *nf* **1.** [saccade] jerk, jolt ■ **elle se dégagea d'une ~** she shook *ou* jerked herself free **2.** *fig* [bouleversement] jolt, shock, upset **3.** GÉOL : **~ (sismique** *ou* **tellurique)** (earth) tremor.

secret, ète [səkrɛ, ɛt] *adj* **1.** [inconnu - accord, code, document etc] secret ■ **cela n'a rien de ~** it's no secret ■ **garder** *ou* **tenir qqch ~** to keep sthg secret
2. [caché - escalier, passage, tiroir] secret ■ **une vie secrète** a secret life
3. [intime - ambition, désir, espoir, pensée] secret, innermost
4. [personne] secretive, reserved.
◆ **secret** *nm* **1.** [confidence] secret ■ **ce n'est un ~ pour personne** it's no secret, everybody knows about it ■ **c'est un bien lourd ~** it's a weighty secret indeed ■ **confier un ~ à qqn** to let sb into a secret ■ **être dans le ~** to be in on the secret ■ **mettre qqn dans le ~** to let sb in on the secret ■ **ne pas avoir de ~s pour qqn** [personne] to have no secrets from sb ; [question, machine] to hold no secret for sb ◐ **~ d'État** state secret ■ **être dans le ~ des dieux** to have privileged information ■ **c'est un ~ de Polichinelle** it's an open secret *ou* not much of a secret
2. [mystère - d'un endroit, d'une discipline] secret
3. [recette] secret, recipe ■ **le ~ du bonheur** the secret of *ou* recipe for happiness ■ **ses ~s de beauté** her beauty secrets *ou* tips ■ **un soufflé dont lui seul a le ~** a soufflé for which he alone knows the secret ◐ **~ de fabrication** COMM trade secret
4. [discrétion] secrecy *(U)* ■ **exiger/promettre le ~ (absolu)** to demand/to promise (absolute) secrecy ■ **je vous demande le ~ sur cette affaire** I want you to keep silent about this matter ◐ **~ professionnel** professional confidence ■ **trahir le ~ professionnel** to commit a breach of (professional) confidence
5. RELIG : **le ~ de la confession** the seal of confession.
◆ **à secret** *loc adj* [cadenas] combination *(modif)* ■ [tiroir] with a secret lock ■ [meuble] with secret drawers.
◆ **au secret** *loc adv* : **être au ~** to be (detained) in solitary confinement ■ **mettre qqn au ~** to detain sb in solitary confinement.
◆ **en secret** *loc adv* **1.** [écrire, économiser] in secret, secretly **2.** [croire, espérer] secretly, privately.

secrétaire [səkretɛr] ◇ *nmf* **1.** [dans une entreprise] secretary ◐ **~ du conseil d'administration** secretary to the Board of Directors ■ **~ de direction** executive secretary, personal assistant ■ **~ général** company secretary ■ **~ juridique** legal secretary ■ **~ médicale** medical secretary ■ **~ de rédaction** [dans l'édition] desk *ou* assistant editor ; PRESSE subeditor **2.** POLIT : **~ général** [auprès d'un ministre] ≃ permanent secretary *UK* ; [dans un parti] general-secretary ■ **~ général de l'ONU** Secretary *ou* Secretary-General of the UN ■ **~ général de l'Assemblée** ≃ Clerk of the House *UK* ■ **~ général du Sénat** ≃ Clerk of the House *UK* ■ **~ d'État** [en France] ≃ Junior Minister *UK* ; [en Grande-Bretagne] Secretary of State ; [aux États-Unis] State Secretary, Secretary of State ■ **~ perpétuel** Permanent Secretary **3.** ADMIN : **~ de mairie** ≃ chief executive *UK*, ≃ town clerk *UK vieilli*.
◇ *nm* [meuble] secrétaire *sout*, writing desk.

secrétariat [səkretarja] *nm* **1.** [fonction] secretaryship ■ **apprendre le ~** to learn to be a secretary, to do a secretarial course ◐ **~ de rédaction** [dans l'édition] desk *ou* assistant-editorship ; PRESSE post of subeditor **2.** [employés] secretarial staff ■ **le budget du ~** budgeting for secretarial services ■ **faire partie du ~** to be a member of the secretariat **3.** [bureau] secretariat **4.** [tâches administratives] secretarial work **5.** POLIT : **~ d'État** [fonction en France] post of Junior Minister ; [ministère français] Junior Minister's Office ; [fonction en Grande-Bretagne] post of Secretary of State ; [ministère britannique] Secretary of State's Office ; [fonction aux États-Unis] post of State Secretary ■ **~ général de l'ONU** UN Secretary-Generalship **6.** ADMIN : **~ de mairie** [fonction] function of chief executive ; [bureau] chief executive's office.

secrètement [səkrɛtmɑ̃] *adv* **1.** [en cachette] secretly, in secret ■ **elle avait vendu ses bijoux ~** she had sold her jewels in secret **2.** [intérieurement] secretly.

sécréter [18] [sekrete] *vt* **1.** BOT & PHYSIOL to secrete **2.** *fig* & *sout* [ennui] to exude *sout*, to ooze ■ [passion, désir] to cause, to release.

sécréteur, euse *ou* **trice** [sekretœr, øz, tris] *adj* secretory.

sécrétion [sekresjɔ̃] *nf* secretion.

sectaire [sɛktɛr] *adj* & *nmf* sectarian.

sectarisme [sɛktarism] *nm* sectarianism.

secte [sɛkt] *nf* sect.

secteur [sɛktœr] *nm* **1.** ÉCON sector ■ **~ d'activité** sector ◐ **~ primaire** primary sector *ou* production ■ **~ privé** private sector *ou* enterprise ■ **~ public** public sector ■ **~ secondaire** manufacturing *ou* secondary sector ■ **~ tertiaire** service *ou* tertiary sector **2.** [zone d'action - d'un policier] beat ; [- d'un représentant] area, patch ; [- de l'urbanisme] district, area ■ MIL & NAUT sector ■ ADMIN *local area covered by the French health and social services department* **3.** *fam* [quartier] : **c'est dans le ~** it's around here ■ **changer de ~** to make o.s. scarce **4.** ÉLECTR : **le ~** the mains (supply) **5.** MATH : **~ (angulaire)** sector ■ **~ sphérique** sector of a sphere **6.** INFORM sector.

section [sɛksjɔ̃] *nf* **1.** [d'une autoroute, d'une rivière] section, stretch ■ [de ligne de bus, de tramway] fare stage ■ [d'un livre] part, section ■ [d'une bibliothèque] section ■ [d'un service] branch, division, department **2.** ÉDUC department ◐ **~ économique/scientifique/littéraire** courses in economics/science/arts **3.** [d'un parti] local branch ■ **~ syndicale** *local branch of a union* ; [dans l'industrie de la presse et du livre] (union) chapel **4.** MATH & GÉOM section ■ **un câble de 12 mm de ~** a 12 mm (section) cable ■ **dessiner la ~ de qqch** to draw the section of sthg *ou* sthg in section ◐ **~ conique/plane** conic/plane section **5.** [coupure] cutting *(U)*, severing *(U)* ■ MÉD amputation **6.** BIOL [groupe, coupe] section **7.** MIL section **8.** MUS : **~ rythmique** rhythm section **9.** POLIT : **~ électorale** ward.

sectionnement [sɛksjɔnmɑ̃] *nm* **1.** [coupure] cutting *(U)*, severing *(U)* **2.** ÉLECTR sectioning (and isolation).

sectionner [3] [sɛksjɔne] *vt* **1.** [tendon, câble, ligne] to sever, to cut ■ MÉD to amputate ■ **la lame avait sectionné le ligament** the blade had cut through the ligament **2.** [diviser] to section, to divide *ou* to split (into sections).

sectionneur [sɛksjɔnœr] *nm* section switch.

sectoriel, elle [sɛktɔrjɛl] *adj* sector-based ■ **application ~le d'une mesure** the application of a measure to a certain sector (only).

sectorisation [sɛktɔrizasjɔ̃] *nf* [gén] division into sectors ■ [des services de santé] *division into areas of responsibility for health and social services.*

sectoriser [3] [sɛktɔrize] *vt* [gén] to sector, to divide into areas *ou* sectors ■ [services de santé] to divide into areas of health and social services responsibility.

Sécu [seky] (*abr de* **Sécurité sociale**) *nf* [système] ≃ Social Security ■ [organisme de remboursement] ≃ DSS *UK*, ≃ Social Security *US*.

séculaire [sekylɛr] *adj* **1.** [vieux] age-old ■ **un chêne ~** an ancient oak ■ [de cent ans] a hundred years' old **2.** [cyclique] secular **3.** ASTRON secular.

sécularisation [sekylarizasjɔ̃] *nf* secularization.

séculariser [3] [sekylarize] *vt* to secularize.

séculier, ère [sekylje, ɛr] *adj* secular.
◆ **séculier** *nm* secular.

secundo [səgɔ̃do] *adv* second, secondly.

sécurisant, e [sekyrizɑ̃, ɑ̃t] *adj* **1.** [qui rassure] reassuring **2.** PSYCHOL security *(modif)*.

sécuriser [3] [sekyrize] *vt* **1.** [rassurer] : **~ qqn** to make sb feel secure *ou* safe, to reassure sb, to give sb a feeling of security **2.** [stabiliser] to (make) secure ■ **des mesures visant à ~ l'emploi** employment-conserving measures.

Securit® [sekyrit] *nm* : **(verre) ~** Triplex glass®.

sécuritaire [sekyritɛr] *adj* : **programme ~** security-conscious programme ▪ **mesures ~s** drastic security measures ▪ **idéologie ~** law-and-order ideology.

sécurité [sekyrite] *nf* **1.** [protection d'une personne - physique] safety, security ; [- matérielle, affective etc] security ▪ **assurer la ~ de qqn** to ensure the safety of sb ▪ **l'installation offre une ~ totale** the plant is completely safe ▪ **mon travail m'apporte une ~ matérielle** my job gives me financial security ▪ **la ~ de l'emploi** job security ⊃ **~ civile** civil defence ▪ **~ publique** public safety ▪ **~ routière** road safety **2.** [surveillance - de bâtiments, d'installations] security **3.** ARM [d'un tank, d'un navire] safety catch *ou* mechanism.
◆ **de sécurité** *loc adj* [dispositif, mesure] safety *(modif)*.
◆ **en sécurité** ⟨⟩ *loc adj* safe ▪ **être/se sentir en ~** to be/to feel safe.
⟨⟩ *loc adv* in a safe place ▪ **mettre qqch en ~ dans un coffre** to keep sthg in a safe.
◆ **en toute sécurité** *loc adv* in complete safety.
◆ **Sécurité sociale** *nf* **1.** [système] *French social security system* **2.** [organisme] ≃ DSS UK.

SÉCURITÉ SOCIALE

The *Sécu*, as it is popularly known, created in 1945-46, provides public health benefits, pensions, maternity leave etc. These benefits are paid for by obligatory insurance contributions (***cotisations***) made by employers (***cotisations patronales***) and employees (***cotisations salariales***). Many French people have complementary health insurance provided by a ***mutuelle***, which guarantees payment of all or part of the expenses not covered by the *Sécurité sociale*.

sédatif, ive [sedatif, iv] *adj* sedative.
◆ **sédatif** *nm* sedative.

sédation [sedasjɔ̃] *nf* sedation, sedating *(U)*.

sédentaire [sedɑ̃tɛr] ⟨⟩ *adj* **1.** [travail, habitude] sedentary ▪ [employé] desk-bound **2.** ANTHR settled, non-nomad, sedentary.
⟨⟩ *nmf* [personne] sedentary person.

sédentarisation [sedɑ̃tarizasjɔ̃] *nf* : **la ~ d'une population** a people's adoption of a sedentary lifestyle.

sédentariser [3] [sedɑ̃tarize] *vt* [tribu] to turn into a sedentary population, to settle.

sédentarité [sedɑ̃tarite] *nf* sedentary lifestyle.

sédiment [sedimɑ̃] *nm* **1.** GÉOL sediment, deposit **2.** MÉD & ŒNOL sediment.

sédimentaire [sedimɑ̃tɛr] *adj* sedimentary.

sédimentation [sedimɑ̃tasjɔ̃] *nf* sedimentation.

séditieux, euse [sedisjø, øz] ⟨⟩ *adj sout* **1.** [propos] seditious, rebellious **2.** [troupe, armée] insurrectionary, insurgent.
⟨⟩ *nm, f* insurgent, rebel.

sédition [sedisjɔ̃] *nf sout* rebellion, revolt, sedition.

séducteur, trice [sedyktœr, tris] ⟨⟩ *adj* [personne, sourire etc] seductive, irresistible.
⟨⟩ *nm, f* seducer (*f* seductress) ▪ **c'est un grand ~** he's a real lady's man ▪ **c'est une grande séductrice** she's a real seductress *ou* a femme fatale.

séduction [sedyksjɔ̃] *nf* **1.** [d'une personne] charm ▪ [d'une musique, d'un tableau] appeal, captivating power ▪ **elle ne manque pas de ~** she's very seductive ▪ **pouvoir de ~** powers of seduction **2.** DR : **~ de mineur** corruption of a minor **3.** [d'une chose] attraction, attractiveness ▪ **le pouvoir de ~ de l'argent** the seductive power of money.

séduire [98] [sedɥir] *vt* **1.** [charmer - suj: personne] to attract, to charm ; [- suj: beauté, gentillesse, sourire] to win over *(sép)* ; [- suj: livre, tableau] to appeal to *(insép)* **2.** [tenter - suj: idée, projet, style de vie] to appeal to *(insép)*, to be tempting to **3.** [tromper - suj: politicien, promesses, publicité] to lure, to seduce **4.** [sexuellement] to seduce.

séduisant, e [sedɥizɑ̃, ɑ̃t] *adj* **1.** [charmant - personne] attractive ; [- beauté] seductive, enticing ; [- sourire, parfum, mode etc] appealing, seductive ▪ **de manière ~e** seductively **2.** [alléchant - offre, idée, projet] attractive, appealing.

séduisit *etc v* ▷ **séduire**.

séduit, e [sedɥi, it] *pp* ▷ **séduire**.

séfarade [sefarad] ⟨⟩ *adj* Sephardic.
⟨⟩ *nmf* Sephardi ▪ **les ~s** the Sephardim.

segment [sɛgmɑ̃] *nm* **1.** ANAT & MATH segment **2.** MÉCAN ring ▪ **~ de piston** piston ring ▪ **~ de frein** AUTO (segmental) brake shoe **3.** INFORM segment ▪ **~ de programme** program segment.

segmentaire [sɛgmɑ̃tɛr] *adj* segmental.

segmentation [sɛgmɑ̃tasjɔ̃] *nf* **1.** BIOL & PHYSIOL segmentation **2.** INFORM segmentation.

segmenter [3] [sɛgmɑ̃te] *vt* [diviser] to segment.
◆ **se segmenter** *vpi* to segment, to break into segments.

ségrégatif, ive [segregatif, iv] *adj* segregative ▪ **lois ségrégatives** laws aimed at maintaining segregation.

ségrégation [segregasjɔ̃] *nf* [discrimination] segregation ▪ **une ~ au niveau des salaires** a discriminatory wage policy ▪ **~ raciale/sociale** racial/social segregation.

ségrégationnisme [segregasjɔnism] *nm* racial segregation.

ségrégationniste [segregasjɔnist] ⟨⟩ *adj* [personne] segregationist ▪ [politique] segregationist, segregational, discriminatory.
⟨⟩ *nmf* segregationist.

ségrégative [segregativ] *f* ▷ **ségrégatif**.

seguia [segja] *nf* open channel *(for bringing water to Saharan oases)*.

seiche [sɛʃ] *nf* ZOOL cuttlefish.

seigle [sɛgl] *nm* rye.

seigneur [sɛɲœr] *nm* **1.** HIST feudal lord *ou* overlord **2.** [maître] lord ▪ **mon ~ et maître** *hum* my lord and master ⊃ **grand ~ : agir en grand ~** to play the fine gentleman ▪ **comme un ~, en grand ~** [avec luxe] like a lord ; [avec noblesse] nobly ▪ **être grand ~, faire le grand ~** to spend money like water *ou* as if there were no tomorrow ▪ **à tout ~ tout honneur** *prov* give honour where honour is due **3.** [magnat] tycoon, baron ▪ **les ~s de l'industrie** captains of industry ▪ **les ~s de la guerre** the war lords **4.** RELIG : **le Seigneur** the Lord ▪ **Notre-Seigneur Jésus-Christ** Our Lord Jesus Christ ▪ **Seigneur (Dieu)!** *litt* Good Lord! ▪ **le jour du Seigneur** the Lord's Day.

seigneurial, e, aux [sɛɲœrjal, o] *adj* **1.** HIST seigniorial **2.** *litt* [digne d'un seigneur] stately, lordly.

seigneurie [sɛɲœri] *nf* **1.** HIST [propriété] seigneury, lord's domain *ou* estate ▪ [pouvoir, droits] seigneury **2.** [titre] : **Votre Seigneurie** Your Lordship.

sein [sɛ̃] *nm* **1.** ANAT breast ▪ **elle se promène les ~s nus** she walks about topless ▪ **donner le ~ à** to breast-feed ▪ **être nourri au ~** to be breast-fed **2.** *litt* [ventre] womb ▪ **porter un enfant dans son ~** to carry a child in one's womb **3.** *litt* [buste] bosom ▪ **serrer qqch/qqn contre son ~** to press sthg/sb against one's bosom ▪ **dans le ~ de** [au centre de] in *ou* at the heart of, in the bosom of *litt*.
◆ **au sein de** *loc prép sout* within ▪ **au ~ de la famille** in the bosom *ou* midst of the family.

Seine [sɛn] *npr f* : **la ~** the (River) Seine.

seing [sɛ̃] *nm* [signature] signature.
◆ **sous seing privé** *loc adj* : **acte sous ~ privé** private agreement, simple contract.

séismal, e, aux [seismal, o] *adj* seismic.

séisme [seism] *nm* **1.** GÉOL earthquake, seism *spéc* ▪ **le ~ a atteint sept degrés sur l'échelle de Richter** the earthquake reached seven on the Richter scale **2.** *fig* [bouleversement] upheaval.

séismique [seismik] = **sismique**.

séismographe [seismɔgraf] = **sismographe**.

SEITA, Seita [seita] (*abr de* **Société nationale d'exploitation industrielle des tabacs et allumettes**) *npr f French government tobacco and matches monopoly.*

seize [sɛz] *dét & nm inv* sixteen, *voir aussi* **cinq**.

seizième [sɛzjɛm] ◇ *adj num* sixteenth, *voir aussi* **cinquième**.
◇ *nmf* sixteenth.
◇ *nm* **1.** [arrondissement] : **le ~** the sixteenth arrondissement *(wealthy district of Paris)* **2.** [partie] : **le ~ de la somme globale** the sixteenth part of the total sum.
◆ **seizièmes** *nmpl* SPORT : **les ~s de finale** the first round *(of a 4-round knockout competition), the second round (of a 5-round knockout competition).*

SEIZIÈME

This term often refers to the upper class social background, lifestyle, way of dressing etc, associated with the sixteenth arrondissement in Paris.

seizièmement [sɛzjɛmmɑ̃] *adv* in the sixteenth place.

séjour [seʒur] *nm* **1.** [durée] stay, sojourn *litt* ■ **il a fait un ~ de deux mois à la mer** he spent two months at the seaside ■ **il fait un ~ linguistique aux États-Unis** he is spending some time in the United States learning the language ■ **je te souhaite un bon ~ à Venise** I hope you have a nice time *ou* I hope you enjoy your stay in Venice ■ **il a fait plusieurs ~s en hôpital psychiatrique** he's been in a psychiatric hospital several times **2.** [pièce] : **(salle de) ~** living *ou* sitting room, lounge *UK* ■ **~-cathédrale** great room *US*, room with a cathedral ceiling *UK* **3.** *litt* [habitation] abode, dwelling place.

séjourner [3] [seʒurne] *vi* **1.** [habiter] to stay, to sojourn *litt* ■ **~ à l'hôtel/chez un ami** to stay at a hotel/with a friend **2.** [eau, brouillard] to lie ■ **les neiges séjournent longtemps en altitude** the snow stays for a long time at high altitude.

sel [sɛl] *nm* **1.** CULIN salt ▶ **gros ~** coarse salt ■ **~ de cuisine** kitchen salt ■ **~ de table, ~ fin** table salt ■ **~ de mer** sea salt **2.** CHIM salt ■ **~ régénérant** dishwasher salt **3.** GÉOL salt ■ **~ gemme** rock salt ■ **le ~ de la terre** BIBLE & *litt* the salt of the earth **4.** PHARM salt **5.** [piquant] wit *(U)* ■ **une remarque pleine de ~** a witty remark ■ **la situation ne manque pas de ~!** the situation is not without a certain piquancy.
◆ **sels** *nmpl* PHARM (smelling) salts ▶ **~s de bain** bath salts.
◆ **sans sel** *loc adj* [régime, biscotte] salt-free ■ [beurre] unsalted.

sélect, e [selɛkt] *adj fam* select, highclass, posh *UK*.

sélecteur [selɛktœr] *nm* **1.** RADIO & TÉLÉCOM selector ■ **~ de programmes** program selector **2.** MÉCAN gear shift ■ [d'une moto] (foot) gearshift control **3.** INFORM chooser.

sélectif, ive [selɛktif, iv] *adj* [mémoire, herbicide, poste de radio] selective.

sélection [selɛksjɔ̃] *nf* **1.** [fait de choisir] selection ■ **opérer une ~ parmi 200 candidats** to make a selection *ou* to choose from 200 candidates ■ **~ à l'entrée** UNIV selective entry *UK ou* admission *US* ▶ **~ professionnelle** professional recruitment **2.** [échantillon] selection, choice **3.** SPORT [équipe] team, squad **4.** BIOL : **~ naturelle** natural selection **5.** RADIO (signal) separation.

sélectionné, e [selɛksjɔne] ◇ *adj* [choisi] selected ■ **des vins ~s** selected *ou* choice wines ‖ INFORM : **le texte ~** the selected text, the selection.
◇ *nm, f* **1.** [candidat] selected candidate *ou* contestant **2.** SPORT squad member, team member.

sélectionner [3] [selɛksjɔne] *vt* **1.** [gén - INFORM] to select **2.** *(en usage absolu)* UNIV : **ils sélectionnent à l'entrée** they have a selection process for admission.

sélectionneur, euse [selɛksjɔnœr, øz] *nm, f* SPORT selector.

sélectivement [selɛktivmɑ̃] *adv* selectively.

sélectivité [selɛktivite] *nf* ÉLECTR, OPT & RADIO selectivity.

sélénium [selenjɔm] *nm* selenium.

sélénologie [selenɔlɔʒi] *nf* selenology.

self [sɛlf] ◇ *nf* ÉLECTR self inductance.
◇ *nm* **1.** PSYCHOL self **2.** *fam* = **self-service**.

self-control [sɛlfkɔ̃trol] (*pl* **self-controls**) *nm* self-control, self-command.

self-induction [sɛlfɛ̃dyksjɔ̃] (*pl* **self-inductions**) *nf* self-induction.

self-made-man [sɛlfmɛdman] (*pl* **self-made-mans** *ou pl* **self-made-men** [-mɛn]) *nm* self-made man.

self-service [sɛlfsɛrvis] (*pl* **self-services**) *nm* **1.** [restaurant] self-service (restaurant), cafeteria **2.** [service] self-service ■ **beaucoup de pompes à essence sont en ~** a lot of petrol pumps are self-service.

selle [sɛl] *nf* **1.** [de cheval] saddle ■ **monter sans ~** to ride bareback ▶ **être bien en ~** *pr & fig* to be firmly in the saddle ■ **mettre qqn en ~** *pr* to put sb in the saddle ; *fig* to give sb a leg up ■ **remettre qqn en ~** *fig* to put sb back on the rails ■ **se mettre en ~** *pr* to get into the saddle, to mount ; *fig* to get down to the job ■ **se remettre en ~** *pr & fig* to get back in *ou* into the saddle **2.** [de bicyclette] saddle **3.** CULIN saddle **4.** [escabeau] turntable **5.** MÉD : **aller à la ~** to have a bowel movement ■ **allez-vous à la ~ régulièrement?** are you regular? **6.** RAIL bearing *ou* sole plate **7.** ZOOL [d'un lombric] saddle.
◆ **selles** *nfpl* [excréments] faeces, stools MÉD.

seller [4] [sele] *vt* to saddle (up).

sellerie [sɛlri] *nf* **1.** [équipement] saddlery **2.** [lieu] saddle room, tack-room **3.** [commerce] saddlery trade.

sellette [sɛlɛt] *nf* **1.** HIST [siège] (high) stand *ou* table ▶ **mettre qqn sur la ~** to put sb in the hot seat ■ **être sur la ~** [critiqué] to be in the hot seat, to come under fire ; [examiné] to be undergoing reappraisal **2.** CONSTR slung cradle **3.** [pour sculpteur] turntable ART.

sellier [selje] *nm* [fabricant, marchand] saddler.

sellier-maroquinier [seljemarɔkinje] (*pl* **selliers-maroquiniers**) *nm* **1.** [fabricant] fancy leather goods manufacturer **2.** [commerçant] dealer in fancy leather goods.

selon [səlɔ̃] *prép* **1.** [conformément à] in accordance with ■ **agir ~ les vœux de qqn** to act in accordance with sb's wishes ■ **~ toute apparence** by *ou* from *ou* to all appearances ■ **~ toute vraisemblance** in all probability **2.** [en fonction de] according to ■ **dépenser ~ ses moyens** to spend according to one's means ■ **~ le cas** as the case may be ■ **~ les circonstances/les cas** depending on the circumstances/each individual case ▶ **on se reverra? – c'est ~!** *fam* shall we see each other again? – it all depends! **3.** [d'après] according to ■ **~ moi/vous** in my/your opinion, to my/your mind ■ **~ vos propres termes** in your own words ■ **~ l'expression consacrée** as the hallowed expression has it.
◆ **selon que** *loc conj* : **~ qu'il fera beau ou qu'il pleuvra** depending on whether it's fine or rainy.

S.Em. (*abr écrite de* **Son Éminence**) HE.

SEM [sɛm] (*abr de* **société d'économie mixte**) *nf company financed by state and private capital.*

semailles [səmaj] *nfpl* **1.** [action] sowing **2.** [graines] seeds **3.** [période] sowing season ■ **les ~ d'automne** autumn sowing.

semaine [səmɛn] *nf* **1.** [sept jours] week ■ **toutes les ~s** [nettoyer, recevoir] every *ou* each week ; [publier, payer] weekly, on a weekly basis ■ **deux visites par ~** two visits a week *ou* per week ■ **dans une ~** in a week's time ■ **faire des ~s de 50 heures** to work a 50-hour week ■ **qui est de ~?** who's on duty this week? ▶ **la ~ anglaise** the five-day (working) week ■ **la ~ de 39 heures** the 39-hour working week ■ **il te remboursera la ~ des quatre jeudis** he'll never pay you back in a month of Sundays
2. RELIG week ■ **la ~ sainte** Holy Week ■ **la ~ pascale** Easter week

3. COMM : **la ~ de la photo** photography week ◗ **~ commerciale** week-long promotion *ou* sale ▪ **c'est sa ~ de bonté** *hum* he's been overcome by a fit of generosity **4.** [argent de poche] : **je lui donne 50 euros pour sa ~** I give her 50 euros a week pocket money **5.** JOAILL [bracelet] seven-band bangle.

◆ **à la petite semaine** *fam* ◇ *loc adj* [politique] short-sighted, day-to-day.
◇ *loc adv* : **prêter à la petite ~** to make short-term loans *(with high interest)* ▪ **vivre à la petite ~** to live from day to day *ou* from hand to month.

◆ **à la semaine** *loc adv* [payer] weekly, on a weekly basis, by the week.

◆ **en semaine** *loc adv* during the week, on weekdays, on a weekday.

semainier, ère [səmenje, ɛr] *nm, f* [personne] weekly worker.
◆ **semainier** *nm* **1.** [calendrier] page-a-week diary **2.** [meuble] semainier (chest) **3.** INDUST weekly time sheet **4.** JOAILL seven-band bangle.

sémanticien, enne [semɑ̃tisjɛ̃, ɛn] *nm, f* semanticist.

sémantique [semɑ̃tik] ◇ *adj* semantic.
◇ *nf* semantics *(sing)* ▪ **~ générative** generative semantics.

sémaphore [semafɔr] *nm* **1.** RAIL semaphore signal **2.** NAUT [poste] signal station.

semblable [sɑ̃blabl] ◇ *adj* **1.** [pareil] similar, alike ▪ **je n'ai rien dit de ~** I said nothing of the sort *ou* no such thing ▪ **je n'avais jamais rien vu de ~** I had never seen anything like it *ou* the like of it ▪ **~ à** similar to, like **2.** GÉOM & MATH similar.
◇ *nmf (avec possessif)* **1.** [être humain] : **vous et vos ~s** you and your kind ▪ **partager le sort de ses ~s** to share the lot of one's fellow man **2.** [animal] related species.

semblablement [sɑ̃blabləmɑ̃] *adv* similarly, likewise.

semblant [sɑ̃blɑ̃] *nm* **1.** [apparence] : **un ~ de : un ~ d'intérêt/d'affection** a semblance of interest/affection ▪ **offrir un ~ de résistance** to put on a show of *ou* to put up a token resistance **2.** [feindre] : **faire ~** to pretend ▪ **ne fais pas ~ d'avoir oublié** don't pretend to have forgotten *ou* (that) you've forgotten ▪ **faire ~ d'être malade** to sham illness, to malinger ◗ **ne faire ~ de rien** to pretend not to notice.

sembler [3] [sɑ̃ble] *vi* to seem, to appear ▪ **elle semble plus âgée que lui** she seems (to be) *ou* she looks older than him ▪ **ils semblaient bien s'entendre** they seemed *ou* appeared to be getting on well ▪ **ça peut ~ drôle à certains** this may seem *ou* sound funny to some.

◆ **il semble** *v impers* **1.** [dire que] : **il semble que...** it seems... ▪ **il semble qu'il y a** *ou* **ait eu un malentendu** it seems that *ou* it looks as if there's been a misunderstanding, there seems to have been a misunderstanding ▪ **il semblerait qu'il ait décidé de démissionner** reports claim *ou* it has been reported that he intends to resign **2.** [croire que] : **il me/te semble (que) : cela ne te semble-t-il pas injuste?** don't you find this unfair?, doesn't this strike you as being unfair? ▪ **c'est bien ce qu'il m'a semblé** I thought as much ▪ **il ne me semblait pas te l'avoir dit** I didn't think I'd told you about it ▪ **il était, me semblait-il, au courant de tout** it seemed *ou* appeared to me that he was aware of everything ▪ **il me semble qu'on s'est déjà vus** I think we've met before ▪ **ce me semble** *sout* : **je vous l'ai déjà dit, ce me semble** it would seem to me that I have already told you that ▪ **comme/quand/qui bon me semble : faites comme bon vous semble** do as you think fit *ou* best, do as you please ▪ **je sors quand/avec qui bon me semble** I go out whenever/with whoever I please.

◆ **à ce qu'il semble, semble-t-il** *loc adv* seemingly, apparently ▪ **ils sont blessés, semble-t-il** they seem to be hurt, it seems (as though) they're hurt, apparently, they're hurt.

sème [sɛm] *nm* seme.

semelle [səmɛl] *nf* **1.** [d'une chaussure, d'un ski] sole ▪ **bottes à ~s fines/épaisses** thin-soled/thick-soled boots ▪ **chaussures à ~s compensées** platform shoes ◗ **~ intérieure** insole, inner sole **2.** *fam* [viande dure] : **c'est de la ~, ce steak!** this steak is like (shoe) leather *ou* old boots UK **3.** *loc* **(pas) d'une ~ : ne la lâchez pas d'une ~** don't let her out of your sight ▪ **on n'a pas avancé** *ou* **bougé d'une ~** we haven't moved a single inch, we haven't made any progress whatsoever ▪ **ne la quitte pas d'une ~** don't loose track of her, keep on her trail **4.** CONSTR [de plancher] sill *ou* sole plate ▪ [de toiture] inferior (roof) purlin ▪ [d'une marche] tread **5.** MIN [élément] sole (piece) ▪ [banc] sole **6.** RAIL : **~ de frein** brake shoe (insert) **7.** TECHNOL bedplate **8.** [d'un fer à repasser] base, sole.

semence [səmɑ̃s] *nf* **1.** [graine] seed **2.** *litt* [germe] : **les ~s d'une révolte** the seeds of a revolt **3.** *litt* [sperme] semen, seed *litt* **4.** JOAILL : **~ de perles** seed pearls ▪ **~ de diamants** diamond sparks **5.** [clou] tack.

semer [19] [səme] *vt* **1.** AGRIC & HORT to sow ▪ **~ un champ** to sow a field ▪ ◗ **Je sème à tout vent** *slogan of the Larousse publishing house* **2.** *fig* [disperser - fleurs, paillettes] to scatter, to strew ▪ **semé de** scattered *ou* strewn with ▪ **parcours semé d'embûches** course littered with obstacles ▪ **il sème ses affaires partout** he leaves his things everywhere **3.** *fam* [laisser tomber] to drop **4.** [distancer] to lose, to shake off *(sép)* ▪ **~ le peloton** to leave the pack behind **5.** [propager] to bring ▪ **~ le désordre** *ou* **la pagaille** to wreak havoc ▪ **~ la discorde** to sow the seeds of discord ▪ **~ le doute dans l'esprit de qqn** to sow *ou* to plant a seed of doubt in sb's mind.

semestre [səmɛstr] *nm* **1.** [dans l'année civile] half-year, six-month period ▪ **pour le premier ~** for the first half of the year *ou* six months of the year **2.** UNIV half-year, semester **3.** [rente] half-yearly pension ▪ [intérêt] half-yearly interest.

semestriel, elle [səmɛstrijɛl] *adj* **1.** [dans l'année civile] half-yearly **2.** UNIV semestral.

semestriellement [səmɛstrijɛlmɑ̃] *adv* **1.** [dans l'année civile] half-yearly, every six months **2.** UNIV per *ou* every semester.

semeur, euse [səmœr, øz] *nm, f* **1.** AGRIC sower **2.** *fig* [propagateur] : **~ de trouble** troublemaker.

semi- [səmi] *préf* semi-.

semi-aride [səmiarid] *adj* semiarid.

semi-automatique [səmiotɔmatik] *adj* semiautomatic.

semi-circulaire [səmisirkylɛr] *adj* semicircular.

semi-conducteur, trice [səmikɔ̃dyktœr, tris] *adj* semiconducting.
◆ **semi-conducteur** *nm* semiconductor.

semi-conserve [səmikɔ̃sɛrv] *nf* semipreserve.

semi-consonne [səmikɔ̃sɔn] *nf* semiconsonant, semivowel.

semi-fini, e [səmifini] *adj* semifinished, semi-manufactured.

semi-grossiste [səmigrosist] *nmf wholesaler who also deals in retail.*

semi-liberté [səmilibɛrte] *nf* temporary release *(from prison).*

sémillant, e [semijɑ̃, ɑ̃t] *adj* sprightly, spirited.

semi-lunaire [səmilynɛr] *adj* half-moon shaped, semilunar ▪ **os ~** semi-lunar.

séminaire [seminɛr] *nm* **1.** [réunion] seminar, workshop **2.** RELIG seminary.

séminal, e, aux [seminal, o] *adj* seminal.

séminariste [seminarist] *nm* seminarist, seminarian US.

semi-nomade [səminɔmad] ◇ *adj* seminomadic.
◇ *nmf* seminomad.

semi-officiel, elle [səmiɔfisjɛl] *adj* semiofficial.

sémiologie [semjɔlɔʒi] *nf* semiology, semeiology.

sémiologue [semjɔlɔg] *nmf* semiologist.

sémioticien, enne [semjɔtisjɛ̃, ɛn] *nm, f* semiotician.

sémiotique [semjɔtik] *nf* semiotics *(sing).*

semi-précieux, euse [səmipresjø, øz] *adj* semi-precious.

semi-professionnel, elle [səmiprɔfɛsjɔnɛl] *adj* semiprofessional.

semi-public, ique [səmipyblik] *adj* semipublic.

sémique [semik] *adj* semic.

semi-remorque [səmirəmɔrk] <> *nf* semitrailer.
<> *nm* articulated lorry *UK*, trailer truck *US*.

semi-rigide [səmiriʒid] *adj* semirigid.

semis [səmi] *nm* **1.** [action] sowing ▪ **~ à la volée** broadcast sowing **2.** [terrain] seedbed **3.** *fig* **c'était un tissu à fond blanc avec un ~ de petites fleurs bleues** the material had a pattern of small blue flowers on a white background.

sémite [semit] *adj* Semitic.
◆ **Sémite** *nmf* Semite.

sémitique [semitik] *adj* Semitic.

sémitisme [semitism] *nm* [études] Semitics *(sing)* ▪ [phénomène] Semitism.

semi-voyelle [səmivwajɛl] *(pl* **semi-voyelles***)* *nf* semivowel, semiconsonant.

semoir [səmwar] *nm* **1.** [panier] seed-bag **2.** [machine] sower, seeder.

semonce [səmɔ̃s] *nf* **1.** *sout* [réprimande] reprimand, rebuke **2.** NAUT : **coup de ~** warning shot.

semoule [səmul] *nf* semolina ▪ **~ de riz** rice flour ▪ **~ de maïs** cornflour ▪ **~ de blé dur** durum wheat flour.

sempiternel, elle [sɑ̃pitɛrnɛl] *adj* neverending, endless.

sempiternellement [sɑ̃pitɛrnɛlmɑ̃] *adv* eternally, forever.

sénat [sena] *nm* **1.** [assemblée] senate ▪ **le Sénat** the (French) Senate **2.** [lieu] senate (house).

SÉNAT

The *Sénat* is the upper house of the French Parliament. Its members, the ***sénateurs*** are elected for a nine-year mandate by the Deputies of the ***Assemblée nationale*** and certain other government officials. The President of the Senate may deputise for the President of the Republic.

sénateur, trice [senatœr, tris] *nm, f* senator.

sénatorial, e, aux [senatɔrjal, o] *adj* senatorial, senate *(modif)*.
◆ **sénatoriales** *nfpl* senatorial elections.

sénéchal, aux [seneʃal, o] *nm* seneschal.

Sénégal [senegal] *npr m* : **le ~** Senegal ▪ **au ~** in Senegal.

sénégalais, e [senegalɛ, ɛz] *adj* Senegalese.
◆ **Sénégalais, e** *nm, f* Senegalese.

Sénèque [senɛk] *npr* Seneca.

sénescence [senesɑ̃s] *nf* senescence.

sénile [senil] *adj* senile.

sénilité [senilite] *nf* senility.

senior [senjɔr] *adj & nmf* **1.** SPORT senior **2.** [tourisme] for the over-50s, for the young at heart ▪ [menu] over 50s' ▪ **notre clientèle ~** our over-50s customers **3.** [personnes de plus de 50 ans] over-50 *(gén pl)*.

senne [sɛn] *nf* seine.

sens [sɑ̃s] <> *v* ▷ **sentir.**
<> *nm* **1.** PHYSIOL sense ▪ **le ~ du toucher** the sense of touch ◐ **sixième ~** sixth sense ▪ **reprendre ses ~** *pr* to come to ; *fig* to come to one's senses
2. [instinct] sense ▪ **avoir le ~ de la nuance** to be subtle ▪ **le ~ de l'humour** a sense of humour ▪ **avoir le ~ de l'orientation** to have a good sense of direction ▪ **ne pas avoir le ~ des réalités** to have no grasp of reality ◐ **bon ~, ~ commun** common sense ▪ **ça tombe sous le ~** it's obvious, it stands to reason
3. [opinion] : **à mon ~, c'est impossible** as I see it *ou* to my mind, it's impossible
4. [signification - d'un mot, d'une phrase] meaning *(C)*, sense ; [- d'une allégorie, d'un symbole] meaning *(C)* ▪ **ce que tu dis n'a pas de ~** [c'est inintelligible, déraisonnable] what you're saying doesn't make sense ▪ **porteur de ~** meaningful ▪ **lourd** *ou* **chargé de ~** meaningful ▪ **vide de ~** meaningless ▪ **au ~ propre/figuré** in the literal/figurative sense ▪ **au ~ strict** strictly speaking
5. [direction] direction ▪ **dans tous les ~** *pr* in all directions, all over the place ▪ **en ~ inverse** the other way round *ou* around ▪ **pose l'équerre dans ce ~-là/l'autre ~** lay the set square down this way/the other way round ▪ **scier une planche dans le ~ de la largeur/longueur** to saw a board widthwise/lengthwise ▪ **dans le ~ nord-sud/est-ouest** in a southerly/westerly direction ▪ **installer qqch dans le bon ~** to fix sthg the right way up ▪ **fais demi-tour, on va dans le mauvais ~!** turn round, we're going the wrong way *ou* in the wrong direction! ▪ **la circulation est bloquée dans le ~ Paris-province** traffic leaving Paris is at a standstill ▪ **dans le ~ de la marche** facing the front *(of a vehicle)* ▪ **dans le ~ contraire de la marche** facing the rear *(of a vehicle)* ▪ **dans le ~ du courant** with the current ▪ **dans le ~ des aiguilles d'une montre** clockwise ▪ **dans le ~ inverse des aiguilles d'une montre** anticlockwise *UK*, counterclockwise *US* ◐ **~ giratoire** TRANSP roundabout *UK*, traffic circle *US* ▪ **~ interdit** [panneau] no-entry sign ; [rue] one-way street ▪ **être** *ou* **rouler en ~ interdit** to be going the wrong way up/down a one-way street ▪ **(rue à) ~ unique** one-way street ▪ **à ~ unique** *fig* [amour] unrequited *sout* ; [décision] unilateral, one-sided
6. *fig* [orientation] line ▪ **des mesures allant dans le ~ d'une plus grande justice** measures directed at greater justice ▪ **nous avons publié une brochure dans ce ~** we have published a brochure along those (same) lines *ou* to that effect ▪ **leur politique ne va pas dans le bon ~** their policy's going down the wrong road.
<> *nmpl* [sensualité] (carnal) senses ▪ **pour le plaisir des ~** for the gratification of the senses.
◆ **dans le sens où** *loc conj* in the sense that, in so far as.
◆ **dans un certain sens** *loc adv* in a way, in a sense, as it were.
◆ **en ce sens que** = **dans le sens où.**
◆ **sens dessus dessous** *loc adv* upside down ▪ **la maison était ~ dessus dessous** [en désordre] the house was all topsy-turvy.
◆ **sens devant derrière** *loc adv* back to front, the wrong way round.

sensass [sɑ̃sas] *adj inv fam* [sensationnel] terrific, sensational.

sensation [sɑ̃sasjɔ̃] *nf* **1.** [impression] sensation, feeling ▪ **~ de fraîcheur** feeling of freshness, fresh sensation ▪ **j'avais la ~ qu'on reculait** I had the feeling we were going backwards ▪ **~s fortes : les amateurs de ~s fortes** people who like thrills **2.** [impact] : **faire ~** to cause a stir *ou* sensation **3.** PHYSIOL sensation.
◆ **à sensation** *loc adj* sensational ▪ **un reportage à ~** a shock *ou* sensation-seeking report.

sensationnalisme [sɑ̃sasjɔnalism] *nm* sensationalism.

sensationnel, elle [sɑ̃sasjɔnɛl] *adj* **1.** [spectaculaire - révélation, image] sensational **2.** *fam* [remarquable] sensational, terrific, great.
◆ **sensationnel** *nm* : **le ~** the sensational ▪ **journal qui donne dans le ~** sensationalist newspaper.

sensé, e [sɑ̃se] *adj* sensible, well-advised, wise ▪ **dire des choses ~es** to talk sense ▪ **ce qu'il a dit n'est pas très ~** what he said doesn't make much sense.

sensément [sɑ̃semɑ̃] *adv litt* sensibly, wisely.

sensibilisateur, trice [sɑ̃sibilizatœr, tris] *adj* sensitizing.
◆ **sensibilisateur** *nm* PHOTO sensitizer.

sensibilisation [sɑ̃sibilizasjɔ̃] *nf* **1.** [prise de conscience] awareness ▪ **il y a une grande ~ des jeunes aux dangers du tabagisme** young people are alert to *ou* aware of the dangers of smoking ▪ **campagne/techniques de ~** consciousness-raising campaign/techniques **2.** MÉD & PHOTO sensitization.

sensibiliser [3] [sɑ̃sibilize] *vt* **1.** [gén] : **~ qqn à qqch** to make sb conscious *ou* aware of sthg ▪ **il faudrait essayer de ~ l'opinion** we'll have to try and make people aware **2.** MÉD & PHOTO to sensitize.

sensibilité [sɑ̃sibilite] *nf* **1.** [physique] sensitiveness, sensitivity ▪ **~ à la douleur/au soleil** sensitivity to pain/to the sun ▮ [intellectuelle] sensibility ▪ [émotive] sensitivity ▪ **tu manques totalement de ~** you're utterly insensitive **2.** ÉCON : **la ~ du marché des changes** the sensitivity of the foreign exchange market **3.** PHOTO, PHYSIOL & RADIO sensitivity.

sensible [sɑ̃sibl] <> *adj* **1.** [physiquement, émotivement] sensitive ▪ **~ à** sensitive to ▪ **trop ~** oversensitive ▪ **sera-t-il ~ à cette preuve d'amour?** will he be touched by this proof of love? ▪ **~ à la beauté de qqn** susceptible to sb's beauty ▪ **personnes ~s s'abstenir** not recommended for people of a nervous disposition **2.** [peau, gencive] delicate, sensitive ▪ [balance, microphone] sensitive, responsive ▪ [direction de voiture] responsive **3.** [phénomène - perceptible] perceptible ; [- notable] noticeable, marked, sensible *sout* ▪ **~ à l'ouïe** perceptible to the ear ▪ **hausse/baisse ~** marked rise/fall **4.** PHILOS sensory ▪ **un être ~** a sentient being ➊ **le monde ~** the world as perceived by the senses **5.** MUS [note] leading **6.** PHOTO sensitive.
<> *nf* MUS leading note, subtonic.

sensiblement [sɑ̃sibləmɑ̃] *adv* **1.** [beaucoup] appreciably, noticeably, markedly ▪ **il fait ~ plus chaud dans ton bureau** it's noticeably warmer in your office **2.** [à peu près] about, approximately, more or less, roughly.

sensiblerie [sɑ̃sibləri] *nf* oversensitiveness, squeamishness.

sensitif, ive [sɑ̃sitif, iv] <> *adj* **1.** ANAT sensory **2.** PSYCHOL oversensitive.
<> *nm, f* PSYCHOL oversensitive subject ▪ **c'est un ~** he's oversensitive.
◆ **sensitive** *nf* BOT sensitive plant.

sensoriel, elle [sɑ̃sɔrjɛl] *adj* [organe, appareil] sense *(modif)* ▪ [nerf, cortex] sensory.

sensualisme [sɑ̃sɥalism] *nm* sensualism.

sensualité [sɑ̃sɥalite] *nf* sensuality.

sensuel, elle [sɑ̃sɥɛl] <> *adj* **1.** [plaisir, personne] sensual, sybaritic *litt* **2.** [musique] sensuous, voluptuous.
<> *nm, f* sensualist, sybarite *litt*.

sente [sɑ̃t] *nf litt* path, footpath, track.

sentence [sɑ̃tɑ̃s] *nf* **1.** [jugement] sentence ▪ **prononcer une ~** to pass *ou* to give *ou* to pronounce sentence **2.** [maxime] maxim, saying.

sentencieusement [sɑ̃tɑ̃sjøzmɑ̃] *adv* sententiously, moralistically.

sentencieux, euse [sɑ̃tɑ̃sjø, øz] *adj* sententious, moralizing.

senteur [sɑ̃tœr] *nf litt* fragrance, scent, aroma.

senti, e [sɑ̃ti] *adj* : **bien ~** [lecture, interprétation] appropriate, apposite *sout* ▪ **c'était une repartie bien ~e** it was a retort that struck home ▪ **une vérité bien ~e** a home truth.

sentier [sɑ̃tje] *nm* **1.** [allée] path, footpath **2.** SPORT : **~ de grande randonnée** long-distance hiking path **3.** *fig* & *litt* path, way ▪ **les ~s de la gloire** the paths of glory ➊ **être sur le ~ de la guerre** *fig* to be on the warpath ▪ **suivre les ~s battus** to keep to well-trodden paths ▪ **sortir des ~s battus** to get *ou* to wander off the beaten track **4.** [le quartier] : **le Sentier** *predominantly Jewish district of Paris famous as a centre for the clothing trade* **5.** POLIT : **le Sentier lumineux** the Shining Path, the Sendero Luminoso.

sentiment [sɑ̃timɑ̃] *nm* **1.** [émotion] feeling ➊ **prendre qqn par les ~s** to appeal to sb's feelings **2.** *(toujours sing)* [sensibilité] feeling *(U)* ▪ **le ~ religieux** religious feeling *ou* fervour ▮ [sensiblerie] (silly) sentimentalism ➊ **ce n'est pas le moment de faire du ~** this is no time to get sentimental ▪ **avoir qqn au ~** to get around sb **3.** [opinion] feeling ▪ **si vous voulez savoir mon ~** if you want to know what I think *ou* feel ▪ **j'ai ce ~-là aussi** my feelings exactly **4.** [conscience] : **avoir le/un ~ de** to have the/a feeling of **5.** CHASSE scent.
◆ **sentiments** *nmpl* **1.** [disposition] : **faire appel aux bons ~s de qqn** to appeal to sb's better *ou* finer feelings ▪ **ramener qqn à de meilleurs ~s** to bring sb round to a more generous point of view ▪ **revenir à de meilleurs ~s** to be in a better frame of mind **2.** [dans la correspondance] : **veuillez agréer l'expression de mes ~s distingués** yours faithfully *esp UK*, sincerely yours *esp US* ▪ **nos ~s les meilleurs** kindest regards.

sentimental, e, aux [sɑ̃timɑ̃tal, o] <> *adj* **1.** [affectif] sentimental ▪ **vie ~e** love life **2.** *péj* sentimental, mawkish *péj*.
<> *nm, f* : **c'est un grand ~** he's a sentimentalist, he's very sentimental.

sentimentalement [sɑ̃timɑ̃talmɑ̃] *adv* sentimentally, mawkishly *péj*.

sentimentalisme [sɑ̃timɑ̃talism] *nm* emotionalism, sentimentalism.

sentimentalité [sɑ̃timɑ̃talite] *nf* sentimentality, mawkishness *péj*.

sentinelle [sɑ̃tinɛl] *nf* MIL sentinel, sentry ▪ **en ~** on guard ▪ **être en ~** to stand sentinel *ou* sentry, to be on sentry duty ▪ **les cambrioleurs ont mis un homme en ~ à la sortie de la banque** the robbers have put a lookout in front of the bank.

sentir [37] [sɑ̃tir] <> *vt*

A. AVOIR UNE IMPRESSION DE
B. EXHALER, DONNER UNE IMPRESSION

A. AVOIR UNE IMPRESSION DE

1. [par l'odorat] to smell ▪ [par le toucher] to feel ▪ [par le goût] to taste ▪ **sens-moi cette soupe!** *fam* just smell this soup! ▪ **je sens une odeur de gaz** I can smell gas ▪ **je n'ai rien senti!** I didn't feel a thing! ▪ **je ne sens plus ma main** [d'ankylose] my hand's gone numb *ou* dead ▪ **je ne sens plus mes jambes** [de fatigue] my legs are killing me ▪ **je sens une lourdeur dans mes jambes** my legs feel heavy ▪ **elle commence à ~ son âge** she's starting to feel her age ▪ **il sentit les larmes lui monter aux yeux** he could feel tears coming to his eyes ▪ **je n'ai pas senti l'après-midi/les années passer** the afternoon/years just flashed by ▪ **j'ai senti qu'on essayait de mettre la main dans ma poche** I was aware *ou* I felt that someone was trying to reach into my pocket ➊ **le ~ passer, la ~ passer** *fam* [douleur, claque] : **je l'ai sentie passer** that really hurt ▪ **vous allez la ~ passer, l'amende!** you'll certainly know about it when you get the fine! ▪ **c'est lui qui a payé le repas, il a dû le ~ passer!** he paid for the meal, it must have cost him an arm and a leg!

2. [avoir l'intuition de - mépris, présence, réticence] to feel, to sense, to be aware of ; [- danger, menace] to be aware *ou* conscious of, to sense ▪ **tu ne sens pas ta force** you don't know your own strength ▪ **je le sentais venir (de loin) avec son petit air innocent!** *fam* I could see him coming (a mile off) with that innocent look on his face! ▪ **je le sentais prêt/résolu** I could feel *ou* tell he was ready/determined ▪ **je sens bien qu'il m'envie** I can feel *ou* tell that he envies me ▪ **j'ai senti qu'on me suivait** I felt *ou* sensed (that) I was being followed ▪ **faire ~ qqch à qqn** to make sb aware of sthg, to show sb sthg ▪ **il m'a fait ~ que j'étais de trop** he made me understand *ou* he hinted that I was in the way ▪ **elle nous le fait ~, qu'elle est le chef!** *fam* she makes sure we know who's the boss! ▪ **les conséquences de votre décision se feront ~ tôt ou tard** the implications of your decision will be felt sooner or later

3. *sout* [éprouver - joie, chagrin, remords] to feel

4. [apprécier - art, musique] to feel, to have a feeling for

5. *fam* [être convaincu par] : **je ne la sens pas pour le rôle** my feeling is that she's not right for the part ▪ **je ne le sens pas, ton projet** I'm not convinced by your project

6. [maîtriser - instrument, outil] to have a feel for ; [- rôle, mouvement à exécuter] to feel at ease with ▪ **~ sa monture** to feel good in the saddle ▪ **je ne sentais pas bien mon service aujourd'hui** [au tennis] my service wasn't up to scratch today

7. *fam* [tolérer] : **je ne peux pas ~ sa sœur** I can't bear the sight of *ou* stand her sister ▪ **je ne peux pas ~ ses blagues sexistes** I can't stomach *ou* I just can't take his sexist jokes

B. EXHALER, DONNER UNE IMPRESSION

1. [dégager - odeur, parfum] to smell (of), to give off a smell of ■ **qu'est-ce que ça sent?** what's that smell? ■ ~ **le gaz** to smell of gas ■ **les roses ne sentent rien** the roses don't smell (of anything) *ou* have no smell ■ **ça sent bon le lilas, ici** there's a nice smell of lilac in here

2. [annoncer] : **ça sent la pluie/neige** it feels like rain/snow ■ **ça sentait la mutinerie** there was mutiny in the air ■ **ses propositions sentent le traquenard** there's something a bit suspect about his proposals ■ **se faire ~** [devenir perceptible] to be felt, to become obvious ■ **la fatigue se fait ~ chez les coureurs** the runners are showing signs of tiredness

3. [laisser deviner] to smack of *(insép)*, to savour of *(insép)* ■ **son interprétation/style sent un peu trop le travail** her performance/style is rather too constrained ■ **il sent le policier à des kilomètres** *fam* you can tell he's a policeman a mile off ■ **ce n'est pas un acte de vandalisme, ça sentirait plutôt la vengeance** it's not pure vandalism, it feels more like revenge ■ **ça sent sa province/les années trente!** *fam* it smacks of provincial life/ the thirties! ■ **son accent sentait bon le terroir** he had a wonderfully earthy accent.

◇ *vi* **1.** [avoir une odeur] to smell ■ **le fromage sent fort** the cheese smells strong ■ **ça sent bon** [fleur, parfum] it smells nice ; [nourriture] it smells good *ou* nice ▶ **ça sent mauvais** *pr* it doesn't smell very nice ■ **ça commence à ~ mauvais, filons!** *fam fig* things are beginning to turn nasty, let's get out of here! **2.** [puer] to smell, to stink, to reek ■ **il sent des pieds** his feet smell, he's got smelly feet.

◆ **se sentir** ◇ *vp (emploi réciproque) fam* **ils ne peuvent pas se ~** they can't stand each other.

◇ *vp (emploi passif)* to show ■ **il ne l'aime pas – ça se sent** he doesn't like her – you can tell (he doesn't) *ou* you can sense it.

◇ *vpi* to feel ■ **se ~ en sécurité/danger** to feel safe/threatened ■ **je me sentais glisser** I could feel myself slipping ■ **se ~ mal** [s'évanouir] to feel faint ; [être indisposé] to feel ill ■ **se ~ bien** to feel good *ou* all right ■ **je ne m'en sens pas capable** I don't feel up to it *ou* equal to it ▶ **non mais, tu te sens bien?** *fam* have you gone mad?, are you off your rocker? ■ **tu te sens d'y aller?** *fam* do you feel up to going? ■ **elle ne se sent plus depuis qu'elle a eu le rôle** *fam* she's been really full of it since she landed the part ■ **ne plus se ~ de joie** to be bursting *ou* beside o.s. with joy.

◇ *vpt* : **je ne me sens pas le courage/la force de marcher** I don't feel up to walking/have the strength to walk.

señorita [seɲɔrita] *nm* [cigare] *French-made cigarillo.*

seoir [67] [swar] ◆ **seoir à** *v+prép litt* **1.** [être seyant] to become, to suit **2.** [convenir] to suit ■ *(tournure impersonnelle)* **il sied de** *litt* [il convient de] it is right *ou* proper to ■ **il sied à qqn de...** it is proper for sb to..., it behoves sb to... *sout* ■ **il ne vous sied pas** *ou* **il vous sied mal de protester** it ill becomes *ou* befits you to complain ■ **comme il sied** as is proper *ou* fitting.

Séoul [seul] *npr* Seoul.

SEP (*abr de* **sclérose en plaques**) *nf* MS.

sépale [sepal] *nm* sepal.

séparable [separabl] *adj* : **~ de** separable from ■ **l'intelligence n'est pas ~ de la sensibilité** intelligence cannot be separated *ou* divorced from the emotions.

séparateur, trice [separatœr, tris] *adj* separating, separative.

◆ **séparateur** *nm* **1.** ÉLECTR & TECHNOL separator ■ **~ d'eau et de vapeur** water trap **2.** INFORM separator, delimiter.

séparation [separasjɔ̃] *nf* **1.** [éloignement] separation, parting ■ **elle n'a pas supporté la ~ d'avec ses enfants** she couldn't bear to be parted *ou* separated from her children ■ **quand arriva le jour de notre ~** when the day of our separation arrived, when the day came for us to part **2.** [rupture] break-up, split-up **3.** DR separation (agreement) ■ **~ amiable** *ou* **de fait** voluntary separation ■ **le régime de la ~ de biens** (marriage settlement based on) separate ownership of property ■ **~ de corps** divorce a mensa et thoro *vieilli* **4.** POLIT : **la ~ des pouvoirs** the separation of powers ■ **la ~ de l'Église et de l'État** the separation of Church and State **5.** [cloison] partition, division **6.** CHIM separating, isolating **7.** NUCL : **~ isotopique** isotope separation.

séparatisme [separatism] *nm* separatism.

séparatiste [separatist] *adj* & *nmf* separatist.

séparé, e [separe] *adj* **1.** [éléments, problèmes, courrier] separate **2.** [époux] separated.

séparément [separemɑ̃] *adv* separately ■ **c'est un problème à traiter ~** this problem must be dealt with separately.

séparer [3] [separe] *vt* **1.** [isoler] to separate ■ **~ les raisins gâtés des raisins sains** to separate the bad grapes from the good ones, to pick the bad grapes out from amongst the good ones ▶ **~ le bon grain de l'ivraie** *allus* & BIBLE to separate the wheat from the chaff **2.** [éloigner - gens] to part, to separate, to pull apart *(sép)* ■ **séparez-les, ils vont se tuer!** pull them apart or they'll kill each other! ■ **~ qqn de** : **on les a séparés de leur père** they were separated from *ou* taken away from their father **3.** [différencier] : **~ l'amour et l'amitié amoureuse** to distinguish between love and a loving friendship ■ **tout les sépare** they're worlds apart, they have nothing in common **4.** [diviser] to separate, to divide ■ **le Nord est séparé du Sud** *ou* **le Nord et le Sud sont séparés par un désert** the North is separated from the South by a desert ■ **deux heures/cinq kilomètres nous séparaient de la frontière** we were two hours/five kilometres away from the border.

◆ **se séparer** ◇ *vp (emploi réciproque)* [se quitter] to break up ■ **les Beatles se sont séparés en 1970** the Beatles split up *ou* broke up in 1970 ■ **on se sépara sur le pas de la porte** we parted on the doorstep.

◇ *vpi* to divide, to branch (off).

◆ **se séparer de** *vp+prép* **1.** [se priver de] to part with ■ **je ne me sépare jamais de mon plan de Paris** I'm never without my Paris street map **2.** [quitter] : **se ~ de son mari** to separate *ou* to part from one's husband.

sépia [sepja] ◇ *nf* **1.** ZOOL cuttlefish ink **2.** ART [couleur] sepia ■ [dessin] sepia (drawing).

◇ *adj inv* sepia, sepia-coloured.

sept [sɛt] ◇ *dét* **1.** seven ■ **les Sept Merveilles du monde** the Seven Wonders of the World, *voir aussi* **cinq 2.** [dans des séries] seventh ■ **le tome ~** volume seven **3.** JEUX : **le jeu des ~ familles** Happy Families.

◇ *nm inv* **1.** [numéro] seven **2.** JEUX [carte] seven **3.** TV : **les Sept d'or** *annual television awards.*

◇ *nf inv* : **la Sept** *former French television channel.*

septantaine [sɛptɑ̃tɛn] *nf Belgique & Suisse* about seventy ■ **il a la ~** he's about seventy.

septante [sɛptɑ̃t] *dét Belgique & Suisse* seventy.

Septante [sɛptɑ̃t] *npr f* : **la (version des) ~** the Septuagint.

septantième [sɛptɑ̃tjɛm] *nmf* & *adj Belgique* seventieth.

septembre [sɛptɑ̃br] *nm* September, *voir aussi* **mars**.

septennal, e, aux [sɛptenal, o] *adj* **1.** [qui a lieu tous les sept ans] septennial **2.** [qui dure sept ans] septennial, seven-year *(avant n).*

septennat [sɛptena] *nm* **1.** POLIT (seven year) term of office ■ **pendant son premier ~** during his first term of office **2.** [période] seven-year period.

septentrion [sɛptɑ̃trijɔ̃] *nm litt* north, septentrion *arch.*

septentrional, e, aux [sɛptɑ̃trijɔnal, o] *adj* northern, septentrional *arch.*

septicémie [sɛptisemi] *nf* blood poisoning, septicaemia *spéc.*

septième [sɛtjɛm] ◇ *adj num* seventh ■ **le ~ art** the cinema ■ **être au ~ ciel** to be in seventh heaven.

◇ *nmf* seventh.

◇ *nm* **1.** [partie] seventh (part) **2.** [étage] seventh floor *UK*, sixth story *US.*

◇ *nf* **1.** ÉDUC senior form *UK ou* fifth grade *US (in primary school)* **2.** MUS seventh.

septièmement [sɛtjɛmmɑ̃] *adv* seventhly, in the seventh place.

septique [sɛptik] *adj* septic.

septuagénaire [sɛptɥaʒenɛr] ◇ *adj* seventy-year-old *(avant n)*, septuagenarian.
◇ *nmf* septuagenarian, seventy-year-old man/woman.

septuor [sɛptɥɔr] *nm* septet, septette.

septuple [sɛptypl] ◇ *adj* septuple, sevenfold.
◇ *nm* septuple.

sépulcral, e, aux [sepylkral, o] *adj litt* sepulchral ■ **un silence ~** the silence of the grave.

sépulcre [sepylkr] *nm litt* sepulchre.

sépulture [sepyltyr] *nf* **1.** [lieu] burial place **2.** *litt* [enterrement] burial, sepulture *litt*.

séquelle [sekɛl] *nf* [d'une maladie] aftereffect ■ [d'un bombardement, d'une guerre] aftermath, sequel ■ **sa bronchite n'a pas laissé de ~** she suffered no aftereffects from her bronchitis.

séquence [sekɑ̃s] *nf* **1.** CINÉ, GÉOL, MUS & RELIG sequence **2.** JEUX : **~ de cartes** run, sequence of cards **3.** INFORM sequence ■ **~ d'appel** call sequence.

séquencer [sekɑ̃se] *vt* BIOL to sequence.

séquenceur [sekɑ̃sœr] *nm* sequencer.

séquentiel, elle [sekɑ̃sjɛl] *adj* **1.** [ordonné] sequential **2.** INFORM [accès] sequential, serial ■ [traitement] sequential.

séquestration [sekɛstrasjɔ̃] *nf* **1.** DR [d'une personne] illegal confinement *ou* restraint ■ [de biens] sequestration (order) **2.** CHIM & MÉD sequestration.

séquestre [sekɛstr] *nm* **1.** DR [saisie] sequestration ■ [personne] sequestrator **2.** MÉD sequestrum.
◆ **sous séquestre** *loc adj & loc adv* : **biens (mis *ou* placés) sous ~** sequestrated property.

séquestrer [3] [sekɛstre] *vt* **1.** [personne] to confine illegally **2.** DR [bien] to sequestrate.

séquoia [sekɔja] *nm* sequoia wellingtonia, giant sequoia.

sera *etc v* ▷ **être**.

sérac [serak] *nm* serac.

sérail [seraj] *nm* **1.** [harem] seraglio, harem **2.** [palais d'un sultan] seraglio ■ **nourri dans le ~, j'en connais les détours** *Racine allus* I've been around long enough to know what I'm talking about ■ **fils de ministre, il a été élevé dans le ~ (politique)** as a cabinet minister's son, he was brought up in a political atmosphere.

séraphin [serafɛ̃] *nm* seraph.

séraphique [serafik] *adj* seraphic, seraphical.

serbe [sɛrb] *adj* Serbian.
◆ **Serbe** *nmf* Serb, Serbian.
◆ **serbe** *nm* LING Serb, Serbian.

Serbie [sɛrbi] *npr f* : **(la) ~** Serbia.

serbo-croate [sɛrbɔkrɔat] (*pl* **serbo-croates**) ◇ *adj* Serbo-Croat, Serbo-Croatian.
◇ *nm* LING Serbo-Croat, Serbo-Croatian.

serein, e [sərɛ̃, ɛn] *adj* **1.** [esprit, visage] serene, peaceful **2.** *litt* [eau, ciel] serene, clear, tranquil **3.** *sout* [jugement] unbiased, dispassionate ■ [réflexion] undisturbed, unclouded.

sereinement [sərɛnmɑ̃] *adv* **1.** [tranquillement] serenely, peacefully **2.** *sout* [impartialement] dispassionately.

sérénade [serenad] *nf* **1.** MUS serenade ■ [concert] serenade ■ **donner une ~ à qqn** to serenade sb **2.** *fam* [scène] row, din.

sérénissime [serenisim] *adj* : **la Sérénissime République** La Serenissima, the Venetian Republic.

sérénité [serenite] *nf* **1.** [d'une personne] serenity, peacefulness ■ [d'un jugement] dispassionateness ■ [des pensées] clarity **2.** *litt* [du ciel] serenity, tranquillity, clarity.

séreux, euse [serø, øz] *adj* serous.

serf, serve [sɛrf, sɛrv] ◇ *adj* **1.** *litt* [soumis] serflike, servile **2.** HIST : **la condition serve** serfdom.
◇ *nm, f* HIST serf.

serge [sɛrʒ] *nf* serge ■ **tailleur en ~** serge suit.

sergent, e [sɛrʒɑ̃, ɑ̃t] *nm, f* MIL sergeant ■ **~ instructeur** drill sergeant
◆ **sergent** *nm vieilli* [agent de police] : **~ de ville** police constable *esp UK*, police officer.

sergent-chef, sergente-chef [sɛrʒɑ̃ʃɛf, sɛrʒɑ̃tʃɛf] (*mpl* **sergents-chefs**, *fpl* **sergentes-chefs**) *nm, f* [de l'armée - de terre] staff sergeant ; [- de l'air] flight sergeant *UK*, senior master sergeant *US*.

sergent-major, sergente-major [sɛrʒɑ̃maʒɔr, sɛrʒɑ̃tmaʒɔr] (*mpl* **sergents-majors**, *fpl* **sergentes-majors**) *nm, f* quartermaster sergeant, sergeant major.

sériciculture [serisikyltyr] *nf* silkworm breeding, sericulture *spéc*.

série [seri] *nf* **1.** [suite - de questions, d'articles] series *(sing)* ; [- d'attentats] series, spate, string ; [- d'échecs] series, run, string ; [- de tests] series, battery ■ **il y a eu récemment une ~ de descentes de police** there's been a spate of police raids recently **2.** [ensemble - de clefs, de mouchoirs] set ; [- de poupées russes, de tables gigognes] nest ■ COMM & INDUST (production) batch ■ **~ limitée** limited run ■ **~ de prix** rates, list of charges **3.** [catégorie] class, category ■ **dans la ~ "scandales de l'été", tu connais la dernière?** *hum* have you heard the latest in the line of summer scandals? **4.** CINÉ : **film de ~ B** B-movie **5.** TV : **~ (télévisée)** television series **6.** SPORT [classement] series ■ [épreuve] qualifying heat *ou* round **7.** GÉOL, MATH, MUS & NUCL series *(sing)*.
◆ **de série** *loc adj* **1.** INDUST mass-produced **2.** COMM [numéro] serial *(modif)* **3.** AUTO [modèle] production *(modif)*.
◆ **en série** ◇ *loc adj* **1.** INDUST [fabrication] mass *(modif)* **2.** ÉLECTR [couplage, enroulement] series *(modif)*.
◇ *loc adv* **1.** INDUST : **fabriquer qqch en ~** to mass-produce sthg **2.** ÉLECTR : **monté en ~** connected in series **3.** [à la file] one after the other.
◆ **série B** *nm* B-movie.
◆ **série noire** *nf* **1.** LITTÉR crime thriller ■ **c'est un vrai personnage de ~ noire** he's like something out of a detective novel **2.** *fig* catalogue of disasters.

sériel, elle [serjɛl] *adj* serial ■ **musique ~le** serial music.

sérier [9] [serje] *vt* to arrange, to classify, to grade.

sérieusement [serjøzmɑ̃] *adv* **1.** [consciencieusement] seriously ■ **as-tu étudié la question ~?** have you looked at the matter thoroughly? **2.** [sans plaisanter] seriously, in earnest ■ **je pense me présenter aux élections – ~?** I think I'll stand in the election – really? **3.** [gravement] seriously, gravely ■ **~ blessé** seriously *ou* severely injured **4.** [vraiment] : **ça commençait à bouchonner ~** traffic was really building up.

sérieux, euse [serjø, øz] *adj* **1.** [grave - ton, visage] serious, solemn ■ **être ~ comme un pape** to look as solemn as a judge ■ **ne prends pas cet air ~!** don't look so serious! ■ [important - lecture, discussion] serious
2. [consciencieux - employé] serious, responsible ; [- élève] serious, serious-minded, earnest ; [- travail] conscientious ■ **être ~ dans son travail** to be a conscientious worker, to take one's work seriously ■ **ça ne fait pas très ~** it doesn't look good
3. [digne de foi - offre] genuine ; [- candidature, revue] serious ; [- personne] reliable, dependable ; [- analyse, enquête] serious, thorough, in-depth
4. [dangereux - situation, maladie] grave, serious ; [- blessure] severe
5. [sincère] serious ■ **'pas ~ s'abstenir'** 'only genuine inquirers need apply', 'no time-wasters' ■ **c'est ~, cette histoire d'augmentation?** *fam* is this talk about getting a rise serious? ■ [vrai] : **c'est ~, cette histoire?** is it all true? ■ **c'est ~, tu pars?** it's true that you are leaving?
6. *(avant le nom)* [important - effort] real ; [- dégâts, difficultés, risques] serious ■ **il a de sérieuses chances de gagner** he stands a good chance of winning ■ **on a de sérieuses raisons de le penser** we have good reasons to think so ■ **de ~ progrès techniques** considerable technical advances ■ **ils ont une sérieuse avance sur nous** they are well ahead of us.
◆ **sérieux** *nm* **1.** [gravité - d'une personne] seriousness ; [- d'une situation] gravity ■ **garder son ~** to keep a straight face

2. [application] seriousness, serious-mindedness ▪ **elle fait son travail avec ~** she's serious about her work
3. [fiabilité - d'une intention] seriousness, earnestness ; [- d'une source de renseignements] reliability, dependability.
◆ **au sérieux** *loc adv* : **prendre qqch/qqn au ~** to take sthg/sb seriously ▪ **se prendre (trop) au ~** to take o.s. (too) seriously.

sérigraphie [serigrafi] *nf* **1.** [procédé] silk-screen *ou* screen process printing **2.** [ouvrage] silk-screen print.

serin, e [sərɛ̃, in] *nm, f* **1.** ZOOL canary **2.** *fam* [personne] nitwit.
◆ **serin** *adj m inv* [couleur] : **jaune ~** bright *ou* canary yellow.

seriner [3] [sərine] *vt fam* [répéter] : **~ qqch à qqn** to drill *ou* to drum *ou* to din sthg into sb ▪ **il m'a seriné ça toute la soirée** he kept telling me the same thing all evening.

seringue [sərɛ̃g] *nf* **1.** MÉD needle, syringe ▪ **~ hypodermique** hypodermic needle **2.** CULIN syringe.

serment [sɛrmɑ̃] *nm* **1.** [parole solennelle] oath ▪ **témoigner sous ~** to testify under oath ▪ **déclarer sous la foi du ~** to declare on *ou* upon oath ▪ **faire un ~ sur l'honneur** to pledge one's word of honour ⊃ **~ d'Hippocrate** MÉD Hippocratic oath ▪ **~ judiciaire** oath *ou* affirmation *(in a court of law)* ▪ **~ politique** oath of allegiance ▪ **le ~ du Jeu de paume** HIST the Tennis Court Oath **2.** [promesse] pledge ▪ **des ~s d'amour** pledges *ou* vows of love ▪ **j'ai fait le ~ de ne rien dire** I'm pledged *ou* sworn to secrecy ⊃ **~ d'ivrogne** *ou* **de joueur** vain promise.

sermon [sɛrmɔ̃] *nm* **1.** RELIG sermon ▪ **faire un ~** to deliver *ou* to preach a sermon **2.** *fig* & *péj* lecture ▪ **épargne-moi tes ~s** spare me the lecture.

sermonner [3] [sɛrmɔne] *vt* [morigéner] to lecture, to sermonize, to preach at.

sermonneur, euse [sɛrmɔnœr, øz] ◇ *adj* sermonizing, lecturing.
◇ *nm, f* sermonizer.

SERNAM, Sernam® [sɛrnam] (*abr de* **Service national des messageries**) *npr m rail delivery service*, ≃ Red Star® *UK*.

sérodiagnostic [serɔdjagnɔstik] *nm* serodiagnosis, serum diagnosis.

sérologie [serɔlɔʒi] *nf* serology.

sérologique [serɔlɔʒik] *adj* serologic, serological.

sérologiste [serɔlɔʒist] *nmf* serologist.

séronégatif, ive [serɔnegatif, iv] ◇ *adj* [gén] seronegative ▪ [HIV] HIV negative.
◇ *nm, f* : **les ~s** HIV negative people.

séronégativité [serɔnegativite] *nf* [gén] seronegativity ▪ [au HIV] HIV-negative status.

séropositif, ive [serɔpozitif, iv] ◇ *adj* [gén] seropositive ▪ [HIV] HIV positive.
◇ *nm, f* : **les ~s** HIV positive people.

séropositivité [serɔpozitivite] *nf* [gén] seropositivity ▪ [HIV] HIV infection.

sérosité [serozite] *nf* serous fluid.

serpe [sɛrp] *nf* bill, billhook ▪ **un visage taillé à la ~** a rough-hewn face.

serpent [sɛrpɑ̃] *nm* **1.** ZOOL snake ⊃ **~ à lunettes** Indian cobra ▪ **~ de mer** MYTHOL sea monster *ou* serpent ; PRESSE silly-season story *UK*, flupp story *US* ▪ **~ à sonnette** rattlesnake ▪ **c'est (comme) le ~ qui se mord la queue** it's a vicious circle **2.** *litt* [personne] viper **3.** [forme sinueuse] : **~ de fumée** ribbon of smoke **4.** FIN : **le ~ monétaire européen** the (European currency) Snake **5.** MUS serpent.

serpentaire [sɛrpɑ̃tɛr] ◇ *nm* ORNITH secretary bird.
◇ *nf* BOT snakeroot.

serpenter [3] [sɛrpɑ̃te] *vi* to wind along, to meander.

serpentin, e [sɛrpɑ̃tɛ̃, in] *adj litt* twisting, winding, sinuous.
◆ **serpentin** *nm* **1.** [de papier] (paper) streamer **2.** PHYS coil.
◆ **serpentine** *nf* MINÉR serpentine.

serpillière [sɛrpijɛr] *nf* [torchon] floorcloth ▪ **il faudrait passer la ~ dans la cuisine** the kitchen floor needs cleaning.

serpolet [sɛrpɔlɛ] *nm* mother-of-thyme, wild thyme.

serrage [sɛraʒ] *nm* [d'une vis] screwing down, tightening ▪ [d'un joint] clamping.

serre [sɛr] *nf* **1.** HORT & AGRIC [en verre] greenhouse, glasshouse *UK* ▪ [en plastique] greenhouse ▪ **cultures en ~** greenhouse plants ▪ **légumes poussés en ~** vegetables grown under glass ⊃ **~ chaude** hothouse ▪ **effet de ~** greenhouse effect **2.** ORNITH claw, talon **3.** TECHNOL [d'une substance] pressing, squeezing **4.** MÉTALL ramming **5.** NAUT stringer.

serré, e [sere] *adj* **1.** [nœud, ceinture] tight **2.** [vêtement] : **~ à la taille** fitted at the waist, tight-waisted **3.** [contracté] : **les lèvres/dents ~es** with set lips/clenched teeth ▪ **c'est le cœur ~ que j'y repense** when I think of it, it gives me a lump in my throat **4.** [dense - style] tight, concise ; [- emploi du temps] tight, busy ; [- réseau] dense ; [- débat] closely-conducted, closely-argued ; [- écriture] cramped **5.** [café] strong **6.** SPORT [arrivée, peloton] close ▪ [match] tight, close-fought ▪ **jouer** *ou* **mener un jeu ~** to play a tight game.
◆ **serré** *adv* : **jouer ~** to play a tight game.

serre-file [sɛrfil] (*pl* **serre-files**) *nm* MIL serrefile.

serre-fils [sɛrfil] *nm inv* [vis] binding screw ▪ [pince] wire grip.

serre-joint(s) [sɛrʒwɛ̃] *nm inv* (builder's) clamp.

serre-livres [sɛrlivr] *nm inv* bookend ▪ **deux ~** a pair of bookends.

serrement [sɛrmɑ̃] *nm* **1.** *sout* [action] : **~ de cœur** pang of anguish, tug at the heartstrings ▪ **~ de main** handshake **2.** MIN dam.

serrer [4] [sere] ◇ *vt* **1.** [presser] to hold tight ▪ **serre-moi fort dans tes bras** hold me tight in your arms ▪ **~ qqch contre son cœur** to clasp sthg to one's breast ▪ **~ qqn contre son cœur** to clasp sb to one's bosom ▪ **~ qqn à la gorge** to grab sb by the throat ▪ **~ le kiki à qqn** *fam* to try to strangle sb ▪ **~ la main** *ou* **la pince** *fam* **à qqn** to shake hands with sb, to shake sb's hand
2. [suj: vêtement] to be tight ▪ **la chaussure droite/le col me serre un peu** the right shoe/the collar is a bit tight
3. [bien fermer - nœud, lacets] to tighten, to pull tight ; [- joint] to clamp ; [- écrou] to tighten (up) ; [- frein à main] to put on tight ▪ **~ la vis à qqn** *fam* to crack down hard on sb
4. [contracter] to clench ▪ **~ les lèvres** to set *ou* to tighten one's lips ▪ **~ les dents** to clench *ou* to set *ou* to grit one's teeth ▪ **~ les mâchoires** to clench one's jaws ▪ **en serrant les poings** *pr* clenching one's fists ; *fig* barely containing one's anger ▪ **avoir la gorge serrée par l'émotion** to be choked with emotion ⊃ **~ les fesses** *fam* to have the jitters
5. [rapprocher] : **~ les rangs** *fig* & MIL to close ranks ▪ **~ le jeu** SPORT to play a tight game ⊃ **être serrés comme des sardines** *ou* **des harengs** to be squashed up like sardines
6. [suivre] : **~ le trottoir** AUTO to hug the kerb ▪ **~ qqn de près** to follow close behind sb, to follow sb closely ▪ **~ un problème de plus près** to study a problem more closely
7. NAUT : **~ le vent** to sail close to *ou* to hug the wind
8. *litt* [enfermer] to put away.
◇ *vi* AUTO : **~ à droite/gauche** to keep to the right/left.
◆ **se serrer** ◇ *vpi* **1.** [se rapprocher] to squeeze up ▪ **se ~ contre qqn** [par affection] to cuddle *ou* to snuggle up to sb ; [pour se protéger] to huddle up against sb ▪ **se ~ les uns contre les autres** to huddle together
2. [se contracter] to tighten up ▪ **je sentais ma gorge se ~** I could feel a lump in my throat ▪ **mon cœur se serra en les voyant** my heart sank when I saw them.
◇ *vpt* : **se ~ la main** to shake hands.

serre-tête [sɛrtɛt] *nm inv* **1.** [accessoire] headband, hairband **2.** SPORT [d'athlète] headband ▪ [de rugbyman] scrum cap.

serrure [seryr] *nf* lock ▪ **laisser la clef dans la ~** to leave the key in the lock *ou* door ⊃ **~ encastrée** mortise lock ▪ **~ de sécurité** AUTO childproof lock ▪ **~ de sûreté** safety lock.

serrurerie [seryrri] *nf* **1.** [métier] locksmithing, locksmithery **2.** [ferronnerie] ironwork ▪ **~ d'art** decorative ironwork.

serrurier [seryrje] *nm* **1.** [qui pose des serrures] locksmith **2.** [en ferronnerie] iron manufacturer.

sert *etc v* ⊳ **servir.**

sertir [32] [sɛrtir] *vt* **1.** JOAILL to set ▪ **couronne sertie de diamants** crown set with diamonds **2.** MÉTALL [tôles] to crimp over *(sép)* ▪ [rivet] to clinch **3.** ARM to crimp.

sertissage [sɛrtisaʒ] *nm* **1.** JOAILL setting **2.** MÉTALL [de tôles] crimping together ▪ [d'un rivet] clinching.

sertisseur, euse [sɛrtisœr, øz] *nm, f* **1.** JOAILL (jewel) setter **2.** MÉTALL crimper.
◆ **sertisseur** *nm* [appareil] closing *ou* sealing *ou* double seaming machine.

sérum [serɔm] *nm* **1.** PHYSIOL : **~ (sanguin)** (blood) serum **2.** PHARM serum ▪ **~ antivenimeux** antivenin serum ▪ **~ physiologique** saline ▪ **~ de vérité** truth drug.

servage [sɛrvaʒ] *nm* **1.** HIST serfdom **2.** *litt* [esclavage] bondage, thraldom.

servant [sɛrvɑ̃] ◇ *adj m* RELIG : **frère ~** lay brother *(with domestic tasks).*
◇ *nm* RELIG : **~ (de messe)** server.

servante [sɛrvɑ̃t] *nf* [domestique] servant, maidservant.

serve [sɛrv] *f* ⊳ **serf.**

serveur [sɛrvœr] *nm* **1.** [de restaurant] waiter ▪ [de bar] barman **2.** SPORT server **3.** JEUX dealer **4.** INDUST [ouvrier] feeder (worker) **5.** INFORM server ▪ **(centre) ~** information retrieval centre ▪ **~ de données** on-line data service ▪ **~ de réseau** network server.

serveuse [sɛrvøz] *nf* waitress.

serviabilité [sɛrvjabilite] *nf* helpfulness.

serviable [sɛrvjabl] *adj* helpful, obliging, amenable.

service [sɛrvis] *nm* **1.** [travail] duty, shift ▪ **mon ~ commence à 18 h** I go on duty *ou* I start my shift *ou* I start work at 6 p.m ▪ **l'alcool est interdit pendant le ~** drinking is forbidden while on duty ▪ **il n'a pu assurer son ~** he wasn't able to go to work ▪ **être de ~ : qui est de ~ ce soir?** who's on duty tonight? ▪ **il n'est pas de ~** he's off-duty ▪ **elle a 22 ans de ~ dans l'entreprise** she's been with the company for 22 years ▪ **finir son ~** to come off duty ▪ **prendre son ~** to go on *ou* to report for duty ▪ **reprendre du ~** to be employed for a supplementary period ▪ **mon vieux manteau a repris du ~** *fam hum* my old coat has been saved from the bin ▮ [pour la collectivité] service, serving ▪ **le ~ de l'État** public service, the service of the state ▪ **ses états de ~** his service record
2. [pour un client, un maître] service ▪ **prendre qqn à son ~** to take sb into service ▪ **elle a deux ans de ~ comme femme de chambre** she's been in service for two years as a chambermaid ▪ **à votre ~** at your service ▪ **elle a passé sa vie au ~ des autres** she spent her life helping others ▪ **il a mis son savoir-faire au ~ de la société** he put his expertise at the disposal of the company ▪ **je ne suis pas à ton ~!** I'm not your slave! ▪ **qu'y a-t-il pour votre ~?** what can I do for you? ▪ **'~ compris/non compris'** 'service included/not included' ▪ **prends ces cacahuètes et fais le ~** take these peanuts and hand them round ⊙ **après dix ans de bons et loyaux ~s** after ten years of good and faithful service
3. [série de repas] sitting ▪ **nous irons au premier/deuxième ~** we'll go to the first/second sitting
4. [département - d'une entreprise, d'un hôpital] department ▪ **~ clientèle** customer services ▪ **~ du contentieux** [département] legal department ; [personnes] legal experts ▪ **les ~s commerciaux** the sales department *ou* division ▪ **~ du personnel** personnel department *ou* division ▪ **~ de presse** [département] press office ; [personnes] press officers, press office staff ▪ **~ des urgences** casualty (department) *UK*, emergency room *US* ; ADMIN : **~ postal** postal service
5. [aide] favour ▪ **rendre un ~ à qqn** [suj: personne] to do sb a favour, to help sb out ▪ **elle n'aime pas rendre ~** she's not very helpful ▪ **tu m'as bien rendu ~** you were a great help to me ▪ **rendre un mauvais ~ à qqn** to do sb a disservice ▪ **lui faire tous ses devoirs, c'est un mauvais ~ à lui rendre!** it won't do her any good if you do all her homework for her! ▪ **ton dictionnaire m'a bien rendu ~** your dictionary was of great use to me ▪ **ça peut encore/toujours rendre ~** it can still/it'll always come in handy
6. [assortiment - de linge, de vaisselle] set ▪ **acheter un ~ de 6 couverts en argent** to buy a 6-place canteen of silver cutlery
7. TRANSP service ▪ **~ d'été/d'hiver** summer/winter timetable ▪ **~ non assuré le dimanche** no service on Sundays, no Sunday service
8. MIL : **~ militaire** *ou* **national** military/national service ▪ **~ actif** active service ▪ **~ civil** non-military national service ▪ **bon pour le ~** fit for military duties ▪ **allez, bon/bons pour le ~!** *fig & hum* it'll/they'll do! ▪ **en ~ commandé** on an official assignment ▪ **le ~ de santé** the (army) medical corps ▪ **le ~ des transmissions** signals
9. SPORT service, serve ▪ **Pichot au ~!, ~ Pichot!** Pichot to serve! ▪ **prendre le ~ de qqn** to break sb's serve *ou* service
10. ÉLECTR duty
11. FIN servicing ▪ **assurer le ~ de la dette** to service the debt
12. RELIG : **~ (divin)** service ▪ **~ funèbre** funeral service.
◆ **services** *nmpl* **1.** ÉCON services, service industries, tertiary sector ▪ **biens et ~s** goods and services
2. [collaboration] services ▪ **se passer des ~s de qqn** to do without sb's help ; *euphém* [le licencier] to dispense with sb's services ▪ **offrir ses ~s à qqn** to offer one's services to sb, to offer to help sb out
3. POLIT : **~s secrets** *ou* **spéciaux** secret service
4. *Suisse* [couverts] knives and forks *(for laying at table).*
◆ **en service** ◇ *loc adj* in service, in use.
◇ *loc adv* : **mettre un appareil en ~** to put a machine into service ▪ **cet hélicoptère/cette presse entrera en ~ en mai** this helicopter will be put into service/this press will come on stream in May.
◆ **service après-vente** *nm* **1.** [prestation] after-sales service
2. [département] after-sales department ▪ [personnes] after-sales staff.
◆ **service d'ordre** *nm* **1.** [système] policing ▪ **assurer le ~ d'ordre dans un périmètre** to police a perimeter ▪ **mettre en place un ~ d'ordre dans un quartier** to establish a strong police presence in an area
2. [gendarmes] police (contingent) ▪ [syndiqués, manifestants] stewards.
◆ **service public** *nm* public service *ou* utility ▪ **~ public de l'audiovisuel** the publicly-owned channels *(on French television)* ▪ **la poste est un ~ public** postal services are state-controlled.

SERVICE MILITAIRE OU NATIONAL

Until 1996, all French men aged 18 and over were required to do ten months national service unless declared unfit. The system has been phased out and replaced by an obligatory *journée d'appel de préparation à la défense*, one day spent learning about the army and army career opportunities. The *JAPD* is obligatory for men and for women. The object of this reform is to professionalize the army.

serviette [sɛrvjɛt] *nf* **1.** [linge] : **~ de bain** bath towel ▪ **~ hygiénique** sanitary towel *UK ou* napkin *US* ▪ **~ en papier** paper napkin ▪ **~ de table** table napkin ▪ **~ de toilette** towel ; [pour s'essuyer les mains] (hand) towel **2.** [cartable] briefcase.

serviette-éponge [sɛrvjɛtepɔ̃ʒ] *(pl* **serviettes-éponges***) nf* (terry) towel.

servile [sɛrvil] *adj* **1.** [esprit, attitude] servile, subservient, sycophantic *sout* ▪ [manières] servile, cringing, fawning **2.** *vieilli* [d'esclave] servile.

servilement [sɛrvilmɑ̃] *adv* **1.** [bassement] obsequiously, subserviently **2.** *sout* [sans originalité] slavishly.

servilité [sɛrvilite] *nf* **1.** [bassesse] obsequiousness, subservience **2.** [manque d'originalité] slavish imitativeness.

servir [38] [sɛrvir] ◇ *vt* **1.** [dans un magasin] to serve ▪ **on vous sert?** [dans un café, une boutique] are you being attended to *sout ou* served? ▪ **~ qqn de** *ou* **en qqch** to serve sb with sthg, to serve sthg to sb ▪ **c'est une bonne cliente, sers-la bien** [en poids] be generous, she's a good customer ; [en qualité] give her the best, she's a good customer ▪ **c'est difficile de se faire ~ ici** it's

difficult to get served here ▪ **tu voulais du changement, tu es** *ou* **te voilà servi!** *fig* you wanted some changes, now you've got more than you bargained for *ou* now how do you like it? ▮ [approvisionner] : ~ **qqn en** to supply sb with
2. [donner - boisson, mets] to serve ▪ [dans le verre] to pour (out) *(sép)* ▪ [dans l'assiette] to dish out *ou* up *(sép)*, to serve up *(sép)* ▪ **sers le café** pour the coffee ▪ **puis-je te ~ du poulet?** can I help you to some chicken? ▪ **elle nous a servi un très bon cassoulet** she gave us *ou* served up some lovely cassoulet ▪ **le dîner est servi!** dinner's ready *ou* served! ▪ **Monsieur est servi** *sout* [au dîner] dinner is served, Sir ▪ ~ **qqch à qqn** to serve sb with *ou* to help sb to sthg ▪ **sers-moi à boire** give *ou* pour me a drink ▪ **faîtes-vous ~ à boire** get the waiter to pour you a drink ▪ **vous nous servirez le thé au salon** we'll take tea in the drawing room ▪ *(en usage absolu)* **nous ne servons plus après 23 h** we don't take orders after 11 p.m., last orders are at 11 p.m ▪ **servez chaud** serve hot
3. *fam* [raconter] to give ▪ **ils nous servent toujours les mêmes histoires aux informations** they always dish out the same old stories on the news
4. [travailler pour - famille] to be in service with ; [- communauté, pays, parti] to serve ; [- justice] to be at the service of ; [- patrie, cause] to serve ▪ **j'aime bien me faire ~** I like to be waited on ▪ **vous avez bien/mal servi votre entreprise** you have served your company well/haven't given your company good service ▪ ~ **l'intérêt public** [loi, mesure] to be in the public interest ; [personne] to serve the public interest ▪ ~ **l'État** POLIT to serve the state ; [être fonctionnaire] to be employed by the state ▪ **Charles Albert, pour vous ~** *hum* Charles Albert, at your service ➋ **on n'est jamais si bien servi que par soi-même** *prov* if you want something doing, do it yourself
5. [aider - suj: circonstances] to be of service to, to be *ou* to work to the advantage of ▪ ~ **les ambitions de qqn** to serve *ou* to aid *ou* to further sb's ambitions ▪ **le mauvais temps l'a servi** the bad weather served him well *ou* worked to his advantage *ou* was on his side ▪ **sa mémoire la sert beaucoup** her memory's a great help to her ▪ **finalement, son culot ne l'a pas servi** *fam* his cheek didn't get him anywhere in the end
6. [payer - pension, rente] to pay (out) *(sép)* ▪ ~ **les intérêts d'une dette** to service a debt
7. SPORT to serve
8. [préparer - arme] to serve
9. RELIG : ~ **la messe** to serve mass
10. JEUX [cartes] to deal (out) *(sép)* ▪ [joueur] to serve, to deal to *(sép)*
11. CHASSE to dispatch
12. VÉTÉR & ZOOL [saillir] to cover, to serve
13. *Suisse* [utiliser] to use.
◇ *vi* **1.** [être utile - outil, vêtement, appareil] to be useful *ou* of use, to come in handy ▪ **garde la malle, ça peut toujours ~** keep the trunk, you might need it *ou* it might come in handy one day ▪ **ça me servira pour ranger mes lettres** I can use it to put my letters in ▪ **il a servi, ce manteau!** I got a lot of use out of this coat! ▪ **cet argument a beaucoup servi** this argument has been put forward many times ▪ **ça n'a jamais servi** it's never been used
2. [travailler] : **elle sert au château depuis 40 ans** she's worked as a servant *ou* been in service at the castle for 40 years ▪ ~ **dans un café/restaurant** [homme] to be a waiter (in a) café/restaurant ; [femme] to be a waitress (in a) café/restaurant ▮ MIL to serve
3. SPORT to serve ▪ **à toi de ~!** your serve *ou* service! ▪ **elle sert bien** [gén] she has a good service *ou* serve ; [dans ce match] she's serving well.
◆ **servir à** *v+prép* **1.** [être destiné à] to be used for
2. [avoir pour conséquence] : ~ **à qqch : ça ne sert à rien de lui en parler** it's useless *ou* of no use to talk about it with him ▪ **ne pleure pas, ça ne sert à rien** don't cry, it won't make any difference ▪ **crier ne sert à rien** there's no point in shouting ▪ **à quoi servirait de lui en parler?** what would be the good *ou* point of killing him? ▪ **tu vois bien que ça a servi à quelque chose de faire une pétition!** as you see, getting up a petition did serve some purpose! ▪ **ça n'a servi qu'à le rendre encore plus furieux** it only served to make him *ou* it only made him even more furious
3. [être utile à] : ~ **à qqn : merci, ça m'a beaucoup servi** thanks, it was really useful *ou* a great help ▪ **sa connaissance du russe lui a servi dans son métier** her knowledge of Russian helped her *ou* was of use to her in her job ▪ **les circonstances m'ont beaucoup servi** the circumstances were in my favour ▪ **ça me servira à couper la pâte** I'll use it to cut the dough.
◆ **servir de** *v+prép* [article, appareil] to be used as ▪ [personne] to act as, to be ▪ **le coffre me sert aussi de table** I also use the trunk as a table ▪ **le proverbe qui sert d'exergue au chapitre** the proverb which heads the chapter ▪ **je lui ai servi d'interprète** I acted as his interpreter.
◆ **se servir** ◇ *vp (emploi réfléchi)* [à table, dans un magasin] to help o.s. ▪ **servez-vous de** *ou* **en légumes** help yourself to vegetables ▪ **je me suis servi un verre de lait** I poured myself a glass of milk ▪ **sers-toi!** help yourself! ▪ **il s'est servi dans la caisse** *euphém* he helped himself to the money in the till ▮ [s'approvisionner] : **je me sers chez le boucher de l'avenue** I buy my meat at the butcher's on the avenue.
◇ *vp (emploi passif)* CULIN to be served ▪ **le vin rouge se sert chambré** red wine should be served at room temperature.
◆ **se servir de** *vp+prép* : **se ~ de qqch** to use sthg ▪ **il ne peut plus se ~ de son bras droit** he can't use his right arm anymore ▪ **c'est une arme dont on ne se sert plus** it's a weapon which is no longer used *ou* in use ▪ **se ~ de qqch comme** to use sthg as ▪ **se ~ de qqn** to make use of *ou* to use sb.

serviteur [sɛrvitœr] *nm* (male) servant ▪ **votre (humble) ~!** *hum* your (humble) servant!, at your service!

servitude [sɛrvityd] *nf* **1.** [soumission] servitude **2.** [contrainte] constraint ▪ **se plier aux ~s de la mode** to be a slave to fashion **3.** DR easement ▪ ~ **de passage** right of way.

servocommande [sɛrvɔkɔmɑ̃d] *nf* servocontrol, power-assisted control, power booster *US*.

servofrein [sɛrvɔfrɛ̃] *nm* servo brake, servo-assisted brake.

ses [se] *pl* ⊳ **son**.

sésame [sezam] *nm* **1.** BOT & CULIN sesame ▪ **graine de ~** sesame seed **2.** *loc* **Sésame, ouvre-toi!** open, Sesame! ▪ **le ~ (ouvre-toi) de la réussite** the key to success.

session [sesjɔ̃] *nf* **1.** [réunion - d'une assemblée] session, sitting **2.** UNIV exam period ▪ **il a été collé à la ~ de juin** he failed the June exams ▪ **la ~ de repêchage** the repeat examinations, the resits *UK*.

set [sɛt] *nm* **1.** [objet] : ~ **(de table)** table mat ▪ **six ~s de table** a set of six table mats **2.** SPORT set ▪ **balle de ~** set point.

setter [setɛr] *nm* ZOOL setter ▪ ~ **anglais/irlandais** English/Irish setter.

seuil [sœj] *nm* **1.** [dalle] doorstep ▪ [entrée] doorway, threshold **2.** *sout* [début] threshold, brink ▪ **être au ~ de la mort** to be on the verge of death **3.** [limite] threshold ▪ **la population a atteint le ~ critique d'un milliard** population has reached the critical level *ou* threshold of one billion **4.** SC threshold ▪ ~ **de tolérance** threshold of tolerance **5.** PSYCHOL threshold, limen *spéc* **6.** ÉCON : ~ **de rentabilité/saturation** break-even/saturation point ▪ **le ~ de pauvreté** the poverty line **7.** GÉOGR sill.

seul, e [sœl] ◇ *adj* **1.** [sans compagnie] alone, on one's own ▪ ~ **au monde** *ou* **sur la terre** (all) alone in the world ▪ **il n'est bien que ~** he prefers his own company ▪ **enfin ~s!** alone at last! ▪ ~ **à ~** [en privé] in private, privately ▪ **je voudrais te parler ~ à ~** I'd like to talk to you in private ▪ **se retrouver ~ à ~ avec qqn** to find o.s. alone with sb ▪ **elle vit ~e avec sa mère** she lives alone with her mother ▪ **un homme ~ a peu de chances de réussir** [sans aucune aide] it's unlikely that anybody could succeed on their own ▪ **tu seras ~ à défendre le budget** you'll be the only one speaking for the budget ▪ **tout ~, toute ~e : elle parle toute ~e** she's talking to herself ▪ **il a bâti sa maison tout ~** he built his house all by himself ▪ **leur entrevue ne s'est pas passée toute ~e!** their meeting didn't go smoothly! ▪ **le dîner ne se préparera pas tout ~!** dinner isn't going to make itself! ▪ **laisse des pommes de terre, t'es pas tout ~!** *fam* leave some potatoes, you're not the only one eating!
2. [abandonné, esseulé] lonely, lonesome *US*
3. [sans partenaire, non marié] alone, on one's own ▪ **un homme ~** [non accompagné] a man on his own ; [célibataire] a single man, a bachelor ▪ **elle est ~e avec trois enfants** she's bringing up three children on her own ▪ **les personnes ~es ne touche-**

ront pas l'allocation single *ou* unmarried people will not be eligible for the allowance ▪ **un club pour personnes ~es** a singles club
4. *(avant le n)* [unique] only, single, sole ▪ **c'est l'homme d'une ~e passion** he's a man with one overriding *ou* ruling passion ▪ **c'est l'homme d'une ~e femme** he's a one-woman man ▪ **un ~ mot et tu es mort** one word and you're dead ▪ **il n'a qu'un ~ défaut** he's only got one fault ▪ **je n'ai été en retard qu'une ~e fois** I was late only once ▪ **pas un ~..., pas une ~e...** not one..., not a single... ▪ **un ~ et même..., une ~e et même...** one and the same... ▪ **un ~ et unique..., une ~e et unique...** only one (and one only)... ▪ **je l'ai vue une ~e et unique fois** I saw her only once ▪ **le ~ et unique exemplaire** the one and only copy ▪ **la ~e fois que je l'ai vue** the only *ou* one time I saw her
5. [sans autre chose] : **mon salaire ~** *ou soutmon* **~ salaire ne suffit pas à faire vivre ma famille** my salary alone is not enough to support my family ▪ **le vase ~ vaut combien?** how much is it for just the vase? ▪ **la propriété à elle ~e leur donne de quoi vivre** the property alone brings in enough for them to live on
6. *(comme adverbe)* only ▪ **~ Pierre a refusé** only Pierre refused, Pierre was the only one to refuse
7. *(avant le n)* [simple] mere ▪ **la ~e évocation de la scène lui donnait des frissons** the mere mention of *ou* merely talking about the scene gave him goose pimples.
◇ *nm, f* **1.** [personne] only one (person) ▪ **je te crois mais je dois être la ~e!** I believe you, but thousands wouldn't! ▪ **tu voudrais t'arrêter de travailler? t'es pas le ~!** *fam* you'd like to stop work? you're not the only one! ▪ **pas un ~ (de ses camarades) n'était prêt à l'épauler** not a single one (of her friends) was prepared to help her
2. [animal, objet] only one.

seulement [sœlmɑ̃] *adv* **1.** [uniquement] only **2.** [dans le temps] : **il arrive ~ ce soir** he won't arrive before this evening ▪ **il est arrivé ~ ce matin** he only arrived this morning ▪ **je viens ~ de finir** I've only just finished **3.** [même] even ▪ **sais-tu ~ de quoi tu parles?** do you even know what you're talking about? **4.** [mais] only, but ▪ **je veux y aller, ~ voilà, avec qui?** I'd love to go, but *ou* only the problem is who with?
◆ **non seulement..., mais encore** *loc corrélative* not only... but also.

seulet, ette [sœlɛ, ɛt] *adj vieilli & hum* (all) on one's own ▪ **j'étais toute ~te ce jour-là** I was all by myself *ou* all alone that day.

sève [sɛv] *nf* **1.** BOT sap ▪ **plein de ~** full of sap, sappy **2.** [énergie] : **la ~ de la jeunesse** the vigour of youth.

sévère [sevɛr] *adj* **1.** [personne, caractère, règlement] strict, stern, severe **2.** [critique, verdict] severe, harsh ▪ **ne sois pas trop ~ avec lui** don't be too hard on him **3.** [style, uniforme] severe, austere, unadorned **4.** [important - pertes] severe, heavy ; [- dégâts] major.

sévèrement [sevɛrmɑ̃] *adv* severely, harshly, strictly.

sévérité [severite] *nf* **1.** [d'un parent, d'un juge] severity, harshness **2.** [d'un verdict, d'un code, d'une éducation] severity, rigidness, strictness **3.** [d'une tenue, d'un style] severity, austerity.

sévices [sevis] *nmpl* : **exposer qqn à des ~** to expose sb to ill-treatment *ou* physical cruelty ▪ **être victime de ~** to suffer cruelty, to be ill-treated ▪ **faire subir des ~ à qqn** to ill-treat sb.

sévillan, e [sevijɑ̃, an] *adj* from Seville.
◆ **Sévillan, e** *nm, f inhabitant of or person from Seville.*

Séville [sevij] *npr* Seville.

sévir [32] [sevir] *vi* **1.** [personne] : **si tu continues à tricher, je vais devoir ~** if you keep on cheating, I'll have to do something about it ▪ **~ contre la fraude fiscale** to deal ruthlessly with tax evasion **2.** [fléau, épidémie] to rage, to be rampant *ou* rife, to reign supreme ▪ **Morin ne sévira pas longtemps comme directeur à la comptabilité** *hum* Morin won't reign long as head of accounts ▪ **c'est une idée qui sévit encore dans les milieux économiques** unfortunately the idea still has currency among economists.

sevrage [səvraʒ] *nm* **1.** [d'un bébé] weaning **2.** [d'un drogué] coming off (drugs) ▪ **quand je me suis retrouvé en prison, le ~ a été brutal** when I found myself in prison, I had to come off drugs suddenly.

sevrer [19] [səvre] *vt* **1.** [bébé] to wean **2.** [drogué] : **~ qqn** to get sb off drugs **3.** *fig* **~ qqn de** to deprive sb of **4.** HORT to sever *(a layer).*

sèvres [sɛvr] *nm* **1.** [matière] Sèvres (china) ▪ **un service de ~** a Sèvres china service **2.** [objet] piece of Sèvres china.

sexagénaire [sɛksaʒenɛr] ◇ *adj* sixty-year-old *(avant n),* sexagenarian.
◇ *nmf* sexagenarian, sixty-year-old person.

sex-appeal [sɛksapil] *(pl* **sex-appeals***) nm* sex appeal ▪ **avoir du ~** to be sexy, to have sex appeal.

S. Exc. *(abr écrite de* **Son Excellence***)* HE.

sexe [sɛks] *nm* **1.** [caractéristique] sex ▪ **enfant du ~ masculin/féminin** male/female child ➔ **le (beau) ~** the fair *ou* gentle sex ▪ **le ~ fort/faible** the stronger/weaker sex **2.** ANAT sex (organs), genitals **3.** [sexualité] : **le ~** sex.

sexisme [sɛksism] *nm* **1.** [idéologie] sexism **2.** [politique] sexual discrimination.

sexiste [sɛksist] *adj & nmf* sexist.

sexologie [sɛksɔlɔʒi] *nf* sexology.

sexologue [sɛksɔlɔg] *nmf* sexologist.

sex-shop [sɛksʃɔp] *(pl* **sex-shops***) nm* sex shop.

sextant [sɛkstɑ̃] *nm* sextant.

sextet [sɛkstɛt] *nm* six-bit byte.

sexto [sɛksto] *adv* sixthly, in the sixth place.

sextuor [sɛkstɥɔr] *nm* sextet, sextette.

sextuple [sɛkstypl] ◇ *adj* sextuple, sixfold.
◇ *nm* sextuple.

sextupler [3] [sɛkstyple] ◇ *vt* : **~ qqch** to sextuple sthg, to increase sthg sixfold.
◇ *vi* to sextuple, to increase sixfold.

sextuplés, es [sɛkstyple] *nmf pl* sextuplets.

sexualisation [sɛksɥalizasjɔ̃] *nf* sexualization.

sexualiser [3] [sɛksɥalize] *vt* to sexualize ▪ **~ la publicité** to put sex into advertising.

sexualité [sɛksɥalite] *nf* sexuality.

sexué, e [sɛksɥe] *adj* [animal] sexed ▪ [reproduction] sexual.

sexuel, elle [sɛksɥɛl] *adj* [comportement] sexual ▪ [organes, éducation, hormone] sex *(modif)* ▪ **l'acte ~** the sex *ou* sexual act.

sexuellement [sɛksɥɛlmɑ̃] *adv* sexually.

sexy [sɛksi] *adj inv fam* sexy.

seyait *etc v* ▷ **seoir.**

seyant, e [sɛjɑ̃, ɑ̃t] *adj* becoming ▪ **peu ~** unbecoming ▪ **sa nouvelle coiffure est peu ~e** his new hairstyle doesn't suit him.

Seychelles [sɛʃɛl] *npr fpl* : **les (îles) ~** the Seychelles ▪ **aux ~** in the Seychelles, *voir aussi* **île.**

SFIO *(abr de* **Section française de l'Internationale ouvrière***) npr f the French Socialist Party between 1905 and 1971.*

SG *nm* = **secrétaire général.**

SGA *nm* = **secrétaire général adjoint.**

SGBD *(abr de* **système de gestion de base de données***) nm* DBMS.

SGEN *(abr de* **Syndicat général de l'Éducation nationale***) npr m teachers' trade union.*

SGML *(abr de* **Standard Generalized Mark-up Language***) nm* SGML.

shah [ʃa] *nm* shah, Shah.

shaker [ʃɛkœr] *nm* (cocktail) shaker.

shakespearien, enne [ʃɛkspirjɛ̃, ɛn] *adj* Shakespearean, Shakespearian.

shampoing, shampooing [ʃɑ̃pwɛ̃] *nm* **1.** [produit] shampoo ▪ **~ traitant** medicated shampoo ▪ **~ pour moquettes** carpet shampoo **2.** [lavage] shampoo ▪ **se faire un ~** to shampoo *ou* to wash one's hair.

shampouiner [3] [ʃɑ̃pwine] *vt* to shampoo.

shampouineur, euse [ʃɑ̃pwinœr, øz] *nm, f* [personne] shampooer.
◆ **shampouineur** *nm*, **shampouineuse** *nf* [machine] carpet cleaner *ou* shampooer.

Shanghai [ʃɑ̃gaj] *npr* Shanghai.

shérif [ʃerif] *nm* **1.** [aux États-Unis] sheriff **2.** [en Grande-Bretagne] sheriff *(representative of the Crown).*

sherry [ʃeri] (*pl* **sherrys** *ou pl* **sherries**) *nm* sherry.

shetland [ʃɛtlɑ̃d] *nm* **1.** TEXT Shetland (wool) **2.** [vêtement] Shetland jumper **3.** ZOOL Shetland pony.

Shetland [ʃɛtlɑ̃d] *npr fpl* : **les (îles) ~** the Shetland Islands, the Shetlands.

shilling [ʃiliŋ] *nm* shilling.

shingle [ʃingœl] *nm* (roofing) shingle.

shinto [ʃinto], **shintoïsme** [ʃintɔism] *nm* Shinto.

shog(o)un [ʃɔgun] *nm* shogun.

shoot [ʃut] *nm* **1.** SPORT shot **2.** △ [injection] fix△.

shooter [3] [ʃute] *vi* SPORT to shoot.
◆ **se shooter**△ *vpi* [drogué] to shoot up△, to fix△ ▪ **se ~ à l'héroïne** to shoot△ *ou* to mainline△ heroin ▪ **il se shoote au café** *hum* he has to have his fix of coffee.

shopping [ʃɔpiŋ] *nm* shopping ▪ **faire du ~** to go shopping ▪ **je fais toujours mon ~ chez eux** I always shop there.

short [ʃɔrt] *nm* (pair of) shorts ▪ **être en ~** to be in *ou* wearing shorts.

show [ʃo] *nm* **1.** [variétés] show **2.** [d'un homme politique] performance ▪ **le ~ télévisé du Premier ministre** the Prime Minister's TV performance.

show-business [ʃobiznɛs] *nm inv* show business.

shunter [3] [ʃœte] *vt* ÉLECTR to shunt.

si [1] [si] *nm inv* MUS B ▪ [chanté] si, ti, *voir aussi* **fa**.

si [2] [si] <> *adv* **1.** [tellement - avec un adjectif attribut, un adverbe, un nom] so ; [- avec un adjectif épithète] such ▪ **il est si mignon!** he's (ever) so sweet! ▪ **je la vois si peu** I see so little of her, I see her so rarely ▪ **ça fait si mal!** it hurts so much! ▪ **elle a de si beaux cheveux!** she has such beautiful hair! ▪ *(en corrélation avec 'que')* **si... que** so... that ▪ **elle travaille si bien qu'on l'a augmentée** she works so well that she got a rise
2. [exprimant la concession] however ▪ **si aimable soit-il...** however nice he may be... ▪ *(en corrélation avec 'que')* **si dur que ça puisse paraître, je ne céderai pas** however hard it may seem *ou* hard as it may seem I won't give way ▪ **si vous le vexez si peu que ce soit, il fond en larmes** if you upset him even the slightest bit, he bursts into tears
3. [dans une comparaison] : **si... que** as... as ▪ **il n'est pas si bête qu'il en a l'air** he's not as stupid as he seems
4. [en réponse affirmative] yes ▪ **ce n'est pas fermé? – si** isn't it closed? – yes (it is) ▪ **ça n'a pas d'importance – si, ça en a!** it doesn't matter – it DOES *ou* yes it does! ▪ **tu n'aimes pas ça? – si, si!** don't you like that? – oh yes I DO! ▪ **je ne veux pas que tu me rembourses – si, si, voici ce que je te dois** I don't want you to pay me back – no, I insist, here's what I owe you ▪ **je n'y arriverai jamais – mais si!** I'll never manage – of course you will! ▪ **le spectacle n'est pas gratuit – il paraît que si** the show isn't free – apparently it is ▪ **tu ne vas quand même pas lui dire? – oh que si!** still, you're not going to tell him, are you? – oh yes I am!
<> *conj (devant 'il' ou 'ils' s'* [s]*)* **1.** [exprimant une condition] if ▪ **si tu veux, on y va** we'll go if you want ▪ **si tu ne réfléchis pas par toi-même et si** *ou* **que tu crois tout ce qu'on te dit...** if you don't think for yourself and you believe everything people tell you... ▪ **je ne lui dirai que si tu es d'accord** I'll tell him only if you agree, I won't tell him unless you agree ▪ **si tu oses...!** [ton menaçant] don't you dare! ▪ **avez-vous des enfants? si oui, remplissez le cadre ci-dessous** do you have any children? if yes, fill in the box below
2. [exprimant une hypothèse] if ▪ **si tu venais de bonne heure, on pourrait finir avant midi** if you came early we would be able to finish before midday ▪ **s'il m'arrivait quelque chose, prévenez John** should anything happen to me *ou* if anything should happen to me, call John ▪ **ah toi, si je ne me retenais pas...!** just count yourself lucky I'm restraining myself! ▪ **si j'avais su, je me serais méfié** if I had known *ou* had I known, I would have been more cautious
3. [exprimant une éventualité] what if ▪ **et si tu te trompais?** what if you were wrong?
4. [exprimant une suggestion] what about ▪ **et si on jouait aux cartes?** what about playing cards?
5. [exprimant un souhait, un regret] : **ah, si j'étais plus jeune!** I wish *ou* if only I were younger!
6. [dans l'interrogation indirecte] if, whether ▪ **dites-moi si vous venez** tell me if *ou* whether you're coming
7. [introduisant une complétive] if, that ▪ **ne sois pas surprise s'il a échoué** don't be surprised that *ou* if he failed
8. [introduisant une explication] if ▪ **si quelqu'un a le droit de se plaindre, c'est bien moi!** if anyone has reason to complain, it's me!
9. [exprimant la répétition] if, when ▪ **si je prends une initiative, elle la désapprouve** whenever *ou* every time I take the initiative, she disapproves (of it)
10. [exprimant la concession, l'opposition] : **comment faire des économies si je gagne le salaire minimum?** how can I save if I'm only earning the minimum wage? ▪ **si son premier roman a été un succès, le second a été éreinté par la critique** though her first novel was a success, the second was slated by the critics
11. [emploi exclamatif] : **tu penses s'il était déçu/heureux!** you can imagine how disappointed/happy he was! ▪ **tu as l'intention de continuer? – si j'ai l'intention de continuer? bien sûr!** do you intend to go on? – of course I do *ou* I certainly do *ou* I do indeed! ▪ **si ce n'est pas mignon à cet âge-là!** aren't they cute at that age! ▪ **si je m'attendais à te voir ici!** well, I (certainly) didn't expect to meet you here *ou* fancy meeting you here!
<> *nm inv* : **avec des si, on mettrait Paris en bouteille** *prov* if ifs and buts were pots and pans, there'd be no trade for tinkers *prov*.
◆ **si bien que** *loc conj* [de telle sorte que] so ▪ **il ne sait pas lire une carte, si bien qu'on s'est perdus** he can't read a map, and so we got lost.
◆ **si ce n'est** *loc prép* **1.** [pour rectifier] if not ▪ **ça a duré une bonne heure, si ce n'est deux** it lasted at least an hour, if not two
2. [excepté] apart from, except ▪ **tout vous convient? – oui, si ce n'est le prix** is everything to your satisfaction? – yes, apart from *ou* except the price ▪ **si ce n'était sa timidité, c'est un garçon très agréable** he's a nice young man, if a little shy ▪ **si ce n'est toi, c'est donc ton frère** *La Fontaine allus* if it's not you, then it must be your double *ou* your twin brother *hum*.
◆ **si ce n'est que** *loc conj* apart from the fact that, except (for the fact) that ▪ **il n'a pas de régime, si ce n'est qu'il ne doit pas fumer** he has no special diet, except that he mustn't smoke.
◆ **si tant est que** *loc conj* provided that ▪ **on se retrouvera à 18 h, si tant est que l'avion arrive à l'heure** we'll meet at 6 p.m. provided (that) *ou* if the plane arrives on time.

SI 1. = **syndicat d'initiative 2.** (*abr de* **Système International**) SI.

sial [sjal] *nm* sial.

Siam [sjam] *npr m* : **le ~** Siam ▪ **au ~** in Siam.

siamois, e [sjamwa, az] *adj* **1.** GÉOGR Siamese **2.** MÉD Siamese ▪ **frères ~** (male) Siamese twins ▪ **sœurs ~es** (female) Siamese twins.
◆ **siamois** *nm* ZOOL Siamese (cat).

Sibérie [siberi] *npr f* : **(la) ~** Siberia.

sibérien, enne [siberjɛ̃, ɛn] *adj* Siberian.

◆ **Sibérien, enne** *nm, f* Siberian.

sibylle [sibil] *nf* sibyl.

sibyllin, e [sibilɛ̃, in] *adj* **1.** *litt* [mystérieux] enigmatic, cryptic **2.** MYTHOL sibylic, sibyllic **3.** ANTIQ : **livres ~s** Sibylline Books ■ **oracles ~s** Sibylline Prophecies.

sic [sik] *adv* sic.

SICAV, Sicav [sikav] (*abr de* **société d'investissement à capital variable**) *nf* **1.** [société] open-ended investment trust, ≃ unit trust *UK*, ≃ mutual fund *US* ■ **~ monétaire** money market fund **2.** [action] *share in an open-ended investment trust.*

Sicile [sisil] *npr f* : **(la) ~** Sicily.

sicilien, enne [sisiljɛ̃, ɛn] *adj* Sicilian.
◆ **Sicilien, enne** *nm, f* Sicilian.
◆ **sicilien** *nm* LING Sicilian.
◆ **sicilienne** *nf* MUS siciliano.

SICOB, Sicob [sikɔb] (*abr de* **Salon des industries du commerce et de l'organisation du bureau**) *npr m* : **le ~** *annual information technology trade fair in Paris.*

SIDA, Sida [sida] (*abr de* **syndrome immuno-déficitaire acquis**) *nm* AIDS, Aids ■ **~ déclaré** full-blown Aids.

side-car [sidkar, sajdkar] (*pl* **side-cars**) *nm* **1.** [habitacle] sidecar **2.** [moto] motorbike and sidecar.

sidéen, enne [sideɛ̃, ɛn] ◇ *adj* suffering from Aids.
◇ *nm, f* Aids sufferer.

sidéral, e, aux [sideral, o] *adj* sidereal.

sidérant, e [siderɑ̃, ɑ̃t] *adj fam* staggering, amazing ■ **c'est ~!** it's mind-blowing!

sidérer [18] [sidere] *vt fam* [abasourdir] to stagger ■ **j'étais sidéré d'apprendre cela** I was staggered to hear that, you could have knocked me down with a feather when I heard that.

sidérurgie [sideryrʒi] *nf* **1.** [technique] (iron and) steel metallurgy **2.** [industrie] (iron and) steel industry.

sidérurgique [sideryrʒik] *adj* (iron and) steel *(modif)* ■ **usine ~** steelworks, steel factory.

sidérurgiste [sideryrʒist] *nmf* **1.** [ouvrier] steel worker **2.** [industriel] steelworks owner.

sidologue [sidɔlɔg] *nmf* Aids specialist.

siècle [sjɛkl] *nm* **1.** [100 ans] century ■ **l'église a plus de quatre ~s** the church is more than four centuries old ■ **au début du ~** at the turn of the century ■ **au IIᵉ ~ avant/après J.-C.** in the 2nd century BC/AD ■ **les écrivains du seizième ~** sixteenth-century writers **2.** [époque] age ■ **vivre avec son ~** to keep up with the times, to be in tune with one's age ■ **ça fait des ~s que je ne suis pas allé à la patinoire** *fam* I haven't been to the ice-rink for ages ■ **l'affaire du ~** the bargain of the century ▶ **le ~ des Lumières** the Enlightenment, the Age of Reason ■ **le Grand Siècle, le ~ de Louis XIV** the grand siècle, the age of Louis XIV **3.** RELIG : **le ~** worldly life, the world.

sied *etc v* ▷ **seoir**.

siège [sjɛʒ] *nm* **1.** [chaise] seat ■ **prenez donc un ~** (do) take a seat, do sit down ▶ **~ avant/arrière/baquet** AUTO front/back/bucket seat ■ **~ éjectable** AÉRON ejector seat ■ **~ de voiture pour bébé** baby car seat
2. POLIT seat ■ **perdre/gagner des ~s** to lose/to win seats ▶ **~ vacant** *ou* **à pourvoir** vacant seat
3. [centre - gén] seat ; [- d'un parti] headquarters ■ **le ~ du gouvernement** the seat of government ▶ **~ d'exploitation** COMM (company) works ■ **~ social** registered *ou* head office
4. MIL siege ■ **faire le ~ d'une ville** to lay siege to *ou* to besiege a town ■ **lever le ~** to raise a siege
5. MÉD : **l'enfant s'est présenté par le ~** it was a breech birth
6. DR : **le ~** the bench
7. RELIG : **~ épiscopal** (episcopal) see.

siéger [22] [sjeʒe] *vi* **1.** [député] to sit ■ **~ au Parlement** to have a seat *ou* to sit in Parliament ■ **~ à un comité** to sit on a committee **2.** [organisme] to be based in **3.** *sout* [se trouver] to be located in ■ **chercher où siège la difficulté/l'infection** to seek to locate the difficulty/the infection.

sien [sjɛ̃] (*f* **sienne** [sjɛn], *mpl* **siens** [sjɛ̃], *fpl* **siennes** [sjɛn]) *adj poss* : **il a fait sienne cette maxime** *sout* he made this maxim his own ■ **une sienne cousine** *litt* a cousin of his/hers.
◆ **le sien** (*f* **la sienne**, *mpl* **les siens**, *fpl* **les siennes**) *pron poss* his *m*, hers *f* ■ [en se référant à un objet, un animal] its ■ **elle est partie avec une valise qui n'était pas la sienne** she left with a suitcase that wasn't hers *ou* that didn't belong to her ■ *(emploi nominal)* **les ~s** one's family and friends ▶ **y mettre du ~** [faire un effort] to make an effort ; [être compréhensif] to be understanding ■ **faire des siennes** *fam* : **Jacques a encore fait des siennes** Jacques has (gone and) done it again ■ **ma voiture ne cesse de faire des siennes!** my car's always playing up!

Sienne [sjɛn] *npr* Sienna.

siéra *etc v* ▷ **seoir**.

sierra [sjera] *nf* sierra ■ **la ~ Nevada** the Sierra Nevada.

sieste [sjɛst] *nf* [repos] (afternoon) nap *ou* rest ■ **faire la ~** to have *ou* to take a nap (in the afternoon).

sieur [sjœr] *nm* **1.** DR : **le ~ Pichard** Mr Pichard Esquire **2.** *fam hum* **le ~ Dupond** old Dupond.

sifflant, e [siflɑ̃, ɑ̃t] *adj* **1.** [respiration] hissing, whistling, wheezing **2.** LING sibilant.
◆ **sifflante** *nf* LING sibilant.

sifflement [sifləmɑ̃] *nm* **1.** [action - gén] whistling *(U)* ; [- d'un serpent] hiss, hissing **2.** [bruit] whistle ■ **~ d'oreilles** ringing in the ears.

siffler [3] [sifle] ◇ *vi* **1.** [serpent] to hiss ■ [oiseau] to whistle ■ **~ comme un merle** *ou* **un pinson** *fig* to sing like a lark **2.** [personne] to whistle ■ [gendarme, arbitre] to blow one's whistle **3.** [respirer difficilement] to wheeze **4.** [vent, train, bouilloire] to whistle ■ **les balles sifflaient de tous côtés** bullets were whistling all around us.
◇ *vt* **1.** [chanson] to whistle **2.** [chien, personne] to whistle for ■ **~ les filles** to whistle at girls **3.** [suj: gendarme] to blow one's whistle at ■ [suj: arbitre] to whistle for ■ **~ la mi-temps** to blow the half-time whistle, to whistle for half-time **4.** [orateur, pièce] to hiss, to boo, to catcall **5.** *fam* [boire] to swill down *(sép)*, to swig, to knock back *(sép)*.

sifflet [siflɛ] *nm* [instrument] whistle ■ **donner un coup de ~** to (blow the) whistle.
◆ **sifflets** *nmpl* [huées] hisses, catcalls ■ **quitter la scène sous les ~s** to be booed off the stage.

siffleur, euse [siflœr, øz] ◇ *adj* [oiseau] whistling ■ [serpent] hissing ■ **merle ~** whistling blackbird.
◇ *nm, f* [à un spectacle] catcaller, heckler.
◆ **siffleur** *nm* ORNITH wigeon, widgeon.

siffleux [siflø] *nm Québec* [marmotte] groundhog, woodchuck.

sifflotement [siflɔtmɑ̃] *nm* whistling.

siffloter [3] [siflɔte] ◇ *vt* : **~ qqch** [doucement] to whistle sthg to o.s. ; [gaiement] to whistle sthg happily.
◇ *vi* [doucement] to whistle to o.s. ■ [gaiement] to whistle away happily.

sigle [sigl] *nm* acronym, initials.

sigma [sigma] *nm* **1.** [lettre] sigma **2.** CHIM sigma bond.

signal, aux [siɲal, o] *nm* **1.** [signe] signal ▶ **donner le ~ du départ** to give the signal for departure ; SPORT to give the starting signal ■ **envoyer un ~ de détresse** to send out a distress signal *ou* an SOS **2.** [annonce] : **cette loi a été le ~ d'un changement de politique** this law signalled *ou* was the signal for a shift in policy **3.** [dispositif] signal ■ **~ d'alarme/d'incendie** alarm/fire signal ■ **actionner le ~ d'alarme** to pull the alarm cord ■ **~ sonore/lumineux** sound/light signal ■ **~ d'arrêt** stop sign ■ **signaux lumineux** AUTO traffic signals *ou* lights **4.** NAUT signal ■ **signaux de port** port *ou* harbour signals **5.** RAIL signal ■ **~ fermé/ouvert** on/off signal **6.** INFORM & TÉLÉCOM signal ■ **~ analogique/numérique** analog/digital signal ■ **~ d'appel** call waiting function **7.** ÉCON : **~ du marché** market indicator.

signalé, e [siɲale] *adj litt* [remarquable] signal, notable.

signalement [siɲalmɑ̃] *nm* description, particulars ■ **donner le ~ de son agresseur** to describe one's attacker.

signaler [3] [siɲale] *vt* **1.** [faire remarquer - faute, détail] to point out *(sép)*, to indicate, to draw attention to ; [- événement important] to draw attention to ; [- accident, cambriolage] to report ; [- changement d'adresse] to notify ■ **~ qqch à la police** to report sthg to the police ■ **rien à ~** nothing to report ■ **à ~ encore, une exposition à Beaubourg** another event worth mentioning is an exhibition at Beaubourg ■ **permettez-moi de vous ~ qu'il est interdit de...** allow me to draw your attention to the fact that *ou* to point out that it's forbidden to... ■ **il est déjà 11 h, je te signale!** for your information, it's already 11 o'clock! ■ **son ouvrage n'est signalé nulle part dans votre thèse** his book is not mentioned anywhere in your thesis **2.** [suj: drapeau, sonnerie] to signal ■ [suj: panneau indicateur] to signpost, to point to *(insép)* ■ **passage à niveau non signalé** unsignalled level crossing ■ **le village n'est même pas signalé au croisement** the village is not even signposted *ou* there's not even a signpost for the village at the junction ■ **la chapelle n'est pas signalée sur le plan** the chapel isn't indicated *ou* marked *ou* shown on the map ■ **il n'a pas signalé qu'il tournait** he didn't signal *ou* indicate that he was turning **3.** [dénoter] to indicate, to be the sign of ■ **c'est le symptôme qui nous signale la présence du virus** this symptom tells us that the virus is present.

◆ **se signaler à** *vp+prép* : **se ~ à l'attention de qqn** to draw sb's attention to o.s.

◆ **se signaler par** *vp+prép* : **elle se signale surtout par son absence** she's remarkable mostly by her absence ■ **elle se signale surtout par sa bonne volonté** what sets her apart is her willingness to cooperate.

signalétique [siɲaletik] *adj* [plaque] descriptive, identification *(modif)*.

signaleur [siɲalœr] *nm* **1.** MIL signaller **2.** RAIL signalman.

signalisateur, trice [siɲalizatœr, tris] *adj* signalling.

signalisation [siɲalizasjɔ̃] *nf* **1.** [matériel] : **~ aérienne** markings and beacons ■ **~ routière** [sur la chaussée] (road) markings ; [panneaux] roadsigns **2.** [aménagement] : **faire la ~ d'une section de voie ferrée** to put signals along a stretch of railway line **3.** PSYCHOL signals **4.** RAIL signals ■ **~ automatique** automatic signalling.

signaliser [3] [siɲalize] *vt* [route] to provide with roadsigns and markings ■ [voie ferrée] to equip with signals ■ [piste d'aéroport] to provide with markings and beacons ■ **c'est bien/mal signalisé** [route] it's been well/badly signposted.

signataire [siɲatɛr] ◇ *adj* signatory.

◇ *nmf* signatory ■ **les ~s du traité** the signatories of the treaty.

signature [siɲatyr] *nf* **1.** [signe] signature ■ **elle a apposé sa ~ au bas de la lettre** she signed the letter at the bottom of the page ■ **avoir la ~** DR to be an authorized signatory *(on behalf of a company)* ■ **~ électronique** INFORM e-signature, digital signature **2.** [marque distinctive] signature ■ **cet attentat à la bombe porte leur ~** this bomb attack bears their mark *ou* imprint **3.** [artiste] : **les plus grandes ~s de la mode sont représentées dans le défilé** the greatest fashion houses *ou* designers are represented on the catwalk **4.** [acte] signing ■ **vous serez payé à la ~ du contrat** you'll be paid once the contract has been signed **5.** IMPR signature, quire.

signe [siɲ] *nm* **1.** [geste] sign, gesture ■ **parler par ~s** to communicate by sign language *ou* signs ■ **faire un ~ à qqn** to make a sign *ou* to signal to sb ■ **faire un ~ de tête à qqn** [affirmatif] to nod to sb ; [négatif] to shake one's head at sb ■ **faire un ~ de la main à qqn** [pour saluer, attirer l'attention] to wave to sb, to wave one's hand at sb ■ **agiter la main en ~ d'adieu** to wave goodbye ■ **faire ~ à qqn** to signal to sb ■ **il m'a fait ~ d'entrer** he beckoned me in ■ **fais-lui ~ de se taire** signal (to) him to be quiet ■ **faire ~ que oui** to nod (in agreement) ■ **faire ~ que non** [de la tête] to shake one's head (in refusal) ; [du doigt] to wave one's finger in refusal ■ **quand vous serez à Paris, faites-moi ~** *fig* when you're in Paris, let me know ▶ **~ de la croix** RELIG sign of the cross ■ **faire un ~ de croix** *ou* **le ~ de la croix** to cross o.s., to make the sign of the cross

2. [indication] sign ■ **c'est un ~** [mauvais] that's ominous ; [bon] that's a good sign ■ **c'est ~ de : c'est ~ de pluie/de beau temps** it's a sign of rain/of good weather ■ **c'est ~ que...** it's a sign that... ■ **c'est bon ~** it's a good sign, it augurs well *sout* ■ **c'est mauvais ~** it's a bad sign, it's ominous ■ **(un) ~ de : il n'y a aucun ~ d'amélioration** there's no sign of (any) improvement ■ **c'est un ~ des temps/des dieux** it's a sign of the times/from the Gods ■ **il n'a pas donné ~ de vie depuis janvier** there's been no sign of him since January ■ **donner des ~s d'impatience** to give *ou* to show signs of impatience ■ **la voiture donne des ~s de fatigue** the car is beginning to show its age ▶ **~ annonciateur** *ou* **avant-coureur** *ou* **précurseur** forerunner, portent *litt* ■ **~s extérieurs de richesse** DR outward signs of wealth

3. [marque] mark ■ **~ cabalistique** cabalistic sign ■ **~s particuliers** ADMIN distinguishing marks, special peculiarities ■ **'~s particuliers: néant'** 'distinguishing marks: none'

4. LING, MATH, MÉD & MUS sign ■ **le ~ moins/plus** the minus/plus sign

5. IMPR : **~ de correction** proofreading mark *ou* symbol ■ **~ de ponctuation** punctuation mark

6. ASTROL : **~ (du zodiaque)** sign (of the zodiac).

◆ **en signe de** *loc prép* as a sign *ou* mark of ■ **mettre un brassard en ~ de deuil** to wear an armband as a sign of mourning.

◆ **sous le signe de** *loc prép* **1.** ASTROL under the sign of **2.** *fig* **la réunion s'est tenue sous le ~ de la bonne humeur** the atmosphere at the meeting was good-humoured.

signé, e [siɲe] *adj* [exemplaire] signed ■ [argenterie, bijoux] hallmarked.

signer [3] [siɲe] ◇ *vt* **1.** [chèque, formulaire, lettre] to sign ■ [pétition] to sign, to put one's name to ■ **'~ ici'** '(please) sign here' ■ **~ son arrêt de mort** *fig* to sign one's (own) death warrant **2.** [laisser sa marque personnelle] to sign, to put one's signature to ▶ **c'est signé!** it's easy to guess who did that! ■ **cette pagaille, c'est signé Maud!** *fam* this mess is obviously Maud's handiwork! **3.** [officialiser - contrat, traité] to sign **4.** [être l'auteur de - argenterie] to hallmark ; [- pièce, film] to be the author of ; [- tableau] to sign ; [- ligne de vêtements] to be the creator of ■ **elle a signé les meilleures chansons de l'époque** she wrote all the best songs of that era **5.** [dédicacer - livre] to sign copies of.

◇ *vi* **1.** [tracer un signe] to sign ■ **~ d'une croix/de son sang** to sign with a cross/in one's blood **2.** [établir un acte officiel] to sign.

◆ **se signer** *vpi* to cross o.s.

signet [siɲɛ] *nm* [d'un livre] bookmark.

signifiant [siɲifjɑ̃] *nm* signifier.

significatif, ive [siɲifikatif, iv] *adj* **1.** [riche de sens - remarque, geste, symbole] significant ; [- regard] significant, meaningful ■ **de façon significative** significantly **2.** [révélateur] : **~ de** revealing *ou* suggestive of ■ **c'est très ~ de son caractère/ses goûts** it says a lot about her character/her taste **3.** [important - écart, différence, changement] significant.

signification [siɲifikasjɔ̃] *nf* **1.** [sens - d'un terme, d'une phrase, d'un symbole] meaning, signification *sout* ; [- d'une action] meaning ■ **lourd de ~** pregnant with meaning *sout* **2.** [importance - d'un événement, d'une déclaration] import, significance **3.** DR (official) notification **4.** LING : **la ~** signifying, the signifying processes.

signifié [siɲifje] *nm* : **le ~** the signified.

signifier [9] [siɲifje] *vt* **1.** [avoir tel sens - suj: mot, symbole] to mean, to signify

2. [indiquer - suj: mimique, geste, acte] to mean ■ **il ne m'a pas encore téléphoné – cela ne signifie rien** he hasn't phoned me yet – that doesn't mean anything ■ **de telles menaces ne signifient rien de sa part** such threats mean nothing coming from him ■ [pour exprimer l'irritation] : **que signifie ceci?** what's the meaning of this?

3. [être le signe avant-coureur de] to mean, to betoken *sout* ■ **cela signifierait sa ruine** that would spell ruin for her

4. [impliquer] to mean, to imply

5. *sout* [notifier] to notify ■ **~ ses intentions à qqn** to make one's intentions known *ou* to state one's intentions to sb ■ **il m'a**

signifié son départ/son accord he has informed me that he is leaving/that he agrees ■ **~ son congé à qqn** to give sb notice of dismissal *sout*, to give sb his/her notice
6. DR [jugement] to notify ■ **~ à qqn que...** to serve notice on *ou* upon sb that...

sikh [sik] *adj* & *nm* Sikh.

sil [sil] *nm* ochreous clay.

silence [silɑ̃s] *nm* **1.** [absence de bruit] silence ■ **un peu de ~, s'il vous plaît!** [avant un discours] (be) quiet please! ; [dans une bibliothèque, une salle d'étude] quiet *ou* silence, please! ■ **demander** *ou* **réclamer le ~** to call for silence ■ **à son arrivée, tout le monde fit ~** there was a hush *ou* everyone fell silent when she arrived ■ **garder le ~** to keep silent *ou* quiet ■ **faire** *ou* **obtenir le ~** to make everyone keep quiet ■ **~ on tourne!** CINÉ quiet on the set! ■ **dans le ~ de la nuit** in the still *ou* silence of the night ■ **il régnait un ~ de mort** it was as quiet *ou* silent as the grave ▶ **~ radio** radio silence **2.** [secret] : **acheter le ~ de qqn** to buy sb's silence, to pay sb to keep quiet ■ **garder le ~ sur qqch** to keep quiet about sthg ■ **imposer le ~ à qqn** to shut sb up ■ **passer qqch sous ~** to pass over sthg in silence, to keep quiet about sthg **3.** [lacune] : **le ~ de la loi en la matière** the absence of legislation regarding this matter **4.** [pause] silence ■ [dans la conversation] : **son récit était entrecoupé de nombreux ~s** his story was interrupted by numerous pauses ■ **~ radio** not a peep, (complete) radio silence ■ **il devait me rappeler après son voyage mais depuis silence radio** he was supposed to call me back after his trip but I haven't heard a peep *ou* a dicky bird *vieilli* out of him since a month **5.** MUS rest.
◆ **en silence** *loc adv* [se regarder] in silence, silently ■ [se déplacer] silently, noiselessly ■ [souffrir] in silence, uncomplainingly.

silencieusement [silɑ̃sjøzmɑ̃] *adv* [se regarder] silently, in silence ■ [se déplacer] in silence, noiselessly ■ [souffrir] in silence, uncomplainingly.

silencieux, euse [silɑ̃sjø, øz] *adj* **1.** [où règne le calme - trajet, repas, salle] quiet, silent **2.** [qui ne fait pas de bruit - pendule, voiture] quiet, noiseless ; [- mouvement] noiseless **3.** [qui ne parle pas] silent, quiet ■ **la majorité silencieuse** the silent majority ▮ [taciturne] quiet, silent, uncommunicative *péj*.
◆ **silencieux** *nm* **1.** ARM silencer **2.** AUTO silencer *UK*, muffler *US*.

Silésie [silezi] *npr f* : **(la) ~** Silesia ■ **(la) basse/haute ~** Lower/Upper Silesia.

silex [silɛks] *nm* **1.** GÉOL flint, flintstone **2.** ARCHÉOL flint, flint tool.

silhouette [silwɛt] *nf* **1.** [ligne générale - du corps] figure ; [- d'un véhicule] lines ■ **elle a une jolie ~** she's got a nice *ou* good figure **2.** [contours] silhouette, outline ■ [forme indistincte] (vague) form ■ **leurs ~s se détachaient sur le soleil couchant** they were silhouetted against the sunset ■ **je vis une ~ dans le brouillard/derrière les rideaux** I saw a shape in the fog/behind the curtains **3.** ART silhouette.

silhouetter [4] [silwete] *vt* ART [dessiner les contours de] to outline ■ [découper dans du papier] to silhouette.
◆ **se silhouetter sur** *vp+prép litt* to stand out *ou* to be silhouetted against.

silicate [silikat] *nm* silicate.

silice [silis] *nf* silica ■ **verre de ~** silica glass, vitreous silica.

siliceux, euse [silisø, øz] *adj* siliceous ■ **roches siliceuses** siliceous deposits.

silicium [silisjɔm] *nm* silicon.

silicone [silikon] *nf* silicone.

silicose [silikoz] *nf* silicosis.

sillage [sijaʒ] *nm* **1.** NAUT [trace] wake ■ [remous] wash **2.** [d'une personne, d'un véhicule] wake ■ **cette mesure entraîne dans son ~ une refonte de nos structures hospitalières** this decision carries along with it a restructuring of our hospital system ▶ **marcher dans le ~ de qqn** *pr* & *fig* to follow in sb's footsteps *ou* wake **3.** AÉRON [trace] (vapour) trail ■ [remous] wake **4.** PHYS wake.

sillon [sijɔ̃] *nm* **1.** AGRIC [de gros labours] furrow ■ [petite rigole] drill **2.** *litt* [ride] furrow **3.** [d'un disque] groove **4.** ANAT [du cerveau] fissure, sulcus ■ **~ fessier** anal cleft.

sillonner [3] [sijɔne] *vt* **1.** [parcourir - suj: canaux, voies] to cross, to criss-cross ■ **j'ai sillonné la Bretagne** I've visited every corner of *ou* I've travelled the length and breadth of Brittany ■ **il sillonnait les mers depuis 20 ans** he'd been ploughing the (ocean) waves for 20 years ■ **le pays est sillonné de rivières** the country is criss-crossed by rivers **2.** *sout* [marquer] to furrow, to groove ■ **son visage sillonné de rides** his furrowed *ou* deeply lined face **3.** AGRIC to furrow.

silo [silo] *nm* **1.** AGRIC silo ■ **mettre en ~** to silo **2.** MIL silo.

silotage [silɔtaʒ] *nm* ensilage.

silt [silt] *nm* silt.

simagrées [simagre] *nfpl* : **faire des ~** [minauder] to put on airs ■ **tu l'aurais vue faire ses ~!** you should've seen her simpering!

simien, enne [simjɛ̃, ɛn] *adj* ZOOL simian.
◆ **simien** *nm* simian, ape.

simiesque [simjɛsk] *adj* monkey-like, ape-like, simian.

similaire [similɛr] *adj* similar.

similarité [similarite] *nf sout* similarity, likeness.

simili [simili] ◇ *préf* : **~ marbre** imitation marble ■ **~ pierre** artificial stone.
◇ *nm* **1.** [imitation] : **c'est du ~** it's artificial *ou* an imitation **2.** [cliché] half-tone engraving.
◇ *nf* [procédé] half-tone process.

similicuir [similikɥir] *nm* imitation leather, Leatherette®.

similigravure [similigravyr] *nf* **1.** [procédé] half-tone process **2.** [cliché] half-tone engraving.

similitude [similityd] *nf* **1.** [d'idées, de style] similarity, similitude *sout* ■ [de personnes] similarity, likeness ■ **leur ~** the likeness between them **2.** MATH similarity.

simoun [simun] *nm* simoon.

simple [sɛ̃pl] ◇ *adj* **1.** [facile - exercice, système] straightforward, simple, easy ■ **c'est très ~ à utiliser** it's very easy *ou* simple to use ▶ **c'est ~ comme bonjour** it's as easy as ABC *ou* as pie **2.** *(avant le n)* [avec une valeur restrictive] mere, simple ■ **c'est une ~ question d'argent** it's simply *ou* only a matter of money ■ **pour la ~ raison que...** for the simple reason that... ■ **réduit à sa plus ~ expression** reduced to its simplest form ■ **vous aurez une démonstration gratuite sur ~ appel** all you need do is (to) *ou* simply phone this number for a free demonstration ■ **ce n'est qu'une ~ formalité** it's merely a *ou* it's a mere formality ■ **ça s'ouvre d'une ~ pression du doigt** it opens simply by pressing on it ■ **ce n'est qu'un ~ employé de bureau** he's just an ordinary office worker **3.** [non raffiné - gens] unaffected, uncomplicated ; [- objets, nourriture, goûts] plain, simple ▶ **elle est apparue dans le plus ~ appareil** she appeared in her birthday suit *hum* **4.** [ingénu] simple, simple-minded **5.** [non composé - mot, élément, fleur, fracture] simple ; [- chaînette, nœud] single.
◇ *nm* **1.** [ce qui est facile] : **aller du ~ au complexe** to progress from the simple to the complex **2.** [proportion] : **les prix varient du ~ au double** prices can double **3.** SPORT singles ■ **jouer en ~** to play a singles match ▶ **~ messieurs/dames** men's/ladies' singles.
◆ **simples** *nmpl* medicinal herbs *ou* plants.
◆ **simple d'esprit** ◇ *nm* simpleton, halfwit.
◇ *loc adj* : **il est un peu ~ d'esprit** he's a bit simple.

simplement [sɛ̃pləmɑ̃] *adv* **1.** [seulement] simply, merely, just **2.** [sans apprêt - parler] unaffectedly, simply ; [- s'habiller] simply, plainly ■ **elle nous a reçus très ~** she received us simply *ou* without ceremony ■ **la chambre est décorée très ~** the room is plainly decorated **3.** [clairement] : **expliquer qqch ~** to explain sthg in simple *ou* straightforward terms.

simplet, ette [sɛ̃plɛ, ɛt] *adj* **1.** [personne - peu intelligente] simple, simple-minded ; [- ingénue] naïve ■ **elle est un peu ~te** she's a bit simple **2.** [sans finesse - jugement, réponse, scénario] simplistic, black-and-white.

simplicité [sɛ̃plisite] *nf* **1.** [facilité] simplicity, straightforwardness ■ **l'exercice est d'une ~ enfantine** the exercise is child's play ■ **l'opération est d'une grande ~** the operation is very straightforward **2.** [de vêtements, d'un décor, d'un repas] plainness, simplicity ■ **avec ~** simply, plainly ■ **nous avons dîné en toute ~** we had a very simple dinner **3.** [naturel] unaffectedness, lack of affectation **4.** [naïveté] naivety.

simplifiable [sɛ̃plifjabl] *adj* **1.** MATH reducible **2.** [procédé] which can be simplified *ou* made simpler.

simplificateur, trice [sɛ̃plifikatœr, tris] *adj* simplifying.

simplification [sɛ̃plifikasjɔ̃] *nf* **1.** MATH reduction **2.** [d'un système] simplification, simplifying.

simplifier [9] [sɛ̃plifje] *vt* **1.** [procédé] to simplify ■ [explication] to simplify, to make simpler ■ **en simplifiant le texte à outrance** *ou* **à l'excès** by oversimplifying the text ■ **si tu me disais la vérité, cela simplifierait les choses** it would make things easier if you told me the truth **2.** MATH [fraction] to reduce, to simplify ■ [équation] to simplify.
◆ **se simplifier** ◇ *vpi* to become simplified *ou* simpler.
◇ *vpt* to simplify ■ **elle se simplifie l'existence en refusant de prendre des responsabilités** she makes her life simpler by refusing to take any responsibility.

simplisme [sɛ̃plism] *nm* simplism.

simpliste [sɛ̃plist] *adj* simplistic, oversimple.

simulacre [simylakr] *nm* **1.** [par jeu, comme méthode] imitation **2.** [pour tromper] : **un ~ de négociations** mock *ou* sham negotiations ■ **ce n'était qu'un ~ de procès** it was a mockery of a trial.

simulateur, trice [simylatœr, tris] *nm, f* **1.** [imitateur] simulator ■ **~, va!** *hum* you're such a fraud! **2.** [faux malade] malingerer.
◆ **simulateur** *nm* AÉRON, INFORM & MIL simulator ■ **~ de vol** flight simulator.

simulation [simylasjɔ̃] *nf* **1.** [d'un sentiment] feigning, faking, simulation ■ [d'une maladie] malingering **2.** MIL & TECHNOL simulation ■ **~ sur ordinateur** computer simulation **3.** DR nondisclosure *ou* concealment of contract.

simulé, e [simyle] *adj* **1.** [pitié, douleur] faked, feigned **2.** AÉRON, INFORM & MIL simulated **3.** DR : **acte ~** bogus deed *(concealing a contract).*

simuler [3] [simyle] *vt* **1.** [feindre - douleur, ivresse, folie] to feign ■ **~ l'innocence** to put on an air *ou* a show of innocence ■ **~ la maladie** [appelé, employé] to malinger ; [enfant] to pretend to be ill ■ **l'animal simule la mort** the animal is playing dead ■ *(en usage absolu)* **je ne pense pas qu'elle simule** I don't think she's pretending **2.** MIL & TECHNOL to simulate **3.** DR [acte] to deceive *(by nondisclosure of a contract).*

simultané, e [simyltane] *adj* simultaneous.
◆ **simultanée** *nf* JEUX simultaneous game (of chess).

simultanéité [simyltaneite] *nf* simultaneity, simultaneousness.

simultanément [simyltanemɑ̃] *adv* simultaneously.

Sinaï [sinaj] *npr m* : **le ~** Sinai ■ **le mont ~** Mount Sinai.

sincère [sɛ̃sɛr] *adj* **1.** [amitié, chagrin, remords] sincere, genuine, true ■ [personne] sincere, genuine ■ [réponse] honest, sincere **2.** [dans les formules de politesse] : **nos vœux les plus ~s** our very best wishes ■ **je vous présente mes ~s condoléances** please accept my sincere *ou* heartfelt condolences ■ **veuillez agréer mes ~s salutations** yours sincerely, yours truly *US* **3.** DR [acte] genuine, authentic.

sincèrement [sɛ̃sɛrmɑ̃] *adv* **1.** [franchement] sincerely, genuinely, truly **2.** *(en tête de phrase)* [réellement] honestly, frankly ■ **~, tu me déçois** you really disappoint me ■ **~, ça ne valait pas le coup** to tell you the truth, it wasn't worth it.

sincérité [sɛ̃serite] *nf* **1.** [franchise] sincerity ■ **en toute ~** in all sincerity, to be quite honest ■ **manque de ~** lack of sincerity, disingenuousness **2.** [authenticité - d'une amitié, de remords] genuineness ; [- d'une réponse] honesty.

sinécure [sinekyr] *nf* sinecure ■ **ce n'est pas une ~** *fam* it's no picnic.

sine die [sinedje] *loc adv* sine die ■ **remettre qqch ~** to postpone sthg indefinitely.

sine qua non [sinekwanɔn] *loc adj inv* : **condition ~** essential condition ■ **c'est la condition ~ de ma participation** it's an essential condition if I am to take part at all.

Singapour [sɛ̃gapur] *npr* Singapore ■ **à ~** in Singapore.

singapourien, enne [sɛ̃gapurjɛ̃, ɛn] *adj* Singaporean.
◆ **Singapourien, enne** *nm, f* Singaporean.

singe [sɛ̃ʒ] *nm* ZOOL [à longue queue] monkey ■ [sans queue] ape ■ **les grands ~s** the (great) apes ■ **faire le ~** [faire des grimaces] to make faces ; [faire des pitreries] to clown *ou* to monkey around.

singer [17] [sɛ̃ʒe] *vt* **1.** [personne] to ape, to mimic **2.** [manières distinguées, passion] to feign, to fake.

singerie [sɛ̃ʒri] *nf* [section d'un zoo] monkey *ou* ape house.
◆ **singeries** *nfpl* [tours et grimaces] clowning ■ [d'un clown] antics ■ *péj* [manières affectées] affectedness, airs and graces ■ **faire des ~s** to clown *ou* to monkey around.

single [siŋgəl] *nm* **1.** [disque] single **2.** RAIL single sleeper **3.** SPORT singles (game) **4.** [dans un hôtel] single (room).

singleton [sɛ̃glətɔ̃] *nm* **1.** CARTES singleton **2.** MATH singleton (set).

singulariser [3] [sɛ̃gylarize] *vt* : **~ qqn** to make sb conspicuous *ou* stand out.
◆ **se singulariser** ◇ *vp (emploi réfléchi)* [se faire remarquer] to make o.s. conspicuous ■ **il faut toujours que tu te singularises!** you always have to be different from everyone else, don't you?
◇ *vpi* [être remarquable] : **il s'est singularisé par son courage** he stood out thanks to his courage.

singularité [sɛ̃gylarite] *nf* **1.** [étrangeté - d'un comportement, d'idées, d'une tenue] oddness, strangeness **2.** [trait distinctif - d'une personne] peculiarity ; [- d'un système] distinctive feature, peculiarity ■ **la boîte présentait cette ~ de s'ouvrir par l'arrière** the box was unusual in that it opened at the back **3.** *litt* [unicité] uniqueness **4.** MATH & PHYS singularity.

singulier, ère [sɛ̃gylje, ɛr] *adj* **1.** [comportement, idées] odd, strange, singular *sout* ■ **je trouve ~ que...** I find it odd *ou* strange that... **2.** [courage, beauté] remarkable, rare, unique **3.** LING singular, *voir aussi* **pluriel 4.** [d'un seul] singular, single.
◆ **singulier** *nm* LING singular.

singulièrement [sɛ̃gyljɛrmɑ̃] *adv* **1.** [beaucoup] very much ■ **il m'a ~ déçu** I was extremely disappointed in him ■ **~ beau** extremely *ou* remarkably handsome ■ **~ réussi** hugely successful **2.** [bizarrement] oddly, in a strange *ou* peculiar way **3.** [notamment] especially, particularly.

sinistre [sinistr] ◇ *adj* **1.** [inquiétant - lieu, bruit] sinister ; [- personnage] sinister, evil-looking ■ **un ~ présage** an ill omen **2.** [triste - personne, soirée] dismal **3.** *(avant le n)* [en intensif] : **c'est un ~ imbécile/une ~ canaille** he's a total idiot/crook.
◇ *nm* **1.** [incendie] fire, blaze ■ [inondation, séisme] disaster **2.** DR [incendie] fire ■ [accident de la circulation] accident ■ **déclarer un ~** to put in a claim ■ **évaluer un ~** to estimate a claim.

sinistré, e [sinistre] ◇ *adj* [bâtiment, village, quartier - gén] damaged, stricken ; [- brûlé] burnt-out ; [- bombardé] bombed-out ; [- inondé] flooded ■ **la ville est ~e** [après un tremblement de terre] the town has been devastated by the earthquake ■ **les personnes ~es** the disaster victims ; [après des inondations] the flood victims ➲ **région** *ou* **zone (déclarée) ~e** ADMIN disaster area.
◇ *nm, f* disaster victim.

sinistrement [sinistrəmɑ̃] *adv* sinisterly, in a sinister way ▪ **rire ~** to give a sinister laugh.

sinistrose [sinistroz] *nf fam* (systematic) pessimism ▪ **le pays est en proie à la ~** the country's morale is very low.

sinologue [sinɔlɔg] *nmf* specialist in Chinese studies, sinologist.

sinon [sinɔ̃] *conj* **1.** [sans cela] otherwise, or else ▪ **je ne peux pas me joindre à vous, ~ je l'aurais fait avec plaisir** I can't join you, otherwise I would have come with pleasure ▪ **j'essaierai d'être à l'heure, ~ partez sans moi** I'll try to be on time, but if I'm not go without me ▪ **tais-toi, ~...!** be quiet or else...! **2.** [si ce n'est] if not ▪ **elle était, ~ jolie, du moins gracieuse** she was, if not pretty, at least graceful ▪ **elle l'a, ~ aimé, du moins apprécié** although *ou* if she didn't like it she did at least appreciate it **3.** [excepté] except, other than ▪ **que faire, ~ attendre?** what can we do other than *ou* except wait?
◆ **sinon que** *loc conj* except that.

sinoque△ [sinɔk] *adj* nutty△, loony△ ▪ **t'es ~!** you're off your rocker!△.

sino-tibétain, e [sinɔtibetɛ̃, ɛn] (*mpl* **sino-tibétains**, *fpl* **sino-tibétaines**) *adj* Sino-Tibetan.
◆ **sino-tibétain** *nm* LING Sino-Tibetan.

sinueux, euse [sinɥø, øz] *adj* **1.** [chemin] winding, sinuous ▪ [fleuve] winding, meandering ▪ **rivière au cours ~** meandering *ou* sinuous river **2.** [pensée] convoluted, tortuous.

sinuosité [sinɥozite] *nf* **1.** [fait d'être courbé - chemin] winding ; [- rivière] winding, meandering **2.** [courbe - d'un chemin] curve, bend ; [- d'une rivière] meander.
◆ **sinuosités** *nfpl fig* tortuousness, convolutions.

sinus [sinys] *nm* **1.** ANAT sinus ▪ **~ du cœur** sinus venosus **2.** MATH sine.

sinusite [sinyzit] *nf* sinusitis.

sinusoïdal, e, aux [sinyzɔidal, o] *adj* sinusoidal.

sinusoïde [sinyzɔid] ◇ *nm* ANAT sinusoid.
◇ *nf* MATH sine curve.

Sion [sjɔ̃] *npr* Zion, Sion.

sionisme [sjɔnism] *nm* Zionism.

sioniste [sjɔnist] *adj* & *nmf* Zionist.

sioux [sju] *adj* ANTHR Siouan.
◆ **Sioux** *nmf* Sioux ▪ **les Sioux** the Sioux (Indians).
◆ **sioux** *nm* LING Sioux.

siphon [sifɔ̃] *nm* **1.** MÉD, PHYS & ZOOL siphon **2.** [d'appareils sanitaires] trap, U-bend **3.** [carafe] soda siphon *UK*, siphon bottle *US* **4.** TRAV PUB (inverted) siphon.

siphonné, e [sifɔne] *adj fam* [fou] batty, crackers.

siphonner [3] [sifɔne] *vt* to siphon ▪ **~ de l'eau/un réservoir** to siphon off water/a reservoir.

sire [sir] *nm* **1.** [seigneur] lord ▪ **un triste ~** a dubious character **2.** [titre] : **Sire** [roi] Sire *arch*, Your Majesty ; [empereur] Sire *arch*, Your Imperial Majesty.

sirène [sirɛn] *nf* **1.** [des pompiers] fire siren ▪ [d'une voiture de police, d'une ambulance, d'une usine] siren ▪ [d'un navire] siren, (fog) horn **2.** MYTHOL siren **3.** [femme séduisante] siren.

sirocco [sirɔko] *nm* sirocco.

sirop [siro] *nm* **1.** CULIN [concentré] syrup, cordial ▪ [dilué] (fruit) cordial *ou* drink ▪ **~ d'érable** maple syrup ▪ **~ de fraise/de menthe** strawberry/mint cordial ▪ **~ d'orgeat** barley water **2.** PHARM syrup ▪ **~ pour** *ou* **contre la toux** cough mixture.

siroter [3] [sirɔte] ◇ *vt* to sip, to take sips of.
◇ *vi fam* to booze.

SIRPA, Sirpa [sirpa] (*abr de* **Service d'information et de relations publiques des armées**) *npr m French army public information service.*

sirupeux, euse [sirypø, øz] *adj* **1.** [visqueux et sucré] syrupy **2.** *sout* & *péj* [sentiment] schmaltzy *péj*, syrupy *péj*.

sis, e [si, siz] *adj sout* & DR : **~ à** located *ou* situated at.

sismal, e, aux [sismal, o] = **séismal**.

sismicité [sismisite] *nf* seismicity.

sismique [sismik] *adj* seismic.

sismographe [sismɔgraf] *nm* seismograph.

sismologie [sismɔlɔʒi] *nf* seismology.

sismologue [sismɔlɔg] *nmf* seismologist.

Sisyphe [sizif] *npr* Sisyphus ▪ **le mythe de ~** the myth of Sisyphus ⊙ **un travail de ~** a never-ending task.

sitar [sitar] *nm* sitar.

sitcom [sitkɔm] *nm* & *nf* sitcom.

site [sit] *nm* **1.** [panorama] beauty spot ▪ **il y a plusieurs ~s touristiques par ici** there are several tourist spots *ou* places of interest for tourists round here ⊙ **~ classé** ADMIN conservation area, ≃ National Trust area *UK* ▪ **~ historique** historical site **2.** [environnement] setting **3.** [emplacement] site, siting ▪ **le choix du ~ de la centrale a posé problème** the siting of the power station has caused problems ⊙ **~ archéologique** [gén] archeological site ; [en cours d'excavation] archeological dig ▪ **~ de lancement** launch area **4.** CHIM & ÉCON site **5.** INFORM site ▪ **~ miroir** mirror (site) ▪ **~ web** website.
◆ **de site** *loc adj* MIL : **angle/ligne de ~** angle/line of sight.

sit-in [sitin] *nm inv* sit-in ▪ **faire un ~** to stage a sit-in.

sitôt [sito] ◇ *adv* **1.** [avec une participiale] : **~ levé, je me mettais au travail** no sooner was I up than I'd start work, I'd start work as soon as I was up ⊙ **~ dit, ~ fait** no sooner said than done **2.** *litt* [aussitôt] immediately ▪ **~ après la gare** just *ou* immediately past the station **3.** *litt* [si rapidement] : **une rose épanouie et ~ fanée** a rose in full bloom and yet so quick to wither.
◇ *prép litt* : **~ son élection...** as soon as she was elected..., no sooner was she elected...
◆ **pas de sitôt** *loc adv* : **on ne se reverra pas de ~** we won't be seeing each other again for a while ▪ **je n'y retournerai pas de ~!** I won't go back there *ou* you won't catch me going back there in a hurry!
◆ **sitôt que** *loc conj litt* as soon as ▪ **~ qu'il la vit, il se mit à rire** as soon as he saw her he started to laugh.

situation [sitɥasjɔ̃] *nf* **1.** [circonstances] situation ▪ **ma ~ financière n'est pas brillante!** my financial situation is *ou* my finances are none too healthy! ▪ **se trouver dans une ~ délicate** to find o.s. in an awkward situation *ou* position ▪ **je n'aimerais pas être dans ta ~** I wouldn't like to be in your position ▪ **tu vois un peu la ~!** do you get the picture? ▪ **c'est l'homme de la ~** he's the right man for the job ⊙ **~ de famille** ADMIN marital status **2.** [emploi rémunéré] job ▪ **avoir une bonne ~** [être bien payé] to have a well-paid job ; [être puissant] to have a high-powered job ▪ **elle s'est fait une belle ~** she worked her way up to a very good position **3.** [lieu] situation, position, location **4.** FIN report of assets ▪ **~ de trésorerie** cash budget **5.** LITTÉR & THÉÂTRE situation ▪ **comique de ~** situation comedy.
◆ **en situation** *loc adv* in real life ▪ **voyons comment elle va aborder les choses en ~** let's see how she gets on in real life *ou* when faced with the real thing.
◆ **en situation de** *loc prép* : **être en ~ de faire qqch** to be in a position to do sthg.

situé, e [sitɥe] *adj* : **maison bien/mal ~e** well-/poorly-situated house.

situer [7] [sitɥe] *vt* **1.** [dans l'espace, le temps - gén] to place ; [- roman, film *etc*] to set **2.** [classer] to place, to situate **3.** *fam* [cerner - personne] to define ▪ **on a du mal à la ~** it's difficult to know what makes her tick.
◆ **se situer** ◇ *vp (emploi réfléchi)* : **se ~ par rapport à qqn/qqch** to place o.s. in relation to sb/sthg ▪ **où vous situez-vous dans ce conflit?** where do you stand in this conflict?
◇ *vpi* [gén] to be situated *ou* located ▪ [scène, action] to take place ▪ **où se situe-t-elle dans le mouvement expressionniste?**

where would you place her in the expressionist movement? ■ **l'augmentation se situera aux alentours de 3 %** the increase will be in the region of 3%.

SIVOM, Sivom [sivɔm] (*abr de* **Syndicat intercommunal à vocation multiple**) *npr m group of local authorities pooling public services.*

SIVP *nm* (*abr de* **stage d'initiation à la vie professionnelle**) *vieilli* ■ = **stage d'insertion à la vie professionnelle**.

six [(*en fin de phrase* [sis], *devant consonne ou h aspiré* [si], *devant voyelle ou h muet* [siz])] ◇ *dét* **1.** six **2.** [dans des séries] : **tout le chapitre ~** all of chapter six, *voir aussi* **cinq**.
◇ *nm inv* six, *voir aussi* **cinq**.

sixain [sizɛ̃] = **sizain**.

sixième [sizjɛm] ◇ *adj num* sixth.
◇ *nmf* sixth.
◇ *nm* **1.** [partie] sixth **2.** [étage] sixth floor *UK*, seventh floor *US*.
◇ *nf* ÉDUC first form *UK*, sixth grade *US*.

sixièmement [sizjɛmmɑ̃] *adv* sixthly, in the sixth place.

six-quatre-deux [siskatdø] ◆ **à la six-quatre-deux** *loc adv fam* **faire qqch à la ~** to do sthg in a slapdash way, to bungle sthg.

sixte [sikst] *nf* **1.** MUS sixth **2.** ESCRIME sixte.

Sixtine [sikstin] *npr* : **la chapelle ~** the Sistine Chapel.

sixtus [sikstys] *nm inv Suisse* hairpin.

sizain [sizɛ̃] *nm* **1.** LITTÉR sextain **2.** CARTES set of six packs of cards.

Skaï® [skaj] *nm* Skai®, Leatherette®.

skate [skɛt], **skateboard** [skɛtbɔrd] *nm* skateboard ■ **faire du ~** to skateboard.

sketch [skɛtʃ] (*pl* **sketchs** *ou pl* **sketches**) *nm* CINÉ, THÉÂTRE & TV sketch.

ski [ski] *nm* **1.** LOISIRS & SPORT [activité] skiing ■ **faire du ~** to go skiing ▶ **~ alpin/nordique** Alpine/Nordic skiing ■ **~ acrobatique** hot-dogging ■ **~ de descente** downhill skiing ■ **~ de fond** cross-country skiing ■ **~ nautique** water-skiing ■ **faire du ~ nautique** to water-ski ■ **~ de randonnée** ski-touring ■ **~ sauvage** *ou* **hors piste** off-piste skiing **2.** [matériel] ski ■ **~ compact** *ou* **court** short ski **3.** AÉRON landing skid.
◆ **de ski** *loc adj* [chaussures, lunettes] ski *(modif)* ■ [vacances, séjour] skiing *(modif)*.

skiable [skjabl] *adj* skiable ■ **la piste noire n'est plus ~** it's now impossible to ski down *ou* to use the black run.

ski-bob [skibɔb] (*pl* **ski-bobs**) *nm* skibob ■ **faire du ~** to go skibobbing.

skier [10] [skje] *vi* to ski ■ **je vais ~ tous les dimanches** I go skiing every Sunday.

skieur, euse [skjœr, øz] *nm, f* skier.

skiff [skif] *nm* skiff.

skinhead [skinɛd] *nm* skinhead.

skip [skip] *nm* INDUST skip.

skipper [skipœr] *nm* NAUT skipper.

slalom [slalɔm] *nm* **1.** SPORT [course] slalom ■ **descendre une piste en ~** to slalom down a slope ▶ **~ spécial/géant** special/giant slalom **2.** *fam* [zigzags] zigzagging ■ **faire du ~ entre** to zigzag between.

slalomer [3] [slalɔme] *vi* **1.** SPORT to slalom **2.** *fam* [zigzaguer] : **~ entre** to zigzag *ou* to weave in and out of.

slalomeur, euse [slalɔmœr, øz] *nm, f* slalom skier.

slave [slav] *adj* Slavonic, Slavic *US*.
◆ **Slave** *nmf* Slav ■ **les Slaves** the Slavs.
◆ **slave** *nm* LING Slavonic, Slavic.

slavisant, e [slavizɑ̃, ɑ̃t] *nm, f* Slavicist, Slavist.

slaviser [3] [slavize] *vt* to submit to a Slavonic influence, to Slavonicize.

slaviste [slavist] = **slavisant**.

Slavonie [slavɔni] *npr f* : **(la) ~** Slavonia.

slavophile [slavɔfil] *adj* & *nmf* Slavophil, Slavophile.

slibard△ [slibar] *nm* underpants.

slip [slip] *nm* **1.** [pour homme] (pair of) underpants, shorts *US* ■ [pour femme] briefs *UK*, panties, knickers ▶ **~ de bain** [d'homme] bathing *ou* swimming trunks **2.** NAUT slip, slipway.

s.l.n.d. (*abr écrite de* **sans lieu ni date**) *date and origin unknown.*

slogan [slɔgɑ̃] *nm* slogan.

sloop [slup] *nm* sloop.

slovaque [slɔvak] *adj* Slovak, Slovakian.
◆ **Slovaque** *nmf* Slovak, Slovakian.
◆ **slovaque** *nm* LING Slovak.

Slovaquie [slɔvaki] *npr f* : **(la) ~** Slovakia.

slovène [slɔvɛn] *adj* Slovene, Slovenian.
◆ **Slovène** *nmf* Slovene, Slovenian.
◆ **slovène** *nm* LING Slovene.

Slovénie [slɔveni] *npr f* : **(la) ~** Slovenia.

slow [slo] *nm* **1.** [gén] slow number ■ **danser un ~ avec qqn** to dance (to) a slow number with sb **2.** [fox-trot] slow fox trot.

SM ◇ (*abr écrite de* **Sa Majesté**) HM.
◇ *nm* (*abr de* **sado-masochisme**) SM.

SMAG, Smag [smag] (*abr de* **salaire minimum agricole garanti**) *nm guaranteed minimum agricultural wage.*

smala(h) [smala] *nf* **1.** [d'un chef arabe] retinue **2.** *fam* [famille] : **avec toute sa ~** with her whole tribe.

smart [smart] *adj inv fam vieilli* chic, smart.

smash [smaʃ] (*pl* **smashs** *ou pl* **smashes**) *nm* SPORT smash ■ **faire un ~** to smash (the ball).

smasher [3] [smaʃe] *vi* & *vt* SPORT to smash.

SME (*abr de* **Système monétaire européen**) *npr m* EMS.

SMIC, Smic [smik] (*abr de* **salaire minimum interprofessionnel de croissance**) *nm index-linked guaranteed minimum wage.*

smicard, e [smikar, ard] *nm, f fam* minimum-wage earner ■ **les ~s** people earning *ou* on the minimum wage.

smiley [smaɪlɪ] *nm* smiley.

smocks [smɔk] *nmpl* COUT smocking ■ **faire des ~ sur une robe** to smock a dress.

smoking [smɔkiŋ] *nm* dinner suit *UK*, tuxedo *US* ■ **veste de ~** dinner jacket, tuxedo *US*.

SMUR, Smur [smyr] (*abr de* **Service médical d'urgence et de réanimation**) *npr m French ambulance and emergency unit.*

smurf [smœrf] *nm* break-dancing.

smurfer [3] [smœrfe] *vi* to break-dance.

Smyrne [smirn] *npr* Smyrna.

snack [snak] *nm* **1.** = **snack-bar 2.** [collation] snack.

snack-bar [snakbar] (*pl* **snack-bars**), **snack** [snak] *nm* snack bar, self-service restaurant, cafeteria.

SNC = **service non compris**.

SNCF (*abr de* **Société nationale des chemins de fer français**) *npr f French railways board* ■ **la ~ est en grève** the (French) railwaymen are on strike ■ **il travaille à la ~** he works for the (French) railways.

SNES, Snes [snɛs] (*abr de* **Syndicat national de l'enseignement secondaire**) *npr m secondary school teachers' union.*

Sne-sup [snɛsyp] (*abr de* **Syndicat national de l'enseignement supérieur**) *npr m university teachers' union.*

SNI [sni] (*abr de* **Syndicat national des instituteurs**) *npr m primary school teachers' union.*

sniff [snif] ◇ *interj* boo hoo.
◇ *nm*△ [de cocaïne] snort△.

sniffer [3] △[snife] ◇ *vi* to snort△.
◇ *vt* [cocaïne] to snort△ ■ **~ de la colle** to gluesniff, to sniff glue.

SNJ (*abr de* **Syndicat national des journalistes**) *npr m national union of journalists.*

snob [snɔb] ◇ *adj* snobbish, snobby.
◇ *nmf* snob.

snober [3] [snɔbe] *vt* [personne] to snub ■ [chose] to turn one's nose up at ■ **certains libraires snobent les bandes dessinées** some booksellers think it beneath them to stock comics.

snobinard, e [snɔbinar, ard] *fam* ◇ *adj* snobbish, hoity-toity.
◇ *nm, f* snob.

snobisme [snɔbism] *nm* snobbery, snobbishness ■ **il joue au golf par ~** he plays golf out of snobbery *ou* purely for the snob value.

snow-boot [snobut] (*pl* **snow-boots**) *nm* snow boot.

s.o. (*abr écrite de* **sans objet**) na.

S-O (*abr écrite de* **Sud-Ouest**) SW.

sobre [sɔbr] *adj* **1.** [personne - tempérante] abstemious ; [- non ivre] sober **2.** [modéré, discret - architecture, tenue, style] sober, restrained ; [- vêtement] simple.

sobrement [sɔbrəmɑ̃] *adv* **1.** [avec modération] temperately, soberly **2.** [avec discrétion, retenue] soberly.

sobriété [sɔbrijete] *nf* **1.** [tempérance] soberness, temperance **2.** [discrétion, retenue] soberness ■ **il mit de la ~ dans ses félicitations** he was restrained in his congratulations **3.** [dépouillement - d'un style, d'un décor] bearness.

sobriquet [sɔbrikɛ] *nm* nickname ■ **un petit ~ affectueux** a pet name.

soc [sɔk] *nm* ploughshare.

sociabiliser [1] [sɔsjabilize] *vt* to make sociable.

sociabilité [sɔsjabilite] *nf* sociableness, sociability.

sociable [sɔsjabl] *adj* **1.** [individu, tempérament] sociable, gregarious ■ **j'ai été un enfant très ~** I was a very outgoing child **2.** [vivant en société] social.

social, e, aux [sɔsjal, o] *adj* **1.** [réformes, problèmes, ordre, politique] social ■ **c'est une menace ~e** it represents a threat to society **2.** ADMIN social, welfare *(modif)* ■ **avantages sociaux** welfare benefits ■ **logements sociaux** public housing ■ **services sociaux** social services **3.** ENTOM & ZOOL social **4.** DR company *(modif)* ■ **un associé peut être tenu responsable des dettes ~es** a partner may be liable for company debts.
➤ **social** *nm* : **le ~** social issues *ou* matters.

social-démocrate [sɔsjaldemɔkrat] (*pl* **sociaux-démocrates** [sɔsjodemɔkrat]) ◇ *adj* social democratic.
◇ *nmf* [gén] social democrat ■ [adhérent d'un parti] Social Democrat.

social-démocratie [sɔsjaldemɔkrasi] (*pl* **social-démocraties**) *nf* social democracy.

socialement [sɔsjalmɑ̃] *adv* socially.

socialisant, e [sɔsjalizɑ̃, ɑ̃t] ◇ *adj* **1.** POLIT left-leaning, with left-wing tendencies **2.** [préoccupé de justice sociale] socialistic.
◇ *nm, f* **1.** POLIT socialist sympathizer **2.** [contestataire social] advocate of social equality.

socialisation [sɔsjalizasjɔ̃] *nf* **1.** ÉCON collectivization **2.** POLIT : **depuis la ~ du pays** since the country went socialist **3.** PSYCHOL socialization.

socialiser [3] [sɔsjalize] *vt* **1.** ÉCON to collectivize **2.** PSYCHOL to socialize.

socialisme [sɔsjalism] *nm* socialism ■ **~ d'État** State socialism.

socialiste [sɔsjalist] *adj* & *nmf* socialist.

social-révolutionnaire [sɔsjalrevɔlysjɔnɛr] (*pl* **sociaux-révolutionnaires** [sɔsjorevɔlysjɔnɛr]) *adj* & *nmf* social-revolutionary.

sociétaire [sɔsjetɛr] *nmf* [d'une association] member ■ **~ de la Comédie-Française** *actor co-opted as a full member of the Comédie-Française.*

société [sɔsjete] *nf* **1.** SOCIOL : **la ~** society ■ **vivre en ~** to live in society ■ **les insectes qui vivent en ~** social insects ▶ **la ~ d'abondance** the affluent society ■ **la ~ de consommation** the consumer society
2. *litt* [présence] company, society ■ **rechercher la ~ de qqn** to seek (out) sb's company
3. *fam* [personnes réunies] company, gathering
4. [catégorie de gens] society ■ **cela ne se fait pas dans la bonne ~** it's not done in good company *ou* in the best society ■ **la haute ~** high society
5. [association - de gens de lettres, de savants] society ; [- de sportifs] club ■ **~ littéraire/savante** literary/learned society ■ **~ secrète** secret society ■ **la Société des Amis** the Society of Friends, the Quakers ■ **la Société de Jésus** the Society of Jesus ■ **la Société des Nations** the League of Nations ■ **la Société protectrice des animaux = SPA**
6. COMM, DR & ÉCON company, firm ▶ **~ anonyme** (public) limited company ■ **~ à capital variable** company with variable capital ■ **~ de capitaux (à responsabilité limitée)** limited liability company ■ **~ (de capitaux) par actions (à responsabilité limitée)** (limited liability) joint-stock company ■ **~ civile professionnelle** professional *ou* non-trading partnership ■ **~ en commandite** limited partnership ■ **~ en commandite simple** ≃ general partnership ■ **~ d'économie mixte** government-controlled corporation ■ **~ d'intérêt collectif agricole** agricultural cooperative ■ **~ d'investissement à capital variable = SICAV** ■ **~ en nom collectif** ≃ (unlimited) private company ■ **~ de personnes** partnership ■ **~ de prévoyance** provident society ■ **~ à responsabilité limitée** ≃ limited liability company ■ **~ de services** service company ■ **Société nationale des chemins de fer français = SNCF**
7. BANQUE : **~ financière/de crédit** finance/credit company ■ **~ de crédit immobilier** building society UK, savings and loan association US
8. DR : **~ d'acquêts** joint (matrimonial) assets
9. INFORM : **~ de services et d'ingénierie informatique** services and software organization
10. LOISIRS : **jeux de ~** games *(for playing indoors, often with boards or cards).*

sociobiologie [sɔsjɔbjɔlɔʒi] *nf* sociobiology.

socioculturel, elle [sɔsjɔkyltyrɛl] *adj* sociocultural.

sociodrame [sɔsjɔdram] *nm* sociodrama.

socio-économique [sɔsjɔekɔnɔmik] (*pl* **socio-économiques**) *adj* socioeconomic.

socio-éducatif, ive [sɔsjɔedykatif, iv] (*mpl* **socio-éducatifs**, *fpl* **socio-éducatives**) *adj* socioeducational.

sociolinguistique [sɔsjɔlɛ̃gɥistik] *nf* sociolinguistics *(U).*

sociologie [sɔsjɔlɔʒi] *nf* sociology ■ **~ religieuse** sociology of religion.

sociologique [sɔsjɔlɔʒik] *adj* sociological.

sociologue [sɔsjɔlɔg] *nmf* sociologist.

socioprofessionnel, elle [sɔsjɔprɔfɛsjɔnɛl] *adj* socio-professional.

socle [sɔkl] *nm* **1.** ARCHIT [piédestal] pedestal, base ■ [stylobate] stylobate **2.** CONSTR [d'un bâtiment] plinth, socle ■ [d'un mur] footing **3.** GÉOL (large) block **4.** MENUIS [de chambranle] skirting, capping ■ [de marche] string, stairstring.

socque [sɔk] *nm* **1.** ANTIQ sock **2.** [chaussure] clog.

socquette [sɔkɛt] *nf* ankle sock, bobby sock *US*.

Socrate [sɔkrat] *npr* Socrates.

socratique [sɔkratik] *adj* Socratic.

soda [sɔda] *nm* **1.** [boisson gazeuse] fizzy drink, soda *US* ▪ **~ à l'orange** orangeade, orange soda *US* **2.** [eau de Seltz] soda (water) ▪ **whisky ~** whisky and soda.

sodé, e [sɔde] *adj* sodium *(modif)*.

sodique [sɔdik] *adj* sodic, sodium *(modif)*.

sodium [sɔdjɔm] *nm* sodium.

Sodome [sɔdɔm] *npr* Sodom ▪ **~ et Gomorrhe** Sodom and Gomorrah.

sodomie [sɔdɔmi] *nf* sodomy.

sodomiser [3] [sɔdɔmize] *vt* to sodomize, to bugger.

sodomite [sɔdɔmit] *nm* sodomite.

sœur [sœr] *nf* **1.** [parenté] sister ▪ **c'est une vraie ~ pour moi** she's like a sister to me ▪ **l'envie et la calomnie sont ~s** envy and slander are sisters ⊳ **ma grande ~** my big sister ▪ **ma petite ~** my little sister ▪ **ma ~ aînée** my elder *ou* older sister ▪ **ma ~ cadette** my younger sister ▪ **~ de lait** foster sister ▪ **~ de sang** blood sister ▪ **et ta ~!**△ mind your own (damn) business! **2.** RELIG sister, nun ▪ **chez les ~s** with the nuns, in a convent ▪ **bien, ma ~** very well, sister ▪ **~ Thérèse** Sister Theresa ⊳ **bonne ~** *fam* nun ▪ **les Petites Sœurs des pauvres** the Little Sisters of the Poor.

sœurette [sœrɛt] *nf fam* (little) sister ▪ **ça va, ~?** alright, sis?

sofa [sɔfa] *nm* sofa.

Sofia [sɔfja] *npr* Sofia.

SOFRES, Sofres [sɔfrɛs] (*abr de* **Société française d'enquêtes par sondages**) *npr f French market research company*.

soft [sɔft] ◇ *nm inv fam* INFORM software.
◇ *adj inv* [film, roman] softcore.

software [sɔftwɛr] *nm* software.

soi [swa] ◇ *pron pers* **1.** [représentant un sujet indéterminé] oneself ▪ **être content de ~** to be pleased with oneself ▪ **il ne faut pas penser qu'à ~** one shouldn't think only of oneself ▪ **ne pas regarder derrière ~** not to look back ▪ **prendre sur ~** to get a grip on oneself ▪ **prendre sur ~ de faire qqch** to take it upon oneself to do sthg **2.** [représentant un sujet déterminé] : **on ne pouvait lui reprocher de ne penser qu'à ~** he couldn't be reproached for thinking only of himself **3.** *loc* **en ~** in itself, per se *sout* ▪ **cela va de ~** that goes without saying.
◇ *nm* : **le ~** the self.

soi-disant [swadizɑ̃] ◇ *adj inv* **1.** [qu'on prétend tel - liberté, gratuité] so-called ; [- coupable, responsable] alleged **2.** [qui se prétend tel - aristocrate] self-styled ; [- ami, héritier, génie] so-called.
◇ *adv fam* [à ce qu'on prétend] supposedly ▪ **elle l'a ~ tué** they say she killed *ou* she's alleged to have killed him ▪ **tu étais ~ absent!** you were supposed to be out! ▪ **elle est sortie, ~ pour acheter du fromage** she went out, ostensibly to get some cheese *ou* to get some cheese, she said.
◆ **soi-disant que** *loc conj fam* apparently ▪ **~ qu'il ne nous aurait pas vus!** he didn't see us, or so he said!

soie [swa] *nf* **1.** TEXT silk ▪ **~ grège/naturelle/sauvage** raw/natural/wild silk ▪ **~ moirée** watered silk **2.** ZOOL [de sanglier, de chenille] bristle ▪ [de bivalves] byssus **3.** [d'un couteau] tang.
◆ **de soie** *loc adj* [étoffe, tapis] silk *(modif)* ▪ [peau] silky.

soierie [swari] *nf* **1.** [étoffe] silk **2.** [activité] silk trade.

soif [swaf] *nf* **1.** [envie de boire] thirst ▪ **avoir ~** to be thirsty ▪ **avoir grand-~** to be parched ▪ **ça m'a donné ~** it made me thirsty ⊳ **jusqu'à plus ~** [boire] till one's thirst is quenched ; *fig* till one can take no more **2.** *fig* **~ de pouvoir/de richesses** craving for power/wealth ▪ **~ de connaissances** thirst for knowledge ▪ **avoir ~ de sang** to thirst for blood.

soiffard, e [swafar, ard] *nm, f fam* boozer, alkie.

soignant, e [swaɲɑ̃, ɑ̃t] *adj* caring ▪ **le personnel ~ est en grève** the nursing staff are on strike.

soigné, e [swaɲe] *adj* **1.** [propre - apparence, personne] neat, tidy, well-groomed ; [- vêtements] neat ; [- ongles] well kept ; [- mains] well cared for ▪ **être très ~ de sa personne** to be very well-groomed ▪ **peu ~** [apparence, personne, tenue] untidy ; [coiffure] unkempt **2.** [fait avec soin - décoration] carefully done ; [- style] polished ; [- écriture, coiffure] neat, tidy ; [- travail] neat, careful ; [- dîner] carefully prepared ; [- jardin] neat, well-kept ▪ **peu ~** [jardin] badly kept ; [dîner] carelessly put together ; [écriture] untidy ; [travail] careless, shoddy **3.** *fam* [en intensif] : **j'ai un mal de tête ~!** I've got a splitting headache! ▪ **le devoir de chimie était ~!** the chemistry paper was a real stinker!

soigner [3] [swaɲe] *vt* **1.** [malade] to treat, to nurse, to look after *(insép)* ▪ [maladie] to treat ▪ **il ne veut pas se faire ~** he refuses (any) treatment ▪ **ils m'ont soigné aux antibiotiques** they treated me with antibiotics ▪ **c'est le docteur Jean qui la soigne** [d'habitude] she's under *ou* in the care of Dr. Jean ▪ **je n'arrive pas à ~ mon rhume** I can't get rid of my cold ▪ **il faut te faire ~!** *fam* you need (to get) your head examined! **2.** [bien traiter - ami, animal, plantes] to look after *(insép)*, to take care of ; [- jardin] to look after **3.** [être attentif à - apparence, tenue, présentation, prononciation] to take care *ou* trouble over ; [- écriture, style] to polish (up) ; [- image de marque] to take good care of, to nurse ; [- repas] to prepare carefully, to take trouble over (the preparation of) ▪ **~ sa mise** to dress with care **4.** *fam* [exagérer] : **ils ont soigné l'addition!** the bill's a bit steep! **5.** *fam* [frapper] : **tu aurais vu ses bleus, le mec l'a soigné!** you should've seen his bruises, the guy made mincemeat of him!
◆ **se soigner** ◇ *vp (emploi réfléchi)* : **il se soigne à l'homéopathie** he relies on homeopathic treatment when he's ill ▪ **je suis timide mais je me soigne!** *hum* I'm shy but I'm doing my best to get over it!
◇ *vp (emploi passif)* to be susceptible to treatment ▪ **ça se soigne bien** it can be easily treated ▪ **ça se soigne difficilement** it's difficult to treat (it) ▪ **ça se soigne, tu sais!** *fam hum* they have a cure for that these days, you know!

soigneur [swaɲœr] *nm* [d'un boxeur] second ▪ [d'un cycliste] trainer ▪ [d'une équipe de football, de rugby] physiotherapist *UK*, physical therapist *US*.

soigneusement [swaɲøzmɑ̃] *adv* [écrire, plier] neatly, carefully ▪ [rincer, laver] carefully ▪ **sa chambre est toujours rangée très ~** his room is always very neat (and tidy).

soigneux, euse [swaɲø, øz] *adj* **1.** [propre et ordonné] tidy ▪ **il n'est pas du tout ~ dans son travail** he's quite untidy *ou* messy in his work ▪ **tu n'es pas assez ~ de tes habits** you're not careful enough with *ou* you don't take enough care of your clothes **2.** [consciencieux - employé] meticulous ; [- recherches, travail] careful, meticulous ▪ **elle est très soigneuse dans ce qu'elle fait** she's very careful in what she does, she takes great care over her work **3.** [soucieux de] : **~ de** : **~ de sa réputation** mindful of his reputation.

soi-même [swamɛm] *pron pers* oneself ▪ **être/rester ~** to be/to remain oneself ▪ **il faut tout faire ~ ici** you have to do everything yourself around here ▪ **c'est Antoine? – ~!** *fam hum* is it Antoine? – in person *ou* none other! ▪ **faire qqch de ~** to do sthg spontaneously ▪ **par ~** by oneself, on one's own ▪ **se replier sur ~** to withdraw into oneself.

soin [swɛ̃] *nm* **1.** [attention] care ▪ **avoir *ou* prendre ~ de qqch** to take care of sthg ▪ **prendre ~ de qqn** to look after *ou* to take care of sb ▪ **avoir *ou* prendre ~ de faire qqch** to take care to do *ou* to make a point of doing sthg ▪ **on dirait qu'elle met un ~ tout particulier à m'agacer** it's as if she was making a point of annoying me ▪ **avec ~** carefully, with care ▪ **faire qqch sans ~** to do sthg carelessly
2. *sout* [souci] care, concern ▪ **mon premier ~ fut de tout ranger** my first concern *ou* the first thing I did was to put everything back into place
3. [propreté] neatness ▪ **avec ~** neatly, tidily ▪ **sa maison est toujours rangée avec ~** his house is always very neat *ou* tidy ▪ **être sans ~** to be untidy ▪ **il a peint le cadre sans aucun ~** he made a mess of painting the frame
4. [responsabilité] task ▪ **je te laisse le ~ de la convaincre** I leave it (up) to you to convince her ▪ **confier à qqn le ~ de faire qqch**

to entrust sb with the task of doing sthg ■ **il lui a confié le ~ de gérer son garage** he entrusted her with the management of his garage.

◆ **soins** *nmpl* **1.** [de routine] care ■ [médicaments] treatment ■ **donner** *ou* **dispenser des ~s à** [médicaux] to give medical care to ■ **prodiguer des ~s à un nouveau-né** to care for a newborn baby ➊ **premiers ~s, ~s d'urgence** first aid ■ **~s de beauté** beauty care ■ **~s dentaires** dental treatment *ou* care ■ **~s intensifs** intensive care ■ **~s (médicaux)** medical care *ou* treatment ■ **~s palliatifs** palliative care ■ **~s du visage** skin care *(for the face)*
2. [attention] care, attention ■ **nous apporterons tous nos ~s au règlement de cette affaire** we'll do our utmost to settle this matter ■ **confier qqn aux (bons) ~s de qqn** to leave sb in the care of sb ■ **aux bons ~s de** [dans le courrier] care of ➊ **sa grand-mère est aux petits ~s pour lui** *fam* his grandma waits on him hand and foot.

soir [swar] *nm* **1.** [fin du jour] evening ■ [début de la nuit] night ■ **le ~ tombe** night is falling, the evening is drawing in ■ **le ~ de ses 20 ans** on the evening of her 20th birthday **2.** [dans des expressions de temps] : **ce ~** tonight, this evening ■ **lundi ~** Monday evening *ou* night ■ **hier ~** yesterday evening, last night ■ **le 11 au ~** on the 11th in the evening, on the evening of the 11th ■ **le ~** in the evening, in the evenings ■ **tous les ~s, chaque ~** every evening ■ **vers 6 h du ~** around 6 (o'clock) in the evening, around 6 p.m ■ **à 10 h du ~** at 10 (o'clock) at night, at 10 p.m **3.** PRESSE : **Le Soir** *Belgian daily newspaper.*

◆ **du soir** *loc adj* **1.** [journal] evening *(modif)* ■ [prière] night *(modif)* **2.** *fam* [personne] : **il est du ~** he's a night owl.

soirée [sware] *nf* **1.** [fin de la journée] evening ■ **bonne ~!** have a nice evening!, enjoy your evening! **2.** [fête, réunion] party ■ **~ dansante** (evening) dance **3.** CINÉ & THÉÂTRE evening performance.

sois *etc v* ⊳ **être**.

soit [swa] ◇ *conj* **1.** [c'est-à-dire] that is to say **2.** [introduisant une hypothèse] : **~ une droite AB** let AB be a line, given a line AB.
◇ *adv* : **~, j'accepte vos conditions** very well then, I accept your conditions ■ **tu préfères cela? eh bien ~!** all right *ou* very well then, if that's what you prefer!

◆ **soit que... ou que** *loc corrélative* either... or.

◆ **soit que..., soit que** *loc corrélative* either... or ■ **~ que vous veniez chez moi, ~ que j'aille chez vous, nous nous retrouverons demain** either you come to my place or I'll go to yours, but we'll meet up tomorrow.

◆ **soit..., soit** *loc corrélative* either... or ■ **c'est ~ l'un, ~ l'autre** it's (either) one or the other.

soixantaine [swasɑ̃tɛn] *nf* : **une ~** about sixty ■ **avoir la ~** to be about sixty, *voir aussi* **cinquantaine**.

soixante [swasɑ̃t] *dét & nm inv* sixty, *voir aussi* **cinquante**.

soixante-dix [swasɑ̃tdis] *dét & nm inv* seventy, *voir aussi* **cinquante**.

soixante-dixième [swasɑ̃tdizjɛm] *adj num, nmf & nm* seventieth, *voir aussi* **cinquième**.

soixante-huitard, e [swasɑ̃tɥitar, ard] ◇ *adj* [réforme] *brought about by the students' revolt of 1968* ■ [tendance] anti-establishment.
◇ *nm, f* veteran of the 1968 students' revolt.

soixantième [swasɑ̃tjɛm] *adj num, nmf & nm* sixtieth, *voir aussi* **cinquième**.

soja [sɔʒa] *nm* **1.** BOT soya **2.** CULIN : **graines de ~** soya beans *UK*, soybeans *US* ■ **germes de ~** bean sprouts.

sol [sɔl] ◇ *nm inv* MUS G ■ [chanté] sol, so, soh, *voir aussi* **fa**, *voir aussi* **clef**.
◇ *nm* **1.** AGRIC & HORT [terre] soil **2.** [surface - de la Terre] ground ; [- d'une planète] surface ■ **l'avion s'est écrasé au ~** the plane crashed ■ **le ~ lunaire** the surface of the Moon **3.** [surface aménagée - à l'intérieur] floor ■ **spécialiste des ~s** flooring specialist **4.** *litt* [patrie] soil ■ **sur le ~ américain** on American soil **5.** GÉOL soil, solum *spéc* **6.** SPORT floor **7.** CHIM sol.

◆ **au sol** *loc adj* **1.** SPORT [exercice] floor *(modif)* **2.** AÉRON [vitesse, ravitaillement] ground *(modif)*.

sol-air [sɔlɛr] *adj inv* ground-to-air.

solaire [sɔlɛr] ◇ *adj* **1.** ASTRON solar ■ **le rayonnement ~** the Sun's radiation **2.** [qui a trait au soleil] solar **3.** [qui utilise le soleil - capteur, four] solar ; [- habitat] solar, solar-heated **4.** [qui protège du soleil] sun *(modif)* ■ **crème/huile ~** suntan lotion/oil **5.** ANAT ⊳ **plexus**.
◇ *nm* : **le ~** solar energy.

solarium [sɔlarjɔm] *nm* solarium.

soldat [sɔlda] *nm* **1.** MIL soldier, serviceman ■ **simple ~, ~ de deuxième classe** [armée de terre] private ; [armée de l'air] aircraftman *UK*, airman basic *US* ■ **~ de première classe** [armée de terre] lance corporal *UK*, private first class *US* ; [armée de l'air] leading aircraftman *UK*, airman third class *US* ■ **le Soldat inconnu** the Unknown Soldier *ou* Warrior **2.** JEUX : **(petits) ~s de plomb** tin *ou* lead *ou* toy soldiers ■ **jouer aux petits ~s** to play with toy soldiers ■ **jouer au petit ~** *fam* to swagger **3.** ENTOM soldier (ant).

soldate [sɔldat] *nf fam* woman soldier, servicewoman.

soldatesque [sɔldatɛsk] *litt* ◇ *adj* : **des manières ~s** rough soldierly manners.
◇ *nf péj* : **la ~** army rabble.

solde[1] [sɔld] *nf* **1.** MIL pay **2.** *Belgique* [salaire] salary, wages.

◆ **à la solde de** *loc prép péj* in the pay of ■ **avoir qqn à sa ~** to be sb's paymaster.

solde[2] [sɔld] *nm* **1.** FIN [d'un compte] (bank) balance ■ [à payer] outstanding balance ■ **vous serez remboursés du ~ en janvier** you'll be paid the balance in January ➊ **~ créditeur** credit balance, balance in hand ■ **~ débiteur** debit balance, balance owed ■ **~ à reporter** balance carried forward ■ **pour ~ de tout compte** in (full) settlement **2.** COMM [vente] sale, sales, clearance sale ■ [marchandise] sale item *ou* article ■ **acheter** *ou* **avoir qqch en ~** to buy sthg in the sales *UK ou* on sale *US ou* at sale price ■ **le bonnet était en ~** the hat was reduced ■ **mettre qqch en ~** to sell sthg at sale price.

◆ **soldes** *nmpl* sale, sales ■ **au moment des ~s** during the sales, when the sales are on.

solder [3] [sɔlde] *vt* **1.** COMM to sell (off) at sale price *ou* at a reduced price ■ **toutes nos chemises sont soldées** all our shirts are at a reduced *ou* at sale price ■ **elle me l'a soldé pour 100 euros** she knocked the price down to 100 euros, she let me have it for 100 euros ■ **tout est soldé à dix euros** everything is reduced to ten euros ■ *(en usage absolu)* **on solde!** the sales are on!, there's a sale on! **2.** [dette] to settle **3.** BANQUE [compte] to close.

◆ **se solder par** *vp+prép* **1.** [se terminer par] to result in ■ **se ~ par un échec** to result in failure, to come to nothing **2.** COMM, ÉCON & FIN : **se ~ par un excédent/un déficit de** to show a surplus/a deficit of.

solderie [sɔldəri] *nf* discount store.

soldeur, euse [sɔldœr, øz] *nm, f* discount trader.

sole [sɔl] *nf* **1.** [d'un four] hearth **2.** AGRIC break (field) **3.** [d'un cheval] sole **4.** MÉCAN sole piece **5.** CONSTR (trowel) throw **6.** CULIN & ZOOL sole.

solécisme [sɔlesism] *nm* solecism.

soleil [sɔlɛj] *nm* **1.** [étoile qui éclaire la Terre] : **le Soleil** the Sun ■ **se lever avec le ~** to be up with the lark ➊ **le ~ levant/couchant** the rising/setting sun ■ **au ~ levant/couchant** at sunrise/sunset ■ **le ~ de minuit** the midnight sun ■ **le ~ brille pour tout le monde** *prov* the sun shines for everyone **2.** [chaleur] sun, sunshine ■ [clarté] sun, sunlight, sunshine ■ **quelques brèves apparitions du ~** some sunny spells ■ **il y aura beaucoup de ~ sur le sud de la France** it'll be very sunny in *ou* over southern France ■ **une journée sans ~** a day with no sunshine ■ **un ~ de plomb** a blazing sun ■ **ma chambre manque de ~** my room doesn't get enough sun *ou* sunlight ■ **on a le ~ sur le balcon jusqu'à midi** the balcony gets the sun until noon ■ **au ~** in the sun ■ **tu es en plein ~** you're right in the sun ■ **prendre le ~** to sunbathe **3.** BOT sunflower **4.** SPORT (backward) grand circle **5.** [feu d'artifice] Catherine wheel **6.** HÉRALD sol.

solennel, elle [sɔlanɛl] *adj* **1.** [obsèques, honneurs, silence] solemn **2.** [déclaration, occasion, personne, ton] solemn, formal **3.** DR [contrat] solemn.

solennellement [sɔlanɛlmɑ̃] *adv* **1.** [en grande pompe] formally, ceremoniously **2.** [cérémonieusement] solemnly, in a solemn voice **3.** [officiellement] solemnly.

solenniser [3] [sɔlanize] *vt* to solemnize.

solennité [sɔlanite] *nf* **1.** [d'une réception] solemnity **2.** [d'un ton, d'une personne] solemnity, formality **3.** *sout* [fête] solemn ceremony *ou* celebration ▪ **la ~ de Pâques** the solemn celebration of Easter **4.** DR solemnity.

Solex® [sɔlɛks] *nm* ≃ moped.

solfège [sɔlfɛʒ] *nm* **1.** [notation] musical notation ▪ [déchiffrage] sight-reading ▪ **faire du ~** to study musical notation **2.** [manuel] music primer.

solfier [9] [sɔlfje] *vt* to sol-fa ▪ **solfiez correctement le morceau suivant** sol-fa the following piece of music accurately.

solidaire [sɔlidɛr] *adj* **1.** [personnes] : **être ~s** [les uns des autres] to stand *ou* to stick together ; [l'un de l'autre] to show solidarity with each other ▪ **nous sommes ~s de nos camarades** we support *ou* stand by our comrades ▪ **deux syndicats peu ~s** two unions showing little solidarity **2.** [reliés - processus, pièces mécaniques] interdependent ▪ **être ~ de** to interact with **3.** [interdépendants] interdependent **4.** DR joint and several.

solidairement [sɔlidɛrmɑ̃] *adv* **1.** [conjointement] jointly, in solidarity with each other **2.** *fig* **les processus fonctionnent ~** the processes are interdependent **3.** MÉCAN [par engrenage] in a mesh ▪ [directement] locked (together) **4.** DR jointly and severally.

solidariser [3] [sɔlidarize] *vt* **1.** [faire partager les mêmes intérêts] to unify, to bring together **2.** [relier - processus] to make interdependent **3.** MÉCAN [par engrenage] to mesh ▪ [directement] to lock (together), to interlock.
◆ **se solidariser avec** *vp+prép* to show solidarity with.

solidarité [sɔlidarite] *nf* **1.** [entre personnes] solidarity ▪ **par ~ avec** out of a fellow-feeling for, in order to show solidarity with ➔ **~ ministérielle** ministerial responsibility ▪ **Solidarité** [syndicat polonais] Solidarity **2.** [de processus] interdependence **3.** MÉCAN [engrenage] meshing ▪ [entraînement] locking, interlocking **4.** DR joint and several liability.

solide [sɔlid] ◇ *adj* **1.** [résistant - meubles, matériel] solid, sturdy, strong ; [- papier] tough, strong ; [- vêtements] hardwearing ; [- bâtiment] solid, strong ; [- verrou, nœud] secure ▪ **peu ~** [chaise, pont] rickety
2. [établi, stable - formation, culture, technique] sound ; [- entreprise] well-established ; [- institution, argument] solid, sound ; [- professionnalisme, réputation] solid ; [- bases] sound, firm ; [- amitié] firm, enduring ; [- foi] firm, staunch ; [- principes, qualités] staunch, sound, sterling *(modif)* ; [- monnaie] strong, firm ▪ **attitude empreinte d'un ~ bon sens** no-nonsense attitude, attitude based on sound common sense ▪ **elle s'est entourée d'une ~ équipe de chercheurs** she's surrounded herself with a reliable *ou* strong research team
3. [robuste - personne, membre] sturdy, robust ; [- santé] sound ▪ **avoir une ~ constitution** to have an iron constitution ▪ **le poulain n'est pas encore très ~ sur ses pattes** the foal isn't very steady on its legs yet ▪ **le cœur n'est plus très ~** the heart's getting weaker
4. *fam (avant le n) fam* [substantiel] substantial, solid ▪ **un ~ petit déjeuner** a substantial *ou* solid breakfast ▪ **un ~ coup de poing** a mighty punch ▪ **avoir une ~ avance sur ses concurrents** to enjoy a secure *ou* comfortable lead over one's rivals ➔ **avoir un ~coup de fourchette** to have a hearty appetite
5. [non liquide - aliments, corps, état] solid
6. TEXT [tissu] resistant ▪ [teinture] fast
7. MATH solid.
◇ *nm* **1.** [ce qui est robuste] : **les voitures suédoises, c'est du ~** Swedish cars are built to last ▪ **son dernier argument, c'est du ~!** *fam* her last argument is rock solid!
2. [sol ferme] solid ground ▪ **marcher sur du ~** to walk on solid ground
3. [aliments solides] solids, solid food
4. MATH & PHYS solid.

solidement [sɔlidmɑ̃] *adv* **1.** [fortement] securely, firmly **2.** [profondément] firmly ▪ **c'est une croyance ~ ancrée** it's a deeply-rooted *ou* deep-seated idea **3.** *fam* [en intensif] seriously ▪ **je l'ai ~ grondé** I gave him a good talking-to.

solidification [sɔlidifikasjɔ̃] *nf* solidification.

solidifier [9] [sɔlidifje] *vt* to solidify, to harden.
◆ **se solidifier** *vpi* to solidify, to harden.

solidité [sɔlidite] *nf* **1.** [d'un meuble] solidity, sturdiness ▪ [d'un vêtement] sturdiness, durability ▪ [d'un bâtiment] solidity **2.** [d'une institution, de principes, d'arguments] solidity, soundness ▪ [d'une équipe] reliability ▪ [d'une monnaie] strength ▪ **la ~ technique de son jeu** the soundness of her playing technique **3.** [force d'une personne] sturdiness, robustness.

soliloque [sɔlilɔk] *nm* soliloquy.

soliloquer [3] [sɔlilɔke] *vi* to soliloquize.

solipsisme [sɔlipsism] *nm* solipsism.

soliste [sɔlist] *nmf* soloist.

solitaire [sɔlitɛr] ◇ *adj* **1.** [personne, existence, activité] solitary, lonely **2.** [isolé - île, quartier, retraite] solitary, lone **3.** ARCHIT [colonne] isolated.
◇ *nmf* **1.** [misanthrope] loner, lone wolf **2.** [navigateur, voyageur] : **c'est une course de ~s** it's a single-handed race.
◇ *nm* **1.** [anachorète] hermit, recluse **2.** JEUX & JOAILL solitaire **3.** CHASSE old boar.
◆ **en solitaire** ◇ *loc adj* [course, vol] solo *(modif)* ▪ [navigation] single-handed.
◇ *loc adv* [vivre, travailler] on one's own ▪ [naviguer] single-handed ▪ **il vit en ~ dans sa vieille maison** he lives on his own in his old house.

solitairement [sɔlitɛrmɑ̃] *adv* : **vivre ~** to lead a solitary life.

solitude [sɔlityd] *nf* **1.** [d'une personne - momentanée] solitude ; [- habituelle] loneliness ▪ **j'aime la ~** I like to be alone *ou* on my own ▪ **dans une grande ~ morale** morally isolated ▪ **la ~ à deux** the loneliness of a couple *(when the two stop communicating with each other)* **2.** [d'une forêt, d'un paysage] loneliness, solitude.

solive [sɔliv] *nf* CONSTR joist ▪ **~ apparente** exposed joist.

Soljenitsyne [sɔlʒenitsin] *npr* Solzhenitsyn.

sollicitation [sɔlisitasjɔ̃] *nf* **1.** [requête] request, entreaty **2.** [tentation] temptation **3.** [poussée, traction] : **les freins répondent à la moindre ~** the brakes are extremely responsive **4.** CONSTR stress.

solliciter [3] [sɔlisite] *vt* **1.** [requérir - entrevue] to request, to solicit, to beg the favour of *sout* ; [- aide, conseils] to solicit, to seek (urgently) ; [- emploi] to apply for *(insép)* ▪ **~ qqch de qqn** to request sthg from sb ▪ **je me permets de ~ votre bienveillance** may I appeal to your kindness **2.** [mettre en éveil - curiosité, attention] to arouse ; [- élève] to spur *ou* to urge on *(sép)* ▪ **le problème qui nous sollicite** *ou* **qui sollicite notre attention actuellement** the problem currently before us **3.** [texte] to overinterpret **4.** [faire appel à] to approach, to appeal to *(insép)* ▪ **être très sollicité** to be (very much) in demand ▪ **sollicité par les chasseurs de tête** head-hunted **5.** [faire fonctionner - mécanisme] to put a strain on ▪ **dès que les freins sont sollicités** as soon as you touch the brakes **6.** ÉQUIT [cheval] to spur *ou* to urge on *(sép)*.

solliciteur, euse [sɔlisitœr, øz] *nm, f* [quémandeur] supplicant, supplicant.

sollicitude [sɔlisityd] *nf* [intérêt - affectueux] (excessive) care, solicitude *sout* ; [- soucieux] concern, solicitude *sout* ▪ **être plein de ~ envers qqn** to be very attentive to *ou* towards sb.

solo [sɔlo] (*pl* **solos** *ou pl* **soli** [-li]) ◇ *nm* **1.** [entreprise] one-man *ou* one-woman business, sole trader **2.** MUS solo ▪ **elle joue/chante en ~** she plays/sings solo ▪ **une escalade en ~** *fig* a solo climb **3.** THÉÂTRE [spectacle] one-man-show.
◇ *nmf* [célibataire] single person.

sol-sol [sɔlsɔl] *adj inv* ground-to-ground.

solstice [sɔlstis] *nm* solstice ■ **~ d'été/d'hiver** summer/winter solstice.

solubiliser [3] [sɔlybilize] *vt* to solubilize.

solubilité [sɔlybilite] *nf* solubility ■ **produit de ~** solubility product.

soluble [sɔlybl] *adj* **1.** CHIM soluble ■ **~ dans l'eau** water-soluble **2.** [problème] solvable, soluble.

soluté [sɔlyte] *nm* solute ■ **~ physiologique** saline solution, (artificial) serum.

solution [sɔlysjɔ̃] *nf* **1.** [résolution, clé] solution, answer ■ **apporter une ~ à un problème** to find a solution to *ou* to solve a problem ▶ **une ~ de facilité** an easy way out **2.** [terme - d'une crise] resolution, settling ; [- d'une situation complexe] resolution **3.** HIST : **la ~ finale** the Final Solution **4.** MATH solution **5.** *sout* [gén - MÉD] : **~ de continuité** solution of continuity **6.** CHIM & PHARM solution ■ **en ~** dissolved, in (a) solution.

solutionner [3] [sɔlysjɔne] *vt* to solve, to resolve.

solvabilité [sɔlvabilite] *nf* solvency ■ **degré de ~** credit rating.

solvable [sɔlvabl] *adj* solvent.

solvant [sɔlvɑ̃] *nm* solvent.

soma [sɔma] *nm* BIOL soma.

somali, e [sɔmali] *adj* Somalian, Somali.
◆ **Somali, e** *nm, f* Somali.
◆ **somali** *nm* LING Somali.

Somalie [sɔmali] *npr f* : **(la) ~** [république] Somalia ; [bassin] Somaliland.

somalien, enne [sɔmaljɛ̃, ɛn] = **somali.**

somatique [sɔmatik] *adj* somatic ■ **affection ~** somatic disorder.

somatiser [3] [sɔmatize] *vt* to somatize.

sombre [sɔ̃br] *adj* **1.** [pièce, ruelle, couleur, robe] dark ■ **il fait très ~** it's very dark **2.** [personne, caractère, humeur, regard] gloomy, melancholy, sombre ■ [avenir, perspectives] gloomy ■ **les jours les plus ~s de notre histoire** the gloomiest *ou* darkest days of our history **3.** *fam (avant le n) fam* [en intensif] : **c'est une ~ crapule/un ~ crétin** he's the scum of the earth/a prize idiot ■ **il m'a raconté une ~ histoire de fraude fiscale** he told me some murky story about tax evasion **4.** LING [voyelle] dark.

sombrement [sɔ̃brəmɑ̃] *adv* gloomily, sombrely ■ **"rien", fit-il ~** "nothing", he said gloomily.

sombrer [3] [sɔ̃bre] *vi* **1.** [bateau] to sink, to founder **2.** *sout* [être anéanti - civilisation] to fall, to decline, to collapse ; [- entreprise] to go bankrupt, to fail, to collapse ; [- projet] to collapse, to fail ; [- espoir] to fade, to be dashed ■ **sa raison a sombré** he lost his reason **3.** [s'abandonner à] : **~ dans** to sink into ■ **~ dans le sommeil/le désespoir** to sink into sleep/despair.

sombrero [sɔ̃brero] *nm* sombrero.

sommaire [sɔmɛr] ◇ *adj* **1.** [succinct] brief, succinct **2.** [rudimentaire - réparation] makeshift ■ **il n'a reçu qu'une éducation ~** his education was rudimentary, to say the least **3.** [superficiel - analyse] summary, basic ; [- examen] superficial, perfunctory **4.** [expéditif - procès] summary.
◇ *nm* [d'un magazine] summary ■ [d'un livre] summary, synopsis ■ **au ~ de notre journal ce soir** our main news stories tonight.

sommairement [sɔmɛrmɑ̃] *adv* **1.** [brièvement] briefly **2.** [rudimentairement] basically **3.** [rapidement] hastily, rapidly ■ **il a ~ inventorié le contenu des poches de la victime** he made a rapid inventory of the contents of the victim's pockets **4.** [expéditivement] summarily.

sommation [sɔmasjɔ̃] *nf* **1.** MIL [avant de tirer] warning, challenge ■ **faire une ~** to challenge ■ **après les ~s d'usage** after the standard warning (had been given) **2.** DR summons ■ **~ sans frais** (tax) reminder **3.** *sout* [requête] demand **4.** MATH summation **5.** PHYSIOL convergence.

somme[1] [sɔm] *nm* nap ■ **faire un (petit) ~** to have a nap.

somme[2] [sɔm] *nf* **1.** FIN : **~ (d'argent)** sum *ou* amount (of money) ■ **pour la ~ de 200 euros** for (the sum of) 200 euros ■ **elle me doit une ~ importante** she owes me quite a large sum *ou* quite a lot of money ■ **j'ai dépensé des ~s folles** I spent huge amounts of money ■ **c'est une ~!** that's a lot of money! **2.** MATH sum ■ **la ~ totale** the grand total ■ **faire une ~** to add up (figures) ■ **faire la ~ de 15 et de 16** to add (up) 15 and 16 ▶ **~ algébrique** algebraic sum **3.** [quantité] : **~ de travail/d'énergie** amount of work/energy ■ **ça représente une ~ de sacrifices/d'efforts importante** it means great sacrifices/a lot of effort ■ **quand on fait la ~ de tout ce que j'ai remué comme archives** when you add up the number of archive documents I've handled **4.** [œuvre] general survey.
◆ **en somme** *loc adv* **1.** [en bref] in short ■ **en ~, tu refuses** in short, your answer is no **2.** [en définitive] all in all ■ **c'est assez simple en ~** all in all, it's quite easy.
◆ **somme toute** *loc adv* all things considered, when all is said and done ■ **~ toute, tu as eu de la chance** all things considered, you've been lucky.

sommeil [sɔmɛj] *nm* **1.** PHYSIOL [repos] sleep ■ **je manque de ~** I haven't been getting enough sleep ■ **il cherchait le ~** he was trying to sleep ■ **j'ai le ~ léger/profond** I'm a light/heavy sleeper ■ **une nuit sans ~** a sleepless night, a night without sleep ■ **avoir ~** to be *ou* to feel sleepy ■ **tomber de ~** to be ready to drop, to be falling asleep (on one's feet) ▶ **~ lent/paradoxal** NREM/REM sleep ■ **le premier ~** the first hours of sleep ■ **dormir d'un ~ de plomb** [d'habitude] to be a heavy sleeper, to sleep like a log ; [ponctuellement] to be sleeping like a log *ou* fast asleep **2.** *fig* [inactivité] inactivity, lethargy, sluggishness.
◆ **en sommeil** ◇ *loc adj* [volcan, économie] inactive, dormant.
◇ *loc adv* : **rester en ~** to remain dormant *ou* inactive ■ **mettre un secteur économique en ~** to put an economic sector in abeyance.

sommeiller [4] [sɔmeje] *vi* **1.** [personne] to doze ■ **je commençais à ~ au volant** I was falling asleep at the wheel **2.** [affaire, passion, volcan] to lie dormant.

sommelier, ère [sɔməlje, ɛr] *nm, f* sommelier, wine waiter (*f* waitress).
◆ **sommelière** *nf Suisse* waitress.

sommer [3] [sɔme] *vt* **1.** DR : **~ qqn de faire qqch** to summon sb to do sthg **2.** *sout* [ordonner à] : **~ qqn de faire qqch** to order sb to do sthg **3.** ARCHIT to crown, to top **4.** MATH to add up *(sép).*

sommes *v* ▷ **être.**

sommet [sɔmɛ] *nm* **1.** [plus haut point - d'un mont] summit, highest point, top ; [- d'un bâtiment, d'un arbre] top **2.** [partie supérieure - d'un arbre, d'une colline] crown ; [- d'une montagne] top, summit ; [- d'une vague] crest ; [- de la tête] crown, vertex *spéc* ■ **leurs émissions n'atteignent pas des ~s** *fig* their programmes don't aim very high *ou* aren't exactly intellectually ambitious **3.** [degré suprême - d'une hiérarchie] summit, top ; [- d'une carrière] top, summit, acme *sout* ■ **une décision prise au ~** a decision taken from the top ■ **le ~ de la gloire** the pinnacle of fame ■ **elle est au ~ de son talent** she's at the height of her talent **4.** MATH [d'un angle, d'une hyperbole] vertex **5.** POLIT summit (meeting).

sommier [sɔmje] *nm* **1.** [de lit] (bed) base ■ **~ à lattes** slatted base ■ **~ métallique** wire mattress **2.** ARCHIT [d'une voûte - poutre] springer, skewback ; [- pierre] impost ■ [d'un clocher] stock **3.** CONSTR [d'une porte] lintel ■ [d'une grille] crossbar **4.** MUS [d'un orgue] windchest ■ [d'un piano] frame **5.** [de comptabilité] register, ledger.

sommité [sɔmite] *nf* authority ■ **les ~s de la médecine** leading medical experts.

somnambule [sɔmnɑ̃byl] ◇ *adj* : **être ~** to sleepwalk, to be a sleepwalker.

<> *nmf* sleepwalker, somnambulist *spéc.*

somnambulisme [sɔmnɑ̃bylism] *nm* sleepwalking, somnambulism *spéc.*

somnifère [sɔmnifɛr] <> *adj* soporific, sleep-inducing. <> *nm* [substance] soporific ▪ [comprimé] sleeping pill *ou* tablet.

somnolence [sɔmnɔlɑ̃s] *nf* **1.** [d'une personne] drowsiness, sleepiness, somnolence *sout* **2.** [d'une économie] lethargy, sluggishness.

somnolent, e [sɔmnɔlɑ̃, ɑ̃t] *adj* **1.** [personne] drowsy, sleepy, somnolent *sout* **2.** [village] sleepy ▪ [voix] droning ▪ [esprit] dull, lethargic, apathetic ▪ [économie] lethargic, sluggish ▪ [faculté intellectuelle] dormant.

somnoler [3] [sɔmnɔle] *vi* **1.** [personne] to doze **2.** [ville] to be sleepy ▪ [économie] to be lethargic *ou* in the doldrums ▪ [faculté intellectuelle] to lie dormant, to slumber.

somptuaire [sɔ̃ptɥɛr] *adj* **1.** [dépenses] extravagant **2.** ART : **arts ~s** decorative arts **3.** ANTIQ & HIST sumptuary.

somptueusement [sɔ̃ptɥøzmɑ̃] *adv* [décorer, illustrer] sumptuously, lavishly, richly ▪ [vêtir] sumptuously, magnificently.

somptueux, euse [sɔ̃ptɥø, øz] *adj* **1.** [luxueux - vêtements, cadeau] sumptuous, splendid ; [- décor, salon, palais] magnificent, splendid **2.** [superbe - banquet] sumptuous, lavish ; [- illustration] lavish ▪ **la pièce a une somptueuse distribution** the play has a glittering cast.

somptuosité [sɔ̃ptɥozite] *nf litt* [d'une toilette] sumptuousness, magnificence ▪ [d'un décor, d'une pièce, d'illustrations] sumptuousness, splendour, lavishness.

son[1] [sɔ̃] *nm* **1.** LING, MUS & PHYS sound ▪ **un ~ sourd** a thump, a thud ▪ **un ~ strident** [klaxon, trompette] a blast ▪ **émettre** *ou* **produire un ~** to give out a sound ▪ **le mur rend un ~ creux** the wall has a hollow sound ➊ **~ de cloche : c'est un autre ~ de cloche** that's (quite) another story ▪ **j'ai entendu plusieurs ~s de cloche** I've heard several variants *ou* versions of that story ▪ **spectacle ~ et lumière** son et lumière **2.** AUDIO sound, volume ▪ **baisser/monter le ~** to turn the sound up/down ▪ **~ seul** sound only, wild track ▪ **le ~ était épouvantable** CINÉ the soundtrack was terrible ▪ **au ~, Marcel Blot** sound (engineer), Marcel Blot **3.** AGRIC bran ▪ **~ d'avoine** oat bran ▪ **pain au ~** bran loaf.

◆ **au son de** *loc prép* to the sound of.

son[2] [sɔ̃], **sa** [sa], **ses** [se] *(devant nf ou adj f commençant par voyelle ou h muet son* [sɔ̃]*) dét (adj poss)* **1.** [d'un homme] his ▪ [d'une femme] her ▪ [d'une chose] its ▪ [d'un bateau, d'une nation] its, her ▪ **~ frère et sa sœur, ses frère et sœur** his/her brother and sister ▪ **un de ses amis** a friend of his/hers, one of his/her friends ▪ **donne-lui ~ biberon** [à un petit garçon] give him his bottle ; [à une petite fille] give her her bottle ▪ **le bébé, dès ses premiers contacts avec le monde** the baby, from its first experience of the world ▪ **à sa vue, elle s'évanouit** on seeing him/her, she fainted ▪ **dans sa maison à lui** *fam* in HIS house, in his own house

2. [d'un sujet indéfini] : **il faut faire ses preuves** one has to show one's mettle *sout*, you have to show your mettle ▪ **tout le monde a ses problèmes** everybody has (his *ou* their) problems **3.** [dans des titres] : **Son Altesse Royale** His/Her Royal Highness **4.** [d'une abstraction] : **avant de prendre une décision, il faut penser à ses conséquences** before taking a decision, one *sout ou* you must think about the consequences (of it) ▪ **dans cette affaire, tout a ~ importance** in this affair everything is of importance

5. [emploi expressif] : **ça a ~ charme** it's got its own charm *ou* a certain charm ▪ **il fait ~ intéressant** *fam* he's trying to draw attention to himself ▪ **elle se fait ses 2 800 euros par mois** *fam* she brings in 2,800 euros a month ▪ **il va encore piquer sa colère!** he's going to have another one of his outbursts! ▪ **il a réussi à avoir ~ samedi** *fam* he managed to get Saturday off.

sonar [sɔnar] *nm* sonar.

sonate [sɔnat] *nf* sonata.

sonatine [sɔnatin] *nf* sonatina.

sondage [sɔ̃daʒ] *nm* **1.** [enquête] poll, survey ▪ **faire un ~ auprès d'un groupe** to poll a group, to carry out a survey among a group ▪ **j'ai fait un petit ~ parmi mes amis** I sounded out some of my friends ➊ **~ d'opinion** opinion poll **2.** [d'un terrain] sampling, sounding **3.** MÉD probe, probing **4.** MIN & PÉTR [puits] bore hole **5.** NAUT sounding.

sonde [sɔ̃d] *nf* **1.** ASTRON & MÉTÉOR sonde ▪ **~ aérienne** balloon sonde ▪ **~ spatiale** ASTRONAUT (space) probe **2.** NAUT : **(ligne de) ~** lead (line), sounding line ▪ **être sur les ~s** to be on soundings **3.** MÉD probe, sound ▪ **~ (d'alimentation)** feeding tube ▪ **~ (creuse)** catheter **4.** COMM [pour les liquides, le beurre] taster ▪ [pour les grains] sampler ▪ [de douanier] probe **5.** PÉTR drill.

sondé, e [sɔ̃de] *nm, f* person (who has been) polled.

sonder [3] [sɔ̃de] *vt* **1.** [personne - gén] to sound out *(sép)* ; [- dans une enquête] to poll ▪ **je vais tâcher de la ~ là-dessus** I'll try and sound her out on that ▪ **~ l'opinion** to make a survey of public opinion **2.** NAUT to sound ▪ **~ la côte** to take soundings along the coast **3.** MÉTÉOR to probe **4.** MÉD [plaie] to probe ▪ [malade, vessie] to catheterize **5.** INDUST du pétrole to bore, to drill ▪ **~ le terrain** *fig* to test the ground *ou* the waters **6.** [bagages] to probe ▪ [fromage, liquides] to taste ▪ [grains] to sample **7.** [âme] to sound out *(sép)*, to probe.

sondeur, euse [sɔ̃dœr, øz] *nm, f* **1.** [pour une enquête] pollster **2.** GÉOL probe.

◆ **sondeur** *nm* **1.** NAUT depth finder, sounder **2.** MÉTÉOR : **~ acoustique** echo sounder.

◆ **sondeuse** *nf* INDUST du pétrole boring *ou* drilling machine.

songe [sɔ̃ʒ] *nm litt* **1.** [rêve] dream ▪ **voir qqch/qqn en ~** to see sthg/sb in one's dreams ➊ **'le Songe d'une nuit d'été'** ***Shakespeare*** 'A Midsummer Night's Dream' **2.** [chimère] dream, daydream, illusion.

songer [17] [sɔ̃ʒe] *sout* <> *vt* to muse, to reflect, to think ▪ **comment aurais-je pu ~ qu'ils nous trahiraient?** how could I have imagined that they'd betray us?

<> *vi* [rêver] to dream.

◆ **songer à** *v+prép sout* **1.** [penser à] to think about *(insép)* ▪ [en se souvenant] to muse over *(insép)*, to think back to **2.** [prendre en considération - carrière, personne] to think of *(insép)*, to have regard for ▪ **songe un peu plus aux autres!** be a bit more considerate (of others)! **3.** [envisager] to contemplate, to think of *(insép)* ▪ **voyons, vous n'y songez pas!** come now, you can't mean it *ou* be serious! ▪ **il songe sérieusement à se remarier** he's seriously considering *ou* contemplating remarriage **4.** [s'occuper de] to remember ▪ **as-tu songé aux réservations?** did you remember to make reservations? **5.** [réfléchir à - offre, suggestion] to think over *(sép)*, to consider.

songerie [sɔ̃ʒri] *nf litt* daydreaming.

songeur, euse [sɔ̃ʒœr, øz] *adj* pensive, thoughtful, reflective ▪ **d'un air ~** dreamily ▪ **ça vous laisse ~** it makes you wonder.

sonnaille [sɔnaj] *nf* **1.** [pour le bétail] cowbell **2.** [bruit] jangling.

sonnant, e [sɔnɑ̃, ɑ̃t] *adj* sharp ▪ **à trois heures ~es** at three (o'clock) sharp, at three on the dot, at the stroke of three (o'clock).

sonné, e [sɔne] *adj* **1.** [annoncé par la cloche] gone, past ▪ **il est midi ~** it's gone *UK ou* past twelve **2.** *fam* [révolu] : **elle a la cinquantaine bien ~e** she's on the wrong side of fifty **3.** *fam* [fou] cracked, nuts **4.** *fam* [assommé] groggy, punch-drunk.

sonner [3] [sɔne] <> *vi* **1.** [téléphone, cloche] to ring ▪ [minuterie, réveil] to go off ▪ [carillon, pendule] to chime ▪ [glas, tocsin] to toll, to sound ▪ **j'ai mis le réveil à ~ pour** *ou* **à 8 h** I've set the alarm for 8 o'clock

2. [instrument en cuivre] to sound ▪ [clefs, pièces métalliques] to jingle, to jangle ▪ [pièces de monnaie] to jingle, to chink ▪ [enclume, marteau] to ring, to resound ▪ [rire] to ring, to peal (out) ▪ [voix] to resound, to ring ▪ [personne] : **~ du cor** to sound the horn ▪ **~ clair** [monnaie] to ring true ; [marteau] to give *ou* to have a clear ring ▪ **~ creux** to sound hollow, to give a hollow sound ; *fig* to have a hollow ring ▪ **~ faux** *pr & fig* to ring false

3. [heure] to strike ■ **4 h ont sonné** it has struck 4 o'clock, 4 o'clock has struck ■ **attendez que la fin du cours sonne!** wait for the bell!, wait till the bell goes *ou* rings! ■ **l'heure de la vengeance a sonné** *fig* the time for revenge has come
4. [personne] to ring ■ **on a sonné** there's someone at the door ■ **~ chez qqn** to ring sb's doorbell ■ **~ puis entrer** please ring before entering
5. [accentuer] : **faire ~** : **faire ~ une consonne** to sound a consonant.
◇ *vt* **1.** [cloche] to ring, to chime ■ [glas, tocsin] to sound, to toll ■ **~ les cloches à qqn** *fam* to give sb a telling-off *ou* roasting ■ **tu vas te faire ~ les cloches!** you'll catch it!
2. [pour faire venir - infirmière, valet] to ring for ■ **je ne t'ai pas sonné!** *fam* who asked you? ■ *(en usage absolu)* **Madame a sonné?** you rang, Madam?
3. [pour annoncer - messe, vêpres] to ring (the bells) for ■ MIL [- charge, retraite, rassemblement] to sound ■ **~ le réveil** MIL to sound the reveille
4. [suj: horloge] to strike
5. *fam* [assommer] to knock out *(sép)*, to stun ■ [abasourdir] to stun, to stagger, to knock (out) ■ **ça l'a sonné!** he was reeling under the shock!
6. TECHNOL [sonder - installation, monnaie] to sound
7. *Belgique* [appeler] to telephone.

sonnerie [sɔnri] *nf* **1.** [son] ring ■ **la ~ du téléphone/réveil la fit sursauter** the telephone/alarm clock gave her a start ■ **~ de clairon** bugle call **2.** MIL call ■ **la ~ du réveil** the sounding of reveille **3.** [mécanisme - d'un réveil] alarm, bell ; [- d'une pendule] chimes ; [- d'une sonnette] bell **4.** [alarme] alarm (bell).

sonnet [sɔnɛ] *nm* sonnet.

sonnette [sɔnɛt] *nf* **1.** [avertisseur] bell ■ **~ d'alarme** alarm bell ■ **tirer la ~ d'alarme** RAIL to pull the communication cord ; *fig* to blow the whistle **2.** [son] : **(coup de) ~** ring (of the bell) **3.** TRAV PUB piledriver.

sonneur [sɔnœr] *nm* **1.** [de cloches] bell-ringer **2.** MUS player **3.** TECHNOL pile-driver operator.

sono [sɔno] *nf* [d'un groupe, d'une discothèque] sound system, sound ■ [d'une salle de conférences] public-address system, PA (system).

sonore [sɔnɔr] ◇ *adj* **1.** ACOUST [signal] acoustic, sound *(modif)* ■ [onde] sound **2.** [bruyant - rire, voix] loud, ringing, resounding ; [- claque, baiser] loud, resounding **3.** [résonnant - escalier, voûte] echoing ■ **le vestibule est ~** sound reverberates *ou* echoes in the hall **4.** LING [phonème] voiced.
◇ *nf* LING voiced consonant.

sonorisation [sɔnɔrizasjɔ̃] *nf* **1.** [action] wiring for sound **2.** [équipement] sound system **3.** CINÉ : **la ~ d'un film** dubbing a film **4.** LING voicing.

sonoriser [3] [sɔnɔrize] *vt* **1.** [discothèque] to fit with a sound system ■ [salle de conférences] to fit with a PA system ■ [film] to (add the) sound track (to) **2.** LING to voice.

sonorité [sɔnɔrite] *nf* **1.** [d'un instrument de musique] tone ■ [de la voix] sonority *sout*, tone ■ [d'une langue] sonority *sout* **2.** [résonance - de l'air] resonance, sonority *sout* ; [- d'une pièce] acoustics *(U)* ; [- d'un lieu] sonority *sout* **3.** LING voicing.

sonothèque [sɔnɔtɛk] *nf* sound (effects) library.

sont *v* ▷ **être**.

Sopalin® [sɔpalɛ̃] *nm* kitchen paper.

sophisme [sɔfism] *nm* sophism.

sophiste [sɔfist] *nmf* **1.** [raisonneur] sophist **2.** ANTIQ Sophist.

sophistication [sɔfistikasjɔ̃] *nf* **1.** [raffinement] refinement, sophistication **2.** [affectation] affectation, sophistication **3.** [complexité technique] sophistication, complexity.

sophistique [sɔfistik] ◇ *adj* sophistic.
◇ *nf* sophistry.

sophistiqué, e [sɔfistike] *adj* **1.** [raffiné] sophisticated, refined **2.** [affecté] affected, sophisticated **3.** [complexe] complex, sophisticated.

sophistiquer [3] [sɔfistike] *vt* **1.** [raffiner à l'extrême] to refine **2.** [perfectionner] to make more sophisticated, to perfect.

Sophocle [sɔfɔkl] *npr* Sophocles.

sophrologie [sɔfrɔlɔʒi] *nf* sophrology *(form of autogenic relaxation)*.

sophrologue [sɔfrɔlɔg] *nmf* sophrologist *(practitioner of sophrology)*.

soporifique [sɔpɔrifik] ◇ *adj* **1.** PHARM soporific **2.** [ennuyeux] boring, soporific.
◇ *nm vieilli* soporific.

soprano [sɔprano] (*pl* **sopranos** *ou pl* **soprani** [-ni]) ◇ *nm* [voix - de femme] soprano ; [- d'enfant] soprano, treble.
◇ *nmf* soprano.

sorbet [sɔrbɛ] *nm* sorbet *UK*, sherbet *US*.

sorbetière [sɔrbətjɛr] *nf* [de glacier] ice-cream churn ■ [de ménage] ice-cream maker.

sorbier [sɔrbje] *nm* sorb ■ **~ des oiseleurs** rowan tree, mountain ash.

sorbitol [sɔrbitɔl] *nm* sorbitol.

sorbonnard, e [sɔrbɔnar, ard] *fam* ◇ *adj* [esprit] niggling, pedantic.
◇ *nm, f* [professeur] Sorbonne academic ■ [étudiant] Sorbonne student.

Sorbonne [sɔrbɔn] *npr f* : **la ~** the Sorbonne.

sorcellerie [sɔrsɛlri] *nf* **1.** [pratique] sorcery, witchcraft **2.** *fam* [effet surprenant] bewitchment, magic ■ **c'est de la ~!** it's magic!

sorcier, ère [sɔrsje, ɛr] *nm, f* **1.** [magicien] wizard (*f* witch) ■ **il ne faut pas être (grand) ~ pour comprendre cela** *fam* you don't need to be a genius to understand that **2.** ANTHR sorcerer (*f* sorceress).
◆ **sorcier** *adj m fam* **ce n'est pourtant pas ~** you don't need to be a genius to understand.
◆ **sorcière** *nf* [mégère] harpy, witch.

sordide [sɔrdid] *adj* **1.** [misérable - taudis, vêtements] wretched, squalid **2.** [vil - égoïsme] petty ; [- crime] foul, vile **3.** [mesquin - motif] squalid, sordid ■ **de ~s bagarres autour de l'héritage** sordid arguments over the legacy.

sordidement [sɔrdidmɑ̃] *adv* sordidly, squalidly.

Sorel [sɔrɛl] *npr* : **Julien ~** *the hero of Stendhal's 'le Rouge et le Noir', a working-class intellectual exasperated with the bourgeois mediocrity around him.*

sorgho [sɔrgo] *nm* sorghum.

Sorlingues [sɔrlɛ̃g] *npr fpl* : **les (îles) ~** the Scilly Isles, *voir aussi* **île**.

sornettes [sɔrnɛt] *nfpl* balderdash *(U)*, twaddle *(U)* ■ **débiter** *ou* **raconter des ~s** to talk nonsense.

sors *etc v* ▷ **sortir**.

sort [sɔr] *nm* **1.** [condition] fate, lot ■ **être content de son ~** to be happy with one's lot ■ **des mesures ont été prises pour améliorer le ~ des immigrés** steps were taken to improve the lot *ou* status of immigrants ■ **je n'envie pas son ~!** I wouldn't like to be in her shoes! ■ **tu m'abandonnes à mon triste ~!** you've left me to my fate! ▶ **faire un ~ à** *fam* [plat] to make short work of, to polish off ; [bouteille] to polish off, to drink up **2.** [destin] fate, destiny ■ **mon ~ est entre vos mains** my future depends on you, my fate is in your hands *sout* ■ **toutes les demandes d'emploi subissent le même ~** all letters of application meet with the same fate *ou* receive the same treatment **3.** [puissance surnaturelle] : **le ~** Fate, Fortune, Destiny ■ **mais le ~ en a décidé autrement** but fate decided otherwise ▶ **le mauvais ~** misfortune ■ **le ~ en est jeté** the die is cast **4.** [sortilège - gén] spell ; [- défavorable] curse ■ **jeter un ~ à qqn** to cast a spell on sb.

sortable [sɔrtabl] *adj* : **tu n'es vraiment pas ~!** I can't take you anywhere!

sortant, e [sɔrtɑ̃, ɑ̃t] ◇ *adj* **1.** POLIT outgoing ■ **le maire ~** the outgoing mayor **2.** JEUX : **les numéros ~ s** the numbers chosen **3.** INFORM output *(modif)*.
◇ *nm, f* **1.** POLIT incumbent **2.** [personne qui sort] : **on contrôle également les ~s** those leaving are also screened.

sorte [sɔrt] *nf* **1.** [genre] sort, kind, type ■ **toutes ~s de** all kinds *ou* sorts *ou* manner of **2.** [pour exprimer une approximation] : **une ~ de** a sort *ou* kind of ■ **une ~ de grand dadais** *péj* a big clumsy oaf **3.** IMPR sort.
◆ **de la sorte** *loc adv* that way ■ **comment osez-vous me traiter de la ~?** how dare you treat me in that way *ou* like that! ■ **je n'ai jamais été humiliée de la ~!** I've never been so humiliated!
◆ **de sorte à** *loc conj* in order to, so as to.
◆ **de (telle) sorte que** *loc conj* **1.** *(suivi du subj)* [de manière à ce que] so that, in such a way that ■ **disposez vos plantes de telle ~ qu'elles reçoivent beaucoup de lumière** arrange your plants so that they receive maximum light **2.** *(suivi de l'indic)* [si bien que] so that.
◆ **en aucune sorte** *loc adv litt* not in the least.
◆ **en (quelque) sorte** *loc adv* as it were, in a way, somewhat ■ **immobile, pétrifié en quelque ~** motionless, as it were paralysed ■ **alors, on repart à zéro? – oui, en quelque ~** so, we're back to square one? – yes, in a manner of speaking.
◆ **en sorte de** *loc conj* so as to ■ **fais en ~ d'arriver à l'heure** try to be there on time.
◆ **en sorte que** *litt* = **de (telle) sorte que**.

sortie [sɔrti] *nf* **1.** [action] exit ■ THÉÂTRE exit ■ **sa ~ fut très remarquée** her exit *ou* departure did not go unnoticed ■ **faire sa ~** THÉÂTRE to leave the stage, to exit ■ **faire une fausse ~** to make as if to leave
2. [moment] : **à ma ~ de prison/d'hôpital** when I come (*ou* came) out of prison/hospital, on my release from prison/discharge from hospital ■ **les journalistes l'ont assaillie dès sa ~ de l'hôtel** the journalists thronged round her as soon as she stepped *ou* came out of the hotel ■ **à la ~ des bureaux/usines, la circulation est infernale** when the offices/factories come out, the traffic is hell ■ **retrouvons-nous à la ~ du travail/spectacle** let's meet after work/the show ■ **il s'est retourné à la ~ du virage** he rolled (his car) over just after *ou* as he came out of the bend
3. [fin] end ■ **à la ~ de l'hiver** when winter was (nearly) over ■ **à ma ~ de l'école** [à la fin de mes études] when I left school
4. [excursion, promenade] outing ■ [soirée en ville] evening *ou* night out ■ **on a organisé une petite ~ en famille/à vélo** we've organized a little family outing/cycle ride ■ **ils m'ont privé de ~ trois dimanches de suite** they kept me in for three Sundays in a row ➜ **~ éducative** *ou* **scolaire** school outing
5. AÉRON & MIL sortie ■ **faire une ~** to make a sortie ■ **les pompiers font jusqu'à vingt ~s par semaine** the firemen are called out up to twenty times a week
6. [porte, issue - d'une école, d'une usine] gates ; [- d'une salle de spectacles] exit, way out ■ **par ici la ~!** this way out, please! ■ **poussé vers la ~** pushed towards the exit ■ **attends-moi à la ~** wait for me outside ■ **gagner la ~** to reach the exit ■ **il gagna la ~ sans encombre** he made his way out unimpeded ■ **le supermarché se trouve à la ~ de la ville** the supermarket is on the outskirts of the town ■ **'attention, ~ de garage/véhicules'** 'caution, garage entrance/vehicle exit' ➜ **~ de secours** emergency exit ■ **~ de service** service entrance ■ **~ des artistes** stage door
7. [sur route] exit ■ **~ (de route)** turnoff ■ **à toutes les ~s de Paris** at every major exit from Paris
8. BANQUE & ÉCON [de produits, de devises] export ■ [de capital] outflow ■ [sujet de dépense] item of expenditure ■ [dépense] outgoing
9. [d'un disque, d'un film] release ■ [d'un roman] publication ■ [d'un modèle] launch
10. INFORM [de données] output, readout ■ [option sur programme] exit ■ **~ sur imprimante** printout ■ **~ papier** output
11. SPORT [aux jeux de ballon] : **~ en touche** going out of play *ou* into touch ■ **faire une ~** [gardien de but] to come out of goal, to leave the goalmouth ❙ [en gymnastique] exit
12. [d'un cheval] outing
13. *fam* [remarque] quip, sally ■ [emportement] outburst ■ **elle a parfois de ces ~s!** she sometimes comes out with the most amazing stuff!
14. [d'eau, de gaz] outflow, outlet
15. IMPR [des presses] delivery.
◆ **de sortie** *loc adj* : **c'est son jour de ~** [d'un domestique] it's his/her day off ■ **être de ~** [domestique] to have one's day off ■ **je suis de ~ demain** *fam* [au restaurant, au spectacle] I'm going out tomorrow.

sortie-de-bain [sɔrtidbɛ̃] (*pl* **sorties-de-bain**) *nf* bathrobe.

sortilège [sɔrtilɛʒ] *nm* charm, spell.

sortir¹ [sɔrtir] *nm litt* [fin] : **dès le ~ de l'enfance, il dut apprendre à se défendre** he was barely out of his childhood when he had to learn to fend for himself.
◆ **au sortir de** *loc prép* **1.** [dans le temps] : **au ~ de l'hiver** as winter draws to a close ■ **au ~ de la guerre** towards the end of the war **2.** [dans l'espace] : **je vis la cabane au ~ du bois** as I was coming out of the woods, I saw the hut.

sortir² [32] [sɔrtir] ◇ *vi (aux être)* **1.** [quitter un lieu - vu de l'intérieur] to go out ; [- vu de l'extérieur] to come out ■ **vous trouverez la boîte aux lettres en sortant** you'll find the letter box on your way out ■ **~ par la fenêtre** to get out *ou* to leave by the window ■ **sors!** get out (of here)! ■ **fais ~ la guêpe** get the wasp out (of here) ■ **Madame, je peux ~?** please Miss, may I leave the room? ■ **une méchante grippe l'empêche de ~** a bad bout of flu is keeping him indoors *ou* at home ■ **vivement que je puisse ~!** I can't wait to get out! ■ **elle est sortie déjeuner/se promener** she's gone (out) for lunch/for a walk ■ **si elle se présente, dites-lui que je suis sorti** if she calls, tell her I'm out *ou* I've gone out *ou* I'm not in ■ **il était si mauvais que le public est sorti** he was so bad that the audience walked out (on him) ■ **~ de : ~ d'une pièce** to leave a room ■ **~ d'une voiture** to get out of a car ■ **je l'ai vu qui sortait de l'hôpital/l'école vers 16 h** I saw him coming out of the hospital/school at about 4 pm ■ **fais ~ ce chien de la voiture** get that dog out of the car ■ **faites-les ~!** send them out! ■ **~ du lit** to get out of bed ➜ **il est sorti de sa vie** he's out of her life ■ **ça me sort par les yeux** *fam* I'm sick and tired of it, I've had it up to here
2. [marquant la fin d'une activité, d'une période] : **~ de table** to leave the table ■ **elle sort de l'hôpital demain** she's coming out of hospital tomorrow ■ **~ de l'école/du bureau** [finir sa journée] to finish school/work ■ **~ de prison** to come out of *ou* to be released from prison
3. [pour se distraire] : **je sors très peu** I hardly ever go out ■ **~ avec qqn** to go out with sb ■ **ils sortent ensemble depuis trois ans** *fam* they've been going out together for three years
4. [apparaître - dent, bouton] to come through ; [- pousse] to come up, to peep through
5. [se répandre] to come out ■ **le son sort par là** the sound comes out here ■ **c'est pour que la fumée sorte** it's to let the smoke out *ou* for the smoke to escape
6. [s'échapper] to get out ■ **~ de : aucun dossier ne doit ~ de l'ambassade** no file may be taken out of *ou* leave the embassy ■ **faire ~ qqn/des marchandises d'un pays** to smuggle sb/goods out of a country ■ **je vais te confier quelque chose, mais cela ne doit pas ~ d'ici** I'm going to tell you something, but it mustn't go any further than these four walls
7. [être mis en vente - disque, film] to be released, to come out ; [- livre] to be published, to come out ■ **ça vient de ~!** it's just (come) out!, it's (brand) new!
8. [être révélé au public - sujet d'examen] to come up ; [- numéro de loterie] to be drawn ; [- numéro à la roulette] to turn *ou* to come up ; [- tarif, barème] to be out
9. *fam* [être dit] to come out ■ **il fallait que ça sorte!** it had to come out *ou* to be said!
10. INFORM : **~ (d'un système)** to exit (from a system)
11. NAUT & AÉRON : **~ du port** to leave harbour ■ **~ en mer** to put out to sea ■ **aujourd'hui, les avions/bateaux ne sont pas sortis** the planes were grounded/the boats stayed in port today
12. SPORT [balle] to go out ■ **le ballon est sorti en corner/touche** the ball went out for a corner/went into touch ■ **on a fait ~ le joueur (du terrain)** [pour faute] the player was sent off ; [il est blessé] the player had to go off because of injury
13. THÉÂTRE : **le roi sort** exit the King ■ **les sorcières sortent** exeunt (the) witches.
◇ *vt (aux avoir)* **1.** [mener dehors - pour se promener, se divertir] to take out *(sép)* ■ **il faut ~ les chiens régulièrement** dogs have to be walked regularly ■ **viens avec nous au concert, ça te sortira** come with us to the concert, that'll get you out (of the house)

2. [mettre dehors - vu de l'intérieur] to put out *ou* outside ; [- vu de l'extérieur] to bring out *ou* outside *(sép)* ▪ **~ la poubelle** to take out the rubbish bin *UK ou* the trash *US*
3. [présenter - crayon, outil] to take out *(sép)* ; [- pistolet] to pull out ; [- papiers d'identité] to produce ▪ **on va bientôt pouvoir ~ les vêtements d'été** we'll soon be able to get out our summer clothes ◗ **il a toujours du mal à les ~** *fam* he's never too keen to put his hand in his pocket
4. [extraire] : **~ qqch de** to take *ou* to get sthg out of ▪ **des mesures ont été prises pour ~ le pays de la crise** measures have been taken in order to get the country out of *ou* to rescue the country from the present crisis ▪ **~ qqn de** to get *ou* to pull sb out of ▪ **j'ai eu du mal à le ~ de son lit** [le faire lever] I had trouble getting him out of bed ◗ **je vais te ~ d'affaire** *ou* **d'embarras** *ou* **de là** I'll get you out of it
5. *fam* [expulser] to get *ou* to throw out *(sép)* ▪ **sortez-le ou je fais un malheur!** get him out of here before I do something I'll regret! ▪ **elle a sorti la Suédoise en trois sets** she disposed of *ou* beat the Swedish player in three sets
6. [mettre sur le marché] to launch, to bring out ▪ **~ un disque/film** [auteur] to bring out a record/film ; [distributeur] to release a record/film ▪ **~ un livre** to bring out *ou* to publish a book
7. *fam* [dire] to say, to come out with ▪ **tu sais ce qu'elle m'a sorti?** you know what she came out with? ▪ **il m'a sorti que j'étais trop vieille!** he told me I was too old, just like that!
8. [roue, train d'atterrissage] to drop ▪ [volet] to raise.

◆ **sortir de** *v+prép* **1.** [emplacement, position] to come out of, to come off ▪ **~ des rails** to go off *ou* to jump the rails ▪ **~ de la piste** [voiture] to come off *ou* to leave the track ; [skieur] to come off the piste ◗ **ça m'était complètement sorti de la tête** *ou* **de l'esprit** it had gone right out of my head *ou* mind ▪ **l'incident est sorti de ma mémoire** *ou* **m'est sorti de la mémoire** I've forgotten the incident
2. [venir récemment de] to have (just) come from ▪ **elle sort de chez moi** she's just left my place ▪ **d'où sors-tu?** *fam* where have you been? ▪ **je sors d'une grippe** I'm just recovering from a bout of flu ▪ **~ de faire qqch** *fam* to have just done sthg ◗ **je sors d'en prendre** *fam* I've had quite enough of that, thank you
3. [venir à bout de] to come out of ▪ **nous avons eu une période difficile mais heureusement nous en sortons** we've had a difficult time but fortunately we're now emerging from it *ou* we're seeing the end of it now ◗ **est-ce qu'on va enfin en ~?** *fam* when are we going to see an end to all this?
4. [se tirer de, se dégager de] : **elle est sortie indemne de l'accident** she came out of the accident unscathed ▪ **qui sortira victorieux de ce match?** who will win this match? ▪ **~ de sa rêverie** to emerge from one's reverie ▪ **lorsqu'on sort de l'adolescence pour entrer dans l'âge adulte** when one leaves adolescence (behind) to become an adult
5. [se départir de] : **il est sorti de sa réserve après quelques verres de vin** he opened *ou* loosened up after a few glasses of wine ▪ **elle est sortie de son silence pour écrire son second roman** she broke her silence to write her second novel
6. [s'écarter de] : **attention à ne pas ~ du sujet!** be careful not to get off *ou* to stray from the subject! ▪ **~ de l'ordinaire** to be out of the ordinary ◗ **il ne veut pas ~** *ou* **il ne sort pas de là** he won't budge ▪ **il n'y a pas à ~ de là** [c'est inévitable] there's no way round it, there's no getting away from it
7. [être issu de] : **~ d'une bonne famille** to come from *ou* to be of a good family ▪ **pour ceux qui sortent des grandes écoles** for those who have studied at *ou* are the products of the grandes écoles ▪ **il ne faut pas être sorti de Polytechnique pour savoir ça** you don't need a PhD to know that ◗ **mais d'où sors-tu?** [tu es mal élevé] where did you learn such manners?, where were you brought up? ; [tu ne connais rien] where have you been all this time?
8. [être produit par] to come from ▪ **la veste sortait de chez un grand couturier** the jacket was made by a famous designer
9. *(tournure impersonnelle)* [résulter de] : **que sortira-t-il de tout cela?** what will come of all this? ▪ **il n'est rien sorti de son interrogatoire** his interrogation revealed nothing.

◆ **se sortir de** *vp+prép* to get out of ▪ **se ~ d'une situation embarrassante** to get (o.s.) out of *ou sout* to extricate o.s. from an embarrassing situation ◗ **s'en ~** *fam* : **aide-moi à finir, je ne m'en sortirai jamais seul!** give me a hand, I'll never get this finished on my own ▪ **donne-lui une fourchette, il ne s'en sort pas avec des baguettes** give him a fork, he can't manage with chopsticks ▪ **tu t'en es très bien sorti** you did very well ▪ **elle s'en est sortie avec quelques bleus** she got away with a few bruises ▪ **il s'en est finalement sorti** [il a survécu] he pulled through in the end ; [il a réussi] he won through in the end ▪ **on ne s'en sort pas avec une seule paie** it's impossible to manage on *ou* to get by on a single wage ▪ **malgré les allocations, on ne s'en sort pas** in spite of the benefit, we're not making ends meet ▪ **s'en ~ pour** *fam* [avoir à payer] to be stung for ▪ **tu t'en es sorti pour combien?** how much were you stung for?

SOS (*abr de* **save our souls**) *nm* **1.** [signal de détresse] SOS ▪ **lancer un ~** to put *ou* to send out an SOS **2.** [dans des noms de sociétés] : **~-Amitié** *charity providing support for people in despair* ▪ **~ médecins/dépannage** emergency medical/repair service ▪ **~-Racisme** *voluntary organization set up to combat racism in French society.*

sosie [sozi] *nm* double, doppelganger ▪ **c'est ton ~!** he's the spitting image of you!

sot, sotte [so, sɔt] ◇ *adj* **1.** [idiot] stupid ▪ **il n'est pas ~** he's no fool **2.** *litt* [embarrassé] dumbfounded.
◇ *nm, f* fool, idiot.

sot-l'y-laisse [solilɛs] *nm inv* oyster *(in poultry).*

sottement [sɔtmɑ̃] *adv* foolishly, stupidly.

sottise [sɔtiz] *nf* **1.** [caractère] stupidity, silliness **2.** [acte] stupid *ou* foolish action ▪ **arrête de faire des ~s** [à un enfant] stop messing about ▪ **je viens de faire une grosse ~** I've just done something very stupid *ou* silly **3.** [parole] stupid remark ▪ **ne dis pas de ~s, le soleil se couche à l'ouest** don't be silly *ou* talk nonsense, the sun sets in the west.
◆ **sottises** *nfpl* [injures] insults ▪ **elle m'a dit des ~s** she insulted me.

sottisier [sɔtizje] *nm* collection of howlers.

sou [su] *nm* **1.** HIST [sol] sol, sou ▪ [5 centimes] five centimes ▪ **cent ~s** five francs **2.** *fam* [argent] penny, cent *US* ▪ **tu n'auras pas un ~!** you won't get a penny! ▪ **ça ne vaut pas un ~** *fam* it's not worth tuppence *UK ou* a red cent *US* ▪ **économiser ~ à** *ou* **par ~** to save every spare penny ▪ **il a dépensé jusqu'à son dernier ~** he's spent every last penny he had ◗ **être sans le ~** to be broke ▪ **je suis sans un ~** I haven't got any money (on me) ▪ **elle n'a jamais eu un ~ vaillant** she never had two pennies to rub together ▪ **un ~ est un ~** a penny saved is a penny gained **3.** *loc* **elle n'a pas (pour) un ~** *ou* **deux ~s de jugeote** *fam* she hasn't an ounce of sense ▪ **elle n'est pas méfiante pour un ~** *ou* **deux ~s** she's not in the least suspicious ▪ **être propre comme un ~ neuf** to be as clean as a new pin.
◆ **sous** *nmpl fam* [argent] cash ▪ **des ~s, toujours des ~s!** money for this, money for that! ◗ **c'est une affaire** *ou* **une histoire de gros ~s** there's a lot of cash involved.

Souabe [swab] *npr f* : **(la) ~** Swabia.

souahéli, e [swaeli] = **swahili**.

soubassement [subasmɑ̃] *nm* **1.** ARCHIT & CONSTR foundation **2.** GÉOL bedrock **3.** [base - d'une théorie] basis, underpinnings.

soubresaut [subrəso] *nm* **1.** [secousse] jerk, jolt **2.** [haut-le-corps] shudder, convulsion.

soubrette [subrɛt] *nf* THÉÂTRE soubrette, maid ▪ **jouer les ~s** to play minor roles.

souche [suʃ] *nf* **1.** BOT [d'un arbre en terre] stock, bole ▪ [d'un arbre coupé] stump ▪ [d'une vigne] stock ▪ **ne reste pas là planté comme une ~!** don't just stand there like a lemon *UK ou* a turkey *US* **2.** [d'un carnet] stub, counterfoil *UK* **3.** [origine] descent, stock ▪ **faire ~** [ancêtre] to found *ou* to start a line ▪ **un mot de ~ indo-européenne** a word with an indo-european root **4.** *fam* [crétin] idiot, dumbo **5.** CONSTR base ▪ **~ de cheminée** chimney stack **6.** BIOL strain **7.** DR stock.
◆ **de souche** *loc adj* : **ils sont français de ~** they're of French extraction *ou* origin.
◆ **de vieille souche** *loc adj* of old stock.

souci [susi] *nm* **1.** [inquiétude] worry ▪ **se faire du ~** to worry, to fret ▪ **se faire du ~ pour** to worry *ou* to be worried about

■ **donner du ~ à qqn** to worry sb ■ **mon fils me donne bien du ~!** my son is a great worry to me ■ **eh oui, tout ça c'est bien du ~!** oh dear, what a worry it all is! **2.** [préoccupation] worry ■ **avoir des ~s** to have worries ■ **c'est un ~ de moins!** that's one thing less to worry about! ■ **des ~s d'argent/de santé** money/health worries ■ **c'est le dernier** *ou* **le cadet de mes ~s!** it's the least of my worries!, I couldn't care less! ■ **avoir le ~ de bien faire** to be concerned *ou* to care about doing things well **3.** BOT marigold.

◆ **dans le souci de** *loc conj* : **je l'ai fait dans le ~ de t'aider** I was (only) trying to help you when I did it.

◆ **sans souci** ◇ *loc adj* [vie, personne - insouciant] carefree ■ **être sans ~** [sans tracas] to be free of worries.

◇ *loc adv* : **vivre sans ~** [de façon insouciante] to live a carefree life ; [sans tracas] to live a life free of worries.

soucier [9] [susje] ◆ **se soucier de** *vp+prép* [s'inquiéter de] to worry about ■ [s'intéresser à] to care about ▶ **il s'en soucie comme d'une guigne** *ou* **de sa première chemise** *ou* **de l'an quarante** *fam* he doesn't give a damn about it.

soucieusement [susjøzmɑ̃] *adv* anxiously, worriedly.

soucieux, euse [susjø, øz] *adj* **1.** [préoccupé] worried, preoccupied ■ **elle m'a regardé d'un air ~** she looked at me worriedly **2.** [attaché à] : **~ de** concerned about, mindful of *litt* ■ **peu ~ du qu'en dira-t-on** indifferent to *ou* unconcerned about what people (may) say ■ **~ que** [attentif à] anxious that.

soucoupe [sukup] *nf* saucer ■ **~ volante** flying saucer ■ **faire** *ou* **ouvrir des yeux comme des ~s** to open one's eyes wide.

soudage [sudaʒ] *nm* : **~ autogène** welding ■ **~ hétérogène** soldering.

soudain, e [sudɛ̃, ɛn] *adj* sudden, unexpected ■ **un revirement ~ de la situation** an unexpected reversal of the situation.

◆ **soudain** *adv* all of a sudden, suddenly ■ **~ la porte s'ouvrit** all of a sudden *ou* suddenly, the door opened.

soudainement [sudɛnmɑ̃] *adv* suddenly, all of a sudden ■ **pourquoi est-il parti si ~?** why did he leave so hurriedly?

soudaineté [sudɛnte] *nf* suddenness ■ **la ~ de son départ** her hurried *ou* sudden departure.

Soudan [sudɑ̃] *npr m* : **le ~** the Sudan ■ **au ~** in the Sudan.

soudanais, e [sudanɛ, ɛz], **soudanien, enne** [sudanjɛ̃, ɛn] *adj* GÉOGR Sudanese.

◆ **Soudanais, e, Soudanien, enne** *nm, f* Sudanese (person) ■ **les Soudanais** the Sudanese.

soudard [sudar] *nm* **1.** HIST ill-disciplined soldier **2.** *litt* [individu grossier et brutal] brute.

soude [sud] *nf* **1.** CHIM soda ■ **~ caustique** caustic soda **2.** BOT barilla.

souder [3] [sude] *vt* **1.** TECHNOL [par soudure - hétérogène] to solder ; [- autogène] to weld ■ **~ à l'arc** to arc-weld **2.** [unir] to bring *ou* to bind *ou* to join together.

◆ **se souder** *vpi* [vertèbres, mots] to become fused.

soudeur, euse [sudœr, øz] *nm, f* [par soudure - hétérogène] solderer ; [- autogène] welder.

◆ **soudeuse** *nf* [machine] welder, welding machine.

soudoyer [13] [sudwaje] *vt* to bribe ■ **on a su par la suite que le gardien s'était fait ~** we discovered later that the guard had been bribed.

soudure [sudyr] *nf* **1.** [soudage - autogène] welding ; [- hétérogène] soldering **2.** [résultat - autogène] weld ; [- hétérogène] soldered joint **3.** [jonction] join ▶ **assurer** *ou* **faire la ~** to bridge the gap **4.** [soudage - autogène] weld ; [- hétérogène] solder.

souffert, e [sufɛr, ɛrt] *pp* ▷ **souffrir**.

soufflage [suflaʒ] *nm* **1.** [modelage - du verre] blowing ; [- des polymères] inflation **2.** MIN heave **3.** MÉTALL blow.

soufflant, e [suflɑ̃, ɑ̃t] *adj* **1.** [appareil] : **radiateur ~** fan heater **2.** *fam* [étonnant] staggering, amazing.

souffle [sufl] *nm* **1.** [air expiré - par une personne] blow ■ **elle dit oui dans un ~** she breathed her assent ▶ **dernier ~** *litt* last breath ■ **jusqu'à mon dernier ~** as long as I live and breathe, to my dying day

2. [respiration] breath ■ [rythme respiratoire] breathing ■ **avoir du ~** to have a lot of breath ■ **avoir le ~ court, manquer de ~** to be short-winded ■ **être à bout de ~, n'avoir plus de ~** [haletant] to be out of breath ■ **l'entreprise est à bout de ~** *fig* the company is on its last legs ■ **reprendre son ~** to get one's breath *ou* wind back ■ **retenir son ~** *pr* & *fig* to hold one's breath ▶ **trouver un deuxième** *ou* **second ~** *pr* to get *ou* to find one's second wind ; *fig* to get a new lease of life

3. [courant d'air] : **~ d'air** *ou* **de vent** breath of air

4. *litt* [force] breath, spirit

5. [d'une explosion] blast

6. AUDIO (thermal) noise ■ **~ du signal** modulation noise

7. MÉD : **~ au cœur** heart murmur.

soufflé, e [sufle] *adj* **1.** TECHNOL blown **2.** *fam* [étonné] amazed, staggered, dumbfounded ■ **j'étais soufflé!** I was speechless!, you could have knocked me down with a feather! **3.** CULIN soufflé *(modif)* **4.** [boursouflé - visage, main] puffy, swollen.

◆ **soufflé** *nm* CULIN soufflé ■ **~ au fromage** cheese soufflé.

souffler [3] [sufle] ◇ *vi* **1.** [expirer - personne] to breathe out ■ **soufflez dans le ballon** [Alcootest] blow into the bag ■ **ils m'ont fait ~ dans le ballon** they gave me a breath test ■ **~ dans un cor/trombone** to blow (into) a horn/trombone ▶ **~ sur le feu** *pr* to blow on the fire ; *fig* to add fuel to the flames

2. MÉTÉOR [vent] to blow ■ **le vent soufflera sur tout le pays** it'll be windy all over the country ■ **le vent soufflait en rafales** *ou* **bourrasques** there were gusts of wind, the wind was gusting ■ **quand le vent souffle de l'ouest** when the wind blows *ou* comes from the west

3. [respirer avec difficulté] to blow, to puff, to breathe hard ■ **suant et soufflant** puffing and blowing ■ **~ comme un bœuf** *ou* **un cachalot** *ou* **une forge** *ou* **une locomotive** *ou* **un phoque** *fam* to wheeze like a pair of old bagpipes

4. [retrouver sa respiration - personne] to get one's breath back ; [- cheval] to get its breath back ■ **laisser ~ son cheval** to blow *ou* to wind one's horse

5. [se reposer] to have a break ■ **au bureau, on n'a pas le temps de ~!** it's all go at the office!

6. ZOOL [cétacé] to blow.

◇ *vt* **1.** [bougie] to blow out *(sép)*

2. [exhaler] : **va ~ ta fumée de cigarette ailleurs** blow your smoke elsewhere ▶ **~ le chaud et le froid** to blow hot and cold

3. [murmurer - mot, réponse] to whisper ■ THÉÂTRE to prompt ■ **~ qqch à qqn** to whisper sthg to sb ■ **il a fallu qu'on lui souffle son rôle** she had to have a prompt ■ *(en usage absolu)* **on ne souffle pas!** no whispering!, don't whisper (the answer)! ▶ **ne pas ~ mot (de qqch)** not to breathe a word (about sthg)

4. [suggérer - idée, conseil] to whisper, to suggest

5. *fam* [époustoufler - suj: événement, personne] to take aback, to stagger, to knock out *(sép)* ■ **son insolence m'a vraiment soufflé!** I was quite staggered at her rudeness!

6. *fam* [dérober] : **~ qqch à qqn** to pinch sthg from sb ■ **je me suis fait ~ ma place** someone's pinched my seat

7. JEUX [pion] to huff

8. [suj: bombe, explosion] to blow up *(sép)*, to blast away *(sép)*

9. MÉTALL & TECHNOL to blow.

soufflerie [sufləri] *nf* **1.** AÉRON wind tunnel **2.** INDUST blower ■ [d'une forge] bellows **3.** MUS [d'un orgue] bellows.

soufflet [suflɛ] *nm* **1.** [instrument] (pair of) bellows ■ **~ de forge** (forge *ou* blacksmith's) bellows **2.** [d'un cartable] extensible pocket **3.** *litt* [gifle] slap ■ [affront] snub **4.** COUT (pocket) gusset **5.** PHOTO bellows **6.** RAIL (wagon) communication bellows.

souffleter [27] [suflәte] *vt litt* to slap in the face.

souffleur, euse [suflœr, øz] *nm, f* **1.** THÉÂTRE prompter **2.** TECHNOL : **~ de verre** glassblower.

◆ **souffleur** *nm* ZOOL blower dolphin.

◆ **souffleuse** *nf* *Québec* [chasse-neige] snowblower, snow thrower.

souffrance [sufrɑ̃s] *nf* **1.** [fait de souffrir] suffering **2.** [mal - physique] pain ; [- psychologique] pain, torment ■ **abréger les** *OU* **mettre fin aux ~s de qqn** to put an end to sb's suffering.
◆ **en souffrance** *loc adv* : **être** *OU* **rester en ~** to be held up ■ **dossiers en ~** files pending.

souffrant, e [sufrɑ̃, ɑ̃t] *adj* **1.** [malade] : **être ~** to be unwell **2.** [malheureux] suffering ■ **l'humanité ~e** the downtrodden masses.

souffre-douleur [sufrədulœr] *nm inv* scapegoat ■ **à l'école, c'était toujours lui le ~** at school, he was always the one who got bullied.

souffreteux, euse [sufrətø, øz] *adj* **1.** [malingre] sickly, puny *péj* ■ **un enfant ~** a sickly *OU* delicate child **2.** [maladif - air] sickly **3.** [rabougri - plante] stunted, scrubby.

souffrir [34] [sufrir] ◇ *vt* **1.** [endurer - épreuves] to endure, to suffer ■ **si tu avais souffert ce que j'ai souffert!** if you'd suffered as much as I have!, if you had gone through what I have! ■ **~ le martyre** to go through *OU* to suffer agonies ■ **son dos lui fait ~ le martyre** he has terrible trouble with his back
2. *litt* [tolérer] : **elle ne souffre pas d'être critiquée** *OU* **qu'on la critique** she can't stand *OU* take criticism
3. *litt* [admettre - suj: personne] to allow, to tolerate ; [- suj: règlement] to allow (for), to admit of ■ **le règlement de son dossier ne peut ~ aucun délai** the settlement of his case simply cannot be postponed.
◇ *vi* **1.** [avoir mal] to be in pain, to suffer ■ **tu souffres?** are you in pain?, does it hurt? ■ **où souffrez-vous?** where is the pain?, where does it hurt? ■ **elle a beaucoup souffert lors de son accouchement** she had a very painful delivery ■ **c'est une intervention bénigne, vous ne souffrirez pas** it's a very minor operation, you won't feel any pain ■ **~ en silence** to suffer in silence ■ **il est mort sans ~** he felt no pain when he died ■ **elle a cessé de ~** *euphém*, **elle ne souffrira plus** *euphém* she's out of pain (now) ■ **il faut ~ pour être belle!** *hum* one must suffer to be beautiful! ■ **faire ~** [faire mal] to cause pain to, to hurt ■ **mon dos me fait ~ ces temps-ci** my back's been hurting (me) lately
2. [avoir mal pour une raison] : **~ de** : **~ de la hanche** to have trouble with one's hip ■ **pour tous les gens qui souffrent du dos/du diabète** for all people with back problems/diabetes sufferers ■ **~ de la faim/soif** to suffer from hunger/thirst ■ **~ de la chaleur** [être très sensible à] to suffer in the heat ; [être atteint par] to suffer from the heat ■ **~ de** *fig* [pâtir de] : **sa renommée a souffert du scandale** his reputation suffered from the scandal ■ **dût ton amour-propre en ~** even though your pride may be hurt by it ■ *(en usage absolu)* **les récoltes n'ont pas trop souffert** the crops didn't suffer too much *OU* weren't too badly damaged ■ **c'est le sud du pays qui a le plus souffert** the southern part of the country was the worst hit
3. *fam* [peiner] to toil, to have a hard time (of it).
◆ **se souffrir** *vp (emploi réciproque) litt* : **ils ne peuvent pas se ~** they can't stand *OU* bear each other.

soufi [sufi] *nm* Sufi.

soufisme [sufism] *nm* Sufism.

soufre [sufr] ◇ *nm* **1.** CHIM sulphur ■ **~ octaédrique/prismatique** monoclinic/rhombic sulphur **2.** *loc* **sentir le ~** to be highly unorthodox.
◇ *adj inv* sulphur (yellow).

soufrer [3] [sufre] *vt* **1.** [allumettes] to sulphur **2.** AGRIC to (treat *OU* spray with) sulphur **3.** TEXT to sulphurate.

soufrière [sufrijɛr] *nf* sulphur mine.

souhait [swɛ] *nm* wish ■ **si je pouvais formuler un ~** if I had one wish ■ **tous nos ~s de bonheur** all our best wishes for your future happiness ■ **envoyer ses ~s de bonne année** to send New Year greetings ■ **à tes ~s!, à vos ~s!** bless you! *(after a sneeze)*.
◆ **à souhait** *loc adv litt* extremely well, perfectly ■ **rôti à ~** cooked to perfection *OU* a turn.
Voir module d'usage

souhaitable [swɛtabl] *adj* desirable ■ **ce n'est guère ~** this is not to be desired.

souhaiter [4] [swete] *vt* **1.** [espérer] to wish *OU* to hope for *(insép)* ■ **il ne reviendra plus – souhaitons-le** *OU* **c'est à ~!** he won't come back – let's hope not! ■ **ce n'est pas à ~!** it's not something we would wish for! ■ **~ la mort/la ruine/le bonheur de qqn** to wish sb dead/for sb's ruin/for sb's happiness ■ **je souhaiterais pouvoir t'aider** I wish I could *OU* I'd like to be able to help (you) ■ **~ que** to hope that ■ **souhaitons que tout aille bien** let's hope everything goes all right ■ **il est à ~ que...** it's to be hoped that... **2.** [formuler un vœu de] to wish ■ **nous vous souhaitons un joyeux Noël** with our best wishes for a happy Christmas ■ **~ sa fête/son anniversaire à qqn** to wish sb a happy saint's day/a happy birthday ■ **je te souhaite beaucoup de réussite/d'être heureux** I wish you every success/happiness ■ **souhaite-moi bonne chance!** wish me luck! ■ **je vous souhaite bonne nuit** I'll say good night to you ■ **je te souhaite bien du plaisir!** *fam*, **je t'en souhaite!** *iron* best of luck to you!
◆ **se souhaiter** *vp (emploi réciproque)* : **nous nous sommes souhaité la bonne année** we wished each other a happy New Year.

souiller [3] [suje] *vt litt* **1.** [maculer] to soil **2.** [polluer] to contaminate, to pollute, to taint **3.** [entacher - réputation] to ruin, to sully *litt*, to tarnish *litt* ; [- innocence] to defile *litt*, to taint *litt*.

souillon [sujɔ̃] *nmf* [gén] slob ■ [femme] slut.

souillure [sujyr] *nf* **1.** *litt* [tache] stain **2.** *litt* [flétrissure] blemish, taint ■ **la ~ du péché** the stain of sin.

souk [suk] *nm* **1.** [marché] souk **2.** *fam* [désordre] shambles *(sing)* ■ **c'est le ~ ici!** what a mess *OU* shambles here!

soul [sul] ◇ *adj inv* MUS soul *(modif)*.
◇ *nm* [jazz] hard bop.
◇ *nf* [pop] soul (music).

soûl, e [su, sul] *adj* **1.** [ivre] drunk ■ **~ comme une bourrique** *OU* **un cochon** *OU* **une grive** *OU* **un Polonais** *fam* (as) drunk as a lord *esp UK*, stewed to the gills *US* **2.** *fig* **~ de** [rassasié de] sated with ; [étourdi par] drunk *OU* intoxicated with *fig*.

LES SOUHAITS

I'd love *OU* **I'd so like you to meet them.** J'aimerais tellement que vous fassiez leur connaissance.

Wouldn't it be wonderful if we could all go? Ça ne serait pas formidable si nous pouvions tous y aller ?

I'd like nothing better than to talk to him. J'aimerais vraiment lui parler.

I'd give anything to be there now! Je donnerais n'importe quoi pour être là-bas !

I wish I were on a Greek island... J'aimerais tellement être sur une île grecque...

I wish it would stop raining. Si seulement il pouvait arrêter de pleuvoir !

I wish you could have seen her face! J'aurais voulu que tu voies sa tête !

I just wish this was all over. Je voudrais que tout ça soit terminé.

All I want is for you to tell the truth. Tout ce que je veux, c'est que tu dises la vérité.

If only he were here! Si seulement il était là !

If only she would accept! Si seulement elle acceptait !

◆ **soûl** *nm* : **tout son ~** to one's heart's content ▪ **en avoir tout son ~** to have one's fill ▪ **dormir tout son ~** to sleep as much as one wants.

soulagement [sulaʒmɑ̃] *nm* relief, solace *sout* ▪ **c'est un ~ de t'avoir ici** it helps *ou* it's a comfort to have you around ▪ **à mon grand ~, il partit enfin** I was greatly relieved when he left at last.

soulager [17] [sulaʒe] *vt* **1.** [personne - physiquement] to relieve, to bring relief to ▪ **cela devrait vous ~ de votre mal de tête** this should relieve *ou* help your headache ▪ **on l'a soulagée de son chéquier** *hum* she was relieved of her chequebook **2.** [personne - moralement] to relieve, to soothe ▪ **pleure, ça te soulagera** have a good cry, you'll feel better afterwards ▪ **ça me soulage de savoir qu'il est bien arrivé** it's a relief to know he got there safely ▪ **~ la conscience de qqn** to ease sb's conscience **3.** [diminuer - misère, souffrances] to relieve ; [- douleur] to relieve, to soothe **4.** [décharger] to relieve ▪ **mon collègue me soulage parfois d'une partie de mon travail** my colleague sometimes relieves me of part of my work **5.** CONSTR [étayer] to shore up *(sép)* **6.** NAUT [ancre] to weigh.
◆ **se soulager** ◇ *vp (emploi réfléchi)* [d'une charge de travail] to lessen the strain on o.s. ▪ **prends un collaborateur pour te ~** take somebody on to take some of the pressure of work off you.
◇ *vpi* **1.** [moralement] to get *ou* to find relief, to take comfort ▪ **il m'arrive de crier pour me ~** sometimes I shout to let *ou* to blow off steam **2.** *fam euphém* to relieve o.s.

soûlant, e [sulɑ̃, ɑ̃t] *adj fam* exhausting, harrassing ▪ **elle parle, elle parle, c'en est ~!** she goes on and on, it makes your head spin!

soûlard, e [sular, ard], **soûlaud, e** [sulo, od] *nm, f fam* boozer, drunkard ▪ **c'est une vieille ~e** she's an old soak.

soûler [3] [sule] *vt* **1.** *fam* [rendre ivre] : **~ qqn** to get sb drunk **2.** [étourdir] to make dizzy *ou* giddy ▪ **tu me soûles, avec tes questions!** you're making me dizzy with all these questions!
◆ **se soûler** *vpi* **1.** *fam* [s'enivrer] to get drunk, to booze **2.** [s'étourdir] : **se ~ de** to get intoxicated with *fig* ▪ **il se soûle de paroles** he talks so much that it goes to his head.

soûlerie [sulri] *nf fam* bender, drinking session.

soulèvement [sulɛvmɑ̃] *nm* **1.** [mouvement] : **déclenché par le ~ du clapet** triggered by the lifting of the valve **2.** [insurrection] uprising **3.** GÉOL : **~ de terrain** upheaval *ou* uplift (of the ground).

soulever [19] [sulve] *vt* **1.** [pour porter, élever - charge] to lift (up) ; [- couvercle, loquet] to lift ; [- capot] to lift, to open ; [- personne allongée] to raise (up) ; [- personne debout] to lift (up) ; [- voile] to lift ; [- chapeau] to raise ; [- voiture] to lift ; [- voiture sur cric] to jack up *(sép)* ; [- avec effort] to heave ▪ **de gros sanglots soulevaient sa poitrine** his chest was heaving with sobs ▪ **~ qqn/qqch de terre** to lift sb/sthg off the ground **2.** [remuer - poussière, sable] to raise ▪ **le vent soulevait les feuilles mortes** the wind was stirring up dead leaves **3.** [provoquer - protestations, tollé] to raise ; [- enthousiasme, émotion] to arouse ; [- difficulté] to bring up *(sép)*, to raise ▪ **son imitation souleva une tempête de rires** her impersonation caused gales of laughter **4.** [poser - question, objection] to raise, to bring up *(sép)* **5.** [pousser à se révolter - population] to stir up *(sép)* **6.** [retourner] : **~ le cœur : ça m'a soulevé le cœur** it turned my stomach, it made me sick **7.** △ [prendre - chose] to pinch ; [- mari, maîtresse] to steal.
◆ **se soulever** *vpi* **1.** [se redresser] to lift *ou* to raise o.s. up ▪ **il l'aida à se ~** he helped her to sit up **2.** [mer] to swell (up), to heave ▪ [poitrine] to heave **3.** [peuple] to rise up *(insép)*, to revolt.

soulier [sulje] *nm* **1.** [chaussure] shoe **2.** *fam loc* **être dans ses petits ~s** to feel (very) small.

souligner [3] [suliɲe] *vt* **1.** [mettre un trait sous] to underline **2.** [accentuer] to enhance, to emphasize ▪ **une robe qui souligne la taille** a dress which emphasizes *ou* sets off the waist **3.** [faire remarquer] to emphasize, to stress.

soûlographie [sulɔgrafi] *nf fam* [ivrognerie] drunkenness.

soûlot, ote [sulo, ɔt] *fam* = **soûlard, e**.

soumettre [84] [sumɛtr] *vt* **1.** [se rendre maître de - nation] to subjugate ; [- mutins] to take control of, to subdue, to bring to heel ; [- passion] to control, to tame **2.** [à une épreuve, à un règlement] : **~ qqn à** to subject sb to ▪ **~ qqch à un examen** to subject sthg to an examination **3.** [présenter - loi, suggestion, texte] to submit ▪ **je lui soumettrai votre demande** I'll refer your request to her ▪ **je voulais d'abord le ~ à votre approbation** I wanted to submit it for your approval first ▪ **le projet de loi sera ensuite soumis au Sénat** the bill will then be brought before the Senate *ou* be submitted to the Senate (for approval).
◆ **se soumettre** *vpi* to give in, to submit, to yield ▪ **se ~ à** [se plier à] to submit *ou* to subject o.s. to ; [s'en remettre à] to abide by ▪ **se ~ à la décision de qqn** to abide by sb's decision ▶ **il faudra se ~ ou se démettre!** *Gambetta allus* give in or go!

soumis, e [sumi, iz] *adj* submissive, obedient, dutiful.

soumission [sumisjɔ̃] *nf* **1.** [obéissance - à un pouvoir] submission, submitting ; [- à une autorité] acquiescence, acquiescing ▪ **faire acte de ~** to submit **2.** [asservissement] submissiveness ▪ **vivre dans la ~** to live a submissive life, to live one's life in a state of submission **3.** COMM tender ▪ **par (voie de) ~** by tender.

soumissionnaire [sumisjɔnɛr] *nmf* tenderer.

soumissionner [3] [sumisjɔne] *vt* to bid *ou* to tender for *(insép)*.

soumit *etc v* ▷ **soumettre**.

soupape [supap] *nf* **1.** AUTO & MÉCAN valve ▪ **~ d'admission/d'échappement** inlet/outlet valve ▪ **~ automatique** automatic control ▪ **~ de sécurité** *ou* **sûreté** *pr & fig* safety valve **2.** [bonde] plug **3.** ÉLECTR valve, tube **4.** MUS pallet.

soupçon [supsɔ̃] *nm* **1.** [suspicion] suspicion ▪ **éveiller les ~s** to arouse *ou* to excite suspicion ▪ **avoir des ~s sur qqn/qqch** to be suspicious of sb/sthg ▪ **j'ai eu des ~s dès le début** I suspected something from the beginning ▪ **être à l'abri** *ou* **au-dessus de tout ~** to be free from *ou* above all suspicion **2.** [idée, pressentiment] suspicion, inkling **3.** [petite quantité] : **un ~ de : un ~ de crème** a touch *ou* dash of cream ▪ **un ~ de maquillage** a hint *ou* touch of make-up ▪ **un ~ d'ironie** a touch *ou* hint of irony ▪ **un ~ de rhum** a dash *ou* a (tiny) drop of rum.

soupçonnable [supsɔnabl] *adj* open to suspicion.

soupçonner [3] [supsɔne] *vt* **1.** [suspecter] to suspect ▪ **~ qqn de meurtre/trahison** to suspect sb of murder/treason **2.** [pressentir - piège] to suspect ▪ **je ne lui aurais jamais soupçonné autant de talent** I would never have suspected *ou* thought that he was so talented ▪ **~ que** to have a feeling *ou* to suspect that **3.** [douter de] to doubt **4.** [imaginer] to imagine, to suspect.

soupçonneusement [supsɔnøzmɑ̃] *adv* suspiciously, with suspicion.

soupçonneux, euse [supsɔnø, øz] *adj* suspicious ▪ **il la regarda d'un air ~** he looked at her suspiciously.

soupe [sup] *nf* **1.** CULIN soup ▪ **~ aux choux/au crabe** cabbage/crab soup ▪ **~ au lait** *pr* bread and milk ▪ **c'est une ~ au lait, elle est (très) ~ au lait** *fig* she flies off the handle easily ▪ **il est rentré tard hier soir et a eu droit à la ~ à la grimace** he got home late last night, so now he's in the doghouse **2.** *fam* [repas] grub, nosh ▪ **~ populaire** soup kitchen ▪ **je suis bon pour la ~ populaire!** *hum* I might as well go and beg on the streets! ▪ **à la ~!** grub's up!, come and get it! **3.** *fam* [neige] slushy snow.

soupente [supɑ̃t] *nf* **1.** [dans un grenier] loft ▪ [sous un escalier] cupboard *ou* closet US *(under the stairs)* **2.** TECHNOL [barre de soutien] supporting bar.

souper[1] [supe] *nm* **1.** [dialecte: dîner] dinner, supper **2.** [après le spectacle] (late) supper.

souper[2] [3] [supe] *vi* **1.** [dialecte] *vieilli* [dîner] to have dinner ▪ **~ de** to dine on **2.** [après le spectacle] to have a late supper **3.** *fam loc* **en avoir soupé de** to be sick of *ou* fed up with.

soupeser [19] [supəze] *vt* **1.** [en soulevant] to feel the weight of, to weigh in one's hand *ou* hands **2.** [juger] to weigh up *(sép)*.

soupière [supjɛr] *nf* (soup) tureen.

soupir [supir] *nm* **1.** [expiration] sigh ■ **~ de soulagement** sigh of relief ■ **pousser des ~s** to sigh ▶ **dernier ~** *litt* last breath ■ **rendre le dernier ~** to breathe one's last **2.** MUS crotchet rest *UK*, quarter *ou* quarter-note rest *US*.
◆ **soupirs** *nmpl litt* [désirs] : **l'objet de mes ~s** the one I yearn for.

soupirail, aux [supiraj, o] *nm* [d'une cave] (cellar) ventilator ■ [d'une pièce] basement window.

soupirant [supirɑ̃] *nm* suitor.

soupiraux [supiro] *pl* ▷ **soupirail**.

soupirer [3] [supire] ◇ *vi* **1.** [pousser un soupir] to sigh ■ **~ d'aise** to sigh with contentment **2.** *litt* [être amoureux] to sigh, to yearn.
◇ *vt* [dire] to sigh.
◆ **soupirer après** *v+prép litt* to long *ou* to sigh *ou* to yearn for.

souple [supl] *adj* **1.** [lame] flexible, pliable, supple ■ [plastique] non-rigid **2.** [malléable] : **argile ~** plastic clay **3.** [agile - athlète, danseur, corps] supple ; [- démarche] fluid, flowing **4.** [doux - cuir, peau, brosse à dents] soft ■ **gel fixation ~** light-hold hair gel ■ **voiture dotée d'une suspension ~** car with smooth suspension **5.** [aménageable] flexible, adaptable ■ **la réglementation/l'horaire est ~** the rules/hours are flexible **6.** [qui sait s'adapter] flexible, adaptable **7.** [docile] docile, obedient ■ **être ~ comme un gant** to be very docile **8.** [écriture, style] flowing **9.** AÉRON non-rigid.

souplement [supləmɑ̃] *adv* smoothly ■ **le chat retomba ~ sur ses pattes** the cat landed smoothly on its feet.

souplesse [suplɛs] *nf* **1.** [d'une personne, d'un félin, d'un corps] suppleness ■ [d'une démarche] suppleness, springiness **2.** [douceur - d'un cuir, d'un tissu] softness ; [- de la peau] smoothness **3.** [malléabilité - d'une matière] flexibility, pliability ■ **~ d'esprit** [agilité] nimble-mindeness ; [adaptabilité] versatility ■ *péj* [servilité] servility **4.** [d'un horaire, d'une méthode] flexibility, adaptability.
◆ **en souplesse** *loc adv* smoothly ■ **retomber en ~ sur ses jambes** [après une chute] to land nimbly on one's feet ; [en gymnastique] to make a smooth landing.

souquer [3] [suke] ◇ *vt* **1.** [amarrage] to pull taut **2.** [bateau] to push to its limits.
◇ *vi* to pull at the oars, to stretch out ■ **~ ferme** to pull hard at the oars.

sourate [surat] = **surate**.

source [surs] *nf* **1.** [point d'eau] spring ▶ **~ chaude** hot spring **2.** [origine] spring, source ■ **où la Seine prend-elle sa ~?** where is the source of the Seine?, where does the Seine originate? ■ **remonter jusqu'à la ~** [d'un fleuve] to go upriver until one finds the source ; [d'une habitude, d'un problème] to go back to the root ■ **à la ~** [au commencement] at the source, in the beginning ■ **retenir les impôts à la ~** to deduct tax at source, to operate a pay-as-you-earn system *UK*
3. [cause] source ■ **une ~ de revenus** a source of income ■ **cette maison n'a été qu'une ~ d'ennuis** this house has been nothing but trouble ■ **être ~ de** to give rise to ■ **cette formulation peut être ~ de malentendus** the way it's worded could give rise to misinterpretations
4. PRESSE : **tenir ses renseignements de bonne ~** *ou* **de ~ sûre** *ou* **de ~ bien informée** to have information on good authority ■ **nous savons** *ou* **tenons de ~ sûre que...** we have it on good authority that..., we are reliably informed that... ■ **de ~ officielle/officieuse, on apprend que...** official/unofficial sources reveal that... ■ **quelles sont vos ~s?** what sources did you use?
5. ÉLECTR : **~ de courant** power supply
6. INFORM source
7. LING *(comme adj)* source *(modif)*
8. NUCL : **~ radioactive** radioactive source
9. PHYS : **~ lumineuse** *ou* **de lumière** light source ■ **~ de chaleur/d'énergie** source of heat/energy, heat/energy source
10. PÉTR oil deposit.

sourcier, ère [sursje, ɛr] *nm, f* dowser, water-diviner.

sourcil [sursi] *nm* eyebrow ■ **il a des ~s bien fournis** he's beetle-browed.

sourcilier, ère [sursilje, ɛr] *adj* superciliary.

sourciller [3] [sursije] *vi* to frown ■ **sans ~** without batting an eyelid *ou* turning a hair.

sourcilleux, euse [sursijø, øz] *adj litt* [pointilleux] pernickety, finicky.

sourd, e [sur, surd] ◇ *adj* **1.** [personne] deaf ■ **être ~ de naissance** to be born deaf ■ **~ de l'oreille gauche** deaf in the left ear ■ **arrête de crier, je ne suis pas ~!** stop shouting, I'm not deaf *ou* I can hear (you)! ▶ **faire la ~e oreille** to pretend not to hear ■ **être ~ comme un pot** *fam* to be as deaf as a post **2.** [indifférent] : **le gouvernement est resté ~ à leurs revendications** the government turned a deaf ear to their demands **3.** [atténué - son, voix] muffled, muted **4.** [vague - douleur] dull ; [- sentiment] muted, subdued ■ **j'éprouvais une ~e inquiétude** I felt vaguely worried **5.** [clandestin] hidden, secret **6.** LING unvoiced, voiceless.
◇ *nm, f* deaf person ■ **les ~s** the deaf ■ **c'est comme si on parlait à un ~** it's like talking to a brick wall ▶ **crier** *ou* **hurler comme un ~** to scream *ou* to shout at the top of one's voice ■ **frapper** *ou* **taper comme un ~** to bang with all one's might.
◆ **sourde** *nf* LING unvoiced *ou* voiceless consonant.

sourdement [surdəmɑ̃] *adv litt* **1.** [sans bruit] dully, with a muffled noise **2.** [secrètement] silently.

sourdine [surdin] *nf* MUS [d'une trompette, d'un violon] mute ■ [d'un piano] soft pedal ■ **mettre la ~** *fig* to tone it down.
◆ **en sourdine** ◇ *loc adj* muted.
◇ *loc adv* **1.** MUS [jouer] quietly, softly ■ **mets-la en ~!** *fam fig* shut up! **2.** [en secret] quietly, on the quiet.

sourdingue△ [surdɛ̃g] ◇ *adj* clotheared.
◇ *nmf* clothears.

sourd-muet, sourde-muette [surmɥɛ, surdmɥɛt] (*mpl* **sourds-muets**, *fpl* **sourdes-muettes**) ◇ *adj* deaf and dumb.
◇ *nm, f* deaf-mute, deaf-and-dumb person.

sourdre [73] [surdr] *vi litt* **1.** [liquide] to rise (up) **2.** [idée, sentiment] to well up ■ **le mécontentement commençait à ~ dans la population** discontent was beginning to make itself felt among the population.

souri [suri] *pp* ▷ **sourire**.

souriant, e [surjɑ̃, ɑ̃t] *adj* **1.** [regard, visage] smiling, beaming ■ [personne] cheerful **2.** *sout* [agréable - paysage] pleasant, welcoming ; [- pensée] agreeable ■ **un avenir ~** a bright future.

souriceau, x [suriso] *nm* baby mouse.

souricière [surisjɛr] *nf* **1.** [ratière] mousetrap **2.** [piège] trap ■ **se jeter dans la ~** to fall into a trap.

sourire[1] [surir] *nm* smile ■ **elle esquissa un ~** she smiled faintly ■ **il entra, le ~ aux lèvres** he came in with a smile on his lips *ou* face ■ **avec un grand** *ou* **large ~** beaming, with a broad smile ■ **faire un ~ à qqn** to smile at sb ■ **fais-moi un petit ~** give me a smile! ■ **elle était tout ~** she was wreathed in *ou* all smiles ■ **avoir le ~** to have a smile on one's face ■ **il a toujours le ~!** he always looks cheerful! ■ **il a pris la nouvelle avec le ~** he took the news cheerfully ■ **il faut savoir garder le ~** you have to learn to keep smiling.

sourire[2] [95] [surir] *vi* to smile ■ **souriez!** [pour une photo] smile! ■ **la remarque peut faire ~** this remark may bring a smile to your face *ou* make you smile ■ **~ à qqn** to smile at sb, to give sb a smile.
◆ **sourire à** *v+prép* **1.** [être favorable à] to smile on ■ **la fortune lui sourit enfin** fortune is smiling on him at last ■ **la chance ne te sourira pas toujours!** you won't always be (so) lucky! **2.** [plaire à - suj: idée, perspective] to appeal to.

◆ **sourire de** *v+prép* [se moquer de] to smile *ou* to laugh at ■ **il souriait de mon entêtement** my stubbornness made him smile.

souris [suri] ◇ *nf* **1.** ZOOL mouse ■ **~ blanche** white mouse ■ **j'aurais aimé être une petite ~!** I'd like to have been a fly on the wall! ■ **on entendrait trotter une ~** you could hear a pin drop **2.** △ [femme] bird, chick **3.** CULIN [de gigot] knuckle-joint **4.** INFORM mouse.
◇ *adj inv* mousy, mouse-coloured.
◆ **souris d'hôtel** *nf* (female) hotel thief.

sournois, e [surnwa, az] ◇ *adj* **1.** [personne, regard] cunning, shifty, sly **2.** [attaque, procédé] underhand **3.** [douleur] dull, gnawing.
◇ *nm, f* sly person.

sournoisement [surnwazmɑ̃] *adv* slyly ■ **regarder ~ qqn** to look shiftily at sb.

sournoiserie [surnwazri] *nf* **1.** [caractère] shiftiness, slyness, underhand manner **2.** [acte] sly piece of work ■ [parole] sly remark.

sous [su] *prép* **1.** [dans l'espace] under, underneath, beneath ■ **être ~ la douche** to be in the *ou* having a shower ■ **se promener ~ la pluie** to walk in the rain ■ **un paysage ~ la neige** a snow-covered landscape ■ **nager ~ l'eau** to swim underwater ■ **~ terre** underground, below ground ■ **assis ~ le parasol** sitting under *ou* underneath *ou* beneath the parasol ■ **enlève ça de ~ la table** *fam* get it out from under the table ■ **~ les tropiques** in the Tropics ■ **ça s'est passé ~ nos yeux** it took place before our very eyes
2. *fig* [derrière] behind, under, beneath ■ **~ des dehors taciturnes** behind a stern exterior ■ **~ son air calme...** beneath his calm appearance...
3. [à l'époque de] : **~ Louis XV** during the reign of *ou* under Louis XV ■ **~ sa présidence/son ministère** under his presidency/ministry ■ **~ la Commune** during *ou* at the time of the Paris Commune
4. [dans un délai de] within ■ **~ huitaine/quinzaine** within a week/fortnight
5. [marquant un rapport de dépendance] under ■ **~ ses ordres** under his command ■ **il est placé ~ ma responsabilité** I'm in charge of him ■ **~ caution** on bail
6. MÉD : **être ~ anesthésie** to be under anaesthetic ■ **être ~ antibiotiques/perfusion** to be on antibiotics/a drip
7. [marquant la manière] : **emballé ~ vide** vacuum-packed ■ **~ verre** under glass ■ **~ pli scellé** in a sealed envelope ■ **elle a acheté le billet ~ un faux nom** she bought the ticket under an assumed name ■ **elle se présente aux élections ~ l'étiquette libérale** she's running as a candidate on the liberal ticket ■ **vu ~ cet angle** seen from this angle ■ **vu ~ cet éclairage nouveau** considered in this new light ■ **parfait ~ tous rapports** perfect in every respect
8. [avec une valeur causale] under ■ **~ la torture/canonnade** under torture/fire ■ **~ le coup du choc...** with the shock... ■ **~ le coup de l'émotion** in the grip of the emotion.

sous-alimentation [suzalimɑ̃tasjɔ̃] *nf* malnutrition, undernourishment.

sous-alimenté, e [suzalimɑ̃te] *adj* undernourished, underfed ■ **des enfants ~s** children suffering from malnutrition.

sous-alimenter [3] [suzalimɑ̃te] *vt* to undernourish.

sous-bois [subwa] *nm inv* undergrowth, underwood ■ **se promener dans les ~** to walk in the undergrowth.

sous-brigadier [subrigadje] *nm* deputy sergeant.

sous-catégorie [sukategɔri] *nf* subcategory.

sous-chef [suʃɛf] *nm* **1.** [gén] second-in-command **2.** [dans un restaurant] sous-chef, underchef **3.** RAIL : **~ de gare** assistant station master.

sous-comité [sukɔmite] *nm* subcommittee.

sous-commission [sukɔmisjɔ̃] *nf* subcommittee.

sous-consommation [sukɔ̃sɔmasjɔ̃] *nf* underconsumption, underconsuming *(U)*.

sous-continent [sukɔ̃tinɑ̃] *nm* subcontinent ■ **~ indien** Indian subcontinent.

sous-couche [sukuʃ] *nf* [de peinture, de vernis] undercoat.

souscripteur [suskriptœr] *nm* FIN subscriber.

souscription [suskripsjɔ̃] *nf* **1.** [engagement] subscription, subscribing *(U)* **2.** [somme] subscription ■ **lancer** *ou* **ouvrir une ~** to start a fund **3.** [signature] signing *(U)* **4.** BOURSE & ÉCON application, subscription.
◆ **en souscription** *loc adv* : **publier une revue en ~** to publish a journal on a subscription basis ■ **uniquement en ~** available to subscribers only.

souscrire [99] [suskrir] *vt* **1.** DR [signer - acte] to sign, to put one's signature to, to subscribe *sout* ; [- billet, chèque] to draw, to sign **2.** [abonnement, police d'assurance] to take out *(insép)*.
◆ **souscrire à** *v+prép* **1.** [approuver] to approve, to subscribe to, to go along with ■ **je souscris entièrement à ce qui vient d'être dit** I go along totally with what's just been said **2.** [suj: lecteur] to take out a subscription to **3.** BOURSE & ÉCON [emprunt] to subscribe to ■ *(en usage absolu)* **pour combien souscrivez-vous?** how much will you subscribe?

sous-cutané, e [sukytane] *adj* subcutaneous.

sous-développé, e [sudevlɔpe] *adj* underdeveloped.

sous-développement [sudevlɔpmɑ̃] *nm* underdevelopment.

sous-directeur, trice [sudirɛktœr, tris] *nm, f* assistant manager (*f* manageress).

sous-emploi [suzɑ̃plwa] *nm* underemployment.

sous-employer [13] [suzɑ̃plwaje] *vt* [travailleur] to underemploy ■ [appareil] to underuse.

sous-ensemble [suzɑ̃sɑ̃bl] *nm* subset.

sous-entendre [73] [suzɑ̃tɑ̃dr] *vt* to imply ■ **que sous-entendez-vous par là?** what are you hinting *ou* driving at?, what are you trying to imply? ■ **sous-entendu, je m'en moque!** meaning I don't care!

sous-entendu [suzɑ̃tɑ̃dy] *nm* innuendo, hint, insinuation ■ **en fixant sur moi un regard lourd de ~s** giving me a meaningful look.

sous-équipé, e [suzekipe] *adj* underequipped.

sous-équipement [suzekipmɑ̃] *nm* underequipment.

sous-espèce [suzɛspɛs] *nf* subspecies.

sous-estimation [suzɛstimasjɔ̃] *nf* **1.** [jugement] underestimation **2.** FIN [d'un revenu] underestimation, underassessment ■ [d'un bien] undervaluation.

sous-estimer [3] [suzɛstime] *vt* **1.** [une qualité, un bien] to underestimate, to underrate **2.** FIN to undervalue.

sous-évaluation [suzevalɥasjɔ̃] *nf* FIN undervaluation.

sous-évaluer [7] [suzevalɥe] *vt* FIN to undervalue.

sous-exploitation [suzɛksplwatasjɔ̃] *nf* underexploitation, underexploiting *(U)*, underuse.

sous-exploiter [3] [suzɛksplwate] *vt* to underexploit.

sous-exposer [3] [suzɛkspoze] *vt* to underexpose.

sous-exposition [suzɛkspozisjɔ̃] *nf* underexposure.

sous-fifre [sufifr] *nm* underling, minion.

sous-industrialisé, e [suzɛ̃dystrijalize] *adj* underindustrialized.

sous-jacent, e [suʒasɑ̃, ɑ̃t] *adj* **1.** [caché] underlying ■ **l'urbanisation et les problèmes ~s** urbanization and its underlying problems **2.** GÉOL subjacent.

Sous-le-Vent [suləvɑ̃] *npr* : **les îles ~** [en Polynésie] the Leeward Islands, the Western Society Islands ; [aux Antilles] the Netherlands (and Venezuelan) Antilles *voir aussi* **île**.

sous-lieutenant [suljøtnɑ̃] *nm* [dans l'armée de terre] second lieutenant ▪ [dans l'aviation] pilot officer *UK*, second lieutenant *US* ▪ [dans la marine] sublieutenant *UK*, lieutenant junior grade *US*.

sous-locataire [sulɔkatɛr] *nmf* subtenant.

sous-location [sulɔkasjɔ̃] *nf* **1.** [action] subletting **2.** [bail] subtenancy.

sous-louer [6] [sulwe] *vt* to sublet.

sous-main [sumɛ̃] *nm inv* **1.** [buvard] desk blotter **2.** [carton, plastique] pad.
◆ **en sous-main** *loc adv* secretly ▪ **il y a eu des tractations en ~** some underhand deals were struck.

sous-marin, e [sumarɛ̃, in] *adj* [câble, plante] submarine, underwater ▪ [navigation] submarine ▪ [courant] submarine, undersea ▪ [photographie] underwater, undersea.
◆ **sous-marin** *nm* **1.** NAUT submarine **2.** *fam* [espion] mole **3.** *Québec* [sandwich] long sandwich, sub *US*.

sous-marque [sumark] *nf* sub-brand.

sous-médicalisé, e [sumedikalize] *adj* with insufficient medical facilities.

sous-ministre [suministr] *nm Québec* undersecretary (of state).

sous-multiple [sumyltipl] *nm* submultiple.

sous-munitions [sumynisjɔ̃] *nfpl* MIL submunition.

sous-nappe [sunap] *nf* undercloth.

sous-nutrition [sunytrisjɔ̃] *nf* malnutrition.

sous-œuvre [suzœvr] *nm* : **reprendre un bâtiment en ~** to underpin a building ▪ **reprise en ~** underpinning.

sous-officier [suzɔfisje] *nm* non-commissioned officer.

sous-ordre [suzɔrdr] *nm* **1.** ZOOL suborder **2.** [subordonné] subordinate, underling, minion.
◆ **en sous-ordre** *loc adj* [opposant, créancier] subsidiary.

sous-payer [11] [supeje] *vt* to underpay.

sous-peuplé, e [supœple] *adj* underpopulated.

sous-peuplement [supœpləmɑ̃] *nm* underpopulation.

sous-préfecture [suprefɛktyr] *nf* subprefecture.

sous-préfet [suprefɛ] *nm* subprefect.

sous-préfète [suprefɛt] *nf* **1.** [fonctionnaire] (female) subprefect **2.** [épouse] subprefect's wife.

sous-production [suprɔdyksjɔ̃] *nf* underproduction.

sous-produit [suprɔdɥi] *nm* **1.** INDUST by-product **2.** [ersatz] poor imitation, (inferior) derivative.

sous-programme [suprɔgram] *nm* subroutine ▪ **~ ouvert** open subroutine.

sous-prolétaire [suprɔletɛr] *nmf* member of the urban underclass.

sous-prolétariat [suprɔletarja] *nm* urban underclass.

sous-pull [supyl] *nm* (light-weight) sweater.

sous-répertoire (*pl* **sous-répertoires**) [surepɛrtwar] *nm* INFORM sub-directory.

sous-secrétaire [susəkretɛr] *nm* : **~ (d'État)** Under-Secretary (of State).

sous-secrétariat [susəkretarja] *nm* **1.** [bureau] Under-Secretary's office **2.** [poste] Under-Secretaryship.

sous-secteur [susɛktœr] *nm* subsection.

soussigné, e [susiɲe] <> *adj* undersigned ▪ **je ~ Robert Brand, déclare avoir pris connaissance de l'article 4** I, the undersigned Robert Brand, declare that I have read clause 4.
<> *nm, f* : **le ~/les ~s déclarent que...** the undersigned declares/declare that...

sous-sol [susɔl] *nm* **1.** GÉOL subsoil **2.** [d'une maison] cellar ▪ [d'un magasin] basement, lower ground floor ▪ **voir notre grand choix d'affaires au ~** visit our bargain basement!

sous-tasse [sutas] *nf* saucer.

sous-tendre [73] [sutɑ̃dr] *vt* **1.** GÉOM to subtend **2.** [être à la base de] to underlie, to underpin.

sous-tension [sutɑ̃sjɔ̃] *nf* undervoltage.

sous-titrage [sutitraʒ] *nm* subtitling ▪ **le ~ est excellent** the subtitles are very good.

sous-titre [sutitr] *nm* **1.** PRESSE subtitle, subheading, subhead **2.** CINÉ subtitle.

sous-titré, e [sutitre] *adj* subtitled, with subtitles.

sous-titrer [3] [sutitre] *vt* **1.** [article de journal] to subtitle, to subhead ▪ [livre] to subtitle **2.** [film] to subtitle.

soustracteur [sustraktœr] *nm* subtracter.

soustractif, ive [sustraktif, iv] *adj* subtractive.

soustraction [sustraksjɔ̃] *nf* **1.** MATH subtraction ▪ **il ne sait pas encore faire les ~s** he can't subtract yet **2.** DR [vol] removal, removing *(U)*, purloining *(U)* *sout* ▪ **~ de documents** abstraction of documents.

soustraire [112] [sustrɛr] *vt* **1.** MATH to subtract, to take away *(sép)* ▪ **~ 10 de 30** to take 10 away from 30 **2.** *sout* [enlever] : **~ qqn/qqch à** to take sb/sthg away from ▪ **~ qqn à la justice** to shield sb from justice, to protect sb from the law ▪ **~ qqn/qqch aux regards indiscrets** to hide sb/sthg from prying eyes **3.** [subtiliser] to remove.
◆ **se soustraire à** *vp+prép sout* **se ~ à l'impôt/une obligation/un devoir** to evade tax/an obligation/a duty ▪ **se ~ à la justice** to escape the law.

sous-traitance [sutrɛtɑ̃s] *nf* subcontracting ▪ **donner un travail en ~** to subcontract a job ▪ **je fais ce travail en ~** I'm on this job as subcontractor.

sous-traitant, e [sutrɛtɑ̃, ɑ̃t] *nm, f* subcontractor ▪ **donner un travail à un ~** to farm out a piece of work.

sous-traiter [4] [sutrete] *vt* : **~ un travail** [entrepreneur principal] to subcontract a job, to contract a job out ; [sous-entrepreneur] to contract into *ou* to subcontract a job.

soustrayait *etc v* ▷ **soustraire**.

sous-utiliser [3] [suzytilize] *vt* to underuse, to underutilize.

sous-verre [suvɛr] *nm inv* glass mount.

sous-vêtement [suvɛtmɑ̃] *nm* piece of underwear, undergarment ▪ **en ~s** in one's underwear *ou* underclothes.

soutane [sutan] *nf* cassock ▪ **prendre la ~** to enter the Church, to take (Holy) Orders.

soute [sut] *nf* hold ▪ **~ à bagages** luggage hold ▪ **~ à charbon** coal hole *UK*, coal bunker ▪ **~ à mazout** oil tank.
◆ **soutes** *nfpl* [combustible] fuel oil.

soutenable [sutnabl] *adj* **1.** [défendable] defensible, tenable **2.** [supportable] bearable.

soutenance [sutnɑ̃s] *nf* : **~ (de thèse)** *oral examination for thesis* viva *UK*.

soutènement [sutɛnmɑ̃] *nm* **1.** CONSTR support **2.** MIN timbering.
◆ **de soutènement** *loc adj* support *(modif)*, supporting.

souteneur [sutnœr] *nm* [proxénète] pimp.

soutenir [40] [sutnir] *vt* **1.** [maintenir - suj: pilier, poutre] to hold up *(sép)*, to support ; [- suj: attelle, gaine, soutien-gorge] to support ▪ **un médicament pour ~ le cœur** a drug to sustain the heart *ou* to keep the heart going **2.** [réconforter] to support, to give (moral) support to ▪ **sa présence m'a beaucoup soutenue dans cette épreuve** his presence was a great comfort to me in this ordeal **3.** [être partisan de - candidature, cause, politique *etc*] to support, to back (up), to stand by *(insép)* ▪ **tu soutiens toujours ta fille contre moi!** you always stand up for *ou* you're always siding with your daughter against me! ▪ **~ une**

équipe to be a fan of *ou* to support a team **4.** [faire valoir - droits] to uphold, to defend ; [- argument, théorie] to uphold, to support **5.** [affirmer] to assert, to claim ▪ **je pense que nous sommes libres mais elle soutient le contraire** I think that we are free but she claims (that) the opposite is true ▪ **il soutient que tu mens** he keeps saying that you're a liar ▪ **elle m'a soutenu mordicus qu'il était venu ici** *fam* she swore blind *ou* she insisted that he'd been here **6.** [résister à - attaque] to withstand ; [- regard] to bear, to support ▪ **~ la comparaison avec** to stand *ou* to bear comparison with ▪ **~ un siège** MIL to last out *ou* to withstand a siege **7.** [prolonger - attention, discussion, suspense *etc*] to keep up *(sép)*, to sustain ; [- réputation] to maintain, to keep up ▪ **il est difficile de ~ une conversation lorsque les enfants sont présents** it's difficult to keep a conversation going *ou* to keep up a conversation when the children are around **8.** MUS [note] to sustain, to hold **9.** UNIV : **~ sa thèse** to defend one's thesis, to take one's viva *UK*.

◆ **se soutenir** ◇ *vp (emploi réciproque)* to stand by each other, to stick together.

◇ *vpi* **1.** [se tenir] to hold o.s. up, to support o.s. ▪ **le vieillard n'arrivait plus à se ~ sur ses jambes** the old man's legs could no longer support *ou* carry him ▪ **elle se soutenait avec peine** she could hardly stay upright **2.** [se prolonger - attention, intérêt, suspense] to be kept up *ou* maintained.

soutenu, e [sutny] *adj* **1.** [sans faiblesse - couleur] intense, deep ; [- note de musique] sustained ; [- attention, effort] unfailing, sustained, unremitting ; [- rythme] steady, sustained **2.** LING formal ▪ **en langue ~e** in formal speech.

souterrain, e [sutɛrɛ̃, ɛn] *adj* **1.** [sous la terre] underground, subterranean ▪ **câble ~** underground cable ▪ **des eaux ~es** ground water **2.** [dissimulé] hidden, secret **3.** MIN deep, underground.

◆ **souterrain** *nm* **1.** [galerie] underground *ou* subterranean passage **2.** [en ville] subway *UK*, underpass *US*.

soutien [sutjɛ̃] *nm* **1.** [soubassement] supporting structure, support **2.** [aide] support ▪ **apporter son ~ à qqn** to support sb, to back sb up ▪ **~ financier** financial backing ▪ **mesures de ~ à l'économie** measures to bolster the economy **3.** [défenseur] supporter ▪ **c'est l'un des plus sûrs ~s du gouvernement** he's one of the mainstays of the government **4.** DR : **~ de famille** (main) wage earner ▪ **être ~ de famille** to have dependents *(and receive special treatment as regards French National Service)* **5.** ÉCON : **~ des prix** price support **6.** MIL support.

soutien-gorge [sutjɛ̃gɔrʒ] (*pl* **soutiens-gorge**) *nm* bra, brassiere *sout* ▪ **~ d'allaitement** nursing bra.

soutient *etc v* ▷ **soutenir**.

soutint *etc v* ▷ **soutenir**.

soutirer [3] [sutire] *vt* **1.** [vin] to draw off *(sép)*, to decant **2.** [extorquer] : **~ qqch à qqn** to get sthg from *ou* out of sb ▪ **~ une promesse à qqn** to extract a promise from sb ▪ **~ des renseignements à qqn** to get *ou* to squeeze some information out of sb ▪ **il s'est fait ~ pas mal d'argent par ses petits enfants** his grandchildren managed to squeeze a lot of money out of him.

souvenance [suvnɑ̃s] *nf litt* **à ma ~** as far as I can recall *ou* recollect.

souvenir¹ [suvnir] *nm* **1.** [impression] memory, recollection ▪ **votre opération ne sera bientôt plus qu'un mauvais ~** your operation will soon be nothing but a bad memory ▪ **je garde un excellent ~ de ce voyage** I have excellent memories of that trip ▪ **n'avoir aucun ~ de** to have no remembrance *ou* recollection of ▪ **elle n'en a qu'un vague ~** she has only a dim *ou* vague recollection of it ▪ **cela n'éveille donc aucun ~ en toi?** doesn't it remind you of anything? ▪ **mes ~s d'enfance** my childhood memories ▪ **au ~ de ces événements, il se mit à pleurer** when he thought back to the events, he started to cry ▪ **avoir le ~ de** to have a memory of, to remember **2.** [dans des formules de politesse] : **avec mon affectueux ~** yours (ever) ▪ **mes meilleurs ~s à votre sœur** (my) kindest regards to your sister ▪ **meilleurs ~s de Rome** greetings from Rome **3.** [objet - donné par qqn] keepsake ; [- rappelant une occasion] memento ; [- pour touristes] souvenir **4.** *(comme adj; avec ou sans trait d'union)* souvenir *(modif)* ▪ **poser pour la photo-~** to pose for a commemorative photograph.

◆ **en souvenir de** *loc prép* [afin de se remémorer] : **prenez ce livre en ~ de cet été/de moi** take this book as a souvenir of this summer/as something to remember me by.

souvenir² [40] [suvnir] ◆ **se souvenir de** *vp+prép* [date, événement] to remember, to recollect, to recall ▪ [personne, lieu] to remember ▪ **on se souviendra d'elle comme d'une grande essayiste** she'll be remembered as a great essay-writer ▪ **je ne me souviens jamais de son adresse** I keep forgetting *ou* I can never remember his address ▪ **je ne me souviens pas de l'avoir lu** I can't remember *ou* I don't recall *ou* I don't recollect having read it ▪ **je m'en souviendrai, de ses week-ends reposants à la campagne!** *fam iron* I won't forget his restful weekends in the countryside in a hurry! ▪ *(en usage absolu)* **mais si, souviens-toi, elle était toujours au premier rang** come on, you must remember her, she was always sitting in the front row.

◆ **il me souvient, il lui souvient** *etc v impers litt* **il me souvient un détail/de l'avoir aperçu** I remember a detail/having seen him.

souvent [suvɑ̃] *adv* often ▪ **on se voit de moins en moins ~** we see less and less of each other ▪ **il ne vient pas ~ nous voir** he doesn't often come and see us, he seldom comes to see us ▪ **le plus ~ c'est elle qui conduit** most often *ou* more often than not *ou* usually, she's the one who does the driving ➔ **plus ~ qu'à son tour** far too often.

souvenu, e [suvny] *pp* ▷ **souvenir**.

souverain, e [suvrɛ̃, ɛn] ◇ *adj* **1.** [efficace - remède] excellent, sovereign **2.** POLIT [pouvoir, peuple] sovereign **3.** [suprême] supreme ▪ **avoir un ~ mépris pour qqch** to utterly despise sthg ▪ **avec une ~e méconnaissance des faits** supremely ignorant of the facts **4.** PHILOS : **le ~ bien** the sovereign good **5.** RELIG : **le ~ pontife** the Pope, the Supreme Pontiff.

◇ *nm, f* monarch, sovereign ▪ **notre ~e** our Sovereign.

◆ **souverain** *nm* [monnaie] sovereign (coin).

souverainement [suvrɛnmɑ̃] *adv* **1.** [suprêmement] utterly, totally, intensely ▪ **être ~ indifférent à** to be utterly *ou* supremely indifferent to **2.** [sans appel] with sovereign *ou* final power.

souveraineté [suvrɛnte] *nf* sovereignty.

souvient, souvint *etc v* ▷ **souvenir**.

soviet [sɔvjɛt] *nm* [assemblée] soviet ▪ **le Soviet Suprême** the Supreme Soviet.

soviétique [sɔvjetik] *adj* Soviet.

◆ **Soviétique** *nmf* Soviet.

soviétisation [sɔvjetizasjɔ̃] *nf* sovietization, sovietizing *(U)*.

soviétiser [3] [sɔvjetize] *vt* to sovietize.

soviétologue [sɔvjetɔlɔg] *nmf* Sovietologist.

sovkhoze [sɔvkoz] *nm* sovkhoz.

soyeux, euse [swajø, øz] *adj* silky.

◆ **soyeux** *nm* [dialecte] **1.** [fabricant] silk manufacturer **2.** [négociant] silk merchant.

soyons *v* ▷ **être**.

SPA (*abr de* **Société protectrice des animaux**) *npr f society for the protection of animals*, ≃ RSPCA *UK*, ≃ SPCA *US*.

spacieusement [spasjøzmɑ̃] *adv* : **ils sont très ~ installés** they've got a very roomy *ou* spacious place.

spacieux, euse [spasjø, øz] *adj* spacious, roomy.

spadassin [spadasɛ̃] *nm* **1.** *arch* swordsman **2.** *litt* [tueur] (hired) killer ▪ **un mafioso et ses ~s** a Mafia boss and his hitmen.

spaghetti [spagɛti] (*pl inv ou pl* **spaghettis**) *nm* : **des ~, des ~s** spaghetti ▪ **un ~** a strand of spaghetti.

sparadrap [sparadra] *nm* (sticking) plaster *UK*, band aid, Band aid® *US*.

Spartacus [spartakys] *npr* Spartacus.

spartakisme [spartakism] *nm* Spartacism.

Sparte [spart] *npr* Sparta.

spartiate [sparsjat] *adj* **1.** [de Sparte] Spartan *pr* **2.** [austère] Spartan *fig*, ascetic.
◆ **Spartiate** *nmf* Spartan.
◆ **spartiates** *nfpl* [sandales] (Roman) sandals.
◆ **à la spartiate** *loc adv* austerely ▪ **élever ses enfants à la ~** to give one's children a Spartan upbringing.

spasme [spasm] *nm* spasm.

spasmodique [spasmɔdik] *adj* spasmodic.

spasmophile [spasmɔfil] ◇ *adj* suffering from spasmophilia.
◇ *nmf person suffering from spasmophilia.*

spasmophilie [spasmɔfili] *nf* spasmophilia.

spath [spat] *nm* spar ▪ **~ fluor** fluor spar, fluorite ▪ **~ pesant** barytes, barite.

spatial, e, aux [spasjal, o] *adj* **1.** [de l'espace] spatial **2.** ASTRONAUT, AUDIO & MIL space *(modif)*.
◆ **spatial** *nm* space industry.

spationaute [spasjɔnot] *nmf* spaceman (*f* spacewoman).

spationef [spasjɔnɛf] *nm* spaceship.

spatio-temporel, elle [spasjɔtɑ̃pɔrɛl] (*mpl* **spatio-temporels**, *fpl* **spatio-temporelles**) *adj* spatiotemporal.

spatule [spatyl] *nf* **1.** CULIN spatula **2.** [d'un ski] tip **3.** ART (pallet) knife **4.** CONSTR jointer **5.** ZOOL [poisson] spoonbill, paddle-fish ▪ [oiseau] spoonbill.

speaker, speakerine [spikœr, spikrin] *nm, f* announcer, link man (*f* woman) *UK*.
◆ **speaker** *nm* POLIT [en Grande-Bretagne, aux États-Unis] : **le ~** the Speaker.

spécial, e, aux [spesjal, o] *adj* **1.** [d'une catégorie particulière] special, particular, specific, distinctive **2.** [exceptionnel - gén] special, extraordinary, exceptional ; [- numéro, édition] special ▪ **bénéficier d'une faveur ~e** to be especially favoured **3.** [bizarre] peculiar, odd ▪ **ils ont une mentalité ~e** they're a bit eccentric *ou* strange ▪ **toi, t'es ~!** you're a bit weird! **4.** ÉCON : **commerce ~** import-export trade (balance) **5.** SPORT [slalom] special.
◆ **spécial, aux** *nm* *fam* SPORT (special) slalom.
◆ **spéciale** *nf* **1.** ÉDUC *second year of a two year entrance course for a grande école* **2.** [huître] *type of cultivated oyster* **3.** SPORT (short) off-road rally.

spécialement [spesjalmɑ̃] *adv* **1.** [à une fin particulière] specially, especially ▪ **je me suis fait faire un costume ~ pour le mariage** I had a suit made specially for the wedding ▪ **parlez-nous de l'Italie et (plus) ~ de Florence** tell us about Italy, especially Florence **2.** [très] particularly, specially ▪ **ça n'a pas été ~ drôle** it wasn't particularly amusing ▪ **pas ~ : tu veux lui parler? – pas ~** do you want to talk to her? – not particularly.

spécialisation [spesjalizasjɔ̃] *nf* specialization, specializing.

spécialisé, e [spesjalize] *adj* [gén] specialized ▪ INFORM dedicated, special-purpose ▪ **des chercheurs ~s dans l'intelligence artificielle** researchers specializing in artificial intelligence.

spécialiser [3] [spesjalize] *vt* **1.** [étudiant, travailleur] to turn *ou* to make into a specialist ▪ **nous spécialisons des biochimistes** we train specialists in biochemistry **2.** [usine, activité] to make more specialized.
◆ **se spécialiser** *vpi* to specialize ▪ **14 ans, c'est trop tôt pour se ~** ÉDUC 14 is too young to start specializing ▪ **se ~ dans la dermatologie** to specialize in dermatology.

spécialiste [spesjalist] *nmf* **1.** [gén - MÉD] specialist **2.** *fam* [habitué] : **c'est un ~ des gaffes** he's an expert at putting his foot in it.

spécialité [spesjalite] *nf* **1.** CULIN speciality ▪ **~s de la région** local specialities *ou* products ▪ **fais-nous une de tes ~s** cook us one of your special recipes *ou* dishes **2.** PHARM : **~ pharmaceutique** branded pharmaceutical *ou* (patented) pharmaceutical product **3.** SC & UNIV field, area, specialism ▪ **~ médicale** area of medicine ▪ **le meilleur dans** *ou* **de sa ~** the best in his field **4.** [manie, habitude] : **le vin, c'est sa ~** he's the wine expert.

spécieux, euse [spesjø, øz] *adj* specious, fallacious.

spécification [spesifikasjɔ̃] *nf* specification ▪ **sans ~ de** without specifying, without mention of.

spécificité [spesifisite] *nf* specificity.

spécifier [9] [spesifje] *vt* to specify, to state, to indicate ▪ **~ les conditions d'un prêt** to specify *ou* to indicate the conditions of a loan ▪ **je lui ai bien spécifié l'heure du rendez-vous** I made sure I told him the time of the appointment.

spécifique [spesifik] *adj* specific.

spécifiquement [spesifikmɑ̃] *adv* specifically.

spécimen [spesimɛn] *nm* **1.** [élément typique] specimen, example **2.** IMPR specimen ▪ **~ gratuit** [d'un livre] presentation copy **3.** *fam* [individu bizarre] queer fish *UK*, odd duck *US*.

spectacle [spɛktakl] *nm* **1.** CINÉ, DANSE, MUS & THÉÂTRE show ▪ **aller au ~** to go to (see) a show ▪ **faire un ~** to do a show ▪ **monter un ~** to put on a show ▪ **consulter la page (des) ~s** to check the entertainment *ou* entertainments page ▪ **le ~** show business ➊ **le ~ continue** the show must go on **2.** [ce qui se présente au regard] sight, scene ▪ **le ~ qui s'offrait à nous** the sight before our eyes ▪ **elle présentait un bien triste/curieux ~** she looked a rather sorry/odd sight ▪ **au ~ de** at the sight of.
◆ **à grand spectacle** *loc adj* grandiose ▪ **film à grand ~** blockbuster.
◆ **en spectacle** *loc adv* : **se donner** *ou* **s'offrir en ~** to make an exhibition *ou* a spectacle of o.s.

spectaculaire [spɛktakylɛr] *adj* **1.** [exceptionnel, frappant] spectacular, impressive ▪ **de manière ~** dramatically **2.** [notable] spectacular.

spectateur, trice [spɛktatœr, tris] *nm, f* **1.** CINÉ, DANSE, MUS & THÉÂTRE spectator, member of the audience ▪ **les ~s** the audience **2.** [d'un accident, d'un événement] spectator, witness **3.** [simple observateur] onlooker ▪ **il a participé à nos réunions en ~** he just came to our meetings as an onlooker.

spectral, e, aux [spɛktral, o] *adj* **1.** *litt* [fantomatique] ghostly, ghostlike, spectral *litt* **2.** PHYS spectral ▪ **analyse ~e** spectrum *ou* spectroscopic analysis.

spectre [spɛktr] *nm* **1.** [fantôme] ghost, phantom, spectre **2.** *fam* [personne maigre] ghostly figure, apparition **3.** [représentation effrayante] : **le ~ de** the spectre of **4.** CHIM, ÉLECTR & PHYS spectrum **5.** PHARM [d'un antibiotique] spectrum.

spectrographe [spɛktrɔgraf] *nm* spectrograph.

spectromètre [spɛktrɔmɛtr] *nm* spectrometer.

spectroscope [spɛktrɔskɔp] *nm* spectroscope.

spéculaire [spekylɛr] ◇ *adj* specular ▪ **image ~** mirror image.
◇ *nf* BOT Venus's looking glass.

spéculateur, trice [spekylatœr, tris] *nm, f* speculator ▪ **~ à la baisse** bear ▪ **~ à la hausse** bull ▪ **~ sur devises** currency speculator.

spéculatif, ive [spekylatif, iv] *adj* speculative.

spéculation [spekylasjɔ̃] *nf* speculation.

spéculer [3] [spekyle] *vi* **1.** BOURSE to speculate ▪ **~ en Bourse** to speculate on the stock exchange ▪ **~ sur l'or** to speculate in gold **2.** *litt* [méditer] to speculate.
◆ **spéculer sur** *v+prép* [compter sur] to count *ou* to bank *ou* to rely on *(insép)* ▪ **le gouvernement spécule sur une hausse de la natalité** the government is banking *ou* relying on a rise in the birthrate.

spéculoos [spekylos] *nm* *Belgique* *ginger biscuit.*

spéculum [spekylɔm] *nm* MÉD speculum.

speech [spitʃ] (*pl* **speechs** *ou pl* **speeches**) *nm fam* (short) speech ▪ **il nous a refait son ~ sur l'importance des bonnes manières** he made the same old speech about the importance of good manners.

speed [spid] *adj fam* hyper ▪ **il est complètement ~** he's really hyper.

speedé, e [spide] *adj fam* hyper.

speeder *vi fam* to hurry, to rush ▪ **elle est toujours en train de ~** she's always in a mad rush ▪ **il faut ~** we've got to get a move on *UK ou* to move it *US*.

spéléologie [speleɔlɔʒi] *nf* [science et étude] speleology ▪ [sport] potholing *UK*, spelunking *US*.

spéléologique [speleɔlɔʒik] *adj* speleologic.

spéléologue [speleɔlɔg] *nmf* [savant, chercheur] speleologist ▪ [sportif] potholer *UK*, spelunker *US*.

spencer [spɛnsœr] *nm* [vêtement] spencer.

spermatocyte [spɛrmatɔsit] *nm* spermatocyte.

spermatogenèse [spɛrmatɔʒenɛz] *nf* spermatogenesis.

spermatozoïde [spɛrmatɔzɔid] *nm* spermatozoid.

sperme [spɛrm] *nm* sperm.

spermicide [spɛrmisid] <> *adj* spermicidal.
<> *nm* spermicide, spermatocide.

spermophile [spɛrmɔfil] *nm* spermophile.

sphère [sfɛr] *nf* **1.** ASTRON & GÉOM sphere **2.** [zone] field, area, sphere ▪ **~ d'activité** field *ou* sphere of activity ▪ **~ d'influence** sphere of influence ▪ **les hautes ~s** the higher realms *litt*.

sphérique [sferik] *adj* spheric, spherical.

sphincter [sfɛ̃ktɛr] *nm* sphincter.

sphinx [sfɛ̃ks] *nm* **1.** ART & MYTHOL sphinx ▪ **le Sphinx** the Sphinx **2.** [personne énigmatique] sphinx ▪ **son impassibilité de ~ me déroutait** his sphinx-like inscrutability disconcerted me **3.** ENTOM hawkmoth, sphinx (moth).

spi [spi] = **spinnaker**.

spina-bifida [spinabifida] *nm inv* spina bifida.

spinal, e, aux [spinal, o] *adj* spinal.

spinnaker [spinekər] *nm* spinnaker.

spiral, e, aux [spiral, o] *adj* spiral, helical.
◆ **spiral, aux** *nm* [ressort] spiral, spring ▪ [d'une montre] hairspring.
◆ **spirale** *nf* **1.** [circonvolution] spiral, helix ▪ **des ~es de fumée** coils of smoke **2.** [hausse rapide] spiral.
◆ **à spirale** *loc adj* [cahier] spiral, spiralbound.
◆ **en spirale** <> *loc adj* [escalier, descente] spiral.
<> *loc adv* in a spiral, spirally ▪ **s'élever/retomber en ~e** to spiral upwards/downwards.

spire [spir] *nf* [d'un coquillage] whorl ▪ [d'une spirale, d'une hélice] turn, spire.

spirite [spirit] <> *adj* spiritualistic.
<> *nmf* spiritualist.

spiritisme [spiritism] *nm* spiritualism, spiritism.

spiritualiser [3] [spiritɥalize] *vt* to give a spiritual dimension to, to spiritualize.

spiritualisme [spiritɥalism] *nm* spiritualism.

spiritualiste [spiritɥalist] <> *adj* spiritualistic.
<> *nmf* spiritualist.

spiritualité [spiritɥalite] *nf* spirituality.

spirituel, elle [spiritɥɛl] *adj* **1.** PHILOS spiritual **2.** [non physique] spiritual ▪ **père ~** spiritual father **3.** [plein d'esprit] witty ▪ **comme c'est ~!** how clever! **4.** RELIG spiritual ▪ **chef ~** spiritual head ▪ **pouvoir ~** spiritual power ▪ **concert ~** concert of sacred music.
◆ **spirituel** *nm* RELIG spiritual.

spirituellement [spiritɥɛlmɑ̃] *adv* **1.** PHILOS & RELIG spiritually **2.** [brillamment] wittily.

spiritueux, euse [spiritɥø, øz] *adj* [boisson] spirituous *spéc*, strong.
◆ **spiritueux** *nm* spirit ▪ **vins et ~** wines and spirits.

spiroïdal, e, aux [spirɔidal, o] *adj* spiroid.

spiromètre [spirɔmɛtr] *nm* spirometer.

Spirou [spiru] *npr* PRESSE *popular weekly cartoon magazine*.

spitant, e [spitɑ̃, ɑ̃t] *adj Belgique* **1.** [personne] lively **2.** [gazeux] : **eau ~e** carbonated water.

spleen [splin] *nm litt* spleen *arch*, melancholy.

splendeur [splɑ̃dœr] *nf* **1.** [somptuosité] magnificence, splendour **2.** [merveille] : **son collier est une ~** her necklace is splendid *ou* magnificent ▪ **les ~s des églises baroques** the magnificence of baroque churches **3.** [prospérité, gloire] grandeur, splendour ▪ **Rome, au temps de sa ~** Rome at her apogee *litt* ▪ **voilà le macho dans toute sa ~** *hum* that's macho man in all his glory.

splendide [splɑ̃did] *adj* **1.** [somptueux - décor, fête, étoffe] splendid, magnificent **2.** [beau] magnificent, wonderful, splendid ▪ **elle avait une mine ~** she was blooming **3.** [rayonnant - soleil] radiant **4.** *litt* [glorieux] splendid.

splendidement [splɑ̃didmɑ̃] *adv* splendidly, magnificently.

spoliateur, trice [spɔljatœr, tris] <> *adj litt* spoliatory, despoiling.
<> *nm, f sout* spoliator *litt*, despoiler *litt*.

spoliation [spɔljasjɔ̃] *nf sout* spoliation *litt*, despoilment *litt*.

spolier [9] [spɔlje] *vt sout* to spoliate *litt*, to despoil *litt* ▪ **spoliés de leurs droits/possessions** stripped of their rights/possessions.

spondée [spɔ̃de] *nm* spondee.

spongieux, euse [spɔ̃ʒjø, øz] *adj* **1.** ANAT spongy **2.** [sol, matière] spongy, sponge-like.

sponsor [spɔ̃sɔr] *nm* (commercial) sponsor.

sponsoring [spɔ̃sɔriŋ], **sponsorat** [spɔ̃sɔra] *nm* (commercial) sponsorship.

sponsoriser [3] [spɔ̃sɔrize] *vt* to sponsor (commercially).

spontané, e [spɔ̃tane] *adj* spontaneous.

spontanéité [spɔ̃taneite] *nf* spontaneity, spontaneousness.

spontanément [spɔ̃tanemɑ̃] *adv* spontaneously ▪ **elle a avoué ~** she owned up of her own accord.

sporadique [spɔradik] *adj* [attaque, effort] sporadic, occasional ▪ [symptôme, crise] sporadic, isolated ▪ [averse] scattered.

sporadiquement [spɔradikmɑ̃] *adv* sporadically.

spore [spɔr] *nf* spore.

sport [spɔr] <> *adj inv* **1.** [vêtement pratique, de détente] casual **2.** [fair-play] sporting.
<> *nm* **1.** [ensemble d'activités, exercice physique] sport ▪ [activité de compétition] (competitive) sport ▪ **faire du ~** to do sport ▪ **un peu de ~ te ferait du bien** some physical exercise would do you good ➔ **~s aquatiques** water sports ▪ **~ de combat** combat sport ▪ **~ de contact** contact sport ▪ **~ équestre** equestrian sport, equestrianism ▪ **~ individuel** individual sport ▪ **~s d'équipe** team sports ▪ **~s d'hiver** winter sports ▪ **aller aux ~s d'hiver** to go skiing, to go on a winter sports holiday *UK ou* vacation *US* ▪ **~s nautiques** water sports ▪ **le journal des ~s** TV the sports news ▪ **la page des ~s** the sports page **2.** *fam loc* **c'est du ~** it's no picnic ▪ **il va y avoir du ~!** the sparks are going to fly! ▪ **faire qqch pour le ~** to do sthg for the fun *ou* the hell of it.
◆ **de sport** *loc adj* [terrain, vêtement] sports *(modif)*.

sportif, ive [spɔrtif, iv] <> *adj* **1.** [association, club, magazine, reportage] sports *(modif)* ▪ **reporter ~** sports reporter, sportscaster **2.** [événement, exploit] sporting **3.** [personne] sporty ▪ **elle est très sportive** she does a lot of sport ▪ **je ne suis pas**

très ~ I'm not very sporty ■ **avoir une allure sportive** to look athletic **4.** [loyal - public] sporting, fair ; [- attitude, geste] sporting, sportsmanlike ■ **avoir l'esprit ~** to show sportsmanship.
◇ *nm, f* sportsman (*f* sportswoman).

sportivement [spɔrtivmɑ̃] *adv* sportingly ■ **très ~, il l'a aidé à se relever** he helped him up, which was very sporting of him.

sportivité [spɔrtivite] *nf* [d'une personne] sportsmanship ■ **le match a manqué de ~** it wasn't a very sporting match.

spot [spɔt] *nm* **1.** [projecteur, petite lampe] spotlight **2.** PHYS light spot **3.** ÉLECTRON spot **4.** [publicité] : **~ (publicitaire)** commercial.

SPOT, Spot [spɔt] (*abr de* **satellite pour l'observation de la Terre**) *npr m* earth observation satellite.

Spoutnik [sputnik] *npr m* Sputnik.

spray [sprɛ] *nm* spray ■ **parfum en ~** spray *ou* spray-on perfume.

sprint [sprint] *nm* SPORT [course] sprint (race) ■ [pointe de vitesse - gén] spurt ; [- en fin de parcours] final spurt *ou* sprint ■ **piquer un ~** to put on a spurt, to sprint.

sprinter[1] [sprintœr] *nm* sprinter.

sprinter[2] [3] [sprinte] *vi* to sprint ■ [en fin de parcours] to put on a burst of speed.

squale [skwal] *nm* shark.

squame [skwam] *nm* MÉD scale, squama *spéc.*

square [skwar] *nm* **1.** [jardin] (small) public garden *ou* gardens **2.** [place] square ■ **il habite ~ Blériot** he lives in Blériot Square.

squash [skwaʃ] *nm* squash ■ **jouer au ~** to play squash.

squat [skwat] *nm* [habitation] squat.

squatter[1] [skwatœr] *nm* squatter.

squatter[2] [skwate], **squattériser** [3] [skwaterize] *vt* [bâtiment] to squat in (*inSép*).

squelette [skəlɛt] *nm* **1.** ANAT skeleton ■ **c'est un ~ ambulant** he's nothing but skin and bone, he's a walking skeleton **2.** [d'un discours] skeleton, broad outline **3.** CHIM skeleton **4.** CONSTR & NAUT carcass, skeleton.

squelettique [skəletik] *adj* **1.** [animal, enfant] skeleton-like, skeletal ■ [plante] stunted ■ **elle a des jambes ~s** she's got legs like matchsticks **2.** [troupes] decimated ■ [équipe] skeleton (*modif*) **3.** ANAT skeletal.

Sri Lanka [srilɑ̃ka] *npr m* : **le ~** Sri Lanka ■ **au ~** in Sri Lanka.

sri lankais, e [srilɑ̃kɛ, ɛz] *adj* Sri Lankan.
◆ **Sri Lankais, e** *nm, f* Sri Lankan.

SS ◇ **1.** (*abr écrite de* **Sécurité sociale**) SS, ≃ DSS *UK*, ≃ SSA *US* **2.** (*abr écrite de* **Sa Sainteté**) HH.
◇ *npr f* (*abr de* **SchutzStaffel**) SS.
◇ *nm* (*abr de* **SchutzStaffel**) ■ **un ~** a member of the SS.

S/S (*abr écrite de* **steamship**) S/S.

S-S-E (*abr écrite de* **sud-sud-est**) SSE.

S-S-O (*abr écrite de* **sud-sud-ouest**) SSW.

SSR (*abr de* **Société suisse de Radiodiffusion et de Télévision**) *npr f French-speaking Swiss broadcasting company.*

St (*abr écrite de* **saint**) St, St.

stabilisant, e [stabilizɑ̃, ɑ̃t] *adj* stabilizing.
◆ **stabilisant** *nm* stabilizing agent, stabilizer.

stabilisateur, trice [stabilizatœr, tris] *adj* stabilizing.
◆ **stabilisateur** *nm* **1.** [de vélo] stabilizer **2.** AÉRON [horizontal] horizontal stabilizer *US*, tail plane ■ [vertical] vertical stabilizer *US*, fin **3.** AUTO antiroll *ou* torsion bar **4.** CHIM stabilizer.

stabilisation [stabilizasjɔ̃] *nf* **1.** AÉRON & ASTRONAUT stabilization, stabilizing (*U*) **2.** CHIM stabilization **3.** ÉCON supporting (*U*).

stabiliser [3] [stabilize] *vt* **1.** [échafaudage - donner un équilibre à] to stabilize ; [- maintenir en place] to hold steady **2.** [consolider - situation] to stabilize, to normalize **3.** [personne] : **son mariage va le ~** marriage will make him settle down **4.** [monnaie, devise, prix] to stabilize **5.** [malade, maladie] to stabilize.
◆ **se stabiliser** *vpi* **1.** [situation] to stabilize ■ [objet] to steady ■ [athlète] to regain one's balance ■ **la situation militaire semble se ~** the military situation seems to be stabilizing **2.** [personne] to settle down.

stabilité [stabilite] *nf* **1.** [d'un véhicule, d'un échafaudage, d'une monnaie, d'un marché] stability, steadiness **2.** [d'un caractère] stability, steadiness **3.** CHIM, MÉTÉOR & PHYS stability **4.** POLIT : **~ gouvernementale** (governmental) stability.

stable [stabl] *adj* **1.** [qui ne bouge pas - position, structure] steady, stable ■ **la table n'est pas très ~** the table's a bit rocky **2.** [constant - personne, marché, emploi] stable, steady **3.** CHIM & PHYS stable.

stade [stad] *nm* **1.** SPORT stadium **2.** [étape, phase] stage ■ **j'en suis arrivé au ~ où...** I've reached the stage where... **3.** ANTIQ stadium **4.** PSYCHOL stage ■ **le ~ oral** the oral stage.

stadier, ière [stadje, ɛr] *nm, f* steward (*at sports stadium*).

staff [staf] *nm* **1.** CONSTR staff **2.** [personnel] staff.

stage [staʒ] *nm* **1.** COMM work placement ■ [sur le temps de travail] in-service training ■ **un ~ de trois mois** a three-month training period ■ **faire un ~** [cours] to go on a training course ; [expérience professionnelle] to go on a work placement ■ **faire un ~ de traitement de texte** to do a word-processing course ■ **~ en entreprise** work experience *ou* placement ■ **faire un ~ en entreprise** to do an internship in a company ■ **~ de formation** training course ■ **~ de recyclage** retraining period ■ **~ d'insertion à la vie professionnelle** training scheme for young unemployed people **2.** LOISIRS : **faire un ~ de plongée** [cours] to have scuba diving lessons ; [vacances] to go on a scuba diving holiday *UK ou* vacation *US*.

stagflation [stagflasjɔ̃] *nf* stagflation.

stagiaire [staʒjɛr] ◇ *adj* [officier] trainee (*avant n*) ■ [avocat] pupil ■ [journaliste] cub ■ **un instituteur ~** a student teacher.
◇ *nmf* [gén] trainee ■ **un ~ en comptabilité** a trainee accountant.

stagnant, e [stagnɑ̃, ɑ̃t] *adj* **1.** [eau] stagnant **2.** [affaires] sluggish.

stagnation [stagnasjɔ̃] *nf* stagnation, stagnating.

stagner [3] [stagne] *vi* **1.** [liquide] to stagnate **2.** [économie, affaires] to stagnate, to be sluggish **3.** [personne] to stagnate, to get into a rut ■ **~ dans son ignorance** to be bogged down in one's own ignorance.

stakhanovisme [stakanɔvism] *nm* Stakhanovism.

stakhanoviste [stakanɔvist] *adj* & *nmf* Stakhanovite.

stalactite [stalaktit] *nf* stalactite.

stalag [stalag] *nm* stalag.

stalagmite [stalagmit] *nf* stalagmite.

Staline [stalin] *npr* Stalin.

stalinien, enne [stalinjɛ̃, ɛn] *adj* & *nm, f* Stalinist.

stalinisme [stalinism] *nm* Stalinism.

stalle [stal] *nf* [de cheval, d'église] stall.

stance [stɑ̃s] *nf* LITTÉR stanza.
◆ **stances** *nfpl lyrical poem composed of stanzas.*

stand [stɑ̃d] *nm* **1.** [de foire] stall, stand **2.** JEUX & MIL : **~ (de tir)** (shooting) range **3.** SPORT : **~ (de ravitaillement)** pit.

standard [stɑ̃dar] ◇ *adj* **1.** [normalisé - modèle, pièce, taille] standard (*modif*) **2.** [non original - discours, goûts] commonplace, unoriginal, standard **3.** LING standard.
◇ *nm* **1.** COMM & INDUST standard **2.** ÉCON : **~ de vie** living standard **3.** TÉLÉCOM switchboard **4.** MUS (jazz) standard.

standardisation [stɑ̃dardizasjɔ̃] *nf* standardization, standardizing.

standardiser [3] [stɑ̃dardize] *vt* [normaliser, uniformiser] to standardize.

standardiste [stɑ̃dardist] *nmf* (switchboard) operator.

stand-by [stɑ̃dbaj] ◇ *adj inv* **1.** AÉRON [billet, passager, siège] standby *(modif)* **2.** FIN standby *(modif)* ■ **crédit ~** standby credit.
◇ *nmf* standby.

standing [stɑ̃diŋ] *nm* **1.** [d'une personne - position sociale] social status *OU* standing ; [- réputation] (good) reputation, standing **2.** [confort] : **appartement (de) grand ~** luxury flat.

staphylocoque [stafilɔkɔk] *nm* staphylococcus ■ **~ doré** staphylococcus aureus.

star [star] *nf* **1.** CINÉ (film) star ■ MUS & THÉÂTRE star ■ **en une semaine, elle était devenue une ~** within one week, she'd risen to stardom **2.** [du monde politique, sportif] star **3.** [favorite] number one.

starlette [starlɛt] *nf* starlet.

star-system [starsistɛm] (*pl* **star-systems**) *nm* CINÉ, MUS & THÉÂTRE star system.

starter [startɛr] *nm* **1.** AUTO choke ■ **mettre le ~** to pull the choke out **2.** SPORT starter.

starting-block [startiŋblɔk] (*pl* **starting-blocks**) *nm* starting block.

station [stasjɔ̃] *nf* **1.** TRANSP : **~ d'autobus** bus stop ■ **~ de métro** underground *UK OU* subway *US* station ■ **~ de taxis** taxi rank *UK OU* stand *US* **2.** [centre] : **~ d'épuration** sewerage plant ■ **~ de lavage** carwash ■ **~ météorologique** weather station **3.** RADIO & TV station ■ **~ d'émission** broadcasting station ■ **~ périphérique** private radio station ■ **~ de télévision** television station **4.** [lieu de séjour] resort ■ **~ balnéaire** sea *OU* seaside resort ■ **~ de sports d'hiver** ski resort ■ **~ thermale** (thermal) spa **5.** INFORM : **~ de travail** workstation **6.** [position] posture ■ **~ verticale** upright position ■ **la ~ debout est déconseillée** standing is not advisable **7.** ASTRON stationary point **8.** ASTRONAUT : **~ orbitale** orbital station ■ **~ spatiale** space station.

station-aval [stasjɔ̃aval] (*pl* **stations-aval**) *nf* ASTRONAUT down-range station.

stationnaire [stasjɔnɛr] *adj* **1.** MATH & SC stationary **2.** MÉD [état] stable ■ ASTRON : **théorie de l'état** *OU* **de l'Univers ~** steady-state theory **3.** PHYS [phénomène] stable ■ [onde] stationary, standing ■ [état] stationary.

stationnement [stasjɔnmɑ̃] *nm* **1.** [arrêt] parking ■ **~ bilatéral** parking on both sides of the road ■ **~ en double file** double-parking ■ **~ unilatéral** parking on one side (only) ■ **~ payant** parking fee payable ■ **'~ interdit'** 'no parking' ■ **'~ gênant'** 'restricted parking' **2.** *Québec* car park.
◆ **en stationnement** *loc adj* **1.** [véhicule] parked **2.** MIL stationed.

stationner [3] [stasjɔne] *vi* **1.** [véhicule] to be parked **2.** MIL : **les troupes stationnées en Allemagne** troops stationed in Germany **3.** [rester sur place - personne] to stay, to remain ■ **'ne pas ~ devant la sortie'** 'keep exit clear'.

station-service [stasjɔ̃sɛrvis] (*pl* **stations-service**) *nf* petrol station *UK*, gas station *(U)*.

statique [statik] ◇ *adj* **1.** [immobile] static ■ **tu es trop ~ dans cette scène** you don't move around enough during the scene **2.** [inchangé] static, unimaginative **3.** ÉLECTR static.
◇ *nf* statics *(U)*.

statisticien, enne [statistisjɛ̃, ɛn] *nm, f* statistician.

statistique [statistik] ◇ *adj* statistical.
◇ *nf* **1.** [étude] statistics *(U)* **2.** [donnée] statistic, figure ■ **des ~s** statistics, a set of figures.

statistiquement [statistikmɑ̃] *adv* statistically.

statuaire [statɥɛr] ◇ *adj* statuary.
◇ *nf* statuary.

statue [staty] *nf* **1.** ART statue ■ **~ équestre** equestrian statue ■ **~ en pied** *OU* **pédestre** standing *OU* pedestrian statue ■ **droit** *OU* **raide comme une ~** stiff as a poker **2.** *fig* ▶ **~ de sel** pillar of salt.

statuer [7] [statɥe] *vt* to rule ■ **le tribunal a statué qu'il y avait eu faute** the court ruled that misconduct had taken place.
◆ **statuer sur** *v+prép* : **~ sur un litige** to rule on a lawsuit ■ **la cour n'a pas statué sur le fond** the court pronounced no judgement *OU* gave no ruling on the merits of the case.

statuette [statɥɛt] *nf* statuette.

statufier [9] [statyfje] *vt* **1.** [représenter en statue] to erect a statue of *OU* to **2.** [faire un éloge excessif de] to lionize **3.** *litt* [pétrifier] to petrify ■ **statufié par la peur** transfixed with fear, petrified.

statu quo [statykwo] *nm inv* [état actuel des choses] status quo ■ **maintenir le ~** to maintain the status quo.

stature [statyr] *nf* **1.** [carrure] stature **2.** [envergure] stature, calibre.

statut [staty] *nm* DR & SOCIOL status ■ **mon ~ de femme mariée** my status as a married woman ■ **~ social** social status.
◆ **statuts** *nmpl* [règlements] statutes, ≃ Articles (and Memorandum) of Association.

statutaire [statytɛr] *adj* **1.** [conforme aux statuts] statutory **2.** [désigné par les statuts - gérant] registered.

statutairement [statytɛrmɑ̃] *adv* statutorily.

Stavisky [staviski] *npr m* : **l'affaire ~** the Stavisky case.

Ste (*abr écrite de* **sainte**) St, St.

Sté (*abr écrite de* **société**) Co.

steak [stɛk] *nm* steak ■ **un ~ haché** a beefburger *UK*, a hamburger *US* ■ **~ au poivre** pepper steak ■ **~ tartare** steak tartare.

steeple(-chase) [stip(ə)l(tʃɛz)] (*pl* **steeple-chases**) *nm* steeplechase.

stèle [stɛl] *nf* stele.

stellaire [stelɛr] ◇ *adj* **1.** ASTRON stellar **2.** ANAT [ganglion] stellate.
◇ *nf* BOT stitchwort.

stem(m) [stɛm] *nm* SPORT stem (turn).

stencil [stɛnsil] *nm* stencil.

sténo [steno] ◇ *nmf* = **sténographe**.
◇ *nf* = **sténographie**.

sténodactylo [stenɔdaktilo] ◇ *nmf* [personne] shorthand typist.
◇ *nf* [activité] shorthand typing.

sténodactylographie [stenɔdaktilɔgrafi] *nf* shorthand typing.

sténographe [stenɔgraf] *nmf* stenographer, shorthand note-taker.

sténographie [stenɔgrafi] *nf* shorthand.

sténographier [9] [stenɔgrafje] *vt* to take down in shorthand ■ **notes sténographiées** shorthand notes, notes in shorthand.

sténographique [stenɔgrafik] *adj* shorthand *(modif)*.

sténotype [stenɔtip] *nf* Stenotype®.

sténotyper [3] [stenɔtipe] *vt* to take down on a Stenotype®.

sténotypie [stenɔtipi] *nf* stenotypy.

sténotypiste [stenɔtipist] *nmf* stenotypist.

stentor [stɑ̃tɔr] *nm* ZOOL stentor.

stéphanois, e [stefanwa, az] *adj* from Saint-Étienne.
◆ **Stéphanois, e** *nm, f inhabitant of Saint-Étienne.*

steppe [stɛp] *nf* steppe.

stère [stɛr] *nm* stere *(cubic metre of wood)*.

stéréo [stereo] ◇ *adj inv* stereo.

<> *nf* **1.** [procédé] stereo **2.** *fam* [récepteur] stereo.
◆ **en stéréo** <> *loc adj* stereo *(modif).*
<> *loc adv* in stereo.

stéréophonie [stereɔfɔni] *nf* stereophony.
◆ **en stéréophonie** <> *loc adj* stereo *(modif).*
<> *loc adv* in stereo, in stereophonic sound.

stéréophonique [stereɔfɔnik] *adj* stereophonic.

stéréoscope [stereɔskɔp] *nm* stereoscope.

stéréoscopie [stereɔskɔpi] *nf* stereoscopy.

stéréoscopique [stereɔskɔpik] *adj* stereoscopic.

stéréotype [stereɔtip] *nm* **1.** [formule banale] stereotype, cliché **2.** IMPR stereotype.

stéréotypé, e [stereɔtipe] *adj* [comportement] stereotyped ▪ [tournure] clichéd, hackneyed.

stéréovision [stereɔvizjɔ̃] *nf* stereovision.

stérile [steril] <> *adj* **1.** [femme] infertile, sterile, barren *litt* ▪ [homme] sterile ▪ [sol] barren ▪ [végétal] sterile **2.** [improductif - artiste] unproductive ; [- imagination] infertile, barren ; [- hypothèse] unproductive, vain ; [- rêve] vain, hopeless ; [- effort] vain, fruitless **3.** MÉD [aseptique] sterile, sterilized **4.** MIN & MINÉR dead.
<> *nm* MIN & MINÉR dead ground.
◆ **stériles** *nmpl* GÉOL deads, waste rock.

stérilet [sterilɛ] *nm* IUD, coil ▪ **se faire poser/enlever un ~** to have a coil put in/taken out.

stérilisant, e [sterilizɑ̃, ɑ̃t] *adj* **1.** [procédure, technique] sterilizing **2.** [idéologie, mode de vie] numbing, brain-numbing.

stérilisateur [sterilizatœr] *nm* sterilizer.

stérilisation [sterilizasjɔ̃] *nf* **1.** [action de rendre infécond] sterilization **2.** [désinfection] sterilization.

stérilisé, e [sterilize] *adj* sterilized.

stériliser [3] [sterilize] *vt* **1.** [rendre infécond] to sterilize **2.** [rendre aseptique] to sterilize.

stérilité [sterilite] *nf* **1.** [d'une femme] sterility, infertility, barrenness *litt* ▪ [d'un homme] infertility, sterility ▪ [d'un sol] barrenness **2.** [de l'esprit] barrenness, unproductiveness **3.** MÉD [asepsie] sterility.

sterling [stɛrliŋ] *adj inv* & *nm inv* sterling.

sternum [stɛrnɔm] *nm* **1.** ANAT breastbone, sternum *spéc* **2.** ZOOL sternum.

stéroïde [sterɔid] <> *adj* steroidal.
<> *nm* steroid.

stéthoscope [stetɔskɔp] *nm* stethoscope.

steward [stiwart] *nm* AÉRON steward.

stick [stik] *nm* [de fard, de colle] stick.

stigmate [stigmat] *nm* **1.** MÉD mark, stigma *spéc* **2.** [marque] : **porter les ~s de la guerre/débauche** to bear the cruel marks of war/the marks of debauchery **3.** BOT eyespot, stigma **4.** ZOOL (respiratory) stigma.
◆ **stigmates** *nmpl* RELIG stigmata.

stigmatique [stigmatik] *adj* stigmatic.

stigmatisation [stigmatizasjɔ̃] *nf* stigmatization, stigmatizing.

stigmatiser [3] [stigmatize] *vt* **1.** [dénoncer] to stigmatize, to condemn, to pillory *fig* **2.** *litt* [marquer - condamné] to brand, to stigmatize.

stimulant, e [stimylɑ̃, ɑ̃t] *adj* **1.** [fortifiant - climat] bracing, stimulating ; [- boisson] stimulant *(modif)* **2.** [encourageant - résultat, paroles] encouraging.
◆ **stimulant** *nm* **1.** [remontant, tonique] stimulant **2.** [aiguillon] stimulus, spur.

stimulateur, trice [stimylatœr, tris] *adj* stimulative.
◆ **stimulateur** *nm* MÉD stimulator ▪ **~ (cardiaque)** pacemaker.

stimulation [stimylasjɔ̃] *nf* **1.** CHIM, PHYSIOL & PSYCHOL stimulation, stimulus **2.** [d'une fonction organique] stimulation ▪ **pour la ~ de leur appétit** to stimulate *ou* to whet their appetite **3.** [incitation] stimulus.

stimuler [3] [stimyle] *vt* **1.** [activer - fonction organique] to stimulate **2.** [enflammer - sentiment] to stimulate **3.** [encourager - personne] to encourage, to motivate **4.** [intensifier - activité] to stimulate ▪ **~ l'industrie/l'économie** to stimulate industry/the economy.

stimulus [stimylys] (*pl inv ou pl* **stimuli** [-li]) *nm* stimulus.

stipendié, e [stipɑ̃dje] *adj litt* & *péj* venal, corrupt.

stipendier [9] [stipɑ̃dje] *vt litt* & *péj* to bribe, to buy.

stipulation [stipylasjɔ̃] *nf* **1.** *sout* stipulation, stipulating **2.** DR stipulation.

stipuler [3] [stipyle] *vt* **1.** DR to stipulate **2.** [spécifier] to stipulate, to specify ▪ **la circulaire stipule que l'augmentation sera appliquée à partir du mois prochain** the circular stipulates that the rise will be applicable as from next month.

STO (*abr de* **service du travail obligatoire**) *nm* HIST forced labour *(by French workers requisitioned during the Second World War).*

stock [stɔk] *nm* **1.** COMM stock ▪ ÉCON stock, supply **2.** [réserve personnelle] stock, collection, supply ▪ **faire des ~s (de)** to stock up (on).
◆ **en stock** <> *loc adj* [marchandise] in stock.
<> *loc adv* : **avoir qqch en ~** to have sthg in stock.

stockage [stɔkaʒ] *nm* **1.** [constitution d'un stock] stocking (up) **2.** [conservation - d'énergie, d'informations, de liquides, d'armes] storage **3.** TECHNOL storage ▪ **~ dynamique** flow storage.

stock-car [stɔkkar] (*pl* **stock-cars**) *nm* [voiture] stock car ▪ [course] stock car racing ▪ **faire du ~** to go stock car racing.

stocker [3] [stɔke] *vt* [s'approvisionner en] to stock up on *ou* with ▪ [avoir - en réserve] to (keep in) stock ; [- en grande quantité] to stockpile, to hoard.

Stockholm [stɔkɔlm] *npr* Stockholm.

stock-option [stɔkɔpsjɔ̃] *nf* stock option.

stoïcien, enne [stɔisjɛ̃, ɛn] <> *adj* **1.** PHILOS Stoic **2.** *litt* [courageux, impassible] stoic, stoical.
<> *nm, f* PHILOS Stoic.

stoïcisme [stɔisism] *nm* stoicism.

stoïque [stɔik] <> *adj* stoical.
<> *nmf* stoic.

stoïquement [stɔikmɑ̃] *adv* stoically.

stomacal, e, aux [stɔmakal, o] *adj* stomach *(modif)*, gastric.

stomatologie [stɔmatɔlɔʒi] *nf* stomatology.

stomatologiste [stɔmatɔlɔʒist], **stomatologue** [stɔmatɔlɔg] *nmf* stomatologist.

stomisé, e [stɔmize] *nmf* ostomate.

stop [stɔp] <> *nm* **1.** [panneau] stop sign **2.** [lumière] brake light, stoplight **3.** *fam* [auto-stop] hitchhiking ▪ **faire du ~** to hitch, to thumb a lift *ou* it **4.** [dans un télégramme] stop.
<> *interj* stop (it) ▪ **tu me diras stop – stop!** [en versant à boire] say when – when!

stop-and-go [stɔpɛndgo] *nm inv* ÉCON stop-and-go method.

stopper [3] [stɔpe] <> *vt* **1.** [train, voiture] to stop, to bring to a halt ▪ [engin, maladie] to stop ▪ [développement, processus, production] to stop, to halt ▪ [pratique] to put a stop to, to stop **2.** TEXT to mend *(using invisible mending).*
<> *vi* [marcheur, véhicule, machine, processus, production] to stop, to come to a halt *ou* standstill ▪ **la voiture a stoppé net** the car stopped dead.

stoppeur, euse [stɔpœr, øz] *nm, f* **1.** *fam* [en voiture] hitchhiker, hitcher **2.** TEXT invisible mender.

store [stɔr] *nm* [intérieur] blind ▪ [extérieur - d'un magasin] awning ▪ **~ vénitien** Venetian blind.

story-board [stɔribɔrd] *nm* storyboard.

strabisme [strabism] *nm* squint, strabismus *spéc* ▪ **elle a un léger ~** she has a slight squint ◐ **~ convergent** esotropia, convergent strabismus ▪ **~ divergent** exotropia, divergent strabismus.

stradivarius [stradivarjys] *nm* Stradivarius.

strangulation [strɑ̃gylasjɔ̃] *nf* strangulation, strangling *(U)* ▪ **il est mort par ~** he died by strangulation, he was strangled to death.

strapontin [strapɔ̃tɛ̃] *nm* **1.** [siège] jump *ou* folding seat **2.** *loc* **avoir un ~** to hold a minor position.

stras [stras] = **strass**.

strass [stras] *nm* paste *(U)*, strass.

stratagème [strataʒɛm] *nm* stratagem, ruse.

strate [strat] *nf* **1.** GÉOL stratum **2.** *sout* [niveau] layer ▪ **les ~s de la personnalité** the layers *ou* strata of the personality **3.** BOT zone.

stratège [stratɛʒ] *nm* **1.** MIL strategist **2.** *fig* **un fin ~** a cunning strategist.

stratégie [strateʒi] *nf* **1.** JEUX & MIL strategy **2.** *fig* **sa ~ électorale** her electoral strategy.

stratégique [strateʒik] *adj* **1.** MIL strategic, strategical **2.** *fig* **un repli ~** a strategic retreat.

stratification [stratifikasjɔ̃] *nf* stratification, stratifying *(U)*.

stratifié, e [stratifje] *adj* stratified.
⬌ **stratifié** *nm* laminate.

stratifier [9] [stratifje] *vt* to stratify.

stratocumulus [stratɔkymylys] *nm* stratocumulus.

stratosphère [stratɔsfɛr] *nf* stratosphere.

stratus [stratys] *nm* stratus.

Stravinski [stravinski] *npr* Stravinsky.

streptocoque [strɛptɔkɔk] *nm* streptococcus.

stress [strɛs] *nm inv* stress ▪ **les maladies liées au ~** stress-related illnesses.

stressant, e [strɛsɑ̃, ɑ̃t] *adj* stressful, stress-inducing.

stressé, e [strɛse] *adj* stressed ▪ **les gens ~s** people under stress.

stresser [4] [strɛse] *vt* to put under stress.

Stretch® [strɛtʃ] ◇ *adj inv* stretch *(modif)*, stretchy.
◇ *nm inv* stretch material.

stretching [strɛtʃiŋ] *nm* stretching ▪ **cours de ~** stretch class ▪ **faire du ~** to do stretching exercises.

strict, e [strikt] *adj* **1.** [astreignant, précis - contrôle, ordre, règle, principe] strict, exacting **2.** [minimal] strict ▪ **le ~ nécessaire** *ou* **minimum** the bare minimum ▪ **les obsèques seront célébrées dans la plus ~e intimité** the funeral will take place strictly in private **3.** [sévère - éducation, personne] strict ; [- discipline] strict, rigorous **4.** [austère - intérieur, vêtement] severe, austere **5.** [rigoureux, absolu] strict, absolute ▪ **c'est ton droit le plus ~** it's your lawful right ▪ **c'est la ~e vérité!** it's absolutely true!

strictement [striktəmɑ̃] *adv* **1.** [rigoureusement] strictly, scrupulously **2.** [absolument] strictly, absolutely ▪ **c'est ~ confidentiel** it's strictly *ou* highly confidential **3.** [sobrement] severely.

stricto sensu [striktosɛ̃sy] *loc adv* strictly speaking, stricto sensu *sout*.

strident, e [stridɑ̃, ɑ̃t] *adj* [son, voix] strident, shrill, piercing.

stridulation [stridylasjɔ̃] *nf* stridulation, stridulating.

strie [stri] *nf* **1.** [sillon] stria *spéc*, (thin) groove **2.** [ligne de couleur] streak **3.** GÉOL & MINÉR stria.

strié, e [strije] *adj* **1.** [cannelé - roche, tige] striated **2.** [veiné - étoffe, marbre] streaked **3.** ANAT striated.

strier [10] [strije] *vt* **1.** [creuser] to striate, to groove **2.** [veiner] to streak ▪ **strié de bleu** streaked with blue.

string [striŋ] *nm* G-string.

strip [strip] *nm fam* striptease.

stripping [stripiŋ] *nm* MÉD & PÉTR stripping.

strip-tease [striptiz] *(pl* **strip-teases***)* *nm* striptease act ▪ **faire un ~** to do a strip-tease.

strip-teaseur, strip-teaseuse [striptizœr, øz] *(mpl* **strip-teaseurs**, *fpl* **strip-teaseuses***)* *nm, f* stripper, striptease artist.

striure [strijyr] *nf* striation.

stroboscope [strɔbɔskɔp] *nm* stroboscope, strobe (light).

strophe [strɔf] *nf* **1.** [d'un poème] stanza **2.** [de tragédie grecque] strophe.

structural, e, aux [stryktyral, o] *adj* structural.

structuralisme [stryktyralism] *nm* structuralism.

structuration [stryktyrasjɔ̃] *nf* [action] structuring ▪ [résultat] structure.

structure [stryktyr] *nf* **1.** [organisation - d'un service, d'une société, d'un texte] structure **2.** [institution] system, organization ▪ **~s administratives/politiques** administrative/political structures **3.** [ensemble de services] facility ▪ **~s d'accueil** reception facilities *(for recently arrived tourists, refugees etc)* **4.** CONSTR building, structure **5.** LING structure.

structuré, e [stryktyre] *adj* structured, organized.

structurel, elle [stryktyrɛl] *adj* structural.

structurer [3] [stryktyre] *vt* to structure, to organize ▪ **c'est une ébauche de scénario qu'il faudrait ~** it's the idea for a scenario which needs to be given some shape.
⬌ **se structurer** *vpi* to take shape.

strychnine [striknin] *nf* strychnine.

stuc [styk] *nm* stucco.
⬌ **en stuc** *loc adj* stucco *(modif)*.

studette [stydɛt] *nf* small studio flat *UK ou* apartment *US*, bedsitter *UK*.

studieux, euse [stydjø, øz] *adj* **1.** [appliqué - élève] hard-working, studious **2.** [consacré à l'étude] studious ▪ **une soirée studieuse** an evening of study, a studious evening.

studio [stydjo] *nm* **1.** [appartement] studio flat *UK*, studio apartment *US* **2.** AUDIO, CINÉ & TV studio ▪ **~ d'enregistrement** recording studio **3.** PHOTO photography *ou* photographic studio.
⬌ **en studio** *loc adv* : **tourné en ~** shot in studio ▪ **scène tournée en ~** studio scene.

stupéfaction [stypefaksjɔ̃] *nf* stupefaction *litt*, astonishment ▪ **à sa/ma (grande) ~** to his/my utter amazement.

stupéfaire [109] [stypefɛr] *vt* to amaze, to astound.

stupéfait, e [stypefɛ, ɛt] *adj* [personne] astounded, stunned, stupefied *litt* ▪ **je suis ~ de voir qu'il est revenu** I'm amazed to see he came back.

stupéfiant, e [stypefjɑ̃, ɑ̃t] *adj* **1.** [nouvelle, réaction] astounding, amazing, stupefying *litt* **2.** PHARM narcotic.
⬌ **stupéfiant** *nm* [drogue] drug, narcotic.

stupéfier [9] [stypefje] *vt* **1.** [abasourdir] to astound, to stun ▪ **sa décision a stupéfié sa famille** his family was stunned by his decision **2.** *litt* [suj: froid, peur] to stupefy.

stupeur [stypœr] *nf* **1.** [ahurissement] amazement, astonishment ▪ **le public était plongé dans la ~** the audience was dumbfounded *ou* stunned **2.** MÉD & PSYCHOL stupor.

stupide [stypid] *adj* **1.** [inintelligent - personne, jeu, initiative, réponse, suggestion] stupid, silly, foolish ; [- raisonnement] stupid ▪ **il eut un rire ~** he laughed stupidly **2.** [absurde - accident, mort] stupid **3.** [ahuri] stunned, dumbfounded.

stupidement [stypidmɑ̃] *adv* stupidly, absurdly, foolishly.

stupidité [stypidite] *nf* **1.** [d'une action, d'une personne, d'un propos] stupidity, foolishness **2.** [acte] piece of foolish behaviour **3.** [parole] stupid *ou* foolish remark ▪ **arrête de dire des ~s!** stop talking nonsense!

stupre [stypr] *nm litt* depravity.

stups[△] [styp] *nmpl arg crime* **les ~** the narcotics *ou* drugs squad.

style [stil] *nm* **1.** [d'un écrivain, d'un journal] style ▪ **c'est écrit dans le plus pur ~ administratif/journalistique** it's written in purest bureaucratic jargon *péj*/journalese *péj* **2.** [d'un artiste, d'un sportif] style, (characteristic) approach, touch ▪ **son ~ de jeu** his (particular) way of playing, his style **3.** ART style ➲ **~ gothique/Régence** Gothic/Regency style **4.** [genre, ordre d'idée] style ▪ **dis-lui que tu vas réfléchir, ou quelque chose dans** *ou* **de ce ~** tell him you'll think about it, or something along those lines *ou* in that vein **5.** *fam* [manière d'agir] style ▪ **tu aurais pu l'avoir dénoncé – ce n'est pas mon ~** you could have denounced him – it's not my style *ou* that's not the sort of thing I'd do ➲ **~ de vie** lifestyle **6.** [élégance] style, class ▪ **avoir du ~** to have style ▪ **elle a beaucoup de ~** she's very stylish *ou* chic **7.** BOT & ENTOM style **8.** [d'un cadran solaire] style, gnomon ▪ [d'un cylindre enregistreur] needle, stylus ▪ ANTIQ & HIST [poinçon] style, stylus **9.** ENTOM [d'une antenne] style, seta **10.** LING : **~ direct/indirect** direct/indirect speech.
◆ **de style** *loc adj* [meuble, objet] period *(modif).*

stylé, e [stile] *adj* [personnel] well-trained.

stylet [stilɛ] *nm* **1.** MÉD stilet, stylet **2.** [dague] stiletto **3.** INFORM stylus.

styliser [3] [stilize] *vt* to stylize ▪ **oiseau stylisé** stylized (drawing of a) bird.

stylisme [stilism] *nm* fashion design.

styliste [stilist] *nmf* **1.** [de mode, dans l'industrie] designer **2.** [auteur] stylist.

stylistique [stilistik] ◇ *adj* stylistic.
◇ *nf* stylistics *(sing).*

stylo [stilo] *nm* pen ▪ **~ (à bille)** ballpoint (pen), Biro® *UK* ▪ **~ à encre/cartouche** fountain/cartridge pen.

stylo-feutre [stiloføtr] (*pl* **stylos-feutres**) *nm* felt-tip pen.

su, e [sy] *pp* ▷ **savoir.**
◆ **su** *nm* : **au vu et au ~ de tout le monde** in front of everybody, quite openly.

suaire [sɥɛr] *nm* shroud.

suant, e [sɥɑ̃, sɥɑ̃t] *adj* **1.** *fam* [ennuyeux] dull, boring ▪ [énervant] annoying ▪ **ce que tu peux être ~!** you're a pain (in the neck)! **2.** [en sueur] sweaty.

suave [sɥav] *adj* [manières, ton] suave, sophisticated ▪ [senteur] sweet ▪ [teintes] subdued, mellow ▪ **de sa voix ~** in his suave voice, in dulcet tones *hum.*

suavité [sɥavite] *nf* [de manières, d'un ton] suaveness, suavity, smoothness ▪ [d'une musique, de senteurs] sweetness ▪ [de teintes] mellowness.

subalpin, e [sybalpɛ̃, in] *adj* subalpine.

subalterne [sybaltɛrn] ◇ *adj* **1.** [position] secondary ▪ **un rôle ~** a secondary *ou* minor role **2.** [personne] subordinate, junior *(modif).*
◇ *nmf* subordinate, underling *péj.*

subaquatique [sybakwatik] *adj* subaquatic.

subconscient, e [sybkɔ̃sjɑ̃, ɑ̃t] *adj* subconscious.
◆ **subconscient** *nm* subconscious.

subdéléguer [18] [sybdelege] *vt* to subdelegate.

subdésertique [sybdezɛrtik] *adj* semi-desert *(modif).*

subdiviser [3] [sybdivize] *vt* to subdivide ▪ **chapitre subdivisé en deux parties** chapter subdivided into two parts.
◆ **se subdiviser** *vpi* : **se ~ (en)** to subdivide (into).

subdivision [sybdivizjɔ̃] *nf* **1.** [processus] subdivision, subdividing **2.** [catégorie] subdivision.

subdivisionnaire [sybdivizjɔnɛr] *adj* subdivisional.

subduction [sybdyksjɔ̃] *nf* subduction.

subéquatorial, e, aux [sybekwatɔrjal, o] *adj* subequatorial.

subir [32] [sybir] *vt* **1.** [dommages, pertes] to suffer, to sustain ▪ [conséquences, défaite] to suffer ▪ [attaque, humiliation, insultes, sévices] to be subjected to, to suffer ▪ **faire ~ une torture à qqn** to subject sb to torture ▪ **après tout ce qu'elle m'a fait ~** after all she inflicted on me *ou* made me go through **2.** [influence] to be under ▪ [situation, personne] to put up with ▪ **je ne pouvais que ~ son envoûtement** I could not free myself of her spell ▪ **il a l'air de ~ le match** he looks as though he's just letting the match go on around him **3.** [opération, transformation] to undergo.

subit, e [sybi, it] *adj* sudden.

subitement [sybitmɑ̃] *adv* suddenly, all of a sudden.

subito [sybito] *adv fam* **1.** [tout à coup] suddenly, all of a sudden **2.** *loc* **~ presto** [tout de suite] at once, immediately.

subjacent, e [sybʒasɑ̃, ɑ̃t] *adj* subjacent.

subjectif, ive [sybʒɛktif, iv] *adj* subjective.

subjectivement [sybʒɛktivmɑ̃] *adv* subjectively.

subjectivisme [sybʒɛktivism] *nm* subjectivism.

subjectiviste [sybʒɛktivist] ◇ *adj* subjectivistic.
◇ *nmf* subjectivist.

subjectivité [sybʒɛktivite] *nf* subjectivity, subjectiveness.

subjonctif, ive [sybʒɔ̃ktif, iv] *adj* subjunctive.
◆ **subjonctif** *nm* subjunctive, *voir aussi* **pluriel.**

subjuguer [3] [sybʒyge] *vt sout* [suj: discours, lecture] to enthral, to captivate ▪ [suj: beauté, charme, regard] to enthral, to beguile ▪ [suj: éloquence] to enthral ▪ **elle le subjuguait** she held him spellbound ▪ **je restai subjugué devant tant de grâce** I was enthralled by so much grace.

sublimation [syblimasjɔ̃] *nf* **1.** [élévation morale] sublimation, sublimating **2.** CHIM & PSYCHOL sublimation.

sublime [syblim] ◇ *adj* **1.** *sout* [noble, grand] sublime, elevated ▪ **une beauté ~** sublime beauty **2.** [exceptionnel, parfait] sublime, wonderful, magnificent ▪ **tu as été ~** you were magnificent ▪ **un repas ~** a wonderful meal.
◇ *nm* : **le ~** the sublime.

sublimé, e [syblime] *adj* sublimated.
◆ **sublimé** *nm* CHIM sublimate.

sublimer [3] [syblime] *vt* **1.** PSYCHOL to sublimate **2.** CHIM to sublimate, to sublime.

subliminal, e, aux [sybliminal, o], **subliminaire** [sybliminɛr] *adj* subliminal.

submergé, e [sybmɛrʒe] *adj* **1.** [rochers] submerged ▪ [champs] submerged, flooded **2.** [surchargé, accablé] inundated ▪ **~ de travail** snowed under with work ▪ **~ de réclamations** inundated with complaints **3.** [incapable de faire face] swamped, up to one's eyes ▪ **depuis que ma secrétaire est partie, je suis ~** since my secretary left, I've been up to my eyes in work.

submerger [17] [sybmɛrʒe] *vt* **1.** [inonder] to flood, to submerge **2.** [envahir - suj: angoisse, joie] to overcome, to overwhelm ; [- suj: réclamations] to inundate, to swamp ; [- suj: dettes] to overwhelm, to swamp ▪ **notre standard est submergé d'appels** our switchboard's swamped with *ou* jammed by calls ▪ **je suis submergé de travail** I'm snowed under with work ▪ **se laisser ~** to allow o.s. to be overcome **3.** [écraser - défenseur] to overwhelm, to overrun ■ **le service d'ordre fut rapidement submergé par les manifestants** the police were soon unable to contain the demonstrators.

submersible [sybmɛrsibl] ◇ *adj* submersible, submergible.
◇ *nm* submersible.

submersion [sybmɛrsjɔ̃] *nf* ***litt*** submersion, submerging.

subodorer [3] [sybɔdɔre] *vt* ***hum*** [danger] to scent, to smell, to sense ■ **je subodore un canular** I can smell a hoax.

subordination [sybɔrdinasjɔ̃] *nf* **1.** [dans une hiérarchie] subordination, subordinating ■ **il a refusé sa ~ au directeur commercial** he refused to work under the sales manager **2.** LING & LOGIQUE subordination.
◆ **de subordination** *loc adj* : **relation de ~** relation of subordination.

subordonnant [sybɔrdɔnɑ̃] *nm* subordinating word.

subordonné, e [sybɔrdɔne] ◇ *adj* **1.** [subalterne] subordinate **2.** LING subordinate, dependent.
◇ *nm, f* [subalterne] subordinate, subaltern.
◆ **subordonnée** *nf* LING subordinate *ou* dependent clause.

subordonner [3] [sybɔrdɔne] *vt* **1.** [hiérarchiquement] : **~ qqn à** to subordinate sb to ■ **les statuts subordonnent le directeur au conseil d'administration** the director is answerable to the board **2.** [faire dépendre] : **~ qqch à** to subordinate sthg to, to make sthg dependent on **3.** [faire passer après] : **~ qqch à** to subordinate sthg to **4.** LING [proposition] to subordinate.

subornation [sybɔrnasjɔ̃] *nf* subornation ■ **~ de témoins** subornation of witnesses.

suborner [3] [sybɔrne] *vt* **1.** DR [témoin] to suborn **2.** ***vieilli*** [avec des pots-de-vin] to bribe **3.** ***litt*** [jeune fille] to seduce.

suborneur, euse [sybɔrnœr, øz] *nm, f* DR suborner.
◆ **suborneur** *nm* ***litt*** seducer.

subreptice [sybrɛptis] *adj* ***litt*** [manœuvre] surreptitious, stealthy.

subrepticement [sybrɛptismɑ̃] *adv* ***litt*** surreptitiously, stealthily.

subrogation [sybrɔgasjɔ̃] *nf* subrogation, subrogating *(U)*.

subrogé, e [sybrɔʒe] *adj* **1.** [remplaçant] surrogate **2.** DR : **~ tuteur** deputy *ou* surrogate guardian.

subroger [17] [sybrɔʒe] *vt* to subrogate.

subséquent, e [sybsekɑ̃, ɑ̃t] *adj* **1.** ***litt*** [qui suit] subsequent **2.** GÉOGR : **affluent ~** subsequent stream.

subside [sypsid] *nm* [de l'État] grant, subsidy ■ **il vivait des ~s de ses parents** he lived on the allowance he received from his parents.

subsidiaire [sybzidjɛr] *adj* subsidiary.

subsidiarité [sybzidjarite] *nf* subsidiarity.

subsistance [sybzistɑ̃s] *nf* [existence matérielle] subsistence ■ **pourvoir à** *ou* **assurer la ~ de qqn** to support *ou* to maintain *ou* to keep sb ■ **elle arrive tout juste à assurer sa ~** she just manages to survive, she has just enough to keep body and soul together.

subsistant, e [sybzistɑ̃, ɑ̃t] ◇ *adj* remaining, subsisting.
◇ *nm, f* [assuré social] transferred (benefit) claimant.
◆ **subsistant** *nm* MIL [soldat] seconded soldier ■ [officier] seconded officer.

subsister [3] [sybziste] *vi* **1.** [demeurer - doute, espoir, rancœur, traces] to remain, to subsist ***litt*** ; [- tradition] to live on ■ **quelques questions subsistent auxquelles on n'a pas répondu** there are still a few questions which remain unanswered **2.** [survivre] to survive ■ **je n'ai que 100 euros par semaine pour ~** I only have 100 euros a week to live on.

subsonique [sypsɔnik] *adj* subsonic.

substance [sypstɑ̃s] *nf* **1.** [matière] substance ■ **~ biodégradable/solide/liquide** biodegradable/solid/liquid substance ■ **~ organique/vivante** organic/living matter ■ **~ alimentaire** food **2.** [essentiel - d'un texte] substance, gist ; [- d'une idéologie] substance **3.** [profondeur, signification] substance ■ **des mots vides de toute ~** words empty of substance, meaningless words **4.** PHILOS & RELIG substance ■ [matérialité] substance, reality.
◆ **en substance** *loc adv* in substance ■ **c'est, en ~, ce qu'elle m'a raconté** that's the gist of what she told me.

substantialisme [sypstɑ̃sjalism] *nm* substantialism.

substantiel, elle [sypstɑ̃sjɛl] *adj* **1.** [nourriture, repas] substantial, filling **2.** [argument] substantial, sound ■ **je cherche des lectures un peu plus ~les** I'm looking for books with a bit more substance (to them) **3.** [avantage, différence] substantial, significant, important ■ [somme] substantial, considerable.

substantiellement [sypstɑ̃sjɛlmɑ̃] *adv* substantially.

substantif, ive [sypstɑ̃tif, iv] *adj* substantive.
◆ **substantif** *nm* substantive.

substantivation [sypstɑ̃tivasjɔ̃] *nf* substantivization, substantivizing.

substantiver [3] [sypstɑ̃tive] *vt* to turn into a substantive.

substituer [7] [sypstitɥe] *vt* **1.** [remplacer] : **~ qqch à** to substitute sthg for, to replace by sthg **2.** CHIM to substitute **3.** DR : **~ un héritage** to entail an estate.
◆ **se substituer à** *vp+prép* [pour aider, représenter] to substitute for, to stand in for, to replace ■ [de façon déloyale] to substitute o.s. for ■ **personne ne peut se ~ à la mère** no one can replace the mother.

substitut [sypstity] *nm* **1.** [produit, personne] : **~ de** substitute for **2.** DR deputy *ou* assistant public prosecutor.

substitutif, ive [sypstitytif, iv] *adj* substitutive.

substitution [sypstitysjɔ̃] *nf* **1.** [d'objets, de personnes] substitution ■ **il y a eu ~ de documents** documents have been substituted ■ **il y a eu ~ d'enfant** the babies were switched round **2.** CHIM, LING & MATH substitution.
◆ **de substitution** *loc adj* [réaction] substitution *(modif)* ■ **produit de ~** substitute.

substrat [sypstra] *nm* **1.** CHIM & ÉLECTRON substrate **2.** LING & PHILOS substratum.

substructure [sypstryktyr] *nf* substructure.

subterfuge [syptɛrfyʒ] *nm* subterfuge, ruse, trick.

subtil, e [syptil] *adj* **1.** [argument, esprit, raisonnement, personne] subtle, discerning ■ **ses plaisanteries ne sont pas très ~es** his jokes aren't very subtle *ou* are a bit heavy-handed **2.** [allusion, différence] subtle ■ [nuance, distinction] subtle, fine, nice **3.** [arôme, goût, parfum] subtle, delicate **4.** [alambiqué] subtle, over-fine.

subtilement [syptilmɑ̃] *adv* subtly.

subtilisation [syptilizasjɔ̃] *nf* spiriting away.

subtiliser [3] [syptilize] ◇ *vt* [voler] to steal, to spirit away *(sép)* ■ **ils lui ont subtilisé sa montre** they relieved him of his watch ***hum***.
◇ *vi* ***litt*** & ***péj*** to subtilize.

subtilité [syptilite] *nf* **1.** [d'un raisonnement, d'un parfum, d'une nuance] subtlety, subtleness, delicacy **2.** [argutie] hairsplitting ■ **je ne comprends rien à ces ~s** all these fine *ou* fine-drawn distinctions are beyond me.

subtropical, e, aux [syptrɔpikal, o] *adj* subtropical.

suburbain, e [sybyrbɛ̃, ɛn] *adj* suburban.

subvenir [40] [sybvənir] ◆ **subvenir à** *v+prép* [besoins] to provide for ■ [dépenses] to meet.

subvention [sybvɑ̃sjɔ̃] *nf* subsidy ■ **notre troupe reçoit une ~ de la mairie** our company gets a subsidy from *ou* is subsidized by the city council.

subventionné, e [sybvɑ̃sjɔne] *adj* [cinéma, théâtre, recherches] subsidized ■ **école privée ~e** ≃ grant-aided *ou* state-aided private school.

subventionner [3] [sybvɑ̃sjɔne] *vt* [entreprise, théâtre] to subsidize, to grant funds to ■ [recherche] to subsidize, to grant funds towards.

subvenu [sybvəny] *pp* ▷ **subvenir**.

subversif, ive [sybvɛrsif, iv] *adj* subversive.

subversion [sybvɛrsjɔ̃] *nf* subversion, subverting *(U)*.

subvertir [32] [sybvɛrtir] *vt litt* to overthrow, to subvert.

subvient, subvint *etc v* ▷ **subvenir**.

suc [syk] *nm* BOT & PHYSIOL juice ■ **~s gastriques** gastric juices.

succédané [syksedane] *nm* **1.** [ersatz] substitute ■ **un ~ de café** coffee substitute, ersatz coffee **2.** [personne ou chose de second ordre] second rate **3.** PHARM substitute.

succéder [18] [syksede] ◆ **succéder à** *v+prép* **1.** [remplacer dans une fonction] to succeed, to take over from ■ **tous ceux qui lui ont succédé** all his successors, all those who came after him ■ **~ à qqn sur le trône** to succeed sb to the throne **2.** [suivre] to follow ■ **un épais brouillard a succédé au soleil** the sun gave way to thick fog ■ **puis les défaites succédèrent aux victoires** after the victories came defeats **3.** DR [hériter de] to inherit from.

◆ **se succéder** *vpi* **1.** [se suivre] to follow each other ■ **les crises se succèdent** it's just one crisis after another **2.** [alterner] : **les Ravit se sont succédé à la tête de l'entreprise depuis 50 ans** the Ravit family has been running the company for 50 years.

succès [syksɛ] *nm* **1.** [heureux résultat, réussite personnelle] success ■ **être couronné de ~** to be crowned with success, to be successful **2.** [exploit, performance] success ■ [en amour] conquest ■ **l'opération est un ~ total** the operation is a complete success ■ **aller** *ou* **voler de ~ en ~** to go from one success to another ■ **leurs nombreux ~ en coupe d'Europe** their many victories in the European Cup **3.** [approbation - du public] success, popularity ; [- d'un groupe] success ■ **remporter un immense ~** to be a huge success ■ **avoir du ~** [œuvre, artiste] to be successful ; [suggestion] to be very well received ■ **avoir du ~ auprès de qqn : sa pièce a eu beaucoup de ~ auprès des critiques mais peu auprès du public** his play was acclaimed by the critics but the public was less than enthusiastic ■ **il a beaucoup de ~ auprès des femmes/jeunes** he's very popular with women/young people ■ **eh bien, il a du ~, mon soufflé!** well, I see you like my soufflé *ou* my soufflé appears to be a success! **4.** [chanson] hit ■ [film, pièce] (box-office) hit *ou* success ■ [livre] success, bestseller ■ **~ d'estime** critical acclaim, succès d'estime ■ **l'ouvrage a été un ~ d'estime** the book was well-received by the critics (but not by the public) ■ **~ de librairie** bestseller ■ **sa comédie musicale a été un immense ~ commercial** his musical was a box office hit *ou* a runaway success ■ **un gros ~** [film] a big success ; [livre] a best-seller ; [disque] a hit.

◆ **à succès** *loc adj* [auteur, chanteur] popular ■ **chanson à ~** hit record *ou* song ■ **romancier à ~** popular *ou* best-selling novelist.

◆ **avec succès** *loc adv* successfully, with success.

◆ **sans succès** *loc adv* [essayer] unsuccessfully, without (any) success ■ **elle s'est présentée plusieurs fois sans ~ à ce poste** she made several unsuccessful applications for this job.

successeur [syksesœr] *nm* **1.** [remplaçant] successor ■ **ses ~s** her successors, the people who succeeded her **2.** DR heir **3.** MATH successor.

successible [syksesibl] ◇ *adj* **1.** [qui a droit à la succession] entitled to inherit **2.** [qui donne droit à la succession] : **à défaut de parents au degré ~** in the absence of relations close enough to inherit the estate.
◇ *nmf* eventual heir, remainderman *spéc.*

successif, ive [syksesif, iv] *adj* successive ■ **trois essais ~s** three successive attempts.

succession [syksesjɔ̃] *nf* **1.** DR [héritage] succession, inheritance ■ [biens] estate ■ **liquider une ~** to settle a succession **2.** [remplacement] succession ■ **prendre la ~ d'un directeur** to take over from *ou* to succeed a manager ■ **prendre la ~ d'un monarque** to succeed a monarch (to the throne) **3.** [suite] succession, series *(sing)* ■ **la ~ des événements est difficile à suivre** the succession of events is difficult to follow.

successivement [syksesivmɑ̃] *adv* successively, one after the other.

succinct, e [syksɛ̃, ɛ̃t] *adj* **1.** [bref, concis] succinct, brief, concise ■ **un rapport ~** a brief *ou* concise report **2.** [laconique] brief, laconic **3.** [sommaire, réduit] : **un auditoire ~** a sparse audience ■ **un repas ~** a light meal.

succinctement [syksɛ̃tmɑ̃] *adv* **1.** [brièvement] briefly, succinctly **2.** [sommairement] frugally ■ **déjeuner ~** to have a light lunch.

succion [sy(k)sjɔ̃] *nf* [aspiration] sucking, suction ■ **des bruits de ~** sucking noises.

succomber [3] [sykɔ̃be] *vi sout* **1.** [décéder] to die, to succumb *sout* **2.** [céder - personne] to succumb ■ **il a succombé sous le nombre** he was forced to yield to greater numbers *ou* because he was outnumbered ■ **~ sous un fardeau** to collapse under a burden ■ **l'entreprise a succombé sous la concurrence** the company couldn't hold out against the competition ■ **~ à** [désir] to succumb to *sout*, to yield to ; [désespoir, émotion] to succumb to *sout*, to give way to ; [fatigue, sommeil] to succumb to *sout* ; [blessures] to die from, to succumb to *sout* ■ **j'ai succombé à ses charmes** I fell (a) victim *ou* I succumbed to her charms.

succube [sykyb] *nm* succubus.

succulence [sykylɑ̃s] *nf litt* succulence, succulency.

succulent, e [sykylɑ̃, ɑ̃t] *adj* [savoureux - mets, viande] succulent ■ **son autobiographie est remplie d'anecdotes ~es** *fig* her autobiography is full of delicious anecdotes.

succursale [sykyrsal] *nf* COMM branch.

succursalisme [sykyrsalism] *nm* retail chain.

sucement [sysmɑ̃] *nm* sucking.

sucer [16] [syse] *vt* **1.** [liquide] to suck ■ [bonbon, glace, sucette] to eat, to suck ■ **pastilles à ~** lozenges to be sucked **2.** [doigt, stylo] to suck (on) ■ **~ son pouce** to suck one's thumb **3.** ▲ [comme pratique sexuelle] to suck off ▲ *(sép)* **4.** △ [boisson] to tipple.

◆ **se sucer** *vpt* : **se ~ les doigts** to suck one's fingers ● **se ~ la pomme**△ *ou* **la poire**△ *ou* **le museau**△ to neck, to snog△ *UK*, to make out *US*.

sucette [sysɛt] *nf* **1.** [friandise] lollipop, lolly *UK* **2.** [tétine] dummy *UK*, pacifier *US*.

suceur, euse [sysœr, øz] ◇ *adj* sucking.
◇ *nm, f litt* **~ de sang** bloodsucker.

suçon [sysɔ̃] *nm* lovebite, hickey *US* ■ **faire un ~ à qqn** to give sb a lovebite.

suçoter [3] [sysɔte] *vt* to suck (slowly) ■ **il suçotait sa pipe** he was sucking at his pipe.

sucrage [sykraʒ] *nm* **1.** [gén] sugaring **2.** ŒNOL chaptalization.

sucrant, e [sykrɑ̃, ɑ̃t] *adj* sweetening ■ **agent ~** sweetener.

sucre [sykr] *nm* **1.** [produit de consommation] sugar ■ **enrobé de ~** sugar-coated ■ **confiture sans ~** sugar-free jam ● **~ de betterave/canne** beet/cane sugar ■ **~ roux** *ou* **brun** brown sugar ■ **~ candi** candy sugar ■ **~ cristallisé** (coarse) granulated sugar ■ **~ d'érable** maple sugar ■ **~ glace** icing sugar *UK*, confectioner's *ou* powdered sugar *US* ■ **~ en morceaux** lump *ou* cube sugar ■ **~ d'orge** [produit] barley sugar ; [bâton] stick of barley sugar ■ **~ en poudre** (fine) caster sugar ■ **~ semoule** (fine) caster sugar ■ **~ vanillé** vanilla sugar **2.** [sucreries] : **évitez le ~** avoid sugar *ou* sweet things **3.** [cube] sugar lump *ou* cube ■ **tu prends ton café avec un ou deux ~s?** do you take your coffee with one or two sugars *ou* lumps? ■ **je prends toujours mon thé sans ~** I always take my tea unsweetened *ou* without sugar **4.** *(comme adj)* **confiture pur ~** jam made with pure sugar ● **il est tout ~ tout miel** he's all sweetness and light.

◆ **au sucre** *loc adj* [fruits, crêpes] (sprinkled) with sugar.
◆ **en sucre** *loc adj* **1.** [confiserie] sugar *(modif)*, made with sugar **2.** *fam fig* **ne touche pas au bébé – il n'est pas en ~!** don't touch the baby – don't worry, he's not made of glass!

sucré, e [sykre] ◇ *adj* **1.** [naturellement] sweet ▪ [artificiellement] sweetened ▪ **je n'aime pas le café ~** I don't like sugar in my coffee ▪ **un verre d'eau ~e** a glass of sugar water ▪ **non ~** unsweetened **2.** [doucereux - paroles] sugary, sweet, honeyed ; [- voix] suave, sugary.
◇ *nm, f* : **faire le ~/la ~e** to go all coy.
◆ **sucré** *nm* : **le ~** sweet things ▪ **j'ai envie de ~** I'd like something sweet to eat ▪ **aimer le ~** to have a sweet tooth.

sucrer [3] [sykre] ◇ *vt* **1.** [avec du sucre - café, thé] to sugar, to put sugar in ; [- vin] to add sugar to, to chaptalize ; [- fruits] to sprinkle with sugar ▪ **sucrez à volonté** add sugar to taste ▪ **je ne sucre jamais mon thé** I never put sugar in my tea ➤ **~ les fraises**△ to be doddery **2.** [avec une matière sucrante] to sweeten **3.**△ [supprimer - prime] to stop ; [- réplique, passage] to do away with *(insép)* ▪ **on lui a sucré son permis de conduire après son accident** his driving licence was revoked after the accident.
◇ *vi* : **le miel sucre moins bien que le sucre** sugar is a better sweetener than honey.
◆ **se sucrer**△ *vpi* [s'enrichir] to feather one's own nest.

sucrerie [sykrəri] *nf* **1.** [friandise] sweet thing, sweetmeat ▪ **elle adore les ~s** she has a sweet tooth *ou* loves sweet things **2.** [raffinerie] sugar refinery ▪ [usine] sugar house **3.** *Québec* [forêt d'érables] maple forest.

Sucrette® [sykrɛt] *nf* (artificial) sweetener.

sucrier, ère [sykrije, ɛr] *adj* [industrie, betterave] sugar *(modif)* ▪ [région] sugar-producing.
◆ **sucrier** *nm* **1.** [pot] sugar basin *ou* bowl **2.** [producteur] sugar producer.

sud [syd] ◇ *nm inv* **1.** [point cardinal] south ▪ **où est le ~?** which way is south? ▪ **la partie la plus au ~ de l'île** the southernmost part of the island ▪ **il habite dans le ~ de Paris** he lives in the South of Paris ▪ **il habite au ~ de Paris** he lives to the south of Paris ▪ **aller au** *ou* **vers le ~** to go south *ou* southwards ▪ **les trains qui vont vers le ~** trains going south, southbound trains ▪ **rouler vers le ~** to drive south *ou* southwards ▪ **la cuisine est plein ~** *ou* **exposée au ~** the kitchen faces due south *ou* has a southerly aspect *sout* ▪ **le vent est au ~** MÉTÉOR the wind is blowing from the south, a southerly wind is blowing **2.** [partie d'un pays, d'un continent] south, southern area *ou* regions ▪ **le Sud de l'Italie** Southern Italy ▪ **elle habite dans le Sud** she lives in the south *ou* down south ▪ **les gens du Sud** Southerners.
◇ *adj inv* **1.** [qui est au sud - façade de maison] south, southfacing ; [- côte, côté, versant] south, southern ; [- portail] south ▪ **dans la partie ~ de la France** in the South of France, in southern France **2.** [dans des noms géographiques] : **Sud** South ▪ **le Pacifique Sud** the South Pacific.

sud-africain, e [sydafrikɛ̃, ɛn] *(mpl* **sud-africains**, *fpl* **sud-africaines)** *adj* South African.
◆ **Sud-Africain, e** *nm, f* South African.

sud-américain, e [sydamerikɛ̃, ɛn] *(mpl* **sud-américains**, *fpl* **sud-américaines)** *adj* South American.
◆ **Sud-Américain, e** *nm, f* South American.

sudation [sydasjɔ̃] *nf* sweating, sudation *spéc.*

sudatoire [sydatwar] *adj* sudatory.

sud-coréen, enne [sydkɔreɛ̃, ɛn] *(mpl* **sud-coréens**, *fpl* **sud-coréennes)** *adj* South Korean.
◆ **Sud-Coréen, enne** *nm, f* South Korean.

sud-est [sydɛst] ◇ *adj inv* southeast.
◇ *nm inv* **1.** [point cardinal] southeast ▪ **au ~ de Lyon** southeast of Lyons ▪ **vent de ~** southeast *ou* southeasterly wind **2.** GÉOGR : **le Sud-Est asiatique** South East Asia.

sudiste [sydist] *adj & nmf* HIST Confederate.

sudorifique [sydɔrifik] *adj & nm* sudorific.

sudoripare [sydɔripar] *adj* sudoriferous.

sud-ouest [sydwɛst] ◇ *adj inv* southwest.
◇ *nm inv* southwest ▪ **au ~ de Tokyo** southwest of Tokyo ▪ **vent de ~** southwest *ou* southwesterly wind.

sud-sud-est [sydsydɛst] *adj inv & nm inv* south-southeast.

sud-sud-ouest [sydsydwɛst] *adj inv & nm inv* south-southwest.

Sud Viêt-nam [sydvjɛtnam] *npr m* HIST : **le ~** South Vietnam.

suède [sɥɛd] *nm* suede ▪ **des gants en ~** suede *ou* kid gloves.

Suède [sɥɛd] *npr f* : **(la) ~** Sweden.

suédine [sɥedin] *nf* suedette.

suédois, e [sɥedwa, az] *adj* Swedish.
◆ **Suédois, e** *nm, f* Swede.
◆ **suédois** *nm* LING Swedish.

suée [sɥe] *nf fam* [transpiration] sweat ▪ **attraper** *ou* **prendre une (bonne) ~** [en faisant un effort] to work up quite a sweat.

suer [7] [sɥe] ◇ *vi* **1.** [transpirer - personne] to sweat, to get sweaty ▪ **~ à grosses gouttes** to be streaming with sweat, to be sweating profusely **2.** [bois, plâtres] to ooze, to sweat ▪ **faire ~ des oignons** CULIN to sweat onions **3.** *fam* [fournir un gros effort] to slog *UK*, to slave (away) ▪ **j'en ai sué pour faire démarrer la tondeuse!** I had the devil's own job trying to get the mower started! ➤ **faire ~ le burnous**△ to use sweated labour **4.** *fam loc* **faire ~** [importuner] : **il nous fait ~!** he's a pain in the neck! ▪ **ça me ferait ~ de devoir y retourner** I'd hate to have to go back there ▪ **elle m'a fait ~ toute la matinée pour que je joue avec elle** she pestered me all morning to play with her ▪ **je me suis fait ~ toute la journée** I was bored stiff all day long.
◇ *vt* **1.** [sueur] to sweat ▪ **~ sang et eau** [faire de grands efforts] to sweat blood **2.** [humidité] to ooze **3.** *litt* [laisser paraître - bêtise, ennui, égoïsme] to exude, to reek of.

sueur [sɥœr] *nf* **1.** [transpiration] sweat ▪ **sa chemise était mouillée par la ~** his shirt was sweaty *ou* was damp with sweat ➤ **~s froides : j'en ai eu des ~s froides** I was in a cold sweat ▪ **donner des ~s froides à qqn** to put sb in a cold sweat **2.** [effort intense] sweat ▪ **à la ~ de son front** by the sweat of one's brow ▪ **gagner qqch à la ~ de son front** to earn sthg with the sweat of one's brow.
◆ **en sueur** *loc adj* in a sweat ▪ **être en ~** to be in a sweat, to be sweating.

Suez [sɥɛz] *npr* Suez.

suffire [100] [syfir] *vi* **1.** [en quantité] to be enough, to be sufficient, to suffice *sout* ▪ **une cuillerée, ça te suffit?** is one spoonful enough for you? ▪ **~ à** *ou* **pour faire qqch : deux minutes suffisent pour le cuire** it just takes two minutes to cook ▪ **une heure me suffira pour tout ranger** one hour will be enough for me to put everything away ▪ **je ne lui rendrai plus service, cette expérience m'a suffi** I won't help her again, I've learned my lesson ▪ **y ~ : il faut doubler l'effectif – le budget n'y suffira jamais** the staff has to be doubled – the budget won't cover it **2.** [en qualité] to be (good) enough ▪ **parler ne suffit pas, il faut agir** words aren't enough, we must act ▪ **des excuses ne me suffisent pas** I'm not satisfied with an apology ▪ **ma parole devrait vous ~** my word should be good enough for you ▪ **pas besoin de tralala, un sandwich me suffit** there's no need for anything fancy, a sandwich will do ▪ **~ à qqch : ~ aux besoins de qqn** to meet sb's needs ▪ **ça suffit à mon bonheur** it's enough to make me happy **3.** *(tournure impersonnelle)* **il suffit de** *(suivi d'un n)* : **je n'avais jamais volé – il suffit d'une fois!** I've never stolen before – once is enough! ▪ **il suffit d'une erreur pour que tout soit à recommencer** one single mistake means starting all over again ▪ **il suffirait de peu pour que le régime s'écroule** it wouldn't take much to bring down the regime ▪ **il suffit de** *(suivi de l'infin)* : **s'il suffisait de travailler pour réussir!** if only work was enough to guarantee success! ▪ **il te suffit de dire que nous arriverons en retard** just say we'll be late ▪ **il suffit que : il suffit qu'on me dise ce que je dois faire** I just have *ou* need to be told what to do ▪ **il suffit que je tourne le dos pour qu'elle fasse des bêtises** I only have to turn my back and she's up to some mischief ▪ **(ça) suffit!** *fam* (that's) enough! ▪ **ça suffit comme ça!** that's enough now! ▪ **il suffit!** *sout* it's enough!

se suffire <> *vp (emploi réciproque)* : **ils se suffisent l'un à l'autre** they've got each other and that's all they need.
<> *vpi* : **se ~ à soi-même** [matériellement] to be self-sufficient ; [moralement] to be quite happy with one's own company.

suffisamment [syfizamɑ̃] *adv* sufficiently, enough ▪ **je t'ai ~ prévenu** I've warned you often enough.

suffisance [syfizɑ̃s] *nf* **1.** [vanité] self-importance, self-satisfaction ▪ **c'est un homme plein de ~** he's a very self-satisfied man **2.** *litt* **avoir sa ~ de qqch, avoir qqch à ~** to have plenty of sthg.
en suffisance *loc adv litt* **de l'argent en ~** plenty of *ou* sufficient money.

suffisant, e [syfizɑ̃, ɑ̃t] *adj* **1.** [en quantité] sufficient ▪ **sa retraite est ~e pour deux** his pension's sufficient *ou* enough for two ▪ **trois bouteilles pour cinq, c'est bien *ou* amplement ~** three bottles for five, that's plenty *ou* that's quite enough **2.** [en qualité] sufficient, good enough ▪ **votre accord n'est pas ~, nous avons aussi besoin de celui de son père** your consent isn't enough, we also need his father's ▪ **des excuses ne seront pas ~es, il veut un démenti** apologies won't be sufficient *ou* won't do, he wants a denial ▪ **tes résultats à l'école sont tout juste ~s** your school results are just about satisfactory ▪ **c'est une raison ~e pour qu'il accepte** it's a good enough reason *ou* it's reason enough to make him accept **3.** [arrogant - air, personne] self-important, conceited ▪ **d'un air ~** smugly.

suffisons *etc v* ▷ **suffire**.

suffixation [syfiksasjɔ̃] *nf* suffixation, suffixing *(U)*.

suffixe [syfiks] *nm* suffix.

suffocant, e [syfɔkɑ̃, ɑ̃t] *adj* **1.** [atmosphère, chaleur, odeur] suffocating, stifling **2.** [ahurissant] astounding, staggering, stunning.

suffocation [syfɔkasjɔ̃] *nf* suffocation ▪ **j'ai des ~s** I feel as if I am choking.

suffoquer [3] [syfɔke] <> *vi* [étouffer] to suffocate, to choke ▪ **on suffoque ici!** it's stifling in here! ▪ **~ de colère** to be choking with anger ▪ **~ de joie** to be overcome with happiness.
<> *vt* **1.** [suj: atmosphère, fumée, odeur] to suffocate, to choke **2.** [causer une vive émotion à] to choke ▪ **la colère le suffoquait** he was choking with anger **3.** [choquer - suj: attitude, prix] to stagger, to stun, to confound.

suffrage [syfraʒ] *nm* **1.** POLIT [système] vote ▪ **~ censitaire** HIST suffrage with property qualification *ou* for householders (only) ▪ **être élu au ~ direct/indirect** to be elected by direct/ indirect suffrage ▪ **~ restreint** restricted suffrage ▪ **~ universel** universal suffrage **2.** [voix] vote ▪ **obtenir beaucoup/peu de ~s** to poll heavily/badly ▪ **c'est leur parti qui a eu le plus de ~s** their party headed the poll **3.** *litt* [approbation] approval, approbation, suffrage *litt* ▪ **sa dernière pièce a enlevé *ou* remporté tous les ~s** his last play was an unqualified success ▪ **accorder son ~ à** to give one's approval to.

suffragette [syfraʒɛt] *nf* suffragette.

suggérer [18] [sygʒere] *vt* **1.** [conseiller, proposer - acte] to suggest ; [- nom, solution] to suggest, to put forward *(sép)*, to propose ▪ **nous lui avons suggéré de renoncer** we suggested he should give up ▪ **je suggère que nous partions tout de suite** I suggest that we go right away **2.** [évoquer] to suggest, to evoke ▪ **sa peinture suggère plus qu'elle ne représente** his painting is more evocative than figurative.

suggestible [sygʒɛstibl] *adj* suggestible.

suggestif, ive [sygʒɛstif, iv] *adj* **1.** [évocateur] suggestive, evocative ▪ **de façon suggestive** suggestively **2.** [érotique] suggestive, provocative.

suggestion [sygʒɛstjɔ̃] *nf* **1.** [conseil, proposition] suggestion ▪ **faire une ~** to make a suggestion **2.** PSYCHOL suggestion.
Voir module d'usage

suggestionner [3] [sygʒɛstjɔne] *vt* to influence by suggestion.

suggestivité [sygʒɛstivite] *nf* **1.** [évocation] evocativeness **2.** [érotisme] suggestiveness.

suicidaire [sɥisidɛr] <> *adj* **1.** [instinct, personne, tendance] suicidal **2.** [qui conduit à l'échec] suicidal ▪ **de si gros investissements, ce serait ~!** such large investments would be suicidal *ou* courting disaster!
<> *nmf* suicidal person, potential suicide.

suicide [sɥisid] *nm* **1.** [mort] suicide ▪ **faire une tentative de ~** to try to commit suicide, to attempt suicide ▪ **~ assisté** assisted suicide **2.** [désastre] suicide ▪ **n'y va pas, c'est du ~!** *fig* don't go, it would be madness *ou* it's suicide!

suicidé, e [sɥiside] *nm, f* suicide.

suicider [3] [sɥiside] *vt* : **le prisonnier a été suicidé dans sa cellule** the murder of the prisoner in his cell was made to look like suicide.
se suicider *vpi* **1.** [se tuer] to commit suicide, to kill o.s. ▪ **tenter de se ~** to attempt suicide, to try to commit suicide **2.** *fig* [causer soi-même sa perte] to commit suicide.

suie [sɥi] *nf* soot ▪ **être couvert *ou* noir de ~** to be all sooty *ou* black with soot.

suif [sɥif] *nm* **1.** [de bétail] fat ▪ CULIN suet ▪ [pour chandelle] tallow **2.** *fam* [bagarre] : **il va y avoir du ~** there's going to be a scrap.

sui generis [sɥiʒeneris] *loc adj* sui generis, unique ▪ **une odeur ~** *euphém* a rather distinctive smell.

suint [sɥɛ̃] *nm* suint.

suintant, e [sɥɛ̃tɑ̃, ɑ̃t] *adj* sweating, oozing ▪ **des murs ~s** damp walls.

suintement [sɥɛ̃tmɑ̃] *nm* **1.** [écoulement] sweating *(U)*, oozing *(U)* **2.** INDUST **du pétrole** oozing (forth) *(U)*.

suinter [3] [sɥɛ̃te] <> *vi* **1.** [s'écouler] to ooze, to seep ▪ **l'humidité suinte des murailles** the walls are dripping with

LA SUGGESTION

Let's go swimming! Allons nager !

Why don't you phone him? Pourquoi tu ne l'appelles pas ?

Why not go and see her? Pourquoi est-ce que tu n'irais pas la voir ?

Perhaps we could buy him a watch. On pourrait peut-être lui acheter une montre ?

What about a CD? *(comme idée de cadeau)* Un CD, peut-être ?

What if I spoke to him first? Et si je lui parlais d'abord ?

How about a game of cards? Une partie de cartes, ça te dit ?

Have you ever thought about changing jobs? Et si tu changeais de travail ?

What would you say to *ou* **How would you feel about a trip abroad?** Qu'est-ce que tu dirais d'un voyage à l'étranger ?

You could always write to them. Tu pourrais leur écrire.

I suggest telling him *ou* **(that) we tell him.** Je suggère qu'on le lui dise.

moisture **2.** [laisser échapper un liquide - plaie] to weep ■ **ce mur suinte** this wall is running with moisture **3.** *litt* [se manifester] to ooze.
◇ *vt litt* to ooze.

suis *v* **1.** ▷ **être 2.** ▷ **suivre.**

suisse [sɥis] ◇ *adj* Swiss ■ **~ allemand/romand** Swiss German/French.
◇ *nm* **1.** [au Vatican] Swiss guard **2.** [bedeau] beadle **3.** *Québec* chipmunk.
◆ **Suisse** *nmf* Swiss (person) ■ **Suisse allemand/romand** German-speaking/French-speaking Swiss ■ **les Suisses** the Swiss.
◆ **en suisse** *loc adv* : **boire/manger en ~** to drink/to eat on one's own.

Suisse [sɥis] *npr f* : **(la) ~** Switzerland ■ **la ~ allemande/romande** the German-speaking/French-speaking part of Switzerland.

Suissesse [sɥisɛs] *nf* Swiss woman.

suit *etc v* ▷ **suivre.**

suite [sɥit] *nf* **1.** [prolongation - gén] continuation ; [- d'un film, d'un roman] sequel ; [- d'une émission] follow-up ■ **~ page 17** continued on page 17 ■ **la ~ au prochain numéro** to be continued (in our next issue) ■ **~ et fin** final instalment ■ **apportez-moi la ~** [pendant un repas] bring me the next course ■ **écoute la ~** [du discours] listen to what comes next ; [de mon histoire] listen to what happened next ■ **je n'ai pas pu entendre la ~** I couldn't hear the rest ■ **attendons la ~ des événements** let's wait to see what happens next ■ **faire ~ à** to follow ■ **de violents orages ont fait ~ à la sécheresse** the drought was followed by violent storms ■ **prendre la ~ de qqn** to take over from sb, to succeed sb
2. [série] series, succession ■ **une ~ de malheurs** a run *ou* series of misfortunes
3. [cortège] suite, retinue
4. [dans un hôtel] suite
5. [répercussion] consequence ■ **la ~ logique/naturelle de mon adhésion au parti** the logical/natural consequence of my joining the party ■ **donner ~ à** [commande, lettre, réclamation] to follow up *(sép)*, to deal with *(insép)* ; [projet] to carry on with ■ **avoir des ~s** to have repercussions ■ **elle est morte des ~s de ses blessures** she died of her wounds
6. [lien logique] coherence ■ **ses propos n'avaient guère de ~** what he said wasn't very logical ■ **avoir de la ~ dans les idées** to be coherent *ou* consistent ■ **tu as de la ~ dans les idées!** *hum* you certainly know what you want!
7. DR pursuit
8. LING & MATH sequence
9. MUS suite.
◆ **à la suite** *loc adv* **1.** [en succession] one after the other
2. [après] : **un nom avec plusieurs chiffres inscrits à la ~** a name followed by a string of numbers.
◆ **à la suite de** *loc prép* **1.** [derrière - dans l'espace] behind ; [- dans un écrit] after ■ **cinq chambres les unes à la ~ des autres** five rooms in a row
2. [à cause de] following ■ **à la ~ de son discours télévisé, sa cote a remonté** following her speech on TV, her popularity rating went up.
◆ **de suite** *loc adv* **1.** *fam* [immédiatement] straightaway, right away ■ **il revient de ~** he'll be right back
2. [à la file] in a row, one after the other, in succession ■ **elle est restée de garde 48 heures de ~** she was on duty for 48 hours on end ■ **on n'a pas eu d'électricité pendant cinq jours de ~** we didn't have any electricity for five whole days *ou* five days running.
◆ **par la suite** *loc adv* [dans le passé] afterwards, later ■ [dans le futur] later ■ **ils se sont mariés par la ~** they eventually got married.
◆ **par suite** *loc adv* therefore.
◆ **par suite de** *loc prép* due to, owing to ■ **par ~ d'un arrêt de travail des techniciens** due to industrial action by technical staff.
◆ **sans suite** *loc adj* **1.** [incohérent] disconnected ■ **il tenait des propos sans ~** his talk was incoherent
2. COMM discontinued.
◆ **suite à** *loc prép* ADMIN : **~ à votre lettre** further to *ou* in response to *ou* with reference to your letter ■ **~ à votre appel téléphonique** further to your phone call.

suivait *etc v* ▷ **suivre.**

suivant[1] [sɥivɑ̃] *prép* **1.** [le long de] : **découper ~ le pointillé** cut out following the dotted line **2.** [d'après] according to ■ **~ son habitude, elle s'est levée très tôt** as is her habit *ou* wont *sout*, she got up very early **3.** [en fonction de] according to, depending on ■ **vous donnerez ~ vos possibilités** you'll give according to your means ■ **~ votre âge/vos besoins** depending on your age/your needs.
◆ **suivant que** *loc conj* according to whether ■ **~ que vous parlez avec l'un ou l'autre** according to which one you talk to.

suivant[2]**, e** [sɥivɑ̃, ɑ̃t] ◇ *adj* **1.** [qui vient après - chapitre, mois, semaine] following, next ; [- échelon, train] next ■ **quel est le chiffre ~?** what's the next number?, what number comes next? ■ **quelle est la personne ~e?** [dans une file d'attente] who's next? **2.** [qui va être précisé] following ■ **il m'a raconté l'histoire ~e** he told me the following story ■ **procédez de la manière ~e** follow these instructions.
◇ *nm, f* **1.** [dans une succession] next one ■ **(au) ~, s'il vous plaît** next, please ■ **son premier roman, et même les ~s** his first novel and even the following ones *ou* the ones that followed ■ **pas mardi prochain mais le ~** not this coming Tuesday but the next one *ou* the one after **2.** *(comme adj)* [ce qui va être précisé] : **les résultats sont les ~s** here are the results, the results are as follows.
◆ **suivant** *nm* [membre d'une escorte] attendant.
◆ **suivante** *nf* THÉÂTRE lady's maid.

suiveur, euse [sɥivœr, øz] *adj* [véhicule] following.
◆ **suiveur** *nm* **1.** [de femmes - gén] skirt-chaser ; [- en voiture] kerb-crawler **2.** SPORT follower, fan **3.** [inconditionnel, imitateur] slave, uncritical follower.

suivi, e [sɥivi] ◇ *pp* ▷ **suivre.**
◇ *adj* **1.** [ininterrompu - effort] sustained, consistent ; [- correspondance] regular ; [- qualité] consistent ; [- activité] steady ■ **nous avons eu une correspondance très ~e pendant des années** we wrote to each other very regularly for years **2.** [logique - propos, raisonnement] coherent ; [- politique] consistent **3.** [qui a la faveur du public] : **mode très ~e** very popular fashion ■ **conférence peu/très ~e** poorly attended/well-attended conference ■ **la grève a été peu/très ~e** there was little/a lot of support for the strike.
◆ **suivi** *nm* [d'un cas, d'un dossier] follow-up ■ **assurer le ~ de** [cas, dossier] to follow through *(sép)* ; [commande] to deal with *(insép)* ; COMM [article] to continue to stock ■ **le travail en petits groupes assure un meilleur ~** working in small groups means that individual participants can be monitored more successfully.

suivisme [sɥivism] *nm* [attitude d'imitation servile] follow-my-leader attitude.

suivre [89] [sɥivr] ◇ *vt*

A. DANS L'ESPACE, LE TEMPS **B.** ADOPTER, OBÉIR À

A. DANS L'ESPACE, LE TEMPS

1. [pour escorter, espionner, rattraper] to follow ■ **les enfants suivaient leurs parents en courant** the children were running behind their parents ■ **suivez le guide** this way (for the guided tour), please ■ **la police les a suivis sur plusieurs kilomètres** the police chased them for several kilometres ■ **il l'a fait ~ par un détective privé** he had her followed by a private detective ■ **~ qqn de près** [gén] to follow close behind sb ; [pour le protéger] to stick close to sb ■ **le coureur anglais, suivi de très près par le Belge** the English runner, with the Belgian close on his heels ■ **~ la piste de qqn** to follow sb's trail ■ **~ qqn à la trace** to follow sb's tracks ■ **~ qqn comme son ombre** to follow sb like a shadow ■ **~ qqn des yeux *ou* du regard** to follow sb with one's eyes ■ **il suivait des yeux ses moindres gestes** he was watching her every move ■ **certaines personnes, suivez mon regard, n'ont pas fait leur travail** certain people, who shall be *ou* remain

nameless, haven't done their work ■ *(en usage absolu)* **marche moins vite, je ne peux pas ~** slow down, I can't keep up ■ **ils ne suivent plus** they're not behind (us) any more
2. [se dérouler après] to follow (on from), to come after ■ **la réunion sera suivie d'une collation** refreshments will be served after the meeting ■ *(en usage absolu)* **le jour qui suivit** (the) next day, the following day ■ *(tournure impersonnelle)* **il suit de votre déclaration que le témoin ment** it follows from your statement that the witness is lying
3. [être placé après] to follow, to come after ■ **votre nom suit le mien sur la liste** your name is right after mine on the list ■ **les conjonctions toujours suivies du subjonctif** the conjunctions always followed by *ou* that always govern the subjunctive ■ *(en usage absolu)* **suit un résumé du roman précédent** then comes a summary of the previous novel ■ **dans les pages qui suivent** in the following pages

B. ADOPTER, OBÉIR À
1. [emprunter - itinéraire, rue] to follow
2. [longer - à pied] to walk along ; [- en voiture] to drive along ; [- en bateau] to sail along ■ **la route suit la rivière sur plusieurs kilomètres** the road runs along *ou* follows (the course of) the river for several kilometres ■ **le circuit suit ce tracé** here is the outline of the course ■ **découper en suivant les pointillés** cut along the dotted line
3. [se soumettre à - traitement] to undergo ■ **~ des cours de cuisine** to attend a cookery course ■ **~ un régime** to be on a diet
4. [se conformer à - conseil, personne, instructions] to follow ■ [règlement] to comply with *(insép)* ■ **vous n'avez qu'à ~ les panneaux** just follow the signs ■ **son exemple n'est pas à ~** he's not a good example ■ **je préfère ~ mon idée** I prefer to do it my way ■ **~ le mouvement** *fam* to (just) go *ou* tag along with the crowd ■ *(en usage absolu)* **la majorité n'a pas suivi** the majority didn't follow
5. CARTES : **je suis** I'm in
6. COMM [stocker] to stock ■ [produire] to produce

C.
1. [observer - carrière, progrès, feuilleton] to follow ; [- actualité] to keep up with *(insép)* ■ **il suit le feuilleton à la radio tous les jours** he tunes in to the serial every day
2. [se concentrer sur - exposé, messe] to listen to *(insép)*, to pay attention to ■ **maintenant, suivez-moi bien** now, listen to me carefully *ou* pay close attention ■ **suis bien mes gestes** watch my gestures closely ■ *(en usage absolu)* **encore un qui ne suivait pas!** [distrait] so, someone else wasn't paying attention! ■ **je vais ~ avec Pierre** [sur son livre] I'll share Pierre's book
3. [comprendre - explications, raisonnement] to follow ■ **je ne te suis plus** I'm not with you any more
4. [s'occuper de - dossier, commande] to deal with *(insép)* ; [- élève] to follow the progress of ■ **elle suit ses patients de près** she follows her patients' progress closely ■ **je suis suivie par un très bon médecin** I'm with *ou* under a very good doctor.
◇ *vi* **1.** ÉDUC [assimiler le programme] to keep up ■ **il a du mal à ~ en physique** he's having difficulty keeping up in physics **2.** [être acheminé après] : **'lettre suit'** 'will write soon, letter follows' ■ **faire ~** [lettre] to forward, to send on ■ **faire ~ son courrier** to have one's mail forwarded **3.** [être ci-après] to follow ■ **sont reçus les candidats dont les noms suivent** the names of the successful candidates are as follows ■ **procéder comme suit** proceed as follows.
◆ **se suivre** *vpi* **1.** [être l'un derrière l'autre - personnes, lettres] to follow one another ■ **par temps de brouillard, ne vous suivez pas de trop près** in foggy conditions, keep your distance (from other vehicles) ■ **les trois coureurs se suivent de très près** the three runners are very close behind one another *ou* are tightly bunched **2.** [être dans l'ordre - pages] to be in the right order, to follow on from one another **3.** [se succéder dans le temps] : **les jours se suivent et ne se ressemblent pas** *prov* who knows what tomorrow holds *loc*, every day is a new beginning *ou* dawn.
◆ **à suivre** ◇ *loc adj* : **c'est une affaire à ~** it's something we should keep an eye on.
◇ *loc adv* : **'à ~'** 'to be continued'.

sujet, ette [syʒɛ, ɛt] ◇ *adj* **1.** : **~ à** [susceptible de] : **~ à des attaques cardiaques/à des migraines** subject to heart attacks/ migraines ■ **~ au mal de mer** liable to become seasick, prone to seasickness ■ **nous sommes tous ~s à l'erreur** we're all prone to making mistakes
2. [franchise, honnêteté, moralité] : **~ à** : **~ à caution** questionable ■ **leurs informations sont ~tes à caution** their information should be taken warily
3. *litt* [assujetti] subjugated, enslaved.
◇ *nm, f* [citoyen] subject.
◆ **sujet** *nm* **1.** [thème - d'une discussion] subject, topic ; [- d'une pièce, d'un roman] subject ; [- d'un exposé, d'une recherche] subject ■ **le ~ de notre débat ce soir est...** the question we'll be debating tonight is... ■ **quel est le ~ du livre?** what's the book about? ■ **~ de conversation** topic (of conversation) ■ **changeons de ~** let's change the subject ■ **~ de plainte** grievance ■ **c'est devenu un ~ de plaisanterie** it has become a standing joke ■ **~ d'examen** examination question
2. [motif] : **~ de** cause of, ground for, grounds for ■ **ils ont de nombreux ~s de discorde** they have many reasons to disagree ■ **leur salaire est leur principal ~ de mécontentement** the main cause of their dissatisfaction is their salary ■ **sa santé est devenue un gros ~ de préoccupation** her condition is now giving serious grounds for concern *ou* has become a great source of anxiety ■ **tu n'as pas ~ de te plaindre** you have no cause *ou* grounds for complaint
3. ART & MUS subject
4. [figurine] figurine
5. GRAMM [fonction] subject ■ LING : **le ~ parlant** the speaker
6. MÉD, PHILOS & PSYCHOL subject ■ **~ d'expérience** experimental subject
7. HORT stock.
◆ **au sujet de** *loc prép* about, concerning ■ **c'est au ~ de Martha?** is it about Martha? ■ **j'aimerais vous faire remarquer, à ce ~, que...** concerning this matter, I'd like to point out to you that... ■ **je voudrais parler au directeur – c'est à quel ~?** I'd like to talk to the manager – what about?
Voir module d'usage

CHANGER DE SUJET

Incidentally, has anyone heard from John lately? Au fait, est-ce que quelqu'un a des nouvelles de John ?

By the way, you still owe me for the train ticket. Au fait, tu me dois toujours le billet de train.

Talking of ghosts, did anyone see that film on TV last night? À propos de fantômes, est-ce que quelqu'un a vu le film à la télé hier soir ?

While I remember, did you ever find your ring? Tant que j'y pense, est-ce que tu as retrouvé ta bague finalement ?

Before I forget, who won the match? Avant que j'oublie, qui a gagné le match ?

Anyway, as I was saying,... Bref, comme je disais tout à l'heure,...

Changing the subject completely, does anyone know a good dentist? Je change complètement de sujet, mais est-ce que quelqu'un connaîtrait un bon dentiste ?

sujétion [syʒesjɔ̃] *nf* **1.** POLIT [d'un peuple] subjection, enslavement ▪ **tenir en ~** to hold *ou* to have in one's power **2.** *sout* [à une règle] subjection, subjecting *(U)*.

sulfate [sylfat] *nm* sulphate.

sulfater [3] [sylfate] *vt* **1.** AGRIC to spray with sulphur **2.** ÉLECTR to sulphate.

sulfateuse [sylfatøz] *nf* **1.** AGRIC sulphur sprayer **2.**△ *arg mil* [mitrailleuse] typewriter △ *UK*, submachine *ou* machine gun.

sulfite [sylfit] *nm* sulphite.

sulfurage [sylfyraʒ] *nm* sulphuration.

sulfure [sylfyr] *nm* sulphide.

sulfuré, e [sylfyre] *adj* sulphuret.

sulfurer [3] [sylfyre] *vt* to sulphuret.

sulfureux, euse [sylfyrø, øz] *adj* **1.** CHIM sulphurous **2.** [démoniaque] demonic.

sulfurique [sylfyrik] *adj* sulphuric.

sulfurisé, e [sylfyrize] *adj* sulphurized.

sulky [sylki] *nm* sulky.

sultan [syltɑ̃] *nm* sultan.

sultanat [syltana] *nm* sultanate.

sultane [syltan] *nf* **1.** [titre] sultana, sultaness **2.** [canapé] sultana.

Sumatra [symatra] *npr* Sumatra ▪ **à ~** in Sumatra.

sumérien, enne [symerjɛ̃, ɛn] *adj* Sumerian.
◆ **Sumérien, enne** *nm, f* Sumerian.

summum [sɔmmɔm] *nm* **1.** [d'une carrière] peak, zenith *sout* ▪ [d'une civilisation] acme ▪ [de l'élégance, du luxe, de l'arrogance] height ▪ **au ~ de sa puissance** at the peak of its power ▪ **elle était au ~ de son art quand elle peignit ce tableau** her art was at its peak *ou* height when she painted this picture **2.** *fam loc* **c'est le ~!** [on ne peut faire mieux] it's the tops! ; [on ne peut faire pire] it's the end!

sumo [sumo] *nm* sumo.

sunnite [synit] ◇ *adj* Sunni.
◇ *nmf* Sunnit, Sunnite.

sup [syp] *adj inv fam* [supplémentaire] : **faire des heures ~** to work overtime.

super [sypɛr] *fam* ◇ *adj inv* [personne, idée] great, terrific ▪ [maison, moto] fantastic, great ▪ **c'est de la ~ qualité** it's exceptional quality ▪ **~ réductions sur tout le stock!** massive reductions on the whole stock!
◇ *adv* [compliqué, bon, cher, propre] really, amazingly ▪ [gentil] really.
◇ *nm* [essence] four-star (petrol) *UK*, premium *US*.

super- [sypɛr] *préf* **1.** [en intensif] super ▪ **des collants ~fins** extra-fine tights ▪ **~rapide** superfast **2.** *fam* [exceptionnel] super ▪ **~flic** supercop.

superalliage [sypɛraljaʒ] *nm* superalloy.

superbe [sypɛrb] ◇ *adj* **1.** [magnifique - yeux, bijou, ville] superb, beautiful ; [- bébé, femme] beautiful, gorgeous ; [- homme] good-looking, handsome ; [- voix] superb, beautiful ; [- journée] glorious, beautiful ; [- temps] wonderful ▪ **tu as une mine ~ aujourd'hui** you look radiant today **2.** [sublime] : **~ de : il a été ~ de cynisme/d'indifférence** he was superbly cynical/indifferent **3.** *litt* [altier - air] haughty.
◇ *nf litt* haughtiness ▪ **cela va lui faire perdre de sa ~** he won't be quite so proud after this.

superbement [sypɛrbəmɑ̃] *adv* **1.** [splendidement] superbly, magnificently, beautifully **2.** *litt* [arrogamment] arrogantly, haughtily.

supercalculateur [sypɛrkalkylatœr] *nm* INFORM supercomputer.

supercarburant [sypɛrkarbyrɑ̃] *nm* four-star *ou* high-octane petrol *UK*, premium *US*.

superchampion, onne [sypɛrʃɑ̃pjɔ̃, ɔn] *nm, f* sports superstar.

supercherie [sypɛrʃəri] *nf* [tromperie] deception, trick ▪ [fraude] fraud ▪ **~ littéraire** literary hoax.

supérette [syperɛt] *nf* mini-market, superette *US*.

superfétatoire [sypɛrfetatwar] *adj litt* superfluous, unnecessary, redundant.

superficie [sypɛrfisi] *nf* **1.** [d'un champ] acreage, area ▪ [d'une maison] surface area, floor space ▪ **l'entrepôt fait 3 000 m^2 de ~ *ou* a une ~ de 3 000 m^2** the warehouse has a surface area of 3,000 m^2 **2.** *litt* [apparence] superficial *ou* external appearance **3.** AGRIC : **~ agricole utile *ou* utilisée** utilized agricultural area.

superficiel, elle [sypɛrfisjɛl] *adj* **1.** [brûlure] superficial, surface *(modif)* **2.** [connaissances, personne] shallow, insubstantial ▪ [étude, travail] superficial, perfunctory ▪ [contrôle] superficial, cursory.

superficiellement [sypɛrfisjɛlmɑ̃] *adv* **1.** [blesser] superficially **2.** [inspecter, corriger] cursorily, superficially.

superfin, e [sypɛrfɛ̃, in] *adj* extrafine.

superflu, e [sypɛrfly] *adj* **1.** [non nécessaire - biens, excuse, recommandation] superfluous, unnecessary **2.** [en trop - détails, exemple] redundant, superfluous ▪ **un grand lessivage ne serait pas ~** a good scrub wouldn't do any harm! ▪ **pour vous débarrasser de vos poils ~s** to get rid of unwanted hair.
◆ **superflu** *nm* : **le ~** that which is superfluous ▪ **se passer du ~** to do without non-essentials.

superforme [sypɛrfɔrm] *nf fam* **être en ~, tenir la ~** to be in great form *ou* on top form *ou* bursting with health.

supergéante [sypɛrʒeɑ̃t] *nf* ASTRON supergiant.

supergrand [sypɛrgrɑ̃] *nm fam* superpower.

super-huit [sypɛrɥit] ◇ *adj inv* super eight.
◇ *nm inv* [format] super eight.
◇ *nf inv* [caméra] super-eight (film) camera.

supérieur, e [syperjœr] ◇ *adj* **1.** [plus haut que le reste - étagère, étage] upper, top ; [- ligne] top ▪ **le bord ~ droit de la page** the top right-hand corner of the page ▪ [juste au-dessus - étagère, ligne] above ▪ **les jouets sont à l'étage ~** toys are on the next floor *ou* the floor above
2. [quantitativement - efficacité] higher, greater ; [- prix, rendement, vitesse] higher ; [- volume] bigger, greater ▪ **~ en nombre : troupes ~es en nombre** troops superior in number ▪ **leurs joueurs se retrouvent maintenant ~s en nombre** their players now outnumber the opposition ▪ **~ à** [prix] higher than ; [volume] bigger than ▪ **donne-moi un chiffre ~ à huit** give me a number higher than eight ▪ **taux légèrement ~ à 8 %** rate slightly over 8% ▪ **une note ~e à 10** a mark above 10 ▪ **d'une longueur/largeur ~e à...** longer/wider than... ▪ **il est d'une taille ~e à la moyenne** he's taller than average
3. [dans une hiérarchie - échelons] upper, topmost ; [- classes sociales] upper ▪ **enseignement ~** higher education ▪ **les autorités ~es** the powers above ▪ [juste au-dessus - niveau] next ; [- grade, rang] senior ; [- autorité] higher ▪ **passer dans la classe ~e** ÉDUC to move up one class ▪ **je lui suis hiérarchiquement ~** I'm his superior *ou* senior
4. [dans une échelle de valeurs - intelligence, esprit, être] superior ; [- intérêts] higher ▪ **de qualité ~e** top quality ▪ **~ à : intelligence ~e à la moyenne** above-average intelligence ▪ **leur lessive est-elle vraiment ~e à toutes les autres?** is their washing powder really better than all the others? ▪ **il est techniquement ~ au Suédois** SPORT his technique is superior to that of the Swedish player
5. [hautain - air, ton] superior ▪ **ne prends pas cet air ~!** don't look so superior!
6. ANAT [membre, mâchoire] upper
7. BIOL [animal, espèce, végétal] higher
8. GÉOGR [en amont] upper
9. MATH superior ▪ **~ ou égal à** superior or equal to, greater than or equal to
10. RELIG : **le Père ~** the father superior ▪ **la Mère ~e** the mother superior.

◇ *nm, f* [dans une hiérarchie] : ~ **(hiérarchique)** superior.
◆ **supérieur** *nm* UNIV : **le ~** higher education.
◆ **Supérieur, e** ◇ *nm, f* RELIG father (*f* mother) superior.
◇ *adj* : **le lac Supérieur** Lake Superior.

supérieurement [syperjœrmɑ̃] *adv* exceptionally ▪ **elle est ~ douée** she's exceptionally gifted.

supériorité [syperjɔrite] *nf* **1.** [en qualité] superiority **2.** [en quantité] superiority ▪ **~ numérique** superiority in numbers ▪ **la ~ que donne l'argent** the power that money confers **3.** [arrogance] patronizing attitude, superiority ▪ **un air de ~** a superior air.

superlatif, ive [syperlatif, iv] *adj* superlative.
◆ **superlatif** *nm* LING superlative ▪ **~ relatif/absolu** relative/absolute superlative, *voir aussi* **pluriel**.
◆ **au superlatif** *loc adv* **1.** LING in the superlative **2.** [très] extremely ▪ **il est paresseux au ~** he's extremely lazy.

superléger [syperleʒe] *nm* light welterweight.

superman [syperman] (*pl* **supermans** *ou pl* **supermen** [-mɛn]) *nm fam* superman.

supermarché [sypermarʃe] *nm* supermarket.

supernova [sypernɔva] *nf* supernova.

superordinateur [syperɔrdinatœr] *nm* supercomputer.

superpétrolier [syperpetrɔlje] *nm* supertanker.

Superphénix [syperfeniks] *npr the fast-breeder reactor at Creys-Malville.*

superposable [syperpozabl] *adj* **1.** GÉOM superposable **2.** [chaise, lit] stacking (*avant n*).

superposer [3] [syperpoze] *vt* **1.** [meubles] to stack (up) ▪ [images, couleurs] to superimpose ▪ **cette année la mode superpose les épaisseurs** layered fabrics are fashionable this year **2.** GÉOM to superpose.
◆ **se superposer** ◇ *vp (emploi passif)* [étagères] to stack.
◇ *vpi* **1.** [se mêler - images, sons, couleurs] to be superimposed ▪ **leurs deux visages se superposent dans ma mémoire** their two faces have become indistinguishable in my memory **2.** GÉOM to be superposed.

superposition [syperpozisjɔ̃] *nf* **1.** [d'étagères, de plats] stacking **2.** GÉOM superposition **3.** [de photos, de sons] superimposition, superimposing (*U*).

superproduction [syperprɔdyksjɔ̃] *nf* CINÉ big-budget film UK *ou* movie US.

superprofit [syperprɔfi] *nm* enormous profit.

superpuissance [syperpɥisɑ̃s] *nf* superpower.

supersonique [sypersɔnik] ◇ *adj* supersonic.
◇ *nm* supersonic aircraft.

superstar [syperstar] *nf* superstar.

superstitieusement [syperstisjøzmɑ̃] *adv* superstitiously.

superstitieux, euse [syperstisjø, øz] ◇ *adj* superstitious ▪ **ils ont un attachement ~ aux traditions** they have an exaggerated respect for tradition.
◇ *nm, f* superstitious person.

superstition [syperstisjɔ̃] *nf* superstition ▪ **j'évite les échelles par pure ~** I walk round ladders simply because I'm superstitious.

superstructure [syperstryktyr] *nf* superstructure.

supertanker [sypertɑ̃kœr] *nm* supertanker.

superviser [3] [sypervize] *vt* to supervise, to oversee.

superviseur [sypervizœr] *nm* **1.** [personne] supervisor **2.** INFORM supervisor, scheduler.

supervision [sypervizjɔ̃] *nf* supervision ▪ **être sous la ~ de qqn** to be supervised by sb, to be under sb's supervision.

super-welter [syperweltœr] (*pl* **super-welters**) *nm* light middleweight.

supin [sypɛ̃] *nm* LING supine.

supplanter [3] [syplɑ̃te] *vt* **1.** [rival] to supplant, to displace, to supersede **2.** [machine, système] to supplant, to take over from (*insép*).

suppléance [sypleɑ̃s] *nf* **1.** ÉDUC [poste de remplaçant] supply post UK, substitute post US ▪ [poste d'adjoint] assistantship ▪ **assurer la ~ de qqn** [le remplacer] to deputize for sb ; [l'assister] to assist sb ▮ [activité - de remplaçant] supply UK *ou* substitute US teaching ; [- d'adjoint] assistantship **2.** DR & POLIT deputy **3.** LING suppletion.

suppléant, e [sypleɑ̃, ɑ̃t] ◇ *adj* **1.** ÉDUC [remplaçant] supply UK, substitute US ▪ [adjoint] assistant **2.** DR & POLIT deputy.
◇ *nm, f* **1.** ÉDUC [remplaçant] supply teacher UK, substitute teacher US ▪ [adjoint] assistant teacher **2.** DR & POLIT deputy.

suppléer [15] [syplee] *vt* **1.** *litt* [remédier à - manque] to make up for (*insép*), to compensate for (*insép*) ; [- lacune] to fill in (*sép*) **2.** [compléter] to complement, to supplement ▪ **~ qqch par** to complete sthg with **3.** ÉDUC to replace, to stand in for (*insép*) **4.** DR & POLIT to deputize for.
◆ **suppléer à** *v+prép* **1.** [remédier à - insuffisance] to make up for, to compensate for **2.** [remplacer - suj: personne] to replace ▪ **l'énergie nucléaire a peu à peu suppléé aux énergies traditionnelles** nuclear energy has gradually taken over from *ou* replaced traditional forms of energy.

supplément [syplemɑ̃] *nm* **1.** [coût] extra *ou* additional charge ▪ **ils demandent un ~ de deux euros pour le vin** they charge two euros extra for wine ▪ **payer un ~** to pay extra **2.** RAIL [réservation] supplement ▪ **un train à ~** a train with a fare surcharge *ou* supplement **3.** [de nourriture] extra portion ▪ [de crédits] additional facility ▪ **un ~ d'informations** additional *ou* further information ▪ **le juge a demandé un ~ d'enquête** the judge asked that the investigation be pursued further **4.** [à un livre, un journal] supplement ▪ **~ détachable** pullout **5.** DR : **~ de revenu familial** ≃ family income supplement **6.** MATH supplement.
◆ **en supplément** *loc adv* extra ▪ **c'est en ~** it comes as an extra, it's an extra ▪ **menu douze euros, boisson en ~** menu twelve euros, drinks extra.

supplémentaire [syplemɑ̃tɛr] *adj* **1.** [crédit, dépense] additional, supplementary, extra ▪ **un délai ~** an extension (of deadline) ▪ **ce sera une charge ~ pour les contribuables** it will mean even more of a burden to the taxpayer **2.** RAIL relief (*modif*) **3.** MATH supplementary.

supplétif, ive [sypletif, iv] *adj* **1.** [gén] auxiliary, additional **2.** DR [loi] supplementary **3.** MIL auxiliary **4.** LING suppletive.
◆ **supplétif** *nm* MIL auxiliary.

suppliant, e [syplijɑ̃, ɑ̃t] ◇ *adj* begging, imploring, beseeching *litt* ▪ **d'un ton ~** imploringly, pleadingly.
◇ *nm, f* supplicant.

supplication [syplikasjɔ̃] *nf* entreaty, supplication *sout* ▪ **malgré toutes mes ~s** despite all my pleading.

supplice [syplis] *nm* **1.** HIST torture ▪ **il va à l'école comme au ~** when he goes to school, it's as if he was going to his own funeral ▶ **~ chinois** *pr* Chinese water torture ; *fig* extreme torment ▪ **subir le ~ de la roue** to be broken on the wheel ▪ **le ~ de Tantale** the punishment of Tantalus ▪ **le dernier ~** [la peine de mort] execution **2.** [douleur physique] agony, torture ▪ **ce mal de tête est un vrai ~** I'm going through agony *ou* agonies with this headache ▮ [douleur morale] torture, torment, agony ▶ **être au ~** to be in agonies ▪ **mettre qqn au ~** to torture sb.

supplicié, e [syplisje] *nm, f* [personne - qui a subi la peine de mort] execution victim ; [- qui a été torturée] torture victim ▪ **les corps des ~s étaient entassés dans des charrettes** the bodies of those executed were piled onto carts.

supplicier [9] [syplisje] *vt* **1.** *litt* [exécuter] to execute ▪ [torturer] to torture **2.** [tourmenter] to torment, to rack, to plague.

supplier [10] [syplije] *vt* to beg, to implore, to beseech *litt* ▪ **~ qqn (à genoux) de faire qqch** to beg sb (on bended knee) to do sthg.

supplique [syplik] *nf* DR & RELIG petition ▪ **présenter une ~ à qqn** to petition sb.

support [sypɔr] *nm* **1.** [de colonne, de meuble] base, support ▪ [de statuette] stand, pedestal ▪ [pour un échafaudage] support ▪ **~ mural** wall bracket **2.** [de communication] medium ➲ **~ publicitaire** advertising medium **3.** ACOUST : **~ magnétique** magnetic support **4.** CULIN base **5.** IMPR support ▪ **~ d'impression** *material on which printing is done* **6.** INFORM medium ▪ **~ de données** data carrier ▪ **~ d'information** data support ▪ **~ individuel d'information** smart card, individual data support ▪ **sur ~ papier** hard copy **7.** MATH & PHOTO support.

supportable [sypɔrtabl] *adj* **1.** [douleur] bearable ▪ **il fait froid, mais c'est ~** it's cold but not unbearably so **2.** [conduite, personne] tolerable ▪ **tu n'es plus ~!** I can't take any more of this from you!

supporter[1] [sypɔrtɛr] *nm* SPORT supporter.

supporter[2] [3] [sypɔrte] *vt* **1.** [servir d'assise à] to support, to hold up *(sép)* ▪ **cinq piliers supportent la voûte** the roof is held up by five pillars
2. [assumer - responsabilité, obligation] to assume ▪ [prendre en charge - dépense] to bear ▪ **l'acheteur supporte les frais** the fees are borne by the purchaser
3. [être assujetti à - impôt] to be subject to
4. [résister à] to stand up to *(insép)*, to withstand ▪ **des plantes qui supportent/ne supportent pas le froid** plants that do well/badly in the cold ▪ **bien ~ une opération** to come through an operation in good shape ▪ **mal ~ une opération** to have trouble recovering from an operation ▪ **je ne supporte pas l'alcool/la pilule** drink/the pill doesn't agree with me
5. [subir sans faillir - épreuve, privation] to bear, to endure, to put up with *(insép)* ; [- insulte, menace] to bear ▪ **elle supporte mal la douleur** she can't cope with pain
6. [tolérer, accepter] to bear, to stand ▪ **je ne supporte pas de perdre** I can't stand losing ▮ [personne] to put up with *(insép)*, to stand, to bear ▪ **il faudra le ~ encore deux jours** we'll have to put up with him for two more days ▪ **j'arrive tout juste à les ~** I can just about tolerate them
7. [résister à] to withstand ▪ **leur nouvelle voiture supporte la comparaison avec la concurrence** their new car will bear *ou* stand comparison with anything produced by their competitors ▪ **sa théorie ne supporte pas une critique sérieuse** his theory won't stand up to serious criticism
8. SPORT [encourager] to support.
◆ **se supporter** ◇ *vp (emploi réfléchi)* **je ne me supporte plus en blonde/en noir** blonde hair/black just isn't right for me any more.
◇ *vp (emploi réciproque)* to bear *ou* to stand each other.
◇ *vp (emploi passif)* to be bearable.

supposé, e [sypoze] *adj* **1.** [faux - testament] false, forged ; [- nom] assumed **2.** [admis] : **la vitesse est ~e constante** the speed is assumed to be constant **3.** [présumé - vainqueur] supposed, presumed ; [- père] putative ; [- dimension] estimated ▪ **l'auteur ~ du pamphlet** the supposed author of the pamphlet.
◆ **supposé que** *loc conj* supposing (that), assuming that.

supposer [3] [sypoze] *vt* **1.** [conjecturer, imaginer] to suppose, to assume ▪ **je suppose que tu n'es pas prêt** I take it *ou* I suppose you're not ready ▪ **sa réponse laisse ~ qu'il était au courant** his answer leads one to assume he knew all about it ▪ **tout laisse ~ qu'il avait été contacté par la CIA** everything points to his having been contacted by the CIA ▪ **en supposant que tu échoues** suppose (that) *ou* supposing (that) *ou* let's suppose (that) you fail ▪ **à ~ que** assuming that, supposing **2.** [estimer, penser] : **et tu la supposes assez bête pour se laisser faire?** so you think she's stupid enough to let it happen? ▪ **~ qqch à qqn** to credit sb with sthg **3.** [impliquer] to imply, to require, to presuppose ▪ **une mission qui suppose de la discrétion** an assignment where discretion is required *ou* is a must.

supposition [sypozisjɔ̃] *nf* **1.** [hypothèse] supposition, assumption ▪ **faire des ~s** to speculate ▪ **dans cette ~** if this is the case ▪ **une ~: il s'enfuit** *fam* suppose he runs away **2.** DR : **~ de nom** false personation.
Voir module d'usage

suppositoire [sypozitwar] *nm* suppository.

suppôt [sypo] *nm litt* henchman ▪ **~ de Satan** *ou* **du diable** fiend.

suppression [sypresjɔ̃] *nf* **1.** [abrogation] abolition ▪ **la ~ de la peine de mort** the abolition of the death penalty **2.** [dans un texte] deletion **3.** [élimination] elimination ▪ **~ de la douleur par piqûres** elimination of pain by injections **4.** [assassinat] elimination, liquidation **5.** ÉCON : **il y a eu beaucoup de ~s d'emploi dans la région** there were many job losses in the area **6.** DR : **~ d'état** *destruction of proof of somebody's civil status.*

supprimer [3] [syprime] *vt* **1.** [faire cesser - cause, effet] to do away with *(insép)* ; [- habitude, obstacle] to get rid of *(insép)* ; [- pauvreté, racisme] to put an end to *(insép)*, to do away with *(insép)* ; [- douleur] to kill, to stop ; [- fatigue] to eliminate **2.** [démolir - mur, quartier] to knock *ou* to pull down *(sép)*, to demolish **3.** [annuler - loi] to repeal, to annul ; [- projet] to do away with *(insép)* ; [- allocation, prime] to withdraw, to stop **4.** [retirer] : **~ des emplois** to lay people off, to make people redundant *UK* ▪ **on va te ~ ton permis de conduire** they'll take away *ou* they'll withdraw your driving licence ▪ **j'ai partiellement supprimé le sel** I cut down on salt ▪ **j'ai totalement supprimé le sel** I cut out salt (altogether) ▪ **ils vont ~ des trains dans les zones rurales** train services will be cut in rural areas **5.** [enlever - opération, séquence] to cut (out), to take out *(sép)* ; [- mot, passage] to delete ▪ **~ les étapes/intermédiaires** to do away with the intermediate stages/the middlemen **6.** INFORM to delete **7.** [tuer] to eliminate, to do away with *(insép)* ▪ **il s'est fait ~ par la mafia** the mafia did away with him.
◆ **se supprimer** *vp (emploi réfléchi)* to take one's own life.

suppurer [3] [sypyre] *vi* to suppurate.

supputation [sypytasjɔ̃] *nf sout* calculation, estimation.

supputer [3] [sypyte] *vt* [quantité] to estimate ▪ [possibilités] to assess ▪ **~ les possibilités d'aboutir à un accord** to assess the likelihood of reaching an agreement.

supra [sypra] *adv* supra ▪ **voir ~** supra, see above.

supraconducteur, trice [syprakɔ̃dyktœr, tris] *adj* superconductive.
◆ **supraconducteur** *nm* superconductor.

LA SUPPOSITION

Let's suppose we finish on time. Supposons que nous finissions dans les délais.

Supposing he was right and she does resign... Supposons qu'il a raison et qu'elle démissionne...

Suppose he can't come? Supposons qu'il ne puisse pas venir ?

What if he doesn't succeed? Et s'il ne réussit pas ?

Assuming we start tomorrow, will we still meet the deadline? En admettant qu'on commence demain, est-ce que nous respecterons les délais ?

supranational, e, aux [sypranasjɔnal, o] *adj* supranational.

supranationalité [sypranasjɔnalite] *nf* supranationality.

suprématie [sypremasi] *nf* supremacy.

suprême [syprɛm] <> *adj* **1.** [supérieur] supreme ▪ **le pouvoir ~** the supreme power ▶ **l'Être ~** RELIG the Supreme Being **2.** [extrême - importance, bonheur, plaisir] extreme, supreme ; [- ignorance] utter, blissful, sublime ; [- mépris] sublime **3.** [dernier] supreme, final ▪ **dans un ~ effort** in a final attempt ▪ **à l'heure** *ou* **au moment ~** *sout* at the hour of reckoning, at the moment of truth **4.** CULIN supreme.
<> *nm* CULIN suprême ▪ **~ de volaille** chicken suprême.

suprêmement [syprɛmmɑ̃] *adv* supremely.

sur[1] [syr] *prép* **1.** [dans l'espace - dessus] on ; [- par-dessus] over ; [- au sommet de] on top of ; [- contre] against ▪ **~ la table** on the table ▪ **un visage est dessiné ~ le sable** a face has been drawn in the sand ▪ **elle avait des bleus ~ tout le visage** she had bruises all over her face, her face was covered in bruises ▪ **il a jeté ses affaires ~ le lit** he threw his things onto the bed ▪ **monter ~ un escabeau** to climb (up) a stepladder ▪ **monter ~ un manège/une bicyclette** to get on a roundabout/bicycle ▪ **retire tes pieds de ~ la chaise** *fam* take your feet off the chair ▪ **demain, du soleil ~ le nord** tomorrow, there will be sunshine in the north ▪ **ouragan ~ la ville** hurricane over the city ▪ **une chambre avec vue ~ la mer** a room with a view of *ou* over the sea ▪ **des fenêtres qui donnent ~ la rue** windows giving onto *ou* overlooking the street ▪ **~ la cime de l'arbre** at the top of the tree ▪ **mettre un doigt ~ sa bouche** to put a finger to one's lips ▪ **la peinture est appliquée directement ~ le plâtre** the paint is applied directly onto the plaster ▪ **sa silhouette se détachait ~ le ciel** he was silhouetted against the sky ▪ **je n'ai pas d'argent ~ moi** I haven't got any money on me ▪ **il y avait un monde fou, on était tous les uns ~ les autres** there was a huge crowd, we were all crushed up together *ou* one on top of the other ▪ **la clef est ~ la porte** the key's in the door ▪ **je n'ai plus d'argent ~ mon compte** I haven't any money left in my account ▪ **sculpture ~ bois** ART wood carving ▪ **sculpture ~ marbre** ART marble sculpture ▪ **je cherche un logement ~ Paris** I'm looking for somewhere to live in Paris
2. [indiquant la direction] : **~ votre gauche, le Panthéon** on *ou* to your left, the Pantheon ▪ **en allant ~ Rennes** going towards Rennes ▪ **obliquer ~ la droite** to turn *ou* to bear right ▪ **diriger son regard ~ qqn** to look in sb's direction ▪ **tirer ~ qqn** to shoot at sb ▪ **le malheur s'est abattu ~ cette famille** unhappiness has fallen upon this family ▪ **la porte s'est refermée ~ elle** the door closed behind *ou* after her
3. [indiquant une distance] over, for ▪ **'virages ~ 3 km'** 'bends for 3 km' ▪ **il est le plus rapide ~ 400 mètres** he's the fastest over 400 metres ▪ **la foire s'étend ~ 3 000 m²** the fair covers 3,000 m²
4. [dans le temps - indiquant l'approximation] towards, around ▪ **~ les quatre heures, quelqu'un a téléphoné** (at) around *ou* about four, somebody phoned ▪ [indiquant la proximité] : **~ le moment** *ou* **le coup, je me suis étonné** at the time *ou* at first, I was surprised ▪ **être ~ le départ** to be about to leave ▪ **il va ~ ses 40 ans** he's approaching *ou* nearly 40
5. [indiquant la durée] : **c'est un contrat ~ cinq ans** it's a five-year contract, the contract runs for five years ▪ **les versements sont étalés ~ plusieurs mois** the instalments are spread over several months
6. [indiquant la répétition] after, upon ▪ **je lui ai envoyé lettre ~ lettre** I sent him letter after *ou* upon letter ▪ **elle écrit roman ~ roman** she writes one novel after another
7. [indiquant la cause] : **condamné ~ faux témoignage** condemned on false evidence ▪ **juger qqn ~ ses propos/son apparence** to judge sb by his words/appearance ▪ **j'ai agi ~ vos ordres** I acted on your orders ▪ **il est venu ~ votre invitation** he came at your invitation
8. [indiquant la manière, l'état, la situation] : **avoir un effet ~ qqn/qqch** to have an effect on sb/sthg ▪ **être ~ ses gardes/la défensive/le qui-vive** to be on one's guard/the defensive/the lookout ▪ **danser ~ un air connu** to dance to a well-known tune ▪ **~ le mode majeur/mineur** MUS in the major/minor key ▪ **c'est ~ la première chaîne/France Inter** it's on channel one/France Inter
9. [indiquant le moyen] : **vivre ~ ses économies/un héritage** to live off one's savings/a legacy ▪ **je n'aime pas choisir ~ catalogue** I don't like choosing from a catalogue ▪ **on peut tailler deux jupes ~ le même patron** you can make two skirts out of *ou* from the same pattern ▪ **ça s'ouvre ~ simple pression** you open it by just pressing it ▪ **fait ~ traitement de texte** done on a word-processor ▪ **le film se termine ~ une vue du Lido** the film ends with *ou* on a view of the Lido
10. [indiquant le domaine, le sujet] : **on a un dossier ~ lui** we've got a file on him ▪ **je sais peu de choses ~ elle** I don't know much about her ▪ **~ ce point, nous sommes d'accord** we agree on that point ▪ **140 personnes sont ~ le projet** there are 140 people on *ou* involved in the project ▪ **faire des recherches ~ qqch** to do some research into sthg ▪ **un poème ~ la solitude** a poem about solitude ▪ **elle s'est expliquée ~ ses choix politiques** she explained her political choices ▪ **elle pleurait ~ ses jeunes années** she was crying over her lost youth ▪ **s'apitoyer ~ soi-même** to feel sorry for oneself
11. [indiquant - une proportion] out of ; [- une mesure] by ▪ **un homme ~ deux** one man in two, every second man ▪ **un jour ~ deux** every other day ▪ **un lundi ~ trois** every third Monday ▪ **~ 100 candidats, 15 ont été retenus** 15 out of 100 candidates were shortlisted ▪ **tu as une chance ~ deux de gagner** you've got a 50-50 chance of winning ▪ **cinq mètres ~ trois** five metres by three ▪ **12 ~ 3 égale 4** MATH 12 divided by *ou* over 3 equals 4 ▪ **j'ai eu 12 ~ 20** I got 12 out of 20 ▪ **faire une enquête ~ 1 000 personnes** to do a survey of *ou* involving 1,000 people
12. [indiquant une relation de supériorité] over ▪ **régner ~ un pays** to rule over a country ▪ **l'emporter ~ qqn** to defeat sb.

sur[2], e [syr] *adj* sour.

sûr, e [syr] *adj* **1.** [certain, convaincu] sure, certain ▪ **j'en suis tout à fait ~, j'en suis ~ et certain** I'm absolutely sure, I'm positive ▪ **c'est ~ et certain** it's 100% sure ▪ **j'en étais ~!** I knew it! ▪ **c'est ~ qu'il pleuvra** it's bound to rain ▪ **c'est ~ qu'ils ne viendront pas** it's certain that they won't come ▪ **une chose est ~e** one thing's for sure ▪ **rien n'est moins ~** nothing is less certain ▪ **être ~ de** to be sure of ▪ **être ~ de son fait** to be positive ▪ **elle est ~e du succès** [du sien propre] she's sure she'll succeed ; [de celui d'autrui] she's sure it'll be a success ▪ **je suis ~ d'avoir raison** I'm sure I'm right **2.** [confiant] sure, confident ▪ **être ~ de qqn** to have (every) confidence in sb ▪ **être ~ de soi** [en général] to be self-assured *ou* self-confident ; [sur un point particulier] to be confident ▪ **il n'est plus ~ de ses réflexes** he has lost confidence in his reflexes **3.** [fiable - personne, ami] trustworthy, reliable ; [- données, mémoire, raisonnement] reliable, sound ; [- alarme, investissement] safe ; [- main, pied] steady ; [- oreille] keen ; [- goût] reliable ▪ **avoir le coup d'œil/de crayon ~** to be good at sizing things up/at capturing a likeness *(in drawing)* ▪ **le temps n'est pas ~** the weather is unreliable **4.** [sans danger] safe ▪ **des rues peu ~es** unsafe streets ▪ **le plus ~ est de...** the safest thing is to... ▪ **appelle-moi, c'est plus ~!** call me, just to be on the safe side!
◆ **sûr** *adv fam* **~ qu'il va gagner!** he's bound to win! ▪ **il va accepter – pas ~!** he'll accept – don't count on it!
◆ **à coup sûr** *loc adv* definitely, no doubt ▪ **elle sera à coup ~ en retard** she's sure to be late.
◆ **pour sûr** *loc adv fam* for sure.

surabondance [syrabɔ̃dɑ̃s] *nf* overabundance, profusion, wealth ▪ **une ~ de céréales** an overabundance of cereals.

surabondant, e [syrabɔ̃dɑ̃, ɑ̃t] *adj* overabundant, profuse.

surabonder [3] [syrabɔ̃de] *vi* : **les minéraux surabondent dans la région** the region is rich in minerals ▪ **les activités culturelles surabondent dans cette ville** the town offers a wide range of cultural activities.
◆ **surabonder de, surabonder en** *v+prép* to abound with *ou* in.

suraccumulation [syrakymylasjɔ̃] *nf* overaccumulation.

suractivité [syraktivite] *nf* hyperactivity.

suraigu, ë [syregy] *adj* **1.** [voix, son] very shrill **2.** [douleur] intense, acute.

surajouter [3] [syraʒute] *vt* to add ▪ **il surajoute toujours des détails inutiles** he always adds unnecessary details.
◆ **se surajouter** *vpi* to come on top ▪ **se ~ à** to come on top of.

suralimentation [syralimɑ̃tasjɔ̃] *nf* **1.** [d'une personne] overeating ▪ [d'un animal] overfeeding **2.** MÉCAN boosting, supercharging **3.** MÉD superalimentation.

suralimenté, e [syralimɑ̃te] *adj* **1.** [personne] overfed **2.** [moteur] supercharged.

suralimenter [3] [syralimɑ̃te] *vt* **1.** [personne, animal] to overfeed **2.** MÉCAN to supercharge.

suranné, e [syrane] *adj* [style] old-fashioned, outmoded ▪ **une mode ~e** an outdated fashion.

surarmement [syrarməmɑ̃] *nm* stockpiling of weapons.

surate [syrat] *nf* sura.

surbaissé, e [syrbese] *adj* **1.** [plafond] lowered ▪ [arc, voûte] surbased **2.** AUTO : **voiture à carrosserie ~e** car with a low (wheelbase) clearance.

surbaisser [4] [syrbese] *vt* [plafond] to lower ▪ [arc, voûte] to surbase.

surbooké, e [syrbuke] *adj* overbooked.

surboum [syrbum] *nf* *vieilli* party *(amongst adolescents)*.

surcapacité [syrkapasite] *nf* overcapacity.

surcapitalisation [syrkapitalizasjɔ̃] *nf* overcapitalization, overcapitalizing *(U)*.

surcharge [syrʃarʒ] *nf* **1.** [excédent de poids] overload, overloading ▪ **~ de bagages** excess luggage **2.** [excès] overabundance, surfeit ▪ **~ de travail** extra work ▪ **les parents se plaignent de la ~ des programmes scolaires** parents are complaining that the school curriculum is overloaded **3.** [sur un mot] alteration **4.** [sur un timbre] surcharge, overprint **5.** CONSTR [d'un enduit] overthick coat ▪ [ornementation] frills, over-embellishment **6.** ÉLECTR overload **7.** IMPR overprint **8.** [d'un cheval de course] (weight) handicap.
◆ **en surcharge** *loc adj* excess *(avant n)*, extra *(avant n)*.

surcharger [17] [syrʃarʒe] *vt* **1.** [véhicule] to overload **2.** [accabler] to overburden ▪ **surchargé de travail** overworked **3.** [alourdir] to weigh down **4.** [raturer] to alter ▪ **un rapport surchargé de ratures** a report containing too many deletions.

surchauffe [syrʃof] *nf* **1.** PHYS superheating **2.** [d'un moteur, d'un appareil] overheating **3.** ÉCON overheating **4.** MÉTALL [technique] superheating ▪ [défaut] overheating.

surchauffé, e [syrʃofe] *adj* **1.** [trop chauffé] overheated ▪ **l'air était toujours ~ dans l'atelier** the air in the workshop was always too hot **2.** [surexcité] overexcited ▪ **des esprits ~s** reckless individuals.

surchauffer [3] [syrʃofe] *vt* **1.** [pièce, appareil] to overheat **2.** PHYS to superheat.

surchauffeur [syrʃofœr] *nm* superheater.

surchemise [syrʃəmiz] *nf* overshirt.

surchoix [syrʃwa] *nm* best *ou* top quality, choice *(avant n)*.

surclasser [3] [syrklase] *vt* to outclass.

surcomprimer [3] [syrkɔ̃prime] *vt* to supercharge.

surconsommation [syrkɔ̃sɔmasjɔ̃] *nf* overconsumption, excess *ou* excessive consumption.

surcouper [3] [syrkupe] *vt* CARTES to overtrump.

surcoût [syrku] *nm* [supplément prévu] surcharge, overcharge ▪ [dépense] overspend, overexpenditure.

surcroît [syrkrwa] *nm* : **un ~ de travail** extra *ou* additional work.
◆ **de surcroît** *loc adv* moreover, what's more ▪ **il est beau, et intelligent de ~** he is handsome, and moreover *ou* what's more, he's bright.
◆ **en surcroît** *loc adv* [en plus] in addition ▪ **venir** *ou* **être donné en ~** to come on top.
◆ **par surcroît** = **de surcroît**.

surdéveloppé, e [syrdevlɔpe] *adj* overdeveloped.

surdéveloppement [syrdevlɔpmɑ̃] *nm* over-development.

surdévelopper [syrdevlɔpe] *vt* to overdevelop.

surdimensionné, e [syrdimɑ̃sjɔne] *adj* oversized.

surdi-mutité [syrdimytite] (*pl* **surdi-mutités**) *nf* deaf-muteness, deaf-mutism.

surdiplômé, e [syrdiplome] *adj* overqualified.

surdité [syrdite] *nf* deafness ▪ **~ de perception/transmission** perceptive/conductive deafness.

surdosage [syrdozaʒ] *nm* overdosage, overdosing.

surdose [syrdoz] *nf* overdose.

surdoué, e [syrdwe] ◇ *adj* hyperintelligent *spéc*, gifted.
◇ *nm, f* hyperintelligent *spéc ou* gifted child.

sureau, x [syro] *nm* elder, elderberry tree.

sureffectif [syrefɛktif] *nm* overmanning *(U)* ▪ **en ~** [entreprise] overstaffed.

surélévation [syrelevasjɔ̃] *nf* CONSTR [action] heightening ▪ [état] additional *ou* extra height.

surélever [19] [syrelve] *vt* CONSTR [mur] to heighten, to raise ▪ **on a surélevé la voie ferrée** the railway has been raised above ground level.

sûrement [syrmɑ̃] *adv* **1.** [en sécurité] safely **2.** [efficacement] efficiently, with a sure hand **3.** [certainement] certainly, surely ▪ **il sera ~ en retard** he's bound to *ou* sure to be late ▪ **ils ont ~ été pris dans les embouteillages** they must have been caught in the traffic ▪ **oui, ~, il vaudrait mieux le prévenir** yes, no doubt, it would be better to warn him ▪ **~ qu'il vaudrait mieux attendre, mais...** *fam* sure it's better to wait, but... **4.** [oui] : **va-t-elle accepter? – ~** will she accept? – she certainly will *ou* she's bound to ▪ **~ pas!** certainly not!

suremploi [syrɑ̃plwa] *nm* overemployment.

surenchère [syrɑ̃ʃɛr] *nf* **1.** [prix] higher bid, overbid ▪ **faire une ~** to overbid **2.** *fig* **la ~ électorale** exaggerated political promises *(during an election campaign)* ▪ **la ~ publicitaire/médiatique** advertising/media exaggeration ▶ **faire de la ~** to go one better than everybody else.

surenchérir [32] [syrɑ̃ʃerir] *vi* **1.** [offrir de payer plus] to overbid, to raise one's bid, to make a higher bid ▪ **il y aura un délai pour ~** a period of time will be set aside for any higher bids **2.** *fig* **~ sur** to go one better than ▪ **~ sur une offre** to make a better offer.

surendetté, e [syrɑ̃dɛte] *adj* heavily *ou* deeply indebted.

surendettement [surɑ̃dɛtmɑ̃] *nm* debt burden.

surentraîner [4] [syrɑ̃trɛne] *vt* to overtrain.

suréquipement [syrekipmɑ̃] *nm* [action] overequipping ▪ [état] overequipment ▪ [excès] excess equipment.

suréquiper [3] [syrekipe] *vt* to overequip.

surestimation [syrɛstimasjɔ̃] *nf* **1.** [action] overestimation ▪ COMM overvaluing **2.** [résultat] overestimate ▪ COMM overvaluation.

surestimer [3] [syrɛstime] *vt* **1.** [objet] to overvalue **2.** [valeur, personne] to overestimate.

suret, ette [syrɛ, ɛt] *adj* sourish, slightly tart ▪ **un petit vin ~** a wine with a hint of tartness.

sûreté [syrte] *nf* **1.** [sécurité] safety ▪ **la ~ de l'État** state security ▪ **par mesure de ~, pour plus de ~** as a precaution **2.** [fiabilité - de la mémoire, d'une méthode, d'un diagnostic, des freins] reliability ; [- d'une serrure] security **3.** [système de protection] safety device **4.** DR : **~ personnelle** guarantee, surety ▪ **~ individuelle** (rights of) personal security *(against arbitrary detention)* ▪ **~ réelle** (valuable) security ▪ **la Sûreté (nationale)** *the French criminal investigation department* ▪ ≃ CID UK, ≃ FBI US.
◆ **de sûreté** *loc adj* safety *(modif)*.
◆ **en sûreté** *loc adv* : **mettre qqch en ~** to put sthg in a safe place *ou* away for safekeeping.

surévaluation [syrevalɥasjɔ̃] *nf* overvaluation, overestimation.

surévaluer [7] [syrevalɥe] *vt* **1.** [donner une valeur supérieure à] to overvalue ▪ **le conseil municipal a surévalué les terrains** the council overvalued the land **2.** [accorder une importance excessive à] to overestimate.

surexcitable [syrɛksitabl] *adj* **1.** [gén] overexcitable **2.** PSYCHOL hyperexcitable.

surexcitant, e [syrɛksitɑ̃, ɑ̃t] *adj* overexciting.

surexcitation [syrɛksitasjɔ̃] *nf* overexcitement.

surexcité, e [syrɛksite] *adj* overexcited.

surexciter [3] [syrɛksite] *vt* **1.** [personne] to overexcite **2.** [sentiment, faculté] to overexcite, to overstimulate, to inflame ▪ **~ l'imagination de qqn** to overexcite *ou* to overstimulate sb's imagination.

surexploiter [3] [syrɛksplwate] *vt* **1.** [terre, ressources] to overexploit **2.** [ouvrier] to exploit **3.** [idée] to overuse.

surexposer [3] [syrɛkspoze] *vt* to overexpose.

surexposition [syrɛkspozisjɔ̃] *nf* overexposure.

surf [sœrf] *nm* **1.** [planche] surfboard **2.** [sport] surfing ▪ **faire du ~** to go surfing.

surface [syrfas] *nf* **1.** [aire] (surface) area ➊ **~ corrigée** DR surface area *(used in the evaluation of a reasonable rent)* **2.** [espace utilisé] surface ▪ **quelle est la ~ de l'entrepôt?** how big is the warehouse? **3.** [partie extérieure] surface, outside ▪ **la ~ de la Terre** the Earth's surface ▪ **une peau se forme à la ~ du lait** skin forms on the surface *ou* on top of the milk ▪ **remonter à la ~, faire ~** [sous-marin, nageur] to surface ▪ **refaire ~, revenir à la ~** [après évanouissement] to come to *ou* round ; [après anesthésie] to come out of anaesthetic, to come round ; [après une dépression] to pull out of it ; [après une absence] to reappear **4.** [apparence] surface, (outward) appearance ▪ **la ~ des choses** the surface of things **5.** AÉRON : **~ portante** aerofoil *UK*, airfoil *US* **6.** SPORT : **~ de réparation** penalty area **7.** TECHNOL : **~ de chauffe** heating surface.

➡ **de surface** *loc adj* **1.** NAUT & PHYS surface *(modif)* **2.** [amabilité, regrets] superficial, outward.

➡ **en surface** *loc adv* **1.** [à l'extérieur] on the surface **2.** [superficiellement] on the face of things, superficially.

surfait, e [syrfɛ, ɛt] *adj* [auteur, œuvre] overrated ▪ [réputation] inflated ▪ **c'est un peu ~** it's not what it's cracked up to be.

surfer [3] [sœrfe] *vi* to surf.

surfeur, euse [sœrfœr, øz] *nm, f* surfer.

surfil [syrfil] *nm* [technique] whipping ▪ [point] overcasting stitch.

surfiler [3] [syrfile] *vt* COUT to whip.

surfin, e [syrfɛ̃, in] *adj* superfine.

surgélation [syrʒelasjɔ̃] *nf* (industrial) deep-freezing.

surgelé, e [syrʒəle] *adj* frozen, deep-frozen.

➡ **surgelé** *nm* frozen food ▪ **j'ai acheté un ~ pour ce soir** I've bought a frozen dinner for tonight.

surgeler [25] [syrʒəle] *vt* to deep-freeze *(industrially)*.

surgénérateur [syrʒeneratœr] = **surrégénérateur**.

surgir [32] [syrʒir] *vi* **1.** [personne, animal, objet] to appear *ou* to materialize suddenly, to loom up ▪ [hors du sol et rapidement] to shoot *ou* to spring up ▪ **des gens, surgis d'on ne sait où** people who had sprung from nowhere ▪ **l'eau surgit du sol entre deux rochers** the water springs *ou* gushes out of the ground between two rocks **2.** [conflit] to arise ▪ [difficultés] to crop up, to arise.

surhausser [3] [syrose] *vt* CONSTR to raise.

surhomme [syrɔm] *nm* **1.** [gén] superman **2.** PHILOS übermensch, overman.

surhumain, e [syrymɛ̃, ɛn] *adj* superhuman ▪ **ce qu'on me demande est ~** I'm being asked to do something beyond human endurance.

surimi [syrimi] *nm* surimi.

surimposition [syrɛ̃pozisjɔ̃] *nf* **1.** FIN overtaxation **2.** GÉOGR superimposition.

surimpression [syrɛ̃presjɔ̃] *nf* superimposition.

➡ **en surimpression** *loc adj* superimposed ▪ **les deux images sont en ~** the two pictures are superimposed.

Surinam(e) [syrinam] *npr m* : **le ~** Surinam ▪ **au ~** in Surinam.

surinfection [syrɛ̃fɛksjɔ̃] *nf* secondary infection.

surintendant, e [syrɛ̃tɑ̃dɑ̃, ɑ̃t] *nm, f* (in-house) social worker.

➡ **surintendant** *nm* HIST : **~ général des finances** ≃ Lord High Treasurer ▪ **~ général des bâtiments du roi** ≃ Surveyor General of the King's Works.

surinvestissement [syrɛ̃vɛstismɑ̃] *nm* FIN & PSYCHOL overinvestment.

surir [32] [syrir] *vi* to (become *ou* turn) sour.

surjet [syrʒɛ] *nm* [point] overcast stitch ▪ [couture] overcast seam.

surjeter [27] [syrʒəte] *vt* to overcast.

sur-le-champ [syrləʃɑ̃] *loc adv* immediately, at once, straightaway.

surlendemain [syrlɑ̃dmɛ̃] *nm* : **le ~ de la fête** two days after the party ▪ **il m'a appelé le lendemain, et le ~** he called me the next day, and the day after ▪ **et le ~, j'étais à Paris** and two days later, I was in Paris.

surligner [3] [syrliɲe] *vt* to highlight *(with a fluorescent pen)*.

surligneur [syrliɲœr] *nm* highlighter.

surmédicalisation [syrmedikalizasjɔ̃] *nf* overmedicalization.

surmenage [syrmənaʒ] *nm* [nerveux] overstrain, overexertion ▪ [au travail] overwork, overworking ▪ **souffrir de ~** to be overworked, to suffer from overwork ➊ **~ intellectuel** mental strain.

surmené, e [syrməne] *nm, f* [nerveusement] person suffering from nervous exhaustion ▪ [par le travail] overworked person.

surmener [19] [syrməne] *vt* **1.** [bête de somme, cheval] to overwork, to drive too hard **2.** [personne - physiquement] to overwork ; [- nerveusement] to overtax.

➡ **se surmener** *vp (emploi réfléchi)* to overtax o.s., to work too hard, to overdo it.

surmoi [syrmwa] *nm inv* superego.

surmontable [syrmɔ̃tabl] *adj* surmountable, superable *sout*, which can be overcome.

surmonter [3] [syrmɔ̃te] *vt* **1.** [être situé sur] to surmount, to top ▪ **un dôme surmonte l'édifice** the building is crowned by a dome **2.** [triompher de - difficulté] to get over, to surmount, to overcome ; [- peur, émotion] to overcome, to get the better of, to master ; [- fatigue] to overcome.

surmortalité [syrmɔrtalite] *nf* comparatively high death rate.

surmultiplié, e [syrmyltiplije] *adj* : **vitesse ~e** overdrive.

surnager [17] [syrnaʒe] *vi* **1.** [flotter] to float ▪ **le pétrole surnage à la surface de la mer** oil is floating on the sea **2.** [subsister - ouvrage] to remain ; [- souvenir] to linger on.

surnatalité [syrnatalite] *nf* comparatively high birth rate.

surnaturel, elle [syrnatyrɛl] *adj* **1.** [d'un autre monde] supernatural **2.** [fabuleux, prodigieux] uncanny **3.** [divin] spiritual ▪ **la vie ~le** the spiritual life.

➡ **surnaturel** *nm* : **le ~** the supernatural.

surnom [syrnɔ̃] *nm* **1.** [appellation] nickname ▪ **Cœur de lion était le ~ du roi Richard** King Richard was known as the Lionheart **2.** ANTIQ agnomen.

surnombre [syrnɔ̃br] *nm* excessive numbers.
◆ **en surnombre** *loc adj* redundant, excess *(avant n)* ▪ **nous étions en ~** there were too many of us.

surnommer [3] [syrnɔme] *vt* to nickname ▪ **dans sa famille, on la surnomme "Rosita"** her family's pet name for her is "Rosita".

surnuméraire [syrnymerɛr] *adj* & *nmf* supernumerary.

suroffre [syrɔfr] *nf* **1.** [offre plus avantageuse] higher bid *OU* offer **2.** ÉCON oversupply.

surpaie *etc v* ▷ **surpayer**.

surpassement [syrpasmɑ̃] *nm* : **le ~ de soi** *OU* **de soi-même** excelling o.s.

surpasser [3] [syrpase] *vt* **1.** [surclasser] to surpass, to outdo ▪ **~ qqn en habileté** to be more skilful than sb **2.** [aller au-delà de] to surpass, to go beyond ▪ **leur enthousiasme surpasse toutes mes espérances** their enthusiasm is beyond all my expectations, they're far more enthusiastic than I expected.
◆ **se surpasser** *vp (emploi réfléchi)* to excel o.s. ▪ **quel gâteau, tu t'es surpassé!** what a cake, you've really surpassed yourself!

surpayer [11] [syrpeje] *vt* **1.** [employé] to overpay **2.** [marchandise] to be overcharged for.

surpeuplé, e [syrpœple] *adj* overpopulated.

surpeuplement [syrpœpləmɑ̃] *nm* overpopulation.

surpiquer [3] [syrpike] *vt* to oversew.

surpiqûre [syrpikyr] *nf* oversewn seam.

surplace [syrplas] *nm* : **faire du ~** [à vélo] to go dead slow ; [en voiture] to come to a standstill *OU* a complete stop ▪ **l'économie fait du ~** *fig* the economy is marking time *OU* treading water.

surplis [syrpli] *nm* surplice.

surplomb [syrplɔ̃] *nm* overhang.
◆ **en surplomb** *loc adj* overhanging.

surplombant, e [syrplɔ̃bɑ̃, ɑ̃t] *adj* overhanging.

surplomber [3] [syrplɔ̃be] ◇ *vt* to overhang ▪ **des falaises qui surplombent la mer** overhanging cliffs ▪ **de chez elle on surplombe tout Paris** from her window you have a bird's-eye view of the whole of Paris.
◇ *vi* to overhang.

surplus [syrply] *nm* **1.** [excédent] surplus, extra ▪ **le ~ de la récolte** the surplus crop **2.** [supplément - à une quantité] supplement ; [- à un prix] surcharge ▪ **vous paierez le ~ le mois prochain** you'll pay the extra next month **3.** ÉCON [stock excédentaire] surplus (stock) ▪ [gain] surplus **4.** [boutique] (army) surplus (store) ▪ **les ~ américains** US army surplus.
◆ **au surplus** *loc adv* moreover, what's more.

surpopulation [syrpɔpylasjɔ̃] *nf* overpopulation.

surprenait *etc v* ▷ **surprendre**.

surprenant, e [syrprənɑ̃, ɑ̃t] *adj* **1.** [inattendu, étonnant] surprising, odd **2.** [exceptionnel] astonishing, amazing.

surprendre [79] [syrprɑ̃dr] *vt* **1.** [dans un acte délictueux] : **~ qqn** to catch sb in the act ▪ **on l'a surprise à falsifier la comptabilité** she was caught (in the act of) falsifying the accounts **2.** [prendre au dépourvu] : **ils sont venus nous ~ à la maison** they paid us a surprise visit at home ▪ **ils réussirent à ~ la sentinelle** they managed to take the sentry by surprise ▪ **~ qqn au saut du lit** to catch sb when he/she has just got up ▪ **se laisser ~ par** [orage] to get caught in ; [marée] to get caught by ; [crépuscule] to be overtaken by **3.** [conversation] to overhear ▪ **j'ai surpris leur regard entendu** I happened to see the knowing look they gave each other **4.** [déconcerter] to surprise ▪ **être surpris de qqch** to be surprised at sthg ▪ **cela ne surprendra personne** this will come as a surprise to nobody.
◆ **se surprendre à** *vp+prép* : **se ~ à faire** to find *OU* to catch o.s. doing.

surpression [syrpresjɔ̃] *nf* very high pressure.

surprime [syrprim] *nf* extra *OU* additional premium.

surpris, e [syrpri, iz] ◇ *pp* ▷ **surprendre**.
◇ *adj* **1.** [pris au dépourvu] surprised ▪ **l'ennemi, ~, n'opposa aucune résistance** caught off their guard, the enemy put up no resistance
2. [déconcerté] surprised ▪ **je suis ~ de son absence/de ne pas la voir/qu'elle ne réponde pas/de ce qu'elle ne réagisse pas** I'm surprised (that) she's not here/not to see her/(that) she doesn't reply/(that) she hasn't reacted ▪ **être agréablement/désagréablement ~** to be pleasantly/unpleasantly surprised ▪ **je serais bien ~ si elle ne demandait pas une augmentation** I'd be surprised if she didn't ask for a rise
3. [vu, entendu par hasard] : **quelques mots ~ entre deux portes** a snatch of overheard conversation.
◆ **surprise** *nf* **1.** [étonnement, stupéfaction] surprise ▪ **cette information causa une grande ~e** this information was received with amazement *OU* caused much surprise ▪ **à la grande ~e de** to the great surprise of ▪ **à la ~e générale** to everybody's surprise ▪ **regarder qqn avec ~e** to look at sb in surprise ▪ **on va de ~e en ~e avec eux** with them it's just one surprise after another
2. [événement inattendu] surprise ▪ **quelle (bonne) ~e!** what a (nice *OU* pleasant) surprise! ▪ **avoir une ~e** to be surprised ▪ **tout le monde a eu la ~e d'avoir une prime** everyone was surprised to get a bonus ▪ **faire une ~e à qqn** to spring a surprise on sb ▪ **ne lui dis pas, je veux lui faire la ~e** don't tell him, I want it to be a surprise ▪ **on a souvent de mauvaises ~es avec lui** you often have unpleasant surprises with him ❯ **attaque ~e** surprise attack ▪ **visite ~e** surprise *OU* unexpected visit ▪ **voyage ~e** unplanned trip
3. [cadeau] surprise ▪ [pour les enfants] lucky bag
4. MIL surprise.
◆ **par surprise** *loc adv* MIL : **prendre une ville par ~e** to take a town by surprise.
◆ **sans surprise(s)** *loc adj* : **ce fut un voyage sans ~e** it was an uneventful trip ▪ **son père est sans ~e** his father is very predictable.
Voir module d'usage

LA SURPRISE

What a (nice) surprise! Quelle (bonne) surprise !
Really? Ah, bon ?
Never! Non !
Well I never! Ça alors !
Oh my God! Oh mon Dieu !
I don't know what to say! Je ne sais vraiment pas quoi dire !
You can't be serious? C'est une plaisanterie !
You must be joking! Tu plaisantes !
Would you believe it! C'est incroyable !
That's amazing *OU* **incredible!** C'est incroyable !
He can't be married! Ce n'est pas possible qu'il soit marié !
I can't believe it! Je n'arrive pas à le croire !
I could hardly believe my eyes/ears. Je n'en croyais pas mes yeux/mes oreilles.
I can't get over it! Je n'en reviens pas !
Well, I'll be blowed! Ça alors !
I was totally speechless. J'étais bouche bée.
Much to my surprise *OU* **Surprisingly enough, she agreed.** À ma grande surprise, elle a accepté.
You'll never guess who was there! Tu ne devineras jamais qui était là !

surprise-partie [syrprizparti] (*pl* **surprises-parties**) *nf vieilli* party.

surprit *etc v* ▻ **surprendre.**

surproduction [syrprɔdyksjɔ̃] *nf* overproduction.

surproduire [98] [syrprɔdɥir] *vt* to overproduce.

surprotéger [22] [syrprɔteʒe] *vt* to overprotect.

surpuissant, e [syrpɥisɑ̃, ɑ̃t] *adj* MÉCAN ultra-powerful.

surqualifié, e [syrkalifje] *adj* overqualified.

surréalisme [syrrealism] *nm* surrealism.

surréaliste [syrrealist] ◇ *adj* **1.** ART & LITTÉR surrealist **2.** [magique] surreal.
◇ *nmf* surrealist.

surréel [syrreɛl] *nm* surreal.

surrégénérateur [syrreʒeneratœr] ◇ *nm* breeder reactor ▪ **~ à neutrons rapides** fast breeder reactor.
◇ *adj m* fast breeder *(modif).*

surrénal, e, aux [syrrenal, o] *adj* suprarenal, adrenal.
◆ **surrénale** *nf* suprarenal *ou* adrenal gland.

surréservation [syrrezɛrvasjɔ̃] *nf* overbooking.

sursalaire [syrsalɛr] *nm* bonus.

sursaturé, e [syrsatyre] *adj* oversaturated.

sursaturer [3] [syrsatyre] *vt* **1.** ÉCON to oversaturate **2.** PHYS to supersaturate.

sursaut [syrso] *nm* **1.** [tressaillement] start, jump ▪ **elle eut un ~ de peur** she jumped in alarm **2.** [regain subit] burst ▪ **un ~ d'énergie** a burst of energy.
◆ **en sursaut** *loc adv* [brusquement] with a start ▪ **elle se réveilla en ~** she woke up with a start.

sursauter [3] [syrsote] *vi* to start, to jump ▪ **faire ~ qqn** to give sb a start, to make sb start *ou* jump.

surseoir [66] [syrswar] ◆ **surseoir à** *v+prép* **1.** *litt* [différer - publication, décision] to postpone, to defer **2.** DR : **~ à statuer** to defer a judgment ▪ **~ à une exécution** to stay an execution.

sursis, e [syrsi, iz] *pp* ▻ **surseoir.**
◆ **sursis** *nm* **1.** [délai] reprieve, extension ▪ **ils bénéficient d'un ~ pour payer leurs dettes** they've been granted an extension of the time limit for paying their debts **2.** DR reprieve ▪ **bénéficier d'un ~** to be granted *ou* given a reprieve **3.** [ajournement] deferment, extension ▪ **~ d'incorporation** MIL deferment *ou* deferral of call-up.
◆ **avec sursis** *loc adj* suspended ▪ **il est condamné à (une peine de) cinq ans avec ~** he's been given a five year suspended (prison) sentence.
◆ **en sursis** *loc adj* **1.** DR in remission **2.** [en attente] : **c'est un mort en ~** he's living on borrowed time.

sursitaire [syrsitɛr] *nm* MIL provisionally exempted conscript.

sursoit, sursoyait *etc v* ▻ **surseoir.**

surtaxe [syrtaks] *nf* surcharge.

surtaxer [3] [syrtakse] *vt* [frapper d'une taxe - supplémentaire] to surcharge ; [- excessive] to overcharge.

surtension [syrtɑ̃sjɔ̃] *nf* (voltage) overload, overvoltage.

surtitre [syrtitr] *nm* PRESSE head.

surtout[1] [syrtu] *adv* **1.** [avant tout, par-dessus tout] above all ▪ [plus particulièrement] particularly, especially ▪ **il y avait ~ des touristes dans la salle** most of the audience were tourists **2.** [renforçant un conseil, un ordre] : **~, dis au médecin que tu as de l'asthme** be sure to tell the doctor that you've got asthma ▪ **~, pas de panique!** whatever you do, don't panic! ▪ **ne faites ~ pas de bruit** don't you make ANY noise ▪ **je vais lui dire – ~ pas!** I'll tell her – you'll do nothing of the sort!
◆ **surtout que** *loc conj fam* especially as.

surtout[2] [syrtu] *nm* [décor de table] epergne, centrepiece.

survécu *pp* ▻ **survivre.**

surveillance [syrvɛjɑ̃s] *nf* **1.** [contrôle - de travaux] supervision, overseeing ; [- médical] monitoring ▪ **tromper** *ou* **déjouer la ~ de qqn** to evade sb *sout*, to give sb the slip **2.** ADMIN & DR surveillance ▪ **~ légale** sequestration (by the courts) ▪ **~ du territoire** counterespionage *ou* counterintelligence section.
◆ **de surveillance** *loc adj* **1.** [service, salle] security *(modif)* ▪ [avion, équipe] surveillance *(modif)* ▪ [appareil] supervisory ▪ [caméra] surveillance *(modif)*, closed-circuit *(avant n)* **2.** MÉD monitoring.
◆ **en surveillance** *loc adv* : **le malade est en ~ à l'hôpital** the patient's progress is being monitored in hospital.
◆ **sans surveillance** *loc adj* & *loc adv* unattended, unsupervised.
◆ **sous la surveillance de** *loc prép* under the surveillance of, under observation by ▪ **sous la ~ de la police** under police surveillance.
◆ **sous surveillance** *loc adv* **1.** [par la police] under surveillance ▪ **mettre** *ou* **placer qqch sous ~** to put sthg under surveillance **2.** MÉD under observation.

surveillant, e [syrvɛjɑ̃, ɑ̃t] *nm, f* **1.** [de prison] prison guard ▪ [d'hôpital] charge nurse *UK*, sister *UK*, head nurse *US* ▪ [de magasin] store detective ▪ [de chantier] supervisor, overseer **2.** ÉDUC (paid) monitor ▪ [d'examen] invigilator *UK*, proctor *US* ▪ **~ d'internat** boarders' supervisor ▪ **~ général** *vieilli* head supervisor *(person who was in charge of discipline in a school).*

surveiller [4] [syrvɛje] *vt* **1.** [garder - bébé, bagages] to watch, to keep an eye on ; [- prisonnier] to guard ▪ **~ un malade** [personne] to watch over a patient ; [avec une machine] to monitor a patient ▪ **j'aurais dû le ~ davantage** I should have kept a closer watch on him **2.** [épier] to watch ▪ **on nous surveille** we're being watched ▪ *(en usage absolu)* to keep watch ▪ **je surveille, vous pouvez y aller** go ahead, I'm keeping watch **3.** [contrôler - travaux, ouvriers] to oversee, to surpervise ; [- cuisson] to watch ; [- examen] to invigilate *UK*, to proctor *US* ▪ **vous devriez ~ les fréquentations de vos enfants** you should keep an eye on the company your children keep **4.** [observer] to watch, to keep watch on *ou* over ▪ **~ qqn de près** [gén] to watch sb closely ; [police] to keep sb under close surveillance ▪ **la situation est à ~ de près** the situation should be very closely monitored **5.** [prendre soin de - santé, ligne] to watch.
◆ **se surveiller** *vp (emploi réfléchi)* **1.** [se contrôler] to be careful what one does **2.** [se restreindre] to watch o.s., to keep a watch on o.s. ▪ **tu as grossi, tu devrais te ~** you've put on weight, you should watch yourself.

survenir [40] [syrvənir] *vi* **1.** [problème, complication] to arise, to crop up ▪ [événement, incident] to happen, to occur, to take place **2.** *litt* [personne] to appear *ou* to arrive unexpectedly.

survente [syrvɑ̃t] *nf* **1.** COMM overcharging **2.** NAUT increase of wind force.

survêt [syrvɛt] *nm fam* tracksuit.

survêtement [syrvɛtmɑ̃] *nm* SPORT & LOISIRS tracksuit.

survie [syrvi] *nf* **1.** [continuation de la vie] survival ▪ **quelques jours de ~** a few more days to live ▪ **donner à un malade quelques mois de ~** to prolong a patient's life for a few more months ▪ **la ~ d'une tradition** the continuance *ou* survival of a tradition ➊ **expérience de ~** survival experiment **2.** [au-delà de la mort] afterlife **3.** DR : **droits** *ou* **gains de ~** (stipulated *ou* contractual) rights of survivorship **4.** ÉCOL survival.

survient, survint *etc v* ▻ **survenir.**

survit *etc v* ▻ **survivre.**

survitrage [syrvitraʒ] *nm* double glazing ▪ **poser un ~** to fit double glazing.

survivance [syrvivɑ̃s] *nf* **1.** [d'une coutume] trace, survival ▪ **c'est une ~ des rites païens** it's a relic *ou* a survival from pagan rites **2.** *litt* [survie] survival **3.** LING archaicism.

survivant, e [syrvivɑ̃, ɑ̃t] ◇ *adj* [conjoint, coutume] surviving *(avant n).*
◇ *nm, f* **1.** [rescapé] survivor **2.** *fig* survivor ▪ **un ~ du surréalisme** a survivor from the surrealist era.

survivre [90] [syrvivr] *vi* **1.** [réchapper] to survive, to live on **2.** [continuer à exister] to survive ▪ **une coutume qui a survécu à travers les siècles** a custom that has survived *ou* endured through the ages ▪ **dans le monde des affaires, il faut lutter pour ~** in business, it's a struggle for survival ▪ **~ à** [accident] to survive ‖ [personne] to survive, to outlive.
◆ **se survivre** *vpi* **1.** [artiste, célébrité] to outlive one's fame *ou* success **2.** *litt* **se ~ dans qqn/qqch** to live through sb/sthg.

survol [syrvɔl] *nm* **1.** AÉRON : **l'Espagne a refusé le ~ de son territoire** Spain refused to allow the aircraft to fly over *ou* to overfly its territory **2.** [d'un texte] skimming through ▪ [d'une question] skimming over.

survoler [3] [syrvɔle] *vt* **1.** AÉRON to overfly, to fly over **2.** [texte] to skim through ▪ [question] to skim over ▪ **vous ne faites que ~ la question** your treatment of the question is (too) cursory *ou* superficial.

survoltage [syrvɔltaʒ] *nm* (voltage) overload, overvoltage.

survolter [3] [syrvɔlte] *vt* **1.** ÉLECTR to boost **2.** [exciter] to work *ou* to stir up, to overexcite.

sus [sy(s)] ◇ *adv litt* **courir ~ à qqn** to give chase to sb.
◇ *interj arch* **~, mes amis!** come, my friends! ▪ **~ à l'ennemi!** have at them!
◆ **en sus** *loc adv sout* in addition.
◆ **en sus de** *loc prép sout* in addition to.

susceptibilité [sysɛptibilite] *nf* [sensibilité] touchiness, sensitiveness ▪ **ménager la ~ de qqn** to humour sb.

susceptible [sysɛptibl] *adj* **1.** [sensible] touchy, oversensitive, thinskinned ▪ **ne sois pas si ~** don't be so ready to take offence **2.** [exprime la possibilité] : **~ de : ce cheval est ~ de gagner** that horse is capable of winning ▪ **votre offre est ~ de m'intéresser** I might be interested in your offer ▪ **une situation ~ de se produire** a situation likely to occur ▪ **texte ~ de plusieurs interprétations** text open to a number of interpretations.

susciter [3] [sysite] *vt* **1.** [envie, jalousie, haine, intérêt, sympathie] to arouse ▪ [mécontentement, incompréhension, étonnement] to cause, to give rise to *(insép)* ▪ [problèmes] to give rise to *(insép)*, to create **2.** [déclencher - révolte] to stir up *(sép)* ; [- dispute] to provoke ; [- malveillance] to incite.

suscription [syskripsjɔ̃] *nf* **1.** [adresse] address, superscription *sout* **2.** [sur un acte diplomatique] superscription.

sus-dénommé, e [sysdenɔme] *adj* & *nm, f* DR above-named, aforenamed.

susdit, e [sysdi, it] *adj* & *nm, f* DR aforesaid.

susmentionné, e [sysmɑ̃sjɔne] *adj* above-mentioned, aforementioned DR.

susnommé, e [sysnɔme] *adj* & *nm, f* above-named, aforenamed DR.

suspect, e [syspɛ, ɛkt] ◇ *adj* **1.** [attitude, objet] suspicious, suspect **2.** [dont on peut douter] : **je trouve ses progrès soudains très ~s** I'm rather suspicious of her sudden progress **3.** [suspecté] : **être ~ de qqch** to be suspected *ou* under suspicion of sthg ‖ [susceptible] : **elle était peu ~e de sympathie envers le terrorisme** she was hardly likely to approve of terrorism.
◇ *nm, f* suspect.

suspecter [4] [syspɛkte] *vt* **1.** [soupçonner] to suspect ▪ **on le suspecte d'avoir commis un meurtre** he's suspected of murder, he's under suspicion of murder **2.** [douter de] to doubt, to have doubts about *(insép)* ▪ **~ la sincérité de qqn** to doubt sb's sincerity.

suspendre [73] [syspɑ̃dr] *vt* **1.** [accrocher - lustre, vêtement] to hang ▪ **suspends ta veste à la patère** hang your jacket (up) on the hook **2.** [dépendre de] : **être suspendu à** to depend *ou* to be dependent on **3.** [interrompre - hostilités] to suspend ; [- négociations] to break off *(sép)* ; [- séance, audience] to adjourn ; [- récit] to interrupt **4.** [différer - décision] to defer, to postpone **5.** [interdire - émission, journal] to ban ▪ [révoquer - fonctionnaire, prêtre, juge] to suspend.
◆ **se suspendre à** *vp+prép* to hang from.

suspendu, e [syspɑ̃dy] *adj* **1.** CONSTR hanging *(modif)* **2.** TRAV PUB [pont] suspension *(modif)* **3.** AUTO : **voiture bien/mal ~e** car with good/bad suspension **4.** BOT suspended **5.** GÉOGR : **vallée ~e** hanging valley.

suspens [syspɑ̃] *adj m* RELIG suspended.
◆ **en suspens** ◇ *loc adj* **1.** [affaire, dossier] pending, unfinished ▪ [intrigue] unresolved ▪ [lecteur] uncertain **2.** [flocons, planeur] suspended, hanging.
◇ *loc adv* : **tenir qqn en ~** to keep sb in suspense ▪ **laisser un dossier en ~** to keep a file pending ▪ **laisser une question en ~** to leave a question unanswered *ou* unresolved.

suspense[1] [syspɑ̃s] *nf* RELIG suspension.

suspense[2] [syspɛns] *nm* suspense ▪ **il y a un ~ terrible dans le livre** the book's full of suspense ▪ **prolonger** *ou* **faire durer le ~** to prolong the suspense.
◆ **à suspense** *loc adj* suspense *(modif)* ▪ **film à ~** thriller ▪ **roman à ~** thriller, suspense story.

suspensif, ive [syspɑ̃sif, iv] *adj* DR suspensive.

suspension [syspɑ̃sjɔ̃] *nf* **1.** [d'un objet] hanging **2.** DR [interruption] suspension ▪ **~ d'audience** adjournment (of hearing) ▪ **~ d'instance** deferment of proceedings ▪ **~ de paiement** suspension *ou* withholding of payment ▪ **~ de peine** ≃ deferred sentence ▪ **~ de séance** adjournment **3.** ADMIN [sanction] suspension **4.** AUTO, CHIM, GÉOGR, MUS & RAIL suspension **5.** IMPR : **points de ~** suspension points **6.** [luminaire] ceiling light fitting.
◆ **en suspension** *loc adj* **1.** [poussière] hanging ▪ **en ~ dans l'air** hanging in the air **2.** CHIM in suspension.

suspente [syspɑ̃t] *nf* **1.** NAUT sling **2.** [de parachute] suspending ropes **3.** CONSTR (wire) support **4.** TRAV PUB suspender.

suspicieux, euse [syspisjø, øz] *adj litt* suspicious, suspecting.

suspicion [syspisjɔ̃] *nf* **1.** [défiance] suspicion, suspiciousness ▪ **jeter la ~ sur qqn** to cast suspicion on sb **2.** DR [supposition d'un délit] suspicion ▪ **~ de fraude** suspicion of fraud.

sustentation [systɑ̃tasjɔ̃] *nf* **1.** AÉRON lift **2.** PHYS sustentation.

sustenter [3] [systɑ̃te] *vt* **1.** *vieilli* [nourrir - personne] to sustain **2.** AÉRON to lift.
◆ **se sustenter** *vp (emploi réfléchi) hum* to feed, to take sustenance ▪ **nous nous sustentions de quelques morceaux de pain** we fed on a few pieces of bread.

susurrant, e [sysyrɑ̃, ɑ̃t] *adj* susurrant *litt*, whispering, softly murmuring.

susurrement [sysyrmɑ̃] *nm* whispering.

susurrer [3] [sysyre] ◇ *vt* [chuchoter] to whisper ▪ **~ des mots doux à l'oreille de qqn** to whisper sweet nothings in sb's ear.
◇ *vi* **1.** [bruire - vent] to whisper **2.** [chuchoter] to whisper.

sut *etc v* ⊳ **savoir**.

suture [sytyr] *nf* **1.** BOT, GÉOL & ZOOL suture **2.** ANAT & MÉD suture ▪ **point de ~** stitch ▪ **on lui a fait cinq points de ~** he had five stitches (put in).

suturer [3] [sytyre] *vt* to stitch up *(sép)*, to suture *spéc.*

suzerain, e [syzrɛ̃, ɛn] ◇ *adj* suzerain.
◇ *nm, f* suzerain, (feudal) overlord.

suzeraineté [syzrɛnte] *nf* suzerainty.

svastika [zvastika] *nm* swastika.

svelte [zvɛlt] *adj* [membre] slender ▪ [personne] slender, slim.

sveltesse [zvɛltɛs] *nf litt* svelteness, slenderness, slimness.

SVP = **s'il vous plaît**.

swahili, e [swaili] *adj* Swahili.
◆ **swahili** *nm* LING Swahili.

swastika [swastika] = **svastika**.

Swaziland [swazilɑ̃d] *npr m* : **le ~** Swaziland.

sweater [switœr] *nm* sweater.

sweat-shirt [switʃœrt] *(pl* **sweat-shirts***)* *nm* sweat shirt.

swing [swiŋ] *nm* **1.** MUS [rythme] swing, swinging ■ [style] swing **2.** SPORT swing.

swinguer [3] [swiŋge] *vi* to swing ■ **quel orchestre, ça swingue!** that band really swings!

sycomore [sikɔmɔr] *nm* sycamore.

Sydney [sidnɛ] *npr* Sydney.

syllabe [silab] *nf* **1.** LING syllable **2.** [parole] : **elle n'a pas prononcé une ~** she never opened her mouth.

syllabique [silabik] *adj* syllabic.

syllabus [silabys] *nm* *Belgique* [polycopié] handout *(for a university class)*.

syllogisme [silɔʒism] *nm* syllogism.

syllogistique [silɔʒistik] ◇ *adj* syllogistic, syllogistical.
◇ *nf* syllogistic.

sylphe [silf] *nm* MYTHOL sylph.

sylphide [silfid] *nf* MYTHOL & *litt* sylph.
◆ **de sylphide** *loc adj* [corps, taille] sylph-like.

sylvaner [silvanɛr] *nm* **1.** BOT Sylvaner grape **2.** ŒNOL Sylvaner.

sylvestre [silvɛstr] *adj* *litt* sylvan *litt*, forest *(modif)*.

Sylvestre [silvɛstr] *npr* : **saint ~** Saint Sylvester.

sylvicole [silvikɔl] *adj* forestry *(modif)*, silvicultural *spéc*.

sylviculteur, trice [silvikyltœr, tris] *nm, f* forester, silviculturist *spéc*.

sylviculture [silvikyltyr] *nf* forestry, silviculture *spéc*.

symbiose [sɛ̃bjoz] *nf* BIOL & *fig* symbiosis.
◆ **en symbiose** *loc adv* in symbiosis, symbiotically ■ **ils vivent en ~** *fig* they're inseparable.

symbiotique [sɛ̃bjɔtik] *adj* symbiotic.

symbole [sɛ̃bɔl] *nm* **1.** [signe] symbol **2.** [personnification] symbol, embodiment ■ **il est le ~ du respect filial** he's the embodiment of filial duty, he's filial duty personified **3.** RELIG : **Symbole** Creed **4.** CHIM, INFORM & MATH symbol.

symbolique [sɛ̃bɔlik] ◇ *adj* **1.** [fait avec des symboles] symbolic ■ **langage/logique ~** symbolic language/logic **2.** [sans valeur réelle] token, nominal ■ **une somme ~** a nominal amount ■ **un geste ~** a symbolic *ou* token gesture.
◇ *nm* : **le ~** the symbolic.
◇ *nf* **1.** [ensemble des symboles] symbolic system, symbolism **2.** [étude des symboles] interpretation of symbols, symbology.

symboliquement [sɛ̃bɔlikmɑ̃] *adv* symbolically ■ **on leur a donné ~ un euro à chacun** they each got a token one-euro piece.

symbolisation [sɛ̃bɔlizasjɔ̃] *nf* **1.** [mise en symboles] symbolization **2.** MATH symbolization.

symboliser [3] [sɛ̃bɔlize] *vt* to symbolize ■ **la colombe symbolise la paix** the dove symbolizes peace *ou* is the symbol of peace.

symbolisme [sɛ̃bɔlism] *nm* **1.** [système] symbolism **2.** ART & LITTÉR Sy mbolism.

symboliste [sɛ̃bɔlist] ◇ *adj* **1.** [relatif aux symboles] symbolistic **2.** ART & LITTÉR Symbolist.
◇ *nmf* Symbolist.

symétrie [simetri] *nf* [gén] symmetry ■ **la parfaite ~ des fenêtres sur la façade** the perfect symmetry of the windows on the front of the building.

symétrique [simetrik] ◇ *adj* **1.** [gén] symmetrical ■ **une rangée ~ de l'autre** one row symmetrical to the other **2.** GÉOM symmetrical ■ MATH symmetric.
◇ *nm* & *nf* [point] symmetrical point ■ [figure] symmetrical figure.
◇ *nm* symmetrical element.

symétriquement [simetrikmɑ̃] *adv* symmetrically.

sympa [sɛ̃pa] *adj fam* [personne, attitude] friendly, nice ■ [lieu] nice, pleasant ■ [idée, mets] nice ■ **il n'est vraiment pas ~** he's not very nice at all.

sympathie [sɛ̃pati] *nf* **1.** [cordialité] friendship, fellow feeling ■ **il y a une grande ~ entre eux** they get on very well ■ **être en ~ avec qqn** to be on friendly terms with sb **2.** [penchant] liking *(C)* ■ **je n'ai aucune ~ pour lui** I don't like him at all, I have no liking for him at all ■ **inspirer la ~** to be likeable **3.** [bienveillance] sympathy *(U)* ■ **recevoir des témoignages de ~** to receive expressions of sympathy **4.** [pour une idée] sympathy ■ **je n'ai pas beaucoup de ~ pour ce genre d'attitude** I don't have much time for that kind of attitude **5.** MÉD sympathy.
◆ **sympathies** *nfpl* [tendances] sympathies ■ **ses ~s vont vers les républicains** his sympathies are *ou* lie with the Republicans.

sympathique [sɛ̃patik] ◇ *adj* **1.** [personne] nice, pleasant, likeable ■ **elle m'est très ~** I like her very much **2.** [visage] friendly ■ [idée] good ■ [lieu] pleasant, nice ■ [mets] appetizing ■ [ambiance, réunion, spectacle] pleasant ■ [attitude] kind, friendly ■ **il est bien ~, ce petit vin/fromage!** nice little wine/cheese, this! **3.** PHYSIOL sympathetic.
◇ *nm* ANAT sympathetic nervous system.

sympathiquement [sɛ̃patikmɑ̃] *adv* nicely, in a kindly way.

sympathisant, e [sɛ̃patizɑ̃, ɑ̃t] ◇ *adj* sympathizing.
◇ *nm, f* sympathizer.

sympathiser [3] [sɛ̃patize] *vi* **1.** [s'entendre] : **~ avec** to get on with *esp UK*, to get along with *esp US* ■ **il n'a pas sympathisé avec les autres enfants** he didn't get on with the other children ■ **nous avons tout de suite sympathisé** we took to *ou* liked each other right away **2.** POLIT : **elle sympathise avec les communistes** she's a communist sympathizer.

symphonie [sɛ̃fɔni] *nf* **1.** MUS symphony ▶ **'Symphonie du Nouveau Monde'** ***Dvorak*** 'New World Symphony' ■ **~ concertante** sinfonia concertante ■ **'Symphonie fantastique'** ***Berlioz*** 'Symphonie fantastique' ■ **'Symphonie héroïque'** ***Beethoven*** 'Eroica Symphony' ■ **'Symphonie inachevée'** ***Schubert*** 'Unfinished Symphony' ■ **'Symphonie pastorale'** ***Beethoven*** 'Pastoral Symphony' **2.** *litt* [harmonie] symphony.

symphonique [sɛ̃fɔnik] *adj* symphonic.

symphoniste [sɛ̃fɔnist] *nmf* symphonist.

symposium [sɛ̃pozjɔm] *nm* [colloque] symposium.

symptomatique [sɛ̃ptɔmatik] *adj* **1.** MÉD symptomatic **2.** [caractéristique] symptomatic, indicative ■ **c'est ~ de leurs relations** it's symptomatic of *ou* it tells you something about their relationship.

symptomatologie [sɛ̃ptɔmatɔlɔʒi] *nf* symptomatology.

symptôme [sɛ̃ptom] *nm* **1.** MÉD symptom **2.** [signe] symptom, sign ■ **les premiers ~s de qqch** the forerunners *ou* first signs of sthg.

synagogue [sinagɔg] *nf* synagogue.

synapse [sinaps] *nf* **1.** ANAT synapse **2.** BIOL synapsis.

synarthrose [sinartroz] *nf* synarthrosis.

synchrone [sɛ̃kron] *adj* synchronous.

synchronie [sɛ̃krɔni] *nf* synchrony.

synchronique [sɛ̃krɔnik] *adj* synchronic.

synchronisation [sɛ̃krɔnizasjɔ̃] *nf* synchronization.

synchroniser [3] [sɛ̃krɔnize] *vt* to synchronize.

synchroniseur [sɛ̃krɔnizœr] *nm* **1.** AUTO synchromesh (device) **2.** CINÉ, ÉLECTR & PHOTO synchronizer **3.** ÉCOL biorhythm trigger *ou* signal.

synchronisme [sɛ̃krɔnism] *nm* synchronism.

synchrotron [sɛ̃krɔtrɔ̃] *nm* synchrotron.

synclinal, e, aux [sɛ̃klinal, o] *adj* synclinal.

syncope [sɛ̃kɔp] *nf* **1.** MÉD syncope faint ■ **tomber en ~, avoir une ~** to faint **2.** LING syncope **3.** MUS syncopation.

syncopé, e [sɛ̃kɔpe] *adj* syncopated.

syncrétisme [sɛ̃kretism] *nm* syncretism.

syndic [sɛ̃dik] *nm* **1.** ADMIN : **~ (d'immeuble)** managing agent **2.** DR [de faillite] (official) receiver *(before 1985)* **3.** HIST syndic **4.** BOURSE president **5.** *Suisse* [président de commune] *high-ranking civic official, similar to a mayor, in certain Swiss cantons.*

SYNDIC

A *syndic* is an administrative body which represents the interests of the owners of all the flats in a building, collectively known as the *syndicat de copropriété*. The role of the *syndic* is to ensure the upkeep of the building and to organize meetings during which a vote is taken on any repairs, improvements etc, that are deemed necessary. The services of the *syndic* are paid for by the owners of the flats.

syndical, e, aux [sɛ̃dikal, o] *adj* **1.** POLIT (trade) union *(modif)* **2.** ADMIN management *(modif)* ■ **droit ~** right of association.

syndicalisation [sɛ̃dikalizasjɔ̃] *nf* unionization.

syndicaliser [3] [sɛ̃dikalize] *vt* to unionize.

syndicalisme [sɛ̃dikalism] *nm* **1.** [mouvement] (trade) unionism **2.** [ensemble des syndicats] trade unions **3.** [action] union activities ■ **faire du ~** to be active in a union **4.** [doctrine] unionism.

syndicaliste [sɛ̃dikalist] ◇ *adj* **1.** [mouvement] (trade) union *(modif)* **2.** [doctrine] unionist.
◇ *nmf* (trade) unionist.

syndicat [sɛ̃dika] *nm* **1.** POLIT [travailleurs] union ■ **se former** *ou* **se regrouper en ~** to form a trade union ➤ **~ ouvrier** trade union ■ **~ patronal** employers' confederation *ou* association **2.** DR [association] association ■ **~ de communes** association of communes ■ **~ interdépartemental** association of regional administrators ■ **~ de copropriétaires** co-owners' association **3.** FIN : **~ d'émission/de garantie** issuing/underwriting syndicate ■ **~ financier** financial syndicate.
◆ **syndicat d'initiative** *nm* tourist office, tourist information bureau.

syndiqué, e [sɛ̃dike] ◇ *adj* (belonging to a trade) union ■ **ouvriers ~s/non ~s** union/non-union workers.
◇ *nm, f* (trade) unionist.

syndiquer [3] [sɛ̃dike] *vt* to unionize, to organize ■ **~ les travailleurs d'un atelier** to organize the workers in a workshop.
◆ **se syndiquer** *vp (emploi réfléchi)* to join a union.

syndrome [sɛ̃drom] *nm* syndrome ■ **~ immunodéficitaire acquis** acquired immunodeficiency syndrome ■ **~ prémenstruel** premenstrual tension *ou* syndrome ■ **~ du choc toxique** toxic shock syndrome.

synergie [sinɛrʒi] *nf* **1.** MÉD & PHYSIOL synergism **2.** ÉCON synergy.

synesthésie [sinɛstezi] *nf* synaesthesia.

synode [sinɔd] *nm* RELIG synod.

synodique [sinɔdik] *adj* ASTRON & RELIG synodic.

synonyme [sinɔnim] ◇ *adj* synonymous ■ **être ~ de** to be synonymous with.
◇ *nm* synonym.

synonymie [sinɔnimi] *nf* synonymy.

synonymique [sinɔnimik] *adj* synonymic, synonymous.

synopsis [sinɔpsis] ◇ *nf* SC & ÉDUC [bref aperçu] synopsis.
◇ *nm* CINÉ synopsis.

synoptique [sinɔptik] *adj* synoptic, synoptical.
◆ **synoptiques** *nmpl* : **les ~s** the Synoptic Gospels.

synovial, e, aux [sinɔvjal, o] *adj* synovial.

synovie [sinɔvi] *nf* synovia, synovial fluid.

synovite [sinɔvit] *nf* synovitis.

syntagmatique [sɛ̃tagmatik] ◇ *adj* syntagmatic.
◇ *nf* syntagmatic analysis.

syntagme [sɛ̃tagm] *nm* phrase, syntagm *spéc* ■ **~ nominal/verbal/adjectival** noun/verb/adjectival phrase.

syntaxe [sɛ̃taks] *nf* INFORM & LING syntax.

syntaxique [sɛ̃taksik] *adj* INFORM & LING syntactic.

synthé [sɛ̃te] *nm fam* synthesizer.

synthèse [sɛ̃tɛz] *nf* **1.** [structuration de connaissances] synthesis **2.** [exposé, ouvrage] summary, résumé ■ **écrire une ~ sur l'histoire de l'après-guerre** to write a brief history of the post-war years **3.** BIOL, CHIM & PHILOS synthesis **4.** INFORM synthesis ■ **~ de la parole** speech synthesis.
◆ **de synthèse** *loc adj* **1.** [non analytique] : **avoir l'esprit de ~** to have a systematic mind **2.** [fibre, parole] synthetic.

synthétique [sɛ̃tetik] ◇ *adj* **1.** [raisonnement, approche] synthetic, synthesizing **2.** CHIM [fibre] synthetic, man-made, artificial **3.** LING & PHILOS synthetic.
◇ *nm* [matière] synthetic *ou* man-made fibres.

synthétiquement [sɛ̃tetikmɑ̃] *adv* synthetically.

synthétiser [3] [sɛ̃tetize] *vt* **1.** [idées, résultats, relevés] to synthesize, to bring together **2.** CHIM to synthesize.

synthétiseur [sɛ̃tetizœr] *nm* synthesizer.

synthétisme [sɛ̃tetism] *nm* Synthetism.

syntonie [sɛ̃tɔni] *nf* PSYCHOL & RADIO syntony.

syntoniseur [sɛ̃tɔnizœr] *nm* tuner.

syphilis [sifilis] *nf* syphilis.

syphilitique [sifilitik] *adj* & *nmf* syphilitic.

syriaque [sirjak] *adj* & *nm* Syriac.

Syrie [siri] *npr f* : **(la) ~** Syria.

syrien, enne [sirjɛ̃, ɛn] *adj* Syrian.
◆ **Syrien, enne** *nm, f* Syrian.
◆ **syrien** *nm* LING Syrian.

systématicien, enne [sistematisjɛ̃, ɛn] *nm, f* taxonomist, systematist.

systématique [sistematik] ◇ *adj* **1.** [méthodique] methodical, orderly, systematic ■ **de façon ~** systematically **2.** [invariable - réaction] automatic, invariable ; [- refus] automatic ■ **c'est ~, quand je dis oui, il dit non** when I say yes, he invariably says no **3.** [inconditionnel - soutien] unconditional, solid **4.** MÉD systemic.
◇ *nf* SC systematics *(sing)*.

systématiquement [sistematikmɑ̃] *adv* systematically.

systématisation [sistematizasjɔ̃] *nf* systematization.

systématisé, e [sistematize] *adj* PSYCHOL systematized.

systématiser [3] [sistematize] *vt* **1.** [organiser en système] to systemize, to systematize **2.** *(en usage absolu)* [être de parti pris] to systemize, to systematize ■ **il ne faut pas ~** we mustn't generalize.

système [sistɛm] *nm* **1.** [structure] system ■ **~ de production** system of production ■ **~ de valeurs** system of values ■ **il refuse d'entrer dans le ~** he refuses to be part of the system ➤ **~ solaire** solar system **2.** [méthode] way, means ■ **je connais un bon ~ pour faire fortune** I know a good way of making a fortune ➤ **~ D** resourcefulness **3.** [appareillage] system ■ **~ de chauffage/d'éclairage** heating/lighting system **4.** ANAT & MÉD system ■ **~ nerveux/digestif** nervous/digestive system ■ **~ pileux** hair *(on body and head)* ■ **~ végétatif** vegetative system **5.** CONSTR : **~ de construction** system **6.** ÉCON : **~ monétaire européen** European Monetary System ■ **analyse de ~** systems analysis **7.** GÉOL system **8.** INFORM system ■ **~ d'information** information system ■ **~ expert** expert system ■ **~ d'exploitation** (operating) system ■ **~ de navigation** navigation system **9.** SC : **~ international d'unités** SI unit ■ **~ métrique** metric system **10.** *fam loc* **il me court** *ou* **porte** *ou* **tape sur le ~** he's really getting on my nerves.

systémique [sistemik] ◇ *adj* systemic.
◇ *nf* systems analysis.

T

t, T [te] *nm* [lettre] t, T, *voir aussi* **g**.
◆ **en T** *loc adj* T-shaped ▪ **bandages en ~** T bandage.

t (*abr écrite de* **tonne**) t.

t. (*abr écrite de* **tome**) vol.

t' [t] *pron pers* ▷ **te**, ▷ **tu**.

ta [ta] *f* ▷ **ton**.

TAA (*abr de* **train autos accompagnées**) *nm car sleeper train*, ≃ Motorail *UK*.

tabac [taba] ◇ *adj inv* [couleur] tobacco brown, tobacco-coloured.
◇ *nm* **1.** BOT tobacco plant **2.** [produit] tobacco ▪ **campagne contre le ~** anti-smoking campaign ◗ **~ blond/brun** mild/dark tobacco ▪ **~ à chiquer** chewing tobacco ▪ **~ à priser** snuff **3.** [magasin] tobacconist's *UK*, tobacco store *US* ▪ **un bar ~, un bar-~** *a bar with a tobacco counter* **4.** MÉTÉOR : **coup de ~** squall, gale **5.** *fam loc* **c'est toujours le même ~** it's always the same old thing *ou* story ▪ **faire un ~** to be a smash hit ▪ **passer qqn à ~** to beat sb up, to lay into sb.
◆ **du même tabac** *loc adj fam* of the same kind ▪ **ils sont du même ~** they're tarred with the same brush ▪ **et autres ennuis du même ~** and troubles of that ilk.

tabagie [tabaʒi] *nf* **1.** [lieu enfumé] : **c'est une vraie ~ ici** you can't see for smoke around here **2.** *Québec* [magasin] tobacconist's *UK*, tobacco store *US*.

tabagique [tabaʒik] ◇ *adj* tobacco *(modif)*, nicotine-related.
◇ *nmf* tobacco addict, chain-smoker.

tabagisme [tabaʒism] *nm* tobacco addiction, nicotinism *spéc*.

tabasser [3] [tabase] *vt fam* to beat *ou* to rough up *(sép)*, to thrash, to beat black and blue ▪ **se faire ~** to be *ou* get beaten up.

tabatière [tabatjɛr] *nf* **1.** [boîte] snuffbox **2.** CONSTR skylight (opening), roof light.

tabellion [tabeljɔ̃] *nm* **1.** HIST scrivener, tabellion **2.** *litt & péj* [notaire] lawyer.

tabernacle [tabɛrnakl] *nm* NAUT & RELIG tabernacle.

tablar(d) [tablar] *nm Suisse* shelf.

tablature [tablatyr] *nf* tablature.

table [tabl] *nf* **1.** [pour les repas] table ▪ **débarrasser** *ou* **desservir la ~** to clear the table ▪ **dresser** *ou* **mettre la ~** to set the table ▪ **une ~ de six couverts** a table set for six ▪ **qui sera mon voisin de ~?** who will I be sitting next to (for the meal)? ▪ **sortir** *ou* **se lever de ~** to leave the table, to get up from the table ◗ **la ~ d'honneur** the top *ou* head table ▪ **~ d'hôte** table d'hôte ▪ **nous avons pris notre repas à la ~ d'hôte** we ate with the other guests in the hotel dining room ▪ **tenir ~ ouverte** to keep open house
2. [nourriture] : **la ~** food ▪ **aimer la ~** to enjoy *ou* to like good food ▮ [restaurant] : **une des meilleures ~s de Paris** one of the best restaurants in Paris
3. [tablée] table, tableful ▪ **présider la ~** to preside over the guests *(at a meal)* ▪ **il a fait rire toute la ~** he made the whole table laugh
4. [meuble à usages divers] table ▪ **~ de chevet** *ou* **de nuit** bedside table ▪ **~ de cuisine/de salle à manger** kitchen/dining-room table ▪ **~ basse** coffee table ▪ **~ de billard** billiard table ▪ **~ de cuisson** hob ▪ **~ à dessin** drawing board ▪ **~ de jeu** gambling table ▪ **~ à langer** baby changing table ▪ **~ de lecture** turntable ▪ **~ de montage** IMPR & PHOTO light table ; CINÉ cutting table ▪ **~ d'opération** operating table ▪ **~ d'orientation** viewpoint indicator ▪ **~ de ping-pong** table-tennis table ▪ **~ à rallonges** extension *ou* draw table ▪ **~ à repasser** ironing board ▪ **~ ronde** *pr & fig* round table ▪ **~ roulante** trolley *UK*, tea wagon *US* ▪ **~ tournante** *table used for séances* ▪ **faire tourner les ~s** to hold a séance ▪ **~ de travail** work surface ▪ **~ à volets** drop-leaf table ▪ **~s gigognes** nest of tables
5. [liste, recueil] table ▪ **~ de logarithmes/mortalité/multiplication** log/mortality/multiplication table ▪ **~ alphabétique** alphabetical table *ou* list ▪ **~ des matières** (table of) contents ▪ **les Tables de la Loi** BIBLE The Tables of the Law ▪ **~ rase** PHILOS tabula rasa ▪ **faire ~ rase** to wipe the slate clean, to make a fresh start
6. CONSTR [plaque] panel ▪ [panneau] panel, table
7. GÉOL table, mesa
8. IMPR table ▪ **~ de réception** delivery table
9. INFORM table ▪ **~ traçante** plotter
10. JOAILL table
11. MUS : **~ d'harmonie** soundboard
12. RAIL : **~ de roulement** running *ou* rail surface
13. RELIG : **~ d'autel** (altar) table ▪ **la ~ de communion, la sainte ~** the communion *ou* the Lord's table.
◆ **à table** ◇ *loc adv* at table ▪ **passer à** *ou* **se mettre à ~** to sit down to a meal ▪ **nous pouvons passer à ~** the meal is ready now ▪ **nous serons dix à ~** there will be ten of us at table ▪ **je te rappelle plus tard, je suis à ~** I'll call you later, I'm eating ◗ **se mettre à ~**△ *arg crime* [parler] to spill the beans.
◇ *interj* : **à ~!** it's ready!
◆ **table d'écoute** *nf* wiretapping set *ou* equipment ▪ **elle est sur ~ d'écoute** her phone is tapped ▪ **mettre qqn sur ~ d'écoute** to tap sb's phone.

tableau, x [tablo] *nm* **1.** ÉDUC : **aller au ~** to go to the front of the classroom *(and answer questions or recite a lesson)* ◗ **~ noir** blackboard
2. [support mural] rack, board ▪ **~ pour fusibles** fuseboard
3. [panneau d'information] board ▪ **~ d'affichage** notice board ▪ **~ des arrivées/départs** arrivals/departures board

4. ART painting, picture ■ **un ~ de Goya** a painting by Goya ■ **un ~ ancien** an old master
5. [spectacle] scene, picture ■ **ils formaient un ~ touchant** they were a touching sight ■ **vous voyez d'ici le ~!** *fam* you can imagine *ou* picture the scene!
6. [description] picture ■ **vous nous faites un ~ très alarmant de la situation** you've painted an alarming picture of the situation ▶ **pour achever le ~** to cap it all
7. [diagramme] table ■ **remplir un ~** to fill in a table
8. [liste - gén] list, table ; [- d'une profession] roll ■ **~ d'avancement** promotions roster *ou* list ■ **~ des avocats** roll of lawyers ■ **~ des éléments** CHIM periodic table ■ **~ de gonflage** tyre-pressure table ■ **~ horaire** [des trains] timetable
9. ÉLECTR : **~ de contrôle** control board
10. INFORM array
11. MATH table
12. MÉD : **~ clinique** overall clinical picture
13. PHARM (French) drugs classification ■ **~ A** toxic drugs (list) ■ **~ B** narcotics (list) ■ **~ C** dangerous drugs (list)
14. THÉÂTRE scene ▶ **~ de service** [répétitions] rehearsal roster ; [représentations] performances roster ■ **~ vivant** tableau vivant
15. *loc* **gagner sur les deux/tous les ~x** to win on both/all counts
16. INFORM : **~ de bord** control panel.
◆ **tableau de bord** *nm* **1.** AUTO dashboard
2. AÉRON & NAUT instrument panel
3. ÉCON (list of) indicators, control panel.
◆ **tableau de chasse** *nm* **1.** CHASSE bag
2. AÉRON list of kills
3. *fam* [conquêtes amoureuses] conquests.
◆ **tableau d'honneur** *nm* ÉDUC roll of honour ■ **elle a eu le ~ d'honneur ce mois-ci** she was on the roll of honour this month.

tablée [table] *nf* table ■ **une ~ de jeunes** a tableful *ou* party of youngsters.

tabler [3] [table] ◆ **tabler sur** *v+prép* to bank *ou* to count on ■ **ne table pas sur une augmentation** don't bank on getting a rise.

tablette [tablɛt] *nf* **1.** [petite planche] shelf **2.** CULIN [de chewing-gum] stick ■ [de chocolat] bar **3.** CONSTR slab ■ [de radiateur] top ■ [de cheminée] mantelpiece ■ [d'une maçonnerie] coping **4.** PHARM tablet **5.** INFORM : **~ graphique** graphic tablet.
◆ **tablettes** *nfpl* ANTIQ tablets ■ **je vais l'inscrire** *ou* **le noter dans mes ~s** *fig* I'll make a note of it.

tableur [tablœr] *nm* spreadsheet.

tablier [tablije] *nm* **1.** [vêtement] apron ■ [blouse] overall *UK*, work coat *US* ■ [d'enfant] smock ▶ **rendre son ~** [démissionner] to hand in one's resignation ; *fig* to give up, to throw in the towel **2.** [rideau - de cheminée] register ; [- de magasin] steel shutter **3.** TRAV PUB deck and beams, superstructure *(of a bridge)* **4.** AUTO [d'une voiture] cowl ■ [d'un scooter] footrest **5.** RAIL foot plate **6.** TECHNOL [de machine-outil] apron.

tabloïd(e) [tablɔid] *adj* & *nm* tabloid.

tabou, e [tabu] *adj* **1.** ANTHR & RELIG taboo **2.** [à ne pas évoquer] forbidden, taboo.
◆ **tabou** *nm* ANTHR & RELIG taboo ■ **ce sont des ~s** these are taboo subjects.

taboulé [tabule] *nm* tabbouleh.

tabouret [taburɛ] *nm* **1.** [siège] stool ■ **~ de bar/cuisine/piano** bar/kitchen/piano stool **2.** [pour les pieds] foot stool.

tabulaire [tabylɛr] *adj* tabular.

tabulateur [tabylatœr] *nm* tabulator.

tabulation [tabylasjɔ̃] *nf* **1.** [positionnement] tabulation **2.** [taquets] tabs.

tabulatrice [tabylatris] *nf* tabulator.

tac [tak] *interj* **1.** [bruit sec] tap, rat-a-tat **2.** *loc* **et ~!** so there! ■ **du ~ au ~** tit for tat ■ **répondre du ~ au ~** to answer tit for tat.

TAC = **train auto-couchettes**.

tacaud [tako] *nm* bib, pout.

tachant, e [taʃɑ̃, ɑ̃t] *adj* **1.** [qui tache] staining **2.** [qui se tache] easily soiled.

tache [taʃ] *nf* **1.** [marque] stain ■ **~ de graisse** grease stain *ou* mark ■ **je me suis fait une ~** I've stained my clothes ▶ **faire ~** *fam* to jar ■ **le piano moderne fait ~ dans le salon** the modern piano looks out of place in the living room ■ **faire ~ d'huile** to spread **2.** [partie colorée] patch, spot ■ **le soleil faisait des ~s de lumière sur le sol** the sun dappled the ground with light **3.** [sur un fruit] mark, blemish **4.** [sur la peau] mark, spot ▶ **~ de rousseur** *ou* **de son** freckle ■ **~ de vin** strawberry mark *(birthmark)* **5.** [souillure morale] blot, stain, blemish ■ **cette fraude est une ~ à sa réputation** this fraud has stained his reputation ▶ **~ originelle** RELIG stain of original sin **6.** ASTRON : **~ solaire** sunspot **7.** ART patch, tache **8.** MÉD [sur une radiographie] opacity ■ [coloration anormale] spot **9.** ZOOL patch, spot, mark.
◆ **sans tache** *loc adj* **1.** [fruit] unblemished **2.** [réputation] spotless.

tâche [taʃ] *nf* **1.** [travail] task, job ■ **remplir une ~** to fulfil a task ■ **assigner une ~ à qqn** to give sb a task *ou* a job *ou* a piece of work to do ■ **faciliter/compliquer la ~ à qqn** to make things easier/more complicated for sb ▶ **~s ménagères** housework **2.** [mission, rôle] task, mission ▶ **prendre à ~ de faire qqch** *litt* to undertake to do sthg **3.** INFORM task.
◆ **à la tâche** <> *loc adj* : **travail à la ~** piecework.
<> *loc adv* INDUST : **travailler à la ~** to be on piecework ■ **il est à la ~** he's a pieceworker ■ **on n'est pas à la ~!** *fam* what's the rush? ■ **mourir à la ~** to die in harness.

tacher [3] [taʃe] <> *vt* **1.** [salir - vêtement, tapis] to stain ■ **taché de sang** blood-stained **2.** *sout* [ternir - réputation, nom, honneur] to stain **3.** *sout* [colorer] to spot, to dot.
<> *vi* [encre, sauce, vin *etc*] to stain.
◆ **se tacher** <> *vp (emploi réfléchi)* to get o.s. dirty, to stain one's clothes.
<> *vp (emploi passif)* [tissu] to soil ■ [bois, peinture, moquette] to mark ■ [fruit] to become marked ■ **le blanc se tache facilement** white soils *ou* gets dirty easily.

tâcher [3] [taʃe] *vt* : **~ que** to make sure that ■ **tâche qu'elle ne l'apprenne pas** make sure she doesn't hear about it.
◆ **tâcher de** *v+prép* to try to ■ **tâche d'être à l'heure** try to be on time.

tâcheron [taʃrɔ̃] *nm* **1.** [petit entrepreneur] jobber ■ [ouvrier agricole] hired hand, journeyman **2.** *péj* [travailleur] drudge, workhorse *péj* ■ [écrivaillon] hack ■ **les ~s d'Hollywood** Hollywood hacks.

tacheter [27] [taʃte] *vt* to spot, to speckle, to fleck ■ **un chat blanc tacheté de noir** a white cat with black markings.

tachisme [taʃism] *nm* tachism, tachisme.

tachiste [taʃist] *adj* & *nmf* tachist, tachiste.

tachycardie [takikardi] *nf* tachycardia.

tachygraphe [takigraf] *nm* tachograph.

tacite [tasit] *adj* tacit ■ **c'était un aveu ~** it was a tacit admission ▶ **(par) ~ reconduction** (by) tacit agreement to renew.

Tacite [tasit] *npr* Tacitus.

tacitement [tasitmɑ̃] *adv* tacitly.

taciturne [tasityrn] *adj* taciturn, silent, uncommunicative.

tacot [tako] *nm* *fam* banger *UK*, (old) heap.

TacOTac® [takɔtak] *npr m public lottery with a weekly prize draw.*

tact [takt] *nm* **1.** PHYSIOL (sense of) touch **2.** [délicatesse] tact, delicacy ■ **avoir du ~** to be tactful ■ **manque de ~** tactlessness ■ **manquer de ~** to be tactless ■ **annoncer la nouvelle avec/sans ~** to break the news tactfully/tactlessly.

tacticien, enne [taktisjɛ̃, ɛn] *nm, f* **1.** MIL (military) tactician **2.** *fig* [stratège] strategist.

tactile [taktil] *adj* tactile.

tactique [taktik] <> *adj* tactical.
<> *nf* **1.** MIL tactics *(sing)* **2.** [moyens] tactics *(pl)*.

tadjik [tadʒik] *adj* Tadzhiki.

◆ **Tadjik** *nmf* Tadzhik.
◆ **tadjik** *nm* LING Tadzhiki.

Tadjikistan [tadʒikistɑ̃] *npr m* : **le ~** Tadzhikistan.

Tadj Mahall [tadʒmaal] = **Taj Mahal**.

tænia [tenja] = **ténia**.

taffe [taf] *nf fam* [de cigarette] drag, puff.

taffetas [tafta] *nm* TEXT taffeta ▪ **une robe en** *ou* **de ~** a taffeta dress.

tag [tag] *nm* tag *(graffiti)*.

Tage [taʒ] *npr m* : **le ~** the (River) Tagus.

tagliatelle [tagljatɛl] (*pl inv ou pl* **tagliatelles**) *nf* tagliatelle *(U)*.

taguer [3] [tage] *vt* to tag *(with graffiti)*.

tagueur, euse [tagœr, øz] *nm, f* tagger *(graffitist)*.

Tahiti [taiti] *npr* Tahiti ▪ **à ~** in Tahiti.

tahitien, enne [taisjɛ̃, ɛn] *adj* Tahitian.
◆ **Tahitien, enne** *nm, f* Tahitian.
◆ **tahitien** *nm* LING Tahitian.

taïaut [tajo] *interj* tally-ho.

tai-chi(-chuan) [tajʃiʃwan] *nm inv* T'ai Chi (Ch'uan).

taie [tɛ] *nf* **1.** [enveloppe] : **~ d'oreiller** pillowcase, pillow slip ▪ **~ de traversin** bolster case **2.** MÉD leucoma.

taïga [tajga] *nf* taiga.

taillade [tajad] *nf* **1.** [estafilade] slash, gash **2.** HORT [sur un arbre] gash.

taillader [3] [tajade] *vt* to gash *ou* to slash (through).
◆ **se taillader** *vpt* : **se ~ les poignets** to slash one's wrists.

taillanderie [tajɑ̃dri] *nf* [fabrication, commerce] edge-tool industry.

taillant [tajɑ̃] *nm* [tranchant] (cutting) edge.

taille [taj] *nf*

A.

1. HORT [d'un arbre - gén] pruning ; [- importante] cutting back ; [- légère] trimming ▪ [d'une haie] trimming, clipping ▪ [de la vigne] pruning
2. ARM [tranchant] edge ▪ **frapper de ~** to strike *ou* to slash with the edge of one's sword
3. ART [du bois, du marbre] carving ▪ [en gravure] etching ▪ **l'art de la ~** carving
4. CONSTR [à la carrière] hewing, cutting ▪ [sur le chantier] dressing
5. HIST [impôt] taille, tallage
6. INDUST [d'un engrenage] milling, cutting
7. JOAILL cutting
8. MIN longwall, working face
9. MUS tenor (line)

B.

1. [d'une personne, d'un animal] height ▪ **une femme de haute ~** a tall woman, a woman of considerable height ▪ **un homme de petite ~** a short man ▪ **un enfant de ~ moyenne** a child of average height ▪ **ils ont à peu près la même ~** they're about the same height ▪ **de la ~ de** as big as, the size of
2. [d'un endroit, d'un objet] size ▪ **une pièce de ~ moyenne** an average-sized room
3. [importance] size ▪ **une erreur de cette ~ est impardonnable** a mistake of this magnitude is unforgivable
4. [vêtement] size ▪ **quelle est votre ~?** what size do you take? ▪ **ce n'est pas ma ~** it's not my size ▪ **donnez-moi la ~ en dessous/au-dessus** give me one size down/up ▪ **les grandes/petites ~s** the large/small sizes ▪ **elles font toutes deux la même ~** they both wear the same size ▪ **~ XL** size XL ▪ **deux ~s de plus/de moins** two sizes bigger/smaller ▪ **je n'ai plus votre ~** I'm out of your size ▶ **elle a la ~ mannequin** she's got a real model's figure
5. [partie du corps] waist ▪ **avoir la ~ longue/courte** to be long-/short-waisted ▪ **avoir la ~ fine** to be slim-waisted *ou* slender-waisted ▪ **sa robe est serrée/trop serrée à la ~** her dress is fitted/too tight at the waist ▶ **avoir une ~ de guêpe** *ou* **de nymphe** to have an hourglass figure ▪ **avoir la ~ bien prise** to have a nice *ou* good figure
6. [partie d'un vêtement] waist ▪ **robe à ~ haute/basse** high-/low-waisted dress ▪ **un jean (à) ~ basse** low-waisted *ou* hipster *UK ou* hip-hugger *US* jeans
7. INFORM : **~ mémoire** storage capacity.

◆ **à la taille de** *loc prép* in keeping with ▪ **ses moyens ne sont pas à la ~ de ses ambitions** his ambitions far exceed his means.

◆ **de taille** *loc adj* **1.** [énorme] huge, great ▪ **le risque est de ~** the risk is considerable ▪ **une surprise de ~** a big surprise **2.** [capable] : **être de ~** to measure up ▪ **face à un adversaire comme lui, tu n'es pas de ~** you're no match for an opponent like him ▪ **de ~ à** capable of, able to.

taillé, e [taje] *adj* **1.** [bâti] : **un homme bien ~** a well-built man ▪ **~ en** *ou* **comme : un gaillard ~ en hercule** a great hulk of a man **2.** [apte à] : **~ pour** cut out for ▪ **tu n'es pas ~ pour ce métier** you're not cut out for this job **3.** [coupé - arbre] trimmed, pruned ; [- haie] trimmed, clipped ; [- cristal] cut ; [- crayon] sharpened ; [- barbe, moustache] trimmed ▪ **une barbe ~e en pointe** a goatee (beard) ▪ **un costume bien/mal ~** a well-cut/badly-cut suit.

taille-crayon [tajkrɛjɔ̃] (*pl inv ou pl* **taille-crayons**) *nm* pencil sharpener.

taille-douce [tajdus] (*pl* **tailles-douces**) *nf* intaglio ▪ **une gravure** *ou* **impression en ~** an intaglio.

taille-haie [tajəɛ] (*pl inv ou pl* **taille-haies**) *nm* hedge trimmer.

tailler [3] [taje] ◇ *vt* **1.** [ciseler - pierre] to cut, to hew *sout* ; [- verre] to engrave ; [- bois, marbre] to carve ; [- diamant] to cut ▪ **~ en pièces** *fig* : **~ en pièces une armée** to cut an army to pieces ▪ **la critique l'a taillé en pièces** the reviewers made mincemeat out of him **2.** [barbe, moustache] to trim ▪ [crayon] to sharpen **3.** [façonner] to cut, to hew *sout* ▪ **il a taillé un escalier dans la pente** he cut some steps into the hillside **4.** COUT [vêtement] to cut (out) ▶ **~ une bavette** *fam* to have a chat *ou* a chinwag **5.** HORT [arbre] to prune, to cut back *(sép)* ▪ [haie] to trim, to clip ▪ [vigne] to prune **6.** INDUST [engrenage] to mill, to cut.
◇ *vi* **1.** [inciser] to cut ▪ **~ dans les chairs avec un scalpel** to cut into the flesh with a scalpel **2.** [vêtement] : **cette robe taille grand/petit** this dress is cut *UK ou* runs *US* large/small.
◆ **se tailler** ◇ *vpi*[△] [partir] to scram ▪ **allez, on se taille!** come on, let's clear off! ▪ **taille-toi!** scram!, beat it!
◇ *vpt* : **se ~ un chemin à travers les ronces** to hack one's way through the brambles ▪ **se ~ un chemin à travers la foule** to force one's way through the crowd ▪ **se ~ un (beau) succès** to be a great success.

tailleur [tajœr] *nm* **1.** COUT [artisan] tailor ▪ **~ pour dames** ladies' tailor **2.** [vêtement] (lady's) suit **3.** [ouvrier] : **~ de diamants** diamond *ou* gem cutter ▪ **~ de pierres/de pavés/de marbre** stone/paving stone/marble cutter ▪ **~ de verre** glass engraver.
◆ **en tailleur** *loc adv* cross-legged.

tailleur-pantalon [tajœrpɑ̃talɔ̃] (*pl* **tailleurs-pantalons**) *nm* trouser suit *UK*, pantsuit *US*.

taillis [taji] *nm* coppice, copse, thicket ▪ **~ sous futaie** coppice with standards.

tain [tɛ̃] *nm* [pour miroir] silvering.

taire [111] [tɛr] *vt* **1.** [passer sous silence - raisons] to conceal, to say nothing about ; [- information] to hush up *(sép)* ; [- plan, projet] to keep secret, to say nothing about, to keep quiet about ▪ **je tairai le nom de cette personne** I won't mention this person's name ▪ **il a préféré ~ ses projets** he preferred to keep his plans secret ▪ **faire ~ qqn** [empêcher qqn de parler] to silence sb, to force sb to be quiet ▪ **faites ~ les enfants** make the children be quiet ▪ **faire ~ qqch** to stifle sthg ▪ **fais ~ tes scrupules** forget your scruples **2.** *litt* [cacher - sentiment] : **elle sait ~ ses émotions** she's able to keep her emotions to herself.
◆ **se taire** *vpi* **1.** [s'abstenir de parler] to be *ou* to keep quiet ▪ **tais-toi!** be quiet! ▪ **elle sait se ~ et écouter les autres** she

knows when to be silent and listen to others **2.** [cesser de s'exprimer] to fall silent ▪ **l'opposition s'est tue** the opposition has gone very quiet **3.** *litt* [cesser de faire du bruit] to fall *litt ou* to become silent **4.** *fam loc* **et quand il t'a invitée à danser? – tais-toi, je ne savais plus où me mettre!** and when he asked you to dance? – don't, I felt so embarrassed!

taisons *etc v* ▻ **taire**.

Taïwan [tajwan] *npr* Taiwan ▪ **à ~** in Taiwan.

taïwanais, e [tajwanɛ, ɛz] *adj* Taiwanese.
◆ **Taïwanais, e** *nm, f* Taiwanese ▪ **les Taïwanais** the Taiwanese.

tajine [taʒin] *nm* **1.** [mets] *Moroccan lamb (or chicken) stew* **2.** [récipient] tajine.

Taj Mahal [taʒmaal] *npr m* : **le ~** the Taj Mahal.

talc [talk] *nm* talcum powder, talc.

talé, e [tale] *adj* [fruit] bruised.

talent [talɑ̃] *nm* **1.** [capacité artistique] talent ▪ **avoir du ~** to have talent, to be talented **2.** [don, aptitude particulière] talent, skill, gift ▪ **ses ~s de communicateur** his talents as a communicator **3.** [personne] talent ▪ **il est à la recherche de jeunes/nouveaux ~s** he's looking for young/new talent **4.** HIST talent.
◆ **de talent** *loc adj* talented ▪ **un styliste de grand ~** a designer of great talent, a highly talented designer.
◆ **sans talent** *loc adj* untalented.

talentueux, euse [talɑ̃tɥø, øz] *adj fam* talented, gifted.

talion [taljɔ̃] *nm* talion.

talisman [talismɑ̃] *nm* **1.** [amulette] talisman **2.** *litt* [sortilège] spell, charm.

talkie-walkie [tɔkiwɔki] (*pl* **talkies-walkies**) *nm* walkie-talkie.

talk-show [tɔkʃo] *nm* talk-show.

Talmud [talmyd] *npr m* Talmud.

talmudique [talmydik] *adj* Talmudic.

taloche [talɔʃ] *nf* **1.** CONSTR float **2.** *fam* [gifle] cuff, wallop ▪ **filer une ~ à qqn** to clout sb.

talocher [3] [talɔʃe] *vt fam* **~ qqn** to clip *ou* to cuff sb round the ear.

talon [talɔ̃] *nm* **1.** ANAT heel ▪ **accroupi sur ses ~s** crouching (on his haunches *ou* heels) ➊ **~ d'Achille : son ~ d'Achille** his Achilles' heel ▪ **être** *ou* **marcher sur les ~s de qqn** to follow close on sb's heels ▪ **montrer** *ou* **tourner les ~s** [s'enfuir] to show a clean pair of heels ▪ **tourner les ~s** [faire demi-tour] to (turn round and) walk away **2.** [d'une chaussure] heel ➊ **~s aiguilles** spike *ou* stiletto *UK* heels ▪ **~s bottiers** medium heels ▪ **porter des ~s hauts** *ou* **des hauts ~s** to wear high heels ▪ **chaussures à ~s hauts** high-heeled shoes ▪ **porter des ~s plats** to wear flat heels **3.** [d'une chaussette] heel **4.** [d'un fromage, d'un jambon] heel **5.** [d'un chèque] stub, counterfoil ▪ [d'un carnet à souches] counterfoil **6.** CARTES stock, talon **7.** MUS heel, nut **8.** RAIL heel **9.** TECHNOL [de quille, de serrure, de ski] heel.

talonnage [talɔnaʒ] *nm* SPORT heeling *(U)* ▪ **faire un ~** to heel (the ball).

talonner [3] [talɔne] ◇ *vt* **1.** [poursuivre] : **~ qqn** to follow on sb's heels ▪ **le coureur marocain, talonné par l'Anglais** the Moroccan runner, with the Englishman close on his heels **2.** [harceler - suj: créancier] to hound ; [- suj: gêneur] to pester ▪ **le directeur me talonne pour que je remette mon rapport** the manager's after me to get my report in **3.** [tourmenter - suj: faim] to gnaw at *(insép)* **4.** [cheval] to spur with one's heels **5.** SPORT to heel, to hook.
◇ *vi* NAUT [navire] to touch the bottom.

talonnette [talɔnɛt] *nf* **1.** [d'une chaussure] heelpiece, heel cap **2.** [d'un pantalon] binding strip.

talquer [3] [talke] *vt* to put talcum powder *ou* talc on.

talus [taly] *nm* **1.** [d'un chemin] (side) slope **2.** CONSTR [de mur] batter, talus **3.** MIL talus.

tamanoir [tamanwar] *nm* (great) anteater.

tamarin [tamarɛ̃] *nm* **1.** ZOOL tamarin **2.** BOT tamarind.

tamarinier [tamarinje] *nm* tamarind (tree).

tamaris [tamaris], **tamarix** [tamariks] *nm* tamarisk.

tambouille^△ [tɑ̃buj] *nf* grub ▪ **faire la ~** to cook (the grub).

tambour [tɑ̃bur] *nm* **1.** MUS [instrument] drum ▪ **jouer du ~** to play the drum ▪ **on entendait les ~s de la fanfare** we could hear the drumming of the band ➊ **~ de basque** tambourine ▪ **au son du ~** [bruyamment] noisily ▪ **sans ~ ni trompette** discreetly, unobtrusively ▪ **~ battant** briskly ▪ **'le Tambour'** ***Grass*** 'The Tin Drum' **2.** [son] drumbeat ▪ **le matin on les réveille au ~** they're woken in the morning by the sound of a drum **3.** [joueur] drummer ▪ **~ de ville** town crier **4.** ARCHIT, AUTO & ÉLECTR drum **5.** CONSTR [sas] tambour (door) **6.** COUT [à broder] tambour **7.** INFORM : **~ magnétique** magnetic drum **8.** TECHNOL [de lave-linge] drum ▪ [en horlogerie] barrel.

tambourin [tɑ̃burɛ̃] *nm* [de basque] tambourine ▪ [provençal] tambourin.

tambourinage [tɑ̃burinaʒ] *nm* drumming.

tambourinement [tɑ̃burinmɑ̃] *nm* = **tambourinage**.

tambouriner [3] [tɑ̃burine] ◇ *vi* **1.** [frapper] to drum (on) ▪ **il est venu ~ à notre porte à six heures du matin** he came beating *ou* hammering on our door at six in the morning ▪ **la grêle tambourinait à la fenêtre** hailstones were drumming on *ou* beating against the window pane **2.** MUS & *vieilli* to drum.
◇ *vt* **1.** MUS [air, cadence] to drum (out) **2.** [proclamer] to cry out *(sép)*.

tambourineur, euse [tɑ̃burinœr, øz] *nm, f* tambourine player.

Tamerlan [tamɛrlɑ̃] *npr* : **~ le Grand** Tamerlane *ou* Tamburlaine the Great.

tamis [tami] *nm* **1.** [à farine] sieve ▪ [en fil de soie, de coton] tammy (cloth), tamis ▪ **passer au ~** [farine, sucre] to put through a sieve, to sift, to sieve ; [dossier] to go through with a fine-tooth comb **2.** CONSTR [à sable] sifter, riddle *spéc* **3.** SPORT [d'une raquette] strings.

Tamise [tamiz] *npr f* : **la ~** the Thames.

tamisé, e [tamize] *adj* **1.** [farine, terre] sifted, sieved **2.** [éclairage] soft, subdued ▪ [lumière naturelle] soft.

tamiser [3] [tamize] *vt* **1.** [farine, poudre] to sift, to sieve **2.** [lumière naturelle] to filter ▪ [éclairage] to subdue **3.** CONSTR [sable] to sift, to riddle *spéc*.

tamoul, e [tamul] *adj* Tamil.
◆ **Tamoul, e** *nm, f* Tamil.
◆ **tamoul** *nm* LING Tamil.

tampon [tɑ̃pɔ̃] ◇ *nm* **1.** [pour absorber] wad ▪ **~ périodique** tampon **2.** [pour imprégner] pad ▪ **~ encreur** ink pad **3.** [pour nettoyer] pad ▪ **~ Jex**® Brillo pad® ▪ **~ à récurer** scouring pad, scourer **4.** [pour obturer] plug, bung ▪ **il a bouché la fissure avec un ~ de papier** he stopped up the crack with a wad of paper **5.** [plaque gravée] rubber stamp ▪ [oblitération] stamp ▪ **le ~ de la poste** the postmark ➊ **~ dateur** date stamp **6.** *fig* buffer **7.** ART dabber, dauber **8.** CONSTR [dalle] cover ▪ [cheville] wall plug **9.** INFORM & RAIL buffer **10.** MÉCAN plug gauge **11.** MÉD swab, tampon.
◇ *adj inv* POLIT : **État/zone ~** buffer state/zone.

tampon-buvard [tɑ̃pɔ̃byvar] (*pl* **tampons-buvards**) *nm* blotter.

tamponner [3] [tɑ̃pɔne] *vt* **1.** [document, passeport] to stamp ▪ [lettre timbrée] to postmark **2.** [télescoper] to collide with *(insép)*, to hit, to bump into *(insép)* ▪ [violemment] to crash into *(insép)* **3.** [sécher - front, lèvres, yeux] to dab (at) **4.** [enduire - meuble] to dab **5.** CHIM to buffer **6.** CONSTR [mur] to plug **7.** MÉD [plaie] to tampon.
◆ **se tamponner** ◇ *vp (emploi réciproque)* to collide, to bump into one another ▪ **ils se sont tamponnés** they collided.
◇ *vp (emploi réfléchi)*^△ : **je m'en tamponne (le coquillard)!** I don't give a damn!

tamponneur, euse [tãpɔnœr, øz] *adj* colliding.

tam-tam [tamtam] (*pl* **tam-tams**) *nm* MUS [d'Afrique] tom-tom ▪ [gong] tam-tam.

tan [tã] *nm* tanbark.

Tananarive [tananariv] *npr* Antananarivo.

tancer [16] [tãse] *vt litt* to scold ▪ **~ vertement qqn** to berate sb *sout.*

tanche [tãʃ] *nf* tench.

tandem [tãdɛm] *nm* **1.** [vélo] tandem **2.** [couple] pair ▪ **le ~ qu'ils forment est redoutable** together, they make a formidable pair.
◆ **en tandem** ◇ *loc adj* [attelage] tandem *(modif).*
◇ *loc adv* [agir, travailler] in tandem, as a pair.

tandis que [tãdikə], **tandis qu'** [tãdik] *loc conj* **1.** [pendant que] while, whilst *sout* ▪ [au même moment que] as **2.** [alors que] whereas.

tangage [tãgaʒ] *nm* AÉRON & NAUT pitching ▪ **il y avait du ~** the boat was pitching.

tangence [tãʒãs] *nf* tangency ▪ **point de ~** point of tangency *spéc* OU contact.

tangent, e [tãʒã, ãt] *adj* **1.** GÉOM & MATH tangent, tangential **2.** *fam* [limite - cas, candidat] borderline ▪ **ses notes sont ~es** her grades put her on the borderline ▪ **je ne l'ai pas renvoyé, mais c'était ~** I didn't fire him but I was very close to doing so.
◆ **tangente** *nf* **1.** GÉOM & MATH tangent ▪ **une ~e à la courbe** a tangent to the curve **2.** *loc* **prendre la ~e** *fam* [se sauver] to make off ; [esquiver une question] to dodge the issue.

tangentiel, elle [tãʒãsjɛl] *adj* tangential.

Tanger [tãʒe] *npr* Tangier, Tangiers.

tangerine [tãʒərin] *nf* tangerine.

tangibilité [tãʒibilite] *nf* tangibility, tangibleness.

tangible [tãʒibl] *adj* **1.** [palpable] tangible, palpable *sout* **2.** [évident] tangible, real ▪ **l'amélioration des résultats est ~** there has been a real improvement in the results.

tango [tãgo] ◇ *adj inv* bright orange.
◇ *nm* tango.

tangue [tãg] *nf* sea sand.

tanguer [3] [tãge] *vi* **1.** NAUT to pitch ▪ **la tempête faisait ~ le navire** the storm was tossing the boat around, the boat was tossed about in the storm **2.** *fam* [tituber] to reel, to sway **3.** *fam* [vaciller - décor] to spin.

tanière [tanjɛr] *nf* **1.** [d'un animal] den, lair **2.** [habitation] retreat ▪ **il ne sort jamais de sa ~** he never leaves his den.

tanin [tanɛ̃] *nm* tannin.

tank [tãk] *nm* INDUST & MIL tank.

tanker [tãkœr] *nm* NAUT tanker.

tannage [tanaʒ] *nm* tanning.

tannant, e [tanã, ãt] *adj* **1.** [produit] tanning **2.** *fam* [importun] annoying ▪ [énervant] maddening ▪ **ce que tu peux être ~ avec tes questions!** you're a real pain with all these questions!

tanné, e [tane] *adj* **1.** [traité - cuir] tanned **2.** [hâlé - peau] weathered, weather-beaten.
◆ **tannée** *nf* **1.** [écorce] tanbark **2.** △ [correction] hiding, thrashing ▪ **prendre une ~e** to get a hiding **3.** △ [défaite humiliante] drubbing, trouncing ▪ **il a pris** OU **s'est ramassé une ~e aux présidentielles** he got well and truly thrashed in the presidential election.

tanner [3] [tane] *vt* **1.** [traiter - cuir] to tan **2.** [hâler - peau] to tan **3.** *fam* [harceler] to pester, to hassle ▪ **son fils le tanne pour avoir une moto** his son keeps pestering him for a motorbike.

tannerie [tanri] *nf* **1.** [établissement] tannery **2.** [industrie, opérations] tanning.

tanneur, euse [tanœr, øz] *nm, f* tanner.

tannin [tanɛ̃] = **tanin**.

tant [tã] ◇ *adv* **1.** [avec un verbe] : **il l'aime ~** he loves her so much ▪ **il a ~ travaillé sur son projet** he's worked so hard on his project ▮ [en corrélation avec 'que'] : **ils ont ~ fait qu'ils ont obtenu tout ce qu'ils voulaient** they worked so hard that they ended up getting everything they wanted ▪ **j'ai ~ crié que je suis enroué** I shouted so much that I've lost my voice ▶ **~ va la cruche à l'eau (qu'à la fin elle se casse)** *prov* the pitcher will go to the well once too often
2. [avec un participe passé] : **le jour ~ attendu arriva enfin** the long-awaited day arrived at last
3. *sout* [introduisant la cause] : **deux personnes se sont évanouies, ~ il faisait chaud** it was so hot (that) two people fainted
4. [exprimant une quantité imprécise] so much ▪ **il gagne ~ de l'heure** he earns so much per hour
5. [introduisant une comparaison] : **~... que : pour des raisons ~ économiques que politiques** for economic as well as political reasons ▪ **ce n'est pas ~ sa colère qui me fait mal que son mépris** it is not much her anger that hurts me as her contempt
6. *loc* **vous m'en direz ~!** *fam,* **tu m'en diras ~!** *fam* you don't say! ▪ **comme il y en a ~ : une maison de banlieue comme il y en a ~** one of those suburban houses that you come across so often.
◇ *nm* : **suite à votre lettre du ~** with reference to your letter of such and such a date ▪ **vous serez payé le ~ de chaque mois** you'll be paid on such and such a date every month.
◆ **en tant que** *loc conj* **1.** [en qualité de] as
2. [dans la mesure où] as long as.
◆ **tant bien que mal** *loc adv* after a fashion ▪ **le moteur est reparti, ~ bien que mal** somehow, the engine started up again.
◆ **tant de** *loc dét* **1.** [tellement de] *(suivi d'un n non comptable)* so much, such ▪ *(suivi d'un n comptable)* so many ▪ **~ de gens** so many people ▮ [en corrélation avec 'que'] : **elle a ~ de travail qu'elle n'a même plus le temps de faire les courses** she has so much work that she doesn't even have the time to go shopping anymore ▪ **vous m'avez reçu avec ~ de générosité que je ne sais quoi dire** you've made me so welcome that I'm lost for words ▪ **~ d'années ont passé que j'ai oublié** so many years have gone by that I've forgotten
2. [exprimant une quantité imprécise] : **il y a ~ de lignes par page** there are so many lines to a page.
◆ **tant et plus** *loc adv* over and over again, time and time again.
◆ **tant et si bien que** *loc conj* : **ils ont fait ~ et si bien qu'ils ont réussi** they worked so hard that they succeeded ▪ **~ et si bien que je ne lui parle plus** so much so that we're no longer on speaking terms.
◆ **tant il est vrai que** *loc conj* : **il s'en remettra, ~ il est vrai que le temps guérit tout** he'll get over it, for it's true that time is a great healer.
◆ **tant mieux** *loc adv* good, fine, so much the better ▪ **vous n'avez rien à payer – ~ mieux!** you don't have anything to pay – good OU fine! ▪ **il est parti et c'est ~ mieux** he's left and just as well OU and a good thing too ▪ **~ mieux pour lui** good for him.
◆ **tant pis** *loc adv* never mind, too bad ▪ **je reste, ~ pis s'il n'est pas content** I'm staying, too bad if he doesn't like it ▪ **~ pis pour lui** too bad (for him).
◆ **tant soit peu** *loc adv* : **s'il est ~ soit peu intelligent, il comprendra** if he is even the slightest bit intelligent, he'll understand.
◆ **tant que** *loc conj* **1.** [autant que] as OU so much as ▪ **elle ne travaille pas ~ que les autres** she doesn't work as much OU as hard as the others ▪ **manges-en ~ que tu veux** have as many OU much as you like ▶ **tu l'aimes ~ que ça?** do you love him that much? ▪ **elle est jolie – pas ~ que ça** she's pretty – not really ▪ **il y a 15 ans – ~ que ça?** that was 15 years ago – that long ago? ▪ **vous irez, tous ~ que vous êtes** every last one of you will go ▪ **tous ~ que nous sommes** all of us, every single OU last one of us
2. [aussi longtemps que] as long as ▪ [pendant que] while ▪ **tu peux rester ~ que tu veux** you can stay as long as you like ▪ **~ qu'on y est** while we're at it ▪ **~ que j'y pense, as-tu reçu ma carte?** while I think of it, did you get my card? ▪ **~ que ce n'est pas grave!** *fam* as long as it's not serious! ▶ **pourquoi pas un château avec piscine ~ que tu y es!** why not a castle with a swimming pool while you're at it! ▪ **~ qu'il y a de la vie, il y a de l'espoir** while there's life there's hope.

◆ **tant qu'à** *loc conj* : **~ qu'à partir, autant partir tout de suite** if I/you *etc* must go, I/you *etc* might as well do it right away ■ **~ qu'à m'expatrier, j'aime mieux que ce soit dans un beau pays** if I have to go and live abroad, I'd rather go somewhere nice ▶ **~ qu'à faire : ~ qu'à faire, je préférerais du poisson** I'd rather have fish if I have the choice ■ **~ qu'à faire, sortons maintenant** we might as well go out now.
◆ **un tant soit peu** *loc adv* : **si tu étais un ~ soit peu observateur** if you were the least bit observant ■ **si elle avait un ~ soit peu de bon sens** if she had the slightest bit of common sense ■ **s'il voulait être un ~ soit peu plus aimable** if he would only be just the slightest *ou* tiniest bit more friendly.

Tantale [tɑ̃tal] *npr* Tantalus.

tante [tɑ̃t] *nf* **1.** [dans une famille] aunt ■ **~ Marie** Aunt Marie **2.** △ [mont-de-piété] : **chez ma ~** at my uncle's, at the pawnshop **3.** △ [homosexuel] fairy.

tantième [tɑ̃tjɛm] ◇ *adj* : **la ~ partie des bénéfices** so much of the profits.
◇ *nm* [part proportionnelle] proportion ■ [quote-part de bénéfice] director's fee *ou* percentage.

tantine [tɑ̃tin] *nf* *fam* aunty.

tantinet [tɑ̃tinɛ] *nm* tiny bit.
◆ **un tantinet** *loc adv* a tiny (little) bit ■ **un ~ stupide** a tiny bit stupid.

tantôt [tɑ̃to] *adv* **1.** *fam* [cet après-midi] this afternoon **2.** [dialecte: plus tard] later ■ **à ~** see you later **3.** [dialecte: plus tôt] earlier.
◆ **tantôt..., tantôt** *loc corrélative* sometimes..., sometimes.

tantouze△ [tɑ̃tuz] *nf péj* fairy, queen△.

tantrique [tɑ̃trik] *adj* Tantric.

tantrisme [tɑ̃trism] *nm* Tantrism.

Tanzanie [tɑ̃zani] *npr f* : **(la) ~** Tanzania.

tanzanien, enne [tɑ̃zanjɛ̃, ɛn] *adj* Tanzanian.
◆ **Tanzanien, enne** *nm, f* Tanzanian.

tao [tao] *nm* Tao.

TAO (*abr de* **traduction assistée par ordinateur**) *nf* CAT.

taoïsme [taɔism] *nm* Taoism.

taoïste [taɔist] *adj & nmf* Taoist.

taon [tɑ̃] *nm* horsefly.

tapage [tapaʒ] *nm* **1.** [bruit] din, uproar ■ **faire du ~** to make a racket **2.** [scandale] scandal, fuss ■ **ça a fait tout un ~** there was quite a fuss about it **3.** DR : **~ nocturne** *disturbance of the peace at night.*

tapageur, euse [tapaʒœr, øz] *adj* **1.** [bruyant] noisy, rowdy **2.** [voyant - vêtement] showy, flashy ; [- publicité] obtrusive **3.** [dont on parle beaucoup] : **une liaison tapageuse** a much-talked-about affair.

tapageusement [tapaʒøzmɑ̃] *adv* flashily, showily.

tapant, e [tapɑ̃, ɑ̃t] *adj* : **je serai là à dix heures ~es** I'll be there at ten o'clock sharp *ou* on the dot ■ **il est rentré à minuit ~** he came home on the stroke of midnight.

tape [tap] *nf* **1.** [pour punir] (little) slap, tap **2.** [amicale] pat ■ **donner une petite ~ sur le dos/bras de qqn** to pat sb's back/arm **3.** [pour attirer l'attention] tap ■ **donner une petite ~ sur l'épaule de qqn** to tap sb's shoulder.

tapé, e [tape] *adj* **1.** *fam* [fou] crackers, cracked **2.** [fruit - abîmé] bruised **3.** *fam* [juste et vigoureux - réplique] smart **4.** *fam* [marqué par l'âge - visage] aged.
◆ **tapée** *nf fam* [multitude] : **une ~e de dossiers** heaps of files ■ **il y avait une ~e de photographes** there was a swarm of photographers.

tape-à-l'œil [tapalœj] ◇ *adj inv* [couleur, bijoux, toilette] flashy, showy.
◇ *nm inv* : **c'est du ~** [objets, toilette] it's all show ■ **il aime le ~** he likes showy things.

tape-cul (*pl* **tape-culs**), **tapecul** [tapky] *nm* **1.** [tilbury] gig **2.** *fam* [voiture] rattletrap **3.** *fam* [balançoire] seesaw **4.** *fam* NAUT [voile] jigger ■ [mât] jigger mast.

tapée [tape] *f* ▷ **tapé.**

tapement [tapmɑ̃] *nm* **1.** [action] tapping, drumming **2.** [bruit] tapping.

tapenade [tapənad] *nf* tapenade *(hors d'œuvre made from olives, anchovies and capers, blended with olive oil and lemon juice and served on toast).*

taper [3] [tape] ◇ *vt* **1.** [personne - gén] to hit ; [- d'un revers de main] to slap
2. [marteler - doucement] to tap ; [- fort] to hammer, to bang
3. [heurter] : **~ un coup à une porte** to knock once on a door
4. [dactylographier] to type ■ **~ un document à la machine** to type (out) a document ■ **~ 40 mots à la minute** to type 40 words per minute
5. TÉLÉCOM [code] to dial
6. △ [demander de l'argent à] : **il m'a tapé de 300 euros** he touched me for 300 euros, he cadged *UK ou* bummed *US* 300 euros off me.
◇ *vi* **1.** [donner un coup à quelque chose] : **~ sur** [clavier] to bang *ou* to thump away at ; [clou, pieu] to hit ; [avec un marteau] to hammer (away at) ■ **elle a tapé du poing sur la table** she banged *ou* thumped her fist on the table ■ **~ dans une balle** [lui donner un coup] to kick a ball ; [s'amuser avec] to kick a ball around ■ **~ du pied** *ou* **des pieds** to stamp one's foot *ou* feet ■ **~ des mains** to clap one's hands
2. [battre, frapper] : **~ sur qqn** [une fois] to hit sb ; [à coups répétés] to beat sb up ■ **c'est un bon boxeur et il tape dur** he's a good boxer and he hits hard *ou* packs a powerful punch ▶ **se faire ~ sur les doigts** to get rapped over the knuckles ■ **la petite veste rose m'avait tapé dans l'œil** *fam* I was really taken with the little pink jacket ■ **elle lui a tapé dans l'œil dès le premier jour** *fam* he fancied her from day one
3. [dactylographier] : **il tape bien/mal** he types well/badly, he's a good/bad typist ■ **tape sur cette touche** press this key
4. *fam* [soleil] to beat down ■ **le vin rouge m'a tapé sur la tête** the red wine knocked me out
5. *fam* [critiquer] : **~ sur** [personne, film] to run down *(sép)*, to knock ■ **elle s'est fait ~ dessus dans la presse** *ou* **par les journaux** the newspapers really panned her
6. *fam* [puiser] : **~ dans** [réserves, économies] to dig into *(insép)* ; [tiroir-caisse] to help o.s. from.
◆ **se taper** ◇ *vp (emploi réciproque)* to hit each other ■ **ils ont fini par se ~ dessus** eventually, they came to blows ▶ **se ~ sur le ventre**△ [être en bonnes relations] to be very close.
◇ *vpt* **1.** *fam* [consommer - dîner, petits fours] to put away *(sép)*, to scoff *UK* ; [- boisson] to knock back *(sép)*
2. △ [sexuellement] to lay, to have it off with△
3. *fam* [subir - corvée, travail, gêneur] to get landed *UK ou* lumbered *UK ou* stuck with ■ **je me suis tapé les cinq étages à pied** I had to walk up the five floors
4. *loc* **se ~ les cuisses** *fam* [de satisfaction, de rire] to slap one's thighs ■ **c'était à se ~ le derrière** *fam ou* **le cul** △ **par terre** it was a scream *ou* hoot ■ **c'est à se ~ la tête contre les murs** *fam* it's enough to drive you stark raving mad ■ **se ~ la cloche** *fam* to have a blow-out△ *UK*, to pig out.
◇ *vpi* : **se ~ sur les cuisses** [de satisfaction, de rire] to slap one's thighs ■ **je m'en tape**△ I don't give a damn(about it) ■ **tu peux (toujours) te ~ !**△ you can whistle for it!

tapette [tapɛt] *nf* **1.** [petite tape] pat, tap **2.** [piège à souris] mousetrap **3.** △ *péj* [homosexuel] poof *UK*, fag *US* **4.** [contre les mouches] flyswatter ■ [pour les tapis] carpet beater.

tapeur, euse [tapœr, øz] *nm, f fam* cadger *UK*, scrounger, mooch *US*.

tapi, e [tapi] *adj* **1.** [accroupi] crouching, hunched up ■ [en embuscade] lurking **2.** *litt* [blotti, dissimulé] lurking, skulking, lying low ■ **une chaumière ~e au cœur de la forêt** a cottage hidden *ou* lying in the heart of the forest **3.** [retiré] buried, shut away.

tapin△ [tapɛ̃] *nm* : **faire le ~** to be on the game△ *UK*, to work the streets *US*.

tapiner [3] △ [tapine] *vi* to be on the game△ *UK*, to work the streets *US*.

tapinois [tapinwa] ◆ **en tapinois** *loc adv* [entrer, se glisser] sneakily, furtively.

tapioca [tapjɔka] *nm* tapioca ▪ **potage au ~** tapioca soup.

tapir[1] [tapir] *nm* tapir.

tapir[2] [32] [tapir] ◆ **se tapir** *vpi* **1.** [se baisser] to crouch (down) ▪ [se dissimuler - par peur] to hide ; [- en embuscade] to lurk ▪ **il se tapit derrière un buisson et l'attendit** he lay in wait for her behind a bush **2.** *sout* [se retirer] to hide away.

tapis [tapi] *nm* **1.** [pièce de tissu - gén] carpet ; [- de taille moyenne] rug ; [- de petite taille] mat ▶ **~ de bain** bath mat ▪ **~ de haute laine** deep-pile carpet ▪ **~ d'Orient** oriental carpet ▪ **~ de prière** prayer mat ▪ **~ rouge** *pr* & *fig* red carpet ▪ **~ de selle** saddlecloth ▪ **~ de sol** ground sheet ▪ **~ de souris** INFORM mouse mat *OU* pad ▪ **~ volant** flying *OU* magic carpet **2.** *litt* [couche - de feuilles, de neige] carpet ▪ **~ de verdure** grassy expanse **3.** GÉOGR : **~ végétal** plant cover **4.** JEUX [de billard, d'une table de jeu] cloth, baize ▪ **~ vert** [table de jeu] green baize ; [de conférence] baize ▪ **Tapis Vert** *game of chance organized by the French national lottery* **5.** SPORT [dans une salle de sport] mat ▪ [à la boxe] canvas ▪ **aller au ~** [boxeur] to be knocked down ▪ **envoyer son adversaire au ~** to floor one's opponent **6.** TECHNOL : **~ roulant** [pour piétons] moving pavement *UK OU* sidewalk *US*, travolator ▪ **~ transporteur** [pour bagages, pièces de montage] conveyor (belt).
◆ **sur le tapis** *loc adv* **1.** JEUX on the table **2.** *fig* **l'affaire est de nouveau sur le ~** the matter is being discussed again ▪ **à quoi bon remettre toutes nos vieilles querelles sur le ~?** what's the use of bringing up *OU* raking over all our old quarrels again?

tapis-brosse [tapibrɔs] (*pl* **tapis-brosses**) *nm* doormat.

tapisser [3] [tapise] *vt* **1.** [mur - avec du papier peint] to wallpaper ; [- avec du tissu] to hang with material ; [- avec des tentures] to hang with curtains *OU* drapes *US* ▪ [fauteuil, étagère] to cover ▪ **~ une cloison de posters** to cover a partition with posters **2.** CULIN [garnir] to line **3.** *litt* [couvrir - suj: bruyère, neige] to cover, to carpet ▪ **un nid tapissé de feuilles** a nest lined with leaves **4.** ANAT & BOT to line.

tapisserie [tapisri] *nf* **1.** [art, panneau] tapestry ▪ **les ~s des Gobelins** the Gobelins tapestries ▶ **faire ~** [dans une réunion] to be left out ; [au bal] to be a wallflower **2.** [petit ouvrage] tapestry ▪ **faire de la ~** to do tapestry *OU* tapestry-work ▶ **point de ~** canvas stitch **3.** [papier peint] wallpaper *(U)* ▪ **refaire les ~s d'une chambre** to repaper a bedroom **4.** [métier] tapestry-making.

tapissier, ère [tapisje, ɛr] *nm, f* **1.** [fabricant] tapestry-maker **2.** [vendeur] upholsterer **3.** [décorateur] interior decorator.

tapotement [tapɔtmɑ̃] *nm* [avec les doigts] tapping ▪ [avec la main] patting.

tapoter [3] [tapɔte] ◇ *vt* **1.** [dos, joue] to pat ▪ [surface] to tap **2.** [air de musique] to bang out.
◇ *vi* **1.** [tambouriner] to tap ▪ **elle tapotait sur la table avec un crayon** she was drumming (on) the table with a pencil **2.** [jouer médiocrement] : **il tapotait sur le vieux piano** he was banging out a tune on the old piano.

tapuscrit [tapyskri] *nm* typescript.

taquet [takɛ] *nm* **1.** [cale - de meuble] wedge ; [- de porte] wedge, stop **2.** CONSTR [coin en bois] (wood) angle block ▪ [d'une porte] catch **3.** IMPR jogger **4.** NAUT cleat **5.** RAIL : **~ d'arrêt** Scotch block **6.** TECHNOL [d'une machine à écrire] tabulator stop **7.** TEXT picker.

taquin, e [takɛ̃, in] ◇ *adj* teasing ▪ **il est un peu ~ par moments** he's a bit of a tease sometimes.
◇ *nm, f* [personne] teaser, tease.
◆ **taquin** *nm* JEUX *puzzle consisting of sliding plates in a frame which have to be arranged in a set order.*

taquiner [3] [takine] *vt* **1.** [faire enrager] to tease ▪ **cesse de la ~** stop teasing her **2.** [être légèrement douloureux] to bother **3.** *fam loc* **~ le piano/violon** to play the piano/violin a bit ▪ **~ le goujon** to do a bit of fishing.
◆ **se taquiner** *vp (emploi réciproque)* to tease each other.

taquinerie [takinri] *nf* **1.** [action] teasing **2.** [parole] : **cesse tes ~s** stop teasing.

tarabiscoté, e [tarabiskɔte] *adj* **1.** [bijou] overornate **2.** [style, phrases] fussy, affected **3.** [explication, récit] complicated, involved, convoluted ▪ **ton histoire est bien ~e!** your story is pretty complicated!

tarabuster [3] [tarabyste] *vt* **1.** [houspiller - personne] to pester, to badger ▪ **elle m'a tarabusté jusqu'à ce que j'accepte** she just wouldn't leave me alone until I said yes **2.** [tracasser] to bother.

tarama [tarama] *nm* taramasalata.

taratata [taratata] *interj fam* [exprime - la méfiance, l'incrédulité] nonsense, rubbish ; [- la contrariété] fiddlesticks ▪ **~, tu as dit que tu viendrais, tu viendras!** no, no, you said you'd come, so come you will!

taraud [taro] *nm* [pour filetage] tap, screw tap.

tarauder [3] [tarode] *vt* to tap, to thread.

tard [tar] *adv* **1.** [à la fin de la journée, d'une période] late ▪ **il se fait ~** it's getting late ▪ **~ dans la matinée/l'après-midi** late in the morning/afternoon **2.** [après le moment fixé ou opportun] late ▪ **les magasins restent ouverts ~** the shops stay open late *OU* keep late opening hours ▪ **c'est trop ~** it's too late ▪ **plus ~** later ▪ **il est arrivé encore plus ~ que moi** he came in even later than I did ▪ **je m'en occuperai un peu plus ~** I'll deal with it a little later ▪ **nous parlions de lui pas plus ~ que ce matin** we were talking about him only *OU* just this morning ▪ **elle est venue ~ à la danse classique** she was a latecomer to ballet.
◆ **au plus tard** *loc adv* at the latest.
◆ **sur le tard** *loc adv* late (on) in life.

tarder [3] [tarde] *vi* **1.** [être lent à se décider - personne] to delay ▪ **je n'aurais pas dû tant ~** I shouldn't have left it so late *OU* have put it off so long ▪ **ne pars pas maintenant – j'ai déjà trop tardé** don't go now – I should be gone already **2.** [être long à venir - événement] to be a long time coming, to take a long time to come ▪ **sa décision n'a pas tardé** his decision wasn't long coming ▪ **ça ne tardera plus maintenant** it won't be long now ▪ **je t'avais dit qu'on le reverrait, ça n'a pas tardé!** I told you we'd see him again, we didn't have to wait long! ▪ **la réponse tardait à venir** the answer took a long time to come ▪ **un conflit ne tardera pas à éclater entre les deux pays** it won't be long before the two countries enter into conflict ▪ [mettre du temps - personne] : **elle devrait être rentrée, elle ne va pas ~** she should be back by now, she won't be long ▪ **il a trop tardé à donner son accord** he waited too long before giving his approval ▪ **ne pas ~ à : nous ne tarderons pas à le savoir** we'll soon know ▪ **elle n'a pas tardé à se rendre compte que...** it didn't take her long to realize that..., she soon realized that...
◆ **il tarde** *v impers* : **il me tarde d'avoir les résultats** I'm longing to get the results ▪ **il nous tarde tant que tu reviennes** we are so longing for your return.
◆ **sans (plus) tarder** *loc adv* without delay ▪ **partons sans plus ~** let's leave without further delay.

tardif, ive [tardif, iv] *adj* **1.** [arrivée] late ▪ [remords] belated *sout*, tardy *litt* ▪ **l'arrivée tardive des secours sur le lieu de l'accident** the late arrival of the emergency services at the scene of the accident **2.** [heure] late, advanced *sout* **3.** AGRIC late, late-developing.

tardivement [tardivmɑ̃] *adv* **1.** [à une heure tardive] late **2.** [trop tard] belatedly, tardily *litt*.

tare [tar] *nf* **1.** [défectuosité - physique] (physical) defect ; [- psychique] abnormality **2.** *fig* defect, flaw ▪ **l'agressivité est la ~ de la société moderne** aggressiveness is the ugliest feature of modern society **3.** COMM [perte de valeur] loss, shrinkage **4.** [d'une balance, d'un poids brut, d'un prix] tare.

taré, e [tare] ◇ *adj* **1.** [gâté - fruit] imperfect **2.** [atteint d'une tare] abnormal **3.** [corrompu] corrupt ■ **un politicien ~** a corrupt politician **4.** *fam* [fou] soft in the head, touched, mad ■ [imbécile] stupid.
◇ *nm, f* **1.** MÉD imbecile **2.** [vicieux] pervert **3.** *fam* [fou] loony, nutter ■ [imbécile] moron, idiot.

tarentelle [tarɑ̃tɛl] *nf* tarantella.

tarentule [tarɑ̃tyl] *nf* (European) tarantula.

tarer [3] [tare] *vt* COMM to tare.

targette [tarʒɛt] *nf* small bolt.

targuer [3] [targe] ◆ **se targuer de** *vp+prép sout* [se vanter de] to boast about *ou* of ■ [s'enorgueillir de] to pride o.s. on ■ **il se targue de connaître plusieurs langues** he claims he knows *ou* to know several languages ■ **un risque que je me targue d'avoir pris** a risk I'm proud to have taken *ou* I pride myself on having taken.

tarif [tarif] *nm* **1.** [liste de prix] price list ■ [barème] rate, rates ■ **~ douanier** customs rate ■ **~ postal** postal *ou* postage rates ■ **il est payé au ~ syndical** he's paid the union rate ■ **augmentation du ~ horaire** increase in *ou* of the hourly rate **2.** [prix pratiqué] : **quel est votre ~?, quels sont vos ~s?** [femme de ménage, baby-sitter, mécanicien, professeur particulier] how much do you charge? ; [conseiller, avocat] what fee do you charge?, what are your fees? ■ **quel est le ~ courant pour une traduction?** what's the usual *ou* going rate for translation? ➜ **~ heures creuses/pleines** [gaz, électricité] off-peak/full tariff rate ■ **le ~ étudiant est de 40 euros** the price for students is 40 euros ■ **~ normal** standard rate ■ **à plein ~** TRANSP full-fare ; LOISIRS full-price ■ **à ~ réduit** TRANSP reduced-fare ; LOISIRS reduced-price ■ **~ réduit le lundi** reduced price on Mondays ■ **'~ réduit pour étudiants'** 'concessions for students' **3.** *fam* [sanction] fine, penalty ■ **10 jours de prison, c'est le ~** 10 days in the cooler is what it's usually worth *ou* what you usually get.

tarifaire [tarifɛr] *adj* [disposition, réforme] tariff *(modif)*.

tarifé, e [tarife] *adj* fixed-price.

tarifer [3] [tarife] *vt* [marchandises] to fix the price of.

tarification [tarifikasjɔ̃] *nf* pricing.

tarin [tarɛ̃] *nm*△ [nez] hooter *UK*, conk *UK*, shnozz *US*.

tarir [32] [tarir] ◇ *vi* **1.** [cesser de couler] to dry up, to run dry **2.** *sout* [pleurs] to dry (up) **3.** [s'épuiser - conversation] to dry up ; [- enthousiasme, inspiration] to dry up, to run dry ■ **ne pas ~ de** to be full of, to bubble with ■ **ne pas ~ d'éloges sur qqn** to be full of praise for sb ■ **elle ne tarissait pas de détails** she gave a wealth of detail ■ **ne pas ~ sur : les journaux ne tarissent pas sur la jeune vedette** the papers are full of stories about the young star.
◇ *vt* **1.** [assécher - puits, source] to dry up *(insép)* **2.** *sout* [faire cesser - pleurs] to dry **3.** [épuiser - fortune, inspiration] to dry up *(insép)*.
◆ **se tarir** *vpi* **1.** [mare, puits] to dry up ■ [rivière] to run dry ■ **son lait s'est tari** her milk dried up **2.** [inspiration, enthousiasme, fortune] to dry up, to peter out.

tarissable [tarisabl] *adj* : **une source ~** a spring which can dry up.

tarmac [tarmak] *nm* tarmac.

tarot [taro] *nm* **1.** JEUX [carte, jeu] tarot ■ **jouer au ~** to play tarot **2.** [cartomancie] Tarot, tarot.

tarse [tars] *nm* tarsus.

tarsien, enne [tarsjɛ̃, ɛn] *adj* tarsal.

tartan [tartɑ̃] *nm* tartan.

Tartan® [tartɑ̃] *nm* Tartan®.

tartare [tartar] ◇ *adj* **1.** HIST Tatar, Tartar **2.** CULIN tartar, tartare.
◇ *nm* CULIN steak tartare.
◆ **Tartare** *nmf* HIST Tartar.

tarte [tart] ◇ *nf* **1.** CULIN tart ■ **~ aux pommes** apple tart *ou* pie ■ **~ aux prunes/fraises** plum/strawberry tart ➜ **~ à la crème** CULIN custard pie *ou* tart ■ *fam* [cliché] stock reply, cliché ■ **humour ~ à la crème** custard pie humour *UK*, slapstick ■ **~ Tatin** *upside-down apple tart* **2.** △ [gifle] clip, clout **3.** *fam loc* **c'est pas de la ~** it's easier said than done, it's no picnic.
◇ *adj fam* **1.** [ridicule - personne] plain-looking *UK*, plain *UK*, homely *US* ; [- chapeau, robe] naff *UK*, stupid-looking ■ **ce que tu as l'air ~!** you look a (real) idiot! **2.** [stupide - personne] dim, dumb *US* ; [- film, histoire, roman] daft, dumb *US*.

tartelette [tartəlɛt] *nf* tartlet, little tart.

Tartempion [tartɑ̃pjɔ̃] *npr fam* so-and-so ■ **c'est euh, ~, qui me l'a donné** it's er... what's-his-name who gave it to me.

tartiflette [tartiflɛt] *nf cheese and potato gratin from the Savoy region.*

tartine [tartin] *nf* **1.** CULIN slice of bread ■ **une ~ de beurre/pâté** a slice of bread and butter/with pâté **2.** *fam fig* **c'est juste une carte postale, pas la peine d'en mettre une ~** *ou* **des ~s** it's only a postcard, there's no need to write your life story.

tartiner [3] [tartine] *vt* **1.** CULIN to spread ■ **sors le beurre et tartine les toasts** take the butter out and spread it on the toast **2.** *fam fig* to churn out ■ **il a fallu qu'elle tartine des pages et des pages** she had to write page after page.

tartre [tartr] *nm* **1.** [dans une bouilloire, une machine à laver] fur, scale **2.** [sur les dents] tartar **3.** [sur un tonneau] tartar, argol.

tartré, e [tartre] *adj* tartarized.

tartrique [tartrik] *adj* tartaric.

tartuf(f)e [tartyf] ◇ *adj litt* [hypocrite] : **il est un peu ~** he's a bit of a hypocrite *ou* Tartuffe *litt*.
◇ *nm* hypocrite, Tartuffe *litt*.
◆ **Tartuffe** *npr main character in Molière's play of the same name: the archetypal hypocrite.*

tartuf(f)erie [tartyfri] *nf* **1.** [caractère] hypocrisy **2.** [parole, acte] piece of hypocrisy.

Tarzan [tarzɑ̃] *npr* Tarzan.

tas [ta] *nm* [amoncellement - de dossiers, de vêtements] heap, pile ; [- de sable, de cailloux] heap ; [- de planches, de foin] stack ■ **mettre en ~** [feuilles, objets] to pile *ou* to heap up ■ **faites des petits ~ de pâte** shape the dough into small mounds ■ **~ de fumier** dung heap ■ **~ d'ordures** rubbish *UK ou* garbage *US* heap ■ **son vieux ~ de boue** *fam ou* **ferraille** *fam* his rusty old heap ➜ **un ~** *ou* **des ~ de** [beaucoup de] a lot of ■ **~ de paresseux/menteurs!** *fam* you lazy/lying lot! *UK*, you bunch of lazybones/liars!
◆ **dans le tas** *loc adv fam* **1.** [dans un ensemble] : **il y aura bien quelqu'un dans le ~ qui pourra me renseigner** one of them's bound to be able to tell me ■ **l'armoire est pleine de vêtements, tu en trouveras bien un ou deux qui t'iront dans le ~** the wardrobe's full of clothes, you're bound to find something there that will fit you **2.** [au hasard] : **la police a tiré/tapé dans le ~** the police fired into the crowd/hit out at random.
◆ **sur le tas** *fam* ◇ *loc adj* **1.** [formation] on-the-job **2.** CONSTR on-site.
◇ *loc adv* **1.** [se former] on the job ■ **il a appris son métier sur le ~** he learned his trade as he went along **2.** CONSTR [tailler] on site.

Tasmanie [tasmani] *npr f* : **(la) ~** Tasmania.

tasmanien, enne [tasmanjɛ̃, ɛn] *adj* Tasmanian.
◆ **Tasmanien, enne** *nm, f* Tasmanian.

tasse [tas] *nf* **1.** [récipient] cup ■ **~ à café** coffee cup ■ **~ à thé** teacup **2.** [contenu] cup, cupful ■ **ajouter deux ~s de farine** add two cupfuls of flour ■ **voulez-vous une ~ de thé?** would you like a cup of tea? ■ **ce n'est pas ma ~ de thé** it's not my cup of tea.

tassé, e [tase] *adj* **1.** [serrés - voyageurs] packed *ou* crammed in **2.** [ratatiné, voûté - personne] wizened.
◆ **bien tassé, e** *loc adj fam* **1.** [café] strong ■ [scotch, pastis] stiff ■ [verre] full (to the brim), well-filled **2.** [dépassé - âge] : **elle a soixante ans bien ~s** she's sixty if she's a day **3.** [féroce - remarque] well-chosen ■ [grave - maladie] bad, nasty.

tasseau, x [taso] *nm* MENUIS [de lattis] brace, strut ■ [de tiroir] batten, strip.

tassement [tasmɑ̃] *nm* **1.** [affaissement - de neige, de terre] packing down **2.** [récession] slight drop, downturn ▪ **un ~ des voix de gauche aux dernières élections** a slight fall in the numbers of votes for the left in the last elections **3.** BOURSE easing, falling back **4.** CONSTR subsidence **5.** MÉD : **~ de vertèbres** compression of the vertebrae.

tasser [3] [tase] <> *vt* **1.** [neige, terre] to pack *ou* to tamp down *(sép)* **2.** [entasser] to cram, to squeeze ▪ **tasse les vêtements dans le sac** press the clothes down in the bag **3.** [faire paraître plus petit] to shrink ▪ **cette robe la tasse** that dress makes her look dumpy **4.** SPORT to box in *(sép)*.
<> *vi* HORT to thicken.
◆ **se tasser** *vpi* **1.** [s'effondrer - fondations, terrain] to subside **2.** [se voûter - personne] to shrink **3.** [s'entasser - voyageurs, spectateurs] to cram, to squeeze up ▪ **en se tassant on peut tenir à quatre à l'arrière (de la voiture)** if we squeeze up, four of us can get in the back (of the car) **4.** *fam* [s'arranger - situation] to settle down ▪ **je crois que les choses vont se ~** I think things will settle down **5.** [ralentir - demande, vente] to fall, to drop ; [- production] to slow down ▪ **le marché des valeurs s'est tassé** the securities market has levelled off.

taste-vin [tastəvɛ̃] *nm inv* [tasse] taster (cup).

tata [tata] *nf* **1.** *langage enfantin* [tante] aunty, auntie **2.** △ *péj* [homosexuel] poofter *UK*, fag *US*.

tatami [tatami] *nm* tatami.

tatane△ [tatan] *nf* shoe.

Tataouine-les-Bains [tatawinlebɛ̃] *npr fam* **à ~** in the middle of nowhere.

tâter [3] [tate] *vt* **1.** [fruit, membre, tissu] to feel **2.** *fig* [sonder] : **~ le terrain** to see how the land lies ▪ **tâte le terrain avant de leur faire une proposition** put some feelers out before making them an offer ▪ **tu lui as demandé une augmentation? – non, mais j'ai tâté le terrain** did you ask him for a rise? – no, but I tried to sound him out **3.** [tester - personne] to sound out *(sép)* ▪ **~ l'opinion** to sound out attitudes, to put out feelers.
◆ **tâter de** *v+prép* **1.** *hum* [nourriture, vin] to try, to taste **2.** [faire l'expérience de] : **elle a déjà tâté de la prison** she's already had a taste of prison ▪ **il a tâté de plusieurs métiers** he's tried his hand at several jobs.
◆ **se tâter** <> *vp (emploi réfléchi)* [après un accident] to feel o.s. ▪ **se ~ la jambe/le bras** to feel one's leg/one's arm.
<> *vpi* to be in *UK ou* of *US* two minds ▪ **je ne sais pas si je vais accepter, je me tâte encore** I don't know whether I'll accept, I haven't made up my mind (about it) yet.

tâte-vin [tatvɛ̃] = **taste-vin**.

Tati® [tati] *npr name of a chain of cut-price stores.*

tatie [tati] *nf fam* auntie.

tatillon, onne [tatijɔ̃, ɔn] *fam* <> *adj* [vétilleux] pernickety ▪ **son côté ~ m'exaspère** his fussiness really gets on my nerves.
<> *nm, f* [personne] nitpicker, fusspot.

tâtonnant, e [tatɔnɑ̃, ɑ̃t] *adj* **1.** [personne] groping **2.** [style] hesitant ▪ **nos recherches sont encore ~es** our research is still proceeding by trial and error.

tâtonnement [tatɔnmɑ̃] *nm* : **avancer par ~s** *pr* to grope one's way along ; *fig* to proceed by trial and error ▪ **nous n'en sommes encore qu'aux ~s** we're still trying to find our way.

tâtonner [3] [tatɔne] *vi* **1.** [pour marcher] to grope *ou* to feel one's way (along) ▪ [à la recherche de qqch] to grope about *ou* around **2.** [hésiter] to grope around ▪ [expérimenter] to proceed by trial and error ▪ **nous avons beaucoup tâtonné avant de trouver l'explication** we groped around a lot before finding the solution.

tâtons [tatɔ̃] ◆ **à tâtons** *loc adv* **1.** [à l'aveuglette] : **avancer à ~** to grope *ou* to feel one's way along ▪ **elle chercha l'interrupteur à ~** she felt *ou* groped around for the switch **2.** *fig* **c'est un domaine nouveau, nous devons avancer à ~** it's a new field, we have to feel our way (along).

tatou [tatu] *nm* armadillo.

tatouage [tatwaʒ] *nm* **1.** [action] tattooing ▪ **se faire faire un ~** to get tattooed **2.** [dessin] tattoo ▪ **il est couvert de ~s** he's tattooed all over.

tatouer [6] [tatwe] *vt* [dessin, personne] to tattoo.

tatoueur [tatwœr] *nm* tattoo artist, tattooist.

tau [to] *nm inv* **1.** [lettre grecque] tau **2.** HÉRALD tau cross, Saint Anthony's cross.

taudis [todi] *nm* slum, hovel ▪ **c'est un vrai ~ chez lui!** his place is a real slum *ou* pigsty!

taulard, e△ [tolar, ard] *nm, f arg crime* convict, jailbird.

taule△ [tol] *nf* **1.** [prison] nick△ *UK*, clink△ ▪ **elle a fait un an de ~** she did a one year stretch (inside) **2.** [chambre] pad△.
◆ **en taule**△ *loc adv* inside ▪ **je ne veux pas me retrouver en ~** I don't want to wind up inside.

taulier, ère△ [tolje, ɛr] *nm, f* owner *ou* boss *(of a hotel or restaurant).*

taupe [top] *nf* **1.** ZOOL [mammifère] mole ▪ [poisson] porbeagle ▪ **vieille ~** *fam* old hag *ou* bat **2.** [fourrure] moleskin **3.** △ *arg scol second year of a two-year entrance course for the Science sections of the Grandes Écoles* **4.** △ *arg mil* sapper **5.** *fam* [agent secret] mole **6.** TRAV PUB mole.

taupière [topjɛr] *nf* [piège] mole trap.

taupin [topɛ̃] *nm arg scol pupil preparing for entry to the Science sections of the Grandes Écoles.*

taupinière [topinjɛr], **taupinée** [topine] *nf* [monticule] molehill ▪ [tunnel] (mole) burrow.

taureau, x [tɔro] *nm* bull ▪ **~ de combat** fighting bull ▪ **il a un cou de ~** he's got a neck like a bull ▪ **son frère a une force de ~** his brother is as strong as an ox ▪ **prendre le ~ par les cornes** to take the bull by the horns.

Taureau, x [tɔro] *npr m* **1.** ASTRON Taurus **2.** ASTROL Taurus ▪ **elle est ~** she's (a) Taurus *ou* a Taurean.

taurillon [tɔrijɔ̃] *nm* bull calf.

taurin, e [tɔrɛ̃, in] *adj* bull-fighting.

tauromachie [tɔrɔmaʃi] *nf* bullfighting, tauromachy *spéc.*

tautologie [totɔlɔʒi] *nf* tautology.

tautologique [totɔlɔʒik] *adj* tautological.

taux [to] *nm* **1.** [tarif] rate **2.** [proportion] rate ▪ **~ d'échec/de réussite** failure/success rate ▪ **~ de mortalité/natalité** death/birth rate ▪ **~ de fécondité** reproduction rate ▪ **~ d'absentéisme** ÉDUC truancy rate **3.** COMM rate ▪ **~ d'escompte** discount rate ▪ **~ de marque** mark-up (percentage) **4.** ÉCON : **à quel ~ prêtent-ils?** what is their lending rate? ◐ **~ de base bancaire** bank base lending rate ▪ **~ de change** exchange rate ▪ **~ de crédit** lending rate ▪ **~ de croissance** growth rate ▪ **~ directeur** intervention rate ▪ **~ d'escompte** discount rate ▪ **~ d'inflation** inflation rate ▪ **~ d'intérêt** interest rate, rate of interest **5.** INDUST : **~ horaire** hourly rate **6.** MÉD [d'albumine, de cholestérol] level ▪ **son ~ d'invalidité est de 50 %** he's 50% disabled.

taveler [24] [tavle] *vt* **1.** [fruit] to mark **2.** [peau] to speckle.
◆ **se taveler** *vpi* [fruit] to become marked.

taverne [tavɛrn] *nf* **1.** HIST inn, public house **2.** *Québec* [bistrot] tavern.

tavernier, ère [tavɛrnje, ɛr] *nm, f* HIST innkeeper.

tavillon [tavijɔ̃] *nm Suisse* [bardeau] *thin, rounded wooden slat used for covering walls and roofs in Switzerland.*

taxable [taksabl] *adj* ÉCON taxable, liable to duty.

taxation [taksasjɔ̃] *nf* **1.** FIN taxation, taxing *(U)* ▪ **~ d'office** estimation of tax *(in the case of failure to file a tax return)* **2.** DR [réglementation - des prix] statutory price fixing ; [- des salaires] statutory wage fixing.

taxe [taks] *nf* **1.** FIN tax ▪ **toutes ~s comprises** inclusive of tax ◐ **~ sur le chiffre d'affaires** sales *ou* turnover tax ▪ **~ de luxe** luxury tax ▪ **~ à la valeur ajoutée** value added tax **2.** ADMIN tax ▪ **~ de douane** customs duty ▪ **~ foncière** property tax ■ ~ **d'habitation** *tax paid on residence*, ≃ council tax *UK* ■ ~ **parafiscale** additional levy ■ ~ **professionnelle** business tax ■ ~ **de séjour** visitor's *ou* tourist tax ■ ~ **Tobin** Tobin tax **3.** DR [montant des dépens] costs.

taxer [3] [takse] *vt* **1.** ÉCON & FIN to tax ■ ~ **les disques à 10 %** to tax records at 10%, to put a 10% tax on records **2.** DR : ~ **les dépens** to fix *ou* to tax costs **3.** [accuser] : ~ **qqn de** to accuse sb of, to tax sb with *sout* ■ **vous m'avez taxé d'hypocrisie** you accused me of being a hypocrite **4.** [qualifier] : **on l'a taxé d'opportuniste** he's been called an opportunist **5.** *fam* [emprunter] to cadge.

taxi [taksi] *nm* **1.** [voiture] taxi, cab **2.** *fam* [conducteur] cabby, taxi *ou* cab driver ■ **faire le** ~ to be a taxi driver **3.** *(comme adj; avec ou sans trait d'union)* **avion-~** taxi plane.

taxi-brousse [taksibrus] (*pl* **taxis-brousse**) *nm Belgique* bush taxi.

taxidermie [taksidɛrmi] *nf* taxidermy.

taxidermiste [taksidɛrmist] *nmf* taxidermist.

taxi-girl [taksigœrl] (*pl* **taxi-girls**) *nf* taxi-dancer, hostess *(hired for dancing)*.

taximètre [taksimɛtr] *nm* taximeter.

taxinomie [taksinɔmi] *nf* taxonomy.

Taxiphone® [taksifɔn] *nm* public phone, pay-phone.

taxiway [taksiwɛ] *nm* taxiway, taxi strip *ou* track.

taxonomie [taksɔnɔmi] = **taxinomie**.

taylorisme [telɔrism] *nm* Taylorism.

TB, tb (*abr écrite de* **très bien**) vg.

TBE, tbe (*abr écrite de* **très bon état**) vgc.

Tchad [tʃad] *npr m* : **le** ~ Chad ■ **au** ~ in Chad ■ **le lac** ~ Lake Chad.

tchadien, enne [tʃadjɛ̃, ɛn] *adj* Chadian.
◆ **Tchadien, enne** *nm, f* Chadian.

tchador [tʃadɔr] *nm* chador, chuddar.

Tchaïkovski [tʃajkɔfski] *npr* Tchaikovsky.

tchao [tʃao] *fam* = **ciao**.

tchatche [tʃaʃ] *nf fam* : **avoir la** ~ to have the gift of the gab.

tchatcher [tʃaʃe] *vi fam* to chatter *UK*, to jazz *US*.

tchécoslovaque [tʃekɔslɔvak] *adj* Czechoslovakian, Czechoslovak.
◆ **Tchécoslovaque** *nmf* Czechoslovakian, Czechoslovak.

Tchécoslovaquie [tʃekɔslɔvaki] *npr f* : **(la)** ~ Czechoslovakia.

Tchekhov [tʃekɔf] *npr* : **Anton** ~ Anton Chekhov.

tchèque [tʃɛk] *adj* Czech ■ **(la) République** ~ (the) Czech Republic.
◆ **Tchèque** *nmf* Czech.

Tchernobyl [tʃɛrnɔbil] *npr* Chernobyl.

tchétchène [tʃetʃɛn] *adj* Chechen.

tchétchène [tʃetʃɛn] *adj* Chechen.

tchin-tchin [tʃintʃin] *interj fam* cheers.

TD (*abr de* **travaux dirigés**) *nmpl* **1.** ÉDUC *supervised practical work* **2.** UNIV *university class where students do exercises set by the teacher*.

TdF (*abr de* **Télévision de France**) *npr French broadcasting authority*.

te [tə] *(devant voyelle ou h muet t'* [t]*) pron pers (2e pers sing)* **1.** [avec un verbe pronominal] : **tu te lèves tard** you get up late ■ **tu te prends pour qui?** who do you think you are? ■ **tu vas te faire mal** you'll hurt yourself **2.** [complément] you ■ **elle t'a envoyé un colis** she's sent you a parcel ■ **elle t'est devenue indispensable** she has become indispensable to you ■ **ne te laisse pas faire** don't let yourself be pushed around **3.** *fam* [emploi expressif] : **je te l'ai envoyé balader, celui-là!** I sent HIM packing!

té [te] ◇ *nm* **1.** [équerre] T-square **2.** MENUIS tee.
◇ *interj* [dialecte] : **té! voilà Martin!** hey, here comes Martin!
◆ **en té** *loc adj* T-shaped.

technicien, enne [tɛknisjɛ̃, ɛn] ◇ *adj* [esprit, civilisation] technically-oriented.
◇ *nm, f* **1.** [en entreprise] technician, engineer ■ **il est ~ en informatique** he's a computer technician **2.** [dans un art, un sport] : **c'est une excellente ~ne mais elle gagne peu de matchs** she's got an excellent technique *ou* technically speaking, she's excellent but she doesn't win many matches.

technicité [tɛknisite] *nf* **1.** [d'un mot, d'un texte] technical nature *ou* quality, technicality *sout* **2.** [avance technologique] technological sophistication ■ **matériel d'une haute ~** very advanced equipment **3.** [savoir-faire] skill.

technico-commercial, e [tɛknikokɔmɛrsjal, o] (*mpl* **technico-commerciaux**, *fpl* **technico-commerciales**) *adj* : **notre personnel** ~ our technical salesmen ▶ **agent** ~ sales technician, sales engineer.

Technicolor® [tɛknikɔlɔr] *nm* Technicolor® ■ **en** ~ Technicolor *(modif)*.

technique [tɛknik] ◇ *adj* **1.** [pratique] technical, practical ■ **elle a une certaine habileté** ~ she's got a certain knack of doing things **2.** [mécanique] technical ■ **incident** ~ technical hitch **3.** [technologique] technical ■ **les progrès ~s en informatique** technical advances in computer science **4.** [spécialisé] technical ■ **le sens ~ d'un mot** the technical sense *ou* meaning of a word.
◇ *nm* ÉDUC : **le** ~ vocational education.
◇ *nf* **1.** [d'un art, d'un métier] technique ■ **la ~ de l'aquarelle** the technique of watercolour painting **2.** [savoir-faire] technique **3.** [méthode] technique ■ **c'est toute une ~ d'ouvrir les huîtres** there's quite an art to opening oysters ■ **répondre à une question par une autre question, c'est sa ~** answering a question by another question is his speciality **4.** [de production] technique ▶ ~ **de pointe** state-of-the-art technique **5.** [applications de la science] : **la** ~ applied science.

techniquement [tɛknikmɑ̃] *adv* technically ■ ~ **faisable** technically feasible.

technocrate [tɛknɔkrat] *nmf* technocrat.

technocratie [tɛknɔkrasi] *nf* technocracy.

technocratique [tɛknɔkratik] *adj* technocratic.

technocratiser [3] [tɛknɔkratize] *vt* [pays] to turn into a technocracy ■ [système, processus] to make technocratic.

technologie [tɛknɔlɔʒi] *nf* **1.** ÉDUC technology, applied science **2.** [technique] technology ▶ **nouvelle** ~ new technology ■ **~s avancées** advanced technology, high technology **3.** [théorie] technology, technological theory, technologies.

technologique [tɛknɔlɔʒik] *adj* technological.

technologue [tɛknɔlɔg], **technologiste** [tɛknɔlɔʒist] *nmf* technologist.

technopole [tɛknɔpɔl] *nf large urban centre with teaching and research facilities to support development of hi-tech industries*.

technopôle [tɛknɔpol] *nm area specially designated to accommodate and foster hi-tech industries*.

teck [tɛk] *nm* teak.
◆ **en teck** *loc adj* teak *(modif)*.

teckel [tekɛl] *nm* dachshund.

tectonique [tɛktɔnik] ◇ *adj* tectonic.
◇ *nf* tectonics *(sing)* ■ ~ **des plaques** plate tectonics.

Te Deum [tedeɔm] *nm inv* Te Deum.

tee [ti] *nm* SPORT tee ■ **poser la balle sur le** ~ to tee up ■ **partir du** ~ to tee off.

teen-ager [tinedʒœr] (*pl* **teen-agers**) *nmf* teenager.

tee-shirt [tiʃœrt] (*pl* **tee-shirts**) *nm* tee-shirt, T-shirt.

Téflon® [teflɔ̃] *nm* Teflon®.

tégument [tegymɑ̃] *nm* BOT & ZOOL tegument.

Téhéran [teerɑ̃] *npr* Tehran, Teheran.

teignait *etc v* ⊳ **teindre**.

teigne [tɛɲ] *nf* **1.** ENTOM tineid **2.** MÉD ringworm, tinea *spéc* **3.** *fam* [homme] louse ▪ [femme] vixen ▪ **quelle ~, celle-là!** wretched woman! ▶ **être mauvais** *ou* **méchant comme une ~** to be a nasty piece of work *UK*, to be real ornery *US*.

teigneux, euse [tɛɲø, øz] ◇ *adj* **1.** MÉD suffering from ringworm **2.** *fam* [hargneux] nasty, ornery *US*.
◇ *nm, f* **1.** MÉD ringworm sufferer **2.** *fam* [homme] bastard ▪ [femme] cow *UK*, bitch.

teindre [81] [tɛ̃dr] *vt* **1.** [soumettre à la teinture] to dye ▪ **se faire ~ les cheveux** to have one's hair dyed **2.** *litt* [colorer] to tint.
◆ **se teindre** ◇ *vp (emploi passif)* : **c'est une étoffe qui se teint facilement** it's a material which is easy to dye *ou* which takes dye well *ou* which dyes well.
◇ *vp (emploi réfléchi)* : **se ~ les cheveux/la barbe en roux** to dye one's hair/beard red ▪ **elle se teint pour paraître plus jeune** she dyes her hair to make herself look younger.
◆ **se teindre de** *vp+prép litt* [se colorer en] : **au coucher du soleil, les cimes se teignent de rose et d'or** at sunset, the mountain tops are tinted pink and gold.

teint [tɛ̃] *nm* [habituel] complexion ▪ [momentané] colour, colouring ▪ **avoir le ~ pâle/jaune/mat** to have a pale/sallow/matt complexion.
◆ **bon teint** *loc adj* **1.** TEXT colour-fast **2.** [pur] staunch ▪ **des royalistes bon ~** staunch *ou* dyed-in-the-wool royalists.
◆ **grand teint** *loc adj* [couleur] fast ▪ [tissu] colour-fast.

teinte [tɛ̃t] *nf* **1.** [couleur franche] colour ▪ [ton] shade, tint, hue ▪ **du tissu aux ~s vives** brightly coloured material **2.** [petite quantité - de libéralisme, de sadisme] tinge ; [- d'ironie, de mépris] hint.

teinté, e [tɛ̃te] *adj* **1.** [lunettes] tinted ▪ [verre] tinted, stained **2.** [bois] stained.

teinter [3] [tɛ̃te] *vt* **1.** [verre] to tint, to stain ▪ [lunettes, papier] to tint ▪ [boiseries] to stain **2.** [mêler] to tinge ▪ **son amitié était teintée de pitié** her friendship was tinged with pity, there was a hint of pity in her friendship **3.** [colorer] to tint ▪ **le soleil couchant teintait le lac de rose** the setting sun gave the lake a pinkish tinge.
◆ **se teinter de** *vp+prép* **1.** [se colorer en] : **se ~ d'ocre** to take on an ochre tinge *ou* hue **2.** *fig* [être nuancé de] to be tinged with ▪ [se nuancer de] to become tinged with.

teinture [tɛ̃tyr] *nf* **1.** [action] dyeing ▪ **se faire faire une ~** to have one's hair dyed **2.** [produit] dye **3.** PHARM tincture ▪ **~ d'arnica/d'iode** tincture of arnica/of iodine **4.** *sout* [connaissance superficielle] smattering ▪ **elle a une ~ d'histoire** she has a vague knowledge of history.

teinturerie [tɛ̃tyrri] *nf* **1.** [activité] dyeing **2.** [boutique] dry cleaner's.

teinturier, ère [tɛ̃tyrje, ɛr] *nm, f* [qui nettoie] dry cleaner ▪ [qui colore] dyer.

tek [tɛk] = **teck**.

tel [tɛl] (*f* **telle**, *mpl* **tels**, *fpl* **telles**) ◇ *dét (adj indéf)*

> **A.** EMPLOYÉ SEUL
> **B.** EN CORRÉLATION AVEC 'QUE'

A. EMPLOYÉ SEUL

1. [avec une valeur indéterminée] : **~ jour, ~ endroit, à telle heure** on such and such a day, at such and such a place, at such and such a time ▪ **il m'a demandé de lui acheter ~ et ~ livres** he asked me to buy him such and such books ▪ **pourrais-tu me conseiller ~ ou ~ plat?** could you recommend any particular dish? ▪ **cela peut se produire dans telle ou telle circonstance** it can happen under certain circumstances
2. [semblable] such ▪ **je n'ai rien dit de ~** I never said such a thing, I said nothing of the sort ▪ **un ~ homme peut être dangereux** a man like that can be dangerous ▪ **il était médecin et comme ~, il avait des passe-droits** he was doctor and as such he had special dispensations ▪ **il n'est pas avare, mais il passe pour ~** he's not mean, but people think he is ▪ **en tant que ~** as such
3. [ainsi] : **telle fut l'histoire qu'il nous raconta** such was the story he told us ▪ **telle avait été sa vie, telle fut sa fin** as had been his/her life, such was his/her death ▶ **pourquoi ça? – parce que ~ est mon bon plaisir!** *hum* and why is that? – because I say so!
4. [introduisant un exemple, une énumération, une comparaison] like ▪ **des métaux ~s le cuivre et le fer** metals such as copper and iron ▪ **les révolutionnaires qui, ~ Danton, croyaient à la démocratie** the revolutionaries who, like Danton, believed in democracy ▪ **elle a filé ~ l'éclair** she shot off like a bolt of lightning ▶ **~ père, ~ fils** *prov* like father, like son *prov*
5. [en intensif] such ▪ **c'est un ~ honneur pour nous...** it is such an honour for us...

B. EN CORRÉLATION AVEC 'QUE'

1. [introduisant une comparaison] : **il est ~ que je l'ai toujours connu** he's just the same as when I knew him ▪ **un homme ~ que lui** a man like him ▪ **telle que je la connais, elle va être en retard** knowing her, she's bound to be late ▪ **~ que tu me vois, je viens de décrocher un rôle** the person you see before you has just got a part ▶ **tu prends le lot ~ que** *fam* take the batch as it is ▪ **il me l'a dit ~ que!** *fam* he told me just like that!
2. [introduisant un exemple ou une énumération] : **~ que** such as, like
3. [avec une valeur intensive] : **son bonheur était ~ qu'il ne pouvait y croire** his happiness was such that he could hardly believe it ▪ **la douleur fut telle que je faillis m'évanouir** the pain was so bad that I nearly fainted ▪ **il a fait un ~ bruit qu'il a réveillé toute la maisonnée** he made such a noise *ou* so much noise that he woke the whole house up.
◇ *pron indéf* **1.** [désignant des personnes ou des choses non précisées] : **telle ou telle de ses idées aurait pu prévaloir** one or other of his ideas might have prevailed ▪ **c'est en manœuvrant ~ et ~ qu'il a réussi à se faire élire** he managed to get himself elected by manipulating various people ▶ **~ est pris qui croyait prendre** *prov* it's the biter bitten ▪ **~ qui rit vendredi, dimanche pleurera** *prov* you can be laughing one day and crying the next **2.** [en remplacement d'un nom propre] : **a-t-il rencontré un** *ou* **Un ~?** did he meet so-and-so?
◆ **tel quel, telle quelle** *loc adj* : **tout est resté ~ quel depuis son départ** everything is just as he left it ▪ **tu peux manger les huîtres telles quelles ou avec du citron** you can eat oysters on their own or with lemon.

tél. (*abr écrite de* **téléphone**) tel.

Tel-Aviv [tɛlaviv] *npr* Tel Aviv ▪ **~-Jaffa** Tel Aviv-Jaffa.

télé [tele] *nf fam* [poste, émissions] TV ▪ **il n'y a rien ce soir à la ~** there's nothing on TV *ou* telly tonight.
◆ **de télé** *loc adj fam* [chaîne, émission] TV *(modif)*.

téléachat [teleaʃa] *nm* [à la télévision] teleshopping ▪ [via Internet] online shopping.

téléacheteur, euse [teleaʃtœr, øz] *nm, f* [à la télévision] television shopper ▪ [via Internet] online shopper *ou* purchaser *ou* customer.

téléacteur, trice [teleaktœr, tris] *nm, f* telesales *ou* telemarketing operator.

téléaffichage [teleafiʃaʒ] *nm* telecontrolled signboarding.

télébenne [telebɛn] *nf* cable car.

Téléboutique® [telebutik] *nf* ≃ Telecom shop® *UK*, ≃ telephone store *US*.

télécabine [telekabin] *nf* **1.** [cabine] cable car ▪ **les skieurs montent en ~** skiers go up in a cable car **2.** [installation] cableway.

Télécarte® [telekart] *nf* phonecard.

téléchargeable [teleʃarʒabl] *adj* downloadable.

téléchargement [teleʃarʒəmɑ̃] *nm* INFORM downloading.

télécharger [teleʃarʒe] *vt* to download.

télécommande [telekɔmɑ̃d] *nf* **1.** AUDIO [procédé, appareil] remote control **2.** [par radio] radio-control **3.** INFORM telecommand.

télécommandé, e [telekɔmɑ̃de] *adj* **1.** TECHNOL [engin, mise à feu] remote-controlled ▪ **la porte du garage est ~e** the garage door is remote-controlled *ou* works by remote control **2.** *fig* [ordonné de loin] masterminded *ou* manipulated from afar.

télécommander [3] [telekɔmɑ̃de] *vt* **1.** [engin, mise à feu, télévision] to operate by remote control **2.** [ordonner de loin] to mastermind, to manipulate ▪ **ces mouvements ont été télécommandés depuis l'Europe** these movements have been masterminded from Europe.

télécommunication [telekɔmynikasjɔ̃] *nf* telecommunication ▪ **les ~s** telecommunications.

téléconférence [telekɔ̃ferɑ̃s] *nf* **1.** [procédé] teleconferencing **2.** [conférence] teleconference.

télécopie [telekɔpi] *nf* fax ▪ **envoyer qqch par ~** to fax sthg.

télécopier [9] [telekɔpje] *vt* to fax.

télécopieur [telekɔpjœr] *nm* facsimile machine *spéc*, fax (machine).

télédétection [teledetɛksjɔ̃] *nf* remote sensing ▪ **satellite de ~** spy satellite.

télédiffuser [3] [teledifyze] *vt* to broadcast (by television), to televise.

télédiffusion [teledifyzjɔ̃] *nf* (television) broadcasting.

télédistribution [teledistribysjɔ̃] *nf* cable television.

télé-enseignement [teleɑ̃sɛɲmɑ̃] (*pl* **télé-enseignements**) *nm* distance learning.

téléfilm [telefilm] *nm* film made for television.

télégénique [teleʒenik] *adj* telegenic ▪ **être ~** to look good on television.

télégestion [teleʒɛstjɔ̃] *nf* teleprocessing.

télégramme [telegram] *nm* telegram, cable ▪ **~ téléphoné** *telegram delivered over the phone*, ≃ Telemessage® *UK*.

télégraphe [telegraf] *nm* telegraph.

télégraphier [9] [telegrafje] *vt* to cable, to telegraph ▪ **~ qqch à qqn** to cable sb sthg.

télégraphique [telegrafik] *adj* **1.** TÉLÉCOM [poteau] telegraph *(modif)* ▪ [message] telegraphic **2.** *fig* **(en) langage** *ou* **style ~** (in) telegraphic language *ou* style.

télégraphiste [telegrafist] *nmf* telegrapher, telegraphist.

téléguidage [telegidaʒ] *nm* radio control.

téléguidé, e [telegide] *adj* **1.** [piloté à distance - engin, avion] radiocontrolled **2.** *fig* [manipulé] manipulated.

téléguider [3] [telegide] *vt* **1.** TECHNOL [maquette] to control by radio **2.** [inspirer] to manipulate ▪ **c'est lui qui a téléguidé la campagne de presse** he's the one who masterminded the press campaign from behind the scenes.

téléimprimeur [teleɛ̃primœr] *nm* teleprinter.

téléinformatique [teleɛ̃fɔrmatik] *nf* teleprocessing.

télékinésie [telekinezi] *nf* telekinesis.

télémarketing [telemarkɔtiŋ] *nm* telemarketing, telesales.

télématique [telematik] ◇ *adj* telematic.
◇ *nf* data communications, telematics *(U)*.

télématiser [3] [telematize] *vt* to provide with telematic facilities.
◆ **se télématiser** *vp (emploi réfléchi)* to equip o.s. with telematic facilities.

télémessage [telemɛsaʒ] *nm* TÉLÉCOM text message.

télémessagerie [telemesaʒri] *nf* electronic mail, e-mail.

téléobjectif [teleɔbʒɛktif] *nm* telephoto (lens).

téléologie [teleɔlɔʒi] *nf* teleology.

télépaiement [telepemɑ̃] *nm* electronic payment.

télépathie [telepati] *nf* telepathy ▪ **communiquer par ~** to communicate via telepathy.

télépathique [telepatik] *adj* telepathic.

téléphérique [teleferik] *nm* cable car.

téléphone [telefɔn] *nm* **1.** [instrument] phone, telephone ▪ **repose le ~** put down the receiver ➲ **~ à carte** cardphone ▪ **~ cellulaire** cellphone, cellular phone ▪ **~ de courtoisie** courtesy phone ▪ **~ à manivelle/sans fil/à touches** magneto/cordless/pushbutton telephone ▪ **~ mobile** mobile phone ▪ **~ portable** mobile phone ▪ **~ public** public telephone, pay-phone ▪ **le ~ rouge** [entre présidents] the hot line ▪ **~ de voiture** carphone **2.** [installation] phone, telephone ▪ **il a/n'a pas le ~** he's/he isn't on the phone *UK*, he has a/has no phone *US* ▪ **j'ai demandé à avoir le ~** I asked to have a phone put in ▪ **installer le ~** to connect the phone **3.** [service] : **le ~ marche plutôt mal chez nous** we have a rather bad telephone service **4.** *fam* [numéro] (phone) number.
◆ **au téléphone** *loc adv* : **je suis au ~** I'm on the phone ▪ **je l'ai eu au ~** I talked to him on the phone.
◆ **de téléphone** *loc adj* [facture, numéro] phone *(modif)*, telephone *(modif)*.
◆ **par téléphone** *loc adv* : **il a réservé par ~** he booked over the phone ▪ **réservation possible par ~** phone booking available ▪ **faites vos achats par ~** do your shopping by phone.
◆ **téléphone arabe** *nm* grapevine ▪ **j'ai appris par le ~ arabe qu'il était rentré** I heard on the grapevine that he was back.

téléphoné, e [telefɔne] *adj fam* [prévisible] predictable, obvious ▪ **des gags ~s** jokes that you can see coming a mile off.

téléphoner [3] [telefɔne] ◇ *vi* to make a phone call ▪ **puis-je ~?** can I make a phone call?, may I use the phone? ▪ **combien est-ce que ça coûte pour ~ en Angleterre?** how much does it cost to call England? ▪ **ne me dérangez pas quand je téléphone** please do not disturb me when I'm on the phone ▪ **~ à qqn** to phone sb, to call sb.
◇ *vt* to phone ▪ **je te téléphonerai la nouvelle dès que je la connaîtrai** I'll phone and tell you the news as soon as I get it ▪ **elle m'a téléphoné de venir les rejoindre pour dîner** she called to ask me to join them for dinner.
◆ **se téléphoner** *vp (emploi réciproque)* to call each other ▪ **on se téléphone, d'accord?** we'll talk on the phone later, OK?

téléphonie [telefɔni] *nf* telephony ▪ **~ sans fil** wireless telephony.

téléphonique [telefɔnik] *adj* [message, ligne, réseau] telephone *(modif)*, phone *(modif)* ▪ **nous avons eu un entretien ~** we had a discussion over the phone.

téléphoniste [telefɔnist] *nmf* telephonist *UK*, (telephone) operator *US*.

téléporter [telepɔrte] *vt* to teleport.

téléprompteur [teleprɔ̃ptœr] *nm* Teleprompter®, Autocue®.

téléprospecteur, trice [teleprɔspɛktœr, tris] *nm, f* telesalesperson.

téléreportage [telerəpɔrtaʒ] *nm* **1.** [émission] television report **2.** [activité] television reporting.

téléreporter [telerəpɔrtɛr] *nm* television reporter.

télescopage [teleskɔpaʒ] *nm* **1.** [de véhicules] collision **2.** [d'idées, de souvenirs] intermingling **3.** LING telescoping, blending.

télescope [teleskɔp] *nm* telescope ▪ **~ électronique** electron telescope.

télescoper [3] [teleskɔpe] *vt* [véhicule] to collide with, to crash into *(insép)*.
◆ **se télescoper** *vp (emploi réciproque)* **1.** [véhicules] to crash into one another **2.** [idées, souvenirs] to intermingle.

télescopique [teleskɔpik] *adj* [antenne] telescopic.

téléscripteur [teleskriptœr] *nm* teleprinter ■ **une nouvelle vient de tomber sur nos ~s** some news has just come through on our teleprinters.

téléservice [teleservis] *nf* on-line service.

télésiège [telesjɛʒ] *nm* chair *ou* ski lift ■ **on y monte en ~** you get there by chair lift, you take the chair lift up there.

téléski [teleski] *nm* drag lift, ski tow.

téléspectateur, trice [telespɛktatœr, tris] *nm, f* television *ou* TV viewer ■ **la majorité des ~s** the majority of viewers *ou* of the viewing audience.

télésurveillance [telesyrvejɑ̃s] *nf* (security) telemonitoring.

Télétel® [teletel] *nm (French) public videotex.*

Télétex® [teletɛks] *nm* teletex.

télétexte [teletɛkst] *nm* teletext.

télétraitement [teletrɛtmɑ̃] *nm* teleprocessing.

télétransmission [teletrɑ̃smisjɔ̃] *nf* remote transmission.

télétravail, aux [teletravaj, o] *nm* teleworking, telecommuting.

télétravailler [teletravaje] *vi* to telework, to telecommute.

télétravailleur, euse [teletravajœr, øz] *nm, f* teleworker, telecommuter.

Télétype [teletip] *nm* Teletype®.

télévente [televɑ̃t] *nf* [à la télévision] television selling ■ [via Internet] online selling *ou* commerce, e-commerce.

télévisé, e [televize] *adj* [discours, match] televised.

téléviser [3] [televize] *vt* to televise.

téléviseur [televizœr] *nm* television *ou* TV set.

télévision [televizjɔ̃] *nf* **1.** [entreprise, système] television ■ **il regarde trop la ~** he watches too much television ■ **les ~s européennes** European television companies ◆ **~ câblée** *ou* **par câble** cable television ■ **~ en circuit fermé** closed circuit television ■ **la ~ à péage** *ou* **à accès conditionnel** pay-TV ■ **~ par satellite** satellite television **2.** [appareil] television ■ **allumer la ~** to turn the television on.
◆ **à la télévision** *loc adv* on television *ou* TV ■ **passer à la ~** to go on television.

télévision-réalité [televizjɔ̃realite] *nf* TV reality TV, fly-on-the-wall television ■ **une émission de ~** fly-on-the-wall documentary ; [de style feuilleton] docusoap.

télévisuel, elle [televizɥɛl] *adj* televisual.

télex [telɛks] *nm* telex ■ **envoyer un ~** to (send a) telex.

télexer [4] [telekse] *vt* to telex.

tellement [tɛlmɑ̃] *adv* **1.** [avec un adverbe, un adjectif] : **c'est ~ loin** it's so far ■ **je n'ai pas ~ mal** it doesn't hurt that *ou* so much ■ **il est ~ têtu** he's so stubborn ■ **c'est ~ mieux comme ça** it's so much better like that **2.** [avec un verbe] : **j'ai ~ pleuré!** I cried so much! ‖ [en corrélation avec 'que'] : **j'en ai ~ rêvé que j'ai l'impression d'y être déjà allée** I've dreamt about it so much *ou* so often that I feel I've been there already **3.** [introduisant la cause] : **personne ne l'invite plus ~ il est ennuyeux** he's so boring (that) nobody invites him anymore ■ **j'ai mal aux yeux ~ j'ai lu** my eyes hurt from reading so much **4.** *loc* **pas ~** *fam* not really ■ **plus ~** *fam* not really any more ■ **je n'aime plus ~ ça** I don't really like that any more ■ **des jeunes au chômage, comme on en voit ~ dans la rue** young people on the dole such as you often come across on the street.
◆ **tellement de** *loc dét* : **j'ai ~ de travail/de soucis en ce moment** I've got so much work/so many worries at the moment ‖ [en corrélation avec 'que'] : **il y avait ~ de bruit que l'on ne s'entendait plus** there was so much noise that we could no longer hear ourselves speak ■ **il y a ~ d'hôtels que je ne sais lequel choisir** there are so many hotels that I don't know which one to choose.

tellurien, enne [telyrjɛ̃, ɛn] *adj* tellurian.

tellurique [telyrik] *adj* telluric ■ **courants ~s** telluric currents.

téloche [telɔʃ] *nf fam* telly.

téméraire [temerɛr] *adj* **1.** [imprudent - personne] foolhardy, rash, reckless **2.** [aventuré - tentative] rash, reckless **3.** [fait à la légère] rash ■ **voici une remarque bien ~** this is an extremely rash comment.

témérité [temerite] *nf* **1.** [hardiesse] boldness, temerity *litt* **2.** [imprudence - d'une initiative, d'une personne] foolhardiness, recklessness ; [- d'un jugement] rashness.

témoignage [temwaɲaʒ] *nm* **1.** DR [action de témoigner] testimony, evidence ◆ **faux ~** perjury, false evidence, false witness ■ **faire un faux ~** to give false evidence ■ **condamné pour faux ~** found guilty of perjury *ou* of giving false evidence ■ **rendre ~ à qqch** [rendre hommage] to pay tribute to *ou* to hail *sout ou* to salute sthg ■ **rendre ~ à qqn** [témoigner publiquement en sa faveur] to testify in sb's favour **2.** [contenu des déclarations] deposition, (piece of) evidence ■ **le ~ du chauffeur de taxi est accablant pour elle** the taxi driver's statement is conclusive evidence against her ■ **porter ~ de qqch** to bear witness to sthg **3.** [preuve] gesture, expression, token ■ **un ~ d'amitié** a token of friendship ■ **recevoir des ~s de sympathie** [après un deuil] to receive messages of sympathy ; [pendant une épreuve] to receive messages of support **4.** [récit - d'un participant, d'un observateur] (eyewitness) account ■ **cette pièce sera un jour considérée comme un ~ sur la vie des années 80** this play will one day be considered as an authentic account of life in the 80s.

témoigner [3] [temwaɲe] ◇ *vi* DR to testify, to give evidence ■ **~ en faveur de/contre l'accusé** to give evidence for/against the defendant ■ **~ contre ses complices** to turn King's *ou* Queen's evidence *UK*, to turn State's evidence *US*.
◇ *vt* **1.** DR [certifier] : **~ que** to testify that ■ **il a témoigné avoir passé la soirée avec l'accusé** he testified to spending the evening with the defendant **2.** [montrer - sympathie] to show ; [- dégoût, goût] to show ; [- intérêt] to show, to evince *sout* ■ **il ne m'a témoigné que du mépris en retour** he showed me nothing but contempt in return.
◆ **témoigner de** *v+prép* **1.** DR to testify to **2.** [indiquer - bonté, générosité, intérêt] to show, to indicate ■ [prouver] to show, to bear witness *ou* to testify to, to attest *sout* ■ **le problème ne fait qu'empirer, comme en témoignent ces statistiques** the problem is only getting worse, witness these statistics *ou* as these statistics show.

témoin [temwɛ̃] *nm* **1.** DR [qui fait une déposition] witness ■ **il a été cité comme ~** he was called as a witness ■ **le ~ est à vous** your witness ◆ **~ auriculaire** ear witness ■ **~ à charge/décharge** witness for the prosecution/defence ■ **~ instrumentaire** witness to a deed ■ **~ oculaire** eyewitness ■ **faux ~** perjurer
2. [à un mariage, à la signature d'un contrat] witness ■ [à un duel] second ■ **c'est le ~ du marié** he's the best man ■ **devant ~s** in front of witnesses
3. [spectateur] witness, eyewitness ■ **l'accident s'est passé sans ~** there were no witnesses to the accident ■ **être ~ de qqch** to be witness to *ou* to witness sthg ■ **prendre qqn à ~** to call upon sb as a witness ■ **Dieu/le ciel m'est ~ que j'ai tout fait pour l'en empêcher** as God/heaven is my witness, I did all I could to stop him
4. [preuve] witness ■ **elle a bien mené sa carrière, ~ sa réussite** she has managed her career well, her success is a testimony to that
5. CONSTR (plaster) tell-tale
6. RELIG : **Témoin de Jéhovah** Jehovah's Witness
7. SPORT baton ■ **passer le ~** to hand over *ou* to pass the baton
8. *(comme adj)* **appartements ~s** show flats *UK*, model apartments *US* ■ **groupe/sujet ~** SC control group/subject
9. INFORM : **~ de connexion** cookie.

tempe [tɑ̃p] *nf* temple ■ **un coup à la ~** a blow to the side of the head ■ **ses ~s commencent à grisonner** he's going grey at the temples.

tempérament [tɑ̃peramɑ̃] *nm* **1.** [caractère] temperament, disposition, nature ■ **ce n'est pas dans mon ~** it's not like me, it's not in my nature ■ **il est d'un ~ plutôt anxieux** he's the worrying kind ■ **il est d'un ~ plutôt instable** he's got a rather unstable character **2.** [disposition physique] temperament, constitution ■ **~ bilieux/sanguin** bilious/sanguine temperament ■ **~ lymphatique/nerveux** lymphatic/nervous disposition ▶ **s'abîmer** *fam* *ou* **s'esquinter** *fam* *ou* **se crever** △ **le ~à faire qqch** to wreck one's health doing sthg **3.** *fam* [sensualité] sexual nature ■ **être d'un ~ fougueux/exigeant** to be an ardent/a demanding lover ■ **il a du ~!** *euphém* he's hot-blooded! **4.** *fam* [forte personnalité] strong-willed person **5.** MUS temperament.
◆ **à tempérament** ◇ *loc adj* [achat] on deferred payment.
◇ *loc adv* [acheter] on hire purchase *UK*, on an installment plan *US*.
◆ **par tempérament** *loc adv* naturally, by nature ■ **plus musicien que son frère par ~** more musical than his brother by nature.

tempérance [tɑ̃perɑ̃s] *nf* **1.** RELIG temperance **2.** [sobriété] temperance, moderation.

tempérant, e [tɑ̃perɑ̃, ɑ̃t] *adj* temperate, sober.

tempérant, e [tɑ̃perɑ̃, ɑ̃t] *adj* temperate, sober.

température [tɑ̃peratyr] *nf* **1.** MÉD & PHYSIOL temperature ■ **avoir** *ou* **faire** *fam* **de la ~** to have a temperature ■ **prendre la ~ de** [patient] to take the temperature of ; [assemblée, public] to gauge (the feelings of) **2.** MÉTÉOR temperature ■ **il y eut une brusque chute de la ~** *ou* **des ~s** there was a sudden drop in temperature ■ **on a atteint des ~s de 67 °C/40 °C** temperatures went down to 67 °C/reached 40 °C **3.** [d'une pièce, d'une serre, d'un bain] temperature ■ **avant d'aller nager, je prends la ~ de l'eau** before going swimming, I test the water **4.** PHYS temperature ■ **~ absolue/critique/thermodynamique** absolute/critical/thermodynamic temperature.

tempéré, e [tɑ̃pere] *adj* **1.** GÉOGR [climat, région] temperate **2.** MUS [gamme] tempered.

tempérer [18] [tɑ̃pere] *vt* **1.** *litt* [température excessive] to temper *sout*, to ease **2.** [atténuer - colère] to soften, to appease ; [- ardeurs, passion, sévérité] to soften, to temper *sout* ■ **tempère ton enthousiasme, je n'ai pas encore dit oui** don't get carried away, I haven't said yes yet.
◆ **se tempérer** *vp (emploi réfléchi)* to restrain o.s.
◆ **se tempérer de** *vp+prép* to be softened *ou* tempered with ■ **sa colère se tempérait d'un peu de pitié** a hint of pity softened his anger.

tempête [tɑ̃pɛt] *nf* **1.** MÉTÉOR storm, tempest *litt* ▶ **~ de neige** snowstorm ■ **~ de sable** sandstorm **2.** [troubles] storm ■ **son livre a provoqué une véritable ~ dans les milieux politiques** his book raised quite a storm in political circles ▶ **une ~ dans un verre d'eau** a storm in a teacup *UK*, a tempest in a teapot *US* **3.** [déferlement] wave, tempest, storm ■ **~ d'applaudissements/de critiques/de protestations** storm of applause/criticism/protest ■ **~ d'insultes** hail of abuse.

tempêter [4] [tɑ̃pete] *vi* to rage, to rant (and rave) ■ **ils ne cessent de ~ contre les syndicats** they're always railing against the unions.

tempétueux, euse [tɑ̃petɥø, øz] *adj litt* **1.** [côte, mer] tempestuous *litt*, stormy ■ [courant] turbulent **2.** [amour, passion] tempestuous, stormy.

temple [tɑ̃pl] *nm* **1.** RELIG [gén] temple ■ [chez les protestants] church ■ **le Temple** [ordre] the Order of the Temple, the Knights Templar ; [à Paris] *densely-populated district in the 3rd arrondissement of Paris, well known for the gardens and covered market built on the site of the old stronghold of the Knights Templars* **2.** [haut lieu] : **le ~ de la mode/musique** the Mecca of fashion/music.

templier [tɑ̃plije] *nm* HIST (Knight) Templar.

tempo [tɛmpo] *nm* **1.** MUS tempo **2.** [rythme - d'un film, d'un roman] tempo, pace ; [- de la vie] pace.

temporaire [tɑ̃pɔrɛr] *adj* temporary ■ **c'est une employée ~** she's a temporary worker.

temporairement [tɑ̃pɔrɛrmɑ̃] *adv* temporarily.

temporal, e, aux [tɑ̃pɔral, o] *adj* ANAT temporal.
◆ **temporal, aux** *nm* ANAT temporal bone.

temporalité [tɑ̃pɔralite] *nf litt* temporality, temporalness.

temporel, elle [tɑ̃pɔrɛl] *adj* **1.** RELIG [autorité, pouvoir] temporal ■ [bonheur] temporal, earthly ■ [biens] worldly, temporal **2.** LING temporal.

temporisateur, trice [tɑ̃pɔrizatœr, tris] ◇ *adj* [politique, tendance] temporizing *sout*, delaying ■ [stratégie, tactique] delaying.
◇ *nm, f* temporizer *sout*.
◆ **temporisateur** *nm* **1.** SC retarder **2.** INFORM timer.

temporiser [3] [tɑ̃pɔrize] *vi* to use delaying tactics, to temporize *sout* ■ **notre équipe devrait ~ pour conserver son but d'avance** our team should now play for time to retain its one-goal lead.

temps [tɑ̃] ◇ *nm*

A. CLIMAT
B. DURÉE

A. CLIMAT

weather ■ **quel ~ fait-il à Nîmes?** what's the weather like in Nîmes? ■ **avec le ~ qu'il fait, par ce ~** in this weather ■ **il fait un ~ gris** it's overcast, the weather's dull *UK* *ou* gloomy ■ **par beau ~** *ou* **par ~ clair, on voit la côte anglaise** when it's fine *ou* on a clear day, you can see the English coast

B. DURÉE

1. [écoulement des jours] : **le ~** time ■ **comme le ~ passe!, comme** *ou* **que le ~ passe vite!** how time flies! ■ **le Temps** Old Father Time

2. [durée indéterminée] time *(U)* ■ **c'est du ~ perdu** it's a waste of time ■ **mettre du ~ à faire qqch** to take time to do sthg ■ **mettre du ~ à se décider** to take a long time deciding *ou* to decide ■ **passer son ~ à : je passe mon ~ à lire** I spend (all) my time reading ■ **pour passer le ~** to while away *ou* to pass the time ■ **prendre du ~** to take time ■ **ça prendra le ~ qu'il faudra** *ou* **que ça prendra** *fam* it'll take as long as it takes ■ **trouver le ~ long** to feel time dragging by

3. [durée nécessaire] time *(C)* ■ **le ~ que : calculer le ~ que met la lumière pour aller du Soleil à la Terre** to compute the time that light takes to go from the Sun to the Earth ■ **va chercher du lait, le ~ que je fasse du thé** go and get some milk while I make some tea ■ **le ~ de : le ~ de faire qqch** (the) time to do sthg ■ **le ~ d'enfiler un manteau et j'arrive** just let me put on a coat and I'll be with you ■ **juste le ~ de les entendre** just long enough to hear them ■ **avoir le ~ de faire qqch** to have (the) time to do sthg ■ **prendre son ~** to take one's time ■ **surtout prends ton ~!** *iron* take your time, won't you?, don't hurry, will you? ■ **prendre le ~ de faire qqch** to take the time to do sthg ▶ **~ de cuisson/préparation** CULIN cooking/preparation time ■ **un ~ partiel** a part-time job ■ **un ~ plein** *ou* **plein ~** a full-time job ■ **être** *ou* **travailler à ~ partiel** to work part-time ■ **être** *ou* **travailler à plein ~** *ou* **à ~ plein** to work full-time ■ **travailler à ~ complet** to work full-time ■ **faire un trois quarts (de) ~** ≃ to work 30 hours per week ■ **le ~ de la réflexion** time to think ■ **diminuer le ~ de travail** to reduce working hours

4. [loisir] time *(C)* ■ **maintenant qu'elle est à la retraite, elle ne sait plus quoi faire de son ~** now that she's retired, she doesn't know how to fill her time ■ **avoir du ~** *ou* **le ~** to have time ■ **mon train est à 7 h, j'ai grandement** *ou* **tout le ~** my train is at 7, I've plenty of time (to spare) ■ **avoir tout son ~** to have all the time in the world ■ **ne nous pressons pas, on a tout notre ~!** *iron* couldn't you go (just) a little bit slower? ■ **avoir du ~ devant soi** to have time to spare *ou* on one's hands ▶ **~ libre** free time ■ **avoir du ~ libre** to have some spare time

5. [moment favorable] : **il est ~ : il est (grand) ~!** it's high time!, it's about time! ■ **la voilà – il était ~!** here she is – it's about time *ou* and not a minute too soon *ou* and about time too! ■ **il était ~, le bol allait tomber** that was close, the bowl was about to fall ■ **il n'est plus ~** time's run out ■ **il est ~ de** now's the time for ■ **il n'est plus ~ de discuter, il faut agir** the time for discussion is past *ou* enough talking, we must act ■ **il est ~**

que tu t'inscrives you'd better enrol soon, it's time you enrolled ▪ le ~ était venu pour moi de partir the time had come for me to *ou* it was time for me to leave

6. [époque déterminée] time *(C)* ▪ **le ~ n'est plus aux querelles** we should put quarrels behind us, the time for quarelling is past ▪ **il fut un ~ où...** there was a time when... ▪ **le ~ n'est plus où...** gone are the days when... ▪ **la plus grande découverte de notre ~** the biggest discovery of our time ▪ **être en avance/en retard sur son ~** to be ahead of/behind one's time ▪ **être de son ~** to move with the times ▪ **il n'était pas de son ~** [en retard] he was out of step with his time ; [en avance] he was ahead of his time ▪ **dans mon jeune ~** when I was young, in my younger days ▪ **j'ai cru, un ~, que...** I thought, for a while, that... ▪ **il y a un ~ pour tout** there's a time for everything ▪ **elle est fidèle – ça n'aura** *ou* **ne durera qu'un ~** she's faithful – it won't last ▪ **faire son ~** [détenu, soldat] to do *ou* to serve one's time ▪ **la cafetière/mon manteau a fait son ~** *fam* the coffee machine's/my coat's seen better days ▪ **des idées qui ont fait leur ~** outmoded ideas ▪ **en ~ normal** *ou* **ordinaire** usually, in normal circumstances ▪ **en ~ voulu** in good time ▪ **en ~ utile** in due time *ou* course ▪ **en son ~** in due course ▪ **chaque chose en son ~** there's a right time for everything

7. [saison, période de l'année] time *(C)*, season ▪ **le ~ des moissons** harvest (time) ▪ **le ~ des cerises/pêches** the cherry/peach season

8. [phase - d'une action, d'un mouvement] stage ▪ **dans un premier ~** first ▪ **dans un deuxième ~** secondly ▪ **dans un troisième ~** thirdly

9. INFORM time ▪ **~ d'accès/d'amorçage** access/start-up time ▪ **~ partagé** time sharing ▪ **~ réel** real time ▪ **traitement en ~ réel** real-time processing ▪ **travailler en ~ réel** to work in real time

10. LING tense

11. MÉCAN stroke

12. MUS beat ▪ **valse à trois ~** waltz in three-four time

13. RELIG : **le ~ de l'avent/du carême** (the season of) Advent/Lent ▪ **le ~ pascal** Easter time, Eastertide

14. SPORT [d'une course] time ▪ **elle a fait le meilleur ~ aux essais** hers was the best time *ou* she was the fastest in the trials ‖ ESCRIME [durée - d'une action] time, temps ; [- d'un combat] bout.

◇ *nmpl* [époque] times, days ▪ **les ~ sont durs** *ou* **difficiles!** times are hard! ▪ **les ~ modernes/préhistoriques** modern/prehistoric times.

◆ **à temps** *loc adv* in time ▪ **je n'arriverai/je ne finirai jamais à ~!** I'll never make it/I'll never finish in time!

◆ **à temps perdu** *loc adv* in one's spare time, in a spare moment.

◆ **au même temps** = **en même temps**.

◆ **au même temps que** = **en même temps que**.

◆ **au temps de** *loc prép* in *ou* at the time of, in the days of ▪ **au ~ de Voltaire** in Voltaire's time *ou* day.

◆ **au temps jadis** *loc adv* in times past, in the old days.

◆ **au temps où, au temps que** *loc conj* in the days when, at the time when.

◆ **avec le temps** *loc adv* with the passing of time ▪ **avec le ~, tout s'arrange** time is a great healer.

◆ **ces temps-ci** *loc adv* these days, lately.

◆ **dans ce temps-là** *loc adv* in those days, at that time.

◆ **dans le même temps** = **en même temps**.

◆ **dans le même temps que** = **en même temps que**.

◆ **dans le temps** *loc adv* before, in the old days.

◆ **dans les temps** *loc adv* on time ▪ **être dans les ~** [pour un travail] to be on schedule *ou* time ; [pour une course] to be within the time (limit).

◆ **de temps à autre, de temps en temps** *loc adv* from time to time, occasionally, (every) now and then.

◆ **du temps de** *loc prép* : **du ~ de Louis XIV** in the days of Louis the XIVth ▪ **du ~ de notre père, tu n'aurais pas osé** when our father was (still) alive, you wouldn't have dared ▪ **de mon ~, ça n'existait pas** when I was young *ou* in my day, there was no such thing.

◆ **du temps où, du temps que** = **au temps où**.

◆ **en ce temps-là** = **dans ce temps-là**.

◆ **en même temps** *loc adv* at the same time.

◆ **en même temps que** *loc conj* at the same time as.

◆ **en temps de** *loc prép* : **en ~ de guerre/paix** in wartime/peacetime ▪ **en ~ de prospérité/récession** in times of prosperity/recession.

◆ **en temps et lieu** *loc adv* in due course *ou* time, at the proper time and place.

◆ **en un temps où** *loc conj* at a time when.

◆ **par les temps qui courent** *loc adv fam* (things being as they are) these days *ou* nowadays.

◆ **tout le temps** *loc adv* all the time, always ▪ **ne me harcèle pas tout le ~!** don't keep on pestering me!

◆ **temps fort** *nm* MUS strong beat ▪ *fig* high point, highlight ▪ **un des ~ forts du festival** one of the high points *ou* highlights of the festival.

◆ **temps mort** *nm* **1.** [au basketball, au volleyball] time-out **2.** *fig* lull, slack period ▪ [dans une conversation] lull, pause.

tenable [tənabl] *adj* **1.** [supportable] bearable ▪ **la situation n'est plus ~, il faut agir** the situation's become untenable *ou* unbearable, we must take action **2.** [contrôlable] : **à l'approche de Noël, les enfants ne sont plus ~s** as Christmas gets nearer, the children are going wild.

tenace [tənas] *adj* **1.** [obstiné - travailleur] tenacious, obstinate ; [- chercheur] tenacious, dogged ; [- ennemi] relentless ; [- résistance, volonté] tenacious ; [- refus] dogged ; [- vendeur] tenacious, insistent **2.** [durable - fièvre, grippe, toux] persistent, stubborn ; [- parfum, odeur] persistent, lingering ; [- tache] stubborn ; [- préjugé, impression, superstition] deep-rooted, stubborn, tenacious **3.** [qui adhère fortement - colle] strong ; [- plante, lierre] clinging.

ténacité [tenasite] *nf* **1.** [d'une personne, d'une volonté] tenacity, tenaciousness ▪ **avec ~** doggedly ▪ **faire preuve de ~** to be persistent **2.** [d'une fièvre, d'une toux, d'une odeur] persistence ▪ [d'une tache] stubbornness ▪ [d'un préjugé, d'une superstition] deep-rootedness, persistence **3.** TECHNOL resilience.

tenaille [tənaj] *nf* **1.** [outil] : **~, ~s** [de charpentier, de menuisier] pincers ; [de cordonnier] pincers, nippers ; [de forgeron] tongs **2.** [fortification] tenaille.

◆ **en tenaille(s)** *loc adv* : **prendre qqn en ~** *ou* **~s** to catch *ou* to trap sb in a pincer movement.

tenailler [3] [tənaje] *vt sout* [faim, soif] to gnaw ▪ [doute, inquiétude, remords] to gnaw (at), to rack, to torment ▪ **être tenaillé par la faim/par le remords** to be racked with hunger/tormented by remorse.

tenancier, ère [tənɑ̃sje, ɛr] *nm, f* **1.** [d'un café, d'un hôtel, d'une maison de jeu] manager **2.** [fermier] tenant farmer **3.** HIST (feudal) tenant.

tenant, e [tənɑ̃, ɑ̃t] *nm, f* SPORT : **~ (du titre)** holder, titleholder.

◆ **tenant** *nm* **1.** [d'une doctrine, d'une idéologie, d'un principe] supporter, upholder **2.** HÉRALD supporter.

◆ **tenants** *nmpl* [d'une terre] adjacent parts DR abuttals ▪ **les ~s et les aboutissants** [d'une affaire] the ins and outs, the full details.

◆ **d'un (seul) tenant** *loc adj* all in one block ▪ **trois hectares d'un seul ~** three adjoining hectares.

tendance [tɑ̃dɑ̃s] *nf* **1.** [disposition, propension] tendency ▪ **avoir ~ à** to tend to, to have a tendency to ▪ **tu as un peu trop ~ à croire que tout t'est dû** you're too inclined to think that the world owes you a living

2. [orientation, évolution - gén] trend ; [- d'un créateur] leanings ; [- d'un livre, d'un discours] drift, tenor ▪ **les nouvelles ~s de l'art/la mode** the new trends in art/fashion ▪ **~s de l'automne** [vêtement] the autumn fashions ▪ *(comme adj)* **une coupe très ~** a very fashionable cut

3. [position, opinion] allegiance, leaning, sympathy ▪ **un parti de ~ libérale** a party with liberal tendencies ▪ **des partis de toutes ~s étaient représentés** the whole spectrum of political opinion was represented ‖ [fraction d'un parti] : **la ~ centriste au sein du parti** the middle-of-the-road tendency within the party ▪ **le groupe a décidé, toutes ~s réunies, de voter l'amendement** all the factions within the group voted in favour of supporting the amendment ▪ **à quelle ~ appartiens-tu?** what are your political leanings?, where do your (political) sympathies lie?

4. BOURSE & ÉCON trend ■ **~ inflationniste** inflationary trend ■ **une ~ baissière** *ou* **à la baisse** a downward trend, a downswing ■ **une ~ haussière** *ou* **à la hausse** an upward trend, an upswing
5. [résultat d'une étude] trend ■ **~ générale** (general) trend.

tendanciel, elle [tɑ̃dɑ̃sjɛl] *adj* : **une évolution ~le** a trend-setting development.

tendancieux, euse [tɑ̃dɑ̃sjø, øz] *adj* [film, récit, interprétation] tendentious, tendencious ■ [question] loaded.

tendeur [tɑ̃dœr] *nm* **1.** [pour tendre - un câble] tensioner ; [- une toile de tente] guy rope ; [- une chaîne de bicyclette] chain adjuster **2.** [pour porte-bagages] luggage strap.

tendinite [tɑ̃dinit] *nf* tendinitis.

tendon [tɑ̃dɔ̃] *nm* tendon, sinew ■ **~ d'Achille** Achilles' tendon.

tendre[1] [tɑ̃dr] ◇ *adj* **1.** [aimant - personne] loving, gentle, tender ; [- voix] gentle ; [- yeux] gentle, loving ■ [affectueux - lettre] loving, affectionate ■ **elle n'est pas ~ avec lui** she's hard on him ■ **la presse n'est pas ~ pour elle ce matin** she's been given a rough ride in the papers this morning **2.** [moelleux - viande, légumes] tender ➲ **~ comme la rosée** (as) fresh as the morning dew **3.** [mou - roche, mine de crayon, métal] soft ■ **bois ~** softwood **4.** *litt* [délicat - feuillage, bourgeons] tender, delicate ; [- herbe] soft **5.** [doux - teinte] soft, delicate ■ **un tissu rose/vert ~** a soft pink/green material **6.** [jeune] early ■ **nos ~s années** our early years ■ **âge ~, ~ enfance** early childhood ■ **dès sa plus ~ enfance** since his earliest childhood.
◇ *nmf* tender-hearted person.

tendre[2] [73] [tɑ̃dr] *vt* **1.** [étirer - câble, corde de raquette] to tighten, to tauten ; [- élastique, ressort] to stretch ; [- corde d'arc] to draw back *(sép)* ; [- arc] to bend ; [- arbalète] to arm ; [- voile] to stretch, to brace ; [- peau d'un tambour] to pull, to stretch **2.** [disposer - hamac, fil à linge, tapisserie] to hang ; [- collet, souricière] to set ■ **~ une embuscade** *ou* **un piège à qqn** to set an ambush *ou* a trap for sb ➲ **~ ses filets** *pr* to set one's nets ; *fig* to set a trap **3.** [revêtir - mur] to cover ■ **~ une pièce de toile de jute** to cover the walls of a room with hessian **4.** [allonger - partie du corps] : **~ le cou** to crane *ou* to stretch one's neck ■ **elle tendit son front/sa joue à sa mère pour qu'elle l'embrasse** she offered her forehead/her cheek for her mother to kiss ■ **~ les bras (vers qqn)** to stretch out one's arms (towards sb) ■ **assieds-toi, il y a un fauteuil qui te tend les bras** sit down, there's an armchair waiting for you ■ **vas-y, le poste de directeur te tend les bras** go ahead, the director's job is yours for the taking ■ **~ la main** [pour recevoir qqch] to hold out one's hand ■ **~ la main à qqn** [pour dire bonjour] to hold out one's hand to sb ; [pour aider] to offer a helping hand to sb ; [pour se réconcilier] to extend a *ou* the hand of friendship to sb ➲ **~ l'autre joue** *allus* & BIBLE to turn the other cheek **5.** [offrir, présenter] to offer **6.** [concentrer] : **~ sa volonté vers la réussite** to strive for success ■ **~ ses efforts vers un but** to strive to achieve an aim.
◆ **tendre à** *v+prép* **1.** [avoir tendance à] : **c'est une pratique qui tend à disparaître** it's a custom which is dying out **2.** [contribuer à] : **cela tendrait à prouver que j'ai raison** this would seem to prove that I'm right **3.** [aspirer à] : **~ à la perfection** to aim at perfection **4.** [arriver à] : **~ à sa fin** to near an end.
◆ **tendre vers** *v+prép* **1.** [viser à] : **~ vers la perfection** to aim at perfection, to strive towards perfection **2.** [approcher de] : **le rythme de la production tend vers son maximum** maximum output is close to being reached **3.** MATH : **~ vers zéro/l'infini** to tend to zero/infinity.
◆ **se tendre** *vpi* **1.** [courroie, câble] to tighten (up), to become taut, to tauten **2.** [atmosphère, relations] to become strained.

tendrement [tɑ̃drəmɑ̃] *adv* [embrasser, regarder, sourire] tenderly, lovingly ■ **ils s'aiment ~** they love each other dearly.

tendresse [tɑ̃drɛs] *nf* **1.** [attachement - d'un amant] tenderness ; [- d'un parent] affection, tenderness ■ **avec ~** tenderly ■ **avoir de la ~ pour qqn** to feel affection for sb **2.** [inclination, penchant] : **je n'ai aucune ~ pour les menteurs** I have no love for liars, I don't think much of liars.
◆ **tendresses** *nfpl* : **je vous envoie mille ~s ainsi qu'aux enfants** much love to you and to the children.

tendron [tɑ̃drɔ̃] *nm* **1.** CULIN : **~ de veau** middle-cut breast of veal **2.** BOT shoot.

tendu, e [tɑ̃dy] ◇ *pp* ▷ **tendre.**
◇ *adj* **1.** [nerveux - de tempérament] tense ; [- dans une situation] tense, strained, fraught ; [- avant un événement, un match] keyed up, tense ■ **jamais, dit-il d'une voix ~e** never, he said in a strained voice **2.** [atmosphère] strained ■ [rapports] strained, fraught *UK* ■ [situation] tense, fraught *UK* **3.** [partie du corps, muscle] tensed up **4.** [étiré - corde, courroie] tight, taut ; [- corde d'arc] drawn ; [- arc] drawn, bent ; [- voile, peau de tambour] stretched ■ **ma raquette de tennis est trop ~ e/n'est pas assez ~e** my tennis racket strings are too tight/too slack **5.** [allongé] : **avancer le doigt ~/le poing ~/les bras ~s** to advance with pointed finger/raised fist/outstretched arms **6.** LING tense.

ténèbres [tenɛbr] *nfpl* **1.** [nuit, obscurité] darkness *(U)*, dark *(U)* ■ **être plongé dans les ~** to be in total darkness **2.** *fig* **les ~ de la superstition** the dark age of superstition **3.** RELIG Tenebrae.

ténébreux, euse [tenebrø, øz] ◇ *adj litt* **1.** [forêt, maison, pièce] dark, gloomy, tenebrous *litt* ■ [recoin, cachot] dark, murky **2.** [inquiétant - intrigue, complot] dark ; [- époque, situation] obscure, murky ■ **de ~ projets** devious plans **3.** [incompréhensible] mysterious, unfathomable ■ **une ténébreuse affaire** a shady business ■ **le ~ langage de la loi** the obscure language of the legal profession **4.** [personne, caractère] melancholic, saturnine *litt.*
◇ *nm, f hum* **un beau ~** a tall, dark, handsome stranger.

Tenerife, Ténériffe [tenerif] *npr* Tenerife.

ténia [tenja] *nm* tapeworm, taenia *spéc.*

tenir [40] [tənir] ◇ *vt*

> **A.** AVOIR DANS LES MAINS
> **B.** CONSERVER
> **C.** POSSÉDER
> **D.** CONTRÔLER, AVOIR LA RESPONSABILITÉ DE
> **E.** EXPRIME UNE MESURE
> **F.** ÊTRE CONSTANT DANS
> **G.** CONSIDÉRER

A. AVOIR DANS LES MAINS
1. [retenir] to hold (on to) ■ **~ la main de qqn** to hold sb's hand ■ **je tenais mal la bouteille et elle m'a échappé** I wasn't holding the bottle tightly enough and it slipped
2. [manier] to hold ■ **tu tiens mal ta raquette/ton arc** you're not holding your racket/your bow properly

B. CONSERVER
1. [maintenir - dans une position] to hold, to keep ; [- dans un état] to keep ■ **enlève les vis qui tiennent le panneau** undo the screws which hold the panel in place ■ **tiens-lui la porte, il est chargé** hold the door open for him, he's got his hands full ■ **tenez-lui la tête hors de l'eau** hold her head above the water ■ **elle tient ses chiens attachés** she keeps her dogs tied up ■ **~ chaud** to keep warm ■ **je veux une robe qui tienne chaud** I'd like a warm dress ■ **tenez-le prêt (à partir)** make sure he's ready (to leave)
2. [garder - note] to hold ■ **~ l'accord** to stay in tune ■ **'tenez votre droite'** [sur la route] 'keep (to the) right' ; [sur un Escalator] 'keep to the right'
3. *vieilli* [conserver - dans un lieu] to keep
4. *Belgique* [collectionner] to collect

C. POSSÉDER
1. [avoir reçu] : **~ qqch de qqn** [par hérédité] to get sthg from sb ■ **les propriétés que je tenais de ma mère** [par héritage] the properties I'd inherited from my mother
2. [avoir capturé] to have caught, to have got hold of ■ [avoir à sa merci] to have got ■ **ah, ah, petit coquin, je te tiens!** got you, you little devil! ■ **si je tenais celui qui a défoncé ma portière!** just let me get *ou* lay my hands on whoever smashed in my car door! ■ **elle m'a tenu une heure avec ses histoires de divorce** I had to listen to her going on about her divorce for a whole hour ■ **pendant que je vous tiens (au téléphone), pourrais-je vous demander un service?** since I'm speaking to you (on the phone), may I ask you a favour?

3. [détenir - indice, information, preuve] to have ; [- contrat] to have, to have won ; [- réponse, solution] to have (found) *OU* got ■ **je crois que je tiens un scoop!** I think I've got a scoop! ■ **~ qqch de** [l'apprendre] to have (got) sthg from ■ **il a eu des troubles psychologiques – de qui tenez-vous cela?** he's had psychological problems – who told you that? ■ **nous tenons de source sûre/soviétique que...** we have it on good authority/we hear from Soviet sources that... ■ **~ qqch de** [le tirer de] : **je tiens mon autorité de l'État** I derive my power from the state ■ **qu'est-ce que je tiens comme rhume!** *fam* I've got a stinking *UK OU* horrible cold! ⊳ **elle en tient une couche!** *fam* she's as thick as two short planks *UK*, what a dumb bell! *US* ■ **il en tient une bonne ce soir** *fam* he's had a skinful *UK OU* he's three sheets to the wind tonight ■ **qu'est-ce qu'il tient!** *fam* [il est stupide] what a twit *UK OU* blockhead! ; [il est ivre] he's really plastered! ; [il est enrhumé] he's got a stinking *UK OU* horrible cold!
4. [transmettre] : **nous vous ferons ~ une copie des documents** *sout* we will make sure you receive a copy of the documents

D. CONTRÔLER, AVOIR LA RESPONSABILITÉ DE
1. [avoir prise sur, dominer] to hold ■ **quand la colère le tient, il peut être dangereux** he can be dangerous when he's angry ■ **la jalousie le tenait** jealousy had him in its grip, he was gripped by jealousy ■ **ce rhume me tient depuis deux semaines** I've had this cold for two weeks ▮ MIL to control ■ [avoir de l'autorité sur - classe, élève] to (keep under) control
2. [diriger, s'occuper de - commerce, maison, hôtel] to run ; [- comptabilité, registre] to keep ■ **~ la caisse** to be at the cash desk, to be the cashier ■ **elle tient la rubrique artistique à "Madame"** she has a regular Arts column in "Madame" ■ **le soir, il tenait le bar** at night he used to serve behind the bar ■ **~ la marque** JEUX & SPORT to keep score
3. [donner - assemblée, conférence, séance] to hold, to have ■ **le tribunal tiendra audience dans le nouveau bâtiment** the court hearings will be held in the new building
4. [prononcer - discours] to give ; [- raisonnement] to have ; [- langage] to use ■ **il me tint à peu près ce langage** *La Fontaine allus* here's roughly what he said to me ■ **~ des propos désobligeants/élogieux** to make offensive/appreciative remarks ■ **comment peux-tu ~ un tel raisonnement?** how can you possibly think this way?
5. [astreint à] : **être tenu à qqch : être tenu au secret professionnel** to be bound by professional secrecy ■ **nous sommes tenus à la discrétion** we're obliged to be very discreet ■ **je me sens tenu de la prévenir** I feel morally obliged *OU* duty-bound to warn her
6. THÉÂTRE [rôle] to play, to have ■ **~ un rôle dans** *fig* to play a part in
7. ÉQUIT [cheval] to keep in hand

E. EXPRIME UNE MESURE
1. [occuper] to take up *(sép)*, to occupy ■ **le fauteuil tient trop de place** the armchair takes up too much room ■ **~ une place importante** to have *OU* to hold an important place
2. [contenir] to hold

F. ÊTRE CONSTANT DANS
1. [résister à] (to be able) to take ■ **il tient l'alcool** he can take *esp UK OU* hold his drink ⊳ **~ le coup** *fam* [assemblage, vêtements] to hold out ; [digue] to hold (out) ; [personne] (to be able) to take it ■ **le soir, je ne tiens pas le coup** I can't take late nights ■ **~ la route** [véhicule] to have good road-holding *UK*, to hold the road well ■ **ton raisonnement ne tient pas la route** *fig* your argument doesn't stand up to scrutiny
2. [respecter] to keep to, to stand by, to uphold ■ **~ une promesse** to keep *OU* to fulfil a promise ▮ [s'engager dans - pari] : **je tiens la gageure** *OU* **le pari!** I'll take up the challenge! ■ **tenu!, je tiens!** JEUX you're on!

G. CONSIDÉRER
sout to hold, to consider ■ **~ qqn/qqch pour** to consider sb/sthg to be, to look upon sb/sthg as.

◇ *vi* **1.** [rester en position - attache] to hold ; [- chignon] to stay up, to hold ; [- bouton, trombone] to stay on ; [- empilement, tas] to stay up ■ **~ en place** to stay in place ■ **mets du gel, tes cheveux tiendront mieux** use gel, your hair'll hold its shape better ■ **la porte du placard ne tient pas fermée** the cupboard door won't stay shut ■ **tout ça tient avec de la colle** all this is held together with glue ■ **le porridge vous tient au corps** *OU* **à l'estomac** porridge keeps you going ■ **faire ~ qqch avec de la colle/des clous** to glue/to nail sthg into position ■ **~ à** [être fixé à] to be fixed on *OU* to ; [être contigu à] to be next to ■ [personne] : **il ne tient pas encore bien sur sa bicyclette/ses skis/ses jambes** he's not very steady on his bike/his skis/his legs yet ■ **je ne tiens plus sur mes jambes** [de fatigue] I can hardly stand up any more ■ **cet enfant ne tient pas sur sa chaise** this child can't sit still *OU* is always fidgeting in his chair ■ **elle ne tient pas en place** she can't sit still
2. [résister - union] to last, to hold out ; [- chaise, vêtements] to hold *OU* to last out ; [- digue] to hold out ; [- personne] to hold *OU* to last out ■ **je ne tiens plus au soleil, je rentre** I can't stand the sun any more, I'm going in ■ **le cœur ne tiendra pas** his heart won't take it ■ **tes arguments ne tiendront pas longtemps face à la réalité** your arguments won't hold for very long when faced with reality ⊳ **~ bon** *OU* **ferme** [s'agripper] to hold firm *OU* tight ; [ne pas céder] to hold out ■ **tenez bon, les secours arrivent** hold *OU* hang on, help's on its way ■ **il me refusait une augmentation, mais j'ai tenu bon** he wouldn't give me a rise but I held out *OU* stood my ground ■ **le dollar tient toujours bon** the dollar is still holding firm ■ **ne pas y ~, ne (pas) pouvoir y ~ : n'y tenant plus, je l'appelai au téléphone** unable to stand it any longer, I phoned him ■ **ça sent si bon le chocolat, je ne vais pas pouvoir y ~** there's such a gorgeous smell of chocolate, I just won't be able to resist it
3. [durer, ne pas s'altérer - fleurs] to keep, to last ; [- tissu] to last (well) ; [- beau temps] to last, to hold out ; [- bronzage] to last ; [- neige] to settle, to stay ■ **aucun parfum ne tient sur moi** perfumes don't stay on me
4. [être valable, être d'actualité - offre, pari, rendez-vous] to stand ; [- promesse] to hold ■ **ça tient toujours pour demain?** is it still on for tomorrow? ■ **il n'y a pas de... qui tienne : il n'y a pas de congé qui tienne** there's no question of having leave ■ **il n'y a pas de "mais ma tante" qui tienne, tu vas te coucher!** there's no "but Auntie" about it, off to bed with you!
5. [pouvoir être logé] to fit ■ **le compte rendu tient en une page** the report takes up one page ■ **~ en hauteur/largeur (dans)** to fit vertically/widthwise (in) ■ **on tient facilement à cinq dans la barque** the boat sits five in comfort ■ **son histoire tient en peu de mots** his story can be summed up in a few words
6. *loc* **en ~ pour qqn** *fam* to have a crush on sb ■ **en ~ pour qqch** *fam* [aimer] to be hooked on sthg ; [ne considérer que] to stick to sthg ■ **elle en tient vraiment pour l'hypothèse de l'assassinat** she seems convinced it was murder ■ **tiens, tenez** [en donnant qqch] here ■ **tiens, tenez** [pour attirer l'attention, pour insister] : **tiens, le tonnerre gronde** listen, it's thundering ■ **tiens, rends-toi utile** here, make yourself useful ■ **tenez, je ne vous ferai même pas payer l'électricité** look, I won't even charge you for the electricity ■ **s'il est intéressé par le salaire? tiens, bien sûr que oui!** is he interested in the salary? you bet he is! ■ **tiens, tenez** [exprime la surprise, l'incrédulité] : **tiens, Bruno! que fais-tu ici?** (hello) Bruno, what are you doing here? ■ **tiens, je n'aurais jamais cru ça de lui** well, well, I'd never have expected it of him ■ **elle a refusé? tiens donc!** *fam iron* she said no? you amaze me! *OU* surprise, surprise! ■ **un tiens vaut mieux que deux tu l'auras** *prov* a bird in the hand is worth two in the bush *prov.*

➡ **tenir à** *v+prép* **1.** [être attaché à - personne] to care for, to be very fond of ; [- objet] to be attached to ; [- réputation] to care about ; [- indépendance, liberté] to value ■ **si tu tiens à la vie...** if you value your life...
2. [vouloir] : **~ à faire qqch** to be eager to do *OU* to be keen on doing sthg ■ **je tiens à être présent à la signature du contrat** I insist on being there when the contract is signed ■ **tu veux lui parler? – je n'y tiens pas vraiment** would you like to talk to him? – not really *OU* not particularly ■ **~ à ce que : je tiens à ce qu'ils aient une bonne éducation** I'm most concerned that they should have a good education ■ **tiens-tu à ce que cela se sache?** do you really want it to become known? ■ **je voudrais t'aider – je n'y tiens pas** I'd like to help you – I'd rather you didn't ■ **venez dîner, j'y tiens absolument!** come and have dinner, I insist!
3. [résulter de] to stem *OU* to result from, to be due to, to be caused by ■ **le bonheur tient parfois à peu de chose** sometimes it's the little things that give people the most happiness ■ **à quoi ça tient?** *fam* what's the reason for it?, what's it due to? ⊳ **qu'à cela ne tienne** never mind, fear not *hum*

4. *(tournure impersonnelle)* [être du ressort de] : **il ne tient qu'à toi de mettre fin à ce désordre** it's entirely up to you to sort out this shambles ▪ **s'il ne tenait qu'à moi** if it was up to me *ou* my decision.

◆ **tenir de** *v+prép* **1.** [ressembler à] to take after ▪ **ce chien tient à la fois de l'épagneul et du setter** this dog is a sort of cross between a spaniel and a setter ▶ **elle est vraiment têtue/douée – elle a de qui ~!** she's so stubborn/gifted – it runs in the family! **2.** [relever de] : **sa guérison tient du miracle** his recovery is something of a miracle ▪ **des propos qui tiennent de l'injure** remarks verging on the insulting.

◆ **se tenir** ◇ *vp (emploi réciproque)* : **ils marchaient en se tenant la main** they were walking hand in hand ▪ **se ~ par le cou/la taille** to have one's arms round each other's shoulders/waists.

◇ *vp (emploi passif)* [se dérouler - conférence] to be held, to take place ; [- festival, foire] to take place ▪ **le festival se tient en plusieurs endroits** there are several venues for the festival.

◇ *vpt* : **se ~ la tête à deux mains** to hold *ou* to clutch one's head in one's hands.

◇ *vpi* **1.** [se retenir] to hold on (tight) ▪ **se ~ à** to hold on to ; [fortement] to cling to, to clutch, to grip
2. [se trouver - en position debout] to stand, to be standing ; [- en position assise] to sit, to be sitting *ou* seated ▪ **se ~ (légèrement) en retrait** to stand back (slightly) ▪ **se ~ debout** to be standing (up) ▪ **se ~ droit** [debout] to stand up straight ; [assis] to sit up straight ▪ **tiens-toi mieux sur ta chaise** sit properly on your chair ▪ **c'est parce que tu te tiens mal que tu as mal au dos** you get backaches because of bad posture ▪ **se ~ aux aguets** to be on the lookout, to watch out ▪ **se ~ coi** to remain silent
3. [se conduire] to behave ▪ **bien se ~** to behave o.s. ▪ **mal se ~** to behave o.s. badly
4. [être cohérent] : **se ~ (bien)** [argumentation, intrigue] to hold together, to stand up ; [raisonnement] to hold water, to hold together ▪ **je voudrais trouver un alibi qui se tienne** I'm looking for a plausible excuse ‖ [coïncider - indices, événements] to hang together, to be linked
5. *loc* **s'en ~ à** : **tenez-vous-en aux ordres** confine yourself to carrying out orders ▪ **d'abord ingénieur puis directrice d'usine, elle ne s'en est pas tenue là** she started out as an engineer, then became a factory manager, but she didn't stop there ▪ **je ne m'en tiendrai pas à ses excuses** I won't be content with a mere apology from him ▪ **ne pas se ~ de** [joie, impatience] to be beside o.s. with ▪ **on ne se tenait plus de rire** we were in absolute fits (of laughter) ▪ **tiens-toi bien, tenez-vous bien : ils ont détourné, tiens-toi bien, deux millions d'euros!** they embezzled, wait for it, 2 million euros! ▪ **elle a battu le record, tenez-vous bien, de plus de deux secondes!** she broke the previous record and by over two seconds, would you believe!

◆ **se tenir pour** *vp+prép* **1.** [se considérer comme] : **je ne me tiens pas encore pour battu** I don't reckon I'm *ou* I don't consider myself defeated yet ▪ **se ~ pour satisfait** to feel satisfied ▪ **je ne me tiens pas pour un génie** I don't regard myself as *ou* think of myself as *ou* consider myself a genius **2.** *loc* **je ne supporterai pas tes insolences, tiens-le-toi pour dit!** I'll say this only once, I won't put up with your rudeness!

Tennessee [tenesi] *npr m* : **le ~** Tennessee.

tennis [tenis] ◇ *nm* **1.** [activité] tennis ▪ **jouer au ~** to play tennis ▶ **~ sur gazon** lawn tennis ▪ **~ en salle** indoor tennis **2.** [court] (tennis) court.

◇ *nmpl & nfpl* [chaussures - pour le tennis] tennis shoes ; [- pour la marche] sneakers, trainers.

◆ **tennis de table** *nm* table tennis.

tennis-elbow [teniselbo] (*pl* **tennis-elbows**) *nm* tennis elbow.

tennisman [tenisman] (*pl* **tennismans** *ou pl* **tennismen** [-men]) *nm* (male) tennis player.

tenon [tənɔ̃] *nm* TECHNOL tenon.

ténor [tenɔr] *nm* **1.** MUS tenor ▪ **fort ~** operatic tenor **2.** [vedette] big name ▪ **tous les grands ~s de la politique seront là** all the big political names will be there.

tenseur [tɑ̃sœr] ◇ *adj m* ANAT tensor.

◇ *nm* ANAT & MATH tensor.

tensiomètre [tɑ̃sjɔmɛtr] *nm* **1.** MÉCAN tensometer, tensiometer **2.** MÉD sphygmomanometer **3.** PHYS & TEXT tensiometer.

tension [tɑ̃sjɔ̃] *nf* **1.** [étirement] tension, tightness **2.** [état psychique] : **elle est dans un tel état de ~ qu'un rien la met en colère** she's so tense that the slightest thing makes her lose her temper ▶ **~ (nerveuse)** tension, strain, nervous stress **3.** [désaccord, conflit, difficulté] tension ▪ **des ~s au sein de la majorité** tension *ou* strained relationships within the majority **4.** ÉLECTR voltage, tension ▪ **basse ~** low voltage ▪ **'danger, haute ~'** 'beware, high voltage' **5.** MÉD : **avoir** *ou* **faire** *fam* **de la ~** to have high blood pressure ▪ **prendre la ~ de qqn** to check sb's blood pressure ▶ **~ artérielle** *ou* **vasculaire** blood pressure **6.** PHON tenseness **7.** PHYS [d'un liquide] tension ▪ [d'un gaz] pressure.

◆ **à basse tension** *loc adj* ÉLECTR low-voltage, low-tension.

◆ **à haute tension** *loc adj* ÉLECTR high-tension.

◆ **sous tension** ◇ *loc adj* **1.** ÉLECTR [fil] live ▪ **la télécommande s'utilise quand le récepteur est sous ~** use the remote control switch when the set is in standby mode **2.** [nerveux] tense, under stress.

◇ *loc adv* : **mettre un appareil sous ~** to switch on an appliance.

tentaculaire [tɑ̃takylɛr] *adj* **1.** ZOOL tentacular **2.** [ville] sprawling ▪ [industrie, structure] gigantic ▪ **une entreprise ~** a massive *ou* gigantic organization.

tentacule [tɑ̃takyl] *nm* ZOOL tentacle.

tentant, e [tɑ̃tɑ̃, ɑ̃t] *adj* [nourriture] tempting ▪ [projet, pari, idée] tempting ▪ [offre, suggestion] tempting, attractive ▪ **ce que tu me proposes est très ~** I'm very tempted by your offer.

tentateur, trice [tɑ̃tatœr, tris] ◇ *adj* [propos] tempting ▪ [sourire, charme] alluring.

◇ *nm, f* tempter ▪ **le Tentateur** RELIG the Tempter.

tentation [tɑ̃tasjɔ̃] *nf* **1.** [attrait, désir] temptation ▪ **céder** *ou* **succomber à la ~** to yield to temptation ▪ **avoir** *ou* **éprouver la ~ de faire** to be tempted to do **2.** RELIG : **induire qqn en ~** to lead sb into temptation *sout.*

tentative [tɑ̃tativ] *nf* **1.** [essai] attempt ▪ **faire une ~** to make an attempt ▪ **une ~ d'évasion** an escape attempt, an attempted escape ▪ **une ~ de suicide** a suicide attempt, an attempted suicide ▪ **faire une ~ de suicide** to try to commit suicide **2.** DR : **~ de meurtre** attempted murder.

tente [tɑ̃t] *nf* **1.** [de camping] tent ▪ [à une garden-party] marquee ▪ **monter une ~** to put up *ou* to pitch a tent ▪ **passer une semaine sous la ~** to go camping for a week ‖ [chapiteau de cirque] (circus) tent ▪ **la grande ~** the big top **2.** MÉD : **~ à oxygène** oxygen tent.

tenter [3] [tɑ̃te] *vt* **1.** [risquer, essayer] to try, to attempt ▪ **~ une expédition de secours** to mount a rescue attempt ▪ **~ une ascension difficile** to attempt a difficult climb ▪ **je vais tout ~ pour la convaincre** I'll try everything to convince her ▪ **~ de faire** [chercher à faire] to try *ou* to attempt *ou* to endeavour *sout* to do ▶ **~ le diable** to tempt fate ▪ **~ (la) fortune** *ou* **la chance** *ou* **le sort** to try one's luck **2.** [soumettre à une tentation] to tempt ▪ **le gâteau me tentait** the cake looked very tempting ▪ **une petite jupe noire m'avait tentée** my eye had been caught by a little black skirt ▪ **le mariage, cela ne te tente pas?** don't you ever feel like getting married? ▪ **se laisser ~** to give in to temptation ▪ **il te propose une sortie, laisse-toi ~** he's offering to take you out, why not accept? ▪ **être tenté de** to be tempted *ou* to feel inclined to.

tenture [tɑ̃tyr] *nf* **1.** [tapisserie] hanging ▪ **~ murale** wallcovering **2.** [rideaux] curtain, drape *US* **3.** [pour un service funèbre] funeral hanging.

tenu, e [təny] ◇ *pp* ▷ **tenir**.

◇ *adj* **1.** [soigné, propre] : **bien ~** tidy, well-kept ▪ **une maison mal ~e** an untidy *ou* a badly kept house ▪ **des enfants bien/mal ~s** well/poorly turned-out children ▪ **des comptes bien ~s** well-kept accounts **2.** [soumis à une stricte surveillance] : **les élèves sont très ~s** the pupils are kept on a tight rein **3.** BOURSE [actions] firm **4.** MUS sustained, held **5.** PHON tense.

◆ **tenu** *nm* SPORT play-the-ball.

ténu, e [teny] *adj* **1.** [mince - fil, pointe] fine, slender ; [- voix, air, brume] thin **2.** [subtil - raison, distinction] tenuous.

tenue [təny] *nf*

A.

1. [d'une séance, d'un rassemblement] : **ils ont interdit la ~ de la réunion dans nos locaux** they banned the meeting from being held on our premises
2. [gestion - d'une maison, d'un établissement] running ■ **l'école est réputée pour sa ~** the school is renowned for being well-run
3. AUTO : **~ de route** road holding ■ **avoir une bonne ~ de route** to hold the road well ■ **avoir une mauvaise ~ de route** to have poor road holding
4. BOURSE [fermeté] firmness ■ **la bonne/mauvaise ~ des valeurs** the strong/poor performance of the stock market
5. COMM : **~ des livres** bookkeeping
6. ÉQUIT [d'un cheval] stamina
7. MUS holding
8. PHON tenseness

B.

1. [attitude corporelle] posture, position
2. [comportement, conduite] behaviour ■ **manquer totalement de ~** to behave appallingly ■ **voyons, un peu de ~!** come now, behave yourself!
3. [aspect extérieur d'une personne] appearance ■ **ils exigent de leurs employés une ~ correcte** they require their employees to be smartly dressed
4. [habits - gén] clothes, outfit, dress ; [- de policier, de militaire, de pompier] uniform ■ **une ~ de sport** sports gear *ou* kit ■ **dans ma ~ de travail** in my work clothes ■ **'~ correcte exigée'** 'dress code' ➲ **~ de cérémonie, grande ~** full-dress *ou* dress uniform ■ **~ de soirée** evening dress
5. [rigueur intellectuelle] quality ■ **un magazine d'une haute ~** a quality magazine
6. ÉQUIT [d'un cavalier] seat
7. TEXT firmness.

◆ **en grande tenue** *loc adj* MIL in full dress *ou* dress uniform ■ **officiers en grande ~** officers in dress uniform.
◆ **en petite tenue** *loc adj* scantily dressed *ou* clad, in one's underwear ■ **se promener en petite ~** to walk around with hardly a stitch on.
◆ **en tenue** *loc adj* [militaire, policier] uniformed ■ **ce jour-là, je n'étais pas en ~** [militaire] I was in civilian clothes that day ; [policier] I was in plain clothes that day.
◆ **en tenue légère** = **en petite tenue**.

TEP (*abr de* **tomographie à émission de positrons**) *nf* MÉD PET.

tequila [tekila] *nf* tequila.

TER (*abr de* **transport express régional**) *nm French regional network of trains and coaches.*

ter [tɛr] *adv* **1.** [dans des numéros de rue] b **2.** [à répéter trois fois] three times.

tératogène [teratɔʒɛn] *adj* teratogenic.

tératologique [teratɔlɔʒik] *adj* teratological.

tercet [tɛrsɛ] *nm* tercet.

térébenthine [terebɑ̃tin] *nf* turpentine.

Tergal® [tɛrgal] *nm* Tergal® *(synthetic fibre made in France).*

tergiversation [tɛrʒiversasjɔ̃] *nf* prevarication ■ **cessez vos ~s** stop avoiding the issue *ou* beating about the bush.

tergiverser [3] [tɛrʒivɛrse] *vi* to prevaricate.

terme [tɛrm] *nm* **1.** [dans l'espace] end, term *sout* ■ **ils arrivèrent enfin au ~ de leur voyage** they finally reached the end of their journey
2. [dans le temps] end, term *sout* ■ **sa convalescence touche à son ~** his convalescence will soon be over ■ **parvenir à son ~** [aventure, relation] to reach its conclusion *ou* term *sout* ■ **la restructuration doit aller jusqu'à son ~** the restructuring must be carried through to its conclusion ■ **mettre un ~ à qqch** to put an end to sthg
3. [date-butoir] term, deadline ■ **passé ce ~, vous devrez payer des intérêts** after that date, interest becomes due
4. [échéance d'un loyer] date for payment of rent ■ [montant du loyer] rent ■ **l'augmentation prendra effet au ~ de janvier** the increase applies to rent paid as from January ■ **payer à ~ échu** to pay at the end of the rental period ■ **avoir plusieurs ~s de retard** to be several months behind (with one's rent)
5. [date d'un accouchement] : **le ~ est prévu pour le 16 juin** the baby is due on the 16th June ■ **elle a dépassé le ~** she is overdue
6. BANQUE & BOURSE term, date for payment
7. DR term ■ **~ de rigueur** latest due date ■ **~ de grâce** days of grace *sout*
8. [mot] term, word ■ **ce furent ses propres ~s** those were her very words ■ **en ~s simples** in plain *ou* simple terms ■ **puis, elle s'exprima en ces ~s** then she said this ■ **en d'autres ~s** in other words ■ **s'exprimer en ~s orduriers** to use filthy language ■ **parler de qqn en bons/mauvais ~s** to speak well/ill of sb ■ **~ technique** technical term ■ **~ argotique** slang expression ■ **~ de métier** professional *ou* technical term
9. ART, LOGIQUE & MATH term.

◆ **termes** *nmpl* **1.** [sens littéral d'un écrit] wording *(U)*, terms **2.** [relations] terms ■ **être en bons/mauvais ~s avec qqn** to be on good/bad terms with sb ■ **nous sommes en très bons ~s** we get along splendidly.
◆ **à court terme** ◇ *loc adj* [prêt, projet] short-term.
◇ *loc adv* in the short term *ou* run.
◆ **à long terme** ◇ *loc adj* [prêt, projet] long-term.
◇ *loc adv* in the long term *ou* run.
◆ **à terme** ◇ *loc adj* **1.** BANQUE : **compte à ~** *deposit account requiring notice for withdrawals* time deposit *US* ■ **compte à ~ de 30 jours** 30-days account ■ **assurance à ~** term insurance **2.** BOURSE : **opérations à ~** forward transactions ■ **marché à ~** forward market ; [change] futures market.
◇ *loc adv* **1.** [à la fin] to the end, to its conclusion ■ **arriver à ~** [délai] to expire ; [travail] to reach completion ; [paiement] to fall due ■ **conduire** *ou* **mener à ~ une entreprise** to bring an undertaking to a successful conclusion, to carry an undertaking through successfully
2. [tôt ou tard] sooner or later, in the end, in the long run
3. COMM [à la date prévue] on credit
4. FIN : **acheter à ~** to buy forward
5. MÉD at term ■ **bébé né à ~** baby born at full term.
◆ **au terme de** *loc prép* [à la fin de] at the end of, in the final stage of ■ **parvenir au ~ de son existence/aventure** to reach the end of one's life/adventure.
◆ **aux termes de** *loc prép* [selon] under the terms of ■ **aux ~s de la loi/du traité** under the terms of the law/of the treaty.
◆ **avant terme** *loc adv* prematurely ■ **bébé né avant ~** premature baby ■ **il est né six semaines avant ~** he was six weeks premature.

terminaison [tɛrminɛzɔ̃] *nf* **1.** ANAT : **~s nerveuses** nerve endings **2.** LING ending ■ **mot à ~ en "al"** word ending in "al".

terminal, e, aux [tɛrminal, o] *adj* **1.** [qui forme l'extrémité] terminal **2.** [final] last, final **3.** MÉD terminal **4.** ÉDUC : **classe ~e** final year *(in a lycée)*, ≃ (upper) sixth form *UK*, ≃ senior year *US*.
◆ **terminal, aux** *nm* **1.** INFORM terminal ■ **~ bancaire/industriel** bank/manufacturing terminal ■ **~ portable/vocal** portable/voice terminal ■ **~ graphique** graphic terminal, graphic display device ■ **~ intelligent** smart terminal, remote station ■ **~ lourd** high-speed terminal ■ **~ point de vente** point of sale terminal **2.** INDUST du pétrole : **~ pétrolier** oil terminal **3.** TRANSP terminal.
◆ **terminale** *nf* ÉDUC final year *(in a lycée)*, ≃ (upper) sixth form *UK*, ≃ senior year *US*.

terminer [3] [tɛrmine] *vt* **1.** [mener à sa fin - repas, tâche, lecture] to finish (off), to end ■ **c'est terminé, rendez vos copies** time's up, hand in your papers ■ *(en usage absolu)* **j'ai presque terminé** I've nearly finished ■ **pour ~, je remercie tous les participants** finally, let me thank all those who took part **2.** [stopper - séance, débat] to end, to close, to bring to an end *ou* a close **3.** [être le dernier élément de] to end ■ **le volume qui termine la série comprend un index** the last volume in the series includes an index ■ **un clip termine l'émission** the programme ends with a pop video **4.** [finir - plat, boisson] to finish (off), to eat up *(sép)*.

◆ **(en) terminer avec** *v+prép* to finish with ■ **je suis bien soulagé d'en avoir terminé avec cette affaire** I'm really glad to have seen the end of this business.

◆ **se terminer** *vpi* **1.** [arriver à sa fin - durée, période, saison] to draw to a close ■ **la chanson/guerre vient de se ~** the song/war has just finished ■ **heureusement que ça se termine, j'ai hâte de retrouver ma maison** thank God the end is in sight, I can't wait to get back home **2.** [se conclure] : **se ~ bien/mal** [film, histoire] to have a happy/an unhappy ending ; [équipée, menée] to turn out well/disastrously ■ **comment tout cela va-t-il se ~?** where's it all going to end? ■ **leur aventure s'est terminée au poste** the adventure wound up with them down at the (police) station ■ **ça s'est terminé en drame** it ended in a tragedy ■ **se ~ par** to end in ■ **l'histoire se termine par la mort du héros** the story ends with the death of the hero.

terminologie [tɛrminɔlɔʒi] *nf* terminology.

terminus [tɛrminys] *nm* terminus ■ **~! tout le monde descend!** last stop! all change!

termite [tɛrmit] *nm* termite.

termitière [tɛrmitjɛr] *nf* termite mound, termitarium *spéc.*

ternaire [tɛrnɛr] *adj* ternary.

terne [tɛrn] *adj* **1.** [sans éclat - cheveux, regard] dull ■ [teint] sallow ■ **les dorures sont devenues ~s avec le temps** the gilt has become tarnished over the years ■ **mes cheveux sont ~s en ce moment** my hair's lost it's shine **2.** [ennuyeux] dull, dreary **3.** [inintéressant] dull ■ **un élève ~** a slow pupil.

ternir [32] [tɛrnir] *vt* **1.** [métal, argenterie] to tarnish ■ [glace] to dull **2.** [honneur, réputation] to tarnish, to stain, to smear ■ [souvenir, beauté] to cloud, to dull ■ **un amour que les ans n'ont pu ~** a love undimmed by the passing years.

◆ **se ternir** *vpi* **1.** [métal] to tarnish ■ [miroir] to dull ■ **l'argenterie se ternit si on ne l'entretient pas** silverware loses its shine *OU* becomes tarnished unless it is regularly cleaned **2.** [honneur, réputation] to become tarnished *OU* stained ■ [beauté, nouveauté] to fade ■ [souvenir] to fade, to grow dim.

ternissement [tɛrnismɑ̃] *nm* [d'un métal] tarnishing ■ [d'une glace] dulling.

ternissure [tɛrnisyr] *nf* **1.** [condition] tarnish, tarnished appearance **2.** [tache] tarnished *OU* dull spot.

terrain [tɛrɛ̃] *nm*

A. SOL, TERRE
B. LIEU À USAGE SPÉCIFIQUE
C. SENS ABSTRAIT

A. SOL, TERRE

1. GÉOL soil, ground ■ **~s calcaires** limestone soil *OU* areas ■ **~ sédimentaire/volcanique** sedimentary/volcanic formations
2. AGRIC soil
3. [relief] ground, terrain ■ **~ accidenté** uneven terrain ■ **~ en pente** sloping ground

B. LIEU À USAGE SPÉCIFIQUE

1. CONSTR piece *OU* plot of land ■ **le ~ coûte cher à Genève** land is expensive in Geneva ➊ **~ à bâtir** development land *(U)*, building plot ■ **~ loti** developed site
2. AGRIC land ■ **~ cultivé/en friche** cultivated/uncultivated land
3. LOISIRS & SPORT [lieu du jeu] field, pitch *UK* ■ [moitié défendue par une équipe] half ■ [installations] ground ■ **~ de football/rugby** football/rugby pitch *UK OU* field ■ **notre correspondant sur le ~** SPORT our correspondent on the spot ■ **~ de golf** golf course *OU* links ➊ **~ d'aventure** adventure playground ■ **~ de boules** *ground for playing boules* ■ **~ de camping** campsite ■ **~ de jeux** playground ■ **~ de sports** sports field *OU* ground
4. AÉRON field ■ **~ (d'aviation)** airfield ■ **~ d'atterrissage** landing field
5. MIL ground ■ **~ d'exercice** *OU* **militaire** training ground ■ **~ miné** minefield ■ *(toujours sing)* [d'une bataille] battleground ■ [d'une guerre] war *OU* combat zone ■ **l'armée occupe le ~ conquis** the army is occupying the captured territory ■ **la prochaine offensive nous permettra de gagner du ~** the next offensive will enable us to gain ground
6. [lieu d'un duel] duelling place

C. SENS ABSTRAIT

1. [lieux d'étude] field ■ **les jeunes députés n'hésitent pas à aller sur le ~** young MPs are always ready to go out and meet people ➊ **un homme de ~** a man with practical experience
2. [domaine de connaissances] : **être sur son ~** to be on familiar ground *fig* ■ **ils discutent de chiffres et je ne peux pas les suivre sur ce ~** they're discussing figures, so I'm out of my depth ■ **situons la discussion sur le ~ juridique/psychologique** let's discuss this from the legal/psychological angle
3. [ensemble de circonstances] : **il a trouvé là un ~ favorable à ses idées** he found there a breeding ground for his ideas ■ **elle connaît le ~, laissons-la décider** she knows the situation, let her decide ■ **sonde le ~ avant d'agir** see how the land lies before making a move ■ **être en ~ neutre/sur un ~ glissant** to be on neutral/on a dangerous ground ■ **être sur un ~ mouvant** to be on shaky ground ■ **trouver un ~ d'entente** to find common ground
4. MÉD ground ■ **l'enfant présente un ~ favorable aux angines** the child is susceptible to throat infections ■ **quand le virus trouve un ~ favorable** when the virus finds its ideal breeding conditions.

◆ **terrain vague** *nm* piece of waste ground *OU* land, empty lot *US.*

terrassant, e [tɛrasɑ̃, ɑ̃t] *adj* **1.** [nouvelle, révélation] staggering, stunning, crushing **2.** [coup] staggering, crushing.

terrasse [tɛras] *nf* **1.** [grand balcon] balcony ■ [entre maison et jardin] terrace, patio ■ [sur le toit] (roof) terrace **2.** [d'un café, d'un restaurant] : **être assis à la ~** to sit outside ■ **elle attendait à la ~ d'un café** she was waiting at a table outside a café **3.** [d'un jardin, d'un parc] terrace, terraced garden.

◆ **en terrasse** ◇ *loc adj* : **cultures en ~** terrace cultivation ■ **rizières en ~** terraced rice fields.
◇ *loc adv* : **nous prendrons le café en ~** we'll have our coffee at one of the outside tables.

terrassement [tɛrasmɑ̃] *nm* TRAV PUB excavation, excavation work, earthworks.

◆ **de terrassement** *loc adj* [travail] excavation *(modif)* ■ [engin] earth-moving ■ [outil] digging.

terrasser [3] [tɛrase] *vt* **1.** [jeter à terre, renverser] to bring *OU* to strike down *(sép)* **2.** [foudroyer] to strike down *(sép)* ■ **être terrassé par une crise cardiaque** to be struck down by a heart attack **3.** [atterrer, accabler] to crush, to shatter ■ **l'annonce de leur mort l'a terrassé** he was shattered by the news of their death **4.** TRAV PUB to excavate, to dig.

terrassier [tɛrasje] *nm* workman *(employed for excavation work).*

terre [tɛr] *nf*

A. GLOBE
B. SOL
C. MATIÈRE

A. GLOBE

1. [planète] : **la Terre** the Earth ➊ **sciences de la Terre** earth sciences
2. [monde terrestre] earth ■ **le bonheur existe-t-il sur la ~?** is there such a thing as happiness on this earth *OU* in this world? ■ **si je suis encore sur cette ~** if I am still alive

B. SOL

1. [surface du sol] ground ■ **elle souleva l'enfant de ~** she picked the child up (from the ground) ➊ **~ battue** [dans une habitation] earth *OU* hard-earth *OU* mud floor ; [dans une cour] bare ground ; [sur un court de tennis] clay (surface) ■ **mettre qqn plus bas que ~** [en actes] to treat sb like dirt ; [en paroles] to tear sb to shreds
2. [élément opposé à la mer] land *(U)* ■ **on les transporte par voie de ~** they are transported overland *OU* by land ■ **nous sommes en vue de la ~** we are in sight of land ■ **nous avons navigué sans nous éloigner des ~s** we sailed close to the coast ■ **~!** NAUT land ahoy! ■ **prendre ~** to make land ➊ **sur la ~ ferme** on dry land, on terra firma
3. [région du monde] land ■ **les ~s arctiques** the Arctic regions ■ **il reste des ~s inexplorées** there are still some unexplored regions

4. [pays] land, country ■ **la ~ de France** French soil ▶ **(la) ~ Adélie** Adelie Land ■ **(la) ~ de Baffin** Baffin Island ■ **~ d'accueil** host country ■ **~ d'exil** place of exile ■ **~ natale** native land *ou* country ■ **la Terre promise** the Promised Land ■ **la Terre sainte** the Holy Land
5. [terrain] land *(U)*, estate ■ **acheter une ~** to buy a piece of land
6. [symbole de la vie rurale] **: la ~** the land, the soil ■ **homme de la ~** man of the soil ■ **revenir à/quitter la ~** to return to/to leave the land
7. ÉLECTR earth *UK*, ground *US* ■ **mettre** *ou* **relier qqch à la ~** to earth *UK ou* to ground *US* sthg

C. MATIÈRE

1. [substance - gén] earth, soil ■ **ne joue pas avec la ~** don't play in the dirt ■ **mettre** *ou* **porter qqn en ~** to bury sb ■ AGRIC earth, soil ■ **~ à vigne/à blé** soil suitable for wine-growing/for wheat ■ **~ arable** farmland ■ **~ de bruyère** peaty soil ■ **~ grasse** heavy *ou* clayey soil
2. [matière première] clay, earth ■ **~ glaise** (brick) clay, brick-earth *UK* ■ **~ cuite** earthenware ■ **en ~ cuite** earthenware *(modif)*
3. [pigment] **: ~ de Sienne** sienna ■ **~ d'ombre** terra ombra, raw umber.
◆ **terres** *nfpl* [domaine, propriété] estate, estates ■ **vivre sur/de ses ~s** to live on/off one's estates.
◆ **à terre** *loc adv* **1.** [sur le sol] on the ground ■ **frapper qqn à ~** to strike sb when he's down **2.** NAUT on land ■ **descendre à ~** to land ■ **vous pourrez rester à ~ deux heures** you may stay ashore for two hours.
◆ **en pleine terre** *loc adv* AGRIC in the open, in open ground.
◆ **par terre** ◇ *loc adj* [ruiné, anéanti] spoilt, wrecked ■ **avec la pluie, notre promenade est par ~** the rain has put paid to our walk *UK ou* ruined our plans for a walk.
◇ *loc adv* [sur le plancher] on the floor ■ [sur le sol] on the ground ■ **tomber par ~** to fall down ■ **j'ai lavé par ~** *fam* I've washed the floor.
◆ **sous terre** *loc adv* **1.** [sous le sol] underground ■ **ils durent établir des abris sous ~** they had to build shelters underground *ou* underground shelters **2.** *loc* **j'aurais voulu être à cent pieds sous ~** *ou* **rentrer sous ~** I wished the earth would swallow me up.
◆ **sur terre** *loc adv* **1.** [ici-bas] on (this) earth **2.** *loc* **revenir** *ou* **redescendre sur ~** to come back to earth (with a bump).

terre à terre [tɛratɛr] *loc adj inv* [esprit, personne] down-to-earth, matter-of-fact ■ [pensée, occupation, vie] mundane.

terreau, x [tɛro] *nm* compost *(U)* ■ **~ de feuilles** leaf mould.

Terre de Feu [tɛrdəfø] *npr f* **: (la) ~** Tierra del Fuego ■ **en ~** in Tierra del Fuego.

terre-neuvas [tɛrnœva] *nm inv* **1.** [navire] fishing boat (off Newfoundland) **2.** [marin] fisherman (off Newfoundland).

terre-neuve [tɛrnœv] *nm inv* **1.** ZOOL Newfoundland terrier **2.** [personne dévouée] **: avoir une mentalité de ~** to be a Good Samaritan.

Terre-Neuve [tɛrnœv] *npr* Newfoundland ■ **à ~** in Newfoundland.

terre-plein [tɛrplɛ̃] *(pl* **terre-pleins**) *nm* **1.** [sur route] **: ~ central** central reservation *UK*, center divider strip *US* **2.** CONSTR backing, (relieving) platform **3.** MIL terreplein.

terrer [4] [tere] *vt* **1.** AGRIC & HORT [arbre, plante] to earth up *(sép)* ■ [recouvrir de terre] to cover over with soil ■ [semis] to earth over *(sép)* **2.** TEXT to full.
◆ **se terrer** *vpi* **1.** [se mettre à l'abri, se cacher] to go to ground *ou* to earth, to lie low ■ [se retirer du monde] to hide away **2.** [dans un terrier] to go to ground *ou* to earth, to burrow.

terrestre [tɛrɛstr] *adj* **1.** [qui appartient à notre planète] earth *(modif)*, earthly, terrestrial ■ **la croûte** *ou* **l'écorce ~** the Earth's crust ■ **le globe ~** the terrestrial globe **2.** [qui se passe sur la terre] earthly, terrestrial ■ **durant notre vie ~** during our life on earth **3.** [vivant sur la terre ferme] land *(modif)* ■ **animaux/plantes ~s** land animals/plants **4.** [établi au sol - transport] land *(modif)* **5.** [d'ici-bas - joie, plaisir] worldly, earthly.

terreur [tɛrœr] *nf* **1.** [effroi] terror, dread ■ **vivre dans la ~ de** to live in dread of ■ **avoir la ~ de faire qqch** to have a terror of doing sthg **2.** [terrorisme] **: la ~** terror (tactics) ■ **la Terreur** HIST the (Reign of) Terror **3.** [voyou] **: jouer les ~s** to act the bully **4.** [personne ou chose effrayante] **: le patron est sa ~** she's terrified of the boss ■ **le bac est sa ~** the baccalaureat exam is her greatest fear.

terreux, euse [tɛrø, øz] *adj* **1.** [couvert de terre - chaussure, vêtement] muddy ; [- mains] dirty ; [- légume] caked with soil **2.** [brun - couleur, teint] muddy ■ **avoir le visage ~** to be ashen faced **3.** [qui rappelle la terre - odeur, goût] earthy.

terrible [tɛribl] ◇ *adj* **1.** [affreux - nouvelle, accident, catastrophe] terrible, dreadful **2.** [insupportable - chaleur, douleur] terrible, unbearable ; [- déception, conditions de vie] terrible **3.** [en intensif - bruit, vent, orage] terrific, tremendous ■ **elle a eu une chance ~** she's been incredibly lucky **4.** [terrifiant - colère, cri, rage] terrible **5.** [pitoyable] terrible, awful, dreadful ■ **ce qui est ~, c'est de dire que...** the terrible thing about it is saying that... ■ **le plus ~, c'est de savoir que...** the worst thing *ou* part of it is knowing that... **6.** *fam* [fantastique] terrific, great ■ **son concert? pas ~!** her concert? it was nothing to write home about!
◇ *adv fam* [très bien] great.

terriblement [tɛribləmɑ̃] *adv* terribly, dreadfully.

terrien, enne [tɛrjɛ̃, ɛn] ◇ *adj* **1.** [qui possède des terres] landowning ■ **noblesse ~ne** landed aristocracy ■ **propriétaire ~** landowner **2.** [rural] rural.
◇ *nm, f* **1.** [habitant de la Terre] inhabitant of the Earth ■ [dans un récit de science-fiction] earthling **2.** [paysan] countryman **3.** [opposé au marin] landsman, landlubber *péj.*

terrier [tɛrje] *nm* **1.** [abri - d'un lapin] (rabbit) hole *ou* burrow ; [- d'un renard] earth, hole, foxhole ; [- d'un blaireau] set **2.** [chien] terrier.

terrifiant, e [tɛrifjɑ̃, ɑ̃t] *adj* **1.** [effrayant] terrifying **2.** *fam* [extraordinaire] amazing ■ **c'est ~ ce qu'il a grandi en quelques mois!** it's amazing how much he's grown in just a few months!

terrifier [9] [tɛrifje] *vt* to terrify ■ **absolument terrifié** absolutely terrified.

terril [tɛril] *nm* slag heap.

terrine [tɛrin] *nf* **1.** [récipient] terrine dish **2.** CULIN terrine ■ **~ de lapin** rabbit terrine *ou* pâté.

territoire [tɛritwar] *nm* **1.** GÉOGR territory ■ **sur le ~ français** on French territory ■ **en ~ ennemi** in enemy territory ■ **les ~s occupés** POLIT the occupied territories **2.** ADMIN area ■ **~s d'outre-mer** (French) overseas territories **3.** DR jurisdiction **4.** ZOOL territory ■ **marquer son ~** [animal] to mark its territory ; *fig* to mark one's territory **5.** [secteur, fief] territory ■ **sa chambre, c'est son ~** his room is his kingdom ■ **défendre son ~** to defend one's patch.

territorial, e, aux [tɛritɔrjal, o] *adj* territorial.
◆ **territorial, aux** *nm* territorial.
◆ **territoriale** *nf* territorial army.

territorialité [tɛritɔrjalite] *nf* DR territoriality ■ **~ des lois/de l'impôt** *laws/tax regulations applying to people in a given territory.*

terroir [tɛrwar] *nm* **1.** [région agricole] region ■ **le ~ de la Beauce** the Beauce region **2.** [campagne, ruralité] country ■ **il a gardé l'accent du ~** he has retained his rural accent ■ **c'est un écrivain du ~** he's a regional author ■ **avoir un goût de ~** *fig* to be evocative *ou* redolent of the soil.

terroriser [3] [tɛrɔrize] *vt* **1.** [martyriser] to terrorize **2.** [épouvanter] to terrify ■ **l'idée de la mort la terrorise** the idea of death terrifies her.

terrorisme [tɛrɔrism] *nm* terrorism.

terroriste [tɛrɔrist] *adj* & *nmf* terrorist.

tertiaire [tɛrsjɛr] ◇ *adj* **1.** CHIM & MÉD tertiary ■ GÉOL **: ère ~** Tertiary era **2.** ADMIN & ÉCON **: secteur ~** tertiary sector, service industries.
◇ *nm* **1.** GÉOL **: le ~** the Tertiary era **2.** ADMIN & ÉCON **: le ~** the tertiary sector.

tertiairisation [tɛrsjɛrizasjɔ̃], **tertiarisation** [tɛrsjarizasjɔ̃] *nf* expansion of the tertiary sector.

tertio [tɛrsjo] *adv* third, thirdly ▪ **~, je n'ai pas le temps** thirdly, I haven't got time.

tertre [tɛrtr] *nm* **1.** [monticule] hillock, mound **2.** [sépulture] : **~ (funéraire)** burial mound.

tes [te] *pl* ▷ **ton** *(adj poss)*.

Tessin [tɛsɛ̃] *npr m* **1.** [rivière] : **le ~** the (River) Ticino **2.** [canton] : **le ~** Ticino.

tessiture [tɛsityr] *nf* tessitura.

tesson [tɛsɔ̃] *nm* [de verre, de poterie] fragment ▪ **un mur hérissé de ~s de bouteille** a wall with broken glass all along the top.

test [tɛst] *nm* **1.** [essai, vérification] test ▪ **soumettre qqn à un ~, faire passer un ~ à qqn** to give sb a test ▶ **~ d'aptitude** aptitude test ▪ **~ du lendemain** [en publicité] day after recall **2.** INFORM test ▪ **~ automatique** automatic testing **3.** MÉD test ▪ **~ de grossesse** pregnancy test ▪ **~ allergologique** allergy test ▪ **~ cutané** cutaneous reaction test ▪ **~ de dépistage du SIDA** AIDS test **4.** PSYCHOL test ▪ **~ projectif** projective test **5.** *(comme adj; avec ou sans trait d'union)* test *(modif)* ▪ **population ~** test population ▪ **région ~** test region **6.** SPORT [test-match] (rugby) test (match) **7.** ZOOL test.

testament [tɛstamɑ̃] *nm* DR will, testament ▪ **faire son ~** to make one's will ▪ **ceci est mon ~** this is my last will and testament ▪ **il peut faire son ~!** *fam fig* he'd better make (out) his will! ▶ **~ authentique** *ou* **public** executed will.

testamentaire [tɛstamɑ̃tɛr] *adj* testamental.

testateur, trice [tɛstatœr, tris] *nm, f* testator.

tester [3] [tɛste] ◇ *vt* **1.** [déterminer les aptitudes de - élèves] to test **2.** [vérifier le fonctionnement de - appareil, produit] to test **3.** [mettre à l'épreuve] to put to the test ▪ **elle a voulu ~ ma loyauté/sa collègue** she wanted to put my loyalty/her colleague to the test.
◇ *vi* DR to make out one's will.

testeur [tɛstœr] *nm* [personne, machine] tester.

testicule [tɛstikyl] *nm* testicle, testis *spéc.*

testimonial, e, aux [tɛstimɔnjal, o] *adj* testimonial.

test-match [tɛstmatʃ] (*pl* **test-match(e)s**) *nm* (rugby) test (match).

testostérone [tɛstɔsterɔn] *nf* testosterone.

tétanie [tetani] *nf* tetany.

tétanique [tetanik] ◇ *adj* tetanic ▪ **bacille ~** tetanus bacillus.
◇ *nmf* tetanus sufferer.

tétanisation [tetanizasjɔ̃] *nf* tetanization.

tétaniser [3] [tetanize] *vt* **1.** MÉD to tetanize **2.** [paralyser - de peur] to petrify ; [- d'étonnement] to stun ▪ **la fureur de leur père les avait tétanisés** they were stunned by their father's anger.

tétanos [tetanos] *nm* lockjaw, tetanus *spéc.*

têtard [tɛtar] *nm* ZOOL tadpole.

tête [tɛt] *nf*

> **A.** PARTIE DU CORPS
> **B.** SIÈGE DE LA PENSÉE
> **C.** PERSONNE, ANIMAL
> **D.** PARTIE HAUTE, PARTIE AVANT, DÉBUT

A. PARTIE DU CORPS

1. ANAT head ▪ **la ~ haute** with (one's) head held high ▪ **la ~ la première** head first ▪ **de la ~ aux pieds** from head to foot *ou* toe ▪ **avoir mal à la ~** to have a headache ▪ **avoir la ~ lourde** to have a thick head *UK*, to feel fuzzy ▪ **j'ai la ~ qui tourne** [malaise] my head is spinning ▪ **ne tourne pas la ~, elle nous regarde** don't look round, she's watching us ▪ **dès qu'il m'a vu, il a tourné la ~** as soon as he saw me, he looked away ▶ **en avoir par-dessus la ~** *fam* to be sick (and tired) of it ▪ **avoir la ~ sur les épaules** to have a good head on one's shoulders ▪ **faire une grosse ~** *fam ou* **la ~ au carré** *fam* **à qqn** to smash sb's head *ou* face in ▪ **j'en donnerais** *ou* **j'en mettrais ma ~ à couper** I'd stake my life on it ▪ **être tombé sur la ~** *fam* to have a screw loose ▪ **il ne réfléchit jamais, il fonce ~ baissée** he always charges in *ou* ahead without thinking ▪ **se cogner** *ou* **se taper la ~ contre les murs** to bang one's head against a (brick) wall ▪ **se jeter à la ~ de qqn** to throw o.s. at sb

2. [en référence à la chevelure, à la coiffure] : **se laver la ~** to wash one's hair ▪ **~ nue** bareheaded ▶ **nos chères ~s blondes** [les enfants] our little darlings

3. [visage, expression] face ▪ **avoir une bonne ~** to look like a nice person ▪ **ne fais pas cette ~!** don't pull *UK ou* make such a long face! ▪ **il a fait une de ces ~s quand je lui ai dit!** you should have seen his face when I told him! ▪ **elle n'a pas une ~ à se laisser faire** she doesn't look the sort to be pushed around ▶ **il a** *ou* **c'est une ~ à claques** *fam* you just want to smack him in the mouth ▪ **~ de nœud**▲ dickhead▲ ▪ **faire la ~** to sulk ▪ **faire la ~ à qqn** to ignore sb ▪ **avec lui, c'est à la ~ du client** [restaurant] he charges what he feels like ; [professeur] he gives you a good mark if he likes your face

4. [mesure] head ▪ **il a une ~ de plus que son frère** he's a head taller than his brother

5. CULIN head ▪ **~ pressée** *Belgique* [fromage de tête] pork brawn *UK*, headcheese *US*

6. SPORT header

B. SIÈGE DE LA PENSÉE

1. [siège des pensées, de l'imagination, de la mémoire] mind, head ▪ **il a des rêves plein la ~** he's a dreamer ▪ **une drôle d'idée m'est passée par la ~** I had a strange idea ▪ **se mettre dans la ~ que** to get it into one's head that ▪ **se mettre dans la ~** *ou* **en ~ de faire qqch** to make up one's mind to do sthg ▶ **une ~ bien faite** *Montaigne allus* a good mind ▪ **avoir la grosse ~** *fam* to be big-headed ▪ **avoir toute sa ~** to have all one's faculties ▪ **faire sa mauvaise ~** to dig one's heels in ▪ **avoir la ~ chaude, avoir la ~ près du bonnet** to be quick-tempered ▪ **monter la ~ à qqn** to give sb (big) ideas ▪ **monter à la ~ de qqn** [succès] to go to sb's head ; [chagrin] to unbalance sb ▪ **se monter la ~** to get carried away ▪ **tourner la ~ à qqn** to turn sb's head ▪ **avoir la ~ vide/dure** to be empty-headed/stubborn ▪ **il est ~ en l'air** he's got his head in the clouds ▪ **excuse-moi, j'avais la ~ ailleurs** sorry, I was thinking about something else *ou* I was miles away ▪ **il n'a pas de ~** [il est étourdi] he is scatterbrained *ou* a scatterbrain ▪ **ça m'est sorti de la ~** I forgot, it slipped my mind ▪ **il ne sait plus où donner de la ~** he doesn't know whether he's coming or going ▪ **n'en faire qu'à sa ~** to do exactly as one pleases ▪ **je le lirai à ~ reposée** I'll take the time to read it in a quiet moment

2. [sang-froid, présence d'esprit] head ▪ **avoir** *ou* **garder la ~ froide** to keep a cool head

C. PERSONNE, ANIMAL

1. [individu] person ▪ **plusieurs ~s connues** several familiar faces ▪ **prendre une assurance sur la ~ de qqn** to take out an insurance policy on sb ▶ **être une ~ de lard** *ou* **de mule** to be as stubborn as a mule, to be pig-headed ▪ **~ de linotte** *ou* **d'oiseau** *ou* **sans cervelle** scatterbrain ▪ **~ de cochon** bloody-minded individual ▪ **~ couronnée** crowned head ▪ **forte ~** rebel ▪ **une grosse ~** *fam* a brain ▪ **petite ~** *fam* pinhead ▪ **avoir ses ~s** *fam* to have one's favourites

2. [vie d'une personne] head, neck ▪ **le procureur réclame la ~ de l'accusé** the prosecution is demanding the prisoner's execution ▶ **jouer** *ou* **risquer sa ~** to risk one's skin ▪ **sauver sa ~** to save one's skin *ou* neck

3. [meneur, leader] head, leader ▶ **les ~s pensantes du comité** the brains of the committee

4. [animal d'un troupeau] head *(inv)*

D. PARTIE HAUTE, PARTIE AVANT, DÉBUT

1. [faîte] top ▪ **la ~ d'un arbre** a treetop

2. [partie avant] front end ▪ **la ~ du train** the front of the train ▪ **~ de lit** bedhead ▪ **mets la ~ du lit vers le nord** turn the head of the bed towards the north ▪ **prendre la ~ du défilé** to head *ou* to lead the procession ▪ **prendre la ~** [marcher au premier rang] to take the lead ; [commander, diriger] to take over ▶ **~ de ligne** [gén] terminus, end of the line ; RAIL railhead

3. [début] : **faites ressortir les ~s de chapitres** make the chapter headings stand out

4. [dans un classement] top, head ▪ **les dix élèves qui forment la ~ de la classe** the ten best pupils in the class ◗ **~ d'affiche** top of the bill ▪ **~ de série** SPORT seeded player ▪ **~ de série numéro huit** number eight seed
5. [extrémité - d'un objet, d'un organe] head ; [- d'un os] head, caput ◗ **~ d'ail** head of garlic ▪ **~ de bielle** big end ▪ **~ d'épingle** pinhead ▪ **gros comme une ~ d'épingle** the size of a pinhead
6. ACOUST head ▪ **~ d'effacement** erase head ▪ **~ de lecture** head
7. IMPR head, top
8. INFORM head
9. MIL head ▪ **~ de pont** [sur rivière] bridgehead ; [sur plage] beachhead
10. NUCL head ▪ **~ chercheuse** homing device ▪ **~ nucléaire** nuclear warhead.

◆ **à la tête de** *loc prép* **1.** [en possession de] : **elle s'est trouvée à la ~ d'une grosse fortune** she found herself in possession of a great fortune **2.** [au premier rang de] at the head *ou* front of ▪ **à la ~ d'un groupe de mécontents** heading a group of protesters **3.** [à la direction de] in charge of, at the head of ▪ **être à la ~ d'une société** to head a company ▪ **il est à la ~ d'un cabinet d'assurances** he runs an insurance firm.

◆ **de tête** ◇ *loc adj* **1.** [femme, homme] able **2.** [convoi, voiture] front *(avant n)* **3.** IMPR head *(modif)*.
◇ *loc adv* [calculer] in one's head ▪ **de ~, je dirais que nous étions vingt** at a guess I'd say there were twenty of us.

◆ **en tête** *loc adv* **1.** [devant] : **monter en ~** to go to the front ▪ **être en ~** [gén] to be at the front ; [dans une course, une compétition] to (be in the) lead **2.** [à l'esprit] : **avoir qqch en ~** to have sthg in mind ▪ **je ne l'ai plus en ~** I can't remember it.

◆ **en tête à tête** *loc adv* alone together ▪ **dîner en ~ à ~ avec qqn** to have a quiet dinner (alone) with sb.

◆ **en tête de** *loc prép* **1.** [au début de] at the beginning *ou* start of ▪ **tous les mots placés en ~ de phrase** the first word of every sentence **2.** [à l'avant de] at the head *ou* front of ▪ **les dirigeants syndicaux marchent en ~ du défilé** the union leaders are marching at the head of the procession **3.** [au premier rang de] at the top of ▪ **en ~ des sondages** leading the polls.

◆ **par tête** *loc adv* per head, a head, apiece ▪ **ça coûtera 40 euros par ~** it'll cost 40 euros a head *ou* per head *ou* apiece.

◆ **par tête de pipe** *fam* = **par tête.**

◆ **sur la tête de** *loc prép* **1.** [sur la personne de] : **le mécontentement populaire s'est répercuté sur la ~ du Premier ministre** popular discontent turned towards the Prime Minister **2.** [au nom de] in the name of **3.** [en prêtant serment] : **je le jure sur la ~ de mes enfants** I swear on my mother's grave.

◆ **tête brûlée** *nf* hothead.

◆ **tête de mort** *nf* **1.** [crâne] skull **2.** [emblème] death's head, skull and crossbones.

◆ **tête de nègre** = **tête-de-nègre** *(nf)*.

◆ **tête de Turc** *nf* whipping boy, scapegoat.

tête-à-queue [tɛtakø] *nm inv* (180°) spin ▪ **faire un ~** to spin round, to spin 180°.

tête-à-tête [tɛtatɛt] *nm inv* **1.** [réunion] tête-à-tête, private talk ▪ **avoir un ~ avec qqn** to have a tête-à-tête with sb **2.** [sofa] tête-à-tête, vis-à-vis **3.** [service - à thé] tea set for two ; [- à café] coffee set for two.

tête-bêche [tɛtbɛʃ] ◇ *adv* [lits, personnes] head to foot *ou* to tail.
◇ *nm inv* tête-bêche stamp.

tête-de-loup [tɛtdəlu] (*pl* **têtes-de-loup**) *nf* ceiling brush.

tête-de-nègre [tɛtdənɛgr] (*pl* **têtes-de-nègre**) ◇ *adj inv* dark brown, chocolate-brown.
◇ *nm inv* [couleur] dark brown.
◇ *nf* **1.** CULIN chocolate-coated meringue **2.** BOT Boletus - aereus.

tétée [tete] *nf* **1.** [action de téter] feeding, breast-feeding **2.** [repas] feed *UK*, feeding *US* ▪ **l'heure de la ~** feeding time *UK*, nursing time *US*.

téter [8] [tete] *vt* **1.** [sein, biberon] to suck (at) ▪ **~ sa mère** to suck (at) one's mother's breast, to feed *ou* to breast-feed from one's mother ▪ *(en usage absolu)* **il tète encore** he's still being breast-fed, he's still suckling *ou US* nursing **2.** [crayon] to suck on ▪ [pouce] to suck.

têtière [tɛtjɛr] *nf* **1.** [d'un fauteuil, d'un sofa] antimacassar **2.** NAUT [d'une voile] head.

tétine [tetin] *nf* **1.** ZOOL [mamelle] teat **2.** [d'un biberon] teat *UK*, nipple *US* ▪ [sucette] dummy *UK*, pacifier *US*.

téton [tetɔ̃] *nm* **1.** *fam* [sein] tit△ **2.** MÉCAN stud, nipple.

tétrachlorure [tetraklɔryr] *nm* tetrachloride ▪ **~ de carbone** carbon tetrachloride.

tétraèdre [tetraɛdr] *nm* tetrahedron.

tétralogie [tetralɔʒi] *nf* tetralogy ▪ **'la Tétralogie'** *Wagner* '(The) Ring Cycle'.

tétraplégie [tetrapleʒi] *nf* quadriplegia, tetraplegia.

tétraplégique [tetrapleʒik] ◇ *adj* quadriplegic, tetraplegic.
◇ *nmf* quadriplegic.

tétrapode [tetrapɔd] ◇ *adj* tetrapod.
◇ *nm* ZOOL tetrapod.

tétras [tetra] *nm* grouse ▪ **grand ~** capercaillie.

tétrasyllabe [tetrasilab] ◇ *adj* tetrasyllabic.
◇ *nm* tetrasyllable.

têtu, e [tety] *adj* stubborn, obstinate ▪ **~ comme une mule** *ou* **un âne** *ou* **une bourrique** stubborn as a mule.

teuf [tœf] *fam nf* party, rave.

teuf-teuf [tœftœf] (*pl* **teufs-teufs**) *fam* ◇ *nm* [train] choo-choo train.
◇ *nm & nf* [vieille voiture] old banger *esp UK*, jalopy.
◇ *onomat* [bruit du train] puff-puff, choo-choo.

teuton, onne [tøtɔ̃, ɔn] *adj* Teutonic.
◆ **Teuton, onne** *nm, f* **1.** HIST Teuton **2.** *péj* [Allemand] Jerry *injur*.

teutonique [tøtɔnik] *adj* Teutonic ▪ **les chevaliers ~s** the Teutonic knights.

texan, e [tɛksɑ̃, an] *adj* Texan.
◆ **Texan, e** *nm, f* Texan.

Texas [tɛksas] *npr m* : **le ~** Texas ▪ **au ~** in Texas.

texte [tɛkst] *nm* **1.** [écrit] text ▪ **reportez-vous au ~ original** consult the original ▪ **commenter/résumer un ~** to do a commentary on/to do a précis of a text **2.** [œuvre littéraire] text ▪ **les grands ~s classiques** the great classical texts *ou* works ❙ [extrait d'une œuvre] passage ▪ **~s choisis** selected passages **3.** MUS [paroles d'une chanson] lyrics ▪ CINÉ & THÉÂTRE lines **4.** DR [teneur d'une loi, d'un traité] text, terms, wording ▪ [la loi elle-même] law, act ▪ [le traité lui-même] treaty ▪ **selon le ~ de la loi/du traité** according to the terms of the law/treaty ▪ **le ~ est paru au Journal officiel** the act was published in the official gazette **5.** IMPR [opposé aux marges, aux illustrations] text **6.** LING [corpus, énoncé] text **7.** LITTÉR text, work ▪ **elle a proposé son ~ à plusieurs éditeurs** she sent her work to several publishers ▪ **écrire un court ~ d'introduction** to write a short introduction **8.** ÉDUC & UNIV [sujet de devoir] question *(for work in class or homework)* ▪ **je vais vous lire le ~ de la dissertation** I'll give you the essay question ◗ **~ libre** free composition.
◆ **dans le texte** *loc adv* in the original ◗ **en français dans le ~** *pr* in French in the original ; *fig* to quote the very words used.

textile [tɛkstil] ◇ *adj* textile ▪ **fibre/verre ~** textile fibre/glass.
◇ *nm* **1.** [tissu] fabric, material ▪ **les ~s synthétiques** synthetic *ou* man-made fibres **2.** [industrie] : **le ~, les ~s** the textile industry.

texto [tɛksto] ◇ *adv fam* word for word, verbatim.
◇ *nm* TÉLÉCOM text (message).

textuel, elle [tɛkstɥɛl] *adj* **1.** [conforme - à ce qui est écrit] literal, word-for-word ; [- à ce qui a été dit] verbatim **2.** LITTÉR textual ▪ **analyse ~le** textual analysis.
◆ **textuel** *adv fam* quote unquote ▪ **elle m'a dit qu'elle s'en fichait, ~** she told me she didn't care, those were her exact words.

textuellement [tɛkstɥɛlmɑ̃] *adv* word for word.

texture [tɛkstyr] *nf* [d'un bois, de la peau] texture.

TF1 (*abr de* **Télévision Française 1**) *npr French independent television company.*

TGV (*abr de* **train à grande vitesse**) *nm French high-speed train.*

thaï, e [taj] *adj* Thai.
◆ **Thaï, e** *nm, f* Thai.

thaïlandais, e [tajlɑ̃dɛ, ɛz] *adj* Thai ■ **un ressortissant ~** a Thai (national).
◆ **Thaïlandais, e** *nm, f* Thai ■ **j'ai rencontré un Thaïlandais** I met someone from Thailand.

Thaïlande [tajlɑ̃d] *npr f* : **(la) ~** Thailand ■ **le golfe de ~** the Gulf of Siam.

thalamus [talamys] *nm* thalamus.

thalasso [talasɔ] *nf fam* = **thalassothérapie**.

thalassothérapie [talasɔterapi] *nf* seawater therapy, thalassotherapy *spéc.*

thanatos [tanatɔs] *nm* Thanatos.

thatchérien, enne [tatʃerjɛ̃, ɛn] *adj & nm, f* Thatcherite.

thatchérisme [tatʃerism] *nm* Thatcherism.

thaumaturge [tomatyrʒ] *nmf* thaumaturge, thaumaturgist.

thé [te] *nm* **1.** [boisson] tea ■ **faire du ~** to make (a pot of) tea ■ **prendre le ~** to have tea ■ **boire du ~** to drink tea ⊙ **~ de Chine/Ceylan** China/Ceylon tea ■ **~ noir/vert** black (leaf)/ green tea ■ **~ citron** lemon tea *UK*, tea with lemon ■ **~ au lait** tea with milk ■ **~ à la menthe** mint tea ■ **~ nature** tea without milk **2.** [feuilles] tea, tea-leaves ■ **une cuillerée de ~** a spoonful of tea **3.** [réception] tea party ■ [repas] (afternoon) tea **4.** BOT tea, tea-plant.

théâtral, e, aux [teatral, o] *adj* **1.** [relatif au théâtre] theatrical, stage *(modif)*, theatre *(modif)* ■ **une représentation ~e** theatrical production ■ **production ~e** stage production **2.** [scénique] stage *(modif)* ■ **il aurait fallu utiliser une écriture ~e** it should have been written in a style more suitable for the stage **3.** [spectaculaire - geste, action] dramatic, theatrical ■ **avec de grands gestes théâtraux** with a lot of histrionics *ou* drama.

théâtralement [teatralmɑ̃] *adv* [avec affectation] theatrically.

théâtraliser [3] [teatralize] *vt* to theatricalize.

théâtralité [teatralite] *nf* LITTÉR stageworthiness.

théâtre [teatr] *nm*

A.

1. [édifice - gén] theatre ■ ANTIQ amphitheatre ■ **aller au ~** to go to the theatre ■ **elle va souvent au ~** she's a regular theatre-goer ⊙ **le Théâtre-Français** the Comédie Française ■ **~ lyrique** opera house ■ **~ d'ombres** shadow theatre ■ **~ de poche** small theatre ■ **~ en rond** theatre-in-the-round ■ **~ de verdure** open-air theatre

2. [compagnie théâtrale] theatre company ■ **~ municipal** local theatre ■ **~ national** national theatre ■ **~s subventionnés** state-subsidized theatres

3. [art, profession] drama, theatre ■ **elle veut faire du ~** she wants to go on the stage *ou* to become an actress *ou* to act ■ **je vis pour le ~** [acteur] I live for the theatre *ou* stage ■ **quand j'étais étudiant j'ai fait un peu de ~** when I was a student I did some acting ⊙ **~ filmé** film of a play

4. [genre] drama, theatre ■ **je préfère le ~ au cinéma** I prefer theatre *ou* plays to films ■ **le ~ dans le ~** a play within a play ⊙ **le ~ élisabéthain/romantique** Elizabethan/Romantic theatre *ou* drama ■ **le ~ de l'absurde** the theatre of the absurd ■ **le ~ de boulevard** mainstream popular theatre *(as first played in theatres on the Paris boulevards)* ■ **~ musical** musicals ■ **le ~ de rue** street theatre ■ **~ total** total theatre

5. [œuvres d'un auteur] works, plays

6. [attitude pleine d'outrance] histrionics ■ **le voilà qui fait son ~** there he goes, putting on his usual act

B.

1. [lieu d'un événement] scene ■ **notre région a été le ~ de nombreuses mutations** our part of the country has seen a lot of changes

2. MIL : **~ d'opérations** *ou* **des opérations** the theatre of operations.

◆ **de théâtre** *loc adj* [critique, troupe] drama *(modif)*, theatre *(modif)* ■ [cours] drama *(modif)* ■ [agence] booking ■ [jumelles] opera *(modif)* ■ [accessoire, décor] stage *(modif)* ■ **une femme de ~** a woman of the stage *ou* theatre ■ **metteur en scène de ~** (stage) director.

théâtreux, euse [teatrø, øz] *nm, f péj & hum* [comédien amateur] amateur actor, Thespian *hum.*

théier, ère [teje, ɛr] *adj* tea *(modif)* ■ **la production théière** tea production.
◆ **théier** *nm* tea plant.
◆ **théière** *nf* teapot.

théine [tein] *nf* theine.

thématique [tematik] <> *adj* thematic.
<> *nf* **1.** LITTÉR themes ■ **la ~ des contes de fées** the themes developed in fairy tales ■ **la ~ de Kafka** themes in Kafka **2.** MUS themes.

thème [tɛm] *nm* **1.** ART, LITTÉR & MUS theme ■ **sur le ~ de** on the theme of **2.** [traduction] translation into a foreign language ■ ÉDUC prose ■ **~ latin/allemand** translation *(from one's language) into Latin/German* ■ **faire du ~** to translate into a foreign language **3.** LING stem, theme.
◆ **thème astral** *nm* ASTROL birth chart.

théocratie [teɔkrasi] *nf* theocracy.

théologal, e, aux [teɔlɔgal, o] *adj* theological.

théologie [teɔlɔʒi] *nf* theology.

théologien, enne [teɔlɔʒjɛ̃, ɛn] *nm, f* theologian.

théologique [teɔlɔʒik] *adj* theological.

théorème [teɔrɛm] *nm* theorem ■ **le ~ de Pythagore** Pythagoras' theorem.

théoricien, enne [teɔrisjɛ̃, ɛn] *nm, f* **1.** [philosophe, chercheur etc] theorist, theoretician ■ **un ~ de la mécanique quantique** an expert in quantum theory **2.** [adepte - d'une doctrine] theorist.

théorie [teɔri] *nf* **1.** SC theory ■ **~ des ensembles** set theory ■ **la ~ de la relativité** the theory of relativity **2.** [ensemble de concepts] theory ■ **la ~ du surréalisme** the theory of surrealism **3.** [ensemble des règles] theory ■ **il possède bien la ~ des échecs** he has a good theoretical knowledge of chess **4.** [opinion] theory ■ **c'est la ~ du gouvernement** that's the government's theory *ou* that's what the government claims **5.** [connaissance spéculative] theory ■ **tout cela, c'est de la ~** this is all purely theoretical **6.** *litt* [défilé] procession **7.** ANTIQ theory.
◆ **en théorie** *loc adv* in theory, theoretically ■ **en ~, tu as raison, en fait le système est inapplicable** in theory you're right, but in actual fact the system is unworkable.

théorique [teɔrik] *adj* theoretical.

théoriquement [teɔrikmɑ̃] *adv* **1.** *sout* [d'un point de vue spéculatif] theoretically, in theory **2.** [en toute hypothèse] in theory ■ **~, je devrais arriver à 21 h** in theory, I ought to arrive at 9 p.m.

théoriser [3] [teɔrize] <> *vt* to theorize.
<> *vi* to theorize, to speculate.

théosophie [teɔzɔfi] *nf* theosophy.

thérapeute [terapøt] *nmf* **1.** [spécialiste des traitements] therapist **2.** *litt* [médecin] doctor, physician **3.** [psychothérapeute] therapist.

thérapeutique [terapøtik] <> *adj* therapeutic.
<> *nf* **1.** [traitement] therapy, treatment ■ **le choix entre plusieurs ~s** the choice between several courses of treatment **2.** [discipline médicale] therapeutics *(U)*.

thérapie [terapi] *nf* **1.** [traitement] therapy, treatment ▪ **~ cellulaire** cell *ou* cellular therapy ▪ **~ génique** gene therapy **2.** PSYCHOL therapy ▪ **~ cognitive** cognitive therapy ▪ **~ familiale** family therapy ▪ **~ de groupe** group therapy.

Thérèse [terɛz] *npr* : **sainte ~ d'Avila** Saint Teresa of Avila.

thermal, e, aux [tɛrmal, o] *adj* [eau] thermal ▪ [source] thermal, hot.

thermalisme [tɛrmalism] *nm* balneology ▪ **l'argent de la commune provient du ~** the commune derives its revenue from its spa facilities.

thermes [tɛrm] *nmpl* **1.** [établissement de cure] thermal baths **2.** ANTIQ thermae.

thermidor [tɛrmidɔr] *nm 11th month of the French Revolutionary calendar (from July 19 to Aug 17).*

thermidorien, enne [tɛrmidɔrjɛ̃, ɛn] *adj* Thermidorian, of the 9th Thermidor.
◆ **Thermidoriens** *nmpl* revolutionaries of the 9th Thermidor, Thermidorians.

thermique [tɛrmik] ◇ *adj* [réacteur, équilibre, signature, papier] thermal ▪ [énergie] thermic.
◇ *nf* heat sciences.
◇ *nm* thermal.

thermodurcissable [tɛrmɔdyrsisabl] ◇ *adj* thermosetting.
◇ *nm* thermoset (substance).

thermodynamique [tɛrmɔdinamik] ◇ *adj* thermodynamic.
◇ *nf* thermodynamics *(U)*.

thermoélectricité [tɛrmɔelɛktrisite] *nf* thermoelectricity.

thermoélectrique [tɛrmɔelɛktrik] *adj* thermoelectric.

thermogène [tɛrmɔʒɛn] *adj* thermogenous, thermogenetic.

Thermolactyl® [tɛrmɔlaktil] *nm thermal clothing fabric.*

thermomètre [tɛrmɔmɛtr] *nm* **1.** [appareil] thermometer ▪ **le ~ monte/descend** the temperature (on the thermometer) is rising/falling ⊃ **~ digital/médical** digital/clinical thermometer ▪ **~ à maximum et minimum** maximum and minimum thermometer **2.** [indice] barometer *fig*, gauge.

thermométrie [tɛrmɔmetri] *nf* thermometry.

thermonucléaire [tɛrmɔnykleɛr] *adj* thermonuclear.

thermoplastique [tɛrmɔplastik] *adj* thermoplastic.

thermopropulsion [tɛrmɔprɔpylsjɔ̃] *nf* thermopropulsion.

thermorégulateur, trice [tɛrmɔregylatœr, tris] *adj* thermoregulator.

thermorésistant, e [tɛrmɔrezistɑ̃, ɑ̃t] *adj* heat-resistant, thermoresistant.

Thermos® [tɛrmos] *nf* ▻ **bouteille.**

thermostat [tɛrmɔsta] *nm* thermostat.

thermothérapie [tɛrmɔterapi] *nf* thermotherapy.

thésard, e [tezar, ard] *nm, f fam* research student, postgrad.

thésaurisation [tezɔrizasjɔ̃] *nf* [gén - ÉCON] hoarding.

thésauriser [3] [tezɔrize] ◇ *vi* to hoard money.
◇ *vt* to hoard (up).

thésaurus [tezɔrys] *nm* **1.** [lexique] lexicon **2.** [outil de classement] thesaurus.

thèse [tɛz] *nf* **1.** ÉDUC thesis ▪ **~ de doctorat d'État** ≃ PhD, ≃ doctoral thesis *UK*, ≃ doctoral *ou* PhD dissertation *US* ▪ **~ de troisième cycle** [en lettres] ≃ MA *UK* ≃ master's thesis *US* ; [en sciences] ≃ MSc *UK* ≃ master's thesis *US* **2.** [théorie] argument, thesis, theory ▪ **~, antithèse, synthèse** thesis, antithesis, synthesis ▪ **la ~ de l'accident n'est pas écartée** the possibility that it may have been an accident hasn't been ruled out.

Thésée [teze] *npr* Theseus.

Thessalonique [tɛsalɔnik] *npr* Salonika, Salonica.

thêta [tɛta] *nm* theta.

Thomas [tɔma] *npr* : **saint ~ d'Aquin** Thomas Aquinas.

thomisme [tɔmism] *nm* Thomism.

thon [tɔ̃] *nm* tuna (fish), tunny *UK* ▪ **~ blanc** long-fin *ou* white-meat tuna ▪ **~ en boîte** tinned tuna fish ▪ **~ à l'huile** tuna in oil ▪ **~ au naturel** tuna in brine.

thonier [tɔnje] *nm* tuna boat.

thoracique [tɔrasik] *adj* thoracic.

thorax [tɔraks] *nm* thorax.

thriller [srilœr, trilœr] *nm* thriller.

thrombose [trɔ̃boz] *nf* thrombosis.

THS [teaʃɛs] (*abr de* **traitement hormonal substitutif**) *nm* HRT.

thune△ [tyn] *nf* [argent] : **je n'avais pas une ~** I was broke.

thuriféraire [tyriferɛr] *nm* **1.** RELIG thurifer **2.** *litt* flatterer, sycophant *litt*.

thuya [tyja] *nm* thuja ▪ **~ occidental** white cedar.

thym [tɛ̃] *nm* thyme.

thymus [timys] *nm* thymus.

thyroïde [tirɔid] ◇ *adj* thyroid.
◇ *nf* thyroid (gland).

thyroïdien, enne [tirɔidjɛ̃, ɛn] *adj* thyroid *(modif)*.

tiare [tjar] *nf* **1.** [coiffure] tiara **2.** [dignité papale] : **la ~** the Papal tiara.

Tibère [tibɛr] *npr* Tiberius.

Tibériade [tiberjad] *npr* : **le lac de ~** Lake Tiberias, the Sea of Galilee.

Tibet [tibɛ] *npr m* : **le ~** Tibet ▪ **au ~** in Tibet.

tibétain, e [tibetɛ̃, ɛn] *adj* Tibetan.
◆ **Tibétain, e** *nm, f* Tibetan.

tibia [tibja] *nm* **1.** ANAT [os] shinbone, tibia *spéc* ▪ [devant de la jambe] shin ▪ **donner à qqn un coup de pied dans les ~s** to kick sb in the shins **2.** ZOOL tibia.

Tibre [tibr] *npr m* : **le ~** the (River) Tiber.

tic [tic] *nm* **1.** [au visage] tic, (nervous) twitch ▪ **son visage était agité de ~s** his face twitched nervously **2.** [manie gestuelle] (nervous) tic, twitch ▪ **il est bourré de ~s** *fam* he's got a lot of nervous tics **3.** [répétition stéréotypée] habit ▪ **un ~ de langage** a (speech) mannerism **4.** VÉTÉR [avec déglutition d'air] wind sucking.

ticket [tikɛ] *nm* **1.** [de bus, de métro] ticket ▪ [de vestiaire, de consigne] slip, ticket ⊃ **~ de caisse** sales receipt, bill ▪ **~ de quai** platform ticket **2.** [coupon - de rationnement, de pain] coupon **3.** *fam loc* **il a un ~ avec elle** she fancies him *UK*, she's sweet on him *US* **4.** POLIT [aux États-Unis] ticket.
◆ **ticket modérateur** *nm* [pour la Sécurité sociale] *proportion of medical expenses payable by the patient.*

Ticket-Restaurant® [tikɛrɛstɔrɑ̃] (*pl* **Tickets-Restaurant**) *nm voucher given to employees to cover part of luncheon expenses,* ≃ Luncheon Voucher® *UK*.

tic-tac [tiktak] *nm inv* [d'une pendule, d'une bombe] ticking *(U)*, tick-tock ▪ **faire ~** to tick (away), to go tick-tock.

tie-break [tajbrɛk] (*pl* **tie-breaks**) *nm* tie break.

tiédasse [tjedas] *adj* lukewarm, tepid.

tiède [tjɛd] ◇ *adj* **1.** [ni chaud ni froid] lukewarm, warm, tepid ▪ **salade ~** warm salad ▌[pas suffisamment chaud] lukewarm, not hot enough ▪ **le thé va être ~, bois-le vite** drink your tea before it gets cold *ou* while it's hot **2.** *fig* [peu enthousiaste - accueil, réaction] lukewarm, unenthusiastic, half-hearted ; [- sentiment] half-hearted ▪ **les syndicalistes sont ~s** the union members lack conviction *ou* are apathetic.
◇ *nmf fam* [indifférent, mou] wet *UK*, wimp.
◇ *adv* : **je préfère boire/manger ~** I don't like drinking/eating very hot things ▪ **il fait ~ aujourd'hui** it's mild *ou* warm today.

tièdement [tjɛdmɑ̃] *adv* [accueillir] coolly, unenthusiastically ▪ [soutenir] half-heartedly.

tiédeur [tjedœr] *nf* **1.** [d'un liquide] lukewarmness ▪ [d'un solide] warmth ▪ [de l'air] mildness ▪ **la ~ d'un matin de juin** the mildness of a June morning **2.** *fig* [d'un accueil] lukewarmness, coolness ▪ [d'un sentiment] half-heartedness.

tiédir [32] [tjedir] ◇ *vi* **1.** [se refroidir - boisson, métal, air] to cool (down) ▪ **laisser ~ le gâteau/lait** leave the cake/milk to cool down **2.** [se réchauffer] to grow warmer ▪ **faire ~ du lait** to warm up some milk.
◇ *vt* **1.** [refroidir légèrement] to cool (down) **2.** [réchauffer légèrement] to warm (up).

tiédissement [tjedismɑ̃] *nm* **1.** [refroidissement] cooling (down *ou* off) **2.** [réchauffement] warming (up).

tien [tjɛ̃] (*f* **tienne** [tjɛn], *mpl* **tiens** [tjɛ̃], *fpl* **tiennes** [tjɛn]) *adj poss litt* : **je suis tienne pour toujours** I am yours forever ▪ **ce devait être un ~ cousin** it must have been a cousin of yours.
◆ **le tien** (*f* **la tienne**, *mpl* **les tiens**, *fpl* **les tiennes**) *pron poss* yours ▪ **ce parapluie n'est pas le ~** this is not your umbrella, this umbrella is not yours *ou* doesn't belong to you ▪ *(emploi nominal)* **les ~s** your family and friends ➤ **à la tienne!** *fam* [à ta santé] good health!, cheers! ; [bon courage] all the best! ▪ **tu comptes la convaincre? eh bien, à la tienne!** so you think you can convince her? well all I can say is, good luck to you *ou* rather you than me! ▪ **mets-y du ~** [fais un effort] make an effort ; [sois compréhensif] try to be understanding ▪ **tu as encore fait des tiennes!** *fam* you've (gone and) done it again! ▪ **ici il n'y a pas de ~ et de mien** it's share and share alike here.

tient *etc v* ▷ **tenir**.

tierce [tjɛrs] *f* ▷ **tiers adj**.

tiercé, e [tjɛrse] *adj* **1.** AGRIC third ploughed **2.** HÉRALD tierced, en tierce.
◆ **tiercé** ◇ *adj m* : **pari ~** triple forecast.
◇ *nm* **1.** LOISIRS triple forecast ▪ **gagner le ~ (dans l'ordre/le désordre)** to win on three horses (with the right placings/without the right placings) ▪ **toucher un gros ~** to win a lot of money on the horses **2.** [gén - trois gagnants] : **le ~ gagnant** *pr* the first three, the three winners ; *fig* the winning three *ou* trio ▪ **toucher le ~ gagnant** *pr* to win on horses ; *fig* to hit the jackpot.

tiers[1] [tjɛr] *nm* **1.** [partie d'un tout divisé en trois] third ▪ **elle en a lu un ~** she's a third of the way through (reading it) ▪ **la maison était brûlée aux deux ~** two-thirds of the house had been destroyed by fire **2.** *sout* [troisième personne] third person ▪ [personne étrangère à un groupe] stranger, outsider, third party ➤ **il se fiche** *ou* **se moque du ~ comme du quart** he couldn't care less **3.** DR third party ▪ **les dommages causés à un ~** third party damages ➤ **~ acquéreur** subsequent purchaser ▪ **~ opposant** (opposing) third party **4.** COMM : **~ porteur** holder in due course, (second) endorser **5.** FIN : **~ provisionnel** *thrice-yearly income tax payment based on estimated tax due for the previous year* **6.** HIST : **le Tiers** the Third Estate **7.** [pour la Sécurité sociale] : **~ payant** *system by which a proportion of the fee for medical treatment is paid directly to the hospital, doctor or pharmacist by the patient's insurer*.
◆ **au tiers** *loc adj* DR third-party *(modif)*.

tiers[2], tierce [tjɛr, tjɛrs] *adj* **1.** [étranger à un groupe] third ▪ **tierce personne** third party **2.** [dans l'Union européenne] : **pays ~** third *ou* non-EC country ▪ **produits ~** non-community products **3.** DR : **tierce collision** third-party *(modif)* **4.** HIST : **le ~ état** the Third Estate **5.** MATH : **a tierce, a'''** "a" triple dash **6.** RELIG : **~ ordre** third order.
◆ **tierce** *nf* **1.** JEUX tierce ▪ **tierce à la dame** three-card run with queen as the highest card ▪ **tierce majeure** tierce major **2.** ESCRIME & HÉRALD tierce **3.** IMPR press proof **4.** MUS third ▪ **tierce majeure/mineure** major/minor third.

tiers-monde [tjɛrmɔ̃d] (*pl* **tiers-mondes**) *nm* Third World.

tiers-mondialisation [tjɛrmɔ̃djalizasjɔ̃], **tiers-mondisation** [tjɛrmɔ̃dizasjɔ̃] *nf* : **la ~ du pays** the country's economic decline to Third World levels.

tiers-mondisme [tjɛrmɔ̃dism] (*pl* **tiers-mondismes**) *nm* *support for the Third World*.

tiers-mondiste [tjɛrmɔ̃dist] (*pl* **tiers-mondistes**) ◇ *adj* **1.** [du tiers-mondisme] pro-Third World **2.** [du tiers-monde] Third World *(modif)*.
◇ *nmf* **1.** [spécialiste du tiers-monde] Third World expert **2.** [idéologue du tiers-mondisme] Third Worldist.

tif(fe)s [tif] *nmpl fam* hair ▪ **mes ~s** my hair.

TIG (*abr de* **travail d'intérêt général**) *nm* ≃ community service.

tige [tiʒ] *nf* **1.** BOT [d'une feuille] stem, stalk ▪ [de blé, de maïs] stalk ▪ [d'une fleur] stem ▪ **tulipe à longue ~** long-stemmed tulip ▮ [arbre] : **haute/basse ~** tall/half standard **2.** [axe - d'une épingle, d'une aiguille, d'un clou, d'un candélabre, d'une flèche] shaft ; [- d'un cadran solaire] finger, pointer ; [- d'un guéridon] pedestal ▪ **une ~ de fer** an iron rod ➤ **clef à ~ creuse/pleine** key with a hollow/solid shank **3.** *fam* [cigarette] fag *UK*, smoke *US* **4.** [d'une chaussure] upper ▪ **bottes à ~ basse** ankle boots ▪ **baskets à ~ haute** high tops **5.** [origine d'une famille] stock, line **6.** ARCHIT [de colonne] shaft **7.** AUTO rod **8.** INDUST du pétrole : **~ de forage** drill pipe.

tignasse [tiɲas] *nf fam* **1.** [chevelure mal peignée] mop *ou* shock (of hair) **2.** [chevelure] hair ▪ **il l'a attrapée par la ~** he grabbed (hold of) her by the hair.

tigre [tigr] *nm* **1.** ZOOL tiger ▪ **un ~ royal** *ou* **du Bengale** a Bengal tiger **2.** *litt* [homme cruel] : **c'est un vrai ~** he's a real ogre ➤ **~ de papier** paper tiger.

Tigre [tigr] *npr m* GÉOGR : **le ~** the (River) Tigris.

tigré, e [tigre] *adj* [pelage] striped, streaked ▪ [chat] tabby *(modif)*, tiger *(modif)*.

tigresse [tigrɛs] *nf* **1.** ZOOL tigress **2.** *litt* [femme très jalouse] tigress.

tilbury [tilbyri] *nm* tilbury.

tilde [tild] *nm* [en espagnol] tilde ▪ [en phonétique, pour remplacer un mot] swung dash.

tilleul [tijœl] ◇ *nm* **1.** BOT lime (tree) **2.** [feuilles séchées] lime-blossom *(U)* ▪ [infusion] lime *ou* lime-blossom tea.
◇ *adj inv* : **(vert) ~** lime green.

tilt [tilt] *nm* **1.** JEUX tilt signal **2.** *fam loc* **le mot a fait ~** [je me suis souvenu] the word rang a bell ▪ **et soudain, ça a fait ~** [j'ai compris] and suddenly it clicked *ou* the penny dropped *UK*.

timbale [tɛ̃bal] *nf* **1.** [gobelet] (metal) cup **2.** CULIN [moule] timbale mould ▪ [préparation] timbale ▪ **~ de saumon** salmon timbale **3.** MUS kettledrum ▪ **une paire de ~s** tympani, a set of kettledrums.

timbre [tɛ̃br] *nm*

A.

1. = **timbre-poste**
2. [vignette - au profit d'une œuvre] sticker *(given in exchange for a donation to charity)* ; [- attestant un paiement] stamp *(certifying receipt of payment)*
3. [sceau, marque] stamp
4. [instrument marqueur] stamp ▪ **~ dateur** date stamp ▪ **~ en caoutchouc** rubber stamp
5. DR : **~ fiscal** revenue stamp
6. MÉD : **~ tuberculinique** tuberculosis patch

B.

1. ACOUST [qualité sonore - d'un instrument] tone, timbre, colour ; [- d'une voix] tone, resonance ▪ **un beau ~ de voix** beautiful mellow tones, a beautiful rich voice
2. [sonnette] bell ▪ [de porte] doorbell ▪ **~ de bicyclette** bicycle bell
3. MUS [instrument] (small) bell.

TIMBRE FISCAL

These stamps are sold at most tobacconists and are used to pay fees due for obtaining official documents (driving licence, passport etc) and to pay fines (notably for driving and parking offences).

timbré, e [tɛ̃bre] *adj* **1.** *fam* [fou] nuts, cracked **2.** DR stamped **3.** [d'une bonne sonorité] : **de sa voix bien ~e** in his mellow *ou* rich tones.

timbre-amende [tɛ̃bramɑ̃d] (*pl* **timbres-amendes**) *nm stamp purchased to certify payment of a fine.*

timbre-poste [tɛ̃brəpɔst] (*pl* **timbres-poste**) *nm* (postage) stamp.

timbre-quittance [tɛ̃brəkitɑ̃s] (*pl* **timbres-quittances**) *nm* receipt stamp.

timbrer [3] [tɛ̃bre] *vt* **1.** [lettre, colis] to stamp, to stick *ou* to put a stamp on **2.** DR [document] to stamp, to put a stamp on, to affix a stamp to *sout*.

time-sharing [tajmʃɛriŋ] (*pl* **time-sharings**) *nm* INFORM time sharing.

timide [timid] <> *adj* **1.** [embarrassé - sourire, air, regard] timid, shy ; [- personne] bashful, diffident ▪ **il est ~ avec les femmes** he's shy of *ou* he shrinks away from women ▪ **faussement ~** coy **2.** [faible] slight, feeble, tiny ▪ **une critique ~** hesitant criticism ▪ **l'auteur de quelques ~s réformes** the author of a handful of half-hearted *ou* feeble reforms.
<> *nmf* shy person.

timidement [timidmɑ̃] *adv* **1.** [avec embarras] timidly, shyly ▪ [gauchement] self-consciously, bashfully **2.** [de façon peu perceptible] slightly, feebly *péj*, faint-heartedly *péj* ▪ **l'euro remonte ~** the euro is rising slightly.

timidité [timidite] *nf* **1.** [manque d'assurance] timidity, shyness, diffidence ▪ [gaucherie] self-consciousness, bashfulness **2.** [d'un projet, d'une réforme] feebleness *péj*, half-heartedness *péj*.

timing [tajmiŋ] *nm* timing *(of a technical process).*

timon [timɔ̃] *nm* **1.** AGRIC [d'une charrette] shaft ▪ [d'une charrue] (draught) beam **2.** NAUT & *vieilli* tiller.

timonerie [timɔnri] *nf* **1.** NAUT [abri] wheelhouse ▪ [service] wheelhouse, steering ▪ [personnel] wheelhouse crew **2.** AUTO steering and braking gear.

timonier [timɔnje] *nm* **1.** NAUT helmsman **2.** AGRIC wheelhorse, wheeler **3.** HIST : **le grand ~** the Great Helmsman.

timoré, e [timɔre] <> *adj* timorous, fearful, unadventurous.
<> *nm, f* timorous *ou* fearful *ou* unadventurous person.

tint *etc v* ▻ **tenir**.

tintamarre [tɛ̃tamar] *nm* [vacarme] racket, din ▪ **on a fait du ~ autour de son livre** there was a lot of hooha *ou* a big to-do about his book.

tintement [tɛ̃tmɑ̃] *nm* **1.** [d'une cloche, d'une sonnette] ringing *(U)* ▪ [d'un lustre] tinkling *(U)* ▪ [de clefs, de pièces de monnaie] jingle, jingling *(U)* ▪ [de verres] chink, clinking *(U)* **2.** MÉD : **~ d'oreilles** ringing in the ears, tinnitus *spéc*.

tinter [3] [tɛ̃te] <> *vi* **1.** [sonner lentement] to ring (out), to peal **2.** [produire des sons clairs] to tinkle, to jingle ▪ **tous les verres tintaient sur le plateau** all the glasses were clinking on the tray ▪ **faire ~ des pièces de monnaie** to jingle coins **3.** *loc* **les oreilles doivent lui ~** his ears must be burning.
<> *vt* **1.** [sonner - cloche] to chime **2.** [coup] : **la cloche du village tintait les coups de midi** the church bell was striking twelve **3.** [annoncer - glas, messe] to toll the bell for ▪ **~ le tocsin** to sound the tocsin.

tintin [tɛ̃tɛ̃] *interj fam* no go, no way ▪ **les cadres ont eu une augmentation, et nous ~!** the executives got a rise, and we didn't get a blessed thing! ⊃ **tu peux faire ~ pour tes places gratuites!** as for your free tickets, forget it *ou* no way!

Tintoret [tɛ̃tɔrɛ] *npr* : **le ~** Tintoretto ▪ **un tableau du ~** a painting by Tintoretto.

tintouin [tɛ̃twɛ̃] *nm fam* **1.** [inquiétude, souci] hassle, (fuss and) bother ▪ **se faire du ~** to get all worked up **2.** [vacarme] racket, din ▪ **quel ~ à côté!** what a racket they're making next door! **3.** *loc* **sa canne à pêche, ses bottes, son chapeau et tout le ~** his fishing rod, boots, hat and all the rest of it.

TIP [tip] (*abr de* **titre interbancaire de paiement**) *nm payment slip for bills.*

TIPP (*abr de* **taxe intérieure sur les produits pétroliers**) *nf* domestic tax on petroleum products.

tipi [tipi] *nm* tepee, teepee.

tique [tik] *nf* tick.

tiquer [3] [tike] *vi* [réagir] to flinch ▪ **le prix l'a fait ~** he flinched *ou* baulked when he saw the price ▪ **~ sur qqch** to baulk at sthg.

tir [tir] *nm* **1.** ARM & MIL [action de lancer au moyen d'une arme] shooting, firing ▪ [projectiles envoyés] fire ▪ **un ~ intense/nourri/sporadique** heavy/sustained/sporadic fire ⊃ **~ direct/indirect** direct/indirect fire ▪ **~ précis** *ou* **groupé** grouped fire ▪ **~ de barrage** barrage fire ▪ **~ courbe** high-angle fire ▪ **~ par rafales** firing in bursts ▪ **~ de roquette** rocket attack ▪ **rectifier le ~** to change one's angle of attache, to change one's approach to a problem **2.** [endroit - pour l'entraînement] rifle *ou* shooting range ; [- à la foire] shooting gallery **3.** MIN & TRAV PUB blasting **4.** SPORT : **le ~** [discipline olympique] shooting ⊃ **~ à la carabine/au pistolet** rifle-/pistol-shooting ▪ **~ à l'arc** archery ▪ **~ aux pigeons** clay pigeon shooting **5.** FOOTBALL shot ▪ **~ (au but)** shot at goal.
◆ **de tir** *loc adj* [concours, champion] shooting ▪ [position, vitesse] firing ▪ **angle/ligne de ~** angle/line of fire.

TIR [teiɛr, tir] (*abr écrite de* **transport international routier**) TIR.

tirade [tirad] *nf* **1.** CINÉ & THÉÂTRE monologue, speech **2.** *péj* [discours] speech, tirade *péj*.

tirage [tiraʒ] *nm* **1.** IMPR [action] printing ▪ [ensemble d'exemplaires] print run, impression ▪ [d'une gravure] edition ▪ **un ~ de 50 000 exemplaires** a print run of 50,000 ▪ **écrivain qui fait de gros ~s** bestselling author ⊃ **~ limité/numéroté** limited/numbered edition ▪ **~ à part** offprint **2.** PRESSE [action] printing, running ▪ [exemplaires mis en vente] circulation ▪ **un ~ de 50 000** circulation figures *ou* a circulation of 50,000 ▪ **à fort** *ou* **grand ~** with large circulation figures ▪ **la presse à grand ~** the popular press **3.** INFORM [sur imprimante] printout **4.** PHOTO [action] printing ▪ [copies] prints **5.** BANQUE drawing ▪ **droits de ~ spéciaux** ÉCON special drawing rights **6.** JEUX [d'une carte] taking, picking ▪ [d'une tombola] draw ▪ **~ au sort** drawing of lots ▪ **nous t'avons désigné par ~ au sort** we drew lots and your name came up **7.** [d'une cheminée, d'un poêle] draught ▪ **le ~ est bon/mauvais** it draws well/doesn't draw well **8.** MÉTALL drawing **9.** *fam loc* **il y a du ~ entre eux** there's some friction between them.

tiraillement [tirajmɑ̃] *nm* **1.** [sur une corde] tug **2.** [d'estomac] gnawing pain ▪ [de la peau, d'un muscle] tightness ▪ **sentir les ~s de la faim** to feel pangs of hunger.
◆ **tiraillements** *nmpl* [conflit] struggle, conflict ▪ **il y a des ~s dans la famille/le syndicat** there is friction within the family/the union.

tirailler [3] [tiraje] <> *vt* **1.** [tirer sur] to tug at, to pull on, to give little pulls on **2.** [faire souffrir légèrement] to prick ▪ **la faim lui tiraillait l'estomac** he was feeling pangs of hunger **3.** [solliciter] to dog, to plague ▪ **être tiraillé entre l'espoir et l'inquiétude** to be torn between hope and anxiety.
<> *vi* to fire at random ▪ **on entendait ~ dans les bois** random fire could be heard in the woods, people could be heard firing away in the woods.

tirailleur [tirajœr] *nm* **1.** [éclaireur] scout **2.** HIST & MIL (native) infantryman **3.** *fig* [personne qui agit isolément] : **dans une grève, il y a toujours quelques ~s** during a strike, there are always some who don't play by the book.
◆ **en tirailleurs(s)** *loc adv* [avancer] in extended order.

tirant [tirɑ̃] *nm* **1.** NAUT : **~ d'eau** draught ▪ **avoir cinq pieds de ~ d'eau** to draw five feet (of water) **2.** [d'une botte] (boot) strap ▪ [d'une chaussure] (heel) strap **3.** CONSTR [entrait] tie beam ▪ [fer plat] rod **4.** MIN strap, tie beam.

tire [tir] *nf* **1.** △ [voiture] car **2.** *Québec* [friandise] maple toffee *ou* taffy ▪ **~ d'érable** maple candy.

tiré, e [tire] *adj* **1.** [fatigué et amaigri - visage] drawn, pinched ▪ **avoir les traits ~s** to look drawn **2.** *loc* **~ par les cheveux** contrived, far-fetched.

◆ **tiré** *nm* **1.** BANQUE drawee **2.** PRESSE : ~ **à part** off-print **3.** MUS down-bow.

tire-au-cul△ [tiroky] = **tire-au-flanc**.

tire-au-flanc [tiroflɑ̃] *nm inv fam* skiver, dodger, shirker.

tire-botte [tirbɔt] (*pl* **tire-bottes**) *nm* **1.** [pour mettre] boot hook **2.** [pour enlever] bootjack.

tire-bouchon [tirbuʃɔ̃] (*pl* **tire-bouchons**) *nm* corkscrew.
◆ **en tire-bouchon** *loc adj* corkscrew *(modif)* ■ **cochon à la queue en** ~ pig with a corkscrew tail.

tire-bouchonner [3] [tirbuʃɔne] *vi* to twist round and round ■ **ses chaussettes tire-bouchonnent** his socks are all twisted round his ankles.

tire-d'aile [tirdɛl] ◆ **à tire-d'aile** *loc adv* **1.** [en volant] : **les corbeaux passèrent au-dessus de la maison à** ~ the crows flew over the house with strong, regular wingbeats **2.** *fig* [à toute vitesse] : **il s'est enfui à** ~ he took to his heels.

tire-fesses [tirfɛs] *nm inv fam* ski tow.

tire-fond [tirfɔ̃] *nm inv* **1.** CONSTR [vis] long screw ■ [anneau] eye bolt **2.** RAIL sleeper screw.

tire-jus△ [tirʒy] *nm inv* snot rag△.

tire-lait [tirlɛ] *nm inv* breast-pump.

tire-larigot [tirlarigo] ◆ **à tire-larigot** *loc adv fam* **boire à** ~ to drink *ou* to have one's fill.

tirelire [tirlir] *nf* **1.** [en forme de cochon] piggy bank ■ [boîte] moneybox **2.** △ [estomac] belly, gut **3.** *fam* [tête] mug.

tirer [3] [tire] ◇ *vt*

> **A.** DÉPLACER
> **B.** EXTRAIRE, OBTENIR
> **C.** PROJETER
> **E.** TRACER, IMPRIMER

A. DÉPLACER

1. [traîner - avec ou sans effort] to pull, to drag ; [- en remorquant] to draw, to tow ■ **tire la table au milieu de la pièce** pull the table out into the centre of the room ■ **tiré par un cheval** horse-drawn ■ ~ **qqn par le bras/les cheveux/les pieds** to drag sb by the arm/hair/feet

2. [amener à soi] to pull ■ [étirer - vers le haut] to pull (up) ; [- vers le bas] to pull (down) ■ **je sentis que quelqu'un tirait ma veste** I felt a tug at my jacket ■ **elle me tira doucement par la manche** she tugged *ou* pulled at my sleeve ■ ~ **les cheveux à qqn** to pull sb's hair ■ ~ **ses cheveux en arrière** to draw *ou* to pull one's hair back ■ **tire bien le drap** stretch the sheet (taut) ■ ~ **un fil** [accidentellement] to pull a thread ; [pour faire un jour] to draw a thread ➊ ~ **la couverture à soi** [s'attribuer le mérite] to take all the credit ; [s'attribuer le profit] to take the lion's share

3. [pour actionner - cordon d'appel, élastique] to pull ; [- tiroir] to pull (open *ou* out) ■ ~ **les rideaux** to pull *ou* to draw the curtains ■ **tire le portail derrière toi** close the gates behind you, pull the gates to ■ ~ **un verrou** [pour ouvrir] to slide a bolt open ; [pour fermer] to slide a bolt to, to shoot a bolt ■ ~ **la chasse d'eau** to flush the toilet

4. NAUT to draw

B. EXTRAIRE, OBTENIR

1. [faire sortir] : ~ **qqch de** to pull *ou* to draw sthg out of ■ ~ **le vin/cidre (du tonneau)** to draw wine/cider (off from the barrel) ■ ~ **qqn de** [le faire sortir de] to get sb out of ■ ~ **qqn d'un cauchemar** *fig* to rouse sb from a nightmare ■ ~ **qqn du sommeil** to wake sb up ■ ~ **qqn du coma** to pull sb out of a coma ■ ~ **qqn de son silence** to draw sb out (of his/her silence) ■ ~ **une œuvre de l'oubli** to rescue a work from oblivion ■ **tire-moi de là** help me out

2. [fabriquer] : ~ **qqch de** to derive *ou* to get *ou* to make sthg from ■ **les produits que l'on tire du pétrole** oil-based products ■ ~ **des sons d'un instrument** to get *ou* to draw sounds from an instrument ■ ~ **un film d'une pièce de théâtre** to adapt a play for the screen ■ **photos tirées d'un film** movie stills

3. [percevoir - argent] : **elle tire sa fortune de ses terres** she makes her money from her land ■ **tu ne tireras pas grand-chose de ta vieille montre** you won't get much (money) for your old watch ■ [retirer - chèque, argent liquide] to draw ■ ~ **de l'argent d'un compte** to draw money out of *ou* to withdraw money from an account

4. [extraire, dégager] : **tirer la morale/un enseignement de qqch** to learn a lesson from sthg ■ **ce vers est tiré d'un poème de Villon** this line is (taken) from a poem by Villon ■ **ce que j'ai tiré de ce livre/cet article** what I got out of this book/article ■ **ce roman tire son titre d'une chanson populaire** the title of this novel is taken from a popular song ■ ~ **satisfaction de** to derive satisfaction from ■ ~ **vanité de** to be proud of ■ ~ **vengeance de qqch** to avenge sthg

5. [obtenir, soutirer] : ~ **qqch de** : ~ **de l'argent de qqn** to extract money from sb, to get money out of sb ■ **la police n'a rien pu ~ de lui** the police couldn't get anything out of him ■ **tu auras du mal à lui ~ des remerciements** you'll get no thanks from her ■ ~ **des larmes à qqn** to make sb cry ■ **on n'en tirera jamais rien, de ce gosse** *fam* [il n'est bon à rien] we'll never make anything out of this kid ; [il ne parlera pas] we'll never get this kid to talk, we'll never get anything out of this kid ■ **je n'ai pas pu en ~ davantage** I couldn't get any more out of her

6. *fam* [voler] : **je me suis fait ~ mon portefeuille au cinéma!** somebody nicked *UK ou* swiped *US* my wallet at the cinema!

7. JEUX [billet, numéro] to draw, to pick ■ [loterie] to draw, to carry out the draw for ■ [carte] to draw, to take ■ **tirez une carte postale au hasard** pick any postcard ■ **qui va ~ le nom du gagnant?** who will draw (out) the name of the winner? ■ **le gagnant sera tiré au sort** there will be a draw to decide the winner

C. PROJETER

1. ARM [coup de fusil, missile] to fire ■ [balle, flèche] to shoot ■ ~ **un coup de feu** to fire a shot

2. [feu d'artifice] to set off ■ **ce soir, on tirera un feu d'artifice** there will be a fireworks display tonight

3. CHASSE [lapin, faisan] to shoot

4. [à la pétanque, boule en main] to throw ■ [boule placée] to knock out *(sép)* ■ FOOTBALL to take ■ ~ **un corner** to take a corner ■ **le penalty va être tiré par le capitaine** the penalty will be taken by the captain ‖ TENNIS [passing-shot, volée] to hit ■ [en haltérophilie] to lift ■ ESCRIME : ~ **des armes** to fence

5. *loc* ~ **un coup avec qqn**▲ to have it off with sb△

D. PASSER

fam to spend, to do, to get through *(insép)* ■ **j'ai encore trois semaines à ~ avant mon congé** I've another three weeks to go before my leave

E. TRACER, IMPRIMER

1. [dessiner - ligne] to draw ; [- plan] to draw up *(sép)* ■ **tirez deux traits sous les verbes** underline the verbs twice

2. PHOTO to print ■ **je voudrais que cette photo soit tirée sur du papier mat** I'd like a matt print of this picture

3. IMPR [livre] to print ■ [estampe, lithographie] to print, to draw ■ [tract] to print, to run ■ [gravure] to strike, to pull, to print ■ **ce magazine est tiré à plus de 200 000 exemplaires** this magazine has a print run *ou* a circulation of 200,000 ➊ **'bon à ~'** 'passed for press' ■ **un bon à ~** [épreuve] a press proof

4. *Belgique loc* **tu es assez grand, tu tires ton plan** you're old enough to look after yourself.

◇ *vi* **1.** MIL [faire feu] to fire, to shoot ■ **ne tirez pas, je me rends!** don't shoot, I surrender! ■ **tirez dans les jambes** shoot at *ou* aim at the legs ■ **il tire mal** he's a bad shot ■ ~ **à balles/à blanc** to fire bullets/blanks ■ ~ **sur qqn** to take a shot *ou* to shoot *ou* to fire at sb ■ **ils ont l'ordre de ~ sur tout ce qui bouge** they've been ordered to shoot *ou* to fire at anything that moves ■ **on m'a tiré dessus** I was fired *ou* shot at **2.** ARM & SPORT : ~ **à l'arc/l'arbalète** [activité sportive] to do archery/crossbow archery ; [action ponctuelle] to shoot a bow/crossbow ■ ~ **à la carabine/au pistolet** [activité sportive] to do rifle/pistol shooting ; [action ponctuelle] to shoot with a rifle/pistol **3.** FOOTBALL [au golf] to shoot ■ **il a tiré dans le mur/petit filet** he sent the ball against the wall/into the side netting ‖ ESCRIME to fence **4.** [exercer une traction] to pull ■ **tire!** pull!, heave! ■ **ça tire dans les genoux à la montée** *fam* going up is tough on the knees ■ **elle tire bien, ta voiture!** *fam* it goes well, your car! ■ **la moto tire à droite** the motorbike pulls to the right ■ **ne tire pas sur ton gilet** don't pull your cardigan out of shape ■ **il tira violemment sur le fil du téléphone** he gave the phone wire a sharp pull ■ ~ **sur** *fig* [délais, budget] to stretch ➊ ~ **sur la ficelle** to go a bit far **5.** [aspirer - fumeur] : ~ **sur une pipe** to draw on *ou* to pull at a pipe

■ ~ **sur une cigarette** to puff at *ou* to draw on a cigarette **6.** [avoir un bon tirage - cheminée, poêle] : ~ **(bien)** to draw (well) ■ **la cheminée/pipe tire mal** the fireplace/pipe doesn't draw properly **7.** [peau] to feel tight ■ [points de suture] to pull ■ **ma peau me tire** *fam* my skin feels tight ■ **aïe, ça tire!** ouch, it's pulling! **8.** JEUX : ~ **au sort** to draw *ou* to cast lots **9.** IMPR : ~ **à 50 000 exemplaires** to have a circulation of *ou* to have a (print) run of 50,000 (copies) ■ **à combien le journal tire-t-il?** what are the paper's circulation figures? **10.** *loc Belgique* & *Suisse* **ça tire** there's a draught.

◆ **tirer à** *v+prép* **1.** PRESSE : ~ **à la ligne** to pad out an article *(because it is being paid by the line)* **2.** NAUT : ~ **au large** to make for the open sea **3.** *loc* ~ **à sa fin** to come to an end.

◆ **tirer sur** *v+prép* [couleur] to verge *ou* to border on ■ **ses cheveux tirent sur le roux** his hair is reddish *ou* almost red.

◆ **se tirer** ◇ *vp (emploi passif)* : **le store se tire avec un cordon** the blind pulls down with a cord.

◇ *vpi fam* **1.** [partir, quitter un endroit] to clear off, to make tracks ■ [s'enfuir] to beat it, to clear off ■ **s'il n'est pas là dans 5 minutes, je me tire** if he's not here in 5 minutes I'm going ■ **tire-toi!** [ton menaçant] beat it!, clear *ou* push off! ■ **il s'est tiré de chez lui** he's left home ■ **dès que je peux, je me tire de cette boîte** as soon as I can, I'll get out of this dump **2.** [toucher à sa fin - emprisonnement, service militaire] to draw to a close ■ **plus qu'une semaine, ça se tire quand même!** only a week to go, it's nearly over after all!

◆ **se tirer de** *vp+prép* [se sortir de] to get out of ■ **il s'est bien/mal tiré de l'entrevue** he did well/badly at the interview ▶ **s'en** ~ *fam* [s'en sortir] : **avec son culot, elle s'en tirera toujours** with her cheek, she'll always come out on top ■ **si tu ne m'avais pas aidé à finir la maquette, je ne m'en serais jamais tiré** if you hadn't given me a hand with the model, I'd never have managed ■ **rien à faire, je ne m'en tire pas!** [financièrement] it's impossible, I just can't make ends meet! ■ **il y a peu de chances qu'il s'en tire** [qu'il survive] the odds are against him pulling through ■ **tu ne t'en tireras pas avec de simples excuses** [être quitte] you won't get away *ou* off with just a few words of apology ■ **je m'en suis tiré avec une suspension de permis** I got away with my licence being suspended ■ **s'en** ~ **à** *ou* **avec** *ou* **pour** [devoir payer] to have to pay ■ **à quatre, on ne s'en tirera pas à moins de 150 euros le repas** the meal will cost at least 150 euros for the four of us ■ **il ne s'en tirera pas comme ça** he won't get off so lightly, he won't get away with it ■ **on n'a encaissé qu'un seul but, on ne s'en est pas trop mal tirés** they scored only one goal against us, we didn't do too badly ■ **je n'aime pas faire de discours – tu t'en es très bien tiré** I don't like to make speeches – you did very well.

tiret [tirɛ] *nm* **1.** IMPR [de dialogue] dash ■ [en fin de ligne] rule **2.** [trait d'union] hyphen.

tirette [tirɛt] *nf* **1.** ÉLECTR pull knob **2.** [d'un meuble] (sliding) leaf.

tireur, euse [tirœr, øz] *nm, f* **1.** [criminel, terroriste] gunman ■ [de la police] marksman ■ **bon/mauvais** ~ good/bad shot ▶ ~ **isolé** *ou* **embusqué** sniper ■ ~ **d'élite** sharpshooter **2.** [aux boules] driver **3.** BANQUE drawer **4.** ESCRIME fencer **5.** FOOTBALL shooter **6.** PHOTO printer **7.** : ~ **de cartes, tireuse de cartes** fortune-teller *(who reads cards)*.

◆ **tireuse** *nf* **1.** PHOTO printer **2.** [pour le vin] bottle filling machine.

tiroir [tirwar] *nm* **1.** [de meuble] drawer **2.** MÉCAN slide valve ■ ~ **rond** *ou* **à pistons** piston valve.

◆ **à tiroirs** *loc adj* **1.** [à épisodes] *containing episodes independent of the main action* **2.** *fam* [à rallonge] : **un nom à ~s** a double-barrelled name.

tiroir-caisse [tirwarkɛs] *(pl* **tiroirs-caisses**) *nm* till.

tisane [tizan] *nf* [infusion] herb tea, herbal tea.

tisanière [tizanjɛr] *nf* teapot *(for herbal tea)*.

tison [tizɔ̃] *nm* brand.

tisonner [3] [tizɔne] *vt* to poke.

tisonnier [tizɔnje] *nm* poker ■ **donner un coup de ~ dans le feu** to give the fire a poke.

tissage [tisaʒ] *nm* **1.** [procédé] weaving ■ [entrecroisement de fils] weave ■ **un ~ serré/lâche** a close/loose weave **2.** [bâtiment] cloth mill.

tisser [3] [tise] *vt* **1.** TEXT [laine, coton, tissu] to weave ■ **l'habitude tisse des liens** [entre des personnes] the more you get to know someone, the closer you feel to them **2.** [toile d'araignée] to spin **3.** *sout* [élaborer] to weave, to construct ■ **l'auteur a subtilement tissé son intrigue** the playwright subtly wove *ou* constructed the plot.

tisserand, e [tisrɑ̃, ɑ̃d] *nm, f* weaver.

tisseur, euse [tisœr, øz] *nm, f* **1.** [artisan] weaver **2.** [industriel] mill owner.

tissu [tisy] *nm* **1.** TEXT fabric, material, cloth ■ **une longueur de ~** a length of fabric ▶ **du ~ d'ameublement** furnishing fabric *ou* material ■ **le rayon des ~s d'ameublement** the soft furnishings department ■ ~ **matelassé** quilted material **2.** *fig* & *sout* [enchevêtrement] : **un ~ de mensonges** a pack *ou* tissue *sout* of lies ■ **un ~ d'incohérences** a mass of contradictions **3.** SOCIOL fabric, make-up ■ **le ~ social** the social fabric ■ **le ~ urbain** the urban infrastructure **4.** BIOL tissue ■ ~ **musculaire** muscle tissue **5.** BOT tissue.

◆ **de tissu, en tissu** *loc adj* fabric *(modif)*, cloth *(modif)*.

tissu-éponge [tisyepɔ̃ʒ] *(pl* **tissus-éponges**) *nm* terry, terry-towelling ■ **en ~** terry *(modif)*, terry-towelling *(modif)*, terry cloth US.

titan [titɑ̃] *nm litt* [colosse] titan ■ **c'est un ~** he's got superhuman strength.

◆ **de titan** *loc adj* [travail] Herculean.

Titan [titɑ̃] *npr* **1.** ASTRON Titan **2.** ARM : **(missile)** ~ Titan missile.

titane [titan] *nm* titanium.

titanesque [titanɛsk], **titanique** [titanik] *adj litt* [force] massive, superhuman ■ [travail] Herculean ■ [ouvrage] monumental.

Tite [tit] *npr* Titus.

Tite-Live [titliv] *npr* Livy.

titi [titi] *nm fam* ~ **parisien** Parisian urchin.

Titicaca [titikaka] *npr* : **le lac ~** Lake Titicaca.

Titien [tisjɛ̃] *npr* : **(le) ~** Titian.

titillation [titijasjɔ̃] *nf* **1.** [léger chatouillement] tickling, tickle **2.** *fig* [excitation de l'esprit] titillation.

titiller [3] [titije] *vt* **1.** [chatouiller agréablement] to tickle ■ **le champagne me titillait le palais** the champagne tickled my palate **2.** *fig* [exciter légèrement] to titillate.

titrage [titraʒ] *nm* **1.** [d'un film] titling **2.** CHIM titration, titrating **3.** MIN [d'un minerai] assaying **4.** TEXT counting.

titre [titr] *nm*

A.

1. [d'un roman, d'un poème] title ■ [d'un chapitre] title, heading
2. IMPR : ~ **courant** running title ■ **grand ~** full title ■ **(page de) ~** title page
3. PRESSE headline ■ ~ **sur cinq colonnes à la une** five column front page headline ▶ **les gros ~s** the main headlines ■ **faire les gros ~s des quotidiens** to hit *ou* to make the front page of the daily newspapers

B.

1. [désignation d'un rang, d'une dignité] title ■ **porter un ~** to have a title, to be titled ■ **porter le ~ de duc** to have the title of duke ▶ **un ~ de noblesse** *ou* **nobiliaire** a title ■ **avoir des ~s de noblesse** to be titled
2. [nom de charge, de grade] qualification ■ **conférer le ~ de docteur à qqn** to confer the title of doctor on *ou* upon sb
3. SPORT title ■ **mettre son ~ en jeu** to risk one's title

C.

1. [certificat] credentials ■ **voici les ~s à présenter à l'appui de votre demande** the following documents must accompany your application ■ **décliner ses ~s universitaires** to list one's academic *ou* university qualifications ■ **recruter sur ~s** to recruit on the basis of (paper) qualifications ▶ **~ de pension** pension book ▪ **~ de permission** (leave) pass ▪ **~ de transport** ticket

2. *fig* ▶ **son ~ de gloire est d'avoir introduit l'informatique dans l'entreprise** his proudest achievement is to have computerized the company

3. BANQUE (transferable) security ▪ **avance sur ~s** advance on *ou* against securities

4. BOURSE [certificat] certificate ▪ [valeur] security ▪ **les ~s** securities, bonds ▶ **~ nominatif** registered bond ▪ **~ au porteur** [action] bearer share ; [obligation] floater *ou* bearer security

5. DR title ▪ **~ de propriété** title deed, document of title ▪ **juste ~** good title

6. FIN : **~ budgétaire** ≃ budget item *(one of the seven categories into which public spending is divided in the French budget)*

D.

1. JOAILL fineness, titre *spéc* ▪ **le ~ des monnaies d'or et d'argent est fixé par la loi** the precious metal content of gold and silver coins is determined by law

2. PHARM titre

3. TEXT count

E.

[locutions] : **à ~ amical** as a friend ▪ **à ~ consultatif** in an advisory capacity ▪ **à ~ d'essai** on a trial basis ▪ **à ~ exceptionnel** exceptionally ▪ **à ~ privé/professionnel** in a private/professional capacity ▪ **décoration attribuée à ~ posthume** posthumous award ▪ **à ~ provisoire** on a provisional basis ▪ **présidence accordée à ~ honorifique** honorary title of president ▪ **à ~ gracieux** free of charge, without charge ▪ **à ~ onéreux** for a fee *ou* consideration ▪ **à ~ de** [en tant que] : **consulter qqn à ~ d'ami** to consult sb as a friend ▪ **demander une somme à ~ d'avance** to ask for some money by way of an advance ▪ **à ~ d'exemple** by way of an example, as an example ▪ **à ~ indicatif** for information only ▪ **à quel ~?** [en vertu de quel droit] in what capacity? ; [pour quelle raison] on what grounds? ▪ **à quel ~ vous occupez-vous de ses affaires?** [gén] in what capacity are you looking after his affairs? ; [avec irritation] who told you you could *ou* who gave you permission to look after his affairs?

◆ **à aucun titre** *loc adv* on no account ▪ **il n'est à aucun ~ mon ami** he is no friend of mine.

◆ **à ce titre** *loc adv* [pour cette raison] for this reason, on this account ▪ **l'accord est signé et à ce ~ je suis satisfait** the agreement has been signed and for this reason I am satisfied.

◆ **à de nombreux titres, à divers titres** *loc adv* for several reasons, on more than one account ▪ **je me félicite à plus d'un ~ du résultat de ces négociations** I have more than one reason to be pleased with the outcome of these negotiations.

◆ **à juste titre** *loc adv* [préférer] understandably, rightly ▪ [croire] correctly, justly, rightly ▪ **elle s'est emportée, (et) à juste ~** she lost her temper and understandably *ou* rightly so.

◆ **à plus d'un titre** = **à de nombreux titres.**

◆ **au même titre** *loc adv* for the same reasons ▪ **elle a obtenu une prime, j'en réclame une au même ~** she got a bonus, I think I should have one too for the same reasons.

◆ **au même titre que** *loc conj* for the same reasons as ▪ **je proteste au même ~ que mon voisin** I protest for the same reasons as my neighbour.

◆ **en titre** *loc adj* **1.** ADMIN titular **2.** [officiel - fournisseur, marchand] usual, appointed ▪ **le fournisseur en ~ de la cour de Hollande** the official *ou* appointed supplier to the Dutch Court.

titré, e [titre] *adj* **1.** [anobli] titled **2.** PHARM [liqueur, solution] standard *(modif).*

titrer [3] [titre] *vt* **1.** PRESSE : **~ qqch** to run sthg as a headline **2.** PHARM to titrate **3.** [anoblir] to confer a title upon **4.** [œuvre d'art, roman] to give a title to, to entitle.

titubant, e [titybɑ̃, ɑ̃t] *adj* [démarche] unsteady, wobbly ▪ **un ivrogne ~** a drunkard staggering about.

tituber [3] [titybe] *vi* [ivrogne] to stagger *ou* to reel *ou* (along) ▪ [malade] to stagger (along).

titulaire [titylɛr] ◇ *adj* **1.** [enseignant] tenured ▪ [évêque] titular ▪ **être ~** [professeur d'université] to have tenure ; [sportif] to be under contract **2.** [détenteur] : **être ~ de** [permis, document, passeport] to hold ▪ **être ~ d'un compte en banque** to be an account holder **3.** DR : **être ~ d'un droit** to be entitled to a right. ◇ *nmf* **1.** ADMIN incumbent **2.** [détenteur - d'un permis] holder ; [- d'un passeport] bearer, holder **3.** DR : **le ~ d'un droit** the person entitled to a right **4.** SPORT player under contract.

titularisation [titylarizasjɔ̃] *nf* [d'un professeur d'université] granting tenure to ▪ [d'un enseignant] appointment to a permanent post ▪ [d'un sportif] giving a contract to.

titulariser [3] [titylarize] *vt* [enseignant] to appoint to a permanent post ▪ [sportif] to give a contract to ▪ [professeur d'université] : **être titularisé** to be given *ou* to be granted tenure ▪ **il attend d'être titularisé** he's waiting for tenure.

TMS [teɛmɛs] (*abr de* **troubles musculo-squelettiques**) *nmpl* MÉD RSI.

TNP (*abr de* **Théâtre national populaire**) *npr m* : **le ~** the French National Theatre *(based at the Palais de Chaillot in Paris until 1972 and at Villeurbanne near Lyon since then).*

TNT ◇ *nm* (*abr de* **trinitrotoluène**) TNT.
◇ *nf* (*abr de* **télévision numérique terrestre**) digital television, DTT.

toast [tost] *nm* **1.** [en buvant] toast ▪ **~ de bienvenue** toast of welcome ▪ **porter un ~** to propose a toast ▪ **porter un ~ à qqn** to drink (a toast) to sb, to toast sb **2.** [pain grillé] piece of toast ▪ **des ~s au saumon** salmon canapés.

toaste(u)r [tostɛr] *nm* toaster.

toboggan [tɔbɔgɑ̃] *nm* **1.** [glissière - sur terre] slide ; [- dans l'eau] chute ▪ **les enfants qui font du ~** the children going down the slide ▪ **tu veux faire du ~?** do you want to go on the slide? ▶ **~ de secours** escape chute **2.** AUTO [armature de pneu] (type) casing reinforcement.

toc [tɔk] ◇ *nm fam* **1.** [imitation sans valeur - d'un matériau] fake, worthless imitation ; [- d'une pierre] rhinestone, paste ; [- d'un bijou] fake ▪ **en ~** fake, imitation ▪ **sa bague, c'est du ~** her ring is fake **2.** *fig* [ce qui est factice] sham ▪ **sa culture/son amitié, c'est du ~** his so-called education/friendship is just a sham *ou* is all on the surface.
◇ *adj inv fam* rubbishy *UK*, trashy, tacky ▪ **ça fait ~** it looks cheap *ou* tacky.
◇ *interj* **1.** [coups à la porte] : **~~!** knock knock! **2.** *fam* [après une remarque] : **et ~!** so there!, put that in your pipe and smoke it! ▪ **et ~, bien fait pour toi/lui/eux!** and (it) serves you/him/them right!

TOC (*abr de* **troubles obsessionnels compulsifs**) [teose] *ou* [tɔk] *nmpl* MÉD OCD.

tocade [tɔkad] = **toquade.**

tocard, e [tɔkar, ard] *adj fam* [tableau, décor] naff *UK*, tacky.
◆ **tocard** *nm fam* **1.** [cheval] old nag **2.** [personne] dead loss, (born) loser.

toccata [tɔkata] *nf* toccata.

tocsin [tɔksɛ̃] *nm* alarm bell, tocsin *sout* ▪ **sonner le ~** to ring the alarm, to sound the tocsin *sout.*

toge [tɔʒ] *nf* **1.** ANTIQ toga ▪ **~ prétexte/virile** toga praetexta/virilis **2.** [de magistrat] gown.

Togo [tɔgo] *npr m* : **le ~** Togo ▪ **au ~** in Togo.

togolais, e [tɔgɔlɛ, ɛz] *adj* Togolese.
◆ **Togolais, e** *nm, f* Togolese ▪ **les Togolais** the Togolese.

tohu-bohu [tɔybɔy] *nm inv* **1.** [désordre et confusion] confusion, chaos **2.** [bruit - de voitures, d'enfants] racket, din ; [- d'un marché, d'une gare] hustle and bustle ; [- d'une foule] hubbub ; [- d'une foire] hurly-burly.

toi [twa] *pron pers* **1.** [après un impératif] : **dis-~ bien que...** bear in mind that... ▪ **réveille-~!** wake up! ▪ **habille-~!** get dressed!
2. [sujet] you ▪ **qui va le faire? – ~** who's going to do it? – you (are) ▪ **~ parti, il ne restera personne** when you're gone there'll be nobody left ▪ **qu'est-ce que tu en sais, ~?** what do YOU know about it? ▪ **tu t'amuses, ~, au moins** at least YOU'RE having fun ▪ **~ et moi** you and I ▪ **~ seul peux la convaincre** you're the only one who can persuade her
3. [avec un présentatif] you ▪ **c'est ~?** is it you? ▪ **c'est ~ qui le dis!** that's what YOU say!

4. [complément] you ▪ **il vous a invités, Pierre et ~** he's invited you and Pierre ▪ **~, je te connais!** I know you! ▮ [après une préposition] : **c'est à ~ qu'on l'a demandé** you were the one who was asked, YOU were asked ▪ **qui te l'a dit, à ~?** who told YOU about it? ▪ **je te fais confiance, à ~** I trust you ▪ **eh, je te parle, à ~!** hey, I'm talking to you! ▪ **un ami à ~** *fam* a friend of yours ▪ **c'est à ~?** is this yours? ▪ **à ~ de jouer!** your turn! **5.** [pronom réfléchi] yourself ▪ **alors, tu es content de ~?** I hope you're pleased with yourself, then!

toile [twal] *nf* **1.** TEXT [matériau brut] canvas, (plain) fabric ▪ **~ de coton/lin** cotton/linen cloth ▪ **~ à bâches** tarpaulin ▪ **~ de jute** gunny, (jute) hessian ▪ **~ à matelas** ticking ▪ **~ métis** cotton-linen mix ▪ **~ à sac** sackcloth, sacking ▪ **grosse ~** rough *ou* coarse canvas ▮ [tissu apprêté] cloth ▪ **~ cirée** waxcloth ▪ **~ émeri** emery cloth ▪ **~ plastifiée** plastic-coated cloth ▪ **~ de tente** tent canvas **2.** *fam* [film] : **se payer une ~** to go to the flicks **3.** ART [vierge] canvas ▪ [peinte] canvas, painting **4.** COUT cloth ▪ **~ à patron** toile **5.** NAUT [ensemble des voiles d'un navire] sails **6.** [couverture d'un livre] cloth **7.** THÉÂTRE (painted) curtain ▪ **~ de fond** *pr & fig* backdrop **8.** ZOOL web ▪ **~ d'araignée** cobweb, spider's web.
◆ **Toile** *nf* : **la Toile** the Web.
◆ **de toile, en toile** *loc adj* [robe, pantalon] cotton *(modif)* ▪ [sac] canvas *(modif)*.

toilerie [twalri] *nf* **1.** [atelier] canvas mill **2.** [commerce] canvas trade ▪ [fabrication] canvas manufacturing, canvas-making.

toilettage [twalɛtaʒ] *nm* [d'un chat, d'un chien] grooming.

toilette [twalɛt] *nf* **1.** [soins de propreté] : **faire sa ~** to have a wash, to get washed ▪ **faire une ~ de chat** to give o.s. a lick and a promise ▪ **faire la ~ d'un malade** to wash a sick person ▪ **faire la ~ d'un mort** to lay out a corpse ▪ **produits pour la ~ de bébé** baby-care products ▪ **articles** *ou* **produits de ~** toiletries **2.** [lustrage du pelage, des plumes] grooming ▪ **le chat fait sa ~** the cat's washing *ou* licking itself **3.** *sout* [tenue vestimentaire] clothes, outfit ▪ **elle est en grande ~** she is (dressed) in all her finery **4.** [table] dressing table ▪ [avec vasque] washstand.
◆ **toilettes** *nfpl* [chez un particulier] toilet *UK*, bathroom *US* ▪ [dans un café] toilet, toilets *UK*, restroom *US* ▪ **~s (publiques)** (public) toilets *UK*, restroom *US* ▪ **aller aux ~s** to go to the toilet ▪ **je cherche les ~s** [pour dames] I'm looking for the ladies *UK ou* ladies room *US* ; [pour hommes] I'm looking for the gents *UK ou* the men's room *US*.

toiletter [4] [twalete] *vt* **1.** [chien, chat] to groom ▪ **je fais ~ le chien au moins une fois par mois** I take the dog to be groomed at least once a month **2.** *fam* [modifier légèrement - texte] to amend, to doctor.

toi-même [twamɛm] *pron pers* yourself ▪ **tu l'as vu ~** you saw it yourself ▪ **vérifie par ~** check for yourself ▪ **imbécile ~!** *fam* same to you!, look who's talking!

toise [twaz] *nf* **1.** [règle graduée] height gauge ▪ **passer qqn à la ~** to measure sb's height **2.** *arch former French unit of measure equal to 1.949m.*

toiser [3] [twaze] *vt* **1.** *vieilli* [personne] to measure sb's height **2.** *fig* **~ qqn** to look sb up and down, to eye sb from head to foot.

toison [twazɔ̃] *nf* **1.** ZOOL fleece **2.** [chevelure] mane **3.** *fam* [poils] bushy (tuft of) hair **4.** MYTHOL : **la Toison d'or** the Golden Fleece.

toit [twa] *nm* **1.** ARCHIT & CONSTR roof ▪ **habiter sous les ~s** [dans une chambre] to live in an attic room *ou* in a garret ; [dans un appartement] to live in a top-floor flat *UK ou* top-storey apartment *US* with a sloping ceiling ▶ **~ plat/en pente** flat/sloping roof ▪ **~ d'ardoises** slate roof ▪ **~ de chaume** thatched roof ▪ **~ en terrasse** terrace roof ▪ **~ de tuiles** tiled roof **2.** [demeure] roof ▪ **avoir un ~** to have a roof over one's head ▪ **chercher un ~** to look for somewhere to live ▪ **vivre sous le même ~** to live under the same roof **3.** AUTO : **~ ouvrant** sunroof ▪ **une voiture à ~ ouvrant** a car with a sunroof **4.** MIN roof.

toiture [twatyr] *nf* [ensemble des matériaux] roofing ▪ [couverture] roof ▪ **toute la ~ du manoir** all the roofs of the manor house.

tokaj [tɔkaj] *nm* (Hungarian) Tokay.

tokay [tɔkɛ] *nm* ŒNOL (Alsatian) Tokay.

Tokyo [tɔkjo] *npr* Tokyo.

tôlard, e△ [tolar, ard] *arg crime* = **taulard**.

tôle [tol] *nf* **1.** MÉTALL [non découpée] sheet metal ▪ [morceau] metal sheet ▪ **~ d'acier/d'aluminium** sheet steel/aluminium ▪ **~ ondulée** corrugated iron ▪ **~ galvanisée/laminée** galvanized/laminated iron **2.** *fam* [mauvais revêtement de route] uneven surface **3.** ÉLECTR : **~ magnétique** magnetized strip **4.** △ = **taule**.

tôlé, e [tole] *adj* AUTO metal-panelled.

Tolède [tɔlɛd] *npr* Toledo.

tolérable [tɔlerabl] *adj* [bruit, chaleur, douleur] bearable, tolerable ▪ [attitude, entorse à une règle] tolerable, permissible ▪ **son impertinence n'est plus ~** her impertinence can no longer be tolerated.

tolérance [tɔlerɑ̃s] *nf* **1.** [à l'égard d'une personne] tolerance ▪ [à l'égard d'un règlement] latitude ▪ **ce n'est pas un droit, c'est une simple ~** this is not a right, it is merely something which is tolerated ▪ **il y a une ~ d'un litre d'alcool par personne** each person is allowed to bring in a litre of spirits free of duty ▶ **~ orthographique** permitted variation in spelling **2.** BOT & PHYSIOL tolerance ▪ **~ au bruit/à la chaleur/à une drogue** tolerance to noise/to heat/to a drug ▪ **~ des greffes tissulaires** acceptance *ou* tolerance of tissue grafts ▶ **~ immunitaire** immunological tolerance **3.** MÉCAN tolerance ▪ **affecter une ~ à une cote** to allow a margin of tolerance *(when determining dimensions)* **4.** RELIG toleration.

tolérant, e [tɔlerɑ̃, ɑ̃t] *adj* **1.** [non sectaire] tolerant, broad-minded ▪ **il est ~ et éloigné de tout fanatisme** he is tolerant and a stranger to all forms of extremism **2.** [indulgent] lenient, indulgent, easygoing ▪ **une mère trop ~e** an overindulgent *ou* excessively lenient mother.

tolérer [18] [tɔlere] *vt* **1.** [permettre - infraction] to tolerate, to allow ▪ **ils tolèrent le stationnement bilatéral à certaines heures** you're allowed to park on both sides of the street at certain times of the day ▪ **le directeur ne tolère pas les retards** the boss will not have people arriving late **2.** [admettre - attitude, personne] to tolerate, to put up with *(insép)* ▪ **je ne tolérerai pas son insolence** I won't stand for *ou* put up with *ou* tolerate his rudeness ▪ **elle ne l'aimait pas, elle tolérait juste sa présence à ses côtés** she didn't like him, she just put up with having him around **3.** [supporter - médicament, traitement] to tolerate ▪ **les femmes enceintes tolèrent bien ce médicament** pregnant women can take this drug without adverse effects.

tôlerie [tolri] *nf* **1.** [fabrique] sheet metal workshop **2.** [technique] sheet metal manufacture **3.** [commerce] sheet metal trade **4.** [d'un véhicule] panels, bodywork ▪ [d'un réservoir] plates, (steel) cladding.

tôlier, ère△ [tolje, ɛr] = **taulier**.
◆ **tôlier** ◇ *nm* INDUST sheet metal worker ▪ AUTO panel beater.
◇ *adj m* : **ouvrier ~** sheet metal worker.

tollé [tɔle] *nm* general outcry ▪ **soulever un ~ général** to provoke a general outcry.

Tolstoï [tɔlstɔj] *npr* : **Léon ~** Leon Tolstoy.

TOM [tɔm] *(abr de* **Territoire d'Outre-Mer***) nm inv French overseas territory, created in 1946 and abolished in 2003.*

tomate [tɔmat] *nf* **1.** BOT [plante] tomato (plant) ▪ [fruit] tomato ▶ **~ cerise** cherry tomato ▪ **~s farcies** CULIN stuffed tomatoes ▪ **envoyer des ~s (pourries) à qqn** [conspuer] to boo sb **2.** *fam* [boisson] *pastis drink with grenadine.*
◆ **à la tomate** *loc adj* [soupe, sauce] tomato *(modif)*.

tombal, e, als *ou* **aux** [tɔ̃bal, o] *adj* funerary, tomb *(modif)*, tombstone *(modif)* ▪ **inscription ~e** funerary *ou* tomb *ou* tombstone inscription.

tombant, e [tɔ̃bɑ̃, ɑ̃t] *adj* **1.** [oreille, moustache] floppy ▪ [seins, fesses] sagging ▪ [épaules] sloping ▪ [tentures] hanging **2.** [jour] failing, dwindling.

tombe [tɔ̃b] *nf* [fosse] grave ▪ [dalle] tombstone ▪ [monument] tomb ▪ **aller sur la ~ de qqn** [pour se recueillir] to visit sb's grave

▪ **muet** *ou* **silencieux comme une ~** as silent *ou* quiet as the grave ▪ **sa femme est morte, il la suivra sans doute d'ici peu dans la ~** his wife has died, he probably won't outlive her long.

tombeau, x [tɔ̃bo] *nm* **1.** [sépulcre] grave, tomb, sepulchre *litt* ▪ **descendre au ~** to go to one's grave ▪ **conduire** *ou* **mettre qqn au ~** [causer sa mort] to send sb to his/her grave **2.** *loc* **à ~ ouvert** at breakneck speed.

tombée [tɔ̃be] *nf* **: à la ~ du jour** *ou* **de la nuit** at nightfall *ou* dusk.

tomber[1] [3] [tɔ̃be] ◇ *vi (aux être)*

> **A.** CHANGER DE NIVEAU - SENS PROPRE ET FIGURÉ
> **B.** SE PRODUIRE, ARRIVER

A. CHANGER DE NIVEAU - SENS PROPRE ET FIGURÉ

1. [personne] to fall (down), to fall over ▪ [meuble, pile de livres] to fall over, to topple over ▪ [cloison] to fall down, to collapse ▪ [avion, bombe, projectile] to fall ▪ **~ par terre** to fall on the floor, to fall down ▪ **~ à plat ventre** to fall flat on one's face ▪ **~ dans un fauteuil** to fall *ou* to collapse into an armchair ▪ **~ de fatigue** to be ready to drop (from exhaustion) ▪ **~ de sommeil** to be asleep on one's feet ▪ **ne monte pas à l'échelle, tu vas ~** don't go up the ladder, you'll fall off ▪ **~ dans l'escalier** to fall down the stairs ▪ **~ de cheval** to fall off *ou* from a horse ▪ **~ d'un arbre** to fall out of a tree *ou* from a tree ▪ **faire ~ qqn** [en lui faisant un croche-pied] to trip sb up ; [en le bousculant] to knock *ou* to push sb over ▪ **le vent a fait ~ des arbres** the wind blew some trees over *ou* down ▪ **elle l'a fait ~ de la table** she pushed him off the table ▪ **faire ~ qqch** [en poussant] to push sthg over ; [en renversant] to knock sthg over ; [en lâchant] to drop sthg ; [en donnant un coup de pied] to kick sthg over ▪ **j'ai fait ~ mes lunettes** I've dropped my glasses ▸ **tu es tombé bien bas** *fig* you've sunk very low
2. *sout* [mourir] to fall, to die ▪ **~ sur le champ de bataille** to fall on the battlefield ▪ **ceux qui sont tombés au champ d'honneur** those killed in action
3. [se détacher - feuille, pétale, fruit] to fall *ou* to drop off ; [- cheveu, dent] to fall *ou* to come out ▪ **ne ramasse pas les cerises qui sont tombées** don't pick the cherries which are on the ground
4. [pendre - cheveux, tentures] to hang ; [- moustaches] to droop ; [- seins] to sag, to droop ▪ **ses longs cheveux lui tombaient dans le dos** her long hair hung down her back ▪ **une mèche lui tombait sur un œil** a lock of hair hung over one eye ▪ **il a les épaules qui tombent** he's got sloping shoulders ▪ **la robe tombe bien sur toi** the dress hangs well *ou* nicely on you
5. [s'abattre, descendre - rayon de soleil, radiations, nuit] to fall ; [- brouillard, gifle, coup] to come down ▪ **la neige/pluie tombait** it was snowing/raining ▪ **une goutte est tombée dans mon cou** a drop trickled *ou* rolled down my neck ▪ *(tournure impersonnelle)* **il tombe en moyenne 3 mm d'eau par jour** the average daily rainfall is 3 mm ▪ **il en est tombé, de la pluie!** *fam* it tipped *ou* threw it down! *UK*, it poured! ▪ **il tombera de la neige sur l'est** there will be snow in the east ▪ **il tombe quelques gouttes** it's spitting ▪ **il tombe de grosses gouttes/gros flocons** big drops/flakes are falling ▪ **il tombe de la grêle** it's hailing ▪ **toi, tu as ta paie qui tombe tous les mois** *fam* you have a regular salary coming in (every month) ▪ **il lui tombe au moins 3 000 euros par mois** *fam* he has at least 3,000 euros coming in every month ▸ **ça va ~!** [il va pleuvoir] it's going to pour (with rain)! ; [il va y avoir des coups] you're/we're *etc* going to get it! ▪ **des têtes vont ~!** heads will roll! ▪ **~ sous les yeux de qqn** to come to sb's attention
6. [déboucher] **: là où la rue Daneau tombe dans le boulevard Lamain** at the point where Rue Daneau joins *ou* meets Boulevard Lamain ▪ **continuez tout droit et vous tomberez sur le marché** keep going straight on and you'll come to the market
7. [diminuer - prix, température, voix, ton] to fall, to drop ; [- fréquentation] to drop (off) ; [- fièvre] to come down, to drop ; [- colère] to die down, to subside ; [- inquiétude] to melt away, to vanish ; [- enthousiasme, agitation, intérêt] to fall *ou* to fade away, to subside ; [- tempête] to subside, to abate, to die away ; [- vent] to drop, to fall, to die down ; [- jour] to draw to a close ▪ **la température est tombée de 10 degrés** the temperature has dropped *ou* fallen (by) 10 degrees ▪ **sa cote de popularité est tombée très bas/à 28 %** his popularity rating has plummeted/has dropped to 28% ▪ **faire ~ la fièvre** to bring down *ou* to reduce sb's temperature
8. [disparaître - obstacle] to disappear, to vanish ; [- objection, soupçon] to vanish, to fade ▪ **sa réticence est tombée devant mes arguments** she gave way in the face of my arguments ▪ **sa joie tomba brusquement** his happiness suddenly vanished *ou* evaporated ▪ **ses défenses sont tombées** he dropped his guard
9. [s'effondrer - cité] to fall ; [- dictature, gouvernement, empire] to fall, to be brought down, to be toppled ; [- record] to be broken ; [- concurrent] to go out, to be defeated ; [- plan, projet] to fall through ▪ **les candidats de droite sont tombés au premier tour** the right-wing candidates were eliminated in the first round ▪ **le chef du gang est tombé hier** the ringleader was arrested yesterday ▪ **faire ~** [cité] to bring down ; [gouvernement] to bring down, to topple ; [record] to break ; [concurrent] to defeat
10. [devenir] **: ~ amoureux** to fall in love ▪ **~ enceinte** to become pregnant ▪ **~ malade** to become *ou* to fall ill ▪ **~ fou** *fam* to go mad ▪ **~ (raide) mort** to drop dead, to fall down dead
11. JEUX [carte] **: tous les atouts sont tombés** all the trumps have been played

B. SE PRODUIRE, ARRIVER

1. [événement] to fall *ou* to be on ▪ **mon anniversaire tombe un dimanche** my birthday is *ou* falls on a Sunday ▪ **~ juste** [calcul] to work out exactly ▪ **bien ~** to come at the right moment *ou* time ▪ **ton bureau l'intéresse – ça tombe bien, je voulais m'en débarrasser** he's interested in your desk – that's good, I wanted to get rid of it ▪ **mal ~** to come at the wrong moment *ou* at a bad time ▪ **le mardi tombe assez mal pour moi** Tuesday's not a good day *ou* very convenient for me ‖ [personne] **: on est tombés en plein pendant la grève des trains** we got there right in the middle of the rail strike ▪ **~ juste** [deviner] to guess right ▪ **bien ~** [opportunément] to turn up at the right moment ; [avoir de la chance] to be lucky *ou* in luck ▪ **ah, vous tombez bien, je voulais justement vous parler** ah, you've come just at the right moment, I wanted to speak to you ▪ **tu ne pouvais pas mieux ~!** you couldn't have come at a better time! ▪ **il est excellent, ce melon, je suis bien tombé** this melon's excellent, I was lucky ▪ **mal ~** [inopportunément] to turn up at the wrong moment ; [ne pas avoir de chance] to be unlucky *ou* out of luck ▪ **il ne pouvait pas plus mal ~** he couldn't have picked a worse time ▪ **travailler pour Fanget? tu aurais pu plus mal ~** working for Fanget? it could be worse ▪ **tu tombes à point!** you've timed it perfectly!, perfect timing!
2. [nouvelles] to be *ou* to come out ▪ **les dernières nouvelles qui viennent de ~ font état de 143 victimes** news just out *ou* released puts the number of victims at 143 ▪ **à 20 h, la nouvelle est tombée** the news came through at 8 p.m.

◇ *vt (aux avoir)* **1.** [triompher de - candidat, challenger] to defeat **2.** *fam* [séduire] to seduce ▪ **il les tombe toutes** he's got them falling at his feet **3.** *fam loc* **~ la veste** to slip off one's jacket.

◆ **tomber dans** *v+prép* [se laisser aller à - découragement, désespoir] to sink *ou* to lapse into *(insép)* ▪ **sans ~ dans l'excès inverse** without going to the other extreme ▪ **des traditions qui tombent dans l'oubli** traditions which are falling into oblivion ▪ **~ dans la dépression** to become depressed ▪ **~ dans l'erreur** to commit an error.

◆ **tomber en** *v+prép* **: ~ en lambeaux** to fall to bits *ou* pieces ▪ **~ en ruine** to go to rack and ruin ▪ **~ en morceaux** to fall to pieces.

◆ **tomber sur** *v+prép fam* **1.** [trouver par hasard - personne] to come across, to run *ou* to bump into, to meet up with *US* ; [- objet perdu, trouvaille] to come across *ou* upon, to stumble across ▪ **je suis tombé sur ton article dans le journal** I came across your article in the newspaper ▪ **je suis tombé sur une arête** I bit on a fishbone ▪ **on a tiré au sort et c'est tombé sur elle** lots were drawn and her name came up **2.** [avoir affaire à - examinateur, sujet d'examen] to get ▪ **quand j'ai téléphoné, je suis tombé sur sa mère/un répondeur** when I phoned, it was her mother who answered (me)/I got an answering machine **3.** [assaillir - personne] to set about, to go for ▪ **il tombe sur les nouveaux pour la moindre erreur** he comes down on the newcomers (like a ton of bricks) if they make the slightest mistake ▸ **il a fallu que ça tombe sur moi!** it had to be me! **4.** [se porter sur - regard, soupçon] to fall on ; [- conversation] to turn to.

tomber[2] [tɔ̃be] *nm litt* **au ~ du jour** *ou* **de la nuit** at nightfall *ou* dusk.

tombereau, x [tɔ̃bro] *nm* **1.** [benne] dumper, dump truck **2.** [contenu] truckload.

tombeur [tɔ̃bœr] *nm fam* **1.** [séducteur] ladykiller **2.** SPORT : **le ~ du champion d'Europe** the man who defeated the European champion.

tombola [tɔ̃bɔla] *nf* raffle, tombola.

Tombouctou [tɔ̃buktu] *npr* Timbuktu.

tome [tɔm] ◇ *nm* [section d'un ouvrage] part ▪ [volume entier] volume.
◇ *nf* = **tomme**.

tomette [tɔmɛt] = **tommette**.

tomme [tɔm] *nf* Tomme cheese.

tommette [tɔmɛt] *nf red hexagonal floor tile.*

ton[1] [tɔ̃] *nm*

A.
1. [qualité de la voix] tone ▪ **~ monocorde** drone ▪ **sur un ~ monocorde** monotonously
2. [hauteur de la voix] pitch (of voice) ▪ **~ nasillard** twang
3. [intonation] tone, intonation ▪ **d'un ~ sec** curtly ▪ **hausser le ~** to up the tone ▪ **pas la peine de prendre un ~ ironique/méchant pour me répondre!** there's no need to be so ironic/spiteful when you answer me! ▪ **ne me parle pas sur ce ~!** don't speak to me like that *ou* in that tone of voice! ▪ **ne le prends pas sur ce ~!** don't take it like that!
4. [style - d'une lettre, d'une œuvre artistique] tone, tenor
5. [manière de se comporter] ➊ **le bon ~** good form
6. LING [en phonétique] tone, pitch ▪ [dans une langue tonale] pitch ▪ **les langues à ~** tonal languages

B.
1. ACOUST tone
2. MUS [d'une voix, d'un instrument] tone ▪ [tube] crook, shank ▪ **prendre le ~** to tune (up) ▪ **baisser/élever le ~ en chantant** to lower/to raise the pitch while singing ▮ [mode musical] key ▪ **le ~ majeur/mineur** major/minor key ▪ **donner le ~** MUS to give the chord ; *fig* to set the tone ▪ **elle a très vite donné le ~ de la conversation** she quickly set the tone of the conversation

C.
1. [couleur] tone, shade ▪ **les verts sont en ~s dégradés** the greens are shaded (from dark to light) ▪ **être dans le même ~ que** to tone in with
2. ART shade ▪ **les ~s chauds/froids** warm/cold tones.

➡ **dans le ton** *loc adv* : **tu crois que je serai dans le ~?** do you think I'll fit in? ▪ **ici on ne fait pas de manières, il faudra te mettre dans le ~** we don't stand on ceremony here, you'll just have to take us as you find us.

➡ **de bon ton** *loc adj* in good taste ▪ **il est de bon ~ de mépriser l'argent** it's quite the thing *ou* good form to despise money.

➡ **sur le ton de** *loc prép* : **sur le ~ de la conversation** conversationally, in a conversational tone ▪ **sur le ~ de la plaisanterie** jokingly, in jest, in a joking tone.

➡ **sur tous les tons** *loc adv* in every possible way ▪ **on nous répète sur tous les ~s que...** we're being told over and over again that..., it's being drummed into us that...

➡ **ton sur ton** *loc adj* [en camaïeu] in matching tones *ou* shades.

ton[2] [tɔ̃] *(f ta* [ta], *devant n ou adj commençant par voyelle ou h muet ton* [tɔ̃n], *pl tes* [te]*) dét (adj poss)* **1.** [indiquant la possession] your ▪ **ta meilleure amie** your best friend ▪ **~ père et ta mère** your father and mother ▪ **tes frères et sœurs** your brothers and sisters ▪ **un de tes amis** one of your friends, a friend of yours **2.** *fam* [emploi expressif] : **eh bien regarde-la, TON émission!** all right then, watch your (damned) programme! ▪ **arrête de faire ~ intéressant!** stop trying to draw attention to yourself! ▪ **alors, tu as réussi à avoir ~ lundi?** so you managed to get Monday off, then? **3.** RELIG Thy.

tonal, e, als [tɔnal] *adj* **1.** LING pitch *(modif)* **2.** MUS tonal.

tonalité [tɔnalite] *nf* **1.** ART tonality **2.** MUS [organisation] tonality ▪ [d'un morceau] key **3.** [atmosphère] tone ▪ **le film prend vite une ~ tragique** the film soon becomes tragic in tone **4.** ACOUST tonality ▪ [d'une radio] tone **5.** TÉLÉCOM : **~ (d'invitation à numéroter)** dialling tone ▪ **je n'ai pas de ~** I'm not getting a *ou* there's no dialling tone ▪ **~ d'appel** ringing tone.

tondeur, euse [tɔ̃dœr, øz] *nm, f* shearer.
➡ **tondeuse** *nf* **1.** HORT : **tondeuse (à gazon)** (lawn) mower ▪ **tondeuse électrique/à main** electric/hand mower **2.** [de coiffeur] (pair of) clippers **3.** [pour moutons] (pair of) sheep shears **4.** TEXT (pair of) shears.

tondre [75] [tɔ̃dr] *vt* **1.** [cheveux] to crop ▪ [laine de mouton] to shear (off) ▪ **il a les cheveux tondus** he's got close-cropped hair *ou* a crew cut **2.** [mouton] to shear ▪ [chien] to clip **3.** [pelouse] to mow, to cut ▪ [haie] to clip **4.** *fam* [dépouiller, voler] to fleece ▪ [exploiter] to fleece, to take to the cleaners ▪ **~ qqn** [au jeu] to clean sb out.

tondu, e [tɔ̃dy] ◇ *adj* **1.** [crâne] closely cropped **2.** [mouton] shorn ▪ [caniche] clipped **3.** [pelouse] mowed, mown ▪ [haie] clipped.
◇ *nm, f* [personne tondue] *person with close-cropped hair.*
➡ **tondu** *nm fam vieilli* [moine] monk.
➡ **tondue** *nf* HIST : **les ~es** *French women whose heads were shaved at the end of World War II for fraternizing with Germans.*

tong [tɔ̃g] *nf* flip-flop ▪ **des ~s** (a pair of) flip-flops.

tonicité [tɔnisite] *nf* **1.** PHYSIOL tonicity *spéc,* muscular tone **2.** [de l'air, de la mer] tonic *ou* bracing effect.

tonifiant, e [tɔnifjɑ̃, ɑ̃t] *adj* **1.** [air, climat] bracing, invigorating ▪ [promenade] invigorating ▪ [crème, exercice, massage] tonic, toning **2.** [influence, conseils] stimulating, inspiring.

tonifier [9] [tɔnifje] *vt* [corps, peau] to tone up *(sép)* ▪ [cheveux] to give new life to ▪ [esprit] to stimulate ▪ **une marche au grand air tonifie l'organisme** a walk in the open air does wonders for the constitution.

tonique [tɔnik] ◇ *adj* **1.** [air, climat] bracing ▪ [médicament] tonic, fortifying ▪ [lotion] toning, tonic ▪ [boisson] tonic ▪ [activité] stimulating, invigorating **2.** PHYSIOL tonic **3.** LING [syllabe] tonic, stressed.
◇ *nm* **1.** MÉD tonic **2.** [lotion] toning lotion, skin tonic.
◇ *nf* MUS tonic, keynote.

tonitruant, e [tɔnitryɑ̃, ɑ̃t] *adj* thundering, resounding.

tonitruer [3] [tɔnitrye] *vi* to thunder, to resound.

tonnage [tɔnaʒ] *nm* **1.** [d'un bateau] : **~ brut/net** gross/net tonnage **2.** [d'un port] tonnage.

tonnant, e [tɔnɑ̃, ɑ̃t] *adj* [voix] thundering.

tonne [tɔn] *nf* **1.** [unité de masse] ton, tonne ▪ **un bateau de mille ~s** a thousand-ton ship ➊ **~ (métrique)** (metric) ton *ou* tonne ▪ **un (camion de) deux ~s** a two-ton lorry *UK ou* truck *US* **2.** *fam* **des ~s** [beaucoup] tons, heaps, loads ▪ **j'ai des ~s de choses à vous raconter** I've loads of things to tell you ▪ **en faire des ~s** [en rajouter] to lay it on (really) thick **3.** AGRIC [réservoir] tank ▪ [grand tonneau] large cask *ou* barrel ▪ [son contenu] cask, barrel.

tonneau, x [tɔno] *nm* **1.** [contenant pour liquide] cask, barrel ▪ **vin au ~** wine from the barrel *ou* cask ▪ **mettre du vin en ~** to pour wine in *ou* into barrels ➊ **c'est le ~ des Danaïdes** [travail interminable] it's an endless task ; [gouffre financier] it's a bottomless pit ▪ **le ~ de Diogène** Diogenes' tub **2.** [quantité de liquide] caskful, barrelful **3.** [accident] somersault ▪ **faire un ~** to roll over, to somersault.
➡ **du même tonneau** *loc adj fam* of the same ilk *péj.*

tonnelet [tɔnlɛ] *nm* keg, small cask.

tonnelier [tɔnəlje] *nm* cooper.

tonnelle [tɔnɛl] *nf* **1.** [abri] bower, arbour **2.** CHASSE tunnel net *(for partridges).*

tonnellerie [tɔnɛlri] *nf* [fabrication] cooperage.

tonner [3] [tɔne] ◇ *vi* [artillerie] to thunder, to roar, to boom ▪ **on entendait ~ les canons** you could hear the thunder *ou* roar of the cannons.
◇ *v impers* : **il tonne** it's thundering.

◆ **tonner contre** *v+prép* [suj: personne] to fulminate against.

tonnerre [tɔnɛr] ◇ *nm* **1.** [bruit de la foudre] thunder ■ **le ~ gronda dans le lointain** there was a rumble of thunder in the distance ■ **une voix de ~** a thunderous voice ▶ **coup de ~** *pr* thunderclap ■ **ce fut un véritable coup de ~** *fig* it caused a real storm ■ **ses révélations ont eu l'effet d'un coup de ~ dans l'assemblée** the meeting was thunderstruck by her revelations **2.** [tumulte soudain] storm, tumult, commotion ■ **un ~ d'applaudissements** thunderous applause.
◇ *interj fam* **~ (de Dieu)!** hell and damnation! ■ **~ de Brest!, mille ~s!** hang *ou* damn it all!
◆ **du tonnerre (de Dieu)** *fam vieilli* ◇ *loc adj* [voiture, fille] terrific, great ■ [repas, spectacle] terrific, fantastic ■ **un solo de batterie du ~** a really mean drum solo.
◇ *loc adv* tremendously *ou* terrifically well ■ **ça a marché du ~** it went like a dream.

tonsure [tɔ̃syr] *nf* **1.** RELIG [partie rasée] tonsure ■ [cérémonie] tonsuring ■ **porter la ~** to be tonsured **2.** *fam* [calvitie] bald patch ■ **il commence à avoir une petite ~** he's going a bit thin on top.

tonsuré [tɔ̃syre] ◇ *adj m* tonsured.
◇ *nm* monk, cleric.

tonsurer [3] [tɔ̃syre] *vt* to tonsure.

tonte [tɔ̃t] *nf* **1.** [de moutons - activité] shearing ; [- époque] shearing time **2.** [laine tondue] fleece **3.** [d'une pelouse] mowing.

tontine [tɔ̃tin] *nf* DR tontine.

tonton [tɔ̃tɔ̃] *nm* **1.** *fam* [oncle] uncle **2.** HIST : **~ macoute** Tonton Macoute, Haitian secret policeman *(under the Duvalier regime)*.

tonus [tɔnys] *nm* **1.** [dynamisme] dynamism, energy ■ **avoir du ~** to be full of energy **2.** PHYSIOL tonus ■ **~ musculaire** muscle tone.

top [tɔp] ◇ *nm* **1.** [signal sonore] pip, beep ■ **au quatrième ~ il sera exactement 1 h** at the fourth stroke, it will be 1 o'clock precisely **2.** [dans une course] : **~, partez!** ready, steady, go! ■ **donner le ~ de départ** to give the starting signal.
◇ *adj* **1.** [personne] : **~ modèle** top model **2.** [excellent] *fam* **c'est ~!** that's brilliant!

topaze [tɔpaz] *nf* topaz ■ **couleur ~** topaz.

toper [3] [tɔpe] *vi* : **tope là!** *fam* it's a deal!, you're on!

topinambour [tɔpinɑ̃bur] *nm* Jerusalem artichoke.

topique [tɔpik] ◇ *adj* **1.** *sout* [argument] relevant ■ [remarque] pertinent, apposite, relevant **2.** PHARM topical.
◇ *nm* **1.** LING topic **2.** PHARM topical remedy.
◇ *nf* PHILOS topics *(U)*.

topless [tɔplɛs] ◇ *adj* topless.
◇ *nm* : **faire du ~** to go topless.

top niveau [tɔpnivo] (*pl* **top niveaux**) *nm fam* **elle est au ~** [sportive] she's a top-level sportswoman ; [cadre] she's a top-flight executive.

topo [tɔpo] *nm fam* **1.** [discours, exposé] report ■ **il a fait un long ~ sur la situation financière** he gave an extensive report on the financial situation ▶ **c'est toujours le même ~!** it's always the same old story! ■ **tu vois (d'ici) le ~!** (do) you get the picture? **2.** *vieilli* [croquis] sketch, draft.

topographie [tɔpɔgrafi] *nf* topography.

topographique [tɔpɔgrafik] *adj* topographic, topographical.

topologie [tɔpɔlɔʒi] *nf* topology.

topologique [tɔpɔlɔʒik] *adj* topologic(al).

toponymie [tɔpɔnimi] *nf* toponymy ■ **elle s'intéresse à la ~** she's interested in place names.

top secret [tɔpsəkrɛ] *adj inv* top secret, highly confidential.

toquade [tɔkad] *nf* **1.** [lubie] fad, whim **2.** [passade] crush ■ **avoir une ~ pour qqn** to have a crush on sb.

toquard, e [tɔkar, ard] *fam* = **tocard**.

toque [tɔk] *nf* **1.** [de femme] pill-box hat, toque ■ **~ de fourrure** (pill-box shaped) fur-hat **2.** [de liftier, de jockey, de magistrat] cap ■ **~ de cuisinier** chef's hat.

toqué, e [tɔke] *fam* ◇ *adj* **1.** [cinglé] dotty *UK*, flaky *US* ■ **un vieil oncle un peu ~** a slightly dotty old uncle **2.** [passionné de] : **~ de : être ~ de qqn** to be mad *ou* nuts about sb.
◇ *nm, f* loony, nutter *UK*, screwball *US* ■ **un ~ d'écologie** an ecology crank *ou* freak.

toquer [3] [tɔke] ◆ **toquer à** *v+prép vieilli* **~ à la porte** to tap on *ou* to knock on the door.
◆ **se toquer de** *vp+prép fam* **se ~ de qqn** to become besotted with sb ■ **se ~ de qqch** to have a sudden passion for sthg.

Tora(h) [tɔra] *npr f* : **la ~** the Torah.

torche [tɔrʃ] *nf* **1.** [bâton résineux] torch ■ **elle n'était plus qu'une ~ vivante** *ou* **vive** she'd become a human torch, her whole body was ablaze **2.** ÉLECTR & TECHNOL : **~ électrique** (electric) torch *UK*, flashlight ■ **~ de soudage** soldering torch **3.** AÉRON : **le parachute s'est mis en ~** the parachute didn't open properly **4.** PÉTR flare.

torcher [3] [tɔrʃe] *vt* **1.** *fam* [essuyer - plat, casserole] to wipe clean **2.** △ [nettoyer - fesses] to wipe **3.** *fam* [bâcler - lettre, exposé] to botch ; [- réparation] to make a pig's ear of, to botch **4.** CONSTR to cob.
◆ **se torcher**△ *vp (emploi réfléchi)* to wipe one's bottom.

torchère [tɔrʃɛr] *nf* **1.** INDUST du pétrole flare **2.** [candélabre] candle-stand, torchère.

torchis [tɔrʃi] *nm* CONSTR cob.

torchon [tɔrʃɔ̃] *nm* **1.** [linge de maison] : **~ (à vaisselle)** tea towel ■ **le ~ brûle** [dans un parti, un gouvernement, une entreprise] tempers are getting frayed ; [dans un couple, entre des collègues, des amis] there's a bit of friction between them **2.** *fam* [écrit mal présenté] mess ■ **qu'est-ce que c'est que ce ~?** [devoir scolaire] do you call that mess homework? **3.** *fam* [mauvais journal] rag.

tordant, e [tɔrdɑ̃, ɑ̃t] *adj fam* hilarious ■ **elle est ~e, ta fille** your daughter's a scream *ou* riot *ou* hoot.

tord-boyaux [tɔrbwajo] *nm inv fam* rotgut, hooch *US*.

tordre [76] [tɔrdr] *vt* **1.** [déformer - en courbant, en pliant] to bend ; [- en vrillant] to twist **2.** [linge mouillé] to wring (out) ■ **elle tordait nerveusement son mouchoir** she was playing with *ou* twiddling her handkerchief nervously **3.** [membre] to twist ■ **~ le bras à qqn** to twist sb's arm ■ **~ le cou à une volaille** to wring a bird's neck ■ **~ le cou à qqn** *fam* to wring sb's neck **4.** [défigurer] : **les traits tordus par la douleur** his features twisted *ou* his face contorted with pain **5.** [faire mal à] : **les brûlures qui lui tordaient l'estomac** the burning pains which were knotting his stomach **6.** TEXT to twist.
◆ **se tordre** ◇ *vpi* [ver] to twist ■ [pare-chocs] to buckle ▶ **se ~ de douleur** to be doubled up with pain ■ **se ~ (de rire)** to be doubled *ou* creased *UK* up with laughter.
◇ *vpt* : **se ~ le pied** to sprain *ou* to twist one's foot ■ **se ~ les mains (de désespoir)** to wring one's hands (in despair).

tordu, e [tɔrdy] ◇ *adj* **1.** [déformé - bouche] twisted ; [- doigt] crooked **2.** [plié, recourbé - clef] bent ; [- roue de vélo, pare-chocs] buckled ■ [vrillé] twisted **3.** *fam* [extravagant - idée, logique] twisted, weird ; [- esprit] twisted, warped ■ **tu es complètement ~!** you're off your head! ■ **c'est un plan ~** it's a crazy idea **4.** *fam* [vicieux] : **coup ~** [acte malveillant] mean *ou* nasty *ou* dirty trick ■ **c'est la spécialiste des coups ~s** she's always playing dirty tricks on people.
◇ *nm, f fam* [personne bizarre ou folle] loony, nutter *UK*, screwball *US* ■ **où il va, l'autre ~?** where's that idiot off to?

tore [tɔr] *nm* **1.** ARCHIT & MATH torus **2.** INFORM : **~ magnétique** magnetic core.

toréador [tɔreadɔr] *nm vieilli* toreador, torero.

toréer [15] [tɔree] *vi* [professionnel] to be a bullfighter ■ **il doit ~ demain** he'll be bullfighting tomorrow.

torero, a [tɔrero, a] *nm, f* bullfighter, torero.

torgnole△ [tɔrɲɔl] *nf* wallop.

toril [tɔril] *nm* toril, bull pen.

tornade [tɔrnad] *nf* MÉTÉOR tornado.

Toronto [tɔrɔ̃to] *npr* Toronto.

torpédo [tɔrpedo] *nf* open tourer *UK*, open touring car *US*.

torpeur [tɔrpœr] *nf* torpor ▪ **sortir de sa ~** to shake o.s. up, to rouse o.s.

torpillage [tɔrpijaʒ] *nm* **1.** MIL torpedoing **2.** *fig* [sabotage] scuppering *UK*, sabotage ▪ **le ~ de la négociation** the wrecking of the negotiations.

torpille [tɔrpij] *nf* **1.** ARM [projectile sous-marin] torpedo ▪ **~ aérienne** aerial torpedo **2.** ZOOL torpedo (ray).

torpiller [3] [tɔrpije] *vt* **1.** MIL to torpedo **2.** [projet] to torpedo, to scupper.

torpilleur [tɔrpijœr] *nm* torpedo boat.

torréfacteur [tɔrefaktœr] *nm* **1.** [machine - pour le café] roaster, coffee-roaster ; [- pour le tabac] (tobacco) toaster **2.** [commerçant] coffee merchant.

torréfaction [tɔrefaksjɔ̃] *nf* [du café, du cacao] roasting ▪ [du tabac] toasting.

torréfier [9] [tɔrefje] *vt* [café, cacao] to roast ▪ [tabac] to toast ▪ **grains torréfiés** roasted beans.

torrent [tɔrɑ̃] *nm* **1.** [ruisseau de montagne] torrent, (fast) mountain stream **2.** [écoulement abondant] torrent, stream ▪ **des ~s d'eau** [inondation] a flood ; [pluie] torrential rain, a torrential downpour ▪ **des ~s de larmes** floods of tears ▪ **un ~ d'injures** a stream *OU* torrent of abuse ▪ **des ~s de lumière** a flood of light.
◆ **à torrents** *loc adv* : **il pleut à ~s** it's pouring down.

torrentiel, elle [tɔrɑ̃sjɛl] *adj* **1.** [d'un torrent - eau, allure] torrential **2.** [très abondant] : **des pluies ~les** torrential rain.

torrentueux, euse [tɔrɑ̃tɥø, øz] *adj litt* **1.** [rivière] rushing, onrushing, fast **2.** [rythme] frantic ▪ [vie] hectic.

torride [tɔrid] *adj* [chaleur, après-midi] torrid, scorching ▪ [soleil] scorching ▪ [région, climat] torrid.

tors, e [tɔr, tɔrs] *adj* **1.** [laine, soie] twisted **2.** [colonne] wreathed ▪ [pied de meuble] twisted **3.** [membre] crooked, bent.

torsade [tɔrsad] *nf* **1.** [de cordes] twist ▪ **~ de cheveux** twist *OU* coil of hair ▪ **cheveux en ~s** braided *OU* twisted hair **2.** [en tricot] : **(point) ~** cable stitch **3.** ARCHIT cabling, cable moulding.
◆ **à torsades** *loc adj* **1.** ARCHIT cabled **2.** [vêtement] : **pull à ~s** cablestitch sweater.

torsadé, e [tɔrsade] *adj* **1.** ARCHIT : **colonne torsadée** cabled column **2.** ÉLECTR : **paire ~e** twisted pair.

torsader [3] [tɔrsade] *vt* [fil] to twist ▪ [cheveux] to twist, to coil.

torse [tɔrs] ◇ *f* ▷ **tors.**
◇ *nm* **1.** ANAT trunk, torso ▪ **~ nu : mettez-vous ~ nu, s'il vous plaît** strip to the waist, please ▪ **il était ~ nu** he was barechested **2.** ART torso.

torseur [tɔrsœr] *nm* torque.

torsion [tɔrsjɔ̃] *nf* **1.** [d'un cordage, d'un bras] twisting **2.** MATH, PHYS & TECHNOL torsion **3.** TEXT twist (level).

tort [tɔr] *nm* **1.** *(sans article)* **avoir ~** [se tromper] to be wrong ▪ **tu as ~ de ne pas la prendre au sérieux** you're making a mistake in not taking her seriously, you're wrong not to take her seriously ▪ **tu n'avais pas tout à fait ~/pas ~ de te méfier** you weren't entirely wrong/you were quite right to be suspicious ▪ **donner ~ à qqn** [désapprouver] to disagree with sb ▪ **elle me donne toujours ~ contre son fils** she always sides with her son against me ▪ **les faits lui ont donné ~** events proved her (to be) wrong *OU* showed that she was (in the) wrong
2. [défaut, travers] fault, shortcoming ▪ **je reconnais mes ~s** I admit I was wrong ▪ **elle a le ~ d'être trop franche** the trouble *OU* problem with her is (that) she's too direct ▪ **c'est un ~ (de)** it's a mistake (to) ▪ **tu ne fais pas de sport? c'est un ~** don't you do any exercise? you definitely ought to *OU* should ▪ **avoir le ~ de** to make the mistake of ▪ **il a eu le ~ de lui faire confiance** he made the mistake of trusting her
3. [dommage] wrong ▪ **réparer le ~ qu'on a causé** to right the wrong one has caused, to make good the wrong one has done ▪ **réparer un ~** to make amends ▪ **faire du ~ à qqn** to do harm to sb, to wrong sb, to harm sb ▪ **faire du ~ à une cause** [personne] to harm a cause ; [initiative] to be detrimental to a cause
4. [part de responsabilité] fault ▪ **avoir tous les ~s** [gén] to be entirely to blame ; [dans un accident] to be fully responsible ; [dans un divorce] to be the guilty party ▪ **les ~s sont partagés** both parties are equally to blame ▪ **j'ai des ~s envers eux** I have done them wrong.
◆ **à tort** *loc adv* **1.** [faussement] wrongly, mistakenly ▪ **croire/affirmer qqch à ~** to believe/to state sthg wrongly
2. [injustement] wrongly ▪ **condamner qqn à ~** to blame sb wrongly.
◆ **à tort ou à raison** *loc adv* right or wrong, rightly or wrongly.
◆ **à tort et à travers** *loc adv* : **tu parles à ~ et à travers** you're talking nonsense ▪ **elle dépense son argent à ~ et à travers** money burns a hole in her pocket, she spends money like water.
◆ **dans mon tort, dans son tort** *etc loc adv* : **être dans son ~** to be in the wrong ▪ **mettre qqn dans son ~** to make sb appear to be in the wrong.
◆ **en tort** *loc adv* in the wrong ▪ **dans cet accident, c'est lui qui est en ~** he is to blame for the accident.
Voir module d'usage

torticolis [tɔrtikɔli] *nm* stiff neck, torticollis *spéc* ▪ **avoir un ~** to have a stiff neck.

tortillard [tɔrtijar] *nm fam* slow (local) train ▪ **ce train est un vrai ~** this train stops at every cowshed *UK OU* cow town *US*.

tortiller [3] [tɔrtije] ◇ *vt* **1.** [mèche, mouchoir, fil, papier] to twist ▪ [doigts] to twiddle ▪ [moustache] to twirl **2.** [fesses] to wiggle.
◇ *vi* **1.** [onduler] : **~ des fesses/hanches** to wiggle one's bottom/hips **2.** *fam loc* **il n'y a pas à ~** there's no getting out of *OU* away from it.

DONNER TORT À QUELQU'UN

I'm sorry, but you're wrong. Je regrette, mais vous avez tort.

You've got it all wrong. Vous vous trompez complètement.

You're completely missing the point. Vous n'y êtes pas du tout.

With all due respect, I think you're mistaken. Si je peux me permettre, je pense que vous vous trompez.

That can't be right, surely. Ça ne peut pas être ça, si?

Actually, that's not strictly true. En fait, ce n'est pas tout à fait exact.

I think you'll find it's French, not Spanish. Je pense que c'est du français, et pas de l'espagnol.

No, that's not what I meant at all. Non, ce n'est pas du tout ce que je voulais dire.

That's nonsense *OU* **rubbish** *fam* **!** N'importe quoi!

◆ **se tortiller** *vpi* [ver] to wriggle, to squirm ■ [personne - par gêne, de douleur] to squirm ; [- d'impatience] to fidget, to wriggle ■ **se ~ sur sa chaise comme un ver** to wriggle in one's chair like a worm.

tortillon [tɔrtijɔ̃] *nm* [de papier] twist ■ **des ~s de pâte à choux** choux pastry twists.

tortionnaire [tɔrsjɔnɛr] *nmf* torturer.

tortue [tɔrty] *nf* **1.** ZOOL tortoise ■ **~ marine** turtle ■ **~ d'eau douce** terrapin **2.** *fam* [traînard] slowcoach *UK*, slowpoke *US* ■ **avancer comme une ~** to go at a snail's pace, to crawl along.

tortueux, euse [tɔrtɥø, øz] *adj* **1.** [en lacets - sentier] winding, tortuous *sout* ; [- ruisseau] meandering, winding, sinuous *litt* **2.** [compliqué - raisonnement, esprit] tortuous, devious ; [- moyens] crooked, devious, tortuous ; [- style] convoluted, involved.

torturant, e [tɔrtyrɑ̃, ɑ̃t] *adj* [pensée] tormenting, agonising.

torture [tɔrtyr] *nf* **1.** [supplice infligé] torture **2.** *fig* [souffrance] torture, torment ■ **l'attente des résultats fut pour lui une véritable ~** he suffered agonies waiting for the results.

◆ **à la torture** *loc adv* : **être à la ~** to suffer agonies ■ **mettre qqn à la ~** to put sb through hell.

◆ **sous la torture** *loc adv* under torture ■ **elle n'a pas parlé, même sous la ~** she refused to talk, even under torture.

torturé, e [tɔrtyre] *adj* [marqué par la souffrance] tortured, tormented ■ **un regard ~** a tormented look.

torturer [3] [tɔrtyre] *vt* **1.** [supplicier - suj: bourreau] to torture **2.** [tourmenter - suj: angoisse, faim] to torture, to torment, to rack ; [- suj: personne] : **~ qqn** to put sb through torture ■ **la jalousie le torturait** he was tortured by jealousy ■ **torturé par sa conscience** tormented by his conscience **3.** [style, texte] to labour.

◆ **se torturer** *vp (emploi réfléchi)* to torture o.s., to worry o.s. sick ■ **ne te torture pas l'esprit!** don't rack your brains (too much)!

torve [tɔrv] *adj* : **il m'a lancé un regard ~** he shot me a murderous sideways look.

Toscane [tɔskan] *npr f* : **(la) ~** Tuscany.

tôt [to] *adv* **1.** [de bonne heure le matin] early ■ **se lever ~** [ponctuellement] to get up early ; [habituellement] to be an early riser ▮ [de bonne heure le soir] : **se coucher ~** to go to bed early ▮ [au début d'une période] : **~ dans l'après-midi** early in the afternoon, in the early afternoon
2. [avant le moment prévu ou habituel] soon ■ **il est trop ~ pour le dire** it's too early *ou* soon to say that ■ **arrive suffisamment ~ ou il n'y aura pas de place** be there in good time or there won't be any seats left ■ **il fallait y penser plus ~** you should have thought about it earlier *ou* before ■ **je voudrais passer les prendre plus ~** I would like to come and collect them sooner *ou* earlier ■ **elle a dû partir plus ~ que prévu** she had to leave earlier than expected ■ **ce n'est pas trop ~!** at last!, (it's) about time too!
3. [rapidement] soon ■ **le plus ~ possible** as early *ou* as soon as possible ■ **le plus ~ sera le mieux** the sooner, the better ⊙ **avoir ~ fait de** *sout* to be quick to ■ **je n'avais pas plus ~ raccroché qu'il me rappela** no sooner had I put the receiver down than he phoned me back ■ **je n'y retournerai pas de si ~!** I won't go back there in a hurry!

◆ **au plus tôt** *loc adv* **1.** [rapidement] as soon as possible **2.** [pas avant] at the earliest ■ **samedi au plus ~** on Saturday at the earliest, no earlier than Saturday.

◆ **tôt ou tard** *loc adv* sooner or later ■ **~ ou tard, quelqu'un se plaindra** sooner or later *ou* one of these days, someone's bound to complain.

total, e, aux [tɔtal, o] *adj* **1.** [entier - liberté] total, complete ■ **j'ai une confiance ~e en elle** I trust her totally *ou* implicitly **2.** [généralisé - destruction, échec] total, utter, complete **3.** [global - hauteur, poids, dépenses] total ■ **somme ~e** total (amount) **4.** ASTRON [éclipse] total **5.** THÉÂTRE : **spectacle ~** total theatre.

◆ **total** *adv fam* the net result is that ■ **~, je n'ai plus qu'à recommencer** the net result (of all that) is that I've got to start all over again.

◆ **total, aux** *nm* total (amount) ■ **faire le ~** to work out the total ■ **faire le ~ de** to total up, to add up, to reckon up ■ **fais le ~ de ce que je te dois** work out everything I owe you ⊙ **~ général** sum total, grand total ■ **~ partiel** subtotal.

◆ **totale** *nf fam* (total) hysterectomy.

◆ **au total** *loc adv* **1.** [addition faite] in total ■ **au ~, il vous revient 2 000 euros** in total you are entitled to 2,000 euros **2.** [tout bien considéré] all in all, all things (being) considered, on the whole.

totalement [tɔtalmɑ̃] *adv* [ignorant, libre, ruiné] totally, completely ■ [détruit] utterly ■ **il est ~ incapable de gagner sa vie** he is totally *ou* quite incapable of earning a living.

totalisant, e [tɔtalizɑ̃, ɑ̃t] *adj* PHILOS synthetic.

totaliser [3] [tɔtalize] *vt* **1.** [dépenses, recettes] to add up *(sép)*, to total up *(sép)*, to reckon up *(sép)*, to totalize **2.** [atteindre le total de] to have a total of, to total ■ **il totalise 15 victoires** he has won a total of 15 times ■ **qui totalise le plus grand nombre de points?** who has the highest score?

totalitaire [tɔtalitɛr] *adj* totalitarian.

totalitarisme [tɔtalitarism] *nm* totalitarianism.

totalité [tɔtalite] *nf* **1.** [ensemble] : **la ~ des marchandises** all the goods ■ **la presque ~ des tableaux** almost all the paintings **2.** [intégralité] whole ■ **la ~ de la somme** the whole (of the) sum **3.** PHILOS totality, wholeness.

◆ **en totalité** *loc adv* : **somme remboursée en ~** sum paid back in full ■ **le navire a été détruit en ~** the ship was completely destroyed, the whole ship was destroyed.

totem [tɔtɛm] *nm* totem.

toto [toto] *nm fam* [pou] louse.

touareg, ègue [twarɛg] *adj* Tuareg.

◆ **Touareg, ègue** *nm, f* Tuareg.

toubib [tubib] *nm fam* doctor.

toucan [tukɑ̃] *nm* toucan.

touchant[1] [tuʃɑ̃] *prep* [concernant] concerning, about.

touchant[2], **e** [tuʃɑ̃, ɑ̃t] *adj* [émouvant] touching, moving ■ **une scène ~e** a sight to melt the heart ■ **être ~ de maladresse/sincérité** to be touchingly awkward/earnest.

touche [tuʃ] *nf*

A.

1. [gén] key ■ [d'un téléviseur] button ■ **~ sourdine** mute button *ou* key ▮ [d'un téléphone] key, button ■ [d'une machine à écrire] key ■ **~ entrée/contrôle** enter/controlkey
2. ÉLECTR [plot de contact] contact
3. MUS [de clavier] key ■ [d'instrument à cordes] fingerboard

B.

1. ESCRIME hit
2. JOAILL touch
3. PÊCHE bite ⊙ **avoir une ~ avec qqn** *fam* to have something going with sb ■ **faire une ~** *fam* to score

C.

1. [coup de pinceau] touch, (brush) stroke ■ **du vert en ~s légères** light strokes of green ⊙ **mettre la ~ finale à qqch** to put the finishing touches to sthg
2. [cachet, style] touch
3. [trace] note, touch ■ **une ~ de couleur** a touch of colour ■ **une ~ de cynisme** a touch *ou* tinge *ou* hint of cynicism
4. *fam* [apparence] look ■ **on avait une de ces ~s avec nos cheveux mouillés!** we did look funny with our hair all wet!

D.

SPORT [ligne] touchline ■ [remise en jeu - RUGBY] line-out ■ FOOTBALL throw-in ■ [sortie de ballon] : **il y a ~** the ball is in touch *ou* is out ■ **jouer la ~** to play for time *(by putting the ball into touch)*.

◆ **en touche** *loc adv* into touch ■ **envoyer le ballon en ~** to kick the ball into touch.

◆ **sur la touche** *loc adv* SPORT : **rester sur la ~** to stay on the bench ■ **être** *ou* **rester sur la ~** *fam fig* to be left out, to be/remain on the sidelines ■ **quand il a eu 50 ans, ils l'ont mis sur la ~** when he was fifty, they put him out to grass *ou* they threw him on the scrap heap.

touche-à-tout [tuʃatu] *nmf* **1.** [importun] meddler **2.** [dilettante] dabbler, Jack-of-all-trades (and master of none).

toucher[1] [tuʃe] *nm* **1.** [sens] (sense of) touch ■ [palpation] touch **2.** [sensation] feel ■ **le ~ onctueux de l'argile** the smooth feel of clay **3.** [manière de toucher] touch ■ **avoir un ~ délicat/vigoureux** [gén - MUS] to have a light/energetic touch **4.** MÉD (digital) palpation *spéc*, examination **5.** SPORT touch ■ **il a un bon ~ de balle** he's got a nice touch.
◆ **au toucher** *loc adv* : **doux/rude au ~** soft/rough to the touch ■ **c'est facile à reconnaître au ~** it's easy to tell what it is by touching it *ou* by the feel of it.

toucher[2] [3] [tuʃe] ◇ *vt*

A.

1. [pour caresser, saisir] to touch ■ [pour examiner] to feel ■ **ne me touche pas!** get your hands off me!, don't touch me! ■ **le parchemin s'effrite dès qu'on le touche** the parchment crumbles at the first touch ■ **~ qqch du pied** to touch sthg with one's foot ▶ **pas touche!** *fam* hands off! ■ **touchez avec les yeux!** don't touch, just look!
2. [entrer en contact avec] to touch ■ **ma main a touché sa main** my hand brushed (against) his ■ **au moment où la navette spatiale touche le sol** when the space shuttle touches down *ou* lands
3. *fam* [joindre - suj: personne] to contact, to reach, to get in touch with ■ **où peut-on vous ~ en cas d'urgence?** where can you be contacted *ou* reached in an emergency? ■ [suj: lettre] to reach ■ **si notre message l'avait touché** if our message had got (through) to him *ou* reached him
4. MÉD to palpate *spéc*, to examine
5. NAUT [port] to put in at, to call at ■ [rochers, fonds] to hit, to strike

B.

1. [se servir de - accessoire, instrument] to touch ■ **son service est si puissant que je ne touche pas une balle** *fam* his serve is so powerful I can't get anywhere near the ball
2. [consommer] to touch ■ **il n'a même pas touché son repas/la bouteille** he never even touched his meal/the bottle
3. [blesser] to hit ■ **touché à l'épaule** hit in the shoulder ■ **touché!** ESCRIME touché! ▶ **touché, coulé!** JEUX hit, sunk!
4. [atteindre - suj: mesure] to concern, to affect, to apply to ; [- suj: crise, krach boursier, famine] to affect, to hit ; [- suj: incendie, épidémie] to spread to *(insép)* ■ **la marée noire a touché tout le littoral** the oil slick spread all along the coast ■ **reste-t-il un secteur que l'informatique n'ait pas touché?** are there still any areas untouched by computerization? ■ **les personnes touchées par l'impôt sur les grandes fortunes** people in the top tax bracket
5. [émouvoir - suj: film, geste, gentillesse, spectacle] to move, to touch ■ **ses chansons ne me touchent pas** her songs leave me cold ■ **vos compliments me touchent beaucoup** I'm very touched by your kind words ■ **ses prières avaient touché mon cœur** her entreaties had moved *ou* stirred me ■ [affecter - suj: décès] to affect, to shake ; [- suj: critique, propos désobligeants] to affect, to have an effect on ■ **elle a été très touchée par sa disparition** she was badly shaken by his death
6. *fam* [s'en prendre à - personne] to touch
7. [percevoir - allocation, honoraires, pension, salaire] to receive, to get, to draw ; [- indemnité, ration] to receive, to get ; [- chèque] to cash (in) *(sép)* ■ **elle touche 30 000 euros par an** she earns 30,000 euros a year ■ **~ gros** *fam* to line one's pockets, to make a packet ■ **touchez-vous les allocations familiales?** do you get child benefit? ■ **il a dû ~ pas mal d'argent** *fam* he must've been slipped a tidy sum ■ **~ le tiercé** to win the tiercé ■ **~ le chômage** to be on the dole *UK*, to be on welfare *US*

C.

1. [être contigu à] to join onto, to adjoin *sout*, to be adjacent to *sout*
2. [concerner] : **une affaire qui touche la Défense nationale** a matter related to defence, a defence-related matter
3. [être parent avec] to be related to.

◇ *vi* **1.** NAUT to touch bottom **2.** PÊCHE to bite **3.** △ [exceller] : **elle touche en informatique!** she's a wizard at *ou* she knows a thing or two about computers! ■ **ça y est, au saxo, je commence à ~!** I'm beginning to get the hang of the sax now! **4.** *loc* **touchez là!** it's a deal!, (let's) shake on it!
◆ **toucher à** *v+prép* **1.** [porter la main sur - objet] to touch ■ **évitez de ~ aux fruits** try not to handle the fruit ■ **que je ne te reprenne pas à ~ aux allumettes!** don't let me catch you playing with matches again! ; [- adversaire, élève] to touch, to lay hands *ou* a finger on ■ **si tu touches à un seul cheveu de sa tête...!** if you so much as lay a finger on her...! ■ [porter atteinte à] to interfere with *(insép)*, to harm, to touch ■ **ils ne veulent pas vraiment ~ au gouvernement** their aim isn't really to harm the government ■ **ne touchez pas aux parcs nationaux!** hands off the national parks! **2.** [modifier - appareil, documents, législation] to tamper *ou* to interfere with ■ **ton dessin est parfait, n'y touche plus** your drawing is perfect, leave it as it is **3.** [utiliser - aliment, instrument] to touch ; [- somme d'argent] to touch, to break into ■ **je n'ai jamais touché à la drogue** I've never been on *ou* touched drugs ▶ **~ à tout** *pr* to fiddle with *ou* to touch everything ; *fig* to dabble (in everything) ■ **je touche un peu à tout** [artisan] I'm a Jack-of-all-trades, I do a little bit of everything ; [artiste] I'm a man of many parts **4.** [être proche de - suj: pays, champ] to adjoin *sout*, to border (upon) ; [- suj: maison, salle] to join on *(insép)* to, to adjoin *sout* ■ **notre propriété touche aux salines** our property borders on the salt marsh ■ [confiner à] : **~ à la perfection** to be close to perfection **5.** [concerner, se rapporter à - activité, sujet] to have to do with, to concern ■ **tout ce qui touche au sexe est tabou** everything connected *ou* to do with sex is taboo **6.** [aborder - sujet, question] to bring up *(sép)*, to come onto *(insép)*, to broach ■ **vous venez de ~ au point essentiel du débat** you've put your finger on the key issue in the debate **7.** *sout* [atteindre - un point dans l'espace, dans le temps] to reach ■ **le navire touche au port ce soir** the ship will enter *ou* reach harbour tonight ■ **le projet touche à son terme** the project is nearing its end ■ **notre séjour touche à sa fin** our stay is nearing its end.
◆ **se toucher** ◇ *vp (emploi réciproque)* [être en contact] to touch, to be in contact ■ [entrer en contact] to touch, to come into contact ■ [jardins, communes] to touch, to be adjacent (to each other), to adjoin each other *sout* ■ **ils se touchèrent de l'épaule** their shoulders touched.
◇ *vp (emploi réfléchi)* *euphém* [se masturber] to play with o.s.

touche-touche [tuʃtuʃ] ◆ **à touche-touche** *loc adv* *fam* **être à ~** to be nose to tail *ou* bumper to bumper.

touffe [tuf] *nf* **1.** [de cheveux, de poils] tuft **2.** [d'arbustes] clump, cluster **3.** [de fleurs] clump ■ **~ d'herbe** tussock.

touffeur [tufœr] *nf litt* sultry *ou* sweltering heat.

touffu, e [tufy] *adj* **1.** [bois, feuillage, haie] thick, dense ■ [barbe, sourcils] thick, bushy ■ [arbre] thickly-covered, with dense foliage **2.** [texte] dense.

touillage [tujaʒ] *nm fam* [d'une sauce] stirring ■ [d'une salade] tossing.

touiller [3] [tuje] *vt fam* [sauce] to stir ■ [salade] to toss.

toujours [tuʒur] *adv* **1.** [exprimant la continuité dans le temps] always ■ **je l'ai ~ dit/cru** I've always said/thought so ■ **il est ~ à se plaindre** he's always *ou* he never stops complaining ■ **ils n'ont pas ~ été aussi riches** they haven't always been so rich ■ **ça ne durera pas ~** it won't last forever ■ **le ciel ~ bleu** the eternally blue sky ■ **Sophie, ~ plus belle** Sophie, ever more beautiful ■ **~ plus haut, ~ plus vite, ~ plus loin** ever higher, ever faster, ever farther ■ **ils sont ~ plus exigeants** they are more and more demanding **2.** [marquant la fréquence, la répétition] always ■ **elle est ~ en retard** she is always late ■ **les erreurs ne sont pas ~ où on les attend** mistakes sometimes occur where we least expect them ■ **tu as ~ raison, enfin presque ~** you're always right, well, nearly always! **3.** [encore] still ■ **tu travailles ~?** are you still working? ■ **il fait ~ aussi chaud** it is as hot as ever ■ **tu es ~ aussi serviable!** *iron* you're just *ou* still as helpful as ever(, I see)! ■ **~ pas** still not ■ **ta leçon n'est ~ pas sue** you still don't know your lesson ■ **elle n'a ~ pas téléphoné** she hasn't phoned yet, she still hasn't phoned **4.** [dans des emplois expressifs] : **tu peux ~ essayer** you can always try, you might as well try ■ **prends-le, tu peux ~ en avoir besoin** take it, you may *ou* might need it (some day) ■ **ça peut ~ servir** it might come in handy *ou* useful ■ **c'est ~ mieux que rien** still, it's better than nothing ■ **on trouvera ~ un moyen** we're sure *ou* bound to find a way ■ **tu peux ~ pleurer, je ne céderai pas** (you can) cry as much as you like, I won't give in ■ **tu lui fais confiance? – pas dans le travail, ~!** do you trust him? – not when it comes to work, anyway! ■ **c'est ~ ça de pris** that's something (at least).

◆ **comme toujours** *loc adv* as always, as ever ■ **il a été charmant, comme ~** he was charming as always.

◆ **de toujours** *loc adj* : **elle se retrouvait face à son public de ~** she found herself before her faithful audience of old ■ **une amitié de ~** a lifelong friendship.

◆ **pour toujours** *loc adv* forever ■ **tu me le donnes pour ~?** can I keep it forever *ou* for good?

◆ **toujours est-il que** *loc conj* the fact remains that ■ **j'ignore pourquoi elle a refusé, ~ est-il que le projet tombe à l'eau** I don't know why she refused, but the fact remains that the plan has had to be abandoned.

toundra [tundra] *nf* tundra.

toupet [tupɛ] *nm* **1.** *fam* [audace] impudence, nerve, cheek *UK* ■ **elle a du ~** *ou* **un sacré ~** she's got some nerve *ou UK* cheek! ■ **il a eu le ~ de...** he had the nerve *ou UK* cheek to... **2.** [de cheveux] tuft of hair, quiff *UK* **3.** ZOOL [d'un cheval] forelock.

toupie [tupi] *nf* **1.** JEUX (spinning) top ■ **tourner comme une ~** to spin like a top ■ **vieille ~** *fam* [harpie] old ratbag *UK*, old hen *US* **2.** MENUIS spindle moulder.

tour[1] [tur] *nf* **1.** ARCHIT & CONSTR tower ■ **la ~ de Babel** BIBLE the Tower of Babel ■ **~ de bureaux** office (tower) block ■ **~ de contrôle** AÉRON control tower ■ **la ~ Eiffel** the Eiffel tower ■ **~ de guet** observation tower ■ **~ d'habitation** tower *ou* high-rise block ■ **~ d'ivoire** *fig* ivory tower ■ **la ~ de Londres** the Tower of London ■ **la ~ (penchée) de Pise** the Leaning Tower of Pisa ■ **immeuble ~** tower block **2.** *fam* [personne grande et corpulente] : **c'est une vraie ~** he's/she's built like the side of a house **3.** JEUX castle, rook **4.** CHIM : **~ de fractionnement** fractionating column **5.** INDUST du pétrole : **~ de forage** drilling rig.

tour[2] [tur] *nm*

A. CERCLE
B. PÉRIODE, ÉTAPE
C. ACTION HABILE OU MALICIEUSE
D. ASPECT
E. ROTATION
F. TECHNOL

A. CERCLE

1. [circonférence - d'un fût, d'un arbre] girth ; [- d'un objet, d'une étendue] circumference

2. [mensuration] : **~ de taille/hanches** waist/hip measurement ■ **prends ton ~ de taille** measure (round) your waist ■ **quel est votre ~ de taille/hanches?** what size waist/hips are you? ■ **~ de cou** collar size ■ **il fait (un) 42 de ~ de cou** he takes a size 42 collar ■ **~ de poitrine** [d'une femme] bust measurement *ou* size ; [d'un homme] chest measurement *ou* size ■ **~ de tête** hat size

3. [parure] : **~ de cou** JOAILL choker ; [vêtement en fourrure] fur collar ■ **~ de lit** (bed) valance

4. [circuit] tour, circuit ■ **j'ai fait le grand ~ pour venir ici** I came here the long way round ■ **faire le ~ de** *pr* : **faire le ~ d'un parc** to go round a park ; [à pied] to walk round a park ; [en voiture] to drive round a park ■ **faire le ~ du monde** to go round the world ■ **faire le ~ du monde en auto-stop/voilier** to hitch-hike/to sail round the world ■ **faire le ~ de** *fig* : **l'anecdote a fait le ~ des bureaux** the story went round the offices *ou* did the rounds of the offices ■ **faire le ~ d'une question** to consider a problem from all angles ■ **j'ai fait le ~ de toutes les options** I've explored all the possibilities ■ **je sais ce qu'il vaut, j'en ai vite fait le ~** I know what he's worth, it didn't take me long to size him up ▶ **~ de circuit** lap ■ **le Tour de France** [cycliste] the Tour de France ; [des compagnons] the Tour de France *(carried out by an apprentice to become a journeyman)* ■ **~ d'honneur** lap of honour ■ **~ de piste** SPORT [athlétisme] lap ; ÉQUIT round ■ **faire un ~ de piste sans faute** ÉQUIT to have a clear round ■ **le ~ du propriétaire : on a fait le ~ du propriétaire** we went *ou* looked round the property ■ **fais-moi faire le ~ du propriétaire** show me round your property ■ **j'ai fait le ~ du cadran** *fam* I slept round the clock ■ **faire un ~ d'horizon** to deal with all aspects of a problem

5. [promenade - à pied] walk, stroll ; [- en voiture] drive, ride ; [- à bicyclette, à cheval, en hélicoptère] ride ■ [court voyage] trip, outing *(U)* ■ **faire un ~** [à pied] to go for a walk ; [en voiture] to go for a drive *ou* ride ; [à vélo] to go for a ride ■ **faire un ~ en ville** to go into town ■ **nous irons faire un ~ dans les Pyrénées** we'll go for a trip in the Pyrenees

B. PÉRIODE, ÉTAPE

1. [moment dans une succession] turn ■ JEUX [gén] turn, go ■ [aux échecs] move ■ **c'est (à) ton ~** [gén] it's your turn *ou* go ; [échecs] it's your move ■ **à qui le ~** whose turn is it?, who's next? ■ **chacun son ~** everyone will have his turn ■ **laisser passer son ~** to miss one's turn ■ **attendre son ~** to wait one's turn ■ **c'est à ton ~ de mettre la table** it's your turn to lay *ou* to set the table ■ **tu parleras à ton ~** you'll have your chance to say something ■ **nous veillons chacun à notre ~** we take turns to be on watch ▶ **~ de garde** [d'un médecin] spell *ou* turn of duty ■ **~ de scrutin** ballot ■ **au premier ~** in the first ballot *ou* round

2. SPORT [série de matches] round ■ **le second ~ de la coupe d'Europe** the second round of the European Cup

C. ACTION HABILE OU MALICIEUSE

1. [stratagème] trick ■ **elle prépare un mauvais ~** she's up to some mischief ■ **jouer un ~ à qqn** to play a trick on sb ■ **jouer un sale** *ou* **mauvais ~ à qqn** to play a nasty *ou* dirty trick on sb ■ **ça vous jouera un mauvais** *ou* **vilain ~** you'll be sorry for it!, it'll catch up with you (one day)! ■ **ma mémoire/vue me joue des ~s** my memory/sight is playing tricks on me ▶ **et le ~ est joué!** and there you have it! ■ **avoir plus d'un ~ dans son sac** to have more than one trick up one's sleeve

2. [numéro, technique] : **~ d'adresse** skilful trick, feat of skill ■ **~ de cartes** card trick ■ **~ de passe-passe** sleight of hand

D. ASPECT

1. [orientation] turn ■ **cette affaire prend un très mauvais ~** this business is going very wrong ■ **la discussion prend un très mauvais ~** the discussion is taking a nasty turn ▶ **~ d'esprit** turn *ou* cast of mind ■ **donner le ~** *Suisse* [maladie] to take a turn for the better ; [personne] to wrap up

2. LING [expression] expression, phrase ■ [en syntaxe] construction ■ **un ~ de phrase maladroit** an awkward turn of phrase

E. ROTATION

1. [d'une roue, d'un cylindre] turn, revolution ■ [d'un outil] turn ■ ASTRON revolution ■ **faire un ~/trois ~s sur soi-même** to spin round once/three times (on o.s.) ▶ **il n'y a qu'un ~ de clef** the key's only been turned once ■ **donner deux ~s de clef** to give a key two turns, to turn a key twice ■ **n'oublie pas de donner un ~ de clef (à la porte)** don't forget to lock the door ■ **~ de manège** ride on a roundabout *UK ou* a merry-go-round ■ **~ de vis** (turn of the) screw

2. AUTO revolution, rev

3. MÉD : **~ de reins : attraper** *ou* **se donner un ~ de reins** to put one's back out, to rick one's back

F. TECHNOL

lathe ■ **~ de potier** potter's wheel ■ **fait au ~** *fig* beautifully made.

◆ **à tour de bras** *loc adv* [frapper] with all one's strength *ou* might.

◆ **à tour de rôle** *loc adv* in turn ■ **on peut le faire à ~ de rôle si tu veux** we can take (it in) turns if you like.

◆ **tour à tour** *loc adv* alternately, by turns.

◆ **tour de chant** *nm* (song) recital.

◆ **tour de force** *nm* tour de force, (amazing) feat ■ **il a réussi le ~ de force de la convaincre** he managed to convince her, and it was quite a tour de force *ou* quite an achievement.

◆ **tour de main** *nm* **1.** [savoir-faire] knack ■ **avoir/prendre le ~ de main** to have/to pick up the knack ■ **c'est un ~ (de main) à prendre** it's just a knack one has to pick up **2.** *loc* **en un ~ de main** in no time (at all), in the twinkling of an eye.

◆ **tour de table** *nm* **1.** ÉCON *a meeting of shareholders or investors to decide a course of action* **2.** [débat] : **faisons un ~**

de table I'd like each of you in turn to give his or her comments ■ **réunir un ~ de table** to organize a brainstorming session.

TOUR DE FRANCE

The world-famous annual cycle race starts in a different town each year, but the home stretch is always the Champs-Élysées in Paris. The widespread excitement caused by the race, along with the heroic status of many *coureurs-cyclistes*, reflects the continuing fondness of the French towards cycling in general.

Touraine [turɛn] *npr f*: **(la) ~** the Touraine (region).

tourangeau, elle, x [turɑ̃ʒo, ɛl] *adj* [de Touraine] from the Touraine.

◆ **Tourangeau, elle, x** *nm, f* [de Touraine] *inhabitant of or person from the Touraine.*

tourbe [turb] *nf* [matière] peat, turf.

tourbeux, euse [turbø, øz] *adj* [sol] peat *(modif)*, peaty, boggy.

tourbière [turbjɛr] *nf* peat bog.

tourbillon [turbijɔ̃] *nm* **1.** MÉTÉOR [vent tournoyant] whirlwind, vortex *litt* **2.** [masse d'air, de particules] : **~ de poussière/sable** eddy of dust/sand ■ **~ de fumée** twist *ou* coil *ou* eddy of smoke ■ **~ de feuilles** flutter of whirling leaves ■ **~ de neige** snow flurry **3.** [dans l'eau - important] whirlpool ; [- petit] swirl ■ **l'eau faisait des ~s** the water was eddying *ou* swirling **4.** [rotation rapide] whirling, spinning ■ **les ~s de la valse** the whirling motion of a waltz **5.** *litt* [vertige, griserie] whirl **6.** MÉCAN & PHYS vortex.

◆ **en tourbillons** *loc adv* : **monter/descendre en ~s** to swirl up/down.

tourbillonnant, e [turbijɔnɑ̃, ɑ̃t] *adj* **1.** [vent, poussière] whirling ■ [feuilles, flocons] swirling, whirling, fluttering **2.** [existence] whirlwind *(modif)*, hectic.

tourbillonner [3] [turbijɔne] *vi* **1.** [eau, rivière] to swirl, to make eddies **2.** [tournoyer - flocons, feuilles, sable] to whirl, to swirl, to flutter ; [- fumée] to whirl, to eddy ; [- danseur] to spin *ou* to whirl *ou* to twirl (round) **3.** [défiler rapidement - pensées] : **les idées tourbillonnaient dans sa tête** ideas were whirling *ou* dancing around in his head.

tourelle [turɛl] *nf* **1.** ARCHIT turret, tourelle **2.** MIL [abri] (gun) turret ■ [d'un bateau] conning tower.

Tourgueniev [turgenjɛf] *npr* Turgenev.

tourière [turjɛr] *adj f & nf* : **(sœur) ~** *sister responsible for a convent's external relations.*

tourisme [turism] *nm* **1.** [fait de voyager] touring ■ **faire du ~** [dans un pays] to go touring ; [dans une ville] to go sightseeing **2.** [commerce] : **le ~** tourism, the tourist industry ■ **notre région vit du ~** we are a tourist area.

◆ **de tourisme** *loc adj* **1.** [ville] tourist *(modif)* ■ [agence] travel *(modif)* **2.** [à usage personnel - avion, voiture] private.

tourista [turista] *nf fam* traveller's tummy.

touriste [turist] *nmf* **1.** [gén] tourist ■ [pour la journée] day-tripper **2.** *fam* [dilettante, amateur] (outside) observer ■ **vous allez participer au débat? – non, je suis là en ~** are you going to take part in the discussion? – no, I'm just watching *ou* just an observer *ou* just sitting in.

touristique [turistik] *adj* **1.** [pour le tourisme - brochure, guide] tourist *(modif)* ■ **route ~** scenic route ■ **pendant la saison ~** in season, during the tourist season **2.** [qui attire les touristes] tourist *(modif)* ■ **c'est un village très ~** this village is very popular with tourists *ou* is a very popular spot ■ **cette ville est beaucoup trop ~ à mon goût** there are too many tourists in this town for my taste.

tourment [turmɑ̃] *nm* **1.** *litt* [physique] intense suffering, agony ■ **les ~s de la maladie** the torments *ou* throes of illness **2.** *sout* [moral] agony, torment.

tourmente [turmɑ̃t] *nf litt* **1.** [tempête] tempest *litt*, storm ■ **~ de neige** blizzard **2.** *fig* [bouleversements] turmoil.

tourmenté, e [turmɑ̃te] *adj* **1.** [angoissé - personne] tormented, troubled, anguished ; [- conscience] tormented, troubled **2.** [visage] tormented ■ **un regard ~** a haunted *ou* tormented look **3.** [agité - époque] troubled **4.** *sout* [accidenté - paysage, côte] wild, rugged, craggy ■ [changeant - ciel] changing, shifting ■ **un paysage d'orage sous un ciel ~** a stormy landscape under a shifting sky **5.** LITTÉR & ART tortuous **6.** MÉTÉOR & NAUT : **mer ~e** rough *ou* heavy sea.

tourmenter [3] [turmɑ̃te] *vt sout* **1.** [martyriser - animal, personne] to torment, to ill-treat **2.** [harceler] to harass ■ **tourmenté par ses héritiers** plagued *ou* harassed by his heirs **3.** [suj: faim, soif, douleur] to torment, to plague, to rack ■ [suj: incertitude, remords] to torment, to haunt, to rack ■ [suj: jalousie] to plague, to torment ■ [suj: obsession] to torment, to haunt ■ **ses rhumatismes le tourmentent** he's plagued by rheumatism.

◆ **se tourmenter** *vpi sout* [s'inquiéter] to worry o.s., to fret, to be anxious ■ **elle se tourmente pour son fils** she's worried sick about her son.

tournage [turnaʒ] *nm* **1.** CINÉ shooting, filming ■ **sur le ~** during filming **2.** TECHNOL turning.

tournailler [3] [turnaje] *vi fam* to wander round and round ■ **~ autour de** to hang *ou* to prowl around.

tournant[1] [turnɑ̃] *nm* **1.** [virage] bend, turn **2.** *fig* turning point, watershed ➊ **marquer un ~** to indicate *ou* to mark a change of direction ■ **prendre le** *ou* **un ~** to adapt to changing circumstances ■ **attendre qqn au ~** *fam* to be waiting for a chance to get even with sb, to have it in for sb ■ **avoir** *ou* **attraper qqn au ~** *fam* to get one's own back on sb, to get even with sb.

tournant[2]**, e** [turnɑ̃, ɑ̃t] *adj* **1.** [dispositif, siège] swivel *(modif)*, swivelling **2.** [scène] revolving ■ [escalier, route] winding **3.** MIL [manœuvre] outflanking.

tournante [turnɑ̃t] *nf* gang rape, gangbang.

tourné, e [turne] *adj* **1.** [façonné au tour] turned ■ **un pied de lampe en bois ~** hand-turned wooden lamp base **2.** CULIN [altéré - produits laitiers] sour, curdled ; [- vin] sour ■ **ce lait est ~** this milk is off *UK ou* bad *US ou* has gone off *UK ou* bad *US* ■ **ce bouillon est ~** this soup has gone bad *ou* off *UK* **3.** *loc* **bien ~** [taille] neat ; [remarque, missive] well-phrased ■ **avoir l'esprit mal ~** to have a dirty mind.

tournebouler [3] [turnəbule] *vt fam* [troubler] to confuse, to mix up *(sép)* ■ **il était tout tourneboulé** he was in a real dither.

tournebroche [turnəbrɔʃ] *nm* [gén] roasting jack *ou* spit ■ [d'un four] rotisserie ■ **canard/agneau au ~** spit-roasted duck/lamb.

tourne-disque [turnədisk] (*pl* **tourne-disques**) *nm* record-player.

tournedos [turnədo] *nm* tournedos.

tournée [turne] ◇ *f* ▻ **tourné.**

◇ *nf* **1.** [d'un facteur, d'un commerçant] round ■ **faire sa ~** [facteur, livreur] to do *ou* to make one's round ; [représentant] to be on the road ➊ **~ de conférences** lecture tour ■ **faire une ~ électorale** [candidat député] to canvass one's constituency ; [dans une élection présidentielle] to go on the campaign trail ■ **~ d'inspection** tour of inspection **2.** [d'un artiste, d'une troupe] tour ■ **faire une ~** to go on tour ■ **faire une ~ en Europe** to go on a European tour **3.** [visite] : **faire la ~ des galeries** to do the rounds of *ou* to go round the art galleries ➊ **faire la ~ des grands ducs** to go out on the town **4.** *fam* [au bar] round ■ **~ générale!** drinks all round! ■ **c'est ma ~** it's my round ■ **c'est la ~ du patron** drinks are on the house **5.** *fam* [volée de coups] hiding.

◆ **en tournée** *loc adv* : **être en ~** [facteur, représentant] to be off on one's rounds ; [chanteur] to be on tour.

tournemain [turnəmɛ̃] ◆ **en un tournemain** *loc adv* in no time at all.

tourner [3] [turne] <> *vi*

A. DÉCRIRE DES CERCLES
B. CHANGER D'ORIENTATION, D'ÉTAT
C. MARCHER, RÉUSSIR

A. DÉCRIRE DES CERCLES

1. [se mouvoir autour d'un axe - girouette] to turn, to revolve ; [- disque] to revolve, to spin ; [- aiguille de montre, manège] to turn, to go round *UK OU* around ; [- objet suspendu, rouet, toupie] to spin (round *UK*) *OU* around ; [- aile de moulin] to turn *OU* to spin round *UK OU* around ; [- clef, pédale, poignée] to turn ; [- hélice, roue, tour] to spin, to rotate ▪ **~ sur soi-même** to turn round ; [vite] to spin (round and round) ▪ **la Terre tourne sur elle-même** the Earth spins on its axis ▪ **je voyais tout ~** everything was spinning *OU* swimming ▪ **faire ~** [pièce de monnaie, manège, roue] to spin ; [clef] to turn ▪ **faire ~ les tables** to do table-turning ▪ **j'ai la tête qui tourne** my head's spinning ▪ **ça me fait ~ la tête** it makes my head spin ● **~ de l'œil** *fam* to pass out, to faint
2. [se déplacer en cercle - personne] to go round *UK OU* around ; [- oiseau] to fly *OU* to wheel round *UK OU* around, to circle (round *UK*) *OU* around ; [- insecte] to fly *OU* to buzz round *UK OU* around ; [- avion] to fly round *UK OU* around (in circles), to circle ; [- astre, satellite] to revolve, to go round *UK OU* around ▪ **les prisonniers tournaient dans la cour** the prisoners were walking round (and round) the yard ▪ **j'ai tourné 10 minutes avant de trouver à me garer** I drove round for 10 minutes before I found a parking space
3. *fam* [être en tournée - chanteur] to (be on) tour ▪ **notre représentant tourne dans votre région en ce moment** our representative is in your area at the moment

B. CHANGER D'ORIENTATION, D'ÉTAT

1. [changer de direction - vent] to turn, to veer, to shift ; [- personne] to turn (off) ; [- véhicule] to turn (off), to make a turn ; [- route] to turn, to bend ▪ **tournez à droite** turn (off to the) right ▪ **tourne dans l'allée** turn into the drive ▪ **~ au coin de la rue** to turn at the corner (of the street) ● **la chance** *OU* **la fortune a tourné (pour eux)** their luck has changed
2. [faire demi-tour] to turn (round *UK*) *OU* around ▪ **tourne dans le parking** turn round in the car park *UK OU* parking lot *US*
3. *fam* [se succéder - équipes] to rotate ▪ **les médecins tournent pour assurer les urgences** the doctors operate a rota system to cover emergencies
4. [évoluer] to go, to turn out ▪ **bien ~** [situation, personne] to turn out well *OU* satisfactorily ▪ **mal ~** [initiative, plaisanterie] to turn out badly, to go wrong ▪ **tout ça va mal ~!** no good will come of it! ▪ **la conversation a très mal tourné** the discussion took a very nasty turn ▪ **un jeune qui a mal tourné** a youngster who turned out badly *OU* went off the straight and narrow
5. [s'altérer - lait] to go off *UK OU* bad *US*, to turn (sour) ; [- viande] to go off *UK OU* bad ; [- crème, mayonnaise] to curdle ▪ **faire ~ du lait/une mayonnaise** to curdle milk/mayonnaise

C. MARCHER, RÉUSSIR

1. [fonctionner - compteur] to go round *UK OU* around ; [- taximètre] to tick away ; [- programme informatique] to run ▪ **le moteur tourne** the engine's running *OU* going ▪ **faire ~ un moteur (à plein régime)** to run an engine (at full throttle) ▪ **l'heure** *OU* **la pendule tourne** time passes ▪ **l'usine tourne à plein (rendement)** the factory's working at full capacity ▪ **faire ~ une entreprise** [directeur] to run a business ▪ **ce sont les commandes étrangères qui font ~ l'entreprise** orders from abroad keep the business going
2. [réussir - affaire, entreprise, économie] to be running well ▪ **alors, les affaires, ça tourne?** *fam* so, how's business (going)? ▪ **ça ne tourne pas très bien entre eux** *fam* it's not going too well between them.

<> *vt*

A. FAIRE CHANGER D'ORIENTATION
B. CINÉ & TV
C. METTRE EN FORME

A. FAIRE CHANGER D'ORIENTATION

1. [faire pivoter - bouton, clé, poignée, volant] to turn ▪ **tourne le bouton jusqu'au 7** turn the knob to 7 ▪ **il faut ~ le couvercle pour ouvrir le bocal** it's a jar with a twist-off top
2. [mélanger - sauce, café] to (give a) stir ; [- salade] to toss
3. [diriger - antenne, visage, yeux] to turn ▪ **~ son regard** *OU* **les yeux vers** to turn one's eyes *OU* to look towards ▪ **~ ses pensées vers** to turn one's thoughts to *OU* towards ▪ **~ son attention vers** to focus one's attention on, to turn one's attention to
4. [retourner - carte] to turn over *OU* up *(sép)* ; [- page] to turn (over) *(sép)* ; [- brochette, grillade] to give a turn, to turn (over) *(sép)* ▪ **~ qqch contre un mur** to turn sthg against *OU* to face a wall ▪ **~ et retourner, ~ dans tous les sens** [boîte, gadget] to turn over and over ; [problème] to turn over and over (in one's mind), to mull over ● **~ la mêlée** SPORT to wheel the scrum (round)
5. [contourner - cap] to round ; [- coin de rue] to turn ; [- ennemi] to get round *(insép)* ▪ **~ la difficulté/le règlement/la loi** *fig* to get round the problem/regulations/law
6. *loc* **~ le cœur à qqn** *pr* to nauseate sb, to turn sb's stomach ; *fig* to break sb's heart

B. CINÉ & TV

1. [cinéaste] **: ~ un film** to shoot *OU* to make a film *UK OU* movie *US* ; [acteur] to make a film *UK OU* movie *US* ▪ **~ une scène** [cinéaste] to shoot *OU* to film a scene ; [acteur] to play *OU* to act a scene
2. *(en usage absolu)* **elle a tourné plusieurs fois avec Pasolini** she played in several of Pasolini's films *UK OU* movies *US* ● **silence, on tourne!** quiet please, action!

C. METTRE EN FORME

1. MENUIS & MÉTALL to turn
2. [formuler - compliment] to turn ; [- critique] to phrase, to express ▪ **je ne sais pas comment ~ cela** I don't know how to put it ▪ **il tourne bien ses phrases** he's got a neat turn of phrase
3. [transformer] **: elle tourne tout au tragique** she always makes a drama out of everything ▪ **~ qqch à son avantage/désavantage** to turn sthg to one's advantage/disadvantage ▪ **~ qqch/qqn en ridicule** to ridicule sthg/sb, to make fun of sthg/sb.

◆ **tourner à** *v+prép* **: ~ au burlesque/drame** to take a ludicrous/tragic turn ▪ **~ à la catastrophe** to take a disastrous turn ▪ **~ au ridicule** to become ridiculous ▪ **ça tourne à la farce!** it's turning into a farce! ▪ **le temps tourne à la pluie/neige** it looks like rain/snow.

◆ **tourner autour de** *v+prép* **1.** [axe] to move *OU* to turn round ▪ **les planètes qui tournent autour du Soleil** the planets revolving round the Sun ▪ **l'escalier tourne autour de l'ascenseur** the staircase spirals *OU* winds round the lift **2.** [rôder] **: ~ autour de qqn** [gén] to hang *OU* to hover round sb ; [pour le courtiser] to hang round sb ▪ **les enfants tournaient autour du magasin depuis un moment** [par désœuvrement] the children had been hanging around outside the shop for a while ; [avec de mauvaises intentions] the children had been loitering outside the shop for a while **3.** [valoir environ] to be around *OU* about, to be in the region of ▪ **les réparations devraient ~ autour de 200 euro** the repairs should cost around *OU* should cost about *OU* should be in the region of 200 euro **4.** [concerner - suj: conversation] to revolve round, to centre *OU* to focus on ; [- suj: enquête policière] to centre on.

◆ **tourner en** *v+prép* to turn *OU* to change into ▪ **la neige tourne en gadoue** the snow's turning into slush.

◆ **se tourner** *vpi* **1.** [faire un demi-tour] to turn round ▪ **tourne-toi, je me déshabille** turn round *OU* turn your back, I'm getting undressed **2.** [changer de position] to turn ▪ **il se tournait et se retournait dans son lit** he was tossing and turning in his bed ▪ **tourne-toi sur le ventre** turn over onto your belly ‖ *fig* **de quelque côté qu'on se tourne** wherever *OU* whichever way you turn ▪ **je ne sais plus de quel côté me ~** I don't know which way to turn any more.

◆ **se tourner contre** *vp+prép* to turn against.

◆ **se tourner en** *vp+prép* *litt* to turn into.

◆ **se tourner vers** *vp+prép* **1.** [s'orienter vers] to turn towards ▪ **tous les regards se tournèrent vers elle** all eyes turned to look at her **2.** *fig* **se ~ vers qqn/Dieu** to turn to sb/God ▪ **se ~ vers une carrière** to take up a career.

tournesol [turnəsɔl] *nm* BOT sunflower.

tourneur, euse [turnœr, øz] *nm, f* turner ▪ **~ sur bois/métal** wood/metal turner.

tournevis [turnəvis] *nm* screwdriver ■ **~ cruciforme** Phillips screwdriver®.

tournicoter [3] [turnikɔte], **tourniquer** [3] [turnike] *vi fam* to flit *ou* to buzz around.

tourniquet [turnikɛ] *nm* **1.** [à l'entrée d'un établissement] turnstile **2.** [présentoir] revolving (display) stand **3.** [pour arroser] rotary sprinkler **4.** MÉD tourniquet.

tournis [turni] *nm* **1.** VÉTÉR turnsick, gid, coenuriasis *spéc* **2.** *loc* **avoir le ~** to feel giddy *ou* dizzy ■ **donner le ~ à qqn** to make sb (feel) giddy.

tournoi [turnwa] *nm* **1.** JEUX & SPORT tournament ▶ **~ open** open (tournament) ■ **le Tournoi des Cinq Nations** the Five Nations Tournament **2.** HIST tournament, tourney **3.** *litt* [compétition] challenge ■ **~ d'éloquence** contest of eloquence.

tournoie *etc v* ▻ **tournoyer.**

tournoiement [turnwamɑ̃] *nm* [de feuilles, de papiers] whirling, swirling ■ [d'un danseur] twirling, swirling, whirling.

tournoyer [13] [turnwaje] *vi* [feuilles, fumée, flocons] to whirl, to swirl ■ [aigle] to wheel *ou* to circle round ■ [danseur] to swirl *ou* to twirl *ou* to whirl round ■ **le radeau tournoyait dans les rapides** the raft was tossed round (and round) in the rapids ■ **faire ~ qqch** to whirl *ou* to swing sthg.

tournure [turnyr] *nf* **1.** [allure, aspect] demeanour **2.** [évolution, tendance] trend, tendency ■ **d'après la ~ que prend la situation** from the way the situation is developing *ou* going ■ **attendons de voir quelle ~ prennent les événements** let's wait and see how the situation develops ■ **prendre ~** to take shape ▶ **~ d'esprit** turn *ou* cast of mind **3.** LING [expression] turn of phrase, expression ■ [en syntaxe] form, construction ■ **~ impersonnelle/interrogative** impersonal/interrogative form **4.** MÉTALL turning, turnings **5.** [vêtement] bustle.

tour-opérateur [turɔperatœr] (*pl* **tour-opérateurs**) *nm* tour operator.

tourte [turt] *nf* **1.** [tarte] pie ■ **~ aux poires/épinards** pear/spinach pie **2.** *fam vieilli* [balourd] dumbo, thicko *UK*, dumbbell *US*.

tourteau, x [turto] *nm* **1.** [crabe] : **~ (dormeur)** (edible) crab **2.** AGRIC oil cake, cattle-cake **3.** CULIN : **~ fromagé** ≃ baked cheesecake.

tourtereau, x [turtəro] *nm* ORNITH young turtledove.
◆ **tourtereaux** *nmpl hum* lovebirds ■ **où sont les ~x?** [à un mariage] where's the happy couple?

tourterelle [turtərɛl] *nf* turtledove ■ **~ turque** collared dove.

tourtière [turtjɛr] *nf* **1.** [plat] pie dish *ou* plate **2.** *Québec* CULIN meat pie.

tous [*adj* tu, *pron* tus] *adj & pron indéf mpl* ▻ **tout** *(dét pron).*

Toussaint [tusɛ̃] *nf* RELIG : **(le) jour de la ~** All Saints' Day.

TOUSSAINT

All Saints' Day is a public holiday in France. It is the traditional occasion for a visit to the cemetery to lay flowers (usually chrysanthemums) on the graves.

tousser [3] [tuse] *vi* **1.** MÉD to cough ■ **je tousse beaucoup/un peu** I have a bad/slight cough **2.** [moteur] to splutter ■ **le moteur toussa plusieurs fois puis démarra** the engine spluttered several times then came to life.

toussotement [tusɔtmɑ̃] *nm* (slight) coughing *ou* cough.

toussoter [3] [tusɔte] *vi* **1.** MÉD to have a bit of a cough *ou* a slight cough **2.** [pour prévenir] to give a little *ou* discreet cough.

tout [tu *devant voyelle ou h muet* tut] (*f* **toute** [tut], *mpl* **tous** [*adj* tu, *pron* tus], *fpl* **toutes** [tut]) ◇ *adj qualificatif (au singulier)* **1.** [entier] all (the), the whole (of the) ■ **~e la nuit** all night ■ **elle a parcouru ~e la distance en 2 heures** she covered the full distance in 2 hours ■ **il se plaint ~e la journée** he complains all the time *ou* the whole day long ■ **~ le village a participé** the whole village took part ■ **~e une journée** a whole day ■ **~ ceci/cela** all (of) this/that ■ **~ ce travail pour rien!** all this work for nothing! ■ **j'ai ~ mon temps** I've plenty of time *ou* all the time in the world ■ **~e ma fortune** my whole fortune ■ **ils se sont aimés ~e leur vie** they loved each other all their lives ▶ **avec lui, c'est ~ l'un ou ~ l'autre** with him, it's either (all) black or (all) white **2.** [devant un nom propre] all ■ **j'ai visité ~ Paris en huit jours** I saw all *ou* the whole of Paris in a week **3.** [devant un nom sans article] : **on a ~ intérêt à y aller** it's in our every interest to go ■ **c'est en ~e liberté que j'ai choisi** I made the choice completely of my own free will ■ **rouler à ~e vitesse** to drive at full *ou* top speed ■ **en ~e franchise/simplicité** in all sincerity/simplicity ■ **c'est de ~e beauté** it's extremely beautiful **4.** [avec une valeur emphatique] : **c'est ~e une affaire!** it's quite a to-do! ■ **c'est ~e une expédition pour y aller!** getting there involves quite a trek! **5.** *(comme adv)* [entièrement] completely ■ **elle était ~e à son travail** she was completely absorbed in her work **6.** [unique, seul] only ■ **c'est ~ l'effet que ça te fait?** is that all it means to you? ■ **ma fille est ~ mon bonheur** my daughter is my sole *ou* only source of happiness ■ **pour ~ remerciement on m'a renvoyé** by way of thanks I got fired ■ **pour ~e famille il n'avait qu'une cousine éloignée** one distant cousin was all the family he had **7.** [suivi d'une relative] : **~ ce qu'on dit** everything people say ■ **~ ce qui me gêne, c'est la différence d'âge** the only thing *ou* all I'm worried about is the age difference ■ **~ ce que l'entreprise compte de personnel qualifié** the company's entire qualified workforce ▶ **ils s'amusaient ~ ce qu'ils savaient** they were having a whale of a time ■ **~ ce qu'il y a de : ses enfants sont ~ ce qu'il y a de bien élevés** his children are very well-behaved *ou* are models of good behaviour ■ **ce projet est ~ ce qu'il y a de plus sérieux** this project couldn't be more serious.
◇ *dét (adj indéf)*

A. AU SINGULIER
B. AU PLURIEL

A. AU SINGULIER

[chaque, n'importe quel] any, all, every ■ **~ citoyen a des droits** every citizen has rights, all citizens have rights ■ **~e personne ayant vu l'accident** any person who witnessed the accident ■ **~ changement les inquiète** the slightest change worries them ■ **pour ~ renseignement, écrivez-nous** for further information, write to us ■ **à ~ âge** at any age ■ **à ~e heure du jour et de la nuit** at any hour of the day or night ■ **de ~ temps** since time immemorial, from the beginning of time ■ **en ~ temps** throughout *ou* all through history ■ **~ autre** anybody else ■ **~ autre que lui aurait refusé** anyone other than him *ou* anybody else would have refused ▶ **~e peine mérite salaire** *prov* the labourer is worthy of his hire *prov*

B. AU PLURIEL

1. [exprimant la totalité] all ■ **tous les hommes** all men, the whole of mankind ■ **tous les gens** everybody, everyone ■ **je veux tous les détails** I want all the details *ou* the full details ■ **ça se vend maintenant à tous les coins de rue** it's now sold on every street corner

2. [devant un nom sans article] : **ils étaient 150 000, ~es disciplines/races confondues** there were 150,000 of them, taking all disciplines/races together ■ **champion ~es catégories** overall champion ■ **il roulait tous feux éteints** he was driving with his lights off ■ **je dois le rencontrer ~es affaires cessantes** I must meet him forthwith ■ **il est mon préféré à tous égards** I like him best in every respect

3. [exprimant la périodicité] every ■ **tous les jours** every day ■ **~es les deux semaines** every other week, every second week, every two weeks ■ **à prendre ~es les quatre heures** to be taken every four hours *ou* at four-hourly intervals ■ **~es les fois qu'on s'est rencontrés** every time we've met.
◇ *pron indéf*

A. AU SINGULIER
B. AU PLURIEL

A. AU SINGULIER

everything, all ■ [n'importe quoi] anything ■ **j'ai ~ jeté** I threw everything away ■ **dis-moi ~** tell me all about it ■ **t'as ~ compris!** *fam* that's it!, that's right! ■ **c'est ~ dire** that says it all ■ **il**

mange de ~ he eats anything ▪ **il est prêt à ~** he's ready for anything ▪ **capable de ~** capable of anything ▪ **c'est ~** that's all ▪ **ce sera ~?** [dans un magasin] will be that all?, anything else? ▪ **ce n'est pas ~** that's not all ▪ **ce n'est pas ~ de faire des enfants, il faut les élever ensuite** having children is one thing, but then you've got to bring them up ▪ **être ~ pour qqn** to be everything for sb, to mean everything to sb ▪ **et ~ et ~** *fam* and all that (sort of thing) ▪ **on aura ~ vu!** now I've *ou* we've seen everything! ▪ **~ est là** [objets] that's everything ; [problème] that's the whole point *ou* the crux of the matter ▪ **vous serez remboursé ~ ou partie** you'll get all or part of your money back ▪ **avec toi c'est ~ ou rien** with you, it's all or nothing *ou* one extreme or the other ▪ **c'est ~ sauf du foie gras** it's anything but foie gras ▪ **il est ~ sauf un génie** call him anything but not a genius ▪ **~ se passe comme si...** it's as though... ▪ **à ~ faire** [produit] all-purpose ▪ **~ bien considéré, ~ bien réfléchi** all things considered ▪ **~ bien pesé** after weighing up the pros and the cons ▪ **il a ~ de son père** he's every bit like his father

B. AU PLURIEL

1. [désignant ce dont on a parlé] : **il y a plusieurs points de vue, tous sont intéressants** there are several points of view, they are all interesting ▪ **j'adore les prunes – prends-les ~es** I love plums – take them all *ou* all of them

2. [avec une valeur récapitulative] all ▪ **Jean, Pierre, Jacques, tous voulaient la voir** Jean, Pierre, Jacques, they all wanted to see her ▪ **c'est tous feignants et compagnie!** *fam* they're just a bunch of idlers!

3. [tout le monde] : **vous m'entendez tous?** can you all hear me? ▪ **à vous tous qui m'avez aidé, merci** to all of you who helped me, thank you ▪ **des émissions pour tous** programmes suitable for all (audiences) ▪ **tous ensemble** all together ▪ **tous tant** *ou* **autant que nous sommes** all of us, every (single) one of us.

◆ **tout** (*f* **toute**, *fpl* **toutes**) *adv (s'accorde en genre et en nombre devant un adj f commençant par une consonne ou un h aspiré)* **1.** [entièrement, tout à fait] quite, very, completely ▪ **ils étaient ~ seuls** they were quite *ou* completely alone ▪ **la ville ~ entière** the whole town ▪ **~ neuf** brand new ▪ **~ nu** stark naked ▪ **~ cru** (totally) raw ▪ **un ~ jeune homme** a very young man ▪ **sa chevelure était ~e hérissée** his/her hair was all messy ▪ **ses ~ premiers mots** his/her very first words ▪ **les ~ premiers temps** at the very beginning ▪ **une robe ~ en dentelle** a dress made of lace ▪ **le jardin est ~ en longueur** the garden is just one long strip ▪ **un de nos ~ meilleurs acteurs** one of our very best actors ▪ **~ mouillé** wet *ou* soaked through, drenched ▪ **être ~ occupé à faire qqch** to be very busy doing sthg ▪ **je t'aime ~ autant qu'autrefois** I love you just as much as I did before ▪ **~ simplement/autrement** quite simply/differently ▪ **téléphone-moi, ~ simplement** just phone me, that's the easiest (way) ▪ **une toile ~ coton** a 100% cotton cloth, an all cotton material ▪ **il est ~e bonté/générosité** he is goodness/generosity itself ▪ **ça, c'est ~ lui!** that's typical of him *ou* just like him! **2.** [en intensif] : **~ en haut/bas** right at the top/bottom ▪ **c'est ~ près** it's very close ▪ **~ à côté de moi** right next to me ▪ **~ contre le mur** right up against the wall ▪ **c'est ~ le contraire!** it's quite the opposite! **3.** [déjà] : **~ prêt** *ou* **préparé** ready-made ▪ **~ bébé, elle dansait déjà** even as a baby, she was already dancing ⊙ **on verra – c'est ~ vu!** we'll see – it's already decided! **4.** *(avec un gérondif)* [indiquant la simultanéité] : **on mangera ~ en marchant** we'll eat while we're walking ❙ [indiquant la concession] : **~ en avouant son ignorance dans ce domaine, il continuait à me contredire** although he'd confessed his ignorance in that field, he kept on contradicting me.

◆ **tout** *nm* **1.** [ensemble] whole ▪ **former un ~** to make up a whole ▪ **mon ~ est un instrument de musique** [dans une charade] my whole *ou* all is a musical instrument **2.** [l'essentiel] : **le ~** the main *ou* the most important thing ▪ **le ~ c'est de ne pas bafouiller** the most important thing is not to stutter ⊙ **ce n'est pas le ~, mais je dois partir** *fam* that's all very well, but I've got to go now ▪ **ce n'est pas le ~ de critiquer, il faut pouvoir proposer autre chose** it's not enough to criticize, you've got to be able to suggest something else ▪ **jouer** *ou* **risquer le ~ pour le ~** to risk (one's) all ▪ **tenter le ~ pour le ~** to make a (final) desperate attempt *ou* a last ditch effort ▪ **c'est un ~** it's all the same, it makes no difference ▪ **à quand le ~ informatique?** when will everything be computerized? ▪ **la politique du ~ ou rien** an all-or-nothing policy ▪ **changer du ~ au ~** to change completely.

◆ **du tout** *loc adv* not at all ▪ **je vous dérange? – du ~, du ~!** am I disturbing you? – not at all *ou* not in the least! ▪ **elle finissait son café sans du ~ se soucier de notre présence** she was finishing her coffee without paying any attention to us at all *ou* whatsoever.

◆ **en tout** *loc adv* **1.** [au total] in total, in all ▪ **cela fait 95 euros en ~** that comes to 95 euros in all *ou* in total **2.** [exactement] exactly, entirely ▪ **la copie est conforme en ~ à l'original** the copy matches the original exactly.

◆ **en tout et pour tout** *loc adv* (all) in all ▪ **en ~ et pour ~, nous avons dépensé 300 euros** all in all, we've spent 300 euros.

◆ **tout à coup** *loc adv* all of a sudden, suddenly.

◆ **tout à fait** *loc adv* **1.** [complètement] quite, fully, absolutely ▪ **en es-tu ~ à fait conscient?** are you fully aware of it? ▪ **je vous comprends ~ à fait** I understand you perfectly well ▪ **ce n'est pas ~ à fait exact** it's not quite correct ▪ **n'ai-je pas raison? – ~ à fait!** am I right? – absolutely! **2.** [exactement] exactly ▪ **c'est ~ à fait ce que je cherche/le même** it's exactly what I've been looking for/the same **3.** [oui] certainly ▪ **vous faites les retouches? – ~ à fait** do you do alterations? – certainly (we do).

◆ **tout de même** *loc adv* **1.** [malgré tout] all the same, even so ▪ **j'irai ~ de même** all the same, I'll still go **2.** [en intensif] : **~ de même, tu exagères!** steady on!, that's a bit much!

◆ **tout de suite** *loc adv* **1.** [dans le temps] straight away, right away, at once ▪ **apporte du pain – ~ de suite!** bring some bread – right away! **2.** [dans l'espace] immediately ▪ **tournez à gauche ~ de suite après le pont** turn left immediately after the bridge.

◆ **tout... que** *loc conj* : **~ directeur qu'il est** *ou* **qu'il soit,...** he may well be the boss,...

---

tout-à-l'égout [tutalegu] *nm inv* main *ou* mains drainage, main sewer ▪ **avez-vous le ~?** are you connected to the main sewer?

Toutankhamon [tutɑ̃kamɔ̃] *npr* Tutankhamen, Tutankhamun.

toute [tut] ▻ **tout** *(adj qualificatif, dét, pron etc).*

toutefois [tutfwa] *adv* however, nevertheless ▪ **c'est un homme généreux, ~ peu l'apprécient** he's a generous man, yet he's disliked by many ▪ **je lui parlerai, si ~ il veut bien me recevoir** I'll talk to him, that is, if he'll see me ▪ **elle n'est guère patiente, sauf, ~, avec ses enfants** she's not exactly patient, except, however, with her children.

toute-puissance [tutpɥisɑ̃s] *nf inv* omnipotence, all-powerful influence.

toutes [tut] *fpl* ▻ **tout** *(dét et pron indéf).*

toutou [tutu] *nm fam* **1.** [chien] doggie, bow-wow **2.** [personne docile] lapdog ▪ **filer** *ou* **obéir comme un (petit) ~** to be a lapdog.

Tout-Paris [tupari] *nm* : **le ~** the Parisian smart set.

tout-petit [tup(ə)ti] (*pl* **tout-petits**) *nm* [qui ne marche pas] infant ▪ [qui marche] toddler ▪ **un livre/une émission pour les ~ s** a book/a programme for the very young.

tout-puissant, toute-puissante [tupɥisɑ̃, tutpɥisɑ̃t] (*mpl* **tout-puissants**, *fpl* **toutes-puissantes**) *adj* **1.** [influent] omnipotent, all-powerful **2.** RELIG almighty.

Tout-Puissant [tupɥisɑ̃] *npr m* : **le ~** the Almighty.

tout(-)terrain [tutɛrɛ̃] (*pl* **tous(-)terrains**) ◇ *adj* cross-country *(modif).*
◇ *nm* dirt-track driving *ou* riding.
◇ *nf* cross-country car *ou* vehicle.

tout-venant [tuvnɑ̃] *nm inv* [choses] everyday things ▪ [personnes] ordinary people ▪ **des places d'opéra qui ne sont pas pour le ~** opera tickets that are beyond the means of ordinary people.

toux [tu] *nf* cough ▪ **~ grasse/nerveuse/sèche** loose/nervous/dry cough.

toxicité [tɔksisite] *nf* toxicity.

toxico [tɔksiko] *nmf fam* druggie.

toxicologie [tɔksikɔlɔʒi] *nf* toxicology.

toxicologue [tɔksikɔlɔg] *nmf* toxicologist.

toxicomane [tɔksikɔman] ◇ *adj* drug-addicted.
◇ *nmf* drug addict.

toxicomanie [tɔksikɔmani] *nf* drug addiction.

toxine [tɔksin] *nf* toxin.

toxique [tɔksik] ◇ *adj* toxic, poisonous.
◇ *nm* poison, toxin.

toxoplasmose [tɔksɔplasmoz] *nf* toxoplasmosis.

TP ◇ *nmpl* **1.** = **travaux pratiques 2.** = **travaux publics**.
◇ *npr m* = **Trésor public**.

TPE [tepeø] ◇ *nmpl* (*abr de* **travaux personnels encadrés**) ÉDUC GIS.
◇ *nf* (*abr de* **très petite entreprise**) VSB.

TPG *nm* = **trésorier payeur général**.

tr (*abr écrite de* **tour**) rev.

trac[1] [trak] *nm* [devant un public] stage fright *ou* nerves ▪ [à un examen] exam nerves ▪ **avoir le ~** to have the jitters.

trac[2] [trak] ◆ **tout à trac** *loc adv vieilli* out of the blue, just like that ▪ **elle a dit ça tout à ~** she just came out with it, she blurted it out all of a sudden.

traçabilité [trasabilite] *nf* traceability.

traçage [trasaʒ] *nm* **1.** [d'un trait, d'une figure] drawing ▪ [d'une inscription] writing *ou* tracing (out) ▪ [d'un itinéraire] plotting (out) **2.** TECHNOL marking, scribing.

traçant, e [trasɑ̃, ɑ̃t] *adj* ARM [projectile] tracer (*modif*).

tracas [traka] ◇ *nm* [ennui, embarras] : **cette affaire lui cause bien du ~** this business is causing her a lot of worry *ou* upset.
◇ *nmpl* [soucis matériels ou financiers] troubles.

tracasser [3] [trakase] *vt* [suj: situation] to worry, to bother ▪ [suj: enfant] to worry ▪ **son état de santé actuel me tracasse** I'm worried about the current state of his health.
◆ **se tracasser** *vpi* to worry ▪ **ne te tracasse plus pour cela** don't give it another thought.

tracasserie [trakasri] *nf* (*souvent pl*) petty annoyance ▪ **faire face à des ~s administratives** to put up with a lot of frustrating redtape.

tracassier, ère [trakasje, ɛr] *adj* [administration, fonctionnaire] pettifogging ▪ [personne] awkward, difficult.

trace [tras] *nf* **1.** [empreinte - d'un animal] track, trail, spoor ; [- d'un fugitif] trail ▪ **des ~s de pas** footprints, footmarks ▪ **des ~s de pneus** tyre *ou* wheel marks ▪ **suivre la ~** *ou* **les ~s de qqn, marcher sur les ~s de qqn** *fig* to follow in sb's footsteps
2. [d'un coup, de brûlures, d'une maladie] mark ▪ **il portait des ~s de coups** his body showed signs of having been beaten
3. [marque, indice] trace, smear ▪ **il y a des ~s de doigts sur la vitre** there are fingermarks on the window pane ▪ **sans laisser de ~s** without (a) trace ▪ **pas la moindre ~ d'effraction** no sign *ou* evidence *ou* trace of a break-in ▪ **elle a laissé des ~s de son passage** you can see she's been here ▪ **il n'y a pas ~ d'elle** *ou* **aucune ~ d'elle** no sign of her (anywhere) ▪ **on ne trouve pas ~ de votre dossier** your file cannot be traced, there's no trace of your file
4. [quantité infime] trace ▪ **elle parle sans la moindre ~ d'accent** she speaks without the slightest trace *ou* hint of an accent
5. [vestige] trace ▪ **on y a retrouvé les ~s d'une civilisation très ancienne** traces of a very ancient civilization have been discovered there
6. [marque psychique] mark ▪ **une telle épreuve laisse forcément des ~s** such an ordeal is bound to take its toll
7. MATH & PSYCHOL trace
8. SPORT trail ▪ **faire la ~** to break a trail ➔ **~ directe** straight running.
◆ **à la trace** *loc adv* **1.** [d'après les empreintes] : **suivre à la ~** [fuyard, gibier] to track (down)
2. *fam fig* **on peut le suivre à la ~, il sème ses stylos partout** he's easy to track down, he leaves his pens lying around all over the place.
◆ **sur la trace de** *loc prép* [à la recherche de] on the trail of *ou* track of ▪ **ils sont sur la ~ du bandit/d'un manuscrit** they are on the bandit's trail/tracking down a manuscript.

tracé [trase] *nm* **1.** [représentation - d'une ville, d'un réseau] layout, plan ▪ **faire le ~ d'une route** to lay out *ou* to plan a road (*on paper*) **2.** [chemin suivi - par un fleuve] course ; [- par une voie] route **3.** [ligne - dans un graphique] line ; [- dans un dessin] stroke, line ▪ [contour - d'un littoral] outline **4.** TRAV PUB tracing, marking out (*on site*).

tracer [16] [trase] ◇ *vt* **1.** [trait, cercle, motif] to draw ▪ **vous nous tracez un tableau pessimiste de l'avenir** you're painting a less than rosy picture of our future **2.** [inscription, mot] to write **3.** [marquer l'emplacement de - itinéraire] to trace, to plot ; [- chemin, terrain] to mark *ou* to stake *ou* to lay out (*sép*) **4.** *fig* [indiquer] to map out (*sép*), to plot ▪ **~ une ligne de conduite pour qqn** to plot a course of action for sb ➔ **~ le chemin** *ou* **la route** *ou* **la voie à qqn** to mark out *ou* to pave the way for sb **5.** MIN to open up (*sép*) **6.** TECHNOL to mark, to scribe.
◇ *vi fam* [aller très vite] to shift *UK*, to barrel along *US* ▪ **elle trace, ta bagnole!** your car goes like a bomb!, your car doesn't half shift *UK ou* barrels right along *US*.

traceur, euse [trasœr, øz] ◇ *adj* ARM & PHYS tracer (*modif*).
◇ *nm, f* TECHNOL scriber.
◆ **traceur** *nm* **1.** NUCL & PHYS tracer **2.** INFORM : **~ de courbes** graph plotter.

trachée [traʃe] *nf* **1.** ANAT trachea *spéc*, windpipe **2.** ZOOL trachea.

trachée-artère [traʃeartɛr] (*pl* **trachées-artères**) *nf* ANAT trachea.

trachéite [trakeit] *nf* tracheitis.

trachéotomie [trakeɔtɔmi] *nf* tracheotomy.

tract [trakt] *nm* pamphlet, leaflet, tract ▪ **distribuer des ~s (à)** to leaflet.

tractations [traktasjɔ̃] *nfpl* dealings, negotiations ▪ **des ~ eurent lieu et l'affaire fut étouffée** negotiations took place and the whole business was hushed up.

tracté, e [trakte] *adj* motor-drawn.

tracter [3] [trakte] *vt* to tow, to pull.

tracteur, trice [traktœr, tris] *adj* AUTO towing (*avant n*).
◆ **tracteur** *nm* **1.** AGRIC tractor **2.** AUTO : **~ routier** tractor.

traction [traksjɔ̃] *nf* **1.** [mode de déplacement] traction, haulage ▪ **~ animale/mécanique** animal/mechanical traction, animal/mechanical haulage **2.** AUTO : **une Traction** a vintage Citroën, an old front-wheel drive Citroën ➔ **~ avant** [système] front-wheel drive **3.** MÉD traction **4.** PHYS traction ▪ **force de ~** tractive force **5.** RAIL [force] traction ➔ **~ électrique/à vapeur** electric/steam traction **6.** SPORT [sur une barre] pull-up ▪ [au sol] press-up, push-up.

tractus [traktys] *nm* tract ▪ **~ digestif** digestive tract.

tradition [tradisjɔ̃] *nf* **1.** [ensemble des coutumes] tradition ▪ **la ~ veut qu'elle soit née ici** tradition has it that she was born here ▪ **c'est dans la plus pure ~ écossaise** it's in the best Scottish tradition **2.** [usage] tradition, custom **3.** DR tradition, transfer **4.** RELIG : **la Tradition** Tradition.
◆ **de tradition** *loc adj* traditional ▪ **il est de ~ de/que...** it's a tradition to/that...

traditionalisme [tradisjɔnalism] *nm* **1.** [gén] traditionalism **2.** RELIG Traditionalism.

traditionaliste [tradisjɔnalist] *adj* & *nmf* traditionalist.

traditionnel, elle [tradisjɔnɛl] *adj* **1.** [fondé sur la tradition] traditional ▪ **une interprétation ~le d'un texte** a conventional interpretation of a text **2.** [passé dans les habitudes] usual, traditional ▪ **le ~ baiser de la mariée** the time-honoured tradition of kissing the bride.

traditionnellement [tradisjɔnɛlmɑ̃] *adv* **1.** [selon la tradition] traditionally **2.** [comme d'habitude] as usual, as always ▪ **un secteur industriel ~ déficitaire** an industrial sector which usually *ou* traditionally runs at a loss.

traducteur, trice [tradyktœr, tris] *nm, f* translator.
◆ **traducteur** *nm* **1.** TECHNOL transducer **2.** INFORM translator.

traduction [tradyksjɔ̃] *nf* **1.** [processus] translating, translation ■ **~ de l'espagnol en allemand** translation from Spanish into German ▶ **~ assistée par ordinateur** computer *ou* machine (assisted) translation ■ **~ automatique** automatic translation ■ **~ littérale** literal *ou* word-for-word translation ■ **~ simultanée** simultaneous translation **2.** [texte] translation **3.** [transposition] expression ■ **la ~ musicale de sa passion** the expression of his passion in music, the musical expression of his passion.

traduire [98] [tradɥir] *vt* **1.** [écrivain, roman, terme] to translate ■ **livre traduit de l'anglais** book translated from (the) English ■ **~ du russe en chinois** to translate from Russian *ou* out of Russian into Chinese ■ **elle est peu traduite en Europe** very few of her works are translated in Europe **2.** [exprimer - pensée, sentiment] to express, to reflect, to convey ; [- colère, peur] to reveal, to indicate **3.** DR : **~ qqn en justice** to bring sb before the courts, to prosecute sb.
◆ **se traduire** *vp (emploi passif)* : **la phrase peut se ~ de différentes façons** the sentence can be translated *ou* rendered in different ways.
◆ **se traduire par** *vp+prép* **1.** [avoir pour résultat] : **cela se traduit par des changements climatiques profonds** it results in *ou* entails radical changes in the climate ■ **la sécheresse s'est traduite par une baisse de la production agricole** agricultural production fell as a result of the drought **2.** [être exprimé par] : **son émotion se traduisit par des larmes** his emotion found expression in tears.

traduisible [tradɥizibl] *adj* translatable ■ **le proverbe n'est pas ~** the proverb cannot be translated.

traduisons *etc v* ▷ **traduire.**

traduit, e [tradɥi, itɒ] *pp* ▷ **traduire.**

trafic [trafik] *nm* **1.** [commerce illicite] traffic, trafficking ■ **~ d'armes** arms dealing, gunrunning ■ **le ~ de drogue** *ou* **de stupéfiants** drug trafficking ■ **faire du ~ de drogue** [gén] to be involved in drug trafficking ; [organisateur] to traffic in drugs ; [revendeur] to deal in *ou* to push *ou* to peddle drugs **2.** *fam* [manigance] fishy business **3.** DR : **~ d'influence** (bribery and) corruption *ou* corrupt receiving **4.** TRANSP traffic ■ **~ aérien/ferroviaire/maritime/portuaire/routier** air/rail/sea/port/road traffic.

traficoter [3] [trafikɔte] *fam* ◇ *vi* : **il traficote** he's a small-time crook, he's into petty dealing.
◇ *vt* [manigancer] to be up to ■ **qu'est-ce que tu traficotes dans ma chambre?** what do you think you're up to in my room?

trafiquant, e [trafikɑ̃, ɑ̃t] *nm, f* dealer, trafficker ■ **~ de drogue** drug dealer *ou* trafficker ■ **~ d'armes** gunrunner, arms dealer.

trafiquer [3] [trafike] ◇ *vi* [faire du commerce illicite] to traffic, to racketeer.
◇ *vt fam* **1.** [falsifier, altérer - comptabilité, résultats électoraux] to doctor ; [- vin] to adulterate ; [- compteur électrique] to tamper with *(insép)* ; [- compteur kilométrique] to rig **2.** *fam* [manigancer] to be up to ■ **je me demande ce qu'ils trafiquent** I wonder what they're up to.

tragédie [traʒedi] *nf* **1.** LITTÉR tragedy **2.** THÉÂTRE tragedy ■ **c'est dans la ~ qu'elle a atteint au sublime** she reached the summit of her art in tragic roles **3.** [événement funeste] tragedy, disaster, calamity ■ **l'émeute a tourné à la ~** the riot had a tragic outcome.

tragédien, enne [traʒedjɛ̃, ɛn] *nm, f* tragedian (*f* tragedienne), tragic actor (*f* actress).

tragi-comédie [traʒikɔmedi] (*pl* **tragi-comédies**) *nf* **1.** LITTÉR tragi-comedy **2.** *fig* tragi-comic saga ■ **leur liaison est une perpétuelle ~** their love affair is one long series of ups and downs.

tragi-comique [traʒikɔmik] (*pl* **tragi-comiques**) ◇ *adj* LITTÉR & *fig* tragicomic ■ **un incident ~** an incident that inspires both laughter and tears *ou* that makes you laugh and cry.
◇ *nm* LITTÉR : **le ~** the tragicomic.

tragique [traʒik] ◇ *adj* **1.** LITTÉR tragic ■ **le genre ~** the tragic genre ■ **un auteur ~** a tragic author, an author of tragedies, a tragedian **2.** [dramatique] tragic ■ **elle a eu une fin ~** she came to a sad *ou* tragic end ■ **ce n'est pas ~** it's not the end of the world **3.** [angoissé - regard] anguished.
◇ *nm* **1.** LITTÉR : **le ~** tragedy, tragic art **2.** [auteur de tragédies] tragic author, tragedian **3.** *fig* tragedy ■ **le ~ de sa situation** the tragic side *ou* the tragedy of his situation ■ **prendre qqch au ~** to make a tragedy out of sthg ■ **elle ne prend jamais rien au ~** she never looks on the dark side of things, she never makes a drama out of things ■ **tourner au ~** to take a tragic turn, to go tragically wrong.

tragiquement [traʒikmɑ̃] *adv* tragically.

trahir [32] [trair] *vt*

A.

1. [son camp] to betray ■ *(en usage absolu)* **ceux qui trahissent** traitors, those who betray their country
2. [renier - idéal, foi] to betray
3. *litt* [tromper - ami, amant] : **~ qqn** to deceive sb, to be unfaithful to sb
4. [manquer à] to break, to go against ■ **~ sa promesse/ses engagements** to break one's promise/one's commitments ■ **~ la vérité** to distort *ou* to twist the truth
5. *sout* [décevoir] to betray ■ **~ l'attente de qqn** to fail to live up to sb's expectations ■ **~ les intérêts de qqn** to betray sb's interests
6. [dénaturer - pensée] to misinterpret, to distort, to do an injustice to ; [- en traduisant] to give a false rendering of
7. [ne pas correspondre à] : **mes paroles ont trahi ma pensée** my words failed to express my true thoughts
8. [faire défaut à - suj: forces, mémoire] to fail ■ **si ma mémoire ne me trahit pas** if my memory serves me right

B.

1. [révéler] to betray, to give away *(sép)* ■ **je faillis ~ mes sentiments** I almost revealed my feelings ■ **~ un secret** to give away a secret
2. [démasquer] to give away *(sép)* ■ **son silence l'a trahie** her silence gave her away
3. [exprimer] to betray ■ **son visage ne trahit aucun émoi** he remained stony-faced.
◆ **se trahir** *vpi* **1.** [se révéler] : **l'angoisse se trahissait dans sa voix** her voice betrayed her anxiety **2.** [laisser voir une émotion] to betray o.s., to give o.s. away **3.** [se faire découvrir] to give o.s. away ■ **il s'est trahi en faisant du bruit** he gave himself away by making a noise.

trahison [traizɔ̃] *nf* **1.** DR treason ■ **haute ~** MIL high treason ; POLIT high treason *(by the President)* **2.** [infidélité] infidelity, unfaithfulness ■ **elle me soupçonne des pires ~s** she thinks I'm always being unfaithful to her **3.** [déloyauté] betrayal, disloyalty ■ **acte de ~** betrayal.

train [trɛ̃] *nm*

A.

1. [convoi] train ■ **j'irai t'attendre au ~** I'll wait for you at the station ■ **le ~ de 9 h 40** the 9:40 train ■ **il y a beaucoup de ~s pour Lyon** there's a very good train service to Lyons ■ **je prends le ~ à Arpajon** I catch the train at Arpajon ■ **être dans le ~** to be on the train ▶ **~ autocouchette** car-sleeper train ■ **~ de banlieue** suburban *ou* commuter train ■ **~ direct** non-stop *ou* through train ■ **~ électrique** JEUX train set ■ **~ express** express train ■ **~ de grande ligne** long distance train, intercity train *UK* ■ **~ à grande vitesse** high-speed train ■ **~ de marchandises** goods *UK ou* freight train ■ **~ omnibus** slow *ou* local train ■ **ce ~ est omnibus entre Paris et Vierzon** this train stops *ou* calls at all stations between Paris and Vierzon ■ **~ rapide** fast train ■ **~ postal** mail train ■ **~ supplémentaire** relief train ■ **~ de voyageurs** passenger train ■ **monter dans** *ou* **prendre le ~ en marche** to climb onto *ou* to jump on the bandwagon
2. [moyen de transport] : **le ~** rail (transport), train ■ **j'irai par le** *ou* **en ~** I'll go (there) by train ■ **elle voyage beaucoup en ~** she travels by train a great deal
3. [voyageurs] train

4. [file de véhicules] line (of cars) ■ **~ de camions** convoy *ou* line of lorries *UK ou* trucks *US* ■ **~ de péniches** train *ou* string of barges
5. [ensemble, série] set, batch ■ **~ de réformes** set of reforms
6. AÉRON : **~ d'atterrissage** landing gear, undercarriage
7. ASTRONAUT : **~ spatial** space train
8. AUTO : **~ avant/arrière** front/rear wheel-axle unit
9. MIL : **~ de combat** (combat *ou* unit) train ■ **~ régimentaire** supply train ■ **~ sanitaire** hospital train
10. INFORM [de travaux] stream
11. MÉTALL : **~ de laminoirs** (mill) train
12. INDUST du pétrole : **~ de forage** *ou* **de sonde** (set of) drilling pipes

B.
1. [allure] pace ■ **accélérer le ~** [marcheur, animal] to quicken the pace ; [véhicule] to speed up ■ **au** *ou* **du ~ où vont les choses** the way things are going, at this rate ▶ **aller à fond de ~** *ou* **à un ~ d'enfer** to speed *ou* to race along ■ **aller bon ~** [en marchant] to walk at a brisk pace ■ **les négociations ont été menées bon ~** the negotiations made good progress ■ **aller son petit ~** [marcher] to jog along ; [agir posément] to do things at one's own pace ■ **aller son ~** to carry on (as normal)
2. [manière de vivre] : **~ de vie** lifestyle, standard of living ■ **mener grand ~** to live in grand style
3. SPORT [dans une course - de personnes, de chevaux] pacemaker ■ **gagner au ~** to win after setting the pace throughout the race ■ **mener le ~** to set the pace

C.
1. ZOOL quarters ■ **~ avant** *ou* **de devant** forequarters ■ **~ arrière** *ou* **de derrière** hindquarters
2. *fam* [fesses] backside ■ **il nous faisait avancer à coups de pied dans le ~** he pushed us on with the occasional kick up the backside ■ **courir** *ou* **filer au ~ de qqn** [le suivre partout] to stick to sb like glue ; [le prendre en filature] to tail *ou* to shadow sb.
◆ **en train** ◇ *loc adj* **1.** [en cours] : **être en ~** [ouvrage, travaux] to be under way ■ **j'ai un tricot en ~** I'm knitting something **2.** [personne] : **être en ~** [plein d'allant] to be full of energy ; [de bonne humeur] to be in good spirits *ou* in a good mood ■ **je ne me sens pas vraiment en ~ en ce moment** I don't feel my usual perky self, I am not feeling especially perky at the moment.
◇ *loc adv* **1.** [en route] : **mettre un roman en ~** to start a novel ■ **se mettre en ~** to warm up **2.** [en forme] : **le repas m'avait mis en ~** the meal had put me in good spirits.
◆ **en train de** *loc prép* : **être en ~ de faire qqch** to be (busy) doing sthg ■ **il est toujours en ~ de taquiner sa sœur** he's always teasing his sister ■ **l'opinion publique est en ~ d'évoluer** public opinion is changing.

traînailler [trɛnaje] *fam* = **traînasser**.

traînant, e [trɛnɑ̃, ɑ̃t] *adj* **1.** [lent - élocution] drawling, lazy ■ **je m'en moque, dit-elle d'une voix ~e** I don't care, she drawled **2.** [qui traîne à terre] trailing.

traînard, e [trɛnar, ard] *nm, f fam* **1.** [lambin] slowcoach *UK*, slowpoke *US* **2.** [dans une marche] straggler.

traînasser [3] [trɛnase] *vi fam* **1.** [errer paresseusement] to loaf *ou* to hang about ■ **elle est toujours à ~ dans les rues** she's always hanging around in the streets **2.** [lambiner dans son travail] to fall behind **3.** [élocution] to drawl.

train-auto [trɛ̃oto] (*pl* **trains-autos**) *nm* car-sleeper train.

traîne [trɛn] *nf* **1.** [vêtement] train **2.** NAUT tow **3.** PÊCHE dragnet ■ **pêche à la ~** trolling **4.** *Québec* **~ sauvage** toboggan.
◆ **à la traîne** *loc adj* : **être** *ou* **rester à la ~** [coureur, pays, élève] to lag *ou* to drag behind.

traîneau, x [trɛno] *nm* [véhicule] sleigh, sledge *UK*, sled *US*.

traînée [trene] *nf* **1.** [trace - au sol, sur un mur] trail, streak ; [- dans le ciel] trail ■ **une ~ de fumée** a trail of smoke ▶ **se propager** *ou* **se répandre comme une ~ de poudre** to spread like wildfire **2.** *fam péj* [prostituée] tart *UK*, whore.

traîner [4] [trene] ◇ *vt* **1.** [tirer - gén] to pull ; [- avec effort] to drag, to haul ■ **~ qqn par les pieds** to drag sb (along) by the feet ■ **~ les pieds** to shuffle along, to drag one's feet *pr* ▶ **~ la jambe** *ou* *fam* **patte** to hobble *ou* to limp along ■ **~ qqn dans la boue** *ou* **la fange** *fig* to drag sb's name through the mud ■ **~ un boulet** to have a millstone round one's neck ■ **~ ses guêtres** *fam ou* **bottes** *fam* to loaf *ou* to hang about
2. [emmener - personne réticente] to drag along *(sép)* ; [- personne non désirée] to trail, to drag about *(sép)*
3. [garder avec soi - fétiche, jouet] to drag around *(sép)*
4. *fam* [avoir] : **toute ma jeunesse, j'ai traîné ce sentiment de culpabilité** throughout my youth I carried around this sense of guilt ■ **ça fait des semaines que je traîne cette angine** this sore throat has been with *ou* plaguing me for weeks.
◇ *vi* **1.** [pendre] : **~ (par terre)** to drag on the floor *ou* ground
2. *fam* [ne pas être rangé - documents, vêtements] to lie around, to be scattered around ■ **laisser ~ qqch** to leave sthg lying around
3. [s'attarder, flâner] to dawdle ■ [rester en arrière] to lag *ou* to drag behind ■ **ne traîne pas, Mamie nous attend** stop dawdling *ou* do hurry up, Grandma's expecting us ■ **~ en chemin** *ou* **en route** to dawdle on the way ■ **j'aime bien ~ sur les quais** *fam* I like strolling along the banks of the river ■ *péj* [errer] to hang about *ou* around ■ **il traîne dans tous les bistrots** he hangs around in all the bars ■ **des chiens traînent dans le village** dogs roam around the village
4. *fig* & *péj* [maladie, idée] : **elle attrape toutes les maladies qui traînent** she catches every bug that's going around
5. *fam péj* [s'éterniser - affaire, conversation, procédure] to drag on ; [- superstition, maladie] to linger *ou* to drag on ■ **~ en longueur** [discours, négociations] to drag on ■ **ça n'a pas traîné!** it didn't take long!, it wasn't long coming! ■ **faire ~ des pourparlers/un procès** to drag out negotiations/a trial
6. [ralentir - voix] to drawl (out) ■ **elle a la voix qui traîne** she drawls.
◆ **se traîner** *vpi* **1.** [blessé] to crawl ■ **se ~ par terre** to crawl on the floor *ou* ground ■ **je me suis traînée jusque chez le docteur** *fig* I dragged myself to the doctor's ■ [manquer d'énergie] : **depuis sa mort, elle se traîne** she just mopes around the place now he's dead
2. *fam* [conducteur, véhicule] to crawl along, to go at a crawl.

traîne-savates [trɛnsavat] *nmf fam* dosser *UK*, bum *US*.

train-ferry [trɛ̃feri] (*pl* **trains-ferries**) *nm* train ferry.

training [trɛniŋ] *nm* **1.** [chaussure] sports shoe, trainer ■ [survêtement] tracksuit **2.** PSYCHOL : **~ autogène** self-induced relaxation.

train-train, traintrain [trɛ̃trɛ̃] *nm inv* routine ■ **le ~ quotidien** the daily grind.

traire [112] [trɛr] *vt* [vache] to milk ■ [lait] to draw ■ **machine à ~** milking machine.

trait [trɛ] *nm* **1.** [ligne] line ■ **tirer** *ou* **tracer un ~ (à la règle)** to draw a line (with a ruler) ■ **d'un ~ de plume** with a stroke of the pen ■ **~ de soulignement** underscore ▶ **tirer un ~ sur** : **tirons un ~ sur cette dispute** let's forget this argument, let's put this argument behind us ■ **tirer un ~ sur le passé** to turn over a new leaf, to make a complete break with the past
2. [marque distinctive - d'un système, d'une œuvre, d'un style] (characteristic) feature ■ **~ de caractère** (character) trait ▶ **~ pertinent** LING significant feature
3. [acte] : **~ d'esprit** witticism, flash of wit ■ **~ de générosité** act of generosity ■ **~ de génie** stroke of genius
4. *litt* [projectile] shaft, spear ■ **partir** *ou* **filer comme un ~** to set off like a shot
5. [repartie] shaft ■ **~ satirique** shaft of satire ■ **~ railleur** taunt, gibe
6. *loc* **avoir ~ à** [avoir un rapport avec] to have to do *ou* to be connected with ■ **ayant ~ à** regarding, concerning.
◆ **traits** *nmpl* [du visage] features ■ **il a des ~s fins/grossiers** he has delicate/coarse features ■ **avoir les ~s tirés** to look drawn ■ **on l'a présenté sous les ~s d'un maniaque** he was portrayed as a maniac.
◆ **à grands traits** *loc adv* [dessiner, esquisser] roughly, in broad outline ■ **voici l'intrigue, résumée à grands ~s** here's a broad *ou* rough outline of the plot.
◆ **à longs traits** *loc adv* [boire] in long draughts.
◆ **de trait** *loc adj* [bête, cheval] draught.
◆ **d'un (seul) trait** *loc adv* [avaler] in one gulp, in one go ■ [réciter] (all) in one breath ■ [dormir] uninterruptedly.

◆ **trait pour trait** *loc adv* [exactement] exactly ■ **c'est sa mère ~ pour ~** she's the spitting image of her mother.
◆ **trait d'union** *nm* hyphen ■ ***fig*** link ■ **ce mot prend un ~ d'union** this word is hyphenated *ou* takes a hyphen, this is a hyphenated word ■ **servir de ~ d'union entre *fig*** to bridge the gap between, to link.

traitable [trɛtabl] *adj* **1.** [sujet, question] treatable ■ [problème] manageable ■ **la question n'est pas ~ en une demi-heure** the question cannot be dealt with in half an hour **2.** ***litt*** [accommodant] amenable, helpful.

traitant, e [trɛtɑ̃, ɑ̃t] *adj* [shampooing] medicated.

traite [trɛt] *nf* **1.** COMM, FIN & DR draft, bill ■ [lettre de change] bill of exchange ■ **tirer une ~ sur** to draw a bill *ou* draft on **2.** [versement] instalment, payment ■ **on n'arrive plus à payer les ~s de la maison** we can't pay the mortgage (on the house) any longer **3.** [commerce, trafic] **: ~ des Noirs** slave trade ■ **~ des Blanches** white slave trade *ou* traffic **4.** AGRIC [action] milking *(U)* ■ [lait] milk (yield).
◆ **de traite** *loc adj* [poste, salle] milking.
◆ **d'une (seule) traite** *loc adv* [voyager] in one go, without stopping ■ [avaler] at one go, in one gulp ■ [lire, réciter] in one stretch *ou* breath ■ [dormir] uninterruptedly ■ [travailler] without interruption, at a stretch.

traité [trete] *nm* **1.** [accord] treaty ■ **~ de paix** peace treaty ■ **le ~ de Rome** the Treaty of Rome **2.** [ouvrage] treatise.

traitement [trɛtmɑ̃] *nm* **1.** MÉD & PHARM treatment ■ **un bon ~ contre les poux** a cure for lice ■ **donner un ~ à qqn** to prescribe (a treatment) for sb **2.** [d'un fonctionnaire] salary, wage, wages **3.** [façon d'agir envers quelqu'un] treatment ■ **mauvais ~s** ill-treatment ■ **faire subir de mauvais ~s à qqn** to ill-treat sb ⊙ **~ de choc** shock treatment ■ **avoir un *ou* bénéficier d'un ~ de faveur** to enjoy preferential treatment **4.** INFORM processing ■ **~ de données** data processing ■ **~ différé** off-line processing ■ **~ par lots** batch processing ■ **~ d'images** image processing ■ **~ de texte** word processing ; [logiciel] word processing package **5.** INDUST treatment, processing **6.** [d'un problème, d'une question] treatment, presentation.
◆ **en traitement, sous traitement** *loc adj* under treatment ■ **être en *ou* sous ~** to be being treated *ou* having treatment *ou* under treatment.

traiter [4] [trete] *vt* **1.** [se comporter avec] to treat ■ **~ qqn avec égard** to treat sb with consideration, to show consideration to sb ■ **~ qqn durement/complaisamment** to be harsh/accommodating towards sb ■ **il me traite comme un ami/gamin *fam*** he treats me like a friend/kid ■ **bien ~ qqn** to treat sb well ■ **mal ~ qqn** to treat sb badly, to ill-treat sb ■ **~ qqn d'égal à égal** to treat sb as an equal
2. [soigner - patient, maladie] to treat ■ **se faire ~ pour** to undergo treatment *ou* to be treated for ■ **on me traite à l'homéopathie** I'm having homeopathy
3. INDUST to treat, to process ■ [aliments] to process ■ [récoltes - gén] to treat ; [- par avion] to spray ■ [lentille] to coat
4. [qualifier] **: ~ qqn de : ~ qqn d'imbécile** to call sb an idiot ■ **se faire ~ de menteur** to be called a liar ■ **~ qqn de tous les noms** to call sb all the names under the sun
5. COMM [affaire, demande, dossier] to deal with *(insép)*, to handle
6. [étudier - thème] to treat, to deal with *(insép)* ■ **vous ne traitez pas le sujet** you're not addressing the question
7. INFORM [données, texte, images] to process ■ **~ qqch par lots** to batch process sthg.
◆ **traiter avec** *v+prép* to negotiate *ou* to deal ■ **nous ne traiterons pas avec des terroristes** we won't bargain *ou* negotiate with terrorists.
◆ **traiter de** *v+prép* [suj: roman, film, thèse] to deal with *(insép)*, to be about ■ [suj: auteur] to deal with.
◆ **se traiter** ◇ *vp (emploi passif)* [maladie] **: ça se traite aux antibiotiques** it can be treated with antibiotics.
◇ *vp (emploi réciproque)* [personne] **: ils se traitaient de menteurs** they were calling each other liars.

traiteur [trɛtœr] *nm* [qui livre] caterer ■ **chez le ~** [magasin] at the delicatessen.

traître, esse [trɛtr, ɛs] ◇ *adj* **1.** [déloyal - personne] traitorous, treacherous ■ **être ~ à sa patrie** to be a traitor to *ou* to betray one's country **2.** [trompeur - visage, sourire] deceptive ; [- paroles] treacherous ■ **il est ~, ce petit vin de pays! *fam*** this little local wine is stronger than you'd think! **3.** ***loc*** **pas un ~ mot** not a single word ■ **elle n'a pas dit un ~ mot** she didn't breathe *ou* say a (single) word.
◇ *nm, f* **1.** [gén - POLIT] traitor (*f* traitress) **2.** THÉÂTRE villain.
◆ **en traître** *loc adv* **: prendre qqn en ~** to play an underhand trick on sb ■ **agir en ~** to act treacherously.

traîtreusement [trɛtrøzmɑ̃] *adv* treacherously, traitorously, perfidiously ***sout.***

traîtrise [trɛtriz] *nf* **1.** [caractère] treacherousness, treachery **2.** [acte - perfide] (piece of) treachery ; [- déloyal] betrayal.

trajectoire [traʒɛktwar] *nf* **1.** [d'une balle, d'un missile] trajectory, path ■ [d'une planète, d'un avion] path ■ **~ de vol** flight path **2.** [carrière professionnelle] career path.

trajet [traʒɛ] *nm* **1.** [chemin parcouru] distance ■ [voyage] journey ■ [d'un car, d'un autobus] route ■ **je fais tous les jours le ~ Paris-Egly** I commute everyday between Paris and Egly ■ **il a fait le ~ en huit heures** he covered the distance in eight hours ■ **~ par mer** crossing **2.** ANAT course **3.** ARM [d'un projectile] path.

tralala [tralala] *nm* ***fam*** fuss, frills ■ **pas besoin de tant de ~** no need to make so much fuss ■ **(et) tout le ~ : il y avait des petits fours, du champagne, tout le ~!** there were petits fours, champagne, the (whole) works!

tram [tram] *nm* **1.** [moyen de transport] tram *UK*, streetcar *US* **2.** [véhicule] tram *UK*, tramcar *UK*, streetcar *US*.

trame [tram] *nf* **1.** TEXT [base] weft, woof ■ [fil] weft, weft thread, pick **2.** [d'un livre, d'un film] thread, basic outline *ou* framework **3.** ARCHIT & IMPR screen **4.** TV [lignes] raster ■ [ensemble] field ■ [pour lignes paires et impaires] frame.

tramer [3] [trame] *vt* **1.** [conspiration] to hatch ■ [soulèvement] to plot ■ **elle trame quelque chose! *fig*** she's plotting something! **2.** TEXT to weave **3.** IMPR & PHOTO to screen.
◆ **se tramer** *vp (emploi passif)* to be afoot ■ **un complot se tramait contre l'empereur** a plot was being hatched against the emperor ■ **il se trame quelque chose** something's afoot.

tramontane [tramɔ̃tan] *nf* tramontane, transmontane.

trampoline [trɑ̃pɔlin] *nm* trampoline ■ **faire du ~** to do trampolining.

tramway [tramwɛ] *nm* **1.** [moyen de transport] tramway (system) **2.** [véhicule] tramcar *UK*, streetcar *US* ■ **'Un tramway nommé Désir' *Williams*** 'A Streetcar Named Desire'.

tranchant, e [trɑ̃ʃɑ̃, ɑ̃t] *adj* **1.** [lame] sharp, keen, cutting ■ [outil] cutting ■ [bord] sharp, cutting **2.** [personne, réponse, ton] curt, sharp.
◆ **tranchant** *nm* [d'une lame] sharp *ou* cutting edge ■ **le ~ de la main** the edge of the hand.

tranche [trɑ̃ʃ] *nf* **1.** [de pain, de viande, de pastèque] slice ■ **~ de bacon** [à frire] rasher (of bacon) ■ **~ de saumon** [darne] salmon steak ; [fumée] slice *ou* leaf of (smoked) salmon ■ **une ~ fine** a sliver, a thin slice ■ **une ~ de rôti** a slice cut off the joint ⊙ **~ napolitaine** CULIN Neapolitan slice *ou* ice-cream ■ **une ~ de vie** a slice of life **2.** [subdivision - d'un programme de construction] stage, phase ■ **~ horaire** ADMIN period of time ■ **~ d'âge** age bracket ■ **~ de salaires/de revenus** salary/income bracket ■ **~ d'imposition** tax bracket **3.** BOURSE & FIN [d'actions] block, tranche ■ [d'emprunt] instalment ■ [loterie] **: ~ d'émission** issue **4.** RADIO & TV slot **5.** [bord - d'un livre] edge ; [- d'une médaille, d'une pièce] edge, rim ■ **doré sur ~** gilt-edged.
◆ **en tranche(s)** ◇ *loc adj* [pain, saucisson] sliced.
◇ *loc adv* **: débiter *ou* couper qqch en ~s** to slice sthg (up), to cut sthg into slices.

tranché, e [trɑ̃ʃe] *adj* **1.** [sans nuances - couleurs] distinct, clear, sharply contrasted **2.** [distinct - catégories] distinct ; [- caractères] distinct, well-defined, clear-cut **3.** [péremptoire - position] clear-cut, uncompromising, unequivocal.
◆ **tranché** *nm* HÉRALD tranché, party per bend.

◆ **tranchée** *nf* **1.** MIL & TRAV PUB trench ▪ **creuser une ~e** to (dig a) trench ▪ **il était dans les ~es pendant la guerre** he fought in the trenches **2.** [en forêt] cutting *(U)* ▪ [pare-feu] firebreak.
◆ **tranchées** *nfpl* MÉD colic *(U)*, gripe *(U)*, gripes ▪ **~es utérines** after-pains.

trancher [3] [trɑ̃ʃe] ◇ *vt* **1.** [couper] to cut, to sever *sout*, to slice through ▪ **~ la gorge de qqn** to cut *ou* to slit sb's throat **2.** [différend] to settle ▪ [difficulté] to solve ▪ [question] to decide **3.** *sout* [discussion] to bring to a sudden end, to cut short *(sép)*.
◇ *vi* [décider] to make *ou* to take a decision, to decide ▪ **~ dans le vif** to take drastic action.
◆ **trancher avec, trancher sur** *v+prép* [suj: couleur] to stand out against, to contrast sharply with ▪ [suj: attitude] to be in sharp contrast *ou* to contrast strongly with ▪ **sa déclaration tranche avec les propos apaisants du gouvernement** his remarks are in sharp contrast to the pacifying words of his government.
◆ **se trancher** *vpt* : **se ~ le doigt** to chop one's finger off.

tranquille [trɑ̃kil] *adj* **1.** [sans agitation - quartier, rue] quiet ; [- campagne] quiet, peaceful, tranquil *litt* ; [- soirée] calm, quiet, peaceful ; [- sommeil, vie] peaceful, tranquil *litt* ; [- air, eau] still, quiet, tranquil *litt* ▪ **aller** *ou* **marcher d'un pas ~** to stroll unhurriedly
2. [en paix] : **on ne peut même plus être ~ chez soi!** you can't even get some peace and quiet at home any more! ▪ **allons dans mon bureau, nous y serons plus ~s pour discuter** let's go into my office, we can talk there without being disturbed ▪ **laisser qqn ~** to leave sb alone *ou* in peace ▪ **le bébé ne la laisse jamais ~** the baby gives her no peace ▪ **laisse-le ~ avec tes problèmes!** stop bothering him with your problems! ▪ **laisse-moi ~, je suis assez grand pour ouvrir la boîte tout seul!** leave me alone, I'm old enough to open the box on my own! ▪ **laisser qqch ~** *fam* [ne pas y toucher] to leave sthg alone ▪ **laisse ma vie de famille ~!** leave my family life out of it!
3. [calme, sage] quiet ▪ **se tenir** *ou* **rester ~** to keep quiet *ou* still ; [ne pas se faire remarquer] to keep a low profile
4. [serein - personne, foi] calm, serene
5. [rassuré] : **être ~** to feel *ou* to be easy in one's mind ▪ **sois ~, elle va bien** don't worry *ou* set your mind at rest, she's all right ▪ **je ne suis pas** *ou* **ne me sens pas ~ quand il est sur les routes** I worry when he's on the road ▪ **je serais plus ~ s'il n'était pas seul** I'd feel easier in my mind knowing that he wasn't on his own
6. [sûr] : **tu peux être ~ (que)...** you can rest assured (that)... ▪ **ils n'auront pas mon argent, sois ~!** they won't get my money, that's for sure!

tranquillement [trɑ̃kilmɑ̃] *adv* **1.** [calmement - dormir, jouer] quietly, peacefully ; [- répondre, regarder] calmly, quietly **2.** [sans se presser - marcher, travailler] unhurriedly ▪ **on est allés ~ jusqu'à l'église avec grand-mère** we walked slowly to the church with grandma.

tranquillisant, e [trɑ̃kilizɑ̃, ɑ̃t] *adj* [paroles, voix, présence] soothing, reassuring.
◆ **tranquillisant** *nm* PHARM tranquillizer ▪ **bourré de ~s** *fam* doped up to the eyeballs (with tranquillizers).

tranquilliser [3] [trɑ̃kilize] *vt* : **~ qqn** to set sb's mind at rest, to reassure sb.
◆ **se tranquilliser** *vp (emploi réfléchi)* to stop worrying ▪ **tranquillise-toi, je ne rentrerai pas en auto-stop** don't worry, I won't hitch-hike home.

tranquillité [trɑ̃kilite] *nf* **1.** [calme - d'un lieu] quietness, peacefulness, tranquillity *sout* ; [- d'une personne] peace, tranquillity *sout* ▪ **les enfants ne me laissent pas un seul moment de ~** the children don't give me a single moment's peace **2.** [sérénité] : **~ d'esprit** peace of mind.
◆ **en toute tranquillité** *loc adv* [sereinement] with complete peace of mind.

transaction [trɑ̃zaksjɔ̃] *nf* **1.** BOURSE, COMM & ÉCON transaction, deal ▪ **~s** transactions, dealings **2.** DR (formal) settlement **3.** INFORM transaction.

transalpin, e [trɑ̃zalpɛ̃, in] *adj* transalpine.

transat [trɑ̃zat] ◇ *nm* deck chair.
◇ *nf* SPORT transatlantic race ▪ **la ~ en solitaire** the single-handed transatlantic race.

transatlantique [trɑ̃zatlɑ̃tik] ◇ *adj* transatlantic.
◇ *nm* **1.** NAUT (transatlantic) liner **2.** [chaise longue] deck chair.
◇ *nf* SPORT transatlantic race.

transbahuter [3] [trɑ̃sbayte] *vt fam* to move, to shift, to cart ▪ **les bagages ont été transbahutés dans une autre voiture** the luggage was shoved into another car.
◆ **se transbahuter** *vpi fam* to shift o.s.

transbordement [trɑ̃sbɔrdəmɑ̃] *nm* [de marchandises] transshipment ▪ [de voyageurs] transferring *(of passengers to another vessel or vehicle)*.

transborder [3] [trɑ̃sbɔrde] *vt* [marchandises] to transship ▪ [voyageurs] to transfer.

transbordeur [trɑ̃sbɔrdœr] ◇ *nm* [navire] transporter bridge.
◇ *adj m* : **pont ~** transporter bridge.

transcanadien, enne [trɑ̃skanadjɛ̃, ɛn] *adj* trans-Canadian, trans-Canada *(avant n)*.

transcendance [trɑ̃sɑ̃dɑ̃s] *nf* **1.** PHILOS transcendence, transcendency **2.** MATH transcendence.

transcendant, e [trɑ̃sɑ̃dɑ̃, ɑ̃t] *adj* **1.** *fam* [génial] brilliant ▪ **ce n'est pas ~!** [livre, film] it's not exactly brilliant! **2.** MATH & PHILOS transcendental.

transcendantal, e, aux [trɑ̃sɑ̃dɑ̃tal] *adj* transcendental.

transcender [3] [trɑ̃sɑ̃de] *vt* to transcend.
◆ **se transcender** *vpi* to transcend o.s.

transcodage [trɑ̃skɔdaʒ] *nm* [gén] transcoding, code translation ▪ INFORM compiling.

transcontinental, e, aux [trɑ̃skɔ̃tinɑ̃tal, o] *adj* transcontinental.

transcripteur [trɑ̃skriptœr] *nm* transcriber.

transcription [trɑ̃skripsjɔ̃] *nf* **1.** [fait d'écrire - gén] transcription, transcribing, noting (down) ; [- des notes] copying out (in longhand) ; [- un document officiel] recording **2.** [copie] copy, transcript ▪ [document officiel] record **3.** LING & MUS [gén] transcribing, transcription ▪ [translittération] transliteration.

transcrire [99] [trɑ̃skrir] *vt* **1.** [conversation] to transcribe, to note *ou* to take down *(sép)* ▪ [notes] to copy *ou* to write out (in longhand) *(sép)* ▪ [dans un registre] to record **2.** LING : **~ un mot d'un alphabet dans un autre** to transliterate a word ▪ **~ un nom russe/chinois en caractères romains** to Romanize a Russian/Chinese name **3.** MUS to transcribe.

transculturel, elle [trɑ̃skyltyrɛl] *adj* transcultural, cross-cultural.

transe [trɑ̃s] *nf* **1.** [état d'hypnose] trance **2.** [exaltation] trance, exaltation.
◆ **transes** *nfpl* [mouvements] convulsions ▪ **être pris de ~s** to go into convulsions.
◆ **en transe(s)** *loc adj & loc adv* : **être en ~** to be in a trance ▪ **entrer en ~** [médium] to go *ou* to fall into a trance ; *fig & hum* to get all worked up.

transept [trɑ̃sɛpt] *nm* transept.

transférer [18] [trɑ̃sfere] *vt* **1.** [prisonnier, sportif] to transfer ▪ [diplomate] to transfer, to move ▪ [évêque] to translate ▪ **~ qqn de... à** to transfer sb from... to ▪ [magasin, siège social] to transfer, to move ▪ [fonds] to transfer ▪ [reliques] to translate ▪ **'succursale transférée au n° 42'** 'our branch is now at no. 42' **2.** INFORM [information] to transfer **3.** DR [droits] to transfer, to convey ▪ [propriété - gén] to transfer, to convey ; [- par legs] to demise ▪ [pouvoirs] to transfer, to pass on *(sép)* **4.** PSYCHOL : **~ qqch sur qqn** to transfer sthg onto sb **5.** ART : **~ un motif sur** to transfer a design on *ou* onto.

transfert [trɑ̃sfɛr] *nm* **1.** [gén - COMM] transfer ▪ **~ de fonds** transfer of funds **2.** INFORM transfer ▪ **~ de données** data transfer **3.** DR [de propriété] transfer, conveyance ▪ [de droits, de pouvoirs] transfer ▪ **~ par legs** demise **4.** PSYCHOL transference ▪ **elle fait un ~ sur toi** she's using you as the object of her transference **5.** TÉLÉCOM : **~ d'appel** call forwarding.

transfiguration [trɑ̃sfigyrasjɔ̃] *nf* **1.** [changement profond] transfiguration **2.** RELIG : **la Transfiguration** the Transfiguration.

transfigurer [3] [trɑ̃sfigyre] *vt* to transfigure.

transfo [trɑ̃sfo] *nm fam* = **transformateur.**

transformable [trɑ̃sfɔrmabl] *adj* **1.** [modifiable] changeable, alterable ▪ **des décors ~s** flexible sets **2.** SPORT convertible.

transformateur, trice [trɑ̃sfɔrmatœr, tris] *adj* [influence] transforming.
◆ **transformateur** *nm* ÉLECTR transformer ▪ **~ de traversée** bushing (current) transformer.

transformation [trɑ̃sfɔrmasjɔ̃] *nf* **1.** [d'une personnalité, d'un environnement] transformation ▪ [d'une matière première, d'énergie] conversion **2.** [résultat d'un changement] transformation, alteration, change ▪ **nous avons fait des ~s dans la maison** [travaux] we've made some alterations to the house ; [décor, ameublement] we've made some changes in the house **3.** SPORT conversion.

transformer [3] [trɑ̃sfɔrme] *vt* **1.** [faire changer - bâtiment, personnalité, institution, paysage] to transform, to change, to alter ; [- matière première] to transform, to convert ; [- vêtement] to make over *(sép)*, to alter ▪ **~ qqch en** [faire devenir] to convert sthg into **2.** SPORT to convert.
◆ **se transformer** *vpi* [quartier, personnalité, paysage, institution] to change ▪ **l'environnement se transforme lentement/rapidement** the environment is changing slowly/rapidly ▪ **ce voyage se transformait en cauchemar** the trip was turning into a nightmare.

transfrontalier, ère [trɑ̃sfrɔ̃talje, ɛr] *adj* cross-border *(epith)*.

transfuge [trɑ̃sfyʒ] *nmf* MIL & POLIT renegade, turncoat ▪ [qui change de camp] defector.

transfuser [3] [trɑ̃sfyze] *vt* **1.** MÉD [sang] to transfuse ▪ **elle se fait ~ régulièrement à cause de sa maladie** she has regular blood transfusions because of her illness **2.** *litt* [sentiment] to instill, to communicate, to pass on *(sép)*.

transfusion [trɑ̃sfyzjɔ̃] *nf* : **~ sanguine** *ou* **de sang** blood transfusion ▪ **faire une ~ à qqn** to give sb a (blood) transfusion.

transgénique [trɑ̃sʒenik] *adj* transgenic.

transgresser [4] [trɑ̃sgrese] *vt* [loi, règle] to infringe, to contravene, to break ▪ [ordre] to disobey, to go against ▪ **~ les interdits** to break the taboos.

transgression [trɑ̃sgrɛsjɔ̃] *nf* [d'une règle, d'une loi] infringement, contravention, transgression ▪ [d'un ordre] contravention.

transhumance [trɑ̃zymɑ̃s] *nf* [de troupeaux] seasonal migration, transhumance *spéc* ▪ **au moment de la ~** when the herds are moved to the grazing grounds.

transhumant, e [trɑ̃zymɑ̃, ɑ̃t] *adj* transhumant *spéc*.

transhumer [3] [trɑ̃zyme] ◇ *vi* [vers les pâturages] to move up to (summer) grazing grounds ▪ [vers la vallée] to move down to the wintering grounds.
◇ *vt* [troupeaux] to move.

transi, e [trɑ̃zi] *adj* : **être ~ (de froid)** to be chilled to the bone *ou* to the marrow ▪ **être ~ de peur** to be paralysed *ou* transfixed by fear.

transiger [17] [trɑ̃ziʒe] *vi* to (come to a) compromise ▪ **~ avec qqn** to seek a compromise *ou* to bargain with sb ▪ **~ avec sa conscience** to make a deal with one's conscience ▪ **ne pas ~ sur la ponctualité** to be uncompromising in matters of punctuality, to be a stickler for punctuality.

transir [32] [trɑ̃zir] *vt* : **le froid m'avait transi** the cold had gone right through me.

transistor [trɑ̃zistɔr] *nm* **1.** RADIO transistor (radio) **2.** ÉLECTRON transistor ▪ **~ à effet de champ** field-effect transistor, FET.
◆ **à transistors** *loc adj* transistorized.

transit [trɑ̃zit] *nm* **1.** COMM [de marchandises, de touristes] transit **2.** PHYSIOL : **~ intestinal** intestinal transit ▪ **'favorise le ~ intestinal'** 'relieves constipation'.
◆ **de transit** *loc adj* transit *(modif)* ▪ **salle de ~** [d'un aéroport] transit lounge.
◆ **en transit** *loc adj* in transit, transitting.

transitaire [trɑ̃zitɛr] ◇ *adj* [commerce, port] transit *(modif)*.
◇ *nmf* forwarding agent.

transiter [3] [trɑ̃zite] ◇ *vt* [marchandises] to pass through *(sép)*, to transit.
◇ *vi* [voyageurs, marchandises] : **~ par** to pass through in in transit ▪ **ces dossiers transitent par mon service** those files come through my department.

transitif, ive [trɑ̃zitif, iv] *adj* transitive.
◆ **transitif** *nm* LING transitive verb.

transition [trɑ̃zisjɔ̃] *nf* **1.** [entre deux états] transition **2.** [entre deux paragraphes, deux scènes] transition, link **3.** [entre deux gouvernements] interim **4.** PHYS transition.
◆ **de transition** *loc adj* **1.** [administration, gouvernement] interim *(modif)* ▪ **période de ~** period of transition, transition *ou* transitional period **2.** AÉRON & CHIM transition *(modif)*.
◆ **sans transition** *loc adv* without transition ▪ **elle passait sans ~ de l'enthousiasme à la fureur** her mood used to change *ou* to switch abruptly from enthusiasm to rage.

transitionnel, elle [trɑ̃zisjɔnɛl] *adj* [gén] transitional.

transitivité [trɑ̃zitivite] *nf* transitivity.

transitoire [trɑ̃zitwar] *adj* **1.** [administration, dispositions, régime] interim, transitional ▪ [charge] temporary **2.** [situation] transitory, transient.

Transjordanie [trɑ̃sʒɔrdani] *npr f* HIST : **(la) ~** Transjordan.

translation [trɑ̃slasjɔ̃] *nf* **1.** DR [d'une juridiction, d'un dignitaire] transfer ▪ [de propriété] conveyance, transfer **2.** INFORM : **~ dynamique** dynamic relocation **3.** MATH & PHYS translation ▪ **mouvement de ~** translation movement.

translucide [trɑ̃slysid] *adj* translucent.

transmanche [trɑ̃smɑ̃ʃ] *adj inv* cross-Channel.

transmet *etc v* ▷ **transmettre.**

transmetteur [trɑ̃smɛtœr] *nm* **1.** TÉLÉCOM transmitter **2.** MIL ≃ soldier in the Signals Corps.

transmettre [84] [trɑ̃smɛtr] *vt* **1.** TÉLÉCOM to transmit **2.** RADIO & TV [émission] to transmit, to relay, to broadcast **3.** PHYS to transmit ▪ **~ un mouvement à qqch** to set sthg in motion **4.** [de la main à la main] to hand (on), to pass on *(sép)* ▪ **l'ailier transmet le ballon à l'avant-centre** the wing-forward passes the ball to the centre-forward ▪ [de génération en génération] to pass on *(sép)*, to hand down *(sép)* **5.** [communiquer - information, ordre, remerciement] to pass on *(sép)*, to convey *sout* ; [- pli] to send on *(sép)*, to forward ; [- secret] to pass on *(sép)* ▪ **transmettez mes amitiés/mes respects à votre frère** [à l'oral] please remember me to/convey my respects to *sout* your brother ; [dans une lettre] please send my regards/my respects to your brother ▪ *(en usage absolu)* **écrire au journal, qui transmettra** write care of the newspaper **6.** [faire partager - goût, émotion] to pass on *(sép)*, to put over *(sép)* ▪ **il m'a transmis son enthousiasme pour l'art abstrait** he communicated his enthusiasm for abstract art to me **7.** MÉD to transmit, to pass on *(sép)* **8.** DR [propriété] to pass on *(sép)*, to transfer ▪ [pouvoirs] to pass on *(sép)*, to hand over *(sép)*, to transfer.
◆ **se transmettre** *vp (emploi passif)* to be transmitted ▪ **le virus se transmet par contact/par la salive** the virus is transmitted by (direct) contact/through saliva ▪ **la vibration se transmet à la membrane** the vibration spreads *ou* is transmitted to the membrane.

transmigrer [3] [trɑ̃smigre] *vi* **1.** *litt* [émigrer] to migrate **2.** [âme] to transmigrate.

transmis, e [trɑ̃smi, iz] *pp* ▻ **transmettre**.

transmissible [trɑ̃smisibl] *adj* **1.** MÉD transmittable, transmissible ▪ **c'est ~ par contact/par la salive** it can be transmitted by (direct) contact/through saliva **2.** DR [biens, droit] transferable, transmissible.

transmission [trɑ̃smisjɔ̃] *nf* **1.** AUTO & MÉCAN [pièces] : **organes de ~** transmission (system) **2.** PHYS [de chaleur, de son] transmission **3.** TÉLÉCOM transmission ▪ RADIO & TV [d'une émission] transmission, relaying, broadcasting **4.** MÉD passing on, transmission, transmitting **5.** [d'une information, d'un ordre] passing on, conveying ▪ [d'un secret] passing on ▪ [d'une lettre] forwarding, sending on ▪ **~ de pensée** telepathy, thought transference **6.** [legs - d'un bijou, d'une histoire] handing down, passing on ; [- d'un état d'esprit] passing on **7.** DR [de pouvoirs, de biens] transfer.

◆ **transmissions** *nfpl* MIL : **les ~s** ≃ the Signals Corps.

transmit *etc v* ▻ **transmettre**.

transmuer [trɑ̃smɥe] *vt* to transmute ▪ **~ qqch en** to transmute sthg into.

◆ **se transmuer** *vpi* to be transmuted.

transmutation [trɑ̃smytasjɔ̃] *nf* transmutation.

transocéanique [trɑ̃zɔseanik] *adj* transoceanic.

Transpac [trɑ̃spak] *npr the French packet-switching network.*

transpalette [trɑ̃spalɛt] *nf* pallet truck, stacker.

transparaître [91] [trɑ̃sparɛtr] *vi* [lumière, couleur, sentiment] to show *ou* to filter through ▪ **son visage ne laissa rien ~** he remained impassive, his face showed no emotion.

transparence [trɑ̃sparɑ̃s] *nf* **1.** [propriété - d'une porcelaine, d'une surface] transparence, transparency ; [- d'une peau] clearness, transparence, transparency ; [- d'un regard, d'un liquide] transparency, clearness ▪ **regarder qqch par ~** to look at sthg against the light ▪ **on voit son soutien-gorge par ~** her bra is showing through **2.** *sout* [caractère d'évidence - d'un dessein, d'une personnalité] transparency, obviousness **3.** [caractère public - de transactions, d'une comptabilité] public accountability **4.** CINÉ backprojection.

transparent, e [trɑ̃sparɑ̃, ɑ̃t] *adj* **1.** [translucide - porcelaine, papier, surface] transparent ; [- regard, eau] transparent, limpid ; [- vêtement] transparent, see-through ▪ **ta robe est très ~e** your dress is very transparent *ou* see-through ▪ [lumineux, clair - peau] transparent, clear **2.** [évident - dessein, motif] obvious, transparent **3.** [public - comptabilité, transaction] open.

◆ **transparent** *nm* [de projection] transparency.

transparu [trɑ̃spary] *pp* ▻ **transparaître**.

transpercer [16] [trɑ̃spɛrse] *vt* **1.** [suj: flèche, épée] to pierce (through), to transfix *litt* ▪ **~ qqn d'un coup d'épée** to run sb through with a sword **2.** [pénétrer - suj: pluie] to get through *(insép)* ▪ **un froid qui transperce** piercing cold.

transpiration [trɑ̃spirasjɔ̃] *nf* **1.** PHYSIOL [sudation] perspiration ▪ [sueur] perspiration, sweat **2.** BOT transpiration.

transpirer [3] [trɑ̃spire] *vi* **1.** PHYSIOL to perspire, to sweat ▪ **~ des mains/pieds** to have sweaty hands/feet ▪ **je transpirais à grosses gouttes** great drops *ou* beads of sweat were rolling off my forehead ▮ *fig* [faire des efforts] to sweat blood, to be hard at it ▪ **~ sur qqch** to sweat over sthg **2.** [être divulgué] to leak out, to come to light.

transplant [trɑ̃splɑ̃] *nm* [avant l'opération] organ for transplant ▪ [après l'opération] transplant, transplanted organ.

transplantation [trɑ̃splɑ̃tasjɔ̃] *nf* **1.** MÉD [d'un organe - méthode] transplantation ; [- opération] transplant ▪ **~ cardiaque/rénale/hépatique** heart/kidney/liver transplant ▪ **~ embryonnaire** surgical transplantation of an embryo **2.** AGRIC & HORT transplantation, transplanting **3.** [déplacement - de personnes] moving, resettling ; [- d'animaux] transplantation.

transplanté, e [trɑ̃splɑ̃te] *nm, f* receiver *(of a transplant)*.

transplanter [3] [trɑ̃splɑ̃te] *vt* **1.** MÉD [organe] to transplant ▪ [embryon] to implant **2.** AGRIC & HORT to transplant **3.** [populations] to move, to transplant ▪ *péj* to uproot.

transport [trɑ̃spɔr] *nm* **1.** [acheminement - de personnes, de marchandises] transport *UK*, transportation *US* ; [- d'énergie] conveyance, conveying ▪ **~ par air** *ou* **avion** air transport ▪ **~ par mer** shipping ▪ **~ par route** road transport *ou* haulage ⊙ **~ de troupes** MIL [acheminement] troop transportation ; [navire, avion] (troop) carrier, troop transport **2.** [émotion] transport, burst ▪ **~ de joie** transport *ou* burst of joy ▪ **~ d'enthousiasme** burst *ou* gush of enthusiasm ▪ **~ de colère** burst *ou* outburst of anger ▪ **~s amoureux** *litt* & *hum* amorous transports.

◆ **transports** *nmpl* ADMIN transport network ▪ **~s (publics** *ou* **en commun)** public transport *(U)* ▪ **je passe beaucoup de temps dans les ~s pour aller au travail** I spend a lot of time commuting ▪ **prendre les ~s en commun** to use public transport ▪ **les ~s aériens** (the) airlines ▪ **les ~s ferroviaires** the rail (transport) network ▪ **les ~s maritimes** the shipping lines ▪ **les ~s routiers** road transport ▪ **les ~s urbains** the urban transport system.

◆ **de transport** *loc adj* transport *UK (modif)*, transportation *US (modif)*.

transportable [trɑ̃spɔrtabl] *adj* [denrées] transportable ▪ [blessé] fit to be moved.

transporter [3] [trɑ̃spɔrte] *vt* **1.** [faire changer d'endroit - cargaison, passager, troupes] to carry, to transport, to convey *sout* ; [- blessé] to move ▪ **~ des vivres par avion/par bateau** to fly/to ship food supplies ▪ **~ qqch par camion** to send sthg by lorry *UK ou* by truck *US* ▪ **~ qqch par train** to transport sthg by rail ▪ **~ qqn à l'hôpital/d'urgence à l'hôpital** to take/to rush sb to hospital ▪ *fig* [par l'imaginaire] to take ▪ **le premier acte nous transporte en Géorgie/au XVI**[e] **siècle** the first act takes us to Georgia/takes us back to the 16th century **2.** [porter] to carry ▪ **les alluvions transportées par le fleuve** the sediment carried (along) by the river **3.** PHYS to convey **4.** *litt* [enthousiasmer] to carry away *(sép)*, to send into raptures ▪ **être transporté de joie** to be overjoyed *ou* in transports of delight **5.** FIN [fonds] to transfer **6.** HIST [condamné] to transport.

◆ **se transporter** *vpi* **1.** [se déplacer] to move **2.** *fig* [en imagination] to imagine o.s.

transporteur, euse [trɑ̃spɔrtœr, øz] *adj* carrying ▪ **benne transporteuse** skip.

◆ **transporteur** *nm* **1.** [entreprise] haulage contractor, haulier *UK*, hauler *US* ▪ [en langage juridique] carrier ▪ **~ routier** road haulage contractor, road haulier *UK ou* hauler *US* **2.** [outil] conveyor **3.** NAUT : **~ de vrac** bulk carrier **4.** INDUST du pétrole : **~ de gaz** gas transporter (ship).

transposable [trɑ̃spozabl] *adj* transposable.

transposer [3] [trɑ̃spoze] *vt* **1.** [intervertir - mots] to switch (round), to transpose **2.** [adapter] : **~ un sujet antique à l'époque moderne** to adapt an ancient play to a contemporary setting **3.** MUS to transpose.

transposition [trɑ̃spozisjɔ̃] *nf* **1.** [commutation] transposition **2.** [adaptation] adaptation **3.** ÉLECTR, IMPR, MATH, MÉD & MUS transposition.

transsaharien, enne [trɑ̃ssaarjɛ̃, ɛn] *adj* Transsaharan.

transsexuel, elle [trɑ̃ssɛksɥɛl] *adj* transexual, transsexual.

transsibérien, enne [trɑ̃ssiberjɛ̃, ɛn] *adj* Trans-Siberian ▪ **le Transsibérien** the Trans-Siberian (Railway).

transsubstantiation [trɑ̃ssypstɑ̃sjasjɔ̃] *nf* transsubstantiation.

transvasement [trɑ̃svazmɑ̃] *nm* [d'un liquide] decanting.

transvaser [3] [trɑ̃svaze] *vt* to decant ▪ **transvasez le bouillon dans un verre gradué** pour the stock into a measuring jug.

transversal, e, aux [trɑ̃svɛrsal, o] *adj* [coupe, fil, poutre, trait] cross, transverse, transversal ▪ [onde, axe, moteur] transverse ▪ [voie] which runs *ou* cuts across ▪ **rue ~e** side road.

◆ **transversale** *nf* **1.** FOOTBALL [barre] crossbar **2.** GÉOM transversal **3.** [route] cross-country trunk road *UK ou* highway *US* **4.** RAIL [entre régions] cross-country line ■ [de ville à ville] Inter-City *UK ou* interurban *US* line.

transversalement [trɑ̃svɛrsalmɑ̃] *adv* transversally, across.

transverse [trɑ̃svɛrs] *adj* ANAT & GÉOM transverse.

Transylvanie [trɑ̃silvani] *npr f* : **(la) ~** Transylvania.

trapèze [trapɛz] ◇ *nm* **1.** GÉOM trapezium *UK*, trapezoid *US* **2.** ANAT [muscle] trapezius **3.** LOISIRS trapeze ■ **faire du ~** to perform on the trapeze ▶ **~ volant** flying trapeze.
◇ *adj* ANAT : **muscle ~** trapezius ■ **os ~** trapezium.

trapéziste [trapezist] *nmf* trapezist, trapeze artist.

trappe [trap] *nf* **1.** [piège] trap **2.** [sur le sol - porte] trap door ; [- ouverture] hatch ■ [d'une scène de théâtre] trap opening ■ [pour parachutiste] exit door ■ **passer à la ~** to be whisked away (without trace).

Trappe [trap] *npr f* **1.** [abbaye] Trappist monastery **2.** [ordre] : **la ~** the Trappist order.

trapper [3] [trape] *vt & vi Québec* to trap.

trappeur [trapœr] *nm* trapper.

trappiste [trapist] *nm* [moine] Trappist monk.

trapu, e [trapy] *adj* **1.** [personne] stocky, thickset **2.** [bâtiment] squat **3.** *fam* [difficile - devoir, exercice] tough, stiff ■ **l'examen était vraiment ~!** the exam was a real stinker! **4.** *fam* [savant] brainy ■ **il est ~ en chimie** he's brilliant at chemistry.

traque [trak] *nf* CHASSE : **la ~** beating (game).

traquenard [traknar] *nm* **1.** [machination] snare, trap ■ **tomber dans un ~** to fall into a trap **2.** [pour les oiseaux] bird trap ■ [pour les souris] trap **3.** ÉQUIT [trot] rack ■ [cheval] racker.

traquer [3] [trake] *vt* **1.** [criminel, fuyard] to track *ou* to hunt down *(sép)* ■ [vedette] to hound ■ [erreur] to hunt down *(sép)* ■ **en le traquant, ils ont découvert où il habitait** they tracked him down to his home **2.** CHASSE [rechercher] to track down *(sép)* ■ [rabattre] to drive ■ **animal traqué** hunted animal.

trauma [troma] *nm* trauma.

traumatique [tromatik] *adj* traumatic.

traumatisant, e [tromatizɑ̃, ɑ̃t] *adj* traumatizing.

traumatiser [3] [tromatize] *vt* to traumatize.

traumatisme [tromatism] *nm* trauma, traumatism ■ **~ crânien** cranial trauma.

traumatologie [tromatɔlɔʒi] *nf* traumatology.

travail[1], ails [travaj] *nm* VÉTÉR trave.

travail[2], aux [travaj, o] *nm*

> **A.** ACTION
> **B.** RÉSULTAT, EFFET
> **C.** LIEU D'ACTIVITÉ PROFESSIONNELLE

A. ACTION

1. [occupation] : **le ~** work ■ **le ~ de bureau** office work ■ **le ~ de jour/nuit** day/night work ■ **je finis le ~ à cinq heures** I stop *ou* finish work at five ■ **écrire un dictionnaire est un ~ collectif** writing a dictionary involves working as a team ■ **~ de force** hard physical work ■ **un ~ de longue haleine** a long-term work *ou* project ▶ **le ~ posté** *ou* **par roulement** shift work ■ **le ~ à domicile** outwork ■ **~ d'intérêt général** DR community service ■ **le ~ manuel** manual work *ou* labour ■ **le ~ au noir** [occasionnel] undeclared casual work, moonlighting ; [comme pratique généralisée] black economy ■ **~ à la pièce** piecework ■ **le ~ saisonnier** seasonal work ■ **le ~ salarié** paid work ■ **le ~ temporaire** [gén] temporary work ; [dans un bureau] temping
2. [tâches imposées] work ■ **donner du ~ à qqn** to give sb (some) work to do
3. [tâche déterminée] job ■ **faire un ~ de recherche/traduction** to do a piece of research/a translation ▶ **c'est un ~ de bagnard** *ou* **forçat** it's back-breaking work *ou* a back-breaking job ■ **c'est un ~ de fourmi** it's a painstaking task ■ **c'est un ~ de Romain** *ou* **de Titan** it's a colossal job ■ **et voilà le ~!** *familier* and Bob's your uncle!
4. [efforts] (hard) work ■ **c'est du ~ d'élever cinq enfants!** bringing up five children is a lot of (hard) work! ■ **il a encore du ~ s'il veut devenir champion** he's still got a lot of work to do if he wants to be champion
5. [exécution] work ■ **admirez le ~ du pinceau** admire the brushwork ■ **on lui a confié les peintures et elle a fait du bon/mauvais ~** she was responsible for doing the painting and she made a good/bad job of it ▶ **regarde-moi ce ~!** just look at this mess! ■ **je ne retrouve pas une seule disquette, qu'est-ce que c'est que ce ~?** I can't find a single floppy disc, what's going on here? ■ **et voilà le ~!** *fam* and Bob's your uncle!
6. [façonnage] working ■ **elle est attirée par le ~ du bois/de la soie** she's interested in working with wood/with silk
7. [poste] job, occupation, post ■ [responsabilité] job ■ **chercher du** *ou* **un ~** to be job-hunting, to be looking for a job ■ **sans ~** unemployed, jobless, out of work
8. [dans le système capitaliste] labour
9. [contrainte exercée - par la chaleur, l'érosion] action
10. PHYSIOL [accouchement] labour ■ **le ~ n'est pas commencé/est commencé** the patient has not yet gone/has gone into labour ■ [activité] work ■ **réduire le ~ du cœur/des reins** to lighten the strain on the heart/on the kidneys
11. MÉCAN & PHYS work
12. PSYCHOL work, working through ■ **~ du deuil** grieving process

B. RÉSULTAT, EFFET

1. [écrit] piece ■ **il a publié un ~ très intéressant sur Proust** he published a very interesting piece on Proust
2. [transformation - gén] work ■ [modification interne - dans le bois] warping ; [- dans le fromage] maturing ; [- dans le vin] working

C. LIEU D'ACTIVITÉ PROFESSIONNELLE

work, workplace ■ **aller à son ~** to go to (one's) work.

◆ **travaux** *nmpl* **1.** [tâches] work, working ■ **gros travaux** heavy work ■ **j'ai fait des petits travaux** I did some odd jobs ■ **ils font des travaux après le pont** there are roadworks after the bridge ■ **'fermé pendant les travaux'** 'closed for *ou* during alterations' ■ **'attention, travaux'** 'caution, work in progress' ▶ **travaux domestiques** *ou* **ménagers** housework ■ **travaux d'aiguille** COUT needlework ■ **travaux d'approche** MIL approaches ; *fig* manoeuvring ■ **travaux de construction** building work ■ **travaux forcés** hard labour ■ **travaux d'Hercule** MYTHOL labours of Hercules ; *fig* Herculean tasks ■ **travaux manuels** [gén] arts and crafts ; ÉDUC handicraft ■ **travaux d'utilité collective** ≃ YTS ■ **grands travaux** large-scale public works ■ **entrer aux Travaux publics** to become a civil engineer **2.** [d'une commission] work ■ **nous publierons le résultat de nos travaux** we'll publish our findings.

◆ **au travail** *loc adv* **1.** [en activité] at work, working ■ **se mettre au ~** to get down *ou* to set to work ■ **allez, au ~!** come on, get to work! **2.** [sur le lieu d'activité] at work, in the workplace ■ **je vous donne mon numéro au ~** I'll give you my work number.

◆ **de travail** *loc adj* **1.** [horaire, séance] working ■ [vêtement, camarade, permis] work *(modif)* ■ **mes instruments de ~** the tools of my trade ▶ **contrat de ~** employment contract **2.** [d'accouchement - période] labour *(modif)* ; [- salle] labour *(modif)*, delivery *(modif)*.

◆ **du travail** *loc adj* [accident, sociologie, législation] industrial ■ **conflit du ~** employment dispute ■ **droit du ~** employment law.

◆ **en travail** *adv* PHYSIOL in labour ■ **entrer en ~** to go into *ou* to start labour.

travaillé, e [travaje] *adj* [élaboré - style] polished ; [- façade, meuble] finely *ou* elaborately worked ; [- fer] wrought.

travailler [3] [travaje] ◇ *vi* **1.** [être actif] to work ■ **tu as le temps de ~ avant dîner** you've got time to do some work *ou* to get some work done before dinner ■ **~ dur** to work hard ■ **elle travaille vite** she's a fast worker ■ **le maçon a bien travaillé** the bricklayer made a good job of it ■ **~ à** *ou* **sur une chanson** to work at *ou* on a song ■ **~ sur ordinateur** to work on a computer ➤ **~ comme un bœuf** *ou* **forçat** to slave away, to work like a Trojan ■ **~ du chapeau** *fam* *ou* **de la touffe** *fam* to have a screw loose

2. [avoir une profession] to work ■ **vous travaillez?** do you work?, do you have a job? ■ **j'ai arrêté de ~ à 55 ans** I stopped work *ou* retired at 55 ■ **~ pour payer ses études** to work one's way through college/university ■ **aller ~** to go to work ■ **~ en free-lance** to do freelance work, to be a freelancer ■ **~ en usine** to work in a factory ■ **~ dans un bureau** to work in an office ■ **~ à la pièce** to do piecework ■ **~ à son compte** to have one's own business ■ **elle travaille dans l'informatique** she works with computers ■ **elle travaille dans la maroquinerie** she's in the leather trade

3. [faire des affaires] to do (good) business ■ **entreprise qui travaille bien/mal/à perte** thriving/stagnating/lossmaking firm

4. [pratiquer son activité - artiste, athlète] to practise, to train ; [- boxeur] to work out, to train ■ **faire ~ ses jambes** to make one's legs work, to exercise one's legs ■ **faire ~ son argent** *fig* to make one's money work ■ **c'est ton imagination qui travaille** your imagination's working overtime, you're imagining things

5. [changer de forme, de nature - armature, poutre] to warp ; [- fondations, vin] to work

6. [suivi d'une préposition] : **~ à** [succès] to work *ou* to strive for ■ **~ contre/pour** to work against/for ■ **le temps travaille contre/pour nous** time is working against us/is on our side.

◇ *vt* **1.** [façonner - bois, bronze, glaise] to work ■ CULIN [- mélange, sauce] to stir ■ **~ la pâte** CULIN to knead *ou* to work the dough ; [peintre] to work the paste ■ **~ la terre** to work *ou* to till *sout* the land

2. [perfectionner - discours, style] to work on *(insép)*, to polish up *(sép)*, to hone ; [- matière scolaire] to work at *ou* on *(insép)*, to go over *(insép)* ; [- concerto, scène] to work on, to rehearse ■ SPORT [- mouvement] to practise, to work on ; [- balle] to put (a) spin on

3. [obséder] to worry ■ **ça me travaille de le savoir malheureux** it worries me to know that he's unhappy ■ **l'idée de la mort le travaillait** (the idea of) death haunted him ■ **être travaillé par le remords/l'angoisse** to be tormented by remorse/anxiety

4. [tenter d'influencer] to work on *(insép)*.

travailleur, euse [travajœr, øz] ◇ *adj* hardworking, industrious.

◇ *nm, f* **1.** [exerçant un métier] worker ■ **~ intellectuel** white-collar worker ■ **~ manuel** manual *ou* *esp US* blue-collar worker ■ **les ~s** [gén] working people, the workers ; [ouvriers] labour ; [prolétariat] the working classes ➤ **~ agricole** agricultural *ou* farm worker ■ **~ à domicile** outworker, homeworker ■ **~ immigré** migrant *ou* immigrant worker ■ **les ~s immigrés** immigrant labour ■ **~ indépendant** self-employed person, freelance worker ■ **~ au noir** [gén] undeclared worker ; [en plus de son activité principale] moonlighter ■ **~ posté** shift worker ■ **~ saisonnier** casual worker **2.** ADMIN : **~ social** social worker ■ **travailleuse familiale** home help **3.** [personne laborieuse] hard worker ■ **c'est un gros ~** he's a hard worker *ou* very hard-working.

travaillisme [travajism] *nm* Labour doctrine *ou* philosophy.

travailliste [travajist] ◇ *adj* Labour *(modif)* ■ **être ~** to be a member of the Labour Party *ou* party ➤ **le parti ~** the Labour Party *ou* party.

◇ *nmf* member of the Labour Party ■ **les ~s se sont opposés à cette mesure** Labour opposed the move.

travée [trave] *nf* **1.** [rangée de sièges, de personnes assises] row **2.** ARCHIT & CONSTR [d'une voûte, d'une nef] bay ■ [solivage] girder ■ [d'un pont] span.

traveller's cheque, traveller's check [travlœrʃɛk] *(pl* **traveller's cheques** *ou pl* **traveller's checks***)* *nm* traveller's cheque *UK*, traveler's check *US*.

travelling [travliŋ] *nm* CINÉ **1.** [déplacement - gén] tracking ; [- sur plate-forme] dollying ■ **faire un ~** [caméra, cameraman] to track, to dolly ➤ **~ avant/arrière/latéral** tracking *ou* dollying in/out/sideways **2.** [plate-forme] dolly, travelling platform **3.** [prise de vue] tracking shot.

travelo[△] [travlo] *nm* transvestite, drag queen ■ **habillé en ~** in drag.

travers [travɛr] *nm* **1.** [largeur] breadth ■ **sa voiture m'a heurté par le ~** her car hit me broadside on **2.** [viande] : **~ (de porc)** spare rib **3.** NAUT : **par le ~** abeam, on the beam **4.** *sout* [défaut] fault, shortcoming, failing ■ **elle tombait dans les mêmes ~ que ses prédécesseurs** she displayed the same shortcomings as her predecessors ■ **un petit ~** a minor fault.

◆ **à travers** *loc prép* through, across ■ **à ~ la fenêtre/le plancher/les barreaux** through the window/the floor/the bars ■ **à ~ les âges** throughout the centuries ■ **prendre** *ou* **passer à ~ champs** to go through the fields *ou* across country ■ **ils ont prêché à ~ tout le pays** they went preaching throughout the length and breadth of the country ■ **passer à ~ les mailles du filet** PÊCHE & *fig* to slip through the net ■ **j'ai réussi à passer à ~ le contrôle fiscal** I managed to escape the tax inspection.

◆ **au travers de** *loc prép* **1.** [en franchissant] through ■ **passer au ~ des dangers** to escape danger **2.** [par l'intermédiaire de] through, by means of ■ **son idée se comprend mieux au ~ de cette comparaison** his idea is easier to understand by means of this comparison.

◆ **de travers** ◇ *loc adj* crooked.

◇ *loc adv* **1.** [en biais - couper] askew, aslant ; [- accrocher] askew ■ **marcher de ~** [ivrogne] to stagger *ou* to totter along ■ **la remorque du camion s'est mise de ~** the truck jack-knifed ■ **j'ai avalé mon pain de ~** the bread went down the wrong way **2.** [mal] : **tu fais tout de ~!** you do everything wrong! ■ **elle comprend tout de ~!** she gets everything wrong!, she always gets the wrong end of the stick! ■ **regarder qqn de ~** to give sb a funny look ■ **tout va de ~** everything's going wrong ■ **répondre de ~** to give the wrong answer ■ **il prend tout ce qu'on lui dit de ~** he takes everything the wrong way.

◆ **en travers** *loc adv* **1.** [en largeur] sideways, across, crosswise ■ **le wagon s'est mis en ~** the carriage ended up sideways (across the tracks) ■ **la remorque du camion s'est mise en ~** the truck jack-knifed **2.** NAUT abeam.

◆ **en travers de** *loc prép* across ■ **s'il se met en ~ de mon chemin** *ou* **de ma route** *fig* if he stands in my way.

traversable [traversabl] *adj* which can be crossed ■ **la rivière est ~** [à gué] the river is fordable ; [en bateau] the river can be crossed by boat.

traverse [travɛrs] *nf* **1.** RAIL sleeper *UK*, crosstie *US* **2.** CONSTR [de charpente] crossbeam, crosspiece ■ [entre deux montants] (cross) strut.

traversée [travɛrse] *nf* **1.** [d'une route, d'un pont, d'une frontière] crossing ■ [d'une agglomération, d'un pays] going *ou* getting through *ou* across ➤ **faire sa ~ du désert** [politicien] to be in the political wilderness **2.** SPORT [en alpinisme - épreuve] through route ; [- passage] traverse ■ [au ski] traverse ■ **faire une ~** to traverse **3.** RAIL crossing point.

traverser [3] [travɛrse] *vt* **1.** [parcourir - mer, pièce, route] to go across *(insép)*, to cross, to traverse *sout* ; [- pont] to go over *ou* across *(insép)* ; [- tunnel] to go *ou* to pass through *(insép)* ■ **~ qqch à la nage/à cheval/en voiture/en bateau/en avion** to swim/to ride/to drive/to sail/to fly across sthg ■ **~ une pièce en courant/en sautillant** to run/to skip through a room ■ **aider qqn à ~ la route** to help sb across the road ■ **faire ~ une vieille dame** to help an old lady across the road ■ **il n'a fait que ~ ma vie** *fig* he only passed through my life **2.** [s'étirer d'un côté à l'autre de - suj: voie] to cross, to run *ou* to go across *(insép)* ; [- suj: pont] to cross, to span ; [- suj: tunnel] to cross, to run *ou* to go under *(insép)* **3.** [vivre - époque] to live *ou* to go through *(insép)* ; [- difficultés] to pass *ou* to go through *(insép)* **4.** [transpercer - suj: épée] to run through *(insép)*, to pierce ; [- suj: balle] to go through *(insép)* ; [- suj: pluie, froid] to come *ou* to go through *(insép)* ■ **une image me traversa l'esprit** an image passed *ou* flashed through my mind.

traversier [travɛrsje] *nm* *Québec* ferry.

traversin [travɛrsɛ̃] *nm* [oreiller] bolster.

travesti, e [travɛsti] *adj* **1.** [pour tromper] in disguise, disguised ■ [pour s'amuser] dressed up (in fancy dress) **2.** THÉÂTRE [comédien] playing a female part ■ **rôle ~** female part played by a man **3.** [vérité] distorted ■ [propos] twisted, misrepresented.

◆ **travesti** *nm* **1.** THÉÂTRE actor playing a female part ■ [dans un cabaret] female impersonator, drag artist ■ **numéro** *ou* **spectacle de ~** drag act **2.** [homosexuel] transvestite **3.** [vêtement - d'homosexuel] drag *(U)* ; [- de bal] fancy dress *(U)*.

travestir [32] [travɛstir] *vt* **1.** [pour une fête] to dress up *(sép)* ■ [comédien] to cast in a female part ■ **~ qqn en** to dress sb up as **2.** [pensées] to misrepresent ■ [vérité] to distort ■ [propos] to twist.
◆ **se travestir** *vp (emploi réfléchi)* **1.** [homme] to dress as a woman, to put on drag ■ [femme] to dress as a man **2.** [pour une fête] to dress up (in fancy dress), to put fancy dress on ■ **se ~ en punk** to dress up as a punk.

travestisme [travɛstism] *nm* transvestism.

travestissement [travɛstismɑ̃] *nm* **1.** [pour une fête] dressing up, wearing fancy dress **2.** PSYCHOL cross-dressing **3.** [de propos, de la vérité] twisting, distortion, distorting ■ [de pensées] misrepresentation.

traviole [travjɔl] ◆ **de traviole** *fam* ◇ *loc adj* [tableau] aslant, crooked ■ [dents] crooked, badly set.
◇ *loc adv* **1.** [en biais] : **marcher de ~** [ivrogne] to stagger *ou* to totter along ■ **j'écris de ~** my handwriting's all crooked *ou* cockeyed ■ **tu as mis ton chapeau de ~** you've put your hat on crooked *ou UK* skew-wiff **2.** [mal] : **il fait tout de ~** he can't do anything right ■ **tout va de ~** everything's going wrong ■ **tu comprends toujours tout de ~** you always get hold of the wrong end of the stick.

trax [traks] *nm Suisse* bulldozer.

trayait *etc v* ▷ **traire**.

trayeur, euse [trɛjœr, øz] *nm, f* milker, milkman (*f* milkwoman) *US*.
◆ **trayeuse** *nf* milking machine.

trébuchant, e [trebyʃɑ̃, ɑ̃t] *adj* staggering, stumbling, tottering.

trébucher [3] [trebyʃe] ◇ *vi* **1.** [perdre l'équilibre] to stumble, to totter, to stagger ■ **~ contre une marche** to trip over a step ■ **faire ~ qqn** to trip sb up **2.** [achopper] to stumble ■ **~ sur un mot** to stumble over a word.
◇ *vt* TECHNOL to weigh.

trèfle [trɛfl] *nm* **1.** BOT clover, trefoil ■ **~ à quatre feuilles** four-leaf clover **2.** JEUX clubs ■ **la dame de ~** the Queen of clubs **3.** ARCHIT trefoil **4.** [emblème irlandais] shamrock.

tréfonds [trefɔ̃] *nm* **1.** *litt* [partie profonde] : **être ému jusqu'au ~ de son être** to be moved to the depths of one's soul ■ **dans le ~ de son âme** in the (innermost) depths of her soul **2.** DR subsoil.

treillage [trɛjaʒ] *nm* HORT trellis *ou* lattice (work) ■ [d'une vigne] wire trellis.

treille [trɛj] *nf* **1.** [vigne] climbing vine **2.** [tonnelle] arbour.

treillis [trɛji] *nm* **1.** TEXT canvas **2.** MIL (usual) outfit **3.** [en lattes] trellis ■ [en fer] wire-mesh.

treize [trɛz] ◇ *dét* thirteen ■ **acheter/vendre qqch ~ à la douzaine** to buy/to sell thirteen of sthg for the price of twelve ■ **il y en a ~ à la douzaine** it's a baker's dozen, *voir aussi* **cinq**.
◇ *nm inv* thirteen, *voir aussi* **cinq**.

treizième [trɛzjɛm] *adj num* & *nmf* thirteenth, *voir aussi* **cinquième**.

treizièmement [trɛzjɛmmɑ̃] *adv* in the thirteenth place.

trek [trɛk], **trekking** [trɛkiŋ] *nm* trekking.

tréma [trema] *nm* diaeresis ■ **e ~** e (with) diaeresis.

tremblant, e [trɑ̃blɑ̃, ɑ̃t] *adj* [flamme] trembling, flickering ■ [feuilles] fluttering, quivering ■ [main, jambes] shaking, trembling, wobbly ■ [voix] tremulous, quavering, shaky ■ **~ de peur** trembling *ou* shaking *ou* shuddering with fear ■ **~ de froid** trembling *ou* shivering with cold ■ **écrire d'une main ~e** to write shakily ■ **répondre d'une voix ~e** to answer tremulously.

tremble [trɑ̃bl] *nm* aspen.

tremblé, e [trɑ̃ble] *adj* [écriture] shaky, wobbly ■ [trait] wobbly, wavy, shaky.
◆ **tremblé** *nm* IMPR wavy rule.

tremblement [trɑ̃bləmɑ̃] *nm* **1.** [d'une personne - de froid] shiver ; [- de peur] tremor, shudder ■ **son corps était secoué** *ou* **parcouru de ~s** his whole body was shaking *ou* trembling **2.** [de la main] shaking, trembling, tremor ■ [de la voix] trembling, quavering, tremor ■ [des paupières] twitch, twitching ■ [des lèvres] trembling, tremble ■ **avoir des ~s** to shake ▶ **et tout le ~** and all the rest **3.** [du feuillage] trembling, fluttering ■ [d'une lueur, d'une flamme] trembling, flickering ■ [d'une cloison, de vitres] shaking, rattling.
◆ **tremblement de terre** *nm* earthquake.

trembler [3] [trɑ̃ble] *vi* **1.** [personne] : **~ de peur** to tremble *ou* to shake *ou* to shudder with fear ■ **~ de froid** to shiver *ou* to tremble with cold ■ **~ de rage** to tremble *ou* to quiver with anger ■ **~ de tout son corps** *ou* **de tous ses membres** to be shaking *ou* to be trembling all over, to be all of a tremble ▶ **~ comme une feuille** to be shaking like a leaf **2.** [main, jambes] to shake, to tremble ■ [voix] to tremble, to shake, to quaver ■ [menton] to tremble, to quiver ■ [paupière] to twitch **3.** [feuillage] to tremble, to quiver, to flutter ■ [flamme, lueur] to flicker ■ [gelée] to wobble ■ [cloison, vitre] to shake, to rattle ■ [terre] to quake, to shake ■ **les trains font ~ la maison** the trains are shaking the house ■ **la terre a tremblé** there's been an earthquake *ou* an earth tremor **4.** [avoir peur] to tremble (with fear) ■ **~ devant qqn/qqch** to stand in fear of sb/sthg ■ **~ pour (la vie de) qqn** to fear for sb *ou* sb's life ■ **~ à la pensée de/que** [de crainte] to tremble at the thought of/that ; [d'horreur] to shiver at the thought of/that.

tremblotant, e [trɑ̃blɔtɑ̃, ɑ̃t] *adj* [main] shaking, trembling ■ [voix] tremulous, quavering, shaking ■ [lueur] flickering, trembling.

tremblote [trɑ̃blɔt] *nf fam* **avoir la ~** to have the shakes ; [de peur] to have the jitters ; [de froid] to have the shivers.

tremblotement [trɑ̃blɔtmɑ̃] *nm* **1.** [d'une personne - gén] shaking ; [- de fièvre, de froid] shivering ; [- de peur] shivering, shuddering **2.** [d'une main] (faint) shaking *ou* trembling ■ [d'une voix] slight tremor *ou* quavering ■ [d'une lueur] flicker.

trembloter [3] [trɑ̃blɔte] *vi* [gén] to tremble ■ [vieillard, main] to shake ■ [voix] to quaver ■ [lueur] to flicker ■ [de froid] to shiver ■ [de peur] to shudder (with fear).

trémie [tremi] *nf* **1.** [pour les raisins, les betteraves] hopper ■ [pour le blé] tank ■ [pour les volailles] feed hopper **2.** CONSTR [pour béton] tremie ■ **~ d'ascenseur** lift *UK ou* elevator *US* shaft ■ **~ de cheminée** hearth cavity ■ **~ d'escalier** stair well **3.** [de sel] pyramid salt formation **4.** [accès à un tunnel] mouth, well, entrance.

trémière [tremjɛr] *adj f* ▷ **rose**.

trémolo [tremɔlo] *nm* **1.** MUS tremolo **2.** [de la voix] : **avec des ~s dans la voix** with a tremor in his voice.

trémousser [3] [tremuse] ◆ **se trémousser** *vpi* to wiggle, to wriggle ■ **elle marchait en se trémoussant** she wiggled her hips as she walked.

trempe [trɑ̃p] *nf* **1.** [caractère] : **une femme de sa ~** a woman with such moral fibre ■ **son frère est d'une autre ~** his brother is cast in a different mould **2.** *fam* [punition] hiding, thrashing, belting ■ **recevoir une bonne ~** to get a good hiding *ou* thrashing **3.** MÉTALL [traitement] quenching ■ [résultat] temper ■ **de bonne ~** well-tempered.

trempé, e [trɑ̃pe] *adj* **1.** [personne, vêtements] soaked, drenched ■ [chaussures, jardin] waterlogged ■ **~ de sueur** soaked with sweat ■ **~ de larmes** [mouchoir] tear-stained ▶ **~ jusqu'aux os** *ou* **comme une soupe** *fam* soaked to the skin, wet through **2.** [vin, lait] watered-down **3.** [énergique] : **avoir le caractère bien ~** to be resilient **4.** MÉTALL quenched **5.** [verre] toughened.

tremper [3] [trɑ̃pe] ◇ *vt* **1.** [plonger - chiffon] to dip, to soak ; [- sucre, tartine] to dip, to dunk ; [- linge, vaisselle] to soak ■ **je n'ai fait que ~ mes lèvres dans le champagne** I just had a taste *ou* took a sip of the champagne ■ **je n'ai fait que ~ mes pieds**

dans l'eau I only dipped my feet in the water **2.** [mouiller] : **j'ai trempé ma chemise tellement je transpirais** I sweated so much (that) my shirt got soaked **3.** MÉTALL to quench **4.** *litt* [affermir - personnalité, caractère] to steel *litt*, to toughen, to harden ■ **cela va lui ~ le caractère** this'll toughen him up.
<> *vi* [vêtement, vaisselle, lentilles] to soak ■ **faire ~ qqch : j'ai fait ~ les draps** I put the sheets in to soak ■ **faire ~ des haricots** to soak beans, to leave beans to soak ■ **~ dans : les clichés trempent dans un bain spécial** the photographs (are left to) soak in a special solution ■ **attention, tes manches trempent dans la soupe** careful, you've got your sleeves in the soup.
◆ **tremper dans** *v+prép* [être impliqué dans] to be involved in, to have a hand in ■ **elle a trempé dans une sordide affaire** she was involved in a sordid affair.
◆ **se tremper** <> *vpi* to have a quick dip.
<> *vpt* : **il s'est trempé les pieds en marchant dans l'eau** he stepped into a puddle and got his feet wet.

trempette [trɑ̃pɛt] *nf fam* **faire ~** to have a (quick) dip.

tremplin [trɑ̃plɛ̃] *nm* **1.** SPORT [de gymnastique] springboard ■ [de plongeon] diving-board, springboard ■ **~ de ski** ski-jump **2.** [impulsion initiale] springboard, stepping stone, launching pad ■ **servir de ~ à qqn** to be a springboard for sb.

trémulation [tremylasjɔ̃] *nf* tremulousness.

trench-coat [trɛnʃkot] (*pl* **trench-coats**), **trench** [trɛnʃ] *nm* trench coat.

trentaine [trɑ̃tɛn] *nf* : **une ~ (de)** around *ou* about thirty ■ **avoir la ~** to be thirtyish *ou* thirty-something.

trente [trɑ̃t] *dét & nm inv* thirty ■ **être sur son ~ et un** to be dressed up to the nines ■ **se mettre sur son ~ et un** to get all dressed up, *voir aussi* **cinq**.

trentenaire [trɑ̃tnɛr] *adj & nmf* thirty-year-old.

trente-six (*en fin de phrase* [trɑ̃tsis], *devant consonne ou h aspiré* [trɑ̃tsi], *devant voyelle ou h muet* [trɑ̃tsiz]) <> *dét* **1.** [gén] thirty six, *voir aussi* **cinquante** **2.** *fam* [pour exprimer la multitude] umpteen, dozens of ■ **il n'y a pas ~ solutions!** there aren't all that many solutions! ■ **j'ai ~ mille choses à faire** I've a hundred and one things to do ▶ **voir ~ chandelles** to see stars.
<> *nm inv fam* **tous les ~ du mois** once in a blue moon.

trente-sixième [trɑ̃tsizjɛm] *adj num* **1.** [gén] thirty-sixth **2.** *fam loc* **être dans le ~ dessous** to feel really down.

trente-trois-tours [trɑ̃ttrwatur] *nm inv* LP.

trentième [trɑ̃tjɛm] *adj num & nmf* thirtieth, *voir aussi* **cinquième**.

trépanation [trepanasjɔ̃] *nf* trephination, trepanation, trepanning.

trépaner [3] [trepane] *vt* to trephine, to trepan.

trépas [trepa] *nm litt* **le ~** death.

trépassé, e [trepase] *nm, f* **1.** *litt* deceased ■ **les ~s** the departed *sout*, the dead **2.** RELIG : **le jour** *ou* **la fête des Trépassés** All Souls' Day.

trépasser [3] [trepase] *vi litt* to depart this life, to pass away *ou* on *euphém*.

trépidant, e [trepidɑ̃, ɑ̃t] *adj* **1.** [animé - époque] frantic, hectic ; [- vie] hectic ; [- danse, rythme] wild, frenzied **2.** [véhicule] vibrating, throbbing.

trépidation [trepidasjɔ̃] *nf* **1.** [d'un moteur] vibration **2.** MÉD tremor **3.** [agitation] bustle, whirl.

trépider [3] [trepide] *vi* [moteur] to vibrate, to throb ■ [surface] to vibrate.

trépied [trepje] *nm* tripod.

trépignement [trepiɲmɑ̃] *nm* stamping (of feet) ■ **dès qu'on lui refuse quelque chose, ce sont des ~s** when he can't get his own way, he throws a tantrum.

trépigner [3] [trepiɲe] *vi* to stamp one's feet ■ **~ de colère** to stamp one's feet in anger ■ **~ d'impatience** to be hopping up and down with impatience.

très [trɛ] *adv* **1.** [avec un adverbe, un adjectif] very ■ **une entreprise ~ compétitive** a highly competitive company ■ **il est ~ snob** he's a real snob ■ **je ne l'ai pas vu depuis ~ longtemps** I haven't seen him for ages *ou* for a very long time ■ **~ bien payé** very well *ou* highly paid ■ **tu comprends ce que je veux dire? – non, pas ~ bien** do you see what I mean? – not very well *ou* not really ■ **~ bien, je m'en vais** all right (then) *ou* very well (then) *ou* OK (then), I'm going ■ **nous sommes tous ~ famille** we're all very much into family life **2.** [dans des locutions verbales] : **avoir ~ peur/faim** to be very frightened/hungry ■ **j'ai ~ envie de lui dire ses quatre vérités** I very much want to give him a few home truths **3.** [employé seul, en réponse] very ■ **il y a longtemps qu'il est parti? – non, pas ~** has he been gone long? – no, not very ▶ **faire des heures supplémentaires? ~ peu pour moi!** me, do overtime? not likely!

Très-Haut [trɛo] *npr m* : **le ~** God, the Almighty.

trésor [trezɔr] *nm* **1.** [argent] treasure **2.** DR treasure trove **3.** [chose précieuse] treasure **4.** ARCHÉOL [d'un sanctuaire] treasure, treasury **5.** *(gén pl)* [grande quantité] : **des ~s de bienfaits/de patience** a wealth of good/patience **6.** *fam* [terme d'affection] : **mon (petit) ~** my treasure *ou* darling *ou* pet ■ **tu es un ~** you're a treasure *ou* a darling *ou* an angel **7.** FIN : **le Trésor (public)** [service] *department dealing with the state budget* ≃ the Treasury ; [moyens financiers] state finances **8.** HIST exchequer.

trésorerie [trezɔrri] *nf* **1.** [argent - gén] treasury, finances ; [- d'une entreprise] liquid assets ; [- d'une personne] budget ■ **ses problèmes de ~** his cash (flow) problems **2.** [gestion] accounts **3.** [bureaux - gouvernementaux] public revenue office ; [- privés] accounts department **4.** [fonction - gén] treasurership ; [- d'un trésorier-payeur] paymastership.

trésorier, ère [trezɔrje, ɛr] *nm, f* **1.** ADMIN treasurer **2.** MIL paymaster.

trésorier-payeur [trezɔrjepɛjœr] (*pl* **trésoriers-payeurs**) *nm* : **~ général** paymaster *(for a 'département' or 'région')*.

tressage [trɛsaʒ] *nm* [de rotin] weaving ■ [de cheveux] plaiting, braiding.

tressaillement [tresajmɑ̃] *nm* [de joie] thrill ■ [de peur] shudder, quiver, quivering.

tressaillir [47] [tresajir] *vi* [personne, animal - de surprise, de peur] to (give a) start ; [- de douleur] to flinch, to wince ■ **~ de joie** to thrill.

tressautement [tresotmɑ̃] *nm* **1.** [sursaut] start, jump **2.** [secousse] jolting ■ **les ~s du vieux tramway** the jolting *ou* juddering *UK* of the old tram.

tressauter [3] [tresote] *vi* **1.** [sursauter] to jump, to start ■ **la sonnette m'a fait ~** the bell made me jump *ou* startled me **2.** [être cahoté - passager] to be tossed about ■ **les cahots du chemin faisaient ~ les voyageurs** the passengers were thrown *ou* jolted around by the bumps in the road.

tresse [trɛs] *nf* **1.** [de cheveux, de fils] plait, braid **2.** ARCHIT strapwork *(U)* **3.** ÉLECTR braid, braiding **4.** NAUT vinnet.

tresser [4] [trese] *vt* [cheveux, rubans, fils] to plait, to braid ■ [corbeille] to weave ■ [câble] to twist ■ [guirlande] to wreathe ■ **~ des couronnes à qqn** *fig* to praise sb to the skies.

tréteau, x [treto] *nm* trestle.

treuil [trœj] *nm* winch, windlass.

treuillage [trœjaʒ] *nm* winching.

treuiller [5] [trœje] *vt* to winch ■ **~ une charge** [vers le haut] to winch up a load ; [vers le bas] to winch down a load.

trêve [trɛv] *nf* **1.** MIL truce **2.** [repos] rest, break ■ **ses rhumatismes ne lui laissent aucune ~** his rheumatisms give him no respite ■ **elle s'est accordée une ~ dans la rédaction de sa thèse** she took a break from writing her thesis ▶ **la ~ des confiseurs** *the lull in political activities between Christmas and the New Year in France.*

◆ **trêve de** *loc prép* enough ■ **~ de bavardages!** we must stop chatting!, enough of this chatting! ■ **allez, ~ de plaisanteries, où est la clef?** come on, stop messing about, where's the key?
◆ **sans trêve** *loc adv* unceasingly, without end, neverendingly.

Trèves [trɛv] *npr* Trier.

tri [tri] *nm* **1.** [de fiches] sorting out, sorting, classifying ■ [de renseignements] sorting out, selecting ■ [de candidats] picking out, screening ■ **il faut faire le ~ dans ce qu'il dit** you have to sift out the truth in what he says **2.** [postal] sorting **3.** [déchets] : **~ sélectif (des ordures)** *sorting of rubbish into different types for recycling.*

triade [trijad] *nf* [groupe de trois] triad.

triage [trijaʒ] *nm* **1.** [pour répartir] sorting (out) ■ **~ à la main** hand sorting **2.** [pour choisir] grading, selecting, sifting **3.** MIN picking *(U)* **4.** [en papeterie] assorting, sorting **5.** RAIL marshalling *(U)*.

trial, s [trijal] ◇ *nm* (motorbike) trial *ou* trials.
◇ *nf* trial motorbike.

triangle [trijɑ̃gl] *nm* **1.** GÉOM triangle **2.** GÉOGR : **le ~ des Bermudes** the Bermuda Triangle ■ **le Triangle d'or** the Golden Triangle **3.** MUS triangle **4.** AUTO : **~ de sécurité** warning triangle.
◆ **en triangle** *loc adv* in a triangle ■ **le jardin se termine en ~** the garden ends in a triangle.

triangulaire [trijɑ̃gylɛr] *adj* **1.** [gén - GÉOM] triangular ■ [tissu, salle] triangular, triangular-shaped **2.** [à trois éléments] triangular ■ **élection ~** three-cornered election.

trias [trijas] *nm* : **le ~** the Triassic *ou* Trias.

triathlon [trijatlɔ̃] *nm* triathlon.

tribal, e, aux [tribal, o] *adj* tribal.

tribalisme [tribalism] *nm* tribalism.

tribord [tribɔr] *nm* starboard ■ **à ~** (to) starboard, on the starboard side.

tribu [triby] *nf* **1.** ANTHR & ANTIQ tribe **2.** *fam* [groupe nombreux] : **toute la ~** [famille] the entire clan *hum* ; [amis] the (whole) crowd *ou* gang *hum* **3.** [d'animaux] tribe, swarm.

tribulations [tribylasjɔ̃] *nfpl* (trials and) tribulations *litt* ■ **tu n'es pas au bout de tes ~!** you're not out of the woods yet!

tribun [tribœ̃] *nm* **1.** [orateur] eloquent (public) speaker **2.** ANTIQ tribune.
◆ **de tribun** *loc adj* [éloquence] spellbinding ■ **il a un talent de ~** he's very good at public speaking.

tribunal, aux [tribynal, o] *nm* **1.** DR [édifice] court, courthouse ■ [magistrats] court, bench ■ **porter une affaire devant le ~** *ou* **les tribunaux** to take a matter to court *ou* before the Courts ■ **comparaître devant le ~** to appear before the Court ■ **traîner qqn devant les tribunaux** to take sb to court ➤ **~ administratif** *court which deals with internal French civil service matters* ■ **~ de commerce** [litiges] commercial court ; [liquidations] bankruptcy court ■ **~ des conflits** jurisdictional court ■ **~ pour enfants** juvenile court ■ **~ d'exception** special court ■ **~ de grande instance** ≃ Crown Court ■ **~ d'instance** magistrates' court ■ **~ de police** police court **2.** MIL : **~ militaire** court martial ■ **passer devant le ~ militaire** to be court-martialled.

tribune [tribyn] *nf* **1.** [places - assises] grandstand ; [- debout] stand ; [- dans un stade de football] terraces, bleachers *US* **2.** [estrade] rostrum, platform, tribune *sout* ■ **monter à la ~** [gén] to go to the rostrum ; [au Parlement] to address the House **3.** [lieu de discussions] forum ■ **notre émission offre une ~ aux écologistes** our program provides a platform for the green party ■ **à la ~ de ce soir, le racisme** on the agenda of tonight's debate, racism **4.** PRESSE : **~ libre** [colonne] opinion column ; [page] opinions page **5.** ARCHIT gallery, tribune.

tribut [triby] *nm* **1.** *litt* tribute ■ **la population a payé un lourd ~ à l'épidémie** the epidemic took a heavy toll of the population **2.** HIST tribute.

tributaire [tribytɛr] ◇ *adj* **1.** [dépendant] : **~ de** reliant *ou* dependent on **2.** GÉOGR : **être ~ de** to be a tributary of, to flow into **3.** HIST tributary.
◇ *nm* GÉOGR tributary.

tricentenaire [trisɑ̃tnɛr] ◇ *adj* three-hundred-year-old.
◇ *nm* tercentenary.

tricéphale [trisefal] *adj* three-headed.

triceps [trisɛps] *nm* triceps (muscle) ■ **~ brachial** triceps brachii.

triche [triʃ] *nf fam* **c'est le roi de la ~** he's a prize cheat ■ **c'est de la ~** that's cheating.

tricher [3] [triʃe] *vi* to cheat ■ **~ sur** to cheat on ■ **~ sur le poids** to give short weight ■ **~ sur les prix** to overcharge ■ **il triche sur son âge** he lies about his age ■ **~ avec** to play around with.

tricherie [triʃri] *nf* cheating *(U)*.

tricheur, euse [triʃœr, øz] *nm, f* [au jeu, aux examens] cheat, cheater ■ [en affaires] trickster, con man ■ [en amour] cheat.

trichloréthylène [triklɔretilɛn] *nm* trichlorethylene, trichloroethylene.

trichromie [trikromi] *nf* **1.** IMPR trichromatism *spéc*, three-colour printing **2.** TEXT trichrome printing **3.** TV three-colour process.

tricolore [trikɔlɔr] ◇ *adj* **1.** [aux couleurs françaises] red, white and blue **2.** [français] French ■ **l'équipe ~** the French team **3.** [à trois couleurs] three-coloured.
◇ *nm* French player ■ **les ~s** the French (team).

tricorne [trikɔrn] *nm* tricorn, cocked hat.

tricot [triko] *nm* **1.** [technique] knitting ■ **faire du ~** to knit, to do some knitting **2.** [étoffe] knitted *ou* worsted fabric **3.** [vêtement] knitted garment ■ [pull] pullover, sweater ■ [gilet] cardigan ➤ **~ de corps** *ou* **de peau** vest *UK*, undershirt *US*.
◆ **en tricot** *loc adj* [cravate, bonnet] knitted.

tricoter [3] [trikɔte] ◇ *vt* [laine, maille] to knit ■ [vêtement] to knit (up) ■ **tricotez une maille à l'endroit, une maille à l'envers** knit one, purl one.
◇ *vi* **1.** TEXT to knit ■ **~ à la machine** to machine-knit **2.** *fam* [s'activer - coureur] to scramble ; [- danseur, cheval] to prance ; [- cycliste] to peddle hard.
◆ **à tricoter** *loc adj* [aiguille, laine, machine] knitting.

trictrac [triktrak] *nm* **1.** [activité] trictrac, tricktrack **2.** [plateau] trictrac *ou* tricktrack board.

tricycle [trisikl] ◇ *nm* tricycle.
◇ *adj* AÉRON tricycle.

tricyclique [trisiklik] *adj* tricyclic.

trident [tridɑ̃] *nm* **1.** PÊCHE three-pronged fish spear, trident **2.** AGRIC three-pronged (pitch) fork **3.** GÉOM & MYTHOL trident.

tridimensionnel, elle [tridimɑ̃sjɔnɛl] *adj* [gén - CHIM] three-dimensional.

triennal, e, aux [trijenal, o] *adj* **1.** [ayant lieu tous les trois ans] triennial *sout*, three-yearly **2.** [qui dure trois ans] three-year, three-year-long, triennial *sout* ■ **comité ~** committee appointed for three years **3.** AGRIC three-yearly.

trier [10] [trije] *vt* **1.** [sortir d'un lot - fruits] to pick (out) ; [- photos, candidats] to select ➤ **ses amis sont triés sur le volet** his friends are hand-picked **2.** [répartir par catégories - lettres] to sort (out) *(sép)* ; [- œufs] to grade ; [- lentilles] to pick over *(sép)* **3.** RAIL [wagons] to marshal.

trieur, euse [trijœr, øz] *nm, f* sorter, grader.
◆ **trieur** *nm* **1.** AGRIC sorting *ou* grading machine **2.** MIN picker (machine) ■ **~ magnétique** magnetic separator.
◆ **trieuse** *nf* INFORM sorting machine.

trifouiller [3] [trifuje] *vt fam* [papiers] to mess *ou* to jumble up *(sép)*.

◆ **trifouiller dans** *v+prép fam* **1.** [fouiller dans - papiers, vêtements] to rummage, to rifle through **2.** [tripoter - moteur] to tinker with.

triglycéride [trigliserid] *nm* triglyceride.

trigonométrie [trigɔnɔmetri] *nf* trigonometry.

trijumeau, x [triʒymo] ◇ *adj m* trigeminal.
◇ *nm* trigeminal nerve.

trilatéral, e, aux [trilateral, o] *adj* trilateral, three-sided.

trilingue [trilɛ̃g] ◇ *adj* trilingual.
◇ *nmf* trilingual person.

trille [trij] *nm* trill ■ **faire des ~s** to trill.

trilogie [trilɔʒi] *nf* **1.** [groupe de trois] triad **2.** ANTIQ & LITTÉR trilogy ■ **son roman est une ~** her novel is a trilogy.

trim. 1. = **trimestre 2.** = **trimestriel.**

trimaran [trimarɑ̃] *nm* trimaran.

trimbal(l)age [trɛ̃balaʒ], **trimbal(l)ement** [trɛ̃balmɑ̃] *nm fam* lugging *ou* dragging *ou* carting around ■ **le ~ du matériel a duré toute la nuit** it took all night to shift the equipment.

trimbal(l)er [3] [trɛ̃bale] *vt fam* **1.** [porter] to lug *ou* to cart around **2.** [emmener] to take **3.** *loc* **qu'est-ce qu'elle trimballe!**△ she's as thick as two short planks! *UK*, what a lamebrain! *US*.

◆ **se trimbal(l)er** *vpi fam* **1.** [aller et venir] to go about **2.** [se déplacer] to go ■ **elle se trimballe toujours avec son frère** she drags that brother of hers around with her everywhere.

trimer [3] [trime] *vi fam* to slave away ■ **il a trimé toute sa vie** he's spent his entire life slaving away *ou* working his fingers to the bone.

trimestre [trimɛstr] *nm* **1.** ÉDUC term ■ **premier ~** Autumn term ■ **deuxième ~** Spring term ■ **troisième ~** Summer term **2.** [trois mois] quarter ■ **payer tous les ~s** to pay on a quarterly basis **3.** [somme payée ou reçue] quarterly instalment.

trimestriel, elle [trimɛstrijɛl] *adj* **1.** ÉDUC [bulletin] end-of-term ■ [réunion] termly **2.** [réunion, magazine, loyer] quarterly.

trimestriellement [trimɛstrijɛlmɑ̃] *adv* **1.** ÉDUC once a term, on a termly basis **2.** [payer, publier] quarterly, on a quarterly basis, every three months.

trimoteur [trimɔtœr] ◇ *adj m* three-engined.
◇ *nm* three-engined aircraft.

tringle [trɛ̃gl] *nf* **1.** [pour pendre] rail ■ **~ à rideaux** curtain rail **2.** [pour tenir] rod ■ **~ de tapis d'escalier** stair rod **3.** [d'une crémone] rod **4.** ARCHIT tringle.

tringler [3] ▲ [trɛ̃gle] *vt* to screw▲.

trinitaire [trinitɛr] *adj* Trinitarian.

trinité [trinite] *nf* **1.** RELIG : **la Trinité** the (Holy) Trinity ; [fête] Trinity Sunday **2.** *litt* [trois éléments] trinity.

Trinité-et-Tobago [triniteetɔbago] *npr* Trinidad and Tobago ■ **à ~** in Trinidad and Tobago, *voir aussi* **île.**

trinôme [trinom] *adj* & *nm* MATH trinomial.

trinquer [3] [trɛ̃ke] *vi* **1.** [choquer les verres] : **~ à qqch/qqn** to drink (a toast) to sthg/sb ■ **trinquons!** let's drink to that! **2.** *fam* [subir un dommage] to get the worst of it, to get it in the neck, to cop it *UK* ■ **c'est lui qui va ~** he'll be the one who suffers **3.** *fam* [boire] to drink.

trio [trijo] *nm* **1.** [trois personnes] trio, threesome ■ **notre ~ n'en eut pas pour longtemps à résoudre le mystère** our three heroes solved the mystery in no time **2.** MUS trio.

triode [trijɔd] ◇ *adj* triode *(modif)*.
◇ *nf* triode.

triolet [trijɔlɛ] *nm* MUS & LITTÉR triolet.

triomphal, e, aux [trijɔ̃fal, o] *adj* [entrée] triumphant ■ [victoire, succès] resounding ■ [arc, procession] triumphal.

triomphalement [trijɔ̃falmɑ̃] *adv* [sourire, dire] triumphantly ■ [traiter, recevoir] in triumph ■ **descendre ~ les Champs-Élysées** to parade down the Champs-Élysées in triumph.

triomphalisme [trijɔ̃falism] *nm* overconfidence ■ **dans un moment de ~** in a moment of self-congratulation.

triomphaliste [trijɔ̃falist] *adj* [discours, vainqueur] complacent, self-congratulatory, gloating ■ [attitude] overconfident.

triomphant, e [trijɔ̃fɑ̃, ɑ̃t] *adj* triumphant ■ **il est sorti ~ de l'épreuve** he came out the winner.

triomphateur, trice [trijɔ̃fatœr, tris] ◇ *adj* triumphant.
◇ *nm, f* winner, victor *litt.*

triomphe [trijɔ̃f] *nm* **1.** [d'une armée, d'un groupe] triumph, victory ■ [d'un artiste, d'une idée] triumph ■ **l'album est un ~** the album is a great success **2.** [jubilation] triumph ■ **son ~ fut de courte durée** his triumph was short-lived **3.** [ovation] : **faire un ~ à qqn** to give sb a triumphant welcome.

triompher [3] [trijɔ̃fe] *vi* **1.** [armée] to triumph ■ [parti] to win (decisively) **2.** [idée] to triumph, to prevail ■ [bêtise, corruption, racisme] to be rife **3.** [artiste] to be a great success **4.** [jubiler] to rejoice, to exult *litt*, to gloat **5.** ANTIQ to triumph.

◆ **triompher de** *v+prép* [ennemi, rival] to triumph over *(insép)*, to beat, to vanquish *litt* ■ [malaise, obstacle] to triumph over, to overcome ■ **sa persévérance l'a fait ~ de toutes ces épreuves** his perseverance helped him through all these ordeals.

trip△ [trip] *nm arg crime* trip ■ **faire un mauvais ~** *pr* to have a bad trip ; *fig* to have a rough time.

tripant, e [tripɑ̃, ɑ̃t] *adj Québec fam* great, fantastic.

triparti, e [triparti] *adj* [traité] tripartite ■ [négociations] three-way ■ [alliance électorale] three-party *(avant n)*.

tripartisme [tripartism] *nm* three-party government.

tripartite [tripartit] = **triparti.**

tripatouillage [tripatujaʒ] *nm fam* **1.** [malaxage] messing around **2.** [truquage] tampering, fiddling *UK*, fiddle *UK* ■ **~ des comptes** cooking the books ■ **~ des résultats** massaging *ou* fixing the results.

tripatouiller [3] [tripatuje] *fam* ◇ *vt* **1.** [truquer - document] to tamper with *(insép)* ; [- chiffres, résultats] to fiddle *UK*, to doctor *US* ■ **~ les comptes** to cook the books ■ **~ les statistiques** to massage the figures **2.** [modifier - textes] to alter **3.** [nourriture] to play with *(insép)*.
◇ *vi* : **les enfants adorent ~ dans le sable** children love messing around in the sand.

tripatouilleur, euse [tripatujœr, øz] *nm, f fam* **c'est un ~** [mauvais bricoleur] he's a botcher ; [mauvais écrivain] he's a hack, he just cobbles other people's ideas together.

triperie [tripri] *nf* **1.** [boutique] tripe and offal shop **2.** [activité] tripe (and offal) trade **3.** [abats] offal.

tripes [trip] *nfpl* **1.** CULIN : **des ~** tripe **2.** *fam* ANAT guts, insides ■ **la peur m'a pris aux ~** *fig* I was petrified with fear ▶ **rendre ~ et boyaux** to throw one's guts up.

tripette [tripɛt] *nf fam* **ça ne vaut pas ~** it's not worth a straw *ou* bean *UK ou* red cent *US*.

triphasé, e [trifaze] *adj* three-phase.

triphtongue [triftɔ̃g] *nf* triphthong.

tripier, ère [tripje, ɛr] *nm, f* tripe (and offal) butcher.

triplace [triplas] ◇ *adj* three-seater.
◇ *nm* AÉRON three-seater (plane).

triplan [triplɑ̃] *nm* triplane.

triple [tripl] ◇ *adj* **1.** [à trois éléments] triple ■ **une ~ collision ferroviaire** a crash involving three trains ■ **une ~ semelle** a three-layer sole ■ **un ~ menton** a triple chin ■ **un ~ rang de perles** three rows *ou* a triple row of pearls ■ **en ~ exemplaire** in triplicate ▶ **~ saut périlleux** triple somersault **2.** [trois fois

plus grand] treble, triple ▪ **ton jardin est ~ du mien** your garden is treble the size of mine ▪ **une ~ dose** three times the usual amount **3.** *fam* [en intensif] : ~ **imbécile!** you stupid idiot! **4.** MUS : ~ **croche** demi-semiquaver *UK*, thirty-second note *US*.
◇ *nm* : **neuf est le ~ de trois** nine is three times three ▪ **il fait le ~ de travail** he does three times as much work ▪ **on a payé le ~** we paid three times that amount ▪ **le ~ de poids/longueur** three times as heavy/long ▪ **ça coûte le ~** it's three times the price.
◆ **en triple** *loc adv* [copier, signer] in triplicate.

triplé [triple] *nm* **1.** [aux courses] treble ▪ **gagner le ~** to win a treble **2.** [d'un athlète] triple win.

triplement [tripləmɑ̃] ◇ *adv* in three ways, on three counts.
◇ *nm* trebling, tripling ▪ **le ~ de mes ressources** the threefold increase in *ou* the trebling of my income.

tripler [3] [triple] ◇ *vt* **1.** [dépenses, dose] to treble, to triple **2.** ÉDUC : ~ **une classe** to repeat a year *UK ou* class *US* for a second time, to do a year *UK ou* class *US* for a third time.
◇ *vi* to treble, to triple.

triplés, ées [triple] *nmf pl* triplets.

triplet [triplɛ] *nm* **1.** MATH triplet **2.** OPT & PHOTO triple lens **3.** ARCHIT triplet.

triplex [triplɛks] *nm* **1.** [carton] triplex **2.** [papier] three-sheet paper **3.** [appartement] three-storey flat *UK*, triplex (apartment) *US*.

triporteur [triportœr] *nm* delivery tricycle.

tripot [tripo] *nm péj* **1.** [lieu mal famé] *disreputable bar, nightclub etc* **2.** [maison de jeu] gambling den.

tripotée [tripɔte] *nf fam* **1.** [grand nombre] crowd ▪ **une ~ de** lots of ▪ **ils ont toute une ~ d'enfants** they've got loads of kids **2.** [coups] thrashing, belting ▪ [défaite] thrashing, clobbering.

tripoter [3] [tripɔte] *fam* ◇ *vt* **1.** [toucher distraitement - crayon, cheveux] to twiddle, to play *ou* to fiddle with **2.** [palper - fruit, objet] to handle, to finger ▪ **ne tripote pas ton bouton** don't keep picking at *ou* touching your spot **3.** [personne] to fondle, to grope.
◇ *vi* **1.** [fouiller] to rummage *ou* to root around, to root about **2.** [en affaires] to be up to some dodgy *UK ou* funny *US* business.
◆ **se tripoter** *vp (emploi réfléchi) fam* to play with o.s.

tripoteur, euse [tripɔtœr, øz] *nm, f fam* **1.** [qui trafique] shady dealer, crook **2.** [qui caresse] fondler, groper.

triptyque [triptik] *nm* triptych.

trique [trik] *nf* [bâton] cudgel ▪ **donner des coups de ~ à qqn** to thrash sb ▪ **elle nous mène à la ~** *fig* she rules us with a rod of iron.

trisaïeul, e [trizajœl] *nm, f* great-great-grandfather (*f* great-great-grandmother).

trisannuel, elle [trizanɥɛl] *adj* **1.** [qui a lieu tous les trois ans] three-yearly, triennial *sout* **2.** [qui dure trois ans] three-year-long, triennial *sout*.

trisomie [trizɔmi] *nf* trisomy ▪ ~ **21** trisomy 21.

trisomique [trizɔmik] ◇ *adj* : **enfant ~** Down's syndrome child.
◇ *nmf* Down's syndrome child.

Tristan [tristɑ̃] *npr* **1.** LITTÉR : ~ **et Iseut** Tristram *ou* Tristan and Iseult **2.** MUS : **'~ et Isolde'** *Wagner* 'Tristan and Isolde'.

triste [trist] *adj* **1.** [déprimé - personne] sad ; [- sourire, visage] sad, unhappy, sorrowful ▪ **un clown ~** a sad-looking clown ▪ **d'un air ~** bleakly ▪ **ne prends pas cet air ~** don't look so glum ⊙ ~ **comme un bonnet de nuit** as miserable as sin ▪ ~ **comme la mort** utterly dejected ▪ **faire ~ figure** *ou* **mine** *litt* to look pitiful ▪ **faire ~ figure** *ou* **mine à qqn** to give sb a cold reception
2. [pénible] sad, unhappy ▪ **son ~ sort** his sad *ou* unhappy fate **3.** [attristant] sad ▪ **c'est ~ à dire** it's sad to say ⊙ ~ **comme un lendemain de fête** a real anticlimax ▪ **c'est pas triste!** *fam* what a hoot *ou* laugh! ▪ **il est pas ~, avec sa chemise à fleurs** he's a scream in his flowery shirt ▪ **ils font voter les réformes sans avoir le financement, ça va pas être ~!** they're pushing the reforms through without funds, what a farce!
4. [terne - couleur] drab, dull ▪ [morne - rue, saison] bleak ▪ **une ville ~ à pleurer** a dreadfully bleak town
5. *(avant le n)* [déplorable] deplorable, sorry, sad ▪ **elle était dans un ~ état** she was in a sorry state ▪ **nous vivons une bien ~ époque** we're living through pretty grim times ▮ [méprisable] : **un ~ sire** an unsavoury character.

tristement [tristəmɑ̃] *adv* **1.** [en étant triste] sadly **2.** [de façon terne] drearily **3.** [de manière pénible] sadly, regrettably ▪ ~ **célèbre** notorious.

tristesse [tristɛs] *nf* **1.** [sentiment] sadness ▪ **sourire avec ~** to smile sadly ▪ **quelle ~ de voir une telle déchéance!** how sad to see such decrepitude! **2.** [d'un livre, d'une vie] sadness ▪ **la ~ du paysage** the bleakness of the landscape **3.** [manque de vitalité] dreariness, dullness.

tristounet, ette [tristunɛ, ɛt] *adj fam* **1.** [triste] down, low ▪ **une petite figure ~te** a sad little face **2.** [qui rend triste] gloomy, dreary, depressing **3.** [terne] dull.

trisyllabique [trisilabik] *adj* trisyllabic.

trithérapie [triterapi] *nf* combination therapy, tritherapy, triple therapy.

triton [tritɔ̃] *nm* **1.** ZOOL [amphibien] newt, triton *spéc* ▪ [gastropode] triton, Triton's shell **2.** MUS tritone **3.** PHYS triton.

triturer [3] [trityre] *vt* **1.** [pétrir - bras, corps, pâte] to knead **2.** [manipuler - gants, breloque] to fiddle with **3.** [influencer] to manipulate, to distort ▪ **les grands groupes de presse triturent l'opinion publique** the big newspaper groups distort public opinion **4.** PHARM [médicament] to crush, to grind, to triturate *spéc*.
◆ **se triturer** *vpt* : **se ~ les méninges** *ou* **la cervelle** *fam* to rack one's brains.

triumvir [trijɔmvir] *nm* triumvir.

triumvirat [trijɔmvira] *nm* **1.** [groupe] triumvirate, troika **2.** ANTIQ triumvirate.

trivial, e, aux [trivjal, o] *adj* **1.** [grossier] crude, offensive **2.** [banal] trivial, trite ▪ **un détail ~** a minor detail ▪ **une remarque ~e** a commonplace, a mundane remark **3.** MATH trivial.

trivialement [trivjalmɑ̃] *adv* **1.** [vulgairement] crudely, coarsely **2.** [banalement] trivially, tritely.

trivialité [trivjalite] *nf* **1.** [caractère vulgaire] crudeness, coarseness **2.** [parole vulgaire] crude remark **3.** [caractère banal] triviality, banality.

tr/mn, tr/min (*abr écrite de* **tour par minute**) rpm.

troc [trɔk] *nm* **1.** [système économique] barter ▪ **(économie de) ~** barter economy **2.** [échange] swap.

troène [trɔɛn] *nm* privet.

troglodyte [trɔglɔdit] *nm* **1.** ANTHR cave dweller, troglodyte *spéc* **2.** ZOOL wren, troglodyte *spéc*.

troglodytique [trɔglɔditik] *adj* [population] cave-dwelling, troglodytic *spéc* ▪ **habitations ~s** cave dwellings.

trogne [trɔɲ] *nf fam* face ▪ **il avait une ~ d'ivrogne** he had the look of a wino about him.

trognon [trɔɲɔ̃] ◇ *adj fam* cute ▪ **elles sont vraiment ~s** they're so cute.
◇ *nm* **1.** [d'une pomme] core ▪ [d'un chou] stem ▪ **il t'exploitera jusqu'au ~** he'll squeeze you dry **2.** *fam* [terme d'affection] sweetie.

Troie [trwa] *npr* Troy ▪ **le cheval/la guerre de ~** the Trojan Horse/War.

troïka [trɔika] *nf* **1.** [traîneau] troika **2.** [trois personnes] troika ▪ **la ~ qui dirige maintenant le journal** the newspaper's new management trio.

trois [trwa] ◇ *dét* **1.** three ■ **frapper les ~ coups** *to announce the beginning of a theatre performance by knocking three times* ■ **~ dimensions : maquette en ~ dimensions** model in three dimensions, three-dimensional model ■ **à ~ temps** in triple *ou* three-four time ▶ **les ~ jours** [à l'armée] *in France, induction course preceding military service (now lasting one day)* ■ **haut comme ~ pommes** knee-high to a grasshopper ■ **Les Trois Suisses®** *French mail order company* ■ **'les Trois Mousquetaires'** *Alexandre Dumas* 'The Three Musketeers', *voir aussi* **cinq 2.** [exprimant une approximation] : **dans ~ minutes** in a couple of minutes ■ **il n'a pas dit ~ mots** he hardly said a word ■ **deux ou ~, ~ ou quatre** a few, a handful.
◇ *nm inv* **1.** [chiffre] three **2.** JEUX three.

trois-étoiles [trwazetwal] ◇ *adj inv* three-star.
◇ *nm* [hôtel] three-star hotel ■ [restaurant] three-star restaurant.

trois-huit [trwaɥit] ◇ *nm inv* MUS three-eight (time).
◇ *nmpl* INDUST : **les ~** *shift system based on three eight-hour shifts* ■ **faire les ~** to work in shifts of eight hours.

troisième [trwazjɛm] ◇ *adj num* third ■ **la ~ personne du singulier** GRAMM the third person singular ▶ **~ dimension** third dimension ■ **le ~ larron : il était le ~ larron dans cette affaire** he took advantage of the quarrel the other two were having, *voir aussi* **cinquième**.
◇ *nmf* third.
◇ *nf* **1.** ÉDUC fourth year *UK*, eighth grade *US* **2.** AUTO third gear.

troisièmement [trwazjɛmmɑ̃] *adv* thirdly, in the third place.

trois-mâts [trwama] *nm inv* three-master.

trois-pièces [trwapjɛs] *nm inv* [costume] three-piece suit.

trois-quarts [trwakar] ◇ *adj inv* three-quarter.
◇ *nm inv* **1.** [manteau] three-quarter (length) coat **2.** SPORT three-quarter ■ **~ aile/centre** wing/centre (three-quarter) **3.** MUS [violon] three-quarter violin.

troll [trɔl] *nm* MYTHOL troll.

trolley [trɔlɛ] *nm* **1.** TRANSP trolley bus **2.** [chariot] truck *(on cableway)* **3.** ÉLECTR trolley.

trolleybus [trɔlɛbys] = **trolley** *(sens 1)*.

trombe [trɔ̃b] *nf* MÉTÉOR [sur mer] waterspout ■ [sur terre] whirlwind ■ **~ d'eau** downpour.
▶ **en trombe** *loc adv* briskly and noisily ■ **elle entra en ~** she burst in ■ **la voiture passa en ~** the car shot past ■ **partir en ~** to shoot off.

trombine△ [trɔ̃bin] *nf* [visage] mug△ ■ [physionomie] look ■ **si tu avais vu sa ~!** you should have seen his face!

trombinoscope [trɔ̃binɔskɔp] *nm fam hum* rogues' gallery.

trombone [trɔ̃bɔn] *nm* **1.** MUS [instrument] trombone ■ [musicien] trombonist, trombone (player) ■ **~ à coulisse/pistons** slide/valve trombone **2.** [agrafe] paper clip.

trompe [trɔ̃p] *nf* **1.** ENTOM & ZOOL [d'éléphant] trunk, proboscis *spéc* ■ [de papillon] proboscis ■ [de tapir] snout, proboscis *spéc* **2.** MUS horn **3.** AUTO [avertisseur] horn **4.** ANAT : **~ d'Eustache** Eustachian tube ■ **~ utérine** *ou* **de Fallope** Fallopian tube **5.** ARCHIT squinch.

trompe-la-mort [trɔ̃plamɔr] *nmf* daredevil.

trompe-l'œil [trɔ̃plœj] *nm inv* **1.** ART [style] trompe l'œil **2.** [faux-semblant] window dressing ■ **son discours antiraciste n'était qu'un ~** his antiracist speech was mere window-dressing.
▶ **en trompe-l'œil** *loc adj* ART : **peinture en ~** trompe l'œil painting.

tromper [3] [trɔ̃pe] *vt* **1.** [conjoint] to be unfaithful to, to deceive *sout*, to betray *sout* ■ **elle le trompe avec Thomas** she's having an affair with Thomas behind his back
2. [donner le change à] to fool, to trick, to deceive ■ **~ qqn sur ses intentions** to mislead sb as to one's intentions ▶ **~ son monde : avec ses airs affables, il trompe bien son monde** everybody is taken in by his kindly manner
3. [berner, flouer] to dupe, to cheat ■ **il m'a trompé dans la vente de la maison** he cheated me on the sale of the house ■ **on m'a trompé sur la qualité** I was misinformed as to the quality
4. [échapper à] : **~ la vigilance de qqn** to elude sb ▶ **~ l'ennui** to stave off boredom
5. [induire en erreur] to mislead ■ **mon instinct ne me trompe jamais** my instincts never let me down *ou* fail me ■ **ne te laisse pas ~ par les apparences** don't be taken in by appearances ■ *(en usage absolu)* **c'est un signe qui ne trompe pas** it's a sure sign
6. *litt* [décevoir] : **~ l'espoir de qqn** to disappoint sb
7. [apaiser - faim] to appease.
▶ **se tromper** *vpi* **1.** [commettre une erreur] to make a mistake ■ **se ~ dans une addition/dictée** to get a sum/dictation wrong ■ **je me suis trompé de 11 euros** I was 11 euros out *UK ou* off *US* ■ **je ne m'étais pas trompé de beaucoup** I wasn't far wrong *ou* far off *US*
2. [prendre une chose pour une autre] : **se ~ de jour** to get the day wrong ■ **se ~ de bus** to get on the wrong bus ▶ **se ~ d'adresse** *pr* to go to the wrong address ■ **se ~ d'adresse** *ou* **de porte** *fam fig* : **si c'est un complice que tu cherches, tu te trompes d'adresse** if it's an accomplice you want, you've come to the wrong address
3. [s'illusionner] to make a mistake, to be wrong ■ **tout le monde peut se ~** anyone can make a mistake, nobody's infallible ■ **se ~ sur les motifs de qqn** to misunderstand sb's motives ■ **si je ne me trompe** if I'm not mistaken ■ **c'était en 1989 si je ne me trompe** it was in 1989, correct me if I'm wrong ■ **s'y ~ : que l'on ne s'y trompe pas** let there be no misunderstanding about that ■ **au fond, elle était malheureuse et ses amis ne s'y trompaient pas** deep down she was unhappy and her friends could tell.

tromperie [trɔ̃pri] *nf* [supercherie] deception ■ **il y a ~ sur la qualité** the quality hasn't been described accurately.

trompeter [27] [trɔ̃pəte] ◇ *vt* [fait] to trumpet, to shout from the rooftops.
◇ *vi vieilli* [musicien - gén] to play the trumpet, to trumpet ■ [aigle] to scream.

trompette [trɔ̃pɛt] ◇ *nf* **1.** [instrument] trumpet ■ **~ bouchée** muted trumpet ■ **~ à pistons** valve trumpet ■ **les ~s de Jéricho** BIBLE the trumpets of Jericho ■ **la Trompette du Jugement dernier** (the sound of) the Last Judgment **2.** AUTO rear axle tube.
◇ *nm* [musicien - gén] trumpet player, trumpet, trumpeter ■ MIL trumpeter.

trompette-des-morts [trɔ̃pɛtdemɔr] (*pl* **trompettes-des-morts**), **trompette-de-la-mort** [trɔ̃pɛtdəlamɔr] (*pl* **trompettes-de-la-mort**) *nf* BOT horn of plenty.

trompettiste [trɔ̃petist] *nmf* trumpet player, trumpet, trumpeter.

trompeur, euse [trɔ̃pœr, øz] ◇ *adj* **1.** [personne] lying, deceitful **2.** [signe, air, apparence] deceptive, misleading ■ **le vent faiblit mais c'est ~** the wind's dropping but you can't rely on that.
◇ *nm, f* deceiver ■ **à ~, ~ et demi** *prov* the biter is sometimes bit.

trompeusement [trɔ̃pøzmɑ̃] *adv* [en apparence] deceptively ■ [traîtreusement] deceitfully *péj*.

tronc [trɔ̃] *nm* **1.** BOT trunk **2.** ANAT [d'un être humain] trunk, torso ■ [d'un animal] trunk, barrel ■ [d'un nerf, d'une artère] trunk, truncus *spéc* **3.** [boîte pour collectes] offertory box ■ **~ des pauvres** alms box **4.** *(comme adj; avec ou sans trait d'union)* limbless.
▶ **tronc commun** *nm* [d'une famille] common stock, ancestry ■ ÉDUC compulsory subjects, core curriculum.

tronche [trɔ̃ʃ] *nf fam* **1.** [visage] face ■ [expression] look ■ **t'aurais vu la ~ qu'il faisait!** you should have seen the look on his face! **2.** [tête] head.

tronçon [trɔ̃sɔ̃] *nm* **1.** [morceau coupé] segment, section ■ **un tuyau divisé en ~s** a pipe divided into segments **2.** TRANSP [de voie] section ■ [de route] section, stretch **3.** [d'un texte] part, section **4.** ARCHIT frustrum **5.** MENUIS log, block.

tronçonner [3] [trɔ̃sɔne] *vt* to cut *ou* to chop (into sections) ▪ **~ un arbre** to saw a tree (into sections).

tronçonneuse [trɔ̃sɔnøz] *nf* motor saw ▪ **~ à chaîne** chain saw.

trône [tron] *nm* **1.** [siège, pouvoir] throne ▪ **monter sur le ~** to ascend *ou* to come to the throne **2.** *fam fig* & *hum* throne ▪ **être sur le ~** to be on the throne.

trôner [3] [trone] *vi* **1.** [personne] to sit enthroned *hum ou* in state **2.** [bouquet, œuvre d'art] to sit prominently *ou* imposingly ▪ **son portrait trônait dans le salon** his portrait was displayed in a prominent position in the drawing room.

tronquer [3] [trɔ̃ke] *vt* **1.** [phrase, récit] to shorten **2.** [pilier, statue] to truncate.

trop [tro] *adv* **1.** [excessivement - devant un adjectif, un adverbe] too ; [- avec un verbe] too much ▪ **de la viande ~ cuite** overcooked meat ▪ **et en plus, c'est moi qui paye, c'est ~ fort!** and what's more I'm the one who's paying, it really is too much! ▪ **elle sort ~ peu** she doesn't go out enough ▪ **on a ~ chargé la voiture** we've overloaded the car ▪ **tu manges (beaucoup) ~** you eat (far) too much ▪ **ne fais pas ~ le difficile** don't be too awkward ▪ **cela n'a que ~ duré** it's been going on far too long ▪ **il ne le sait que ~** he knows (it) only too well ▪ [en corrélation avec 'pour'] : **tu es ~ intelligent pour croire cela** you're too intelligent to believe that ▪ **~ belle pour toi** too beautiful for you ▪ **~ beau pour être vrai** too good to be true ▪ **il a ~ tardé à répondre pour qu'elle lui écrive encore** he has taken too long in replying for her to write to him again ⊙ **il est ~, lui!** *fam* he really is too much!
2. [emploi nominal] : **ne demande pas ~** don't ask for too much ▪ **prends la dernière part – non, c'est ~** have the last slice – no, it's too much ⊙ **c'est ~!, c'en est ~!** that's it!, I've had enough! ▪ **~ c'est ~!** enough is enough! ▪ **je sors, ~ c'est ~** I'm leaving, I've had enough!
3. [très, beaucoup] so ▪ **ce bébé est ~ mignon!** this baby is so cute! ▪ **c'est ~ bête!** how stupid! ▪ **vous êtes ~ aimable** how very kind of you, you're very *ou* too kind ‖ [dans des phrases négatives] : **il n'est pas ~ content** he's not very happy ▪ **je ne sais ~** I'm not sure ▪ **je ne le connais pas ~** I don't know him very *ou* that well ▪ **on ne se voit plus ~** we don't see much of each other any more ▪ **sans ~ savoir pourquoi** without really knowing why.
◆ **de trop** *loc adv* : **j'ai payé 11 euros de ~** I paid 11 euros too much ▪ **il y a une assiette de ~** there's one plate too many ▪ **votre remarque était de ~** that remark of yours was uncalled for ▪ **je suis de ~, peut-être?** are you telling me I'm in the way *ou* not wanted? ▪ **deux jours ne seront pas de ~ pour tout terminer** two days should just about be enough to finish everything ▪ **un rafraîchissement ne serait pas de ~!** a drink wouldn't go amiss!
◆ **en trop** *loc adv* : **tu as des vêtements en ~ à me donner?** have you got any spare clothes to give me? ▪ **j'ai payé 11 euros en ~** I paid 11 euros too much ▪ **il y a un verre en ~** there's a *ou* one glass too many ▪ **se sentir en ~** to feel in the way.
◆ **par trop** *loc adv litt* much too, far too ▪ **c'est par ~ injuste** it's simply too unfair (for words).
◆ **trop de** *loc dét* **1.** [suivi d'un nom non comptable] too much ▪ [suivi d'un nom comptable] too many ▪ **ils ont ~ d'argent** they've got too much money ▪ **il y a beaucoup ~ de monde** there are far too many people ▪ **nous ne serons pas ~ de cinq pour soulever le piano** it'll take at least five of us to lift the piano ‖ [en corrélation avec 'pour'] : **j'ai ~ de soucis pour me charger des vôtres** I've too many worries of my own to deal with yours ▪ *(comme nom)* **le ~ d'énergie des enfants** the children's excess *ou* surplus energy
2. *loc* **en faire ~** [travailler] to overdo things ; [pour plaire] to overdo it.

trope [trɔp] *nm* trope.

trophée [trɔfe] *nm* trophy.

tropical, e, aux [trɔpikal, o] *adj* tropical.

tropique [trɔpik] ◇ *adj* tropical.
◇ *nm* ASTRON & GÉOGR tropic ▪ **le ~ du Cancer/Capricorne** the tropic of Cancer/Capricorn.
◆ **tropiques** *nmpl* GÉOGR : **les ~s** the tropics ▪ **sous les ~s** in the tropics.

tropisme [trɔpism] *nm* tropism.

troposphère [trɔpɔsfɛr] *nf* troposphere.

trop-perçu [trɔpɛrsy] (*pl* **trop-perçus**) *nm* overpayment (of taxes), excess payment (of taxes).

trop-plein [trɔplɛ̃] (*pl* **trop-pleins**) *nm* **1.** [de forces, d'émotion] overflow, surplus ▪ **ton ~ d'énergie** your surplus energy **2.** [d'eau, de graines] overflow ▪ [de vin] surplus **3.** TECHNOL overflow.

troquer [3] [trɔke] *vt* **1.** [échanger] to exchange, to swop, to swap ▪ **je troquerais bien mon manteau contre le tien** I wouldn't mind swapping coats with you **2.** COMM to barter, to trade ▪ **ils troquent les fruits contre de la soie** they trade fruit for silk.

troquet [trɔkɛ] *nm fam* bar.

trot [tro] *nm* ÉQUIT trot, trotting ▪ **~ assis/enlevé** sitting/rising trot ▪ **~ attelé** trotting (with a sulky) ▪ **~ monté** saddle-trot, saddle-trotting.
◆ **au trot** *loc adv* **1.** ÉQUIT at a trot *ou* trotting pace ▪ **au petit ~** at a jogging pace **2.** *fam* [vite] on the double ▪ **allez, et au ~!** come on, jump to it!

Trotski [trɔtski] *npr* Trotsky.

trotskisme [trɔtskism] *nm* Trotskyism.

trotskiste [trɔtskist] *adj* & *nmf* Trotskyist.

trotte [trɔt] *nf fam* **il y a une bonne ~ d'ici à la plage** it's a fair distance *ou* it's quite a step from here to the beach.

trotter [3] [trɔte] *vi* **1.** [cheval] to trot **2.** [marcher vite - enfant] to trot *ou* to run along ; [- souris] to scurry along **3.** *fam* [marcher beaucoup] to do a lot of walking, to cover quite a distance on foot **4.** *fig* **une idée qui me trotte dans la tête** an idea which keeps running through my mind ▪ **cet air me trotte continuellement dans la tête!** I can't get that tune out of my head!

trotteur, euse [trɔtœr, øz] ◇ *adj* **1.** ÉQUIT : **cheval ~** trotter **2.** [vêtement] : **talon ~** low heel.
◇ *nm, f* trotter.
◆ **trotteurs** *nmpl* [chaussures] flat shoes.
◆ **trotteuse** *nf* [d'une montre] second hand.

trottinement [trɔtinmɑ̃] *nm* [marche rapide] trotting, scurrying ▪ [d'un enfant] toddling ▪ [bruit de pas] patter.

trottiner [3] [trɔtine] *vi* **1.** [souris] to scurry (along) ▪ [cheval] to jog-trot (along) **2.** [personne] to trot along ▪ **la petite trottinait près de son père** the child trotted along next to her father.

trottinette [trɔtinɛt] *nf* **1.** [patinette] scooter **2.** *fam* [petite voiture] little car.

trottoir [trɔtwar] *nm* **1.** [bord de chaussée] pavement *UK*, sidewalk *US* ⊙ **faire le ~** to walk the streets *euphém* **2.** TECHNOL : **~ roulant** travelator, travolator, moving walkway.

trou [tru] *nm* **1.** [cavité - gén] hole ; [- sur la route] pothole ▪ **faire un ~ dans les économies de qqn** to make a hole in sb's savings ⊙ **~ de mémoire** memory lapse, lapse of memory ▪ **j'ai eu un ~ (de mémoire) en scène** I dried up on stage ▪ **~ noir** ASTRON black hole ; *fig* depths of despair ▪ **~ normand** *glass of Calvados taken between courses* ▪ **faire le ~ normand** *to take a break between courses with a glass of Calvados* ▪ **un ~ de souris** a tiny place ▪ **j'étais tellement gênée que j'aurais voulu disparaître dans un ~ de souris** I was so embarrassed I wished the earth would swallow me up ▪ **faire son ~ : parti de rien, il a fait son ~** he made his way in the world from very humble beginnings ▪ **elle a fait son ~ dans l'édition** she has made a nice little niche for herself in publishing ▪ **sortir de son ~** to go out into the big wide world
2. [ouverture - dans une clôture, dans les nuages] hole, gap ; [- d'une aiguille] eye ; [- dans du cuir] eyelet ⊙ **le ~ de la serrure** the keyhole ▪ **regarder par le ~ de la serrure** to watch through the keyhole

3. [déchirure] hole, tear, rip ■ **faire un ~ à son collant** to make a hole in *ou* to rip one's tights ■ **il a fini par faire un ~ à son pull à l'endroit du coude** he finally wore a hole in the elbow of his jumper ■ **drap plein de ~s** tattered sheet, sheet full of holes **4.** [moment] gap ■ **un ~ dans son emploi du temps** [élève] a free period ; [dans la reconstitution d'un crime] *a period of time during which one's movements cannot be accounted for* **5.** *fam* [endroit reculé] (little) place, hole *péj*, one-horse-town *hum* ■ **pas même un café, quel ~!** not even a café, what a dump! ■ **il n'est jamais sorti de son ~** he's never been away from home **6.** *fam* [tombe] grave ■ **quand je serai dans le ~** when I've kicked the bucket *ou* I'm six foot under **7.** *fam* [prison] : **être au ~** to be inside **8.** *fam* [déficit] deficit ■ **un ~ dans le budget** a budget deficit ■ **le ~ de la Sécurité sociale** the deficit in the French Social Security budget **9.** ANAT hole, foramen *spéc* ■ **~ de l'oreille** earhole ■ **~s de nez** nostrils ■ **ça me sort par les ~s de nez** *fam* I've had it up to here ■ **~ du cul▲** *ou* **de balle▲** arsehole△ *UK*, asshole△ *US* ■ **il n'a pas les yeux en face des ~s** *fam* [il n'est pas observateur] he's pretty unobservant ; [il est à moitié endormi] he's still half asleep **10.** AÉRON : **~ d'air** air pocket ■ **des ~s d'air** turbulence **11.** [au golf] hole ■ **faire un ~** to get a hole.

troubadour [trubadur] *nm* troubadour.

troublant, e [trublɑ̃, ɑ̃t] *adj* **1.** [événement] disturbing, unsettling, disquieting ■ [question, ressemblance] disconcerting **2.** [déshabillé, sourire] thrilling, arousing ■ **une femme ~e** a desirable woman.

trouble¹ [trubl] ◇ *adj* **1.** [eau] cloudy, murky ■ [vin] cloudy ■ [image] blurred ■ [photo] blurred, out-of-focus ■ [regard, verre] misty, dull **2.** [confus] vague, unclear, imprecise **3.** [équivoque] equivocal, ambiguous ■ [peu honnête] dubious ■ **une affaire ~** a murky business ■ **personnage ~** suspicious character.
◇ *adv* through a blur ■ **je vois ~** everything *ou* my vision is blurred.

trouble² [trubl] *nm* **1.** [sentiment - de gêne] confusion, embarrassment ; [- de perplexité] confusion ; [- de peine] distress, turmoil ■ **la nouvelle sema le ~ dans les esprits** the news sowed confusion in people's minds *ou* threw people's minds into confusion **2.** MÉD disorder ■ **~ caractériel** emotional disorder ■ **un ~ du comportement** a behaviour problem ■ **~s du langage** speech disorders ■ **~s circulatoires** circulation problems, trouble with one's circulation ■ **elle souffre de ~s digestifs** she has trouble with her digestion ■ **~s de la personnalité** personality problems ; PSYCHOL personality disorders ■ **~s respiratoires** respiratory disorders ■ **~s visuels** *ou* **de la vue** eye trouble **3.** [désaccord] discord, trouble ■ **jeter** *ou* **semer le ~ dans une famille** to sow discord within a family ■ **ne viens pas jeter** *ou* **semer le ~ ici!** don't you come stirring up trouble (around here)! **4.** DR disturbance (of rights).
➡ **troubles** *nmpl* [agitation sociale] unrest.

trouble-fête [trubləfɛt] *nmf* killjoy, spoilsport ■ **je ne veux pas jouer les ~, mais...** I don't want to be a spoilsport *ou* to put a damper on the proceedings but...

troubler [3] [truble] *vt* **1.** [eau] to cloud **2.** [rendre moins net] to blur, to dim, to cloud ■ **~ la vue de qqn** to blur *ou* to cloud sb's vision **3.** [sommeil] to disturb ■ [paix] to disturb, to disrupt ■ [silence] to break ■ [digestion] to upset **4.** [fête, réunion] to disrupt ■ [plan] to upset, to disrupt ■ **une époque troublée** troubled times ■ **~ l'ordre public** to cause a breach of the peace *UK*, to disturb the peace **5.** [déconcerter] to confuse, to disconcert ■ **un détail nous trouble encore** one detail is still baffling us ■ **ses remarques m'avaient troublé** her remarks had unsettled me ■ **la question semble te ~** you seem put out *ou* disconcerted by the question **6.** [mettre en émoi - personne] to thrill, to arouse ; [- imagination] to stir ■ **ce film m'a vraiment troublé** I found the film quite disturbing ■ **sa présence le troublait profondément** her presence aroused *ou* excited him profoundly.
➡ **se troubler** *vpi* **1.** [eau] to become cloudy *ou* turbid *litt* ■ [vue] to become blurred **2.** [perdre contenance] to get confused ■ **continuez sans vous ~** carry on and don't let yourself get ruffled.

troué, e [true] *adj* : **un vieux châle ~** a tatty *UK ou* raggedy *US* old shawl ■ **la chaussette est ~e** the sock's got a hole in ■ **des chaussettes toutes ~es** socks full of holes ▶ **~ comme une écumoire** *ou* **une passoire** full of *ou* riddled with holes.

trouée [true] *nf* **1.** [ouverture] gap ■ **une ~ de ciel bleu** a patch of blue sky ■ **une ~ dans les nuages** a break in the clouds ■ **la ~ du chemin** the opening formed by the path **2.** GÉOGR gap **3.** MIL breach ■ **effectuer une ~** to break through.

trouer [3] [true] *vt* **1.** [percer - carton, tissu] to make a hole in ; [- tôle] to pierce ; [- cloison] to make *ou* to bore a hole in ■ **la balle lui a troué le corps** the bullet pierced his body **2.** *sout* [traverser] to pierce ■ **le soleil trouait les nuages** the sun was breaking through the clouds **3.** [cribler] to pit ■ **surface trouée de balles** surface pitted with bullet holes.
➡ **se trouer** *vpi* [d'un seul trou] to get a hole ■ [de plusieurs trous] to go into *UK ou* get holes.

troufion△ [trufjɔ̃] *nm* soldier, private, squaddy *UK*.

trouillard, e△ [trujar, ard] ◇ *adj* chicken-livered, chicken-hearted.
◇ *nm, f* chicken.

trouille△ [truj] *nf* fear, fright ■ **ça va lui flanquer** *ou* **ficher la ~** it'll scare the living daylights out of her ▶ **j'avais une ~ bleue** I was scared stiff *ou* to death.

trouillomètre△ [trujɔmɛtr] *nm* : **avoir le ~ à zéro** to be scared stiff *ou* to death.

troupe [trup] *nf* **1.** [de touristes, d'enfants] troop ■ **ils se déplacent toujours en ~** they always go round as a group **2.** MIL [formation, régiment] troop ■ **la ~, les ~s** the troops *ou* men ▶ **~s de choc** shock troops **3.** THÉÂTRE company, troupe ■ **monter une ~** to set up a company ■ **final avec toute la ~** grand finale (with all the cast) **4.** [de scouts] troop **5.** [d'éléphants] herd.

troupeau, x [trupo] *nm* **1.** [de vaches] herd ■ [de moutons] flock ■ [d'oies] gaggle ■ [d'éléphants] herd ■ **il garde le ~** [de vaches] he's tending the herd ; [de moutons] he's tending the flock **2.** RELIG : **le ~ des fidèles** the flock **3.** *péj* [multitude passive] herd *péj* ■ **quel ~ d'imbéciles!** what a load of idiots!

troupier [trupje] ◇ *adj m* ▷ **comique**.
◇ *nm* soldier.

trousse [trus] *nf* [étui] case ■ [d'écolier] pencil case ■ **~ de maquillage** make-up bag ■ **~ de médecin** medical bag ■ **~ à ongles** manicure set ■ **~ à outils** tool kit ■ **~ de secours** first-aid kit ■ **~ de toilette** sponge bag.
➡ **aux trousses de** *loc prép* : **avoir qqn à ses ~s** to be followed by sb ■ **le fisc est à ses ~s** he's got the taxman after him ■ **il a la police aux ~s** the police are after him.

trousseau, x [truso] *nm* **1.** [assortiment] : **~ (de clés)** bunch of keys **2.** [d'une mariée] trousseau *(including linen)*.

trousser [3] [truse] *vt* **1.** CULIN to truss (up) **2.** [rédiger avec brio] : **en deux minutes, il troussait un poème** he could dash off a poem in a couple of minutes ■ **un petit refrain bien troussé** a neatly turned refrain ■ **un petit slogan bien troussé** a snappy slogan **3.** △ [femme] to have△ **4.** *vieilli* [retrousser - vêtement] to hitch up *(sép)*.
➡ **se trousser** *vpi vieilli* to hitch up one's skirts.

trousseur [trusœr] *nm fam vieilli* **~ de jupons** womanizer, philanderer.

trou-trou [trutru] (*pl* **trou-trous**) *nm embroidery of ribbon-leading eyelets* ■ **jupon/corsage à ~s** broderie anglaise petticoat/blouse, frilly petticoat/blouse.

trouvaille [truvaj] *nf* [objet, lieu] find ■ [idée, méthode] brainwave ■ [expression] coinage ■ **une émission pleine de ~s** a programme full of good ideas.

trouvé, e [truve] *adj* **1.** [découvert] ▷ **enfant 2.** *loc* **bien ~** [original] well-chosen, apposite ■ **voilà une réponse bien ~e!** that's a (pretty) good answer! ■ **tout ~** ready-made ■ **voici un moyen tout ~ de gagner de l'argent** here's a ready-made way of making money.

trouver [3] [truve] *vt*

A. APRÈS UNE RECHERCHE
B. INVOLONTAIREMENT
C. PAR L'ESPRIT, LA VOLONTÉ
D. AVOIR COMME OPINION

A. APRÈS UNE RECHERCHE

1. [objet perdu, personne, emploi] to find ▪ [empreintes, trésor] to find, to discover ▪ [pétrole] to strike, to find ▪ **où pourrais-je la ~ mardi?** where could I find *ou* contact her on Tuesday? ▪ **~ où** [découvrir un lieu approprié pour] **: j'ai trouvé où faire reproduire des cartes postales anciennes** I've found a place where they do reproductions of old postcards ▪ **il faut que je trouve 5 000 euros avant demain** I must get hold of *ou* find 5,000 euros before tomorrow ▪ **j'ai trouvé en elle la sœur/l'amie que je cherchais** in her I found the sister/the friend I'd been looking for
2. [détecter] to find, to discover ▪ **ils lui ont trouvé quelque chose au sein** they found a lump in her breast
3. [acheter] to find, to get ▪ **du safran, on en trouve dans les épiceries fines** you can get *ou* find saffron in good delicatessens
4. [rendre visite à] **: aller ~ qqn** to go to sb, to go and see sb ▪ **il faut que tu ailles ~ un spécialiste** you should go and see a specialist ▪ **venir ~ qqn** to come to sb, to come and see sb

B. INVOLONTAIREMENT

1. [tomber sur - personne, lettre, trésor] to find ▪ **j'ai trouvé ce livre en faisant du rangement** I found *ou* came across this book while I was tidying up ▪ **à notre grande surprise, nous avons trouvé le beau temps en arrivant** when we got there we were surprised to find that the weather was good ▪ **si je m'attendais à te ~ là!** fancy meeting you here! ▪ **si je trouve celui qui m'a cabossé ma portière!** just let me lay my hands on whoever dented my car door! ▪ **~ qqch par hasard** to chance *ou* to stumble upon sthg ▪ **j'ai trouvé ma maison cambriolée** I found my house burgled *ou* that my house had been burgled ▪ **on l'a trouvé mort dans la cuisine** he was found dead in the kitchen ▶ **~ à qui parler** [un confident] to find a friend ▪ **s'il continue comme ça, il va ~ à qui parler!** if he goes on like that, I'll give him what for!
2. [surprendre] to find, to catch ▪ **je l'ai trouvé fouillant** *ou* **qui fouillait dans mes tiroirs** I found *ou* I caught him searching through my drawers

C. PAR L'ESPRIT, LA VOLONTÉ

1. [inventer - prétexte, méthode etc] to find ▪ **où as-tu trouvé cette idée?** where did you get that idea from? ▪ **je ne savais pas ce que je faisais – c'est tout ce que tu as trouvé?** I didn't know what I was doing – is that the best you can come up with? ▪ **~ qqch à répondre** to find an answer ▪ **je n'ai rien trouvé à répondre** I was stuck for an answer
2. [deviner - solution] to find ; [- réponse, mot de passe] to find (out), to discover ; [- code] to break, to crack ▪ **j'ai trouvé!** I've got it!, I know! ▪ **39 moins 7, il fallait ~ 32** 39 take away 7, the correct result was 32
3. [parvenir à] to find ▪ **ça y est, j'ai trouvé ce que je voulais te dire!** I know what I wanted to tell you! ▪ **je n'arrivais pas à ~ mes mots** I couldn't find the right words, I was lost for words ▪ **là, tu as trouvé le mot juste!** you've said it! ▪ **tu as trouvé ça tout seul?** *hum* did you come up with that all on your own? ▪ **~ à : ~ à se loger** to find accommodation *ou* somewhere to live ▪ **je trouverai à me faire remplacer** I'll find someone to stand in for me ▪ **~ à vendre sa voiture** to find a buyer for one's car ▪ **le chien a encore trouvé à s'échapper** the dog's managed to run away again
4. [se ménager] to find ▪ **~ le temps de lire** to find time to read ▪ **je n'ai pas le temps – trouve-le!** I haven't got time – (then you must) make time!
5. [ressentir] to find ▪ **~ du plaisir à (faire) qqch** to take pleasure in (doing) sthg, to enjoy (doing) sthg ▪ **nous trouvions de la satisfaction à remplir notre devoir** we used to find it satisfying to do our duty

D. AVOIR COMME OPINION

1. [juger, estimer] to find, to think ▪ **~ qqch remarquable** to find sthg remarkable, to think that sthg is remarkable ▪ **tu vas me ~ vieilli** you'll think *ou* find I've aged ▪ **comment me trouves-tu dans cette robe?** how do you like me in this dress? ▪ **~ que** to think *ou* to find that ▪ **il est prétentieux – je ne trouve pas** he's pretentious – I don't think so ▪ **la soupe manque de sel, tu ne trouves pas?** the soup needs more salt, don't you think? ▪ **tu trouves?** do you think so?
2. [reconnaître] **: ~ qqch à qqn/qqch : je lui trouve du charme** I think he's got charm ▪ **tu ne lui trouves pas une petite ressemblance avec ta sœur?** don't you think *ou* wouldn't you say that she looks a bit like your sister? ▪ **mais enfin, qu'est-ce que tu lui trouves, à ce type?** *fam* for goodness' sake, what do you see in this guy? ▪ **je lui ai trouvé mauvaise mine hier** he didn't look very well to me yesterday.

◆ **se trouver** ◇ *v impers* **1.** *(suivi d'un sing)* **il se trouve** [il existe, il y a] there is ▪ *(suivi d'un pl)* there are ▪ **il se trouvera toujours quelqu'un pour te renseigner** you'll always find somebody *ou* there'll always be someone you can ask ▪ **il s'est trouvé peu de gens pour accepter** only a few people said yes *ou* accepted **2.** [fait du hasard] **: il se trouve que...** as it happens... ▪ **il se trouve que quelqu'un vous a vu dans mon bureau** as it happens, somebody saw you in my office ▪ **il s'est trouvé que je les ai entendus** I chanced to overhear them, by chance I overheard them ▪ **il s'est trouvé que c'était lui le fautif** it turned out that HE was to blame.
◇ *vp (emploi réfléchi)* [s'estimer] **: je me trouve trop mince** I think I'm too thin.
◇ *vp (emploi passif)* to be found, to exist ▪ **de bons artisans, cela se trouve difficilement** it's not easy to find *ou* to get good craftsmen.
◇ *vpi* **1.** [en un lieu, une circonstance - personne] to be ; [- bâtiment, ville] to be (situated) *ou* located ▪ **je me trouvais là par hasard** I just happened to be there ▪ **qu'est-ce que tu dirais si tu te trouvais face à face avec lui?** what would you say if you suddenly found yourself face to face with him? ▪ **où se trouve la gare?** where's the station? ▪ **A se trouve à égale distance de B et de C** B and C are equidistant from A ▪ **se ~ sur** [figurer] to appear *ou* to be shown on ▪ [résider - intérêt, problème] to be, to lie **2.** [arriver] **: quand vous vous trouverez sur la place, tournez à droite** when you arrive at the square, turn right **3.** [dans une situation] to find o.s., to be ▪ **je me trouve devant un choix** I'm faced with a choice ▪ **se ~ dans l'impossibilité de faire qqch** to find o.s. *ou* to be unable to do sthg ▪ **se ~ dans l'obligation de faire qqch** to have no option but to do sthg **4.** [se sentir] to feel ▪ **je me suis trouvé bête d'avoir crié** I felt stupid for having screamed ▪ **se ~ bien/mieux** [du point de vue de la santé] to feel good/better ; [dans un siège] to feel comfortable/more comfortable ; [avec quelqu'un] to feel at ease/more at ease ; [dans un vêtement élégant] to feel (that one looks) good/better ▪ **se ~ mal** [s'évanouir] to pass out, to faint ▪ **se ~ bien/mal de qqch : elle a suivi mes conseils et s'en est bien/mal trouvée** she followed my advice, and benefited from it/and lived to regret it ▪ **se ~ mieux de qqch : qu'il parte, je ne m'en trouverai que mieux!** let him leave, see if I care! **5.** [se réaliser] to find o.s. ▪ **en tant qu'écrivain, elle ne s'est pas encore trouvée** as a writer, she hasn't found her individual voice *ou* style yet **6.** [exprime la fortuité d'un événement, d'une situation] to happen ▪ **ils se trouvaient appartenir au même club** they happened to belong *ou* it turned out that they belonged to the same club ▪ **je me trouve être libre ce jour-là** it so happens that I'm free that day ▶ **si ça se trouve** *fam* maybe.

trouvère [truvɛr] *nm* trouvère ▪ **'le Trouvère'** *Verdi* 'Il Trovatore'.

troyen, enne [trwajɛ̃, ɛn] *adj* Trojan.
◆ **Troyen, enne** *nm, f* Trojan.

tr/s (*abr écrite de* **tours par seconde**) revs/s.

truand [tryɑ̃] *nm* crook, gangster ▪ **les commerçants du coin, tous des ~s!** *fig* the local shopkeepers are all crooks!

truander [3] [tryɑ̃de] *fam* ◇ *vt* to con, to swindle ▪ **se faire ~** to be *ou* get conned.
◇ *vi* [aux examens] to cheat.

trublion [tryblijɔ̃] *nm* troublemaker.

truc [tryk] *nm fam* **1.** [astuce] trick ▪ **les ~s du métier** the tricks of the trade ▪ **il doit y avoir un ~, c'est trop beau** there's bound to be a catch, it's too good to be true ▪ **j'ai un ~ pour rentrer sans payer** I know a way of getting in without paying
2. CINÉ & THÉÂTRE (special) effect, trick

3. [chose précise] thing ■ **je pense à un ~** I've just thought of something ■ **j'ai plein de ~s à faire** I've got lots to do ■ **tu devrais t'acheter un ~ pour nettoyer ton four** you ought to buy something to clean your oven with ‖ *péj* thing, business, stuff ■ **mange pas de ce ~-là!** don't eat any of that (stuff)! ■ **sa maladie, c'est un sale ~** her illness is a nasty business ◆ **ce n'est pas/c'est mon ~** it's not/it's my cup of tea ■ **le rock, c'est pas mon ~** rock is not my (kind of) thing, rock doesn't turn me on ■ **l'écologie, c'est vraiment son ~** he's really into environmental issues
4. [objet dont on a oublié le nom] thing, thingie *UK*, whachamacallit
5. [personne dont on a oublié le nom] : **Truc** What's-his-name (*f* What's-her-name), Thingie *UK*.

trucage [trykaʒ] = **truquage**.

truchement [tryʃmɑ̃] *nm* : **par le ~ de son ami** through *ou* via his friend.

trucider [3] [tryside] *vt fam* to kill ■ **une heure de retard, on va se faire ~!** we're an hour late, they'll kill us!

trucmuche [trykmyʃ] *nm fam* **1.** [chose] thingy *UK*, thingumajig, thingamabob **2.** : **Trucmuche** [personne] What's-his-name (*f* What's-her-name), Thingie *UK*.

truculence [trykylɑ̃s] *nf* vividness, colourfulness.

truculent, e [trykylɑ̃, ɑ̃t] *adj* [personne] colourful, larger than life ■ [prose] vivid, colourful ■ [plaisanterie] racy.

truelle [tryɛl] *nf* [du maçon] trowel.

truffe [tryf] *nf* **1.** [champignon] truffle **2.** [friandise] (chocolate) truffle **3.** [de chien, de chat] nose **4.** *fam* [nez] snout **5.** *fam* [personne] clot, dumbbell *US*.

truffer [3] [tryfe] *vt* **1.** CULIN to garnish with truffles **2.** [emplir] to fill ■ **truffé de mines** riddled with mines ■ **truffé d'anecdotes** peppered with anecdotes.

truffier, ère [tryfje, ɛr] *adj* : **chien ~** truffle hound ■ **chêne ~** *oak on whose roots truffles grow.*

truie [trɥi] *nf* ZOOL sow.

truisme [tryism] *nm* truism ■ **c'est un ~!** it's obvious!, it goes without saying!

truite [trɥit] *nf* trout ■ **~ arc-en-ciel/saumonée** rainbow/salmon trout ■ **~ de rivière** brown trout ■ **~ de mer** sea trout.

trumeau, x [trymo] *nm* **1.** [entre des fenêtres] (window) pier **2.** [panneau de lambris, de peinture, de glace] pier glass ■ [d'une cheminée] overmantel **3.** ARCHIT pier.

truquage [trykaʒ] *nm* **1.** CINÉ [action] (use of) special effects ■ [résultat] special effect **2.** [d'élections, de résultats] rigging.

truquer [3] [tryke] *vt* **1.** [élection, statistiques] to rig ■ [entretien] to set up *(sép)* ■ [tableau] to fake **2.** CINÉ : **~ une scène** to use special effects in a scene.

truqueur, euse [trykœr, øz] *nm, f* [escroc] cheat.

truquiste [trykist] *nmf* CINÉ special effects man (*f* woman).

trust [trœst] *nm* **1.** ÉCON trust **2.** [entreprise] corporation.

truster [trœste] *vt* [marché] to corner, to monopolize.

trypanosome [tripanozom] *nm* trypanosome ■ **les ~s** the Trypanosoma.

ts = **tous**.

tsar [tsar, dzar] *nm* tsar, czar.

tsarine [tsarin, dzarin] *nf* tsarina, czarina.

tsarisme [tsarism, dzarism] *nm* tsarism, czarism.

tsariste [tsarist, dzarist] *adj* & *nmf* tsarist, czarist.

tsé-tsé [tsetse] *nf inv* tsetse (fly).

TSF (*abr de* **télégraphie sans fil**) *nf vieilli* [appareil] wireless ■ [procédé] wireless telegraphy.

T-shirt [tiʃœrt] = **tee-shirt**.

tsigane [tsigan] *adj* Gypsyish.
◆ **Tsigane** *nmf* (Hungarian) Gypsy.

tsunami [tsynami] *nm* tsunami.

TSVP (*abr écrite de* **tournez s'il vous plaît**) PTO.

tt = **tout**.

TT(A) (*abr de* **transit temporaire (autorisé)**) *registration for vehicles bought in France for tax-free export by non-residents.*

TTC (*abr de* **toutes taxes comprises**) *loc adj* inclusive of all tax, including tax.

tt conf = **tout confort**.

ttes = **toutes**.

TTX (*abr écrite de* **traitement de texte**) WP.

tu[1]**, e** [ty] *pp* ▭ **taire**.

tu[2] [ty] *pron pers (2e pers sing)* **1.** [sujet d'un verbe] you ■ *(élidé en 't' devant voyelle ou h muet)* **t'es bête!** *fam* you're stupid! **2.** RELIG thou ■ [en s'adressant à Dieu] : **Tu** Thou **3.** [emploi nominal] : **dire tu à qqn** to use the familiar form *ou* the "tu" form with *ou* to sb ■ **allez, on va se dire tu** ≃ come on, let's not stand on ceremony ◆ **être à tu et à toi avec qqn** to be on first-name terms with sb.

TU (*abr de* **temps universel**) *nm* UT, GMT.

tuant, e [tɥɑ̃, ɑ̃t] *adj fam* **1.** [épuisant] exhausting **2.** [ennuyeux] deadly dull *ou* boring.

tub [tœb] *nm* **1.** [objet] tub, bathtub **2.** [bain] bath.

tuba [tyba] *nm* **1.** MUS tuba **2.** SPORT snorkel.

tubage [tybaʒ] *nm* **1.** MÉD intubation, cannulation ■ **~ gastrique** gastric intubation **2.** INDUST **du pétrole** casing.

tube [tyb] *nm* **1.** [conduit] tube, pipe ■ **~ lance-torpilles** torpedo tube **2.** ÉLECTR : **~ cathodique** cathode-ray tube ■ **~ au néon** neon tube **3.** [contenant] tube ■ **~ de peinture** tube of paint ◆ **~ à essai** test tube **4.** ANAT & BOT tube ■ **~ digestif** digestive tract **5.** *fam* [chanson] (smash) hit, chart-topper ■ **le ~ de l'été** this summer's chart-topper.

tubercule [tybɛrkyl] *nm* **1.** BOT tuber **2.** ANAT & MÉD tubercle.

tuberculeux, euse [tybɛrkylø, øz] ◇ *adj* **1.** [malade] tuberculous ■ [symptôme] tuberculous, tubercular **2.** BOT tuberous.
◇ *nm, f* tuberculosis sufferer, tubercular.

tuberculine [tybɛrkylin] *nf* tuberculin.

tuberculose [tybɛrkyloz] *nf* tuberculosis, TB.

tubéreux, euse [tyberø, øz] *adj* tuberous.
◆ **tubéreuse** *nf* tuberose.

tubulaire [tybylɛr] *adj* **1.** ANAT & CONSTR tubular **2.** [chaudière] tubulous.

tubulé, e [tybyle] *adj* BOT tubulate.

tubuleux, euse [tybylø, øz] *adj* BOT tubulous.

tubulure [tybylyr] *nf* **1.** [ouverture d'un flacon] tubulure **2.** [tuyauterie] piping ■ [tube] pipe **3.** AUTO : **~ d'admission** inlet *ou* induction manifold ■ **~ d'échappement** exhaust manifold.

TUC, Tuc [tyk] (*abr de* **travaux d'utilité collective**) *nmpl community work scheme for unemployed young people.*

tuciste [tysist] *nmf person involved in a "TUC" scheme.*

tudieu [tydjø] *interj fam arch* zounds.

tué, e [tɥe] *nm, f* [dans un accident] : **11 ~s et 25 blessés** 11 dead *ou* 11 people killed and 25 injured.

tue-mouches [tymuʃ] *adj inv* **1.** [insecticide] : **papier ~** flypaper **2.** BOT : **amanite ~** fly agaric.

tuer [7] [tɥe] *vt* **1.** [personne] to kill ■ **~ qqn à coups de couteau** to stab sb *ou* to knife sb to death ■ **se faire ~** to be killed ■ **je t'assure, il est à ~!** [exaspérant] honestly, I could (cheerfully) strangle him! ■ **ta fille me tuera!** [dit par énervement] your daughter will be the death of me! ■ **ce voyage m'a tué** this trip's worn me out *ou* killed me ■ **qu'il ne comprenne pas, ça me tue** *fam* it amazes me he doesn't understand ■ *(en usage absolu)* **le tabac tue** tobacco kills *ou* is a killer **2.** [plante] to

kill (off) ▪ [animal de boucherie] to kill, to slaughter ▪ [gibier] to shoot ▪ **~ le veau gras** to kill the fatted calf ▪ **~ la poule aux œufs d'or** to kill the goose that lays the golden eggs ▪ **~ qqch dans l'œuf** to nip sthg in the bud **3.** [anéantir - tourisme, espoir] to ruin, to spoil, to kill **4.** *loc* **~ le temps** to kill time.
◆ **se tuer** <> *vp (emploi réfléchi)* [volontairement] to kill o.s.
<> *vpi* [par accident] to die, to be killed.
◆ **se tuer à** *vp+prép* **1.** [s'épuiser à] : **elle se tue à la tâche** *OU* **à la peine** *litt OU* **au travail** she's working herself to death **2.** [s'évertuer à] : **comme je me tue à te le répéter** as I keep telling you again and again.

tuerie [tyri] *nf* slaughter, massacre, bloodbath.

tue-tête [tytɛt] ◆ **à tue-tête** *loc adv* at the top of one's voice ▪ **chantant l'hymne national à ~** bellowing out the national anthem.

tueur, euse [tɥœr, øz] *nm, f* **1.** [meurtrier] killer ▪ **~ professionnel** *OU* **à gages** hired *OU* professional killer ▪ **~ en série** serial killer ▪ **~ fou** psychopath **2.** CHASSE pothunter **3.** [aux abattoirs] slaughterer.

tuf [tyf] *nm* : **~ calcaire** tufa ▪ **~ volcanique** tuff.

tuile [tɥil] *nf* **1.** CONSTR (roofing) tile ➊ **~ creuse** *OU* **canal** *OU* **romaine** curved tile ▪ **~ faîtière** ridge tile ▪ **~ plate** plain tile **2.** CULIN biscuit *UK*, cookie *US (in the shape of a curved tile)* **3.** *fam* [événement désagréable] stroke of bad luck, blow ▪ **il nous arrive une (grosse) ~** we're in big trouble ▪ **on n'a plus de gaz, la ~!** we're out of gas, what a pain! **4.** JEUX [au mah-jong] tile.

tuilerie [tɥilri] *nf* **1.** [industrie] tile industry **2.** [fabrique] tilery.

tulipe [tylip] *nf* **1.** BOT tulip **2.** [abat-jour] tulip-shaped lampshade.

tulle [tyl] *nm* **1.** TEXT tulle **2.** PHARM : **~ gras** tulle gras.

tuméfaction [tymefaksjɔ̃] *nf* **1.** [fait d'enfler] swelling, tumefaction *spéc* **2.** [partie enflée] swelling, swollen area *OU* part.

tuméfié, e [tymefje] *adj* swollen, tumid *spéc.*

tuméfier [9] [tymefje] *vt* to cause to swell, to tumefy *spéc.*
◆ **se tuméfier** *vpi* to swell up, to tumefy *spéc.*

tumescence [tymesɑ̃s] *nf* tumescence.

tumeur [tymœr] *nf* MÉD tumour ▪ **~ bénigne/maligne/blanche** benign/malignant/white tumour ▪ **~ au cerveau** brain tumour.

tumoral, e, aux [tymɔral, o] *adj* tumorous, tumoral.

tumulte [tymylt] *nm* [activité - soudaine] commotion, tumult ; [- incessante] hurly-burly, turmoil ▪ **le ~ des flots** *litt* the tumult of the waves.

tumultueusement [tymyltɥøzmɑ̃] *adv* stormily, tumultuously.

tumultueux, euse [tymyltɥø, øz] *adj* [discussion] stormy, turbulent, tumultuous ▪ [foule] boisterous, turbulent ▪ [vie] stormy, turbulent ▪ [passion] tumultuous, turbulent ▪ [flots] turbulent.

tumulus [tymylys] *nm* tumulus.

tune [tyn] *fam* = **thune**.

tuner [tynɛr] *nm* RADIO tuner.

tungstène [tœ̃kstɛn] *nm* tungsten.

tunique [tynik] *nf* **1.** [vêtement] tunic **2.** ANAT tunic, tunica **3.** BOT tunic.

Tunis [tynis] *npr* Tunis.

Tunisie [tynizi] *npr f* : **(la) ~** Tunisia.

tunisien, enne [tynizjɛ̃, ɛn] *adj* Tunisian.
◆ **Tunisien, enne** *nm, f* Tunisian.
◆ **tunisien** *nm* LING Tunisian.

tunnel [tynɛl] *nm* tunnel ▪ **percer un ~ (sous)** to tunnel (under) ➊ **le ~ sous la Manche** the Channel Tunnel.

tunnelier [tynəlje] *nm* tunneller.

TUP [typ] *nm* = **titre universel de paiement**.

Tupperware® [typɛrwɛr] <> *npr* Tupperware®.
<> *nm* [récipient] a Tupperware container.

tuque [tyk] *nf Québec* wool hat, tuque.

turban [tyrbɑ̃] *nm* **1.** [couvre-chef] turban **2.** CULIN ring-shaped mould.

turbin△ [tyrbɛ̃] *nm* work ▪ **après le ~** after work, after a day's grind.

turbine [tyrbin] *nf* turbine ▪ **~ hydraulique/à gaz/à vapeur** water/gas/steam turbine.

turbiner [3] △ [tyrbine] *vi* to grind *OU* to slog away, to graft *UK*.

turbo [tyrbo] <> *adj inv* turbine-driven, turbo *(modif).*
<> *nm* AUTO turbo.
<> *nf* turbo.

turbocompresseur [tyrbɔkɔ̃presœr] *nm* turbocharger ▪ **~ de suralimentation** turbosupercharger.

turbomoteur [tyrbɔmɔtœr] *nm* turboshaft engine.

turbopompe [tyrbɔpɔ̃p] *nf* turbopump, turbine pump.

turbopropulseur [tyrbɔpropylsœr] *nm* turboprop.

turboréacteur [tyrbɔreaktœr] *nm* turbojet (engine) ▪ **~ à double flux** by-pass turbojet.

turbot [tyrbo] *nm* turbot.

turbotrain [tyrbɔtrɛ̃] *nm* turbotrain.

turbulence [tyrbylɑ̃s] *nf* **1.** [d'un enfant] boisterousness, unruliness **2.** *litt* [d'une foule, d'une fête] rowdiness ▪ [de l'océan] turbulence *litt* **3.** MÉTÉOR turbulence, turbulency.

turbulent, e [tyrbylɑ̃, ɑ̃t] *adj* **1.** [enfant] boisterous, unruly **2.** *litt* [foule, fête] rowdy ▪ [époque] stormy ▪ [eaux] turbulent **3.** PHYS turbulent.

turc, turque [tyrk] *adj* Turkish.
◆ **Turc, Turque** *nm, f* Turk ▪ **le Grand Turc** the Grand Turk ▪ **les Jeunes-Turcs** HIST the Young Turks ▪ **fort comme un Turc** as strong as a horse.
◆ **turc** *nm* LING Turkish ▪ POLIT : **jeunes ~s** young radicals.
◆ **à la turque** <> *loc adj* **1.** [cabinets] seatless, hole-in-the-ground **2.** ART Turkish.
<> *loc adv* [s'asseoir] cross-legged.

turf [tœrf] *nm* **1.** [activité] horse racing **2.** [terrain] turf, racecourse **3.** △ [boulot] daily bread ▪ [lieu de travail] work.

turfiste [tœrfist] *nmf* racegoer.

turgescence [tyrʒesɑ̃s] *nf* turgescence.

Turkestan [tyrkɛstɑ̃] *npr m* : **(le) ~** Turkestan, Turkistan.

turkmène [tyrkmɛn] *adj* Turkoman.
◆ **Turkmène** *nmf* Turkoman.
◆ **turkmène** *nm* LING Turkmen.

Turkménistan [tyrkmenistɑ̃] *npr m* : **(le) ~** Turkmenistan.

turlupiner [3] [tyrlypine] *vt fam* to worry, to bug, to bother ▪ **c'est ce qui me turlupine** that's what's bugging me *OU* what's on my mind.

turlututu [tyrlytyty] *interj* fiddlesticks.

turne△ [tyrn] *nf* [chambre d'étudiant] room ▪ [logement d'étudiant] digs ▪ [taudis] dive△.

turpitude [tyrpityd] *nf litt* **1.** [caractère vil] turpitude *litt*, depravity **2.** [acte] base *OU* vile *OU* depraved act.

turque [tyrk] *f* ⊳ **turc**.

Turquie [tyrki] *npr f* : **(la) ~** Turkey.

turquoise [tyrkwaz] <> *nf* turquoise.
<> *adj inv* turquoise (blue).

tut *etc v* ⊳ **taire**.

tutélaire [tytelɛr] *adj* **1.** *litt* [divinité, rôle] guardian, tutelary *litt* **2.** DR tutelary.

tutelle [tytɛl] *nf* **1.** DR guardianship, tutelage ▪ **il est en** *ou* **sous ~** he has a guardian, he's under tutelage ▪ **placer** *ou* **mettre qqn en** *ou* **sous ~** to put sb into the care of a guardian ▶ **~ légale, ~ d'État** wardship (order) **2.** ADMIN : **~ administrative** administrative supervision **3.** POLIT trusteeship ▪ **territoire sous ~** trust territory **4.** [protection] care, protection ▪ [contrainte] control ▪ **tenir un pays en ~** *ou* **sous sa ~** to hold sway over a country.

tuteur, trice [tytœr, tris] *nm, f* **1.** DR guardian ▪ **~ ad hoc** *specially appointed guardian (ad litem)* **2.** *litt* [appui, protection] guardian, guarantee ▪ **la loi est la tutrice de nos libertés** the law is the guardian *ou* guarantee of our liberty.
◆ **tuteur** *nm* prop, support, stake HORT.

tutoie *etc v* ▷ **tutoyer**.

tutoiement [tytwamɑ̃] *nm use of the familiar "tu".*

tutorat [tytɔra] *nm* guardianship, tutelage.

tutoyer [13] [tytwaje] *vt to use the familiar "tu" form with* ▪ **elle tutoie son professeur** ≃ she's on first-name terms with her teacher.

tutti quanti [tutikwɑ̃ti] *loc adv* : **et ~** and the rest ▪ **la grand-mère, le cousin et ~** the grandmother, the cousin and the whole brood.

tutu [tyty] *nm* tutu.

tuyau, x [tɥijo] *nm* **1.** [conduit] pipe ▪ **~ d'arrosage** (garden) hose, hosepipe ▪ **~ d'échappement** exhaust (pipe) **2.** BOT [d'une tige] stalk **3.** [d'une plume] quill **4.** *fam* [information] tip ▪ **c'est lui qui m'a filé les ~x** I got the info *ou* gen *UK* from him **5.** COUT flute.

tuyautage [tɥijotaʒ] *nm* **1.** *fam* [fait de renseigner] tipping off **2.** COUT fluting **3.** TECHNOL plumbing.

tuyauter [3] [tɥijote] *vt* **1.** *fam* [informer] to tip off *(sép)* ▪ **je me suis fait ~ pour la prochaine course, on ne peut pas perdre** someone's given me a tip for the next race, we can't lose **2.** [plisser] to flute.

tuyauterie [tɥijotri] *nf* **1.** [canalisations] pipes, piping **2.** [d'un orgue] pipes **3.** △ [vessie] waterworks *euphém.*

tuyère [tyjɛr] *nf* **1.** [d'une turbine] nozzle **2.** [d'un haut-fourneau] tuyere, tuyère.

TV (*abr de* **télévision**) *nf* TV.

TVA (*abr de* **taxe à la valeur ajoutée**) *nf* ≃ VAT.

TVHD (*abr de* **télévision haute définition**) *nf* HDTV.

tweed [twid] *nm* tweed.

twin-set [twinsɛt] (*pl* **twin-sets**) *nm* twinset.

twist [twist] *nm* twist (dance).

tympan [tɛ̃pɑ̃] *nm* **1.** ANAT eardrum, tympanum *spéc* ▪ **un bruit à crever** *ou* **à déchirer les ~s** an earsplitting noise **2.** ARCHIT tympanum.

tympanon [tɛ̃panɔ̃] *nm* dulcimer.

type [tip] *nm* **1.** *fam* [homme] man, guy, bloke *UK* ▪ **c'est un drôle de ~!** [bizarre] he's a pretty weird bloke! ; [louche] he's a shady character! ▪ **quel sale ~!** what a nasty piece of work! *UK*, what an SOB! *US* ▪ **c'est un chic ~** he's a decent sort **2.** [genre] kind, type ▪ **c'est le ~ d'homme à partir sans payer** he's the type *ou* sort of man who would leave without paying ▪ **elle a le ~ indien** she looks Indian ▪ **c'est pas mon ~** she's not my type ▪ **c'est le ~ même du romantique** he's the typical romantic ▪ **un écrou du ~ X** a type X nut **3.** *(comme adj; avec ou sans trait d'union)* typical ▪ **contrat ~** model contract ▪ **erreur ~** typical *ou* classic mistake **4.** BOT type **5.** IMPR [ensemble de caractères] type ▪ [empreinte] type face.

typé, e [tipe] *adj* : **elle est indienne mais pas très ~e** she's Indian but doesn't have typical Indian features ▪ **une femme brune très ~e** a dark-haired woman with very distinctive looks.

typhoïde [tifɔid] *adj & nf* typhoid.

typhon [tifɔ̃] *nm* typhoon.

typhus [tifys] *nm* **1.** MÉD typhus (fever) **2.** VÉTÉR typhoid.

typique [tipik] *adj* [caractéristique] typical, characteristic ▪ **c'est ~ d'elle d'être en retard** it's typical of *ou* just like her to be late.

typiquement [tipikmɑ̃] *adv* typically.

typo[1] [tipo] *nf fam* typography.

typo[2]**, ote** [tipo, ɔt] *nm, f fam* typographer.

typographe [tipɔgraf] *nmf* [compositeur - sur machine] typographer ; [- à la main] hand compositor.

typographie [tipɔgrafi] *nf* **1.** [technique] letterpress (printing) **2.** [présentation] typography ▪ **la ~ est confuse** the page is badly set out.

typographique [tipɔgrafik] *adj* [procédé] letterpress *(modif)* ▪ [caractère] typographic.

typologie [tipɔlɔʒi] *nf* typology.

tyran [tirɑ̃] *nm* **1.** [despote] tyrant ▪ **faire le ~** to tyrannise *ou* to bully people **2.** ORNITH tyrant flycatcher.

tyrannie [tirani] *nf* tyranny ▪ **exercer sa ~ sur** to exercise one's tyranny over, to tyrannize.

tyrannique [tiranik] *adj* tyrannical.

tyranniser [3] [tiranize] *vt* to tyrannize, to bully ▪ **se faire ~** to be bullied.

Tyrol [tirɔl] *npr m* : **le ~** the Tyrol *ou* Tirol ▪ **au ~** in the Tyrol *ou* Tirol.

tyrolien, enne [tirɔljɛ̃, ɛn] *adj* Tyrolean, Tyrolese.
◆ **tyrolienne** *nf* **1.** [air] Tyrolienne, yodel ▪ **chanter une ~** to yodel **2.** [danse] Tyrolienne.

tzar [tsar, dzar] = **tsar**.

tzigane [dzigan] = **tsigane**.

u, U [y] *nm* u, U, *voir aussi* **g**.
◆ **en U** *loc adj* U-shaped ▪ **virage en U** U turn.

u (*abr écrite de* **unité**) [dix mille euros] : **300 u** three million euros.

UAP [yape] (*abr de* **unité d'appui psychologique**) *nf* trauma counselling service.

ubac [ybak] *nm northern side of a valley.*

ubiquité [ybikɥite] *nf* ubiquity, ubiquitousness ▪ **avoir le don d'~** *hum* to be ubiquitous *ou* everywhere at once.

Ubu [yby] *npr* : **le père ~** *the grotesque and disreputable character in a number of plays by Alfred Jarry, especially 'Ubu roi' (1896); the origin of the adjective 'ubuesque'.*

ubuesque [ybyɛsk] *adj* **1.** LITTÉR Ubuesque **2.** [grotesque] grotesque, farcical.

UDF (*abr de* **Union pour la démocratie française**) *npr f right-wing French political party.*

UDR (*abr de* **Union pour la défense de la République**) *npr f right-wing French political party.*

UE (*abr de* **Union Européenne**) *nf* EU.

UEFA (*abr de* **Union of European Football Associations**) *npr f* UEFA ▪ **la coupe de l'~** the UEFA cup.

UEO (*abr de* **Union de l'Europe occidentale**) *npr f* WEU.

UER ◇ *nf* (*abr de* **unité d'enseignement et de recherche**) *former name for a university department.*
◇ *npr f* (*abr de* **Union européenne de radiodiffusion**) EBU.

UFC (*abr de* **Union fédérale des consommateurs**) *npr f French consumers' association.*

UFR (*abr de* **unité de formation et de recherche**) *nf university department.*

UHF (*abr de* **ultra-haute fréquence**) *nf* UHF.

UHT (*abr de* **ultra-haute température**) *adj* UHT ▪ **lait stérilisé ~** UHT sterilized milk.

ukase [ykaz] *nm* HIST & *fig* ukase.

Ukraine [ykrɛn] *npr f* Ukraine.

ukrainien, enne [ykrɛnjɛ̃, ɛn] *adj* Ukrainian.
◆ **Ukrainien, enne** *nm, f* Ukrainian.
◆ **ukrainien** *nm* LING Ukrainian.

ulcère [ylsɛr] *nm* ulcer ▪ **~ à** *ou* **de l'estomac** stomach ulcer.

ulcérer [18] [ylsere] *vt* **1.** [indigner] to appal, to sicken ▪ **ulcéré par tant d'ingratitude** appalled *ou* sickened by such ungratefulness **2.** MÉD to ulcerate.

◆ **s'ulcérer** *vpi* to ulcerate, to form an ulcer ▪ **la plaie commence à s'~** the wound is beginning to ulcerate *ou* to fester *litt.*

ulcéreux, euse [ylserø, øz] *adj* [couvert d'ulcères] ulcerous ▪ [de la nature d'un ulcère] ulcer-like.

uléma [ylema] *nm* ulema.

ULM (*abr de* **ultra-léger motorisé**) *nm* microlight.

Ulster [ylstɛr] *npr m* : **(l')~** Ulster.

ultérieur, e [ylterjœr] *adj* later ▪ **à une date ~e** at a later date.

ultérieurement [ylterjœrmɑ̃] *adv* later ▪ **nous déciderons ~** we'll make up our minds at a later stage.

ultimatum [yltimatɔm] *nm* ultimatum ▪ **adresser un ~ à qqn** to present sb with an ultimatum.

ultime [yltim] *adj* [dernier] ultimate, final ▪ **ce furent là ses ~s paroles** those were her last *ou* final words.

ultra [yltra] ◇ *adj* extremist, reactionary.
◇ *nmf* **1.** [extrémiste] extremist, reactionary **2.** HIST ultra-royalist.

ultra-confidentiel, elle [yltrakɔ̃fidɑ̃sjɛl] *adj* top secret, highly confidential.

ultraconservateur, trice [yltrakɔ̃sɛrvatœr, tris] *adj* ultraconservative.

ultracourt, e [yltrakur, kurt] *adj* ultra-short.

ultraléger, ère [yltraleʒe, ɛr] *adj* superlight, extralight.

ultramoderne [yltramɔdɛrn] *adj* ultramodern, state-of-the-art *(avant n).*

ultra-perfectionné, e [yltrapɛrfɛksjɔne] *adj* ultra-high performance *(modif).*

ultraportatif [yltrapɔrtatif] *nm* notebook computer.

ultrarapide [yltrarapid] *adj* high-speed.

ultrasensible [yltrasɑ̃sibl] *adj* **1.** [instrument] ultrasensitive ▪ [peau] highly sensitive **2.** PHOTO high-speed *(avant n).*

ultrason [yltrasɔ̃] *nm* ultrasound, ultrasonic sound.

ultrasonique [yltrasɔnik], **ultrasonore** [yltrasɔnɔr] *adj* ultrasonic.

ultraviolet, ette [yltravjɔlɛ, ɛt] *adj* ultraviolet.
◆ **ultraviolet** *nm* ultraviolet ray.

ululer [3] [ylyle] *vi* to hoot.

Ulysse [ylis] *npr* Ulysses ▪ **'Ulysse'** ***Joyce*** 'Ulysses'.

UMP [yɛmpe] (*abr de* **Union pour un mouvement populaire**) *nf* POLIT *French right-wing political party.*

un, une [œ̃ (*devant nm commençant par voyelle ou h muet* œ̃n), yn] (*mpl* **uns** [œ̃], *fpl* **unes** [yn], *pl* **des** [de]) ◇ *dét (art indéfini)* **1.** [avec une valeur indéterminée] a, an (*devant une voyelle*) ▪ **un homme a appelé ce matin** a man called this morning ▪ **il doit y avoir une erreur** there must be a *ou* some mistake ▪ **un jour, ce sera permis** one day *ou* someday, it will be allowed ▪ **il y a des enfants qui jouent dans la rue** there are (some) children playing in the street ▪ **as-tu des livres à me prêter?** do you have any books you can lend me?

2. [avec une valeur particularisante] a, an (*devant une voyelle*) ▪ **j'irai plutôt un mardi** I'll go on a Tuesday instead ▪ **c'est avec un grand plaisir que...** it's with great pleasure that... ▪ **tu es une idiote** you're an idiot ▪ **elle a fait preuve d'une réelle gentillesse** she showed real kindness ▪ **un grand voyage se prépare des mois à l'avance** a *ou* any long journey needs months of preparation

3. [avec une valeur emphatique] : **il est d'une bêtise/d'un drôle!** he's so stupid/funny! ▪ **j'ai eu une frousse, mais une frousse!** *fam* I was absolutely terrified! ▪ **il y avait une foule!** there was such a crowd! ▪ **j'ai une de ces migraines!** I've got a splitting headache! ▪ **j'ai attendu des heures!** I waited for hours! ▪ **il travaille jusqu'à des trois heures du matin** he works as late as three in the morning ▪ **il gagne des 2 000 ou 3 000 euros par mois** he makes up to 2,000 or 3,000 euros a month

4. [avec un nom propre] : **un M. Baloi vous demande au téléphone** there's a Mr Baloi for you (on the phone) ▪ **tout le monde ne peut pas être un Rimbaud** we can't all be Rimbauds ▪ **c'est une future Callas** she will be another *ou* she's the next Callas ▪ **c'est un Apollon** he's a real Adonis ▮ [désignant une œuvre] : **faire l'acquisition d'un Picasso/d'un Van Gogh** to acquire a Picasso/a Van Gogh.

◇ *pron indéf* **1.** [dans un ensemble] one ▪ [en corrélation avec 'de'] : **un des seuls** one of the few ▪ **appelle-le un de ces jours** give him a call one of these days ▪ **un des événements qui a le plus retenu mon attention** one of the events that really grabbed my attention ▮ [avec l'article défini] : **c'est l'un des concerts les plus réussis de ma carrière** it's one of the most successful concerts of my career ▪ **l'un de mes amis** one of my friends, a friend of mine ▪ **l'un des deux** one of the two ▪ **l'un de vous deux est de trop** one of you is not needed

2. [en corrélation avec 'en'] one ▪ **on demanda un médecin, il y en avait un dans la salle** they called for a doctor, there was one in the room ▪ **parmi les enfants, il y en a un qui...** one of the children... ▪ **mais bien sûr que j'en ai une, de voiture!** *fam* of course I've got a car!

3. (*emploi nominal*) [quelqu'un] one person, someone ▪ **j'en connais une qui va être surprise!** I know someone who's going to get a surprise!

◇ *dét (adj num)* **1.** one ▪ **les enfants de un à sept ans** children (aged) from one to seven ▪ **une femme sur cinq** one woman out of *ou* in five ▪ **il y a un problème, un seul** there's just one problem ▪ **ils n'ont même pas marqué un (seul) but** they didn't even score one *ou* a single goal ▪ **je ne resterai pas une minute de plus ici** I won't stay here another minute ▪ **j'ai fait plus d'une erreur dans ma jeunesse** I made many mistakes *ou* more than one mistake in my youth ▪ **une à une, les lumières s'éteignaient** the lights were going out one by one *ou* one after the other ▪ **avale les cachets un par un** swallow the tablets one by one *ou* one at a time ▪ **vingt et un ans** twenty one years ▪ **deux heures une** one minute past two ◐ **la cuisine ne fait qu'un avec le salon** there is an open-plan kitchen cum living-room ▪ **il ne faisait qu'un avec sa monture** horse and rider were as one ▪ **et d'un, et de deux!** that's one, and another (one)!

2. [dans des séries] one ▪ **page un** *ou* **une** page one ▪ **il est une heure** it's one o'clock ▪ **le trente et un mars** on March the thirty-first *UK*, March thirty-first *US* ◐ **une, deux! une, deux!** left, right! left, right! ▪ **et d'une** *fam* firstly, first of all, for a start.

◇ *adj qualificatif sout* : **Dieu est un** God is one.

◆ **un** *nm inv* : **donnez-moi deux chiffres entre un et dix** give me two numbers between one and ten ▪ **tu fais mal tes un** your ones don't look right ▪ **la clef du un est perdue** the key for number one has been lost ▪ **on répète la dernière scène du un** THÉÂTRE we're rehearsing the last scene of act one.

unanime [ynanim] *adj* **1.** [commun, général - vote, décision] unanimous **2.** [du même avis] : **la presse ~ a condamné ce geste** the press unanimously condemned this gesture.

unanimement [ynanimmɑ̃] *adv* unanimously.

unanimité [ynanimite] *nf* unanimity ▪ **voter à l'~ pour qqn** to vote unanimously for sb ▪ **élu à l'~ moins une voix** elected with only one dissenting vote ▪ **faire l'~** to win unanimous support ▪ **un candidat qui fait l'~ contre lui** a candidate who has no support from anyone.

underground [œndœrgraund] ◇ *adj inv* underground.
◇ *nm inv* underground (culture), counter-culture.

une [yn] ◇ *dét (art indéfini f)* ⊳ **un**.
◇ *nf* **1.** PRESSE : **la ~** page one, the front page ▪ **faire la ~** to make the headlines ▪ **la naissance de la princesse fait la** *ou* **est à la ~ de tous les quotidiens** the birth of the princess is on the front page of all the dailies ▪ **ce sujet sera à la ~ de notre dernier journal télévisé ce soir** this will be one of the main items in our late news bulletin **2.** TV : **la Une** *France's channel one* ▪ **sur la Une** on channel one **3.** *fam* [histoire, nouvelle] one ▪ **j'en ai ~ (bonne) à t'apprendre** wait till you hear this **4.** *fam* [fessée, claque] : **tu vas en recevoir ~!** you're going to get a slap! ▪ **j'en ai pris ~ en pleine poire** I got one right across the face **5.** *fam* THÉÂTRE scene one.

UNEDIC [ynedik] (*abr de* **Union nationale interprofessionnelle pour l'emploi dans l'industrie et le commerce**) *npr f the department controlling the ASSEDIC.*

UNEF, Unef [ynɛf] (*abr de* **Union nationale des étudiants de France**) *npr f* ≃ National Union of Students.

UNESCO, Unesco [ynɛsko] (*abr de* **United Nations Educational Scientific and Cultural Organisation**) *npr f* UNESCO, Unesco.

unetelle [yntɛl] *f* ⊳ **untel**.

uni, e [yni] *adj* **1.** [d'une seule couleur] plain, self-coloured *UK*, solid *US* ▪ [sans motif] plain **2.** [sable] smooth, fine ▪ [terrain] even, level, smooth ▪ [mer] smooth, unruffled **3.** [soudé - couple] close ; [- famille, société] close-knit ▪ **~s derrière le chef** united behind the leader ▪ **tous ~s face aux pollueurs!** let's unite (in the fight) against pollution!
◆ **uni** *nm* [étoffe] plain fabric.

UNICEF, Unicef [ynisɛf] (*abr de* **United Nations International Children's Emergency Fund**) *npr f* UNICEF, Unicef.

unicellulaire [yniselylɛr] *adj* unicellular.

unicité [ynisite] *nf sout* uniqueness.

unicolore [ynikɔlɔr] *adj* plain, self-coloured *UK*, solid *US*.

unidirectionnel, elle [ynidirɛksjɔnɛl] *adj* unidirectional.

unième [ynjɛm] *adj num ord* first ▪ **quarante et ~** forty-first ▪ **cent ~** hundred and first, *voir aussi* **cinquième**.

unificateur, trice [ynifikatœr, tris] ◇ *adj* unifying, uniting.
◇ *nm, f* unifier.

unification [ynifikasjɔ̃] *nf* **1.** [d'un pays] unification, unifying **2.** [uniformisation] standardization, standardizing.

unifier [9] [ynifje] *vt* **1.** [réunir - provinces] to unify, to unite **2.** [uniformiser - tarifs] to standardize, to bring into line with each other.
◆ **s'unifier** *vpi* [parti, pays] to become united.

uniforme [ynifɔrm] ◇ *adj* **1.** [régulier - vitesse] uniform, regular, steady ; [- surface] even, smooth, level **2.** [identique] : **horaire ~ pour tout le personnel** the same timetable for all members of staff **3.** [monotone] uniform, unvarying, unchanging ▪ **une vie ~** a humdrum existence ▪ **un paysage ~** an unchanging *ou* a monotonous landscape.
◇ *nm* uniform ▪ **endosser/quitter l'~** [de l'armée] to join/to leave the forces.
◆ **en uniforme** *loc adj* in uniform ▪ **un policier en ~** a uniformed policeman ▪ **en grand ~** in full uniform *ou* regalia.

uniformément [ynifɔrmemɑ̃] *adv* **1.** [sans aspérités] uniformly, evenly ▪ **paysage ~ plat** uniformly flat landscape **2.** [identiquement] : **des femmes ~ vêtues de noir** women all dressed in the same black clothes **3.** [sans changement] regularly, steadily, uniformly ▪ **la vie s'écoulait ~** life went on in its usual way.

uniformisation [ynifɔrmizasjɔ̃] *nf* standardization, standardizing.

uniformiser [3] [ynifɔrmize] *vt* to standardize.

uniformité [ynifɔrmite] *nf* **1.** [régularité] uniformity, evenness **2.** [monotonie] monotony ▪ **l'~ de sa vie** the monotony of her life.

unijambiste [yniʒɑ̃bist] ◇ *adj* one-legged.
◇ *nmf* one-legged person.

unilatéral, e, aux [ynilateral, o] *adj* unilateral.

unilatéralement [ynilateralmɑ̃] *adv* unilaterally.

unilingue [ynilɛ̃g] *adj* unilingual, monolingual.

uninominal, e, aux [yninɔminal, o] *adj* ⊳ **scrutin.**

union [ynjɔ̃] *nf* **1.** [fait de mélanger] union, combination ▪ [mélange] union, integration
2. [solidarité] union, unity ▪ **~ nationale** national coalition ◗ **faire l'~ sacrée** [être solidaires] to show *ou* to present a united front ; HIST to unite in the face of the aggressor *(in 1914)* ▪ **Union de la gauche** *union of left-wing parties founded in 1972* ▪ **l'Union européenne** the European union ▪ **Union monétaire européenne** European Monetary Union ▪ **l'~ fait la force** *prov* unity is strength
3. [harmonie - dans un groupe] harmony ; [- dans une famille, un couple] closeness
4. [liaison entre un homme et une femme] union ▪ **~ charnelle** *litt* union of the flesh ▪ **~ conjugale** marital union ◗ **~ libre** free love ▪ **vivre en ~ libre** to cohabit
5. [regroupement] union, association ▪ **~ de consommateurs** consumer association ◗ **~ douanière** customs union
6. GÉOGR : **l'Union soviétique** *ou* **des républiques socialistes soviétiques** the Soviet Union, the Union of Soviet Socialist Republics ▪ **l'ex-Union soviétique** the former Soviet Union.

unionisme [ynjɔnism] *nm* **1.** *arch* [syndicalisme] unionism **2.** HIST Unionism.

unioniste [ynjɔnist] *adj* & *nmf* **1.** *arch* [syndicaliste] unionist **2.** HIST Unionist.

unipare [ynipar] *adj* uniparous.

unipersonnel, elle [ynipɛrsɔnɛl] *adj* **1.** LING impersonal **2.** COMM : **entreprise** *ou* **société ~le** one-person business, sole proprietorship.

unique [ynik] *adj* **1.** [seul] (one and) only, one ▪ **c'est mon ~ recours** it's the only recourse I have *ou* my sole recourse ▪ **l'~ explication possible** the only possible explanation **2.** [exceptionnel] unique ▪ **il est ~ au monde** it's unique **3.** *fam* [étonnant] priceless ▪ **il est vraiment ~, lui!** he's priceless, he is! **4.** [dans une famille] : **être fils/fille/enfant ~** to be an only son/daughter/child.

uniquement [ynikmɑ̃] *adv* only, solely ▪ **nous nous occupons ~ de prêts à court terme** we deal only *ou* solely *ou* exclusively in short-term loans.

unir [32] [ynir] *vt* **1.** [lier] to unite, to bring together *(sép)* ▪ **~ deux pays** to unite two countries **2.** *sout* [marier] to join in marriage *ou* matrimony **3.** [villes] to link, to connect **4.** [combiner] to combine ▪ **son style unit l'aisance à** *ou* **et la rigueur** her style combines both ease and precision.
◆ **s'unir** *vpi* **1.** [se regrouper] to unite ▪ **s'~ contre un ennemi commun** to unite against a common enemy **2.** *sout* [se marier] to become joined in marriage *ou* matrimony **3.** [être compatible] to match.

unisexe [ynisɛks] *adj* unisex.

unisexué, e [ynisɛksɥe], **unisexuel, elle** [ynisɛksɥɛl] *adj* unisexual.

unisson [ynisɔ̃] *nm* unison.
◆ **à l'unisson** *loc adv* in unison ▪ **nos cœurs battaient à l'~** our hearts were beating as one *ou* in unison.

unitaire [ynitɛr] ◇ *adj* **1.** [principe, slogan] uniting ▪ [politique] unitarian **2.** MATH [matrice, vecteur] unit **3.** COMM : **prix ~** unit price ▪ **tarification ~** tariff based on the price per unit **4.** RELIG Unitarian.
◇ *nmf* RELIG Unitarian.

unité [ynite] *nf* **1.** [cohésion] unity ▪ **arriver à une certaine ~ de pensée** *ou* **vues** to reach a certain consensus ◗ **~ budgétaire** FIN yearly budget *(presented before Parliament)* ▪ **l'~ nationale** POLIT national unity ▪ **les trois ~s, l'~ d'action, l'~ de temps et l'~ de lieu** HIST & THÉÂTRE the three unities, unity of action, unity of time, and unity of place **2.** [étalon] unit, measure ▪ **~ de masse** weight ▪ **~ de temps** unit for measuring time *ou* time measure **3.** [élément, module] unit, item ▪ **~ d'entrée/de sortie** INFORM input/output device ▪ **~ centrale (de traitement)** INFORM central processor unit, mainframe ▪ **~ de commande** INFORM control unit ▪ **~ pilote** experimental unit ▪ **~ de production** INDUST production unit ‖ LING (distinctive) feature ▪ UNIV : **~ de valeur** course credit *ou* unit **4.** MATH unit **5.** MIL unit **6.** PHARM unit.
◆ **à l'unité** ◇ *loc adj* : **prix à l'~** unit price.
◇ *loc adv* [acheter, vendre] by the unit, singly, individually.

univers [ynivɛr] *nm* **1.** ASTRON : **l'Univers** the Universe ▪ **l'~** [notre planète] the world ▪ **l'~ entier a salué cet exploit** people all over the world admired this exploit **2.** [domaine] world, universe ▪ **l'~ poétique de Mallarmé** Mallarmé's poetic world ▪ **l'~ carcéral** life in prison ◗ **~ du discours** LOGIQUE universe of discourse.

universalisation [yniversalizasjɔ̃] *nf* universalization.

universaliser [3] [yniversalize] *vt* to universalize, to make universal.
◆ **s'universaliser** *vpi* to become universal.

universalisme [yniversalism] *nm* **1.** PHILOS universalism **2.** RELIG Universalism.

universalité [yniversalite] *nf* universality.

universaux [ynivɛrso] *nmpl* : **les ~** the universals, the five predictables.

universel, elle [ynivɛrsɛl] *adj* **1.** [mondial] universal ▪ **produit de réputation ~le** world-famous product ▪ **paix ~le** world peace **2.** [partagé par tous - sentiment] universal, general **3.** [à usages multiples] : **remède ~** panacea, universal remedy.
◆ **universel** *nm* : **l'~** the universal.

universellement [ynivɛrsɛlmɑ̃] *adv* universally ▪ **~ reconnu** recognized by all ▪ **~ admiré** universally admired.

universitaire [ynivɛrsitɛr] ◇ *adj* [carrière, études] academic, university *(modif)* ▪ [année, centre, titre] academic ▪ [restaurant] university *(modif)*.
◇ *nmf* **1.** [enseignant] academic, don *UK* **2.** *Belgique* graduate *ou* post-graduate student.

université [ynivɛrsite] *nf* **1.** [institution, bâtiment] university ▪ **enseigner à l'~** to be a university teacher, to teach college *US* ▪ **l'Université** the teaching profession ◗ **~ d'été** UNIV summer school ▪ **~ du troisième âge** post-retirement *ou* senior citizens' university **2.** POLIT : **les ~s d'été du parti socialiste** socialist party summer school *(during which party leaders meet younger members)*.

univoque [ynivɔk] *adj* **1.** LING unequivocal **2.** [relation, rapport] one-to-one.

untel, unetelle, Untel, Unetelle [œ̃tɛl, yntɛl] *nm, f* Mr. So-and-so (*f* Mrs. So-and-so) ▪ **tu dis "bonjour Mademoiselle Unetelle, puis-je parler au directeur?"** you say "good morning Miss so-and-so *ou* Miss Whatever-her-name-is, may I speak to the manager?".

UPF (*abr de* **Union pour la France**) *npr f French political party.*

uppercut [ypɛrkyt] *nm* uppercut.

UPU (*abr de* **Union postale universelle**) *npr f* UPU.

uranium [yranjɔm] *nm* uranium ▪ **~ enrichi/épuisé** enriched/depleted uranium.

Uranus [yranys] *npr* ASTRON & MYTHOL Uranus.

urbain, e [yrbɛ̃, ɛn] *adj* **1.** [de la ville] urban, city *(modif)* ▶ **un grand centre ~** a big city **2.** *litt* [courtois] urbane, worldly.

urbanisation [yrbanizasjɔ̃] *nf* urbanization, urbanizing.

urbaniser [3] [yrbanize] *vt* to urbanize.

urbanisme [yrbanism] *nm* town planning.

urbaniste[1] [yrbanist] *nmf* town planner.

urbaniste[2] [yrbanist], **urbanistique** [yrbanistik] *adj* town planning *(modif)*.

urbanité [yrbanite] *nf litt* urbanity.

urdu [urdu] *nm* Urdu.

urée [yre] *nf* urea ▪ **avoir de l'~** to have excess urea.

urémie [yremi] *nf* uraemia.

uretère [yrtɛr] *nm* ureter.

urètre [yrɛtr] *nm* urethra.

urgence [yrʒɑ̃s] *nf* **1.** [caractère pressant] urgency ▪ **il n'y a pas ~** it's not urgent, there's no urgency ▪ **bois ton café tranquillement, il n'y a pas ~** *fam* drink your coffee, there's no (desperate) rush ▪ **il y a ~ à ce que vous preniez une décision** it's urgent for you to come to a decision ▪ **en cas d'~** in case of *ou* in an emergency **2.** [incident] emergency.
◆ **urgences** *nfpl* MÉD casualty department *UK*.
◆ **d'urgence** ◇ *loc adj* **1.** [mesures, soins] emergency *(modif)* ▪ **c'est un cas d'~** it's an emergency **2.** POLIT : **état d'~** state of emergency ▪ **procédure d'~** emergency *ou* special powers.
◇ *loc adv* as a matter of emergency ▪ **opérer d'~** to perform an emergency operation ▪ **on l'a transporté d'~ à l'hôpital** he was rushed (off) to hospital ▪ **faites-le venir d'~** ask him to come straightaway.
◆ **de toute urgence** *loc adv* most urgently.

urgent, e [yrʒɑ̃, ɑ̃t] *adj* urgent ▪ **la situation est ~e** this is an emergency ▪ **commençons par le plus ~** let's start with the most urgent thing ▪ **il est ~ que je le voie** I must see him urgently ▪ **ce n'est pas ~** it's not urgent, there's no (desperate) rush ▶ **pli ~** urgent letter.

urgentiste [yrʒɑ̃tist] *nmf* MÉD A&E doctor.

urger [17] [yrʒe] *vi fam* **ça urge?** is it urgent?, how urgent is it?

urinaire [yrinɛr] *adj* urinary.

urinal, aux [yrinal, o] *nm* (bed) urinal.

urine [yrin] *nf* urine ▪ **dans les ~s du patient** in the patient's urine.

uriner [3] [yrine] *vi* to urinate, to pass water.

urinoir [yrinwar] *nm* (public) urinal.

urique [yrik] *adj* uric.

urne [yrn] *nf* **1.** POLIT ballot box ▪ **se rendre aux ~s** to go to the polls **2.** [vase] urn ▪ **~ funéraire** (funeral) urn.

uro-génital, e [yrɔʒenital, o] *(mpl* **uro-génitaux**, *fpl* **uro-génitales)** *adj* urogenital, urinogenital.

urologie [yrɔlɔʒi] *nf* urology.

urologue [yrɔlɔg] *nmf* urologist.

URSS [yrs, yɛrɛsɛs] *(abr de* **Union des républiques socialistes soviétiques)** *npr f* : **(l')~** the USSR ▪ **l'ex-~** the former USSR.

URSSAF, Urssaf [yrsaf] *(abr de* **Union pour le recouvrement des cotisations de Sécurité sociale et d'Allocations familiales)** *npr f administrative body responsible for collecting social security payments.*

urticaire [yrtikɛr] *nf* nettle rash, hives, urticaria *spéc* ▪ **avoir de l'~** to have nettle rash ▶ **donner de l'~ : les huîtres me donnent de l'~** oysters bring me out in spots ▪ **cette musique, ça me donne de l'~** that music makes my skin crawl.

Uruguay [yrygwɛ] *npr m* : **l'~** [pays] Uruguay ; [fleuve] the Uruguay (River).

uruguayen, enne [yrygwejɛ̃, ɛn] *adj* Uruguayan.
◆ **Uruguayen, enne** *nm, f* Uruguayan.

us [ys] *nmpl litt* customs ▪ **les ~ et coutumes** habits and customs.

US *(abr de* **union sportive)** *nf* sports club *ou* association ▪ **l'~ (de) Liévin** the Liévin Sports Association *ou* SA.

USA *(abr de* **United States of America)** *npr mpl* : **les ~** the USA, the US, the States.

usage [yzaʒ] *nm* **1.** [utilisation] use ▪ **faire ~ de qqch** to use sthg ▪ **faire bon ~ de qqch** to put sthg to good use ▪ **faire mauvais ~ de qqch** to misuse sthg ▪ **faire un ~ abusif du pouvoir** to abuse power ▪ **faire de l'~** to stand up to a lot of use ▪ **mon imperméable a fait de l'~** my raincoat has seen good service ▪ **avoir l'~ de** to have the use of ▪ **une maison dont elle n'a pas la propriété mais l'~** DR a house which she doesn't own, but which she is legally entitled to use ▪ **je n'en ai aucun ~** I have no use for it ▪ **à mon ~ personnel** for my private *ou* own personal use ▶ **droit d'~** right of use
2. [contrôle] use ▪ **il a encore l'~ de son bras** he can still use his arm ▪ **perdre l'~ des yeux/d'un bras** to lose the use of one's eyes/an arm ▪ **perdre l'~ de la parole** to lose one's power of speech
3. [fonction] use, purpose ▪ **appareil d'~ courant** household appliance ▪ **à divers ~s** multi-purpose ▪ **à ~ intensif** heavy-duty ▪ **à ~ unique** [seringue, produit] use-once-then-throw-away ▪ **locaux à ~ administratif** office space ▪ **à ~s multiples** multi-purpose ▪ **'à ~ interne'** 'for internal use, to be taken internally' ▪ **'à ~ externe'** 'not to be taken internally'
4. LING (accepted) usage ▪ **~ écrit/oral** written/spoken usage ▪ **le mot est entré dans l'~** the word is now in common use ▪ **le mot est sorti de l'~** the word has become obsolete *ou* is no longer used ▶ **le bon ~** correct usage
5. [coutume] habit, habitual practice ▪ **selon un ~ bien établi** following a well-established habit ▪ **l'~, les ~s** accepted *ou* established custom, (the rules of) etiquette ▪ **c'est l'~** it's the done thing ▪ **ce n'est pas l'~ d'applaudir au milieu d'un air** it's not done to clap *ou* you just don't clap in the middle of an aria ▪ **c'est conforme à l'~** *ou* **aux ~s** it's in accordance with the rules of etiquette ▪ **c'est contraire à l'~** *ou* **aux ~s, c'est contre l'~** *ou* **les ~s** it's not the done thing, it's contrary to the rules of etiquette.
◆ **à l'usage** *loc adv* with use ▪ **c'est à l'~ qu'on s'aperçoit des défauts d'une cuisine** you only realize what the shortcomings of a kitchen are after you've used it for a while ▪ **nous verrons à l'~!** let's wait and see!
◆ **à l'usage de** *loc prép* : **un livre de cuisine à l'~ des enfants** a cookery book aimed at *ou* intended for children.
◆ **d'usage** *loc adj* **1.** [habituel] customary, usual ▪ **finir une lettre avec la formule d'~** to end a letter in the usual *ou* accepted manner ▪ **échanger les banalités d'~** to exchange the customary platitudes ▪ **il est d'~ de laisser un pourboire** it is customary to leave a tip
2. LING : **l'orthographe d'~** the generally accepted spelling.
◆ **en usage** *loc adv* in use ▪ **cette technique n'est plus en ~** this technique is now obsolete *ou* is no longer in use.

usagé, e [yzaʒe] *adj* **1.** [usé - costume] worn, old ; [- verre] used, old **2.** [d'occasion] used, secondhand.

usager, ère [yzaʒe, ɛr] *nm, f* **1.** [utilisateur] user ▪ **les ~s du téléphone/de la route** telephone/road users **2.** [locuteur] : **les ~s de l'espagnol** Spanish language speakers, speakers of the Spanish language.

usant, e [yzɑ̃, ɑ̃t] *adj* [tâche] gruelling, wearing ▪ [enfant] wearing, tiresome ▪ **c'est ~** it really wears you down.

usé, e [yze] *adj* **1.** [vieux - habit] worn, worn-out ; [- pile] worn, old ; [- lame] blunt ; [- pneu] worn ▶ **~ jusqu'à la corde** *ou* **trame** threadbare **2.** [rebattu - sujet] hackneyed, well-worn ; [- plaisanterie] old ▪ **c'est ~! essaye une autre excuse** I've heard that one before! try another excuse **3.** [affaibli - vieillard] worn-out, weary.

user [3] [yze] ◇ *vt* **1.** [détériorer - terrain, métal] to wear away *(sép)* ; [- pneu] to wear smooth ; [- veste, couverture] to wear out *(sép)* ▪ **~ un jean jusqu'à la corde** *ou* **trame** to wear out a pair of jeans ▪ **on avait usé nos fonds de culottes sur les mêmes bancs**

we'd been at school together **2.** [utiliser - eau, poudre] to use ; [- gaz, charbon] to use, to burn ; [- réserves] to use, to go through *(insép)* **3.** [fatiguer] to wear out *(sép)* ■ **usé par des années de vie politique** worn out by years in politics ■ **tu m'uses la santé!** *fam* you'll be the death of me!

◇ *vi litt* **en ~ : en ~ bien avec qqn** to treat sb well, to do well by sb ■ **en ~ mal avec qqn** to treat sb badly, to mistreat sb.

◆ **user de** *v+prép sout* [utiliser - autorité, droits] to exercise ; [- mot, tournure] to use ; [- outil] to use ; [- audace, diplomatie] to use, to employ ■ **l'alcool? j'en ai usé et abusé** alcohol? I've used and abused it.

◆ **s'user** ◇ *vpi* **1.** [se détériorer - gén] to wear out ; [- pile] to run down ; [- lame] to go blunt ■ **les semelles en cuir ne s'usent pas vite** there's a lot of wear in leather soles **2.** [s'affaiblir] : **ma patience commence à s'~** my patience is wearing thin.

◇ *vpt* [se fatiguer] to wear o.s. out ■ **s'~ la santé** *fam* to exhaust o.s., to wear o.s. out ■ **s'~ les yeux** *ou* **la vue** to strain one's eyes.

usinage [yzinaʒ] *nm* machining.

usine [yzin] *nf* **1.** INDUST factory, plant, mill ■ **~ sidérurgique** steel mill, steelworks ■ **~ métallurgique** ironworks ■ **~ à gaz** gasworks; *fig* overly complicated system ■ **~ pilote** pilot plant **2.** *fig & péj* **à la fac, c'est l'~!** it's just a production line at college! ■ **ce restaurant, une vraie ~!** they get you in and out as quick as they can in that restaurant!

usiner [3] [yzine] ◇ *vt* to machine.

◇ *vi fam* [travailler dur] : **ça usinait dans la cuisine** they were slogging away *ou* hard at it in the kitchen.

usité, e [yzite] *adj* [terme] commonly used ■ **l'expression n'est plus ~e** the phrase has gone out of use *ou* is no longer in common use.

USP [yɛspe] (*abr de* **unité de soins palliatifs**) *nf* MÉD palliative care unit.

ustensile [ystɑ̃sil] *nm* utensil, implement ■ **~s de cuisine** cooking *ou* kitchen utensils ■ **~s de jardinage** garden tools.

usuel, elle [yzɥɛl] *adj* [ustensile, vêtement] everyday *(avant n)* ■ [vocabulaire, terme] common, everyday *(avant n)* ■ **le procédé ~ est de...** it's common practice to...

usuellement [yzɥɛlmɑ̃] *adv* ordinarily, commonly.

usufruit [yzyfrɥi] *nm* usufruct.

usufruitier, ère [yzyfrɥitje, ɛr] *adj & nm, f* usufructuary.

usuraire [yzyrɛr] *adj* usurious.

usure [yzyr] *nf* **1.** [action de s'user] wear (and tear) ■ **matière résistante à l'~** material that stands up to wear (and tear), material that wears well, hard-wearing material ■ **l'~ des roches** erosion suffered by the rock **2.** [affaiblissement] : **l'~ des forces/sentiments** the erosion of one's strength/feelings ■ **notre mariage a résisté à l'~ du temps** our marriage has stood the test of time ■ **victime de l'~ du pouvoir** worn down by the exercise of power ➊ **avoir qqn à l'~** *fam* to wear *ou* to grind sb down (until he gives in) **3.** [intérêt de prêt] usury ■ **prêter à ~** to lend upon usury *ou* at usurious rates of interest.

usurier, ère [yzyrje, ɛr] *nm, f* usurer.

usurpateur, trice [yzyrpatœr, tris] ◇ *adj litt* usurping.

◇ *nm, f* usurper.

usurpation [yzyrpasjɔ̃] *nf* usurpation, usurping ■ **~ de pouvoir** usurpation *ou* usurping of power.

usurpatoire [yzyrpatwar] *adj* usurpatory.

usurper [3] [yzyrpe] *vt* [droit, identité] to usurp ■ **sa gloire est usurpée** *fig* her fame isn't rightfully hers.

◆ **usurper sur** *v+prép litt* to encroach on *ou* upon.

ut [yt] *nm inv* MUS C.

UTA (*abr de* **Union des transporteurs aériens**) *npr f French airline company.*

Utah [yta] *npr m* : **l'~** Utah.

utérin, e [yterɛ̃, in] *adj* **1.** ANAT uterine **2.** [de la même mère] : **frères ~s** uterine brothers ■ **sœurs ~es** uterine sisters.

utérus [yterys] *nm* womb, uterus *spéc.*

utile [ytil] ◇ *adj* **1.** [qui sert beaucoup] useful ■ **ça peut (toujours) être ~** it might come in handy ■ **cela m'a été ~ de connaître la langue** my knowledge of the language was very useful to me **2.** [nécessaire] necessary ■ **il n'est pas ~ d'avertir la police** there's no need to notify the police **3.** [serviable] useful ■ **il cherche toujours à se rendre ~** he always tries to make himself useful ■ **puis-je t'être ~ à quelque chose?** can I be of any help to you?, can I help you with anything?

◇ *nm* : **l'~** that which is useful ■ **joindre l'~ à l'agréable** to combine business with pleasure.

utilement [ytilmɑ̃] *adv* usefully, profitably ■ **employer son temps ~** to spend one's time profitably, to make good use of one's time.

utilisable [ytilizabl] *adj* **1.** [objet, appareil] usable ■ **ce vieux réveil est encore ~?** is this old alarm clock still working? **2.** [billet] valid.

utilisateur, trice [ytilizatœr, tris] *nm, f* [d'un appareil] user ■ [d'un service] user, consumer.

utilisation [ytilizasjɔ̃] *nf* use, utilization ■ **la sorbetière est d'~ simple** the ice-cream maker is simple *ou* easy to use ➊ **notice d'~** instructions for use.

utiliser [3] [ytilize] *vt* [appareil, carte, expression] to use ■ [moyens, tactique] to use, to employ ■ **je n'ai pas su ~ les possibilités qui m'étaient offertes** I didn't make the most of the opportunities I was given ■ **il sait ~ son monde** he knows how to make the best use of his connections.

utilitaire [ytilitɛr] ◇ *adj* utilitarian.

◇ *nm* INFORM utility (program) ■ **~s de programmation** utilities.

utilitarisme [ytilitarism] *nm* utilitarianism.

utilitariste [ytilitarist] *adj & nmf* utilitarian.

utilité [ytilite] *nf* **1.** [caractère utile] use, usefulness ■ **chaque ustensile a son ~** every implement has its specific use ■ **des objets sans ~** useless objects ■ **ça ne t'est plus d'aucune ~** it's no longer of any use to you, you no longer need it ■ **la carte de la région m'a été de peu d'~/d'une grande ~** the map of the area was of little/great use to me ■ **quelle est l'~ d'avoir une voiture dans Paris?** what's the use of having a car in Paris? ■ **en as-tu l'~?** can you make use of it?, do you need it? ■ **je ne vois pas l'~ de lui en parler** I don't see any point in mentioning it to her ➊ **reconnu d'~ publique** *officially recognized as beneficial to the public at large* **2.** ÉCON utility.

◆ **utilités** *nfpl* THÉÂTRE : **jouer les ~s** *pr* to play minor *ou* small parts ; *fig* to play second fiddle.

utopie [ytɔpi] *nf* **1.** PHILOS utopia, utopian ideal **2.** [chimère] utopian idea ■ **c'est de l'~!** that's all pie in the sky! ■ **votre programme politique relève de l'~** your political programme is rather utopian.

utopique [ytɔpik] *adj* utopian.

utopiste [ytɔpist] ◇ *adj* utopian.

◇ *nmf* **1.** [rêveur] utopian **2.** PHILOS Utopian.

Utrecht [ytrɛkt] *npr* Utrecht.

UV ◇ *nf* = **unité de valeur.**

◇ *nm* (*abr de* **ultraviolet**) UV ■ **faire des UVs** to go to a solarium.

UVA (*abr de* **ultraviolet A**) *nm* UVA ■ **bronzage ~** sunlamp tan.

uvéite [yveit] *nf* MÉD uveitis, iritis.

uzbek [yzbɛk] = **ouzbek.**

V

v, V [ve] *nm* **1.** [lettre] v, V, *voir aussi* **g** **2.** [forme] V (shape) ▪ **faire le V de la victoire** to make the victory sign.
◆ **en V** *loc adj* V-shaped ▪ **un pull (à col) en V** a V-necked sweater ▪ **décolleté en V** plunging neckline.

v. 1. (*abr écrite de* **verset**) v. (*verse*) **2.** = **vers** (*adv*).

v° = **verso**.

V (*abr écrite de* **volt**) V.

V., v. = **voir**.

V1 *nm* V-1.

V2 *nm* V-2.

va *v* ▷ **aller**.

vacance [vakɑ̃s] *nf* **1.** [d'un emploi] vacancy **2.** [d'une fonction politique] : **pendant la ~ du siège** while the seat is empty ▪ **pendant la ~ du pouvoir** while there is no one officially in power ▪ **élection provoquée par la ~ du siège** election made necessary because the seat became vacant **3.** DR : **~ de succession** abeyance of succession.
◆ **vacances** *nfpl* **1.** [période de loisirs] holidays *UK*, vacation *US* ▪ **prendre des ~s** to take a holiday, to go on holiday ▪ **prendre deux mois de ~s** to take two months off, to have a two-month holiday ▪ **rentrer de ~s** to come back from one's holiday *ou* vacation ➔ **~s actives** adventure holiday ▪ **~s de neige** skiing holidays *ou* vacation ▪ **~s à thème** special-interest holiday **2.** [période du calendrier] : **~s judiciaires** recess (of the Courts) ▪ **~s parlementaires** Parliamentary recess ▪ **~s scolaires** school holidays *UK ou* break *US* ▪ **~s universitaires** vacation *UK*, university recess *US* ▪ **un job pendant les ~s (universitaires)** a summer job ▪ **les ~s de Noël** ÉDUC & UNIV the Christmas holidays *UK ou* vacation *US* ; [pour les salariés] the Christmas break ▪ **les grandes ~s** the summer holidays *UK*, the long vacation *US*.
◆ **en vacances** *loc adv* on holiday *UK ou* vacation *US* ▪ **partir en ~s** to go (off) on holiday.

vacancier, ère [vakɑ̃sje, ɛr] *nm, f* holidaymaker *UK*, vacationist *US*, vacationer *US*.

vacant, e [vakɑ̃, ɑ̃t] *adj* **1.** [libre - logement] vacant, unoccupied ; [- siège, trône] vacant ▪ **il y a un poste d'ingénieur ~** there's a vacancy for an engineer ➔ **succession ~e** DR estate in abeyance **2.** *litt* [vague - regard] vacant, empty.

vacarme [vakarm] *nm* racket, din, row ▪ **les enfants faisaient un ~ infernal** the children were making a terrible racket *ou* an awful din.

vacataire [vakatɛr] *nmf* [remplaçant] stand-in, temporary replacement ▪ UNIV part-time lecturer ▪ **avoir un poste de ~ à l'Unesco** to be under temporary contract to UNESCO.

vacation [vakasjɔ̃] *nf* ÉDUC & UNIV : **être payé à la ~** to be paid on a sessional basis.
◆ **vacations** *nfpl* **1.** DR recess **2.** [honoraires] fees.

vaccin [vaksɛ̃] *nm* **1.** [produit] vaccine ▪ **~ informatique** computer vaccine **2.** [injection] vaccination, inoculation ▪ **faire un ~ à qqn** to vaccinate sb.

vaccinable [vaksinabl] *adj* : **à quel âge sont-ils ~s?** how old do they have to be before they can be vaccinated?

vaccination [vaksinasjɔ̃] *nf* vaccination, inoculation ▪ **~ préventive** protective inoculation.

vaccine [vaksin] *nf* cowpox, vaccinia *spéc* ▪ **fausse ~** vaccinella, false vaccinia.

vacciner [3] [vaksine] *vt* **1.** MÉD to vaccinate ▪ **se faire ~ contre la rage** to get vaccinated against rabies **2.** *fig* **je suis vacciné contre ce genre de remarque** I've become immune to that kind of remark ▪ **plus de ski, je suis vaccinée pour un moment** no more skiing, I've had my fill of that for the time being.

vachard, e [vaʃar, ard] *adj fam* [coup] nasty, foul, dirty ▪ [question] nasty ▪ **il était ~, l'examen!** the exam was a real stinker!

vache [vaʃ] ◇ *adj fam* rotten, nasty ▪ **faire un coup ~ à qqn** to play a dirty trick on sb ▪ **c'est ~ de ta part** it's rotten of you ▪ **allez, ne sois pas ~** come on, don't be rotten, come on, be a sport *UK*.
◇ *nf* **1.** ZOOL cow ▪ **~ sacrée** sacred cow ▪ **~ laitière** *ou* **à lait** milker, dairy cow ▪ **~ à lait** *fig* milch cow ▪ **dans la famille, c'est moi qui suis la ~ à lait** *fam* I have to fork out for everybody in this family ▪ **parler français comme une ~ espagnole** *fam* to murder the French language **2.** [cuir] cowhide **3.** [récipient] : **~ à eau** water bag **4.** *fam* [homme] swine ▪ [femme] cow ▪ **ah les ~s, ils ne m'ont pas invité!** the swines didn't invite me! ➔ **cette ~ de bagnole!**△ that bloody car!△ ▪ **une ~ de moto**△ one hell of a motorbike△ **5.** △ *arg crime* [policier] cop, pig△ **6.** *(comme interj)* **(ah) la ~!** *fam* [étonnement] wow!, gosh! ; [indignation, douleur] oh hell!
◆ **en vache** *loc adv* on the sly ▪ **faire un coup en ~ à qqn** to stab sb in the back.

vachement△ [vaʃmɑ̃] *adv* really, bloody△ *UK*, real *US* ▪ **elle est ~ belle, ta robe** that's a great dress you're wearing ▪ **ça fait une sacrée différence! – oui, ~!** it makes a difference! – you can say that again! ▪ **mais je t'assure qu'il t'aime – oui, ~!** *iron* but I'm telling you he loves you – like hell he does!△.

Vache-qui-rit® [vaʃkiri] *npr f* : **la ~** *famous brand of cheese spread triangles.*

vacher, ère [vaʃe, ɛr] *nm, f* cowboy (*f* cowgirl).

vacherie [vaʃri] *nf fam* **1.** [caractère méchant] meanness, rottenness **2.** [acte] dirty *ou* rotten trick ▪ **faire une ~ à qqn** to play a dirty *ou* rotten trick on sb **3.** [propos] nasty remark ■ **il me disait des ~s** he was saying really nasty things to me, he was being really horrible to me.

vacherin [vaʃʀɛ̃] *nm* **1.** [dessert] vacherin **2.** [fromage] vacherin cheese.

vachette [vaʃɛt] *nf* **1.** [animal] young cow **2.** [peau] calfskin.
◆ **en vachette** *loc adj* calfskin *(modif).*

vacillant, e [vasijɑ̃, ɑ̃t] *adj* **1.** [titubant - démarche] unsteady, shaky **2.** [qui bouge - flamme] flickering **3.** [courage] faltering, wavering ■ [mémoire] failing, faltering ■ **sa raison ~e** her failing reason **4.** [caractère] wavering, irresolute, indecisive.

vacillation [vasijasjɔ̃] *nf* **1.** [d'une lueur, d'une flamme] flickering **2.** *litt* [irrésolution] hesitations, hesitating ■ **après bien des ~s, j'ai pris ma décision** after changing my mind several times, I made a decision.

vacillement [vasijmɑ̃] *nm* **1.** [d'un poteau, d'une pile de livres] wobbling **2.** *fig* [indécision, doute] indecision, vacillating.

vaciller [3] [vasije] *vi* **1.** [tituber - bébé] to totter ; [- ivrogne] to sway, to stagger ■ **~ sur ses jambes** to be unsteady on one's legs ■ **elle vacilla sur ses jambes** her legs nearly gave way under her **2.** [chaise, pile de livres] to wobble **3.** [flamme] to flicker **4.** [raison, courage] to falter, to waver ■ [voix] to falter, to shake ■ [mémoire] to be failing, to falter ■ **elle n'a jamais vacillé dans ses prises de position** she has never wavered in her attitude.

va-comme-je-te-pousse [vakɔmʃtəpus] ◆ **à la va-comme-je-te-pousse** *loc adv fam* any old how ■ **ça a été fait à la ~** [ouvrage] it was thrown together any old how ; [lit] it was made in a hurry ; [repas] it was just thrown together ; [réforme] it was just pushed through (any old how).

vacuité [vakɥite] *nf litt* **1.** [vide] vacuity *litt*, emptiness **2.** [inanité] vacuity, vacuousness, inanity ■ **un roman d'une effrayante ~** a dreadfully inane novel.

vade-mecum [vademekɔm] *nm inv litt* vade mecum.

vadrouille [vadʀuj] *nf* **1.** *fam* [excursion] ramble, jaunt ■ **faire une ~ en Italie** to go off for a jaunt in Italy **2.** *Québec* [balai] *long-handled mop used for dusting.*
◆ **en vadrouille** *loc adv* : **partir en ~** to go (off) on a jaunt ■ **il est toujours en ~ quelque part** he's always gadding about somewhere.

vadrouiller [3] [vadʀuje] *vi fam* to rove about ■ **~ de par le monde** to rove *ou* to knock about the world.

vadrouilleur, euse [vadʀujœʀ, øz] *nm, f fam* rover ■ **j'ai toujours été une vadrouilleuse** I've always been a bit of a rover.

va-et-vient [vaevjɛ̃] *nm inv* **1.** [circulation] comings and goings, toings and froings **2.** [aller et retour] : **faire le ~** to go back and forth *ou* backwards and forwards **3.** MÉCAN [latéral] to-and-fro motion ■ [vertical] up-and-down movement ■ **dispositif de ~** reciprocating device **4.** ÉLECTR : **(interrupteur de) ~** two-way switch **5.** [charnière de porte] helical hinge ■ **porte/battant à ~** swing door/panel **6.** [bac] small ferry *ou* ferryboat.

vagabond, e [vagabɔ̃, ɔ̃d] ◇ *adj* [mode de vie, personne] wandering, roving ■ [pensée] wandering, roaming.
◇ *nm, f* tramp, vagabond, vagrant.

vagabondage [vagabɔ̃daʒ] *nm* **1.** [errance] roaming, roving, wandering **2.** DR vagrancy.

vagabonder [3] [vagabɔ̃de] *vi* to wander, to roam ■ **ses pensées vagabondent sans parvenir à se fixer** *fig* her thoughts wander *ou* drift without any focus.

vagin [vaʒɛ̃] *nm* vagina.

vaginal, e, aux [vaʒinal, o] *adj* vaginal.

vaginite [vaʒinit] *nf* vaginitis.

vagir [32] [vaʒiʀ] *vi* [crier - bébé] to cry, to wail.

vagissant, e [vaʒisɑ̃, ɑ̃t] *adj* crying.

vagissement [vaʒismɑ̃] *nm* cry ■ **attiré par de faibles ~s** alerted by the sound of whimpering.

vague[1] [vag] *nf* **1.** [dans la mer] wave ■ **grosse ~** roller ■ **courir dans les ~s** to run into the waves *ou* surf ▶ **~ de fond** *pr & fig* groundswell ■ **faire des ~s** *pr & fig* to make waves ■ **je ne veux pas de ~s** I don't want any scandal **2.** *litt* [des blés, des cheveux] wave, ripple ■ **effet de ~** ripple effect ; ARCHIT waved motif **3.** [mouvement] wave ■ **~ de colère** wave *ou* surge of anger ■ **~ de protestations/grèves** wave of protest/strikes ■ **la première ~ de départs** the first wave of departures ■ **~ d'immigrants** wave of immigrants **4.** MÉTÉOR : **~ de chaleur** heatwave ■ **~ de froid** cold spell.

vague[2] [vag] ◇ *adj* **1.** [peu marqué - sourire, détail] vague ; [- souvenir, connaissances] vague, hazy ; [- contour, sensation] vague, indistinct ■ [vacant - regard, expression] vacant, abstracted ■ **avoir l'air ~** to look vague, to have a vacant expression (on one's face) ■ **esquisser un ~ sourire** to smile faintly **2.** *(avant le n)* [non précisé] vague ■ **un ~ cousin à moi** some distant cousin of mine ■ **ils ont eu une ~ liaison** they had some sort *ou* kind of an affair ■ **il habite du côté de la Grande Place – c'est plutôt ~!** he lives somewhere near the Grande Place – that's a bit vague! **3.** [vêtement] loose, loose-fitting, generously-cut **4.** ANAT [nerf] vagal.
◇ *nm* **1.** [flou] vagueness, indistinctness ■ [imprécision] vagueness ■ **laisser une question dans le ~** to be vague about a matter ■ **rester dans le ~** to be (as) vague (as possible), to avoid giving any details **2.** [vide] : **regarder dans le ~** to gaze vacantly into space *ou* the blue.
◆ **vague à l'âme** *nm* melancholy ■ **avoir du ~ à l'âme** to be melancholy.

vaguelette [vaglɛt] *nf* wavelet.

vaguement [vagmɑ̃] *adv* **1.** [de façon imprécise] vaguely ■ **ils se ressemblent ~** they look vaguely alike, there is a vague resemblance between them ■ **tu as prévu le repas de ce soir? – ~!** have you thought of what to cook tonight? – sort of! ■ **elle est ~ actrice** *péj* she's some kind of actress **2.** [un peu] vaguely, mildly.

vaguemestre [vagmɛstʀ] *nm* MIL & NAUT mail orderly.

vaguer [3] [vage] *vi litt* [vagabonder - personne] to wander, to roam ; [- pensée] to rove, to wander ■ **laisser ~ son imagination** to allow one's imagination free rein.

vahiné [vaine] *nf* Tahitian woman.

vaillamment [vajamɑ̃] *adv* valiantly, bravely, gallantly ■ **se défendre ~** to put up stout resistance.

vaillance [vajɑ̃s] *nf* [courage - moral] courage, bravery, stout-heartedness ; [- physique] valiance ■ **elle a beaucoup de ~** she's very brave.

vaillant, e [vajɑ̃, ɑ̃t] *adj* **1.** [courageux - moralement] courageous, brave, stout-hearted ; [- physiquement] valiant ■ **à cœur ~, rien d'impossible** *prov* nothing is impossible to a valiant heart **2.** [bien portant] strong, healthy ■ **il est encore ~** he's still in good health ■ **elle n'est plus bien ~e** she's not very strong these days.

vaille *etc v* ▷ **valoir.**

vain, e [vɛ̃, vɛn] *adj* **1.** [inutile] vain, fruitless, pointless ■ **tous nos efforts ont été ~s** all our efforts were fruitless *ou* in vain ■ **il est ~ de continuer** it is pointless to continue **2.** *litt* [superficiel] shallow, superficial ■ [vaniteux] vain, conceited **3.** *(avant le n)* [serment, espérance] empty, vain ■ [promesse] empty, hollow, worthless ■ **socialisme n'est pas un ~ mot pour moi** to me, socialism is not an empty *ou* idle word **4.** DR : **~e pâture** common grazing land.
◆ **en vain** *loc adv* in vain, vainly, fruitlessly.

vaincre [114] [vɛ̃kʀ] *vt* **1.** [équipe, adversaire] to beat, to defeat ■ [armée] to defeat ■ **s'avouer vaincu** to admit defeat ■ **les joueurs partaient vaincus d'avance** the players felt beaten *ou* defeated before they began ■ **nous vaincrons!** we shall overcome! **2.** [peur, douleur, inhibition] to overcome, to conquer, to master ■ [mal de tête, maladie] to overcome ■ [hostilité, réticences] to overcome, to triumph over *(insép)* ■ **~ toutes les résistances** to carry all before one ■ **être vaincu par le sommeil/la fatigue** to be overcome with sleep/exhaustion.

vaincu, e [vɛ̃ky] *nm, f* defeated man (*f* woman) ■ **les ~s** the defeated, the vanquished *litt* ■ **les ~s ne participeront pas aux demi-finales** the losers will not take part in the semi-finals.

vainement [vɛnmɑ̃] *adv* in vain, vainly, fruitlessly ■ **on l'a ~ cherché** we looked for him in vain.

vainquait *etc v* ▻ **vaincre**.

vainqueur [vɛ̃kœr] ◇ *adj m* winning, victorious, triumphant, conquering ■ **sortir ~ d'une épreuve** to emerge (as) the winner of a contest.
◇ *nm* [gagnant - SPORT] winner ■ MIL victor.

vair [vɛr] *nm* vair ■ **la pantoufle de ~ de Cendrillon** Cinderella's glass slipper.

vairon [vɛrɔ̃] ◇ *adj m* : **yeux ~s** wall-eyes ■ **aux yeux ~s** wall-eyed.
◇ *nm* ZOOL minnow.

vais *v* ▻ **aller**.

vaisseau, x [vɛso] *nm* **1.** [navire] ship, vessel *sout* ■ **~ amiral** flagship ■ **~ de guerre** warship, man-of-war ■ **~ fantôme** ghost ship **2.** ANAT vessel ■ **~ capillaire/lymphatique/sanguin** capillary/lymphatic/blood vessel **3.** BOT vessel ■ **plantes à ~x** vascular plants **4.** ASTRONAUT : **~ spatial** spacecraft ■ **~ spatial habité** spaceship, manned spacecraft **5.** ARCHIT nave.

vaisselier [vɛsəlje] *nm* dresser *UK*, buffet *US*.

vaisselle [vɛsɛl] *nf* **1.** [service] crockery ■ **acheter de la belle ~** to buy some nice tableware ◐ **~ de porcelaine** china tableware **2.** [ustensiles sales] (dirty) dishes ■ **faire la ~** to do the washing-up *UK*, to do *OU* to wash the dishes.

val, s *OU* **vaux** [val, vo] *nm* [vallée] valley ■ **le Val d'Aoste** the Valle d'Aosta ■ **le Val de Loire** the Loire Valley, the Val de Loire.

Val [val] (*abr de* **véhicule automatique léger**) *nm* automatic urban train service.

valable [valabl] *adj* **1.** [valide - ticket, acte] valid ■ **non ~** invalid **2.** [acceptable - schéma, argument] valid, good ; [- excuse, raison] valid, good, legitimate **3.** [excellent - musicien, athlète] really good ■ **trouver un interlocuteur ~** [gén] to find someone who'll know what you're talking about ; POLIT to find an authorized representative.

valablement [valabləmɑ̃] *adv* **1.** [à bon droit] validly, justifiably, legitimately ■ **peut-on ~ invoquer la légitime défense?** can we justifiably plead self-defence? **2.** [efficacement] usefully.

Valais [valɛ] *npr m* : **le ~** Valais.

valaisan, anne [valɛzɑ̃, an] *adj* from Valais.

Val-de-Grâce [valdəgras] *npr m* : **le ~** *military hospital in Paris.*

valdinguer [3] [valdɛ̃ge] *vi fam* [tomber] : **il est allé ~ contre le parcmètre** he went sprawling against the parking meter ■ **envoyer ~ qqch** to send sthg flying ■ **envoyer ~ qqn** to send sb packing.

Valence [valɑ̃s] *npr* [en Espagne] Valencia.

valenciennes [valɑ̃sjɛn] *nf* (Valenciennes) lace.

valériane [valerjan] *nf* valerian.

valet [valɛ] *nm* **1.** [serviteur] : **jouer les ~s de comédie** THÉÂTRE to play servants ◐ **~ de chambre** manservant ■ **~ d'écurie** groom, stable boy ■ **~ de ferme** farm hand ■ **~ de pied** footman **2.** JEUX jack, knave ■ **~ de pique** jack *OU* knave of spades **3.** [cintre] : **~ (de nuit)** valet **4.** MENUIS clamp.

valetaille [valtaj] *nf litt & péj* flunkeys ■ **toute une ~ s'empressait autour de nous** a whole crowd of flunkeys was fussing around us.

valétudinaire [valetydinɛr] *litt* ◇ *adj* valetudinarian, valetudinary.
◇ *nmf* valetudinarian.

valeur [valœr] *nf* **1.** [prix] value, worth ■ **cette statue a-t-elle une quelconque ~?** is this statue worth anything? ■ **la ~ en a été fixée à 500 euros** its value has been put at 500 euros, it's been valued at 500 euros ■ **prendre/perdre de la ~** to increase/to decrease in value ■ **estimer qqch au-dessus/au-dessous de sa ~** to overvalue/to undervalue sthg ■ **bijoux sans ~** *OU* **qui n'ont aucune ~** worthless jewels ■ **manuscrit d'une ~ inestimable** invaluable manuscript ◐ **mettre en ~** [terre] to exploit ; [capital] to get the best return out of ; [connaissances] to put to good use ; [taille, minceur] to enhance ; [talent, qualités] to bring out, to highlight ■ **le noir est la couleur qui me met le plus en ~** black is the colour that suits me best
2. COMM, ÉCON, FIN & MATH value ■ **~ marchande/vénale** market/monetary value ■ **~ absolue** absolute value ■ **en ~ absolue** in absolute terms ■ **~ ajoutée** added value ■ **~ approchée** approximate value ■ **~ en bourse** *OU* **boursière** market value ■ **~ déclarée** declared value ■ **~ d'échange** exchange value ■ **~ d'usage** use value ■ **~ refuge** [gén] sound *OU* safe investment ; BOURSE currency-safe investment
3. [importance subjective] value ■ **attacher** *OU* **accorder une grande ~ à qqch** to prize sthg, to set great value by sthg ■ **attacher** *OU* **accorder de la ~ aux traditions** to value traditions ■ **ton opinion n'a aucune ~ pour moi** as far as I'm concerned, your opinion is worthless ■ **la ~ sentimentale d'un collier** the sentimental value of a necklace
4. [mérite] worth, merit ■ **avoir conscience de sa ~** to know one's own worth
5. *litt* [bravoure] valour, bravery ■ **la ~ n'attend pas le nombre des années** ***Corneille allus*** there is no age for courage
6. *litt* [personne de mérite] : **une ~** a great name ■ **~ sûre : une ~ sûre de la sculpture française** one of the top French sculptors
7. [validité - d'une méthode, d'une découverte] value ■ **sa déposition enlève toute ~ à la vôtre** her testimony renders yours invalid *OU* worthless
8. [équivalent] : **donnez-lui la ~ d'une cuillère à soupe de sirop** give him the equivalent of a tablespoonful of syrup.
◆ **valeurs** *nfpl* **1.** [normes morales] values ■ **~s morales/sociales/familiales** moral/social/family values
2. BOURSE : **~s (mobilières)** stocks and shares, securities ■ **~s à revenu fixe/variable** fixed/variable income securities ■ **~s disponibles** liquid *OU* tangible assets ■ **~s minières/pétrolières/stannifères** mining/oil/tin shares ■ **~s vedettes** leading shares.
◆ **de valeur** *loc adj* **1.** COMM & FIN [bague, tableau] valuable ■ **des objets de ~** valuables, items of value, valuable items ■ **de grande ~** precious, very valuable
2. [de mérite] : **personnes de ~** people of merit ■ **un collaborateur de ~** a prized colleague.

valeureusement [valœrøzmɑ̃] *adv litt* bravely, gallantly, valiantly.

valeureux, euse [valœrø, øz] *adj litt* [vaillant] brave, gallant, valiant.

validation [validasjɔ̃] *nf* [d'un billet] validation ■ [d'un document] authentication.

valide [valid] *adj* **1.** [permis, titre de transport] valid ■ **non ~** invalid **2.** [bien portant] fit, (well and) strong ■ [non blessé] able-bodied ■ **il n'avait qu'un bras ~** he had only one good arm.

validement [validmɑ̃] *adv* validly.

valider [3] [valide] *vt* [traité] to ratify ■ [document] to authenticate ■ [testament] to prove, to probate *US* ■ [billet, passeport] to validate ■ **il faut faire ~ le bulletin de Loto dans un bureau de tabac** you have to get the Loto ticket stamped in a newsagent's.

validité [validite] *nf* **1.** ADMIN & TRANSP validity ■ **durée de ~** period of validity ■ **proroger la ~ d'un visa** to extend a visa ■ **établir la ~ d'un document** to authenticate a document ■ **établir la ~ d'un testament** to prove *OU* to probate a will ◐ **date (limite) de ~** expiry date **2.** [bien-fondé - d'un argument, d'un témoignage] validity.

valise [valiz] *nf* **1.** [bagage] suitcase, bag ■ **mes ~s** my suitcases *OU* bags *OU* luggage ■ **défaire ses ~s** to unpack (one's bags) ◐ **faire ses ~s** *pr* to pack (one's bags) ■ **faire sa ~** *OU* **ses**

~s [partir] to pack one's bags and go **2.** *fam* [sous les yeux] : **avoir des ~s (sous les yeux)** to have bags under one's eyes **3.** DR : **la ~ diplomatique** the diplomatic bag *ou* US pouch ■ **expédier du courrier par la ~ diplomatique** to send mail via the diplomatic bag.

valium [valjɔm] *nm* valium.

vallée [vale] *nf* **1.** GÉOGR valley ■ **les gens de la ~** people who live in the valley ⊃ **~ glaciaire** *ou* **en U** glaciated *ou* U-shaped valley ■ **~ suspendue** hanging valley **2.** BIBLE : **cette ~ de larmes** *litt* this vale of tears.

vallon [valɔ̃] *nm* small valley.

vallonné, e [valɔne] *adj* undulating, hilly.

valoche△ [valɔʃ] *nf* [valise] case, bag ■ *fig* [sous les yeux] : **avoir des ~s (sous les yeux)** to have bags under one's eyes.

valoir [60] [valwar] ◇ *vi* **1.** [avoir tel prix] to be worth ■ **as-tu une idée de ce que peut ~ ce guéridon?** have you any idea how much this little table might be worth? ■ **une famille qui vaut plusieurs milliards de dollars** *fam* a family worth several billion dollars ‖ [coûter] to cost ■ **~ très cher** to cost a lot, to be very expensive, to be very dear ■ **ne pas ~ cher** to be cheap *ou* inexpensive ■ **ces gens-là ne valent pas cher** *fig* those people are just worthless *ou* contemptible
2. [avoir telle qualité] to be worth ■ **que vaut ton jeune élève?** how good is your young pupil? ■ **je sais ce que je vaux** I know my worth *ou* what I'm worth ■ **que vaut une vie d'artiste sans la reconnaissance du public?** what's the point of being an artist without public recognition? ■ **ne rien ~ : son idée/projet ne vaut rien** her idea/project is worthless ■ **quand je manque de sommeil, je ne vaux rien** if I haven't had enough sleep I'm useless ■ **ne pas ~ grand-chose : l'émission d'hier ne valait pas grand-chose** yesterday's programme wasn't up to much ■ **~ mieux que : elle vaut mieux que la réputation qu'on lui fait** she's much better than her reputation would suggest ■ **vous ne valez pas mieux l'un que l'autre** you're as bad as each other ■ **et il t'a quittée? tu vaux mieux que ça** and he left you? you deserve better than that
3. [origine de la valeuré] : **~ par : ma bague ne vaut que par les souvenirs qu'elle représente** my ring has only sentimental value ■ **son initiative vaut surtout par son audace** the main merit of his initiative is its boldness
4. [être valable, applicable] : **~ pour** to apply to, to hold for ■ **le règlement vaut pour tout le monde** the rules hold for everyone
5. COMM : **à ~ sur : il y a deux euros à ~ sur votre prochain achat** you'll get two euros off your next purchase ■ **verser un acompte à ~ sur une somme** to pay a deposit to be set off against a sum
6. *loc* **faire ~** [argument] to emphasize, to put forward *(sép)* ; [opinion, raisons] to put forward *(sép)* ; [droit] to assert, to enforce ; [qualité] to highlight, to bring out *(sép)* ■ **faire ~ ses droits à la retraite** to provide evidence for one's entitlement to a pension ■ **elle fait ~ sa fille** she pushes her daughter forward ■ **se faire ~** to show o.s. off to advantage ■ **faire ~ un capital** ÉCON to turn a sum of money to (good) account, to make a sum of money yield a good profit ■ **faire ~ des terres/une propriété** to derive profit from land/a property ■ *(tournure impersonnelle)* **dans ce cas, mieux vaut s'abstenir** in that case, it's better to do nothing ■ **il vaut mieux ne pas répondre** it's best *ou* better not to answer ■ **il vaudrait mieux que tu y réfléchisses** you'd do better to *ou* you should think about it ■ **ça vaut mieux : appelle le médecin, ça vaut mieux** it would be better *ou* safer if you called the doctor ■ **je vais lui dire – je crois que ça vaut mieux** I'm going to tell him – I think that would be the best thing to do ■ **ça vaut mieux ainsi/pour lui** it's better that way/for him ■ **je vais te rembourser – ça vaudrait mieux pour toi!** I'll pay you back – you'd better!
◇ *vt* **1.** [procurer] : **~ qqch à qqn** to earn sb sthg, to bring sthg to sb ■ **ses efforts lui ont valu une médaille aux jeux Olympiques** his efforts earned him a medal at the Olympic Games ■ **tous les soucis que m'a valus ce club** all the worries that club cost me ■ **voilà ce que ça m'a valu de l'aider!** that's all I got for helping her! ■ **qu'est-ce qui me vaut l'honneur/le plaisir de ta visite?** to what do I owe the honour/pleasure of your visit? ■ **l'émission d'hier soir nous a valu une avalanche de coups de téléphone** we were deluged with telephone calls after last night's programme ■ **ne rien ~ à qqn** [ne pas lui convenir] to be no good for sb, not to agree with sb, not to suit sb ■ **son exploit lui a valu d'être admiré par tous** his achievement earned him widespread admiration
2. [représenter] to be equivalent to, to be worth ■ **un essai vaut trois points** a try is worth three points ■ **chaque faute de grammaire vaut quatre points** you lose four points for each grammatical mistake
3. [mériter] to be worth ■ **le village vaut le détour/déplacement** the village is worth the detour/journey ■ **ça vaut le coup d'œil** it's worth seeing ■ **sa cuisine vaut d'être goûtée** her cooking's worth sampling ■ **l'enjeu de l'affaire vaut que l'on prenne le temps de la réflexion** it's worth taking time to reflect when you see what's at stake in the deal ⊃ **~ la peine** *ou* **le coup** *fam* to be worth it, to be worthwhile ■ **ça vaut le coup d'essayer** it's worth trying *ou* a try ■ **quand je paie 40 euros pour un spectacle, je veux que ça en vaille la peine** if I spend 40 euros on a show I like to get my money's worth ■ **j'ai gagné 3 000 euros – dis donc, ça vaut le coup!** I won 3,000 euros – well, that was certainly worth it! ■ **à ce prix-là, ça vaut le coup** at that price, you can't go wrong
4. [dans une comparaison] to be as good as, to match up (to) ■ **son idée en vaut une autre** her idea is as good as any other ■ **tu la vaux largement** you're every bit as good as her ■ **ah, rien ne vaut les confitures de grand-mère!** there's nothing like grandma's jam! ■ **ça ne vaut pas Éric, tu sais ce qu'il m'a dit?** *fam* what about Eric then? do you know what he told me?
◆ **se valoir** *vp (emploi réciproque)* to be equivalent ■ **nous nous valons au sprint** we're both equally good (as) sprinters ■ **vous vous valez bien!** you're both as bad as each other! ■ **tu vas voter Dupond ou Dufort? – tout ça se vaut!** are you going to vote Dupond or Dufort? – it's six of one and half a dozen of the other *ou* it's all the same thing!
◆ **vaille que vaille** *loc adv* somehow (or other).

valorisant, e [valɔrizɑ̃, ɑ̃t] *adj* **1.** [satisfaisant moralement] : **il fait un travail ~** his work brings him a lot of job satisfaction **2.** [donnant du prestige] : **une situation ~e** a situation which increases one's prestige.

valorisation [valɔrizasjɔ̃] *nf* **1.** ÉCON [mise en valeur] economic development ■ [valeur] enhanced value ■ **on observe une ~ des tâches manuelles** *fig* manual work is becoming more highly valued **2.** ÉCOL [des déchets] recovering.

valoriser [3] [valɔrize] *vt* **1.** ÉCON [région] to develop the economy of ■ **une nouvelle gare valorisera les terrains avoisinants** a new railway station will enhance the value of local land **2.** ÉCOL [déchets] to recover **3.** [augmenter le prestige de] : **son succès l'a valorisé aux yeux de ses amis** his success has increased his standing in the eyes of his friends ■ **cherchez un travail qui vous valorise** look for a job which will give you personal satisfaction.

valse [vals] *nf* **1.** DANSE waltz ■ **~ viennoise** Viennese waltz **2.** *fam* [succession rapide] (game of) musical chairs ■ **la ~ des ministres** ministerial musical chairs **3.** *fam* [modification] : **la ~ des prix** *ou* **étiquettes** spiralling prices.

valse-hésitation [valsezitasjɔ̃] (*pl* **valses-hésitations**) *nf* [tergiversation] shilly-shallying, dithering (about) ■ **après une interminable ~** after much shilly-shallying.

valser [3] [valse] *vi* **1.** [danser] to waltz ■ **faire ~ qqn** to waltz with sb **2.** *fam* [tomber] to career, to hurtle ■ **envoyer ~ qqch** to send sthg flying ■ **envoyer ~ qqn** to show sb the door ⊃ **faire ~ l'argent** *ou* **les billets** to throw money about *ou* around **3.** *fam* **faire ~ le personnel** [déplacer, congédier] to play musical chairs with the staff *fig*.

valseur, euse [valsœr, øz] *nm, f* waltzer.
◆ **valseuses**▲ *nfpl* balls△.
◆ **valseur**△ *nm* bum UK, fanny US.

valu, e [valy] *pp* ▷ **valoir**.

valve [valv] *nf* **1.** ANAT, BOT & ZOOL valve **2.** TECHNOL [clapet] valve ■ [soupape à clapet] valve **3.** ÉLECTRON valve.

valvule [valvyl] *nf* **1.** ANAT valve ■ **~ mitrale** mitral valve **2.** BOT valve, valvule.

vamp [vɑ̃p] *nf* vamp ■ **elle se prend pour une ~** she thinks she's some kind of vamp.

vamper [3] [vɑ̃pe] *vt fam* to vamp.

vampire [vɑ̃pir] *nm* **1.** [mort] vampire **2.** *litt & péj* [parasite] vampire, vulture, bloodsucker **3.** ZOOL vampire bat.

vampiriser [3] [vɑ̃pirize] *vt* **1.** [suj: vampire] to suck the blood of **2.** *fam* [dominer] to have under one's sway, to subjugate ▪ **ayant vampirisé la presse écrite, il s'attaque maintenant à la télévision** having subjugated the print media, he's now preparing for an assault on television.

vampirisme [vɑ̃pirism] *nm* **1.** [croyance, pratique] vampirism **2.** *litt* [rapacité] vampirism.

van [vɑ̃] *nm* **1.** [corbeille] winnowing basket, fan **2.** [véhicule] horse box *UK ou* trailer *US*.

Vancouver [vɑ̃kuvɛr] *npr* Vancouver.

vandale [vɑ̃dal] *nm* **1.** [voyou] vandal ▪ **et mon parquet, bande de ~s!** look what you've done to my floor, you vandals! **2.** HIST Vandal.

vandaliser [3] [vɑ̃dalize] *vt* to vandalize ▪ **~ une cabine téléphonique** to vandalize *ou* to wreck a telephone booth.

vandalisme [vɑ̃dalism] *nm* vandalism, hooliganism ▪ **commettre des actes de ~** to commit acts of vandalism.

vanille [vanij] *nf* vanilla.
◆ **à la vanille** *loc adj* vanilla *(modif)*, vanilla-flavoured.

vanillé, e [vanije] *adj* vanilla-flavoured.

vanillier [vanije] *nm* vanilla plant.

vanilline [vanilin] *nf* vanillin.

vanité [vanite] *nf* **1.** [orgueil] vanity, pride, conceit ▪ **tirer ~ de qqch** to pride o.s. on sthg, to take pride in sthg ▪ **sans ~, je crois pouvoir faire mieux** with all due modesty *ou* without wishing to boast, I think I can do better **2.** [futilité] pointlessness, futility **3.** ART vanitas.

vaniteux, euse [vanitø, øz] ◇ *adj* [orgueilleux] vain, conceited, self-important.
◇ *nm, f* conceited man (*f* woman).

vanity-case [vanitikɛz] (*pl* **vanity-cases**) *nm* vanity case.

vanne [van] *nf* **1.** [d'une écluse] sluicegate ▪ [d'un moulin] hatch ▪ **ouvrir les ~s** *pr* to open the sluicegates ; *fig* to open the floodgates **2.** [robinet] stopcock **3.** *fam* [plaisanterie] dig, jibe ▪ **lancer** *ou* **envoyer une ~ à qqn** to have a dig at sb.

vanné, e [vane] *adj fam* worn out, beat ▪ **je suis ~!** I've had it!, I'm beat!

vanneau, x [vano] *nm* green plover, peewit.

vanner [3] [vane] *vt* **1.** AGRIC to winnow **2.** *fam* [épuiser] to wear out *(sép)*.

vannerie [vanri] *nf* [tressage] basketwork, basketry ▪ **faire de la ~** [paniers] to weave baskets.
◆ **en vannerie** *loc adj* wicker, wickerwork *(modif)*.

vanneur, euse [vanœr, øz] *nm, f* winnower.

vannier [vanje] *nm* basket maker.

vantail, aux [vɑ̃taj, o] *nm* [de porte] leaf ▪ [de fenêtre] casement ▪ **porte à double ~** *ou* **à vantaux** stable *UK ou* Dutch *US* door.

vantard, e [vɑ̃tar, ard] ◇ *adj* boastful, boasting, bragging.
◇ *nm, f* bragger, braggart.

vantardise [vɑ̃tardiz] *nf* **1.** [glorification de soi] boastfulness, bragging **2.** [remarque] boast.

vanter [3] [vɑ̃te] *vt* [louer, exalter] to praise ▪ *sout* to extol ▪ **~ les mérites de qqch** to sing the praises of sthg ▪ **~ les mérites de qqn** to sing sb's praises ➊ **~ sa marchandise** *hum* to boast.
◆ **se vanter** *vpi* to boast, to brag ▪ **se ~ de : il s'est vanté de gagner la course** he boasted that he would win the race ▪ **il s'est vanté d'avoir gagné la course** he bragged that he had won the race ▪ **elle l'a fait renvoyer mais elle ne s'en vante pas** she had him fired, but she keeps quiet about it ▪ **il n'y a pas de quoi se ~** this is nothing to be proud of *ou* to boast about ▪ **sans (vouloir) me ~, j'avais déjà compris** I don't wish to boast, but I'd got the idea already.

Vanuatu [vanwatu] *npr* Vanuatu.

va-nu-pieds [vanypje] *nmf péj* [clochard] tramp, beggar.

vapes [vap] *nfpl fam* **être dans les ~** [évanoui] to be out for the count ; [rêveur] to be miles away ▪ **je suis encore un peu dans les ~** I'm still in a daze ▪ **elle est constamment dans les ~** her head is always in the clouds ▪ **tomber dans les ~** [s'évanouir] to pass out, to faint.

vapeur [vapœr] ◇ *nf* **1.** [gén] steam ▪ **~ (d'eau)** steam, (water) vapour ▪ **~ atmosphérique** atmospheric vapour **2.** CHIM & PHYS vapour ▪ **~ sèche/saturante** dry/saturated vapour ▪ **~s de pétrole** petrol *UK ou* gas *US* fumes **3.** *litt* [brouillard] haze, vapour *litt*.
◇ *nm* NAUT steamship, steamer.
◆ **vapeurs** *nfpl vieilli* **avoir des** *ou* **ses ~s** to have a fit of the vapours.
◆ **à la vapeur** *loc adv & adj* : **ça marche à la ~** it's steam-driven ▪ **cuit à la ~** steam-cooked ▪ **cuire des légumes à la ~** to steam vegetables ▪ **repassage à la ~** steam ironing.
◆ **à toute vapeur** *loc adv fam* **aller à toute ~** [navire] to sail full steam ahead ; [train] to go full steam ahead *ou* at full speed ; *fig* to go as fast as one can.
◆ **à vapeur** *loc adj* steam *(modif)*, steam-driven ▪ **machine à ~** steam engine ▪ **bateau à ~** steamboat, steamer ▪ **train à ~** steam train ▪ **marine à ~** steamers, steamships.

vapocuiseur [vapokɥizœr] *nm* pressure cooker.

vaporeux, euse [vapɔrø, øz] *adj* **1.** [voilé - lumière, paysage] hazy, misty **2.** [léger - tissu] filmy, diaphanous ; [- robe] flimsy.

vaporisateur [vapɔrizatœr] *nm* **1.** [pulvérisateur] spray ▪ [atomiseur] spray, atomizer ▪ **parfum en ~** spray perfume **2.** TECHNOL [échangeur] vaporizer.

vaporisation [vapɔrizasjɔ̃] *nf* **1.** [pulvérisation] spraying **2.** TECHNOL [volatilisation] vaporization.

vaporiser [3] [vapɔrize] *vt* **1.** [pulvériser] to spray ▪ **'ne pas ~ vers une flamme'** 'do not spray onto a naked flame' **2.** TECHNOL [volatiliser] to vaporize.
◆ **se vaporiser** *vpi* to vaporize, to turn to vapour.

vaquer [3] [vake] *vi* ADMIN [être en vacances] to be on vacation.
◆ **vaquer à** *v+prép sout* to attend to, to see to ▪ **~ à ses occupations** to attend to *ou* to go about one's business ▪ **~ aux tâches ménagères** to see to *ou* to attend to the household chores.

varappe [varap] *nf* [activités] rock climbing ▪ [course] rock climb ▪ **faire de la ~** to go rock-climbing.

varapper [3] [varape] *vi* to rock-climb, to go rock-climbing.

varappeur, euse [varapœr, øz] *nm, f* rock climber.

varech [varɛk] *nm* kelp, varec.

vareuse [varøz] *nf* **1.** NAUT fisherman's smock **2.** COUT loose-fitting jacket.

variable [varjabl] ◇ *adj* **1.** [changeant - temps] unsettled ; [- taux] variable ▪ **être d'humeur ~** to be moody **2.** GRAMM : **mot ~** inflected *ou* inflectional word ▪ **mot ~ en genre/nombre** word inflected in gender/number **3.** [varié - composition, forme] varied, diverse **4.** ASTRON [étoile] variable.
◇ *nf* CHIM, ÉCON, MATH & PHYS variable ▪ **~ aléatoire/discrète/continue** random/discrete/continuous variable.
◇ *nm* MÉTÉOR : **le baromètre est au "~"** the barometer is at *ou* reads "change".

variance [varjɑ̃s] *nf* variance ▪ **~ de l'échantillon** sample variance.

variante [varjɑ̃t] *nf* **1.** [gén - LING] variant ▪ **la 305 est une ~ du modèle précédent** the 305 is a variation on the previous model **2.** [aux échecs] opening move.

variateur [varjatœr] *nm* **1.** MÉCAN : **~ de vitesse** speed variator **2.** ÉLECTR : **~ (de lumière)** dimmer (switch).

variation [varjasjɔ̃] *nf* **1.** [fluctuation] variation, change ■ ~ **d'intensité/de poids** variation in intensity/weight ■ **pour vos plantes, attention aux ~s de température** your plants do not like changes in temperature ➊ **en fonction des ~s saisonnières** ÉCON on a seasonally adjusted basis **2.** MUS variation ■ **~ sur un thème de Paganini** variation on a theme by Paganini **3.** ASTRON variation **4.** BIOL variation.
◆ **variations** *nfpl* [modifications] changes, modifications ■ **subir des ~s** to undergo change *ou* changes.

varice [varis] *nf* varicose vein, varix *spéc* ■ **avoir des ~s** to have varicose veins.

varicelle [varisɛl] *nf* chickenpox, varicella *spéc.*

varié, e [varje] *adj* **1.** [non uniforme - style, répertoire] varied ■ **une gamme ~e de papiers peints** a wide range of wallpapers **2.** *(au pl)* [différents] various, diverse, miscellaneous ■ **objets divers et ~s** various *ou* miscellaneous objects ■ **hors-d'œuvre ~s** CULIN selection of hors d'oeuvres **3.** MUS : **thème ~** theme and variations.

varier [9] [varje] ◇ *vt* [diversifier - cursus, menu, occupations] to vary, to diversify ■ **pour ~ les plaisirs** just for a change ➊ **~ le menu** *pr* to vary the (basic) menu ; *fig* to ring the changes.
◇ *vi* **1.** [changer - temps, poids, humeur] to vary, to change ■ **les produits varient en qualité** products vary in quality ■ **les prix varient de 50 à 150 euros** prices vary *ou* range from 50 to 150 euros **2.** MATH : **faire ~ une fonction** to vary a function **3.** [diverger] to differ ■ **les médecins varient dans le choix du traitement** doctors differ in *ou* are at variance on the choice of the treatment.

variété [varjete] *nf* **1.** [diversité] variety, diversity ■ **nos châles existent dans une ~ de coloris** our shawls come in a variety *ou* a wide range of colours **2.** [sorte, genre] variety, kind, sort, type ■ **toutes les ~s possibles et imaginables d'escroquerie** every conceivable type of swindle **3.** BOT variety ■ [de maïs, de blé] (crop) strain ➊ **les ~s cultivées** cultivars **4.** MUS : **la ~** [industrie] the commercial music business ; [genre] commercial music.
◆ **variétés** *nfpl* LITTÉR miscellanies ■ MUS easy listening, light music.
◆ **de variétés** *loc adj* [spectacle, émission] variety ■ [musique] light ■ **disque de ~s** easy listening *ou* light music record.

variole [varjɔl] *nf* smallpox, variola *spéc.*

variqueux, euse [varikø, øz] *adj* varicose.

varois, e [varwa, az] *adj* from the Var.

Varsovie [varsɔvi] *npr* Warsaw ■ **le pacte de ~** the Warsaw Pact.

vas *v* ▷ **aller.**

vasculaire [vaskylɛr] *adj* ANAT & BOT vascular.

vascularisation [vaskylarizasjɔ̃] *nf* **1.** MÉD vascularization **2.** ANAT vascularity.

vascularisé, e [vaskylarize] *adj* vascular.

vase [vaz] ◇ *nf* [boue] mud, silt, sludge ■ **banc de ~** mudbank.
◇ *nm* **1.** [récipient décoratif] vase **2.** CHIM & PHYS vessel ■ **~s communicants** connecting vessels ■ **~ d'expansion** surge tank **3.** [objet] : **~ de nuit** chamber pot.
◆ **en vase clos** *loc adv* : **nous vivions en ~ clos** we led an isolated existence ■ **la recherche ne peut se faire en ~ clos** research cannot be carried out in isolation *ou* in a vacuum.

vasectomie [vazɛktɔmi] *nf* vasectomy.

vaseline [vazlin] *nf* petroleum jelly, Vaseline®.

vaseux, euse [vazø, øz] *adj* **1.** [boueux] muddy, silty, sludgy **2.** *fam* [confus - idée, plan] hazy, woolly **3.** *fam* [malade] : **se sentir tout ~** [affaibli] to feel under the weather, to feel off colour ; [étourdi] to feel woozy **4.** *fam* [médiocre] pathetic ■ **ses blagues vaseuses** his pathetic jokes.

vasistas [vazistas] *nm* fanlight, transom *US.*

vasoconstricteur, trice [vazɔkɔ̃striktœr, tris] *adj* vasoconstrictor.

vasodilatateur, trice [vazɔdilatatœr, tris] *adj* vasodilator.

vasodilatation [vazɔdilatasjɔ̃] *nf* vasodilation.

vasomoteur, trice [vazɔmɔtœr, tris] *adj* vasomotor.

vasouiller [3] [vazuje] *vi fam* to flounder ■ **et votre projet? – ça vasouille** what about your project? – we're struggling.

vasque [vask] *nf* **1.** [bassin] basin (of fountain) **2.** [coupe] bowl.

vassal, e, aux [vasal, o] *adj* vassal *(modif).*
◆ **vassal, aux** *nm* vassal.

vaste [vast] *adj* **1.** [immense - vêtement] enormous, huge ; [- domaine, sujet] vast, far-reaching ; [- palais, gouffre] vast, huge, immense ■ **de par le ~ monde** *sout* the world over **2.** [de grande ampleur] huge.

Vatican [vatikɑ̃] *npr m* : **le ~** the Vatican ■ **l'État de la cité du ~** Vatican City ■ **au ~** in Vatican City.

vaticiner [3] [vatisine] *vi litt* to vaticinate.

va-tout [vatu] *nm inv* : **jouer son ~** to risk *ou* to stake one's all.

vauclusien, enne [voklyzjɛ̃, ɛn] *adj* from the Vaucluse.

vaudeville [vodvil] *nm* vaudeville, light comedy.

vaudevillesque [vodvilɛsk] *adj* **1.** THÉÂTRE vaudeville *(modif)* **2.** [grotesque] farcical, ludicrous, preposterous.

vaudois, e [vodwa, az] *adj* **1.** GÉOGR from the canton of Vaud **2.** HIST & RELIG Waldensian.
◆ **Vaudois, e** *nm, f* **1.** GÉOGR Vaudois **2.** HIST & RELIG Waldensian.

vaudou, e [vodu] *adj* voodoo.
◆ **vaudou** *nm* voodoo, voodooism.

vaudra *etc v* ▷ **valoir.**

vau-l'eau [volo] ◆ **à vau-l'eau** *loc adv* : **aller à ~** [barque] to go with the stream *ou* current ; [affaire, projet] to be going downhill *ou* to the dogs.

vaurien, enne [vorjɛ̃, ɛn] *nm, f* **1.** [voyou] good-for-nothing, scoundrel, rogue **2.** [enfant] : **petit ~!** you little devil!

vaut *etc v* ▷ **valoir.**

vautour [votur] *nm* **1.** ORNITH vulture **2.** [personne cupide] vulture, shark.

vautré, e [votre] *pp* : **il était ~ sur son lit** he was sprawling on his bed.

vautrer [3] [votre] ◆ **se vautrer** *vpi* **1.** [se rouler] to wallow ■ **se ~ par terre** to grovel **2.** [s'affaler] to sprawl, to be sprawled ■ **se ~ dans un fauteuil** to loll in an armchair.

vaux *etc v* ▷ **valoir.**

va-vite [vavit] ◆ **à la va-vite** *loc adv* in a rush *ou* hurry ■ **travail fait à la ~** slapdash work.

vd = **vend,** = **vendre.**

VDQS (*abr de* **vin délimité de qualité supérieure**) *label indicating quality of wine.*

vds *nm* = **vends,** = **vendre.**

veau, x [vo] *nm* **1.** ZOOL calf ■ **le ~ d'or** BIBLE the golden calf ■ **adorer le ~ d'or** *fig* to worship Mammon **2.** CULIN veal ■ **escalope/côtelette de ~** veal escalope/cutlet **3.** [cuir] calf, calfskin **4.** *fam péj* [personne] lump, clot *UK* ■ [voiture] banger *UK*, old crate *US* ■ **cette voiture est un vrai ~** this car is a real heap.
◆ **en veau** *loc adj* calf, calfskin *(modif).*

vécés [vese] *nmpl fam* [toilettes] : **les ~** the loo *UK*, the john *US.*

vecteur [vɛktœr] *nm* **1.** MATH vector **2.** MÉD carrier, vector **3.** MIL carrier.

vectoriel, elle [vɛktɔrjɛl] *adj* vector *(modif)*, vectorial ■ **fonction ~le** vector function.

vécu, e [veky] ◇ *pp* ▷ **vivre.**
◇ *adj* **1.** [réel] real, real-life, true ■ **c'est une histoire ~e** it's a true story **2.** PHILOS : **temps ~, durée ~e** time as experienced.

◆ **vécu** *nm* : **le ~ de qqn** sb's (real-life) experiences.

vedettariat [vədɛtarja] *nm* stardom ▪ **accéder au ~** to achieve stardom *ou* star-status.

vedette [vədɛt] *nf* **1.** [artiste] star ▪ **~ du petit écran/du cinéma** TV/film star ◐ **~ américaine** *performer who warms up the audience for the main star* **2.** [célébrité] star, celebrity ▪ **une ~ de la politique/du rugby** a big name in politics/rugby ◐ **présentateur-~** star presenter ▪ **produit ~** leading product **3.** [première place] : **avoir** *ou* **tenir la ~** THÉÂTRE to top the bill, to have star billing ; *fig* to be in the limelight ▪ **partager la ~ avec qqn** THÉÂTRE to share star billing with sb ; *fig* to share the limelight with sb ▪ **ravir** *ou* **souffler la ~ à qqn** to upstage sb **4.** NAUT launch ▪ **~ de la douane** customs patrol boat **5.** MIL sentinel **6.** [dans un texte] heading ▪ [dans un dictionnaire] headword.
◆ **en vedette** *loc adv* : **mettre qqn/qqch en ~** to put the spotlight on sb/sthg.

vedettisation [vədɛtizasjɔ̃] *nf* : **la ~ de qqn** turning sb into a celebrity.

végétal, e, aux [veʒetal, o] *adj* [fibre] plant ▪ [huile] vegetable ▪ **règne ~** plant kingdom.
◆ **végétal, aux** *nm* plant, vegetable.

végétalien, enne [veʒetaljɛ̃, ɛn] *adj* & *nm, f* vegan.

végétalisme [veʒetalism] *nm* veganism.

végétarien, enne [veʒetarjɛ̃, ɛn] *adj* & *nm, f* vegetarian.

végétarisme [veʒetarism] *nm* vegetarianism.

végétatif, ive [veʒetatif, iv] *adj* **1.** ANAT, BOT & MÉD vegetative **2.** [inactif] : **mener une vie végétative** to sit around all day.

végétation [veʒetasjɔ̃] *nf* BOT vegetation ▪ **des arbres en pleine ~** trees in full growth.
◆ **végétations** *nfpl* MÉD : **~s (adénoïdes)** adenoids.

végéter [18] [veʒete] *vi* to vegetate, to stagnate ▪ **le marché végète** trading is slow.

véhémence [veemɑ̃s] *nf* vehemence.
◆ **avec véhémence** *loc adv* vehemently, passionately.

véhément, e [veemɑ̃, ɑ̃t] *adj* [plaidoyer] vehement, passionate ▪ [dénégation] vehement, vociferous.

véhiculaire [veikylɛr] *adj* ▭▷ **langue**.

véhicule [veikyl] *nm* **1.** TRANSP vehicle ▪ **~ automobile/hippomobile** motor/horse-drawn vehicle ▪ **~ de tourisme** private car ▪ **~ utilitaire** commercial vehicle ▪ **~ à deux roues** two-wheeler ▪ **~ spatial** spacecraft, spaceship ▪ **'~ lent'** 'slow vehicle' **2.** [moyen de transmission] vehicle ▪ **le ~ de** a vehicle for **3.** ART & PHARM vehicle **4.** RELIG : **petit ~** Hinayana ▪ **grand ~** Mahayana.

véhiculer [3] [veikyle] *vt* **1.** TRANSP to convey, to transport **2.** [transmettre - idée, message] to convey, to serve as *ou* to be a vehicle for.

veille [vɛj] *nf* **1.** [jour d'avant] : **la ~, je lui avais dit...** the day before, I'd said to him... ▪ **la ~ au soir** the night before ▪ **la ~ de** the eve of, the day before ▪ **la ~ de Noël** Christmas Eve ▪ **la ~ du jour de l'an** New Year's Eve ▪ **la ~ de son départ/sa mort** the day before he left/died ▪ **à la ~ de : à la ~ des présidentielles/de la visite du pape** on the eve of the presidential elections/of the Pope's visit ▪ **on était à la ~ d'entrer en guerre** we were on the brink of war *ou* on the point of declaring war **2.** [éveil] : **état de ~** waking state ▪ **être entre la ~ et le sommeil** between waking and sleeping **3.** [garde] vigil ▪ MIL night watch ▪ **homme de ~** NAUT lookout ▪ **~ technologique** monitoring of technological development.
◆ **en veille** ◇ *loc adj* [ordinateur] in sleep mode.
◇ *loc adv* : **mettre en ~** [ordinateur] to put in sleep mode.

veillée [veje] *nf* **1.** [soir] evening **2.** [réunion] evening gathering ▪ **faire une ~ autour d'un feu** to spend the evening round a fire **3.** [en colonie de vacances] evening activities **4.** [garde] vigil, watch ▪ **~ d'armes** HIST knightly vigil ▪ **c'est notre ~ d'armes avant le concours** *fig* it's the last night before our exam.

veiller [4] [veje] ◇ *vt* [un malade] to watch over, to sit up with ▪ [un mort] to keep watch *ou* vigil over.
◇ *vi* **1.** [rester éveillé] to sit *ou* to stay up *(insép)* ▪ **ne veille pas trop tard** don't stay up too late **2.** [être de garde] to keep watch, to be on watch **3.** [être sur ses gardes] to be watchful *ou* vigilant **4.** [entre amis] to spend the evening in company.
◆ **veiller sur** *v+prép* [surveiller - enfant] to watch (over), to look after, to take care of ; [- santé] to watch, to take care of.
◆ **veiller à** *v+prép* to see to ▪ **~ aux intérêts du pays** to attend to *ou* to see to *ou* to look after the interests of the country ▪ **je veillais au bon déroulement des opérations** I saw to it that everything was running smoothly ▪ **veillez à ce qu'il ne tombe pas** be careful *ou* watch that he doesn't fall ▪ **je veillerai à ce qu'elle arrive à l'heure** I'll see (to it) *ou* make sure that she gets there on time ▪ **veillez à ne pas refaire la même faute** take care *ou* be careful not to make the same mistake again ◐ **~ au grain** to keep one's weather eye open.

veilleur [vejœr] *nm* **1.** MIL [soldat] lookout **2.** [gardien] : **~ de nuit** night watchman.

veilleuse [vejøz] *nf* [lampe] night-light ▪ [flamme] pilot light ▪ **mettre en ~** [lumière] to dim, to turn down low ▪ *fam fig* [projet] to put off temporarily, to put on the back burner, to shelve ▪ **mets-la en ~!**^△^ just pipe down, will you!
◆ **veilleuses** *nfpl* AUTO sidelights.

veinard, e [vɛnar, ard] *fam* ◇ *adj* [chanceux] lucky, jammy *UK*.
◇ *nm, f* lucky devil *ou* so-and-so ▪ **sacré ~, va!** you lucky devil!

veine [vɛn] *nf* **1.** ANAT vein ▪ **s'ouvrir les ~s** to slash one's wrists ◐ **~ cave** vena cava **2.** [d'un minerai] vein, lode ▪ [du bois] grain ▪ [d'une feuille] vein **3.** [inspiration] vein, inspiration ▪ **les deux récits sont de la même ~** the two stories are in the same vein **4.** *fam* [chance] luck ▪ **avoir de la ~** to be lucky ▪ **quel coup de ~!** what a stroke of luck!, what a fluke! ▪ **pas de ~!** hard *ou* tough luck! ▪ **c'est bien ma ~!** *iron* just my luck! ◐ **avoir une ~ de cocu**^△^ *ou* **de pendu** to have the luck of the devil **5.** *loc* **être en ~ de générosité** to be in a generous mood ▪ **je suis en ~ d'inspiration ce matin** I'm feeling inspired this morning.

veiné, e [vene] *adj* [bras, main] veiny ▪ [bois] grained ▪ [feuille, marbre] veined ▪ **~ de rose** pink-veined.

veiner [4] [vene] *vt* to vein.

veineux, euse [venø, øz] *adj* **1.** ANAT venous **2.** [strié - bois] grainy.

veinule [venyl] *nf* venule, veinlet.

veinure [venyr] *nf* veining ▪ **le bois présente des ~s** the wood is veined.

vélaire [velɛr] *adj* & *nf* velar.

velche [vɛlʃ] *Suisse* ◇ *adj* French-speaking Swiss.
◇ *nmf* French-speaking Swiss *(person)*.

Velcro® [vɛlkro] *nm* Velcro®.

vêler [4] [vele] *vi* to calve.

vélin [velɛ̃] *nm* vellum, ▭▷ **papier**.

véliplanchiste [veliplɑ̃ʃist] *nmf* windsurfer.

velléitaire [veleitɛr] ◇ *adj* indecisive.
◇ *nmf* : **c'est une ~** she has ideas but never carries them through.

velléité [veleite] *nf* vague desire, stray impulse ▪ **il lui vient des ~s de repeindre la cuisine** he sometimes gets the urge to redecorate the kitchen (but never gets round to it) ▪ **des ~s littéraires** a vague desire to write.

vélo [velo] *nm* **1.** [bicyclette] bike, bicycle ▪ **faire du ~, monter à ~** to ride a bike ▪ **aller à ~** to go by bike, to cycle ▪ **on a fait un tour à ~** we went for a ride (on our bikes) ◐ **~ d'appartement** exercise bike ▪ **~ de course** racing bike ▪ **~ tout terrain** mountain bike **2.** LOISIRS & SPORT : **le ~** cycling.

véloce [velɔs] *adj litt* [rapide] swift, fleet *litt* ▪ [agile] nimble, deft.

vélocité [velɔsite] *nf* **1.** *litt* [rapidité] velocity, speed, swiftness ▪ **exercice de ~** MUS finger exercise **2.** PHYS velocity.

vélocross [velɔkrɔs] *nm* cyclo-cross ▪ **faire du ~** to go cross-country cycling.

vélodrome [velɔdrom] *nm* velodrome.

vélomoteur [velɔmɔtœr] *nm* lightweight motorcycle, moped *UK*.

véloski [velɔski] *nm* skibob.

velours [vəlur] *nm* TEXT velvet ▪ **~ côtelé, ~ à côtes** corduroy ▪ **pantalons en ~ côtelé** *ou* **~ à côtes** corduroy trousers, cords.

velouté, e [vəlute] *adj* **1.** [doux - peau] velvet *(modif)*, silky **2.** TEXT [tissu] raised-nap *(modif)* ▪ [papier peint] flocked.
◆ **velouté** *nm* **1.** CULIN [potage] cream soup ▪ [sauce] velouté (sauce) ▪ **~ de poulet** cream of chicken (soup) **2.** [douceur - de la peau] velvetiness, silkiness.

velouter [3] [vəlute] *vt* **1.** TEXT to raise, to nap **2.** [papier peint] to flock.
◆ **se velouter** *vpi* [voix] to soften.

velouteux, euse [vəlutø, øz] *adj* velvety, soft, silky.

Velpeau [vɛlpo] *npr* ▷ **bande.**

velu, e [vəly] *adj* **1.** [homme, poitrine] hairy **2.** BOT hairy, downy, villous *spéc* **3.** TEXT raised-nap.

vélum [velɔm] *nm* **1.** [protection] awning **2.** ANTIQ velarium **3.** ZOOL velum.

Vélux® [velyks] *nm* roof light.

venaison [vənɛzɔ̃] *nf* venison.

vénal, e, aux [venal, o] *adj* **1.** [corrompu] venal, corrupt **2.** [intéressé] venal, mercenary.

vénalité [venalite] *nf* venality.

venant [vənɑ̃] *nm* : **à tout ~, à tous ~s** [au premier venu] to all and sundry ▪ **à tout ~** [à tout propos] constantly.

vendable [vɑ̃dabl] *adj* saleable, marketable ▪ **ma voiture n'est pas ~** my car has no market value.

vendange [vɑ̃dɑ̃ʒ] *nf* **1.** [cueillette] grape-picking, grape-harvesting, grape-harvest ▪ **faire la ~** *ou* **les ~s** [vigneron] to harvest the grapes ; [journalier] to go grape-picking **2.** [quantité récoltée] grape-harvest, grape-yield ▪ [qualité récoltée] vintage.
◆ **vendanges** *nfpl* [saison] grape-harvesting time.

vendanger [17] [vɑ̃dɑ̃ʒe] ◇ *vt* to harvest, to pick.
◇ *vi* to harvest grapes.

vendangeur, euse [vɑ̃dɑ̃ʒœr, øz] *nm, f* grape-picker.
◆ **vendangeur** *nm* harvest mite, chigger.
◆ **vendangeuse** *nf* **1.** [machine] grape-picker **2.** BOT aster.

vendéen, enne [vɑ̃deɛ̃, ɛn] *adj* Vendean.

vendémiaire [vɑ̃demjɛr] *nm 1st month in the French Revolutionary calendar (from Sept 22nd/23rd/24th to Oct 21st/22nd/23rd).*

vendetta [vɑ̃deta] *nf* vendetta.

vendeur, euse [vɑ̃dœr, øz] ◇ *adj* selling ▪ **si ma maison vous intéresse, je suis vendeuse** if you're interested in my house, I'm willing to sell ▶ **commissionnaire ~** selling agent.
◇ *nm, f* **1.** [dans un magasin] salesperson, shop assistant *UK*, (sales) clerk *US* ▪ **'recherche ~s'** 'sales staff wanted' **2.** [dans une entreprise] (sales) representative ▪ **il est bon ~** he's a good salesman **3.** [marchand] seller ▪ **~ de journaux** news *ou* newspaper man ▪ **~ de chaussures** shoe seller.
◆ **vendeur** *nm* DR vendor, seller.

vendre [73] [vɑ̃dr] *vt* **1.** [céder - propriété, brevet, marchandise] to sell ▪ **il vend ses melons (à) 2 euros** he sells his melons at *ou* for 2 euros each ▪ **~ qqch à la pièce/à la douzaine/au poids** to sell sthg by unit/by the dozen/by weight ▪ **~ (qqch) au détail** to retail (sthg) ▪ **~ (qqch) en gros** to sell (sthg) wholesale ▪ **~ qqch au prix fort** to price sthg high ▪ **~ qqch à perte** to sell sthg at a loss ▪ **~ qqch aux enchères** [gén] to auction sthg ; [pour s'en débarrasser] to auction sthg off ▪ **~ qqch à qqn** to sell sb sthg, to sell sthg to sb ▪ **elle m'a vendu sa montre (pour) 10 euros** she sold me her watch for 10 euros ▪ **tu me la vendrais combien?** how much would you sell it (to me) for? ▪ **'à ~'** 'for sale' ▪ *(en usage absolu)* **ils vendent cher/ne vendent pas cher chez Zapp** Zapp's is expensive/cheap ▶ **~ sa salade** *fam* to sell one's line *ou* o.s. ▪ **il vendrait père et mère** he'd sell his own grandmother ▪ **il ne faut jamais ~ la peau de l'ours avant de l'avoir tué** *prov* don't count your chickens before they are hatched *prov* **2.** [commercialiser] to sell ▪ **~ ses charmes** *euphém* to sell one's body ▪ *(en usage absolu)* **ce qui les intéresse, c'est de ~** they're interested in selling *ou* sales ▪ **nous vendons beaucoup à l'étranger** we sell a lot abroad, we get a lot of sales abroad ▪ **la publicité fait ~** advertising sells
3. [trahir - secret] to sell ; [- associé, confident] to sell down the river ▪ **~ son âme au diable** to sell one's soul to the devil ▶ **~ la mèche** [exprès] to give the game *ou* show away ; [par accident] to let the cat out of the bag.
◆ **se vendre** ◇ *vp (emploi passif)* to sell ▪ **ça se vend bien/mal actuellement** it is/isn't selling well at the moment ▶ **se ~ comme des petits pains** to sell *ou* to go like hot cakes.
◇ *vp (emploi réfléchi)* **1.** [se mettre en valeur] to sell o.s. **2.** [traître] to sell o.s. ▪ **se ~ à l'adversaire** to sell o.s. to *ou* to sell out to the opposite side.

vendredi [vɑ̃drədi] *nm* Friday ▪ **le ~ saint** Good Friday, *voir aussi* **mardi.**

Vendredi [vɑ̃drədi] *npr* [dans "Robinson Crusoé"] Man Friday.

vendu, e [vɑ̃dy] ◇ *pp* ▷ **vendre.**
◇ *adj* [vénal] corrupt.
◇ *nm, f péj* turncoat, traitor.

vénéneux, euse [venenø, øz] *adj* **1.** [toxique] poisonous, toxic **2.** *litt* [pernicieux] : **elle nourrissait des pensées vénéneuses** malignant thoughts were going through her mind.

vénérable [venerabl] *adj* venerable ▪ **d'un âge ~** ancient *hum.*

vénération [venerasjɔ̃] *nf* **1.** RELIG reverence **2.** [admiration] veneration, reverence, respect ▪ **avoir de la ~ pour qqn** to revere sb.

vénérer [18] [venere] *vt* **1.** RELIG to worship, to revere **2.** [admirer] to revere, to worship, to venerate.

vénerie [vɛnri] *nf* hunting ▪ **la grande ~** *hunting with hounds* ▪ **la petite ~** *hunting with small dogs.*

vénérien, enne [venerjɛ̃, ɛn] *adj* venereal.

vénérologie [venerɔlɔʒi] *nf* venereology.

vénérologue [venerɔlɔg] *nmf* venereologist.

veneur [vənœr] *nm* **1.** [chasseur] hunter **2.** [maître des chiens] master of hounds **3.** HIST : **le Grand ~** ≃ the Master of the Royal Hunt.

Venezuela [venezɥela] *npr m* : **le ~** Venezuela ▪ **au ~** in Venezuela.

vénézuélien, enne [venezɥeljɛ̃, ɛn] *adj* Venezuelan.
◆ **Vénézuélien, enne** *nm, f* Venezuelan.

vengeance [vɑ̃ʒɑ̃s] *nf* revenge, vengeance ▪ **crier** *ou* **demander** *ou* **réclamer ~** to cry out for revenge ▪ **tirer ~ d'une injustice** to avenge an injustice ▪ **il a menti par ~** he lied for the sake of revenge ▪ **soif** *ou* **désir de ~** revengefulness, vengefulness ▪ **avoir sa ~** to get one's own back, to have one's revenge ▶ **c'est la ~ divine** *ou* **du ciel** *hum* it's divine retribution ▪ **la ~ est un plat qui se mange froid** *prov* vengeance is a meal best eaten cold *prov.*

venger [17] [vɑ̃ʒe] *vt* **1.** [réparer] to avenge **2.** [dédommager] : **~ qqn de qqch** to avenge sb for sthg.
◆ **se venger** *vp (emploi réfléchi)* **1.** [tirer réparation] to revenge *ou* to avenge o.s., to take vengeance ▪ **je me vengerai!** I'll get my own back! ▪ **se ~ de qqn/qqch** to take one's revenge on sb/for sthg **2.** [calmer sa colère] : **ne te venge pas sur moi** don't take it out on me.

vengeur, eresse [vɑ̃ʒœr, vɑ̃ʒrɛs] ◇ *adj* avenging, revengeful, vengeful ■ **dit-elle d'un ton ~** she said, vindictively. ◇ *nm, f* avenger.

véniel, elle [venjɛl] *adj* **1.** [excusable] minor, slight **2.** RELIG venial.

venimeux, euse [vənimø, øz] *adj* **1.** [toxique] venomous, poisonous **2.** [méchant] venomous, malevolent ■ **des commentaires ~** barbs, barbed remarks.

venin [vənɛ̃] *nm* **1.** [poison] venom **2.** *litt* [malveillance] : **cracher** *ou* **jeter son ~** to vent one's spleen ■ **répandre son ~ contre qqn/qqch** to speak viciously about sb/sthg.

venir [40] [vənir] ◇ *v aux* **1.** [se rendre quelque part pour] to come and *ou* to ■ **Roger viendra me chercher** Roger will come and collect me ■ **je suis venu m'excuser** I've come to apologize ■ **venez manger!** dinner's ready! ■ **~ voir qqn** to come and see *ou* to visit sb, to visit with sb *US* ■ **~ voir qqch** to come and see sthg ■ *(à valeur d'insistance)* **tu l'as bien cherché, alors ne viens pas te plaindre!** you asked for it, so now don't come moaning to me about it! ■ **qu'est-ce que tu viens nous raconter** *ou* **chanter là?** *fam* what on earth are you on about *UK ou* talking about? **2.** [avoir fini de] : **~ de : ~ de faire qqch** to have just done sthg ■ **je viens de l'avoir au téléphone** I was on the phone to her just a few minutes *ou* a short while ago **3.** *sout* **~ à** [exprime un hasard] to happen to ■ **si les vivres venaient à manquer** should food supplies run out, if food supplies were to run out.
◇ *vi*

A. AVEC IDÉE DE MOUVEMENT
B. SANS IDÉE DE MOUVEMENT
C. SURGIR, SE MANIFESTER

A. AVEC IDÉE DE MOUVEMENT

1. [se déplacer, se rendre] to come ■ **viens plus près** come closer ■ **ils sont venus nombreux** they came in droves ■ **il est reparti** *ou* **il s'en est allé comme il était venu** *pr* he left just as he had come ; [il est mort] he died without having made his mark ■ **comment êtes-vous venus?** how did you get here? ■ **je l'ai rencontrée en venant ici** I met her on my way here ■ **viens au lit** come to bed ■ **alors, tu viens?** are you coming? ■ **on va au restaurant, tu viens avec nous?** we're off to the restaurant, are you coming with us *ou* along? ■ **~ de : d'où viens-tu?** where have you been? ■ **je viens de Paris et je repars à New York** I've just been in Paris and now I'm off to New York ■ **~ sur** [prédateur, véhicule] to move in on, to bear down upon ■ **la moto venait droit sur nous** the motorbike was heading straight for us ■ **~ vers qqn** [s'approcher] to come up to *ou* towards sb ■ **~ à qqn** [s'adresser à qqn] to come to sb ; [atteindre qqn] to reach sb

2. [emmener, appeler] : **faire ~** [médecin, police, réparateur] to send for, to call ; [parasites, touristes] to attract ■ **faire ~ une personne chez soi** to have somebody come round ■ **faites ~ le prévenu chez le juge** bring the accused to the judge's office ■ **je fais ~ mon foie gras directement du Périgord** I have my foie gras sent straight from Périgord ■ **faire ~ les larmes aux yeux de qqn** to bring tears to sb's eyes

B. SANS IDÉE DE MOUVEMENT

[distance] : **~ à** *ou* **jusqu'à** [vers le haut] to come up to, to reach (up to) ; [vers le bas] to come down to, to reach (down to) ; [en largeur, en longueur] to come out to, to stretch to, to reach

C. SURGIR, SE MANIFESTER

1. [arriver - moment, saison] to come ■ **le moment est venu de** the time has come to ■ **quand vient l'hiver** when winter comes ■ **l'aube vint enfin** dawn broke at last ■ **voici ~ la nuit** it's nearly night *ou* nighttime ■ **puis il vient un âge/moment où...** then comes an age/a time when... ■ **ça va ~ : je ne suis jamais tombé amoureux – non, mais ça va ~!** I've never fallen in love – (no, but) you will one day! ■ **alors, elle vient cette bière?** am I getting that beer or not?, how long do I have to wait for my beer? ■ **alors, ça vient?** hurry up! ■ **ça vient, ça vient!** alright, it's coming!

2. [apparaître - inspiration, idée, boutons] to come ■ **la prudence vient avec l'âge** wisdom comes with age ■ **prendre la vie comme elle vient** *ou* **les choses comme elles viennent** *ou* **les événements comme ils viennent** to take things in one's stride *ou* as they come, to take life as it comes ■ **~ à qqn : l'envie m'est soudain venue d'aller me baigner** I suddenly felt like going swimming *ou* fancied a swim ■ **une idée géniale m'était venue** a great idea had dawned on me ■ **les mots semblaient lui ~ si facilement!** her words seemed to flow so effortlessly! ■ **les mots ne me venaient pas** I was at a loss for words, I couldn't find the words ■ **des rougeurs me sont venues sur tout le corps** I came out in red blotches all over ■ **~ à l'esprit de qqn** *ou* **à l'idée de qqn** to come to *ou* to dawn on sb ■ **rien ne lui venait à l'esprit** *ou* **l'idée** her mind was a blank

3. [dans une chronologie, un ordre, une hiérarchie] to come ■ **le mois/l'année/la décennie qui vient** the coming month/year/decade ■ **le trimestre qui vient** next term ■ **~ après : fais tes devoirs, la télé viendra après** do your homework, we'll see about TV later on ■ **dans ce jeu, l'as vient après le valet** in this game, the ace is worth less than the jack

4. [se développer] to come along *ou* up (well), to do well ■ **~ à fruit** to (go into) fruit ■ **~ à maturité** to reach maturity, to ripen

5. IMPR & PHOTO : **~ bien/mal : les verts viennent bien sur la photo** the green shades come out beautifully in the photograph.

◇ *v impers* **1.** [se déplacer] : **il vient peu de touristes en hiver** few tourists come in winter **2.** [idée, réflexion] : **il me/te** *etc* **vient : il me vient une idée** I've got an idea ■ **il m'est venu à l'idée de faire** I suddenly thought of doing, it dawned on me to do ■ **il m'est venu une envie de tout casser** I suddenly felt like smashing the place up **3.** [exprime un hasard] : **s'il venait à pleuvoir** should it (happen to) rain.

◆ **venir à** *v+prép* **1.** [choisir] to come to ■ **vous êtes venu tôt à la politique** you started your political career early **2.** [atteindre] : **en ~ à** [thème, problème] to come *ou* to turn to ; [conclusion] to come to, to reach ; [décision] to come to ■ **en ~ au fait** *ou* **à l'essentiel** to come *ou* to go straight to the point ■ **je sais certaines choses... – où veux-tu en ~?** I know a thing or two... – what do you mean by that *ou* are you getting at *ou* are you driving at? ■ **en ~ aux mains** *ou* **coups** to come to blows ■ **en ~ à faire** [finir par] to come to ; [en dernière extrémité] to resort *ou* to be reduced to ■ **j'en viens à me demander si...** I'm beginning to wonder whether... ■ **j'en viendrais presque à souhaiter sa mort** I've reached the stage where I almost wish he were dead ■ **si j'en suis venu à voler, c'est que...** I resorted to stealing because... ■ **y ~** [dans une discussion] : **et l'argent? – j'y viens** what about the money? – I'm coming to that ■ **y ~** [s'y résoudre] to come round to it.

◆ **venir de** *v+prép* **1.** [être originaire de - suj: personne] to come from, to be from, to be a native of ; [- suj: plante, fruit, animal] to come *ou* to be *ou* to originate from ■ **une mode qui vient d'Espagne** a fashion which comes from *ou* originated in Spain ■ **le mot vient du latin** the word comes *ou* derives from Latin **2.** [provenir de - suj: marchandise] to originate from ; [- suj: bruit, vent] to come from ■ **ces images nous viennent de Tokyo** these pictures come to you from Tokyo **3.** [être issu de] to come from ■ **venant d'elle, c'est presque un compliment** coming from her it's almost a compliment **4.** [être dû à - suj: problème] to come *ou* to stem from, to lie in *ou* with ■ **le problème vient de la prise** it's the plug ■ **il y a une grosse erreur dans la comptabilité – ça ne vient pas de moi** there's a big discrepancy in the books – it's got nothing to do with me ■ **c'est de là que vient le mal/problème** this is the root of the evil/problem ■ **de là vient son indifférence** hence her indifference, that's why she's indifferent ■ **de là vient que : les travaux sont finis, de là vient que tout est calme** the building work is over, hence the peace and quiet ■ **d'où vient que : je dois terminer pour demain, d'où vient que je n'ai pas de temps à vous consacrer** my deadline is tomorrow, that's why I can't give you any of my time ■ **d'où vient que...?** how is it that ...?

◆ **s'en venir** *vpi litt* to come.

◆ **à venir** *loc adj* : **dans les jours/semaines/mois à ~** in the days/weeks/months to come ■ **les années à ~** the coming years *ou* years to come ■ **les générations à ~** future *ou* coming generations.

Venise [vəniz] *npr* Venice.

vénitien, enne [venisjɛ̃, ɛn] *adj* Venetian.
◆ **Vénitien, enne** *nm, f* Venetian.

vent [vɑ̃] *nm* **1.** MÉTÉOR wind ■ **un ~ du nord/nord-est** a North/North-East wind ■ **le ~ souffle/tourne** the wind is blowing/

changing ▪ **le ~ tombe/se lève** the wind is dropping/rising ▪ **il y a** *ou* **il fait du ~** it's windy *ou* breezy ▪ **un ~ de panique a soufflé sur la foule** *fig* a ripple of panic ran through the crowd ◐ **~ de terre/mer** land/sea breeze ▪ **plante de plein ~** outdoor plant ▪ **il fait un ~ à décorner les bœufs** there is a fierce wind blowing, it's a blustery day
2. NAUT & AÉRON : **au ~ (de)** to windward (of) ▪ **sous le ~ (de)** to leeward (of) ▪ **aller contre le ~** NAUT to head into the wind ; AÉRON to go up the wind ◐ **~ arrière** AÉRON tail wind ; NAUT rear wind ▪ **~ contraire** adverse wind ▪ **~ debout** head wind ▪ **avoir le ~ en poupe** to be up-and-coming, to be going places ▪ **du ~!** *fam* clear off!, get lost! ▪ **bon ~!** good riddance! ▪ **quel bon ~ vous amène?** to what do we owe the pleasure (of your visit)? ▪ **il a réussi contre ~s et marées** he managed against all the odds ▪ **je le ferai contre ~s et marées** I'll do it come hell or high water ▪ **aller** *ou* **filer comme le ~** to fly *ou* to hurtle along ▪ **(éparpillés) à tous les ~s** *ou* **à tout ~** (scattered) far and wide
3. [courant d'air] : **du ~** [de l'air] some air, a breeze ; [des paroles vaines] hot air ; [des actes vains] empty posturing ▪ **il lui a fait un peu de ~ avec son journal** he fanned her with his newspaper ◐ **faire du ~** *fig* : **elle fait beaucoup de ~** she just makes a lot of noise
4. MÉD & PHYSIOL : **des ~s** wind *(U)* ▪ **lâcher des ~s** to break wind
5. CHASSE wind ◐ **avoir ~ de qqch** to (get to) hear of sthg ▪ **elle a eu ~ de l'affaire** she heard about *ou* she got wind of the story
6. [atmosphère] : **le ~ est à la révolte** there is unrest in the air ▪ **prendre le ~** to test the water, to gauge the situation ◐ **sentir** *ou* **voir d'où vient le ~** to see which way the wind blows *ou* how the land lies ▪ **sentir le ~ tourner** to feel the wind change, to realize that the tide is turning
7. ASTRON : **~ solaire** solar wind
8. GÉOGR : **les îles du Vent** the Windward Isles.
◆ **vents** *nmpl* MUS wind instruments ▪ **les ~s jouent trop fort** the wind section is playing too loud.
◆ **dans le vent** *loc adj* up-to-date.
◆ **en plein vent** ◇ *loc adj* [exposé] exposed (to the wind). ◇ *loc adv* [dehors] in the open (air).

ventail, aux [vɑ̃taj, o] *nm*, **ventaille** *nf* [vɑ̃taj] ventail.

vente [vɑ̃t] *nf* **1.** [opération] sale ▪ **technique de ~** selling technique ▪ **retiré de la ~** withdrawn from sale ◐ **~ au détail/en gros/en demi-gros** [par le négociant] retail/wholesale/cash-and-carry selling ; [profession] retail/wholesale/cash-and-carry trade ▪ **~ pour cause d'inventaire** stock-taking sale ▪ **~ pour liquidation avant départ** closing-down sale ▪ **~ à perte** dumping ▪ **lettre/promesse de ~** sales letter/agreement
2. [domaine d'activité] selling ▪ **~ au comptant** cash selling ▪ **~ par correspondance** mail-order selling ▪ **~ à crédit** credit selling ▪ **~ directe** direct selling ▪ **~ à domicile** door-to-door selling ▪ **~ à l'essai** sale on approval ▪ **~ par téléphone** telesales, telemarketing ▪ **~ à tempérament** hire-purchase UK *ou* installment plan US selling ▪ **~ à terme** sale for settlement
3. DR : **~ (par adjudication) forcée/judiciaire** compulsory sale, sale by order of the court
4. [réunion, braderie] sale ▪ **~ à l'encan** *ou* **aux enchères** auction (sale) ▪ **~ à la criée** auction (sale) *(especially of fish or meat)* ▪ **~ paroissiale** church bazaar ▪ **~ publique** public sale
5. BOURSE : **à la ~ : le dollar vaut 1 euro à la ~** the selling rate for the US dollar is 1 euro
6. [part de bois] fellable stand ▪ [arbres] : **asseoir les ~s** to mark trees *(before felling them)*.
◆ **ventes** *nfpl* COMM selling, sales ▪ **achats et ~s** buying and selling ▪ **le responsable des ~s** the sales manager ▪ **~s d'armes** arms sales.
◆ **en vente** *loc adj* & *loc adv* [à vendre] for sale ▪ [disponible] available, on sale ▪ **en ~ en pharmacie** on sale at *ou* available from the chemist's ▪ **en ~ libre** sold without a prescription ▪ **en ~ sur/sans ordonnance** obtainable on prescription/without a prescription ▪ **mettre qqch en ~** [commercialiser qqch] to put sthg on the market ▪ **mettre une maison en ~** to put a house up for sale.

venté, e [vɑ̃te] *adj* **1.** [où le vent souffle] windswept, windy **2.** [exposé] windswept.

venter [3] [vɑ̃te] *v impers* : **il vente** it's windy, the wind is blowing.

venteux, euse [vɑ̃tø, øz] *adj* **1.** [où le vent souffle] windswept, windy **2.** [à courants d'air] draughty.

ventilateur [vɑ̃tilatœr] *nm* **1.** [pour rafraîchir] fan ▪ **~ à pales/de plafond** blade/ceiling fan **2.** AUTO [de radiateur] cooling fan ▪ [de chauffage] heating fan.

ventilation [vɑ̃tilasjɔ̃] *nf* **1.** [appareil] ventilation ▪ **faire marcher la ~** to turn on the fan ▮ [aération] supply of (fresh) air **2.** MÉD & PHYSIOL ventilation ▪ **~ assistée** respiratory assistance **3.** [d'une comptabilité] breakdown **4.** [répartition] allocation, apportionment ▪ **la ~ des revenus** the allocation of income *ou* allocating income.

ventiler [3] [vɑ̃tile] *vt* **1.** [aérer] to air, to ventilate ▪ **mal ventilé** stuffy, airless **2.** MÉD to ventilate, to give respiratory assistance to **3.** [diviser - données] to explode, to scatter ; [- élèves, emplois] to distribute, to spread ▪ **ils ont ventilé les postes sur trois régions différentes** they allocated posts in three different areas **4.** FIN to break down *(sép)*.

ventôse [vɑ̃toz] *nm 6th month in the French Revolutionary calendar (from Feb 20th to Mar 21st)*.

ventouse [vɑ̃tuz] *nf* **1.** [en caoutchouc] suction cup **2.** MÉD cup, cupping glass ▪ **poser des ~s à qqn** to cup sb ▪ **application de ~s** cupping **3.** ZOOL sucker **4.** [déboucheur] plunger ▪ **faire ~** to adhere *ou* to hold fast (through suction) **5.** CONSTR [pour l'aération] air valve, air-vent.

ventral, e, aux [vɑ̃tral, o] *adj* front *(modif)*, ventral *spéc.*

ventre [vɑ̃tr] *nm* **1.** ANAT & ZOOL stomach ▪ **être couché sur le ~** to be lying down *ou* flat on one's stomach ▪ **mettez-vous sur le ~** [de la position debout] lie on your stomach ; [de la position couchée] roll over onto your stomach ▪ **il leur marcherait** *ou* **passerait sur le ~** *fig* he'd trample all over them ▪ **avoir mal au ~** to have (a) stomachache ▪ **avoir le ~ creux** *ou* **vide** to have an empty stomach ▪ **avoir le ~ plein** to be full, to have a full stomach ◐ **il s'est sauvé ~ à terre** you couldn't see him for dust ▪ **rentrer/partir ~ à terre** to get back/to go off on the double ▪ **n'avoir rien dans le ~ : je n'ai rien dans le ~ depuis trois jours** I haven't had anything to eat for three days, I've had to go hungry for the last three days ▪ **il n'a rien dans le ~** *fig* he's got no guts ▪ **je voudrais bien savoir ce qu'elle a dans le ~** [de manière générale] I'd like to know what makes her tick ; [sur un point précis] I'd like to know what she's up to ▪ **lui, professeur? ça me ferait mal au ~!** *fam* a professor, him? like hell he is! ▪ **~ affamé n'a point** *ou* **pas d'oreilles** *prov* there is no reasoning with a starving man **2.** [contenu - d'un appareil, d'un véhicule] innards **3.** [utérus] womb **4.** [renflement - d'un vase, d'un tonneau, d'un pot] bulge, belly ; [- d'un bateau] bilge ; [- d'un avion] belly **5.** PHYS loop, antinode.

ventrée [vɑ̃tre] *nf fam* **on s'est mis une ~ (de saucisses)** we stuffed ourselves (with sausages).

ventricule [vɑ̃trikyl] *nm* ventricle.

ventrière [vɑ̃trijɛr] *nf* **1.** [sangle - ventrale] girth ; [- de levage] sling **2.** CONSTR crosspiece, purlin **3.** NAUT bilge block.

ventriloque [vɑ̃trilɔk] *nmf* ventriloquist.

ventripotent, e [vɑ̃tripɔtɑ̃, ɑ̃t] *adj* potbellied, rotund *euphém.*

ventru, e [vɑ̃try] *adj* **1.** [personne] potbellied, paunchy **2.** [potiche] potbellied.

venu, e [vəny] ◇ *pp* ⊳ **venir.**
◇ *adj* **1.** [enfant, plante, animal] : **bien ~** strong, sturdy, robust ; [conseil, remarque] timely, apposite ; [attitude] appropriate ; [roman] mature ▪ **mal ~** [enfant, animal] sickly ; [plante] stunted ; [remarque, attitude] uncalled for, unwarranted, ill-advised ; [conseil] untimely, unwelcome **2.** [attitude, comportement] : **être bien ~ de** [être bien inspiré de] : **tu serais bien ~ de t'excuser** you'd be well-advised to apologize, it would be a good idea for you to apologize ▪ **être mal ~ de** [n'être pas qualifié pour] : **tu serais mal ~ de te plaindre!** you're hardly in a position to complain! ▪ **il serait mal ~ de la critiquer** it wouldn't be appropriate to criticize her.
◆ **venue** *nf* **1.** [d'une personne] arrival **2.** [d'une saison] approach **3.** [naissance] birth ▪ **la ~e (au monde) d'un enfant** the

arrival *ou* birth of a child **4.** TECHNOL : **~e d'eau/de gaz** water/gas inrush **5.** *loc* **d'une belle ~e** *litt* [arbre] well-grown, sturdy, lush ■ **d'une seule ~e, tout d'une ~e** *litt* grown all in one spurt.

vénus [venys] *nf* ZOOL Venus shell ■ **les ~** the veneridae.

Vénus [venys] ◇ *npr* Venus.
◇ *nf* [belle femme] Venus ■ **ce n'est pas une ~** she's no (great) beauty.

vépéciste [vepesist] *nm* mail-order company.

vêpres [vɛpr] *nfpl* vespers ■ **aller aux ~** to go to vespers ■ **sonner les ~** to ring the bell for vespers.

ver [vɛr] *nm* **1.** [gén] worm ■ [de viande, de fromage, de fruit] maggot ■ **avoir des ~s** MÉD to have worms ■ **cette pomme est pleine de ~s** worms have been at this apple ■ **meuble mangé aux** *ou* **rongé aux** *ou* **piqué des ~s** worm-eaten piece of furniture ◐ **~ à bois** woodworm ■ **~ luisant** glowworm ■ **~ à soie** silkworm ■ **~ solitaire** tapeworm ■ **~ de terre** earthworm ■ **tirer les ~s du nez à qqn** *fam* to worm sthg out of sb ■ **pas moyen de lui tirer les ~s du nez** *fam* he won't give anything away ■ **j'ai fini par lui tirer les ~s du nez** I finally got the truth out of him ■ **le ~ est dans le fruit** *fam* the rot's set in **2.** INFORM : **~ informatique** worm (program).

véracité [verasite] *nf* **1.** *litt* [habitude de dire vrai] veracity *sout*, truthfulness **2.** [authenticité] truth ■ **la ~ de ce témoignage est évidente** this statement is obviously true.

véranda [verɑ̃da] *nf* **1.** [galerie] veranda, verandah, porch *US* **2.** [pièce] conservatory.

verbal, e, aux [vɛrbal, o] *adj* **1.** [dit de vive voix] verbal **2.** [s'exprimant par les mots] : **violence ~e** angry words ■ **elle est en plein délire ~** *péj* she can't stop talking **3.** LING [adjectif, système] verbal ■ [phrase, forme, groupe] verb *(modif)*.

verbalement [vɛrbalmɑ̃] *adv* verbally, orally.

verbalisateur [vɛrbalizatœr] *adj m* : **agent ~** policeman *(in charge of reporting petty offences)*.

verbalisation [vɛrbalizasjɔ̃] *nf* **1.** [amendes] reporting petty offences **2.** PSYCHOL verbalization, verbalizing.

verbaliser [3] [vɛrbalize] ◇ *vi* to report an offender ■ **je suis obligé de ~** I'll have to report you.
◇ *vt* to express verbally, to put into words, to verbalize.

verbe [vɛrb] *nm* **1.** GRAMM verb ■ **~ à particule** phrasal verb **2.** [ton de voix] : **avoir le ~ haut** to lord it *UK*, to take a haughty tone **3.** *litt* [expression de la pensée] words, language **4.** BIBLE : **le Verbe** the Word.

verbeux, euse [vɛrbø, øz] *adj* verbose, wordy, long-winded.

verbiage [vɛrbjaʒ] *nm* verbiage.

verdâtre [vɛrdatr] *adj* greenish, greeny.

verdeur [vɛrdœr] *nf* **1.** [vigueur] vitality, vigour **2.** [crudité] raciness, boldness, sauciness **3.** [acidité - d'un vin, d'un fruit] slight tartness *ou* acidity.

verdict [vɛrdikt] *nm* **1.** DR verdict ■ **rendre son ~** to pass sentence, to return a verdict ■ **le juge a rendu un ~ sévère** the judge brought in a stiff sentence ■ **rendre un ~ de culpabilité/d'acquittement** to return a verdict of guilty/not guilty ■ **quel est votre ~?** how do you find? **2.** [opinion] verdict, pronouncement ■ **le ~ du médecin n'était pas très encourageant** the doctor's prognosis wasn't very hopeful.

verdir [32] [vɛrdir] ◇ *vi* **1.** [devenir vert] to turn green **2.** [de peur] to blench ■ **elle a verdi en apprenant la nouvelle** the blood drained out of her face when she heard the news **3.** [plante, arbre] to have green shoots.
◇ *vt* to add green *ou* a green tinge to.

verdoie *etc v* ▻ **verdoyer**.

verdoiement [vɛrdwamɑ̃] *nm* greenness ■ **le ~ des arbres dans le lointain** the green hue of trees in the distance.

verdoyant, e [vɛrdwajɑ̃, ɑ̃t] *adj* [vert] verdant *litt*, green.

verdoyer [13] [vɛrdwaje] *vi* to be green *ou* *litt* verdant.

Verdun [vɛrdœ̃] *npr* Verdun ■ **la bataille de ~** the Battle of Verdun.

verdure [vɛrdyr] *nf* **1.** [couleur] verdure *litt*, greenness **2.** [végétation] greenery, verdure *litt* ■ [dans un bouquet] greenery, (green) foliage **3.** CULIN salad.
◆ **de verdure** *loc adj* [tapisserie] verdure *(modif)* ■ THÉÂTRE open-air.

véreux, euse [verø, øz] *adj* **1.** [plein de vers - fruit, viande] wormy, maggoty **2.** [malhonnête - affaire, avocat, architecte, policier] dubious, shady.

verge [vɛrʒ] *nf* **1.** [barre] rod **2.** [insigne] rod, wand, staff **3.** ANAT penis **4.** [mesure] yard ■ **~ d'arpenteur** measuring stick ■ *Québec* yard **5.** ACOUST bar.
◆ **verges** *nfpl vieilli* **donner les ~s à qqn** to birch sb ■ **donner des ~s à qqn pour se faire fouetter** to give sb a stick to beat one with, to make a rod for one's own back.

vergeoise [vɛrʒwaz] *nf* brown sugar.

verger [vɛrʒe] *nm* (fruit) orchard.

vergeté, e [vɛrʒəte] *adj* **1.** [peau, cuisse] stretchmarked **2.** HÉRALD paly.

vergetures [vɛrʒətyr] *nfpl* stretchmarks.

verglacé, e [vɛrglase] *adj* : **route ~e** road covered in black ice, icy road.

verglas [vɛrgla] *nm* black ice *UK*, glare ice *US* ■ **il y a du ~ dans l'allée** the drive is iced over ■ **plaques de ~** patches of black ice, icy patches.

vergogne [vɛrgɔɲ] ◆ **sans vergogne** *loc adv* shamelessly ■ **mentir sans ~** to lie shamelessly *ou* without compunction.

vergue [vɛrg] *nf* NAUT yard ■ **~ de misaine** foreyard.

véridique [veridik] *adj* **1.** *litt* [sincère - témoin] truthful, veracious *sout* **2.** [conforme à la vérité] genuine, true ■ **tout cela est parfaitement ~** there's not a word of a lie in all this ■ **elle les a renvoyés, ~!** *fam* she fired them, it's true! **3.** [qui ne trompe pas] genuine, authentic.

vérif [verif] *nf fam* = **vérification**.

vérifiable [verifjabl] *adj* : **son témoignage n'est pas ~** there's no way of checking *ou* verifying his testimony ■ **votre hypothèse n'est pas ~** your hypothesis can't be tested.

vérificateur, trice [verifikatœr, tris] ◇ *adj* testing, checking ■ **instrument ~** testing instrument ■ **mesure vérificatrice** checking measurement.
◇ *nm, f* inspector, controller ■ **~ des comptes** auditor.
◆ **vérificateur** *nm* [contrôleur - de courant, de réseau] tester ; [- de l'altimètre, de filetage] gauge.
◆ **vérificatrice** *nf* [personne] verifier operator ■ [machine] verifier ■ **vérificatrice de cartes** card verifier, verifying punch, key-verifier.

vérificatif, ive [verifikatif, iv] *adj* verificatory ■ **faire une étude vérificative** to carry out a check.

vérification [verifikasjɔ̃] *nf* **1.** [d'identité] check ■ [d'un témoignage, d'un déplacement] check, verification ■ [d'un dossier] examination, scrutiny ■ **~ faite auprès du percepteur** having checked with the tax office **2.** [d'une hypothèse, d'une preuve] checking, verification ■ **faire la ~ d'une hypothèse** to test a hypothesis **3.** FIN checking ■ **~ des comptes** audit **4.** TECHNOL test, check **5.** INFORM check, control.

vérifier [9] [verifje] *vt* **1.** [examiner - mécanisme] to check, to verify ; [- dossier] to check, to go through ■ *(en usage absolu)* **~ plutôt deux fois qu'une** to check and double-check **2.** [preuve, témoignage] to check ■ **vérifie son adresse** check that his address is correct, check his address ■ **~ que** *ou* **si...** to check *ou* to make sure that, to check whether... ■ **je vais ~ que** *ou* **si ce que vous dites est vrai** I'll make sure that you're telling the truth **3.** [confirmer] to confirm, to bear out *(sép)* **4.** MATH : **~ un calcul par total de contrôle** to check a sum.
◆ **se vérifier** *vpi* [craintes, supposition] to be borne out *ou* confirmed.

vérin [verɛ̃] *nm* jack ■ **~ à air comprimé** thrustor ■ **~ hydraulique** hydraulic jack.

véritable [veritabl] *adj* **1.** [d'origine] real, true **2.** [authentique - or] real, genuine ; [- amitié, sentiment] true ■ **c'est de la soie ~** it's real silk **3.** *(avant le n)* [absolu] real ■ **une ~ ordure**△ a real bastard△.

véritablement [veritabləmɑ̃] *adv* **1.** [réellement] genuinely ■ **il est ~ malade** he's genuinely ill **2.** [exactement] really, exactly **3.** [en intensif] truly, really, absolutely.

vérité [verite] *nf* **1.** [ce qui est réel ou exprimé comme réel] **: la ~** the truth ■ **c'est la ~ vraie!** *fam* it's true, honest it is ■ **s'écarter de la ~ historique** to take liberties with history ■ **je sais que c'est la ~** I know it for a fact ■ **la ~, c'est que ça m'est égal** actually *ou* the truth is *ou* in fact I don't care ■ **je finirai bien par savoir la ~** I'll get at the truth eventually ■ **dis-moi la ~** tell me the truth ■ **être loin de la ~** to be wide of the mark ■ **12 millions? vous n'êtes pas loin de la ~** 12 million? you're not far from the truth ⊃ **la ~ toute nue** the plain *ou* naked truth ■ **la ~ n'est pas toujours bonne à dire, toute ~ n'est pas bonne à dire** the truth is sometimes better left unsaid ■ **il n'y a que la ~ qui blesse** nothing hurts like the truth ■ **la ~ sort de la bouche des enfants** *prov* out of the mouths of babes and sucklings (comes forth the truth) *prov* ■ **~ en-deçà des Pyrénées, erreur au-delà** *Pascal allus* what is considered true in one country may be thought of as false in the next **2.** [chose vraie] **: une ~** a true fact **3.** [principe] truth ■ **une ~ première** a basic truth ■ **les ~s éternelles** undying truths, eternal verities *litt* **4.** [ressemblance] **: ses tableaux sont d'une grande ~** his paintings are very true to life **5.** [sincérité] truthfulness, candidness ■ **son récit avait un accent de ~** her story rang true.
◆ **à la vérité, en vérité** *loc adv* to tell the truth.

verjus [vɛrʒy] *nm* **1.** [suc] verjuice **2.** [vin] sour wine.

verlan [vɛrlɑ̃] *nm* ≃ backslang.

VERLAN

This form of slang, popular among young people, involves inverting the syllables of words. The term *verlan* is the word *l'envers* pronounced back to front. Well-known examples of verlan are *ripou* (*pourri*, used to refer to corrupt policemen), *laisse béton !* (*laisse tomber ! -* forget it!), and *meuf* (*femme*). The term *Beur* comes from the *verlan* version of the word *Arabe*.

vermeil, eille [vɛrmɛj] *adj* [rouge - pétale, tenture] vermilion ; [- teint, joue] ruddy, rosy ; [- lèvres] rosy.
◆ **vermeil** *nm* vermeil, gilded silver.

vermicelle [vɛrmisɛl] *nm* **: ~, ~s** vermicelli ■ **~s chinois** Chinese noodles.

vermicide [vɛrmisid] ◇ *adj* vermicidal.
◇ *nm* vermicide.

vermiculaire [vɛrmikylɛr] *adj* **1.** [en forme de ver] wormlike, vermicular *sout* **2.** ANAT **: appendice ~** vermiform appendix.

vermifuge [vɛrmifyʒ] *adj* & *nm* vermifuge, anthelmintic *spéc.*

vermillon [vɛrmijɔ̃] ◇ *adj inv* vermilion, bright red.
◇ *nm* **1.** [cinabre] vermilion, cinnabar **2.** [couleur] vermilion.

vermine [vɛrmin] *nf* **1.** [parasite] vermin **2.** *fig* & *péj* **ces gens-là, c'est de la ~** those people are vermin.

vermisseau, x [vɛrmiso] *nm* small worm.

Vermont [vɛrmɔ̃] *npr m* **: le ~** Vermont.

vermouler [3] [vɛrmule] ◆ **se vermouler** *vpi* to get woodworm.

vermoulu, e [vɛrmuly] *adj* **1.** [piqué des vers] worm-eaten ■ **la plupart des poutres sont ~es** most of the beams are worm-eaten, there's woodworm in most of the beams **2.** *fig* [vieux] antiquated, age-old.

vermoulure [vɛrmulyr] *nf* **1.** [trou] wormhole **2.** [poussière] woodworm dust.

vermouth [vɛrmut] *nm* vermouth.

vernaculaire [vɛrnakylɛr] *adj* vernacular ■ **nom ~** vernacular *ou* common name.

verni, e [vɛrni] ◇ *adj* **1.** [meuble, ongle] varnished ■ [brique, poterie] enamelled, glazed ■ **des souliers ~s** patent leather shoes **2.** [brillant] glossy, shiny **3.** *fam* [chanceux] lucky.
◇ *nm, f fam* lucky thing.
◆ **verni** *nm* patent leather.

vernir [32] [vɛrnir] *vt* [enduire - bois, tableau, ongle] to varnish ; [- céramique] to enamel, to glaze ■ **~ au tampon** to French-polish.

vernis [vɛrni] *nm* **1.** [enduit - sur bois] varnish ; [- sur métal] polish ■ **~ à l'asphalte** asphalt varnish, black japan ; [- sur céramique] enamel ■ **~ au plomb** lead glazing **2.** ÉLECTR **: ~ conducteur** conductive lacquer *ou* varnish ■ **~ isolant** isolac, enamel **3.** [cosmétique] **: ~ à ongles** nail polish **4.** ART **: ~ à l'huile** oil varnish **5.** BOT varnish *ou* lacquer tree **6.** *fig* & *péj* **avoir un ~ de** to have a smattering of ■ **le ~ d'éducation ne cache pas sa vulgarité** a veneer of good manners does nothing to hide his vulgarity.

vernissage [vɛrnisaʒ] *nm* **1.** [d'un tableau, d'un meuble] varnishing ■ [d'une céramique] glazing ■ [du métal] enamelling **2.** [d'une exposition] private viewing ■ **aller à un ~** to go to a private viewing.

vernissé, e [vɛrnise] *adj* **1.** [céramique, tuile] glazed **2.** [luisant - feuilles] glossy.

vernisser [3] [vɛrnise] *vt* to glaze, to enamel.

vérole [verɔl] *nf* **1.** *fam* [syphilis] pox ■ **avoir la ~** to have the pox **2.** [variole] **: petite ~** smallpox.

vérolé, e [verɔle] *adj fam* poxy.

véronal® [verɔnal] *nm* barbitone.

Véronèse [verɔnɛz] *npr* Veronese.

véronique [verɔnik] *nf* **1.** BOT speedwell, veronica *spéc* **2.** [passe de tauromachie] veronica.

verra *etc v* ▷ **voir.**

verrat [vera] *nm* breeding boar.

verre [vɛr] *nm* **1.** [matériau] glass ■ **~ antiballes** bulletproof glass ■ **~ armé** wired glass ■ **~ dépoli** frosted *ou* ground glass ■ **~ double** plate glass ■ **~ filé** spun glass ■ **~ incassable** shatterproof glass ■ **~ moulé** pressed glass ■ **~ optique** optical glass ■ **~ organique** organic glass ■ **~ trempé** tempered *ou* toughened glass
2. [protection] glass ■ **~ de lampe** lamp glass ■ **~ de montre** watch glass
3. [récipient] glass ■ **~ ballon** round wine glass ■ **~ à dents** tooth glass ■ **~ doseur** measuring glass ■ **~ à eau** [droit] tumbler ■ **~ gradué** [en chimie] graduated vessel ; [pour la cuisine] measuring glass ■ **~ à moutarde** mustard jar *(that can be used as a glass when empty)* ■ **~ à pied** stemmed glass ■ **~ à vin** wine-glass
4. [contenu] **: boire un ~** to have a drink ■ **je bois** *ou* **prends juste un petit ~** I'll just have a quick one ■ **~ de** glass of, glassful of ⊃ **avoir un ~ dans le nez** *fam* to have had one too many
5. GÉOL **: ~ volcanique** volcanic glass.
◆ **verres** *nmpl* **1.** OPT glasses ⊃ **~s de contact** contact lenses ■ **~s correcteurs** correcting lenses ■ **~s polarisés** polaroid lenses ■ **~s progressifs** [les verres] varifocal lenses ; [les lunettes elles-mêmes] varifocals
2. [bouteilles] empties.
◆ **de verre** *loc adj* glass *(modif)* ■ **objets de ~** glassware *(U).*
◆ **en verre** *loc adj* [bibelot] glass *(modif)* ■ **ce n'est pas en ~** it won't break.
◆ **sous verre** ◇ *loc adj* [photo, fleurs] glass-framed ■ **une photo sous ~** a glass-mounted photograph.
◇ *loc adv* **: mettre qqch sous ~** to put sthg in a clip frame.

verrée [vere] *nf Suisse* reception.

verrerie [vɛrri] *nf* **1.** [usine] glassworks **2.** [technique] glasswork, glassmaking **3.** [objets] glassware **4.** [industrie] glass trade.

verrier, ère [vɛrje, ɛr] *adj* glass *(modif).*

➜ **verrier** *nm* **1.** [souffleur de verre] glassblower **2.** [artisan - en verrerie] glassmaker ; [- en vitraux] stained-glass maker *ou* artist.
➜ **verrière** *nf* **1.** [toit] glass roof **2.** [baie - à hauteur de plafond] glass wall *ou* partition ; [- à mi-hauteur] glass screen **3.** [vitrail] stained-glass window **4.** AÉRON canopy.

verr num (*abr de* **verrouillage numérique**) [vernym] *nf* INFORM num lock.

verroterie [verɔtri] *nf* [bibelots] glass trinkets ▪ [bijoux] glass jewels ▪ [perles] glass beads.

verrou [veru] *nm* **1.** [fermeture] bolt ▪ **mettre** *ou* **pousser les ~s** to slide the bolts home, to bolt the door ▪ **tirer le ~** to unbolt the door ▶ **~ de sûreté** safety latch, night bolt ▪ **~ trois points** multilock **2.** RAIL lock ▪ **~ d'aiguille** facing point lock **3.** GÉOL glacial cross cliff **4.** ARM breechblock, bolt **5.** MIL blockade.
➜ **sous les verrous** *loc adv* : **être sous les ~s** to be behind bars ▪ **mettre qqn sous les ~s** to put sb behind bars.

verrouillage [verujaʒ] *nm* **1.** [d'une porte] locking, bolting ▪ [d'une portière] locking ▪ **~ automatique** *ou* **central** central locking ▪ **à ~ automatique** self-locking ▪ **~ de sécurité enfants** childproof lock **2.** ARM bolting **3.** MIL blockade **4.** AÉRON : **~ du train d'atterrissage** [procédé] up-and-down locking ; [dispositif] up-and-down lock **5.** RAIL : **~ électrique** electric interlocking **6.** ÉLECTRON [procédé] clamping ▪ [dispositif] clamping device **7.** INFORM [du clavier] locking ▪ [de l'accès] lockout.

verrouiller [3] [veruje] *vt* **1.** [clore - porte] to lock, to bolt **2.** [empêcher l'accès de] to close off *(sép)* ▪ **la police a verrouillé le quartier** the police have cordoned off *ou* closed off the area **3.** [enfermer - personne] to lock in *(sép)* **4.** INFORM [clavier] to lock **5.** MIL to blockade.
➜ **se verrouiller** *vp (emploi réfléchi)* : **se ~ (chez soi)** to shut *ou* to lock o.s. in.

verrue [very] *nf* wart ▪ **~ plantaire** verruca, plantar wart.

verruqueux, euse [verykø, øz] *adj* warty, verrucose *spéc.*

vers[1] [ver] ◇ *nm* LITTÉR **1.** [genre] verse ▪ **~ libres** free verse ▪ **~ métriques/syllabiques/rythmiques** quantitative/syllabic/accentual-syllabic verse **2.** [unité] line ▪ **le dernier ~ est faux** *ou* **boiteux** the last line doesn't tally.
◇ *nmpl* [poème] (lines of) poetry, verse ▪ **écrire** *ou* **faire des ~** to write poetry *ou* verse ▪ **~ de circonstance** occasional verse ▪ **des ~ de mirliton** doggerel.
➜ **en vers** ◇ *loc adj* : **conte/lettre en ~** tale told/letter written in verse.
◇ *loc adv* : **mettre qqch en ~** to put sthg into verse.

vers[2] [ver] *prép* **1.** [dans la direction de] to, towards ▪ **il regarde ~ la mer** he's looking towards the sea ▪ **ma chambre regarde ~ le nord** my bedroom looks *ou* faces north ▪ **~ la gauche** to the left ▪ **le village ~ lequel nous nous dirigions** the village we were heading for ▪ **~ où tu vas?** *fam* which way are you going? ▪ **il s'est tourné ~ moi** *pr* he turned to *ou* towards me ; [pour que je l'aide] he turned *ou* came to me ▪ **un pas ~ la paix** a step towards peace **2.** [indiquant l'approximation - dans le temps] around ; [- dans l'espace] near ▪ **~ midi** around midday ▪ **~ les années 30** in the 30s or thereabouts ▪ **l'accident a eu lieu ~ Ambérieu** the accident happened somewhere near Ambérieu ▪ **~ les 1 800 mètres la végétation se raréfie** around 1,800 metres the vegetation becomes sparse.

versaillais, e [versajɛ, ɛz] *adj* **1.** GÉOGR from Versailles **2.** HIST : **l'armée ~e** the Versailles army *(loyal to the Thiers government in 1871).*

Versailles [versaj] *npr* Versailles ▪ **le château de ~** (the Palace of) Versailles.

VERSAILLES

France's greatest palace, by Le Vau and Mansart, with gardens by Le Nôtre. Built at enormous cost by Louis XIV and added to in the 18th century, it was the home of the French court until the Revolution. Numerous treaties were signed there, including the Treaty of Versailles in 1919 marking the end of the First World War.

versant [versɑ̃] *nm* **1.** GÉOGR [côté - d'une montagne, d'une vallée] side, slope ▪ **un ~ abrupt** a steep slope *ou* hillside **2.** [aspect - d'une position, d'un argument] side, aspect.

versatile [versatil] *adj* [esprit, caractère, personne] fickle.

versatilité [versatilite] *nf* fickleness.

verse [vers] *nf* AGRIC lodging, laying.
➜ **à verse** *loc adv* : **il pleut à ~** it's pouring (with rain), it's pouring down.

versé, e [verse] *adj* *sout* versed ▪ **être très/peu ~ dans la politique** to be well-versed/not particularly well-versed in politics ▪ **être ~/peu ~ dans l'art contemporain** to be conversant with/ignorant of contemporary art.

Verseau [verso] *nm* **1.** ASTRON Aquarius **2.** ASTROL Aquarius ▪ **elle est ~** she's Aquarius *ou* an Aquarian.

versement [versəmɑ̃] *nm* **1.** [paiement] payment ▪ **~s compensatoires** compensatory payments, compensation *(U)* **2.** [paiement partiel] instalment ▪ **effectuer un ~** to pay an instalment ▪ **un premier ~** a down payment **3.** [dépôt] deposit ▪ **effectuer** *ou* **faire un ~ à la banque** to pay money into a bank account ▪ **~ en espèces** cash deposit.

verser [3] [verse] ◇ *vt* **1.** [répandre - sang, larmes] to shed ▪ **~ des larmes** *ou* **pleurs** to cry ▪ **sans qu'une goutte de sang n'ait été versée** without a drop of blood being spilt **2.** [servir - liquide] to pour out *(sép)* ▪ **verse-lui en un peu plus** pour him a bit more, help him to a bit more **3.** [faire basculer - sable, gravier, chargement] to tip ▪ **verse la farine dedans** pour the flour in **4.** [coucher à terre - céréales] to lay *ou* to beat down **5.** [affecter] to assign, to transfer ▪ **elle vient d'être versée à la comptabilité** she's just been assigned to accounts **6.** [payer] to pay ▪ **~ de l'argent sur un compte** to put money into an account ▪ **on vous versera une retraite** you will receive a pension **7.** [apporter] to add, to append ▪ **~ une pièce au dossier** *pr* to add a new item to the file ; *fig* to bring further information to bear on the case.
◇ *vi* to spill, to overturn ▪ **la charrette a versé** the cart tipped over *ou* overturned.
➜ **verser dans** *v+prép* : **nous versons dans le mélodrame** this is becoming melodramatic ▪ **~ dans le ridicule** [personne, film] to become ridiculous.

verset [versɛ] *nm* **1.** [d'un livre sacré, d'un poème] verse ▪ **'les Versets sataniques'** ***Rushdie*** 'The Satanic Verses' **2.** RELIG versicle.

verseur [versœr] *adj m* : **bec ~** [d'une théière] spout ; [d'une casserole, d'une tasse] lip ▪ **camion ~** dump truck.

verseuse [versøz] *nf* coffeepot.

versificateur [versifikatœr] *nm* *péj* versifier, poetaster *péj*, rhymester *péj*.

versification [versifikasjɔ̃] *nf* versification, versifying.

versifier [9] [versifje] ◇ *vt* to versify, to turn into verse, to write in verse.
◇ *vi* **1.** [faire des vers] to versify, to write *ou* to compose verse **2.** *péj* to versify.

version [versjɔ̃] *nf* **1.** ÉDUC & UNIV translation *(from a foreign language into one's mother tongue)* ▪ **~ anglaise** [pour un Français] translation from English into French ▪ **~ latine** translation from Latin **2.** [variante - d'une œuvre] version ; [- d'une automobile] model, version ; [- d'un logiciel] version ▶ **en ~ originale** in the original language ▪ **en ~ originale sous-titrée** with subtitles ▪ **en ~ française** dubbed in French **3.** [interprétation] version ▪ **voici ma ~ des faits** this is my version of the facts, this is how I see what happened ▪ **c'est la ~ officielle des faits** that's the official version of what happened **4.** MÉD version, turning.

verso [verso] *nm* **1.** [envers] verso, other side ▪ **je n'ai pas lu le ~** I haven't read the back of the page **2.** INFORM back.
➜ **au verso** *loc adv* : **voir au ~** see overleaf ▪ **la suite au ~** continued overleaf.

verste [verst] *nf* verst.

vert, e [vɛr, vɛrt] *adj* **1.** [couleur] green ▪ ~ **de** : ~ **de rage** livid ▪ **être ~ de peur** to be white with fear **2.** [vin] tart, acid ▪ [fruit] green, unripe ▪ *fig* [débutant, apprenti] inexperienced ▪ **ils sont trop ~s** *La Fontaine allus* it's a case of sour grapes **3.** [bois] green **4.** [à préparer] : **cuir ~** untanned leather **5.** [vigoureux] sprightly **6.** [agricole, rural] green, agricultural, rural ▪ **l'Europe ~e** farming within the EC ▪ **la livre ~e** the green pound ▪ **station ~e** rural tourist centre **7.** [écologiste] green **8.** [osé] risqué, raunchy ➊ **en dire/en avoir entendu des ~es et des pas mûres** to tell/to have heard some pretty raunchy jokes ▪ **en avoir vu des ~es et des pas mûres** to have been through a lot ▪ **il lui en a fait voir des ~es et des pas mûres!** he's really put her through it! **9.** *(avant le n)* [violent] : **une ~e semonce** a good dressing-down.

◆ **vert** *nm* **1.** [couleur] green ▪ **peint** *ou* **teint en ~** painted *ou* tinted green ➊ ~ **bouteille** bottle green ▪ ~ **d'eau** sea green ▪ ~ **pomme** apple green **2.** TRANSP green light ▪ **passer au ~** : **les voitures doivent passer au ~** motorists must wait for the light to turn green ▪ **le feu est passé au ~** the lights have turned (to) green **3.** *loc* **mettre un cheval au ~** to turn a horse out to grass ▪ **se mettre au ~** to go to the countryside.

◆ **Verts** *nmpl* : **les Verts** SPORT *the Saint-Étienne football team* ; POLIT *the Green Party.*

vert-de-gris [vɛrdəgri] *nm inv* verdigris.

vertébral, e, aux [vɛrtebral, o] *adj* vertebral, spinal.

vertèbre [vɛrtɛbr] *nf* vertebra ▪ ~ **cervicale/dorsale/lombaire** cervical/dorsal/lumbar vertebra ▪ **avoir une ~ déplacée** to have a slipped disc.

vertébré, e [vɛrtebre] *adj* vertebrate.

◆ **vertébré** *nm* vertebrate.

vertement [vɛrtəmɑ̃] *adv* harshly, sharply ▪ **répondre ~** to retort sharply, to give a sharp answer ▪ **se faire tancer ~** *litt & hum* to get a good dressing-down.

vertical, e, aux [vɛrtikal, o] *adj* [droit - position, corps, arbre] vertical, upright ; [- écriture, ligne] vertical.

◆ **vertical** *nm* vertical circle.

◆ **verticale** *nf* vertical line.

◆ **à la verticale** ◇ *loc adj* vertically ▪ **un versant à la ~e** a sheer drop.

◇ *loc adv* vertically ▪ **se mettre à la ~e** to stand vertically *ou* upright ▪ **s'élever/descendre à la ~e** to rise/to descend vertically, to go vertically upwards/downwards.

verticalement [vɛrtikalmɑ̃] *adv* **1.** [tout droit] vertically ▪ **tomber/monter ~** to fall down/to come up in a straight line **2.** [dans les mots croisés] down.

verticalité [vɛrtikalite] *nf* [d'une ligne] verticality ▪ [d'un mur] verticality, uprightness ▪ [d'une falaise] sheerness.

vertige [vɛrtiʒ] *nm* **1.** [peur du vide] vertigo ▪ **avoir le ~** to suffer from vertigo **2.** [malaise] dizzy spell ▪ **avoir un ~** *ou* **des ~s** to feel dizzy *ou* faint ▪ **cela me donne le ~** it's making my head swim, it's making me (feel) dizzy ▪ **des sommes astronomiques qui donnent le ~** huge amounts of money that make one's head swim *ou* that don't bear thinking about **3.** [égarement] giddiness ▪ [tentation] : **céder/résister au ~ de la spéculation** to give in to/to resist the temptations of speculation.

vertigineux, euse [vɛrtiʒinø, øz] *adj* **1.** [effrayant - altitude] vertiginous, dizzy, giddy ; [- vitesse] terrifying, breakneck *(avant n)* ▪ **une baisse vertigineuse des cours** a breathtaking collapse on the stock exchange ▪ **une hausse vertigineuse des prix** a staggering increase in prices ▪ **des sommes vertigineuses** absurdly large sums of money **2.** MÉD vertiginous.

vertu [vɛrty] *nf* **1.** *litt* [conduite morale] virtue, virtuousness, righteousness **2.** [qualité] virtue ▪ **les ~s cardinales** the cardinal virtues ▪ **les ~s théologales** the theological virtues **3.** [propriété] virtue, property, power ▪ **les ~s thérapeutiques des plantes** the healing properties of plants ▪ **réapprenons les ~s de la vie à la campagne** *fig* let us rediscover the virtues of country life **4.** *hum* [chasteté] virtue ▪ **défendre/perdre sa ~** to defend/to lose one's virtue.

◆ **en vertu de** *loc prép* according to ▪ **en ~ des bons principes** following accepted moral principles ▪ **en ~ de la loi** according to the law, in accordance with the law, under the law ▪ **en ~ de quoi...** for which reason...

vertueusement [vɛrtɥøzmɑ̃] *adv* virtuously ▪ **vivre ~** to live virtuously.

vertueux, euse [vɛrtɥø, øz] *adj* **1.** [qui a des qualités morales] virtuous, righteous **2.** *vieilli* [chaste] virtuous.

verve [vɛrv] *nf* **1.** [fougue] verve, gusto ▪ [esprit] wit ▪ **avec ~** with gusto *ou* verve ▪ **exercer sa ~ contre qqn** to use one's wit against sb **2.** *litt* [créativité] inspiration.

◆ **en verve** *loc adj* : **être en ~** to be particularly witty.

verveine [vɛrvɛn] *nf* **1.** BOT vervain, verbena ▪ ~ **officinale** verbena officinalis **2.** [tisane] verbena (tea) **3.** [liqueur] vervein liqueur.

vésiculaire [vezikylɛr] *adj* bladder-like, vesicular *spéc.*

vésicule [vezikyl] *nf* MÉD [ampoule] blister, vesicle ▪ [cavité] bladder ▪ ~ **biliaire/cérébrale** gall/brain bladder.

vespasienne [vɛspazjɛn] *nf vieilli* street urinal.

vespéral, e, aux [vɛsperal, o] *adj litt* evening *(modif)*, vespertine *litt* ▪ **les lueurs ~es** evening lights, the lights at eventide *litt.*

◆ **vespéral, aux** *nm* RELIG vesperal.

vesse-de-loup [vɛsdəlu] (*pl* **vesses-de-loup**) *nf* puffball.

vessie [vesi] *nf* **1.** ANAT & ZOOL bladder ▪ **prendre des ~s pour des lanternes** to be easily hoodwinked ▪ **il voudrait nous faire prendre des ~s pour des lanternes** he's trying to pull the wool over our eyes **2.** [sac] bladder.

vestale [vɛstal] *nf* **1.** [prêtresse] vestal virgin **2.** *litt* [femme chaste] vestal.

veste [vɛst] *nf* jacket ▪ ~ **de pyjama** pyjama jacket *ou* top ▪ ~ **de tailleur** suit jacket ➊ **prendre une ~** to come a cropper ▪ **tomber la ~** *pr* to take off one's jacket ; *fig* to get down to work *ou* business.

vestiaire [vɛstjɛr] *nm* **1.** [placard] locker **2.** [dépôt] cloakroom ▪ **prendre son ~** to collect one's things *ou* belongings from the cloakroom **3.** [pièce] changing room, locker room *US* ▪ **l'arbitre, au ~!** get off, ref!

vestibule [vɛstibyl] *nm* **1.** [d'un bâtiment public, d'une maison] (entrance) hall, vestibule ▪ [d'un hôtel] lobby **2.** MÉD vestibule.

vestige [vɛstiʒ] *nm* [d'une armée] remnant ▪ [d'une ville, d'une société] vestige ▪ [d'une croyance, du passé, d'une coutume] remnant, vestige ▪ [d'une idée, d'un sentiment] remnant, trace, vestige ▪ **il ne reste que des ~s de sa grandeur** only a shadow of his former greatness remains.

vestimentaire [vɛstimɑ̃tɛr] *adj* clothing *(modif)* ▪ **dépenses ~s** clothes expenditure, money spent on clothing ▪ **élégance ~** sartorial elegance *sout* ▪ **c'est le détail ~ qui fait tout** it's the finishing touch that makes the outfit.

veston [vɛstɔ̃] *nm* jacket.

Vésuve [vezyv] *npr m* : **le ~** (Mount) Vesuvius.

vétéciste [vetesist] *nmf* hybrid bike rider.

vêtement [vɛtmɑ̃] *nm* **1.** [habit] piece *ou* article *ou* item of clothing, garment *sout* ▪ **il fait froid, mets un ~ chaud** it's cold, put something warm on ▪ **des ~s en loques** tattered clothes, rags ▪ **~s de travail** work *ou* working clothes ▪ **~s de sport** sportswear ▪ **~s pour homme** menswear ▪ **~s pour femme** ladies' wear ▪ **~s de ski** skiwear ▪ **il portait ses ~s de tous les jours** he was wearing his everyday clothes ▪ **~s habillés** formal dress ▪ **~s de ville** informal clothes ‖ [costume distinctif] dress, garb ▪ **~s ecclésiastiques** clerical garb *ou* dress ▪ **~s sacerdotaux** vestments **2.** [profession] : **l'industrie du ~** the clothing industry ▪ **être dans le ~** *fam* to be in the rag trade *UK ou* garment industry *US* **3.** COMM : **~s hommes** menswear ▪ ~ **dames** *ou* **femmes** ladies' wear ▪ ~ **enfants** children's wear.

vétéran [veterɑ̃] *nm* **1.** [soldat] veteran, old campaigner ▪ [ancien combattant] (war) veteran **2.** [personne expérimentée] veteran, old hand ▪ **un ~ de la politique** a veteran political campaigner **3.** SPORT veteran.

vétérinaire [veterinɛr] ◇ *adj* veterinary ▪ **faire des études ~s** to study veterinary medicine *ou* science.
◇ *nmf* vet, veterinary surgeon *UK*, veterinarian *US*.

vététiste [vetetist] *nmf* mountain biker.

vétille [vetij] *nf* trifle ▪ **perdre son temps à des ~s** to waste time over trifles *ou* trivia *ou* piffling details.

vêtir [44] [vetir] *vt* **1.** *sout* [habiller - enfant, malade] to dress **2.** [prisonnier, malade] to clothe, to provide with clothes, to kit out *UK* **3.** *litt* [revêtir] to put on *(sép)*, to don.
◆ **se vêtir** *vp (emploi réfléchi) sout* to dress (o.s.) ▪ **trouver de quoi se ~** to find something to put on.

vétiver [vetivɛr] *nm* vetiver.

veto [veto] *nm inv* **1.** POLIT veto ▪ **mettre** *ou* **opposer son ~ à une mesure** to veto a measure ➔ **exercer son droit de ~** to use one's power of veto **2.** [interdiction] : **opposer son ~ à qqch** to forbid *ou* to prohibit *ou* to veto sthg.

vêtu, e [vety] ◇ *pp* ⊳ **vêtir**.
◇ *adj* dressed ▪ **être bien/mal ~** to be well/badly dressed ▪ **être chaudement ~** to be warmly dressed *ou* clad ▪ **~ de** dressed in, wearing ▪ **un enfant ~ d'un blouson** a child wearing a jacket ▪ **une femme toute ~e de blanc** a woman all in white ▪ **un homme ~ de haillons** a man in rags ▪ **toute de soie ~e** all dressed in silk.

vétuste [vetyst] *adj* dilapidated, decrepit ▪ **la pompe était ~** the pump had fallen into disrepair.

vétusté [vetyste] *nf* [d'un bâtiment] dilapidated state ▪ [d'une loi] obsolescence ▪ **la ~ de l'installation électrique est en cause** the poor state of the wiring is to blame.

veuf, veuve [vœf, vœv] ◇ *adj* **1.** [personne] : **devenir ~** to be widowed, to become a widower ▪ **devenir veuve** to be widowed, to become a widow ▪ **~ de : il est ~ de plusieurs femmes** he's a widower several times over **2.** [typographie] : **ligne veuve** widow.
◇ *nm, f* widower *(f* widow) ▪ **Madame veuve Dupont** ADMIN Mrs Dupont *(term of address used on official correspondence to widows)* ▪ **la veuve Dupont** Mrs Dupont *(slightly informal way of referring to a widow)*.
◆ **veuve** *nf* ORNITH widow bird, whydah.

veuille *etc v* ⊳ **vouloir**.

veule [vøl] *adj* [personne] spineless, cowardly ▪ [visage, traits] weak.

veulent *v* ⊳ **vouloir**.

veulerie [vølri] *nf* spinelessness.

veut *etc v* ⊳ **vouloir**.

veuvage [vœvaʒ] *nm* [perte d'un mari] widowhood ▪ [perte d'une femme] widowerhood.

veuve [vœv] *f* ⊳ **veuf**.

veux *etc v* ⊳ **vouloir**.

vexant, e [vɛksɑ̃, ɑ̃t] *adj* **1.** [contrariant] annoying ▪ **c'est ~** how infuriating! **2.** [blessant - personne] hurtful ; [- remarque] cutting, slighting, hurtful.

vexation [vɛksasjɔ̃] *nf* snub, slight, humiliation ▪ **essuyer des ~s** to be snubbed.

vexatoire [vɛksatwar] *adj* vexatious, harassing.

vexer [4] [vɛkse] *vt* : **~ qqn** to hurt sb's feelings ▪ **être vexé** to be hurt *ou* offended ▪ **il est vexé de n'avoir pas compris** he's cross because he didn't understand ▪ **elle est vexée que tu ne la croies pas** she feels hurt because you don't believe her.
◆ **se vexer** *vpi* to be hurt *ou* offended *ou* upset, to take offence ▪ **ne te vexe pas mais...** no offence meant, but... ▪ **se ~ facilement** to be easily offended, to be oversensitive.

VF (*abr de* **version française**) *nf indicates that a film is dubbed in French*.

VHF (*abr de* **very high frequency**) *nf* VHF.

VHS (*abr de* **Video Home System**) *nm* VHS.

via [vja] *prép* via, through.

viabiliser [3] [vjabilize] *vt* to service ▪ **terrain viabilisé** piece of land with water, gas and electricity installed *(for building purposes)*.

viabilité [vjabilite] *nf* **1.** [aménagements] utilities, services **2.** [état d'une route] practicability **3.** [d'un organisme, d'un projet] viability ▪ [d'un fœtus] survival potential.

viable [vjabl] *adj* **1.** BIOL viable ▪ **avant 24 semaines de gestation le fœtus n'est pas ~** if born 24 weeks before term, the baby will not survive **2.** [entreprise, projet] viable, practicable, feasible.

viaduc [vjadyk] *nm* viaduct.

via ferrata [vjafɛrata] *nf inv* via ferrata, *high mountain route equipped with fixed climbing aids*.

viager, ère [vjaʒe, ɛr] *adj* life *(modif)*.
◆ **viager** *nm* (life) annuity.
◆ **en viager** *loc adv* : **placer son argent en ~** to buy an annuity ▪ **acheter/vendre une maison en ~** to buy/to sell a house so as to provide the seller with a life annuity.

viande [vjɑ̃d] *nf* **1.** CULIN meat ▪ **~ de bœuf** beef ▪ **~ de cheval** horsemeat ▪ **~ hachée** minced meat, mince *UK*, ground meat *US* ▪ **~ salée** cured *ou* salted meat ▪ **~ fumée** smoked meat ▪ **~ de boucherie** fresh meat *(as sold by the butcher)* ➔ **~ froide** dish of cold meat ▪ **~ rouge/blanche** red/white meat **2.** △ [corps] : **amène ta ~** get your arse△ *UK ou* haul your ass△ *US* over here ▪ **montrer sa ~** to bare one's flesh.

viander [3] [vjɑ̃de] *vi* [cerf, daim, chevreuil] to graze.
◆ **se viander**△ *vpi* to get smashed up.

Viandox® [vjɑ̃dɔks] *nm liquid seasoning containing meat essences*, ≃ Bovril®.

viatique [vjatik] *nm* **1.** RELIG viaticum **2.** *litt* [atout] asset ▪ **il n'a que son savoir pour tout ~** his knowledge is his only asset, his only means to success is his knowledge ‖ [soutien] help **3.** *arch* [pour un voyage] provisions and money (for the journey).

vibrant, e [vibrɑ̃, ɑ̃t] *adj* **1.** [corde, lamelle] vibrating ▪ **consonne ~e** vibrant consonant **2.** [fort - voix, cri] vibrant **3.** [émouvant - accueil, discours] stirring ; [- voix] tremulous ▪ **~ de** ringing *ou* echoing with ▪ **il lui a rendu un hommage ~** he paid him a warm tribute **4.** [sensible - nature, personne, caractère] sensitive.

vibraphone [vibrafɔn] *nm* vibraphone, vibraharp *US*.

vibraphoniste [vibrafɔnist] *nmf* vibraphonist.

vibrateur [vibratœr] *nm* **1.** TECHNOL vibration generator **2.** CONSTR vibrator.

vibratile [vibratil] ⊳ **cil**.

vibration [vibrasjɔ̃] *nf* **1.** [tremblement - d'un moteur, d'une corde] vibration ; [- d'une voix] quaver, tremor, vibration ; [- du sol] vibration **2.** ACOUST & ÉLECTRON vibration.
◆ **vibrations** *nfpl* vibrations ▪ **il y a de bonnes ~s ici** *fam* you get a good feeling *ou* good vibes from this place.

vibrato [vibrato] *nm* vibrato.

vibratoire [vibratwar] *adj* vibratory.

vibrer [3] [vibre] ◇ *vi* **1.** [trembler - diapason, vitre, plancher, voix] to vibrate ▪ **~ d'émotion** to quiver *ou* to quaver with emotion ▪ **faire ~ qqch** to vibrate sthg **2.** *fig* **faire ~ qqn** [l'intéresser] to thrill *ou* to stir sb ▪ **la musique expérimentale, ça ne me fait pas ~** *fam hum* I don't really get off on avant-garde music.
◇ *vt* to vibrate.

vibreur [vibrœr] *nm* TÉLÉCOM VibraCall® (alert *ou* feature).

vibromasseur [vibromasœr] *nm* vibrator.

vicaire [vikɛr] *nm* [auxiliaire - d'un curé] curate ; [- d'un évêque, du pape] vicar ▪ **Grand Vicaire, Vicaire général** vicar-general ▪ **~ apostolique** vicar apostolic.

vice [vis] *nm* **1.** [le mal] vice ▪ **le ~ et la vertu** vice and virtue ▪ **mais c'est du ~!** *fam hum* it's sheer perversion! **2.** [sexuel] : **le ~** perverse tendencies ▪ **un ~ contre nature** an unnatural tendency **3.** [moral] vice ▪ **avoir tous les ~s** to have all the vices ▪ **on ne lui connaît aucun ~** she has no known vice ▮ *hum* [travers] vice **4.** COMM & DR defect, flaw ▪ **~ apparent** conspicuous defect ▪ **~ caché** hidden *ou* latent defect ▪ **~ de construction** structural fault ▪ **annulé pour ~ de forme** DR annulled because of a mistake in the drafting.

vice- [vis] *préf* vice-.

vice-amiral [visamiral, o] (*pl* **vice-amiraux**) *nm* vice-admiral.

vice-consul [viskɔ̃syl] (*pl* **vice-consuls**) *nm* vice-consul.

vice-consulat [viskɔ̃syla] (*pl* **vice-consulats**) *nm* vice-consulate.

vicelard, e[△] [vislar, ard] ◇ *adj* devious, crafty.
◇ *nm, f* **1.** [personne cruelle] sly devil **2.** [pervers] : **un vieux ~** a dirty old man, an old lecher.

vice-présidence [visprezidɑ̃s] (*pl* **vice-présidences**) *nf* [d'un État] vice-presidency ▪ [d'un congrès] vice-chair.

vice-président, e [visprezidɑ̃, ɑ̃t] (*mpl* **vice-présidents**, *fpl* **vice-présidentes**) *nm, f* [d'un État] vice-president ▪ [d'un meeting] vice-chairman (*f* vice-chairwoman), vice-chairperson.

vice-roi [visrwa] (*pl* **vice-rois**) *nm* viceroy.

vice-royauté [visrwajote] (*pl* **vice-royautés**) *nf* vice-royalty.

vice versa [vis(e)vɛrsa] *loc adv* vice versa.

vichy [viʃi] ◇ *nm* **1.** TEXT gingham **2.** [eau] Vichy (water) ▪ **un ~ fraise** *a glass of Vichy water with strawberry syrup* **3.** CULIN vichy ▪ **carottes ~** carrots vichy *(glazed with butter and sugar).*
◇ *nf* bottle of Vichy water.

Vichy [viʃi] *npr* : **le gouvernement de ~** the Vichy Government.

LE GOUVERNEMENT DE VICHY

Seat of the French government under Maréchal Pétain from 1940 to 1944, during the German occupation. Pétain's right-wing traditionalist and authoritarian regime extolled the virtues of a *new order* and a *National Revolution* which would bring back the values of *Work, Family and Fatherland*. The Vichy government collaborated with the Germans and deported French Jews after 1942. Reduced to a puppet regime after the German invasion of the free zone, the government collapsed after the Allied victory.

vichyssois, e [viʃiswa, az] *adj* from Vichy, of Vichy.
◆ **Vichyssois, e** *nm, f* **1.** GÉOGR inhabitant of Vichy, native of Vichy **2.** HIST Vichyist.

vicié, e [visje] *adj* **1.** [pollué - air, sang] polluted, contaminated **2.** *litt* [faussé - raisonnement, débat] warped, vitiated *litt* **3.** DR vitiated.

vicier [9] [visje] *vt* **1.** [polluer - air, sang] to pollute, to contaminate **2.** *litt* [dénaturer - esprit, qualité] to corrupt, to taint ; [- relation, situation] to mar **3.** DR to vitiate.

vicieusement [visjøzmɑ̃] *adv* **1.** [lubriquement] lecherously, licentiously **2.** [incorrectement] faultily, wrongly **3.** [méchamment] maliciously, nastily.

vicieux, euse [visjø, øz] ◇ *adj* **1.** [pervers - livre, film] obscene ; [- regard] depraved ; [- personne] lecherous, depraved ▪ **il faut vraiment être ~ pour trouver ça drôle** you have to have a pretty warped sense of humour to find that funny **2.** [trompeur - coup, balle] nasty ; [- calcul] misleading **3.** [animal] vicious **4.** [incorrect - expression, prononciation, position] incorrect, wrong.
◇ *nm, f* [homme] lecher, pervert ▪ **un vieux ~** a dirty old man, an old lecher ▪ **petite vicieuse!** you little slut *ou* tramp!

vicinal, e, aux [visinal, o] *adj* ⊳ **chemin**.

vicissitude [visisityd] *nf litt* [succession] vicissitude.
◆ **vicissitudes** *nfpl* **1.** [difficultés] tribulations ▪ **après bien des ~s** after many trials and tribulations, taking many hard knocks on the way **2.** [événements] vicissitudes, ups and downs.

vicomte [vikɔ̃t] *nm* viscount.

vicomté [vikɔ̃te] *nf* viscountcy, viscounty.

vicomtesse [vikɔ̃tɛs] *nf* viscountess.

victime [viktim] *nf* **1.** [d'un accident, d'un meurtre] victim, casualty ▪ **les ~s du crash** the victims of the crash ▪ **accident de la route, trois ~s** car crash, three casualties ▪ **l'accident a fait trois ~s** three people died in the accident ▪ **les ~s du SIDA** AIDS victims **2.** RELIG (sacrificial) victim **3.** [bouc émissaire] victim, scapegoat **4.** [d'un préjudice] victim ▪ **être la ~ d'un escroc** to fall prey to *ou* to be the victim of a con man ▪ **être ~ d'hallucinations** to suffer from delusions.

victoire [viktwar] *nf* **1.** [fait de gagner - bataille, compétition] victory, winning ; [- dans une entreprise] victory, success *(U)* **2.** [résultat - militaire] victory ; [- sportif] victory, win ; [- dans une entreprise] victory, success ▪ **remporter une ~** to gain a victory ▪ **remporter une ~ sur soi-même** *fig* to triumph over o.s. ▪ **une ~ à la Pyrrhus** a Pyrrhic victory.

Victoria [viktɔrja] *npr* : **le lac ~** Lake Victoria.

victorien, enne [viktɔrjɛ̃, ɛn] *adj* Victorian.

victorieux, euse [viktɔrjø, øz] *adj* SPORT victorious, winning *(avant n)* ▪ POLIT victorious, winning *(avant n)*, successful ▪ MIL victorious ▪ [air] triumphant ▪ **sortir ~ d'un combat** to come out victorious.

victuailles [viktɥaj] *nfpl* victuals *sout*, food *(U)*, provisions.

vidage [vidaʒ] *nm* **1.** [d'un récipient] emptying **2.** *fam* [d'une personne] kicking out **3.** INFORM : **faire un ~** to (take a) dump ▪ **~ sur disque/de la mémoire** disk/core dump ▪ **gestionnaire de ~** dumper ▪ **~ d'écran (sur imprimante)** screen dump.

Vidal [vidal] *npr* : **le ~** *dictionary used by doctors as a reference book on medicines.*

vidange [vidɑ̃ʒ] *nf* **1.** [d'un récipient, d'un réservoir] emptying **2.** [dispositif] drain, (waste) outlet ▪ **~ du carter** oil pan drain *ou* outlet **3.** AUTO oil change ▪ **faire la ~** to change the oil **4.** AGRIC timber hauling *ou* skidding **5.** *Belgique* [verre consigné] returnable empties.
◆ **vidanges** *nfpl* [eaux usées] sewage *(U)*, liquid waste *(U)*.
◆ **de vidange** *loc adj* [huile, système] waste.

vidanger [17] [vidɑ̃ʒe] *vt* **1.** [eaux usées] to empty **2.** AUTO [huile] to change **3.** AÉRON to defuel.

vidangeur [vidɑ̃ʒœr] *nm* cesspit emptier.

vide [vid] ◇ *adj* **1.** [sans contenu] empty ▪ **tasse à demi ~** half-empty cup ▪ **un espace ~** [entre deux objets] an empty space ; [sur un document] a blank space ▪ **une pièce ~** an empty *ou* unfurnished room ▪ **avoir le ventre** *ou* **l'estomac ~** to have an empty stomach ▪ **j'ai la tête** *ou* **l'esprit complètement ~** I can't think straight ▪ **un regard ~** a vacant stare ▪ **~ de** devoid of ▪ **des remarques ~s de sens** meaningless remarks, remarks devoid of meaning
2. [sans occupant] empty
3. [sans intérêt - personnalité, vie] empty
4. [dénudé - mur] bare, empty.
◇ *nm* **1.** ASTRON : **le ~** (empty) space, the void
2. [néant] space ▪ **regarder dans le ~** to stare into space ▪ **parler dans le ~** [sans auditoire] to address empty space ; [sans contenu] to talk vacuously ▪ **faire des promesses dans le ~** to make empty promises
3. PHYS vacuum ▪ **faire le ~** [dans un vase clos] to create a vacuum ▮ *fig* **faire le ~ autour de soi** to drive all one's friends away ▪ **faire le ~ autour de qqn** to isolate sb ▪ **faire le ~ dans son esprit** to make one's mind go blank
4. [distance qui sépare du sol] (empty) space ▪ **la maison est construite, en partie, au-dessus du ~** part of the house is built over

a drop ■ **avoir peur du ~** to be scared of heights ■ **pendre dans le ~** to hang in mid-air ■ **tomber dans le ~** to fall into (empty) space

5. [trou - entre deux choses] space, gap ; [- entre les mots ou les lignes d'un texte] space, blank

6. [lacune] void, gap, blank ■ **son départ a laissé un grand ~ dans ma vie** she left a gaping void in my life when she went ▶ **~ juridique** DR legal vacuum ■ **il y a un ~ juridique en la matière** the law is not specific on this matter

7. [manque d'intérêt] emptiness, void

8. CONSTR : **~ d'air** air space ■ **~ sanitaire** ventilation space.

◆ **à vide** ◇ *loc adj* **1.** [hors fonctionnement] no-load

2. [sans air] : **cellule/tube/cuve à ~** vacuum photocell/tube/tank.

◇ *loc adv* : **le moteur tourne à ~** the engine's ticking over *ou* idling ■ **les usines tournent à ~** the factories are running but not producing.

◆ **sous vide** ◇ *loc adj* vacuum *(modif)*.

◇ *loc adv* : **emballé sous ~** vacuum-packed.

vidé, e [vide] *adj* **1.** [volaille] drawn, cleaned ■ [poisson] gutted ■ **vendre des poulets ~s** to sell chickens without giblets

2. *fam* [fatigué] exhausted, worn out.

vidéaste [videast] *nmf* video maker.

vide-grenier [vidgrənje] *nm inv* second-hand goods sale, car-boot sale UK, yard sale US.

vidéo [video] ◇ *adj inv* video *(modif)*.

◇ *nf* video (recording) ■ **faire de la ~** to make videos.

vidéocassette [videɔkasɛt] *nf* videocassette, video.

vidéo-clip [videɔklip] (*pl* **vidéo-clips**) *nm* (music) video.

vidéoclub [videɔklœb] *nm* videoclub.

vidéocommunication [videɔkɔmynikasjɔ̃] *nf* video communication.

vidéoconférence [videɔkɔ̃ferɑ̃s] *nf* video conferencing.

vidéodisque [videɔdisk] *nm* videodisk.

vidéofréquence [videɔfrekɑ̃s] *nf* video frequency.

vidéogramme [videɔgram] *nm* videogram.

vidéographie [videɔgrafi] *nf* videography ■ **~ interactive** videotex.

vidéolecteur [videɔlɛktœr] *nm* videoplayer.

vidéophone [videɔfɔn] = **visiophone**.

vidéoprojecteur [videɔprɔʒɛktœr] *nm* video projector.

vide-ordures [vidɔrdyr] *nm inv* rubbish UK *ou* garbage US chute.

vidéotex [videɔtɛks] *nm* videotex.

vidéothèque [videɔtɛk] *nf* video library.

vidéotransmission [videɔtrɑ̃smisjɔ̃] *nf* video transmission.

vide-poches [vidpɔʃ] *nm inv* [meuble] tidy ■ [dans une voiture] glove compartment.

vide-pomme [vidpɔm] *nm inv* apple corer.

vider [3] [vide] *vt* **1.** [le contenu de - seau, verre, sac] to empty (out) *(sép)* ; [- poche, valise] to empty (out) *(sép)* ; [- baignoire] to let the water out of, to empty ■ **~ les ordures** to put out the rubbish UK *ou* garbage US ■ **~ son chargeur** to empty one's magazine ■ **~ de** : **~ une maison de ses meubles** to empty a house of its furniture, to clear the furniture from a house ■ **~ les lieux** to vacate the premises ▶ **~ l'abcès** to clear the air, to make a clean breast of things ■ **~ son sac** to get things off one's chest, to unburden o.s.

2. [le milieu de - pomme] to core ; [- volaille] to empty, to clean (out) *(sép)* ; [- poisson] to gut

3. [boire] to drain ■ **~ son verre** to drain one's glass ■ **~ une bouteille** to empty a bottle ■ **nous avons vidé une bouteille à deux** we downed a bottle between the two of us ■ **~ les fonds de bouteille** to drink the dregs

4. *fam* [épuiser] to do in *(sép)*, to finish off *(sép)* ■ **être vidé** to be exhausted

5. [mettre fin à] to settle (once and for all)

6. DR : **~ un délibéré** to give a verdict after deliberation

7. *fam* [renvoyer] to throw *ou* to kick out *(sép)* ■ **~ qqn** [employé] to sack UK *ou* to fire sb ; [client] to throw sb out, to bounce sb US ; [élève] to throw *ou* to chuck sb out

8. INFORM to dump

9. ÉQUIT : **~ les arçons** *ou* **étriers** to take a tumble (off one's horse).

◆ **se vider** *vpi* **1.** [contenu] to empty *ou* to drain (out)

2. [salle, ville] to empty.

videur, euse [vidœr, øz] *nm, f* [de volaille] cleaner.

◆ **videur** *nm* [de boîte de nuit] bouncer.

viduité [vidɥite] *nf* DR viduity ■ [d'une femme] widowhood ■ [d'un homme] widowerhood ■ **délai de ~** *time a widow or widower must wait before remarrying.*

vie [vi] *nf* **1.** BIOL life ■ **la ~ animale/végétale** animal/plant life ■ **durée de ~** life span

2. [existence] life ■ **il a eu la ~ sauve** he has been spared ■ **laisser la ~ sauve à qqn** to spare sb's life ■ **donner la ~ à un enfant** to give birth to a child ■ **mettre sa ~ en danger** to put one's life in danger ■ **risquer sa ~** to risk one's life ■ **ôter la ~ à qqn** to take sb's life ■ **revenir à la ~** to come back to life ■ **sauver la ~ de qqn** to save sb's life ■ **au début de sa ~** at the beginning of his life ■ **à la fin de sa ~** at the end of his life, late in life ■ **une fois dans sa ~** once in a lifetime ■ **de sa ~ elle n'avait vu un tel sans-gêne** she'd never seen such a complete lack of consideration ■ **l'œuvre de toute une ~** a lifetime's work ■ **à Julie, pour la ~** to Julie, forever *ou* for ever ■ **avoir la ~ devant soi** [ne pas être pressé] to have all the time in the world ; [être jeune] to have one's whole life in front of one ■ **il a dû être danseur dans une autre ~** he must have been a dancer in a previous incarnation ■ **être entre la ~ et la mort** to be hovering between life and death, to be at death's door ■ **passer de ~ à trépas** to pass away ▶ **la ~ continue** life goes on ■ **à la ~ à la mort** for life (and beyond the grave)

3. [personne] life ■ **son rôle est de sauver des ~s** he is there to save lives

4. [entrain] life ■ **mettre un peu de ~ dans** to liven up *(sép)* ■ **plein de ~** [ressemblant] true to life, lifelike ; [énergique] lively, full of life

5. [partie de l'existence] life ■ **~ privée** private life ■ **la ~ affective/intellectuelle/sexuelle** love/intellectual/sex life ■ **entrer dans la ~ active** to start working ■ **la ~ associative** community life

6. [façon de vivre - d'une personne, d'une société] life, lifestyle, way of life ; [- des animaux] life ■ **la ~ en Australie** the Australian lifestyle *ou* way of life ■ **dans la ~, l'important c'est de...** the important thing in life is to... ■ **faire sa ~ avec qqn** to settle down with sb ■ **avoir la ~ dure** to have a hard life ■ **faire** *ou* **mener la ~ dure à qqn** to make life difficult for sb ■ **rater sa ~** to make a mess of one's life ■ **refaire sa ~** to start afresh *ou* all over again ■ **c'est la ~!, la ~ est ainsi faite!** such is *ou* that's life! ▶ **mener une ~ de bâton de chaise** *ou* **de patachon** *fam* to lead a riotous life ■ **~ de bohême** bohemian life ■ **mener une ~ de chanoine** to live the life of Riley ■ **une ~ de chien** *fam* a dog's life ■ **ce n'est pas une ~!** I don't call that living! ■ **c'est la belle ~** *ou* **la ~ de château!** this is the life! ■ **faire la ~** *fam* to live it up ■ **mener joyeuse ~** to lead a merry life

7. [biographie] life ■ **il a écrit une ~ de Flaubert** he wrote a life *ou* biography of Flaubert

8. [conditions économiques] (cost of) living ■ **dans ce pays, la ~ n'est pas chère** prices are very low in this country ■ **le coût de la ~** the cost of living

9. RELIG life ■ **la ~ éternelle** everlasting life ■ **la ~ ici-bas** this life ■ **la ~ terrestre** life on earth

10. TECHNOL life ■ **à courte ~** short-lived ■ **à longue ~** long-lived ■ **~ d'un neutron** neutron lifetime.

◆ **à vie** *loc adj* for life, life *(modif)* ■ **amis à ~** friends for life ■ **membre à ~** life member.

◆ **en vie** *loc adj* alive, living ■ **être toujours en ~** to be still alive *ou* breathing.

◆ **sans vie** *loc adj* [corps] lifeless, inert ■ [œuvre] lifeless, dull.

vieil [vjɛj] *m* ⊳ **vieux**.

vieillard [vjɛjar] *nm* old man ■ **les ~s** old people, the old, the aged.

vieille [vjɛj] *f* ▷ **vieux**.

vieillerie [vjɛjri] *nf* **1.** [objet] old thing **2.** [idée] : **qui s'intéresse à ces ~s?** who's interested in those stale ideas?

vieillesse [vjejɛs] *nf* **1.** [d'une personne] old age ■ **avoir une ~ heureuse** to be happy in old age ■ **mourir de ~** to die of old age **2.** *litt* [d'un bijou, d'un vase] age **3.** [personnes] : **la ~** old people, the old, the aged.

vieilli, e [vjeji] *adj* [démodé] old-fashioned ■ [vieux] : **je l'ai trouvé très ~** I thought he'd aged a lot.

vieillir [32] [vjejir] ◇ *vi* **1.** [prendre de l'âge - personne] to age, to be getting old ; [- vin, fromage] to age, to mature ; [- technique] to become outmoded ■ **tout le monde vieillit** we all grow old ■ **bien ~** to grow old gracefully ■ **il a mal vieilli** he hasn't aged well ■ **ce film vieillit mal** this film doesn't stand the test of time ■ **son roman a beaucoup vieilli** her novel seems really dated now ■ **l'argent vieillit bien** silver ages well **2.** [paraître plus vieux] : **il a vieilli de 20 ans** he looks 20 years older ■ **tu ne vieillis pas** you never seem to look any older.
◇ *vt* **1.** [rendre vieux - personne] to make old, to age **2.** [vin, fromage] to age, to mature ■ [métal] to age-harden **3.** [apparence] : **~ qqn** [suj: vêtement, couleur] to make sb seem older ; [suj: personne] : **vous me vieillissez!** you're making me older than I am! ■ **c'est fou ce que les cheveux longs la vieillissent!** long hair makes her look a lot older!
◆ **se vieillir** *vp (emploi réfléchi)* [en apparence] to make o.s. look older ■ [en mentant] to lie about one's age *(by pretending to be older)*.

vieillissant, e [vjejisɑ̃, ɑ̃t] *adj* ageing ■ **des techniques ~es** techniques that are being superseded.

vieillissement [vjejismɑ̃] *nm* **1.** [naturel] ageing, the ageing process ■ **les signes qui trahissent le ~** the telltale signs of age *ou* of the ageing process **2.** [technique] ageing.

vieillot, otte [vjejo, ɔt] *adj* old-fashioned.

vielle [vjɛl] *nf* hurdy-gurdy.

viendra, vienne *etc v* ▷ **venir**.

Vienne [vjɛn] *npr* **1.** [en Autriche] Vienna ■ **le congrès de ~** the Congress of Vienna **2.** [en France - ville] Vienne ■ **la ~** [rivière] the (river) Vienne ; [département] Vienne *(département in Poitou-Charentes; chef-lieu: Poitiers, code: 86)*.

viennois, e [vjenwa, az] *adj* [Autriche] Viennese.
◆ **Viennois, e** *nm, f* [en Autriche] *inhabitant of or person from Vienna* ■ **les Viennois** the Viennese.

viennoiserie [vjenwazri] *nf pastry made with sweetened dough (croissant, brioche etc)*.

vient *etc v* ▷ **venir**.

vierge [vjɛrʒ] ◇ *adj* **1.** [personne] virgin ■ **elle/il est encore ~** she's/he's still a virgin **2.** [vide - cahier, feuille] blank, clean ; [- casier judiciaire] clean ; [- pellicule, film] unexposed ; [- cassette, disquette] blank **3.** [inexploité - sol, terre] virgin ■ **de la neige ~** fresh snow **4.** [sans additif] : **minerai ~** native ore **5.** *litt* [pur] pure, unsullied, uncorrupted ■ **~ de** devoid of, innocent of *litt*.
◇ *nf* [femme] virgin.

Vierge [vjɛrʒ] *npr f* **1.** RELIG : **la ~ (Marie)** the Virgin (Mary), the Blessed Virgin **2.** ASTROL Virgo **3.** ASTRON Virgo ■ **être ~** to be (a) Virgo *ou* a Virgoan.

Viêt-nam [vjɛtnam] *npr m* : **le ~** Vietnam ■ **au ~** in Vietnam ■ **le Nord/Sud ~** North/South Vietnam ■ **un ancien du ~** a Vietnam veteran.

vietnamien, enne [vjɛtnamjɛ̃, ɛn] *adj* Vietnamese.
◆ **Vietnamien, enne** *nm, f* Vietnamese ■ **les Vietnamiens** the Vietnamese.
◆ **vietnamien** *nm* LING Vietnamese.

vieux [vjø] *(devant nm commençant par voyelle ou h muet* **vieil** [vjɛj] **vieille** [vjɛj]*) adj* **1.** [âgé] old ■ **sa vieille mère** her old *ou* aged mother ■ **un vieil homme** an old *ou* elderly man ■ **les vieilles gens** old people, elderly people, the elderly ■ **devenir ~** to grow old, to get old ■ **vivre ~** [personne, animal] to live to be old, to live to a ripe old age ■ **se faire ~** to be getting on (in years), to be getting old ■ **je deviens frileux sur mes ~ jours** I feel the cold more with age ■ **le plus ~ des deux** the older *ou* elder (of the two) ■ **le plus ~ des trois** the eldest *ou* oldest of the three ■ **faire ~** to look old ■ **être ~ avant l'âge** to be old before one's time
2. *(avant le n)* [de longue date - admirateur, camarade, complicité, passion] old, long-standing ; [- famille, tradition] old, ancient ; [- dicton, recette] old ; [- continent, montagne] old ■ **la vieille ville** the old (part of the) town ● **le Vieux Monde** the Old World
3. [désuet - instrument, méthode] old ■ **c'est un tissu un peu ~ pour une robe de fillette** this material is a bit old-fashioned for a little girl's dress ■ **une vieille expression** [qui n'est plus usitée] an obsolete turn of phrase ; [surannée] an old-fashioned turn of phrase ■ **le ~ français** LING Old French ■ [usé, fané] old ■ **recycler les ~ papiers** to recycle waste paper ■ **un ~ numéro** [de magazine] a back issue ● **vieil or** old gold ■ **~ rose** old rose
4. [précédent] old
5. *fam* [à valeur affectueuse] : **alors, mon ~ chien?** how's my old doggie then? ■ **le ~ père Davril** old Davril ■ **~ farceur!** you old devil! ‖ [à valeur dépréciative] : **il doit bien rester un ~ bout de fromage** there must be an odd bit of cheese left over ■ **t'aurais pas une vieille enveloppe?** got an envelope (, any old one will do)? ■ **~ dégoûtant!** you disgusting old man! ‖ [à valeur intensive] : **ta voiture a pris un ~ coup** your car got a nasty bash ■ **j'ai eu un ~ coup de cafard** I felt really low
6. ŒNOL ▷ **vin**.
◆ **vieux** ◇ *nm* **1.** *fam péj* [homme âgé] old man ● **un ~ de la vieille** [soldat de Napoléon] an old veteran of Napoleon's guard ; [personne d'expérience] an old hand
2.[△] [père] : **mon/son ~** my/his old man
3. *fam* [à valeur affective - entre adultes] : **allez, (mon) ~, ça va s'arranger** come on mate *UK ou* buddy *US*, it'll be all right ■ **débrouille-toi, mon (petit) ~!** you sort it out yourself, pal *ou UK* mate! ■ [pour exprimer la surprise] : **j'en ai eu pour 1 000 euros – ben mon ~!** it cost me 1,000 euros – good heavens!
4. [ce qui est ancien] old things ■ **faire du neuf avec du ~** to turn old into new ■ **le vin sent le** *ou* **a un goût de ~** the wine tastes as though it's past its best
5. *fam loc* **prendre un coup de ~ : elle a pris un sacré coup de ~** she's looking a lot older ■ **le film a pris un coup de ~** the film seems to have dated.
◇ *adv* : **ça fait ~!** it's really old-fashioned! ■ **s'habiller ~** to wear old-fashioned clothes.
◇ *nmpl péj* **1.** *fam* [personnes âgées] : **les ~** old people ■ **les petits ~** old folk
2. [△] [parents] : **les** *ou* **mes ~** my parents, my folks, my Mum *UK ou* Mom *US* and Dad.
◆ **vieille** *nf* **1.** *fam péj* [femme âgée] old woman *ou* girl ■ **une petite vieille** a little old lady
2.[△] [mère] : **la vieille, ma/ta vieille** my/your old lady
3. *fam* [à valeur affective - entre adultes] : **salut, ma vieille!** hi there! ■ **il est trop tard, ma vieille!** it's too late, darling! ■ [exprime l'indignation] : **t'es gonflée, ma vieille!** you've got some nerve, you!
◆ **de vieux, de vieille** *loc adj* old-fashioned, antiquated, geriatric *hum* ■ **tu as des idées de ~** you're so old-fashioned (in your ideas) ■ **ce sont des hantises de ~** those are old people's obsessions.
◆ **vieux de, vieille de** *loc adj* [qui date de] : **c'est un manteau ~ d'au moins 30 ans** it's a coat which is at least 30 years old ■ **une amitié vieille de 20 ans** a friendship that goes back 20 years.
◆ **vieille fille** *nf vieilli & péj* spinster, old maid *péj* ■ **rester vieille fille** to remain unmarried ■ **c'est une manie de vieille fille** it's an old-maidish thing to do *péj*.
◆ **vieux garçon** *nm vieilli & péj* bachelor ■ **rester ~ garçon** to remain single *ou* a bachelor ■ **des manies de ~ garçon** bachelor ways.
◆ **vieux jeu** *loc adj* [personne, attitude] old-fashioned ■ [vêtements, idées] old-fashioned, outmoded ■ **ce que tu peux être ~ jeu!** you're so behind the times!

vif, vive [vif, viv] *adj* **1.** [plein d'énergie - personne] lively, vivacious ; [- musique, imagination, style] lively ■ **avoir le regard ~** to have a lively look in one's eye ■ **marcher d'un pas ~** to walk briskly ■ **rouler à vive allure** to drive at great speed
2. [intelligent - élève] sharp ; [- esprit] sharp, quick ■ **être ~ (d'esprit)** to be quick *ou* quick-witted *ou* sharp

3. [emporté - remarque, discussion, reproche] cutting, biting ; [- geste] brusque, brisk ■ **excusez-moi de ces mots un peu ~s** I apologize for having spoken rather sharply
4. [très intense - froid] biting ; [- couleur] bright, vivid ; [- désir, sentiment] strong ; [- déception, intérêt] keen ; [- félicitations, remerciements] warm ; [- regret, satisfaction] deep, great ; [- douleur] sharp ■ **porter un ~ intérêt à** to be greatly *ou* keenly interested in ■ **avec un ~ soulagement** with a profound sense of relief ■ **c'est avec un ~ plaisir que...** it's with great pleasure that... ■ **à feu ~** over a brisk heat ■ **l'air est ~ ce matin** it's chilly this morning ■ **l'air est ~ au bord de la mer** the sea air is bracing
5. [nu - angle, arête] sharp ; [- joint] dry ; [- pierre] bare
6. [vivant] : **être brûlé/enterré ~** to be burnt/buried alive
7. GÉOGR : **marée de vive eau** spring tide
8. ŒNOL [vin] lively.
◆ **vif** *nm* **1.** [chair vivante] : **le ~** the living flesh, the quick ➲ **piquer qqn au ~** to cut sb to the quick
2. [centre] : **trancher** *ou* **tailler dans le ~** to go straight to the point ■ **entrer dans le ~ du sujet** to get to the heart of the matter
3. DR living person
4. CONSTR sharp edge.
◆ **à vif** *loc adj* [blessure] open ■ **la chair était à ~** the flesh was exposed.
◆ **de vive voix** *loc adv* personally ■ **je le lui dirai de vive voix** I'll tell him personally.
◆ **sur le vif** *loc adv* [peindre] from life ■ [commenter] on the spot ■ **ces photos ont été prises sur le ~** these photos were unposed.

vif-argent [vifarʒɑ̃] (*pl* **vifs-argents**) *nm* quicksilver ■ **c'est du** *ou* **un ~** he's a bundle of energy.

vigie [viʒi] *nf* **1.** RAIL observation box ■ **~ de frein/signaux** brake/signal cabin **2.** NAUT [balise] danger-buoy ■ *vieilli* [guetteur] look-out ■ [poste] look-out post ■ [panier] crow's nest.

vigilance [viʒilɑ̃s] *nf* vigilance, watchfulness ■ **avec ~** watchfully ■ **sa ~ s'est relâchée** he's become less vigilant.

vigilant, e [viʒilɑ̃, ɑ̃t] *adj* [personne, regard] vigilant, watchful ■ [soins] vigilant ■ **soyez ~!** watch out!

vigile [viʒil] ◇ *nm* **1.** [d'une communauté] vigilante ■ [veilleur de nuit] night watchman ■ [surveillant] guard **2.** ANTIQ watch.
◇ *nf* RELIG vigil.

vigne [viɲ] *nf* **1.** AGRIC vine, grapevine ■ [vignoble] vineyard ■ **une région de ~s** a wine-producing region **2.** BOT : **~ vierge** Virginia creeper.

vigneron, onne [viɲərɔ̃, ɔn] *nm, f* wine-grower, wine-producer.

vignette [viɲɛt] *nf* **1.** COMM (manufacturer's) label ■ [sur un médicament] label *ou* sticker *(for reimbursement within the French Social Security system)* **2.** ART [sur un livre, une gravure] vignette.

VIGNETTE

The word *vignette* refers to the removable price sticker on pharmaceutical products which has to be affixed to a claim form for the reimbursement of the medical expenses known as the *feuille de soins* before it is sent to the *Sécurité sociale*.

vignoble [viɲɔbl] *nm* vineyard ■ **le ~ italien/alsacien** the vineyards of Italy/Alsace ■ **une région de ~s** a wine-growing area.

vigoureusement [viguʀøzmɑ̃] *adv* [frapper, frictionner] vigorously, energetically ■ [se défendre] vigorously ■ [protester] forcefully.

vigoureux, euse [viguʀø, øz] *adj* **1.** [fort - homme] vigorous, sturdy ; [- membres] strong, sturdy ; [- arbre, plante] sturdy ; [- santé] robust ; [- poignée de main, répression] vigorous ■ **il est encore ~!** he's still hale and hearty *ou* going strong! **2.** [langage, argument] forceful ■ [opposition, soutien] strong ■ [défense] vigorous, spirited ■ [contestation, effort] vigorous, forceful, powerful ■ [mesures] energetic.

vigueur [vigœʀ] *nf* **1.** [d'une personne, d'une plante] strength, vigour ■ [d'un coup] vigour, strength, power ■ **avec ~** vigorously, energetically **2.** [d'un style, d'une contestation] forcefulness, vigour ■ [d'un argument] forcefulness ■ **se défendre avec ~** to defend o.s. vigorously ■ **protester avec ~** to object forcefully.
◆ **en vigueur** ◇ *loc adj* [décret, loi, règlement] in force ■ [tarif, usage] current ■ **cesser d'être en ~** [loi] to lapse ; [règlement] to cease to apply.
◇ *loc adv* : **entrer en ~** [décret, tarif] to come into force *ou* effect.

VIH (*abr de* **virus d'immunodéficience humaine**) *nm* HIV.

viking [vikiŋ] *adj* Viking.
◆ **Viking** *nmf* Viking ■ **les Vikings** the Vikings.

vil, e [vil] *adj* **1.** *litt* [acte, personne, sentiment] base, vile, despicable **2.** *(avant le n) litt* [métier, condition] lowly, humble **3.** *loc* **à ~ prix** extremely cheap.

vilain, e [vilɛ̃, ɛn] ◇ *adj* **1.** [laid - figure, personne etc] ugly ; [- quartier] ugly, sordid ; [- décoration, bâtiment, habit] ugly, hideous ■ **ils ne sont pas ~s du tout, tes dessins** your drawings aren't bad at all ■ **un ~ petit canard** an ugly duckling **2.** [méchant] naughty ■ **c'est un ~ monsieur** he's a bad man ■ **la ~e bête, elle m'a mordu!** that nasty beast has bitten me! ■ **jouer un ~ tour à qqn** to play a rotten *ou* dirty trick on sb **3.** [sérieux - affaire, blessure, coup, maladie] nasty **4.** [désagréable - odeur] nasty, bad ; [- temps] nasty, awful.
◇ *nm, f* bad *ou* naughty boy (*f* girl) ■ **oh le ~/la ~e!** you naughty boy/girl!
◆ **vilain** *nm* **1.** HIST villein **2.** *fam* [situation désagréable] : **il va y avoir du ~!** there's going to be trouble! ■ **ça tourne au ~!** things are getting nasty!

vilebrequin [vilbʀəkɛ̃] *nm* **1.** TECHNOL (bit) brace **2.** AUTO crankshaft.

vilenie [vileni] *nf* *litt* **1.** [caractère] baseness, villainy **2.** [action] base *ou* vile deed, villainous act.

vilipender [3] [vilipɑ̃de] *vt litt* to disparage, to revile ■ **il a été vilipendé dans la presse** he was pilloried in the press.

villa [vila] *nf* **1.** [résidence secondaire] villa **2.** [pavillon] (detached) house **3.** ANTIQ & HIST villa **4.** [rue] private road.

village [vilaʒ] *nm* **1.** [agglomération, personnes] village **2.** LOISIRS : **~ (de vacances)** holiday *UK ou* vacation *US* village **3.** *loc* **~ global** *ou* **planétaire** the global village.

villageois, e [vilaʒwa, az] ◇ *adj* village *(modif)*, country *(modif)*.
◇ *nm, f* villager, village resident.

ville [vil] *nf* **1.** [moyenne] town ■ [plus grande] city ■ **toute la ~ en parle** it's the talk of the town ■ **à la ~ comme à la scène** in real life as (well as) on stage ➲ **~ d'eau** spa (town) ■ **~ industrielle/universitaire** industrial/university town ■ **~ nouvelle** new town ■ **la Ville éternelle** the Eternal City ■ **la Ville lumière** the City of Light ■ **la Ville sainte** RELIG the Holy City **2.** [quartier] : **~ haute/basse** upper/lower part of town **3.** ADMIN : **la ~** [administration] the local authority ; [représentants] the (town) council **4.** [milieu non rural] : **la ~** towns, cities ■ **les gens de la ~** city-dwellers, townspeople ■ **la vie à la ~** town *ou* city life.
◆ **de ville** *loc adj* [vêtement] : **chaussures/tenue de ~** shoes/outfit for wearing in town.
◆ **en ville** *loc adv* : **aller en ~** to go to *ou* into town *UK*, to go downtown *US* ■ **et si nous dînions en ~?** let's eat out tonight ■ **trouver un studio en ~** to find a flat *UK ou* studio apartment *US* in town.

ville-champignon [vilʃɑ̃piɲɔ̃] (*pl* **villes-champignons**) *nf* fast-expanding town.

ville-dortoir [vildɔʀtwaʀ] (*pl* **villes-dortoirs**) *nf* dormitory town.

villégiature [vileʒjatyʀ] *nf* holiday *UK*, vacation *US* ■ **être en ~** to be on holiday *UK ou* vacation *US* ■ **lieu de ~** holiday resort *UK*, vacation resort *US*.

ville-satellite [vilsatelit] *(pl* **villes-satellites***)* *nf* satellite town.

Villette [vilɛt] *npr f* : **la ~** *cultural complex in the north of Paris (including a science museum, theatre and park).*

Vilnius [vilnjys] *npr* Vilnius.

vin [vɛ̃] *nm* **1.** ŒNOL [boisson] wine ■ [ensemble de récoltes] vintage ◆ **grand ~, ~ de grand cru** vintage wine ■ **~ d'appellation d'origine contrôlée** appellation contrôlée wine ■ **~ blanc** white wine ■ **~ de Bordeaux** [rouge] claret ; [blanc] white Bordeaux ■ **~ de Bourgogne** Burgundy ■ **~ chaud** mulled wine ■ **~ de consommation courante** table wine ■ **~ du cru** local wine ■ **~ cuit** fortified wine ■ **~ gris** pale rosé ■ **~ de messe** altar *ou* communion wine ■ **~ mousseux** sparkling wine ■ **~ nouveau** *ou* **(de) primeur** new wine ■ **~ ordinaire** table wine ■ **~ de pays** local wine ■ **~ pétillant** sparkling wine ■ **~ du Rhin** hock ■ **~ rosé** rosé wine ■ **~ rouge** red wine ■ **~ de table** table wine ■ **~ vieux** aged wine ■ **avoir le ~ gai/triste/mauvais** to get merry/depressed/nasty after a few drinks ■ **être entre deux ~s** to be tiddly *ou* tipsy **2.** [liqueur] : **~ de canne/riz** cane/rice wine.
◆ **vin d'honneur** *nm* reception *(where wine is served).*

vinaigre [vinɛgr] *nm* **1.** [condiment] vinegar ■ **cornichons/oignons au ~** pickled gherkins/onions ◆ **~ d'alcool/de cidre/de vin** spirit/cider/wine vinegar ■ **~ balsamique** balsamic vinegar **2.** *fam loc* **tourner au ~** [vin] to turn sour ■ **les choses ont tourné au ~** things definitely went wrong.

vinaigrer [4] [vinegre] *vt* to add vinegar to ■ **ce n'est pas assez vinaigré** there's too little vinegar ■ **de l'eau vinaigrée** water with a touch of vinegar added.

vinaigrerie [vinɛgrəri] *nf* **1.** [fabrique] vinegar factory **2.** [production] vinegar making **3.** [commerce] vinegar trade.

vinaigrette [vinɛgrɛt] *nf* vinaigrette, French dressing ■ **haricots à la** *ou* **en ~** beans with vinaigrette *ou* French dressing.

vinaigrier [vinɛgrije] *nm* **1.** [bouteille] vinegar bottle **2.** [fabricant] vinegar maker *ou* manufacturer.

vinasse [vinas] *nf* **1.** *fam péj* [vin] plonk *UK*, jug wine *US* **2.** [résidu] vinasse.

vindicatif, ive [vɛ̃dikatif, iv] *adj* vindictive.

vindicte [vɛ̃dikt] *nf* DR : **la ~ publique** prosecution and punishment ■ **désigner** *ou* **livrer qqn à la ~ populaire** to expose sb to trial by the mob.

vineux, euse [vinø, øz] *adj* [rappelant le vin - visage] blotchy ; [- goût] wine-like ; [- haleine] which reeks of wine ; [- melon] wine-flavoured ■ **d'une couleur vineuse** wine-coloured.

vingt [vɛ̃] ◇ *dét* twenty ■ **je te l'ai dit ~ fois!** I've told you a hundred times! ■ **je n'ai plus ~ ans!** I'm not as young as I used to be! ■ **ah, si j'avais encore mes jambes/mon cœur de ~ ans!** if only I still had the legs/the heart of a twenty year-old! ◆ **~ dieux!** *fam vieilli* : RAPPEL-ADRESSE/> **dieux, la belle fille!** strewth *UK ou* Lord *US*, what a beauty! ■ **ne touche pas à ça, ~ dieux!** leave that alone, for God's sake!, *voir aussi* **cinq**.
◇ *nm inv* twenty ■ **il a joué trois fois le ~** he played three times on number twenty ■ **le ~ de chaque mois** the twentieth of the month.

vingtaine [vɛ̃tɛn] *nf* : **une ~** twenty or so, around twenty.

vingt-deux [vɛ̃tdø] *dét* & *nm inv* twenty-two ■ **~ v'là les flics!**△ watch out, here come the cops!

vingt-et-un [vɛ̃teœ̃] *nm* JEUX pontoon *UK*, vingt-et-un, twenty-one.

vingtième [vɛ̃tjɛm] *adj num* & *nmf* twentieth, *voir aussi* **cinquantième**.

vingtièmement [vɛ̃tjɛmmɑ̃] *adv* in the twentieth place.

vingt-quatre [vɛ̃tkatr] *dét* & *nm inv* twenty-four ■ **~ heures sur ~** round the clock ■ **surveillé ~ heures sur ~** under round-the-clock surveillance.

vinicole [vinikɔl] *adj* [pays] wine-growing ■ [industrie, production] wine *(modif)* ■ **entreprise ~** wine-making firm *UK*, winery *US*.

vinification [vinifikasjɔ̃] *nf* [de jus de fruits] vinification ■ [pour l'obtention de vin] wine-making process.

vinifier [9] [vinifje] *vt* to make into wine.

vint *etc v* ⊳ **venir**.

vinyle [vinil] *nm* vinyl.

vioc, vioque△ [vjɔk] *nm, f* **1.** [vieille personne] old codger *(f* biddy), old timer *US* **2.** [père, mère] : **la** *ou* **ma vioque** my old lady ■ **le** *ou* **mon ~** my old man ■ **mes ~s** my old folks.

viol [vjɔl] *nm* [d'une personne] rape ■ [d'un sanctuaire] violation, desecration.

violacé, e [vjɔlase] *adj* purplish-blue ■ **les mains ~es par le froid** hands blue with cold.
◆ **violacée** *nf* member of the Violaceae.

violacer [16] [vjɔlase] ◆ **se violacer** *vpi* [visage] to turn *ou* to go *ou* to become purple ■ [mains] to turn *ou* to go *ou* to become blue.

violateur, trice [vjɔlatœr, tris] *nm, f* [d'une loi, d'une constitution] transgressor ■ [d'un sanctuaire, d'une sépulture] violator, desecrator.

violation [vjɔlasjɔ̃] *nf* **1.** [d'une loi, d'une règle] violation ■ [d'un serment] breach ■ [d'un accord] violation, breach **2.** [d'un sanctuaire, d'une sépulture] violation, desecration ■ **~ de domicile** forcible entry *(into somebody's home).*

viole [vjɔl] *nf* viol ■ **~ d'amour** viola d'amore ■ **~ de gambe** bass viol, viola da gamba.

violemment [vjɔlamɑ̃] *adv* [frapper] violently ■ [protester, critiquer] vehemently ■ [désirer] passionately ■ **il se jeta ~ sur moi** he hurled himself at me.

violence [vjɔlɑ̃s] *nf* **1.** [brutalité - d'un affrontement, d'un coup, d'une personne] violence ; [- d'un sport] roughness, brutality ■ **avec ~** with violence, violently ■ **scène de ~** violent scene ■ **obliger qqn à faire qqch par la ~** to force sb to do sthg by violent means ■ **répondre à la ~ par la ~** to meet violence with violence ■ **faire ~ à une femme** *arch* to violate a woman ■ *fig* **faire ~ à** [principes, sentiments] to do violence to, to go against ; [texte] to do violence to, to distort the meaning of ■ **se faire ~** to force o.s. **2.** [acte] assault, violent act ◆ **~ à agent** assault on (the person of) a police officer ■ **~ routière** dangerous *ou* reckless driving **3.** [intensité - d'un sentiment, d'une sensation] intensity ; [- d'un séisme, du vent etc] violence, fierceness.

violent, e [vjɔlɑ̃, ɑ̃t] ◇ *adj* **1.** [brutal - sport, jeu] rough, brutal ; [- attaque, affrontement] fierce, violent, brutal ; [- personne] violent, brutal ; [- tempérament] violent, fiery ■ **se montrer ~ avec qqn** to be violent with sb ■ **une mort ~e** a violent death **2.** [intense - pluie] driving ; [- vent, tempête] violent, raging ; [- couleur] harsh, glaring ; [- parfum] pungent, overpowering ; [- effort] huge, strenuous ; [- besoin, envie] intense, uncontrollable, urgent ; [- douleur] violent ■ **un ~ mal de tête** a splitting headache.
◇ *nm, f* violent person.

violenter [3] [vjɔlɑ̃te] *vt* **1.** [femme] to assault sexually ■ **elle a été violentée** she was sexually assaulted **2.** *litt* [désir, penchant] to do violence to, to go against.

violer [3] [vjɔle] *vt* **1.** [personne] to rape ■ **se faire ~** to be raped **2.** [loi, règle] to violate ■ [serment] to break ■ [accord, secret professionnel] to violate, to break **3.** [sanctuaire, sépulture] to violate, to desecrate ■ **~ le domicile de qqn** DR to force entry into sb's home ■ **~ les consciences** *fig* to violate people's consciences.

violet, ette [vjɔlɛ, ɛt] *adj* purple, violet ■ **ses mains ~tes de froid** her hands blue with cold.

◆ **violet** *nm* purple, violet (colour).
◆ **violette** *nf* violet ▪ **~te odorante/de Parme** sweet/Parma violet.

violeur, euse [vjɔlœr, øz] *nm, f* rapist.

violine [vjɔlin] *adj* dark purple.

violon [vjɔlɔ̃] *nm* **1.** MUS [instrument - d'orchestre] violin ; [- de violoneux] fiddle ▪ [artiste] : **premier ~ (solo)** first violin ▪ **jouer les seconds** *ou* **troisièmes ~s** *fig* to play second fiddle ▪ **~ d'Ingres** hobby ▪ **accorder ses ~s** to reach an agreement **2.** *fam* [prison] cells.

violoncelle [vjɔlɔ̃sɛl] *nm* cello, violoncello *spéc.*

violoncelliste [vjɔlɔ̃selist] *nmf* cellist, cello player, violoncellist *spéc.*

violoneux [vjɔlɔnø] *nm péj* (mediocre) violinist.

violoniste [vjɔlɔnist] *nmf* violinist, violin-player.

VIP [viajpi, veipe] (*abr de* **very important person**) *nmf* VIP.

vipère [vipɛr] *nf* adder, viper ▪ **~ aspic** asp ▪ **c'est une vraie ~** *fig* & *péj* she's really vicious.

vipérin, e [viperɛ̃, in] *adj* **1.** ZOOL viperine ▪ **couleuvre ~e** viperine grass snake **2.** *litt* [méchant] viperish *sout*, vicious.
◆ **vipérine** *nf* BOT viper's bugloss.

virage [viraʒ] *nm* **1.** [d'une route] bend, curve, turn *US* ▪ **prendre un ~** to take a bend, to go round a bend ▪ **prendre un ~ à la corde** to hug the bend ▪ **prendre un ~ sur les chapeaux de roue** to take a bend *ou* turn on two wheels ◗ **~ en épingle à cheveux** hairpin bend ▪ **~ en S** S-bend *UK*, S-curve *US* ▪ **~ relevé** banked corner **2.** [mouvement - d'un véhicule, au ski] turn ▪ **faire un ~ incliné** *ou* **sur l'aile** AÉRON to bank an aeroplane **3.** [changement - d'attitude, d'idéologie] (drastic) change *ou* shift ▪ **~ à droite/gauche** POLIT shift to the right/left **4.** PHOTO toning *(U)* **5.** CHIM change in colour.

virago [virago] *nf* virago, shrew *fig.*

viral, e, aux [viral, o] *adj* viral ▪ **maladie ~e** viral infection *ou* illness.

virée [vire] *nf fam* **1.** [promenade] : **faire une ~ à vélo/en voiture** to go for a bicycle ride/a drive ▪ **si on faisait une ~ dans les bars du coin?** let's hit the local bars **2.** [court voyage] trip, tour, jaunt ▪ **on a fait une petite ~ en Bretagne** we went for a little jaunt to Brittany.

virement [virmɑ̃] *nm* **1.** BANQUE : **faire un ~ de 400 euros sur un compte** to transfer 400 euros to an account ◗ **~ automatique** standing order ▪ **~ bancaire** bank transfer ▪ **~ de crédit** credit transfer **2.** NAUT : **~ de bord** tacking.

virer [3] [vire] ◇ *vi* **1.** [voiture] to turn ▪ [vent] to veer ▪ [grue] to turn round ▪ [personne] to turn *ou* to pivot round ▪ **~ sur l'aile** AÉRON to bank ▪ **~ de bord** NAUT [gén] to veer ; [voilier] to tack ; *fig* to take a new line *ou* tack **2.** CHIM [liquide] to change colour **3.** MÉD [cuti-réaction] to come up positive **4.** PHOTO to tone.
◇ *vt* **1.** BANQUE to transfer ▪ **~ 300 euros sur un compte** to transfer 300 euros to an account **2.** *fam* [jeter - meuble, papiers] to chuck (out), to ditch ▪ **vire-moi ces journaux de là** get those papers out of there **3.** *fam* [renvoyer - employé] to fire, to sack *UK* ; [- importun] to kick *ou* to chuck out *(sép)* ▪ **se faire ~** [employé] to get the sack *UK ou* the bounce *US* ▪ **je me suis fait ~ de chez moi** I got kicked *ou* thrown out of my place **4.** MÉD : **il a viré sa cuti** *pr* his skin test was positive ; *fig*fam he changed radically **5.** NAUT to veer ▪ **virez l'ancre!** weigh the anchor! **6.** PHOTO to tone.
◆ **virer à** *v+prép* : **~ à l'aigre** [vin] to turn sour ▪ **~ au vert/rouge** to turn green/red.

virevolte [virvɔlt] *nf* **1.** [pirouette] pirouette, twirl **2.** *fig* [changement] volte-face ▪ **faire des ~s** to chop and change.

virevolter [3] [virvɔlte] *vi* **1.** [tourner sur soi] to pirouette, to spin round *(insép)* **2.** [s'agiter] to dance around ▪ **elle virevoltait gaiement dans la maison** she was flitting happily about the house.

Virgile [virʒil] *npr* Virgil.

virginal, e, aux [virʒinal, o] *adj* virginal, maidenly ▪ **d'une blancheur ~e** *litt* virgin *ou* lily white.
◆ **virginal, e** *nm, f* MUS virginals.

Virginie [virʒini] ◇ *nm* Virginia (tobacco).
◇ *npr f* GÉOGR : **(la) ~** Virginia ▪ **(la) ~-Occidentale** West Virginia.

virginité [virʒinite] *nf* **1.** [d'une personne] virginity ▪ **perdre sa ~** to lose one's virginity ▪ **le parti devra se refaire une ~** *fig* the party will have to forge itself a new reputation **2.** *litt* [d'un lys, de la neige] purity.

virgule [virgyl] *nf* **1.** [dans un texte] comma ▪ **copier qqch sans y changer une ~** to copy sthg out without a single alteration **2.** MATH (decimal) point ▪ **4 ~ 9** 4 point 9 ◗ **~ flottante** floating comma.

viril, e [viril] *adj* **1.** [force, langage] manly, virile **2.** [sexuellement] virile.

viriliser [3] [virilize] *vt* **1.** BIOL [suj: médicament] to cause the development of male sexual characteristics in **2.** [en apparence - suj: sport] to make more masculine in appearance.

virilisme [virilism] *nm* virilism.

virilité [virilite] *nf* **1.** [gén] virility, manliness **2.** [vigueur sexuelle] virility.

virologie [virɔlɔʒi] *nf* virology.

virtualiser [virtɥalize] *vt* to virtualize.

virtualité [virtɥalite] *nf* virtuality.

virtuel, elle [virtɥɛl] *adj* **1.** [fait, valeur] potential **2.** INFORM, OPT & PHYS virtual.

virtuellement [virtɥɛlmɑ̃] *adv* **1.** [potentiellement] potentially **2.** [très probablement] virtually, practically.

virtuose [virtɥoz] *nmf* MUS virtuoso ▪ **~ du violon** violin virtuoso ▪ **c'est une ~ du tennis/de l'aiguille** she's a brilliant tennis player/needlewoman.

virtuosité [virtɥozite] *nf* virtuosity ▪ **elle a joué la fugue avec une grande ~** she gave a virtuoso rendering of the fugue ▪ **manier le pinceau avec ~** to be a brilliant painter.

virulence [virylɑ̃s] *nf* **1.** [d'un reproche, d'un discours] virulence, viciousness, venom **2.** MÉD virulence.

virulent, e [virylɑ̃, ɑ̃t] *adj* **1.** [critique, discours] virulent, vicious, venomous ▪ [haine] burning, bitter **2.** MÉD [agent, poison] virulent.

virus [virys] *nm* **1.** BIOL virus ▪ **le ~ de la grippe** the influenza virus ◗ **~ filtrant** filterable virus **2.** *fig* **tout le pays était atteint par le ~ du loto** the whole country was gripped by lottery fever ▪ **elle a attrapé le ~ du deltaplane** *fam* she's completely hooked on hang-gliding, she's got the hang-gliding bug **3.** INFORM virus.

vis [vis] *nf* TECHNOL screw ▪ **~ à bois** woodscrew ▪ **~ platinée** AUTO contact point ▪ **~ sans fin** worm *ou* endless screw ▪ **~ de serrage** setscrew.

visa [viza] *nm* **1.** [sur un passeport] visa ▪ **un ~ pour l'Australie** a visa for Australia ◗ **~ de touriste** *ou* **de visiteur** tourist *UK ou* non-immigrant *US* visa ▪ **~ de sortie** exit visa ▪ **~ de transit** transit visa **2.** [sur un document] stamp ▪ **apposer un ~ sur** to stamp ◗ **~ de censure** CINÉ (censor's) certificate.

Visa® [viza] *nf* : **la (carte) ~** Visa®(card).

visage [vizaʒ] *nm* **1.** [d'une personne] face ▪ **il a soudain changé de ~** his expression suddenly changed ◗ **Visage pâle** paleface ▪ **faire bon ~ à qqn** to put on a show of friendliness for sb ▪ **à ~ découvert** [sans masque] unmasked ; [sans voile] unveiled ; [ouvertement] openly **2.** [aspect] aspect ▪ **l'Afrique aux multiples ~s** the many faces of Africa ▪ **enfin une ville à ~ humain!** at last a town made for people to live in! ▪ **elle révélait enfin son vrai ~** she was revealing her true self *ou* nature at last.

visagiste [vizaʒist] *nmf* hair stylist.

vis-à-vis [vizavi] *nm* **1.** [personne en face] : **mon ~** the person opposite me ■ **faire ~ à qqn** to be opposite sb, to face sb **2.** [immeuble d'en face] : **nous n'avons pas de ~** there are no buildings directly opposite **3.** [canapé] tête-à-tête.
➔ **vis-à-vis de** *loc prép* **1.** [en face de] : **être ~ de qqn** to be opposite sb **2.** [envers] towards, vis-à-vis ■ **quelle position avez-vous ~ de ce problème?** what is your position on this problem? **3.** [par rapport à] by comparison with, next to, against.
➔ **en vis-à-vis** *loc adv* : **être en ~** to be opposite each other, to be facing each other ■ **assis en ~** sitting opposite each other *ou* face-to-face.

viscéral, e, aux [viseral, o] *adj* **1.** PHYSIOL visceral **2.** [dégoût] profound ■ [peur] deep-rooted, profound ■ [jalousie] pathological ■ **je ne l'aime pas, c'est ~** I don't like him, it's a gut feeling.

viscères [visɛr] *nmpl* viscera.

viscose [viskoz] *nf* viscose.

viscosité [viskozite] *nf* [gén - PHYS] viscosity.

visée [vize] *nf* **1.** *(gén pl)* [intention] design, aim ■ **avoir des ~s sur qqn/qqch** to have designs on sb/sthg **2.** ARM aiming, taking aim, sighting **3.** CINÉ & PHOTO viewfinding.

viser [3] [vize] ◇ *vt* **1.** ARM [cible] to (take) aim at *(insép)* ■ [jambe, tête] to aim for ■ **bien visé!** good shot! **2.** [aspirer à - poste] to set one's sights on *(insép)*, to aim for ; [- résultats] to aim at *ou* for *(insép)* **3.** [concerner - suj: réforme] to be aimed *ou* directed at ; [- suj: critique] to be aimed *ou* directed at, to be meant for ■ **je ne vise personne!** I don't mean anybody in particular! ■ **se sentir visé** to feel one is being got at **4.** △ [regarder] to look at, to check out **5.** ADMIN [passeport] to visa ■ [document - gén] to stamp ; [- avec ses initiales] to initial.
◇ *vi* **1.** MIL to (take) aim ■ **~ juste/trop bas** to aim accurately/too low **2.** *fig* **~ (trop) haut** to set one's sights *ou* to aim (too) high.
➔ **viser à** *v+prép* [suj: politique, personne] to aim at ■ **mesures visant à faire payer les pollueurs** measures aimed at making the polluters pay.

viseur [vizœr] *nm* **1.** ARM [gén] sight, sights ■ [à lunette] telescopic sight **2.** OPT telescopic sight **3.** CINÉ & PHOTO viewfinder.

visibilité [vizibilite] *nf* visibility ■ **atterrir sans ~** to make a blind landing, to land blind ■ **~ nulle** zero visibility.

visible [vizibl] ◇ *adj* **1.** [objet] visible ■ **~ à l'œil nu** visible to the naked eye **2.** [évident - gêne, intérêt, mépris] obvious, visible ; [- amélioration, différence] visible, perceptible ■ **il est ~ que...** it's obvious *ou* clear that... **3.** *sout* [prêt à recevoir] : **elle est ~ de midi à 4 h** she receives visitors between 12 and 4.
◇ *nm* : **le ~** that which is visible.

visiblement [viziblәmɑ̃] *adv* [gêné, mécontent] obviously, visibly ■ [amélioré] perceptibly, visibly ■ **~, ils se connaissaient déjà** they'd obviously met before.

visière [vizjɛr] *nf* [gén] eyeshade *UK*, vizor *US* ■ [d'un casque] visor, vizor ■ [d'une casquette] peak ■ **~ de protection** face-guard.

visioconférence [vizjokɔ̃ferɑ̃s] *nf* videoconference.

vision [vizjɔ̃] *nf* **1.** [idée] view, outlook ■ **nous n'avons pas la même ~ des choses** we see things differently ■ **sa ~ du monde** her world view **2.** [image] vision ■ [hallucination] vision, apparition ■ **tu as des ~s!** *fam hum* you're seeing things! **3.** PHYSIOL vision.

visionnaire [vizjɔnɛr] *adj* & *nmf* visionary.

visionner [3] [vizjɔne] *vt* [film, émission] to view ■ [diapositives] to look at.

visionneuse [vizjɔnøz] *nf* viewer.

visiophone [vizjɔfɔn] *nm* videophone, viewphone.

Visitation [vizitasjɔ̃] *nf* RELIG : **la ~** the Visitation.

visite [vizit] *nf* **1.** [chez quelqu'un - gén] visit ; [- courte] call ■ **~ éclair** flying visit ■ **avoir** *ou* **recevoir la ~ de qqn** to have a visit from sb ■ **je m'attendais à sa ~** I was expecting him to call ■ **rendre ~ à qqn** to pay sb a visit, to call on sb, to visit sb ■ **être en ~ chez qqn** to be paying sb a visit, to be visiting sb *ou* with sb *US* ▶ **~ officielle/privée** official/private visit ■ **~ de politesse** courtesy call *ou* visit
2. [à l'hôpital, auprès d'un détenu] visit ■ **heures de ~** visiting hours
3. [visiteur] : **avoir de la ~** to have a visitor ■ **tu attends de la** *fam* *ou* **une ~?** are you expecting a visitor *ou* somebody?
4. [exploration - d'un lieu] visit, tour ■ **~ audioguidée** audio guided tour ■ **~ guidée** guided tour
5. [d'un médecin - chez le patient] visit, call ; [- dans un hôpital] (ward) round ▶ **~ de contrôle** follow-up examination ■ **~ à domicile** house call *ou* visit ■ **~ médicale** medical *ou* physical *US* examination, medical, physical *US* ■ **passer une ~ médicale** to undergo a medical examination, to take a physical examination *US*
6. [inspection - pour acheter] viewing ; [- pour surveiller] inspection ■ **~ de douane** customs inspection ■ **~ d'inspection** visitation, visit ■ **faire une ~ d'inspection de** to visit.

visiter [3] [vizite] *vt* **1.** [se promener dans - région, monument] to visit ; [- caves, musée] to go round *(insép)*, to visit ; [- pour acheter] to view ; [- par curiosité] to look round *(insép)* ■ **une personne de l'agence vous fera ~ l'appartement** somebody from the agency will show you round *ou US*through the flat *UK ou* apartment *US* **2.** [rendre visite à - détenu] to visit ; [- malade, indigent, client] to visit, to call on *(insép)* **3.** [inspecter - matériel, valise] to examine, to inspect ; [- bateau] to inspect **4.** RELIG [diocèse] to visit ■ [suj: Saint-Esprit] to visit **5.** TEXT to perch.

visiteur, euse [vizitœr, øz] *nm, f* **1.** [invité] visitor, caller ■ [d'un musée] visitor **2.** [professionnel] : **~ des douanes** customs inspector ■ **~ de prison** prison visitor **3.** COMM representative, rep ■ **~ médical** representative in pharmaceutical products, medical representative **4.** TEXT percher.

vison [vizɔ̃] *nm* **1.** ZOOL mink **2.** [fourrure] mink **3.** [vêtement] mink (coat).

visqueux, euse [viskø, øz] *adj* **1.** PHYS [matière] viscous ■ [surface] viscid **2.** [peau, personne] slimy.

visser [3] [vise] *vt* **1.** [fixer - planche, support] to screw on *ou* to *(sép)* ; [- couvercle] to screw on *ou* down *(sép)* ■ **le miroir est vissé au mur** the mirror is screwed to the wall ■ *fig* **être vissé sur son siège** to be glued to one's chair **2.** [en tournant - bouchon, embout] to screw on *(sép)* ; [- robinet] to turn off *(sép)* **3.** *fam* [personne] to crack down on *(insép)*, to put the screws on ■ **il a toujours vissé ses gosses** he always kept a tight rein on his kids.
➔ **se visser** *vp (emploi passif)* to screw on *ou* in ■ **ampoule qui se visse** screw-in bulb.

Vistule [vistyl] *npr f* : **la ~** the River Vistula.

visu [vizy] **de visu**.

visualisation [vizɥalizasjɔ̃] *nf* **1.** [mentale] visualization, visualizing **2.** INFORM display ■ **console** *ou* **écran de ~** visual display terminal *ou* unit, VDU.

visualiser [3] [vizɥalize] *vt* **1.** [mentalement] to visualize **2.** INFORM to display.

visuel, elle [vizɥɛl] *adj* [mémoire, support] visual.
➔ **visuel** *nm* INFORM visual display unit *ou* terminal, VDU.

vit *etc v* **1.** ⊳ **vivre 2.** ⊳ **voir**.

vital, e, aux [vital, o] *adj* **1.** BIOL & PHYSIOL vital **2.** [indispensable] vital, essential ■ **l'agriculture est ~e pour notre région** agriculture is vital to this region **3.** [fondamental - problème, question] vital, fundamental.

vitalité [vitalite] *nf* [d'une personne] vitality, energy ■ [d'une économie] dynamism, vitality, buoyancy ■ [d'une expression, d'une théorie] vitality ■ **être plein de ~** to be full of energy.

vitamine [vitamin] *nf* vitamin ■ **~ A/C** vitamin A/C.

vitaminé, e [vitamine] *adj* with added vitamins, vitaminized.

vite [vit] ◇ *adv* **1.** [rapidement - courir, marcher] fast, quickly ; [- se propager] rapidly, quickly ■ **roule moins ~** slow down, don't drive so fast ■ **va plus ~** speed up, go faster ■ **tout s'est**

passé si ~ **que je n'ai pas eu le temps de voir** everything happened so quickly that I didn't see a thing ▪ **comme le temps passe ~!** doesn't time fly! ▪ **elle apprend/travaille ~** she's a quick learner/worker ▪ **il calcule ~** he's quick at calculations ▪ **on fait faire des travaux, mais ça ne va pas ~** we're having some alterations done, but it's taking a long time *ou* it's a long job ▪ **prenons un taxi, ça ira plus ~** let's take a taxi, it'll be quicker ▪ **les exercices vont trop ~ pour moi** I can't keep up *ou* pace with the exercises ▪ **ça a été ~ réglé** it was settled in no time at all, it was soon settled ▪ **fais ~!** hurry up!, be quick (about it)! ▪ **tu retournes en ville? – je fais ~** are you going back into town? – I won't be long ▪ **et plus ~ que ça!** and be quick about it! ⊳ **~ fait** *fam* quickly ▪ **range-moi ta chambre ~ fait!** tidy up your room and be quick about it! ▪ **ça a été du ~ fait!** it didn't take long!, that was quick work! ; *péj* it's slapdash work! ▪ **~ fait, bien fait** *fam* **: on lui a repeint sa grille ~ fait, bien fait** we gave her gate a nice new coat of paint in no time ▪ **je vais l'envoyer se faire voir ~ fait, bien fait!**△ I'll send him packing once and for all! ▪ **aller plus ~ que la musique** *ou* **les violons** to jump the gun

2. [à la hâte] quickly, in a hurry *ou* rush ▪ **manger ~** to bolt one's food (down) ▪ **aller ~** [dans ses conclusions] to be hasty ▪ **ne conclus pas trop ~** don't jump *ou* rush to conclusions ⊳ **ils vont gagner – c'est ~ dit!** they're going to win – I wouldn't be so sure! ▪ **il est assez efficace – il faut le dire ~!** he's quite efficient – well, that's one way of putting it! ▪ **ne parle pas trop ~!** don't speak too soon!

3. [sans tarder] quickly, soon ▪ **envoyez ~ votre bulletin-réponse!** send your entry form now! ▪ **j'ai ~ compris de quoi il s'agissait** I soon realized what it was all about, it didn't take me long to realize what it was all about

4. [facilement] quickly, easily ⊳ **méfie-toi, il a ~ fait de s'énerver** be careful, he loses his temper easily ▪ **on a ~ fait de se brûler avec ça!** it's easy to burn yourself on that thing!

5. *loc* **aller ~ en besogne** [être rapide] to be a quick worker ; [être trop pressé] to be over-hasty ▪ **vous allez un peu ~ en besogne, je ne vous accuse pas!** don't jump to conclusions, I haven't accused you of anything!

<> *adj* [en langage journalistique - coureur] fast.

◆ **au plus vite** *loc adv* as soon as possible.

vitesse [vitɛs] *nf* **1.** [d'un coureur, d'un véhicule] speed ▪ **à la ~ de 180 km/h** at (a speed of) 180 km/h ▪ **la ~ est limitée à 90 km/h** the speed limit is 90 km/h ▪ **faire de la ~** to drive *ou* to go fast ▪ **prendre de la ~** to pick up speed, to speed up ▪ **gagner/perdre de la ~** to gather/to lose speed ⊳ **~ ascensionnelle** AÉRON rate of climb ▪ **~ de circulation de l'argent** ÉCON velocity of circulation of money ▪ **~ de croisière** *pr* & *fig* cruising speed ▪ **le projet a maintenant atteint sa ~ de croisière** the project is now running smoothly along ▪ **~ d'horloge** clock rate *ou* speed ▪ **~ de pointe** top *ou* maximum speed ▪ **~ relative** AÉRON airspeed ▪ **gagner** *ou* **prendre qqn de ~** [à pied] to walk faster than sb ; [en voiture] to go *ou* to drive faster than sb ; *fig* to beat sb to it, to pip sb at the post *UK*, to beat sb by a nose *US* **2.** PHYS [d'un corps] speed, velocity ▪ [de la lumière] speed ▪ **~ acquise** momentum ▪ **~ initiale** [gén] initial speed ; ARM muzzle speed ▪ **~ moyenne** average speed ▪ **~ de réaction** reaction velocity *ou* speed ▪ **la ~ du son** the speed of sound ▪ **à la ~ du son** at the speed of sound **3.** [rythme - d'une action] speed, quickness, rapidity ; [- d'une transformation] speed, rapidity ▪ **ses cheveux poussent à une ~ incroyable!** her hair grows so fast! **4.** AUTO & MÉCAN gear ▪ **première/deuxième/troisième ~** first/second/third gear ▪ **passer les ~s** to go up through the gears ; [en rétrogradant] to go down through the gears ▪ **les ~s ne veulent pas passer** *fam* the gearbox is sticking ▪ **à deux ~s** *fig* two-tier ▪ **à la ~ grand V** *fam* at the double, at a rate of knots *UK*.

◆ **à toute vitesse** *loc adv* in double-quick time ▪ **passer à toute ~** [temps, moto] to fly by.

◆ **en vitesse** *loc adv* [rapidement] quickly ▪ [à la hâte] in a rush *ou* hurry ▪ **déjeuner/se laver en ~** to have a quick lunch/wash ▪ **écrire une lettre en ~** to dash off a letter ▪ **on prend un verre en ~?** shall we have a quick drink? ▪ **sors d'ici, et en ~!** get out of here and be sharp about it! ▪ **il a déguerpi en ~!** he left at the double!, he didn't hang around!

viticole [vitikɔl] *adj* **: région ~** wine-growing *ou* wine-producing region ▪ **entreprise ~** wine-making company *UK*, winery *US*.

viticulteur, trice [vitikyltœr, tris] *nm, f* wine-grower, wine-producer, viticulturist *spéc*.

viticulture [vitikyltyr] *nf* vine-growing, viticulture *spéc*.

vitoulet [vitulɛ] *nm* *Belgique* *veal meatball*.

vitrage [vitraʒ] *nm* **1.** [vitres] windows ▪ [panneau] glass partition **2.** [verre] window glass **3.** [installation] glazing **4.** [rideau] net curtain.

vitrail, aux [vitraj, o] *nm* **1.** [gén] stained-glass window ▪ [non coloré] leaded glass window ▪ **les vitraux de Chartres** the stained-glass windows of Chartres **2.** [technique] **: le ~** stained-glass window making.

vitre [vitr] *nf* **1.** [plaque de verre] (window) pane **2.** [fenêtre] window ⊳ **~ arrière** AUTO rear window.

vitré, e [vitre] *adj* **1.** [porte - complètement] glass *(modif)* ; [- au milieu] glazed ▪ [panneau, toit] glass *(modif)* **2.** [parchemin] vitreous **3.** ANAT [corps, humeur] vitreous.

vitrer [3] [vitre] *vt* [fenêtre, porte] to glaze ▪ [verrière] to fit with glass.

vitrerie [vitrəri] *nf* **1.** [fabrique] glaziery **2.** [commerce] window glass trade *ou* industry **3.** [vitres] window glass.

vitreux, euse [vitrø, øz] *adj* **1.** [terne - œil, regard] glassy, glazed **2.** GÉOL & PHYS vitreous **3.** [porcelaine] vitreous.

vitrier [vitrije] *nm* glazier.

vitrification [vitrifikasjɔ̃] *nf* **1.** [d'un parquet] sealing, varnishing ▪ [de tuiles] glazing **2.** [de sable, de déchets nucléaires] vitrification.

vitrifier [9] [vitrifje] *vt* **1.** [parquet] to varnish ▪ [tuiles] to glaze ▪ **brique vitrifiée** glazed brick **2.** [déchets nucléaires, sable] to vitrify **3.** [ville] to destroy with nuclear weapons.

vitrine [vitrin] *nf* **1.** [devanture] (shop *UK* *ou* store *US*) window, display window ▪ [vitre] shop window ▪ [objets exposés] window display ▪ **faire une ~** to dress a window ▪ **mettre qqch en ~** to put sthg (out) on display *(in the window)* ⊳ **faire** *ou* **lécher les ~s** *fam* to do some window-shopping **2.** [meuble - de maison] display cabinet ; [- de musée] display cabinet, showcase ; [- de magasin] showcase, display case.

vitriol [vitrijɔl] *nm* vitriol ▪ **des propos au ~** caustic *ou* vitriolic remarks.

vitrioler [3] [vitrijɔle] *vt* **1.** [traiter] to vitriolize **2.** [blesser] **: ~ qqn** to attack sb with acid ▪ **il a été vitriolé** he had sulphuric acid thrown in his face.

vitro [vitro] ⊳ **in vitro**.

vitrocéramique [vitroseramik] *adj* **: plaque ~** ceramic hob.

vitupérations [vityperasjɔ̃] *nfpl* *sout* vituperation *sout*, vilification *sout*, verbal abuse.

vitupérer [18] [vitypere] <> *vi* *litt* to vituperate *sout* ▪ **~ contre qqn/qqch** to inveigh against sb/sthg.

<> *vt* *sout* to vituperate *sout*, to inveigh against.

vivable [vivabl] *adj* [situation] bearable ▪ [habitation] fit for living in ▪ [personne] **: elle n'est pas ~** *fam* she's impossible to live with ▪ **ce n'est plus ~ au bureau!** it's unbearable at the office now!

vivace [vivas] *adj* **1.** BOT hardy **2.** [qui dure - croyance, opinion] deep-rooted ; [- souvenir] abiding ; [- foi] steadfast ▪ **son souvenir est encore ~** his memory is still very much alive.

vivacité [vivasite] *nf* **1.** [promptitude - d'une attaque, d'une démarche, d'un geste] briskness ; [- d'une intelligence] sharpness, acuteness ▪ **~ d'esprit** quick-wittedness **2.** [brusquerie - d'une personne, de propos] brusqueness ▪ **~ d'humeur** hotness of temper, quick-temperedness **3.** [entrain - d'une personne, d'un style] vivaciousness, vivacity, liveliness ; [- d'un marché] liveliness, buoyancy ; [- d'une description] vividness, liveliness ; [- d'un regard] vivacity ▪ **parler avec ~** to speak animatedly **4.** [force - d'une douleur] sharpness, intensity ; [- du froid] bitterness, sharpness ; [- d'une impression] vividness, keenness ; [- d'une couleur] brightness, vividness ; [- d'une lumière] brightness.

vivant, e [vivɑ̃, ɑ̃t] *adj* **1.** BIOL [organisme] living ▪ [personne, animal] alive ▪ **enterré ~** buried alive ▪ **j'en suis sorti ~** I lived to tell the tale, I survived ▪ **cuire un homard ~** to cook a live lobster *ou* a lobster alive **2.** [existant - croyance, tradition, souvenir] living ▪ **l'emploi du mot est resté très ~** the term is still very much in use **3.** [animé - enfant, conférence, présentation] lively, spirited ; [- bourg, rue] lively, bustling, full of life **4.** [réaliste - description, style] vivid **5.** [constitué d'humains - rempart] human **6.** [incarné, personnifié - preuve, exemple, témoignage] living.

◆ **vivant** *nm* **1.** [période] **: de son ~** [dans le passé] when he was alive ; [dans le présent] as long as he lives ▪ **je ne verrai pas ça de mon ~!** I won't live to see it! **2.** [personne] **: un bon ~** a bon viveur, a connoisseur of the good things in life.

◆ **vivants** *nmpl* RELIG **: les ~s** the living ▪ **les ~s et les morts** [gén] the living and the dead ; BIBLE the quick and the dead.

vivarium [vivarjɔm] *nm* vivarium.

vivat [viva] ◇ *nm* cheer ▪ **s'avancer sous les ~s** to walk forth through a hail of applause.
◇ *interj arch* hurrah, bravo.

vive[1] [viv] *interj* **: ~ le Canada/la République!** long live Canada/the Republic! ▪ **~ *ou* ~nt les vacances!** three cheers for holidays! ▪ **~ moi!** *fam hum* hurrah for me!

vive[2] [viv] *nf* ZOOL weever.

vivement [vivmɑ̃] *adv* **1.** [exprime un souhait] **: ~ le week-end!** I can't wait for the weekend!, roll on the weekend! *UK*, bring on the weekend! *US* ▪ **~ qu'il s'en aille!** I'll be glad when he's gone! **2.** [extrêmement - ému, troublé] deeply, greatly ; [- intéressé] greatly, keenly ▪ **je souhaite ~ que...** I sincerely wish that... ▪ **féliciter/remercier/recommander qqn ~** to congratulate/thank/recommend sb warmly **3.** [brusquement - interpeller] sharply ▪ **~ rabroué** told off in no uncertain terms **4.** [vite - marcher] briskly.

vivent [viv] ◇ *interj* ▷ **vive**.
◇ *v* ▷ **vivre**.

viveur, euse [vivœr, øz] *nm, f vieilli* bon viveur.

vivier [vivje] *nm* **1.** [d'un commerce] fish tank **2.** PÊCHE [enclos - pour poissons] fishpond ; [- pour homards] crawl ; [- d'un bateau] fish tank *ou* well **3.** *fig* **un véritable ~ d'acteurs** a breeding ground for actors.

vivifiant, e [vivifjɑ̃, ɑ̃t] *adj* [air] bracing, invigorating ▪ [expérience] revivifying *sout*, invigorating ▪ [atmosphère] enlivening, revivifying *sout*.

vivifier [9] [vivifje] ◇ *vt sout* [personne] to revivify *sout*, to invigorate ▪ [industrie, région] to bring life to ▪ [imagination, sentiments] to quicken, to sharpen.
◇ *vi* RELIG to give life.

vivipare [vivipar] ◇ *adj* viviparous.
◇ *nmf* member of the Vivipara.

vivisection [vivisɛksjɔ̃] *nf* vivisection ▪ **être contre la ~** to be an antivivisectionist, to be against live experiments.

vivo [vivo] ▷ **in vivo**.

vivoter [3] [vivɔte] *vi* [personne] to get by *ou* along (with little money) ▪ **il vivotait de ses tableaux** he scraped a living from his paintings.

vivre[1] [vivr] *nm* **: le ~ et le couvert** bed and board.

◆ **vivres** *nmpl* food *(U)*, foodstuffs, provisions.

vivre[2] [90] [vivr] ◇ *vi* **1.** BIOL [personne, animal] to live, to be alive ▪ [cellule, plante] to live ▪ **~ vieux *ou* longtemps** to live to a great age *ou* ripe old age ▪ **elle a vécu jusqu'à 95 ans** she lived to be 95 ▪ **il ne lui reste plus longtemps à ~** she hasn't got much time left (to live) ➲ **avoir vécu** to have had one's day **2.** [mener une existence] to live ▪ **~ en paix** to live in peace ▪ **~ libre et indépendant** to lead a free and independent life ▪ **~ au jour le jour** to take each day as it comes ▪ **~ à l'heure de l'Europe/du XXIe siècle** to live in the world of the European community/of the 21st century ▪ **~ dans le luxe/l'angoisse** to live in luxury/anxiety ▪ **~ dans le péché** to lead a sinful life ▪ **on voit que tu n'as jamais vécu dans la misère** it's obvious you've never experienced poverty ▪ **ne ~ que pour la musique/sa famille** to live only for music/one's family ▪ **une rue qui vit la nuit** a street that comes alive at night ▪ **il fait bon ~ ici** life is good *ou* it's a good life here ▪ **une maison où il fait bon ~** a house that's good to live in ▪ **elle a beaucoup vécu** she's seen life ➲ **on ne vit plus** [on est inquiet] we're worried sick ; [on est harassé] this isn't a life, this isn't what you can call living ▪ **savoir ~ : il ne sait pas ~** [il est impoli] he has no manners ; [il est trop nerveux] he doesn't know how to enjoy life ▪ **ils vécurent heureux et eurent beaucoup d'enfants** (and) they lived happily ever after
3. [résider] to live ▪ **~ au Brésil/dans un château** to live in Brazil/in a castle ▪ **~ dans une *ou* en communauté** to live communally *ou* in a community ▪ **~ avec qqn** [maritalement] to live with sb ; [en amis] to share *ou* to live with sb ▪ **~ ensemble** [couple non marié] to live together ➲ **être facile à ~** to be easy-going *ou* easy to get on with ▪ **être difficile à ~** to be difficult to get on with
4. [subsister] to live ▪ **ils ont tout juste de quoi ~** they've just enough to live on ▪ **~ sur un seul salaire** to live *ou* to exist on just one salary ▪ **faire ~ une famille** [personne] to provide a living for *ou* to support a family ; [commerce] to provide a living for a family ▪ **~ bien/chichement** to have a good/poor standard of living ▪ **~ de** to live on ▪ **ils vivaient de la cueillette et de la chasse** they lived on what they gathered and hunted *ou* off the land ▪ **~ de sa plume** to live by one's pen ▪ **~ de chimères** to live a life of illusion ▪ **~ d'espérance** to live in hope ➲ **l'espoir fait ~!** we all live in hope! ▪ **il faut bien ~!** one's got to keep the wolf from the door *ou* to live (somehow)! ▪ **~ aux crochets de qqn** to sponge off sb ▪ **~ de l'air du temps** to live on thin air ▪ **~ d'amour et d'eau fraîche** to live on love alone
5. [se perpétuer - croyance, coutume] to be alive ▪ **pour que notre entreprise vive** so that our company may continue to exist
6. [donner l'impression de vie - sculpture, tableau] **: voici une description qui vit** here is a description that is full of life.
◇ *vt* **1.** [passer par - époque, événement] to live through *(insép)* ▪ **~ des temps difficiles** to live through *ou* to experience difficult times ▪ **~ des jours heureux/paisibles** to spend one's days happily/peacefully
2. [assumer - divorce, grossesse, retraite] to experience ▪ **elle a mal/bien vécu mon départ** she couldn't cope/she coped well after I left
3. *loc* **~ sa vie** to live one's own life ▪ **~ sa foi** to live intensely through one's faith ▪ **il faut ~ l'instant présent** one must live for the moment.

vivrier, ère [vivrije, ɛr] *adj* **: cultures vivrières** food crops.

vizir [vizir] *nm* vizier ▪ **le grand ~** the grand vizier.

VL (*abr de* **véhicule lourd**) *nm* HGV.

v'là [vla] *prép fam* **: le ~!** here he is!

vlan, v'lan [vlɑ̃] *onomat* [bruit - de porte] bang, wham, slam ; [- de coup] smack, thud, wallop.

VO (*abr de* **version originale**) *nf indicates that a film is in the original language.*

◆ **en VO** *loc adj* in the original version ▪ **en ~ sous-titrée** in the original version with subtitles.

vocable [vɔkabl] *nm* **1.** LING term **2.** RELIG name, patronage ▪ **sous le ~ de** dedicated to.

vocabulaire [vɔkabylɛr] *nm* **1.** LING vocabulary ▪ **avoir du ~** to have a wide vocabulary ➲ **quel ~!** [réprimande] language! **2.** [lexique] lexicon, (specialized) dictionary.

vocal, e, aux [vɔkal, o] *adj* vocal.

vocalique [vɔkalik] *adj* vocalic, vowel *(modif)*.

vocalisation [vɔkalizasjɔ̃] *nf* LING & MUS vocalization, vocalizing.

vocalise [vɔkaliz] *nf* MUS vocalise *spéc*, singing exercise ▪ **faire des ~s** to practise scales.

vocaliser [3] [vɔkalize] ◇ *vi* MUS to vocalize *spéc*, to practise scales.
◇ *vt* PHON to vocalize.

◆ **se vocaliser** *vpi* to become vocalized.

vocatif [vɔkatif] *nm* vocative (case), *voir aussi* **pluriel**.

vocation [vɔkasjɔ̃] *nf* **1.** [d'une personne] vocation, calling ▪ **ne pas avoir/avoir la ~ (de)** to feel no/a vocation (for) ▪ **manquer** *ou* **rater sa ~ : voilà un pansement bien fait, tu as manqué** *ou* **raté ta ~** what a professional-looking bandage, you should have been a nurse *ou* you missed your vocation **2.** [rôle, mission] : **grâce à la ~ touristique de notre région** because our area is dedicated to tourism ▪ **la ~ du nouveau musée est d'éduquer les jeunes** the new museum is designed to be of educational value to young people **3.** ADMIN : **avoir ~ à** *ou* **pour faire** to be empowered to do.

vocifération [vɔsiferasjɔ̃] *nf* vociferation ▪ **des ~s** an outcry, a clamour ▪ **sous les ~s du public** met by boos and hisses from the audience.

vociférer [18] [vɔsifere] ◇ *vi* to yell, to shout, to vociferate *sout* ▪ **~ contre** to inveigh against *sout*, to berate *sout*.
◇ *vt* [injures] to scream, to shout.

vodka [vɔdka] *nf* vodka.

vœu, x [vø] *nm* **1.** [souhait] wish ▪ **faire un ~** to (make a) wish ▪ **faire le ~ que** to wish *ou* to pray that ▪ **exaucer un ~** to grant a wish ▶ **faire un ~ pieux** to make a vain wish **2.** [serment] vow ▪ **faire (le) ~ de faire qqch** to (make a) vow to do sthg **3.** RELIG : **faire ~ de pauvreté/de chasteté/d'obéissance** to take a vow of poverty/of chastity/of obedience ▶ **~x du baptême** baptismal vows ▪ **~x (de religion)** (religious) vows ▪ **prononcer ses ~x** to take one's vows.
◆ **vœux** *nmpl* [de fin d'année] : **meilleurs ~x** [sur une carte] Season's Greetings ▪ **nous vous adressons nos meilleurs ~x** *ou* **nos ~x les plus sincères pour la nouvelle année** our best wishes for the New Year ▪ **le président a présenté ses ~x télévisés** the president made his New Year speech *ou* address on TV ‖ [dans une grande occasion] wishes ▪ **tous nos ~x pour...** our best wishes for..., with all good wishes for... ▪ **meilleurs ~x de la part de...** with all good wishes from... ▪ **tous nos ~x de bonheur** our very best wishes for your happiness ▪ **tous nos ~x de succès** all the best, good luck.
Voir module d'usage

vogue [vɔg] *nf* **1.** [mode] vogue, fashion, trend **2.** [popularité] vogue, popularity ▪ **connaître une grande ~** [style, activité, sport] to be very fashionable ▪ **la ~ que connaissent actuellement les jeux vidéo** the current vogue *ou* craze for video games **3.** *Suisse* [kermesse] village fête.
◆ **en vogue** *loc adj* fashionable ▪ **c'est la coiffure en ~** it's the latest hairstyle ▪ **être en ~** [vêtement] to be fashionable *ou* in vogue ; [activité, personne] to be fashionable.

voguer [3] [vɔge] *vi* **1.** NAUT to sail ▪ **~ vers** [navire] to sail towards ; [personne] to sail for ▶ **et vogue la galère!** *vieilli & hum* whatever will be will be! **2.** *litt* [nuage, image] to drift *ou* to be floating by.

voici [vwasi] *prép* **1.** [désignant ce qui est proche dans l'espace] *(suivi d'un singulier)* here is, this is ▪ *(suivi d'un pluriel)* here are, these are ▪ **~ mes parents** here are my parents ; [dans des présentations] these are my parents ▪ **les ~!** here they are! ▪ **en ~ : j'ai perdu mon crayon – en ~ un** I've lost my pencil – here's one ▪ **du riz? en ~!** rice? here you are *ou* there you are! ▪ **en ~ un qui n'a pas peur!** *fam* HE's certainly got guts! ▪ **en ~ une surprise!** what a surprise! ▪ **nous y ~!** here we are! ; [dans une discussion] now... ▪ **l'homme que ~** this man (here) ▪ *(tournure elliptique)* **as-tu un timbre? – ~!** do you have a stamp? – here (you are)! ▪ **~ madame, ce sera tout?** here you are, madam, will there be anything else? ‖ [opposé à 'voilà'] : **~ ma sœur et voilà mon fils** this is my sister and that's my son
2. [caractérisant un état] : **vous ~ rassuré, j'espère** I hope that's reassured you ▪ **me ~ prêt** I'm ready now ▪ **nous ~ enfin arrivés!** here we are at last! ▪ **le ~ qui veut faire du karaté maintenant!** now he wants to take up karate! ▶ **me/te/nous** *etc* **~ bien!** *fam iron* what a mess!
3. [introduisant ce dont on va parler] *(suivi d'un singulier)* this *ou* here is ▪ *(suivi d'un pluriel)* these *ou* here are ▪ **~ ce que je pense** this is what I think ▪ **~, je crains que ma demande ne vous surprenne beaucoup** now, I'm afraid my request may come as a big surprise to you
4. [pour conclure] : **~ qui m'étonne!** that's a surprise! ▪ **~ ce que c'est que de mentir!** this *ou* that is where lying gets you!
5. [désignant une action proche dans le temps] : **et me ~ à pleurer** and here I am crying ▪ **~ l'heure du départ** it's time to go now ▪ **~ l'orage** here comes the storm ▪ **~ venir le printemps** spring is coming ▪ **~ que la nuit tombe** (now) it's getting dark ▪ **~ qu'ils recommencent avec leur musique!** their music's started (up) again!
6. [exprimant la durée] : **j'y suis allé ~ trois mois** I went there three months ago ▪ **~ une heure qu'il est au téléphone** he's been on the phone for an hour.

voie [vwa] *nf* **1.** [rue] road ▪ **~ express** *ou* **rapide** express way ▪ **~ de passage/raccordement** major/access road ▪ **~ d'accès** access road ▪ **~ à double sens** two-way road ▪ **~ piétonne** pedestrian street ▪ **~ prioritaire** main road ▪ **~ privée** private road ▪ **la ~ publique** ADMIN (public) highway *ou* thoroughfare ▪ **~ sans issue** no through road, cul-de-sac ▪ **~ à sens unique** one-way road ‖ TRANSP (traffic) lane ▪ **(route à) trois ~s** three-lane road ▪ **~ de dégagement** slip road ▪ **les ~s sur berges** [à Paris] *expressway running along the Seine in Paris* ‖ ANTIQ : **~ romaine** Roman way *ou* road
2. [moyen d'accès] way ▪ [itinéraire] route ▪ **par la ~ des airs** by air ▪ **par ~ de terre** overland, by land ‖ *fig* **la ~ est libre** the road is clear ▪ **laisser la ~ libre à qqn** to make way for sb ▪ **ouvrir la ~ à qqn/qqch** to pave the way for sb/sthg, to make way for sb/sthg ▪ **trouver sa ~** to find one's niche in life ▪ **la ~ de la réussite** the road to success ▪ **ta ~ est toute tracée** it's obvious what your next move should be ▶ **~ fluviale** *ou* **navigable** (inland) waterway ▪ **~ aérienne** air route, airway ▪ **~ de communication** communication route ▪ **~s d'eau** watercourses ▪ **~ maritime** sea route, seaway ▪ **entrer dans l'Administration par la ~ royale** to take the most prestigious route into the Civil Service
3. RAIL : **'ne pas traverser les ~s'** 'do not cross the tracks' ▪ **le train 242 est attendu ~ 9** train 242 is due to arrive on platform 9 ▶ **~ de garage** *ou* **de service** *ou* **de dégagement** siding ▪ **mettre sur une ~ de garage** *fig* [projet] to shelve, to table *US* ; [employé] to push aside, to put on the sidelines ▪ **~ (ferrée)** railway *UK*, railroad *US* ▪ **~ principale** main line

LES VŒUX

Happy birthday! Joyeux anniversaire !
Many happy returns! Joyeux anniversaire !
Happy anniversary! Joyeux anniversaire *(de mariage)* !
Happy *ou* **Merry Christmas!** Joyeux Noël !
Happy New Year! Bonne année !
Happy Easter! Joyeuses Pâques !
Best wishes! Meilleurs vœux !
To your health! À votre santé !
May you both be very happy! Tous mes vœux de bonheur !
I wish you every happiness! Je vous souhaite beaucoup de bonheur !
Here's wishing you all the best in your new job. Je te souhaite bonne chance dans tes nouvelles fonctions.
Enjoy your meal! Bon appétit !

4. [procédure, moyen] : **suivre la ~ hiérarchique/diplomatique/normale** to go through the official/diplomatic/usual channels ■ **par des ~s détournées** by devious means, by a circuitous route ▶ **par ~ de conséquence** consequently
5. RELIG : **les ~s du Seigneur sont impénétrables** the Lord works in mysterious ways
6. CHASSE scent, track ■ **mettre qqn sur la ~** *pr* to put sb on the right scent ; *fig* [en devinant] to give sb a clue ; [dans une enquête] to put sb on the right track ■ **être sur la bonne ~** *pr* to have the scent ; *fig* to be on the right track *ou* lines ■ **être sur la mauvaise ~** *fig* to be barking up the wrong tree
7. PHARM : **par ~ orale** *ou* **buccale** orally ■ **par ~ nasale/rectale** through the nose/the rectum
8. ANAT & PHYSIOL tract, duct ■ **par les ~s naturelles** naturally ▶ **~s biliaires** biliary ducts ■ **~s digestives** digestive tract ■ **~s respiratoires** airways, respiratory tract ■ **~s urinaires** urinary tract
9. CHIM : **~ humide/sèche** wet/dry process
10. INFORM & TÉLÉCOM [sur bande] track ■ [de communication] channel ■ **~ d'entrée** input channel ■ **~ de transmission** transmission channel
11. NAUT : **~ d'eau** leak
12. ASTRON : **la Voie lactée** the Milky Way.
◆ **voies** *nfpl* DR : **~s de fait** [coups] assault and battery ■ **se livrer à des ~s de fait sur qqn** to assault sb.
◆ **en bonne voie** *loc adj* : **être en bonne ~** to be going well ■ **maintenant, les affaires sont en bonne ~** business is looking up ■ **votre dossier est en bonne ~** your file is being processed.
◆ **en voie de** *loc prép* : **en ~ d'achèvement** on the way to completion ■ **en ~ de construction** being built, under construction ■ **espèces en ~ de disparition** endangered species ■ **en ~ de guérison** getting better, on the road to recovery.
◆ **par la voie de** *loc prép* through, via ■ **régler un litige par la ~ de la négociation** to settle a conflict through negotiation.

voilà [vwala] *prép* **1.** [désignant ce qui est éloigné] *(suivi d'un singulier)* there *ou* that is ■ *(suivi d'un pluriel)* there *ou* those are ■ **le monument que ~** that monument (there) ‖ [opposé à 'voici'] : **voici mon lit, ~ le tien** here's *ou* this is my bed and there's *ou* that's yours
2. [désignant ce qui est proche] *(suivi d'un singulier)* here *ou* this is ■ *(suivi d'un pluriel)* here *ou* these are ■ **~ mes parents** here are my parents ; [dans des présentations] these are my parents ■ **~ l'homme dont je vous ai parlé** here *ou* this is the man I spoke to you about ■ **tiens, les ~!** look, here *ou* there they are! ■ **ah, te ~ enfin!** so here *ou* there you are at last! ■ **nous y ~!** here we are! ; [dans une discussion] now... ■ **l'homme que ~** this man (here) ■ **en ~ : du riz? en ~!** rice? here *ou* there you are! ■ **je ne trouve pas de marteau – en ~ un** I can't find a hammer – here's one ■ **tu voulais un adversaire à ta mesure? en ~ un!** you wanted an opponent worthy of you? well, you've got one! ■ **en ~ un qui n'a pas peur!** *fam* HE's certainly got guts! ■ **en ~ une surprise/des manières!** what a surprise/way to behave! ■ **vous vouliez la clef, ~** you wanted the key, here it is *ou* here you are ■ **~ madame, ce sera tout?** here you are, madam, will there be anything else?
3. [caractérisant un état] : **la ~ recousue/cassée** now it's sewn up again/broken ■ **me ~ prêt** I'm ready now ■ **les ~ enfin partis!** at last they've gone! ■ **dire que te ~ marié!** to think you're married now! ■ **le ~ qui veut faire du karaté maintenant!** now he wants to take up karate! ■ **te ~ beau, que t'est-il arrivé?** *iron* you're in a fine state, what's happened to you? ▶ **me/te/nous** *etc* **~ bien!** *fam iron* now what a mess!
4. [introduisant ce dont on va parler] *(suivi d'un singulier)* this *ou* here is ■ *(suivi d'un pluriel)* these *ou* here are ■ **~ ce que je lui dirai** this *ou* here is what I'll say to her ■ **que veux-tu dire par là? – eh bien ~,...** what do you mean by that? – well,...
5. [pour conclure] *(suivi d'un singulier)* that's ■ *(suivi d'un pluriel)* those are ■ **~ bien les hommes!** how typical of *ou* how like men! ■ **~ ce que c'est, la jalousie!** that's jealousy for you! ■ **~ ce que c'est que de mentir!** that's where lying gets you! ■ **un hypocrite, ~ ce que tu es!** you're nothing but a hypocrite! ■ **quelques jours de repos, ~ qui devrait te remettre sur pied** a few day's rest, THAT should set you right again ■ **on lui paiera les réparations et ~!** we'll pay for the repairs and that's all (there is to it)! ■ **et ~, il a encore renversé son café!** I don't believe it, he spilt his coffee again! ■ **et ~, ça devait arriver!** what did I tell you! ■ **ah ~, c'est parce qu'il avait peur!** so, that explains it, he was frightened! ■ **~! vous avez tout compris** that's it! you've got it ■ **~ tout** that's all
6. [introduisant une objection, une restriction] : **j'en voudrais bien un, seulement ~, c'est très cher** I'd like one, but the problem is *ou* but you see, it's very expensive ■ **c'est facile, seulement ~, il fallait y penser** it's easy once you've thought of it ■ **~, j'hésitais à vous en parler, mais...** well, yes, I wasn't going to mention it, but...
7. [désignant une action proche dans le temps] : **~ la pluie** [il ne pleut pas encore] here comes the rain ; [il pleut] it's raining ■ **~ venu le moment de s'expliquer** now's the moment to explain ■ **~ que la nuit tombe** (now) it's getting dark ■ **~ qu'ils remettent ça avec leur musique!** *fam* they're at it again with their music! ■ **~ Monsieur, je suis à vous dans un instant** yes, sir, I'll be with you in a minute ■ **il y a quelqu'un? – ~, ~** anybody in? – hang on, I'm coming! ▶ **ne ~-t-il pas que** *fam* : **je descends de voiture et ne ~-t-il pas qu'une contractuelle arrive!** I get out of my car and guess what, a traffic warden turns up! ■ **(ne) ~-t-il pas qu'on deviendrait coquette!** vain, now, are we?
8. [exprimant la durée] : **il est rentré ~ une heure** he's been home for an hour, he came home an hour ago ■ **~ longtemps/deux mois qu'il est parti** he's been gone a long time/two months ■ **~ cinq minutes que je t'appelle!** I've been calling you for five minutes!

voilage [vwalaʒ] *nm* [rideau] net curtain.

voile[1] [vwal] *nm* **1.** [d'une toilette, d'un monument] veil ■ **porter le ~** to wear the veil ▶ **~ de deuil** mourning veil ■ **~ de mariée** marriage veil ■ **prendre le ~** RELIG to take the veil **2.** TEXT [pour rideau] net, (piece of) netting ■ [pour chapeau] (piece of) gauze, veil **3.** *fig* veil ■ **ils ont enfin levé le ~ sur ce mystère** they have at last lifted the curtain on this mystery ■ **jeter** *ou* **mettre** *ou* **tirer un ~ sur** to throw a veil across, to draw a veil over **4.** *litt* [opacité] : **un ~ de brume/fumée** a veil of mist/smoke **5.** MÉD : **~ au poumon** shadow on the lung ■ **j'ai un ~ devant** *ou* **sur les yeux** my vision *ou* sight is blurred **6.** PHOTO fog **7.** ANAT : **~ du palais** velum *spéc*, soft palate **8.** BOT veil **9.** [déformation - du métal] buckle, buckling ; [- du plastique, du bois] warp, warping.
◆ **sous le voile de** *loc prép sout* in the guise of ■ **on voit là l'hypocrisie sous le ~ de la respectabilité** here we have hypocrisy under a cloak of respectability.

voile[2] [vwal] *nf* **1.** NAUT sail ■ **faire ~ vers** to sail towards ■ **être sous ~s** to be under sail ■ **mettre à la ~** to set sail ■ **nous sommes rentrés à la ~** we sailed back ▶ **mettre les ~s** *fam* to clear off **2.** *litt* [bateau] sail, sailing boat **3.** SPORT : **la ~** sailing, yachting ■ **faire de la ~** to sail, to go yachting.
◆ **à voile** *loc adj* **1.** NAUT : **bateau à ~** sailing boat ; HIST clipper ■ **la marine à ~** sailing ships **2.** △ *loc* **marcher à ~ et à vapeur** to be AC/DC *ou* bisexual.
◆ **toutes voiles dehors** *loc adv* **1.** NAUT in full sail, all sail *ou* sails set **2.** *fam* [rapidement] like a bat out of hell.

voilé, e [vwale] *adj* **1.** [monument, visage, personne] veiled ■ **des femmes ~es de noir** women veiled in black **2.** [couvert - lune, soleil] hazy ; [- ciel] overcast ; [- horizon] hazy **3.** [voix] hoarse, husky **4.** [dissimulé - signification] obscure ■ **s'exprimer en termes ~s** to express o.s. in oblique *ou* veiled terms ■ **sa déception à peine ~e** his thinly-veiled disappointment **5.** PHOTO fogged, veiled **6.** [déformé - métal] buckled ; [- bois, plastique] warped.

voiler [3] [vwale] *vt* **1.** [couvrir] to veil, to hide, to cover **2.** [rendre moins net - contours] to veil ; [- lumière] to dim ■ **le regard voilé par les larmes** her eyes misty *ou* blurred with tears ■ [enrouer - voix] to make husky ■ **la voix voilée par l'émotion/l'alcool** his voice husky with emotion/thick with drink **3.** *litt* [dissimuler - fautes] to conceal, to veil ; [- motifs, vérité] to mask, to veil, to disguise **4.** PHOTO to fog **5.** [déformer - métal] to buckle ; [- bois, plastique] to warp.
◆ **se voiler** ◇ *vpt* : **se ~ le visage** [le couvrir] to wear a veil (over one's face) ▶ **se ~ la face** to bury one's head in the sand, to hide from the truth.
◇ *vpi* **1.** [lune, soleil] to become hazy ■ [ciel - de nuages] to cloud over ; [- de brume] to mist over, to become hazy *ou* misty ■ **son regard s'était voilé** [mouillé de larmes] her eyes had misted over

ou become blurred (with tears) ; [terni par la mort] her eyes had become glazed **2.** [voix] to grow *ou* to become husky **3.** [métal] to buckle ■ [bois, plastique] to become warped.

voilerie [vwalri] *nf* NAUT sail maker's.

voilette [vwalɛt] *nf* (hat) veil.

voilier[1] [vwalje] *nm* **1.** NAUT : **~ (de plaisance)** sailing boat, sailboat *US* ; [navire à voiles] sailing ship ■ *(comme adj)* **navire bon/mauvais ~** good/bad sailer **2.** [ouvrier] sail maker **3.** ZOOL [poisson] sailfish ■ [oiseau] : **grand ~** long-flight bird.

voilier[2], ère [vwalje, ɛr] *adj vieilli* [bateau] sailing ■ [oiseau] long-flight bird.

voilure [vwalyr] *nf* NAUT sail, sails ■ **changer de/réduire la ~** to change/to shorten sail ■ **dans la ~** aloft, in the rigging.

voir [62] [vwar] <> *vt*

> **A.** PERCEVOIR AVEC LES YEUX
> **B.** PENSER, CONCEVOIR

A. PERCEVOIR AVEC LES YEUX

1. [distinguer] to see ■ PHYSIOL to (be able to) see ■ **il ne voit rien de l'œil gauche** he can't see anything with his *ou* he's blind in the left eye ■ **grand-mère ne voit plus rien** grandma's lost her sight ■ **je voyais ses cartes** I could see his cards ■ **il faut le ~ pour le croire!** you have to see it to believe it! ■ **à les ~, on ne dirait pas qu'ils roulent sur l'or** to look at them, you wouldn't think they were rolling in it ■ **à la ~ si souriante, on ne dirait pas qu'elle souffre** when you see how cheerful she is, you wouldn't think she's in pain ■ **~ qqn faire** *ou* **qui fait qqch** to see sb do *ou* doing sthg ■ **elle m'a fait ~ sa robe de mariée** she showed me her wedding dress ■ **fais ~!** let me see!, show me! ➊ **~ le jour** [bébé] to be born ; [journal] to come out ; [théorie, invention] to appear ■ **comme je vous vois : je les ai vues comme je vous vois** I saw them with my own eyes ■ **faut ~ (ça)** *fam* **: il était habillé, faut ~!** you should have seen what he was wearing! ■ **il faut la ~ lui répondre, il faut ~ comment elle lui répond** you should see the way she speaks to him ■ **~ venir : je te vois venir, tu veux de l'argent!** *fam* I can see what you're leading up to *ou* getting at, you want some money! ■ **le garagiste m'a fait payer 800 euros – il t'a vu venir!** *fam* the mechanic charged me 800 euros – he saw you coming! ■ **Noël n'est que dans trois semaines, on a le temps de ~ venir!** Christmas isn't for another three weeks, we've got plenty of time!
2. [assister à - accident, événement] to witness, to see ; [- film, spectacle] to see ■ **c'est vrai, je l'ai vue le faire** it's true, I saw her do it ■ **je l'ai vu faire des erreurs** I saw him making *ou* make mistakes ■ **à ~** well worth seeing ■ **c'est un film à ~ absolument** that film is a must ■ **ici, les terrains ont vu leur prix doubler en cinq ans** land prices here doubled over five years ➊ **tu n'as encore rien vu** you haven't seen anything yet ■ **n'avoir rien vu** to be wet behind the ears *ou* green ■ **on aura tout vu!** that beats everything! ■ **en ~ : j'en ai vu d'autres!** I've seen worse!, I've been through worse! ■ **ils en ont vu, avec leur aînée!** their oldest girl really gave them a hard time! ■ **il en a vu de toutes les couleurs** *ou* **des vertes et des pas mûres** *fam ou* **de belles** *ou* **de drôles** he's been through quite a lot ■ **en faire ~ (de toutes les couleurs) à qqn** *fam* to give sb a hard time, to lead sb a merry dance ■ **pour ~ : mets de l'eau dessus pour ~** pour some water on it, just to see what happens ■ **j'ai fait du chinois pendant un an pour ~** I studied Chinese for a year just to see how I got on ■ **répète un peu, pour ~!** (you)DARE say that again! ■ **vas te faire ~!**△ push off!
3. [trouver - spécimen] to see, to find, to encounter *sout* ; [- qualité] to see ➊ **un homme galant comme on n'en voit plus** the kind of gentleman they don't make any more
4. [inspecter - appartement] to see, to view ; [- rapport] to see, to (have a) look at ; [- leçon] to go *ou* to look over ■ [remarquer] to see, to notice ■ **ne pas ~ : il préfère ne pas ~ ses infidélités** he prefers to turn a blind eye to *ou* to shut his eyes to her affairs ■ **elle me regarde mais ne me voit pas** she stares at me but doesn't see me ▌[visiter] to see, to visit ■ **qui n'a pas vu l'Égypte n'a rien vu** unless you've seen Egypt, you haven't lived
5. [consulter, recevoir - ami, médecin] to see ■ **le médecin va vous ~ dans quelques instants** the doctor will be with *ou* see you in a few minutes ■ **il faut ~ un psychiatre, mon vieux!** *fam fig* you need your head examined, old man! ■ **aller ~** to go to ■ **je dois aller ~ le médecin** I've got to go to the doctor's ■ **je vais aller ~ mes amis** I'm going to go and see my friends ■ [fréquenter] to see ■ [être en présence de] : **je la vois chaque jour** I see her every day ■ **va-t-en, je t'ai assez vu!** *fam* go away, I've seen *ou* had enough of you!
6. [se référer à] : **~ illustration p. 7** see diagram p 7 ■ **voyez l'horaire des trains** check *ou* consult the train timetable

B. PENSER, CONCEVOIR

1. [imaginer] to see, to imagine, to picture ■ **le pull est trop large – je te voyais plus carré que cela** the jumper is too big – I thought you had broader shoulders ■ **je nous vois mal gagner le match** I can't see us winning the match ■ **~ d'ici qqn/qqch : lui confier le budget? je vois ça d'ici!** ask him to look after the budget? I can just see it!
2. [concevoir - méthode, solution] to see, to think of ■ **je ne vois pas comment je pourrais t'aider** I can't see how I could help you ■ **vous voyez quelque chose à ajouter?** can you think of anything else (which needs adding)? ■ **je ne vois pas de mal à cela** I don't see any harm in it ■ **~ qqch d'un mauvais œil, ne pas ~ qqch d'un bon œil** to be displeased about sthg ■ **~ qqch/qqn avec les yeux de : elle le voit avec les yeux de l'amour** she sees him through a lover's eyes ■ *(en usage absolu)* **pose-moi n'importe quelle question – bon, je vais ~** ask me anything – let's see *ou* let me think ■ **il faut trouver un moyen! – je ne vois pas** we must find a way! – I can't think of one *ou* anything
3. [comprendre - danger, intérêt] to see ■ **tu vois ce que je veux dire?** do you see *ou* understand what I mean? ■ **je ne vois pas ce qu'il y a de drôle!** I can't see what's so funny!, I don't get the joke! ■ **je n'en vois pas l'utilité** I can't see the point of it ■ **il est directeur de banque – je vois!** he's a bank manager – I see!
4. [constater] to see, to realize ■ **tu vois que mes principes n'ont pas changé** as you can see, my principles haven't changed ➊ **elle ne nous causera plus d'ennuis – c'est** *ou* **ça reste à ~** she won't trouble us any more – that remains to be seen *ou* that's what YOU think!
5. [considérer, prendre en compte] to see, to consider, to take into account ■ **ils ne voient que leur intérêt** they only consider their own interest
6. [examiner] to see, to check ■ **nous prenons rendez-vous? – voyez cela avec ma secrétaire** shall we make an appointment? – arrange that with my secretary ■ **voyez si l'on peut changer l'heure du vol** see *ou* check whether the time of the flight can be changed ■ **c'est à** *ou* **il faut ~ : j'irai peut-être, c'est à ~** I might go, I'll have to see ■ **les photos seraient mieux en noir et blanc – hum, il faut ~** the pictures would look better in black and white – mm, maybe (maybe not)
7. [juger] to see ■ **tu n'es pas sur place, tu vois mal la situation** you're not on the spot, your view of the situation is distorted ■ **se faire bien/mal ~ : se faire bien ~ de qqn** to make o.s. popular with sb ■ **se faire mal ~ de qqn** to make o.s. unpopular with sb
8. *loc* **avoir à ~ avec** [avoir un rapport avec] : **je voudrais vous parler: ça a à ~ avec notre discussion d'hier** I would like to speak to you: it's to do with what we were talking about yesterday ■ **n'avoir rien à ~ avec** [n'avoir aucun rapport avec] : **l'instruction n'a rien à ~ avec l'intelligence** education has nothing to do with intelligence ■ **je n'ai rien à ~ avec la famille des Bellechasse** I'm not related at all to the Bellechasse family ■ **cela n'a rien à ~ avec le sujet** that's irrelevant, that's got nothing to do with it ■ **ça n'a rien à ~ : tu parles de grèves, mais ça n'a rien à ~!** you talk about strikes but that has nothing to do with it! ■ **tu vois, vous voyez : tu vois, je préférais ne rien savoir** I preferred to remain in the dark, you see ■ **je te l'avais dit, tu vois!** what did I tell you! ■ **tu verras, tu verrais : essaie de recommencer et tu verras!** just (you) try it again and see! ■ **tu verrais, si j'avais encore mes jambes!** if my legs were still up to it, there'd be no holding *ou* stopping me! ■ **attendez ~** *fam* hang on, wait a sec ■ **dis ~, où est le calendrier?** *fam* tell me, where's the calendar? ■ **écoute ~, on va y aller ensemble, d'accord?** *fam* listen, let's go together, OK? ■ **essaie ~!** *fam* [encouragement] go on, have a try! ; [défi] (you) just try!, don't you dare! ■ **regardez ~** *fam* (just) look at that ■ **voyons ~** *ou* **regardons ~ ce que tu as comme note** *fam* let's just have a look and see what mark you got ■ **voyez-vous cela** *ou* **ça! : une moto à 14 ans, voyez-vous ça!** a motorbike at 14, whatever next! ■ **voyons!** come (on) now!

■ **un peu de courage, voyons!** come on, be brave! ■ **voyons, tu n'espères pas que je vais te croire!** you don't seriously expect me to believe you, do you?

<> *vi*

A. PERCEVOIR LA RÉALITÉ - SENS PROPRE ET FIGURÉ
B. JEUX

A. PERCEVOIR LA RÉALITÉ - SENS PROPRE ET FIGURÉ

1. PHYSIOL to (be able to) see ■ **il ne voit que d'un œil** he can only see out of one eye ■ **elle ne** *ou* **n'y voit plus** she can't see *ou* she's blind now ‖ [exercer sa vue] to see ■ **il ne sait pas ~** he just doesn't use his powers of observation ■ **~ bien** to see clearly, to have good eyesight ■ **~ mal** to have poor eyesight ■ **~ double** to have double vision

2. [juger] : **encore une fois, tu as vu juste** you were right, once again ■ **~ faux** to have poor judgement ■ **ne ~ que par les yeux de qqn** to see everything through sb's eyes

B. JEUX

[pour une mise] : **aller** *ou* **jouer** *ou* **mettre sans ~** to play *ou* to bet blind ■ **20 euros, pour ~** 20 euros, and I'll see you.

◆ **voir à** *v+prép* [veiller à] : **~ à faire qqch** to see to it *ou* to make sure *ou* to ensure that sthg is done ■ **il faudrait ~ à ranger ta chambre/payer tes dettes** you'd better tidy up your room/clear your debts ■ **~ à ce que qqch soit fait** to see to it *ou* to make sure *ou* to ensure that sthg is done.

◆ **se voir** <> *vp (emploi réfléchi)* **1.** [se contempler] to (be able to) see o.s. ■ **il s'est vu mourir** *fig* he knew he was dying **2.** [s'imaginer] to see *ou* to imagine *ou* to picture o.s. ■ **elle se voyait déjà championne!** she thought the championship was hers already! ■ **je ne me vois pas lui demander une augmentation** I (just) can't see myself asking her for a rise.

<> *vp (emploi réciproque)* [se rencontrer] to see each other.

<> *vp (emploi passif)* **1.** [être visible, évident - défaut] to show, to be visible ; [- émotion, gêne] to be visible, to be obvious, to be apparent ■ **il porte une perruque, ça se voit bien** you can tell he wears a wig **2.** [se manifester - événement] to happen ; [- attitude, coutume] to be seen *ou* found ■ **ça se voit couramment** it's commonplace.

<> *vpi* **1.** [se trouver] : **se ~ dans l'impossibilité de faire qqch** to find o.s. unable to do sthg ■ **se ~ dans l'obligation de...** to find o.s. obliged to... ■ **leur équipe s'est vue reléguée à la 15e place** their team saw themselves drop to 15th position ■ **les crédits se verront affectés à la rénovation des locaux** the funds will be used to renovate the building **2.** *(suivi d'un infin)* **se ~ interdire l'inscription à un club** to be refused membership to a club ■ **il s'est vu retirer son permis de conduire sur-le-champ** he had his driving licence taken away from him on the spot.

voire [vwar] *adv* : **~ (même)** (or) even ■ **certains, ~ la majorité** some, or *ou* perhaps even most ■ **vexé, ~ offensé** upset, not to say offended.

voirie [vwari] *nf* **1.** [entretien des routes] road maintenance ■ **le service de la ~** ADMIN road maintenance and cleaning department (of the local council) **2.** [réseau] public road network **3.** [décharge] refuse dump *UK*, garbage dump *US*.

voisé, e [vwaze] *adj* voiced.

voisin, e [vwazɛ̃, in] <> *adj* **1.** [d'à côté] next, adjoining ■ [qui est à proximité] neighbouring ■ **il habite la maison ~e** he lives next door ■ **nos jardins sont ~s** our gardens are next to each other, we've got adjoining gardens ■ **les pays ~s de l'équateur/de notre territoire** the countries near the equator/bordering on our territory ■ **un prix ~ du million** a price approaching *ou* around one million **2.** [dans le temps] : **~ de** [antérieur à] preceding, before ; [postérieur à] after, following ; [autour de] around **3.** [similaire - idées, langues] similar ; [- espèces] closely related ■ **~ de** akin to ■ **des pratiques ~es du charlatanisme** practices akin to *ou* bordering on quackery.

<> *nm, f* **1.** [habitant à côté] neighbour ■ **~ d'à côté** next-door neighbour ■ **mes ~s du dessus/dessous** the people upstairs/downstairs from me ◗ **~ de palier** neighbour (across the landing) **2.** [placé à côté] neighbour ■ **mon ~ de table** the person next to me *ou* my neighbour at table ■ **nos ~s belges** our Belgian neighbours **3.** [autrui] : **le ~** the next man, one's fellow (man).

voisinage [vwazinaʒ] *nm* **1.** [quartier] vicinity, neighbourhood ■ **les hôtels du ~** the nearby hotels, the hotels in the vicinity **2.** [les alentours] : **le ~ de** : **dans le ~ de** in the vicinity of ■ **ils habitent dans le ~ d'une centrale nucléaire** they live near a nuclear plant ■ **le ~ de la gendarmerie les rassure** they are comforted by the fact that there is a police station nearby **3.** [dans le temps] : **au ~ de Noël** [avant] just before Christmas ; [après] just after Christmas ; [avant et après] around Christmas (time) **4.** [personnes] neighbours ■ **tout le ~ est au courant** the whole neighbourhood knows about it **5.** [rapports] : **être** *ou* **vivre en bon ~ avec qqn** to be on neighbourly terms with sb **6.** MATH neighbourhood.

voisiner [3] [vwazine] *vi* **1.** [être près de] : **~ avec** to be near **2.** *litt* [fréquenter ses voisins] to be on friendly terms with one's neighbours.

voiture [vwatyr] *nf* **1.** [de particulier] car, automobile *US* ■ **on y va en ~?** shall we go (there) by car?, shall we drive (there)? ◗ **~ de fonction** *ou* **de service** company car ■ **~ de course** racing car ■ **~ décapotable** convertible ■ **~ (de) deux places** two-seater ■ **~ d'enfant** *vieilli* [landau] pram *UK*, baby carriage *US* ; [poussette] pushchair *UK*, stroller *US* ■ **~ de livraison** delivery van ■ **~ particulière** private car ■ **~ à pédales** pedal car ■ **~ de police** police car ■ **~ des pompiers** fire engine ■ **~ (de) quatre places** four-seater ■ **~ de sport** sports car ■ **~ de tourisme** private car ■ **~ tout terrain** all terrain vehicle ■ **petite ~** JEUX toy car ; [d'infirme] wheelchair **2.** RAIL coach, carriage *UK*, car *US* ■ **en ~!** all aboard! ◗ **~ de tête/queue** front/rear carriage *UK ou* car *US* **3.** [véhicule sans moteur - pour personnes] carriage, coach ; [- pour marchandises] cart ■ **~ à bras** handcart ■ **~ à cheval** *ou sout* **hippomobile** horsedrawn carriage ■ **~ de louage** *ou* **place** hackney carriage.

voiture-balai [vwatyrbalɛ] (*pl* **voitures-balais**) *nf* SPORT *car which follows a cycle race to pick up competitors who drop out* ■ **faire la ~** *fig* to go round picking up the stragglers.

voiture-bar [vwatyrbar] (*pl* **voitures-bars**) *nf* RAIL buffet-car.

voiture-école [vwatyrekɔl] (*pl* **voitures-écoles**) *nf* driving-school car.

voiture-lit [vwatyrli] (*pl* **voitures-lits**) *nf* RAIL sleeper *UK*, Pullman *US*.

voiturer [3] [vwatyre] *vt hum* & *arch* [transporter - gén] to convey ; [- dans une charrette] to cart.

voiture-restaurant [vwatyrrɛstɔrɑ̃] (*pl* **voitures-restaurants**) *nf* RAIL restaurant *ou* dining car.

voiturier [vwatyrje] *nm* **1.** [d'hôtel] porter *(who parks the guests' cars)* **2.** COMM & DR carrier.

voix [vwa] *nf* **1.** PHYSIOL voice ■ **parler par la ~ de qqn** to speak through sb ■ **prendre une grosse/petite ~** to put on a gruff/tiny voice ◗ **~ artificielle** INFORM synthetized speech ■ **~ off** CINÉ voice over ■ **une ~ de stentor** a stentorian voice ■ **attention, Papa va faire la grosse ~!** *fam* mind now, Daddy's going to get very cross! ■ **donner de la ~** [chien] to bay ; [personne] to shout, to bawl ■ **de la ~ et du geste** with much waving and shouting **2.** MUS [de chanteur] voice ■ [partition] part ■ **avoir de la ~** to have a strong voice ■ **poser sa ~** to train one's voice ■ **chanter à plusieurs/cinq ~** to sing in parts/five parts ■ **fugue à deux/trois ~** fugue for two/three voices ◗ **~ de basse/soprano/ténor** bass/soprano/tenor voice ■ **~ de poitrine/tête** chest/head voice ■ **~ de fausset** falsetto voice

3. [personne] voice ■ **une grande ~ de la radio s'éteint** one of the great voices of radio has disappeared

4. [message] voice ■ **la ~ de la conscience** the voice of one's conscience ■ **écouter la ~ de la raison/de la sagesse/de Dieu** to listen to the voice of reason/of wisdom/of God ■ **la ~ du peuple** the voice of the people ◗ **avoir ~ au chapitre** to have a *ou* one's say in the matter ■ **tu n'as pas ~ au chapitre** you have no say in the matter

5. POLIT vote ■ **un homme, une ~** one man one vote ■ **~ pour/contre** vote for/against ■ **obtenir 1 500 ~** to win *ou* to get

1,500 votes ■ **recueillir** *ou* **remporter 57 % des ~** to win 57% of the vote *ou* votes ■ **donner sa ~ à** to give one's vote to, to vote for ■ **mettre qqch aux ~** to put sthg to the vote ■ **avoir ~ consultative** to have a consultative role ■ **avoir ~ prépondérante** to have a casting vote
6. GRAMM voice ■ **~ active/passive** active/passive voice, *voir aussi* **pluriel**.
◆ **à voix basse** *loc adv* in a low voice ■ **les deux hommes discutaient à ~ basse dans un coin** the two men spoke in lowered tones in a corner.
◆ **à haute voix, à voix haute** *loc adv* **1.** [lire] aloud **2.** [parler] loud, loudly, in a loud voice ■ **à haute (et intelligible) ~** loudly and clearly.
◆ **en voix** *loc adj* : **être en ~** to be in good voice ■ **elle n'est pas en ~ ce soir** she's not in very good voice *ou* singing well tonight.
◆ **sans voix** *loc adj* : **être** *ou* **rester sans ~** [d'épouvante] to be speechless, to be struck dumb ; [d'émotion, de chagrin] to be speechless.

vol [vɔl] *nm* **1.** DR theft, robbery ■ **commettre un ~** to commit a theft, to steal ▶ **~ simple/qualifié** common/aggravated theft ■ **~ à l'arraché** bag snatching ■ **~ avec effraction** breaking and entering, burglary ■ **~ à l'étalage** shoplifting ■ **~ de grand chemin** highway robbery ■ **~ à main armée** armed robbery ■ **~ à la roulotte** theft from parked cars ■ **~ à la tire** pickpocketing ■ **~ de voiture** car theft **2.** [vente à un prix excessif] : **c'est du ~ (manifeste)!** it's daylight robbery! ■ **c'est du ~ organisé!** it's a racket! **3.** AÉRON & ASTRONAUT flight ■ **prendre son ~** to take off ■ **il y a 40 minutes de ~** it's a 40-minute flight ▶ **~ (en) charter** charter flight ■ **~ d'essai** test flight ■ **~ aux instruments** instrument flight ■ **~ libre** hang-gliding ■ **pratiquer le** *ou* **faire du ~ libre** to go hang-gliding ■ **~ en rase-mottes** hedgehopping flight ■ **~ régulier** scheduled flight ■ **~ à voile** gliding ■ **pratiquer le** *ou* **faire du ~ à voile** to glide, to do gliding ■ **~ à vue** sight flight **4.** ZOOL flight ■ **prendre son ~** to fly away, to take wing *litt* ■ **~ plané : faire un ~ plané** *pr* to glide ■ **j'ai fait un ~ plané!** *fam fig* I went flying! ❙ [groupe - d'oiseaux] flight, flock ; [- d'insectes] swarm ■ **~ de perdreaux** flock *ou* covey of partridges ■ **~ de pigeons** flight of pigeons.
◆ **à vol d'oiseau** *loc adv* as the crow flies ■ **c'est loin, à ~ d'oiseau?** is it far, as the crow flies?
◆ **au vol** *loc adv* **1.** [en passant] : **saisir au ~** [ballon, clés] to catch in mid-air ■ **attraper** *ou* **prendre un bus au ~** to jump on to a moving bus ■ **saisir une occasion au ~** to jump at *ou* to seize an opportunity ■ **saisir un nom au ~** to (just) catch a name **2.** CHASSE : **tirer/tuer un oiseau au ~** to shoot/to kill a bird on the wing.
◆ **de haut vol** *loc adj* [artiste, spécialiste] top *(avant n)* ■ [projet] ambitious, far-reaching.

vol. (*abr écrite de* **volume**) vol.

volage [vɔlaʒ] *adj* fickle ■ **le public est ~** *fig* audiences are fickle *ou* unpredictable.

volaille [vɔlaj] *nf* CULIN & ZOOL : **une ~** [oiseau de basse-cour] a fowl ■ **de la ~** poultry.

volailler [vɔlaje] *nm* **1.** [éleveur] poultry *ou* chicken farmer **2.** [marchand] poulterer *UK*, poultryman.

volant[1] [vɔlɑ̃] *nm* **1.** AUTO steering wheel ■ **être au ~** to be at the wheel, to be behind the wheel, to be driving ■ **prendre le** *ou* **se mettre au ~** to take the wheel, to get behind the wheel ■ **peux-tu prendre le ~ après Évreux?** could you take over the driving after Évreux? ■ **donner un coup de ~** to pull on the wheel (sharply) **2.** MÉCAN [manuel] handwheel **3.** [vêtement] flounce ■ **robe à ~s** flounced dress **4.** JEUX [objet] shuttlecock ■ [activité] battledore and shuttlecock **5.** [feuille] tear-off portion **6.** ÉCON & FIN : **~ de sécurité** [financier] reserve funds ; [en personnel] reserve ■ **~ de trésorerie** cashflow **7.** AÉRON member of the cabin crew, crew member.

volant[2], e [vɔlɑ̃, ɑ̃t] *adj* **1.** AÉRON & ZOOL flying ■ **personnel ~** AÉRON cabin crew **2.** [mobile - câble, camp, échafaudage, pont, service] flying ■ **on mettra une table ~e devant le fauteuil** we'll put an occasional table in front of the armchair.

volapük [vɔlapyk] *nm* Volapuk ■ **dans un effroyable ~** *fig & péj* in gobbledygook.

volatil, e [vɔlatil] *adj* **1.** CHIM volatile **2.** [fluctuant - électorat] fickle ; [- situation] volatile ; [- sentiment] volatile.

volatile [vɔlatil] *nm* **1.** *hum* [oiseau] bird, (feathered) creature ■ **le malheureux ~ se retrouva dans la casserole** the wretched bird ended up in the pot **2.** [oiseau de basse-cour] fowl, chicken.

volatiliser [3] [vɔlatilize] *vt* CHIM to volatilize.
◆ **se volatiliser** *vpi* **1.** *fam* [disparaître] to vanish (into thin air) ■ **en une soirée au club, mes 500 euros s'étaient volatilisés** one evening at the club and my 500 euros had gone up in smoke **2.** CHIM to volatilize.

vol-au-vent [vɔlovɑ̃] *nm inv* vol-au-vent.

volcan [vɔlkɑ̃] *nm* **1.** GÉOGR & GÉOL volcano ■ **~ en activité/dormant/éteint** active/dormant/extinct volcano **2.** *fig* **c'est un vrai ~** she's likely to explode at any moment ▶ **être assis** *ou* **danser** *ou* **dormir sur un ~** to be sitting on a powder keg.

volcanique [vɔlkanik] *adj* **1.** GÉOGR & GÉOL volcanic **2.** *litt* [passion] fiery, volcanic, blazing.

volcaniser [3] [vɔlkanize] *vt* to volcanize.

volcanisme [vɔlkanism] *nm* volcanism.

volcanologie [vɔlkanɔlɔʒi] *nf* volcanology, vulcanology.

volcanologue [vɔlkanɔlɔg] *nmf* volcano expert, volcanologist, vulcanologist.

volé, e [vɔle] ◇ *adj* [argent, bijou] stolen.
◇ *nm, f* victim of theft.

volée [vɔle] *nf* **1.** [ce qu'on lance] : **~ d'obus/de pierres** volley of shells/of stones ■ **~ de flèches** volley *ou* flight of arrows ■ **~ de coups** shower of blows ■ **~ d'insultes** *fig* shower of insults ▶ **une ~ de bois vert** a barrage of fierce criticism
2. *fam* [correction] thrashing, hiding, belting ■ **tu vas recevoir la ~!** you're really going to get it!
3. *fam* [défaite] beating, hammering ■ **je lui ai flanqué sa ~ au ping-pong** I licked him at table tennis ■ **il a pris une sacrée ~ en demi-finale** he got trounced *ou* thrashed in the semi-finals
4. SPORT volley ■ **reprendre une balle de ~** to volley a ball, to hit the ball on the volley ■ **monter à la ~** to come to the net ■ **il n'est pas/il est très bon à la ~** he's a bad/he's a good volleyer ▶ **coup de ~** FOOTBALL & RUGBY punt ■ **envoyer une balle d'un coup de ~** to punt a ball
5. ORNITH [formation] flock, flight ■ [distance] flight ■ **une ~ de fillettes** *fig & litt* a crowd of little girls
6. [son de cloche] peal (of bells), pealing bells
7. CONSTR : **~ d'escaliers** flight of stairs
8. *Suisse* [promotion] : **on était de la même ~** we were in the same year.
◆ **à la volée** *loc adv* **1.** [en passant] : **attraper** *ou* **saisir à la ~** [clés, balle] to catch in mid-air ■ **saisir un nom à la ~** to (just) catch a name
2. AGRIC : **semer à la ~** to (sow) broadcast
3. CHASSE : **tirer à la ~** to shoot without aiming first.
◆ **à toute volée** *loc adv* [frapper, projeter] vigorously, with full force ■ **il a lancé le vase à toute ~ contre le mur** he hurled the vase at *ou* flung the vase against the wall ■ **claquer une porte à toute ~** to slam *ou* to bang a door shut ■ **sonner à toute ~** [cloches] to peal (out) ; [carillonneur] to peal all the bells.
◆ **de haute volée** *loc adj* [spécialiste] top *(avant n)* ■ [projet] ambitious, far-reaching.

voler [3] [vɔle] ◇ *vi* **1.** AÉRON & ORNITH to fly ■ **faire ~ un cerf-volant** to fly a kite ▶ **~ de ses propres ailes** to stand on one's own two feet, to fend for o.s.
2. [étincelles, projectile] to fly ■ **il faisait ~ ses adversaires/les assiettes** he was throwing his opponents around/throwing the plates in the air ▶ **~ en éclats** to be smashed to bits *ou* to pieces ■ **ça vole bas!** *fam*, **ça ne vole pas haut!** *fam* VERY funny! *iron*
3. *litt* [nuages, flocons] to fly (along)
4. *sout* [se précipiter] : **~ vers qqn/qqch** to fly to sb/towards sthg ■ **il a volé à sa rencontre** he rushed to meet her ■ **~ au secours de qqn** to fly to sb's assistance ▶ **~ dans les plumes à qqn** *fam* to let fly at sb, to have a go at sb.

<> *vt* **1.** [objet, idée] to steal ■ **~ qqch à qqn** to steal sthg from sb ■ **on m'a volé ma montre!** my watch has been stolen! ■ **il volait de l'argent dans la caisse** he used to steal money from the till ■ **~ un baiser à qqn** *litt* to steal a kiss from sb ■ *(en usage absolu)* to steal ■ **ce n'est pas bien de ~** it's wrong to steal, stealing is wrong ❯ **n'avoir pas volé : je n'ai pas volé mon argent/dîner/week-end** I've certainly earned my money/earned myself some dinner/earned myself a weekend ■ **tu ne l'as pas volé!** [tu es bien puni] you (certainly) asked for it!, it serves you right!
2. [personne] to rob ■ **il s'est fait ~ son portefeuille/tout son matériel hi-fi** his wallet/all his stereo equipment was stolen ‖ [léser] to cheat, to swindle ■ **je me suis fait ~ de 10 euros** I've been swindled out of 10 euros ■ **elle ne t'a pas volé sur le poids de la viande** she gave you a good weight of meat.

volet [vɔlɛ] *nm* **1.** [d'une maison] shutter **2.** [d'un document - section] section ■ ART [d'un polyptyque] wing, volet *spéc* **3.** [d'une politique, d'un projet de loi] point, part ■ [d'une émission] part ❯ **le ~ social** [de la CE] the social chapter **4.** AÉRON flap ■ [de parachute] : **~ de courbure** flap **5.** MÉCAN paddle.

voleter [27] [vɔlte] *vi* **1.** [oiseau, papillon] to flutter *ou* to flit (about) **2.** *litt* [flammèche] to flutter, to dance *litt*.

voleur, euse [vɔlœr, øz] <> *adj* : **être ~** [enfant] to be a (bit of a) thief ; [marchand] to be a crook *ou* a cheat ❯ **il est ~ comme une pie** he's got sticky fingers *fig*.
<> *nm, f* [escroc] thief, robber ■ [marchand] crook, cheat ■ **~ de bétail** cattle thief ■ **~ à l'étalage** shoplifter ■ **~ à la tire** pickpocket ■ **au ~!** stop thief! ■ **partir** *ou* **se sauver comme un ~** [en courant] to take to one's heels ; [discrètement] to slip away.

Volga [vɔlga] *npr f* : **la ~** the (River) Volga.

volière [vɔljɛr] *nf* [enclos] aviary ■ [cage] bird-cage ■ **c'est une vraie ~ dans cette classe!** *fig* it's like a zoo in this class!

volige [vɔliʒ] *nf* lath.

volley-ball [vɔlɛbol] (*pl* **volley-balls**) *nm* volleyball.

volleyer [12] [vɔlɛje] *vi* to volley.

volleyeur, euse [vɔlɛjœr, øz] *nm, f* **1.** [au volleyball] volleyball player **2.** TENNIS volleyer ■ **c'est un bon/mauvais ~** he volleys/doesn't volley well.

volontaire [vɔlɔ̃tɛr] <> *adj* **1.** [déterminé] self-willed ■ [têtu] headstrong, wilful **2.** [voulu - engagement] voluntary ; [- oubli] intentional **3.** [qui agit librement - engagé, travailleur] volunteer *(modif)* ■ **se porter ~ pour** to volunteer for.
<> *nmf* volunteer.

volontairement [vɔlɔ̃tɛrmɑ̃] *adv* **1.** [sans y être obligé] voluntarily, of one's own free will **2.** [intentionnellement] on purpose, intentionally, deliberately ■ **c'est ~ que j'ai supprimé ce passage** I deleted this passage on purpose.

volontariat [vɔlɔ̃tarja] *nm* : **le ~** [gén] voluntary work ; MIL voluntary service.

volontarisme [vɔlɔ̃tarism] *nm* voluntarism, voluntaryism.

volontariste [vɔlɔ̃tarist] <> *adj* voluntaristic.
<> *nmf* voluntarist.

volonté [vɔlɔ̃te] *nf* **1.** [détermination] will, willpower ■ **avoir de la ~/beaucoup de ~** to have willpower/a strong will ■ **avoir une ~ de fer** to have a will of iron *ou* an iron will ■ **il manque de ~** he lacks willpower, he doesn't have enough willpower **2.** [désir] will, wish ■ **faire qqch/aller contre la ~ de qqn** to do sthg/go against sb's will ■ **la ~ de gagner/survivre** the will to win/to survive ■ **montrer sa ~ de faire qqch** to show one's determination to do sthg ❯ **la ~ divine** *ou* **de Dieu** God's will ■ **~ de puissance** PHILOS will-to-power ■ **que Ta/Votre ~ soit faite** Thy will be done **3.** [disposition] : **bonne ~** willingness ■ **faire preuve de bonne ~** to show willing ■ **être plein de bonne ~** to be full of goodwill ■ **il est plein de bonne ~ mais il n'arrive à rien** he tries hard but doesn't achieve anything ■ **faire appel aux bonnes ~s** to appeal for volunteers to come forward ■ **mauvaise ~** unwillingness ■ **faire preuve de mauvaise ~** to be grudging ■ **allez, lève-toi, c'est de la mauvaise ~!** come on, get up, you're not really trying!

◆ **à volonté** <> *loc adj* : **café à ~** as much coffee as you want, unlimited coffee.
<> *loc adv* [arrêter, continuer] at will ■ **poivrez à ~** add pepper to taste ■ **servez-vous à ~** take as much as you want.

volontiers [vɔlɔ̃tje] *adv* **1.** [de bon gré] gladly, willingly ■ [avec plaisir] with pleasure ■ **un café? – très ~** a coffee? – yes please *ou* I'd love one **2.** [souvent] willingly, readily ■ **on croit ~ que...** we are apt to think *ou* ready to believe that... ■ **il ne sourit pas ~** he's not very generous with his smiles.

volt [vɔlt] *nm* volt.

voltage [vɔltaʒ] *nm* voltage.

voltaïque[1] [vɔltaik] *adj* ÉLECTR voltaic, galvanic.

voltaïque[2] [vɔltaik] *adj* **1.** GÉOGR Voltaic, of Burkina-Faso **2.** LING Gur, Voltaic.

voltaire [vɔltɛr] *nm* Voltaire chair.

voltairien, enne [vɔltɛrjɛ̃, ɛn] *adj & nm, f* Voltairean, Voltairian.

voltamètre [vɔltamɛtr] *nm* voltameter.

voltampère [vɔltɑ̃pɛr] *nm* volt-ampere.

volte [vɔlt] *nf* ÉQUIT volt, volte.

volte-face [vɔltəfas] *nf inv* **1.** [fait de pivoter] : **faire ~** to turn round **2.** [changement - d'opinion, d'attitude] volteface, about-turn ■ **le parti a fait une ~** the party did a 180 degrees turn *ou* a U-turn.

voltige [vɔltiʒ] *nf* **1.** [au trapèze] : **la haute ~** acrobatics, flying trapeze exercises **2.** ÉQUIT mounted gymnastics, voltige **3.** AÉRON : **~ (aérienne)** aerobatics **4.** [entreprise difficile] : **la Bourse, c'est de la ~** speculating on the Stock Exchange is a highly risky business.

voltiger [17] [vɔltiʒe] *vi* **1.** [libellule, oiseau] to fly about, to flutter (about) ■ [abeille, mouche] to buzz about **2.** [flocon, papier] to float around in the air, to flutter (about).

voltigeur, euse [vɔltiʒœr, øz] *nm, f* **1.** acrobat. **2.** HIST light infantryman **3.** [au baseball] : **~ gauche/droit** left/right fielder ■ **~ du centre** centre fielder *UK*, center fielder *US*.

voltmètre [vɔltmɛtr] *nm* voltmeter.

volubile [vɔlybil] *adj* **1.** [qui parle - beaucoup] garrulous, voluble ; [- avec aisance] fluent **2.** BOT voluble.

volubilis [vɔlybilis] *nm* morning glory, convolvulus.

volubilité [vɔlybilite] *nf* volubility, garrulousness.

volume [vɔlym] *nm* **1.** [tome] volume
2. ACOUST volume ■ **augmente** *ou* **monte le ~** turn the sound up ■ **baisse** *ou* **descend le ~** turn the sound down ❯ **~ sonore** sound level
3. [quantité globale] volume, amount ■ **le ~ des exportations** the volume of exports ■ **~ d'affaires** volume of trade
4. ART & GÉOM volume
5. [poids, épaisseur] volume ■ **une permanente donnerait du ~ à vos cheveux** a perm would give your hair more body ‖ [cubage] volume ■ **~ (d'eau) du fleuve** volume of water of the river ■ **eau oxygénée (à) 20 ~s** 20-volume hydrogen peroxide ❯ **~ atomique/moléculaire** atomic/molecular volume
6. INFORM [unité] volume ■ **~ mémoire** storage capacity.

volumétrique [vɔlymetrik] *adj* volumetric.

volumineux, euse [vɔlyminø, øz] *adj* [sac] bulky, voluminous ■ [correspondance] voluminous, massive.

volupté [vɔlypte] *nf* **1.** [plaisir] sensual *ou* voluptuous pleasure ■ **la ~** *litt* the pleasures of the flesh **2.** [caractère sensuel] voluptuousness.

voluptueusement [vɔlyptɥøzmɑ̃] *adv* voluptuously.

voluptueux, euse [vɔlyptɥø, øz] *adj* voluptuous.

volute [vɔlyt] *nf* [de fumée] coil ■ [de lianes] curl, scroll ■ [en arts décoratifs] volute.

vomi [vɔmi] *nm* vomit.

vomir [32] [vɔmir] ◇ *vt* **1.** PHYSIOL [repas] to bring up *(sép)*, to vomit ▪ [sang, bile] to bring *ou* to cough up *(sép)* **2.** *fig* [fumée] to spew, to vomit ▪ [foule] to spew forth *(insép)* ▪ [insultes] to spew out *(insép)* **3.** *fig* [rejeter avec dégoût] to have no time for, to feel revulsion for.
◇ *vi* to be sick, to vomit ▪ **une telle hypocrisie me donne envie de ~** such hypocrisy makes me sick.

vomissement [vɔmismɑ̃] *nm* **1.** [action] vomiting ▪ **si l'enfant est pris de ~s** if the child starts to vomit **2.** [substance] vomit.

vomissure [vɔmisyr] *nf* vomit.

vomitif, ive [vɔmitif, iv] *adj* emetic, vomitive.
◆ **vomitif** *nm* emetic, vomitive.

vont *v* ▷ **aller**.

vorace [vɔras] *adj* [mangeur] voracious ▪ [appétit] insatiable, voracious ▪ [lecteur] voracious, avid ▪ **application ~ en mémoire** INFORM memory-intensive application.

voracement [vɔrasmɑ̃] *adv* voraciously.

voracité [vɔrasite] *nf* voracity, voraciousness.

vortex [vɔrteks] *nm* vortex.

vos [vo] *pl* ▷ **votre**.

Vosges [voʒ] *npr fpl* : **les ~** the Vosges *(département in Lorraine; chef-lieu: Épinal, code: 88)*.

vosgien, enne [voʒjɛ̃, ɛn] *adj* from the Vosges.

votant, e [vɔtɑ̃, ɑ̃t] *nm, f* voter.

votation [vɔtasjɔ̃] *nf Suisse* vote.

vote [vɔt] *nm* **1.** [voix] vote **2.** [élection] vote ▪ **procédons** *ou* **passons au ~** let's have *ou* take a vote ⊃ **~ à bulletin secret** secret ballot ▪ **~ par correspondance** postal vote *ou* ballot *UK*, absentee ballot *US* ▪ **~ à main levée** vote by show of hands ▪ **~ obligatoire** compulsory vote ▪ **~ par procuration** proxy vote ▪ **~ secret** secret ballot **3.** [d'une loi] passing ▪ [de crédits] voting ▪ [d'un projet de loi] vote ▪ **~ bloqué** *enforced vote on a text containing only government amendments.*

voter [3] [vɔte] ◇ *vi* to vote ▪ **~ à droite/à gauche/au centre** to vote for the right/left/centre ▪ **~ pour qqn** to vote for sb ▪ **~ pour les conservateurs** to vote Conservative ▪ **~ à main levée** to vote by show of hands ▪ **~ contre/pour qqch** to vote against/for sthg.
◇ *vt* [crédits] to vote ▪ [loi] to pass ▪ [projet de loi] to vote for *(insép)* ▪ **~ la peine de mort** to pass a vote in favour of capital punishment.

votif, ive [vɔtif, iv] *adj* votive.

votre [vɔtr] *(pl* **vos** [vo]) *dét (adj poss)* **1.** [indiquant la possession] your ▪ **~ livre et vos crayons** [d'une personne] your book and your pencils ; [de plusieurs personnes] your books and your pencils ▪ **~ père et ~ mère** your father and mother ▪ **un de vos amis** one of your friends, a friend of yours **2.** [dans des titres] : **Votre Majesté** Your Majesty **3.** [emploi expressif] your ▪ **comment va ~ cher Victor?** how is your dear Victor? **4.** RELIG Thy.

vôtre [votr] *dét (adj poss) sout* yours ▪ **cette maison qui fut ~** this house which was yours *ou* which belonged to you ▪ **mes ambitions, vous les avez faites ~s** you espoused my ambitions.
◆ **le vôtre** *(f* **la vôtre**, *pl* **les vôtres)** *pron poss* : **ma voiture est garée à côté de la ~** my car is parked next to yours ▪ *(emploi nominal)* **les ~s** your family and friends ▪ **vous et les ~s** you and yours ▪ **dans la lutte, je suis des ~s** I'm with you *ou* I'm on your side in the struggle ▪ **je ne pourrai pas être des ~s ce soir** I will not be able to join you tonight ⊃ **si au moins vous y mettiez du ~!** you could at least make an effort! ▪ **vous avez encore fait des ~s!** you've gone and done it again! ▪ **à la (bonne) ~!** (your) good health!

voudra *etc v* ▷ **vouloir**.

vouer [6] [vwe] *vt* **1.** [dédier - vie, énergie] to devote ; [- admiration, fidélité, haine] to vow **2.** [destiner] : **voué à l'échec** destined for failure, doomed to fail **3.** RELIG [enfant] to dedicate ▪ [temple] to vow, to dedicate ▪ **voué à la mémoire de...** sacred to the memory of...
◆ **se vouer à** *vp+prép* to dedicate one's energies *ou* o.s. to ▪ **se ~ à la cause de** to take up the cause of.

vouloir[1] [vulwar] *nm sout* **bon ~** goodwill ▪ **mauvais ~** ill will.

vouloir[2] [57] [vulwar] *vt*

A. AVOIR POUR BUT
B. PRÉFÉRER, SOUHAITER
C. SUJET: CHOSE
D. LOCUTIONS

A. AVOIR POUR BUT

1. [être décidé à obtenir] to want ▪ **je le ferai, que tu le veuilles ou non** I'll do it, whether you like it or not ▪ **~ absolument (obtenir) qqch** to be set on (getting) sthg ▪ **quand elle veut quelque chose, elle le veut!** when she's decided she wants something, she's determined (to get it)! ▪ **si tu veux mon avis** if you ask me ▪ **lui, j'en fais (tout) ce que je veux** I've got him eating out of my hand ▪ **~ que : je ne veux pas que tu lui dises** I don't want you to tell him ▪ **je veux absolument que tu ranges ta chambre** I insist (that) you tidy up your bedroom ▪ **~ faire qqch** to want to do sthg ▪ **elle veut récupérer son enfant/être reçue par le ministre** she's determined to get her child back/that the Minister should see her ▪ **arrangez-vous comme vous voulez, mais je veux être livré demain** I don't mind how you do it but I insist the goods are delivered tomorrow ▪ **je ne veux pas entendre parler de ça!** I won't hear of it *ou* such a thing! ▪ **je ne veux plus en parler** I don't want to talk about it any more ▪ **à ton âge, pourquoi ~ faire le jeune homme?** at your age, why do you try to act like a young man? ▪ **~ qqch de : il veut 45 000 euros de son studio** he wants 45,000 euros for his bedsit ▪ **~ qqch de qqn** to want sthg from sb ▪ **que veux-tu de moi?, qu'est-ce que tu me veux?** what do you want from me? ▪ *(en usage absolu)* **quand tu veux, tu fais très bien la cuisine** you can cook beautifully when you put your mind to it ▪ **il peut être vraiment désagréable quand il veut** he can be a real nuisance when he wants to ⊃ **~, c'est pouvoir** *prov*, **quand on veut, on peut** where there's a will, there's a way *prov*
2. [prétendre - suj: personne] to claim
3. [avoir l'intention de] : **~ faire qqch** to want *ou* to intend *ou* to mean to do sthg ▪ **sans ~ me mêler de tes affaires/te contredire...** I don't want to interfere/to contradict you but... ▪ **je l'ai vexé sans le ~** I offended him unintentionally *ou* without meaning to ▪ **je ne voudrais surtout pas t'empêcher de voir ton match!** I wouldn't dream of preventing you from watching the match! ▪ **~ dire : il ne s'est pas ennuyé ce soir-là – que veux-tu dire par là?** he had some fun that night – what do you mean by that *ou* what are you getting at? ▪ **vous voulez dire qu'on l'a tuée?** do you mean *ou* are you suggesting (that) she was killed?
4. [essayer de] : **~ faire** to want *ou* to try to do ▪ **en voulant la sauver, il s'est noyé** he drowned in his attempt *ou* trying to rescue her ▪ **tu veux me faire peur?** are you trying to frighten me?
5. [s'attendre à] to expect ▪ **tu voudrais peut-être aussi que je te remercie!** you don't expect to be thanked into the bargain, do you? ▪ **pourquoi voudrais-tu qu'on se fasse cambrioler?** why do you assume we might be burgled? ▪ **que veux-tu que j'y fasse?** what do you want me to do about it?, what can I do about it? ▪ **que voulez-vous que je vous dise?** what can I say?, what do you want me to say?
6. *fam* [sexuellement] to want

B. PRÉFÉRER, SOUHAITER

1. [dans un choix] to want, to wish ▪ **jus d'ananas ou d'orange? – ce que tu veux!** pineapple or orange juice? – whatever *ou* I don't mind! ▪ **on prend ma voiture ou la tienne? – c'est comme tu veux** shall we take my car or yours? – as you wish *ou* please *ou* like ▪ **je me débrouillerai seule – comme tu voudras!** I'll manage on my own – suit yourself! ▪ **où va-t-on? – où tu veux** where are we going? – wherever you want ▪ **je pourrai revenir? – bien sûr, quand vous voulez!** may I come again? – of course, any time *ou* whenever you want! ▪ **tu peux dessiner une maison si tu veux** you could draw a house, if you like ▪ **tu l'as** *ou* **l'auras voulu!** you asked for it!
2. [dans une suggestion] to want ▪ **veux-tu de l'aide?** do you want *ou* would you like some help? ▪ **tu veux une fessée?** do you want your bottom smacked? ▪ **voudriez-vous vous joindre à nous?** would you care *ou* like to join us?

3. [dans un souhait] : **je ne veux que ton bonheur** I only want you to be happy ■ **j'aurais tellement voulu être avec vous** I'd have so much liked *ou* loved to have been with you ■ **quand tu me parles, je te voudrais un autre ton** *sout* please don't use that tone when you're talking to me ■ **comme je voudrais avoir des enfants!** how I'd love to have children! ■ **elle voudrait vous dire quelques mots en privé** she'd like a word with you in private ■ **je voudrais vous y voir!** I'd like to see how YOU'd cope with it! ▶ **aller au match sans avoir rangé ta chambre, je voudrais bien voir ça!** *iron* whatever gave you the idea (that) you could go to the match without tidying up your room first?
4. [dans une demande polie] : **veuillez m'excuser un instant** (will you) please excuse me for a moment ■ **veuillez avoir l'obligeance de...** would you kindly *ou* please... ■ **veuillez recevoir, Monsieur, mes salutations distinguées** yours sincerely *UK ou* truly *US* ■ **veuillez vous retirer, Marie** you may go now, Marie ■ **voudriez-vous avoir l'amabilité de me prêter votre crayon?** would you be so kind as to lend me your pencil? ■ **nous voudrions une chambre pour deux personnes** we'd like a double room ■ **je vous serais reconnaissant de bien ~ m'envoyer votre brochure** I should be glad to receive your brochure ■ **voulez-vous me suivre** please follow me
5. [dans un rappel à l'ordre] : **veux-tu (bien) me répondre!** will you (please) answer me? ■ **voulez-vous ne pas toucher à ça!** please don't touch that! ■ **ne m'interromps pas, tu veux!, veuille bien ne pas m'interrompre!** will you please not interrupt me?, would you mind not interrupting me? ■ **un peu de respect, tu veux (bien)** a bit less cheek, if you don't mind!

C. SUJET: CHOSE
1. [se prêter à, être en état de] : **les haricots ne veulent pas cuire** the beans won't cook ■ **la télé ne marche que quand elle veut** *hum* the TV only works when it feels like it
2. [exiger] to require ■ **la tradition voulait que...** it was a tradition that... ■ **la dignité de notre profession veut que...** the dignity of our profession demands that... ■ **comme le veulent les usages** as convention dictates ■ **les lois le veulent ainsi** that is what the law says ‖ [prétendre] : **comme le veut une vieille légende** as an old legend has it
3. [déterminer - suj: destin, hasard, malheur] : **la chance a voulu que...** as luck would have it... ■ **le malheur voulut qu'il fût seul ce soir-là** unfortunately he was alone that night ■ **le calendrier a voulu que cela tombe un lundi** it fell on a Monday, as it so happened
4. [s'efforcer de] : **le décor veut évoquer une ferme normande** the decor strives *ou* tries to suggest a Normandy farmhouse
5. : **~ dire** [avoir comme sens propre] to mean ; [avoir comme implication] to mean, to suggest ■ **je me demande ce que veut dire ce changement d'attitude** I wonder what the meaning of this turn-around is *ou* what this turn-around means ■ **cela ne veut rien dire** it doesn't mean anything ▶ **ça veut tout dire!** that says it all! ■ **ça veut bien dire ce que ça veut dire!** it's clear *ou* plain enough! ■ **tu vas m'obéir, non mais, qu'est-ce que ça veut dire?** *fam* for goodness's sake will you do as I say!
6. GRAMM to take

D. LOCUTIONS
[consenti, accepter] : **bien ~** : **bien ~ faire qqch** to be willing *ou* to be prepared *ou* to be quite happy to do sthg ■ **je veux bien être patient, mais il y a des limites!** I can be patient, but there are limits! ■ **un petit café? – oui, je veux bien** fancy a coffee? – yes please ■ **poussons jusqu'à la prochaine ville – moi je veux bien, mais il est tard!** let's go on to the next town – I don't mind, but it IS late! ■ **bien ~** [admettre] : **je veux bien qu'il y ait des restrictions budgétaires mais...** I understand (that) there are cuts in the budget but... ■ **je veux bien avoir des défauts, mais pas celui-là** granted, I have some shortcomings, but that isn't one of them ■ **moi je veux bien!** (it's) fine by me! ■ **il a dit nous avoir soutenus, moi je veux bien, mais le résultat est là!** he said he supported us, OK *ou* and that may be so, but look at the result! ■ **il t'a cogné? – je veux!** *fam* : **je veux** *fam* did he hit you? – and how *ou* he sure did! ■ **que veux-tu, que voulez-vous : c'est ainsi, que voulez-vous!** that's just the way it is! ■ **j'accepte ses humeurs, que veux-tu!** I (just) put up with his moods, what can I do? ■ **si tu veux, si vous voulez** more or less, if you like.

◆ **vouloir de** *v+prép* **1.** [être prêt à accepter] : **~ de qqn/qqch** to want sb/sthg ■ **je ne veux pas d'une relation sérieuse** I don't want a serious relationship **2.** *loc* **en ~** *fam* : **elle en veut** [elle a de l'ambition] she wants to make it *ou* to win ; [elle a de l'application] she's dead keen ■ **il faut en ~ pour réapprendre à marcher** you need a lot of determination to learn to walk again ■ **en ~ à qqn** [éprouver de la rancune] to bear *ou* to have a grudge against sb ■ **je ne l'ai pas fait exprès, ne m'en veux pas** I didn't do it on purpose, don't be cross with me ■ **décidément, ton chien m'en veut** your dog's definitely got something against me ■ **tu ne m'en veux pas?** no hard feelings? ■ **elle m'en voulait de mon manque d'intérêt pour elle** she resented my lack of interest in her ■ **elle lui en veut d'avoir refusé** she holds it against him that he said no ■ **en ~ à qqn/qqch** [le convoiter] : **elle en veut à ma fortune** she's after my money ■ **en ~ à qqch** [vouloir le détruire] to seek to damage sthg ■ **qui peut en ~ à ma vie/réputation?** who could wish me dead/would want to damage my reputation?

◆ **se vouloir** *vpi* : **je me voudrais plus audacieux** I'd like to be bolder ■ **le livre se veut une satire de l'aristocratie allemande** the book claims *ou* is supposed to be a satire on the German aristocracy.

◆ **s'en vouloir** <> *vp (emploi réfléchi)* to be angry *ou* annoyed with o.s. ■ **je m'en veux de l'avoir laissé partir** I feel bad at having let him go ▶ **je m'en voudrais!** *fam* not likely!
<> *vp (emploi réciproque)* **elles s'en veulent à mort** they really hate each other.

◆ **en veux-tu en voilà** *loc adv fam* [en abondance] : **il y avait des glaces en veux-tu en voilà** there were ice creams galore ■ **il lui faisait des compliments en veux-tu en voilà** he was showering her with compliments.

◆ **si l'on veut** *loc adv* **1.** [approximativement] if you like **2.** [pour exprimer une réserve] : **il est fidèle... si l'on veut!** he's faithful... after a fashion!

voulu, e [vuly] *adj* **1.** [requis] required, desired, requisite *sout* ■ **vous aurez toutes les garanties ~es** you'll have all the required guarantees **2.** [délibéré] deliberate, intentional ■ **c'est ~** it's intentional *ou* (done) on purpose **3.** [décidé d'avance] agreed ■ **au moment ~** at the right time ■ **terminé en temps ~** completed on schedule.

vous [vu] <> *pron pers (2e pers pl)*

> **A.** EN S'ADRESSANT À UNE PERSONNE
> **B.** EN S'ADRESSANT À PLUSIEURS PERSONNES
> **C.** VALEUR INTENSIVE

A. EN S'ADRESSANT À UNE PERSONNE
1. [sujet ou objet direct] you ■ **~ parti, je lui écrirai** once you've gone, I shall write to her ■ **eux m'ont compris, pas ~** they understood me, you didn't ■ **elle a fait comme ~** she did (the same) as you did ‖ [en renforcement] : **et ~ qui aviez toujours peur!** to think YOU're the one who was always scared! ■ **je ~ connais, ~!** I know YOU! ■ **~, ~ restez** as for you, you're staying
2. [objet indirect] : **à ~** [objet] : **c'est à ~** it belongs to you ■ **à ~!** [dans un magasin, un jeu] it's your turn! ■ **une maison bien à ~** a house of your very own, your very own house ■ **pensez un peu à ~** think of yourself a bit ■ **de ~** : **c'est de ~, cette lettre?** is this one of your letters? ■ **de ~ à moi** between (the two of) us *ou* you and me ■ **chez ~** at your house, in your home ■ **ça va, chez ~?** *fam* (are) things OK at home?
3. [dans des formes réfléchies] : **taisez-~!** be quiet! ■ **regardez-~** look at yourself

B. EN S'ADRESSANT À PLUSIEURS PERSONNES
1. [sujet ou objet direct] you ■ **elle ~ a accusés tous les trois** she accused all three of you ‖ [en renforcement] you (people) ■ **~, ~ restez** as for you (people), you're staying ■ **~ (autres), les intellectuels, ~ êtes tous pareils** you're all the same, you intellectuals
2. [après une préposition] : **à ~** [objet] : **c'est à ~** it belongs to you ■ **à ~** RADIO & TV over to you ■ **pensez à ~ et à vos amis** think of yourselves and of your friends ■ **à ~ trois, vous finirez bien la tarte?** surely the three of you can finish the tart? ■ **de ~** : **l'un de ~ trahira** one of you will be a traitor
3. [dans des formes réfléchies] : **taisez-~ tous!** be quiet, all of you! ■ **regardez-~** look at yourselves ‖ [dans des formes réciproques] one another, each other ■ **aidez-~** help one another ■ **battez-~** fight with each other

C. VALEUR INTENSIVE
fam **Il ~ mange tout un poulet** he can put away a whole chicken ■ **elle sait ~ séduire une foule** she does know how to captivate a crowd.
◇ *nm* : **le ~** the "vous" form ■ **leurs enfants leur disent "~"** their children use the "vous" form to them.

vous-même [vumɛm] (*pl* **vous-mêmes**) *pron pers* yourself ■ **~s** yourselves ■ **vous devriez comprendre de ~s** you ought to understand for yourselves ■ **vous pouvez vérifier par ~** you can check for yourself.

voussure [vusyr] *nf* [d'une voûte] spring ■ [d'une baie] arch ■ [d'un plafond] coving.

voûte [vut] *nf* **1.** ARCHIT [construction] vault ■ [passage] archway ■ **~ d'arête** groined vault ■ **~ en éventail** fan *ou* palm vaulting **2.** *litt* vault, canopy ■ **la ~ céleste** *ou* **des cieux** the canopy of heaven ■ **la ~ étoilée** the starry dome **3.** ANAT : **~ crânienne** cranial vault ■ **~ palatine** *ou* **du palais** roof of the mouth ■ **~ plantaire** arch of the foot.
◆ **en voûte** *loc adj* vaulted.

voûté, e [vute] *adj* **1.** [homme] stooping, round-shouldered ■ [dos] bent ■ **avoir le dos ~** to stoop, to have a stoop ■ **ne te tiens pas ~** stand up straight **2.** [galerie] vaulted, arched.

voûter [3] [vute] *vt* **1.** ARCHIT to vault, to arch **2.** [courber] to cause to stoop.
◆ **se voûter** *vpi* to stoop, to become round-shouldered.

vouvoie *etc v* ▷ **vouvoyer**.

vouvoiement [vuvwamɑ̃] *nm* "vous" form of address ■ **ici, le ~ est de rigueur** here people have to address each other as "vous".

vouvoyer [13] [vuvwaje] *vt* to address as "vous" ■ **les parents se faisaient ~ par leurs enfants** the children addressed their parents as "vous".
◆ **se vouvoyer** *vp (emploi réciproque)* to address each other as "vous".

vox populi [vɔkspɔpyli] *nf inv litt* vox populi ■ **écouter la ~** to listen to what the people have to say.

voyage [vwajaʒ] *nm* **1.** [excursion lointaine] journey, trip ■ [circuit] tour, trip ■ **leur ~ en Italie** their trip to Italy ■ **aimer les ~s** to like travelling ■ **faire un ~** to go on a trip ■ **faire un ~ dans le temps** [passé, futur] to journey through time ■ **faire un ~ autour du monde** to go round the world ■ **partir en ~** to go on a trip ■ **nous partons en ~** we're off on a trip, we're going away ■ **vous serez du ~?** [avec eux] are you going on the trip? ; [avec nous] are you coming on the trip? ■ **cela représente deux jours/six mois de ~** it means a two-day/six-month trip ■ **bon ~** have a nice trip! ➲ **~ d'affaires** business trip ■ **~ d'agrément** (pleasure) trip ■ **~ d'études** field trip ■ **~ en mer** sea voyage *litt*, journey by sea ■ **~ de noces** honeymoon ■ **être en ~ de noces** to be honeymooning *ou* on one's honeymoon ■ **~ officiel** [en un endroit] official trip ; [en plusieurs endroits] official tour ■ **~ organisé** package tour ■ **~ de presse** press visit ■ **le grand ~** *euphém* the last journey ■ **les ~s forment la jeunesse** *prov* travel broadens the mind *prov* **2.** [déplacement local] journey ■ **tous les matins, je fais le ~ en train** I do the journey by train every morning ■ **~ aller** outward journey ■ **~ retour** return *ou* homeward journey **3.** [allée et venue] trip ■ **on a fait trois ~s pour vider la maison** we made three trips to empty the house **4.** *fam* [sous drogue] trip.

voyageage [vwajaʒaʒ] *nm Québec* travelling *(back and forth)*.

voyager [17] [vwajaʒe] *vi* **1.** [faire une excursion] to travel ■ [faire un circuit] to tour ■ **aimer ~** to like travelling ■ **~ dans le temps** [passé, futur] to travel through time **2.** [se déplacer] to travel ■ **~ en bateau/en avion** to travel by sea/by air ■ **~ en deuxième classe** to travel second class **3.** [denrées, sacs] to travel ■ **le vin voyage mal** wine doesn't travel well **4.** COMM to travel ■ **~ pour une société** to travel for a firm.

voyageur, euse [vwajaʒœr, øz] ◇ *adj* [caractère] *litt* wayfaring *litt*, travelling.
◇ *nm, f* **1.** [dans les transports en commun] passenger ■ [dans un taxi] fare **2.** [qui explore] traveller ■ **c'est une grande voyageuse** she travels extensively **3.** COMM : **~ (de commerce)** commercial traveller.

voyagiste [vwajaʒist] *nm* tour operator.

voyait *etc v* ▷ **voir**.

voyance [vwajɑ̃s] *nf* clairvoyance.

voyant, e [vwajɑ̃, ɑ̃t] ◇ *adj* [couleur] loud, gaudy, garish ■ [robe] showy, gaudy, garish ■ **peu ~** inconspicuous ■ **trop ~** obtrusive.
◇ *nm, f* **1.** [visionnaire] visionary, seer ■ [spirite] : **~ (extralucide)** clairvoyant **2.** [non aveugle] sighted person.
◆ **voyant** *nm* : **~ (lumineux)** indicator *ou* warning light ■ [d'un signal] mark ■ [plaque de nivellement] vane levelling shaft.

voyelle [vwajɛl] *nf* vowel.

voyeur, euse [vwajœr, øz] *nm, f* voyeur.

voyeurisme [vwajœrism] *nm* voyeurism.

voyou, te [vwaju, ut] *adj* loutish ■ **verve ~te** vulgar wit.
◆ **voyou** *nm* **1.** [jeune délinquant] lout ■ [gangster] gangster **2.** [ton affectueux ou amusé] : **petit ~!** you little rascal!

VPC *nf* = **vente par correspondance**.

vrac [vrak] *nm* **1.** [mode de distribution] bulk **2.** [marchandise] material transported in bulk.
◆ **en vrac** *loc adj* & *loc adv* **1.** [non rangé] in a jumble ■ **ses idées sont en ~ dans sa dissertation** the ideas are just jumbled together in his essay **2.** [non emballé] loose ■ [en gros] in bulk ■ **on invite toute la famille en ~** *fam fig* we're inviting the whole family in one go.

vrai, e [vrɛ] *adj* **1.** [exact] true ■ **il n'y a pas un mot de ~ dans son témoignage** there's not a word of truth in her testimony ■ **ce serait plus facile – c'est ~ mais...** it would be easier – true *ou* certainly *ou* granted but... ■ **ma voiture peut monter jusqu'à 300 km/h – c'est ~?** my car can do up to 300 km/h – can it (really) *ou* oh really? ■ **c'est ~ qu'on n'a pas eu de chance** *fam* true, we were a bit unlucky ■ **pas ~?** *fam* : **il l'a bien mérité, pas ~?** he deserved it, didn't he? ■ **on ira tous les deux, pas ~!** we'll go together, OK? ■ **c'est pas ~!** *fam* [pour nier] it's *ou* that's not true! ; [ton incrédule] you're joking! ; [ton exaspéré] I don't believe this! ; [ton horrifié] my God, no! ■ **c'est si ~ que...** so much so that... ■ **il est ~ que...** it's true (to say) that... ■ **il est très irritable, il est ~ qu'il n'est pas encore habitué à eux** he's very irritable, true, he's not used to them yet ■ **il est bien ~ que...** it's absolutely true *ou* it can't be denied that...
2. [authentique - cuir, denrée] genuine, real ; [- or] real ; [- connaisseur] real, true ; [- royaliste, républicain] true ■ **c'est une copie, ce n'est pas un ~ Modigliani** it's a copy, it's not a real Modigliani ■ **les ~es rousses sont rares** there are few genuine *ou* real redheads ■ **ce ne sont pas ses ~es dents** they're not her own teeth ■ **c'est un ~ gentleman** he's a real gentleman ■ **ça c'est de la bière, de la ~e!** *fam* that's what I call beer! ➲ **c'est ~, ce mensonge?** *fam hum* are you fibbing? ■ **il n'y a que ça de ~ : le soleil, il n'y a que ça de ~** give me sunshine anyday ■ **pour enlever les taches, l'acétone, il n'y a que ça de ~** to remove stains, acetone's the thing ■ **~ de ~ : je pars avec toi – ~ de ~?** I'm going with you – really (and truly)? ■ **ça c'est de la bière, de la ~e de ~e!** that's what I call beer!
3. [non fictif, non inventé - raison] real ■ **c'est une histoire ~e** it's a true story
4. *(avant le n)* [à valeur intensive] real, complete, utter ■ **c'est un ~ désastre** it's a real *ou* an utter disaster ■ **elle a été une ~e sœur pour moi** she was a real sister to me ■ **c'est une ~e folle!** she's completely crazy!
5. [franc, naturel - personne, acteur] straightforward ■ **des dialogues ~s** dialogues that ring true ■ **des personnages ~s** characters that are true to life
6. *(avant le n)* [assigné] true
7. ASTRON : **temps ~** true time.
◆ **vrai** ◇ *adv* **1.** [conformément à la vérité] : **elle dit ~** [elle dit la vérité] she's telling the truth ; [elle a raison] she's right, what she says is right ■ **tu n'en veux plus? – non, ~, j'ai trop mangé** don't you want some more? – no, really, I've eaten too much already

2. [avec vraisemblance] : **des auteurs qui écrivent/acteurs qui jouent ~** authors whose writing/actors whose acting is true to life ■ **faire ~** [décor, prothèse] to look real
3. *fam vieilli* [exprime la surprise, l'irritation] : **~, j'ai cru que je n'en verrais jamais la fin!** I thought I'd never see the back of it, I did!
◇ *nm* : **le ~** [la vérité] the truth ■ **il y a du** *ou* **un peu de ~ dans ses critiques** there's some truth *ou* an element of truth in her criticism ■ **être dans le ~** to be right.
◆ **à dire (le) vrai** = à vrai dire.
◆ **au vrai** *loc adv* to be specific ■ **au ~, voici ce qui s'est passé** specifically, this is what took place.
◆ **à vrai dire** *loc adv* in actual fact, to tell you the truth, to be quite honest.
◆ **pour de vrai** *loc adv fam* really, truly ■ **cette fois-ci, je pars pour de ~** this time I'm really leaving.

vrai-faux, vraie-fausse [vrɛfo, fos] (*mpl* **vrais-faux**, *fpl* **vraies-fausses**) *adj hum* : **de vrais-faux plombiers** professional cowboy plumbers ■ **de vrais-faux passeports** genuine false passports.

vraiment [vrɛmɑ̃] *adv* **1.** [réellement] really ■ **il avait l'air ~ ému** he seemed really *ou* genuinely moved ■ **je vous assure, ~, je dois y aller** no, really, I must go **2.** [en intensif] really ■ **il est ~ bête!** he's really *ou* so stupid! ■ **tu n'as ~ rien compris!** you haven't understood a thing! ■ **tu trouves que j'ai fait des progrès? – ah oui, ~!** do you think I've improved *ou* made any progress? – oh yes, a lot! ■ **~, il exagère!** he really has got a nerve! **3.** [exprimant le doute] : **~? tu en es sûr?** really? are you sure? ■ **elle a dit que c'était moi le meilleur – ~?** *iron* she said I was the best – you don't say *ou* really!

vraisemblable [vrɛsɑ̃blabl] ◇ *adj* [théorie] likely ■ [dénouement, excuse] convincing, plausible ■ **une fin peu ~** a rather implausible ending ■ **il est (très) ~ qu'il ait oublié** he's forgotten, in all likelihood ■ **il n'est pas ~ qu'elle avoue** it wouldn't be like her to own up.
◇ *nm* : **le ~** the plausible.

vraisemblablement [vrɛsɑ̃blabləmɑ̃] *adv* in all likelihood *ou* probability, very likely ■ **est-il là? – ~ non** is he there? – it appears not.

vraisemblance [vrɛsɑ̃blɑ̃s] *nf* **1.** [d'une œuvre] plausibility, verisimilitude *sout* **2.** [d'une hypothèse] likelihood.
◆ **selon toute vraisemblance** *loc adv* in all likelihood ■ **selon toute ~, il est allé se plaindre** he very likely went *ou* in all likehood he went and complained.

V/Réf (*abr écrite de* **Votre référence**) your ref.

vreneli [vrɛnli] *nm Suisse gold coin worth 20 Swiss francs.*

vrille [vrij] *nf* **1.** [outil] gimlet **2.** AÉRON spin.
◆ **en vrille** *loc adv* : **descendre en ~** to spin downwards.

vrillé, e [vrije] *adj* [tordu] twisted.

vriller [3] [vrije] ◇ *vi* [avion, fusée] to spiral, to spin.
◇ *vt* to pierce, to bore into.

vrombir [32] [vrɔ̃bir] *vi* [avion, moteur] to throb, to hum ■ [insecte] to buzz, to hum ■ **faire ~ un moteur** to rev up an engine.

vrombissement [vrɔ̃bismɑ̃] *nm* [d'un avion, d'un moteur] throbbing sound, humming ■ [d'un insecte] buzzing, humming.

VRP (*abr de* **voyageur représentant placier**) *nm* rep.

VTC [vetese] (*abr de* **vélo tout chemin**) *nf* SPORT hybrid bike.

VTT [vetete] (*abr de* **vélo tout terrain**) *nm* SPORT ATB, mountain bike.

vu[1] [vy] *nm inv sout* : **au vu et au su de tous** openly ■ **au vu de son dossier...** looking at his case...

vu[2] [vy] *prép* [en considération de] in view of, considering, given ■ **vu l'article 317 du Code pénal...** DR in view of article 317 of the Penal Code...
◆ **vu que** *loc conj* [étant donné que] in view of the fact that, seeing that, considering that ■ **il lui faudra au moins deux heures pour venir, vu qu'il est à pied** he'll need at least two hours to get here, seeing that he's (coming) on foot.

vu[3]**, e** [vy] ◇ *pp* ▷ **voir**.
◇ *adj* **1.** [bien/mal considéré] : **bien/mal vu : il est bien vu de travailler tard** it's the done thing *ou* it's good form to work late ■ **il veut être bien vu** he wants to be well thought of ■ **fumer, c'est assez mal vu ici** smoking is disapproved of here ■ **être bien vu de qqn** to be well thought-of by sb ■ **être mal vu de qqn** to be not well thought-of by sb **2.** [bien/mal analysé] : **bien/mal vu : personnages bien/mal vus** finely observed/poorly-drawn characters ■ **un problème bien vu** an accurately diagnosed problem ■ **une situation bien vue** a finely judged situation ■ **bien vu!** well spotted! **3.** [compris] : **(c'est) vu?** understood?, get it? ■ **(c'est) vu!** OK!, got it!

vue [vy] *nf* **1.** [sens] eyesight, sight ■ **recouvrer la ~** to get one's sight *ou* eyesight back ■ **perdre la ~** to lose one's sight, to go blind ■ **avoir une bonne ~** to have good eyesight ■ **avoir une mauvaise ~** to have bad *ou* poor eyesight ■ **avoir la ~ basse** to have weak eyes ■ **ma ~ baisse** my eyes are getting weaker ■ **avoir une ~ perçante** to be hawk-eyed
2. [regard] : **se présenter** *ou* **s'offrir à la ~ de qqn** [personne, animal, chose] to appear before sb's eyes ; [spectacle, paysage] to unfold before sb's eyes
3. [fait de voir] sight ■ **je ne supporte pas la ~ du sang** I can't stand the sight of blood
4. [yeux] eyes ■ **tu vas t'abîmer la ~** you'll ruin your eyes ■ **ils ont vérifié ma ~** they checked my eyesight ▶ **en mettre plein la ~ à qqn** *fam* to dazzle sb ■ **on va leur en mettre plein la ~!** let's really impress them *ou* knock' em for six! *UK*
5. [panorama] view ■ **d'ici, vous avez une ~ magnifique** the view (you get) from here is magnificent ■ **~ sur la mer** sea view ■ **une ~ imprenable** an unobstructed view ■ **de ma cuisine, j'ai une ~ plongeante sur leur chambre** from my kitchen I can see straight down into their bedroom ■ **avoir ~ sur** to look out on
6. [aspect] view, aspect ■ **dessiner une ~ latérale de la maison** to draw a side view *ou* the side aspect of the house
7. [image] view ■ **~ du port** [peinture, dessin, photo] view of the harbour ▶ **~ d'ensemble** PHOTO general view ; *fig* overview
8. [idée, opinion] view, opinion ■ **avoir des ~s bien arrêtées sur qqch** to have firm opinions *ou* ideas about sthg ‖ [interprétation] view, understanding, interpretation ▶ **~ de l'esprit** *péj* idle fancy.
◆ **vues** *nfpl* plans, designs ■ **cela n'était** *ou* **n'entrait pas dans nos ~s** this was no part of our plan ▶ **avoir des ~s sur qqn** to have designs on sb ■ **avoir des ~s sur qqch** to covet sthg.
◆ **à courte vue** *loc adj* [idée, plan] short-sighted.
◆ **à la vue de** *loc prép* : **il s'évanouit à la ~ du sang** he faints at the sight of blood ■ **à la ~ de tous** in front of everybody, in full view of everybody.
◆ **à vue** ◇ *loc adj* **1.** BANQUE : **dépôt à ~** call deposit ■ **retrait à ~** withdrawal on demand
2. THÉÂTRE ▷ **changement**.
◇ *loc adv* [atterrir] visually ■ [tirer] on sight ■ [payable] at sight.
◆ **à vue de nez** *loc adv fam* roughly, approximately ■ **on lui donnerait 20 ans, à ~ de nez** at a rough guess, she could be about 20.
◆ **à vue d'œil** *loc adv* : **ton cousin grossit à ~ d'œil** your cousin is getting noticeably *ou* visibly fatter ■ **mes économies disparaissent à ~ d'œil** my savings just disappear before my very eyes.
◆ **de vue** *loc adv* by sight ■ **je le connais de ~** I know his face, I know him by sight.
◆ **en vue** ◇ *loc adj* **1.** [célèbre] prominent ■ **les gens en ~** people in the public eye *ou* in the news
2. [escompté] : **avoir une solution en ~** to have a solution in mind ■ **j'ai quelqu'un en ~ pour racheter ma voiture** I've got somebody who's interested in buying my car.
◇ *loc adv* : **mettre qqch (bien) en ~ dans son salon** to display sthg prominently in one's lounge.
◆ **en vue de** *loc prép* **1.** [tout près de] within sight of
2. [afin de] so as *ou* in order to ■ **j'y vais en ~ de préparer le terrain** I'm going in order to prepare the ground.

vulcain [vylkɛ̃] *nm* red admiral.

Vulcain [vylkɛ̃] *npr* Vulcan.

vulcaniser [3] [vylkanize] *vt* to vulcanize.

vulcanologie [vylkanɔlɔʒi] = **volcanologie**.

vulcanologue [vylkanɔlɔg] = **volcanologue**.

vulgaire [vylgɛr] <> *adj* **1.** [sans goût - meuble, vêtement] vulgar, common, tasteless ; [- couleur] loud, garish ; [- style] crude, coarse, unrefined ; [- personne] uncouth, vulgar **2.** [impoli] crude, coarse ▪ **ne sois pas ~!** no need for that sort of language! **3.** *(avant le n)* [ordinaire] ordinary, common, common-or-garden *hum* ▪ **un ~ employé** a common clerk **4.** [non scientifique] : **nom ~** common name ▮ [non littéraire - langue] vernacular ; [- latin] vulgar.
<> *nm* [vulgarité] : **le ~** vulgarity ▪ **la décoration de son appartement est d'un ~!** the way he's decorated his flat is so vulgar!

vulgairement [vylgɛrmɑ̃] *adv* **1.** [avec mauvais goût] coarsely, vulgarly, tastelessly **2.** [de façon impolie] coarsely, rudely **3.** [de façon non scientifique] commonly.

vulgarisateur, trice [vylgarizatœr, tris] *adj* [ouvrage] popularizing ▪ **l'auteur tente de n'être pas trop ~** the author attempts to avoid over-simplification.

vulgarisation [vylgarizasjɔ̃] *nf* popularization ▪ **un ouvrage de ~** a book for the layman ▪ **la ~ de la pensée d'Einstein** the simplification of Einstein's thought.

vulgariser [3] [vylgarize] *vt* **1.** [faire connaître - œuvre, auteur] to popularize, to make accessible to a large audience ▪ *(en usage absolu)* **il nous faut expliquer sans ~** we have to explain without over-simplifying **2.** *litt* [rendre grossier] to vulgarize, to debase, to make coarser.

vulgarisme [vylgarism] *nm* [tournure] vulgarism.

vulgarité [vylgarite] *nf* **1.** [caractère vulgaire] vulgarity, coarseness **2.** [action] vulgar behaviour ▪ [parole] vulgar *ou* coarse remark.

vulgum pecus [vylgɔmpekys] *nm inv* : **le ~** the hoi polloi.

vulnérabilité [vylnerabilite] *nf* vulnerability.

vulnérable [vylnerabl] *adj* **1.** [fragile] vulnerable ▪ **ne l'attaque pas, il est ~** don't attack him, he's easily hurt **2.** JEUX vulnerable.

vulve [vylv] *nf* vulva.

Vve = **veuve**.

VVF (*abr de* **village vacances famille**) *nm state-subsidized holiday village.*

vx = **vieux**.

w, W [dubləve] *nm* w, W, *voir aussi* **g**.

W 1. (*abr écrite de* **watt**) W **2.** (*abr écrite de* **ouest**) W.

Wagner [vagnɛr] *npr* Wagner.

wagnérien, enne [vagnerjɛ̃, ɛn] *adj* & *nm, f* Wagnerian.

wagon [vagɔ̃] *nm* **1.** [voiture] : ~ **(de passagers)** coach, carriage *UK*, car *US* ▪ ~ **(de marchandises)** wagon, truck *UK*, freight car, boxcar *US* **2.** [contenu] truckload *UK*, wagonload ▪ **des plaintes? on en a reçu tout un ~** ***fam fig*** complaints? they've been coming in by the truckload.

wagon-bar [vagɔ̃bar] (*pl* **wagons-bars**) *nm* buffet car.

wagon-citerne [vagɔ̃sitɛrn] (*pl* **wagons-citernes**) *nm* tank wagon *UK* *OU* car *US*.

wagon-lit [vagɔ̃li] (*pl* **wagons-lits**) *nm* sleeper, sleeping car, wagon-lit.

wagonnet [vagɔnɛ] *nm* truck *UK*, cart *US*.

wagon-poste [vagɔ̃pɔst] (*pl* **wagons-poste**) *nm* mailcoach *UK*, mailcar *US*.

wagon-restaurant [vagɔ̃rɛstɔrɑ̃] (*pl* **wagons-restaurants**) *nm* dining *OU* restaurant car.

wahhabite [waabit] ◇ *adj* Wahhabite.
◇ *nmf* Wahhabi, Wahabi.

Walkman® [wɔkman] *nm* Walkman®, personal stereo.

walk-over [wɔkɔvœr] *nm inv* SPORT **1.** [compétition à un seul concurrent] walkover **2.** *fam* [victoire facile] walkover.

walkyrie [valkiri] *nf* Valkyrie, Walkyrie.

wallingant, e [walɛ̃gɑ̃, ɑ̃t] ◇ *adj* [manifestant, région] in favour of Walloon autonomy.
◇ *nm, f* ***Belgique péj*** Walloon autonomist.

Wallis-et-Futuna [walisefutuna] *npr* Wallis and Futuna.

wallon, onne [walɔ̃, ɔn] *adj* Walloon.
◆ **Wallon, onne** *nm, f* Walloon.
◆ **wallon** *nm* LING Walloon.

Wallonie [walɔni] *npr f* : **(la)** ~ Southern Belgium *(where French and Walloon are spoken)*, Wallonia.

Washington [waʃiŋtɔn] *npr* **1.** [ville] Washington DC **2.** [État] Washington State.

wassingue [vasɛ̃g] *nf* floorcloth.

Watergate [watœrgɛt] *npr m* : **le (scandale du) ~** (the) Watergate (scandal).

water-polo [watɛrpɔlo] (*pl* **water-polos**) *nm* water polo.

waters [watɛr] *nmpl* toilet.

waterzoï [watɛrzɔj] *nm* ***Belgique*** *speciality made from fish or meat in cream sauce.*

watt [wat] *nm* watt.

wattheure [watœr] *nm* watt-hour.

W-C [vese] (*abr de* **water closet**) *nmpl* WC.

Web [wɛb] *nm* : **le ~** the Web.

webmaster [wɛbmastɛr], **webmestre** [wɛbmɛstr] *nm* INFORM Webmaster, webmaster.

week-end [wikɛnd] (*pl* **week-ends**) *nm* weekend ▪ **partir en ~** to go away for the weekend ▪ **~ prolongé** long weekend.

welche [vɛlʃ] = **velche**.

western [wɛstɛrn] *nm* western ▪ **comme dans les ~s** as (they do) in the movies.

western-spaghetti [wɛstɛrnspageti] (*pl* **westerns-spaghettis**) *nm* spaghetti western.

Westphalie [vɛsfali] *npr f* : **(la) ~** Westphalia.

Wh (*abr écrite de* **wattheure**) Wh.

whisky [wiski] (*pl* **whiskys** *OU* *pl* **whiskies**) *nm* [écossais] whisky ▪ [irlandais ou américain] whiskey.

white-spirit [wajtspirit] (*pl inv* *OU* *pl* **white-spirits**) *nm* white spirit.

wienerli [vinɛrli] *nm* ***Suisse*** *small sausage.*

Wight [wajt] *npr* : **l'île de ~** the Isle of Wight.

winchester [wintʃɛstɛr] *nm* Winchester (rifle).

Wisconsin [wiskɔnsin] *npr m* : **le ~** Wisconsin.

wishbone [wiʃbon] *nm* NAUT wishbone.

wisigoth, e [vizigo, ɔt] *adj* Visigothic.
◆ **Wisigoth, e** *nm, f* Visigoth ▪ **les Wisigoths** the Visigoths.

wok [wɔk] *nm* wok.

www (*abr de* **World Wide Web**) *nm* www.

Wyoming [wajɔmiŋ] *npr m* : **le ~** Wyoming.

WYSIWYG [wiziwig] (*abr de* **what you see is what you get**) WYSIWYG.

x, X [iks] <> *nm* [lettre] x, X ▪ MATH x ▪ **j'ai vu la pièce x fois** I've seen the play umpteen times ▪ **ça fait x temps que je te demande de le faire** I've been asking you to do it for ages ▪ **Madame X** Mrs. X ▪ **être né sous X** to be taken into care at birth ▪ **classé X** X-rated, *voir aussi* **g**.
<> *nmf arg scol* (ex) student of the École Polytechnique.
<> *nf arg scol* **l'X** the École Polytechnique.

xénon [gzenɔ̃] *nm* xenon.

xénophobe [gzenɔfɔb] <> *adj* xenophobic.
<> *nmf* xenophobe.

xénophobie [gzenɔfɔbi] *nf* xenophobia.

xérès [gzerɛs, kserɛs] *nm* sherry.

Xérocopie® [gserɔkɔpi] *nf* Xerox® copy.

Xérographie® [gserɔgrafi] *nf* xerography.

Xerxès [gzerksɛs] *npr* Xerxes.

xylographie [ksilɔgrafi] *nf* xylography.

xylophage [ksilɔfaʒ] <> *adj* xylophagous.
<> *nmf* xylophage.

Xylophène® [ksilɔfɛn] *nm* wood preserver.

xylophone [gsilɔfɔn] *nm* xylophone.

y, Y [igrɛk] *nm* y, Y, *voir aussi* **g**.

y [i] *pron* **1.** [représente le lieu] there ▪ **j'y vais souvent** I often go there ▪ **on y entre comment?** how do you get in? ▪ **vas-y, entre!** go on in! ▪ **on n'y voit rien** you can't see a thing (here) ▪ **je n'y suis pour personne** whoever it is, I'm not in **2.** [représente une chose] it ▪ **pensez-y, à mon offre** do think about my offer ▪ **n'y comptez pas** don't count *ou* bank on it ▪ **je n'y manquerai pas** I certainly will **3.** [représente une personne] : **les fantômes, j'y crois** I believe in ghosts **4.** *loc* **il y va de** it's a matter of ▪ **il y va de ma dignité** my dignity's at stake ▪ **chacun y va de sa chansonnette** everyone comes out with a little song ▪ **j'y suis!** [j'ai compris] (I've) got it! ; [je t'ai compris] I'm with you! ▪ **y être pour quelque chose** to have something to do with it ▪ **je n'y suis pour rien, moi!** it's (got) nothing to do with me!, it's not my fault! ▪ **laisse-le choisir, il s'y connaît** let him choose, he knows all about it ▪ **si tu veux un matériel de qualité, il faut y mettre le prix** if you want quality material, you have to pay for it ▪ **avec les petits, il faut savoir s'y prendre** with little children you have to know how to handle them.

Y (*abr écrite de* **yen**) Y.

yacht [jɔt] *nm* yacht ▪ **~ de croisière** cruiser.

yacht-club [jɔtklœb] (*pl* **yacht-clubs**) *nm* yacht club.

ya(c)k [jak] *nm* yak.

Yalta [jalta] *npr* Yalta ▪ **la conférence de ~** the Yalta Conference.

yang [jɑ̃g] *nm* yang.

Yang-tseu-kiang [jɑ̃gtsekjɑ̃g], **Yangzi Jiang** [jɑ̃gzijɑ̃g] *npr m* Yangtze, Yangtze Kiang.

Yaoundé [jaunde] *npr* Yaoundé, Yaunde.

yaourt [jaurt] *nm* yoghurt.

yaourtière [jaurtjɛr] *nf* yoghurt maker.

yass [jas] *nm* Suisse *popular Swiss card game.*

Yellowstone [jelostɔn] *npr* : **le parc national de ~** the Yellowstone National Park.

Yémen [jemɛn] *npr m* : **le ~** Yemen ▪ **au ~** in Yemen.

yéménite [jemenit] *adj* Yemeni.
◆ **Yéménite** *nmf* Yemeni.

yen [jɛn] *nm* yen.

yeti [jeti] *nm* yeti.

Yeu [jø] *npr* : **l'île d'~** the île d'Yeu, *voir aussi* **île**.

yeux [jø] *pl* ▷ **œil**.

yé-yé [jeje] ◇ *adj inv* pop *(in the sixties).*
◇ *nmf* [chanteur] (sixties) pop singer ▪ [garçon, fille] sixties pop fan.

yiddish [jidiʃ] *adj inv* & *nm inv* Yiddish.

yi-king [jikiŋ] *nm* I-ching.

yin [jin] *nm* yin.

ylang-ylang [ilɑ̃gilɑ̃g] (*pl* **ylangs-ylangs**) *nm* ylang-ylang, ilang-ilang.

yodler [3] [jɔdle] *vi* to yodel.

yoga [jɔga] *nm* yoga.

yog(h)ourt [jɔgurt] = **yaourt**.

yogi [jɔgi] *nmf* yogi.

yole [jɔl] *nf* skiff.

Yom Kippour [jɔmkipur] *nm inv* Yom Kippur.

yorkshire [jɔrkʃœr], **yorkshire-terrier** [jɔrkʃœrterje] (*pl* **yorkshires** *ou pl* **yorkshire-terriers**) *nm* Yorkshire terrier.

yougoslave [jugɔslav] *adj* Yugoslav, Yugoslavian.
◆ **Yougoslave** *nmf* Yugoslav, Yugoslavian.

Yougoslavie [jugɔslavi] *npr f* : **(la) ~** Yugoslavia.

youpala [jupala] *nm* baby bouncer.

youpi [jupi] *interj* yippee, hooray.

youpin, e▲ [jupɛ̃, in] *nm, f antisemitic term used with reference to Jewish people,* ≃ yid.

yourte [jurt] *nf* yurt.

yoyo [jojo] *nm* MÉD grommet.

Yo-Yo® [jojo] *nm inv* yo-yo.

ypérite [iperit] *nf* mustard gas.

yucca [juka] *nm* yucca.

yuppie [jupi] *nmf* yuppie.

Z

z, Z [zɛd] *nm* z, Z, *voir aussi* **g**.

ZAC, Zac [zak] (*abr de* **zone d'aménagement concerté**) *nf area earmarked for local government planning project.*

Zacharie [zakari] *npr* **1.** [père de saint Jean-Baptiste] Zacharias **2.** [prophète] Zechariah.

ZAD, Zad [zad] (*abr de* **zone d'aménagement différé**) *nf area earmarked for future development.*

Zagreb [zagrɛb] *npr* Zagreb.

Zaïre [zair] *npr m* : **le ~** [pays] Zaïre ; [fleuve] the (River) Zaïre ■ **au ~** in Zaïre.

zaïrois, e [zairwa, az] *adj* Zaïrese.
◆ **Zaïrois, e** *nm, f* Zaïrese.

zakouski [zakuski] *nmpl* zakuski, zakouski.

Zambèze [zɑ̃bɛz] *npr m* : **le ~** the Zambese *ou* Zambezi (River).

Zambie [zɑ̃bi] *npr f* : **(la) ~** Zambia.

zambien, enne [zɑ̃bjɛ̃, ɛn] *adj* Zambian.

Zanzibar [zɑ̃zibar] *npr* Zanzibar.

zapper [zape] *vi* to zap *(TV channels)* ■ [comportement] to flit *ou* hop from on thing to another.

zappeur [zapœr] *nm* [sur une télévision] (compulsive) channel-hopper ■ [comportement] -hopper, -surfer.

zapping [zapiŋ] *nm* : **le ~** zapping, (constant) channel-hopping.

Zazie [zazi] *npr* LITTÉR *main character in Queneau's novel 'Zazie dans le métro', a little girl who combines the mischievousness and impertinence of a child with the worldliness of an adult.*

zazou [zazu] *fam* ◇ *adj* [dans les années 40] hep *vieilli*.
◇ *nmf* [amateur de jazz] hipster *vieilli*.

zèbre [zɛbr] *nm* **1.** ZOOL zebra ■ **courir** *ou* **filer comme un ~** to go like greased lightning **2.** *fam* [individu] : **c'est un (drôle de) ~, celui-là!** [ton dépréciatif] he's a weirdo! ; [ton amusé ou admiratif] he's quite something! ■ **arrête de faire le ~!** stop being silly!

zébrer [18] [zebre] *vt* [de lignes - irrégulières] to streak ; [- régulières] to stripe.

zébrure [zebryr] *nf* **1.** [du zèbre, du tigre] stripe **2.** [marque de coup] weal **3.** [d'éclair] streak.

zébu [zeby] *nm* zebu.

zélateur, trice [zelatœr, tris] *nm, f* **1.** [adepte] *litt* devotee, partisan **2.** RELIG zealot.

zèle [zɛl] *nm* zeal ■ **elle travaillait avec ~** she worked zealously ■ **fais pas de ~** *fam* don't do more than you have to!, don't overdo it!

zélé, e [zele] *adj* zealous.

zen [zɛn] *adj inv* & *nm* Zen ■ **être ~** to be laid back ■ **rester ~** to keep cool.

zénith [zenit] *nm* **1.** [sommet] zenith, acme ■ **arrivé au ~ de ses pouvoirs** having reached the zenith of his powers **2.** ASTRON zenith.
◆ **Zénith** *npr m* : **le Zénith** modern concert hall in the north of Paris.

ZEP, Zep [zɛp] (*abr de* **zone d'éducation prioritaire**) *nf designated area with special educational needs.*

zéphyr [zefir] *nm* [vent] zephyr, light breeze ■ **Zéphyr** MYTHOL Zephyr.

zeppelin [zɛplɛ̃] *nm* zeppelin.

zéro [zero] ◇ *nm* **1.** MATH zero, nought ■ [dans un numéro de téléphone] 0 ■ [dans une gradation] zero ■ **~~ trente-cinq** double 0 three-five ◑ **'le Zéro et l'Infini'** ***Koestler*** 'Darkness at Noon'
2. ARM zero
3. PHYS zero (degrees centigrade), freezing (point) ■ **~ absolu** absolute zero
4. SPORT zero, nil *UK* ■ **deux buts à ~** two (goals to) nil *UK ou* zero ■ **~ partout** no score ‖ TENNIS love ■ **~ partout** love all
5. ÉDUC nought *UK*, zero ■ **j'ai eu ~** I got (a) nought ◑ **~ de conduite** black mark ■ **~ pointé** nought *UK*, zero
6. *fam* [incapable] dead loss
7. *(comme adj)* [sans intérêt] nil, worthless ■ **au niveau organisation, c'était ~** as far as organisation goes it was useless ■ **ils ont de beaux tissus, mais pour la confection c'est ~** they've got some nice fabrics but when it comes to making clothes they haven't a clue.
◇ *dét* : **~ faute** no mistakes ■ **~ heure** midnight, zero hour *spéc* ■ **~ heure quinze** zero hours fifteen ■ **ça te coûtera ~ centime** it'll cost you nothing at all.
◆ **à zéro** ◇ *loc adj* : **avoir le moral** *ou* **être à ~** *fam* to be at an all-time low.
◇ *loc adv fam* **être réduit à ~** to be reduced ■ **recommencer** *ou* **repartir à ~** [dans sa carrière, dans un raisonnement] to go back to square one *ou* the drawing board ; [sans argent, sans aide] to start again from scratch.

zeste [zɛst] *nm* **1.** [d'un agrume] zest ■ **un ~ de citron** a piece of lemon peel **2.** [petite quantité] pinch ■ **un ~ d'accent** a hint *ou* faint trace of an accent.

Zeus [dzøs] *npr* Zeus.

zézaie *etc v* ▻ **zézayer**.

zézaiement [zezɛmɑ̃] *nm* lisp.

zézayer [11] [zezeje] *vi* to (have a) lisp.

ZI *nf* = **zone industrielle**.

zibeline [ziblin] *nf* [fourrure, animal] sable.

zieuter [3] △ [zjøte] *vt* to eye (up) *(sép)*, to eyeball△ *US* ■ **t'as passé la soirée à ~ ma femme** you've spent the whole evening eyeing up my wife.

zig△ [zig] *nm* guy, bloke *UK*.

zigoto [zigɔto] *nm fam* **c'est un drôle de ~!** he's a funny customer! ■ **faire le ~** to clown around.

zigouiller [3] △ [ziguje] *vt* to knife (to death), to bump off△ *(sép)*, to do in△ *(sép)* ■ **se faire ~** to get done in.

zigue△ [zig] = **zig**.

zigzag [zigzag] *nm* zigzag ■ **la route fait des ~s dans la montée** the road zigzags up ■ **elle marchait en faisant des ~s** she was zigzagging along.
◆ **en zigzag** *loc adj* zigzagging, winding.

zigzaguer [3] [zigzage] *vi* to zigzag ■ **il avançait en zigzaguant** he zigzagged along.

Zimbabwe [zimbabwe] *npr m* : **le ~** Zimbabwe ■ **au ~** in Zimbabwe.

zinc [zɛ̃g] *nm* **1.** [métal] zinc **2.** *fam* [comptoir] bar ■ **on prend un verre sur le ~?** shall we have a drink at the bar? **3.** *fam* [avion] plane.

zingueur [zɛ̃gœr] *nm* zinc worker.

zinnia [zinja] *nm* zinnia.

zinzin [zɛ̃zɛ̃] *fam* ◇ *adj* dotty, batty, nuts.
◇ *nm* **1.** [idiot] nutcase **2.** [truc] thingamajig, thingumajig.

Zip® [zip] *nm* zip *UK*, zipper *US*.

zipper [3] [zipe] *vt* INFORM to zip.

zircon [zirkɔ̃] *nm* zircon.

zizanie [zizani] *nf* discord ■ **c'est la ~ entre les frères** the brothers are at odds *OU* loggerheads ■ **jeter** *OU* **mettre** *OU* **semer la ~ dans un groupe** to stir things up in a group.

zizi [zizi] *nm fam* [sexe] willie *UK*, peter *US*.

zob▲ [zɔb] *nm* prick, cock.

Zodiac® [zɔdjak] *nm* inflatable dinghy.

zodiacal, e, aux [zɔdjakal, o] *adj* [signe] zodiac.

zodiaque [zɔdjak] *nm* ASTRON & ASTROL zodiac.

zombi(e) [zɔ̃bi] *nm* zombie.

zona [zona] *nm* shingles *(U)*, herpes zoster *spéc* ■ **avoir un ~** to suffer from shingles.

zonage [zonaʒ] *nm* zoning.

zonal, e, aux [zonal, o] *adj* GÉOGR zonal.

zonard [zonar] *nm fam* dropout.

zone [zon] *nf* **1.** [domaine] zone, area ■ **~ de flou** *OU* **d'incertitude** *OU* **d'ombre** grey area ■ **la ~ d'activité du directeur commercial** the commercial manager's area ■ **la ~ d'influence de l'Asie** Asia's sphere of influence
2. ANAT : **~ érogène** erogenous zone
3. ADMIN [surface délimitée] area, zone ■ **~ d'aménagement concerté = ZAC** ■ **~ bleue** restricted parking area ■ **~ industrielle** industrial estate *UK OU* park *US* ■ **~ piétonnière** *OU* **piétonne** pedestrian area *OU* precinct *UK* ■ **~ résidentielle** residential area ■ **~ de stationnement interdit** no parking area ■ **~ à urbaniser en priorité = ZUP** ‖ ADMIN & FIN : **~s des salaires** *wage bands subject to the same percentage reduction*
4. HIST : **~ libre/occupée** unoccupied/occupied France
5. GÉOGR : **~ désertique** desert belt ■ **~ forestière** forest belt ■ **~ glaciale/tempérée/torride** frigid/temperate/torrid zone ■ **~ de végétation** vegetation zone
6. MÉTÉOR ▶ **~ de dépression, ~ dépressionnaire** trough of low pressure
7. GÉOL & MATH zone
8. FIN : **~ franc** franc area, *monetary zone where the franc was the principal currency* ■ **~ monétaire** monetary zone
9. INFORM : **~ de données** data field ■ **~ de mémoire** storage area
10. MIL : **~ d'exclusion aérienne** no-fly zone ■ **~ tampon** buffer zone
11. *péj* **c'est la ~** *fam* [quartier pauvre] it's a really rough area ; [désordre] it's a real mess *OU* tip ■ **cette famille, c'est vraiment la ~** they're real dropouts in that family.
◆ **de deuxième zone** *loc adj* second-rate, second-class.
◆ **de troisième zone** *loc adj* third-rate.

ZONE

1. The Paris area is divided into fare zones for public transport. Zones 1 and 2 cover metropolitan Paris and certain areas of the nearby suburbs. The remaining zones cover the outer suburbs: ***j'habite en zone 3, une carte orange quatre zones***.
2. France is divided into three ***zones*** (A, B and C), the schools in the different zones taking their mid-term breaks and Easter holidays at different times to avoid swamping the roads, the public transport system and tourist infrastructure.

zoner [3] [zone] ◇ *vt* to zone.
◇ *vi fam* to doss *UK OU* to bum around.

zoo [zo(o)] *nm* zoo ■ **c'est le ~ ici!** *fig* this place is like a madhouse!

zoologie [zɔɔlɔʒi] *nf* zoology.

zoologique [zɔɔlɔʒik] *adj* zoological.

zoologiste [zɔɔlɔʒist] *nmf* zoologist.

zoom [zum] *nm* [objet] zoom lens ■ [procédé] zoom ■ **faire un ~ sur** to zoom in on.

zoomer [3] [zume] *vi* [pour se rapprocher] to zoom in ■ [pour s'éloigner] to zoom out.

zoophile [zɔɔfil] ◇ *adj* zoophilic.
◇ *nmf* zoophile.

zoophilie [zɔɔfili] *nf* zoophilia, bestiality.

zooplancton [zɔɔplɑ̃ktɔ̃] *nm* zooplankton.

zootechnie [zɔɔtɛkni] *nf* zootechnics *(U)*.

Zoroastre [zɔrɔastr] *npr* Zoroaster.

zoroastrisme [zɔrɔastrism] *nm* Zoroastrianism.

zou [zu] *interj* [pour éloigner] shoo ■ [pour marquer la rapidité] whoosh ■ **allez, ~ les enfants, au lit!** come on, off to bed children! ■ **on ferme la maison et ~, on part pour l'Italie** we'll shut up the house and whizz off to Italy.

zouave [zwav] *nm* **1.** MIL Zouave **2.** *fam loc* **faire le ~** [faire le pitre] to clown about ; [faire le malin] to show off.

zouk [zuk] *nm* MUS zouk *(type of Caribbean music)*.

zoulou, e [zulu] *adj* Zulu.
◆ **Zoulou, e** *nm, f* Zulu.

Zoulouland, Zululand [zululɑ̃d] *npr m* : **le ~** Zululand, Kwazulu.

zozo [zozo] *nm fam* ninny, nitwit.

zozoter [3] [zɔzɔte] *vi* to lisp.

Zululand [zululɑ̃d] = **Zoulouland**.

ZUP, Zup [zyp] (*abr de* **zone à urbaniser par priorité**) *nf area earmarked for urgent urban development.*

Zurich [zyrik] *npr* Zürich ■ **le lac de ~** Lake Zürich.

zut [zyt] *interj fam* drat, blast ■ **~ alors, y a plus de sucre!** blast (it), there's no sugar left! ■ **et puis ~, tant pis, je l'achète!** what the hell, I'll buy it! ■ **dis-lui ~** tell him to get lost.

zwieback [tsɥibak] *nm Suisse sweet biscuit.*

zyeuter△ [zjøte] = **zieuter**.

zygomatique [zigɔmatik] *adj* zygomatic.

zygote [zigɔt] *nm* zygote.

	1 avoir	**2 être**	**3 chanter**
present indicative	j'ai tu as il, elle a nous avons vous avez ils, elles ont	je suis tu es il, elle est nous sommes vous êtes ils, elles sont	je chante tu chantes il, elle chante nous chantons vous chantez ils, elles chantent
imperfect	il, elle avait	il, elle était	il, elle chantait
past historic	il, elle eut ils, elles eurent	il, elle fut ils, elles furent	il, elle chanta ils, elles chantèrent
future	j'aurai il, elle aura	je serai il, elle sera	je chanterai il, elle chantera
present conditional	j'aurais il, elle aurait	je serais il, elle serait	je chanterais il, elle chanterait
present subjunctive	que j'aie qu'il, elle ait que nous ayons qu'ils, elles aient	que je sois qu'il, elle soit que nous soyons qu'ils, elles soient	que je chante qu'il, elle chante que nous chantions qu'ils, elles chantent
imperfect subjunctive	qu'il, elle eût qu'ils, elles eussent	qu'il, elle fût qu'ils, elles fussent	qu'il, elle chantât qu'ils, elles chantassent
imperative	aie ayons ayez	sois soyons soyez	chante chantons chantez
present participle	ayant	étant	chantant
past participle	eu, eue	été	chanté, e

	4 baisser	**5 pleurer**	**6 jouer**
present indicative	je baisse tu baisses il, elle baisse nous baissons vous baissez ils, elles baissent	je pleure tu pleures il, elle pleure nous pleurons vous pleurez ils, elles pleurent	je joue tu joues il, elle joue nous jouons vous jouez ils, elles jouent
imperfect	il, elle baissait	il, elle pleurait	il, elle jouait
past historic	il, elle baissa ils, elles baissèrent	il, elle pleura ils, elles pleurèrent	il, elle joua ils, elles jouèrent
future	je baisserai il, elle baissera	je pleurerai il, elle pleurera	je jouerai il, elle jouera
present conditional	je baisserais il, elle baisserait	je pleurerais il, elle pleurerait	je jouerais il, elle jouerait
present subjunctive	que je baisse qu'il, elle baisse que nous baissions qu'ils, elles baissent	que je pleure qu'il, elle pleure que nous pleurions qu'ils, elles pleurent	que je joue qu'il, elle joue que nous jouions qu'ils, elles jouent
imperfect subjunctive	qu'il, elle baissât qu'ils, elles baissassent	qu'il, elle pleurât qu'ils, elles pleurassent	qu'il, elle jouât qu'ils, elles jouassent
imperative	baisse baissons baissez	pleure pleurons pleurez	joue jouons jouez
present participle	baissant	pleurant	jouant
past participle	baissé, e	pleuré, e	joué, e

	7 saluer	8 arguer	9 copier
present indicative	je salue tu salues il, elle salue nous saluons vous saluez ils, elles saluent	j'argue, arguë tu argues, arguës il, elle argue, arguë nous arguons vous arguez ils, elles arguent, arguënt	je copie tu copies il, elle copie nous copions vous copiez ils, elles copient
imperfect	il, elle saluait	il, elle arguait	il, elle copiait
past historic	il, elle salua ils, elles saluèrent	il, elle argua ils, elles arguèrent	il, elle copia ils, elles copièrent
future	je saluerai il, elle saluera	j'arguerai, arguërai il, elle arguera, arguëra	je copierai il, elle copiera
present conditional	je saluerais il, elle saluerait	j'arguerais, arguërais il, elle arguerait, arguërait	je copierais il, elle copierait
present subjunctive	que je salue qu'il, elle salue que nous saluions qu'ils, elles saluent	que j'argue, arguë qu'il, elle argue, arguë que nous arguions qu'ils, elles arguent, arguënt	que je copie qu'il, elle copie que nous copiions qu'ils, elles copient
imperfect subjunctive	qu'il, elle saluât qu'ils, elles saluassent	qu'il, elle arguât qu'ils, elles arguassent	qu'il, elle copiât qu'ils, elles copiassent
imperative	salue saluons saluez	argue, arguë arguons arguez	copie copions copiez
present participle	saluant	arguant	copiant
past participle	salué, e	argué, e	copié, e

	10 prier *	11 payer **	12 grasseyer
present indicative	je prie tu pries il, elle prie nous prions vous priez ils, elles prient	je paie, paye tu paies, payes il, elle paie, paye nous payons vous payez ils, elles paient, payent	je grasseye tu grasseyes il, elle grasseye nous grasseyons vous grasseyez ils, elles grasseyent
imperfect	il, elle priait	il, elle payait	il, elle grasseyait
past historic	il, elle pria ils, elles prièrent	il, elle paya ils, elles payèrent	il, elle grasseya ils, elles grasseyèrent
future	je prierai il, elle priera	je paierai, payerai il, elle paiera, payera	je grasseyerai il, elle grasseyera
present conditional	je prierais il, elle prierait	je paierais, payerais il, elle paierait, payerait	je grasseyerais il, elle grasseyerait
present subjunctive	que je prie qu'il, elle prie que nous priions qu'ils, elles prient	que je paie, paye qu'il, elle paie, paye que nous payions qu'ils, elles paient, payent	que je grasseye qu'il, elle grasseye que nous grasseyions qu'ils, elles grasseyent
imperfect subjunctive	qu'il, elle priât qu'ils, elles priassent	qu'il, elle payât qu'ils, elles payassent	qu'il, elle grasseyât qu'ils, elles grasseyassent
imperative	prie prions priez	paie, paye payons payez	grasseye grasseyons grasseyez
present participle	priant	payant	grasseyant
past participle	prié, e	payé, e	grasseyé, e

***** Note the presence of two **i**'s in the 1st and 2nd person plural of the imperfect indicative and the present subjunctive: nous *priions, vous priiez.*

****** Verbs in **-ayer** such as *payer* can either keep the **y** in all their forms or replace the **y** by **i** before mute **e** (in the endings : **-e, -es, -ent, -erai**). The pronunciation is different depending on which form is chosen: *je paye* [pεj] or *je paie* [pε].
In the 1st and 2nd person plural of the imperfect indicative and the present subjunctive, there is an **i** after the **y.**

	13 ployer	14 essuyer	15 créer
present indicative	je ploie tu ploies il, elle ploie nous ployons vous ployez ils, elles ploient	j'essuie tu essuies il, elle essuie nous essuyons vous essuyez ils, elles essuient	je crée tu crées il, elle crée nous créons vous créez ils, elles créent
imperfect	il, elle ployait	il, elle essuyait	il, elle créait
past historic	il, elle ploya ils, elles ployèrent	il, elle essuya ils, elles essuyèrent	il, elle créa ils, elles créèrent
future	je ploierai il, elle ploiera	j'essuierai il, elle essuiera	je créerai il, elle créera
present conditional	je ploierais il, elle ploierait	j'essuierais il, elle essuierait	je créerais il, elle créerait
present subjunctive	que je ploie qu'il, elle ploie que nous ployions qu'ils, elles ploient	que j'essuie qu'il, elle essuie que nous essuyions qu'ils, elles essuient	que je crée qu'il, elle crée que nous créions qu'ils, elles créent
imperfect subjunctive	qu'il, elle ployât qu'ils, elles ployassent	qu'il, elle essuyât qu'ils, elles essuyassent	qu'il, elle créât qu'ils, elles créassent
imperative	ploie ployons ployez	essuie essuyons essuyez	crée créons créez
present participle	ployant	essuyant	créant
past participle	ployé, e	essuyé, e	créé, e

	16 avancer *	17 manger **	18 céder
present indicative	j'avance tu avances il, elle avance nous avançons vous avancez ils, elles avancent	je mange tu manges il, elle mange nous mangeons vous mangez ils, elles mangent	je cède tu cèdes il, elle cède nous cédons vous cédez ils, elles cèdent
imperfect	il, elle avançait	il, elle mangeait	il, elle cédait
past historic	il, elle avança ils, elles avancèrent	il, elle mangea ils, elles mangèrent	il, elle céda ils, elles cédèrent
future	j'avancerai il, elle avancera	je mangerai il, elle mangera	je céderai, cèderai il, elle cédera, cèdera
present conditional	j'avancerais il, elle avancerait	je mangerais il, elle mangerait	je céderais, cèderais il, elle céderait, cèderait
present subjunctive	que j'avance qu'il, elle avance que nous avancions qu'ils, elles avancent	que je mange qu'il, elle mange que nous mangions qu'ils, elles mangent	que je cède qu'il, elle cède que nous cédions qu'ils, elles cèdent
imperfect subjunctive	qu'il, elle avançât qu'ils, elles avançassent	qu'il, elle mangeât qu'ils, elles mangeassent	qu'il, elle cédât qu'ils, elles cédassent
imperative	avance avançons avancez	mange mangeons mangez	cède cédons cédez
present participle	avançant	mangeant	cédant
past participle	avancé, e	mangé, e	cédé, e

***** *Annoncer, commencer, déplacer, effacer, lancer* and *placer* are conjugated in the same way as *avancer.* Note that verbs in **–cer** change **c** to **ç** in front of the vowels **a** and **o**: *il avança, nous avançons,* etc.
****** Note that verbs in **–ger**, such as *juger* and *manger,* retain an **e** after the **g** in front of the vowels **a** and **o**: *je mangeais, nous mangeons,* etc.

	19 semer	20 rapiécer	21 acquiescer
present indicative	je sème tu sèmes il, elle sème nous semons vous semez ils, elles sèment	je rapièce tu rapièces il, elle rapièce nous rapiéçons vous rapiécez ils, elles rapiècent	j'acquiesce tu acquiesces il, elle acquiesce nous acquiesçons vous acquiescez ils, elles acquiescent
imperfect	il, elle semait	il, elle rapiéçait	il, elle acquiesçait
past historic	il, elle sema ils, elles semèrent	il, elle rapiéça ils, elles rapiécèrent	il, elle acquiesça ils, elles acquiescèrent
future	je sèmerai il, elle sèmera	je rapiécerai, rapiècerai il, elle rapiécera, rapiècera	j'acquiescerai il, elle acquiescera
present conditional	je sèmerais il, elle sèmerait	je rapiécerais, rapiècerais il, elle rapiécerait, rapiècerait	j'acquiescerais il, elle acquiescerait
present subjunctive	que je sème qu'il, elle sème que nous semions qu'ils, elles sèment	que je rapièce qu'il, elle rapièce que nous rapiécions qu'ils, elles rapiècent	que j'acquiesce qu'il, elle acquiesce que nous acquiescions qu'ils, elles acquiescent
imperfect subjunctive	qu'il, elle semât qu'ils, elles semassent	qu'il, elle rapiéçât qu'ils, elles rapiéçassent	qu'il, elle acquiesçât qu'ils, elles acquiesçassent
imperative	sème semons semez	rapièce rapiéçons rapiécez	acquiesce acquiesçons acquiescez
present participle	semant	rapiéçant	acquiesçant
past participle	semé, e	rapiécé, e	acquiescé

	22 siéger *	23 déneiger	24 appeler**
present indicative	je siège tu sièges il, elle siège nous siégeons vous siégez ils, elles siègent	je déneige tu déneiges il, elle déneige nous déneigeons vous déneigez ils, elles déneigent	j'appelle tu appelles il, elle appelle nous appelons vous appelez ils, elles appellent
imperfect	il, elle siégeait	il, elle déneigeait	il, elle appelait
past historic	il, elle siégea ils, elles siégèrent	il, elle déneigea ils, elles déneigèrent	il, elle appela ils, elles appelèrent
future	je siégerai, siègerai il, elle siégera, siègera	je déneigerai il, elle déneigera	j'appellerai il, elle appellera
present conditional	je siégerais, siègerais il, elle siégerait, siègerait	je déneigerais il, elle déneigerait	j'appellerais il, elle appellerait
present subjunctive	que je siège qu'il, elle siège que nous siégions qu'ils, elles siègent	que je déneige qu'il, elle déneige que nous déneigions qu'ils, elles déneigent	que j'appelle qu'il, elle appelle que nous appelions qu'ils, elles appellent
imperfect subjunctive	qu'il, elle siégeât qu'ils, elles siégeassent	qu'il, elle déneigeât qu'ils, elles déneigeassent	qu'il, elle appelât qu'ils, elles appelassent
imperative	siège siégeons siégez	déneige déneigeons déneigez	appelle appelons appelez
present participle	siégeant	déneigeant	appelant
past participle	siégé	déneigé, e	appelé, e

* *Assiéger* conjugates in the same way as *siéger,* but the past participle is variable: *assiégé, assiégée.*
** Most verbs ending in **–eler** behave like *appeler* and double the final –l before mute **–e**: *j'appelle, tu appelleras,* etc.

	25 peler	26 interpeller	27 jeter *
present indicative	je pèle tu pèles il, elle pèle nous pelons vous pelez ils, elles pèlent	j'interpelle tu interpelles il, elle interpelle nous interpellons vous interpellez ils, elles interpellent	je jette tu jettes il, elle jette nous jetons vous jetez ils, elles jettent
imperfect	il, elle pelait	il, elle interpellait	il, elle jetait
past historic	il, elle pela ils, elles pelèrent	il, elle interpella ils, elles interpellèrent	il, elle jeta ils, elles jetèrent
future	je pèlerai il, elle pèlera	j'interpellerai il, elle interpellera	je jetterai il, elle jettera
present conditional	je pèlerais il, elle pèlerait	j'interpellerais il, elle interpellerait	je jetterais il, elle jetterait
present subjunctive	que je pèle qu'il, elle pèle que nous pelions qu'ils, elles pèlent	que j'interpelle qu'il, elle interpelle que nous interpellions qu'ils, elles interpellent	que je jette qu'il, elle jette que nous jetions qu'ils, elles jettent
imperfect subjunctive	qu'il, elle pelât qu'ils, elles pelassent	qu'il, elle interpellât qu'ils, elles interpellassent	qu'il, elle jetât qu'ils, elles jetassent
imperative	pèle pelons pelez	interpelle interpellons interpellez	jette jetons jetez
present participle	pelant	interpellant	jetant
past participle	pelé, e	interpellé, e	jeté, e

* Most verbs ending in **–eter** behave like *jeter* and double the final **–t** before a mute **–e**: *je jette, tu jetteras,* etc.

	28 acheter	29 dépecer	30 envoyer
present indicative	j'achète tu achètes il, elle achète nous achetons vous achetez ils, elles achètent	je dépèce tu dépèces il, elle dépèce nous dépeçons vous dépecez ils, elles dépècent	j'envoie tu envoies il, elle envoie nous envoyons vous envoyez ils, elles envoient
imperfect	il, elle achetait	il, elle dépeçait	il, elle envoyait
past historic	il, elle acheta ils, elles achetèrent	il, elle dépeça ils, elles dépecèrent	il, elle envoya ils, elles envoyèrent
future	j'achèterai il, elle achètera	je dépècerai il, elle dépècera	j'enverrai il, elle enverra
present conditional	j'achèterais il, elle achèterait	je dépècerais il, elle dépècerait	j'enverrais il, elle enverrait
present subjunctive	que j'achète qu'il, elle achète que nous achetions qu'ils, elles achètent	que je dépèce qu'il, elle dépèce que nous dépecions qu'ils, elles dépècent	que j'envoie qu'il, elle envoie que nous envoyions qu'ils, elles envoient
imperfect subjunctive	qu'il, elle achetât qu'ils, elles achetassent	qu'il, elle dépeçât qu'ils, elles dépeçassent	qu'il, elle envoyât qu'ils, elles envoyassent
imperative	achète achetons achetez	dépèce dépeçons dépecez	envoie envoyons envoyez
present participle	achetant	depeçant	envoyant
past participle	acheté, e	dépecé, e	envoyé, e

	31 aller *	32 finir	33 haïr
present indicative	je vais tu vas il, elle va nous allons vous allez ils, elles vont	je finis tu finis il, elle finit nous finissons vous finissez ils, elles finissent	je hais tu hais il, elle hait nous haïssons vous haïssez ils, elles haïssent
imperfect	il, elle allait	il, elle finissait	il, elle haïssait
past historic	il, elle alla ils, elles allèrent	il, elle finit ils, elles finirent	il, elle haït ils, elles haïrent
future	j'irai il, elle ira	je finirai il, elle finira	je haïrai il, elle haïra
present conditional	j'irais il, elle irait	je finirais il, elle finirait	je haïrais il, elle haïrait
present subjunctive	que j'aille qu'il, elle aille que nous allions qu'ils, elles aillent	que je finisse qu'il, elle finisse que nous finissions qu'ils, elles finissent	que je haïsse qu'il, elle haïsse que nous haïssions qu'ils, elles haïssent
imperfect subjunctive	qu'il, elle allât qu'ils, elles allassent	qu'il, elle finît qu'ils, elles finissent	qu'il, elle haït qu'ils, elles haïssent
imperative	va allons allez	finis finissons finissez	hais haïssons haïssez
present participle	allant	finissant	haïssant
past participle	allé, e	fini, e	haï, e

* *Aller* is conjugated with *être* in compound tenses. The imperative of *aller* is *vas* when it is followed by y: *vas-y.*
S'en aller in the imperative gives: *va-t'en, allons-nous-en, allez-vous-en.*
In compound tenses, *aller* can be replaced by *être* and conjugated with *avoir*: *je suis allé* or *j'ai été.*

	34 ouvrir	35 fuir	36 dormir *
present indicative	j'ouvre tu ouvres il, elle ouvre nous ouvrons vous ouvrez ils, elles ouvrent	je fuis tu fuis il, elle fuit nous fuyons vous fuyez ils, elles fuient	je dors tu dors il, elle dort nous dormons vous dormez ils, elles dorment
imperfect	il, elle ouvrait	il, elle fuyait	il, elle dormait
past historic	il, elle ouvrit ils, elles ouvrirent	il, elle fuit ils, elles fuirent	il, elle dormit ils, elles dormirent
future	j'ouvrirai il, elle ouvrira	je fuirai il, elle fuira	je dormirai il, elle dormira
present conditional	j'ouvrirais il, elle ouvrirait	je fuirais il, elle fuirait	je dormirais il, elle dormirait
present subjunctive	que j'ouvre qu'il, elle ouvre que nous ouvrions qu'ils, elles ouvrent	que je fuie qu'il, elle fuie que nous fuyions qu'ils, elles fuient	que je dorme qu'il, elle dorme que nous dormions qu'ils, elles dorment
imperfect subjunctive	qu'il, elle ouvrît qu'ils, elles ouvrissent	qu'il, elle fuît qu'ils, elles fuissent	qu'il, elle dormît qu'ils, elles dormissent
imperative	ouvre ouvrons ouvrez	fuis fuyons fuyez	dors dormons dormez
present participle	ouvrant	fuyant	dormant
past participle	ouvert, e	fui, e	dormi

* *Endormir* conjugates in the same way as *dormir,* but the past participle is variable: *endormi, endormie.*

	37 mentir *	38 servir	39 acquérir
present indicative	je mens tu mens il, elle ment nous mentons vous mentez ils, elles mentent	je sers tu sers il, elle sert nous servons vous servez ils, elles servent	j'acquiers tu acquiers il, elle acquiert nous acquérons vous acquérez ils, elles acquièrent
imperfect	il, elle mentait	il, elle servait	il, elle acquérait
past historic	il, elle mentit ils, elles mentirent	il, elle servit ils, elles servirent	il, elle acquit ils, elles acquirent
future	je mentirai il, elle mentira	je servirai il, elle servira	j'acquerrai il, elle acquerra
present conditional	je mentirais il, elle mentirait	je servirais il, elle servirait	j'acquerrais il, elle acquerrait
present subjunctive	que je mente qu'il, elle mente que nous mentions qu'ils, elles mentent	que je serve qu'il, elle serve que nous servions qu'ils, elles servent	que j'acquière qu'il, elle acquière que nous acquérions qu'ils, elles acquièrent
imperfect subjunctive	qu'il, elle mentît qu'ils, elles mentissent	qu'il, elle servît qu'ils, elles servissent	qu'il, elle acquît qu'ils, elles acquissent
imperative	mens mentons mentez	sers servons servez	acquiers acquérons acquérez
present participle	mentant	servant	acquérant
past participle	menti	servi, e	acquis, e

* *Démentir* conjugates in the same way as *mentir,* but the past participle is variable: *démenti, démentie.*

	40 venir	41 cueillir	42 mourir
present indicative	je viens tu viens il, elle vient nous venons vous venez ils, elles viennent	je cueille tu cueilles il, elle cueille nous cueillons vous cueillez ils, elles cueillent	je meurs tu meurs il, elle meurt nous mourons vous mourez ils, elles meurent
imperfect	il, elle venait	il, elle cueillait	il, elle mourait
past historic	il, elle vint ils, elles vinrent	il, elle cueillit ils, elles cueillirent	il, elle mourut ils, elles moururent
future	je viendrai il, elle viendra	je cueillerai il, elle cueillera	je mourrai il, elle mourra
present conditional	je viendrais il, elle viendrait	je cueillerais il, elle cueillerait	je mourrais il, elle mourrait
present subjunctive	que je vienne qu'il, elle vienne que nous venions qu'ils, elles viennent	que je cueille qu'il, elle cueille que nous cueillions qu'ils, elles cueillent	que je meure qu'il, elle meure que nous mourions qu'ils, elles meurent
imperfect subjunctive	qu'il, elle vînt qu'ils, elles vinssent	qu'il, elle cueillît qu'ils, elles cueillissent	qu'il, elle mourût qu'ils, elles mourussent
imperative	viens venons venez	cueille cueillons cueillez	meurs mourons mourez
present participle	venant	cueillant	mourant
past participle	venu, e	cueilli, e	mort, e

	43 partir	44 revêtir	45 courir
present indicative	je pars tu pars il, elle part nous partons vous partez ils, elles partent	je revêts tu revêts il, elle revêt nous revêtons vous revêtez ils, elles revêtent	je cours tu cours il, elle court nous courons vous courez ils, elles courent
imperfect	il, elle partait	il, elle revêtait	il, elle courait
past historic	il, elle partit ils, elles partirent	il, elle revêtit ils, elles revêtirent	il, elle courut ils, elles coururent
future	je partirai il, elle partira	je revêtirai il, elle revêtira	je courrai il, elle courra
present conditional	je partirais il, elle partirait	je revêtirais il, elle revêtirait	je courrais il, elle courrait
present subjunctive	que je parte qu'il, elle parte que nous partions qu'ils, elles partent	que je revête qu'il, elle revête que nous revêtions qu'ils, elles revêtent	que je coure qu'il, elle coure que nous courions qu'ils, elles courent
imperfect subjunctive	qu'il, elle partît qu'ils, elles partissent	qu'il, elle revêtît qu'ils, elles revêtissent	qu'il, elle courût qu'ils, elles courussent
imperative	pars partons partez	revêts revêtons revêtez	cours courons courez
present participle	partant	revêtant	courant
past participle	parti, e	revêtu, e	couru, e

	46 faillir *	47 défaillir	48 bouillir
present indicative	je faillis, faux tu faillis, faux il, elle faillit, faut nous faillissons, faillons vous faillissez, faillez ils, elles faillissent, faillent	je défaille tu défailles il, elle défaille nous défaillons vous défaillez ils, elles défaillent	je bous tu bous il, elle bout nous bouillons vous bouillez ils, elles bouillent
imperfect	il, elle faillissait, faillait	il, elle défaillait	il, elle bouillait
past historic	il, elle faillit ils, elles faillirent	il, elle défaillit ils, elles défaillirent	il, elle bouillit ils, elles bouillirent
future	je faillirai, faudrai il, elle faillira, faudra	je défaillirai, défaillerai il, elle défaillira, défaillera	je bouillirai il, elle bouillira
present conditional	je faillirais, faudrais il, elle faillirait, faudrait	je défaillirais, défaillerais il, elle défaillirait, défaillerait	je bouillirais il, elle bouillirait
present subjunctive	que je faillisse, faille qu'il, elle faillisse, faille que nous faillissions, faillions qu'ils, elles faillissent, faillent	que je défaille qu'il, elle défaille que nous défaillions qu'ils, elles défaillent	que je bouille qu'il, elle bouille que nous bouillions qu'ils, elles bouillent
imperfect subjunctive	qu'il, elle faillît qu'ils, elles faillissent	qu'il, elle défaillît qu'ils, elles défaillissent	qu'il, elle bouillît qu'ils, elles bouillissent
imperative	faillis, faux faillissons, faillons faillissez, faillez	défaille défaillons défaillez	bous bouillons bouillez
present participle	faillissant, faillant	défaillant	bouillant
past participle	failli	défailli	bouilli, e

* The most often used conjugation for *faillir* is that which follows the same pattern as *finir*. *Faillir* is rarely used in its conjugated forms.

	49 gésir *	**50 saillir**	**51 ouïr ****
present indicative	je gis tu gis il, elle gît nous gisons vous gisez ils, elles gisent	– – il, elle saille – – ils, elles saillent	j'ouïs, ois tu ouïs, ois il, elle ouït, oit nous ouïssons, oyons vous ouïssez, oyez ils, elles ouïssent, oient
imperfect	il, elle gisait	il, elle saillait	il, elle ouïssait, oyait
past historic	–	il, elle saillit ils, elles saillirent	il, elle ouït ils, elles ouïrent
future	–	– il, elle saillera	j'ouïrai, orrais il, elle ouïra, orra
present conditional	–	– il, elle saillerait	j'ouïrais il, elle ouïrait, orrait
present subjunctive	–	– qu'il, elle saille – qu'ils, elles saillent	que j'ouïsse, oie qu'il, elle ouïsse, oie que nous ouïssions, oyions qu'ils, elles ouïssent, oient
imperfect subjunctive	–	qu'il, elle saillît qu'ils, elles saillissent	qu'il, elle ouït qu'ils, elles ouïssent
imperative	–	–	ouïs, ois ouïssons, oyons ouïssez, oyez
present participle	gisant	saillant	oyant
past participle	–	sailli, e	ouï, e

* *Gésir* is defective in other tenses and modes.
** *Ouïr* is only used in the present infinitive, past participle *ouï(e)* and in compound tenses.

	52 recevoir *	**53 devoir**	**54 mouvoir**
present indicative	je reçois tu reçois il, elle reçoit nous recevons vous recevez ils, elles reçoivent	je dois tu dois il, elle doit nous devons vous devez ils, elles doivent	je meus tu meus il, elle meut nous mouvons vous mouvez ils, elles meuvent
imperfect	il, elle recevait	il, elle devait	il, elle mouvait
past historic	il, elle reçut ils, elles reçurent	il, elle dut ils, elles durent	il, elle mut ils, elles murent
future	je recevrai il, elle recevra	je devrai il, elle devra	je mouvrai il, elle mouvra
present conditional	je recevrais il, elle recevrait	je devrais il, elle devrait	je mouvrais il, elle mouvrait
present subjunctive	que je reçoive qu'il, elle reçoive que nous recevions qu'ils, elles reçoivent	que je doive qu'il, elle doive que nous devions qu'ils, elles doivent	que je meuve qu'il, elle meuve que nous mouvions qu'ils, elles meuvent
imperfect subjunctive	qu'il, elle reçût qu'ils, elles reçussent	qu'il, elle dût qu'ils, elles dussent	qu'il, elle mût qu'ils, elles mussent
imperative	reçois recevons recevez	dois devons devez	meus mouvons mouvez
present participle	recevant	devant	mouvant
past participle	reçu, e	dû, due, dus, dues	mû, mue, mus, mues

* Note that **c** changes to **ç** before **o** or **u**: *je reçois, j'ai reçu,* etc.

	55 émouvoir	56 promouvoir *	57 vouloir
present indicative	j'émeus tu émeus il, elle émeut nous émouvons vous émouvez ils, elles émeuvent	je promeus tu promeus il, elle promeut nous promouvons vous promouvez ils, elles promeuvent	je veux tu veux il, elle veut nous voulons vous voulez ils, elles veulent
imperfect	il, elle émouvait	il, elle promouvait	il, elle voulait
past historic	il, elle émut ils, elles émurent	il, elle promut ils, elles promurent	il, elle voulut ils, elles voulurent
future	j'émouvrai il, elle émouvra	je promouvrai il, elle promouvra	je voudrai il, elle voudra
present conditional	j'émouvrais il, elle émouvrait	je promouvrais il, elle promouvrait	je voudrais il, elle voudrait
present subjunctive	que j'émeuve qu'il, elle émeuve que nous émeuvions qu'ils, elles émeuvent	que je promeuve qu'il, elle promeuve que nous promouvions qu'ils, elles promeuvent	que je veuille qu'il, elle veuille que nous voulions qu'ils, elles veuillent
imperfect subjunctive	qu'il, elle émût qu'ils, elles émussent	qu'il, elle promût qu'ils, elles promussent	qu'il, elle voulût qu'ils, elles voulussent
imperative	émeus émouvons émouvez	promeus promouvons promouvez	veux, veuille voulons, veuillons voulez, veuillez
present participle	émouvant	promouvant	voulant
past participle	ému, e	promu, e	voulu, e

* Conjugated forms of this verb are rare.

	58 pouvoir *	59 savoir	60 valoir
present indicative	je peux, puis tu peux il peut nous pouvons vous pouvez ils, elles peuvent	je sais tu sais il, elle sait nous savons vous savez ils, elles savent	je vaux tu vaux il, elle vaut nous valons vous valez ils, elles valent
imperfect	il, elle pouvait	il, elle savait	il, elle valait
past historic	il, elle put ils, elles purent	il, elle sut ils, elles surent	il, elle valut ils, elles valurent
future	je pourrai il, elle pourra	je saurai il, elle saura	je vaudrai il, elle vaudra
present conditional	je pourrais il, elle pourrait	je saurais il, elle saurait	je vaudrais il, elle vaudrait
present subjunctive	que je puisse qu'il, elle puisse que nous puissions qu'ils, elles puissent	que je sache qu'il, elle sache que nous sachions qu'ils, elles sachent	que je vaille qu'il, elle vaille que nous valions qu'ils, elles vaillent
imperfect subjunctive	qu'il, elle pût qu'ils, elles pussent	qu'il, elle sût qu'ils, elles sussent	qu'il, elle valût qu'ils, elles valussent
imperative	–	sache sachons sachez	vaux valons valez
present participle	pouvant	sachant	valant
past participle	pu	su, e	valu, e

* *Pouvoir* has no imperative. The 1st person singular interrogative, 'can I?', is *puis-je ?* (and not *peux-je ?*).

	61 prévaloir	62 voir	63 prévoir
present indicative	je prévaux tu prévaux il, elle prévaut nous prévalons vous prévalez ils, elles prévalent	je vois tu vois il, elle voit nous voyons vous voyez ils, elles voient	je prévois tu prévois il, elle prévoit nous prévoyons vous prévoyez ils, elles prévoient
imperfect	il, elle prévalait	il, elle voyait	il, elle prévoyait
past historic	il, elle prévalut ils, elles prévalurent	il, elle vit ils, elles virent	il, elle prévit ils, elles prévirent
future	je prévaudrai il, elle prévaudra	je verrai il, elle verra	je prévoirai il, elle prévoira
present conditional	je prévaudrais il, elle prévaudrait	je verrais il, elle verrait	je prévoirais il, elle prévoirait
present subjunctive	que je prévale qu'il, elle prévale que nous prévalions qu'ils, elles prévalent	que je voie qu'il, elle voie que nous voyions qu'ils, elles voient	que je prévoie qu'il, elle prévoie que nous prévoyions qu'ils, elles prévoient
imperfect subjunctive	qu'il, elle prévalût qu'ils, elles prévalussent	qu'il, elle vît qu'ils, elles vissent	qu'il, elle prévît qu'ils, elles prévissent
imperative	prévaux prévalons prévalez	vois voyons voyez	prévois prévoyons prévoyez
present participle	prévalant	voyant	prévoyant
past participle	prévalu, e	vu, e	prévu, e

	64 pourvoir	65 asseoir *	66 surseoir
present indicative	je pourvois tu pourvois il, elle pourvoit nous pourvoyons vous pourvoyez ils, elles pourvoient	j'assieds, j'assois tu assieds, assois il, elle assied, assoit nous asseyons, assoyons vous asseyez, assoyez ils, elles asseyent, assoient	je sursois tu sursois il, elle sursoit nous sursoyons vous sursoyez ils, elles sursoient
imperfect	il, elle pourvoyait	il, elle asseyait, assoyait	il, elle sursoyait
past historic	il, elle pourvut ils, elles pourvurent	il, elle assit ils, elles assirent	il, elle sursit ils, elles sursirent
future	je pourvoirai il, elle pourvoira	j'assiérai, j'assoirai il, elle assiéra, assoira	je surseoirai il, elle surseoira
present conditional	je pourvoirais il, elle pourvoirait	j'assiérais, j'assoirais il, elle assiérait, assoirait	je surseoirais il, elle surseoirait
present subjunctive	que je pourvoie qu'il, elle pourvoie que nous pourvoyions qu'ils, elles pourvoient	que j'asseye, j'assoie qu'il, elle asseye, assoie que nous asseyions, assoyions qu'ils, elles asseyent, assoient	que je sursoie qu'il, elle sursoie que nous sursoyions qu'ils, elles sursoient
imperfect subjunctive	qu'il, elle pourvût qu'ils, elles pourvussent	qu'il, elle assît qu'ils, elles assissent	qu'il, elle sursît qu'ils, elles sursissent
imperative	pourvois pourvoyons pourvoyez	assieds, assois asseyons, assoyons asseyez, assoyez	sursois sursoyons sursoyez
present participle	pourvoyant	asseyant, assoyant	sursoyant
past participle	pourvu, e	assis, e	sursis

* Forms with **oi** are often written **eoi**: je m'asseois, il, elle asseoira, que tu asseoies, ils, elles asseoiraient.

	67 seoir	68 pleuvoir *	69 falloir
present indicative	– – il, elle sied – – ils, elles siéent	– – il pleut – – –	– – il faut – – –
imperfect	il, elle seyait	il pleuvait	il fallait
past historic	–	il plut –	il fallut –
future	– il, elle siéra	– il pleuvra	– il faudra
present conditional	– il, elle siérait	– il pleuvrait	– il faudrait
present subjunctive	– qu'il, elle siée – qu'ils, elles siéent	– qu'il pleuve – –	– qu'il faille – –
imperfect subjunctive	–	qu'il plût –	qu'il fallût –
imperative	–	–	–
present participle	seyant	pleuvant	–
past participle	–	plu	fallu

* *Pleuvoir* is an impersonal verb. It has no imperative. *Pleuvoir* can be used in the plural in the figurative sense: *les injures pleuvent, pleuvaient,* etc.

	70 échoir	71 déchoir	72 choir
present indicative	– – il, elle échoit – – ils, elles échoient	je déchois tu déchois il, elle déchoit nous déchoyons vous déchoyez ils, elles déchoient	je chois tu chois il, elle choit – – ils, elles choient
imperfect	il, elle échoyait	–	–
past historic	il, elle échut ils, elles échurent	il, elle déchut ils, elles déchurent	il, elle chut ils, elles churent
future	– il, elle échoira, écherra	je déchoirai il, elle déchoira	je choirai, cherrai il, elle choira, cherra
present conditional	– il, elle échoirait, écherrait	je déchoirais il, elle déchoirait	je choirais, cherrais il, elle choirait, cherrait
present subjunctive	– qu'il, elle échoie – qu'ils, elles échoient	que je déchoie qu'il, elle déchoie que nous déchoyions qu'ils, elles déchoient	–
imperfect subjunctive	qu'il, elle échût qu'ils, elles échussent	qu'il, elle déchût qu'ils, elles déchussent	qu'il, elle chût –
imperative	–	–	–
present participle	échéant	–	–
past participle	échu, e	déchu, e	chu, e

	73 vendre	74 répandre	75 répondre
present indicative	je vends tu vends il, elle vend nous vendons vous vendez ils, elles vendent	je répands tu répands il, elle répand nous répandons vous répandez ils, elles répandent	je réponds tu réponds il, elle répond nous répondons vous répondez ils, elles répondent
imperfect	il, elle vendait	il, elle répandait	il, elle répondait
past historic	il, elle vendit ils, elles vendirent	il, elle répandit ils, elles répandirent	il, elle répondit ils, elles répondirent
future	je vendrai il, elle vendra	je répandrai il, elle répandra	je répondrai il, elle répondra
present conditional	je vendrais il, elle vendrait	je répandrais il, elle répandrait	je répondrais il, elle répondrait
present subjunctive	que je vende qu'il, elle vende que nous vendions qu'ils, elles vendent	que je répande qu'il, elle répande que nous répandions qu'ils, elles répandent	que je réponde qu'il, elle réponde que nous répondions qu'ils, elles répondent
imperfect subjunctive	qu'il, elle vendît qu'ils, elles vendissent	qu'il, elle répandît qu'ils, elles répandissent	qu'il, elle répondît qu'ils, elles répondissent
imperative	vends vendons vendez	répands répandons répandez	réponds répondons répondez
present participle	vendant	répandant	répondant
past participle	vendu, e	répandu, e	répondu, e

	76 mordre	77 perdre	78 rompre
present indicative	je mords tu mords il, elle mord nous mordons vous mordez ils, elles mordent	je perds tu perds il, elle perd nous perdons vous perdez ils, elles perdent	je romps tu romps il, elle rompt nous rompons vous rompez ils, elles rompent
imperfect	il, elle mordait	il, elle perdait	il, elle rompait
past historic	il, elle mordit ils, elles mordirent	il, elle perdit ils, elles perdirent	il, elle rompit ils, elles rompirent
future	je mordrai il, elle mordra	je perdrai il, elle perdra	je romprai il, elle rompra
present conditional	je mordrais il, elle mordrait	je perdrais il, elle perdrait	je romprais il, elle romprait
present subjunctive	que je morde qu'il, elle morde que nous mordions qu'ils, elles mordent	que je perde qu'il, elle perde que nous perdions qu'ils, elles perdent	que je rompe qu'il, elle rompe que nous rompions qu'ils, elles rompent
imperfect subjunctive	qu'il, elle mordît qu'ils, elles mordissent	qu'il, elle perdît qu'ils, elles perdissent	qu'il, elle rompît qu'ils, elles rompissent
imperative	mords mordons mordez	perds perdons perdez	romps rompons rompez
present participle	mordant	perdant	rompant
past participle	mordu, e	perdu, e	rompu, e

	79 prendre	80 craindre	81 peindre
present indicative	je prends tu prends il, elle prend nous prenons vous prenez ils, elles prennent	je crains tu crains il, elle craint nous craignons vous craignez ils, elles craignent	je peins tu peins il, elle peint nous peignons vous peignez ils, elles peignent
imperfect	il, elle prenait	il, elle craignait	il, elle peignait
past historic	il, elle prit ils, elles prirent	il, elle craignit ils, elles craignirent	il, elle peignit ils, elles peignirent
future	je prendrai il, elle prendra	je craindrai il, elle craindra	je peindrai il, elle peindra
present conditional	je prendrais il, elle prendrait	je craindrais il, elle craindrait	je peindrais il, elle peindrait
present subjunctive	que je prenne qu'il, elle prenne que nous prenions qu'ils, elles prennent	que je craigne qu'il, elle craigne que nous craignions qu'ils, elles craignent	que je peigne qu'il, elle peigne que nous peignions qu'ils, elles peignent
imperfect subjunctive	qu'il, elle prît qu'ils, elles prissent	qu'il, elle craignît qu'ils, elles craignissent	qu'il, elle peignît qu'ils, elles peignissent
imperative	prends prenons prenez	crains craignons craignez	peins peignons peignez
present participle	prenant	craignant	peignant
past participle	pris, e	craint, e	peint, e

	82 joindre	83 battre	84 mettre
present indicative	je joins tu joins il, elle joint nous joignons vous joignez ils, elles joignent	je bats tu bats il, elle bat nous battons vous battez ils, elles battent	je mets tu mets il, elle met nous mettons vous mettez ils, elles mettent
imperfect	il, elle joignait	il, elle battait	il, elle mettait
past historic	il, elle joignit ils, elles joignirent	il, elle battit ils, elles battirent	il, elle mit ils, elles mirent
future	je joindrai il, elle joindra	je battrai il, elle battra	je mettrai il, elle mettra
present conditional	je joindrais il, elle joindrait	je battrais il, elle battrait	je mettrais il, elle mettrait
present subjunctive	que je joigne qu'il, elle joigne que nous joignions qu'ils, elles joignent	que je batte qu'il, elle batte que nous battions qu'ils, elles battent	que je mette qu'il, elle mette que nous mettions qu'ils, elles mettent
imperfect subjunctive	qu'il, elle joignît qu'ils, elles joignissent	qu'il, elle battît qu'ils, elles battissent	qu'il, elle mît qu'ils, elles missent
imperative	joins joignons joignez	bats battons battez	mets mettons mettez
present participle	joignant	battant	mettant
past participle	joint, e	battu, e	mis, e

	85 moudre	86 coudre	87 absoudre *
present indicative	je mouds tu mouds il, elle moud nous moulons vous moulez ils, elles moulent	je couds tu couds il, elle coud nous cousons vous cousez ils, elles cousent	j'absous tu absous il, elle absout nous absolvons vous absolvez ils, elles absolvent
imperfect	il, elle moulait	il, elle cousait	il, elle absolvait
past historic	il, elle moulut ils, elles moulurent	il, elle cousit ils, elles cousirent	il, elle absolut ils, elles absolurent
future	je moudrai il, elle moudra	je coudrai il, elle coudra	j'absoudrai il, elle absoudra
present conditional	je moudrais il, elle moudrait	je coudrais il, elle coudrait	j'absoudrais il, elle absoudrait
present subjunctive	que je moule qu'il, elle moule que nous moulions qu'ils, elles moulent	que je couse qu'il, elle couse que nous cousions qu'ils, elles cousent	que j'absolve qu'il, elle absolve que nous absolvions qu'ils, elles absolvent
imperfect subjunctive	qu'il, elle moulût qu'ils, elles moulussent	qu'il, elle cousît qu'ils, elles cousissent	qu'il, elle absolût qu'ils, elles absolussent
imperative	mouds moulons moulez	couds cousons cousez	absous absolvons absolvez
present participle	moulant	cousant	absolvant
past participle	moulu, e	cousu, e	absous, oute

* The past historic and the imperfect subjunctive are rare.

	88 résoudre	89 suivre	90 vivre *
present indicative	je résous tu résous il, elle résout nous résolvons vous résolvez ils, elles résolvent	je suis tu suis il, elle suit nous suivons vous suivez ils, elles suivent	je vis tu vis il, elle vit nous vivons vous vivez ils, elles vivent
imperfect	il, elle résolvait	il, elle suivait	il, elle vivait
past historic	il, elle résolut ils, elles résolurent	il, elle suivit ils, elles suivirent	il, elle vécut ils, elles vécurent
future	je résoudrai il, elle résoudra	je suivrai il, elle suivra	je vivrai il, elle vivra
present conditional	je résoudrais il, elle résoudrait	je suivrais il, elle suivrait	je vivrais il, elle vivrait
present subjunctive	que je résolve qu'il, elle résolve que nous résolvions qu'ils, elles résolvent	que je suive qu'il, elle suive que nous suivions qu'ils, elles suivent	que je vive qu'il, elle vive que nous vivions qu'ils, elles vivent
imperfect subjunctive	qu'il, elle résolût qu'ils, elles résolussent	qu'il, elle suivît qu'ils, elles suivissent	qu'il, elle vécût qu'ils, elles vécussent
imperative	résous résolvons résolvez	suis suivons suivez	vis vivons vivez
present participle	résolvant	suivant	vivant
past participle	résolu, e	suivi, e	vécu, e

* *Survivre* conjugates in the same way as *vivre,* but the past participle *(survécu)* is invariable.

	91 paraître *	92 naître	93 croître
present indicative	je parais tu parais il, elle paraît nous paraissons vous paraissez ils, elles paraissent	je nais tu nais il, elle naît nous naissons vous naissez ils, elles naissent	je croîs tu croîs il, elle croît nous croissons vous croissez ils, elles croissent
imperfect	il, elle paraissait	il, elle naissait	il, elle croissait
past historic	il, elle parut ils, elles parurent	il, elle naquit ils, elles naquirent	il, elle crût ils, elles crûrent
future	je paraîtrai il, elle paraîtra	je naîtrai il, elle naîtra	je croîtrai il, elle croîtra
present conditional	je paraîtrais il, elle paraîtrait	je naîtrais il, elle naîtrait	je croîtrais il, elle croîtrait
present subjunctive	que je paraisse qu'il, elle paraisse que nous paraissions qu'ils, elles paraissent	que je naisse qu'il, elle naisse que nous naissions qu'ils, elles naissent	que je croisse qu'il, elle croisse que nous croissions qu'ils, elles croissent
imperfect subjunctive	qu'il, elle parût qu'ils, elles parussent	qu'il, elle naquît qu'ils, elles naquissent	qu'il, elle crût qu'ils, elles crûssent
imperative	parais paraissons paraissez	nais naissons naissez	croîs croissons croissez
present participle	paraissant	naissant	croissant
past participle	paru, e	né, e	crû, crue, crus, crues

* Note the circumflex **î** when **i** comes before **t** in verbs ending in **–aître.**

	94 accroître	95 rire *	96 conclure **
present indicative	j'accrois tu accrois il, elle accroît nous accroissons vous accroissez ils, elles accroissent	je ris tu ris il, elle rit nous rions vous riez ils, elles rient	je conclus tu conclus il, elle conclut nous concluons vous concluez ils, elles concluent
imperfect	il, elle accroissait	il, elle riait	il, elle concluait
past historic	il, elle accrut ils, elles accrurent	il, elle rit ils, elles rirent	il, elle conclut ils, elles conclurent
future	j'accroîtrai il, elle accroîtra	je rirai il, elle rira	je conclurai il, elle conclura
present conditional	j'accroîtrais il, elle accroîtrait	je rirais il, elle rirait	je conclurais il, elle conclurait
present subjunctive	que j'accroisse qu'il, elle accroisse que nous accroissions qu'ils, elles accroissent	que je rie qu'il, elle rie que nous riions qu'ils, elles rient	que je conclue qu'il, elle conclue que nous concluions qu'ils, elles concluent
imperfect subjunctive	qu'il, elle accrût qu'ils, elles accrussent	qu'il, elle rît qu'ils, elles rissent	qu'il, elle conclût qu'ils, elles conclussent
imperative	accrois accroissons accroissez	ris rions riez	conclus concluons concluez
present participle	accroissant	riant	concluant
past participle	accru, e	ri	conclu, e

* *Rire* takes two **i**'s in the 1st and 2nd person plural of the imperfect indicative and the present subjunctive: *(que) nous riions, (que) vous riiez.*
** *Inclure* and *occlure* conjugate in the same way as *conclure,* but their past participles are *inclus, incluse, occlus, occluse.*

	97 nuire *	**98 conduire**	**99 écrire**
present indicative	je nuis tu nuis il, elle nuit nous nuisons vous nuisez ils, elles nuisent	je conduis tu conduis il, elle conduit nous conduisons vous conduisez ils, elles conduisent	j'écris tu écris il, elle écrit nous écrivons vous écrivez ils, elles écrivent
imperfect	il, elle nuisait	il, elle conduisait	il, elle écrivait
past historic	il, elle nuisit ils, elles nuisirent	il, elle conduisit ils, elles conduisirent	il, elle écrivit ils, elles écrivirent
future	je nuirai il, elle nuira	je conduirai il, elle conduira	j'écrirai il, elle écrira
present conditional	je nuirais il, elle nuirait	je conduirais il, elle conduirait	j'écrirais il, elle écrirait
present subjunctive	que je nuise qu'il, elle nuise que nous nuisions qu'ils, elles nuisent	que je conduise qu'il, elle conduise que nous conduisions qu'ils, elles conduisent	que j'écrive qu'il, elle écrive que nous écrivions qu'ils, elles écrivent
imperfect subjunctive	qu'il, elle nuisît qu'ils, elles nuisissent	qu'il, elle conduisît qu'ils, elles conduisissent	qu'il, elle écrivît qu'ils, elles écrivissent
imperative	nuis nuisons nuisez	conduis conduisons conduisez	écris écrivons écrivez
present participle	nuisant	conduisant	écrivant
past participle	nui	conduit, e	écrit, e

* *Luire* and *reluire* have an alternative past historic form: *je luis, je reluis,* etc.

	100 suffire	**101 confire ***	**102 dire**
present indicative	je suffis tu suffis il, elle suffit nous suffisons vous suffisez ils, elles suffisent	je confis tu confis il, elle confit nous confisons vous confisez ils, elles confisent	je dis tu dis il, elle dit nous disons vous dites ils, elles disent
imperfect	il, elle suffisait	il, elle confisait	il, elle disait
past historic	il, elle suffit ils, elles suffirent	il, elle confit ils, elles confirent	il, elle dit ils, elles dirent
future	je suffirai il, elle suffira	je confirai il, elle confira	je dirai il, elle dira
present conditional	je suffirais il, elle suffirait	je confirais il, elle confirait	je dirais il, elle dirait
present subjunctive	que je suffise qu'il, elle suffise que nous suffisions qu'ils, elles suffisent	que je confise qu'il, elle confise que nous confisions qu'ils, elles confisent	que je dise qu'il, elle dise que nous disions qu'ils, elles disent
imperfect subjunctive	qu'il, elle suffît qu'ils, elles suffissent	qu'il, elle confît qu'ils, elles confissent	qu'il, elle dît qu'ils, elles dissent
imperative	suffis suffisons suffisez	confis confisons confisez	dis disons dites
present participle	suffisant	confisant	disant
past participle	suffi	confit, e	dit, e

* *Circoncire* conjugates in the same way as *confire,* but its past participle is *circoncis, circoncise.*

	103 contredire	104 maudire	105 bruire *
present indicative	je contredis tu contredis il, elle contredit nous contredisons vous contredisez ils, elles contredisent	je maudis tu maudis il, elle maudit nous maudissons vous maudissez ils, elles maudissent	je bruis tu bruis il, elle bruit – – –
imperfect	il, elle contredisait	il, elle maudissait	il, elle bruyait
past historic	il, elle contredit ils, elles contredirent	il, elle maudit ils, elles maudirent	–
future	je contredirai il, elle contredira	je maudirai il, elle maudira	je bruirai il, elle bruira
present conditional	je contredirais il, elle contredirait	je maudirais il, elle maudirait	je bruirais il, elle bruirait
present subjunctive	que je contredise qu'il, elle contredise que nous contredisions qu'ils, elles contredisent	que je maudisse qu'il, elle maudisse que nous maudissions qu'ils, elles maudissent	–
imperfect subjunctive	qu'il, elle contredît qu'ils, elles contredissent	qu'il, elle maudît qu'ils, elles maudissent	–
imperative	contredis contredisons contredisez	maudis maudissons maudissez	–
present participle	contredisant	maudissant	–
past participle	contredit, e	maudit, e	bruit

* Traditionally *bruire* is only used in the present indicative, imperfect (*je bruyais, tu bruyais,* etc), future and conditional; *bruisser* (conjugation 3) is used more and more to replace *bruire,* especially in all the defective forms.

	106 lire	107 croire	108 boire
present indicative	je lis tu lis il, elle lit nous lisons vous lisez ils, elles lisent	je crois tu crois il, elle croit nous croyons vous croyez ils, elles croient	je bois tu bois il, elle boit nous buvons vous buvez ils, elles boivent
imperfect	il, elle lisait	il, elle croyait	il, elle buvait
past historic	il, elle lut ils, elles lurent	il, elle crut ils, elles crurent	il, elle but ils, elles burent
future	je lirai il, elle lira	je croirai il, elle croira	je boirai il, elle boira
present conditional	je lirais il, elle lirait	je croirais il, elle croirait	je boirais il, elle boirait
present subjunctive	que je lise qu'il, elle lise que nous lisions qu'ils, elles lisent	que je croie qu'il, elle croie que nous croyions qu'ils, elles croient	que je boive qu'il, elle boive que nous buvions qu'ils, elles boivent
imperfect subjunctive	qu'il, elle lût qu'ils, elles lussent	qu'il, elle crût qu'ils, elles crussent	qu'il, elle bût qu'ils, elles bussent
imperative	lis lisons lisez	crois croyons croyez	bois buvons buvez
present participle	lisant	croyant	buvant
past participle	lu, e	cru, e	bu, e

	109 faire	**110 plaire**	**111 taire**
present indicative	je fais tu fais il, elle fait nous faisons vous faites ils, elles font	je plais tu plais il, elle plaît nous plaisons vous plaisez ils, elles plaisent	je tais tu tais il, elle tait nous taisons vous taisez ils, elles taisent
imperfect	il, elle faisait	il, elle plaisait	il, elle taisait
past historic	il, elle fit ils, elles firent	il, elle plut ils, elles plurent	il, elle tut ils, elles turent
future	je ferai il, elle fera	je plairai il, elle plaira	je tairai il, elle taira
present conditional	je ferais il, elle ferait	je plairais il, elle plairait	je tairais il, elle tairait
present subjunctive	que je fasse qu'il, elle fasse que nous fassions qu'ils, elles fassent	que je plaise qu'il, elle plaise que nous plaisions qu'ils, elles plaisent	que je taise qu'il, elle taise que nous taisions qu'ils, elles taisent
imperfect subjunctive	qu'il, elle fît qu'ils, elles fissent	qu'il, elle plût qu'ils, elles plussent	qu'il, elle tût qu'ils, elles tussent
imperative	fais faisons faites	plais plaisons plaisez	tais taisons taisez
present participle	faisant	plaisant	taisant
past participle	fait, e	plu	tu, e

	112 extraire	**113 clore**	**114 vaincre ***
present indicative	j'extrais tu extrais il, elle extrait nous extrayons vous extrayez ils, elles extraient	je clos tu clos il, elle clôt nous closons vous closez ils, elles closent	je vaincs tu vaincs il, elle vainc nous vainquons vous vainquez ils, elles vainquent
imperfect	il, elle extrayait	–	il, elle vainquait
past historic	–	–	il, elle vainquit ils, elles vainquirent
future	j'extrairai il, elle extraira	je clorai il, elle clora	je vaincrai il, elle vaincra
present conditional	j'extrairais il, elle extrairait	je clorais il, elle clorait	je vaincrais il, elle vaincrait
present subjunctive	que j'extraie qu'il, elle extraie que nous extrayions qu'ils, elles extraient	que je close qu'il, elle close que nous closions qu'ils, elles closent	que je vainque qu'il, elle vainque que nous vainquions qu'ils, elles vainquent
imperfect subjunctive	–	–	qu'il, elle vainquît qu'ils, elles vainquissent
imperative	extrais extrayons extrayez	clos – –	vaincs vainquons vainquez
present participle	extrayant	closant	vainquant
past participle	extrait, e	clos, e	vaincu, e

***** The only irregularity of the verb *vaincre* is that it does not take a **t** at the end of the 3rd person singular of the present indicative. Note that **c** becomes **qu** in front of all vowels except **u**.

	115 frire	116 foutre
present indicative	je fris tu fris il, elle frit – – –	je fous tu fous il, elle fout nous foutons vous foutez ils, elles foutent
imperfect	–	il, elle foutait
past historic	–	–
future	je frirai il, elle frira	je foutrai il, elle foutra
present conditional	je frirais il, elle frirait	je foutrais il, elle foutrait
present subjunctive	–	que je foute qu'il, elle foute que nous foutions qu'ils, elles foutent
imperfect subjunctive	–	–
imperative	fris – –	fous foutons foutez
present participle	–	foutant
past participle	frit, e	foutu, e

cultural supplement

cahier culturel

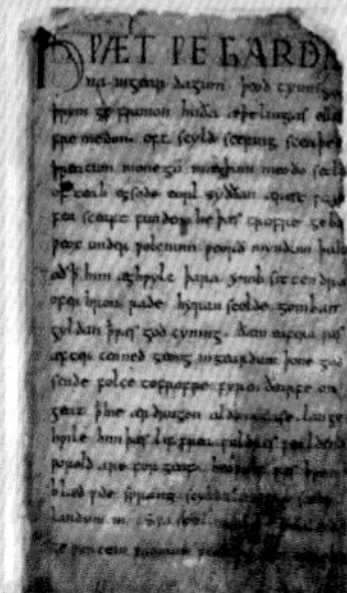

First page of the manuscript of the Old English epic poem Beowulf *(700–1000 A.D.).*
Première page du manuscrit du poème épique Beowulf, *rédigé en vieil anglais (700–1000 ap. J-C.).*

The beginnings of English. Old English, also called Anglo-Saxon, was a West Germanic language spoken in parts of England and the south of Scotland between around the middle of the 5th c. and the middle of the 12th. It was a language unusually rich in literature. In particular, the epic poem *Beowulf* has taken on national emblematic status.

Les origines de la langue anglaise. Le vieil anglais, appelé aussi anglo-saxon, qui appartient à la famille des langues germaniques occidentales, était parlé dans certaines régions d'Angleterre et dans le sud de l'Écosse entre le milieu du Ve siècle et le milieu du XIIe siècle. Cette époque se caractérise par une extrême richesse littéraire. Citons notamment le poème épique *Beowulf*, qui a acquis le statut d'emblème national.

Latin, the administrative language of Europe. The *Domesday Book*, the huge survey of England undertaken by William the Conqueror in 1086, aimed to record every piece of land, its buildings, its inhabitants, its livestock, its crops. The document, written in Latin, but including a great many local terms and annotations in Old English, remains to this day a valuable source of information for historians and genealogists.

Le latin, langue de l'administration à travers toute l'Europe. *Le Domesday Book*, immense travail cadastral décidé par Guillaume le Conquérant en 1086, recense la totalité des terres, maisons, habitants, animaux d'élevage et récoltes du royaume d'Angleterre. Ce document, rédigé en latin mais contenant de nombreux termes locaux ainsi que des annotations en vieil anglais, demeure à ce jour une précieuse source de renseignements pour les historiens et les généalogistes.

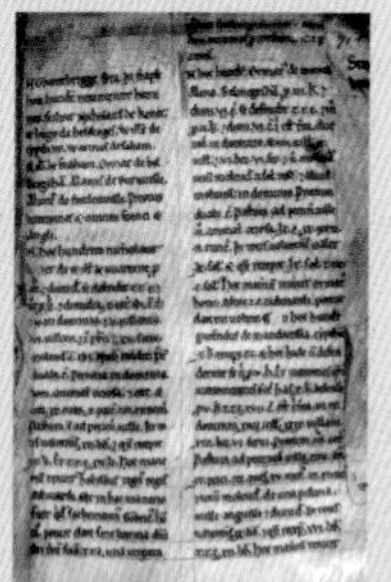

Transcript of notes (12th c.) to the Domesday Book *(1008).*
Transcription de notes (XIIe s.) provenant du Domesday Book *(1008).*

King John signing Magna Carta *(1215).*
La signature de la Magna Carta *par le roi Jean sans Terre (1215).*

English, Norman, Latin. King John (John Lackland: 1165–1216) was forced by his barons to sign the *Magna Carta* (the Great Charter) at Runnymede near Windsor in 1215. Written in Latin, it laid down a number of rights and principles and is considered to be one of the most important documents in the history of democracy. Latin was the official written language but King John spoke Norman French, as did all the English kings, their parliaments, and the entire English ruling class from the Norman Conquest in 1066 until English started to regain the linguistic arena in the 1360s.

Anglais, normand, latin. Le roi Jean sans Terre (1165–1216) fut contraint par ses barons de signer la *Magna Carta* (La Grande Charte) à Runnymede près de Windsor en 1215. Rédigée en latin, elle établit un certain nombre de droits et de principes fondamentaux et est considérée comme l'un des textes majeurs dans l'histoire de la démocratie. Le latin était la langue écrite officielle, mais le roi Jean parlait le franco-normand, à l'instar de tous les souverains anglais, leur parlement et toute la classe dirigeante anglaise à partir de 1066, date de la conquête de l'Angleterre par les Normands, et jusqu'aux années 1360, lorsque l'anglais recommença à s'imposer dans l'arène linguistique.

Middle English. Throughout the three centuries following the Norman Conquest English evolved, taking in a good deal of French, into what we now call Middle English but the language of literature and administration continued to be either Latin or French. Geoffrey Chaucer (1342–1400) is generally credited with being the first writer to show that English could be a language of rich literary expression.

Le moyen anglais. Au cours des trois siècles qui ont suivi la conquête de l'Angleterre par les Normands, la langue anglaise, fortement influencée par le français, a évolué et est devenue ce que les linguistes appellent « le moyen anglais ». Mais la langue de la littérature et de l'administration demeurait soit le latin soit le français. On considère l'œuvre de Geoffrey Chaucer (1342–1400) comme l'une des premières illustrations de la richesse littéraire de la langue anglaise.

A miniature taken from a 15th c. manuscript representing Chaucer's pilgrims.
Miniature provenant d'un manuscrit du XVe s. représentant les pèlerins de Chaucer.

William Shakespeare, as depicted by Louis Coblitz (1814–1863).
William Shakespeare, peint par Louis Coblitz (1814–1863).

Renaissance. Universally recognized as the greatest writer in the English language to the present day, William Shakespeare (1564–1616) was also England's foremost Renaissance figure. As the most frequently quoted writer in the English-speaking world, his influence cannot be over-stated. With Shakespeare and later writers such as John Milton (1608–74) came the emergence of Early Modern English.

La Renaissance. Reconnu universellement comme le plus grand écrivain de la langue anglaise, William Shakespeare (1564–1616) fut également l'une des figures littéraires majeures de la Renaissance en Angleterre. L'influence de cet auteur, le plus souvent cité dans le monde anglophone, a été colossale. C'est avec Shakespeare et, plus tard, dans l'œuvre d'autres écrivains tels que John Milton (1608–1674) qu'apparut « l'anglais moderne naissant ».

The King James Bible. Second only to Shakespeare in terms of impact on the language is the *King James Bible*. It was sponsored by King James VI of Scotland and I of England and published in 1611. Its power and poetry have become part of the fabric of the language.

La Bible du roi Jacques. En termes d'impact sur la langue anglaise, la *Bible du roi Jacques* arrive juste après Shakespeare. Cette traduction fut commandée par le roi Jacques VI d'Écosse, qui devint Jacques Ier d'Angleterre, et publiée en 1611. D'une grande puissance poétique, elle fait partie du patrimoine littéraire anglais.

Frontispiece to the King James Version of the Bible (1611).
Frontispice de la Bible du roi Jacques (1611).

Samuel Pepys Esquire, English Diarist.
Samuel Pepys Esquire, chroniqueur anglais.

England's greatest diarist. English naval administrator and Member of Parliament, Samuel Pepys (1633–1703) was a man of great culture and insatiable curiosity. A fervent bibliophile, he left over 3000 volumes on his death, including the celebrated diary which he kept over one of the most turbulent periods of English history. Endlessly vivid, the diary provides the best account available of London during the Great Plague and the Great Fire that destroyed much of the City of London.

Le plus grand chroniqueur anglais. Officier d'administration navale et membre du Parlement, Samuel Pepys (1633–1703) était un homme d'une grande culture et d'une curiosité insatiable. Fervent bibliophile, il laissa à sa mort plus de 3000 volumes, notamment le célèbre journal qu'il avait tenu durant l'une des époques les plus troublées de l'histoire de l'Angleterre. D'une grande vivacité, son journal nous livre un témoignage précieux et unique sur la grande peste qui frappa Londres et le grand incendie qui ravagea la ville.

Samuel Johnson (1709–1784), the father of modern lexicography.
Samuel Johnson (1709–1784), le père de la lexicographie moderne.

Modern lexicography. One of the intellectual giants of the 18th century, Samuel Johnson, was poet, essayist, philosopher, biographer, literary critic – and, last but not least, lexicographer. Perhaps his best known work, *A Dictionary of the English Language* was astonishingly written single-handed between 1747 and 1755. It remained the authority on the English language until James Murray's great *Oxford English Dictionary*, written between 1860 and 1928.

La lexicographie moderne. Samuel Johnson fut l'une des figures intellectuelles marquantes du XVIIIe siècle en Angleterre. Poète, essayiste, philosophe, critique littéraire, et surtout lexicographe, il est l'auteur d'*Un Dictionnaire de la langue anglaise*, probablement son œuvre la plus célèbre. Ce qui est stupéfiant, c'est qu'il rédigea à lui tout seul ce dictionnaire de 1747 à 1755. Il fit autorité jusqu'à la parution du grand *Oxford English Dictionary* de James Murray, rédigé entre 1860 et 1928.

Modernism. The decades leading up to the First World War (1914–18) gave rise to a number of movements constituting what we now call Modernism. English literature saw a veritable explosion of experimentation in language and form. Notable figures are James Joyce, T.S. Elliott, Virginia Woolf, Gertrude Stein, Ezra Pound, and W.B. Yeats.

La modernité. Au cours des décennies qui ont précédé la Première Guerre mondiale (1914–1918), plusieurs mouvements littéraires ont vu le jour, constituant un courant qu'on appelle « la modernité ». La littérature anglaise connut une véritable explosion d'expérimentations stylistiques et formelles. Ses principaux représentants sont James Joyce, T.S. Eliot, Virginia Woolf, Gertrude Stein, Ezra Pound et W.B. Yeats.

James Joyce (1882–1941), Irish writer, best known as the author of the revolutionary novels Ulysses (1922) and Finnegans Wake (1939).
James Joyce (1882–1941), écrivain irlandais. Ses deux romans les plus célèbres ont révolutionné la littérature : Ulysse (1922) et Finnegans Wake (1939).

In Romance for the first time. In 842, Charles the Bald and Louis the Germanic swore an oath of alliance. Charles the Bold's address to the soldiers is written not in Latin but in Romance, which was the everyday language of the western part of the Carolingian Empire: *Pro Deo amor et pro christiano poblo et nostro comun salvament...* (For the love of God, the salvation of the Christian people and that of us both...).

En roman pour la première fois. En 842, Charles le Chauve et Louis le Germanique prononcent à Strasbourg un serment d'alliance. Le texte qui s'adresse aux soldats de Charles le Chauve n'est pas rédigé en latin, mais en roman, c'est-à-dire dans la langue quotidienne de la partie occidentale de l'Empire carolingien : *Pro Deo amor et pro christiano poblo et nostro comun salvament...* (Pour l'amour de Dieu et le salut commun du peuple chrétien et de nous deux...).

Portrait of the king of France, Charles II the Bold (843–877), brother of Louis the Germanic.
Portrait du roi de France Charles II le Chauve (843–877), frère de Louis le Germanique.

King Philippe VI de Valois receives the homage of Edward III of England.
Le roi Philippe VI de Valois reçoit l'hommage d'Édouard III d'Angleterre.

Norman French in England. King Edward III of England (1327–1377) pays homage to the King of France, Philippe VI de Valois (1328–1350). Like almost all the members of the English aristocracy, Edward III did not speak English. After defeating Philippe VI at the Battle of Crécy (1346), he congratulated his troops, who were all English, in Franco-Norman.

Le franco-normand des Anglais. Le roi d'Angleterre Édouard III (1327–1377) prête hommage au roi de France Philippe VI de Valois (1328–1350). Comme presque tous les membres de l'aristocratie anglaise, d'origine normande, Édouard III ne parlait pas anglais. Vainqueur de Philippe VI à Crécy (1346), il a félicité ses propres soldats, tous anglais, en langue franco-normande.

French as a literary language. For a long time, the French romances of chivalry, particularly those of Chrétien de Troyes (1135–1183), the greatest writer of French romances of the Middle Ages, were read all over Europe in the original French.

Le français, langue littéraire. Longtemps, l'Europe a lu dans leur langue d'origine les romans français de chevalerie, notamment ceux de Chrétien de Troyes (1135–1183), le plus grand romancier français du Moyen Âge.

Illustration from Perceval, a romance of chivalry by Chrétien de Troyes.
Illustration de Perceval, roman de chevalerie de Chrétien de Troyes.

Latin, the language of the university. Throughout Europe, up until the 16th century, university teaching was conducted in Latin rather than in the vernacular. Here, a Parisian teacher delivers a commented reading of a text.

Le latin, langue universitaire. Jusqu'au XVIe siècle, dans toute l'Europe, l'enseignement universitaire a été assuré en latin et non en langue vulgaire. Ici, un maître parisien donne en latin la lecture commentée d'un ouvrage.

A teacher at the University of Paris, miniature taken from the Chronicles of Saint-Denis.
Un maître de l'Université de Paris, miniature extraite des Chroniques de Saint-Denis.

A courtier and a lady drinking chocolate, engraving by Nicolas Guérard (17th c.).
Un cavalier et une dame buvant du chocolat, gravure de Nicolas Guérard (XVIIe s.).

Elegant conversation. In the 18th century, the salons presided over by the "précieuses" were attended by the cream of high society. These cultured women helped to purge the language of clumsiness and vulgarity, but their quest for ingenious modes of expression sometimes led to ridiculous situations.

Parler élégamment. Au XVIIe siècle, les salons animés par les « précieuses » réunissaient les personnes du meilleur monde. Ces femmes cultivées ont aidé à éliminer de la langue lourdeurs et grossièretés, mais leur recherche du langage ingénieux les a menées parfois jusqu'au ridicule.

Portrait of John Calvin by an anonymous artist.
Portrait anonyme de Jean Calvin.

French during the Reformation. Published in Latin in 1536 and then circulated in French after 1541, *The Institutes of the Christian Religion* by Calvin (1509–1564) is an instance of the increasing use of French in theology and religious worship.

La Réforme en français. Publiée en latin en 1536, puis diffusée en français après 1541, *l'Institution de la religion chrétienne* de Calvin (1509–1564) témoigne de l'emploi croissant du français dans le domaine de la théologie et de la pratique religieuse.

The origins of the French Academy, engraving, 17th c.
Les origines de l'Académie française, gravure du XVIIe s.

The systematization of the language. Cardinal Richelieu founded the French Academy in 1634. He assigned to it the task of systematizing the language and producing a dictionary and a grammar. This intervention of the governing power in the language of the land is unique in Europe.

La langue réglementée. Le cardinal de Richelieu institue l'Académie française en 1634 ; il lui donne la mission de réglementer la langue française et de préparer un dictionnaire et une grammaire : une intervention du pouvoir unique en Europe.

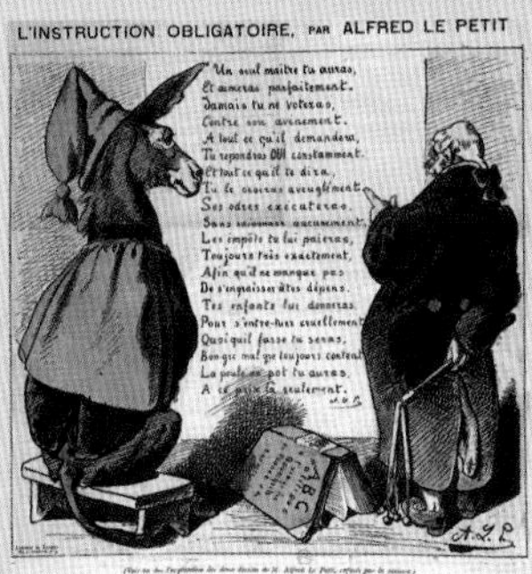

"Compulsory education", cartoon published in L' Éclipse in 1882.
« L'instruction obligatoire », caricature parue dans L'Éclipse en 1882.

One single French language. The "one and indivisible" Republic continued the work of the monarchy in repressing local languages and dialects. In 1881, Jules Ferry put forward legislation establishing free, compulsory primary education. French replaced regional dialects, which from then on were spoken only in the home.

Un français et un seul. La République « une et indivisible » a poursuivi l'œuvre de la monarchie en refoulant l'usage des parlers locaux. En 1881, Jules Ferry fait voter les lois qui établissent la gratuité et l'obligation de l'enseignement primaire. Le français va l'emporter sur les parlers régionaux dont l'emploi se restreint au milieu familial.

Reading chart used in primary schools (c. 1900).
Tableau de lecture à l'usage des écoles communales (v. 1900).

Reading for all. The inauguration of free education went hand in hand with the publication and distribution of a mass of learning materials – textbooks, exercise books, educational charts – to municipal primary schools.

L'égalité devant la lecture. À l'affirmation de la gratuité correspond la fabrication et la distribution d'un abondant matériel scolaire aux écoles des communes : manuels, cahiers, tableaux pédagogiques ...

art of the high Middle Ages

l'art du haut Moyen Âge

With the fall of the Western Roman Empire began a period during which Europe was increasingly split up, resulting in a considerable degree of artistic diversity. In contrast to the Greco-Roman aesthetic, there were moves towards formal stylization and a strong tendency towards decorative abstraction. However, towards the end of the period, the "Carolingian Renaissance" saw a move back towards more classical references.

La chute de l'Empire romain d'Occident marque le début d'une époque durant laquelle l'Europe est de plus en plus divisée. Il en résulte une extrême diversité dans le domaine artistique. On constate une rupture avec l'esthétique gréco-romaine : l'art s'oriente vers une stylisation formelle et tend à privilégier l'abstraction décorative. Cependant, vers la fin de cette période, la « Renaissance carolingienne » coïncide avec un retour à des modèles plus classiques.

Bronze plaque (550–650), Merovingian dynasty.
Plaque de bronze (550–650) de la dynastie mérovingienne.

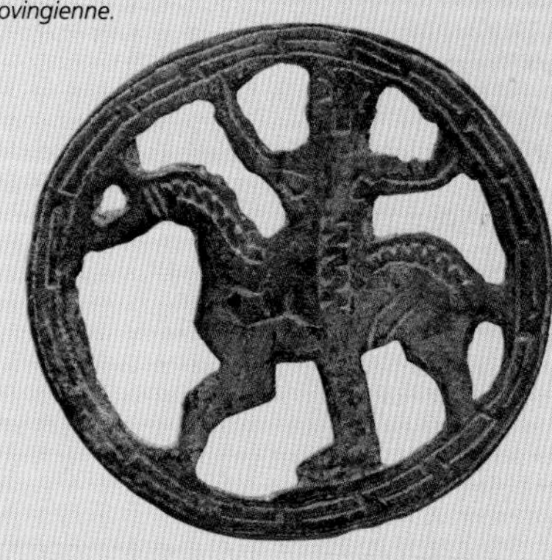

Celtic art in the Middle Ages

l'art celtique au Moyen Âge

The artistic tradition of the Celtic peoples of Britain and Ireland goes back to earliest times. In Britain it was interrupted by the Roman invasion but emerged again subsequently and went on until the Romanesque period. The heritage of Celtic art varies from area to area and covers a wide range of media, from stonecarving and metalwork to the wonderful illuminations of the Irish *Book of Kells*. In sculpture and silversmithing, forms are generally highly stylized and non-representational though it is thought that reference is made to symbols of religious significance. The Pictish stones of eastern Scotland, however, often show hunting and battle scenes.

La tradition artistique des peuples celtes de Grande-Bretagne et d'Irlande remonte à une époque très ancienne. En Grande-Bretagne, elle fut interrompue par l'invasion romaine, mais réapparut par la suite et s'imposa jusqu'à l'émergence de l'art roman. L'héritage de l'art celtique varie d'une région à l'autre et couvre une vaste gamme de supports : pierre, métaux, jusqu'aux magnifiques enluminures du *Livre de Kells*, œuvre irlandaise. En sculpture et en orfèvrerie, les formes sont généralement très stylisées et abstraites, même si l'on pense que les Celtes faisaient référence à des symboles religieux. Cependant, sur les pierres pictes, dans l'est de l'Écosse, on trouve des représentations de scènes de chasse et de batailles.

Jesus on the roof of the temple, miniature from The Book of Kells, *Ireland (600–750).*
Jésus sur le toit du Temple, miniature provenant du Livre de Kells, *Irlande (600–750).*

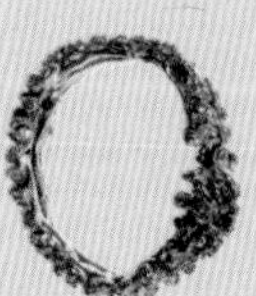

Celtic bracelet (between 299 and 100 BC) found at Aurillac.
Bracelet celte (entre -299 et -100) trouvé à Aurillac.

Romanesque art

l'art roman

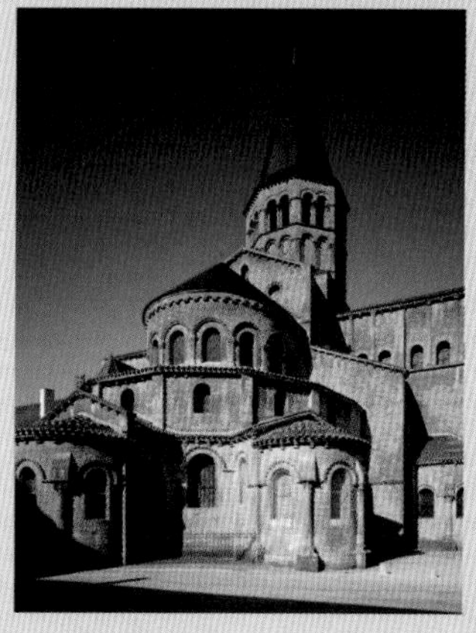

The basilica of Paray le Monial (Saône et Loire).
La basilique de Paray le Monial (Saône et Loire).

It was in the early 19th century that scholars, by analogy with the group of languages known as the "Romance" family, gave the name "Romanesque" to the various types of architecture and art that flowered in Europe from the end of the 10th century. The Church, eager to maintain its control over a rapidly increasing population, directed the contruction or reconstruction of innumerable places of worship. In the words of the chronicler Raoul Glaber (died c. 1050), "It was like a great wave of emulation that surged from one people to another. It seemed as if the whole world, shaking off its old rags, clothed itself in the white robes of these new churches".

C'est au début du XIXe siècle que des érudits, par analogie avec la famille des langues romanes, ont utilisé l'adjectif « roman » pour désigner les différents types d'architecture et d'art qui fleurirent en Europe à partir de la fin du Xe siècle. L'Église, soucieuse de conserver son emprise sur la population, qui croissait rapidement, dirigea la construction ou la reconstruction d'innombrables lieux de culte. Selon les propres termes du chroniqueur Raoul Glaber (qui mourut vers 1050), "ce fut comme une immense vague d'émulation qui s'éleva d'un peuple à l'autre. On eût dit que le monde entier quittait ses vieux oripeaux pour revêtir les blanches robes de ces nouvelles églises".

Norman architecture in Britain

l'architecture normande en Grande-Bretagne

The Norman Conquest of Britain, which started with the arrival of William the Conqueror in 1066, brought in its wake a great flowering of architecture. The Normans built grand castles and fortifications all over the land but it is in the religious architecture of the period that can most clearly be seen the influence of the Romanesque by then established in Normandy. Even before the Conquest, Norman masons had been working in Britain, notably on Westminster Abbey, the first Romanesque building in England. Later came the great cathedrals of Ely, Durham, Peterborough and Winchester as well as hundreds of parish churches, many of which have survived to the present day.

La conquête de la Grande-Bretagne par les Normands, qui débuta avec l'arrivée de Guillaume le Conquérant en 1066, entraîna dans son sillage une floraison d'œuvres architecturales. Les Normands édifièrent de majestueux châteaux et fortifications dans tout le pays, mais c'est dans l'architecture religieuse que l'influence de l'art roman (bien implanté à l'époque en Normandie) est la plus perceptible. Avant même la conquête, des maçons normands avaient déjà travaillé en Grande-Bretagne, et participé notamment à la construction de l'abbaye de Westminster, premier édifice roman en Angleterre. Plus tard, furent érigées les grandes cathédrales d'Ely, de Durham, de Peterborough et de Winchester, ainsi que des centaines d'églises paroissiales, dont beaucoup subsistent encore de nos jours.

The Norman cathedral at Ely, built between c. 1083 and 1130.
La cathédrale normande d'Ely, construite entre 1083 et 1130.

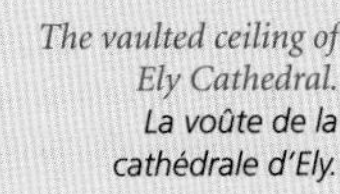

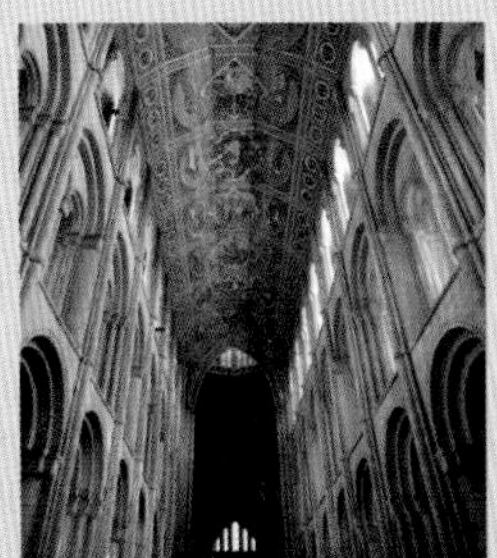

The vaulted ceiling of Ely Cathedral.
La voûte de la cathédrale d'Ely.

Gothic art

l'art gothique

This highly original movement in art and architecture, which Italian scholars of the *quattrocento*, besotted as they were with classical antiquity, pejoratively and entirely incorrectly called "Gothic" with reference to the Goths, who were a Germanic people, first appeared in the Île de France around 1140. By the end of the 12th century, the new style of architecture had already spread well beyond regional boundaries into Picardy, Champagne, Burgundy – and even England. In the course of the 13th century, the Gothic style imposed itself throughout the greater part of the Western world whilst taking on a particular local colour in each country. For three splendid centuries, Gothic art flourished in every branch of the arts.

L'art si original que les érudits italiens du Quattrocento, férus d'Antiquité classique, qualifièrent péjorativement et très improprement de gothique (des Goths, des Germains) est apparu en Île-de-France au cours des années 1140. À la fin du XIIe siècle, ce nouveau style architectural s'est déjà étendu jusqu'en Picardie, en Champagne, en Bourgogne… et même jusqu'en Angleterre. Au cours du XIIIe siècle, le style gothique s'impose à la plus grande partie de l'Occident, tout en prenant dans chaque pays une coloration particulière. Cette floraison, étalée sur trois siècles, concerne l'ensemble des arts.

King's College Chapel, University of Cambridge, England, built for Henry VI c. 1441–1516.
Chapelle du King's College, université de Cambridge, Angleterre, construite pour Henry VI vers 1441–1516.

Sculpture on the facade of Reims Cathedral.
Sculpture de la façade de la cathédrale de Reims.

The Wilton Diptych (c. 1395–1399) was painted for King Richard III and is considered to be one of the finest examples of International Gothic Style.
Le Diptyque de Wilton (vers 1395–1399) peint pour le roi Richard III, est considéré comme l'un des joyaux du gothique rayonnant.

the Renaissance / **la Renaissance**

The artists of the Renaissance sought to rediscover the prestige and the values of the great art of Antiquity, considered to have been in eclipse throughout the dark centuries of the Middle Ages. Though it is from this concept that the name "Renaissance" arose, its polemical overtones have caused it to be set aside in recent times. Nowadays we think of the Renaissance first and foremost as a period of extraordinary intellectual activity, linked to humanism, which questioned all the old accepted values and set to creating new approaches to form and visual representation. Italy was the birthplace of the Renaissance.

Les artistes de la Renaissance ont voulu retrouver le prestige et les vertus du grand art de l'Antiquité, qui aurait subi une éclipse au long des siècles obscurs du Moyen Âge. Cette conception, à l'origine du terme même de *Renaissance*, revêt un aspect polémique et a été écartée ; nous retenons de ce mouvement l'extraordinaire bouillonnement intellectuel, lié au courant humaniste, qui a remis en cause les certitudes acquises et présidé à un nouveau système formel et iconographique. L'Italie fut le berceau de ce phénomène.

Funerary statue of René de Chalon (1547), by Ligier Richier.
Statue funéraire de René de Chalon (1574), par Ligier Richier.

Château de Chambord (1519–1537), Early Renaissance.
Château de Chambord (1519–1537), première Renaissance.

the Tudor era / **l'ère des Tudor**

The Tudor era in England was notable for a move away from grand religious buildings and a focus on more domestic architecture. This is the period of the decorative timbers and brickwork that we now think of as the 'old English style' associated for example with Shakespeare's birthplace, Stratford-upon-Avon. A very noticeable change in this period is the use of brick instead of stone. The craft of brickmaking had recently been imported from the Low Countries and bricks were a luxury item – and consequently a sign of affluence. With the burning of coal for domestic heating came a need for chimneys to evacuate the smoke and it is to this that we owe the tall, decorative chimneys of the Tudor era. Typical too are the tall graceful oriel windows such as that over the entrance to Hampton Court Palace.

Pendant l'ère des Tudor en Angleterre, on construit moins d'édifices religieux et on se tourne davantage vers l'architecture domestique. C'est la période des maisons en brique à colombages : le style « old English », que l'on associe notamment à la ville natale de Shakespeare, Stratford-upon-Avon. On emploie désormais de la brique au lieu de la pierre, ce qui représente un changement considérable dans l'architecture. La fabrication des briques a été récemment importée des Pays-Bas, et les briques sont coûteuses, donc signe de richesse. Avec le chauffage domestique au charbon apparurent les cheminées. Le style Tudor se caractérise notamment par ses hautes cheminées décoratives et par la présence de grands et majestueux oriels (fenêtres en encorbellement), comme celui situé au-dessus du porche d'entrée de Hampton Court Palace.

A Tudor house in Suffolk.
Une demeure de style Tudor dans le Suffolk.

The entrance to Hampton Court Palace (begun 1514), built by Henry VIII.
Le porche d'entrée de Hampton Court Palace (commencé en 1514), dont la construction fut commandée par Henry VIII.

French Classicism — le classicisme français

France was a major centre of Classicism, particulary during the reign of Louis XIV. However, those associated with the movement never referred to themselves as "Classical artists". They felt themselves to be working towards perfection. Their faith in an ideal of balance and beauty was firmly grounded in the study of antiquity (especially Roman) and the observation of nature. These were supposed to be complementary and mutually justifying.

La France, en particulier sous le règne du Louis XIV, est l'un des principaux berceaux du classicisme. Mais ses artistes ne se qualifient jamais eux-mêmes de classiques. Ils ont le sentiment d'œuvrer vers la perfection ; leur foi en un idéal d'équilibre et de beauté a pour fondements l'étude de l'Antiquité (surtout romaine) et l'observation de la nature, censées se corriger et se justifier mutuellement.

The shepherds of Arcadia (1650), painting by Nicolas Poussin.
Les bergers de l'Arcadie (1650), peinture de Nicolas Poussin.

17th century England — l'Angleterre du XVIIe siècle

The west facade of St Paul's Cathedral, London (1675–1710).
La façade ouest de la cathédrale Saint-Paul, Londres (1675–1710).

The 17th century was a turbulent era of English history, taking in as it did the Civil War, the execution of the King, the Commonweath and Protectorate of Cromwell, the Restoration, the Great Plague and the Great Fire of London in 1666 which destroyed two thirds of the city. Undoubtedly the greatest scientific and artistic genius of the century was Sir Christopher Wren (1632–1723), who, in the wake of the Great Fire designed no less than 53 churches and a good many secular buildings as well. His masterpiece is St Paul's Cathedral, rebuilt on the site of Old St Paul's, destroyed in the Fire. Its late Renaissance style is considered to be England's restrained version of the Baroque. Its stunning dome was inspired by St Peter's Basilica in Rome.

Le XVIIe siècle, qui fut l'une des périodes les plus agitées dans l'histoire de l'Angleterre, englobe la Guerre civile, l'exécution du roi, le Commonwealth et le protectorat de Cromwell, la Restauration, la grande peste et le grand incendie de Londres en 1666, qui détruisit les deux tiers de la ville. Le plus grand génie du siècle, à la fois homme de science et artiste, fut sans conteste Sir Christopher Wren (1632–1723). À la suite du grand incendie, il conçut les plans de 53 églises, ainsi que ceux de nombreux bâtiments profanes. Son chef-d'œuvre est indiscutablement la cathédrale Saint-Paul, reconstruite sur le site de l'ancienne cathédrale, détruite par l'incendie. Son style Renaissance tardive est considéré comme une version mesurée du baroque en Angleterre. Son dôme impressionnant a été inspiré par la basilique Saint-Pierre de Rome.

French Neoclassicism — le néoclassicisme français

Amongst the influences leading to this Europe-wide movement were the philosophy of the Enlightenment, the rediscovery of Antiquity thanks to archaeology (excavations in Rome, Pompeii, Paestum and Athens), the engravings of Giovanni Battista Piranesi, the teaching of theoreticians like Joachim Winckelmann and a more profound level of reflection on the nature of art. The stance taken by the Neoclassicists in relation to Baroque and Rococco can also be seen as a moral criticism of aristocratic society.

Parmi les multiples influences qui ont conduit à l'émergence de ce mouvement dans toute l'Europe, on peut citer notamment la philosophie des Lumières, la redécouverte de l'Antiquité grâce à l'archéologie (des fouilles sont conduites à Rome, Pompéi, Paestum et Athènes), les gravures de Giovanni Battista Piranesi, l'enseignement de théoriciens tels que Joachim Winckelmann et une réflexion plus profonde sur la nature de l'art. La position des néoclassiques vis à vis du baroque et du rococo peut être également interprétée comme une critique morale de la société aristocratique.

The Sabine women *(1799), by Louis David.*
Les Sabines *(1799), par Louis David.*

American Georgian Colonial

le style colonial géorgien aux États-Unis

The Corbit-Sharp House (1774) in Odessa, Delaware is a fine example of Georgian style architecture.
La Corbit-Sharp House (1774) à Odessa, dans le Delaware, est un bel exemple d'architecture coloniale géorgienne.

What has come to be known as the *Georgian Colonial* style grew up in the United States as a wealthy elite emerged in the society during the 18th century. The style drew on Renaissance modes and imitated English Georgian but was rather more sober. Houses were, however, designed to give an impression of the prosperity and stability of their owners.

Ce qu'on appelle le style colonial géorgien s'est développé aux États-Unis, à l'époque où naissait une élite fortunée dans la société du XVIIIe siècle. S'inspirant de l'architecture de la Renaissance, ce style imitait le géorgien anglais, mais avec plus de sobriété. Les demeures étaient cependant conçues pour refléter la prospérité et l'influence de leurs propriétaires.

18th century society painters

les peintres de la haute société au XVIIIe siècle

The 18th century was the heyday of British society painting, with Sir Joshua Reynolds as its leading practitioner. He specialized in portraits of society figures in the "Grand Style" which set out to idealize its subjects. Reynolds was the leading portraitist of the second half of the century, painting around three thousand portraits in all. His arch-rival was Thomas Gainsborough, the favourite portrait painter of the royal family, whose style was a little less idealized than was Reynolds'.

Le XVIIIe siècle fut l'âge d'or des peintres de la haute société en Angleterre, dont Sir Joshua Reynolds était le chef de file. Il peignait essentiellement des portraits des gens du monde dans le « grand style », soucieux d'idéaliser les sujets de ses tableaux. Reynolds, qui régna sur le portrait anglais durant la deuxième moitié du siècle, en peignit environ trois mille. Son grand rival était Thomas Gainsborough, le portraitiste préféré de la famille royale, dont les œuvres étaient un peu moins idéalisées.

Thomas Gainsborough (1727–1788), Portrait of Mrs Richard Brinsley Sheridan.
Thomas Gainsborough (1727–1788), portrait de Mme Richard Brinsley Sheridan.

Romanticism

le romantisme

The Romantic movement defined itself in opposition to the academic and neoclassicist tradition and towards the end of the 18th century, and even more so at the beginning of the 19th, the search for perfection and reason was swept aside to give pride of place to spontaneity and revolution. Buoyed up by the hopes raised by the French Revolution and faced with the materialism of the industrial revolution, the Romantic artists claimed their right to be subjective, to draw inspiration from their dream worlds.

En réaction contre la tradition académique et néoclassique, ce courant fait triompher, dès la fin du XVIIIe siècle, mais surtout au début du XIXe, la spontanéité et la révolte là où dominaient souci de perfection et raison. Après les espoirs suscités par la Révolution française, et face au matérialisme de la révolution industrielle, les artistes romantiques réclament le droit à la subjectivité en puisant leur inspiration dans le rêve.

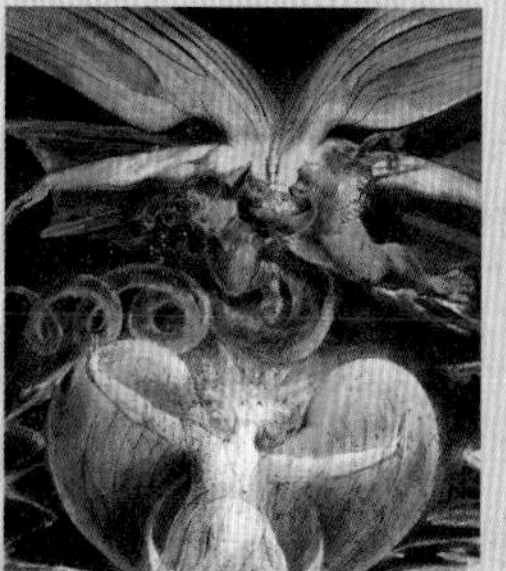

William Blake (1757–1827) The Great Red Dragon and the Woman Clothed in Sun. *Blake, as poet, painter and engraver was one of the leading and most original figures of the Romantic movement in Britain.*
William Blake (1757–1827) Le Grand dragon rouge et la femme vêtue de soleil. *Blake, à la fois poète, peintre et graveur, est l'une des figures les plus marquantes et les plus originales du romantisme anglais.*

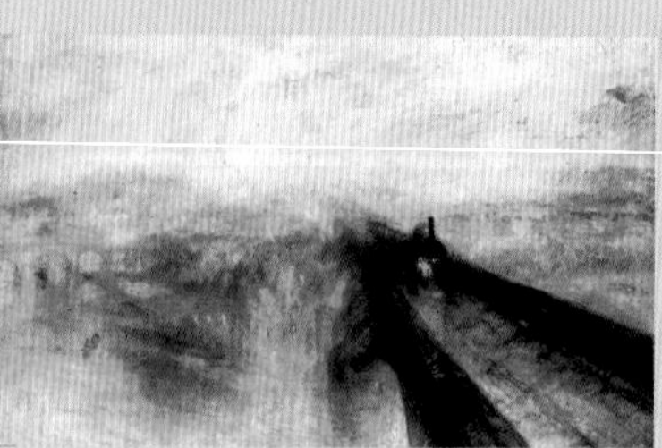

J.M.W. Turner (1775–1851), Rain, Steam and Speed – The Great Western Railway *(1844). An artistic prodigy, Turner had his first painting exhibited at the Royal Academy at the age of fifteen. He painted magnificent oil canvases but was also a stunning watercolourist. He is often called "the painter of light" and in this respect is a precursor of the Impressionists.*
J.M.W. Turner (1775–1851), Pluie, vapeur et vitesse – Le chemin de fer de la Great Western *(1844). Artiste de génie, Turner exposa sa première toile à l'Académie royale dès l'âge de quinze ans. Il réalisa de magnifiques peintures à l'huile, mais fut aussi un prodigieux aquarelliste. Surnommé « le peintre de la lumière », Turner est un précurseur de l'impressionnisme.*

Realism — le réalisme

19th century Realism made new demands on the painter: it required an absolutely objective approach and brought peasants and ordinary people back to centre stage. Such subjects had long been banished from anything but depictions of rural idylls or moralistic caricatures. "Anything that does not inscribe itself on the retina does not belong in the realm of the painter", proclaimed Gustave Courbet, whose monumental painting, *The Artist's Studio*, first exhibited in 1855, provides an excellent illustration of his theories which were considerably influenced by those of Pierre Joseph Prudhon.

Le réalisme du XIXe siècle exige du peintre une approche objective et remet à l'honneur les paysans et les gens du peuple, depuis longtemps écartés de la scène artistique, ou bien représentés uniquement dans des œuvres idylliques ou moralisantes. « Tout ce qui ne se dessine pas sur la rétine est en dehors du domaine de la peinture », proclame Gustave Courbet, dont le monumental *Atelier*, exposé en 1855, exprime les théories, largement inspirées de celles de Pierre Joseph Proudhon.

The Reaper *(1820), pencil drawing by Jean-François Millet.*
Le Faucheur *(1820), dessin au crayon de Jean-François Millet.*

Symbolism — le symbolisme

Pierre Puvis de Chavannes, The Dream *(1883).*
Le Rêve *(1883), par Pierre Puvis de Chavannes.*

In both art and literature, Symbolism can be seen as developing out of Romanticism. The attempt to capture all that is unfathomable in the human spirit, to shed light on everything that cannot be said and cannot even be seen, in more general terms to allow fantasy to take pride of place over reality and the dream world over the everyday world, the endeavour to give ideas priority over matter – all these aspirations, already apparent in William Blake or Caspar David Friedrich, made up the artistic universe of Symbolism.

Dans la peinture comme dans la littérature, le symbolisme apparaît clairement comme l'héritier du romantisme. Les symbolistes tentent de capturer l'insondable dans l'esprit humain, de mettre en évidence ce qui ne peut être dit ou vu. Plus généralement, ils souhaitent faire prévaloir l'imaginaire sur le réel, l'univers du rêve sur la réalité quotidienne. Ils s'efforcent de privilégier les idées et non la matière. L'univers artistique du symbolisme recèle toutes ces aspirations, déjà présentes chez William Blake ou Caspar David Friedrich.

the Pre-Raphaelites — les préraphaélites

Frequently controversial and severely criticized by their contemporaries, the Pre-Raphaelite Brotherhood is considered by some to have been the first avant-garde group in the history of painting. They embraced the ideals of the Romantics, roundly condemning what they considered to be the academic mannerism of the 18th century in general, and of Joshua Reynolds in particular. There is a tension in the movement between the idealization of all things medieval, as practised by such as Dante Gabriel Rossetti and John Everett Millais and the insistence on realism favoured by William Holman Hunt. Common to both strands is the detailed depiction of nature and the development of painting techniques that give jewel-like colour to the paintings.

William Holman Hunt (1827–1910), The Awakening Conscience *(1853).*
William Holman Hunt (1827–1910), L'Éveil de la conscience *(1853).*

Les préraphaélites, peintres souvent sujets à controverse et sévèrement critiqués par leurs contemporains, sont considérés par certains historiens d'art comme le premier groupe d'avant-garde dans l'histoire de la peinture. Acquis aux idéaux des romantiques, ils rejetaient en bloc la peinture du XVIIIe siècle, qualifiée de « maniérisme académique », et en particulier les portraits de Joshua Reynolds. Le mouvement oscille entre la prédilection pour les thèmes moyenâgeux, comme chez Dante Gabriel Rossetti et John Everett Millais, et la veine réaliste, présente chez William Holman Hunt. Ces deux courants se rejoignent dans la représentation détaillée de la nature et l'usage de techniques picturales qui confèrent un éclat chatoyant à leurs tableaux.

Sir John Everett Millais (1829–1896), Ophelia *(1852).*
Sir John Everett Millais (1829–1896), Ophélie *(1852).*

Impressionism — *l'impressionnisme*

Claude Monet,
Water Lilies *(1900).*
Le Bassin aux nymphéas *(1900), par Claude Monet.*

Pierre-Auguste Renoir (1841–1919), The Swing *(1876).*
La balançoire *(1876), de Pierre-Auguste Renoir (1841–1919).*

Paul Cézanne,
Mount Sainte-Victoire *(1906).*
La Montagne Sainte-Victoire *(1906), de Paul Cézanne.*

The real breakthrough of this new generation of painters born around 1835–1840 lay in their spontaneous realization of the the importance of the sensations experienced by the artist painting outdoors. They sought to capture the effects of natural light and its modulations according to the time of day and the season. Impressionism moved progressively away from the traditional conventions that had governed painting up until then, in particular studio lighting, perspective and drawing. The main representatives of Impressionism were Monet, Pissaro, Sisley, Renoir, Cézanne, Berthe Morisot et Degas.

Cette nouvelle génération de peintres, nés dans les années 1835–1840, exécute ses tableaux en plein air. Ils s'attachent à saisir les effets de lumière, observant la nature et ses modulations liées aux heures, aux saisons, au cadrage. L'impressionnisme s'affranchit progressivement des conventions picturales traditionnelles : l'éclairage d'atelier, la perspective, le dessin. Les principaux représentants de ce mouvement sont Monet, Pissaro, Sisley, Renoir, Cézanne, Berthe Morisot et Degas.

the Arts and Crafts Movement — *le mouvement Arts and Crafts*

Inspired largely by the writings of the influential poet, painter, art critic and social reformer, John Ruskin, the *Arts and Crafts Movement* had a tremendous influence on architecture and the decorative arts in Europe and America. Based on ideals of craftsmanship and fiercely opposed to the division of labour increasingly practised in manufacturing, the movement insisted on the importance of the texture of materials and the need to preserve disappearing rural crafts.

Inspiré en grande partie par les écrits de John Ruskin, éminent poète, peintre, critique d'art et réformateur, le *mouvement Arts and Crafts* exerça une influence considérable sur l'architecture et les arts décoratifs en Europe et aux États-Unis. Fondé sur l'artisanat (envisagé comme une force créatrice) et farouchement opposé à la division du travail, pratiquée de plus en plus fréquemment dans l'industrie, ce mouvement insistait sur l'importance de la texture des matériaux et la nécessité de préserver l'artisanat rural en voie de disparition.

William Morris (1834–1896), printed cotton, based on a design by William Blake. Morris was a central figure in the renaissance of English decorative art and produced hundreds of designs in his fabric workshops.
William Morris (1834–1896), coton imprimé, réalisé à partir d'un motif de William Blake. Morris, l'un des chefs de file du mouvement prônant la renaissance des arts décoratifs, produisit des centaines de motifs dans ses ateliers de textile.

Fauvism and Expressionism

le fauvisme et l'expressionnisme

European painting in the first two or three decades of the 20th century was marked by an explosion of colour and an eloquent simplification of form. Fauvism, essentially a French movement, aimed to achieve pure plasticity and refuted the subtleties of the Impressionists, choosing instead to exaggerate everything that stemmed from sensation. Expressionism, on the other hand, was more concerned with content and the human meaning of art. German expressionism made use of aggressive drawing techniques and colours whilst the Flemish version was more restrained.

La peinture européenne des deux ou trois premières décennies du XXe siècle se caractérise notamment par l'explosion de la couleur et la simplification des formes. Le fauvisme, courant français, s'attache à la plastique pure, réfutant les subtilités de l'impressionnisme pour mettre l'accent sur tout ce qui relève de la sensation. L'expressionnisme se préoccupe davantage du contenu et de la dimension humaine des œuvres ; le graphisme et la palette de l'expressionnisme allemand sont assez agressifs, tandis que le courant flamand est plus retenu.

Maurice Vlaminck,
The Bridge at Chatou, *(1906.)*
Le Pont de Chatou *(1906),*
par Maurice de Vlaminck.

André Derain (1880–1954),
Bust of a Woman *(1905).*
Buste de femme *(1905),*
par André Derain (1880–1954).

Art Nouveau

l'Art nouveau

"*Modern style*", as *Art Nouveau* was known in France at the time, started to appear in a number of countries towards the end of the 19th century. The movement had its roots in a rejection of the endless repetition of classical styles. It was very wide-ranging and, from its early manifestations in architecture and the design of furniture and objects, went on to influence many areas of art. Its highly decorative lyrical style whose curving lines were inspired by both plant forms and the female body, became very popular in the years leading up to the First Word War.

L'Art nouveau, appelé aussi « modern style », est apparu dans de nombreux pays vers la fin du XIXe siècle. Ce mouvement s'oppose à la reproduction systématique des styles du passé. Courant d'une grande envergure, dès ses premières manifestations dans l'architecture et la conception de meubles et d'objets, l'Art nouveau exerça son influence dans de nombreux domaines artistiques. Son style, caractérisé par une profusion ornementale où domine la ligne courbe d'inspiration végétale ou féminine, devint très populaire dans les années précédant la Première Guerre mondiale.

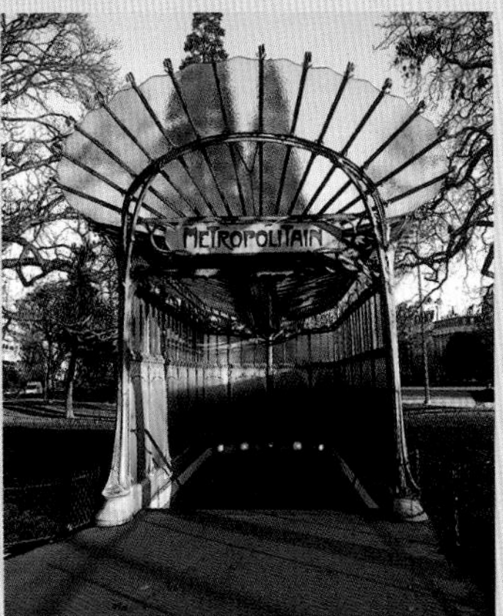

The Porte Dauphine métro station (1900) in Paris, designed by Hector Guimard.
La station de métro de la porte Dauphine (1900) par Hector Guimard.

René Lalique "Dragonfly Woman" brooch (1898).
Broche « La Femme libellule » (1898) par René Lalique.

Cubism

le cubisme

Starting around the year 1907, a number of artists living in Paris, amongst them Picasso, Braque and Gris, in search of a greater degree of rigour in art, set out to "depict nature" not precisely in terms of "the cylinder, the sphere and the cone", as conjectured by Cézanne, but at least by the rectangle, the circle, the pyramid and the cube.

À partir de 1907, en quête de rigueur, quelques artistes parisiens (Picasso, Gris, Braque) entreprennent de « traiter la nature » sinon « par le cylindre, la sphère, le cône », comme Paul Cézanne l'avait imaginé, du moins par le rectangle, le cercle, la pyramide et le cube.

Pablo Ruiz Picasso (1881–1973), Man with Clarinet *(1911).*
Homme à la pipe *(1911), par Pablo Ruiz Picasso (1881–1973).*

Georges Braque (1882–1963), Le Quotidien *(1912–13).*
Le Quotidien *(1912–13), par Georges Braque (1882–1963).*

Dada

le mouvement Dada

Appropriately enough, the term "Dada" (*hobby-horse*) has no meaning in an artistic context and was, it was claimed, chosen by opening a dictionary at random. This is entirely in accord with the emphasis on the absurd – and also the everyday – in the output of its practitioners. It first manifested itself in 1916, fuelled by outrage at the appalling events in Europe at the time, and set out to provide a radical critique of the whole of Western civilization, savagely deriding all existing values and condemning the power of art to deceive.

Le mot « dada », dont le sens, fort à propos, n'a rien à voir avec l'art, fut choisi, aux dires de ces fondateurs, en ouvrant un dictionnaire au hasard. Il est en parfaite adéquation avec le goût pour l'absurde (ainsi que l'intérêt pour le quotidien) omniprésent dans les œuvres dadaïstes. Le dadaïsme se manifesta pour la première fois en 1916, scandalisé par les événements épouvantables qui se déroulaient en Europe à l'époque, et se mit à critiquer violemment la civilisation occidentale dans son ensemble, tournant en ridicule toutes les valeurs établies et condamnant dans l'art sa faculté de tromper.

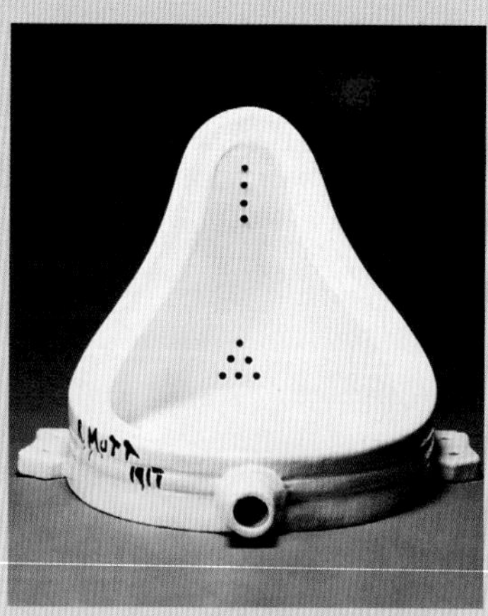

Marcel Duchamp (1887–1968), Fountain *(1917). Best known for his 'ready-mades', in this case a urinal, Duchamp was a leading member of the Dada group.*
Marcel Duchamp (1887–1968), Fontaine *(1917). Célèbre surtout pour ses « ready-made » et notamment cet urinoir, Duchamp était l'un des chefs de file du groupe Dada.*

Surrealism

le surréalisme

Francis Bacon (1909–1992), Person writing, reflected in the mirror *(1976).*
Personnage écrivant reflété dans le miroir *(1976), par Francis Bacon (1909–1992).*

For the Surrealists, a work of art was justified only if it contributed, however slightly, to "changing life". This could only be done by refusing to sacrifice the inventive powers of the artist to the description of the visible world. In France the moving spirit and principal theoretician of the movement was André Breton who in *Surréalisme et peinture* (1925) put forward the theory of the "*modèle intérieur*" (internal model), the aim of which was to turn art away from realist representation which, according to Breton, had held the western world in its sway since the Renaissance: from now on the artist was to focus only on those images that surged up from his innermost being. The surrealist movement had an immense influence on subsequent generations of artists including Francis Bacon, Henry Moore and Edward Hopper.

Max Ernst, The Equivocal Woman *(also known as* The Teetering Woman*) (1923).*
La femme chancelante *par Max Ernst (1923).*

Pour les surréalistes, une œuvre d'art n'était justifiée que si elle contribuait, même modestement, à « transformer la vie ». Cela ne pouvait se produire qu'en refusant de sacrifier le pouvoir inventif de l'artiste au profit de la description du monde visible. En France, la figure de proue et le principal théoricien du mouvement était André Breton. Dans *Surréalisme et peinture* (1925), il exposa la théorie du « modèle intérieur », qui avait pour objectif de détourner l'art de la représentation réaliste sous l'emprise de laquelle se trouvait le monde occidental depuis la Renaissance : désormais, l'artiste devait se concentrer uniquement sur les images qui surgissaient des profondeurs de son être. Le mouvement surréaliste exerça une influence colossale sur les générations suivantes d'artistes, comme par exemple Francis Bacon, Henry Moore ou Edward Hopper.

Abstract Art

l'art abstrait

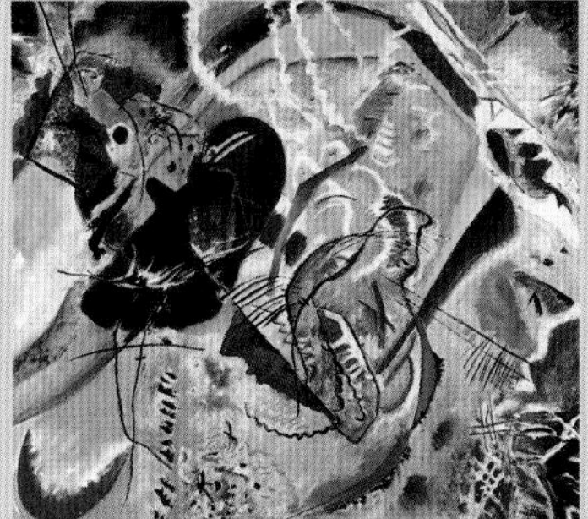

Wassily Kandinsky (1866–1944), Improvisation n° 35 *(1914).*
Improvisation n° 35 *(1914), par Wassily Kandinsky (1866–1944).*

As early as the 1850s Eugène Delacroix wrote that if colour has been properly used in a painting, it should be possible to feel what the painting is expressing through its chromatic effect alone, by looking at it from a distance and without identifying its subject matter. Thus it was inevitable that one day artists would set to wondering whether it was necessary to have a subject at all. So it was that in the 20th century there was a move on the part of some artists towards expression through the evocative powers of colour and the use of non-figurative form.

Dès les années 1850, Eugène Delacroix écrivait que si la couleur avait été bien employée dans un tableau, on devait pouvoir ressentir l'expression de ce tableau uniquement par son effet chromatique, en le regardant de loin, sans en identifier le sujet. Il était inévitable qu'un jour les artistes se demandent s'il était vraiment nécessaire d'avoir un sujet : c'est ainsi que nombre d'entre eux en sont venus au XXe siècle à s'exprimer en accentuant le pouvoir évocateur des couleurs et en n'utilisant que des formes non-figuratives.

Pop Art

le pop art

Easily recognizable by its depiction of everyday household objects, its use of the brash colours and simple lines of comic-strips and of advertising and television images, Pop Art was essentially a product of the post-war society of Britain and America in the 1950s and '60s. Like pop music, it drew its inspiration and energy from popular culture and in America may be seen as a reaction against abstract expressionism. Apparent objectivity and an easily readable style go hand in hand with a certain humour and tongue-in-cheek irony. Perhaps best known are American pop artists Roy Lichtenstein (1923–97) and Andy Warhol (1928–87).

Facilement reconnaissable à sa représentation des objets de la vie quotidienne, son usage des couleurs criardes et ses emprunts à la bande dessinée, ainsi qu'à son goût pour la publicité et les images provenant de la télévision, le pop art s'est développé dans la société britannique et la société américaine de l'après-guerre, au cours des années 1950 et 1960. Comme la pop music, il puise son inspiration et son énergie dans la culture populaire. Aux États-Unis, ce mouvement peut être considéré comme une réaction contre l'expressionnisme abstrait. Une apparente objectivité et un style facilement lisible vont de pair avec un certain humour et une ironie mordante. Les représentants les plus connus du pop art sont Roy Lichtenstein (1923–1997) et Andy Warhol (1928–1987).

Andy Warhol (1928–87), Jacky, (nine panels), *(1964).*
Jacky, (neuf panneaux), *(1964), par Andy Warhol (1928–1987).*

photographic credits

crédits photographiques

page	credit/crédit
2 ht g/top l	Ph. © Heritage Images/LEEMAGE
2 ht d/top r	Ph. © Heritage Images/LEEMAGE
2 m g/middle l	Ph. © Bettmann/CORBIS
2 bas d/bottom r	British Museum, Londres/London. Ph. Fleming © Archives Larbor
3 ht g/top l	Musée du Château de Versailles, Versailles. Ph. © Archives Nathan
3 ht d/top r	© The Art Archive/Bodleian Library Oxford
3 m ht/top middle	Ph. © Bettmann/CORBIS
3 m bas/bottom middle	Ph. © Bettmann/CORBIS
3 bas d/bottom r	Ph. Coll. Archives Larbor
4 ht d/top r	Bibliothèque Nationale de France, Paris. Ph. Coll. Archives Nathan
4 m g/middle l	Bibliothèque Nationale de France, Paris. Ph. Coll. Archives Larbor
4 m d/middle r	Bibliothèque Nationale de France, Paris. Ph. Coll. Archives Larbor
4 bas g/bottom l	Bibliothèque Nationale de France, Paris. Ph. Coll. Archives Nathan
5 ht g/top l	Bibliothèque Nationale de France, Paris. Ph. Coll. Archives Larousse
5 ht d/top r	Collection particulière/Private collection. Ph. © Archives Nathan
5 m/middle	Bibliothèque des Arts Décoratifs, Paris. Ph. Jean-Loup Charmet © Archives Larbor
5 bas g/bottom l	Bibliothèque Nationale de France, Paris. Ph. Jeanbor © Archives Larbor
5 bas d/bottom r	Musée National de l'Éducation, Rouen. © Archives Larbor
6 ht d/top r	Ph. © RMN
6 m/middle	Ph. © Jean Bernard/LEEMAGE
6 bas g/bottom l	Trinity College Library, Dublin. Ph. Coll. Archives Larbor
6 bas m/bottom middle	Bibliothèque Nationale de France, Paris. Ph. Coll. Archives Larousse
7 ht g/top l	Ph. © Philippa Lewis; Edifice/CORBIS
7 ht d/top r	Ph. © Nik Wheeler/CORBIS
7 m d/middle r	Ph. © Brian Harding; EyeUbiquitous/CORBIS
7 bas g/bottom l	Ph. © Jan Butchofsky-Houser/CORBIS
7 bas d/bottom r	National Gallery. Ph. © AKG-images Paris
8 ht d/top r	Église Saint-Étienne, Bar-Le-Duc. Ph. R. Bollaert © Archives Larbor
8 ht g/top l	Ph. © Paul Hardy/CORBIS
8 bas g/bottom l	Ph. © Gillian Darley; Edifice/CORBIS
8 bas d/bottom r	Ph. © Robert Harding World Imagery/CORBIS
9 ht d/top r	Ph. © Angelo Hornak/CORBIS
9 m g/middle l	Musée du Louvre, Paris. Ph. H. Josse © Archives Larbor
9 bas d/bottom r	Musée du Louvre, Paris. Ph. H. Josse © Archives Larbor

page	credit/crédit
10 ht g/top l	Ph. © Lee Snider/Photo Images/CORBIS
10 ht d/top r	National Gallery of Art, Washington. Ph. Coll. Archives Larousse
10 bas d/bottom r	National Gallery of Art, Londres/London. Ph. © Archives Larbor
10 bas g/bottom l	National Gallery of Art, Washington. Ph. Coll. Archives Larousse
11 ht d/top r	Musée du Louvre, Paris. Ph. Hubert Josse © Archives Larbor
11 ht g/top l	Musée d'Orsay, Paris. Ph. H. Josse © Archives Larbor
11 bas d/bottom r	Tate Gallery, Londres/London. Ph. © Archives Larbor
11 bas m/bottom middle	Tate Gallery, Londres/London. Ph. © Archives Larousse
12 ht g/top l	Musée d'Orsay, Paris. Ph. © Archives Larbor
12 ht d/top r	Musée d'Orsay, Paris. Ph. H. Josse © Archives Larbor
12 m g/middle l	Kunsthaus, Zurich. Ph. Walter Dräyer © Archives Larbor
12 bas g/bottom l	Victoria and Albert Museum, Londres/London. Ph. © Archives Larbor
13 ht d/top r	Musée de l'Annonciade, Saint-Tropez. Ph. Jeanbor © Archives Larbor © Adagp, Paris 2007
13 m ht/top middle	Courtesy Galerie Schmit, Paris © Adagp, Paris 2007
13 bas d/bottom r	Ph. Olivier Ploton © Archives Larbor
13 bas g/bottom l	Musée Calouste Gulbenkian, Lisbonne/Lisbon. Ph. Coll. Archives Larbor © ADAGP, Paris 2007
14 ht g/top l	Kimbell Art Museum, Fort Worth, Texas. © Archives Larbor © Succession Picasso Paris 2007
14 ht d/top r	MNAM, Centre Georges-Pompidou, Paris. Ph. Luc Joubert © Archives Larbor © Adagp, Paris 2007
14 m d/middle l	Fondation Dina Vierny-Musée Maillol, Paris. Ph. Jean-Alex Brunelle © Fondation Dina Vierny-Musée; Maillol, Paris © Succession Marcel Duchamp/Adagp, Paris 2007
15 ht g/top l	Collection particulière/Private collection. Ph. Coll. Archives Larbor © Adagp, Paris 2007
15 ht m/top middle	Kunstsamnlung Nordrhein - Westfalen, Dusseldorf, Allemagne/Germany. Ph. X. © Archives Larbor © Adagp, Paris 2007
15 m g/middle l	Kunstumuseum, Bâle. Ph. Coll. Archives Larbor © ADAGP, Paris 2007
15 bas d/bottom r	Collection particulière/Private collection. Ph. Luc Joubert © Archives Larbor © Adagp, Paris 2007

Planches thématiques
Coloured themed plates

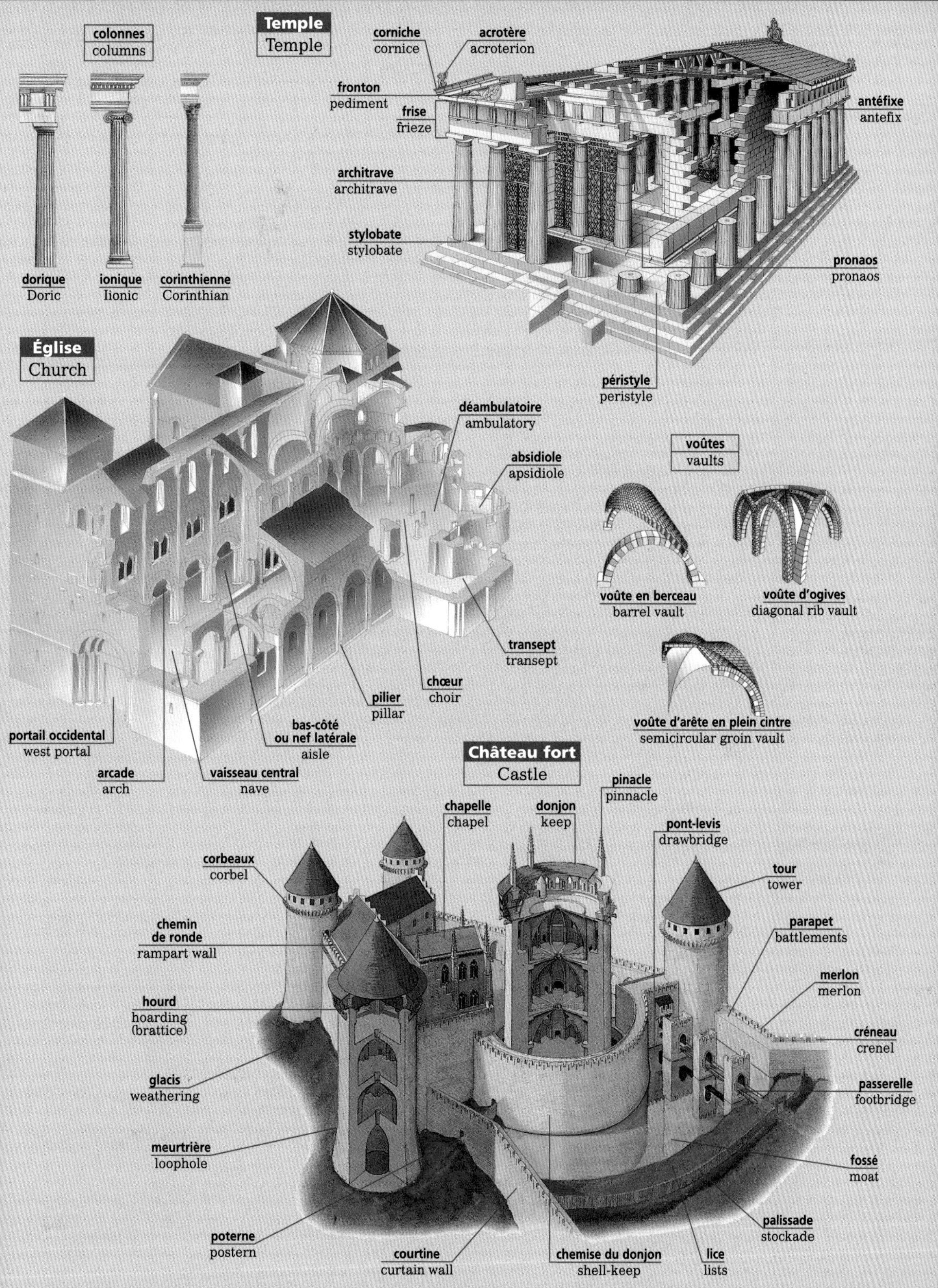
colonnes
columns
dorique
Doric
ionique
Iionic
corinthienne
Corinthian
Temple
Temple
corniche
cornice
acrotère
acroterion
fronton
pediment
frise
frieze
antéfixe
antefix
architrave
architrave
stylobate
stylobate
pronaos
pronaos
péristyle
peristyle
Église
Church
déambulatoire
ambulatory
absidiole
apsidiole
voûtes
vaults
voûte en berceau
barrel vault
voûte d'ogives
diagonal rib vault
transept
transept
chœur
choir
pilier
pillar
voûte d'arête en plein cintre
semicircular groin vault
bas-côté
ou nef latérale
aisle
portail occidental
west portal
arcade
arch
vaisseau central
nave
Château fort
Castle
pinacle
pinnacle
chapelle
chapel
donjon
keep
pont-levis
drawbridge
corbeaux
corbel
tour
tower
chemin
de ronde
rampart wall
parapet
battlements
merlon
merlon
hourd
hoarding
(brattice)
créneau
crenel
glacis
weathering
passerelle
footbridge
meurtrière
loophole
fossé
moat
palissade
stockade
poterne
postern
courtine
curtain wall
chemise du donjon
shell-keep
lice
lists

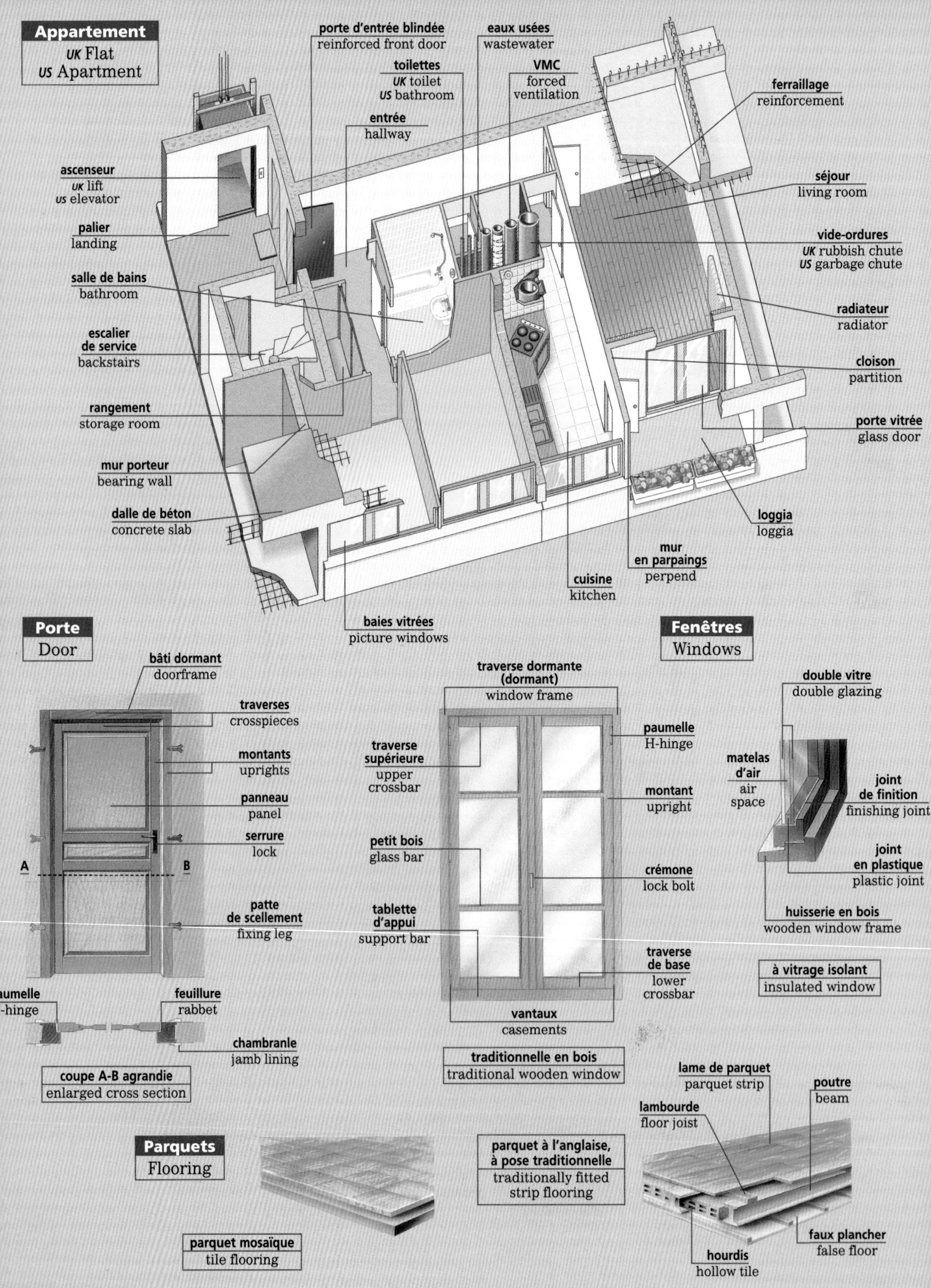
Appartement
UK Flat
US Apartment
porte d'entrée blindée
reinforced front door
eaux usées
wastewater
toilettes
UK toilet
US bathroom
VMC
forced ventilation
entrée
hallway
ferraillage
reinforcement
ascenseur
UK lift
US elevator
séjour
living room
palier
landing
vide-ordures
UK rubbish chute
US garbage chute
salle de bains
bathroom
radiateur
radiator
escalier de service
backstairs
cloison
partition
rangement
storage room
porte vitrée
glass door
mur porteur
bearing wall
dalle de béton
concrete slab
loggia
loggia
mur en parpaings
perpend
cuisine
kitchen
baies vitrées
picture windows
Porte
Door
bâti dormant
doorframe
traverses
crosspieces
montants
uprights
panneau
panel
serrure
lock
A
B
patte de scellement
fixing leg
paumelle
H-hinge
feuillure
rabbet
chambranle
jamb lining
coupe A-B agrandie
enlarged cross section
Fenêtres
Windows
traverse dormante (dormant)
window frame
traverse supérieure
upper crossbar
paumelle
H-hinge
montant
upright
petit bois
glass bar
crémone
lock bolt
tablette d'appui
support bar
traverse de base
lower crossbar
vantaux
casements
traditionnelle en bois
traditional wooden window
double vitre
double glazing
matelas d'air
air space
joint de finition
finishing joint
joint en plastique
plastic joint
huisserie en bois
wooden window frame
à vitrage isolant
insulated window
Parquets
Flooring
parquet mosaïque
tile flooring
parquet à l'anglaise, à pose traditionnelle
traditionally fitted strip flooring
lame de parquet
parquet strip
poutre
beam
lambourde
floor joist
faux plancher
false floor
hourdis
hollow tile

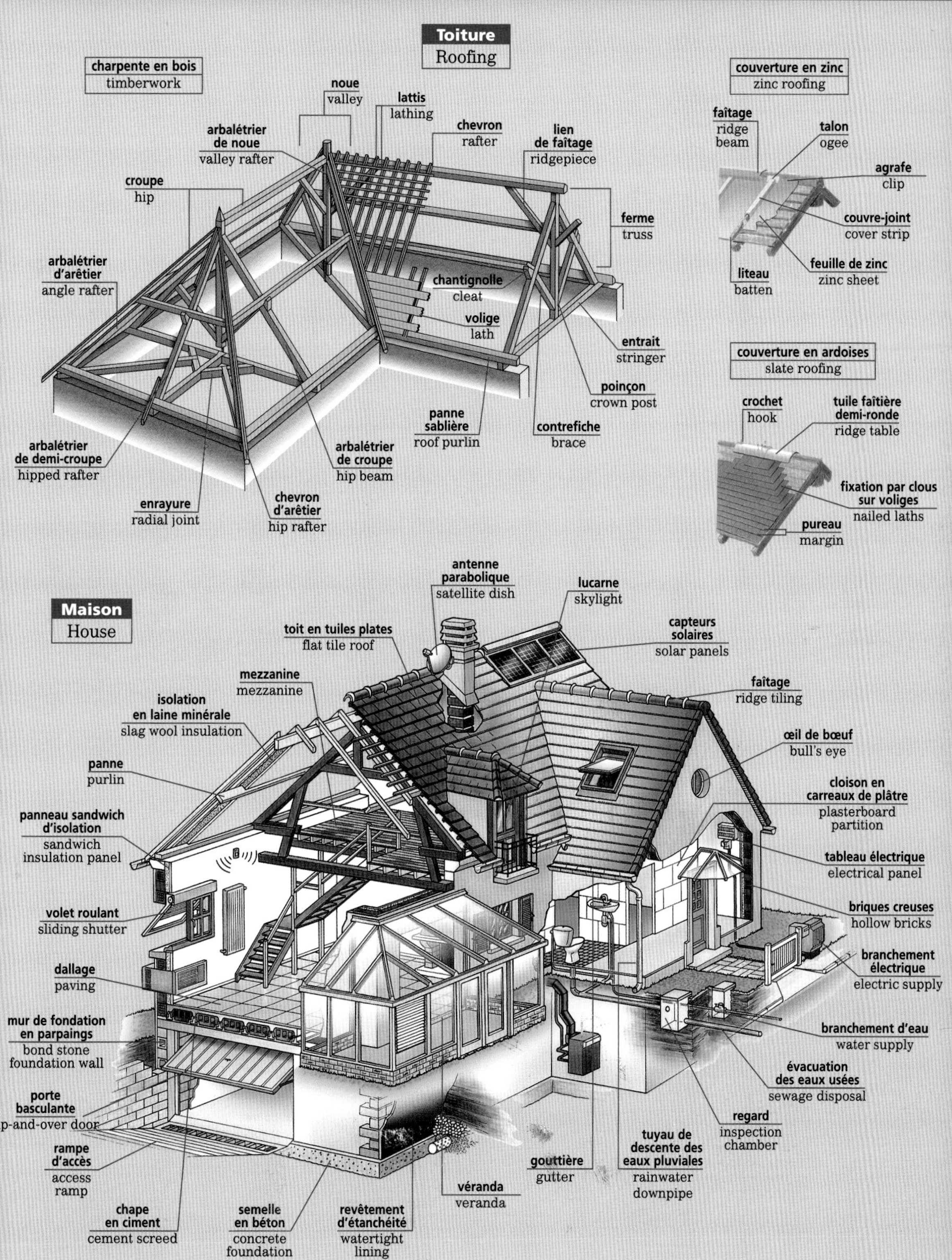
Toiture
Roofing
charpente en bois
timberwork
noue
valley
lattis
lathing
arbalétrier de noue
valley rafter
chevron
rafter
lien de faîtage
ridgepiece
croupe
hip
ferme
truss
arbalétrier d'arêtier
angle rafter
chantignolle
cleat
volige
lath
entrait
stringer
poinçon
crown post
panne sablière
roof purlin
contrefiche
brace
arbalétrier de demi-croupe
hipped rafter
arbalétrier de croupe
hip beam
enrayure
radial joint
chevron d'arêtier
hip rafter
couverture en zinc
zinc roofing
faîtage
ridge beam
talon
ogee
agrafe
clip
couvre-joint
cover strip
feuille de zinc
zinc sheet
liteau
batten
couverture en ardoises
slate roofing
crochet
hook
tuile faîtière demi-ronde
ridge table
fixation par clous sur voliges
nailed laths
pureau
margin
Maison
House
antenne parabolique
satellite dish
lucarne
skylight
toit en tuiles plates
flat tile roof
capteurs solaires
solar panels
mezzanine
mezzanine
faîtage
ridge tiling
isolation en laine minérale
slag wool insulation
œil de bœuf
bull's eye
panne
purlin
cloison en carreaux de plâtre
plasterboard partition
panneau sandwich d'isolation
sandwich insulation panel
tableau électrique
electrical panel
volet roulant
sliding shutter
briques creuses
hollow bricks
dallage
paving
branchement électrique
electric supply
mur de fondation en parpaings
bond stone foundation wall
branchement d'eau
water supply
évacuation des eaux usées
sewage disposal
porte basculante
up-and-over door
regard
inspection chamber
rampe d'accès
access ramp
tuyau de descente des eaux pluviales
rainwater downpipe
gouttière
gutter
véranda
veranda
chape en ciment
cement screed
semelle en béton
concrete foundation
revêtement d'étanchéité
watertight lining

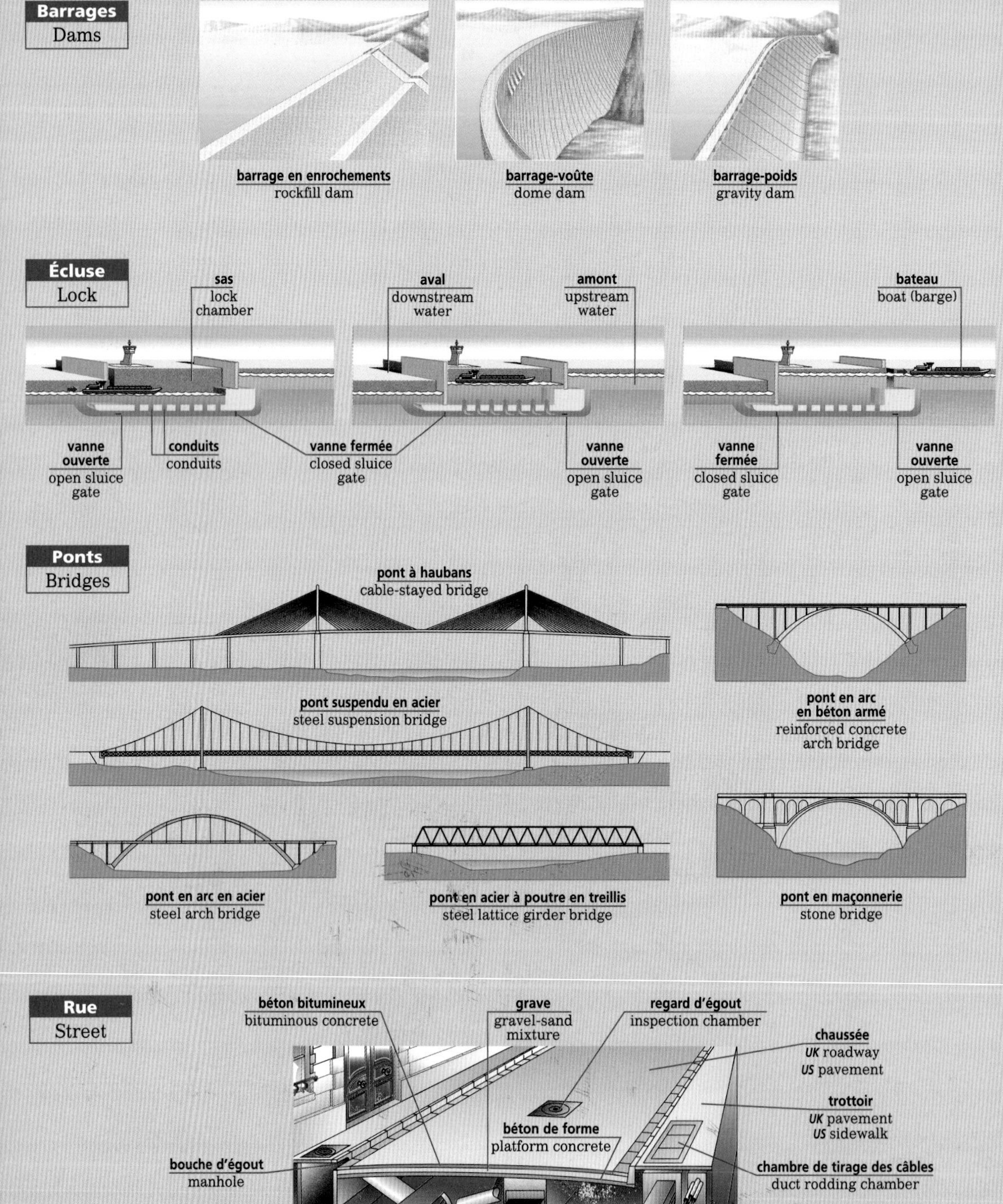
Barrages
Dams
barrage en enrochements
rockfill dam
barrage-voûte
dome dam
barrage-poids
gravity dam
Écluse
Lock
sas
lock chamber
aval
downstream water
amont
upstream water
bateau
boat (barge)
vanne ouverte
open sluice gate
conduits
conduits
vanne fermée
closed sluice gate
vanne ouverte
open sluice gate
vanne fermée
closed sluice gate
vanne ouverte
open sluice gate
Ponts
Bridges
pont à haubans
cable-stayed bridge
pont suspendu en acier
steel suspension bridge
pont en arc en béton armé
reinforced concrete arch bridge
pont en arc en acier
steel arch bridge
pont en acier à poutre en treillis
steel lattice girder bridge
pont en maçonnerie
stone bridge

Rue
Street

béton bitumineux
bituminous concrete
grave
gravel-sand mixture
regard d'égout
inspection chamber
chaussée
UK roadway
US pavement
trottoir
UK pavement
US sidewalk
béton de forme
platform concrete
bouche d'égout
manhole
chambre de tirage des câbles
duct rodding chamber
eau en retour
returning water
chauffage urbain
district heating
vapeur
steam
eau
water
gaz
gas
réseaux câblés
network cabling
égout collecteur
main sewer
grillage avertisseur
protection grate

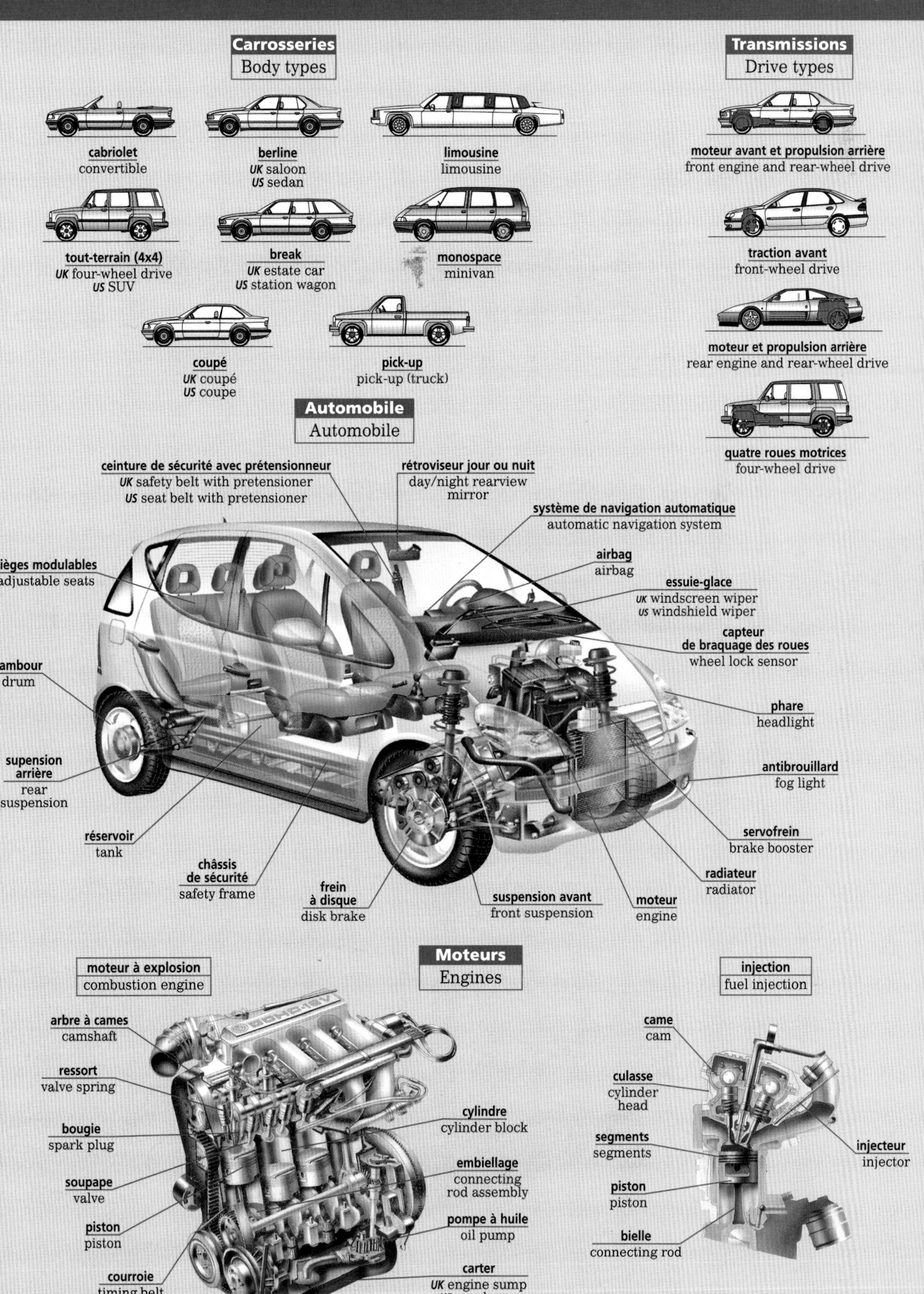
Carrosseries
Body types
cabriolet
convertible
berline
UK saloon
US sedan
limousine
limousine
tout-terrain (4x4)
UK four-wheel drive
US SUV
break
UK estate car
US station wagon
monospace
minivan
coupé
UK coupé
US coupe
pick-up
pick-up (truck)
Transmissions
Drive types
moteur avant et propulsion arrière
front engine and rear-wheel drive
traction avant
front-wheel drive
moteur et propulsion arrière
rear engine and rear-wheel drive
quatre roues motrices
four-wheel drive
Automobile
Automobile
ceinture de sécurité avec prétensionneur
UK safety belt with pretensioner
US seat belt with pretensioner
rétroviseur jour ou nuit
day/night rearview mirror
système de navigation automatique
automatic navigation system
sièges modulables
adjustable seats
airbag
airbag
essuie-glace
UK windscreen wiper
US windshield wiper
capteur de braquage des roues
wheel lock sensor
tambour
drum
phare
headlight
supension arrière
rear suspension
antibrouillard
fog light
réservoir
tank
servofrein
brake booster
châssis de sécurité
safety frame
frein à disque
disk brake
suspension avant
front suspension
moteur
engine
radiateur
radiator
Moteurs
Engines
moteur à explosion
combustion engine
injection
fuel injection
arbre à cames
camshaft
ressort
valve spring
bougie
spark plug
soupape
valve
piston
piston
courroie
timing belt
cylindre
cylinder block
embiellage
connecting rod assembly
pompe à huile
oil pump
carter
UK engine sump
US crankcase
came
cam
culasse
cylinder head
segments
segments
piston
piston
bielle
connecting rod
injecteur
injector

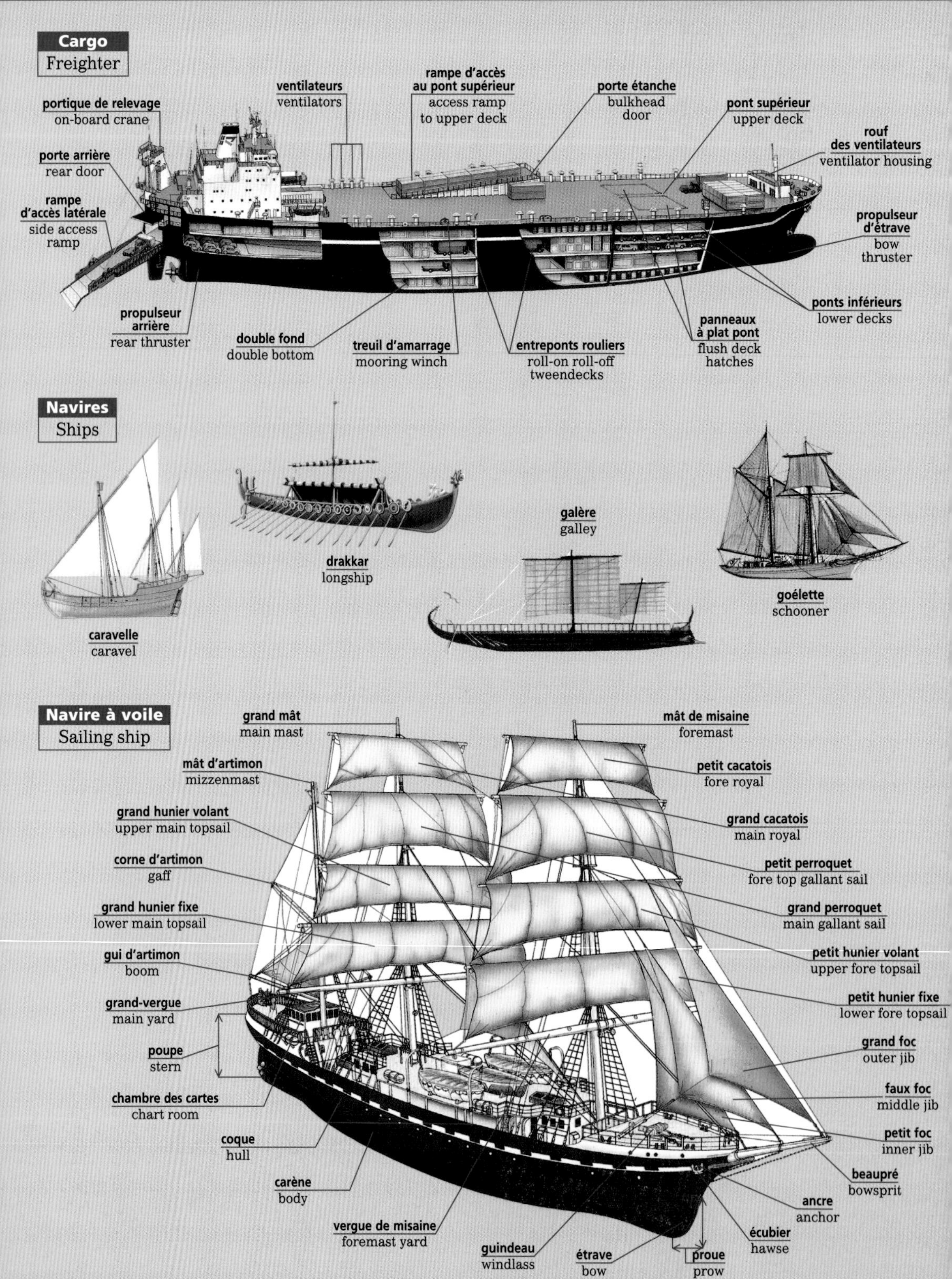
Cargo
Freighter
portique de relevage
on-board crane
ventilateurs
ventilators
rampe d'accès au pont supérieur
access ramp to upper deck
porte étanche
bulkhead door
pont supérieur
upper deck
rouf des ventilateurs
ventilator housing
porte arrière
rear door
rampe d'accès latérale
side access ramp
propulseur d'étrave
bow thruster
ponts inférieurs
lower decks
propulseur arrière
rear thruster
double fond
double bottom
treuil d'amarrage
mooring winch
entreponts rouliers
roll-on roll-off tweendecks
panneaux à plat pont
flush deck hatches
Navires
Ships
caravelle
caravel
drakkar
longship
galère
galley
goélette
schooner
Navire à voile
Sailing ship
grand mât
main mast
mât de misaine
foremast
mât d'artimon
mizzenmast
petit cacatois
fore royal
grand hunier volant
upper main topsail
grand cacatois
main royal
corne d'artimon
gaff
petit perroquet
fore top gallant sail
grand hunier fixe
lower main topsail
grand perroquet
main gallant sail
gui d'artimon
boom
petit hunier volant
upper fore topsail
grand-vergue
main yard
petit hunier fixe
lower fore topsail
poupe
stern
grand foc
outer jib
chambre des cartes
chart room
faux foc
middle jib
petit foc
inner jib
coque
hull
beaupré
bowsprit
carène
body
ancre
anchor
vergue de misaine
foremast yard
écubier
hawse
guindeau
windlass
étrave
bow
proue
prow

Hélicoptère
Helicopter

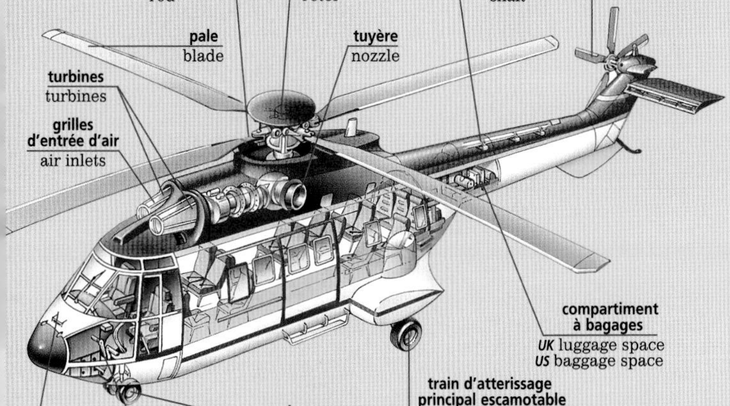

bielle de commande de pas
pitch-control rod

rotor principal
main rotor

arbre de transmission
transmission shaft

rotor anticouple
tail rotor

pale
blade

tuyère
nozzle

turbines
turbines

grilles d'entrée d'air
air inlets

compartiment à bagages
UK luggage space
US baggage space

train d'atterrissage principal escamotable
retractable landing gear

train avant
front landing gear

détecteur de givre
ice detector

palonnier
rudder bar

Montgolfière
Hot-air ballon

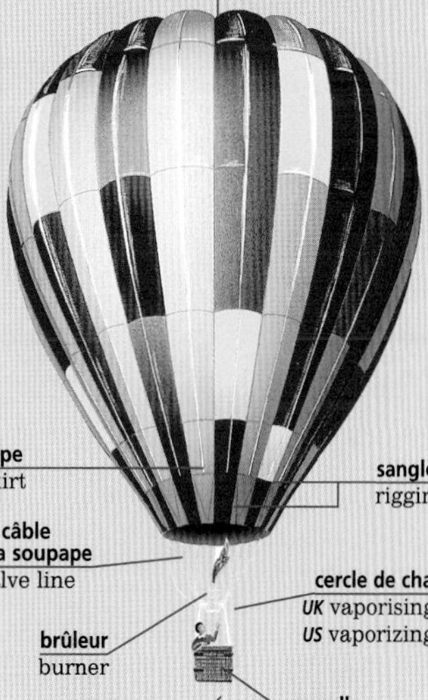

soupape
valve

jupe
skirt

sangles
rigging

câble de la soupape
valve line

cercle de charge
UK vaporising coil
US vaporizing coil

brûleur
burner

nacelle
basket

guiderope
tether line

Avion de transport commercial
Commercial passenger plane

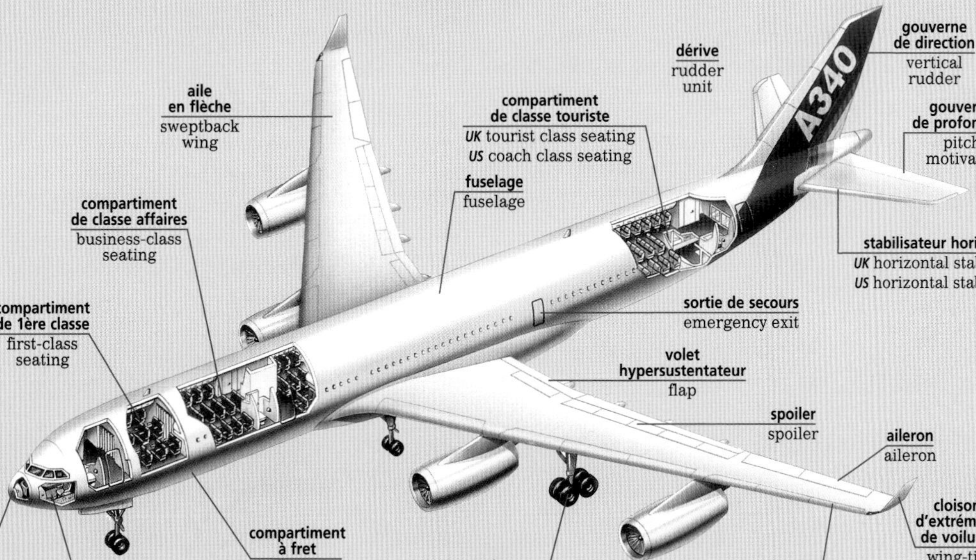

dérive
rudder unit

gouverne de direction
vertical rudder

aile en flèche
sweptback wing

compartiment de classe touriste
UK tourist class seating
US coach class seating

gouverne de profondeur
pitch motivator

fuselage
fuselage

compartiment de classe affaires
business-class seating

stabilisateur horizontal
UK horizontal stabiliser
US horizontal stabilizer

sortie de secours
emergency exit

compartiment de 1ère classe
first-class seating

volet hypersustentateur
flap

spoiler
spoiler

aileron
aileron

cloison d'extrémité de voilure
wing-tip fence

radar
radar

compartiment à fret
cargo hold

train d'atterrissage
landing gear

poste de pilotage (cockpit)
cockpit

bec de bord d'attaque
leading-edge slat

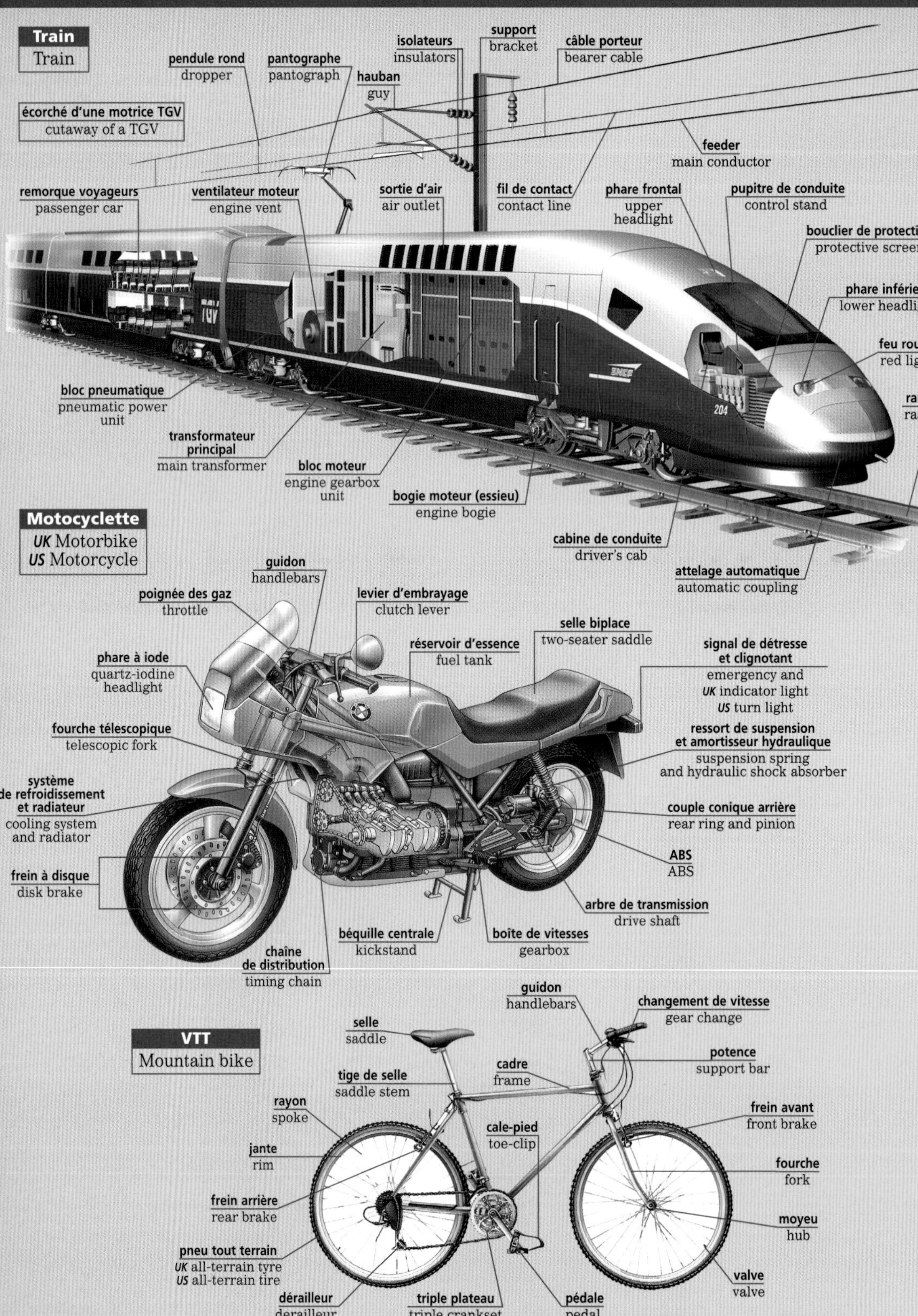
Train
Train
écorché d'une motrice TGV
cutaway of a TGV
pendule rond
dropper
pantographe
pantograph
isolateurs
insulators
hauban
guy
support
bracket
câble porteur
bearer cable
feeder
main conductor
remorque voyageurs
passenger car
ventilateur moteur
engine vent
sortie d'air
air outlet
fil de contact
contact line
phare frontal
upper headlight
pupitre de conduite
control stand
bouclier de protection
protective screen
phare inférieur
lower headlight
feu rouge
red light
rail
rail
bloc pneumatique
pneumatic power unit
transformateur principal
main transformer
bloc moteur
engine gearbox unit
bogie moteur (essieu)
engine bogie
cabine de conduite
driver's cab
attelage automatique
automatic coupling
Motocyclette
UK Motorbike
US Motorcycle
guidon
handlebars
poignée des gaz
throttle
levier d'embrayage
clutch lever
selle biplace
two-seater saddle
réservoir d'essence
fuel tank
phare à iode
quartz-iodine headlight
signal de détresse et clignotant
emergency and UK indicator light US turn light
fourche télescopique
telescopic fork
ressort de suspension et amortisseur hydraulique
suspension spring and hydraulic shock absorber
système de refroidissement et radiateur
cooling system and radiator
couple conique arrière
rear ring and pinion
ABS
ABS
frein à disque
disk brake
arbre de transmission
drive shaft
béquille centrale
kickstand
boîte de vitesses
gearbox
chaîne de distribution
timing chain
VTT
Mountain bike
guidon
handlebars
changement de vitesse
gear change
selle
saddle
potence
support bar
cadre
frame
tige de selle
saddle stem
rayon
spoke
frein avant
front brake
cale-pied
toe-clip
jante
rim
fourche
fork
frein arrière
rear brake
moyeu
hub
pneu tout terrain
UK all-terrain tyre
US all-terrain tire
valve
valve
dérailleur
derailleur
triple plateau
triple crankset
pédale
pedal

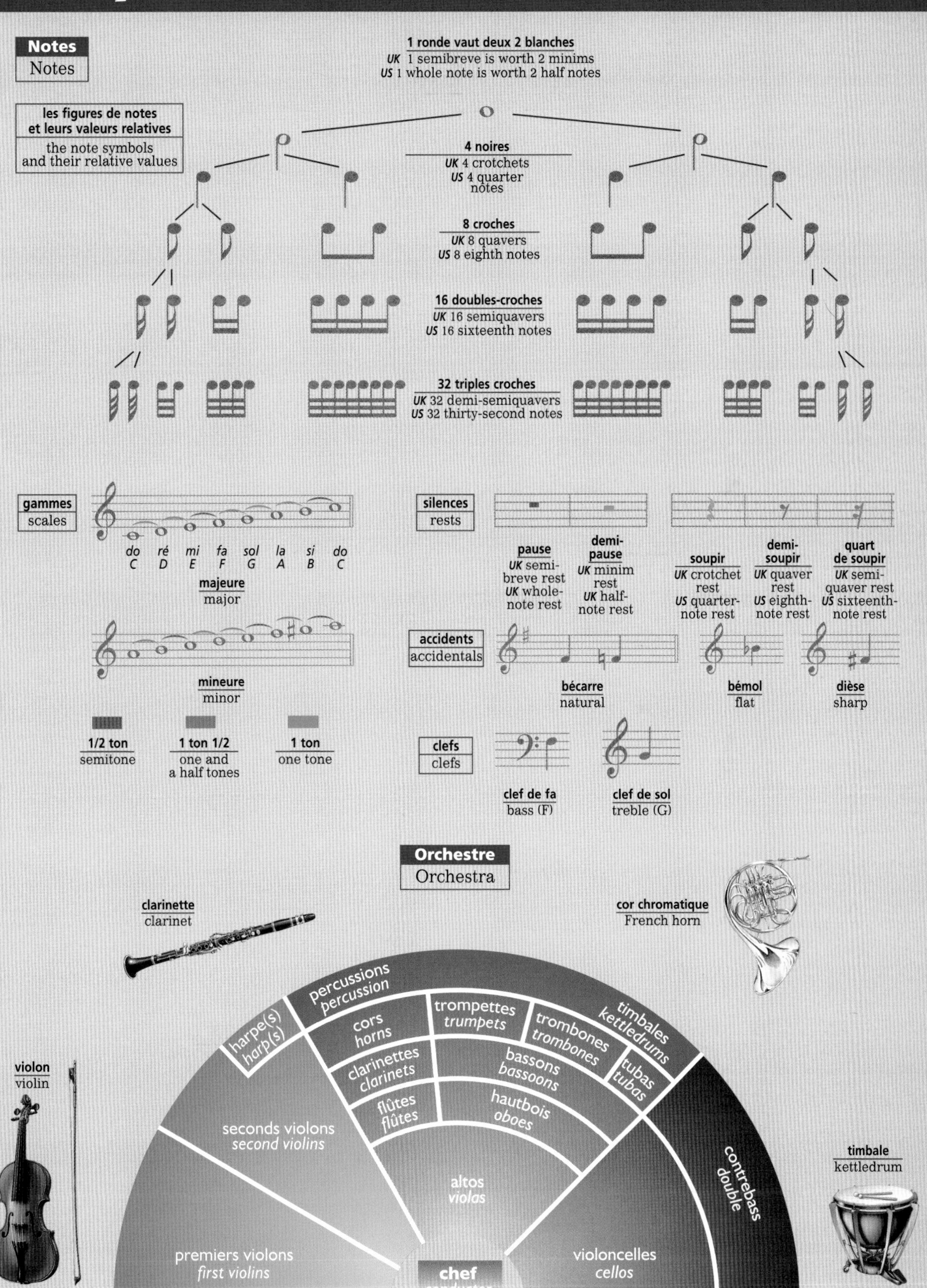
Notes
Notes
les figures de notes et leurs valeurs relatives
the note symbols and their relative values
1 ronde vaut deux 2 blanches
UK 1 semibreve is worth 2 minims
US 1 whole note is worth 2 half notes
4 noires
UK 4 crotchets
US 4 quarter notes
8 croches
UK 8 quavers
US 8 eighth notes
16 doubles-croches
UK 16 semiquavers
US 16 sixteenth notes
32 triples croches
UK 32 demi-semiquavers
US 32 thirty-second notes
gammes
scales
do ré mi fa sol la si do
C D E F G A B C
majeure
major
mineure
minor
1/2 ton
semitone
1 ton 1/2
one and a half tones
1 ton
one tone
silences
rests
pause
UK semibreve rest
UK whole-note rest
demi-pause
UK minim rest
UK half-note rest
soupir
UK crotchet rest
US quarter-note rest
demi-soupir
UK quaver rest
US eighth-note rest
quart de soupir
UK semi-quaver rest
US sixteenth-note rest
accidents
accidentals
bécarre
natural
bémol
flat
dièse
sharp
clefs
clefs
clef de fa
bass (F)
clef de sol
treble (G)
Orchestre
Orchestra
clarinette
clarinet
cor chromatique
French horn
violon
violin
timbale
kettledrum
percussions
percussion
harpe(s)
harp(s)
trompettes
trumpets
trombones
trombones
timbales
kettledrums
cors
horns
clarinettes
clarinets
bassons
bassoons
tubas
tubas
flûtes
flûtes
hautbois
oboes
seconds violons
second violins
altos
violas
contrebass
double
premiers violons
first violins
chef
conductor
violoncelles
cellos

Football
UK Football
US Soccer

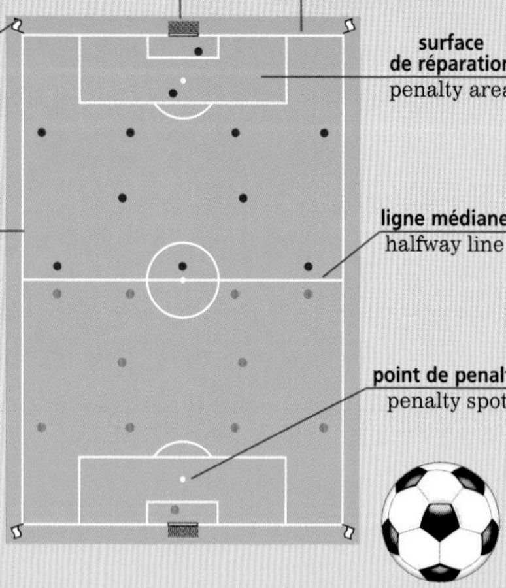

point de corner
corner
but
goal
ligne de but
goal line
surface de réparation
penalty area
ligne de touche
touchline
ligne médiane
halfway line
point de penalty
penalty spot

Rugby
Rugby

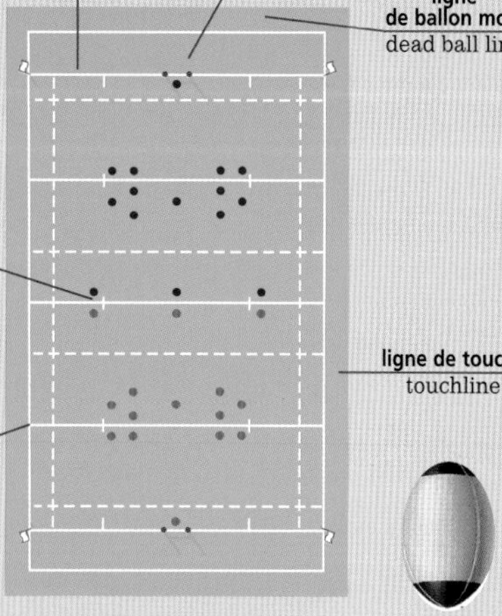

ligne de but
goal line
en-but
in-goal
ligne de ballon mort
dead ball line
ligne de milieu de terrain
halfway line
ligne de touche
touchline
ligne des 22 mètres
UK 22 metre line
US 22 meter line

Basket-ball
Basketball

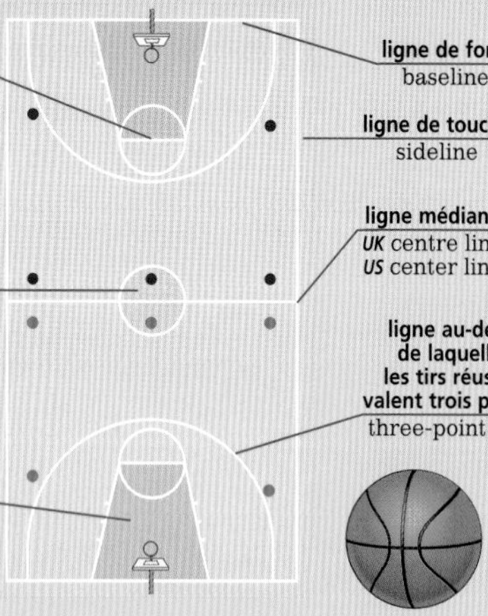

ligne des lancers francs
free-throw line
ligne de fond
baseline
ligne de touche
sideline
ligne médiane
UK centre line
US center line
cercle central
UK centre circle
US center circle
ligne au-delà de laquelle les tirs réussis valent trois points
three-point line
couloir des lancers francs
free-throw lane

Tennis
Tennis

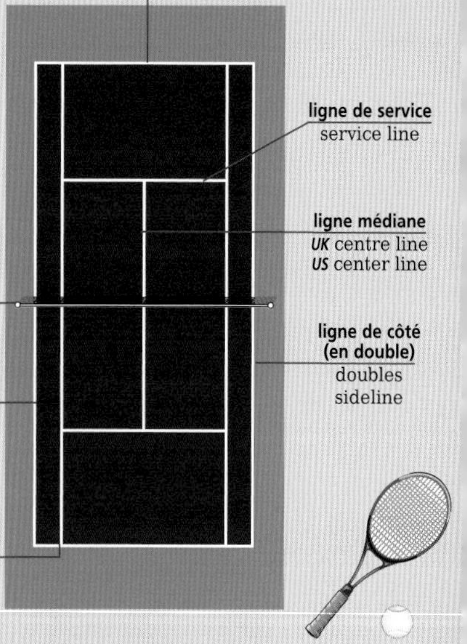

ligne de fond
baseline
ligne de service
service line
ligne médiane
UK centre line
US center line
filet
net
ligne de côté (en double)
doubles sideline
ligne de côté (en simple)
singles sideline
ligne de côté de service
service sideline

Athlétisme
UK Athletics
US Track and field

rivière de steeple
water jump
saut à la perche
pole vault
lancer du disque
discus
lancer du javelot
javelin
saut en hauteur
high jump
lancer du poids
shot put
piste de 400 m
UK 400 metre track
US 400 meter track
saut en longueur et triple saut
long jump and triple jump
lancer du marteau
hammer

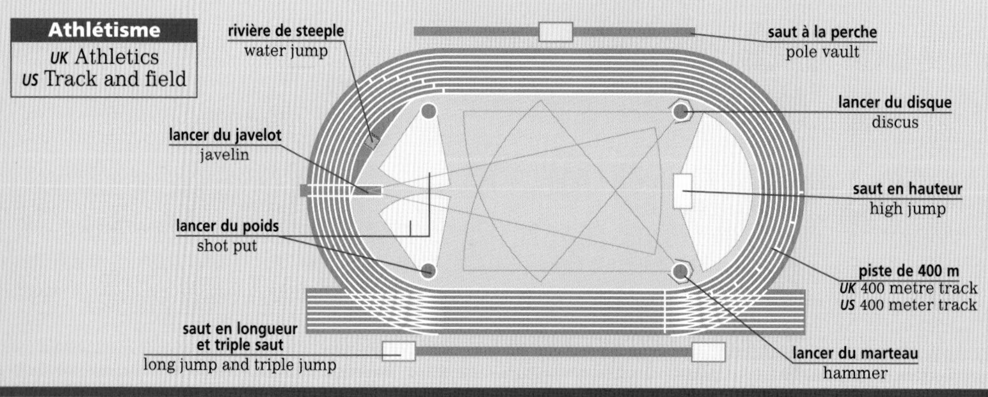

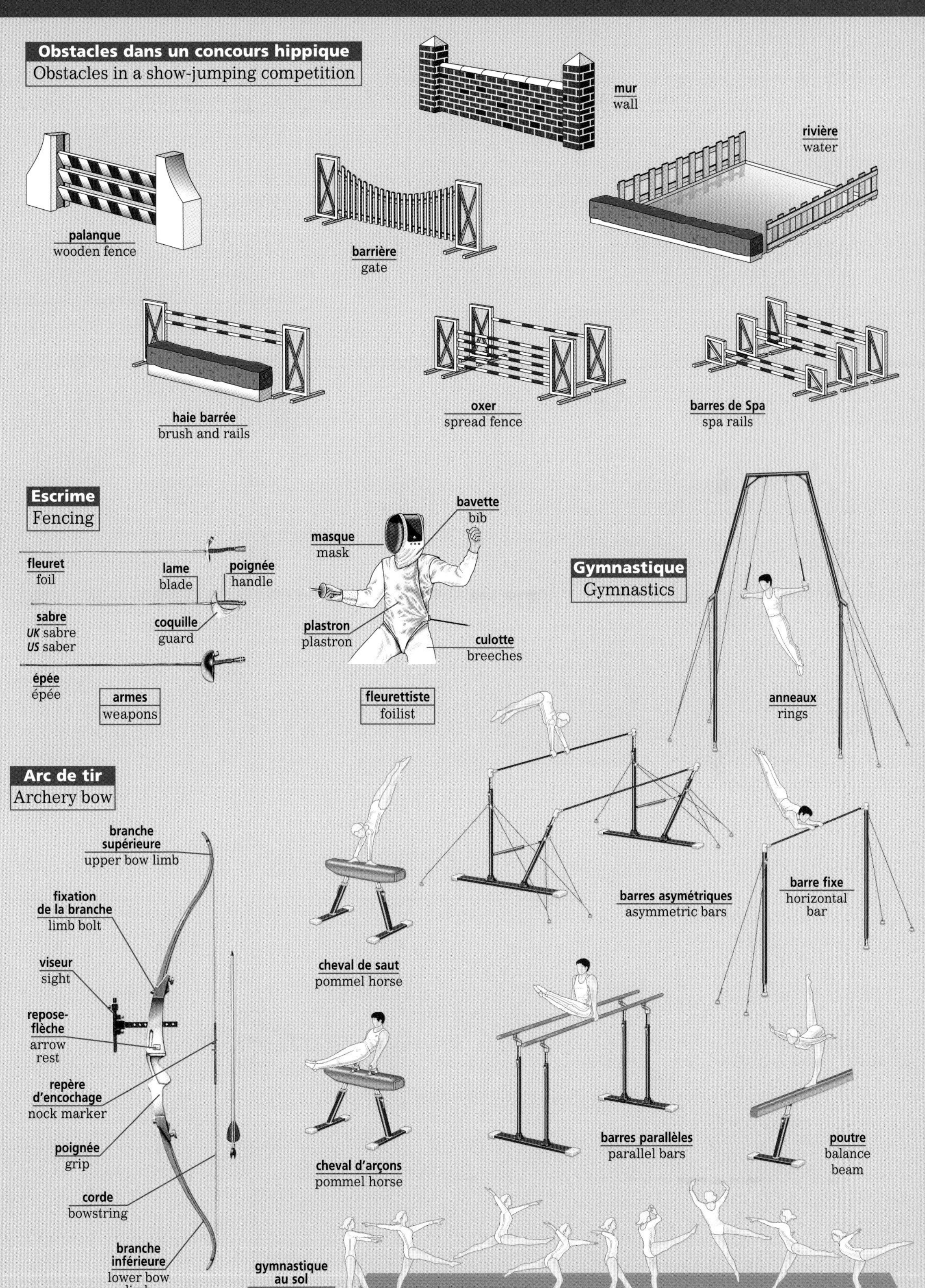
Obstacles dans un concours hippique
Obstacles in a show-jumping competition
mur
wall
rivière
water
palanque
wooden fence
barrière
gate
haie barrée
brush and rails
oxer
spread fence
barres de Spa
spa rails
Escrime
Fencing
fleuret
foil
lame
blade
poignée
handle
sabre
UK sabre
US saber
coquille
guard
épée
épée
armes
weapons
masque
mask
bavette
bib
plastron
plastron
culotte
breeches
fleurettiste
foilist
Gymnastique
Gymnastics
anneaux
rings
Arc de tir
Archery bow
branche supérieure
upper bow limb
fixation de la branche
limb bolt
viseur
sight
repose-flèche
arrow rest
repère d'encochage
nock marker
poignée
grip
corde
bowstring
branche inférieure
lower bow limb
cheval de saut
pommel horse
barres asymétriques
asymmetric bars
barre fixe
horizontal bar
cheval d'arçons
pommel horse
barres parallèles
parallel bars
poutre
balance beam
gymnastique au sol
floor exercises

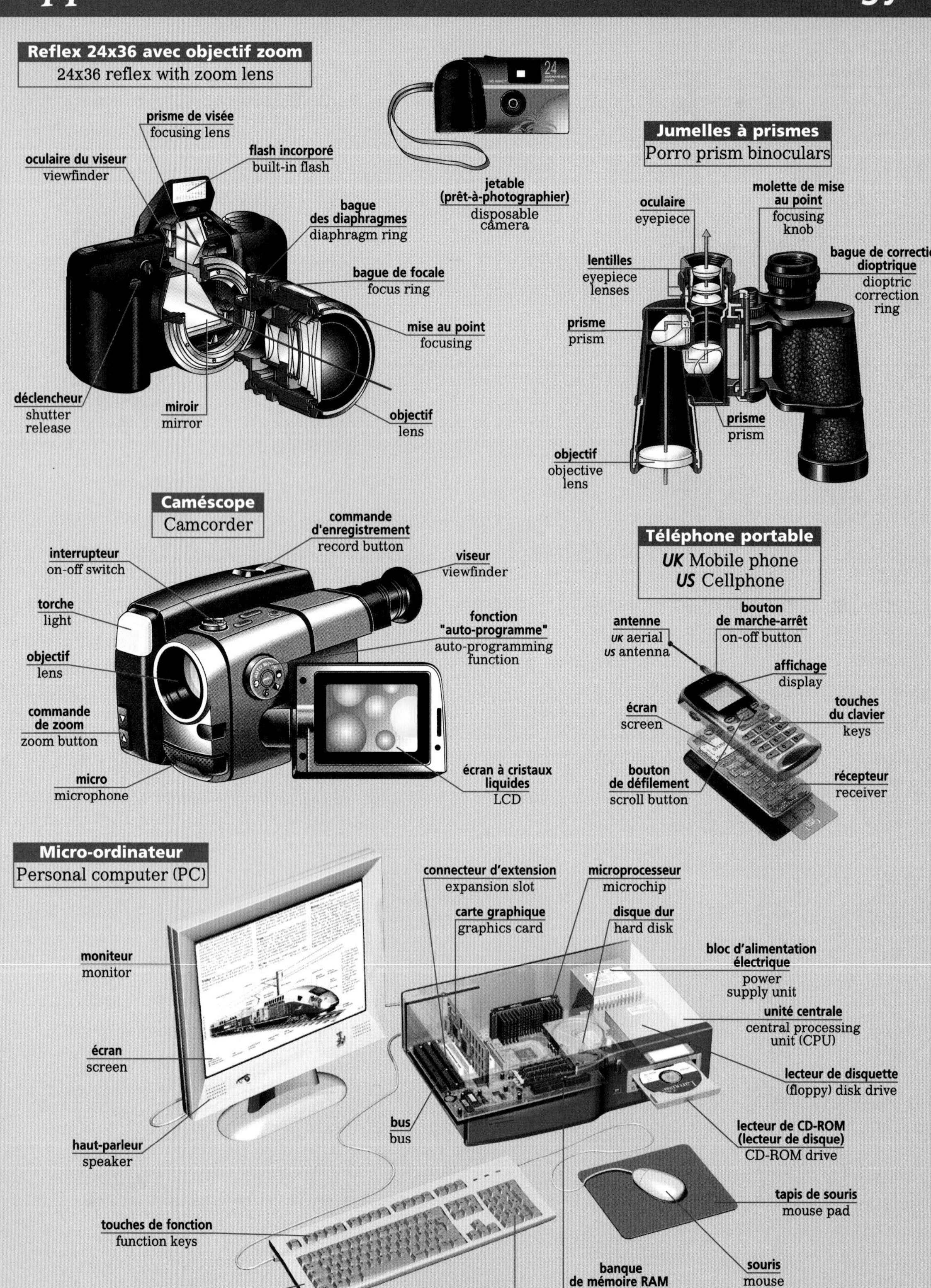

Reflex 24x36 avec objectif zoom
24x36 reflex with zoom lens
prisme de visée
focusing lens
oculaire du viseur
viewfinder
flash incorporé
built-in flash
bague des diaphragmes
diaphragm ring
bague de focale
focus ring
mise au point
focusing
déclencheur
shutter release
miroir
mirror
objectif
lens
jetable (prêt-à-photographier)
disposable camera
Jumelles à prismes
Porro prism binoculars
oculaire
eyepiece
molette de mise au point
focusing knob
bague de correction dioptrique
dioptric correction ring
lentilles
eyepiece lenses
prisme
prism
prisme
prism
objectif
objective lens
Caméscope
Camcorder
commande d'enregistrement
record button
interrupteur
on-off switch
viseur
viewfinder
torche
light
fonction "auto-programme"
auto-programming function
objectif
lens
commande de zoom
zoom button
micro
microphone
écran à cristaux liquides
LCD
Téléphone portable
UK Mobile phone
US Cellphone
antenne
UK aerial
US antenna
bouton de marche-arrêt
on-off button
affichage
display
écran
screen
touches du clavier
keys
bouton de défilement
scroll button
récepteur
receiver
Micro-ordinateur
Personal computer (PC)
connecteur d'extension
expansion slot
microprocesseur
microchip
carte graphique
graphics card
disque dur
hard disk
moniteur
monitor
bloc d'alimentation électrique
power supply unit
unité centrale
central processing unit (CPU)
écran
screen
lecteur de disquette
(floppy) disk drive
bus
bus
lecteur de CD-ROM (lecteur de disque)
CD-ROM drive
haut-parleur
speaker
tapis de souris
mouse pad
touches de fonction
function keys
souris
mouse
banque de mémoire RAM (mémoire vive)
RAM (read only memory)
clavier
keyboard
pavé numérique
numeric keypad

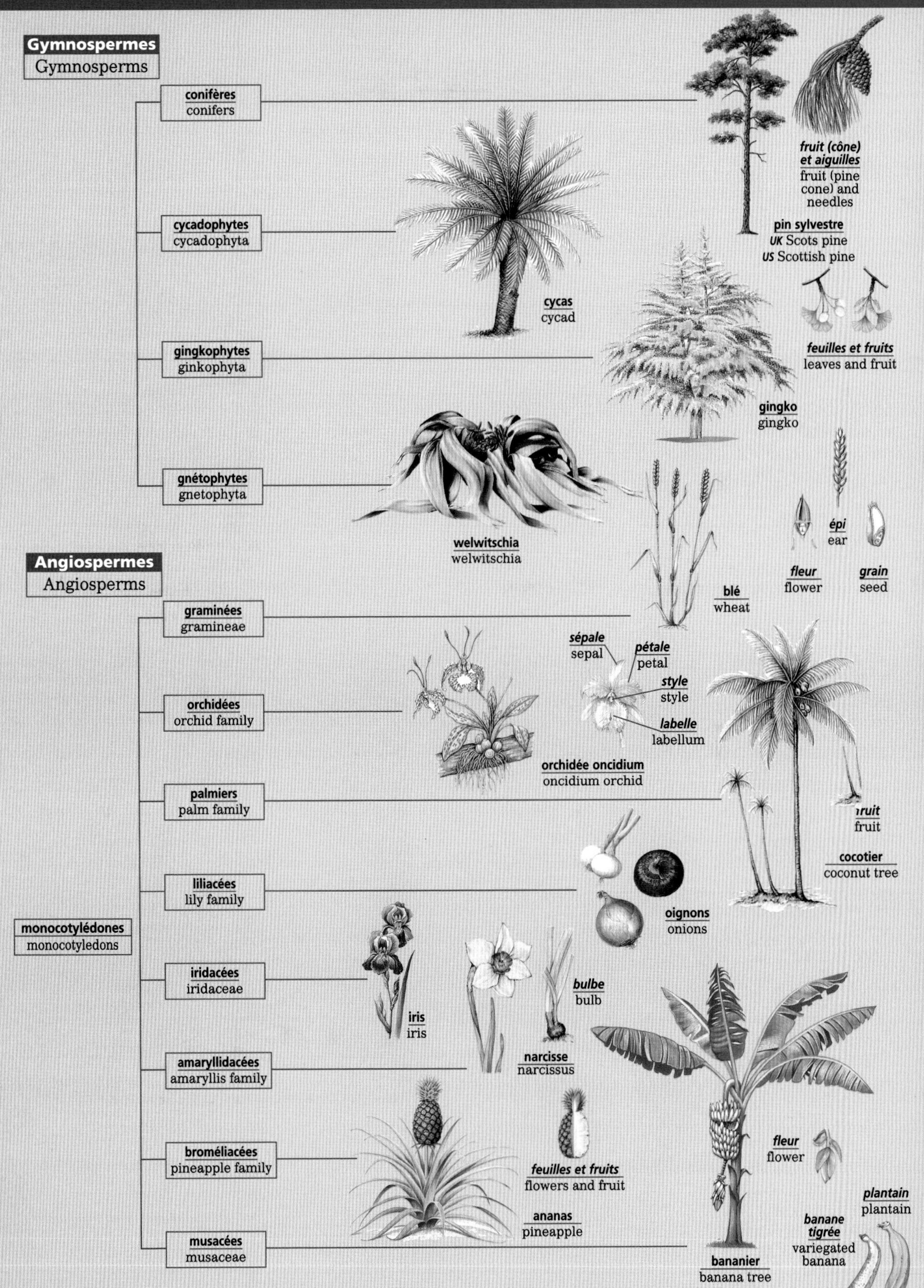
Gymnospermes
Gymnosperms
conifères
conifers
cycadophytes
cycadophyta
gingkophytes
ginkophyta
gnétophytes
gnetophyta
fruit (cône) et aiguilles
fruit (pine cone) and needles
pin sylvestre
UK Scots pine
US Scottish pine
cycas
cycad
feuilles et fruits
leaves and fruit
gingko
gingko
welwitschia
welwitschia
épi
ear
fleur
flower
grain
seed
blé
wheat
Angiospermes
Angiosperms
graminées
gramineae
orchidées
orchid family
sépale
sepal
pétale
petal
style
style
labelle
labellum
orchidée oncidium
oncidium orchid
palmiers
palm family
fruit
cocotier
coconut tree
liliacées
lily family
oignons
onions
monocotylédones
monocotyledons
iridacées
iridaceae
iris
iris
bulbe
bulb
narcisse
narcissus
amaryllidacées
amaryllis family
broméliacées
pineapple family
feuilles et fruits
flowers and fruit
ananas
pineapple
fleur
flower
plantain
plantain
banane tigrée
variegated banana
musacées
musaceae
bananier
banana tree

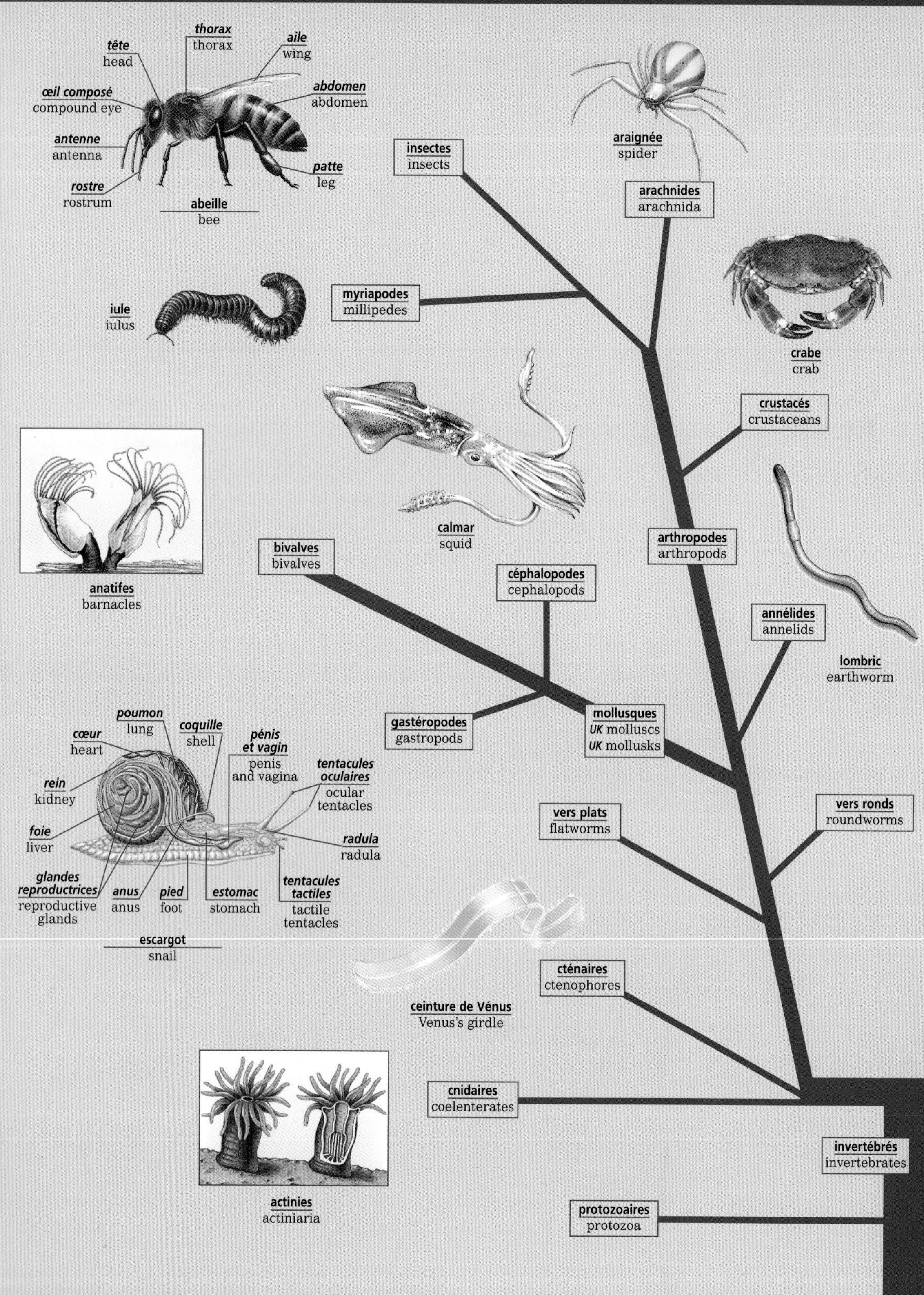
tête
head
thorax
thorax
aile
wing
œil composé
compound eye
abdomen
abdomen
antenne
antenna
patte
leg
rostre
rostrum
abeille
bee
araignée
spider
insectes
insects
arachnides
arachnida
iule
iulus
myriapodes
millipedes
crabe
crab
crustacés
crustaceans
calmar
squid
anatifes
barnacles
bivalves
bivalves
arthropodes
arthropods
céphalopodes
cephalopods
annélides
annelids
lombric
earthworm
gastéropodes
gastropods
mollusques
UK molluscs
UK mollusks
poumon
lung
cœur
heart
coquille
shell
pénis
et vagin
penis
and vagina
tentacules
oculaires
ocular
tentacles
rein
kidney
foie
liver
radula
radula
vers plats
flatworms
vers ronds
roundworms
glandes
reproductrices
reproductive
glands
anus
anus
pied
foot
estomac
stomach
tentacules
tactiles
tactile
tentacles
escargot
snail
cténaires
ctenophores
ceinture de Vénus
Venus's girdle
cnidaires
coelenterates
invertébrés
invertebrates
actinies
actiniaria
protozoaires
protozoa

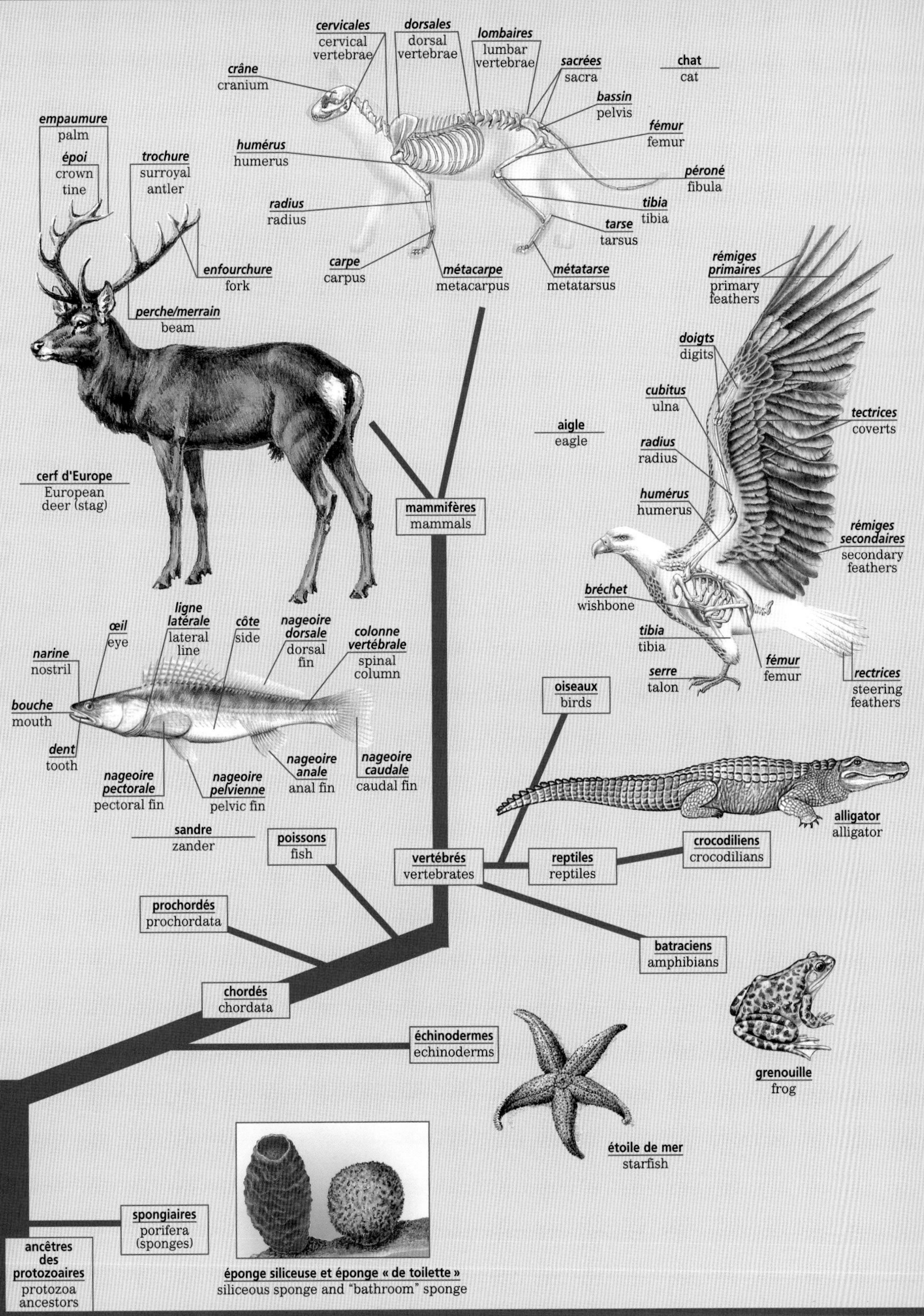
cervicales
cervical vertebrae
dorsales
dorsal vertebrae
lombaires
lumbar vertebrae
crâne
cranium
sacrées
sacra
chat
cat
bassin
pelvis
fémur
femur
humérus
humerus
péroné
fibula
radius
radius
tibia
tibia
tarse
tarsus
carpe
carpus
métacarpe
metacarpus
métatarse
metatarsus
empaumure
palm
époi
crown tine
trochure
surroyal antler
enfourchure
fork
perche/merrain
beam
cerf d'Europe
European deer (stag)
rémiges primaires
primary feathers
doigts
digits
cubitus
ulna
tectrices
coverts
aigle
eagle
radius
radius
humérus
humerus
rémiges secondaires
secondary feathers
bréchet
wishbone
tibia
tibia
serre
talon
fémur
femur
rectrices
steering feathers
mammifères
mammals
ligne latérale
lateral line
œil
eye
côte
side
nageoire dorsale
dorsal fin
colonne vertébrale
spinal column
narine
nostril
bouche
mouth
dent
tooth
nageoire pectorale
pectoral fin
nageoire pelvienne
pelvic fin
nageoire anale
anal fin
nageoire caudale
caudal fin
sandre
zander
oiseaux
birds
alligator
alligator
poissons
fish
vertébrés
vertebrates
reptiles
reptiles
crocodiliens
crocodilians
prochordés
prochordata
batraciens
amphibians
chordés
chordata
échinodermes
echinoderms
grenouille
frog
étoile de mer
starfish
spongiaires
porifera (sponges)
ancêtres des protozoaires
protozoa ancestors
éponge siliceuse et éponge « de toilette »
siliceous sponge and "bathroom" sponge

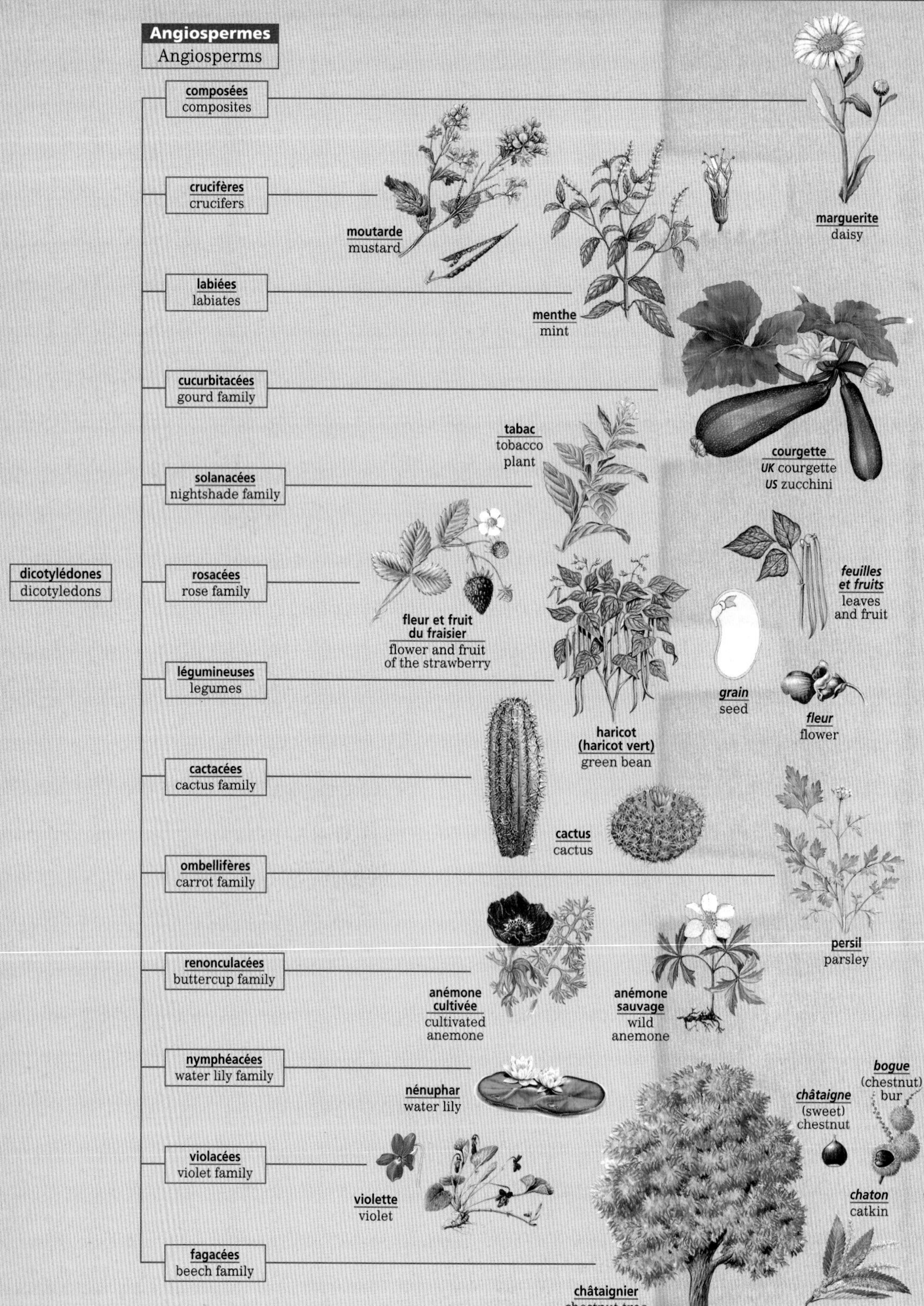
Angiospermes
Angiosperms
dicotylédones
dicotyledons
composées
composites
crucifères
crucifers
labiées
labiates
cucurbitacées
gourd family
solanacées
nightshade family
rosacées
rose family
légumineuses
legumes
cactacées
cactus family
ombellifères
carrot family
renonculacées
buttercup family
nymphéacées
water lily family
violacées
violet family
fagacées
beech family
marguerite
daisy
moutarde
mustard
menthe
mint
courgette
UK courgette
US zucchini
tabac
tobacco plant
fleur et fruit du fraisier
flower and fruit of the strawberry
feuilles et fruits
leaves and fruit
grain
seed
fleur
flower
haricot (haricot vert)
green bean
cactus
cactus
persil
parsley
anémone cultivée
cultivated anemone
anémone sauvage
wild anemone
nénuphar
water lily
bogue
(chestnut) bur
châtaigne
(sweet) chestnut
chaton
catkin
violette
violet
châtaignier
chestnut tree

Atlas des pays anglophones
Atlas of English-speaking countries

Atlas des pays francophones
Atlas of French-speaking countries

le monde anglophone the English-speaking world

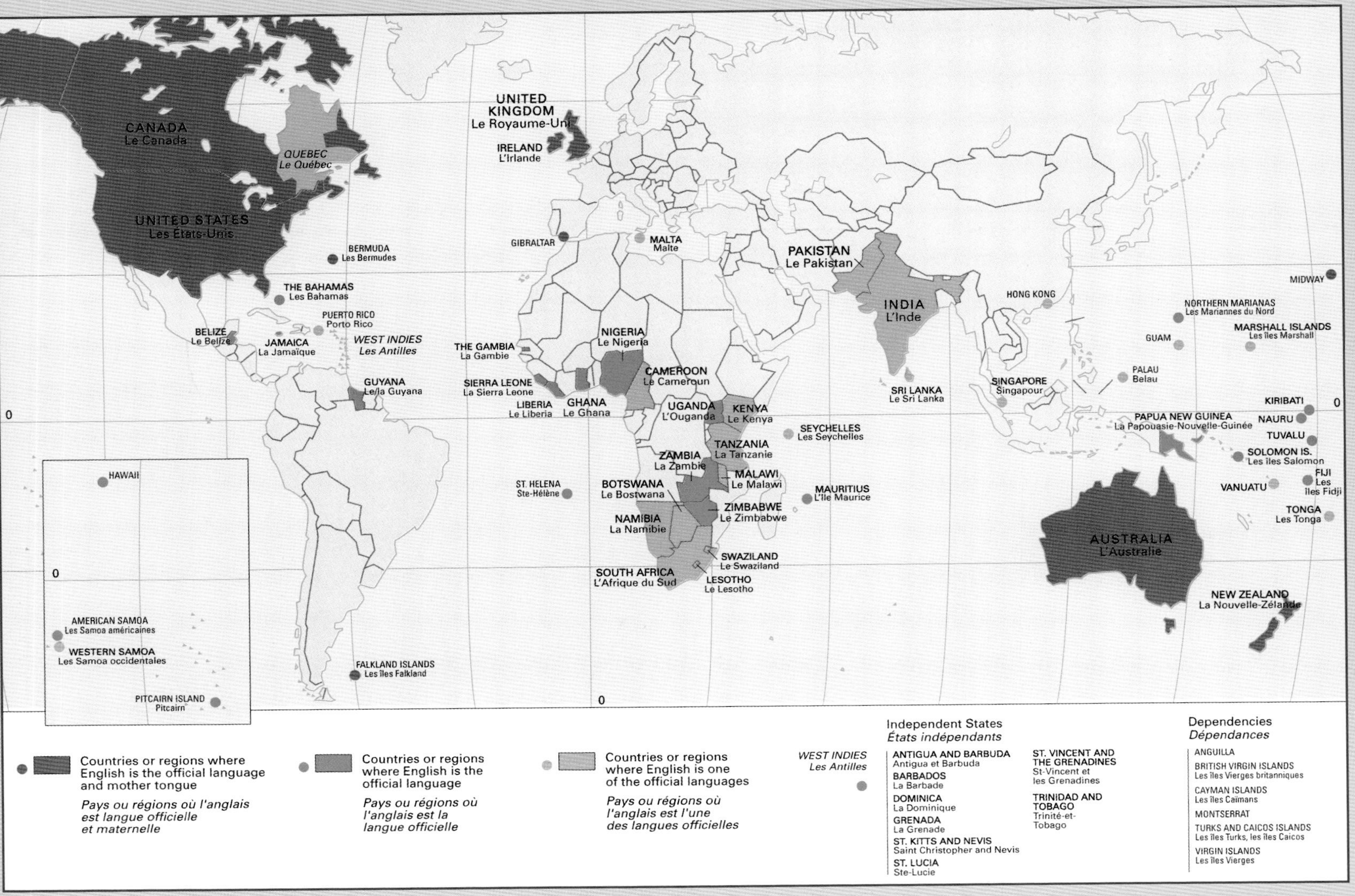
CANADA
Le Canada
UNITED STATES
Les États-Unis
QUEBEC
Le Québec
BERMUDA
Les Bermudes
THE BAHAMAS
Les Bahamas
PUERTO RICO
Porto Rico
WEST INDIES
Les Antilles
JAMAICA
La Jamaïque
BELIZE
Le Belize
GUYANA
Le/la Guyana
FALKLAND ISLANDS
Les îles Falkland
HAWAII
AMERICAN SAMOA
Les Samoa américaines
WESTERN SAMOA
Les Samoa occidentales
PITCAIRN ISLAND
Pitcairn
UNITED KINGDOM
Le Royaume-Uni
IRELAND
L'Irlande
GIBRALTAR
THE GAMBIA
La Gambie
SIERRA LEONE
La Sierra Leone
LIBERIA
Le Liberia
GHANA
Le Ghana
NIGERIA
Le Nigeria
CAMEROON
Le Cameroun
MALTA
Malte
ST. HELENA
Ste-Hélène
UGANDA
L'Ouganda
KENYA
Le Kenya
TANZANIA
La Tanzanie
ZAMBIA
La Zambie
MALAWI
Le Malawi
ZIMBABWE
Le Zimbabwe
BOTSWANA
Le Bostwana
NAMIBIA
La Namibie
SOUTH AFRICA
L'Afrique du Sud
SWAZILAND
Le Swaziland
LESOTHO
Le Lesotho
SEYCHELLES
Les Seychelles
MAURITIUS
L'île Maurice
PAKISTAN
Le Pakistan
INDIA
L'Inde
SRI LANKA
Le Sri Lanka
SINGAPORE
Singapour
HONG KONG
PALAU
Belau
GUAM
NORTHERN MARIANAS
Les Mariannes du Nord
MARSHALL ISLANDS
Les îles Marshall
MIDWAY
KIRIBATI
NAURU
TUVALU
SOLOMON IS.
Les îles Salomon
FIJI
Les îles Fidji
TONGA
Les Tonga
VANUATU
PAPUA NEW GUINEA
La Papouasie-Nouvelle-Guinée
AUSTRALIA
L'Australie
NEW ZEALAND
La Nouvelle-Zélande
0
Countries or regions where English is the official language and mother tongue
Pays ou régions où l'anglais est langue officielle et maternelle
Countries or regions where English is the official language
Pays ou régions où l'anglais est la langue officielle
Countries or regions where English is one of the official languages
Pays ou régions où l'anglais est l'une des langues officielles
WEST INDIES
Les Antilles
Independent States
États indépendants
ANTIGUA AND BARBUDA
Antigua et Barbuda
BARBADOS
La Barbade
DOMINICA
La Dominique
GRENADA
La Grenade
ST. KITTS AND NEVIS
Saint Christopher and Nevis
ST. LUCIA
Ste-Lucie
ST. VINCENT AND THE GRENADINES
St-Vincent et les Grenadines
TRINIDAD AND TOBAGO
Trinité-et-Tobago
Dependencies
Dépendances
ANGUILLA
BRITISH VIRGIN ISLANDS
Les îles Vierges britanniques
CAYMAN ISLANDS
Les îles Caïmans
MONTSERRAT
TURKS AND CAICOS ISLANDS
Les îles Turks, les îles Caïcos
VIRGIN ISLANDS
Les îles Vierges

CANADA
MEXICO
MEXIQUE
ATLANTIC OCEAN
OCÉAN ATLANTIQUE
PACIFIC OCEAN
OCÉAN PACIFIQUE
Gulf of Mexico
Golfe du Mexique
Gulf of California
Golfe de Californie
Straits of Florida
Détroit de Floride
Tropic of Cancer
Tropique du Cancer
Rocky Mountains
Montagnes Rocheuses
Appalachian Mts
Appalaches
Lake Superior
Lac Supérieur
Lake Michigan
Lac Michigan
Lake Huron
Lac Huron
L. Erie
Lac Érié
L. Ontario
Great Salt Lake
Grand Lac Salé
Mississippi
Arkansa
Rio Grande
Colorado
Columbia
Yukon
MAINE (ME)
NEW YORK (NY)
PENNSYLVANIA (PA)
PENNSYLVANIE
WEST VIRGINIA (WV)
VIRGINIE OCCIDENTALE
VIRGINIA (VA)
VIRGINIE
NORTH CAROLINA (NC)
CAROLINE DU NORD
SOUTH CAROLINA (SC)
CAROLINE DU SUD
GEORGIA (GA)
GÉORGIE
FLORIDA (FL)
FLORIDE
ALABAMA (AL)
MISSISSIPPI (MS)
TENNESSEE (TN)
KENTUCKY (KY)
OHIO (OH)
INDIANA (IN)
ILLINOIS (IL)
MICHIGAN (MI)
WISCONSIN (WI)
MINNESOTA (MI)
IOWA (IA)
MISSOURI (MO)
ARKANSAS (AR)
LOUISIANA (LA)
LOUISIANE
TEXAS (TX)
OKLAHOMA (OK)
KANSAS (KS)
NEBRASKA (NE)
SOUTH DAKOTA (SD)
DAKOTA DU SUD
NORTH DAKOTA (ND)
DAKOTA DU NORD
MONTANA (MT)
WYOMING (WY)
COLORADO (CO)
NEW MEXICO (NM)
NOUVEAU-MEXIQUE
ARIZONA (AZ)
UTAH (UT)
IDAHO (ID)
NEVADA (NV)
CALIFORNIA (CA)
CALIFORNIE
OREGON (OR)
WASHINGTON (WA)
ALASKA (AK)
HAWAII (HI)
Augusta
Concord
Boston
Providence
Hartford
Montpelier
Albany
New York
Newark
Trenton
Philadelphia
Philadelphie
Dover
Baltimore
Annapolis
WASHINGTON D.C.
Buffalo
Harrisburg
Pittsburgh
Richmond
Raleigh
Charleston
Columbia
Jacksonville
Miami
Tallahassee
Atlanta
Cleveland
Columbus
Frankfort
Nashville
Birmingham
Montgomery
Detroit
Lansing
Indianapolis
Chicago
Milwaukee
Madison
Springfield
St Louis
Jefferson City
Kansas City
Memphis
Jackson
New Orleans
La Nouvelle-Orléans
Baton Rouge
Little Rock
Des Moines
St Paul
Minneapolis
Houston
Dallas
Fort Worth
Austin
San Antonio
Oklahoma City
Topeka
Lincoln
Pierre
Bismarck
Denver
Cheyenne
Mt Elbert 14431 ft 4398 m
Santa Fe
El Paso
Phoenix
Grand Canyon
Salt Lake City
Helena
Boise
Carson City
Las Vegas
Mt Whitney 14495 ft 4418 m
Sacramento
San Francisco
Oakland
San Jose
Los Angeles
Long Beach
San Diego
Olympia
Seattle
Portland
Salem
Honolulu
Hawaii
Juneau
Mt McKinley 20320 ft 6194 m
40
30
20
60
150
155
160
170
300 km
1000 km
Federal capital
Capitale fédérale
State capital
Capitale d'État
Major city
Ville importante
Other cities
Autres villes
International boundary
Frontière internationale
State boundary
Limite d'État
500 1000 2000 m
1000 km
1 NEW HAMPSHIRE (NH)
2 VERMONT (VT)
3 MASSACHUSETTS (MA)
4 RHODE ISLAND (RI)
5 CONNECTICUT (CT)
6 NEW JERSEY (NJ)
7 MARYLAND (MD)
8 DELAWARE (DE)

les îles Britanniques — the British Isles

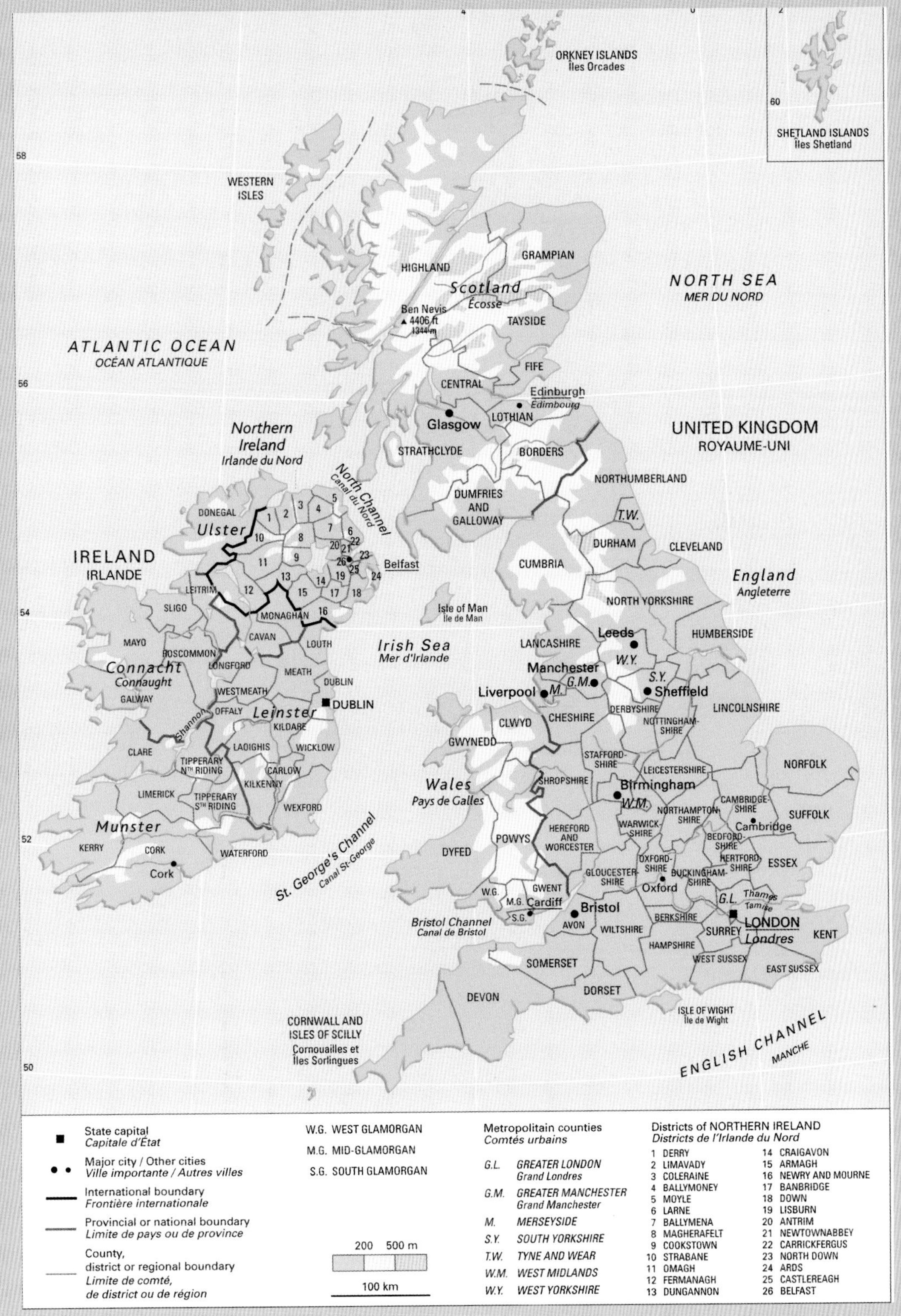

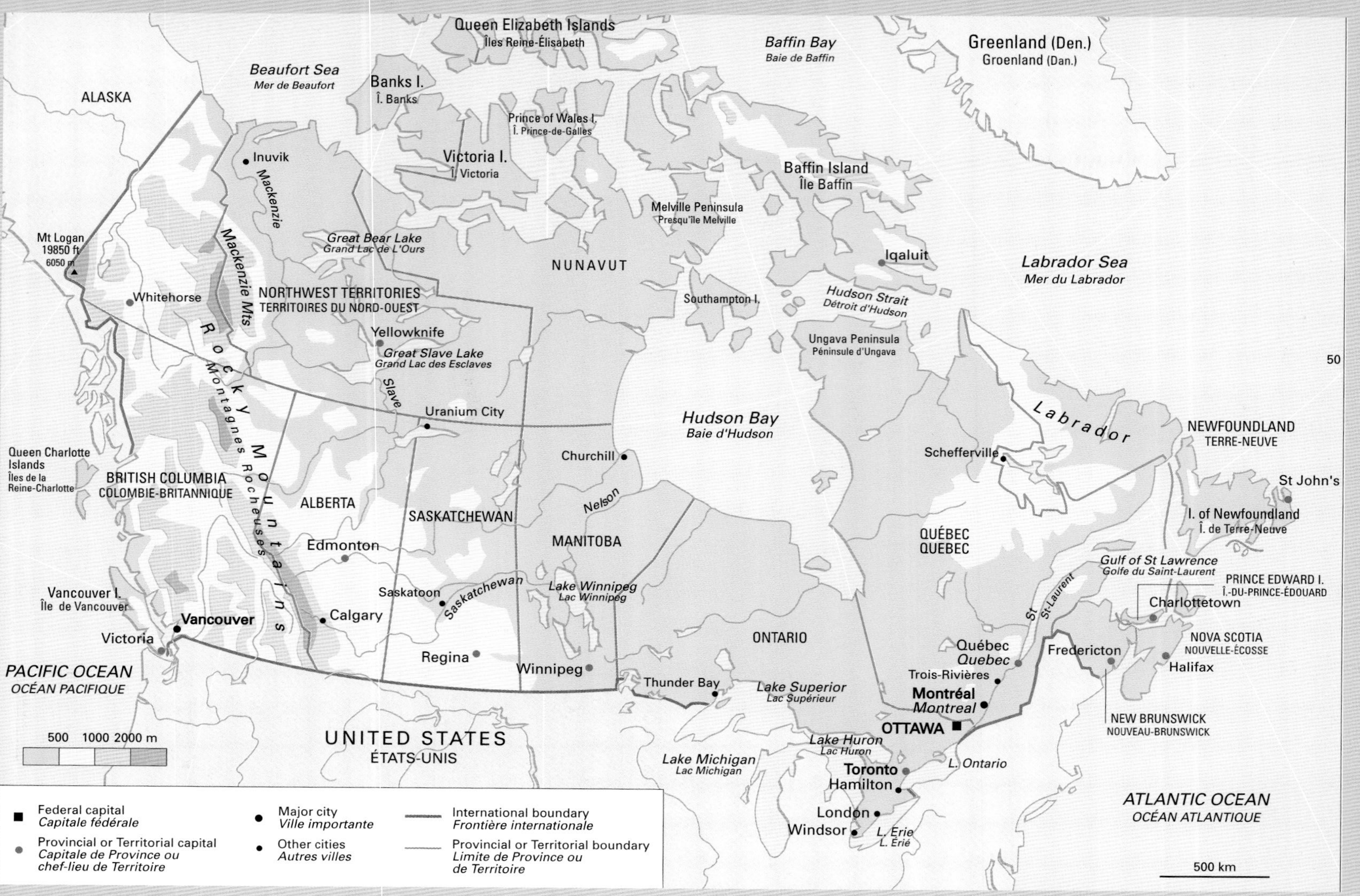

Queen Elizabeth Islands
Îles Reine-Élisabeth
Baffin Bay
Baie de Baffin
Greenland (Den.)
Groenland (Dan.)
Beaufort Sea
Mer de Beaufort
Banks I.
Î. Banks
ALASKA
Prince of Wales I.
Î. Prince-de-Galles
Victoria I.
Î. Victoria
Baffin Island
Île Baffin
Inuvik
Mackenzie
Melville Peninsula
Presqu'île Melville
Great Bear Lake
Grand Lac de L'Ours
Mt Logan
19850 ft
6050 m
NUNAVUT
Iqaluit
Labrador Sea
Mer du Labrador
Mackenzie Mts
Whitehorse
NORTHWEST TERRITORIES
TERRITOIRES DU NORD-OUEST
Southampton I.
Hudson Strait
Détroit d'Hudson
Yellowknife
Great Slave Lake
Grand Lac des Esclaves
Ungava Peninsula
Péninsule d'Ungava
50
Slave
Rocky Mountains
Montagnes Rocheuses
Uranium City
Hudson Bay
Baie d'Hudson
Labrador
NEWFOUNDLAND
TERRE-NEUVE
Queen Charlotte Islands
Îles de la Reine-Charlotte
Churchill
Schefferville
BRITISH COLUMBIA
COLOMBIE-BRITANNIQUE
St John's
ALBERTA
Nelson
SASKATCHEWAN
I. of Newfoundland
Î. de Terre-Neuve
QUÉBEC
QUEBEC
MANITOBA
Edmonton
Gulf of St Lawrence
Golfe du Saint-Laurent
Saskatchewan
Lake Winnipeg
Lac Winnipeg
PRINCE EDWARD I.
Î.-DU-PRINCE-ÉDOUARD
Saskatoon
Vancouver I.
Île de Vancouver
St
St-Laurent
Charlottetown
Calgary
Vancouver
ONTARIO
Victoria
NOVA SCOTIA
NOUVELLE-ÉCOSSE
Québec
Quebec
Fredericton
Regina
Halifax
PACIFIC OCEAN
OCÉAN PACIFIQUE
Winnipeg
Trois-Rivières
Thunder Bay
Lake Superior
Lac Supérieur
Montréal
Montreal
NEW BRUNSWICK
NOUVEAU-BRUNSWICK
OTTAWA
500 1000 2000 m
UNITED STATES
ÉTATS-UNIS
Lake Huron
Lac Huron
Lake Michigan
Lac Michigan
L. Ontario
Toronto
Hamilton
ATLANTIC OCEAN
OCÉAN ATLANTIQUE
London
Windsor
L. Erie
L. Érié
500 km
Federal capital
Capitale fédérale
Provincial or Territorial capital
Capitale de Province ou chef-lieu de Territoire
Major city
Ville importante
Other cities
Autres villes
International boundary
Frontière internationale
Provincial or Territorial boundary
Limite de Province ou de Territoire

Australie

Australia

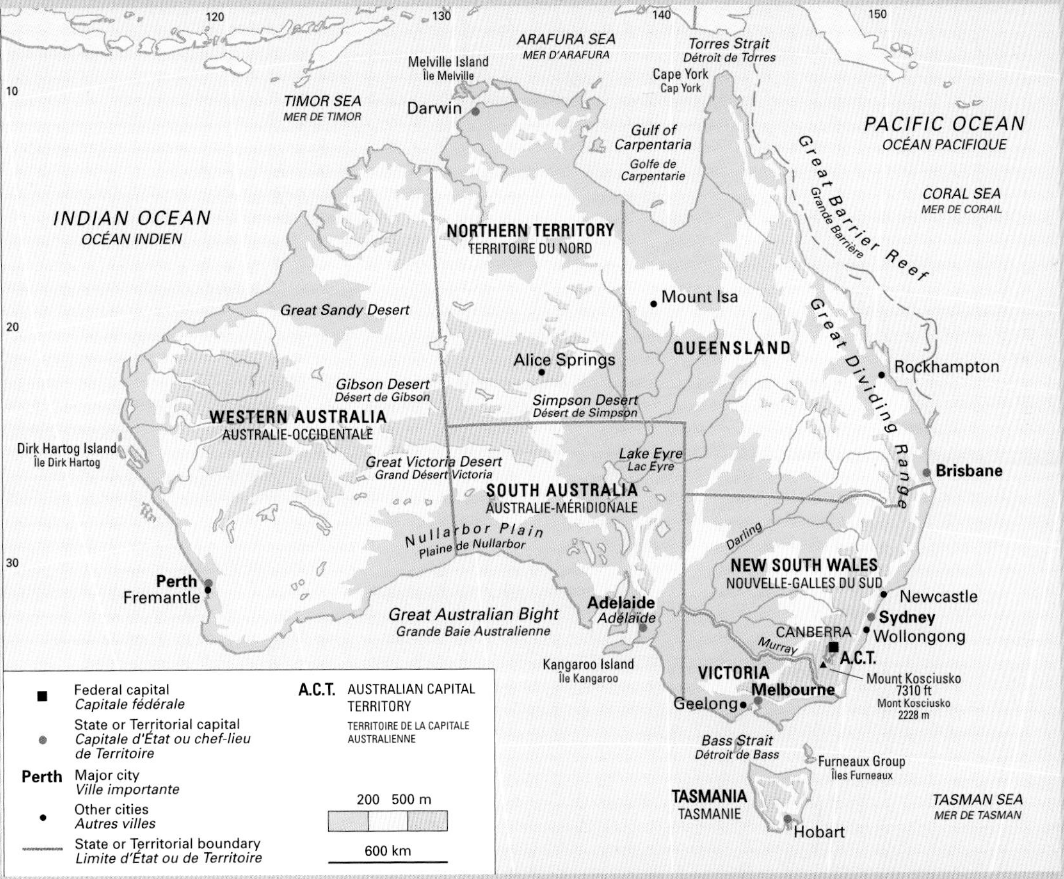

120
130
140
150
10
20
30
ARAFURA SEA
MER D'ARAFURA
Torres Strait
Détroit de Torres
Melville Island
Île Melville
Cape York
Cap York
TIMOR SEA
MER DE TIMOR
Darwin
Gulf of Carpentaria
Golfe de Carpentarie
PACIFIC OCEAN
OCÉAN PACIFIQUE
Great Barrier Reef
Grande Barrière
CORAL SEA
MER DE CORAIL
INDIAN OCEAN
OCÉAN INDIEN
NORTHERN TERRITORY
TERRITOIRE DU NORD
Mount Isa
Great Sandy Desert
Great Dividing Range
QUEENSLAND
Alice Springs
Rockhampton
Gibson Desert
Désert de Gibson
Simpson Desert
Désert de Simpson
WESTERN AUSTRALIA
AUSTRALIE-OCCIDENTALE
Dirk Hartog Island
Île Dirk Hartog
Lake Eyre
Lac Eyre
Great Victoria Desert
Grand Désert Victoria
Brisbane
SOUTH AUSTRALIA
AUSTRALIE-MÉRIDIONALE
Nullarbor Plain
Plaine de Nullarbor
Darling
NEW SOUTH WALES
NOUVELLE-GALLES DU SUD
Perth
Fremantle
Newcastle
Great Australian Bight
Grande Baie Australienne
Adelaide
Adélaïde
Sydney
Wollongong
CANBERRA
Murray
A.C.T.
Kangaroo Island
Île Kangaroo
VICTORIA
Melbourne
Mount Kosciusko
7310 ft
Mont Kosciusko
2228 m
Geelong
Bass Strait
Détroit de Bass
Furneaux Group
Îles Furneaux
TASMANIA
TASMANIE
Hobart
TASMAN SEA
MER DE TASMAN
Federal capital
Capitale fédérale
State or Territorial capital
Capitale d'État ou chef-lieu de Territoire
Perth Major city
Ville importante
Other cities
Autres villes
State or Territorial boundary
Limite d'État ou de Territoire
A.C.T. AUSTRALIAN CAPITAL TERRITORY
TERRITOIRE DE LA CAPITALE AUSTRALIENNE
200 500 m
600 km

Nouvelle-Zélande

New Zealand

164
168
172
176
180
36
40
North Cape
Great Barrier Island
Île Great Barrier
Auckland
TASMAN SEA
MER DE TASMAN
Hamilton
East Cape
North Island
Île du Nord
Lake Taupo
Lac Taupo
Cape Farewell
Cap Farewell
WELLINGTON
South Island
Île du Sud
Cook Strait
Détroit de Cook
PACIFIC OCEAN
OCÉAN PACIFIQUE
Mount Cook
12316 ft
Mont Cook
3754 m
Southern Alps
Alpes du Sud
Christchurch
State capital
Capitale d'État
Major city
Ville importante
Other cities
Autres villes
Chatham Islands
Îles Chatham
500 1000 m
300 km
Dunedin
Stewart Island
Île Stewart
Foveaux Strait
Détroit de Foveaux
Bounty Islands
Îles Bounty

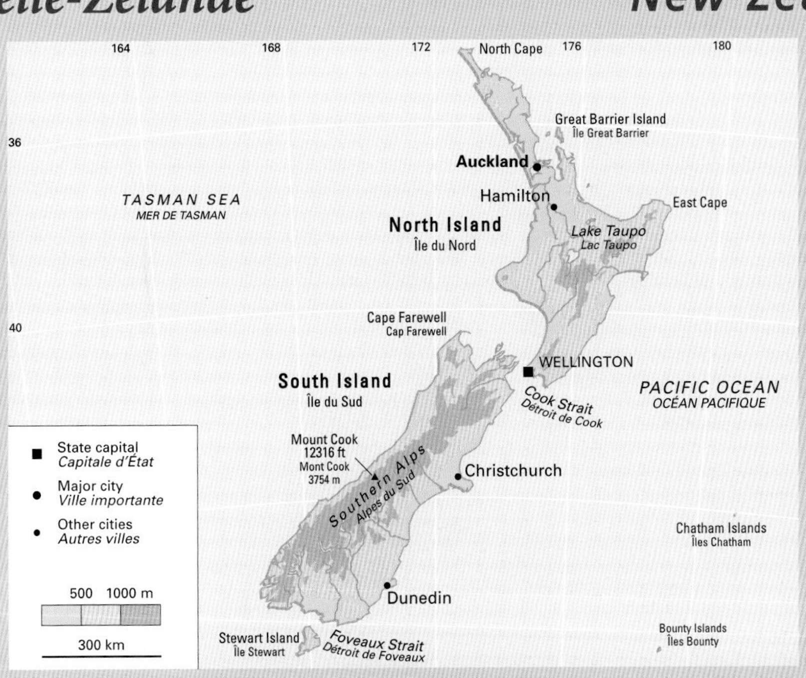

la francophonie — *the French-speaking world*

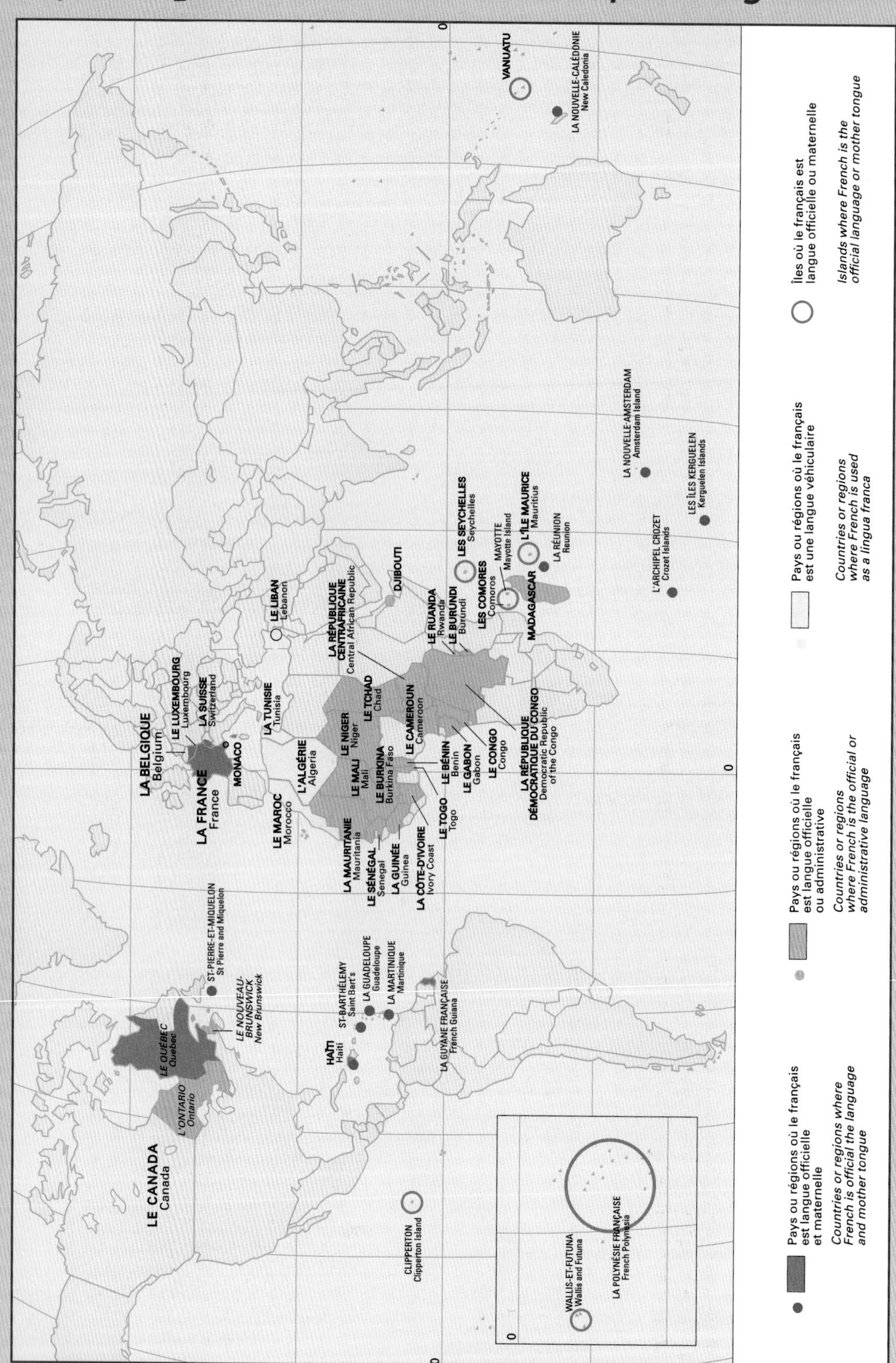

LE CANADA
Canada
L'ONTARIO
Ontario
LE QUÉBEC
Quebec
LE NOUVEAU-BRUNSWICK
New Brunswick
ST-PIERRE-ET-MIQUELON
St Pierre and Miquelon
HAÏTI
Haiti
ST-BARTHÉLEMY
Saint Bart's
LA GUADELOUPE
Guadeloupe
LA MARTINIQUE
Martinique
LA GUYANE FRANÇAISE
French Guiana
CLIPPERTON
Clipperton Island
WALLIS-ET-FUTUNA
Wallis and Futuna
LA POLYNÉSIE FRANÇAISE
French Polynesia
LA BELGIQUE
Belgium
LE LUXEMBOURG
Luxembourg
LA SUISSE
Switzerland
LA FRANCE
France
MONACO
LA TUNISIE
Tunisia
L'ALGÉRIE
Algeria
LE MAROC
Morocco
LE LIBAN
Lebanon
LA MAURITANIE
Mauritania
LE SÉNÉGAL
Senegal
LA GUINÉE
Guinea
LA CÔTE-D'IVOIRE
Ivory Coast
LE MALI
Mali
LE BURKINA
Burkina Faso
LE NIGER
Niger
LE TOGO
Togo
LE BÉNIN
Benin
LE GABON
Gabon
LE CAMEROUN
Cameroon
LE TCHAD
Chad
LA RÉPUBLIQUE CENTRAFRICAINE
Central African Republic
LE CONGO
Congo
LA RÉPUBLIQUE DÉMOCRATIQUE DU CONGO
Democratic Republic of the Congo
LE RUANDA
Rwanda
LE BURUNDI
Burundi
DJIBOUTI
LES SEYCHELLES
Seychelles
LES COMORES
Comoros
MAYOTTE
Mayotte Island
MADAGASCAR
L'ÎLE MAURICE
Mauritius
LA RÉUNION
Reunion
L'ARCHIPEL CROZET
Crozet Islands
LES ÎLES KERGUELEN
Kerguelen Islands
LA NOUVELLE-AMSTERDAM
Amsterdam Island
VANUATU
LA NOUVELLE-CALÉDONIE
New Caledonia
Pays ou régions où le français est langue officielle et maternelle
Countries or regions where French is official the language and mother tongue
Pays ou régions où le français est langue officielle ou administrative
Countries or regions where French is the official or administrative language
Pays ou régions où le français est une langue véhiculaire
Countries or regions where French is used as a lingua franca
Îles où le français est langue officielle ou maternelle
Islands where French is the official language or mother tongue

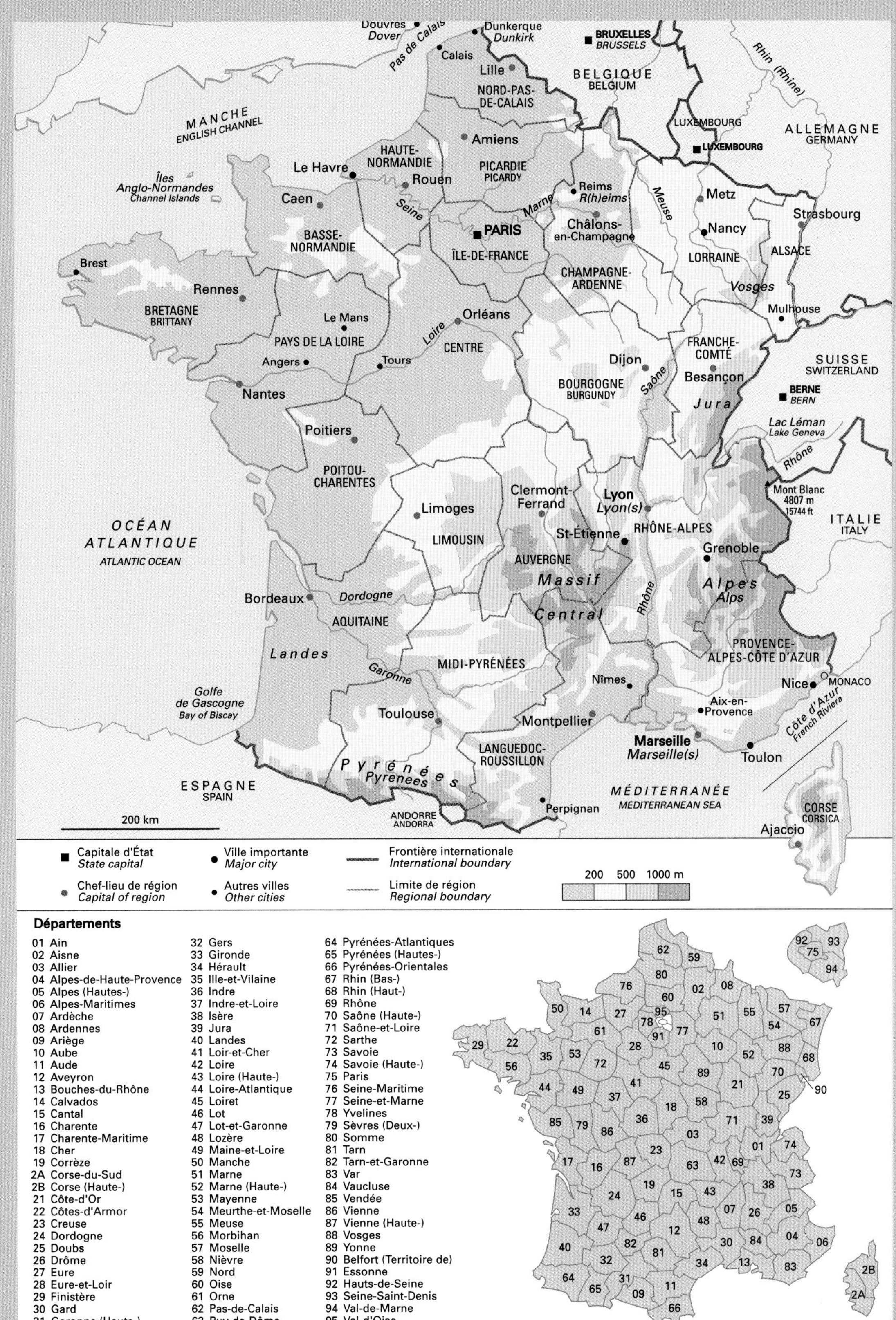
Douvres
Dover
Pas de Calais
Calais
Dunkerque
Dunkirk
BRUXELLES
BRUSSELS
Lille
NORD-PAS-DE-CALAIS
BELGIQUE
BELGIUM
Rhin (Rhine)
MANCHE
ENGLISH CHANNEL
LUXEMBOURG
LUXEMBOURG
ALLEMAGNE
GERMANY
Amiens
HAUTE-NORMANDIE
Le Havre
Rouen
PICARDIE
PICARDY
Îles Anglo-Normandes
Channel Islands
Caen
Seine
Marne
Reims
R(h)eims
Meuse
Metz
Strasbourg
PARIS
Châlons-en-Champagne
Nancy
BASSE-NORMANDIE
ÎLE-DE-FRANCE
LORRAINE
ALSACE
Brest
CHAMPAGNE-ARDENNE
Vosges
Rennes
Mulhouse
BRETAGNE
BRITTANY
Le Mans
Orléans
Loire
PAYS DE LA LOIRE
CENTRE
FRANCHE-COMTÉ
Angers
Tours
Dijon
SUISSE
SWITZERLAND
Saône
Besançon
BOURGOGNE
BURGUNDY
BERNE
BERN
Nantes
Jura
Lac Léman
Lake Geneva
Poitiers
Rhône
POITOU-CHARENTES
Mont Blanc
4807 m
15744 ft
Clermont-Ferrand
Lyon
Lyon(s)
Limoges
OCÉAN ATLANTIQUE
ATLANTIC OCEAN
ITALIE
ITALY
St-Étienne
RHÔNE-ALPES
LIMOUSIN
Grenoble
AUVERGNE
Massif Central
Alpes
Alps
Bordeaux
Dordogne
AQUITAINE
PROVENCE-ALPES-CÔTE D'AZUR
Landes
Garonne
MIDI-PYRÉNÉES
Nîmes
Nice
MONACO
Golfe de Gascogne
Bay of Biscay
Aix-en-Provence
Côte d'Azur
French Riviera
Toulouse
Montpellier
Marseille
Marseille(s)
LANGUEDOC-ROUSSILLON
Toulon
Pyrénées
Pyrenees
ESPAGNE
SPAIN
MÉDITERRANÉE
MEDITERRANEAN SEA
CORSE
CORSICA
Perpignan
200 km
ANDORRE
ANDORRA
Ajaccio
Capitale d'État
State capital
Ville importante
Major city
Frontière internationale
International boundary
Chef-lieu de région
Capital of region
Autres villes
Other cities
Limite de région
Regional boundary
200 500 1000 m
Départements
01 Ain
02 Aisne
03 Allier
04 Alpes-de-Haute-Provence
05 Alpes (Hautes-)
06 Alpes-Maritimes
07 Ardèche
08 Ardennes
09 Ariège
10 Aube
11 Aude
12 Aveyron
13 Bouches-du-Rhône
14 Calvados
15 Cantal
16 Charente
17 Charente-Maritime
18 Cher
19 Corrèze
2A Corse-du-Sud
2B Corse (Haute-)
21 Côte-d'Or
22 Côtes-d'Armor
23 Creuse
24 Dordogne
25 Doubs
26 Drôme
27 Eure
28 Eure-et-Loir
29 Finistère
30 Gard
31 Garonne (Haute-)
32 Gers
33 Gironde
34 Hérault
35 Ille-et-Vilaine
36 Indre
37 Indre-et-Loire
38 Isère
39 Jura
40 Landes
41 Loir-et-Cher
42 Loire
43 Loire (Haute-)
44 Loire-Atlantique
45 Loiret
46 Lot
47 Lot-et-Garonne
48 Lozère
49 Maine-et-Loire
50 Manche
51 Marne
52 Marne (Haute-)
53 Mayenne
54 Meurthe-et-Moselle
55 Meuse
56 Morbihan
57 Moselle
58 Nièvre
59 Nord
60 Oise
61 Orne
62 Pas-de-Calais
63 Puy-de-Dôme
64 Pyrénées-Atlantiques
65 Pyrénées (Hautes-)
66 Pyrénées-Orientales
67 Rhin (Bas-)
68 Rhin (Haut-)
69 Rhône
70 Saône (Haute-)
71 Saône-et-Loire
72 Sarthe
73 Savoie
74 Savoie (Haute-)
75 Paris
76 Seine-Maritime
77 Seine-et-Marne
78 Yvelines
79 Sèvres (Deux-)
80 Somme
81 Tarn
82 Tarn-et-Garonne
83 Var
84 Vaucluse
85 Vendée
86 Vienne
87 Vienne (Haute-)
88 Vosges
89 Yonne
90 Belfort (Territoire de)
91 Essonne
92 Hauts-de-Seine
93 Seine-Saint-Denis
94 Val-de-Marne
95 Val-d'Oise

Belgique

Belgium

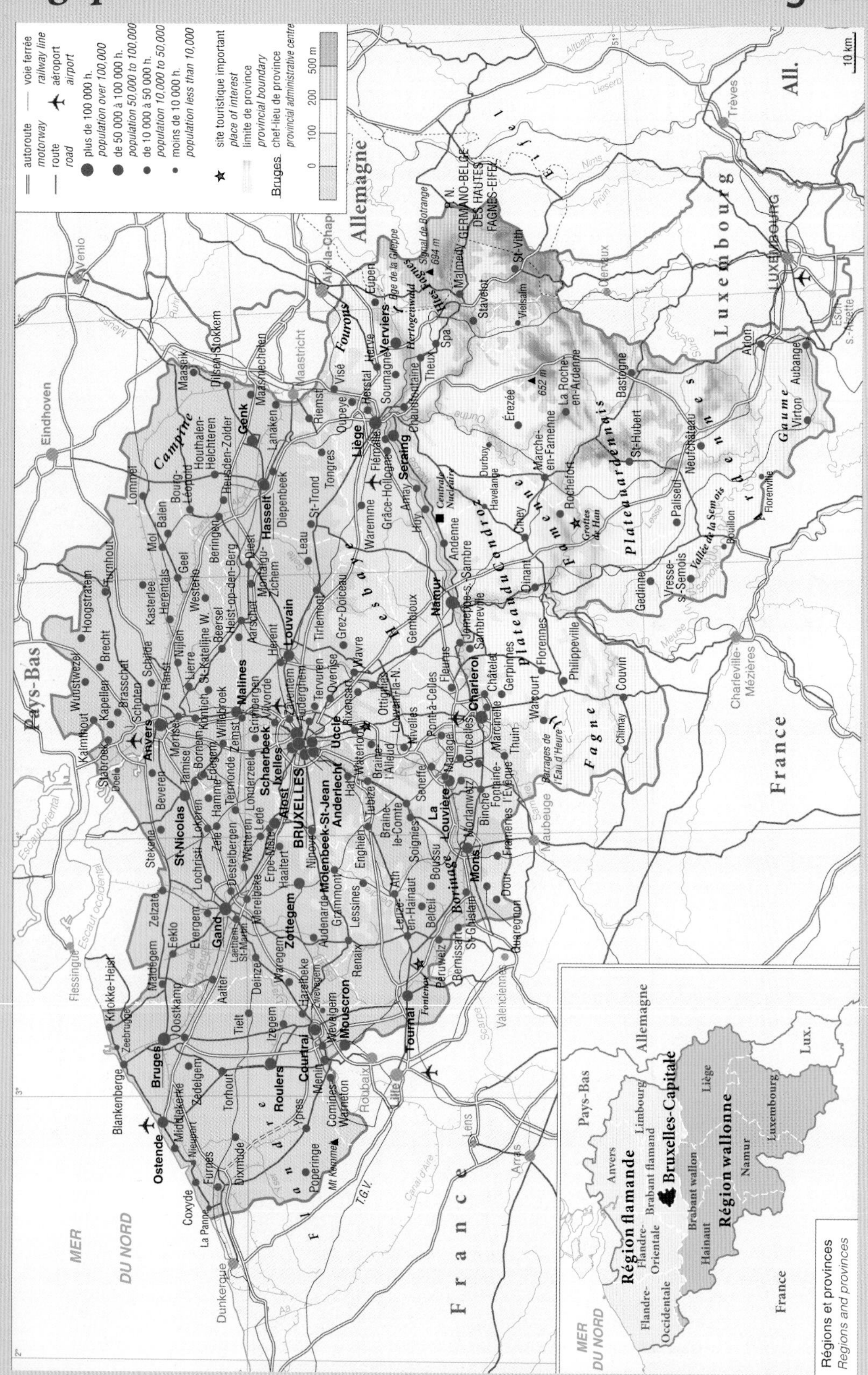

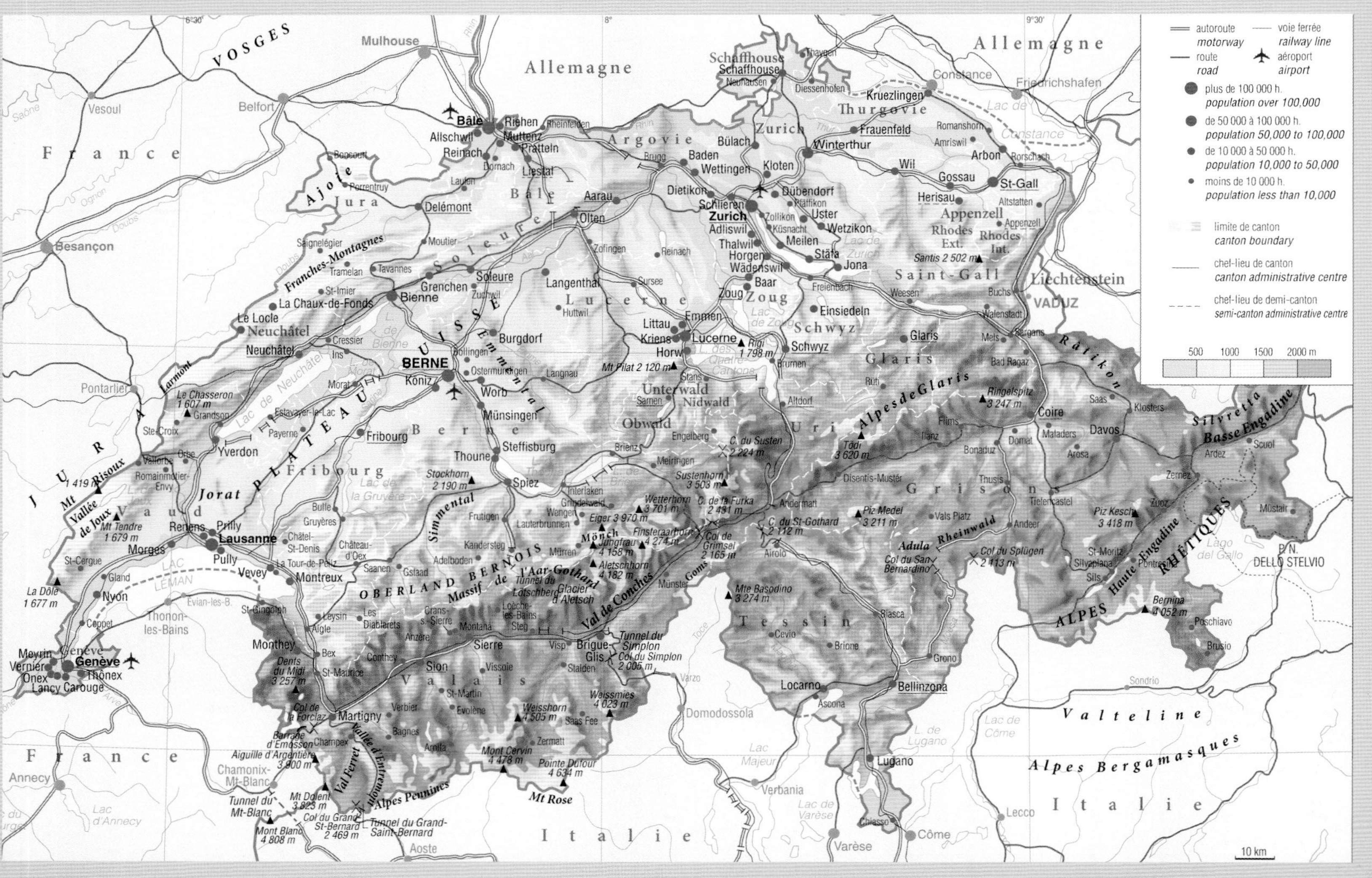
autoroute
motorway
route
road
voie ferrée
railway line
aéroport
airport
plus de 100 000 h.
population over 100,000
de 50 000 à 100 000 h.
population 50,000 to 100,000
de 10 000 à 50 000 h.
population 10,000 to 50,000
moins de 10 000 h.
population less than 10,000
limite de canton
canton boundary
chef-lieu de canton
canton administrative centre
chef-lieu de demi-canton
semi-canton administrative centre
500 1000 1500 2000 m
10 km
Allemagne
France
Italie
Liechtenstein
VADUZ
BERNE
Zurich
Bâle
Genève
Lausanne
Lucerne
St-Gall
Lac Léman
Lac de Neuchâtel
Lac de Constance
Jura
Valais
Tessin
Grisons
Mt Rose
Mt Blanc 4 808 m

Quebec

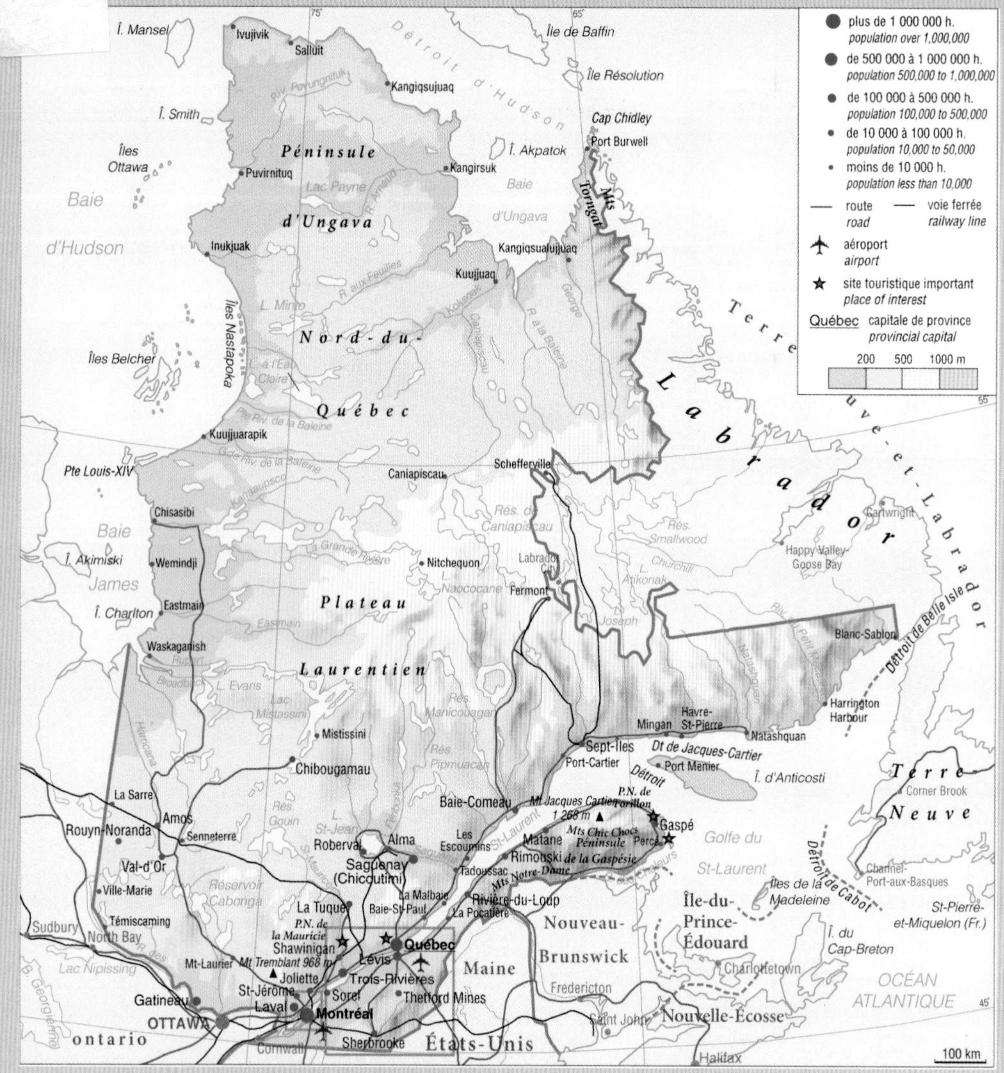
plus de 1 000 000 h.
population over 1,000,000
de 500 000 à 1 000 000 h.
population 500,000 to 1,000,000
de 100 000 à 500 000 h.
population 100,000 to 500,000
de 10 000 à 100 000 h.
population 10,000 to 50,000
moins de 10 000 h.
population less than 10,000
route
road
voie ferrée
railway line
aéroport
airport
site touristique important
place of interest
Québec capitale de province
provincial capital
200 500 1000 m
Péninsule d'Ungava
Nord-du-Québec
Plateau Laurentien
Labrador
Terre-Neuve-et-Labrador
Baie d'Hudson
Baie James
Détroit d'Hudson
Baie d'Ungava
Île de Baffin
Île Résolution
Cap Chidley
Port Burwell
Mts Torngat
Ivujivik
Salluit
Kangiqsujuaq
Kangirsuk
Puvirnituq
Inukjuak
Kuujjuaq
Kangiqsualujjuaq
Kuujjuarapik
Chisasibi
Wemindji
Eastmain
Waskaganish
Caniapiscau
Schefferville
Nitchequon
Fermont
Mistissini
Chibougamau
La Sarre
Amos
Rouyn-Noranda
Senneterre
Val-d'Or
Ville-Marie
Témiscaming
North Bay
Sudbury
Mt-Laurier
Mt Tremblant 968 m
Gatineau
OTTAWA
Joliette
St-Jérôme
Laval
Montréal
Sherbrooke
Thetford Mines
Sorel
Trois-Rivières
Lévis
Québec
Shawinigan
P.N. de la Mauricie
La Tuque
Baie-St-Paul
La Malbaie
Roberval
Alma
Saguenay (Chicoutimi)
Tadoussac
Les Escoumins
Baie-Comeau
Rivière-du-Loup
La Pocatière
Rimouski
Matane
Mt Jacques Cartier 1 268 m
P.N. de Forillon
Gaspé
Percé
Mts Chic Chocs
Péninsule de la Gaspésie
Mts Notre-Dame
Sept-Îles
Port-Cartier
Port Menier
Mingan
Havre-St-Pierre
Natashquan
Harrington Harbour
Blanc-Sablon
Cartwright
Happy Valley-Goose Bay
Labrador City
Détroit de Belle Isle
Dt de Jacques-Cartier
Détroit d'Honguedo
Î. d'Anticosti
Golfe du St-Laurent
Îles de la Madeleine
Détroit de Cabot
Corner Brook
Terre-Neuve
Channel-Port-aux-Basques
St-Pierre-et-Miquelon (Fr.)
Î. du Cap-Breton
Île-du-Prince-Édouard
Charlottetown
Nouveau-Brunswick
Fredericton
Saint John
Nouvelle-Écosse
Halifax
OCÉAN ATLANTIQUE
Maine
États-Unis
ontario
Cornwall
Î. Mansel
Î. Smith
Îles Ottawa
Îles Belcher
Îles Nastapoka
Pte Louis-XIV
Î. Akimiski
Î. Charlton
Î. Akpatok
Lac Payne
L. Minto
L. à l'Eau Claire
Rés. de Caniapiscau
Rés. Smallwood
L. Nacocane
L. Evans
Lac Mistassini
Rés. Manicouagan
Rés. Pipmuacan
Rés. Gouin
L. St-Jean
Réservoir Cabonga
Lac Nipissing
100 km

Guadeloupe

Guadeloupe

Martinique

Martinique

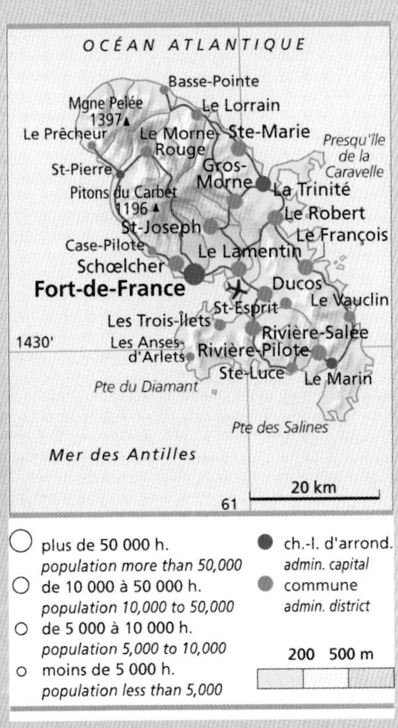

Nouvelle-Calédonie — New Caledonia

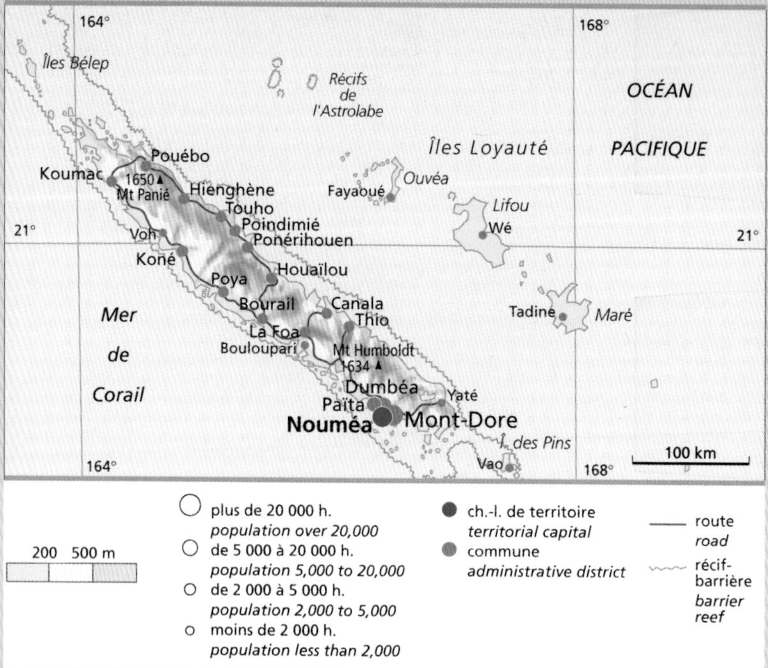

164°
168°
Îles Bélep
Récifs de l'Astrolabe
Îles Loyauté
OCÉAN PACIFIQUE
Pouébo
Koumac
1650 Mt Panié
Hienghène
Touho
Poindimié
Ponérihouen
Fayaoué
Ouvéa
Lifou
Wé
21°
Voh
Koné
Houaïlou
Poya
Bourail
Canala
Thio
Tadine
Maré
Mer de Corail
La Foa
Boulouparí
Mt Humboldt 1634
Dumbéa
Yaté
Païta
Nouméa
Mont-Dore
Î. des Pins
Vao
100 km
200 500 m
plus de 20 000 h.
population over 20,000
de 5 000 à 20 000 h.
population 5,000 to 20,000
de 2 000 à 5 000 h.
population 2,000 to 5,000
moins de 2 000 h.
population less than 2,000
ch.-l. de territoire
territorial capital
commune
administrative district
route
road
récif-barrière
barrier reef

Polynésie Française — French Polynesia

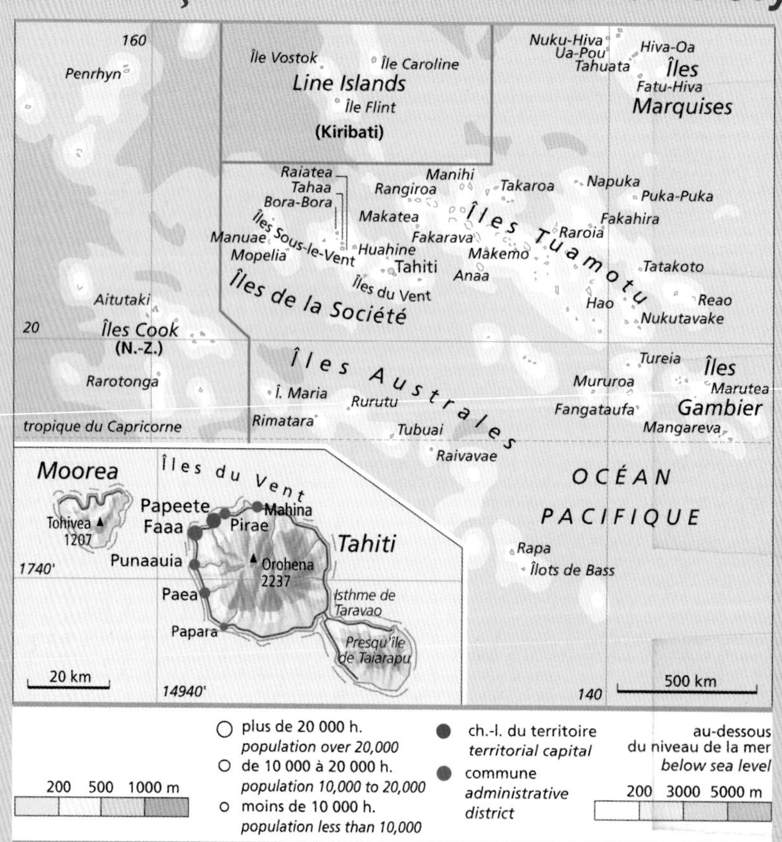

160
Penrhyn
Île Vostok
Île Caroline
Line Islands
Île Flint
(Kiribati)
Nuku-Hiva
Ua-Pou
Tahuata
Hiva-Oa
Fatu-Hiva
Îles Marquises
Raiatea
Tahaa
Bora-Bora
Manihi
Rangiroa
Takaroa
Napuka
Puka-Puka
Makatea
Îles Tuamotu
Fakahira
Raroia
Îles Sous-le-Vent
Manuae
Mopelia
Fakarava
Huahine
Makemo
Tahiti
Anaa
Tatakoto
Îles du Vent
Îles de la Société
Hao
Reao
Nukutavake
Aitutaki
20
Îles Cook (N.-Z.)
Îles Australes
Tureia
Îles Gambier
Rarotonga
Î. Maria
Rurutu
Mururoa
Marutea
Fangataufa
Rimatara
Tubuai
Mangareva
tropique du Capricorne
Raivavae
Moorea
Îles du Vent
Papeete
Mahina
Faaa
Pirae
Tohivea 1207
Tahiti
Punaauia
Orohena 2237
1740'
Paea
Isthme de Taravao
Papara
Presqu'île de Taiarapu
20 km
14940'
OCÉAN PACIFIQUE
Rapa
Îlots de Bass
140
500 km
plus de 20 000 h.
population over 20,000
de 10 000 à 20 000 h.
population 10,000 to 20,000
moins de 10 000 h.
population less than 10,000
ch.-l. du territoire
territorial capital
commune
administrative district
au-dessous du niveau de la mer
below sea level
200 500 1000 m
200 3000 5000 m

COMMUNICATION GUIDE — GUIDE DE COMMUNICATION

Opening and closing formulas

The following table shows the main opening and closing formulas used in French correspondence. Nowadays, the rules governing opening and closing formulas are far more relaxed than they used to be, permitting different combinations from those given below.

	OPENING FORMULAS	CLOSING FORMULAS
To a relative or close friend	Cher Cédric,/Mon cher Cédric, Chère Françoise,/Ma chère Françoise, **You would only use somebody's first name when they are a close friend or relative.** Chère mamie, etc. Ma chère mamie, etc.	Je t'embrasse (très fort) Bises/Grosses bises Bisous/Gros bisous À bientôt
To an acquaintance	Cher Monsieur, **Note that you would never use a person's surname in an opening formula.** Chère Madame, **Used irrespective of a woman's marital status.** Chère Mademoiselle, Cher ami,/Chère amie, **Used to mark respect to the person you are writing to.**	Amicalement Bien amicalement Amitiés Avec mon meilleur souvenir/ toute mon amitié
In formal correspondence, when you know the name and sex of the person you are writing to	Monsieur, **These are the most neutral forms. They can be replaced by *Cher Monsieur, Chère Madame,/ Mademoiselle,* if you wish to show more respect.** **Remember to use the same form in the closing formula.**	Veuillez agréer OR Je vous prie d'agréer, Monsieur, mes salutations distinguées OR l'expression de mes sentiments distingués. **When the sender is a man.** Recevez, Monsieur, mes salutations distinguées. **When the sender is a woman.**
	Madame, Mademoiselle,	Veuillez agréer OR Je vous prie d'agréer, Madame,/Mademoiselle, mes respectueuses salutations. **When the sender is a man.** Veuillez agréer OR Je vous prie d'agréer, Madame,/Mademoiselle, mes salutations distinguées. **When the sender is a woman.** Veuillez agréer OR Je vous prie d'agréer, Monsieur,/Madame,/ Mademoiselle, l'expression de mes sentiments (très) respectueux. **Used to show more respect.**
In formal correspondence, when you do not know the name or sex of the person you are writing to	Messieurs, Madame, Monsieur,	Veuillez agréer OR Je vous prie d'agréer, Messieurs/Madame, Madame, Monsieur, mes salutations distinguées OR l'expression de mes sentiments distingués.

Formules d'appel et formules finales

Le tableau suivant indique les principales formules d'appel et formules finales utilisées dans la correspondance au Royaume-Uni et aux États-Unis.

	FORMULES D'APPEL	FORMULES FINALES
À des amis intimes, membres de la famille	Dear David Dear Lily Dear Mum and Dad Dear Uncle Tony My dearest Jill My dear Alfred	Love With love Love from us both Love to all **Formules employées couramment. Notez qu'un homme s'adressant à un homme préférera des formules plus neutres et évitera d'utiliser *love*.**
		Lots of love All my love With all our love **Formules plus affectueuses.**
		Yours All the best Best wishes **Formules plus neutres.**
À des connaissances, des amis	Dear Harriet Dear Sally and Michael Dear Mrs Simpson Dear Mr Brown Dear Mr and Mrs Adams	With best wishes With kind regards Kindest regards Regards Yours All the best Best wishes
Dans une lettre d'affaires, lorsqu'on connaît le nom du correspondant	Dear Mr Jones Dear Mrs Clarke Dear Ms Fletcher **Dans de nombreuses situations on préfère aujourd'hui l'abréviation *Ms*, qui s'applique aussi bien à une femme mariée qu'à une femme célibataire, plutôt que *Mrs* pour une femme mariée ou *Miss* pour une femme célibataire.** Dear Dr Illingworth	Yours sincerely ***(UK)*** Sincerely ***(US)*** Yours truly (surtout ***US***) With best wishes With kind regards **Formules pouvant être utilisées avant les formules finales ci-dessus, lorsqu'un premier contact a déjà eu lieu et que l'on veut marquer sa sympathie au correspondant.**
Pour s'adresser à quelqu'un dont on ne connaît pas le nom	Dear Sir Dear Madam	Yours faithfully ***(UK)*** Sincerely yours ***(US)***
Pour s'adresser à quelqu'un dont on ne sait si c'est un homme ou une femme, et dont on ignore le nom	Dear Sir or Madam Dear Sir/Madam Dear Sirs ***(UK)*** Gentlemen ***(US)***	Yours faithfully ***(UK)*** Sincerely yours ***(US)***

Model layout of a letter to a friend or relative

Note that in informal and personal correspondence, the name and address of the sender are not given at the top of the letter.

The date is shown in the top right-hand corner and is often preceded by the name of the place where the letter is written. If no place name is given, the date starts with a capital "L" *(Le 2 mars 2007).*

Note that the opening formula is always followed by a comma.

Paragraphs can either be indented or level with the left-hand margin, irrespective of whether they are typed or handwritten.

See table of closing formulas.

The signature is placed several lines below the final line of text, either in the middle or on the right-hand side of the page.

Grenoble, le 2 mars 2007

Cher Laurent,

J'espère que tu vas bien. Je suis désolée de ne pas avoir répondu à ta lettre plus tôt, mais je suis vraiment débordée en ce moment. Je voulais avant tout te remercier pour le livre que tu m'as envoyé pour mon anniversaire. Je l'ai trouvé passionnant.

Je profite également de cette lettre pour t'annoncer que je vais bientôt me marier... Eh oui, tout arrive ! Tu sais peut-être que j'ai rencontré Pierre il y a un an environ, et que nous vivons ensemble depuis quelque temps. Nous avons l'intention d'officialiser tout ça en mai ou en juin. Si je t'en parle, c'est bien sûr parce que j'aimerais beaucoup que tu viennes. Il faudra que tu réserves tous tes week-ends de mai et juin jusqu'à ce qu'une date précise soit fixée !

J'espère avoir de tes nouvelles bientôt.

Je t'embrasse.

Céline

Présentation type de lettre à un ami, un parent

La présence de la virgule après la formule d'appel n'est pas obligatoire.

Remarquez que, dans les lettres manuscrites, chaque nouveau paragraphe commence en retrait.

Au Royaume-Uni, l'adresse de l'expéditeur figure en haut à droite. Notez que le nom ne figure pas. Aux États-Unis, dans la correspondance personnelle, les nom et adresse de l'expéditeur n'apparaissent pas.

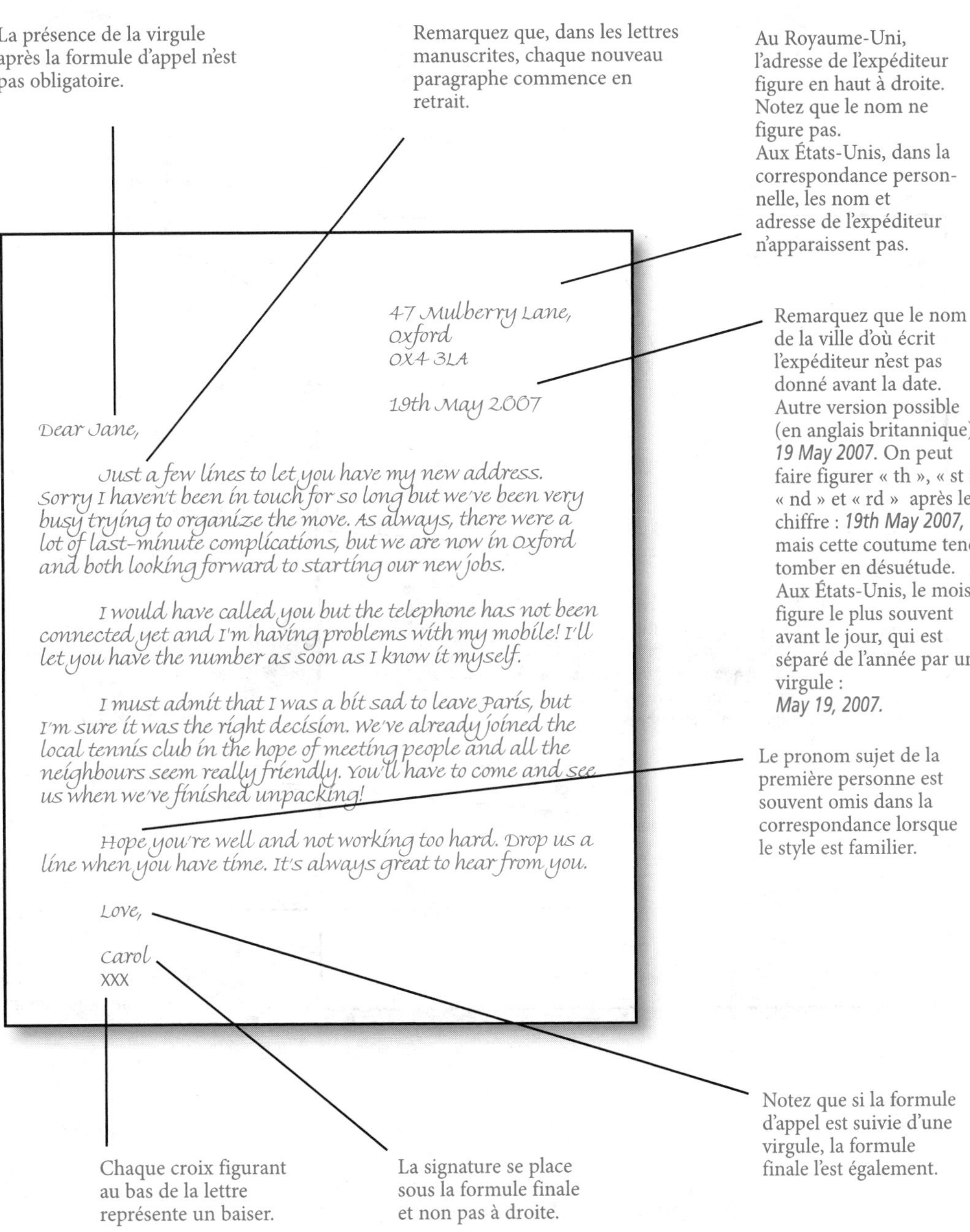

47 Mulberry Lane,
Oxford
OX4 3LA

19th May 2007

Dear Jane,

Just a few lines to let you have my new address. Sorry I haven't been in touch for so long but we've been very busy trying to organize the move. As always, there were a lot of last-minute complications, but we are now in Oxford and both looking forward to starting our new jobs.

I would have called you but the telephone has not been connected yet and I'm having problems with my mobile! I'll let you have the number as soon as I know it myself.

I must admit that I was a bit sad to leave Paris, but I'm sure it was the right decision. We've already joined the local tennis club in the hope of meeting people and all the neighbours seem really friendly. You'll have to come and see us when we've finished unpacking!

Hope you're well and not working too hard. Drop us a line when you have time. It's always great to hear from you.

Love,

Carol
XXX

Remarquez que le nom de la ville d'où écrit l'expéditeur n'est pas donné avant la date. Autre version possible (en anglais britannique) : *19 May 2007*. On peut faire figurer « th », « st », « nd » et « rd » après le chiffre : *19th May 2007*, mais cette coutume tend à tomber en désuétude. Aux États-Unis, le mois figure le plus souvent avant le jour, qui est séparé de l'année par une virgule : *May 19, 2007.*

Le pronom sujet de la première personne est souvent omis dans la correspondance lorsque le style est familier.

Notez que si la formule d'appel est suivie d'une virgule, la formule finale l'est également.

Chaque croix figurant au bas de la lettre représente un baiser.

La signature se place sous la formule finale et non pas à droite.

Model layout of a formal or business letter

The name and address of the sender are placed at the top left-hand side of the page. These can be followed by the sender's telephone and fax numbers.

It is common to give a brief summary of the contents of the letter above the opening formula.

The name and address of the addressee are placed on the right-hand side, below those of the sender and above the date.

J.-P. Salvatore
13 Résidence de la Marmande
28 rue de l'Écureuil
80000 Amiens

Monsieur Torrent
Agence Les Sables
5 rue du Marché
85160 Saint-Jean-de-Monts

Amiens, le 5 juin 2007

Objet : réservation de la villa « Marguerite »

Monsieur,

Suite à notre conversation téléphonique de ce jour, je vous confirme ma réservation de la villa « Marguerite », 10 rue du Rivage, à Saint-Jean-de-Monts, pour la période du 10 au 31 juillet 2007.

J'ai bien noté que cette villa se trouve à 500 mètres de la mer et près des principaux commerçants. « Marguerite » comporte un salon, une salle à manger, deux chambres et une terrasse et la cuisine est équipée d'un lave-vaisselle.

Comme convenu, je vous réglerai la somme de 1200 euros à la réservation et de 800 euros à la remise des clés.

Je vous prie d'agréer, Monsieur, mes salutations distinguées.

J.-P. Salvatore

J.-P. Salvatore

PJ : un chèque de 1200 euros, n° 4209374 sur la BNP.

Note that the name of the addressee is never used in the opening formula of a formal or business letter.

Paragraphs can be indented or level with the left-hand margin.

The wording of the opening formula is always repeated in the closing formula.

The sender's name may be written in capitals (for a handwritten letter) or typed below the signature, especially when the signature is not legible.

"PJ" stands for *pièce(s) jointe(s)* and indicates an enclosure. Note that you should list the document(s) enclosed.

Présentation type de lettre commerciale

Le nom, ou le titre, et l'adresse du destinataire figurent à gauche, au-dessus de la formule d'appel et en dessous d'un numéro de référence éventuel.

L'adresse de l'expéditeur figure en haut à droite, sauf s'il s'agit de papier à en-tête, auquel cas elle apparaît en haut au centre de la page.

On peut également écrire la date en chiffres. Notez toutefois qu'au Royaume-Uni on donne d'abord le jour, puis le mois et l'année : 2.5.07, et qu'aux États-Unis le mois précède le jour et l'année : 5.2.07.

Dans le style britannique, la formule d'appel peut être suivie d'une virgule ou non ; elle est suivie de deux points (:) en style américain.

Il est fréquent de donner, au début de la lettre, un bref résumé de son contenu. Aux États-Unis, ce résumé apparaît avant la formule d'appel.

Les dates ne sont jamais précédées de *of* ou de *the* dans le corps de la lettre. On prononce toutefois *July the seventh* ou *the seventh of July*.

Remarquez que, dans une lettre non manuscrite, les paragraphes ne sont pas en retrait.

Le style britannique veut qu'il n'y ait pas de ponctuation après la formule finale s'il n'y en a pas après la formule d'appel. Aux États-Unis, en revanche, la formule est suivie d'une virgule.

> Harvey & Co
> 29 Mudeford Road
> Manchester
> M14 6FR
> Tel: 0161 543 7644
> E-mail: harvey@uniline.co
>
> The Manager
> Lakelands Hotel
> Windermere
> Cumbria WI6 8YT
>
> 2 May 2007
>
> Dear Sir or Madam
>
> Re: Reservation of conference facilities
>
> Following our telephone conversation of this morning, I am writing to confirm the reservation of your conference facilities for the weekend of July 7 and 8.
>
> There will be a total of sixty-eight participants, most of whom will be arriving on the Saturday morning. As I mentioned on the phone, we would like to have a light lunch provided and a four-course meal in the evening. In addition we would appreciate coffee, tea and biscuits mid-morning and mid-afternoon.
>
> If you need to discuss any details, please do not hesitate to contact me. I enclose a list of the participants for your information.
>
> Thanking you in advance.
>
> Yours faithfully
>
> *Brian Woods*
>
> Mr Brian Woods
>
> Enc

Indique qu'il y a des pièces jointes au courrier.

La signature se place sous la formule finale (et non à droite). Dans les lettres commerciales ou officielles, on peut faire figurer le nom dactylographié sous la signature, notamment si celle-ci est peu lisible.

Addressing an envelope

The name and address are placed in the bottom right-hand corner of the envelope. Each line begins with a capital letter. Note that there is a comma between the number and the name of the street.

The sender's name and address can be placed on the reverse of the envelope at the top. In formal and business correspondence it is usually placed on the front in the top left-hand corner of the envelope.

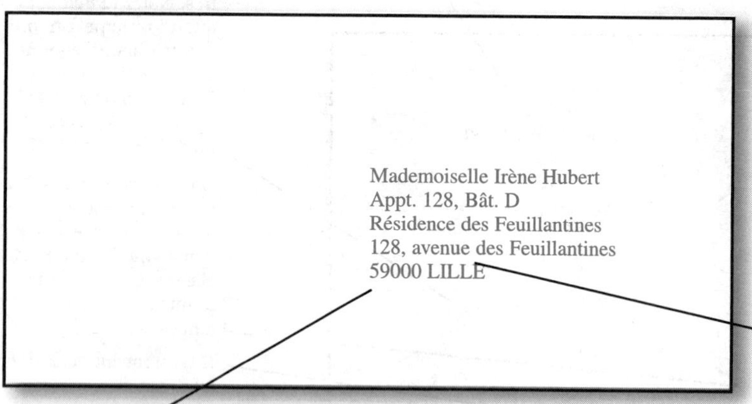

Mademoiselle Irène Hubert
Appt. 128, Bât. D
Résidence des Feuillantines
128, avenue des Feuillantines
59000 LILLE

Or "Av". Other possible abbreviations are: "Bd" (= *Boulevard*). Note that there is no abbreviation for "rue".

French postcodes consist of five numbers written without any spaces. Of these numbers, the first two indicate the *département*. The postcode is written before the name of the town or village which should be written in capital letters.

Note that the first name is always given in full, even in business correspondence.

Mme Francine Liber
Directrice des ressources humaines
EDIMEDIA
5, boulevard du Versant Nord
G1N 4G2 SAINTE FOY QUEBEC
CANADA

In business correspondence abbreviations of titles *(M., Mme, MM., Mmes, Mlle, Mlles)* are possible, although it is preferable to give the title in full *(Monsieur, Madame, Messieurs, Mesdames, Mademoiselle, Mesdemoiselles).*

Rédaction de l'enveloppe

• Au Royaume-Uni

L'adresse se place au milieu de l'enveloppe.
L'expéditeur peut éventuellement écrire son adresse au dos de l'enveloppe, en haut.

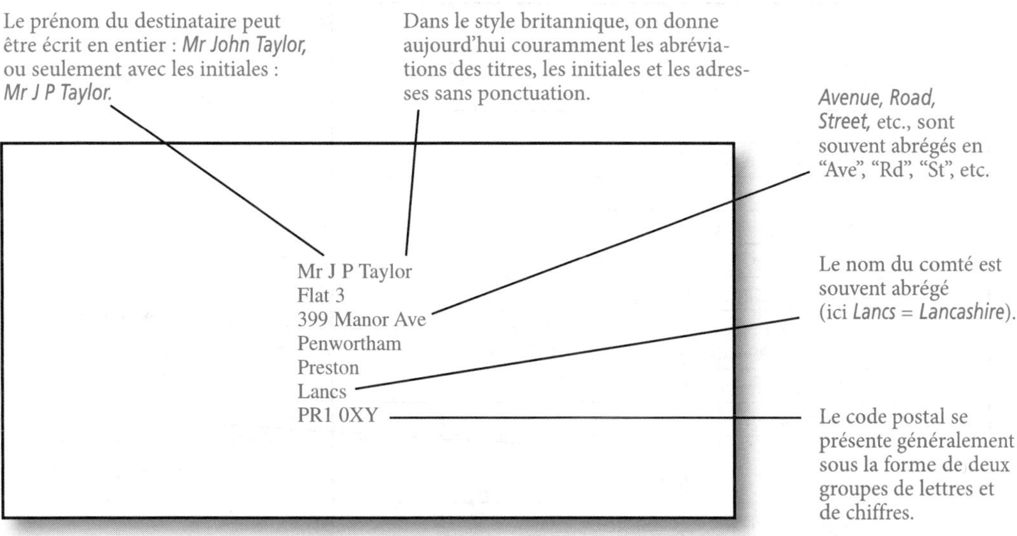

Le prénom du destinataire peut être écrit en entier : *Mr John Taylor,* ou seulement avec les initiales : *Mr J P Taylor.*
Dans le style britannique, on donne aujourd'hui couramment les abréviations des titres, les initiales et les adresses sans ponctuation.
Avenue, Road, Street, etc., sont souvent abrégés en "Ave", "Rd", "St", etc.
Mr J P Taylor
Flat 3
399 Manor Ave
Penwortham
Preston
Lancs
PR1 0XY
Le nom du comté est souvent abrégé (ici *Lancs* = *Lancashire*).
Le code postal se présente généralement sous la forme de deux groupes de lettres et de chiffres.

• Aux États-Unis

L'adresse se place au milieu de l'enveloppe.
L'adresse de l'expéditeur figure en haut à gauche du nom et de l'adresse du destinataire.

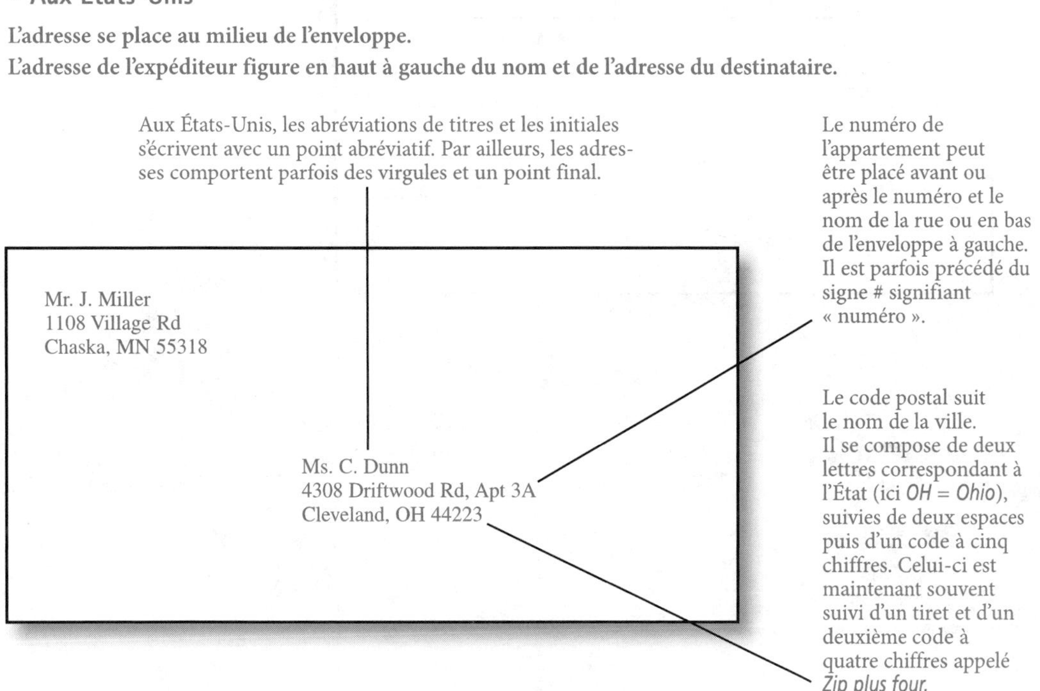

Aux États-Unis, les abréviations de titres et les initiales s'écrivent avec un point abréviatif. Par ailleurs, les adresses comportent parfois des virgules et un point final.
Le numéro de l'appartement peut être placé avant ou après le numéro et le nom de la rue ou en bas de l'enveloppe à gauche. Il est parfois précédé du signe # signifiant « numéro ».
Mr. J. Miller
1108 Village Rd
Chaska, MN 55318
Ms. C. Dunn
4308 Driftwood Rd, Apt 3A
Cleveland, OH 44223
Le code postal suit le nom de la ville. Il se compose de deux lettres correspondant à l'État (ici *OH* = *Ohio*), suivies de deux espaces puis d'un code à cinq chiffres. Celui-ci est maintenant souvent suivi d'un tiret et d'un deuxième code à quatre chiffres appelé *Zip plus four.*

Filling in a form

Note that *nom*, or the alternative *nom de famille*, means surname.

NOM : *LEROY*

NOM DE JEUNE FILLE : *MANIE*

PRÉNOM(S) : *Patricia Gabrielle*

SEXE : Masculin Féminin X

SITUATION DE FAMILLE : Célibataire Marié(e) X Divorcé(e)

ADRESSE : n° : *48* Rue : *Brantôme*

Ville : *Paris* Code postal : *75003*

TÉLÉPHONE : Domicile : *01 49 67 43 22*

Bureau : *01 39 68 92 10*

FAX : *01 39 68 92 11*

E-MAIL : *pleroy@inform.fr*

NATIONALITÉ : *Française*

DATE ET LIEU DE NAISSANCE : *28 février 1956 à Dinan*

N° DE SÉCURITÉ SOCIALE : *256022235068041*

PROFESSION : *Photojournaliste*

NOM DE L'EMPLOYEUR : *L'Explorateur*

ADRESSE DE L'EMPLOYEUR : *3, rue de la Liberté*
94100 SAINT MAUR DES FOSSÉS

PERSONNE À CONTACTER EN CAS DE NÉCESSITÉ :

Nom : *Monsieur Antoine Manie*

Adresse : *22, rue de la Croix Blanche 33000 BORDEAUX*

Téléphone : *05 56 51 83 27*

Fait à *Paris* Le *4 avril 2007*

Signature : *P. Leroy*

French telephone numbers consist of ten digits and are written in groups of twos.

Note that the nationality is given in the feminine form to agree with *nationalité*.

It is common in France to ask for the place of birth as well as the date of birth.

Remplir un formulaire

TITLE: Mr Mrs Ms ✓ Miss

SURNAME: HUTCHINSON

MAIDEN NAME: CLARKE

FIRST NAME(S): Josephine Ann

SEX: Male Female ✓

MARITAL STATUS: Single Married ✓ Divorced

ADDRESS: Street number: 13 Street: Lexford Drive
Town: Woodbridge County: Suffolk
Postcode: IP12 3DG

TELEPHONE: Home: 01394 412431
Office: 01394 430698

FAX: 01394 430621

E-MAIL: jhutchinson@pixie.uk

NATIONALITY: British

DATE OF BIRTH: 19/01/1977

NATIONAL INSURANCE NUMBER: NA191487B

PROFESSION: Legal secretary

EMPLOYER: Brown & Cole

EMPLOYER'S ADDRESS: 3 Church Road, Woodbridge, Suffolk IP11 4AY

PERSON TO BE CONTACTED IN CASE OF AN EMERGENCY:

Full name: Mr James Clarke

Address: 16 Ecclesall Road, Sheffield S11 8PN

Telephone: 01142 621637

Signature: Josephine Hutchinson Date: 4 April 2007

Il n'est pas courant de demander le lieu de naissance.

Aux États-Unis, on donne le mois avant le jour dans la date de naissance : 01/19/1977.

Aux États-Unis, l'équivalent est le *social security number.*

Aux États-Unis, on écrirait *April 4, 2007.*

Par *Full name* on entend le nom et le(s) prénom(s).

Writing to a friend

Toulouse, le 5 mai 2007

Cher Christophe,

Une fois de plus, j'ai laissé passer plusieurs mois avant de te répondre, je suis impardonnable ! J'ai tout de même des circonstances atténuantes : j'ai changé de service dans ma société, et je suis maintenant beaucoup plus souvent en déplacement.

Tu as l'air de bien t'adapter à ton nouveau cadre de vie ; est-ce que tu t'es fait des amis ? C'est certainement beaucoup plus facile de rencontrer des gens dans une petite ville, surtout quand on est sportif comme toi et qu'on peut s'inscrire à tout un tas de clubs et d'associations.

En tout cas, compte sur moi pour venir te rendre visite très bientôt, puisque tu m'invites si gentiment. J'avais justement l'intention de prendre quelques jours de congé début juillet ; est-ce que la semaine du 5 au 11 te conviendrait ?

J'espère que tu ne seras pas aussi fainéant que moi et que tu répondras vite !

Je t'embrasse.

Christine

Meilleur souvenir de Prague, où nous passons une semaine très agréable à admirer la splendide architecture de la ville et à déguster ses nombreuses bières !

À très bientôt.

Jean et Renée

Monsieur et Madame Paul Robin
8, boulevard Alsace-Lorraine
64100 Bayonne
France

Salut les copains ! Quel temps fait-il à Nancy ? Ici, le soleil brille, la mer est bleue, le sable doré, bref c'est le paradis. Enfin, ça serait vraiment le paradis si Anne ne m'obligeait pas à aller visiter les petits villages de l'intérieur à l'heure de la sieste...

On vous racontera tout plus en détail à notre retour.

Bises.

Sandra

Jérôme et Pascale Hulet
25 bis, rue Georges Clemenceau
54000 Nancy
France

Écrire à un ami

Arrived safely after a long flight that was delayed two hours! The hotel and food are wonderful - and the island is spectacular. Spent yesterday on the beach recovering from the five-hour bike ride Dave persuaded me to go on the day before. Never again! Hope you're both well and the dog is behaving itself. See you next Friday.

Love,

Carol

Mr + Mrs P Gordon
29 Marl Ave
Ferndown
DORSET
BH17 8JN
UK

24 Lodge Road
Peterborough
PE7 4QZ

15 January 2007

Dear Anne,

Just a quick note to let you know that everything is fine and to apologize for not having written sooner. As you can see, I have moved since the last time I wrote - and lost your address in the move!

How are things in Paris? You didn't say much about the course in your last letter. I hope everything is going well. As you can imagine, life has been a bit hectic at this end, what with the move and Christmas. The new house is much larger and closer to work. I now have a spare bedroom (for visitors!) and a second bathroom. What luxury!

Did Serge write and tell you that he's getting married? I think the wedding is in August.

Anyway, I must dash. Give my love to Richard and please write again soon.

Lots of love,

Mary

Hi!

Tuesday

Saw this card and thought of you! Having a great time exploring Cairo's markets and museums. Having a few problems with the language – but quite a lot of people seem to understand English. Off to visit the pyramids tomorrow – and maybe a camel ride!

Wish you were here.

All my love,

Isabelle

Andy and Yvonne Birch
52 Moor Grange View
Wellington Heath
HERTFORDSHIRE
HR2 7PJ UK

Invitations and replies

Traditional format. The name of the grandparents can also be added above those of the parents, in which case the following line of text is replaced by: *ont le plaisir de vous faire part du mariage de leurs petits-enfants et enfants.*

The bride's parents.

The groom's parents.

Monsieur et Madame Pierre Degoulet *Monsieur et Madame André Lebeau*

ont le plaisir de vous faire part du mariage de leurs enfants

Sophie et Christophe

et vous prient de leur faire l'honneur d'assister
à la cérémonie religieuse, qui sera célébrée
le samedi 26 juin 2007 à quatorze heures
en l'église Saint-Pierre d'Épernon,
ainsi qu'au dîner organisé à partir de vingt heures
à la Grande Cascade, au Bois de Boulogne.

48, rue des Plantes 75014 Paris *13, rue Beaubourg 75003 Paris*

Address of the bride's parents.

Address of the groom's parents.

Françoise et Jérôme

sont très heureux de vous faire part
de leur mariage, qui aura lieu

le 20 mars 2007

À cette occasion, ils vous invitent à la soirée qu'ils organisent, à partir de 20 heures, à la Petite Ferme, 12 rue du Château, 78000 Versailles

Réponse souhaitée avant le 28 février.

23 rue du Montparnasse, 75006 Paris

Or: *Merci de répondre avant le 28 février.*

More modern format.
The invitation comes from the bride and the groom themselves. The address given is theirs.

Perpignan, le 29 avril 2007

Chers Pierre et Christine,

Nous vous remercions vivement de votre invitation au mariage de Sophie et Christophe et nous nous ferons un plaisir d'assister à la cérémonie religieuse et au dîner, puisque vous nous proposez si gentiment de nous héberger quelques jours.

Il nous tarde de revoir toute la famille et de féliciter Sophie en personne!

Nous vous téléphonerons dès que nous aurons réservé un vol pour Paris.

Amicalement,

Jean-Paul et Marie Dubois

Invitations et réponses

Martin and Isabelle
invite you to
Martin's birthday party
on: **Wednesday May 27**
at: **31 Canning Crescent**
from: **8pm** to: **midnight**
Please bring a bottle
RSVP

Sur une invitation plus classique, il est parfois fait allusion à la tenue requise : *dress formal* ou *black tie* en anglais britannique, *formal attire* en anglais américain, signifient que les hommes doivent porter un costume sombre, et les femmes, une robe de cocktail ; *black tie* signifie que les hommes doivent porter un smoking, et les femmes, une robe du soir.

L'usage classique veut que l'on ne donne que le prénom du mari. Néanmoins, cette pratique n'est plus considérée comme politiquement correcte, notamment aux États-Unis.

Mr & Mrs Peter Harvey request the pleasure of the company of
Margaret Downey
at the marriage of their daughter
Caroline to Mr. Joe Cavanagh
at Oundle Town Hall on Wednesday 19th May 2007

17 Lime Avenue
Oundle
Peterborough PE6 4ED

RSVP
15th April 2007

Date à laquelle le destinataire doit avoir répondu à l'invitation.

17 Lime Avenue
Oundle
Peterborough
PEG 4ED
25 March 2007

Dear Mr & Mrs Harvey,

Thank you so much for the invitation to Caroline's wedding. I would love to come.

Caroline mentioned that it would be possible to arrange accommodation at The Talbot Inn for the night of the reception. Could you let me have their number so that I can book a room.

Thank you once again for the kind invitation. I look forward to seeing you in May.

Yours sincerely,

Margaret Downey

Greetings cards and congratulations

Other possibilities: *Bonne (et heureuse) année (à vous) ! ; Tous nos vœux pour la nouvelle année.*

In France, Season's greetings are sent in the New Year (throughout January) rather than before Christmas.

Juan-Les-Pins, le 6 janvier 2007

Chers Yves et Liliane,

Meilleurs vœux pour la nouvelle année ! Nous espérons que l'an 2007 vous apportera beaucoup de bonnes choses, notamment sur le plan professionnel puisque nous savons que vous envisagez de vous installer à votre compte.

Nous espérons aussi que cette nouvelle année nous donnera l'occasion de vous revoir.

Bien amicalement,

Suzanne et Alain

Other possibility: *que cette nouvelle année vous apporte beaucoup de bonnes choses/beaucoup de bonheur.*

Les Sables-d'Olonne, le 16 juin 2007

Chère Isabelle,

Toute la famille se joint à moi pour te souhaiter un très très joyeux anniversaire. Nous espérons que tu fêteras ça dignement !

Le contenu du colis devrait te rappeler ton dernier séjour ici. Ne mange pas tout d'un coup !

Tout le monde t'embrasse.

Catherine

Cher Marc,

Bravo ! Je te félicite d'avoir réussi ton bac. Je savais que tu l'aurais sans problème. Tu étais d'ailleurs bien le seul à avoir des doutes là-dessus.

J'ai transmis la nouvelle à tous les copains qui te félicitent aussi. Nous t'attendons de pied ferme en août pour fêter ça !

À bientôt !

Benoît

To be more formal, a card written in the third person can be sent: *Ludovic et Sarah Duval adressent à Françoise et Jérôme toutes leurs félicitations et leurs vœux de bonheur à l'occasion de leur mariage.*

Arbois, le 10 mai 2007

Chers Françoise et Jérôme,

C'est avec grand plaisir que nous avons appris votre mariage : toutes nos félicitations et tous nos vœux de bonheur !

Nous espérons vous revoir bientôt pour vous féliciter en personne. Comptez-vous passer quelques jours dans le Jura cet été, comme chaque année ?

Très amicalement,

Ludovic et Sarah

Cartes de vœux et félicitations

Wishing you all a Merry Christmas and a Happy New Year.
Lots of love,
Monique and the family
Ou : *Season's greetings.* Au Royaume-Uni et aux États-Unis, la coutume veut que l'on adresse ses vœux au cours du mois de décembre et non en janvier.
Happy Birthday, Sue!
Have a great day - see you at the party.
Love, Hubert
X
Ou : *Many happy returns* en anglais britannique.
Good luck with your exams.
We'll all be thinking about you and keeping our fingers crossed.
Eric, Bridget and the kids
Good luck in your new home.
I hope you'll both be very happy there.
Love,
Pascale
X
Sorry to hear about your accident.
Hope you're feeling better now.
All my love,
Nathalie
X
Ou : *Congratulations on your engagement.*
Congratulations on getting engaged.
I hope you'll be very happy together.
Have you set a date for the wedding yet?
Lots of love,
Marie-Claude
X
Ou : *Get well soon.*

Thank you letters

Strasbourg, le 11 février 2007

Chère Grand-Mère,

J'ai bien reçu la très belle montre que tu m'as envoyée pour mon anniversaire. C'est tout à fait le genre de montre dont j'avais envie depuis longtemps ! Merci mille fois ! Je vais pouvoir la montrer à mes amis lors de la fête que je donne samedi. C'est vraiment dommage que tu ne puisses pas venir, ce n'est pas tous les jours qu'on a dix-huit ans ! Je t'enverrai quelques photos.

J'espère que tu vas bien et que les chiens ne font pas trop des leurs. Je compte toujours venir te voir à Pâques en Normandie. Je suis sûr que tu prendras bien soin de moi pendant que je prépare mon bac.

Je te remercie encore pour le beau cadeau et te dis à très bientôt au téléphone.

Je t'embrasse.

Laurent

Bristol, le 3 août 2007

Chère Christine,

Me voilà de retour à Bristol, et le Périgord me manque déjà. Je ne sais comment vous remercier de m'avoir accueillie pendant deux semaines, de m'avoir fait visiter tous ces endroits magnifiques et de m'avoir fait rencontrer des personnes charmantes. Tout le monde a été vraiment gentil et patient avec moi, et j'ai l'impression d'avoir fait d'énormes progrès en français !

Grâce à vous j'ai pu recueillir des informations précieuses et vais maintenant pouvoir commencer à rédiger l'article que « Travel Magazine » m'a commandé. Puis-je me permettre de vous l'envoyer pour lecture et commentaires éventuels ?

J'espère pouvoir à mon tour vous recevoir à Bristol. C'est une ville très intéressante et un bon point de départ pour des visites d'une journée, à Bath entre autres. Bien sûr la cuisine anglaise ne vaut pas celle du Périgord, mais je pourrais quand même vous faire goûter nos fameux « English breakfasts » et « cream teas ».

Je vous remercie encore pour tout et vous dis à bientôt.

Amicalement,

Fiona

Lettres de remerciement

2099 Driftwood Drive
Laguna Beach, CA 92677
USA

December 6, 2007

Dear Monique,

Thank you so much for the beautiful bouquet of flowers that arrived this morning, just in time for my birthday. They look wonderful in the living room and will cheer the place up for the party this weekend. You do spoil me!

It was so nice to see you in the fall. Hopefully I shall be able to come to France to visit you sometime next year. Give my regards to all the family. I hope everyone is well.

Thanks again for the flowers. I'll get Bret to take a photo of them so that you can see just how lovely they are!

Take care and write soon.

Love,

Cheryl

Bonnet, Jean-Pierre
56, rue de la Gare
64000 Pau
FRANCE

12 February 2007

Dear Mr Andrews,

I am writing to thank you for your help in organizing our rugby tour of Scotland. Everyone involved was delighted with the transport and accommodation laid on and with the warm welcome given to our party.

The members of the club would also like to take this opportunity to thank your wife and her team of helpers for the refreshments provided at the end of each match.

We are looking forward to seeing you in the summer in Pau and hope that you will enjoy it as much as we enjoyed our stay in Scotland.

Thank you once again for all your help.

Yours sincerely,

Jean-Pierre Bonnet

Business letters

• Asking for a catalogue

E-mails can be less formal.

À : produits@unisecu.fr
De : Jacques Lefur, INTERNET : lefurj@aloha.fr
Date : 12/02/07
Objet : demande de catalogue

Bonjour,

Je souhaiterais recevoir, à l'adresse ci-dessous, un exemplaire de votre catalogue de vêtements et chaussures de sport, ainsi qu'une liste de prix.

Merci d'avance.

Jacques Lefur
21, rue Daguerre
75014 Paris

• Placing an order

Michèle Truchet
Architecte
13 rue Laurent Pichat
75116 Paris
Tél. : 01 48 13 26 55
Télécopie : 01 48 13 26 56
e-mail : mtruchet@architech.com

Universa S.A.
35, rue de Bretagne
95450 Seraincourt

Paris, le 10 septembre 2007

Messieurs,

Je souhaiterais passer commande de plusieurs articles figurant dans votre catalogue 2007. Il s'agit de :
• 10 rames de papier laser haute définition de couleur blanche (Réf LA00HDB)
• 10 rames de papier laser haute définition de couleur grise "Acier" (Réf LA06HDC)
• 10 rames de papier laser « qualité photo » de couleur blanche (RéfLA00PB).

Cette commande étant urgente, j'espère qu'il vous sera possible d'effectuer la livraison sous deux jours, comme cela a été le cas par le passé. Si cela n'était pas possible, veuillez me le faire savoir dès que possible par téléphone pour que je puisse prendre mes dispositions.

Je vous remercie par avance de votre compréhension et vous prie d'agréer, Messieurs, mes salutations distinguées.

Michèle Truchet

• Sending a payment

Martine Santos
24 bis rue de l'Ours
13008 Marseille

Société Informatika
155, rue Linné
75005 Paris

Marseille, le 15 juin 2007

Messieurs,

Veuillez trouver ci-joint, en règlement de votre facture numéro 127B/00016/HK, un chèque d'un montant de 2540 euros.

Vous en souhaitant bonne réception, je vous prie d'agréer, Messieurs, mes salutations distinguées.

Martine Santos

Lettres commerciales

• Demande de catalogue

To: tilecompany@evermail.co
From: John D. Smith INTERNET: johndsmith@inline.co.uk

Date: 16/11/07
Re: catalogue

Dear Sir or Madam,

I would be grateful if you could send me a catalogue and price list to the following address: 24-26 Lime Street, Edinburgh, EH6 2RT.

I am particularly interested in floor tiles for a bathroom and was wondering whether or not you have a distributor in the Edinburgh area. Failing that, I would like to know how much you charge for delivery.

Thanking you in advance.

Yours faithfully,

John D. Smith

• Passer une commande

29 Pennyworth Square
Ringwood
Hampshire
BH24 1DA

Great Outdoors
267 Albion Court
LONDON W1V 5HG

13 November 2007

Dear Sirs,

Following receipt of your latest catalogue, I have pleasure in placing an order for three pairs of walking boots, catalogue number WB109. The sizes and colours are as follows:

Men's UK size 11, black (one pair)
Women's UK size 6, brown (one pair)
Child's UK size 10, brown (one pair)

As mentioned in your catalogue, an order of three or more pairs qualifies for a 20% discount. Please find enclosed a cheque for £120 as payment in full.

I look forward to receiving the order within 28 days.

Yours faithfully,

Matthew Browning

Matthew Browning

• Règlement d'une facture

11 Morecambe Rd
Swansea
Dorset
SA2 OLY

Mr T Price
Gold & Sons
29 Lambert Street
CHESTER CH1 7TY

14 June 2007

Dear Mr Price,

Please find enclosed a cheque to the amount of £398.90 in final payment of order no. GS567-98.

I look forward to doing business with your company again in the future.

Yours sincerely,

Tina Walker

Tina Walker

Making, confirming and cancelling a reservation via Internet

Hazel.Brown

à : laroseraie@worldnet.fr
envoyé : jeudi 4 décembre 2007 18:32
de : hazelbrown@easynet.co.uk
objet : réservation

Bonjour,

J'ai trouvé votre adresse dans la brochure que m'a envoyée l'Office du Tourisme de Villard de Lans.

Je voudrais réserver une chambre avec bain pour deux personnes en demi-pension pour la semaine du 14 au 21 février, de préférence orientation sud et avec balcon.

Salutations

Hazel Brown

Court Place Barn
23 Lea Road
Bakewell DE45 1AR
Royaume-Uni

===============

n@easynet.co.uk
décembre 2007 10:22
worldnet.fr
ation 14-21 février

Madame,

J'ai bien reçu votre message électronique concernant la réservation d'une chambre et je vous en remercie.

Je vous confirme la disponibilité d'une chambre double avec bain pour la semaine du 14 au 21 février.

Le tarif demi-pension pour cette période est de 93 euros par personne et par jour (haute saison).

Merci de bien vouloir me faire parvenir un chèque d'arrhes d'un montant de 300 euros ou de me communiquer votre numéro de carte bancaire et date d'expiration par le moyen qui vous conviendra (téléphone ou télécopie) car nous n'avons pas encore de système de paiement sécurisé sur internet.

Dans l'attente de votre réponse, je vous adresse mes meilleures salutations

Henri Maréchal

Hôtel La Roseraie
38250 Villard de Lans

===============

Hazel.Brown

à : laroseraie@worldnet.fr
envoyé : vendredi 26 décembre 2007 15:41
de : hazelbrown@easynet.co.uk
objet : ma réservation pour février

Monsieur,

J'ai bien reçu votre réponse concernant la disponibilité d'une chambre pour deux. Malheureusement je viens de me casser la jambe et dois renoncer à mon séjour en montagne. J'annule donc notre réservation mais espère bien pouvoir passer quelques jours à Villard de Lans l'année prochaine.

J'espère que cette annulation tardive ne vous causera pas trop de désagrément et vous adresse mes meilleures salutations.

Hazel Brown

Court Place Barn
23 Lea Road
Bakewell DE45 1AR

===============

Faire, confirmer et annuler une réservation sur Internet

Harry.Catte

From: hcat@hotmail.com
Sent: 14 September 2007 10:44
To: info@hoteljacinta.co.uk

Dear Sir or Madam

Having visited your website at www.hoteljacinta.co.uk, I wish to reserve three nights' bed and breakfast accommodation at your hotel from 28-30 October inclusive. I require a double room with en-suite bathroom, and the room should be as quiet as possible. As for dietary requirements, my wife and I are both vegetarians.

Please let me know whether you have a room available for these dates, and also whether your hotel can provide Internet access to guests.

I presume that, at the advertised all-inclusive rate of £37.50 per person per night, the total cost of our stay would be £225. Can you confirm this?

Regards,

Harry Catte
hcat@hotmail.com
18 Prince Edward Street
EDINBURGH
EH10 6AF
0131 423 6561

«Best regards», n'est employé que pour une personne de connaissance.

Hotel Jacinta

From: info@hoteljacinta.co.uk
Sent: 15 September 2007 11:27
To: hcat@hotmail.com
Re: Reservation for 28-30 October 2007

Dear Sir

Thanking you for your e-mail of 14 September, I am pleased to confirm the availability of a double room with en-suite bathroom for the period between 28 and 30 October inclusive (three nights). The room is quiet and our gourmet restaurant offers a choice of vegetarian dishes. All rooms are equipped with Internet access.

The special all-inclusive cost of your three-night stay on a bed-and breakfast basis is indeed £225. For confirmation, we require either a £75 deposit or a credit-card reference that you can send by e-mail, fax or telephone (our website does not yet allow online reservations).

We look forward to welcoming you at the Jacinta.

Yours faithfully,

John Seymour
Manager
Hotel Jacinta

==============

Harry.Catte

From: hcat@hotmail.com
Sent: 17 September 2007 9:12
To: info@hoteljacinta.co.uk

Dear Mr Seymour

I regret to inform you that owing to a change in plans we shall be unable to stay at your hotel between 28 and 30 October 2007.

We hope to choose another date this winter to stay at the Jacinta and consider this unfortunate cancellation a simple postponement. Please accept my apologies for any inconvenience it may have caused.

Yours truly,

Harry Catte

Court Place Barn
23 Lea Road
Bakewell DE45 1AR

==============

Requesting information

Joanna Rice
3 Bramley Court
Farnborough
Hampshire
GU14 6GX
UK

Université de Provence
Service d'enseignement
du français aux étudiants étrangers
29, avenue Robert Schuman
13621 Aix-en-Provence Cedex 1

Farnborough, le 13 janvier 2007

Monsieur, Madame,

Ayant trouvé votre adresse sur Internet, et ayant consulté votre site, je vous écris pour vous demander de bien vouloir m'envoyer de plus amples renseignements sur vos cours d'été pour étrangers.

J'ai 25 ans et j'ai étudié le français jusqu'au « A-level », l'équivalent du baccalauréat. Après une interruption de plusieurs années, j'aimerais me remettre à niveau, pour des raisons professionnelles notamment.

Pourriez-vous m'indiquer les possibilités d'hébergement pendant la durée du cours, en particulier l'hébergement en famille, qui serait un bon moyen de compléter l'enseignement fourni à l'université. À défaut, est-il possible de louer une chambre en cité universitaire ?

Dans l'attente de vous lire, je vous prie d'agréer, Monsieur, Madame, de mes salutations distinguées.

Joanna Rice

Alison Summers
3 Abbey Street
Glastonbury
Somerset
BA6 4AC
UK

Office de Tourisme
Rond-Point de la Tour Mataguerre
26, place Francheville
24000 Périgueux

Glastonbury, le 25 juin 2007

Monsieur, Madame,

Mon mari et moi-même prévoyons de passer les deux premières semaines d'août dans le Périgord et ses environs. Nous hésitons, pour ce qui est de l'hébergement, entre un séjour à l'hôtel qui nous permettrait de faire un circuit, et une location en gîte qui présenterait l'avantage d'une plus grande autonomie. C'est pourquoi nous souhaiterions recevoir des renseignements (prix, description, emplacement) sur ces deux modes d'hébergement.

Nous aimerions visiter principalement, lors de notre séjour, Bergerac, Périgueux, Sarlat et les grottes de Lascaux. Nous vous serions donc reconnaissants de bien vouloir nous faire parvenir une liste d'hôtels et de gîtes d'où ces sites nous seraient accessibles.

Nous avons l'intention de louer une voiture, de préférence à Périgueux, où nous arriverons par le train. Pourriez-vous nous fournir également une liste d'agences de location de voitures ?

Enfin, si vous disposez d'un calendrier des manifestations culturelles dans la région autour de cette période, je vous remercie de bien vouloir le joindre à la documentation ci-dessus.

Dans l'attente de votre envoi, je vous prie d'agréer, Monsieur, Madame, l'expression de mes salutations distinguées.

Alison Summers

If the person sending the lett[er] is a woman, the word 'sentimen[ts]' is avoided if the addressee is a m[an] (and vice versa)

Demande de renseignements

39, rue de la Moselle
67000 Strasbourg
FRANCE

Bloomsbury School of English
92-96 Gordon Square
OXFORD OX6 5DY

5 March 2007

Dear Sir/Madam

I am writing to ask for more information about the language courses advertised in this month's copy of 'Lingua'.

I am currently studying for a law degree and am particularly interested in obtaining a qualification in business English. The advertisement mentions that your school is recognized by the London Chamber of Commerce and prepares candidates for a number of its exams.

I am hoping to come to England for three or four weeks this summer and would like to know if you will be running Chamber of Commerce exam courses at that time. I have the equivalent of an A-Level in English, although my written language is much better than my spoken English.

I would also be grateful if you could send me further information on accommodation. If possible, I would like to stay with a family but I also understand that the university has rooms that they rent out. Could you let me have some idea of the cost of these two options.

Thanking you in anticipation, I look forward to hearing from you in the near future.

Yours faithfully

Laurent Leblanc

68, rue Borie
74100 Thonon-les-Bains
FRANCE

Tourist Information Centre
49-51 Station Road
GLASGOW G20 9SL

17 May 2007

Dear Sir or Madam,

My wife and I are planning to visit Glasgow in July of this year and would be grateful if you could send us information about the different types of accommodation available. We intend to stay for a period of three weeks and have budgeted around £500 for accommodation. Are we likely to find a reasonable hotel or bed and breakfast for that?

We would also like information on hiring a car. We will be travelling to Glasgow by plane and would ideally like to collect a car at the airport on our arrival.

I have already collected a certain amount of information on places of interest to visit in and around Glasgow. I would, however, be grateful if you could send me details about train services between Glasgow and Edinburgh.

I look forward to hearing from you.

Yours faithfully,

Pascal Mondon

Unsolicited applications

Paul Sewell
1222 George Washington Avenue
Salt Lake City, UT 84112
États-Unis

Cabinet d'architecture
et d'urbanisme
25, rue du Chat
69210 Lyon

Salt Lake City, le 7 avril 2007

À l'attention du responsable du recrutement

Monsieur, Madame,

Diplômé depuis peu de la faculté d'architecture de l'Université d'Utah, et amoureux de la France depuis de nombreuses années, je souhaiterais vivement exercer mon activité dans votre pays.

L'expérience acquise à la fois à l'Université d'Utah et comme stagiaire dans le cabinet d'architectes « Johnson Brown » à Salt Lake City, ainsi que les travaux en collaboration réalisés au cours de mes études et les participations à divers colloques, conférences, ateliers, etc. (voir CV ci-joint), m'ont préparé tant aux aspects pratiques qu'aux aspects théoriques du métier d'architecte. Je serais ravi de mettre ces atouts au service de votre cabinet, dont les qualités d'originalité sont évidentes à la vue des divers ouvrages réalisés en région lyonnaise, que j'ai pu admirer lors de mon dernier séjour en France. Je suis particulièrement désireux de m'associer à une société jeune et innovante telle que la vôtre.

Je me tiens à votre disposition pour tous renseignements complémentaires et, vous remerciant de l'attention que vous voudrez bien accorder à ma candidature, je vous prie d'agréer, Monsieur, Madame, l'expression de mes sentiments respectueux.

Paul Sewell

Sarah Fitzpatrick
45 Hilly Road
Uplands
Swansea SA2 0LY
UK

Hôtel du Parc
33, rue Molière
26200 Montélimar

Swansea, le 19 février 2007

À l'attention du responsable du personnel

Monsieur, Madame,

Titulaire d'un diplôme des métiers de l'hôtellerie délivré par le Catering College de Swansea, ainsi que d'un certificat de français sanctionnant des cours du soir, je suis à la recherche d'un emploi temporaire dans l'hôtellerie française, de préférence pour les mois de juin à septembre de cette année.

J'ai déjà effectué plusieurs stages dans des établissements britanniques, comme vous le constaterez à la lecture du CV ci-joint. Les responsables du personnel s'y sont montrés unanimement satisfaits de mes services, et vous pouvez les contacter pour leur demander de plus amples détails (voir références au bas du CV).

Je suis consciente du fait que les mois d'été sont particulièrement chargés dans la plupart des établissements hôteliers, notamment dans les endroits touristiques, et je suis tout à fait disposée à m'adapter aux conditions de travail requises par ce surcroît d'activité.

Dans l'espoir d'une réponse favorable, je vous prie d'agréer, Monsieur, Madame, l'expression de mes salutations distinguées.

Sarah Fitzpatrick

Lettres de candidature spontanée

98, rue Jeanne d'Arc
86000 Poitiers

The Personnel Manager
IES Systems Ltd
37 Holborn Street
London W1 5RT

24 October 2007

Dear Sir or Madam,

I have been given your address by a British colleague who has reason to believe that you may be recruiting staff for your sales team. I enclose my CV for your records and would be grateful if you would consider my application should a suitable post arise.

As you will see, I am currently working for a software company in Poitiers. Having graduated from a business school, I joined the company as a junior sales assistant and have now been an account manager with them for four years. I am in charge of a number of major accounts and manage a team of six.

I understand that you have a number of clients in French-speaking countries and believe that my technical and linguistic knowledge would be of benefit to your company. I am already familiar with many of your computer-based training packages and am therefore aware of the quality of your products.

I am available for interview at any time and would be able to start work within a month of handing in my notice. Please do not hesitate to write to me for further details.

I look forward to hearing from you.

Yours faithfully,

Jean Pinot

Jean Pinot

19, rue de la Convention
45000 Orléans

Sidney House Hotel
23-27 Hampton Street
BATH B12 8TN

18 February 2007

Dear Sirs,

I am writing to inquire about the possibility of summer work in the kitchens of your hotel.

I am currently studying to become a chef at a catering college in Paris. As part of my final year studies, I must find a work placement for two months during the summer break (June to August). Whilst on holiday last year with my family, I stayed in your hotel and was extremely impressed by the food on offer in your restaurant. I have already carried out a three-week placement at a restaurant in Paris and enclose a copy of the reference supplied by the catering manager at the end of that period. I greatly enjoyed working as part of a large team and very much look forward to repeating that experience.

I have the equivalent of an A-level in English and as part of my present studies follow a number of courses that are taught in English. I would, however, like to improve my spoken language which is why I am applying for jobs in Britain.

I will be available for work from June 11 to August 30. Please do not hesitate to contact me at the above address if you require any further information.

Thank you for considering my application.

Yours faithfully,

Carole Roussin

Unsolicited applications

In France, applications are always one page long.

You only use "Cher Monsieur" or "Chère Madame" for a letter addressed to someone you have been introduced to.

John Gardener
28 Cranham Street
Oxford OX3 5GF

A l'attention de Monsieur Dubois
Société Pétrodéveloppements
52, rue du Général Leclerc
78380 Bougival

Oxford, le 3/3/2007

Monsieur,

Votre intervention à la conférence d'Amsterdam m'a fait découvrir de nouveaux aspects de la prospection pétrolière et m'incite à vous écrire pour vous proposer mes services.

J'ai terminé la Royal School of Mines en 1990 et travaillé pendant plusieurs années sur une plate-forme en mer du Nord. J'ai ensuite travaillé dans un bureau d'études à Londres et maintenant j'aimerais de nouveau travailler sur le terrain, dans un environnement à la pointe de la technologie.

Vous avez évoqué un projet sur une plate-forme de forage et mon expérience tant de meneur d'hommes que de spécialiste en forage pourrait vous être très utile. Je peux me libérer rapidement. Je vous joins mon CV où vous trouverez des détails supplémentaires sur ma carrière.

Je reste à votre disposition pour un entretien durant lequel je pourrai vous parler plus en détail de mes motivations.

Dans cette attente, je vous adresse mes salutations les meilleures.

J. Garderner

Applications used to have to be handwritten but this pratice is now less common.

Lettres de candidature spontanée

17, rue Henri Vieuxtemps
4000 Liège
BELGIUM
+32 43 487146

Dans un courrier, l'adresse du destinataire se place à gauche.

Miss Mary Dodd
Snowdon Mountain Railway
Llanberis
Gwynedd (North Wales)
LL55 4TY
UK

6 May 2007

Dear Miss Dodd,

I am writing to inquire about the possibility of gaining work experience with your company this summer. I am currently studying for a degree in Tourism at the University of Liège (Belgium), and hope to gain employment in this field when I graduate in approximately one year's time.

I hope you will forgive my writing to you speculatively. I was given your name by a fellow student, Thomas Lenzen, who did his work experience with you last year. He found it to be an extremely interesting and useful experience and has very positive memories of working with you.

I have already gained considerable experience of working in the tourist industry, most recently at the Musée Opinel at St-Jean-de-Maurienne in France, and at the Boutique Tintin in Brussels. References from these employers are attached along with my CV. I have a good command of English, which forms part of my degree course.

I have also spent some time in the UK, including a brief visit to Wales about eighteen months ago. I found it a beautiful and fascinating country, to which I am very keen to return. I enjoy mountaineering, I am something of a railway enthusiast, and I even have hopes of aquiring a little of the Welsh language!

These are some of the reasons why I believe I would be well suited to working at the Snowdon Mountain Railway, whether in the gift shop, the railway exhibition or the café. I hope you will be able to offer me a position, and look forward very much to hearing from you.

Yours faithfully,

Paul Lambotte

Le texte doit être aligné à gauche non justifié et sans alinéa.

La signature est placée en bas à gauche.

Answering a job advertisement

Groupe de presse cherche

Secrétaire de Rédaction

Bilingue anglais,
maîtrise de l'allemand,
environnement PC.
Disponible immédiatement.

CV, lettre de motivation et prétentions à : Déca Presse (réf. SRBA99), 255-257 avenue de Lille, 92300 Levallois.

Salary expectations.

Helen Ryland
6 Fletcher Close
Castle Eden
Co. Durham TS27 4BL
Irlande

Déca Presse
255-257 avenue de Lille
92300 Levallois

Castle Eden, le 28 mai 2007

Objet : poste de secrétaire de rédaction (Réf. SRBA99)

Monsieur, Madame,

Votre annonce parue dans Le Monde cette semaine a retenu toute mon attention. Je pense en effet être à même d'apporter à votre société les qualités acquises aux différents postes de secrétaire de rédaction bilingue que j'ai occupés en Irlande et au Royaume-Uni : sens du détail, correction de l'expression, rapidité, esprit d'équipe, maîtrise de l'outil informatique (PC et Mac, Quark Xpress).

Comme vous le verrez sur mon CV, je possède une formation en langues appliquées aux médias (français-allemand), et, pour compléter les aspects linguistiques de mon métier, je me suis toujours employée à entretenir mon niveau en français par des cours du soir ainsi que des cours d'été en France.

Je vous remercie par avance de l'attention que vous voudrez bien prêter à ma candidature, et me tiens à votre disposition pour tout renseignement complémentaire et pour un entretien éventuel.

Veuillez agréer, Monsieur, Madame, l'expression de mes sentiments distingués.

Helen Ryland

Réponse à une offre d'emploi

Languages at work
In-house French tutor

Large American IT company seeks native French speaker to teach French presentation and conversation skills to its international sales team. Applicants must have a recognized teaching qualification and experience of teaching to all levels. The post is for an initial period of two years. Salary negotiable.

Applications and résumé to:
The Personnel Officer, InfoSoft US Inc., 2567 Fremont Ave., Boulder CO 80303-2252 or email: pturner@infosoft.co.us.
Closing date: August 15, 2003.

Résumé est l'équivalent américain de *CV*.

56, rue du Bois
78000 Versailles

The Personnel Officer
InfoSoft US Inc.
2567 Fremont Ave.
Boulder CO 80303-2252

August 4, 2007

Re: Post of in-house French tutor

Dear Sir/Madam:

I am writing to apply for the above-mentioned post advertised in the July issue of 'IT News' and enclose my résumé for your consideration.

After graduating in French Language and Literature from the University of Nantes, I prepared the CAPES (a high school teaching qualification) and taught for three years at a high school in Paris. During this time, I also studied for a diploma in FLE (Français Langue Étrangère – the teaching of French as a Foreign language) since it had always been my intention to teach abroad.

After leaving France in 2001, I spent the next five years teaching French in Britain in both private language schools and companies. During this period, I gained a wide range of experience, teaching both beginners and more advanced students, general conversation and business French. As you will see from my résumé, I taught a number of students working in the field of IT and am therefore aware of the needs of such people.

I returned to France in May of this year for personal reasons and have been working as a substitute teacher in Paris since then. I am, however, looking to move abroad again and would particularly welcome the experience of working in the United States.

I remain at your disposal for any further information and look forward to hearing from you in the near future.

Sincerely yours,

Claude Vago

Remarquez la ponctuation, différente du style britannique.

Donnez une explication ou un équivalent pour chaque diplôme obtenu à l'étranger.

Answering a job advertisement

R & M, société de services spécialisée dans l'ingénierie documentaire et la formation technique
recherche un traducteur de langue maternelle anglaise pour faire la traduction en anglais de documents techniques français (domaine des télécoms et de l'informatique).

Ce poste est basé en Rhône-Alpes.

De formation supérieure, bilingue anglais/français, vous justifiez d'une expérience d'un an minimum dans la traduction technique.

Envoyez une lettre de candidature et un CV à drh@ereem.fr

Ian.Butcher

de : ianbutcher@easynet.co.uk
à : ldrh@ereem.fr
envoyé : lundi 5 mai 2007 12:11
Objet : traducteur anglophone

Madame, Monsieur,

Votre annonce concernant un poste de traducteur publiée sur le site de l'APEC m'a vivement intéressé. Je suis en fin de stage dans une société qui produit du matériel de télécommunications et pour laquelle je viens de créer un glossaire bilingue français-anglais.

Après des études secondaires à Oxford, j'ai fait des études de langues (français et allemand) à l'université de Leeds. J'ai ensuite suivi un DESS à l'Ecole de traduction et d'interprétation de Genève (option terminologie). Je suis de langue maternelle anglaise et souhaite vivement m'établir en France dans une région où je pourrai pratiquer le ski.

Je vous envoie mon curriculum vitae en pièce jointe ; il vous fournira une version plus détaillée de mon parcours professionnel à ce jour.

Je me tiens à votre disposition pour un entretien et vous adresse mes meilleures salutations

Ian Butcher

==============

You don't usually add your address and phone numbers.

Réponse à une offre d'emploi

Quality Control Director

A new director is required for our expanding range of products.
Applicants should have experience in the dairy industry and in team management.
Foreign experience would be appreciated.
Applications and résumé to:
Louise Rapple, Human Resources Dept,
Fertnel Cheese Corporation,
1674 Observatory Drive
Madison, WI 53706-1283
USA

Résumé est l'équivalent américain de *CV.*

132, rue Marcadet
75018 Paris
FRANCE
+33 1 42012645

Louise Rapple
Human Resources Dept
Fertnel Cheese Corporation
1674 Observatory Drive
Madison, WI 53706-1283
USA

May 17, 2007

Re: Post of Quality Control Director

Dear Ms Rapple,

I wish to apply for the post of Quality Control Director advertised in "Cheese Reporter" of May 16, 2007.

As you will see from the enclosed résumé, I have worked in the dairy products industry for several years, mostly at the small firm of Fromageries Duval SA here in Paris, where I am currently Head of Quality Control.

I graduated "avec mention très bien" (the French equivalent of Summa Cum Laude) in Food Science from one of France's most respected universities, and have acquired a wide knowledge of cheesemaking processes, from traditional artisanal techniques to high-volume commercial brands.

My experience is principally of traditional French styles, but a period of work experience with Rivageois Inc. in Canada taught me much about the North American industry.

I feel I would be an asset to your organization, and would certainly value the opportunity of working for such a large and prestigious corporation.

Please find attached my résumé.
If you require any further details, please do not hesitate to contact me. I hope to hear from you soon.

Sincerely yours,

Anatole Duplay

French CV, English graduate

There is no one standard layout for a CV. Personal details, in particular, can be presented in a number of different ways (centred, in two columns, left-aligned). The important thing is to be clear and concise.

The surname can be given in capitals.

This information is optional. Other marital statuses include: *marié(e), divorcé(e), séparé(e), pacsé(e), veuf (veuve).*

Daniel Peter Lowe

3 Hilda Cottages
Mansfield
Nottinghamshire NG18 7BF
Royaume-Uni
Téléphone : 0044 1623 29385

Célibataire
22 ans
Nationalité britannique

Age can be replaced by date of birth or both can be indicated.

FORMATION

2004-2007	BSc en multimédia (licence), mention très bien Université de Sheffield. Projet de dernière année : production d'un CD-ROM utilisant des techniques de vidéo numérique
2002-2004	A-levels (baccalauréat). Options : langue anglaise, mathématiques, informatique, français
2000-2002	GCSEs : langue anglaise, littérature anglaise, mathématiques, physique, chimie, dessin industriel, géographie, français

For somebody with little professional experience, educational details should come first.

EXPÉRIENCE PROFESSIONNELLE

2006-2007	Animation d'un cybercafé à Mansfield
2005-2006	Participation à la coordination de conférences sur le multimédia (Nottingham, Sheffield, Manchester)
été 2006	Stage d'un mois chez Nova Média, Bruxelles. Travail sur un système de reconnaissance automatique de la parole

---

DIVERS

- **Connaissance approfondie de nombreux logiciels :**
- Adobe Illustrator 7.0.1, Quark 4.0.4, MS Office, etc.
- Systèmes d'exploitation : Windows (Mac/PC), Linux
- Français lu, écrit, parlé. Nombreux séjours en France.
- Goût pour les voyages, le cinéma, le karaté et la randonnée.

Level of proficiency should be indicated. One or more adjectives can be used (eg: *japonais parlé*). Other possibilities: *notions de japonais, bonne connaissance du japonais, japonais courant.*

CV britannique, diplômé français

L'adresse durant l'année universitaire n'est donnée que si elle est différente de l'adresse permanente.

Remarquez la présentation : style télégraphique, aucune mention du lieu de naissance.

Selon le statut : *married, divorced, separated.*

Lorsqu'on a peu ou n'a pas d'expérience professionnelle, on commence par la formation.

Commencez toujours par la date la plus récente et remontez dans le temps.

Énumérez toutes les matières lorsque l'intitulé des cours suivis ne les mentionne pas expressément. Ne donnez la mention que si elle est supérieure à passable.

Signifie que le titulaire du permis n'a jamais été pénalisé pour infraction.

Name:	Serge Aubain
Term Address:	46, rue Passerat 42000 St Etienne France
Telephone:	0033 5 77 46 98 75
Home Address:	38 avenue Mozart 86000 Poitiers France
Telephone:	0033 5 56 43 87 60
Date of Birth:	17.10.86
Nationality:	French
Marital Status:	Single

EDUCATION AND QUALIFICATIONS

2007	École des mines de St-Étienne, 42023 St-Étienne Cedex 2, France First year of a Diploma in Civil Engineering. Core subjects: Maths, Computing, Physics, Mechanical Engineering, Economics, English. Options: Biotechnology, German.
1997-2005	Lycée Fauriel, 145 -149 Cours Fauriel, 86000 Poitiers Baccalauréat S (equivalent to A-level). Subjects: Maths, Physics, Chemistry, French, Geography, History, English, German.

WORK EXPERIENCE

July 2007- Sept. 2007	Group leader at a children's holiday camp, La Rochelle. Duties included organizing activities for children aged between 10 and 16 years, teaching tennis and swimming, liaising with other leaders.
2005-2007	Part-time work as a lifeguard at the local swimming pool.

INTERESTS AND OTHER QUALIFICATIONS

Life saving award (gold medallion)
Full clean driving licence
Basic word processing
Tennis (captain of the school tennis team 2004-2005)
Swimming
Theatre

REFEREES

Mme Sylvie Pasteur
(Headmistress)
Lycée Fauriel
145-149 Cours Fauriel
86000 Poitiers
France

M. Paul Minoche
(Head Lifeguard)
Piscine de Grouchy
86003 Poitiers
France

En règle générale, si l'on est étudiant, on fournit une référence scolaire ou universitaire et une référence personnelle ou professionnelle.

French CV, English graduate with some experience

Jennifer Susan AXFORD
21 Little Moor Road
Burton-upon-Trent
Staffordshire DE14 5JK
Royaume-Uni
Tél. : 0044 1283 574830

Née le 16 septembre 1983
Nationalité britannique

FORMATION	2005	**Licence en gestion** Université de St Andrews, Écosse
	2001	**A-levels** (baccalauréat). Options : français, mathématiques, économie
	1999	**GCSEs** Options : français, mathématiques, anglais, économie, chimie, allemand, histoire, géographie
EXPÉRIENCE PROFESSIONNELLE	mars 2007	**Vendeuse** Librairie Waterstone's, Burton-upon-Trent - réassort commandes livres de poche - réception de la marchandise et mise en rayon - accueil et vente
	2006	**Aide vendeuse** à temps partiel Boutique du musée d'art d'Auxerre, France - tenue de caisse - mise en rayon
DIVERS		• Travail bénévole pour une organisation caritative britannique (travail en magasin : tri de vêtements, tenue de caisse ; participation aux campagnes ponctuelles : démarchage, distribution de prospectus, etc.). • Séjour d'un an en France, à Auxerre (janvier - décembre 2006), où j'ai suivi une formation de français pour étrangers, travaillé comme aide vendeuse et donné des cours particuliers d'anglais. • Centres d'intérêt : musique (je joue de la basse dans un groupe), yoga, aromathérapie.

CV américain, diplômé français ayant une première expérience

Remarquez qu'aux États-Unis on n'indique ni la situation de famille ni la date de naissance, car ces informations ne sont plus considérées comme devant être connues de l'employeur.

Les diplômes américains et britanniques portent parfois des noms différents et il peut être nécessaire de donner un équivalent.

Anne-Marie Bertheas
20, rue de la Paix
13200 Arles
France
Tél. : 0033 4 46 75 88 09

EMPLOYMENT	2001-	English teacher, Lycée Pothier, 13200 Arles Teaching English to French students aged 13-18 as preparation for the Baccalauréat (equivalent to high school diploma)
	1997-1998	Language assistant, Hutton Comprehensive, Hutton, Lancashire, Great Britain Teaching French to English students aged 11-16 as preparation for the GCSE examination (equivalent to high school diploma)
	1995-1997	Sales assistant, Auchan, Place du Peuple, 13200 Arles Weekend work in the electrical department of a large supermarket.
EDUCATION	1995-2001	University of Lille, Lille, France
	June 2001	CAPES (high school teaching qualification)
	May 1999	Licence d'anglais (equivalent to BA) English Language, Literature and Civilization
	May 1997	Diplôme de Français Langue Étrangère (qualification for teaching French as a foreign language)
LANGUAGES	English	(near-native fluency)
	German	(written and spoken)
	Spanish	(basic knowledge)
OTHER INFORMATION	Word processing (Word for Windows, QuarkXpress) Full clean driver's license Secretary of Arles France-Great Britain Society	
REFERENCES	Available upon request	

Driving licence
en anglais britannique.

French CV, American professional with experience

The CV of somebody with a certain amount of professional experience may begin with a profile summarizing their main skills and/or qualities.

ROSS D. JAGGER

Consultant en gestion d'entreprise

Spécialiste en :
• opérations internationales
• planification stratégique
• investissements

13, rue de Lévy
75017 Paris
Tél. : 01 45 78 93 40
Fax : 01 45 85 03 05
e-mail : djagger@infonie.fr

Date de naissance : 3/6/1965
Double nationalité américaine - française
Marié, 2 enfants

PRINCIPAUX PROJETS

- Planification stratégique, études de concurrence, estimations pour diverses sociétés multinationales.
- Réalisation d'opérations de marketing direct.
- Évaluation de sociétés nouvellement créées. Conseil sur le lancement de nouveaux produits.
- Mise en place d'un système de transactions de devises pour un grand établissement financier.
- Coordination des investissements informatiques pour des sociétés américaines, asiatiques et européennes.
- Travail sur des bases de données client-serveur : bases de vente et de marketing pour divers clients (banque, électronique, agences de publicité).

FORMATION

- **Mastère en Gestion internationale (1993)**
  American Graduate School of International Management, San Diego, Californie, États-Unis
- **Licence d'Économie internationale (1992)**
  Université de l'Illinois

CV britannique, cadre confirmé français

Un candidat ayant déjà une certaine expérience peut commencer son CV par un résumé de ses principales compétences et/ou qualités.

DOMINIQUE PETIT
25 bd St Denis, 69008 Lyon, France.
Tel. : 0033 4 66 54 11 98
e-mail: dominique.petit@compu.fr

- bilingual editor
- proven organizational and interpersonal skills
- meticulous eye for detail

EMPLOYMENT	2003	Senior Editor, Larousse Publishing, Lyon, France Managing and coordinating reference publishing projects for French and international markets: – preparation of timetables and budgets – staff recruitment and training – administration of Lyon office – liaising with freelancers and typesetters
	2000-2003	Editor, Mac Bride, Edinburgh, UK Working on a French-English dictionary: – compilation and translation of text – proofreading
	1998-2000	Translator, Euro Translations, Paris, France – commercial and technical translation
EDUCATION	1996-1998	École supérieure d'Interprètes et de Traducteurs (ESIT), Paris, France
	May 1998	Diplôme d'Études supérieures spécialisées (DESS) (postgraduate qualification in translation)
	1991-1996	Université Lumière-Lyon-II, Lyon, France
	June 1996	Maîtrise d'anglais (equivalent to MA) Research topic: Accents and Class in British Society
	June 1996	Licence d'anglais (equivalent to BA) English
	1984-1991	Lycée Charles de Gaulle, Lyon, France
	June 1991	Baccalauréat L (equivalent to A-level) Subjects: French, English, German, Spanish, Maths, Geography, History
OTHER SKILLS		Word processing (Word for Windows NT) Working knowledge of publishing databases
PERSONAL DETAILS		Date of Birth:14.01.73 Marital Status: Married (2 children) Nationality: French
REFEREES		Available on request

Reference letter

This is a general opening formula used when there is no one particular contact person.
It is the equivalent of: *To whom it may concern.*

The White Horse Inn
11 Lime Street
Wadebridge
Cornwall PL27 4GG
Tel./Fax: 01208 55694

Wadebridge, le 7 juin 2007

À QUI DE DROIT

Mademoiselle Eileen Mockridge a été employée, de février 2006 à avril 2007, comme serveuse au White Horse Inn à Wadebridge. En tant que gérant de cet établissement, j'ai beaucoup apprécié le professionnalisme et la ponctualité de Mademoiselle Mockridge, dont les rapports avec la clientèle et avec le reste du personnel étaient excellents.

Je suis persuadé qu'Eileen saura s'intégrer sans difficulté à un nouvel environnement de travail, et qu'elle donnera entière satisfaction dans un emploi du même type, ou même à un poste impliquant de plus grandes responsabilités.

Michael J. Clark

Michael J. Clark
Gérant

Lettre de recommandation

La lettre de recommandation ne s'adresse à aucun employeur en particulier. Cette formule générale équivaut à : *À qui de droit*. Aux États-Unis, elle est suivie de deux points (:).

On peut choisir de donner, en début de lettre, un bref résumé de son contenu.

Le Petit Prince
Place de l'Église
57000 Metz
Tél. : (0033) 03 89 34 57 85

15 September 2007

To whom it may concern

Susan Clarke

This is to certify that Susan Clarke was employed as a receptionist at the above-mentioned establishment from April 12, 2007 to September 15, 2007.

As a receptionist, Susan's duties included taking bookings for the hotel and restaurant, liaising between the two, welcoming guests and generally ensuring the smooth running of the establishment.

I have found Susan to be a pleasant, reliable and hard-working member of staff who has always carried out her duties to the highest possible level. In addition to excellent interpersonal skills, her French has improved to almost native speaker level during her time with us. She has become a highly valued member of our team, popular with both guests and other staff, and will be greatly missed. I have no reservations about recommending her to future employers.

Yours faithfully

Jean-Christophe Pousset

Jean-Christophe Pousset
Manager

Telephoning

• Calling someone at home

— Allô.
— Oui, allô, est-ce que je suis bien chez Monsieur et Madame Renouet, s'il vous plaît ?

To check that you have dialled the right number.

— Oui, c'est bien ça.
— Ah, bonjour madame, est-ce que je pourrais parler à Anne-Sophie, s'il vous plaît ?

• The person is out

— Ah non, je regrette, elle n'est pas là en ce moment. Est-ce que je peux lui transmettre un message ?
— Oui, d'accord. Est-ce que vous pourriez lui dire que Denis a appelé.
— Bien sûr, je lui dirai. Je lui demande de vous rappeler ?
— Oui, ça serait bien si elle pouvait me rappeler. Je serai chez moi toute la journée. Merci beaucoup. Au revoir, madame.
— Au revoir, monsieur.

• The person is in

— Oui, je vous la passe. C'est de la part de qui ?
— C'est Denis. C'est au sujet de son séjour en Angleterre.
— D'accord, je vais la chercher.

• Getting the wrong number

— Allô.
— Bonjour, est-ce que je pourrais parler à Éric, s'il vous plaît ?
— Ah non, je regrette, vous avez dû vous tromper de numéro.
— Ah bon ? Ce n'est pas le 05 59 35 67 13 ?

When saying a telephone number the figures are pronounced in pairs, so you would say: *zéro cinq, cinquante-neuf, trente-cinq, soixante-sept, treize*

— Non, c'est le 05 59 35 67 12.
— Oh pardon, excusez-moi.
— Ce n'est pas grave, au revoir.
— Au revoir.

• Calling a company

— Jutheau S.A., bonjour.
— Bonjour. Je voudrais le poste 128, s'il vous plaît.
— Oui, ne quittez pas. Je vous le passe.
— Anne-Marie Béchu, service commercial.
— Bonjour, madame. Je voudrais parler à Monsieur Péri, s'il vous plaît.
— Oui, c'est de la part de qui, s'il vous plaît ?
— François Lebeau de chez Lavoisier.
— Je regrette, c'est occupé. Est-ce que vous voulez patienter ou rappeler plus tard ?
— Je vais attendre un peu.
— Très bien... Je regrette, c'est toujours occupé. Est-ce que je peux prendre un message ?
— Oui, pourriez-vous lui dire de rappeler François Lebeau chez Lavoisier au 01 43 22 77 02 ? C'est au sujet de la réunion du 14 avec les représentants.
— Entendu, monsieur.
— Je vous remercie, madame. Au revoir.
— Au revoir, monsieur.

Au téléphone

• Appeler quelqu'un chez lui

— Hello, 0155 915 3678.

Au Royaume-Uni, certaines personnes annoncent leur numéro de téléphone lorsqu'elles décrochent. Aux États-Unis, cela n'est pas courant.

— Hello, could I speak to Jane, please?

• La personne est absente

— No, I'm sorry, she's not in at the moment. Can I give her a message?

— Yes, please. Could you tell her that Fred rang?

Aux États-Unis, on dirait *called.*

— Yes, of course. Shall I ask her to ring you back?

— Yes, please. I'll be at home all day.

— OK, I'll tell her when she comes in.

— Thank you, goodbye.

— Goodbye.

• La personne est là

— Yes. Who's calling?

— It's Fred. I'm calling about the trip to France.

— OK, one moment, I'll just get her for you.

• Se tromper de numéro

— Hello.

— Hello. Could I speak to Tom, please?

— I'm sorry. I think you must have the wrong number.

— Is that not 742215?

Aux États-Unis, on dit : *Is this 742215?* Notez qu'au Royaume-Uni ainsi qu'aux États-Unis les chiffres sont prononcés séparément. Toutefois, lorsque deux chiffres identiques se suivent, on dira au Royaume-Uni *double 2* alors qu'on prononcera ces chiffres deux fois aux États-Unis.

— No, this is 742216.

— Oh, sorry.

— That's OK.

• Appeler une entreprise

— Good morning, Smith Brothers.

— Good morning. Could I have extension 478, please?

Ou : *Could you put me through to extension 478, please?*

— One moment. I'll put you through.

— Good morning, electrical department. Linda speaking. How may I help you?

— Hello. I'd like to speak to someone about the washing machine I've just bought.

— Hold the line, please. I'll transfer you to our after-sales department. Can I say who's calling?

L'équivalent de cette formule britannique est, aux États-Unis : *Would you mind holding a moment? I'll transfer you...*

— Mrs Jones.

— I'm afraid the line's busy. Would you like to hold?

— Yes, please.

— I'm afraid the line's still busy.

Ou : *the line's engaged* en anglais britannique.

Would you like to continue holding or would you like to call back later?

— Could I leave a message?

— Certainly.

— Would you ask someone to call me on 01162 476548. It's quite urgent.

Aux États-Unis, on dirait *at* au lieu de *on.*

— I'll make sure someone calls you back within the next ten minutes, Mrs Jones.

— Thank you very much. Goodbye.

— Goodbye. Thank you for calling.

Text messaging

J'ai acheté le pain ; je rentre aussi vite que possible.

I've bought the bread; I'll be back as soon as possible.

ght le p1, rentr
asap

Salut ! Rendez-vous au cinéma. J'espère bien que tu es d'accord. C'est ce qu'on avait décidé. À plus tard.

Hi! We'll meet up at the UK *cinema,* US *movie theater. Hope that's o.k. It's what we'd decided. See you later.*

slt, rdv o 6ne
GspR b1 q t dak
sete D6D, a+

Aucun message. Je le savais ! Tu es occupé, tu as oublié, qu'est-ce que tu fais ?

I knew it! No messages. Are you too busy, have you forgotten? What are you up to? [I haven't received any messages from you]

O k1 msg G le sa
V, t oqp
ta oublié
kestufé?????

ya 1 blem, l'ordi
e KC Rstp pcq G
c pas keskonfe

On a un problème, l'ordinateur est en panne. S'il te plaît, réponds-moi. Je ne sais pas ce qu'il faut faire.

There's a problem: the computer has broken down. Please get back to me because I don't know what to do.

koi 2 9 Tu l'M
ta télé JKD

Quoi de neuf ? Tu l'aimes ta télévision, je plaisante.

So, what's new? You're in love with your T.V. set! Just kidding.

Le livre T1TRS
TA KPC

Le livre t'intéresse ? Tu n'as qu'à passer.

Are you interested in the book? Just come by.

Je t'aime, qu'est-ce que tu crois ? Je t'attends toujours au restaurant, grosses bises.

Of course, I love you! I'm still waiting for you at the restaurant. Lots of love.

Messages SMS

Please forgive me; the movie finished late. See you at lunch.

Excuse-moi, le film s'est terminé plus tard que prévu. Je te verrai au déjeuner.

pls 4giv me de movie finishd l8, c U @ lch

SBTA on holiday

Sorry, but try again. I'm on holiday.

Désolé, je suis en vacances.

Paul, leave a message as soon as possible, lots of love, Sue.

Paul, laisse un message dès que possible, affectueusement, Sue.

I'd like to see your house, but I can't go in the morning.

J'aimerais bien voir ta maison, mais je ne peux pas venir le matin.

It's never going to happen, so why are you telling everyone how great she is?

Ça n'arrivera jamais, alors pourquoi est-ce que tu racontes à tout le monde à quel point elle est super ?

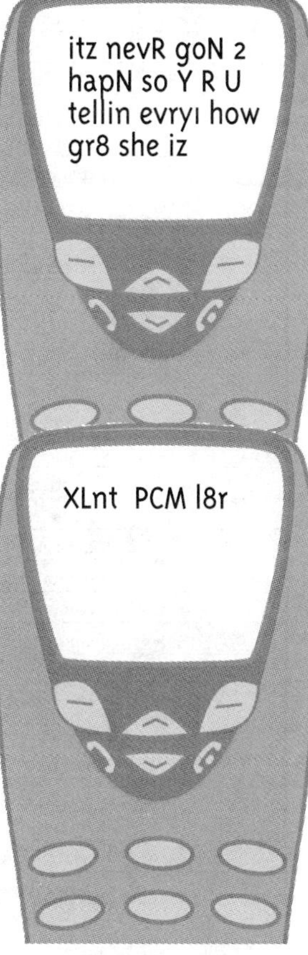

Excellent, please call me later.

Super, rappelle-moi plus tard.

RU wrkN 2day we R goin U d country fry R U frE

Are you working today? We're going to the country on Friday. Are you free?

Tu travailles aujourd'hui ? On va à la campagne vendredi. Est-ce que tu es libre ?

Ordinal numbers

$1^{er}/1^{ère}$	premier/première
$2^{ème}/2^{nd(e)}$	deuxième/second(e)
3ème	troisième
4ème	quatrième
5ème	cinquième
6ème	sixième
7ème	septième
8ème	huitième
9ème	neuvième
10ème	dixième
11ème	onzième
12ème	douzième
13ème	treizième
14ème	quatorzième
15ème	quinzième
16ème	seizième
17ème	dix-septième
18ème	dix-huitième
19ème	dix-neuvième
20ème	vingtième
21ème	vingt et unième
22ème	vingt-deuxième
30ème	trentième
31ème	trente et unième
40ème	quarantième
41ème	quarante et unième
50ème	cinquantième
51ème	cinquante et unième
60ème	soixantième
61ème	soixante et unième
62ème	soixante-deuxième
70ème	soixante-dixième
71ème	soixante et onzième
72ème	soixante-douzième
80ème	quatre-vingtième
81ème	quatre-vingt unième
90ème	quatre-vingt-dixième
91ème	quatre-vingt-onzième
100ème	centième
101ème	cent unième
200ème	deux centième
300ème	trois centième
572ème	cinq cent soixante-douzième
1000ème	millième
1950ème	mille neuf cent cinquantième
2000ème	deux millième
$1\ 000\ 000^{ème}$	millionième
$2\ 000\ 000^{ème}$	deux millionième

Cardinal numbers

0	zéro
1	un
2	deux
3	trois
4	quatre
5	cinq
6	six
7	sept
8	huit
9	neuf
10	dix
11	onze
12	douze
13	treize
14	quatorze
15	quinze
16	seize
17	dix-sept
18	dix-huit
19	dix-neuf
20	vingt
21	vingt et un
22	vingt-deux
30	trente
31	trente et un
40	quarante
41	quarante et un
50	cinquante
51	cinquante et un
60	soixante
61	soixante et un
62	soixante-deux
70	soixante-dix
71	soixante et onze
72	soixante-douze
80	quatre-vingt(s)
81	quatre-vingt-un
90	quatre-vingt-dix
91	quatre-vingt-onze
100	cent
101	cent un
200	deux cents
300	trois cents
572	cinq cent soixante-douze
1000	mille
1066	mille soixante-six
2000	deux mille
2002	deux mille deux
2007	deux mille sept
1 000 000	un million
2 000 000	deux millions
1 000 000 000	un milliard

Les nombres ordinaux

1st	first
2nd	second
3rd	third
4th	fourth
5th	fifth
6th	sixth
7th	seventh
8th	eighth
9th	ninth
10th	tenth
11th	eleventh
12th	twelfth
13th	thirteenth
14th	fourteenth
15th	fifteenth
16th	sixteenth
17th	seventeenth
18th	eighteenth
19th	nineteenth
20th	twentieth
21st	twenty-first
22nd	twenty-second
30th	thirtieth
31st	thirty-first
40th	fortieth
41st	forty-first
50th	fiftieth
51st	fifty-first
60th	sixtieth
61st	sixty-first
62nd	sixty-second
70th	seventieth
71st	seventy-first
72nd	seventy-second
80th	eightieth
81st	eighty-first
90th	ninetieth
91st	ninety-first
100th	(one) hundredth
101st	hundred and first
200th	two hundredth
300th	three hundredth
572nd	five hundred and seventy-second
1000th	(one) thousandth
1950th	nineteen hundred and fiftieth
2000th	two thousandth
1,000,000th	(one) millionth
2,000,000th	two millionth

Les nombres cardinaux

0	zero, nought ***UK***
1	one
2	two
3	three
4	four
5	five
6	six
7	seven
8	eight
9	nine
10	ten
11	eleven
12	twelve
13	thirteen
14	fourteen
15	fifteen
16	sixteen
17	seventeen
18	eighteen
19	nineteen
20	twenty
21	twenty-one
22	twenty-two
30	thirty
31	thirty-one
40	forty
41	forty-one
50	fifty
51	fifty-one
60	sixty
61	sixty-one
62	sixty-two
70	seventy
71	seventy-one
72	seventy-two
80	eighty
81	eighty-one
90	ninety
91	ninety-one
100	a OR one hundred
101	a hundred and one
200	two hundred
300	three hundred
572	five hundred and seventy-two
1000	a OR one thousand
1066	ten sixty-six OR one thousand and sixty-six
2000	two thousand
2002	two thousand and two
2007	two thousand and seven
1,000,000	a OR one million
2,000,000	two million
1,000,000,000	a OR one billion

Fractions and other mathematical functions

1/2	un demi OR une demie OR la moitié	**once**	une fois
1 1/2	un et demi	**twice**	deux fois
2 1/2	deux et demi	**three (four) times**	trois (quatre) fois
1/3	un tiers	**twice as much (many)**	deux fois plus
2/3	deux tiers	**firstly, in the first place**	premièrement, primo
1/4	un quart	**secondly, in the second place**	deuxièmement, deuzio
3/4	trois quarts	**thirdly, in the third place**	troisièmement, tertio
1/5	un cinquième	**7 + 8 = 15**	sept plus huit égalent quinze
3 4/5	trois et quatre cinquièmes	**9 – 4 = 5**	neuf moins quatre égalent cinq
5/8	cinq huitièmes	**2 x 3 = 6**	deux fois trois égalent six
12/20	douze vingtièmes	**20 ÷ 5 = 4**	vingt divisé par cinq égalent quatre
75/100	soixante-quinze centièmes		
0,45	zéro virgule quarante-cinq		
2,5	deux virgule cinq		

Currency

		Coins	Banknotes *UK*, Bills *US*	
British currency	**1p**	un penny	**£5**	cinq livres
	2p	deux pence	**£10**	dix livres
	5p	cinq pence	**£20**	vingt livres
	10p	dix pence	**£50**	cinquante livres
	20p	vingt pence		
	50p	cinquante pence		
	£1	une livre		
American currency	**1 cent (a penny)**	un cent	**$1**	un dollar
	5 cents (a nickel)	cinq cents	**$5**	cinq dollars
	10 cents (a dime)	dix cents	**$10**	dix dollars
	25 cents (a quarter)	vingt-cinq cents	**$20**	vingt dollars
			$50	cinquante dollars
			$100	cent dollars
European currency	**1 cent**	un centime	**5€**	cinq euros
	2 cents	deux centimes	**10€**	dix euros
	5 cents	cinq centimes	**20€**	vingt euros
	10 cents	dix centimes	**50€**	cinquante euros
	20 cents	vingt centimes	**100€**	cent euros
	50 cents	cinquante centimes	**200€**	deux cents euros
	1€	un euro	**500€**	cinq cents euros
	2€	deux euros		

Fractions et autres fonctions mathématiques

1/2	one OU a half	**une fois**	once
1 1/2	one and a half	**deux fois**	twice
2 1/2	two and a half	**trois (quatre) fois**	three (four) times
1/3	one OU a third	**deux fois plus**	twice as much (many)
2/3	two thirds	**premièrement, primo**	firstly, in the first place
1/4	one OU a quarter, one OU a fourth	**deuxièmement, deuzio**	secondly, in the second place
3/4	three quarters, three fourths	**troisièmement, tertio**	thirdly, in the third place
1/5	one OU a fifth	**7 + 8 = 15**	seven plus OU and eight is fifteen
3 4/5	three and four fifths	**9 – 4 = 5**	nine minus OU less four is five
5/8	five eighths	**2 x 3 = 6**	twice OU two times three is six
12/20	twelve twentieths	**3 x 3 = 9**	three times three is nine
75/100	seventy-five hundredths	**20 ÷ 5 = 4**	twenty divided by five is four
0.45	(nought *UK* OU zero *US*) point four five		
2.5	two point five		

Monnaie

	Pièces		Billets	
Monnaie britannique	**1p**	a penny	**£5**	five pounds
	2p	two pence	**£10**	ten pounds
	5p	five pence	**£20**	twenty pounds
	10p	ten pence	**£50**	fifty pounds
	20p	twenty pence		
	50p	fifty pence		
	£1	a pound		
Monnaie américaine	**1 cent**	one cent (a penny)	**$1**	one dollar
	5 cents	five cents (a nickel)	**$5**	five dollars
	10 cents	ten cents (a dime)	**$10**	ten dollars
	25 cents	twenty-five cents (a quarter)	**$20**	twenty dollars
			$50	fifty dollars
			$100	a hundred dollars
Monnaie européenne	**1 cent**	a cent	**5€**	five euros
	2 cents	two cents	**10€**	ten euros
	5 cents	five cents	**20€**	twenty euros
	10 cents	ten cents	**50€**	fifty euros
	20 cents	twenty cents	**100€**	a hundred euros
	50 cents	fifty cents	**200€**	two hundred euros
	1€	a euro	**500€**	five hundred euros
	2€	two euros		

Continental weights and measures

Length	
1 millimètre (mm)	= 0.03937 inches
1 centimètre (cm)	= 10 mm = 0.3937 inches
1 décimètre (dm)	= 10 cm = 3.937 inches
1 mètre (m)	= 10 dm = 1.0936 yards = 3.2809 feet
1 kilomètre (km)	= 1000 m = 1,093 yards = 0.6214 mile

Area	
1 millimètre carré (mm^2)	= 0.00155 square inches
1 centimètre carré (cm^2)	= 100 mm^2 = 0.1550 square inches
1 mètre carré (m^2)	= 10 000 cm^2 = 1.1960 square yards
1 are (a)	= 100 m^2 = 119.60 square yards
1 hectare (ha)	= 100 a = 2.4711 acres
1 kilomètre carré (km^2)	= 100 ha = 0.3861 square mile

Cubic measures	
1 centimètre cube (cm^3)	= 0.0610 cubic inch
1 décimètre cube (dm^3)	= 1000 cm^3 = 0.0351 cubic foot
1 mètre cube (m^3)	= 1000 dm^3 = 1.3080 cubic yards

Capacity		United Kingdom	United States
1 millilitre (ml)		0.0352 fluid ounce	0.0338 fluid ounce
1 centilitre (cl)	= 10 ml	0.352 fluid ounce	0.338 fluid ounce
1 décilitre (dl)	= 10 cl	3.52 fluid ounces	3.38 fluid ounces
1 litre (l)	= 10 dl	1.76 pints = 0.22 gallon	2.113 pints = 0.264 gallon
1 hectolitre (hl)	= 100 l	220 gallons	264 gallons

Weight	
1 milligramme (mg)	= 0.0154 grain
1 gramme (g)	= 1000 mg = 15.43 grains = 0.0353 ounce
1 iivre	= 500 g = 1.1024 pounds
1 kilogramme (kg)	= 1000 g = 2.2046 pounds
1 tonne (t)	= 1000 kg : *UK* = 0.9842 ton ; *US* = 1.1023 tons

Poids et mesures anglo-saxons

Longueur	
1 inch (in.)	= 2,54 cm
1 foot (ft)	= 12 inches = 30,48 cm
1 yard (yd)	= 3 feet = 91,44 cm
1 furlong	= 220 yards = 201,17 m
1 mile (ml, *US* mi.)	= 1609,34 m
Surface	
1 square inch (sq. in.)	= 6,45 cm^2
1 square foot (sq. ft)	= 144 square inches = 929,03 cm^2
1 square yard (sq. yd)	= 9 square feet = 0,836 m^2
1 square rod (sq. rd)	= 30,25 square yards = 25,29 m^2
1 acre (a.)	= 4840 square yards = 4046,9 m^2
1 square mile (sq. ml., *US* sq. mi.)	= 640 acres = 2,59 km^2 = 259 ha
Capacité	
1 cubic inch (cu. in.)	= 16,387 cm^3
1 cubic foot (cu. ft)	= 1728 cubic inches = 0,028 m^3
1 cubic yard (cu. yd)	= 27 cubic feet = 0,765 m^3
1 register ton (reg. tn)	= 100 cubic feet = 2,832 m^3
Capacité (Grande-Bretagne)	
1 imperial gill (gi., gl)	= 0,142 l
1 imperial pint (pt)	= 4 gills = 0,568 l
1 imperial quart (qt)	= 2 imperial pints = 1,136 l
1 imperial gallon (imp. gal.)	= 4 imperial quarts = 4,546 l
1 imperial barrel (bbl., bl.)	= 36 imperial gallons = 1,636 hl
Capacité (États-Unis)	
1 U.S. dry pint	= 0,551 l
1 U.S. dry quart	= 2 dry pints = 1,1 l
1 U.S. liquid gill	= 0,118 l
1 U.S. liquid pint	= 4 gills = 0,473 l
1 U.S. liquid quart	= 2 liquid pints = 0,946 l
1 U.S. gallon	= 8 liquid pints = 3,785 l
1 U.S. barrel	= 31,5 gallons = 119,2 l
1 U.S. barrel oil	= 42 gallons = 158,97 l
Poids	
1 grain (gr.)	= 0,0648 g
1 dram (dr. av.)	= 27,34 grains = 1,77 g
1 ounce (oz av.)	= 16 drams = 28,35 g
1 pound (lb. av.)	= 16 ounces = 0,453 kg
1 stone (st.)	= 14 pounds = 6,35 kg
1 quarter (qr)	*UK* = 28 pounds = 12,7 kg ; *US* = 25 pounds = 11,34 kg
1 hundredweight (cwt)	*UK* = 112 pounds = 50,8 kg ; *US* = 100 pounds = 45,36 kg
1 ton (t, tn)	*UK* = 2240 pounds = 1016 kg ; *US* = 2000 pounds = 907,18 kg

ENGLISH-FRENCH
ANGLAIS-FRANÇAIS

a (*pl* **a's**), **A** (*pl* **A's** *OR pl* **As**) [eɪ] *n* **1.** [letter] a *m*, A *m* ■ **45a** [house, page number] 45 bis, *see also* **f** **2.** [in list] : **I'm not going because a) I've no money and b) I've no time** je n'y vais pas parce que primo je n'ai pas d'argent et secundo je n'ai pas le temps.

a [*(weak form* [ə], *strong form* [eɪ]*)*] *(before vowel an weak form* [ən], *strong form* [æn]*) det* **1.** [before countable nouns] un, une *f* ■ **a book** un livre ■ **I can't see a thing** je ne vois rien ‖ [before professions] : **she's a doctor** elle est médecin ■ **have you seen a doctor?** as-tu vu un médecin?
2. [before numbers] : **a thousand dollars** mille dollars ■ **a dozen eggs** une douzaine d'œufs ■ **a twentieth of a second** un vingtième de seconde ■ **an hour and a half** une heure et demie ‖ [per] : **£2 a dozen/a hundred grams** deux livres la douzaine/les cent grammes ■ **three times a year** trois fois par an
3. [before terms of quantity, amount] : **a few weeks/months** quelques semaines/mois ■ **a lot of money** beaucoup d'argent
4. [before periods of time] un, une *f* ■ **I'm going for a week/month/year** je pars (pour) une semaine/un mois/un an
5. [before days, months, festivals] un, une *f* ■ **it was an exceptionally cold March** ce fut un mois de mars particulièrement froid
6. [in generalizations] : **a cheetah can outrun a lion** le guépard court plus vite que le lion
7. [before uncountable nouns] : **a wide knowledge of the subject** une connaissance approfondie du sujet
8. [before verbal nouns] : **there's been a general falling off in sales** il y a eu une chute des ventes
9. [before personal names] : **a Miss Jones was asking for you** une certaine Miss Jones vous a demandé ‖ [before names of artists] : **it's a genuine Matisse** c'est un Matisse authentique
10. [after half, rather, such, what] : **half a glass of wine** un demi-verre de vin ■ **she's rather an interesting person** c'est quelqu'un d'assez intéressant ■ **what a lovely dress!** quelle jolie robe!
11. [after as, how, so, too + adj] : **that's too big a slice for me** cette tranche est trop grosse pour moi ■ **she's as nice a girl as you could wish to meet** c'est la fille la plus gentille du monde.

a. *written abbr of* **acre.**

A [eɪ] (*pl* **A's** *OR pl* **As**) <> *n* **1.** [letter] A *m* ■ **A5** *UK* **TRANSP** ≃ RN *f* 5 ■ **from A to Z** de A à Z **2.** **SCH** : **to get an A in French** ≃ obtenir plus de 15 sur 20 en français **3.** **MUS** la *m*.
<> *adj* **1.** **MUS** [string] de la **2.** *UK* **TRANSP** : **A road** route *f* nationale *(en Grande-Bretagne)*.
<> (*written abbrev of* **ampere**) A.

A-1 *adj* **1.** [first-class, perfect] : **everything's ~** tout est parfait **2.** [in health] : **to be ~** être en pleine santé *OR* forme **3.** **NAUT** en excellent état.

A4 <> *n* [paper size] format *m* A4.
<> *adj* : **~ paper** papier *m* (format) A4.

AA <> *pr n* **1.** (*abbrev of* **Automobile Association**) *automobile club britannique et compagnie d'assurances, qui garantit le dépannage de ses adhérents et propose des services touristiques et juridiques,* ≃ ACF *m*, ≃ TCF *m* **2.** (*abbrev of* **Alcoholics Anonymous**) Alcooliques Anonymes *mpl*.
<> *n* *US* = **Associate in Arts.**

AAA *pr n* **1.** [ˌθriːˈeɪz] (*abbrev of* **Amateur Athletics Association**) *ancien nom de la fédération britannique d'athlétisme (remplacé en octobre 1991 par la British Athletics Federation)* **2.** [ˌtrɪplˈeɪ] (*abbrev of* **American Automobile Association**) *automobile club américain,* ≃ ACF *m*, ≃ TCF *m*.

Aachen [ˈɑːkən] *pr n* Aix-la-Chapelle.

aardvark [ˈɑːdvɑːk] *n* oryctérope *m*.

Aargau [ˈɑːgaʊ] *pr n* Argovie *f*.

aargh [æː] *excl* aargh.

AAUP (*abbrev of* **American Association of University Professors**) *pr n syndicat américain des professeurs d'université.*

AB <> *n* **1.** *US* **UNIV** (*abbrev of* **Bachelor of Arts**) *(titulaire d'une) licence de lettres* **2.** *UK* **NAUT** = **able-bodied seaman.**
<> *written abbr of* **Alberta.**

aback [əˈbæk] *adv* : **to be taken ~** être pris au dépourvu, être interloqué ; **NAUT** être pris bout au vent ■ **I was quite taken ~ by what he said** j'ai été très surpris par ce qu'il m'a dit.

abacus [ˈæbəkəs] (*pl* **abacuses** *OR pl* **abaci** [ˈæbəsaɪ]) *n* boulier *m*.

abandon [əˈbændən] <> *vt* **1.** [leave - person, object] abandonner ; [- post, place] déserter, quitter ■ **to ~ ship** abandonner *OR* quitter le navire **2.** [give up - search] abandonner, renoncer à ; [- studies, struggle] renoncer à ; [- idea, cause] laisser tomber ■ **several runners ~ed the race** plusieurs coureurs ont abandonné ■ **the match was ~ed because of bad weather** on a interrompu le match en raison du mauvais temps **3.** [for insurance] : **they ~ed the car to the insurance company** ils ont cédé la voiture à la compagnie d'assurances.
<> *n* **1.** [neglect] abandon *m* ■ **in a state of ~** laissé à l'abandon **2.** [lack of inhibition] désinvolture *f*, laisser-aller *m* ■ **they leapt about with wild** *OR* **gay ~** ils sautaient de joie sans aucune retenue.

abandoned [əˈbændənd] *adj* **1.** [person] abandonné, délaissé ■ [house] abandonné **2.** [dissolute - behaviour, person] débauché ; [- life] de débauche **3.** [unrestrained - laughter, gaiety] sans retenue.

abandonment [əˈbændənmənt] *n* **1.** [of place, person, project] abandon *m* **2.** [of right] cession *f*.

abase [əˈbeɪs] *vt* : **to ~ o.s.** s'humilier, s'abaisser.

abasement [əˈbeɪsmənt] *n* humiliation *f*.

abashed [əˈbæʃt] *adj* penaud ■ **to be** *OR* **to feel ~** avoir honte.

abate [əˈbeɪt] ◇ *vi* [storm] s'apaiser ■ [pain] diminuer ■ [noise] s'atténuer.
◇ *vt* [tax] baisser, réduire.

abatement [əˈbeɪtmənt] *n* **1.** [of tax, rent] réduction *f*, abattement *m* **2.** [of noise, strength] diminution *f*, réduction *f*.

abattoir [ˈæbətwɑːʳ] *n* abattoirs *mpl*.

abbess [ˈæbes] *n* abbesse *f*.

abbey [ˈæbɪ] ◇ *n* abbaye *f*.
◇ *comp* [grounds] de l'abbaye.

abbot [ˈæbət] *n* abbé *m (dans un monastère)*.

abbr, abbrev 1. *written abbr of* **abbreviation 2.** *written abbr of* **abbreviated**.

abbreviate [əˈbriːvɪeɪt] *vt* [text, title] abréger ■ **"for example" is ~d to "e.g."** "par exemple" est abrégé en "p. ex.".

abbreviation [əˌbriːvɪˈeɪʃn] *n* [of expression, title, word] abréviation *f* ■ **"Dr" is an ~ for "doctor"** "Dr" est l'abréviation de "docteur".

ABC ◇ *n* **1.** [rudiments] rudiments *mpl*, B.A. Ba *m* **2.** [alphabet] alphabet *m* ■ **it's as easy as ~** c'est simple comme bonjour.
◇ *pr n (abbrev of* **American Broadcasting Company***) chaîne de télévision américaine.*
◆ **ABCs** *npl US* = **ABC** *(n)*.

abdicate [ˈæbdɪkeɪt] ◇ *vt* **1.** [right] renoncer à ■ [responsibility] abandonner **2.** [monarch] : **to ~ the throne** abdiquer.
◇ *vi* abdiquer.

abdication [ˌæbdɪˈkeɪʃn] *n* **1.** [of throne] abdication *f* **2.** [of right] renonciation *f* ■ [of responsibility] abandon *m* ■ **the Abdication** *UK* HIST *abdication d'Édouard VIII d'Angleterre en 1936 devant l'opposition de l'Église anglicane à son mariage avec Wallis Warfield Simpson, Américaine deux fois divorcée.*

abdomen [ˈæbdəmen] *n* abdomen *m*.

abdominal [æbˈdɒmɪnl] *adj* abdominal.

abduct [əbˈdʌkt] *vt* enlever, kidnapper.

abduction [æbˈdʌkʃn] *n* rapt *m*, enlèvement *m*.

abductor [əbˈdʌktəʳ] *n* **1.** [of person] ravisseur *m*, - euse *f* **2.** PHYSIOL (muscle *m*) abducteur *m*.

aberration [ˌæbəˈreɪʃn] *n* **1.** [action, idea] aberration *f* ■ **it's an ~** c'est aberrant ■ **in a moment of ~** dans un moment de folie **2.** ASTRON & OPT aberration *f*.

abet [əˈbet] *(pret & pp* **abetted**, *cont* **abetting***) vt* [aid] aider ■ [encourage] encourager.

abeyance [əˈbeɪəns] *n fml* **1.** [disuse] désuétude *f* ■ **to fall into ~** tomber en désuétude **2.** [suspense] suspens *m* ■ **the question was left in ~** la question a été laissée en suspens.

abhor [əbˈhɔːʳ] *(pret & pp* **abhorred**, *cont* **abhorring***) vt fml* détester, avoir en horreur.

abhorrence [əbˈhɒrəns] *n fml* aversion *f*, horreur *f* ■ **to have an ~ of sthg** avoir horreur de qqch *OR* une aversion pour qqch, avoir qqch en horreur.

abhorrent [əbˈhɒrənt] *adj fml* **1.** [detestable - practice, attitude] odieux ■ **I find their attitude ~, their attitude is ~ to me** je trouve leur attitude détestable **2.** [contrary] contraire ■ [incompatible] incompatible ■ **such economic considerations are ~ to socialism** des considérations économiques de ce genre sont contraires au *OR* incompatibles avec le socialisme.

abide [əˈbaɪd] *(pret & pp* **abided***)* ◇ *vt* supporter ■ **I can't ~ people smoking in restaurants** je ne peux pas supporter les gens qui fument au restaurant.
◇ *vi lit* **1.** *(pret & pp* **abode** [əˈbəʊd]) [live] demeurer, habiter ■ **~ with me** RELIG restez avec moi **2.** [endure] continuer, durer.
◆ **abide by** *vt insep* [decision, law, promise] se conformer à, respecter ■ [result] supporter, assumer.

abiding [əˈbaɪdɪŋ] *adj* constant, permanent.

ability [əˈbɪlətɪ] *(pl* **abilities***) n* **1.** [mental or physical] capacité *f*, capacités *fpl*, aptitude *f* ■ **he has great ~** il a beaucoup de capacités, il est très capable ■ **children at different levels of ~/of different abilities** des enfants de niveaux intellectuels différents/aux compétences diverses ■ **I'll do it to the best of my ~** je le ferai du mieux que je peux, je ferai de mon mieux **2.** [special talent] capacités *fpl*, aptitude *f* ■ [artistic or musical] dons *mpl*, capacités *fpl*.

abject [ˈæbdʒekt] *adj* [person, deed] abject, vil ■ [apology, flattery] servile ■ **they live in ~ poverty** ils vivent dans une misère noire.

abjectly [ˈæbdʒektlɪ] *adv* [act, refuse] de manière abjecte ■ [apologize] avec servilité, servilement.

abjure [əbˈdʒʊəʳ] *vt* [belief] renier ■ [religion] abjurer ■ [right] renoncer à ■ [alliance] refuser, renier.

Abkhazia [æbˈxɑːzɪə] *pr n* : **the ~** l'Abkhazie *f*.

ablative [ˈæblətɪv] ◇ *adj* : **the ~ case** l'ablatif *m*.
◇ *n* ablatif *m*.

ablaze [əˈbleɪz] ◇ *adj* **1.** [on fire] en flammes **2.** [luminous] : **the offices were ~ with light** toutes les lumières brillaient dans les bureaux **3.** [face] brillant ■ [eyes] enflammé, pétillant ■ **her eyes were ~ with anger** ses yeux étaient enflammés de colère.
◇ *adv* : **to set sthg ~** embraser qqch.

able [ˈeɪbl] *(comp* **abler**, *superl* **ablest***) adj* **1.** : **to be ~ to** [to be capable of] : **to be ~ to do sthg** pouvoir faire qqch ■ **I wasn't ~ to see** je ne voyais pas ■ **she wasn't ~ to explain** elle était incapable d'expliquer ■ **I'm not ~ to tell you** je ne suis pas en mesure de vous le dire ■ **she's better** *OR* **more ~ to explain than I am** elle est mieux à même de vous expliquer que moi **2.** [competent] capable **3.** [talented] talentueux, de talent.

able-bodied *adj* robuste, solide.

able-bodied seaman, able seaman *n* NAUT matelot *m* breveté.

ablutions [əˈbluːʃnz] *npl* **1.** *fml* [washing] : **to do** *OR* **to perform one's ~** faire ses ablutions **2.** *mil sl* [building] lavabos *mpl*.

ably [ˈeɪblɪ] *adv* d'une façon compétente.

abnegate [ˈæbnɪgeɪt] *vt* renoncer à.

abnormal [æbˈnɔːml] *adj* anormal ■ **~ psychology** psychopathologie *f*.

abnormality [ˌæbnɔːˈmælətɪ] *(pl* **abnormalities***) n* **1.** [abnormal state, condition etc] anormalité *f*, caractère *m* anormal **2.** [gen - MED & BIOL] anomalie *f* ■ [physical deformity] malformation *f* ■ **behavioural abnormalities** troubles *mpl* du comportement.

abnormally [æbˈnɔːməlɪ] *adv* anormalement.

aboard [əˈbɔːd] ◇ *adv* à bord ■ **to go ~** monter à bord ■ **all ~!** NAUT tout le monde à bord! ; RAIL en voiture!
◇ *prep* à bord de ■ **~ ship** à bord du bateau.

abode [əˈbəʊd] *n fml* demeure *f* ■ **welcome to my ~** bienvenue dans mon humble demeure ■ **one's place of ~** LAW son domicile.

abolish [əˈbɒlɪʃ] *vt* [privilege, slavery] abolir ■ [right] supprimer ■ [law] supprimer, abroger.

abolition [ˌæbəˈlɪʃn] *n* [of privilege, slavery] abolition *f* ■ [of law] suppression *f*, abrogation *f*.

abolitionism [ˌæbəˈlɪʃənɪzm] *n* abolitionnisme *m (dans un contexte américain, ce mot fait le plus souvent référence à l'abolition de l'esclavage aux États-Unis)*.

abolitionist [ˌæbəˈlɪʃənɪst] ◇ *adj* abolitionniste.
◇ *n* abolitionniste *mf*.

abominable [əˈbɒmɪnəbl] *adj* **1.** [very bad] abominable, lamentable, affreux **2.** [odious] abominable, odieux.

abominable snowman *n* : **the ~** l'abominable homme *m* des neiges.

abominably [ə'bɒmɪnəblɪ] *adv* **1.** [write, spell] lamentablement, affreusement **2.** [as intensifier] extrêmement, abominablement **3.** [act, behave] abominablement, odieusement.

abomination [ə,bɒmɪ'neɪʃn] *n* **1.** *fml* [loathing] abomination *f* ■ **we hold such behaviour in ~** ce genre de comportement nous fait horreur *OR* nous horrifie **2.** *fml* [detestable act] abomination *f*, acte *m* abominable **3.** [awful thing] abomination *f*, chose *f* abominable.

aboriginal [,æbə'rɪdʒənl] *adj* **1.** [culture, legend] aborigène, des aborigènes **2.** BOT & ZOOL aborigène.
◆ **Aboriginal** ◇ *adj* aborigène, des aborigènes.
◇ *n* = **Aborigine** *(sense 1)*.

aborigine [,æbə'rɪdʒənɪ] ◇ *n* [original inhabitant] aborigène *mf*.
◇ *adj* aborigène, des aborigènes.
◆ **Aborigine** *n* **1.** [person] aborigène *mf* (d'Australie) **2.** LING langue *f* aborigène.

abort [ə'bɔ:t] ◇ *vi* **1.** [mission, plans] avorter, échouer ■ [flight] avorter ■ **the controller gave the order to ~** l'aiguilleur du ciel a donné l'ordre d'abandonner *OR* de suspendre le vol **2.** MED avorter **3.** COMPUT abandonner, interrompre.
◇ *vt* **1.** [mission, flight] interrompre, mettre un terme à ■ [plan] faire échouer **2.** MED avorter.
◇ *n* **1.** [of mission, spacecraft] interruption *f* **2.** COMPUT abandon *m*.

abortion [ə'bɔ:ʃn] *n* **1.** MED avortement *m*, interruption *f* (volontaire) de grossesse ■ **to have an ~** se faire avorter **2.** [of plans, mission] avortement *m*.

abortionist [ə'bɔ:ʃənɪst] *n* **1.** [practitioner] avorteur *m*, - euse *f* **2.** *pej* [advocate] partisan *m* de l'avortement (légal).

abortive [ə'bɔ:tɪv] *adj* **1.** [attempt] raté, infructueux **2.** [agent, organism, process] abortif.

abound [ə'baʊnd] *vi* [fish, resources] abonder ■ [explanations, ideas] abonder, foisonner ■ **the area ~s in** *OR* **with natural resources** la région abonde en *OR* regorge de ressources naturelles.

about [ə'baʊt] ◇ *prep* **1.** [concerning, on the subject of] à propos de, au sujet de, concernant ■ **I'm worried ~ her** je suis inquiet à son sujet ■ **I'm not happy ~ her going** ça ne me plaît pas qu'elle y aille ■ **there's no doubt ~ it** cela ne fait aucun doute, il n'y a aucun doute là-dessus ■ **now, ~ your request for a salary increase...** bon, en ce qui concerne votre demande d'augmentation... ■ **what's the book ~?** c'est un livre sur quoi? ■ **I don't know what all the fuss is ~** je ne vois pas pourquoi tout le monde se met dans cet état ■ **what do you want to see me ~?** vous voulez me voir à quel sujet? ■ **that's what life's all ~** c'est ça la vie ■ **he asked us ~ the war** il nous a posé des questions sur la guerre ■ **she asked me ~ my mother** elle m'a demandé des nouvelles de ma mère ■ **you should do something ~ your headaches** vous devriez faire quelque chose pour vos maux de tête ■ **I can't do anything ~ it** je n'y peux rien ■ **what do YOU know ~ it?** qu'est-ce que vous en savez, vous? ■ **I don't know much ~ Egyptian art** je ne m'y connais pas beaucoup en art égyptien ■ **I didn't know ~ your accident** je ne savais pas que vous aviez eu un accident ■ **what do you think ~ modern art?** que pensez-vous de l'art moderne? ■ **I was thinking ~ my mother** je pensais à ma mère ■ **I'd like you to think ~ my offer** j'aimerais que vous réfléchissiez à ma proposition ■ **I warned them ~ the political situation** je les ai mis en garde en ce qui concerne la situation politique
2. [in the character of] : **what I like ~ her is her generosity** ce que j'aime en *OR* chez elle, c'est sa générosité ■ **what I don't like ~ the house is all the stairs** ce qui me déplaît dans cette maison, ce sont tous les escaliers ■ **there's something ~ the place that reminds me of Rome** il y a quelque chose ici qui me fait penser à Rome
3. [busy with] : **while I'm ~ it** pendant que j'y suis ■ **be quick ~ it!** faites vite!, dépêchez-vous!
4. [in phrasal verbs] partout ■ **there were clothes lying all ~ the room** il y avait des vêtements qui traînaient partout
5. *lit* [surrounding] autour de
6. *fml* [on one's person] : **he had a dangerous weapon ~ his person** il portait une arme dangereuse.
◇ *adv* **1.** [more or less] environ, à peu près ■ **~ £50** 50 livres environ ■ **~ five o'clock** vers cinq heures ■ **that looks ~ right** ça a l'air d'être à peu près ça ■ **I've just ~ finished** j'ai presque fini ■ **I've had just ~ enough!** j'en ai vraiment assez! ■ **it's ~ time you started** il serait grand temps que vous vous y mettiez ■ **that's ~ it for now** c'est à peu près tout pour l'instant
2. [somewhere near] dans les parages, par ici ■ **is there anyone ~?** il y a quelqu'un? ■ **there was no one ~ when I left the building** il n'y avait personne dans les parages quand j'ai quitté l'immeuble ■ **my keys must be ~ somewhere** mes clés doivent être quelque part par ici
3. [in all directions, places] : **there's a lot of flu ~** il y a beaucoup de grippe en ce moment ■ **watch out, there are pickpockets ~** méfie-toi, il y a beaucoup de pickpockets qui traînent ▮ [in phrasal verbs] : **there are some terrible rumours going ~** il court des rumeurs terribles ■ **don't leave your money ~** ne laissez pas traîner votre argent ■ **they've been sitting ~ all day** ils ont passé toute la journée assis à ne rien faire ■ **stop fooling ~!** *inf* arrête de faire l'imbécile! ■ **she was waving her arms ~** elle agitait les bras dans tous les sens
4. [in opposite direction] : **to turn ~** se retourner.
◇ *adj* **1.** [expressing imminent action] : **to be ~ to do sthg** être sur le point de faire qqch ■ **I was just ~ to leave** j'allais partir, j'étais sur le point de partir
2. [expressing reluctance] : **I'm not ~ to answer that kind of question** je ne suis pas prêt à répondre à ce genre de question.

about-turn *UK*, **about-face** *US* ◇ *interj* : **~!** MIL [to right] demi-tour... droite! ; [to left] demi-tour... gauche!
◇ *vi* **1.** MIL faire un demi-tour **2.** [change opinion] faire volte-face.
◇ *n* **1.** MIL demi-tour *m* **2.** [change of opinion] volte-face *f inv* ■ **to do an ~** faire volte-face.

above [ə'bʌv] ◇ *prep* **1.** [in a higher place or position than] au-dessus de ■ **~ ground** en surface ■ **they live ~ the shop** ils habitent au-dessus du magasin ■ **a village on the river ~ Oxford** un village (situé) en amont d'Oxford
2. [greater in degree or quantity than] au-dessus de ■ **it's ~ my price limit** c'est au-dessus du prix *OR* ça dépasse le prix que je me suis fixé
3. [in preference to] plus que ■ **he values friendship ~ success** il accorde plus d'importance à l'amitié qu'à la réussite ■ **he respected her ~ all others** il la respectait entre toutes
4. [beyond] au-delà de ■ **the discussion was all rather ~ me** la discussion me dépassait complètement ■ **~ and beyond the call of duty** bien au-delà du strict devoir
5. [morally or intellectually superior to] : **she's ~ that sort of thing** elle est au-dessus de ça ■ **~ suspicion/reproach** au-dessus de tout soupçon/reproche ■ **he's not ~ cheating** il irait jusqu'à tricher ■ **I'm not ~ asking for favours** je ne répugne pas à demander des faveurs
6. [superior in rank, quality to] au-dessus de ■ **she's ranked ~ the other athletes** elle se classe devant les autres athlètes ➜ **to get ~ o.s.** se monter la tête
7. [in volume, sound] par-dessus ■ **it's difficult to make oneself heard ~ all this noise** il est difficile de se faire entendre avec tout ce bruit.
◇ *adj fml* ci-dessus ADMIN précité ■ **the ~ facts** les faits cités plus haut ■ **the names on the ~ list** les noms qui figurent sur la liste ci-dessus.
◇ *adv* **1.** [in a higher place or position] au-dessus ■ **the stars ~** le ciel constellé ■ **the people in the flat ~** les voisins du dessus ■ **to fall from ~** tomber d'en haut ■ **two lines ~** deux lignes plus haut
2. [greater in degree or quantity] : **aged 20 and ~** âgé de 20 ans et plus
3. [a higher rank or authority] en haut ■ **we've had orders from ~** nous avons reçu des ordres d'en haut
4. [in a previous place] plus haut ■ **mentioned ~** cité plus haut *OR* ci-dessus
5. [in heaven] là-haut, au ciel
6. MUS [in pitch] : **the note ~** un ton plus haut *OR* au-dessus.

◇ *n fml*: **the ~** [fact, item] ce qui se trouve ci-dessus ; [person] le susnommé, la susnommée *f* ; [persons] les susnommés ■ **can you explain the ~?** pouvez-vous expliquer ce qui précède?
◆ **above all** *adv phr* avant tout, surtout.

aboveboard [ə,bʌv'bɔ:d] ◇ *adj* **1.** [person] honnête, régulier **2.** [action, behaviour] franc, franche *f*, honnête.
◇ *adv* **1.** [openly] ouvertement, au grand jour **2.** [honestly] honnêtement, de façon régulière **3.** [frankly] franchement, cartes sur table.

aboveground [ə,bʌv'graʊnd] *adj* [installation] de surface ■ *US fig* [income, earnings] déclaré.

above-mentioned [-'menʃnd] (*pl inv*) *fml* ◇ *adj* cité plus haut, susmentionné.
◇ *n*: **the ~** [person] le susmentionné, la susmentionnée.

above-named (*pl inv*) *fml* ◇ *adj* susnommé.
◇ *n*: **the ~** le susnommé, la susnommée.

abracadabra [,æbrəkə'dæbrə] ◇ *interj*: **~!** abracadabra!
◇ *n* [magical word] formule *f* magique.

Abraham ['eɪbrəhæm] *pr n* Abraham.

abrasion [ə'breɪʒn] *n* **1.** TECH abrasion *f* **2.** [graze - on skin] éraflure *f*, écorchure *f*.

abrasive [ə'breɪsɪv] ◇ *adj* **1.** TECH abrasif **2.** [character] rêche ■ [criticism, wit] corrosif ■ [voice] caustique.
◇ *n* TECH abrasif *m*.

abreact [,æbrɪ'ækt] ◇ *vt* PSYCHOL libérer par abréaction.
◇ *vi* abréagir.

abreast [ə'brest] *adv* [march, ride] côte à côte, de front ■ **the children were riding three ~** les enfants faisaient du vélo à trois de front.
◆ **abreast of** *prep phr* **1.** [alongside] à la hauteur de, au même niveau que **2.** [in touch with]: **to be ~ of sthg** être au courant de qqch ■ **she likes to keep (herself) ~ of current affairs/the latest fashions** elle aime se tenir au courant de l'actualité/de la dernière mode.

abridge [ə'brɪdʒ] *vt* [book] abréger ■ [article, play, speech] écourter, abréger.

abridged [ə'brɪdʒd] *adj* abrégé.

abroad [ə'brɔ:d] *adv* **1.** [overseas] à l'étranger **2.** [over wide area] au loin ■ [in all directions] de tous côtés, partout ■ **there are rumours ~ about possible redundancies** le bruit court qu'il va y avoir des licenciements **3.** *lit* [out of doors] (au) dehors.

abrogate ['æbrəgeɪt] *vt fml* abroger, abolir.

abrogation [,æbrə'geɪʃn] *n fml* abrogation *f*.

abrupt [ə'brʌpt] *adj* **1.** [sudden - change, drop, movement] brusque, soudain ; [- laugh, question] brusque ; [- departure] brusque, précipité **2.** [behaviour, person] brusque, bourru **3.** [style] haché, décousu **4.** [slope] abrupt, raide.

abruptly [ə'brʌptlɪ] *adv* **1.** [change, move] brusquement, tout à coup ■ [ask, laugh] abruptement ■ [depart] brusquement, précipitamment **2.** [behave, speak] avec brusquerie, brusquement **3.** [fall, rise] en pente raide, à pic.

abruptness [ə'brʌptnɪs] *n* **1.** [of change, movement] soudaineté *f* ■ [of departure] précipitation *f* **2.** [of behaviour, person] brusquerie *f*, rudesse *f*.

ABS (*abbrev of* **Antiblockiersystem**) *n* ABS *m*.

Absalom ['æbsələm] *pr n* Absalon.

abscess ['æbsɪs] *n* abcès *m*.

abscond [əb'skɒnd] *vi fml* s'enfuir, prendre la fuite ■ **to ~ from prison** s'échapper de prison, s'évader.

abseil ['æbseɪl] ◇ *vi* descendre en rappel.
◇ *n* (descente *f* en) rappel *m*.

absence ['æbsəns] *n* **1.** [state of being away] absence *f* ■ **in** *OR* **during my ~** pendant mon absence ▶ **~ makes the heart grow fonder** *prov* l'éloignement renforce l'affection **2.** [instance of being away] absence *f* **3.** [lack] manque *m*, défaut *m* ■ **in the ~ of adequate information** en l'absence d'informations satisfaisantes, faute de renseignements **4.** LAW non-comparution *f*, défaut *m* ■ **he was tried in his ~** il fut jugé par contumace.

absent ◇ *adj* ['æbsənt] **1.** [not present] absent ■ **he was ~ from the meeting** il n'a pas participé à la réunion ▶ **to ~ friends** *formule utilisée pour porter un toast aux absents* ■ **to be** *OR* **to go ~without leave** MIL être absent sans permission, être porté manquant **2.** [lacking] absent **3.** [inattentive - person] distrait ; [- manner] absent, distrait.
◇ *vt* [æb'sent] : **to ~ o.s. (from sthg)** s'absenter (de qqch).

absentee [,æbsən'ti:] ◇ *n* [someone not present] absent *m*, - e *f* ■ [habitually] absentéiste *mf*.
◇ *adj* absentéiste ■ **~ ballot** vote *m* par correspondance ■ **~ rate** taux *m* d'absentéisme.

absenteeism [,æbsən'ti:ɪzm] *n* absentéisme *m*.

absent-minded [,æbsənt-] *adj* [person] distrait ■ [manner] absent, distrait.

absent-mindedly [,æbsənt'maɪndɪdlɪ] *adv* distraitement, d'un air distrait.

absent-mindedness [,æbsənt'maɪndɪdnɪs] *n* distraction *f*, absence *f*.

absinth(e) ['æbsɪnθ] *n* absinthe *f*.

absolute ['æbsəlu:t] ◇ *adj* **1.** [as intensifier] absolu, total ■ **what ~ nonsense!** quelles bêtises, vraiment! ■ **he's an ~ idiot** c'est un parfait crétin *OR* imbécile **2.** [entire - secrecy, truth] absolu **3.** [unlimited - power] absolu, souverain ; [- ruler] absolu **4.** [definite, unconditional - decision, refusal] absolu, formel ; [- fact] indiscutable ; [- proof] formel, irréfutable ■ **~ veto** véto *m* formel **5.** [independent, not relative] absolu ■ **in ~ terms** en valeurs absolues **6.** CHEM [alcohol] absolu, anhydre **7.** GRAM [adjective] substantivé ■ [verb] absolu **8.** LAW [court order, decree] définitif ■ **the decree was made ~** le décret a été prononcé.
◇ *n* absolu *m*.

absolutely ['æbsəlu:tlɪ] *adv* **1.** [as intensifier] vraiment **2.** [in expressing opinions] absolument ■ **I ~ agree** je suis tout à fait d'accord ■ **it's ~ nothing to do with you** cela ne vous regarde absolument pas ■ **do you agree? – ~ not!** êtes-vous d'accord? – absolument pas! **3.** [deny, refuse] absolument, formellement.

absolute majority *n* majorité *f* absolue.

absolute pitch *n US* oreille *f* absolue.

absolute zero *n* zéro *m* absolu.

absolution [,æbsə'lu:ʃn] *n* [forgiveness] absolution *f* ■ RELIG absolution *f*, remise *f* des péchés ■ **to grant sb ~** promettre à qqn l'absolution ▮ [in liturgy] : **the Absolution** l'absoute *f*.

absolutism ['æbsəlu:tɪzm] *n* POL absolutisme *m* ■ RELIG *forme intransigeante de prédestination.*

absolve [əb'zɒlv] *vt* **1.** [from blame, sin etc] absoudre ■ [from obligation] décharger, délier ■ **to ~ sb from** *OR* **of all blame** décharger qqn de toute responsabilité **2.** LAW acquitter ■ **to ~ sb of sthg** acquitter qqn de qqch.

absorb [əb'sɔ:b] *vt* **1.** *liter & fig* [changes, cost, light, liquid] absorber ■ [surplus] absorber, résorber ■ [idea, information] absorber, assimiler ■ **the project ~ed all my time** ce projet a pris tout mon temps **2.** [shock, sound] amortir **3.** [incorporate - company] absorber, incorporer ; [- group, people] absorber, assimiler ■ **the newcomers were quickly ~ed into the community** les nouveaux venus ont été rapidement intégrés *OR* assimilés à la communauté **4.** (*usu passive*) [engross] absorber ■ **to be ~ed in sthg** être absorbé par qqch.

absorbency [əb'sɔ:bənsɪ] *n* [gen] pouvoir *m* absorbant ■ CHEM & PHYS absorptivité *f*.

absorbent [əb'sɔ:bənt] ◇ *adj* absorbant.
◇ *n* absorbant *m*.

absorbent cotton *n US* coton *m* hydrophile.

absorbing [əb'sɔ:bɪŋ] *adj* [activity, book] fascinant, passionnant ■ [work] absorbant, passionnant.

absorption [əb'sɔ:pʃn] *n* **1.** [of light, liquid, smell] absorption *f* ▪ [of surplus] résorption *f* **2.** [of shock, sound] amortissement *m* **3.** [of company] absorption *f*, incorporation *f* ▪ [of group, people] absorption, assimilation *f* **4.** [fascination] passion *f*, fascination *f* ▪ [concentration] concentration *f* (d'esprit).

abstain [əb'steɪn] *vi* **1.** [refrain] s'abstenir ▪ **to ~ from alcohol** s'abstenir de boire de l'alcool **2.** [not vote] s'abstenir.

abstainer [əb'steɪnər] *n* **1.** [teetotaller] abstinent *m*, - e *f* **2.** [person not voting] abstentionniste *mf*.

abstemious [æb'sti:mjəs] *adj* [person] sobre, abstinent ▪ [diet, meal] frugal.

abstention [əb'stenʃn] *n* **1.** [from action] abstention *f* ▪ [from drink, food] abstinence *f* **2.** [in vote] abstention *f*.

abstinence ['æbstɪnəns] *n* abstinence *f*.

abstinent ['æbstɪnənt] *adj lit* [temperate] sobre, frugal ▪ RELIG abstinent.

abstract ◇ *adj* ['æbstrækt] abstrait.
◇ *n* ['æbstrækt] **1.** [idea, term] abstrait *m* ▪ **in the ~** dans l'abstrait **2.** [summary] résumé *m*, abrégé *m* ▪ **an ~ of accounts** FIN un extrait de comptes **3.** ART [painting, sculpture] œuvre *f* abstraite.
◇ *vt* [æb'strækt] **1.** [remove] extraire **2.** *euph* [steal] soustraire, dérober **3.** [regard theoretically] abstraire **4.** [summarize] résumer.

abstracted [æb'stræktɪd] *adj* **1.** [preoccupied] préoccupé, absorbé ▪ [absent-minded] distrait **2.** [extracted] extrait.

abstractedly [æb'stræktɪdlɪ] *adv* distraitement, d'un air distrait.

abstraction [æb'strækʃn] *n* **1.** [concept] idée *f* abstraite, abstraction *f* **2.** PHILOS abstraction *f* **3.** [act of removing] extraction *f* **4.** [preoccupation] préoccupation *f* ▪ [absent-mindedness] distraction *f* **5.** ART [work of art] œuvre *f* abstraite.

abstruse [æb'stru:s] *adj* abstrus.

absurd [əb'sɜ:d] ◇ *adj* [unreasonable] absurde, insensé ▪ [ludicrous] absurde, ridicule.
◇ *n* absurde *m* ▶ **the theatre of the ~** le théâtre de l'absurde.

absurdity [əb'sɜ:dətɪ] (*pl* **absurdities**) *n* absurdité *f*.

absurdly [əb'sɜ:dlɪ] *adv* [behave, dress] d'une manière insensée ▪ [as intensifier] ridiculement.

ABTA ['æbtə] (*abbrev of* **Association of British Travel Agents**) *pr n association des agences de voyage britanniques*.

Abu Dhabi [,æbu:'dɑ:bɪ] *pr n* Abou Dhabi.

abundance [ə'bʌndəns] *n* abondance *f*, profusion *f* ▪ **there was food in ~** il y avait à manger à profusion ▪ **she has an ~ of talent** elle est bourrée de talent.

abundant [ə'bʌndənt] *adj* [plentiful] abondant ▪ **he gave ~ proof of his devotion** il a largement fait la preuve de son dévouement.

abundantly [ə'bʌndəntlɪ] *adv* **1.** [profusely] abondamment ▪ [eat, serve] abondamment, copieusement ▪ [grow] à foison **2.** [as intensifier] extrêmement ▪ **she made it ~ clear that I was not welcome** elle me fit comprendre très clairement que j'étais indésirable.

abuse ◇ *n* [ə'bju:s] **1.** [misuse] abus *m* ▪ **such positions are open to ~** de telles situations incitent aux abus ▶ **drug ~** usage *m* de la drogue **2.** *(U)* [insults] injures *fpl*, insultes *fpl* ▪ **to heap ~ on sb** accabler qqn d'injures **3.** *(U)* [cruel treatment] mauvais traitements *mpl* ▪ **sexual ~** violences *fpl* sexuelles **4.** [unjust practice] abus *m*.
◇ *vt* [ə'bju:z] **1.** [authority, position] abuser de **2.** [insult] injurier, insulter **3.** [treat cruelly] maltraiter, malmener **4.** [masturbate] : **to ~ o.s.** *fml* se masturber.

abuser [ə'bju:zər] *n* **1.** [gen] : **~s of the system** ceux qui profitent du système **2.** [of child] *personne qui a maltraité un enfant physiquement ou psychologiquement* **3.** [of drugs] : **(drug) ~** drogué *m*, - e *f*.

abusive [ə'bju:sɪv] *adj* **1.** [language] offensant, grossier ▪ [person] grossier ▪ [phone call] obscène ▪ **to be ~ to sb** être grossier envers qqn **2.** [behaviour, treatment] brutal **3.** [incorrectly used] abusif, mauvais.

abusively [ə'bju:sɪvlɪ] *adv* **1.** [speak, write] de façon offensante, grossièrement **2.** [behave, treat] brutalement **3.** [use] abusivement.

abut [ə'bʌt] (*pret & pp* **abutted**, *cont* **abutting**) *vi fml* **to ~ on (to) sthg** être adjacent à qqch.

abutment [ə'bʌtmənt], **abuttal** [ə'bʌtl] *n* **1.** [point of junction] jointure *f*, point *m* de jonction **2.** ARCHIT [support] contrefort *m* ▪ [on bridge] butée *f*.

abuzz [ə'bʌz] *adj* bourdonnant ▪ **~ with activity** en effervescence.

abysmal [ə'bɪzml] *adj* **1.** [immeasurable] infini, abyssal ▪ **~ ignorance** une ignorance crasse **2.** [very bad] épouvantable, exécrable.

abysmally [ə'bɪzməlɪ] *adv* atrocement ▪ [fail] lamentablement.

abyss [ə'bɪs] *n* abîme *m*, gouffre *m* ▪ [in sea] abysse *m* ▪ *fig* abîme *m* ▪ **a great ~ seemed to open up between us** *fig* il y avait comme un abîme entre nous.

Abyssinia [,æbɪ'sɪnjə] *pr n* Abyssinie *f* ▪ **in ~** en Abyssinie.

Abyssinian [,æbɪ'sɪnjən] ◇ *adj* abyssinien, abyssin ▪ **~ cat** chat *m* abyssin ▪ **the ~ Empire** l'empire *m* d'Éthiopie.
◇ *n* Abyssinien *m*, - enne *f*.

a/c (*written abbrev of* **account (current)**) *UK* CC.

AC *n* = **alternating current**.

acacia [ə'keɪʃə] *n* acacia *m*.

academia [,ækə'di:mɪə] *n* le milieu universitaire.

academic [,ækə'demɪk] ◇ *adj* **1.** [related to formal study - book, institution, job] universitaire, scolaire ; [- failure, system] scolaire ▪ **~ advisor** *US* directeur *m*, - trice *f* d'études ▪ **~ dress** toge *f* d'étudiant ▪ **~ freedom** liberté *f* d'enseignement ▪ **~ rank** *US* grade *m* ▪ **~ year** année *f* universitaire **2.** [intellectual - standard, style, work] intellectuel ; [- person] studieux, intellectuel **3.** [theoretical] théorique, spéculatif ▪ [not practical] sans intérêt pratique, théorique ▪ **out of ~ interest** par simple curiosité ▪ **whether he comes or not is all ~** qu'il vienne ou pas, cela n'a pas d'importance **4.** [conventional] académique.
◇ *n* universitaire *mf*.

academically [,ækə'demɪklɪ] *adv* [advanced, competent, talented] sur le plan intellectuel ▪ [sound] intellectuellement ▪ **to be ~ qualified** posséder les diplômes requis.

academician [ə,kædə'mɪʃn] *n* académicien *m*, - enne *f*.

academy [ə'kædəmɪ] (*pl* **academies**) *n* **1.** [society] académie *f*, société *f* **2.** [school] école *f* ▪ [private] école *f* privée, collège *m* ▪ **an ~ of music** un conservatoire de musique.

Academy Award *n* oscar *m*.

Acadia [ə'keɪdjə] *pr n* Acadie *f*.

Acadian [ə'keɪdjən] ◇ *n* Acadien *m*, - enne *f*.
◇ *adj* acadien.

acanthus [ə'kænθəs] (*pl* **acanthuses** *OR pl* **acanthi** [-θaɪ]) *n* acanthe *f*.

a cappella [,ɑ:kə'pelə] ◇ *adj* a cappella.
◇ *adv* a cappella.

ACAS ['eɪkæs] (*abbrev of* **Advisory, Conciliation and Arbitration Service**) *pr n organisme britannique de conciliation et d'arbitrage des conflits du travail*, ≃ conseil *m* de prud'hommes.

accede [æk'si:d] *vi fml* **1.** [agree] agréer, accepter ■ **to ~ to sthg** [demand, request] donner suite *OR* accéder à qqch ; [plan, suggestion] accepter *OR* agréer qqch **2.** [attain] accéder ■ **to ~ to the throne** monter sur le trône ■ **to ~ to office** entrer en fonction ■ **to ~ to the directorship** accéder à la direction **3.** LAW : **to ~ to a treaty** adhérer à un traité.

accelerate [ək'seləreɪt] ◇ *vt* [pace, process, rhythm] accélérer ■ [decline, event] précipiter, accélérer ■ [work] activer ■ **~d classes** SCH & UNIV cours *mpl OR* niveaux *mpl* accélérés.
◇ *vi* **1.** [move faster] s'accélérer **2.** AUT accélérer.

acceleration [əkˌselə'reɪʃn] *n* [gen - AUT] accélération *f.*

accelerator [ək'seləreɪtəʳ] *n* AUT & PHYS accélérateur *m* ■ **tu put one's foot on the ~** appuyer sur l'accélérateur.

accelerator board, accelerator card *n* carte *f* accélératrice.

accent ['æksent] ◇ *n* [gen - GRAM & MUS] accent *m* ■ **she has** *OR* **she speaks with a Spanish ~** elle a l'accent espagnol ■ **she speaks French without an ~** elle parle français sans accent ■ **the ~ here is on team work** ici on met l'accent sur le travail d'équipe.
◇ *vt* **1.** [stress - syllable] accentuer, appuyer sur ; [- word] accentuer, mettre l'accent sur ■ [put written mark on] mettre un accent sur, accentuer **2.** *fig* [make stand out] mettre en valeur, accentuer.

accentuate [æk'sentjʊeɪt] *vt* **1.** [word] accentuer, mettre l'accent sur **2.** [feature, importance] souligner, accentuer.

accentuation [ækˌsentjʊ'eɪʃn] *n* accentuation *f.*

accept [ək'sept] *vt* **1.** [agree to receive - apology, gift, invitation] accepter ; [- advice, suggestion] accepter, écouter ■ COMM [- bill] accepter ; [- goods] prendre livraison de ■ **he proposed and she ~ed (him)** il la demanda en mariage et elle accepta ■ **the machine only ~s coins** la machine n'accepte que les pièces **2.** [believe as right, true] accepter, admettre ■ **it is generally ~ed that...** il est généralement reconnu que... **3.** [face up to - danger] faire face à, affronter ; [- challenge] accepter, relever ; [- one's fate] se résigner à ■ **she hasn't really ~ed his death** elle n'a pas vraiment accepté sa mort ■ **you have to ~ the inevitable** il vous faut accepter l'inévitable ■ **they refused to ~ the appalling working conditions** ils ont refusé de travailler dans des conditions aussi épouvantables **4.** [take on - blame, responsibility] accepter, prendre ; [- job, task] se charger de, accepter **5.** [admit - to job, school] accepter, prendre ; [- to club, university] accepter, admettre ■ **she's been ~ed at** *OR US* **to Harvard** elle a été admise à Harvard.

acceptable [ək'septəbl] *adj* **1.** [satisfactory] acceptable, convenable ■ [tolerable] acceptable, admissible ■ **her behaviour just isn't socially ~** son attitude est tout simplement intolérable en société ■ **are these conditions ~ to you?** ces conditions vous conviennent-elles? **2.** [welcome] bienvenu, opportun.

acceptably [ək'septəblɪ] *adv* [suitably] convenablement ■ [tolerably] passablement.

acceptance [ək'septəns] *n* **1.** [of gift, invitation] acceptation *f* ■ **~ speech** discours *m* de réception **2.** [assent - to proposal, suggestion] consentement *m* ■ **his ~ of his fate** sa résignation devant son sort **3.** [to club, school, group] admission *f* **4.** [approval, favour] approbation *f*, réception *f* favorable ■ **the idea is gaining ~** l'idée fait son chemin **5.** [belief] : **there is general ~ now that smoking causes cancer** il est généralement reconnu maintenant que le tabac provoque le cancer **6.** COMM & FIN [of goods] réception *f* ■ [of bill of exchange] acceptation *f* ■ [bill of exchange] traite *f* ■ **~ house** banque *f* d'escompte (d'effets étrangers) *OR* d'acceptation.

accepted [ək'septɪd] *adj* : **~ ideas** les idées généralement répandues *OR* admises ■ **contrary to ~ belief** contrairement à la croyance établie ■ **it's an ~ fact that too much sun ages the skin** il est généralement reconnu que le soleil à haute dose accélère le vieillissement de la peau.

access ['ækses] ◇ *n* **1.** [means of entry] entrée *f*, ouverture *f* ■ [means of approach] accès *m*, abord *m* ■ LAW droit *m* de passage ■ **the kitchen gives ~ to the garage** la cuisine donne accès au garage ■ **how did the thieves gain ~?** comment les voleurs se sont-ils introduits? ■ **'~ only'** 'sauf riverains (et livreurs)' **2.** [right to contact, use] accès *m* ■ **I have ~ to confidential files** j'ai accès à des dossiers confidentiels ■ **he has direct ~ to the minister** il a ses entrées auprès du ministre ■ **the father has ~ to the children at weekends** LAW le père a droit de visite le week-end pour voir ses enfants ➔ **~ rights** [to child] droits *mpl* de visite **3.** *UK lit* [bout - of illness] accès *m*, attaque *f* ; [- of fever, anger] accès *m* **4.** COMPUT accès *m* ■ **to have ~ to a file** avoir accès à un fichier.
◇ *comp* [port, route] d'accès ■ **~ channel** TV canal *m* d'accès.
◇ *vt* accéder à.

access course *n UK* UNIV *cours de mise à niveau permettant aux personnes n'ayant pas le diplôme requis d'entrer à l'université.*

accessibility [əkˌsesə'bɪlətɪ] *n* accessibilité *f.*

accessible [ək'sesəbl] *adj* **1.** [place] accessible, d'accès facile ■ [person] d'un abord facile **2.** [available] accessible ■ **computers are now ~ to everyone** maintenant les ordinateurs sont accessibles à tous **3.** [easily understandable] à la portée de tous, accessible **4.** [open, susceptible] ouvert, accessible.

accession [æk'seʃn] ◇ *n* **1.** [to office, position] accession *f* ■ [to fortune] accession *f*, entrée *f* en possession ■ **Queen Victoria's ~ (to the throne)** l'accession au trône *OR* l'avènement de la reine Victoria **2.** [addition to collection] nouvelle acquisition *f* **3.** [increase] augmentation *f*, accroissement *m* ■ LAW [to property] accession *f* **4.** *fml* [consent] assentiment *m*, accord *m* ■ [of treaty] adhésion *f.*
◇ *vt* enregistrer.

accession number *n* numéro *m* de catalogue.

accessorize, ise [ək'sesəraɪz] *vt* accessoiriser.

accessory [ək'sesərɪ] (*pl* **accessories**) ◇ *n* **1.** (*usu pl*) [supplementary article] accessoire *m* ■ **a suit with matching accessories** un ensemble avec (ses) accessoires coordonnés **2.** LAW complice *mf* ■ **an ~ after/before the fact** un complice par assistance/par instigation **3.** COMPUT accessoire *m.*
◇ *adj* **1.** [supplementary] accessoire **2.** LAW complice.

access road *n* [gen] route *f* d'accès ■ [to motorway] bretelle *f* d'accès *OR* de raccordement.

access time *n* temps *m* d'accès.

accidence ['æksɪdəns] *n* morphologie *f* flexionnelle.

accident ['æksɪdənt] ◇ *n* **1.** [mishap] accident *m*, malheur *m* ■ [unforeseen event] événement *m* fortuit, accident *m* ■ **her son had a car ~** son fils a eu un accident de voiture **2.** [chance] hasard *m*, chance *f* ■ **it was purely by ~ that we met** nous nous sommes rencontrés tout à fait par accident **3.** PHILOS accident *m.*
◇ *comp* [figures, rate] des accidents ■ **~ insurance** assurance *f* (contre les) accidents ■ **~ prevention** AUT la prévention des accidents, la prévention routière.

accidental [ˌæksɪ'dentl] ◇ *adj* **1.** [occurring by chance - death, poisoning] accidentel ; [- meeting] fortuit **2.** *fml* [nonessential] accessoire, extrinsèque ■ PHILOS accidentel **3.** MUS accidentel.
◇ *n* [gen - MUS] accident *m.*

accidentally [ˌæksɪ'dentəlɪ] *adv* [break, drop] accidentellement ■ [meet] par hasard ■ **she ~ tore the page** elle a déchiré la page sans le vouloir ■ **he did it ~ on purpose** *hum* il l'a fait "exprès sans le vouloir".

accident-prone *adj* : **to be ~** être prédisposé aux accidents.

acclaim [ə'kleɪm] ◇ *vt* **1.** [praise] acclamer, faire l'éloge de ■ [applaud] acclamer, applaudir **2.** [proclaim] proclamer.
◇ *n (U)* acclamation *f*, acclamations *fpl* ■ **his play met with great critical ~** sa pièce a été très applaudie par la critique.

acclamation [ˌæklə'meɪʃn] *n (U)* acclamation *f*, acclamations *fpl* ■ **to be elected by ~** être plébiscité.

acclimate ['æklɪmeɪt] *US vt & vi* = **acclimatize.**

acclimation [ˌæklɪ'meɪʃn] *US n* = **acclimatization.**

acclimatization [ə,klaımətaı'zeıʃn] *n* [to climate] acclimatation *f* ■ [to conditions, customs] accoutumance *f*, acclimatement *m*.

acclimatize, ise [ə'klaımətaız] ◇ *vt* [animal, plant] acclimater ■ **to ~ o.s. to** [climate] s'habituer à, s'accoutumer à ; [conditions, customs] s'acclimater à, s'habituer à, s'accoutumer à.
◇ *vi* : **to ~ to** [climate] s'habituer à, s'accoutumer à ; [conditions, customs] s'acclimater à, s'habituer à, s'accoutumer à.

accolade ['ækəleıd] *n* **1.** [praise] acclamation *f*, acclamations *fpl* ■ [approval] marque *f* d'approbation ■ [honour] honneur *m* **2.** [in conferring knighthood] accolade *f* **3.** ARCHIT accolade *f*.

accommodate [ə'kɒmədeıt] ◇ *vt* **1.** [provide lodging for] loger ■ [provide with something needed] équiper, pourvoir ■ [provide with loan] prêter de l'argent à **2.** [have room for - subj: car] contenir ; [- subj: house, room] contenir, recevoir ■ **the cottage ~s up to six people** dans la villa, on peut loger jusqu'à six (personnes) **3.** [oblige] répondre aux besoins de ■ **the bill is designed to ~ special interest groups** cette loi vise à prendre en compte les besoins de groupes d'intérêts particuliers **4.** [adapt] accommoder, adapter ■ **she soon ~d herself to the new working conditions** elle s'est vite adaptée aux nouvelles conditions de travail.
◇ *vi* : **to ~ to sthg** s'accommoder OR s'habituer à qqch.

accommodating [ə'kɒmədeıtıŋ] *adj* [willing to help] obligeant ■ [easy to please] accommodant, complaisant.

accommodation [ə,kɒmə'deıʃn] *n* **1.** *(U)* [lodging] logement *m* ■ [lodging and services] prestations *fpl* ■ **the hotel has no ~ available** l'hôtel est complet ➊ **furnished ~** chambre *f* meublée, (logement *m*) meublé *m* ■ **the high cost of rented ~** le prix élevé des locations ■ **office ~** bureaux *mpl* à louer **2.** *(U)* [facility] équipement *m* ■ **sleeping ~** chambres *fpl* **3.** [settlement of disagreement] accord *m*, accommodement *m* ■ [compromise] compromis *m* **4.** *fml* [willingness to help] obligeance *f* ■ [willingness to please] complaisance *f* **5.** ANAT & PSYCHOL accommodation *f* **6.** COMM & FIN [loan] prêt *m* de complaisance.
◆ **accommodations** *npl* US **1.** [lodging, food and services] hébergement *m* **2.** [on boat, train] place *f*.

accommodation address *n* UK adresse *f (utilisée uniquement pour la correspondance)*.

accommodation agency *n* agence *f* de logement.

accommodation bill *n* effet *m* de complaisance.

accommodation bureau *n* = **accommodation agency**.

accommodation ladder *n* échelle *f* de coupée.

accompaniment [ə'kʌmpənımənt] *n* **1.** [gen] accompagnement *m* ■ **he entered to the ~ of wild applause** il entra sous un tonnerre d'applaudissements **2.** CULIN accompagnement *m*, garniture *f* **3.** MUS accompagnement *m* ■ **guitar/piano ~** accompagnement à la guitare/au piano.

accompanist [ə'kʌmpənıst] *n* accompagnateur *m*, - trice *f*.

accompany [ə'kʌmpənı] (*pret & pp* **accompanied**) *vt* **1.** [escort] accompagner, escorter ■ **she was accompanied by her brother** elle était accompagnée de son frère **2.** [supplement] accompagner ■ CULIN accompagner, garnir **3.** MUS accompagner ■ **he accompanies her on the piano** il l'accompagne au piano.

accompanying [ə'kʌmpənııŋ] *adj* : **the ~ documents** les documents ci-joints ■ **children will not be allowed in without an ~ adult** l'entrée est interdite aux enfants non accompagnés.

accompanyist [ə'kʌmpənııst] *n* US = **accompanist**.

accomplice [ə'kʌmplıs] *n* complice *mf* ■ **to be an ~ to** OR **in sthg** être complice de qqch.

accomplish [ə'kʌmplıʃ] *vt* **1.** [manage to do - task, work] accomplir, exécuter ; [- desire, dream] réaliser ; [- distance, trip] effectuer ■ **the talks ~ed nothing** les pourparlers n'ont pas abouti ■ **we hope to ~ a great deal during our discussions** nous espérons obtenir des résultats durant ces débats **2.** [finish successfully] venir à bout de, mener à bonne fin.

accomplished [ə'kʌmplıʃt] *adj* **1.** [cook, singer] accompli, doué ■ [performance] accompli **2.** [successfully completed] accompli.

accomplishment [ə'kʌmplıʃmənt] *n* **1.** [skill] talent *m* ■ **speaking fluent French is just one of her many ~ s** elle parle français couramment, entre autres talents **2.** [feat] exploit *m*, œuvre *f* (accomplie) **3.** [completion - of task, trip] accomplissement *m* ; [- of ambition] réalisation *f*.

accord [ə'kɔ:d] ◇ *n* **1.** [consent] accord *m*, consentement *m* ■ **to be in ~ with sb** être d'accord avec qqn **2.** [conformity] accord *m*, conformité *f* ■ **to be in ~ with sthg** être en accord OR en conformité avec qqch **3.** [harmony] accord *m*, harmonie *f* **4.** *fml* [agreement] accord *m* ■ [treaty] traité *m*.
◇ *vt* [permission] accorder ■ [welcome] réserver ■ **to ~ sb permission** accorder une autorisation OR une permission à qqn ■ **he ~ed her a warm welcome** il lui a réservé un accueil chaleureux.
◇ *vi* s'accorder, concorder ■ **what he said did not ~ with our instructions** ce qu'il a dit n'était pas conforme à nos instructions.
◆ **of one's own accord** *adv phr* de son plein gré.
◆ **with one accord** *adv phr* d'un commun accord.

accordance [ə'kɔ:dəns] *n* **1.** [conformity] accord *m*, conformité *f* **2.** *fml* [granting] octroi *m*.
◆ **in accordance with** *prep phr* : **in ~ with the law** aux termes de OR conformément à la loi ■ **her statement is not in ~ with company policy** sa déclaration n'est pas dans la ligne de l'entreprise.

according [ə'kɔ:dıŋ] ◆ **according as** *conj phr fml* selon que, suivant que.
◆ **according to** *prep phr* **1.** [on the evidence of] selon, d'après ■ **~ to what you say** d'après ce que vous dites **2.** [in relation to] : **arranged ~ to height** disposés par ordre de taille ■ **prices vary ~ to how long the job will take** le prix varie selon le temps qu'il faut pour effectuer le travail **3.** [in accordance with] suivant, conformément à ■ **everything went ~ to plan** tout s'est passé comme prévu.

accordingly [ə'kɔ:dıŋlı] *adv* **1.** [appropriately] en conséquence **2.** [consequently] par conséquent.

accordion [ə'kɔ:djən] *n* accordéon *m*.

accordionist [ə'kɔ:djənıst] *n* accordéoniste *mf*.

accost [ə'kɒst] *vt* [gen] accoster, aborder ■ [subj: prostitute] racoler.

account [ə'kaʊnt] ◇ *n* **1.** [report] récit *m*, compte rendu *m* ■ **he gave his ~ of the accident** il a donné sa version de l'accident ■ **by his own ~ he had had too much to drink** à l'en croire, il avait trop bu
2. [explanation] compte rendu *m*, explication *f* ■ **to bring** OR **to call sb to ~** demander des comptes à qqn ■ **you will be held to ~ for all damages** il vous faudra rendre des comptes pour tous les dommages causés
3. [consideration] importance *f*, valeur *f* ■ **what you think is of no ~ to me** ce que vous pensez ne m'intéresse pas ■ **to take sthg into ~, to take ~ of sthg** tenir compte de qqch, prendre qqch en compte ■ **he took little ~ of her feelings** il ne tenait pas compte OR faisait peu de cas de ses sentiments
4. [advantage, profit] profit *m* ■ **to put** OR **to turn one's skills to good ~** tirer parti de ses compétences ■ **I started working on my own ~** j'ai commencé à travailler à mon compte
5. [rendition] interprétation *f*, version *f* ■ **to give a good ~ of o.s.** faire bonne impression
6. COMM [in bank, with shop] compte *m* ■ **put it on** OR **charge it to my ~** mettez cela sur mon compte ■ **I'd like to settle my ~** je voudrais régler ma note ■ **to ~ rendered** COMM suivant compte remis ➊ **~ number** numéro *m* de compte ■ **~s payable** comptes *mpl* fournisseurs ■ **~s receivable** comptes *mpl* clients
7. [detailed record of money] compte *m* ■ **his wife keeps the ~s** c'est sa femme qui tient les comptes
8. [business, patronage] appui *m* ■ [in advertising] budget *m*.
◇ *vt fml* considérer.

◆ **by all accounts** *adv phr* aux dires de tous, d'après ce que tout le monde dit.
◆ **on account** *adv phr* à crédit ■ **payment on ~** paiement à compte *OR* à crédit ■ **I paid £100 on ~** j'ai versé un acompte de 100 livres.
◆ **on account of** *prep phr* à cause de ■ **don't leave on ~ of me** *OR* **on my ~** ne partez pas à cause de moi ■ **we didn't go on ~ of there being a storm** nous n'y sommes pas allés à cause de la tempête.
◆ **on no account** *adv phr* en aucun cas, sous aucun prétexte.
◆ **account for** *vt insep* **1.** [explain] expliquer, rendre compte de ■ **there's no ~ing for his recent odd behaviour** il n'y a aucune explication à son comportement bizarre de ces derniers temps ■ **there's no ~ing for taste** des goûts et des couleurs, on ne discute pas, chacun ses goûts
2. [answer for] rendre compte de ■ **he has to ~ for every penny he spends** il doit rendre compte de chaque franc qu'il dépense ■ **all the children are ~ed for** aucun des enfants n'a été oublié ■ **two hostages have not yet been ~ed for** deux otages n'ont toujours pas été retrouvés
3. [represent] représenter ■ **wine ~s for 5% of all exports** le vin représente 5 % des exportations totales
4. *fml* [shoot, kill] abattre, tuer ■ [catch] attraper.

accountability [ə,kaʊntə'bɪlətɪ] *n* : **the public wants more police ~** le public souhaite que la police réponde davantage de ses actes ■ **public ~** transparence *f*.

accountable [ə'kaʊntəbl] *adj* **1.** [responsible] responsable ■ **she is not ~ for her actions** elle n'est pas responsable de ses actes ■ **I'm ~ to your mother for you** je suis responsable de toi devant ta mère ■ **they cannot be held ~ for the accident** on ne peut les tenir responsables de l'accident **2.** [explainable] explicable.

accountancy [ə'kaʊntənsɪ] *n* [subject, work] comptabilité *f* ■ [profession] profession *f* de comptable.

accountant [ə'kaʊntənt] *n* comptable *mf*.

account book *n* livre *m* de comptes.

account day *n* ST. EX jour *m* de liquidation.

account executive *n* responsable *mf* de budget.

accounting [ə'kaʊntɪŋ] *n* comptabilité *f* ■ **she does the ~** [for business] elle fait *OR* tient la comptabilité ; [for the family] elle tient les comptes ■ **~ period** exercice *m*.

accoutrements *UK*, **accouterments** *US* [ə'ku:trəmənts] *npl* [equipment] attirail *m* ■ MIL équipement *m*.

accredit [ə'kredɪt] *vt* **1.** [credit] créditer ■ **they ~ed the discovery to him** on lui a attribué cette découverte ■ **she is ~ed with having discovered radium** on lui attribue la découverte du radium **2.** [provide with credentials] accréditer ■ **ambassador ~ed to Morocco** ambassadeur accrédité au Maroc **3.** [recognize as bona fide] agréer.

accreditation [ə,kredɪ'teɪʃn] *n* : **to seek ~** chercher à se faire accréditer *OR* reconnaître.

accredited [ə'kredɪtɪd] *adj* **1.** [idea, rumour] admis, accepté **2.** [official, person] accrédité, autorisé ■ **the ~ representative to the United Nations** le représentant accrédité aux Nations unies **3.** [recognized as bona fide] agréé ■ **~ dairy herds** troupeaux *mpl* tuberculinés ■ **~ schools** SCH & UNIV *établissements délivrant des diplômes reconnus par l'État*.

accretion [æ'kri:ʃn] *n* **1.** [growth - in size] accroissement *m* ; [- of dirt, wealth] accroissement *m*, accumulation *f* **2.** [addition] addition *f* ■ **~ of property** LAW accumulation de biens **3.** GEOL accrétion *f* **4.** MED [adhesion] accrétion *f* ■ [deposit] concrétion *f*.

accrual [ə'kru:əl] *n fml* accumulation *f* ■ **~s** FIN compte *m* de régularisation (du passif).

accrue [ə'kru:] *fml* ◇ *vi* **1.** [increase] s'accroître, s'accumuler ■ [interest] courir ■ **~d interest** intérêt *m* couru ■ **~d income** recettes *fpl* échues ■ **~d expenses** frais *mpl* à payer **2.** [benefit, gain] : **to ~ to** revenir à.
◇ *vt* accumuler.

accumulate [ə'kju:mjʊleɪt] ◇ *vt* accumuler.
◇ *vi* s'accumuler.

accumulation [ə,kju:mjʊ'leɪʃn] *n* **1.** [process] accumulation *f* **2.** [things collected] amas *m*, tas *m* **3.** FIN [of capital] accroissement *m* ■ [of interest] accumulation *f*.

accumulative [ə'kju:mjʊlətɪv] *adj* cumulatif, qui s'accumule ■ FIN cumulatif.

accumulator [ə'kju:mjʊleɪtə[r]] *n* **1.** [battery] accumulateur *m* **2.** *UK* [bet] *pari dont les gains sont placés sur la course suivante*.

accuracy ['ækjʊrəsɪ] *n* [of aim, description, report, weapon] précision *f* ■ [of figures, watch] exactitude *f* ■ [of memory, translation] fidélité *f*, exactitude *f* ■ [of prediction] justesse *f*.

accurate ['ækjʊrət] *adj* [description, report] précis, juste ■ [instrument, weapon] précis ■ [figures, watch] exact ■ [estimate] juste ■ [memory, translation] fidèle ■ **the report was ~ in every detail** le compte rendu était fidèle jusque dans les moindres détails ■ **to be more ~, there were 15 of them** pour être plus précis, ils étaient 15 ■ **she's very ~ in her calculations** elle est très précise dans ses calculs.

accurately ['ækjʊrətlɪ] *adv* [count, draw] avec précision ■ [tell] exactement ■ [judge, estimate] avec justesse ■ [remember, translate] fidèlement.

accursed [ə'kɜ:sɪd] *adj* [cursed] maudit ■ [hateful] maudit, exécrable.

accusal [ə'kju:zl] *n* accusation *f*.

accusation [,ækju:'zeɪʃn] *n* **1.** [gen] accusation *f* ■ **to make an ~ against sb** porter une accusation contre qqn ■ **there was a note of ~ in her voice** sa voix prenait des accents un tant soit peu accusateurs **2.** LAW accusation *f*, plainte *f* ■ **they brought an ~ of theft against him** ils ont porté plainte contre lui pour vol.

accusative [ə'kju:zətɪv] ◇ *adj* **1.** GRAM accusatif **2.** = **accusatorial**.
◇ *n* accusatif *m* ■ **in the ~** à l'accusatif.

accusatorial [ə,kju:zə'tɔ:rɪəl], **accusatory** [ə'kju:zətrɪ] *adj* **1.** [look, tone] accusateur **2.** LAW [system] accusatoire.

accuse [ə'kju:z] *vt* accuser ■ **to ~ sb of (doing) sthg** accuser qqn de (faire) qqch ■ **he is** *OR* **he stands ~d of tax fraud** il est accusé de fraude fiscale.

accused [ə'kju:zd] (*pl inv*) *n* : **the ~** l'accusé *m*, - e *f*, l'inculpé *m*, - e *f*.

accuser [ə'kju:zə[r]] *n* accusateur *m*, - trice *f*.

accusing [ə'kju:zɪŋ] *adj* accusateur.

accusingly [ə'kju:zɪŋlɪ] *adv* de façon accusatrice.

accustom [ə'kʌstəm] *vt* habituer, accoutumer ■ **to ~ sb to sthg** habituer qqn à qqch.

accustomed [ə'kʌstəmd] *adj* **1.** [familiar] habitué, accoutumé ■ **to get** *OR* **to grow ~ to sthg** s'habituer *OR* s'accoutumer à qqch ■ **I'm not ~ to getting up so early** je n'ai pas l'habitude de me lever si tôt **2.** [regular] habituel, coutumier.

AC/DC ◇ *written abbr of* **alternating current/direct current**.
◇ *adj inf* [bisexual] : **to be ~** marcher à voile et à vapeur.

ace [eɪs] ◇ *n* **1.** GAMES [on card, dice, dominoes] as *m* ■ **the ~ of spades** l'as de pique ➊ **to have an ~ up one's sleeve, to have an ~ in the hole** avoir un atout en réserve ■ **to hold all the ~s** avoir tous les atouts dans son jeu ■ **to come within an ~ of doing sthg** être à deux doigts de faire qqch **2.** [expert] as *m* ■ **she's an ~ at chess** c'est un as aux échecs **3.** [in tennis] ace *m* **4.** [pilot] as *m*.
◇ *adj inf* super, formidable.
◇ *vt* **1.** [in tennis] : **he ~d his opponent** il a servi un ace contre son adversaire ; *fig* il n'a pas laissé une chance à son adversaire **2.** *US* [in golf] : **to ~ a hole** faire un trou en un.

acerbic [ə'sɜːbɪk] *adj* [taste] acerbe ■ [person, tone] acerbe, caustique.

acetate ['æsɪteɪt] *n* acétate *m*.

acetic [ə'siːtɪk] *adj* acétique.

acetic acid *n* acide *m* acétique.

acetone ['æsɪtəʊn] *n* acétone *f*.

acetylene [ə'setɪliːn] ◇ *n* acétylène *m*.
◇ *comp* [burner, lamp, torch] à acétylène ■ [welding] acétylène.

ACGB *pr n* = **Arts Council of Great Britain**.

ache [eɪk] ◇ *vi* **1.** [feel pain] faire mal, être douloureux ■ **I ~ all over** j'ai mal partout ■ **my head/tooth ~s** j'ai mal à la tête/aux dents ■ **her heart ~d to see them so unhappy** *fig* elle souffrait de les voir si malheureux **2.** [feel desire] avoir très envie.
◇ *n* [physical] douleur *f* ■ [emotional] peine *f* ■ **~s and pains** douleurs *fpl*, maux *mpl*.

achieve [ə'tʃiːv] *vt* [gen] accomplir, faire ■ [desire, dream, increase] réaliser ■ [level, objective] arriver à, atteindre ■ [independence, success] obtenir ■ **we really ~d something today** on a vraiment bien avancé aujourd'hui ■ **the demonstration ~d nothing** la manifestation n'a servi à rien.

achievement [ə'tʃiːvmənt] *n* **1.** [deed] exploit *m*, réussite *f* ■ **convincing her to come was quite an ~** c'est un véritable exploit d'avoir réussi à la convaincre de venir **2.** [successful completion] accomplissement *m*, réalisation *f* ■ **I felt a real sense of ~** j'ai vraiment eu le sentiment d'avoir accompli quelque chose **3.** SCH [performance] : **~ tests** tests *mpl* de niveau.

achiever [ə'tʃiːvəʳ] *n* fonceur *m*, - euse *f*.

Achilles [ə'kɪliːz] *pr n* Achille.

Achilles' heel *n* talon *m* d'Achille.

Achilles' tendon *n* tendon *m* d'Achille.

aching ['eɪkɪŋ] *adj* douloureux, endolori.

achy ['eɪkɪ] *adj* douloureux, endolori.

acid ['æsɪd] ◇ *n* **1.** [gen - CHEM] acide *m* **2.** *inf* [LSD] acide *m*.
◇ *adj* **1.** [drink, taste] acide **2.** [remark, tone, wit] mordant, acide ■ [person] revêche, caustique **3.** CHEM acide.

acid drop *n* bonbon *m* acidulé.

acid house *n* MUS house music *f*.

acid house party *n* acid party *f*.

acid jazz [,æsɪd'dʒæz] *n (U)* MUS acid jazz *m*.

acidic [ə'sɪdɪk] *adj* acide.

acidity [ə'sɪdətɪ] *n* CHEM & *fig* acidité *f*.

acid jazz *n* MUS acid jazz *m*.

acid rain *n* pluie *f* acide.

acid test *n* épreuve *f* décisive.

acidulous [ə'sɪdjʊləs] *adj* acidulé.

ack-ack [,æk'æk] *UK dated* ◇ *n* défense *f* contre avions, DCA *f*.
◇ *comp* de DCA, antiaérien.

acknowledge [ək'nɒlɪdʒ] *vt* **1.** [admit truth of] reconnaître, admettre ■ [defeat, mistake] reconnaître, avouer ■ **we ~ (the fact) that we were wrong** nous admettons notre erreur **2.** [show recognition of - person] : **she ~d him with a nod** elle lui a adressé un signe de la tête ■ **they ~d him as their leader** ils l'ont reconnu comme leur chef ■ **he ~d her child (as his)** LAW il a reconnu l'enfant (comme étant le sien) **3.** [confirm receipt of - greeting, message] répondre à ■ ADMIN [- letter, package] accuser réception de **4.** [express gratitude for] : **he ~d the cheers of the crowd** il a salué en réponse aux applaudissements de la foule ■ **I'd like to ~ the help given me by my family** j'aimerais remercier ma famille pour l'aide qu'elle m'a apportée.

acknowledged [ək'nɒlɪdʒd] *adj* [expert, authority] reconnu.

acknowledg(e)ment [ək'nɒlɪdʒmənt] *n* **1.** [admission] reconnaissance *f* ■ [of mistake] reconnaissance *f*, aveu *m* ■ **in ~ of your letter** en réponse à votre lettre ■ **~ of receipt** accusé *m* de réception ■ **he received a watch in ~ of his work** il a reçu une montre en reconnaissance OR remerciement de son travail **2.** [letter, receipt] accusé *m* de réception ■ [for payment] quittance *f*, reçu *m*.
◆ **acknowledg(e)ments** *npl* [in article, book] remerciements *mpl*.

ACLU (*abbrev of* **American Civil Liberties Union**) *pr n ligue américaine des droits du citoyen*.

acme ['ækmɪ] *n* apogée *m*, point *m* culminant.

acne ['æknɪ] *n* acné *f*.

acolyte ['ækəlaɪt] *n* [gen - RELIG] acolyte *m*.

aconite ['ækənaɪt] *n* [plant] aconit *m* ■ [drug] aconitine *f*.

acorn ['eɪkɔːn] *n* gland *m* ■ **~ cup** cupule *f*.

acoustic [ə'kuːstɪk] *adj* [feature, phonetics, nerve] acoustique ■ **~ engineer** acousticien *m*, - enne *f* ■ **~ guitar** guitare *f* sèche.

acoustically [ə'kuːstɪklɪ] *adv* du point de vue de l'acoustique.

acoustic coupler [-'kʌpləʳ] *n* coupleur *m* acoustique.

acoustics [ə'kuːstɪks] ◇ *n (U)* [subject] acoustique *f*.
◇ *npl* [of room, theatre] acoustique *f* ■ **to have bad/good ~** avoir une mauvaise/bonne acoustique.

acoustic tile *n* carreau *m* acoustique.

ACPO ['ækpəʊ] (*abbrev of* **Association of Chief Police Officers**) *n syndicat d'officiers supérieurs de la police britannique*.

acquaint [ə'kweɪnt] *vt* **1.** [inform] aviser, renseigner ■ **I'll ~ you with the facts** je vais vous mettre au courant des faits ■ **she ~ed herself with their customs** elle s'est familiarisée avec leurs habitudes **2.** [familiarize] : **to be ~ed with** [person, place, subject] connaître ; [fact, situation] être au courant de ■ **we were just getting ~ed** on venait juste de faire connaissance.

acquaintance [ə'kweɪntəns] *n* **1.** [person] connaissance *f*, relation *f* ■ **he has a wide circle of ~s** il a des relations très étendues **2.** [knowledge] connaissance *f* ■ **pleased to make your ~** enchanté de faire votre connaissance ■ **on closer** OR **further ~ he seems quite intelligent** quand on le connaît un peu mieux, il semble assez intelligent ■ **to have a nodding** OR **passing ~ with sb/sthg** connaître vaguement qqn/qqch.

acquaintance rape *n viol commis par une personne connue de la victime*.

acquaintanceship [ə'kweɪntənʃɪp] *n* **1.** [relationship] relations *fpl* **2.** [people] relations *fpl*, cercle *m* de connaissances ■ **he has a wide ~** il a de nombreuses relations.

acquiesce [,ækwɪ'es] *vi* acquiescer, consentir ■ **they ~d to our demands** ils ont consenti à nos exigences.

acquiescence [,ækwɪ'esns] *n* acquiescement *m*.

acquiescent [,ækwɪ'esnt] *adj* consentant.

acquire [ə'kwaɪəʳ] *vt* **1.** [advantage, experience, possession, success] acquérir ■ [reputation] se faire **2.** [information, knowledge, language] apprendre **3.** [habit] prendre, contracter ■ **I've ~d a taste for champagne** j'ai pris goût au champagne.

acquired [ə'kwaɪəd] *adj* acquis ■ **an ~ taste** un goût acquis.

acquired immune deficiency syndrome *n* = **AIDS**.

acquisition [,ækwɪ'zɪʃn] *n* acquisition *f* ■ **she's the team's latest ~** elle est la dernière acquisition de l'équipe.

acquisitive [ə'kwɪzɪtɪv] *adj* [for money] âpre au gain ■ [greedy] avide.

acquit [ə'kwɪt] (*pret & pp* **acquitted**, *cont* **acquitting**) *vt* **1.** [release - from duty, responsibility] acquitter, décharger ■ LAW acquitter, relaxer ■ **to ~ sb of sthg** acquitter qqn de qqch **2.** [behave] : **to ~ o.s. well/badly** bien/mal s'en tirer **3.** [debt, duty] s'acquitter de.

acquittal [ə'kwɪtl] *n* **1.** [of duty] accomplissement *m* **2.** LAW acquittement *m* **3.** [of debt, obligation] acquittement *m*.

acre ['eɪkəʳ] *n* ≃ demi-hectare *m*, acre *f* ▪ **they have ~s of room** *fig* ils ont des kilomètres de place.

acreage ['eɪkərɪdʒ] *n* aire *f*, superficie *f* ▪ **how much ~ do you have here?** combien avez-vous d'hectares ici?

acrid ['ækrɪd] *adj* **1.** [smell, taste] âcre **2.** [language, remark] acerbe, mordant.

acrimonious [ˌækrɪ'məʊnjəs] *adj* [person, remark] acrimonieux, hargneux ▪ [attack, dispute] virulent.

acrimoniously [ˌækrɪ'məʊnjəslɪ] *adv* [say] avec amertume ▪ **the meeting ended ~** la réunion s'est terminée dans l'amertume.

acrimony ['ækrɪmənɪ] *n* acrimonie *f*, hargne *f*.

acrobat ['ækrəbæt] *n* acrobate *mf*.

acrobatic [ˌækrə'bætɪk] *adj* acrobatique.

acrobatics [ˌækrə'bætɪks] *npl* acrobatie *f* ▪ **to do** *OR* **to perform ~** faire des acrobaties *OR* de l'acrobatie.

acronym ['ækrənɪm] *n* acronyme *m*.

Acropolis [ə'krɒpəlɪs] *pr n* Acropole *f*.

across [ə'krɒs] ◇ *prep* **1.** [from one side to the other of] d'un côté à l'autre de ▪ **to walk ~ sthg** traverser qqch ▪ **I ran ~ the street** j'ai traversé la rue en courant ▪ **they built a bridge ~ the lake** ils ont construit un pont sur le lac ▪ **he lay ~ the bed** il était couché *OR* allongé en travers du lit ▪ **she felt a pain ~ her chest** une douleur lui a traversé la poitrine ▪ **he's very broad ~ the shoulders** il est très large d'épaules
2. [on or to the other side of] de l'autre côté de ▪ **the house ~ the street** la maison d'en face ▪ **he sat ~ the table from me** il s'assit en face de moi ▪ **can you help me ~ the road?** pouvez-vous m'aider à traverser la rue? ▪ **she glanced ~ the room at us** elle nous lança un regard de l'autre bout de la pièce
3. [so as to cover] : **he leaned ~ my desk** il s'est penché par-dessus mon bureau ▪ **a smile spread ~ her face** un sourire a éclairé son visage
4. [so as to cross] en travers de, à travers ▪ **the study of literature ~ cultures** l'étude de la littérature à travers différentes cultures ▪ **the lines cut ~ each other** les lignes se coupent
5. [throughout] : **he gave speeches all ~ Europe** il a fait des discours dans toute l'Europe
6. [on] : **he hit me ~ the face** il m'a frappé au visage.
◇ *adv* **1.** [from one side to the other] d'un côté à l'autre ▪ **the room is 3 metres ~** la pièce fait 3 mètres de large ▪ **I helped him ~** je l'ai aidé à traverser
2. [on or to the other side] de l'autre côté ▪ **he reached ~ and picked the pen up** il a tendu le bras et a pris le stylo ▪ **she walked ~ to Mary** elle s'est dirigée vers Mary ▪ **I looked ~ at my mother** j'ai regardé ma mère
3. [in crosswords] horizontalement ▪ **what's 23 ~?** [clue] quelle est la définition du 23 horizontal(ement)? ; [solution] qu'est-ce qu'il y a comme *OR* en 23 horizontal(ement)?
◆ **across from** *prep phr* en face de.

across-the-board *adj* général, systématique.
◆ **across the board** *adv phr* systématiquement ▪ **stock prices have fallen across the board** le prix des actions a baissé de façon systématique.

acrostic [ə'krɒstɪk] *n* acrostiche *m*.

acrylic [ə'krɪlɪk] ◇ *adj* acrylique.
◇ *n* acrylique *m*.

act [ækt] ◇ *vi* **1.** [take action] agir ▪ **they ~ed for the best** ils ont agi pour le mieux ▪ **she has a good lawyer ~ing for her** elle est représentée par un bon avocat ▪ **to ~ on behalf of sb, to ~ on sb's behalf** agir au nom de qqn **2.** [serve] : **to ~ as** servir de, faire office de ▪ **she ~ed as my interpreter** elle m'a servi d'interprète **3.** [behave] agir, se comporter ▪ **she just ~s dumb** elle fait l'innocente ▪ **you ~ed like a fool** vous vous êtes conduit comme un imbécile ▪ **he ~s as though he were bored** il agit comme s'il s'ennuyait ▪ **she's just ~ing like she's angry** elle joue à *OR* fait celle qui est en colère **4.** THEAT jouer **5.** [produce an effect, work] agir.
◇ *vt* [part] jouer, tenir ▪ [play] jouer ▪ *fig* **he tries to ~ the dutiful husband** il essaie de jouer les maris parfaits ▪ **stop ~ing the fool!** arrête de faire l'imbécile! ▪ **~ your age!** sois raisonnable!
◇ *n* **1.** [action, deed] acte *m* ▪ **the Acts of the Apostles** les Actes des Apôtres ▪ **an ~ of God** un acte divin ▪ **to be caught in the ~** être pris sur le fait ▪ **to get in on the ~** être dans le coup **2.** [pretence] comédie *f*, numéro *m* ▪ **to put on an ~** jouer la comédie ▪ **I'm not fooled by your worried mother ~!** ton numéro de mère anxieuse ne prendra pas avec moi! **3.** [in circus, show] numéro *m* ▪ **a comedy ~** un numéro de comédie ► **to get one's ~ together** *inf* se reprendre **4.** THEAT [part of play] acte *m* **5.** [law] loi *f* ▪ **an ~ of Congress/Parliament** une loi du Congrès/Parlement ▪ **the Act of Supremacy** l'Acte de suprématie ▪ **the Act of Union** l'Acte d'union.
◆ **act on** *vt insep* **1.** [advice, suggestion] suivre ▪ [order] exécuter ▪ **she ~ed on the information we gave her** elle a suivi les *OR* s'est conformée aux indications que nous lui avons données ▪ **~ing on your instructions, we have cancelled your account** selon vos instructions, nous avons fermé votre compte **2.** [chemical, drug] agir sur.
◆ **act out** ◇ *vt sep* [fantasy] vivre ▪ [emotions] exprimer (par mime) ▪ [event, story] mimer.
◇ *vi insep* PSYCHOL passer à l'acte.
◆ **act up** *vi insep* *inf* [person] faire l'idiot, déconner ▪ [engine, machine] déconner.
◆ **act upon** *vt insep* = **act on**.

ACT (*abbrev of* **American College Test**) *n examen de fin d'études secondaires aux États-Unis.*

acting ['æktɪŋ] ◇ *n* **1.** [profession] profession *f* d'acteur, profession *f* d'actrice ▪ **I've done a bit of ~** [theatre] j'ai fait un peu de théâtre ; [cinema] j'ai fait un peu de cinéma **2.** [performance] interprétation *f*, jeu *m*.
◇ *adj* **1.** [temporary] provisoire, par intérim ▪ **~ director/president** directeur/président par intérim **2.** [lessons, school] de comédien.

action ['ækʃn] ◇ *n* **1.** [process] action *f* ▪ **it's time for ~** il est temps d'agir, passons aux actes ▪ **to go into ~** entrer en action ▪ **to take ~** prendre des mesures ▪ **we must take ~ to stop them** nous devons agir pour les arrêter ▪ **to put sthg into ~** [idea, policy] mettre qqch en pratique ; [plan] mettre qqch à exécution ; [machine] mettre qqch en marche ▪ **she's an excellent dancer, you should see her in ~** c'est une excellente danseuse, vous devriez la voir en action ▪ **the car is out of ~** *UK* la voiture est en panne ▪ **the storm put the telephone out of ~** le téléphone est en dérangement à cause de l'orage ▪ **her accident will put her out of ~ for four months** son accident va la mettre hors de combat pour quatre mois
2. [deed] acte *m*, geste *m*, action *f* ▪ **she defended her ~ in dismissing him** elle a défendu son geste en le congédiant ▪ **he's not responsible for his ~s** il n'est pas responsable de ses actes ▪ **don't judge her by her ~s alone** ne la jugez pas seulement sur ses actes ► **~s speak louder than words** les actes en disent plus long que les mots
3. [of chemical, drug, force] effet *m*, action *f*
4. [activity, events] activité *f* ▪ **he wants to be where the ~ is** *inf* il veut être au cœur de l'action ▪ **~!** CIN silence, on tourne! ▪ **we all want a piece of the ~** *inf* nous voulons tous être dans le coup
5. [of book, film, play] intrigue *f*, action *f*
6. [movement - of person] gestes *mpl* ; [- of animal] allure *f* ; [- of heart] fonctionnement *m*
7. [operating mechanism - of clock] mécanique *f*, mécanisme *m* ; [- of gun] mécanisme *m* ; [- of piano] action *f*, mécanique *f*
8. LAW procès *m*, action *f* en justice ▪ **to bring an ~ against sb** intenter une action contre qqn
9. MIL [fighting] combat *m*, action *f* ▪ **to go into ~** engager le combat ▪ **killed in ~** tué au combat.
◇ *comp* [film, photography] d'action.
◇ *vt* [idea, suggestion] mettre en action *OR* en pratique ▪ [plan] mettre à exécution.

actionable ['ækʃnəbl] *adj* [allegations, deed, person] passible de poursuites ▪ [claim] recevable.

actioner ['akʃ(ə)nəʳ] *n* *inf* film *m* d'action.

action group *n* groupe *m* de pression.

action movie ['ækʃənmu:vɪ] *n* film *m* d'action.

action-packed *adj* [film] bourré d'action ▮ [holiday] rempli d'activités, bien rempli.

action painting *n* peinture *f* gestuelle.

action replay *n* UK TV *répétition immédiate d'une séquence.*

action stations ◇ *npl* MIL postes *mpl* de combat.
◇ *interj* : **~!** à vos postes!

activate ['æktɪveɪt] *vt* **1.** [gen - CHEM] & TECH activer **2.** PHYS rendre radioactif.

activation [,æktɪ'veɪʃn] *n* activation *f*.

active ['æktɪv] ◇ *adj* **1.** [lively - person] actif, dynamique ; [- imagination] vif, actif **2.** [busy, involved - person] actif, énergique ; [- life, stock market] actif ▮ **to be ~ in sthg, to take an ~ part in sthg** prendre une part active à qqch ▮ **to be politically ~** être engagé ▮ **to be sexually ~** avoir une activité sexuelle ▮ **~ minority** minorité *f* agissante **3.** [keen - encouragement, interest] vif ▮ **they took his suggestion into ~ consideration** ils ont soumis sa proposition à une étude attentive ▮ **you have our ~ support** vous avez notre soutien total **4.** [in operation - account] actif ; [- case, file] en cours ; [- law, regulation] en vigueur ; [- volcano] en activité **5.** [chemical, ingredient] actif **6.** GRAM actif ▮ **the ~ voice** la voix active, l'actif *m* **7.** MIL actif ▮ **to be on ~ service** *UK* *OR* **duty** *US* être en service actif ▮ **he saw ~ service in the Far East** il a servi en Extrême-Orient **8.** PHYS actif, radioactif.
◇ *n* GRAM [voice] actif *m* ▮ [verb] verbe *m* actif ▮ **a verb in the ~** un verbe à l'actif.

actively ['æktɪvlɪ] *adv* **1.** [involve, participate] activement **2.** [disagree, discourage] vivement, activement.

activist ['æktɪvɪst] *n* militant *m*, - e *f*, activiste *mf*.

activity [æk'tɪvətɪ] (*pl* **activities**) *n* **1.** [of brain, person] activité *f* ▮ [of place, bank account] mouvement *m* ▮ **economic/political ~** activité économique/politique **2.** [occupation] activité *f* ▮ **leisure activities** des activités de loisir.

activity holiday *n* UK vacances *fpl* actives.

actor ['æktər] *n* acteur *m*, comédien *m*.

actress ['æktrɪs] *n* actrice *f*, comédienne *f*.

actressy ['æktrɪsɪ] *adj pej* théâtral, cabotin *pej*.

ACTT (*abbrev of* **Association of Cinematographic, Television and Allied Technicians**) *pr n ancien syndicat britannique des techniciens du cinéma et de l'audiovisuel, aujourd'hui remplacé par BECTU.*

actual ['æktʃʊəl] *adj* **1.** [genuine] réel, véritable ▮ [existing as a real fact] concret ▮ **what were her ~ words?** quels étaient ses mots exacts? ▮ **to take an ~ example** prendre un exemple concret ▮ **the ~ result was quite different** le résultat véritable était plutôt différent ▮ **the ~ cost was £1,000** le coût exact était de 1 000 livres **2.** [emphatic use] même ▮ **the ~ ceremony doesn't start until 10.30** la cérémonie même ne commence pas avant 10 h 30.
◆ **in actual fact** *adv phr* en fait.

actuality [,æktʃʊ'ælətɪ] (*pl* **actualities**) *n* réalité *f* ▮ **in ~** en réalité ▮ **the actualities of the situation** les conditions réelles de la situation.

actually ['æktʃʊəlɪ] *adv* **1.** [establishing a fact] vraiment ▮ **I haven't ~ read the book** à vrai dire, je n'ai pas lu le livre ▮ **what did he ~ say?** qu'est-ce qu'il a dit vraiment? **2.** [emphatic use] vraiment ▮ **you mean she ~ speaks Latin!** tu veux dire qu'elle parle vraiment le latin! **3.** [contradicting or qualifying] en fait ▮ **she's ~ older than she looks** en fait, elle est plus âgée qu'elle n'en a l'air ▮ **I suppose you've never been there – I have, ~** je suppose que vous n'y êtes jamais allé –si, en fait **4.** [in requests, advice etc] en fait ▮ **~, you could set the table** en fait, tu pourrais mettre la table.

actuarial [,æktjʊ'eərɪəl] *adj* actuariel.

actuary ['æktjʊərɪ] (*pl* **actuaries**) *n* actuaire *mf*.

actuate ['æktjʊeɪt] *vt* **1.** [machine, system] mettre en marche, faire marcher **2.** *fml* [person] faire agir, inciter.

acuity [ə'kju:ətɪ] *n* [of hearing, sight] acuité *f* ▮ [of person, thought] perspicacité *f*.

acumen ['ækjʊmen] *n* perspicacité *f*, flair *m* ▮ **business ~** sens *m* des affaires.

acupuncture ['ækjʊpʌŋktʃər] *n* acupuncture *f*.

acupuncturist ['ækjʊpʌŋktʃərɪst] *n* acupuncteur *m*, - trice *f*.

acute [ə'kju:t] ◇ *adj* **1.** [hearing, sense] fin ▮ [sight] pénétrant, perçant ▮ **an ~ sense of hearing** l'ouïe fine ▮ [smell] subtil, développé **2.** [perceptive - mind, person] perspicace, pénétrant ; [- intelligence] fin, vif ; [- analysis] fin **3.** [severe - pain] aigu, vif ; [- anxiety, distress] vif ; [- shortage] critique, grave **4.** MED [attack, illness] aigu **5.** [angle] aigu **6.** GRAM [accent] aigu(uë) ▮ **it's spelled with an "e" ~** ça s'écrit avec un "e" accent aigu.
◇ *n* accent *m* aigu.

acutely [ə'kju:tlɪ] *adv* **1.** [intensely - be aware, feel] vivement ; [- suffer] intensément **2.** [extremely - embarrassing, unhappy] très, profondément **3.** [shrewdly] avec perspicacité.

ad [æd] (*abbrev of* **advertisement**) *n inf* [in newspaper] petite annonce *f* ▮ [on TV] pub *f* ▮ **to put an ~ in the newspaper** passer une annonce dans le journal.

AD ◇ *adv* (*abbrev of* **Anno Domini**) apr. J.-C.
◇ *n* = **active duty**.

adage ['ædɪdʒ] *n* adage *m*.

Adam ['ædəm] ◇ *pr n* Adam ▮ **I don't know him from ~** je ne le connais ni d'Ève ni d'Adam.
◇ *adj* dans le style Adam *(style architectural créé par les Écossais Robert et James Adam au XVIII*e *siècle).*

adamant ['ædəmənt] *adj* résolu, inflexible.

adamantly ['ædəməntlɪ] *adv* résolument.

Adam's ale *n* UK *hum* flotte *f*, château-la-pompe *m hum*.

Adam's apple *n* pomme *f* d'Adam.

adapt [ə'dæpt] ◇ *vt* **1.** [adjust] adapter, ajuster **2.** [book, play] adapter ▮ **the play was ~ed for television** la pièce a été adaptée pour la télévision.
◇ *vi* s'adapter ▮ **she ~ed well to the change** elle s'est bien adaptée au changement.

adaptability [ə,dæptə'bɪlətɪ] *n* [of person] faculté *f* d'adaptation, adaptabilité *f*.

adaptable [ə'dæptəbl] *adj* adaptable.

adaptation [,ædæp'teɪʃn] *n* [of person, work] adaptation *f*.

adapter, adaptor [ə'dæptər] *n* **1.** [person] adaptateur *m*, - trice *f* **2.** [device] adaptateur *m* ▮ [multiple plug] prise *f* multiple.

ADC *n* **1.** = **aide-de-camp** **2.** (*abbrev of* **analogue-digital converter**) CAN *m*.

add [æd] ◇ *vt* **1.** [put together] ajouter ▮ **~ her name to the list** ajoute son nom à la liste ➲ **to ~ fuel to the fire** jeter de l'huile sur le feu **2.** [say] ajouter **3.** MATHS [figures] additionner ▮ [column of figures] totaliser ▮ **~ 4 and** *OR* **to 9** additionnez 4 et 9 ▮ **it will ~ (on) another £100 to the cost** cela augmentera le coût de 100 livres ▮ **they ~ed (on) 10% for service** ils ont ajouté 10 % pour le service.
◇ *vi* faire des additions.
◆ **add on** *vt sep* = **add** *(sense 3)*.
◆ **add to** *vt insep* ajouter à, accroître.
◆ **add up** ◇ *vt sep* [find the sum of - figures] additionner ; [- bill, column of figures] totaliser ▮ **we ~ed up the advantages and disadvantages** nous avons fait le total des avantages et des inconvénients.
◇ *vi insep* **1.** [figures, results] se recouper ▮ **these figures don't ~ up** ces chiffres ne font pas le compte ▮ **the bill doesn't ~ up** la note n'est pas juste ▮ **it just doesn't ~ up** *fig* il y a quelque chose qui cloche *OR* qui ne marche pas **2.** = **add** *(vi)*.
◆ **add up to** *vt insep* **1.** [subj: figures] s'élever à, se monter à **2.** *fig* [subj: results, situation] signifier, se résumer à ▮ **his qualifications ~ up to an impressive CV** ses qualifications constituent un CV impressionnant.

added ['ædɪd] *adj* supplémentaire.

addend [ə'dend] *n* nombre *m* OR nombres *mpl* à ajouter.

addendum [ə'dendəm] (*pl* **addenda** [-də]) *n* addendum *m*, addenda *mpl*.

adder ['ædəʳ] *n* **1.** [snake] vipère *f* **2.** [machine] additionneur *m*.

addict ['ædɪkt] *n* **1.** MED intoxiqué *m*, - e *f* **2.** *fig* fanatique *mf*, fana *mf*, mordu *m*, - e *f* ■ **she's a film ~** c'est une fana OR mordue de cinéma.

addicted [ə'dɪktɪd] *adj* **1.** MED adonné **2.** *fig* **to be ~ to sthg** s'adonner à qqch, se passionner pour qqch ■ **she's ~ to exercise/hard work** c'est une mordue d'exercice/de travail.

addiction [ə'dɪkʃn] *n* MED dépendance *f* ■ *fig* penchant *m* fort, forte inclination *f*.

addictive [ə'dɪktɪv] *adj* MED qui crée une dépendance ■ **chocolate is very ~** *hum* le chocolat, c'est une vraie drogue, on devient vite accro au chocolat.

add-in ◇ *n* COMPUT [software] add-in *m* ■ [card] carte *f* d'extension.
◇ *adj* : **~ (circuit) card** carte *f* d'extension.

adding machine ['ædɪŋ-] *n* calculatrice *f*, machine *f* à calculer.

Addis Ababa [ˌædɪs'æbəbə] *pr n* Addis-Abeba.

Addison's disease ['ædɪsnz-] *n* maladie *f* bronzée d'Addison.

addition [ə'dɪʃn] *n* **1.** [gen - MATHS] addition *f* **2.** [something or someone added] addition *f*, ajout *m* ■ **they're going to have an ~ to the family** leur famille va s'agrandir ■ **she's a welcome new ~ to our staff** nous sommes heureux de la compter au sein du personnel **3.** *US* [to house] annexe *f*.
◆ **in addition** *adv phr* de plus, de surcroît.
◆ **in addition to** *prep phr* en plus de.

additional [ə'dɪʃənl] *adj* additionnel ■ [supplementary] supplémentaire ■ **there is an ~ charge on certain trains** il y a un supplément à payer pour certains trains.

additionally [ə'dɪʃənəlɪ] *adv* **1.** [further, more] davantage, plus **2.** [moreover] en outre, de plus.

additive ['ædɪtɪv] ◇ *adj* additif.
◇ *n* additif *m*.

addled ['ædld] *adj* **1.** [person] aux idées confuses, brouillon ■ [brain] fumeux, brouillon ■ [ideas] confus **2.** [egg] pourri.

add-on *n* COMPUT dispositif *m* supplémentaire.

address [ə'dres] ◇ *vt* **1.** [envelope, letter, package] adresser, mettre l'adresse sur ■ **the letter is ~ed to you** cette lettre vous est adressée **2.** [direct] adresser ■ **~ all complaints to the manager** adressez vos doléances au directeur **3.** [speak to] s'adresser à ■ [write to] écrire à ■ **she stood up and ~ed the audience** elle s'est levée et a pris la parole devant l'assistance ■ **to ~ the chair** s'adresser au président **4.** [deal with - subject, theme] traiter, examiner ; [- issue, problem] aborder ■ **to ~ o.s. to a task** s'attaquer OR se mettre à une tâche **5.** [take position facing] faire face à.
◇ *n* **1.** [of building, person] adresse *f* ■ **we've changed our ~** nous avons changé d'adresse **2.** [speech] discours *m*, allocution *f* **3.** COMPUT adresse *f* **4.** *UK* POL [message to sovereign] adresse *f* **5.** *arch* [way of speaking] conversation *f* ■ [way of behaving] abord *m*.

address book *n* carnet *m* d'adresses.

addressee [ˌædre'si:] *n* destinataire *mf*.

adduce [ə'dju:s] *vt* [explanation, proof, reason] fournir, apporter ■ [expert] invoquer, citer.

Adelaide ['ædəleɪd] *pr n* Adélaïde.

Adélie Land ['ædeɪlɪ-] *pr n* terre Adélie *f*.

adenoidal [ˌædɪ'nɔɪdl] *adj* adénoïde.

adenoids ['ædɪnɔɪdz] *npl* végétations *fpl* (adénoïdes).

adept ◇ *adj* [ə'dept] habile, adroit ■ **to be ~ at doing sthg** être adroit à faire qqch ■ **she's ~ in mathematics** elle est douée en mathématiques.
◇ *n* ['ædept] expert *m*.

adequacy ['ædɪkwəsɪ] *n* **1.** [of amount, payment, sum] fait *m* d'être suffisant **2.** [of person] compétence *f*, compétences *fpl*, capacité *f*, capacités *fpl* ■ [of description, expression] justesse *f*.

adequate ['ædɪkwət] *adj* **1.** [in amount, quantity] suffisant, adéquat **2.** [appropriate] qui convient, adapté ■ **he proved ~ to the task** il s'est révélé être à la hauteur de la tâche ■ **this flat is hardly ~ for a family of six** cet appartement ne convient guère à une famille de six personnes ■ **this one is quite ~** celui-ci fera très bien l'affaire **3.** [just satisfactory] acceptable, satisfaisant.

adequately ['ædɪkwətlɪ] *adv* **1.** [sufficiently] suffisamment **2.** [satisfactorily] convenablement.

adhere [əd'hɪəʳ] *vi* **1.** [stick] coller, adhérer ■ **to ~ to sthg** coller à qqch **2.** [join] adhérer, s'inscrire ■ **to ~ to a political party** s'inscrire à un parti politique **3.** [remain loyal] : **to ~ to** [party] adhérer à ; [rule] obéir à ; [plan] se conformer à ; [belief, idea] adhérer à, souscrire à.

adherence [əd'hɪərəns] *n* adhésion *f* ■ **~ to sthg** adhésion à qqch.

adherent [əd'hɪərənt] ◇ *adj* adhérent.
◇ *n* [to party] adhérent *m*, - e *f*, partisan *m*, - e *f* ■ [to agreement] adhérent *m*, - e *f* ■ [to belief, religion] adepte *mf*.

adhesion [əd'hi:ʒn] *n* [attachment] adhérence *f* ■ PHYS adhésion *f* ■ MED adhérence *f*.

adhesive [əd'hi:sɪv] ◇ *adj* adhésif, collant ■ **~ tape** [gen] ruban *m* adhésif, Scotch® *m* ; MED sparadrap *m*.
◇ *n* adhésif *m*.

ad hoc [ˌæd'hɒk] ◇ *adj* [committee] ad hoc *(inv)* ■ [decision, solution] adapté aux circonstances, ponctuel ■ **the board meets on an ~ basis** le conseil se réunit de façon ad hoc.
◇ *adv* à l'improviste.

adieu [ə'dju:] (*pl* **adieus** OR *pl* **adieux** [ə'dju:z]) *n* adieu *m*.

ad infinitum [ˌædɪnfɪ'naɪtəm] *adv* à l'infini.

adipose ['ædɪpəʊs] *adj* adipeux.

adjacent [ə'dʒeɪsənt] *adj* **1.** [sharing common boundary - house, room] contigu, voisin ; [- building] qui jouxte, mitoyen ; [- country, territory] limitrophe ■ **their house is ~ to the police station** leur maison jouxte le commissariat de police **2.** [nearby - street] adjacent ; [- town] proche, avoisinant **3.** MATHS adjacent.

adjectival [ˌædʒek'taɪvl] *adj* adjectif, adjectival.

adjective ['ædʒɪktɪv] *n* adjectif *m*.

adjoin [ə'dʒɔɪn] ◇ *vt* [house, land, room] : **they had rooms ~ing mine** leurs chambres étaient contiguës à la mienne.
◇ *vi* être contigu.

adjoining [ə'dʒɔɪnɪŋ] *adj* contigu, attenant ■ **~ rooms** des pièces contiguës ■ **at the ~ table** à la table voisine.

adjourn [ə'dʒɜ:n] ◇ *vi* **1.** [committee, court - break off] suspendre la séance ; [- end] lever la séance **2.** [move elsewhere] se retirer, passer ■ **shall we ~ to the living room for coffee?** passerons-nous au salon pour prendre le café?
◇ *vt* **1.** [break off] suspendre **2.** [defer] ajourner, remettre, reporter ■ **let's ~ this discussion until tomorrow** reportons cette discussion à demain ■ **the president ~ed the meeting** le président a levé la séance.

adjournment [ə'dʒɜ:nmənt] *n* [of discussion, meeting] suspension *f*, ajournement *m* ■ LAW [of trial] remise *f*, renvoi *m* ■ **to call for an ~** demander un renvoi ■ **to move the ~** demander la clôture.

adjudge [ə'dʒʌdʒ] *vt fml* **1.** [pronounce] déclarer **2.** LAW [judge] prononcer, déclarer ■ [award] adjuger, accorder.

adjudicate [ə'dʒu:dɪkeɪt] ◇ *vi* **1.** [give a decision] se prononcer **2.** [serve as judge] arbitrer.
◇ *vt* [claim] décider ■ [competition] juger.

adjudication [ə,dʒu:dɪ'keɪʃn] *n* **1.** [process] jugement *m*, arbitrage *f* ■ **the matter is up for ~** l'affaire est en jugement **2.** [decision] jugement *m*, décision *f* ■ LAW arrêt *m* ■ **~ of bankruptcy** LAW déclaration *f* de faillite.

adjudicator [ə'dʒu:dɪkeɪtər] *n* [of competition] juge *m*, arbitre *m* ■ [of dispute] arbitre *m*.

adjunct ['ædʒʌŋkt] *n* **1.** [addition] accessoire *m* **2.** [subordinate person] adjoint *m*, - e *f*, auxiliaire *mf* **3.** GRAM complément *m* adverbial.

adjust [ə'dʒʌst] ◇ *vt* **1.** [regulate - heat, height, speed] ajuster, régler ; [- knob, loudness] ajuster ; [- brakes, machine, television] régler, mettre au point ; [- clock] régler **2.** [alter - plan, programme] ajuster, mettre au point ; [- length, size] ajuster ; [- salary, wage] rajuster **3.** [correct] rectifier ■ **figures ~ed for inflation** chiffres en monnaie constante **4.** [position of clothing, hat] rajuster ■ **'please ~ your dress before leaving'** rajustez vos vêtements avant de sortir, SVP **5.** [adapt] ajuster, adapter **6.** [insurance] : **to ~ a claim** ajuster une demande d'indemnité.
◇ *vi* **1.** [adapt] s'adapter ■ **to ~ to sthg** s'adapter à qqch **2.** [chair, machine] se régler, s'ajuster.

adjustable [ə'dʒʌstəbl] *adj* [chair, height, speed] ajustable, réglable ■ [shape, size] ajustable, adaptable ■ [hours, rate] flexible ■ **~ spanner** *UK OR* **wrench** *US* clé *f* à molette *OR* anglaise.

adjusted [ə'dʒʌstɪd] *adj* : **well ~** équilibré ■ **badly ~** pas équilibré.

adjustment [ə'dʒʌstmənt] *n* **1.** [to heat, height, speed] ajustement *m*, réglage *m* ■ [to knob, loudness] ajustement *m* ■ [to brakes, machine, television] réglage *m*, mise *f* au point ■ [to clock] réglage *m* **2.** [to plan, programme] ajustement *m*, mise *f* au point ■ [to length, size] ajustement *m* ■ [to salary, wage] rajustement *m* **3.** [correction] rectification *f* **4.** [adaptation - of person] adaptation *f*.

adjutant ['ædʒʊtənt] *n* MIL adjudant-major *m*.

ad-lib [,æd'lɪb] ◇ *vi & vt* (*pret & pp* **ad-libbed**, *cont* **ad-libbing**) improviser.
◇ *adj* improvisé, impromptu.
◆ **ad lib** ◇ *n* [improvised performance] improvisation *f*, improvisations *fpl* ■ [witticism] mot *m* d'esprit.
◇ *adv* **1.** [without preparation] à l'improviste **2.** [without limit] à volonté **3.** MUS ad libitum.

adman ['ædmæn] (*pl* **admen** [-men]) *n* publicitaire *m*.

admin ['ædmɪn] (*abbrev of* **administration**) *n inf* travail *m* administratif.

administer [əd'mɪnɪstər] ◇ *vt* **1.** [manage - business, institution] diriger, administrer, gérer ; [- finances, fund] gérer ; [- country, public institution] administrer ; [- estate] régir **2.** *fml* [dispense - blow, medicine, punishment, test, last rites] administrer ; [- law] appliquer ; [- justice] rendre, dispenser ■ **to ~ an oath (to sb)** faire prêter serment (à qqn).
◇ *vi fml* **to ~ to sb** subvenir aux besoins de qqn.

administrate [əd'mɪnɪstreɪt] *vt* = **administer** (*vt sense 1*).

administration [əd,mɪnɪ'streɪʃn] *n* **1.** [process - of business, institution] direction *f*, administration *f*, gestion *f* ; [- of finances, fund] gestion *f* ; [- of country, public institution] administration *f* ; [- of estate] curatelle *f* **2.** [people - of business, institution] direction *f*, administration *f* ; [- of country, public institution] administration *f* **3.** POL gouvernement *m* ■ **under the last ~** sous le dernier gouvernement **4.** [of help, justice, medicine, punishment] administration *f* **5.** [of oath] prestation *f* **6.** [receivership] : **to go into ~** être placé sous administration judiciaire.

administrative [əd'mɪnɪstrətɪv] *adj* administratif.

administrator [əd'mɪnɪstreɪtər] *n* [of business, institution] directeur *m*, - trice *f*, administrateur *m*, - trice *f* ■ [of area, public institution] administrateur *m*, - trice *f* ■ [of estate] curateur *m*, - trice *f*.

admirable ['ædmərəbl] *adj* admirable, excellent.

admirably ['ædmərəblɪ] *adv* admirablement ■ **she coped ~** elle s'en est tiré admirablement bien.

admiral ['ædmərəl] *n* **1.** NAUT amiral *m* ■ **~ of the fleet, fleet ~** ≃ amiral de France **2.** [butterfly] vanesse *f*.

admiralty ['ædmərəltɪ] (*pl* **admiralties**) *n* amirauté *f* ■ **the Admiralty (Board)** *UK* ≃ le ministère de la Marine ■ **~ court/law** tribunal *m* /droit *m* maritime.

admiration [,ædmə'reɪʃn] *n* **1.** [feeling] admiration *f* **2.** [person, thing] : **she was the ~ of the entire class** elle faisait l'admiration de la classe entière.

admire [əd'maɪər] *vt* admirer ■ **he ~d (her for) the way she dealt with the press** il admirait la façon dont elle savait s'y prendre avec la presse.

admirer [əd'maɪərər] *n* admirateur *m*, - trice *f*.

admiring [əd'maɪərɪŋ] *adj* admiratif.

admiringly [əd'maɪərɪŋlɪ] *adv* avec admiration.

admissibility [əd,mɪsə'bɪlətɪ] *n* [of behaviour, plan] admissibilité *f* ■ LAW recevabilité *f*.

admissible [əd'mɪsəbl] *adj* [behaviour, plan] admissible ■ [document] valable ■ LAW [claim, evidence] recevable.

admission [əd'mɪʃn] *n* **1.** [entry] admission *f*, entrée *f* ■ **the ~ of Portugal to the EC** l'entrée du Portugal dans la CEE ■ **'~ £1.50'** 'entrée £1.50' ■ **to gain ~ to a club** être admis dans un club ■ **they granted women ~ to the club** ils ont admis les femmes dans le club ▮ SCH & UNIV : **~s office** service *m* des inscriptions ■ **~s form** dossier *m* d'inscription **2.** [fee] droit *m* d'entrée **3.** [person admitted - to theatre] entrée *f* ; [- to school] candidat *m* accepté ; [- to club] membre *m* accepté **4.** [statement] déclaration *f* ■ [confession] aveu *m* ■ **an ~ of guilt** un aveu ■ **by** *OR* **on one's own ~** de son propre aveu **5.** LAW [of evidence] acceptation *f*, admission *f*.

admit [əd'mɪt] (*pret & pp* **admitted**, *cont* **admitting**) *vt* **1.** [concede] admettre, reconnaître, avouer ■ **I ~ I was wrong** je reconnais que j'ai eu tort ■ **she refused to ~ defeat** elle a refusé de reconnaître sa défaite ■ **no one would ~ doing it** personne ne voulait admettre l'avoir fait ■ **it is generally admitted that women live longer than men** il est généralement admis que les femmes vivent plus longtemps que les hommes **2.** [confess] avouer ■ **he admitted taking bribes** il a reconnu avoir accepté des pots-de-vin **3.** [allow to enter - person] laisser entrer, faire entrer ; [- air, light] laisser passer, laisser entrer ■ **'~ two'** [on ticket] 'valable pour deux personnes' ■ **he was admitted to hospital** il a été hospitalisé ■ **to be admitted to a university** être admis à l'université ➔ **admitting office** *US* [in hospital] service *m* des admissions **4.** [accommodate] (pouvoir) contenir *OR* recevoir **5.** *fml* [allow] admettre, permettre **6.** LAW [claim] faire droit à ■ [evidence] admettre comme valable.
◆ **admit of** *vt insep UK fml* admettre, permettre ■ **her behaviour ~s of no excuse** son attitude est inexcusable.
◆ **admit to** *vt insep* [acknowledge] admettre, reconnaître ■ [confess] avouer ■ **she did ~ to a feeling of loss** elle a effectivement avoué ressentir un sentiment de perte.

admittance [əd'mɪtəns] *n* admission *f*, entrée *f* ■ **'no ~'** 'accès interdit au public' ■ **his supporters gained ~ to the courtroom/to the president** ses supporters ont réussi à entrer dans le tribunal/à s'approcher du président.

admittedly [əd'mɪtɪdlɪ] *adv* : **~, he's weak on economics, but he's an excellent manager** d'accord, l'économie n'est pas son point fort, mais il fait un excellent gestionnaire ■ **our members, although ~ few in number, are very keen** nos membres, peu nombreux il faut le reconnaître, sont très enthousiastes.

admixture [æd'mɪkstʃər] *n fml* **1.** [mixture] mélange *m* **2.** [ingredient] ingrédient *m*.

admonish [əd'mɒnɪʃ] *vt* **1.** *fml* [rebuke] réprimander, admonester ■ **he was ~ed for not having acted more promptly** il a été réprimandé pour ne pas avoir agi plus rapidement **2.** [warn] avertir, prévenir ■ LAW admonester.

admonition [ˌædmə'nɪʃn] *n* **1.** [rebuke] réprimande *f*, remontrance *f*, admonestation *f* **2.** [warning] avertissement *m* ■ LAW admonition *f*.

ad nauseam [ˌæd'nɔːzɪæm] *adv* *liter* jusqu'à la nausée ■ *fig* à satiété ■ **she went on about her holiday ~** elle nous a raconté ses vacances à n'en plus finir.

ado [ə'duː] *n* : **without more** *OR* **further ~** sans plus de cérémonie *OR* de manières ▶ **'Much Ado About Nothing'** *Shakespeare* 'Beaucoup de bruit pour rien'.

adobe [ə'dəʊbɪ] ◇ *n* adobe *m*.
◇ *comp* [house, wall] d'adobe.

adolescence [ˌædə'lesns] *n* adolescence *f*.

adolescent [ˌædə'lesnt] ◇ *n* adolescent *m*, - e *f*.
◇ *adj* [boy, girl] adolescent ■ *pej* [childish] enfantin, puéril *pej*.

Adonis [ə'dəʊnɪs] *pr n* MYTH Adonis ■ **a young ~** *fig* un jeune Apollon.

adopt [ə'dɒpt] *vt* **1.** [child] adopter **2.** [choose - plan, technique] adopter, suivre, choisir ; [- country, name] adopter, choisir ; [- career] choisir, embrasser ■ POL [- candidate] choisir ■ **he ~ed the suggestion as his own** il a repris la proposition à son compte **3.** [assume - position] prendre ; [- accent, tone] adopter, prendre **4.** *fml* [approve - minutes, report] approuver ; [- motion] adopter.

adopted [ə'dɒptɪd] *adj* [child] adoptif ■ [country] d'adoption, adoptif.

adoption [ə'dɒpʃn] *n* **1.** [of child, country, custom] adoption *f* ■ **she's an American by ~** elle est américaine d'adoption **2.** [of candidate, career, plan] choix *m* **3.** *fml* [of bill, motion] adoption *f*.

adoptive [ə'dɒptɪv] *adj* [child] adoptif ■ [country] d'adoption, adoptif.

adorable [ə'dɔːrəbl] *adj* adorable.

adoration [ˌædə'reɪʃn] *n* adoration *f* ■ **in ~** en adoration ▶ **'The Adoration of the Magi'** 'l'Adoration des Mages'.

adore [ə'dɔːʳ] *vt* **1.** RELIG adorer **2.** *inf* [like] adorer ■ **I ~ walking in the rain** j'adore marcher sous la pluie.

adoring [ə'dɔːrɪŋ] *adj* [look] d'adoration ■ [smile] rempli d'adoration ■ [mother] dévoué ■ [fans] fervent.

adoringly [ə'dɔːrɪŋlɪ] *adv* avec adoration.

adorn [ə'dɔːn] *vt* *fml* & *lit* **1.** [decorate - dress, hair] orner, parer ; [- room, table] orner ■ **~ed with flowers** orné de fleurs ■ **she ~ed herself with jewels** elle s'est parée de bijoux **2.** [story] embellir.

adornment [ə'dɔːnmənt] *n* **1.** [act, art] décoration *f* **2.** [of dress, hair] parure *f* ■ [of room, table] ornement *m*.

ADP *n* = **automatic data processing**.

adrenal gland *n* surrénale *f*.

adrenalin(e) [ə'drenəlɪn] *n* adrénaline *f* ■ **it really gets the ~ flowing** ça donne un bon coup d'adrénaline.

Adriatic [ˌeɪdrɪ'ætɪk] *pr n* : **the ~ (Sea)** l'Adriatique *f*, la mer Adriatique.

adrift [ə'drɪft] ◇ *adv* **1.** NAUT à la dérive ■ **their boat had been cut ~** leur bateau avait été détaché **2.** *UK* [undone] : **to come** *OR* **to go ~** se détacher, se défaire.
◇ *adj* [boat] à la dérive ■ *fig* abandonné ■ **she was (all) ~** elle divaguait complètement.

adroit [ə'drɔɪt] *adj* adroit, habile.

ADSL [ˌeɪdiːes'el] (*abbrev of* **Asymmetric Digital Subscriber Line**) *n* ADSL *m*, RNA *m* *offic.*

ADT (*abbrev of* **Atlantic Daylight Time**) *n heure d'été des Provinces Maritimes du Canada et d'une partie des Caraïbes.*

adulation [ˌædjʊ'leɪʃn] *n* flagornerie *f*.

adulatory ['ædjʊleɪtərɪ] *adj* adulateur.

adult ['ædʌlt] ◇ *n* adulte *mf* ■ **'for ~s only'** 'interdit aux moins de 18 ans'.
◇ *adj* **1.** [fully grown] adulte **2.** [mature] adulte ■ **try and be a little more ~ about this** essaie de faire preuve d'un peu plus de maturité **3.** [book, film, subject] pour adultes.

adult education *n* enseignement *m* pour adultes.

adulterate [ə'dʌltəreɪt] *vt* frelater ■ **they ~d the wine with water** ils ont coupé le vin (avec de l'eau).

adulterer [ə'dʌltərəʳ] *n* adultère *m (personne)*.

adulteress [ə'dʌltərɪs] *n* adultère *f*.

adulterous [ə'dʌltərəs] *adj* adultère.

adultery [ə'dʌltərɪ] *n* adultère *m (acte)*.

adulthood ['ædʌlthʊd] *n* âge *m* adulte.

adumbrate ['ædʌmbreɪt] *vt* *fml* **1.** [outline] ébaucher, esquisser **2.** [foreshadow] faire pressentir **3.** [obscure] obscurcir, voiler.

advance [əd'vɑːns] ◇ *vt* **1.** [clock, tape, film] faire avancer ■ [time, event] avancer ■ **the date of the meeting was ~d by one week** la réunion a été avancée d'une semaine **2.** [further - project, work] avancer ; [- interest, cause] promouvoir **3.** [suggest - idea, proposition] avancer, mettre en avant ; [- opinion] avancer, émettre ; [- explanation] avancer **4.** [money] avancer, faire une avance de ■ **we ~d her £100 on her salary** nous lui avons avancé 100 livres sur son salaire **5.** *fml* [increase] augmenter, hausser.
◇ *vi* **1.** [go forward] avancer, s'avancer ■ **to ~ on** *OR* **towards sthg** avancer *OR* s'avancer vers qqch **2.** [make progress] avancer, progresser, faire des progrès **3.** [time] avancer, s'écouler ■ [evening, winter] avancer **4.** *fml* [price, rent] monter, augmenter **5.** [be promoted] avancer, obtenir de l'avancement ■ MIL monter en grade.
◇ *n* **1.** [forward movement] avance *f*, marche *f* en avant ■ MIL avance *f*, progression *f* ■ **the ~ of old age** *fig* le vieillissement **2.** [progress] progrès *m* **3.** [money] avance *f* ■ **an ~ on his salary** une avance sur son salaire **4.** *fml* [in price, rent] hausse *f*, augmentation *f*.
◇ *comp* **1.** [prior] préalable ■ **~ booking is advisable** il est recommandé de réserver à l'avance ▶ **~ booking office** guichet *m* de location ■ **~ notice** préavis *m*, avertissement *m* ■ **~ payment** paiement *m* anticipé ■ **~ warning** avertissement *m* **2.** [preceding] : **~ copy** [of book] exemplaire *m* de lancement ; [of speech] texte *m* distribué à l'avance ■ **~ group** *OR* **party** [gen] groupe *m* de reconnaissance ; MIL pointe *f* d'avant-garde ■ **~ man** *US* POL organisateur *m* de la publicité *(pour une campagne politique)*.
◆ **advances** *npl* avances *fpl* ■ **to make ~s to sb** faire des avances à qqn.
◆ **in advance** *adv phr* [beforehand - pay, thank] à l'avance, d'avance ; [- prepare, reserve, write] à l'avance ■ **he sent the messenger on in ~** [ahead] il a envoyé le messager devant.
◆ **in advance of** *prep phr* : **their computer technology is far in ~ of anything we have** ils sont très en avance sur nous en matière d'informatique.

advanced [əd'vɑːnst] *adj* **1.** [course, education] supérieur ■ [child, country, pupil] avancé ■ [research, work] poussé ■ [equipment, technology] avancé, de pointe ■ **the system is very ~ technologically** le système est très en avance au niveau technologique ▶ **~ mathematics** mathématiques *fpl* supérieures **2.** [afternoon, season] avancé ■ **a woman of ~ years, a woman ~ in years** une femme d'un âge avancé.

Advanced level *UK* *n* = **A-level**.

advancement [əd'vɑːnsmənt] *n* **1.** [promotion] avancement *m*, promotion *f* **2.** [improvement] progrès *m*, avancement *m*.

advancing [əd'vɑːnsɪŋ] *adj* qui approche, qui avance ■ **the ~ army** l'armée en marche *OR* qui avance ■ **the ~ tide** la marée qui monte.

advantage [əd'vɑ:ntɪdʒ] <> *n* **1.** [benefit] avantage *m* ▪ **they have an ~ over us** *OR* **the ~ of us** ils ont un avantage sur nous ▪ **the plan has the ~ of being extremely cheap** le plan présente l'avantage d'être extrêmement bon marché ▪ **it's to your ~ to learn another language** c'est (dans) ton intérêt d'apprendre une autre langue ▪ **she turned the situation to her ~** elle a tiré parti de la situation, elle a tourné la situation à son avantage ▪ **to take ~ of sthg (to do sthg)** profiter de qqch (pour faire qqch) ▪ **to take ~ of sb** [make use of] profiter de qqn ; [exploit] exploiter qqn ; [abuse sexually] abuser de qqn ▪ **she uses her charm to great ~** elle sait user de son charme ▪ **that colour shows her eyes off to great ~** cette couleur met ses yeux en valeur ▪ **this lighting shows the pictures to their best ~** cet éclairage met les tableaux en valeur ➊ **you have the ~ of** *OR* **over me** *UK fml* à qui ai-je l'honneur? **2.** TENNIS avantage *m* **3.** [in team sports] : **to play the ~ rule** laisser jouer la règle de l'avantage.
<> *vt* avantager.

advantageous [,ædvən'teɪdʒəs] *adj* avantageux ▪ **to be ~ to sb** être avantageux pour qqn, avantager qqn.

advent ['ædvənt] *n fml & lit* [coming] venue *f*, avènement *m*.
◆ **Advent** *n* RELIG l'Avent *m* ▪ **Advent Sunday** le premier dimanche de l'Avent.

Advent calendar *n* calendrier *m* de l'Avent.

adventure [əd'ventʃər] <> *n* **1.** [experience] aventure *f* **2.** [excitement] aventure *f* ▪ **he has no spirit of ~** il n'a pas le goût du risque **3.** [financial operation] spéculation *f* hasardeuse.
<> *comp* [film, novel] d'aventures.

adventure game *n* COMPUT jeu *m* d'aventures.

adventure holiday *n vacances organisées avec des activités sportives.*

adventure playground *n UK sorte d'aire de jeux.*

adventurer [əd'ventʃərər] *n* aventurier *m* ▪ *pej* aventurier *m*, intrigant *m*.

adventuresome [əd'ventʃəsəm] *adj US* aventureux, téméraire.

adventurous [əd'ventʃərəs] *adj* [person, spirit] aventureux, audacieux ▪ [life, project] aventureux, hasardeux.

adverb ['ædvɜ:b] *n* adverbe *m*.

adverbial [əd'vɜ:bɪəl] *adj* adverbial.

adversarial [,ædvə'seərɪəl] *adj* antagoniste, hostile.

adversary ['ædvəsərɪ] (*pl* **adversaries**) *n* adversaire *mf*.

adverse ['ædvɜ:s] *adj* [comment, criticism, opinion] défavorable, hostile ▪ [circumstances, report] défavorable ▪ [effect] opposé, contraire ▪ [wind] contraire, debout ▪ **the match was cancelled due to ~ weather conditions** le match a été annulé à cause du mauvais temps.

adversely ['ædvɜ:slɪ] *adv* [affect] : **the harvest was ~ affected by frost** la récolte a été très touchée par les gelées.

adversity [əd'vɜ:sətɪ] (*pl* **adversities**) *n* **1.** [distress] adversité *f* ▪ **in the face of ~** dans l'adversité **2.** [incident] malheur *m*.

advert[1] ['ædvɜ:t] *n UK inf* [advertisement] (petite) annonce *f* ▪ COMM annonce *f* publicitaire, pub *f* ▪ **the ~s** TV la pub.

advert[2] [əd'vɜ:t] *vi fml* [refer] se rapporter, se référer ▪ **he ~ed to the incident in his report** il a fait allusion à l'incident dans son rapport.

advertise ['ædvətaɪz] <> *vt* **1.** COMM faire de la publicité pour ▪ **I heard his new record ~d on the radio** j'ai entendu la publicité pour son nouveau disque à la radio **2.** [subj: individual, group] mettre une (petite) annonce pour ▪ **we ~d our house in the local paper** nous avons mis *OR* passé une annonce pour vendre notre maison dans le journal local **3.** [make known] afficher ▪ **don't go advertising the fact that we're thinking of leaving** ne va pas crier sur les toits que nous pensons partir.
<> *vi* **1.** COMM faire de la publicité ▪ **to ~ in the press/on radio/on TV** faire de la publicité dans la presse/à la radio/à la télévision **2.** [make an announcement] mettre une (petite) annonce *OR* des annonces **3.** [make a request] chercher par voie d'annonce ▪ **we ~d for a cook** nous avons mis *OR* fait paraître une annonce pour trouver une cuisinière.

advertisement [*UK* əd'vɜ:tɪsmənt, *US* ,ædvər'taɪzmənt] *n* **1.** COMM [in all media] annonce *f* publicitaire, publicité *f* ▪ TV spot *m* publicitaire ▪ **are the ~s effective?** la publicité est-elle efficace? **2.** [for event, house, sale] (petite) annonce *f* ▪ **to put an ~ in the paper** passer une annonce dans le journal ▪ **I got the job through an ~** j'ai eu le poste grâce à une annonce **3.** *fig* [example] : **this company is a good/poor ~ for public ownership** la situation de cette société plaide/ne plaide pas en faveur de la nationalisation.

advertiser ['ædvə,taɪzər] *n* annonceur *m* (publicitaire).

advertising ['ædvətaɪzɪŋ] <> *n (U)* **1.** [promotion] publicité *f* **2.** [advertisements] publicité *f* **3.** [business] publicité *f*.
<> *comp* [rates, revenues] publicitaire ▪ **~ agency** agence *f* de publicité ▪ **~ campaign** campagne *f* publicitaire *OR* de publicité ▪ **~ jingle** jingle *m*, sonal *m offic* ▪ **Advertising Standards Authority** *UK* ≃ Bureau *m* de vérification de la publicité.

advertorial [ædvə'tɔ:rɪəl] *n* publireportage *m*.

advice [əd'vaɪs] *n* **1.** *(U)* [counsel] conseil *m* ▪ **a piece of ~** un conseil ▪ **he asked his father's ~, he asked his father for ~** il a demandé conseil à *OR* a consulté son père ▪ **let me give you**

ADVICE

Asking for advice

Que feriez-vous à ma place ? What would you do, if you were me?

Qu'est-ce que tu en penses ? What do you think?

J'aurais besoin d'un conseil. I could do with some advice.

Tu crois que je devrais lui en parler ? Do you think I should talk to him about it?

Giving advice

Tu veux mon avis ? Do you want to know what I think?

Si tu veux mon avis, je pense que tu devrais y aller. If you want my advice, I think you should go.

Je n'ai pas de conseil à te donner, mais... I'm not in a position to give you advice, but...

Ne le prends pas mal, mais... Don't take this the wrong way, but...

Tu sais, je crois que tu devrais accepter. You know, I think you should accept.

À ta place *OU* **Si j'étais toi, je le lui dirais.** If I were you, I'd tell her.

Je vous conseille de le lui dire. I advise you to tell her.

Tu devrais le lui dire. You really should tell her.

Tu ferais peut-être mieux de le lui dire. Perhaps you should tell her.

Pourquoi tu ne le lui dis pas carrément ? Why don't you just tell her?

Et si tu lui en parlais ? Why don't you talk to her about it?

some ~ permettez que je vous donne un conseil *OR* que je vous conseille ■ **to take** *OR* **follow sb's ~** suivre le conseil de qqn ■ **take my ~ and say nothing to her** suis mon conseil, ne lui dis rien ■ **my ~ to you would be to write a letter of apology** je te conseille d'envoyer une lettre d'excuses ■ **I called him, I took** *OR* **followed your ~ and called him** suivant votre conseil, je l'ai appelé ■ **to take legal/medical ~** consulter un avocat/un médecin **2.** [notification] avis *m* ■ **as per ~** suivant avis ➜ **~ note, letter of ~** avis *m*.

Voir module d'usage page précédente

advisability [əd,vaɪzə'bɪlətɪ] *n* opportunité *f*, bien-fondé *m* ■ **they discussed the ~ of performing another operation** ils ont discuté de l'opportunité d'une nouvelle opération.

advisable [əd'vaɪzəbl] *adj* conseillé, recommandé ■ **it would be ~ to lock the door** il serait prudent *OR* préférable que vous fermiez la porte à clé ■ **I don't think it's ~ to go out** je ne vous conseille pas de sortir.

advise [əd'vaɪz] *vt* **1.** [give advice to] conseiller, donner des conseils à ■ [recommend] recommander ■ **to ~ sb to do sthg** conseiller à qqn de faire qqch ■ **we ~d them to wait** nous leur avons conseillé d'attendre ■ **he ~d them against taking legal action** il leur a déconseillé d'intenter une action en justice **2.** [act as counsel to] conseiller ■ **she ~s the government on education** elle conseille le gouvernement en matière d'éducation **3.** *fml* [inform] aviser, informer ■ **she ~d him of the cost** elle l'a informé du coût.

advisedly [əd'vaɪzɪdlɪ] *adv* délibérément, en connaissance de cause.

advisement [əd'vaɪzmənt] *n* *US* [consultation] : **the matter is still under ~** aucune décision n'a encore été prise.

adviser *UK*, **advisor** *US* [əd'vaɪzə^r] *n* conseiller *m*, - ère *f* ■ SCH & UNIV conseiller *m*, - ère *f* pédagogique.

advisory [əd'vaɪzərɪ] *adj* **1.** [role, work] consultatif, de conseil ■ **he's employed in an ~ capacity** il est employé à titre consultatif ➜ **~ board** *OR* **body** organe *m* consultatif ■ **~ opinion** *US* LAW avis *m* consultatif de la cour **2.** [informative] : **~ bulletin** bulletin *m* de renseignements.

advocacy ['ædvəkəsɪ] *n* soutien *m* appuyé, plaidoyer *m*.

advocate <> *vt* ['ædvəkeɪt] prôner, préconiser ■ **he ~s reducing** *OR* **a reduction in defence spending** il préconise une réduction des dépenses militaires.
<> ['ædvəkət] *n* **1.** [supporter] défenseur *m*, avocat *m*, - e *f* ■ **a strong ~ of free enterprise** un fervent partisan de la libre entreprise **2.** *esp Scotland* [barrister] avocat *m* (plaidant), avocate *f* (plaidante).

advt *written abbr of* **advertisement**.

AEA (*abbrev of* **Atomic Energy Authority**) *pr n UK* ≃ CEA *f*.

AEC (*abbrev of* **Atomic Energy Commission**) *pr n US* ≃ CEA *f*.

AEEU (*abbrev of* **Amalgamated Engineering and Electrical Union**) *pr n syndicat britannique de l'industrie mécanique*.

Aegean [i:'dʒi:ən] <> *pr n* : **the ~** la mer Égée.
<> *adj* égéen ■ **the ~ Sea** la mer Égée ■ **the ~ Islands** les îles *fpl* de la mer Égée.

Aegina [i:'dʒaɪnə] *pr n* Égine.

aegis ['i:dʒɪs] *n fig* & MYTH égide *f* ■ **under the ~ of** sous l'égide de ■ **under the ~ of the European Parliament** sous l'égide du Parlement européen.

Aeneas [ɪ'ni:əs] *pr n* Énée.

Aeneid [ɪ'ni:ɪd] *pr n* : **'The ~' *Virgil*** 'l'Énéide'.

aeolian harp [i:'əʊljən-] *n* harpe *f* éolienne.

aeon ['i:ən] *n* **1.** [age] période *f* incommensurable ■ GEOL ère *f* **2.** PHILOS éon *m*.

aerate ['eəreɪt] *vt* **1.** [liquid] gazéifier ■ [blood] oxygéner **2.** [soil] retourner.

aerial ['eərɪəl] <> *adj* [in the air] aérien ■ **~ cable car, ~ railway** téléphérique *m* ■ **~ photograph** photographie *f* aérienne.
<> *n UK* RADIO & TV antenne *f*.

aerobatics [,eərəʊ'bætɪks] (*pl inv*) *n* acrobatie *f* aérienne, acrobaties *fpl* aériennes.

aerobic [eə'rəʊbɪk] *adj* aérobie.

aerobics [eə'rəʊbɪks] <> *n (U)* aérobic *m* ■ **to do ~** faire de l'aérobic.
<> *comp* [class, teacher] d'aérobic.

aerodrome ['eərədrəʊm] *n* aérodrome *m*.

aerodynamic [,eərəʊdaɪ'næmɪk] *adj* aérodynamique.

aerodynamics [,eərəʊdaɪ'næmɪks] *n (U)* aérodynamique *f*.

aero-engine ['eərəʊ-] *n* aéromoteur *m*.

aerofoil ['eərəʊfɔɪl] *n UK* surface *f* portante, plan *m* de sustention.

aerogram ['eərəgræm] *n* **1.** [letter] aérogramme *m* **2.** [radiotelegram] radiotélégramme *m*.

aeronaut ['eərənɔ:t] *n* aéronaute *mf*.

aeronautic(al) [,eərə'nɔ:tɪk(l)] *adj* aéronautique.

aeronautics [,eərə'nɔ:tɪks] *n (U)* aéronautique *f*.

aeroplane ['eərəpleɪn] *n UK* avion *m*.

aerosol ['eərəsɒl] <> *n* **1.** [suspension system] aérosol *m* **2.** [container] bombe *f*, aérosol *m*.
<> *comp* [container, spray] aérosol ■ [hairspray, paint] en aérosol, en bombe.

aerospace ['eərəʊ,speɪs] <> *n* aérospatiale *f*.
<> *comp* [industry, research] aérospatial.

Aesop ['i:sɒp] *pr n* Ésope ■ **'~'s Fables'** 'les Fables d'Ésope'.

aesthete ['i:sθi:t] *n* esthète *mf*.

aesthetic [i:s'θetɪk] *adj* esthétique.

aesthetically [i:s'θetɪklɪ] *adv* esthétiquement ■ **~ pleasing**.

aestheticism [i:s'θetɪsɪzm] *n* esthétisme *m*.

aesthetics [i:s'θetɪks] *n (U)* esthétique *f*.

afar [ə'fɑ:^r] *adv lit* au loin, à (grande) distance.
◆ **from afar** *adv phr* de loin.

AFDC (*abbrev of* **Aid to Families with Dependent Children**) *n type d'allocations familiales, destinées tout particulièrement aux familles monoparentales*.

affable ['æfəbl] *adj* [person] affable, aimable ■ [conversation, interview] chaleureux.

affably ['æfəblɪ] *adv* affablement, avec affabilité.

affair [ə'feə^r] *n* **1.** [event] affaire *f* ■ **the meeting was a noisy ~** la réunion était bruyante ■ **it was a sorry ~** c'était une histoire lamentable ➜ **the Dreyfus ~** l'affaire Dreyfus **2.** [business, matter] affaire *f* **3.** [concern] affaire *f* ■ **whether I go or not is my ~** que j'y aille ou non ne regarde que moi **4.** [sexual] liaison *f*, aventure *f* **5.** *inf* [thing] truc *m* ■ **he was driving one of those sporty ~s** il conduisait une de ces voitures genre sport.
◆ **affairs** *npl* [business, matters] affaires *fpl* ■ **her financial ~s** ses finances ■ **I'm not interested in your private ~s** je ne m'intéresse pas à votre vie privée ■ **to put one's ~s in order** [business] mettre de l'ordre dans ses affaires ■ **given the current state of ~s** étant donné la situation actuelle, les choses étant ce qu'elles sont ■ **it's an embarrassing state of ~s** la situation est gênante ■ **this is a fine state of ~s!** *iron* c'est du propre! ■ **~s of state** affaires d'État.

affect <> *vt* [ə'fekt] **1.** [have effect on - person, life] avoir un effet sur, affecter ■ [influence - decision, outcome] influer sur, avoir une incidence sur ■ **I don't see how your decision ~s her** je ne vois pas ce que votre décision change pour elle ■ **she doesn't seem to be particularly ~ed by the noise** elle ne semble pas être particulièrement dérangée par le bruit ■ **these plants were badly ~ed by a late frost** ces plantes ont beaucoup souffert des gelées tardives ■ **the bad weather has ~ed sporting events this weekend** le mauvais temps a eu des répercussions sur les événements sportifs du week-end
2. [concern, involve] toucher, concerner

3. [emotionally] affecter, émouvoir, toucher ■ **he was deeply ~ed by her death** il a été très affecté *OR* touché par sa mort ■ **don't let it ~ you** ne vous laissez pas abattre par cela
4. MED [subj: illness, epidemic] atteindre ■ [subj: drug] agir sur ■ **it has been proved that smoking ~s your health** il est prouvé que le tabac est nocif pour la santé ■ **thousands of people are ~ed by this incurable disease** des milliers de gens sont touchés *OR* concernés par cette maladie incurable ■ **a disease that ~s the kidneys** une maladie qui affecte les reins ■ **she has had a stroke, but her speech is not ~ed** elle a eu une attaque, mais les fonctions du langage ne sont pas atteintes
5. *fml* [pretend, feign - indifference, surprise] affecter, feindre ; [- illness] feindre, simuler
6. BOT & ZOOL [climate, habitat] être un habitué *OR* des habitués de, affecter.
◇ *n* ['æfekt] PSYCHOL affect *m*.

affectation [,æfek'teɪʃn] *n* **1.** [in behaviour, manners] affectation *f*, manque *m* de naturel ■ [in language, style] manque *m* de naturel ■ **without ~** simple, sans manières **2.** [mannerism] pose *f* **3.** [pretence] semblant *m*, simulacre *m*.

affected [ə'fektɪd] *adj* [person, behaviour] affecté, maniéré ■ [accent, dress, language] affecté, recherché.

-affected *in cpds* affecté par ■ **famine/drought~** affecté par la famine/sécheresse.

affectedly [ə'fektɪdlɪ] *adv* avec affectation, d'une manière affectée.

affection [ə'fekʃn] *n* **1.** [liking] affection *f*, tendresse *f* ■ **she has (a) deep ~ for him** elle a une profonde affection pour lui, elle l'aime profondément **2.** *(usu pl)* affection *f* ■ **to gain** *OR* **to win (a place in) sb's ~s** gagner l'affection *OR* le cœur de qqn ■ **she transferred her ~s to another man** elle a reporté son affection sur un autre homme **3.** MED affection *f*, maladie *f*.

affectionate [ə'fekʃənət] *adj* affectueux, tendre ■ **your ~ niece** [in letter] votre nièce affectionnée.

affectionately [ə'fekʃənətlɪ] *adv* affectueusement.

affective [ə'fektɪv] *adj* [gen - LING] & PSYCHOL affectif.

affidavit [,æfɪ'deɪvɪt] *n* déclaration *f* sous serment *(écrite)*.

affiliate ◇ *vt* [ə'fɪlɪeɪt] affilier ■ **to ~ o.s. to** *OR* **with** s'affilier à ■ **the local group decided not to ~ itself to the national organization** la section locale a décidé de ne pas s'affilier au mouvement national.
◇ *n* [ə'fɪlɪət] [person] affilié *m*, - e *f* ■ [organization] groupe *m* affilié.
◇ *comp* [member, organization] affilié.

affiliated [ə'fɪlɪeɪtɪd] *adj* [member, organization] affilié ■ **to be ~ to** *OR* **with** être affilié à ■ **an ~ company** une filiale.

affiliation [ə,fɪlɪ'eɪʃn] *n* **1.** ADMIN & COMM affiliation *f* **2.** LAW attribution *f* de paternité ■ **~ order** jugement *m* en reconnaissance de paternité **3.** [connection] attache *f* ■ **his political ~s** ses attaches politiques.

affinity [ə'fɪnətɪ] *(pl* **affinities)** *n* **1.** [connection, link] lien *m*, affinité *f* ■ BIOL affinité *f*, parenté *f* ■ CHEM affinité *f* ■ **the affinities between the English and German languages** la ressemblance *OR* la parenté entre l'anglais et l'allemand **2.** [attraction] affinité *f*, attraction *f* ■ **he has little ~ for** *OR* **with modern art** il est peu attiré par l'art moderne ■ **she feels a strong sense of ~ with** *OR* **for him** elle se sent beaucoup d'affinités avec lui **3.** LAW [relation] affinité *f*.

affinity card [ə'fɪnɪtɪ,kɑ:d] *n* carte *f* affinitaire.

affirm [ə'fɜ:m] *vt* **1.** [state] affirmer, soutenir ■ **"I will be there," he ~ed** "j'y serai", assura-t-il **2.** [profess - belief] professer, proclamer ; [- intention] proclamer ■ **she ~ed her intention to sell** elle proclamait son intention de vendre **3.** [support - person] soutenir.

affirmation [,æfə'meɪʃn] *n* affirmation *f*, assertion *f*.

affirmative [ə'fɜ:mətɪv] ◇ *n* **1.** GRAM affirmatif *m* ■ **in the ~** à l'affirmatif, à la forme affirmative **2.** [in reply] : **the answer is in the ~** la réponse est affirmative.
◇ *adj* affirmatif.
◇ *interj* : **~!** affirmatif!

affirmative action *n US (U)* mesures *fpl* d'embauche antidiscriminatoires *(en faveur des minorités)*.

affix ◇ *vt* [ə'fɪks] [seal, signature] apposer ■ [stamp] coller ■ [poster] afficher, poser.
◇ *n* ['æfɪks] LING affixe *m*.

afflict [ə'flɪkt] *vt* affecter ■ **to be ~ed with a disease** souffrir d'une maladie.

affliction [ə'flɪkʃn] *n* **1.** [suffering] affliction *f* ■ [distress] détresse *f* **2.** [misfortune] affliction *f*, souffrance *f* ■ **blindness is a terrible ~** la cécité est une grande infirmité.

affluence ['æfluəns] *n* [wealth] richesse *f*, aisance ■ **in times of ~** en période de prospérité.

affluent ['æfluənt] ◇ *adj* **1.** [wealthy] aisé, riche ■ **the ~ society** la société d'abondance **2.** *lit* [abundant] abondant.
◇ *n* GEOG affluent *m*.

afford [ə'fɔ:d] *vt* **1.** [money] avoir les moyens de payer ■ **she couldn't ~ to buy a car** elle n'avait pas les moyens d'acheter *OR* elle ne pouvait pas se permettre d'acheter une voiture ■ **how much can you ~?** combien pouvez-vous mettre?, jusqu'à combien pouvez-vous aller? ■ **I can't ~ £50!** je ne peux pas mettre 50 livres! **2.** [time, energy] : **the doctor can only ~ (to spend) a few minutes with each patient** le médecin ne peut pas se permettre de passer plus de quelques minutes avec chaque patient ■ **I'd love to come, but I can't ~ the time** j'aimerais beaucoup venir mais je ne peux absolument pas me libérer **3.** [allow o.s.] se permettre ■ **I can't ~ to take any risks** je ne peux pas me permettre de prendre des risques ■ **we can't ~ another delay** nous ne pouvons pas nous permettre encore un retard **4.** *lit* [provide] fournir, offrir ■ **this ~s me great pleasure** ceci me procure un grand plaisir.

affordable [ə'fɔ:dəbl] *adj* [commodity] (dont le prix est) abordable ■ **at an ~ price** à un prix abordable.

afforestation [æ,fɒrɪ'steɪʃn] *n* boisement *m*.

affray [ə'freɪ] *n* échauffourée *f*.

affricate ['æfrɪkət] *n* affriquée *f*.

affront [ə'frʌnt] ◇ *n* affront *m*, insulte *f* ■ **to suffer an ~** essuyer un affront ■ **it was an ~ to her dignity** c'était un affront à sa dignité.
◇ *vt* [offend] faire un affront à, insulter, offenser ■ **to feel ~ed** se sentir offensé.

Afghan ['æfgæn] ◇ *n* **1.** [person] Afghan *m*, - e *f* **2.** LING afghan *m* **3.** [dog] lévrier *m* afghan **4.** [coat] afghan *m* **5.** *US* [blanket] couverture *f* en lainage.
◇ *adj* afghan ■ **~ hound** lévrier *m* afghan.

Afghani [æf'gænɪ] *n* & *adj* GEOG & LING = **Afghan**.

Afghanistan [æf'gænɪstæn] *pr n* Afghanistan *m*.

aficionado [ə,fɪsjə'nɑ:dəʊ] *(pl* **aficionados)** *n* aficionado *m*, amoureux *m* ■ **theatre ~s, ~s of the theatre** les aficionados du théâtre.

afield [ə'fɪəld] *adv* : **to go far ~** aller loin ■ **people came from as far ~ as Australia** les gens venaient même d'Australie ■ **don't go too far ~** n'allez pas trop loin.

afire [ə'faɪər] *lit* ◇ *adj* **1.** [burning] en feu, en flammes **2.** *fig* [with emotion] enflammé.
◇ *adv* : **to set sthg ~** *liter* mettre le feu à qqch ; *fig* embraser qqch.

aflame [ə'fleɪm] *lit* ◇ *adj* **1.** [burning] en flammes, en feu **2.** [emotionally] enflammé **3.** [in colour] : **the sky was ~ with colour** le ciel flamboyait de couleurs vives.
◇ *adv* : **to set ~** *liter* mettre le feu à ; *fig* exciter, enflammer.

AFL-CIO *(abbrev of* **American Federation of Labor and Congress of Industrial Organizations)** *pr n la plus grande confédération syndicale américaine.*

afloat [ə'fləʊt] ◇ *adj* **1.** [swimmer] qui surnage ■ [boat] à flot ■ [cork, oil] flottant ■ *fig* [business] à flot **2.** [flooded] inondé.

◇ *adv* **1.** [floating] à flot, sur l'eau ▪ **we managed to get** *OR* **to set the raft ~** nous avons réussi à mettre le radeau à flot ▪ **to stay ~** [swimmer] garder la tête hors de l'eau, surnager ; [boat] rester à flot ▪ **to keep sthg/sb ~** maintenir qqch/qqn à flot ▪ *fig* **to get a business ~** [from start] mettre une entreprise à flot ; [from financial difficulties] renflouer une entreprise ▪ **small businesses struggling to stay ~** des petites entreprises qui luttent pour se maintenir à flot **2.** [on boat] : **holiday spent ~** [on barge] des vacances en péniche ; [at sea] des vacances en mer.

aflutter [ə'flʌtər] ◇ *adj* : **to be (all) ~ with excitement** tressaillir d'excitation.
◇ *adv* : **she set my heart ~** elle fit battre mon cœur.

afoot [ə'fʊt] *adj* [in preparation] : **there is something ~** il se prépare *OR* il se trame quelque chose ▪ **there is a scheme ~ to build a new motorway** on a formé le projet *OR* on envisage de construire une nouvelle autoroute.

aforementioned [ə'fɔː,menʃənd] *adj fml* susmentionné, précité ▪ **the ~ persons** lesdites personnes.

aforenamed [ə'fɔːneɪmd] *adj fml* susnommé, précité.

aforesaid [ə'fɔːsed] *adj fml* susdit, précité.

aforethought [ə'fɔːθɔːt] *adj fml* prémédité.

afoul [ə'faʊl] *adv lit* **to run ~ of sb** se mettre qqn à dos, s'attirer le mécontentement de qqn.

afraid [ə'freɪd] *adj* **1.** [frightened] : **to be ~** avoir peur ▪ **to make sb ~** faire peur à qqn ▪ **she is ~ of the dark** elle a peur du noir ▪ **there's nothing to be ~ of** il n'y a rien à craindre ▪ **she was ~ (that) the dog would** *OR* **might bite her** elle avait peur *OR* elle craignait que le chien (ne) la morde ▪ **he is ~ for his life** il craint pour sa vie ▪ **she was ~ for her daughter** elle avait peur pour sa fille **2.** [indicating reluctance, hesitation] : **he isn't ~ of work** le travail ne lui fait pas peur ▪ **don't be ~ to speak** *OR* **of speaking your mind** n'ayez pas peur de dire ce que vous pensez ▪ **I'm ~ (that) I'll say the wrong thing** je crains *OR* j'ai peur de ne pas dire ce qu'il faut **3.** [indicating regret] : **I'm ~ I won't be able to come** je regrette *OR* je suis désolé de ne pouvoir venir ▪ **I'm ~ I can't help you** je regrette *OR* je suis désolé, mais je ne peux pas vous aider ▪ **I'm ~ to say...** j'ai le regret de dire... ▪ **I'm ~ so** j'ai bien peur que oui, j'en ai bien peur ▪ **I'm ~ not** j'ai bien peur que non, j'en ai bien peur.

afresh [ə'freʃ] *adv* de nouveau ▪ **we'll have to start ~** il va falloir recommencer *OR* reprendre à zéro.

Africa ['æfrɪkə] *pr n* Afrique *f* ▪ **in ~** en Afrique ➊ **'Out of ~'** *Blixen* 'la Ferme africaine'.

African ['æfrɪkən] ◇ *n* Africain *m*, - e *f*.
◇ *adj* africain.

African American *n* Noir *m* américain, Noire *f* américaine.

African violet *n* saintpaulia *m*.

Afrikaans [,æfrɪ'kɑːns] *n* afrikaans *m*.

Afrikaner [,æfrɪ'kɑːnər] *n* Afrikaner *mf*.

Afro ['æfrəʊ] (*pl* **Afros**) ◇ *adj* [hairstyle] afro.
◇ *n* coiffure *f* afro.

Afro-American ◇ *n* Afro-Américain *m*, - e *f*.
◇ *adj* afro-américain.

Afro-Asian ◇ *n* Afro-Asiatique *mf*.
◇ *adj* afro-asiatique.

Afro-Caribbean ◇ *n* Afro-antillais *m*, - e *f*.
◇ *adj* afro-antillais.

aft [ɑːft] ◇ *adv* NAUT & AERON à *OR* vers l'arrière.
◇ *adj* [deck] arrière.

after ['ɑːftər] ◇ *prep* **1.** [in time - gen] après ; [- period] après, au bout de ▪ **~ dark** après la tombée de la nuit ▪ **~ which she left** après quoi elle est partie ▪ **it is ~ six o'clock already** il est déjà six heures passées *OR* plus de six heures ▪ **it's twenty ~ eight** *US* il est huit heures vingt ▪ **the day ~ tomorrow** après-demain *m* ▪ **~ this date** ADMIN passé *OR* après cette date **2.** [in space] après ▪ [in series, priority etc] après ▪ **Rothman comes ~ Richardson** Rothman vient après Richardson ▪ **~ you** [politely] après vous (je vous en prie) ▪ **~ you with the paper** tu peux me passer le journal quand tu l'auras fini **3.** [following consecutively] : **day ~ day** jour après jour ▪ **time ~ time** maintes (et maintes) fois ▪ **(for) mile ~ mile** sur des kilomètres et des kilomètres ▪ **he's made mistake ~ mistake** il a fait erreur sur erreur ▪ **generation ~ generation of farmers** des générations entières de fermiers ▪ **it's been one crisis ~ another ever since she arrived** on va de crise en crise depuis son arrivée
4. [behind] après, derrière ▪ **close the door ~ you** fermez la porte derrière vous ▪ **he locked up ~ them** il a tout fermé après leur départ *OR* après qu'ils soient partis
5. [in view of] après ▪ **~ what you told me** après ce que vous m'avez dit
6. [in spite of] : **~ all the trouble I took, no-one came** après *OR* malgré tout le mal que je me suis donné, personne n'est venu
7. [in the manner of] : **~ Rubens** d'après Rubens
8. [in search of] : **to be ~ sb/sthg** chercher qqn/qqch ▪ **she's ~ you** elle te cherche ; [angry with] elle t'en veut ; [attracted to] tu l'intéresses ▪ **the police are ~ him** la police est à ses trousses, il est recherché par la police ▪ **he's ~ her money** il en veut à son argent ▪ **what's he ~?** [want] qu'est-ce qu'il veut? ; [looking for] qu'est-ce qu'il cherche? ; [intend] qu'est-ce qu'il a derrière la tête? ▪ **I know what she's ~** je sais où elle veut en venir
9. [as verb complement] : **to ask** *OR* **to inquire ~ sb** demander des nouvelles de qqn ▪ **to name a child ~ sb** *UK* donner à un enfant le nom de qqn ▪ **they ran ~ him** ils lui ont couru après.
◇ *adv* après, ensuite ▪ **the day ~** le lendemain, le jour suivant ▪ **two days ~** deux jours après *OR* plus tard ▪ **the week ~** la semaine d'après *OR* suivante ▪ **to follow (on) ~** suivre.
◇ *conj* après que ▪ **come and see me ~ you have spoken to him** venez me voir quand vous lui aurez parlé ▪ **I came ~ he had left** je suis arrivé après qu'il est parti ▪ **~ saying goodnight to the children** après avoir dit bonsoir aux enfants.
◇ *adj* [later] : **in ~ life** *OR* **years** plus tard dans la vie.
◆ **afters** *npl UK inf* dessert *m* ▪ **what's for ~s?** qu'est-ce qu'il y a pour le dessert *OR* comme dessert?
◆ **after all** *adv phr* **1.** [when all's said and done] après tout **2.** [against expectation] après *OR* malgré tout ▪ **so she was right ~ all** alors elle avait raison en fait.
◆ **one after another, one after the other** *adv phr* l'un après l'autre ▪ **he made several mistakes one ~ the other** il a fait plusieurs fautes d'affilée *OR* à la file.

afterbirth ['ɑːftəbɜːθ] *n* placenta *m*.

afterburner ['ɑːftəbɜːnər] *n* chambre *f* de postcombustion.

aftercare ['ɑːftəkeər] *n* **1.** MED postcure *f* **2.** [of prisoner] assistance *f (aux anciens détenus)*.

after-dinner *adj* [speaker, speech] de fin de dîner *OR* banquet ▪ **an ~ drink** ≃ un digestif.

aftereffect ['ɑːftərɪ,fekt] *n (usu pl)* [gen] suite *f* ▪ MED séquelle *f*.

afterglow ['ɑːftəgləʊ] *n* [of sunset] dernières lueurs *fpl*, derniers reflets *mpl* ▪ *fig* [of pleasure] sensation *f* de bien-être *(après coup)*.

after-hours *adj* [after closing time] qui suit la fermeture ▪ [after work] qui suit le travail ▪ **an ~ bar** *US* un bar de nuit.
◆ **after hours** *adv phr* [after closing time] après la fermeture ▪ [after work] après le travail.

afterlife ['ɑːftəlaɪf] *n* vie *f* après la mort.

aftermath ['ɑːftəmæθ] *n* **1.** [of event] séquelles *fpl*, suites *fpl* ▪ **in the ~ of the military coup** à la suite du coup d'État militaire ▪ **in the immediate ~** tout de suite après, dans la foulée **2.** AGRIC regain *m*.

afternoon [,ɑːftə'nuːn] ◇ *n* après-midi *m inv OR f inv* ▪ **this ~** cet après-midi ▪ **all ~** tout l'après-midi ▪ **tomorrow/yesterday ~** demain/hier après-midi ▪ **in the ~** [in general] l'après-midi ; [of particular day] (dans) l'après-midi ▪ **on Friday ~s** le vendredi après-midi ▪ **on Friday ~** [in general] le vendredi après-midi ; [of particular day] vendredi après-midi

■ **in the early ~** tôt dans l'après-midi ■ **at 2 o'clock in the ~** à 2 h de l'après-midi ■ **on the ~ of May 16th** (dans) l'après-midi du 16 mai ■ **on a summer ~** par un après-midi d'été ■ **good ~** [hello] bonjour ; [goodbye] au revoir.
<> *comp* [class, train] de l'après-midi ■ [walk] qui a lieu dans l'après-midi ■ **~ performance** CIN & THEAT matinée *f*.
◆ **afternoons** *adv esp US* (dans) l'après-midi.

afternoon tea *n thé pris avec une légère collation dans le cours de l'après-midi.*

afterpains ['ɑːftəpeɪnz] *npl* tranchées *fpl* utérines.

after-sales *adj* après-vente *(inv)*.

after-school *adj* [activities] extrascolaire.

aftershave ['ɑːftəʃeɪv] *n* : **~ (lotion)** (lotion *f*) après-rasage *m*, (lotion *f*) after-shave *m*.

aftershock ['ɑːftəʃɒk] *n* réplique *f* (d'un séisme).

aftersun ['ɑːftəsʌn] *adj* : **~ cream** crème *f* après-soleil.

aftertaste ['ɑːftəteɪst] *n liter & fig* arrière-goût *m*.

after-tax *adj* [profits] après impôts, net d'impôt ■ [salary] net d'impôt.

afterthought ['ɑːftəθɔːt] *n* pensée *f* après coup ■ **I had an ~** j'ai pensé après coup ■ **I only mentioned it as an ~** j'en ai seulement parlé après coup, quand l'idée m'est venue ■ **the west wing was added as an ~** l'aile ouest a été ajoutée après coup.

afterwards ['ɑːftəwədz] *UK*, **afterward** ['æftərwərd] *US adv* après, ensuite ■ **I only realized ~** je n'ai compris qu'après coup *OR* que plus tard.

afterword ['ɑːftəwɜːd] *n* [postscript] postface *f* ■ [epilogue] épilogue *m*.

afterworld ['ɑːftəwɜːld] *n* vie *f* après la mort.

Aga® ['ɑːgə] *n cuisinière en fonte à l'ancienne.*

again [ə'gen] *adv* **1.** [once more] encore une fois, de nouveau ■ **it's me ~!** c'est encore moi!, me revoici! ■ **here we are back home ~!** nous revoilà chez nous! ■ **you'll soon be well ~** vous serez bientôt remis ■ **(the) same ~ please!** [in bar] remettez-nous ça *OR* la même chose s'il vous plaît! ■ **yet ~** encore une fois | [with negative] ne... plus ■ **I didn't see them ~** je ne les ai plus revus ■ **not you ~!** encore vous? ▶ **~ and ~** maintes et maintes fois, à maintes reprises ■ **she read the passage through over and over ~** elle a lu et relu le passage
2. [with verbs] : **to begin ~** recommencer ■ **to come ~** revenir ■ **to do ~** refaire ■ **can you say it ~?** pouvez-vous répéter?
3. [indicating forgetfulness] déjà ■ **what's her name ~?** comment s'appelle-t-elle déjà?
4. [in quantity] : **as much/many ~** encore autant ■ **half as much ~** encore la moitié de ça ■ **half as many pages ~** la moitié plus de pages
5. [furthermore] d'ailleurs, qui plus est.

against [ə'genst] <> *prep* **1.** [indicating position] contre ■ **he leant his bike (up) ~ the wall** il appuya son vélo contre le mur ■ **she had her nose pressed ~ the window** elle avait le nez écrasé au carreau | [indicating impact] contre ■ **I banged my knee ~ the chair** je me suis cogné le genou contre la chaise
2. [in the opposite direction to - current, stream, grain] contre ■ [contrary to - rules, principles] à l'encontre de ■ **to go ~ a trend** s'opposer à une *OR* aller à l'encontre d'une tendance ■ **it's ~ the law to steal** le vol est interdit par la loi ■ **they sold the farm ~ my advice/wishes** ils ont vendu la ferme sans tenir compte de mes conseils/de ce que je souhaitais
3. [indicating opposition to - person, proposal, government] contre ■ **the fight ~ inflation/crime** la lutte contre l'inflation/la criminalité ■ **to decide ~ sthg** décider de ne pas faire qqch ■ **she's ~ telling him** elle trouve qu'on ne devrait pas le lui dire ■ **I advised her ~ going** je lui ai déconseillé d'y aller ■ **what have you got ~ him/the idea?** qu'est-ce que vous avez contre lui/l'idée? ■ **I've nothing ~ it** je n'ai rien contre
4. [unfavourable to] contre ■ **conditions were ~ them** les conditions leur étaient défavorables ■ **his appearance is ~ him** son physique ne joue pas en sa faveur
5. [in competition with] contre ■ **a race ~ time** *OR* **the clock** une course contre la montre
6. [indicating defence, protection, precaution etc] contre ■ **an injection ~ measles** une injection contre la rougeole | *fml* [in preparation for] en vue de, en prévision de ■ **to save money ~ one's retirement** faire des économies en prévision de *OR* pour la retraite
7. [in contrast to] contre, sur ■ **yellow flowers ~ a green background** des fleurs jaunes sur un fond vert ■ **these events took place ~ a background of political violence** *fig* ces événements ont eu lieu dans un climat de violence politique
8. [in comparison to, in relation to] en comparaison de, par rapport à ■ **the dollar fell ~ the yen** FIN le dollar a baissé par rapport au yen
9. [in exchange for] contre, en échange de ■ **cash is available ~ presentation of the voucher** ce bon peut être échangé contre de l'argent.
<> *adv* contre ■ **are you for or ~?** êtes-vous pour ou contre? ■ **the odds are 10 to 1 ~** [gen] il y a une chance sur dix ; [in horse racing] la cote est à 10 contre 1.

agape [ə'geɪp] *adj* bouche bée *(inv)*.

Aga-saga ['ɑːgə,sɑːgə] *n UK hum roman ayant pour thème la vie sentimentale d'une femme au foyer aisée.*

agate ['ægɪt] *n* agate *f*.

age [eɪdʒ] <> *n* **1.** [of person, animal, tree, building] âge *m* ■ **he is 25 years of ~** il est âgé de 25 ans ■ **at the ~ of 25** à l'âge de 25 ans ■ **when I was your ~** quand j'avais votre âge ■ **his wife is only half his ~** sa femme n'a que la moitié de son âge ■ **she's twice my ~** elle a le double de mon âge ■ **I have a son your ~** j'ai un fils de votre âge ■ **she doesn't look her ~** elle ne fait pas son âge ■ **I'm beginning to feel my ~** je commence à me sentir vieux ■ **act** *OR* **be your ~!** [be reasonable] sois raisonnable! ; [don't be silly] ne sois pas stupide! ■ **he is of an ~ when he should consider settling down** il est à un âge où il devrait penser à se ranger ■ **the two of them were of an ~** ils étaient tous les deux à peu près du même âge ■ **to be of ~** LAW être majeur ▶ **the ~ of consent** LAW *âge où les rapports sexuels sont autorisés par la loi britannique (16 ans)* ■ **they are below the ~ of consent** ils tombent sous le coup de la loi sur la protection des mineurs ■ **to come of ~** atteindre sa majorité, devenir majeur
2. [old age - of person] âge *m*, vieillesse *f* ; [- of wood, paper, wine etc] âge *m* ■ **bent with ~** courbé par l'âge ■ **yellow** *OR* **yellowed with ~** jauni par l'âge ▶ **Age Concern** *association caritative britannique d'aide aux personnes âgées*
3. [period - esp historical] époque *f*, âge *m* ■ GEOL âge *m* ■ **through the ~s** à travers les âges
4. *(usu pl)* [long time] éternité *f* ■ **I haven't seen you for** *OR* **in ~s!** cela fait une éternité que je ne vous ai (pas) vu! ■ **it took him ~s to do the work** il a mis très longtemps à faire le travail.
<> *vi* vieillir, prendre de l'âge ■ **he's beginning to ~** il commence à se faire vieux ■ **to ~ well** [person] vieillir bien ; [wine, cheese] s'améliorer en vieillissant.
<> *vt* **1.** [person] vieillir
2. [wine, cheese] laisser vieillir *OR* mûrir ■ **~d in the wood** vieilli en fût.

age bracket *n* = **age group**.

aged <> *adj* **1.** [eɪdʒd] [of the age of] : **a man ~ 50** un homme (âgé) de 50 ans **2.** ['eɪdʒɪd] [old] âgé, vieux *(before vowel or silent 'h' vieil)*, vieille *f* ■ **my ~ aunt** ma vieille tante.
<> *npl* : **the ~** les personnes *fpl* âgées, les vieux *mpl*.

age group *n* tranche *f* d'âge ■ **the 20 to 30 ~** la tranche d'âge des 20 à 30 ans ■ **the younger ~** les jeunes *mpl*.

ageing ['eɪdʒɪŋ] <> *adj* **1.** [person] vieillissant, qui se fait vieux ■ [society] de vieux ■ [machinery, car] (qui se fait) vieux ■ **the ~ process** le processus du vieillissement **2.** [clothes, hairstyle] qui vieillit.
<> *n* **1.** [of society, population] vieillissement *m* **2.** [of wine, cheese] vieillissement *m*.

ageism ['eɪdʒɪzm] *n* âgisme *m*.

ageist ['eɪdʒɪst] <> *adj* [action, policy] qui relève de l'âgisme.
<> *n personne qui fait preuve d'âgisme.*

ageless ['eɪdʒlɪs] *adj* [person] sans âge, qui n'a pas d'âge ■ [work of art] intemporel ■ [beauty] toujours jeune.

age limit *n* limite *f* d'âge.

agency ['eɪdʒənsɪ] (*pl* **agencies**) *n* **1.** COMM [for employment] agence *f*, bureau *m* ■ [for travel, accommodation] agence *f* ■ **dating ~** club *m* de rencontres **2.** ADMIN service *m*, bureau *m* ■ **international aid agencies** des organisations d'aide internationale ■ **a government ~** une agence gouvernementale **3.** [intermediary - of person] intermédiaire *m*, entremise *f* ; [- of fate] jeu *m* ; [- of light, water] action *f* ■ **by the ~ of direct sunlight** par l'action directe des rayons du soleil.

agenda [ə'dʒendə] *n* **1.** [for meeting] ordre *m* du jour ■ [for activities] programme *m* ■ **what's on today's ~?, what's on the ~ (for) today?** [for meeting] quel est l'ordre du jour? ; [for activities] qu'est-ce qu'il y a au programme pour aujourd'hui? ■ **it was top of the ~** *fig* c'était prioritaire ➤ **to set the ~** mener le jeu **2.** [set of priorities] : **to have one's own ~** avoir son propre programme.

agent ['eɪdʒənt] *n* **1.** COMM agent *m*, représentant *m*, - e *f* ■ [for travel, insurance] agent *m* ■ [for firm] concessionnaire *mf* ■ [for brand] dépositaire *mf* ■ **where's the nearest Jaguar ~ ?** où est le concessionnaire Jaguar le plus proche ? **2.** [for actor, sportsman, writer] agent *m* **3.** [spy] agent *m* **4.** [means] agent *m*, moyen *m* ■ [key person] : **an ~ of change** un acteur *m* **5.** CHEM, LING & COMPUT agent *m* ■ **cleaning ~** produit *m* de nettoyage.

age-old *adj* séculaire, antique.

agglomerate ◇ *vt* [ə'glɒməreɪt] agglomérer.
◇ *vi* [ə'glɒməreɪt] s'agglomérer.
◇ *n* [ə'glɒmərət] agglomérat *m*.
◇ *adj* [ə'glɒmərət] aggloméré.

agglomeration [əˌglɒmə'reɪʃn] *n* agglomération *f*.

agglutination [əˌgluːtɪ'neɪʃn] *n* agglutination *f*.

agglutinative [ə'gluːtɪnətɪv] *adj* agglutinant.

aggrandizement [ə'grændɪzmənt] *n pej* agrandissement *m* ■ **personal ~** volonté *f* de se pousser en avant.

aggravate ['ægrəveɪt] *vt* **1.** [worsen - illness, conditions] aggraver ; [- situation, problem] aggraver, envenimer ; [- quarrel] envenimer ■ LAW : **~d assault** coups et blessures ■ **~d burglary** cambriolage *m* aggravé de coups et blessures **2.** [irritate - person] agacer, ennuyer.

aggravating ['ægrəveɪtɪŋ] *adj* **1.** [worsening - situation, illness, conditions] aggravant **2.** [irritating - person, problem] agaçant, exaspérant.

aggravation [ˌægrə'veɪʃn] *n* **1.** [deterioration - of situation, illness, conditions] aggravation *f* ; [- of dispute] enveniment *m* **2.** [irritation] agacement *m*, exaspération *f*.

aggregate ◇ *n* ['ægrɪgət] **1.** [total] ensemble *m*, total *m* ■ **in the ~, on ~** dans l'ensemble, globalement ■ **to win on ~** SPORT gagner au total des points **2.** CONSTR & GEOL agrégat *m*.
◇ *adj* ['ægrɪgət] global, total.
◇ *vt* ['ægrɪgeɪt] **1.** [bring together] rassembler **2.** [add up to] s'élever à, se monter à.

aggression [ə'greʃn] *n* agression *f*.

aggressive [ə'gresɪv] *adj* **1.** [gen - PSYCHOL] agressif **2.** MIL [action, weapon] offensif **3.** COMM [campaign] énergique ■ *US* [businessman] combatif, dynamique.

aggressively [ə'gresɪvlɪ] *adv* [behave] agressivement, avec agressivité ■ [campaign] avec dynamisme.

aggressiveness [ə'gresɪvnɪs] *n* **1.** [gen] agressivité *f* **2.** COMM [of businessman] combativité *f* ■ [of campaign] dynamisme *m*, fougue *f*.

aggressor [ə'gresəʳ] *n* agresseur *m*.

aggrieved [ə'griːvd] *adj* **1.** [gen] affligé, chagriné ■ **to feel ~ at** *OR* **about sthg** être chagriné de *OR* par qqch **2.** LAW lésé.

aggro ['ægrəʊ] *n UK inf (U)* **1.** [violence, fighting] grabuge *m*, bagarre *f* **2.** [fuss, bother] histoires *fpl*.

aghast [ə'gɑːst] *adj* [astounded] interloqué, pantois ■ [horrified] horrifié, atterré ■ **she was ~ at the news** elle était atterrée par la nouvelle.

agile [*UK* 'ædʒaɪl, *US* 'ædʒəl] *adj* **1.** [person, animal] agile, leste **2.** [brain, mind] vif.

agility [ə'dʒɪlətɪ] *n* **1.** [physical] agilité *f*, souplesse *f* **2.** [mental] vivacité *f*.

aging *etc* ['eɪdʒɪŋ] *adj* & *n* = **ageing**.

agitate ['ædʒɪteɪt] ◇ *vi* POL : **to ~ for/against sthg** faire campagne en faveur de/contre qqch ■ **they are agitating for better working conditions** ils réclament de meilleures conditions de travail.
◇ *vt* **1.** [liquid] agiter, remuer **2.** [emotionally] agiter, troubler.

agitated ['ædʒɪteɪtɪd] *adj* agité, troublé ■ **to become** *OR* **to get ~** se mettre dans tous ses états.

agitation [ˌædʒɪ'teɪʃn] *n* **1.** [emotional] agitation *f*, émoi *m*, trouble *m* ■ **to be in a state of ~** être dans tous ses états **2.** [unrest] agitation *f*, troubles *mpl* ■ [campaign] campagne *f* mouvementée **3.** [of sea] agitation *f*.

agitator ['ædʒɪteɪtəʳ] *n* **1.** POL [person] agitateur *m*, - trice *f* **2.** [machine] agitateur *m*.

agitprop ['ædʒɪtprop] ◇ *n* agit-prop *f inv*.
◇ *comp* [art, theatre] de l'agit-prop.

aglow [ə'gləʊ] *adj* [fire] rougeoyant ■ [sky] embrasé ■ **to be ~ with colour** briller de couleurs vives ■ **his face was ~ with excitement/health** *fig* son visage rayonnait d'émotion/de santé.

AGM (*abbrev of* **annual general meeting**) *n UK* AGA *f*.

agnostic [æg'nɒstɪk] ◇ *n* agnostique *mf*.
◇ *adj* agnostique.

agnosticism [æg'nɒstɪsɪzm] *n* agnosticisme *m*.

ago [ə'gəʊ] *adv* : **they moved here ten years ~** ils ont emménagé ici il y a dix ans ■ **how long ~ did this happen?** cela c'est produit il y a combien de temps?, il y a combien de temps que cela s'est produit? ■ **as long ~ as 1900** en 1900 déjà, dès 1900.

agog [ə'gɒg] *adj* en émoi ■ **the children were all ~ (with excitement)** les enfants étaient tout excités ■ **I was ~ to discover what had happened** je brûlais d'impatience de savoir ce qui s'était passé.

agonize, ise ['ægənaɪz] *vi* se tourmenter ■ **to ~ over** *OR* **about a decision** hésiter longuement avant de prendre une décision ■ **don't ~ over it!** n'y passe pas trop de temps! ■ **to ~ over how to do sthg** se ronger les sangs *OR* se tracasser pour savoir comment faire qqch.

agonized ['ægənaɪzd] *adj* [behaviour, reaction] angoissé, d'angoisse ■ [cry] déchirant.

agonizing ['ægənaɪzɪŋ] *adj* [situation] angoissant ■ [decision] déchirant, angoissant ■ [pain] atroce.

agonizingly ['ægənaɪzɪŋlɪ] *adv* atrocement.

agony ['ægənɪ] (*pl* **agonies**) *n* **1.** [physical - pain] douleur *f* atroce ; [- suffering] souffrance *f* atroce, souffrances *fpl* atroces ■ **to be in ~** souffrir le martyre ■ **to cry out in ~** crier de douleur ■ **it was ~ to stand up** je souffrais le martyre pour me lever ➤ **death ~** agonie *f* (de la mort) **2.** [emotional, mental] supplice *m*, angoisse *f* ■ **to be in an ~ of doubt/remorse** être torturé par le doute/le remords.

agony aunt *n UK responsable du courrier du cœur.*

agony column *n* courrier *m* du cœur.

agoraphobia [ˌægərə'fəʊbjə] *n* agoraphobie *f*.

agoraphobic [ˌægərə'fəʊbɪk] ◇ *adj* agoraphobe.
◇ *n* agoraphobe *mf*.

AGR (*abbrev of* **advanced gas-cooled reactor**) *n* AGR *m*.

agrarian [ə'greərɪən] ◇ *adj* agraire.
◇ *n* agrarien *m*, - enne *f*.

agree [ə'griː] ◇ *vi* **1.** [share same opinion] être d'accord ■ **I quite ~** je suis tout à fait d'accord (avec vous) ■ **don't you ~?** n'êtes-vous pas d'accord? ■ **to ~ about sthg** être d'accord sur qqch ■ **I ~ about going on a holiday** je suis d'accord pour partir en vacances ■ **I think we ~ on** *OR* **about the basic**

facts je pense que nous sommes d'accord sur l'essentiel ▪ **to ~ with sb** être d'accord avec *OR* être du même avis que qqn ▪ **I ~ with you about the decor** je suis d'accord avec vous pour ce qui est du décor ▪ **they ~ with me that it's a disgrace** ils trouvent comme moi que c'est une honte ▪ **I couldn't ~ with you more** je partage entièrement votre avis
2. [be in favour] être d'accord ▪ **I don't ~ with censorship** je suis contre *OR* je n'admets pas la censure ▪ **I don't ~ with people smoking in public places** je ne suis pas d'accord pour que les gens fument dans les lieux publics
3. [assent] consentir, donner son adhésion ▪ **to ~ to a proposal** donner son adhésion à *OR* accepter une proposition ▪ **to ~ to sb's request** consentir à la requête de qqn ▪ **her parents have ~d to her going abroad** ses parents ont consenti à ce qu'elle aille *OR* sont d'accord pour qu'elle aille à l'étranger ▪ **they ~d to share the cost** ils se sont mis d'accord pour partager les frais
4. [reach agreement] se mettre d'accord ▪ **to ~ on** *OR* **upon a date** convenir d'une date
5. [correspond - account, estimate] concorder ▪ **your statement doesn't ~ with hers** ta version *OR* ta déclaration ne correspond pas à la sienne, vos deux versions ne concordent pas
6. [be suitable] : **the climate here ~s with me** le climat d'ici me réussit *OR* me convient très bien ▪ **rich food doesn't ~ with me** la nourriture riche ne me réussit pas
7. GRAM s'accorder ▪ **the verb ~s with the subject** le verbe s'accorde avec le sujet.
◇ *vt* **1.** [share opinion] : **to ~ that...** être d'accord avec le fait que... ▪ **we all ~ that he's innocent** nous sommes tous d'accord pour dire qu'il est innocent, nous sommes tous d'avis qu'il est innocent ▪ **I don't ~ that the police should be armed** je ne suis pas d'accord pour que la police soit armée
2. [consent] : **to ~ to do sthg** accepter de *OR* consentir à faire qqch
3. [admit] admettre, reconnaître ▪ **they ~d that they had made a mistake** ils ont reconnu *OR* convenu qu'ils avaient fait une faute
4. [reach agreement on] convenir de ▪ **we ~d to differ** nous sommes restés chacun sur notre position ▪ **it was ~d that the money should be invested** il a été convenu que l'argent serait investi ▪ **to ~ a price** se mettre d'accord sur un prix ▪ **the budget has been ~d** le budget a été adopté ▪ **unless otherwise ~d** LAW sauf accord contraire
5. [accept - statement, plan] accepter.

agreeable [ə'grɪəbl] *adj* **1.** [pleasant - situation] plaisant, agréable ; [- person] agréable **2.** [willing] consentant ▪ **to be ~ to doing sthg** accepter de *OR* bien vouloir faire qqch ▪ **are you ~ to the proposal?** consentez-vous à la proposition?, êtes-vous d'accord avec la proposition? **3.** [acceptable] acceptable, satisfaisant ▪ **I hope the terms are ~ to you** j'espère que les conditions vous conviennent.

agreeably [ə'grɪəblɪ] *adv* agréablement.

agreed [ə'gri:d] ◇ *adj* **1.** [in agreement] d'accord ▪ **is everyone ~?** est-ce que tout le monde est d'accord? ▪ **it's ~ that we leave on Friday** il est entendu *OR* convenu que nous partons vendredi ▪ **we are ~ on** *OR* **about the conditions** nous sommes d'accord sur les conditions **2.** [fixed - time, place, price] convenu ▪ **as ~** comme convenu.
◇ *interj* : **~!** (c'est) d'accord *OR* entendu!

agreement [ə'gri:mənt] *n* **1.** [gen] accord *m* ▪ **to be in ~ with sb about sthg** être d'accord avec qqn sur qqch *OR* au sujet de qqch ▪ **to reach ~** parvenir à un accord ▪ **by ~ with the management** en accord avec la direction **2.** COMM & POL accord *m* ▪ **under the (terms of the) ~** selon les termes de l'accord ▪ **to come to an ~** tomber d'accord, parvenir à un accord **3.** GRAM accord *m*.
Voir module d'usage

agribusiness ['ægrɪ,bɪznɪs] *n (U)* agro-industries *fpl*.

agricultural [,ægrɪ'kʌltʃərəl] *adj* [produce, machinery, land, society] agricole ▪ [expert] agronome ▪ [college] d'agriculture, agricole.

agriculturalist [,ægrɪ'kʌltʃərəlɪst] *n* [specialist] agronome *mf* ▪ [farmer] agriculteur *m*, - trice *f*.

agricultural show *n* [national] salon *m* de l'agriculture ▪ [local] foire *f* agricole.

agriculture ['ægrɪkʌltʃər] *n* agriculture *f*.

agronomist [ə'grɒnəmɪst] *n* agronome *mf*.

agronomy [ə'grɒnəmɪ] *n* agronomie *f*.

aground [ə'graʊnd] ◇ *adj* NAUT échoué.
◇ *adv* : **to run** *OR* **to go ~** s'échouer.

ah [ɑ:] *interj* : **~!** ah!

aha [ɑ:'hɑ:] *interj* : **~!** ah, ah!, tiens!

ahead *etc* [ə'hed] *adv* **1.** [in space] en avant, devant ▪ **the road ~** la route devant nous/eux *etc* ▪ **there's a crossroads about half a mile ~** il y a un croisement à environ 800 mètres (d'ici) ▪ **go/drive on ~ and I'll catch you up** vas-y *OR* pars en avant, je te rattraperai ▪ **to push** *OR* **press ~ with a project** poursuivre un projet **2.** [in time] : **the years ~** les années à venir ▪ **what lies ~?** qu'est-ce qui nous attend? ▪ **looking ~ to the future** en pensant à l'avenir ▪ **to plan ~** faire des projets ▪ **we must think ~** nous devons prévoir **3.** [in competition, race] en avance ▪ **three lengths/five points ~** trois longueurs/cinq points d'avance ▪ **it's better to quit while you're ~** *fig* mieux vaut te retirer du jeu pendant que tu as l'avantage.
◆ **ahead of** *prep phr* **1.** [in front of] devant **2.** [in time] : **he arrived ten minutes ~ of me** il est arrivé dix minutes avant moi ▪ **to finish ~ of schedule** terminer plus tôt que prévu *OR* en avance ▪ **the rest of the team are two months ~ of us** les autres membres de l'équipe ont deux mois d'avance sur nous ▪ **to be ~ of one's time** *fig* être en avance sur son époque

AGREEMENT

Je suis entièrement de votre avis. I couldn't agree with you more.

Je suis tout à fait d'accord. I quite agree.

Je suis assez d'accord (avec toi). I'm inclined to agree (with you).

Vous avez (absolument) raison. You're (absolutely) right.

C'est aussi mon avis. I think so too.

Vous avez eu tout à fait raison de lui dire de partir. You were absolutely right to tell him to leave.

C'est exactement ce que je pensais. That's just what I was thinking.

Je n'aurais pas dit mieux moi-même. I couldn't have put it better myself.

À ta place, j'aurais fait exactement la même chose. I'd have done exactly the same in your situation.

Tu as fait le bon choix. You've made the right choice.

Je partage votre sentiment là-dessus. Those are my feelings exactly.

Absolument ! Absolutely!

Pas de problème. That's fine by me.

Ça me paraît être la bonne solution. That seems to be the best solution.

Pourquoi pas ? I don't see why not.

Bon, d'accord. Go on, then.

3. [in competition, race] : **he is five points ~ of his nearest rival** il a cinq points d'avance sur son rival le plus proche, il devance son rival le plus proche de cinq points.

ahem [ə'hem] *interj* : ~! hum!

ahoy [ə'hɔɪ] *interj* : ~! ohé!, holà! ■ **ship ~!** ohé du navire!

AI ◇ *pr n* (*abbrev of* **Amnesty International**) AI.
◇ *n* **1.** (*abbrev of* **artificial intelligence**) IA *f* **2.** = **artificial insemination**.

AIB (*abbrev of* **Accident Investigation Bureau**) *pr n commission d'enquête sur les accidents en Grande-Bretagne.*

aid [eɪd] ◇ *n* **1.** [help, assistance] aide *f* ■ **I managed to open the tin with the ~ of a screwdriver** à l'aide d'un tournevis, j'ai réussi à ouvrir la boîte ■ **to come to sb's ~** venir à l'aide de qqn ■ **to go to the ~ of sb** se porter au secours de *OR* porter secours à qqn **2.** POL aide *f* ■ **food ~** aide alimentaire ■ **overseas ~** aide au tiers-monde ■ **the government gives ~ to depressed areas** le gouvernement octroie des aides aux régions en déclin **3.** [helpful equipment] aide *f*, support *m* ■ **teaching ~s** supports *OR* aides pédagogiques ■ **visual ~s** supports visuels **4.** [assistant] aide *mf*, assistant *m*, - e *f* **5.** [for climber] piton *m*.
◇ *vt* **1.** [help - person] aider, venir en aide à ; [- financially] aider, secourir ■ **to ~ sb with sthg** aider qqn pour qqch **2.** [give support to - region, industry] aider, soutenir **3.** [encourage - development, understanding] contribuer à **4.** LAW : **to ~ and abet sb** être (le) complice de qqn ■ **~ed and abetted by her sister** *fig* avec la complicité de sa sœur.
◆ **in aid of** *prep phr* : **a collection in ~ of the homeless** une collecte au profit des sans-abri ■ **what are all these levers in ~ of?** *UK inf fig* à quoi servent tous ces leviers? ■ **what are the cakes in ~ of?** *UK inf fig* les gâteaux sont en l'honneur de quoi?

AID ◇ *n* (*abbrev of* **artificial insemination by donor**) IAD *f*.
◇ *pr n* (*abbrev of* **Agency for International Development**) AID *f*.

aide [eɪd] *n* aide *mf*, assistant *m*, - e *f*.

-aided [eɪdɪd] *in cpds* **1.** COMPUT assisté par ■ **computer~ design** conception *f* assistée par ordinateur, CAO *f* **2.** [financially] : **grant~** [student] boursier ; [industry] subventionné ; [school] qui reçoit une subvention.

aide-de-camp [eɪddə'kɑ̃:] (*pl* **aides-de-camp** [,eɪdz-]) *n* aide *m* de camp.

aide-mémoire [,eɪdmem'wɑ:] (*pl* **aides-mémoire** ['eɪdz-]) *n* aide-mémoire *m inv*.

Aids, AIDS [eɪdz] (*abbrev of* **acquired immune deficiency syndrome**) ◇ *n* sida *m*, SIDA *m*, Sida *m*.
◇ *comp* [sufferer] du sida ■ [clinic] pour sidéens ■ **~ specialist** sidologue *mf* ■ **~ patient** sidéen *m*, - enne *f* ■ **the ~ virus** le virus du sida.

aids-related *adj* lié au sida ■ **~ complex** ARC *m*.

aid worker *n* [voluntary] volontaire *mf* ■ [paid] employé *m*, - e *f* d'une organisation humanitaire.

AIH (*abbrev of* **artificial insemination by husband**) *n* IAC *f*.

ail [eɪl] ◇ *vt dial & lit* **what ~s you?** qu'avez-vous?, quelle mouche vous a piqué?
◇ *vi* être souffrant.

aileron ['eɪlərɒn] *n* aileron *m*.

ailing ['eɪlɪŋ] *adj* [person] souffrant, en mauvaise santé ■ [economy, industry] malade.

ailment ['eɪlmənt] *n* mal *m*, affection *f*.

aim [eɪm] ◇ *n* **1.** [intention, purpose] but *m* ■ **with the ~ of** afin de, dans le but de ■ **his ~ is to get rich quickly** il a pour but *OR* il s'est donné comme but de s'enrichir rapidement **2.** [with weapon] : **to take ~ (at sthg/sb)** viser (qqch/qqn) ■ **to have a good ~** bien viser ■ **to miss one's ~** manquer la cible *OR* son but.
◇ *vt* **1.** [gun] braquer ■ [missile] pointer ■ [stone] lancer ■ [blow] allonger, décocher ■ [kick] donner ■ **he ~ed his gun at the man's head** il a braqué son pistolet sur la tête de l'homme **2.** *fig* [criticism, product, programme] destiner ■ **was that remark ~ed at me?** est-ce que cette remarque m'était destinée?
◇ *vi* **1.** [take aim] : **to ~ at** *OR* **for sthg** viser qqch **2.** [have as goal] : **she's ~ing to become a millionaire by the age of 30** son but, c'est d'être millionnaire à 30 ans ■ **we ~ to arrive before midnight** nous avons l'intention *OR* nous nous sommes fixés d'arriver avant minuit ■ **to ~ high** viser haut.

aimless ['eɪmlɪs] *adj* [person] sans but, désœuvré ■ [life] sans but ■ [occupation, task] sans objet, futile.

aimlessly ['eɪmlɪslɪ] *adv* [walk around] sans but ■ [stand around] sans trop savoir quoi faire ■ **he wandered ~ through the streets** il errait dans les rues.

ain't [eɪnt] *inf* **1.** = **am not 2.** = **is not 3.** = **are not 4.** = **has not 5.** = **have not**.

air [eəʳ] ◇ *n* **1.** [gen - PHYS] air *m* ■ **I need some (fresh) ~** j'ai besoin de prendre l'air ■ **I went out for a breath of (fresh) ~** je suis sorti prendre l'air ■ **to take the ~** *lit* prendre le frais ■ **the divers came up for ~** les plongeurs sont remontés à la surface pour respirer ■ **I need a change of ~** *fig* j'ai besoin de changer d'air ■ **to disappear** *OR* **vanish into thin ~** se volatiliser, disparaître sans laisser de traces
2. [sky] air *m*, ciel *m* ■ **the smoke rose into the ~** la fumée s'éleva vers le ciel ■ **to throw sthg up into the ~** lancer qqch en l'air ■ **seen from the ~, the fields looked like a chessboard** vus d'avion, les champs ressemblaient à un échiquier ■ **to take to the ~** [bird] s'envoler ; [plane] décoller
3. AERON : **to travel by ~** voyager par avion ➜ **~ speed** vitesse *f* du vol
4. RADIO & TV : **to be on (the) ~** [person] être à *OR* avoir l'antenne ; [programme] être à l'antenne ; [station] émettre ■ **to go on the ~** [person] passer à l'antenne ; [programme] passer à l'antenne, être diffusé ■ **to go off the ~** [person] rendre l'antenne ; [programme] se terminer ; [station] cesser d'émettre
5. [manner, atmosphere] air *m* ■ **there is an ~ of mystery about her** elle a un air mystérieux ■ **with a triumphant ~** d'un air triomphant
6. MUS air *m*.
◇ *comp* [piracy, traffic] aérien ■ [travel, traveller] par avion.
◇ *vt* **1.** [linen, bed, room] aérer
2. [express - opinion, grievance] exprimer, faire connaître ; [- suggestion, idea] exprimer, avancer
3. *US* RADIO & TV diffuser.
◆ **airs** *npl* : **to put on** *OR* **to give o.s. ~s** se donner de grands airs ■ **~s and graces** *UK* minauderies *fpl*.
◆ **in the air** *adv phr* : **there's a rumour in the ~ that they're going to sell** le bruit court qu'ils vont vendre ■ **there's something in the ~** il se trame quelque chose ■ **the project is still very much (up) in the ~** le projet n'est encore qu'à l'état d'ébauche *OR* est encore vague.

airbag ['eəbæg] *n* AUT Air Bag® *m*, coussin *m* gonflable.

airbase ['eəbeɪs] *n* base *f* aérienne.

airbed ['eəbed] *n* matelas *m* pneumatique.

airborne ['eəbɔ:n] *adj* **1.** [plane] en vol ■ **to become ~** décoller **2.** [troops, division, regiment] aéroporté.

airbrake ['eəbreɪk] *n* AUT frein *m* à air comprimé ■ AERON aérofrein *m*, frein *m* aérodynamique.

air brick *n* brique *f* creuse.

airbrush ['eəbrʌʃ] ◇ *n* pistolet *m (pour peindre)*.
◇ *vt* peindre au pistolet.

air bubble *n* [in wallpaper, liquid] bulle *f* d'air ■ [in plastic, metal] soufflure *f*.

Airbus® ['eəbʌs] *n* Airbus® *m*.

air chief marshal *n UK* général *m* d'armée aérienne.

air commodore *n UK* général *m* de brigade aérienne.

air-conditioned *adj* climatisé.

air-conditioner *n* climatiseur *m*.

air-conditioning *n* climatisation *f*.

air-cooled [-ku:ld] *adj* [engine] à refroidissement par air.

air corridor *n* couloir *m* aérien.

air cover *n* couverture *f* aérienne.

aircraft ['eəkrɑ:ft] *(pl inv) n* avion *m*.

aircraft carrier *n* porte-avions *m inv*.

aircraft(s)man ['eəkrɑ:ft(s)mən] *(pl* **aircraft(s)men** [-mən]*) n UK* MIL soldat *m* de deuxième classe *(dans l'armée de l'air)*.

aircraft(s)woman ['eəkrɑ:ft(s),wʊmən] *(pl* **aircraft(s)women** [-,wɪmɪn]*) n UK* MIL femme *f* soldat de deuxième classe *(dans l'armée de l'air)*.

aircrew ['eəkru:] *n* équipage *m (d'avion)*.

air current *n* courant *m* atmosphérique.

air cushion *n* [gen] coussin *m* pneumatique ▪ TECH coussin *m* OR matelas *m* d'air.

air cylinder *n* cylindre *m* à air comprimé.

airdrome ['eərdrəʊm] *n US* = **aerodrome**.

airdrop ['eədrɒp] ◇ *n* parachutage *m*.
◇ *vt (pret & pp* **airdropped**, *cont* **airdropping**) parachuter.

Airedale terrier [,eədeɪl'terɪəʳ], **Airedale** *n* airedale-terrier *m*.

airfare ['eəfeəʳ] *n* prix *m* du billet (d'avion), tarif *m* aérien.

air ferry *n* avion *m* transbordeur.

airfield ['eəfi:ld] *n* terrain *m* d'aviation, (petit) aérodrome *m*.

airfoil ['eəfɔɪl] *n US* = **aerofoil**.

air force *n* armée *f* de l'air ▪ **~ base** base *f* aérienne.

airframe ['eəfreɪm] *n* cellule *f* (d'avion).

airfreight ['eəfreɪt] *n* [cargo] fret *m* aérien ▪ [transport] transport *m* aérien ▪ **to send sthg by ~** expédier qqch par voie aérienne OR par avion.

air freshener [-'freʃənəʳ] *n* désodorisant *m (pour la maison)*.

airgun ['eəgʌn] *n* [rifle] carabine *f* OR fusil *m* à air comprimé ▪ [pistol] pistolet *m* à air comprimé.

airhead ['eəhed] *n inf* taré *m*, - e *f*.

airhole ['eəhəʊl] *n* trou *m* d'aération.

air hostess ['eə,həʊstɪs] *n* hôtesse *f* de l'air.

airily ['eərəlɪ] *adv* avec désinvolture.

airing ['eərɪŋ] *n* **1.** [of linen, room] aération *f* ▪ **the room needs an ~** la pièce a besoin d'être aérée ▪ **give the sheets a good ~** secouez bien les draps **2.** *fig* **to give an idea an ~** agiter une idée, mettre une idée sur le tapis.

airing cupboard *n placard chauffé faisant office de sèche-linge.*

air-kiss ['eəkɪs] *vi* s'embrasser (avec affectation).

airlane ['eəleɪn] *n* couloir *m* aérien OR de navigation aérienne.

airless ['eəlɪs] *adj* **1.** [room] qui manque d'air, qui sent le renfermé **2.** [weather] lourd.

air letter *n* aérogramme *m*.

airlift ['eəlɪft] ◇ *n* pont *m* aérien.
◇ *vt* [passengers, troops - out] évacuer par pont aérien ; [- in] faire entrer par pont aérien ▪ [supplies, cargo] transporter par pont aérien.

airline ['eəlaɪn] *n* **1.** AERON ligne *f* aérienne **2.** [for compressed air] tuyau *m* d'air.

airliner ['eəlaɪnəʳ] *n* avion *m* de ligne.

airlock ['eəlɒk] *n* **1.** [in spacecraft, submarine] sas *m* **2.** [in pipe] poche *f* OR bulle *f* d'air.

airmail ['eəmeɪl] ◇ *n* poste *f* aérienne ▪ **'by ~'** [on envelope] 'par avion'.
◇ *comp* [letter, parcel] par avion ▪ **~ paper** papier *m* pelure.
◇ *vt* expédier par avion.

airman ['eəmən] *(pl* **airmen** [-mən]*) n* **1.** [gen] aviateur *m* **2.** *US* MIL soldat *m* de première classe (de l'armée de l'air).

air marshal *n* général *m* de corps aérien.

air mattress *n* matelas *m* pneumatique.

airmobile ['eəmə,bi:l] *adj US* aéroporté.

air pistol *n* pistolet *m* à air comprimé.

airplane ['eərpleɪn] *US n* = **aeroplane**.

airplay ['eəpleɪ] *n* : **that record is getting a lot of ~** on entend souvent ce disque à la radio.

air pocket *n* [affecting plane] trou *m* d'air ▪ [in pipe] poche *f* d'air.

air pollution *n* pollution *f* atmosphérique.

airport ['eəpɔ:t] *n* aéroport *m*.

air pressure *n* pression *f* atmosphérique.

air pump *n* compresseur *m*, pompe *f* à air.

air raid *n* [by the ennemy] attaque *f* aérienne, raid *m* aérien.

air-raid shelter *n* abri *m* antiaérien.

air-raid warden *n* préposé *m*, - e *f* à la défense passive.

air-raid warning *n* alerte *f* antiaérienne.

air rifle *n* carabine *f* à air comprimé.

airscrew ['eəskru:] *n UK* hélice *f* (d'avion).

air-sea rescue *n* sauvetage *m* en mer *(par hélicoptère)*.

airship ['eəʃɪp] *n* dirigeable *m*.

air show *n* **1.** COMM [exhibition] salon *m* de l'aéronautique **2.** [display] meeting *m* aérien.

airsick ['eəsɪk] *adj* : **to be** OR **to get ~** avoir le mal de l'air.

airsock ['eəsɒk] *n* manche *f* à air.

airspace ['eəspeɪs] *n* espace *m* aérien.

airstream ['eəstri:m] *n* courant *m* atmosphérique.

airstrike ['eəstraɪk] *n* [by one's forces] raid *m* aérien, attaque *f* aérienne.

airstrip ['eəstrɪp] *n* terrain *m* OR piste *f* d'atterrissage.

air terminal *n* aérogare *f*.

airtight ['eətaɪt] *adj* hermétique, étanche (à l'air) ▪ **I don't think his argument is completely ~** *fig* je ne crois pas que son argument soit totalement irréfutable.

airtime ['eətaɪm] *n* RADIO & TV : **that record is getting a lot of ~** on entend souvent ce disque à la radio.

air-to-air *adj* MIL air-air *(inv)*, avion-avion *(inv)*.

air-to-surface *adj* MIL air-sol *(inv)*.

air-traffic control *n* contrôle *m* du trafic aérien.

air-traffic controller *n* contrôleur *m*, - euse *f* du trafic aérien, aiguilleur *m* du ciel.

air vice-marshal *n UK* général *m* de division aérienne.

airwaves ['eəweɪvz] *npl* ondes *fpl* (hertziennes) ▪ **on the ~** sur les ondes, à la radio.

airway ['eəweɪ] *n* **1.** AERON [route] voie *f* aérienne ▪ [company] ligne *f* aérienne **2.** MED voies *fpl* respiratoires **3.** [shaft] conduit *m* d'air.

airworthy ['eə,wɜ:ðɪ] *adj* en état de navigation.

airy ['eərɪ] *(comp* **airier**, *superl* **airiest**) *adj* **1.** [room] bien aéré, clair **2.** *fig* [casual - manner] insouciant, désinvolte ; [- ideas, plans, promises] en l'air.

airy-fairy *adj UK inf* [person, notion] farfelu.

aisle [aɪl] *n* **1.** [in church] bas-côté *m*, nef *f* latérale ▪ **her father led her up the ~** c'est son père qui l'a menée à l'autel **2.** [in cinema, supermarket, aeroplane] allée *f* ▪ [on train] couloir *m* (central) ▪ **~ seat** [train] siège *m* côté couloir ; [aeroplane] (siège *m* au bord d'une) allée.

aitch [eɪtʃ] *n* H *m inv*, h *m inv*.

ajar [ə'dʒɑ:ʳ] ◇ *adj* [door, window] entrouvert, entrebâillé.
◇ *adv* : **the door stood ~** la porte est restée entrouverte.

AK *written abbr of* **Alaska**.

aka (*abbrev of* **also known as**) *adv* alias, dit.

akimbo [əˈkɪmbəʊ] *adv* : **with arms ~** les mains *OR* poings sur les hanches.

akin [əˈkɪn] *adj* : **~ to** [like] qui ressemble à, qui tient de ; [related to] apparenté à.

AL *written abbr of* **Alabama**.

Alabama [ˌæləˈbæmə] *pr n* Alabama *m* ▪ **in ~** dans l'Alabama.

alabaster [ˌæləˈbɑːstəʳ] <> *n* albâtre *m*.
<> *comp* d'albâtre.

alacrity [əˈlækrətɪ] *n fml* empressement *m* ▪ **with great ~** avec grand empressement.

Aladdin [əˈlædɪn] *pr n* Aladin.

Alamo [ˈæləməʊ] *pr n* : **the ~** [fort] Fort Alamo ; [battle] la bataille de Fort Alamo.

THE ALAMO

Fort texan assiégé par les Mexicains pendant la guerre d'Indépendance du Texas contre le Mexique, en 1836. Défendu par une poignée d'hommes, dont Davy Crockett, il fut totalement détruit et la garnison entière fut tuée. ***Remember the Alamo*** devint le cri de ralliement des Texans au moment de l'indépendance de leur État.

à la mode [ɑːlɑːˈməʊd] *adj US* [with ice cream] (servi) avec de la crème glacée.

alarm [əˈlɑːm] <> *n* **1.** [warning] alarme *f*, alerte *f* ▪ **to sound** *OR* **to raise the ~** donner l'alarme *OR* l'alerte *OR* l'éveil **2.** [for fire, burglary] sonnette *f OR* sonnerie *f* d'alarme **3.** [anxiety] inquiétude *f*, alarme *f* ▪ **there is no cause for ~** il n'y a aucune raison de s'alarmer ▪ **the government viewed events with increasing ~** le gouvernement s'est montré de plus en plus inquiet face à ces événements **4.** = **alarm clock**.
<> *comp* [signal] d'alarme ▪ **~ bell** sonnerie *f* d'alarme ▪ **to set (the) ~ bells ringing** *fig* donner l'alerte ▪ **~ call** [to wake sleeper] réveil *m* téléphonique.
<> *vt* **1.** [frighten, worry - person] alarmer, faire peur à ; [- animal] effaroucher, faire peur à **2.** [warn] alerter.

alarm clock *n* réveil *m*, réveille-matin *m inv* ▪ **he set the ~ for eight o'clock** il a mis le réveil à sonner à huit heures *OR* pour huit heures.

alarmed [əˈlɑːmd] *adj* **1.** [anxious] inquiet ▪ **don't be ~** ne vous alarmez *OR* effrayez pas ▪ **to become ~** [person] s'alarmer ; [animal] s'effaroucher, prendre peur **2.** [vehicle, building] équipé d'une alarme.

alarming [əˈlɑːmɪŋ] *adj* alarmant.

alarmingly [əˈlɑːmɪŋlɪ] *adv* d'une manière alarmante.

alarmist [əˈlɑːmɪst] <> *adj* alarmiste.
<> *n* alarmiste *mf*.

alas [əˈlæs] *interj* : **~!** hélas!

Alaska [əˈlæskə] *pr n* Alaska *m* ▪ **in ~** en Alaska ▪ **the ~ Highway** la route de l'Alaska.

Alaskan [əˈlæskən] <> *n* habitant *m*, - e *f* de l'Alaska.
<> *adj* de l'Alaska.

Alaska Range *pr n* : **the ~** la chaîne de l'Alaska.

Albania [ælˈbeɪnjə] *pr n* Albanie *f* ▪ **in ~** en Albanie.

Albanian [ælˈbeɪnjən] <> *n* **1.** [person] Albanais *m*, - e *f* **2.** LING albanais *m*.
<> *adj* albanais.

albatross [ˈælbətrɒs] *n* **1.** ZOOL & SPORT albatros *m* **2.** *fig* [handicap] boulet *m* ▪ **their past was an ~ round their necks** ils traînaient leur passé comme un boulet.

albeit [ɔːlˈbiːɪt] *conj* bien que, encore que, quoique ▪ **an impressive, ~ flawed work of art** une œuvre impressionnante bien qu'imparfaite *OR* quoiqu'imparfaite.

Alberta [ælˈbɜːtə] *pr n* Alberta *m* ▪ **in ~** dans l'Alberta.

Albert Hall [ˈælbət-] *pr n* : **the ~** *salle de concert à Londres.*

THE ALBERT HALL

Grande salle londonienne accueillant concerts et manifestations diverses ; elle porte le nom du prince Albert, époux de la reine Victoria. Réputée pour sa grande capacité, elle est souvent évoquée dans des comparaisons métaphoriques : ***enough people to fill the Albert Hall***.

albino [ælˈbɪnəʊ] *n* albinos *mf*.

Albion [ˈælbjən] *pr n* Albion.

album [ˈælbəm] *n* [book, LP] album *m*.

albumen [ˈælbjʊmən] *n* **1.** [egg white] albumen *m*, blanc *m* de l'œuf **2.** = **albumin**.

albumin [ˈælbjʊmɪn] *n* albumine *f*.

alchemist [ˈælkəmɪst] *n* alchimiste *m*.

alchemy [ˈælkəmɪ] *n* alchimie *f*.

Alcibiades [ˌælsɪˈbaɪədiːz] *pr n* Alcibiade.

alcohol [ˈælkəhɒl] *n* alcool *m*.

alcoholic [ˌælkəˈhɒlɪk] <> *adj* [drink] alcoolisé ▪ [person] alcoolique.
<> *n* alcoolique *mf*.

Alcoholics Anonymous *pr n* Alcooliques *mpl* anonymes, ligue *f* antialcoolique.

alcoholism [ˈælkəhɒlɪzm] *n* alcoolisme *m*.

alcopop [ˈælkəʊpɒp] *n* limonade *f* alcoolisée *inf*, alcoopop *m*.

alcove [ˈælkəʊv] *n* [in room] alcôve *f* ▪ [in wall] niche *f* ▪ [in garden] tonnelle *f*.

aldehyde [ˈældɪhaɪd] *n* aldéhyde *m*.

alder [ˈɔːldəʳ] *n* aulne *m*, aune *m*.

alderman [ˈɔːldəmən] (*pl* **aldermen** [-mən]) *n* **1.** ADMIN alderman *m*, conseiller *m* municipal **2.** HIST ≃ échevin *m*.

ale [eɪl] *n* bière *f (anglaise)*, ale *f*.

alehouse [ˈeɪlhaʊs] (*pl* [-haʊzɪz]) *n arch* taverne *f* ▪ *inf* pub *m*.

alert [əˈlɜːt] <> *n* alerte *f* ▪ **to give the ~** donner l'alerte ▪ **to be on the ~** [gen] être sur le qui-vive ; MIL être en état d'alerte.
<> *adj* **1.** [vigilant] vigilant, sur le qui-vive ▪ **you should be ~ to the possible dangers** soyez vigilants quant aux éventuels dangers **2.** [lively - child, mind] vif, éveillé.
<> *vt* alerter, donner l'alerte à ▪ **the public should be ~ed to these dangers** on devrait attirer l'attention du public sur ces dangers, on devrait sensibiliser l'opinion publique à ces dangers.

alertness [əˈlɜːtnɪs] *n* **1.** [vigilance] vigilance *f* **2.** [liveliness] vivacité *f*, esprit *m* éveillé.

A-level (*abbrev of* **advanced level**) *n UK* SCH : **~s, ~ exams** ≃ baccalauréat *m* ▪ **he teaches ~ physics** ≃ il est professeur de physique en terminale ▪ **to take one's ~s** ≃ passer son bac.

A-LEVEL

Examen sanctionnant la fin du cycle secondaire en Grande-Bretagne. Il se prépare en deux ans après le ***GCSE*** et donne accès aux études supérieures. Il est beaucoup plus spécialisé que le baccalauréat français, les élèves ne présentant en moyenne que trois matières. Chaque ***A-level*** est noté séparément et les élèves s'efforcent d'obtenir les meilleurs résultats dans chacune des matières car le système d'accès à l'Université est très sélectif.
En Écosse, l'examen équivalent est le ***Higher*** ou le ***Higher Grade***, qui est moins spécialisé et comprend cinq matières.

Alexander [ˌælɪgˈzɑːndəʳ] *pr n* : **~ the Great** Alexandre le Grand.

Alexandra Palace [ˌælɪg'zɑ:ndrə-] *pr n salle d'exposition et de concert de Londres.*

ALEXANDRA PALACE

Cet édifice victorien, situé à Alexandra Park, au nord de Londres, abritait les studios de télévision de la BBC. C'est aujourd'hui un centre d'expositions et de loisirs.

Alexandria [ˌælɪg'zɑ:ndrɪə] *pr n* Alexandrie.

alexandrine [ˌælɪg'zændraɪn] <> *adj* alexandrin.
<> *n* alexandrin *m*.

alfalfa [æl'fælfə] *n* luzerne *f*.

Alfred ['ælfrɪd] *pr n* Alfred ▪ **~ the Great** Alfred le Grand.

alfresco [æl'freskəʊ] *adj* & *adv* en plein air.

algae ['ældʒi:] *npl* algues *fpl*.

algebra ['ældʒɪbrə] *n* algèbre *f*.

algebraic [ˌældʒɪ'breɪɪk] *adj* algébrique.

Algeria [æl'dʒɪərɪə] *pr n* Algérie *f* ▪ **in ~** en Algérie.

Algerian [æl'dʒɪərɪən] <> *n* Algérien *m*, - enne *f*.
<> *adj* algérien.

Algiers [æl'dʒɪəz] *pr n* Alger.

algorithm ['ælgərɪðm] *n* algorithme *m*.

alias ['eɪlɪəs] <> *adv* alias.
<> *n* [name] nom *m* d'emprunt, faux nom *m* ▪ [of author] nom *m* de plume, pseudonyme *m*.

alibi ['ælɪbaɪ] <> *n* LAW alibi *m* ▪ ***fig*** alibi *m*, excuse *f*.
<> *vt* ***US inf*** [person, action] trouver des excuses à.

Alice ['ælɪs] *pr n* : **'~ in Wonderland'** ***Carroll*** 'Alice au pays des merveilles'.

Alice band *n* bandeau *m (pour les cheveux)*.

alien ['eɪljən] <> *n* **1.** ADMIN [foreigner] étranger *m*, - ère *f* **2.** [in science fiction] extraterrestre *mf*.
<> *adj* **1.** [foreign - customs, environment] étranger **2.** [contrary] : **~ to sthg** contraire OR opposé à qqch ▪ **violence is completely ~ to his nature** la violence n'est absolument pas dans sa nature **3.** [in science fiction] extraterrestre ▪ **~ life forms** d'autres formes de vie.

alienate ['eɪljəneɪt] *vt* [gen - LAW] aliéner ▪ **this tax will ~ the people** avec cet impôt, ils vont s'aliéner la population.

alienated ['eɪljəneɪtɪd] *adj* : **many young people feel ~ and alone** beaucoup de jeunes se sentent seuls et rejetés.

alienation [ˌeɪljə'neɪʃn] *n* **1.** [of support, friends] fait *m* de décourager OR d'éloigner **2.** LAW & PSYCHOL aliénation *f*.

alight [ə'laɪt] <> *vi* [bird] se poser ▪ [person - from bus, train] descendre ; [- from bike, horse] descendre, mettre pied à terre.
<> *adj* [fire] allumé ▪ [house] en feu.
<> *adv* : **to set sthg ~** mettre le feu à qqch.
◆ **alight on** *vt insep* ***fml*** [idea] avoir soudain ▪ [information] apprendre par hasard ▪ [lost object] trouver par hasard.

align [ə'laɪn] <> *vt* **1.** [place in line - points, objects] aligner, mettre en ligne **2.** FIN & POL aligner ▪ **to ~ o.s. with sb** s'aligner sur qqn **3.** TECH dégauchir ▪ AUT régler le parallélisme de.
<> *vi* [points, objects] être aligné ▪ [persons, countries] s'aligner.

alignment [ə'laɪnmənt] *n* **1.** [gen - POL] alignement *m* ▪ **to be in/out of ~** être/ne pas être dans l'alignement, être aligné/désaligné **2.** AUT parallélisme *m*.

alike [ə'laɪk] <> *adj* semblable ▪ **no two are ~** il n'y en a pas deux pareils ▪ **they look ~** ils se ressemblent.
<> *adv* [act, speak, dress] de la même façon OR manière ▪ **this affects Peter and his brother ~** cela touche Peter aussi bien que son frère.

alimentary canal *n* tube *m* digestif.

alimony ['ælɪmənɪ] *n* pension *f* alimentaire.

A-line *adj* [skirt, dress] trapèze *(inv)*.

alive [ə'laɪv] *adj* **1.** [living] vivant, en vie ▪ **while he was ~** de son vivant ▪ **to be burnt ~** être brûlé vif ▪ **to bury sb ~** enterrer qqn vivant ▪ **to keep ~** [person] maintenir en vie ; [hope] garder ; [tradition] préserver ▪ **they kept her memory ~** ils sont restés fidèles à sa mémoire ▪ **he felt that he was the luckiest man ~** il se sentit l'homme le plus heureux du monde ▪ **no man ~ could endure such pain** personne au monde ne pourrait endurer de telles souffrances ▪ **it's good to be ~** il fait bon vivre ◉ **~ and kicking : he's still ~ and kicking** ▪ [not dead] il est toujours bien en vie ; [lively] il est toujours d'attaque OR plein de vie **2.** [lively, full of life] plein de vie, vif, actif ▪ **she always comes ~ in the evening** elle se réveille toujours le soir **3.** [alert, aware] conscient, sensible ▪ **to be ~ to the dangers of sthg** être conscient des OR sensible aux dangers de qqch **4.** [full, crowded] : **the evening air was ~ with insects** il y avait des nuées d'insectes dans l'air ce soir-là ▪ **the streets were ~ with people** les rues fourmillaient OR grouillaient de monde.

alkali ['ælkəlaɪ] *n* alcali *m*.

alkaline ['ælkəlaɪn] *adj* alcalin.

alkie, alky [ælkɪ] (*pl* **alkies**) *n* ***inf*** poivrot *m*, - e *f*.

all [ɔ:l] <> *det* **1.** [the whole of] tout *m*, toute *f*, tous *mpl*, toutes *f* ▪ **~ expenses will be reimbursed** tous les frais seront remboursés ▪ **~ day and ~ night** toute la journée et toute la nuit ▪ **~ six of us want to go** nous voulons y aller tous/toutes les six ▮ [every one of a particular type] : **~ kinds of people** toutes sortes de gens ▪ **for children of ~ ages** pour les enfants de tous les âges
2. [the utmost] : **in ~ fairness (to sb)** pour être juste (avec qqn).
<> *predet* **1.** [the whole of] tout *m*, toute *f*, tous *mpl*, toutes *f* ▪ **~ the butter** tout le beurre ▪ **~ five women** les cinq femmes
2. [with comparative adjectives] : **~ the better!** tant mieux! ▪ **you will feel ~ the better for a rest** un peu de repos vous fera le plus grand bien ▪ **it's ~ the more unfair since** OR **as he promised not to put up the rent** c'est d'autant plus injuste qu'il a promis de ne pas augmenter le loyer.
<> *pron* **1.** [everything] tout ▪ **~ I want is to rest** tout ce que je veux c'est du repos ▪ **will that be ~?** ce sera tout? ▪ **it was ~ I could do not to laugh** j'ai eu du mal à m'empêcher de rire ▪ **it's ~ his fault** c'est sa faute à lui ▪ **you men are ~ the same!** vous les hommes, vous êtes tous pareils OR tous les mêmes! ◉ **~ or nothing** tout ou rien ▪ **~ in good time** chaque chose en son temps ▪ **when ~ is said and done** en fin de compte, au bout du compte
2. [everyone] tous ▪ **don't ~ speak at once!** ne parlez pas tous en même temps!
3. SPORT : **the score is 5 ~** le score est de 5 partout ▪ **30 ~** [in tennis] 30 partout
4. [as quantifier] : **~ of the butter/the cakes** tout le beurre, tous les gâteaux ▪ **~ of London** Londres tout entier ▪ **~ of it was sold** (le) tout a été vendu ▪ **how much wine did they drink? – ~ of it** combien de vin ont-ils bu? – tout ce qu'il y avait ▪ **~ of you can come** vous pouvez tous venir ▪ **listen, ~ of you** écoutez-moi tous ◉ **the book cost me ~ of £10** le livre ne m'a coûté que 10 livres ▪ **it's ~ of five minutes' walk away!** ***hum*** c'est AU MOINS à cinq minutes à pied! ***hum.***
<> *adv* [as intensifier] tout ▪ **she was ~ alone** elle était toute seule ▪ **she was ~ excited** elle était tout excitée ▪ **she was ~ dressed** OR **she was dressed ~ in black** elle était habillée tout en noir ▪ **the soup went ~ down my dress** la soupe s'est répandue partout sur ma robe ▪ **the jacket's split ~ up the sleeve** la veste a craqué tout le long de la manche ▪ **don't get your hands ~ dirty** ***inf*** ne va pas te salir les mains! ◉ **~ in one piece** [furniture] tout d'une pièce ; ***fig*** [person] sain et sauf ▪ **I'm ~ for it** moi, je suis tout à fait pour ▪ **it's ~ up with him** ***inf*** il est fichu.
<> *n* tout ▪ **I would give my ~ to be there** je donnerais tout ce que j'ai pour y être ▪ **the team gave their ~** l'équipe a donné son maximum ▪ **to stake one's ~** tout miser.
◆ **all along** *adv phr* depuis le début.
◆ **all at once** *adv phr* **1.** [suddenly] tout d'un coup
2. [all at the same time] à la fois, en même temps.
◆ **all but** *adv phr* presque ▪ **~ but finished** presque OR pratiquement fini ▪ **I ~ but missed it** j'ai bien failli le rater, c'est tout juste si je ne l'ai pas raté.
◆ **all in** <> *adj phr* ***inf*** [exhausted] : **I'm ~ in** je suis mort.
<> *adv phr* [everything included] tout compris.
◆ **all in all** *adv phr* tout compte fait.

◆ **all over** ◇ *adj phr* [finished] fini ▪ **that's ~ over and done with now** tout ça c'est bien terminé maintenant.
◇ *prep phr* partout ▪ **you've got ink ~ over you!** tu t'es mis de l'encre partout! ▪ **~ over the world** dans le monde entier ▪ **we have agencies ~ over Europe** nous avons des agences dans toute l'Europe *OR* partout en Europe ▪ **it'll be ~ over town tomorrow morning!** demain matin, toute la ville sera au courant! ➊ **~ over the place** [everywhere] partout, dans tous les coins ; [very erratic, inaccurate] pas au point *hum* ▪ **he was ~ over her** il ne l'a pas laissée tranquille un instant.
◇ *adv phr* [everywhere] partout ▪ **painted green ~ over** peint tout en vert ➊ **it was like being a child ~ over again** c'était comme retomber en enfance ▪ **that's him ~ over!** *inf* ça c'est lui tout craché!
◆ **all that** *adv phr* : **it isn't ~ that difficult** *OR* **as difficult as ~ that** ce n'est pas si difficile que ça.
◆ **all the more** ◇ *det phr* : **~ the more reason for doing it again** raison de plus pour recommencer.
◇ *adv phr* encore plus.
◆ **all the same** ◇ *adv phr* [nevertheless] tout de même, quand même.
◇ *adj phr* : **it's ~ the same to me** ça m'est complètement égal, peu m'importe ▪ **if it's ~ the same to you** si cela ne vous gêne pas.
◆ **all told** *adv phr* tout compris.
◆ **all too** *adv phr* : **~ too soon** bien trop vite ▪ **the holidays went ~ too quickly** les vacances ne sont passées que trop vite ▪ **it's ~ too easy to forget that** c'est tellement facile de l'oublier.

all- *in cpds* entièrement ▪ **~male/female** entièrement masculin/féminin.

Allah ['ælə] *pr n* Allah.

all-American *adj* cent pour cent américain ▪ **the ~ boy** le jeune américain type.

all-around *adj US* = **all-round**.

allay [ə'leɪ] *vt* [fear] apaiser ▪ [doubt, suspicion] dissiper ▪ [pain, grief] soulager, apaiser.

All Black *n* : **the ~s** les All Blacks *mpl (l'équipe nationale de rugby de la Nouvelle-Zélande)*.

all clear ◇ *n* (signal *m* de) fin *f* d'alerte ▪ **he received** *OR* **was given the ~ on the project** *fig* on lui a donné le feu vert pour le projet.
◇ *interj* : **~!** fin *f* d'alerte!

all-comers *npl* : **the British ~ 100 m record** le record britannique de l'épreuve du 100 m ouverte à tous.

all-day *adj* qui dure toute la journée ▪ **~ breakfast** petit-déjeuner *m* servi toute la journée.

allegation [,ælɪ'geɪʃn] *n* allégation *f*.

allege [ə'ledʒ] *vt* alléguer, prétendre ▪ **he ~s that he was beaten up** il prétend avoir été roué de coups ▪ **the incident is ~d to have taken place the night before** l'incident aurait eu lieu *OR* on prétend que l'incident a eu lieu la veille au soir.

alleged [ə'ledʒd] *adj* [motive, incident, reason] allégué, prétendu ▪ [thief] présumé.

allegedly [ə'ledʒɪdlɪ] *adv* prétendument, paraît-il ▪ **they ~ broke in and stole £300** ils seraient entrés par effraction et auraient volé 300 livres.

allegiance [ə'li:dʒəns] *n* allégeance *f* ▪ **to swear ~** faire serment d'allégeance ▪ **to switch ~** changer de bord.

allegoric(al) [,ælɪ'gɒrɪk(l)] *adj* allégorique.

allegory ['ælɪgərɪ] (*pl* **allegories**) *n* allégorie *f*.

alleluia [,ælɪ'lu:jə] *interj* : **~!** alléluia!

all-embracing [-ɪm'breɪsɪŋ] *adj* exhaustif, complet.

Allen key, Allen wrench *US n* clé *f* (à vis) à six pans creux.

allergen ['ælədʒen] *n* allergène *m*.

allergic [ə'lɜ:dʒɪk] *adj* [reaction, person] allergique ▪ **I'm ~ to cats** je suis allergique aux chats ▪ **he's ~ to hard work** *hum* il est allergique au travail.

allergist ['ælədʒɪst] *n* allergologiste *mf*, allergologue *mf*.

allergy ['ælədʒɪ] (*pl* **allergies**) *n* allergie *f*.

alleviate [ə'li:vɪeɪt] *vt* [pain, suffering] alléger, apaiser, soulager ▪ [problem, difficulties] limiter, réduire ▪ [effect] alléger, atténuer.

alleviation [ə,li:vɪ'eɪʃn] *n* apaisement *m*, soulagement *m*.

alley ['ælɪ] *n* **1.** [street] ruelle *f*, passage *m* ▪ [in park, garden] allée *f* ▪ **that's right up my ~** c'est tout à fait mon rayon **2.** *US* [on tennis court] couloir *m* **3.** [for tenpin bowling, skittles] bowling *m*, prise *f* de jeu **4.** [marble] (grosse) bille *f*, calot *m*.

alley cat *n* chat *m* de gouttière.

alleyway ['ælɪweɪ] *n* ruelle *f*, passage *m*.

All Fools' Day *n* le premier avril.

all fours ◆ **on all fours** *adv phr* à quatre pattes.

Allhallows [,ɔ:l'hæləʊz] *n* Toussaint *f*.

alliance [ə'laɪəns] *n* alliance *f* ▪ **to enter into** *OR* **to form an ~ with sb** s'allier *OR* faire alliance avec qqn.

allied ['ælaɪd] *adj* **1.** POL [force, nations] allié ▪ **Italy was allied with Germany** l'Italie était alliée avec *OR* à l'Allemagne **2.** [related - subjects] connexe, du même ordre ▪ ECON & FIN [product, industry] assimilé ▪ BIOL de la même famille **3.** [connected] allié ▪ **~ with** *OR* **to** allié à ▪ **his natural talent, ~ with** *OR* **to his good looks, made him a star** son talent naturel allié à un physique agréable ont fait de lui une star.
◆ **Allied** *adj* : **the Allied forces** [in World War II] les forces alliées.

alligator ['ælɪgeɪtəʳ] ◇ *n* alligator *m*.
◇ *comp* [bag, shoes] en (peau d')alligator ▪ [skin] d'alligator.

all-important *adj* de la plus haute importance, d'une importance primordiale *OR* capitale ▪ **she found the ~ solution** elle a trouvé la solution essentielle.

all-in *adj UK* **1.** [price, tariff] net, tout compris, forfaitaire ▪ [insurance policy] tous risques **2.** *inf* [exhausted] crevé.
◆ **all in** *adv* tout compris.

all-inclusive *adj* [price, tariff] net, tout compris, forfaitaire ▪ [insurance policy] tous risques.

all-in-one *adj* tout-en-un *(inv)*.

all-in wrestling *n* lutte *f* libre, catch *m*.

alliteration [ə,lɪtə'reɪʃn] *n* allitération *f*.

alliterative [ə'lɪtərətɪv] *adj* allitératif.

all-night *adj* [party, film] qui dure toute la nuit ▪ [shop, restaurant] de nuit, ouvert la nuit ▪ **an ~ sitting of Parliament** une session parlementaire de nuit.

all-nighter [-'naɪtə] *n* : **the party will be an ~** la fête va durer toute la nuit ▪ **we pulled an ~ for the physics exam** *US* on a passé la nuit à réviser l'examen de physique.

allocate ['æləkeɪt] *vt* **1.** [assign - money, duties] allouer, assigner, attribuer ▪ **funds ~d to research** des crédits affectés à la recherche **2.** [share out] répartir, distribuer **3.** LAW & FIN ventiler.

allocation [,ælə'keɪʃn] *n* **1.** [assignment - of money, duties] allocation *f*, affectation *f* ; [- of role, part] attribution *f* **2.** [sharing out] répartition *f* **3.** [share - of money] part *f* ; [- of space] portion *f* **4.** LAW & FIN ventilation *f*.

allomorph ['æləmɔ:f] *n* allomorphe *m*.

allophone ['æləfəʊn] *n* allophone *m*.

allot [ə'lɒt] (*pret & pp* **allotted**, *cont* **allotting**) *vt* **1.** [assign - money, duties, time] allouer, assigner, attribuer ▪ **in the allotted time** dans le délai imparti **2.** [share out] répartir, distribuer.

allotment [ə'lɒtmənt] *n* **1.** [of money, duties, time] allocation *f*, attribution *f* **2.** *UK* [land] jardin *m* ouvrier *OR* familial.

all out *adv* : **to go ~ to do sthg** se donner à fond pour faire qqch.
◆ **all-out** *adj* [strike, war] total ▪ [effort] maximum.

allover [ˈɔːl,əʊvəʳ] *adj* qui s'étend sur toute la surface ▪ **an ~ tan** un bronzage intégral.

allow [əˈlaʊ] *vt* **1.** [permit] permettre, autoriser ▪ **to ~ sb to do sthg** permettre à qqn de faire qqch, autoriser qqn à faire qqch ▪ **he was ~ed a final cigarette** on lui a permis (de fumer) une dernière cigarette ▪ **we weren't ~ed in** on ne nous a pas permis d'entrer ▪ **the dog is not ~ed in the house** on ne laisse pas le chien entrer dans la maison, l'accès de la maison est interdit au chien ▪ **'smoking is not ~ed'** 'défense de fumer' ▪ **she ~ed herself to be manipulated** elle s'est laissée manipuler ▪ **he decided to ~ events to take their course** il a décidé de laisser les événements suivre leur cours ▪ **I won't ~ such behaviour!** je ne tolérerai pas une telle conduite! ▪ **~ me!** vous permettez?
2. [enable] permettre ▪ **the ramp ~s people in wheelchairs to enter the building** la rampe permet l'accès de l'immeuble aux personnes en fauteuil roulant
3. [grant - money, time] accorder, allouer ; [- opportunity] donner ; [- claim] admettre ▪ **she ~ed herself a cream cake as a special treat** comme petit plaisir, elle s'est offert un gâteau à la crème
4. [take into account] prévoir, compter ▪ **~ a week for delivery** il faut prévoir OR compter une semaine pour la livraison
5. *lit* [admit] admettre, convenir.
◆ **allow for** *vt insep* **1.** [take account of] tenir compte de ▪ **~ing for the bad weather** compte tenu du mauvais temps
2. [make allowance or provision for] : **remember to ~ for the time difference** n'oublie pas de compter le décalage horaire ▪ **we hadn't ~ed for these extra costs** nous n'avions pas prévu ces frais supplémentaires ▪ **after ~ing for travel expenses** déduction faite des frais de voyage.
◆ **allow of** *vt insep fml* admettre, souffrir, autoriser.

allowable [əˈlaʊəbl] *adj* admissible, permis ▪ **expenses ~ against tax** dépenses *fpl* fiscalement déductibles.

allowance [əˈlaʊəns] *n* **1.** ADMIN [grant] allocation *f* ▪ [for housing, travel, food] indemnité *f* ▪ [alimony] pension *f* alimentaire ▪ [for student - from state] bourse *f* ; [- from parents] pension *f* alimentaire ▪ [pension] pension *f* ▪ [income, salary] revenu *m*, appointements *mpl* ▪ **his parents give him a monthly ~ of £100** ses parents lui versent une mensualité de 100 livres ➊ **cost-of-living ~** indemnité de vie chère ▪ **rent ~** allocation (de) logement **2.** [discount] rabais *m*, réduction *f* ▪ **tax ~** [deduction] dégrèvement *m* fiscal ; [tax-free part] revenu *m* non imposable ▪ **trade-in ~** (valeur *f* de) reprise *f* **3.** *US* [pocket money] argent *m* de poche **4.** *phr* **to make ~s for sb** être indulgent avec qqn ▪ **to make ~ OR ~s for sthg** tenir compte de qqch, prendre qqch en considération.

alloy ◇ *n* [ˈælɔɪ] alliage *m*.
◇ *comp* [ˈælɔɪ] : **~ steel** acier *m* allié OR spécial ▪ **~ wheels** AUT roues *fpl* en alliage léger.
◇ *vt* [əˈlɔɪ] [metal] allier, faire un alliage de.

all-party committee *n* commission *f* multipartite *(commission où tous les partis sont représentés)*.

all-powerful *adj* tout-puissant.

all-purpose *adj* [gen] qui répond à tous les besoins, passe-partout *(inv)* ▪ [tool, vehicle] polyvalent ▪ **~ cleaning fluid** détachant *m* tous usages.

all right ◇ *adj* **1.** [adequate] (assez) bien, pas mal ▪ **the film was ~** le film n'était pas mal
2. [in good health] en bonne santé ▪ [safe] sain et sauf ▪ **I hope they'll be ~ on their own** j'espère qu'ils sauront se débrouiller tout seuls ▪ **are you ~?** [not hurt] ça va? ▪ **do you think the car will be ~?** tu crois que ça ira avec la voiture? ➊ **I'm ~ Jack** *inf* moi, ça va bien (et vous, je m'en fiche)
3. [indicating agreement, approval] : **is it ~ if they come too?** ça va s'ils viennent aussi? ▪ **it's ~** [no problem] ça va ; [no matter] ça ne fait rien, peu importe ▪ **I've come to see if everything is ~** je suis venu voir si tout va bien ▪ **is everything ~, Madam?** tout va bien, Madame? ▪ **it's ~ by me** moi, ça me va
4. [pleasant] bien, agréable ▪ [nice-looking] chouette ▪ **she's ~** *inf* elle est pas mal
5. [financially] à l'aise, tranquille ▪ **I'll see that you're ~** je veillerai à ce que vous ne manquiez de rien.
◇ *adv* **1.** [well, adequately] bien ▪ **they're doing ~** [progressing well] ça va (pour eux) ; [succeeding in career, life] ils se débrouillent bien
2. [without doubt] : **it's rabies ~** pour être la rage, c'est la rage ▪ **he was listening ~** ça, pour écouter, il écoutait.
◇ *interj* : **~!** [indicating agreement, understanding] entendu!, d'accord! ; [indicating approval] c'est ça!, ça va! ; [indicating impatience] ça va!, ça suffit! ; [indicating change or continuation of activity] bon!
◆ **all-right** *adj esp US* **he's an all-right guy** c'est un type réglo ▪ **it was an all-right film** le film n'était pas mal.

all-round *adj* **1.** [versatile - athlete, player] complet, - ète *f* ; [- ability] complet, polyvalent **2.** [comprehensive - improvement] général, sur toute la ligne.

all round *adv* : **taken ~** à tout prendre.

all-rounder [-ˈraʊndəʳ] *n UK* **he's a good ~** [gen] il est doué dans tous les domaines, il est bon en tout ; SPORT c'est un sportif complet.

All Saints' Day *n* (le jour de) la Toussaint.

all-seater *adj* : **~ stadium** *stade ayant uniquement des places assises.*

all-singing all-dancing *adj* dernier cri.

All Souls' Day *n* le jour OR la Fête des Morts.

all square *adj* **1.** [financially] : **we're ~ now** nous ne sommes plus en compte maintenant **2.** SPORT [level] à égalité.

all-star *adj* [show, performance] avec beaucoup de vedettes, à vedettes ▪ **with an ~ cast** avec un plateau de vedettes.

all-terrain bike *n* vélo *m* tout terrain.

all-terrain vehicle [ɔːltə,reɪnˈviːɪkl] *n* véhicule *m* tout terrain, 4x4 *m*.

all-time *adj* [record] sans précédent ▪ **sales have reached an ~ high/low** les ventes ont connu le niveau le plus élevé jamais atteint/sont tombées au niveau le plus bas jamais atteint ▪ **this film is one of the ~ greats** ce film est l'un des meilleurs de tous les temps.

all told *adv* en tout.

allude [əˈluːd] *vi* : **to ~ to sb/sthg** faire allusion à qqn/qqch.

allure [əˈljʊəʳ] ◇ *vt* attirer, séduire.
◇ *n* attrait *m*, charme *m*.

alluring [əˈljʊərɪŋ] *adj* séduisant, attrayant.

allusion [əˈluːʒn] *n* allusion *f* ▪ **to make an ~ to sthg** faire allusion à qqch.

allusive [əˈluːsɪv] *adj* allusif, qui contient une allusion OR des allusions.

alluvial [əˈluːvjəl] *adj* [ground] alluvial ▪ **~ deposits** alluvions *fpl*, dépôts *mpl* alluvionnaires.

all-weather *adj* [surface] de toute saison, tous temps ▪ **~ court** [tennis] (terrain *m* en) quick *m*.

ally ◇ *vt* [əˈlaɪ] allier, unir ▪ **to ~ o.s. with sb** s'allier avec qqn.
◇ *n* [ˈælaɪ] (*pl* allies) [gen - POL] allié *m*, - e *f* ▪ **the Allies** HIST les Alliés.

Alma Mater, alma mater [,ælməˈmɑːtəʳ] *n* [school] *école ou université où l'on a fait ses études* ▪ *US* [anthem] *hymne d'une école ou d'une université.*

almanac [ˈɔːlmənæk] *n* almanach *m*, agenda *m*.

almighty [ɔːlˈmaɪtɪ] ◇ *adj* **1.** [omnipotent] tout-puissant, omnipotent **2.** *inf* [as intensifier - row, racket] formidable, sacré.
◇ *adv US inf* extrêmement, énormément.
◆ **Almighty** RELIG ◇ *n* : **the Almighty** le Tout-Puissant.
◇ *adj* : **Almighty God, God Almighty** Dieu Tout-Puissant.

almond ['ɑ:mənd] ◇ *n* **1.** [nut] amande **2.** : **~ (tree)** amandier *m*.
◇ *comp* [icing, essence] d'amandes ▪ [cake] aux amandes.

almond paste *n* pâte *f* d'amande.

almost ['ɔ:lməʊst] *adv* presque ▪ **he is ~ 30** il a presque 30 ans ▪ **I ~ cried** j'ai failli pleurer ▪ **he was ~ crying with frustration** il pleurait presque de rage.

alms [ɑ:mz] *npl* aumône *f* ▪ **to give ~ to sb** faire l'aumône *OR* la charité à qqn.

almshouse ['ɑ:mz,haʊs] (*pl* [-,haʊzɪz]) *n* *UK* *résidence pour personnes âgées ou défavorisées, gérée par l'Église ou par une association caritative.*

aloe ['æləʊ] *n* aloès *m*.

aloft [ə'lɒft] *adv* : **(up) ~** [gen] en haut, en l'air ; AERON en l'air ; NAUT dans la mâture.

alone [ə'ləʊn] ◇ *adj* **1.** [on one's own] seul ▪ **I'm not ~ in thinking that it's unfair** je ne suis pas le seul à penser que c'est injuste
2. [only] seul ▪ **she ~ knows the truth** elle seule connaît la vérité ▪ **time ~ will tell** qui vivra verra
3. [lonely] seul.
◇ *adv* **1.** [on one's own] seul ▪ **she managed to open the box ~** elle a réussi à ouvrir la boîte toute seule ▪ **to stand ~** [person] rester seul ; [house] être situé à l'écart ▪ **she stands ~ as the most successful politician this century** *fig* elle est la seule depuis le début du siècle à avoir aussi bien réussi politiquement *OR* en politique ➜ **to go it ~** faire cavalier seul
2. [undisturbed] : **to leave** *OR* **to let sb ~** laisser qqn tranquille ▪ **leave me ~** [on my own] laissez-moi seul ; [in peace] laissez-moi tranquille, laissez-moi en paix ▪ **leave the bag ~!** laissez le sac tranquille!, ne touchez pas au sac! ▪ **if I were you I would leave well ~** si j'étais vous, je ne m'en mêlerais pas.
◆ **let alone** *conj phr* sans parler de ▪ **she can't even walk, let ~ run** elle ne peut même pas marcher, alors encore moins courir.

along [ə'lɒŋ] ◇ *prep* [the length of] le long de ▪ **the railway runs ~ the coast** la voie ferrée longe la côte ▪ [at or to a certain point in] : **could you move further ~ the row** pourriez-vous vous déplacer vers le bout du rang? ▪ **the toilets are just ~ the corridor** les toilettes sont juste un peu plus loin dans le couloir.
◇ *adv* **1.** [in phrasal verbs] : **I was driving/strolling ~ on a sunny afternoon, when...** je roulais/me baladais par un après-midi ensoleillé, quand... ▪ **just then ~ came a policeman** c'est alors qu'un policier est arrivé **2.** [indicating progress] : **how far ~ is the project?** où en est le projet? ▪ **things are going** *OR* **coming ~ nicely, thank you** les choses ne se présentent pas trop mal, merci **3.** [indicating imminent arrival] : **I'll be ~ in a minute** j'arrive tout de suite ▪ **there'll be another bus ~ shortly** un autre bus va passer bientôt.
◆ **along by** *prep phr* en passant par.
◆ **along with** *prep phr* avec ▪ **my house was flooded ~ with hundreds of others** ma maison a été innondée avec des centaines d'autres.

alongshore [ə,lɒŋ'ʃɔ:ʳ] ◇ *adv* le long de la côte.
◇ *adj* [current, tide] côtier.

alongside [ə,lɒŋ'saɪd] ◇ *prep* **1.** [along] le long de ▪ **to come** *OR* **to draw ~ the quay** accoster le quai ▪ **the railway runs ~ the road** la ligne de chemin de fer longe la route **2.** [beside] à côté de ▪ **the car drew up ~ me** la voiture s'est arrêtée à côté de moi **3.** [together with] avec.
◇ *adv* **1.** NAUT : **to come ~** [two ships] naviguer à couple ; [at quayside] accoster **2.** [gen - at side] : **they're going to build a patio with a flower bed ~** ils vont construire un patio bordé d'un parterre de fleurs.

aloof [ə'lu:f] *adj* distant ▪ **to keep** *OR* **to remain ~** se tenir à distance ▪ **I try to keep ~ from such matters** j'essaie de ne pas me mêler à ces histoires.

aloofness [ə'lu:fnɪs] *n* attitude *f* distante, réserve *f*.

alopecia [,ælə'pi:ʃə] *n (U)* alopécie *f*.

aloud [ə'laʊd] *adv* [read] à haute voix, à voix haute, tout haut ▪ [think] tout haut.

alp [ælp] *n* [mountain] montagne *f* ▪ [pasture] alpage *m*, alpe *f*.

alpaca [æl'pækə] *n* alpaga *m*.

alpha ['ælfə] *n* **1.** [Greek letter] alpha *m* **2.** *UK* SCH ≃ mention *f* bien ▪ **~ plus** ≃ mention *f* très bien.

alphabet ['ælfəbet] *n* alphabet *m*.

alphabetic(al) [,ælfə'betɪk(l)] *adj* alphabétique ▪ **in ~ order** par ordre *OR* dans l'ordre alphabétique.

alphabetically [,ælfə'betɪklɪ] *adv* alphabétiquement, par ordre alphabétique.

alphabetize, ise ['ælfəbə,taɪz] *vt* classer par ordre alphabétique.

alphameric [,ælfə'merik] *adj* = **alphanumeric**.

alphanumeric [,ælfənju:'merɪk] *adj* alphanumérique ▪ **~ key** COMPUT touche *f* alphanumérique.

alpha wave *n* rythme *m* alpha.

alpine ['ælpaɪn] *adj* **1.** GEOG des Alpes **2.** [climate, landscape] alpestre ▪ [club, skiing, troops] alpin ▪ **~ plants** [at low altitude] plantes *fpl* alpestres ; [at high altitude] plantes *fpl* alpines.

Alps [ælps] *pr npl* : **the ~** les Alpes *fpl* ▪ **in the ~** dans les Alpes.

al-Qaeda [,ælkæ'i:də] *pr n* Al-Qaida.

already [ɔ:l'redɪ] *adv* déjà.

alright [,ɔ:l'raɪt] *adj, adv* & *interj* = **all right**.

Alsace [æl'sæs] *pr n* Alsace *f* ▪ **in ~** en Alsace.

Alsatian [æl'seɪʃn] ◇ *n* **1.** [person] Alsacien *m*, - enne *f* **2.** LING alsacien *m* **3.** *UK* [dog] berger *m* allemand.
◇ *adj* [person] d'Alsace, alsacien ▪ [wine] d'Alsace.

also ['ɔ:lsəʊ] *adv* **1.** [as well] aussi, également ▪ **she ~ speaks Italian** elle parle aussi *OR* également l'italien ▪ **he's lazy and ~ stupid** il est paresseux et en plus il est bête **2.** [furthermore] en outre, de plus, également ▪ **~, it must be pointed out that...** en outre *OR* de plus, il faut signaler que..., il faut également signaler que...

also-ran *n* **1.** SPORT [gen] concurrent *m* non classé ▪ [in horse-race] cheval *m* non classé **2.** *fig* [person] perdant *m*, - e *f*.

Alta. *written abbr of* **Alberta**.

altar ['ɔ:ltəʳ] *n* autel *m* ▪ **to lead sb to the ~** *fig* conduire *OR* mener qqn à l'autel ➜ **~ boy** enfant *m* de chœur ▪ **~ cloth** nappe *f* d'autel ▪ **at the ~ rail** devant l'autel.

altarpiece ['ɔ:ltəpi:s] *n* retable *m*.

alter ['ɔ:ltəʳ] ◇ *vt* **1.** [change - appearance, plan] changer, modifier ▪ **this ~s matters considerably** cela change vraiment tout ▪ **to ~ course** NAUT & AERON changer de cap *OR* de route **2.** SEW faire une retouche *OR* des retouches à, retoucher **3.** [falsify - evidence, facts, text] falsifier, fausser.
◇ *vi* changer, se modifier ▪ **to ~ for the better** [situation] s'améliorer ; [person] changer en mieux ▪ **to ~ for the worse** [situation] s'aggraver, empirer ; [person] changer en mal.

alteration [,ɔ:ltə'reɪʃn] *n* **1.** [changing] changement *m*, modification *f* ▪ [touching up] retouche *f* **2.** [change] changement *m*, modification *f* ▪ [reorganization] remaniement *m* ▪ [transformation] transformation *f* ▪ **to make an ~ to sthg** modifier qqch, apporter une modification à qqch **3.** SEW retouche *f* ▪ **to make ~s to a dress** faire des retouches à une robe **4.** [falsification - of figures, document] falsification *f* **5.** CONSTR aménagement *m*, transformation *f* ▪ **to have ~s done** faire faire des aménagements ▪ **they've made major ~s to their house** ils ont fait des transformations importantes dans leur maison.

altercation [,ɔ:ltə'keɪʃn] *n* *fml* altercation *f* ▪ **to have an ~ with sb** se disputer *OR* avoir une altercation avec qqn.

alter ego *n* alter ego *m*.

alternate ◇ *adj* [*UK* ɔ:l'tɜ:nət, *US* 'ɔ:ltərnət] **1.** [by turns] alterné ▪ **we visit her on ~ weekends** nous lui rendons visite un week-end sur deux **2.** [every other] tous les deux ▪ **on ~ days** un jour sur deux, tous les deux jours **3.** *US* [alternative] alternatif.

<> *vi* ['ɔ:ltəneɪt] **1.** [happen by turns] alterner ■ **wet days ~d with fine days** les jours pluvieux alternaient avec les beaux jours, les jours pluvieux et les beaux jours se succédaient **2.** [take turns] se relayer ■ **two actors ~d in the leading role** deux acteurs jouaient le rôle principal en alternance *OR* à tour de rôle **3.** [vary] alterner ■ **an economy that ~s between periods of growth and disastrous slumps** une économie où alternent la prospérité et le marasme le plus profond **4.** ELEC changer périodiquement de sens.
<> *vt* ['ɔ:ltəneɪt] (faire) alterner, employer alternativement *OR* tour à tour ■ AGRIC alterner.
<> *n* [*UK* ɔ:l'tɜ:nət, *US* 'ɔ:ltərnət] *US* remplaçant *m*, - e *f*, suppléant *m*, - e *f*.

alternately [ɔ:l'tɜ:nətlɪ] *adv* alternativement, en alternance, tour à tour.

alternating ['ɔ:ltəneɪtɪŋ] *adj* [gen] alternant, en alternance ■ ELEC & TECH alternatif ■ MATHS alterné.

alternating current *n* courant *m* alternatif.

alternation [,ɔ:ltə'neɪʃn] *n* alternance *f*.

alternative [ɔ:l'tɜ:nətɪv] <> *n* **1.** [choice] solution *f*, choix *m* ■ **he had no ~ but to accept** il n'avait pas d'autre solution que d'accepter ■ **you leave me with no ~** vous ne me laissez pas le choix ■ **what's the ~?** quelle est l'autre solution? ■ **there are several ~s** il y a plusieurs possibilités **2.** PHILOS terme *m* d'une alternative.
<> *adj* **1.** [different, other - solution, government] autre, de rechange ■ **an ~ proposal** une contre-proposition ■ **an ~ route** AUT un itinéraire bis *OR* de délestage **2.** [not traditional - lifestyle] peu conventionnel, hors normes ; [- press, theatre] parallèle ■ **~ energy** énergies *fpl* de substitution ■ **~ fuel** combustible *m* propre *OR* alternatif ■ **~ medicine** médecine *f* douce *OR* parallèle ■ **~ technology** technologies *fpl* douces **3.** PHILOS alternatif.

alternatively [ɔ:l'tɜ:nətɪvlɪ] *adv* comme alternative, sinon ■ **you could travel by train or ~ by bus** vous pourriez voyager en train ou bien en autobus.

alternator ['ɔ:ltəneɪtəʳ] *n* alternateur *m*.

although [ɔ:l'ðəʊ] *conj* **1.** [despite the fact that] bien que, quoique ■ **~ I have never liked him, I do respect him** bien que *OR* quoique je ne l'aie jamais aimé je le respecte, je ne l'ai jamais aimé, néanmoins je le respecte **2.** [but, however] mais ■ **I don't think it will work, ~ it's worth a try** je ne crois pas que ça va marcher, mais ça vaut la peine d'essayer.

altimeter ['æltɪmi:təʳ] *n* altimètre *m*.

altitude ['æltɪtju:d] <> *n* [gen - AERON] altitude *f* ■ [in mountains] altitude *f*, hauteur *f* ■ **at high ~** *OR* **~s** en altitude, en hauteur ■ **at these ~s** à cette altitude, à ces hauteurs.
<> *comp* : **~ sickness** mal *m* d'altitude.

alt key [ælt-] *n* touche *f* alt.

alto ['æltəʊ] (*pl* **altos**) <> *adj* [voice - female] de contralto ; [- male] de haute-contre ■ [instrument] alto *(inv)* ■ **~ clef** clef *f* d'ut.
<> *n* **1.** [voice - female] contralto *m* ; [- male] haute-contre *f* **2.** [instrument] alto *m*.

altogether [,ɔ:ltə'geðəʳ] <> *adv* **1.** [entirely] tout à fait, entièrement ■ **I don't ~ agree with you** je ne suis pas tout à fait *OR* entièrement d'accord avec vous ■ **he isn't ~ reliable** on ne peut pas toujours compter sur lui ■ **it's ~ out of the question** il n'en est absolument pas question ■ **that's a different matter ~** c'est un tout autre problème **2.** [as a whole] en tout ■ **taken ~** à tout prendre **3.** [in general] somme toute, tout compte fait ■ **~, it was an enjoyable evening** somme toute, c'était une soirée agréable.
<> *n phr* : **in the ~** *UK inf hum* tout nu, à poil.

altruism ['æltruɪzm] *n* altruisme *m*.

altruist ['æltruɪst] *n* altruiste *mf*.

altruistic [,æltru'ɪstɪk] *adj* altruiste.

aluminium [,ælju'mɪnɪəm] *UK*, **aluminum** [ə'lu:mɪnəm] *US* <> *n* aluminium *m*.
<> *comp* [utensil] en aluminium.

alumna [ə'lʌmnə] (*pl* **alumnae** [-ni:]) *n US* SCH ancienne élève *f* ■ UNIV ancienne étudiante *f*.

alumnus [ə'lʌmnəs] (*pl* **alumni** [-naɪ]) *n US* SCH ancien élève *m* ■ UNIV ancien étudiant *m*.

alveolar [æl'vɪələʳ] *adj* ANAT & LING alvéolaire ■ **~ ridge** alvéoles *fpl* (dentaires).

always ['ɔ:lweɪz] *adv* toujours ■ **has she ~ worn glasses?** a-t-elle toujours porté des lunettes? ■ **you can ~ try phoning** vous pouvez toujours essayer de téléphoner.

always-on [,ɔ:lweɪz'ɑn] *adj* permanent.

Alzheimer's ['æltshaɪməz] *n* maladie *f* d'Alzheimer.

Alzheimer's disease ['ælts,haɪməz-] *n* maladie *f* d'Alzheimer.

am [æm] *vi & aux vb* ▷ **be**.

a.m. (*abbrev of* **ante meridiem**) *adv* du matin.

AM *n* (*abbrev of* **amplitude modulation**) AM.

AMA (*abbrev of* **American Medical Association**) *pr n ordre américain des médecins*.

amalgam [ə'mælgəm] *n* **1.** [gen - METALL] amalgame *m* **2.** DENT amalgame *m*.

amalgamate [ə'mælgə,meɪt] <> *vt* **1.** [firms, businesses] fusionner, unir **2.** [ideas, metals] amalgamer ■ **their findings were ~d with ours to produce the final report** leurs conclusions et les nôtres ont été réunies pour constituer le rapport final.
<> *vi* **1.** [firms] fusionner **2.** [races] se mélanger ■ [metals] s'amalgamer.

amalgamation [ə,mælgə'meɪʃn] *n* **1.** COMM & ECON fusion *f* **2.** [of races] mélange *m* ■ [of metals] amalgamation *f*.

amanuensis [ə,mænju'ensɪs] (*pl* **amanuenses** [-si:z]) *n fml* [secretary] secrétaire *mf*, sténographe *mf* ■ [transcriber, copyist] copiste *mf*.

amaryllis [,æmə'rɪlɪs] *n* amaryllis *f*.

amass [ə'mæs] *vt* [fortune, objects, information] amasser, accumuler.

amateur ['æmətəʳ] <> *n* [gen - SPORT] amateur *m*, -trice *f*.
<> *adj* **1.** [sport, photographer] amateur ■ [painting, psychology] d'amateur ■ **~ dramatics** théâtre *m* amateur ■ **he has an ~ interest in psychology** il s'intéresse à la psychologie en amateur **2.** *pej* = **amateurish**.

amateurish [,æmə'tɜ:rɪʃ] *adj pej* d'amateur, de dilettante.

amateurism ['æmətərɪzəm] *n* **1.** SPORT amateurisme *m* **2.** *pej* [lack of professionalism] amateurisme *m*, dilettantisme *m*.

amatory ['æmətərɪ] *adj lit* [letter, verse] d'amour, galant *fml* ■ [feelings] amoureux.

amaze [ə'meɪz] *vt* stupéfier, ahurir ■ **you ~ me!** pas possible! ■ **I was ~d at** *OR* **by his courage** son courage m'a ahuri, j'ai été ahuri par son courage.

amazed [ə'meɪzd] *adj* [expression, look] de stupéfaction, ahuri, éberlué ■ [person] stupéfait, ahuri ■ **he was ~ to see her there** il était stupéfait de la trouver là.

amazement [ə'meɪzmənt] *n* stupéfaction *f*, stupeur *f* ■ **to our ~** à notre stupéfaction ■ **I watched in ~** j'ai regardé, complètement stupéfait.

amazing [ə'meɪzɪŋ] *adj* **1.** [astonishing] stupéfiant, ahurissant ■ **it's ~ how fast they work** je ne reviens pas de la vitesse à laquelle ils travaillent ■ **that's ~!** je n'en reviens pas! **2.** [brilliant, very good] extraordinaire, sensationnel.

amazingly [ə'meɪzɪŋlɪ] *adv* incroyablement, extraordinairement ■ **he's ~ patient** il est d'une patience extraordinaire *OR* étonnante ■ **he was ~ good as Cyrano** il était absolument extraordinaire dans le rôle de Cyrano ■ **~ enough, she believed him** aussi étonnant que ça puisse paraître, elle l'a cru.

Amazon ['æməzn] *pr n* **1.** [river] : **the ~** l'Amazone *f* **2.** [region] : **the ~ (Basin)** l'Amazonie *f* ▪ **in the ~** en Amazonie ▪ **the ~ rain forest** la forêt (tropicale) amazonienne **3.** MYTH Amazone *f*.
◆ **amazon** *n* : **she's a bit of an ~** *fig* [strong] c'est une grande bonne femme ; [athletic] c'est une vraie athlète ; [aggressive] c'est une vraie virago.

Amazonian [,æmə'zəʊnjən] *adj* amazonien.

ambassador [æm'bæsədər] *n* POL & *fig* ambassadeur *m* ▪ **the Spanish ~ to Morocco** l'ambassadeur d'Espagne au Maroc ▪ **the ~'s wife** l'ambassadrice *f* ◐ **~-at-large** *US* ambassadeur *m* extraordinaire, chargé *m* de mission.

ambassadress [æm'bæsədrɪs] *n* ambassadrice *f*.

amber ['æmbər] <> *n* [colour, resin] ambre *m*.
<> *adj* **1.** [necklace, ring] d'ambre **2.** [dress, eyes] ambré ▪ **~(-coloured)** ambré ▪ **the (traffic) lights turned ~** *UK* le feu est passé à l'orange.

ambergris ['æmbəgri:s] *n* ambre gris *m*.

ambiance ['æmbɪəns] *n* = **ambience**.

ambidextrous [,æmbɪ'dekstrəs] *adj* ambidextre.

ambience ['æmbɪəns] *n* ambiance *f*.

ambient ['æmbɪənt] *adj* ambiant.

ambiguity [,æmbɪ'gju:ətɪ] (*pl* **ambiguities**) *n* **1.** [uncertainty] ambiguïté *f*, équivoque *f* ▪ [of expression, word] ambiguïté *f* ▪ **to avoid any ~** pour éviter tout malentendu **2.** [phrase] expression *f* ambiguë.

ambiguous [æm'bɪgjʊəs] *adj* ambigu, équivoque.

ambiguously [æm'bɪgjʊəslɪ] *adv* de façon ambiguë.

ambit ['æmbɪt] *n* *fml* [of regulation] étendue *f*, portée *f* ▪ [of study] champ *m* ▪ [of person] compétences *fpl*, capacités *fpl*.

ambition [æm'bɪʃn] *n* ambition *f* ▪ **her ~ was to become a physicist** elle avait l'ambition OR son ambition était de devenir physicienne.

ambitious [æm'bɪʃəs] *adj* ambitieux ▪ **she's very ~ for her children** elle a beaucoup d'ambition pour ses enfants.

ambivalence [æm'bɪvələns] *n* ambivalence *f*.

ambivalent [æm'bɪvələnt] *adj* ambivalent ▪ **to be** OR **to feel ~ about sthg** être OR se sentir indécis à propos de qqch ▪ **I have rather ~ feelings about him** j'éprouve des sentiments partagés à son égard.

amble ['æmbl] <> *vi* [person] marcher OR aller d'un pas tranquille ▪ [horse] aller l'amble ▪ **we ~d home** nous sommes rentrés lentement OR sans nous presser.
<> *n* [of person] pas *m* tranquille ▪ [of horse] amble *m*.

ambrosia [æm'brəʊzjə] *n* ambroisie *f*.

ambulance ['æmbjʊləns] <> *n* ambulance *f*.
<> *comp* : **~ driver** ambulancier *m*, - ère *f* ▪ **~ man** [driver] ambulancier ; [nurse] infirmier *m* d'ambulance ; [stretcher carrier] brancardier *m* ▪ **~ nurse** infirmier *m*, - ère *f* d'ambulance.

ambulance chaser *n* *US inf pej* *avocat qui encourage les victimes d'accident à le consulter.*

ambulatory ['æmbjʊlətrɪ] (*pl* **ambulatories**) <> *adj* ambulatoire ▪ **~ medical care** traitement *m* ambulatoire.
<> *n* ARCHIT déambulatoire *m*.

ambush ['æmbʊʃ] <> *vt* [attack] attirer dans une embuscade ▪ **they were ~ed** ils sont tombés OR ils ont donné dans une embuscade.
<> *n* embuscade *f*, guet-apens *m* ▪ **the battalion was caught in an ~** le bataillon est tombé OR a donné dans un guet-apens.

ameliorate [ə'mi:ljə,reɪt] *fml* <> *vt* améliorer.
<> *vi* s'améliorer.

amelioration [ə,mi:ljə'reɪʃn] *n* *fml* amélioration *f*.

amen [,ɑ:'men] <> *n* amen *m inv*.
<> *interj* RELIG : **~!** amen! ▪ **~ to that!** *inf fig* bien dit!

amenable [ə'mi:nəbl] *adj* **1.** [cooperative] accommodant, souple ▪ **to be ~ to sthg** être disposé à qqch ▪ **the disease is ~ to treatment** la maladie peut être traitée **2.** *fml* [accountable] responsable ▪ **she is ~ for her actions to the committee** elle est responsable de ses actes devant le comité **3.** [able to be tested] vérifiable ▪ **data ~ to analysis** données susceptibles d'être vérifiées par analyse.

amend [ə'mend] *vt* **1.** [rectify - mistake, text] rectifier, corriger ; [- behaviour, habits] réformer, amender *fml* **2.** [law, rule] amender, modifier ▪ [constitution] amender.

amendment [ə'mendmənt] *n* **1.** [correction] rectification *f*, correction *f* ▪ [modification] modification *f*, révision *f* **2.** [to bill, constitution, law] amendement *m* ▪ [to contract] avenant *m* ▪ **an ~ to the law** une révision de la loi.

amends [ə'mendz] *npl* réparation *f*, compensation *f* ▪ **to make ~ for sthg** [compensate] faire amende honorable, se racheter ; [apologize] se faire pardonner ▪ **we'll try and make ~** nous allons essayer de réparer nos torts.

amenity [ə'mi:nətɪ] (*pl* **amenities**) *n* [pleasantness] charme *m*, agrément *m*.
◆ **amenities** *npl* **1.** [features] agréments *mpl* ▪ [facilities] équipements *mpl* ▪ **urban amenities** équipements *mpl* collectifs **2.** [social courtesy] civilités *fpl*, politesses *fpl*.

Amerasian <> *n* Amérasien *m*, - enne *f*.
<> *adj* amérasien.

America [ə'merɪkə] *pr n* Amérique *f* ▪ **in ~** en Amérique.
◆ **Americas** *pr npl* : **the ~s** les Amériques.

American [ə'merɪkn] <> *n* Américain *m*, - e *f*.
<> *adj* américain ▪ **the ~ embassy** l'ambassade *f* des États-Unis ◐ **the ~ Dream** le rêve américain ▪ **~ English** (anglais *m*) américain *m*.

Americana [ə,merɪ'kɑ:nə] *npl* *objets ou documents faisant partie de l'héritage culturel américain.*

American eagle *n* aigle *m* d'Amérique.

American football *n* *UK* football *m* américain.

American Indian *n* Indien *m*, - enne *f* d'Amérique, Amérindien *m*, - enne *f*.

Americanism [ə'merɪkənɪzm] *n* américanisme *m*.

americanization [ə,merɪkənaɪ'zeɪʃn], **Americanization** [ə,merɪkənaɪ'zeɪʃn] *n* américanisation *f*.

americanize, ise [ə'merɪkə,naɪz] *vt* américaniser.

American League *pr n* *l'une des deux ligues professionnelles de base-ball aux États-Unis.*

American plan *n* *US* pension *f* complète.

American Samoa *pr n* Samoa américaines *fpl*.

amethyst ['æmɪθɪst] <> *n* **1.** [stone] améthyste *f* **2.** [colour] violet *m* d'améthyste.
<> *adj* **1.** [necklace, ring] d'améthyste **2.** [colour] violet d'améthyste *(inv)*.

Amex ['æmeks] *pr n* (*abbrev of* **American Stock Exchange**) *deuxième place boursière des États-Unis.*

amiability [,eɪmjə'bɪlətɪ] *n* amabilité *f*.

amiable ['eɪmjəbl] *adj* aimable, gentil.

amiably ['eɪmjəblɪ] *adv* avec amabilité OR gentillesse, aimablement.

amicable ['æmɪkəbl] *adj* [feeling, relationship] amical, d'amitié ▪ [agreement, end] à l'amiable ▪ **to settle a dispute in an ~ way** régler un différend à l'amiable.

amicably ['æmɪkəblɪ] *adv* amicalement ▪ **let's try and settle this ~** essayons de régler ce problème à l'amiable.

amid [ə'mɪd] *prep* au milieu de, parmi ▪ **~ all the noise and confusion, she escaped** dans la confusion générale, elle s'est échappée ▪ **share prices fell ~ rumours of a change of**

government le prix des actions a baissé face aux rumeurs selon lesquelles il allait y avoir un changement de gouvernement.

amidships [ə'mɪdʃɪps] *adj & adv* au milieu OR par le milieu du navire.

amidst [ə'mɪdst] *prep* = **amid**.

amino acid [ə'mi:nəʊ-] *n* acide *m* aminé, aminoacide *m*.

Amish ['ɑ:mɪʃ] <> *adj* amish.
<> *npl* : **the ~** les Amish *mpl (communauté mennonite vivant en Pennsylvanie, austère et fidèle aux traditions)*.

amiss [ə'mɪs] <> *adv* **1.** [incorrectly] de travers, mal ■ **to take sthg ~** mal prendre qqch **2.** [out of place] mal à propos ■ **a little tact and diplomacy wouldn't go ~** un peu de tact et de diplomatie seraient les bienvenus OR ne feraient pas de mal.
<> *adj* **1.** [wrong] : **something seems to be ~ with the engine** on dirait qu'il y a quelque chose qui ne va pas dans le moteur **2.** [out of place] déplacé.

amity ['æmətɪ] (*pl* **amities**) *n fml* [friendship] amitié *f* ■ [good relations] bonnes relations *fpl*, bons rapports *mpl*.

ammeter ['æmɪtə^r] *n* ampèremètre *m*.

ammo ['æməʊ] *n (U) inf* munitions *fpl*.

ammonia [ə'məʊnjə] *n* [gas] ammoniac *m* ■ [liquid] ammoniaque *f*.

ammoniac [ə'məʊnɪæk] <> *adj* ammoniacal.
<> *n* ammoniac *m*, gomme-ammoniaque *f*.

ammunition [,æmjʊ'nɪʃn] *n (U)* munitions *fpl* ■ **the letter could be used as ~ against them** *fig* la lettre pourrait être tournée contre eux.

ammunition belt *n* ceinturon *m*.

ammunition dump *n* dépôt *m* de munitions.

amnesia [æm'ni:zjə] *n* amnésie *f* ■ **to have** OR **to suffer (from) ~** être atteint d'amnésie, être amnésique *fig* **to suffer from selective ~** avoir une mémoire sélective.

amnesic [æm'ni:zɪk] <> *adj* amnésique.
<> *n* amnésique *mf*.

amnesty ['æmnəstɪ] (*pl* **amnesties**) *n* amnistie *f* ■ **under an ~** en vertu d'une amnistie.

amniocentesis [,æmnɪəʊsen'ti:sɪs] (*pl* **amniocenteses** [-si:z]) *n* amniocentèse *f*.

amniotic [,æmnɪ'ɒtɪk] *adj* amniotique ■ **~ fluid** liquide *m* amniotique.

amoeba [ə'mi:bə] (*pl* **amoebae** [-bi:] OR *pl* **amoebas**) *n* amibe *f*.

amoebic [ə'mi:bɪk] *adj* amibien.

amoebic dysentery *n* dysenterie *f* amibienne.

amok [ə'mɒk] *adv* : **to run ~** *liter* être pris d'une crise de folie meurtrière OR furieuse ; *fig* devenir fou furieux, se déchaîner ■ **defence spending has run ~** les dépenses militaires ont dérapé.

among(st) [ə'mʌŋ(st)] *prep* **1.** [in the midst of] au milieu de, parmi ■ **I moved ~ the spectators** je circulais parmi les spectateurs ■ **she was lost ~ the crowd** elle était perdue dans la foule ■ **to be ~ friends** être entre amis **2.** [forming part of] parmi ■ **~ those who left was her brother** parmi ceux qui sont partis, il y avait son frère ■ **several members abstained, myself ~ them** plusieurs membres se sont abstenus, dont moi ■ **it is ~ her most important plays** c'est une de ses pièces les plus importantes ■ **~ other things** entre autres (choses) **3.** [within a specified group] parmi, entre ■ **it's a current expression ~ teenagers** c'est une expression courante chez les jeunes ■ **we discussed it ~ ourselves** nous en avons discuté entre nous ■ **I count her ~ my friends** je la compte parmi OR au nombre de mes amis **4.** [to each of] parmi, entre ■ **share the books ~ you** partagez les livres entre vous, partagez-vous les livres.

amoral [,eɪ'mɒrəl] *adj* amoral.

amorous ['æmərəs] *adj* [person] amoureux, porté à l'amour ■ [glance] amoureux, ardent ■ [letter] d'amour ■ **~ advances** des avances.

amorously ['æmərəslɪ] *adv* amoureusement.

amorphous [ə'mɔ:fəs] *adj* CHEM amorphe ■ [shapeless] amorphe ■ *fig* [personality] amorphe, mou *(before vowel or silent 'h'* **mol***)*, molle *f* ■ [ideas] informe, sans forme ■ [plans] vague.

amortization [ə,mɔ:tɪ'zeɪʃn] *n* amortissement *m*.

amortize, ise [ə'mɔ:taɪz] *vt* amortir.

amount [ə'maʊnt] *n* **1.** [quantity] quantité *f* ■ **great** OR **large ~s of money** beaucoup d'argent ■ **in small/large ~ s** en petites/grandes quantités ■ **no ~ of talking can bring him back** on peut lui parler tant qu'on veut, ça ne le fera pas revenir ■ **I have a certain ~ of respect for them** j'ai un certain respect pour eux ■ **any ~ of** des quantités de, énormément de ■ **you'll have any ~ of time for reading on holiday** tu auras tout ton temps pour lire pendant les vacances **2.** [sum, total] montant *m*, total *m* ■ [of money] somme *f* ■ **do you have the exact ~?** avez-vous le compte (exact)? ■ **you're in credit to the ~ of £100** vous avez un crédit de 100 livres ■ **please find enclosed a cheque to the ~ of $100** veuillez trouver ci-joint un chèque (d'un montant) de 100 dollars.

◆ **amount to** *vt insep* **1.** [total] se monter à, s'élever à ■ **after tax it doesn't ~ to much** après impôts ça ne représente pas grand-chose ■ **he'll never ~ to much** il ne fera jamais grand-chose **2.** [be equivalent to] : **it ~s to something not far short of stealing** c'est pratiquement du vol ■ **it ~s to the same thing** cela revient au même ■ **what his speech ~s to is an attack on democracy** en fait, avec ce discours, il attaque la démocratie.

amp [æmp] *n* **1.** = **ampere** **2.** *inf* [amplifier] ampli *m*.

amperage ['æmpərɪdʒ] *n* intensité *f* de courant.

ampere ['æmpeə^r] *n* ampère *m*.

ampersand ['æmpəsænd] *n* esperluette *f*.

amphetamine [æm'fetəmi:n] *n* amphétamine *f*.

amphibian [æm'fɪbɪən] <> *n* **1.** ZOOL amphibie *m* **2.** [plane] avion *m* amphibie ■ [car] voiture *f* amphibie ■ [tank] char *m* amphibie.
<> *adj* amphibie.

amphibious [æm'fɪbɪəs] *adj* amphibie.

amphitheatre *UK*, **amphitheater** *US* ['æmfɪ,θɪətə^r] *n* amphithéâtre *m*.

ample ['æmpl] *adj* **1.** [large - clothing] ample ; [- garden, lawn] grand, vaste ; [- helping, stomach] grand **2.** [more than enough - supplies] bien OR largement assez de ; [- proof, reason] solide ; [- fortune, means] gros, grosse *f* ■ **he was given ~ opportunity to refuse** il a eu largement l'occasion OR il a eu de nombreuses occasions de refuser ■ **we have ~ reason to suspect foul play** nous avons de solides OR de bonnes raisons de soupçonner quelque chose de louche.

amplification [,æmplɪfɪ'keɪʃn] *n* **1.** [of power, sound] amplification *f* **2.** [further explanation] explication *f*, développement *m*.

amplifier ['æmplɪfaɪə^r] *n* amplificateur *m*.

amplify ['æmplɪfaɪ] *vt* **1.** [power, sound] amplifier **2.** [facts, idea, speech] développer.

amplitude ['æmplɪtju:d] *n* [breadth, scope] ampleur *f*, envergure *f* ■ ASTRON & PHYS amplitude *f*.

amplitude modulation *n* modulation *f* d'amplitude.

amply ['æmplɪ] *adv* amplement, largement ■ [person] : **~ built** bien bâti.

ampoule *UK*, **ampule** *US* ['æmpu:l] *n* ampoule *f (de médicament)*.

amputate ['æmpjʊteɪt] *vt* amputer ■ **they had to ~ her arm** ils ont dû l'amputer du bras.

amputation [,æmpjʊ'teɪʃn] *n* amputation *f*.

amputee [,æmpjʊ'ti:] *n* amputé *m*, - e *f*.

Amsterdam [,æmstə'dæm] *pr n* Amsterdam.

amt *written abbr of* **amount**.

Amtrak® ['æmtræk] *pr n société nationale de chemins de fer aux États-Unis.*

amuck [ə'mʌk] *adv* = **amok**.

amulet ['æmjʊlɪt] *n* amulette *f*, fétiche *m*.

amuse [ə'mju:z] *vt* **1.** [occupy] divertir, amuser, distraire ■ **he ~d himself (by) building sandcastles** il s'est amusé à faire des châteaux de sable ■ **you'll have to ~ yourself this afternoon** il va falloir trouver de quoi t'occuper cet après-midi **2.** [make laugh] amuser, faire rire.

amused [ə'mju:zd] *adj* **1.** [occupied] occupé, diverti ■ **to keep o.s. ~** s'occuper, se distraire ■ **the game kept them ~ for hours** le jeu les a occupés pendant des heures **2.** [delighted, entertained] amusé ■ **they were greatly ~ at** *OR* **by the cat's behaviour** le comportement du chat les a bien fait rire ■ **I was greatly ~ to hear about his adventures** cela m'a beaucoup amusé d'entendre parler de ses aventures ■ **she was not (at all) ~** elle n'a pas trouvé ça drôle (du tout) ➔ **we are not ~** très drôle! *iron (expression faisant allusion à une réflexion qu'aurait faite la reine Victoria pour exprimer sa désapprobation).*

amusement [ə'mju:zmənt] *n* **1.** [enjoyment] amusement *m*, divertissement *m* ■ **she smiled in ~** elle a eu un sourire amusé ■ **I listened in ~** amusé, j'ai écouté ■ **much to everyone's ~** au grand amusement de tous ■ **there was much ~ at her untimely entrance** son entrée intempestive a fait rire tout le monde **2.** [pastime] distraction *f*, amusement *m* ■ **what ~s do you have for the children?** qu'est-ce que vous avez pour distraire les enfants? **3.** [at a funfair] attraction *f*.

amusement arcade *n* arcade *f*.

amusement park *n* parc *m* d'attractions.

amusing [ə'mju:zɪŋ] *adj* amusant, drôle.

Amway® ['æmwei] *pr n marque américaine de produits d'entretien vendus à domicile par des particuliers rassemblant leurs amis et connaissances.*

an [*(stressed)*æn *(unstressed)*ən] ◇ *det* ▻ **a**.
◇ *conj* *arch* si.

Anabaptist [,ænə'bæptɪst] ◇ *adj* anabaptiste.
◇ *n* anabaptiste *mf*.

anabolic [,ænə'bɒlɪk] *adj* anabolisant.

anabolic steroid *n* stéroïde *m* anabolisant.

anachronism [ə'nækrənɪzm] *n* anachronisme *m*.

anachronistic [ə,nækrə'nɪstɪk] *adj* anachronique.

anaconda [,ænə'kɒndə] *n* anaconda *m*.

anaemia *UK*, **anemia** *US* [ə'ni:mjə] *n* MED & *fig* anémie *f* ■ **to suffer from ~** être anémique.

anaemic *UK*, **anemic** *US* [ə'ni:mɪk] *adj* **1.** MED & *fig* anémique ■ **to become ~** s'anémier **2.** [pale] anémique, blême.

anaerobic [,ænə'rəʊbɪk] *adj* anaérobie ■ **~ exercise** exercice *m* d'anaérobie.

anaesthesia *etc UK*, **anesthesia** *US* [,ænɪs'θi:zjə] *n* anesthésie *f*.

anaesthetic *UK*, **anesthetic** *US* [,ænɪs'θetɪk] ◇ *n* anesthésique *m*, anesthésiant *m* ■ **under ~** sous anesthésie ■ **to give sb an ~** anesthésier qqn.
◇ *adj* anesthésique, anesthésiant.

anaesthetist *UK*, **anesthetist** *US* [æ'ni:sθətɪst] *n* anesthésiste *mf*.

anaesthetize, ise *UK*, **anesthetize** *US* [æ'ni:sθətaɪz] *vt* MED anesthésier ■ *fig* anesthésier, insensibiliser.

anagram ['ænəgræm] *n* anagramme *f*.

anal ['eɪnl] *adj* **1.** ANAT anal ■ **~ intercourse** sodomie *f* **2.** PSYCHOL anal ■ **he's so ~** *inf* il est vraiment coincé.

analgesia [,ænæl'dʒi:zjə] *n* analgésie *f*.

analgesic [,ænæl'dʒi:sɪk] ◇ *adj* analgésique.
◇ *n* analgésique *m*.

analog *n* & *comp US* = **analogue**.

analogous [ə'næləgəs] *adj* analogue ■ **to be ~ to** *OR* **with sthg** être analogue à qqch.

analogue *UK*, **analog** *US* ['ænəlɒg] ◇ *n* analogue *m*.
◇ *comp* [clock, watch, computer] analogique.

analogy [ə'nælədʒɪ] (*pl* **analogies**) *n* analogie *f* ■ **the author draws an ~ between a fear of falling and the fear of death** l'auteur établit une analogie entre la peur de tomber et la peur de mourir ■ **by ~ with sthg** par analogie avec qqch ■ **reasoning from ~** raisonnement par analogie.

analysable *UK*, **analyzable** *US* ['ænəlaɪzəbl] *adj* analysable.

analysand [ə'nælɪsænd] *n* patient *m* en analyse.

analyse *UK*, **analyze** *US* ['ænəlaɪz] *vt* **1.** [examine] analyser, faire l'analyse de ■ [sentence] analyser, faire l'analyse logique de **2.** PSYCHOL psychanalyser.

analysis [ə'næləsɪs] (*pl* **analyses** [-si:z]) *n* **1.** [examination] analyse *f* ■ [of sentence] analyse *f* logique ■ **in the final** *OR* **last** *OR* **ultimate ~** en dernière analyse, en fin de compte **2.** PSYCHOL psychanalyse *f*, analyse *f* ■ **to be in ~** être en analyse, suivre une analyse.

analyst ['ænəlɪst] *n* **1.** [specialist] analyste *mf* **2.** PSYCHOL analyste *mf*, psychanalyste *mf*.

analytic(al) [,ænə'lɪtɪk(l)] *adj* analytique.

analytical geometry *n* géométrie *f* analytique.

analytical psychology *n* psychologie *f* analytique.

analyze *etc vt US* = **analyse**.

anamorphosis [,ænə'mɔ:fəsɪs] *n* anamorphose *f*.

anaphora [ə'næfərə] *n* LING anaphorique *m* ■ [in rhetoric] anaphore *f*.

anaphoric [,ænə'fɒrɪk] *adj* anaphorique.

anarchic [æ'nɑ:kɪk] *adj* anarchique.

anarchism ['ænəkɪzm] *n* anarchisme *m*.

anarchist ['ænəkɪst] *n* anarchiste *mf*.

anarchistic [,ænə'kɪstɪk] *adj* anarchiste.

anarchy ['ænəkɪ] *n* anarchie *f*.

anathema [ə'næθəmə] *n* **1.** *fml* [detested thing] abomination *f* ■ **such ideas are ~ to the general public** le grand public a horreur de ces idées **2.** RELIG & *fig* anathème *m*.

anathematize, ise [ə'næθəmətaɪz] *vt* RELIG anathématiser, frapper d'anathème ■ *fig* jeter l'anathème sur.

Anatolia [,ænə'təʊljə] *pr n* Anatolie *f*.

Anatolian [,ænə'təʊljən] ◇ *n* Anatolien *m*, - enne *f*.
◇ *adj* anatolien.

anatomical [,ænə'tɒmɪkl] *adj* anatomique.

anatomically [,ænə'tɒmɪklɪ] *adv* anatomiquement ■ **~ correct** [doll, model] réaliste du point de vue anatomique.

anatomize, ise [ə'nætəmaɪz] *vt* MED & *fig* disséquer.

anatomy [ə'nætəmɪ] *n* **1.** BIOL [of animal, person] anatomie *f* ■ *fig* [of situation, society] structure *f* **2.** *fig* [analysis] analyse *f* **3.** *hum* [body] corps *m*, anatomie *f* *hum*.

ANC (*abbrev of* **African National Congress**) *pr n* ANC *m*.

ancestor ['ænsestəʳ] *n* [forefather] ancêtre *m*, aïeul *m* ■ *fig* [of computer, system] ancêtre *m*.

ancestral [æn'sestrəl] *adj* ancestral ■ **~ home** demeure *f* ancestrale.

ancestress ['ænsestrɪs] *n* aïeule *f*.

ancestry ['ænsestrɪ] (*pl* **ancestries**) *n* **1.** [lineage] ascendance *f* **2.** [ancestors] ancêtres *mpl*, aïeux *mpl*.

anchor ['æŋkəʳ] <> *n* **1.** [for boat] ancre *f* ▪ **to cast** *OR* **to come to** *OR* **to drop ~** jeter l'ancre, mouiller ▪ **up** *OR* **weigh ~!** levez l'ancre! **2.** [fastener] attache *f* **3.** *fig* [mainstay] soutien *m*, point *m* d'ancrage **4.** TV présentateur *m*, - trice *f* **5.** SPORT pilier *m*, pivot *m*.
<> *vi* **1.** [boat] jeter l'ancre, mouiller **2.** [fasten] s'ancrer, se fixer **3.** [settle] se fixer, s'installer ▪ **they remain firmly ~ed in tradition** ils restent fermement ancrés dans la tradition.
<> *vt* **1.** [boat] ancrer **2.** [fasten] ancrer, fixer **3.** TV [programme] présenter.

anchorage ['æŋkərɪdʒ] *n* **1.** NAUT [place] mouillage *m*, ancrage *m* ▪ [fee] droits *mpl* de mouillage *OR* d'ancrage **2.** [fastening] ancrage *m*, attache *f* **3.** *fig* [mainstay] soutien *m*, point *m* d'ancrage.

anchorite ['æŋkəraɪt] *n* ermite *m*, solitaire *m* ▪ RELIG anachorète *m*.

anchorman ['æŋkəmæn] (*pl* **anchormen** [-men]) *n* **1.** TV présentateur *m* **2.** SPORT pilier *m*, pivot *m*.

anchorwoman ['æŋkə,wʊmən] (*pl* **anchorwomen** [-,wɪmɪn]) *n* TV présentatrice *f*.

anchovy [*UK* 'æntʃəvɪ, *US* 'æntʃəʊvɪ] (*pl inv OR pl* **anchovies**) *n* anchois *m* ▪ **~ paste** beurre *m* d'anchois.

ancient ['eɪnʃənt] <> *adj* **1.** [custom, ruins] ancien ▪ [civilization, world] antique ▪ [relic] historique ▪ **~ Greece** la Grèce antique ◐ **~ history** *liter & fig* histoire *f* ancienne ▪ **~ monument** monument *m* historique *OR* classé ▪ **~ times** les temps *mpl* anciens, l'antiquité *f* ▪ **'The Rime of the Ancient Mariner'** ***Coleridge*** 'la Chanson du vieux marin' **2.** *hum* [very old - person] très vieux ; [- thing] antique, antédiluvien ▪ **she drives an ~ Volkswagen** elle conduit une Volkswagen qui a fait la guerre.
<> *n* HIST : **the ~s** les anciens *mpl*.

ancillary [æn'sɪlərɪ] <> *adj* **1.** [supplementary] auxiliaire ▪ **local services are ~ to the national programme** les services locaux apportent leur aide *OR* contribution au programme national ▪ **~ staff** [gen] personnel *m* auxiliaire ; [in hospital] personnel *m* des services auxiliaires, agents *mpl* des hôpitaux ; [in school] personnel *m* auxiliaire, auxiliaires *mf pl* **2.** [subsidiary - reason] subsidiaire ; [- advantage, cost] accessoire.
<> *n* (*pl* **ancillaries**) **1.** [helper] auxiliaire *mf* ▪ **hospital ancillaries** personnel *m* des services auxiliaires, agents *mpl* des hôpitaux **2.** [of firm] filiale *f*.

and [(*strong form* [ænd], *weak form* [ənd], [ən])] <> *conj* **1.** [in addition to] et ▪ **get your hat ~ coat** va chercher ton manteau et ton chapeau ▪ **he went out without his shoes ~ socks on** il est sorti sans mettre ses chaussures ni ses chaussettes ▪ **he goes fishing winter ~ summer (alike)** il va à la pêche en hiver comme en été ▪ **you can't work for us AND work for our competitors** vous ne pouvez pas travailler ET pour nous ET pour nos concurrents ▪ **I'm Richard Rogers – ~?** je suis Richard Rogers – (et) alors? ◐ **there are books ~ books** il y a livres et livres
2. [then] : **he opened the door ~ went out** il a ouvert la porte et est sorti ▪ **I fell ~ cut my knee** je me suis ouvert le genou en tombant
3. [with infinitive] : **go ~ look for it** va le chercher ▪ **try ~ understand** essayez de comprendre
4. [but] mais ▪ **I want to go ~ he doesn't** je veux y aller, mais lui ne veut pas
5. [in numbers] : **one hundred ~ three** cent trois ▪ **three ~ a half years** trois ans et demi ▪ **four ~ two thirds** quatre deux tiers
6. [indicating continuity, repetition] : **he cried ~ cried** il n'arrêtait pas de pleurer ▪ **for hours ~ hours** pendant des heures (et des heures) ▪ **he goes on ~ on about politics** quand il commence à parler politique il n'y a plus moyen de l'arrêter ▮ [with comparative adjectives] : **louder ~ louder** de plus en plus fort
7. [as intensifier] : **her room was nice ~ sunny** sa chambre était bien ensoleillée ▪ **he's good ~ mad** *inf* il est fou furieux
8. [with implied conditional] : **one move ~ you're dead** un geste et vous êtes mort
9. [introducing questions] et ▪ **I went to New York – ~ how did you like it?** je suis allé à New York – et alors, ça vous a plu?
10. [introducing statement] : **~ now it's time for "Kaleidoscope"** et maintenant, voici l'heure de "Kaléidoscope" ▪ **~ another thing...!** ah! autre chose *OR* j'oubliais ▮ [what's more] : **~ that's not all...** et ce n'est pas tout...
<> *n* : **I want no ifs, ~s or buts** je ne veux pas de discussion.
◆ **and all** *adv phr* **1.** [and everything] et tout (ce qui s'ensuit) ▪ **the whole lot went flying, plates, cups, teapot ~ all** tout a volé, les assiettes, les tasses, la théière et tout
2. △ *UK* [as well] aussi ▪ **you can wipe that grin off your face ~ all** tu peux aussi arrêter de sourire comme ça.
◆ **and so on (and so forth)** *adv phr* et ainsi de suite.

Andalusia [,ændə'lu:zjə] *pr n* Andalousie *f*.

Andalusian [,ændə'lu:zjən] <> *n* Andalou *m*, - se *f*.
<> *adj* andalou.

Andean [æn'di:ən] *adj* des Andes, andin.

Andes ['ændi:z] *pr npl* : **the ~** les Andes *fpl* ▪ **in the ~** dans les Andes.

andiron ['ændaɪən] *n* chenet *m*.

Andorra [æn'dɔ:rə] *pr n* Andorre *f*.

Andorran [æn'dɔ:rən] <> *n* Andorran *m*, - ane *f*.
<> *adj* andorran.

Andrew ['ændru:] *pr n* : **Saint ~** saint André.

androcentric [,ændrəʊ'sentrɪk] *adj* androcentrique.

Androcles ['ændrə,kli:z] *pr n* Androclès.

androgynous [æn'drɒdʒɪnəs] *adj* BIOL & BOT androgyne.

android ['ændrɔɪd] <> *adj* androïde.
<> *n* androïde *m*.

Andromache [æn'drɒməkɪ] *pr n* Andromaque.

Andromeda [æn'drɒmɪdə] *pr n* Andromède.

Andy Capp [,ændɪ'kæp] *pr n personnage de bande dessinée incarnant, sous une forme caricaturale, un ouvrier machiste, paresseux et irrévérencieux.*

anecdotal [,ænek'dəʊtl] *adj* anecdotique ▪ **~ evidence** preuve *f OR* témoignage *m* anecdotique.

anecdote ['ænɪkdəʊt] *n* anecdote *f*.

anemia *n US* = **anaemia**.

anemometer [,ænɪ'mɒmɪtəʳ] *n* anémomètre *m*.

anemone [ə'nemənɪ] *n* anémone *f*.

aneroid ['ænərɔɪd] *adj* anéroïde.

anesthesia *n US* = **anaesthesia**.

anesthesiologist [ænɪs,θi:zɪ'ɒlədʒɪst] *n US* anesthésiste *mf*.

aneurism ['ænjʊərɪzm] *n* anévrisme *m*, anévrysme *m*.

anew [ə'nju:] *adv lit* **1.** [again] de nouveau, encore ▪ **the fighting began ~** le combat reprit **2.** [in a new way] à nouveau ▪ **to start life ~** repartir à zéro.

angel ['eɪndʒəl] *n* **1.** RELIG ange *m* ▪ **an ~ of mercy** un ange de miséricorde ◐ **the Angel of Darkness** l'ange des ténèbres ▪ **to be on the side of the ~s** être du bon côté ▪ **to go where ~s fear to tread** s'aventurer en terrain dangereux **2.** [person] ange *m*, amour *m* ▪ **be an ~ and fetch me a glass of water** sois gentil, va me chercher un verre d'eau **3.** *inf* THEAT [investor] commanditaire *mf*.

angel cake *n* ≃ gâteau *m* de Savoie.

Angeleno [,ændʒə'li:nəʊ] *n habitant de Los Angeles.*

angelfish ['eɪndʒəlfɪʃ] (*pl inv OR pl* **angelfishes**) *n* [fish] scalaire *m* ▪ [shark] ange *m*.

angelic [æn'dʒelɪk] *adj* angélique ▪ **she looks absolutely ~** elle a vraiment l'air d'un ange *OR* angélique.

angelica [æn'dʒelɪkə] *n* angélique *f*.

angelus ['ændʒələs] *n* [bell, prayer] angélus *m*.

anger ['æŋgəʳ] <> *n* colère *f*, fureur *f* ■ **she felt intense ~** elle était très en colère ■ **in a fit** *OR* **a moment of ~** dans un accès *OR* un mouvement de colère ■ **he later regretted words spoken in ~** il regretta ensuite les mots prononcés sous l'empire de la colère ■ **to move sb to ~** mettre qqn en colère.
<> *vt* mettre en colère, énerver.

anger management *n thérapie pour aider les gens coléreux à mieux se maîtriser.*

angina [æn'dʒaɪnə] *n (U)* angine *f*.

angina pectoris [-'pektərɪs] *n* angine *f* de poitrine.

angle ['æŋgl] <> *n* **1.** [gen - GEOM] angle *m* ■ **the roads intersect at an ~ of 90°** les routes se croisent à angle droit ■ **the car hit us at an ~** la voiture nous a heurtés de biais ■ **she wore her hat at an ~** elle portait son chapeau penché ■ **cut at an ~** coupé en biseau **2.** [corner] angle *m*, coin *m* **3.** *fig* [point of view] angle *m*, aspect *m* ■ **seen from this ~** vu sous cet angle ■ **from an economic ~** d'un point de vue économique ■ **what's your ~ on the situation?** comment voyez-vous la situation? ■ **we need a new ~** il nous faut un éclairage *OR* un point de vue nouveau **4.** *inf* [motive] raison *f*, motif *m* ■ **what's his ~ in all this?** qu'est-ce qu'il espère y gagner?
<> *vt* **1.** [move] orienter ■ **I ~d the light towards the workbench** j'ai orienté *OR* dirigé la lumière sur l'établi **2.** *fig* [slant] présenter sous un certain angle.
<> *vi* **1.** [slant] s'orienter **2.** FISHING pêcher à la ligne ■ **to go angling** aller à la pêche (à la ligne) ‖ *fig* **to ~ for sthg** chercher (à avoir) qqch.

angle bracket *n* crochet *m*.

Anglepoise® ['æŋglpɔɪz] *n* lampe *f* architecte.

angler ['æŋgləʳ] *n* **1.** FISHING pêcheur *m*, - euse *f* (à la ligne) **2.** [fish] lotte *f* de mer, baudroie *f*.

Anglican ['æŋglɪkən] <> *adj* anglican ■ **the ~ Communion** la communauté anglicane.
<> *n* anglican *m*, - e *f*.

Anglicanism ['æŋglɪkənɪzm] *n* anglicanisme *m*.

anglicism ['æŋglɪsɪzm] *n* anglicisme *m*.

anglicize, ise ['æŋglɪsaɪz] *vt* angliciser.

angling ['æŋglɪŋ] *n* pêche *f* à la ligne.

Anglo ['æŋgləʊ] (*pl* **Anglos**) *n* **1.** *US* Américain blanc *m*, Américaine blanche *f* **2.** *Canada* Canadien *m*, - enne *f* anglophone.

Anglo- *in cpds* anglo-.

Anglo-American <> *adj* anglo-américain.
<> *n* Anglo-Américain *m*, - e *f*.

Anglo-Catholic *n anglican acceptant les préceptes de l'Église catholique sans pour autant se convertir.*

Anglo-French *adj* anglo-français, franco-anglais, franco-britannique.

Anglo-Indian <> *adj* anglo-indien.
<> *n* **1.** [person of mixed British and Indian descent] métis *m*, - isse *f* d'origine anglaise et indienne **2.** [English person living in India] Anglais *m*, - e *f* des Indes.

Anglo-Irish <> *adj* anglo-irlandais.
<> *n* LING anglais *m* parlé en Irlande.
<> *npl* : **the ~** les Anglo-Irlandais *mpl*.

anglophile ['æŋgləʊfaɪl] *adj* anglophile.
◆ **Anglophile** *n* anglophile *mf*.

anglophobe ['æŋgləʊfəʊb] *adj* anglophobe.
◆ **Anglophobe** *n* anglophobe *mf*.

Anglo-Saxon <> *n* **1.** [person] Anglo-Saxon *m*, - onne *f* **2.** LING anglo-saxon *m*.
<> *adj* anglo-saxon.

Angola [æŋ'gəʊlə] *pr n* Angola *m* ■ **in ~** en Angola.

Angolan [æŋ'gəʊlən] <> *n* Angolais *m*, - e *f*.
<> *adj* angolais.

angora [æŋ'gɔːrə] <> *n* **1.** [animal] angora *m* ■ **~ (cat/goat/rabbit)** (chat *m* /chèvre *f* /lapin *m*) angora *m* **2.** [cloth, yarn] laine *f* angora, angora *m*.
<> *adj* **1.** [cat, rabbit] angora *(inv)* **2.** [coat, sweater] en angora.

Angostura bitters® [,æŋgə'stjʊərə-] *npl* bitter *m* à base d'angustura.

angrily ['æŋgrəlɪ] *adv* [deny, speak] avec colère *OR* emportement ■ [leave, stand up] en colère.

angry ['æŋgrɪ] (*comp* **angrier**, *superl* **angriest**) *adj* **1.** [person - cross] en colère, fâché ; [- furious] furieux ■ **to be ~ at** *OR* **with sb** être fâché *OR* en colère contre qqn ■ **she's ~ about** *OR* **at not having been invited** elle est en colère parce qu'elle n'a pas été invitée, elle est furieuse de ne pas avoir été invitée ■ **they're ~ at the price increase** ils sont très mécontents de l'augmentation des prix ■ **I'm ~ with myself for having forgotten** je m'en veux d'avoir oublié ■ **to get ~** se mettre en colère, se fâcher ■ **her remarks made me ~** ses observations m'ont mis en colère ▶ **~ young man** jeune rebelle *m* **2.** [look, tone] irrité, furieux ■ [outburst, words] violent ■ **he wrote her an ~ letter** il lui a écrit une lettre dans laquelle il exprimait sa colère **3.** *fig* [sky] menaçant ■ [sea] mauvais, démonté **4.** [inflamed] enflammé, irrité ■ [painful] douloureux.

angst [æŋst] *n* angoisse *f*.

anguish ['æŋgwɪʃ] <> *n* [mental] angoisse *f* ■ [physical] supplice *m* ■ **to be in ~** [worried] être angoissé *OR* dans l'angoisse ; [in pain] souffrir le martyre, être au supplice.
<> *vt* angoisser, inquiéter énormément.

anguished ['æŋgwɪʃt] *adj* angoissé.

angular ['æŋgjʊləʳ] *adj* **1.** [features, room] anguleux ■ [face] anguleux, osseux ■ [body] anguleux, décharné **2.** [movement] saccadé, haché **3.** TECH [distance, speed] angulaire.

anhydrous [æn'haɪdrəs] *adj* anhydre.

aniline ['ænɪliːn] *n* aniline *f* ■ **~ dye** colorant *m* à base d'aniline.

animal ['ænɪml] <> *n* **1.** ZOOL animal *m* ■ [excluding humans] animal *m*, bête *f* ■ **man is a social ~** l'homme est un animal sociable ■ **she's not a political ~** elle n'a pas la politique dans le sang **2.** *pej* [brute] brute *f* **3.** [thing] chose *f* ■ **French socialism is a very different ~** le socialisme à la française est complètement différent ■ **there's no such ~** ça n'existe pas.
<> *adj* **1.** [products, behaviour] animal ■ **~ life** faune *f* ■ **~ lover** ami *m*, - e *f* des animaux *OR* des bêtes ■ **~ rights** droits *mpl* des animaux ▶ ***'Animal Farm' Orwell*** 'la Ferme des animaux' **2.** [desire, needs] animal, bestial ■ [courage, instinct] animal ■ **~ high spirits** vivacité *f*, entrain *m*.

animal husbandry *n* élevage *m*.

animalism ['ænɪməlɪzm] *n* **1.** [animal trait] animalité *f* **2.** [sensuality] animalité *f*, sensualité *f* **3.** [theory] animalisme *m*.

animal magnetism *n* magnétisme *m*, charme *m*.

animate <> *vt* ['ænɪmeɪt] **1.** [give life to] animer **2.** *fig* [enliven - face, look, party] animer, égayer ; [- discussion] animer, stimuler **3.** [move to action] motiver, inciter **4.** CIN & TV animer.
<> *adj* ['ænɪmət] vivant, animé.

animated ['ænɪmeɪtɪd] *adj* animé ■ **to become ~** s'animer.

animated cartoon *n* dessin *m* animé.

animatedly ['ænɪmeɪtɪdlɪ] *adv* [behave, participate] avec vivacité *OR* entrain ■ [talk] d'un ton animé, avec animation.

animation [,ænɪ'meɪʃn] *n* **1.** [of discussion, party] animation *f* ■ [of place, street] activité *f*, animation *f* ■ [of person] vivacité *f*, entrain *m* ■ [of face, look] animation *f* **2.** CIN & TV animation *f*.

animator ['ænɪmeɪtəʳ] *n* animateur *m*, - trice *f*.

animatronics [,ænɪmə'trɒnɪks] *n* animatronique *f* ■ CIN animatique *f*.

animism ['ænɪmɪzm] *n* animisme *m*.

animist ['ænɪmɪst] <> *adj* animiste.
<> *n* animiste *mf*.

animosity [ˌænɪ'mɒsətɪ] (*pl* **animosities**) *n* animosité *f*, antipathie *f* ▪ **she felt great ~ towards politicians** elle avait une grande animosité contre *OR* une antipathie profonde pour les hommes politiques.

animus ['ænɪməs] *n* [hostility] = **animosity**.

anion ['ænaɪən] *n* anion *m*.

anise ['ænɪs] *n* anis *m*.

aniseed ['ænɪsi:d] ◇ *n* graine *f* d'anis.
◇ *comp* à l'anis ▪ **~ ball** bonbon *m* à l'anis.

anisette [ˌænɪ'zet] *n* anisette *f*.

ankle ['æŋkl] ◇ *n* cheville *f*.
◇ *comp* : **~ boot** bottine *f* ▪ **~ sock** socquette *f* ▪ **~ strap** bride *f*.

anklebone ['æŋkəlbəʊn] *n* astragale *m*.

ankle-deep *adj* : **she was ~ in mud** elle était dans la boue jusqu'aux chevilles ▪ **the water is only ~** l'eau monte *OR* vient seulement jusqu'à la cheville.

ankle-length *adj* qui descend jusqu'à la cheville.

ankylosis [æŋkɪ'ləʊsɪs] *n* ankylose *f*.

annalist ['ænəlɪst] *n* annaliste *mf*.

annals ['ænlz] *npl* annales *fpl*.

Anne [æn] *pr n* : **Saint ~** sainte Anne ▪ **~ of Cleves** Anne de Clèves.

anneal [ə'ni:l] *vt* [glass] recuire ▪ [metal] tremper, recuire.

annex ◇ *vt* [æ'neks] annexer.
◇ *n US* = **annexe**.

annexation [ˌænek'seɪʃn] *n* [act] annexion *f* ▪ [country] pays *m* annexé ▪ [document] document *m* annexe, annexe *f*.

annexe *UK*, **annex** *US* ['æneks] *n* [building, supplement to document] annexe *f*.

annihilate [ə'naɪəleɪt] *vt* **1.** [destroy - enemy, race] anéantir, détruire ; [- argument, effort] anéantir, annihiler **2.** *inf* [defeat] écraser.

annihilation [əˌnaɪə'leɪʃn] *n* **1.** [destruction - of argument, enemy, effort] anéantissement *m* **2.** *inf* [defeat] défaite *f* (totale), pâtée *f*.

anniversary [ˌænɪ'vɜ:sərɪ] ◇ *n* (*pl* **anniversaries**) anniversaire *m (d'un événement)*, commémoration *f*.
◇ *comp* [celebration, dinner] anniversaire, commémoratif.

Anno Domini [ˌænəʊ'dɒmɪnaɪ] *adv fml* après Jésus-Christ.

annotate ['ænəteɪt] *vt* annoter.

annotation [ˌænə'teɪʃn] *n* [action] annotation *f* ▪ [note] annotation *f*, note *f*.

announce [ə'naʊns] ◇ *vt* annoncer ▪ **to ~ sthg to sb** annoncer qqch à qqn ▪ **we are pleased to ~ the birth/marriage of our son** nous sommes heureux de vous faire part de la naissance/du mariage de notre fils.
◇ *vi US* **to ~ for the presidency** se déclarer candidat à la présidence.

announcement [ə'naʊnsmənt] *n* [public statement] annonce *f* ▪ ADMIN avis *m* ▪ [notice of birth, marriage] faire-part *m*.

announcer [ə'naʊnsəʳ] *n* [gen] annonceur *m*, - euse *f* ▪ RADIO & TV [newscaster] journaliste *mf* ▪ [introducing programme] speaker *m*, speakerine *f*, annonceur *m*, - euse *f*.

annoy [ə'nɔɪ] *vt* ennuyer, agacer ▪ **is this man ~ing you?** cet homme vous ennuie-t-il *OR* vous importune-t-il? *fml* ▪ **he only did it to ~ you** il l'a fait uniquement pour vous ennuyer *OR* contrarier.

annoyance [ə'nɔɪəns] *n* **1.** [displeasure] contrariété *f*, mécontentement *m* ▪ **with a look of ~** d'un air contrarié *OR* ennuyé ▪ **to my great ~** à mon grand mécontentement *OR* déplaisir **2.** [source of irritation] ennui *m*, désagrément *m*.

annoyed [ə'nɔɪd] *adj* : **to be/to get ~ with sb** être/se mettre en colère contre qqn ▪ **she was ~** elle était mécontente.

annoying [ə'nɔɪɪŋ] *adj* [bothersome] gênant, ennuyeux ▪ [very irritating] énervant, agaçant, fâcheux ▪ **the ~ thing is...** ce qui est énervant dans l'histoire, c'est...

annoyingly [ə'nɔɪɪŋlɪ] *adv* de manière gênante *OR* agaçante ▪ **she was ~ vague** elle était si vague que c'en était agaçant.

annual ['ænjʊəl] ◇ *adj* annuel ▪ **what's your ~ income?** combien gagnez-vous par an?
◇ *n* **1.** [publication] publication *f* annuelle ▪ [of association, firm] annuaire *m* ▪ [for children] album *m* (de bandes dessinées) **2.** BOT plante *f* annuelle.

annual general meeting *n* assemblée *f* générale annuelle.

annualize, ise ['ænjʊəˌlaɪz] *vt* annualiser ▪ **~d percentage rate** taux *m* effectif global.

annually ['ænjʊəlɪ] *adv* annuellement, tous les ans ▪ **he earns £20,000 ~** il gagne 20 000 livres par an.

annual report *n* FIN rapport *m* annuel.

annuity [ə'nju:ɪtɪ] (*pl* **annuities**) *n* [regular income] rente *f* ▪ **~ for life, life ~** viager *m*, rente *f* viagère ▌[investment] viager *m*, rente *f* viagère ▪ **to purchase an ~** placer de l'argent en viager.

annul [ə'nʌl] (*pret & pp* **annulled**, *cont* **annulling**) *vt* [law] abroger, abolir ▪ [agreement, contract] résilier ▪ [marriage] annuler ▪ [judgment] casser, annuler.

annulment [ə'nʌlmənt] *n* [of law] abrogation *f*, abolition *f* ▪ [of agreement, contract] résiliation *f* ▪ [of marriage] annulation *f* ▪ [of judgment] cassation *f*, annulation *f*.

Annunciation [əˌnʌnsɪ'eɪʃn] *n* : **the ~** l'Annonciation *f*.

anode ['ænəʊd] *n* anode *f*.

anodyne ['ænədaɪn] ◇ *n* MED analgésique *m*, calmant *m* ▪ *fig* baume *m*.
◇ *adj* **1.** MED analgésique, antalgique ▪ *fig* apaisant **2.** [inoffensive] anodin.

anoint [ə'nɔɪnt] *vt* [in religious ceremony] oindre, consacrer par l'onction ▪ **they ~ed him king** ils l'ont sacré roi.

anointment [ə'nɔɪntmənt] *n* **1.** [action] onction *f* **2.** [ointment] onguent *m*, pommade *f*.

anomalous [ə'nɒmələs] *adj* [effect, growth, result] anormal, irrégulier ▪ GRAM anormal.

anomaly [ə'nɒməlɪ] (*pl* **anomalies**) *n* anomalie *f*.

anon [ə'nɒn] *adv arch & lit* [soon] bientôt, sous peu ▪ **see you ~** *hum* à bientôt.

anon. (*written abbrev of* **anonymous**) anon.

anonymity [ˌænə'nɪmətɪ] *n* **1.** [namelessness] anonymat *m* **2.** [unexceptional quality] banalité *f*.

anonymous [ə'nɒnɪməs] *adj* anonyme ▪ **to remain ~** garder l'anonymat.

anonymously [ə'nɒnɪməslɪ] *adv* [act, donate] anonymement, en gardant l'anonymat ▪ [publish] anonymement, sans nom d'auteur.

anorak ['ænəræk] *n* **1.** [coat] anorak *m* **2.** *inf* [obsessive person] fada *mf*.

anorexia [ˌænə'reksɪə] *n* anorexie *f*.

anorexia nervosa [-nɜ:'vəʊsə] *n* anorexie *f* mentale.

anorexic [ˌænə'reksɪk] ◇ *adj* anorexique.
◇ *n* anorexique *mf*.

another [ə'nʌðəʳ] ◇ *det* **1.** [additional] un... de plus, une... de plus *f*, encore un, encore une *f* ▪ **have ~ chocolate** prenez un autre *OR* reprenez un chocolat ▪ **~ cup of tea?** vous reprendrez bien une tasse de thé? ▪ **~ 5 miles** encore 5 miles ▪ **~ 5 minutes and we'd have missed the train** 5 minutes de plus et on ratait le train ▪ **without ~ word** sans un mot de plus, sans ajouter un mot ▪ **and for ~ thing, he's ill** et de plus il est

malade **2.** [second] un autre, une autre *f*, un second, une seconde *f* ▪ **it could be ~ Vietnam** ça pourrait être un second *OR* nouveau Viêt-nam **3.** [different] un autre, une autre *f* ▪ **let's do it ~ way** faisons-le autrement ▪ **that's ~ matter entirely!** ça, c'est une tout autre histoire!
◇ *pron* **1.** [a similar one] un autre, une autre *f*, encore un, encore une *f* ▪ **many ~** *lit* bien d'autres, beaucoup d'autres **2.** [a different one] : **~ of the girls** une autre des filles ▪ **bring a dessert of one sort or ~** apportez un dessert (, n'importe lequel) **3.** [somebody else] *arch & lit* un autre, une autre *f*.

A. N. Other [ˌeɪen'ʌðəʳ] *n UK* monsieur X, madame X.

Ansaphone® ['ɑːnsəfəʊn] *n* répondeur *m* (téléphonique).

ANSI (*abbrev of* **American National Standards Institute**) *pr n* ≃ AFNOR *f*.

answer ['ɑːnsəʳ] ◇ *vt* **1.** [letter, person, telephone, advertisement] répondre à ▪ [door] aller *OR* venir ouvrir ▪ **she ~ed with a shy grin** pour toute réponse elle a souri timidement ▪ **I phoned earlier but nobody ~ed** j'ai téléphoné tout à l'heure mais ça ne répondait pas ▪ **to ~ a prayer** exaucer une prière **2.** [respond correctly to] : **he could only ~ two of the questions** il n'a su répondre qu'à deux des questions ▪ **few of the students ~ed this question well** peu d'élèves ont bien traité cette question
3. [fulfil] répondre à, satisfaire
4. [description] répondre à, correspondre à
5. LAW : **the defendant ~ed the charge** l'accusé a répondu à *OR* a réfuté l'accusation.
◇ *vi* répondre, donner une réponse.
◇ *n* **1.** [reply - to letter, person, request] réponse *f* ; [- to criticism, objection] réponse *f*, réfutation *f* ▪ **she made no ~** elle n'a pas répondu ▪ **in ~ to her question he simply grinned** pour toute réponse à sa question, il a eu un large sourire ▪ **I rang the bell but there was no ~** j'ai sonné mais personne n'a répondu *OR* n'a ouvert ▪ **I phoned but there was no ~** j'ai téléphoné mais ça ne répondait pas ▪ **she won't take "no" for an ~** elle n'acceptera pas de refus ▪ **he has an ~ for everything** il a réponse à tout ▪ **it's the ~ to all my prayers** *OR* **dreams!** c'est ce dont j'ai toujours rêvé! ▪ **~ to the charge** LAW réponse à l'accusation
2. [solution] solution *f* ▪ **the (right) ~** la bonne réponse ▪ **there's no easy ~** *liter & fig* il n'y a pas de solution facile
3. [to exam question] réponse *f*
4. [equivalent] : **she's England's ~ to Edith Piaf** elle est *OR* c'est l'Édith Piaf anglaise ▪ **it's the poor man's ~ to lobster** c'est le homard des pauvres.
◆ **answer back** ◇ *vi insep* répondre (avec insolence).
◇ *vt sep* répondre (avec insolence) à, répliquer à.
◆ **answer for** *vt insep* **1.** [be responsible for] répondre de, être responsable de ▪ **she'll ~ to me for his safety** elle se portera garante envers moi de sa sécurité ▪ **this government has a lot to ~ for** ce gouvernement a bien des comptes à rendre ▪ **you'll ~ for that!** vous me le paierez!
2. [vouch for] garantir.
◆ **answer to** *vt insep* **1.** [respond to] : **the cat ~s to (the name of) Frankie** le chat répond au nom de Frankie, le chat s'appelle Frankie
2. [correspond to] répondre à, correspondre à.

answerable ['ɑːnsərəbl] *adj* **1.** [person] responsable, comptable ▪ **to be ~ to sb for sthg** être responsable de qqch devant qqn, être garant de qqch envers qqn ▪ **he's ~ only to the president** il ne relève que du président ▪ **I'm ~ to no one** je n'ai de comptes à rendre à personne **2.** [question] susceptible de réponse, qui admet une réponse ▪ [accusation, argument] réfutable.

answering machine ['ɑːnsərɪŋ-] *n* répondeur *m* (automatique *OR* téléphonique).

answering service *n* permanence *f* téléphonique.

answerphone ['ænsəfəʊn] *n* = **answering machine**.

ant [ænt] *n* fourmi *f* ▪ **to have ~s in one's pants** *inf* avoir la bougeotte.

ANTA *pr n* = **American National Theater and Academy**.

antacid [ˌænt'æsɪd] ◇ *n* (médicament *m*) alcalin *m*, antiacide *m*.
◇ *adj* alcalin, antiacide.

antagonism [æn'tægənɪzm] *n* antagonisme *m*, hostilité *f* ▪ **there is considerable ~ towards the new tax** il y a une opposition considérable au nouvel impôt.

antagonist [æn'tægənɪst] *n* antagoniste *mf*, adversaire *mf*.

antagonistic [ænˌtægə'nɪstɪk] *adj* [person] opposé, hostile ▪ [feelings, ideas] antagoniste, antagonique.

antagonize, ise [æn'tægənaɪz] *vt* contrarier, mettre à dos ▪ **we can't afford to ~ the voters** nous ne pouvons pas nous permettre de nous aliéner les électeurs ▪ **don't ~ him!** ne te le mets pas à dos!

Antarctic [ænt'ɑːktɪk] ◇ *pr n* : **the ~ (Ocean)** l'Antarctique *m*, l'océan *m* Antarctique ▪ **in the ~** dans l'Antarctique.
◇ *adj* antarctique.

Antarctica [ænt'ɑːktɪkə] *pr n* Antarctique *f*, le continent *m* antarctique.

Antarctic Circle *pr n* : **the ~** le cercle polaire antarctique.

ante ['æntɪ] ◇ *n* **1.** CARDS mise *f* ▪ **to up the ~** *inf* augmenter la mise **2.** *inf* [price] part *f*.
◇ *vi* CARDS faire une mise.
◆ **ante up**△ *vt sep & vi insep US* casquer△ ▪ **come on, ~ up!** allez, allonge!

anteater ['æntˌiːtəʳ] *n* fourmilier *m*.

antecedent [ˌæntɪ'siːdənt] ◇ *n* GRAM, LOGIC & MATHS antécédent.
◇ *adj* antérieur, précédent ▪ **~ to sthg** antérieur à qqch.
◆ **antecedents** *npl fml* [family] ancêtres *mpl* ▪ [history] passé *m*, antécédents *mpl*.

antechamber ['æntɪˌtʃeɪmbəʳ] *n* antichambre *f*.

antedate [ˌæntɪ'deɪt] *vt* **1.** [precede in time] précéder, dater d'avant **2.** [give earlier date to] antidater **3.** [set an earlier date for] avancer.

antediluvian [ˌæntɪdɪ'luːvjən] *adj lit & hum* antédiluvien.

antelope ['æntɪləʊp] (*pl inv OR pl* **antelopes**) *n* antilope *f*.

ante meridiem [-mə'rɪdɪəm] *adj fml* du matin.

antenatal [ˌæntɪ'neɪtl] *UK* ◇ *adj* prénatal ▪ **~ care** soins *mpl* prénatals ▪ **~ clinic** service *m* de consultation prénatale.
◇ *n inf* consultation *f* prénatale.

antenna [æn'tenə] (*pl* **antennae** [-niː] *OR pl* **antennas**) *n* antenne *f*.

antepenultimate [ˌæntɪpɪ'nʌltɪmət] ◇ *adj* antépénultième.
◇ *n* antépénultième *f*.

anterior [æn'tɪərɪəʳ] *adj fml* antérieur ▪ **~ to** antérieur à.

anteroom ['æntɪrʊm] *n* antichambre *f*, vestibule *m*.

anthem ['ænθəm] *n* [song] chant *m* ▪ RELIG motet *m*.

anther ['ænθəʳ] *n* anthère *f*.

anthill ['ænthɪl] *n* fourmilière *f*.

anthologist [æn'θɒlədʒɪst] *n* anthologiste *mf*.

anthology [æn'θɒlədʒɪ] (*pl* **anthologies**) *n* anthologie *f*.

Anthony ['æntənɪ] *pr n* : **Saint ~** saint Antoine.

anthracite ['ænθrəˌsaɪt] ◇ *n* anthracite *m*.
◇ *adj* : **~ (grey)** (gris *m*) anthracite *(inv)*.

anthrax ['ænθræks] *n* [disease] charbon *m* ▪ [sore] anthrax *m*.

anthropocentric [ˌænθrəpə'sentrɪk] *adj* anthropocentrique.

anthropoid ['ænθrəpɔɪd] ◇ *adj* anthropoïde.
◇ *n* anthropoïde *m*.

anthropological [ˌænθrəpə'lɒdʒɪkl] *adj* anthropologique.

anthropologist [ˌænθrə'pɒlədʒɪst] *n* anthropologue *mf*.

anthropology [ˌænθrə'pɒlədʒɪ] *n* anthropologie *f*.

anthropomorphic [ˌænθrəpə'mɔːfɪk] *adj* anthropomorphique.

anthropomorphous [ˌænθrəpəˈmɔːfəs] *adj* anthropomorphe.

anthropophagous [ˌænθrəˈpɒfəgəs] *adj* anthropophage.

anti [ˈæntɪ] *adj inf* **he's a bit ~ all that kind of thing** il est un peu contre tout cela *OR* toutes ces choses.

anti- *in cpds* anti- ▪ **~American** antiaméricain.

antiabortion [ˌæntɪəˈbɔːʃn] *adj* : **the ~ movement** le mouvement contre l'avortement.

antiabortionist [ˌæntɪəˈbɔːʃnɪst] *n* adversaire *mf* de l'avortement.

antiaircraft [ˌæntɪˈeəkrɑːft] *adj* [system, weapon] antiaérien ▪ **~ defence** défense *f* contre avions, DCA *f*.

antiapartheid [ˌæntɪəˈpɑːtheɪt] *adj* antiapartheid.

antibacterial [ˌæntɪbækˈtiːrɪəl] *adj* antibactérien.

antiballistic missile [ˌantɪbəˈlɪstɪk-] *n* missile *m* antibalistique.

antibiotic [ˌæntɪbaɪˈɒtɪk] ◇ *adj* antibiotique.
◇ *n* antibiotique *m*.

antibody [ˈæntɪˌbɒdɪ] (*pl* **antibodies**) *n* anticorps *m*.

anticathode [ˌæntɪˈkæθəʊd] *n* anticathode *f*.

Antichrist [ˈæntɪˌkraɪst] *n* : **the ~** l'Antéchrist *m*.

anticipate [ænˈtɪsɪˌpeɪt] ◇ *vt* **1.** [think likely] prévoir, s'attendre à ▪ **they ~ meeting some opposition, they ~ that they will meet some opposition** ils s'attendent à rencontrer une certaine opposition ▪ **I didn't ~ leaving so early** je ne m'attendais pas à ce qu'on parte si tôt ▪ **as ~d** comme prévu **2.** [be prepared for - attack, decision, event] anticiper, anticiper sur ; [- needs, wishes] devancer, prévenir, aller au devant de ▪ **we ~d our competitors by launching our product first** nous avons devancé la concurrence en lançant notre produit les premiers **3.** [act on prematurely - effect, success] escompter ; [- profit, salary] anticiper sur ; [- happiness] anticiper, savourer d'avance ; [- pain] anticiper, éprouver d'avance **4.** [pay in advance - bill] anticiper **5.** [mention prematurely] anticiper, anticiper sur.
◇ *vi* anticiper.

anticipation [ænˌtɪsɪˈpeɪʃn] *n* **1.** [expectation] attente *f* ▪ **they raised their prices in ~ of increased inflation** ils ont augmenté leurs prix en prévision d'une hausse de l'inflation **2.** *fml* [readiness] anticipation *f* ▪ **in ~ of your wishes, I've had the fire made up** pour aller au devant de *OR* pour devancer vos désirs, j'ai demandé qu'on fasse du feu **3.** [eagerness] impatience *f*, empressement *m* ▪ **fans jostled at the gates in eager ~** les fans, ne tenant plus d'impatience, se bousculaient aux grilles d'entrée **4.** [premature experiencing - of inheritance, profits, success] anticipation *f*, attente *f* ; [- of fear, pain] appréhension *f*.

anticipatory [ænˌtɪsɪˈpeɪtərɪ] *adj* d'anticipation.

anticlerical [ˌæntɪˈklerɪkl] ◇ *adj* anticlérical.
◇ *n* anticlérical *m*, - e *f*.

anticlericalism [ˌæntɪˈklerɪkəlɪsm] *n* anticléricalisme *m*.

anticlimactic [ˌæntɪklaɪˈmæktɪk] *adj* décevant.

anticlimax [æntɪˈklaɪmæks] *n* **1.** [disappointment] déception *f* ▪ **the opening ceremony was a bit of an ~** la cérémonie d'ouverture a été quelque peu décevante ▪ **what an ~!** quelle douche froide! **2.** LIT chute *f* (dans le trivial).

anticlockwise [ˌæntɪˈklɒkwaɪz] *UK* ◇ *adv* dans le sens inverse *OR* contraire des aiguilles d'une montre.
◇ *adj* : **turn it in an ~ direction** tournez-le dans le sens inverse des aiguilles d'une montre.

anticoagulant [ˌæntɪkəʊˈægjʊlənt] ◇ *adj* anticoagulant.
◇ *n* anticoagulant *m*.

anticonstitutional [ˈæntɪˌkɒnstɪˈtjuːʃənl] *adj* anticonstitutionnel.

anticonvulsant [ˌæntɪkənˈvʌlsənt] ◇ *adj* antispasmodique.
◇ *n* antispasmodique *m*.

anticorrosive [ˌæntɪkəˈrəʊsɪv] ◇ *adj* anticorrosif.
◇ *n* anticorrosif *m*.

antics [ˈæntɪks] *npl* [absurd behaviour] cabrioles *fpl*, gambades *fpl* ▪ [jokes] bouffonnerie *f*, pitrerie *f* ▪ **I'm fed up with her silly ~** j'en ai assez de son cirque ridicule ▪ **they're up to their (old) ~ again** les voilà repartis avec leurs pitreries.

anticyclone [ˌæntɪˈsaɪkləʊn] *n* anticyclone *m*.

anti-dazzle *adj UK* **~ headlights** phares *mpl* antiéblouissants.

antidepressant [ˌæntɪdəˈpresnt] ◇ *adj* antidépresseur.
◇ *n* antidépresseur *m*.

antidote [ˈæntɪdəʊt] *n* antidote *m* ▪ **work is an ~ to *OR* for unhappiness** le travail est un antidote à *OR* contre la tristesse.

anti-Establishment *adj* anticonformiste.

antifreeze [ˈæntɪfriːz] *n* antigel *m*.

antigen [ˈæntɪdʒən] *n* antigène *m*.

antiglare [ˈæntɪgleəʳ] *adj* : **~ headlights** phares *mpl* antiéblouissants.

Antigone [ænˈtɪgənɪ] *pr n* Antigone.

Antigua [ænˈtiːgə] *pr n* Antigua ▪ **in ~** à Antigua ▪ **~ and Barbuda** Antigua et Barbuda.

Antiguan [ænˈtiːgən] ◇ *n habitant d'Antigua*.
◇ *adj* d'Antigua.

antihero [ˈæntɪˌhɪərəʊ] (*pl* **antiheroes**) *n* antihéros *m*.

antihistamine [ˌæntɪˈhɪstəmɪn] *n* antihistaminique *m*.

anti-imperialist ◇ *adj* anti-impérialiste.
◇ *n* anti-impérialiste *mf*.

anti-inflammatory *adj* anti-inflammatoire.

anti-inflationary *adj* anti-inflationniste.

antiknock [ˌæntɪˈnɒk] *n* antidétonant *m*.

Antilles [ænˈtɪliːz] *pr npl* Antilles *fpl* ▪ **the Greater/Lesser ~** les Grandes/Petites Antilles.

antilog [ˌæntɪlɒg], **antilogarithm** [ˌæntɪˈlɒgərɪðm] *n* antilogarithme *m*.

antimacassar [ˌæntɪməˈkæsəʳ] *n* têtière *f*.

antimagnetic [ˌæntɪmægˈnetɪk] *adj* antimagnétique.

antimatter [ˈæntɪˌmætəʳ] *n* antimatière *f*.

antimilitarism [ˌæntɪˈmɪlɪtərɪzm] *n* antimilitarisme *m*.

antimissile [ˌæntɪˈmɪsaɪl] ◇ *adj* antimissile *(inv)*.
◇ *n* missile *m* antimissile.

antimony [ˈæntɪmənɪ] *n* antimoine *m*.

antinuclear [ˌæntɪˈnjuːklɪəʳ] *adj* antinucléaire.

antiparticle [ˈæntɪˌpɑːtɪkl] *n* antiparticule *f*.

antipathetic [ˌæntɪpəˈθetɪk] *adj* antipathique.

antipathy [ænˈtɪpəθɪ] (*pl* **antipathies**) *n* antipathie *f* ▪ **to feel ~ towards sb/sthg** avoir *OR* éprouver de l'antipathie pour qqn/qqch.

antipersonnel [ˈæntɪˌpɜːsəˈnel] *adj euph* antipersonnel *(inv)*.

antiperspirant [ˌæntɪˈpɜːspərənt] ◇ *adj* antiperspirant.
◇ *n* antiperspirant *m*.

antiphony [ænˈtɪfənɪ] (*pl* **antiphonies**) *n* chant *m* en contre-chant.

antiphrasis [ænˈtɪfrəsɪs] (*pl* **antiphrases** [-siːz]) *n* antiphrase *f*.

antipodean [ænˌtɪpəˈdɪən] *adj* des antipodes.

antipodes [ænˈtɪpədiːz] *npl* antipodes *mpl*.
◆ **Antipodes** *pr npl* : **the Antipodes** l'Australie *f* et la Nouvelle-Zélande.

antipope [ˈæntɪpəʊp] *n* antipape *m*.

antiquarian [ˌæntɪ'kweərɪən] ◇ *adj* [collection, shop] d'antiquités ■ [bookseller, bookshop] spécialisé dans les livres anciens.
◇ *n* [collector] collectionneur *m*, - euse *f* d'antiquités ■ [researcher] archéologue *mf* ■ [merchant] antiquaire *mf*.

antiquary ['æntɪkwərɪ] (*pl* **antiquaries**) *n* = **antiquarian** *(n)*.

antiquated ['æntɪkweɪtɪd] *adj* **1.** [outmoded - machine, method] vieillot, obsolète ; [- building, installation] vétuste ; [- idea, manners] vieillot, suranné ; [- person] vieux jeu *(inv)* **2.** [ancient] très vieux.

antique [æn'ti:k] ◇ *adj* **1.** [very old] ancien ■ [dating from Greek or Roman times] antique ■ **an ~ clock** une pendule ancienne *OR* d'époque **2.** *inf* = **antiquated**.
◇ *n* [furniture] meuble *m* ancien *OR* d'époque ■ [vase] vase *m* ancien *OR* d'époque ■ [work of art] objet *m* d'art ancien.
◇ *comp* [lover, shop] d'antiquités ■ **~ dealer** antiquaire *mf*.

antiquity [æn'tɪkwətɪ] (*pl* **antiquities**) *n* **1.** [ancient times] Antiquité *f* **2.** [building, ruin] monument *m* ancien, antiquité *f* ■ [coin, statue] objet *m* ancien ■ [work of art] objet d'art *m* ancien, antiquité *f* **3.** [oldness] antiquité *f*.

antiracist [ˌæntɪ'reɪsɪst] *adj* antiraciste.

antiriot [ˌæntɪ'raɪət] *adj* anti-émeutes.

anti-roll bar *n* barre *f* antiroulis.

antirrhinum [ˌæntɪ'raɪnəm] *n* muflier *m*, gueule-de-loup *f*.

antirust [ˌæntɪ'rʌst] *adj* antirouille *(inv)*.

anti-Semite *n* antisémite *mf*.

anti-Semitic *adj* antisémite.

anti-Semitism *n* antisémitisme *m*.

antiseptic [ˌæntɪ'septɪk] ◇ *adj* antiseptique.
◇ *n* antiseptique *m*.

antiskid [ˌæntɪ'skɪd] *adj* antidérapant.

antislavery [ˌæntɪ'sleɪvərɪ] *adj* antiesclavagiste.

antisocial [ˌæntɪ'səʊʃl] *adj* **1.** [behaviour, measure] antisocial **2.** [unsociable] sauvage.

antistatic [ˌæntɪ'stætɪk] *adj* antistatique.

antitank [ˌæntɪ'tæŋk] *adj* antichar.

antitheft [ˌæntɪ'θeft] *adj* antivol ■ **an ~ device** un antivol, un dispositif contre le vol *OR* antivol.

antithesis [æn'tɪθɪsɪs] (*pl* **antitheses** [-si:z]) *n* **1.** [exact opposite] contraire *m*, opposé *m* ■ **he is the ~ of a forceful young manager** c'est tout le contraire du jeune cadre dynamique **2.** [contrast, opposition] antithèse *f*, contraste *m*, opposition *f* **3.** LIT antithèse *f*.

antithetic(al) [ˌæntɪ'θetɪk(l)] *adj* antithétique.

antitoxin [ˌæntɪ'tɒksɪn] *n* antitoxine *f*.

antitrust [ˌæntɪ'trʌst] *adj* *US* antitrust *(inv)*.

anti-viral ◇ *adj* COMPUT & MED antiviral.
◇ *n* MED antiviral *m*.

antivivisectionist ['æntɪˌvɪvɪ'sekʃnɪst] *n* adversaire *mf* de la vivisection.

antler ['æntlər] *n* corne *f* ■ **the ~s** les bois *mpl*, la ramure.

antonomasia [ˌæntənə'meɪzɪə] *n* antonomase *f*.

Antony ['æntənɪ] *pr n* : **(Mark) ~** (Marc) Antoine ■ **'~ and Cleopatra'** ***Shakespeare*** 'Antoine et Cléopâtre'.

antonym ['æntənɪm] *n* antonyme *m*.

antsy ['æntsɪ] *adj* *US inf* agité, nerveux ■ **I'm feeling ~** j'ai la bougeotte.

Antwerp ['æntwɜ:p] *pr n* Anvers.

anus ['eɪnəs] *n* anus *m*.

anvil ['ænvɪl] *n* enclume *f*.

anxiety [æŋ'zaɪətɪ] (*pl* **anxieties**) *n* **1.** [feeling of worry] anxiété *f*, appréhension *f* ■ **rising interest rates have caused ~** la hausse des taux d'intérêt a suscité une vive anxiété ■ **a source of deep ~** une source d'angoisse profonde **2.** [source of worry] souci *m* ■ **her son is a great ~ to her** son fils lui donne énormément de soucis *OR* l'inquiète énormément **3.** [intense eagerness] grand désir *m*, désir *m* ardent ■ **in his ~ to please her, he forgot everything else** il tenait tellement à lui faire plaisir qu'il en oubliait tout le reste **4.** PSYCHOL anxiété *f* ■ **~ attack** crise *f* d'angoisse.

anxious ['æŋkʃəs] *adj* **1.** [worried] anxieux, angoissé, inquiet ■ **she's ~ about losing her job** elle a peur de perdre son travail ■ **I'm ~ for their safety** je suis inquiète *OR* je crains pour leur sécurité ■ **she's a very ~ person** c'est une grande angoissée **2.** [worrying] inquiétant, angoissant ■ **these are ~ times** nous vivons une sombre époque ■ **we had one or two ~ moments** nous avons connu quelques moments d'anxiété *OR* d'inquiétude **3.** [eager] anxieux, impatient ■ **they're ~ to start** ils sont impatients *OR* pressés de commencer ■ **he was ~ for them to go** il attendait impatiemment qu'ils partent *OR* leur départ ■ **he was very ~ that we shouldn't be seen together** il tenait beaucoup à ce que l'on ne nous voie pas ensemble ■ **she's very ~ to please** elle est très désireuse *OR* anxieuse de plaire.

anxiously ['æŋkʃəslɪ] *adv* **1.** [nervously] avec inquiétude, anxieusement **2.** [eagerly] impatiemment, avec impatience.

anxiousness ['æŋkʃəsnɪs] *n* = **anxiety**.

any ['enɪ] ◇ *det* **1.** [some - in questions] : **have you ~ money?** avez-vous de l'argent? ■ **have ~ guests arrived?** des invités sont-ils arrivés? ■ **were you in ~ danger?** étiez-vous en danger? ■ **~ news about the application?** *inf* il y a du neuf pour la candidature? ■ [in conditional clauses] : **if there's ~ cake left, can I have some?** s'il reste du gâteau, est-ce que je peux en avoir? ■ **~ nonsense from you and you'll be out!** *inf* tu n'as qu'à bien te tenir, sinon, c'est la porte!
2. [in negative phrases] : **he hasn't ~ change/money/cigarettes** il n'a pas de monnaie/d'argent/de cigarettes ■ **he can't stand ~ noise** il ne supporte pas le moindre bruit, il ne supporte aucun bruit ■ **it's impossible to say with ~ degree of certainty** on ne peut l'affirmer avec aucune certitude ■ **she's forbidden to do ~ work** tout travail lui est interdit ■ **hardly** *OR* **barely** *OR* **scarcely ~** très peu de
3. [no matter which] n'importe quel, n'importe quelle *f* ■ **at ~ time of day** à n'importe quel moment *OR* à tout moment de la journée ■ **~ one of these paintings is worth a fortune** chacun de ces tableaux vaut une fortune ■ **answer ~ two of the questions in section C** répondez à deux des questions de la section C ➲ **~ (old) cup will do** n'importe quelle vieille tasse fera l'affaire
4. [all, every] tout ■ **give me ~ money you've got** donne-moi tout l'argent que tu as ■ **~ latecomers should report to the office** tous les retardataires doivent se présenter au bureau
5. [unlimited] : **there are ~ number of ways of winning** il y a mille façons de gagner.
◇ *adv* **1.** [with comparative - in questions, conditional statements] : **can you walk ~ faster?** peux-tu marcher un peu plus vite? ■ **if she isn't ~ better by tomorrow, call the doctor** si elle ne va pas mieux demain, appelez le médecin ; [- in negative statements] : **he won't be ~ (the) happier** il n'en sera pas plus heureux ■ **we can't go ~ further** nous ne pouvons aller plus loin ■ **it's not getting ~ easier to find good staff** c'est toujours aussi difficile de trouver de bons employés
2. *inf* [at all] : **you're not helping me ~** tu ne m'aides pas du tout ■ **has the situation improved ~?** la situation s'est-elle arrangée un tant soit peu? ■ **she wasn't ~ too pleased with the press coverage she got** elle n'était pas ravie de la publicité que lui ont faite les médias.
◇ *pron* **1.** [in questions, conditional statements - some, someone] : **did you see ~?** en avez-vous vu? ■ **did ~ of them go?** est-ce que certains d'entre eux y sont allés? ■ **if ~ of you wants them, do take them** si quelqu'un parmi vous *OR* si l'un d'entre vous les veut, il n'a qu'à les prendre ■ **few, if ~, of his supporters remained loyal** aucun ou presque aucun de ses supporters ne lui est resté fidèle
2. [in negative statements - even one] : **he won't vote for ~ of the candidates** il ne votera pour aucun des candidats ■ **there was hardly ~ of it left** il n'en restait que très peu ■ **she's learned two foreign languages, I haven't learned ~** elle a étudié deux langues étrangères, je n'en ai étudié aucune ■ **I have**

absolutely no money and don't expect to get ~ je n'ai pas un sou et je ne m'attends pas à en avoir ▶ **he's not having ~ (of it)** *inf* il ne marche pas
3. [no matter which one] n'importe lequel, n'importe laquelle *f* ■ **study ~ of her works and you will discover...** étudie n'importe laquelle de ses œuvres et tu découvriras... | [every one, all] tout ■ **~ of the suspects would fit that description** cette description s'applique à tous les suspects.

anybody ['enɪ,bɒdɪ] *pron* **1.** *(in questions, conditional statements)* [someone] quelqu'un ■ **(is) ~ home?** il y a quelqu'un? ■ **she'll persuade them, if ~ can** si quelqu'un peut les convaincre, c'est bien elle **2.** *(in negative statements)* [someone] personne ■ **there was hardly ~ there** il n'y avait presque personne **3.** [no matter who, everyone] **: ~ who wants can join us** tous ceux qui veulent peuvent se joindre à nous ■ **invite ~ you want** invitez qui vous voulez ■ **it could happen to ~** ça pourrait arriver à tout le monde *OR* n'importe qui ■ **I don't care what ~ thinks** je me fiche de ce que pensent les gens ■ **she's cleverer than ~ I know** c'est la personne la plus intelligente que je connaisse ■ **~ with any sense** *OR* **in their right mind would have...** toute personne un peu sensée aurait... ■ **please, ~ but him!** je t'en prie, pas lui! ■ **~ but him would have...** n'importe qui d'autre que lui *OR* tout autre que lui aurait... ■ **~ will do** n'importe qui *OR* le premier venu fera l'affaire ■ **~ would think you'd just lost your best friend** on croirait que tu viens de perdre ton meilleur ami ▶ **he's not just ~, he's my brother!** ce n'est pas n'importe qui, c'est mon frère! ■ **a couple of gin and tonics and you're ~'s** *hum* deux ou trois gin-tonics et on fait tout ce qu'on veut de toi **4.** [important person] quelqu'un (d'important *OR* de connu) ■ **~ who's ~ will be there** tout le gratin sera là ■ **if you want to be ~, you've got to work** si tu veux devenir quelqu'un tu dois travailler.

anyhow ['enɪhaʊ] ◇ *adv* **1.** = **anyway 2.** [in any manner, by any means] **: you can do it ~, but just get it done!** tu peux le faire n'importe comment, mais fais-le! ■ **I had to persuade her somehow, ~** il fallait que je trouve un moyen de la convaincre, n'importe lequel **3.** *inf* [haphazardly] n'importe comment.
◇ *adj inf* **he left the room all ~** il a laissé la pièce sens dessus dessous.

any more *UK*, **anymore** *US* [,enɪ'mɔːr] *adv* **: they don't live here ~** ils n'habitent plus ici ■ **I won't do it ~** je ne le ferai plus (jamais).

anyone ['enɪwʌn] *pron* = **anybody**.

anyplace ['enɪpleɪs] *adv* & *pron US inf* = **anywhere**.

anyroad ['enɪrəʊd] *adv UK dial* = **anyway**.

anything ['enɪθɪŋ] *pron* **1.** [something - in questions] quelque chose ■ **did you hear ~?** avez-vous entendu quelque chose? ■ **can't we do ~?** est-ce qu'il n'y a rien à faire? ■ **is there ~ in** *OR* **to what she says?** est-ce qu'il y a du vrai dans ce qu'elle dit? ■ **have you heard ~ from them?** avez-vous eu de leurs nouvelles? ■ **did you notice ~ unusual?** avez-vous remarqué quelque chose de bizarre? ■ **~ the matter?** *inf* quelque chose ne va pas? ; [- in conditional statements] **: if ~ should happen, take care of John for me** s'il m'arrivait quelque chose *OR* quoi que ce soit, occupez-vous de John ; [- in negative statements] rien ■ **I didn't say ~** je n'ai rien dit ■ **don't do ~ stupid!** ne fais pas de bêtise! ■ **I don't know ~ about computers** je ne m'y connais pas du tout *OR* je n'y connais rien en informatique ■ **she hasn't written ~ very much since last year** elle n'a pas écrit grand-chose depuis l'année dernière ▶ **she's not angry or ~** elle n'est pas fâchée ni rien ■ **do you want a book or ~?** voulez-vous un livre ou autre chose? ■ **if she feels sick or ~, call the doctor** si elle se sent mal *OR* si ça ne va pas, appelez le médecin **2.** [no matter what] **: just tell him ~** racontez-lui n'importe quoi ■ **~ you like** tout ce que vous voudrez ■ **I'd give ~ to know the truth** je donnerais n'importe quoi pour savoir la vérité ▶ **~ goes!** tout est permis! **3.** [all, everything] tout ■ **her son eats ~** son fils mange de tout ■ **I like ~ with chocolate in it** j'aime tout ce qui est au chocolat ■ **she must earn ~ between £30,000 and £40,000** elle doit gagner dans les 30 000 à 40 000 livres ■ **you can use it to flavour ~ from jam to soup** vous pouvez l'utiliser pour parfumer n'importe quoi, de la confiture à la soupe **4.** [in intensifying phrases] **: he isn't ~ like his father** il ne ressemble en rien à son père ■ **it doesn't taste ~ like a tomato** ça n'a pas du tout le goût de tomate ■ **they aren't producing the goods ~ like fast enough** ils ne produisent pas la marchandise assez vite, loin de là ■ **I wouldn't miss it for ~** je ne le manquerais pour rien au monde ■ **it's as easy as ~** c'est facile comme tout ■ **he worked like ~** il a travaillé comme un fou.
◆ **anything but** *adv phr* tout sauf ■ **that music is ~ but relaxing** cette musique est tout sauf reposante ■ **is he crazy? – ~ but!** est-ce qu'il est fou? – bien au contraire! *OR* il est tout sauf ça!

anyway ['enɪweɪ] *adv* **1.** [in any case - reinforcing] de toute façon ■ **what's to stop them ~?** de toute façon, qu'est-ce qui peut les en empêcher? ; [- summarizing, concluding] en tout cas ■ **~, in the end she left** toujours est-il qu'elle *OR* en tout cas, elle a fini par partir ■ **~, I have to go** [I'll be late] bon, il faut que j'y aille ; [I don't have any choice] enfin, il faut que j'y aille **2.** [nevertheless, notwithstanding] quand même ■ **thanks ~** merci quand même **3.** [qualifying] en tout cas ■ **that's what we all think, well, most of us ~** c'est ce qu'on pense tous, ou presque tous en tout cas **4.** [returning to topic] bref.

anyways ['enɪweɪz] *US adv* = **anyway**.

anywhere ['enɪweər] ◇ *adv* **1.** [in questions] quelque part ■ **have you seen my keys ~?** avez-vous vu mes clés (quelque part)? ■ **are you going ~ at Easter?** vous partez à Pâques? ■ **are you going ~ this evening?** est-ce que vous sortez ce soir?
2. [in positive statements - no matter where] n'importe où ■ **just put it down ~** posez-le n'importe où ■ **sit ~ you like** asseyez-vous où vous voulez ■ **~ you go it's the same story** où que vous alliez, c'est toujours pareil *OR* toujours la même chose ■ **I'd know her ~** je la reconnaîtrais entre mille | [everywhere] partout ■ **you can find that magazine ~** on trouve cette revue partout
3. [in negative statements - any place] nulle part ■ **I can't find my keys ~** je ne trouve mes clés nulle part ■ **look, this isn't getting us ~** écoute, tout ça ne nous mène à rien
4. [any number within a range] **: we might receive ~ between 60 and 600 applications** on peut recevoir entre 60 et 600 demandes
5. *phr* **he isn't ~ near as quick as you are** il est loin d'être aussi rapide que toi ■ **are they ~ near completion?** ont-ils bientôt fini?
◇ *pron* [any place] **: do they need ~ to stay?** ont-ils besoin d'un endroit où loger? ■ **she's looking for a flat, but hasn't found ~ yet** elle cherche un appartement mais elle n'a encore rien trouvé ■ **they live miles from ~** ils habitent en pleine brousse.

A-OK *US inf* ◇ *adj* excellent ■ **everything's ~** tout baigne ■ **he's ~** c'est un type bien.
◇ *adv* parfaitement.

aorta [eɪ'ɔːtə] (*pl* **aortas** *OR pl* **aortae** [-tiː]) *n* aorte *f*.

Aosta [ɑː'ɒstə] *pr n* Aoste.

AP *n* = **American Plan**.

apace [ə'peɪs] *adv lit* rapidement, vite.

Apache [ə'pætʃɪ] ◇ *n* (*pl inv OR pl* **Apaches**) **1.** [person] Apache *mf* **2.** LING apache *m*.
◇ *adj* apache.

apart [ə'pɑːt] ◇ *adv* **1.** [separated - in space] **: the houses were about 10 kilometres ~** les maisons étaient à environ 10 kilomètres l'une de l'autre ■ **cities as far ~ as Johannesburg and Hong Kong** des villes aussi éloignées l'une de l'autre que Johannesburg et Hong Kong ■ **he stood with his legs wide ~** il se tenait (debout) les jambes bien écartées ■ **they can't bear to be ~** ils ne supportent pas d'être loin l'un de l'autre *OR* séparés | [in time] **: the twins were born 3 minutes ~** les jumeaux sont nés à 3 minutes d'intervalle | *fig* **we're miles ~ when it comes to politics** nous avons des points de vue politiques très différents **2.** [in pieces] en pièces, en morceaux ■ **to break ~** s'émietter **3.** [with verbs of motion] **: to push ~** éloigner (en poussant) ■ **they sprang ~ when I entered the room** ils se sont écartés vivement l'un de l'autre quand je suis entré dans la pièce ■ **to grow ~ from sb** s'éloigner de qqn **4.** [isolated] à l'écart ■ **she stood ~ from the others** elle se tenait à l'écart des autres **5.** [aside] à part ■ **joking ~** trêve de plaisanterie.

◇ *adj (after n)* [distinct and special] à part ▪ **they regard it as a thing ~** ils considèrent que c'est quelque chose de complètement différent.

◂ **apart from** *prep phr* **1.** [except for] à part ▪ **it's fine, ~ from a few minor mistakes** à part *OR* sauf quelques fautes sans importance, c'est très bien **2.** [as well as] en plus de ▪ **she has many interests ~ from golf** elle s'intéresse à beaucoup de choses à part le *OR* en plus du golf ▪ **quite ~ from the fact that it's too big, I don't like the colour** outre (le fait) que c'est trop grand, je n'aime pas la couleur.

apartheid [ə'pɑ:theɪt] *n* apartheid *m.*

apartment [ə'pɑ:tmənt] *n* **1.** *UK (usu pl)* [room] pièce *f* ▪ [bedroom] chambre *f* ▪ **the Royal ~s** la résidence royale **2.** [flat] appartement *m*, logement *m* ▪ **a one-bedroom** *OR* **one-bedroomed ~** un deux-pièces.

apartment building *n US* immeuble *m (d'habitation).*

apartment house *n US* immeuble *m (d'habitation).*

apathetic [,æpə'θetɪk] *adj* apathique, indifférent.

apathetically [,æpə'θetɪklɪ] *adv* avec apathie *OR* indifférence.

apathy ['æpəθɪ] *n* apathie *f*, indifférence *f.*

ape [eɪp] ◇ *n* **1.** [monkey] grand singe *m*, anthropoïde *m spec* **2.** *pej* [person] brute *f* **3.** *US inf* **to go ~** devenir fou.
◇ *vt* singer.

ape-man (*pl* **ape-men**) *n* homme-singe *m.*

aperient [ə'pɪərɪənt] MED ◇ *adj* laxatif.
◇ *n* laxatif *m.*

aperitif [əperə'ti:f] *n* apéritif *m.*

aperture ['æpə,tjʊəʳ] *n* **1.** [opening] ouverture *f*, orifice *m* ▪ [gap] brèche *f*, trouée *f* **2.** PHOT ouverture *f* (du diaphragme).

apex ['eɪpeks] (*pl* **apexes** *OR pl* **apices** ['eɪpɪsi:z]) *n* [of triangle] sommet *m*, apex *m* ▪ *fig* point *m* culminant, sommet *m.*

APEX ['eɪpeks] *n UK* (*abbrev of* **advance purchase excursion**) ▪ **~ fare** tarif *m* apex.

aphasia [ə'feɪzjə] *n* aphasie *f.*

aphid ['eɪfɪd] *n* puceron *m.*

aphorism ['æfərɪzm] *n* aphorisme *m.*

aphrodisiac [,æfrə'dɪzɪæk] ◇ *adj* aphrodisiaque.
◇ *n* aphrodisiaque *m.*

API (*abbrev of* **American Press Institute**) *pr n association de journalistes américains.*

apiary ['eɪpjərɪ] (*pl* **apiaries**) *n* rucher *m.*

apices ['eɪpɪsi:z] *pl* ▷ **apex.**

apiculture ['eɪpɪkʌltʃəʳ] *n* apiculture *f.*

apiece [ə'pi:s] *adv* **1.** [for each item] chacun *m*, - e *f*, (la) pièce ▪ **the plants are £3 ~** les plantes coûtent 3 livres (la) pièce *OR* chacune **2.** [for each person] chacun *m*, - e *f*, par personne ▪ **we had two shirts ~** nous avions deux chemises chacun.

aplenty [ə'plentɪ] *adj lit* **she's always had money ~** elle a toujours eu beaucoup *OR* énormément d'argent.

aplomb [ə'plɒm] *n* sang-froid *m*, aplomb *m pej.*

Apocalypse [ə'pɒkəlɪps] *n* Apocalypse *f.*

apocalyptic [ə,pɒkə'lɪptɪk] *adj* apocalyptique.

Apocrypha [ə'pɒkrɪfə] *npl* : **the ~** les Apocryphes *mpl.*

apocryphal [ə'pɒkrɪfl] *adj* apocryphe.

apogee ['æpədʒi:] *n* ASTRON & *fig* apogée *m.*

apolitical [,eɪpə'lɪtɪkəl] *adj* apolitique.

apologetic [ə,pɒlə'dʒetɪk] *adj* **1.** [person] : **she was very ~ for being late** elle s'est excusée plusieurs fois d'être arrivée en retard ▪ **he was most ~** il s'est confondu en excuses **2.** [letter, look, note, smile] d'excuse.

apologetically [ə,pɒlə'dʒetɪklɪ] *adv* [say] en s'excusant, pour s'excuser ▪ [smile] pour s'excuser.

apologist [ə'pɒlədʒɪst] *n* apologiste *mf.*

apologize, ise [ə'pɒlədʒaɪz] *vi* s'excuser ▪ **there's no need to ~** inutile de vous excuser ▪ **he ~d to them for the delay** il leur a demandé de l'excuser pour son retard ▪ **~ to the lady** demande pardon à la dame ▪ **I can't ~ enough** je ne sais comment m'excuser.

apology [ə'pɒlədʒɪ] (*pl* **apologies**) *n* **1.** [expression of regret] excuses *fpl* ▪ **to make one's apologies to sb** s'excuser auprès de qqn ▪ **I owe him an ~** je lui dois des excuses ▪ **the director sends his apologies** le directeur vous prie de l'excuser **2.** [defence] apologie *f* **3.** *UK pej* [poor example] : **he's a mere ~ for a man** c'est un nul.
Voir module d'usage

apoplectic [,æpə'plektɪk] ◇ *adj* apoplectique ▪ **to have an ~ fit** avoir *OR* faire une attaque d'apoplexie ▪ *fig* fou de rage.
◇ *n* apoplectique *mf.*

apoplexy ['æpəpleksɪ] *n* apoplexie *f.*

apostasy [ə'pɒstəsɪ] (*pl* **apostasies**) *n* apostasie *f.*

apostate [ə'pɒsteɪt] ◇ *adj* apostat.
◇ *n* apostat *m*, - e *f.*

apostle [ə'pɒsl] *n* RELIG & *fig* apôtre *m* ▪ **the Apostles' Creed** le Symbole des Apôtres.

apostolic [,æpə'stɒlɪk] *adj* apostolique.

apostrophe [ə'pɒstrəfɪ] *n* apostrophe *f.*

APOLOGIES

Making an apology

Pardon, je ne vous avais pas vu. Sorry, I didn't see you there.

Pardon !/Excusez-moi ! *(eg: after sneezing)* Excuse me!

Pardon ! *(eg: when trying to get past somebody)* Excuse me!

Excusez-moi, je dois vous laisser. Excuse me, I have to go now.

Désolé de vous interrompre, mais je cherche la sortie. Sorry to interrupt, but I'm looking for the exit.

Je suis désolé pour le malentendu de ce matin. I'm sorry about the confusion this morning.

Si je t'ai vexé l'autre jour, je suis (vraiment) désolé. I'm (terribly) sorry if I offended you the other day.

Je regrette de ne pas pouvoir venir samedi. I'm sorry (that) I can't come on Saturday.

J'ai bien peur que nous ne soyons obligés d'annuler le dîner de la semaine prochaine. I'm afraid we're going to have to cancel dinner next week.

Accepting an apology

Ce n'est pas grave. That's OK.

Ça ne fait rien. It doesn't matter.

N'en parlons plus. Let's say no more about it.

Ne t'en fais pas. Don't worry about it.

Vous n'avez pas besoin de vous excuser. There's no need to apologize.

Je vous en prie. Don't mention it.

apostrophize, ise [ə'pɒstrəfaɪz] *vt* apostropher.

apothecary [ə'pɒθəkərɪ] (*pl* **apothecaries**) *n* pharmacien *m*, - enne *f*, apothicaire *m* *arch*.

apothem ['æpəθem] *n* apothème *m*.

apotheosis [ə,pɒθɪ'əʊsɪs] (*pl* **apotheoses** [-si:z]) *n* apothéose *f*.

appal *UK*, **appall** *US* [ə'pɔ:l] (*pret & pp* **appalled**, *cont* **appalling**) *vt* [scandalize] choquer, scandaliser ▪ [horrify] écœurer ▪ **she was appalled at** *OR* **by the very thought** l'idée même l'écœurait.

Appalachian [,æpə'leɪtʃjən] ◇ *pr n* : **the ~s, the ~ Mountains** les (monts *mpl*) Appalaches *mpl*.
◇ *adj* appalachien.

appall *US vt* = **appal**.

appalled [ə'pɔ:ld] *adj* écœuré.

appalling [ə'pɔ:lɪŋ] *adj* épouvantable.

appallingly [ə'pɔ:lɪŋlɪ] *adv* **1.** [badly] de façon écœurante **2.** [as intensifier] effroyablement ▪ **an ~ bad film** un film effroyablement mauvais.

apparatus [,æpə'rætəs] (*pl inv OR pl* **apparatuses**) *n* **1.** *(U)* [equipment] équipement *m* ▪ [set of instruments] instruments *mpl* ▪ **critical ~** LIT appareil *m OR* apparat *m* critique **2.** *(U)* [in gymnasium] agrès *mpl* **3.** [machine] appareil *m* **4.** ANAT appareil *m* **5.** [organization] : **the ~ of government** la machine administrative, l'administration *f*.

apparel [ə'pærəl] ◇ *n* **1.** *lit & arch* [garb] costume *m*, mise *f* **2.** *US* [clothes] habillement *m*, vêtements *mpl* ▪ [industry] confection *f*.
◇ *vt* (*UK pret & pp* **apparelled**, *cont* **apparelling**) (*US pret & pp* **appareled**, *cont* **appareling**) *lit & arch* [dress] vêtir, habiller ▪ [adorn] orner.

apparent [ə'pærənt] *adj* **1.** [obvious] évident, apparent ▪ **the need for better education facilities is becoming increasingly ~** il est de plus en plus évident qu'il faut améliorer le système éducatif ▪ **for no ~ reason** sans raison apparente **2.** [seeming] apparent, supposé.

apparently [ə'pærəntlɪ] *adv* **1.** [seemingly] apparemment, en apparence ▪ **she was ~ quite calm and collected** elle paraissait assez calme et sereine **2.** [according to rumour] à ce qu'il paraît ▪ **is she leaving? – ~ not** elle part? – on dirait que non ▪ **~, they had a huge row** il paraît qu'ils se sont violemment disputés.

apparition [,æpə'rɪʃn] *n* apparition *f*.

appeal [ə'pi:l] ◇ *n* **1.** [request] appel *m* ▪ **she made an ~ on behalf of the victims** elle a lancé un appel au profit des victimes ▪ **an ~ for help** un appel au secours
2. LAW appel *m*, pourvoi *m* ▪ **to enter** *OR* **to lodge an ~** interjeter un appel, se pourvoir en appel ▪ **on ~** en seconde instance ▪ **right of ~** droit *m* d'appel
3. [attraction] attrait *m*, charme *m* ▪ **travelling has lost its ~ for me** je n'aime plus voyager, les voyages ne m'intéressent plus ▪ **the idea does have a certain ~** l'idée est bien séduisante.
◇ *vi* **1.** [make request] faire un appel ▪ [publicly] lancer un appel ▪ [plead] supplier, implorer ▪ **she ~ed to me to be patient** elle m'a prié d'être patient ▪ **they're ~ing for help for the victims** ils lancent un appel au profit des victimes
2. : **to ~ to sthg** [invoke] faire appel à qqch
3. [apply] faire appel ▪ **he ~ed to them for help** il leur a demandé du secours ▪ **they ~ed to the management for better working conditions** ils ont fait appel à la direction pour obtenir de meilleures conditions de travail ▪ **he ~ed against the decision** il a fait appel contre cette décision
4. LAW interjeter appel, se pourvoir en appel ▪ **to ~ against a sentence** appeler d'un jugement
5. [please] plaire ▪ **the idea ~ed to me** l'idée m'a séduit ▪ **it doesn't really ~ to me** ça ne m'attire pas vraiment, ça ne me dit pas grand-chose.

appeal court *n* cour *f* d'appel.

appealing [ə'pi:lɪŋ] *adj* **1.** [attractive - dress, person] joli ; [- idea, plan] intéressant **2.** [moving] émouvant, attendrissant ▪ [imploring] suppliant, implorant.

appealingly [ə'pi:lɪŋlɪ] *adv* **1.** [charmingly] de façon attrayante **2.** [beseechingly] d'un air suppliant *OR* implorant.

appear [ə'pɪər] *vi* **1.** [come into view - person, ghost, stars] apparaître ▪ **the sun ~ed from behind a cloud** le soleil est sorti de derrière un nuage ▪ **she finally ~ed at about eight o'clock** elle est arrivée finalement vers vingt heures **2.** [come into being] apparaître ▪ [new product] apparaître, être mis sur le marché ▪ [publication] paraître, sortir, être publié **3.** [feature] paraître, figurer **4.** [be present officially] se présenter, paraître ▪ [in court] comparaître ▪ **to ~ before the court** *OR* **the judge** comparaître devant le tribunal ▪ **they ~ed as witnesses for the defence** ils ont témoigné pour la défense **5.** [actor] jouer ▪ **she ~ed as Antigone** elle a joué Antigone ▪ **to ~ on TV** passer à la télévision **6.** [seem] paraître, sembler ▪ **she ~ed nervous** elle avait l'air nerveuse ▪ **how does the situation ~ to you?** comment voyez-vous la situation? ▪ **there ~s to have been a mistake** il semble qu'il y ait eu erreur ▪ **so it ~s, so it would ~** c'est ce qu'il semble, on dirait bien ▪ **is she ill? – it ~s so** est-elle malade? – il paraît (que oui) ▪ **it ~ed later that he had killed his wife** il est ensuite apparu qu'il avait assassiné sa femme.

appearance [ə'pɪərəns] *n* **1.** [act of appearing] apparition *f* ▪ **she made a brief ~ at the party** elle a fait une brève apparition à la fête ▪ **the president made a personal ~** le président est apparu en personne ▪ **to put in an ~** faire acte de présence
2. [advent] avènement *m* ▪ [of new product] mise *f* sur le marché ▪ [of publication] parution *f*
3. [in court] comparution *f* ▪ **to make an ~ before a court** *OR* **a judge** comparaître devant un tribunal
4. [performance] : **this was her first ~ on the stage** c'était sa première apparition sur scène ▪ **she's made a number of television ~s** elle est passée plusieurs fois à la télévision ▪ **in order of ~** par ordre d'entrée en scène
5. [outward aspect] apparence *f*, aspect *m* ▪ **to have a good ~** [person] présenter bien ▪ **contrary to all ~s, against all ~s** contrairement à toute apparence ▪ **don't judge by ~s** ne vous fiez pas aux apparences, il ne faut pas se fier aux apparences ▪ **they tried hard to keep up ~s** ils ont tout fait pour sauver les apparences ▪ **for ~s' sake** pour la forme.

appease [ə'pi:z] *vt* apaiser, calmer.

appeasement [ə'pi:zmənt] *n* apaisement *m* ▪ *pej &* POL conciliation *f*.

appellate [ə'pelət] *adj* : **~ court** cour *f* d'appel.

appellation [,æpə'leɪʃn] *n* appellation *f*.

append [ə'pend] *vt fml* [document, note] joindre ▪ [signature] apposer.

appendage [ə'pendɪdʒ] *n* [gen - ZOOL] appendice *m*.

appendectomy [,æpen'dektəmɪ] (*pl* **appendectomies**) *n* appendicectomie *f*.

appendices [ə'pendɪsi:z] *pl* ▷ **appendix**.

appendicitis [ə,pendɪ'saɪtɪs] *n (U)* appendicite *f*.

appendix [ə'pendɪks] (*pl* **appendixes** *OR pl* **appendices** [-si:z]) *n* **1.** ANAT appendice *m* ▪ **to have one's ~ out** se faire opérer de l'appendicite **2.** [to book] appendice *m* ▪ [to report] annexe *f*.

appertain [,æpə'teɪn] *vi fml* [belong] : **to ~ to** appartenir à ▪ [relate] : **to ~ to** relever de ▪ **the responsibilities ~ing to adulthood** les responsabilités de l'âge adulte.

appetite ['æpɪtaɪt] *n* appétit *m* ▪ **I've lost my ~** j'ai perdu l'appétit ▪ **don't have too many sweets, you'll spoil your ~** ne mange pas trop de bonbons, ça va te couper l'appétit ▪ **they've gone for a swim to work up an ~** ils sont allés se baigner pour s'ouvrir l'appétit *OR* se mettre en appétit ▪ **I have no ~ for that kind of thing** *fig* je n'ai pas de goût pour ce genre de chose ▪ **he has an insatiable ~ for work** *fig* c'est un boulimique du travail ➤ **~ suppressant** coupe-faim *m*.

appetizer, iser ['æpɪtaɪzər] *n* [food] hors-d'œuvre *m inv*, amuse-gueule *m* ▪ [drink] apéritif *m*.

appetizing, ising ['æpɪtaɪzɪŋ] *adj* appétissant.

Appian ['æpɪən] *adj* : **the ~ Way** la voie Appienne.

applaud [ə'plɔ:d] ◇ *vi* applaudir.
◇ *vt* applaudir, approuver.

applause [ə'plɔ:z] *n (U)* applaudissements *mpl*, acclamations *fpl* ■ **his performance won enthusiastic ~ from the audience** son interprétation a été chaleureusement applaudie par le public.

apple ['æpl] ◇ *n* [fruit] pomme *f* ■ [tree] pommier *m* ■ **he's a rotten ~** c'est un mauvais sujet ■ **she's the ~ of his eye** il tient à elle comme à la prunelle de ses yeux ■ **an ~ a day keeps the doctor away** *prov* chaque jour une pomme conserve son homme *prov*.
◇ *comp* : **~ blossom** fleur *f* de pommier ■ **~ core** trognon *m* de pomme ■ **~ tree** pommier *m* ■ **don't upset the ~ cart** *inf* ne fiche pas tout par terre.

applejack ['æpldʒæk] *n* eau-de-vie *f* de pommes.

apple pie *n* [covered] tourte *f* aux pommes ■ [open] tarte *f* aux pommes.
➡ **apple-pie** *adj inf* impeccable ■ **in apple-pie order** en ordre parfait ➊ **apple-pie bed** *UK* lit *m* en portefeuille.

apple sauce *UK* [æpl'sɔ:s], **applesauce** *US* ['æplsɔ:s] *n* CULIN compote *f* de pommes *(en Grande-Bretagne, traditionnellement servie avec du porc)*.

applet ['æplət] *n* COMPUT applet *m*, microprogramme *m*.

appliance [ə'plaɪəns] *n* **1.** appareil *m* ■ [small] dispositif *m*, instrument *m* ■ **domestic** *OR* **household ~s** appareils électroménagers ■ **electrical ~s** appareils électriques **2.** [fire engine] autopompe *f*.

applicable ['æplɪkəbl] *adj* applicable.

applicant ['æplɪkənt] *n* **1.** [gen, for patent] demandeur *m*, - euse *f* ■ [for a position] candidat *m*, - e *f*, postulant *m*, - e *f* **2.** LAW requérant *m*, - e *f*.

application [,æplɪ'keɪʃn] ◇ *n* **1.** [use] application *f* ■ [of lotion, paint] application *f* ■ **'for external ~ only'** MED 'réservé à l'usage externe' **2.** [request] demande *f* ■ **a job ~** [spontaneous] une demande d'emploi ; [in answer to advertisement] une candidature à un poste ■ **I submitted my ~ for a scholarship** j'ai fait ma demande de bourse **3.** COMPUT application *f* **4.** [diligence] assiduité *f* **5.** [relevance] pertinence *f*.
◇ *comp* COMPUT [package, program, software] d'application.

application form *n* formulaire *m* ■ [detailed] dossier *m* de candidature ■ UNIV dossier *m* d'inscription.

applicator ['æplɪkeɪtər] *n* applicateur *m*.

applied [ə'plaɪd] *adj* [gen - LING], MATHS & SCI appliqué ■ **~ arts** arts *mpl* décoratifs.

appliqué [æ'pli:keɪ] ◇ *n* [decoration] application *f* ■ [decorative work] travail *m* d'application.
◇ *vt* coudre en application.

apply [ə'plaɪ] *(pret & pp* **applied**) ◇ *vt* **1.** [use] appliquer, mettre en pratique *OR* en application ■ [rule, law] appliquer ■ **we ~ the same rule to all students** nous appliquons la même règle à *OR* pour tous les étudiants
2. [pressure] : **to ~ pressure to sthg** exercer une pression *OR* appuyer sur qqch ■ **she applied the brakes** elle a appuyé sur le frein ■ **the bank applied pressure on him to repay his loan** *fig* la banque a fait pression sur lui pour qu'il rembourse son emprunt
3. [paint, lotion etc] appliquer, mettre ■ **~ antiseptic to the wound** désinfectez la plaie ■ **to ~ heat to sthg** exposer qqch à la chaleur
4. [devote] : **to ~ one's mind to sthg** s'appliquer à qqch ■ **she applied herself to her work** elle s'est lancée dans son travail ■ **he must learn to ~ himself** il faut qu'il apprenne à s'appliquer.
◇ *vi* **1.** [make an application] s'adresser, avoir recours ■ **'~ within'** 's'adresser à l'intérieur *OR* ici' ■ **to ~ for a job/scholarship** faire une demande d'emploi/de bourse ■ **he applied to the Research Council for an award** il s'est adressé au conseil de la recherche pour obtenir une bourse ■ **she has decided to ~ for the job** elle a décidé de poser sa candidature pour cet emploi ■ **we applied for a patent** nous avons déposé une demande de brevet
2. [be relevant] s'appliquer ■ **this law applies to all citizens** cette loi s'applique à tous les citoyens ■ **this doesn't ~ to us** nous ne sommes pas concernés.

appoint [ə'pɔɪnt] *vt* **1.** [assign] nommer, désigner ■ **she was ~ed to the post of director** elle a été nommée directrice ■ **the members ~ed him president** les adhérents l'ont nommé président ■ **the president ~ed a committee** le président a constitué un comité ▮ [hire] : **we have ~ed a new cook** nous avons engagé un nouveau cuisinier **2.** [date, place] fixer, désigner ■ **we met on the ~ed day** nous nous sommes rencontrés au jour dit *OR* convenu ■ **his ~ed agent** son agent attitré **3.** *UK fml* [furnish] aménager, installer.

appointee [əpɔɪn'ti:] *n* candidat *m* retenu, candidate *f* retenue, titulaire *mf*.

appointment [ə'pɔɪntmənt] *n* **1.** [arrangement] rendez-vous *m* ■ **to make an ~ with sb** prendre rendez-vous avec qqn ■ **I made an ~ with the dentist** j'ai pris rendez-vous chez le dentiste ■ **they made an ~ to have lunch together** ils se sont donné rendez-vous pour déjeuner ■ **she only sees people by ~** elle ne reçoit que sur rendez-vous ■ **do you have an ~?** avez-vous (pris) rendez-vous? ■ **she has an important ~ to keep** elle doit aller à un rendez-vous important **2.** [nomination] nomination *f*, désignation *f* ■ [office filled] poste *m* ■ [posting] affectation *f* ■ **there are still some ~s to be made** il y a encore quelques postes à pourvoir ■ **'by ~ to Her Majesty the Queen'** COMM 'fournisseur de S.M. la Reine' ▮ [in newspaper] : **'appointments'** 'offres *fpl* d'emploi'.

apportion [ə'pɔ:ʃn] *vt* [blame] répartir ■ [money] répartir, partager.

apposite ['æpəzɪt] *adj* juste, pertinent.

apposition [,æpə'zɪʃn] *n* apposition *f* ■ **a noun/phrase in ~** un nom/une expression en apposition.

appraisal [ə'preɪzl] *n* appréciation *f*, évaluation *f* ➊ **performance ~** [in company] évaluation *f*.

appraise [ə'preɪz] *vt* [object] estimer, évaluer (la valeur de) ■ [importance, quality] évaluer, apprécier ■ **they ~d the damage after the fire** ils évaluèrent les dégâts après l'incendie.

appraising [ə'preɪzɪŋ] *adj* : **she shot him an ~ glance** elle lui a lancé un coup d'œil pour le jauger.

appreciable [ə'pri:ʃəbl] *adj* sensible, appréciable.

appreciably [ə'pri:ʃəblɪ] *adv* sensiblement, de manière appréciable.

appreciate [ə'pri:ʃɪeɪt] ◇ *vt* **1.** [value] apprécier ■ [art] apprécier, goûter ■ [person] apprécier (à sa juste valeur) ■ **they ~ good food** ils apprécient la bonne nourriture **2.** [be grateful for] être reconnaissant de, être sensible à ■ **I would ~ a prompt reply to this letter** je vous serais obligé de bien vouloir me répondre dans les plus brefs délais ■ **I would ~ it if you didn't smoke in the car** je vous serais reconnaissant *OR* je vous saurais gré de ne pas fumer dans la voiture ■ **thanks, I'd really ~ that** ça me rendrait vraiment service **3.** [realize, understand] se rendre compte de, être conscient de ■ **he never ~d its true worth** il ne l'a jamais estimé à sa juste valeur ■ **I do ~ your concern but...** votre sollicitude me touche beaucoup mais...
◇ *vi* [increase in value - currency] monter ; [- goods, property] prendre de la valeur.

appreciation [ə,pri:ʃɪ'eɪʃn] *n* **1.** [thanks] reconnaissance *f* ■ **in ~ of what you have done** en remerciement *OR* pour vous remercier de ce que vous avez fait **2.** [assessment, understanding] évaluation *f*, estimation *f* ■ [of art, literature] critique *f* ■ **she wrote** *OR* **gave an ~ of the play** elle a fait une critique de la pièce ■ **he has a thorough ~ of the situation** il comprend très bien la situation **3.** [increase in value] hausse *f*, augmentation *f*.

appreciative [ə'pri:ʃjətɪv] *adj* **1.** [admiring] admiratif ■ **after a few ~ comments** après quelques remarques élogieuses **2.** [grateful] reconnaissant ■ **I am very ~ of your help** je vous suis très reconnaissant de votre aide.

appreciatively [ə'pri:ʃjətɪvlɪ] *adv* [with enjoyment] joyeusement ■ **he smiled ~** [gratefully] il eut un sourire reconnaissant ; [admiringly] il eut un sourire appréciatif.

apprehend [,æprɪ'hend] *vt fml* **1.** [arrest] arrêter, appréhender **2.** [understand] comprendre, saisir **3.** [fear, dread] redouter, appréhender.

apprehension [,æprɪ'henʃn] *n* **1.** [fear] inquiétude *f*, appréhension *f* **2.** *fml* [arrest] arrestation *f* **3.** *fml* [understanding] compréhension *f*.

apprehensive [,æprɪ'hensɪv] *adj* inquiet, craintif ■ **he is ~ about the interview** il appréhende l'entrevue.

apprehensively [,æprɪ'hensɪvlɪ] *adv* avec appréhension OR inquiétude.

apprentice [ə'prentɪs] ◇ *n* apprenti *m*, - e *f* ■ [in arts and crafts] élève *mf* ■ **she's an electrician's ~** elle est apprentie électricienne.
◇ *comp* : **an ~ toolmaker/butcher** un apprenti outilleur/boucher ■ **an ~ draughtsman** un élève dessinateur ▶ **the Apprentice Boys' Parade** *manifestation annuelle de protestants en Irlande du Nord.*
◇ *vt* : **to ~ sb to sb** : **he is ~d to a sculptor** il suit une formation chez un sculpteur ■ **she is ~d to a violin-maker** elle est en apprentissage chez un luthier.

apprenticeship [ə'prentɪʃɪp] *n* apprentissage *m*.

apprise [ə'praɪz] *vt fml* informer, prévenir ■ **he was ~d of the danger** on l'a averti du danger.

appro ['æprəʊ] (*abbrev of* **approval**) *n UK inf* **on ~** à OR sous condition, à l'essai.

approach [ə'prəʊtʃ] ◇ *vt* **1.** *liter* [person, place] s'approcher de, s'avancer vers ■ **as we ~ed Boston** comme nous approchions de Boston ‖ *fig* [state, time, quality] approcher de ■ **we are ~ing a time when...** le jour approche où... ■ **we have nothing ~ing that colour** nous n'avons rien qui se rapproche de cette couleur ■ **speeds ~ing the speed of light** des vitesses proches de celle de la lumière ■ **it was ~ing Christmas** Noël approchait
2. [consider] aborder ■ **that's not the way to ~ it** ce n'est pas comme cela qu'il faut s'y prendre
3. [speak to] parler à ■ **a salesman ~ed me** un vendeur m'a abordé ■ **I ~ed him about the job** je lui ai parlé du poste ■ **they ~ed him about doing a deal** ils sont entrés en contact avec lui pour conclure un marché.
◇ *vi* [person, vehicle] s'approcher ■ [time, event] approcher, être proche.
◇ *n* **1.** [of person, vehicle] approche *f*, arrivée *f* ■ **she heard his ~** elle l'a entendu venir ■ **the pilot began his ~ to Heathrow** le pilote commença sa descente sur OR vers Heathrow ‖ [of time, death] approche *f*, approches *fpl* ■ **the ~ of spring** la venue du printemps
2. [way of tackling] façon *f*, approche *f* ■ **another ~ to the problem** une autre façon d'aborder le problème ■ **his ~ is all wrong** il s'y prend mal ■ **a new ~ to dealing with unemployment** une nouvelle conception de la lutte contre le chômage ■ **let's try the direct ~** allons-y sans détours
3. [proposal] proposition *f* ■ **the shopkeeper made an ~ to his suppliers** le commerçant a fait une proposition à ses fournisseurs
4. [access] voie *f* d'accès ■ **the ~es to the town** les approches *fpl* OR les abords *mpl* de la ville ■ **the ~es to the beach** les chemins qui mènent à la plage ■ **the ~ to the summit** le chemin qui mène au sommet
5. *fml* [approximation] ressemblance *f*, apparence *f*.

approachable [ə'prəʊtʃəbl] *adj* [place] accessible, approchable ■ [person] abordable, approchable.

approaching [ə'prəʊtʃɪŋ] *adj* [event] prochain, qui est proche ■ [vehicle] qui vient en sens inverse.

approach road *n UK* route *f* d'accès ■ [to motorway] voie *f* de raccordement, bretelle *f*.

approach shot *n* [in golf] approche *f*.

approbation [,æprə'beɪʃn] *n* approbation *f*, consentement *m* ■ **a nod/smile of ~** un signe de tête/un sourire approbateur.

appropriate ◇ *adj* [ə'prəʊprɪət] [moment, decision] opportun ■ [word] bien venu, juste ■ [name] bien choisi ■ [authority] compétent ■ **the level of contribution ~ for** OR **to each country** la contribution appropriée à chaque pays ■ **music/remarks ~ to the occasion** de la musique/des propos de circonstance ■ **take the ~ action** prenez les mesures appropriées ■ **I am not the ~ person to ask** ce n'est pas à moi qu'il faut poser la question.
◇ *vt* [ə'prəʊprɪeɪt] **1.** [take for o.s.] s'approprier, s'emparer de **2.** [set aside] affecter.

appropriately [ə'prəʊprɪətlɪ] *adv* convenablement ■ [speak] avec à-propos, pertinemment ■ [decide] à juste titre ■ **~ dressed** habillé comme il faut OR pour la circonstance ■ **the restaurant is ~ named** le restaurant porte bien son nom.

appropriateness [ə'prəʊprɪətnɪs] *n* [of moment, decision] opportunité *f* ■ [of remark] justesse *f*.

appropriation [ə,prəʊprɪ'eɪʃn] *n* **1.** [taking for o.s.] appropriation *f* **2.** [allocation of money] dotation *f* ■ *US* POL crédit *m* budgétaire ▶ **~s bill** projet *m* de loi de finances ■ **Appropriations Committee** *commission des finances de la Chambre des Représentants qui examine les dépenses.*

approval [ə'pru:vl] *n* **1.** [favourable opinion] approbation *f*, accord *m* ■ **a gesture of ~** un signe approbateur ■ **the plan has your seal of ~, then?** alors tu donnes ton approbation pour le projet? ■ **to meet with sb's ~** obtenir OR recevoir l'approbation de qqn ■ **does the report meet with your ~?** êtes-vous satisfait du rapport? **2.** [sanction] approbation *f*, autorisation *f* ■ **submit the proposal for his ~** soumettez la proposition à son approbation **3.** COMM : **to buy sthg on ~** acheter qqch à OR sous condition ■ **articles sent on ~** marchandises envoyées à titre d'essai.

approve [ə'pru:v] *vt* [plan, proposal etc] approuver ■ [agreement, treaty] ratifier, homologuer ■ **the plan must be ~d by the committee** il faut que le projet reçoive l'approbation du comité ■ **an appliance ~d by the authorities** un appareil agréé par les autorités.
➡ **approve of** *vt insep* approuver ■ [person] avoir une bonne opinion de ■ **they don't ~ of her going out with that man** ils n'apprécient pas du tout qu'elle sorte avec cet homme.

approved [ə'pru:vd] *adj* **1.** [method, practice] reconnu, admis **2.** [authorized] autorisé, admis.

approved school *n nom anciennement donné en Grande-Bretagne à un centre d'éducation surveillé (aujourd'hui appelé "community home").*

approving [ə'pru:vɪŋ] *adj* approbateur, approbatif.

approvingly [ə'pru:vɪŋlɪ] *adv* d'une façon approbatrice ■ **she looked at him ~** elle l'a regardé d'un air approbateur.

approx. (*written abbrev of* **approximately**) *adv* approx., env.

approximate ◇ *adj* [ə'prɒksɪmət] approximatif ■ **the ~ distance to town is 5 miles** il y a à peu près 5 miles d'ici à la ville ■ **he told the ~ truth** il ne disait qu'une partie de la vérité.
◇ *vi* [ə'prɒksɪmeɪt] : **to ~ to sthg** se rapprocher de qqch.

approximately [ə'prɒksɪmətlɪ] *adv* à peu près, environ.

approximation [ə,prɒksɪ'meɪʃn] *n* approximation *f*.

appurtenance [ə'pɜ:tɪnəns] *n (usu pl) fml* accessoire *m* ■ **the property and its ~s** [buildings, gardens etc] la propriété et ses dépendances ; [legal rights & privileges] la propriété et ses circonstances et dépendances.

Apr. (*written abbrev of* **April**) avr.

APR *n* **1.** (*abbrev of* **annualized percentage rate**) TEG *m* **2.** (*abbrev of* **annual purchase rate**) taux *m* annuel.

après-ski [ˌæpreɪ'ski:] ◇ *n* après-ski *m*.
◇ *comp* [clothing, outfit] d'après-ski.

apricot ['eɪprɪkɒt] ◇ *n* **1.** [fruit] abricot *m* ■ [tree] abricotier *m* **2.** [colour] abricot *m inv*.
◇ *comp* **1.** [jam] d'abricots ■ [pie, tart] aux abricots ■ **~ tree** abricotier *m* **2.** [colour, paint, wallpaper] abricot *(inv)*.

April ['eɪprəl] *n* avril *m* ■ **~ Fools' Day** le premier avril ■ **an ~ fool** [person] *personne à qui l'on a fait un poisson d'avril* ; [trick] un poisson d'avril ■ **~ showers** giboulées *fpl* de mars ■ **~ showers bring forth May flowers** *prov* les giboulées de mars apportent les fleurs du printemps *prov*, *see also* **February**.

APRIL FOOLS' DAY

En Grande-Bretagne, le premier avril est l'occasion de farces en tout genre ; en revanche, la tradition du « poisson d'avril » n'existe pas.

a priori [ˌeɪpraɪ'ɔ:raɪ] *adj* a priori.

apron ['eɪprən] *n* **1.** [gen - TECH] tablier *m* ■ **he is tied to his mother's ~ strings** il est pendu aux jupes de sa mère **2.** AERON aire *f* de stationnement.

apropos ['æprəpəʊ] ◇ *adj* opportun, à propos.
◇ *adv* à propos, opportunément.
◆ **apropos of** *prep phr* à propos de.

apse [æps] *n* [in church] abside *f* ■ ASTRON apside *f*.

apt [æpt] *adj* **1.** [person] : **to be ~ to do sthg** faire qqch facilement, être porté à faire qqch ■ **people are ~ to believe the worst** les gens croient facilement le pire ■ **to be ~ to do sthg** être susceptible de faire qqch ■ **it's the little things that are ~ to get forgotten** ce sont les petites choses sans importance que l'on oublie facilement ■ **buttons are ~ to get lost** les boutons se perdent facilement **2.** [suitable] convenable, approprié ■ [remark] juste, qui convient ■ **an ~ expression** une expression heureuse **3.** [clever] doué, intelligent.

apt. (*written abbrev of* **apartment**) appt.

aptitude ['æptɪtju:d] *n* aptitude *f*, disposition *f* ■ **to have an ~ for sthg** avoir une aptitude à OR disposition pour qqch ■ **she shows great ~** elle promet.

aptitude test *n* test *m* d'aptitude.

aptly ['æptlɪ] *adv* à OR avec propos, avec justesse ■ **the dog, Spot, was ~ named** le chien, Spot, portait OR méritait bien son nom ■ **as you so ~ pointed out...** comme tu l'as si bien fait remarquer...

aptness ['æptnɪs] *n* **1.** [suitability] à-propos *m*, justesse *f* **2.** [tendency] tendance *f* **3.** [talent] aptitude *f*, disposition *f*.

Apulia [ə'pju:ljə] *pr n* Pouille *f*, Pouilles *fpl*.

aquacade ['ækwəkeɪd] *n* US spectacle *m* aquatique.

aqualung ['ækwəlʌŋ] *n* scaphandre *m* autonome.

aquamarine [ˌækwəmə'ri:n] ◇ *n* [stone] aigue-marine *f* ■ [colour] bleu vert *m inv*.
◇ *adj* bleu vert *(inv)*.

aquanaut ['ækwənɔ:t] *n* plongeur *m*, scaphandrier *m*.

aquaplane ['ækwəpleɪn] ◇ *n* aquaplane *m*.
◇ *vi* **1.** SPORT faire de l'aquaplane **2.** UK [car] partir en aquaplanage.

aquarium [ə'kweərɪəm] (*pl* **aquariums** OR *pl* **aquaria** [-rɪə]) *n* aquarium *m*.

Aquarius [ə'kweərɪəs] ◇ *pr n* ASTROL & ASTRON Verseau *m*.
◇ *n* : **he's (an) ~** il est (du signe du) Verseau.

aquarobics [ˌækwə'rəʊbɪks] *n* aquagym *f*.

aquatic [ə'kwætɪk] *adj* aquatique ■ [sport] nautique.

aqueduct ['ækwɪdʌkt] *n* aqueduc *m*.

aqueous ['eɪkwɪəs] *adj* aqueux.

aquilegia [ˌækwɪ'li:dʒjə] *n* BOT ancolie *f*.

aquiline ['ækwɪlaɪn] *adj* aquilin ■ [nose] aquilin, en bec d'aigle.

Aquinas [ə'kwaɪnæs] *pr n* : **Saint Thomas ~** saint Thomas d'Aquin.

AR *written abbr of* **Arkansas**.

Arab ['ærəb] ◇ *n* **1.** [person] Arabe *mf* **2.** [horse] cheval *m* arabe.
◇ *adj* arabe ■ **the ~-Israeli Wars** le conflit israélo-arabe ■ **the ~ League** la Ligue arabe.

ARAB

En anglais, le mot *Arab* désigne l'ensemble des ressortissants des pays de culture arabe, et surtout de l'Arabie saoudite. Il n'a pas le sens restreint de « Maghrébin » que l'on rencontre souvent en français : ***the firm was bought by a wealthy Arab family***.

arabesque [ˌærə'besk] *n* arabesque *f*.

Arabia [ə'reɪbjə] *pr n* Arabie *f*.

Arabian [ə'reɪbjən] ◇ *adj* arabe, d'Arabie ■ **the ~ Desert** le désert d'Arabie ■ **the ~ Peninsula** la péninsule d'Arabie ■ **the ~ Sea** la mer d'Arabie ■ **'the ~ Nights, the ~ Nights' Entertainment'** 'les Mille et Une Nuits'.
◇ *n* Arabe *mf*.

Arabic ['ærəbɪk] ◇ *n* arabe *m* ■ **written ~** l'arabe littéral.
◇ *adj* arabe ■ **~ numerals** chiffres *mpl* arabes.

arable ['ærəbl] *adj* arable, cultivable ■ [crops] cultivable ■ [farm] agricole ■ [farmer] : **~ farmer** cultivateur ■ **~ farming** culture *f*.

arachnid [ə'ræknɪd] *n* : **the ~** les arachnides.

Aral Sea ['ɑ:rəl-] *pr n* : **the ~** la mer d'Aral.

Aran ['ærən] *adj* **1.** : **the ~ Islands** les îles *fpl* Aran **2.** [sweater] Aran *(de grosse laine naturelle)*.

Ararat ['ærəræt] *pr n* : **Mount ~** le mont Ararat.

arbiter ['ɑ:bɪtəʳ] *n* arbitre *mf*, médiateur *m*, - trice *f* ■ **magazines act as ~s of modern taste** *fig* les magazines se font les juges OR les arbitres des goûts de notre société.

arbitrarily [UK 'ɑ:bɪtrərəlɪ, US ˌɑ:rbə'trerəlɪ] *adv* arbitrairement.

arbitrariness ['ɑ:bɪtrərɪnɪs] *n* arbitraire *m*, nature *f* arbitraire.

arbitrary ['ɑ:bɪtrərɪ] *adj* arbitraire.

arbitrate ['ɑ:bɪtreɪt] ◇ *vt* arbitrer, juger.
◇ *vi* décider en qualité d'arbitre, arbitrer.

arbitration [ˌɑ:bɪ'treɪʃn] *n* [gen - INDUST] arbitrage *m* ■ **both parties have gone to ~** les deux parties ont recouru à l'arbitrage ■ **they referred the dispute to ~** ils ont soumis le conflit à l'arbitrage ▶ **~ court** OR **tribunal** instance *f* chargée d'arbitrer les conflits sociaux, tribunal *m* arbitral ■ **~ clause** clause *f* compromissoire.

arbitrator ['ɑ:bɪtreɪtəʳ] *n* arbitre *mf*, médiateur *m*, - trice *f* ■ **the dispute has been referred to the ~** le litige a été soumis à l'arbitrage.

arbor ['ɑ:bəʳ] *n* **1.** US = **arbour 2.** TECH arbre *m*, mandrin *m*.

arboreal [ɑ:'bɔ:rɪəl] *adj* [form] arborescent ■ [animal, technique] arboricole.

arboretum [ˌɑ:bə'ri:təm] (*pl* **arboretums** OR *pl* **arboreta** [-tə]) *n* arboretum *m*.

arbour UK, **arbor** US ['ɑ:bəʳ] *n* tonnelle *f*, charmille *f arch*.

arc [ɑ:k] ◇ *n* arc *m*.
◇ *vi* **1.** [gen] décrire un arc **2.** ELEC projeter OR cracher des étincelles.

ARC [ɑ:k] (*abbrev of* **aids-related complex**) *n* ARC *m*.

arcade [ɑː'keɪd] *n* [set of arches] arcade *f*, galerie *f* ■ [shopping] galerie *f* marchande.

Arcadia [ɑː'keɪdjə] *pr n* Arcadie *f* ■ **in ~** en Arcadie.

Arcadian [ɑː'keɪdjən] ◇ *n* Arcadien *m*, - enne *f*.
◇ *adj* arcadien, d'Arcadie.

Arcady ['ɑːkədɪ] *pr n* = **Arcadia**.

arcane [ɑː'keɪn] *adj* mystérieux, ésotérique.

arch [ɑːtʃ] ◇ *n* **1.** ARCHIT arc *m* ■ [in church] arc *m*, voûte *f* **2.** [of eyebrows] courbe *f* ■ [of foot] cambrure *f*, voûte *f* plantaire ■ **to have fallen ~es** MED avoir les pieds plats *OR* ***spec*** un affaissement de la voûte plantaire.
◇ *vt* arquer, cambrer ■ **the cat ~ed its back** le chat fit le gros dos.
◇ *vi* former voûte, s'arquer.
◇ *adj* **1.** [leading] grand, par excellence ■ **my ~ rival** mon principal adversaire **2.** [mischievous] coquin, espiègle ■ [look, smile, tone] malin, espiègle.

archaeology *etc n UK* = **archeology**.

archaeopteryx [ˌɑːkɪ'ɒptərɪks] *n* archéoptéryx *m*.

archaic [ɑː'keɪɪk] *adj* archaïque.

archaism ['ɑːkeɪɪzm] *n* archaïsme *m*.

archangel ['ɑːkˌeɪndʒəl] *n* archange *m*.

archbishop [ˌɑːtʃ'bɪʃəp] *n* archevêque *m*.

ARCHBISHOP

L'archevêque de Cantorbéry est le chef spirituel de l'Église anglicane ; l'archevêque de Westminster est le chef spirituel de l'Église catholique de Grande-Bretagne.

archdeacon [ˌɑːtʃ'diːkən] *n* archidiacre *m*.

archduchess [ˌɑːtʃ'dʌtʃɪs] *n* archiduchesse *f*.

archduke [ˌɑːtʃ'djuːk] *n* archiduc *m*.

arched [ɑːtʃt] *adj* **1.** [roof, window] cintré **2.** [back, foot] cambré ■ [eyebrows] arqué.

archenemy [ˌɑːtʃ'enɪmɪ] (*pl* **archenemies**) *n* pire ennemi *m* ■ **the Archenemy** RELIG Satan.

archeological [ˌɑːkɪə'lɒdʒɪkl] *adj* archéologique.

archeologist [ˌɑːkɪ'ɒlədʒɪst] *n* archéologue *mf*.

archeology [ˌɑːkɪ'ɒlədʒɪ] *n* archéologie *f*.

archer ['ɑːtʃər] *n* archer *m* ■ **the Archer** ASTROL le Sagittaire.

Archers ['ɑːtʃəz] *pr npl* : **The ~** *feuilleton radiophonique diffusé chaque jour par la BBC depuis 1951, décrivant la vie quotidienne dans un village agricole du sud-ouest de l'Angleterre.*

archery ['ɑːtʃərɪ] *n* tir *m* à l'arc.

archetypal [ˌɑːkɪ'taɪpl] *adj* archétype, archétypique, archétypal.

archetype ['ɑːkɪtaɪp] *n* archétype *m*.

archetypical [ˌɑːkɪ'tɪpɪkl] *adj* = **archetypal**.

Archimedes [ˌɑːkɪ'miːdiːz] *pr n* Archimède ■ **~' principle** le principe d'Archimède ■ **~' screw** vis *f* d'Archimède.

archipelago [ˌɑːkɪ'pelɪgəʊ] (*pl* **archipelagoes** *OR pl* **archipelagos**) *n* archipel *m*.

architect ['ɑːkɪtekt] *n* architecte *mf* ■ ***fig*** artisan *m*, créateur *m*, - trice *f*.

architectural [ˌɑːkɪ'tektʃərəl] *adj* architectural.

architecturally [ˌɑːkɪ'tektʃərəlɪ] *adv* au *OR* du point de vue architectural.

architecture ['ɑːkɪtektʃər] *n* [gen - COMPUT] architecture *f*.

architrave ['ɑːkɪtreɪv] *n* architrave *f*.

archive ['ɑːkaɪv] ◇ *n* [repository] archives *fpl*, dépôt *m* ■ **the ~s** les archives *fpl*.
◇ *comp* [photo] d'archives.
◇ *vt* archiver.

archive file *n* COMPUT fichier *m* archives.

archivist ['ɑːkɪvɪst] *n* archiviste *mf*.

archly ['ɑːtʃlɪ] *adv* d'un air espiègle *OR* malicieux.

archpriest [ˌɑːtʃ'priːst] *n* archiprêtre *m*.

archway ['ɑːtʃweɪ] *n* porche *m* ■ [long] galerie *f*, arcades *fpl*.

arc lamp, arc light *n* lampe *f* à arc ■ CIN & TV sunlight *m*.

arctic ['ɑːktɪk] ◇ *adj* **1.** arctique **2.** ***fig*** [cold] glacial.
◇ *n US* [overshoe] couvre-chaussure *m*.
Arctic ['ɑːktɪk] ◇ *pr n* : **the Arctic (Ocean)** l'(océan *m*) Arctique *m* ■ **in the Arctic** dans l'Arctique.
◇ *adj* arctique.

Arctic Circle *pr n* : **the ~** le cercle polaire arctique.

arctic skua *n* labbe *m* parasite.

arctic tern *n* sterne *f* arctique.

ardent ['ɑːdənt] *adj* [keen] passionné ■ **an ~ admirer** un fervent admirateur.

ardently ['ɑːdəntlɪ] *adv* ardemment, passionnément.

ardour *UK*, **ardor** *US* ['ɑːdər] *n* ardeur *f*, passion *f*.

arduous ['ɑːdjʊəs] *adj* ardu, difficile ■ [work, task] laborieux, pénible ■ [path] ardu, raide ■ [hill] raide, escarpé.

arduously ['ɑːdjʊəslɪ] *adv* péniblement, laborieusement.

are ◇ *(vb weak form* [ər], *strong form* [ɑːr]*)* ▷ **be**.
◇ *n* [ɑːr] are *m*.

area ['eərɪə] ◇ *n* **1.** [surface size] superficie *f*, aire *f* ■ **the garden is 500 m² in ~, the garden has** *OR* **covers an ~ of 500 m²** le jardin a une superficie de 500 m² **2.** [region] région *f* ■ MIL territoire *m* ■ [small] secteur *m*, zone *f* ■ **a residential/shopping ~** un quartier résidentiel/commercial ● **a conservation ~** un site classé ■ **~ of outstanding natural beauty** *zone naturelle protégée* **3.** [part, section] partie *f* ■ [of room] coin *m* ■ **living/eating ~** coin salon/salle à manger **4.** [of study, investigation, experience] domaine *m*, champ *m* ■ **in the foreign policy ~** dans le domaine de la politique étrangère.
◇ *comp* [manager, office] régional.

area code *n UK* code *m* postal ■ *US* TELEC indicatif *m* de zone.

areca ['ærɪkə] *n* : **~ (tree)** aréquier *m* ■ **~ nut** noix *f* d'arec.

arena [ə'riːnə] *n* arène *f* ■ **when he entered the electoral ~** ***fig*** quand il est entré en lice pour les élections.

aren't [ɑːnt] = **are not**.

Argentina [ˌɑːdʒən'tiːnə] *pr n* Argentine *f* ■ **in ~** en Argentine.

Argentine ['ɑːdʒəntaɪn] ◇ *n* Argentin *m*, - e *f* [country] Argentine *f* ■ **the ~** l'Argentine.
◇ *adj* argentin.

Argentinian [ˌɑːdʒən'tɪnɪən] ◇ *n* Argentin *m*, - e *f*.
◇ *adj* argentin ■ **the ~ embassy** l'ambassade *f* d'Argentine.

argon ['ɑːgɒn] *n* argon *m*.

Argonaut ['ɑːgənɔːt] *n* : **the ~s** les Argonautes *mpl*.

argot ['ɑːgəʊ] *n* argot *m*.

arguable ['ɑːgjʊəbl] *adj* **1.** [questionable] discutable, contestable **2.** [plausible] défendable ■ **it is ~ that...** on peut soutenir que...

arguably ['ɑːgjʊəblɪ] *adv* possiblement ■ **the Beatles are ~ the most popular group of all time** on pourrait dire *OR* on peut soutenir que les Beatles sont le groupe le plus populaire de tous les temps.

argue ['ɑːgjuː] ◇ *vi* **1.** [quarrel] se disputer ■ **to ~ (with sb) about sthg** se disputer (avec qqn) au sujet de *OR* à propos de qqch **2.** [reason] argumenter ■ **she ~d for/against raising taxes** elle a soutenu qu'il fallait/ne fallait pas augmenter les impôts ■ **we ~d (about it) all day** nous (en) avons discuté toute la journée ■ **he ~d from the historical aspect** ses arguments étaient de nature historique ■ **the facts ~ for the evolutionary**

theory les faits plaident en faveur de la théorie évolutionniste ▪ LAW témoigner ▪ **the evidence ~s against him** les preuves sont contre lui.
◇ *vt* **1.** [debate] discuter, débattre ▪ **a well-~d case** une cause bien présentée *OR* défendue ▪ **why do you always have to ~ the toss** *inf OR* **point?** pourquoi faut-il toujours que tu ergotes *OR* chicanes? **2.** [person] : **he ~d me into/out of staying** il m'a persuadé/dissuadé de rester **3.** [maintain] soutenir, affirmer **4.** *fml* [indicate] indiquer.
◆ **argue out** *vt sep* régler ▪ **I left them to ~ it out** je les ai laissés chercher une solution.

argument ['ɑ:gjʊmənt] *n* **1.** [quarrel] dispute *f* ▪ **they had an ~ about politics** ils se sont disputés à propos de politique ▪ **he had an ~ with a lamppost** *hum* il a rencontré un réverbère **2.** [debate] discussion *f*, débat *m* ▪ **for the sake of ~** à titre d'exemple ▪ **you should listen to both sides of the ~** vous devriez écouter les deux versions de l'histoire ▪ **she got the better of the ~** elle l'a emporté dans la discussion **3.** [reasoning] argument *m* ▪ **I didn't follow his (line of) ~** je n'ai pas suivi son raisonnement ▪ **their ~ was that the plan was too expensive** ils soutenaient que le projet était trop cher ▪ **there is a strong ~ in favour of the proposal** il y a de bonnes raisons pour soutenir *OR* appuyer cette proposition **4.** [of book, play] argument *m*, sommaire *m*.

argumentation [,ɑ:gjʊmen'teɪʃn] *n* argumentation *f*.

argumentative [,ɑ:gjʊ'mentətɪv] *adj* ergoteur, chicaneur.

argy-bargy [,ɑ:dʒɪ'bɑ:dʒɪ] *n (U) UK* chamailleries *fpl*.

argyle [ɑ:'gaɪl] ◇ *adj* à motifs de losanges.
◇ *n* chaussette *f* avec des losanges.

aria ['ɑ:rɪə] *n* aria *f*.

Ariadne [,ærɪ'ædnɪ] *pr n* Ariane.

Arian ['eərɪən] ◇ *n* Arien *m*, - enne *f*.
◇ *adj* arien.

arid ['ærɪd] *adj* **1.** *liter* sec, sèche *f*, desséché **2.** *fig* [of no interest] aride, ingrat ▪ [fruitless] stérile.

aridity [æ'rɪdətɪ] *n* *liter* & *fig* aridité *f*, stérilité *f*.

Aries ['eəri:z] ◇ *pr n* ASTROL & ASTRON Bélier *m*.
◇ *n* : **I'm an ~** je suis (du signe du) Bélier.

aright [ə'raɪt] *adv* bien, correctement ▪ **to set things ~** arranger les choses.

arise [ə'raɪz] (*pret* **arose** [ə'rəʊz], *pp* **arisen** [ə'rɪzn]) *vi* **1.** [appear, happen] survenir, se présenter ▪ **a doubt arose in his mind** un doute est apparu dans son esprit ▪ **if the need ~s** en cas de besoin ▪ **if the occasion ~s** si l'occasion se présente **2.** [result] résulter ▪ **a problem that ~s from this decision** un problème qui résulte *OR* découle de cette décision ▪ **matters arising from the last meeting** des questions soulevées lors de la dernière réunion **3.** *lit* [person] se lever ▪ [sun] se lever, paraître.

aristocracy [,ærɪ'stɒkrəsɪ] (*pl* **aristocracies**) *n* aristocratie *f*.

aristocrat [*UK* 'ærɪstəkræt, *US* ə'rɪstəkræt] *n* aristocrate *mf*.

aristocratic [*UK* ,ærɪstə'krætɪk, *US* ə,rɪstə'krætɪk] *adj* aristocratique.

Aristotelian [,ærɪstɒ'ti:ljən] ◇ *adj* aristotélicien.
◇ *n* Aristotélicien *m*, - enne *f*.

Aristotle ['ærɪstɒtl] *pr n* Aristote.

arithmetic ◇ *n* [ə'rɪθmətɪk] arithmétique *f*.
◇ *adj* [,ærɪθ'metɪk] arithmétique.

arithmetical [,ærɪθ'metɪkl] *adj* arithmétique.

arithmetician [ə,rɪθmə'tɪʃn] *n* arithméticien *m*, - enne *f*.

Arizona [,ærɪ'zəʊnə] *pr n* Arizona *m* ▪ **in ~** dans l'Arizona.

ark [ɑ:k] *n* arche *f* ▪ **this machine must have come out of the ~** *hum* cet appareil doit remonter au déluge *OR* est vieux comme Hérode ▶ **the Ark of the Covenant** l'arche d'alliance.

Arkansas ['ɑ:kənsɔ:] *pr n* Arkansas *m* ▪ **in ~** dans l'Arkansas.

arm [ɑ:m] ◇ *n* **1.** ANAT bras *m* ▪ **he carried a book under his ~** il portait un livre sous le bras ▪ **to hold sb/sthg in one's ~s** tenir qqn/qqch dans ses bras ▪ **with his wife on his ~** avec sa femme à son bras ▪ **he put his ~ round her** il a passé son bras autour d'elle ▪ **with ~s folded** les bras croisés ▪ **to welcome sb/sthg with open ~s** accueillir qqn/qqch à bras ouverts ▪ **within ~'s reach** à portée de la main ▪ **we kept him at ~'s length** nous l'avons tenu à bout de bras ▶ **a list as long as your ~** une liste qui n'en finit pas *OR* interminable ▪ **the long ~ of the law** le bras de la justice ▪ **I'd give my right ~ for that job** je donnerais cher *OR* n'importe quoi pour obtenir cet emploi ▪ **it cost me an arm and a leg** *inf* ça m'a coûté la peau des fesses **2.** [of sea, machinery] bras *m* ▪ [of clothing] manche *f* ▪ [of spectacle frames] branche *f* ▪ [of furniture] bras *m*, accoudoir *m* ▪ [of record player] bras *m* **3.** [section] section *f*, branche *f* ▪ **BBC Enterprises is the commercial ~ of the BBC** BBC Enterprises est la branche commerciale de la BBC.
◇ *vt* **1.** [person, country] armer ▪ **to ~ o.s. with the facts/evidence** *fig* s'armer de faits/preuves **2.** [missile] munir d'une (tête d')ogive ▪ [bomb, fuse] armer.
◇ *vi* s'armer, prendre les armes.
◆ **arm in arm** *adv phr* bras dessus bras dessous.

armada [ɑ:'mɑ:də] *n* armada *f*.

armadillo [,ɑ:mə'dɪləʊ] (*pl* **armadillos**) *n* tatou *m*.

Armageddon [,ɑ:mə'gedn] *n* Apocalypse *f* ▪ *fig* apocalypse *f*.

armament ['ɑ:məmənt] *n* **1.** [fighting force] force *f* de frappe **2.** [weaponry] armement *m*, matériel *m* de guerre **3.** [preparation for war] armement *m*.
◆ **armaments** *npl* armement *m*.

armature ['ɑ:mə,tjʊəʳ] *n* [gen] armature *f* ▪ [of magnet] armature *f* ▪ [of motor] induit *m* ▪ ZOOL carapace *f*.

armband ['ɑ:mbænd] *n* brassard *m* ▪ [mourning] brassard *m* de deuil, crêpe *m*.

arm candy ['ɑ:mkændɪ] *n* *hum* & *pej* jeune *f* et jolie compagne.

armchair ['ɑ:mtʃeəʳ] ◇ *n* fauteuil *m*.
◇ *comp* en chambre ▪ **an ~ gardener/traveller** un jardinier/voyageur en chambre.

armed [ɑ:md] *adj* **1.** [with weapons] armé ▪ **they were ~ with knives** ils étaient armés de couteaux ▪ **the minister arrived at the press conference ~ with pages of statistics** *fig* le ministre est arrivé à la conférence de presse armé *OR* muni de pages entières de statistiques ▶ **~ conflict** conflit *m* armé ▪ **~ robbery** LAW vol *m* *OR* attaque *f* à main armée ▪ **~ to the teeth** armé jusqu'aux dents **2.** [missile] muni d'une (tête d')ogive ▪ [bomb, fuse] armé.

-armed *in cpds* aux bras... ▪ **long~** aux bras longs ▪ **one~** à un seul bras.

armed forces *npl* forces *fpl* armées.

Armenia [ɑ:'mi:njə] *pr n* Arménie *f* ▪ **in ~** en Arménie.

Armenian [ɑ:'mi:njən] ◇ *n* **1.** [person] Arménien *m*, - enne *f* **2.** LING arménien *m*.
◇ *adj* arménien.

armful ['ɑ:mfʊl] *n* brassée *f* ▪ **in ~s, by the ~** par pleines brassées, par brassées entières.

armhole ['ɑ:mhəʊl] *n* emmanchure *f*.

armistice ['ɑ:mɪstɪs] *n* armistice *m*.

Armistice Day *n* l'Armistice *m*.

armor *US n* = **armour**.

Armorica [ɑ:'mɒrɪkə] *pr n* Armorique *f*.

Armorican [ɑ:'mɒrɪkən] ◇ *n* Armoricain *m*, - e *f*.
◇ *adj* armoricain.

armour *UK*, **armor** *US* ['ɑ:mər] *n* **1.** HIST armure *f* ▪ **in full ~** armé de pied en cap **2.** *(U)* MIL [plating] blindage *m* ▪ [vehicles] blindés *mpl* ▪ [forces] forces *fpl* blindées **3.** [of animal] carapace *f*.

armour-clad *UK*, **armor-clad** *US* *adj* blindé ▪ [ship] blindé, cuirassé.

armoured *UK*, **armored** *US* ['ɑ:məd] *adj* **1.** MIL blindé **2.** [animal] cuirassé, à carapace.

armoured car *n* voiture *f* blindée.

armourer *UK*, **armorer** *US* ['ɑ:mərər] *n* armurier *m*.

armour plate *n* blindage *m* ▪ [on ship] cuirasse *f*.

armour-plated [-'pleɪtɪd] *adj* blindé.

armour plating *n* = **armour plate**.

armoury *UK* (*pl* **armouries**), **armory** *US* (*pl* **armories**) ['ɑ:mərɪ] *n* arsenal *m*, dépôt *m* d'armes ▪ *fig* [resources] arsenal *m* ▪ *US* [arms factory] armurerie *f*, fabrique *f* d'armes.

armpit ['ɑ:mpɪt] *n* aisselle *f*.

armrest ['ɑ:mrest] *n* accoudoir *m*.

arms [ɑ:mz] ◇ *npl* **1.** [weapons] armes *fpl* ▪ **to ~!** aux armes! ▪ **to bear ~** porter les armes ▪ **to take up ~ against sb/sthg** s'insurger contre qqn/qqch ◐ **the unions are up in ~ over the new legislation** les syndicats s'élèvent *OR* partent en guerre contre la nouvelle législation **2.** HERALD armes *fpl*, armoiries *fpl*.
◇ *comp* : **~ control** contrôle *m* des armements ▪ **~ dealer** armurier *m* ▪ **~ manufacturer** fabricant *m* d'armes, armurier *m* ▪ **the ~ trade** le commerce d'armes.

arm's-length *adj* **1.** [not intimate] distant, froid **2.** COMM : **~ price** *prix fixé dans les conditions normales de la concurrence*.

arms race *n* course *f* aux armements.

arm-twisting [-'twɪstɪŋ] *n (U) inf* pressions *fpl*.

arm-wrestle *vi* : **to ~ with sb** faire une partie de bras de fer avec qqn.

arm wrestling *n* bras *m* de fer.

army ['ɑ:mɪ] (*pl* **armies**) ◇ *n* **1.** MIL armée *f* (de terre) ▪ **to go into** *OR* **to join the ~** s'engager ▪ **he was drafted into the ~** il a été appelé sous les drapeaux ▪ **an ~ of occupation** une armée d'occupation **2.** *fig* [multitude] foule *f*, multitude *f*.
◇ *comp* [life, nurse, truck, uniform] militaire ▪ [family] de militaires ▪ **~ corps** corps *m* d'armée ▪ **~ officer** officier *m* de l'armée de terre.

A-road *n UK route nationale*.

aroma [ə'rəʊmə] *n* arôme *m*.

aromatherapy [ə,rəʊmə'θerəpɪ] *n* aromathérapie *f*.

aromatic [,ærə'mætɪk] ◇ *adj* aromatique.
◇ *n* aromate *m*.

arose [ə'rəʊz] *pt* ▷ **arise**.

around [ə'raʊnd] ◇ *adv* **1.** [in all directions] autour ▪ **the fields all ~** les champs tout autour ▪ **for five miles ~** sur *OR* dans un rayon de cinq miles
2. [nearby] pas loin ▪ **stay** *OR* **stick ~** reste dans les parages ▪ **he's ~ somewhere** il n'est pas loin, il est dans le coin ▪ **will you be ~ this afternoon?** tu seras là cet après-midi? ▪ **see you ~!** à un de ces jours!
3. [in existence] : **that firm has been ~ for years** cette société existe depuis des années ▪ **he's one of the most promising actors ~ at the moment** c'est un des acteurs les plus prometteurs que l'on puisse voir en ce moment ▪ **there wasn't much money ~ in those days** les gens n'avaient pas beaucoup d'argent à l'époque
4. [here and there] ici et là ▪ **to travel ~** voyager ◐ **I don't know my way ~ yet** je suis encore un peu perdu ▪ **he's been ~** *inf* [has travelled widely] il a pas mal roulé sa bosse ; [is experienced] il n'est pas né d'hier
5. = **round**.
◇ *prep* **1.** [encircling] autour de ▪ **the area ~ Berlin** les alentours *mpl* *OR* les environs *mpl* de Berlin ▪ **~ the world in 80 days** le tour du monde en 80 jours ▪ **the tree measures two metres ~ the trunk** l'arbre mesure deux mètres de circonférence ‖ *fig* **find a way (to get) ~ the problem** trouvez un moyen de contourner le problème ▪ **my keys are somewhere ~ here** mes clés sont quelque part par ici
2. [through] : **they travelled ~ Europe** ils ont voyagé à travers l'Europe ▪ **we strolled ~ town** nous nous sommes promenés en ville
3. [approximately] autour de ▪ **~ five o'clock** vers cinq heures ▪ **~ 1920** vers *OR* aux alentours de 1920 ▪ **he's ~ your age** il a environ *OR* à peu près votre âge.

around-the-clock *adj* : **~ protection/surveillance** protection *f* /surveillance *f* 24 heures sur 24.

arousal [ə'raʊzl] *n* excitation *f*, stimulation *f*.

arouse [ə'raʊz] *vt* **1.** [stimulate] stimuler, provoquer ▪ **the sound ~d their curiosity/suspicions** le bruit a éveillé leur curiosité/leurs soupçons ▪ **his pleading ~d their contempt** ses implorations n'ont suscité que leur mépris ▪ **sexually ~d** excité (sexuellement) **2.** [awaken] réveiller, éveiller ▪ **he ~d her from a deep sleep** il l'a tirée d'un profond sommeil.

arpeggio [ɑ:'pedʒɪəʊ] *n* arpège *m*.

arraign [ə'reɪn] *vt* traduire en justice ▪ *fig* accuser, mettre en cause.

arrange [ə'reɪndʒ] ◇ *vt* **1.** [put in order] ranger, mettre en ordre ▪ [clothing, room] arranger ▪ [flowers] arranger, disposer **2.** [organize, plan] organiser, arranger ▪ **I can ~ a loan** je peux m'arranger pour obtenir un prêt ▪ **I'll ~ a table for eight o'clock** je vais réserver une table pour vingt heures ▪ **it has been ~d for us to travel by train** il a été décidé *OR* convenu que nous voyagerions en train ▪ **let's ~ a time to meet** fixons (une heure pour) un rendez-vous ▪ **he has something ~d** *OR* **has ~d something for the weekend** il a quelque chose de prévu pour le week-end ▪ **here is the first instalment, as ~d** [money] voici le premier versement, comme convenu ▪ **don't worry, I'll ~ it** ne vous en faites pas, je vais m'en occuper **3.** [dispute] régler, arranger **4.** MUS & THEAT adapter ▪ **he ~d the concerto for guitar** il a adapté le concerto pour la guitare.
◇ *vi* prendre des dispositions, s'arranger ▪ **I've ~d with the boss to leave early tomorrow** je me suis arrangé avec le patron pour partir de bonne heure demain ▪ **he's ~d for the car to be repaired** il a fait le nécessaire pour faire réparer la voiture.

arranged marriage [ə'reɪndʒd-] *n* mariage *m* arrangé.

arrangement [ə'reɪndʒmənt] *n* **1.** *(usu pl)* [plan] disposition *f*, arrangement *m* ▪ **what are the travel ~s?** comment le voyage est-il organisé? ▪ **I haven't made any ~s for the journey yet** je n'ai pas encore fait de *OR* mes préparatifs pour le voyage ▪ **could you make ~s to change the meeting?** pouvez-vous faire le nécessaire pour changer la date de la réunion? ▪ **he made ~s to leave work early** il s'est arrangé pour quitter son travail de bonne heure **2.** [understanding, agreement] arrangement *m* ▪ **we can come to an** *OR* **some ~ on the price** pour le prix, nous pouvons nous arranger ▪ **he came to an ~ with the bank** il est parvenu à un accord avec la banque **3.** [layout] arrangement *m*, disposition *f* ▪ [of room] aménagement *m* ▪ [of clothing, hair] arrangement *m* **4.** MUS & THEAT adaptation *f*, arrangement *m*.
◆ **by arrangement** *adv phr* : **price by ~** prix à débattre ▪ **special designs by ~** autres modèles sur demande ▪ **by ~ with the town hall** avec l'autorisation de la mairie ▪ **viewing by ~ with the owner** pour visiter, prenez rendez-vous avec *OR* contactez le propriétaire.

arranger [ə'reɪndʒər] *n* MUS arrangeur *m*, - euse *f*.

arrant ['ærənt] *adj* fini, parfait.

array [ə'reɪ] ◇ *n* **1.** [collection] ensemble *m* impressionnant, collection *f* ▪ **a distinguished ~ of people** une assemblée de gens distingués ▪ **there was a fine ~ of cakes in the window** il y avait une belle sélection de gâteaux en vitrine ‖ LAW, COMPUT & MATHS tableau *m* **2.** MIL rang *m*, ordre *m* ▪ **in battle ~** en ordre de bataille ▪ **in close ~** en rangs serrés **3.** [fine clothes] parure *f*, atours *mpl* ▪ [ceremonial dress] habit *m* d'apparat.
◇ *vt* **1.** [arrange] disposer, étaler ▪ MIL [troops] déployer, disposer **2.** *lit* [adorn] habiller, revêtir.

arrears [əˈrɪəz] *npl* arriéré *m* ■ **taxes in ~** arriéré d'impôts ■ **I'm worried about getting into ~** j'ai peur de m'endetter ■ **we're 6 months in ~ on the loan payments** nous devons 6 mois de traites ■ **to be paid a month in ~** être payé un mois après ■ **she's in ~ with her correspondence** elle a du retard dans sa correspondance.

arrest [əˈrest] ◇ *vt* **1.** [police] arrêter, appréhender **2.** *fml* [growth, development] arrêter ■ [slow down] entraver, retarder ■ **in an effort to ~ unemployment/inflation** pour essayer d'enrayer le chômage/l'inflation ■ **~ed development** MED [physical] arrêt *m* de croissance ; [mental] atrophie *f* de la personnalité ■ **to ~ judgment** LAW surseoir à un jugement, suspendre l'exécution d'un jugement
3. *fml* [attention] attirer, retenir.
◇ *n* **1.** [detention] arrestation *f* ■ **you're under ~!** vous êtes en état d'arrestation! ■ **he was put under ~** il a été arrêté ■ **they made several ~s** ils ont procédé à plusieurs arrestations ▮ MIL : **to be under ~** être aux arrêts ▶ **open/close ~** arrêts *mpl* simples/de rigueur
2. [sudden stopping] arrêt *m*, suspension *f*.

arrestable [əˈrestəbl] *adj* [offence] répréhensible.

arrester [əˈrestər] *n* AERON : **~ gear** [on aircraft carrier] dispositif *m* d'appontage.

arresting [əˈrestɪŋ] *adj* saisissant, frappant.

arrestingly [əˈrestɪŋlɪ] *adv* : **~ beautiful** d'une beauté frappante.

arresting officer *n policier qui a procédé à l'arrestation.*

arrival [əˈraɪvl] *n* **1.** [of person, train, aeroplane etc] arrivée *f* ■ **on** *OR* **upon ~** à l'arrivée ■ **the ~s board/lounge** le tableau/le salon des arrivées **2.** [newcomer] : **late ~s should report to reception** les retardataires doivent se présenter à la réception ■ **he's a new ~** c'est un nouveau venu ■ **the new** *OR* **latest ~ in their family** leur dernier-né *OR* dernière-née **3.** COMM [of goods] arrivage *m* **4.** [advent] avènement *m*.

arrive [əˈraɪv] *vi* **1.** [person, train, aeroplane etc] arriver ■ **as soon as you ~** dès votre arrivée, dès que vous arriverez ■ **the baby ~d three weeks early** le bébé est arrivé *OR* né avec trois semaines d'avance ■ **to ~ on the scene** survenir ■ **the time has ~d for us to take action, the time for action has ~d** le moment est venu pour nous d'agir **2.** *inf* [achieve success] réussir, arriver ■ **she finally ~d after years of singing in backstreet bars** elle connut enfin le succès après avoir chanté pendant des années dans des bars miteux.
◆ **arrive at** *vt insep* [decision] arriver *OR* parvenir à ■ [perfection] atteindre ■ **we finally ~d at the conclusion that...** nous en sommes finalement arrivés à la conclusion que... ▮ [price] fixer ■ **they finally ~d at a price** ils se sont finalement mis d'accord sur un prix.

arrogance [ˈærəgəns] *n* arrogance *f*, morgue *f*.

arrogant [ˈærəgənt] *adj* arrogant, insolent.

arrogantly [ˈærəgəntlɪ] *adv* de manière arrogante, avec arrogance.

arrogate [ˈærəgeɪt] *vt fml* **1.** [claim unjustly] revendiquer à tort, s'arroger ■ [victory] s'attribuer **2.** [assign unjustly] attribuer injustement.

arrow [ˈærəʊ] ◇ *n* flèche *f* ■ **to loose** *OR* **to shoot** *OR* **to let fly an ~** décocher une flèche ■ **the ball flew as straight as an ~ into the net** la balle alla voler tout droit dans le filet.
◇ *vt* **1.** [indicate - on list] cocher ; [- on road sign] flécher **2.** [in editing] indiquer au moyen d'une flèche.

arrowhead [ˈærəʊhed] *n* fer *m*, pointe *f* de flèche.

arrowroot [ˈærəʊruːt] *n* BOT marante *f* ■ CULIN arrow-root *m*.

arse▲ [ɑːs] *n UK* cul△ *m* ■ **move** *OR* **shift your ~** pousse ton cul△ ■ **he's a pain in the ~** c'est un emmerdeur△ ■ **he fell** *OR* **went ~ over tit** il est tombé cul par-dessus tête△.
◆ **arse about△, arse around△** *vi insep UK* déconner△.

arsehole▲ [ˈɑːshəʊl] *n UK* trou *m* du cul▲ ■ **don't be such an ~** ne sois pas si con△.

arse-licker▲ [-ˌlɪkər] *n UK* lèche-cul▲ *m inv*.

arsenal [ˈɑːsənl] *n* arsenal *m*.

arsenic [ˈɑːsnɪk] ◇ *n* arsenic *m* ■ **'Arsenic and Old Lace'** *Capra* 'Arsenic et vieilles dentelles'.
◇ *comp* : **~ poisoning** empoisonnement *m* à l'arsenic.

arson [ˈɑːsn] *n* incendie *m* criminel *OR* volontaire ■ **to commit ~** provoquer (volontairement) un incendie.

arsonist [ˈɑːsənɪst] *n* incendiaire *mf* ■ [maniac] pyromane *mf*.

art [ɑːt] ◇ *vb arch* ▷ **be**.
◇ *n* **1.** [gen] art *m* ■ [school subject] dessin *m* ■ **she studies ~** elle est étudiante en art, ≃ elle fait les Beaux-Arts ■ **~ for ~'s sake** l'art pour l'art ■ **the ~ of ballet** l'art du ballet ■ **I'd love to go to ~ classes** j'aimerais beaucoup suivre des cours de dessin ■ **a work of ~** une œuvre d'art ▶ **~s and crafts** artisanat *m* (d'art) **2.** [skill] art *m*, habileté *f* ■ **the ~ of survival** l'art de survivre ■ **she has got cooking down to a real** *OR* **fine ~** la cuisine chez elle, c'est du grand art **3.** [cunning] ruse *f*, artifice *m* ■ [trick] artifice *m*, stratagème *m*.
◇ *comp* [collection, critic, exhibition] d'art ■ **~ student** étudiant *m*, - e *f* en art ▶ **~ gallery** [museum] musée *m* d'art ; [shop] galerie *f* d'art ■ **~ school** ≃ école *f* des Beaux-Arts.
◆ **arts** ◇ *npl* UNIV lettres *fpl* ■ **Faculty of Arts (and Letters)** faculté *f* des lettres (et sciences humaines) ■ **the Arts Council (of Great Britain)** *organisme public britannique de promotion des arts.*
◇ *comp* UNIV : **~s student** étudiant *m*, - e *f* de *OR* en lettres (et sciences humaines) ■ **I have an ~s degree** j'ai une licence de lettres ■ **~s centre** ≃ musée *m* d'art.

Art Deco [-ˈdekəʊ] *n* Art *m* déco.

artefact [ˈɑːtɪfækt] *n* = **artifact**.

arterial [ɑːˈtɪərɪəl] *adj* artériel ■ **~ road** *UK* route *f OR* voie *f* à grande circulation ■ **~ line** *UK* RAIL grande ligne *f*.

arteriosclerosis [ɑːˌtɪərɪəʊsklɪəˈrəʊsɪs] *n* artériosclérose *f*.

artery [ˈɑːtərɪ] (*pl* **arteries**) *n* artère *f* ■ [road] artère *f*, route *f OR* voie *f* à grande circulation.

artesian well [ɑːˈtiːzjən] *n* puits *m* artésien.

art form *n* moyen *m* d'expression artistique.

artful [ˈɑːtfʊl] *adj* astucieux, habile ■ [crafty] rusé, malin ■ **~ dodger** rusé *m*, - e *f (du nom d'un jeune voleur habile dans le roman de Dickens 'Oliver Twist').*

artfully [ˈɑːtfʊlɪ] *adv* [skilfully] habilement, avec finesse ■ [craftily] astucieusement, avec astuce.

artfulness [ˈɑːtfʊlnɪs] *n* [skill] habileté *f*, finesse *f* ■ [cunning] astuce *f*, ruse *f*.

arthouse [ˈaːthaʊs] ◇ *n* [cinema] cinéma *m* d'art et d'essai.
◇ *adj* [cinema, film] d'art et d'essai.

arthritic [ɑːˈθrɪtɪk] ◇ *adj* arthritique.
◇ *n* arthritique *mf*.

arthritis [ɑːˈθraɪtɪs] *n* arthrite *f*.

arthropod [ˈɑːθrəpɒd] *n* arthropode *m*.

Arthur [ˈɑːθər] *pr n* [king] Arthur.

Arthurian [ɑːˈθjʊərɪən] *adj* du roi Arthur.

artic [ɑːˈtɪk] *n UK inf* = **articulated lorry**.

artichoke [ˈɑːtɪtʃəʊk] *n* artichaut *m* ■ **~ hearts** cœurs *mpl* d'artichauts.

article [ˈɑːtɪkl] ◇ *n* **1.** [object] objet *m* ■ **an ~ of clothing** un vêtement ▶ **it's the genuine ~!** *inf* c'est du vrai de vrai! **2.** [in press] article *m* **3.** LAW [clause, provision] article *m* ■ **the ~s of a contract** les stipulations d'un contrat ▶ **~ of faith** article de foi ■ **the Thirty-Nine Articles** RELIG *les trente-neuf articles de foi de l'Église anglicane* ■ **~s of war** *US* code *m* de justice militaire **4.** GRAM article *m* **5.** COMM article *m*, marchandise *f*.
◇ *vt UK* [to trade] mettre en apprentissage ■ [to profession] mettre en stage.

◆ **articles** *npl UK* **1.** COMM : **~s of association** statuts *mpl (d'une société à responsabilité limitée)* **2.** LAW : **~s of apprenticeship** contrat *m* d'apprentissage ▪ **to do** *OR* **to serve one's ~s** faire son apprentissage.

articled clerk ['ɑːtɪkld-] *n UK* clerc *m* d'avoué *(lié par un contrat d'apprentissage).*

articulate ◇ *adj* [ɑː'tɪkjʊlət] **1.** [person] qui s'exprime bien ▪ [speech] clair, net **2.** [manner of speech] bien articulé, distinct **3.** ANAT & BOT articulé.
◇ *vt* [ɑː'tɪkjʊleɪt] **1.** [words, syllables] articuler **2.** *fig* [wishes, thoughts] exprimer clairement **3.** ANAT & BOT articuler.
◇ *vi* articuler.

articulated lorry [ɑː'tɪkjʊleɪtɪd-] *n UK* semi-remorque *f.*

articulately [ɑː'tɪkjʊlətlɪ] *adv* [speak] distinctement ▪ [explain] clairement.

articulation [ɑː,tɪkjʊ'leɪʃn] *n* ANAT, BOT & LING articulation *f.*

articulatory [ɑː'tɪkjʊlətrɪ] *adj* articulatoire.

artifact ['ɑːtɪfækt] *n* objet *m (fabriqué).*

artifice ['ɑːtɪfɪs] *n* **1.** [trick] artifice *m*, ruse *f* ▪ [scheme] stratagème *m* **2.** [cleverness] art *m*, adresse *f.*

artificial [,ɑːtɪ'fɪʃl] *adj* **1.** [man-made] artificiel ▪ COMM synthétique, artificiel ▪ **~ fertilizer** engrais *m* chimique ▪ **~ flavouring** parfum *m* artificiel *OR* synthétique ▪ **an ~ leg** une jambe artificielle ▪ **~ light** la lumière artificielle ▪ **~ limb** prothèse *f*, membre *m* artificiel **2.** [affected - person] factice, étudié ▪ **an ~ smile** un sourire forcé **3.** LAW : **~ person** personne *f* morale *OR* civique *OR* juridique.

artificial insemination *n* insémination *f* artificielle.

artificial intelligence *n* intelligence *f* artificielle.

artificiality [,ɑːtɪfɪʃɪ'ælətɪ] *(pl* **artificialities***) n* manque *m* de naturel.

artificially [,ɑːtɪ'fɪʃəlɪ] *adv* artificiellement.

artificial respiration *n* respiration *f* artificielle.

artillery [ɑː'tɪlərɪ] *(pl* **artilleries***) n* artillerie *f.*

artilleryman [ɑː'tɪlərɪmən] *(pl* **artillerymen** [-mən]*) n* artilleur *m.*

artisan [,ɑːtɪ'zæn] *n* artisan *m.*

artist ['ɑːtɪst] *n* [gen - ART] artiste *mf* ▪ *fig* spécialiste *mf.*

artiste [ɑː'tiːst] *n* artiste *mf.*

artistic [ɑː'tɪstɪk] *adj* artistique ▪ [design, product] de bon goût, décoratif ▪ [style, temperament] artiste ▪ **she is an ~ child** cette enfant a des dons artistiques.

artistically [ɑː'tɪstɪklɪ] *adv* avec art, artistiquement.

artistry ['ɑːtɪstrɪ] *n* art *m*, talent *m* artistique.

artless ['ɑːtlɪs] *adj* **1.** [without deceit] naturel, ingénu **2.** [without skill] grossier.

Art Nouveau [ɑːnuː'vəʊ] *n* Art *m* nouveau, Modern Style *m.*

arts [ɑːts] *npl* & *comp* = **art**.

artsy ['ɑːtzɪ] *(comp* **artsier**, *superl* **artsiest***) adj inf* = **arty**.

artsy-craftsy [,ɑːtzɪ'krɑːftzɪ] *adj inf* = **arty-crafty**.

artwork ['ɑːtwɜːk] *n* **1.** [illustration] iconographie *f*, illustration *f* **2.** TYPO documents *mpl.*

arty ['ɑːtɪ] *(comp* **artier**, *superl* **artiest***) adj inf pej* [person] qui se veut artiste *OR* bohème ▪ [clothing] de style bohème ▪ [object, film, style] prétentieux.

arty-crafty [,ɑːtɪ'krɑːftɪ] *adj inf pej* [person] qui se veut artiste *OR* bohème ▪ [object, style] bohème, qui se veut artisanal.

arty-farty [,ɑːtɪ'fɑːtɪ] *adj inf pej* [person] prétentieux, poseur ▪ [play, film] prétentieux.

arum ['eərəm] *n* arum *m* ▪ **~ lily** calla *f.*

Aryan ['eərɪən] ◇ *n* Aryen *m*, - enne *f.*
◇ *adj* aryen.

as [([weak form], [əz]) ([strong form], [æz])] ◇ *conj* **1.** [while] alors que ▪ **the phone rang as I was coming in** le téléphone s'est mis à sonner alors que *OR* au moment où j'entrais ▪ **I listened as she explained the plan to them** je l'ai écoutée leur expliquer le projet ▪ **as a student, he worked part-time** lorsqu'il était étudiant, il travaillait à mi-temps ▪ **as he advanced, I retreated** (au fur et) à mesure qu'il avançait, je reculais ▌ [when] : **take two aspirins as needed** prenez deux aspirines en cas de douleur
2. [like] comme, ainsi que ▪ **A as in Able** a comme Anatole ▪ **as shown by the unemployment rate** comme *OR* ainsi que le montre le taux de chômage ▪ **as is often the case** comme c'est souvent le cas ▪ **as I told you** comme je vous l'ai dit ▪ **leave it as it is** laissez-le tel qu'il est *OR* tel quel ➤ **to buy sthg as is** acheter qqch en l'état ▪ **my mistake! as you were!** c'est moi qui me trompe! faites comme si je n'avais rien dit!
3. [since] puisque ▪ **let her drive, as it's her car** laissez-la conduire, puisque c'est sa voiture
4. *fml* [concessive use] : **try as they might, they couldn't persuade her** malgré tous leurs efforts, ils n'ont pu la convaincre ▪ **powerful as the president is, he cannot stop his country's disintegration** quelque pouvoir qu'ait le président, il ne peut empêcher la ruine de son pays
5. [with 'the same', 'such'] : **at the same time as last week** à la même heure que la semaine dernière ▪ **such a problem as only an expert can solve** un problème que seul un expert peut résoudre.
◇ *prep* en tant que, comme ▪ **as her husband, he cannot testify** étant son mari, il ne peut pas témoigner ▪ **he was dressed as a clown** il était habillé en clown ▪ **with Vivien Leigh as Scarlett O'Hara** avec Vivien Leigh dans le rôle de Scarlett O'Hara.
◇ *adv* [in comparisons] : **it's twice as big** c'est deux fois plus grand ▪ **it costs half as much again** ça coûte la moitié plus ▪ **as... as** aussi... que ▪ **as often as possible** aussi souvent que possible ▪ **I worked as much for you as for me** j'ai travaillé autant pour toi que pour moi.

◆ **as against** *prep phr* contre.

◆ **as and when** ◇ *conj phr* : **we'll buy new equipment as and when it's required** nous achèterons du nouveau matériel en temps voulu *OR* quand ce sera nécessaire.
◇ *adv phr inf* en temps voulu.

◆ **as for** *prep phr* quant à ▪ **as for me, I don't intend to go** pour ma part *OR* quant à moi, je n'ai pas l'intention d'y aller ▪ **as for your threats, they don't scare me in the least** pour ce qui est de *OR* quant à vos menaces, elles ne me font pas peur du tout.

◆ **as from** *prep phr* = **as of**.

◆ **as if** *conj phr* comme si ▪ **he moved as if to strike him** il a fait un mouvement comme pour le frapper ▪ **as if it mattered!** comme si ça avait aucune importance! ▪ **as if!** *hum* tu parles!

◆ **as it is** *adv phr* **1.** [in present circumstances] les choses étant ce qu'elles sont
2. [already] déjà.

◆ **as it were** *adv phr* pour ainsi dire.

◆ **as of** *prep phr* à partir de ▪ **as of yesterday** depuis hier.

◆ **as such** *adv phr* **1.** [properly speaking] véritablement, à proprement parler ▪ **it's not a contract as such, more a gentleman's agreement** ce n'est pas un véritable contrat *OR* pas un contrat à proprement parler *OR* pas véritablement un contrat, mais plutôt un accord entre hommes de parole
2. [in itself] même, en soi ▪ **the place as such isn't great** l'endroit même *OR* en soi n'est pas terrible
3. [in that capacity] à ce titre, en tant que tel ▪ **I'm his father and as such, I insist on knowing** je suis son père et à ce titre j'insiste pour qu'on me mette au courant.

◆ **as though** *conj phr* = **as if**.

◆ **as to** *prep phr* **1.** [regarding] : **I'm still uncertain as to the nature of the problem** j'hésite encore sur la nature du problème
2. = **as for**.

◆ **as well** *adv phr* **1.** [in addition] en plus ▪ [also] aussi ▪ **he bought the house and the land as well** il a acheté la maison et la propriété aussi ▪ **and then the car broke down as well!** et par-dessus le marché la voiture est tombée en panne!
2. [with modal verbs] : **you may as well tell me the truth** autant me dire *OR* tu ferais aussi bien de me dire la vérité ▪ **now that we're here, we might as well stay** puisque nous sommes

là, autant rester ■ **shall we go to the cinema? – we might as well** et si on allait au cinéma? – pourquoi pas? ■ **she was angry, as well she might be** elle était furieuse, et ça n'est pas surprenant ■ **perhaps I'd better leave – that might be as well** peut-être vaudrait-il mieux que je m'en aille – je crois que ça vaut mieux ■ **it would be as well not to break it** ce serait mieux si on pouvait éviter de le casser ■ **I decided not to write back – just as well really** j'ai décidé de ne pas répondre – c'est mieux comme ça ■ **it would be just as well if you were present** il vaudrait mieux que vous soyez là ■ **it's just as well he missed his flight** c'est une bonne chose qu'il ait manqué l'avion.

◆ **as well as** *conj phr* [in addition to] en plus de.

◆ **as yet** *adv phr* encore ■ **I don't have the answer as yet** je n'ai pas encore la réponse ■ **an as yet undisclosed sum** une somme qui n'a pas encore été révélée.

ASA *pr n* **1.** *UK* (*abbrev of* **Advertising Standards Agency**) ≃ BVP *m* **2.** (*abbrev of* **American Standards Association**) ASA *f*.

asafoetida, asafetida *US* [,æsəf'etɪdə] *n* ase *f* fétide.

AS-level [eɪ'eslevl] (*abbrev of* **Advanced Supplementary Level**) *n* SCOL *matière supplémentaire pour l'examen A-level.*

asap (*abbrev of* **as soon as possible**) *adv* aussitôt *OR* dès que possible.

asbestos [æs'bestəs] ◇ *n* amiante *f*, asbeste *f*.
◇ *comp* [board, cord] d'amiante.

asbestosis [,æsbes'təʊsɪs] *n* asbestose *f*.

ascend [ə'send] ◇ *vi* monter ■ [in time] remonter ■ **to ~ (back) to sthg** remonter à qqch.
◇ *vt* [stairs] monter ■ [ladder] monter à ■ [mountain] gravir, faire l'ascension de ■ [river] remonter ■ [throne] monter sur ■ **: their ~ to power** leur ascension jusqu'au pouvoir.

ascendancy, ascendency [ə'sendənsɪ] *n* **1.** [position of power] ascendant *m*, empire *m* ■ **Japan has gained ~ over its competitors in the electronics market** le Japon domine ses concurrents sur le marché de l'électronique **2.** [rise] montée *f*.

ascendant, ascendent [ə'sendənt] ◇ *adj* dominant, puissant ■ ASTROL ascendant.
◇ *n* ascendant *m* ■ **his star is in the ~** ASTROL son étoile est à l'ascendant ■ **his business is in the ~** *fig* ses affaires prospèrent.

ascender [ə'sendəʳ] *n* **1.** [in mountaineering] ascendeur *m*, autobloqueur *m* **2.** TYPO hampe *f* montante.

ascending [ə'sendɪŋ] *adj* **1.** [rising] ascendant **2.** [increasing] : **in ~ order** en ordre croissant **3.** BOT montant.

ascension [ə'senʃn] *n* ascension *f*.
◆ **Ascension** *pr n* = **Ascension Island**.

Ascension Day *n* jour *m OR* fête *f* de l'Ascension.

Ascension Island *pr n* île *f* de l'Ascension.

ascent [ə'sent] *n* **1.** [of mountain] ascension *f* **2.** [incline] montée *f* **3.** [in time] retour *m* ■ **the line of ~** l'ascendance *f* **4.** [in rank] montée *f*, avancement *m* ■ **: their ~ to power** leur ascension jusqu'au pouvoir.

ascertain [,æsə'teɪn] *vt fml* établir, constater ■ **the police ~ed their names and addresses** la police a vérifié leurs nom et adresse ■ **to ~ that sthg is the case** vérifier *OR* s'assurer que qqch est vrai ■ **he ~ed that it was safe to continue** il s'est assuré qu'on pouvait continuer sans danger.

ascetic [ə'setɪk] ◇ *adj* ascétique.
◇ *n* ascète *mf*.

ascetically [ə'setɪklɪ] *adv* [live] comme un/une ascète.

asceticism [ə'setɪsɪzm] *n* ascétisme *m*.

ASCII ['æskɪ] (*abbrev of* **American Standard Code for Information**) *n* ASCII *m* ➲ **~ file** fichier *m* ASCII.

ascorbic acid [ə'skɔːbɪk-] *n* acide *m* ascorbique.

Ascot ['æskət] *pr n champ de courses près de Windsor.*

ascribe [ə'skraɪb] *vt* attribuer ■ [fault, blame] imputer ■ **heart attacks are often ~d to stress** les crises cardiaques sont souvent attribuées *OR* imputées au stress.

ascription [ə'skrɪpʃn] *n* attribution *f*, imputation *f*.

ASE (*abbrev of* **American Stock Exchange**) *pr n deuxième place boursière des États-Unis.*

aseptic [,eɪ'septɪk] *adj* aseptique.

asexual [,eɪ'sekʃʊəl] *adj* asexué.

ash [æʃ] *n* **1.** [from fire, cigarette] cendre *f* ■ **cigarette ~** cendre de cigarette ■ **the fire reduced the house to ~es** l'incendie a réduit la maison en cendres ■ **~es to ~es, dust to dust** RELIG tu n'es que poussière et tu retourneras en poussière ➲ **~ bin** [for ashes] cendrier *m* ; [for rubbish] poubelle *f*, boîte *f* à ordures **2.** [tree, wood] frêne *m*.
◆ **Ashes** *npl* [in cricket] *trophée que se disputent l'Angleterre et l'Australie.*

ASH [æʃ] (*abbrev of* **Action on Smoking and Health**) *pr n ligue antitabac britannique.*

ashamed [ə'ʃeɪmd] *adj* confus, honteux ■ **to be ~ (of oneself)** avoir honte ■ **he's ~ of his behaviour/of having cried** il a honte de sa conduite/d'avoir pleuré ■ **I'm ~ of you** j'ai honte de toi, tu me fais honte ■ **I'm ~ to say that...** j'avoue à ma grande honte que... ■ **there is nothing to be ~ of** il n'y a pas de quoi avoir honte.

ash blond ◇ *adj* blond cendré (*inv*).
◇ *n* blond *m* cendré.

ash can *n US* poubelle *f*.

ashen ['æʃn] *adj* **1.** [ash-coloured] cendré, couleur de cendre ■ [face] blême, livide **2.** [of ashwood] en (bois de) frêne.

ashen-faced *adj* blême.

ashlar ['æʃləʳ] *n* pierre *f* de taille.

ashore [ə'ʃɔːʳ] ◇ *adv* à terre ■ **he swam ~** il a nagé jusqu'à la rive ■ **debris from the wreck was washed ~** des morceaux de l'épave ont été rejetés sur la côte ■ **to go ~** débarquer ■ **the ship put the passengers ~ at Plymouth** le navire a débarqué les passagers à Plymouth.
◇ *adj* à terre.

ashram ['æʃrəm] *n* ashram *m*.

ashtray ['æʃtreɪ] *n* cendrier *m*.

Ash Wednesday *n* mercredi *m* des Cendres.

Asia [*UK* 'eɪʃə, *US* 'eɪʒə] *pr n* Asie *f* ■ **in ~** en Asie.

Asia Minor *pr n* Asie *f* Mineure.

Asian [*UK* 'eɪʃn, *US* 'eɪʒn] ◇ *n* [from Asia] Asiatique *mf* ■ *UK* [from Indian subcontinent] *personne originaire du sous-continent indien.*
◇ *adj* [from Asia] asiatique ■ *UK* [from Indian subcontinent] *originaire du sous-continent indien.*

ASIAN

Les Britanniques emploient le mot *Asian* pour désigner les habitants de l'Inde et des pays limitrophes ; ainsi, l'expression ***the Asian community in Birmingham*** fait référence aux personnes d'origine indienne, pakistanaise et bangladaise qui habitent à Birmingham. Pour traduire « Asiatique », il est souvent préférable de choisir l'expression désignant l'habitant du pays en question : ***a Chinese person, a Japanese person***, etc.

Asian American ◇ *adj* américain d'origine asiatique.
◇ *n* Américain *m*, - e *f* d'origine asiatique.

Asian flu *n* grippe *f* asiatique.

Asiatic [*UK* ,eɪʃɪ'ætɪk, *US* ,eɪʒɪ'ætɪk] ◇ *adj* asiatique.
◇ *n* Asiatique *mf*.

aside [ə'saɪd] ◇ *adv* de côté, à part ■ **these problems ~, we have been very successful** à part ces problèmes, ce fut un véritable succès ■ **I stepped ~ to let her pass** je me suis écarté

pour la laisser passer ▪ **he took her ~** il l'a prise à part ▪ **we've been putting money ~ for the trip** nous avons mis de l'argent de côté pour le voyage.
◇ *n* aparté *m* ▪ **he said something to her in an ~** il lui a dit quelque chose en aparté.
◆ **aside from** *prep phr* **1.** [except for] sauf **2.** *US* [as well as] en plus de.

A-side *n* face *f* A *(d'un disque)*.

asinine ['æsɪnaɪn] *adj* [person, behaviour] stupide, sot, sotte *f*.

ask [ɑ:sk] ◇ *vt* **1.** [for opinion, information] : **to ~ sb sthg** demander qqch à qqn ▪ **she ~ed him about his job** elle lui a posé des questions sur son travail ▪ **may I ~ you a question?** puis-je vous poser une question? ▪ **if you ~ me** si vous voulez mon avis ▪ **but how? I ~ you!** *inf* mais comment? je vous le demande! ▪ **don't ~ me!** *inf* est-ce que je sais, moi? ▪ **no one ~ed you!** *inf* on ne t'a rien demandé! **2.** [request] demander, solliciter ▪ **he ~ed them a favour** il leur a demandé un service ▪ **to ~ sb to do sthg** demander à qqn de faire qqch ▪ **I ~ed them to be quiet** je leur ai demandé de ne pas faire de bruit ▪ **she ~ed to have the bags brought up** elle a demandé que les bagages soient montés ▪ **he ~ed to be admitted** il a demandé à être admis ▪ **that's ~ing too much of me** tu m'en demandes trop | COMM : **to ~ a price** demander un prix ▪ **what are you ~ing for it?** combien en voulez-vous *OR* demandez-vous? **3.** [invite] inviter ▪ **they ~ed her to join them** ils l'ont invitée à se joindre à eux ▪ **he ~ed her to the pictures** il l'a invitée au cinéma.
◇ *vi* demander ▪ **he was ~ing about the job** il s'informait *OR* se renseignait sur le poste ▪ **it's there for the ~ing** il suffit de demander.
◆ **ask after** *vt insep* : **she ~ed after you** elle a demandé de vos nouvelles ▪ **I ~ed after her health** je me suis informé de sa santé.
◆ **ask along** *vt sep* inviter ▪ **we ~ed them along (with us)** nous leur avons proposé de venir avec nous.
◆ **ask around** *vi insep* se renseigner ▪ **I ~ed around about rents** je me suis renseigné sur les loyers.
◆ **ask back** *vt sep* [invite again] réinviter ▪ [for reciprocal visit] inviter ▪ **she ~ed us back for dinner** elle nous a rendu l'invitation à dîner.
◆ **ask for** *vt insep* demander ▪ **she ~ed for her book back** elle a demandé qu'on lui rende son livre ▪ **you're just ~ing for trouble!** tu cherches des ennuis! ▸ **he was ~ing for it!** il l'a cherché! ▪ **she left him – he had ~ed for it** elle l'a quitté – il l'a voulu, il l'a eu!
◆ **ask in** *vt sep* inviter à entrer ▪ **he ~ed us in for a drink** il nous a invités à (entrer) prendre un verre.
◆ **ask out** *vt sep* inviter à sortir ▪ **they ~ed us out for dinner/to the theatre** ils nous ont invités au restaurant/au théâtre.
◆ **ask round** *vt sep UK* inviter (à venir).

askance [ə'skæns] *adv* du coin de l'œil ▪ **he looked ~ at her** il l'a regardée d'un air méfiant.

askew [ə'skju:] ◇ *adv* obliquement, de travers.
◇ *adj US* **something's ~ here** il y a quelque chose qui cloche.

asking price ['ɑ:skɪŋ-] *n* prix *m* de départ, prix *m* demandé.

asleep [ə'sli:p] *adj* endormi ▪ **she's ~** elle dort ▪ **to be fast** *OR* **sound ~** dormir profondément *OR* à poings fermés ▪ **to fall ~** s'endormir.

ASLEF ['æzlef] (*abbrev of* **Associated Society of Locomotive Engineers and Firemen**) *pr n syndicat des cheminots en Grande-Bretagne*.

A/S-level *n examen facultatif complétant les A-levels*.

asocial [,eɪ'səʊʃl] *adj* asocial.

asp [æsp] *n* ZOOL aspic *m*.

asparagus [ə'spærəgəs] *n (U)* asperge *f* ▸ **~ tips** pointes *fpl* d'asperges.

ASPCA (*abbrev of* **American Society for the Prevention of Cruelty to Animals**) *pr n société protectrice des animaux aux États-Unis*.

aspect ['æspekt] *n* **1.** [facet] aspect *m*, côté *m* ▪ **we should examine all ~s of the problem** nous devrions étudier le problème sous tous ses aspects **2.** *lit* [appearance] air *m*, aspect *m* **3.** [outlook] orientation *f*, exposition *f* ▪ **a house with a northern/southern ~** une maison exposée au nord/sud **4.** GRAM aspect *m*.

asperity [æ'sperətɪ] (*pl* **asperities**) *n fml* **1.** [of manner, voice] aspérité *f* **2.** [of person] rudesse *f* **3.** [hardship] rigueur *f*.

aspersions [ə'spɜ:ʃnz] *npl* : **to cast ~ on sb** dénigrer qqn.

asphalt ['æsfælt] ◇ *n* asphalte *m*.
◇ *comp* [road, roof] asphalté.
◇ *vt* asphalter.

asphyxia [əs'fɪksɪə] *n* asphyxie *f*.

asphyxiate [əs'fɪksɪeɪt] ◇ *vi* s'asphyxier.
◇ *vt* asphyxier.

asphyxiating [əs'fɪksɪeɪtɪŋ] *adj* asphyxiant.

asphyxiation [əs,fɪksɪ'eɪʃn] *n* asphyxie *f*.

aspic ['æspɪk] *n* gelée *f* ▪ **eggs in ~** œufs *mpl* en aspic.

aspidistra [,æspɪ'dɪstrə] *n* aspidistra *m*.

aspirant ['æspɪrənt] ◇ *n* ambitieux *m*, - euse *f*.
◇ *adj* ambitieux.

aspirate ◇ *vt* ['æspəreɪt] aspirer.
◇ *adj* ['æspərət] aspiré.
◇ *n* ['æspərət] aspirée *f*.

aspiration [,æspə'reɪʃn] *n* **1.** [ambition] aspiration *f* **2.** LING aspiration *f*.

aspirator ['æspəreɪtər] *n* aspirateur *m*.

aspire [ə'spaɪər] *vi* **1.** aspirer ▪ **he ~s to political power** il aspire au pouvoir politique ▪ **she ~s to** *OR* **after higher things** elle vise plus haut, ses ambitions vont plus loin ▪ **to ~ to fame** briguer la célébrité **2.** *arch* & *lit* [rise] monter, s'élever.

aspirin ['æspərɪn] *n* aspirine *f* ▪ [tablet] (comprimé *m* d') aspirine *f*.

aspiring [ə'spaɪərɪŋ] *adj* ambitieux ▪ *pej* arriviste.

ass [æs] *n* **1.** [donkey] âne *m* ▪ **she-~** ânesse *f* **2.** *inf* [idiot] imbécile *mf* ▪ **he made a complete ~ of himself last night** il s'est conduit en parfait imbécile *OR* s'est parfaitement ridiculisé hier soir **3.** ▲ *US* [bottom] cul△ *m* ▪ **you can bet your ~ I'll do it!** tu peux être sûr que je le ferai! ▪ **get your ~ over here!** amène-toi! ▪ **this weather is a pain in the ~** ce temps me fait vraiment chier▲ ▪ **they want your ~** ils veulent ta peau **4.** ▲ *US phr* **a piece of ~** [sex] une baise▲ ; [woman] une fille baisable▲.

assail [ə'seɪl] *vt* attaquer, assaillir ▪ *fig* **he ~ed her with questions** il l'a harcelée de questions ▪ **~ed by doubt** assailli par le doute.

assailant [ə'seɪlənt] *n fml* agresseur *m*, assaillant *m*, - e *f*.

assassin [ə'sæsɪn] *n* assassin *m*.

assassinate [ə'sæsɪneɪt] *vt* assassiner.

assassination [ə,sæsɪ'neɪʃn] *n* assassinat *m* ▪ **~ attempt** tentative *f* d'assassinat.

assault [ə'sɔ:lt] ◇ *n* **1.** [attack] agression *f* ▪ **he is accused of ~** il est accusé de voie de fait | *fig* **a brave ~ on widely held beliefs** une attaque courageuse contre des croyances très répandues ▸ **common ~** voie *f* de fait simple ▪ **~ and battery** LAW coups *mpl* et blessures *fpl* **2.** MIL assaut *m* ▪ **to lead an ~** se lancer à l'assaut **3.** [climbing] assaut *m*.
◇ *vt* **1.** [gen] agresser ▪ [sexually] violenter ▪ **his rough language ~ed their sensibilities** *fig* son langage grossier blessait leur sensibilité **2.** LAW se livrer à des voies de fait sur ▪ [sexually] se livrer à des violences sexuelles sur.

assault course *n* parcours *m* du combattant.

assault rifle *n* fusil *m* d'assaut.

assay [ə'seɪ] ◇ *vt* **1.** [analyse - metal] essayer **2.** *arch* [attempt] essayer, tenter.
◇ *n* essai *m*.

assemblage [ə'semblɪdʒ] *n* **1.** [collection] collection *f*, groupe *m* ▪ [of people] assemblée *f* **2.** [process] montage *m*, assemblage *m*.

assemble [ə'sembl] ◇ *vt* **1.** assembler, amasser ▪ [people] rassembler, réunir ▪ [troops] rassembler **2.** [put together] monter, assembler.
◇ *vi* se rassembler, se réunir.

assembler [ə'semblər] *n* assembleur *m*.

assembly [ə'semblɪ] (*pl* **assemblies**) *n* **1.** [meeting - gen] réunion *f*, assemblée *f* ▪ **the right of ~** la liberté de réunion **2.** POL assemblée *f* ▪ **National Assembly** l'Assemblée *f* nationale **3.** SCH *réunion de tous les élèves de l'établissement* ▪ **~ hall** *hall où les enfants se réunissent le matin avant d'entrer en classe* **4.** MIL rassemblement *m* **5.** [building - process] montage *m*, assemblage *m* ; [- end product] assemblage *m* ▪ **the engine ~** le bloc moteur **6.** COMPUT assemblage *m*.

assembly language *n* langage *m* d'assemblage.

assembly line *n* chaîne *f* de montage ▪ **to work on an ~** travailler à la chaîne.

assembly point *n* point *m* de rassemblement.

assembly room *n* **1.** [gen] salle *f* de réunion ▪ [at town hall] salle *f* des fêtes **2.** [industrial] atelier *m* de montage.

assent [ə'sent] ◇ *vi* consentir, acquiescer ▪ **they finally ~ed to the proposition** ils ont fini par donner leur assentiment à la proposition.
◇ *n* consentement *m*, assentiment *m* ▪ **to give one's ~ to sthg** donner son assentiment à qqch.

assert [ə'sɜːt] *vt* **1.** [proclaim] affirmer, maintenir ▪ [innocence] affirmer, protester de **2.** [insist on] défendre, revendiquer ▪ **we must ~ our right to speak** nous devons faire valoir notre droit à la parole ▮ [impose] : **to ~ o.s.** se faire respecter, s'imposer ▪ **I had to ~ my authority** il a fallu que j'affirme mon autorité *OR* que je m'impose.

assertion [ə'sɜːʃn] *n* affirmation *f*, assertion *f* ▪ [of rights] revendication *f*.

assertive [ə'sɜːtɪv] *adj* assuré, autoritaire ▪ *pej* péremptoire.

assertively [ə'sɜːtɪvlɪ] *adv* fermement ▪ *pej* de façon péremptoire.

assertiveness [ə'sɜːtɪvnɪs] *n* manière *f* assurée ▪ *pej* arrogance *f*.

assertiveness training *n* stage *m* d'affirmation de soi.

assess [ə'ses] *vt* **1.** [judge] estimer, évaluer **2.** [value] fixer *OR* déterminer la valeur de ▪ **to ~ a property for taxation** évaluer *OR* calculer la valeur imposable d'une propriété **3.** [taxes] évaluer ▪ **~ed income** revenu *m* imposable.

assessment [ə'sesmənt] *n* **1.** [judgment] estimation *f*, évaluation *f* ▪ **what's your ~ of the situation?** comment voyez-vous *OR* jugez-vous la situation? **2.** *UK* SCH contrôle *m* des connaissances ▪ [on report card] appréciation *f* des professeurs ▪ **methods of ~** méthodes *fpl* d'évaluation **3.** [valuation - of amount due] détermination *f*, évaluation *f* ; [- of tax] calcul *m* (de la valeur imposable).

assessor [ə'sesər] *n* **1.** expert *m* ▪ **~ of taxes** *US* inspecteur *m* des contributions directes **2.** LAW (juge *m*) assesseur *m*.

asset ['æset] *n* avantage *m*, atout *m*.
◆ **assets** *npl* [possession] avoir *m*, capital *m* ▪ COMM, FIN & LAW actif *m* ▪ **our total ~s** tous nos biens ▪ **~s and liabilities** l'actif *m* et le passif.

asset-stripper *n* dépeceur *m* d'entreprise.

asset-stripping [-,strɪpɪŋ] *n achat d'entreprises pour revente des actifs*.

asseveration [ə,sevə'reɪʃn] *n fml* déclaration *f* ▪ [of good faith, innocence] protestation *f*.

asshole▲ ['æshəʊl] *n US* = **arsehole**.

assiduous [ə'sɪdjʊəs] *adj* assidu.

assiduously [ə'sɪdjʊəslɪ] *adv* assidûment.

assign [ə'saɪn] ◇ *vt* **1.** [allot] assigner, attribuer ▪ **the room was ~ed to study groups** la salle fut affectée *OR* réservée aux groupes d'étude ▪ **I ~ed her the task of writing the report** je l'ai chargée de la rédaction du rapport **2.** [appoint] nommer, désigner ▪ **he's been ~ed to Moscow** il a été affecté à Moscou **3.** [ascribe] : **to ~ a reason for sthg** donner la raison de qqch ▪ **we ~ a value to X** nous attribuons *OR* assignons une valeur à X **4.** LAW céder, transférer ▪ **she ~ed the copyright to the school** elle a fait cession du droit d'auteur à l'école.
◇ *n* cessionnaire *mf*.

assignation [,æsɪg'neɪʃn] *n* **1.** [meeting] rendez-vous *m* clandestin **2.** [assignment] attribution *f* ▪ [of money] allocation *f* ▪ [of person] affectation *f* **3.** LAW cession *f*, transfert *m*.

assignee [,æsaɪ'niː] *n* cessionnaire *mf*.

assignment [ə'saɪnmənt] *n* **1.** tâche *f* ▪ [official] mission *f* ▪ SCH devoir *m* **2.** [appointment] attribution *f* ▪ [of money] allocation *f* ▪ [of person] affectation *f* **3.** LAW cession *f*, transfert *m* ▪ **~ of contract** *cession des droits et obligations découlant d'un contrat*.

assignor [ə'saɪnər] *n* cédant *m*, - e *f*.

assimilate [ə'sɪmɪleɪt] ◇ *vt* **1.** [food, information] assimiler **2.** [immigrants] intégrer.
◇ *vi* s'assimiler, s'intégrer ▪ **foreigners find it difficult to ~ into a new culture** les étrangers ont du mal à s'adapter *OR* s'intégrer à une autre culture.

assimilation [ə,sɪmɪ'leɪʃn] *n* [gen - LING] assimilation *f*.

assist [ə'sɪst] ◇ *vt* **1.** [help] aider, assister ▪ **a man is ~ing police with their enquiries** un homme aide la police dans ses investigations **2.** [with money] : **~ed by the town hall** avec le concours de la mairie ▪ **~ed passage** billet *m* subventionné.
◇ *vi* **1.** [help] aider, prêter secours ▪ **she ~ed at the operation** elle a apporté son assistance pendant l'opération **2.** *arch* [attend] assister.

assistance [ə'sɪstəns] *n* aide *f*, secours *m* ▪ **may I be of ~ to you?** puis-je vous être utile? ▪ **to come to sb's ~** venir au secours de qqn ▪ **with the financial ~ of the university** avec le concours financier de l'université.

assistant [ə'sɪstənt] ◇ *n* assistant *m*, - e *f*, aide *mf* ▪ **foreign language ~** SCH assistant *m*, - e *f* (en langue étrangère) ; UNIV lecteur *m*, - trice *f* (en langue étrangère) ▪ **teaching ~** SCH auxiliaire *mf*.
◇ *comp* [director, judge, librarian, secretary] adjoint ▪ **~ manager** sous-directeur *m*, directeur *m* adjoint ▪ **~ professor** *US* ≃ maître-assistant *m* ▪ **~ teacher** [primary] instituteur *m*, - trice *f* ; [secondary] professeur *mf (qui ne dirige pas de section)*.

assistant referee *n* SPORT assistant-arbitre *m*.

assisted suicide *n* suicide *m* assisté.

assize [ə'saɪz] *n* réunion *f* ▪ LAW assises *fpl* ▪ **~ court, court of ~s** cour *f* d'assises.

assoc 1. *written abbr of* **association 2.** *written abbr of* **associated**.

associate ◇ *vt* [ə'səʊʃɪeɪt] associer ▪ **the problems ~d with nuclear power** les problèmes relatifs à l'énergie nucléaire ▪ **I don't ~ you with that kind of activity** je ne t'imagine pas dans ce genre d'activité ▪ **that kind of behaviour is often ~d with an unhappy childhood** ce type de comportement est souvent lié à une enfance malheureuse.
◇ *vi* [ə'səʊʃɪeɪt] : **to ~ with sb** fréquenter qqn.
◇ *n* [ə'səʊʃɪət] **1.** [partner] associé *m*, - e *f* ▪ LAW complice *mf* **2.** [of club] membre *m*, associé *m*, - e *f* ➊ **Associate in Arts (degree)** *(titulaire d'un) diplôme universitaire américain de lettres*, ≃ DEUG ▪ **Associate in Science (degree)** *(titulaire d'un) diplôme universitaire américain de sciences*, ≃ DEUG.
◇ *adj* [ə'səʊʃɪət] associé, allié ▪ **I'm only an ~ member of the organisation** je suis seulement membre associé de l'organisation ➊ **~ judge** juge *m* assesseur ▪ **Associate Justice** *US* juge *m* de la Cour Suprême.

associated [ə'səʊʃɪeɪtɪd] *adj* associé.

associate professor *n US* ≃ maître *m* de conférences.

association [əˌsəʊsɪ'eɪʃn] *n* **1.** [grouping] association *f*, société *f* **2.** [involvement] association *f*, fréquentation *f* ▪ **through long ~ with the medical profession** à force de fréquenter la profession médicale ▪ **this programme was made in ~ with Belgian television** ce programme a été fait en collaboration avec la télévision belge **3.** [of ideas] association *f* ▪ **by ~ of ideas** par association d'idées, de fil en aiguille ▪ **that trip has many unhappy ~s for me** ce voyage me rappelle bien des choses pénibles.

Association football *n UK fml* football *m* association.

associative [ə'səʊʃjətɪv] *adj* [gen - COMPUT] associatif.

assonance ['æsənəns] *n* assonance *f*.

assort [ə'sɔːt] ◇ *vt* classer, ranger.
◇ *vi* s'assortir ▪ **to ~ with sthg** s'assortir à qqch.

assorted [ə'sɔːtɪd] *adj* **1.** [various] varié, divers ▪ **in ~ sizes** en différentes tailles **2.** [matched] assorti.

assortment [ə'sɔːtmənt] *n* assortiment *m*, collection *f* ▪ [of people] mélange *m* ▪ **there was a good ~ of cakes** il y avait un grand choix *OR* une bonne sélection de gâteaux.

asst *written abbr of* **assistant**.

assuage [ə'sweɪdʒ] *vt fml* [grief, pain] soulager, apaiser ▪ [hunger, thirst] assouvir ▪ [person] apaiser, calmer.

assume [ə'sjuːm] *vt* **1.** [presume] supposer, présumer ▪ **let's ~ that to be the case** mettons *OR* supposons que ce soit le cas ▪ **he's ~d to be rich** on le suppose riche **2.** [undertake] assumer, endosser ▪ **he ~d management of the firm** il a pris la direction de l'entreprise **3.** [usurp - power] prendre ; [- right, title] s'approprier, s'arroger **4.** [adopt] prendre ▪ **she ~d a look of indifference** elle affectait un air d'indifférence ▪ **unemployment is assuming frightening proportions** le chômage commence à prendre d'inquiétantes proportions.

assumed [ə'sjuːmd] *adj* feint, faux, fausse *f* ▪ **~ name** nom *m* d'emprunt.

assuming [ə'sjuːmɪŋ] *conj* en admettant *OR* supposant que.

assumption [ə'sʌmpʃn] *n* **1.** [supposition] supposition *f*, hypothèse *f* ▪ **our cultural ~s** nos présupposés ▪ **on the ~ that he agrees, we can go ahead** en supposant *OR* admettant qu'il soit d'accord, nous pouvons aller de l'avant ▪ **we're working on the ~ that what she says is true** nous partons du principe qu'elle dit la vérité **2.** [of power] appropriation *f* ▪ **~ of office** entrée *f* en fonctions **3.** [of attitude] affectation *f*.
◆ **Assumption** *n* RELIG : **the Assumption** l'Assomption *f*.

Assumption Day *n* jour *m OR* fête *f* de l'Assomption.

assurance [ə'ʃʊərəns] *n* **1.** [assertion] affirmation *f*, assurance *f* ▪ [pledge] promesse *f*, assurance *f* ▪ **she gave repeated ~s that she would not try to escape** elle a promis à plusieurs reprises qu'elle n'essaierait pas de s'enfuir **2.** [confidence] assurance *f*, confiance *f* en soi ▪ [overconfidence] arrogance *f* ▪ **they set out with absolute ~ of their success** ils partirent, sûrs de leur réussite **3.** *UK* [insurance] assurance *f*.

assure [ə'ʃʊəʳ] *vt* **1.** [affirm] affirmer, assurer ▪ [convince] convaincre, assurer ▪ [guarantee] assurer, certifier ▪ **he ~d them of his sincerity** il les a assurés de sa sincérité ▪ **they ~d her it was true** ils lui ont certifié que c'était vrai ▪ **we've never had anyone like that here, I can ~ you** je peux vous assurer que nous n'avons jamais eu quelqu'un comme ça ici **2.** *UK* [insure] assurer.

assured [ə'ʃʊəd] ◇ *adj* **1.** [certain] assuré, certain ▪ **I am ~ of her loyalty** je suis convaincu *OR* certain de sa loyauté **2.** [self-confident] assuré, sûr de soi ▪ [overconfident] arrogant, effronté **3.** *UK* [insured] assuré.
◇ *n* assuré *m*, - e *f*.

assuredly [ə'ʃʊərɪdlɪ] *adv* assurément, sûrement, sans aucun doute.

AST (*abbrev of* **Atlantic Standard Time**) *n heure d'hiver des Provinces Maritimes du Canada et d'une partie des Caraïbes.*

asterisk ['æstərɪsk] ◇ *n* astérisque *m*.
◇ *vt* marquer d'un astérisque.

astern [ə'stɜːn] ◇ *adv* à *OR* sur l'arrière, en poupe.
◇ *adj* à *OR* sur l'arrière.

asteroid ['æstərɔɪd] *n* astéroïde *m*.

asthenosphere [əs'θiːnəˌsfɪəʳ] *n* asthénosphère *f*.

asthma ['æsmə] ◇ *n* asthme *m* ▪ **she has ~** elle est asthmatique.
◇ *comp* : **~ attack** crise *f* d'asthme ▪ **~ sufferer** asthmatique *mf*.

asthmatic [æs'mætɪk] ◇ *adj* asthmatique ▪ **an ~ attack** une crise d'asthme.
◇ *n* asthmatique *mf*.

astigmatic [ˌæstɪg'mætɪk] ◇ *adj* astigmate.
◇ *n* astigmate *mf*.

astigmatism [æ'stɪgmətɪzm] *n* astigmatisme *m*.

astir [ə'stɜːʳ] *adj lit* **1.** [out of bed] debout *(inv)*, levé **2.** [in motion] animé.

ASTMS ['æstiːmz, eɪestiːemes] (*abbrev of* **Association of Scientific, Technical and Managerial Staffs**) *pr n ancien syndicat britannique des personnels scientifiques, techniques et administratifs.*

astonish [ə'stɒnɪʃ] *vt* [surprise] étonner ▪ [amaze] stupéfier, ahurir ▪ **we were ~ed that she had come** nous étions stupéfaits qu'elle soit venue ▪ **she was ~ed to hear from him** *OR* **at hearing from him** elle était stupéfaite d'avoir de ses nouvelles.

astonished [ə'stɒnɪʃt] *adj* surpris.

astonishing [ə'stɒnɪʃɪŋ] *adj* [surprising] étonnant ▪ [amazing] stupéfiant, ahurissant.

astonishingly [ə'stɒnɪʃɪŋlɪ] *adv* incroyablement ▪ **~, they both decided to leave** aussi étonnant que cela paraisse, ils ont tous les deux décidé de partir.

astonishment [ə'stɒnɪʃmənt] *n* [surprise] étonnement *m* ▪ [amazement] stupéfaction *f*, ahurissement *m* ▪ **they stared in ~** ils avaient l'air stupéfait ▪ **a look of ~** un regard stupéfait *OR* ahuri.

astound [ə'staʊnd] *vt* stupéfier, abasourdir ▪ **we were ~ed to hear the news** la nouvelle nous a stupéfaits ▪ **I was ~ed when she left like that** j'étais stupéfait qu'elle parte comme ça.

astounded [ə'staʊndɪd] *adj* stupéfait.

astounding [ə'staʊndɪŋ] *adj* stupéfiant, ahurissant.

astoundingly [ə'staʊndɪŋlɪ] *adv* incroyablement ▪ **~ beautiful** d'une beauté incroyable ▪ **~ enough, they'd already met** chose extraordinaire, ils s'étaient déjà rencontrés.

astral ['æstrəl] *adj* astral.

astray [ə'streɪ] *adv* **1.** [lost] : **to go ~** s'égarer, se perdre **2.** *phr* **to lead sb ~** [misinform] mettre *OR* diriger qqn sur une fausse piste ; [morally] détourner qqn du droit chemin ▪ **he's easily led ~** il se laisse facilement entraîner hors du droit chemin.

astride [ə'straɪd] *prep* à califourchon *OR* à cheval sur.

astringent [ə'strɪndʒənt] ◇ *adj* **1.** [remark] acerbe, caustique ▪ [criticism] dur, sévère **2.** [lotion] astringent.
◇ *n* astringent *m*.

astrologer [ə'strɒlədʒəʳ] *n* astrologue *mf*.

astrological [ˌæstrə'lɒdʒɪkl] *adj* astrologique.

astrologist [ə'strɒlədʒɪst] *n* astrologue *mf*.

astrology [ə'strɒlədʒɪ] *n* astrologie *f*.

astronaut ['æstrənɔːt] *n* astronaute *mf*.

astronautic(al) [ˌæstrə'nɔːtɪk(l)] *adj* astronautique.

astronomer [ə'strɒnəməʳ] *n* astronome *mf*.

astronomic(al) [,æstrə'nɒmɪk(l)] *adj* ASTRON & *fig* astronomique.

astronomically [,æstrə'nɒmɪklɪ] *adv* astronomiquement ▪ *fig* **prices have risen** ~ les prix ont atteint des sommets astronomiques.

astronomy [ə'strɒnəmɪ] *n* astronomie *f*.

astrophysics [,æstrəʊ'fɪzɪks] *n (U)* astrophysique *f*.

Astroturf® ['æstrəʊ,tɜ:f] *n* gazon *m* artificiel.

astute [ə'stju:t] *adj* [person - shrewd] astucieux, fin, perspicace ; [- crafty] malin, rusé ▪ [investment, management] astucieux.

astutely [ə'stju:tlɪ] *adv* astucieusement, avec finesse OR perspicacité.

astuteness [ə'stju:tnɪs] *n* finesse *f*, perspicacité *f*.

asunder [ə'sʌndəʳ] *adj* & *adv lit* [apart] écartés, éloignés (l'un de l'autre) ▪ [in pieces] en morceaux ▪ **to be torn** ~ être mis en pièces.

asylum [ə'saɪləm] *n* **1.** [refuge] asile *m*, refuge *m* ▪ **to give ~ to sb** donner asile à qqn ▪ **to grant sb political** ~ accorder l'asile politique à qqn **2.** [mental hospital] asile *m* (d'aliénés).

asylum-seeker *n* demandeur *m*, - euse *f* d'asile.

asymmetric(al) [,eɪsɪ'metrɪk(l)] *adj* asymétrique.

asymmetry [,eɪ'sɪmətrɪ] *n* asymétrie *f*.

asynchronous [,eɪ'sɪŋkrənəs] *adj* asynchrone.

at [*(weak form)* ət *(strong form)* æt] *prep* **1.** [indicating point in space] à ▪ **at the door/the bus stop** à la porte/l'arrêt de bus ▪ **at my house/the dentist's** chez moi/le dentiste ▪ **she's at a wedding/committee meeting** [attending] elle est à un mariage/en réunion avec le comité ▪ **where are you at with that report?** *US* où en êtes-vous avec ce rapport? ◗ **this club is where it's at** *inf* ce club est très chic OR dans le vent
2. [indicating point in time] à ▪ **at noon/six o'clock** à midi/six heures ▪ **I work at night** je travaille de nuit ▪ **I like to work at night** j'aime travailler la nuit ▪ **I'm busy at the moment** je suis occupé en ce moment ▮ [indicating age] : **he started working at 15** il a commencé à travailler à (l'âge de) 15 ans
3. [indicating direction] vers, dans la direction de ▪ **look at this!** regarde ça! ▪ **he shot at the rabbit** il a tiré sur le lapin ▪ **she grabbed at the purse** elle a essayé de s'emparer du porte-monnaie ▪ **don't shout at me!** ne me crie pas dessus!
4. [indicating activity] : **my parents are at work** mes parents sont au travail ▪ **he was at lunch** il était allé déjeuner ◗ **get me some coffee while you're at it** *inf* prenez-moi du café pendant que vous y êtes ▪ **she's at it again!** *inf* la voilà qui recommence! ▪ **don't let me catch you at it again!** *inf* que je ne t'y reprenne pas!
5. [indicating level, rate] : **the temperature stands at 30°** la température est de 30° ▪ **at 50 mph** à 80 km/h ▪ **he drove at 50 mph** il faisait du 80 (à l'heure) ▪ **the rise worked out at £1 an hour** l'augmentation correspondait à 1 livre de l'heure
6. [indicating price] à ▪ **it's a bargain at £5** à 5 livres, c'est une bonne affaire
7. [with superlative] à ▪ **she's at her most/least effective in such situations** c'est là qu'elle est le plus/le moins efficace
8. [as adjective complement] en ▪ **he's brilliant/hopeless at maths** il est excellent/nul en maths
9. *phr* **to be (on) at sb** *inf* harceler qqn.
◆ **at all** *adv phr* : **he's not at all patient** il n'est pas du tout patient ▪ **thank you for your help – not at all** merci de votre aide – je vous en prie OR il n'y a pas de quoi ▪ **nothing at all** rien du tout ▪ **he comes rarely if at all** il vient très rarement, voire jamais ▪ **if you had any feelings at all** si vous aviez le moindre sentiment ▪ **if you do any travelling at all, you'll know what I mean** si vous voyagez un tant soit peu, vous comprendrez ce que je veux dire.
◆ **at once** *adv phr* **1.** [immediately] tout de suite, immédiatement
2. [simultaneously] en même temps.

atavistic [,ætə'vɪstɪk] *adj* atavique.

ATB (*abbrev of* **all terrain bike**) *n* VTT *m*.

ATC ◇ *n* = **air traffic control**.
◇ *pr n* (*abbrev of* **Air Training Corps**) *unité de formation de l'armée de l'air britannique*.

ate [*UK* et, *US* eɪt] *pt* ⊳ **eat**.

a tempo [ɑ:'tempəʊ] *adj* & *adv* a tempo.

atheism ['eɪθɪɪzm] *n* athéisme *m*.

atheist ['eɪθɪɪst] ◇ *adj* athée.
◇ *n* athée *mf*.

atheistic [,eɪθɪ'ɪstɪk] *adj* athée.

Athenian [ə'θi:njən] ◇ *n* Athénien *m*, - enne *f*.
◇ *adj* athénien.

Athens ['æθɪnz] *pr n* Athènes.

athlete ['æθli:t] *n* [gen] sportif *m*, - ive *f* ▪ [track & field competitor] athlète *mf*.

athlete's foot *n (U)* mycose *f*.

athletic [æθ'letɪk] *adj* [sporty] sportif ▪ [muscular] athlétique.

athletics [æθ'letɪks] ◇ *n (U)* athlétisme *m*.
◇ *comp* [club, meeting] d'athlétisme ▪ [activity - track & field] athlétique ; [- other sport] sportif ▪ ~ **coach** *US* SCH & UNIV entraîneur *m* (sportif).

at-home *n réception chez soi*.

atishoo [ə'tɪʃu:] *onom* atchoum!

Atlantic [ət'læntɪk] ◇ *adj* [coast, community] atlantique ▪ [wind] de l'Atlantique ▪ **the ~ Ocean** l'Atlantique *m*, l'océan *m* Atlantique ▪ ~ **liner** transatlantique *m* ▪ **the ~ Provinces** [in Canada] les Provinces *fpl* atlantiques.
◇ *pr n* : **the** ~ l'Atlantique *m*, l'océan *m* Atlantique.

Atlantis [ət'læntɪs] *pr n* Atlantide *f*.

atlas ['ætləs] *n* atlas *m*.

Atlas ['ætləs] *pr n* **1.** GEOG : **the ~ Mountains** l'Atlas *m* **2.** MYTH Atlas.

atm. (*written abbrev of* **atmosphere**) atm.

ATM (*abbrev of* **automated teller machine**) *n* DAB *m*.

atmosphere ['ætmə,sfɪəʳ] *n* **1.** [air] atmosphère *f* **2.** [feeling, mood] ambiance *f*, atmosphère *f* ▪ **the place has no** ~ l'endroit est impersonnel.

atmospheric [,ætməs'ferɪk] *adj* **1.** [pollution, pressure] atmosphérique **2.** [full of atmosphere] : **the film was very** ~ il y avait beaucoup d'atmosphère dans ce film.

atmospherics [,ætməs'ferɪks] *npl* parasites *mpl*.

atoll ['ætɒl] *n* atoll *m*.

atom ['ætəm] *n* **1.** SCI atome *m* **2.** *fig* **there's not an ~ of truth in what you say** il n'y a pas une once OR un brin de vérité dans ce que tu dis ▪ **they haven't one ~ of common sense** ils n'ont pas le moindre bon sens.

atom bomb *n* bombe *f* atomique.

atomic [ə'tɒmɪk] *adj* [age, bomb, theory] atomique ▪ **~-powered** (fonctionnant à l'énergie) nucléaire OR atomique ◗ ~ **power station** centrale *f* nucléaire ▪ ~ **warfare** guerre *f* nucléaire OR atomique.

atomic energy *n* énergie *f* nucléaire OR atomique.

atomic number *n* nombre *m* OR numéro *m* atomique.

atomic reactor *n* réacteur *m* nucléaire.

atomic weight *n* masse *f* OR poids *m* atomique.

atomize, ise ['ætəmaɪz] *vt* **1.** [liquid] pulvériser, atomiser, vaporiser ▪ [solid] atomiser **2.** [bomb] atomiser.

atomizer ['ætəmaɪzəʳ] *n* atomiseur *m*.

atonal [eɪ'təʊnl] *adj* atonal.

atone [ə'təʊn] ◇ *vi* : **to ~ for** : **to ~ for one's sins** expier ses péchés ▪ **to ~ for a mistake** réparer OR racheter une faute.
◇ *vt* [guilt, sin] expier.

atonement [ə'təʊnmənt] *n* [of crime, sin] expiation *f* ■ [of mistake] réparation *f* ■ **to make ~ for one's sins** expier ses péchés ■ **they made ~ for their past mistakes** ils ont racheté leurs erreurs passées ➔ **Day of Atonement** (fête *f* du) Grand Pardon *m*.

atop [ə'tɒp] *lit* ◇ *adv* en haut.
◇ *prep* en haut de, sur.

A to Z *n* plan *m* de ville.

atrium ['eɪtrɪəm] (*pl* **atria** [-trɪə] *OR pl* **atriums**) *n* **1.** [court] cour *f* ■ ANTIQ atrium *m* **2.** ANAT orifice *m* de l'oreillette.

atrocious [ə'trəʊʃəs] *adj* **1.** [cruel, evil] atroce, horrible **2.** [very bad] affreux, atroce.

atrociously [ə'trəʊʃəslɪ] *adv* **1.** [cruelly] atrocement, horriblement **2.** [badly] affreusement, atrocement.

atrocity [ə'trɒsətɪ] (*pl* **atrocities**) *n* atrocité *f*.

atrophy ['ætrəfɪ] ◇ *n* atrophie *f*.
◇ *vi* (*pret & pp* **atrophied**) s'atrophier.
◇ *vt* (*pret & pp* **atrophied**) atrophier.

attaboy ['ætəbɔɪ] *interj US inf* **~!** bravo! vas-y mon petit!

attach [ə'tætʃ] ◇ *vt* **1.** [connect - handle, label] attacher, fixer ; [- appendix, document] joindre ■ **the ~ed letter** la lettre ci-jointe **2.** [associate with] : **he ~ed himself to a group of walkers** il s'est joint à un groupe de randonneurs **3.** [be part of] : **the research centre is ~ed to the science department** le centre de recherche dépend du *OR* est rattaché au département des sciences **4.** [attribute] attacher, attribuer ■ **don't ~ too much importance to this survey** n'accordez pas trop d'importance à cette enquête **5.** [place on temporary duty] affecter **6.** LAW [person] arrêter, appréhender ■ [property, salary] saisir.
◇ *vi fml* être attribué, être imputé ■ **no blame ~es to you for what happened** la responsabilité de ce qui s'est produit ne repose nullement sur vous.

attaché [ə'tæʃeɪ] *n* attaché *m*, - e *f*.

attaché case *n* mallette *f*, attaché-case *m*.

attached [ə'tætʃt] *adj* attaché ■ **he's very ~ to his family** il est très attaché *OR* il tient beaucoup à sa famille ■ **she's (already) ~** elle a déjà quelqu'un dans sa vie.

attachment [ə'tætʃmənt] *n* **1.** [fastening] fixation *f* **2.** [accessory, part] accessoire *m* **3.** [affection] attachement *m*, affection *f* ■ [loyalty] attachement *m* ■ **she has a strong ~ to her grandfather** elle est très attachée à son grand-père **4.** [temporary duty] détachement *m* ■ **he's on ~ to the hospital** il est en détachement à l'hôpital **5.** LAW [of person] arrestation *f* ■ [of property] saisie *f* **6.** COMPUT pièce *f* jointe.

attack [ə'tæk] ◇ *vt* **1.** [assault - physically] attaquer ; [- verbally] attaquer, s'attaquer à ■ MIL attaquer, assaillir **2.** [tackle] s'attaquer à ■ **a campaign to ~ racism** une campagne pour combattre le racisme **3.** [damage] attaquer, ronger ■ **the disease mainly ~s the very young** la maladie atteint essentiellement les très jeunes enfants ■ **this apathy ~s the very roots of democracy** cette apathie menace les racines mêmes de la démocratie.
◇ *n* **1.** [gen - SPORT] attaque *f* ■ MIL attaque *f*, assaut *m* ■ **~s on old people are on the increase** les agressions contre les personnes âgées sont de plus en plus nombreuses ■ **to launch an ~ on** *liter* donner l'assaut à ; *fig* [crime] lancer une opération contre ; [problem, policy] s'attaquer à ■ **the ~ on her life failed** l'attentat contre elle a échoué ■ **the ~ on drugs** le combat contre la drogue ■ **to return to the ~** revenir à la charge ■ **to go on the ~** passer à l'attaque ■ **the infantry was under ~** l'infanterie subissait un assaut *OR* était attaquée ■ **to come under ~** être en butte aux attaques ■ **to leave o.s. wide open to ~** prêter le flanc à la critique **2.** [of illness] crise *f* ■ **an ~ of fever** un accès de fièvre **3.** MUS attaque *f*.

attacker [ə'tækəʳ] *n* [gen] agresseur *m*, attaquant *m*, - e *f* ■ SPORT attaquant *m*.

attain [ə'teɪn] *vt* **1.** [achieve - ambition, hopes, objectives] réaliser ; [- happiness] atteindre à ; [- independence, success] obtenir ; [- knowledge] acquérir **2.** [arrive at, reach] atteindre, arriver à.
◆ **attain to** *vt insep* : **to ~ to power** arriver au pouvoir.

attainable [ə'teɪnəbl] *adj* [level, objective, profits] réalisable ■ [position] accessible ■ **a growth rate ~ by industrialized countries** un taux de croissance à la portée des *OR* accessible aux pays industrialisés.

attainment [ə'teɪnmənt] *n* **1.** [of ambition, hopes, objectives] réalisation *f* ■ [of independence, success] obtention *f* ■ [of happiness] conquête *f* ■ [of knowledge] acquisition *f* **2.** [accomplishment] résultat *m* (obtenu) ■ [knowledge, skill] connaissance *f*.

attempt [ə'tempt] ◇ *n* **1.** [effort, try] tentative *f*, essai *m*, effort *m* ■ **to make an ~ at doing sthg** *OR* **to do sthg** essayer de faire qqch ■ **we made our first ~ in January** nous avons fait notre coup d'essai *OR* nous avons essayé pour la première fois en janvier ■ **she made every ~ to put him at ease** elle a tout fait pour le mettre à l'aise ■ **he made no ~ to help** il n'a rien fait pour (nous) aider ■ **we made another ~** nous avons renouvelé nos tentatives, nous sommes revenus à la charge ■ **he made an ~ on the record** il a essayé de battre le record ■ **he made a feeble ~ at a joke** il a essayé de plaisanter sans y parvenir ■ **he made it at the first ~** il a réussi du premier coup ■ **I passed the test at my third ~** j'ai réussi l'examen la troisième fois ■ **he was shot in an ~ to escape** il fut tué lors d'une tentative d'évasion *OR* en essayant de s'évader **2.** [attack] attentat *m* ■ **he survived the ~ on his life** il a survécu à l'attentat perpétré contre lui.
◇ *vt* **1.** [try] tenter, essayer ■ [undertake - job, task] entreprendre, s'attaquer à ■ **he ~ed to cross the street, he ~ed crossing the street** il a essayé de traverser la rue ■ **she plans to ~ the record again in June** elle a l'intention de s'attaquer de nouveau au record en juin ■ **he has already ~ed suicide once** il a déjà fait une tentative de suicide **2.** [in mountaineering - ascent, climb] entreprendre ; [- mountain] entreprendre l'escalade de.

attempted [ə'temptɪd] *adj* tenté ■ **~ murder/suicide** tentative *f* de meurtre/de suicide.

attend [ə'tend] ◇ *vt* **1.** [go to - conference, meeting] assister à ; [- church, school] aller à ■ **she ~s the same course as me** elle suit les mêmes cours que moi ■ **the concert was well ~ed** il y avait beaucoup de monde au concert **2.** [look after, care for] servir, être au service de ■ **he was always ~ed by a manservant** un valet de chambre l'accompagnait partout ■ **a doctor ~ed the children** un médecin a soigné les enfants **3.** *fml* [accompany] accompagner ■ **the mission was ~ed by great difficulties** la mission comportait de grandes difficultés.
◇ *vi* [be present] être présent ■ **let us know if you are unable to ~** prévenez-nous si vous ne pouvez pas venir.
◆ **attend on** *vt insep* **1.** [subj: maid] servir, être au service de ■ [subj: bodyguard] accompagner ■ [subj: doctor] soigner ■ **she ~ed on her guests** elle s'est occupée de ses invités **2.** *fml* [be consequence of] résulter de.
◆ **attend to** *vt insep* **1.** [pay attention to] faire *OR* prêter attention à ■ **she ~ed closely to the instructions** elle a suivi les instructions attentivement **2.** [deal with - business, problem] s'occuper de ; [- studies] s'appliquer à ; [- customer] s'occuper de, servir ; [- wound] (faire) soigner.
◆ **attend upon** *vt insep* = **attend on**.

attendance [ə'tendəns] ◇ *n* **1.** [number of people present] assistance *f* ■ **there was a record ~ of over 500 people** il y avait plus de 500 personnes, ce qui est un record **2.** [presence] présence *f* ■ **~ at classes is obligatory** la présence aux cours est obligatoire ■ **his poor ~ made a bad impression** ses nombreuses absences ont fait mauvaise impression ■ **your ~ is requested** vous êtes prié d'y assister ■ **regular ~** assiduité *f* **3.** [service] service *m* ■ **several servants were in ~ on her** plusieurs domestiques l'escortaient *OR* l'accompagnaient.
◇ *comp* [record] d'appel.

attendance allowance *n UK allocation pour les handicapés*.

attendance centre *n UK* ≃ centre *m* de réinsertion.

attendant [ə'tendənt] ◇ *n* [in museum, park] gardien *m*, - enne *f* ■ [in petrol station] pompiste *mf* ■ [servant] domestique *mf*.
◇ *adj fml* **1.** [person - accompanying] qui accompagne ; [- on duty] en service ■ **the salesman ~ on us was a Mr Jones** le vendeur qui nous servait *OR* s'occupait de nous était un certain

M. Jones **2.** [related] : **he talked about marriage and its ~ problems** il parla du mariage et des problèmes qui l'accompagnent.

attention [ə'tenʃn] ◇ *n* **1.** [concentration, thought] attention *f* ■ **may I have your ~ for a moment?** pourriez-vous m'accorder votre attention un instant? ■ **we listened to him with close ~** nous l'avons écouté très attentivement ■ **she knows how to hold an audience's ~** elle sait retenir l'attention d'un auditoire ■ **to pay ~** prêter attention ■ **I paid little ~ to what she said** j'ai accordé peu d'attention à *OR* j'ai fait peu de cas de ce qu'elle a dit ■ **we paid no ~ to the survey** nous n'avons tenu aucun compte de l'enquête ■ **~ to detail** précision *f*, minutie *f* ■ **she switched her ~ back to her book** elle est retournée à son livre ◆ **~ span** capacité *f* d'attention **2.** [notice] attention *f* ■ **the news came to his ~** il a appris la nouvelle ■ **let me bring** *OR* **direct** *OR* **draw your ~ to the matter of punctuality** permettez que j'attire votre attention sur le problème de la ponctualité ■ **let us now turn our ~ to the population problem** considérons maintenant le problème démographique ■ **for the ~ of Mr Smith** à l'attention de M. Smith **3.** [care] : **they need medical ~** ils ont besoin de soins médicaux ■ **the furnace requires constant ~** la chaudière demande un entretien régulier **4.** MIL garde-à-vous *m inv* ■ **to stand at/to come to ~** se tenir/se mettre au garde-à-vous.
◇ *interj* : **~!** garde-à-vous!
◆ **attentions** *npl* attentions *fpl*, égards *mpl*.

attentive [ə'tentɪv] *adj* **1.** [paying attention] attentif ■ **~ to detail** méticuleux **2.** [considerate] attentionné, prévenant ■ **to be ~ to sb** être prévenant envers qqn ■ **she was ~ to our every need** elle était attentive à tous nos besoins.

attentively [ə'tentɪvlɪ] *adv* **1.** [listen, read] attentivement, avec attention **2.** [solicitously] avec beaucoup d'égards.

attenuate ◇ *vt* **1.** [attack, remark] atténuer, modérer ■ [pain] apaiser **2.** [form, line] amincir, affiner **3.** [gas] raréfier.
◇ *vi* [ə'tenjʊeɪt] s'atténuer, diminuer.
◇ *adj* [ə'tenjʊɪt] BOT atténué.

attenuation [ə,tenjʊ'eɪʃn] *n* **1.** [of attack, remark] atténuation *f*, modération *f* ■ [of pain] atténuation *f*, apaisement *m* **2.** [of form] amincissement *m*.

attest [ə'test] *fml* ◇ *vt* **1.** [affirm] attester, certifier ■ [under oath] affirmer sous serment **2.** [be proof of] démontrer, témoigner de **3.** [bear witness to] témoigner ■ **to ~ a signature** légaliser une signature **4.** [put oath to] faire prêter serment à.
◇ *vi* témoigner, prêter serment ■ **she ~ed to the truth of the report** elle a témoigné de la véracité du rapport ■ **to ~ to sb's honesty** se porter garant (de l'honnêteté) de qqn.

attestation [,æte'steɪʃn] *n fml* **1.** [statement] attestation *f* ■ [in court] attestation *f*, témoignage *m* **2.** [proof] attestation *f*, preuve *f* **3.** [of signature] légalisation *f* **4.** [taking of oath] assermentation *f*, prestation *f* de serment.

attic ['ætɪk] *n* [space] grenier *m* ■ [room] mansarde *f*.

Attic ['ætɪk] ◇ *adj* attique.
◇ *n* LING attique *m*, dialecte *m* attique.

Attica ['ætɪkə] *pr n* Attique *f*.

Attila [ə'tɪlə] *pr n* : **~ the Hun** Attila roi des Huns.

attire [ə'taɪəʳ] *fml* ◇ *n (U)* habits *mpl*, vêtements *mpl* ■ [formal] tenue *f*.
◇ *vt* vêtir, habiller, parer.

attitude ['ætɪtju:d] *n* **1.** [way of thinking] attitude *f*, disposition *f* ■ **what's your ~ to** *OR* **towards him?** que pensez-vous de lui? ■ **she took the ~ that...** elle est partie du principe que... ■ **an ~ of mind** un état d'esprit ■ **~s towards homosexuality are changing** les comportements à l'égard de l'homosexualité sont en train de changer **2.** [behaviour, manner] attitude *f*, manière *f* ■ **I don't like your ~, young man** je n'aime pas vos manières, jeune homme ■ **well, if that's your ~ you can go** eh bien, si c'est comme ça que tu le prends, tu peux t'en aller ■ **he's got an ~ problem** il a des problèmes relationnels **3.** *fml* [posture] attitude *f*, position *f* ■ **to strike an ~** poser, prendre une pose affectée **4.** *inf* **to have ~** [to be stylish] avoir du cran ; [to be arrogant] être frimeur ■ **don't give me that ~** ne sois pas si négatif.

attitudinize, ise [,ætɪ'tju:dɪnaɪz] *vi pej* prendre des attitudes, poser.

attn (*written abbrev of* **for the attention of**) attn, à l'attention de.

attorney [ə'tɜ:nɪ] (*pl* **attorneys**) *n* **1.** [representative] mandataire *mf*, représentant *m*, - e *f* **2.** *US* [solicitor - for documents, sales etc] notaire *m* ; [- for court cases] avocat *m*, - e *f* ■ [barrister] avocat *m*, - e *f*.

Attorney General (*pl* **Attorneys General** *OR pl* **Attorney Generals**) *n* [in England, Wales and Northern Ireland] *principal avocat de la couronne* ■ [in US] ≃ ministre *m* de la Justice.

attract [ə'trækt] ◇ *vt* **1.** [draw, cause to come near] attirer ■ **the proposal ~ed a lot of attention/interest** la proposition a attiré l'attention/a éveillé l'intérêt de beaucoup de gens ■ **to ~ criticism** s'attirer des critiques **2.** [be attractive to] attirer, séduire, plaire ■ **she's ~ed to men with beards** elle est attirée par les barbus ■ **what is it that ~s you about skiing?** qu'est-ce qui vous plaît *OR* séduit dans le ski?
◇ *vi* s'attirer ■ **opposites ~** les contraires s'attirent.

attraction [ə'trækʃn] *n* **1.** PHYS [pull] attraction *f* ■ *fig* attraction *f*, attirance *f* ■ **I don't understand your ~ for** *OR* **to her** je ne comprends pas ce qui te plaît chez *OR* en elle ■ **the idea holds no ~ for me** cette idée ne me dit rien **2.** [appeal - of place, plan] attrait *m*, fascination *f* ; [- of person] charme *m*, charmes *mpl* ■ **the ~s of living in the country** les charmes de la vie à la campagne ■ **the main ~ of our show** le clou *OR* la grande attraction de notre spectacle ■ **a tourist ~** un site touristique.

attractive [ə'træktɪv] *adj* **1.** [pretty - person, smile] séduisant ; [- dress, picture] attrayant, beau *(before vowel or silent 'h'* **bel***)*, belle *f* **2.** [interesting - idea, price] intéressant ; [- offer, opportunity] intéressant, attrayant **3.** PHYS [force] attractif.

attractively [ə'træktɪvlɪ] *adv* de manière attrayante ■ **to dress ~** s'habiller de façon séduisante ■ **the meal was very ~ presented** le repas était très agréablement présenté.

attributable [ə'trɪbjʊtəbl] *adj* attribuable, imputable, dû ■ **to be ~ to sthg** être attribuable *OR* imputable *OR* dû à qqch.

attribute ◇ *vt* [ə'trɪbju:t] [ascribe - accident, failure] attribuer, imputer ; [- invention, painting, quotation] prêter, attribuer ; [- success] attribuer ■ **to what do you ~ your success?** à quoi attribuez-vous votre réussite?
◇ *n* ['ætrɪbju:t] **1.** [feature, quality] attribut *m* ■ [object] attribut *m*, emblème *m* **2.** LING & LOGIC attribut *m*.

attribution [,ætrɪ'bju:ʃn] *n* attribution *f*.

attributive [ə'trɪbjʊtɪv] ◇ *n* attribut *m*.
◇ *adj* [gen - GRAM] attributif.

attributively [ə'trɪbjʊtɪvlɪ] *adv* LING comme épithète.

attrition [ə'trɪʃn] *n* [wearing down] usure *f* (par friction) ■ INDUST & RELIG attrition *f*.

attune [ə'tju:n] *vt* MUS accorder ■ *fig* accorder, habituer ■ **her ideas are closely ~d to his** ses idées sont en parfait accord avec les siennes ■ **my ears are not really ~d to this modern music** mes oreilles ne sont pas vraiment habituées à cette musique moderne.

Atty. Gen. *written abbr of* **Attorney General**.

ATV *n* (*abbrev of* **all terrain vehicle**) véhicule *m* tout terrain.

atypical [,eɪ'tɪpɪkl] *adj* atypique.

aubergine ['əʊbəʒi:n] *n UK* aubergine *f*.

auburn ['ɔ:bən] ◇ *adj* auburn *(inv)*.
◇ *n* (couleur *f*) auburn *m*.

auction ['ɔ:kʃn] ◇ *n* (vente *f* aux) enchères *fpl* ■ **to put sthg up for ~** mettre qqch en vente aux enchères.
◇ *vt* : **to ~ sthg (off)** vendre qqch aux enchères.

auctioneer [,ɔ:kʃə'nɪəʳ] *n* commissaire-priseur *m*.

auction room *n* salle *f* des ventes.

audacious [ɔ:'deɪʃəs] *adj* **1.** [daring] audacieux, intrépide **2.** [impudent] effronté, impudent.

audacity [ɔ:'dæsətɪ] *n* **1.** [daring] audace *f*, intrépidité *f* **2.** [impudence] effronterie *f*, impudence *f* ▪ **he had the ~ to ask for a pay rise** il a eu l'audace de demander une augmentation (de salaire).

audible ['ɔ:dəbl] *adj* [sound] audible, perceptible ▪ [words] intelligible, distinct ▪ **the music was barely ~** on entendait à peine la musique.

audibly ['ɔ:dəblɪ] *adv* distinctement.

audience ['ɔ:djəns] ◇ *n* **1.** [at film, match, play] spectateurs *mpl*, public *m* ▪ [at concert, lecture] auditoire *m*, public *m* ▪ [of author] lecteurs *mpl* ▪ [of artist] public *m* ▪ **someone in the ~ laughed** il y eut un rire dans la salle ▪ **was there a large ~ at the play?** y avait-il beaucoup de monde au théâtre? ▪ **his books reach a wide ~** ses livres sont lus par beaucoup de gens **2.** RADIO auditeurs *mpl*, audience *f* ▪ TV téléspectateurs *mpl*, audience *f* **3.** *fml* [meeting] audience *f* ▪ **to grant sb an ~** accorder audience à qqn.
◇ *comp* [figures] de l'assistance, du public ▪ **~ participation** participation *f* de l'assistance (à ce qui se passe sur la scène) ▪ **~ research** études *fpl* d'audience.

audio ['ɔ:dɪəʊ] ◇ *n* son *m*, acoustique *f*.
◇ *comp* : **~ cassette** cassette *f* audio ▪ **~ conference** audioconférence *f* ▪ **~ equipment** équipement *m* acoustique ▪ **~ recording** enregistrement *m* sonore ▪ **~ system** système *m* audio.

audiotypist ['ɔ:dɪəʊ,taɪpɪst] *n* audiotypiste *mf*.

audiovisual [,ɔ:dɪəʊ'vɪzjʊəl] *adj* audiovisuel ▪ **~ methods** l'audiovisuel, les méthodes audiovisuelles.

audit ['ɔ:dɪt] ◇ *n* vérification *f* des comptes, audit *m*.
◇ *vt* **1.** [accounts] vérifier, apurer **2.** *US* UNIV : **he ~s several courses** il assiste à plusieurs cours en tant qu'auditeur libre.

audition [ɔ:'dɪʃn] ◇ *n* **1.** THEAT audition *f* ▪ CIN & TV (séance *f* d')essai *m* ▪ **the director gave her an ~** THEAT le metteur en scène l'a auditionnée ; CIN & TV le metteur en scène lui a fait faire un essai ▪ **to hold ~s** THEAT organiser des auditions ; CIN & TV organiser des essais **2.** [hearing] ouïe *f*, audition *f*.
◇ *vt* THEAT auditionner ▪ CIN & TV faire faire un essai à.
◇ *vi* THEAT [director] auditionner ▪ [actor] passer une audition ▪ CIN & TV faire un essai ▪ **I ~ed for "Woyzeck"** THEAT j'ai passé une audition pour un rôle dans "Woyzeck" ; CIN & TV j'ai fait un essai pour un rôle dans "Woyzeck".

auditor ['ɔ:dɪtəʳ] *n* **1.** [accountant] commissaire *m* aux comptes, auditeur *m*, - trice *f*, audit *m* **2.** *fml* [listener] auditeur *m*, - trice *f* **3.** *US* [student] auditeur *m*, - trice *f* libre.

auditorium [,ɔ:dɪ'tɔ:rɪəm] (*pl* **auditoriums** *OR pl* **auditoria** [-rɪə]) *n* **1.** [of concert hall, theatre] salle *f* **2.** [large meeting room] amphithéâtre *m*.

auditory ['ɔ:dɪtrɪ] *adj* auditif ▪ **~ phonetics** phonétique *f* auditive.

au fait [,əʊ'feɪ] *adj* : **to be ~ with sthg** être au courant de qqch.

Aug. *written abbr of* **August**.

auger ['ɔ:gəʳ] *n* [hand tool] vrille *f* ▪ TECH foreuse *f*.

aught [ɔ:t] *arch & lit* ◇ *pron* ce que ▪ **for ~ I know** (pour) autant que je sache.
◇ *n* zéro *m*.

augment [ɔ:g'ment] ◇ *vt* **1.** [increase] augmenter, accroître ▪ **her salary is ~ed by** *OR* **with gratuities** à son salaire s'ajoutent les pourboires **2.** MUS augmenter.
◇ *vi* augmenter, s'accroître.

augmentation [,ɔ:gmen'teɪʃn] *n* **1.** [increase] augmentation *f*, accroissement *m* **2.** MUS augmentation *f*.

augmented [ɔ:g'mentɪd] *adj* augmenté.

augur ['ɔ:gəʳ] ◇ *vi* : **this weather ~s ill/well for our holiday** ce temps est de mauvais/bon augure pour nos vacances.
◇ *vt* [predict] prédire, prévoir ▪ [be omen of] présager.
◇ *n* augure *m*.

augury ['ɔ:gjʊrɪ] (*pl* **auguries**) *n* **1.** [art] art *m* augural ▪ [rite] rite *m* augural **2.** [omen] augure *m*, présage *m* ▪ [prediction] prédiction *f*.

august [ɔ:'gʌst] *adj lit* [dignified] auguste, vénérable ▪ [noble] noble.

August ['ɔ:gəst] *n* août *m* ▪ **~ Bank Holiday** *jour férié tombant le dernier lundi d'août en Angleterre et au pays de Galles, le premier lundi d'août en Écosse, see also* **February**.

Augustan [ɔ:'gʌstən] *adj* d'Auguste ▪ **the ~ Period** [in Latin literature] le siècle d'Auguste ; [in English literature] l'époque *f* d'Auguste.

Augustine [ɔ:'gʌstɪn] *pr n* : **Saint ~** saint Augustin.

Augustus [ɔ:'gʌstəs] *pr n* Auguste.

auk [ɔ:k] *n* pingouin *m*.

Auld Lang Syne [,ɔ:ldlæŋ'saɪn] *pr n chanson sur l'air de "Ce n'est qu'un au revoir" que l'on chante à minuit le soir du 31 décembre en Grande-Bretagne.*

aunt [ɑ:nt] *n* tante *f*.

auntie ['ɑ:ntɪ] *n UK inf* tantine *f*, tata *f*, tatie *f*.

Aunt Sally [-'sælɪ] (*pl* **Aunt Sallies**) *n UK* [at fairground] ≃ jeu *m* de massacre ▪ *fig* [person] tête *f* de Turc.

aunty ['ɑ:ntɪ] (*pl* **aunties**) *n* = **auntie**.

au pair [,əʊ'peəʳ] (*pl* **au pairs**) ◇ *n* (jeune fille *f*) au pair *f*.
◇ *adj* au pair.
◇ *adv* : **to work ~** travailler au pair.
◇ *vi* travailler au pair.

aura ['ɔ:rə] (*pl* **auras** *OR pl* **aurae** ['ɔ:ri:]) *n* **1.** [of person] aura *f*, émanation *f* ▪ [of place] atmosphère *f*, ambiance *f* ▪ **there's an ~ of mystery about her** il y a quelque chose de mystérieux chez elle **2.** MED aura *f*.

aural ['ɔ:rəl] *adj* **1.** [relating to hearing] auditif, sonore ▪ **~ comprehension** compréhension *f* orale **2.** [relating to the ear] auriculaire.

aurally ['ɔ:rəlɪ] *adv* : **~ handicapped** mal entendant.

auricle ['ɔ:rɪkl] *n* **1.** [of ear] auricule *f* **2.** [of heart] oreillette *f*.

aurora australis [ɔ:,rɔ:rə -ɒ'streɪlɪs] *n* aurore *f* australe.

aurora borealis [-,bɔ:rɪ'eɪlɪs] *n* aurore *f* boréale.

auspices ['ɔ:spɪsɪz] *npl* : **under the ~ of the UN** sous les auspices de l'ONU.

auspicious [ɔ:'spɪʃəs] *adj* [event, start, occasion] propice, favorable ▪ [sign] de bon augure.

auspiciously [ɔ:'spɪʃəslɪ] *adv* favorablement, sous d'heureux auspices.

Aussie ['ɒzɪ] *inf* ◇ *n* Australien *m*, - enne *f*.
◇ *adj* australien.

austere [ɒ'stɪəʳ] *adj* **1.** [person] austère, sévère ▪ [life] austère, sobre, ascétique **2.** [design, interior] austère, sobre.

austerity [ɒ'sterətɪ] ◇ *n* (*pl* **austerities**) **1.** [simplicity] austérité *f*, sobriété *f* **2.** [hardship] austérité *f* **3.** (*usu pl*) [practice] austérité *f*, pratique *f* austère.
◇ *comp* [budget, measure] d'austérité.

Australasia [,ɒstrə'leɪʒjə] *pr n* Australasie *f*.

Australasian [,ɒstrə'leɪʒn] ◇ *n* natif *m*, - ive *f* de l'Australasie.
◇ *adj* d'Australasie.

Australia [ɒ'streɪljə] *pr n* Australie *f* ▪ **in ~** en Australie ▪ **the Commonwealth of ~** l'Australie.

Australian [ɒ'streɪljən] ◇ *n* **1.** [person] Australien *m*, - enne *f* **2.** LING australien *m*.
◇ *adj* australien.

Austral Islands ['ɔ:strəl-] *pr npl*: **the ~** les îles *fpl* Australes.

Austria ['ɒstrɪə] *pr n* Autriche *f* ▪ **in ~** en Autriche.

Austria-Hungary *pr n* Autriche-Hongrie *f*.

Austrian ['ɒstrɪən] <> *n* Autrichien *m*, - enne *f*.
<> *adj* autrichien.

Austrian blind *n* store *m* autrichien.

Austro-Hungarian [,ɒstrəʊ-] *adj* austro-hongrois.

AUT (*abbrev of* **Association of University Teachers**) *pr n syndicat britannique d'enseignants universitaires.*

autarchy ['ɔ:tɑ:kɪ] (*pl* **autarchies**) *n* **1.** = **autocracy 2.** [self-rule] autocratie *f*.

autarky ['ɔ:tɑ:kɪ] (*pl* **autarkies**) *n* **1.** [system] autarcie *f* **2.** [country] pays *m* en autarcie.

authentic [ɔ:'θentɪk] *adj* [genuine] authentique ▪ [accurate, reliable] authentique, véridique.

authenticate [ɔ:'θentɪkeɪt] *vt* [painting] établir l'authenticité de ▪ [signature] légaliser.

authentication [ɔ:,θentɪ'keɪʃn] *n* authentification *f*, certification *f*.

authenticity [,ɔ:θen'tɪsətɪ] *n* authenticité *f*.

author ['ɔ:θər] <> *n* **1.** [writer] auteur *mf*, écrivain *mf* **2.** [of idea, plan] auteur *mf* ▪ [of painting, sculpture] auteur *mf*, créateur *m*.
<> *vt* être l'auteur de.

authoress ['ɔ:θərɪs] *n* **1.** [writer] *femme auteur d'ouvrages s'adressant au grand public* **2.** [of idea, plan] auteur *m* ▪ [of painting, sculpture] auteur *m*, créatrice *f*.

authoritarian [ɔ:,θɒrɪ'teərɪən] <> *adj* autoritaire.
<> *n* personne *f* autoritaire.

authoritative [ɔ:'θɒrɪtətɪv] *adj* **1.** [manner, person] autoritaire **2.** [article, report] qui fait autorité **3.** [official] autorisé, officiel.

authoritatively [ɔ:'θɒrɪtətɪvlɪ] *adv* avec autorité, de manière autoritaire *pej*.

authority [ɔ:'θɒrətɪ] (*pl* **authorities**) *n* **1.** [power] autorité *f*, pouvoir *m* ▪ **she has ~** *or* **she is in ~ over all the staff** elle a autorité sur tout le personnel ▪ **those in ~ in Haiti** ceux qui gouvernent en Haïti
2. [forcefulness] autorité *f*, assurance *f* ▪ **her conviction gave ~ to her argument** sa conviction a donné du poids à son raisonnement ▪ **his opinions carry a lot of ~** ses opinions font autorité
3. [permission] autorisation *f*, droit *m* ▪ **who gave him (the) ~ to enter?** qui lui a donné l'autorisation d'entrer?, qui l'a autorisé à entrer? ▪ **they had no ~ to answer** ils n'étaient pas habilités à répondre ▪ **I decided on my own ~** j'ai décidé de ma propre autorité *or* de mon propre chef ▪ **on his ~** avec son autorisation ▪ **without ~** sans autorisation
4. (*usu pl*) [people in command] autorité *f* ▪ **the authorities** les autorités, l'administration *f* ▪ **the proper authorities** qui de droit, les autorités compétentes ▪ **the education/housing ~** *services chargés de l'éducation/du logement*
5. [expert] autorité *f*, expert *m* ▪ [article, book] autorité *f* ▪ **he's an ~ on China** c'est un grand spécialiste de la Chine
6. [testimony] : **I have it on his ~ that she was there** il m'a certifié qu'elle était présente ▪ **we have it on good ~ that...** nous tenons de source sûre *or* de bonne source que...
7. [permit] autorisation *f*.

authorization [,ɔ:θəraɪ'zeɪʃn] *n* [act, permission] autorisation *f* ▪ [official sanction] pouvoir *m*, mandat *m* ▪ **he has ~ to leave the country** il est autorisé à quitter le pays.

authorize, ise ['ɔ:θəraɪz] *vt* **1.** [empower] autoriser **2.** [sanction] autoriser, sanctionner ▪ **to ~ a loan** consentir un prêt.

authorized ['ɔ:θəraɪzd] *adj* autorisé ▪ **~ dealer** COMM distributeur *m* agréé ▪ **~ capital** FIN capital *m* social *or* nominal.

Authorized Version *n*: **the ~** *la version anglaise de la Bible de 1611 "autorisée" par le roi Jacques Ier d'Angleterre.*

authorship ['ɔ:θəʃɪp] *n* **1.** [of book] auteur *m*, paternité *f* ▪ [of invention] paternité *f* **2.** [profession] profession *f* d'auteur *or* d'écrivain.

autism ['ɔ:tɪzm] *n* autisme *m*.

autistic [ɔ:'tɪstɪk] *adj* autiste.

auto ['ɔ:təʊ] *US* <> *n* voiture *f*, auto *f*.
<> *comp* d'auto, automobile ▪ **~ accident** accident *m* de voiture ▪ **~ parts** pièces *fpl* détachées (pour voiture).

autobank ['ɔ:təʊ,bæŋk] *n* distributeur *m* automatique de billets (de banque).

autobiographic ['ɔ:tə,baɪə'græfɪk] *adj* autobiographique.

autobiography [,ɔ:təbaɪ'ɒgrəfɪ] (*pl* **autobiographies**) *n* autobiographie *f*.

autocracy [ɔ:'tɒkrəsɪ] (*pl* **autocracies**) *n* autocratie *f*.

autocrat ['ɔ:təkræt] *n* autocrate *m*.

autocratic [,ɔ:tə'krætɪk] *adj* autocratique.

autocross ['ɔ:təʊkrɒs] *n* autocross *m*.

Autocue® ['ɔ:təʊkju:] *n UK* téléprompteur *m*.

auto-da-fé [,ɔ:təʊdɑ:'feɪ] (*pl* **autos-da-fé** [,ɔ:təʊz-]) *n* autodafé *m*.

autodestruct [,ɔ:təʊdɪ'strʌkt] <> *vi* s'autodétruire.
<> *adj* qui s'autodétruit.

auto-dial ['ɔ:təʊ,daɪəl] *n* : **a phone with ~** un poste à numérotation automatique.

autodidact ['ɔ:təʊdaɪdækt] *n* autodidacte *mf*.

autofocus ['ɔ:təʊ,fəʊkəs] *n* autofocus *m inv*.

autograph ['ɔ:təgrɑ:f] <> *n* autographe *m*.
<> *comp* [letter] autographe ▪ [album, hunter] d'autographes.
<> *vt* [book, picture, record] dédicacer ▪ [letter, object] signer.

autoimmune [,ɔ:təʊɪ'mju:n] *adj* auto-immun.

automat ['ɔ:təmæt] *n* [machine] distributeur *m* automatique ▪ *US* [room] cafétéria *f* équipée de distributeurs automatiques.

automata [ɔ:'tɒmətə] *pl* ▷ **automaton**.

automate ['ɔ:təmeɪt] *vt* automatiser.

automated ['ɔ:təmeɪtɪd] *adj* automatisé ▪ **~ telling machine, ~ teller** distributeur *m* automatique (de billets).

automatic [,ɔ:tə'mætɪk] <> *adj* [machine] automatique ▪ [answer, smile] automatique, machinal ▪ **~ data processing** COMPUT traitement *m* automatique des données.
<> *n* **1.** [weapon] automatique *m* **2.** AUT voiture *f* à boîte *or* à transmission automatique.

automatically [,ɔ:tə'mætɪklɪ] *adv liter* automatiquement ▪ *fig* automatiquement, machinalement ▪ **teachers are ~ retired at the age of 65** les enseignants sont mis à la retraite d'office à l'âge de 65 ans.

automatic pilot *n* pilote *m* automatique ▪ **on ~** en pilotage automatique ▪ **I just went onto ~** *fig* j'ai poursuivi machinalement.

automation [,ɔ:tə'meɪʃn] *n* [process of making automatic] automatisation *f* ▪ [state of being automatic] automation *f* ▪ **factory** *or* **industrial ~** productique *f*.

automatism [ɔ:'tɒmətɪzm] *n* automatisme *m*.

automatize, ise [ɔ:'tɒmətaɪz] *vt* automatiser.

automaton [ɔ:'tɒmətən] (*pl* **automatons** *or pl* **automata** [-tə]) *n* automate *m*.

automobile ['ɔ:təməbi:l] *n US* automobile *f*, voiture *f*.

automotive [,ɔ:tə'məʊtɪv] *adj* **1.** AUT [engineering, industry] (de l')automobile **2.** [self-propelled] automoteur.

autonomous [ɔ:'tɒnəməs] *adj* autonome.

autonomy [ɔː'tɒnəmɪ] (*pl* **autonomies**) *n* **1.** [self-government] autonomie *f* **2.** [country] pays *m* autonome.

autopilot [,ɔːtəʊ'paɪlət] *n* = **automatic pilot**.

autopsy ['ɔːtɒpsɪ] (*pl* **autopsies**) *n* autopsie *f*.

autosave ['ɔːtəʊ,seɪv] *n* COMPUT sauvegarde *f* automatique.

autosuggestion [,ɔːtəʊsə'dʒestʃn] *n* autosuggestion *f*.

autotimer ['ɔːtəʊ,taɪmər] *n* programmateur *m*.

autumn ['ɔːtəm] ◇ *n* automne *m* ■ **in (the) ~** en automne.
◇ *comp* [colours, weather] d'automne, automnal ■ **~ leaves** [on tree] feuilles *fpl* d'automne ; [dead] feuilles *fpl* mortes.

autumnal [ɔː'tʌmnəl] *adj* automnal, d'automne.

auxiliary [ɔːg'zɪljərɪ] (*pl* **auxiliaries**) ◇ *adj* auxiliaire, supplémentaire ■ **~ staff** [gen] le personnel auxiliaire, les auxiliaires *mpl* ; UK SCH personnel *m* auxiliaire non enseignant.
◇ *n* **1.** [assistant, subordinate] auxiliaire *mf* ■ **nursing ~** infirmier *m*, - ère *f* auxiliaire, aide-soignant *m*, - e *f* **2.** MIL : **auxiliaries** auxiliaires *mpl* **3.** GRAM (verbe *m*) auxiliaire *m*.

auxiliary verb *n* (verbe *m*) auxiliaire *m*.

av. (*abbrev of* **average**) *adj* moyen (*f* ne).

Av. (*written abbrev of* **avenue**) av.

AV *n* = **Authorized Version**.

avail [ə'veɪl] ◇ *n* : **of no ~** : **it is of no ~ to complain** il est inutile de se plaindre ■ **his efforts were of no ~** ses efforts n'ont eu aucun effet ■ **to no ~** sans effet ■ **they argued with her to no ~** ils ont essayé en vain de la convaincre ■ **to little ~** sans grand effet.
◇ *vt* : **to ~ o.s. of sthg** se servir OR profiter de qqch.
◇ *vi lit* servir.

availability [ə,veɪlə'bɪlətɪ] (*pl* **availabilities**) *n* **1.** [accessibility] disponibilité *f* **2.** US *pej* & POL [of candidate] caractère *m* valable.

available [ə'veɪləbl] *adj* **1.** [accessible, to hand] disponible ■ **they made the data ~ to us** ils ont mis les données à notre disposition ■ **we tried every ~ means** nous avons essayé (par) tous les moyens possibles **2.** [free] libre, disponible ■ **the minister in charge was not ~ for comment** le ministre responsable s'est refusé à toute déclaration **3.** US *pej* & POL [candidate] valable *(en raison de son caractère inoffensif)*.

avalanche ['ævəlɑːnʃ] ◇ *n liter* & *fig* avalanche *f*.
◇ *vi* tomber en avalanche.

avant-garde [,ævɒŋ'gɑːd] ◇ *n* avant-garde *f*.
◇ *adj* d'avant-garde, avant-gardiste.

avarice ['ævərɪs] *n* avarice *f*, pingrerie *f*.

avaricious [,ævə'rɪʃəs] *adj* avare, pingre.

Ave (Maria) ['ɑːvɪ(mə'rɪə)] *n* Ave *m* (Maria) *(inv)*.

Ave. (*written abbrev of* **avenue**) av.

avenge [ə'vendʒ] *vt* venger ■ **he ~d his brother's death** il a vengé la mort de son frère ■ **he intends to ~ himself on his enemy** il a l'intention de se venger de OR de prendre sa revanche sur son ennemi.

avenger [ə'vendʒər] *n* vengeur *m*, - eresse *f* ■ **'The Avengers'** [TV series] 'Chapeau melon et bottes de cuir'.

avenging [ə'vendʒɪŋ] *adj* vengeur ■ **an ~ angel** un ange exterminateur.

Aventine Hill ['ævən,taɪn-] *pr n* : **the ~** le mont Aventin.

avenue ['ævənjuː] *n* **1.** [public] avenue *f*, boulevard *m* ■ [private] avenue *f*, allée *f (bordée d'arbres)* **2.** *fig* possibilité *f* ■ **we must explore every ~** il faut explorer toutes les possibilités.

aver [ə'vɜːr] (*pret* & *pp* **averred**, *cont* **averring**) *vi fml* affirmer, déclarer.

average ['ævərɪdʒ] ◇ *n* **1.** [standard amount, quality etc] moyenne *f* ■ **above/below ~** au-dessus/au-dessous de la moyenne ■ **on (an)** OR **on the ~** en moyenne ■ **we travelled an ~ of 100 miles a day** nous avons fait une moyenne de 100 miles par jour OR 100 miles par jour en moyenne ■ **the law of ~s** la loi de la probabilité **2.** MATHS moyenne *f*.
◇ *adj* moyen ■ **ask the ~ man in the street** demandez à l'homme de la rue.
◇ *vt* **1.** MATHS établir OR faire la moyenne de **2.** [perform typical number of] atteindre la moyenne de ■ **the factory ~s 10 machines a day** l'usine produit en moyenne 10 machines par jour ■ **we ~ two letters a day** nous recevons en moyenne deux lettres par jour ■ **he ~d 100 km/h** AUT il a fait du 100 km/h de moyenne **3.** [divide up] partager.

◆ **average out** ◇ *vi insep* : **profits ~ out at 10%** les bénéfices s'élèvent en moyenne à 10 % ■ **factory production ~s out at 120 cars a day** l'usine produit en moyenne 120 voitures par jour.
◇ *vt sep* faire la moyenne de.

averse [ə'vɜːs] *adj* : **she's not ~ to the occasional glass of wine** elle boit volontiers un verre de vin de temps à autre ■ **he's not ~ to making money out of the crisis** ça ne le gêne pas de profiter de la crise pour se faire de l'argent.

aversion [ə'vɜːʃn] *n* **1.** [dislike] aversion *f* ■ **to have an ~ to** avoir une aversion pour OR contre ■ **she has an ~ to smoking** elle a horreur du tabac **2.** [object of dislike] objet *m* d'aversion.

aversion therapy *n* thérapie *f* d'aversion.

avert [ə'vɜːt] *vt* **1.** [prevent] prévenir, éviter **2.** [turn aside - eyes, thoughts] détourner ; [- blow] détourner, parer ; [- suspicion] écarter ■ **I ~ed my gaze** j'ai détourné les yeux.

aviary ['eɪvjərɪ] (*pl* **aviaries**) *n* volière *f*.

aviation [,eɪvɪ'eɪʃn] ◇ *n* aviation *f*.
◇ *comp* [design] d'aviation ■ **the ~ industry** l'aéronautique *f* ■ **~ fuel** kérosène *m*.

aviator ['eɪvɪeɪtər] ◇ *n* aviateur *m*, - trice *f*, pilote *m*.
◇ *comp* : **~ glasses** lunettes *fpl* de soleil sport.

avid ['ævɪd] *adj* avide ■ **~ to learn** avide d'apprendre.

avidly ['ævɪdlɪ] *adv* avidement, avec avidité.

avionics [,eɪvɪ'ɒnɪks] ◇ *n (U)* [science] avionique *f*.
◇ *npl* [instruments] avionique *f*.

avocado [,ævə'kɑːdəʊ] (*pl* **avocados** OR *pl* **avocadoes**) *n* [fruit] : **~ (pear)** avocat *m* ; [tree] avocatier *m*.

avocation [,ævə'keɪʃn] *n* US activité *f* de loisir.

avocet ['ævə,set] *n* avocette *f*.

avoid [ə'vɔɪd] *vt* **1.** [object, person] éviter ■ [danger, task] éviter, échapper à ■ **she ~ed my eyes** elle évita mon regard ■ **we can't ~ inviting them** nous ne pouvons pas faire autrement que de les inviter ■ **they couldn't ~ hitting the car** ils n'ont pas pu éviter la voiture ■ **~ giving them too much information** évitez de leur donner trop d'informations ■ **don't ~ the issue** n'essaie pas d'éviter OR d'éluder la question ■ **to ~ (paying) taxes** [legally] se soustraire à l'impôt ; [illegally] frauder le fisc **2.** LAW [void] annuler, rendre nul.

avoidable [ə'vɔɪdəbl] *adj* évitable.

avoidance [ə'vɔɪdəns] *n* : **~ of work** le soin que l'on met à éviter le travail ■ **~ of duty** manquements *mpl* au devoir ➔ **tax ~** évasion *f* fiscale.

avoirdupois [,ævədə'pɔɪz] ◇ *n* **1.** [system] avoirdupoids *m* **2.** US [of person] embonpoint *m*.
◇ *comp* [ounce, pound] *conforme aux poids et mesures officiellement établis* ■ **~ weight** avoirdupoids *m*.

avow [ə'vaʊ] *vt fml* [state] affirmer, déclarer ■ [admit] admettre, reconnaître, confesser.

avowal [ə'vaʊəl] *n* aveu *m*.

avowed [ə'vaʊd] *adj* déclaré ■ **she's an ~ feminist** elle avoue OR reconnaît être féministe.

avuncular [ə'vʌŋkjʊlər] *adj* avunculaire.

aw [ɔː] *interj* US **~!** oh!

await [ə'weɪt] *vt* **1.** [wait for] attendre ■ **a long-~ed holiday** des vacances qui se sont fait attendre ■ **she's ~ing trial** elle est dans l'attente de son procès **2.** [be in store for] attendre, être réservé à ■ **a warm welcome ~ed them** un accueil chaleureux leur fut réservé.

awake [ə'weɪk] ◇ *adj* **1.** [not sleeping] éveillé, réveillé ■ **to be ~** être réveillé, ne pas dormir ■ **the noise kept me ~** le bruit m'a empêché de dormir ■ **I lay ~ all night** je n'ai pas fermé l'œil de la nuit ■ **his mother stayed ~ all night** sa mère a veillé toute la nuit ■ **he was wide ~** il était bien éveillé **2.** [aware] attentif, vigilant ■ **is the minister ~ to the dangers inherent to the system?** le ministre a-t-il conscience *OR* se rend-il compte des dangers inhérents au système?
◇ *vi* (*pret* **awoke** [ə'wəʊk], *pp* **awoken** [ə'wəʊkn]) **1.** [emerge from sleep] se réveiller, s'éveiller ■ **I awoke from a deep sleep** je suis sorti *OR* je me suis réveillé d'un sommeil profond **2.** [become aware] prendre conscience, se rendre compte ■ **he finally awoke from his illusions** il est enfin revenu de ses illusions.
◇ *vt* (*pret* **awoke** [ə'wəʊk], *pp* **awoken** [ə'wəʊkn]) **1.** [person] réveiller, éveiller **2.** *fig* [curiosity, suspicions] éveiller ■ [memories] réveiller, faire renaître ■ [hope] éveiller, faire naître.

awaken [ə'weɪkn] ◇ *vt* éveiller.
◇ *vi* s'éveiller.

awakening [ə'weɪknɪŋ] ◇ *n* **1.** *liter & fig* [arousal] réveil *m* ■ **it was a rude ~** c'était un réveil brutal *OR* pénible **2.** [beginning] début *m*, commencement *m*.
◇ *adj* naissant.

award [ə'wɔːd] ◇ *n* **1.** [prize] prix *m* ■ [medal] médaille *f* ■ **~ for bravery** décoration *f*, médaille *f* **2.** [scholarship] bourse *f* **3.** LAW [damages] dommages-intérêts *mpl* accordés par le juge ■ [decision] décision *f*, sentence *f* (arbitrale).
◇ *vt* [give - mark] accorder ; [- medal, prize] décerner, attribuer ; [- scholarship] attribuer, allouer ■ LAW [- damages] accorder.

award-winner *n* [person] lauréat *m*, - e *f* ■ [film] film *m* primé ■ [book] livre *m* primé.

award-winning *adj* qui a reçu un prix ■ **he gave an ~ performance in...** il a reçu un prix pour son rôle dans...

aware [ə'weər] *adj* **1.** [cognizant, conscious] conscient ■ [informed] au courant, informé ■ **to be ~ of sthg** être conscient de qqch ■ **I am quite ~ of his feelings** je connais *OR* je n'ignore pas ses sentiments ■ **to become ~ of sthg** se rendre compte *OR* prendre conscience de qqch ■ **she made us ~ of the problem** elle nous a fait prendre conscience du problème ■ **as far as I am ~** autant que je sache ■ **not that I am ~ of** pas que je sache ■ **without being ~ of it** sans s'en rendre compte ■ **politically ~** politisé ■ **socially ~** au courant des problèmes sociaux **2.** [sensitive] sensible.

awareness [ə'weənɪs] *n* [gen] conscience *f* ■ **a heightened ~ of colour** une sensibilité plus aiguë à la couleur ■ **political ~** politisation *f*.

awash [ə'wɒʃ] *adj* **1.** *liter & fig* [flooded] inondé ■ **~ with oil** inondé de pétrole **2.** NAUT à fleur d'eau, qui affleure.

away [ə'weɪ] ◇ *adv* **1.** [indicating movement] : **he drove ~** il s'est éloigné (en voiture) ■ **they're ~!** [at start of race] ils sont partis ▮ [indicating position] : **the village is 10 miles ~** le village est à 10 miles ▮ [in time] : **the holidays are only three weeks ~** les vacances sont dans trois semaines seulement ■ **~ back in the 20s** il y a bien longtemps dans les années 20 **2.** [absent] absent ■ **the boss is ~ on business this week** le patron est en déplacement cette semaine ■ **they're ~ on holiday/in Madrid** ils sont (partis) en vacances/à Madrid **3.** [indicating disappearance, decline etc] : **the water had boiled ~** l'eau s'était évaporée (à force de bouillir) ■ **we danced the night ~** nous avons passé toute la nuit à danser **4.** [continuously] : **he was singing ~ to himself** il fredonnait ■ **she's working ~ on her novel** elle travaille d'arrache-pied à son roman **5.** SPORT : **the team is (playing) ~ this Saturday** l'équipe joue à l'extérieur *OR* en déplacement samedi **6.** *phr* **~ with** *fml* assez de ■ **~ with petty restrictions!** assez de restrictions mesquines!
◇ *adj* SPORT à l'extérieur ■ **an ~ match** un match à l'extérieur ■ **the ~ team** l'équipe (qui est) en déplacement.
◆ **away from** *prep phr* [indicating precise distance] à... de ■ **two metres ~ from us** à deux mètres de nous ▮ [not at, not in] loin de ■ **somewhere well ~ from the city** quelque part très loin de la ville ■ **when we're ~ from home** quand nous partons, quand nous ne sommes pas chez nous.

awe [ɔː] *n* effroi *m* mêlé d'admiration et de respect ■ **to be** *OR* **to stand in ~ of** être impressionné *OR* intimidé par ■ **I stared at her in ~** je l'ai regardée avec la plus grande admiration.

awed [ɔːd] *adj* : **she spoke in an ~ whisper** elle chuchotait d'une voix respectueuse et intimidée.

awe-inspiring *adj* [impressive] impressionnant, imposant ■ [amazing] stupéfiant ■ [frightening] terrifiant.

awesome ['ɔːsəm] *adj* **1.** = **awe-inspiring 2.** *inf* [great] génial.

awe-struck *adj* [intimidated] intimidé, impressionné ■ [amazed] stupéfait ■ [frightened] frappé de terreur.

awful ['ɔːfʊl] ◇ *adj* **1.** [bad] affreux, atroce ■ **she was simply ~ to him** elle a été absolument infecte avec lui ■ **I feel ~** je me sens très mal ■ **she looks ~** [ill] elle a l'air malade ; [badly dressed] elle est affreusement mal habillée ■ **how ~ for you!** ça a dû être vraiment terrible (pour vous)! **2.** [horrific] épouvantable, effroyable **3.** [as intensifier] : **I have an ~ lot of work** j'ai énormément de travail ■ **they took an ~ chance** ils ont pris un risque énorme *OR* considérable.
◇ *adv US inf* = **awfully**.

awfully ['ɔːflɪ] *adv* [very] très, terriblement ■ **~ funny/nice** extrêmement drôle/gentil ■ **he's an ~ good writer** il écrit merveilleusement bien ■ **I'm ~ sorry** je suis vraiment *OR* sincèrement désolé ■ **thanks ~** merci infiniment *OR* mille fois.

awfulness ['ɔːfʊlnɪs] *n* **1.** [of behaviour, treatment] atrocité *f* **2.** [of accident, crime] horreur *f*.

awhile [ə'waɪl] *adv lit* (pendant) un instant *OR* un moment.

awkward ['ɔːkwəd] *adj* **1.** [clumsy - person] maladroit, gauche ; [- gesture] maladroit, peu élégant ; [- style] lourd, gauche ■ **the ~ age** l'âge ingrat **2.** [embarrassed - person] gêné, ennuyé ; [- silence] gêné, embarrassé ■ **she felt ~ about going** cela la gênait d'y aller **3.** [difficult - problem, situation] délicat, fâcheux ; [- task] délicat ; [- question] gênant, embarrassant ; [- person] peu commode, difficile ■ **it's an ~ time for me to leave** cela me serait difficile de partir en ce moment ■ **you've come at an ~ time** vous êtes arrivé au mauvais moment ■ **they could make things ~ for her** ils pourraient lui mettre des bâtons dans les roues ■ **he's an ~ customer** *inf* il faut se le farcir ■ **it's ~ to use** ça n'est pas facile à utiliser ■ **the table is at an ~ angle** la table est mal placée ■ [uncooperative] peu coopératif ■ **he's just being ~** il essaie seulement de compliquer les choses.

awkwardly ['ɔːkwədlɪ] *adv* **1.** [clumsily - dance, move] maladroitement, peu élégamment ; [- handle, speak] maladroitement, gauchement ■ **an ~ phrased sentence** une phrase lourde *OR* mal formulée **2.** [with embarrassment - behave] d'une façon gênée *OR* embarrassée ; [- reply, speak] d'un ton embarrassé *OR* gêné, avec gêne.

awkwardness ['ɔːkwədnɪs] *n* **1.** [clumsiness - of movement, person] maladresse *f*, gaucherie *f* ; [- of style] lourdeur *f*, inélégance *f* **2.** [unease] embarras *m*, gêne *f* ■ **the ~ of the situation** le côté gênant *OR* embarrassant de la situation.

awl [ɔːl] *n* alène *f*, poinçon *m*.

awning ['ɔːnɪŋ] *n* **1.** [over window] store *m* ■ [on shop display] banne *f*, store *m* ■ [at door] marquise *f*, auvent *m* ■ NAUT taud *m*, taude *f* **2.** [tent] auvent *m*.

awoke [ə'wəʊk] *pt* ▷ **awake**.

awoken [ə'wəʊkn] *pp* ▷ **awake**.

AWOL ['eɪwɒl] (*abbrev of* **absent without leave**) *adj* : **to be/to go ~** MIL être absent/s'absenter sans permission ; *fig & hum* disparaître.

awry [ə'raɪ] ◇ *adj* de travers, de guingois.
◇ *adv* de travers ■ **to go ~** mal tourner, aller de travers.

axe *UK*, **ax** *US* [æks] ◇ *n* (*pl* **axes**) [tool] hache *f* ■ **to have an ~ to grind** [ulterior motive] prêcher pour sa paroisse, être intéressé ; [complaint] avoir un compte à régler ■ **to get the ~** *inf* [person] être licencié *OR* viré ; [programme, plan etc] être annulé *OR* supprimé ■ **when the ~ falls** quand le couperet tombe.
◇ *vt* **1.** *liter* [wood] couper, hacher TECH **2.** *fig* [person] licencier, virer ■ [project] annuler, abandonner ■ [job, position] supprimer.

axeman ['æksmæn] *n liter* tueur *m* à la hache ■ *fig* [in company] *cadre chargé des licenciements.*

axes ['æksi:z] *pl* ▷ **axis**.

axiom ['æksɪəm] *n* axiome *m*.

axiomatic [,æksɪə'mætɪk] *adj* axiomatique.

axis ['æksɪs] (*pl* **axes** ['æksi:z]) *n* [gen - ANAT], BOT & GEOM axe *m*.
◆ **Axis** *n* HIST : **the Axis** l'Axe *m*.

axle ['æksl] *n* [gen] axe *m* ■ AUT essieu *m*.

ay [aɪ] *interj* & *n* = **aye** *(interj n)*.

ayatollah [,aɪə'tɒlə] *n* ayatollah *m*.

aye ◇ *adv* [eɪ] *arch* & *lit* toujours.
◇ *interj* [aɪ] *arch* & *dial* **~!** oui ■ **~, ~ sir!** NAUT oui, mon commandant!
◇ *n* [aɪ] oui *m inv* ■ **the ~s have it** les oui l'emportent.

aye-aye ['aɪ,aɪ] *interj UK* **~!** tiens donc!

AZ *written abbr of* **Arizona**.

azalea [ə'zeɪljə] *n* azalée *f*.

Azerbaijan [,æzəbaɪ'dʒɑ:n] *pr n* Azerbaïdjan *m*.

Azerbaijani [,æzəbaɪ'd ʒɑ:nɪ] ◇ *n* Azerbaïdjanais *m*, - e *f*.
◇ *adj* azerbaïdjanais.

Azeri [ə'zerɪ] ◇ *n* Azeri *mf*.
◇ *adj* azeri.

Azores [ə'zɔ:z] *pr npl* : **the ~** les Açores *fpl*.

AZT (*abbrev of* **azidothymidine**) *n* AZT *f*.

Aztec ['æztek] ◇ *n* Aztèque *mf*.
◇ *adj* aztèque.

azure ['æʒə[r]] *lit* ◇ *adj* azuré, d'azur.
◇ *n* azur *m*.

B

b (*pl* **b's** *OR pl* **bs**), **B** (*pl* **B's** *OR pl* **Bs**) [biː] *n* [letter] b *m*, B *m* ■ **B for Bob** B comme Bob ■ **6B Racine Street** 6 ter, rue Racine, *see also* **f**.

b 1. *written abbr of* **billion 2.** *written abbr of* **born**.

B 1. [indicating secondary importance] : **B-movie, B-film, B-picture** film *m* de série B ■ **the B-team** SPORT l'équipe secondaire **2.** SCH & UNIV [mark] bien *(= 12 à 14 sur 20)* **3.** MUS [note] si *m*.

B2B [ˌbiːtəˈbiː] (*abbrev of* **business to business**) *n* B to B.

B2C [ˌbiːtəˈsiː] (*abbrev of* **business to customer**) *n* B to C.

BA ◇ *n* (*abbrev of* **Bachelor of Arts**) *(titulaire d'une) licence de lettres*.
◇ *pr n* **1.** = **British Academy 2.** (*abbrev of* **British Airways**) *compagnie aérienne britannique*.

baa [bɑː] ◇ *n* bêlement *m* ■ **~!** bêê!
◇ *vi* bêler.

BAA (*abbrev of* **British Airports Authority**) *pr n organisme autonome responsable des aéroports en Grande-Bretagne*.

baa-lamb *n baby* petit agneau *m*.

baba [ˈbɑːbɑː] *n* baba *m*.

babble [ˈbæbl] ◇ *vi* **1.** [baby] gazouiller, babiller ■ [person - quickly] bredouiller ; [- foolishly] bavarder, babiller **2.** [stream] jaser, gazouiller.
◇ *vt* [say quickly] bredouiller ■ [say foolishly] bavarder, babiller.
◇ *n* **1.** [of voices] rumeur *f* ■ [of baby] babillage *m*, babil *m* ■ [of stream] gazouillement *m*, babil *m* **2.** [chatter] bavardage *m*.

babbling [ˈbæblɪŋ] ◇ *n* **1.** [of voices] rumeur *f* ■ [of baby] babillage *m*, babil *m* ■ [of stream] gazouillement *m*, babil *m* **2.** [chatter] bavardage *m*.
◇ *adj* babillard.

babe [beɪb] *n* **1.** *liter* [baby] bébé *m* ■ *fig* [naive person] innocent *m*, - e *f*, naïf *m*, - ïve *f* ■ **~ in arms** *liter* enfant *m* au berceau ■ **she's a ~ in arms** *fig* elle est comme l'enfant qui vient de naître **2.** *inf* [young woman] belle gosse *f*, minette *f* **3.** *inf* [term of endearment] chéri *m*, - e *f*.

babel [ˈbeɪbl] *n* brouhaha *m*.
◆ **Babel** *n* : **the tower of Babel** la tour de Babel.

baboon [bəˈbuːn] *n* babouin *m*.

baby [ˈbeɪbɪ] ◇ *n* (*pl* **babies**) **1.** [infant] bébé *m* ■ **we've known her since she was a ~** nous l'avons connue toute petite *OR* bébé ■ **don't be such a ~!** ne fais pas l'enfant! ▶ **they left him holding the ~** il lui ont laissé payer les pots cassés, ils lui ont tout fait retomber dessus ■ **to throw the ~ out with the bathwater** jeter le bébé avec l'eau du bain **2.** *US inf* [young woman] belle gosse *f*, minette *f* **3.** *US inf* [term of endearment] chéri *m*, - e *f* **4.** *inf* [pet project] bébé *m* ■ **the new project is his ~** le nouveau projet, c'est son bébé ■ **it's not my ~** je n'ai rien à voir là-dedans **5.** *US inf* [machine] merveille *f* ■ **this ~ drives like a dream** cette voiture est une pure merveille à conduire.
◇ *comp* [care, food, shampoo] pour bébés ■ **~ battering** *violences commises sur un bébé* ■ **~'s bottle** *UK*, **~ bottle** *US* biberon *m* ■ **~ changing area** relais-bébé *m* ■ **~ linen, ~ clothes** layette *f* ■ **~ seat** siège *m* pour bébés.
◇ *vt* (*pret & pp* **babied**) dorloter, bichonner.
◇ *adj* [animal] bébé, petit ■ [mushroom, tomato] petit ■ **~ elephant** éléphanteau *m*, bébé *m* éléphant ■ **~ girl** petite fille *f*.

baby boom *n* baby boom *m*.

baby boomer [-ˌbuːməʳ] *n* enfant *m* du baby boom.

Baby-bouncer® *n* trotteur *m*, youpala *m*.

baby buggy *n* **1.** *US* = **baby carriage 2.** *UK* [pushchair] : **Baby buggy**® poussette *f*.

baby carriage *n US* voiture *f* d'enfant, landau *m*.

baby doll *n* poupée *f*.
◆ **baby-doll** *adj* : **baby-doll pyjamas, baby-doll nightdress** baby-doll *m*.

baby face *n* visage *m* de bébé.
◆ **baby-face** *adj* au visage de bébé.

baby grand *n* (piano *m*) demi-queue *m*.

Baby-gro® [ˈbeɪbɪgrəʊ] *n* grenouillère *f*.

babyish [ˈbeɪbɪɪʃ] *adj pej* [features, voice] puéril, enfantin ■ [behaviour] puéril, enfantin, infantile.

Babylon [ˈbæbɪlən] *pr n* Babylone.

Babylonia [ˌbæbɪˈləʊnjə] *pr n* Babylonie *f*.

Babylonian [ˌbæbɪˈləʊnjən] ◇ *n* [person] Babylonien *m*, - enne *f*.
◇ *adj* babylonien.

baby-minder *n* nourrice *f*.

baby-sit *vi* garder des enfants, faire du baby-sitting ■ **she ~s for them** elle garde leurs enfants.

baby-sitter *n* baby-sitter *mf*.

baby-sitting *n* garde *f* d'enfants, baby-sitting *m*.

baby sling *n* porte-bébé *m*, Kangourou® *m*.

baby-snatcher *n* ravisseur *m*, - euse *f* de bébés.

baby-snatching [-ˌsnætʃɪŋ] *n* rapt *m OR* enlèvement *m* de bébés.

baby talk *n* langage *m* enfantin *OR* de bébé.

baby-walker *n* trotteur *m*.

babywipe [ˈbeɪbɪwaɪp] *n* lingette *f*.

baccalaureate [ˌbækəˈlɔːrɪət] *n* UNIV ≃ licence *f*.

Bacchae ['bæki:] *pr npl* : **the ~** les Bacchantes *fpl*.

bacchanalia [,bækə'neɪljə] *npl* [rite] bacchanales *fpl* ▪ [party] bacchanale *f*.

bacchanalian [,bækə'neɪljən] *adj* bachique.

baccy△ ['bækɪ] *n UK* tabac *m*.

Bach [bɑ:x] *pr n* Bach.

bachelor ['bætʃələr] ◇ *n* **1.** [man] célibataire *m* ▪ **confirmed ~** célibataire endurci **2.** UNIV ≃ licencié *m*, - e *f* ▪ **~'s degree** ≃ licence *f* ▪ **Bachelor of Arts/Science** [degree] ≃ licence *f* de lettres/de sciences ; [person] ≃ licencié *m*, - e *f* ès lettres/ès sciences.
◇ *adj* [brother, uncle] célibataire ▪ [life] de célibataire.

bachelor flat *n* garçonnière *f*.

bachelor girl *n* célibataire *f*.

bachelorhood ['bætʃələhʊd] *n* [gen] célibat *m* ▪ [of men] vie *f* de garçon.

bacillus [bə'sɪləs] (*pl* **bacilli** [-laɪ]) *n* bacille *m*.

back [bæk] ◇ *adv* **1.** [towards the rear] vers l'arrière, en arrière ▪ **he stepped ~** il a reculé d'un pas, il a fait un pas en arrière ▪ **I pushed ~ my chair** j'ai reculé ma chaise ▪ **she tied her hair ~** elle a attaché ses cheveux ▪ **he glanced ~** il a regardé derrière lui ▪ **their house sits ~ from the road** leur maison est en retrait par rapport à la route
2. [into or in previous place] : **my headache's ~** j'ai de nouveau mal à la tête, mon mal de tête a recommencé ▪ **they'll be ~ on Monday** ils rentrent *OR* ils seront de retour lundi ▪ **I'll be right ~** je reviens tout de suite ▪ **is he ~ at work?** a-t-il repris le travail? ▪ **he went to his aunt's and ~** il a fait l'aller et retour chez sa tante ▪ **meanwhile, ~ in Washington** entre-temps, à Washington ▪ **~ home there's no school on Saturdays** chez moi *OR* nous, il n'y a pas d'école le samedi ⊙ **the ~-to-school sales** les soldes de la rentrée
3. [indicating return to previous state] : **she wants her children ~** elle veut qu'on lui rende ses enfants ▪ **he went ~ to sleep** il s'est rendormi ▪ **business soon got ~ to normal** les affaires ont vite repris leur cours normal ▪ **miniskirts are coming ~ (in fashion)** les minijupes reviennent à la mode
4. [earlier] : **six pages ~** six pages plus haut ▪ **~ in the 17th century** au 17e siècle ▪ **as far ~ as I can remember** d'aussi loin que je m'en souvienne ▪ **~ in November** déjà au mois de novembre ▪ **ten years ~** *inf* il y a dix ans
5. [in reply, in return] : **you should ask for your money ~** vous devriez demander un remboursement *OR* qu'on vous rembourse ▪ **I hit him ~** je lui ai rendu son coup ▪ **she smiled ~ at him** elle lui a répondu par un sourire.
◇ *adj* **1.** [rear - door, garden] de derrière ; [- wheel] arrière *(inv)* ; [- seat] arrière *(inv)*, de derrière ▪ **the ~ legs of a horse** les pattes arrière d'un cheval ▪ **the ~ room is the quietest** la pièce qui donne sur l'arrière est la plus calme ▪ **the ~ page of the newspaper** la dernière page du journal ⊙ **to put sthg on the ~ burner** mettre qqch en attente
2. [quiet - lane, road] écarté, isolé ▪ **~ street** petite rue *f* ▪ **I grew up in the ~ streets of Chicago** j'ai été élevé dans les mauvais quartiers de Chicago
3. [overdue] arriéré ▪ **~ rent/taxes** arriéré *m* de loyer/d'impôts ▪ **~ pay** rappel *m* (de salaire)
4. LING [vowel] postérieur.
◇ *n* **1.** ANAT [of animal, person] dos *m* ▪ **~ pain** mal *m* de dos ▪ **my ~ aches** j'ai mal au dos ▪ **I fell flat on my ~** je suis tombé à la renverse *OR* sur le dos ▪ **we lay on our ~s** nous étions allongés sur le dos ▪ **I only saw them from the ~** je ne les ai vus que de dos ▪ **you had your ~ to me** tu me tournais le dos ⊙ **they have the police at their ~s** [in support] ils ont la police avec eux ; [in pursuit] ils ont la police à leurs trousses ▪ **the decision was taken behind my ~** la décision a été prise derrière mon dos ▪ **to be flat on one's ~** [bedridden] être alité *OR* cloué au lit ▪ **he's always on my ~** *inf* il me critique *OR* harcèle toujours ▪ **get off my ~!** *inf* fiche-moi la paix! ▪ **to have one's ~ to the wall** être au pied du mur ▪ **the rich live off the ~s of the poor** les riches vivent sur le dos des pauvres ▪ **to put sb's ~ up** énerver qqn ▪ **to put one's ~ into sthg** mettre toute son énergie à faire qqch ▪ **to put one's ~ out** se faire mal au dos ▪ **I'll be glad to see the ~ of her** je serai content de la voir partir *OR* d'être débarrassé d'elle
2. [part opposite the front - gen] dos *m*, derrière *m* ; [- of coat, shirt, door] dos *m* ; [- of vehicle, building, head] arrière *m* ; [- of train] queue *f* ; [- of book] fin *f* ▪ **the garden is out *OR* round the ~** le jardin se trouve derrière la maison ⊙ **she's got a face like the ~ of a bus** *inf* c'est un boudin
3. [other side - of hand, spoon, envelope, cheque] dos *m* ; [- of carpet, coin, medal] revers *m* ; [- of page] verso *m* ▪ **I know this town like the ~ of my hand** je connais cette ville comme ma poche
4. [farthest from the front - of cupboard, room, stage] fond *m* ▪ **we'd like a table at the *OR* in the very ~** nous voudrions une table tout au fond ⊙ **in the ~ of beyond** en pleine brousse, au diable vauvert ▪ **I've had it *OR* it's been at the ~ of my mind for ages** j'y pense depuis longtemps, ça fait longtemps que ça me travaille
5. [of chair] dos *m*, dossier *m*
6. SPORT arrière *m*.
◇ *vt* **1.** [move backwards - bicycle, car] reculer ; [- horse] faire reculer ; [- train] refouler ▪ **I ~ed the car into the garage** j'ai mis la voiture dans le garage en marche arrière
2. [support financially - company, venture] financer, commanditer ; [- loan] garantir ▪ [encourage - efforts, person, venture] encourager, appuyer, soutenir ; [- candidate, bill] soutenir
3. [bet on] parier sur, miser sur ⊙ **to ~ a winner** SPORT [horse, team] parier sur un gagnant ; FIN [company, stock] bien placer son argent ; *fig* jouer la bonne carte
4. [strengthen, provide backing for - curtain, material] doubler ; [- picture, paper] renforcer
5. MUS [accompany] accompagner.
◇ *vi* [go in reverse - car, train] faire marche arrière ; [- horse, person] reculer ▪ **the car ~ed into the driveway** la voiture est entrée en marche arrière dans l'allée ▪ **I ~ed into a corner** je me suis retiré dans un coin.
◆ **back and forth** *adv phr* : **to go ~ and forth** [person] faire des allées et venues ; [machine, piston] faire un mouvement de va-et-vient ▪ **his eyes darted ~ and forth** il regardait de droite à gauche.
◆ **back to back** *adv phr liter & fig* dos à dos ▪ **they're showing both films ~ to ~** ils montrent deux films l'un après l'autre.
◆ **back to front** *adv phr* devant derrière.
◆ **in back of** *prep phr US* derrière.
◆ **back away** *vi insep* **1.** [car] faire marche arrière
2. [person] (se) reculer ▪ **she ~ed away from him** elle a reculé devant lui ▪ **they have ~ed away from making a decision** *fig* ils se sont abstenus de prendre une décision.
◆ **back down** *vi insep* [accept defeat] céder.
◆ **back off** *vi insep* **1.** [withdraw] reculer ▪ **~ off, will you!** *inf* fiche-moi la paix!, lâche-moi les baskets!
2. *US* = **back down**.
◆ **back onto** *vt insep* [have back facing towards] donner sur (à l'arrière).
◆ **back out** *vi insep* **1.** [car] sortir en marche arrière ▪ [person] sortir à reculons
2. *fig* [withdraw] se dérober, tirer son épingle du jeu ▪ **don't ~ out now!** ne faites pas marche arrière maintenant! ▪ **to ~ out of a contract** se rétracter *OR* se retirer d'un contrat.
◆ **back up** ◇ *vi insep* **1.** [car] faire marche arrière
2. [drain] se boucher ▪ [water] remonter.
◇ *vt sep* **1.** [car, horse] faire reculer ▪ [train] refouler
2. [support - claim, story] appuyer, soutenir ; [- person] soutenir, épauler, seconder ▪ **her story is ~ed up by eye witnesses** sa version des faits est confirmée par des témoins oculaires ▪ **he ~ed this up with a few facts** il a étayé ça avec quelques faits
3. COMPUT sauvegarder
4. TRANSP : **traffic is ~ed up for 5 miles** il y a un embouteillage sur 8 km.

backache ['bækeɪk] *n* mal *m* de dos.

backbench ['bækbentʃ] ◇ *n banc des membres du Parlement britannique qui n'ont pas de portefeuille*.
◇ *comp* [opinion, support] des "backbenchers".

backbencher [,bæk'bentʃər] *n parlementaire sans fonction ministérielle*.

BACKBENCHER

Les *backbenchers* sont les députés qui n'occupent pas de poste officiel au gouvernement ou dans le cabinet fantôme. Ils sont assis aux derniers rangs de la Chambre des communes, les premiers rangs étant réservés aux différents ministres.

backbiting ['bækbaɪtɪŋ] *n* médisance *f*.

backbone ['bækbəʊn] *n* **1.** ANAT colonne *f* vertébrale ▪ ZOOL épine *f* dorsale **2.** [of country, organization] pivot *m*, épine *f* dorsale **3.** *fig* [strength of character] fermeté *f*, caractère *m* ▪ **he has no ~** il n'a rien dans le ventre **4.** COMPUT épine *f* dorsale, pivot *m*.

backbreaking ['bæk,breɪkɪŋ] *adj* éreintant ▪ **~ work** un travail à vous casser les reins.

backchat ['bæktʃæt] *n* *UK* impertinence *f*, insolence *f*.

backcloth ['bækklɒθ] *n* THEAT toile *f* de fond ▪ *fig* toile *f* de fond, fond *m*.

backcomb ['bækkəʊm] *vt* crêper.

back copy *n* vieux numéro *m*.

backdate [,bæk'deɪt] *vt* [cheque, document] antidater ▪ **the pay rise is ~d to March** l'augmentation de salaire a un effet rétroactif à compter de mars.

back door *n* porte *f* arrière ▪ **to get in through** *OR* **by the ~** *fig* entrer par la petite porte.
◆ **backdoor** *adj* louche, suspect.

backdrop ['bækdrɒp] *n* = **backcloth**.

-backed [bækt] *in cpds* **1.** [chair] à dos, à dossier ▪ **a broad~ man** un homme qui a le dos large **2.** [supported by] : **US~ rebels** des rebelles soutenus par les États-Unis.

back end *n* **1.** [of car, bus] arrière *m* ▪ [of train] queue *f* **2.** *UK inf* [autumn] : **the ~ of the year** l'arrière-saison.

backer ['bækəʳ] *n* **1.** [supporter] partisan *m*, - e *f* ▪ [financial supporter] commanditaire *mf*, bailleur *m* de fonds **2.** SPORT [punter] parieur *m*, - euse *f*.

backfill ['bækfɪl] *vt* remplir.

backfire [,bæk'faɪəʳ] ◇ *vi* **1.** [car] pétarader **2.** [plan] avoir un effet inattendu ▪ **the plan ~d on him** le projet s'est retourné contre lui *OR* lui est retombé sur le nez.
◇ *n* **1.** [noise] pétarade *f* ▪ [explosion] retour *m* d'allumage **2.** [controlled fire] contre-feu *m*.

backflip ['bækflɪp] *n* [in gymnastics] culbute *f* à l'envers.

backgammon ['bæk,gæmən] *n* backgammon *m*.

background ['bækgraʊnd] ◇ *n* **1.** [scene, view] fond *m*, arrière-plan *m* ▪ [sound] fond *m* sonore ▪ THEAT fond *m* ▪ **yellow flowers on a green ~** des fleurs jaunes sur fond vert ▪ **in the ~** dans le fond, à l'arrière-plan ▪ **his wife remains very much in the ~** *fig* sa femme est très effacée *OR* reste à l'écart **2.** [of person - history] antécédents *mpl* ; [- family] milieu *m* socioculturel ; [- experience] formation *f*, acquis *m* ; [- education] formation *f*, bagage *m* ▪ **people from a working-class ~** gens *mpl* de milieu ouvrier ▪ **she has a good ~ in history** elle a une bonne formation en histoire **3.** [of event, situation] contexte *m*, climat *m* ▪ **the economic ~ to the crisis** les raisons économiques de la crise ▪ **the talks are taking place against a ~ of political tensions** les débats ont lieu dans un climat de tension politique ▪ **the report looks at the ~ to the unrest** le rapport examine l'historique de l'agitation.
◇ *adj* **1.** [unobtrusive - music, noise] de fond **2.** [facts, material] de base, de fond ▪ **~ information** éléments de référence *OR* de base ▪ **~ reading** bibliographie *f* **3.** COMPUT : **~ processing** traitement *m* de données en tâches de fond **4.** PHYS : **~ radiation** rayonnement *m* naturel.

backhand ['bækhænd] ◇ *n* revers *m* ▪ **keep serving to his ~** continue de servir sur son revers.
◇ *adj* [stroke] en revers ▪ [volley] de revers.
◇ *adv* en revers.

backhanded ['bækhændɪd] *adj* **1.** [blow, slap] donné avec le revers de la main ▪ **~ stroke** SPORT revers *m* **2.** [compliment, remark] équivoque.

backhander ['bækhændəʳ] *n* **1.** [blow, stroke] coup *m* du revers de la main ▪ SPORT revers *m* **2.** [comment] remarque *f* équivoque **3.** *UK inf* [bribe] pot-de-vin *m*, dessous-de-table *m inv*.

backing ['bækɪŋ] *n* **1.** [support] soutien *m*, appui *m* ▪ [financial support] soutien *m* financier **2.** [material] renforcement *m*, support *m* **3.** MUS [accompaniment] accompagnement *m*.

backing group *n* *UK* *musiciens qui accompagnent un chanteur*.

back issue *n* vieux numéro *m*.

backlash ['bæklæʃ] *n* contrecoup *m* ▪ **a ~ of violence** une réaction de violence.

backless ['bæklɪs] *adj* [dress] (très) décolleté dans le dos ▪ [chair] sans dos, sans dossier.

backlit ['bæklɪt] *adj* [screen] rétro-éclairé.

backlog ['bæklɒg] *n* accumulation *f*, arriéré *m* ▪ **a ~ of orders** COMM des commandes inexécutées *OR* en souffrance.

back number *n* vieux numéro *m*.

backpack ['bækpæk] ◇ *n* sac *m* à dos.
◇ *vi* voyager sac au dos.
◇ *vt* transporter dans un sac à dos.

backpacker ['bækpækəʳ] *n* routard *m*, - e *f*.

backpacking ['bækpækɪŋ] *n* : **to go ~** voyager sac au dos.

back passage *n* **1.** [rectum] rectum *m* **2.** [alley] ruelle *f*.

backpedal [,bæk'pedl] (*UK pret & pp* **backpedalled**, *cont* **backpedalling**) (*US pret & pp* **backpedaled**, *cont* **backpedaling**) *vi* **1.** [on bicycle] rétropédaler **2.** [change mind] faire marche arrière *fig*.

backrest ['bækrest] *n* dossier *m*.

back room *n* **1.** [in house] pièce *f* de derrière ▪ [in shop] arrière-boutique *f* **2.** [for research] laboratoire *m* de recherche secret.
◆ **backroom** *adj* [research, work] secret, - ète *f* ▪ **backroom boys** [gen] ceux qui restent dans l'ombre *OR* dans les coulisses ; [researchers] chercheurs *mpl* qui travaillent dans l'anonymat.

back-scratcher *n* [implement] gratte-dos *m inv*.

back seat *n* siège *m* arrière ▪ **to take a ~** *fig* passer au second plan.

back-seat driver *n pej* [in car] *personne qui donne toujours des conseils au conducteur* ▪ [interfering person] donneur *m*, - euse *f* de leçons.

backside ['bæksaɪd] *n inf* derrière *m*.

backslapping ['bæk,slæpɪŋ] ◇ *n* [heartiness] (excessive) jovialité *f* ▪ [congratulations] encensement *m*.
◇ *adj* jovial.

backslash ['bækslæʃ] *n* barre *f* oblique inversée, antislash *m*.

backslide [,bæk'slaɪd] (*pret* **backslid** [-'slɪd], *pp* **backslid** [-'slɪd] *OR* **backslidden** [-'slɪdn]) *vi* retomber, récidiver.

backslider [,bæk'slaɪdəʳ] *n* récidiviste *mf*.

backspace ['bækspeɪs] ◇ *vi* faire un retour arrière.
◇ *vt* rappeler.
◇ *n* espacement *m* *OR* retour *m* arrière.

backspin ['bækspɪn] *n* effet *m* contraire ▪ **to put ~ on a ball** couper une balle.

backstage [,bæk'steɪdʒ] THEAT & *fig* ◇ *n* coulisse *f*, coulisses *fpl*.
◇ *adv* THEAT dans la coulisse *OR* les coulisses, derrière la scène ▪ *fig* en coulisses, en secret.
◇ *adj* secret, furtif.

backstairs [,bæk'steəz] ◇ *npl* [secondary] escalier *m* de service ■ [secret] escalier *m* secret *OR* dérobé.
◇ *adj* [secret] secret, furtif ■ [unfair] déloyal ■ **~ gossip** bruits *mpl* de couloirs.

backstitch ['bækstɪtʃ] ◇ *n* point *m* arrière.
◇ *vi* & *vt* coudre en point arrière.

backstop ['bækstɒp] *n* SPORT **1.** [screen] panneau *m* **2.** [in baseball] attrapeur *m*.

back straight *n* ligne *f* (droite) d'en face.

backstreet ['bækstri:t] *adj* [secret] secret, furtif ■ [underhanded] louche ■ **~ abortionist** faiseuse *f* d'anges.

backstroke ['bækstrəʊk] *n* [in swimming] dos *m* crawlé.

backswing ['bækswɪŋ] *n* swing *m* (en arrière).

back talk *n US* impertinence *f*.

back-to-back ◇ *adj liter* & *fig* dos à dos.
◇ *n* : **~s** [houses] *rangée de maisons construites dos à dos et séparées par un passage étroit, typique des régions industrielles du nord de l'Angleterre.*

backtrack ['bæktræk] *vi liter* revenir sur ses pas, rebrousser chemin ■ *fig* faire marche arrière ■ **he's already ~ing from** *OR* **on his agreement** il est déjà en train de revenir sur son accord.

backup ['bækʌp] ◇ *n* **1.** [support] soutien *m*, appui *m* **2.** [reserve] réserve *f* ■ [substitute] remplaçant *m* **3.** COMPUT sauvegarde *f* **4.** *US* MUS *musiciens qui accompagnent un chanteur.*
◇ *adj* **1.** [furnace] de secours, de réserve ■ [plan] de secours ■ [supplies] supplémentaire, de réserve ■ [team] remplaçant ■ **~ troops** MIL réserves *fpl* **2.** COMPUT : **~ disk** sauvegarde *f* ■ **~ storage** mémoire *f* auxiliaire **3.** *US* AUT : **~ light** phare *m* de recul.

backward ['bækwəd] ◇ *adj* **1.** [directed towards the rear] en arrière, rétrograde ■ **without a ~ look** sans jeter un regard en arrière **2.** [late in development - country, society, child] arriéré **3.** [reluctant] hésitant, peu disposé ■ **he's not ~ about giving his opinion** il n'hésite pas à donner son avis ■ **she's not exactly ~ in coming forward** *hum* elle n'hésite pas à se mettre en avant.
◇ *adv US* = **backwards**.

backwardness ['bækwədnɪs] *n* **1.** [of development - country] sous-développement *m* ; [- person] retard *m* mental ; [- of economy] retard *m* **2.** [reluctance] hésitation *f*, lenteur *f*.

backwards ['bækwədz] *adv* **1.** [towards the rear] en arrière ■ **I fell ~** je suis tombé en arrière *OR* à la renverse **2.** [towards the past] en arrière, vers le passé ■ **looking ~ in time** en remontant dans le temps **3.** [with the back foremost] : **to walk ~** marcher à reculons ■ **you've got your sweater on ~** tu as mis ton pull à l'envers *OR* devant derrière **4.** [in reverse] à l'envers ■ **now say it ~** dis-le à l'envers maintenant **5.** [thoroughly] à fond, sur le bout des doigts.
◆ **backwards and forwards** *adv phr* : **to go ~ and forwards** [person] aller et venir ; [machine, piston] faire un mouvement de va-et-vient ; [pendulum] osciller ■ **she goes ~ and forwards between London and Paris** elle fait la navette entre Londres et Paris.

backwater ['bæk,wɔ:tər] *n* [of river] bras *m* mort ■ *fig* [remote spot] coin *m* tranquille ■ *pej* coin *m* perdu ■ **a cultural ~** un désert culturel.

backwoods ['bækwʊdz] *adj* [remote] isolé ■ [backward] peu avancé.

back yard *n UK* [courtyard] cour *f* de derrière, arrière-cour *f* ■ *US* [garden] jardin *m* de derrière.

bacon ['beɪkən] *n* lard *m* (maigre), bacon *m* ■ **a slice** *OR* **rasher of ~** une tranche de lard ■ **~ and eggs** œufs *mpl* au bacon *OR* au lard ■ **~ slicer** coupe-jambon *m inv* ■ **to bring home the ~** *inf* [be the breadwinner] faire bouillir la marmite ; [succeed] décrocher la timbale *OR* le gros lot.

bacteria [bæk'tɪərɪə] *npl* bactéries *fpl*.

bacterial [bæk'tɪərɪəl] *adj* bactérien.

bacteriologist [bæk,tɪərɪ'ɒlədʒɪst] *n* bactériologiste *mf*.

bacteriology [bæk,tɪərɪ'ɒlədʒɪ] *n* bactériologie *f*.

bacterium [bæk'tɪərɪəm] (*pl* **bacteria** [-rɪə]) *n* bactérie *f*.

bad [bæd] (*comp* **worse** [wɜ:s], *superl* **worst** [wɜ:st]) ◇ *adj* **1.** [unpleasant - breath, news, terms, weather] mauvais ; [- smell, taste] mauvais, désagréable ■ **that's too ~!** [regrettable] c'est *OR* quel dommage! ; [hard luck] tant pis pour toi! ■ **it's too ~ he had to leave** quel dommage qu'il ait été obligé de partir ■ **I have a ~ feeling about this** j'ai le pressentiment que ça va mal tourner ■ **I feel ~ about leaving you alone** cela m'ennuie de te laisser tout seul ■ **he felt ~ about the way he'd treated her** il s'en voulait de l'avoir traitée comme ça ■ **he's in a ~ mood** *OR* **~ temper** il est de mauvaise humeur ■ **she has a ~ temper** elle a un sale caractère, elle a un caractère de chien *OR* de cochon ■ **I'm on ~ terms with her** nous sommes fâchés ■ **to come to a ~ end** mal finir ■ **it's a ~ business** [unpleasant] c'est une sale affaire ; [unhappy] c'est une triste affaire ■ **things went from ~ to worse** les choses se sont gâtées *OR* sont allées de mal en pis
2. [unfavourable - effect, result] mauvais, malheureux ; [- omen, report] mauvais, défavorable ; [- opinion] mauvais *(before n)* ■ **things look ~** la situation n'est pas brillante ■ **it happened at the worst possible time** ça ne pouvait pas tomber plus mal ■ **he's in a ~ way** [ill, unhappy] il va mal, il est en piteux état ; [in trouble] il est dans de sales draps
3. [severe - accident, mistake] grave ; [- pain] violent, aigu *(uë)* ; [- headache] violent ; [- climate, winter] rude, dur ■ **I have a ~ cold** j'ai un gros rhume ■ **she has a ~ case of flu** elle a une mauvaise grippe
4. [evil, wicked - person] méchant, mauvais ; [- behaviour, habit] mauvais, odieux ■ **you've been a ~ girl!** tu as été vilaine *OR* méchante! ■ **~ boy!** vilain! ➲ **~ language** gros mots *mpl*, grossièretés *fpl*
5. [harmful] mauvais, néfaste ■ **smoking is ~ for your health** le tabac est mauvais pour la santé ■ **eating all these sweets is ~ for him** c'est mauvais pour lui *OR* ça ne lui vaut rien de manger autant de sucreries
6. [unhealthy - leg, arm, person] malade ; [- tooth] malade, carié ■ **how are you? – not so ~** comment allez-vous? – on fait aller *OR* pas trop mal ■ **he was taken ~ at the office** *inf* il a eu un malaise au bureau ■ **to have a ~ heart** être cardiaque
7. [poor - light, work] mauvais, de mauvaise qualité ; [- actor, pay, performance, road] mauvais ■ **that's not ~ for a beginner** ce n'est pas mal pour un débutant ■ **your painting isn't half ~** *inf* ton tableau n'est pas mal du tout ■ **he speaks rather ~ Spanish** il parle plutôt mal espagnol *OR* un espagnol plutôt mauvais ■ **it would be ~ form** *OR* **manners to refuse** ce serait impoli de refuser ■ **I've always been ~ at maths** je n'ai jamais été doué pour les maths, j'ai toujours été mauvais en maths ■ **she's ~ about paying bills on time** elle ne paie jamais ses factures à temps ■ **~ debt** créance *f* douteuse *OR* irrécouvrable
8. [food] mauvais, pourri ■ **to go ~** [milk] tourner ; [meat] pourrir, se gâter
9. △ [very good] terrible.
◇ *n* mauvais *m* ■ **he's gone to the ~** il a mal tourné ■ **we're £100 to the ~** nous sommes débiteurs *OR* nous avons un découvert de 100 livres ■ **she got in ~ with her boss** *inf* elle n'a pas la cote avec son patron.
◇ *npl* [people] : **the ~** les mauvais *mpl*.
◇ *adv inf* **he wants it ~** il en meurt d'envie ■ **she's got it ~ for him** elle l'a dans la peau ■ **he was beaten ~** *US* il s'est fait méchamment tabasser.

baddie, baddy ['bædɪ] *n inf* méchant *m*.

bade [bæd, beɪd] *pt* ▷ **bid**.

badge [bædʒ] *n* **1.** [gen] insigne *m* ■ [metal, plastic] badge *m* ■ [fabric] écusson *m* ■ [on lapel] pin's *m inv* ■ [of scout] badge *m* ■ MIL insigne *m* ■ **a ~ of office** un insigne de fonction **2.** *fig* signe *m*, marque *f*.

badger ['bædʒər] ◇ *n* blaireau *m* ■ **the Badger State** le Wisconsin.
◇ *vt* harceler, persécuter ■ **she ~ed us into going** elle nous a harcelés jusqu'à ce que nous y allions.

badly ['bædlɪ] (*comp* **worse** [wɜ:s], *superl* **worst** [wɜ:st]) *adv* **1.** [poorly] mal ■ **~ made/organized** mal fait/organisé ■ **things aren't going too ~** ça ne va pas trop mal ■ **the candidate did** *OR* **came off ~ in the exams** le candidat n'a pas bien marché à ses examens ■ **we came off worst in the deal** c'est nous qui nous en sommes le plus mal sortis dans l'affaire ▪ **I feel ~ about it** [sorry] je le regrette beaucoup ; [embarrassed] cela me gêne beaucoup ▪ **don't think ~ of him for what he did** ne lui en voulez pas de ce qu'il a fait ▪ **to be ~ off** être dans la misère ▪ **we're ~ off for supplies** nous manquons de provisions **2.** [behave - improperly] mal ; [- cruelly] méchamment, avec cruauté **3.** [severely - burn, damage] gravement, sérieusement ; [- hurt] gravement, grièvement ▪ **she had been ~ beaten** elle avait reçu des coups violents ▪ **the army was ~ defeated** l'armée a subi une sévère défaite **4.** [very much] énormément ▪ **he ~ needs** *OR* **he's ~ in need of a holiday** il a grand *OR* sérieusement besoin de (prendre des) vacances ▪ **we ~ want to see her** nous avons très envie de la voir.

badman ['bædmæn] (*pl* **badmen** [-men]) *n* **US** [crook] bandit *m* ▪ [in movie] méchant *m*.

bad-mannered *adj* mal élevé.

badminton ['bædmɪntən] *n* badminton *m*.

Badminton Horse Trials *pr n prestigieux concours hippique en Angleterre.*

badmouth ['bædmaʊθ] *vt* médire de, dénigrer.

badness ['bædnɪs] *n* **1.** [wickedness] méchanceté *f* ▪ [cruelty] cruauté *f* **2.** [inferior quality] mauvaise qualité *f*, mauvais état *m*.

bad-tempered *adj* [as character trait] qui a mauvais caractère ▪ [temporarily] de mauvaise humeur.

baffle ['bæfl] ◇ *vt* **1.** [puzzle] déconcerter, dérouter **2.** *fml* [frustrate - effort, plans] faire échouer, déjouer ; [- expectations, hopes] décevoir, tromper.
◇ *n* [deflector] déflecteur *m* ▪ [acoustic] baffle *m*, écran *m*.

baffling ['bæflɪŋ] *adj* déconcertant, déroutant.

Bafta (*abbrev of* **British Academy of Film and Television Awards**) *n* : **~ (award)** *prix récompensant les meilleurs films et émissions de télévision en Grande-Bretagne.*

bag [bæg] ◇ *n* **1.** [container] sac *m* ▪ **paper/plastic ~** sac en papier/en plastique ➡ **he was left holding the ~** **US** *inf* tout lui est retombé dessus ▪ **her promotion is in the ~** *inf* son avancement, c'est dans la poche *OR* dans le sac *OR* du tout cuit ▪ **to pull sthg out of the ~** sortir qqch du chapeau ▪ **the whole ~ of tricks** *inf* tout le tralala
2. [handbag] sac *m* (à main) ▪ [suitcase] valise *f* ▪ **~s** valises, bagages *mpl* ▪ **it's time to pack our ~s** *fig* c'est le moment de plier bagage ▪ **they threw her out ~ and baggage** *inf* ils l'ont mise à la porte avec toutes ses affaires
3. [of cloth, skin] poche *f* ▪ **to have ~s under one's eyes** avoir des poches sous les yeux
4. HUNT prise *f*
5. *inf pej* [woman] : **old ~** vieille peau
6. △ [interest] : **it's not my ~** ce n'est pas mon truc.
◇ *vt* (*pret & pp* **bagged**, *cont* **bagging**) **1.** [books, groceries] mettre dans un sac
2. *inf* [seize] mettre le grappin sur, s'emparer de ▪ [steal] piquer, faucher ▪ **he bagged the best seat for himself** il s'est réservé la meilleure place
3. HUNT tuer.
◇ *vi* (*pret & pp* **bagged**, *cont* **bagging**) goder, faire des poches.
➨ **bags** *inf npl* **UK** **1.** [trousers] pantalon *m*, fute *m*
2. [lots] : **there are ~s of things to do** il y a plein de choses à faire.

bagatelle [ˌbægə'tel] *n* **1.** [trinket] bagatelle *f*, babiole *f* **2.** GAMES [board game] (sorte *f* de) flipper *m* ▪ [billiards] billard *m* anglais **3.** MUS bagatelle *f*.

bagel ['beɪgəl] *n* petit pain *m* en couronne *(de la cuisine juive)*.

bagful ['bægfʊl] *n* sac *m* plein, plein sac *m*.

baggage ['bægɪdʒ] *n* **1.** [luggage] valises *fpl*, bagages *mpl* ▪ **~ car** **US** fourgon *m (d'un train)* ▪ **~ room** *OR* **checkroom** **US** consigne *f* ▪ **~ handler** bagagiste *mf* ▪ **~ reclaim** livraison *f* des bagages ▪ **~ tag** **US** bulletin *m* de consigne **2.** MIL équipement *m* (portatif).

Baggie® ['bægɪ] *n* **US** *petit sachet hermétique en plastique.*

baggy ['bægɪ] (*comp* **baggier**, *superl* **baggiest**) *adj* [clothing - too big] trop ample *OR* grand ; [- loose-fitting] ample ▪ **~ trousers** un pantalon bouffant.

Baghdad [bæg'dæd] *pr n* Bagdad.

bag lady *n* clocharde *f*.

bagpiper ['bægpaɪpəʳ] *n* joueur *m*, - euse *f* de cornemuse.

bagpipes ['bægpaɪps] *npl* cornemuse *f*.

bag-snatcher [-snætʃəʳ] *n* voleur *m*, - euse *f* à la tire.

bag-snatching [-ˌsnætʃɪŋ] *n* vol *m* à l'arraché.

bah [bɑː] *interj* : **~!** bah!

Bahamas [bə'hɑːməz] *pr npl* Bahamas *fpl*.

Bahamian [bə'heɪmɪən] ◇ *n* habitant *m*, - e *f* des Bahamas.
◇ *adj* des Bahamas.

Bahrain [bɑː'reɪn] *pr n* Bahreïn, Bahrayn ▪ **the ~ Islands** les îles *fpl* Bahreïn.

Bahraini [bɑː'reɪnɪ] ◇ *n* Bahreïni *m*, - e *f*.
◇ *adj* bahreïni.

Bahrein [bɑː'reɪn] *pr n* = **Bahrain**.

Baikal [baɪ'kɑːl] *pr n* : **Lake ~** le lac Baïkal.

bail [beɪl] ◇ *n* **1.** LAW [money] caution *f* ▪ [guarantor] caution *f*, répondant *m*, - e *f* ▪ [release] mise *f* en liberté provisoire sous caution ▪ **on ~** sous caution ▪ **the judge granted/refused ~** le juge a accordé/refusé la mise en liberté provisoire sous caution ▪ **she was released on £2,000 ~** elle a été mise en liberté provisoire après avoir payé une caution de 2 000 livres ▪ **to stand** *OR* **to go ~ for sb** se porter garant de qqn ▪ **who put up ~?** qui a payé la caution? ▪ **the prisoner jumped** *OR* **forfeited ~** le prisonnier s'est soustrait à la justice *(à la faveur d'une mise en liberté provisoire)* **2.** [in cricket] barrette *f*.
◇ *vt* **1.** LAW [subj: guarantor] payer la caution pour, se porter garant de ▪ [subj: judge] mettre en liberté provisoire sous caution **2.** [water] vider.
➨ **bail out** ◇ *vt sep* **1.** LAW = **bail** *(vt sense 1)* **2.** [help] tirer *OR* sortir d'affaire **3.** [boat] écoper ▪ [cellar, water] vider.
◇ *vi insep* [parachute] sauter en parachute.

bailiff ['beɪlɪf] *n* **1.** LAW huissier *m* **2.** **UK** [on estate, farm] régisseur *m*, intendant *m* **3.** [official - formerly] bailli *m*.

bailout ['beɪlaʊt] *n* [of company] renflouement *m*, sauvetage *m*.

bairn [beən] *n* **UK** *dial* enfant *mf*.

bait [beɪt] ◇ *n* FISHING & HUNT appât *m*, amorce *f* ▪ *fig* appât *m*, leurre *m* ▪ **to rise to** *OR* **to take the ~** *liter & fig* mordre (à l'hameçon).
◇ *vt* **1.** [hook, trap] amorcer **2.** [tease] harceler, tourmenter **3.** [badger, bear] lâcher les chiens sur **4.** [entice] tenter.

baize [beɪz] ◇ *n* [fabric] feutre *m* ▪ [on billiard table] tapis *m*.
◇ *adj* [cloth, lining] de feutre ▪ **~-covered** feutré.

bake [beɪk] ◇ *vt* **1.** CULIN faire cuire au four ▪ **she's baking a cake for me** elle me fait un gâteau **2.** [dry, harden] cuire ▪ **the land was ~d dry** la terre était desséchée.
◇ *vi* **1.** [person - cook] : **she got busy baking** [bread] elle s'est mise à faire du pain ; [cake] elle s'est mise à faire de la pâtisserie **2.** [cake, pottery] cuire (au four) ▪ **the ground was baking in the sun** le sol se desséchait au soleil **3.** *inf* [be hot] : **it's baking in here!** il fait une de ces chaleurs ici! ▪ **I'm baking!** j'étouffe!, je crève de chaleur!
◇ *n* **1.** [batch of food] fournée *f* **2.** **US** *fête où l'on sert un repas cuit au four.*

baked Alaska ['beɪkt-] *n* omelette *f* norvégienne.

baked beans ['beɪkt-] *npl* haricots *mpl* blancs à la sauce tomate.

baked potato ['beɪkt-] *n* pomme *f* de terre en robe de chambre.

Bakelite® ['beɪkəlaɪt] ◇ *n* Bakélite® *f*.
◇ *adj* en Bakélite®.

baker ['beɪkəʳ] *n* boulanger *m*, - ère *f* ▪ **I'm going to the ~'s (shop)** je vais à la boulangerie ▪ **a ~'s dozen** treize à la douzaine.

bakery ['beɪkərɪ] (*pl* **bakeries**) *n* boulangerie *f*.

baking ['beɪkɪŋ] <> *n* **1.** [process] cuisson *f* (au four) **2.** [bread] pain *m* ▪ [pastry] pâtisserie *f*, pâtisseries *fpl*.
<> *adj* **1.** [for cooking] : **~ potatoes** pommes *fpl* de terre à cuire au four ▪ **~ dish** plat *m* allant au four ▪ **~ tray** plaque *f* de four **2.** [hot - pavement, sun] brûlant ; [- day, weather] torride.
<> *adv* : **a ~ hot afternoon** un après-midi torride.

baking powder *n* levure *f* (chimique).

baking soda *n* bicarbonate *m* de soude.

baking tin *n* moule *m* à gâteau.

balaclava (helmet) [bælə'klɑːvə-] *n* passe-montagne *m*.

balalaika [ˌbælə'laɪkə] *n* balalaïka *f*.

balance ['bæləns] <> *n* **1.** [of person - physical] équilibre *m*, aplomb *m* ; [- mental] calme *m*, équilibre *m* ▪ **she tried to keep her ~** elle a essayé de garder l'équilibre *OR* son équilibre ▪ **off ~** [physically, mentally] déséquilibré ▪ **he threw me off ~** *liter* il m'a fait perdre l'équilibre ; *fig* il m'a pris par surprise **2.** [of situation] équilibre *m* ▪ [of painting, sculpture] harmonie *f* ▪ **she tried to strike a ~ between the practical and the idealistic** elle a essayé de trouver un juste milieu entre la réalité et l'idéal ▪ **~ of power** [in government] balance *OR* équilibre des pouvoirs ; [between states] balance *OR* équilibre des forces ▪ **he holds the ~ of power** il peut faire pencher la balance, tout dépend de lui **3.** [scales] balance *f* ▪ **everything is still (hanging) in the ~** rien n'est encore certain ▪ **our future hangs *OR* lies in the ~** notre avenir est en jeu ▪ **his remark tipped the ~ in his favour** sa remarque a fait pencher la balance en sa faveur **4.** [weight, force] poids *m*, contrepoids *m* ▪ **the ~ of evidence is against him** la plupart des preuves lui sont défavorables ▪ **she acts as a ~ to his impulsiveness** elle sert de contrepoids à *OR* elle contrebalance son impulsivité **5.** [remainder] solde *m*, reste *m* ▪ COMM & FIN solde *m* ▪ **~ due** solde débiteur ▪ **I'd like to pay the ~ of my account** j'aimerais solder mon compte ➔ **bank ~** solde (d'un compte) ▪ **~ of payments** balance *f* des paiements ▪ **~ of trade** balance *f* commerciale.
<> *vt* **1.** [put in stable position] mettre en équilibre ▪ [hold in stable position] tenir en équilibre **2.** [act as counterbalance, offset] équilibrer, contrebalancer ▪ **we have to ~ the right to privacy against the public's right to know** nous devons trouver le juste milieu entre le respect de la vie privée et le droit du public à être informé **3.** [weigh] peser ▪ *fig* mettre en balance, comparer ▪ **you have to ~ its usefulness against the actual cost** vous devez mettre en balance *OR* comparer son utilité et le coût réel **4.** [equation, finances] équilibrer ▪ **to ~ the books** dresser le bilan, arrêter les comptes **5.** [settle, pay] régler, solder ▪ **to ~ an account** solder un compte.
<> *vi* **1.** [remain in stable position] se maintenir en équilibre ▪ [be in stable position] être en équilibre **2.** [act as counterbalance] : **the weights ~** les poids s'équilibrent **3.** [budget, finances] s'équilibrer, être équilibré.
◆ **on balance** *adv phr* à tout prendre, tout bien considéré.
◆ **balance out** *vi insep* : **the advantages and disadvantages ~ out** les avantages contrebalancent *OR* compensent les inconvénients ▪ **the debits and credits should ~ out** les débits et les crédits devraient s'équilibrer.

balanced ['bælənst] *adj* **1.** [diet, scales, person] équilibré ▪ **the two teams were pretty well ~** les deux équipes étaient de force à peu près égale ▪ **a ~ view** une vue impartiale *OR* objective **2.** [programme, report] impartial, objectif.

balance sheet *n* bilan *m*.

balancing ['bælənsɪŋ] *adj* **1.** [physical effort] stabilisation *f* ▪ **a ~ act** un numéro d'équilibriste ▪ **it was a real ~ act keeping everyone happy** *fig* il fallait jongler pour pouvoir satisfaire tout le monde **2.** FIN [account, books - equalizing] balance *f* ; [- settlement] règlement *m*, solde *m*.

balcony ['bælkənɪ] (*pl* **balconies**) *n* **1.** [of flat, house] balcon *m* **2.** THEAT balcon *m*.

bald [bɔːld] *adj* **1.** [having no hair] chauve ▪ **he's going ~** il devient chauve, il perd ses cheveux ▪ **a ~ patch** [on person] une calvitie ; [on animal] un endroit sans poils ➔ **as ~ as a coot** *inf* *OR* **as an egg** *inf* chauve comme un œuf *OR* comme une boule de billard **2.** [carpet] usé ▪ [mountain top] pelé ▪ [tyre] lisse **3.** [unadorned] brutal ▪ **the ~ truth** la pure vérité ▪ **a ~ statement** une simple exposition des faits.

bald eagle *n* aigle *m* d'Amérique.

BALD EAGLE

Cet oiseau est le symbole des États-Unis. Il figure sur le sceau officiel.

balderdash ['bɔːldədæʃ] *n (U) dated* âneries *fpl*, bêtises *fpl*.

bald-faced *adj US* [liar, thief] effronté ▪ [lie] flagrant.

bald-headed *adj* chauve.

balding ['bɔːldɪŋ] *adj* qui devient chauve.

baldly ['bɔːldlɪ] *adv* brutalement.

baldness ['bɔːldnɪs] *n* **1.** [of person] calvitie *f* ▪ [of animal] absence *f* de poils **2.** [of mountain top] nudité *f* ▪ [of tyre] usure *f* **3.** [of statement] brutalité *f*.

bale [beɪl] <> *n* [of cloth, hay] balle *f*.
<> *vt* **1.** [hay] mettre en balles ▪ [cotton, merchandise] emballer, empaqueter **2.** = **bail** *(vt sense 2)*.

Balearic Islands [ˌbælɪ'ærɪk-] *pr npl* : **the ~** les Baléares *fpl*.

baleful ['beɪlfʊl] *adj* **1.** [menacing] menaçant ▪ [wicked] sinistre, méchant **2.** [gloomy] lugubre.

balefully ['beɪlfʊlɪ] *adv* **1.** [menacingly - look] d'un sale œil ; [- say] d'un ton menaçant **2.** [gloomily] d'une façon lugubre.

Bali ['bɑːlɪ] *pr n* Bali ▪ **in ~** à Bali.

Balinese [ˌbɑːlɪ'niːz] (*pl inv*) <> *n* **1.** [person] Balinais *m*, - e *f* **2.** LING balinais *m*.
<> *adj* balinais, de Bali.

balk [bɔːk] <> *vi* : **to ~ at sthg** : **the horse ~ed at the fence** le cheval a refusé la barrière ▪ **he ~ed at the idea of murder** il a reculé devant l'idée du meurtre.
<> *vt* **1.** [thwart] contrecarrer, contrarier **2.** [avoid] éviter.
<> *n* **1.** [beam] bille *f* ▪ [of roof] solive *f* **2.** [hindrance] obstacle *m* **3.** [in baseball] feinte *f* irrégulière d'un lanceur.

Balkan ['bɔːlkən] *adj* balkanique ▪ **~ States** États *mpl* balkaniques, Balkans *mpl* ▪ **~ Peninsula** péninsule *f* balkanique, Balkans *mpl*.

Balkans ['bɔːlkənz] *pr npl* Balkans *mpl*.

ball [bɔːl] <> *n* **1.** [sphere] boule *f* ▪ [of wool] pelote *f* ▪ **he rolled up the jersey into a ~** il a roulé le pullover en boule **2.** SPORT [small] balle *f* ▪ [large] ballon *m* ▪ [in snooker] bille *f*, boule *f* ▪ [in croquet] boule *f* ▪ [in golf, tennis] balle *f* ▪ [in rugby] ballon *m* ▪ **the children were playing ~** les enfants jouaient au ballon **3.** [shot - in golf, tennis] coup *m* ; [- in football] passe *f* ; [- in hockey] tir *m* ▪ **a long ~** FTBL une passe longue, une balle en profondeur ▪ **it was a good ~** c'était bien joué **4.** ANAT [of foot] plante *f* ▪ [of thumb] partie *f* charnue ▪ **the ~ of the thumb** la partie charnue du pouce **5.** [dance] bal *m* ▪ **to have *OR* to hold *OR* to organize a ~** donner un bal ▮ *fig* **to have a ~** *inf* se marrer comme des fous **6.** *phr* **the ~ is in his court now** c'est à lui de jouer maintenant, la balle est dans son camp ▪ **to be on the ~** [capable] être à la hauteur de la situation ; [alert] être sur le qui-vive ▪ **to keep the ~ rolling** [maintain interest] maintenir l'intérêt ; [maintain activity] assurer la continuité ; [maintain conversation] alimenter la conversation ▪ **to start *OR* to set the ~ rolling** [in conversation] lancer la conversation ; [in deal] faire démarrer l'affaire ▪ **to play ~** *liter* jouer au ballon ; *fig* coopérer ▪ **that's the way the ~ bounces!** *US inf* c'est la vie!
<> *vi* **1.** [wool] boulocher **2.** ▲ *US* [have sex] baiser▲.
<> *vt* [wool] mettre en pelote ▪ [fists] serrer.
◆ **balls**▲ <> *npl* **1.** [testicles] couilles▲ *fpl* ▪ **they've got you by the ~s** *fig* t'es bien baisé▲ **2.** [courage] : **to have ~s** avoir des couilles au cul▲, en avoir△ **3.** [rubbish] : **what a load of ~s!** c'est des conneries, tout ça!△.
<> *interj* : **~s!** quelles conneries!△.

◆ **ball(s) up**△ *UK vt sep* foutre la merde dans△ ▪ **he completely ~ed** *OR* **~ sed up the job** il a complètement salopé le boulot△.

ballad ['bæləd] *n* [song - narrative] ballade *f* ; [- popular, sentimental] romance *f* ▪ [musical piece] ballade *f*.

ball-and-socket *adj* [joint] à rotule.

ballast ['bæləst] ◇ *n (U)* **1.** [in balloon, ship] lest *m* **2.** [in road] pierraille *f* ▪ RAIL ballast *m*.
◇ *vt* **1.** [balloon, ship] lester **2.** [road] empierrer, caillouter ▪ [railway] ballaster.

ball bearing *n* bille *f* de roulement ▪ **~s** roulement *m* à billes.

ball boy *n* ramasseur *m* de balles.

ballbreaker△ ['bɔ:lˌbreɪkəʳ] *n* **1.** [task] boulot *m* très difficile **2.** *pej* [woman] chieuse△ *f*.

ballcock ['bɔ:lkɒk] *n* robinet *m* à flotteur.

ballerina [ˌbælə'ri:nə] *n* ballerine *f (danseuse)*.

ballet ['bæleɪ] *n* ballet *m* ▪ **~ shoe** chausson *m* de danse.

ballet dancer *n* danseur *m*, - euse *f* de ballet.

ball game *n* **1.** SPORT [with small ball] jeu *m* de balle ▪ [with large ball] jeu *m* de ballon ▪ [baseball] match *m* de base-ball **2.** *inf fig* [activity] : **it's a whole new ~, it's a different ~ altogether** c'est une tout autre histoire.

ball girl *n* ramasseuse *f* de balles.

ballistic [bə'lɪstɪk] *adj* balistique ▪ **to go ~** *inf* péter les plombs.

ballistic missile *n* missile *m* balistique.

ballistics [bə'lɪstɪks] *n (U)* balistique *f*.

ball joint *n* joint *m* à rotule.

balloon [bə'lu:n] ◇ *n* **1.** [toy] ballon *m* **2.** AERON ballon *m*, aérostat *m* ▪ **to go up in a ~** monter en ballon ▪ **when the ~ goes up** *inf fig* quand ça démarre ▪ **the ~ went up** *inf fig* l'affaire a éclaté **3.** [in comic strip] bulle *f* **4.** CHEM [flask] ballon *m* **5.** [brandy glass] (verre *m*) ballon *m*.
◇ *vi* **1.** [billow - sail, trousers] gonfler **2.** *fig* [grow dramatically] augmenter démesurément.
◇ *vt UK* SPORT [ball] projeter très haut en l'air.

ballooning [bə'lu:nɪŋ] *n* : **to go ~** [regularly] pratiquer la montgolfière ; [on one occasion] faire un tour en montgolfière *OR* en ballon.

balloonist [bə'lu:nɪst] *n* aéronaute *mf*.

ballot ['bælət] ◇ *n* **1.** [secret vote] scrutin *m* ▪ **to vote by ~** voter à bulletin secret ▪ **in the second ~** au deuxième tour de scrutin ▪ **to take a ~** procéder à un scrutin *OR* à un vote **2.** [voting paper] bulletin *m* de vote.
◇ *vt* (*pret & pp* **ballotted**, *cont* **ballotting**) sonder au moyen d'un vote.

ballot box *n* **1.** [for ballot papers] urne *f* ▪ **~ stuffing** *US* fraude *f* électorale **2.** *fig* système *m* électoral *OR* démocratique.

ballot paper *n* bulletin *m* de vote.

ball park *n* **1.** [stadium] stade *m* de base-ball **2.** *inf* [approximate range] ordre *m* de grandeur ▪ **his guess was in the right ~** il avait plutôt bien deviné.
◆ **ball-park** *comp inf* **a ~ figure** un chiffre approximatif.

ballpoint ['bɔ:lpɔɪnt] ◇ *adj* à bille ▪ **~ pen** stylo *m* (à) bille.
◇ *n* stylo *m* (à) bille, Bic® *m*.

ballroom ['bɔ:lrʊm] *n* salle *f* de bal.

ballroom dancing *n* danse *f* de salon.

balls [bɔ:lz] *npl & interj* = **ball**.

balls-up△ *UK*, **ball-up**△ *US n* bordel△ *m* ▪ **to make a ~ of sthg** merder qqch△.

ballyhoo [ˌbælɪ'hu:] *n inf* [commotion] tapage *m* ▪ [publicity] battage *m*.

balm [bɑ:m] *n* **1.** *liter & fig* baume *m* **2.** BOT mélisse *f* officinale.

balmy ['bɑ:mɪ] *adj* **1.** [weather] doux, douce *f* **2.** [scented] embaumé, parfumé ▪ BOT balsamique.

baloney [bə'ləʊnɪ] *n inf (U)* [nonsense] idioties *fpl*, balivernes *fpl*.

balsa ['bɒlsə] *n* balsa *m*.

balsam ['bɔ:lsəm] *n* **1.** [balm] baume *m* **2.** [plant] balsamine *f* **3.** [turpentine] oléorésine *f*.

balsamic vinegar [bɔ:l'sæmɪk-] *n* vinaigre *m* balsamique.

balsawood ['bɒlsəwʊd] *n* balsa *m*.

Balthazar [bæl'θæzəʳ] ◇ *pr n* BIBLE Balthazar.
◇ *n* [bottle] balthazar *m*.

Balti ['bɔ:ltɪ] *n* balti.

Baltic ['bɔ:ltɪk] ◇ *pr n* : **the ~ (Sea)** la Baltique.
◇ *adj* [port, coast] de la Baltique ▪ **the ~ Republics** les républiques *fpl* baltes ▪ **the ~ States** les pays *mpl* baltes.

balustrade [ˌbælə'streɪd] *n* balustrade *f*.

bamboo [bæm'bu:] ◇ *n* bambou *m*.
◇ *comp* [screen, table] de *OR* en bambou ▪ **~ shoots** pousses *fpl* de bambou.

bamboozle [bæm'bu:zl] *vt* **1.** [cheat] avoir, embobiner ▪ **they were ~d into signing the contract** on a fait pression sur eux pour qu'ils signent le contrat **2.** [confuse] déboussoler.

ban [bæn] ◇ *n* **1.** [prohibition] interdiction *f*, interdit *m* ▪ **they've put a ~ on smoking in the office** ils ont interdit de fumer dans le bureau ▪ **the nuclear test ~** l'interdiction des essais nucléaires **2.** COMM [embargo] embargo *m* ▪ [sanction] sanctions *fpl* économiques.
◇ *vt* (*pret & pp* **banned**, *cont* **banning**) interdire ▪ **they are banned from the club** ils sont exclus du club ▪ **he was banned from driving for a year** il a eu une suspension de permis de conduire d'un an.

banal [bə'nɑ:l] *adj* banal.

banality [bə'nælətɪ] *n* banalité *f*.

banana [bə'nɑ:nə] ◇ *n* [fruit] banane *f* ▪ [plant] bananier *m* ▪ **a bunch of ~s** un régime de bananes.
◇ *comp* [milk shake, ice cream] à la banane ▪ **~ plantation** bananeraie *f*.
◆ **bananas** *adj inf* maboul, dingue ▪ **to go ~s** [crazy] devenir dingue ; [angry] piquer une crise.

banana boat *n* bananier *m (bateau)*.

banana republic *n pej* république *f* bananière.

banana skin *n* peau *f* de banane, *fig* gaffe ▪ **he slipped on a ~** *fig* il a fait une gaffe.

banana split *n* banana split *m*.

band [bænd] *n* **1.** [musicians - folk, rock] groupe *m* ; [- brass, military] fanfare *f* **2.** [group] bande *f*, troupe *f* **3.** [strip - of cloth, metal] bande *f* ; [- on hat] ruban *m* ; [- of leather] lanière *f* **4.** [stripe - of colour] bande *f* ; [- of sunlight] rai *m* ; [- small] bandelette *f* **5.** [as binding - around wheel] bandage *m* ; [- around books] sangle *f* ; [- on cigar] bague *f* ; [- on barrel] cercle *m* **6.** MECH [drive belt] courroie *f* de transmission **7.** RADIO [range of frequency] bande *f* ▪ OPT [in spectrum] bande *f* ▪ COMPUT bande *f* magnétique **8.** *UK* [range - in age, price] tranche *f* **9.** [ring] anneau *m* ▪ **wedding ~** alliance *f*.
◆ **band together** *vi insep* [unite] se grouper ▪ [gang together] former une bande.

bandage ['bændɪdʒ] ◇ *n* **1.** [strip of cloth] bande *f*, bandage *m* **2.** [prepared dressing] pansement *m*.
◇ *vt* [head, limb] bander ▪ [wound] mettre un bandage sur ▪ [with prepared dressing] panser.
◆ **bandage up** *vt sep* = **bandage** *(vt)*.

Band-Aid® ['bændeɪd] *n* sparadrap *m*.

bandan(n)a [bæn'dænə] *n* bandana *m*.

b and b, B and B *n UK* = **bed and breakfast**.

bandit ['bændɪt] *n liter & fig* bandit *m*.

bandleader ['bænd,li:dər] *n* chef *m* d'orchestre ■ MIL chef *m* de fanfare ■ [of pop group] leader *m*.

bandmaster ['bænd,mɑ:stər] *n* chef *m* d'orchestre.

bandoleer, bandolier [,bændə'lɪər] *n* cartouchière *f*.

band saw *n* scie *f* à ruban.

bandsman ['bændzmən] (*pl* **bandsmen** [-mən]) *n* membre *m* d'un orchestre ■ MIL membre *m* d'une fanfare.

bandstand ['bændstænd] *n* kiosque *m* à musique.

bandwagon ['bændwægən] *n* : **to jump** *OR* **to climb on the ~** prendre le train en marche ; *pej* suivre le mouvement.

bandwidth ['bændwɪdθ] *n* **1.** RADIO largeur *f* de bande **2.** ACOUST bande *f* passante.

bandy ['bændɪ] ◇ *vt* (*pret & pp* **bandied**) **1.** [blows] échanger **2.** [ideas, witticisms, insults] échanger ■ **don't ~ words with me** ne discute pas avec moi.
◇ *adj* (*comp* **bandier**, *superl* **bandiest**) [person] aux jambes arquées ■ [leg - of animal, person] arqué.
◆ **bandy about** *UK*, **bandy around** *vt insep* [expression, story] faire circuler ■ **his name is often bandied about** on parle souvent de lui ■ **this is just one of the explanations being bandied around** c'est une des nombreuses explications qui circulent.

bandy-legged *adj* : **to be ~** avoir les jambes arquées.

bane [beɪn] *n* [scourge, trial] fléau *m* ■ **it's/he's the ~ of my life** ça/il m'empoisonne la vie.

bang [bæŋ] ◇ *n* **1.** [loud noise - explosion] détonation *f* ; [- clatter] fracas *m* ; [- slam] claquement *m* ; [- supersonic] bang *m* ■ **she shut the door with a ~** elle a claqué la porte ■ **there was a big ~** il y a eu une forte détonation *OR* une explosion ➔ **to go over** *OR* **out with a ~** *US*, **to go with a ~** *inf* avoir un succès fou ■ **the show went (off) with a ~** *inf* le spectacle a eu un succès fou ■ **to get a ~ out of sthg** *US inf* : **I got a ~ out of it** ça m'a fait marrer **2.** [bump] coup *m* violent ■ **he got a nasty ~ on the head** il s'est cogné la tête assez violemment.
◇ *adv* **1.** : **to go ~** [explode] éclater ❙ *fig* **~ go my chances of winning!** *inf* envolées, mes chances de gagner! ■ **~ goes another £10!** *inf* et pan, encore 10 livres de parties! **2.** [right] en plein ■ **~ in the middle** au beau milieu, en plein milieu ■ **I walked ~ into him** je suis tombé en plein sur lui.
◇ *onom* [gun] pan! ■ [blow, slam] vlan! ■ [explosion] boum!
◇ *vt* **1.** [hit - table, window] frapper violemment ■ **he ~ed his fist on the table** il a frappé la table du poing ■ **I ~ed my head on the ceiling** je me suis cogné la tête contre le *OR* au plafond ■ **we're ~ing our heads against a brick wall** *fig* nous perdons notre temps **2.** [slam - door, window] claquer **3.** ▲ [have sex with] baiser▲.
◇ *vi* **1.** [slam] claquer **2.** [detonate - gun] détoner.
◆ **bangs** *npl US* frange *f*.
◆ **bang about** *UK*, **bang around** *inf* ◇ *vi insep* faire du bruit, faire du pétard.
◇ *vt sep* [books, crockery] cogner les uns contre les autres ■ [person] tabasser, cogner.
◆ **bang away** *vi insep* **1.** [detonate - guns] tonner **2.** [keep firing - soldier] tirer sans arrêt ■ [keep hammering - workmen] faire du vacarme ■ *fig* [keep working] continuer à travailler.
◆ **bang down** *vt sep* [books] jeter violemment ■ [dish] poser brutalement.
◆ **bang into** *vt insep* [collide with] se cogner contre, heurter.
◆ **bang on** *vi insep UK inf* **he's always ~ing on about his personal problems** il n'arrête pas de casser les pieds à tout le monde avec ses problèmes personnels.
◆ **bang out** *vt sep inf* [tune] jouer fort et mal.
◆ **bang together** *vt sep* cogner l'un contre l'autre ■ **I could have ~ed their heads together!** j'aurais pu prendre l'un pour taper sur l'autre!
◆ **bang up**△ *vt sep* [prisoner] boucler pour la nuit.

banger ['bæŋər] *n UK inf* **1.** [sausage] saucisse *f* ■ **~s and mash** *inf* saucisses-purée *(considérées comme le plat britannique par excellence)* **2.** [car] tacot *m*, vieux clou *m* **3.** [firework] pétard *m*.

Bangkok [,bæŋ'kɒk] *pr n* Bangkok.

Bangladesh [,bæŋglə'deʃ] *pr n* Bangladesh *m*.

Bangladeshi [,bæŋglə'deʃɪ] ◇ *n* Bangladais *m*, - e *f*, Bangladeshi *mf*.
◇ *adj* bangladais, bangladeshi.

bangle ['bæŋgl] *n* bracelet *m*.

bang-on *inf* ◇ *adv UK* **1.** [exactly] pile ■ **to hit sthg ~** frapper qqch en plein dans le mille **2.** [punctually] à l'heure.
◇ *adj* : **his answers were ~** ses réponses étaient percutantes.

banish ['bænɪʃ] *vt* [person] exiler ■ [thought] bannir, chasser.

banishment ['bænɪʃmənt] *n* [of thoughts] bannissement *m* ■ [of person] exil *m*, bannissement *m*.

banister ['bænɪstər] *n* rampe *f* (de l'escalier).

banjo ['bændʒəʊ] (*UK pl* **banjoes**, *US pl* **banjos**) *n* banjo *m*.

bank [bæŋk] ◇ *n* **1.** FIN banque *f* ■ **I asked the ~ for a loan** j'ai demandé un crédit à ma banque ■ **she has £10,000 in the ~** elle a 10 000 livres à la banque ■ **the ~ of issue** la banque d'émission **2.** GAMES banque *f* ■ [in casino] *argent qui appartient à la maison de jeu* ■ **to break the ~** faire sauter la banque ■ **£10 isn't going to break the ~** 10 livres, ce n'est pas la fin du monde **3.** [reserve - of blood, data] banque *f* **4.** [of lake, river] bord *m*, rive *f* ■ [above water] berge *f* ■ [of canal] bord *m*, berge *f* ■ **the Left Bank** [in Paris] la rive gauche **5.** [embankment, mound - of earth, snow] talus *m* ; [- on railway] remblai *m* ■ [hill] pente *f* **6.** [ridge - on racetrack, road] bord *m* relevé ; [- of sand] banc *m* ; [- by sea] digue *f* **7.** [mass - of flowers, shrubs] massif *m* ; [- of cloud, coal] amoncellement *m* ; [- of fog] couche *f* **8.** MIN [pithead] carreau *m* ■ [face of coal, ore] front *m* de taille **9.** AERON virage *m* incliné *OR* sur l'aile **10.** [row - of levers, switches] rangée *f*.
◇ *vt* **1.** [enclose - railway, road] relever *(dans un virage)* ; [- river] endiguer **2.** [heap up - earth, stone] amonceler ; [- fire] couvrir **3.** AERON : **to ~ an aeroplane** faire faire à un avion un virage sur l'aile **4.** [cheque, money] déposer à la banque.
◇ *vi* : **where do you ~?, who do you ~ with?** quelle est votre banque?
◆ **bank on, bank upon** *vt insep* [count on] compter sur ■ **I'm ~ing on it** je compte là-dessus.
◆ **bank up** ◇ *vt sep* **1.** [road] relever *(dans un virage)* ■ [river] endiguer **2.** [fire] couvrir ■ [earth] amonceler.
◇ *vi insep* [cloud] s'amonceler.

bankable ['bæŋkəbl] *adj* bancable, escomptable ■ **to be ~** *fig* être une valeur sûre.

bank account *n* compte *m* bancaire.

bank balance *n* solde *m* bancaire.

bankbook ['bæŋkbʊk] *n* livret *m* (d'épargne).

bank card *n* carte *f* bancaire.

bank charges *npl* frais *mpl* bancaires.

bank clerk *n* employé *m*, - e *f* de banque.

bank discount *n* escompte *m* bancaire.

banker ['bæŋkər] *n* **1.** FIN banquier *m* **2.** [in betting] banquier *m*.

banker's card *n* carte *f* bancaire.

banker's draft *n* traite *f* bancaire.

banker's order *n UK* ordre *m* de virement bancaire.

bank holiday *n* **1.** [in UK] jour *m* férié ■ **~ Monday** lundi férié **2.** [in US] jour *m* de fermeture des banques.

banking ['bæŋkɪŋ] *n (U)* **1.** FIN [profession] profession *f* de banquier, la banque ■ [activity] opérations *fpl* bancaires ■ **international ~** opérations bancaires internationales **2.** [embankment - on river] berge *f* ; [- on racetrack] bords *mpl* relevés **3.** AERON virage *m* sur l'aile.

banking hours *npl* heures *fpl* d'ouverture des banques.

banking house *n* établissement *m* bancaire.

bank loan *n* [money lent] prêt *m* bancaire ■ [money borrowed] emprunt *m* bancaire ■ **to take out a ~** obtenir un prêt bancaire ■ **to pay off a ~** rembourser un emprunt bancaire.

bank manager *n* [head of bank] directeur *m*, - trice *f* d'agence ▪ **my** *OR* **the ~** [head of bank] le directeur de l'agence où j'ai mon compte ; [in charge of account] le responsable de mon compte.

bank note *n* billet *m* de banque.

bank rate *n* taux *m* d'escompte *OR* de l'escompte.

bank robber *n* cambrioleur *m*, - euse *f* de banque.

bankroll ['bæŋkrəʊl] *US inf* ◇ *n* fonds *mpl*, finances *fpl*.
◇ *vt* financer.

bankrupt ['bæŋkrʌpt] ◇ *n* LAW failli *m*, - e *f* ▪ **~'s estate** actif *m* de la faillite ▪ **~'s certificate** concordat *m*.
◇ *adj* LAW [insolvent] failli ▪ *fig* [person] ruiné ▪ **to go ~** faire faillite ▪ **to be ~** être en faillite ▪ **the firm was declared ~** la firme a été déclarée *OR* mise en faillite ▮ *fig* **he is completely ~ of ideas** il est complètement à court d'idées ▪ **morally ~** sans moralité.
◇ *vt* [company, person] mettre en faillite ▪ *fig* [person] ruiner.

bankruptcy ['bæŋkrəptsɪ] *n* LAW faillite *f* ▪ *fig* [destitution] ruine *f* ▪ **~ proceedings** procédure *f* de faillite.

bankruptcy court *n UK* ≃ tribunal *m* de commerce.

bank statement *n* relevé *m* de compte.

banner ['bænəʳ] *n* [flag] étendard *m* ▪ COMPUT bandeau *m* ▪ [placard] bannière *f* ▪ *fig* **to march/to campaign under sb's ~** se ranger/faire campagne sous la bannière de qqn.

banner headline *n* gros titre *m*.

bannister ['bænɪstəʳ] *n* = **banister**.

banns [bænz] *npl* bans *mpl*.

banoffee [bə'nɑfi:] *n (U)* banoffee *m*, caramel *m* banane.

banquet ['bæŋkwɪt] ◇ *n* [formal dinner] banquet *m* ▪ [big meal] festin *m*.
◇ *vi* [dine formally] faire un banquet ▪ [dine lavishly] faire un festin.
◇ *vt* [dignitary] offrir un banquet à ▪ [treat lavishly] offrir un festin à.

bans [bænz] *npl* = **banns**.

banshee ['bænʃ:] *n personnage mythique féminin dont les cris présagent la mort* ▪ **the child was wailing like a ~** l'enfant hurlait comme un putois.

bantam ['bæntəm] *n* [hen] poule *f* naine ▪ [cock] coq *m* nain.

bantamweight ['bæntəmweɪt] ◇ *n* [boxer] poids coq *m inv*.
◇ *adj* [boxer] poids coq *(inv)*.

banter ['bæntəʳ] ◇ *n (U)* badinage *m*, plaisanterie *f*.
◇ *vi* badiner.

bantering ['bæntərɪŋ] *adj* [tone] de plaisanterie, badin.

Bantu [,bæn'tu:] ◇ *n* **1.** (*pl* Bantu *OR pl* Bantus) [person] Bantou *m*, - e *f* **2.** LING bantou *m*.
◇ *adj* bantou.

bap [bæp] *n UK pain rond que l'on utilise pour faire un sandwich.*

baptism ['bæptɪzm] *n* baptême *m* ▪ **~ of fire** *fig* baptême du feu.

baptismal [bæp'tɪzml] *adj* baptismal, de baptême ▪ **~ font** fonts *mpl* baptismaux.

Baptist ['bæptɪst] ◇ *n* **1.** [member of sect] baptiste *mf* **2.** BIBLE : **St John the ~** saint Jean-Baptiste.
◇ *adj* [sect] : **the ~ Church** l'Église *f* baptiste.

baptist(e)ry ['bæptɪstrɪ] (*pl* **baptistries** *OR pl* **baptisteries**) *n* baptistère *m* ▪ [font in Baptist church] fonts *mpl* baptismaux.

baptize, ise [*UK* bæp'taɪz, *US* 'bæptaɪz] *vt* RELIG & *fig* baptiser.

bar [bɑ:] ◇ *n* **1.** [pub] bar *m*, café *m* ▪ [in hotel, club] bar *m* ▪ [in station] café *m*, bar *m* ▪ [counter] bar *m* **2.** [small shop - for coffee, tea] buvette *f* ; [- for sandwiches] snack *m* **3.** [long piece of metal] barre *f* ▪ [on grating, cage] barreau *m* ▪ [on door] bâcle *f* ▪ ELEC [element] barre *f* ▪ **an iron ~** une barre de fer ▪ **'push ~ to open'** [on exit doors] 'appuyer sur la barre pour sortir' ▶ **to be behind ~s** être sous les verrous *OR* derrière les barreaux **4.** [ban] interdiction *f* ▪ **there is no ~ on foreign athletes** les athlètes étrangers sont autorisés à participer aux compétitions **5.** [bank - in lake, river] banc *m* ▪ *US* [alluvial deposit] barre *f* **6.** [slab - of chocolate] tablette *f* ; [- of gold] lingot *m* ▪ **a ~ of soap** une savonnette, un pain de savon **7.** [stripe] raie *f* ▪ [of sunlight] rayon *m* **8.** [in court] barre *f* ▪ **the prisoner at the ~** l'accusé *m*, - e *f* **9.** [authority, tribunal] tribunal *m* **10.** *UK* POL *endroit au Parlement où le public peut venir s'adresser aux députés ou aux Lords* **11.** MUS mesure *f* **12.** MIL *UK* barrette *f (portée sur le ruban d'une médaille)* ▪ *US* galon *m* **13.** [unit of pressure] bar *m*.
◇ *vt* (*pret & pp* **barred**, *cont* **barring**) **1.** [put bars on - window] munir de barreaux ▪ **~ the door** mettez la barre *OR* la bâcle à la porte ▪ **they barred the door against intruders** *fig* ils ont barré la porte aux intrus **2.** [obstruct] barrer ▪ **he barred her way** *OR* **her path** il lui barra le passage ▪ **high interest rates are barring our way out of the recession** *fig* le niveau élevé des taux d'intérêt empêche la reprise (économique) **3.** [ban - person] exclure ; [- activity] interdire ▪ **members of the sect were barred from entering the country** l'entrée du pays était interdite aux membres de la secte ▪ **he was barred from the club** il a été exclu du club **4.** [stripe] rayer.
◇ *prep* excepté, sauf ▪ **~ accidents** sauf accident, sauf imprévu ▪ **~ none** sans exception.
◆ **Bar** *n* LAW : **the Bar** *UK* le barreau ; *US* les avocats ▪ **to call sb to the Bar** *UK*, **to admit sb to the Bar** *US* inscrire qqn au barreau.

-bar [bɑ:] *in cpds* : **a three~ gate** une barrière à trois barreaux ▪ **a two~ electric fire** un radiateur électrique à deux résistances.

barb [bɑ:b] *n* **1.** [on fishhook] ardillon *m* ▪ [on barbed wire] barbe *f*, pointe *f* ▪ [on arrow] barbelure *f* ▪ [feather] barbe *f* **2.** [dig, gibe] trait *m*, pointe *f* **3.** [horse] cheval *m* barbe, barbe *m*.

banoffee [bə'nɑfi:] *n (U)* banoffee *m*, caramel *m* banane.

Barbados [bɑ:'beɪdɒs] *pr n* Barbade *f*.

barbarian [bɑ:'beərɪən] *n* [boor, savage] barbare *mf*.

barbaric [bɑ:'bærɪk] *adj liter* & *fig* barbare.

barbarism ['bɑ:bərɪzm] *n* **1.** [state] barbarie *f* **2.** [in language] barbarisme *m*.

barbarity [bɑ:'bærətɪ] *n* **1.** [brutality] barbarie *f*, inhumanité *f* **2.** [atrocity] atrocité *f*.

Barbarossa [,bɑ:bə'rɒsə] *pr n* Barberousse.

barbarous ['bɑ:bərəs] *adj* [language, manners, tribe] barbare.

Barbary ['bɑ:bərɪ] *pr n* Barbarie *f*, États *mpl* barbaresques.

Barbary coast *pr n* : **the ~** les côtes *fpl* de Barbarie.

barbecue ['bɑ:bɪkju:] ◇ *n* [grill, meal, party] barbecue *m* ▪ **to have a ~** faire un barbecue ▪ **~ sauce** sauce *f* barbecue.
◇ *vt* (*pret & pp* **barbecued**, *cont* **barbecuing**) [steak] griller au charbon de bois ▪ [pig, sheep] rôtir tout entier.

barbed [bɑ:bd] *adj* [arrow, hook] barbelé ▪ [comment] acéré.

barbed wire *n* (fil *m* de fer) barbelé *m* ▪ **a ~ fence** une haie de barbelés.

barber ['bɑ:bəʳ] *n* coiffeur *m* (pour hommes) ▪ **to go to the ~'s** aller chez le coiffeur (pour hommes).

barbershop ['bɑ:bəʃɒp] ◇ *n US* salon *m* de coiffure (pour hommes).
◇ *adj* MUS [songs] *chanté en harmonie étroite* ▪ **~ quartet** *quatuor d'hommes chantant en harmonie étroite.*

barber's pole *n* enseigne *f* de coiffeur.

barbican ['bɑ:bɪkən] *n* barbacane *f*.

BARBICAN

Le *Barbican Centre*, à Londres, réunit une salle de concert, un théâtre, un cinéma, un musée, une bibliothèque et des salles d'exposition.

bar billiards *n UK version du jeu de billard, couramment pratiquée dans les pubs.*

barbiturate [bɑ:'bɪtjʊrət] *n* barbiturique *m* ▪ **~ poisoning** barbiturisme *m*.

Barbour jacket® ['bɑ:bəʳ-] *n veste en toile cirée à col de velours souvent associée à un style de vie BCBG en Grande-Bretagne.*

barbwire ['bɑ:bwaɪəʳ] *n US* = **barbed wire.**

Barcelona [,bɑ:sɪ'ləʊnə] *pr n* Barcelone.

bar chart *n* histogramme *m.*

Barclaycard® ['bɑ:klɪkɑ:d] *n carte de crédit britannique.*

bar code <> *n* code-barres *m* ■ **~ reader** lecteur *m* de code-barres.
<> *vt* mettre un code-barres sur.

bard [bɑ:d] <> *n* **1.** [Celtic] barde *m* ■ [Greek] aède *m* ■ ***lit*** [poet] poète *m* ■ **the Bard (of Avon)** le Barde (de l'Avon) *(surnom de William Shakespeare)* **2.** CULIN barde *f* (de lard).
<> *vt* barder.

bar diagram *n* histogramme *m.*

bare [beəʳ] (*comp* **barer**, *superl* **barest**) <> *adj* **1.** [naked - body, feet] nu ■ **he killed a tiger with his ~ hands** il a tué un tigre à mains nues ■ **to fight with ~ hands** SPORT boxer à main nue **2.** [unadorned, uncovered] nu ■ ELEC [wire] dénudé ■ **we had to sleep on ~ floorboards** nous avons dû coucher à même le plancher ■ **his head was ~** il était nu-tête ■ **~ wood** bois *m* naturel ■ **the lawn was just a ~ patch of grass** la pelouse consistait en un maigre carré d'herbe ■ **to lay ~ one's heart** mettre son cœur à nu ■ **to lay ~ a plot** révéler un complot
3. [empty] vide ■ **the cupboard was ~** le garde-manger était vide
4. [basic, plain] simple, dépouillé ■ **I just told him the barest details** je lui ai donné le minimum de détails ■ **the ~ facts** les faits bruts ■ **the ~ bones of the story** ***fig*** le squelette de l'histoire
5. [absolute] absolu, strict ■ **the ~ necessities of life** le minimum vital
6. [meagre] **: a ~ 20% of the population is literate** à peine 20 % de la population est alphabétisée ■ **they won by a ~ majority** ils ont gagné de justesse.
<> *vt* **1.** [part of body] découvrir ■ ELEC [wire] dénuder ■ [teeth] montrer ■ **to ~ one's head** se découvrir la tête ■ **to ~ one's soul** mettre son âme à nu
2. [unsheath - dagger, sword] dégainer, tirer du fourreau.

bareback ['beəbæk] <> *adj* [rider] qui monte à cru.
<> *adv* [ride] à nu, à cru.

barefaced ['beəfeɪst] *adj* [liar] effronté, éhonté ■ [lie] impudent.

barefoot ['beəfʊt] *adj* aux pieds nus.

barefooted [,beə'fʊtɪd] <> *adj* aux pieds nus.
<> *adv* nu-pieds, (les) pieds nus.

bare-handed <> *adv* [fight] à mains nues.
<> *adj* aux mains nues.

bareheaded [,beə'hedɪd] <> *adv* nu-tête, (la) tête nue.
<> *adj* nu-tête *(inv).*

barelegged [,beə'legd] <> *adv* nu-jambes, (les) jambes nues.
<> *adj* aux jambes nues.

barely ['beəlɪ] *adv* **1.** [only just] à peine, tout juste ■ **I had ~ arrived when I heard the news** j'étais à peine arrivé que j'ai entendu la nouvelle **2.** [sparsely] très peu ■ [poorly] pauvrement.

bareness ['beənɪs] *n* **1.** [nakedness - of person] nudité *f* **2.** [sparseness - of style] sécheresse *f*, dépouillement *m* ; [- of furnishings] pauvreté *f* ; [- of room] dénuement *m* **3.** [simplicity] dépouillement *m.*

Barents Sea ['bærənts-] *pr n* **: the ~** la mer de Barents.

barfly ['bɑ:flaɪ] *n* ***US inf*** pilier *m* de bistrot.

bargain ['bɑ:gɪn] <> *n* **1.** [deal] marché *m*, affaire *f* ■ **you keep your end of the ~ and I'll keep mine** vous respectez vos engagements et je respecterai les miens ■ **to strike** *OR* **to make a ~ with sb** conclure un marché avec qqn ■ **to drive a hard ~** marchander d'une façon acharnée **2.** [good buy] occasion *f* ■ **it's a real ~!** c'est une bonne affaire!, c'est une occasion!
<> *comp* **: ~ offer** promotion *f*, offre *f* exceptionnelle ■ **~ price** prix *m* avantageux ■ **~ sale** soldes *mpl* exceptionnels.
<> *vi* **1.** [haggle] marchander ■ **she ~ed with me over the price of the shoes** elle a marchandé avec moi au sujet du prix des chaussures **2.** [negotiate] négocier ■ **the unions are ~ing with management for an 8% pay rise** les syndicats négocient une hausse de salaire de 8 % avec la direction ■ **I won't ~ with you** je ne parlementerai pas avec vous.
◆ **into the bargain** *adv phr* par-dessus le marché.
◆ **bargain away** *vt sep* [rights] renoncer à, vendre.
◆ **bargain for** *vt insep* [anticipate] s'attendre à ■ **they got more than they ~ed for** ils ne s'attendaient pas à un coup pareil ■ **things happened more quickly than he had ~ed for** les choses sont allées plus vite qu'il n'avait pensé.
◆ **bargain on** *vt insep* [depend on] compter sur ■ **I hadn't ~ed on this happening!** je ne m'attendais pas à cela!

bargain basement *n* [in shop] *dans certains grands magasins, sous-sol où sont regroupés les articles en solde et autres bonnes affaires.*

bargain-hunter *n* dénicheur *m*, -euse *f* de bonnes affaires.

bargaining ['bɑ:gɪnɪŋ] *n* [haggling] marchandage *m* ■ [negotiating] négociations *fpl* ■ **they have considerable ~ power** ils ont beaucoup de poids dans les négociations.

barge [bɑ:dʒ] <> *n* **1.** [on canal] chaland *m* ■ [larger - on river] péniche *f* ■ **motor ~** chaland *m* automoteur, péniche *f* automotrice **2.** [ceremonial boat] barque *f.*
<> *vi* **: they ~ about as if they owned the place** ils vont et viennent comme si l'endroit leur appartenait ■ **he ~d into the room** il fit irruption dans la pièce ■ **she ~d past me** elle m'a bousculé en passant.
<> *vt* **: to ~ one's way into a room** faire irruption dans une pièce ■ **to ~ one's way through the crowd** foncer à travers la foule.
◆ **barge in** *vi insep* [enter] faire irruption ■ [meddle] **: he keeps barging in on our conversation** il n'arrête pas de nous interrompre dans notre conversation.
◆ **barge into** *vt insep* [bump into - person] rentrer dans ; [- piece of furniture] rentrer dans, se cogner contre.

barge pole *n* gaffe *f* ■ **I wouldn't touch it with a ~** ***UK*** [disgusting object] je n'y toucherais pas avec des pincettes ; [risky business] je ne m'en mêlerais pour rien au monde.

barista [bə'ri:stə] *n* barman *m*, serveuse *f.*

baritone ['bærɪtəʊn] <> *n* [singer, voice] baryton *m.*
<> *adj* [part, voice] de baryton.

barium ['beərɪəm] *n* baryum *m.*

barium meal *n* MED bouillie *f* barylée.

bark [bɑ:k] <> *n* **1.** [of dog] aboiement *m* ■ [of fox] glapissement *m* ■ ***fig*** [cough] toux *f* sèche ■ **his ~ is worse than his bite** il fait plus de bruit que de mal **2.** [of tree] écorce *f* ■ **to take the ~ off a tree** écorcer un arbre.
<> *vi* [dog] aboyer ■ [fox] glapir ■ ***fig*** [cough] tousser ■ [speak harshly] crier, aboyer.
<> *vt* **1.** [order] aboyer **2.** [tree] écorcer ■ [skin] écorcher.
◆ **bark out** *vt sep* [order] aboyer.

barkeep ['bɑ:ki:p] *n* ***US inf*** barman *m.*

barking ['bɑ:kɪŋ] *n (U)* aboiements *m* ■ **: ~ mad** complètement fou.

barley ['bɑ:lɪ] *n* **1.** AGRIC [crop, grain] orge *f* **2.** [in cooking, distilling] orge *m* ■ [in soup] orge *m* perlé ■ [for whisky] orge *m* mondé.

barleycorn ['bɑ:lɪkɔ:n] *n* **1.** [grain] grain *m* d'orge **2.** [barley] orge *f.*

barley sugar *n* sucre *m* d'orge.

barley water *n* ***UK*** *boisson à base d'orge.*

barley wine *n* ***UK*** *bière très forte en alcool.*

barmaid ['bɑ:meɪd] *n* barmaid *f*, serveuse *f (de bar).*

barman ['bɑ:mən] (*pl* **barmen** [-mən]) *n* barman *m*, serveur *m* (de bar).

bar mitzvah [ˌbɑːˈmɪtsvə] *n* [ceremony] bar-mitsva *f inv* ■ [boy] garçon *m* qui fait sa bar-mitsva.

barmy [ˈbɑːmɪ] (*comp* **barmier**, *superl* **barmiest**) *adj UK inf* maboul, dingue.

barn [bɑːn] *n* **1.** [for hay] grange *f* ■ [for horses] écurie *f* ■ [for cows] étable *f* **2.** [for railroad trucks] dépôt *m*.

Barnabas [ˈbɑːnəbəs] *pr n* Barnabé.

barnacle [ˈbɑːnəkl] *n* bernache *f (crustacé)*.

Barnardos [bəˈnɑːdəʊz] *pr n association caritative britannique*.

BARNARDOS

Cette association, fondée par le docteur Barnardo, gère des écoles et des foyers pour orphelins et enfants handicapés ou défavorisés.

barn dance *n bal de campagne où l'on danse des quadrilles*.

barney [ˈbɑːnɪ] *n UK inf* engueulade *f*.

barn owl *n* chouette effraie *f*.

barnstorm [ˈbɑːnˌstɔːm] *vi* **1.** SPORT faire une tournée à la campagne ■ THEAT jouer sur les tréteaux **2.** *US* POL *faire une tournée électorale (dans les circonscriptions rurales)*.

barnstormer [ˈbɑːnˌstɔːməʳ] *n* **1.** [actor] comédien *m* ambulant, comédienne *f* ambulante ■ [acrobat] acrobate *m* ambulant, acrobate *f* ambulante **2.** *US* POL orateur *m* électoral.

barnyard [ˈbɑːnjɑːd] ◇ *n* cour *f* de ferme.
◇ *adj* [animals] de basse-cour ■ *fig* [humour] rustre.

barometer [bəˈrɒmɪtəʳ] *n* baromètre *m* ■ **the ~ is showing fair** le baromètre est au beau ■ **the poll is a clear ~ of public reaction** *fig* le sondage est un parfait baromètre des réactions du public.

barometric [ˌbærəˈmetrɪk] *adj* barométrique ■ **~ pressure** pression *f* atmosphérique.

baron [ˈbærən] *n* **1.** [noble] baron *m* **2.** [magnate] magnat *m* ■ **a press ~** un magnat de la presse **3.** CULIN : **a ~ of beef** un double aloyau de bœuf.

baroness [ˈbærənɪs] *n* baronne *f*.

baronet [ˈbærənɪt] *n* baronnet *m*.

baronetcy [ˈbærənɪtsɪ] *n* [patent] titre *m* de baronnet ■ [position] rang *m* de baronnet.

baronial [bəˈrəʊnjəl] *adj* de baron ■ **~ hall** demeure *f* seigneuriale.

baroque [bəˈrɒk] ◇ *adj* baroque.
◇ *n* baroque *m*.

barrack [ˈbærək] *vt* **1.** [soldiers] caserner **2.** *UK* [heckle] chahuter.
◆ **barracks** *n* caserne *f* ■ **infantry ~s** quartier *m* d'infanterie ■ **in ~s** à la caserne.

barracking [ˈbærəkɪŋ] *n* chahut *m* ■ **he got** *OR* **they gave him a terrible ~** on l'a chahuté violemment.

barrack-room *adj* [humour, joke] de caserne.

barracuda [ˌbærəˈkuːdə] *n* barracuda *m*.

barrage [ˈbærɑːʒ] *n* **1.** MIL tir *m* de barrage **2.** *fig* [of punches, questions] pluie *f*, déluge *m* ■ [of insults, words] déluge *m*, flot *m* **3.** [dam] barrage *m*.

barrage balloon *n* ballon *m* de barrage.

barred [bɑːd] *adj* [window, opening] à barreaux.

barrel [ˈbærəl] ◇ *n* **1.** [cask, unit of capacity - of wine] tonneau *m*, fût *m* ; [- of cider] fût *m* ; [- of beer] tonneau *m* ; [- of oil, tar] baril *m* ; [- of fish] caque *f* ▶ **to have sb over a ~** *inf* tenir qqn à sa merci **2.** [hollow cylinder - of gun, key] canon *m* ; [- of clock, lock] barillet *m* ; [- of pen] corps *m* ■ **to give sb both ~s** *inf* passer un savon à qqn **3.** *inf* [lot] : **we had a ~ of fun** *OR* **a ~ of laughs** on s'est vachement amusés ■ **it wasn't exactly a ~ of laughs** c'était très sérieux *OR* déprimant.
◇ *vt* (*UK pret & pp* **barrelled**, *cont* **barrelling**) (*US pret & pp* **barreled**, *cont* **barreling**) [beer] mettre en tonneau ■ [oil] mettre en baril.
◇ *vi* (*UK pret & pp* **barrelled**, *cont* **barrelling**) (*US pret & pp* **barreled**, *cont* **barreling**) *inf US inf* **to ~ (along)** foncer, aller à toute pompe.

barrel-chested [-ˈtʃestɪd] *adj* : **he is ~** il a le torse bombé.

barrel organ *n* orgue *m* de Barbarie.

barren [ˈbærən] ◇ *adj* **1.** [land - infertile] stérile, improductif ; [- bare] désertique ; [- dry] aride **2.** [sterile - plant, woman] stérile **3.** [dull - film, play] aride ; [- discussion] stérile ; [- writing] aride, sec, sèche *f*.
◇ *n* lande *f*.

barricade [ˌbærɪˈkeɪd] ◇ *n* barricade *f*.
◇ *vt* [door, street] barricader.

barrier [ˈbærɪəʳ] *n* **1.** [fence, gate] barrière *f* ■ [at railway station] portillon *m* **2.** [obstacle] obstacle *m* ■ **the language ~** le barrage *OR* la barrière de la langue ■ **~ method** méthode *f* de contraception locale.

barrier cream *n* crème *f* protectrice.

barrier reef *n* barrière *f* de corail.

barring [ˈbɑːrɪŋ] *prep* excepté, sauf ■ **~ rain the concert will take place tomorrow** à moins qu'il ne pleuve, le concert aura lieu demain ■ **~ accidents** sauf accident, sauf imprévu.

barrister [ˈbærɪstəʳ] *n UK* ≃ avocat *m*, - e *f*.

barroom [ˈbɑːrʊm] *n US* bar *m*.

barrow [ˈbærəʊ] *n* **1.** [wheelbarrow] brouette *f* ■ [fruitseller's] voiture *f* des quatre saisons ■ [for luggage] diable *m* ■ MIN wagonnet *m* **2.** [mound] tumulus *m*.

barrow boy *n UK* marchand *m* ambulant.

barrowload [ˈbærəʊləʊd] *n* brouettée *f*.

bar snack *n repas léger pris dans un pub*.

bar stool *n* tabouret *m* de bar.

bartend [ˈbɑːtend] *vi US* être barman *OR* serveur *(de bar)*, être barmaid *OR* serveuse *(de bar)*.

bartender [ˈbɑːtendəʳ] *n US* barman *m*, barmaid *f*, serveur *m (de bar)*, serveuse *f (de bar)*.

barter [ˈbɑːtəʳ] ◇ *n (U)* échange *m*, troc *m* ■ **a system of ~, a ~ system** une économie de troc.
◇ *vt* échanger, troquer ■ **they ~ed animals for cloth** ils ont échangé des animaux contre du tissu.
◇ *vi* [exchange] faire un échange *OR* un troc ■ [haggle] marchander.

Bartholomew [bɑːˈθɒləmjuː] *pr n* : **Saint ~** saint Barthélemy.

Bart's [bɑːts] *pr n surnom du Saint Bartholomew's Hospital à Londres*.

barysphere [ˈbærɪˌsfɪəʳ] *n* barysphère *f*.

basal [ˈbeɪsl] *adj* PHYSIOL basal ■ [gen] fondamental.

basalt [ˈbæsɔːlt] *n* basalte *m*.

base [beɪs] (*comp* **baser**, *superl* **basest**) ◇ *n* **1.** [bottom - gen] partie *f* inférieure, base *f* ; [- of tree, column] pied *m* ; [- of bowl, glass] fond *m* ; [- of triangle] base *f* **2.** [support, stand] socle *m* **3.** [of food, paint] base *f* ■ **the stock forms the ~ of your sauce** le fond constitue la base de votre sauce **4.** [basis - of knowledge] base *f* ; [- of experience] réserve *f* **5.** ECON & POL base *f* ■ **an industrial ~** une zone industrielle **6.** [centre of activities] point *m* de départ ■ MIL base *f* ■ **the explorers returned to ~** les explorateurs sont retournés au camp de base **7.** CHEM, COMPUT, GEOM & MATHS base *f* **8.** [in baseball & rounders] base *f* ■ **he's way off ~** *US inf fig* il n'y est pas du tout ■ **first ~** *US* SPORT première base ■ **to get to first ~** réussir la première étape ■ **to touch ~ : I just thought I'd touch ~** je voulais juste garder le contact.
◇ *vt* **1.** [found - opinion, project] baser, fonder ■ **the project is ~d on cooperation from all regions** le projet est fondé sur la coopération de toutes les régions **2.** [locate] baser ■ **where are you ~d?** où êtes-vous installé? ■ **the job is ~d in Tokyo** le poste est basé à Tokyo.

◇ *adj* [motive, thoughts, conduct] bas, indigne ▪ [origins] bas ▪ [ingratitude, outlook] mesquin ▪ [coinage] faux, fausse *f*.

baseball ['beɪsbɔ:l] *n* base-ball *m* ▪ **~ cap** casquette *f* de base-ball.

baseboard ['beɪsbɔ:d] *n* US CONSTR plinthe *f*.

base burner *n* US *poêle où le charbon alimente le feu automatiquement.*

base camp *n* camp *m* de base.

base component *n* LING composant *m* de base.

-based [beɪst] *in cpds* **1.** [located] : **the company is Tokyo~** le centre d'opérations de la firme est à Tokyo **2.** [centred] : **a science~ curriculum** un programme basé sur les sciences ▪ **an oil~ economy** une économie fondée sur le pétrole **3.** [composed] : **a water~ paint** une peinture à l'eau.

Basel ['bɑ:zl], **Basle** [bɑ:l] *pr n* Bâle.

base lending rate *n taux de base du crédit bancaire.*

baseless ['beɪslɪs] *adj* [gossip] sans fondement ▪ [suspicion] injustifié ▪ [fear, superstition] déraisonnable.

baseline ['beɪslaɪn] *n* **1.** [in tennis] ligne *f* de fond ▪ [in baseball] ligne *f* des bases **2.** [in surveying] base *f* ▪ [in diagram] ligne *f* zéro ▪ ART ligne *f* de fuite **3.** [standard] point *m* de comparaison ▪ **~ costs** FIN coûts *mpl* de base.

basement ['beɪsmənt] *n* sous-sol *m* ▪ **in the ~** au sous-sol ▪ **a ~ kitchen** une cuisine en sous-sol.

base metal *n* métal *m* vil.

base rate *n* FIN taux *m* de base *(utilisé par les banques pour déterminer leur taux de prêt).*

bases ['beɪsi:z] *pl* ▷ **basis**.

bash [bæʃ] *inf* ◇ *n* **1.** [blow] coup *m* ▪ [with fist] coup *m* de poing **2.** [dent - in wood] entaille *f* ; [- in metal] bosse *f*, bosselure *f* **3.** [party] fête *f* **4.** [attempt] : **to have a ~ at sthg, to give sthg a ~** essayer de faire qqch.
◇ *vt* **1.** [person, one's head] frapper, cogner **2.** [dent - wooden box, table] entailler ; [- car] cabosser, bosseler **3.** *fig* [criticize] critiquer ▪ **it's part of their campaign to ~ the unions** *fig* leur campagne a en partie pour but d'enfoncer les syndicats.
◆ **bash about** UK, **bash around** *inf vt sep* **1.** [hit - person] flanquer des coups à ▪ [punch] flanquer des coups de poing à **2.** [ill-treat - person] maltraiter, rudoyer ; [- car] maltraiter ▪ **the package has been bashed about** OR **around** le paquet a souffert.
◆ **bash in** *vt sep inf* [door] enfoncer ▪ [lid] défoncer ▪ [car, hat] cabosser.
◆ **bash on** *vi insep* UK *inf* [with journey, task] continuer (tant bien que mal).
◆ **bash up** *vt sep inf* [car] bousiller ▪ [person] tabasser.

-basher ['bæʃər] *in cpds inf* **a union~** un anti-syndicaliste, une anti-syndicaliste.

bashful ['bæʃful] *adj* [shy] timide ▪ [modest] pudique.

-bashing ['bæʃɪŋ] *in cpds inf* **media~** dénigration *f* systématique des médias.

basic ['beɪsɪk] *adj* **1.** [fundamental - problem, theme] fondamental ; [- aim, belief] principal ▪ **these things are ~ to a good marriage** ces choses sont fondamentales OR vitales pour un mariage heureux **2.** [elementary - rule, skill] élémentaire ; [- knowledge, vocabulary] de base ▪ **~ English** anglais *m* de base ▪ **the four ~ operations** MATHS les quatre opérations *fpl* fondamentales **3.** [essential] essentiel ▪ **~ foodstuffs** denrées *fpl* de base ▪ **the ~ necessities of life** les besoins *mpl* vitaux **4.** [primitive] rudimentaire **5.** [as a starting point - hours, salary] de base ▪ **this is the ~ model of the car** voici la voiture dans son modèle de base **6.** CHEM basique.
◆ **basics** *npl* : **the ~s** l'essentiel *m* ▪ **let's get down to ~s** venons-en à l'essentiel ▪ **I learned the ~s of computing** j'ai acquis les notions de base en informatique ▪ **they learned to cook with just the ~s** ils ont appris à faire la cuisine avec un minimum.

BASIC ['beɪsɪk] (*abbrev of* **beginner's all-purpose symbolic instruction code**) *n* COMPUT basic *m*.

basically ['beɪsɪklɪ] *adv* au fond ▪ **~ I agree with you** dans l'ensemble OR en gros je suis d'accord avec vous ▪ **she's ~ a very shy person, she's ~ shy** c'est une personne foncièrement timide ▪ **~, I think this war is wrong** cette guerre me paraît fondamentalement injuste ▪ **~, she doesn't know what to think** dans le fond, elle ne sait pas quoi penser.

basic rate *n* UK taux *m* de base ▪ **most people are ~ taxpayers** la plupart des gens sont imposés au taux de base.

basil ['beɪzl] *n* BOT basilic *m*.

basilica [bə'zɪlɪkə] *n* basilique *f*.

basin ['beɪsn] *n* **1.** CULIN bol *m* ▪ [for cream] jatte *f* **2.** [for washing] cuvette *f* ▪ [plumbed in] lavabo *m* **3.** GEOG [of river] bassin *m* ▪ [of valley] cuvette *f* **4.** [for fountain] vasque *f* ▪ [in harbour] bassin *m*.

basis ['beɪsɪs] (*pl* **bases** [-si:z]) *n* **1.** [foundation] base *f* ▪ **he can't survive on that ~** il ne peut pas survivre dans ces conditions-là ▪ **on the ~ of what I was told** d'après ce qu'on m'a dit ▪ **the ~ for assessing income tax** l'assiette de l'impôt sur le revenu **2.** [reason] raison *f* ▪ [grounds] motif *m* ▪ **he did it on the ~ that he'd nothing to lose** il l'a fait en partant du principe qu'il n'avait rien à perdre ▪ **there was no rational ~ for his decision** sa décision n'avait aucun fondement rationnel **3.** [system] : **employed on a part-time ~** employé à mi-temps ▪ **paid on a weekly ~** payé à la semaine ▪ **the centre is organized on a voluntary ~** le centre fonctionne sur la base du bénévolat.

bask [bɑ:sk] *vi* **1.** [lie] : **to ~ in the sun** se prélasser au soleil, lézarder ▪ **a cat ~ing in the sunshine** un chat se chauffant au soleil **2.** [revel] se réjouir, se délecter ▪ **he ~ed in all the unexpected publicity** il se réjouissait de toute cette publicité imprévue.

basket ['bɑ:skɪt] *n* **1.** [container - gen] corbeille *f* ; [- for wastepaper] corbeille *f* à papier ; [- for shopping] panier *m* ; [- for linen] corbeille *f* OR panier *m* à linge ; [- for baby] couffin *m* ; [- on donkey] panier *m* ; [- on someone's back] hotte *f* **2.** [quantity] panier *m* **3.** [group] assortiment *m* ▪ **a ~ of European currencies** un panier de devises européennes **4.** [in basketball - net, point] panier *m* **5.** [on ski stick] rondelle *f* de ski.

basketball ['bɑ:skɪtbɔ:l] *n* basket-ball *m*, basket *m* ▪ **~ player** basketteur *m*, - euse *f*.

basket case△ *n* [nervous wreck] paquet *m* de nerfs ▪ [mad person] bon à enfermer.

basket chair *n* chaise *f* en osier.

basket maker *n* vannier *m*.

basketry ['bɑ:skɪtrɪ] *n* vannerie *f*.

basket weave *n* TEX armure *f* nattée.

basketwork ['bɑ:skɪtwɜ:k] *n (U)* [objects] objets *mpl* en osier ▪ [skill] vannerie *f*.

Basle [bɑ:l] *pr n* = **Basel**.

basmati (rice) [bæz'mɑ:tɪ] *n (U)* CULIN (riz *m*) basmati *m*.

basque [bɑ:sk] *n* corsage *m* très ajusté.

Basque [bɑ:sk] ◇ *n* **1.** [person] Basque *mf* **2.** LING basque *m*.
◇ *adj* basque.

Basque Country *pr n* : **the ~** le Pays basque.

bass[1] [beɪs] ◇ *n* **1.** [part, singer] basse *f* **2.** [bass guitar] basse *f* ▪ [double bass] contrebasse *f* **3.** ACOUST [on stereo] basses *fpl*, graves *mpl* ▪ [knob] bouton *m* de réglage des graves.
◇ *adj* grave, bas ▪ **a part for a ~ voice** une partie pour une voix de basse.

bass[2] [bæs] *n* [freshwater fish] perche *f* ▪ [sea fish] bar *m*, loup *m*.

bass clef [beɪs-] *n* clef *f* de fa.

bass drum [beɪs-] *n* grosse caisse *f*.

basset (hound) [bæsɪt-] *n* basset *m (chien).*

bass guitar [beɪs-] *n* guitare *f* basse.

bassist ['beɪsɪst] *n* bassiste *mf*.

bassoon [bə'su:n] *n* basson *m*.

bastard ['bɑːstəd] ◇ *n* **1.** *lit & pej* [child] bâtard *m*, - e *f* **2.** △ *pej* [nasty person] salaud△ *m* **3.** △ [affectionate use] : **you lucky ~!** sacré veinard! ▪ **poor ~!** pauvre type! **4.** △ [difficult case, job] : **it's a ~ of a book to translate** ce livre est vachement dur à traduire.
◇ *adj* **1.** *lit & pej* [child] bâtard **2.** [language] corrompu **3.** TYPO [character] d'un autre œil.

bastardize, ise ['bɑːstədaɪz] *vt* **1.** [language, style] corrompre **2.** [child] déclarer illégitime *OR* naturel.

baste [beɪst] *vt* **1.** CULIN arroser **2.** SEW bâtir, faufiler.

basting ['beɪstɪŋ] *n* **1.** CULIN arrosage *m* **2.** SEW bâtissage *m*.

bastion ['bæstɪən] *n liter & fig* bastion *m* ▪ **the last ~ of Stalinism** le dernier bastion du stalinisme.

bat [bæt] ◇ *n* **1.** [in baseball & cricket] batte *f* ▪ [in table tennis] raquette *f* ➡ **right off the ~** *US inf* sur-le-champ ▪ **to do sthg off one's own ~** *UK inf* faire qqch de sa propre initiative **2.** [shot, blow] coup *m* **3.** ZOOL chauve-souris *f* ▪ **she's an old ~** *inf pej* c'est une vieille bique *OR* chouette ▪ **to have ~s in the** *OR* **one's belfry** *inf* avoir une araignée au plafond ▪ **to run/to drive like a ~ out of hell** *inf* courir/conduire comme si l'on avait le diable à ses trousses.
◇ *vi* (*pret & pp* **batted**, *cont* **batting**) [baseball player, cricketer - play] manier la batte ; [- take one's turn at playing] être à la batte ▪ **to go in to ~** aller à la batte ▪ **to go to ~ for sb** *US inf* intervenir en faveur de qqn.
◇ *vt* (*pret & pp* **batted**, *cont* **batting**) **1.** [hit] donner un coup à **2.** [blink] : **she batted her eyelids at him** elle battit des paupières en le regardant ▪ **he didn't ~ an eyelid** *fig* il n'a pas sourcillé *OR* bronché.

batch [bætʃ] ◇ *n* [of letters] paquet *m*, liasse *f* ▪ [of people] groupe *m* ▪ [of refugees] convoi *m* ▪ [of bread] fournée *f* ▪ [of recruits] contingent *m* ▪ COMM lot *m*.
◇ *vt* grouper.

batch file *n* COMPUT fichier *m* de commandes.

batch processing *n* COMPUT traitement *m* par lots.

bated ['beɪtɪd] *adj* : **we waited with ~ breath** nous avons attendu en retenant notre souffle.

bath [bɑːθ] ◇ *n* (*pl* **baths** [bɑːðz]) **1.** [wash] bain *m* ▪ [tub] baignoire *f* ▪ **to give sb a ~** donner un bain à qqn ▪ **to have** *UK OR* **to take a ~** prendre un bain ▪ **she's in the ~** elle prend son bain, elle est dans son bain ▪ **to run** *OR fml* **to draw a ~** se faire couler un bain ▪ **a room with ~** une chambre avec salle de bains **2.** [for chemicals, dye] bain *m* ▪ PHOT cuvette *f*.
◇ *vt* (*pret & pp* **bathed**) [baby, person] baigner, donner un bain à.
◇ *vi* (*pret & pp* **bathed**) *UK* prendre un bain.
◆ **baths** *npl* [swimming pool] piscine *f* ▪ [public baths] bains-douches *mpl* ▪ [at spa] thermes *mpl*.

bath bun *n petit pain rond aux raisins secs souvent servi chaud et beurré.*

bath chair *n* fauteuil *m* roulant.

bath cube *n* cube *m* de sels de bain.

bathe [beɪð] ◇ *vi* (*pret & pp* **bathed**) **1.** *UK* [swim] se baigner **2.** *US* [bath] prendre un bain.
◇ *vt* (*pret & pp* **bathed**) **1.** [wound] laver ▪ [eyes, feet] baigner **2.** [covered] : **I was ~d in sweat** j'étais en nage, je ruisselais de sueur ▪ **the hills were ~d in light** les collines étaient éclairées d'une lumière douce ▪ **her face was ~d in tears** son visage était baigné de larmes **3.** *US* [bath] baigner, donner un bain à.
◇ *n* bain *m (dans la mer, dans une rivière)* ▪ **to have a ~** se baigner.

bather ['beɪðəʳ] *n* [swimmer] baigneur *m*, - euse *f*.

bathhouse ['bɑːθhaʊs] (*pl* [-haʊzɪz]) *n* bains-douches *mpl (bâtiment).*

bathing ['beɪ̤ɪŋ] *n (U)* **1.** *UK* [swimming] baignade *f* **2.** [washing] bain *m*.

bathing beauty *n* belle *f* baigneuse.

bathing cap *n* bonnet *m* de bain.

bathing costume *n* maillot *m* de bain.

bathing hut *n* cabine *f* de bains.

bathing machine *n* cabine *f* de bains roulante.

bathing suit *n* = **bathing costume**.

bathing trunks *npl UK* maillot *m* de bain.

bath mat *n* tapis *m* de bain.

bath oil *n* huile *f* de bain.

bathos ['beɪθɒs] *n (U)* LIT chute *f* du sublime au ridicule.

bathrobe ['bɑːθrəʊb] *n* **1.** [for bathroom, swimming pool] peignoir *m* de bain **2.** *US* [dressing gown] robe *f* de chambre.

bathroom ['bɑːθrʊm] *n* salle *f* de bains ▪ **to use** *OR* **to go to the ~** *euph* aller aux toilettes.

bath salts *npl* sels *mpl* de bain.

Bathsheba [bæθ'ʃiːbə] *pr n* Bethsabée.

bath towel *n* serviette *f* de bain.

bathtub ['bɑːθtʌb] *n* baignoire *f*.

bathwater ['bɑːθ,wɔːtəʳ] *n* eau *f* du bain.

bathysphere ['bæθɪ,sfɪəʳ] *n* bathysphère *f*.

batik [bə'tiːk] *n* [cloth, technique] batik *m*.

batman ['bætmən] (*pl* **batmen** [-mən]) *n UK* MIL ordonnance *m f*.

baton ['bætən] *n* **1.** [conductor's] baguette *f* **2.** [policeman's - in traffic] bâton *m* ; [- in riots] matraque *f* **3.** SPORT témoin *m* ▪ **to pass the ~ to sb** *fig* passer le relais à qqn ▪ **to take up the ~** *fig* prendre le relais.

baton charge *n* charge *f* à la matraque.

baton round *n* balle *f* en plastique.

bats [bæts] *adj inf* timbré, cinglé.

batsman ['bætsmən] (*pl* **batsmen** [-mən]) *n* SPORT batteur *m*.

battalion [bə'tæljən] *n* MIL & *fig* bataillon *m*.

batten ['bætn] ◇ *n* [board] latte *f* ▪ [in roof] volige *f* ▪ [in floor] latte *f*, lame *f* de parquet ▪ NAUT latte *f* de voile ▪ THEAT herse *f*.
◇ *vt* CONSTR latter ▪ [floor] planchéier ▪ [roof] voliger.
◆ **batten down** *vt sep* : **to ~ down the hatches** *liter* fermer les écoutilles, condamner les panneaux ; *fig* dresser ses batteries.
◆ **batten on** *vt insep UK* **she immediately ~ed on me for help** elle s'est immédiatement accrochée à moi comme une sangsue pour que je l'aide.

batter ['bætəʳ] ◇ *vt* **1.** [beat - person] battre, maltraiter **2.** [hammer - door, wall] frapper sur **3.** [buffet] : **the ship was ~ed by the waves** le vaisseau était battu par les vagues ▪ **he felt ~ed by the experience** *fig* il se sentait ravagé par l'expérience.
◇ *vi* [hammer] : **to ~ at** *OR* **on the door** frapper à la porte à coups redoublés.
◇ *n* **1.** TYPO [plate] cliché *m* endommagé ▪ [print] tirage *m* défectueux **2.** CULIN pâte *f* à crêpes **3.** [in baseball] batteur *m*.
◆ **batter about** *vt sep* **1.** [person] maltraiter, rouer de coups **2.** [ship] battre.
◆ **batter down** *vt sep* [vegetation] fouler ▪ [wall] démolir ▪ [tree] abattre.
◆ **batter in** *vt sep* [skull] défoncer ▪ [door] enfoncer ▪ [nail] enfoncer à grands coups.

battered ['bætəd] *adj* [building] délabré ▪ [car, hat] cabossé, bosselé ▪ [briefcase, suitcase] cabossé ▪ [face - beaten] meurtri ; [- ravaged] buriné ▪ **a ~ child** un enfant martyr ▪ **a refuge for ~ wives** un refuge pour femmes battues.

battering ['bætərɪŋ] *n* **1.** [beating] : **he got a bad ~** on l'a rossé sévèrement **2.** [hammering] : **the building took a ~ in the war** le bâtiment a été durement éprouvé ▪ **the team took a ~** l'équipe a été battue à plate couture.

battering ram *n* bélier *m*.

battery ['bætərɪ] (*pl* **batteries**) *n* **1.** ELEC [in clock, radio] pile *f* ▪ [in car] batterie *f*, accumulateurs *mpl* **2.** [of guns, missiles] batterie *f* **3.** [barrage] tir *m* de barrage ▪ **a ~ of insults** une pluie d'insultes **4.** LAW ⊳ **assault 5.** AGRIC batterie *f*.

battery charger *n* chargeur *m*.

battery farming *n* élevage *m* intensif *OR* en batterie.

battery hen *n* poule *f* de batterie.

batting ['bætɪŋ] *n* **1.** [wadding] bourre *f (pour matelas, couettes)* **2.** SPORT maniement *m* de la batte.

battle ['bætl] <> *n* **1.** [fight] bataille *f* ▪ **he was killed in ~** il a été tué au combat ▪ **to do** *OR* **to give** *OR* **to join ~** livrer bataille ▮ *fig* lutte *f* ▪ **the ~ between** *OR* **of the sexes** la lutte des sexes ▪ **a ~ of wits** une joute d'esprit ➜ **the Battle of Britain** la bataille d'Angleterre **2.** [struggle] lutte *f* ▪ **the ~ for freedom** la lutte pour la liberté ▪ **to do ~ for** lutter pour ▪ **to do ~ against** *OR* **with** lutter contre ▪ **we're fighting the same ~** nous nous battons pour la même cause ▪ **don't fight his ~s for him** ne te bats pas à sa place ➜ **it's half the ~** la partie est presque gagnée.
<> *comp* [dress, zone] de combat ▪ **in ~ order** en bataille.
<> *vi* se battre, lutter ▪ **she ~d to save his life** elle s'est battue pour lui sauver la vie.
<> *vt US* combattre.

battleaxe *UK*, **battleax** *US* ['bætəlæks] *n* **1.** [weapon] hache *f* d'armes **2.** *pej* & *hum* [woman] virago *f*.

battle cruiser *n* croiseur *m* cuirassé.

battle cry *n* cri *m* de guerre.

battledress ['bætldres] *n* tenue *f* de combat.

battle fatigue *n* psychose *f* traumatique.

battlefield ['bætlfi:ld], **battleground** ['bætlgra nd] *n* MIL & *fig* champ *m* de bataille.

battlement ['bætlmənt] *n* [crenellation] créneau *m*.
◆ **battlements** *npl* [wall] remparts *mpl*.

battle royal *n fml* & *lit* **1.** [fight] bagarre *f* **2.** [argument] querelle *f*.

battle-scarred *adj* [army, landscape] marqué par les combats ▪ [person] marqué par la vie ▪ *hum* [car, table] abîmé.

battleship ['bætlʃɪp] *n* cuirassé *m*.

batty ['bætɪ] (*comp* **battier**, *superl* **battiest**) *adj inf* [crazy] cinglé, dingue ▪ [eccentric] bizarre.

bauble ['bɔ:bl] *n* [trinket] babiole *f*, colifichet *m* ▪ [jester's] marotte *f*.

baud [bɔ:d] *n* COMPUT & ELEC baud *m* ▪ **~ rate** vitesse *f* de transmission (en bauds).

baulk [bɔ:k] <> *n* **1.** [in snooker] *espace entre la bande et la ligne* **2.** = **balk**.
<> *vi* & *vt* = **balk**.

bauxite ['bɔ:ksaɪt] *n* bauxite *f*.

Bavaria [bə'veərɪə] *pr n* Bavière *f* ▪ **in ~** en Bavière.

Bavarian [bə'veərɪən] <> *n* Bavarois *m*, - e *f*.
<> *adj* bavarois ▪ **~ cream** CULIN bavaroise *f*.

bawdy ['bɔ:dɪ] *adj* paillard.

bawl [bɔ:l] <> *vi* **1.** [yell] brailler ▪ **to ~ at sb** crier après qqn **2.** [cry] brailler.
<> *vt* [slogan, word] brailler, hurler.
◆ **bawl out** *vt sep* **1.** [yell] = **bawl** *(vt)* **2.** *inf* [reprimand] passer un savon à **3.** *phr* **the child was ~ing his eyes out** *inf* l'enfant braillait à pleins poumons.

bay [beɪ] <> *n* **1.** [on shoreline] baie *f* ▪ **the Bay State** le Massachusetts ▮ [smaller] anse *f* **2.** [recess - ARCHIT] travée *f* ▪ [window] baie *f* ▪ RAIL voie *f* d'arrêt **3.** BOT & CULIN laurier *m* **4.** HUNT & *fig* **to be at ~** être aux abois ▪ **to keep** *OR* **to hold sb at ~** tenir qqn à distance ▪ **to keep** *OR* **to hold hunger at ~** tromper la faim **5.** [horse] cheval *m* bai.
<> *vi* [bark] aboyer, donner de la voix.
<> *adj* [colour] bai.

bay leaf *n* feuille *f* de laurier.

Bay of Pigs *pr n* : **the ~** la baie des Cochons.

THE BAY OF PIGS

En 1961, la baie des Cochons à Cuba fut le site d'une tentative d'invasion pour renverser le régime de Fidel Castro. L'opération conduite par des Cubains exilés aux États-Unis, équipés et entraînés par la CIA, tourna au désastre.

bayonet ['beɪənɪt] <> *n* baïonnette *f*.
<> *vt* (*pret* & *pp* **bayoneted** *OR* **bayonetted**, *cont* **bayoneting** *OR* **bayonetting**) passer à la baïonnette.

bayonet charge *n* charge *f* à la baïonnette.

bayonet socket *n* douille *f* à baïonnette.

bayou ['baɪu:] *n US* bayou *m*, marécages *mpl*.

bay tree *n* laurier *m*.

bay window *n* **1.** fenêtre *f* en saillie **2.** *US inf* [stomach] gros bide *m*.

bazaar [bə'zɑ:r] *n* [in East] bazar *m* ▪ [sale for charity] vente *f* de charité ▪ [shop] bazar *m*.

bazooka [bə'zu:kə] *n* bazooka *m*.

BB *n* (*abbrev of* **double black**) *sur un crayon à papier, indique une mine grasse.*

B & B *n* = **bed and breakfast**.

BBC (*abbrev of* **British Broadcasting Corporation**) *pr n office national britannique de radiodiffusion* ▪ **the ~** la BBC ▪ **~1** *chaîne généraliste (sans publicité) de la BBC* ▪ **~2** *chaîne à vocation culturelle de la BBC* ▪ **~ World Service** *émissions radiophoniques de la BBC diffusées dans le monde entier* ▪ **~ English** *l'anglais tel qu'il était parlé sur la BBC et qui servait de référence pour la "bonne" prononciation.*

BB gun *n US* carabine *f* à air comprimé.

BBQ *n* = **barbecue**.

BBS *n* = **bulletin board system**.

BC <> *adv* (*abbrev of* **before Christ**) av. J.C.
<> *written abbr of* **British Columbia**.

bcc [,bi:si:'si:] (*abbrev of* **blind carbon copy**) *n* CCI *m*.

BD (*abbrev of* **Bachelor of Divinity**) *n (titulaire d'une) licence de théologie.*

BDS (*abbrev of* **Bachelor of Dental Science**) *n (titulaire d'une) licence de chirurgie dentaire.*

be [bi:] *(pres 1st sing* **am**, *weak form* [əm], *strong form* [æm], *pres 2nd sing* **are** *weak form* [ə], *strong form* [ɑ:], *pres 3rd sing* **is** [ɪz], *pres pl* **are** *weak form* [ə], *strong form* [ɑ:], *pt 1st sing* **was** *weak form* [wəz], *strong form* [wɒz], *pt 2nd sing* **were** *weak form* [wə], *strong form* [wɜ:], *pt 3rd sing* **was** *weak form* [wəz], *strong form* [wɒz], *pt pl* **were** *weak form* [wə], *strong form* [wɜ:]) (*pp* **been** [bi:n], *cont* **being** ['bi:ɪŋ]) <> *vi* **1.** [exist, live] être, exister ▪ **to be or not to be** être ou ne pas être ▪ **God is** Dieu existe ▪ **the greatest scientist that ever was** le plus grand savant qui ait jamais existé *OR* de tous les temps ▪ **as happy as can be** heureux comme un roi ▪ **that may be, but...** cela se peut, mais..., peut-être, mais...
2. [used to identify, describe] être ▪ **I'm Bill** je suis *OR* je m'appelle Bill ▪ **she's a doctor/engineer** elle est médecin/ingénieur ▪ **the glasses were crystal** les verres étaient en cristal ▪ **he is American** il est américain, c'est un Américain ▪ **be careful!** soyez prudent! ➜ **just be yourself** soyez vous-même, soyez naturel
3. [indicating temporary state or condition] : **he was angry/tired** il était fâché/fatigué ▪ **I am hungry/thirsty/afraid** j'ai faim/soif/peur ▪ **my feet/hands are frozen** j'ai les pieds gelés/mains gelées
4. [indicating health] aller, se porter ▪ **how are you?** comment allez-vous?, comment ça va? ▪ **I am fine** ça va
5. [indicating age] avoir ▪ **how old are you?** quel âge avez-vous?
6. [indicating location] être ▪ **the hotel is next to the river** l'hôtel se trouve *OR* est près de la rivière ▪ **where was I?** *liter* où étais-je? ; *fig* [in book, speech] où en étais-je?
7. [indicating measurement] : **the table is one metre long** la table fait un mètre de long ▪ **how tall is he?** combien mesure-t-il? ▪ **the school is two kilometres from here** l'école est à deux kilomètres d'ici

8. [indicating time, date] être ■ **it's 5 o'clock** il est 5 h ■ **yesterday was Monday** hier on était *OR* c'était lundi
9. [happen, occur] être, avoir lieu ■ **the concert is on Saturday night** le concert est *OR* a lieu samedi soir ■ **when is your birthday?** quand est *OR* c'est quand ton anniversaire? ■ **the spring holidays are in March this year** les vacances de printemps tombent en mars cette année ■ **how is it that you arrived so quickly?** comment se fait-il que vous soyez arrivé si vite?
10. [indicating cost] coûter ■ **it is expensive** ça coûte *OR* c'est cher ▮ [add up to] : **the phone bill is £25** la facture de téléphone est de 25 livres
11. [with 'there'] : **there is, there are** il y a, il est *lit* ■ **there is** *OR* **has been no snow** il n'y a pas de neige ■ **there are six of them** ils sont *OR* il y en a six ■ **there will be swimming** on nagera ■ **there's no telling what she'll do** il est impossible de prévoir ce qu'elle va faire
12. [calling attention to] : **this is my friend John** voici mon ami John ■ **there are the others** voilà les autres ■ **there you are!** [I've found you] ah, te voilà! ; [take this] tiens/tenez, voilà! ■ **now there's an idea!** voilà une bonne idée!
13. [with 'it'] : **who is it? – it's us!** qui est-ce? – c'est nous! ■ **it was your mother who decided** c'est ta mère qui a décidé
14. [indicating weather] faire ■ **it is cold/hot/grey** il fait froid/chaud/gris ■ **it is windy** il y a du vent
15. [go] aller, être ■ **she's been to visit her mother** elle a été *OR* est allée rendre visite à sa mère ■ **has the plumber been?** le plombier est-il (déjà) passé? ■ **he was into/out of the house in a flash** il est entré dans/sorti de la maison en coup de vent ■ **I know, I've been there** *liter* je sais, j'y suis allé ; *fig* je sais, j'ai connu ça ▮ [come] être, venir ■ **she is from Egypt** elle vient d'Égypte ■ **your brother has been and gone** votre frère est venu et reparti ▶ **he's only been and wrecked the car!** *inf* il est allé casser la voiture! ■ **now you've been (and gone) and done it!** *inf* et voilà, c'est réussi! *iron*
16. [indicating hypothesis, supposition] : **if I were you** si j'étais vous *OR* à votre place ■ **were it not for their contribution, the school would close** *fml* sans leur assistance, l'école serait obligée de fermer
17. MATHS faire ■ **1 and 1 are 2** 1 et 1 font 2.
◇ *aux vb* **1.** [forming continuous tenses] : **he is having breakfast** il prend *OR* il est en train de prendre son petit déjeuner ■ **a problem which is getting worse and worse** un problème qui s'aggrave ■ **what are you going to do about it?** qu'est-ce que vous allez *OR* comptez faire? ■ **why aren't you working? – but I am working!** pourquoi ne travaillez-vous pas? – mais je travaille!
2. [forming passive voice] : **she is known as a good negotiator** elle est connue pour ses talents de négociatrice ■ **plans are being made** on fait des projets ■ **what is left to do?** qu'est-ce qui reste à faire? ■ **socks are sold by the pair** les chaussettes se vendent par deux ■ **it is said/thought/assumed that...** on dit/pense/suppose que... ■ **'to be continued'** 'à suivre' ■ **not to be confused with** à ne pas confondre avec
3. *(with infinitive)* [indicating future event] : **the next meeting is to take place on Wednesday** la prochaine réunion aura lieu mercredi ■ **she was to become a famous pianist** elle allait devenir une pianiste renommée ▮ [indicating expected event] : **they were to have been married in June** ils devaient se marier en juin
4. *(with infinitive)* [indicating obligation] : **I'm to be home by 10 o'clock** il faut que je rentre avant 10 h ▮ [expressing opinion] : **you are to be congratulated** on doit vous féliciter ■ **they are to be pitied** ils sont à plaindre ▮ [requesting information] : **what am I to say to them?** qu'est-ce que je vais leur dire?
5. *(with passive infinitive)* [indicating possibility] : **bargains are to be found even in the West End** on peut faire de bonnes affaires même dans le West End ■ **she was not to be dissuaded** rien ne devait *OR* il fut impossible de lui faire changer d'avis
6. *(with infinitive)* [indicating hypothesis] : **if he were** *OR* **were he to die** *fml* s'il venait à mourir, à supposer qu'il meure
7. [in tag questions] : **he's always causing trouble, isn't he? – yes, he is** il est toujours en train de créer des problèmes, n'est-ce pas? – oui, toujours ■ **you're back, are you?** vous êtes revenu alors?
8. [in ellipsis] : **is she satisfied? – she is** est-elle satisfaite? – oui (, elle l'est) ■ **you're angry – no I'm not – oh yes you are!** tu es fâché – non – mais si! ■ **I was pleased to see him but the children weren't** (moi,) j'étais content de le voir mais pas les enfants
9. [forming perfect tenses] : **we're finished** nous avons terminé ■ **when I looked again, they were gone** quand j'ai regardé de nouveau, ils étaient partis
10. [as suffix] : **the husband-to-be** le futur mari ■ **the father-to-be** le futur père.
◆ **be that as it may** *adv phr* quoi qu'il en soit.

B/E *written abbr of* **bill of exchange**.

beach [biːtʃ] ◇ *n* [seaside] plage *f* ■ [shore - sand, shingle] grève *f* ■ [at lake] rivage *m*.
◇ *comp* [ball, towel, hut] de plage ■ **~ umbrella** parasol *m*.
◇ *vt* **1.** [boat] échouer **2.** [whale] *(usu passive)* échouer.

beach buggy *n* buggy *m*.

beachchair [ˈbiːtʃˌtʃeə] *n* US chaise *f* longue, transat *m*.

beachcomber [ˈbiːtʃˌkəʊməʳ] *n* [collector] *personne qui ramasse des objets sur les plages* ■ [wave] vague *f* déferlante.

beachhead [ˈbiːtʃhed] *n* tête *f* de pont ■ **to establish** *OR* **to secure a ~** mettre en place une tête de pont sur la plage.

beachwear [ˈbiːtʃweəʳ] *n (U)* [one outfit] tenue *f* de plage ■ [several outfits] articles *mpl* de plage.

beacon [ˈbiːkən] *n* **1.** [warning signal] phare *m*, signal *m* lumineux ■ [lantern] fanal *m* ■ AERON & NAUT balise *f* **2.** [bonfire on hill] feu *m* d'alarme **3.** [in place names] colline *f*.

bead [biːd] ◇ *n* **1.** [of glass, wood] perle *f* ■ [for rosary] grain *m* ■ **where are my ~s?** où est mon collier? **2.** [drop - of sweat] goutte *f* ; [- of water, dew] perle *f* ■ [bubble] bulle *f* ■ **~s of sweat stood out on her forehead** la sueur perlait sur son front **3.** [on gun] guidon *m*.
◇ *vi* [form drops] perler.
◇ *vt* [decorate] décorer de perles.

beaded [ˈbiːdɪd] *adj* **1.** [decorated] couvert *OR* orné de perles **2.** [with moisture] couvert de gouttelettes d'eau.

beading [ˈbiːdɪŋ] *n* **1.** ARCHIT astragale *m* ■ [in carpentry] baguette *f* **2.** SEW [trim] garniture *f* de perles ■ [over cloth] broderie *f* perlée.

beadle [ˈbiːdl] *n* **1.** RELIG bedeau *m* **2.** *UK* UNIV appariteur *m*.

beady [ˈbiːdɪ] (*comp* **beadier**, *superl* **beadiest**) *adj* [eyes, gaze] perçant ■ **I had to keep a ~ eye on the sweets** il fallait que je surveille les bonbons de près.

beady-eyed *adj* aux yeux perçants.

beagle [ˈbiːgl] ◇ *n* beagle *m*.
◇ *vi* chasser avec des beagles.

beak [biːk] *n* **1.** [of bird] bec *m* **2.** *inf* [nose] nez *m* crochu.

beaker [ˈbiːkəʳ] *n* gobelet *m* ■ CHEM vase *m* à bec.

be-all *n phr* : **the ~ and end-all** la raison d'être.

beam [biːm] ◇ *n* **1.** [bar of wood - in house] poutre *f* ; [- big] madrier *m* ; [- small] poutrelle *f* ; [- in gymnastics] poutre *f* **2.** NAUT [cross member] barrot *m* ■ [breadth] largeur *f* ■ **on the ~** par le travers ■ **on the port ~** à babord ■ **on the starboard ~** à tribord **3.** [of scales] fléau *m* ■ [of engine] balancier *m* ■ [of loom] ensouple *f*, rouleau *m* ■ [of plough] age *m* **4.** [ray - of sunlight] rayon *m* ; [- of searchlight, headlamp] faisceau *m* lumineux ■ PHYS faisceau *m* ■ AERON & NAUT chenal *m* de radioguidage ■ **he's way off ~** *UK inf* il déraille complètement **5.** [smile] sourire *m* radieux **6.** *US* AUT : **high ~s** phares *mpl* ■ **low ~s** codes *mpl*.
◇ *vi* **1.** [smile] : **faces ~ing with pleasure** des visages rayonnants de plaisir ■ **he ~ed when he saw us** il eut un sourire radieux en nous apercevant **2.** [shine - sun] briller, darder ses rayons.
◇ *vt* RADIO & TV [message] transmettre par émission dirigée ■ **the pictures were ~ed all over the world** les images ont été diffusées dans le monde entier.

beam-ends *npl* : **on her ~** NAUT couché sur le flanc ■ **to be on one's ~** *UK inf* tirer le diable par la queue.

beaming [ˈbiːmɪŋ] *adj* radieux, resplendissant.

bean [biːn] ◇ *n* **1.** BOT & CULIN haricot *m* **2.** *inf phr* **to be full of ~s** péter le feu ■ **I haven't got a ~** je n'ai pas un rond ■ **that car isn't worth a ~** cette voiture-là ne vaut rien ■ **he doesn't know ~s about it** *US* il n'y connaît rien.

◇ *vt US* **to ~ sb** frapper qqn (sur la tête).

beanbag ['bi:nbæg] *n* [in game] balle *f* lestée ▪ [seat] sacco *m*.

bean curd *n* pâte *f* de soja.

beanfeast ['bi:nfi:st] *n UK inf* gueuleton *m*.

beanie ['bi:nɪ] *n* [skullcap] calotte *f*.

beanpole ['bi:npəʊl] *n liter* rame *f* ▪ *fig* (grande) perche *f*.

beanshoot ['bi:nʃu:t], **beansprout** ['bi:nspra t] *n* germe *m* de soja.

beanstalk ['bi:nstɔ:k] *n* tige *f* de haricot.

bear [beəʳ]) ◇ *vt* (*pret* **bore** [bɔ:ʳ], *pp* **borne** [bɔ:n]) **1.** [carry - goods, burden] porter ; [- gift, message] apporter ; [- sound] porter, transporter ▪ **a convoy of lorries bore the refugees away** *OR* **off** un convoi de camions emmena les réfugiés ▪ **they bore him aloft on their shoulders** ils le portèrent en triomphe ▪ **they arrived ~ing fruit** ils sont arrivés, chargés de fruits ▪ **she bore her head high** elle avait un port de tête altier
2. [sustain - weight] supporter ▪ **the system can only ~ a certain amount of pressure** *fig* le système ne peut supporter qu'une certaine pression
3. [endure] tolérer, supporter ▪ **the news was more than she could ~** elle n'a pas pu supporter la nouvelle ▪ **I can't ~ to see you go** je ne supporte pas que tu t'en ailles ▪ **I can't ~ the suspense** ce suspense est insupportable
4. [accept - responsibility, blame] assumer ; [- costs] supporter
5. [allow - examination] soutenir, supporter ▪ **his theory doesn't really ~ close analysis** sa théorie ne supporte pas une analyse approfondie ▪ **it doesn't ~ thinking about** je n'ose pas *OR* je préfère ne pas y penser
6. [show - mark, name, sign etc] porter ▪ **I still ~ the scars** j'en porte encore les cicatrices ▪ **he ~s no resemblance to his father** il ne ressemble pas du tout à son père ▪ **his statement bore no relation to the facts** sa déclaration n'avait aucun rapport avec les faits ▪ **to ~ witness to sthg** [person] attester qqch ; [thing, quality] témoigner de qqch
7. [give birth to] donner naissance à ▪ **she bore him two sons** elle lui donna deux fils
8. [produce] porter, produire ▪ **the cherry tree ~s beautiful blossom in spring** le cerisier donne de belles fleurs au printemps ▪ **all my efforts have borne fruit** *fig* mes efforts ont porté leurs fruits ▪ **his investment bore 8% interest** FIN ses investissements lui ont rapporté 8 % d'intérêt
9. [feel] porter, avoir en soi ▪ **to ~ love/hatred for sb** éprouver de l'amour/de la haine pour qqn ▪ **I ~ you no ill will** je ne t'en veux pas ▪ **to ~ a grudge against sb** en vouloir *OR* garder rancune à qqn ▪ **to ~ sthg in mind** ne pas oublier qqch ▪ **thanks for the suggestion, I'll ~ it in mind** merci de ta suggestion, j'en tiendrai compte
10. [behave] : **he bore himself like a man** il s'est comporté en homme
11. ST. EX [market, security] chercher à faire baisser.
◇ *vi* (*pret* **bore** [bɔ:ʳ], *pp* **borne** [bɔ:n]) **1.** [move] diriger ▪ **~ (to your) left** prenez sur la gauche *OR* à gauche ▪ **'~ left ahead'** *US* 'tournez à gauche', 'filez à gauche'
2. [tree - fruit] produire, donner ; [- flower] fleurir
3. [be oppressive] peser ▪ **grief bore heavily on her** le chagrin l'accablait
4. ST. EX jouer à la baisse
5. *phr* **to bring a gun to ~ on a target** pointer un canon sur un objectif ▪ **to bring pressure to ~ on sb** faire pression sur qqn ▪ **to bring one's mind to ~ on sthg** s'appliquer à qqch.
◇ *n* **1.** [animal] ours *m*, - e *f* ▪ **~ cub** ourson *m* ▪ **he's like a ~ with a sore head** *UK inf* il est d'une humeur de dogue
2. *pej* [person] ours *m*
3. ST. EX [person] baissier *m*, - ère *f* ▪ **~ market** marché *m* en baisse
4. [toy] ours *m* (en peluche).
◆ **bear down** *vi insep* **1.** [approach] : **to ~ down on** *OR* **upon** [ship] venir sur ; [person] foncer sur
2. [press] appuyer ▪ [in childbirth] pousser.
◆ **bear on** *vt insep* [be relevant to] se rapporter à, être relatif à ▪ [concern] intéresser, concerner.
◆ **bear out** *vt sep UK* confirmer, corroborer ▪ **to ~ sb out, to ~ out what sb says** corroborer ce que qqn dit.
◆ **bear up** *vi insep UK* tenir le coup, garder le moral ▪ **she's ~ing up under the pressure** elle ne se laisse pas décourager par le stress.
◆ **bear upon** *vt insep* = **bear on.**
◆ **bear with** *vt insep* [be patient with] supporter patiemment ▪ **if you'll just ~ with me a minute** je vous demande un peu de patience.

bearable ['beərəbl] *adj* supportable, tolérable.

bearbaiting ['beə,beɪtɪŋ] *n* combat *m* d'ours et de chiens.

beard [bɪəd] ◇ *n* **1.** [on person] barbe *f* ▪ [goatee] barbiche *f* ▪ **to have a ~** avoir la barbe ▪ **a man with a ~** un (homme) barbu ▪ **to grow a ~** se laisser pousser la barbe **2.** [on goat] barbiche *f* ▪ [on fish, oyster] barbe *f* ▪ [on plant] arête *f*, barbe *f* **3.** TYPO talus *m*.
◇ *vt lit* [confront] affronter, braver.

bearded ['bɪədɪd] *adj* barbu ▪ **~ lady** femme *f* à barbe.

beardless ['bɪədlɪs] *adj* imberbe, sans barbe.

bearer ['beərəʳ] ◇ *n* **1.** [of news, letter] porteur *m*, - euse *f* ▪ [of load, coffin] porteur *m* ▪ [servant] serviteur *m* ▪ **I hate to be the ~ of bad tidings** j'ai horreur d'annoncer les mauvaises nouvelles **2.** [of cheque, title] porteur *m*, - euse *f* ▪ [of passport] titulaire *mf* **3.** CONSTR support *m*.
◇ *comp* FIN [bond, cheque] au porteur.

bear garden *n* pétaudière *f*.

bear hug *n* : **to give sb a ~** serrer qqn très fort dans ses bras.

bearing ['beərɪŋ] *n* **1.** [relevance] rapport *m*, relation *f* ▪ **his comments have some** *OR* **a ~ on the present situation** ses remarques ont un certain rapport avec la situation actuelle ▪ **the event had no ~ on the outcome of the war** l'événement n'eut aucune incidence sur l'issue de la guerre **2.** [deportment] maintien *m*, port *m* **3.** [endurance] : **it's beyond** *OR* **past all ~** c'est absolument insupportable **4.** [direction] position *f* ▪ **to take a (compass) ~ (on sthg)** relever la position (de qqch) au compas ▪ **to take a ship's ~** NAUT faire le point ▪ **to get** *OR* **to find one's ~s** *fig* se repérer, s'orienter ▪ **to lose one's ~s** *fig* perdre le nord **5.** MECH palier *m*.
◆ **bearings** *npl* HERALD armoiries *fpl*.

-bearing *in cpds* : **rain~ clouds** des nuages chargés de pluie ▪ **fruit~ trees** des arbres fructifères.

bear pit *n* fosse *f* aux ours.

bearskin ['beəskɪn] *n* **1.** [piece of fur] peau *f* d'ours **2.** MIL [hat] bonnet *m* à poils.

beast [bi:st] *n* **1.** [animal] bête *f*, animal *m* ▪ **the king of the ~s** le roi des animaux ▪ **the Beast** BIBLE l'Antéchrist, la bête de l'Apocalypse ➊ **~ of burden** bête de somme ▪ **~ of prey** bête de proie **2.** [savage nature] : **the ~ in man** la bête en l'homme **3.** [person - unpleasant] cochon *m* ; [- cruel] brute *f* **4.** [difficult task] : **a ~ of a job** un sale boulot.

beastly ['bi:stlɪ] *UK inf* ◇ *adj* [person, behaviour] mauvais ▪ **he's a ~ child** c'est un enfant insupportable ▪ **he was ~ to her** il a été infect avec elle.
◇ *adv* vachement.

beat [bi:t] ◇ *vt* (*pret* **beat**, *pp* **beaten** ['bi:tn]) **1.** [hit - dog, person] frapper, battre ; [- carpet, metal] battre ▪ CULIN [eggs] battre, fouetter ▪ **to ~ sb with a stick** donner des coups de bâton à qqn ▪ **to ~ sb black and blue** battre qqn comme plâtre
2. MUS : **to ~ time** battre la mesure ▪ **to ~ a drum** battre du tambour
3. [move - wing] battre ▪ **the bird was ~ing its wings** l'oiseau battait des ailes
4. [defeat - at game, sport] battre, vaincre ▪ **she ~ him at poker** elle l'a battu au poker ▪ **Liverpool were beaten** Liverpool a perdu ▪ **to ~ the world record** battre le record mondial ▮ *fig* **~ the rush hour, travel early** évitez l'heure de pointe, voyagez plus tôt ▪ **to ~ the system** trouver le joint *fig* ▪ **we've got to ~ racism** il faut en finir avec le racisme ▪ **the problem has me ~** *inf OR* **~en** le problème me dépasse complètement ▪ **she just ~ me to it** elle m'a devancé de peu ▮ [outdo] : **you can't ~ the Chinese for inventiveness** on ne peut pas trouver plus inventifs que les Chinois ▪ **nothing ~s a cup of tea** rien ne vaut une tasse de thé ▪ **~ that!** *liter* voyons si tu peux faire mieux! ; *fig* pas mal, hein? ▪ **that ~s the lot!** *inf*, **that takes some ~ing!** *inf* ça,

c'est le bouquet! ■ **his answer takes some ~ing!** *inf* [critically] c'est le comble! ; [admiringly] on n'aurait pas pu mieux dire! ▶ **to ~ the charge** *US inf* LAW échapper à l'accusation ■ **to ~ the rap** *US inf* échapper à la tôle ■ **if you can't ~ them, join them** si on ne peut pas les battre, alors il faut faire comme eux *OR* entrer dans leur jeu ■ **to ~ sb hollow** *inf OR* **hands down** *UK inf*, **to ~ the pants off sb** *inf* battre qqn à plate couture ■ **(it) ~s me** *inf* cela me dépasse ■ **it ~s me** *OR* **what ~s me is how he gets away with it** *inf* je ne comprends pas *OR* ça me dépasse qu'il s'en tire à chaque fois ■ **can you ~ it!** *inf* tu as déjà vu ça, toi!
5. [path] se frayer ■ **the new doctor soon had people ~ing a path to his door** *fig* très vite, les gens se pressèrent chez le nouveau docteur
6. [retreat] : **to ~ the retreat** MIL battre la retraite ■ **they ~ a hasty retreat when they saw the police arrive** *fig* ils ont décampé en vitesse quand ils ont vu arriver la police
7. *phr* **~ it!** *inf* dégage!
◇ *vi* (*pret* **beat**, *pp* **beaten** ['bi:tn]) **1.** [rain] battre ■ [sun] taper ■ [wind] souffler en rafales ■ **to ~ on** *OR* **at the door** cogner à la porte ▶ **he doesn't ~ about** *UK OR* **around** *US* **the bush** il n'y va pas par quatre chemins ■ **so, not to ~ about** *UK OR* **around** *US* **the bush, I've lost my job** enfin bref, j'ai perdu mon emploi
2. [heart, pulse, wing] battre ■ **with ~ing heart** le cœur battant ■ **his heart was ~ing with terror** son cœur palpitait de terreur ■ **I heard the drums ~ing** j'entendis le roulement des tambours
3. NAUT : **to ~ to windward** louvoyer au plus près.
◇ *n* **1.** [of heart, pulse, wing] battement *m*, pulsation *f* ■ [of drums] battement *m* ■ ACOUST battement *m* ■ **to march to the ~ of the drum** marcher au son du tambour
2. MUS [time] temps *m* ■ [in jazz and pop] rythme *m*
3. [of policeman] ronde *f*, secteur *m* ■ [of sentry] ronde *f* ■ **we need more policemen on the ~** il faudrait qu'il y ait plus de policiers à faire des rondes ■ **he saw the robbery when he was on his ~** il a été témoin du vol pendant qu'il effectuait sa ronde
4. HUNT battue *f*.
◇ *adj inf* [exhausted] crevé, vidé.
◆ **beat back** *vt sep* [enemy, flames] repousser.
◆ **beat down** ◇ *vt sep* **1.** [grass] : **the wind had beaten the grass down** le vent avait couché les herbes ■ **the horses had beaten down the crops** les chevaux avaient foulé les récoltes
2. *UK* [seller] faire baisser ■ **I ~ him down to £20** je lui ai fait baisser son prix à 20 livres.
◇ *vi insep* [sun] taper ■ [rain] tomber à verse *OR* à torrents.
◆ **beat in** *vt sep* [door] défoncer ■ **I'll ~ his head in!** je lui défoncerai le crâne!
◆ **beat off** *vt sep* [enemy, attack] repousser.
◆ **beat out** *vt sep* **1.** [flames] étouffer
2. [metal] étaler au marteau ■ *fig* **to ~ one's brains out** *inf* se creuser la cervelle ■ **to ~ sb's brains out** *inf* défoncer le crâne à qqn
3. [rhythm] marquer.
◆ **beat up** *vt sep* **1.** *inf* [person] tabasser, passer à tabac
2. [eggwhite] faire monter ■ [cream, egg] fouetter, battre
3. [drum up - help, volunteers] racoler, recruter
4. *inf* culpabiliser ■ **to beat o.s. up (about sth)** culpabiliser (à propos de qch).

beaten ['bi:tn] ◇ *pp* ▷ **beat**.
◇ *adj* **1.** [gold] battu, martelé ■ [earth, path] battu ■ CULIN [eggs, cream etc] battu, fouetté ■ **off the ~ track** *fig* hors des sentiers battus **2.** [defeated] vaincu, battu **3.** [exhausted] éreinté, épuisé.

beaten-up *adj* cabossé.

beater ['bi:təʳ] *n* **1.** CULIN [manual] fouet *m* ■ [electric] batteur *m* **2.** TEX peigne *m* ■ [for carpet] tapette *f* **3.** HUNT rabatteur *m*.

Beat generation *n* : **the ~** *mouvement littéraire et culturel américain des années 1950-1960 dont les adeptes (les 'beatniks') refusaient les conventions de la société moderne.*

beatific [bi:ə'tɪfɪk] *adj* béat.

beatification [bi:,ætɪfɪ'keɪʃn] *n* béatification *f*.

beatify [bi:'ætɪfaɪ] *vt* béatifier.

beating ['bi:tɪŋ] *n* **1.** [thrashing] correction *f* ■ **to give sb a ~** donner une correction à qqn **2.** [defeat] défaite *f* ■ **to take a ~** [gen - SPORT] se faire battre à plate couture **3.** [of wings, heart] battement *m* **4.** *(U)* [of metal] batte *f* ■ [of drums] battement *m*, roulement *m* ■ [of carpet] battage *m* **5.** HUNT battue *f*.

beatitude [bi:'ætɪtju:d] *n* béatitude *f*.
◆ **Beatitudes** *npl* : **the Beatitudes** les Béatitudes.

beatnik ['bi:tnɪk] ◇ *n* beatnik *mf*.
◇ *adj* beatnik.

beat-up *adj inf* [car] bousillé, déglingué ■ *US* [person] amoché.

beau [bəʊ] (*pl* **beaux** [bəʊz]) *n* [dandy] dandy *m* ■ [suitor] galant *m*.

Beaufort scale ['bəʊfət] *n* échelle *f* de Beaufort.

beauteous ['bju:tjəs] *adj lit* = **beautiful** *(adj)*.

beautician [bju:'tɪʃn] *n* esthéticien *m*, - enne *f*.

beautiful ['bju:tɪfʊl] ◇ *adj* **1.** [attractive - person, dress] beau *(before vowel or silent 'h'* **bel***)*, belle *f* **2.** [splendid - weather, meal] magnifique, superbe.
◇ *npl* : **fashions for the ~ and the rich** des modes destinées aux gens beaux et riches.

beautifully ['bju:təflɪ] *adv* **1.** [sing, dress] admirablement, à la perfection **2.** [splendidly] : **it was a ~ played shot** c'était bien joué, c'était une belle balle **3.** [as intensifier - peaceful, warm] merveilleusement.

beautify ['bju:tɪfaɪ] (*pret & pp* **beautified**) *vt* embellir, orner ■ **to ~ o.s.** se faire une beauté.

beauty ['bju:tɪ] ◇ *n* (*pl* **beauties**) **1.** [loveliness] beauté *f* ■ **a thing of ~** un objet d'une rare beauté ■ **to spoil the ~ of sthg** déparer qqch ▶ **~ is in the eye of the beholder** *prov* il n'y a pas de laides amours *prov* ■ **~ is only skin-deep** *prov* la beauté n'est pas tout *prov* **2.** [beautiful person] beauté *f* ■ **the beauties of nature** les merveilles de la nature ▶ **'Beauty and the Beast'** 'la Belle et la Bête' **3.** *inf* [excellent thing] merveille *f* **4.** [attraction] : **the ~ of the system is its simplicity** ce qui est bien dans ce système, c'est sa simplicité ■ **that's the ~ of it** c'est ça qui est formidable.
◇ *comp* [cream, product, treatment] de beauté ■ **~ specialist** *OR* **therapist** esthéticien *m*, - enne *f*.

beauty competition, beauty contest *n* concours *m* de beauté.

beauty parade *n* défilé *m* d'un concours de beauté.

beauty parlour *n* institut *m* de beauté.

beauty queen *n* reine *f* de beauté.

beauty salon *n* = **beauty parlour**.

beauty shop *n* *US* institut *m* de beauté.

beauty sleep *n* : **I need my ~** *hum* j'ai besoin de mon compte de sommeil pour être frais le matin.

beauty spot *n* **1.** [on skin] grain *m* de beauté ■ [artificial] mouche *f* **2.** [scenic place] site *m* touristique.

beaver ['bi:vəʳ] ◇ *n* [animal] castor *m* ■ **the Beaver State** l'Oregon *m* ■ [coat] fourrure *f* de castor, castor *m* ■ [hat] chapeau *m* de castor, castor *m*.
◇ *comp* [coat, hat] de castor.
◆ **beaver away** *vi insep UK inf* **to ~ away at sthg** travailler d'arrache-pied à qqch.

bebop ['bi:bɒp] *n* [music, dance] be-bop *m*.

becalm [bɪ'kɑ:m] *vt (usu passive)* **to be ~ed** être encalminé.

became [bɪ'keɪm] *pt* ▷ **become**.

because [bɪ'kɒz] *conj* parce que ■ **if she won it was ~ she deserved to** si elle a gagné, c'est qu'elle le méritait ■ **it was all the more difficult ~ he was sick** c'était d'autant plus difficile qu'il était malade ■ **why can't I go? – ~ (you can't)!** pourquoi est-ce que je ne peux pas y aller? – parce que (c'est comme ça)!
◆ **because of** *prep phr* à cause de ■ **we couldn't move ~ of the snow** nous étions bloqués par la neige ■ **it was all ~ of a silly misunderstanding** tout ça à cause d'un *OR* tout provenait d'un petit malentendu.

béchamel sauce [,beʃə'mel-] *n* (sauce *f*) béchamel *f*.

beck [bek] *n* **1.** *dial* [stream] ruisseau *m*, ru *m lit* **2.** *phr* **to be at sb's ~ and call** être constamment à la disposition de qqn ■ **she has him at her ~ and call** elle le fait marcher à la baguette, il lui obéit au doigt et à l'œil.

beckon ['bekən] ◇ *vi* faire signe ■ **to ~ to sb** faire signe à qqn ■ **a glittering career ~ed for the young singer** *fig* la jeune chanteuse avait devant elle une brillante carrière.
◇ *vt* **1.** [motion] faire signe à ■ **I ~ed them over to me** je leur ai fait signe d'approcher **2.** [attract, call] attirer ■ **the bright lights ~ed me to the city** j'ai été attiré par les lumières de la ville.

become [bɪ'kʌm] (*pret* **became** [bɪ'keɪm], *pp* **become**) ◇ *vi* **1.** [grow] devenir, se faire ■ **to ~ old** vieillir ■ **to ~ fat** grossir ■ **to ~ weak** s'affaiblir ■ **it became clear that we were wrong** il s'est avéré que nous nous trompions ■ **we became friends** nous sommes devenus amis **2.** [acquire post of] devenir ■ **she's ~ an accountant** elle est devenue comptable.
◇ *vt fml* **1.** [suit - subj: hat, dress] aller à **2.** [befit] convenir à, être digne de ■ **such behaviour doesn't ~ him** une telle conduite n'est pas digne de lui.
◆ **become of** *vt insep (only following 'what', 'whatever')* **whatever will ~ of us?** qu'allons-nous devenir? ■ **what became of your hat?** où est passé ton chapeau?

becoming [bɪ'kʌmɪŋ] *adj fml* **1.** [fetching] qui va bien, seyant ■ **that's a very ~ hat** ce chapeau vous va très bien **2.** [suitable] convenable, bienséant ■ **such language is hardly ~ for a young lady!** un tel langage n'est guère convenable chez une jeune fille!

BECTU ['bektu:] (*abbrev of* **Broadcasting, Entertainment, Cinematograph and Theatre Union**) *pr n syndicat britannique des techniciens du cinéma, du théâtre et de l'audiovisuel.*

bed [bed] ◇ *n* **1.** [furniture] lit *m* ■ **we asked for a room with two ~s** nous avons demandé une chambre à deux lits ■ **they sleep in separate ~s** ils font lit à part ■ **it's time to go to** *OR* **time for ~** il est l'heure d'aller au lit *OR* de se coucher ■ **to get out of ~** se lever ■ **did I get you out of ~?** est-ce que je vous ai tiré du lit? ■ **she got** *OR* **put the children to ~** elle a couché les enfants *OR* mis les enfants au lit ■ **to make the ~** faire le lit ■ **they made me up a ~** ils m'ont préparé un lit ■ **he's in ~ with the flu** il est au lit avec la grippe ■ **she took to her ~ with pneumonia** elle a dû s'aliter à cause d'une pneumonie ■ **to go to ~ with sb** coucher avec qqn ➤ **~ and board** pension *f* complète ■ **~ and breakfast** chambre *f* d'hôte *OR* chez l'habitant ■ **'~ and breakfast'** 'chambres avec petit déjeuner' ■ **to get out on the wrong side of (the) ~** se lever du pied gauche *OR* du mauvais pied ■ **you've made your ~, now you must lie in it** *prov* comme on fait son lit, on se couche *prov* **2.** [plot - of flowers] parterre *m*, plate-bande *f* ; [- of vegetables] planche *f* ; [- of coral, oysters] banc *m* **3.** [bottom - of river] lit *m* ; [- of lake, sea] fond *m* **4.** [layer - of clay, rock] couche *f*, lit *m* ; [- of ore] gisement *m* ; [- of ashes] lit *m* ■ [-of mortar] CONSTR bain *m* ■ **~ of nails** lit à clous **5.** TECH [of machine] base *f*, bâti *m* ■ [of lorry] plateau *m* ■ TYPO [of printing press] marbre *m*, plateau *m* ■ **to put a newspaper to ~** *UK* boucler un journal.
◇ *comp* : **~ linen** draps *mpl* de lit (et taies *fpl* d'oreiller) ■ **~ frame** châlit *m* ■ **the doctor recommended complete ~ rest** le médecin a conseillé l'immobilité totale.
◇ *vt* (*pret & pp* **bedded**, *cont* **bedding**) **1.** [embed] fixer, enfoncer ■ CONSTR asseoir **2.** HORT repiquer **3.** *lit* [have sex with] prendre *(sexuellement)*.
◆ **bed down** ◇ *vi insep* [go to bed] se coucher ■ [spend the night] coucher.
◇ *vt sep* **1.** [children] mettre au lit, coucher ■ [animal] installer pour la nuit **2.** [embed] fixer, enfoncer ■ CONSTR asseoir.

BEd [,bi:'ed] (*abbrev of* **Bachelor of Education**) *n (titulaire d'une) licence de sciences de l'éducation.*

bedazzle [bɪ'dæzl] *vt* [dazzle] éblouir, aveugler ■ [fascinate] éblouir.

bed bath *n* toilette *f (d'un malade)*.

bedbug ['bedbʌg] *n* punaise *f* des lits.

bedclothes ['bedkləʊðz] *npl* draps *mpl* et couvertures *fpl*.

bedcover ['bed,kʌvəʳ] *n* dessus-de-lit *m*, couvre-lit *m*.

-bedded [,bedɪd] *in cpds* : **single~ room** chambre *f* à un lit.

bedding ['bedɪŋ] ◇ *n* **1.** [bedclothes] draps *mpl* et couvertures *fpl* ■ [including mattress] literie *f* ■ MIL matériel *m* de couchage **2.** [for animals] litière *f*.
◇ *adj* : **~ plant** plante *f* à repiquer.

Bede [bi:d] *pr n* : **the Venerable ~** Bède le Vénérable.

bedeck [bɪ'dek] *vt lit* orner, parer.

bedevil [bɪ'devl] (*UK pret & pp* **bedevilled**, *cont* **bedevilling**) (*US pret & pp* **bedeviled**, *cont* **bedeviling**) *vt* **1.** [plague - plans, project] déranger, gêner ; [- person] harceler, tourmenter ■ **bedevilled by** *OR* **with problems** assailli par les problèmes **2.** [confuse] embrouiller **3.** [bewitch] ensorceler.

bedfellow ['bed,feləʊ] *n* [associate] associé *m*, - e *f*, collègue *mf* ■ **they make strange ~s** ils forment une drôle d'association *OR* de paire.

bedhead ['bedhed] *n UK* tête *f* de lit.

bed jacket *n UK* liseuse *f*.

bedlam ['bedləm] *n* tohu-bohu *m* ■ **utter ~ broke out after her speech** un véritable tumulte éclata après son discours ■ **it's absolute ~ in town today!** quelle anarchie aujourd'hui en ville!

Bedouin ['bedʊɪn] (*pl inv OR pl* **Bedouins**) ◇ *n* Bédouin *m*, - e *f*.
◇ *adj* bédouin.

bedpan ['bedpæn] *n* bassin *m* (hygiénique).

bedpost ['bedpəʊst] *n* colonne *f* de lit ■ **(just) between you, me and the ~** *hum* entre nous.

bedraggled [bɪ'drægld] *adj* [clothing, person] débraillé ■ [hair] ébouriffé, échevelé.

bedridden ['bed,rɪdn] *adj* alité, cloué au lit.

bedrock ['bedrɒk] *n* GEOL soubassement *m*, substratum *m* ■ *fig* base *f*, fondation *f*.

bedroll ['bedrəʊl] *n* matériel *m* de couchage *(enroulé)*.

bedroom ['bedrʊm] ◇ *n* chambre *f* (à coucher).
◇ *comp* [scene] d'amour ■ **~ comedy** THEAT comédie *f* de boulevard ■ **~ community** *US* cité-dortoir *f* ■ **~ eyes** regard *m* sexy.

-bedroomed [,bedrʊmd] *in cpds* : **two~ flat** trois-pièces *m*.

Beds *written abbr of* **Bedfordshire**.

bedsettee [,bedse'ti:] *n UK* canapé-lit *m*.

bedside ['bedsaɪd] ◇ *adj* [lamp, table] de chevet ■ **~ manner** comportement *m* envers les malades.
◇ *n* chevet *m* ■ **at** *OR* **by your ~** à votre chevet ■ **to rush to sb's ~** courir au chevet de qqn.

bedsit ['bed,sɪt], **bedsitter** ['bedˈsɪtəʳ], **bedsitting room** ['bed'sɪtɪŋ] *n UK* chambre *f* meublée.

bedsocks ['bedsɒks] *npl* chaussettes *fpl* (de lit).

bedsore ['bedsɔ:ʳ] *n* escarre *f*.

bedspread ['bedspred] *n* dessus-de-lit *m inv*, couvre-lit *m*.

bedsprings ['bedsprɪŋz] *npl* [springs] ressorts *mpl* de sommier ■ [frame] sommier *m* à ressorts.

bedstead ['bedsted] *n* châlit *m*.

bedtime ['bedtaɪm] ◇ *n* heure *f* du coucher ■ **what's his ~?** à quelle heure se couche-t-il? ■ **it's your ~** il est l'heure d'aller te coucher ■ **her mother reads to her at ~** sa mère lui lit une histoire avant qu'elle s'endorme.
◇ *comp* : **~ story** histoire *f (qu'on lit à l'heure du coucher)* ■ **I'll read you a ~ story** je vais te lire une histoire avant que tu t'endormes.

bedwarmer ['bed,wɔ:məʳ] *n* bassinoire *f*.

bed-wetting [-,wetɪŋ] *n* incontinence *f* nocturne.

bee [bi:] *n* [insect] abeille *f* ■ **he is a busy little ~** *inf* [he is energetic] il déborde d'énergie ; [he has a lot of work] il a énormément de choses à faire ➤ **to have a ~ in one's bonnet (about sthg)** être obsédé (par qqch) ■ **it's the ~'s knees!** *inf* c'est formidable *OR* super ! ■ **he thinks he's the ~'s knees** *inf* il ne se prend pas pour n'importe qui.

Beeb [bi:b] *pr n UK inf hum* **the ~** *surnom courant de la BBC.*

beech [bi:tʃ] (*pl inv* OR *pl* **beeches**) ◇ *n* [tree] hêtre *m* ■ [wood] (bois *m* de) hêtre *m*.
◇ *comp* [chair, table] de hêtre ■ **~ nut** faine *f* ■ **~ tree** hêtre *m*.

beechwood ['bi:tʃwʊd] *n* [substance] (bois *m* de) hêtre *m* ■ [forest] bois *m* de hêtres.

beef [bi:f] ◇ *n* **1.** [meat] bœuf *m* ■ **joint of ~** rôti *m* (de bœuf), rosbif *m* **2.** (*UKpl* beeves [bi:vz]) [animal] bœuf *m* **3.** *inf* [complaint] grief *m* ■ **what's your ~?** tu as un problème? ■ **to have a ~ with sb/sthg** *US* avoir des ennuis avec qqn/qqch.
◇ *comp* [sausage, stew] de bœuf ■ **~ cattle** bœufs *mpl* de boucherie.
◇ *vi inf* râler ■ **to ~ about sthg** râler contre qqch.
◆ **beef up** *vt sep inf* [army, campaign] renforcer ■ [report, story] étoffer.

beefburger ['bi:f,bɜ:gər] *n* hamburger *m*.

beefcake ['bi:fkeɪk] *n (U) inf hum* beau mâle *m*, beaux mâles *mpl*.

Beefeater ['bi:f,i:tər] *n surnom des gardiens de la Tour de Londres.*

beefsteak ['bi:f,steɪk] *n* bifteck *m*, steak *m*.

beef tea *n* bouillon *m* de bœuf.

beefy ['bi:fɪ] (*comp* **beefier**, *superl* **beefiest**) *adj* **1.** [consistency, taste] de viande, de bœuf **2.** *inf* [brawny] costaud ■ [fat] grassouillet.

beehive ['bi:haɪv] *n* **1.** [for bees] ruche *f* ■ **the Beehive State** l'Utah *m* **2.** [hairstyle] *coiffure très haute maintenue avec de la laque.*

beekeeper ['bi:,ki:pər] *n* apiculteur *m*, - trice *f*.

beekeeping ['bi:,ki:pɪŋ] *n* apiculture *f*.

beeline ['bi:laɪn] *n* ligne *f* droite ■ **he made a ~ for the kitchen** [headed straight to] il s'est dirigé tout droit vers la cuisine ; [rushed to] il s'est précipité OR a filé tout droit à la cuisine.

been [bi:n] *pp* ⊳ **be**.

beep [bi:p] ◇ *n* [of car horn] coup *m* de Klaxon® ■ [of alarm, timer] signal *m* sonore, bip *m*.
◇ *vi* [car horn] klaxonner ■ [alarm, timer] sonner, faire bip.
◇ *vt* : **to ~ one's horn** klaxonner.

beer [bɪər] ◇ *n* bière *f* ■ **his life is not all ~ and skittles** *UK* sa vie n'est pas toujours rose.
◇ *comp* : **~ barrel** tonneau *m* à bière ■ **~ belly** *inf* brioche *f*, bide *m* ■ **~ bottle** canette *f* ■ **~ can** boîte *f* de bière ■ **~ gut** *inf* brioche *f*, bide *m* ■ **~ money** argent *m* de poche ■ **~ tent** *grande tente abritant la buvette lors des manifestations sportives en plein air en Grande-Bretagne.*

beery ['bɪərɪ] (*comp* **beerier**, *superl* **beeriest**) *adj* [atmosphere, smell, taste] qui sent la bière ■ [party] où l'on boit beaucoup de bière.

beeswax ['bi:zwæks] ◇ *n* cire *f* d'abeille.
◇ *vt* cirer *(avec de la cire d'abeille).*

beet [bi:t] *n* betterave *f* (potagère) ■ **red ~** *US* betterave *f* (rouge).

Beethoven ['beɪt,həʊvn] *pr n* Beethoven.

beetle ['bi:tl] ◇ *n* **1.** [insect] scarabée *m*, coléoptère *m* **2.** GAMES *jeu de dés où l'on essaie de dessiner un scarabée* **3.** [hammer] mailloche *f* ■ [machine] mouton *m*.
◇ *vi inf UK inf* courir précipitamment ■ **to ~ along** filer à toute vitesse.
◆ **Beetle**® *n* : **(Volkswagen) ~** AUT Coccinelle® *f*.
◆ **beetle off** *vi insep inf* filer.

beetle-browed [-braʊd] *adj UK* [with bushy eyebrows] aux sourcils broussailleux ■ [scowling] renfrogné.

beetling ['bi:tlɪŋ] *adj* [cliff, crag] qui surplombe, surplombant ■ [brow] proéminent ■ [eyebrows] broussailleux.

beetroot ['bi:tru:t] *n* betterave *f* (potagère OR rouge) ■ **to go (as red as a) ~** devenir rouge comme une tomate.

beet sugar *n* sucre *m* de betterave.

befall [bɪ'fɔ:l] (*pret* **befell** [-'fel], *pp* **befallen** [-'fɔ:lən]) *fml & lit*
◇ *vt* arriver à, survenir à.
◇ *vi* **1.** [happen] arriver, se passer **2.** [be due] échoir.

befit [bɪ'fɪt] (*pret & pp* **befitted**, *cont* **befitting**) *vt fml* convenir à, seoir à *fml* ■ **as ~s a woman of her eminence** comme il sied à une femme de son rang.

befitting [bɪ'fɪtɪŋ] *adj fml* convenable, seyant ■ **in a manner ~ a statesman** d'une façon qui sied à un homme d'État.

before [bɪ'fɔ:r] ◇ *adv* **1.** [at a previous time] avant ■ **haven't we met ~?** est-ce que nous ne nous sommes pas OR ne nous sommes-nous pas déjà rencontrés? ■ **I have never seen this film ~** c'est la première fois que je vois ce film ■ **he's made mistakes ~** ce n'est pas la première fois qu'il se trompe **2.** *lit* [ahead] en avant, devant.
◇ *prep* **1.** [in time] avant ■ **the day ~ the meeting** la veille de la réunion ■ **the day ~ yesterday** avant-hier ■ **it should have been done ~ now** ça devrait déjà être fait ❯ **that was ~ your time** [you had not been born] vous n'étiez pas encore né ; [you had not arrived, joined etc] vous n'étiez pas encore là
2. [in order, preference] avant ■ **the welfare of the people comes ~ private concerns** le bien-être du peuple passe avant tout intérêt privé
3. [in space] devant ■ **on the table ~ them** *fml* sur la table devant eux ■ **we have a difficult task ~ us** *fig* nous avons une tâche difficile devant nous ■ **~ my very eyes** sous mes propres yeux
4. [in the presence of] devant, en présence de ■ **to appear ~ the court/judge** comparaître devant le tribunal/juge
5. [for the consideration of] devant ■ **the problem ~ us** la question qui nous occupe ■ **the case ~ the court** l'affaire portée devant le tribunal ■ **the matter went ~ the council** l'affaire est passée devant le conseil.
◇ *conj* **1.** [in time] avant de, avant que ■ **she hesitated ~ answering** elle a hésité avant de répondre ■ **may I see you ~ you leave?** puis-je vous voir avant que vous ne partiez OR avant votre départ? ■ **it'll be a long time ~ he tries that again** il ne recommencera pas de sitôt, il n'est pas près de recommencer ■ **it'll be two years ~ the school is built** l'école ne sera pas construite avant deux ans ■ **it was almost an hour ~ the ambulance arrived** il a fallu presque une heure avant que l'ambulance n'arrive ❯ **~ you know it** avant qu'on ait le temps de dire "ouf"
2. [rather than] plutôt que de ■ **I'll die ~ I let him marry my daughter** je mourrai plutôt que de le laisser épouser ma fille.
◇ *adj* d'avant, précédent ■ **the day ~** la veille ■ **the night ~** la veille au soir ■ **the week ~** la semaine d'avant OR précédente.

beforehand [bɪ'fɔ:hænd] *adv* auparavant, à l'avance ■ **if you're coming let me know ~** prévenez-moi si vous décidez de venir.

befriend [bɪ'frend] *vt* [make friends with] prendre en amitié, se prendre d'amitié pour ■ **he was ~ed by a colleague** un de ses collègues s'est pris d'amitié pour lui ▮ [assist] venir en aide à, aider.

befuddle [bɪ'fʌdl] *vt* **1.** [confuse - person] brouiller l'esprit OR les idées de, embrouiller ; [- mind] embrouiller **2.** [muddle with alcohol] griser, enivrer.

beg [beg] (*pret & pp* **begged**, *cont* **begging**) ◇ *vi* **1.** [solicit charity] mendier ■ **to ~ for food** mendier de la nourriture **2.** [ask, plead] supplier ■ **to ~ for forgiveness/mercy** demander pardon/grâce **3.** [dog] faire le beau **4.** *UK phr* **to be going begging : I'll have that last sandwich if it's going begging** je prendrai bien ce dernier sandwich si personne d'autre ne le veut.
◇ *vt* **1.** [solicit as charity] mendier ■ **she begged money from the passers-by** elle mendiait auprès des passants **2.** [ask for] demander, solliciter ■ [plead with] supplier ■ **she begged a favour of her sister** elle a demandé à sa sœur de lui rendre un service ■ **to ~ sb's forgiveness** OR **pardon** demander pardon à qqn ❯ **I ~ your pardon** [excuse me] je vous demande pardon ; [I didn't hear you] pardon? ; [indignantly] pardon! **3.** *fml* [request politely] : **I ~ to differ** permettez-moi de ne pas être de votre avis ■ **I ~ to inform you that...** je tiens à OR j'ai l'honneur de

vous informer que... **4.** *phr* **to ~ the question** [evade the issue] éluder la question ; [assume something proved] considérer que la question est résolue.

began [bɪ'gæn] *pt* ▭> **begin**.

beget [bɪ'get] (*pret* **begot** [-'gɒt] *OR* **begat** [-'gæt], *pp* **begotten** [-'gɒtn], *cont* **begetting**) *vt arch* & *lit* [sire] engendrer ▪ *fig* [cause] engendrer, causer.

beggar ['begəʳ] <> *n* **1.** [mendicant] mendiant *m*, - e *f* ▪ [pauper] indigent *m*, - e *f* ▪ **~s can't be choosers** *prov* faute de merles, mangeons des grives *prov*, nécessité fait loi *prov* ▪ **'The Beggar's Opera'** *Gay* 'l'Opéra du gueux' **2.** *UK inf* [so-and-so] type *m* ▪ **you lucky ~!** sacré veinard! ▪ **poor ~!** pauvre diable! ▪ **you naughty little ~!** petit coquin!
<> *vt* **1.** *fml* [impoverish] réduire à la mendicité, appauvrir **2.** [defy] : **to ~ (all) description** défier toute description ▪ **it ~s belief** c'est invraisemblable, ça dépasse l'entendement.

begging ['begɪŋ] <> *n* mendicité *f*.
<> *adj* : **~ letter** lettre *f* de requête *(demandant de l'argent)*.

begging bowl *n* sébile *f (de mendiant)*.

begin [bɪ'gɪn] (*pret* **began** [bɪ'gæn], *pp* **begun** [-'gʌn], *cont* **beginning**) <> *vt* **1.** [start] commencer ▪ [career, term] commencer, débuter ▪ [task] entreprendre, s'attaquer à ▪ [work] commencer, se mettre à ▪ **to ~ to do** *OR* **doing sthg** commencer à faire qqch, se mettre à faire qqch ▪ **the quotation beginning this chapter** la citation qui ouvre ce chapitre ▪ **she began life as a waitress** elle a débuté comme serveuse ▪ **he soon began to complain** il n'a pas tardé à se plaindre ▪ **the film doesn't ~ to compare with the book** le film est loin de valoir le livre ▪ **I can't ~ to explain** c'est trop difficile à expliquer
2. [start to say] commencer
3. [found - institution, club] fonder, inaugurer ▪ [initiate - business, fashion] lancer ; [- argument, fight, war] déclencher, faire naître ; [- conversation] engager, amorcer ; [- discussion, speech] commencer, ouvrir.
<> *vi* **1.** [start - subj: person, career, concert, project, speech] commencer ▪ **the day began badly/well** la journée s'annonçait mal/bien ▪ **to ~ again** *OR* **afresh** recommencer (à zéro) ▪ **when does school ~?** quand est la rentrée? ▪ **after the film ~s** après le début du film ▪ **he began in politics** il a commencé par faire de la politique ▪ **let me ~ by thanking our host** permettez-moi tout d'abord de remercier notre hôte ▪ **the play ~s with a murder** la pièce débute par un meurtre ▪ **I began with the idea of buying a flat** au départ *OR* au début je voulais acheter un appartement ⊳ **well begun is half done** *UK prov* ce qui commence bien est à moitié fait
2. [originate - club, country, institution] être fondé ; [- fire, epidemic] commencer ; [- war] éclater, commencer ; [- trouble] commencer ; [- river] prendre sa source ; [- road] commencer ; [- fashion] commencer, débuter ▪ **the magazine began as a freesheet** la revue a débuté comme publication gratuite.
◆ **to begin with** *adv phr* [in the first place] d'abord, pour commencer ▪ [initially] au départ ▪ **everything went well to ~ with** tout s'est bien passé au début *OR* au départ ▪ **the plate was cracked to ~ with** l'assiette était déjà fêlée au départ.

beginner [bɪ'gɪnəʳ] *n* débutant *m*, - e *f* ▪ **it's ~'s luck!** on a toujours de la chance au début! ▪ **French for ~s** français pour débutants.

beginning [bɪ'gɪnɪŋ] <> *n* **1.** [start - of book, career, project] commencement *m*, début *m* ▪ **in** *OR* **at the ~** au début, au commencement ▪ **this is just the ~ of our troubles** nos ennuis ne font que commencer ▪ **begin at the ~** commencez par le commencement ▪ **let's start again from the ~** reprenons depuis le début ▪ **from ~ to end** du début à la fin, d'un bout à l'autre ▪ **it's the ~ of the end** c'est le début de la fin **2.** [early part, stage - of book, career, war] commencement *m*, début *m* ; [- of negotiations] début *m*, ouverture *f* ▪ **since the ~ of time** depuis la nuit des temps **3.** [origin - of event] origine *f*, commencement *m* ▪ **Protestantism had its ~s in Germany** le protestantisme a pris naissance en Allemagne ▪ **his assassination signalled the ~ of the war** son assassinat a marqué le déclenchement de la guerre.
<> *adj* : **~ student** débutant *m*, - e *f*.

begone [bɪ'gɒn] *vi lit* **~ !** hors d'ici!

begonia [bɪ'gəʊnjə] *n* bégonia *m*.

begot [-'gɒt] *pt* ▭> **beget**.

begotten [-'gɒtn] *pp* ▭> **beget**.

begrudge [bɪ'grʌdʒ] *vt* **1.** [envy] envier ▪ **she ~s him his success** elle lui en veut de sa réussite **2.** [give grudgingly] donner *OR* accorder à regret ▪ **he ~s every minute spent away from his family** il rechigne à passer une seule minute loin de sa famille ▪ **I ~ spending so much on rent** ça me fait mal au cœur de payer un loyer aussi cher.

beguile [bɪ'gaɪl] *vt* **1.** [charm] envoûter, séduire **2.** [delude] enjôler, tromper ▪ **to ~ sb into doing sthg** amener qqn à faire qqch **3.** [pass pleasantly] : **to ~ (away) the hours** faire passer le temps *(agréablement)*.

beguiling [bɪ'gaɪlɪŋ] *adj* charmant, séduisant.

begun [-'gʌn] *pp* ▭> **begin**.

behalf [bɪ'hɑːf] ◆ **in behalf of** *prep phr US* = **on behalf of**.
◆ **on behalf of** *prep phr* : **on ~ of sb** [as their representative] de la part de *OR* au nom de qqn ; [in their interest] dans l'intérêt de *OR* pour qqn ▪ **she acted on his ~ when he was ill** c'est elle qui l'a représenté quand il était malade ▪ **your lawyer acts on your ~** votre avocat agit en votre nom ▪ **the commission decided on their ~** la commission a décidé en leur nom ▪ **don't worry on my ~** ne vous inquiétez pas à mon sujet.

behave [bɪ'heɪv] <> *vi* **1.** [act] se comporter, se conduire ▪ **why are you behaving this way?** pourquoi agis-tu de cette façon? ▪ **he ~d badly towards her** il s'est mal conduit envers elle ▪ **she was sorry for the way she'd ~d towards him** elle regrettait la façon dont elle l'avait traité **2.** [act properly] se tenir bien, *inf* bien se conduire ▪ **will you ~!** sois sage!, tiens-toi bien! **3.** [function] fonctionner, marcher ▪ **she studies how matter ~s in extremes of cold and heat** elle étudie le comportement de la matière dans des conditions de froid ou de chaleur extrêmes ▪ **the car ~s well on curves** la voiture tient bien la route dans les virages.
<> *vt* : **to ~ o.s.** se tenir bien ▪ **~ yourself!** sois sage!, tiens-toi bien!

behaviour *UK*, **behavior** *US* [bɪ'heɪvjəʳ] <> *n* **1.** [of person] comportement *m*, conduite *f* ▪ [of animal] comportement *m* ▪ **her ~ towards her mother was unforgivable** la façon dont elle s'est comportée avec sa mère était impardonnable ▪ **to be on one's best ~** se tenir *OR* se conduire de son mieux **2.** [of atom, chemical, light] comportement *m* ▪ [of machine] fonctionnement *m*.
<> *comp* [modification, problem] du comportement ▪ [pattern] de comportement.

behavioural *UK*, **behavioral** *US* [bɪ'heɪvjərəl] *adj* de comportement, comportemental.

behavioural science *n* science *f* du comportement, comportementalisme *m*.

behaviourism *UK*, **behaviorism** *US* [bɪ'heɪvjərɪzm] *n* behaviorisme *m*.

behaviourist *UK*, **behaviorist** *US* [bɪ'heɪvjərɪst] <> *adj* behavioriste.
<> *n* behavioriste *mf*.

behead [bɪ'hed] *vt* décapiter.

beheld [bɪ'held] *pt* & *pp* ▭> **behold**.

behest [bɪ'hest] *n fml* commandement *m*, ordre *m* ▪ **at the ~ of the Queen** sur ordre de la reine.

behind [bɪ'haɪnd] <> *prep* **1.** [at the back of] derrière ▪ **she came out from ~ the bushes** elle est sortie de derrière les buissons ▪ **lock the door ~ you** fermez la porte à clé (derrière vous) **2.** [indicating past time] derrière ▪ **you have to put the incident ~ you** il faut que tu oublies cet incident **3.** [indicating deficiency, delay] en retard sur, derrière ▪ **she is ~ the other pupils** elle est en retard sur les autres élèves ▪ **the trains are running ~ schedule** *OR* **~ time** les trains ont du retard (sur l'horaire) **4.** [responsible for] derrière ▪ **who was ~ the plot?** qui était derrière le complot *OR* à l'origine du complot? ▪ **what's ~ all this?** qu'est-ce que ça cache? **5.** [supporting] : **we're right ~ you on this** vous avez tout notre soutien dans cette affaire.

◇ *adv* **1.** [at, in the back] derrière, en arrière ■ **he attacked them from ~** il les a attaqués par derrière ■ **disaster was not far ~** la catastrophe était imminente **2.** [late] en retard ■ **I'm ~ in** *OR* **with my rent** je suis en retard sur mon loyer ■ **I'm ~ in** *OR* **with my work** j'ai du retard dans mon travail ■ **she's too far ~ to catch up with the others** elle a pris trop de retard pour pouvoir rattraper les autres ■ **our team is three points ~** notre équipe a trois points de moins.
◇ *n euph* derrière *m*, postérieur *m*.

behindhand [bɪ'haɪndhænd] *adv* en retard.

behind-the-scenes *adj* secret, - ète *f* ■ **a ~ look at politics** un regard en coulisse sur la politique.

behold [bɪ'həʊld] (*pret & pp* **beheld** [bɪ'held]) *vt arch & lit* [see] regarder, voir ■ [notice] apercevoir ■ **~ your king** voici votre roi.

beholden [bɪ'həʊldən] *adj* redevable ■ **I am deeply ~ to him** je lui suis infiniment redevable.

behove *UK* [bɪ'həʊv], **behoove** *US* [bɪ'hu:v] *vt arch & lit* **it ~s them to be prudent** il leur appartient d'être prudents.

beige [beɪʒ] ◇ *adj* beige.
◇ *n* beige *m*.

Beijing [,beɪ'dʒɪŋ] *pr n* Beijing.

being ['bi:ɪŋ] ◇ *cont* ▷ **be**.
◇ *n* **1.** [creature] être *m*, créature *f* ■ **a human ~** un être humain **2.** [essential nature] être *m* ■ **her whole ~ rebelled** tout son être se révoltait **3.** [existence] existence *f* ■ **already in ~** déjà existant, qui existe déjà ■ **to bring** *OR* **to call sthg into ~** faire naître qqch, susciter qqch ■ **the movement came into ~ in the 1920s** le mouvement est apparu *OR* fut créé dans les années 20.

Beirut [,beɪ'ru:t] *pr n* Beyrouth.

bejewelled *UK*, **bejeweled** *US* [bɪ'dʒu:əld] *adj* [person] paré *OR* couvert de bijoux ■ [box, purse] incrusté de bijoux.

belabour *UK*, **belabor** *US* [bɪ'leɪbər] *vt* **1.** [beat] rouer de coups **2.** [criticize] injurier, invectiver.

Belarus [,belə'ru:s] *pr n* : **the Republic of ~** la république de Biélorussie.

belated [bɪ'leɪtɪd] *adj* tardif.

belatedly [bɪ'leɪtɪdlɪ] *adv* tardivement.

belay [bɪ'leɪ] ◇ *vt & vi* **1.** NAUT amarrer **2.** CLIMBING assurer.
◇ *n* assurance *f*.

belaying pin [bɪ'leɪɪŋ-] *n* cabillot *m*.

belch [beltʃ] ◇ *n* renvoi *m*, rot *m*.
◇ *vi* roter.
◇ *vt* [expel] cracher, vomir.

beleaguer [bɪ'li:gər] *vt* **1.** [harass] harceler, assaillir ■ **reporters ~ed him with questions** les journalistes le harcelèrent de questions **2.** [besiege - city] assiéger ; [- army, group] encercler, cerner.

beleaguered [bɪ'li:gəd] *adj* **1.** *liter* assiégé **2.** *fig* en difficulté.

belfry ['belfrɪ] (*pl* **belfries**) *n* [of church] beffroi *m*, clocher *m* ■ [of tower] beffroi *m*.

Belgian ['beldʒən] ◇ *n* Belge *mf*.
◇ *adj* belge.

Belgium ['beldʒəm] *pr n* Belgique *f* ■ **in ~** en Belgique.

Belgrade [,bel'greɪd] *pr n* Belgrade.

Belgrano [belgra:nəʊ] *pr n* : **the ~ affair** *conflit politique pendant la guerre des Malouines consécutif à la décision prise par le gouvernement britannique de couler un navire argentin.*

belie [bɪ'laɪ] (*pret & pp* **belied**, *cont* **belying**) *vt fml* [misrepresent] donner une fausse idée *OR* impression de ■ [contradict - hope, impression] démentir, tromper ; [- promise] démentir, donner le démenti à ■ **her youthful figure ~d her age** la jeunesse de sa silhouette démentait son âge.

belief [bɪ'li:f] *n* **1.** [feeling of certainty] croyance *f* ■ **~ in God** croyance en Dieu ■ **I've lost any ~ I had in human kindness** je ne crois plus du tout en la bonté humaine ■ **contrary to popular ~** contrairement à ce qu'on croit ■ **it's beyond ~** c'est incroyable **2.** [conviction, opinion] conviction *f*, certitude *f* ■ **it's my ~ he's lying** je suis certain *OR* convaincu qu'il ment ■ **in the ~ that he would help them** certain *OR* persuadé qu'il allait les aider ■ **in the mistaken ~ that...** persuadé à tort que... ■ **to the best of my ~** autant que je sache **3.** [religious faith] foi *f*, croyance *f* ■ [political faith] dogme *m*, doctrine *f* **4.** [confidence, trust] confiance *f*, foi *f*.

believable [bɪ'li:vəbl] *adj* croyable.

believe [bɪ'li:v] ◇ *vt* **1.** [consider as real or true] croire ■ **I don't ~ a word of it** je n'en crois rien *OR* pas un mot ■ **don't you ~ it!** détrompe-toi! ■ **he's getting married! – I don't ~ it!** il va se marier! – c'est pas vrai! ■ **she's fifty, would you ~ it!** elle a cinquante ans, figure-toi! ■ **he couldn't ~ his ears/his eyes** il n'en croyait pas ses oreilles/ses yeux ■ **and, ~ it or not, she left** et, crois-le si tu veux, elle est partie
2. [accept statement or opinion of] croire ■ **if she is to be ~d, she was born a duchess** à l'en croire, elle est duchesse ■ **and ~ (you) me, I know what I'm talking about!** et croyez-moi, je sais de quoi je parle!
3. [hold as opinion, suppose] croire ■ **I don't know what to ~** je ne sais que croire, je ne sais pas à quoi m'en tenir ■ **it is widely ~d that the prisoners have been killed** on pense généralement que les prisonniers ont été tués ■ **she is, I ~, our greatest novelist** elle est, je crois *OR* à mon avis, notre meilleure romancière ■ **he'd have her ~ it's an antique** il voudrait lui faire croire que c'est un objet d'époque ■ **I ~ not** je crois que non, je ne crois pas ■ **I ~ so** je crois que oui, je crois ■ **I wouldn't have ~d it of him** je n'aurais pas cru cela de lui.
◇ *vi* [have religious faith] être croyant, avoir la foi.
◆ **believe in** *vt insep* **1.** [be convinced of existence or truth of] : **to ~ in miracles/in God** croire aux miracles/en Dieu ■ **seeing is believing** voir c'est croire
2. [be convinced of value of] : **I ~ in free enterprise** je crois à la libre entreprise ■ **they ~ in their president** ils ont confiance en *OR* font confiance à *OR* croient en leur président ■ **he ~s in giving the public greater access to information** il est d'avis qu'il faut donner au public un plus grand accès à l'information.

believer [bɪ'li:vər] *n* **1.** [supporter] partisan *m*, adepte *mf* ■ **he's a great ~ in taking exercise** il est convaincu qu'il faut faire de l'exercice **2.** RELIG croyant *m*, - e *f*.

Belisha beacon [bɪ'li:ʃə-] *n UK globe orange clignotant marquant un passage clouté.*

belittle [bɪ'lɪtl] *vt* rabaisser, dénigrer.

Belize [be'li:z] *pr n* Belize *m* ■ **in ~** au Belize.

Belizean [be'li:zɪən] ◇ *n* Bélizien *m*, - enne *f*.
◇ *adj* bélizien.

bell [bel] ◇ *n* **1.** [in church] cloche *f* ■ [handheld] clochette *f* ■ [on bicycle] sonnette *f* ■ [for cows] cloche *f*, clarine *f* ■ [on boots, toys] grelot *m* ■ [sound] coup *m* (de cloche) ■ **there goes the dinner ~** c'est la cloche qui annonce le dîner ➊ **saved by the ~!** sauvé par le gong! ■ **~s and whistles** accessoires *mpl* ■ **'For Whom the Bell Tolls'** *Hemingway* 'Pour qui sonne le glas' **2.** [electrical device - on door] sonnette *f* ■ **there's the ~** il y a quelqu'un à la porte, on sonne (à la porte) **3.** *UK inf* [telephone call] : **I'll give you a ~** je te passe un coup de fil **4.** [of flower] calice *m*, clochette *f* ■ [of oboe, trumpet] pavillon *m* **5.** [of stag] bramement *m* ■ [of hound] aboiement *m*.
◇ *vi* **1.** [stag] bramer ■ [hound] aboyer **2.** [bloat, distend] ballonner.

belladonna [,belə'dɒnə] *n* belladone *f*.

bell-bottoms *npl* pantalon *m* à pattes d'éléphant.

bellboy ['belbɔɪ] *n* chasseur *m*, porteur *m*.

bell buoy *n* bouée *f* à cloche.

belle [bel] *n* belle *f*, beauté *f* ■ **the ~ of the ball** la reine du bal ■ **Southern ~** *dame de haut rang dans les États du sud des États-Unis.*

bellhop ['belhɒp] *n US* = **bellboy**.

bellicose ['belɪkəʊs] *adj* belliqueux.

belligerence [bɪ'lɪdʒərəns], **belligerency** [bɪ'lɪdʒərənsɪ] *n* belligérance *f*.

belligerent [bɪ'lɪdʒərənt] ◇ *adj* belligérant.
◇ *n* belligérant *m*, - e *f*.

bell jar *n* cloche *f* de verre.

bellow ['beləʊ] ◇ *vi* [bull] beugler, meugler ■ [elephant] barrir ■ [person] brailler.
◇ *vt* : **to ~ (out) sthg** brailler qqch.
◇ *n* [of bull] beuglement *m*, meuglement *m* ■ [of elephant] barrissement *m* ■ [of person] braillement *m*.

bellows ['beləʊz] *npl* **1.** [for fire] soufflet *m* ■ **a pair of ~** un soufflet **2.** [for accordion, organ] soufflerie *f*.

bellpull ['belpʊl] *n* [for servant] cordon *m* de sonnette ■ [on door] poignée *f* de sonnette.

bell push *n* bouton *m* de sonnette.

bell-ringer *n* sonneur *m*, carillonneur *m*.

bell-ringing *n* carillonnement *m*.

bell rope *n* [to call servant] cordon *m* de sonnette ■ [in belfry] corde *f* de cloche.

bell tent *n* tente *f* conique.

bell tower *n* clocher *m*.

bellwether ['bel,weðər] *n* [sheep] sonnailler *m* ■ *fig* [person] meneur *m*, - euse *f*, chef *m*.

belly ['belɪ] ◇ *n* (*pl* **bellies**) **1.** [stomach] ventre *m* **2.** [of plane, ship] ventre *m* ■ [of sail] creux *m* **3.** [of cello, guitar] table *f* d'harmonie **4.** CULIN : **~ of pork, pork ~** poitrine *f* de porc.
◇ *vi* (*pret & pp* **bellied**) : **to ~ (out)** s'enfler, se gonfler ‖ *inf* **to ~ up** tomber à plat, foirer, faire faillite.
◇ *vt* (*pret & pp* **bellied**) enfler, gonfler.

bellyache ['belɪeɪk] *inf* ◇ *n* **1.** [pain] mal *m* au *OR* de ventre **2.** [complaint] rogne *f*, rouspétance *f*.
◇ *vi* râler.

bellyaching ['belɪ,eɪkɪŋ] *n (U) inf* ronchonnements *mpl*, rouspétances *fpl*.

belly button *n inf* nombril *m*.

belly dance *n* danse *f* du ventre.
◆ **belly-dance** *vi* danser *OR* faire la danse du ventre.

belly dancer *n* danseuse *f* du ventre *OR* orientale.

belly flop *n* : **to do a ~** faire un plat.

bellyful ['belɪfʊl] *n inf* [of food] ventre *m* plein ■ *fig* **I've had a ~ of your complaints** j'en ai ras le bol de tes rouspétances.

belly-landing *n* AERON *inf* atterrissage *m* sur le ventre.

belly laugh *n inf* gros rire *m*.

belong [bɪ'lɒŋ] *vi* **1.** [as property] : **to ~ to sb** appartenir à *OR* être à qqn **2.** [as member] : **he ~s to a trade union** il fait partie *OR* il est membre d'un syndicat, il est syndiqué **3.** [as part, component] appartenir ■ **the field ~s to that house** le champ dépend de cette maison ■ **this jacket ~s with those trousers** cette veste va avec ce pantalon **4.** [be in proper place] être à sa place ■ **the dishes ~ in that cupboard** les assiettes vont dans ce placard ■ **the two of them ~ together** ces deux-là sont faits pour être ensemble ■ **I don't ~ here** je ne suis pas à ma place ici ■ **go back home where you ~** rentrez chez vous ■ **he ~s in teaching** sa place est dans l'enseignement ■ **these issues ~ in a court of law** ces questions relèvent d'un tribunal.

belonging [bɪ'lɒŋɪŋ] *n* : **a sense of ~** un sentiment d'appartenance.
◆ **belongings** *npl* affaires *fpl*, possessions *fpl* ■ **personal ~s** objets *mpl OR* effets *mpl* personnels.

Belorussia [,belə'rʌsən] ◇ *pr n* GEOG Biélorussie *f*, = **Byelorussia** ■ LING biélorusse *m*.
◇ *adj* GEOG biélorusse.

beloved [bɪ'lʌvd] ◇ *adj* chéri, bien-aimé ■ **my ~ father** mon très cher père, mon père bien-aimé.
◇ *n* bien-aimé *m*, - e *f*, amour *m* ■ **dearly ~, we are gathered here today...** mes très chers amis, nous sommes ici aujourd'hui...

below [bɪ'ləʊ] ◇ *prep* **1.** [at, to a lower position than] au-dessous de, en dessous de ■ [under] sous ■ **the flat ~ ours** l'appartement au-dessous *OR* en dessous du nôtre ■ **her skirt came to ~ her knees** sa jupe lui descendait au-dessous du genou **2.** [inferior to] au-dessous de, inférieur à ■ **~ the poverty line** en dessous du seuil de pauvreté ■ **children ~ the age of five** des enfants de moins de cinq ans **3.** [downstream of] en aval de **4.** [south of] au sud de.
◇ *adv* **1.** [in lower place, on lower level] en dessous, plus bas ■ **we looked down onto the town ~** nous contemplions la ville à nos pieds ■ **the flat ~** l'appartement d'en dessous *OR* du dessous ■ **he could hear two men talking ~** il entendait deux hommes parler en bas ➔ **here ~** *arch & lit* [on earth] ici-bas **2.** [with numbers, quantities] moins ■ **it was twenty ~** *inf* il faisait moins vingt ■ **children of five and ~** les enfants de cinq ans et moins **3.** [in text] plus bas, ci-dessous **4.** NAUT en bas ■ **to go ~** descendre dans l'entrepont ■ **she went ~ to her cabin** elle est descendue à sa cabine.

belt [belt] ◇ *n* **1.** [gen - SPORT] ceinture *f* ■ MIL ceinturon *m*, ceinture *f* ■ **to give sb the ~** donner une correction à qqn ■ **a black ~** SPORT une ceinture noire ➔ **she now has a doctoral degree under her ~** elle a maintenant un doctorat en poche ■ **no hitting below the ~** *liter* il est interdit de porter des coups bas ; *fig* pas de coups bas! ■ **that was a bit below the ~** c'était un peu déloyal comme procédé ■ **to pull in** *OR* **to tighten one's ~** se serrer la ceinture **2.** [of machine] courroie *f* **3.** [area, zone] région *f* **4.** *inf* [sharp blow] coup *m* **5.** *inf* [of whisky] gorgée *f*.
◇ *vt* **1.** [dress, trousers] ceinturer, mettre une ceinture à ■ **he had a gun ~ed to his waist** il avait un revolver à la ceinture ■ **a ~ed raincoat** un imperméable à ceinture **2.** [hit with belt] donner des coups de ceinture à ■ [as punishment] donner une correction à **3.** *inf* [hit] donner *OR* flanquer un coup à ■ **she ~ed the ball** elle a donné un grand coup dans la balle.
◇ *vi inf UK inf* filer ■ **they went ~ing along** ils fonçaient.
◆ **belt down** *vt sep UK inf* [food] engloutir, enfourner ■ [drink] avaler, descendre.
◆ **belt out** *vt sep inf* **she ~ed out the last song** elle s'est donnée à fond dans la dernière chanson.
◆ **belt up** *vi insep* **1.** [in car, plane] attacher sa ceinture **2.** *UK inf* [be quiet] la fermer, la boucler.

belt-driven *adj* actionné par courroie.

belting ['beltɪŋ] *n* : **to give sb a ~** [as punishment] donner des coups de ceinture *OR* administrer une correction à qqn ; [in fight] rouer qqn de coups.

beltway ['belt,weɪ] *n US* (boulevard *m*) périphérique *m* ■ *fig* **inside** *OR* **outside the Beltway** *expressions servant à distinguer la classe politique américaine du grand public.*

bemoan [bɪ'məʊn] *vt* pleurer, se lamenter sur ■ **to ~ one's fate** pleurer sur son sort.

bemused [bɪ'mju:zd] *adj* déconcerté, dérouté.

bench [bentʃ] ◇ *n* **1.** [seat] banc *m* ■ [caned, padded] banquette *f* ■ [in auditorium] gradin *m* ■ **park ~** banc public ■ **on the ~** SPORT en réserve **2.** *UK* [in Parliament] banc *m* ■ **the government ~es** les bancs du gouvernement **3.** [work table] établi *m*, plan *m* de travail **4.** LAW [seat] banc *m* ■ **the ~** [judge] la cour, le juge ‖ [judges as group] : **the ~** les juges, les magistrats ■ **she has been raised to the ~** elle a été nommée juge ■ **he serves** *OR* **sits on the ~** [permanent office] il est juge ; [for particular case] il siège au tribunal.
◇ *comp* [lathe, vice] d'établi.
◇ *vt US* SPORT retirer du jeu.

benchmark ['bentʃ,mɑ:k] ◇ *n liter* repère *m* ■ [in surveying] repère *m* de nivellement ■ *fig* repère *m*, point *m* de référence.
◇ *comp* : **~ test** COMPUT test *m* d'évaluation (de programme).

bend [bend] ◇ *vt* (*pret & pp* **bent** [bent]) **1.** [arm, finger] plier ■ [knee, leg] plier, fléchir ■ [back, body] courber ■ [head] pencher, baisser ■ **they bent their heads over their books** ils se penchèrent sur leurs livres ■ **to ~ one's head in prayer** baisser

la tête pour prier ▪ **he went down on ~ed knee** il se mit à genoux, il s'agenouilla ▪ **to ~ sb to one's will** plier qqn à sa volonté ➲ **to ~ sb's ear** casser les oreilles à qqn
2. [pipe, wire] tordre, courber ▪ [branch, tree] courber, faire ployer ▪ [bow] bander, arquer ▪ **to ~ sthg at right angles** plier qqch à angle droit ▪ **he bent the rod out of shape** il a tordu la barre ➲ **to ~ the rules** faire une entorse au règlement
3. [deflect - light, ray] réfracter ; [- stream] dériver, détourner
4. *lit* [direct, turn] diriger ▪ **he bent his attention** *OR* **his mind to solving the problem** il s'appliqua à résoudre le problème
5. NAUT [fasten - cable, rope] étalinguer ; [- sail] enverguer.
◇ *vi* (*pret & pp* **bent** [bent]) **1.** [arm, knee, leg] plier ▪ [person] se courber, se pencher ▪ [head] se pencher ▪ [rod, wire] plier, se courber ▪ [branch, tree] ployer, plier ▪ **to ~ under the burden/the weight** ployer sous le fardeau/le poids ▪ **she bent over the counter** elle s'est penchée par-dessus le comptoir ▪ **he bent backwards/forwards** il s'est penché en arrière/en avant
2. [river, road] faire un coude, tourner ▪ **the road ~s to the left** la route tourne à gauche
3. [submit] céder ▪ **the people refused to ~ to the colonial forces** le peuple a refusé de se soumettre aux forces coloniales.
◇ *n* **1.** [in road] coude *m*, virage *m* ▪ [in river] méandre *m*, coude *m* ▪ [in pipe, rod] coude *m* ▪ **'~s for 7 miles'** 'virages sur 10 km' ➲ **to drive sb round the ~** *inf* rendre qqn fou
2. [in arm] pli *m*, saignée *f* ▪ [in knee] pli *m*, flexion *f* ▪ **she did a couple of forward ~s** elle s'est penchée plusieurs fois en avant
3. NAUT [knot] nœud *m* (de jonction).
◆ **bends** *npl* : **the ~** la maladie des caissons.
◆ **bend back** ◇ *vi insep* **1.** [person] se pencher en arrière **2.** [blade, tube] se recourber.
◇ *vt sep* replier, recourber.
◆ **bend down** ◇ *vi insep* **1.** [person] se courber, se baisser
2. [branch, tree] plier, ployer.
◇ *vt sep* [branch, tree] faire ployer ▪ [blade, tube] replier, recourber.
◆ **bend over** ◇ *vi insep* se pencher ▪ **to ~ over backwards to please (sb)** *fig* se donner beaucoup de mal pour faire plaisir (à qqn).
◇ *vt sep* replier, recourber.

bender ['bendər] *n inf* beuverie *f* ▪ **to go on a ~** faire la noce.

bendy ['bendɪ] (*comp* **bendier**, *superl* **bendiest**) *adj* **1.** [road] sinueux **2.** [flexible] souple, flexible.

beneath [bɪ'ni:θ] ◇ *prep* **1.** [under] sous ▪ **the ground ~ my feet** le sol sous mes pieds ▪ **the ship sank ~ the waves** le navire a sombré sous les vagues **2.** [below] : **the valley was spread out ~ us** la vallée s'étalait sous nos pieds **3.** [unworthy of] indigne de ▪ **she thinks the work is ~ her** elle estime que le travail est indigne d'elle **4.** [socially inferior to] inférieur *(socialement)* ▪ **he married ~ him** il a fait une mésalliance *fml*, il n'a pas fait un bon mariage.
◇ *adv* [underneath] en bas ▪ **from ~** d'en dessous.

Benedictine ◇ *n* **1.** [,benɪ'dɪktɪn] RELIG bénédictin *m*, - e *f* **2.** [,benɪ'dɪkti:n] [liqueur] Bénédictine® *f*.
◇ *adj* [,benɪ'dɪktɪn] bénédictin.

benediction [,benɪ'dɪkʃn] *n* **1.** RELIG & *fig* [blessing] bénédiction *f* **2.** [service] salut *m*.

benefaction [,benɪ'fækʃn] *n* **1.** [good deed] acte *m* de bienfaisance **2.** [donation] don *m*, donation *f*.

benefactor ['benɪfæktər] *n* bienfaiteur *m*.

benefactress ['benɪfæktrɪs] *n* bienfaitrice *f*.

beneficent [bɪ'nefɪsnt] *adj lit* [person, regime] bienfaisant, généreux ▪ [change, effect] bienfaisant, salutaire.

beneficial [,benɪ'fɪʃl] *adj* [good, useful] avantageux, profitable ▪ **legislation ~ to the self-employed** des lois favorables aux travailleurs non-salariés ▪ **the holiday proved highly ~** les vacances ont été extrêmement bénéfiques ▪ **vitamins are ~ to health** les vitamines sont bonnes pour la santé ▪ **~ effects** des effets salutaires.

beneficiary [,benɪ'fɪʃərɪ] (*pl* **beneficiaries**) *n* **1.** [of insurance policy, trust] bénéficiaire *mf* ▪ [of will] bénéficiaire *mf*, légataire *mf* **2.** RELIG bénéficier *m*.

benefit ['benɪfɪt] ◇ *n* **1.** [advantage] avantage *m* ▪ **she is starting to feel the ~s of the treatment** elle commence à ressentir les bienfaits du traitement ▪ **she did it for the ~ of the whole family** elle a agi pour le bien-être de toute la famille ▪ **I'm saying this for your ~** je dis cela pour toi *OR* pour ton bien ▪ **for the ~ of those who arrived late** pour les retardataires *OR* ceux qui sont arrivés en retard ▪ **the speech she made was all for his ~** le discours qu'elle a prononcé ne s'adressait qu'à lui ▪ **the holiday wasn't of much ~ to him** les vacances ne lui ont pas fait tellement de bien ▪ **it's to your ~ to watch your diet** il est dans votre intérêt de surveiller ce que vous mangez ▪ **with the ~ of hindsight, I now see I was wrong** avec le recul *OR* rétrospectivement, je m'aperçois que j'avais tort ▪ **to give sb the ~ of the doubt** laisser *OR* accorder à qqn le bénéfice du doute **2.** [payment] allocation *f*, prestation *f* ▪ **social security ~s** prestations sociales ▪ **tax ~** *US* dégrèvement *m*, allègement *m* fiscal **3.** [performance] spectacle *m (au profit d'une association caritative)* ▪ **~ concert** concert *m (au profit d'une association caritative)* ▪ **~ match** match *m (au profit d'une association caritative)*.
◇ *vt* (*pret & pp* **benefited**, *cont* **benefiting**) [do good to] faire du bien à ▪ [bring financial profit to] profiter à.
◇ *vi* (*pret & pp* **benefited**, *cont* **benefiting**) : **he will ~ from the experience** l'expérience lui sera bénéfique ▪ **no-one is likely to ~ by** *OR* **from the closures** personne n'a de chance de tirer avantage des fermetures ▪ **the novel would ~ greatly from judicious editing** le roman gagnerait beaucoup à être révisé de façon judicieuse ▪ **you would ~ from a stay in the country** un séjour à la campagne vous ferait du bien.

Benelux ['benɪlʌks] *pr n* Benelux *m* ▪ **the ~ countries** les pays du Benelux ▪ **in the ~ countries** au Benelux.

benevolence [bɪ'nevələns] *n* **1.** [kindness] bienveillance *f*, bienfaisance *f* **2.** [good deed] acte *m* de bienfaisance, bienfait *m*.

benevolent [bɪ'nevələnt] *adj* **1.** [kindly] bienveillant **2.** [donor] généreux, charitable.

benevolently [bɪ'nevələntlɪ] *adv* avec bienveillance.

BEng [,bi:'eŋ] (*abbrev of* **Bachelor of Engineering**) *n (titulaire d'une) licence d'ingénierie*.

Bengal [,beŋ'gɔ:l] *pr n* Bengale *m* ▪ **Bay of ~** golfe *m* du Bengale.

Bengali [beŋ'gɔ:lɪ] ◇ *n* **1.** [person] Bengali *mf* **2.** LING bengali *m*.
◇ *adj* bengali.

benighted [bɪ'naɪtɪd] *adj lit* [ignorant - person] plongé dans (les ténèbres de) l'ignorance ; [- policy] aveugle.

benign [bɪ'naɪn] *adj* **1.** [kind - person] affable, aimable ; [- smile] bienveillant ; [- power, system] bienfaisant, salutaire **2.** [harmless] bénin, - igne *f* ▪ **~ tumour** tumeur *f* bénigne **3.** [temperate- climate] doux, douce *f*, clément.

Benin [be'nɪn] *pr n* Bénin *m*.

Beninese [,benɪ'ni:z] ◇ *n* Béninois *m*, - e *f*.
◇ *adj* béninois.

Ben Nevis [-'nevɪs] *pr n point culminant de la Grande-Bretagne, en Écosse (1343m)*.

bent [bent] ◇ *pt & pp* ▷ **bend**.
◇ *adj* **1.** [curved - tree, tube, wire] tordu, courbé ; [- branch] courbé ; [- back] voûté ; [- person] voûté, tassé **2.** [dented] cabossé, bosselé **3.** [determined] : **he's ~ on becoming an actor** il est décidé à *OR* veut absolument devenir acteur ▪ **to be ~ on self-destruction** être porté à l'autodestruction **4.** *UK inf* [dishonest] véreux **5.** △ *UK pej* [homosexual] homo, gay.
◇ *n* **1.** [liking] penchant *m*, goût *m* ▪ [aptitude] aptitudes *fpl*, dispositions *fpl* ▪ **they're of an artistic ~** ils sont tournés vers les arts ▪ **she has a natural ~ for music** [liking] elle a un goût naturel pour la musique ; [talent] elle a des dispositions naturelles pour la musique **2.** *UK* [endurance] endurance *f*.

bento ['bentəʊ] *n (U)* bento *m*.

bento box *n* CULIN boîte *f* à bento.

bentwood ['bentwʊd] *n* bois *m* courbé.

benumbed [bɪ'nʌmd] *adj lit* **~ed by the** *OR* **with cold** [person] transi de froid ; [fingers, toes] engourdi par le froid.

Benzedrine® ['benzədri:n] *n* Benzédrine® *f*.

benzene ['benzi:n] *n* benzène *m*.

benzine ['benzi:n] *n* benzine *f*.

benzoin ['benzəuɪn] *n* **1.** [resin] benjoin *m* **2.** [tree] styrax *m* benjoin.

bequeath [bɪ'kwi:ð] *vt* [pass on] transmettre, léguer ▪ LAW [in will] léguer ▪ **her father ~ed her his fortune** *OR* **his fortune to her** son père lui a légué sa fortune.

bequest [bɪ'kwest] *n* legs *m*.

berate [bɪ'reɪt] *vt* réprimander.

Berber ['bɜ:bəʳ] <> *n* **1.** [person] Berbère *mf* **2.** LING berbère *m*.
<> *adj* berbère.

bereave [bɪ'ri:v] (*pret & pp* **bereaved** *OR* **bereft** [-'reft]) *vt* priver, déposséder.

bereaved [bɪ'ri:vd] <> *adj* affligé, endeuillé ▪ **a ~ mother** une mère qui vient de perdre son enfant ▪ **he's recently ~** il a perdu quelqu'un récemment.
<> *npl* : **the ~** la famille du défunt.

bereavement [bɪ'ri:vmənt] <> *n* [loss] perte *f* ▪ [grief] deuil *m* ▪ **in his ~** dans son deuil.
<> *comp* : **~ counselling** *service d'aide psychologique aux personnes frappées par un deuil*.

bereft [-'reft] *fml & lit* <> *pt & pp* ▷ **bereave**.
<> *adj* privé ▪ **~ of all hope** complètement désespéré ▪ **to be ~ of reason** avoir perdu la raison ▪ **I feel utterly ~** je me sens totalement seul.

beret ['bereɪ] *n* béret *m*.

bergamot ['bɜ:gəmɒt] *n* bergamote *f*.

beriberi [ˌberɪ'berɪ] *n* béribéri *m*.

Bering Sea ['beərɪŋ-] *pr n* : **the ~** la mer de Béring.

Bering Strait *pr n* : **the ~** le détroit de Béring.

berk [bɜ:k] *n* **UK** *inf* idiot *m*, - e *f*.

Berks. *written abbr of* **Berkshire**.

Berlin [bɜ:'lɪn] *pr n* Berlin ▪ **East ~** Berlin-Est ▪ **West ~** Berlin-Ouest ▪ **the ~ Wall** le mur de Berlin.

Berliner [bɜ:'lɪnəʳ] *n* Berlinois *m*, - e *f*.

berm(e) [bɜ:m] *n* berme *f*.

Bermuda [bə'mju:də] *pr n* Bermudes *fpl* ▪ **in ~** aux Bermudes ▪ **the ~ Triangle** le triangle des Bermudes.

Bermudan [bə'mju:dən] <> *adj* GEOG bermudien (*f* ne).
<> *n* Bermudien *m*, - ne *f*.

Bermudas [bə'mju:dəz], **Bermuda shorts** *npl* bermuda *m*.

Bern [bɜ:n] *pr n* Berne.

Bernese [ˌbɜ:'ni:z] <> *n* Bernois *m*, - e *f*.
<> *adj* bernois.

berry ['berɪ] <> *n* (*pret & pp* **berried**) baie *f*.
<> *vi* (*pl* **berries**) **1.** [bush] produire des baies **2.** [person] cueillir des baies ▪ **to go ~ing** aller cueillir des baies.

berserk [bə'zɜ:k] *adj* fou furieux ▪ **to go ~** [person] devenir fou furieux ; [crowd] se déchaîner.

berth [bɜ:θ] <> *n* **1.** [bunk] couchette *f* **2.** NAUT [in harbour] mouillage *m*, poste *m* d'amarrage ▪ [distance] distance *f* **3.** *phr* **to give sb a wide ~** *UK* éviter qqn (à tout prix) ▪ **I'd give him a wide ~ if I were you** je l'éviterais (à tout prix) *OR* je me tiendrais à distance si j'étais vous.
<> *vi* [at dock] venir à quai, accoster ▪ [at anchor] mouiller.
<> *vt* [dock] amarrer, faire accoster ▪ [assign place to] donner un poste d'amarrage à.

beryl ['berəl] *n* béryl *m*.

beseech [bɪ'si:tʃ] (*pret & pp* **beseeched** *OR* **besought** [-'sɔ:t]) *vt fml & lit* **1.** [ask for] solliciter, implorer **2.** [entreat] implorer, supplier ▪ **to ~ sb to do sthg** implorer *OR* supplier qqn de faire qqch ▪ **please, I ~ you** s'il vous plaît, je vous en supplie.

beseeching [bɪ'si:tʃɪŋ] *adj* suppliant, implorant.

beset [bɪ'set] (*pret & pp* **beset**, *cont* **besetting**) *vt (usu passive)* **1.** [assail] assaillir, harceler ▪ **I was ~ by** *OR* **with doubt** j'étais assailli par le doute ▪ **the whole project is ~ with financial difficulties** le projet pose énormément de problèmes sur le plan financier ▪ **they are ~ with problems** ils sont assaillis de problèmes **2.** [surround] encercler.

besetting [bɪ'setɪŋ] *adj* : **his ~ sin was greed** la cupidité était son plus grand défaut.

beside [bɪ'saɪd] *prep* **1.** [next to] à côté de, auprès de ▪ **walk ~ me** marchez à côté de moi ▪ **a house ~ the sea** une maison au bord de la mer **2.** [as compared with] à côté de, par rapport à **3.** [in addition to] en plus de, outre ▪ [apart from] à part, excepté **4.** *phr* **to be ~ o.s. with rage/excitement/joy** être hors de soi/surexcité/fou de joie.

besides [bɪ'saɪdz] <> *prep* **1.** [in addition to] en plus de, outre ▪ **there are three (other) candidates ~ yourself** il y a trois (autres) candidats à part vous ▪ **~ being old, she's also extremely deaf** non seulement elle est vieille, mais elle est également très sourde ▪ **~ which that book is out of print** sans compter que ce livre est épuisé **2.** *(with negatives)* [apart from] hormis, excepté ▪ **nobody ~ me** personne à part moi.
<> *adv* **1.** [in addition] en plus, en outre ▪ **and more ~** et d'autres encore **2.** [furthermore] en plus ▪ **~, I don't even like funfairs** d'ailleurs *OR* en plus, je n'aime pas les foires.

besiege [bɪ'si:dʒ] *vt* **1.** [surround - town] assiéger ▪ *fig* [- person, office] assaillir **2.** [harass] assaillir, harceler ▪ **we've been ~d by requests for help** nous avons été assaillis de demandes d'aide.

besieger [bɪ'si:dʒəʳ] *n* assiégeant *m*.

besmirch [bɪ'smɜ:tʃ] *vt lit* [make dirty] souiller ▪ *fig* [tarnish] souiller.

besom ['bi:zəm] *n* [broom] balai *m*.

besotted [bɪ'sɒtɪd] *adj* **1.** [infatuated] fou *(before vowel or silent 'h'* **fol***)*, folle *f*, épris ▪ **to be ~ with sb** être fou *OR* follement épris de qqn **2.** [foolish] idiot.

besought [-'sɔ:t] *pt & pp* ▷ **beseech**.

bespatter [bɪ'spætəʳ] *vt lit* [splash] éclabousser ▪ *fig* [tarnish] souiller, éclabousser.

bespeak [bɪ'spi:k] (*pret* **bespoke** [-'spəuk], *pp* **bespoke** *OR* **bespoken** [-'spəukən]) *vt lit* [be sign of] démontrer, témoigner de.

bespectacled [bɪ'spektəkld] *adj* qui porte des lunettes, à lunettes.

bespoke [-'spəuk] <> *pt & pp* ▷ **bespeak**.
<> *adj* [shoemaker, tailor] à façon ▪ [shoes, suit] fait sur mesure.

bespoken [-'spəukən] *pp* ▷ **bespeak**.

Bessemer converter ['besɪməʳ] *n* convertisseur *m* Bessemer.

best [best] (*pl inv*) <> *adj* **1.** *(superl of* **good***)* meilleur ▪ **may the ~ man win** que le meilleur gagne ▪ **she gave him the ~ years of her life** elle lui a sacrifié les plus belles années de sa vie ▪ **I'm doing what is ~ for the family** je fais ce qu'il y a de mieux pour la famille ▪ **she knows what's ~ for her** elle sait ce qui lui va *OR* convient le mieux ▪ **they think it ~ not to answer** ils croient qu'il vaut mieux ne pas répondre ▪ **the ~ thing (to do) is to keep quiet** le mieux, c'est de ne rien dire ▪ **~ of all** le meilleur de tout ▪ **'~ before 1995'** COMM 'à consommer de préférence avant 1995'
2. [reserved for special occasions] plus beau ▪ **she was dressed in her ~ clothes** elle portait ses plus beaux vêtements
3. *phr* **the ~ part of** la plus grande partie de ▪ **she spent the ~ part of the day working** elle a passé le plus clair de la journée à travailler ▪ **I waited for the ~ part of an hour** j'ai attendu près d'une heure *OR* presque une heure.

◇ *adv (superl of well)* mieux ■ **he does it ~** c'est lui qui le fait le mieux ■ **which film did you like ~?** quel est le film que vous avez préféré? ■ **I comforted her as ~ I could** je l'ai consolée de mon mieux *OR* du mieux que j'ai pu ➲ **you had ~ apologize to her** vous feriez mieux de lui présenter vos excuses.
◇ *n* **1.** [most outstanding person, thing, part etc] le meilleur *m*, la meilleure *f*, les meilleurs *mpl*, les meilleures *f* ■ **it/she is the ~ there is** c'est le meilleur/la meilleure qui soit ■ **he wants her to have the ~** il veut qu'elle ait ce qu'il y a de mieux, il veut ce qu'il y a de mieux pour elle ■ **the ~ you can say about him is that...** le mieux qu'on puisse dire à son sujet c'est que... ■ **even the ~ of us can make mistakes** tout le monde peut se tromper ■ **to get** *OR* **to have the ~ of the bargain** avoir la part belle ➲ **she wants the ~ of both worlds** elle veut tout avoir **2.** [greatest, highest degree] le mieux, le meilleur ■ **they're the ~ of friends** ce sont les meilleurs amis du monde ■ **to the ~ of my knowledge/recollection** autant que je sache/je me souvienne ■ **the ~ of luck!** bonne chance! ■ **she's not the calmest of people, even at the ~ of times** ce n'est pas quelqu'un de très calme de toute façon ■ **it was the ~ we could do** nous ne pouvions pas faire mieux ■ **it's journalism at its ~** c'est du journalisme de haut niveau ■ **the garden is at its ~ in spring** c'est au printemps que le jardin est le plus beau ■ **I'm not at my ~ in the morning** je ne suis pas en forme le matin ■ **this is Shakespeare at his ~** voilà du meilleur Shakespeare ■ **to do one's ~** faire de son mieux *OR* tout son possible ■ **to get the ~ out of sb/sthg** tirer un maximum de qqn/qqch ■ **to look one's ~** [gen] être resplendissant ■ **we'll have to make the ~ of the situation** il faudra nous accommoder de la situation (du mieux que nous pouvons) ■ **to make the ~ of a bad bargain** *OR* **job** faire contre mauvaise fortune bon cœur
3. [nicest clothes] : **they were in their Sunday~** ils étaient endimanchés *OR* portaient leurs habits du dimanche
4. [good wishes] : **(I wish you) all the ~** (je vous souhaite) bonne chance
5. [winning majority] : **we played the ~ of three games** le jeu consistait à gagner *OR* il fallait gagner deux parties sur trois.
◇ *vt arch* [get advantage over] l'emporter sur ■ [defeat] vaincre.
◆ **at best** *adv phr* au mieux ■ **his performance has been at ~ mediocre** ses résultats ont été, au mieux, médiocres.
◆ **for the best** *adv phr* pour le mieux ■ **it's all for the ~** c'est pour le mieux ■ **he meant it for the ~** il avait les meilleures intentions du monde.

best-case *adj* : **this is the ~ scenario** c'est le scénario le plus optimiste.

bestial ['bestjəl] *adj* bestial.

bestiality [ˌbestɪ'ælətɪ] *(pl* **bestialities***)* *n* **1.** [of behaviour, character] bestialité *f* **2.** [act] acte *m* bestial **3.** [sexual practice] bestialité *f*.

bestiary ['bestɪərɪ] *(pl* **bestiaries***)* *n* bestiaire *m (recueil)*.

bestir [bɪ'stɜːʳ] *(pret & pp* **bestirred**, *cont* **bestirring***)* *vt* : **to ~ o.s.** s'activer.

best man *n* garçon *m* d'honneur.

BEST MAN

Dans les pays anglo-saxons, le garçon d'honneur est responsable du bon déroulement de la cérémonie du mariage. C'est lui qui présente l'alliance au marié et prononce un discours pendant la réception. La tradition veut que ce discours soit agrémenté de commentaires et de vieilles histoires drôles sur le marié.

bestow [bɪ'stəʊ] *vt fml* [favour, gift, praise] accorder ■ [award, honour] conférer, accorder ■ **to ~ sthg on sb** accorder *OR* conférer qqch à qqn.

bestowal [bɪ'stəʊəl] *n fml* [of favour, honour, title] octroi *m*.

bestride [bɪ'straɪd] *(pret* **bestrode** [-'strəʊd], *pp* **bestridden** [-'strɪdn]) *vt lit* **1.** [straddle - bicycle, horse] enfourcher ; [- chair] se mettre à califourchon *OR* à cheval sur **2.** [span - river] enjamber, franchir ; [- obstacle] enjamber.

best-seller *n* **1.** [book] best-seller *m*, succès *m* de librairie ■ [hi-fi, record] article *m* qui se vend bien **2.** [author] auteur *m* à succès.

best-selling *adj* [book, item] à fort tirage ■ [author] à succès.

bet [bet] ◇ *n* pari *m* ■ **to win/to lose a ~** gagner/perdre un pari ■ **he lay** *OR* **put** *OR* **placed a ~ on the race** il a parié *OR* il a fait un pari sur la course ■ **place your ~s!** faites vos jeux! ■ **they're taking ~s** ils prennent des paris ■ **it's a good** *OR* **safe ~ that they'll win** *fig* ils vont gagner à coup sûr ■ **your best ~ is to take a taxi** *inf fig* tu ferais mieux de prendre un taxi ■ **she's a bad/good ~ as a prospective leader** *fig* elle ferait un mauvais/bon leader.
◇ *vt (pret & pp* **bet** *OR* **betted**, *cont* **betting***)* parier ■ **how much did you ~ on the race?** combien as-tu parié *OR* misé sur la course? ■ **I ~ her £5 he wouldn't come** j'ai parié 5 livres avec elle qu'il ne viendrait pas ■ **I'll ~ you anything you want** je te parie tout ce que tu veux ■ **I ~ you won't do it!** *inf* (t'es pas) chiche! ➲ **I'll ~ my bottom dollar** *OR* **my boots he loses** *inf* il va perdre, j'en mettrais ma main au feu ■ **are you going to the party? – you ~!** *inf* tu vas à la soirée? – et comment! *OR* qu'est-ce que tu crois? ■ **I'll tell him off – I'll ~!** *inf* [you will] je vais lui dire ses quatre vérités -- j'en doute pas! ; [you won't] je vais lui dire ses quatre vérités – mon œil!
◇ *vi (pret & pp* **bet** *OR* **betted**, *cont* **betting***)* parier ■ **to ~ against/on sthg** parier contre/sur qqch ■ **he ~s on the races** il parie *OR* joue aux courses ■ **which horse did you ~ on?** quel cheval as-tu joué?, sur quel cheval as-tu misé? ■ **to ~ 5 to 1** parier *OR* miser à 5 contre 1 ■ **he said he'd phone me – well, I wouldn't ~ on it!** *inf* il a dit qu'il me téléphonerait – à ta place, je ne me ferais pas trop d'illusions!

beta ['biːtə] *n* bêta *m inv*.

beta-blocker [-ˌblɒkəʳ] *n* bêtabloquant *m*.

betake [bɪ'teɪk] *(pret* **betook** [-'tʊk], *pp* **betaken** [-'teɪkn]) *vt lit* **to ~ o.s. to** se rendre à.

betel nut *n* noix *f* d'arec.

betel palm *n* aréquier *m*, arec *m*.

bethel, Bethel ['beθl] *n lieu de recueillement pour les marins.*

bethink [bɪ'θɪŋk] *(pret & pp* **bethought** [-'θɔːt]) *vt arch & dial* **to ~ o.s. of sthg** [consider] considérer qqch, songer à qqch ; [remember] se rappeler qqch, se souvenir de qqch.

Bethlehem ['beθlɪhem] *pr n* Bethléem.

bethought [-'θɔːt] *pt & pp* ▷ **bethink**.

betide [bɪ'taɪd] *vi lit* advenir.

betoken [bɪ'təʊkn] *vt fml* [indicate] être l'indice de, révéler ■ [augur] présager, annoncer.

betook [-'tʊk] *pt* ▷ **betake**.

betray [bɪ'treɪ] *vt* **1.** [be disloyal to - friend, principle] trahir ; [- husband, wife] tromper, trahir ; [- country] trahir, être traître à **2.** [denounce] trahir, dénoncer ■ [hand over] trahir, livrer **3.** [confidence, hope, trust] trahir, tromper **4.** [disclose - secret, truth] trahir, divulguer ; [- grief, happiness] trahir, laisser voir ■ **her voice ~ed her nervousness** sa voix laissait deviner son inquiétude.

betrayal [bɪ'treɪəl] *n* **1.** [of person, principle] trahison *f* **2.** [act] (acte *m* de) trahison *f* ■ **it's a ~ of one's country** c'est une trahison envers son pays **3.** [of confidence, trust] abus *m*, trahison *f* **4.** [of secret, truth] trahison *f*, divulgation *f*.

betrayer [bɪ'treɪəʳ] *n* traître *m*, - esse *f*.

betrothal [bɪ'trəʊðl] *n arch* fiançailles *fpl*.

betrothed [bɪ'trəʊðd] *arch* ◇ *adj* fiancé, promis.
◇ *n* fiancé *m*, - e *f*, promis *m*, - e *f*.

better ['betəʳ] ◇ *adj* **1.** *(compar of good)* [superior] meilleur ■ **that's ~!** voilà qui est mieux! ■ **I'm ~ at languages than he is** je suis meilleur *OR* plus fort en langues que lui ■ **he's a ~ cook than you are** il cuisine mieux que toi ■ **I had hoped for ~ things** j'avais espéré mieux ■ **business is (getting) ~** les affaires vont mieux ■ **it couldn't** *OR* **nothing could be ~ !** c'est on ne peut mieux! ■ **it's ~ if I don't see them** il vaut mieux *OR* il est préférable que je ne les voie pas ■ **you're far ~ leaving now** il vaut beaucoup mieux que tu partes maintenant ➲ **to be all the ~ for having done sthg** se trouver mieux d'avoir fait qqch ■ **you'll be all the ~ for a holiday** des vacances vous feront le plus grand bien ■ **~ off** mieux ■ **they're ~ off than we are** [richer] ils ont plus d'argent que nous ; [in a more advantageous posi-

tion] ils sont dans une meilleure position que nous ▪ **he'd have been ~ off staying where he was** il aurait mieux fait de rester où il était
2. *(compar of well)* [improved in health] : **to get ~** commencer à aller mieux ▪ **now that he's ~** maintenant qu'il va mieux
3. [morally] : **she's a ~ person for it** ça lui a fait beaucoup de bien ▪ **you're a ~ man than I am!** *hum* mieux vaut toi que moi! ▪ **you're no ~ than a liar!** tu n'es qu'un menteur!
4. *phr* **the ~ part of sthg** la plus grande partie de qqch ▪ **I waited for the ~ part of an hour** j'ai attendu presque une heure.
◇ *adv* **1.** *(compar of well)* [more proficiently, aptly etc] mieux ▪ **he swims ~ than I do** il nage mieux que moi ▪ **the town would be ~ described as a backwater** la ville est plutôt un coin perdu ▪ **he held it up to the light, the ~ to see the colours** il l'a mis dans la lumière afin de mieux voir les couleurs ▶ **to go one ~ (than sb)** renchérir (sur qqn)
2. [indicating preference] : **I liked his last book ~** j'ai préféré son dernier livre ▪ **I'd like nothing ~ than to talk to him** je ne demande pas mieux que de lui parler ▪ **so much the ~** tant mieux ▪ **the less he knows the ~** moins il en saura, mieux ça vaudra ▶ **~ late than never** *prov* mieux vaut tard que jamais *prov*
3. [with adj] mieux, plus ▪ **~ looking** plus beau ▪ **~ paid/prepared** mieux payé/préparé ▪ **she's one of Canada's ~-known authors** c'est un des auteurs canadiens les plus OR mieux connus
4. *phr* **we'd ~ be going** [must go] il faut que nous partions ; [would be preferable] il vaut mieux que nous partions ▪ **it'll be ready tomorrow – it'd ~ be!** ce sera prêt demain – il vaudrait mieux! ▪ **you'd ~ be on time!** tu as intérêt à être à l'heure!
◇ *n* **1.** [superior of two] le meilleur *m*, la meilleure *f* ▪ **there's been a change for the ~ in his health** son état de santé s'est amélioré ▪ **the situation has taken a turn for the ~** la situation a pris une meilleure tournure ▶ **for ~ or worse** pour le meilleur ou pour le pire
2. *(usu pl)* [person] supérieur *m*, - e *f*
3. *phr* **to get the ~ of sb : curiosity got the ~ of me** ma curiosité l'a emporté ▪ **we got the ~ of them in the deal** nous l'avons emporté sur eux dans l'affaire
4. [gambler] parieur *m*, - euse *f*.
◇ *vt* [position, status, situation] améliorer ▪ [achievement, sales figure] dépasser ▪ **she's eager to ~ herself** elle a vraiment envie d'améliorer sa situation.

better half *n inf hum* moitié *f*.

betterment ['betəmənt] *n* amélioration *f* ▪ LAW [of property] plus-value *f*.

better-off ◇ *adj* aisé, riche.
◇ *npl* : **the ~** les riches *mpl*.

betting ['betɪŋ] ◇ *n* **1.** [bets] pari *m*, paris *mpl* ▪ **the ~ was heavy** les paris allaient bon train ▪ **what's the ~ they refuse to go?** je suis prêt à parier qu'ils ne voudront pas y aller **2.** [odds] cote *f*.
◇ *adj* : **I'm not a ~ man** je n'aime pas parier ▪ **~ slip** *UK* bulletin *m* de pari individuel.

betting office *n* ≃ (bureau *m* de) PMU *m*.

betting shop *n* bureau *m* de paris *(appartenant à un bookmaker)*.

bettor ['betəʳ] *US n* = **better** *(n sense 4)*.

Betty Ford Clinic ['betɪ-] *pr n centre de désintoxication pour alcooliques et toxicomanes situé en Californie et fréquenté par des personnalités riches et célèbres.*

between [bɪ'twiːn] ◇ *prep* **1.** [in space or time] entre ▪ **the crowd stood ~ him and the door** la foule le séparait de la porte ▪ **~ now and this evening** d'ici ce soir ▪ **I'm ~ jobs at the moment** je suis entre deux emplois en ce moment
2. [in the range that separates] entre ▪ **children ~ the ages of 5 and 10** les enfants de 5 à 10 ans
3. [indicating connection, relation] entre ▪ **a bus runs ~ the airport and the hotel** un bus fait la navette entre l'aéroport et l'hôtel ▪ *fig* **a treaty ~ the two nations** un traité entre les deux États ▶ **~ you and me, ~ ourselves** entre nous
4. [indicating alternatives] entre ▪ **I had to choose ~ going with them and staying at home** il fallait que je choisisse entre les accompagner et rester à la maison
5. [added together] : **~ us we saved enough money for the trip** à nous tous nous avons économisé assez d'argent pour le voyage ▪ **the 5 groups collected £1,000 ~ them** les 5 groupes ont recueilli 1 000 livres en tout ▪ **(in) ~ painting, writing and looking after the children, she was kept very busy** entre la peinture, l'écriture et les enfants, elle était très occupée
6. [indicating division] entre ▪ **they shared the cake ~ them** ils se sont partagé le gâteau.
◇ *adv* = **in between**.

◆ **in between** ◇ *adv phr* **1.** [in intermediate position] : **a row of bushes with little clumps of flowers in ~** une rangée d'arbustes intercalés de petits bouquets de fleurs ▪ **he's neither right nor left but somewhere in ~** il n'est ni de droite ni de gauche mais quelque part entre les deux
2. [in time] entre-temps, dans l'intervalle.
◇ *prep phr* entre.

betweentimes [bɪ'twiːntaɪmz] *adv* dans l'intervalle, entre-temps.

bevel ['bevl] ◇ *vt* (*UK pret & pp* **bevelled**, *cont* **bevelling**) (*US pret & pp* **beveled**, *cont* **beveling**) biseauter, tailler en biseau OR de biais.
◇ *n* [surface] surface *f* oblique ▪ [angle] angle *m* oblique ▪ **~ (edge)** biseau *m*.

beveled *adj US* = **bevelled**.

bevelled *UK*, **beveled** *US* ['bevld] *adj* biseauté.

beverage ['bevərɪdʒ] *n* boisson *f*.

bevvy ['bevɪ] (*pl* **bevvies**) *UK n dial* [drink] boisson *f* (alcoolisée) ▪ [drinking bout] beuverie *f*.

bevy ['bevɪ] (*pl* **bevies**) *n* [of people] bande *f*, troupeau *m pej* ▪ [of quails] volée *f* ▪ [of roe deer] harde *f*.

bewail [bɪ'weɪl] *vt lit* pleurer.

beware [bɪ'weəʳ] *(infinitive and imperative only)* ◇ *vi* prendre garde ▪ **~ of married men** méfiez-vous des hommes mariés ▪ **~ of making hasty decisions** gardez-vous de prendre des décisions hâtives ▪ **'~ of the dog!'** 'chien méchant!'
◇ *vt* prendre garde ▪ **~ what you say to her** prenez garde OR faites attention à ce que vous lui dites.

bewhiskered [bɪ'wɪskəd] *adj lit* [with side whiskers] qui a des favoris ▪ [bearded] barbu.

bewilder [bɪ'wɪldəʳ] *vt* rendre perplexe, dérouter.

bewildered [bɪ'wɪldəd] *adj* perplexe.

bewildering [bɪ'wɪldərɪŋ] *adj* déconcertant, déroutant.

bewilderment [bɪ'wɪldəmənt] *n* confusion *f*, perplexité *f* ▪ **to my complete ~ he refused** à mon grand étonnement, il a refusé.

bewitch [bɪ'wɪtʃ] *vt* **1.** [cast spell over] ensorceler, enchanter **2.** [fascinate] enchanter, charmer.

bewitched [bɪ'wɪtʃt] *adj* ensorcelé, enchanté.

bewitching [bɪ'wɪtʃɪŋ] *adj* [smile] enchanteur, charmeur ▪ [beauty, person] charmant, séduisant.

bewitchingly [bɪ'wɪtʃɪŋlɪ] *adv* d'une façon séduisante ▪ **~ beautiful** beau à ravir.

beyond [bɪ'jɒnd] ◇ *prep* **1.** [on the further side of] au-delà de, de l'autre côté de ▪ **the museum is a few yards ~ the church** le musée se trouve à quelques mètres après l'église **2.** [outside the range of] au-delà de, au-dessus de ▪ **do your duties extend ~ teaching?** est-ce que vos fonctions s'étendent au-delà de l'enseignement? ▪ **~ belief** incroyable ▪ **due to circumstances ~ our control** dû à des circonstances indépendantes de notre volonté ▪ **his guilt has been established ~ (all reasonable) doubt** sa culpabilité a été établie sans aucun OR sans le moindre doute ▪ **it's (gone) ~ a joke** cela dépasse les bornes ▶ **to be ~ sb : economics is completely ~ me** je ne comprends rien à l'économie **3.** [later than] au-delà de, plus de ▪ **the deadline has been extended to ~ 1999** l'échéance a été repoussée au-delà de 1999 ▪ **~ 1995 that law will no longer be valid** après OR à partir de 1995, cette loi ne sera plus applicable **4.** [apart from, other than] sauf, excepté ▪ **I know nothing ~ what I've already told you** je ne sais rien de plus que ce que je vous ai déjà dit.

◇ *adv* **1.** [on the other side] au-delà, plus loin ■ **the room ~ was smaller** la pièce suivante était plus petite **2.** [after] au-delà ■ **major changes are foreseen for 1999 and ~** des changements importants sont prévus pour 1999 et au-delà.
◇ *n* au-delà *m.*

Beyrouth [ˌbeɪ'ru:t] *pr n* = **Beirut**.

bezel ['bezl] ◇ *n* **1.** [face - of tool] biseau *m* ; [- of gem] facette *f* **2.** [rim - for gem] chaton *m* ; [- for watch crystal] portée *f.*
◇ *vt* (*UK pret & pp* **bezelled**, *cont* **bezelling**) (*US pret & pp* **bezeled**, *cont* **bezeling**) biseauter, tailler en biseau.

bf (*written abbrev of* **boldface**) TYPO caractères *mpl* gras.

b/f *written abbr of* **brought forward**.

bhangra ['bæŋgrə] *n* MUS *combinaison de musique traditionnelle du Pendjab et de musique pop occidentale.*

bhp *n* = **brake horsepower**.

Bhutan [ˌbu:'tɑ:n] *pr n* Bhoutan *m.*

bi△ [baɪ] ◇ *adj* bi *(inv).*
◇ *n* bisexuel *m*, - elle *f.*

bi- [baɪ] *in cpds* bi-.

Biafran [bɪ'æfrən] ◇ *n* Biafrais *m*, - e *f.*
◇ *adj* biafrais.

biannual [baɪ'ænjʊəl] *adj* semestriel.

bias ['baɪəs] ◇ *n* **1.** [prejudice] préjugé *m* ■ **there is still considerable ~ against women candidates** les femmes qui se présentent sont encore victimes d'un fort préjugé **2.** [tendency] tendance *f*, penchant *m* ■ **the school has a scientific ~** l'école favorise les sciences **3.** SEW biais *m* ■ **cut on the ~** taillé dans le biais **4.** [in bowls - weight] *poids ou renflement d'une boule qui l'empêche d'aller droit* ; [- curved course] déviation *f* **5.** MATHS biais *m.*
◇ *vt* (*pret & pp* **biased** *OR* **biassed**) [influence] influencer ■ [prejudice] prévenir ■ **his experience ~ed him against/towards them** son expérience l'a prévenu contre eux/en leur faveur ■ **the course is ~ed towards the arts** l'enseignement est plutôt orienté sur les lettres.
◇ *adj* en biais.
◇ *adv* en biais, de biais.

bias binding *n* biais *m (ruban).*

biased, biassed ['baɪəst] *adj* **1.** [partial] partial **2.** [ball] décentré.

biathlon [baɪ'æθlɒn] *n* biathlon *m.*

bib [bɪb] *n* **1.** [for child] bavoir *m*, bavette *f* **2.** [of apron, dungarees] bavette *f* ■ **in one's best ~ and tucker** *UK inf* sur son trente et un **3.** [of feathers, fur] tache *f*, touche *f.*

Bible ['baɪbl] ◇ *n* Bible *f.*
◇ *comp* : **the ~ Belt** *états du sud des États-Unis où l'évangélisme est très répandu* ■ **~ class** [in school] classe *f* d'instruction religieuse ; [Catholic church] catéchisme *m* ■ **~ study** étude *f* de la Bible.
➡ **bible** *n fig* [manual] bible *f*, évangile *m.*

bible-basher *n inf* = **bible-thumper**.

bible-thumper [-ˌθʌmpəʳ] *n inf pej* évangéliste *m* de carrefour.

biblical, Biblical ['bɪblɪkl] *adj* biblique.

bibliographer [ˌbɪblɪ'ɒgrəfəʳ] *n* bibliographe *mf.*

bibliographical [ˌbɪblɪə'græfɪkl] *adj* bibliographique.

bibliography [ˌbɪblɪ'ɒgrəfɪ] (*pl* **bibliographies**) *n* bibliographie *f.*

bibliophile ['bɪblɪəʊfaɪl] *n* bibliophile *mf.*

bicameral [ˌbaɪ'kæmərəl] *adj* bicaméral.

bicarb [baɪ'kɑ:b] *n inf* bicarbonate *m* (de soude).

bicarbonate [baɪ'kɑ:bənət] *n* bicarbonate *m* ■ **~ of soda** bicarbonate *m* de soude.

bicentenary [ˌbaɪsen'ti:nərɪ] *UK* ◇ *adj* bicentenaire.
◇ *n* (*pl* **bicentenaries**) bicentenaire *m.*

bicentennial [ˌbaɪsen'tenjəl] ◇ *adj* bicentenaire.
◇ *n US* bicentenaire *m.*

biceps ['baɪseps] (*pl inv*) *n* biceps *m.*

bicker ['bɪkəʳ] *vi* se chamailler ■ **to ~ about** *OR* **over sthg** se chamailler à propos de qqch.

bickering ['bɪkərɪŋ] ◇ *n* chamailleries *fpl.*
◇ *adj* chamailleur.

bickie ['bɪkɪ] *n inf UK* [biscuit] petit gâteau *m.*

bicultural [ˌbaɪ'kʌltʃərəl] *adj* biculturel.

bicycle ['baɪsɪkl] ◇ *n* vélo *m*, bicyclette *f* ■ **I go to work by ~** je vais travailler à bicyclette *OR* à vélo ■ **do you know how to ride a ~?** sais-tu faire du vélo *OR* de la bicyclette? ■ **he went for a ride on his ~** il est allé faire un tour à vélo.
◇ *comp* [bell, chain, lamp] de vélo, de bicyclette.
◇ *vi* faire du vélo *OR* de la bicyclette ■ **she ~s to work** elle va travailler à bicyclette *OR* à vélo.

bicycle clip *n* pince *f* à vélo.

bicycle pump *n* pompe *f* à bicyclette *OR* à vélo.

bicycle rack *n* [for parking] ratelier *m* à bicyclettes *OR* à vélos ■ [on car roof] porte-vélos *m inv.*

bicycle track *n* piste *f* cyclable.

bid [bɪd] ◇ *vi* (*pret & pp* **bid**, *cont* **bidding**) **1.** [offer to pay] faire une offre, offrir ■ **to ~ for sthg** faire une offre pour qqch ■ **they ~ against us** ils ont surenchéri sur notre offre
2. COMM faire une soumission, répondre à un appel d'offres
3. [make attempt] : **he's bidding for the presidency** il vise la présidence
4. *phr* **to ~ fair to do sthg** promettre de faire qqch.
◇ *vt* (*pret & pp* **bid**, *cont* **bidding**) **1.** [offer to pay] faire une offre de, offrir ■ [at auction] faire une enchère de ■ **what am I ~ for this table?** combien m'offre-t-on pour cette table?
2. CARDS demander, annoncer
3. (*pret* **bade** [bæd] *pp* **bidden** ['bɪdn]) *lit* [say] dire ■ **they bade him farewell** ils lui firent leurs adieux ■ **she bade them welcome** elle leur souhaita la bienvenue ‖ *lit* [order, tell] ordonner, enjoindre ■ **he bade them enter** il les pria d'entrer ‖ *arch* [invite] inviter, convier.
◇ *n* **1.** [offer to pay] offre *f* ■ [at auction] enchère *f* ■ **I made a ~ of £100** [gen] j'ai fait une offre de 100 livres ; [at auction] j'ai fait une enchère de 100 livres ■ **a higher ~** une surenchère
2. COMM [tender] soumission *f* ■ **the firm made** *OR* **put in a ~ for the contract** l'entreprise a fait une soumission *OR* a soumissionné pour le contrat ■ **the State invited ~s for** *OR* **on the project** l'État a mis le projet en adjudication
3. CARDS demande *f*, annonce *f* ■ **it's your ~** c'est à vous d'annoncer ■ **"no ~"** "passe", "parole" ■ **he raised the ~** il a monté *OR* enchéri
4. [attempt] tentative *f* ■ **they made a ~ to gain control of the movement** ils ont tenté de prendre la tête du mouvement ■ **the prisoners made a ~ for freedom** les prisonniers ont fait une tentative d'évasion ■ **a rescue ~** une tentative de sauvetage.

biddable ['bɪdəbl] *adj* **1.** CARDS demandable **2.** *UK* [docile] docile, obéissant.

bidden ['bɪdn] *pp* ▷ **bid**.

bidder ['bɪdəʳ] *n* **1.** [at auction] enchérisseur *m*, - euse *f* ■ **there were no ~s** il n'y a pas eu de preneurs, personne n'a fait d'offre ■ **sold to the highest ~** vendu au plus offrant **2.** COMM soumissionnaire *mf* ■ **the highest/lowest ~** le soumissionnaire le plus/le moins offrant.

bidding ['bɪdɪŋ] *n* **1.** [at auction] enchères *fpl* ■ **the ~ went against me** on avait enchéri sur mon offre ■ **to raise the ~** faire monter les enchères ■ **the ~ is closed** l'enchère est faite, c'est adjugé **2.** COMM [tenders] soumissions *fpl* **3.** CARDS enchères *fpl* **4.** *lit* [request] demande *f* ■ [order] ordre *m*, ordres *mpl* ■ **he did his mother's ~** il respecta les volontés de sa mère ■ **at her brother's ~** sur la requête de son frère.

biddy ['bɪdɪ] (*pl* **biddies**) *n inf pej* [old woman] vieille bonne femme *f* ■ [gossip] commère *f pej.*

bide [baɪd] (*pret* **bided** *OR* **bode** [bəʊd], *pp* **bided**) *vt* : **to ~ one's time** attendre son heure *OR* le bon moment.

bidet ['bi:deɪ] *n* bidet *m*.

bid price *n prix auquel un acheteur accepte d'acheter des actions.*

Biel [bi:l] *pr n* Bienne.

biennial [baɪ'enɪəl] ◇ *adj* **1.** [every two years] biennal, bisannuel **2.** [lasting two years] biennal.
◇ *n* **1.** [event] biennale *f* **2.** [plant] plante *f* bisannuelle.

bier [bɪəʳ] *n* [for corpse] bière *f* ■ [for coffin] brancards *mpl*.

biff [bɪf] *inf* ◇ *vt* flanquer un coup de poing à.
◇ *n* coup *m* de poing, gnon *m*.

bifocal [,baɪ'fəʊkl] *adj* bifocal.
◆ **bifocals** *npl* lunettes *fpl* bifocales *OR* à double foyer.

BIFU ['bɪfu:] *(abbrev of* **The Banking, Insurance and Finance Union***)* *pr n syndicat britannique des employés du secteur financier.*

bifunctional [,baɪ'fʌŋkʃnəl] *adj* bifonctionnel.

bifurcate ['baɪfəkeɪt] ◇ *vi* bifurquer.
◇ *adj* à deux branches.

bifurcation [,baɪfə'keɪʃn] *n* bifurcation *f*.

big [bɪg] *(comp* **bigger**, *superl* **biggest***)* ◇ *adj* **1.** [in size - car, hat, majority] grand, gros, grosse *f* ; [- crowd, field, room] grand ; [- person] grand, fort ■ **the crowd got bigger** la foule a grossi ■ **to earn ~ money** gagner gros ■ **he has a ~ head** *fig* il a la grosse tête ■ **we're not ~ eaters** nous ne sommes pas de gros mangeurs ■ **he has a ~ mouth** *inf fig* il faut toujours qu'il l'ouvre ■ **why did you have to open your ~ mouth?** *inf* tu ne pouvais pas la fermer, non? ➤ **she's too ~ for her boots** *OR* **her breeches** *inf* elle ne se prend pas pour n'importe qui ■ **'The Big Sleep'** ***Chandler, Hawks*** 'le Grand Sommeil'
2. [in height] grand ■ **to get** *OR* **to grow bigger** grandir
3. [older] aîné, plus grand ■ **my ~ sister** ma grande sœur
4. *(as intensifier)* grand, énorme ■ **he's just a ~ bully** ce n'est qu'une grosse brute
5. [important, significant - decision, problem] grand, important ; [- drop, increase] fort, important ■ **the ~ day** le grand jour ■ **he's ~ in publishing, he's a ~ man in publishing** c'est quelqu'un d'important dans l'édition ■ **we're onto something ~!** nous sommes sur une piste intéressante!
6. [grandiose] grand ■ **he went into politics in a ~ way** il est entré dans la politique par la grande porte ■ **they entertain in a ~ way** ils font les choses en grand quand ils reçoivent ■ **~ words!** ce sont de bien grands mots!
7. [generous] grand, généreux ■ **he has a ~ heart** il a du cœur *OR* bon cœur ■ **that's ~ of you!** *iron* quelle générosité!
8. *inf* [popular] à la mode
9. *inf* [enthusiastic] : **to be ~ on sthg** adorer *OR* être fana de qqch ■ **the company is ~ on research** l'entreprise investit beaucoup dans la recherche.
◇ *adv* **1.** [grandly] : **he talks ~** il se vante, il fanfaronne ■ **to think ~** voir grand
2. *inf* [well] : **their music goes over ~ with teenagers** les adolescents adorent leur musique ■ **they made it ~ in the pop world** ce sont maintenant des stars de la musique pop.
◆ **big up** *vt sep UK inf* **1.** [publicize] faire du battage à propos de.
2. [greet] saluer.

bigamist ['bɪgəmɪst] *n* bigame *mf*.

bigamous ['bɪgəməs] *adj* bigame.

bigamy ['bɪgəmɪ] *n* bigamie *f*.

Big Apple *pr n inf* **the ~** New York *(la ville)*.

big bang *n* : **the ~** le big-bang, le big bang ■ **the Big Bang** ST. EX le Big Bang *(réforme et informatisation du système boursier à Londres, entrée en vigueur le 27 octobre 1986)*.

big bang theory *n* la théorie du big-bang *OR* big bang.

Big Ben [-ben] *pr n* Big Ben, *Nom de la cloche de la Tour de l'horloge à Westminster, souvent donné à tort à la tour ou à l'horloge elle-même.*

big-boned *adj* fortement charpenté.

Big Brother *pr n* Big Brother ■ **~ is watching you** Big Brother vous regarde.

big business *n (U)* les grandes entreprises *fpl*.

big cat *n* fauve *m*, grand félin *m*.

big deal *inf* ◇ *interj* : **~!** tu parles!
◇ *n* : **it's no ~** il n'y a pas de quoi en faire un plat!

Big Dipper *pr n US* ASTRON : **the ~** la Grande Ourse.
◆ **big dipper** *n* [in fairground] : **the big dipper** les montagnes *fpl* russes.

big end *n UK* tête *f* de bielle.

Bigfoot ['bɪgfʊt] *pr n sorte d'abominable homme des neiges qui vivrait dans le nord des États-Unis et au Canada.*

big game ◇ *n* gros gibier *m*.
◇ *comp* : **~ hunter** chasseur *m* de gros gibier.

biggie ['bɪgɪ] *n inf* [success - song] tube *m* ; [- film, record] succès *m*.

big gun *n inf* gros bonnet *m*.

bighead ['bɪghed] *n inf* crâneur *m*, - euse *f*.

bigheaded [,bɪg'hedɪd] *adj inf* crâneur ■ **to be ~** avoir la grosse tête.

bighearted [,bɪg'hɑ:tɪd] *adj* au grand cœur ■ **to be ~** avoir le cœur sur la main, avoir bon *OR* du cœur.

bight [baɪt] *n* **1.** [of shoreline] baie *f* **2.** [in rope - slack] mou *m* ; [- coil] boucle *f*.

Big Issue *pr n UK* PRESS : **the ~** *journal des sans-abri.*

bigmouth ['bɪgmaʊθ] *(pl* [-maʊðz]*)* *n inf* grande gueule *f* ■ **she's such a ~** elle ne sait pas la fermer.

big name *n* grand nom *m*.

big noise *n UK inf* gros bonnet *m*.

bigot ['bɪgət] *n* [gen] sectaire *mf*, intolérant *m*, - e *f* ■ RELIG bigot *m*, - e *f*, sectaire *mf*.

bigoted ['bɪgətɪd] *adj* [gen - person] sectaire, intolérant ; [- attitude, opinion] fanatique ■ RELIG bigot.

bigotry ['bɪgətrɪ] *n* [gen] sectarisme *m*, intolérance *f* ■ RELIG bigoterie *f*.

big screen *n* : **the ~** le grand écran, le cinéma.

big shot *n inf* gros bonnet *m*.

big smoke *n UK inf* : **the ~** [gen] la grande ville ; [London] Londres.

big stick *n* : **the ~** le bâton, la force ■ **~ diplomacy** politique *f* musclée.

big time *n inf* **to hit** *OR* **to make** *OR* **to reach the ~** arriver, réussir.
◆ **big-time** *adj inf* [actor, singer] à succès ■ [businessman, politician] de haut vol ■ [project] ambitieux, de grande échelle.

big-timer *n inf* gros bonnet *m*.

big toe *n* gros orteil *m*.

big top *n* [tent] grand chapiteau *m* ■ [circus] cirque *m*.

big wheel, bigwig ['bɪgwɪg] *n inf* gros bonnet *m*.

bijou ['bi:ʒu:] *adj UK pej & hum* chic.

bike [baɪk] *inf* ◇ *n* [bicycle] vélo *m*, bicyclette *f* ■ [motorcycle] moto *f* ■ **to ride a ~** [bicycle] faire du vélo *OR* de la bicyclette ; [motorcycle] faire de la moto ➤ **on your ~!** *UK inf* [go away] dégage! ; [don't be ridiculous] mais oui, c'est ça!
◇ *vi* [bicycle] faire du vélo ■ [motorcycle] faire de la moto.

biker ['baɪkəʳ] *n inf* motard *m*, motocycliste *mf*.

bikeway ['baɪkweɪ] *n US* piste *f* cyclable.

bikini [bɪ'ki:nɪ] *n* bikini *m*.

bikini line *n* : **to have one's ~ done** se faire faire une épilation maillot.

bilabial [,baɪ'leɪbjəl] ◇ *adj* bilabial.
◇ *n* bilabiale *f*.

bilateral [,baɪ'lætərəl] *adj* bilatéral.

bilberry ['bɪlbərɪ] *(pl* **bilberries***)* *n* myrtille *f*.

bile [baɪl] *n* **1.** ANAT bile *f* **2.** *lit* [irritability] mauvaise humeur *f*, irascibilité *f*.

bilge [bɪldʒ] *n* **1.** NAUT [hull] bouchain *m*, renflement *m* ▪ [hold] fond *m* de cale, sentine *f* ▪ [water] eau *f* de cale *OR* de sentine **2.** *inf (U) inf fig* [nonsense] âneries *fpl*, idioties *fpl*.

bilge water *n (U)* **1.** NAUT eau *f* de cale *OR* de sentine **2.** *inf fig* [nonsense] âneries *fpl*, idioties *fpl*.

bilharzia [bɪl'hɑːtsɪə] *n (U)* bilharziose *f*.

bilinear [baɪ'lɪnɪəʳ] *adj* bilinéaire.

bilingual [baɪ'lɪŋgwəl] *adj* bilingue ▪ **to be ~ in French and English** être bilingue français-anglais.

bilingualism [baɪ'lɪŋgwəlɪzm] *n* bilinguisme *m*.

bilious ['bɪljəs] *adj* MED bilieux ▪ **~ attack** crise *f* de foie.

bilk [bɪlk] *vt UK* **1.** [thwart - person] contrecarrer, contrarier les projets de ; [- plan] contrecarrer, contrarier **2.** [cheat] escroquer.

bill [bɪl] ◇ *n* **1.** [for gas, telephone] facture *f*, note *f* ▪ [for product] facture *f* ▪ [in restaurant] addition *f*, note *f* ▪ [in hotel] note *f* ▪ **may I have the ~ please?** l'addition, s'il vous plaît ▪ **put it on my ~** mettez-le sur ma note
2. [draft of law] projet *m* de loi ▪ **to introduce a ~ in Parliament** présenter un projet de loi au Parlement ▪ **to vote on a ~** mettre un projet de loi au vote
3. [poster] affiche *f*, placard *m*
4. THEAT affiche *f* ▪ **to head** *OR* **to top the ~** être en tête d'affiche *OR* en vedette
5. [list, statement] liste *f* ▪ **~ of fare** carte *f* (du jour) ▪ **~ of health** NAUT patente *f* (de santé) ▪ **the doctor gave him a clean ~ of health** *inf* le médecin l'a trouvé en parfaite santé ▪ **~ of lading** COMM connaissement *m* ▪ **to sell sb a ~ of goods** *inf US* rouler *OR* avoir qqn
6. COMM & FIN [promissory note] effet *m*, traite *f* ▪ **~s payable** effets à payer ▪ **~s receivable** effets à recevoir ➊ **~ of exchange** lettre *f OR* effet de change
7. *US* [banknote] billet *m* (de banque)
8. LAW : **~ of indictment** acte *m* d'accusation ▪ **~ of sale** acte *m OR* contrat *m* de vente
9. [beak] bec *m*
10. GEOG promontoire *m*, bec *m*
11. [weapon] hallebarde *f*
12. = **billhook**.
◇ *vt* **1.** [invoice] facturer ▪ **he ~s his company for his travel expenses** il se fait rembourser ses frais de voyage par son entreprise ▪ **~ me for the newspaper at the end of the month** envoyez-moi la facture pour le journal à la fin du mois
2. [advertise] annoncer ▪ **they're ~ed as the best band in the world** on les présente comme le meilleur groupe du monde
3. THEAT mettre à l'affiche, annoncer.
◇ *vi* : **to ~ and coo** [birds] se becqueter ; [people] roucouler.

billboard ['bɪlbɔːd] *n* panneau *m* (d'affichage).

bill broker *n* agent *m OR* courtier *m* de change.

billet ['bɪlɪt] ◇ *n* **1.** [accommodation] cantonnement *m* (chez l'habitant) ▪ [document] billet *m* de logement **2.** ARCHIT billette *f*.
◇ *vt* [gen] loger ▪ MIL cantonner, loger.

billfold ['bɪlfəʊld] *n US* portefeuille *m*.

billhook ['bɪlhʊk] *n* serpe *f*, serpette *f*.

billiard ['bɪljəd] *comp* de billard ▪ **~ table/hall** (table *f* /salle *f* de) billard *m*.
◆ **billiards** *n (U)* (jeu *m* de) billard *m* ▪ **to play (a game of) ~** jouer au billard.

billing ['bɪlɪŋ] *n* **1.** THEAT : **to get** *OR* **to have top/second ~** être en tête d'affiche/en deuxième place à l'affiche **2.** *US* [advertising] : **to give sthg advance ~** annoncer qqch **3.** *liter & fig* [sound] : **~ and cooing** roucoulements *mpl*.

billion ['bɪljən] (*pl inv OR pl* **billions**) *n* [thousand million] milliard *m* ▪ *UK dated* [million million] billion *m*.

billionaire [ˌbɪljə'neəʳ] *n* milliardaire *mf*.

Bill of Rights ◇ *n* déclaration *f* des droits de l'homme.
◇ *pr n* : **the ~** *les dix premiers amendements à la Constitution américaine garantissant, entre autres droits, la liberté d'expression, de religion et de réunion.*

billow ['bɪləʊ] ◇ *vi* [cloth, flag] onduler ▪ [sail] se gonfler ▪ [cloud, smoke] tourbillonner, tournoyer.
◇ *n* **1.** [of smoke] tourbillon *m*, volute *f* **2.** [wave] grosse vague *f*.
◆ **billow out** *vi insep* [sail, cloth] se gonfler.

billposter ['bɪlˌpəʊstəʳ], **billsticker** ['bɪlˌstɪkəʳ] *n* afficheur *m*, - euse *f*, colleur *m*, - euse *f* d'affiches.

billy ['bɪlɪ] (*pl* **billies**) *n* **1.** *US* [weapon] : **~ (club)** matraque *f* **2.** *UK & Australia* [pan] gamelle *f* **3.** *inf* [goat] bouc *m*.

billycan ['bɪlɪkæn] *n UK & Australia* gamelle *f*.

billy goat *n* bouc *m*.

billy-o(h) ['bɪlɪəʊ] *n UK inf* **he ran like ~** il a couru comme un dératé.

bimbo ['bɪmbəʊ] (*pl* **bimbos** *OR pl* **bimboes**) *n inf pej jeune femme sexy et un peu bête.*

bimetallism [ˌbaɪ'metəlɪzm] *n* bimétallisme *m*.

bimonthly [ˌbaɪ'mʌnθlɪ] ◇ *adj* [every two months] bimestriel ▪ [twice monthly] bimensuel.
◇ *adv* [every two months] tous les deux mois ▪ [twice monthly] deux fois par mois.
◇ *n* (*pl* **bimonthlies**) bimestriel *m*.

bin [bɪn] ◇ *n* **1.** *UK* [for rubbish] poubelle *f*, boîte *f* à ordures **2.** [for coal, grain] coffre *m* ▪ [for bread] huche *f* **3.** *UK* [for wine] casier *m* (à bouteilles).
◇ *vt* (*pret & pp* **binned**, *cont* **binning**) **1.** [coal, grain] mettre dans un coffre ▪ *UK* [wine] mettre à vieillir **2.** *UK inf* [discard] flanquer à la poubelle.

binal ['baɪnəl] *adj* double.

binary ['baɪnərɪ] *adj* [number, system] binaire.

binary star *n* binaire *f*.

binbag ['bɪnbæg] *n* sac-poubelle *m*.

bind [baɪnd] ◇ *vt* (*pret & pp* **bound** [baʊnd]) **1.** [tie] attacher, lier ▪ **he was bound hand and foot** il avait les pieds et les poings liés **2.** [encircle] entourer, ceindre ▪ **to ~ a wound** bander *OR* panser une blessure **3.** [provide with border] border **4.** [book] relier ▪ **the book is bound in leather** le livre est relié en cuir **5.** [stick together] lier, agglutiner ▪ **add eggs to ~ the sauce** CULIN ajouter des œufs pour lier la sauce **6.** *fig* [bond, unite] lier, attacher ▪ **they are bound by friendship** c'est l'amitié qui les unit ▪ **the two companies are bound by commercial interests** des intérêts commerciaux lient les deux sociétés **7.** [oblige] obliger, contraindre ▪ **we are bound to tell the truth** nous sommes obligés *OR* tenus de dire la vérité ▪ **to be bound by oath** être lié par serment **8.** [apprentice] mettre en apprentissage.
◇ *vi* (*pret & pp* **bound** [baʊnd]) **1.** [agreement, promise] engager ▪ [rule] être obligatoire **2.** [sauce] se lier ▪ [cement] durcir, prendre **3.** [mechanism] se gripper.
◇ *n* **1.** [bond] lien *m*, liens *mpl* **2.** MUS liaison *f* **3.** *inf* [annoying situation] corvée *f* ▪ **we're in a bit of a ~** nous sommes plutôt dans le pétrin.
◆ **bind over** *vt sep* **1.** [apprentice] mettre en apprentissage **2.** *UK* LAW [order] sommer ▪ **they were bound over to keep the peace** ils ont été sommés de ne pas troubler l'ordre public.
◆ **bind up** *vt sep* [tie - gen] attacher, lier ; [- wound] bander, panser.

binder ['baɪndəʳ] *n* **1.** [folder] classeur *m* **2.** [bookbinder] relieur *m*, - euse *f* **3.** [glue] colle *f* ▪ TECH liant *m*, aggloméTrant *m* **4.** AGRIC [machine] lieuse *f*.

binding ['baɪndɪŋ] ◇ *n* **1.** [for book] reliure *f* **2.** [folder] classeur *m* **3.** [for sewing] extrafort *m* **4.** [on skis] fixation *f*.
◇ *adj* **1.** [law] obligatoire ▪ [contract, promise] qui engage *OR* lie ▪ **the agreement is ~ on all parties** l'accord engage chaque partie ▪ **it is ~ on the buyer to make immediate payment** l'acheteur est tenu de payer immédiatement **2.** [food] constipant.

bindweed ['baɪndwiːd] *n* liseron *m*.

bin-end *n* fin *f* de série *(de vin)*.

binge [bɪndʒ] *inf* ◇ *n* **1.** [spree] : **to go on a ~** faire la bringue ■ **they went on a shopping ~** ils sont allés dépenser du fric dans les magasins ■ **an eating ~** une grosse bouffe **2.** [drinking bout] beuverie *f*, bringue *f*.
◇ *vi* **1.** [overindulge] faire des folies **2.** [overeat] faire des excès *(de nourriture)*.

binge drinking *n fait de boire de très grandes quantités d'alcool en une soirée, de façon régulière.*

bingo ['bɪŋgəʊ] ◇ *n* ≃ loto *m*.
◇ *interj* : **~!** ça y est!

BINGO

Ce jeu, très populaire en Grande-Bretagne et aux États-Unis, consiste à cocher des chiffres sur une carte jusqu'à ce qu'elle soit remplie ; les salles de bingo sont souvent d'anciens cinémas ou des salles municipales.

bin liner *n UK* sac *m* (à) poubelle.

binman ['bɪnmæn] (*pl* **binmen** [-men]) *n UK* éboueur *m*.

binnacle ['bɪnəkl] *n* habitacle *m*.

binocular [bɪ'nɒkjʊlər] *adj* binoculaire.
◆ **binoculars** *npl* jumelles *fpl*.

binomial [,baɪ'nəʊmjəl] ◇ *adj* binomial.
◇ *n* binôme *m*.

bint△ [bɪnt] *n UK pej* nana△ *f*.

bio ['baɪəʊ] *adj* bio *inv*.

bioactive [,baɪəʊ'æktɪv] *adj* bioactif.

biochemical [,baɪəʊ'kemɪkl] ◇ *adj* biochimique.
◇ *n* produit *m* biochimique.

biochemist [,baɪəʊ'kemɪst] *n* biochimiste *mf*.

biochemistry [,baɪəʊ'kemɪstrɪ] *n* biochimie *f*.

biodegradable [,baɪəʊdɪ'greɪdəbl] *adj* biodégradable.

biodiversity [,baɪəʊdaɪ'vɜ:sətɪ] *n* biodiversité *f*.

bioengineering ['baɪəʊ,endʒɪ'nɪərɪŋ] *n* génie *f* biologique.

bioethics [,baɪəʊ'eθɪks] *n (sg)* bioéthique *f*.

biofeedback [,baɪəʊ'fi:dbæk] *n* biofeedback *m*.

biographer [baɪ'ɒgrəfər] *n* biographe *mf*.

biographical [,baɪə'græfɪkl] *adj* biographique.

biography [baɪ'ɒgrəfɪ] *n* biographie *f*.

biological [,baɪə'lɒdʒɪkl] *adj* biologique ■ **~ warfare** guerre *f* bactériologique.

biological clock *n* horloge *f* interne biologique.

biological mother *n* mère *f* biologique.

biological weapon *n* arme *f* biologique.

biologist [baɪ'ɒlədʒɪst] *n* biologiste *mf*.

biology [baɪ'ɒlədʒɪ] *n* biologie *f*.

biome ['baɪəʊm] *n* biome *m*.

biometric [,baɪəʊ'metrɪk] *adj* [data, identifier, reader] biométrique.

bionic [baɪ'ɒnɪk] *adj* bionique.

bionics [baɪ'ɒnɪks] *n (U)* bionique *f*.

biophysicist [,baɪəʊ'fɪzɪsɪst] *n* biophysicien *m*, - enne *f*.

biophysics [,baɪəʊ'fɪzɪks] *n (U)* biophysique *f*.

biopsy ['baɪɒpsɪ] (*pl* **biopsies**) *n* biopsie *f*.

biorhythm ['baɪəʊ,rɪðm] *n* biorythme *m*.

biosphere ['baɪəʊ,sfɪər] *n* biosphère *f*.

biotech [,baɪəʊtek] ◇ *n* biotechnologie *f*.
◇ *adj* [industry] des biotechnologies ■ [company] spécialisé dans les biotechnologies.

biotechnology [,baɪəʊtek'nɒlədʒɪ] *n* biotechnologie *f*.

bioterrorism [,baɪəʊ'terərɪzm] *n* bioterrorisme *m*.

biotype ['baɪətaɪp] *n* biotype *m*.

biowarfare [,baɪəʊ'wɔ:feə] *n* guerre *f* biologique.

bipartisan [,baɪpɑ:tɪ'zæn] *adj* biparti, bipartite.

bipartite [,baɪ'pɑ:taɪt] *adj* BIOL & POL biparti, bipartite.

biped ['baɪped] ◇ *adj* bipède.
◇ *n* bipède *m*.

biplane ['baɪpleɪn] *n* biplan *m*.

bipolar disorder [baɪ'pəʊlədɪs,ɔ:dər] *n* MED trouble *m* bipolaire.

birch [bɜ:tʃ] ◇ *n* **1.** [tree] bouleau *m* ■ [wood] (bois *m* de) bouleau **2.** *UK* [rod for whipping] verge *f* ■ **to give sb the ~** fouetter qqn.
◇ *comp* [forest, furniture] de bouleau.
◇ *vt* fouetter.

birching ['bɜ:tʃɪŋ] *n UK* correction *f*.

bird [bɜ:d] *n* **1.** [gen] oiseau *m* ■ CULIN volaille *f* ■ **she eats like a ~** elle a un appétit d'oiseau ▶ **~ of paradise** [bird, flower] oiseau de paradis ■ **~ of passage** *liter & fig* oiseau de passage ■ **~ of prey** oiseau de proie, rapace *m* ■ **a little ~ told me** mon petit doigt me l'a dit ■ **strictly for the ~s** bon pour les imbéciles ■ **the ~s and the bees** *euph & hum* les choses de la vie ■ **the ~ has flown** l'oiseau s'est envolé ■ **to give sb the ~** *UK inf* [gen] envoyer paître qqn ; THEAT siffler qqn ■ **~s of a feather flock together** *prov* qui se ressemble s'assemble *prov* ■ **a ~ in the hand is worth two in the bush** *prov* un tiens vaut mieux que deux tu l'auras *prov* **2.** *UK inf* [chap] type *m* **3.** *UK inf* [woman] nana△ *f*.

birdbath ['bɜ:dbɑ:θ] (*pl* [-bɑ:ðz]) *n* vasque *f (pour les oiseaux)*.

bird brain *n inf pej* tête *f* de linotte, écervelé *m*, - e *f*.

bird-brained [-breɪnd] *adj inf* [person] écervelé, qui a une cervelle d'oiseau ■ [idea] insensé.

birdcage ['bɜ:dkeɪdʒ] *n* [small] cage *f* à oiseaux ■ [large] volière *f*.

birdcall ['bɜ:dkɔ:l] *n* cri *m* d'oiseau.

bird dog *n* chien *m* d'arrêt *(pour le gibier à plumes)*.

bird fancier *n UK* [interested in birds] ornithologue *mf* amateur ■ [breeder] aviculteur *m*, - trice *f*.

bird flu *n* grippe *f* aviaire.

birdhouse ['bɜ:dhaʊs] (*pl* [-haʊzɪz]) *n US* volière *f*.

birdie ['bɜ:dɪ] *n* **1.** *inf* [small bird] petit oiseau *m*, oisillon *m* ■ **watch the ~!** PHOT le petit oiseau va sortir! **2.** [in golf] birdie *m*.

bird-nesting *n* : **to go ~** aller dénicher des oiseaux.

bird sanctuary *n* réserve *f* OR refuge *m* d'oiseaux.

birdseed ['bɜ:dsi:d] *n* graine *f* pour les oiseaux.

bird's-eye ◇ *adj* : **a ~ view of sthg** *liter* une vue panoramique de qqch ; *fig* une vue d'ensemble de qqch.
◇ *n* **1.** BOT [primrose] primevère *f* farineuse **2.** [cloth] œil-de-perdrix *m*.

bird's-foot *n* BOT pied-d'oiseau *m*.

bird's-nest soup *n* soupe *f* aux nids d'hirondelles.

birdsong ['bɜ:dsɒŋ] *n* chant *m* d'oiseau.

birdtable ['bɜ:d,teɪbl] *n* mangeoire *f (pour oiseaux)*.

bird-watcher *n* ornithologue *mf* amateur.

bird-watching *n* ornithologie *f* ■ **to go ~** aller observer les oiseaux.

biretta [bɪ'retə] *n* barrette *f (d'un ecclésiastique)*.

Biro® ['baɪərəʊ] (*pl* **biros**) *n UK* stylo *m* (à) bille, ≃ Bic® *m*.

birth [bɜ:θ] *n* **1.** [nativity] naissance *f* ■ **deaf from ~** sourd de naissance **2.** [of child] accouchement *m*, couches *fpl* ■ [of animal] mise *f* bas ■ **to give ~** [woman] accoucher ; [animal] mettre bas ■ **she gave ~ to a boy** elle a accouché d'un garçon ▶ **~ pangs** douleurs *fpl* de l'accouchement ■ **the ~ pangs of democracy** *fig* la naissance difficile de la démocratie **3.** *fig* [origin - of movement, nation] naissance *f*, origine *f* ; [- of era, industry] naissance *f*, commencement *m* ; [- of product, radio] apparition *f* **4.** [ancestry, lineage] naissance *f*, ascendance *f* ■ **he's Chinese by ~** il est chinois de naissance ■ **of high ~** de bonne famille, bien né ■ **of low ~** de basse extraction.

birth certificate *n* acte *m* OR extrait *m* de naissance.

birth control *n* **1.** [contraception] contraception *f* ■ **to practise ~** utiliser un contraceptif *OR* un moyen de contraception **2.** [family planning] contrôle *m* des naissances.

birthday [ˈbɜːθdeɪ] ◇ *n* anniversaire *m* ■ **her 21st ~** ses 21 ans.
◇ *comp* [cake, card, present] d'anniversaire ■ **they're giving him a ~ party** ils organisent une fête pour son anniversaire.

Birthday Honours *npl* : **the ~** *titres honorifiques et autres distinctions décernés chaque année le jour de l'anniversaire officiel du souverain britannique.*

birthday suit *n inf hum* [of man] costume *m* d'Adam ■ [of woman] costume *m* d'Ève.

birthmark [ˈbɜːθmɑːk] *n* tache *f* de vin.

birth mother *n* mère *f* gestationnelle.

birthplace [ˈbɜːθpleɪs] *n* [town] lieu *m* de naissance ■ [house] maison *f* natale ■ *fig* berceau *m*.

birthrate [ˈbɜːθreɪt] *n* (taux *m* de) natalité *f*.

birthright [ˈbɜːθraɪt] *n* droit *m* (acquis à la naissance) ■ **freedom of speech is every citizen's ~** la liberté d'expression constitue un droit pour chaque citoyen.

birthstone [ˈbɜːθstəʊn] *n* pierre *f* porte-bonheur *(selon la date de naissance).*

Biscay [ˈbɪskeɪ] *pr n* Biscaye ■ **the Bay of ~** le golfe de Gascogne.

biscuit [ˈbɪskɪt] ◇ *n* **1.** *UK* CULIN biscuit *m*, petit gâteau *m* ■ **that really takes the ~!** *inf* ça, c'est vraiment le bouquet! **2.** *US* CULIN *petit gâteau que l'on mange avec de la confiture ou avec un plat salé* **3.** [colour] beige *m* **4.** [ceramics] biscuit *m*.
◇ *adj* (de couleur) beige.

bisect [baɪˈsekt] *vt* [gen] couper en deux ■ MATHS diviser en deux parties égales.

bisexual [ˌbaɪˈsekʃʊəl] ◇ *adj* **1.** [person, tendency] bisexuel **2.** BIOL & ZOOL bisexué, hermaphrodite.
◇ *n* **1.** [person] bisexuel *m*, - elle *f* **2.** BIOL & ZOOL hermaphrodite *m*.

bisexuality [baɪˌseksjʊˈælɪtɪ] *n* bisexualité *f*.

bishop [ˈbɪʃəp] *n* **1.** RELIG évêque *m* **2.** [in chess] fou *m*.

bishopric [ˈbɪʃəprɪk] *n* [position] épiscopat *m* ■ [diocese] évêché *m*.

Bismarck [ˈbɪzmɑːk] *pr n* Bismarck.

bison [ˈbaɪsn] *n* bison *m*.

bisque [bɪsk] *n* **1.** [colour] beige-rosé *m* **2.** [ceramics] biscuit *m* **3.** [soup] bisque *f*.

bistro [ˈbiːstrəʊ] (*pl* **bistros**) *n* bistro *m*.

bit[1] [bɪt] *n* **1.** [piece - of cake, puzzle, wood, land, string] bout *m* ; [- of book] passage *m* ; [- of film] séquence *f* ■ **you missed out the best ~s** [of story, joke] tu as oublié le meilleur ■ **~s and pieces of sthg** des morceaux de qqch ■ **she picked up her ~s and pieces** elle a ramassé ses affaires ■ **in ~s** en morceaux ■ **to take sthg to ~s** démonter qqch ■ **to fall to ~s** [book, clothes] tomber en lambeaux
2. [unspecified (small) quantity] : **a ~ of money/time** un peu d'argent/de temps ■ **there's been a ~ of trouble at home** il y a eu quelques problèmes à la maison ■ **it's a ~ of a problem** cela pose un problème ■ **he's a ~ of a crook** il est un peu escroc sur les bords ▶ **to do one's ~** y mettre du sien, faire un effort ■ **everyone did their ~** tout le monde y a mis du sien *OR* a fait un effort ■ **we did our ~ to help the children** nous avons fait ce qu'il fallait pour aider les enfants ■ **she's every ~ as competent as he is** elle est tout aussi compétente que lui ■ **to have a ~ on the side** *inf* avoir un amant/une maîtresse ■ **he's/she's a ~ of all right!**△ *UK* il/elle est chouette!
3. *inf* [role] numéro *m*
4. *inf* [small coin] pièce *f*
5. *US* [coin] *ancienne pièce de 12,5 cents*
6. [for horse] mors *m* ■ **to take the ~ between one's teeth** *fig* prendre le mors aux dents
7. [of drill] mèche *f*
8. COMPUT bit *m*.

◆ **a bit** *adv phr* **1.** [some time] quelque temps ■ **let's sit down for a ~** asseyons-nous un instant *OR* un peu ■ **he's away quite a ~** il est souvent absent
2. [slightly] un peu ■ **she's a good/little ~ older than he is** elle est beaucoup/un peu plus âgée que lui ■ [at all] : **they haven't changed a ~** ils n'ont pas du tout changé ■ **not a ~ of it!** pas le moins du monde! ▶ **it's asking a ~ much to expect her to apologize** il ne faut pas s'attendre à des excuses, c'est trop lui demander ■ **that's a ~ much** *OR* **a ~ steep!** ça c'est un peu fort!

◆ **bit by bit** *adv phr* petit à petit.

bit[2] [bɪt] *pt* ▷ **bite**.

bitch [bɪtʃ] ◇ *n* **1.** [female canine - gen] femelle *f* ■ [dog] chienne *f* ■ [fox] renarde *f* ■ [wolf] louve *f* **2.** △ *pej* [woman] garce△ *f* **3.** *inf* [thing] saloperie△ *f* ■ **a ~ of a job** une saloperie de boulot ■ **this problem's a real ~** c'est un vrai casse-tête! **4.** *inf* [complaint] motif *m* de râler.
◇ *vi inf* râler, rouspéter ■ **to ~ about sb/sthg** râler *OR* rouspéter contre qqn/qqch.

bitchy [ˈbɪtʃɪ] (*comp* **bitchier**, *superl* **bitchiest**) *adj inf UK* ▲ *US* vache ■ **a ~ remark** une vacherie ■ **he's in a ~ mood** il est dans une sale humeur.

bite [baɪt] (*pret* **bit** [bɪt], *pp* **bitten** [ˈbɪtn]) ◇ *vt* **1.** [subj: animal, person] mordre ■ [subj: insect, snake] piquer, mordre ■ **the dog bit him on the leg** le chien l'a mordu à la jambe ■ **the dog bit the rope in two** le chien a coupé la corde en deux avec ses dents ■ **to ~ one's nails** se ronger les ongles ■ **he bit his lip** il s'est mordu la lèvre ■ **they've been bitten by the photography bug** *fig* ils sont devenus des mordus de photographie ▶ **to ~ one's tongue** *liter* se mordre la langue ; *fig* se retenir de dire qqch ■ **to ~ the bullet** serrer les dents ■ **to ~ the dust** mordre la poussière ■ **theirs is the latest plan to ~ the dust** leur projet est le dernier à être tombé à l'eau ■ **to ~ the hand that feeds one** montrer de l'ingratitude envers qqn qui vous veut du bien ■ **once bitten, twice shy** *prov* chat échaudé craint l'eau froide *prov* **2.** *inf fig* [bother] agacer, contrarier.
◇ *vi* **1.** [animal, person] mordre ■ [insect, snake] piquer, mordre ■ [fish] mordre (à l'hameçon) ■ **I bit into the apple** j'ai mordu dans la pomme ■ **he bit through the cord** il coupa la ficelle avec ses dents **2.** [mustard, spice] piquer **3.** [air, wind] mordre, cingler **4.** [clutch, screw] mordre ■ [tyre] adhérer (à la route) ■ **the acid bit into the metal** l'acide a attaqué le métal ■ **the rope bit into his wrists** la corde mordait dans la chair de ses poignets **5.** [take effet] : **the law is beginning to ~** les effets de la loi commencent à se faire sentir.
◇ *n* **1.** [of animal, person] morsure *f* ■ [of insect, snake] piqûre *f*, morsure *f* **2.** [piece] bouchée *f* ■ **to take a ~ of sthg** [bite into] mordre dans qqch ; [taste] goûter (à) qqch ▶ **to have** *OR* **to get another** *OR* **a second ~ at the cherry** *UK* s'y reprendre à deux fois **3.** *inf* [something to eat] : **we stopped for a ~ (to eat)** nous nous sommes arrêtés pour manger un morceau ■ **I haven't had a ~ all day** je n'ai rien mangé de la journée **4.** FISHING touche *f* ■ **did you get a ~?** ça a mordu? **5.** [sharpness - of mustard, spice] piquant *m* ; [- of speech, wit] mordant *m* ; [- of air, wind] caractère *m* cinglant *OR* mordant **6.** DENT articulé *m* dentaire.

◆ **bite back** *vt sep* : **to ~ sthg back** se retenir de dire qqch.

◆ **bite off** *vt sep* arracher d'un coup de dents ▶ **to ~ off more than one can chew** avoir les yeux plus grands *OR* gros que le ventre ■ **to ~ sb's head off** *inf* enguirlander qqn.

bite-sized [-ˌsaɪzd] *adj* : **cut the meat into ~ pieces** coupez la viande en petits dés.

biting [ˈbaɪtɪŋ] *adj* **1.** [insect] piqueur, vorace **2.** *fig* [remark, wit] mordant, cinglant ■ [wind] cinglant, mordant ■ [cold] mordant, perçant.

bitingly [ˈbaɪtɪŋlɪ] *adj* d'un ton mordant *OR* cinglant ■ [as intensifier] : **a ~ cold wind** un vent glacial.

bit map [ˈbɪtmæp] *n* mode *m* points ■ **~ screen** écran *m* pixel.

bitmapped [ˈbɪtmæpt] *adj* [image] en mode points.

bit part *n* THEAT petit rôle *m*.

bitten [ˈbɪtn] *pp* ▷ **bite**.

bitter [ˈbɪtəʳ] ◇ *adj* **1.** [taste] amer, âpre ▶ **it's a ~ pill (to swallow)** c'est difficile à avaler **2.** [resentful - person] amer ; [- look, tone] amer, plein d'amertume ; [- reproach, tears] amer ■ **to be ~ about sthg** être amer *OR* plein d'amertume au sujet

de qqch **3.** [unpleasant - disappointment, experience] amer, cruel ; [- argument, struggle] violent ; [- blow] dur ■ **we fought to the ~ end** nous avons lutté jusqu'au bout **4.** [extreme - enemy] acharné ; [- opposition] violent, acharné ; [- remorse] cuisant **5.** [cold - wind] cinglant, glacial ; [- weather] glacial ; [- winter] rude, dur.
◇ *n* [beer] *bière pression relativement amère, à forte teneur en houblon.*
◆ **bitters** *npl* bitter *m*, amer *m* ■ PHARM amer *m*.

bitter lemon *n* Schweppes® *m* au citron.

bitterly ['bɪtəlɪ] *adv* **1.** [speak] amèrement, avec amertume ■ [criticize] âprement ■ [weep] amèrement **2.** [intensely - ashamed, unhappy] profondément ; [- disappointed] cruellement ■ **it was a ~ cold day** il faisait un froid de loup.

bittern ['bɪtən] *n* butor *m (oiseau).*

bitterness ['bɪtənɪs] *n* **1.** [of disappointment, person, taste] amertume *f* ■ [of criticism, remark] âpreté *f* **2.** [of opposition] violence *f*.

bittersweet ['bɪtəswi:t] ◇ *adj* [memory, taste] aigre-doux.
◇ *n* BOT douce-amère *f*.

bitty ['bɪtɪ] (*comp* **bittier**, *superl* **bittiest**) *adj* *UK inf* décousu.

bitumen ['bɪtjumɪn] *n* bitume *m*.

bivalent ['baɪ,veɪlənt] *adj* bivalent.

bivalve ['baɪvælv] ◇ *adj* bivalve.
◇ *n* bivalve *m*.

bivouac ['bɪvʊæk] ◇ *n* bivouac *m*.
◇ *vi* (*pret & pp* **bivouacked**, *cont* **bivouacking**) bivouaquer.

biweekly [,baɪ'wi:klɪ] ◇ *adj* [every two weeks] bimensuel ■ [twice weekly] bihebdomadaire.
◇ *adv* [every two weeks] tous les quinze jours ■ [twice weekly] deux fois par semaine.
◇ *n* (*pl* **biweeklies**) bimensuel *m*.

biyearly [,baɪ'jɪəlɪ] ◇ *adj* [every two years] biennal ■ [twice yearly] semestriel.
◇ *adv* [every two years] tous les deux ans ■ [twice yearly] deux fois par an.
◇ *n* (*pl* **biyearlies**) biennale *f*.

biz [bɪz] *n inf* commerce *m*.

bizarre [bɪ'zɑ:ʳ] *adj* bizarre.

bk *written abbr of* **book**.

bl *written abbr of* **bill of lading**.

BL *n* **1.** (*abbrev of* **Bachelor of Law(s)**) *(titulaire d'une) licence de droit* **2.** (*abbrev of* **Bachelor of Letters**) *(titulaire d'une) licence de lettres.*

blab [blæb] (*pret & pp* **blabbed**, *cont* **blabbing**) *inf* ◇ *vi* **1.** [tell secret] vendre la mèche **2.** [prattle] jaser, babiller.
◇ *vt* laisser échapper, divulguer.

blabber ['blæbəʳ] *inf* ◇ *vi* jaser, babiller ■ **to ~ on about sthg** parler de qqch à n'en plus finir.
◇ *n* **1.** [person] moulin *m* à paroles **2.** [prattle] bavardage *m*, papotage *m*.

blabbermouth ['blæbə,maʊθ] (*pl* [,maʊðz]) *n inf* pipelette *f*.

black [blæk] ◇ *adj* **1.** [colour] noir ■ **as ~ as ink** noir comme du jais *OR* de l'encre
2. [race] noir ■ **he won the ~ vote** il a gagné les voix de l'électorat noir ➊ **~ man** Noir *m* ■ **~ woman** Noire *f* ■ **~ Africa** l'Afrique *f* noire ■ **~ American** Afro-Américain *m*, - e *f* ■ **~ consciousness** négritude *f* ■ **Black Nationalism** *mouvement nationaliste noir américain* ■ **Black Studies** UNIV *études afro-américaines*
3. [coffee] noir ■ [tea] nature *(inv)*
4. [dark] noir, sans lumière ■ **the room was as ~ as pitch** *UK OR* **as ~ as tar** *US* dans la pièce il faisait noir comme dans un four
5. [gloomy - future, mood] noir ; [- despair] sombre ■ **they painted a ~ picture of our prospects** ils ont peint un sombre tableau de notre avenir ■ **in a fit of ~ despair** dans un moment d'extrême désespoir ➊ **~ comedy** comédie *f* noire ■ **~ humour** humour *m* noir
6. [angry] furieux, menaçant ■ **he gave her a ~ look** il lui a jeté *OR* lancé un regard noir
7. [wicked] noir, mauvais ■ **a ~ deed** un crime, un forfait ■ **he's not as ~ as he's painted** il n'est pas aussi mauvais qu'on le dit ➊ **the ~ art** *OR* **arts** la magie noire
8. [dirty] noir, sale ■ **her hands were ~ with ink** elle avait les mains pleines d'encre
9. *UK* INDUST [factory, goods] boycotté ■ **~ economy** économie *f* noire.
◇ *n* **1.** [colour] noir *m* ■ **to be dressed in ~** [gen] être habillé de *OR* en noir ; [in mourning] porter le deuil
2. [darkness] obscurité *f*, noir *m*
3. *phr* **to be in the ~** être créditeur.
◇ *vt* **1.** [make black] noircir ■ [shoes] cirer *(avec du cirage noir)* ■ **he ~ed his attacker's eye** il a poché l'œil de son agresseur
2. *UK* INDUST boycotter.
◆ **Black** *n* [person] Noir *m*, - e *f*.
◆ **black out** ◇ *vt sep* **1.** [extinguish lights] plonger dans l'obscurité ■ [in wartime] faire le black-out dans
2. RADIO & TV [programme] interdire la diffusion de
3. [memory] effacer (de son esprit), oublier.
◇ *vi* s'évanouir.

black and blue *adj* couvert de bleus ■ **they beat him ~** ils l'ont roué de coups.

black and white ◇ *adj* **1.** [photograph, television] noir et blanc ■ **a black-and-white film** un film en noir et blanc **2.** *fig* [clear-cut] précis, net ■ **there's no black-and-white solution** le problème n'est pas simple.
◇ *n* **1.** [drawing, print] dessin *m* en noir et blanc ■ [photograph] photographie *f* en noir et blanc **2.** [written down] : **to put sthg down in ~** écrire qqch noir sur blanc.

blackball ['blækbɔ:l] ◇ *vt* blackbouler.
◇ *n* vote *m* contre.

black beetle *n* cafard *m*, blatte *f*.

black belt *n* ceinture *f* noire ■ **she's a ~ in judo** elle est ceinture noire de judo.

blackberry ['blækbərɪ] ◇ *n* (*pl* **blackberries**) mûre *f*.
◇ *vi* cueillir des mûres ■ **to go ~ing** aller ramasser *OR* cueillir des mûres.

Blackberry® *n* Blackberry® *m*.

blackbird ['blækbɜ:d] *n* merle *m* ■ [in North America] étourneau *m*.

blackboard ['blækbɔ:d] *n* tableau *m* (noir).

black box *n* boîte *f* noire.

black cab *n* taxi *m* londonien.

blackcap ['blækkæp] *n* **1.** ORNITH fauvette *f* à tête noire **2.** *UK* [of judge] bonnet *m* noir.

Black Country *pr n* : **the ~** le Pays noir.

THE BLACK COUNTRY

Le *Black Country* désigne, en Grande-Bretagne, la région industrielle des West Midlands, à l'ouest de Birmingham.

blackcurrant [,blæk'kʌrənt] *n* [bush, fruit] cassis *m*.

Black Death *n* peste *f* noire.

blacken ['blækn] ◇ *vt* **1.** [make black - house, wall] noircir ; [- shoes] cirer *(avec du cirage noir)* ■ **he ~ed his face** il s'est noirci le visage **2.** [make dirty] noircir, salir **3.** *fig* [name, reputation] noircir, ternir.
◇ *vi* [cloud, sky] s'assombrir, (se) noircir ■ [colour, fruit] (se) noircir, devenir noir.

black eye *n* œil *m* poché *OR* au beurre noir ■ **I'll give him a ~!** je vais lui faire un œil au beurre noir!

black-eyed pea *n* dolique *m*, dolic *m*, niébé *m*.

blackfly ['blækflaɪ] (*pl inv OR pl* **blackflies**) *n* puceron *m* noir.

Black Forest *pr n* : **the ~** la Forêt noire.

Black Forest gateau *n* forêt-noire *f*.

blackguard ['blægɑ:d] *n dated & hum* canaille *f*.

blackhead ['blækhed] *n* point *m* noir.

black hole *n* ASTRON trou *m* noir.

black ice *n* verglas *m*.

blacking ['blækɪŋ] *n* [for shoes] cirage *m* noir ■ [for stove] pâte *f* à noircir.

blackjack ['blækdʒæk] *n* [card game] vingt-et-un *m*.

blackleg ['blækleg] <> *n UK pej* jaune *m*, briseur *m* de grève.
<> *vi* (*pret & pp* **blacklegged**, *cont* **blacklegging**) briser la grève.

blacklist ['blæklɪst] <> *n* liste *f* noire.
<> *vt* mettre sur la liste noire.

black magic *n* magie *f* noire.

blackmail ['blækmeɪl] <> *vt* faire chanter ■ **he ~ed them into meeting his demands** il les a contraints par le chantage à satisfaire ses exigences.
<> *n* chantage *m*.

blackmailer ['blækmeɪlər] *n* maître chanteur *m*.

Black Maria [-mə'raɪə] *n inf* panier *m* à salade *(fourgon)*.

black mark *n* mauvais point *m* ■ **it's a ~ against her** ça joue contre elle.

black market *n* marché *m* noir ■ **on the ~** au marché noir.

black marketeer *n* vendeur *m*, - euse *f* au marché noir.

Black Monday *n* lundi *m* noir.

Black Muslim *n* Black Muslim *mf (membre d'un mouvement séparatiste noir se réclamant de l'Islam)*.

blackness ['blæknɪs] *n* [of colour] noir *m*, couleur *f* noire ■ *fig* [of deed] atrocité *f*, noirceur *f*.

blackout ['blækaʊt] *n* **1.** [in wartime] black-out *m inv* ■ [power failure] panne *f* d'électricité **2.** [loss of consciousness] évanouissement *m*, étourdissement *m* ■ [amnesia] trou *m* de mémoire ■ **I must have had a ~** j'ai dû m'évanouir **3.** RADIO & TV black-out *m inv*, censure *f* ■ **the army imposed a news ~ on the war** l'armée a fait le black-out sur la guerre.

Black Panther *n* HIST Panthère *f* noire.

black pepper *n* poivre *m* gris.

Blackpool ['blækpu:l] *pr n station balnéaire du nord-ouest de l'Angleterre, célèbre pour ses attractions et pour ses illuminations nocturnes.*

Black Power *n* POL Black Power *m (mouvement séparatiste noir né dans les années 60 aux États-Unis)*.

black pudding *n* boudin *m* (noir).

Black Sea *pr n* : **the ~** la mer Noire.

black sheep *n* brebis *f* galeuse.

Blackshirt ['blækʃɜ:t] *n* POL Chemise *f* noire.

blacksmith ['blæksmɪθ] *n* [for horses] maréchal-ferrant *m* ■ [for tools] forgeron *m*.

black spot *n UK fig* & AUT point *m* noir.

blackthorn ['blækθɔ:n] *n* prunelier *m*, épine *f* noire.

black tie *n nœud papillon noir porté avec une tenue de soirée* ■ **'black tie'** [on invitation card] 'tenue de soirée exigée'.
◆ **black-tie** *adj* : **it's black-tie** il faut être en smoking.

blacktop ['blæktɒp] *n US* bitume *m*, asphalte *m*.

black velvet *n* **1.** *liter* velours *m* noir **2.** [cocktail] *cocktail de champagne et de stout*.

black widow *n* latrodecte *m*, veuve *f* noire.

bladder ['blædər] <> *n* **1.** ANAT vessie *f* ■ **to have a weak ~** devoir uriner fréquemment **2.** [of leather, skin] vessie *f* **3.** BOT vésicule *f*.
<> *comp* : **~ infection** cystite *f*.

blade [bleɪd] *n* **1.** [cutting edge - of knife, razor, tool] lame *f* ; [- of guillotine] couperet *m* **2.** [of fan] pale *f* ■ [of propeller] pale *f*, aile *f* ■ [of helicopter] hélice *f* ■ [of turbine motor] aube *f* ■ [of plough] soc *m* (tranchant) ■ [of ice skates] lame *f* ■ [of oar, paddle] plat *m*, pale *f* **3.** [of grass] brin *m* ■ [of wheat] pousse *f* ■ [of leaf] limbe *m* ■ **wheat in the ~** blé *m* en herbe **4.** *lit* [sword] lame *f* **5.** *arch* [young man] gaillard *m* **6.** [of tongue] dos *m* **7.** [of shoulder] omoplate *f*.

-bladed [bleɪdɪd] *in cpds* **1.** [knife, razor] à lame... ■ **sharp~ knife** couteau *m* aiguisé **2.** [fan, propeller] à pale... **3.** [plant] à limbe... ■ **broad~ leaf** feuille *f* à limbe large.

blaeberry ['bleɪbərɪ] (*pl* **blaeberries**) *n UK* myrtille *f*.

blah [blɑ:] *inf* <> *n* **1.** [talk] baratin *m*, bla-bla-bla *m inv* **2.** *US* [blues] : **to have the ~s** avoir le cafard.
<> *adj US* **1.** [uninteresting] insipide, ennuyeux **2.** [blue] : **to feel ~** avoir le cafard.

Blairism ['bleərɪzm] *n politique du Premier ministre britannique socialiste Tony Blair.*

Blairite ['bleəraɪt] <> *n* partisan *m* de la politique de Tony Blair.
<> *adj* [views, policies] du gouvernement de Tony Blair.

blamable ['bleɪməbl] *adj* blâmable.

blame [bleɪm] <> *n* **1.** [responsibility] responsabilité *f*, faute *f* ■ **they laid** *OR* **put the ~ for the incident on the secretary** ils ont rejeté la responsabilité de l'incident sur la secrétaire ■ **we had to bear** *OR* **to take the ~** nous avons dû endosser la responsabilité **2.** [reproof] blâme *m*, réprimande *f* ■ **her conduct has been without ~** sa conduite a été irréprochable.
<> *vt* **1.** [consider as responsible] rejeter la responsabilité sur ■ **he is not to ~** ce n'est pas de sa faute ■ **you have only yourself to ~** tu ne peux t'en prendre qu'à toi-même, tu l'as voulu *OR* cherché **2.** [reproach] critiquer, reprocher ■ **I ~ myself for having left her alone** je m'en veux de l'avoir laissée seule ■ **you have nothing to ~ yourself for** tu n'as rien à te reprocher ■ **he left in disgust – I don't ~ him!** il est parti dégoûté – ça se comprend!

blamed [bleɪmd] *adj US* damné, maudit.

blameless ['bleɪmlɪs] *adj* irréprochable, sans reproche.

blamelessly ['bleɪmlɪslɪ] *adv* d'une façon irréprochable.

blameworthy ['bleɪm,wɜ:ðɪ] *adj fml* [person] fautif, coupable ■ [action] répréhensible.

blanch [blɑ:ntʃ] <> *vt* [gen] décolorer, blanchir ■ AGRIC & CULIN blanchir ■ **~ed almonds** amandes *fpl* mondées *OR* épluchées.
<> *vi* blêmir.

blancmange [blə'mɒndʒ] *n entremets généralement préparé à partir d'une poudre*, ≃ flan *m* instantané.

bland [blænd] *adj* **1.** [flavour, food] fade, insipide ■ [diet] fade **2.** [person - dull] insipide, ennuyeux ; [- ingratiating] mielleux, doucereux **3.** [weather] doux, douce *f*.

blandishment ['blændɪʃmənt] *n (usu pl)* [coaxing] cajoleries *fpl* ■ [flattery] flatterie *f*.

blandly ['blændlɪ] *adv* [say - dully] affablement, avec affabilité ; [- ingratiatingly] d'un ton mielleux.

blank [blæŋk] <> *adj* **1.** [paper - with no writing] vierge, blanc, blanche *f* ; [- unruled] blanc, blanche *f* ■ [form] vierge, à remplir ■ **fill in the ~ spaces** remplissez les blancs *OR* les (espaces) vides ■ **leave this line ~** n'écrivez rien sur cette ligne **2.** [empty - screen, wall] vide ; [- cassette] vierge ; [- cartridge] à blanc ■ **to go ~** [screen] s'éteindre ; [face] se vider de toute expression ■ **my mind went ~** j'ai eu un trou **3.** [face, look - expressionless] vide, sans expression ; [- confused] déconcerté, dérouté **4.** [absolute - protest, refusal] absolu, net ; [- dismay] absolu, profond.
<> *n* **1.** [empty space, void] blanc *m*, (espace *m*) vide *m* ■ **she filled in the ~s of her education** elle a comblé les lacunes de son éducation ■ **the rest of his life is a ~** on ne sait rien du reste de sa vie ■ **my mind was a total ~** j'ai eu un passage à vide complet ▶ **to draw a ~** avoir un trou *OR* un passage à vide ■ **she searched everywhere for him but drew a ~** elle l'a cherché partout mais sans succès **2.** [form] formulaire *m* (vierge *OR* à remplir), imprimé *m* **3.** [cartridge] cartouche *f* à blanc **4.** [in dominoes] blanc *m*.
◆ **blank out** *vt sep* [writing] rayer, effacer ■ [memory] oublier, effacer de son esprit.

blank cheque *n* chèque *m* en blanc ■ **to write sb a ~** *fig* donner carte blanche à qqn.

blanket ['blæŋkɪt] ◇ *n* **1.** [for bed] couverture *f* **2.** *fig* [of clouds, snow] couche *f* ▪ [of fog] manteau *m*, nappe *f* ▪ [of smoke] voile *m*, nuage *m* ▪ [of despair, sadness] manteau *m*.
◇ *vt* **1.** [subj: snow] recouvrir ▪ [subj: fog, smoke] envelopper, voiler **2.** [noise] étouffer, assourdir.
◇ *adj* général, global ▪ **our insurance policy guarantees ~ coverage** notre police d'assurance couvre tous les risques.

blanket bath *n* grande toilette *f (d'un malade alité)*.

blanket stitch *n* point *m* de feston.

blankly ['blæŋklɪ] *adv* **1.** [look - without expression] avec le regard vide ; [- with confusion] d'un air ahuri OR interdit **2.** [answer, state] carrément ▪ [refuse] tout net, sans ambages.

blank verse *n* vers *mpl* blancs OR sans rime.

blare [bleəʳ] ◇ *vi* [siren, music] beugler ▪ [voice] brailler.
◇ *n* [gen] vacarme *m* ▪ [of car horn, siren] bruit *m* strident ▪ [of radio, television] beuglement *m* ▪ [of trumpet] sonnerie *f*.
◆ **blare out** ◇ *vi insep* [radio, television] beugler, brailler ▪ [person, voice] brailler, hurler.
◇ *vt sep* [subj: radio, television] beugler, brailler ▪ [subj: person] brailler, hurler.

blarney ['blɑ:nɪ] *inf* ◇ *n* [smooth talk] baratin *m* ▪ [flattery] flatterie *f*.
◇ *vt* [smooth talk] baratiner ▪ [wheedle] embobiner ▪ [flatter] flatter.

blasé [*UK* 'blɑ:zeɪ, *US* ˌblɑ:'zeɪ] *adj* blasé.

blaspheme [blæs'fi:m] ◇ *vi* blasphémer.
◇ *vt* blasphémer.

blasphemous ['blæsfəməs] *adj* [poem, talk] blasphématoire ▪ [person] blasphémateur.

blasphemy ['blæsfəmɪ] (*pl* **blasphemies**) *n* blasphème *m*.

blast [blɑ:st] ◇ *n* **1.** [explosion] explosion *f* ▪ [shock wave] souffle *m* **2.** [of air] bouffée *f* ▪ [of steam] jet *m* ▪ **a ~ (of wind)** un coup de vent, une rafale **3.** [sound - of car horn, whistle] coup *m* strident ; [- of trumpet] sonnerie *f* ; [- of explosion] détonation *f* ; [- of rocket] rugissement *m* ▪ **a whistle ~** un coup de sifflet **4.** *US inf* [fun] : **we had a ~** on s'est vraiment marrés **5.** *phr* **at full ~ : she had the radio on (at) full ~** elle faisait marcher la radio à fond ▪ **the machine was going at full ~** la machine avançait à toute allure.
◇ *vt* **1.** [with explosives] faire sauter ▪ **they ~ed a tunnel through the mountain** ils ont creusé un tunnel à travers la montagne avec des explosifs **2.** [with gun] tirer sur ▪ **the thieves ~ed their way through the roadblock** les voleurs ont forcé le barrage routier en tirant des coups de feu **3.** [subj: radio, television] beugler **4.** BOT [blight] flétrir **5.** [criticize] attaquer OR critiquer violemment **6.** [plan] détruire ▪ [hope] briser, anéantir.
◇ *vi* [radio, television] beugler ▪ [music] retentir ▪ **the radio was ~ing away** la radio marchait à fond.
◇ *interj inf* **~!** zut! ▪ **~ her!** ce qu'elle peut être embêtante!
◆ **blast off** *vi insep* [rocket] décoller.
◆ **blast out** ◇ *vt sep* [music] beugler.
◇ *vi insep* [radio, television] beugler ▪ [music] retentir.

blasted ['blɑ:stɪd] *adj* **1.** [plant] flétri ▪ **a ~ oak** un chêne foudroyé **2.** *inf* [as intensifier] fichu, sacré ▪ **you ~ fool!** espèce d'imbécile! ▪ **it's a ~ nuisance!** c'est vraiment casse-pieds!

blast furnace *n* haut-fourneau *m*.

blasting ['blɑ:stɪŋ] *n* **1.** [explosions] travail *m* aux explosifs, explosions *fpl* ▪ TECH minage *m* ▪ **'beware ~ in progress!'** 'attention, tirs de mines!' **2.** *UK inf* [verbal attack] attaque *f* ▪ **he got a ~ from the boss** le patron lui a passé un sacré savon.

blast-off *n* lancement *m*, mise *f* à feu *(d'une fusée spatiale)*.

blatant ['bleɪtənt] *adj* [discrimination, injustice] évident, flagrant ▪ [lie] manifeste.

blatantly ['bleɪtəntlɪ] *adv* [discriminate, disregard] de façon flagrante ▪ [cheat, lie] de façon éhontée.

blather ['blæðəʳ] *US* ◇ *n (U)* âneries *fpl*, bêtises *fpl*.
◇ *vi* raconter des bêtises OR des âneries.

blaze [bleɪz] ◇ *n* **1.** [flame] flamme *f*, flammes *fpl*, feu *m* ▪ [large fire] incendie *m* ▪ **five die in ~** [in headline] un incendie a fait cinq morts
2. [burst - of colour] éclat *m*, flamboiement *m* ; [- of light] éclat *m* ; [- of eloquence, enthusiasm] élan *m*, transport *m* ; [- of sunlight] torrent *m* ▪ **a ~ of gunfire** des coups de feu, une fusillade ▪ **in a sudden ~ of anger** sous le coup de la colère ▪ **she married in a ~ of publicity** elle s'est mariée sous les feux des projecteurs ▪ **he finished in a ~ of glory** il a terminé en beauté
3. [of gems] éclat *m*, brillance *f*
4. [mark - on tree] marque *f*, encoche *f* ; [- on animal, horse] étoile *f*
5. *UK inf phr* **what the ~s are you doing here?** qu'est-ce que tu fabriques ici? ▪ **we ran like ~s** nous avons couru à toutes jambes ▪ **go to ~s!** *inf* va te faire voir!
◇ *vi* **1.** [fire] flamber ▪ **he suddenly ~d with anger** il s'est enflammé de colère
2. [colour, light, sun] flamboyer ▪ [gem] resplendir, briller
3. [gun] tirer, faire feu.
◇ *vt* **1.** [proclaim] proclamer, claironner ▪ [publish] publier ▪ **the news was ~d across the front page** la nouvelle faisait la une du journal ▪ **it's not the kind of thing you want ~d abroad** ce n'est pas le genre de chose qu'on veut crier sur les toits
2. *phr* **to ~ a trail** frayer un chemin ▪ **they're blazing a trail in biotechnology** ils font un travail de pionniers dans le domaine de la biotechnologie.
◆ **blaze away** *vi insep* **1.** [fire] (continuer de) flamber
2. *UK* [gun] faire feu ▪ **the gangsters ~d away at the police** les gangsters maintenaient un feu nourri contre la police.

blazer ['bleɪzəʳ] *n* blazer *m*.

blazing ['bleɪzɪŋ] *adj* **1.** [building, town] en flammes, embrasé ▪ **to sit in front of a ~ fire** s'installer devant une bonne flambée **2.** [sun] brûlant, ardent ▪ [heat] torride ▪ **a ~ hot day** une journée de chaleur torride **3.** [light] éclatant ▪ [colour] très vif ▪ [gem] brillant, étincelant ▪ [eyes] qui jette des éclairs **4.** [argument] violent **5.** [angry] furieux.

blazon ['bleɪzn] ◇ *n* blason *m*.
◇ *vt* **1.** [proclaim] proclamer, claironner **2.** [mark] marquer ▪ HERALD blasonner.

bleach [bli:tʃ] ◇ *n* [gen] décolorant *m* ▪ **household ~** eau *f* de Javel.
◇ *vt* **1.** [gen] blanchir ▪ **~ing agent** produit *m* à blanchir, décolorant *m* **2.** [hair - chemically] décolorer, oxygéner ; [- with sun] éclaircir ▪ **to ~ one's hair** se décolorer les cheveux ▪ **a ~ed blonde** une fausse blonde, une blonde décolorée.
◇ *vi* blanchir.

bleachers ['bli:tʃəz] *npl US dans un stade, places les moins chères car non abritées.*

bleak [bli:k] ◇ *adj* **1.** [place, room] froid, austère ▪ [landscape] morne, désolé **2.** [weather] morne, maussade ▪ [winter] rude, rigoureux **3.** [situation] sombre, morne ▪ [life] morne, monotone ▪ **the ~ facts** la vérité toute nue OR sans fard ▪ **the future looks ~** l'avenir se présente plutôt mal **4.** [mood, person] lugubre, morne ▪ [smile] pâle ▪ [tone, voice] monocorde, morne.
◇ *n* [fish] ablette *f*.

bleakness ['bli:knɪs] *n* **1.** [of furnishings, room] austérité *f* ▪ [of landscape] caractère *m* morne OR désolé **2.** [of weather] caractère *m* morne OR maussade ▪ [of winter] rigueurs *fpl* **3.** [of situation] caractère *m* sombre OR peu prometteur ▪ [of life] monotonie *f* **4.** [of mood, person] tristesse *f* ▪ [of voice] ton *m* monocorde OR morne.

bleary ['blɪərɪ] (*comp* **blearier**, *superl* **bleariest**) *adj* **1.** [eyes - from fatigue] trouble, voilé ; [- watery] larmoyant ▪ [vision] trouble **2.** [indistinct] indécis, vague.

bleary-eyed [-'aɪd] *adj* [from sleep] aux yeux troubles ▪ [watery-eyed] aux yeux vitreux.

bleat [bli:t] ◇ *vi* **1.** [sheep] bêler ▪ [goat] bêler, chevroter **2.** [person - speak] bêler, chevroter ; [- whine] geindre, bêler.
◇ *vt* [say] dire d'un ton bêlant ▪ [whine] geindre, bêler.
◇ *n* **1.** [of sheep] bêlement *m* ▪ [of goat] bêlement, chevrotement *m* **2.** [of person - voice] bêlement *m* ; [- complaint] gémissement *m*.

bled [bled] *pt* & *pp* ▷ **bleed**.

bleed [bli:d] ◇ *vi* (*pret* & *pp* **bled** [bled]) **1.** [lose blood] saigner, perdre du sang ▪ **to ~ to death** saigner à mort ▪ **my nose is**

~ing je saigne du nez ▪ **my heart ~s for you!** *fig & iron* tu me fends le cœur! **2.** [plant] pleurer, perdre sa sève **3.** [cloth, colour] déteindre.
◇ *vt* (*pret & pp* **bled** [bled]) **1.** [person] saigner **2.** *fig* [extort money from] saigner ▪ **to ~ sb dry** *OR* **white** saigner qqn à blanc **3.** [brake, radiator] purger.
◇ *n* TYPO fond *m* perdu, plein papier *m*.

bleeder ['bli:dər] *n UK inf* [person - gen] type *m* ; [- disagreeable] salaud△ *m*.

bleeding ['bli:dɪŋ] ◇ *n* **1.** [loss of blood] saignement *m* ▪ [haemorrhage] hémorragie *f* ▪ [taking of blood] saignée *f* **2.** [of plant] écoulement *m* de sève.
◇ *adj* **1.** [wound] saignant, qui saigne ▪ [person] qui saigne **2.** △ *UK* [as intensifier] fichu, sacré.
◇ *adv*△ vachement.

bleeding heart *n pej* [gen - POL] sentimental *m*.

bleep [bli:p] ◇ *n* bip *m*, bip-bip *m*.
◇ *vi* émettre un bip *OR* un bip-bip.
◇ *vt* **1.** [doctor] appeler (au moyen d'un bip *OR* d'un bip-bip) **2.** RADIO & TV : **to ~ words (out)** masquer des paroles (par un bip).

bleeper ['bli:pər] *n* bip *m*, bip-bip *m*.

blemish ['blemɪʃ] ◇ *n* **1.** [flaw] défaut *m*, imperfection *f* **2.** [on face - pimple] bouton *m* **3.** [on fruit] tache *f* **4.** *fig* [on name, reputation] tache *f*, souillure *f lit*.
◇ *vt* **1.** [beauty, landscape] gâter ▪ [fruit] tacher **2.** *fig* [reputation] tacher, souiller *lit*.

blench [blentʃ] *vi* [recoil in fear] reculer ▪ [turn pale] blêmir.

blend [blend] ◇ *vt* **1.** [mix together - gen] mélanger, mêler ; [- cultures, races] fusionner ; [- feelings, qualities] joindre, unir ▪ **~ the butter and sugar (together), ~ the sugar into the butter** mélangez le beurre au *OR* avec le sucre ▪ **~ed whisky** blend *m (whisky obtenu par mélange de whiskies de grain industriels et de whiskies pur malt)* **2.** [colours - mix together] mêler, mélanger ; [- put together] marier ▪ **to ~ white and black** mélanger du blanc avec du noir.
◇ *vi* **1.** [mix together - gen] se mélanger, se mêler ; [- cultures, races] fusionner ; [- feelings, sounds] se confondre, se mêler ; [- perfumes] se marier ▪ **the new student ~ed in well** le nouvel étudiant s'est bien intégré **2.** [colours - form one shade] se fondre ; [- go well together] aller ensemble.
◇ *n* **1.** [mixture] mélange *m* ▪ **'house ~'** 'mélange (spécial de la) maison' **2.** *fig* [of feelings, qualities] alliance *f*, mélange *m* **3.** LING mot-valise *m*.

blender ['blendər] *n* CULIN mixer *m* ▪ TECH malaxeur *m*.

bless [bles] (*pret & pp* **blessed**) *vt* **1.** [subj: God, priest] bénir ▪ **God ~ (you)!, ~ you!** *liter* que Dieu vous bénisse! ▪ **~ you!** [after sneeze] à vos/tes souhaits! ; [in thanks] merci mille fois! ▪ **he remembered her birthday, ~ his heart!** et il n'a pas oublié son anniversaire, le petit chéri! ▪ **~ my soul!, ~ me!** *dated* Seigneur!, mon Dieu! ▪ **~ me if I didn't forget her name!** figurez-vous que j'avais oublié son nom! ▪ **I'm ~ed if I know!** *inf* que le diable m'emporte si je sais! ▪ **God ~ America** *phrase traditionnellement prononcée par le président des États-Unis pour terminer une allocution* **2.** *(usu passive) fml* [endow, grant] douer, doter ▪ **she is ~ed with excellent health** elle a le bonheur d'avoir une excellente santé.

blessed ◇ *pt & pp* ▻ **bless**.
◇ *adj* ['blesɪd] **1.** [holy] béni, sacré ▪ **the Blessed Virgin** la Sainte Vierge **2.** [favoured by God] bienheureux, heureux **3.** [wonderful - day, freedom, rain] béni **4.** *inf* [as intensifier] sacré, fichu ▪ **every ~ day** chaque jour que le bon Dieu fait.
◇ *npl* [blest] : **the ~** les bienheureux *mpl*.

blessing ['blesɪŋ] *n* **1.** [God's favour] grâce *f*, faveur *f* **2.** [prayer] bénédiction *f* ▪ [before meal] bénédicité *m* ▪ **the priest said the ~** le prêtre a donné la bénédiction **3.** *fig* [approval] bénédiction *f*, approbation *f* **4.** [advantage] bienfait *m*, avantage *m* ▪ [godsend] aubaine *f*, bénédiction *f* ▪ **it was a ~ that no one was hurt** c'était une chance que personne ne soit blessé ▪ **the rain was a ~ for the farmers** la pluie était un don du ciel *OR* une bénédiction pour les agriculteurs ▪ **what a ~!** quelle chance! ▪ **it was a ~ in disguise** c'était une bonne chose, en fin de compte.

blether ['bleðər] ◇ *n* âneries *fpl*, bêtises *fpl*.
◇ *vi* dire des âneries *OR* des bêtises.

blew [blu:] *pt* ▻ **blow**.

blight [blaɪt] ◇ *n* **1.** BOT [of flowering plants] rouille *f* ▪ [of fruit trees] cloque *f* ▪ [of cereals] rouille, nielle *f* ▪ [of potato plants] mildiou *m* **2.** [curse] malheur *m*, fléau *m* ▪ **the accident cast a ~ on our holiday** l'accident a gâché nos vacances **3.** [condition of decay] : **inner-city ~** la dégradation des quartiers pauvres.
◇ *vt* **1.** BOT [plants - gen] rouiller ▪ [cereals] nieller, rouiller **2.** [spoil - happiness, holiday] gâcher ; [- career, life] gâcher, briser ; [- hopes] anéantir, détruire ; [- plans] déjouer.

blighter ['blaɪtər] *n UK inf* type *m*.

blighty, Blighty ['blaɪtɪ] *n UK inf dated* l'Angleterre *f*.

blimey ['blaɪmɪ] *interj UK inf* **~!** ça alors!, mon Dieu!

blind [blaɪnd] ◇ *adj* **1.** [sightless] aveugle, non voyant ▪ **to go ~** devenir aveugle ▪ **he's ~ in one eye** il est aveugle d'un œil *OR* borgne ➤ **as ~ as a bat** myope comme une taupe ▪ **~ man's buff** colin-maillard *m* ▪ **to turn a ~ eye to sthg** fermer les yeux sur qqch
2. [unthinking] aveugle ▪ **he flew into a ~ rage** il s'est mis dans une colère noire ▪ **~ with anger** aveuglé par la colère ▪ **she was ~ to the consequences** elle ignorait les conséquences, elle ne voyait pas les conséquences ▪ **love is ~** l'amour est aveugle
3. [hidden from sight - corner, turning] sans visibilité
4. AERON [landing, take-off] aux appareils
5. [as intensifier] : **he was ~ drunk** il était ivre mort ▪ **he didn't take a ~ bit of notice of what I said** *inf* il n'a pas fait la moindre attention à ce que j'ai dit ▪ **it doesn't make a ~ bit of difference to me** *inf* cela m'est complètement égal.
◇ *vt* **1.** [deprive of sight] aveugler, rendre aveugle ▪ [subj: flash of light] aveugler, éblouir
2. [deprive of judgment, reason] aveugler ▪ **vanity ~ed him to her real motives** sa vanité l'empêchait de discerner ses véritables intentions ▪ **to ~ sb with science** *hum* éblouir qqn par sa science.
◇ *n* **1.** [for window] store *m*, jalousie *f*
2. *UK inf* [trick] prétexte *m*, feinte *f*
3. *US* [hiding place] cachette *f* ▪ HUNT affût *m*.
◇ *npl* : **the ~** les aveugles *mpl*, les non-voyants *mpl* ▪ **it's a case of the ~ leading the ~** c'est l'aveugle qui conduit l'aveugle.
◇ *adv* **1.** [drive, fly - without visibility] sans visibilité ; [- using only instruments] aux instruments
2. [purchase] sans avoir vu ▪ [decide] à l'aveuglette
3. [as intensifier] : **I would swear ~ he was there** j'aurais donné ma tête à couper *OR* j'aurais juré qu'il était là.

blind alley *n UK* impasse *f*, cul-de-sac *m* ▪ **the government's new idea is just another ~** *fig* encore une idée du gouvernement qui n'aboutira à rien *OR* ne mènera nulle part.

blind date *n* rendez-vous *m OR* rencontre *f* arrangée *(avec quelqu'un qu'on ne connaît pas)*.

blinders ['blaɪndərz] *npl US* œillères *fpl*.

blindfold ['blaɪndfəʊld] ◇ *n* bandeau *m*.
◇ *vt* bander les yeux à *OR* de.
◇ *adv* les yeux bandés ▪ **I could do the job ~** je pourrais faire ce travail les yeux bandés *OR* fermés.
◇ *adj* : **~** *OR* **~ed prisoners** prisonniers aux yeux bandés.

blinding ['blaɪndɪŋ] ◇ *adj* [light] aveuglant, éblouissant ▪ *fig* [speed] éblouissant.
◇ *n* **1.** [of person, animal] aveuglement *m* **2.** CONSTR [on road] couche *f* de sable.

blindingly ['blaɪndɪŋlɪ] *adv* de façon aveuglante ▪ **it was ~ obvious** ça sautait aux yeux.

blindly ['blaɪndlɪ] *adv* [unseeingly] en aveugle, à l'aveuglette ▪ [without thinking] à l'aveuglette, aveuglément.

blindness ['blaɪndnɪs] *n* cécité *f* ▪ *fig* aveuglement *m*.

blind side *n* AUT angle *m* mort ▪ **on my ~** dans mon angle mort.

blind spot *n* **1.** AUT [in mirror] angle *m* mort ■ [in road] endroit *m* sans visibilité **2.** MED point *m* aveugle **3.** *fig* [weak area] côté *m* faible, faiblesse *f* ■ **I have a ~ about mathematics** je ne comprends rien aux mathématiques.

blindworm ['blaɪndwɜ:m] *n* orvet *m*.

bling (bling) ['blɪŋ ('blɪŋ)] *inf* <> *n* [jewellery] bijoux *mpl*, quincaillerie *f*.
<> *adj* [ostentatious] tape-à-l'œil.

blink [blɪŋk] <> *vi* **1.** [person] cligner *OR* clignoter des yeux ■ [eyes] cligner, clignoter ■ **she didn't even ~ at the news** *fig* elle n'a même pas sourcillé en apprenant la nouvelle **2.** [light] clignoter, vaciller.
<> *vt* **1.** : **to ~ one's eyes** cligner les *OR* des yeux ■ **to ~ away** *OR* **to ~ back one's tears** refouler ses larmes *(en clignant des yeux)* **2.** *US* **to ~ one's lights** faire un appel de phares.
<> *n* **1.** [of eyelid] clignement *m* (des yeux), battement *m* de paupières ■ **in the ~ of an eye** *OR* **eyelid** en un clin d'œil, en un rien de temps **2.** [glimpse] coup *m* d'œil **3.** [of light] lueur *f* ■ [of sunlight] rayon *m* **4.** *inf phr* **on the ~** *inf* en panne.

blinker ['blɪŋkər] <> *n* AUT : **~ (light)** [turn signal] clignotant *m* ; [warning light] feu *m* de détresse.
<> *vt* mettre des œillères à.
◆ **blinkers** *npl* [for eyes] œillères *fpl* ■ **when it comes to her family she wears ~s** elle a des œillères quand il s'agit de sa famille.

blinkered ['blɪŋkəd] *adj* **1.** [horse] qui porte des œillères **2.** [opinion, view] borné.

blinking ['blɪnkɪŋ] *inf* <> *adj UK euph* sacré, fichu ■ **~ idiot!** espèce d'idiot!
<> *adv* sacrément, fichtrement.

blip [blɪp] <> *n* **1.** [sound] bip *m*, bip-bip *m* ■ [spot of light] spot *m* ■ [on graph, screen etc] sommet *m* **2.** [temporary problem] mauvais moment *m* (à passer).
<> *vi* faire bip *OR* bip-bip.

bliss [blɪs] *n* **1.** [happiness] bonheur *m* (complet *OR* absolu), contentement *m*, félicité *f lit* ■ **our holiday was absolute ~!** on a passé des vacances absolument merveilleuses *OR* divines! ■ **married ~** le bonheur conjugal **2.** RELIG béatitude *f*.

blissful ['blɪsfʊl] *adj* **1.** [happy] bienheureux ■ [peaceful] serein ■ **she remained in ~ ignorance** elle était heureuse dans son ignorance **2.** RELIG bienheureux.

blissfully ['blɪsfʊlɪ] *adv* [agree, smile] d'un air heureux ■ [peaceful, quiet] merveilleusement ■ **he was ~ happy** il était comblé de bonheur ■ **we were ~ unaware of the danger** nous étions dans l'ignorance la plus totale du danger.

blister ['blɪstər] <> *n* **1.** [on skin] ampoule *f*, cloque *f* **2.** [on painted surface] boursouflure *f* ■ [in glass] soufflure *f*, bulle *f* ■ [in metal] soufflure *f*.
<> *vi* **1.** [skin] se couvrir d'ampoules **2.** [paint] se boursoufler ■ [glass] former des soufflures *OR* des bulles ■ [metal] former des soufflures.
<> *vt* **1.** [skin] donner des ampoules à **2.** [paint] boursoufler ■ [glass] former des soufflures *OR* des bulles dans ■ [metal] former des soufflures dans **3.** [attack verbally] critiquer sévèrement.

blistering ['blɪstərɪŋ] *adj* **1.** [sun] brûlant, de plomb ■ [heat] torride **2.** [attack, criticism] cinglant, virulent ■ [remark] caustique, cinglant.

blister pack *n UK* [for light bulb, pens] emballage *m* bulle, blister (pack) *m* ■ [for pills] plaquette *f*.

BLit [ˌbi:'lɪt] (*abbrev of* **Bachelor of Literature**) *n (titulaire d'une) licence de littérature.*

blithe [blaɪð] *adj* [cheerful] gai, joyeux ■ [carefree] insouciant.

blithely ['blaɪðlɪ] *adv* [cheerfully] gaiement, joyeusement ■ [carelessly] avec insouciance.

blithering ['blɪðərɪŋ] *adj inf* sacré ■ **a ~ idiot** un crétin fini.

BLitt [ˌbi:'lɪt] (*abbrev of* **Bachelor of Letters**) *n UK (titulaire d'une) licence de littérature.*

blitz [blɪts] <> *n* [attack] attaque *f* éclair ■ [bombing] bombardement *m* ■ **an advertising ~** une campagne publicitaire de choc ■ **let's have a ~ and get this work done** attaquons-nous à ce travail pour en finir.
<> *vt* [attack] pilonner ■ [bomb] bombarder.
◆ **Blitz** *n* HIST : **the Blitz** le Blitz.

blizzard ['blɪzəd] *n* tempête *f* de neige, blizzard *m*.

bloated ['bləʊtɪd] *adj* [gen] gonflé, boursouflé ■ [stomach] gonflé, ballonné ■ **to feel ~** se sentir ballonné.

blob [blɒb] *n* [drop] goutte *f* ■ [stain] tache *f*.

bloc [blɒk] *n* bloc *m*.

block [blɒk] <> *n* **1.** [of ice, stone, wood] bloc *m* ■ [for butcher, executioner] billot *m* ■ **the painting was on the (auctioneer's) ~** *US* le tableau était mis aux enchères ➊ **to put** *OR* **to lay one's head on the ~** prendre des risques **2.** [toy] : **(building) ~s** jeu *m* de construction, (jeu de) cubes *mpl* **3.** [of seats] groupe *m* ■ [of shares] tranche *f* ■ [of tickets] série *f* ■ COMPUT bloc *m* **4.** [area of land] pâté *m* de maisons ■ **the school is five ~s away** *US* l'école est cinq rues plus loin ➊ **the new kid on the ~** le petit nouveau **5.** *UK* [building] immeuble *m* ■ [of barracks, prison] quartier *m* ■ [of hospital] pavillon *m* ■ **~ of flats** immeuble (d'habitation) **6.** [obstruction - in pipe, tube] obstruction *f* ; [- in traffic] embouteillage *m* ■ MED & PSYCHOL blocage *m* ■ **to have a (mental) ~ about sthg** faire un blocage sur qqch ➊ **he's suffering from writer's ~** il n'arrive pas à écrire, c'est le vide *OR* le blocage total **7.** SPORT obstruction *f* **8.** *inf* [head] caboche *f* ■ **I'll knock your ~ off!** je vais te démolir le portrait! **9.** [of paper] bloc *m* **10.** TECH : **~ (and tackle)** palan *m*, moufles *mpl*.
<> *comp* [booking, vote] groupé.
<> *vt* **1.** [obstruct - pipe, tube] boucher ; [- road] bloquer, barrer ; [- view] boucher, cacher ■ MED [-artery] obstruer ■ **don't ~ the door!** dégagez la porte! ■ **to ~ sb's way** barrer le chemin à qqn **2.** [hinder - traffic] bloquer, gêner ; [- progress] gêner, enrayer ; [- credit, deal, funds] bloquer ■ MED [pain] anesthésier ■ SPORT [opponent] faire obstruction à **3.** [hat, knitting] mettre en forme.
<> *vi* SPORT faire de l'obstruction.
◆ **block in** *vt sep* **1.** [car] bloquer ■ **I've been ~ed in** ma voiture est bloquée **2.** [drawing, figure] colorer ■ *fig* [plan, scheme] ébaucher.
◆ **block off** *vt sep* [road] bloquer, barrer ■ [door, part of road, window] condamner ■ [view] boucher, cacher ■ [sun] cacher.
◆ **block out** *vt sep* **1.** [light, sun] empêcher d'entrer ■ [view] cacher, boucher **2.** [ideas] empêcher ■ [information] interdire, censurer **3.** [outline] ébaucher.
◆ **block up** *vt sep* **1.** [pipe, tube] boucher, bloquer ■ [sink] boucher **2.** [door, window] condamner.

blockade [blɒ'keɪd] <> *n* **1.** MIL blocus *m* ■ **to lift** *OR* **to raise a ~** lever un blocus ■ **to be under ~** être en état de blocus **2.** *fig* [obstacle] obstacle *m*.
<> *vt* **1.** MIL faire le blocus de **2.** *fig* [obstruct] bloquer, obstruer.

blockage ['blɒkɪdʒ] *n* [gen] obstruction *f* ■ [in pipe] obstruction *f*, bouchon *m* ■ MED [in heart] blocage *m*, obstruction *f* ■ [in intestine] occlusion *f* ■ PSYCHOL blocage *m*.

blockbuster ['blɒkbʌstər] *n inf* **1.** [success - book] best-seller *m*, livre *m* à succès ; [- film] superproduction *f* **2.** [bomb] bombe *f* de gros calibre.

block capital *n* (caractère *m*) majuscule *f* ■ **in ~s** en majuscules.

block diagram *n* COMPUT & GEOG bloc-diagramme *m* ■ ELECTRON schéma *m* (de principe).

blockhead ['blɒkhed] *n inf* imbécile *mf*, idiot *m*, - e *f*.

block vote *n mode de scrutin utilisé par les syndicats britanniques par opposition au mode de scrutin "OMOV".*

BLOCK VOTE

Le *block vote* donne au vote d'un délégué syndical la valeur de toutes les voix de la section qu'il représente.

blog ['blɒg] *n* COMPUT blogue *m*.

blogger ['blɒgər] *n* COMPUT bloggeur *m*, - euse *f*.

blogging ['blɒgɪŋ] *n* COMPUT blogging *m*, création *f* de blogs.

bloke [bləʊk] *n UK inf* type *m*.

blokeish ['bləʊkɪʃ], **blokey** ['bləʊkɪ] *adj inf* [behaviour, humour] de mec ▪ [joke] macho.

blond [blɒnd] <> *adj* blond.
<> *n* blond *m*.

blonde [blɒnd] <> *adj* blond.
<> *n* blond *m*, - e *f*.

blood [blʌd] <> *n* **1.** [fluid] sang *m* ▪ **to donate** *OR* **to give ~** donner son sang ▪ **to spill ~** verser *OR* faire couler du sang ▪ **she bit him and drew ~** elle l'a mordu (jusqu')au sang ▪ **his last question drew ~** *fig* sa dernière question a fait mouche ▪ **he has ~ on his hands** *fig* il a du sang sur les mains ▶ **the mafia are after his ~** *inf* la mafia veut sa peau ▪ **there is bad ~ between the two families** le torchon brûle entre les deux familles ▪ **the argument made for bad ~ between them** la dispute les a brouillés ▪ **his attitude makes my ~ boil** son attitude me met hors de moi ▪ **it's like getting ~ out of a stone** ce n'est pas une mince affaire ▪ **her ~ froze** *OR* **ran cold at the thought** rien qu'à y penser son sang s'est figé dans ses veines ▪ **the town's ~ is up over these new taxes** la ville s'élève *OR* part en guerre contre les nouveaux impôts ▪ **to do sthg in cold ~** faire qqch de sang-froid ▪ **travelling is** *OR* **runs in her ~** elle a le voyage dans le sang *OR* dans la peau ▪ **what we need is new** *OR* **fresh** *OR* **young ~** nous avons besoin d'un *OR* de sang nouveau ▪ **they're out for ~** ils cherchent à se venger ▪ **~ is thicker than water** *prov* la voix du sang est la plus forte **2.** [breeding, kinship] : **of noble/Italian ~** de sang noble/italien.
<> *vt* **1.** HUNT [hound] acharner, donner le goût du sang à ▪ [person] donner le goût du sang à **2.** *fig* [beginner, soldier] donner le baptême du feu à.

blood-and-thunder *adj* [adventure] à sensation ▪ [melodramatic] mélodramatique.

blood bank *n* banque *f* du sang.

bloodbath ['blʌdbɑ:θ] (*pl* [-bɑ:ðz]) *n* massacre *m*, bain *m* de sang.

blood blister *n* pinçon *m*.

blood brother *n* frère *m* de sang.

blood cell *n* cellule *f* sanguine, globule *m* (du sang).

blood count *n* numération *f* globulaire.

bloodcurdling ['blʌd,kɜ:dlɪŋ] *adj* terrifiant ▪ **a ~ scream** un cri à vous glacer *OR* figer le sang.

blood donor *n* donneur *m*, - euse *f* de sang.

blood feud *n* vendetta *f*.

blood group *n* groupe *m* sanguin.

bloodhound ['blʌdhaʊnd] *n* **1.** [dog] limier *m* **2.** *inf* [detective] limier *m*, détective *m*.

bloodiness ['blʌdɪnɪs] *n* état *m* sanglant ▪ **the ~ of war** les carnages de la guerre.

bloodless ['blʌdlɪs] *adj* **1.** [without blood] exsangue **2.** [battle, victory] sans effusion de sang ▪ **the Bloodless Revolution** HIST la Seconde Révolution d'Angleterre *(1688-1689)* **3.** [cheeks, face] pâle.

bloodletting ['blʌd,letɪŋ] *n* **1.** [bloodshed] carnage *m*, massacre *m* **2.** MED saignée *f*.

blood money *n* prix *m* du sang.

blood orange *n* (orange *f*) sanguine *f*.

blood plasma *n* plasma *m* sanguin.

blood poisoning *n* septicémie *f*.

blood pressure *n* tension *f* (artérielle) ▪ **the doctor took my ~** le médecin m'a pris la tension ▪ **to have high/low ~** faire de l'hypertension/de l'hypotension ▪ **her ~ goes up every time she talks politics** *fig* elle se met en colère chaque fois qu'elle parle politique.

blood red *adj* rouge sang *(inv)*.

blood relation *n* parent *m*, - e *f* par le sang.

blood serum *n* sérum *m* sanguin.

bloodshed ['blʌdʃed] *n* carnage *m*, massacre *m* ▪ **without ~** sans effusion *f* de sang.

bloodshot ['blʌdʃɒt] *adj* injecté (de sang).

blood sport *n UK* sport *m* sanguinaire.

bloodstain ['blʌdsteɪn] *n* tache *f* de sang.

bloodstained ['blʌdsteɪnd] *adj* taché de sang.

bloodstream ['blʌdstri:m] *n* sang *m*, système *m* sanguin.

bloodsucker ['blʌd,sʌkər] *n* ZOOL & *fig* sangsue *f*.

blood sugar *n* glycémie *f* ▪ **blood-sugar level** taux *m* de glycémie.

blood test *n* analyse *f* de sang.

bloodthirsty ['blʌd,θɜ:stɪ] (*comp* **bloodthirstier**, *superl* **bloodthirstiest**) *adj* [animal, person] assoiffé *OR* avide de sang, sanguinaire *lit* ▪ [film] violent, sanguinaire *lit*.

blood transfusion *n* transfusion *f* sanguine *OR* de sang.

blood type *n* groupe *m* sanguin.

bloody ['blʌdɪ] (*comp* **bloodier**, *superl* **bloodiest**) <> *adj* **1.** [wound] sanglant, saignant ▪ [bandage, clothing, hand] taché *OR* couvert de sang ▪ [nose] en sang **2.** [battle, fight] sanglant, meurtrier **3.** [blood-coloured] rouge, rouge sang *(inv)* **4.** △ *UK* [as intensifier] foutu△ ▪ **you ~ fool!** espèce de crétin! ▪ **~ hell!** et merde!△ ▪ **it's a ~ shame she didn't come** c'est vachement dommage qu'elle n'ait pas pu venir **5.** *inf* [unpleasant] affreux, désagréable.
<> *adv*△ *UK* vachement ▪ **you can ~ well do it yourself!** tu n'as qu'à te démerder (tout seul)!△ ▪ **are you coming? – not ~ likely!** est-ce que tu viens? – pas question!
<> *vt* ensanglanter, couvrir de sang ▪ **they came out of it bloodied but unbowed** ils s'en sont sortis meurtris mais avec la tête haute.

Bloody Mary <> *pr n* [queen] *surnom de la reine Marie Tudor, donné par les protestants qu'elle persécuta.*
<> *n* [cocktail] bloody mary *m inv*.

bloody-minded *adj UK inf* [person] vache ▪ [attitude, behaviour] buté, têtu.

bloody-mindedness [-'maɪndɪdnɪs] *n UK inf* caractère *m* difficile ▪ **it's sheer ~ on your part** tu le fais uniquement pour emmerder le monde.

Bloody Sunday *n* HIST *dimanche sanglant (30 janvier 1972) au cours duquel des soldats britanniques abattirent 13 Irlandais qui manifestaient contre la détention de présumés terroristes.*

bloom [blu:m] <> *n* **1.** [flower] fleur *f* **2.** [state] : **the roses are just coming into ~** les roses commencent tout juste à fleurir *OR* à s'épanouir ▪ **to be in ~** [lily, rose] être éclos ; [bush, garden, tree] être en floraison *OR* en fleurs **3.** [of cheeks, face] éclat *m* ▪ **in the ~ of youth** dans la fleur de l'âge, en pleine jeunesse **4.** [on fruit] velouté *m*.
<> *vi* **1.** [flower] éclore ▪ [bush, tree] fleurir ▪ [garden] se couvrir de fleurs **2.** *fig* [person] être en pleine forme ▪ [arts, industry] prospérer.

bloomer ['blu:mər] *n UK inf* [blunder] gaffe *f*, faux pas *m*.

bloomers ['blu:məz] *npl* : **(a pair of) ~** une culotte bouffante.

blooming ['blu:mɪŋ] <> *adj* **1.** [flower] éclos ▪ [bush, garden, tree] en fleur, fleuri **2.** [glowing - with health] resplendissant, florissant ; [- with happiness] épanoui, rayonnant **3.** *UK inf* [as intensifier] sacré, fichu ▪ **you ~ idiot!** espèce d'imbécile!
<> *adv UK inf* sacrément, vachement ▪ **you can ~ well do it yourself!** tu n'as qu'à te débrouiller tout seul!

Bloomsbury Group ['blu:mzbrɪ-] *pr n* : **the ~** *groupe d'écrivains, d'artistes et d'intellectuels anglais du début du XXe siècle.*

BLOOMSBURY GROUP

Les membres du *Bloomsbury Group* habitaient, au début du siècle, le quartier du même nom à Londres ; ce groupe d'intellectuels comprenait, entre autres, l'économiste John Maynard Keynes et l'écrivain Virginia Woolf.

blooper ['blu:pər] *n US inf* gaffe *f*, faux pas *m*.

blossom ['blɒsəm] <> *n* **1.** [flower] fleur *f* **2.** [state] : **the cherry trees are just coming into ~** les cerisiers commencent tout juste à fleurir ▪ **to be in ~** être en fleurs.

◇ *vi* **1.** [flower] éclore ■ [bush, tree] fleurir **2.** *fig* [person] s'épanouir ■ [arts, industry] prospérer ■ **she ~ed into a talented writer** elle est devenue un écrivain doué.

blot [blɒt] ◇ *n* **1.** [spot - gen] tache *f* ; [- of ink] tache *f*, pâté *m* **2.** *fig* [on character, name] tache *f*, souillure *f* ■ [on civilization, system] tare *f* ■ **it's a ~ on the landscape** ça gâche le paysage.
◇ *vt* (*pret & pp* **blotted**, *cont* **blotting**) **1.** [dry] sécher **2.** [spot] tacher ■ [with ink] tacher, faire des pâtés sur ■ **to ~ one's copybook** salir sa réputation.
◆ **blot out** *vt sep* [obscure - light, sun] cacher, masquer ; [- memory, thought] effacer ; [- act, event] éclipser.
◆ **blot up** *vt sep* [subj: person] éponger, essuyer ■ [subj: blotting paper, sponge] boire.

blotch [blɒtʃ] ◇ *n* [spot - of colour, ink] tache *f* ; [- on skin] tache *f*, marbrure *f*.
◇ *vi* **1.** [skin] se couvrir de taches *OR* de marbrures **2.** [pen] faire des pâtés.
◇ *vt* **1.** [clothing, paper] tacher, faire des taches sur **2.** [skin] marbrer.

blotchy ['blɒtʃɪ] (*comp* **blotchier**, *superl* **blotchiest**) *adj* [complexion, skin] marbré, couvert de taches *OR* de marbrures ■ [cloth, paper, report] couvert de taches.

blotter ['blɒtər] *n* **1.** [paper] buvard *m* ■ [desk pad] sous-main *m inv* ■ **hand ~** tampon *m* buvard **2.** *US* [register] registre *m* (*provisoire*).

blotting paper *n* (papier *m*) buvard *m*.

blotto ['blɒtəʊ] *adj inf* parti.

blouse [blaʊz] ◇ *n* [for woman] chemisier *m*, corsage *m* ■ [for farmer, worker] blouse *f*.
◇ *vt* faire blouser ■ **a ~d top** un haut blousant.

blouson ['blu:zɒn] *n UK* blouson *m*.

blow [bləʊ] ◇ *n* **1.** [hit] coup *m* ■ [with fist] coup *m* de poing ■ **to come to ~s** en venir aux mains ■ **without striking a ~** sans coup férir ■ **to strike a ~ for freedom** *fig* rompre une lance pour la liberté
2. [setback] coup *m*, malheur *m* ■ [shock] coup *m*, choc *m* ■ **to soften** *OR* **to cushion the ~** amortir le choc ■ **to deal sb/sthg a (serious) ~** porter un coup (terrible) à qqn/qqch ■ **it was a big ~ to her pride** son orgueil en a pris un coup
3. [blast of wind] coup *m* de vent ■ [stronger] bourrasque *f*
4. [puff] souffle *m* ■ [through nose] : **have a good ~** mouche-toi bien
5. △ *drug sl UK* [marijuana] herbe *f* ■ *US* [cocaine] cocaïne *f*.
◇ *vi* (*pret* **blew** [blu:], *pp* **blown** [bləʊn]) **1.** [wind] souffler ■ **it's ~ing a gale out there** le vent souffle en tempête là-bas ■ **let's wait and see which way the wind ~s** *fig* attendons de voir de quel côté *OR* d'où souffle le vent
2. [person] souffler ■ **she blew on her hands/on her coffee** elle a soufflé dans ses mains/sur son café ▶ **he ~s hot and cold** il souffle le chaud et le froid
3. [move with wind] : **the trees were ~ing in the wind** le vent soufflait dans les arbres ■ **papers blew all over the yard** des papiers se sont envolés à travers la cour ■ **the window blew open/shut** un coup de vent a ouvert/fermé la fenêtre
4. [wind instrument] sonner ■ [whistle] siffler
5. [explode - tyre] éclater
6. [whale] souffler
7. *inf* [leave] filer
8. *US* & *Australia* [brag] se vanter
9. [bloom] fleurir ■ [open out] s'épanouir.
◇ *vt* (*pret* **blew** [blu:], *pp* **blown** [bləʊn]) **1.** [wind] faire bouger ■ [leaves] chasser, faire envoler ■ **the wind blew the door open/shut** un coup de vent a ouvert/fermé la porte ■ **the hurricane blew the ship off course** l'ouragan a fait dévier *OR* a dérouté le navire
2. [subj: person] souffler ■ **~ your nose!** mouche-toi! ■ **he blew the dust off the book** il a soufflé sur le livre pour enlever la poussière ■ **to ~ sb a kiss** envoyer un baiser à qqn
3. [bubbles, glass] : **to ~ bubbles/smoke rings** faire des bulles/ronds de fumée ■ **to ~ glass** souffler le verre
4. [wind instrument] jouer de ■ [whistle] faire retentir ■ **the policeman blew his whistle** le policier a sifflé *OR* a donné un coup de sifflet ■ **the referee blew his whistle for time** l'arbitre a sifflé la fin du match ▶ **to ~ the gaff** *inf* vendre la mèche ■ **to ~ one's own trumpet** se vanter ■ **to ~ the whistle on sthg** dévoiler qqch
5. [tyre] faire éclater ■ [fuse, safe] faire sauter ■ **the house was blown to pieces** la maison a été entièrement détruite par l'explosion ■ **the blast almost blew his hand off** l'explosion lui a presque emporté la main ■ **their plans were blown sky-high** *fig* leurs projets sont tombés à l'eau ▶ **he blew a gasket** *UK* *OR* **a fuse when he found out** quand il l'a appris, il a piqué une crise
6. *inf* [squander - money] claquer ■ **he blew all his savings on a new car** il a claqué toutes ses économies pour s'acheter une nouvelle voiture
7. [spoil - chance] gâcher ■ **I blew it!** j'ai tout gâché!
8. *inf* [reveal, expose] révéler ■ **to ~ sb's cover** griller qqn ■ **her article blew the whole thing wide open** son article a exposé toute l'affaire au grand jour ▶ **to ~ the lid off sthg** *inf* faire des révélations sur qqch, découvrir le pot aux roses
9. *US inf* [leave] quitter
10. *UK inf* [disregard] : **let's go anyway, and ~ what he thinks** allons-y quand même, je me moque de ce qu'il pense *OR* il peut penser ce qu'il veut ■ **~ the expense, we're going out to dinner** au diable l'avarice, on sort dîner ce soir
11. *inf phr* **the idea blew his mind** l'idée l'a fait flipper ■ **oh, ~ (it)!** *UK* la barbe!, mince! ■ **to ~ one's lid** *OR* **stack** *OR* **top** exploser de rage ■ **don't ~ your cool** ne t'emballe pas ■ **well, I'll be ~ed!** *UK*, **~ me down!** ça par exemple! ■ **I'll be** *OR* **I'm ~ed if I'm going to apologize!** *UK* pas question que je fasse des excuses!, il peut toujours courir pour que je lui fasse des excuses!
◆ **blow away** *vt sep* **1.** [subj: wind] chasser, disperser ■ **let's take a walk to ~ away the cobwebs** *UK* allons nous promener pour nous changer les idées
2. *inf* [astound] sidérer
3. *inf* [kill] abattre.
◆ **blow down** ◇ *vi insep* être abattu par le vent, tomber.
◇ *vt sep* [subj: wind] faire tomber, renverser ■ [subj: person] faire tomber *OR* abattre (en soufflant).
◆ **blow in** ◇ *vi insep inf* débarquer à l'improviste, s'amener.
◇ *vt sep* [door, window] enfoncer.
◆ **blow off** ◇ *vi insep* [hat, roof] s'envoler.
◇ *vt sep* **1.** [subj: wind] emporter
2. [release] laisser échapper, lâcher ■ **to ~ off steam** *inf* dire ce qu'on a sur le cœur.
◆ **blow out** ◇ *vt sep* **1.** [extinguish - candle] souffler ; [- fuse] faire sauter ■ **to ~ one's brains out** se faire sauter *OR* se brûler la cervelle
2. [subj: storm] : **the hurricane eventually blew itself out** l'ouragan s'est finalement calmé
3. [cheeks] gonfler.
◇ *vi insep* [fuse] sauter ■ [candle] s'éteindre ■ [tyre] éclater.
◆ **blow over** ◇ *vi insep* **1.** [storm] se calmer, passer ■ *fig* **the scandal soon blew over** le scandale fut vite oublié
2. [tree] s'abattre, se renverser.
◇ *vt sep* [tree] abattre, renverser.
◆ **blow up** ◇ *vt sep* **1.** [explode - bomb] faire exploser *OR* sauter ; [- building] faire sauter
2. [inflate] gonfler
3. [enlarge] agrandir ■ [exaggerate] exagérer ■ **the whole issue was blown up out of all proportion** la question a été exagérée hors de (toute) proportion.
◇ *vi insep* **1.** [explode] exploser, sauter ■ **the plan blew up in their faces** *fig* le projet leur a claqué dans les doigts
2. [begin - wind] se lever ; [- storm] se préparer ; [- crisis] se déclencher
3. *inf* [lose one's temper] exploser, se mettre en boule ■ **to ~ up at sb** engueuler qqn.

blow-by-blow *adj* détaillé ■ **she gave me a ~ account** elle m'a tout raconté en détail.

blow-dry ◇ *vt* faire un brushing à.
◇ *n* brushing *m*.

blower ['bləʊər] *n* **1.** [device] soufflante *f* **2.** [grate] tablier *m* *OR* rideau *m* de cheminée **3.** MIN jet *m* de grisou **4.** *inf* [whale] baleine *f* **5.** *UK inf* [telephone] bigophone *m*.

blowfly ['bləʊflaɪ] (*pl* **blowflies**) *n* mouche *f* à viande.

blowgun ['bləʊgʌn] *n US* sarbacane *f*.

blowhole ['bləʊhəʊl] *n* **1.** [of whale] évent *m* **2.** TECH bouche *f* d'aération, évent *m*.

blow job▲ *n* : **to give sb a ~** tailler une pipe à qqn▲.

blowlamp ['bləʊlæmp] *n UK* lampe *f* à souder, chalumeau *m*.

blown [bləʊn] *pp* ⊳ **blow**.

blowout ['bləʊaʊt] *n* **1.** [of fuse] : **there's been a ~** les plombs ont sauté **2.** [of tyre] éclatement *m* ▪ **I had a ~** j'ai un pneu qui a éclaté **3.** [of gas] éruption *f* **4.** *UK inf* [meal] gueuleton *m*.

blowpipe ['bləʊpaɪp] *n* **1.** *UK* [weapon] sarbacane *f* **2.** CHEM & INDUST [tube] chalumeau *m* ▪ [glassmaking] canne *f* de souffleur, fêle *f*.

blowtorch ['bləʊtɔ:tʃ] *n* lampe *f* à souder, chalumeau *m*.

blow-up *n* **1.** [explosion] explosion *f* **2.** *inf* [argument] engueulade *f* **3.** PHOT agrandissement *m*.

blow wave ◇ *n* brushing *m*.
◇ *vt* faire un brushing à.

blowy ['bləʊɪ] (*comp* **blowier**, *superl* **blowiest**) *adj* venté, venteux.

blub [blʌb] (*pret & pp* **blubbed**, *cont* **blubbing**) *vi UK inf* pleurer comme un veau *OR* une Madeleine.

blubber ['blʌbəʳ] ◇ *n* [of whale] blanc *m* de baleine ▪ *inf pej* [of person] *inf* graisse *f*.
◇ *vi* pleurer comme un veau *OR* une Madeleine.
◇ *adj* plein de graisse.

blubbery ['blʌbərɪ] *adj* plein de graisse.

bludgeon ['blʌdʒən] ◇ *n* gourdin *m*, matraque *f*.
◇ *vt* **1.** [beat] matraquer **2.** [force] contraindre, forcer ▪ **they ~ed him into selling the house** ils lui ont forcé la main pour qu'il vende la maison.

blue [blu:] (*cont* **blueing** *OR* **bluing**) ◇ *n* **1.** [colour] bleu *m*, azur *m* **2.** : **the ~** [sky] le ciel, l'azur *m lit* ▪ **they set off into the ~** ils sont partis à l'aventure **3.** POL *membre du parti conservateur britannique* **4.** *UK* UNIV : **the Dark/Light Blues** l'équipe *f* universitaire d'Oxford/de Cambridge ▪ **he got a ~ for cricket** il a représenté son université au cricket **5.** [for laundry] bleu *m*.
◇ *adj* **1.** [colour] bleu ▪ **to be ~ with cold** être bleu de froid ➊ **you can argue until you're ~ in the face but she still won't give in** vous pouvez vous tuer à discuter, elle ne s'avouera pas vaincue pour autant **2.** *inf* [depressed] triste, cafardeux ▪ **to feel ~** avoir le cafard **3.** [obscene - language] obscène, cochon ; [- book, movie] porno **4.** *inf phr* **to have a ~ fit** *UK* piquer une crise ▪ **to scream** *OR* **to shout ~ murder** crier comme un putois ▪ **once in a ~ moon** tous les trente-six du mois.
◇ *vt* **1.** *UK inf* [squander - money] claquer **2.** [laundry] passer au bleu.
◆ **blues** *n* **1.** *inf* **the ~s** [depression] le cafard ▪ **to get** *OR* **to have the ~s** avoir le cafard **2.** MUS : **the ~s** le blues.
◆ **Blues** *pr npl* : **the Blues and Royals** section de la Cavalerie de la Maison du Souverain britannique.
◆ **out of the blue** *adv phr* sans prévenir ▪ **the job offer came out of the ~** la proposition de travail est tombée du ciel.

blue baby *n* enfant *m* bleu, enfant *f* bleue.

bluebell ['blu:bel] *n* jacinthe *f* des bois.

blue berets *npl* casques *mpl* bleus.

blueberry ['blu:bərɪ] (*pl* **blueberries**) *n* myrtille *f* ▪ *Canada* bleuet *m*.

bluebird ['blu:bɜ:d] *n* oiseau *m* bleu.

blue blood *n* sang *m* bleu *OR* noble.

blue-blooded *adj* aristocratique, de sang noble.

bluebottle ['blu:ˌbɒtl] *n* **1.** [fly] mouche *f* bleue *OR* de la viande **2.** BOT bleuet *m*.

blue chip *n* [stock] valeur *f* de premier ordre ▪ [property] placement *m* de bon rapport.
◆ **blue-chip** *comp* [securities, stock] de premier ordre.

blue-collar *adj* [gen] ouvrier ▪ [area, background] populaire, ouvrier ▪ **~ worker** col *m* bleu.

blue-eyed *adj* aux yeux bleus ▪ **the ~ boy** *UK inf* le chouchou.

blue-green algae *npl* cyanophycées *fpl spec*, algues *fpl* bleues.

blue jeans *npl* jean *m*.

blue laws *npl US inf lois qui, au nom de la morale, limitent certaines activités telles que l'ouverture des commerces le dimanche, la vente d'alcool etc.*

blue peter *n* pavillon *m* de partance.

blueprint ['blu:prɪnt] ◇ *n* **1.** [photographic] bleu *m* **2.** *fig* [programme] plan *m*, projet *m* ▪ [prototype] prototype *m* ▪ **the ~ for democratic government** le modèle démocratique.
◇ *vt* tirer des bleus.

blue rib(b)and, blue ribbon ◇ *n premier prix d'une compétition.*
◇ *adj* de première classe.

blue rinse *n* rinçage *m* bleu.

blue shark *n* requin *m* bleu.

blue-sky *comp* : **~ research** recherches *fpl* sans applications immédiates.

bluetit ['blu:tɪt] *n* mésange *f* bleue.

blue whale *n* baleine *f* bleue.

bluff [blʌf] ◇ *n* **1.** [deception] bluff *m* **2.** [cliff] falaise *f*, promontoire *m* **3.** *phr* **to call sb's ~** défier qqn.
◇ *adj* [person] direct, franc, franche *f* ▪ [landscape] escarpé, à pic.
◇ *vi* bluffer.
◇ *vt* bluffer ▪ **to ~ one's way through things** marcher au bluff.

bluish ['blu:ɪʃ] *adj* qui tire sur le bleu ▪ *pej* bleuâtre.

blunder ['blʌndəʳ] ◇ *n* [mistake] bourde *f* ▪ [remark] gaffe *f*, impair *m* ▪ **I made a terrible ~** j'ai fait une gaffe *OR* une bévue épouvantable.
◇ *vi* **1.** [make a mistake] faire une gaffe *OR* un impair **2.** [move clumsily] avancer à l'aveuglette, tâtonner.

blunderbuss ['blʌndəbʌs] *n* tromblon *m*.

blundering ['blʌndərɪŋ] ◇ *adj* [person] maladroit, gaffeur ▪ [action, remark] maladroit, malavisé.
◇ *n* maladresse *f*, gaucherie *f*.

blunt [blʌnt] ◇ *adj* **1.** [blade] peu tranchant, émoussé ▪ [point] émoussé, épointé ▪ [pencil] mal taillé, épointé ▪ LAW [instrument] contondant **2.** [frank] brusque, direct ▪ **let me be ~** permettez que je parle franchement.
◇ *vt* [blade] émousser ▪ [pencil, point] épointer ▪ *fig* [feelings, senses] blaser, lasser.

bluntly ['blʌntlɪ] *adv* carrément, franchement.

bluntness ['blʌntnɪs] *n* **1.** [of blade] manque *m* de tranchant, état *m* émoussé **2.** [frankness] franchise *f*, brusquerie *f*.

blur [blɜ:ʳ] ◇ *n* **1.** [vague shape] masse *f* confuse, tache *f* floue ▪ **my childhood is all a ~ to me now** maintenant mon enfance n'est plus qu'un vague souvenir **2.** [smudge] tache *f* ▪ [of ink] pâté *m*, bavure *f*.
◇ *vt* (*pret & pp* **blurred**, *cont* **blurring**) **1.** [writing] estomper, effacer ▪ [outline] estomper **2.** [judgment, memory, sight] troubler, brouiller ▪ **tears blurred my eyes** mes yeux étaient voilés de larmes.
◇ *vi* (*pret & pp* **blurred**, *cont* **blurring**) [inscription, outline] s'estomper ▪ [judgment, memory, sight] se troubler, se brouiller.

blurb [blɜ:b] *n* notice *f* publicitaire, argumentaire *m* ▪ [on book] (texte *m* de) présentation *f*.

blurred [blɜ:d], **blurry** ['blɜ:rɪ] *adj* flou, indistinct.

blurt [blɜ:t] *vt* lâcher, jeter.
◆ **blurt out** *vt sep* [secret] laisser échapper.

blush [blʌʃ] ◇ *vi* [turn red - gen] rougir, devenir rouge; [- with embarrassment] rougir ▪ **the ~ing bride** l'heureuse élue.
◇ *n* rougeur *f* ▪ **the ~ of a peach** la couleur rosée de la pêche ▪ **"thank you", she said with a ~** "merci", dit-elle en rougissant ▪ **please, spare our ~es** *hum* ne nous faites pas rougir, s'il vous plaît ▪ **she was in the first ~ of youth** elle était dans la prime fleur de l'âge.

blusher ['blʌʃəʳ] *n* fard *m* à joues.

bluster ['blʌstəʳ] ◇ *vi* **1.** [wind] faire rage, souffler en rafales ■ [storm] faire rage, se déchaîner **2.** [speak angrily] fulminer, tempêter **3.** [boast] se vanter, fanfaronner.
◇ *vt* [person] intimider ■ **he tried to ~ his way out of doing it** il a essayé de se défiler avec de grandes phrases.
◇ *n (U)* **1.** [boasting] fanfaronnade *f*, fanfaronnades *fpl*, vantardise *f* **2.** [wind] rafale *f*.

blustering ['blʌstərɪŋ] ◇ *n (U)* fanfaronnade *f*, fanfaronnades *fpl*.
◇ *adj* fanfaron.

blustery ['blʌstərɪ] *adj* [weather] venteux, à bourrasques ■ [wind] qui souffle en rafales, de tempête.

BM *n* (*abbrev of* **Bachelor of Medicine**) *(titulaire d'une) licence de médecine*.

BMA (*abbrev of* **British Medical Association**) *pr n ordre britannique des médecins*.

B-movie *n* film *m* de série B.

BMus ['bi:'mʌz] (*abbrev of* **Bachelor of Music**) *n (titulaire d'une) licence de musique*.

BMX (*abbrev of* **bicycle motorcross**) *n* **1.** [bicycle] VTT *m* **2.** SPORT cyclo-cross *m inv*.

bn *written abbr of* **billion**.

BNP (*abbrev of* **British National Party**) *pr n parti d'extrême-droite britannique*.

BO *n* **1.** (*abbrev of* **body odour**) odeur *f* corporelle ■ **he's got ~** il sent mauvais **2.** = **box office**.

boa ['bəʊə] *n* **1.** : **(feather) ~** boa *m* **2.** : **~ constrictor** boa constricteur *m*, constrictor *m*.

boar [bɔ:ʳ] *n* [male pig] verrat *m* ■ [wild pig] sanglier *m*.

board [bɔ:d] ◇ *n* **1.** [plank] planche *f* ■ **the ~s** THEAT la scène, les planches ➤ **the policy applies to everybody in the company across the ~** cette politique concerne tous les employés de l'entreprise quelle que soit leur position
2. [cardboard] carton *m* ■ [for games] tableau *m*
3. [notice board] tableau *m*
4. ADMIN conseil *m*, commission *f* ■ **~ of directors** conseil d'administration ■ **who's on the ~?** qui siège au conseil d'administration? ■ **~ of inquiry** commission d'enquête ■ **the ~ of health** *US* le service municipal d'hygiène ; MIL le conseil de révision
5. SCH & UNIV : **~ of education** *US* ≃ conseil *m* d'administration *(d'un établissement scolaire)* ■ **~ of examiners** jury *m* d'examen ■ **~ of governors** *UK* ≃ conseil *m* d'administration *(d'un lycée ou d'un collège)* ■ **~ of regents** *US* ≃ conseil *m* d'université
6. [meals provided] pension *f* ■ *arch* [table] table *f* ■ **~ and lodging** (chambre *f* et) pension
7. AERON & NAUT bord *m* ■ **to go on ~** monter à bord de ■ **we're on ~** nous sommes à bord ■ **they took provisions on ~** ils ont embarqué des provisions ➤ **to go by the ~** *UK* être abandonné *OR* oublié ■ **to take sthg on ~** tenir compte de qqch.
◇ *comp* [decision, meeting] du conseil d'administration.
◇ *vt* **1.** [plane, ship] monter à bord de ■ [bus, train] monter dans ■ NAUT [in attack] monter *OR* prendre à l'abordage
2. [cover with planks] couvrir de planches
3. [provide meals, lodging] prendre en pension.
◇ *vi* [lodge] être en pension ■ **to ~ with sb** être pensionnaire chez qqn ■ [plane] **the flight is now ~ing at gate 3** embarquement immédiat du vol porte 3.
◆ **board up** *vt sep* couvrir de planches ■ [door, window] boucher, obturer.

boarder ['bɔ:dəʳ] *n* pensionnaire *mf* ■ SCH interne *mf*, pensionnaire *mf*.

board game *n* jeu *m* de société.

boarding ['bɔ:dɪŋ] *n* **1.** *(U)* [gen & fence] planches *fpl* ■ [floor] planchéiage *m* **2.** [embarking] embarquement *m* ■ NAUT [in attack] abordage *m*.

boarding card *n* carte *f* d'embarquement.

boarding house *n* pension *f* ■ SCH internat *m*.

boarding school *n* internat *m*, pensionnat *m* ■ **to go to ~** être interne ■ **they sent their children to ~** ils ont mis leurs enfants en internat.

Board of Trade *pr n* : **the ~** *UK* le ministère du Commerce ; *US* la chambre de commerce.

boardroom ['bɔ:drʊm] ◇ *n* salle *f* de conférence ■ *fig* [management] administration *f*.
◇ *comp* : **the decision was taken at ~ level** la décision a été prise au niveau de la direction.

boardwalk ['bɔ:dwɔ:k] *n US* passage *m* en bois ■ [on beach] promenade *f* (en planches).

boast [bəʊst] ◇ *n* **1.** fanfaronnade *f*, fanfaronnades *fpl* ■ **it's his proud ~ that he has never lost a game** il se vante de n'avoir jamais perdu un jeu **2.** [in squash] bosse *f*.
◇ *vi* se vanter, fanfaronner.
◇ *vt* **1.** [brag] se vanter de **2.** [possess] être fier d'avoir ■ **the town ~s an excellent symphony orchestra** la ville se glorifie d'avoir un excellent orchestre symphonique.

boaster ['bəʊstəʳ] *n* fanfaron *m*, - onne *f*.

boastful ['bəʊstfʊl] *adj* fanfaron, vantard.

boasting ['bəʊstɪŋ] *n (U)* vantardise *f*, fanfaronnade *f*, fanfaronnades *fpl*.

boat [bəʊt] ◇ *n* [gen] bateau *m* ■ [for rowing] barque *f*, canot *m* ■ [for sailing] voilier *m* ■ [ship] navire *m*, paquebot *m* ■ **to go by ~** prendre le bateau ■ **to take to the ~s** monter dans les canots de sauvetage ➤ **we're all in the same ~** nous sommes tous logés à la même enseigne.
◇ *vi* voyager en bateau ■ **to go ~ing** aller se promener en bateau.

boatbuilder ['bəʊt,bɪldəʳ] *n* constructeur *m* naval.

boat deck *n* pont *m* des embarcations.

boater ['bəʊtəʳ] *n* canotier *m*.

boathouse ['bəʊthaʊs] (*pl* [-haʊzɪz]) *n* abri *m OR* hangar *m* à bateaux.

boating ['bəʊtɪŋ] ◇ *n* canotage *m*.
◇ *comp* [accident, enthusiast, trip] de canotage.

boatload ['bəʊtləʊd] *n* [merchandise] cargaison *f* ■ [people] plein bateau *m*.

boatman ['bəʊtmən] (*pl* **boatmen** [-mən]) *n* [rower] passeur *m* ■ [renter of boats] loueur *m* de canots.

boat people *npl* boat people *mpl*.

boat race *n* ROWING course *f* d'avirons ■ SAIL régates *fpl* ■ **the Boat Race** *course universitaire annuelle d'avirons entre les universités d'Oxford et de Cambridge*.

boatswain ['bəʊsn] *n* maître *m* d'équipage.

boat train *n train qui assure la correspondance avec un bateau*.

boatyard ['bəʊtjɑ:d] *n* chantier *m* de construction navale.

bob [bɒb] ◇ *vi* (*pret & pp* **bobbed**, *cont* **bobbing**,) **1.** [cork, buoy] : **to ~ up and down** danser sur l'eau ■ **I could see his head bobbing up and down behind the wall** je voyais par moments sa tête surgir de derrière le mur **2.** [curtsy] faire une petite révérence **3.** [move quickly] : **to ~ in/out** entrer/sortir rapidement **4.** [bobsleigh] faire du bobsleigh.
◇ *vt* (*pret & pp* **bobbed**, *cont* **bobbing**,) **1.** [move up and down] faire monter et descendre **2.** [hair] couper court **3.** [horse's tail] écourter.
◇ *n* **1.** [abrupt movement] petit coup *m*, petite secousse *f* ■ [of head] hochement *m OR* salut *m* de tête ■ [curtsy] petite révérence *f* **2.** [hairstyle] (coupe *f* au) carré *m* **3.** [horse's tail] queue *f* écourtée **4.** [fishing float] flotteur *m*, bouchon *m* ■ [weight] plomb *m* **5.** *inf phr* **all my bits and ~s** toutes mes petites affaires **6.** [bobsleigh] bobsleigh *m*, bob *m* ■ [runner] patin *m* **7.** (*pl* bob) *inf UK dated* [shilling] shilling *m*.

Bob [bɒb] *pr n* : **~'s your uncle!** *inf* et voilà le travail!

bobbin ['bɒbɪn] *n* [gen] bobine *f* ■ [for lace] fuseau *m* ■ **~ lace** dentelle *f* aux fuseaux.

bobble ['bɒbl] <> *n* **1.** [bobbing movement] secousse *f*, saccade *f* **2.** [pompom] pompon *m* ▪ **~ hat** chapeau *m* à pompon **3.** *US inf* [mistake] boulette *f*.
<> *vi* : **the ball ~d and the player mishit his shot** il y a eu un faux rebond et le joueur a raté son tir.

bobby ['bɒbɪ] (*pl* **bobbies**) *n UK inf dated* flic *m*.

bobby pin *n US* pince *f* à cheveux.

bobby socks, bobby sox *npl US* socquettes *fpl (de fille)*.

bobcat ['bɒbkæt] *n* lynx *m*.

bobsled ['bɒbsled], **bobsleigh** ['bɒbsleɪ] <> *n* bobsleigh *m*, bob *m*.
<> *vi* faire du bobsleigh.

bobtail ['bɒbteɪl] *n* [tail] queue *f* écourtée ▪ [cat] chat *m* écourté ▪ [dog] chien *m* écourté.

Boche△ [bɒʃ] *dated & offens* <> *n* Boche *mf*.
<> *adj* boche.

bod [bɒd] *n inf* **1.** *UK* [person] type *m* ▪ **he's a bit of an odd ~** c'est plutôt un drôle d'oiseau **2.** [body] physique *m*, corps *m*.

bode [bəʊd] <> *pt* ▷ **bide**.
<> *vi* [presage] augurer, présager ▪ **it ~s well for him** cela est de bon augure pour lui ▪ **that ~s ill for us** cela ne présage rien de bon pour nous.

bodge [bɒdʒ] *vt UK inf* **1.** [spoil] saboter, bousiller **2.** [mend clumsily] rafistoler.

bodice ['bɒdɪs] *n* [of dress] corsage *m* ▪ [corset] corset *m*.

bodice ripper *n hum roman grivois à trame historique*.

bodily ['bɒdɪlɪ] <> *adj* matériel ▪ **~ functions** fonctions *fpl* corporelles ▪ **to cause sb ~ harm** blesser qqn.
<> *adv* **1.** [carry, seize] à bras-le-corps **2.** [entirely] entièrement.

bodkin ['bɒdkɪn] *n* [needle] grosse aiguille *f* ▪ [for tape] passe-lacet *m*.

body ['bɒdɪ] (*pl* **bodies**) *n* **1.** [human, animal] corps *m* ⊳ **to keep ~ and soul together** subsister, survivre
2. [corpse] cadavre *m*, corps *m* ▪ **over my dead ~!** *inf* il faudra me passer sur le corps!
3. [group] ensemble *m*, corps *m* ▪ [organization] organisme *m* ▪ **the main ~ of voters** le gros des électeurs ▪ **a large ~ of people** une foule énorme ▪ **they came in one ~** ils sont venus en masse ▪ **taken as a ~** dans leur ensemble, pris ensemble ⊳ **~ politic** corps *m* politique
4. [mass] masse *f* ▪ **a ~ of water** un plan d'eau ▪ **a growing ~ of evidence** une accumulation de preuves ▪ **the ~ of public opinion** la majorité de l'opinion publique
5. [largest part - of document, speech] fond *m*, corps *m*
6. [of car] carrosserie *f* ▪ [of plane] fuselage *m* ▪ [of ship] coque *f* ▪ [of camera] boîtier *m* ▪ [of dress] corsage *m* ▪ [of building] corps *m*
7. [fullness - wine] corps *m* ▪ **a shampoo that gives your hair ~** un shampooing qui donne du volume à vos cheveux
8. *inf* [man] bonhomme *m* ▪ [woman] bonne femme *f*
9. [garment] body *m*
10. PHYS corps *m*.

body bag *n* sac *m* mortuaire.

body blow *n* coup *m* dur.

bodybuilder ['bɒdɪbɪldəʳ] *n* [person] culturiste *mf* ▪ [machine] extenseur *m* ▪ [food] aliment *m* énergétique.

body building *n* culturisme *m*.

body clock *n* horloge *f* biologique.

bodyguard ['bɒdɪgɑ:d] *n* garde *m* du corps.

body language *n* langage *m* du corps.

body lotion *n* lait *m* corporel.

body odour *n* odeur *f* corporelle.

body piercing *n* piercing *m*.

body search *n* fouille *f* corporelle.

body shop *n* atelier *m* de carrosserie.

body snatcher *n* déterreur *m*, - euse *f* de cadavres.

body stocking *n* body *m*.

body warmer [-ˌwɔ:məʳ] *n* gilet *m* matelassé.

bodywork ['bɒdɪwɜ:k] *n* carrosserie *f*.

Boer [bɔ:] <> *n* Boer *mf*.
<> *adj* boer ▪ **the ~ War** HIST la guerre des Boers.

THE BOER WAR

Conflit qui opposa, à la fin du XIXe siècle, les Britanniques aux colons d'origine néerlandaise, installés en Afrique australe (*Boer republics*), et défendant leur indépendance contre les ambitions de la *British South Africa Company* et la suzeraineté britannique. Il prit fin en 1902 par la victoire des Britanniques.

boffin ['bɒfɪn] *n UK inf* chercheur *m* scientifique *OR* technique.

bog [bɒg] *n* **1.** [area] marécage *m*, marais *m* ▪ [peat] tourbière *f* **2.** △ *UK* [lavatory] chiottes△ *fpl*.
◆ **bog down** *vt sep* (*pret & pp* **bogged**, *cont* **bogging**) empêcher, entraver ▪ [vehicle] embourber, enliser ▪ **I got bogged down in paperwork** *fig* je me suis laissé déborder par la paperasserie.

bogey ['bəʊgɪ] *n* **1.** [monster] démon *m*, fantôme *m* ▪ [pet worry] bête *f* noire **2.** GOLF bogey *m*, bogée *m* **3.** *inf* [in nose] crotte *f* de nez **4.** = **bogie**.

bogeyman ['bəʊgɪmæn] (*pl* **bogeymen** [-men]) *n* croque-mitaine *m*, père *m* fouettard.

boggle ['bɒgl] *vi* **1.** [be amazed] être abasourdi ▪ **the mind ~s!** ça laisse perplexe! **2.** [hesitate] hésiter.

boggy ['bɒgɪ] (*comp* **boggier**, *superl* **boggiest**) *adj* [swampy] marécageux ▪ [peaty] tourbeux.

bogie ['bəʊgɪ] *n* RAIL bogie *m* ▪ [trolley] diable *m*.

Bognor Regis ['bɒgnə'ri:dʒɪs] *pr n station balnéaire de la côte sud de l'Angleterre, surtout fréquentée par des personnes âgées*.

bogroll△ ['bɒgrəʊl] *n* PQ *m*.

bog-standard *adj UK inf* [restaurant, food] ordinaire, médiocre ▪ [film, book] sans intérêt, médiocre ▪ [hotel] standard *inv*, médiocre.

bogus ['bəʊgəs] *adj* faux, fausse *f*.

bogy ['bəʊgɪ] (*pl* **bogies**) *n* = **bogie**.

Bohemia [bəʊ'hi:mjə] *pr n* Bohême *f*.

bohemian [bəʊhi:mjən] <> *n* bohème *mf*.
<> *adj* bohème.

Bohemian [bəʊ'hi:mjən] <> *n* [from Bohemia] Bohémien *m*, - enne *f* ▪ [gypsy] bohémien *m*, - enne *f*.
<> *adj* [of Bohemia] bohémien ▪ [gypsy] bohémien.

boil [bɔɪl] <> *n* **1.** [on face, body] furoncle *m* **2.** [boiling point] : **bring the sauce to the ~** amenez la sauce à ébullition ▪ **the water's on the ~** *UK* l'eau bout *OR* est bouillante ▪ **the project has gone off the ~** *UK fig* le projet a été mis en attente.
<> *vt* **1.** [liquid] faire bouillir, amener à ébullition **2.** [laundry] faire bouillir **3.** [food] cuire à l'eau, faire bouillir.
<> *vi* **1.** [liquid] bouillir ▪ **the kettle's ~ing** l'eau bout (dans la bouilloire) ▪ **the pot ~ed dry** *UK* toute l'eau de la casserole s'est évaporée **2.** [seethe - ocean] bouillonner ; [- person] bouillir ▪ **I was ~ing with anger** je bouillais de rage.
◆ **boil down** *vt sep* CULIN faire réduire ▪ *fig* réduire à l'essentiel.
◆ **boil down to** *vt insep* revenir à ▪ **it all ~s down to money** tout cela revient à une question d'argent ▪ **it ~s down to the same thing** ça revient au même.
◆ **boil over** *vi insep* **1.** [overflow] déborder ▪ [milk] se sauver, déborder **2.** *fig* [with anger] bouillir ▪ **he ~ed over with rage** il bouillait de rage ▪ **the unrest ~ed over into violence** l'agitation a débouché sur la violence.

boiled ['bɔɪld] *adj* : **~ beef** [alone] bœuf *m* bouilli ; [dish] pot-au-feu *m inv* ▪ **~ egg** œuf *m* à la coque ▪ **~ ham** jambon *m* cuit (à l'eau) ▪ **~ potatoes** pommes de terre *fpl* à l'eau *OR* bouillies ▪ **~ sweets** *UK* bonbons *mpl* à sucer.

boiler ['bɔɪlər] *n* **1.** [furnace] chaudière *f* ■ [domestic] chaudière *f* ■ *UK* [washing machine] lessiveuse *f* ■ [pot] casserole *f* **2.** [chicken] poule *f* à faire au pot.

boilerhouse ['bɔɪləhaʊs] (*pl* [-haʊzɪz]) *n* bâtiment *m* des chaudières.

boilermaker ['bɔɪlə,meɪkər] *n* [workman] chaudronnier *m*.

boilerman ['bɔɪlə,mæn] (*pl* **boilermen** [-,men]) *n* chauffeur *m*.

boiler room *n* salle *f* des chaudières, chaufferie *f* ■ NAUT chaufferie *f*, chambre *f* de chauffe.

boiler suit *n UK* [for work] bleu *m OR* bleus *mpl* (de travail) ■ [fashion garment] salopette *f*.

boiling ['bɔɪlɪŋ] <> *adj* [very hot] bouillant ■ **the weather here is ~** il fait une chaleur infernale ici ■ **I'm ~** *inf* je crève de chaleur.
<> *adv* : **~ hot** tout bouillant ■ **it's ~ hot today** *inf* il fait une chaleur à crever aujourd'hui.
<> *n* [action] ébullition *f* ■ [bubbling] bouillonnement *m*.

boiling point *n* point *m* d'ébullition ■ **to reach ~** *liter* arriver à ébullition ; *fig* être en ébullition.

boil-in-the-bag *adj* en sachet-cuisson.

boisterous ['bɔɪstərəs] *adj* **1.** [exuberant] tapageur, plein d'entrain **2.** [sea] tumultueux, turbulent ■ [wind] violent, furieux.

bold [bəʊld] <> *adj* **1.** [courageous] intrépide, hardi ■ **a ~ plan** un projet audacieux *OR* osé ■ **a ~ stroke** un coup d'audace ■ **he grew ~er in his efforts** il s'est enhardi dans ses tentatives **2.** [not shy] assuré ■ [brazen] effronté ■ **may I be so ~ as to ask your name?** puis-je me permettre de vous demander qui vous êtes? ◗ **as ~ as brass** *UK* culotté **3.** ART & LIT [vigorous] puissant, hardi ■ **a ~ style of writing** un style (d'écriture) hardi ■ **in ~ relief** en puissant relief **4.** [colours] vif, éclatant **5.** TYPO : **in ~** en gras.
<> *n* caractères *mpl* gras, gras *m*.

bold face *n* caractères *mpl* gras, gras *m* ■ **in ~** en gras.
◆ **boldface** *adj* gras, grasse *f*.

boldfaced ['bəʊldfeɪst] *adj* impudent ■ **a ~ lie** un mensonge éhonté.

boldly ['bəʊldlɪ] *adv* **1.** [bravely] intrépidement, audacieusement **2.** [impudently] avec impudence, effrontément **3.** [forcefully] avec vigueur, vigoureusement.

boldness ['bəʊldnɪs] *n* **1.** [courage] intrépidité *f*, audace *f* **2.** [impudence] impudence *f*, effronterie *f* **3.** [force] vigueur *f*, hardiesse *f*.

Bolivia [bə'lɪvɪə] *pr n* Bolivie *f* ■ **in ~** en Bolivie.

Bolivian [bə'lɪvɪən] <> *n* Bolivien *m*, - enne *f*.
<> *adj* bolivien.

bollard ['bɒlɑːd] *n* [on wharf] bollard *m* ■ *UK* [on road] borne *f*.

bollocking△ ['bɒləkɪŋ] *n UK* engueulade *f* ■ **he got/she gave him a right ~** il a reçu/elle lui a passé un sacré savon.

bollocks▲ ['bɒləks] <> *npl UK* [testicles] couilles△ *fpl*.
<> *n (U)* [rubbish] conneries *fpl*, couillonnades△ *fpl*.
<> *interj* : **~!** quelles conneries!

boll weevil *n* anthonome *m (du cotonnier)*.

Bologna [bə'ləʊnjə] *pr n* Bologne.

boloney [bə'ləʊnɪ] *n* **1.** *US* [sausage] *saucisson fumé* **2.** = **baloney**.

Bolshevik ['bɒlʃɪvɪk] <> *n* bolchevik *mf*.
<> *adj* bolchevique.

bolshie, bolshy ['bɒlʃɪ] *inf* <> *n UK* rouge *mf*.
<> *adj* **1.** [intractable] ronchon **2.** POL rouge.

bolster ['bəʊlstər] <> *vt* **1.** [strengthen] soutenir ■ **he ~ed my morale** il m'a remonté le moral ■ **these laws simply ~ up the system** ces lois ne font que renforcer le système **2.** [pad] rembourrer.
<> *n* **1.** [cushion] traversin *m* **2.** ARCHIT racinal *m*, sous-poutre *f*.

bolt [bəʊlt] <> *vi* **1.** [move quickly] se précipiter ■ **a rabbit ~ed across the lawn** un lapin a traversé la pelouse à toute allure **2.** [escape] déguerpir ■ [horse] s'emballer **3.** [plants] monter en graine.
<> *vt* **1.** [lock] fermer à clé, verrouiller ■ **did you ~ the door?** avez-vous poussé *OR* mis les verrous? **2.** [food] engloutir **3.** *US* [break away from] abandonner, laisser tomber **4.** TECH [fasten] boulonner **5.** [sift] tamiser, passer au tamis ■ *fig* [examine] passer au crible *OR* tamis.
<> *n* **1.** [sliding bar to door, window] verrou *m* ■ [in lock] pêne *m* **2.** [screw] boulon *m* **3.** [dash] : **we made a ~ for the door** nous nous sommes rués sur la porte ■ **she made a ~ for it** elle s'est sauvée à toutes jambes **4.** [lightning] éclair *m* ■ **the news came like a ~ from the blue** *UK* la nouvelle est arrivée comme un coup de tonnerre **5.** [of cloth] rouleau *m* **6.** SPORT [of crossbow] carreau *m* ■ [of firearm] culasse *f* mobile ■ **(expansion) ~** [for climbing] piton *m* (à expansion).
<> *adv* : **~ upright** droit comme un i.
◆ **bolt down** *vt sep* [food, meal] avaler à toute vitesse.

bolt hole *n* abri *m*, refuge *m*.

bomb [bɒm] <> *n* **1.** [explosive] bombe *f* ■ **the ~** la bombe atomique **2.** *UK inf* [large sum of money] fortune *f* ■ **the repairs cost a ~** les réparations ont coûté les yeux de la tête **3.** *US inf* [failure] fiasco *m*, bide *m* **4.** *inf phr* **like a ~** elle fonce ■ **this car goes like a ~** cette voiture ■ **the show went like a ~** *inf UK* le spectacle a eu un succès du tonnerre.
<> *comp* : **~ scare** alerte *f* à la bombe ■ **~ shelter** abri *m*.
<> *vt* bombarder.
<> *vi inf* **1.** [go quickly] filer à toute vitesse **2.** *US* [fail] être un fiasco *OR* bide.
◆ **bomb out** <> *vt sep* détruire par bombardement ■ **he was ~ed out (of his house)** il a perdu sa maison dans le bombardement.
<> *vi insep inf US* [fail] foirer.

bombard [bɒm'bɑːd] *vt* bombarder ■ **to ~ sb with questions** bombarder *OR* assaillir qqn de questions.

bombardier [,bɒmbə'dɪər] *n* [in Air Force] bombardier *m (aviateur)* ■ *UK* [in Royal Artillery] caporal *m* d'artillerie.

bombardment [bɒm'bɑːdmənt] *n* bombardement *m*.

bombast ['bɒmbæst] *n* grandiloquence *f*, boursouflure *f*.

bombastic [bɒm'bæstɪk] *adj* [style] ampoulé, grandiloquent ■ [person] grandiloquent, pompeux.

Bombay duck [,bom'beɪ-] *n petit poisson séché utilisé comme accompagnement dans la cuisine indienne.*

bomb disposal *n* déminage *m* ■ **~ expert** démineur *m* ■ **~ squad** *OR* **team** équipe *f* de déminage.

bomber ['bɒmər] *n* **1.** [aircraft] bombardier *m* ■ **~ pilot** pilote *m* de bombardier **2.** [terrorist] plastiqueur *m*, - euse *f*.

bomber jacket *n* blouson *m* d'aviateur.

bombing ['bɒmɪŋ] <> *n* [by aircraft] bombardement *m* ■ [by terrorist] attentat *m* à la bombe.
<> *comp* [mission, raid] de bombardement.

bombshell ['bɒmʃel] *n* **1.** [explosive] obus *m* **2.** *fig* [shock] : **her death came as a real ~** sa mort nous a fait un grand choc *OR* nous a atterrés ■ **their wedding announcement came as a complete ~** l'annonce de leur mariage a fait l'effet d'une bombe **3.** *inf* [woman] : **a blonde ~** une blonde incendiaire.

bombsight ['bɒmsaɪt] *n* viseur *m* de bombardement.

bombsite ['bɒmsaɪt] *n* lieu *m* bombardé.

bona fide [,bəʊnə'faɪdɪ] *adj* [genuine] véritable, authentique ■ [agreement] sérieux.

bonanza [bə'nænzə] <> *n* aubaine *f*, filon *m* ■ *US* MIN riche filon *m*.
<> *comp* exceptionnel.

bonce [bɒns] *n UK inf* caboche *f*.

bond [bɒnd] <> *n* **1.** [link] lien *m*, liens *mpl*, attachement *m* ■ **the marriage ~** les liens conjugaux **2.** [agreement] engagement *m*, contrat *m* ■ **we entered into a ~ to buy the land** nous nous sommes engagés à acheter la terre ■ **my word is my ~** je n'ai qu'une parole **3.** LAW caution *f* financière **4.** FIN [certificate] bon *m*, titre *m* **5.** [adhesion] adhérence *f* **6.** [paper] papier *m* à lettres (de luxe) **7.** CHEM liaison *f* **8.** CONSTR appareil *m* **9.** COMM : **in ~** en entrepôt ■ **he put the merchandise in ~** il a entreposé les marchandises en douane.

◇ *vt* **1.** [hold together] lier, unir **2.** COMM [goods] entreposer **3.** LAW [place under bond] placer sous caution ■ [put up bond for] se porter caution pour **4.** FIN lier (par garantie financière) **5.** CONSTR liaisonner.
◇ *vi* **1.** [with adhesive] : **the surfaces have ~ed** les surfaces ont adhéré l'une à l'autre **2.** PSYCHOL former des liens affectifs.
◆ **bonds** *npl* [fetters] chaînes *fpl*, fers *mpl* ■ *fig* liens *mpl*, contraintes *fpl*.

bondage ['bɒndɪdʒ] *n* **1.** *liter* esclavage *m* ■ *fig* esclavage *m*, servitude *f* **2.** [sexual] bondage *m*.

bonded ['bɒndɪd] *adj* FIN titré ■ COMM (entreposé) sous douane ■ **~ warehouse** entrepôt *m* sous douane.

bonding ['bɒndɪŋ] *n* **1.** PSYCHOL liens *mpl* affectifs ■ **~ session** réunion amicale, relax **2.** [of two objects] collage *m* **3.** ELEC système *m* OR circuit *m* régulateur de tension **4.** CONSTR liaison *f*.

Bond Street [bɒnd-] *pr n grande rue commerçante de Londres.*

BOND STREET

Cette rue commerçante de Londres, dans le quartier de Mayfair, est connue pour ses boutiques de mode, ses bijouteries et ses galeries d'art.

bone [bəʊn] ◇ *n* **1.** os *m* ■ [of fish] arête *f* ■ **she's got good ~ structure** elle a les pommettes saillantes ➜ **~ of contention** pomme *f* de discorde ■ **chilled** OR **frozen to the ~** glacé jusqu'à la moelle (des os) ■ **his comments were a bit close to** OR **near the ~** ses commentaires frôlaient l'indécence ■ **I have a ~ to pick with you** j'ai un compte à régler avec toi ■ **to make no ~s about sthg** ne pas y aller de main morte OR avec le dos de la cuillère ■ **he'll never make old ~s** il ne fera sûrement pas de vieux os ■ **he's nothing but skin and ~** OR **~s, he's nothing but a bag of ~s** il est maigre comme un clou **2.** [substance] os *m* ■ [in corset] baleine *f* **3.** [essential] essentiel *m* ■ **to cut spending (down) to the ~** réduire les dépenses au strict minimum.
◇ *vt* [meat] désosser ■ [fish] ôter les arêtes de.
◆ **bones** *npl* ossements *mpl*, os *mpl* ■ **to lay sb's ~s to rest** enterrer qqn.
◆ **bone up on** *vt insep UK inf* : **he has to ~ up on his history** il faut qu'il bûche son histoire.

bone china *n* porcelaine *f* tendre.

boned [bəʊnd] *adj* **1.** CULIN [meat, poultry] désossé **2.** [corset] baleiné.

bone-dry *adj* absolument sec.

bonehead ['bəʊnhed] *n inf* crétin *m*, - e *f*, imbécile *mf*.

bone-idle *adj UK* paresseux comme une couleuvre.

boneless ['bəʊnlɪs] *adj* [meat] désossé, sans os ■ [fish] sans arêtes.

bone marrow *n* moëlle *f* ■ **bone-marrow transplant** greffe *f* de moëlle.

boner ['bəʊnər] *n US* **1.** [blunder] gaffe *f*, bourde *f* ■ **to pull a ~** faire une gaffe **2.** ▲ [erection] : **to have a ~** bander.

boneshaker ['bəʊn,ʃeɪkər] *n inf* [car] tacot *m* ■ HIST [bicycle] vélocipède *m*.

bonfire ['bɒn,faɪər] *n* (grand) feu *m*.

Bonfire Night *n UK* le 5 novembre *(commémoration de la tentative de Guy Fawkes de faire sauter le Parlement en 1605).*

bongo ['bɒŋgəʊ] (*pl* **bongos** OR *pl* **bongoes**) *n* bongo *m*.

bonhomie ['bɒnəmi:] *n* bonhomie *f*.

bonk△ [bɒŋk] *hum* ◇ *vi* s'envoyer en l'air.
◇ *vt* s'envoyer en l'air avec.
◇ *n* partie *f* de jambes en l'air.

bonkers ['bɒŋkəz] *adj UK inf* fou *(before vowel or silent 'h' fol)*, folle *f*, cinglé.

bonnet ['bɒnɪt] *n* **1.** [hat - woman's] bonnet *m*, chapeau *m* à brides ; [- child's] béguin *m*, bonnet *m* ■ *Scotland* [- man's] béret *m*, bonnet *m* **2.** AUT *UK* capot *m* **3.** ARCHIT [awning] auvent *m* ■ [of chimney] capuchon *m* **4.** NAUT bonnette *f*.

Bonnie Prince Charlie [,bɒnɪprɪns'tʃɑ:lɪ] *pr n surnom donné à Charles Édouard Stuart, le Jeune Prétendant.*

bonny ['bɒnɪ] (*comp* **bonnier**, *superl* **bonniest**) *adj UK dial* [pretty] joli, beau *(before vowel or silent 'h' bel)*, belle *f*.

bonobo [bə'nəʊbəʊ] (*pl* **bonobos**) *n* ZOOL bonobo *m*.

bonsai ['bɒnsaɪ] *n* bonsaï *m*.

bonus ['bəʊnəs] *n* **1.** [gen - COMM] prime *f* ■ **the holiday was an added ~** *fig* les vacances étaient en prime **2.** *UK* FIN [dividend] dividende *m* exceptionnel.

bony ['bəʊnɪ] (*comp* **bonier**, *superl* **boniest**) *adj* **1.** ANAT osseux ■ [knees, person] anguleux, décharné **2.** [fish] plein d'arêtes ■ [meat] plein d'os.

boo [bu:] ◇ *vt* huer, siffler ■ **the audience ~ed him off the stage** il a quitté la scène sous les huées OR les sifflets du public.
◇ *vi* pousser des huées, siffler ■ **to ~ at sb** huer OR siffler qqn.
◇ *n* huée *f*.
◇ *interj* hou ■ **he wouldn't say ~ to a goose** *UK inf* c'est un grand timide.

boob [bu:b] *inf* ◇ *n* **1.** [idiot] ballot *m* **2.** [mistake] gaffe *f* **3.** [breast] sein *m*.
◇ *vi* gaffer.

boo-boo ['bu:bu:] (*pl* **boo-boos**) *n inf* [blunder] gaffe *f*, bourde *f*.

boob tube *n inf* **1.** *US* [television set] télé *f* **2.** [strapless top] bustier *m* moulant.

booby ['bu:bɪ] (*pl* **boobies**) *n* **1.** *inf* [idiot] nigaud *m*, - e *f*, ballot *m* **2.** ORNITH fou *m* (de Bassan).

booby hatch *n* **1.** NAUT écoutillon *m* **2.** *US inf* [mental hospital] asile *m* de dingues.

booby prize *n* prix *m* de consolation *(attribué par plaisanterie au dernier).*

booby trap (*pret & pp* **booby-trapped**, *cont* **booby-trapping**) *n* MIL objet *m* piégé ■ [practical joke] farce *f*.
◆ **booby-trap** *vt* piéger.

boodle ['bu:dl] *n inf* **1.** *US* [money] pognon *m*, fric *m* **2.** [bribe] pot-de-vin *m* **3.** *US* **the whole ~** tout le bazar.

boogie ['bu:gɪ] *inf* ◇ *vi* [dance] danser ■ [party] faire la fête.
◇ *n* boogie *m*.

boogie-woogie [-,wu:gɪ] *n* boogie-woogie *m*.

boohoo [,bu:'hu:] *inf* ◇ *vi* pleurer à chaudes larmes, chialer.
◇ *interj hum* sniff.

booing ['bu:ɪŋ] *n (U)* huées *fpl*.

book [bʊk] ◇ *n* **1.** *liter* livre *m* ■ **~ lover** bibliophile *mf* ■ **his little black ~** *hum* son carnet d'adresses ■ *fig* **her face is an open ~** toutes ses émotions se voient sur son visage ■ **his life is an open ~** il n'a rien à cacher ■ **mathematics is a closed ~ to me** je ne comprends rien aux mathématiques ➜ **to bring sb to ~** *UK* obliger qqn à rendre des comptes ■ **to do things** OR **to go by the ~** faire qqch selon les règles ■ **to be in sb's good ~s** être dans les petits papiers de qqn ■ **to be in sb's bad ~s** être mal vu de qqn ■ **in my ~** *inf* à mon avis ■ **he can read her like a ~** pour lui elle est transparente ■ **that's one for the ~** OR **~s!** il faudra marquer ça d'une pierre blanche! ■ **that provision is already on the ~s** cette disposition figure déjà dans les textes ■ **that law went on the ~s in 1979** cette loi est entrée en vigueur en 1979 ■ **that suits my ~** *UK* cela me va tout à fait ■ **to throw the ~ at sb** donner le maximum à qqn
2. [section of work] livre *m* ■ [of poem] chant *m*
3. [of stamps, tickets] carnet *m* ■ [of matches] pochette *f*
4. COMM [of samples] jeu *m*, album *m*
5. [betting] pari *m* ■ **to make/to start/to keep a ~ on sthg** inscrire/engager/tenir un pari sur qqch
6. [script, libretto] livret *m*
7. CARDS contrat *m*.
◇ *vt* **1.** [reserve] réserver, retenir ■ *UK* [tickets] prendre ■ **have you already ~ed your trip?** avez-vous déjà fait les réservations pour votre voyage? ■ **the tour is fully ~ed** l'excursion est com-

plète ■ **the performance is ~ed up** *OR* **fully ~ed** on joue à bureaux *OR* guichets fermés ■ **the restaurant is fully ~ ed** le restaurant est complet
2. [engage] embaucher, engager ■ **he's ~ed solid until next week** il est complètement pris jusqu'à la semaine prochaine
3. [subj: police] : **he was ~ed for speeding** il a attrapé une contravention pour excès de vitesse
4. SPORT prendre le nom de
5. COMM [order] enregistrer.
<> *vi* réserver.
◆ **books** *npl* **1.** COMM & FIN [accounts] livre *m* de comptes ■ **to keep the ~s** tenir les comptes *OR* la comptabilité ➊ **the ~s and records** la comptabilité ■ **to cook the ~s** *inf* trafiquer les comptes
2. [of club] registre *m* ■ **she's on the association's ~s** elle est membre de l'association.
◆ **book in** <> *vi insep UK* se faire enregistrer ■ [at hotel] prendre une chambre.
<> *vt sep* inscrire ■ [at hotel] réserver une chambre pour.
◆ **book out** <> *vi insep* quitter une chambre, partir.
<> *vt sep UK* [library book] emprunter.
◆ **book up** <> *vt sep* réserver, retenir ■ **the restaurant is ~ed up** le restaurant est complet ■ **she's ~ed up (all) next week** elle est prise (toute) la semaine prochaine.
<> *vi insep* réserver.

bookable ['bʊkəbl] *adj* **1.** *UK* [seat] qui peut être réservé d'avance **2.** [offence] passible d'une contravention.

bookbinding ['bʊk,baɪndɪŋ] *n* reliure *f*.

bookcase ['bʊkkeɪs] *n* bibliothèque *f (meuble)*.

book club *n* club *m* du livre, cercle *m* de lecture.

bookend ['bʊkend] *n* serre-livres *m inv*.

Booker Prize ['bʊkə-] *pr n* : **the ~** *prix littéraire britannique*.

BOOKER PRIZE

Le *Booker Prize* est le prix littéraire britannique le plus connu ; créé en 1969, il est accordé chaque année au meilleur roman d'expression anglaise découvert par un éditeur britannique.

bookie ['bʊkɪ] *n inf* bookmaker *m*.

booking ['bʊkɪŋ] *n* **1.** [reservation] réservation *f* **2.** [of actor, singer] engagement *m*.

booking clerk *n* préposé *m*, - e *f* aux réservations.

booking office *n* bureau *m* de location.

bookish ['bʊkɪʃ] *adj* [person] qui aime la lecture, studieux ■ [style] livresque.

bookkeeper ['bʊk,ki:pər] *n* comptable *mf*.

bookkeeping ['bʊk,ki:pɪŋ] *n* comptabilité *f*.

book-learning *n (U)* connaissances *fpl* livresques.

booklet ['bʊklɪt] *n* petit livre *m*, brochure *f*, plaquette *f*.

bookmaker ['bʊk,meɪkər] *n* bookmaker *m*.

bookmark ['bʊkmɑ:k] *n* signet *m*, marque-page *m* ■ COMPUT signet *m*.

bookmobile ['bʊkməbi:l] *n US* bibliobus *m*.

bookplate ['bʊkpleɪt] *n* ex-libris *m*.

bookrest ['bʊkrest] *n* lutrin *m*, support *m* à livres.

bookseller ['bʊk,selər] *n* libraire *mf*.

bookshelf ['bʊkʃelf] (*pl* **bookshelves** [-ʃelvz]) *n* étagère *f* à livres, rayon *m* (de bibliothèque).

bookshop ['bʊkʃɒp] *n UK* librairie *f*.

bookstall ['bʊkstɔ:l] *n* étalage *m* de bouquiniste ■ *UK* [in station] kiosque *m* à journaux.

bookstand ['bʊkstænd] *n US* [furniture] bibliothèque *f* ■ [small shop] étalage *m* de bouquiniste ■ [in station] kiosque *m* à journaux.

bookstore ['bʊkstɔ:r] *n US* librairie *f*.

book token *n UK bon d'achat de livres*.

bookworm ['bʊkwɜ:m] *n* **1.** *liter* ver *m* du papier **2.** *fig* rat *m* de bibliothèque.

boom [bu:m] <> *vi* **1.** [resonate - gen] retentir, résonner ; [- guns, thunder] tonner, gronder ; [- waves] gronder, mugir ; [- organ] ronfler ; [- voice] tonner, tonitruer **2.** [prosper] prospérer, réussir ■ **business was ~ing** les affaires étaient en plein essor ■ **car sales are ~ing** les ventes de voitures connaissent une forte progression.
<> *vt* **1.** [say loudly] tonner **2.** *US* [develop] développer ■ [publicize] promouvoir.
<> *n* **1.** [sound - gen] retentissement *m* ; [- of guns, thunder] grondement *m* ; [- of waves] grondement *m*, mugissement *m* ; [- of organ] ronflement *m* ; [- of voice] rugissement *m*, grondement *m* ■ **sonic ~** bang *m* **2.** [period of expansion] (vague *f* de) prospérité *f*, boom *m* ■ [of trade] forte hausse *f* *OR* progression *f* ■ [of prices, sales] brusque *OR* très forte hausse, montée *f* en flèche ■ [of product] popularité *f*, vogue *f* **3.** NAUT [spar] gui *m* **4.** [for camera, microphone] perche *f*, girafe *f* ■ [for crane] flèche *f* **5.** TECH [of derrick] bras *m* **6.** [barrier] barrage *m* (de radeaux *OR* de chaînes), estacade *f*.

boom box *n US inf* radiocassette *f*.

boomerang ['bu:məræŋ] <> *n* boomerang *m*.
<> *vi* faire boomerang ■ **his tricks will ~ on him one day** un jour ses tours lui retomberont sur le nez.

booming ['bu:mɪŋ] <> *adj* **1.** [sound] retentissant **2.** [business] prospère, en plein essor.
<> *n* [gen] retentissement *m* ■ [of guns, thunder] grondement *m* ■ [of waves] grondement *m*, mugissement *m* ■ [of organ] ronflement *m* ■ [of voice] rugissement *m*, grondement *m*.

boom town *n* ville *f* en plein essor, ville-champignon *f*.

boon [bu:n] *n* [blessing] aubaine *f*, bénédiction *f*.

boondocks ['bu:ndɒks], **boonies** ['bu:nɪz] *npl US inf* **the ~** le bled, la cambrousse.

boor [bʊər] *n* [rough] rustre *m* ■ [uncouth] goujat *m*, malotru *m*, - e *f*.

boorish ['bʊərɪʃ] *adj* grossier, rustre.

boost [bu:st] <> *vt* **1.** [sales] faire monter, augmenter ■ [productivity] développer, accroître ■ [morale, confidence] renforcer ■ [economy] relancer **2.** ELEC survolter ■ AUT suralimenter **3.** [promote] faire de la réclame *OR* de la publicité pour.
<> *n* **1.** [increase] augmentation *f*, croissance *f* ■ [improvement] amélioration *f* ■ **the announcement gave the pound a ~ on the foreign exchanges** la nouvelle a fait grimper la livre sur le marché des changes **2.** [promotion] : **the review gave his play a ~** la critique a fait de la publicité pour *OR* du battage autour de sa pièce **3.** [leg-up] : **to give sb a ~** *liter* faire la courte échelle à qqn ; *fig* donner un coup *m* de pouce à qqn ■ **the success gave her morale a ~** le succès lui a remonté le moral.

booster ['bu:stər] *n* **1.** AERON : **~ (rocket)** fusée *f* de lancement, moteur *m* auxiliaire **2.** RADIO amplificateur *m* **3.** ELEC [device] survolteur *m* ■ [charge] charge *f* d'appoint **4.** *US inf* [supporter] supporter *m* **5.** = **booster shot**.

booster shot *n* piqûre *f* de rappel.

boot [bu:t] <> *n* **1.** botte *f* ■ [ankle-length] bottillon *m* ■ [for babies, women] bottine *f* ■ [of soldier, workman] brodequin *m* ■ **to give sb the ~** *inf* flanquer qqn à la porte ■ **they put the ~ in** *UK inf liter* ils lui ont balancé des coups de pied ; *fig* ils ont enfoncé méchamment le clou **2.** *UK* AUT coffre *m*, malle *f* **3.** *inf* [kick] coup *m* de pied **4.** [instrument of torture] brodequin *m*.
<> *vt* **1.** [kick] donner des coups de pied à **2.** [equip with boots] botter **3.** COMPUT : **to ~ (up) the system** initialiser le système.
◆ **to boot** *adv phr* en plus, par-dessus le marché.
◆ **boot out** *vt sep inf* flanquer à la porte.
◆ **boot up** *vt sep* COMPUT = **boot** *(vt, sense 3)*.

bootblack ['bu:tblæk] *n* cireur *m* de chaussures.

boot camp *n US inf* MIL camp *m* d'entraînement pour nouvelles recrues.

bootee ['bu:ti:] *n* [for babies] petit chausson *m*, bottine *f* ■ [for women] bottine *f*, bottillon *m*.

booth [bu:ð] *n* **1.** [at fair] baraque *f*, stand *m* **2.** [cubicle - for telephone, language laboratory] cabine *f* ; [- for voting] isoloir *m* **3.** *US* [in restaurant] box *m*.

bootlace ['bu:tleɪs] *n* lacet *m* (de chaussure).

bootleg ['bu:t,leg] ◇ *vi* (*pret & pp* **bootlegged**, *cont* **bootlegging**) faire de la contrebande de boissons alcoolisées.
◇ *vt* (*pret & pp* **bootlegged**, *cont* **bootlegging**) [make] fabriquer illicitement ▪ [sell] vendre en contrebande.
◇ *n* [gen] marchandise *f* illicite ▪ [liquor] alcool *m* de contrebande ▪ [record, cassette] pirate *m*.
◇ *adj* de contrebande ▪ **~ cassette/record** cassette *f* / disque *m* pirate.

bootlegger ['bu:t,legəʳ] *n* bootlegger *m*.

bootless ['bu:tlɪs] *adj* **1.** [without boots] sans bottes **2.** *lit* [fruitless] vain, infructueux.

bootlicker ['bu:t,lɪkəʳ] *n inf* lèche-bottes *mf inv*.

bootmaker ['bu:t,meɪkəʳ] *n* bottier *m*.

boot polish *n* cirage *m*.

bootstrap ['bu:tstræp] ◇ *n* **1.** [on boot] tirant *m* de botte ▪ **she pulled herself up by her own ~s** *fig* elle a réussi par ses propres moyens **2.** COMPUT programme *m* amorce, amorce *f*.
◇ *adj* autonome ▪ **~ program** COMPUT programme *m* amorce.

booty ['bu:tɪ] *n* butin *m*.

booze [bu:z] *inf* ◇ *n (U)* alcool *m*, boissons *fpl* alcoolisées ▪ **she's off the ~** elle a arrêté de picoler.
◇ *vi* picoler.

boozer ['bu:zəʳ] *n inf* **1.** [drunkard] poivrot *m*, - e *f* **2.** *UK* [pub] bistro *m*.

booze-up *n UK inf* beuverie *f*, soûlerie *f*.

boozy ['bu:zɪ] (*comp* **boozier**, *superl* **booziest**) *adj inf* [person] soûlard ▪ [party, evening] de soûlographie.

bop [bɒp] ◇ *n* **1.** [music] bop *m* **2.** *inf* [dance] danse *f* **3.** *inf* [punch] coup *m* de poing.
◇ *vt* (*pret & pp* **bopped**, *cont* **bopping**) *inf* [hit] cogner.
◇ *vi* (*pret & pp* **bopped**, *cont* **bopping**) *inf* [dance] danser le bop ▪ **we bopped (away) all night** on a dansé toute la nuit.

Bordeaux [bɔ:'dəʊ] ◇ *pr n* [region] le Bordelais.
◇ *n* [wine] bordeaux *m*.

border ['bɔ:dəʳ] ◇ *n* **1.** [boundary] frontière *f* ▪ **on the ~ between Norway and Sweden** à la frontière entre la Norvège et la Suède **2.** [outer edge - of lake] bord *m*, rive *f* ; [- of field] bordure *f*, limite *f* ; [- of forest] lisière *f*, limite *f* **3.** [edging - of dress, handkerchief] bord *m*, bordure *f* ; [- of plate, notepaper] liséré *m* **4.** [in garden] bordure *f*, plate-bande *f*.
◇ *comp* [state, post, guard] frontière *(inv)* ▪ [town, zone] frontière *(inv)*, frontalier ▪ [search] à la frontière ▪ [dispute, patrol] frontalier ▪ **~ police** police *f* des frontières.
◇ *vt* **1.** [line edges of] border ▪ [encircle] entourer, encadrer **2.** [be adjacent to] toucher.
◆ **Borders** *pr npl UK* **the Borders** *région frontalière du sud-est de l'Écosse.*
◆ **border on, border upon** *vt insep* **1.** [be adjacent to] toucher, avoisiner **2.** [verge on] frôler ▪ **his remark ~s on slander** sa remarque frise la calomnie.

Border collie *n* colley *m* berger.

borderland ['bɔ:dəlænd] *n* [country] pays *m* frontière ▪ *liter & fig* [area] région *f* limitrophe.

borderline ['bɔ:dəlaɪn] ◇ *n* limite *f*, ligne *f* de démarcation ▪ **to be on the ~** être à la limite ▪ **the ~ between acceptable and unacceptable behaviour** ce qui sépare un comportement acceptable d'un comportement inacceptable.
◇ *adj* limite ▪ **he is a ~ candidate** il est à la limite.

bore [bɔ:ʳ] ◇ *pt* ▷ **bear**.
◇ *vt* **1.** [tire] ennuyer ▪ **housework ~s me stiff** *inf* OR **to tears** *inf* OR **to death** *inf* faire le ménage m'ennuie à mourir **2.** [drill - hole] percer ; [- well] forer, creuser ; [- tunnel] creuser.
◇ *vi* forer, sonder ▪ **they're boring for coal** ils forent pour extraire du charbon, ils recherchent du charbon par forage ▪ **I felt his eyes boring into me** *fig* je sentais son regard me transpercer.
◇ *n* **1.** [person] raseur *m*, - euse *f* ▪ [event, thing] ennui *m*, corvée *f* ▪ **visiting them is such a ~!** quelle barbe de leur rendre visite! **2.** [from drilling] trou *m* de sonde ▪ MECH alésage *m* **3.** [diameter of gun, tube] calibre *m* ▪ **a twelve-~ shotgun** un fusil de calibre douze **4.** [tidal flood] mascaret *m*.

bored [bɔ:d] *adj* [person] qui s'ennuie ▪ [expression] d'ennui ▪ **to be ~ with doing sthg** s'ennuyer à faire qqch ▪ **I'm ~ with my job** j'en ai assez de mon travail ▪ **to be ~ stiff** *inf* OR **to tears** *inf* OR **to death** *inf* s'ennuyer ferme OR à mourir.

boredom ['bɔ:dəm] *n* ennui *m*.

borehole ['bɔ:həʊl] *n* trou *m* de sonde.

borer ['bɔ:rəʳ] *n* **1.** [person] foreur *m*, perceur *m* ▪ TECH [for wood] vrille *f*, foret *m* ▪ [for metal] alésoir *m* ▪ [for mine, well] foret, sonde *f* **2.** [insect] insecte *m* térébrant.

boring ['bɔ:rɪŋ] ◇ *adj* **1.** [tiresome] ennuyeux ▪ [uninteresting] sans intérêt ▪ **the meeting was so ~** cette réunion était assommante **2.** TECH [for wood] : **~ machine** perceuse *f* ; [for metal] alésoir *m*.
◇ *n* TECH [in wood] perforation *f*, forage *m* ▪ [in metal] alésage *m* ▪ [in ground] forage *m*, sondage *m*.

born [bɔ:n] *adj* **1.** *liter* né ▪ **to be ~** naître ▪ **she was ~ blind** elle est née aveugle ▪ **Victor Hugo was ~ in 1802** Victor Hugo est né en 1802 ▪ **~ of an American father** né d'un père américain ▪ **~ and bred** né et élevé ▮ *fig* **the place where communism was ~** le lieu où est né le communisme ▪ **anger ~ of frustration** une colère née de OR due à la frustration ▶ **in all my ~ days** *inf* de toute ma vie ▪ **I wasn't ~ yesterday!** *inf* je ne suis pas né d'hier OR de la dernière pluie! ▪ **she was ~ with a silver spoon in her mouth** elle est née avec une cuillère en argent dans la bouche ▪ **there's one ~ every minute!** *inf* il y en a toujours un qui tombe dans le panneau! **2.** [as intensifier] : **he's a ~ musician** il est né musicien, c'est un musicien né ▪ **she's a ~ worrier** elle s'inquiète à tout propos.

-born *in cpds* originaire de.

born-again *adj* RELIG & *fig* rené.

borne [bɔ:n] *pp* ▷ **bear**.

-borne *in cpds* transporté par ▪ **water~ organisms** organismes *mpl* véhiculés par l'eau.

Bornean ['bɔ:nɪən] ◇ *n habitant de Bornéo.*
◇ *adj* de Bornéo.

Borneo ['bɔ:nɪəʊ] *pr n* Bornéo ▪ **in ~** à Bornéo.

Borodin ['bɒrədɪn] *pr n* Borodine.

borough ['bʌrəʊ] *n* **1.** [British town] *ville représentée à la Chambre des communes par un ou plusieurs députés* **2.** [in London] *une des 32 subdivisions administratives de Londres* **3.** [in New York] *une des 5 subdivisions administratives de New York.*

borough council *n conseil municipal d'un "borough".*

borrow ['bɒrəʊ] *vt* **1.** [gen - FIN] emprunter ▪ **to ~ sthg from sb** emprunter qqch à qqn ▪ **an artist who ~s his ideas from nature** un artiste qui trouve ses idées dans la nature ▪ **a word ~ed from Russian** un mot emprunté du russe ▶ **to live on ~ed time** avoir peu de temps à vivre **2.** *UK* MATHS [in subtraction] : **I ~ one** je retiens un.

borrower ['bɒrəʊəʳ] *n* emprunteur *m*, - euse *f* ▪ **neither a ~ nor a lender be** *prov* il ne faut ni emprunter ni prêter d'argent.

borrowing ['bɒrəʊɪŋ] *n* FIN & LING emprunt *m* ▪ **the ~ rate** le taux d'intérêt des emprunts.

borstal ['bɔ:stl] *n UK ancien nom d'une institution pour jeunes délinquants, aujourd'hui appelée "young offenders' institution".*

borzoi ['bɔ:zɔɪ] *n* barzoï *m*, lévrier *m* russe.

BOS *n* = **bulletin board system**.

Bosnia ['bɒznɪə] *pr n* Bosnie *f* ▪ **in ~** en Bosnie.

Bosnia-Herzegovina [-,heətsəgə'vi:nə] *pr n* Bosnie-Herzégovine *f*.

Bosnian ['bɒznɪən] ◇ *n* Bosnien *m*, - enne *f*, Bosniaque *mf*.

◇ *adj* bosnien, bosniaque.

bosom ['bʊzəm] *n* **1.** [of person] poitrine *f* ■ [of woman] seins *mpl* ■ *fig & lit* **she took the child to her ~** elle prit l'enfant sous son aile ■ **he harboured in his ~ feelings of deep insecurity** il nourrissait en son sein un sentiment de profonde insécurité ■ **a ~ friend** un ami intime **2.** [of dress] corsage *m* **3.** *fig* [centre] sein *m*, fond *m* ■ **in the ~ of his family** au sein de sa famille.

Bosporus ['bɒspərəs], **Bosphorus** ['bɒsfərəs] *pr n* Bosphore *m*.

boss [bɒs] ◇ *n* **1.** *inf* [person in charge] patron *m*, -onne *f*, chef *m* ■ **who's the ~ around here?** qui est-ce qui commande ici? ■ **I'll show you who's ~!** je vais te montrer qui est le chef! ■ **he enjoys being his own ~** il aime être son propre patron **2.** *inf* [of gang] caïd *m* ■ *US* [politician] manitou *m* (du parti) **3.** [knob] bossage *m* ■ [on shield] ombon *m* **4.** ARCHIT bossage *m* **5.** BIOL bosse *f* **6.** TECH mamelon *m*, bossage *m* ■ [of propeller] moyeu *m*.
◇ *vt inf* [person] commander, donner des ordres à ■ [organization] diriger, faire marcher.
◆ **boss about** *UK*, **boss around** *vt sep inf* mener à la baguette ■ **stop ~ing me around!** j'en ai assez que vous me donniez des ordres!

boss-eyed *adj UK inf* qui louche.

bossily ['bɒsɪlɪ] *adv inf* d'une manière autoritaire.

bossiness ['bɒsɪnɪs] *n inf* comportement *m* autoritaire.

bossy ['bɒsɪ] (*comp* **bossier**, *superl* **bossiest**) *adj inf* autoritaire, dictatorial.

Boston ['bɒstn] *pr n* Boston.

Bostonian [bɒ'stəʊnjən] ◇ *n* Bostonien *m*, - enne *f*.
◇ *adj* bostonien.

Boston Tea Party *pr n* : **the ~** la "Boston Tea Party".

BOSTON TEA PARTY

Insurrection menée en 1773 par les Bostoniens, qui jetèrent à la mer des cargaisons de thé pour protester contre les droits de douane imposés par l'Angleterre. Cette *Tea Party* fut suivie d'autres dans quelques colonies. Elle durcit les fronts entre ***Loyalists*** et ***Patriots***.

bosun ['bəʊsn] *n* = **boatswain**.

botanic(al) [bə'tænɪk(l)] *adj* botanique ■ **~ garden** jardin *m* botanique.

botanist ['bɒtənɪst] *n* botaniste *mf*.

botany ['bɒtənɪ] *n* botanique *f*.

botch [bɒtʃ] *inf* ◇ *vt* [spoil] saboter, bâcler ■ [repair clumsily] rafistoler ■ **to make a ~ed job of sthg** *UK* bousiller qqch.
◇ *n* : **those workmen made a real ~** *OR* **~-up of the job** ces ouvriers ont fait un travail de cochon *OR* ont tout salopé.

both [bəʊθ] ◇ *predet* les deux, l'un *OR* l'autre et l'autre ■ **~ dresses are pretty** les deux robes sont jolies ▶ **you can't have it ~ ways!** il faut te décider!
◇ *pron* tous (les) deux *mpl*, toutes (les) deux *f* ■ **~ are to blame** c'est leur faute à tous les deux ■ **why not do ~?** pourquoi ne pas faire les deux? ■ **Claire and I ~ went** Claire et moi y sommes allés tous les deux.
◆ **both... and** *conj phr* : **her job is ~ interesting and well-paid** son travail est à la fois intéressant et bien payé ■ **I ~ read and write Spanish** je sais lire et écrire l'espagnol ■ **~ the rich and the poor voted for him** les riches et les pauvres ont voté pour lui.

bother ['bɒðəʳ] ◇ *vi* prendre la peine ■ **don't ~ to answer the phone** ce n'est pas la peine de répondre au téléphone ■ **please don't ~ getting up!** ne vous donnez pas la peine de vous lever! ■ **don't ~ about me** ne vous en faites pas *OR* ne vous inquiétez pas pour moi ■ **let's not ~ with the housework** laissons tomber le ménage.
◇ *vt* **1.** [irritate] ennuyer, embêter ■ [pester] harceler ■ [disturb] déranger ■ **would it ~ you if I opened the window?** cela vous dérange *OR* ennuie si j'ouvre la fenêtre? **2.** [worry] tracasser ■ **don't ~ yourself** *OR* **your head about it** ne vous tracassez pas à ce sujet ■ **it doesn't ~ me whether they come or not** cela m'est bien égal qu'ils viennent ou pas **3.** [hurt] faire souffrir ■ **his leg is ~ing him again** sa jambe le fait de nouveau souffrir.
◇ *n* **1.** [trouble] ennui *m* ■ **to have** *OR* **to have a spot of ~ (with sb)** *UK* avoir des ennuis (avec qqn) ■ **he doesn't give her any ~** il ne la dérange pas ■ **the trip isn't worth the ~** le voyage ne vaut pas la peine ■ **thanks for babysitting – it's no ~!** merci pour le babysitting – de rien! **2.** [nuisance] ennui *m* ■ **homework is such a ~!** quelle corvée, les devoirs! ■ **sorry to be a ~** excusez-moi de vous déranger.
◇ *interj inf UK inf* flûte, mince.

bothered ['bɒðəd] *adj* : **to be ~ about sb/sthg** s'inquiéter de qqn/qqch ■ **I can't be ~ to write letters tonight** je n'ai pas le courage d'écrire des lettres ce soir ■ **he can't be ~ to do his own laundry** il a la flemme de laver son linge lui-même ■ **I'm not ~** ça m'est égal.

bothersome ['bɒðəsəm] *adj* ennuyeux, gênant.

Bothnia ['bɒθnɪə] *pr n* ▷ **gulf**.

Botox® ['bəʊtɑks] *n (U)* MED Botox *m*.

Botswana [bɒ'tswɑːnə] *pr n* Botswana *m*.

bottle ['bɒtl] ◇ *n* **1.** [container, contents] bouteille *f* ■ [of perfume] flacon *m* ■ [of medicine] flacon *m*, fiole *f* ■ [jar] bocal *m* ■ [made of stone] cruche *f*, cruchon *m* ■ **a wine ~** une bouteille à vin ■ **we ordered a ~ of wine** nous avons commandé une bouteille de vin ▮ *fig* **he was too fond of the ~** *inf* il levait bien le coude, il aimait la bouteille ■ **to hit the ~** *inf* picoler dur **2.** [for baby] biberon *m* **3.** *UK inf* [nerve] : **he lost his ~** il s'est dégonflé ■ **she's got a lot of ~** elle a un sacré cran.
◇ *vt* [wine] mettre en bouteille ■ [fruit] mettre en bocal *OR* conserve, conserver.
◆ **bottle out**△ *vi insep UK* se dégonfler.
◆ **bottle up** *vt sep* **1.** [emotions] refouler, ravaler **2.** [army] embouteiller, contenir.

bottle bank *n conteneur pour la collecte du verre usagé.*

bottled ['bɒtld] *adj* en bouteille *OR* bouteilles.

bottle-fed *adj* élevé *OR* allaité au biberon.

bottle-feed *vt* allaiter *OR* nourrir au biberon.

bottle green *n* vert *m* bouteille.
◆ **bottle-green** *adj* vert bouteille *(inv)*.

bottleneck ['bɒtlnek] ◇ *n* [in road] rétrécissement *m* de la chaussée, étranglement *m* ■ [of traffic] embouteillage *m*, bouchon *m* ■ [in industry] goulet *m OR* goulot *m* d'étranglement.
◇ *vt US* **strikes have ~ed production** les grèves ont ralenti la production.

bottle opener *n* ouvre-bouteilles *m inv*, décapsuleur *m*.

bottle rack *n* casier *m* à bouteilles.

bottle tan *n* bronzage *m* artificiel.

bottom ['bɒtəm] ◇ *n* **1.** [lowest part - of garment, heap] bas *m* ; [- of water] fond *m* ; [- of hill, stairs] bas *m*, pied *m* ; [- of outside of container] bas *m* ; [- of inside of container] fond *m* ; [- of chair] siège *m*, fond *m* ; [- of ship] carène *f* ■ **at the ~ of page one** au bas de la *OR* en bas de page un ■ **the ship touched (the) ~** le navire a touché le fond ■ *fig* **I believe, at the ~ of my heart, that...** je crois, au fond de moi-même, que... ■ **he thanked them from the ~ of his heart** il les a remerciés du fond du cœur ■ **the ~ fell out of the grain market** FIN le marché des grains s'est effondré ■ **the ~ dropped out of her world when he died** lorsqu'il est mort, pour elle le monde s'est effondré ▶ **~s up!** *inf* cul sec!
2. [last place] : **he's (at the) ~ of his class** il est le dernier de sa classe ■ **you're at the ~ of the list** vous êtes en queue de liste ■ **you have to start at the ~ and work your way up** vous devez commencer au plus bas et monter dans la hiérarchie à la force du poignet
3. [far end] fond *m*, bas *m* ■ **at the ~ of the street/garden** au bout de la rue/du jardin
4. *fig* [origin, source] base *f*, origine *f* ■ **I'm sure she's at the ~ of all this** je suis sûr que c'est elle qui est à l'origine de cette histoire ■ **I intend to get to the ~ of this affair** j'entends aller au fin fond de cette affaire *OR* découvrir le pot aux roses
5. [buttocks] derrière *m*, fesses *fpl*

6. [of two-piece garment] bas *m* ■ **pyjama ~s** bas de pyjama.
◇ *adj* : **the ~ half of the chart** la partie inférieure du tableau ■ **the ~ half of the class/list** la deuxième moitié de la classe/liste ■ **the ~ floor** le rez-de-chaussée ■ **the ~ end of the table** le bas de la table ■ **~ gear** *UK* AUT première *f* (vitesse *f*) ▶ **~ land** *OR* **lands** *US* terre *f* *OR* plaine *f* alluviale ■ **~ round** *US* CULIN gîte *m* à la noix.
◇ *vi* [ship] toucher le fond.
◆ **at bottom** *adv phr* au fond.
◆ **bottom out** *vi insep* [prices] atteindre son niveau plancher ■ [recession] atteindre son plus bas niveau.

bottom drawer *n UK* : **she's collecting things for her ~** elle réunit des choses pour son trousseau.

bottomless ['bɒtəmlɪs] *adj* sans fond, insondable ■ [unlimited - funds, supply] inépuisable ■ [- quantity] *esp US* à volonté.

bottom line *n* FIN résultat *m* net ■ *fig* **the ~** l'essentiel.

bottommost ['bɒtəmməʊst] *adj* le plus bas.

botulism ['bɒtjʊlɪzm] *n* botulisme *m*.

boudoir ['buːdwɑːʳ] *n* boudoir *m*.

bouffant ['buːfɔːŋ] *adj* [hairstyle] gonflant ■ [sleeve] bouffant.

bougainvill(a)ea [ˌbuːgən'vɪlɪə] *n* bougainvillée *f*, bougainvillier *m*.

bough [baʊ] *n lit* branche *f*.

bought [bɔːt] *pt* & *pp* ▷ **buy**.

boulder ['bəʊldəʳ] *n* bloc *m* de roche, boulder *m spec* ■ [smaller] gros galet *m*.

boulevard ['buːləvɑːd] *n* boulevard *m*.

bounce [baʊns] ◇ *n* **1.** [rebound] bond *m*, rebond *m* ■ **he caught the ball on the ~** il a pris la balle au bond **2.** [spring] : **there isn't much ~ in this ball** cette balle ne rebondit pas beaucoup ■ **I'd like to put some ~ in my hair** je voudrais donner du volume à mes cheveux **3.** *US inf* [dismissal] : **to give sb the ~** virer qqn.
◇ *vi* **1.** [object] rebondir ■ **the ball ~d down the steps** la balle a rebondi de marche en marche ■ **the knapsack ~d up and down on his back** le sac à dos tressautait sur ses épaules ■ **the bicycle ~d along the bumpy path** le vélo faisait des bonds sur le chemin cahoteux **2.** [person] bondir, sauter ■ **she came bouncing into/out of the room** elle est entrée dans/sortie de la pièce d'un bond **3.** *inf* [cheque] être refusé pour non-provision ■ **I hope this cheque doesn't ~** j'espère que ce chèque n'est pas sans provision.
◇ *vt* **1.** [cause to spring] faire rebondir ■ **she ~d the ball against** *OR* **off the wall** elle fit rebondir la balle sur le mur ■ **he ~d the baby on his knee** il a fait sauter l'enfant sur son genou ■ **signals are ~d off a satellite** les signaux sont renvoyés *OR* retransmis par satellite ■ **they ~d ideas off each other** *fig* leur échange de vues créait une émulation réciproque **2.** *inf* [cheque] : **the bank ~d my cheque** la banque a refusé mon chèque **3.** *inf* [throw out] flanquer à la porte, vider.
◆ **bounce back** *vi insep* [after illness] se remettre rapidement.

bouncer ['baʊnsəʳ] *n inf* videur *m*.

bouncing ['baʊnsɪŋ] *adj* **1.** [healthy] qui respire la santé ■ **a ~ baby** un bébé en pleine santé **2.** [ball] qui rebondit.

bouncy ['baʊnsɪ] (*comp* **bouncier**, *superl* **bounciest**) *adj* **1.** [ball, bed] élastique ■ [hair] souple, qui a du volume **2.** [person] plein d'entrain, dynamique.

bouncy castle *n grand château gonflable utilisé comme trampoline par les enfants.*

bound [baʊnd] ◇ *pt* & *pp* ▷ **bind**.
◇ *adj* **1.** [certain] sûr, certain ■ **it was ~ to happen** c'était à prévoir ■ **but he's ~ to say that** mais il est certain que c'est cela qu'il va dire ▶ **she's up to no good, I'll be ~** je parie qu'elle ne mijote rien de bon
2. [compelled] obligé ■ **they are ~ by the treaty to take action** l'accord les oblige à prendre des mesures ■ **the teacher felt ~ to report them** l'enseignant s'est cru obligé de les dénoncer ▶ **I'm ~ to say I disagree** je dois dire que je ne suis pas d'accord
3. [connected] : **~ up** lié ■ **his frustration is ~ up with his work** sa frustration est directement liée à son travail
4. [heading towards] : **~ for** [person] en route pour ; [shipment, cargo etc] à destination de ; [train] à destination *OR* en direction de ■ **on a plane ~ for Tokyo** dans un avion à destination de *OR* en route pour Tokyo
5. [tied] lié ■ LING lié ■ **~ hand and foot** pieds et poings liés
6. [book] relié ■ **~ in boards** cartonné.
◇ *n* **1.** [leap] saut *m*, bond *m*
2. MATHS : **lower ~** minorant *m* ■ **upper ~** majorant *m*.
◇ *vi* [person] sauter, bondir ■ [animal] faire un bond *OR* des bonds, bondir ■ **the children ~ed into/out of the classroom** les enfants sont entrés dans/sortis de la salle de classe en faisant des bonds.
◇ *vt* borner, limiter ■ **a country ~ed on two sides by the sea** un pays limité par la mer de deux côtés.
◆ **bounds** *npl* limite *f*, borne *f* ■ **the situation has gone beyond the ~s of all reason** la situation est devenue complètement aberrante *OR* insensée ■ **her rage knew no ~s** sa colère était sans bornes ■ **within the ~s of possibility** dans la limite du possible ▶ **out of ~s** [gen] dont l'accès est interdit ; SPORT hors du jeu ■ **the castle gardens are out of ~s to visitors** les jardins du château sont interdits au public.

-bound *in cpds* **1.** [restricted] confiné ■ **house~** confiné à la maison ■ **snow~ road** route *f* complètement enneigée **2.** [heading towards] : **a south~ train** un train en partance pour le Sud ■ **city~ traffic** circulation *f* en direction du centre-ville.

boundary ['baʊndərɪ] (*pl* **boundaries**) *n* limite *f*, frontière *f* ■ **~ (line)** ligne *f* frontière ; SPORT limites *fpl* du terrain ; [in basketball] ligne *f* de touche.

boundary stone *n* borne *f*, pierre *f* de bornage.

bounder ['baʊndəʳ] *n UK inf dated* goujat *m*, malotru *m*.

boundless ['baʊndlɪs] *adj* [energy, wealth] illimité ■ [ambition, gratitude] sans bornes ■ [space] infini.

bounteous ['baʊntɪəs], **bountiful** ['baʊntɪfʊl] *adj lit* [person] généreux, libéral ■ [supply] abondant ■ [rain] bienfaisant.

bounty ['baʊntɪ] (*pl* **bounties**) *n* **1.** *lit* [generosity] munificence *f* **2.** [gift] don *m* **3.** [reward] prime *f*.

bounty hunter *n* chasseur *m* de primes.

bouquet [bʊ'keɪ] *n* bouquet *m*.

bourbon ['bɜːbən] *n* [whisky] bourbon *m*.

Bourbon ['bʊəbən] ◇ *adj* Bourbon.
◇ *n* Bourbon *mf*.

bourgeois ['bɔːʒwɑː] ◇ *n* bourgeois *m*, - e *f*.
◇ *adj* bourgeois.

bourgeoisie [ˌbɔːʒwɑː'ziː] *n* bourgeoisie *f*.

bout [baʊt] *n* **1.** [period] période *f* ■ **a ~ of drinking** une soûlerie, une beuverie **2.** [of illness] attaque *f* ■ [of fever] accès *m* ■ [of rheumatism] crise *f* ■ **a ~ of bronchitis** une bronchite ■ **a ~ of flu** une grippe **3.** [boxing, wrestling] combat *m* ■ [fencing] assaut *m*.

boutique [buː'tiːk] *n* [shop] boutique *f* ■ [in department store] rayon *m*.

bovine ['bəʊvaɪn] ◇ *adj liter* & *fig* bovin.
◇ *n* bovin *m*.

bovver boots *npl UK inf dated* brodequins *mpl*, rangers *mpl*.

bovver boy *n UK inf dated* loubard *m*.

bow[1] [baʊ] ◇ *vi* **1.** [in greeting] incliner la tête, saluer ■ **I ~ed to him** je l'ai salué de la tête ▶ **he refuses to ~ and scrape to anyone** il refuse de faire des courbettes *OR* des salamalecs à qui que ce soit **2.** [bend] se courber ■ [under load] ployer **3.** *fig* [yield] s'incliner ■ **to ~ to the inevitable** s'incliner devant l'inévitable ■ **the government is ~ing under** *OR* **to pressure from the unions** l'administration s'incline sous la pression des syndicats ■ **I'll ~ to your greater knowledge** je m'incline devant tant de savoir *OR* de science.
◇ *vt* [bend] incliner, courber ■ [knee] fléchir ■ [head - in shame] baisser ; [- in prayer] incliner ; [- in contemplation] pencher.

<> *n* **1.** [gen] salut *m* ▪ **to take a ~** saluer **2.** [of ship] avant *m*, proue *f* ▪ **on the port/starboard ~** par bâbord/tribord avant **3.** [oarsman] nageur *m* de l'avant.
◆ **bow down** <> *vi insep* s'incliner ▪ **he ~ed down to her** il s'est incliné devant elle.
<> *vt sep* faire plier ▪ *fig* écraser, briser.
◆ **bow out** *vi insep fig* tirer sa révérence.

bow² [bəʊ] <> *n* **1.** [curve] arc *m* **2.** [for arrows] arc *m* **3.** MUS [stick] archet *m* ▪ [stroke] coup *m* d'archet **4.** [in ribbon] nœud *m*, boucle *f* ▪ **tie it in a ~** faites un nœud.
<> *vi* MUS manier l'archet.

Bow Bells [bəʊ-] *pr npl cloches de l'église Saint Mary-Le-Bow à Londres.*

BOW BELLS

Selon la tradition, un « vrai Londonien » (un Cockney) se doit d'être né dans le périmètre couvert par le son des cloches de l'église de St Mary-Le-Bow.

bowed [baʊd] *adj* [back] courbé ▪ [head] baissé.

bowel ['baʊəl] *n (usu pl)* **1.** ANAT [human] intestin *m*, intestins *mpl* ▪ [animal] boyau *m*, boyaux *mpl*, intestins *mpl* ▪ **a ~ disorder** troubles *mpl* intestinaux **2.** *fig* **the ~s of the earth** les entrailles *fpl* de la terre.

bower ['baʊəʳ] *n* **1.** [arbour] berceau *m* de verdure, charmille *f* **2.** *lit* [cottage] chaumière *f* ▪ [boudoir] boudoir *m*.

bowing¹ ['baʊɪŋ] *n (U)* [greeting] saluts *mpl* ▪ **~ and scraping** salamalecs *mpl*, courbettes *fpl*.

bowing² ['bəʊɪŋ] *n* MUS technique *f* d'archet.

bowl [bəʊl] <> *n* **1.** [receptacle] bol *m* ▪ [larger] bassin *m*, cuvette *f* ▪ [shallow] jatte *f* ▪ [made of glass] coupe *f* ▪ [for washing-up] cuvette *f* ▪ [of beggar] sébile *f* ▪ [contents] bol *m* **2.** [rounded part - of spoon] creux *m* ; [- of pipe] fourneau *m* ; [- of wine glass] coupe *f* ; [- of sink, toilet] cuvette *f* **3.** GEOG bassin *m*, cuvette *f* **4.** *US* SPORT [arena] amphithéâtre *m* ▪ [championship] championnat *m*, coupe *f* ▪ [trophy] coupe *f* **5.** [ball] boule *f* ▪ **(game of) ~s** *UK* (jeu *m* de) boules *fpl*.
<> *vi* **1.** [play bowls] jouer aux boules ▪ [play tenpin bowling] jouer au bowling ▪ [in cricket] lancer (la balle) **2.** [move quickly] filer, aller bon train ▪ **the bus ~ed along the country lanes** l'autocar roulait à toute vitesse sur les petites routes de campagne.
<> *vt* **1.** [ball, bowl] lancer, faire rouler ▪ [hoop] faire rouler **2.** SPORT [score] : **I ~ed 160** j'ai marqué 160 points ▮ [in cricket] : **to ~ the ball** servir ▪ **he ~ed (out) the batsman** il a mis le batteur hors jeu.
◆ **bowl over** *vt sep* **1.** [knock down] renverser, faire tomber **2.** *inf fig* [amaze] stupéfier, sidérer ▪ **I was ~ed over by the news** la nouvelle m'a abasourdi.

bow-legged [bəʊ-] *adj* à jambes arquées.

bow legs [bəʊ-] *npl* jambes *fpl* arquées.

bowler ['bəʊləʳ] *n* **1.** SPORT [in bowls] joueur *m*, - euse *f* de boules *OR* pétanque, bouliste *mf* ▪ [in tenpin bowling] joueur *m*, - euse *f* de bowling ▪ [in cricket] lanceur *m*, - euse *f* **2.** = **bowler hat**.

bowler hat *n UK* (chapeau *m*) melon *m*.

bowlful ['bəʊlfʊl] *n* bol *m*.

bowline ['bəʊlɪn] *n* [rope] bouline *f* ▪ [knot] nœud *m* de chaise.

bowling ['bəʊlɪŋ] *n* [bowls] jeu *m* de boules, pétanque *f* ▪ [tenpin] bowling *m* ▪ [in cricket] service *m* ▪ **to go ~** [bowls] (aller) jouer à la pétanque ; [tenpin bowling] (aller) faire du bowling.

bowling alley *n* bowling *m*.

bowling green *n* terrain *m* de boules *(sur gazon)*.

bowman ['bəʊmən] (*pl* **bowmen** [-mən]) *n lit* [archer] archer *m* ▪ NAUT nageur *m* de l'avant.

bowsprit ['bəʊsprɪt] *n* beaupré *m*.

bowstring ['bəʊstrɪŋ] *n* corde *f*.

bow tie [bəʊ-] *n* nœud *m* papillon.

bow window [bəʊ-] *n UK* fenêtre *f* en saillie, oriel *m*, bow-window *m*.

bow-wow [ˌbaʊ'waʊ] <> *n baby* toutou *m*.
<> *onom* ouâ ouâ.

box [bɒks] (*pl* **boxes**) <> *n* **1.** [container, contents] boîte *f* ▪ [with lock] coffret *m* ▪ [cardboard box] carton *m* ▪ [crate] caisse *f* ▪ [for money] caisse *f* ▪ [collecting box] tronc *m* ▪ **how can people live in these little ~es?** *fig* comment les gens font-ils pour vivre dans ces trous de souris? **2.** [compartment] compartiment *m* ▪ THEAT loge *f* ▪ LAW [for jury, reporters] banc *m* ▪ [for witness] barre *f* ▪ [in stable] box *m* ▪ [of coachman] siège *m* (de cocher) ▪ **the Royal ~** *loge réservée aux membres de la famille royale* **3.** [designated area - on form] case *f* ; [- in newspaper] encadré *m* ; [- on road, sportsfield] zone *f* quadrillée **4.** AUT & TECH [casing] boîte *f*, carter *m* **5.** *inf* [television] téléviseur *m* **6.** [postal address] boîte *f* postale **7.** [blow] : **a ~ on the ears** une gifle, une claque **8.** SPORT [protector] coquille *f* **9.** BOT buis *m*.
<> *comp* [border, hedge] de *OR* en buis.
<> *vi* [fight] faire de la boxe, boxer.
<> *vt* **1.** [fight] boxer avec, boxer **2.** *phr* **to ~ sb's ears** gifler qqn **3.** [put in box] mettre en boîte *OR* caisse **4.** NAUT : **to ~ the compass** réciter les aires du vent.
◆ **box in** *vt sep* [enclose] enfermer, confiner ▪ [pipes] encastrer ▪ **the car was ~ed in between two vans** la voiture était coincée entre deux camionnettes ▪ **to feel ~ed in** se sentir à l'étroit.
◆ **box up** *vt sep* mettre en boîte *OR* caisse ▪ *fig* enfermer.

box calf *n* box *m*, box-calf *m*.

box camera *n* appareil *m* photographique rudimentaire.

boxcar ['bɒkskɑːr] *n US* wagon *m* de marchandises (couvert).

boxed [bɒkst] *adj* COMM en boîte ▪ **a ~ set** un coffret.

box end wrench *n US* clef *f* polygonale.

boxer ['bɒksəʳ] *n* [fighter] boxeur *m* ▪ [dog] boxer *m*.

boxer shorts *npl* boxer-short *m*.

boxing ['bɒksɪŋ] *n* boxe *f*.

Boxing Day *n UK le 26 décembre.*

boxing glove *n* gant *m* de boxe.

boxing ring *n* ring *m*.

box junction *n UK* carrefour *m (matérialisé sur la chaussée par des bandes croisées).*

box kite *n* cerf-volant *m* cellulaire.

box number *n* [in newspaper] numéro *m* d'annonce ▪ [at post office] numéro *m* de boîte à lettres.

box office *n* [office] bureau *m* de location ▪ [window] guichet *m* (de location) ▪ **the play was a big success at the ~** la pièce a fait recette.
◆ **box-office** *comp* : **to be a box-office success** être en tête du box-office.

box pleat *n* pli *m* creux.

boxroom ['bɒksrʊm] *n UK* débarras *m*, capharnaüm *m*.

box spanner *n* clef *f OR* clé *f* en douille.

boxwood ['bɒkswʊd] *n* buis *m*.

boy [bɔɪ] <> *n* **1.** [male child] garçon *m*, enfant *m* ▪ **when I was a ~** quand j'étais petit *OR* jeune ▪ **be a good ~!** sois sage! ▪ **the Smiths' ~** le petit Smith ▪ **sit down, my ~** assieds-toi, mon petit *OR* mon grand ▪ **I've known them since they were ~s** je les connais depuis leur enfance *OR* depuis qu'ils sont petits ▪ **~s will be ~s** un garçon, c'est un garçon ▮ [son] garçon *m*, fils *m* ▪ **he's a mother's ~** c'est le petit garçon à sa maman **2.** *UK* SCH [student] élève *m* ▪ **day ~** externe *m* **3.** *inf* [term of address] : **that's my ~!** je te reconnais bien là! ▪ **my dear ~** mon cher ami ▪ **how are you, old ~?** *UK* ça va mon vieux? **4.** [male adult] : **a local ~** un gars du coin ▪ **a night out with the ~s** une virée entre copains ▶ **the ~s in blue** *inf* les flics *mpl* ▪ **the backroom ~s** ceux qui restent dans les coulisses **5.** *offens* [native servant] boy *m* **6.** [used to address dog, horse etc] mon beau ▪ **down, ~!** couché, mon beau!
<> *interj* : **(oh) ~!** dis donc!

boycott ['bɔɪkɒt] <> *n* boycottage *m*, boycott *m*.
<> *vt* boycotter.

boyfriend ['bɔɪfrend] *n* petit ami *m*.

boyhood ['bɔɪhʊd] *n* enfance *f*.

boyish ['bɔɪɪʃ] *adj* **1.** [youthful] d'enfant, de garçon ■ [childish] enfantin, puéril **2.** [tomboyish - girl] garçonnier ; [- behaviour] garçonnier, de garçon.

Boys' Brigade *pr n organisation protestante de scoutisme pour garçons.*

boy scout *n* scout *m*.

bozo ['bəʊzəʊ] *n inf pej* type *m*.

Bp (*written abbrev of* **bishop**) Mgr.

Br 1. *written abbr of* **British 2.** [preceding name of monk] (*written abbrev of* **brother**) F.

BR (*abbrev of* **British Rail**) *pr n société des chemins de fer britanniques.*

bra [brɑː] *n* soutien-gorge *m*.

Brabant [brə'bænt] *pr n* Brabant *m*.

brace [breɪs] (*pl* **braces**) <> *vt* **1.** [strengthen] renforcer, consolider ■ [support] soutenir ■ CONSTR entretoiser ■ [beam] armer **2.** [steady, prepare] : **he ~d his body/himself for the impact** il raidit son corps/s'arc-bouta en préparation du choc ■ **he ~d himself to try again** il a rassemblé ses forces pour une nouvelle tentative ■ **the family ~d itself for the funeral** la famille s'est armée de courage pour les funérailles ■ **~ yourself for some bad news** préparez-vous à de mauvaises nouvelles.
<> *n* **1.** [supporting or fastening device] attache *f*, agrafe *f* **2.** MED appareil *m* orthopédique ■ [for teeth] appareil *m* dentaire *OR* orthodontique **3.** CONSTR entretoise *f* **4.** TECH [drill] : **~ (and bit)** vilebrequin *m* à main **5.** (*pl* brace) [of game birds, pistols] paire *f* **6.** MUS & TYPO [bracket] accolade *f*.
◆ **braces** *npl* **1.** *UK* [for trousers] bretelles *fpl* **2.** MED [for teeth] appareil *m* dentaire *OR* orthodontique.

bracelet ['breɪslɪt] *n* bracelet *m*.

bracing ['breɪsɪŋ] <> *adj* fortifiant, tonifiant ■ **a ~ wind** un vent vivifiant.
<> *n* CONSTR entretoisement *m*.

bracken ['brækn] *n* fougère *f*.

bracket ['brækɪt] <> *n* **1.** [L-shaped support] équerre *f*, support *m* ■ [for shelf] équerre *f*, tasseau *m* ■ [lamp fixture] fixation *f* ■ ARCHIT console *f*, corbeau *m* **2.** [category] groupe *m*, classe *f* ■ **the high/low income ~** la tranche des gros/petits revenus **3.** MATHS & TYPO [parenthesis] parenthèse *f* ■ [square] crochet *m* ■ **in** *OR* **between ~s** entre parenthèses ■ **(brace) ~** MUS & TYPO accolade *f*.
<> *vt* **1.** [put in parentheses] mettre entre parenthèses ■ [put in square brackets] mettre entre crochets **2.** [link by brackets] réunir par une accolade **3.** *fig* [categorize] associer, mettre dans la même catégorie ■ **he is often~ed with the Surrealists** on le range souvent parmi les surréalistes.

brackish ['brækɪʃ] *adj* saumâtre.

bract [brækt] *n* BOT bractée *f*.

brad [bræd] *n* semence *f*, clou *m* de tapissier.

bradawl ['brædɔːl] *n* poinçon *m*.

brag [bræg] <> *vi* (*pret & pp* **bragged**, *cont* **bragging**) se vanter ■ **to ~ about sthg** se vanter de qqch.
<> *n* **1.** [boasting] vantardise *f*, fanfaronnades *fpl* **2.** [person] = **braggart 3.** [card game] *jeu de cartes qui ressemble au poker.*

braggart ['brægət] *n* vantard *m*, - e *f*, fanfaron *m*, - onne *f*.

Brahma ['brɑːmə] *pr n* Brahma.

Brahman ['brɑːmən] *n* [person] brahmane *m*.

braid [breɪd] <> *n* **1.** [trimming] ganse *f*, soutache *f* ■ [on uniform] galon *m* **2.** [of hair] tresse *f*, natte *f*.
<> *vt* **1.** [plait] tresser, natter **2.** [decorate with] soutacher, galonner.

braided ['breɪdɪd] *adj* [clothing] passementé ■ [hair] tressé.

braille, Braille [breɪl] <> *adj* braille.
<> *n* braille *m*.

brailled [breɪld] *adj* [switches, instructions] en braille.

brain [breɪn] <> *n* **1.** ANAT cerveau *m* ■ [mind] cerveau *m*, tête *f* ■ CULIN cervelle **2.** *inf fig* **to blow one's ~s out** se faire sauter la cervelle ● **you've got money on the ~** tu es obsédé par l'argent **3.** [intelligence] intelligence *f* ■ **he's got ~s** il est intelligent ● **can I pick your ~s for a minute?** j'ai besoin de tes lumières **4.** *inf* [clever person] = **brains**.
<> *comp* [damage, disease, surgery, tumour] cérébral ■ **~ surgeon** chirurgien *m* du cerveau.
<> *vt inf* [hit] assommer.
◆ **brains** *n inf* [clever person] cerveau *m* ■ **she's the ~s of the family** c'est elle le cerveau de la famille.

brainbox ['breɪnbɒks] *n inf* [skull] crâne *m* ■ [person] cerveau *m*.

brainchild ['breɪn,tʃaɪld] *n inf* bébé *m* ■ **the scheme is his ~** le projet est son bébé.

brain dead *adj* dans un coma dépassé ■ **he's ~** *inf pej* il n'a rien dans le cerveau.

brain death *n* mort *f* cérébrale.

brain drain *n* fuite *f OR* exode *m* des cerveaux.

brainless ['breɪnlɪs] *adj* [person] écervelé, stupide ■ [idea] stupide.

brainpower ['breɪn,paʊər] *n* intelligence *f*.

brainstorm ['breɪnstɔːm] <> *n* **1.** MED congestion *f* cérébrale **2.** *UK inf fig* [mental aberration] idée *f* insensée *OR* loufoque **3.** *US inf fig* [brilliant idea] idée *f* géniale.
<> *vi* faire du brainstorming.
<> *vt* plancher sur.

brainstorming ['breɪn,stɔːmɪŋ] *n* brainstorming *m*, remue-méninges *m inv*.

brains trust *n UK* [panel of experts] groupe *m* d'experts.

brainteaser ['breɪn,tiːzər] *n inf* problème *m* difficile, colle *f*.

brain trust *n US* [advisory panel] brain-trust *m*.

brainwash ['breɪnwɒʃ] *vt* faire un lavage de cerveau à ■ **advertisements can ~ people into believing anything** la publicité peut faire croire n'importe quoi aux gens.

brainwashing ['breɪnwɒʃɪŋ] *n* lavage *m* de cerveau.

brainwave ['breɪnweɪv] *n* **1.** MED onde *f* cérébrale **2.** *inf* [brilliant idea] inspiration *f*, idée *f OR* trait *m* de génie ■ **I've had a ~!** j'ai eu un éclair de génie!

brainy ['breɪnɪ] (*comp* **brainier**, *superl* **brainiest**) *adj inf* intelligent, futé.

braise [breɪz] *vt* braiser.

braising beef ['breɪzɪŋ-] *n* bœuf *m* à braiser.

brake [breɪk] <> *n* **1.** [gen - AUT] frein *m* ■ **to put on** *OR* **to apply the ~s** freiner ■ *fig* **high interest rates acted as a ~ on borrowing** des taux d'intérêt élevés ont freiné les emprunts **2.** [carriage] break *m* **3.** [bracken] fougère *f* ■ [thicket] fourré *m*.
<> *comp* [block, cable, drum, pedal] de frein.
<> *vi* freiner, mettre le frein.

brake fluid *n* liquide *m* de freins, Lockheed® *m*.

brake horsepower *n* puissance *f* au frein.

brake light *n* feu *m* de stop.

brake shoe *n* mâchoire *f* de frein.

brakesman ['breɪksmən] (*pl* **brakesmen** [-mən]) *n* machiniste *m OR* mécanicien *m* d'extraction.

brake van *n UK* RAIL fourgon *m* à frein.

braking ['breɪkɪŋ] *n* freinage *m* ■ **~ distance** distance *f* de freinage.

bramble ['bræmbl] *n* **1.** [prickly shrub] roncier *m*, roncière *f* **2.** [blackberry bush] ronce *f* des haies, mûrier *m* sauvage ■ [berry] mûre *f* sauvage.

bran [bræn] *n* son *m* (de blé), bran *m*.

branch [brɑːntʃ] <> *n* **1.** [of tree] branche *f* **2.** [secondary part - of road] embranchement *m* ; [- of river] bras *m* ; [- of railway] bifurcation *f*, raccordement *m* ; [- of pipe] branchement *m* **3.** [division - gen] division *f*, section *f* ; [- of family] ramifi-

cation *f*, branche *f* ; [- of science] branche *f* ; [- of police force] antenne *f* ; [- of government, civil service] service *m* ▪ LING rameau *m* **4.** COMM [of company] succursale *f*, filiale *f* ▪ [of bank] agence *f*, succursale *f* ▪ **~ manager** [of bank] directeur *m*, - trice *f* d'agence **5.** COMPUT branchement *m* **6.** *US* [stream] ruisseau *m*.
◇ *vi* **1.** [tree] se ramifier **2.** [road, river] bifurquer.
◆ **branch off** *vi insep* [road] bifurquer ▪ **a smaller path ~es off to the left** un chemin plus petit bifurque vers la gauche.
◆ **branch out** *vi insep* étendre ses activités ▪ **they're ~ing out into the restaurant business** ils étendent leurs activités à *OR* se lancent dans la restauration.

branch line *n* ligne *f* secondaire.

branch office *n* [of company] succursale *f* ▪ [of bank] agence *f*, succursale *f*.

brand [brænd] ◇ *n* **1.** COMM [trademark] marque *f* (de fabrique) ▪ **he has his own ~ of humour** *fig* il a un sens de l'humour particulier ◐ **~ leader** marque *f* dominante **2.** [identifying mark - on cattle] marque *f* ; [- on prisoners] flétrissure *f* **3.** [branding iron] fer *m* à marquer **4.** [burning wood] tison *m*, brandon *m* ▪ *lit* [torch] flambeau *m*.
◇ *vt* **1.** [cattle] marquer (au fer rouge) **2.** *fig* [label] étiqueter, stigmatiser ▪ **she was ~ed (as) a thief** on lui a collé une étiquette de voleuse.

branded ['brændɪd] *adj* : **~ goods** produits *mpl* de marque.

Brandenburg ['brændənbɜ:g] *pr n* Brandebourg ▪ **'The ~ Concertos'** ***Bach*** 'les Concertos brandebourgeois'.

brand image *n* image *f* de marque.

branding iron ['brændɪŋ-] *n* fer *m* à marquer.

brandish ['brændɪʃ] ◇ *vt* brandir.
◇ *n* brandissement *m*.

brand name *n* marque *f* (de fabrique).

brand-new *adj* tout *OR* flambant neuf.

Brand's Hatch *pr n circuit de courses automobiles en Angleterre.*

brandy ['brændɪ] (*pl* **brandies**) *n* [made from grapes] ≃ cognac *m* ▪ [made of fruit] eau-de-vie *f*.

brandy butter *n UK beurre mélangé avec du sucre et parfumé au cognac.*

brandy snap *n UK* galette *f* au gingembre.

bran loaf *n* pain *m* au son.

bran tub *n UK* pêche *f* miraculeuse *(jeu)*.

brash [bræʃ] *adj* **1.** [showy] impétueux, casse-cou *(inv)* ▪ [impudent] effronté, impertinent **2.** [colour] criard.

brass [brɑ:s] ◇ *n* **1.** [metal] cuivre *m* (jaune), laiton *m* ▪ [objects] : **the ~ is cleaned once a week** les cuivres sont faits une fois par semaine **2.** *UK* [memorial] plaque *f* mortuaire (en cuivre) **3.** MUS : **the ~** les cuivres *mpl* **4.** *UK inf* [nerve] toupet *m*, culot *m* **5.** *UK inf dial* [money] pognon *m*.
◇ *comp* [object, ornament] de *OR* en cuivre ▪ **the ~ section** MUS les cuivres *mpl* ▪ **to get down to ~ tacks** en venir au fait *OR* aux choses sérieuses.

brass band *n* fanfare *f*, orchestre *m* de cuivres.

brassed off [brɑ:st-] *adj UK inf* **I'm ~ with waiting** j'en ai marre d'attendre ▪ **I'm ~ with their complaints** j'en ai plein le dos de leurs récriminations.

brasserie ['bræsərɪ] *n* brasserie *f*.

brass farthing *n UK* **it's not worth a ~** *inf* ça ne vaut pas un clou.

brassiere [*UK* 'bræsɪəʳ, *US* brə'zɪr] *n* soutien-gorge *m*.

brass knuckles *npl US* coup-de-poing *m* américain.

brass-monkey△ *adj UK* **it's ~ weather** on se les gèle, on se les caille.

brass rubbing *n* [picture] décalque *m* ▪ [action] décalquage *m* par frottement.

brassy ['brɑ:sɪ] (*comp* **brassier**, *superl* **brassiest**) *adj* **1.** [colour] cuivré ▪ [sound] cuivré, claironnant **2.** *inf* [brazen] effronté, impertinent.

brat [bræt] *n pej* morveux *m*, - euse *f*, galopin *m*.

brat pack *n* [gen] jeunes loups *mpl* ▪ CIN *terme désignant les jeunes acteurs populaires des années 80.*

bravado [brə'vɑ:dəʊ] *n* bravade *f*.

brave [breɪv] ◇ *adj* **1.** [courageous] courageux, brave ▪ **be ~!** sois courageux!, du courage! ▪ **to put on a ~ face, to put a ~ face on it** faire bonne contenance **2.** *lit* [splendid] beau *(before vowel or silent 'h'* **bel***)*, belle *f*, excellent ▪ **a ~ new world** une utopie, un monde *OR* une société utopique ◐ **'Brave New World'** ***Huxley*** 'le Meilleur des mondes'.
◇ *vt* [person] braver, défier ▪ [danger, storm] braver, affronter.
◇ *npl* [people] : **the ~** les courageux *mpl*.
◇ *n* [Indian warrior] brave *m*, guerrier *m* indien.
◆ **brave out** *vt sep* faire face à.

bravely ['breɪvlɪ] *adv* courageusement, bravement.

bravery ['breɪvərɪ] *n* courage *m*, vaillance *f*.

bravo [ˌbrɑ:'vəʊ] ◇ *interj* bravo.
◇ *n* (*pl* **bravos**) bravo *m*.

bravura [brə'vʊərə] *n* [gen - MUS] bravoure *f*.

brawl [brɔ:l] ◇ *n* **1.** [fight] bagarre *f*, rixe *f* **2.** *US inf* [party] java *f*.
◇ *vi* se bagarrer.

brawn [brɔ:n] *n (U)* **1.** [muscle] muscles *mpl* ▪ [strength] muscle *m* ▪ **all ~ and no brains** tout dans les bras et rien dans la tête **2.** *UK* CULIN fromage *m* de tête.

brawny ['brɔ:nɪ] (*comp* **brawnier**, *superl* **brawniest**) *adj* [arm] musculeux ▪ [person] musclé.

bray [breɪ] ◇ *vi* [donkey] braire ▪ *pej* [person] brailler ▪ [trumpet] beugler, retentir.
◇ *n* [of donkey] braiment *m* ▪ *pej* [of person] braillement *m* ▪ [of trumpet] beuglement *m*, bruit *m* strident.

brazen ['breɪzn] *adj* **1.** [bold] effronté, impudent **2.** [brass] de cuivre (jaune), de laiton ▪ [sound] cuivré.
◆ **brazen out** *vt sep* : **you'll have to ~ it out** il va falloir que tu t'en tires par des fanfaronnades.

brazier ['breɪzjəʳ] *n* **1.** [for fire] brasero *m* **2.** [brass worker] chaudronnier *m*.

brazil [brə'zɪl] *n* : **~ (nut)** noix *f* du Brézil.

Brazil [brə'zɪl] *pr n* Brésil *m* ▪ **in ~** au Brésil.

Brazilian [brə'zɪljən] ◇ *n* Brésilien *m*, - enne *f*.
◇ *adj* brésilien.

breach [bri:tʃ] ◇ *n* **1.** [gap] brèche *f*, trou *m* ▪ **our troops made a ~ in the enemy lines** nos troupes ont percé les lignes ennemies ▪ **she stepped into the ~ when I fell ill** *fig* elle m'a remplacé au pied levé quand je suis tombé malade **2.** [violation - of law] violation *f* ; [- of discipline, order, rules] infraction *f* ; [- of etiquette, friendship] manquement *m* ; [- of confidence, trust] abus *m* ▪ **a ~ of discipline** une infraction *OR* un manquement à la discipline ▪ **~ of privilege** POL atteinte *f* aux privilèges parlementaires ▪ **~ of contract** rupture *f* de contrat ▪ **~ of the peace** LAW atteinte *f* à l'ordre public ▪ **~ of promise** [gen] manque de parole ; [of marriage] violation *f* de promesse de mariage **3.** [rift] brouille *f*, désaccord *m* **4.** [of whale] saut *m*.
◇ *vt* **1.** [make gap in] ouvrir une brèche dans, faire un trou dans ▪ **we ~ed the enemy lines** nous avons percé les lignes ennemies **2.** [agreement] violer, rompre ▪ [promise] manquer à.
◇ *vi* [whale] sauter hors de l'eau.

bread [bred] *n (U)* **1.** [food] pain *m* ▪ **a loaf of ~** un pain, une miche ▪ **~ and butter** du pain beurré ▪ **a slice of ~ and butter** une tartine (beurrée) ◐ **the ~ and wine** RELIG les espèces *fpl* ▪ **to earn one's daily ~** gagner sa vie *OR* sa croûte ▪ **translation is her ~ and butter** la traduction est son gagne-pain ▪ **to take the ~ out of sb's mouth** ôter le pain de la bouche à qqn ▪ **I know which side my ~ is buttered** je sais où est mon intérêt **2.** *inf* [money] pognon *m*, fric *m*.

bread-and-butter *adj inf* **1.** [basic] : **a ~ job** un travail qui assure le nécessaire ■ **the ~ issues** les questions les plus terre-à-terre **2.** [reliable - person] sur qui l'on peut compter **3.** [expressing gratitude] : **a ~ letter** une lettre de remerciements.

breadbasket ['bred,bɑ:skɪt] *n* **1.** [basket] corbeille *f* à pain **2.** GEOG région *f* céréalière.

bread bin *n UK* [small] boîte *f* à pain ■ [larger] huche *f* à pain.

breadboard ['bredbɔ:d] *n* planche *f* à pain.

bread box *US* = **bread bin**.

breadcrumb ['bredkrʌm] *n* miette *f* de pain.
◆ **breadcrumbs** *npl* CULIN chapelure *f*, panure *f* ■ **fish fried in ~s** du poisson pané.

breaded ['bredɪd] *adj* enrobé de chapelure.

breadfruit ['bredfru:t] *n* [tree] arbre *m* à pain ■ [fruit] fruit *m* à pain.

breadknife ['brednaɪf] (*pl* **breadknives** [-naɪvz]) *n* couteau *m* à pain.

breadline ['bredlaɪn] *n* : **to live** *OR* **to be on the ~** *fig* être sans le sou *OR* indigent.

bread sauce *n UK* sauce *f* à la mie de pain.

breadstick ['bredstɪk] *n* gressin *m*.

breadth [bredθ] *n* **1.** [width] largeur *f* ■ [of cloth] lé *m* ■ **the stage is 60 metres in ~** la scène a 60 mètres de large **2.** [scope - of mind, thought] largeur *f* ; [- of style] ampleur *f* ■ ART largeur *f* d'exécution ■ MUS jeu *m* large.

breadwinner ['bred,wɪnər] *n* soutien *m* de famille.

break [breɪk] ◇ *vt* (*pret* **broke** [brəʊk], *pp* **broken** ['brəʊkn])
1. [split into pieces - glass, furniture] casser, briser ; [- branch, lace, string] casser ■ **to ~ bread** RELIG [priest] administrer la communion ; [congregation] recevoir la communion ■ **to ~ sb's heart** *fig* briser le cœur à qqn ▶ **to ~ the ice** rompre *OR* briser la glace
2. [fracture] casser, fracturer ■ **to ~ one's leg** se casser *OR* se fracturer la jambe ■ **to ~ one's neck** se casser *OR* se rompre le cou ■ **the fall broke his back** la chute lui a brisé les reins ‖ *fig* **to ~ one's back** *inf* s'échiner ■ **we've broken the back of the job** nous avons fait le plus gros du travail ■ **I'll ~ his neck if I catch him doing it again!** *inf* je lui tords le cou si je le reprends à faire ça! ▶ **~ a leg!** *inf* merde! *(pour souhaiter bonne chance à un acteur)*
3. [render inoperable - appliance, machine] casser
4. [cut surface of - ground] entamer ; [- skin] écorcher ■ **the seal on the coffee jar was broken** le pot de café avait été ouvert ▶ **to ~ new** *OR* **fresh ground** innover, faire œuvre de pionnier ■ **scientists are ~ing new** *OR* **fresh ground in cancer research** les savants font une percée dans la recherche contre le cancer
5. [force a way through] enfoncer ■ **the river broke its banks** la rivière est sortie de son lit ■ **to ~ the sound barrier** franchir le mur du son ■ **to ~ surface** [diver, whale] remonter à la surface ; [submarine] faire surface
6. [violate - law, rule] violer, enfreindre ; [- speed limit] dépasser ; [- agreement, treaty] violer ; [- contract] rompre ; [- promise] manquer à ■ RELIG [- commandment] désobéir à ; [- sabbath] ne pas respecter ■ **he broke his word to her** *lit* il a manqué à la parole qu'il lui avait donnée ■ **to ~ parole** LAW *commettre un délit qui entraîne la révocation de la mise en liberté conditionnelle*
7. [escape from, leave suddenly] : **to ~ jail** s'évader (de prison) ■ **to ~ camp** lever le camp ■ **to ~ cover** [animal] être débusqué ; [person] sortir à découvert
8. [interrupt - fast, monotony, spell] rompre ■ **we broke our journey at Brussels** nous avons fait une étape à Bruxelles ■ **a cry broke the silence** un cri a déchiré *OR* percé le silence ■ **the plain was broken only by an occasional small settlement** la plaine n'était interrompue que par de rares petits hameaux ■ **to ~ step** rompre le pas ■ **to ~ sb's service** [in tennis] prendre le service de qqn ■ ELEC [circuit, current] couper
9. [put an end to - strike] briser ; [- uprising] mater ■ **the new offer broke the deadlock** la nouvelle proposition a permis de sortir de l'impasse ■ **he's tried to stop smoking but he can't ~ the habit** il a essayé d'arrêter de fumer mais il n'arrive pas à se débarrasser *OR* se défaire de l'habitude
10. [wear down, destroy - enemy] détruire ; [- person, will, courage, resistance] briser ; [- witness] réfuter ; [- health] abîmer ■ **this scandal could ~ them** ce scandale pourrait signer leur perte ■ **the experience will either make or ~ him** l'expérience lui sera ou salutaire ou fatale
11. [bankrupt] ruiner ■ **her new business will either make or ~ her** sa nouvelle affaire la rendra riche ou la ruinera ▶ **to ~ the bank** [exhaust funds] faire sauter la banque ■ **buying a book won't ~ the bank!** *hum* acheter un livre ne nous ruinera pas!
12. [soften - fall] amortir, adoucir ■ **we planted a row of trees to ~ the wind** nous avons planté une rangée d'arbres pour couper le vent
13. [reveal, tell] annoncer, révéler ■ **~ it to her gently** annonce-le lui avec ménagement
14. [beat, improve on] battre
15. [solve - code] déchiffrer
16. [divide into parts - collection] dépareiller ; [- bank note] entamer ■ **can you ~ a £10 note?** pouvez-vous faire de la monnaie sur un billet de 10 livres?
17. [horse] dresser
18. MIL [demote] casser
19. NAUT [flag] déferler
20. *euph* **to ~ wind** lâcher un vent.
◇ *vi* (*pret* **broke** [brəʊk], *pp* **broken** ['brəʊkn]) **1.** [split into pieces - glass, furniture] se casser, se briser ; [- branch, stick] se casser, se rompre ; [- lace, string] se casser
2. [fracture - bone, limb] se fracturer ■ **is the bone broken?** y a-t-il une fracture?
3. [become inoperable - lock, tool] casser ; [- machine] tomber en panne
4. [disperse - clouds] se disperser, se dissiper ; [- troops] rompre les rangs ; [- ranks] se rompre
5. [escape] : **to ~ free** se libérer ■ **the ship broke loose from its moorings** le bateau a rompu ses amarres
6. [fail - health, person, spirit] se détériorer ■ **she** *OR* **her spirit did not ~** elle ne s'est pas laissée abattre ■ **their courage finally broke** leur courage a fini par les abandonner
7. [take a break] faire une pause ■ **let's ~ for coffee** arrêtons-nous pour prendre un café
8. [arise suddenly - day] se lever, poindre ; [- dawn] poindre ; [- news] être annoncé ; [- scandal, war] éclater
9. [move suddenly] se précipiter, foncer
10. [weather] changer ■ [storm] éclater ■ [wave] déferler
11. [voice - of boy] muer ; [- with emotion] se briser
12. MED : **her waters have broken** elle a perdu les eaux
13. *phr* **to ~ even** [gen] s'y retrouver ; FIN rentrer dans ses frais
14. *US inf* [happen] se passer, arriver ■ **to ~ right/badly** bien/mal se passer
15. LING [vowel] se diphtonguer
16. SPORT [boxers] se dégager ■ [ball] dévier ■ [in billiards, pool *etc*] donner l'acquit.
◇ *n* **1.** [in china, glass] cassure *f*, brisure *f* ■ [in wood] cassure *f*, rupture *f* ■ [in bone, limb] fracture *f* ■ **a clean ~** [in object] une cassure nette ; [in bone] une fracture simple ‖ *fig* [with friend, group] rupture *f* ■ [in marriage] séparation *f* ■ **to make a clean ~ with the past** rompre avec le passé
2. [crack] fissure *f*, fente *f*
3. [gap - in hedge, wall] trouée *f*, ouverture *f* ; [- in rock] faille *f* ; [- in line] interruption *f*, rupture *f* ■ **a ~ in the clouds** une éclaircie
4. [interruption - in conversation] interruption *f*, pause *f* ; [- in payment] interruption *f*, suspension *f* ; [- in trip] arrêt *m* ; [- in production] suspension *f*, rupture *f* ■ **a ~ for commercials, a (commercial) ~** RADIO un intermède de publicité ; TV un écran publicitaire, une page de publicité ■ **a ~ in transmission** une interruption des programmes (due à un incident technique) ■ LIT & MUS pause *f* ■ [in jazz] break *m* ■ ELEC : **a ~ in the circuit** une coupure de courant
5. [rest] pause *f* ■ [holiday] vacances *fpl* ■ *UK* SCH récréation *f* ■ **let's take a ~** on fait une pause? ■ **he drove for three hours without a ~** il a conduit trois heures de suite ■ **you need a ~** [short rest] tu as besoin de faire une pause ; [holiday] tu as be-

soin de vacances ➜ **lunch ~** pause *f* de midi ▪ **do you get a lunch ~?** tu as une pause à midi? ▪ **give me a ~!** *inf* laisse-moi respirer!
6. [escape] évasion *f*, fuite *f* ▪ **jail ~** évasion (de prison) ▪ **she made a ~ for the woods** elle s'est élancée vers le bois ➜ **to make a ~ for it** prendre la fuite
7. *inf* [opportunity] chance *f* ▪ [luck] (coup *m* de) veine *f* ▪ **to have a lucky ~** avoir de la veine ▪ **to have a bad ~** manquer de veine
8. [change] changement *m* ▪ **a ~ in the weather** un changement de temps ▪ **the decision signalled a ~ with tradition** la décision marquait une rupture avec la tradition
9. [carriage] break *m*
10. *lit* **at ~ of day** au point du jour, à l'aube
11. SPORT : **to have a service ~** *OR* **a ~ (of serve)** [in tennis] avoir une rupture de service *(de l'adversaire)* ▪ **he made a 70 ~** *OR* **a ~ of 70** [in snooker, pool etc] il a fait une série de 70.

◆ **break away** ◇ *vi insep* **1.** [move away] se détacher ▪ **I broke away from the crowd** je me suis éloigné de la foule
2. [end association with] rompre ▪ **a group of MPs broke away from the party** un groupe de députés a quitté le parti
3. SPORT [in racing, cycling] s'échapper, se détacher du peloton.
◇ *vt sep* détacher.

◆ **break down** ◇ *vi insep* **1.** [vehicle, machine] tomber en panne
2. [fail - health] se détériorer ; [- authority] disparaître ; [- argument, system] s'effondrer ; [- negotiations, relations, plan] échouer ▪ **radio communications broke down** le contact radio a été coupé
3. [lose one's composure] s'effondrer ▪ **to ~ down in tears** fondre en larmes
4. [divide] se diviser ▪ **the report ~s down into three parts** le rapport comprend *OR* est composé de trois parties
5. CHEM se décomposer ▪ **to ~ down into** se décomposer en.
◇ *vt sep* **1.** [destroy - barrier] démolir, abattre ; [- door] enfoncer ▪ *fig* [- resistance] briser ▪ **we must ~ down old prejudices** il faut mettre fin aux vieux préjugés
2. [analyse - idea] analyser ; [- reasons] décomposer ; [- accounts] analyser, détailler ▪ COMM [- costs, figures] ventiler ▪ CHEM [- substance] décomposer.

◆ **break in** ◇ *vt sep* **1.** [train - person] former ; [- horse] dresser
2. [clothing] porter *(pour user)* ▪ **I want to ~ these shoes in** je veux que ces chaussures se fassent
3. [knock down - door] enfoncer.
◇ *vi insep* **1.** [burglar] entrer par effraction
2. [speaker] interrompre ▪ **to ~ in on sb/sthg** interrompre qqn/qqch.

◆ **break into** *vt insep* **1.** [subj: burglar] entrer par effraction dans ▪ [drawer, safe] forcer
2. [begin suddenly] : **the audience broke into applause** le public s'est mis à applaudir ▪ **the horse broke into a gallop** le cheval a pris le galop
3. [conversation] interrompre
4. [start to spend - savings] entamer
5. COMM percer sur.

◆ **break off** ◇ *vi insep* **1.** [separate] se détacher, se casser
2. [stop] s'arrêter brusquement ▪ **he broke off in mid-sentence** il s'est arrêté au milieu d'une phrase ▪ **they broke off from work** [for rest] ils ont fait une pause ; [for day] ils ont cessé le travail
3. [end relationship] rompre ▪ **she's broken off with him** elle a rompu avec lui.
◇ *vt sep* **1.** [separate] détacher, casser ▪ **to ~ sthg off sthg** casser *OR* détacher qqch de qqch
2. [end - agreement, relationship] rompre ▪ **they've broken off their engagement** ils ont rompu leurs fiançailles.

◆ **break out** ◇ *vi insep* **1.** [begin - war, storm] éclater ; [- disease] se déclarer
2. [become covered] : **to ~ out in spots** *OR* **in a rash** avoir une éruption de boutons ▪ **to ~ out in a sweat** se mettre à transpirer
3. [escape] s'échapper ▪ **to ~ out from** *OR* **of prison** s'évader (de prison) ▪ **we have to ~ out of this vicious circle** il faut que nous sortions de ce cercle vicieux.
◇ *vt sep* [bottle, champagne] ouvrir.

◆ **break through** ◇ *vt insep* [sun] percer ▪ **I broke through the crowd** je me suis frayé un chemin à travers la foule ▪ **the troops broke through enemy lines** les troupes ont enfoncé les lignes ennemies ▪ **she eventually broke through his reserve** elle a fini par le faire sortir de sa réserve.
◇ *vi insep liter* percer ▪ *fig* & MIL faire une percée.

◆ **break up** ◇ *vt sep* **1.** [divide up - rocks] briser, morceler ; [- property] morceler ; [- soil] ameublir ; [- bread, cake] partager ▪ **illustrations ~ up the text** le texte est aéré par des illustrations
2. [destroy - house] démolir ; [- road] défoncer
3. [end - fight, party] mettre fin à, arrêter ; [- coalition] briser, rompre ; [- organization] dissoudre ; [- empire] démembrer ; [- family] séparer ▪ **his drinking broke up their marriage** le fait qu'il buvait a brisé *OR* détruit leur mariage
4. [disperse - crowd] disperser ▪ **~ it up!** [people fighting or arguing] arrêtez! ; [said by policeman] circulez!
5. *inf* [distress] bouleverser, retourner.
◇ *vi insep* **1.** [split into pieces - road, system] se désagréger ; [- ice] craquer, se fissurer ; [- ship] se disloquer
2. [come to an end - meeting, party] se terminer, prendre fin ; [- partnership] cesser, prendre fin ▪ **their marriage broke up** leur mariage n'a pas marché
3. [boyfriend, girlfriend] rompre ▪ **she broke up with her boyfriend** elle a rompu avec son petit ami ▪ **they've broken up** ils se sont séparés
4. [disperse - clouds] se disperser ; [- group] se disperser ; [- friends] se quitter, se séparer
5. *UK* SCH être en vacances ▪ **we ~ up for Christmas on the 22nd** les vacances de Noël commencent le 22
6. [lose one's composure] s'effondrer
7. *US inf* [laugh] se tordre de rire.

◆ **break with** *vt insep* **1.** [end association with - person, organization] rompre avec
2. [depart from - belief, values] rompre avec ▪ **she broke with tradition by getting married away from her village** elle a rompu avec la tradition en ne se mariant pas dans son village.

breakable ['breɪkəbl] *adj* fragile, cassable.
◆ **breakables** *npl* : **put away all ~s** rangez tout objet fragile.

breakage ['breɪkɪdʒ] *n* **1.** [of metal] rupture *f* ▪ [of glass] casse *f*, bris *m* **2.** [damages] casse *f* ▪ **the insurance pays for all ~** *OR* **~s** l'assurance paye toute la casse.

breakaway ['breɪkəweɪ] ◇ *n* **1.** [of people] séparation *f* ▪ [of group] rupture *f* ▪ SPORT [in cycling] échappée *f* ▪ [in boxing] dégagement *m* **2.** CIN accessoire *m* cassable.
◇ *adj* séparatiste, dissident ▪ **a ~ republic** une république séparatiste.

breakdance ['breɪkdɑːns] *n* smurf *m*.
◆ **break-dance** *vi* danser le smurf.

break dancing *n* smurf *m*.

breakdown ['breɪkdaʊn] *n* **1.** [mechanical] panne *f* ▪ **to have a ~** tomber en panne **2.** [of communications, negotiations] rupture *f* ▪ [of railway system] arrêt *m* complet ▪ [of tradition, state of affairs] détérioration *f*, dégradation *f* **3.** MED [nervous] dépression *f* nerveuse ▪ **to have a ~** faire une dépression (nerveuse) ▪ [physical] effondrement *m* **4.** [analysis] analyse *f* ▪ [into parts] décomposition *f* ▪ COMM [of costs, figures] ventilation *f* ▪ **a ~ of the population by age** une répartition de la population par âge.

breakdown lorry, breakdown truck *n UK* dépanneuse *f*.

breaker ['breɪkər] *n* **1.** [scrap merchant] : **the ship was sent to the ~'s** le navire a été envoyé à la démolition **2.** [wave] brisant *m* **3.** ELECTRON = **circuit breaker 4.** [machine] concasseur *m*, broyeur *m* **5.** [CB operator] cibiste *mf*.

break-even *adj* : **~ point** seuil *m* de rentabilité, point mort *m* ▪ **~ price** prix *m* d'équilibre.

breakfast ['brekfəst] ◇ *n* petit déjeuner *m* ▪ **to have ~** prendre le petit déjeuner.
◇ *comp* [service, set] à petit déjeuner ▪ [tea, time] du petit déjeuner.
◇ *vi* prendre le petit déjeuner, déjeuner.

breakfast cereal *n* céréales *fpl*.

breakfast room *n* salle *f* du petit déjeuner.

breakfast television *n* télévision *f* du matin.

break-in *n* cambriolage *m*.

breaking ['breɪkɪŋ] *n* **1.** [shattering] bris *m* ■ [of bone] fracture *f* ■ LAW [of seal] bris *m* ■ **~ and entering** effraction *f* **2.** [violation - of treaty, rule, law] violation *f* ■ **~ of a promise** manquement à une promesse ■ **~ of a commandment** désobéissance à un commandement **3.** [interruption - of journey] interruption *f* ; [- of silence] rupture *f* **4.** LING fracture *f*.

breaking point *n liter* point *m* de rupture ■ *fig* **I've reached ~** je suis à bout, je n'en peux plus ■ **you're trying my patience to ~** tu pousses à bout ma patience ■ **the situation has reached ~** la situation est devenue critique.

breakneck ['breɪknek] *adj* : **at ~ speed** à une allure folle, à tombeau ouvert.

breakout ['breɪkaʊt] *n* [from prison] évasion *f* (de prison).

breakpoint ['breɪkpɔɪnt] *n* **1.** [in tennis] point *m* d'avantage **2.** COMPUT point *m* de rupture.

breakthrough ['breɪkθru:] *n* **1.** [advance, discovery] découverte *f* capitale, percée *f* (technologique) **2.** [in enemy lines] percée *f*.

breakup ['breɪkʌp] *n* **1.** [disintegration - of association] démembrement *m*, dissolution *f* ; [- of relationship] rupture *f* **2.** [end - of meeting, activity] fin *f* **3.** [of ship] dislocation *f* **4.** [of ice] débâcle *f*.

breakup value *n* COMM valeur *f* liquidative.

breakwater ['breɪk,wɔ:tər] *n* digue *f*, brise-lames *m inv*.

bream [bri:m] (*pl inv* OR *pl* **breams**) *n* brème *f*.

breast [brest] ◇ *n* **1.** [chest] poitrine *f* ■ [of animal] poitrine, poitrail *m* ■ CULIN [of chicken] blanc *m* **2.** [bosom - of woman] sein *m*, poitrine *f* ■ *arch* [- of man] sein *m* ■ **she put the baby to her ~** elle porta le bébé à son sein **3.** MIN front *m* de taille.
◇ *vt* **1.** [face - waves, storm] affronter, faire front à **2.** [reach summit of] atteindre le sommet de ■ **the runner ~ed the tape** SPORT le coureur a franchi la ligne d'arrivée (en vainqueur).

breastbone ['brestbəʊn] *n* ANAT sternum *m* ■ [of bird] bréchet *m*.

breast-fed *adj* nourri au sein.

breast-feed ◇ *vt* allaiter, donner le sein à.
◇ *vi* allaiter, nourrir au sein.

breast-feeding *n* allaitement *m* au sein.

breast milk *n* (*U*) lait *m* maternel.

breastplate ['brestpleɪt] *n* [armour] plastron *m* (de cuirasse) ■ [of priest] pectoral *m*.

breast pocket *n* poche *f* de poitrine.

breaststroke ['breststrəʊk] *n* brasse *f* ■ **to swim (the) ~** nager la brasse.

breath [breθ] *n* **1.** [of human, animal] haleine *f*, souffle *m* ■ **to have bad ~** avoir mauvaise haleine ■ **take a ~** respirez ■ **he took a deep ~** il a respiré à fond ■ **let me get my ~ back** laissez-moi retrouver mon souffle OR reprendre haleine ■ **she stopped for ~** elle s'est arrêtée pour reprendre haleine ■ **to be out of ~** être essoufflé OR à bout de souffle ■ **to be short of ~** avoir le souffle court ■ **he said it all in one ~** il l'a dit d'un trait ■ **they are not to be mentioned in the same ~** on ne saurait les comparer ■ **under one's ~** à voix basse, tout bas ■ **he drew his last ~** il a rendu l'âme OR le dernier soupir ■ **to hold one's ~** retenir son souffle ■ **don't hold your ~ waiting for the money** si c'est l'argent que tu attends, ne compte pas dessus OR tu perds ton temps ■ **save your ~!** inutile de gaspiller ta salive! ■ **the sight took his ~ away** la vue OR le spectacle lui a coupé le souffle **2.** [gust] souffle *m* ■ **there isn't a ~ of air** il n'y a pas un souffle d'air ■ **we went out for a ~ of fresh air** nous sommes sortis prendre l'air **3.** [hint] trace *f* ■ **the first ~ of spring** les premiers effluves du printemps.

breathable ['bri:ðəbl] *adj* respirable.

breathalyse UK, **breathalyze** US ['breθəlaɪz] *vt* faire passer l'Alcootest® à.

Breathalyser®, **Breathalyzer®** ['breθəlaɪzər] *n* Alcootest® *m*.

breathe [bri:ð] ◇ *vi* **1.** [person] respirer ■ **to ~ heavily** OR **deeply** [after exertion] souffler OR respirer bruyamment ; [during illness] il respirait péniblement ■ **I ~d more easily** OR **again after the exam** *fig* après l'examen j'ai enfin pu respirer ■ **how can I work with you breathing down my neck?** *fig* comment veux-tu que je travaille si tu es toujours derrière moi? **2.** [wine] respirer.
◇ *vt* **1.** PHYSIOL respirer ■ **she ~d a sigh of relief** elle poussa un soupir de soulagement ■ **to ~ one's last** rendre le dernier soupir OR l'âme ■ **she ~d new life into the project** elle a insufflé de nouvelles forces au projet **2.** [whisper] murmurer ■ **don't ~ a word!** ne soufflez pas mot! **3.** LING aspirer.
◆ **breathe in** *vi insep* & *vt sep* inspirer.
◆ **breathe out** *vi insep* & *vt sep* expirer.

breather ['bri:ðər] *n* moment *m* de repos OR de répit ■ **let's take a ~** prenons le temps de souffler un peu ■ **I went out for a ~** je suis sorti prendre l'air.

breathing ['bri:ðɪŋ] *n* **1.** [gen] respiration *f*, souffle *m* ■ [of musician] respiration *f* ■ **heavy ~** respiration bruyante **2.** LING aspiration *f*.

breathing space *n* moment *m* de répit.

breathless ['breθlɪs] *adj* **1.** [from exertion] essoufflé, hors d'haleine ■ [from illness] oppressé, qui a du mal à respirer **2.** [from emotion] : **his kiss left her ~** son baiser lui a coupé le souffle ■ **the film held us ~** le film nous a tenus en haleine **3.** [atmosphere] étouffant.

breathtaking ['breθ,teɪkɪŋ] *adj* impressionnant ■ **a ~ view** une vue à (vous) couper le souffle.

breath test *n* Alcootest® *m*.

breathy ['breθɪ] (*comp* **breathier**, *superl* **breathiest**) *adj* qui respire bruyamment ■ MUS qui manque d'attaque.

Brechtian ['brektɪən] ◇ *adj* brechtien.
◇ *n* brechtien *m*, - enne *f*.

bred [bred] ◇ *pt* & *pp* ▷ **breed**.
◇ *adj* élevé.

breech [bri:tʃ] ◇ *n* **1.** [of gun] culasse *f* **2.** [of person] derrière *m*.
◇ *vt* [gun] munir d'une culasse.

breech birth *n* accouchement *m* par le siège.

breech delivery = **breech birth**.

breeches ['brɪtʃɪz] *npl* pantalon *m* ■ [knee-length] haut-de-chausses *m* ■ [for riding] culotte *f*.

breechloader ['bri:tʃ,ləʊdər] *n* arme *f* chargée par la culasse.

breed [bri:d] ◇ *n* **1.** ZOOL [race] race *f*, espèce *f* ■ [within race] type *m* ■ BOT [of plant] espèce *f* **2.** *fig* [kind] sorte *f*, espèce *f* ■ **he's one of a dying ~** il fait partie d'une espèce en voie de disparition.
◇ *vt* (*pret & pp* **bred** [bred]) **1.** [raise - animals] élever, faire l'élevage de ; [- plants] cultiver ; [- children] *lit* & *hum* élever **2.** *fig* [cause] engendrer, faire naître.
◇ *vi* (*pret & pp* **bred** [bred]) se reproduire, se multiplier.

breeder ['bri:dər] *n* [farmer] éleveur *m*, - euse *f* ■ [animal] reproducteur *m*, - trice *f*.

breeder reactor *n* surgénérateur *m*, surrégénérateur *m*.

breeding ['bri:dɪŋ] *n* **1.** AGRIC [raising - of animals] élevage *m* ; [- of plants] culture *f* **2.** [reproduction] reproduction *f*, procréation *f* ■ **the ~ season** [for animals] la saison des amours ; [for birds] la saison des nids **3.** [upbringing] éducation *f* **4.** PHYS surgénération *f*, surrégénération *f*.

breeding-ground *n* **1.** [for wild animals, birds] lieu *m* de prédilection pour l'accouplement OR la ponte **2.** *fig* **a ~ for terrorists** une pépinière de terroristes.

breeze [bri:z] <> *n* **1.** [wind] brise *f* ▪ **a gentle** *OR* **light ~** une petite *OR* légère brise ▪ **a stiff ~** un vent frais ▪ **there's quite a ~** ça souffle **2.** *US inf* [easy task] : **that's a ~** c'est l'enfance de l'art, c'est du gâteau **3.** [charcoal] cendres *fpl* (de charbon).
<> *vi* **1.** [move quickly] aller vite **2.** [do easily] : **I ~d through the exam** *inf* j'ai passé l'examen les doigts dans le nez.
◆ **breeze in** *vi insep* : **she ~d in** [quickly] elle est entrée en coup de vent ; [casually] elle est entrée d'un air désinvolte.

breezeblock ['bri:zblɒk] *n UK* parpaing *m*.

breezily ['bri:zɪlɪ] *adv* [casually] avec désinvolture ▪ [cheerfully] joyeusement, jovialement.

breezy ['bri:zɪ] (*comp* **breezier**, *superl* **breeziest**) *adj* **1.** [weather, day] venteux ▪ [place, spot] éventé **2.** [person - casual] désinvolte ; [- cheerful] jovial, enjoué.

Bremen ['breɪmən] *pr n* Brême.

brethren ['breðrən] *npl fml* [fellow members] camarades *mpl* ▪ RELIG frères *mpl*.

Breton ['bretɒn] <> *n* **1.** [person] Breton *m*, - onne *f* **2.** LING breton *m*.
<> *adj* breton.

breve [bri:v] *n* MUS & TYPO brève *f*.

breviary ['bri:vjərɪ] (*pl* **breviaries**) *n* bréviaire *m*.

brevity ['brevɪtɪ] *n* **1.** [shortness] brièveté *f* **2.** [succinctness] concision *f* ▪ [terseness] laconisme *m* ▪ **~ is the soul of wit** *prov* la concision est le secret d'un bon mot d'esprit.

brew [bru:] <> *n* **1.** [infusion] infusion *f* ▪ [herbal] tisane *f* ▪ **a witch's ~** un brouet de sorcière **2.** [beer] brassage *m* ▪ [amount made] brassin *m*.
<> *vt* **1.** [make - tea] préparer, faire infuser ; [- beer] brasser **2.** *fig* [scheme] tramer, mijoter.
<> *vi* **1.** [tea] infuser ▪ [beer] fermenter **2.** [make beer] brasser, faire de la bière **3.** *fig* [storm] couver, se préparer ▪ [scheme] se tramer, mijoter ▪ **there's trouble ~ing** il y a de l'orage dans l'air.
◆ **brew up** *vi insep* **1.** [storm] couver, se préparer ▪ [trouble] se préparer, se tramer **2.** *UK inf* [make tea] préparer *OR* faire du thé.

brewer ['bru:əʳ] *n* brasseur *m*.

brewer's yeast *n* levure *f* de bière.

brewery ['brʊərɪ] (*pl* **breweries**) *n* brasserie *f (fabrique)*.

briar ['braɪəʳ] **1.** = **brier 2.** = **briar pipe**.

briar pipe *n* pipe *f* de bruyère.

bribe [braɪb] <> *vt* soudoyer, acheter ▪ [witness] suborner ▪ **we ~d the guard to tell us** nous avons soudoyé le garde pour qu'il nous le dise.
<> *n* pot-de-vin *m* ▪ **to take ~s** se laisser corrompre.

bribery ['braɪbərɪ] *n* corruption *f* ▪ [of witness] subornation *f* ▪ **open to ~** corruptible ➊ **~ and corruption** LAW corruption.

bric-à-brac ['brɪkəbræk] <> *n* bric-à-brac *m*.
<> *comp* : **a ~ shop/stall** une boutique/un éventaire de brocanteur.

brick [brɪk] <> *n* **1.** [for building] brique *f* ➊ **to come down on sb like a ton of ~s** *inf* passer un savon à qqn ▪ **you can't make ~s without straw** *prov* à l'impossible nul n'est tenu *prov* **2.** [of ice cream] pavé *m* (de glace) **3.** *UK* [toy] cube *m* (de construction).
<> *comp* [building] en brique *OR* briques ▪ **it's like talking to a ~ wall** autant (vaut) parler à un mur *OR* un sourd.
◆ **brick up** *vt sep* murer.

brickbat ['brɪkbæt] *n* [weapon] morceau *m* de brique ▪ *fig* [criticism] critique *f*.

brickie ['brɪkɪ] *n UK inf* maçon *m*, ouvrier-maçon *m*.

bricklayer ['brɪk,leɪəʳ] *n* maçon *m*, ouvrier-maçon *m*.

brick red *n* rouge *m* brique.

brick-red *adj* rouge brique *(inv)*.

brickwork ['brɪkwɜ:k] *n* [structure] briquetage *m*, brique *f*.

brickworks ['brɪkwɜ:ks] (*pl inv*), **brickyard** ['brɪkjɑ:d] *n* briqueterie *f*.

bridal ['braɪdl] *adj* [gown, veil] de mariée ▪ [chamber, procession] nuptial ▪ [feast] de noce ▪ **the ~ suite** la suite réservée aux jeunes mariés.

bride [braɪd] *n* [before wedding] (future) mariée *f* ▪ [after wedding] (jeune) mariée *f* ▪ **the ~ and groom** les (jeunes) mariés *mpl* ➊ **the ~ of Christ** RELIG l'épouse *f* du Christ.

bridegroom ['braɪdgrʊm] *n* [before wedding] (futur) marié *m* ▪ [after wedding] (jeune) marié *m*.

bridesmaid ['braɪdzmeɪd] *n* demoiselle *f* d'honneur.

bride-to-be *n* future mariée *f*.

bridge [brɪdʒ] <> *n* **1.** [structure] pont *m* ▪ **the engineers built** *OR* **put a ~ across the river** le génie a construit *OR* jeté un pont sur le fleuve **2.** *fig* [link] rapprochement *m* **3.** [of ship] passerelle *f* (de commandement) **4.** [of nose] arête *f* ▪ [of glasses] arcade *f* **5.** [of stringed instrument] chevalet *m* **6.** [dentures] bridge *m* **7.** [card game] bridge *m*.
<> *comp* [party, tournament] de bridge.
<> *vt* [river] construire *OR* jeter un pont sur ▪ *fig* **a composer whose work ~d two centuries** un compositeur dont l'œuvre est à cheval sur deux siècles ▪ **to ~ the generation gap** combler le fossé entre les générations ▪ **in order to ~ the gap in our knowledge/in our resources** pour combler la lacune dans notre savoir/le trou dans nos ressources.

bridgehead ['brɪdʒhed] *n* tête *f* de pont.

bridge loan *US* = **bridging loan**.

bridgework ['brɪdʒwɜ:k] *n (U)* [in dentistry] : **to have ~ done** se faire faire un bridge.

bridging loan *n UK* prêt-relais *m*.

bridle ['braɪdl] <> *n* [harness] bride *f* ▪ *fig* [constraint] frein *m*, contrainte *f*.
<> *vt* [horse] brider ▪ *fig* [emotions] refréner ▪ **to ~ one's tongue** tenir sa langue.
<> *vi* [in anger] se rebiffer, prendre la mouche ▪ [in indignation] redresser la tête.

bridle path, bridleway ['braɪdlweɪ] *n* piste *f* cavalière.

brief [bri:f] <> *adj* **1.** [short in duration] bref, court **2.** [succinct] concis, bref ▪ **to be ~, I think you're right** en bref, je crois que tu as raison ▪ **a ~ account** un exposé sommaire **3.** [terse - person, reply] laconique ▪ [abrupt] brusque.
<> *vt* **1.** [bring up to date] mettre au courant ▪ **the boss ~ed me on the latest developments** le patron m'a mis au courant des derniers développements ▮ [give orders to] donner des instructions à ▪ **the soldiers were ~ed on their mission** les soldats ont reçu leurs ordres pour la mission **2.** LAW [lawyer] confier une cause à ▪ [case] établir le dossier de.
<> *n* **1.** LAW dossier *m*, affaire *f* ▪ **he took our ~** il a accepté de plaider notre cause ➊ **to hold a watching ~ for sb/sthg** veiller (en justice) aux intérêts de qqn/qqch ▪ **to hold no ~ for sb/sthg** ne pas se faire l'avocat de qqn/qqch ▪ **he holds no ~ for those who take drugs** *fig* il ne prend pas la défense de ceux qui se droguent **2.** [instructions] briefing *m* ▪ **my ~ was to develop sales** la tâche *OR* la mission qui m'a été confiée était de développer les ventes.
◆ **briefs** *npl* [underwear] slip *m*.
◆ **in brief** *adv phr* en résumé.

briefcase ['bri:fkeɪs] *n* serviette *f*, mallette *f*.

briefing ['bri:fɪŋ] *n* MIL [meeting] briefing *m*, instructions *fpl*.

briefly ['bri:flɪ] *adv* **1.** [for a short time] un court instant ▪ **I visited her ~ on the way home** au retour, je lui ai rendu visite en coup de vent **2.** [succinctly] brièvement ▪ [tersely] laconiquement ▪ **she told them ~ what had happened** elle leur a résumé ce qui s'était passé ▪ **put ~, the situation is a mess** en bref, la situation est très embrouillée.

brier ['braɪəʳ] *n* **1.** [thorny plant] ronces *fpl* ▪ [thorn] épine *f* **2.** [heather] bruyère *f* ▪ [wood] (racine *f* de) bruyère *f*.

brier rose *n* églantine *f*.

brigade [brɪ'geɪd] *n* [gen - MIL] brigade *f* ▪ **one of the old ~** *fig* un vieux de la vieille.

brigadier [,brɪgə'dɪəʳ] *n UK* général *m*, -e *f* de brigade.

brigadier general *n US* [in army] général *m*, -e *f* de brigade ■ [in air force] général *m*, -e *f* de brigade aérienne.

brigand ['brɪgənd] *n* brigand *m*, bandit *m*.

brigantine ['brɪgənti:n] *n* brigantin *m*.

bright [braɪt] ◇ *adj* **1.** [weather, day] clair, radieux ■ [sunshine] éclatant ■ **the weather will get ~er later** le temps s'améliorera en cours de journée ■ **cloudy with ~ intervals** nuageux avec des éclaircies ■ **~ and early** *fig* tôt le matin, de bon *OR* grand matin ‖ [room] clair ■ [fire, light] vif ■ [colour] vif, éclatant
2. [shining - diamond, star] brillant ; [- metal] poli, luisant ; [- eyes] brillant, vif ■ **it was one of the few ~ spots of our visit** *fig* ce fut l'un des rares bons moments de notre visite ▶ **she likes the ~ lights** elle aime la grande ville ■ **the ~ lights of London** les attractions de Londres
3. [clever] intelligent ■ [child] éveillé, vif ■ **a ~ idea** une idée géniale *OR* lumineuse
4. [cheerful] gai, joyeux ■ [lively] animé, vif ■ **to be ~ and breezy** avoir l'air en pleine forme
5. [promising] brillant ■ **there are ~er days ahead** des jours meilleurs nous attendent ■ **the future's looking ~** l'avenir est plein de promesses *OR* s'annonce bien ▶ **to look on the ~ side** prendre les choses du bon côté, être optimiste.
◇ *adv lit* [burn, shine] avec éclat, brillamment.
◆ **brights** *npl US* [headlights] : **to put the ~s on** se mettre en pleins phares.

brighten ['braɪtn] ◇ *vi* **1.** [weather] s'améliorer **2.** [person] s'animer ■ [face] s'éclairer ■ [eyes] s'allumer, s'éclairer **3.** [prospects] s'améliorer.
◇ *vt* **1.** [decorate - place, person] égayer ■ [enliven - conversation] animer, égayer **2.** [prospects] améliorer, faire paraître sous un meilleur jour **3.** [polish - metal] astiquer, faire reluire **4.** [colour] aviver.
◆ **brighten up** *vi insep & vt sep* = **brighten**.

bright-eyed *adj liter* aux yeux brillants ■ *fig* [eager] enthousiaste ■ **~ and bushy-tailed** *hum* frais comme la rosée.

brightly ['braɪtlɪ] *adv* **1.** [shine] avec éclat ■ **the stars were shining ~** les étoiles scintillaient ■ **the fire burned ~** le feu flambait ■ **~ polished** reluisant **2.** [cheerfully] gaiement, joyeusement ■ **to smile ~** sourire d'un air radieux.

brightness ['braɪtnɪs] *n* **1.** [of sun] éclat *m* ■ [of light] intensité *f* ■ [of room] clarté *f*, luminosité *f* ■ [of colour] éclat *m* **2.** [cheerfulness] gaieté *f*, joie *f* ■ [liveliness] vivacité *f* ■ [of smile] éclat *m* **3.** [cleverness] intelligence *f*.

Bright's disease [braɪts-] *n* mal *m* de Bright, néphrite *f* chronique *spec*.

bright spark *n UK inf* [clever person] lumière *f*.

brill [brɪl] (*pl inv*) *n* [fish] barbue *f*.

brilliance ['brɪljəns], **brilliancy** ['brɪljənsɪ] *n* **1.** [of light, smile, career] éclat *m*, brillant *m* **2.** [cleverness] intelligence *f* ■ **no one doubts her ~** il ne fait pas de doute que c'est un esprit brillant *OR* qu'elle est d'une intelligence supérieure.

brilliant ['brɪljənt] ◇ *adj* **1.** [light, sunshine] éclatant, intense ■ [smile] éclatant, rayonnant ■ [colour] vif, éclatant **2.** [outstanding - mind, musician, writer] brillant, exceptionnel ; [- film, novel, piece of work] brillant, exceptionnel ; [- success] éclatant **3.** *inf* [terrific] sensationnel, super **4.** [intelligent] brillant ■ **that's a ~ idea** c'est une idée lumineuse *OR* de génie.
◇ *n* brillant *m*.

brilliantly ['brɪljəntlɪ] *adv* **1.** [shine] avec éclat ■ **~ coloured** d'une couleur vive **2.** [perform, talk] brillamment.

Brillo pad® ['brɪləʊ-] *n* ≃ tampon *m* Jex®.

brim [brɪm] ◇ *n* [of hat] bord *m* ■ [of bowl, cup] bord *m* ■ **full to the ~** plein à ras bord.
◇ *vi* (*pret & pp* **brimmed**, *cont* **brimming**) déborder ■ **eyes brimming with tears** des yeux pleins *OR* noyés de larmes ■ **the newcomers were brimming with ideas** *fig* les nouveaux venus avaient des idées à revendre.
◆ **brim over** *vi insep* déborder ■ **to be brimming over with enthusiasm** *fig* déborder d'enthousiasme.

brimful [,brɪm'fʊl] *adj UK* [cup] plein à déborder *OR* jusqu'au bord ■ *fig* débordant ■ **~ of confidence** très *OR* excessivement confiant.

brimstone ['brɪmstəʊn] *n* **1.** [sulphur] soufre *m* **2.** [butterfly] citron *m*.

brine [braɪn] *n* **1.** [salty water] eau *f* salée ■ CULIN saumure *f* **2.** *lit* [sea] mer *f* ■ [sea water] eau *f* de mer ■ **mussels in ~** moules saumurées.

bring [brɪŋ] (*pret & pp* **brought** [brɔ:t]) *vt* **1.** [take - animal, person, vehicle] amener ; [- object] apporter ■ **I'll ~ the books (across) tomorrow** j'apporterai les livres demain ■ **her father's ~ing her home today** son père la ramène à la maison aujourd'hui ■ **that ~s the total to £350** cela fait 350 livres en tout ■ **he brought his dog with him** il a emmené son chien ■ **did you ~ anything with you** as-tu apporté quelque chose? ■ [fashion, idea, product] introduire, lancer ■ **black musicians brought jazz to Europe** les musiciens noirs ont introduit le jazz en Europe ■ **this programme is brought to you by the BBC** ce programme est diffusé par la BBC
2. [into specified state] entraîner, amener ■ **to ~ sthg into question** mettre *OR* remettre qqch en question ■ **to ~ sb to his/her senses** ramener qqn à la raison ■ **to ~ sthg to an end** *OR* **a close** *OR* **a halt** mettre fin à qqch ■ **to ~ sthg to sb's attention** *OR* **knowledge** *OR* **notice** attirer l'attention de qqn sur qqch ■ **to ~ a child into the world** mettre un enfant au monde ■ **to ~ sthg to light** mettre qqch en lumière, révéler qqch
3. [produce] provoquer, causer ■ **to ~ sthg upon sb** attirer qqch sur qqn ■ **you ~ credit to the firm** vous faites honneur à la société ■ **it ~s bad/good luck** ça porte malheur/bonheur ■ **he brought a sense of urgency to the project** il a fait accélérer le projet ■ **the story brought tears to my eyes** l'histoire m'a fait venir les larmes aux yeux ■ **his speech brought jeers from the audience** son discours lui a valu les huées de l'assistance ■ **money does not always ~ happiness** l'argent ne fait pas toujours le bonheur ■ **the winter brought more wind and rain** l'hiver a amené encore plus de vent et de pluie ■ **tourism has brought prosperity to the area** le tourisme a enrichi la région ■ **who knows what the future will ~?** qui sait ce que l'avenir nous/lui *etc* réserve?
4. [force] amener ■ **she can't ~ herself to speak about it** elle n'arrive pas à en parler ■ **her performance brought the audience to its feet** les spectateurs se sont levés pour l'applaudir
5. [lead] mener, amener ■ **the shock brought him to the verge of a breakdown** le choc l'a mené au bord de la dépression nerveuse ■ **to ~ sb into a conversation/discussion** faire participer qqn à une conversation/discussion ■ **that ~s us to the next question** cela nous amène à la question suivante
6. LAW : **to ~ an action** *OR* **a suit against sb** intenter un procès à *OR* contre qqn ■ **to ~ a charge against sb** porter une accusation contre qqn ■ **the case was brought before the court** l'affaire a été déférée au tribunal ■ **he was brought before the court** il a comparu devant le tribunal ■ **the murderer must be brought to justice** l'assassin doit être traduit en justice
7. [financially] rapporter ■ **her painting only ~s her a few thousand pounds a year** ses peintures ne lui rapportent que quelques milliers de livres par an.
◆ **bring about** *vt sep* **1.** [cause - changes, war] provoquer, amener, entraîner ■ **what brought about his dismissal?** pourquoi a-t-il été renvoyé exactement?, quel est le motif de son renvoi?
2. NAUT faire virer de bord.
◆ **bring along** *vt sep* [person] amener ■ [thing] apporter.
◆ **bring around** = **bring round**.
◆ **bring back** *vt sep* **1.** [fetch - person] ramener ; [- thing] rapporter ■ **no amount of crying will ~ him back** pleurer ne le ramènera pas à la vie
2. [restore] restaurer ■ **the news brought a smile back to her face** la nouvelle lui a rendu le sourire ■ **they're ~ing back miniskirts** ils relancent la minijupe
3. [evoke - memory] rappeler (à la mémoire) ■ **that ~s it all back to me** ça réveille tous mes souvenirs.
◆ **bring down** *vt sep* **1.** [fetch - person] amener ; [- thing] descendre, apporter
2. [reduce - prices, temperature] faire baisser ; [- swelling] réduire
3. [cause to land - kite] ramener (au sol) ; [- plane] faire atterrir
4. [cause to fall - prey] descendre ; [- plane, enemy, tree] abattre

5. [overthrow] faire tomber, renverser
6. MATHS [carry] abaisser
7. *inf* [depress] déprimer, donner le cafard à
8. *lit* [provoke - anger] attirer.

➜ **bring forth** *vt sep fml* **1.** [produce - fruit] produire ; [- child] mettre au monde ; [- animal] mettre bas
2. [elicit] provoquer.

➜ **bring forward** *vt sep* **1.** [present - person] faire avancer ; [- witness] produire ; [- evidence] avancer, présenter
2. [move - date, meeting] avancer
3. [in accounting] reporter.

➜ **bring in** *vt sep* **1.** [fetch in - person] faire entrer ; [- thing] rentrer ■ **we will have to ~ in the police** il faudra faire intervenir la *OR* faire appel à la police
2. [introduce - laws, system] introduire, présenter ; [- fashion] lancer
3. [yield, produce] rapporter ■ **tourism ~s in millions of dollars each year** le tourisme rapporte des millions de dollars tous les ans
4. LAW [verdict] rendre ■ **they brought in a verdict of guilty** ils l'ont déclaré coupable.

➜ **bring off** *vt sep UK inf* [trick] réussir ■ [plan] réaliser ■ [deal] conclure, mener à bien ■ **did you manage to ~ it off?** avez-vous réussi votre coup?

➜ **bring on** *vt sep* **1.** [induce] provoquer, causer
2. [encourage] encourager ■ **the warm weather has really brought on the flowers** la chaleur a bien fait pousser les fleurs
3. THEAT [person] amener sur scène ■ [thing] apporter sur scène.

➜ **bring out** *vt sep* **1.** [take out - person] faire sortir ; [- thing] sortir
2. [commercially - product, style] lancer ; [- record] sortir ; [- book] publier
3. [accentuate] souligner ■ **that colour ~s out the green in her eyes** cette couleur met en valeur le vert de ses yeux ■ **her performance brought out the character's comic side** son interprétation a fait ressortir le côté comique du personnage ■ **to ~ out the best/worst in sb** faire apparaître qqn sous son meilleur/plus mauvais jour
4. *UK* [in rash, spots] : **strawberries ~ me out in spots** les fraises me donnent des boutons
5. [encourage - person] encourager ■ **he's very good at ~ing people out (of themselves)** il sait très bien s'y prendre pour mettre les gens à l'aise
6. [workers] appeler à la grève.

➜ **bring over** *vt sep* [take - person] amener ; [- thing] apporter.

➜ **bring round** *vt sep* **1.** [take - person] amener ; [- thing] apporter ■ **I brought the conversation round to marriage** *fig* j'ai amené la conversation sur le mariage
2. [revive] ranimer
3. [persuade] convaincre, convertir ■ **to ~ sb round to a point of view** convertir *OR* amener qqn à un point de vue.

➜ **bring through** *vt sep* : **he brought the country through the depression** il a réussi à faire sortir le pays de la dépression ■ **the doctors brought me through my illness** grâce aux médecins, j'ai survécu à ma maladie.

➜ **bring to** *vt sep* **1.** [revive] ranimer
2. NAUT mettre en panne.

➜ **bring together** *vt sep* **1.** [people] réunir ■ [facts] rassembler
2. [introduce] mettre en contact, faire se rencontrer
3. [reconcile] réconcilier.

➜ **bring up** *vt sep* **1.** [take - person] amener ; [- thing] monter
2. [child] élever ■ **to be well/badly brought up** être bien/mal élevé
3. [mention - fact, problem] signaler, mentionner ; [- question] soulever ■ **don't ~ that up again** ne remettez pas cela sur le tapis ■ **we won't ~ it up again** nous n'en reparlerons plus
4. [vomit] vomir, rendre
5. LAW : **to ~ sb up before a judge** citer *OR* faire comparaître qqn devant un juge.

bring-and-buy *n UK* ~ **(sale)** *brocante de particuliers en Grande-Bretagne.*

BRING-AND-BUY SALE

Ces brocantes sont en général destinées à réunir des fonds pour une œuvre de charité. On y vend des objets d'occasion et des produits faits maison.

brink [brɪŋk] *n* bord *m* ■ **the country is on the ~ of war/of a recession** le pays est au bord *OR* à la veille de la guerre/d'une récession ■ **to be on the ~ of doing sthg** être sur le point de faire qqch.

brink(s)manship ['brɪŋk(s)mənʃɪp] *n* stratégie *f* du bord de l'abîme.

briny ['braɪnɪ] (*comp* **brinier**, *superl* **briniest**) ◇ *adj* saumâtre, salé.
◇ *n lit* **the ~** la mer.

briquet(te) [brɪ'ket] *n* [of coal] briquette *f*, aggloméré *m* ■ [of ice cream] pavé *m*.

brisk [brɪsk] *adj* **1.** [person] vif, alerte ■ [manner] brusque **2.** [quick] rapide, vif ■ **to go for a ~ walk** se promener d'un bon pas ■ **at a ~ pace** à vive allure **3.** COMM florissant ■ **business is ~** les affaires marchent bien ■ **bidding at the auction was ~** les enchères étaient animées **4.** [weather] vivifiant, frais, fraîche *f* ■ [day, wind] frais, fraîche *f*.

brisket ['brɪskɪt] *n* [of animal] poitrine *f* ■ CULIN poitrine *f* de bœuf.

briskly ['brɪsklɪ] *adv* **1.** [move] vivement ■ [walk] d'un bon pas ■ [speak] brusquement ■ [act] sans délai *OR* tarder **2.** COMM : **cold drinks were selling ~** les boissons fraîches se vendaient très bien *OR* comme des petits pains.

bristle ['brɪsl] ◇ *vi* **1.** [hair] se redresser, se hérisser **2.** *fig* [show anger] s'irriter, se hérisser.
◇ *n* [of beard, brush] poil *m* ■ [of boar, pig] soie *f* ■ [of plant] poil *m*, soie *f* ■ **a brush with nylon/natural ~s** une brosse en nylon/soie.
◇ *comp* [hairbrush, paintbrush] : **a pure ~ brush** une brosse pur sanglier.

➜ **bristle with** *vt insep UK* [swarm with] grouiller de.

bristling ['brɪslɪŋ] *adj* hérissé, en bataille.

bristly ['brɪslɪ] (*comp* **bristlier**, *superl* **bristliest**) *adj* [beard - in appearance] aux poils raides ; [- to touch] qui pique ■ [chin] piquant ■ **his face was all ~** il avait une barbe de trois jours.

Bristol Channel ['brɪstl-] *pr n* : **the ~** le canal de Bristol.

Brit [brɪt] *n inf* Britannique *mf*, *written abbr of* **British.**

Britain ['brɪtn] *pr n* : **(Great) ~** Grande-Bretagne *f* ■ **in ~** en Grande-Bretagne ■ **the Battle of ~** la bataille d'Angleterre.

THE BATTLE OF BRITAIN

Lutte aérienne qui opposa, d'août à octobre 1940, la Luftwaffe à la RAF, l'objectif allemand étant de neutraliser l'espace aérien britannique et d'envahir la Grande-Bretagne. La résistance des forces aériennes britanniques mit un terme au projet des nazis.

Britannia [brɪ'tænjə] *pr n* **1.** [figure] *femme assise portant un casque et tenant un trident, qui personnifie la Grande-Bretagne sur certaines pièces de monnaie* **2.** : **(the Royal Yacht) ~** *yacht de la famille royale britannique.*

Britannic [brɪ'tænɪk] *adj fml* **His** *OR* **Her ~ Majesty** Sa Majesté Britannique.

britches ['brɪtʃɪz] *US* = **breeches.**

briticism ['brɪtɪsɪzm] *n* anglicisme *m*.

British ['brɪtɪʃ] ◇ *adj* britannique, anglais ■ **~ English** anglais *m* britannique ■ **the ~ Embassy** l'ambassade *f* de Grande-Bretagne ■ **the ~ Empire** l'Empire *m* britannique.
◇ *npl* : **the ~** les Britanniques *mpl*, les Anglais *mpl*.

British Academy *pr n* : **the ~** *organisme public d'aide à la recherche dans le domaine des lettres.*

British Broadcasting Corporation *pr n* : **the ~** la BBC.

British Columbia *pr n* Colombie-Britannique *f*.

British Columbian ◇ *n habitant ou natif de la Colombie-Britannique.*

◇ *adj* de la Colombie-Britannique.

British Commonwealth *pr n* : **the ~** le Commonwealth.

British Council *pr n* : **the ~** *organisme public chargé de promouvoir la langue et la culture anglaises.*

BRITISH COUNCIL

La vocation du *British Council* est de promouvoir la langue et la culture anglaises, et de renforcer les liens culturels entre la Grande-Bretagne et les autres pays.

British East India Company *pr n* : **the ~** la Compagnie britannique des Indes orientales.

British Gas *pr n société de production et de distribution du gaz, privatisée en 1986.*

British Isles *pr npl* : **the ~** les îles *fpl* Britanniques ■ **in the ~** aux îles Britanniques.

British Legion *pr n organisme d'aide aux anciens combattants.*

British Library *pr n la bibliothèque nationale britannique.*

BRITISH LIBRARY

La bibliothèque nationale britannique héberge plus de 15 millions de volumes et reçoit automatiquement un exemplaire de chaque ouvrage qui est publié au Royaume-Uni. Son nouveau siège principal, qui a ouvert ses portes en 1997, se situe entre les gares de Euston et King's Cross à Londres. Avant, elle occupait la très pittoresque salle de lecture du British Museum.

British Museum *pr n grand musée et bibliothèque londoniens.*

British Rail *pr n ancienne société des chemins de fers britanniques,* ≃ SNCF *f*.

British Summer Time *n heure d'été britannique.*

British Telecom [-'telɪkɒm] *pr n société britannique de télécommunications.*

BRITISH TELECOM

Les Télécoms britanniques, qui gèrent notamment les services téléphoniques, ont été privatisées en 1984.

Briton ['brɪtn] *n* Britannique *mf*, Anglais *m*, - e *f* ■ HIST Breton *m*, - onne *f* (d'Angleterre).

Brittany ['brɪtənɪ] *pr n* Bretagne *f* ■ **in ~** en Bretagne.

brittle ['brɪtl] *adj* **1.** [breakable] cassant, fragile **2.** [person] froid, indifférent ■ [humour] mordant, caustique ■ [reply] sec, sèche *f* **3.** [sound] strident, aigu, - uë *f*.

bro [brəʊ] (*abbrev of* **brother**) *n inf* **my ~** mon frangin.

broach [brəʊtʃ] ◇ *vt* **1.** [subject] aborder, entamer **2.** [barrel] percer, mettre en perce ■ [supplies] entamer.

◇ *vi* NAUT venir *OR* tomber en travers.

◇ *n* **1.** *US* = **brooch 2.** CONSTR perçoir *m*, foret *m* **3.** CULIN broche *f*.

broad [brɔːd] ◇ *adj* **1.** [wide] large ■ **she has a ~ back** elle a une forte carrure ■ **to be ~ in the shoulders, to have ~ shoulders** être large d'épaules ▶ **he has ~ shoulders, he can take it** il a les reins solides, il peut encaisser ■ **it's as ~ as it's long** *UK* c'est bonnet blanc et blanc bonnet, c'est du pareil au même **2.** [extensive] vaste, immense ■ **a ~ syllabus** un programme très divers ■ **we offer a ~ range of products** nous offrons une large *OR* grande gamme de produits ▶ **in ~ daylight** *liter* au grand jour, en plein jour ; *fig* au vu et au su de tout le monde, au grand jour **3.** [general] général ■ **here is a ~ outline** voilà les grandes lignes ■ **in the ~est sense of the word** au sens le plus large du mot ■ **his books still have a very ~ appeal** ses livres plaisent toujours à *OR* intéressent toujours un vaste public ■ **~ construction** *US* LAW interprétation *f* large

4. [not subtle] évident ■ **a ~ hint** une allusion transparente ■ **"surely not", she said with ~ sarcasm** "pas possible", dit-elle d'un ton des plus sarcastiques ■ **he speaks with a ~ Scots accent** il a un accent écossais prononcé *OR* un fort accent écossais

5. [liberal] libéral ■ **she has very ~ tastes in literature** elle a des goûts littéraires très éclectiques ▶ **Broad Church** *groupe libéral à l'intérieur de l'Église anglicane*

6. [coarse] grossier, vulgaire

7. PHON large ■ **~ transcription** transcription *f* large.

◇ *n* **1.** [widest part] : **the ~ of the back** le milieu du dos **2.** △ *US* [woman] gonzesse△ *f*.

B-road *n UK* ≃ route *f* départementale *OR* secondaire.

broadband ['brɔːdbænd] ◇ *n* diffusion *f* en larges bandes de fréquence.

◇ *adj* à larges bandes.

broad bean *n* fève *f*.

broad-brimmed [-'brɪmd] *adj* à bords larges.

broad-brush *adj* : **a ~ approach** une approche grossière.

broadcast ['brɔːdkɑːst] ◇ *n* émission *f* ■ **repeat ~** rediffusion *f*.

◇ *vt* (*pret & pp* **broadcast** *OR* **broadcasted**) **1.** RADIO diffuser, radiodiffuser, émettre ■ TV téléviser, émettre ■ **you don't have to ~ it!** *fig* ce n'est pas la peine de le crier sur les toits *OR* le carillonner partout! **2.** AGRIC semer à la volée.

◇ *vi* (*pret & pp* **broadcast** *OR* **broadcasted**) [station] émettre ■ [actor] participer à une émission ■ TV paraître à la télévision ■ [show host] faire une émission.

◇ *adj* RADIO radiodiffusé ■ TV télévisé ■ **~ signal/satellite** signal *m* /satellite *m* de radiodiffusion.

◇ *adv* AGRIC à la volée.

broadcaster ['brɔːdkɑːstəʳ] *n* personnalité *f* de la radio *OR* de la télévision.

broadcasting ['brɔːdkɑːstɪŋ] *n* RADIO radiodiffusion *f* ■ TV télévision *f* ■ **he wants to go into ~** il veut faire une carrière à la radio ou à la télévision.

Broadcasting Complaints Commission *pr n organisme britannique traitant les plaintes concernant les émissions de télévision et de radio.*

Broadcasting House *pr n siège de la BBC à Londres.*

Broadcasting Standards Council *pr n organisme britannique de contrôle des émissions de télévision et de radio.*

broaden ['brɔːdn] ◇ *vi* s'élargir.

◇ *vt* élargir.

broad jump *n US* saut *m* en longueur.

broadly ['brɔːdlɪ] *adv* **1.** [widely] largement ■ **to smile ~** faire un grand sourire **2.** [generally] en général ■ **~ speaking** d'une façon générale, en gros.

broadly-based *adj* composé d'éléments variés *OR* divers.

broad-minded *adj* : **to be ~** avoir les idées larges ■ **he has very ~ parents** ses parents sont très tolérants *OR* larges d'esprit.

broad-mindedness [-'maɪndɪdnɪs] *n* largeur *f* d'esprit.

broadsheet ['brɔːdʃiːt] *n* **1.** [newspaper] journal *m* plein format ■ **the ~s** *UK* PRESS les journaux *mpl* de qualité **2.** HIST & TYPO placard *m*.

BROADSHEET

Le terme *Broadsheet* (Grande-Bretagne) ou *Broadside* (États-Unis) désigne les journaux de qualité, imprimés sur des feuilles grand format, qui contiennent des informations sérieuses et des rubriques culturelles, sportives et financières de bon niveau. En Grande-Bretagne, les principaux journaux nationaux de qualité sont : *The Guardian* (tendance centre gauche), *The Independent*, *The Daily Telegraph* (tendance conservatrice), *The Times* (tendance centre droit), *The Financial Times*. Cependant, la majorité de ces quotidiens ont aujourd'hui adopté un format réduit, plus pratique pour les usagers des transports en commun, ce qui a eu pour effet d'augmenter considérablement les ventes. Aux États-Unis, les grands journaux nationaux sont le *Christian Science Monitor* et le *Wall Street Journal* ainsi que le *New York Times*, le *Washington Post* et le *Los Angeles Times* dans leurs éditions nationales.

broadside ['brɔ:dsaɪd] ◇ *n* **1.** [of ship] flanc *m* **2.** [volley of shots] bordée *f* ▪ *fig* [tirade] attaque *f* cinglante ▪ [of insults] bordée *f* d'injures ▪ **to fire a ~ at sb/sthg** s'en prendre violemment à qqn/qqch.
◇ *adv* : **~ (on)** par le travers.

Broadway ['brɔ:dweɪ] *pr n* Broadway *(rue des théâtres à Manhattan)*.

brocade [brə'keɪd] ◇ *n* brocart *m*.
◇ *vt* brocher.

broccoli ['brɒkəlɪ] *n (U)* brocolis *mpl*.

brochure [*UK* 'brəʊʃəʳ, *US* brəʊ'ʃʊr] *n* [gen] brochure *f*, dépliant *m* ▪ SCH & UNIV prospectus *m*.

brogue [brəʊg] *n* [accent] accent *m* du terroir ▪ [Irish] accent *m* irlandais.
◆ **brogues** *npl chaussures basses assez lourdes ornées de petits trous.*

broil [brɔɪl] *US* ◇ *vt* griller, faire cuire sur le gril ▪ *fig* griller.
◇ *vi* griller ▪ **~ing sun** soleil brûlant.

broiler ['brɔɪləʳ] *n* [chicken] poulet *m* (à rôtir).

broke [brəʊk] ◇ *pt* ▻ **break**.
◇ *adj inf* fauché, à sec ▪ **to go ~** faire faillite ➊ **to go for ~** risquer le tout pour le tout ▪ **to be flat** *OR* **dead** *OR* **stony** *UK* **~** être fauché comme les blés, être raide comme un passe-lacet.

broken ['brəʊkn] ◇ *pp* ▻ **break**.
◇ *adj* **1.** [damaged - chair, toy, window] cassé, brisé ; [- leg, rib] fracturé, cassé ; [- back] brisé, cassé ; [- biscuits] brisé ▪ *fig* **~ heart** cœur brisé ▪ **to die of a ~ heart** mourir de chagrin ▪ **she's from a ~ home** elle vient d'un foyer désuni ▪ **a ~ marriage** un mariage brisé, un ménage désuni
2. [sleep - disturbed] interrompu ; [- restless] agité
3. [speech] mauvais, imparfait ▪ **in ~ French** en mauvais français
4. [agreement, promise] rompu, violé ▪ [appointment] manqué
5. [health] délabré ▪ **her spirit is ~** elle est abattue ▪ **he's a ~ man since his wife's death** [emotionally] il a le cœur brisé *OR* il est très abattu depuis la mort de sa femme ▪ **the scandal left him a ~ man** [financially] le scandale l'a ruiné
6. [incomplete - set] incomplet, - ète *f*
7. [uneven - ground] accidenté ; [- coastline] dentelé ; [- line] brisé, discontinu ▪ **~ cloud** *(U)* éclaircie *f*
8. [tamed - animal] dressé, maté
9. LING [vowel] diphtongué
10. MATHS : **~ numbers** fractions *fpl*
11. MUS : **~ chord** arpège *m*.

broken-down *adj* **1.** [damaged - machine] détraqué ; [- car] en panne **2.** [worn out] fini, à bout.

brokenhearted [,brəʊkn'hɑ:tɪd] *adj* au cœur brisé.

broken-winded [-'wɪndɪd] *adj* [horse] poussif.

broker ['brəʊkəʳ] *n* **1.** COMM courtier *m* ▪ NAUT courtier *m* maritime ▪ ST. EX ≃ courtier *m* (en Bourse), ≃ agent *m* de change **2.** [second-hand dealer] brocanteur *m*.

brokerage ['brəʊkərɪdʒ], **broking** ['brəʊkɪŋ] *n* courtage *m*.

brolly ['brɒlɪ] *(pl* **brollies**) *n UK inf* pépin *m (parapluie)*.

bromide ['brəʊmaɪd] *n* **1.** CHEM bromure *m* ▪ [sedative] bromure *m* (de potassium) **2.** *dated* [remark] banalité *f*, platitude *f* **3.** PRINT bromure *m*.

Bromo® ['brəʊməʊ] *n US médicament contre les maux d'estomac et les troubles digestifs.*

bronchial ['brɒŋkjəl] *adj* des bronches, bronchique.

bronchial tubes *npl* bronches *fpl*.

bronchitic [brɒŋ'kɪtɪk] ◇ *adj* bronchitique.
◇ *n* bronchitique *mf*.

bronchitis [brɒŋ'kaɪtɪs] *n (U)* bronchite *f* ▪ **to have (an attack of) ~** avoir *OR* faire une bronchite.

bronchopneumonia [,brɒŋkəʊnju:'məʊnjə] *n* bronchopneumonie *f*.

bronco ['brɒŋkəʊ] *(pl* **broncos**) *n US* cheval *m* sauvage *(de l'Ouest)*.

broncobuster ['brɒŋkəʊ,bʌstəʳ] *n US cowboy qui dompte les chevaux sauvages.*

brontosaurus [,brɒntə'sɔ:rəs] *(pl* **brontosauruses** *OR pl* **brontosauri** [-raɪ]) *n* brontosaure *m*.

Bronx cheer [brɒŋks] *n US inf* [rude noise] : **to give sb a ~** ≃ faire "prout" à qqn.

bronze [brɒnz] ◇ *n* **1.** [alloy] bronze *m* **2.** [statue] bronze *m*, statue *f* de *OR* en bronze.
◇ *comp* **1.** [lamp, medal, statue] de *OR* en bronze **2.** [colour, skin] (couleur *f* de) bronze *(inv)*.
◇ *vi* se bronzer, brunir.
◇ *vt* [metal] bronzer ▪ [skin] faire bronzer, brunir.

Bronze Age *n* : **the ~** l'âge *m* du bronze.

bronzed [brɒnzd] *adj* bronzé, hâlé.

bronze medal *n* médaille *f* de bronze.

bronze medallist *n* : **he's the ~** il a remporté la médaille de bronze.

brooch [brəʊtʃ] *(pl* **brooches**) *n* broche *f (bijou)*.

brood [bru:d] ◇ *n* **1.** [of birds] couvée *f*, nichée *f* ▪ [of animals] nichée *f*, portée *f* ▪ **a ~ mare** une (jument) poulinière **2.** *hum* [children] progéniture *f hum*.
◇ *vi* **1.** [bird] couver **2.** [danger, storm] couver, menacer ▪ **the monument ~s over the town's main square** *fig* le monument domine la grand-place de la ville **3.** [person] ruminer, broyer du noir ▪ **it's no use ~ing on** *OR* **over the past** cela ne sert à rien de s'appesantir sur *OR* remâcher le passé.

brooding ['bru:dɪŋ] ◇ *adj* menaçant, inquiétant.
◇ *n* : **he's done a lot of ~ since he got home** depuis son retour à la maison, il a passé beaucoup de temps à ruminer.

broody ['bru:dɪ] *(comp* **broodier**, *superl* **broodiest**) *adj* **1.** [reflective] pensif ▪ [gloomy] mélancolique, cafardeux **2.** [motherly] : **a ~ hen** une (poule) couveuse ▪ **to feel ~** *UK inf fig* être en mal d'enfant.

brook [brʊk] ◇ *vt (usu neg)* [tolerate] supporter, tolérer ▪ [answer, delay] admettre, souffrir.
◇ *n* [stream] ruisseau *m*.

broom [bru:m] *n* **1.** [brush] balai *m* **2.** BOT genêt *m*.

broomstick ['bru:mstɪk] *n* manche *m* à balai.

bros., Bros. [brɒs] *(abbrev of* **brothers**) COMM Frères.

broth [brɒθ] *n* **1.** CULIN bouillon *m (de viande et de légumes)* **2.** BIOL bouillon *m* de culture.

brothel ['brɒθl] *n* maison *f* close *OR* de passe.

brother ['brʌðəʳ] ◇ *n* **1.** [relative] frère *m* ▪ **older/younger ~** frère aîné/cadet ➊ **'The Brothers Karamazov'** ***Dostoievski*** 'les Frères Karamazov' **2.** *(pl* brethren ['breðrən] *OR pl* brothers) [fellow member - of trade union] camarade *m* ; [- of professional group] collègue *mf* ▪ **~s in arms** compagnons *mpl OR* frères *mpl* d'armes **3.** *US inf* [mate] : **hey, ~!** [stranger] eh, camarade! ; [friend] eh, mon vieux!
◇ *interj inf* dis donc, bigre.

brotherhood ['brʌðəhʊd] *n* **1.** [relationship] fraternité *f* ■ *fig* [fellowship] fraternité *f*, confraternité *f* ■ RELIG confrérie *f* ■ **the ~ of man** la communauté humaine **2.** [association] confrérie *f* ■ **the Brotherhood** [in Freemasonry] la franc-maçonnerie **3.** *US* [entire profession] corporation *f*.

brother-in-law (*pl* **brothers-in-law**) *n* beau-frère *m*.

brotherly ['brʌðəlɪ] *adj* fraternel.

brougham ['bru:əm] *n* [carriage] voiture *f* à chevaux ■ [car] coupé *m* de ville.

brought [brɔ:t] *pt* & *pp* ▷ **bring**.

brouhaha ['bru:hɑ:hɑ:] *n* brouhaha *m*, vacarme *m*.

brow [braʊ] *n* **1.** [forehead] front *m* ■ **her troubled ~** son air inquiet **2.** [eyebrow] sourcil *m* **3.** [of hill] sommet *m* **4.** MIN [pithead] tour *m* d'extraction.

browbeat ['braʊbi:t] (*pret* **browbeat**, *pp* **browbeaten** [-bi:tn]) *vt* intimider, brusquer ■ **to ~ sb into doing sthg** forcer qqn à faire qqch en usant d'intimidation.

brown [braʊn] ◇ *n* brun *m*, marron *m*.
◇ *adj* **1.** [gen] brun, marron ■ [leather] marron ■ [hair] châtain ■ [eyes] marron ■ **she has ~ hair** elle est brune *OR* châtain ■ **the leaves are turning ~** les feuilles commencent à jaunir ⊙ **we'll do it up ~!** *US inf* nous allons fignoler ça! ■ **in a ~ study** plongé dans ses pensées, pensif **2.** [tanned] bronzé, bruni ■ **as ~ as a berry** tout bronzé.
◇ *vi* **1.** CULIN dorer **2.** [skin] bronzer, brunir **3.** [plant] roussir.
◇ *vt* **1.** CULIN faire dorer ■ [sauce] faire roussir **2.** [tan] bronzer, brunir.

brown ale *n* bière *f* brune.

brown bear *n* ours *m* brun.

brown bread *n (U)* pain *m* complet *OR* bis.

browned-off *adj UK inf* **to be ~** [bored] en avoir marre ; [discouraged] ne plus avoir le moral ■ **she's ~ with her job** elle en a marre *OR* ras le bol de son travail.

brown goods *npl* COMM *biens de consommation de taille moyenne tels que téléviseur, radio ou magnétoscope.*

brownie ['braʊnɪ] *n* **1.** [elf] lutin *m*, farfadet *m* **2.** [cake] brownie *m* **3.** : **Brownie®** [camera] Brownie® *m* Kodak.
◆ **Brownie (Guide)** *n* ≃ jeannette *f*.

brownie point *n inf hum* bon point *m* ■ **doing the ironing should earn you a few ~ s** tu seras bien vu si tu fais le repassage.

browning ['braʊnɪŋ] *n UK* CULIN *colorant brun pour les sauces.*

brownout ['braʊnaʊt] *n US* [electric failure] baisse *f* de tension.

brown owl *n* chat-huant *m*.

brown paper *n* papier *m* d'emballage.

brown rice *n* riz *m* complet.

Brown Shirt *n* fasciste *mf* ■ HIST [Nazi] chemise *f* brune.

brown sugar *n* cassonade *f*, sucre *m* roux.

browse [braʊz] ◇ *vi* **1.** [person] regarder, jeter un œil ■ **she ~d through the book** elle a feuilleté le livre **2.** [animal] brouter, paître **3.** COMPUT naviguer.
◇ *vt* COMPUT [disc, file] parcourir.
◇ *n* **1.** [look] : **I popped into the shop to have a ~ around** je suis passée au magasin pour jeter un coup d'œil *OR* regarder **2.** COMPUT navigation *f*.

browser ['braʊzəʳ] *n* COMPUT navigateur *m*, logiciel *m* de navigation, browser *m*.

brucellosis [,bru:sɪ'ləʊsɪs] *n* brucellose *f*.

bruise [bru:z] ◇ *n* [on person] bleu *m*, contusion *f* ■ [on fruit] meurtrissure *f*, talure *f*.
◇ *vi* [fruit] se taler, s'abîmer ■ **to ~ easily** [person] se faire facilement des bleus.
◇ *vt* **1.** [person] faire un bleu à, contusionner ■ **to ~ one's arm** se faire un bleu au bras ‖ *fig* blesser ■ **his ego was bruised** son amour-propre en a pris un coup ‖ [fruit] taler, abîmer ■ [lettuce] flétrir **2.** CULIN [crush] écraser, piler.

bruiser ['bru:zəʳ] *n inf* [big man] malabar *m* ■ [fighter] cogneur *m*.

bruising ['bru:zɪŋ] ◇ *n (U)* contusion *f*, bleu *m* ■ **he suffered ~ to his arm** il a eu le bras contusionné.
◇ *adj fig* pénible, douloureux.

Brum [brʌm] *pr n UK inf nom familier de Birmingham.*

Brummie ['brʌmɪ] *UK inf* ◇ *n nom familier désignant un habitant de Birmingham.*
◇ *adj* de Birmingham.

Brummy ['brʌmɪ] = **Brummie**.

brunch [brʌntʃ] *n* brunch *m*.

Brunei ['bru:naɪ] *pr n* Brunei *m* ■ **in ~** au Brunei.

brunet [bru:'net] *US* ◇ *n* brun *m*, brune *f*.
◇ *adj* [hair] châtain.

brunette [bru:'net] *n* brune *f*, brunette *f* ■ **she's a ~** elle est brune.

brunt [brʌnt] *n* : **the village bore the full ~ of the attack** le village a essuyé le plus fort de l'attaque ■ **she bore the ~ of his anger** c'est sur elle que sa colère a éclaté.

bruschetta [brʊs'ketə] *n* CULIN bruschette *f*.

brush [brʌʃ] ◇ *n* (*pl* **brushes**) **1.** [gen] brosse *f* ■ [paintbrush] pinceau *m*, brosse *f* ■ [shaving brush] blaireau *m* ■ [scrubbing brush] brosse *f* dure ■ [broom] balai *m* ■ [short-handled brush] balayette *f* ■ **hair/nail/tooth ~** brosse à cheveux/à ongles/à dents **2.** [sweep] coup *m* de brosse **3.** [encounter, skirmish] accrochage *m*, escarmouche *f* ■ *fig* **to have a ~ with death** frôler la mort ■ **to have a ~ with the law** avoir des démêlés avec la justice **4.** [of fox] queue *f* **5.** ELEC [in generator, dynamo] balai *m* ■ [discharge] aigrette *f* **6.** *(U)* [undergrowth] broussailles *fpl* ■ [scrubland] brousse *f*.
◇ *vt* **1.** [clean - teeth] brosser ■ [tidy - hair] brosser, donner un coup de brosse à ■ **she ~ed her hair back from her face** elle a brossé ses cheveux en arrière ■ [sweep - floor] balayer **2.** [touch lightly] effleurer, frôler ■ [surface] raser **3.** TEX [wool] gratter.
◇ *vi* effleurer, frôler ■ **her hair ~ed against his cheek** ses cheveux ont effleuré *OR* frôlé sa joue.
◆ **brush aside** *vt sep* **1.** [move aside] écarter, repousser **2.** [ignore - remark] balayer d'un geste ; [- report] ignorer.
◆ **brush away** *vt sep* [remove - tears] essuyer ; [- insect] chasser.
◆ **brush down** *vt sep* [clothing] donner un coup de brosse à ■ [horse] brosser.
◆ **brush off** ◇ *vt sep* **1.** [remove] enlever *(à la brosse ou à la main)* ■ [insect] chasser **2.** [dismiss - remark] balayer *OR* écarter (d'un geste) ; [- person] écarter, repousser.
◇ *vi insep* [dirt] s'enlever.
◆ **brush past** *vt insep* frôler en passant.
◆ **brush up** *vt sep* **1.** *inf* [revise] revoir, réviser ■ **I have to ~ up my maths** il faut que je me remette aux maths **2.** [sweep up] ramasser à la balayette **3.** TEX [wool] gratter.
◆ **brush up on** *vt insep inf* réviser.

brushed [brʌʃt] *adj* gratté ■ **~ cotton** pilou *m*, finette *f*.

brush fire *n* **1.** [fire] feu *m* de brousse, incendie *m* de broussailles **2.** [minor war] conflit *m* armé.

brush-off *n inf* **to give sb the ~** envoyer promener *OR* balader qqn.

brush stroke *n* [gen] coup *m* de brosse ■ ART coup *m OR* trait *m* de pinceau.

brush-up *n* **1.** *UK* [cleanup] coup *m* de brosse **2.** *inf* [revision] révision *f*.

brushwood ['brʌʃwʊd] *n (U)* [undergrowth] broussailles *fpl* ■ [cuttings] menu bois *m*, brindilles *fpl*.

brushwork ['brʌʃwɜ:k] *n (U)* [gen] travail *m* au pinceau ■ ART touche *f*.

brusque [bru:sk] *adj* [abrupt] brusque ▪ [curt] brusque, bourru.

brusquely ['bru:sklɪ] *adv* [abruptly] avec brusquerie ▪ [curtly] avec brusquerie *OR* rudesse, brutalement.

Brussels ['brʌslz] *pr n* Bruxelles.

Brussel(s) sprout *n* chou *m* de Bruxelles.

brutal ['bru:tl] *adj* [cruel - action, behaviour, person] brutal, cruel ▪ [uncompromising - honesty] franc, franche *f*, brutal ▪ [severe - climate, cold] rude, rigoureux.

brutality [bru:'tælətɪ] (*pl* **brutalities**) *n* **1.** [cruelty] brutalité *f*, cruauté *f* **2.** [act of cruelty] brutalité *f*.

brutalize, ise ['bru:təlaɪz] *vt* **1.** [ill-treat] brutaliser **2.** [make brutal] rendre brutal.

brutally ['bru:təlɪ] *adv* [attack, kill, treat] brutalement, sauvagement ▪ [say] brutalement, franchement ▪ [cold] extrêmement ▪ **she gave a ~ honest account of events** elle a raconté les événements avec une franchise brutale *OR* un réalisme brutal.

brute [bru:t] <> *n* **1.** [animal] brute *f*, bête *f* **2.** [person - violent] brute *f* ; [- coarse] brute *f* (épaisse), rustre *m*.
<> *adj* **1.** [animal-like] animal, bestial **2.** [purely physical] brutal ▪ **~ force** *OR* **strength** force *f* brutale **3.** [mindless] brut ▪ **an act of ~ stupidity** un acte d'une bêtise sans nom.

brutish ['bru:tɪʃ] *adj* **1.** [animal-like] animal, bestial **2.** [cruel] brutal, violent ▪ [coarse] grossier.

Brylcreem® [brɪlkri:m] *n marque de brillantine.*

bs *written abbr of* **bill of sale**.

BS *n* **1.** *UK* (*abbrev of* **British Standard/Standards**) *indique que le chiffre qui suit renvoie au numéro de la norme fixée par l'Institut britannique de normalisation* **2.** *US* UNIV (*abbrev of* **Bachelor of Science**) *(titulaire d'une) licence de sciences.*

BSc (*abbrev of* **Bachelor of Science**) *n UK* UNIV *(titulaire d'une) licence de sciences.*

BSE (*abbrev of* **bovine spongiform encephalopathy**) *n* EBS *f*.

BSI (*abbrev of* **British Standards Institution**) *pr n association britannique de normalisation,* ≃ AFNOR *f*.

B-side *n* face *f* B *OR* 2 *(d'un disque).*

BST *n* = **British Summer Time**.

BT *pr n* = **British Telecom**.

btu (*abbrev of* **British thermal unit**) *n unité de chaleur (1054,2 joules).*

BTW (*abbrev of* **by the way**) *adv inf* à propos.

bub [bʌb] *n US inf* **hi, ~!** [man] salut, mon vieux! ; [woman] salut, ma vieille!

bubble ['bʌbl] <> *n* **1.** [of foam] bulle *f* ▪ [in liquid] bouillon *m* ▪ [in champagne] bulle *f* ▪ [in glass] bulle *f*, soufflure *f* ▪ [in paint] boursouflure *f*, cloque *f* ▪ [in metal] soufflure *f* **2.** [transparent cover] cloche *f* **3.** *fig* [illusion] : **to prick** *OR* **to burst sb's ~** réduire à néant les illusions de qqn, enlever ses illusions à qqn **4.** COMM : **~ (scheme)** affaire *f* pourrie **5.** [sound] glouglou *m*.
<> *vi* **1.** [liquid] bouillonner, faire des bulles ▪ [champagne] pétiller ▪ [gas] barboter ▪ **her real feelings ~d beneath the surface** *fig* ses sentiments véritables bouillonnaient en elle **2.** [gurgle] gargouiller, glouglouter **3.** [brim] déborder ▪ **the children were bubbling with excitement** les enfants étaient tout excités *OR* surexcités.
◆ **bubble over** *vi insep liter & fig* déborder ▪ **to ~ over with enthusiasm** déborder d'enthousiasme.
◆ **bubble up** *vi insep* [liquid] monter en bouillonnant ▪ *fig* [feeling] monter.

bubble and squeak *n UK plat à base de pommes de terre et de choux, servi réchauffé.*

bubble bath *n* bain *m* moussant.

bubble car *n UK petite voiture à trois roues.*

bubble gum <> *n* bubble-gum *m*.
<> *adj inf* **~ music** *musique destinée aux jeunes adolescents.*

bubble head *n US inf* imbécile *mf*.

bubblejet printer ['bʌbldʒet-] *n* imprimante *f* à jet d'encre.

bubble pack *n* [for toy, batteries] emballage *m* pelliculé ▪ [for pills] plaquette *f*.

bubbly ['bʌblɪ] (*comp* **bubblier**, *superl* **bubbliest**) *UK* <> *adj* **1.** [liquid] pétillant, plein de bulles **2.** [person] pétillant, plein d'entrain.
<> *n inf* champ *m*.

bubonic [bju:'bɒnɪk] *adj* bubonique.

buccaneer [ˌbʌkə'nɪər] *n* **1.** HIST boucanier *m* **2.** [unscrupulous person] flibustier *m*, pirate *m*.

buccaneering [ˌbʌkə'nɪərɪŋ] *adj* entreprenant.

buck [bʌk] <> *n* **1.** [male animal] mâle *m* **2.** *inf* [young man] jeune mec *m* ▪ *arch* [dandy] dandy *m* **3.** *US inf* [dollar] dollar *m* ▪ **to make a fast** *OR* **quick ~** gagner du fric facilement **4.** *inf* [responsibility] responsabilité *f* ▪ **to pass the ~** faire porter le chapeau à qqn ▪ **the ~ stops here** en dernier ressort, c'est moi le responsable **5.** [jump] ruade *f*.
<> *comp* [goat, hare, kangaroo, rabbit] mâle ▪ **~ deer** daim *m*, chevreuil *m*.
<> *vi* **1.** [horse] donner une ruade ▪ *US* [car] cahoter, tressauter **2.** *US* [charge] donner un coup de tête **3.** *US inf* [resist] : **to ~ against change** se rebiffer contre les changements **4.** *US inf* [strive] rechercher.
<> *vt* **1.** [subj: horse] : **the horse ~ed his rider (off)** le cheval a désarçonné *OR* jeté bas son cavalier **2.** *inf* [resist] : **to ~ the system** se rebiffer contre le système.
◆ **buck up** *UK inf* <> *vt sep* **1.** [cheer up] remonter le moral à **2.** [improve] améliorer ▪ **you'd better ~ up your ideas** tu as intérêt à te remuer *OR* à en mettre un coup.
<> *vi insep* **1.** [cheer up] se secouer **2.** [hurry up] se grouiller, se magner.

buckboard ['bʌkbɔ:d] *n voiture hippomobile à quatre roues très répandue aux États-Unis à la fin du XIX*[e] *siècle.*

bucket ['bʌkɪt] <> *n* **1.** [container, contents] seau *m* ▶ **it rained ~s** *inf* il a plu à seaux ▪ **to cry** *OR* **to weep ~s** *inf* pleurer comme une Madeleine *OR* un veau ▪ **a ~ and spade** un seau et une pelle *(symbole, pour un Britannique, de vacances familiales au bord de la mer)* **2.** TECH [of dredger, grain elevator] godet *m* ▪ [of pump] piston *m* ▪ [of wheel] auget *m*.
<> *vt* **1.** [put in bucket] mettre dans un seau ▪ [carry] transporter dans un seau **2.** *UK* [horse] surmener ▪ [car] conduire brutalement.
<> *vi UK inf* **1.** [rain] pleuvoir à seaux **2.** [move hurriedly] aller à fond de train ▪ [car] rouler à fond la caisse.
◆ **bucket down** *vi insep UK inf* pleuvoir à seaux.

bucketful ['bʌkɪtfʊl] *n* plein seau *m* ▪ **a ~ of water** un seau plein d'eau.

bucket seat *n* baquet *m*, siège-baquet *m*, siège *m* cuve.

bucket shop *n* **1.** FIN bureau *m* *OR* maison *f* de contrepartie, bureau *m* de courtiers marrons **2.** *UK* [travel agency] *organisme de vente de billets d'avion à prix réduit.*

Buck House [bʌk-] *pr n inf nom familier du palais de Buckingham.*

Buckingham Palace ['bʌkɪŋəm-] *pr n* le palais de Buckingham *(résidence officielle du souverain britannique).*

buckle ['bʌkl] <> *n* **1.** [clasp] boucle *f* **2.** [kink - in metal] gauchissement *m* ; [- in wheel] voilure *f*.
<> *vi* **1.** [fasten] se boucler, s'attacher **2.** [distort - metal] gauchir, se déformer ; [- wheel] se voiler **3.** [give way - knees, legs] se dérober.
<> *vt* **1.** [fasten] boucler, attacher **2.** [distort] déformer, fausser ▪ [metal] gauchir, fausser ▪ [wheel] voiler.
◆ **buckle down** *vi insep inf* s'appliquer ▪ **to ~ down to work** se mettre au travail.
◆ **buckle in** *vt sep* [person] attacher.
◆ **buckle on** *vt sep* [gunbelt, sword] attacher, ceindre.
◆ **buckle to** *vi insep inf* s'y mettre, s'y atteler.

buckram ['bʌkrəm] *n* bougran *m*.

Bucks *written abbr of* **Buckinghamshire**.

bucksaw ['bʌksɔ:] *n* scie *f* à bûches.

buck's fizz *n UK cocktail composé de champagne et de jus d'orange.*

buckshot ['bʌkʃɒt] *n* chevrotine *f*, gros plomb *m*.

buckskin ['bʌkskɪn] *n* peau *f* de daim.

bucktooth ['bʌk,tu:θ] (*pl* **buckteeth** [-,ti:θ]) *n* dent *f* proéminente *OR* qui avance.

buckwheat ['bʌkwi:t] *n* sarrasin *m*, blé *m* noir ■ **~ flour** farine *f* de blé noir *OR* de sarrasin.

bucolic [bju:'kɒlɪk] ◇ *adj* bucolique, pastoral.
◇ *n* bucolique *f*.

bud [bʌd] ◇ *n* **1.** [shoot on plant] bourgeon *m*, il *m* ■ **the trees are in ~** les arbres bourgeonnent ▮ [for grafting] écusson *m* **2.** [flower] bouton *m* ■ **the roses are in ~** les roses sont en bouton **3.** ANAT papille *f* **4.** *US inf* [term of address] : **hey, ~!** [to stranger] eh, vous là-bas! ; [to friend] eh, mon vieux!
◇ *vi* (*pret & pp* **budded**, *cont* **budding**) **1.** BOT [plant] bourgeonner ■ [flower] former des boutons **2.** [horns] (commencer à) poindre *OR* percer **3.** [talent] (commencer à) se révéler *OR* percer.
◇ *vt* (*pret & pp* **budded**, *cont* **budding**) greffer, écussonner.

Buddha [*UK* 'bʊdə, *US* bʊ:də] *pr n* Bouddha.

Buddhism [*UK* 'bʊdɪzm, *US* bʊ:dɪzm] *n* bouddhisme *m*.

Buddhist [*UK* 'bʊdɪst, *US* bʊdɪst] ◇ *n* Bouddhiste *mf*.
◇ *adj* [country, priest] bouddhiste ■ [art, philosophy] bouddhique.

budding ['bʌdɪŋ] *adj* **1.** BOT [plant] bourgeonnant, couvert de bourgeons ■ [flower] en bouton **2.** *fig* [artist, genius] en herbe, prometteur ■ [love] naissant.

buddleia ['bʌdlɪə] *n* buddleia *m*.

buddy ['bʌdɪ] (*pl* **buddies**) *n inf* [friend] copain *m*, copine *f* ■ [for Aids patient] compagnon *m*, compagne *f* (d'un sidéen).

budge [bʌdʒ] ◇ *vi* **1.** [move] bouger ■ **it won't ~** c'est coincé, c'est bloqué **2.** *fig* [yield] céder, changer d'avis ■ **he wouldn't ~ an inch** il a tenu bon.
◇ *vt* **1.** [move] faire bouger **2.** [convince] convaincre, faire changer d'avis.

budgerigar ['bʌdʒərɪgɑ:ʳ] *n UK* perruche *f*.

budget ['bʌdʒɪt] ◇ *n* **1.** [gen - FIN] budget *m* ■ **to be on a tight ~** disposer d'un budget serré *OR* modeste **2.** [law] budget *m* ■ **~ speech** discours *m* de présentation du budget.
◇ *vt* budgétiser, inscrire au budget ■ **to ~ one's time** bien organiser son temps.
◇ *vi* dresser *OR* préparer un budget.
◇ *adj* **1.** [inexpensive] économique, pour petits budgets ■ **~ prices** prix *mpl* avantageux *OR* modiques **2.** ECON & FIN budgétaire.
◆ **budget for** *vt insep* [gen] prévoir des frais de, budgétiser ■ ECON & FIN inscrire *OR* porter au budget, budgétiser.

budget account *n* [with store] compte-crédit *m* ■ [with bank] ≃ compte *m* permanent.

budgetary ['bʌdʒɪtrɪ] *adj* budgétaire.

Budget Day *n* [in UK] *jour de la présentation du budget par le chancelier de l'Échiquier.*

budgie ['bʌdʒɪ] *n inf* perruche *f*.

buff [bʌf] ◇ *n* **1.** [colour] (couleur *f*) chamois *m* **2.** [leather] peau *f* de buffle ■ [polishing cloth] polissoir *m* **3.** *inf* [enthusiast] : **a wine ~** un amateur de vin ■ **a history ~** un mordu d'histoire.
◇ *vt* polir.
◇ *adj* [coloured] (couleur) chamois ■ [leather] de *OR* en buffle.

buffalo ['bʌfələʊ] (*pl inv OR pl* **buffaloes**) ◇ *n* buffle *m*, bufflesse *f*, bufflonne *f* ■ *US* bison *m* ■ **a herd of ~** un troupeau de buffles.
◇ *vt US inf* [intimidate] intimider.

buffalo grass *n herbe courte poussant dans les régions sèches au centre des États-Unis.*

buffer ['bʌfəʳ] ◇ *n* **1.** [protection] tampon *m* ■ [on car] *US* pare-chocs *m inv* ■ RAIL [on train] tampon *m* ■ [at station] butoir *m* ■ COMPUT mémoire *f* tampon ■ **a ~ against inflation** *fig* une mesure de protection contre l'inflation **2.** *UK inf* [fool] imbécile *mf* ■ **old ~** vieille ganache *f* **3.** [for polishing] polissoir *m*.
◇ *vt* tamponner, amortir (le choc) ■ **to be ~ed against reality** être protégé de la réalité *OR* des réalités (de la vie).

buffer memory *n* mémoire *f* tampon.

buffer state *n* état *m* tampon.

buffer zone *n* région *f* tampon.

buffet[1] [*UK* 'bʊfeɪ, *US* bə'feɪ] ['bʌfɪt] ◇ *n* **1.** [refreshments] buffet *m* **2.** [sideboard] buffet *m* **3.** [restaurant] buvette *f*, cafétéria *f* ■ [in station] buffet *m* *OR* café *m* de gare ■ [on train] wagon-restaurant *m*.
◇ *comp* [lunch, dinner] -buffet.

buffet[2] [*UK* 'bʊfeɪ, *US* bə'feɪ] ['bʌfɪt] *vt* [batter] : **~ed by the waves** ballotté par les vagues ■ **the trees were ~ed by the wind** les arbres étaient secoués par le vent.

buffet car ['bʊfeɪ-] *n* wagon-restaurant *m*.

buffeting ['bʌfɪtɪŋ] ◇ *n* [of rain, wind] assaut *m* ■ **the waves gave the boat a real ~** le navire a été violemment ballotté par les vagues.
◇ *adj* violent.

buffoon [bə'fu:n] *n* bouffon *m*, pitre *m* ■ **to act *OR* to play the ~** faire le clown *OR* le pitre.

buffoonery [bə'fu:nərɪ] *n* (*U*) bouffonnerie *f*, bouffonneries *fpl*.

bug [bʌg] ◇ *n* **1.** [insect] insecte *m* ■ [bedbug] punaise *f* ■ *fig* **she's been bitten by the film ~** *inf* c'est une mordue de cinéma **2.** *inf* [germ] microbe *m* ■ **I've got a stomach ~** j'ai des problèmes intestinaux **3.** *inf* [defect] défaut *m*, erreur *f* ■ COMPUT bogue *m* **4.** *inf* [microphone] micro *m* (caché) **5.** *US inf* [car] coccinelle *f*.
◇ *vt* (*pret & pp* **bugged**, *cont* **bugging**) **1.** *inf* [bother] taper sur les nerfs de ■ **what's bugging him?** qu'est-ce qu'il a? **2.** [wiretap - room] poser *OR* installer des appareils d'écoute (clandestins) dans ; [- phone] brancher sur table d'écoute.
◆ **bug out** *vi insep US inf* **1.** [leave hurriedly] ficher le camp **2.** [eyes] être globuleux *OR* exorbité.

bugbear ['bʌgbeəʳ] *n* [monster] épouvantail *m*, croque-mitaine *m* ■ *fig* [worry] bête noire *f*, cauchemar *m*.

bug-eyed *adj US* aux yeux globuleux *OR* exorbités.

bugger ['bʌgəʳ] ◇ *n* **1.** △ [unpleasant person] salaud△ *m* ■ **silly ~!** pauvre conard!△ ■ **you little ~!** petite fripouille! **2.** △ *UK* [job] : **this job's a real ~** c'est une saloperie de boulot△ **3.** △ *UK* [damn] : **I don't give a ~** je m'en tape△ **4.** *dated* [sodomite] pédéraste *m*.
◇ *interj*△ *UK* merde alors!△.
◇ *vt* **1.** [sodomize] sodomiser ■ LAW se livrer à la pédérastie avec **2.** △ *UK* [damn] : **~ him!** je l'emmerde!△ ■ **oh, ~ it!** oh, merde!△ **3.** △ *UK* [damage] bousiller△.
◆ **bugger off**△ *vi insep UK* foutre le camp△.
◆ **bugger up**△ *vt sep UK* saloper△.

bugger all△ *n UK* que dalle△.

buggered△ ['bʌgəd] *adj UK* **1.** [broken] foutu△ **2.** [in surprise] : **well, I'll be ~!** merde alors!△ **3.** [in annoyance] : **~ if I know** j'en sais foutre rien△.

buggery ['bʌgərɪ] ◇ *n* sodomie *f*.
◇ *interj*△ *UK* merde!△.

bugging ['bʌgɪŋ] *n* [of room] utilisation *f* d'appareils d'écoute (clandestins) ■ [of telephone] mise *f* sur écoute ■ **~ device** appareil *m* d'écoute (clandestin).

buggy ['bʌgɪ] ◇ *n* (*pl* **buggies**) **1.** [carriage] boghei *m* ■ [for baby] poussette *f*, poussette-canne *f* ■ *US* [pram] voiture *f* d'enfant **2.** *inf* [car] bagnole *f*.
◇ *adj* (*comp* **buggier**, *superl* **buggiest**) *inf US* [crazy] cinglé.

bugle ['bju:gl] ◇ *n* clairon *m*.
◇ *vi* jouer du clairon, sonner le clairon.

bugler ['bju:gləʳ] *n* (joueur *m* de) clairon *m*.

build [bɪld] ◇ *vt (pret & pp* **built** [bɪlt]) **1.** [dwelling] bâtir, construire ■ [temple] bâtir, édifier ■ [bridge, machine, ship] construire ■ [nest] faire, bâtir ■ **houses are being built** des maisons sont en construction ■ **this bed wasn't built for two people** ce lit n'a pas été conçu pour deux personnes ➤ **to ~ castles in the air** bâtir des châteaux en Espagne **2.** [found] bâtir, fonder.
◇ *vi (pret & pp* **built** [bɪlt]) **1.** [construct] bâtir **2.** [increase] augmenter, monter.
◇ *n* carrure *f*, charpente *f* ■ **of strong ~** solidement bâti *OR* charpenté ■ **of heavy ~** de forte corpulence *OR* taille ■ **of medium ~** de taille *OR* corpulence moyenne ■ **a man of slight ~** un homme fluet ■ **she's about the same ~ as I am** elle est à peu près de ma taille.
◆ **build in** *vt sep* CONSTR [incorporate] encastrer ■ *fig* [include - special features] intégrer.
◆ **build into** *vt sep* [incorporate] intégrer à.
◆ **build on** ◇ *vt sep* **1.** CONSTR ajouter **2.** *fig* **his success is built on hard work** sa réussite repose sur un travail acharné.
◇ *vt insep* : **we need to ~ on our achievements** il faut consolider nos succès.
◆ **build up** ◇ *vt sep* **1.** [develop - business, theory] établir, développer ; [- reputation] établir, bâtir ; [- confidence] donner, redonner ; [- strength] accroître, prendre ■ **you need to ~ up your strength, you need ~ing up** vous avez besoin de prendre des forces **2.** [increase - production] accroître, augmenter ; [- excitement] faire monter, accroître ; [- pressure] accumuler **3.** [promote] faire de la publicité pour.
◇ *vi insep* **1.** [business] se développer **2.** [excitement] monter, augmenter ■ [pressure] s'accumuler ■ **traffic is ~ing up** il commence à y avoir beaucoup de circulation.
◆ **build upon** *vt sep* = **build on** *(vt sense 2)*.

builder ['bɪldəʳ] *n* **1.** CONSTR [contractor] entrepreneur *m* ■ [worker] ouvrier *m* du bâtiment ■ [of machines, ships] constructeur *m* **2.** *fig* [founder] fondateur *m*, - trice *f*.

building ['bɪldɪŋ] ◇ *n* **1.** [structure] bâtiment *m*, construction *f* ■ [monumental] édifice *m* ■ [apartment, office] immeuble *m* **2.** [work] construction *f*.
◇ *comp* [land, plot] à bâtir ■ [materials] de construction ■ **~ industry** *OR* **trade** (industrie *f* du) bâtiment *m*.

building and loan association *n US* = **building society**.

building block *n* [toy] cube *m* ■ *fig* composante *f*.

building contractor *n* entrepreneur *m* (en bâtiment *OR* construction).

building site *n* chantier *m* (de construction).

building society *n UK société d'investissement et de crédit immobilier*.

buildup ['bɪldʌp] *n* **1.** [increase - in pressure] intensification *f* ; [- in excitement] montée *f* ■ COMM [- in production] accroissement *m* ; [- in stock] accumulation *f* ■ MIL [- in troops] rassemblement *m* ■ **nuclear arms ~** accumulation des armes nucléaires **2.** [publicity] campagne *f* publicitaire.

built [bɪlt] ◇ *pt & pp* ▷ **build**.
◇ *adj* [building] bâti, construit ■ [person] charpenté ■ **brick-~** en *OR* de brique ■ **to be powerfully ~** être puissamment *OR* solidement charpenté ■ **to be slightly ~** être fluet.

built-in *adj* [beam, wardrobe] encastré ■ [device, safeguard] intégré ■ *fig* [feature] inné, ancré ■ **~ obsolescence** obsolescence *f* programmée.

built-up *adj* **1.** [land] bâti ■ **a ~ area** une agglomération (urbaine) **2.** [in clothing] : **~ shoulders** épaules *fpl* surhaussées ■ **~ shoes** chaussures *fpl* à semelles compensées.

bulb [bʌlb] *n* **1.** BOT bulbe *m*, oignon *m* ■ **tulip ~** bulbe de tulipe **2.** ELEC ampoule *f* ■ **a light ~** une ampoule **3.** [of thermometer] réservoir *m*.

bulbous ['bʌlbəs] *adj* bulbeux.

Bulgaria [bʌl'geərɪə] *pr n* Bulgarie *f* ■ **in ~** en Bulgarie.

Bulgarian [bʌl'geərɪən] ◇ *n* **1.** [person] Bulgare *mf* **2.** LING bulgare *m*.
◇ *adj* bulgare.

bulge [bʌldʒ] ◇ *n* **1.** [lump, swelling] renflement *m* ■ [on vase, jug] panse *f*, ventre *m* ■ *UK* MIL saillant *m* ■ **he noticed a ~ in her pocket** il remarqua quelque chose qui faisait saillie dans sa poche **2.** [increase] poussée *f* ■ **a population ~** une explosion démographique.
◇ *vi* [swell] se gonfler, se renfler ■ **his suitcase was bulging with gifts** sa valise était bourrée de cadeaux ■ [stick out] faire saillie, saillir ■ **his eyes ~d** il avait les yeux saillants *OR* globuleux.

bulging ['bʌldʒɪŋ] *adj* [eyes] saillant, globuleux ■ [muscles, waist] saillant ■ [bag, pockets] gonflé.

bulimia [bjʊ'lɪmɪə] *n* boulimie *f*.

bulimic [bjʊ'lɪmɪk] ◇ *adj* boulimique.
◇ *n* boulimique *mf*.

bulk [bʌlk] ◇ *n* **1.** [mass] masse *f* ■ [stoutness] corpulence *f* ■ **the great ~ of the cathedral loomed out of the darkness** la silhouette massive de la cathédrale se dessina dans l'obscurité ■ **a man of enormous ~** un homme très corpulent **2.** [main part] : **the ~** la plus grande partie, la majeure partie ■ **she left the ~ of her fortune to charity** elle légua le plus gros de sa fortune aux bonnes œuvres **3.** [in food] fibre *f* (végétale) **4.** NAUT [goods] cargaison *f*.
◇ *comp* [order, supplies] en gros.
◇ *vi* : **to ~ large** *UK* occuper une place importante ■ **the prospect of a further drop in prices ~ed large in their minds** la perspective d'une autre baisse des prix les préoccupait vivement *OR* était au premier plan de leurs préoccupations.
◆ **in bulk** *adv phr* par grosses quantités ■ COMM en gros ■ NAUT en vrac.

bulk buying *n (U)* achat *m* par grosses quantités ■ COMM achat *m* en gros.

bulkhead ['bʌlkhed] *n* cloison *f (d'avion, de navire)*.

bulk mail *n (U)* envois *mpl* en nombre.

bulk rate *n* affranchissement *m* à forfait.

bulky ['bʌlkɪ] *adj* **1.** [massive, large] volumineux ■ [cumbersome] encombrant **2.** [corpulent, stout] corpulent, gros, grosse *f* ■ [solidly built] massif.

bull [bʊl] ◇ *n* **1.** [male cow] taureau *m* ■ **like a ~ in a china shop** comme un éléphant dans un magasin de porcelaine ■ **to take the ~ by the horns** prendre le taureau par les cornes **2.** [male of a species] mâle *m* **3.** *inf* [large, strong man] costaud *m*, malabar *m* **4.** ST. EX haussier *m*, spéculateur *m* à la hausse **5.** [centre of target] centre *m* de la cible ■ **to hit the ~** faire mouche, mettre dans le mille **6.** △ [nonsense] connerie△ *f*, conneries△ *fpl* ■ **that's a lot** *OR* **load of ~** c'est des conneries tout ça△ **7.** RELIG bulle *f*.
◇ *comp* [elephant, whale] mâle *m* ■ **~ calf** jeune taureau *m*, taurillon *m*.
◇ *vt* ST. EX [market, prices, shares] pousser à la hausse.

bulldog ['bʊldɒg] *n* ZOOL bouledogue *m*.

bulldog clip *n* pince *f* à dessin.

bulldoze ['bʊldəʊz] *vt* **1.** [building] démolir au bulldozer ■ [earth, stone] passer au bulldozer ■ **whole villages have been ~d out of existence** des villages entiers ont été rasés au bulldozer **2.** *fig* [push] : **to ~ sb into doing sthg** forcer qqn à faire qqch, faire pression sur qqn pour lui faire faire qqch.

bulldozer ['bʊldəʊzəʳ] *n* bulldozer *m*.

bullet ['bʊlɪt] ◇ *n* **1.** balle *f* ■ **to get the ~** *UK inf* se faire virer, se faire sacquer **2.** TYPO puce *f*.
◇ *comp* [hole] de balle ■ [wound] par balle.

bulletin ['bʊlətɪn] *n* [announcement] bulletin *m*, communiqué *m* ■ [newsletter] bulletin *m*.

bulletin board *n* **1.** *US* [gen] tableau *m* d'affichage **2.** COMPUT : **~ (system)** babillards *mpl*.

bulletproof ['bʊlɪtpruːf] ◇ *adj* [glass, vest] pare-balles *(inv)* ■ [vehicle] blindé.
◇ *vt* [door, vehicle] blinder.

bullfight ['bʊlfaɪt] *n* corrida *f*, course *f* de taureaux.

bullfighter ['bʊl,faɪtəʳ] *n* torero *m*, -a *f*, matador *m*.

bullfighting ['bʊl,faɪtɪŋ] *n (U)* courses *fpl* de taureaux, tauromachie *f*.

bullfinch ['bʊlfɪntʃ] *n* bouvreuil *m*.

bullfrog ['bʊlfrɒg] *n* grenouille *f* mugissante.

bullhorn ['bʊlhɔ:n] *n US* mégaphone *m*, porte-voix *m inv*.

bullion ['bʊljən] *n* [gold] or *m* en lingots *OR* en barres ▪ [silver] argent *m* en lingots *OR* en barres.

bullish ['bʊlɪʃ] *adj* **1.** ST. EX : **the market is ~** les cours *OR* valeurs sont en hausse **2.** *UK inf* [optimistic] : **to be in a ~ mood** être confiant *OR* optimiste.

bull market *n* marché *m* à la hausse.

bull mastiff *n chien issu d'un métissage entre le bouledogue et le mastiff.*

bullock ['bʊlək] *n* [castrated] bœuf *m* ▪ [young] bouvillon *m*.

bullring ['bʊlrɪŋ] *n* arène *f (pour la corrida)*.

bull's-eye *n* **1.** [centre of target] mille *m*, centre *m* de la cible ▪ **to hit the ~** *liter & fig* faire mouche, mettre dans le mille **2.** [sweet] gros bonbon *m* à la menthe **3.** [window] il-de-b uf *m*, oculus *m*.

bullshit▲ ['bʊlʃɪt] ◇ *n (U)* connerie△ *f*, conneries△ *fpl*.
◇ *vt* raconter des conneries△ à.
◇ *vi* déconner, raconter des conneries△.

bull terrier *n* bull-terrier *m*.

bully ['bʊlɪ] ◇ *n* **1.** [adult] tyran *m* ▪ [child] petite brute *f* **2.** [in hockey] bully *m*.
◇ *vt* [intimidate - spouse, employee] malmener ▪ **she bullies her little sister** elle est tyrannique avec sa petite s ur ▪ **they bullied me into going** on a fait pression sur moi pour que j'y aille.
◇ *interj inf* **~ for you!** chapeau! ; *iron* quel exploit!, bravo!
◆ **bully off** *vi insep* [in hockey] engager le jeu, mettre la balle en jeu.

bully beef *n UK* corned-beef *m*.

bullyboy ['bʊlɪbɔɪ] *n UK* brute *f*, voyou *m*.

bullying ['bʊlɪɪŋ] ◇ *adj* [intimidating] agressif, brutal.
◇ *n (U)* brimades *fpl*.

bully-off *n* bully *m*.

bulrush ['bʊlrʌʃ] *n* jonc *m*, scirpe *m*.

bulwark ['bʊlwək] *n* ARCHIT rempart *m*, fortification *f* ▪ [breakwater] digue *f*, môle *m* ▪ *fig* [protection] rempart *m* ▪ **a ~ against inflation** une mesure de protection contre l'inflation.
◆ **bulwarks** *npl* NAUT bastingage *m*, pavois *m*.

bum [bʌm] *inf* ◇ *n* **1.** *UK* [buttocks] fesses *fpl*, pétard *m* **2.** [tramp] clochard *m*, - e *f*, clodo *m* ▪ [lazy person] fainéant *m*, - e *f*, flemmard *m*, - e *f* ▪ [worthless person] minable *mf*, minus *m* **3.** [sports fanatic] fana *m*, mordu *m*, - e *f* ▪ **a beach ~** un fana *OR* mordu des plages **4.** *US* [vagrancy] : **he went on the ~** il s'est mis à dormir sous les ponts.
◇ *adj* [worthless] minable, nul ▪ [injured, disabled] patraque, mal fichu ▪ [untrue] faux, fausse *f* ▪ **he got a bit of a ~ deal** il a été très mal traité ▪ **he was in jail on a ~ rap** *US* il était en prison pour un délit qu'il n'avait pas commis ➔ **~ steer** tuyau *m* percé.
◇ *vt* (*pret & pp* **bummed**, *cont* **bumming**) *US* [beg, borrow] : **to ~ sthg off sb** emprunter qqch à qqn, taper qqn de qqch ▪ **to ~ a lift** *OR* **ride** se faire accompagner en voiture.
◇ *vi* (*pret & pp* **bummed**, *cont* **bumming**) *US* [be disappointed] être déprimé ▪ [laze about] traîner.
◆ **bum about** *UK*, **bum around** *vi insep inf* **1.** [drift, wander] vagabonder, se balader **2.** [loaf, idle] fainéanter, flemmarder.

bumble ['bʌmbl] *vi* **1.** [speak incoherently] bafouiller **2.** [move clumsily] : **he came bumbling in** il entra, l'air gauche.

bumblebee ['bʌmblbi:] *n* bourdon *m*.

bumbler ['bʌmblər] *n* empoté *m*, - e *f*, maladroit *m*, - e *f*.

bumbling ['bʌmblɪŋ] *adj* [person] empoté, maladroit ▪ [behaviour] maladroit.

bumf [bʌmf] *n UK inf* **1.** [documentation] doc *f* **2.** *pej* [useless papers] paperasse *f* **3.** [toilet paper] papier cul△ *m*.

bummed [bʌmd] *adj US inf* **to be ~ (out) with sthg** être déprimé par qqch.

bummer△ ['bʌmər] *n* [bad experience] poisse *f* ▪ **the film's a real ~** ce film est vraiment nul *OR* un vrai navet ▪ **what a ~!** les boules!△.

bump [bʌmp] ◇ *n* **1.** [lump] bosse *f* ▪ **a ~ in the road** une bosse sur la route **2.** [blow, knock] choc *m*, coup *m* ▪ [noise from blow] bruit *m* sourd, choc *m* sourd **3.** AERON [air current] courant *m* ascendant.
◇ *vt* heurter ▪ [elbow, head, knee] cogner.
◇ *vi* **1.** [move with jerks] cahoter **2.** [collide] se heurter ▪ **the boat ~ed against the pier** le bateau a buté contre l'embarcadère.
◇ *adv* : **the driver went ~ into the car in front** le conducteur est rentré en plein dans la voiture de devant.
◆ **bump into** *vt insep* [object] rentrer dedans, tamponner ▪ [person] rencontrer par hasard, tomber sur.
◆ **bump off** *vt sep inf* [murder] liquider, supprimer ▪ [with a gun] descendre.
◆ **bump up** *vt sep inf* [increase] faire grimper ▪ [prices] gonfler, faire grimper.

bumper ['bʌmpər] ◇ *n* **1.** AUT pare-chocs *m inv* **2.** [full glass] rasade *f*.
◇ *adj* [crop, harvest] exceptionnel, formidable ▪ **a ~ issue** *UK* un numéro exceptionnel.

bumper car *n* auto *f* tamponneuse.

bumper sticker *n* autocollant *m (pour voiture)*.

bumper-to-bumper *adj* : **the cars are ~ on the bridge** les voitures roulent pare-chocs contre pare-chocs sur le pont.

bumph *n inf* = **bumf**.

bumpkin ['bʌmpkɪn] *n inf pej* plouc *m*, péquenaud *m*.

bump start *n démarrage d'un véhicule en le poussant.*
◆ **bump-start** *vt* démarrer en poussant.

bumptious ['bʌmpʃəs] *adj* suffisant, prétentieux.

bumpy ['bʌmpɪ] (*comp* **bumpier**, *superl* **bumpiest**) *adj* [road] cahoteux ▪ [flight, ride] agité (de secousses) ▪ [surface, wall] bosselé ▪ **we've got a ~ ride ahead of us** *fig* on va traverser une mauvaise passe.

bun [bʌn] *n* **1.** [bread] petit pain *m* (au lait) ▪ **she's got a ~ in the oven**△ *UK* elle a un polichinelle dans le tiroir△ **2.** [hair] chignon *m*.

bunch [bʌntʃ] ◇ *n* **1.** [of flowers, straw] bouquet *m*, botte *f* ▪ [of grapes] grappe *f* ▪ [of bananas, dates] régime *m* ▪ [of feathers, hair] touffe *f* ▪ [of sticks, twigs] faisceau *m*, poignée *f* ▪ [of keys] trousseau *m* ▪ **do you want a ~ of fives?** *inf* tu veux mon poing sur la gueule? **2.** *inf* [of people] bande *f* ▪ **her family are a strange ~** elle a une drôle de famille ▪ **he's the best of a bad ~** c'est le moins mauvais de la bande ▪ [of things] : **he took out a ~ of papers from the drawer** il sortit un tas de papiers du tiroir **3.** CYCL peloton *m* **4.** *phr* **thanks a ~!** *inf iron* merci beaucoup!
◇ *vt* [straw, vegetables] mettre en bottes, botteler ▪ [flowers] botteler, mettre en bouquets.
◆ **bunches** *npl UK* couettes *fpl* ▪ **she wears her hair in ~es** elle porte des couettes.
◆ **bunch together** ◇ *vi insep* [people] se serrer, se presser.
◇ *vt sep* mettre ensemble ▪ [flowers] botteler, mettre en bouquets.
◆ **bunch up** ◇ *vi insep* **1.** [group of people] se serrer **2.** [clothing] se retrousser.
◇ *vt sep* mettre ensemble ▪ [flowers] mettre en bouquets, botteler ▪ [dress, skirt] retrousser ▪ **your dress is ~ed up at the back** le derrière de ta robe est tout retroussé.

bundle ['bʌndl] ◇ *n* **1.** [of clothes, linen] paquet *m* ▪ [wrapped in a cloth] paquet *m* ▪ [of goods] paquet *m*, ballot *m* ▪ [of sticks, twigs] faisceau *m*, poignée *f* ▪ [of banknotes, papers] liasse *f* ▪ **he's a ~ of nerves** c'est un paquet de nerfs ▪ **a ~ of firewood** un fagot ➔ **a ~ of fun** *OR* **laughs** *inf* marrant, amusant

2. COMPUT lot *m* **3.** *US inf* [money] : **to make a ~** faire son beurre **4.** [baby] bout *m* de chou **5.** *UK phr* **to go a ~ on sthg** *inf* s'emballer pour qqch ■ **thanks a ~!** *inf iron* merci beaucoup!
◇ *vt* **1.** [clothes] mettre en paquet ■ [for a journey] empaqueter ■ [linen] mettre en paquet ■ [goods] mettre en paquet ■ [banknotes, papers] mettre en liasses ■ [sticks, twigs] mettre en faisceaux ■ [firewood] mettre en fagots ■ [straw] botteler, mettre en bottes **2.** [shove] : **he was ~d into the car** on l'a poussé dans la voiture brusquement *OR* sans ménagement.
◆ **bundle off** *vt sep* : **the children were ~d off to school** les enfants furent envoyés *OR* expédiés à l'école vite fait.
◆ **bundle up** ◇ *vt sep* **1.** [tie up] mettre en paquet **2.** [dress warmly] emmitoufler.
◇ *vi insep* s'emmitoufler.

bundled ['bʌndld] *adj* COMPUT : **~ software** logiciel *m* livré avec le matériel.

bun fight *n UK inf hum* [gathering] réception *f*.

bung [bʌŋ] ◇ *n* **1.** [stopper] bondon *m*, bonde *f* **2.** [hole] bonde *f*.
◇ *vt* **1.** [hole] boucher **2.** *UK inf* [put carelessly] balancer ■ **just ~ it in the rubbish bin** fiche-le à la poubelle **3.** *UK inf* [add] rajouter ■ **~ it on the bill** rajoutez-le sur la note.
◆ **bung up** *vt sep UK inf* boucher ■ **my nose is/my eyes are ~ed up** j'ai le nez bouché/les yeux gonflés.

bungalow ['bʌŋgələʊ] *n* [one storey house] maison *f* sans étage ■ [in India] bungalow *m*.

bungee-jumping ['bʌndʒiː-] *n* saut *m* à l'élastique.

bungle ['bʌŋgl] *vt* gâcher.

bungler ['bʌŋglər] *n* incapable *mf*.

bungling ['bʌŋglɪŋ] ◇ *adj* [person] incompétent, incapable ■ [action] maladroit, gauche.
◇ *n* incompétence *f*.

bunion ['bʌnjən] *n* oignon *m (cor)*.

bunk [bʌŋk] ◇ *n* **1.** [berth] couchette *f* ■ [bed] lit *m* **2.** *UK inf* **to do a ~** se tirer△, se faire la malle△ **3.** *inf* [nonsense] foutaise *f*, foutaises *fpl*.
◇ *vi inf* **1.** [sleep] coucher **2.** [escape] se tailler△.
◆ **bunk down** *vi insep* coucher.
◆ **bunk off** *vi insep UK inf* **1.** [scram] décamper, filer **2.** [from school] faire le mur.

bunk bed *n* lits *mpl* superposés.

bunker ['bʌŋkər] ◇ *n* **1.** MIL blockhaus *m*, bunker *m* **2.** [for coal] coffre *m* ■ NAUT soute *f* **3.** GOLF bunker *m*.
◇ *vt* **1.** NAUT [coal, oil, ship] mettre en soute **2.** GOLF envoyer la balle dans un bunker.

bunkhouse ['bʌŋkhaʊs] (*pl* [-haʊzɪz]) *n US* baraquement *m* (pour ouvriers).

bunkum ['bʌŋkəm] *n* *(U)* *inf* [nonsense] foutaise *f*, foutaises *fpl*.

bunk-up *n UK* **to give sb a ~** faire la courte échelle à qqn.

bunny ['bʌnɪ] *n* : **~ (rabbit)** (petit) lapin *m*, Jeannot lapin *m*.

bunny girl *n* hôtesse *f* de boîte de nuit.

bunny hill *n US* [in skiing] piste *f* pour débutants.

Bunsen burner ['bʌnsn-] *n* (bec *m*) Bunsen *m*.

bunting ['bʌntɪŋ] *n* **1.** [fabric] étamine *f* **2.** *(U)* [flags] fanions *mpl*, drapeaux *mpl* **3.** ORNITH bruant *m*.

buoy [*UK* bɔɪ, *US* 'buːɪ] ◇ *n* bouée *f*, balise *f*.
◇ *vt* [waterway] baliser ■ [vessel, obstacle] marquer d'une bouée.
◆ **buoy up** *vt sep* **1.** NAUT faire flotter, maintenir à flot **2.** *fig* [support, sustain] soutenir ■ [person] remonter ■ **her son's visit ~ed her up** *OR* **~ed up her spirits** la visite de son fils l'a remontée *OR* lui a remonté le moral.

buoyancy ['bɔɪənsɪ] *n* **1.** [ability to float] flottabilité *f* ■ [of gas, liquid] poussée *f* **2.** *fig* [resilience] ressort *m*, force *f* morale ■ [cheerfulness] entrain *m*, allant *m* **3.** ST. EX : **the ~ of the market** la fermeté du marché.

buoyant ['bɔɪənt] *adj* **1.** [floatable] flottable, capable de flotter ■ [causing to float] qui fait flotter ■ **sea water is very ~** l'eau de mer porte très bien **2.** *fig* [cheerful] plein d'allant *OR* d'entrain ■ [mood] gai, allègre **3.** FIN [economy, sector] sain, robuste ■ ST. EX [market] soutenu.

buoyantly ['bɔɪəntlɪ] *adv* [walk] d'un pas allègre ■ [float, rise] légèrement ■ [speak] avec allant, avec entrain.

bur [bɜːr] ◇ *n* BOT bardane *f*.
◇ *vt* [clothing] enlever les bardanes de.

burble ['bɜːbl] ◇ *vi* **1.** [liquid] glouglouter, faire glouglou ■ [stream] murmurer **2.** *pej* [person] jacasser ■ **he's always burbling on about moral values** il est toujours à jacasser *OR* dégoiser sur les valeurs morales.
◇ *n* **1.** [of a liquid] glouglou *m* ■ [of a stream] murmure *m* **2.** *pej* [chatter] jacasserie *f*, jacassement *m*.

burden ['bɜːdn] ◇ *n* **1.** *fml* [heavy weight, load] fardeau *m*, charge *f* **2.** *fig* [heavy responsibility, strain] fardeau *m*, charge *f* ■ **to be a ~ to sb** être un fardeau pour qqn ■ **his guilt was a heavy ~ to bear** sa culpabilité était un lourd fardeau ■ **to increase/to relieve the tax ~** augmenter/alléger le fardeau *OR* le poids des impôts ▶ **the ~ of proof** LAW la charge de la preuve **3.** NAUT tonnage *m*, jauge *f* **4.** *UK* [chorus, refrain] refrain *m* ■ *fig* [theme, central idea] fond *m*, substance *f*.
◇ *vt* [weigh down] charger ■ **to be ~ed with sthg** être chargé de qqch ■ **to ~ sb with taxes** *fig* accabler qqn d'impôts.

burdensome ['bɜːdnsəm] *adj fml* [load] pesant ■ [taxes] lourd.

burdock ['bɜːdɒk] *n* bardane *f*.

bureau ['bjʊərəʊ] (*pl* **bureaus** *OR pl* **bureaux** [-rəʊz]) *n* **1.** ADMIN service *m*, office *m* ■ [in private enterprise] bureau *m* **2.** *UK* [desk] secrétaire *m*, bureau *m* **3.** *US* [chest of drawers] commode *f*.

bureaucracy [bjʊə'rɒkrəsɪ] *n* bureaucratie *f*.

bureaucrat ['bjʊərəkræt] *n* bureaucrate *mf*.

bureaucratic [ˌbjʊərə'krætɪk] *adj* bureaucratique.

bureaucratize, ise [bjʊə'rɒkrətaɪz] *vt* bureaucratiser.

Bureau of Indian Affairs *pr n services fédéraux américains responsables des affaires indiennes.*

burette *UK*, **buret** *US* [bjʊ'ret] *n* éprouvette *f* graduée, burette *f*.

burgeon ['bɜːdʒən] *vi* BOT & *lit* bourgeonner ■ [leaf, flower] éclore ■ **a ~ing romance** un amour naissant.

burger ['bɜːgər] *n* hamburger *m*.

burgess ['bɜːdʒɪs] *n* HIST [elected representative] député *m*, représentant *m* ■ *arch* [citizen] bourgeois *m*.

burgher ['bɜːgər] *n* HIST bourgeois *m*, - e *f*.

burglar ['bɜːglər] *n* cambrioleur *m*, - euse *f*.

burglar alarm *n* dispositif *m* d'alarme contre le vol, antivol *m*.

burglarize ['bɜːgləraɪz] *vt US* cambrioler.

burglarproof ['bɜːgləpruːf] *adj* anti-effraction *(inv)*.

burglary ['bɜːglərɪ] (*pl* **burglaries**) *n* cambriolage *m*.

burgle ['bɜːgl] *vt* cambrioler.

burgundy ['bɜːgəndɪ] *n* [colour] bordeaux.

Burgundy ['bɜːgəndɪ] *pr n* **1.** [region] Bourgogne *f* ■ **in ~** en Bourgogne **2.** VINIC bourgogne *m*.

burial ['berɪəl] ◇ *n* enterrement *m*, inhumation *f* ■ **a Christian ~** une sépulture ecclésiastique.
◇ *comp* [place, service] d'inhumation.

burial ground *n* cimetière *m*.

burial mound *n* tumulus *m*.

burk [bɜːk] *n* = **berk**.

Burke's Peerage [bɜːks-] *pr n annuaire de l'aristocratie britannique.*

Burkina-Faso [bɜːˌkiːnə'fæsəʊ], **Burkina** *pr n* Burkina *m* ■ **in ~** au Burkina.

burlap ['bɜːlæp] *n* toile *f* à sac, gros canevas *m*.

burlesque [bɜː'lesk] <> *n* **1.** LIT & THEAT burlesque *m*, parodie *f* **2.** *US* [bawdy comedy] revue *f* déshabillée, striptease *m*.
<> *adj* burlesque.
<> *vt* parodier.

burly ['bɜːlɪ] (*comp* **burlier**, *superl* **burliest**) *adj* de forte carrure.

Burma ['bɜːmə] *pr n* Birmanie *f*.

Burmese [,bɜː'miːz] <> *n* **1.** [person] Birman *m*, - e *f* **2.** LING birman *m*.
<> *adj* birman.

burn [bɜːn] <> *n* **1.** [injury] brûlure *f* **2.** AERON (durée *f* de) combustion *f* **3.** *inf* PHYSIOL : **the ~** la sensation de brûlure.
<> *vi* (*UK pret & pp* **burned** *OR* **burnt** [bɜːnt]) (*US pret & pp* **burned**) **1.** *liter* brûler ▪ **this material won't ~** ce tissu est ininflammable ▪ **the church ~ed to the ground** l'église a été réduite en cendres **2.** *fig* [face, person] : **my face was ~ing** [with embarrassment] j'avais le visage en feu, j'étais tout rouge ▪ **I'm ~ing** [from sun] je brûle ; [from fever] je suis brûlant, je brûle ▪ **she was ~ing with anger** elle bouillait de colère ▪ **she was ~ing for adventure** elle brûlait du désir d'aventure **3.** *inf* [travel at speed] filer, foncer.
<> *vt* (*UK pret & pp* **burned** *OR* **burnt** [bɜːnt]) (*US pret & pp* **burned**) **1.** [paper, logs, food] brûler ▪ [car, crop, forest] brûler, incendier ▪ **three people were burnt to death** trois personnes sont mortes carbonisées *OR* ont été brûlées vives ▪ **to be burnt alive** être brûlé vif ▪ **his cigarette burnt a hole in the carpet** sa cigarette a fait un trou dans la moquette ▪ **did you ~ yourself?** est-ce que tu t'es brûlé? ▪ **I burnt my mouth drinking hot tea** je me suis brûlé (la langue) en buvant du thé chaud ▪ **I've burnt the potatoes** j'ai laissé brûler les pommes de terre ▪ **the house was burnt to the ground** la maison fut réduite en cendres *OR* brûla entièrement ➊ **to ~ one's boats** *OR* **bridges** brûler ses vaisseaux *OR* les ponts ▪ **to ~ one's fingers, to get one's fingers burnt** se brûler les doigts ▪ **to have money to ~** avoir de l'argent à ne pas savoir qu'en faire ▪ **money ~s a hole in his pocket** l'argent lui file entre les doigts **2.** COMPUT graver.

◆ **burn away** <> *vi insep* **1.** [continue burning] : **the bonfire ~ed away for several hours** le feu a brûlé pendant plusieurs heures **2.** [be destroyed by fire] se consumer.
<> *vt sep* [gen] brûler ▪ [paint] brûler, décaper au chalumeau.

◆ **burn down** <> *vi insep* **1.** [be destroyed by fire] brûler complètement **2.** [die down] : **the fire in the stove has ~ed down** le feu dans le poêle est presque éteint ▮ [grow smaller] diminuer, baisser.
<> *vt sep* [building] détruire par le feu, incendier.

◆ **burn off** *vt sep* [vegetation] brûler, détruire par le feu ▪ [gas] brûler ▪ [paint] décaper au chalumeau.

◆ **burn out** <> *vt sep* **1.** [destroy by fire - building] détruire par le feu **2.** ELEC [wear out - bulb] griller ; [- fuse] faire sauter ▪ MECH [- engine] griller ▪ **to ~ o.s. out** *fig* s'épuiser **3.** [die down] diminuer, éteindre ▪ **after twelve hours the forest fire burnt itself out** au bout de douze heures l'incendie de forêt s'est éteint.
<> *vi insep* ELEC [bulb] griller ▪ [fuse] sauter ▪ MECH [brakes, engine] griller ▪ [candle, fire] s'éteindre.

◆ **burn up** <> *vt sep* **1.** [destroy by fire] brûler **2.** *fig* [person - consume] brûler, dévorer ▪ *US inf* [worry] : **it really ~s me up to see you like this** ça me bouffe de te voir comme ça **3.** [consume] : **this car ~s up a lot of petrol** cette voiture consomme beaucoup d'essence ▪ **to ~ up a lot of calories/energy** dépenser *OR* brûler beaucoup de calories/d'énergie ➊ **to ~ up the miles** aller à toute vitesse, foncer.
<> *vi insep* **1.** [fire] flamber **2.** AERON se consumer, se désintégrer.

burned-out ['bɜːnd-] *adj* = **burnt-out**.

burner ['bɜːnəʳ] *n* [on a stove] brûleur *m* ▪ [on a lamp] bec *m*.

burning ['bɜːnɪŋ] <> *adj* **1.** [on fire] en flammes ▪ [arrow, fire, torch] ardent ▪ **the ~ bush** BIBLE le buisson ardent **2.** [hot] ardent, brûlant ▪ **I have a ~ sensation in my stomach** j'ai des brûlures à l'estomac ▮ *fig* [intense] ardent, brûlant ▪ **he had a ~ desire to be a writer** il désirait ardemment être écrivain **3.** [crucial, vital] brûlant ▪ **a ~ issue** une question brûlante.
<> *adv* : **~ hot coals** des charbons ardents ▪ **her forehead is ~ hot** elle a le front brûlant.
<> *n* **1.** [sensation, smell] : **a smell of ~** une odeur de brûlé ▪ **he felt a ~ in his chest** il sentit une brûlure à la poitrine **2.** [destruction by fire] : **he witnessed the ~ of hundreds of books** il a été témoin de l'autodafé de centaines de livres **3.** METALL [overheating] brûlure *f*.

burnished ['bɜːnɪʃt] *adj* **1.** METALL bruni, poli **2.** *lit* [bright, shiny] lustré.

burnout ['bɜːnaʊt] *n* **1.** AERON *arrêt par suite d'épuisement du combustible* **2.** ELEC : **what caused the ~ ?** qu'est-ce qui a fait griller les circuits? **3.** [exhaustion] épuisement *m* total.

Burns' Night [bɜːnz-] *n fête célébrée en l'honneur du poète écossais Robert Burns, le 25 janvier*.

burnt [bɜːnt] <> *pt & pp* ▷ **burn**.
<> *adj* **1.** [charred] brûlé, carbonisé **2.** [dark] : **~ orange/red** orange/rouge foncé.

burnt offering *n* [sacrifice] holocauste *m* ▪ *hum* plat *m* calciné *OR* carbonisé.

burnt-out ['bɜːnt-] *adj* **1.** [destroyed by fire] incendié, brûlé **2.** *inf* [person] lessivé, vidé ▪ **she was ~ by thirty** elle était usée avant (l'âge de) trente ans.

burp [bɜːp] *inf* <> *n* rot *m* ▪ **"cheers", he said with a ~** " à ta santé ", dit-il en rotant.
<> *vi* roter.
<> *vt* : **to ~ a baby** faire faire son rot à un bébé.

burqa [bɜːkə] *n* burqa *f*.

burr [bɜːʳ] <> *n* **1.** [rough edge] barbe *f*, bavure *f* **2.** [tool] fraise *f* **3.** [on tree trunk] broussin *m* **4.** PHON grasseyement *m* ▪ **he speaks with a soft Devon ~** il a un léger accent du Devon **5.** [noise] ronflement *m*, vrombissement *m* **6.** = **bur**.
<> *vt* **1.** [file] ébarber, ébavurer **2.** = **bur**.
<> *vi* **1.** PHON grasseyer **2.** [make a noise] ronfler, vrombir.

burrito [bə'riːtəʊ] *n tortilla fourrée à la viande*.

burrow ['bʌrəʊ] <> *n* terrier *m*.
<> *vt* **1.** [subj: person] creuser ▪ [subj: animal, insect] creuser, fouir ▪ **he ~ed his way underneath the prison wall** il a creusé un tunnel sous le mur de la prison **2.** *fig* [nestle] enfouir ▪ **the cat ~ed its head into my shoulder** le chat a blotti sa tête contre mon épaule.
<> *vi* **1.** [dig] creuser ▪ **they found moles ~ing through the soil** ils ont trouvé des taupes qui creusaient des galeries dans le sol **2.** [search] fouiller **3.** [nestle] s'enfouir, s'enfoncer.

bursar ['bɜːsəʳ] *n* **1.** [treasurer] intendant *m*, - e *f*, économe *mf* **2.** *Scotland* [student] boursier *m*, - ère *f*.

bursary ['bɜːsərɪ] (*pl* **bursaries**) *n* **1.** [grant, scholarship] bourse *f* (d'études) **2.** *UK* [treasury] intendance *f*.

burst [bɜːst] <> *n* **1.** [explosion] éclatement *m*, explosion *f* ▪ [puncture] éclatement *m*, crevaison *f* **2.** [sudden eruption - of laughter] éclat *m* ; [- of emotion] accès *m*, explosion *f* ; [- of ideas] jaillissement *m* ; [- of thunder] coup *m* ; [- of flame] jet *m*, jaillissement *m* ; [- of applause] salve *f* ▪ **a ~of gunfire** une rafale ▪ **he had a sudden ~ of energy** il a eu un sursaut d'énergie ▪ **a ~ of activity** une poussée d'activité.
<> *vi* (*pret & pp* **burst**) **1.** [break, explode - balloon] éclater ; [- abscess] crever ; [- tyre] crever, éclater ; [- bottle] éclater, voler en éclats ▪ **his heart felt as if it would ~ with joy/grief** *fig* il crut que son cœur allait éclater de joie/se briser de chagrin **2.** [enter, move suddenly] : **two policemen ~ into the house** deux policiers ont fait irruption dans la maison ▪ **the front door ~ open** la porte d'entrée s'est ouverte brusquement ▪ **the sun suddenly ~ through the clouds** le soleil perça *OR* apparut soudain à travers les nuages.
<> *vt* (*pret & pp* **burst**) [balloon, bubble] crever, faire éclater ▪ [pipe] faire éclater ▪ [boiler] faire éclater, faire sauter ▪ [tyre] crever, faire éclater ▪ [abscess] crever, percer ▪ **the river is about to ~ its banks** le fleuve est sur le point de déborder ▪ **to ~ a blood vessel** se faire éclater une veine, se rompre un vaisseau sanguin ▪ **don't ~ a blood vessel to get it done** *UK inf hum* ce n'est pas la peine de te crever pour finir, ce n'est pas la peine de te tuer à la tâche.

◆ **burst forth** *vi insep lit* [liquid] jaillir ▪ [person] sortir précipitamment, apparaître.

◆ **burst in** *vi insep* [enter violently] faire irruption ▪ [interrupt] interrompre brutalement la discussion ▪ [intrude] entrer précipitamment ▪ **it was very rude of you to ~ in on** *OR* **upon us like that** c'était très mal élevé de ta part de faire irruption chez nous comme ça.

◆ **burst into** *vt insep* [begin suddenly] : **to ~ into laughter** éclater de rire ▪ **to ~ into tears** éclater en sanglots, fondre en larmes ▪ **to ~ into song** se mettre à chanter ▪ **to ~ into flames** prendre feu, s'enflammer.

◆ **burst out** <> *vi insep* [leave suddenly] sortir précipitamment ▪ **two men suddenly ~ out of the room** deux hommes sortirent en trombe de la pièce.
<> *vt insep* [exclaim] s'exclamer, s'écrier ▪ **to ~ out laughing** éclater de rire ▪ **they all ~ out singing** ils se sont tous mis à chanter d'un coup.

bursting ['bɜ:stɪŋ] *adj* **1.** [full] plein à craquer ▪ **to be ~ at the seams** se défaire aux coutures, se découdre ▪ **the place was ~ at the seams (with people)** *fig* l'endroit était plein à craquer ▪ **to be ~ with joy/pride** déborder de joie/d'orgueil **2.** [longing, yearning] : **to be ~ to do sthg** mourir d'envie de faire qqch **3.** *inf* [desperate to urinate] : **I'm ~** je ne peux plus attendre, ça presse.

Burundi [bʊ'rʊndɪ] *pr n* Burundi *m* ▪ **in ~** au Burundi.

Burundian [bʊ'rʊndjən] <> *n* Burundais *m*, - e *f*.
<> *adj* burundais.

bury ['berɪ] (*pret & pp* **buried**) *vt* **1.** [in the ground] enterrer ▪ [in water] immerger ▪ **to be buried alive** être enterré vivant ▪ **to be buried at sea** être immergé en haute mer ▪ **we agreed to ~ our differences** nous avons convenu d'oublier *OR* d'enterrer nos différends ⊳ **to ~ the hatchet** enterrer la hache de guerre **2.** [cover completely] ensevelir, enterrer ▪ **she buried her feet in the sand** elle a enfoncé ses pieds dans le sable ⊳ **to ~ one's head in the sand** faire l'autruche **3.** [hide] : **she buried her face in the pillow** elle enfouit *OR* enfonça son visage dans l'oreiller ▪ **to ~ one's face in one's hands** enfouir son visage dans ses mains ▪ **he always has his nose buried in a book** il a toujours le nez fourré dans un livre **4.** [occupy] : **to ~ o.s. in (one's) work** se plonger dans son travail **5.** [thrust, plunge - knife] enfoncer, plonger ▪ **he buried his hands in his pockets** il a fourré les mains dans ses poches.

bus [bʌs] <> *n* (*pl* **buses** *OR pl* **busses**) **1.** [vehicle] bus *m* ▪ *US* [coach] car *m* **2.** *UK inf* [old car] (vieille) bagnole **3.** COMPUT bus *m*.
<> *comp* [route, service, strike, ticket] d'autobus, de bus.
<> *vt* (*pret & pp* **bused** *OR* **bussed**, *cont* **busing** *OR* **bussing**) : **we can walk or ~ it home** nous pouvons rentrer à pied ou en autobus. : **the children are bussed to school** les enfants vont à l'école en autobus ▪ *US* SCH [for purposes of racial integration] emmener à l'école en autobus *(pour favoriser l'intégration raciale)*.

busbar ['bʌsbɑ:] *n* COMPUT & ELEC bus *m*.

busboy ['bʌsbɔɪ] *n US* aide-serveur *m*.

busby ['bʌzbɪ] (*pl* **busbies**) *n UK* bonnet *m* de hussard.

bus conductor *n UK* receveur *m*, - euse *f* d'autobus.

bus driver *n* conducteur *m*, - trice *f* d'autobus.

bush [bʊʃ] *n* **1.** [shrub] buisson *m*, arbuste *m* ▪ **the children hid in the ~es** les enfants se cachèrent dans les fourrés ▪ **a ~ of black hair** *fig* une tignasse de cheveux noirs **2.** [scrubland] : **the ~** la brousse **3.** MECH bague *f*.

bushbaby ['bʊʃ,beɪbɪ] *n* galago *m*.

bushed [bʊʃt] *adj inf* [exhausted] crevé, claqué.

bushel ['bʊʃl] (*pret & pp* **busheled**, *cont* **busheling**) *n* [measure] boisseau *m*.

bushfire ['bʊʃ,faɪə^r] *n* feu *m* de brousse.

bushing ['bʊʃɪŋ] *n (U)* TECH bague *f*.

bush jacket *n* saharienne *f*.

Bushman ['bʊʃmən] (*pl inv OR pl* **Bushmen** [-mən]) *n* [in southern Africa] Bochiman *m*.

bushmeat ['bʊʃmi:t] *n (U)* viande *f* de brousse.

bush telegraph *n liter* téléphone *m* de brousse ▪ *UK fig & hum* [grapevine] téléphone *m* arabe.

bushwhack ['bʊʃwæk] <> *vi* **1.** [clear a path] se frayer un passage à travers la brousse **2.** [live in the bush] vivre dans la brousse.
<> *vt US* [ambush] tendre une embuscade à.

bushwhacker ['bʊʃ,wækə^r] *n* **1.** *US & Australia* [backwoodsman] broussard *m*, - e *f* **2.** *US* [guerrilla] guérillero *m*.

bushy ['bʊʃɪ] (*comp* **bushier**, *superl* **bushiest**) *adj* **1.** [area] broussailleux **2.** [tree] touffu ▪ [beard, eyebrows, hair] touffu, fourni.

busily ['bɪzɪlɪ] *adv* activement ▪ **to be ~ engaged in sthg/in doing sthg** être très occupé à qqch/à faire qqch ▪ **he was ~ scribbling in his notebook** il griffonnait sur son calepin d'un air affairé.

business ['bɪznɪs] <> *n* **1.** [firm] entreprise *f* ▪ **would you like to have** *OR* **to run your own ~?** aimeriez-vous travailler à votre compte?
2. *(U)* [trade] affaires *fpl* ▪ **~ is good/bad** les affaires vont bien/mal ▪ **we have lost ~ to foreign competitors** nous avons perdu une partie de notre clientèle au profit de concurrents étrangers ▪ **the travel ~** les métiers *OR* le secteur du tourisme ▪ **she's in the fashion ~** elle est dans la mode ▪ **he's in ~** il est dans les affaires ▪ **this firm has been in ~ for 25 years** cette entreprise tourne depuis 25 ans ▪ **she's in ~ for herself** elle travaille à son compte ▪ **these high interest rates will put us out of ~** ces taux d'intérêt élevés vont nous obliger à fermer ▪ **to go out of ~** cesser une activité ▪ **he's got no ~ sense** il n'a pas le sens des affaires ▪ **to do ~ with** travailler *OR* traiter avec ▪ **he's a man we can do ~ with** *fig* c'est un homme avec lequel nous pouvons traiter ▪ **I've come on ~** je suis venu pour le travail *OR* pour affaires ▪ **big ~ is running the country** le gros commerce gouverne le pays ▪ **selling weapons is big ~** la vente d'armes rapporte beaucoup d'argent ▪ **from now on I'll take my ~ elsewhere** désormais j'irai voir *OR* je m'adresserai ailleurs ▪ **we're not in the ~ of providing free meals** ce n'est pas notre rôle de fournir des repas gratuits ⊳ **a degree in ~, a ~ degree** un diplôme de gestion ▪ **let's get down to ~** passons aux choses sérieuses ▪ **(now) we're in ~!** nous voilà partis!
3. [concern] : **it's my (own) ~ if I decide not to go** c'est mon affaire *OR* cela ne regarde que moi si je décide de ne pas y aller ▪ **it's none of your ~** cela ne vous regarde pas ▪ **tell him to mind his own ~** dis-lui de se mêler de ses affaires ▪ **you had no ~ reading that letter** vous n'aviez pas à lire cette lettre ⊳ **I could see she meant ~** je voyais qu'elle ne plaisantait pas ▪ **she worked like nobody's ~ to get it finished** *inf* elle a travaillé comme un forçat pour tout terminer ▪ **I soon sent him about his ~** je l'ai vite envoyé promener
4. [matter, task] : **any other ~** [on agenda] points *mpl* divers ▪ **any other ~?** d'autres questions à l'ordre du jour? ▪ **she had important ~ to discuss** elle avait à parler d'affaires importantes ▪ **this strike ~ has gone on long enough** cette histoire de grève a assez duré ▪ **I'm tired of the whole ~** je suis las de toute cette histoire
5. [rigmarole] : **it was a real ~ getting tickets for the concert** ça a été toute une affaire pour avoir des billets pour le concert
6. THEAT jeux *mpl* de scène
7. *inf euph* **the dog did his ~ and ran off** le chien a fait ses besoins et a détalé.
<> *comp* [lunch, trip] d'affaires ▪ **~ associate** associé *m*, - e *f* ▪ **~ expenses** [for individual]frais *mpl* professionnels ; [for firm] frais *mpl* généraux ▪ **~ hours** [of office] heures *fpl* de bureau ; [of shop, public service] heures *fpl* d'ouverture.

business address *n* adresse *f* au lieu de travail.

business card *n* carte *f* de visite.

business centre *n* centre *m* des affaires.

business class *n* [on aeroplane] classe *f* affaires.

business college *n UK* école *f* de commerce ▪ [for management training] école *f* (supérieure) de gestion.

business end *n inf* [of knife] partie *f* coupante ▪ [of gun] gueule△ *f*.

businesslike ['bɪznɪslaɪk] *adj* **1.** [systematic, methodical] systématique, méthodique ■ **I was amazed at the ~ way in which she handled the funeral arrangements** j'ai été étonné de voir avec quelle efficacité elle s'est occupée de l'enterrement **2.** [impersonal, formal] : **her manner was cold and ~** son comportement était froid et direct ■ **our conversation was courteous and ~** notre entretien a été courtois et franc.

businessman ['bɪznɪsmæn] (*pl* **businessmen** [-men]) *n* homme *m* d'affaires.

business manager *n* COMM & INDUST directeur *m* commercial ■ SPORT manager *m* ■ THEAT directeur *m*.

business park *n* zone *f* d'activités.

business plan *n* projet *m* d'entreprise.

business school *n* *US* = **business college**.

businesswoman ['bɪznɪs,wʊmən] (*pl* **businesswomen** [-,wɪmɪn]) *n* femme *f* d'affaires.

busing ['bʌsɪŋ] *n* *US* *système de ramassage scolaire aux États-Unis, qui organise la répartition des enfants noirs et des enfants blancs dans les écoles afin de lutter contre la ségrégation raciale.*

busk [bʌsk] *vi* *UK* jouer de la musique *(dans la rue ou le métro)*.

busker ['bʌskəʳ] *n* *UK* musicien *m*, - enne *f* de rue.

bus lane *n* voie *f* *OR* couloir *m* d'autobus.

busload ['bʌsləʊd] *n* : **a ~ of workers** un autobus plein d'ouvriers ■ **the tourists arrived by the ~** *OR* **in ~s** les touristes sont arrivés par cars entiers.

busman ['bʌsmən] (*pl* **busmen** [-mən]) *n* *UK* **to have a ~'s holiday** passer ses vacances à travailler.

bus shelter *n* Abribus® *m*.

bus station *n* gare *f* routière.

bus stop *n* arrêt *m* d'autobus *OR* de bus.

bust [bʌst] ◇ *adj* *inf* **1.** [broken] fichu **2.** [bankrupt] : **to go ~** faire faillite **3.** [broke] : **I'm ~** je suis fauché **4.** *phr...* **or ~!** *expression indiquant la détermination à arriver quelque part.*
◇ *n* **1.** [breasts] poitrine *f*, buste *m* ■ **she has a small ~** elle a peu de poitrine **2.** ART buste *m* **3.** *inf* [police raid, arrest] : **there was a big drugs ~ in Chicago** il y a eu un beau coup de filet chez les trafiquants de drogue de Chicago **4.** *US inf* [failure] fiasco *m*.
◇ *vt* (*pret & pp* **busted** *OR* **bust**) *inf* **1.** [break] bousiller, abîmer ■ *fig* **to ~ a gut** *OR* **blood vessel** se casser la nénette **2.** [arrest, raid] : **he was ~ed on a drugs charge** il s'est fait choper *OR* embarquer pour une affaire de drogue **3.** *US* [catch] découvrir.
◆ **bust out** *vi insep inf* [escape] se tirer.
◆ **bust up** *inf* ◇ *vi insep* [boyfriend, girlfriend] rompre (après une dispute).
◇ *vt sep* [disrupt] : **demonstrators ~ed up the meeting** des manifestants sont venus semer la pagaïe dans la réunion.

bustard ['bʌstəd] *n* outarde *f*.

buster ['bʌstəʳ] *n* *inf US* [pal] : **thanks, ~** merci, mon (petit) gars.

bustle ['bʌsl] ◇ *vi* [hurry] : **he ~d about** *OR* **around the kitchen** il s'affairait dans la cuisine ■ **the nurse came bustling in** l'infirmière entra d'un air affairé.
◇ *n* **1.** [activity] agitation *f* ■ **I enjoy the hustle and ~ of working in a bank** j'aime bien travailler dans une banque à cause de tout le va-et-vient qui y règne **2.** [on dress] tournure *f*.

bustling ['bʌslɪŋ] ◇ *adj* [person] affairé ■ [place] animé ■ **the streets were ~ with Christmas shoppers** les rues grouillaient de gens faisant leurs achats de Noël.
◇ *n* [activity] agitation *f*.

bust-up *n inf* **1.** [quarrel] engueulade *f* **2.** [brawl] bagarre *f*.

busty ['bʌstɪ] (*comp* **bustier**, *superl* **bustiest**) *adj* qui a une forte poitrine.

busy ['bɪzɪ] ◇ *adj* (*comp* **busier**, *superl* **busiest**) **1.** [person] occupé ■ **she was ~ painting the kitchen** elle était occupée à peindre la cuisine ■ **he likes to keep (himself) ~** il aime bien s'occuper ■ **the packing kept me ~ all afternoon** j'ai été occupé à faire les valises tout l'après-midi ■ **I'm afraid I'm ~ tomorrow** malheureusement je suis pris demain ● **she's as ~ as a bee, she's a ~ bee** elle est très occupée **2.** [port, road, street] très fréquenté ■ [time, period, schedule] chargé, plein ■ **I've had a ~ day** j'ai eu une journée chargée ■ **this is our busiest period** [business, shop] c'est la période où nous sommes en pleine activité ■ **the office is very ~ at the moment** nous avons beaucoup de travail au bureau en ce moment ■ **the shops are very ~ today** les magasins sont pleins (de monde) aujourd'hui **3.** *US* [telephone line] occupé ■ **I got the ~ signal** ça sonnait occupé **4.** *pej* [excessively elaborate] chargé.
◇ *vt* (*pret & pp* **busied**) : **he busied himself with household chores** il s'est occupé à des tâches ménagères.

busybody ['bɪzɪ,bɒdɪ] (*pl* **busybodies**) *n* *inf* fouineur *m*, - euse *f*, fouinard *m*, - e *f*.

busy lizzie [-'lɪzɪ] *n* balsamine *f*, impatiente *f*.

but [bʌt] ◇ *conj* **1.** [to express contrast] mais ■ **my husband smokes, ~ I don't** mon mari fume, mais moi non **2.** [in exclamations] mais ■ **~ that's absurd!** mais c'est absurde! **3.** [when addressing sb politely] : **sorry, ~ I think that's MY umbrella** pardon, mais je crois que c'est mon parapluie **4.** [used for emphasis] : **nobody, ~ nobody, gets in without a ticket** personne, absolument personne n'entre sans ticket **5.** [except, only] mais ■ **it tastes like a grapefruit, ~ sweeter** ça a le goût d'un pamplemousse, mais en plus sucré **6.** *lit* **barely a day goes by ~ he receives another invitation** il ne se passe pas un jour sans qu'il reçoive une nouvelle invitation.
◇ *adv* **1.** [only] ne... que ■ **I can ~ try** je ne peux qu'essayer ■ **his resignation cannot ~ confirm such suspicions** *fml* sa démission ne fait que confirmer de tels soupçons **2.** *US inf* [used for emphasis] et ■ **get them down here ~ fast!** descends-les et vite!
◇ *prep* **1.** [except] sauf, à part ■ **she wouldn't see anyone ~ her lawyer** elle ne voulait voir personne sauf *OR* à part son avocat ■ **nothing ~ a miracle could have saved her** seul un miracle aurait pu la sauver **2.** *UK* [with numbers] : **turn right at the next corner ~ one** tournez à droite au deuxième carrefour ■ **I was the last ~ two to finish** j'étais l'avant-avant-dernier à finir.
◇ *n* : **you're coming and no ~s!** tu viens, et pas de mais!
◆ **but for** *prep phr* sans ■ **~ for her courage, many more people would have drowned** sans son courage, il y aurait eu beaucoup plus de noyés.
◆ **but that** *conj phr fml* **I do not doubt ~ that we shall succeed** je ne doute pas de notre réussite.
◆ **but then** *adv phr* enfin ■ **~ then, that's just the way it goes** enfin, c'est comme ça.

butane ['bju:teɪn] *n* butane *m* ■ **~ gas** gaz *m* butane, butane.

butch [bʊtʃ] *inf* ◇ *adj* [woman] hommasse ■ [man] macho.
◇ *n* [lesbian] *lesbienne d'apparence masculine.*

butcher ['bʊtʃəʳ] ◇ *n* **1.** COMM boucher *m* ■ **she's gone to the ~'s** elle est partie chez le boucher ■ **~'s shop** boucherie *f* **2.** [murderer] boucher *m* **3.** *UK phr* **let's have a ~'s (at it)!** *inf* montre un peu!
◇ *vt* **1.** [animal] abattre, tuer **2.** [person] massacrer **3.** *inf* [story, joke] massacrer.

butchery ['bʊtʃərɪ] *n* **1.** COMM boucherie *f* ■ *UK* [slaughterhouse] abattoir *m* **2.** *fig* [massacre] boucherie *f*, massacre *m*.

butler ['bʌtləʳ] *n* maître *m* d'hôtel ■ [in large household] majordome *m*.

Butlin's ['bʌtlɪnz] *pr n* *chaîne de villages de vacances en Grande Bretagne.*

butt [bʌt] ◇ *n* **1.** [end] bout *m* ■ [of rifle] crosse *f* ■ [of cigarette] mégot *m* **2.** *US inf* [buttocks] fesses *fpl* **3.** [in archery - target] but *m* ; [- mound] butte *f* ■ **the ~s** MIL le champ *OR* la butte de tir **4.** [person] : **he was the ~ of all the office jokes** il était la cible de toutes les plaisanteries du bureau **5.** [barrel] tonneau *m*.
◇ *vt* **1.** [subj: animal] donner un coup de corne à ■ [subj: person] donner un coup de tête à **2.** TECH [abut] abouter.
◆ **butt in** *vi insep* [interrupt] : **excuse me for ~ing in** excusez-moi de m'en mêler *OR* de vous interrompre ■ **she is always ~ing in on people's conversations** elle s'immisce toujours dans les conversations des autres.

butte [bju:t] *n* *US* butte *f*, tertre *m*.

butter ['bʌtəʳ] ◇ *n* beurre *m* ▪ **~ dish** beurrier *m* ▪ **she looked as if ~ wouldn't melt in her mouth** on lui aurait donné le bon Dieu sans confession.
◇ *vt* beurrer.
◆ **butter up** *vt sep inf* passer de la pommade à.

butterball ['bʌtəbɔːl] *n* **US** *inf* **he's a ~** il est un peu grassouillet.

butter bean *n sorte de haricot de Lima.*

buttercup ['bʌtəkʌp] *n* bouton *m* d'or.

buttered ['bʌtəd] *adj* [bread] beurré.

butterfat ['bʌtəfæt] *n* matière *f* grasse.

butterfingers ['bʌtə,fɪŋgəz] *n inf* maladroit *m*, - e *f (de ses mains).*

butterfly ['bʌtəflaɪ] (*pl* **butterflies**) *n* **1.** ENTOM papillon *m* ▪ **she always has** *OR* **gets butterflies (in her stomach) before a performance** elle a toujours le trac avant une représentation **2.** SPORT : **(the) ~** la brasse papillon.

butterfly net *n* filet *m* à papillons.

butterfly nut *n* papillon *m*, écrou *m* à ailettes.

butter icing *n* glaçage *m* au beurre.

butter knife *n* couteau *m* à beurre.

buttermilk ['bʌtəmɪlk] *n* [sour liquid] babeurre *m*.

butterscotch ['bʌtəskɒtʃ] *n* caramel *m* dur au beurre.

buttery ['bʌtərɪ] ◇ *adj* **1.** [smell, taste] de beurre ▪ [fingers] couvert de beurre ▪ [biscuits] fait avec beaucoup de beurre **2.** *inf fig* [obsequious] mielleux.
◇ *n* (*pl* **butteries**) **1.** [storeroom] office *m ou f* **2.** [snackbar] buffet *m*, buvette *f*.

butt naked *adj* **US** *inf* à poil.

buttock ['bʌtək] *n* fesse *f*.

button ['bʌtn] ◇ *n* **1.** [on clothing] bouton *m* ▪ MECH bouton *m* ▪ FENCING bouton *m* ▪ **on the ~** *inf* exactement **2.** **US** [badge] badge *m*.
◇ *vt* [gen - FENCING] boutonner ▪ **~ it** *OR* **your lip** *OR* **your mouth!** *inf* ferme-là!, boucle-la!
◇ *vi* boutonner ▪ **the blouse ~s at the back** le chemisier se boutonne par derrière *OR* dans le dos.
◆ **button up** ◇ *vt sep* **1.** [piece of clothing] boutonner **2.** *inf fig* [conclude] régler.
◇ *vi insep* **1.** [piece of clothing] se boutonner **2.** *inf* [shut up] : **~ up!** ferme-la!, boucle-la!

button-down *adj* **1.** [collar] boutonné ▪ [shirt] à col boutonné **2.** **US** *fig* [conventional] : **a ~ businessman** un homme d'affaires très comme il faut.

buttonhole ['bʌtnhəʊl] ◇ *n* **1.** [in clothing] boutonnière *f* **2.** **UK** [flower] : **she was wearing a pink ~** elle portait une fleur rose à la boutonnière.
◇ *vt* **1.** [make buttonholes in] faire des boutonnières sur ▪ [sew with buttonhole stitch] coudre au point de boutonnière **2.** *inf fig* [detain - person] retenir, coincer.

button mushroom *n* champignon *m* de couche *OR* de Paris.

buttress ['bʌtrɪs] ◇ *n* **1.** ARCHIT contrefort *m* **2.** *fig* pilier *m*.
◇ *vt* **1.** ARCHIT étayer ▪ [cathedral] arc-bouter **2.** *fig* [argument, system] étayer, renforcer.

butty ['bʌtɪ] (*pl* **butties**) *n* **UK** *inf* **1.** [sandwich] sandwich *m*, casse-croûte *m* **2.** [friend] copain *m*.

buxom ['bʌksəm] *adj* [plump] plantureux, bien en chair ▪ [busty] à la poitrine plantureuse.

buy [baɪ] ◇ *vt* (*pret & pp* **bought** [bɔːt]) **1.** [purchase] acheter ▪ **to ~ sthg for sb, to ~ sb sthg** acheter qqch à *OR* pour qqn ▪ **can I ~ you a coffee?** puis-je t'offrir un café? ▪ **she bought her car from her sister** elle a racheté la voiture de sa sœur ▪ **I'll ~ it from you** je te le rachète ▪ **they bought it for £100** ils l'ont payé 100 livres ▪ **have you bought the plane tickets?** avez-vous pris les billets d'avion? ▪ **she bought herself a pair of skis** elle s'est acheté une paire de skis ▪ **£20 won't ~ you very much these days** avec 20 livres, on ne va pas très loin de nos jours **2.** [gain, obtain] : **to ~ time** gagner du temps ▪ **she bought their freedom with her life** elle paya leur liberté de sa vie **3.** [bribe] acheter **4.** *inf* [believe] : **she'll never ~ that story** elle n'avalera *OR* ne gobera jamais cette histoire ▪ **OK, I'll ~ that!** d'accord, je marche! **5.** *phr* **to ~ it**△ [die] : **he bought it in the final attack** à la dernière attaque, il a passé l'arme à gauche.
◇ *n* affaire *f* ▪ **this car was a great ~** cette voiture était une très bonne affaire.
◆ **buy back** *vt sep* racheter ▪ **can I ~ my bicycle back from you?** puis-je te racheter mon vélo?
◆ **buy in** ◇ *vt sep* **1.** **UK** [stockpile] stocker **2.** ST. EX acheter, acquérir **3.** [at auction] racheter.
◇ *vi insep* acheter.
◆ **buy into** *vt insep* FIN acheter une participation dans.
◆ **buy off** *vt sep* [bribe] acheter.
◆ **buy out** *vt sep* **1.** FIN racheter la part de, désintéresser **2.** MIL racheter ▪ **he bought himself out (of the army)** il a payé pour pouvoir rompre son contrat avec l'armée.
◆ **buy over** *vt sep* = **buy off**.
◆ **buy up** *vt sep* acheter en quantité ▪ FIN [firm, shares, stock] racheter.

buyer ['baɪəʳ] *n* acheteur *m*, -euse *f* ▪ **she's a ~ at** *OR* **for Harrod's** elle est responsable des achats chez Harrod's ▪ **~s' market** FIN marché *m* demandeur *OR* à la hausse ; [for house buyers] marché *m* d'offre *OR* offreur.

buying ['baɪɪŋ] *n* achat *m*.

buyout ['baɪaʊt] *n* rachat *m*.

buzz [bʌz] ◇ *n* **1.** [of insect] bourdonnement *m*, vrombissement *m* ▪ *fig* **there was a ~ of conversation in the room** la pièce résonnait du brouhaha des conversations ▪ **the announcement caused a ~ of excitement** l'annonce provoqua un murmure d'excitation **2.** [of buzzer] coup *m* de sonnette **3.** *inf* [telephone call] coup *m* de fil **4.** [activity] : **I love the ~ of London** j'adore l'animation de Londres **5.** *inf* [strong sensation] : **I get quite a ~ out of being on the stage** je prends vraiment mon pied sur scène.
◇ *vi* **1.** [insect] bourdonner, vrombir ▪ **the theatre ~ed with excitement** *fig* le théâtre était tout bourdonnant d'excitation **2.** [ears] bourdonner, tinter ▪ **his head was ~ing with ideas** les idées bourdonnaient dans sa tête **3.** [with buzzer] : **he ~ed for his secretary** il appela sa secrétaire (à l'interphone) **4.** *inf* [be lively - person] tenir la forme.
◇ *vt* **1.** [with buzzer] : **he ~ed the nurse** il appela l'infirmière d'un coup de sonnette **2.** **US** *inf* [telephone] passer un coup de fil à **3.** *inf* AERON [building, town etc] raser, frôler ▪ [aircraft] frôler.
◆ **buzz about** *vi insep inf* s'affairer, s'agiter.
◆ **buzz off** *vi insep inf* décamper, dégager.

buzzard ['bʌzəd] *n* **UK** buse *f* ▪ **US** urubu *m*.

buzzer ['bʌzəʳ] *n* sonnette *f*.

buzzing ['bʌzɪŋ] ◇ *n* [of insects] bourdonnement *m*, vrombissement *m* ▪ [in ears] bourdonnement *m*, tintement *m*.
◇ *adj* [insect] bourdonnant, vrombissant ▪ **a ~ noise** *OR* **sound** un bourdonnement *OR* vrombissement.

buzzword ['bʌzwɜːd] *n inf* mot *m* à la mode.

BVDs® *npl* **US** sous-vêtements *mpl (pour hommes).*

b/w (*abbrev of* **black and white**) *adj* NB.

by [baɪ] ◇ *adv* **1.** [past] : **she drove by without stopping** elle est passée (en voiture) sans s'arrêter ▪ **he managed to squeeze by** il a réussi à passer (en se faufilant) ▪ **two hours have gone by** deux heures ont passé ▪ **as time went by he became less bitter** avec le temps il est devenu moins amer **2.** [aside, away] : **she put some money by for her old age** elle a mis de l'argent de côté pour ses vieux jours **3.** [nearby] : **is there a bank close by?** y a-t-il une banque près d'ici? **4.** [to, at someone's home] : **I'll stop** *OR* **drop by this evening** je passerai ce soir.
◇ *prep*

A.
1. [near, beside] près de, à côté de ■ **by the sea** au bord de la mer ■ **come and sit by me** *OR* **my side** viens t'asseoir près *OR* auprès de moi ■ **don't stand by the door** ne restez pas debout près de la porte
2. [past] devant ■ **she walked right by me** elle passa juste devant moi
3. [through] par ■ **she left by the back door** elle est partie par la porte de derrière

B.
1. [indicating means, method] : **by letter/phone** par courrier/téléphone ■ **to go by bus/car/plane/train** aller en autobus/voiture/avion/train ■ **send it by plane/ship** envoyez-le par avion/bateau ■ **I know her by name/sight** je la connais de nom/vue ■ **by candlelight** à la lumière d'une bougie ■ **by moonlight** au clair de lune ➲ **I can do it by myself** je peux le faire (tout) seul ■ **I'm all by myself tonight** je suis tout seul ce soir
2. [indicating agent or cause] par ■ **it was built by the Romans** il fut construit par les Romains ■ **I was shocked by his reaction** sa réaction m'a choqué ■ **she had two daughters by him** elle a eu deux filles de lui
3. [as a result of] par ■ [with present participle] en ■ **he learned to cook by watching his mother** il a appris à faire la cuisine en regardant sa mère
4. [indicating authorship] de ■ **a book by Toni Morrison** un livre de Toni Morrison
5. [indicating part of person, thing held] par ■ **she took her by the hand** elle l'a prise par la main

C.
1. [not later than, before] : **she'll be here by tonight/five o'clock** elle sera ici avant ce soir/pour cinq heures ■ **I'll have finished by Friday** j'aurai fini pour vendredi ■ **by 1960 most Americans had television sets** en 1960 la plupart des Américains avaient déjà un poste de télévision ■ **by the time you read this letter I'll be in California** lorsque tu liras cette lettre, je serai en Californie ■ **he should be in India by now** il devrait être en Inde maintenant ■ **she had already married by then** à ce moment-là elle était déjà mariée
2. [during] : **he works by night and sleeps by day** il travaille la nuit et dort le jour

D.
1. [according to] d'après ■ **they're rich, even by American standards** ils sont riches même par rapport aux normes américaines ■ **it's 6:15 by my watch** il est 6 h 15 à *OR* d'après ma montre ■ **you can tell he's lying by the expression on his face** on voit qu'il ment à l'expression de son visage
2. [in accordance with] selon, d'après ■ **to play by the rules** faire les choses dans les règles
3. [with regard to] de ■ **he's an actor by trade** *OR* **profession** il est acteur de profession ■ **it's all right by me** *inf* moi, je suis d'accord *OR* je n'ai rien contre

E.
1. [indicating degree, extent] de ■ **she won by five points** elle a gagné de cinq points ■ **his second book is better by far** son deuxième livre est nettement meilleur
2. [in calculations, measurements] : **multiply/divide 12 by 6** multipliez/divisez 12 par 6 ■ **the room is 6 metres by 3 (metres)** la pièce fait 6 mètres sur 3 (mètres)
3. [indicating specific amount, duration] : **to be paid by the hour/week/month** être payé à l'heure/à la semaine/au mois ■ **it sold by the thousand** ça s'est vendu par milliers
4. [indicating rate or speed] : **little by little** peu à peu ■ **year by year** d'année en année ■ **two by two** deux par deux
5. [used with points of the compass] quart.

◆ **by and by** *adv phr lit* bientôt.

◆ **by the by** ◇ *adv phr* à propos.
◇ *adj phr* : **that's by the by** ça n'a pas d'importance.

bye [baɪ] ◇ *n* CRICKET balle *f* passée.
◇ *interj inf inf* au revoir, salut ■ **~ for now!** à bientôt!

bye-bye *interj inf* au revoir, salut.

byelaw ['baɪlɔː] *n* = **bylaw**.

by-election, bye-election *n* élection *f* (législative) partielle *(en Grande-Bretagne)*.

Byelorussia [bɪˌeləʊ'rʌʃə] *pr n* Biélorussie *f* ■ **in ~** en Biélorussie.

Byelorussian [bɪˌeləʊ'rʌʃn] ◇ *n* Biélorusse *mf*.
◇ *adj* biélorusse.

bygone ['baɪgɒn] ◇ *adj lit* passé, révolu ■ **he displayed the gallantry of a ~ age** il faisait preuve d'une galanterie qui n'a plus cours aujourd'hui ■ **in ~ days** autrefois, jadis.
◇ *n* **1.** [object] vieillerie *f* **2.** *phr* **let ~s be ~ s** oublions le passé.

bylaw ['baɪlɔː] *n* **1.** *UK* ADMIN arrêté *m* municipal **2.** *US* [of club, company] statut *m*.

by-line *n* signature *f (en tête d'un article)*.

bypass ['baɪpɑːs] ◇ *n* **1.** [road] rocade *f* ■ **the Oxford ~** la route qui contourne Oxford **2.** TECH [pipe] conduit *m* de dérivation, by-pass *m* **3.** ELEC dérivation *f* **4.** MED pontage *m*, by-pass *m* ■ **~ operation, ~ surgery** pontage, by-pass ■ **he's had a heart ~** il a subi un pontage coronarien.
◇ *vt* [avoid - town] contourner, éviter ; [- problem, regulation] contourner, éluder ; [- superior] court-circuiter ■ **I ~ed the personnel officer and spoke directly to the boss** je suis allé parler directement au directeur sans passer par le chef du personnel.

by-product *n* sous-produit *m*, (produit *m*) dérivé *m* ■ *fig* conséquence *f* indirecte, effet *m* secondaire.

byre ['baɪəʳ] *n UK* étable *f* (à vaches).

byroad ['baɪrəʊd] *n* = **byway**.

Byronic [baɪ'rɒnɪk] *adj* byronien.

bystander ['baɪˌstændəʳ] *n* spectateur *m*, - trice *f*.

byte [baɪt] *n* octet *m*.

byway ['baɪweɪ] *n* **1.** [road] chemin *m* détourné *OR* écarté **2.** *fig* [of subject] à-côté *m*.

byword ['baɪwɜːd] *n* symbole *m*, illustration *f* ■ **the company has become a ~ for inefficiency** le nom de cette entreprise est devenu synonyme d'inefficacité.

by-your-leave *n lit & hum* **without so much as a ~** sans même demander la permission.

Byzantine [*UK* bɪ'zæntaɪn, *US* 'bɪzntiːn] ◇ *n* Byzantin *m*, - e *f*.
◇ *adj* byzantin, de Byzance.

Byzantium [bɪ'zæntɪəm] *pr n* Byzance.

C

c 1. (*written abbrev of* **cent(s)**) ct **2.** (*written abbrev of* **century**) s **3.** (*written abbrev of* **circa**) vers.

c (*pl* **c's** *OR pl* **cs**), **C** (*pl* **C's** *OR pl* **Cs**) [siː] *n* [letter] c *m*, C *m*, *see also* **f**.

C ◇ *n* **1.** MUS do *m*, ut *m* **2.** SCH & UNIV assez bien ■ **I got a C in geography** j'ai eu assez bien en géographie **3.** [Roman numeral] C *m*.
◇ (*written abbrev of* **Celsius, Centigrade**) C.

ca. (*written abbrev of* **circa**) vers.

c/a 1. *written abbr of* **capital account 2.** *written abbr of* **credit account 3.** *written abbr of* **current account**.

CA ◇ *n* = **Consumers' Association**.
◇ **1.** *written abbr of* **chartered accountant 2.** *written abbr of* **Central America 3.** *written abbr of* **California**.

CAA *pr n* **1.** (*abbrev of* **Civil Aviation Authority**) *organisme britannique de réglementation de l'aviation civile* **2.** *US* = **Civil Aeronautics Authority**.

cab [kæb] *n* **1.** [taxi] taxi *m* **2.** [of lorry, train] cabine *f* **3.** [horse-drawn] fiacre *m*.

CAB *pr n* **1.** *UK* = **Citizens' Advice Bureau 2.** (*abbrev of* **Civil Aeronautics Board**) *organisme américain de réglementation de l'aviation civile*.

cabal [kəˈbæl] *n* cabale *f*.

cabaret [ˈkæbəreɪ] *n* [nightclub] cabaret *m* ■ [show] spectacle *m*.

cabbage [ˈkæbɪdʒ] *n* chou *m*.

cabbage white *n* piéride *f*.

cabby, cabbie [ˈkæbɪ] *n inf* [taxi-driver] chauffeur *m* de taxi.

caber [ˈkeɪbəʳ] *n* SPORT tronc *m* ■ **tossing the ~** le lancer de troncs.

cabin [ˈkæbɪn] *n* **1.** [hut] cabane *f*, hutte *f* **2.** NAUT cabine *f* **3.** AERON cabine *f* ■ **the First Class ~** la cabine de première classe **4.** *UK* [signal box] cabine *f* d'aiguillage **5.** *UK* [of lorry, train] cabine *f*.

cabin class *n* deuxième classe *f*.

cabin crew *n* équipage *m*.

cabin cruiser *n* cruiser *m*.

cabinet [ˈkæbɪnɪt] *n* **1.** [furniture] meuble *m* (de rangement) ■ [for bottles] bar *m* ■ [radio, television] coffret *m* ■ [for precious objects] cabinet *m* ■ [with glass doors] vitrine *f* ■ **filing ~** classeur *m* **2.** POL cabinet *m* ■ **they took the decision in ~** ils ont pris la décision en Conseil des ministres.

cabinet-maker *n* ébéniste *m*.

cabinet minister *n* ministre *m* siégeant au cabinet.

cabinetwork [ˈkæbɪnɪtwɜːk] *n* ébénisterie *f*.

cabin trunk *n* malle-cabine *f*.

cable [ˈkeɪbl] ◇ *n* **1.** [rope, wire] câble *m* **2.** [telegram] télégramme *m* **3.** NAUT [measure] encablure *f* **4.** [in knitting] point *m* de torsade ■ **~ needle** aiguille *f* à torsades **5.** TV le câble.
◇ *vt* **1.** [lay cables in] câbler **2.** [telegraph] télégraphier à.

cable car *n* téléphérique *m*.

cable company *n* câblo-opérateur *m*.

cable railway *n* funiculaire *m*.

cable stitch *n* point *m* de torsade.

cable television, cable TV *n* câble *m*, télévision *f* par câble.

cablevision [ˈkeɪblvɪʒn] *n* télévision *f* par câble, câblodistribution *f*.

cableway [ˈkeɪblweɪ] *n* téléphérique *m*.

cabling [ˈkeɪblɪŋ] *n* câblage *m*.

caboodle [kəˈbuːdl] *n inf* **the whole (kit and) ~** tout le bataclan *OR* bazar.

caboose [kəˈbuːs] *n* **1.** *US* RAIL fourgon *m* de queue **2.** NAUT coquerie *f*.

cab rank *n* station *f* de taxis.

cabriolet [ˈkæbrɪəʊleɪ] *n* cabriolet *m*.

cabstand [ˈkæbstænd] *n* = **cab rank**.

cacao [kəˈkɑːəʊ] (*pl* **cacaos**) *n* [bean] cacao *m* ■ [tree] cacaoyer *m*, cacaotier *m*.

cache [kæʃ] ◇ *n* [hidden supply] cache *f* ■ **a ~ of weapons, an arms ~** une cache d'armes ■ **~ (memory)** COMPUT antémémoire *f*, mémoire-cache *f*.
◇ *vt* mettre dans une cachette.

cache memory [ˈkæʃˌmemərɪ] *n* COMPUT antémémoire *f*, mémoire *f* cache.

cachet [ˈkæʃeɪ] *n liter & fig* cachet *m*.

cack-handed [kæk-] *adj UK inf* maladroit, gauche.

cackle [ˈkækl] ◇ *vi* **1.** [hen] caqueter **2.** [person - chatter] caqueter, jacasser ; [- laugh] glousser.
◇ *vt* : **"you're trapped!", ~d the old witch** "je te tiens!", gloussa la vieille sorcière.
◇ *n* **1.** [of hen] caquet *m* **2.** [of person - chatter] caquetage *m*, jacasserie *f* ; [- laugh] gloussement *m* ■ **cut the ~!** *inf* assez bavardé!

cacophony [kæˈkɒfənɪ] (*pl* **cacophonies**) *n* cacophonie *f*.

cactus ['kæktəs] (*pl* **cactuses** *OR pl* **cacti** [-taɪ]) *n* cactus *m*.

cad [kæd] *n dated* goujat *m*.

CAD (*abbrev of* **computer-aided design**) *n* CAO *f*.

cadastral [kə'dæstrəl] *adj* cadastral ▪ **~ register** (registre *m* du) cadastre *m*.

cadaver [kə'dɑ:vər] *n* MED cadavre *m*.

CADCAM (*abbrev of* **computer-aided design and manufacture**) *n* CFAO *f*.

caddie ['kædɪ] ◇ *n* **1.** SPORT caddie *m* **2.** = **caddy**.
◇ *vi* : **to ~ for sb** être le caddie de qqn.

caddie car, caddie cart *n* poussette *f (pour cannes de golf)*.

caddy ['kædɪ] *n* **1.** *UK* [container - for tea] boîte *f* **2.** *US* [cart] chariot *m*, Caddie® *m*.

cadence ['keɪdəns] *n* cadence *f*.

cadenza [kə'denzə] *n* cadence *f*.

cadet [kə'det] ◇ *n* **1.** MIL élève *m* officier ▪ [police] élève *m* policier ▪ *UK* SCH *élève qui reçoit une formation militaire* **2.** [younger brother, son] cadet *m*.
◇ *adj* cadet.

cadet corps *n* [for military training] peloton *m* d'instruction militaire ▪ [for police training] corps *m* d'élèves policiers.

cadge [kædʒ] *inf* ◇ *vt* [food, money] se procurer *(en quémandant)* ▪ **he ~d a meal from** *OR* **off his aunt** il s'est invité à manger chez sa tante.
◇ *vi* : **she's always cadging off her friends** elle est toujours en train de taper ses amis.
◇ *n UK* **1.** = **cadger 2.** *phr* **to be on the ~** chercher à se faire payer quelque chose.

cadger ['kædʒər] *n inf* pique-assiette *mf inv*, parasite *m*.

Cadiz [kə'dɪz] *pr n* Cadix.

cadmium ['kædmɪəm] *n* cadmium *m*.

CAE (*abbrev of* **computer-aided engineering**) *n* IAO *f*.

Caesar ['si:zər] *pr n* César ▪ **Julius ~** Jules César.

Caesarean *UK*, **Cesarean** *US* [sɪ'zeərɪən] ◇ *adj* césarien ▪ **~ birth** MED césarienne *f*.
◇ *n* = **Caesarean section**.

Caesarean section *n* césarienne *f* ▪ **to be born** *OR* **delivered by ~** naître par césarienne.

Caesar salad *n salade de laitue, anchois, croûtons et parmesan*.

caesura [sɪ'zjʊərə] (*pl* **caesuras** *OR pl* **caesurae** [-ri:]) *n* césure *f*.

CAF (*written abbrev of* **cost and freight**) C et F.

cafe, café ['kæfeɪ] *n* [in UK] snack *m* ▪ [in rest of Europe] café *m*.

cafeteria [,kæfɪ'tɪərɪə] *n* [self-service restaurant] restaurant *m* self-service, self *m* ▪ *US* [canteen] cantine *f*.

cafetière [kæf'tjeər] *n* cafetière *f* à piston.

caff△ [kæf] *n* snack *m*.

caffeine ['kæfi:n] *n* caféine *f*.

caffeine-free *adj* sans caféine.

caftan ['kæftæn] *n* caftan *m*.

cage [keɪdʒ] ◇ *n* **1.** [with bars] cage *f* **2.** [lift] cabine *f* ▪ MIN cage *f* (d'extraction) **3.** SPORT [in basketball] panier *m* ▪ [in ice hockey] cage *f*.
◇ *vt* mettre en cage, encager.

cage bird *n* oiseau *m* d'agrément *OR* d'appartement.

caged [keɪdʒd] *adj* en cage.

cagey ['keɪdʒɪ] (*comp* **cagier**, *superl* **cagiest**) *adj inf* [cautious] mesuré, circonspect ▪ [reticent] réticent ▪ **he was being ~ about his salary** il s'est montré évasif lorsqu'il s'est agi de son salaire.

cagoule [kə'gu:l] *n* veste *f* imperméable *(à capuche)*.

cagy ['keɪdʒɪ] (*comp* **cagier**, *superl* **cagiest**) *adj* = **cagey**.

cahoots [kə'hu:ts] *npl inf* **to be in ~ (with sb)** être de mèche (avec qqn) ▮ *phr* **they discovered that the bank manager was in ~ with the gang** *inf* on a découvert que le directeur de la banque était de mèche avec les voleurs.

Caiaphas ['kaɪəfæs] *pr n* Caïphe.

Cain [keɪn] *pr n* Caïn ▪ **to raise ~** *US inf* faire du foin.

cairn [keən] *n* cairn *m*.

Cairo ['kaɪərəʊ] *pr n* Le Caire.

caisson ['keɪsɒn] *n* caisson *m*.

cajole [kə'dʒəʊl] *vt* enjôler ▪ **he ~d her into accepting** il l'a amenée à accepter à force de cajoleries.

Cajun ['keɪdʒən] ◇ *n* Cajun *mf inv*.
◇ *adj* cajun *(inv)*.

cake [keɪk] ◇ *n* **1.** CULIN [sweet] gâteau *m* ▪ [pastry] pâtisserie *f* ▪ [savoury] croquette *f* ▪ **a chocolate/cherry ~** un gâteau au chocolat/aux cerises ➊ **it's a piece of ~** *inf* c'est du gâteau *OR* de la tarte ▪ **you can't have your ~ and eat it** *prov* on ne peut pas avoir le beurre et l'argent du beurre *prov* **2.** [block - of soap, wax] pain *m* ; [- of chocolate] plaquette *f*.
◇ *comp* [dish] à gâteau ▪ **~ shop** pâtisserie *f* ▪ **~ stand** assiette *f* montée à gâteaux ▪ **~ pan** *US OR* **tin** moule *m* à gateau.
◇ *vt* : **his boots were ~d with mud** ses bottes étaient pleines de boue ▪ **her hair was ~d with blood** elle avait du sang séché dans les cheveux.
◇ *vi* durcir.

cake mix *n* préparation *f* (instantanée) pour gâteau.

cakewalk ['keɪkwɔ:k] *n* **1.** [dance] cake-walk *m* **2.** *inf fig* [easy task] : **the exam was a ~** l'examen, c'était du gâteau.

cal. (*written abbrev of* **calorie**) cal.

CAL (*abbrev of* **computer-assisted learning** *OR* **computer-aided learning**) *n* EAO *m*.

Calabria [kə'læbrɪə] *pr n* Calabre *f* ▪ **in ~** en Calabre.

Calabrian [kə'læbrɪən] ◇ *n* Calabrais *m*, - e *f*.
◇ *adj* calabrais.

calamine ['kæləmaɪn] *n* calamine *f* ▪ **~ lotion** lotion calmante à la calamine.

calamitous [kə'læmɪtəs] *adj* calamiteux.

calamity [kə'læmətɪ] (*pl* **calamities**) *n* calamité *f*.

calcify ['kælsɪfaɪ] (*pret & pp* **calcified**) ◇ *vt* calcifier.
◇ *vi* se calcifier.

calcination [,kælsɪ'neɪʃn] *n* calcination *f*.

calcium ['kælsɪəm] *n* calcium *m*.

calculate ['kælkjʊleɪt] ◇ *vt* **1.** MATHS calculer ▪ [estimate, evaluate] calculer, évaluer **2.** [design, intend] : **her remark was ~d to offend the guests** sa réflexion était destinée à offenser les invités ▪ **the price of the house was scarcely ~d to attract potential buyers** le prix de la maison n'a guère été calculé pour attirer d'éventuels acheteurs.
◇ *vi* **1.** MATHS calculer, faire des calculs **2.** [count, depend] : **I ~d on George lending me the money** je comptais sur George pour me prêter l'argent.

calculated ['kælkjʊleɪtɪd] *adj* **1.** [considered] calculé, mesuré ▪ **a ~ risk** un risque calculé **2.** [deliberate, intentional] délibéré, voulu ▪ **a ~ insult** une insulte délibérée.

calculating ['kælkjʊleɪtɪŋ] *adj* **1.** *pej* calculateur **2.** [adding] : **~ machine** machine *f* à calculer.

calculation [,kælkjʊ'leɪʃn] *n* MATHS & *fig* calcul *m* ▪ **by** *OR* **according to my ~s** selon *OR* d'après mes calculs.

calculator ['kælkjʊleɪtər] *n* **1.** [machine] calculateur *m* ▪ [small] calculatrice *f* **2.** MATHS [table] table *f*.

calculus ['kælkjʊləs] *n* calcul *m*.

caldron ['kɔ:ldrən] *n* = **cauldron**.

Caledonia [,kælɪ'dəʊnjə] *pr n* HIST Calédonie *f*.

calendar ['kælɪndəʳ] ◇ *n* **1.** [of dates] calendrier *m* **2.** [register] annuaire *m* **3.** *US* [planner] agenda *m*.
◇ *comp* [day, month, year] civil, calendaire.
◇ *vt* [event] inscrire sur le calendrier ▪ *US* [put in planner] noter *(dans son agenda)*.

calf [kɑ:f] (*pl* **calves** [kɑ:vz]) *n* **1.** [young cow, bull] veau *m* ▪ **the cow is in ~** la vache est pleine **2.** [skin] veau *m*, vachette *f* **3.** [buffalo] bufflon *m*, buffletin *m* ▪ [elephant] éléphanteau *m* ▪ [giraffe] girafeau *m*, girafon *m* ▪ [whale] baleineau *m* **4.** ANAT mollet *m*.

calf love *n* premier amour *m*.

calfskin ['kɑ:fskɪn] *n* veau *m*, vachette *f* ▪ **~ gloves** gants *mpl* en veau *OR* vachette.

caliber *US n* = **calibre**.

calibrate ['kælɪbreɪt] *vt* étalonner, calibrer.

calibration [ˌkælɪ'breɪʃn] *n* étalonnage *m*, calibrage *m*.

calibre *UK*, **caliber** *US* ['kælɪbəʳ] *n* **1.** [of gun, tube] calibre *m* ▪ **a high ~ revolver** un revolver de gros calibre **2.** [quality] qualité *f* ▪ **their work is of the highest ~** ils font un travail de grande qualité ▪ **the two applicants are not of the same ~** les deux candidats ne sont pas du même calibre *OR* n'ont pas la même envergure.

calico ['kælɪkəʊ] ◇ *n* (*pl* **calicoes** *OR pl* **calicos**) TEX *UK* calicot *m* blanc ▪ *US* calicot *m* imprimé, indienne *f*.
◇ *comp* de calicot.

California [ˌkælɪ'fɔ:njə] *pr n* Californie *f* ▪ **in ~** en Californie.

Californian [ˌkælɪ'fɔ:njən] ◇ *n* Californien *m*, - enne *f*.
◇ *adj* californien.

Caligula [kə'lɪgjʊlə] *pr n* Caligula.

caliper *US n* = **calliper**.

caliph, Caliph ['keɪlɪf] *n* calife *m*.

calisthenics [ˌkælɪs'θenɪks] *n* = **callisthenics**.

calix ['keɪlɪks] (*pl* **calices** [-lɪsi:z]) *n* calice *m (récipient)*.

call [kɔ:l] ◇ *vi* **1.** [with one's voice] appeler ▪ **to ~ for help** appeler à l'aide *OR* au secours
2. [on the telephone] appeler ▪ **where are you ~ing from?** d'où appelles-tu? ▪ **who's ~ing?** qui est à l'appareil?, c'est de la part de qui?
3. [animal, bird] pousser un cri
4. *UK* [visit] passer ▪ **I was out when they ~ed** je n'étais pas là quand ils sont passés
5. *UK* [stop] s'arrêter ▪ **to ~ at** [train] s'arrêter à ; [ship] faire escale à
6. BRIDGE annoncer.
◇ *vt* **1.** [with one's voice] appeler ▪ **can you ~ the children to the table?** pouvez-vous appeler les enfants pour qu'ils viennent à table? ▪ **he was ~ed to the phone** on l'a demandé au téléphone
2. [telephone] appeler ▪ **don't ~ me at work** ne m'appelle pas au bureau ▪ **we ~ed his house** nous avons appelé chez lui ▪ **to ~ the police/fire brigade** appeler la police/les pompiers ▶ **don't ~ us, we'll ~ you** *hum* on vous écrira
3. [wake up] réveiller
4. [name or describe as] appeler ▪ **he has a cat ~ed Felix** *UK* il a un chat qui s'appelle Félix ▪ **what's this ~ed?** comment est-ce qu'on appelle ça?, comment est-ce que ça s'appelle? ▪ **she ~ed him a crook** elle l'a traité d'escroc
5. [consider] : **Denver is where I ~ home** c'est à Denver que je me sens chez moi ▪ **she had no time to ~ her own** elle n'avait pas de temps à elle ▪ **(and you) ~ yourself a Christian!** et tu te dis chrétien! ▪ **I don't ~ that clean** ce n'est pas ce que j'appelle propre ▪ **let's ~ it a day** si on s'arrêtait là pour aujourd'hui?
6. [announce] : **to ~ an election** annoncer des élections ▪ **to ~ a meeting** convoquer une assemblée ▪ **to ~ a strike** appeler à la grève
7. [send for, summon] appeler, convoquer *fml* ▪ **she was suddenly ~ed home** elle a été rappelée soudainement chez elle ▪ **she was ~ed as a witness** elle a été citée comme témoin ▪ **he ~ed me over** il m'a appelé
8. SPORT [declare, judge] juger ▪ **he ~ed it out** il a jugé qu'elle était dehors
9. BRIDGE annoncer, demander
10. : **to ~ heads/tails** choisir face/pile
11. *phr* **to ~ sthg to mind** rappeler qqch ▪ **to ~ sthg into play** faire jouer qqch ▪ **to ~ sthg into question** remettre qqch en question.
◇ *n* **1.** [cry, shout] appel *m* ▪ [of animal, bird] cri *m* ▪ [of bugle, drum] appel *m* ▪ *fig* **the ~ of the sea** l'appel du large ▪ **a ~ for help** un appel à l'aide *OR* au secours
2. [on the telephone] appel *m* ▪ **to put a ~ through** passer une communication ▪ **to make a ~** passer un coup de téléphone ▪ **there's a ~ for you** on vous demande au téléphone ▪ **to take a ~** prendre un appel ▪ **I'll give you a ~ tomorrow** je t'appelle demain ▶ **~ waiting** signal *m* d'appel ▪ **~ diversion** transfert *m* d'appel
3. [visit] visite *f* ▪ **to make** *OR* **pay a ~ on sb** *UK* rendre visite à qqn
4. [stop] : **the ship made a ~ at Genoa** *UK* le navire a fait escale à Gênes
5. [demand, need] : **there have been renewed ~s for a return to capital punishment** il y a des gens qui demandent à nouveau le rétablissement de la peine de mort ▪ **there is little ~ for unskilled labour** il n'y a qu'une faible demande de travailleurs non spécialisés
6. ST. EX échéance *f*
7. SPORT [decision] jugement *m*
8. BRIDGE annonce *f*
9. [heads or tails] : **your ~** pile ou face?

◆ **on call** *adj phr* [doctor, nurse] de garde ▪ [police, troops] en éveil ▪ [car] disponible ▪ FIN [loan] remboursable sur demande.

◆ **call aside** *vt sep* prendre à part.

◆ **call away** *vt sep* : **she was ~ed away from the office** on l'a appelée et elle a dû quitter le bureau ▪ **she's often ~ed away on business** elle doit souvent partir en déplacement *OR* s'absenter pour affaires.

◆ **call back** ◇ *vt sep* **1.** [on telephone] rappeler
2. [ask to return] rappeler.
◇ *vi insep* **1.** [on telephone] rappeler
2. [visit again] revenir, repasser.

◆ **call down** *vt sep* **1.** *lit* [invoke] : **he ~ed down the wrath of God on the killers** il appela la colère de Dieu sur la tête des tueurs
2. *US inf* [reprimand] engueuler.

◆ **call for** *vt insep* **1.** *UK* [collect] : **he ~ed for her at her parents' house** il est allé la chercher chez ses parents ▪ **whose is this parcel? – someone's ~ing for it later** à qui est ce paquet? – quelqu'un passera le prendre plus tard
2. [put forward as demand] appeler, demander ▪ [subj: agreement, treaty] prévoir
3. [require] exiger ▪ **the situation ~ed for quick thinking** la situation demandait *OR* exigeait qu'on réfléchisse vite.

◆ **call in** ◇ *vt sep* **1.** [send for] faire venir ▪ **the army was ~ed in to assist with the evacuation** on a fait appel à l'armée pour aider à l'évacuation
2. [recall - defective goods] rappeler ; [- banknotes] retirer de la circulation ; [- library books] faire rentrer
3. FIN [debt, loan] rappeler.
◇ *vi insep* **1.** *UK* [pay a visit] passer
2. [telephone] appeler.

◆ **call off** *vt sep* **1.** [appointment, meeting, strike] annuler
2. [dog, person] rappeler.

◆ **call on** *vt insep UK* **1.** [request, summon] faire appel à ▪ **she ~ed on the government to take action** elle a demandé que le gouvernement agisse
2. [visit] rendre visite à.

◆ **call out** ◇ *vt sep* **1.** [cry out] : **"over here" he ~ed out** "par ici" appela-t-il
2. [summon] appeler, faire appel à ▪ **the union ~ed out its members for 24 hours** le syndicat appela ses adhérents à une grève de 24 heures.
◇ *vi insep* [shout] appeler ▪ **she ~ed out to a policeman** elle appela un agent de police.

◆ **call out for** *vt insep* exiger.

◆ **call round** *vi insep UK* : **can I ~ round this evening?** puis-je passer ce soir? ▪ **your mother ~ed round for the parcel** votre mère est passée prendre le paquet.

◆ **call up** ◇ *vt sep* **1.** [telephone] appeler **2.** MIL appeler ▪ [reservists] rappeler **3.** [evoke] évoquer, faire venir à l'esprit **4.** [summon] appeler, convoquer **5.** COMPUT rappeler.
◇ *vi insep* appeler.
◆ **call upon** *vt insep fml* [request, summon] faire appel à ▪ **she may be ~ed upon to give evidence** il est possible qu'elle soit citée comme témoin.

CALL (*abbrev of* **computer-assisted (or -aided) language learning**) *n* enseignement *m* des langues assisté par ordinateur.

call box *n UK* cabine *f* téléphonique.

callboy ['kɔ:lbɔɪ] *n* THEAT avertisseur *m*.

call diversion *n* transfert *m* d'appel.

caller ['kɔ:ləʳ] *n* **1.** [visitor] visiteur *m*, - euse *f* **2.** TELEC demandeur *m*, - euse *f* **3.** [in bingo] ≃ animateur *m*, - trice *f*.

caller ID display, caller display *n* TELEC présentation *f* du numéro.

call girl *n* call-girl *f*.

calligraphy [kə'lɪgrəfɪ] *n* calligraphie *f*.

call-in *n* émission *f* à ligne ouverte.

calling ['kɔ:lɪŋ] *n* **1.** [vocation] appel *m* intérieur, vocation *f* **2.** *fml* [profession] métier *m*, profession *f*.

calling card *n US* [visiting card] carte *f* de visite.

calliper *UK*, **caliper** *US* ['kælɪpəʳ] *n* **1.** MATHS : **a pair of ~ compasses** *OR* **~s** un compas **2.** MED : **~ (splint)** attelle-étrier *f* **3.** TECH [for brake] étrier *m*.

callisthenics [,kælɪs'θenɪks] *n (U)* gymnastique *f* rythmique.

call letters *npl US* indicatif *m* d'appel *(d'une station de radio)*.

callous ['kæləs] *adj* [unfeeling] dur, sans cœur ▪ [behaviour, remark] dur, impitoyable.

calloused ['kæləst] *adj* [feet, hands] calleux, corné.

callously ['kæləslɪ] *adv* durement.

callousness ['kæləsnɪs] *n* dureté *f*.

callow ['kæləʊ] *adj* [immature] sans expérience, sans maturité ▪ **a ~ youth** un jeune homme sans expérience *OR* maturité.

call sign *n* indicatif *m* d'appel *(d'une station de radio)*.

call-up *n UK* [conscription] convocation *f* (au service militaire), ordre *m* d'incorporation ▪ **~ papers** ordre *m* d'incorporation.

callus ['kæləs] *n* [on feet, hands] cal *m*, durillon *m*.

call waiting *n* signal *m* d'appel.

calm [kɑ:m] ◇ *adj* calme ▪ **keep ~!** du calme!, restons calmes! ▪ **she tried to keep ~** elle essaya de garder son calme *OR* sang-froid ▪ **to be ~ and collected** être maître de soi, garder son sang-froid.
◇ *n* calme *m* ▪ [after upset, excitement] accalmie *f* ▪ **the ~ before the storm** le calme qui précède la tempête.
◇ *vt* calmer ▪ [fears] apaiser, calmer ▪ **she tried to ~ her nerves** elle essaya de se calmer.
◆ **calm down** ◇ *vi insep* se calmer ▪ **~ down!** calmez-vous!, ne vous énervez pas!
◇ *vt sep* calmer.

calming ['kɑ:mɪŋ] *adj* calmant.

calmly ['kɑ:mlɪ] *adv* calmement.

calmness ['kɑ:mnɪs] *n* calme *m*.

Calor gas® ['kæləʳ-] *n UK* butane *m*, Butagaz® *m*.

calorie ['kælərɪ] *n* calorie *f*.

calorific [,kælə'rɪfɪk] *adj* calorifique.

calumny ['kæləmnɪ] (*pl* **calumnies**) *n fml* calomnie *f*.

calvary ['kælvərɪ] *n* calvaire *m*.
◆ **Calvary** *pr n* RELIG le Calvaire.

calve [kɑ:v] *vi* vêler.

calves [kɑ:vz] *pl* ▷ **calf**.

Calvinism ['kælvɪnɪzm] *n* calvinisme *m*.

calypso [kə'lɪpsəʊ] (*pl* **calypsos**) *n* calypso *m*.
◆ **Calypso** *pr n* MYTH Calypso.

calyx ['keɪlɪks] (*pl* **calyxes** *OR pl* **calyces** [-si:z]) *n* BOT calice *m*.

cam [kæm] *n* came *f*.

CAM (*abbrev of* **computer-aided manufacturing**) *n* FAO *f*.

camaraderie [,kæmə'rɑ:dərɪ] *n* camaraderie *f*.

camber ['kæmbəʳ] ◇ *n* [in road] bombement *m* ▪ [in beam, girder] cambre *f*, cambrure *f* ▪ [in ship's deck] tonture *f*.
◇ *vi* [road] bomber, être bombé ▪ [beam, girder] être cambré ▪ [ship's deck] avoir une tonture.

Cambodia [kæm'bəʊdjə] *pr n* Cambodge *m* ▪ **in ~** au Cambodge.

Cambodian [kæm'bəʊdjən] ◇ *n* Cambodgien *m*, - enne *f*.
◇ *adj* cambodgien.

cambric ['keɪmbrɪk] *n* batiste *f*.

Cambs. *written abbr of* **Cambridgeshire**.

camcorder ['kæm,kɔ:dəʳ] *n* Caméscope® *m*.

came [keɪm] *pt* ▷ **come**.

camel ['kæml] ◇ *n* **1.** ZOOL chameau *m* ▪ [with one hump] dromadaire *m* ▪ [female] chamelle *f* **2.** [colour] fauve *m inv*.
◇ *comp* **1.** [train] de chameaux ▪ **~ driver** chamelier *m* **2.** [coat, jacket - of camel hair] en poil de chameau ; [- coloured] fauve *(inv)*.

camelhair ['kæmlheəʳ] ◇ *n* poil *m* de chameau.
◇ *comp* [coat, jacket] en poil de chameau.

camellia [kə'mi:ljə] *n* camélia *m*.

cameo ['kæmɪəʊ] ◇ *n* (*pl* **cameos**) **1.** [piece of jewellery] camée *m* **2.** [piece of writing] morceau *m* bref, court texte *m* ▪ CIN, THEAT & TV [appearance] brève apparition *f*.
◇ *comp* **1.** [jewellery] : **a ~ brooch** un camée monté en broche **2.** CIN, THEAT & TV : **a ~ performance** *OR* **role** un petit rôle *(joué par un acteur célèbre)*.

camera ['kæmərə] *n* **1.** [device - for still photos] appareil *m* (photographique), appareil photo *m* ; [- for film, video] caméra *f* ▪ **to be on ~** être à l'écran ▪ **off ~** hors champ **2.** LAW : **in ~** à huis clos.

cameraman ['kæmərəmæn] (*pl* **cameramen** [-men]) *n* cadreur *m*, cameraman *m*.

camera-shy *adj* qui n'aime pas être photographié.

camerawoman ['kæmərə,wʊmən] (*pl* **camerawomen** [-,wɪmɪn]) *n* cadreuse *f*.

camerawork ['kæmərəwɜ:k] *n* prise *f* de vue.

Cameroon [,kæmə'ru:n] *pr n* Cameroun *m* ▪ **in ~** au Cameroun.

Cameroonian [,kæmə'ru:nɪən] ◇ *adj* camerounais.
◇ *n* Camerounais *m*, - e *f*.

camiknickers ['kæmɪ,nɪkəz] *npl UK* combinaison-culotte *f*.

camisole ['kæmɪsəʊl] *n* caraco *m*.

camomile ['kæməmaɪl] *n* camomille *f* ▪ **~ tea** infusion *f* de camomille.

camouflage ['kæməflɑ:ʒ] ◇ *n* camouflage *m*.
◇ *vt* camoufler.

camp [kæmp] ◇ *n* **1.** [place] camp *m* ▪ [not permanent] campement *m* ▪ **to make** *OR* **to pitch** *OR* **to set up ~** établir un camp **2.** [group] camp *m*, parti *m* ▪ **to be in the same ~** être du même bord **3.** *inf* [kitsch] : **(high) ~** kitsch *m*.
◇ *vi* camper.

◇ *adj inf* **1.** [effeminate] efféminé **2.** [affected] affecté, maniéré ▪ [theatrical - person] cabotin ; [- manners] théâtral **3.** [in dubious taste] kitsch *(inv)*.

◆ **camp out** *vi insep* camper, faire du camping.

◆ **camp up** *vt sep phr* **to ~ it up** *inf* [overdramatize] cabotiner ; [effeminate man] en rajouter dans le genre efféminé.

campaign [kæm'peɪn] ◇ *n* MIL & POL & *fig* campagne *f* ▪ **to conduct** *OR* **to lead a ~ against drugs** mener une campagne *OR* faire campagne contre la drogue.
◇ *vi* mener une campagne, faire campagne ▪ **to ~ against/for sthg** mener une campagne contre/en faveur de qqch.

campaigner [kæm'peɪnə^r] *n* POL & *fig* militant *m*, - e *f* ▪ MIL vétéran *m* ▪ **~s in favour of/against nuclear power** des militants pronucléaires/antinucléaires.

campanologist [ˌkæmpə'nɒlədʒɪst] *n* carillonneur *m*.

camp bed *n* lit *m* de camp.

camper ['kæmpə^r] *n* **1.** [person] campeur *m*, - euse *f* **2.** [vehicle] : **~ (van)** camping-car *m*.

campfire ['kæmpˌfaɪə^r] *n* feu *m* de camp.

campground ['kæmpgraʊnd] *n US* [private] camp *m* ▪ [commercial] terrain *m* de camping, camping *m* ▪ [clearing] emplacement *m* de camping, endroit *m* où camper.

camphor ['kæmfə^r] *n* camphre *m*.

camphorated ['kæmfəreɪtɪd] *adj* camphré.

camping ['kæmpɪŋ] ◇ *n* camping *m* ▪ **to go ~** camper, faire du camping.
◇ *comp* [equipment, stove] de camping ▪ **~ gas** butane *m* ▪ **~ ground** *OR* **grounds** *OR* **site** [private] camp *m* ; [commercial] terrain *m* de camping, camping *m* ; [clearing] emplacement *m* de camping, endroit *m* où camper.

campsite ['kæmpsaɪt] *n* [commercial] terrain *m* de camping, camping *m* ▪ [clearing] emplacement *m* de camping, endroit *m* où camper.

campus ['kæmpəs] (*pl* **campuses**) *n* UNIV [grounds] campus *m* ▪ [buildings] campus *m*, complexe *m* universitaire ▪ **to live on ~** habiter sur le campus ▪ **to live off ~** habiter en dehors du campus ▶ **~ university** université *f* regroupée sur un campus.

camshaft ['kæmʃɑːft] *n* arbre *m* à cames.

can[1] [*(weak form* [kən], *strong form* [kæn]*)*] (*pret* **could** [*(weak form* [kəd], *strong form* [kʊd]*)*]) (*negative forms :* **cannot**, *weak form* ['kænət], *strong form* ['kænɒt], *frequently shortened to* **can't** [kɑːnt]; **could not**, *frequently shortened to* **couldn't** ['kʊdnt]*)* *modal vb* **1.** [be able to] pouvoir ▪ **I'll come if I ~** je viendrai si je (le) peux ▪ **I'll come as soon as I ~** je viendrai aussitôt que possible *OR* aussitôt que je pourrai ▪ **we'll do everything we ~ to help** nous ferons tout ce que nous pourrons *OR* tout notre possible pour aider
2. [with verbs of perception or understanding] : **~ you feel it?** tu le sens? ▪ **we ~ hear everything our neighbours say** nous entendons tout ce que disent nos voisins ▪ **I can't understand you when you mumble** je ne te comprends pas *OR* je ne comprends pas ce que tu dis quand tu marmonnes ▪ **there ~ be no doubt about his guilt** sa culpabilité ne fait aucun doute
3. [indicating ability or skill] savoir ▪ **~ you drive/sew?** savez-vous conduire/coudre? ▪ **she ~ speak three languages** elle parle trois langues
4. [giving or asking for permission] pouvoir ▪ **~ I borrow your sweater? – yes, you ~** puis-je emprunter ton pull? – (mais oui,) bien sûr
5. [used to interrupt, intervene] : **~ I just say something here?** est-ce que je peux dire quelque chose?
6. [in offers of help] pouvoir ▪ **~ I be of any assistance?** puis-je vous aider?
7. [indicating reluctance] pouvoir ▪ **we can't leave the children alone** nous ne pouvons pas laisser *OR* il nous est impossible de laisser les enfants seuls ▮ [indicating refusal] pouvoir ▪ **we cannot tolerate such behaviour** nous ne pouvons pas tolérer ce genre de comportement
8. [expressing opinions] : **you can't blame her for leaving him!** tu ne peux pas lui reprocher de l'avoir quitté! ▪ **you'll have to leave, it can't be helped** il faudra que tu partes, il n'y a rien à faire
9. [used to urge or insist] : **can't we at least talk about it?** est-ce que nous pouvons au moins en discuter?
10. [indicating possibility or likelihood] pouvoir ▪ **the contract ~ still be cancelled** il est toujours possible d'annuler *OR* on peut encore annuler le contrat ▪ **the job can't be finished in one day** il est impossible de finir le travail *OR* le travail ne peut pas se faire en un jour ▪ **what ~ I have done with the keys?** qu'est-ce que j'ai bien pu faire des clés? ▶ **I'm as happy as ~ be** je suis on ne peut plus heureux
11. [indicating disbelief or doubt] : **you can't be serious!** (ce n'est pas possible!) vous ne parlez pas sérieusement! ▪ **he can't possibly have finished already!** ce n'est pas possible qu'il ait déjà fini! ▪ **the house can't have been that expensive** la maison n'a pas dû coûter si cher que ça ▪ **how ~ you say that?** comment pouvez-vous *OR* osez-vous dire ça?
12. *phr* **cannot but : his resignation cannot but confirm such suspicions** *fml* sa démission ne fait que confirmer de tels soupçons.

can[2] [*weak form* [kən], *strong form* [kæn]] ◇ *n* **1.** [container - for liquid] bidon *m* ; [- for tinned food] boîte *f* (de conserve) ▪ *US* [- for rubbish] poubelle *f*, boîte *f* à ordures ▪ **a ~ of beer/soda** une boîte de bière/de soda ▶ **a (real) ~ of worms** un vrai casse-tête ▪ **the film is in the ~** CIN le film est dans la boîte ▪ **the deal's in the ~** *inf* l'affaire est conclue **2.** *US inf* [prison] taule *f* **3.** *US inf* [toilet] W-C *mpl*, waters *mpl* ▪ [buttocks] fesses *fpl* **4.** *phr* **to carry the ~** *UK inf* payer les pots cassés.
◇ *vt* (*pret & pp* **canned**, *cont* **canning**) **1.** [food] mettre en boîte *OR* en conserve, conserver (en boîte) **2.** *US inf* [dismiss from job] virer, renvoyer.

Can. *written abbr of* **Canada**.

Cana ['keɪnə] *pr n* : **~ (of Galilee)** Cana (de Galilée).

Canada ['kænədə] *pr n* Canada *m* ▪ **in ~** au Canada.

Canada goose *n* bernache *f* du Canada.

Canadian [kə'neɪdjən] ◇ *n* Canadien *m*, - enne *f*.
◇ *adj* [gen] canadien ▪ [embassy, prime minister] canadien, du Canada ▪ **~ English** anglais *m* du Canada.

Canadianism [kə'neɪdjənɪzm] *n* [expression] canadianisme *m*.

canal [kə'næl] *n* **1.** [waterway] canal *m* ▪ **~ barge** *OR* **boat** péniche *f*, chaland *m* **2.** ANAT canal *m*, conduit *m*.

canapé ['kænəpeɪ] *n* canapé *m (petit four)*.

canard [kæ'nɑːd] *n* [false report] fausse nouvelle *f*, canard *m*.

Canaries [kə'neərɪz] *pr npl* : **the ~** les Canaries *fpl*.

canary [kə'neərɪ] (*pl* **canaries**) *n* **1.** [bird] canari *m*, serin *m* **2.** [colour] : **~ (yellow)** jaune serin *m inv*, jaune canari *m inv*.

Canary Islands *pr npl* : **the ~** les (îles *fpl*) Canaries *fpl* ▪ **in the ~** aux Canaries.

Canary Wharf *pr n quartier d'affaires dans l'est de Londres, dominé par la Canary Wharf Tower, le plus grand immeuble de Grande-Bretagne.*

canasta [kə'næstə] *n* canasta *f*.

Canaveral [kə'nævərəl] *pr n* : **Cape ~** cap Canaveral.

cancan ['kænkæn] *n* cancan *m*, french cancan *m*.

cancel ['kænsl] (*UK pret & pp* **cancelled**, *cont* **cancelling**) (*US pret & pp* **canceled**, *cont* **canceling**) *vt* **1.** [call off - event, order, reservation, flight] annuler ; [- appointment] annuler, décommander **2.** [revoke - agreement, contract] résilier, annuler ; [- cheque] faire opposition à **3.** [mark as no longer valid - by stamping] oblitérer ; [- by punching] poinçonner **4.** [cross out] barrer, rayer, biffer **5.** MATHS éliminer.

◆ **cancel out** *vt sep* **1.** [counterbalance] neutraliser, compenser ▪ **the factors ~ each other out** les facteurs se neutralisent *OR* se compensent **2.** MATHS éliminer, annuler.

cancellation [ˌkænsə'leɪʃn] *n* **1.** [calling off - of event, reservation] annulation *f* ▪ [annulment - of agreement, contract] résiliation *f*, annulation *f* ; [- of cheque] opposition *f* ▪ **we only got a table because there had been a ~** nous n'avons eu une table que parce que quelqu'un avait annulé sa réservation **2.** [act of invalidating - by punching] poinçonnage *m* ; [- by stamping] oblitération *f* **3.** [crossing out] biffage *m* **4.** MATHS élimination *f*.

cancer ['kænsəʳ] <> *n* MED & *fig* cancer *m* ▪ **to die of ~** mourir (à la suite) d'un cancer ▪ **cigarettes cause ~** les cigarettes sont cancérigènes *OR* carcinogènes.
<> *comp* : **~ patient** cancéreux *m*, - euse *f* ▪ **~ research** oncologie *f*, cancérologie *f* ▪ **we're collecting money for ~ research** nous recueillons des fonds pour la recherche contre le cancer ▪ **~ ward** [wing] service *m* oncologique ; [building] pavillon *m* oncologique ▪ **'Cancer Ward'** ***Solzhenitsyn*** 'le Pavillon des cancéreux'.

Cancer ['kænsəʳ] *pr n* ASTROL & ASTRON Cancer *m* ▪ **he's a ~** il est (du signe du) Cancer.

cancerous ['kænsərəs] *adj* cancéreux.

cancer stick *n* ***inf hum*** cigarette *f*.

candelabra [,kændɪ'lɑ:brə] (*pl inv OR pl* **candelabras**), **candelabrum** [,kændɪ'lɑ:brəm] (*pl inv OR pl* **candelabrums**) *n* candélabre *m*.

candid ['kændɪd] *adj* [person] franc, franche *f*, sincère ▪ [smile] franc, franche *f* ▪ [account, report] qui ne cache rien ▪ **I'd like your ~ opinion** j'aimerais que vous me disiez franchement ce que vous en pensez.

candidacy ['kændɪdəsɪ] *n* candidature *f*.

candidate ['kændɪdət] *n* candidat *m*, - e *f* ▪ **to be a** *OR* **to stand as ~ for mayor** être candidat à la mairie.

candidature ['kændɪdətʃəʳ] *n* candidature *f*.

Candid Camera *n* TV la Caméra Cachée.

candidly ['kændɪdlɪ] *adv* [speak] franchement ▪ [smile] candidement, avec candeur.

candidness ['kændɪdnɪs] *n* franchise *f*.

candied ['kændɪd] *adj* [piece of fruit, peel] confit ▪ [whole fruit] confit, glacé.

candle ['kændl] *n* **1.** [of wax - gen] bougie *f*, chandelle *f* ; [- in church] cierge *m*, chandelle *f* ▪ **no one can hold a ~ to her when it comes to dancing** pour ce qui est de la danse, personne ne lui arrive à la cheville ▪ **to burn the ~ at both ends** brûler la chandelle par les deux bouts **2.** PHYS [former unit] bougie *f* ▪ [candela] candela *f*.

candleholder ['kændl,həʊldəʳ] *n* [single] bougeoir *m* ▪ [branched] chandelier *m*.

candlelight ['kændllaɪt] <> *n* lueur *f* d'une bougie *OR* d'une chandelle ▪ **they had dinner by ~** ils ont dîné aux chandelles ▪ **she read by ~** elle lisait à la lueur d'une bougie.
<> *comp* [dinner, supper] aux chandelles.

candlelit ['kændllɪt] *adj* éclairé aux bougies *OR* aux chandelles.

Candlemas ['kændlməs] *n* la Chandeleur.

candlestick ['kændlstɪk] *n* [single] bougeoir *m* ▪ [branched] chandelier *m*.

candlewick ['kændlwɪk] <> *n* [yarn] chenille *f* (de coton).
<> *comp* [bedspread] en chenille (de coton).

candour *UK*, **candor** *US* ['kændəʳ] *n* candeur *f*, franchise *f*.

candy ['kændɪ] <> *n* (*pl* **candies**) **1.** *US* [piece] bonbon *m* ▪ *(U)* [sweets in general] bonbons *mpl*, confiserie *f* ▪ **~ bar** [chocolate] barre *f* de chocolat ; [muesli] barre *f* de céréale **2.** CULIN [sugar] sucre *m* candi.
<> *vt* (*pl pret & pp* **candied**) [ginger, pieces of fruit, orange peel] confire ▪ [whole fruit] glacer, confire ▪ [sugar] faire candir.
<> *vi* (*pl pret & pp* **candied**) se candir, se cristalliser.

candy corn *n (U) US bonbons que l'on mange à Halloween.*

candyfloss ['kændɪflɒs] *n UK* barbe *f* à papa.

candy-striped *adj* à rayures multicolores.

candy striper [-,straɪpəʳ] *n US bénévole qui travaille aux œuvres de bienfaisance dans un hôpital.*

cane [keɪn] <> *n* **1.** [stem of plant] canne *f* ▪ [in making baskets, furniture] rotin *m*, jonc *m* **2.** [rod - for walking] canne *f* ; [- for punishment] verge *f*, baguette *f* ▪ **to give sb the ~** fouetter qqn **3.** [for supporting plant] tuteur *m*.
<> *comp* [furniture] en rotin ▪ [chair - entirely in cane] en rotin ; [- with cane back, seat] canné.
<> *vt* **1.** [beat with rod] donner des coups de bâton à, fouetter **2.** ***inf*** [defeat] battre à plate couture.

cane sugar *n* sucre *m* de canne.

canine ['keɪnaɪn] <> *adj* **1.** [gen] canin ▪ ZOOL de la famille des canidés **2.** ANAT : **~ tooth** canine *f*.
<> *n* **1.** [animal] canidé *m* **2.** [tooth] canine *f*.

caning ['keɪnɪŋ] *n* **1.** [beating] : **to give sb a ~** [gen] donner des coups de bâton *OR* de trique à qqn ; SCH fouetter qqn **2.** ***inf*** [defeat] : **to get a ~** être battu à plate couture.

canister ['kænɪstəʳ] *n* **1.** [for flour, sugar] boîte *f* **2.** [for gas, shaving cream] bombe *f* ▪ **tear gas ~** bombe lacrymogène.

canker ['kæŋkəʳ] *n* **1.** *(U)* MED ulcère *m*, chancre *m* **2.** BOT & ***fig*** chancre *m*.

cannabis ['kænəbɪs] *n* [plant] chanvre *m* indien ▪ [drug] cannabis *m*.

canned [kænd] *adj* **1.** [food] en boîte, en conserve ▪ **~ goods** conserves *fpl* **2.** ***pej*** [pre-prepared, pre-recorded] : **~ laughter** rires *mpl* préenregistrés ▪ **~ music** musique *f* en conserve ***hum*** & ***pej*** *OR* enregistrée **3.** ***inf*** [drunk] paf *(inv)*, rond.

cannelloni [,kænɪ'ləʊnɪ] *n (U)* cannelloni *mpl*.

cannery ['kænərɪ] (*pl* **canneries**) *n* conserverie *f*, fabrique *f* de conserves ▪ **'Cannery Row'** ***Steinbeck*** 'Rue de la sardine'.

cannibal ['kænɪbl] <> *adj* cannibale, anthropophage.
<> *n* cannibale *mf*, anthropophage *mf*.

cannibalism ['kænɪbəlɪzm] *n* cannibalisme *m*, anthropophagie *f*.

cannibalize, *UK* **ise** ['kænɪbəlaɪz] *vt* [car] cannibaliser, récupérer des pièces détachées de ▪ [text] récupérer des parties de.

cannily ['kænɪlɪ] *adv* [assess] avec perspicacité ▪ [reason] habilement, astucieusement.

canning ['kænɪŋ] <> *n* mise *f* en boîte *OR* en conserve.
<> *comp* [process] de mise en boîte *OR* en conserve ▪ **~ industry** conserverie *f*, industrie *f* de la conserve.

cannon ['kænən] <> *n* (*pl inv OR pl* **cannons**) **1.** [weapon] canon *m* **2.** TECH [barrel of gun, syringe] canon *m* **3.** *UK* [in billiards] carambolage *m*.
<> *vi* **1.** [bump] : **to ~ into sthg/sb** se heurter contre qqch/qqn **2.** *UK* [in billiards] caramboler.

cannonade [,kænə'neɪd] *n* canonnade *f*.

cannonball ['kænənbɔ:l] *n* **1.** [ammunition] boulet *m* de canon **2.** SPORT : **a ~ (service)** un service en boulet de canon.

cannon fodder *n* chair *f* à canon.

cannonshot ['kænənʃɒt] *n* [firing] coup *m* de canon ▪ [range] : **within ~** à portée de canon.

cannot ['kænɒt] *vb* ▷ **can**.

canny ['kænɪ] (*comp* **cannier**, *superl* **canniest**) *adj* **1.** [astute] astucieux, habile ▪ [shrewd] malin, - igne *f*, rusé **2.** [wary] prudent, circonspect **3.** *UK* ***dial*** [person - thrifty] économe ; [- nice] sympathique.

canoe [kə'nu:] <> *n* canoë *m* ▪ [dugout] pirogue *f* ▪ SPORT canoë *m*, canoë-kayak *m*.
<> *vi* (*cont* **canoeing**) [gen] faire du canoë ▪ SPORT faire du canoë *OR* du canoë-kayak.

canoeing [kə'nu:ɪŋ] *n* SPORT canoë-kayak *m* ▪ **to go ~** faire du canoë-kayak.

canoeist [kə'nu:ɪst] *n* canoéiste *mf*.

canon ['kænən] *n* **1.** RELIG [decree, prayer] canon *m* ▪ [clergyman] chanoine *m* **2.** LIT œuvre *f* **3.** MUS canon *m* **4.** *fig* [rule] canon *m*, règle *f*, règles *fpl*.

canonical [kə'nɒnɪkl] *adj* **1.** RELIG [text] canonique ▪ [dress, robe] sacerdotal **2.** MUS en canon **3.** *fig* [accepted] canonique, autorisé.

canonize, *UK* **ise** ['kænənaɪz] *vt* RELIG & *fig* canoniser.

canon law *n* droit *m* canon.

canoodle [kə'nu:dl] *vi UK inf* se faire des mamours.

can opener *n* ouvre-boîtes *m inv*.

canopy ['kænəpɪ] (*pl* **canopies**) *n* **1.** [over bed] baldaquin *m*, ciel *m* de lit ▪ [over balcony, passageway] auvent *m*, marquise *f* ▪ [over throne] dais *m* ▪ ARCHIT [with columns] baldaquin *m* **2.** [of parachute] voilure *f* **3.** AERON [of cockpit] verrière *f* **4.** *fig* [branches, sky] voûte *f*.

cant [kænt] ◇ *n* **1.** *(U)* [insincere talk] paroles *fpl* hypocrites ▪ [clichés] clichés *mpl*, phrases *fpl* toutes faites **2.** [jargon] argot *m* de métier, jargon *m* **3.** [slope] pente *f*, inclinaison *f* ▪ [oblique surface] surface *f* oblique, plan *m* incliné **4.** [movement] secousse *f*, cahot *m*.
◇ *vi* **1.** [talk - insincerely] parler avec hypocrisie ; [- in clichés] débiter des clichés **2.** [use jargon] parler en argot de métier, jargonner **3.** [tip slightly] se pencher, s'incliner ▪ [overturn] se renverser *OR* se retourner (d'un seul coup).
◇ *vt* [tip slightly] pencher, incliner ▪ [overturn] renverser *OR* retourner (d'un seul coup).

can't [kɑ:nt] = **can**.

Cantab. (*written abbrev of* **Cantabrigiensis**) *de l'université de Cambridge*.

cantaloup *UK*, **cantaloupe** *US* ['kæntəlu:p] *n* cantaloup *m*.

cantankerous [kæn'tæŋkərəs] *adj* **1.** [bad-tempered - habitually] acariâtre, qui a mauvais caractère, grincheux ; [- temporarily] de mauvaise humeur **2.** [quarrelsome] querelleur.

cantata [kæn'tɑ:tə] *n* cantate *f*.

canteen [kæn'ti:n] *n* **1.** [restaurant] cantine *f* **2.** *US* [flask] flasque *f*, gourde *f* **3.** [box for cutlery] coffret *m* ▪ **~ of cutlery** ménagère *f* **4.** MIL [mess tin] gamelle *f*.

canter ['kæntəʳ] ◇ *n* petit galop *m*.
◇ *vi* aller au petit galop.
◇ *vt* faire aller au petit galop.

Canterbury ['kæntəbrɪ] *n* Canterbury.

canticle ['kæntɪkl] *n* cantique *m* ▪ **the Canticle of Canticles** le Cantique des cantiques.

cantilever ['kæntɪli:vəʳ] ◇ *n* **1.** [beam, girder] cantilever *m* ▪ [projecting beam] corbeau *m*, console *f* **2.** AERON cantilever *m*.
◇ *comp* [beam, girder] en cantilever, cantilever *(inv)*.

cantilever bridge *n* pont *m* cantilever.

canton ◇ *n* **1.** ['kæntɒn] ADMIN canton *m* **2.** ['kæntən] HERALD canton *m*.
◇ *vt* **1.** [kæn'tɒn] ADMIN [land] diviser en cantons **2.** [kæn'tu:n] MIL [soldiers] cantonner.

Canton [kæn'tɒn] *pr n* Canton.

cantonal ['kæntənl] *adj* cantonal.

Cantonese [,kæntə'ni:z] (*pl inv*) ◇ *n* **1.** [person] Cantonais *m*, - e *f* **2.** LING cantonais *m*.
◇ *adj* cantonais.

Canute [kə'nju:t] *pr n* Knud.

canvas ['kænvəs] ◇ *n* (*pl inv OR pl* **canvasses**) **1.** [cloth] toile *f* ▪ [for tapestry] canevas *m* ▪ **under ~** [in tent] sous une tente ; NAUT sous voiles **2.** [painting] toile *f*, tableau *m*.
◇ *comp* [bag, cloth] de *OR* en toile.

canvass ['kænvəs] ◇ *vi* **1.** [seek opinions] faire un sondage **2.** COMM [seek orders] visiter la clientèle, faire la place ▪ [door to door] faire du démarchage *OR* du porte-à-porte **3.** POL [candidate, campaign worker] solliciter des voix.
◇ *vt* **1.** [seek opinion of] sonder **2.** COMM [person] démarcher, solliciter des commandes de ▪ [area] prospecter **3.** POL [person] solliciter la voix de ▪ [area] faire du démarchage électoral dans **4.** *US* POL [ballots] pointer.
◇ *n* **1.** [gen - COMM] démarchage *m* ▪ POL démarchage *m* électoral **2.** *US* POL [of ballots] pointage *m*.

canvasser ['kænvəsəʳ] *n* **1.** [pollster] sondeur *m*, enquêteur *m*, - euse *f* **2.** COMM [salesman] placier *m* ▪ [door to door] démarcheur *m* **3.** POL agent *m* électoral *(qui sollicite des voix)* **4.** *US* [of ballots] scrutateur *m*, - trice *f*.

canvassing ['kænvəsɪŋ] *n* **1.** [gen - COMM] démarchage *m* **2.** POL démarchage *m* électoral.

canyon ['kænjən] *n* ca~non *m*, canyon *m*, gorge *f*.

canyoning ['kænjənɪŋ] *n* SPORT canyoning *m*.

cap [kæp] ◇ *n* **1.** [hat - with peak] casquette *f* ; [- without peak] bonnet *m* ; [- of jockey, judge] toque *f* ; [- of nurse, traditional costume] coiffe *f* ; [- of soldier] calot *m* ; [- of officer] képi *m* ▪ **~ and bells** marotte *f* (de bouffon) ▪ **~ and gown** *expression britannique évoquant le milieu universitaire* ▪ **if the ~ fits, wear it** qui se sent morveux (qu'il) se mouche ▪ **to go to sb ~ in hand** aller vers qqn chapeau bas ▪ **to set one's ~ at sb** jeter son dévolu sur qqn **2.** *UK* SPORT : **he has three England ~s** il a été sélectionné trois fois dans l'équipe d'Angleterre **3.** [cover, lid - of bottle, container] capsule *f* ; [- of lens] cache *m* ; [- of tyre valve] bouchon *m* ; [- of pen] capuchon *m* ; [- of mushroom] chapeau *m* ; [- of tooth] couronne *f* ; [- of column, pedestal] chapiteau *m* **4.** [for toy gun] amorce *f* **5.** [contraceptive device] diaphragme *m*.
◇ *vt* (*pret & pp* **capped**, *cont* **capping**) **1.** [cover] couvrir, recouvrir **2.** [tooth] couronner **3.** [outdo] surpasser ▪ **he capped that story with an even funnier one** il a raconté une histoire encore plus drôle que celle-là ▪ **to ~ it all** pour couronner le tout, pour comble **4.** [spending] limiter, restreindre **5.** *UK* SPORT sélectionner (dans l'équipe nationale).

CAP [kæp, si:eɪ'pi:] (*abbrev of* **Common Agricultural Policy**) *n* PAC *f*.

capability [,keɪpə'bɪlətɪ] (*pl* **capabilities**) *n* **1.** [gen] aptitude *f*, capacité *f* ▪ **the work is beyond his capabilities** ce travail est au-dessus de ses capacités **2.** MIL capacité *f*, potentiel *m* ▪ **nuclear ~** puissance *f OR* potentiel *m* nucléaire.

capable ['keɪpəbl] *adj* **1.** [able] capable ▪ **they are quite ~ of looking after themselves** ils sont parfaitement capables de *OR* ils peuvent très bien se débrouiller tout seuls **2.** [competent] capable, compétent.

capably ['keɪpəblɪ] *adv* avec compétence, de façon compétente.

capacious [kə'peɪʃəs] *adj fml* [container] de grande capacité *OR* contenance.

capacitance [kə'pæsɪtəns] *n* ELEC capacité *f*.

capacitor [kə'pæsɪtəʳ] *n* ELEC condensateur *m*.

capacity [kə'pæsɪtɪ] ◇ *n* (*pl* **capacities**) **1.** [size - of container] contenance *f*, capacité *f* ; [- of room] capacité *f* ▪ **filled to ~** [bottle, tank] plein ; [ship, theatre] plein, comble **2.** [aptitude] aptitude *f*, capacité *f* ▪ **~ to learn** aptitude à apprendre, capacité d'apprendre ▪ **the work is well within our ~** nous sommes tout à fait en mesure *OR* capables de faire ce travail **3.** [position] qualité *f*, titre *m* ▪ LAW [legal competence] pouvoir *m* légal ▪ **she spoke in her ~ as government representative** elle s'est exprimée en sa qualité de *OR* en tant que représentante du gouvernement ▪ **they are here in an official ~** ils sont ici à titre officiel **4.** [of factory, industry] moyens *mpl* de production ▪ [output] rendement *m* ▪ **the factory is (working) at full ~** l'usine produit à plein rendement **5.** [of engine] capacité *f* **6.** ELEC capacité *f*.
◇ *comp* : **a ~ audience** une salle comble ▪ **they played to a ~ crowd** ils ont joué à guichets fermés.

cape [keɪp] *n* **1.** [cloak] cape *f*, pèlerine *f* **2.** GEOG [headland] cap *m* ■ [promontory] promontoire *m*.

CAPE

Cape Bon le cap Bon ;
Cape Canaveral cap Canaveral ;
Cape Cod cap Cod ;
the Cape of Good Hope le cap de Bonne-Espérance ;
Cape Horn le cap Horn.

caper ['keɪpəʳ] <> *vi* **1.** [jump, skip] cabrioler, gambader, faire des cabrioles *OR* des gambades **2.** [frolic] faire le fou.
<> *n* **1.** [jump, skip] cabriole *f*, gambade *f* **2.** [practical joke] farce *f* **3.** *inf* [nonsense] : **I haven't time for all that ~** je n'ai pas de temps à perdre avec des âneries pareilles **4.** *inf* [illegal activity] coup *m* **5.** CULIN câpre *f* ■ [shrub] câprier *m*.
<> *comp* : **~ sauce** sauce *f* aux câpres.

Capernaum [kə'pɜːnjəm] *pr n* Capharnaüm.

Cape Town *pr n* Le Cap.

Cape Verde [-vɜːd] *pr n* : **the ~ Islands** les îles *fpl* du Cap-Vert ■ **in ~** au Cap-Vert.

capful ['kæpfʊl] *n* [of liquid] capsule *f* (pleine).

capillary ['kæpəlerɪ] <> *adj* capillaire.
<> *n* (*pl* **capillaries**) capillaire *m*.

capital ['kæpɪtl] <> *adj* **1.** [chief, primary] capital, principal ■ **it's of ~ importance** c'est d'une importance capitale, c'est de la plus haute importance ■ **~ city** capitale *f* **2.** LAW capital ■ **~ offence** crime *m* passible de la peine de mort **3.** [upper case] majuscule ■ **~ D** D majuscule ■ **in ~ letters** en majuscules, en capitales ■ **he's an idiot with a ~ "I"** c'est un imbécile avec un grand "I" **4.** *UK inf dated* [wonderful] chouette, fameux.
<> *n* **1.** [city] capitale *f* **2.** [letter] majuscule *f*, capitale *f* ■ **write in ~s** écrivez en (lettres) majuscules *OR* en capitales **3.** *(U)* [funds] capital *m*, capitaux *mpl*, fonds *mpl* ■ ECON & FIN [funds and assets] capital *m* (en espèces et en nature) ■ **to raise ~** réunir des capitaux ■ **to try and make ~ (out) of a situation** essayer de tirer profit *OR* parti d'une situation **4.** FIN [principal] capital *m*, principal *m* **5.** ARCHIT [of column] chapiteau *m*.
<> *comp* de capital ■ **~ allowances** amortissements *mpl* admis par le fisc ■ **~ income** revenu *m* du capital ■ **~ investment** mise *f* de fonds ■ **~ reserves** réserves *fpl* et provisions *fpl* ■ **~ sum** capital *m*.

capital assets *npl* actif *m* immobilisé, immobilisations *fpl*.

capital expenditure *n (U)* dépenses *fpl* d'investissement.

capital gains *npl* gains *mpl* en capital, plus-values *fpl* (en capital).

capital gains tax *n impôt sur les plus-values.*

capital goods *npl* biens *mpl* d'équipement *OR* d'investissement.

capital-intensive *adj* à forte intensité de capital.

capitalism ['kæpɪtəlɪzm] *n* capitalisme *m*.

capitalist ['kæpɪtəlɪst] <> *adj* capitaliste.
<> *n* capitaliste *mf*.

capitalistic [,kæpɪtə'lɪstɪk] *adj* capitaliste.

capitalization [,kæpɪtəlaɪ'zeɪʃn] *n* capitalisation *f*.

capitalize, *UK* ise ['kæpɪtəlaɪz] <> *vt* **1.** [write in upper case] mettre en majuscules **2.** ECON [convert into capital] capitaliser ■ [raise capital through issue of stock] constituer le capital social de (par émission d'actions) ■ [provide with capital] pourvoir de fonds *OR* de capital ■ **under-/over-~d** sous-/sur-capitalisé **3.** FIN [estimate value of] capitaliser.
<> *vi* : **to ~ on sthg** [take advantage of] tirer profit *OR* parti de qqch ; [make money on] monnayer qqch.

capital levy *n* impôt *m OR* prélèvement *m* sur le capital.

capital punishment *n* peine *f* capitale, peine *f* de mort.

capital stock *n* capital *m* social, fonds *mpl* propres.

capital transfer tax *n* impôt *m* sur le transfert de capitaux.

capitation [,kæpɪ'teɪʃn] *n* **1.** FIN capitation *f* ■ **~ (tax)** capitation **2.** *esp UK* SCH : **~ (allowance *OR* expenditure)** dotation *f* forfaitaire par élève *(accordée à un établissement scolaire)*.

Capitol ['kæpɪtl] *pr n* **1.** [in Rome] : **the ~** le Capitole **2.** [in US] : **the ~** [national] le Capitole *(siège du Congrès américain)* ; [state] le Capitole *(siège du Congrès de l'État)*.

Capitol Hill *pr n la colline du Capitole, à Washington, où se trouve le Congrès américain.*

CAPITOL HILL

Ce nom désigne, par extension, le Congrès américain : *The proposal will not be welcomed on Capitol Hill.*

capitulate [kə'pɪtjʊleɪt] *vi* MIL & *fig* capituler.

capitulation [kə,pɪtjʊ'leɪʃn] *n* MIL & *fig* capitulation *f*.

capon ['keɪpən] *n* chapon *m*.

cappuccino [,kæpʊ'tʃiːnəʊ] (*pl* **cappuccinos**) *n* cappuccino *m*.

caprice [kə'priːs] *n* [whim] caprice *m* ■ [change of mood] saute *f* d'humeur.

capricious [kə'prɪʃəs] *adj* [person] capricieux, fantasque ■ [weather] capricieux, changeant.

Capricorn ['kæprɪkɔːn] *pr n* ASTROL & ASTRON Capricorne *m* ■ **he's a ~** il est (du signe du) Capricorne.

caps [kæps] (*abbrev of* **capital letters**) *npl* cap.

capsicum ['kæpsɪkəm] *n* [fruit & plant - sweet] poivron *m*, piment *m* doux ; [- hot] piment *m*.

capsize [kæp'saɪz] <> *vi* [gen] se renverser ■ [boat] chavirer.
<> *vt* [gen] renverser ■ [boat] faire chavirer.

capstan ['kæpstən] *n* cabestan *m*.

capsule ['kæpsjuːl] <> *n* **1.** [gen - AERON], ANAT & BOT capsule *f* **2.** PHARM capsule *f*, gélule *f*.
<> *adj* concis, bref.

Capt. (*written abbrev of* **captain**) cap.

captain ['kæptɪn] <> *n* **1.** [of boat] capitaine *mf* ■ MIL capitaine *mf* **2.** [of group, team] chef *m*, capitaine *mf* ■ SPORT capitaine *mf* (d'équipe) ■ **~ of industry** capitaine d'industrie **3.** *US* [of police] ≃ commissaire *m* (de police) de quartier **4.** *US* [head waiter] maître *m* d'hôtel ■ [of bell boys] responsable *m* des grooms.
<> *vt* [gen] diriger ■ MIL commander ■ SPORT être le capitaine de.

captaincy ['kæptɪnsɪ] *n* **1.** MIL grade *m* de capitaine ■ **to receive one's ~** être promu *OR* passer capitaine **2.** SPORT poste *m* de capitaine ■ **under the ~ of Rogers** avec Rogers comme capitaine.

caption ['kæpʃn] <> *n* **1.** [under illustration] légende *f* **2.** [in article, chapter] sous-titre *m* **3.** CIN sous-titre *m*.
<> *vt* **1.** [illustration] mettre une légende à, légender **2.** CIN sous-titrer.

captious ['kæpʃəs] *adj fml* [person] qui trouve toujours à redire, chicanier ■ [attitude] chicanier.

captivate ['kæptɪveɪt] *vt* captiver, fasciner.

captivating ['kæptɪveɪtɪŋ] *adj* captivant, fascinant.

captive ['kæptɪv] <> *n* captif *m*, - ive *f*, prisonnier *m*, - ère *f* ■ **to take sb ~** faire qqn prisonnier ■ **to hold sb ~** garder qqn en captivité.
<> *adj* [person] captif, prisonnier ■ [animal, balloon] captif ■ **a ~ audience** un public captif.

captivity [kæp'tɪvətɪ] *n* captivité *f* ■ **in ~** en captivité.

captor ['kæptəʳ] *n* [gen] personne *f* qui capture ■ [unlawfully] ravisseur *m*, - euse *f*.

capture ['kæptʃəʳ] ◇ *vt* **1.** [take prisoner - animal, criminal, enemy] capturer, prendre ; [- runaway] reprendre ; [- city] prendre, s'emparer de ■ GAMES prendre **2.** [gain control of - market] conquérir, s'emparer de ; [- attention, imagination] captiver ; [- admiration, interest] gagner **3.** [succeed in representing] rendre, reproduire.
◇ *n* capture *f*, prise *f*.

car [kɑːʳ] ◇ *n* **1.** [automobile] voiture *f*, automobile *f*, auto *f* ■ **to go by ~** aller en voiture **2.** *US* [of train] wagon *m*, voiture *f* **3.** *US* [tram] tramway *m*, tram *m* **4.** [of lift] cabine *f (d'ascenseur)* **5.** [of airship, balloon] nacelle *f*.
◇ *comp* [engine, tyre, wheel] de voiture, d'automobile ■ [journey, trip] en voiture ■ **~ allowance** *UK* indemnité *f* de déplacement (en voiture) ■ **~ boot sale** *UK marché où chacun vient avec sa voiture (dont le coffre sert de stand) pour vendre des objets de toute sorte* ■ **~ chase** course-poursuite *f* ■ **~ industry** industrie *f* (de l')automobile ■ **~ radio** autoradio *m* ■ **~ worker** ouvrier *m*, - ère *f* de l'industrie automobile.

carafe [kə'ræf] *n* carafe *f*.

car alarm *n* AUT alarme *f* de voiture.

carambola [,kærəm'bəʊlə] *n* carambole *f*.

caramel ['kærəmel] ◇ *n* caramel *m*.
◇ *comp* : **a ~ (candy)** *US*, **a (piece of) ~** un caramel ■ **~ cream, ~ custard** crème *f* (au) caramel.

caramelize, *UK* **ise** ['kærəməlaɪz] ◇ *vt* caraméliser.
◇ *vi* se caraméliser.

carat *UK*, **karat** *US* ['kærət] *n* carat *m* ■ **an 18 ~ gold ring** une bague en or 18 carats.

Caravaggio [,kærə'vædʒɪəʊ] *pr n* le Caravage.

caravan ['kærəvæn] ◇ *n* **1.** *UK* [vehicle] caravane *f* **2.** [of gipsy] roulotte *f* **3.** [group of travellers] caravane *f*.
◇ *vi UK* (*pret & pp* **caravanned**, *cont* **caravanning**) : **to go caravanning** faire du caravaning *OR offic* du caravanage.

caravanner *UK*, **caravaner** *US* ['kærəvænəʳ] *n* caravanier *m*, - ère *f*.

caravanning ['kærəvænɪŋ] *n* caravaning *m*, caravanage *offic*.

caravan site *n UK* [for campers] camping *m* (pour caravanes) ■ [of gipsies] campement *m*.

caravel ['kærəvel] *n* NAUT caravelle *f*.

caraway ['kærəweɪ] *n* [plant] carvi *m*, cumin *m* des prés ■ **~ seeds** (graines *fpl* de) carvi.

carbine ['kɑːbaɪn] *n* carabine *f*.

carbohydrate [,kɑːbəʊ'haɪdreɪt] *n* **1.** CHEM hydrate *m* de carbone **2.** *(usu pl)* [foodstuff] : **~s** glucides *mpl*.

carbolic [kɑː'bɒlɪk] *adj* phéniqué ■ **~ acid** phénol *m*.

car bomb *n* voiture *f* piégée.

carbon ['kɑːbən] *n* **1.** CHEM carbone *m* **2.** [copy, paper] carbone *m*.

carbonate ['kɑːbənɪt] *n* carbonate *m*.

carbonated ['kɑːbəneɪtɪd] *adj* carbonaté ■ **~ soft drinks** boissons *fpl* gazeuses.

carbon copy *n* TYPO carbone *m* ■ *fig* réplique *f*.

carbon dating *n* datation *f* au carbone 14.

carbon dioxide *n* gaz *m* carbonique, dioxyde *m* de carbone.

carbon fibre *n* fibre *f* de carbone.

carbon footprint *n* empreinte *f* carbone.

carbonize, *UK* **ise** ['kɑːbənaɪz] *vt* carboniser.

carbon monoxide *n* monoxyde *m* de carbone.

carbon paper *n* TYPO (papier *m*) carbone *m*.

carbon steel *n* acier *m* carburé.

carbuncle ['kɑː,bʌŋkl] *n* **1.** MED furoncle *m* **2.** [gemstone] escarboucle *f*.

carburettor *UK*, **carburetor** *US* [,kɑːbə'retəʳ] *n* carburateur *m*.

carcass, carcase ['kɑːkəs] *n* **1.** [of animal] carcasse *f*, cadavre *m* ■ [for food] carcasse *f* **2.** [of person - dead] cadavre *m* ■ **move your ~** *inf hum* pousse un peu ta viande **3.** [of building] carcasse *f*, charpente *f* ■ [of car] carcasse *f*.

carcinogen [kɑː'sɪnədʒən] *n* (agent *m*) carcinogène *m OR* cancérogène *m*.

carcinogenic [,kɑːsɪnə'dʒenɪk] *adj* carcinogène, cancérogène.

carcinoma [,kɑːsɪ'nəʊmə] (*pl* **carcinomas** *OR pl* **carcinomata** [-mətə]) *n* carcinome *m*.

car coat *n UK* manteau *m* trois-quarts.

card [kɑːd] ◇ *n* **1.** GAMES carte *f* ■ **to play ~s** jouer aux cartes ◐ **to play one's ~s right** mener bien son jeu *OR* sa barque ■ **to play one's best** *OR* **strongest** *OR* **trump ~** jouer sa meilleure carte ■ **I still have a couple of ~s up my sleeve** j'ai encore quelques atouts dans mon jeu ■ **he holds all the (winning) ~s** il a tous les atouts (en main *OR* dans son jeu) ■ **to lay** *OR* **to place one's ~s on the table** jouer cartes sur table ■ **it was on the ~s** *UK OR* **in the ~s** *US* **that the project would fail** il était dit *OR* prévisible que le projet échouerait
2. [with written information - gen] carte *f* ; [- for business] carte *f* (de visite) ; [- for index] fiche *f* ; [- for membership] carte *f* de membre *OR* d'adhérent ; [- for library] carte *f* (d'abonnement) ■ [postcard] carte *f* (postale) ■ [programme] programme *m*
3. [cardboard] carton *m*
4. COMPUT carte *f*
5. *inf dated* [person] plaisantin *m*
6. TEX carde *f*.
◇ *vt* **1.** [information] ficher, mettre sur fiche
2. SPORT [score] marquer
3. TEX carder.
◆ **cards** *npl UK phr* **to ask for one's ~ s** quitter son travail.

cardamom, cardamum ['kɑːdəməm] *n* cardamome *f* ■ **~ seeds** (graines *fpl* de) cardamome *f*.

cardamon ['kɑːdəmən] *n* = **cardamom**.

cardboard ['kɑːdbɔːd] ◇ *n* carton *m*.
◇ *adj* **1.** [container, partition] de *OR* en carton ■ **~ box** (boîte *f* en) carton *m* ■ **~ city** *quartier où dorment les sans-abri* **2.** *fig* [unreal - character, leader] de carton-pâte, faux, fausse *f*.

card-carrying *adj* : **~ member** membre *m*, adhérent *m*, - e *f*.

card catalogue *n* fichier *m* (de bibliothèque).

card file *n* fichier *m*.

card holder *n* [of library] abonné *m*, - e *f* ■ [of credit card] titulaire *mf* d'une carte de crédit.

cardiac ['kɑːdɪæk] ◇ *adj* cardiaque.
◇ *n* cardiaque *mf*.

cardiac arrest *n* arrêt *m* cardiaque.

cardie ['kɑːdɪ] *n UK inf* cardigan *m*.

cardigan, cardigan sweater *US* ['kɑːdɪgən] *n* cardigan *m*.

cardinal ['kɑːdɪnl] ◇ *adj* **1.** [essential] cardinal **2.** [colour] : **~ (red)** rouge cardinal *(inv)*, écarlate.
◇ *n* **1.** MATHS, ORNITH & RELIG cardinal *m* **2.** [colour] : **~ (red)** rouge cardinal *m inv*, écarlate *f*.

cardinal number *n* MATHS nombre *m* cardinal.

cardinal points *npl* : **the ~** les (quatre) points *mpl* cardinaux.

card index *n* fichier *m*.
◆ **card-index** *vt* : **to card-index information** ficher des renseignements, mettre des renseignements sur fichier.

cardiogram ['kɑːdɪəgræm] *n* cardiogramme *m*.

cardiograph ['kɑːdɪəgrɑːf] *n* cardiographe *m*.

cardiologist [,kɑːdɪ'ɒlədʒɪst] *n* cardiologue *mf*.

cardiology [,kɑːdɪ'ɒlədʒɪ] *n* cardiologie *f*.

cardiovascular [ˌkɑːdɪəʊˈvæskjʊləʳ] *adj* cardiovasculaire.

cardphone [ˈkɑːdfəʊn] *n UK* téléphone *m* à carte.

cardplayer [ˈkɑːdˌpleɪəʳ] *n* joueur *m*, - euse *f* de cartes.

cardpunch [ˈkɑːdpʌntʃ] *n* perforatrice *f* de cartes.

cardsharp(er) [ˈkɑːdˌʃɑːp(əʳ)] *n* tricheur *m* (professionnel aux cartes), tricheuse *f* (professionnelle aux cartes).

card table *n* table *f* de jeu.

card trick *n* tour *m* de cartes.

card vote *n UK* vote *m* sur carte *(chaque voix représentant le nombre de voix d'adhérents représentés)*.

care [keəʳ] <> *vi* **1.** [feel concern] : **to ~ about sthg** s'intéresser à *OR* se soucier de qqch ▪ **they really do ~ about the project** le projet est vraiment important pour eux ▪ **a book for all those who ~ about the environment** un livre pour tous ceux qui s'intéressent à l'environnement *OR* qui se sentent concernés par les problèmes d'environnement ▪ **I don't ~ what people think** je me moque de ce que pensent les gens ▪ **I couldn't** *OR* **could** *US inf* **~ less if he comes or not** ça m'est complètement égal qu'il vienne ou non ▪ **what do I ~?** qu'est-ce que ça peut me faire? ▪ **we could be dead for all he ~s** pour lui, nous pourrions aussi bien être morts ▪ **who ~s?** qu'est-ce que ça peut bien faire?
2. [feel affection] : **to ~ about** *OR* **for sb** aimer qqn ▪ **she ~s a lot about her family** elle est très attachée *OR* elle tient beaucoup à sa famille
3. *fml* [like] : **would you ~ to join us?** voulez-vous vous joindre à nous? ▪ **I was more nervous than I ~d to admit** j'étais plus intimidé qu'il n'y paraissait.
<> *n* **1.** [worry] ennui *m*, souci *m* ▪ **you look as though you haven't a ~ in the world** on dirait que tu n'as pas le moindre souci
2. *(U)* [treatment - of person] soin *m*, soins *mpl*, traitement *m* ; [- of machine, material] entretien *m* ▪ **you should take ~ of that cough** vous devriez (faire) soigner cette toux
3. *(U)* [attention] attention *f*, soin *m* ▪ **'handle with ~'** [on package] 'fragile' ▪ **take ~ not to offend her** faites attention à *OR* prenez soin de ne pas la vexer ▪ **drive with ~** conduisez prudemment ▪ **he was charged with driving without due ~ and attention** il a été accusé de conduite négligente
4. [protection, supervision] charge *f*, garde *f* ▪ **I'm leaving the matter in your ~** je vous confie l'affaire, je confie l'affaire à vos soins ▪ **the children are in the ~ of a nanny** on a laissé *OR* confié les enfants à une nurse *OR* à la garde d'une nurse ▪ **who will take ~ of your cat?** qui va s'occuper *OR* prendre soin de ton chat? ▪ **I'll take ~ of the reservations** je me charge des réservations *OR* de faire les réservations, je vais m'occuper des réservations ▪ **I have important business to take ~ of** j'ai une affaire importante à expédier ▪ **take ~ (of yourself)** *expression affectueuse que l'on utilise lorsque l'on quitte quelqu'un* ▪ **I can take ~ of myself** je peux *OR* je sais me débrouiller (tout seul) ▪ **the problem will take ~ of itself** le problème va s'arranger tout seul ▪ **address the letter to me (in) ~ of Mrs Dodd** adressez-moi la lettre chez Mme Dodd
5. *UK* ADMIN : **the baby was put in ~** *OR* **taken into ~** on a retiré aux parents la garde de leur bébé.
◆ **care for** *vt insep* **1.** [look after - child] s'occuper de ; [- invalid] soigner
2. [like] aimer ▪ **he still ~s for her** [loves, affection] il l'aime toujours ▪ **she didn't ~ for the way he spoke** la façon dont il a parlé lui a déplu ▪ **would you ~ for a cup of coffee?** *fml* aimeriez-vous *OR* voudriez-vous une tasse de café?

CARE [keəʳ] (*abbrev of* **Cooperative for American Relief Everywhere**) *pr n organisation humanitaire américaine.*

care attendant *n UK* ADMIN infirmier *m*, - ère *f* à domicile.

career [kəˈrɪəʳ] <> *n* **1.** [profession] carrière *f*, profession *f* ▪ **she made a ~ (for herself) in politics** elle a fait carrière dans la politique **2.** [life] vie *f*, carrière *f* ▪ **he spent most of his ~ working as a journalist** il a travaillé presque toute sa vie comme journaliste ▪ **her university ~** son parcours universitaire.
<> *comp* [diplomat, soldier] de carrière ▪ **to be ~-minded** être ambitieux ▪ **good ~ prospects** de bonnes possibilités d'avancement.
<> *vi UK* **the car ~ed wildly down the hill** la voiture a descendu la colline à toute vitesse ▪ **to ~ along** aller à toute vitesse *OR* à toute allure.
◆ **careers** *comp* SCH & UNIV : **~s advisor** *OR* **adviser** *OR* **officer** conseiller *m*, - ère *f* d'orientation professionnelle ▪ **~s guidance** orientation *f* professionnelle ▪ **~s office** centre *m* d'orientation professionnelle.

careerist [kəˈrɪərɪst] *n pej* carriériste *mf*.

career woman *n femme qui attache de l'importance à sa carrière.*

carefree [ˈkeəfriː] *adj* [person] sans souci, insouciant ▪ [look, smile] insouciant.

careful [ˈkeəfʊl] *adj* **1.** [cautious] prudent ▪ **be ~!** (faites) attention! ▪ **be ~ of the wet floor!** attention au sol mouillé! ▪ **be ~ not to** *OR* **be ~ you don't hurt her feelings** faites attention à *OR* prenez soin de ne pas la froisser ▪ **be ~ (that) the boss doesn't find out** faites attention *OR* prenez garde que le patron n'en sache rien ▪ **you can't be too ~** [gen] on n'est jamais assez prudent ; [in double-checking sthg] deux précautions valent mieux qu'une ▪ **to be ~ with one's money** [gen] être parcimonieux ; *pej* être près de ses sous ▪ **we have to be ~ with money this month** il faut que nous surveillions nos dépenses ce mois-ci **2.** [thorough - person, work] soigneux, consciencieux ; [- consideration, examination] approfondi ▪ **they showed ~ attention to detail** ils se sont montrés très attentifs aux détails.

carefully [ˈkeəflɪ] *adv* **1.** [cautiously] avec prudence *OR* précaution, prudemment ▪ **she chose her words ~** elle a pesé ses mots **2.** [thoroughly - work] soigneusement, avec soin ; [- consider, examine] de façon approfondie, à fond ; [- listen, watch] attentivement.

careless [ˈkeəlɪs] *adj* **1.** [negligent - person] négligent, peu soigneux ; [- work] peu soigné ▪ **a ~ mistake** une faute d'inattention ▪ **to be ~ with money** dépenser à tort et à travers **2.** [thoughtless - remark] irréfléchi **3.** [carefree - person] sans souci, insouciant ; [- look, smile] insouciant.

carelessly [ˈkeəlɪslɪ] *adv* **1.** [negligently - work, write] sans soin, sans faire attention ▪ **to drive ~** conduire avec négligence **2.** [thoughtlessly - act, speak] sans réfléchir, à la légère ; [- dress] sans soin, sans recherche **3.** [in carefree way] avec insouciance.

carelessness [ˈkeəlɪsnɪs] *n (U)* **1.** [negligence] négligence *f*, manque *m* de soin *OR* d'attention **2.** [thoughtlessness - of dress] négligence *f* ; [- of behaviour] désinvolture *f* ; [- of remark] légèreté *f*.

carer [ˈkeərəʳ] *n terme administratif désignant toute personne qui s'occupe d'un malade ou d'un handicapé.*

caress [kəˈres] <> *vt* caresser.
<> *n* caresse *f*.

caret [ˈkærət] *n* TYPO signe *m* d'insertion.

caretaker [ˈkeəˌteɪkəʳ] <> *n* **1.** [of building] concierge *mf*, gardien *m*, - enne *f* **2.** *US* [carer] : **he's his grandmother's ~** il a sa grande-mère à charge.
<> *adj* [government] intérimaire.

careworn [ˈkeəwɔːn] *adj* accablé de soucis, rongé par les soucis.

carfare [ˈkɑːfeəʳ] *n US* prix *m* du trajet.

car ferry *n* ferry-boat *m*.

cargo [ˈkɑːgəʊ] <> *n* (*pl* **cargoes** *OR pl* **cargos**) cargaison *f*, chargement *m*.
<> *comp* : **~ boat** *OR* **vessel** cargo *m*.

car hire *UK*, **car rental** *US n* location *f* de voitures.

Carib [ˈkærɪb] *n* **1.** [person] Caraïbe *mf* **2.** LING caraïbe *m*.

Caribbean [*UK* kærɪˈbiːən, *US* kəˈrɪbɪən] <> *adj* des Caraïbes ▪ **the ~ islands** les Antilles *fpl*.
<> *n* : **the ~ (Sea)** la mer des Caraïbes *OR* des Antilles ▪ **in the ~** dans les Caraïbes, aux Antilles.

caribou [ˈkærɪbuː] (*pl inv OR pl* **caribous**) *n* caribou *m*.

caricature ['kærɪkəˌtjʊəʳ] ◇ *n liter & fig* caricature *f*.
◇ *vt* [depict] caricaturer ■ [parody] caricaturer, parodier.

caricaturist ['kærɪkəˌtjʊərɪst] *n* caricaturiste *mf*.

caring ['keərɪŋ] ◇ *adj* **1.** [loving] aimant ■ [kindly] bienveillant ■ **a more ~ society** une société plus chaleureuse *OR* humaine **2.** [organization] à vocation sociale ■ **the ~ professions** les métiers *mpl* du social.
◇ *n* [loving] affection *f* ■ [kindliness] bienveillance *f*.

carjack ['kɑːˌdʒæk] *vt* : **to be ~ed** se faire voler sa voiture sous la menace d'une arme.

carjacking ['kɑːˌdʒækɪŋ] *n* vol *m* de voiture sous la menace d'une arme.

carload ['kɑːˌləʊd] *n* : **a ~ of boxes/people** une voiture pleine de cartons/de gens.

Carmel ['kɑːməl] *pr n* : **Mount ~** le mont Carmel.

Carmelite ['kɑːmɪlaɪt] ◇ *adj* carmélite.
◇ *n* [nun] carmélite *f* ■ [friar] carme *m*.

carmine ['kɑːmaɪn] ◇ *adj* carmin *(inv)*, carminé.
◇ *n* carmin *m*.

Carnaby Street ['kɑːnəbɪ-] *pr n rue de Londres.*

CARNABY STREET

Carnaby Street était, dans les années 60, le haut lieu des milieux à la mode londoniens ; depuis, elle a été envahie par des boutiques de fripes.

carnage ['kɑːnɪdʒ] *n* carnage *m* ■ **the annual ~ on Britain's motorways.**

carnal ['kɑːnl] *adj* charnel ■ **to have ~ knowledge of sb** *fml* & LAW avoir des rapports sexuels avec qqn.

carnation [kɑː'neɪʃn] ◇ *n* œillet *m*.
◇ *adj* [pink] rose ■ [reddish-pink] incarnat.

Carnegie Hall [kɑː'negɪ-] *pr n grande salle de concert à New York.*

carnival ['kɑːnɪvl] ◇ *n* **1.** [festival] carnaval *m* **2.** [fun fair] fête *f* foraine.
◇ *comp* [atmosphere, parade] de carnaval.

carnivore ['kɑːnɪvɔːʳ] *n* carnivore *m*, carnassier *m*.

carnivorous [kɑː'nɪvərəs] *adj* carnivore, carnassier.

carob ['kærəb] ◇ *n* [tree] caroubier *m* ■ [pod] caroube *f*.
◇ *comp* : **~ bean** caroube *f* ■ **~ powder** farine *f* de caroube.

carol ['kærəl] ◇ *n* chant *m* (joyeux) ■ **~ service** *office religieux qui précède Noël* ■ **~ singer** *personne qui, à l'époque de Noël, va chanter et quêter au profit des bonnes œuvres* ■ **Christmas ~** chant de Noël, noël *m*.
◇ *vi* (*UK pret & pp* **carolled**, *cont* **carolling**) (*US pret & pp* **caroled**, *cont* **caroling**) [person] chanter (joyeusement) ■ [baby, bird] gazouiller.
◇ *vt* (*UK pret & pp* **carolled**, *cont* **carolling**) (*US pret & pp* **caroled**, *cont* **caroling**) **1.** [sing - subj: person] chanter (joyeusement) ; [- subj: bird] chanter **2.** [praise] célébrer (par des chants).

CAROL SERVICE

Ce service traditionnel a lieu juste avant Noël et se compose de chants de Noël et d'une lecture de passages de la Bible.

Carolina [ˌkærə'laɪnə] *pr n* Caroline *f*.

carousel [ˌkærə'sel] *n* **1.** PHOT [for slides] carrousel *m* **2.** [for luggage] carrousel *m*, tapis *m* roulant (à bagages) **3.** [merry-go-round] manège *m* (de chevaux de bois).

carp [kɑːp] (*pl inv OR pl* **carps**) ◇ *n* [fish] carpe *f*.
◇ *vi inf* [complain] se plaindre ■ [find fault] critiquer ■ **he's always ~ing on about his work** il se plaint toujours de son travail.

car park *n UK* parking *m*, parc *m* de stationnement ■ **long/short stay ~** parking *m* longue/courte durée.

Carpathian Mountains [kɑː'peɪθɪən-], **Carpathians** [kɑː'peɪθɪənz] *pr npl* : **the ~** les Carpates *fpl* ■ **in the ~** dans les Carpates.

carpel ['kɑːpel] *n* BOT carpelle *m*.

carpenter ['kɑːpəntəʳ] *n* [for houses, large-scale works] charpentier *m*, -ère *f* ■ [for doors, furniture] menuisier *m*.

carpentry ['kɑːpəntrɪ] *n* [large-scale work] charpenterie *f* ■ [doors, furniture] menuiserie *f*.

carpet ['kɑːpɪt] ◇ *n* **1.** [not fitted] tapis *m* ■ [fitted] moquette *f* ■ **to be on the ~** *fig* être sur le tapis **2.** *fig* [of leaves, snow] tapis *m*.
◇ *vt* **1.** [floor] recouvrir d'un tapis ■ [with fitted carpet] recouvrir d'une moquette, moquetter ■ [house, room] mettre de la moquette dans, moquetter ■ **~ed hallway** couloir moquetté *OR* avec de la moquette ■ **~ed with leaves/snow** *fig* tapissé de feuilles/de neige **2.** *UK inf* [scold] réprimander.

carpetbag ['kɑːpɪtˌbæg] *n* sac *m* de voyage *(recouvert de tapisserie)*.

carpetbagger ['kɑːpɪtˌbægəʳ] *n pej* **1.** POL candidat *m* parachuté **2.** *US* HIST *nom donné aux nordistes qui s'installèrent dans le sud des États-Unis après la guerre de Sécession pour y faire fortune.*

carpet-bomb *vt* bombarder, arroser de bombes.

carpeting ['kɑːpɪtɪŋ] *n* moquette *f*.

carpet slipper *n* pantoufle *f (recouverte de tapisserie)*.

carpet sweeper *n* [mechanical] balai *m* mécanique ■ [electric] aspirateur *m*.

carpet tile *n* carreau *m* de moquette.

carphone ['kɑːˌfəʊn] *n* téléphone *m* de voiture.

carping ['kɑːpɪŋ] ◇ *adj* [person - complaining] qui se plaint tout le temps ; [- faultfinding] qui trouve toujours à redire, chicanier ■ [attitude] chicanier, grincheux ■ [criticism, voice] malveillant.
◇ *n (U)* [complaining] plaintes *fpl* (continuelles) ■ [faultfinding] chicanerie *f*, critiques *fpl* (malveillantes).

car pool *n groupe de personnes qui s'organise pour utiliser la même voiture afin de se rendre à une destination commune.*

carport ['kɑːˌpɔːt] *n* auvent *m* (pour voiture).

car rental *n US* = **car hire**.

carriage ['kærɪdʒ] *n* **1.** [vehicle - horse-drawn] calèche *f*, voiture *f* à cheval ■ *UK* RAIL voiture *f*, wagon *m* (de voyageurs) **2.** *UK* COMM [cost of transportation] transport *m*, fret *m* ■ **~ forward** (en) port *m* dû ■ **~ paid** (en) port *m* payé ■ **~ free** franco de port **3.** [bearing, posture] port *m*, maintien *m* **4.** [of typewriter] chariot *m* ■ [of gun] affût *m*.

carriage clock *n UK* horloge *f* de voyage (d'ancienne facture).

carriage return *n* retour *m* chariot.

carriage trade *n UK* COMM clientèle *f* riche.

carriageway ['kærɪdʒweɪ] *n UK* chaussée *f*.

carrier ['kærɪəʳ] *n* **1.** [device, mechanism] : **luggage ~** porte-bagages *m inv* **2.** COMM [transporter - company] entreprise *f* de transport, transporteur *m*, société *f* aérienne ; [- aeroplane] appareil *m*, avion *m* ; [- ship] navire *m* ■ **sent by ~** [by road] expédié par camion *OR* par transporteur ; [by rail] expédié par chemin de fer ; [by air] expédié par avion **3.** MED [of disease] porteur *m*, - euse *f*.

carrier bag *n UK* sac *m* en plastique.

carrier pigeon *n* pigeon *m* voyageur.

carrion ['kærɪən] *n* charogne *f*.

carrot ['kærət] ◇ *n* **1.** [plant & vegetable] carotte *f* **2.** *fig* [motivation] carotte *f* ■ **the boss used the promise of promotion as a ~** le patron a promis une promotion pour nous encourager ■ **the ~ and stick approach** la méthode de la carotte et du bâton.

◇ *comp* : **~ coloured** (de couleur) carotte *(inv)* ▪ **~ cake** gâteau *m* aux carottes ▪ **~ juice** jus *m* de carotte.

carroty ['kærətɪ] *adj* roux, rousse *f*.

carrousel [,kærə'sel] *n* = **carousel**.

carry ['kærɪ] (*pret & pp* **carried**) ◇ *vt* **1.** [bear - subj: person] porter ▪ [- heavy load] porter, transporter ▪ **she carried her baby on her back/in her arms** elle portait son enfant sur son dos/dans ses bras ▪ **could you ~ the groceries into the kitchen?** pourrais-tu porter les provisions jusqu'à la cuisine? ▪ **the porter carried the suitcases downstairs/upstairs** le porteur a descendu/monté les bagages
2. [convey, transport - subj: vehicle] transporter ; [- subj: river, wind] porter, emporter ; [- subj: pipe] acheminer, amener ; [- subj: airwaves, telephone wire] transmettre, conduire ▪ **she ran as fast as her legs would ~ her** elle a couru à toutes jambes ▪ **she carries all the facts in her head** elle a tous les faits en mémoire ▶ **to ~ a tune** chanter juste ▪ **to ~ coals to Newcastle** porter de l'eau à la rivière
3. [be medium for - message, news] porter, transmettre ▪ MED [- disease, virus] porter
4. [have on one's person - identity card, papers] porter, avoir (sur soi) ; [- cash] avoir (sur soi) ; [- gun] porter
5. [comprise, include] porter, comporter ▪ **our products ~ a 6-month warranty** nos produits sont accompagnés d'une garantie de 6 mois ▮ [have as consequence] entraîner ▪ **the crime carries a long sentence** ce crime est passible d'une longue peine
6. [subj: magazine, newspaper] rapporter ▪ [subj: radio, television] transmettre ▪ **all the newspapers carried the story** l'histoire était dans tous les journaux
7. [bear, hold] porter ▪ **to ~ o.s. well** [sit, stand] se tenir droit ; [behave] bien se conduire *OR* se tenir
8. [hold up, support - roof, weight] porter, supporter, soutenir ▪ **to ~ a heavy load** *liter & fig* porter un lourd fardeau
9. [win] : **she carried the audience with her** le public était avec elle ▪ **the motion was carried** la motion a été votée ▶ **he carried all before him** ce fut un triomphe pour lui
10. COMM [deal in - stock] vendre, stocker
11. MATHS retenir
12. [be pregnant with] attendre ▪ **she's ~ing their fourth child** elle est enceinte de leur quatrième enfant.
◇ *vi* [ball, sound] porter.
◆ **carry away** *vt sep* **1.** [remove] emporter, enlever ▪ [subj: waves, wind] emporter
2. *(usu passive)* [excite] : **he was carried away by his enthusiasm/imagination** il s'est laissé emporter par son enthousiasme/imagination ▪ **I got a bit carried away and spent all my money** je me suis emballé et j'ai dépensé tout mon argent.
◆ **carry forward** *vt sep* FIN reporter.
◆ **carry off** *vt sep* **1.** [remove forcibly - goods] emporter, enlever ; [- person] enlever
2. [award, prize] remporter
3. [do successfully - aim, plan] réaliser ; [- deal, meeting] mener à bien ▪ **she carried it off beautifully** elle s'en est très bien tirée
4. *euph* [kill - subj: disease] emporter.
◆ **carry on** ◇ *vi insep* **1.** *UK* [continue] continuer ▪ **I carried on working** *OR* **with my work** j'ai continué à travailler, j'ai continué mon travail
2. *inf* [make a fuss] faire une histoire *OR* des histoires ▪ **the way you ~ on, you'd think I never did anything around the house** à t'entendre, je n'ai jamais rien fait dans cette maison
3. *inf* [have affair] : **to ~ on with sb** avoir une liaison avec qqn.
◇ *vt insep* **1.** *UK* [continue - conversation, work] continuer, poursuivre ; [- tradition] entretenir, perpétuer
2. [conduct - work] effectuer, réaliser ; [- negotiations] mener ; [- discussion] avoir ; [- correspondence] entretenir.
◆ **carry out** *vt sep* **1.** [take away] emporter
2. [perform - programme, raid] effectuer ; [- idea, plan] réaliser, mettre à exécution ; [- experiment] effectuer, conduire ; [- investigation, research, survey] conduire, mener ; [- instruction, order] exécuter
3. [fulfil - obligation] s'acquitter de ▪ **he failed to ~ out his promise** il a manqué à sa parole, il n'a pas tenu *OR* respecté sa promesse ▪ **to ~ out one's (professional) duties** s'acquitter de ses fonctions.
◆ **carry over** *vt sep* **1.** *liter* [transport] faire traverser ▪ *fig* [transfer] reporter, transférer
2. [defer, postpone] reporter
3. FIN reporter ▪ **to ~ over a loss to the following year** reporter une perte sur l'année suivante
4. COMM : **to ~ over goods from one season to another** stocker des marchandises d'une saison sur l'autre.
◆ **carry through** *vt sep* **1.** [accomplish] réaliser, mener à bien *OR* à bonne fin
2. [support] soutenir (dans une épreuve) ▪ **her love of life carried her through her illness** sa volonté de vivre lui a permis de vaincre sa maladie.

carryall ['kærɪɔ:l] *n US* fourre-tout *m inv (sac)*.

carrycot ['kærɪkɒt] *n UK* couffin *m*.

carrying case ['kærɪɪŋ-] *n US* boîte *f*, étui *m*.

carrying-on (*pl* **carryings-on**) *n inf* [fuss] histoires *fpl* ▪ [commotion] tapage *m*, agitation *f*.

carry-on ◇ *n UK inf* [fuss] histoires *fpl* ▪ [commotion] tapage *m*, agitation *f*.
◇ *adj* : **~ items, ~ luggage** bagages *mpl* à main.

carryout ['kærɪaʊt] *US & Scotland* ◇ *n* [restaurant] *restaurant qui fait des plats à emporter* ▪ [meal] plat *m* à emporter.
◇ *adj* [dish, food] à emporter.

carry-over *n* [habit, influence, trace] vestige *m*.

carsick ['kɑ:,sɪk] *adj* : **to be** *OR* **to feel ~** avoir le mal de la route.

car sickness *n* mal *m* de la route ▪ **to suffer from ~** être malade en voiture.

cart [kɑ:t] ◇ *n* **1.** [horse-drawn - for farming] charrette *f* ; [- for passengers] charrette *f* (anglaise), voiture *f* ▪ **to put the ~ before the horse** mettre la charrue avant les bœufs **2.** [handcart] charrette *f* à bras.
◇ *vt* **1.** [transport by cart] charrier, charroyer, transporter en charrette **2.** *inf fig* [haul] transporter, trimballer ▪ **I've been ~ing this suitcase around all day** j'ai passé la journée à trimballer cette valise.
◆ **cart away, cart off** *vt sep* [rubbish, wood] emporter ▪ *inf* [person] emmener.

carte blanche [,kɑ:t'blɑ̃ʃ] *n* carte *f* blanche ▪ **to give sb ~ (to do sthg)** donner carte blanche à qqn (pour faire qqch).

cartel [kɑ:'tel] *n* COMM & POL cartel *m*.

carter ['kɑ:tər] *n* charretier *m*, - ère *f*.

Cartesian [kɑ:'ti:zjən] ◇ *adj* cartésien.
◇ *n* cartésien *m*, - enne *f*.

carthorse ['kɑ:thɔ:s] *n* cheval *m* de trait.

Carthusian [kɑ:'θju:zjən] ◇ *adj* de *OR* des chartreux.
◇ *n* chartreux *m*, - euse *f*.

cartilage ['kɑ:tɪlɪdʒ] *n* cartilage *m*.

cartographer [kɑ:'tɒgrəfər] *n* cartographe *mf*.

cartography [kɑ:'tɒgrəfɪ] *n* cartographie *f*.

carton ['kɑ:tn] *n* [cardboard box] boîte *f* (en carton), carton *m* ▪ [of juice, milk] carton *m*, brique *f* ▪ [of cream, yoghurt] pot *m* ▪ [of cigarettes] cartouche *f*.

cartoon [kɑ:'tu:n] *n* **1.** [drawing] dessin *m* humoristique ▪ [series of drawings] bande *f* dessinée **2.** [film] dessin *m* animé **3.** ART [sketch] carton *m*.

cartoonist [kɑ:'tu:nɪst] *n* [of drawings] dessinateur *m*, - trice *f* humoristique ▪ [of series of drawings] dessinateur *m*, - trice *f* de bandes dessinées ▪ [for films] dessinateur *m*, - trice *f* de dessins animés, animateur *m*, - trice *f*.

cartridge ['kɑ:trɪdʒ] *n* **1.** [for explosive, gun] cartouche *f* **2.** [for pen, tape deck, typewriter etc] cartouche *f* **3.** [for stylus] cellule *f* **4.** PHOT chargeur *m* (d'appareil photo).

cartridge belt *n* [for hunter, soldier] cartouchière *f* ▪ [for machine gun] bande *f* (de mitrailleuse).

cartridge paper *n* papier *m* à cartouche.

cartridge pen *n* stylo *m* à cartouche.

cartwheel ['kɑ:twi:l] <> *n* **1.** [of cart] roue *f* de charrette **2.** [movement] roue *f* ▪ **to do** *OR* **to turn a ~** faire la roue.
<> *vi* faire la roue.

cartwright ['kɑ:traɪt] *n* charron *m*.

carve [kɑ:v] *vt* **1.** [stone, wood] tailler ▪ **he ~d the wood into the form of a horse, he ~d a horse from the** *OR* **out of the wood** il a sculpté *OR* taillé un cheval dans le bois ▪ **she ~d their names on the tree trunk** elle a gravé leurs noms sur le tronc de l'arbre **2.** CULIN découper.
◆ **carve out** *vt sep* [piece] découper, tailler ▪ [shape] sculpter, tailler ▪ **she ~d out a career for herself in the arts** *fig* elle a fait carrière.
◆ **carve up** *vt sep* **1.** [cut up - meat] découper ▪ *fig* [- country, estate] morceler, démembrer ▪ **they ~d up the profits among them** ils se sont partagé les profits **2.** *inf* [person] amocher à coups de couteau ▪ [face] balafrer, taillader **3.** *UK inf* AUT faire une queue de poisson à.

carver ['kɑ:vər] *n* couteau *m* à découper.

carvery ['kɑ:vərɪ] (*pl* **carveries**) *n restaurant où l'on mange de la viande découpée à table.*

carve-up *n inf* [of booty, inheritance] fractionnement *m* ▪ [of country, estate] morcellement *m*, démembrement *m*.

carving ['kɑ:vɪŋ] *n* **1.** [sculpture] sculpture *f* ▪ [engraving] gravure *f* **2.** [act] taille *f* ▪ [skill] taille *f*, art *m* de la taille **3.** CULIN découpage *m*.

carving knife *n* couteau *m* à découper.

car wash *n* [place] portique *m* de lavage automatique (de voitures) ▪ [action] lavage *m* de voitures.

Casanova [,kæsə'nəʊvə] <> *pr n* Casanova.
<> *n* : **he's a real ~** c'est un vrai Don Juan.

cascade [kæ'skeɪd] <> *n liter* cascade *f*, chute *f* d'eau ▪ *fig* [of hair] flot *m*.
<> *vi* [water] tomber en cascade ▪ [hair] ruisseler.

case [keɪs] <> *n*

A.

1. [container] caisse *f*, boîte *f* ▪ [for bottles] caisse *f* ▪ [for fruit, vegetables] cageot *m* ▪ [chest] coffre *m* ▪ [for jewellery] coffret *m* ▪ [for necklace, watch] écrin *m* ▪ [for camera, guitar] étui *m*
2. [for display] vitrine *f*
3. *UK* [suitcase] valise *f*
4. TYPO casse *f*

B.

1. [instance, situation] cas *m*, exemple *m* ▪ **it's a clear ~ of mismanagement** c'est un exemple manifeste de mauvaise gestion ▪ **it was a ~ of having to decide on the spur of the moment** il fallait décider sur-le-champ ▪ **in that ~** dans *OR* en ce cas ▪ **in this particular ~** en l'occurrence ▪ **in which ~** auquel cas ▪ **in your ~** en ce qui vous concerne, dans votre cas ▪ **in some ~s** dans certains cas ➔ **the current crisis is a ~ in point** la crise actuelle est un exemple typique *OR* un bon exemple
2. [actual state of affairs] cas *m* ▪ **can we assume that this is in fact the ~?** pouvons-nous considérer que c'est bien le cas? ▪ **as the ~** *OR* **whatever the ~ may be** selon le cas
3. [investigation] affaire *f* ▪ **the ~ is closed** c'est une affaire classée ➔ **he's on the ~** [working on it] il s'en occupe ; [alert, informed] il est très au courant ▪ **to be on sb's ~** *inf* être sur le dos de qqn
4. LAW affaire *f*, cause *f*, procès *m* ▪ **her ~ comes up next week** son procès a lieu la semaine prochaine ▪ **to try a ~** juger une affaire
5. [argument] arguments *mpl* ▪ **there is no ~ against him** aucune preuve n'a pu être retenue contre lui ▪ **the ~ against/for the defendant** les arguments contre/en faveur de l'accusé ▪ **there is a good ~ against/for establishing quotas** il y a beaucoup à dire contre/en faveur de l'établissement de quotas ▪ **to make (out) a ~ for sthg** présenter des arguments pour *OR* en faveur de qqch
6. MED [disease] cas *m* ▪ [person] malade *mf* ▪ **there have been several ~s of meningitis recently** il y a eu plusieurs cas de méningite récemment
7. *inf* [person] cas *m* ▪ **he's a sad ~** c'est vraiment un pauvre type
8. GRAM cas *m*.
<> *vt* **1.** [put in box] mettre en boîte *OR* caisse **2.** [cover] couvrir, envelopper ▪ **~d in ice** couvert de glace **3.** *inf* [inspect] examiner ▪ **the robbers had thoroughly ~d the joint** les voleurs avaient bien examiné les lieux (avant de faire leur coup).
◆ **in any case** *adv phr* **1.** [besides] en tout cas ▪ **in any ~ I shan't be coming** je ne viendrai pas en tout cas *OR* de toute façon **2.** [at least] du moins, en tout cas ▪ **that's what I was told, or in any ~ was led to believe** c'est ce qu'on m'a dit ou en tout cas *OR* ou du moins, ce qu'on m'a fait croire.
◆ **in case** <> *adv phr* au cas où ▪ **I'll take my umbrella (just) in ~** je vais prendre mon parapluie au cas où.
<> *conj phr* au cas où ▪ **I kept a place for you, in ~ you were late** je t'ai gardé une place, au cas où tu serais en retard.
◆ **in case of** *prep phr* en cas de ▪ **in ~ of emergency/fire** en cas d'urgence/d'incendie.

casefile ['keɪsfaɪl] *n* dossier *m*.

case grammar *n* grammaire *f* des cas.

case-hardened *adj* METALL cémenté ▪ *fig* endurci.

case history *n* antécédents *mpl*.

case law *n* jurisprudence *f*.

case load *n* (nombre *m* de) dossiers *mpl* à traiter.

casement ['keɪsmənt] <> *n* [window] fenêtre *f* à battant *OR* battants, croisée *f* ▪ [window frame] châssis *m* de fenêtre (à deux battants) ▪ *lit* fenêtre *f*.
<> *comp* : **~ window** fenêtre *f* à battant *OR* battants, croisée *f*.

case study *n* étude *f* de cas.

casework ['keɪswɜ:k] *n travail social personnalisé.*

caseworker ['keɪs,wɜ:kər] *n travailleur social s'occupant de cas individuels et familiaux.*

cash [kæʃ] <> *n* **1.** [coins and banknotes] espèces *fpl*, (argent *m*) liquide *m* ▪ **to pay (in) ~** payer en liquide *OR* en espèces ▪ **hard** *OR* **ready ~** liquide *m* ➔ **to pay ~ on the nail** payer rubis sur ongle **2.** [money in general] argent *m* ▪ **to be short of ~** être à court (d'argent) **3.** [immediate payment] : **discount for ~** escompte *m* de caisse ▪ **to pay ~ (down)** payer comptant ➔ **~ on delivery** paiement *m* à la livraison, (livraison *f*) contre remboursement ▪ **~ with order** payable à la commande ▪ **~ on shipment** comptant *m* à l'expédition.
<> *comp* **1.** [problems, worries] d'argent **2.** [price, purchase, sale, transaction] (au) comptant ▪ **~ bar** *US* bar *m* payant *(à une réception)* ▪ **she made us a ~ offer for the flat** elle nous a proposé de payer l'appartement (au) comptant ▪ **~ payment** [immediate] paiement *m* comptant ; [in cash] paiement *m* en espèces *OR* en liquide ▪ **~ prize** prix *m* en espèces ▪ **~ sale** vente *f* au comptant.
<> *vt* [cheque] encaisser, toucher ▪ **could you ~ this cheque for me?** [friend] peux-tu me donner de l'argent contre ce chèque? ; [bank] voudriez-vous m'encaisser ce chèque?
◆ **cash in** <> *vt sep* [bond, certificate] réaliser, se faire rembourser ▪ [coupon] se faire rembourser.
<> *vi insep inf* [take advantage] : **to ~ in on a situation** profiter *OR* tirer profit d'une situation.
◆ **cash up** *vi insep UK* COMM faire ses comptes.

cash and carry *n UK* libre-service *m* de gros, cash and carry *m inv*.
◆ **cash-and-carry** *UK adj* de libre-service de gros, de cash and carry.

cashback ['kæʃbæk] *n (U)* COMM reprise *f*, argent *m* liquide *(remis à la caisse d'un magasin et débité avec les achats).*

cashbook ['kæʃbʊk] *n* livre *m* de caisse.

cashbox ['kæʃbɒks] *n* caisse *f*.

cash card *n* carte *f* de retrait.

cash cow *n* vache *f* à lait.

cash crop *n* culture *f* de rapport *OR* commerciale.

cash desk *n* caisse *f*.

cash discount *n* escompte *m* de caisse.

cash dispenser *n* distributeur *m* automatique (de billets), DAB *m*.

cashew ['kæʃuː] *n* [tree] anacardier *m* ■ ~ **(nut)** (noix *f* de) cajou *m*.

cash flow *n* marge *f* brute d'autofinancement, cash-flow *m* ■ ~ **problems** ***liter*** & ***hum*** problèmes *mpl* de trésorerie.

cashier [kæ'ʃɪəʳ] ◇ *n* BANK & COMM caissier *m*, - ère *f*.
◇ *vt* MIL casser ■ ***fig*** renvoyer, congédier.

cashless ['kæʃlɪs] *adj* sans argent.

cash machine *n* distributeur *m* de billets.

cashmere [kæʃ'mɪəʳ] ◇ *n* cachemire *m*.
◇ *comp* [coat, sweater] de *OR* en cachemire.

cashpoint ['kæʃpɔɪnt] *n* ***UK*** distributeur *m* automatique (de billets), DAB *m*.

cash price *n* prix *m* comptant.

cash register *n* caisse *f* (enregistreuse).

casing ['keɪsɪŋ] *n* **1.** [gen] revêtement *m*, enveloppe *f* ■ [for tyre] enveloppe *f* extérieure **2.** [of window] chambranle *m*, châssis *m* ■ [of door] encadrement *m*, chambranle *m*.

casino [kə'siːnəʊ] (*pl* **casinos**) *n* casino *m*.

cask [kɑːsk] *n* [barrel - gen] tonneau *m*, fût *m* ; [- large] barrique *f* ; [- small] baril *m*.

casket ['kɑːskɪt] *n* **1.** [small box] coffret *m*, boîte *f* **2.** ***US*** [coffin] cercueil *m*.

Caspian Sea ['kæspɪən-] *pr n* : **the ~** la (mer) Caspienne.

Cassandra [kə'sændrə] *pr n* MYTH & ***fig*** Cassandre.

casserole ['kæsərəʊl] ◇ *n* **1.** [pan] cocotte *f* **2.** [stew] ragoût *m*.
◇ *vt* (faire) cuire en ragoût.

cassette [kæ'set] *n* **1.** [tape] cassette *f* **2.** PHOT [cartridge] chargeur *m*.

cassette deck *n* lecteur *m* de cassettes.

cassette player *n* lecteur *m* de cassettes.

cassette recorder *n* magnétophone *m* à cassettes.

cassock ['kæsək] *n* soutane *f*.

cast [kɑːst] ◇ *vt* (*pret & pp* **cast**) **1.** [throw] jeter, lancer ■ **to ~ lots *UK*** tirer au sort ■ **to ~ a spell on *OR* over sb** [subj: witch] jeter un sort à qqn, ensorceler qqn ; ***fig*** ensorceler *OR* envoûter qqn ■ **to ~ one's vote for sb** voter pour qqn ■ **the number of votes ~** le nombre de voix *OR* de suffrages ■ **we'll have to ~ our net wide to find the right candidate *fig*** il va falloir ratisser large pour trouver le bon candidat
2. [direct - light, shadow] projeter ; [- look] jeter, diriger ■ **the accident ~ a shadow over their lives** l'accident a jeté une ombre sur leur existence ■ **could you ~ an eye over this report?** voulez-vous jeter un œil sur ce rapport? ■ **he ~ an eye over the audience** il a promené son regard sur l'auditoire ■ **the evidence ~ suspicion on him** les preuves ont jeté la suspicion sur lui
3. [shed, throw off] perdre ■ **~ all fear/thought of revenge from your mind** oubliez toute crainte/toute idée de revanche
4. [film, play] distribuer les rôles de ■ [performer] : **the director ~ her in the role of the mother** le metteur en scène lui a attribué le rôle de la mère
5. ART & TECH [form, statue] mouler ■ [metal] couler, fondre ■ [plaster] couler ■ **they are all ~ in the same mould *fig*** ils sont tous faits sur *OR* sont tous coulés dans le même moule
6. [horoscope] tirer.
◇ *n* **1.** CIN & THEAT [actors] distribution *f*, acteurs *mpl* ■ **~ list** CIN & TV générique *m* ; THEAT distribution *f*
2. ART [colour, shade] nuance *f*, teinte *f*
3. ART & TECH [act of moulding - metal] coulage *m*, coulée *f* ; [- plaster] moulage *m* ; [- coin, medallion] empreinte *f* ■ [mould] moule *m* ■ [object moulded] moulage *m* ■ **to make a bronze ~ of a statue** mouler une statue en bronze
4. MED [for broken limb] plâtre *m* ■ **her arm was in a ~** elle avait un bras dans le plâtre
5. MED [squint] strabisme *m* ■ **he had a ~ in his eye** il louchait d'un œil, il avait un œil qui louchait
6. ***fml*** [type] : **the delicate ~ of her features** la finesse de ses traits ■ **a peculiar ~ of mind** une drôle de mentalité *OR* de tournure d'esprit.
◆ **cast about** *vi insep* ***UK*** : **she ~ about for an idea/an excuse to leave** elle essaya de trouver une idée/un prétexte pour partir.
◆ **cast aside** *vt sep* ***lit*** [book] mettre de côté ■ [shirt, shoes] se débarrasser de ■ ***fig*** [person, suggestion] rejeter, écarter.
◆ **cast away** *vt sep* **1.** [book, letter] jeter ■ ***fig*** [cares, principle] se défaire de
2. NAUT : **to be ~ away** être naufragé.
◆ **cast back** *vt sep* : **~ your mind back to the day we met** souviens-toi du *OR* rappelle-toi le jour de notre première rencontre.
◆ **cast down** *vt sep* **1.** ***fml*** [weapon] déposer, mettre bas **2.** ***fig*** & ***lit*** **to be ~ down** être démoralisé *OR* découragé.
◆ **cast off** ◇ *vt sep* **1.** [undo] défaire ■ [untie] délier, dénouer ■ [in knitting] rabattre ■ NAUT [lines, rope] larguer, lâcher ■ [boat] larguer *OR* lâcher les amarres de
2. ***lit*** [rid oneself of - clothing] enlever, se débarrasser de ■ ***fig*** [- bonds] se défaire de, se libérer de ; [- cares, habit, tradition] se défaire de, abandonner.
◇ *vi insep* **1.** NAUT larguer les amarres, appareiller
2. [in knitting] rabattre les mailles.
◆ **cast on** ◇ *vi insep* monter les mailles.
◇ *vt sep* [stitches] monter.
◆ **cast out** *vt sep* ***arch*** & ***lit*** [person] renvoyer, chasser ■ ***fig*** [fear, guilt] bannir.
◆ **cast up** *vt sep* [subj: sea, tide, waves] rejeter.

castanets [,kæstə'nets] *npl* castagnettes *fpl*.

castaway ['kɑːstəweɪ] NAUT ◇ *n* naufragé *m*, - e *f* ■ ***fig*** naufragé *m*, - e *f*, laissé-pour-compte *m*, laissée-pour-compte *f*.
◇ *adj* naufragé.

caste [kɑːst] *n* [gen] caste *f*, classe *f* sociale ■ [in Hindu society] caste *f*.

caster ['kɑːstəʳ] *n* **1.** [sifter] saupoudroir *m*, saupoudreuse *f* **2.** [wheel] roulette *f*.

caster sugar *n* ***UK*** sucre *m* en poudre.

castigate ['kæstɪgeɪt] *vt* ***fml*** **1.** [punish] corriger, punir ■ [scold] réprimander, tancer ***fml*** **2.** [criticize - person] critiquer sévèrement, fustiger ***fml*** ; [- book, play] éreinter.

castigation [,kæstɪ'geɪʃn] *n* ***fml*** [punishment] correction *f*, punition *f* ■ [scolding] réprimande *f* ■ [criticism] critique *f* sévère.

Castile [kæ'stiːl] *pr n* Castille *f*.

Castilian [kæ'stɪljən] ◇ *n* **1.** [person] Castillan *m*, - e *f* **2.** LING castillan *m*.
◇ *adj* castillan.

casting ['kɑːstɪŋ] *n* **1.** ART [act & object] moulage *m* ■ TECH [act] coulée *f*, coulage *m*, fonte *f* ■ [object] pièce *f* fondue **2.** CIN & THEAT [selection of actors] attribution *f* des rôles, casting *m*.

casting couch *n* ***inf*** **she denied having got the part on the ~** elle a nié avoir couché avec le metteur en scène pour obtenir le rôle.

casting vote *n* voix *f* prépondérante ■ **the president has a *OR* the ~** le président a voix prépondérante.

cast iron *n* fonte *f*.
◆ **cast-iron** *comp* **1.** [pot, stove] de *OR* en fonte **2.** ***fig*** [alibi] inattaquable, en béton.

castle ['kɑːsl] ◇ *n* **1.** [building] château *m* (fort) ■ **to build ~s in the air** bâtir des châteaux en Espagne ■ **'The Castle' *Kafka*** 'le Château' **2.** [in chess] tour *f*.

◇ *vi* [in chess] roquer.

castling [ˈkɑːslɪŋ] *n* [in chess] roque *m*.

castoff [ˈkɑːstɒf] *n (usu pl)* [piece of clothing] vieux vêtement *m* ▪ *fig* [person] laissé-pour-compte *m*, laissée-pour-compte *f*.
◆ **cast-off** *adj* dont personne ne veut ▪ **cast-off clothes** vieux vêtements *mpl*.

castor [ˈkɑːstəʳ] *n* = **caster**.

castor oil *n* huile *f* de ricin.

castrate [kæˈstreɪt] *vt liter* châtrer, castrer ▪ *fig* [weaken - person, political movement] émasculer.

castration [kæˈstreɪʃn] *n liter* castration *f* ▪ *fig* [of political movement] émasculation *f*.

castrato [kæˈstrɑːtəʊ] (*pl* **castratos** *OR pl* **castrati** [-tiː]) *n* castrat *m*.

cast steel *n* acier *m* moulé.

casual [ˈkæʒʊəl] ◇ *adj* **1.** [unconcerned] désinvolte, nonchalant ▪ [natural] simple, naturel ▪ **they're very ~ about the way they dress** ils attachent très peu d'importance à leurs vêtements *OR* à la façon dont ils s'habillent ▪ **I tried to appear ~ when talking about it** j'ai essayé d'en parler avec désinvolture **2.** [informal - dinner] simple, détendu ; [- clothing] sport *(inv)* **3.** [superficial] superficiel ▪ **I took a ~ glance at the paper** j'ai jeté un coup d'œil (rapide) au journal ▪ **to make ~ conversation** parler de choses et d'autres, parler à bâtons rompus ▪ **it was just a ~ suggestion** c'était seulement une suggestion en passant ▪ **she's just a ~ acquaintance of mine** c'est quelqu'un que je connais très peu ▪ **a ~ love affair** une aventure ▪ **~ sex** rapports *mpl* sexuels de rencontre **4.** [happening by chance - meeting] de hasard ; [- onlooker] venu par hasard **5.** [occasional - job] intermittent ; [- worker] temporaire ▪ **~ labourer** *UK* [for one day] journalier *m*, - ère *f* ; [for harvest, season] (travailleur *m*) saisonnier *m*, (travailleuse *f*) saisonnière *f* ; [in construction work] ouvrier *m*, - ère *f* temporaire.
◇ *n* [farmworker - for one day] journalier *m*, - ère *f* ; [- for harvest, season] (travailleur *m*) saisonnier *m*, (travailleuse *f*) saisonnière *f* ; [- in construction work] ouvrier *m*, - ère *f* temporaire.
◆ **casuals** *npl* [clothing] vêtements *mpl* sport ▪ [shoes] chaussures *fpl* sport.

casually [ˈkæʒʊəlɪ] *adv* **1.** [unconcernedly] avec désinvolture, nonchalamment **2.** [informally] simplement ▪ **to dress ~** s'habiller sport **3.** [glance, remark, suggest] en passant **4.** [by chance] par hasard.

casualty [ˈkæʒjʊəltɪ] (*pl* **casualties**) *n* **1.** [wounded] blessé *m*, - e *f* ▪ [dead] mort *m*, - e *f* ▪ **there were heavy casualties** [gen] il y avait beaucoup de victimes *OR* de morts et de blessés ; [dead] il y avait beaucoup de pertes ▪ **truth is often a ~ in political debates** *fig* la vérité est souvent sacrifiée dans les débats politiques **2.** *(U)* = **casualty department**.

casualty department *n* MED [emergency ward] service *m* des urgences ▪ [accident ward] salle *f* des accidentés.

casualty list *n* [gen] liste *f* des victimes ▪ MIL état *m* des pertes.

casualty ward *n* [for emergencies] service *m* des urgences ▪ [for accident victims] salle *f* des accidentés.

casuistry [ˈkæzjʊɪstrɪ] *n* [philosophy] casuistique *f* ▪ *(U)* [reasoning] arguments *mpl* de casuiste.

cat [kæt] *n* **1.** ZOOL chat *m*, chatte *f* ▪ **to let the ~ out of the bag** vendre la mèche ▪ **to be like a ~ on hot bricks** *UK OR* **on a hot tin roof** être sur des charbons ardents ▪ **there isn't enough room to swing a ~** il n'y a pas la place de se retourner ▪ **he looked like something the ~ brought in** il était dégoûtant ▪ **has the ~ got your tongue?** tu as perdu ta langue? ▪ **to fight like ~ and dog** se battre comme des chiffonniers ▪ **to put** *OR* **to set the ~ among the pigeons** *UK* jeter un pavé dans la mare ▪ **to play (a game of) ~ and mouse with sb** jouer au chat et à la souris avec qqn ▪ **when the ~'s away the mice will play** *prov* quand le chat n'est pas là les souris dansent *prov* ▪ **'Cat on a Hot Tin Roof'** *Williams, Brooks* 'la Chatte sur un toit brûlant' **2.** *pej* [woman] rosse *f*, chipie *f* **3.** *inf US dated* [man] mec *m* **4.** *inf* [boat] catamaran *m* **5.** *inf* AUT pot *m* catalytique.

CAT *n* **1.** *UK* (*abbrev of* **computer-aided teaching**) EAO *m* **2.** [kæt] (*abbrev of* **computerized axial tomography**) CAT *f* ▪ **~ scan** scanographie *f*.

cataclysm [ˈkætəklɪzm] *n* cataclysme *m*.

cataclysmic [ˌkætəˈklɪzmɪk] *adj* cataclysmique.

catacomb [ˈkætəkuːm] *n (usu pl)* catacombe *f*.

catafalque [ˈkætəfælk] *n* catafalque *m*.

Catalan [ˈkætəˌlæn] ◇ *n* **1.** [person] catalan *m*, - e *f* **2.** LING catalan *m*.
◇ *adj* catalan.

catalepsy [ˈkætəlepsɪ] *n* catalepsie *f*.

catalogue *UK*, **catalog** *US* [ˈkætəlɒg] ◇ *n* catalogue *m* ▪ [in library] fichier *m* ▪ *US* UNIV guide *m* de l'étudiant ▪ **his life story was a ~ of disasters** *fig* l'histoire de sa vie a été un catalogue de malheurs.
◇ *vt* cataloguer, faire le catalogue de.

Catalonia [ˌkætəˈləʊnɪə] *pr n* Catalogne *f* ▪ **in ~** en Catalogne.

Catalonian [ˌkætəˈləʊnʃən] ◇ *adj* catalan.
◇ *n* [person] catalan *m*, - e *f*.

catalyse *UK*, **catalyze** *US* [ˈkætəlaɪz] *vt* catalyser.

catalyst [ˈkætəlɪst] *n* catalyseur *m*.

catalytic [ˌkætəˈlɪtɪk] *adj* catalytique.

catalytic converter *n* pot *m* catalytique.

catalyze [ˈkætəlaɪz] *US vt* = **catalyse**.

catamaran [ˌkætəməˈræn] *n* catamaran *m*.

cataphora [kəˈtæfrə] *n* cataphore *f*.

catapult [ˈkætəpʌlt] ◇ *n* **1.** *UK* [child's] lance-pierres *m inv* **2.** AERON & MIL catapulte *f* ▪ **~ launching** catapultage *m*.
◇ *vt* [gen - AERON] catapulter ▪ **she was ~ed into the leadership job** *fig* elle a été catapultée à la direction.

cataract [ˈkætərækt] *n* **1.** [waterfall] cataracte *f*, cascade *f* **2.** [downpour] déluge *m* **3.** MED cataracte *f*.

catarrh [kəˈtɑːʳ] *n* catarrhe *m* ▪ **to have bad ~** *UK* être très catarrheux.

catastrophe [kəˈtæstrəfɪ] *n* catastrophe *f*.

catastrophic [ˌkætəˈstrɒfɪk] *adj* catastrophique.

catatonic [ˌkætəˈtɒnɪk] *adj* catatonique.

cat burglar *n* monte-en-l'air *m inv*.

catcall [ˈkætkɔːl] ◇ *n* THEAT sifflet *m*.
◇ *vi* siffler.

catch [kætʃ] ◇ *vt* (*pret & pp* **caught** [kɔːt]) **1.** [ball, thrown object] attraper ▪ **to ~ hold of sthg** attraper qqch ▪ [take hold of] : **to ~ sb's arm** saisir *OR* prendre qqn par le bras
2. [trap - fish, mouse, thief] attraper, prendre ▪ **he got caught by the police** il s'est fait attraper par la police ▪ **to get caught in a traffic jam** être pris dans un embouteillage ▪ **we got caught in a shower/thunderstorm** nous avons été surpris par une averse/l'orage ▪ **to ~ sb doing sthg** surprendre qqn à faire qqch ▪ **you won't ~ me doing the washing-up!** aucun danger de me surprendre en train de faire la vaisselle! ▪ **don't let me ~ you at it again!** que je ne t'y reprenne pas! ➔ **you'll ~ it when you get home!** *UK inf* qu'est-ce que tu vas prendre en rentrant! ▪ **to ~ sb napping** prendre qqn en défaut
3. [disease, infection] attraper ▪ **to ~ a cold** attraper un rhume ▪ **to ~ cold** attraper *OR* prendre froid ▪ **he'll ~ his death (of cold)!** *inf* il va attraper la crève!
4. [bus, train] attraper, prendre ▪ [person] attraper ▪ **to ~ the last post** *UK* arriver à temps pour la dernière levée (du courrier) ▪ **I just caught the end of the film** j'ai juste vu la fin du film
5. [on nail, obstacle] : **he caught his finger in the door** il s'est pris le doigt dans la porte ▪ **she caught her skirt in the door** sa jupe s'est prise dans la porte ▪ **he caught his coat on the brambles** son manteau s'est accroché aux ronces

6. [hear clearly, understand] saisir, comprendre ▪ **I didn't quite ~ what you said** je n'ai pas bien entendu ce que vous avez dit
7. [attract] : **to ~ sb's attention** *OR* **sb's eye** attirer l'attention de qqn ▪ **the idea caught her imagination** l'idée a enflammé son imagination
8. [in portrait, writing - likeness, mood] saisir
9. [hit] : **to ~ sb a blow** *UK* donner *OR* flanquer un coup à qqn ▪ **the wave caught her sideways** la vague l'a frappée de côté ▪ **he fell and caught his head on the radiator** il est tombé et s'est cogné la tête contre le radiateur
10. [notice] remarquer ▪ **did you ~ the look on his face?** vous avez remarqué l'expression de son visage?
11. *phr* **to ~ one's breath** reprendre son souffle.
◇ *vi* (*pret & pp* **caught** [kɔ:t]) **1.** [ignite - fire, wood] prendre ; [- engine] démarrer
2. [bolt, lock] fermer ▪ [gears] mordre
3. [on obstacle] : **her skirt caught on a nail** sa jupe s'est accrochée à un clou ▪ **his coat caught in the door** son manteau s'est pris dans la porte.
◇ *n* **1.** [act] prise *f* ▪ **good ~!** SPORT bien rattrapé!
2. [of fish] prise *f* ▪ **he's a good ~** *hum & fig* [man] c'est une belle prise
3. [snag] piège *m* ▪ **where's** *OR* **what's the ~?** qu'est-ce que ça cache?, où est le piège?
4. [on lock, door] loquet *m* ▪ [on window] loqueteau *m* ▪ [on shoebuckle] ardillon *m*
5. [in voice] : **with a ~ in his voice** d'une voix entrecoupée
6. GAMES jeu *m* de balle ▪ **to play ~** jouer à la balle
7. MUS canon *m*.
◆ **catch at** *vt insep* (essayer d')attraper.
◆ **catch on** *vi insep* **1.** [fashion, trend, slogan] devenir populaire ▪ **this dance style caught on in the fifties** cette danse a fait un tabac *OR* était très populaire dans les années cinquante
2. *inf* [understand] piger, saisir, comprendre.
◆ **catch out** *vt sep UK* [by trickery] prendre en défaut ▪ [in the act] prendre sur le fait ▪ **I won't be caught out like that again!** on ne m'y prendra plus!
◆ **catch up** ◇ *vi insep* **1.** [as verb of movement] : **to ~ up with sb** rattraper qqn ▪ **his past will ~ up with him one day** *fig* il finira par être rattrapé par son passé
2. [on lost time] combler *OR* rattraper son retard ▪ [on studies] rattraper son retard, se remettre au niveau ▪ **to ~ up on** *OR* **with one's work** rattraper le retard qu'on a pris dans son travail ▪ **I need to ~ up on some sleep** j'ai du sommeil à rattraper ▪ **we had a lot of news to ~ up on** nous avions beaucoup de choses à nous dire.
◇ *vt sep* **1.** [entangle] : **the material got caught up in the machinery** le tissu s'est pris dans la machine
2. [absorb, involve] : **to get caught up in a wave of enthusiasm** être gagné par une vague d'enthousiasme ▪ **he was too caught up in the film to notice what was happening** il était trop absorbé par le film pour remarquer ce qui se passait ▪ **I refuse to get caught up in their private quarrel** je refuse de me laisser entraîner dans leurs querelles personnelles
3. [seize] ramasser vivement, s'emparer de
4. [person] rattraper.

catch-22 [-twentɪ'tu:] *n* : **~ situation** situation *f* sans issue, cercle *m* vicieux.

catch-all ◇ *n* fourre-tout *m inv*.
◇ *adj* fourre-tout (*inv*), qui pare à toute éventualité ▪ **~ phrase** expression *f* passe-partout.

catcher ['kætʃər] *n* [gen & in baseball] attrapeur *m*.

catching ['kætʃɪŋ] *adj* **1.** MED contagieux **2.** *fig* [enthusiasm] contagieux, communicatif ▪ [habit] contagieux.

catchment ['kætʃmənt] *n* captage *m*.

catchment area *n* **1.** [drainage area] bassin *m* hydrographique **2.** ADMIN [for hospital] *circonscription hospitalière* ▪ [for school] secteur *m* de recrutement scolaire.

catchment basin *n* = **catchment area**.

catchphrase ['kætʃfreɪz] *n* [in advertising] accroche *f* ▪ [set phrase] formule *f* toute faite ▪ [of performer] petite phrase *f*.

catch question *n* question-piège *f*, colle *f*.

catchword ['kætʃwɜ:d] *n* **1.** [slogan] slogan *m* ▪ POL mot *m* d'ordre, slogan *m* **2.** [in printing - at top of page] mot-vedette *m* ; [- at foot of page] réclame *f* **3.** THEAT réclame *f*.

catchy ['kætʃɪ] (*comp* **catchier**, *superl* **catchiest**) *adj* [tune] qui trotte dans la tête, facile à retenir ▪ [title] facile à retenir.

catechism ['kætəkɪzm] *n* catéchisme *m*.

categorical [,kætɪ'gɒrɪkl] *adj* catégorique.

categorically [,kætɪ'gɒrɪklɪ] *adv* catégoriquement.

categorization [,kætəgəraɪ'zeɪʃn] *n* catégorisation *f*.

categorize, *UK* **ise** ['kætəgəraɪz] *vt* catégoriser.

category ['kætəgərɪ] (*pl* **categories**) *n* catégorie *f*.

cater ['keɪtər] ◇ *vi* s'occuper de la nourriture, fournir des repas.
◇ *vt US* s'occuper de la nourriture pour.
◆ **cater for** *vt insep* **1.** [with food] s'occuper de la nourriture pour ▪ **'coach parties ~ed for'** 'accueil de groupes' **2.** *fig* [needs] répondre à, pourvoir à ▪ [tastes] satisfaire.
◆ **cater to** *vt insep* **1.** [needs, demands] satisfaire, répondre à **2.** *US* = **cater for**.

caterer ['keɪtərər] *n* traiteur *m*.

catering ['keɪtərɪŋ] ◇ *n* restauration *f* ▪ **who did the ~ for the wedding?** qui a fourni le repas pour le mariage?
◇ *comp* [industry] de la restauration ▪ [college] hôtelier ▪ **~ manager** chef *m* *OR* responsable *m* de la restauration.

caterpillar ['kætəpɪlər] *n* ZOOL & TECH chenille *f*.

caterpillar track *n* TECH chenille *f*.

caterwaul ['kætəwɔ:l] ◇ *vi* [cat] miauler ▪ [person] brailler.
◇ *n* [of cat] miaulement *m* ▪ [of person] braillement *m*.

caterwauling ['kætəwɔ:lɪŋ] *n (U)* [of cat] miaulements *mpl* ▪ [of person] braillements *mpl*.

catfish ['kætfɪʃ] (*pl inv OR pl* **catfishes**) *n* poisson-chat *m*.

cat flap *n* chatière *f*.

cat food *n (U)* nourriture *f* pour chats.

catgut ['kætgʌt] *n* [for musical instrument, racket] boyau *m* (de chat) ▪ MED catgut *m*.

catharsis [kə'θɑ:sɪs] (*pl* **catharses** [-si:z]) *n* catharsis *f*.

cathartic [kə'θɑ:tɪk] ◇ *adj* cathartique.
◇ *n* MED purgatif *m*, cathartique *m*.

cathedral [kə'θi:drəl] *n* cathédrale *f*.

cathedral city *n* évêché *m*, ville *f* épiscopale.

Catherine ['kæθrɪn] *pr n* : **Saint ~'s Day** la Sainte-Catherine ▪ **~ the Great** Catherine la Grande ▪ **~ of Aragon** Catherine d'Aragon.

catherine wheel *n* [firework] soleil *m*.

catheter ['kæθɪtər] *n* cathéter *m*, sonde *f* creuse.

cathode ['kæθəud] *n* cathode *f*.

cathode rays *n* rayons *mpl* cathodiques.

cathode ray tube *n* tube *m* cathodique.

catholic ['kæθlɪk] *adj* **1.** [broad - tastes] éclectique **2.** [liberal - views] libéral **3.** [universal] universel.
◆ **Catholic** ◇ *adj* RELIG catholique ▪ **the Catholic Church** l'Église *f* catholique.
◇ *n* catholique *mf*.

Catholicism [kə'θɒlɪsɪzm] *n* catholicisme *m*.

catkin ['kætkɪn] *n* BOT chaton *m*.

cat lick *n inf* toilette *f* de chat, brin *m* de toilette.

catlike ['kætlaɪk] *adj* félin.

cat litter *n* litière *f* (pour chats).

catnap ['kætnæp] *inf* ◇ *n* (petit) somme *m* ▪ **to have a ~** faire un petit somme.
◇ *vi* sommeiller, faire un petit somme.

catnip ['kætnɪp] *n* herbe *f* à chats.

cat-o'-nine-tails *n* chat à neuf queues *m*, martinet *m*.

cat's-eye *n* **1.** TRANSP = **Catseye 2.** [gem] œil-de-chat *m*.

Catseye® ['kæts,aɪ] *n* *UK* TRANSP catadioptre *m (marquant le milieu de la chaussée)*.

cat's-paw *n* [person] dupe *f* ▪ **to be sb's ~** tirer les marrons du feu.

catsuit ['kætsu:t] *n* combinaison-pantalon *f*.

catsup ['kætsəp] *n* *US* ketchup *m*.

cat's whisker *n* **1.** RADIO chercheur *m* (de détecteur à galène) **2.** *inf phr* **he thinks he's the ~s** il se prend pour le nombril du monde.

cattery ['kætərɪ] (*pl* **catteries**) *n* pension *f* pour chats.

cattle ['kætl] *npl (U)* bétail *m*, bestiaux *mpl*, bovins *mpl* ▪ **~ breeder** éleveur *m* (de bétail) ▪ **~ ranch** ranch *m (pour l'élevage du bétail)* ▪ **~ shed** étable *f* ▪ **~ show** concours *m* agricole ▪ **~ truck** fourgon *m* à bestiaux.

cattle grid, cattle guard *US* *n* [sur une route] *grille destinée à empêcher le passage du bétail mais non celui des voitures*.

cattleman ['kætlmən] (*pl* **cattlemen** [-mən]) *n* vacher *m*, bouvier *m*.

cattle market *n* marché *m* *OR* foire *f* aux bestiaux ▪ **this beauty contest is just a ~** *fig* ce concours de beauté n'est qu'un marché aux bestiaux.

catty ['kætɪ] (*comp* **cattier**, *superl* **cattiest**) *adj* *pej* [person, gossip] méchant, vache ▪ **a ~ remark** une réflexion désagréable.

catwalk ['kætwɔ:k] *n* passerelle *f*.

Caucasia [kɔ:'keɪzjə] *pr n* Caucase *m*.

Caucasian [kɔ:'keɪzjən], **Caucasic** [kɔ:'keɪzɪk] ◇ *n* **1.** [from Caucasia] Caucasien *m*, -enne *f* **2.** [white person] Blanc *m*, Blanche *f* **3.** LING caucasien *m*.
◇ *adj* **1.** [from Caucasia] caucasien **2.** [race, man] blanc, blanche *f* **3.** LING caucasien, caucasique.

Caucasus ['kɔ:kəsəs] *pr n* : **the ~** le Caucase ▪ **in the ~** dans le Caucase.

caucus ['kɔ:kəs] *n* **1.** *US* POL [committee] caucus *m* ▪ **the Democratic ~** le groupe *OR* le lobby démocrate **2.** *UK* POL [party organization] comité *m* ▪ **the Black ~ of the Labour Party** *les personnalités noires du parti travailliste*.

CAUCUS

Au Canada et aux États-Unis, les *Caucus* sont les réunions des dirigeants des partis politiques.

caudal ['kɔ:dl] *adj* caudal.

caught [kɔ:t] *pt* & *pp* ▷ **catch**.

cauldron ['kɔ:ldrən] *n* chaudron *m*.

cauliflower ['kɒlɪ,flaʊəʳ] *n* chou-fleur *m*.

cauliflower cheese *n* chou-fleur *m* au gratin.

cauliflower ear *n* oreille *f* en chou-fleur.

caulk [kɔ:k] *vt* [gen] calfeutrer ▪ NAUT calfater.

causal ['kɔ:zl] *adj* [gen] causal ▪ GRAM causal, causatif.

causality [kɔ:'zælətɪ] *n* causalité *f*.

causally ['kɔ:zəlɪ] *adv* : **the two events are ~ linked** les deux événements ont la même cause.

causation [kɔ:'zeɪʃn] *n* [causing] causalité *f* ▪ [cause-effect relationship] relation *f* de cause à effet.

causative ['kɔ:zətɪv] ◇ *adj* [gen] causal ▪ GRAM causal, causatif.
◇ *n* GRAM causatif *m*.

cause [kɔ:z] ◇ *n* **1.** [reason] cause *f* ▪ **to be the ~ of sthg** être (la) cause de qqch ▪ **he was the ~ of all our trouble** c'est lui qui a été la cause *OR* qui a été à l'origine de tous nos ennuis ▪ **the relation of ~ and effect** la relation de cause à effet **2.** [justification] raison *f*, motif *m* ▪ **there is ~ for anxiety** il y a lieu d'être inquiet, il y a de quoi s'inquiéter ▪ **with (good) ~** à juste titre ▪ **without good ~** sans cause *OR* raison valable **3.** [principle] cause *f* ▪ **in the ~ of justice** pour la cause de la justice ▪ **to make common ~ with sb** *fml* faire cause commune avec qqn ▪ **it's all in a good ~!** c'est pour une bonne cause! **4.** LAW cause *f* ▪ **~ of action** fondement *m* d'une action en justice.
◇ *vt* causer, provoquer ▪ **smoking can ~ cancer** le tabac peut provoquer des cancers ▪ **he has ~d us a lot of trouble** il nous a créé beaucoup d'ennuis ▪ **it will only ~ trouble** cela ne servira qu'à semer la zizanie ▪ **what ~d him to change his mind?** qu'est-ce qui l'a fait changer d'avis? ▪ **this ~d me to lose my job** à cause de cela, j'ai perdu mon emploi.

causeway ['kɔ:zweɪ] *n* GEOG chaussée *f*.

caustic ['kɔ:stɪk] ◇ *adj* CHEM & *fig* caustique.
◇ *n* caustique *m*, substance *f* caustique.

caustic soda *n* soude *f* caustique.

cauterize, *UK* **ise** ['kɔ:təraɪz] *vt* cautériser.

caution ['kɔ:ʃn] ◇ *n* **1.** [care] circonspection *f*, prudence *f* ▪ **to proceed with ~** [gen] agir avec circonspection *OR* avec prudence ; [in car] avancer lentement ▪ **'caution!'** 'attention!' ❯ **to throw ~ to the wind** faire fi de toute prudence **2.** [warning] avertissement *m* ▪ [reprimand] réprimande *f* **3.** LAW avertissement *m*.
◇ *vt* **1.** [warn] avertir, mettre en garde ▪ **to ~ sb against doing sthg** déconseiller à qqn de faire qqch ▪ **he ~ed them against the evils of drink** il les a mis en garde contre les dangers de la boisson **2.** LAW : **to ~ a prisoner** informer un prisonnier de ses droits.
◇ *vi* : **to ~ against sthg** déconseiller qqch.

cautionary ['kɔ:ʃənərɪ] *adj* qui sert d'avertissement ▪ **as a ~ measure** par mesure de précaution ▪ **a ~ tale** un récit édifiant.

cautious ['kɔ:ʃəs] *adj* circonspect, prudent ▪ **to be ~ about doing sthg** faire qqch avec circonspection.

cautiously ['kɔ:ʃəslɪ] *adv* avec prudence, prudemment.

cavalcade [,kævl'keɪd] *n* cavalcade *f*.

cavalier [,kævə'lɪəʳ] ◇ *n* [gen - MIL] cavalier *m*.
◇ *adj* cavalier, désinvolte.
◆ **Cavalier** *UK* HIST *n* Cavalier *m (partisan de Charles Ier d'Angleterre pendant la guerre civile anglaise, de 1642 à 1646)*.

cavalry ['kævlrɪ] *n* cavalerie *f*.

cavalry charge *n* charge *f* de cavalerie.

cavalryman ['kævlrɪmən] (*pl* **cavalrymen** [-mən]) *n* cavalier *m (soldat)*.

cavalry officer *n* officier *m* de cavalerie.

cave [keɪv] ◇ *n* caverne *f*, grotte *f*.
◇ *vi* : **to go caving** faire de la spéléologie.
◆ **cave in** *vi insep* **1.** [ceiling, floor] s'écrouler, s'effondrer, s'affaisser ▪ [wall] s'écrouler, s'effondrer, céder **2.** *inf* [person] flancher, céder.

caveat ['kævɪæt] *n* avertissement *m* ▪ LAW notification *f* d'opposition.

cave dweller [keɪv-] *n* [in prehistory] homme *m* des cavernes ▪ [troglodyte] troglodyte *m*.

cave-in [keɪv-] *n* [of ceiling, floor] effondrement *m*, affaissement *m*.

caveman ['keɪvmæn] (*pl* **cavemen** [-men]) *n* *liter* homme *m* des cavernes ▪ *fig* brute *f*.

cave painting [keɪv-] *n* peinture *f* rupestre.

cavern ['kævən] *n* caverne *f*.

cavernous ['kævənəs] *adj* **1.** *fig* **a ~ building** un bâtiment très vaste à l'intérieur ▪ **~ depths** des profondeurs insondables **2.** GEOL plein de cavernes.

caviar(e) ['kævɪɑ:ʳ] *n* caviar *m*.

cavil ['kævl] (*UK pret & pp* **cavilled**, *cont* **cavilling**) (*US pret & pp* **caviled**, *cont* **caviling**) *vi* chicaner, ergoter ■ **to ~ at sthg** chicaner *OR* ergoter sur qqch.

caving ['keɪvɪŋ] *n* spéléologie *f*.

cavity ['kævətɪ] (*pl* **cavities**) *n* **1.** [in rock, wood] cavité *f*, creux *m* **2.** ANAT cavité *f* ■ [in tooth] cavité *f*.

cavity wall ◇ *n* mur *m* creux *OR* à double paroi.
◇ *comp* : **~ insulation** isolation *f* en murs creux.

cavort [kə'vɔːt] *vi* **1.** *liter* cabrioler, gambader, faire des cabrioles **2.** *fig* **while his wife was off ~ing around Europe** pendant que sa femme menait une vie de bâton de chaise en Europe.

caw [kɔː] ◇ *vi* croasser.
◇ *n* croassement *m*.

cayenne pepper *n* poivre *m* de cayenne.

cayman ['keɪmən] *n* caïman *m*.

Cayman Islands, Caymans *pl prn* GEOG : **the ~** les Îles *fpl* Cayman.

CB *n* (*abbrev of* **Citizens' Band**) CB *f*.

CBC (*abbrev of* **Canadian Broadcasting Corporation**) *pr n office national canadien de radiodiffusion.*

CBE (*abbrev of* **Companion of (the Order of) the British Empire**) *n distinction honorifique britannique.*

CBI (*abbrev of* **Confederation of British Industry**) *pr n association du patronat britannique,* ≃ CNPF *m*.

CBS (*abbrev of* **Columbia Broadcasting System**) *pr n chaîne de télévision américaine.*

cc ◇ *n* (*abbrev of* **cubic centimetre**) cm³.
◇ (*written abbrev of* **carbon copy**) pcc.

CC *written abbr of* **county council**.

CCTV *n* = **closed-circuit television**.

CD ◇ *n* **1.** (*abbrev of* **compact disc**) CD *m* **2.** = **Civil Defence**.
◇ (*written abbrev of* **Corps Diplomatique**) CD.

CD burner, burner *n* COMPUT graveur *m* (de CD).

CDI (*abbrev of* **compact disc interactive**) *n* CDI *m*.

CD player *n* lecteur *m* de CD.

CD-R [,siːdiː'ɑːʳ] (*abbrev of* **compact disc recordable**) *n* CD-R *m*.

CD-R drive [,siːdiː'ɑː,draɪv] *n* lecteur-graveur *m* de CD.

CD-ROM [,siːdiː'rɒm] (*abbrev of* **compact disc read only memory**) *n* CD-ROM *m*, CD-Rom *m*, DOC *m offic.*

CD-RW [,siːdiːɑː'dʌbljuː] (*abbrev of* **compact disc rewriteable**) *n* CD-RW *m*.

CDT *n* = **Central Daylight Time**.

CD tower *n* colonne *f* (de rangement) pour CD.

CDV (*abbrev of* **compact disc video**) *n* CDV *m*, CD vidéo *m*.

CE *n* = **Church of England**.

cease [siːs] ◇ *vi fml* [activity, noise] cesser, s'arrêter ■ **the rain eventually ~d** il a finalement cessé de pleuvoir ■ **to ~ and desist** LAW se désister.
◇ *vt* [activity, efforts, work] cesser, arrêter ■ **to ~ to do** *OR* **to ~ doing sthg** cesser de *OR* arrêter de faire qqch ■ **a county that ~d to exist in 1974** un comté qui n'existe plus depuis 1974 ■ **to ~ fire** MIL cesser le feu.
◇ *n* : **without ~** *fml* sans cesse.

ceasefire [,siːs'faɪəʳ] *n* cessez-le-feu *m inv* ■ **to agree to a ~** accepter un cessez-le-feu.

ceaseless ['siːslɪs] *adj* incessant, continuel.

ceaselessly ['siːslɪslɪ] *adv* sans cesse, continuellement.

cedar ['siːdəʳ] ◇ *n* cèdre *m*.
◇ *comp* de *OR* en cèdre.

cede [siːd] *vt* céder.

cedilla [sɪ'dɪlə] *n* cédille *f*.

CEEB (*abbrev of* **College Entry Examination Board**) *pr n commission d'admission dans l'enseignement supérieur aux États-Unis.*

Ceefax® ['siːfæks] *pr n service de télétexte de la BBC.*

ceilidh ['keɪlɪ] *n soirée de danse et de musique folklorique (en Irlande et en Écosse).*

ceiling ['siːlɪŋ] ◇ *n* **1.** [of room] plafond *m* **2.** AERON & METEOR plafond *m* **3.** COMM & ECON plafond *m* ■ **the government has set a 3% ~ on wage rises** le gouvernement a limité à 3 % les augmentations de salaire.
◇ *comp* [charge, price] plafond *(inv)*.

celebrant ['selɪbrənt] *n* RELIG célébrant *m*, officiant *m*.

celebrate ['selɪbreɪt] ◇ *vt* **1.** [birthday, Christmas] fêter, célébrer ■ [event, victory] célébrer **2.** [praise - person, sb's beauty] célébrer, glorifier **3.** RELIG : **to ~ mass** célébrer la messe.
◇ *vi* : **let's ~!** [gen] il faut fêter ça! ; [with drinks] il faut arroser ça!

celebrated ['selɪbreɪtɪd] *adj* célèbre.

celebration [,selɪ'breɪʃn] *n* **1.** [of birthday, Christmas] célébration *f* ■ [of anniversary, past event] commémoration *f* ■ **in ~ of Christmas** pour fêter *OR* célébrer Noël **2.** MUS & POET éloge *m*, louange *f* **3.** RELIG célébration *f* **4.** *(often pl)* [occasion - of birthday, Christmas] fête *f*, fêtes *fpl* ; [- of historical event] cérémonies *fpl*, fête *f* ■ **this calls for a ~!** il faut fêter ça!, il faut arroser ça!

celebratory [,selə'breɪtərɪ] *adj* [dinner] de fête ■ [marking official occasion] commémoratif ■ [atmosphere, mood] de fête, festif.

celebrity [sɪ'lebrətɪ] (*pl* **celebrities**) *n* **1.** [fame] célébrité *f* **2.** [person] vedette *f*, célébrité *f*.

celeriac [sɪ'lerɪæk] *n* céleri-rave *m*.

celery ['selərɪ] ◇ *n* céleri *m*.
◇ *comp* [salt, plant] de céleri.

celestial [sɪ'lestjəl] *adj liter* & *fig* céleste.

celibacy ['selɪbəsɪ] *n* célibat *m*.

celibate ['selɪbət] ◇ *adj* chaste ■ [unmarried] célibataire.
◇ *n* RELIG *personne ayant fait vœu de chasteté.*

cell [sel] ◇ *n* **1.** BIOL & BOT cellule *f* **2.** [in prison, convent] cellule *f* ■ **he spent the night in the ~s** il a passé la nuit en cellule **3.** ELEC élément *m* (de pile) **4.** POL cellule *f*.
◇ *comp* BIOL [wall] cellulaire ■ **~ division** division *f* cellulaire ■ **~ structure** structure *f* cellulaire.

cellar ['seləʳ] *n* [for wine] cave *f*, cellier *m* ■ [for coal, bric-à-brac] cave *f* ■ [for food] cellier *m*.

cellist ['tʃelɪst] *n* violoncelliste *mf*.

cello ['tʃeləʊ] *n* violoncelle *m*.

Cellophane® ['seləfeɪn] *n* Cellophane® *f*.

cellphone ['selfəʊn] *n* = **cellular telephone**.

cellular ['seljʊləʳ] *adj* **1.** ANAT & BIOL cellulaire **2.** CONSTR cellulaire **3.** TEX [blanket] en cellular.

cellular telephone *n* téléphone *m* cellulaire.

cellulite ['seljʊlaɪt] *n* cellulite *f*.

Celluloid® ['seljʊlɔɪd] ◇ *n* Celluloïd® *m* ■ **to capture sthg/sb on ~** *fig* filmer qqch/qqn.
◇ *adj* en Celluloïd®.

cellulose ['seljʊləʊs] ◇ *n* cellulose *f*.
◇ *adj* en *OR* de cellulose, cellulosique.

Celsius ['selsɪəs] *adj* Celsius ■ **25 degrees ~** 25 degrés Celsius.

Celt [kelt] *n* Celte *mf*.

Celtic ['keltɪk] ◇ *n* LING celtique *m*.
◇ *adj* celtique, celte.

cement [sɪ'ment] <> *n* **1.** CONSTR & *fig* ciment *m* **2.** [in dentistry] amalgame *m* **3.** [glue] colle *f*.
<> *vt* **1.** CONSTR & *fig* cimenter **2.** [in dentistry] obturer.

cement mixer *n* bétonnière *f*.

cemetery ['semɪtrɪ] (*pl* **cemeteries**) *n* cimetière *m*.

cenotaph ['senətɑːf] *n* cénotaphe *m*.

censer ['sensəʳ] *n* encensoir *m*.

censor ['sensəʳ] <> *n* CIN & THEAT censeur *m*.
<> *vt* censurer.

censorious [sen'sɔːrɪəs] *adj fml* [comments, criticism] sévère ▪ [person] porté à la censure.

censorship ['sensəʃɪp] *n* **1.** [act, practice] censure *f* **2.** [office of censor] censorat *m*.

censure ['senʃəʳ] <> *n* blâme *m*, critique *f*.
<> *vt* blâmer, critiquer.

census ['sensəs] *n* recensement *m* ▪ **to conduct** *OR* **to take a population ~** faire le recensement de la population, recenser la population.

cent [sent] *n* [coin] [- France] (euro)centime *m* ; [- United States] cent *m* ◆ **it's not worth a ~** *US fig* ça ne vaut rien ▪ **I haven't got a ~** je n'ai pas un sou.

centaur ['sentɔːʳ] *n* centaure *m*.

centenarian [ˌsentɪ'neərɪən] <> *n* centenaire *mf*.
<> *adj* centenaire.

centenary [sen'tiːnərɪ] <> *n* (*pl* **centenaries**) [anniversary] centenaire *m*, centième anniversaire *m*.
<> *comp* centenaire ▪ **~ celebrations** fêtes *fpl* du centenaire.

centennial [sen'tenjəl] <> *n US* centenaire *m*, centième anniversaire *m* ▪ **the Centennial State** le Colorado.
<> *adj* **1.** [in age] centenaire, séculaire **2.** [every hundred years] séculaire.

center *etc US n, comp, vt & vt insep* = **centre**.

centigrade ['sentɪgreɪd] *adj* centigrade ▪ **25 degrees ~** 25 degrés centigrades.

centigram(me) ['sentɪgræm] *n* centigramme *m*.

centilitre *UK*, **centiliter** *US* ['sentɪˌliːtəʳ] *n* centilitre *m*.

centimetre *UK*, **centimeter** *US* ['sentɪˌmiːtəʳ] *n* centimètre *m*.

centipede ['sentɪpiːd] *n* mille-pattes *m inv*.

central ['sentrəl] *adj* central ▪ **this concept is ~ to his theory** ce concept est au centre de sa théorie.

Central African <> *n* Centrafricain *m*, - e *f*.
<> *adj* centrafricain.

Central African Republic *pr n* : **the ~** la République centrafricaine ▪ **in the ~** en République centrafricaine.

Central America *pr n* Amérique *f* centrale ▪ **in ~** en Amérique centrale.

Central American <> *n* Centraméricain *m*, - e *f*.
<> *adj* centraméricain.

Central Asia *pr n* Asie *f* centrale ▪ **in ~** en Asie centrale.

central bank *n* banque *f* centrale.

Central Daylight Time *n* heure *f* d'été du centre des États-Unis.

Central Europe *pr n* Europe *f* centrale.

Central European <> *n* habitant *m*, - e *f* de l'Europe centrale.
<> *adj* d'Europe centrale.

Central European Time *n* heure *f* de l'Europe centrale.

central government *n* gouvernement *m* central.

central heating *n* chauffage *m* central.

centralism ['sentrəlɪzm] *n* centralisme *m*.

centrality [sen'trælətɪ] (*pl* **centralities**) *n* [of argument, idea] caractère *m* essentiel ▪ [of location] situation *f* centrale.

centralization [ˌsentrəlaɪ'zeɪʃn] *n* centralisation *f*.

centralize, *UK* **ise** ['sentrəlaɪz] <> *vt* centraliser.
<> *vi* se centraliser.

centralized ['sentrəlaɪzd] *adj* centralisé ▪ **~ data processing** traitement *m* centralisé de l'information.

central locking *n* AUT verrouillage *m* central.

centrally ['sentrəlɪ] *adv* [located] au centre ▪ [organized] de façon centralisée ▪ **~ heated** ayant le chauffage central ▪ **a ~ planned economy** ECON une économie dirigée.

central nervous system *n* système *m* nerveux central.

Central Office *pr n UK* POL *siège du parti conservateur britannique*.

Central Office of Information *pr n organisme public qui édite des documents d'information sur la Grande-Bretagne*.

central processing unit *n* COMPUT unité *f* centrale.

central reservation *n UK* AUT [with grass] terre-plein *m* central ▪ [with barrier] bande *f* médiane.

Central Standard Time *n* heure *f* d'hiver du centre des États-Unis.

centre *UK*, **center** *US* ['sentəʳ] <> *n* **1.** [gen - GEOM] centre *m* ▪ **in the ~** au centre ◆ **~ of gravity** centre de gravité ▪ **~ of infection** MED foyer *m* infectueux **2.** [of town] centre *m* ▪ **she lives in the city ~** elle habite dans le centre-ville **3.** *fig* [of unrest] foyer *m* ▪ [of debate] cœur *m*, centre *m* ▪ **the ~ of attention** le centre d'attention **4.** [place, building] centre *m* ▪ **a sports/health ~** un centre sportif/médical **5.** POL centre *m* ▪ **to be left/right of ~** être du centre gauche/droit **6.** TECH : **to be off ~** être décentré **7.** SPORT [pass] centre *m*.
<> *comp* **1.** [central] central ▪ **the ~ court** [in tennis] le court central **2.** POL du centre.
<> *vt* **1.** [place in centre] centrer **2.** CIN & PHOT cadrer **3.** *fig* [attention] concentrer, fixer ▪ **to ~ one's hopes on sthg** mettre *OR* fonder tous ses espoirs sur qqch **4.** SPORT : **to ~ the ball** centrer.

⬥ **centre around** *vt insep* tourner autour de.

⬥ **centre on** *vt insep* se concentrer sur ▪ **all their attention was ~d on the World Cup** toute leur attention était concentrée sur la coupe du monde ▪ **the conversation ~d on politics** la conversation tournait autour de la politique.

⬥ **centre round** *vt insep* = **centre around**.

centre-back *n* arrière *m* central.

centreboard *UK*, **centerboard** *US* ['sentəbɔːd] *n* dérive *f* *(d'un bateau)*.

centrefold *UK*, **centerfold** *US* ['sentəˌfəʊld] *n* grande photo *f* de pin-up *(au milieu d'un magazine)*.

centre-forward *n* avant-centre *m*.

centre-half *n* demi-centre *m*.

centreline *UK*, **centerline** *US* ['sentəlaɪn] *n* axe *m*, ligne *f* médiane.

centrepiece *UK*, **centerpiece** *US* ['sentəpiːs] *n* [outstanding feature] joyau *m* ▪ [on table] milieu *m* de table ▪ [of meal] pièce *f* de résistance.

centre-spread *n* = **centrefold**.

centre three-quarter *n* trois-quarts *m* centre.

centrifugal [sentrɪ'fjʊgl] *adj* centrifuge.

centrifuge ['sentrɪfjuːdʒ] <> *n* TECH centrifugeur *m*, centrifugeuse *f*.
<> *vt* centrifuger.

centripetal [sen'trɪpɪtl] *adj* centripète.

centrism ['sentrɪzm] *n* centrisme *m*.

centrist ['sentrɪst] <> *adj* centriste.
<> *n* centriste *mf*.

centurion [sen'tjʊərɪən] *n* centurion *m*.

century ['sentʃʊrɪ] (*pl* **centuries**) *n* **1.** [time] siècle *m* ▪ **in the 20th ~** au XXᵉ siècle ▪ **centuries old** séculaire, vieux de plusieurs siècles **2.** MIL centurie *f*.

CEO *n* = **chief executive officer**.

ceramic [sɪ'ræmɪk] <> *adj* [art] céramique ▪ [vase] en céramique ▪ **~ hob** *UK* plaque *f* vitrocéramique.
<> *n* **1.** = **ceramics 2.** [object] (objet *m* en) céramique *f*.

ceramics [sɪ'ræmɪks] *n (U)* céramique *f*.

cereal ['sɪərɪəl] <> *n* **1.** AGRIC [plant] céréale *f* ▪ [grain] grain *m* (de céréale) **2.** CULIN : **(breakfast) ~** céréales *fpl* ▪ **baby ~** bouillie *f*.
<> *adj* [farming] céréalier ▪ **~ crops** céréales *fpl*.

cerebellum [ˌserɪ'beləm] (*pl* **cerebellums** *OR pl* **cerebella** [-lə]) *n* cervelet *m*.

cerebral ['serɪbrəl] *adj* cérébral.

cerebral palsy *n* paralysie *f* cérébrale.

cerebrum ['serɪbrəm] (*pl* **cerebrums** *OR pl* **cerebra** [-brə]) *n* cerveau *m*.

ceremonial [ˌserɪ'məʊnjəl] <> *adj* **1.** [rite, visit] cérémoniel ▪ [robes] de cérémonie **2.** *US* [post] honorifique.
<> *n* cérémonial *m* ▪ RELIG cérémonial *m*, rituel *m*.

ceremonially [ˌserɪ'məʊnjəlɪ] *adv* selon le cérémonial d'usage.

ceremonious [ˌserɪ'məʊnjəs] *adj* solennel ▪ [mock-solemn] cérémonieux.

ceremoniously [ˌserɪ'məʊnjəslɪ] *adv* solennellement, avec cérémonie ▪ [mock-solemnly] cérémonieusement.

ceremony [*UK* 'serɪmənɪ, *US* 'serəməʊnɪ] (*pl* **ceremonies**) *n* **1.** *(U)* [formality] cérémonie *f*, cérémonies *fpl* ▪ **we don't stand on ~** nous ne faisons pas de cérémonies **2.** [gen - RELIG] cérémonie *f*.

Ceres ['sɪəri:z] *pr n* Cérès.

cerise [sə'ri:z] *adj* (de) couleur cerise, cerise *(inv)*.

cert [sɜ:t] *n UK inf* certitude *f* ▪ **it's a dead ~ that he'll win** il va gagner, ça ne fait pas un pli *OR* c'est couru d'avance ▪ **he's a ~ for the job** il est sûr d'obtenir le poste.

cert. *written abbr of* **certificate**.

certain ['sɜ:tn] <> *adj* **1.** [sure] certain, sûr ▪ **to be ~ of sthg** être sûr de qqch ▪ **he was ~ (that) she was there** il était certain qu'elle était là ▪ **it's ~ that she will get the job** il est sûr qu'elle aura le poste ▪ **he's ~ to come** il ne manquera pas de venir, il viendra sûrement ▪ **to make ~ of sthg** [check] vérifier qqch, s'assurer de qqch ; [be sure to have] s'assurer qqch ▪ **he made ~ that all the doors were locked** il a vérifié que toutes les portes étaient fermées **2.** [inevitable - death, failure] certain, inévitable ▪ **the soldiers faced ~ death** les soldats allaient à une mort certaine **3.** [definite, infallible - cure] sûr, infaillible.
<> *det* **1.** [particular but unspecified] certain ▪ **on a ~ day in June** un certain jour de juin ▪ **he has a ~ something about him** il a un certain je ne sais quoi **2.** [not known personally] certain ▪ **a ~ Mr Roberts** un certain M. Roberts **3.** [some] certain ▪ **to a ~ extent** *OR* **degree** dans une certaine mesure.
<> *pron* certains *mpl*, certaines *f* ▪ **~ of his colleagues** certains *OR* quelques-uns de ses collègues.
◆ **for certain** *adv phr* : **I don't know for ~** je n'en suis pas certain ▪ **I can't say for ~** je ne peux pas l'affirmer ▪ **you'll have it tomorrow for ~** vous l'aurez demain sans faute ▪ **that's for ~!** c'est sûr et certain!, cela ne fait pas de doute!

certainly ['sɜ:tnlɪ] *adv* **1.** [without doubt] certainement, assurément ▪ **he is ~ very handsome** il est très beau, ça ne fait pas de doute ▪ **I will ~ come** je ne manquerai pas de venir, je viendrai, c'est sûr ▪ **it will ~ be ready tomorrow** cela sera prêt demain sans faute **2.** [of course] certainement, bien sûr ▪ **can you help me? – ~!** pouvez-vous m'aider? – bien sûr *OR* volontiers! ▪ **~ not!** bien sûr que non!, certainement pas!

certainty ['sɜ:tntɪ] (*pl* **certainties**) *n* **1.** [conviction] certitude *f*, conviction *f* ▪ **I cannot say with any ~ when I shall arrive** je ne peux pas dire exactement à quelle heure j'arriverai **2.** [fact] certitude *f*, fait *m* certain ▪ [event] certitude *f*, événement *m* certain ▪ **I know for a ~ that he's leaving** je sais à coup sûr qu'il part ▪ **their victory is now a ~** leur victoire est maintenant assurée *OR* ne fait aucun doute ▪ **it's an absolute** *OR* **a racing~** c'est une chose certaine, c'est une certitude absolue.
Voir module d'usage

CertEd [sɜ:t'ed] (*abbrev of* **Certificate in Education**) *n diplôme universitaire britannique en sciences de l'éducation.*

certifiable [ˌsɜ:tɪ'faɪəbl] *adj* **1.** [gen - LAW] qu'on peut certifier **2.** [insane] bon à enfermer (à l'asile).

certificate [sə'tɪfɪkət] *n* **1.** [gen - ADMIN] certificat *m* ▪ **~ of origin** COMM certificat d'origine **2.** [academic] diplôme *m* ▪ [vocational - of apprenticeship] brevet *m* ▪ **Certificate of Pre-vocational Education** *UK* SCH *examen d'accès à une formation professionnelle pour les élèves désirant poursuivre leurs études après le GCSE mais ne souhaitant pas passer les 'A-levels'.*

certification [ˌsɜ:tɪfɪ'keɪʃn] *n* **1.** [act] certification *f*, authentification *f* **2.** [certificate] certificat *m*.

certified ['sɜ:tɪfaɪd] *adj US* SCH : **~ teacher** [in state school] professeur *m* diplômé ; [in private school] professeur *m* habilité.

certified mail *n US* envoi *m* recommandé ▪ **to send sthg by ~** envoyer qqch en recommandé avec accusé de réception.

certified public accountant *n US* ≃ expert-comptable *mf*.

certify ['sɜ:tɪfaɪ] (*pret & pp* **certified**) <> *vt* **1.** [gen - ADMIN] certifier, attester ▪ MED [death] constater ▪ **to ~ that sthg is true**

CERTAINTY

Elle va réussir, j'en suis sûr et certain. I'm convinced she'll pass.

Je suis persuadé qu'il va revenir. I'm sure he'll come back.

Je suis convaincu de sa bonne foi. I'm sure he acted in good faith.

Tu es sûr que c'était elle ? Are you sure it was her?

On va les retrouver, c'est sûr. We'll definitely find them.

Bien sûr qu'il va venir. Of course he'll come.

Je sais pertinemment qu'il ne le fera pas. I know for a fact that he won't do it.

Je t'assure, c'est quelqu'un de très bien. Believe me, he's/she's a really nice person.

Je parie que c'est elle qui lui a tout répété. I bet it was her that told him.

Je suis pratiquement certain que c'est lui. I'm almost sure it's him.

Il n'y a pas de doute, c'est bien lui. There's no doubt about it, it is him.

attester que qqch est vrai ▪ **to ~ sb (insane)** PSYCHOL déclarer qqn atteint d'aliénation mentale ▪ **he ought to be certified!** *inf fig* il est bon à enfermer! **2.** *US* FIN [cheque] certifier **3.** COMM [goods] garantir.
◇ *vi* : **to ~ to sthg** attester qqch.

certitude ['sɜ:tɪtju:d] *n fml* certitude *f*.

cervical [*UK* sə'vaɪkl, *US* 'sɜ:rvɪkl] *adj* cervical.

cervical cancer *n* cancer *m* du col de l'utérus.

cervical smear *n* frottis *m* vaginal.

cervix ['sɜ:vɪks] (*pl* **cervixes** *OR pl* **cervices** [-si:z]) *n* col *m* de l'utérus.

Cesarean, Cesarian *US adj* & *n* = **Caesarean**.

cessation [se'seɪʃn] *n fml* cessation *f*, suspension *f*.

cession ['seʃn] *n* LAW cession *f*.

cesspit ['sespɪt] *n* fosse *f* d'aisances ▪ *fig* cloaque *m*.

cesspool ['sespu:l] *n* = **cesspit**.

cesura [sɪ'zjʊərə] (*pl* **cesuras** *OR pl* **cesurae** [-ri:]) *n* = **caesura**.

CET *n* = **Central European Time**.

cetacean [sɪ'teɪʃjən] ◇ *adj* cétacé.
◇ *n* cétacé *m*.

c & f (*written abbrev of* **cost and freight**) c et f.

cf. (*written abbrev of* **confer**) cf.

c/f *written abbr of* **carried forward**.

CFC (*abbrev of* **chlorofluorocarbon**) *n* CFC *m*.

cfi, CFI (*abbrev of* **cost, freight and insurance**) *adj* & *adv* caf, CAF.

CG *n* = **coastguard**.

C & G (*abbrev of* **City and Guilds**) *n diplôme britannique d'enseignement technique*.

CGA (*abbrev of* **colour graphics adapter**) *n* adaptateur *m* graphique couleur CGA.

CGT *n* = **capital gains tax**.

ch (*written abbrev of* **central heating**) ch. cent.

ch. (*written abbrev of* **chapter**) chap.

cha-cha(cha) ['tʃɑ:tʃɑ:, ˌtʃɑ:tʃɑ:'tʃɑ:] ◇ *n* cha-cha-cha *m inv*.
◇ *vi* danser le cha-cha-cha.

Chad [tʃæd] *pr n* Tchad *m* ▪ **in ~** au Tchad ▪ **Lake ~** le lac Tchad.

Chadian ['tʃædɪən] ◇ *n* Tchadien *m*, - enne *f*.
◇ *adj* tchadien.

chador ['tʃɑ:dɔ:] *n* tchador *m*.

chafe [tʃeɪf] ◇ *vt* **1.** [rub] frictionner, frotter **2.** [irritate] frotter contre, irriter **3.** [wear away - collar] élimer, user (par le frottement) ▪ [paint] érafler ▪ [rope] raguer.
◇ *vi* **1.** [become worn - gen] s'user (par le frottement) ▪ [rope] raguer **2.** [skin] s'irriter ▪ *fig* [person] s'irriter, s'impatienter ▪ **to ~ at** *OR* **under sthg** s'irriter de qqch ▪ **the media ~d under the military censorship** soumis à la censure militaire, les médias rongeaient leur frein.
◇ *n* friction *f*, usure *f*.

chaff [tʃɑ:f] ◇ *n* [of grain] balle *f* ▪ [hay, straw] menue paille *f*.
◇ *vt dated* [tease] taquiner.

chaffinch ['tʃæfɪntʃ] *n* pinson *m*.

chagrin ['ʃægrɪn] ◇ *n lit* (vif) dépit *m*, (vive) déception *f OR* contrariété *f* ▪ **much to my ~** à mon grand dépit.
◇ *vt* contrarier, décevoir.

chain [tʃeɪn] ◇ *n* **1.** [gen] chaîne *f* ▪ **we keep the dog on a ~** notre chien est toujours attaché ▪ **to pull the ~** tirer la chasse d'eau ▪ **to form a human ~** former une chaîne humaine ➊ **bicycle ~** chaîne de bicyclette ▪ **(snow) ~s** AUT chaînes (à neige) **2.** ADMIN : **~ of office** ≃ écharpe *f* de maire **3.** [of mountains] chaîne *f* ▪ [of islands] chapelet *m* **4.** [of events] série *f*, suite *f* ▪ [of ideas] suite *f* **5.** COMM [of shops] chaîne *f* **6.** TECH [for surveying] chaîne *f* d'arpenteur **7.** [measure of length] chaînée *f (22 yards, soit environ 20 m 10)*.
◇ *vt liter* & *fig* enchaîner ▪ [door] mettre la chaîne à ▪ **the dog was ~ed to the post** le chien était attaché au poteau (par une chaîne) ▪ **to be ~ed to one's desk** *fig* être rivé à son bureau.
⇨ **chains** *npl* [for prisoner] chaînes *fpl*, entraves *fpl* ▪ **a prisoner in ~s** un prisonnier enchaîné.
⇨ **chain down** *vt sep* enchaîner, attacher avec une chaîne.
⇨ **chain up** *vt sep* [prisoner] enchaîner ▪ [dog] mettre à l'attache, attacher.

chain drive *n* transmission *f* par chaîne.

chain gang *n* chaîne *f* de forçats.

chain letter *n* lettre *f* faisant partie d'une chaîne.

chain lightning *n (U)* éclairs *mpl* en zigzag.

chain mail *n (U)* cotte *f* de mailles.

chain reaction *n* réaction *f* en chaîne ▪ **to set off a ~** provoquer une réaction en chaîne.

chain saw *n* tronçonneuse *f*.

chain-smoke *vi* fumer cigarette sur cigarette.

chain smoker *n* fumeur invétéré *m*, fumeuse invétérée *f*, gros fumeur *m*, grosse fumeuse *f*.

chain stitch *n* point *m* de chaînette.

chain store *n* magasin *m* à succursales multiples.

chainwheel ['tʃeɪnwi:l] *n* roue *f* dentée *(de vélo)*, pignon *m*.

chair [tʃeəʳ] ◇ *n* **1.** [seat] chaise *f* ▪ [armchair] fauteuil *m* ▪ **please take a ~** asseyez-vous, je vous prie **2.** [chairperson] président *m*, - e *f* ▪ **to be in the ~** présider **3.** UNIV chaire *f* **4.** [for execution] : **to go** *OR* **to be sent to the ~** *US inf* passer à la chaise électrique.
◇ *comp* : **~ leg** pied *m* de chaise.
◇ *vt* **1.** ADMIN [meeting] présider **2.** *UK* [hero, victor] porter en triomphe.

chairlift ['tʃeəlɪft] *n* télésiège *m*.

chairman ['tʃeəmən] (*pl* **chairmen** [-mən]) *n* **1.** [at meeting] président *m (d'un comité)* ▪ **to act as ~** présider la séance **2.** COMM président-directeur *m* général, P-DG *m* **3.** POL : **Chairman Mao** le président Mao.

chairmanship ['tʃeəmənʃɪp] *n* présidence *f (d'un comité, etc)*.

chairperson ['tʃeəˌpɜ:sn] *n* président *m*, - e *f (d'un comité)*.

chairwoman ['tʃeəˌwʊmən] (*pl* **chairwomen** [-ˌwɪmɪn]) *n* présidente *f (d'un comité)*.

chaise [ʃeɪz] *n* cabriolet *m*.

chaise longue [-'lɒŋ] (*pl* **chaises longues**) *n* méridienne *f*.

chalet ['ʃæleɪ] *n* chalet *m*.

chalice ['tʃælɪs] *n* **1.** RELIG calice *m* **2.** [goblet] coupe *f*.

chalk [tʃɔ:k] ◇ *n* **1.** [substance] craie *f* ▪ **a piece of ~** un morceau de craie ➊ **~ and talk** *UK méthode d'enseignement traditionnelle* ▪ **they're as different as ~ and cheese** *UK* c'est le jour et la nuit **2.** [piece] craie *f* **3.** *phr* **by a long ~** *UK* de beaucoup, de loin ▪ **not by a long ~** loin de là, tant s'en faut.
◇ *vt* [write] écrire à la craie ▪ [mark] marquer à la craie ▪ [rub with chalk - gen] frotter de craie ; [- billiard cue] enduire de craie.
⇨ **chalk up** *vt sep* **1.** [write in chalk] écrire à la craie **2.** [credit] : **~ that one up to me** mettez cela sur mon compte ▪ **to ~ sthg up to experience** *fig* mettre qqch au compte de l'expérience **3.** [add up -points, score] totaliser, marquer **4.** [attain - victory] remporter ; [- profits] encaisser.

chalkboard ['tʃɔ:kbɔ:d] *n US* tableau *m* (noir).

chalkface ['tʃɔ:kfeɪs] *n hum* & SCH expérience *f* pratique (de l'enseignement).

chalky [ˈtʃɔːkɪ] (*comp* **chalkier**, *superl* **chalkiest**) *adj* [earth, water] calcaire ■ [hands] couvert de craie ■ [complexion] crayeux, blafard ■ [taste] de craie.

challenge [ˈtʃælɪndʒ] ◇ *vt* **1.** [gen - defy] défier ■ **to ~ sb** lancer un défi à qqn ■ **to ~ sb to do sthg** défier qqn de faire qqch ■ **to ~ sb to a game of tennis** inviter qqn à faire une partie de tennis ■ **to ~ sb to a duel** provoquer qqn en duel
2. [demand effort from] mettre à l'épreuve ■ **she needs a job that really ~s her** elle a besoin d'un travail qui soit pour elle une gageure *OR* un challenge
3. [contest - authority, findings] contester, mettre en cause ■ **to ~ sb's right to do sthg** contester à qqn le droit de faire qqch
4. MIL [subj: sentry] faire une sommation à
5. LAW [juror] récuser.
◇ *n* **1.** [in contest] défi *m* ■ **to issue a ~** lancer un défi ■ **to take up the ~** relever le défi ■ **Jackson's ~ for the leadership of the party** la tentative de Jackson pour s'emparer de la direction du parti
2. [in job, activity] défi *m* ■ **he needs a job that presents more of a ~** il a besoin d'un emploi plus stimulant
3. [to right, authority] mise *f* en question, contestation *f*
4. MIL [by sentry] sommation *f*
5. LAW récusation *f*.

challenged [ˈtʃælɪndʒd] *adj* ***euph*** **physically ~** handicapé ■ **visually ~** malvoyant ‖ ***hum*** **vertically ~** de petite taille ■ **cerebrally ~** limité.

challenger [ˈtʃælɪndʒəʳ] *n* [gen] provocateur *m*, - trice *f* ■ POL & SPORT challenger *m*.

challenging [ˈtʃælɪndʒɪŋ] *adj* **1.** [defiant] de défi **2.** [demanding - ideas, theory] provocateur, stimulant, exaltant ; [- job, activity] stimulant, qui met à l'épreuve ■ **to find o.s. in a ~ situation** se trouver face à un défi.

challengingly [ˈtʃælɪndʒɪŋlɪ] *adv* avec défiance.

chamber [ˈtʃeɪmbəʳ] *n* **1.** [hall, room] chambre *f* ■ **the upper/lower Chamber** ***UK*** POL la Chambre haute/basse **2.** ***arch*** [lodgings] logement *m*, appartement *m* **3.** [of a gun] chambre *f* **4.** ANAT [of the heart] cavité *f* ■ [of the eye] chambre *f*.
◆ **chambers** *npl* [of barrister, judge] cabinet *m* ■ [of solicitor] cabinet *m*, étude *f* ■ **the case was heard in ~s** LAW l'affaire a été jugée en référé.

chamberlain [ˈtʃeɪmbəlɪn] *n* chambellan *m*.

chambermaid [ˈtʃeɪmbəmeɪd] *n* femme *f* de chambre.

chamber music *n* musique *f* de chambre.

chamber of commerce *n* chambre *f* de commerce.

Chamber of Horrors *pr n* : **the ~** *la Chambre des horreurs du musée de cire de Madame Tussaud (à Londres), spécialement consacrée aux meurtres et aux criminels célèbres.*

chamber of trade *n* chambre *f* des métiers.

chamber orchestra *n* orchestre *m* de chambre.

chamber pot *n* pot *m* de chambre.

chambray [ˈʃæmbreɪ] *n* batiste *f*.

chameleon [kəˈmiːljən] *n* ZOOL & ***fig*** caméléon *m*.

chamfer [ˈtʃæmfəʳ] ◇ *n* chanfrein *m*.
◇ *vt* chanfreiner.

chammy [ˈʃæmɪ] (*pl* **chammies**) *n* peau *f* de chamois.

chamois [ˈʃæmwɑː] (*pl inv*) ◇ *n* ZOOL chamois *m* ■ [hide] peau *f* de chamois ■ **(a)~ leather** (une) peau de chamois.
◇ *vt* **1.** [leather, skin] chamoiser **2.** [polish] polir à la peau de chamois.

champ [tʃæmp] ◇ *vt* mâchonner.
◇ *vi* **1.** [munch] mâchonner **2.** ***phr*** **to ~ at the bit : we were all ~ing at the bit to get started** on rongeait tous notre frein en attendant de commencer.
◇ *n* ***inf*** crack *m*.

champagne [ˌʃæmˈpeɪn] ◇ *n* [wine] champagne *m* ■ **a ~ glass** une coupe à champagne.
◇ *comp* : **~ socialism** la gauche caviar.
◇ *adj* [colour] champagne *(inv)*.

champers [ˈʃæmpəz] *n* ***UK inf*** champ' *m*.

champion [ˈtʃæmpjən] ◇ *n* **1.** [winner] champion *m*, - onne *f* ■ **the world chess ~** le champion du monde d'échecs ■ **she's a ~ runner** elle est championne de course **2.** [supporter] champion *m*, - onne *f*.
◇ *vt* défendre, soutenir ■ **she ~ed the cause of birth control** elle s'est faite la championne de la régulation des naissances.

championship [ˈtʃæmpjənʃɪp] *n* **1.** GAMES & SPORT championnat *m* ■ **he plays ~ tennis** il participe aux championnats de tennis **2.** [support] défense *f*.

chance [tʃɑːns] ◇ *n* **1.** [possibility, likelihood] : **is there any ~ of seeing you again?** serait-il possible de vous revoir? ■ **there was little ~ of him finding work** il y avait peu de chances qu'il trouve du travail ■ **we have an outside ~ of success** nous avons une très faible chance de réussir ■ **she's got a good** *OR* **strong ~ of being accepted** elle a de fortes chances d'être acceptée *OR* reçue ■ **to be in with a ~ : he's in with a ~ of getting the job** il a une chance d'obtenir le poste
2. [fortune, luck] hasard *m* ■ **it was pure ~ that I found it** je l'ai trouvé tout à fait par hasard ■ **to leave things to ~** laisser faire les choses ■ **to leave nothing to ~** ne rien laisser au hasard
3. [opportunity] : **I haven't had a ~ to write to him** je n'ai pas trouvé l'occasion de lui écrire ■ **give her a ~ to defend herself** donnez-lui l'occasion de se défendre ■ **it's a ~ in a million** c'est une occasion unique ■ **I'm offering you the ~ of a lifetime** je vous offre la chance de votre vie ■ **the poor man never had** *OR* **stood a ~** le pauvre homme n'avait aucune chance de s'en tirer ■ **this is your last ~** c'est votre dernière chance
4. [risk] risque *m* ■ **I don't want to take the ~ of losing** je ne veux pas prendre le risque de perdre ■ **he took a ~ on a racehorse** il a parié sur un cheval de course.
◇ *adj* de hasard ■ **I was a ~ witness to the robbery** j'ai été un témoin accidentel du vol.
◇ *vi* ***fml*** & ***lit*** [happen] : **I ~d to be at the same table as Sir Sydney** je me suis trouvé par hasard à la même table que sir Sydney.
◇ *vt* [risk] ***lit*** hasarder ■ **he ~d his savings on the venture** il a risqué ses économies dans l'entreprise ■ **let's ~ it** *OR* **our luck** tentons notre chance ➊ **to ~ one's arm** risquer le coup.
◆ **chances** *npl* [possibility, likelihood] chances *fpl* ■ **(the) ~s are (that) he'll never find out** il y a de fortes *OR* grandes chances qu'il ne l'apprenne jamais ■ **what are her ~s of making a full recovery?** quelles sont ses chances de se rétablir complètement?
◆ **by chance** *adv phr* par hasard ■ **by pure** *OR* **sheer ~ we were both staying at the same hotel** il se trouvait que nous logions au même hôtel ■ **would you by any ~ know who that man is?** sauriez-vous par hasard qui est cet homme?
◆ **chance on, chance upon** *vt insep* [person] rencontrer par hasard ■ [thing] trouver par hasard.

chancel [ˈtʃɑːnsl] *n* chœur *m*.

chancellery [ˈtʃɑːnsələrɪ] (*pl* **chancelleries**) *n* chancellerie *f* ■ ***fig*** **in the chancelleries of Europe** dans les hauts-lieux de la politique européenne.

chancellor [ˈtʃɑːnsələʳ] *n* **1.** POL chancelier *m*, -ère *f* ■ **the Chancellor of the Exchequer** POL le Chancelier de l'Échiquier, ≃ le ministre des Finances *(en Grande-Bretagne)* **2.** UNIV ***UK*** président *m*, - e *f* honoraire ■ ***US*** président *m*, - e *f* (d'université).

chancellorship [ˈtʃɑːnsələʃɪp] *n* **1.** ***UK*** ADMIN direction *f* des finances ■ **the economy had done extremely well under Mr Smith's ~** l'économie avait montré d'excellents résultats lorsque M. Smith était au ministère des Finances **2.** ***US*** UNIV présidence *f* (d'université).

chancer [ˈtʃɑːnsəʳ] *n* ***UK inf*** filou *m*.

chancery [ˈtʃɑːnsərɪ] (*pl* **chanceries**) *n* LAW **1.** [in UK] : **the suit is in ~** l'action est en instance ➊ **Chancery (Division)** cour *f* de la chancellerie *(une des trois divisions de la Haute cour de justice en Angleterre)* ■ **ward in ~** pupille *mf* de l'État **2.** [in US] : **Court of Chancery** ≃ cour *f* d'équité **3.** [in wrestling] clé *f*, clef *f*.

chancy [ˈtʃɑːnsɪ] (*comp* **chancier**, *superl* **chanciest**) *adj* ***inf*** risqué.

chandelier [ˌʃændəˈlɪəʳ] *n* lustre *m (pour éclairer).*

chandler [ˈtʃɑːndləʳ] *n* **1.** [supplier] fournisseur *m* ▪ **ship's ~** shipchandler *m* **2.** [candlemaker] chandelier *m*.

change [tʃeɪndʒ] ◇ *n* **1.** [alteration] changement *m* ▪ **we expect a ~ in the weather** nous nous attendons à un changement de temps ▪ **a survey showed a radical ~ in public opinion** un sondage a montré un revirement de l'opinion publique ▪ **a ~ for the better/worse** un changement en mieux/pire, une amélioration/dégradation ▪ **walking to work makes a pleasant ~ from driving** c'est agréable d'aller travailler à pied plutôt qu'en voiture ▪ **it'll be** *OR* **make a nice ~ for them not to have the children in the house** cela les changera agréablement de ne pas avoir les enfants à la maison ▪ **that makes a ~!** voilà qui change! ▪ **there's been little ~ in his condition** son état n'a guère évolué ▪ **to have a ~ of heart** changer d'avis ▪ **I need a ~ of scene** *OR* **scenery** *fig* j'ai besoin de changer de décor *OR* d'air
2. [fresh set or supply] : **a ~ of clothes** des vêtements de rechange
3. [in journey] changement *m*, correspondance *f*
4. [money] monnaie *f* ▪ **can you give me ~ for five pounds?** pouvez-vous me faire la monnaie de cinq livres? ▪ **I don't have any loose** *OR* **small ~** je n'ai pas de petite monnaie ▶ **you'll get no ~ out of him** *UK inf* on ne peut rien en tirer
5. *euph* & PHYSIOL = **change of life**.
◇ *vt* **1.** [substitute, switch] changer, changer de ▪ **to ~ one's name** changer de nom ▪ **she's going to ~ her name to Parker** elle va prendre le nom de Parker ▪ **to ~ one's clothes** changer de vêtements, se changer ▪ **to ~ trains** changer de train ▪ **to ~ ends** SPORT changer de camp ▪ **to ~ one's mind** changer d'avis ▪ **you'd better ~ your ways** tu ferais bien de t'amender ▶ **to ~ one's tune** changer de ton
2. [exchange] changer ▪ **if the shoes are too small we'll ~ them for you** si les chaussures sont trop petites nous vous les changerons ▪ **to ~ places with sb** changer de place avec qqn ▪ **I wouldn't want to ~ places with him!** *fig* je n'aimerais pas être à sa place! ▪ **I'd like to ~ my pounds into dollars** FIN j'aimerais changer mes livres contre des *OR* en dollars ▪ **can you ~ a ten-pound note?** [into coins] pouvez-vous me donner la monnaie d'un billet de dix livres?
3. [alter, modify] changer ▪ **he won't ~ anything in the text** il ne changera rien au texte ▪ **the illness completely ~d his personality** la maladie a complètement transformé son caractère ▶ **to ~ one's spots** changer *OR* modifier totalement son caractère
4. [transform] changer, transformer ▪ **to ~sthg/sb into sthg** changer qqch/qqn en qqch ▪ **to ~ water into wine** BIBLE changer l'eau en vin ▪ **the liquid/her hair has ~d colour** le liquide a/ses cheveux ont changé de couleur
5. [baby, bed] changer
6. AUT : **to ~ gear** changer de vitesse.
◇ *vi* **1.** [alter, turn] changer ▪ **to ~ for the better/worse** changer en mieux/pire ▪ **nothing will make him ~** rien ne le changera, il ne changera jamais ▪ **wait for the lights to ~** attendez que le feu passe au vert ▪ **the wind has ~d** le vent a changé *OR* tourné
2. [become transformed] se changer, se transformer ▪ **to ~ into sthg** se transformer en qqch
3. [change clothing] se changer ▪ **they ~d out of their uniforms** ils ont enlevé leurs uniformes ▪ **he ~d into a pair of jeans** il s'est changé et a mis un jean ▪ **I'm going to ~ into something warmer** je vais mettre quelque chose de plus chaud
4. [transportation] changer ▪ **all ~!** [announcement] tout le monde descend!
5. *UK* AUT : **she ~d into fourth gear** elle a passé la quatrième
6. [moon] entrer dans une nouvelle phase.
◆ **for a change** *adv phr* : **it's nice to see you smiling for a ~** c'est bien de te voir sourire pour une fois.
◆ **change down** *vi insep* AUT rétrograder ▪ **he ~ed down into third** il est passé en troisième.
◆ **change over** *vi insep* **1.** *UK* [switch] : **he ~d over from smoking cigarettes to smoking cigars** il s'est mis à fumer des cigares à la place de cigarettes ▪ **the country has ~d over to nuclear power** le pays est passé au nucléaire
2. SPORT [change positions] changer de côté.
◆ **change up** *vi insep* AUT passer la vitesse supérieure ▪ **he ~d up into third** il a passé la troisième, il est passé en troisième.

changeability [ˌtʃeɪndʒəˈbɪlətɪ] *n* variabilité *f*.

changeable [ˈtʃeɪndʒəbl] *adj* **1.** [variable] variable ▪ **~ weather** temps variable *OR* instable **2.** [capricious, fickle] changeant, inconstant.

changed [tʃeɪndʒd] *adj* changé, différent ▪ **he's a ~ man** c'est un autre homme.

changeling [ˈtʃeɪndʒlɪŋ] *n enfant substitué par les fées au véritable enfant d'un couple.*

change machine *n* distributeur *m* de monnaie.

change of life *n* : **the ~** le retour d'âge.

changeover [ˈtʃeɪndʒˌəʊvəʳ] *n* **1.** [switch] changement *m*, passage *m* ▪ **the ~ to computers went smoothly** le passage à l'informatisation s'est fait en douceur **2.** *UK* SPORT changement *m* de côté.

change purse *n US* porte-monnaie *m inv*.

changing [ˈtʃeɪndʒɪŋ] ◇ *adj* qui change ▪ **we're living in a ~ world** nous vivons dans un monde en évolution.
◇ *n* changement *m* ▪ **the Changing of the Guard** la relève de la garde.

changing room *n UK* SPORT vestiaire *m* ▪ [in shop] cabine *f* d'essayage.

channel [ˈtʃænl] ◇ *n* **1.** [broad strait] détroit *m*, bras *m* de mer ▪ **the Channel** la Manche ▪ **a Channel** *OR* **cross-Channel ferry** un ferry qui traverse la Manche **2.** [river bed] lit *m* ▪ NAUT [navigable course] chenal *m*, passe *f* **3.** [passage - for gases, liquids] canal *m*, conduite *f* ; [- for electrical signals] piste *f* **4.** [furrow, groove] sillon *m* ▪ [on a column] cannelure *f* ▪ [in a street] caniveau *m* **5.** TV chaîne *f* ▪ **the film is on Channel 2** le film est sur la deuxième chaîne **6.** RADIO bande *f* **7.** *fig* [means] canal *m*, voie *f* ▪ **to go through (the) official ~s** suivre la filière officielle **8.** COMPUT canal *m*.
◇ *vt* (*UK pret & pp* **channelled**, *cont* **channelling**) (*US pret & pp* **channeled**, *cont* **channeling**) **1.** [land] creuser des rigoles dans ▪ [river] canaliser ▪ [street] construire des caniveaux dans ▪ [gas, water] acheminer (par des conduites) ▪ [column] canneler **2.** *fig* [direct] canaliser, diriger ▪ **the government wants to ~ resources to those who need them most** le gouvernement veut affecter les ressources en priorité à ceux qui en ont le plus besoin ▪ **she needs to ~ her energies into some useful work** elle a besoin de canaliser son énergie à effectuer du travail utile.

channel hop *vi* zapper.

Channel Islander *n habitant des îles Anglo-Normandes.*

Channel Islands *pr npl* : **the ~** les îles *fpl* Anglo-Normandes ▪ **in the ~** dans les îles Anglo-Normandes.

Channel Tunnel *n* : **the ~** le tunnel sous la Manche.

chant [tʃɑːnt] ◇ *n* **1.** MUS mélopée *f* ▪ RELIG psalmodie *f* **2.** [slogan, cry] chant *m* scandé.
◇ *vi* **1.** MUS chanter une mélopée ▪ RELIG psalmodier **2.** [crowd, demonstrators] scander des slogans.
◇ *vt* **1.** MUS chanter ▪ RELIG psalmodier **2.** [slogans] scander.

Chanukah [ˈhænʊkə] *n* Hanoukka *f*.

chaos [ˈkeɪɒs] *n* chaos *m*.

chaos theory *n* théorie *f* du chaos.

chaotic [keɪˈɒtɪk] *adj* chaotique.

chaotically [keɪˈɒtɪklɪ] *adv* chaotiquement.

chap [tʃæp] ◇ *n* **1.** *UK inf* [man] type *m* ▪ **be a good ~ and tell him I'm not in** sois sympa et dis-lui que je ne suis pas là ▪ **what do you think, ~s?** qu'en pensez-vous, les amis? ▪ **how are you, old ~?** *dated* comment allez-vous, mon vieux? **2.** [sore] gerçure *f*, crevasse *f*.
◇ *vt* (*pret & pp* **chapped**, *cont* **chapping**) gercer, crevasser.
◇ *vi* (*pret & pp* **chapped**, *cont* **chapping**) (se) gercer, se crevasser.

chapat(t)i [tʃə'pætɪ] *n* galette *f* de pain indienne.

chapel ['tʃæpl] ◇ *n* **1.** [in church, school etc] chapelle *f* **2.** *UK* [Nonconformist church] temple *m* **3.** *UK* [of trade unionists] *membres du syndicat dans une maison d'édition.*
◇ *adj* *UK* RELIG non-conformiste.

chapel of rest *n chambre mortuaire dans une entreprise de pompes funèbres.*

chaperon(e) ['ʃæpərəʊn] ◇ *n* chaperon *m*.
◇ *vt* chaperonner.

chaplain ['tʃæplɪn] *n* aumônier *m* ■ [in private chapel] chapelain *m*.

chaplaincy ['tʃæplɪnsɪ] *n* aumônerie *f*.

chaplet ['tʃæplɪt] *n* **1.** [wreath] guirlande *f* **2.** RELIG chapelet *m*.

Chappaquiddick [tʃæpə'kwɪdɪk] *pr n* : **~, the ~ incident** l'affaire *f* de Chappaquiddick *(accident ayant coûté la vie, en 1973, à Mary-Jo Kopechne, collaboratrice du sénateur américain Edward Kennedy, dans des circonstances mal élucidées).*

chapped [tʃæpt] *adj* [hands, lips] gercé.

chappie ['tʃæpɪ] *UK n inf dated* = **chap** *(n sense 1).*

chaps [tʃæps] *npl* jambières *fpl* de cuir.

chapstick® ['tʃæpstɪk] *n* *US* bâton *m* de pommade pour les lèvres.

chapter ['tʃæptəʳ] *n* **1.** [of book] chapitre *m* ■ **it's in ~ three** c'est dans le troisième chapitre ➲ **she can give** *OR* **quote(you) ~ and verse on the subject** elle peut citer toutes les autorités en la matière **2.** [era] chapitre *m* ■ **this closed a particularly violent ~ in our history** ceci marqua la fin d'un chapitre particulièrement violent de notre histoire **3.** [series] succession *f*, cascade *f* ■ **a ~ of accidents** une série d'accidents *OR* de malheurs, une série noire **4.** [of organization] branche *f*, section *f* **5.** RELIG chapitre *m*.

chapter house *n* chapitre *m*.

char [tʃɑːʳ] ◇ *vt* (*pret & pp* **charred**, *cont* **charring**) **1.** [reduce to charcoal] carboniser, réduire en charbon **2.** [scorch] griller, brûler légèrement.
◇ *vi* (*pret & pp* **charred**, *cont* **charring**) **1.** [scorch] brûler ■ [blacken] noircir **2.** *UK inf dated* [clean] faire des ménages.
◇ *n* **1.** *UK inf dated* [cleaner] femme *f* de ménage **2.** *UK inf dated* thé *m* **3.** [fish] omble *m* chevalier.

charabanc ['ʃærəbæŋ] *n dated* autocar *m* (de tourisme).

character ['kærəktəʳ] ◇ *n* **1.** [nature, temperament] caractère *m* ■ **his remark was quite in/out of ~** cette remarque lui ressemblait tout à fait/ne lui ressemblait pas du tout **2.** [aspect, quality] caractère *m* **3.** [determination, integrity] caractère *m* ■ **she's a woman of great ~** c'est une femme qui a beaucoup de caractère **4.** [distinction, originality] caractère *m* ■ **the house had (great) ~** la maison avait beaucoup de caractère **5.** [unusual person] personnage *m* ■ **she seems to attract all sorts of ~s** elle semble attirer toutes sortes d'individus ■ **he's quite a ~!** c'est un phénomène *OR* un sacré numéro! **6.** *pej* [person] individu *m* **7.** CIN, LIT & THEAT personnage *m* ■ **the main ~** le personnage principal, le protagoniste ■ **Chaplin plays two different ~s in "The Great Dictator"** Chaplin joue deux rôles différents dans "Le Dictateur" **8.** TYPO caractère *m* **9.** *lit* [handwriting] écriture *f*.
◇ *comp* **1.** CIN & THEAT : **~ part** *OR* **role** rôle *m* de composition **2.** COMPUT : **~ code** code *m* de caractère ■ **~ set** jeu *m* de caractères.

character actor *n* acteur *m* de genre.

character assassination *n* diffamation *f*.

characteristic [ˌkærəktə'rɪstɪk] ◇ *adj* caractéristique ■ **she refused all honours with ~ humility** elle refusa tous les honneurs avec l'humilité qui la caractérisait.
◇ *n* caractéristique *f* ■ **national ~s** les caractères *mpl* nationaux.

characteristically [ˌkærəktə'rɪstɪklɪ] *adv* : **he was ~ generous with his praise** comme on pouvait s'y attendre, il fut prodigue de ses compliments *OR* il ne ménagea pas ses éloges.

characterization [ˌkærəktəraɪ'zeɪʃn] *n* **1.** *fml* [description] caractérisation *f* **2.** LIT & THEAT représentation *f* *OR* peinture *f* des personnages.

characterize, *UK* **ise** ['kærəktəraɪz] *vt* caractériser ■ **his music is ~d by a sense of joy** sa musique se caractérise par une impression de joie ■ **Shakespeare ~d Henry VI as a weak but pious king** Shakespeare a dépeint Henri VI comme un roi faible mais pieux.

characterless ['kærəktəlɪs] *adj* sans caractère.

character sketch *n* portrait *m* *OR* description *f* rapide.

character witness *n* témoin *m* de moralité.

charade [ʃə'rɑːd] *n* [pretence] feinte *f* ■ **the trial was a complete ~!** c'était une véritable parodie de procès !
◆ **charades** *npl* GAMES charade *f* en action ■ **let's play ~s** jouons aux charades.

charcoal ['tʃɑːkəʊl] ◇ *n* **1.** [fuel] charbon *m* de bois **2.** ART fusain *m* ■ **he drew her in ~** il l'a dessinée au fusain.
◇ *comp* **1.** [fuel] à charbon **2.** ART au charbon, au fusain ■ **a ~ pencil** un (crayon) fusain ■ **a ~ drawing** un croquis au fusain.

charcoal burner *n* charbonnier *m*.

charcoal grey ◇ *n* gris *m* foncé.
◇ *adj* gris foncé *(inv)*, (gris) anthracite *(inv)*.

chard [tʃɑːd] *n* blette *f*, bette *f*.

charge [tʃɑːdʒ] ◇ *n* **1.** [fee, cost] frais *mpl* ■ **postal/telephone ~s** frais postaux/téléphoniques ■ **there's a ~ of one pound for use of the locker** il faut payer une livre pour utiliser la consigne automatique ■ **is there any extra ~ for a single room?** est-ce qu'il faut payer un supplément pour une chambre à un lit? ■ **what's the ~ for delivery?** la livraison coûte combien? ■ **there's no ~ for children** c'est gratuit pour les enfants ■ **free of ~** gratuitement ■ **there's a small admission ~ to the museum** il y a un petit droit d'entrée au musée ■ **cash or ~?** *US* comptant ou crédit? ➲ **carriage ~** *OR* **~s** COMM frais de port **2.** LAW [accusation] chef *m* d'accusation, inculpation *f* ■ **he was arrested on a ~ of conspiracy** il a été arrêté sous l'inculpation d'association criminelle ■ **you are under arrest – on what ~?** vous êtes en état d'arrestation – pour quel motif? ■ **to file ~s against sb** déposer une plainte contre qqn ■ **a ~ of drunk driving was brought against the driver** le conducteur a été mis en examen pour conduite en état d'ivresse ■ **he pleaded guilty to the ~ of robbery** il a plaidé coupable à l'accusation de vol **3.** [allegation] accusation *f* ■ **the government rejected ~s that it was mismanaging the economy** le gouvernement a rejeté l'accusation selon laquelle il gérait mal l'économie ■ **~s of torture have been brought** *OR* **made against the regime** des accusations de torture ont été portées contre le régime
4. [command, control] : **who's in ~ here?** qui est-ce qui commande ici? ■ **she's in ~ of public relations** elle s'occupe des relations publiques ■ **can I leave you in ~ of the shop?** puis-je vous laisser la responsabilité du magasin? ■ **I was put in ~ of the investigation** on m'a confié la responsabilité de l'enquête ■ **to take ~ of sthg** prendre en charge qqch, prendre *OR* assumer la direction de qqch ■ **he had a dozen salesmen under his ~** il avait une douzaine de vendeurs sous sa responsabilité
5. *fml* [burden] : **to be a ~ on sb** être une charge pour qqn
6. *fml* [dependent] *personne confiée à la garde d'une autre* ■ [pupil] élève *mf* ■ **the governess instructed her two ~s in French and Italian** la gouvernante apprit le français et l'italien à ses deux élèves
7. [duty, mission] charge *f* ■ **he was given the ~ of preparing the defence** on l'a chargé de préparer la défense ■ **the judge's ~ to the jury** LAW les recommandations du juge au jury
8. MIL [attack] charge *f* ■ **the Charge of the Light Brigade** *UK* HIST la Charge de la brigade légère
9. ELEC & PHYS charge *f*
10. HERALD meuble *m*.
◇ *vt* **1.** [money] faire payer ■ [demand payment from] demander, prendre ■ **the doctor ~d her $90 for a visit** le médecin lui a fait payer *OR* lui a pris 90 dollars pour une consultation

■ **how much would you ~ to take us to the airport?** combien prendriez-vous pour nous emmener à l'aéroport? ■ **they didn't ~ us for the coffee** ils ne nous ont pas fait payer les cafés ■ **you will be ~d for postage** COMM les frais postaux seront à votre charge
2. [defer payment of] : **~ the bill to my account** mettez le montant de la facture sur mon compte ■ **I ~d all my expenses to the company** j'ai mis tous mes frais sur le compte de la société ■ **can I ~ this jacket?** *US* [with a credit card] puis-je payer cette veste avec ma carte (de crédit) ? ■ **~ it** *US* mettez-le sur mon compte
3. [allege] : **to ~ that sb has done sthg** accuser qqn d'avoir fait qqch
4. LAW inculper ■ **I'm charging you with the murder of X** je vous inculpe du meurtre de X
5. [attack] charger ■ **the troops ~d the building** les troupes donnèrent l'assaut au bâtiment
6. *fml* [command, entrust] : **I was ~d with guarding the prisoner** je fus chargé de la surveillance du prisonnier
7. ELEC & MIL charger
8. *fml* [fill] charger ■ **to ~ sb's glass** remplir le verre de qqn.
◇ *vi* **1.** [demand in payment] demander, prendre ■ **do you ~ for delivery?** est-ce que vous faites payer la livraison? ■ **he doesn't ~** il ne demande *OR* prend rien
2. [rush] se précipiter ■ **the rhino suddenly ~d** tout d'un coup le rhinocéros a chargé ■ **suddenly two policemen ~d into the room** tout d'un coup deux policiers ont fait irruption dans la pièce ■ **she ~d into/out of her office** elle entra dans son/sortit de son bureau au pas de charge
3. MIL [attack] charger, donner l'assaut ■ **~!** à l'assaut!
4. ELEC se charger *OR* recharger.
◆ **charge up** *vt sep* **1.** [bill] : **she ~d everything up to her account** elle a mis tous les frais sur son compte
2. ELEC charger, recharger.

THE CHARGE OF THE LIGHT BRIGADE

Célèbre poème de lord Tennyson, inspiré d'un épisode de la guerre de Crimée, au cours duquel, en 1854, une poignée de soldats britanniques se sacrifia pour sauver le port de Balaklava (qu'ils contrôlaient avec les Français et les Turcs) attaqué par les Russes.

chargeable [ˈtʃɑːdʒəbl] *adj* **1.** FIN : **the item is ~ with duty of £10** l'article est soumis à une taxe de 10 livres ■ **travelling expenses are ~ to the employer** les frais de déplacement sont à la charge de l'employeur ■ **~ expenses** frais déductibles **2.** LAW : **a ~ offence** un délit.

charge account *n US* compte *m* permanent *(dans un magasin)*.

charge card *n* carte *f* de crédit.

charged [tʃɑːdʒd] *adj* **1.** [atmosphere] chargé ■ **a voice ~ with emotion** une voix pleine d'émotion **2.** ELEC chargé.

chargé d'affaires [ˌʃɑːʒeɪdæˈfeəʳ] (*pl* **chargés d'affaires**) *n* chargé *m* d'affaires.

charge hand *n UK* sous-chef *m* d'équipe.

charge nurse *n UK* infirmier *m*, - ère *f* en chef.

charger [ˈtʃɑːdʒəʳ] *n* **1.** ELEC chargeur *m* **2.** *arch* & *lit* [horse] cheval *m* de bataille.

charge sheet *n UK* procès-verbal *m*.

chariot [ˈtʃærɪət] *n* char *m*.

charioteer [ˌtʃærɪəˈtɪəʳ] *n* aurige *m*.

charisma [kəˈrɪzmə] *n* charisme *m*.

charismatic [ˌkærɪzˈmætɪk] *adj* charismatique.

charitable [ˈtʃærətəbl] *adj* **1.** [generous, kind] charitable **2.** [cause, institution] de bienfaisance, de charité ■ **~ organizations** œuvres *fpl* de bienfaisance *OR* de charité ■ **~ works** les bonnes œuvres ■ **a ~ donation** un don fait par charité.

charitably [ˈtʃærətəblɪ] *adv* charitablement.

charity [ˈtʃærətɪ] (*pl* **charities**) *n* **1.** RELIG charité *f* ■ [generosity, kindness] charité ■ **an act of ~** une action charitable, un acte de charité **2.** [help to the needy] charité *f* ■ **they raised £10,000 for ~** ils ont collecté 10 000 livres pour les bonnes œuvres **3.** [organization] association *f* caritative, œuvre *f* de bienfaisance ■ **Catholic charities** les associations caritatives catholiques ■ **~ work** bénévolat *m* ➲ **~ shop** *magasin dont les employés sont des bénévoles et dont les bénéfices servent à subventionner une œuvre d'utilité publique* ■ **the Charity Commission** *commission gouvernementale britannique contrôlant les associations caritatives.*

charlady [ˈtʃɑːˌleɪdɪ] (*pl* **charladies**) *UK n dated* = **char** *(n sense 1)*.

charlatan [ˈʃɑːlətən] ◇ *n* charlatan *m*.
◇ *adj* charlatanesque.

Charlemagne [ˈʃɑːləmeɪn] *pr n* Charlemagne.

Charles [tʃɑːlz] *pr n* : **~ the Bold** Charles le Téméraire ■ **~ V** Charles Quint.

charleston [ˈtʃɑːlstən] *n* charleston *m*.

charley horse [ˈtʃɑːlɪ-] *n (U) US inf* crampe *f*.

charlie [ˈtʃɑːlɪ] *n* **1.** *UK inf* cloche *f* ■ **I felt a proper** *OR* **right ~** je me suis senti vraiment bête **2.** △ *drug sl* [cocaine] coke *f*.

Charlie Chaplin [ˈtʃɑːlɪˈtʃæplɪn] *pr n* [in real life] Charlie Chaplin ■ [in films] Charlot.

charlotte [ˈʃɑːlət] *n* [baked] charlotte *f* ■ **apple ~** charlotte aux pommes.

charm [tʃɑːm] ◇ *n* **1.** [appeal, attraction] charme *m* ■ **to turn on the ~** faire du charme **2.** [in sorcery] charme *m*, sortilège *m* ■ **a lucky ~** un porte-bonheur ■ **to work like a ~** marcher à merveille *OR* à la perfection **3.** [piece of jewellery] breloque *f* ■ **a ~ bracelet** un bracelet à breloques.
◇ *vt* **1.** [please, delight] charmer, séduire ■ **she ~ed him into accepting the invitation** elle l'a si bien enjôlé qu'il a accepté l'invitation **2.** [subj: magician] charmer, ensorceler ■ [subj: snake charmer] charmer.
◆ **charms** *npl* charmes *mpl*.

charmed [tʃɑːmd] *adj* **1.** [delighted] enchanté **2.** [by magic] charmé ■ **to lead a ~ life** *fig* être béni des dieux.

charmer [ˈtʃɑːməʳ] *n* charmeur *m*, - euse *f*.

charming [ˈtʃɑːmɪŋ] *adj* charmant ■ **~!** *iron* c'est charmant!

charmingly [ˈtʃɑːmɪŋlɪ] *adv* de façon charmante.

charr [tʃɑːʳ] *n* = **char** *(n 3)*.

charred [tʃɑːd] *adj* noirci (par le feu).

chart [tʃɑːt] ◇ *n* **1.** NAUT carte *f* marine ■ ASTRON carte *f* (du ciel) **2.** [table] tableau *m* ■ [graph] courbe *f* ■ MED courbe *f* **3.** ASTROL horoscope *m*.
◇ *vt* **1.** NAUT [seas, waterway] établir la carte de, faire un levé hydrographique de ■ ASTRON [stars] porter sur la carte **2.** [record - on a table, graph] faire la courbe de ■ *fig* [- progress, development] rendre compte de **3.** *fig* [make a plan of] tracer ■ **the director ~ed a way out of financial collapse** le directeur a établi *OR* mis au point un plan pour éviter un effondrement financier.
◇ *vi inf* être au hit-parade.
◆ **charts** *npl* MUS hit-parade *m* ■ **she's (got a record) in the ~s** elle est au hit-parade.

charter [ˈtʃɑːtəʳ] ◇ *n* **1.** [statement of rights] charte *f* ■ [of a business, organization, university] statuts *mpl* **2.** [lease, licence] affrètement *m* ■ [charter flight] charter *m* ■ **we've hired three coaches on ~** *UK* nous avons affrété trois autocars.
◇ *vt* **1.** [establish] accorder une charte à **2.** [hire, rent] affréter.

chartered [ˈtʃɑːtəd] *adj* **1.** [hired, rented] affrété **2.** *UK* [qualified] : **a ~ accountant** un expert-comptable ■ **a ~ surveyor** un expert immobilier.

charter flight *n* (vol *m*) charter *m*.

charter plane *n* (avion *m*) charter *m*.

Chartist [ˈtʃɑːtɪst] ◇ *n* chartiste *mf*.
◇ *adj* chartiste.

chart-topping *adj UK qui est en tête de hit-parade.*

charwoman ['tʃɑ:ˌwʊmən] (*pl* **charwomen** [-ˌwɪmɪn]) *n dated* = **char** *(n sense 1)*.

chary ['tʃeərɪ] *adj* **1.** [cautious] précautionneux ■ **he's ~ of allowing strangers into his home** il hésite à accueillir des gens qu'il ne connaît pas chez lui **2.** [ungenerous] parcimonieux ■ **he was ~ of praise** il faisait rarement des éloges, il était avare de compliments.

chase [tʃeɪs] <> *vt* **1.** [pursue] poursuivre ■ **two police cars ~d the van** deux voitures de police ont pris la camionnette en chasse **2.** [amorously] courir (après) **3.** [metal] ciseler, repousser.
<> *vi* [rush] : **she ~d all around London to find a wedding dress** elle a parcouru *OR* fait tout Londres pour trouver une robe de mariée.
<> *n* **1.** [pursuit] poursuite *f* ■ **the hounds gave ~ to the fox** la meute a pris le renard en chasse ■ **the prisoner climbed over the wall and the guards gave ~** le prisonnier escalada le mur et les gardiens se lancèrent à sa poursuite **2.** HUNT [sport, land, game] chasse *f* **3.** [groove] saignée **4.** TYPO châssis *m*.
◆ **chase after** *vt insep* courir après.
◆ **chase away, chase off** *vt sep* chasser.
◆ **chase up** *vt sep UK* **1.** [information] rechercher **2.** [organization, person] : **can you ~ up the manager for me?** pouvez-vous relancer le directeur à propos de ce que je lui ai demandé? ■ **I had to ~ him up for the £50 he owed me** j'ai dû lui réclamer les 50 livres qu'il me devait.

chaser ['tʃeɪsər] *n* **1.** [drink] : **they drank scotch with beer ~s** ils ont bu du scotch suivi par de la bière **2.** [pursuer] chasseur *m* **3.** [horse] cheval *m* de course.

chasm ['kæzm] *n* abîme *m*, gouffre *m*.

chassis ['ʃæsɪ] (*pl inv* ['ʃæsɪ]) *n* **1.** AUT châssis *m* ■ AERON train *m* d'atterrissage **2.** *inf* [body] châssis *m*.

chaste [tʃeɪst] *adj* chaste.

chasten ['tʃeɪsn] *vt fml* **1.** [subdue, humble] corriger, maîtriser ■ [pride] rabaisser ■ **she was ~ed by her failure** elle fut abattue par son échec **2.** [punish, reprimand] châtier, punir.

chastened ['tʃeɪsnd] *adj* abattu.

chastening ['tʃeɪsənɪŋ] *adj* : **prison had a ~ effect on him** la prison l'a assagi ■ **it's a ~ thought** c'était une pensée plutôt décourageante.

chastise [tʃæ'staɪz] *vt fml* [punish, beat] châtier, punir ■ [reprimand] fustiger.

chastisement ['tʃæstɪzmənt] *n fml* châtiment *m*.

chastity ['tʃæstətɪ] *n* chasteté *f*.

chastity belt *n* ceinture *f* de chasteté.

chasuble ['tʃæzjʊbl] *n* chasuble *f*.

chat [tʃæt] <> *vi* (*pret & pp* **chatted**, *cont* **chatting**) bavarder, causer ■ **we were just chatting about this and that** nous causions de choses et d'autres.
<> *n* : **we had a nice ~ over lunch** nous avons eu une conversation agréable pendant le déjeuner ■ **she came over for a ~** elle est venue bavarder un peu.
◆ **chat up** *vt sep UK inf* baratiner, draguer.

chatline ['tʃætlaɪn] *n* [gen] réseau *m* téléphonique *(payant)* ■ [for sexual encounters] téléphone *m* rose.

chat room, chatroom *n* COMPUT forum *m* de discussion.

chat show *n UK* causerie *f* télévisée.

chattel ['tʃætl] *n* bien *m* meuble ■ **a ~ mortgage** *US* FIN un nantissement de biens meubles.

chatter ['tʃætər] <> *vi* **1.** [person] papoter, bavarder, palabrer ■ [bird] jaser, jacasser ■ [monkey] babiller ➊ **the ~ing classes** *pej* les intellos *mpl* **2.** [machine] cliqueter **3.** [teeth] claquer ■ **my teeth were ~ing from** *OR* **with the cold** j'avais tellement froid que je claquais des dents.
<> *n* **1.** [of people] bavardage *m*, papotage *m* ■ [of birds, monkeys] jacassement *m* **2.** [of machines] cliquetis *m* **3.** [of teeth] claquement *m*.

chatterbox ['tʃætəbɒks] *n inf* moulin *m* à paroles.

chatterer ['tʃætərər] *n* [talkative person] bavard *m*, - e *f*.

chatty ['tʃætɪ] *adj* [person] bavard ■ [letter] plein de bavardages.

chauffeur ['ʃəʊfər] <> *n* chauffeur *m*.
<> *vi* travailler comme chauffeur.
<> *vt* conduire.

chauffeur-driven *adj* conduit par un chauffeur.

chauvinism ['ʃəʊvɪnɪzm] *n* [nationalism] chauvinisme *m* ■ [sexism] machisme *m*, phallocratie *f*.

chauvinist ['ʃəʊvɪnɪst] *n* [nationalist] chauvin *m*, - e *f* ■ [sexist] phallocrate *m*, machiste *m*.

chauvinistic ['ʃəʊvɪ'nɪstɪk] *adj* [nationalistic] chauvin ■ [sexist] machiste, phallocrate.

chav ['tʃæv] *n UK inf pej* racaille *f*, lascar *m*.

cheap [tʃi:p] <> *adj* **1.** [inexpensive] bon marché ■ **labour is ~er in the Far East** la main-d'œuvre est moins chère en Extrême-Orient ■ **he bought a ~ ticket to Australia** il a acheté un billet à prix *OR* tarif réduit pour l'Australie ■ **it was the ~est piano in the shop** c'était le piano le moins cher du magasin ➊ **~ and cheerful** sans prétentions **2.** [poor quality] de mauvaise qualité ■ **the furniture was ~ and nasty** *UK* les meubles étaient de très mauvaise qualité **3.** [of little value] : **human life is ~ in many countries** il y a beaucoup de pays où la vie humaine a peu de valeur ■ **that's how he gets his ~ thrills** c'est ça qui l'excite **4.** [low, despicable] : **a ~ joke** une plaisanterie de mauvais goût ■ **he made the girl feel ~** il fit en sorte que la fille eût honte **5.** *US* [stingy] mesquin.
<> *adv* [buy, get, sell] bon marché ■ **I can get it for you ~er** je peux vous le trouver pour moins cher ■ **clothes of that quality don't come ~** des vêtements de cette qualité coûtent cher.
◆ **on the cheap** *adv phr inf* : **she furnished the house on the ~** elle a meublé la maison pour pas cher ■ **they've got immigrants working for them on the ~** ils ont des immigrés qui travaillent pour eux au rabais.

cheapen ['tʃi:pn] <> *vt* **1.** [lower, debase] abaisser ■ **I wouldn't ~ myself by accepting a bribe** je ne m'abaisserais pas à accepter un pot-de-vin **2.** [reduce the price of] baisser le prix de.
<> *vi* devenir moins cher.

cheaply ['tʃi:plɪ] *adv* à bon marché ■ **I can do the job more ~** je peux faire le travail à meilleur marché *OR* pour moins cher.

cheapness ['tʃi:pnɪs] *n* **1.** [low price] bas prix *m* **2.** [poor quality] mauvaise qualité *f*.

cheapo ['tʃi:pəʊ] *adj inf* pas cher.

cheapskate ['tʃi:pskeɪt] *n inf* radin *m*, - e *f*, grippe-sou *m*.

cheat [tʃi:t] <> *vt* **1.** [defraud, swindle] escroquer, léser ■ **to ~ sb out of sthg** escroquer qqch à qqn ■ **to feel ~ed** se sentir lésé *OR* frustré **2.** *fig & lit* [deceive, trick] duper ■ **to ~ death** échapper à la mort.
<> *vi* tricher.
<> *n* **1.** [dishonest person] tricheur *m*, - euse *f* ■ [crook, swindler] escroc *m*, fraudeur *m*, - euse *f* **2.** [dishonest practice] tricherie *f*, tromperie *f*.
◆ **cheat on** *vt insep* **1.** [falsify] tricher sur **2.** [be unfaithful to] tromper.

cheating ['tʃi:tɪŋ] <> *n* **1.** [at cards, games] tricherie *f* ■ [in exams] copiage *m* **2.** [fraud] fraude *f* **3.** *(U)* [infidelity] infidélité *f*, infidélités *fpl*.
<> *adj* **1.** [dishonest] malhonnête, trompeur **2.** [unfaithful, disloyal] infidèle.

cheat sheet *n US inf* antisèche *f*.

Chechen ['tʃetʃen] <> *adj* tchétchène.
<> *n* Tchétchène *mf*.

Chechenia [ˌtʃetʃen'jɑ:], **Chechnya** [ˌtʃetʃen'jɑ:] *pr n* Tchétchénie *f* ■ **in ~** en Tchétchénie.

check [tʃek] <> *vt* **1.** [inspect, examine] contrôler, vérifier ■ [confirm, substantiate] vérifier ■ **the doctor ~ed my blood pressure** le médecin a pris ma tension ■ **the inspector ~ed our**

tickets le contrôleur a contrôlé nos billets **2.** [contain, limit] enrayer ▪ [emotions, troops] contenir ▪ [urge] réprimer ▪ **to ~ o.s.** se retenir **3.** *US* [coat, hat] mettre au vestiaire ▪ [luggage] mettre à la consigne **4.** *US* [mark, tick] cocher **5.** [in chess] faire échec à.
◇ *vi* **1.** [confirm] vérifier ▪ [correspond] correspondre, s'accorder ▪ **I'll have to ~ with the accountant** je vais devoir vérifier auprès du comptable ▪ **his description of the killer ~ed with forensic evidence** sa description du tueur s'accordait avec l'expertise médico-légale **2.** [pause, halt] s'arrêter.
◇ *n* **1.** [examination, inspection] contrôle *m*, vérification *f* ▪ **the airline ordered ~s on all their 747s** la compagnie aérienne a ordonné que des contrôles soient faits sur tous ses 747 **2.** [inquiry, investigation] enquête *f* ▪ **to do** *OR* **to run a ~ on sb** se renseigner sur qqn ▪ **to keep a ~ on sb** surveiller qqn **3.** [restraint] frein *m* ▪ **the House of Lords acts as a ~ upon the House of Commons** la Chambre des lords met un frein au pouvoir de la Chambre des communes ▪ **~s and balances** POL *Aux États-Unis, système d'équilibre des pouvoirs* ▪ **he kept** *OR* **held his anger in ~** il a contenu *OR* maîtrisé sa colère ▪ **we could no longer hold** *OR* **keep the enemy in ~** MIL nous ne pouvions plus contenir l'ennemi **4.** [in chess] échec *m* ▪ **in ~** en échec ▪ **~!** échec au roi! **5.** *US* [bill] addition *f* ▪ [receipt for coats, luggage] ticket *m* **6.** [squares] carreaux *mpl* **7.** *US* [mark, tick] coche *f* **8.** *US* = **cheque**.
◇ *adj* [pattern, skirt] à carreaux.
◆ **check in** ◇ *vi insep* **1.** [at airport] se présenter à l'enregistrement **2.** [at hotel] se présenter à la réception **3.** [phone] : **it's a little late, I'd better ~ in with my parents** il se fait tard, il faudrait que je passe un coup de fil à mes parents.
◇ *vt sep* **1.** [at airport] enregistrer **2.** [at hotel] inscrire **3.** [at cloakroom] mettre au vestiaire ▪ [at left-luggage office] mettre à la consigne **4.** *US* [at library] : **to ~ in a book at the library** rapporter un livre à la bibliothèque.
◆ **check into** *vt insep* : **to ~ into a hotel** descendre dans un hôtel.
◆ **check off** *vt sep US* cocher.
◆ **check on** *vt insep* **1.** [facts] vérifier **2.** [person] : **the doctor ~ed on two patients before leaving** le médecin est allé voir deux patients avant de partir.
◆ **check out** ◇ *vi insep* **1.** [pay hotel bill] régler sa note ▪ [leave hotel] quitter l'hôtel **2.** [prove to be correct] s'avérer exact ▪ [correspond, match] s'accorder, correspondre.
◇ *vt sep* **1.** [library book] faire tamponner ▪ [hotel guest] faire régler sa note à **2.** [investigate - person] enquêter sur, se renseigner sur ; [- information, machine, place] vérifier **3.** *inf* [try] essayer **4.** *inf* **~ this out** [look] vise un peu ça ; [listen] écoute-moi ça.
◆ **check over** *vt sep* examiner, vérifier.
◆ **check up on** *vt insep* : **to ~ up on sb** enquêter *OR* se renseigner sur qqn ▪ **to ~ up on sthg** vérifier qqch ▪ **the social worker ~ed up on reports of child abuse** l'assistante sociale a enquêté sur les allégations de mauvais traitements à enfant.

CHECKS AND BALANCES

Ce système de contrôle mutuel, garanti par la Constitution, est l'un des principes fondamentaux du gouvernement américain. Il a été élaboré afin d'assurer l'équilibre entre les pouvoirs législatif, exécutif et judiciaire.

checkbook *n US* = **chequebook**.

checked [tʃekt] *adj* **1.** [pattern, tablecloth] à carreaux **2.** LING [syllable] fermé, entravé.

checker ['tʃekəʳ] *n US* **1.** GAMES pion *m* **2.** [in supermarket] caissier *m*, - ère *f* ▪ [in left-luggage office] préposé *m*, - e *f* à la consigne ▪ [in cloakroom] préposé *m*, - e *f* au vestiaire.

Checker cab *n taxi américain reconnaissable au motif de damier qui en décore la carrosserie.*

checkered *adj US* = **chequered**.

checkers *n US* = **chequers**.

check guarantee card *n* = **cheque card**.

check-in *n* enregistrement *m* ▪ **~ desk** [airport] comptoir *m* d'enregistrement ; [hotel] réception *f*.

checking account ['tʃekɪŋ-] *n US* compte *m* chèque *OR* chèques.

checklist ['tʃeklɪst] *n* liste *f* de vérification ▪ AERON check-list *f*.

checkmate ['tʃekmeɪt] ◇ *n* **1.** [in chess] échec et mat *m* **2.** *fig* [deadlock, standstill] impasse *f* ▪ [defeat] échec *m* total.
◇ *vt* **1.** [in chess] faire échec et mat à **2.** *fig* [frustrate, obstruct] contrecarrer ▪ [defeat] vaincre.

checkout ['tʃekaʊt] ◇ *n* **1.** [in supermarket] caisse *f* **2.** [in hotel] : **~ (time) is at 11 a.m.** les chambres doivent être libérées avant 11 h.
◇ *comp* : **the ~ counter** la caisse, le comptoir-caisse ▪ **~ girl** caissière *f*.

checkpoint ['tʃekpɔɪnt] *n* (poste *m* de) contrôle *m*.

checkroom ['tʃekrʊm] *n US* [for coats, hats] vestiaire *m* ▪ [for luggage] consigne *f*.

checkup ['tʃekʌp] *n* MED bilan *m* de santé, check-up *m* ▪ **to give sb a ~** faire un bilan de santé à qqn ▪ **to go for** *OR* **to have a ~** faire faire un bilan de santé.

cheek [tʃi:k] ◇ *n* **1.** [of face] joue *f* ▪ **~ to ~** joue contre joue ▪ **to be/to live ~ by jowl with sb** être/vivre tout près de qqn ▪ **to turn the other ~** tendre *OR* présenter l'autre joue **2.** *inf* [buttock] fesse *f* **3.** *UK inf* [impudence] culot *m*, toupet *m* ▪ **he had the ~ to ask her age!** il a eu le culot *OR* le toupet de lui demander son âge!
◇ *vt UK inf* être insolent avec.

cheekbone ['tʃi:kbəʊn] *n* pommette *f*.

-cheeked [tʃi:kt] *in cpds* aux joues... ▪ **rosy~** aux joues roses *OR* rouges ▪ **round~** aux joues rebondies *OR* rondes, joufflu.

cheekily ['tʃi:kɪlɪ] *adv UK* avec effronterie *OR* impudence, effrontément.

cheekiness ['tʃi:kɪnɪs] *n UK* effronterie *f*, audace *f*.

cheeky ['tʃi:kɪ] *adj UK* [person] effronté, impudent ▪ [attitude, behaviour] impertinent.

cheep [tʃi:p] ◇ *n* pépiement *m*.
◇ *vi* pépier.

cheer [tʃɪəʳ] ◇ *n* **1.** [cry] hourra *m*, bravo *m* ▪ **I heard a ~ go up** j'ai entendu des acclamations ▪ **three ~s for the winner!** un ban *OR* hourra pour le gagnant! **2.** *lit* [good spirits] bonne humeur *f*, gaieté *f*.
◇ *vt* **1.** [make cheerful - person] remonter le moral à, réconforter **2.** [encourage by shouts] acclamer.
◇ *vi* pousser des acclamations *OR* des hourras.
◆ **cheer on** *vt sep* encourager (par des acclamations) ▪ **his supporters ~ed him on to victory** les acclamations de ses supporters l'ont encouragé jusqu'à la victoire.
◆ **cheer up** ◇ *vt sep* [person] remonter le moral à, réconforter ▪ [house, room] égayer.
◇ *vi insep* s'égayer, se dérider ▪ **~ up!** courage!

cheerful ['tʃɪəfʊl] *adj* **1.** [happy - person] de bonne humeur ; [- smile] joyeux, gai ; [- atmosphere, mood] gai, joyeux ; [- colour, wallpaper] gai, riant ; [- news] réjouissant **2.** [enthusiastic, willing - helper, worker] de bonne volonté ; [- dedication] grand.

cheerfully ['tʃɪəfʊlɪ] *adv* **1.** [happily] joyeusement, avec entrain **2.** [willingly] de plein gré, avec bonne volonté ▪ **I could ~ have hit him!** je l'aurais bien frappé!

cheerily ['tʃɪərəlɪ] *adv* joyeusement, avec entrain.

cheering ['tʃɪərɪŋ] ◇ *n (U)* acclamations *fpl*, hourras *mpl*.
◇ *adj* [remark, thought] encourageant, qui remonte le moral ▪ [news, sight] encourageant, réconfortant.

cheerio [,tʃɪərɪ'əʊ] *interj UK inf* [goodbye] salut, tchao.

cheerleader ['tʃɪə,li:dəʳ] *n majorette qui stimule l'enthousiasme des supporters des équipes sportives, surtout aux États-Unis.*

cheers [tʃɪəz] *interj UK inf* **1.** [toast] à la tienne **2.** [goodbye] salut, tchao **3.** [thanks] merci.

cheery [ˈtʃɪərɪ] (*comp* **cheerier**, *superl* **cheeriest**) *adj* [person] de bonne humeur ■ [smile] joyeux, gai.

cheese [tʃi:z] ◇ *n* fromage *m* ■ **say ~!** PHOT souriez!
◇ *comp* [omelette, sandwich] au fromage ■ [knife] à fromage ■ **the ~ industry** l'industrie fromagère.

cheeseboard [ˈtʃi:zbɔ:d] *n* [board] plateau *m* à fromage OR fromages ■ [on menu] plateau *m* de fromages.

cheeseburger [ˈtʃi:zˌbɜ:gəʳ] *n* hamburger *m* au fromage.

cheesecake [ˈtʃi:zkeɪk] *n* [dessert] gâteau *m* au fromage (blanc).

cheesecloth [ˈtʃi:zklɒθ] *n* CULIN & TEX étamine *f*.

cheesed off [tʃi:zd-] *adj* UK *inf* : **to be ~** en avoir marre ■ **I'm ~ with this job** j'en ai marre de ce boulot.

cheese straw *n* allumette *f* au fromage.

cheesy [ˈtʃi:zɪ] (*comp* **cheesier**, *superl* **cheesiest**) *adj* **1.** [flavour] qui a un goût de fromage, qui sent le fromage ■ [smell] qui sent le fromage **2.** US *inf* [excuse] nul.

cheetah [ˈtʃi:tə] *n* guépard *m*.

chef [ʃef] *n* CULIN chef *m* (de cuisine), cuisinier *m*, - ère *f*.

Chelsea bun *n petit pain rond aux raisins secs.*

Chelsea Pensioner *n ancien combattant résidant au Chelsea Royal Hospital, à Londres.*

chemical [ˈkemɪkl] ◇ *n* produit *m* chimique.
◇ *adj* chimique ■ **~ engineer** ingénieur *m* chimiste ■ **~ engineering** génie *m* chimique ■ **~ warfare** guerre *f* chimique ■ **~ weapons** armes *fpl* chimiques.

chemically [ˈkemɪklɪ] *adv* chimiquement.

chemise [ʃəˈmi:z] *n* [dress] robe-chemisier *f* ■ [undergarment] chemise *f (de femme)*.

chemist [ˈkemɪst] *n* **1.** [scientist] chimiste *mf* **2.** UK [pharmacist] pharmacien *m*, - enne *f* ■ **~'s (shop)** pharmacie *f*.

chemistry [ˈkemɪstrɪ] ◇ *n* chimie *f* ■ **sexual ~** *fig* (bonne) entente *f* sexuelle.
◇ *comp* : **~ set** panoplie *f* de chimiste.

chemotherapy [ˌki:məʊˈθerəpɪ] *n* chimiothérapie *f*.

cheque UK, **check** US [tʃek] *n* chèque *m* ■ **a ~ for £7** OR **to the amount of £7** un chèque de 7 livres ■ **who should I make the ~ payable to?** à quel nom dois-je libeller le chèque? ■ **to pay by ~** payer par chèque ■ **to write sb a ~** faire un chèque à qqn.

cheque account *n* UK compte *m* chèques.

chequebook UK, **checkbook** US [ˈtʃekbʊk] *n* carnet *m* de chèques, chéquier *m*.

chequebook journalism *n dans les milieux de la presse, pratique qui consiste à payer des sommes importantes pour le témoignage d'une personne impliquée dans une affaire.*

cheque card *n* UK *carte d'identité bancaire sans laquelle les chèques ne sont pas acceptés en Grande-Bretagne.*

chequered UK, **checkered** US [ˈtʃekəd] *adj* **1.** [pattern] à carreaux, à damiers **2.** [varied] varié ■ **she's had a ~ career** sa carrière a connu des hauts et des bas.

chequers, checkers US [ˈtʃekəz] *n (U)* jeu *m* de dames.

Chequers [ˈtʃekəz] *pr n résidence secondaire officielle du Premier ministre britannique.*

cherish [ˈtʃerɪʃ] *vt* [person] chérir, aimer ■ [ambition, hope] caresser, nourrir ■ [experience, memory] chérir ■ [right, value] tenir à ■ **one of my most ~ed memories** un de mes souvenirs les plus chers.

Chernobyl [tʃɜ:ˈnəʊbl] *pr n* Tchernobyl.

Cherokee [ˌtʃerəˈki:] (*pl inv* OR *pl* **Cherokees**) ◇ *n* **1.** [person] Cherokee *mf* **2.** LING cherokee *m*.
◇ *adj* cherokee ■ **~ Indian** Indien *m*, - enne *f* cherokee, Cherokee *mf*.

cheroot [ʃəˈru:t] *n* petit cigare *m (à bouts coupés)*.

cherry [ˈtʃerɪ] (*pl* **cherries**) ◇ *n* **1.** [fruit] cerise *f* ■ [tree] cerisier *m* **2.** = **cherry red**.
◇ *comp* [blossom, wood] de cerisier ■ [pie, tart] aux cerises ■ **~ orchard** cerisaie *f* ■ **~ tree** cerisier *m*.

cherry brandy *n* cherry *m*.

cherry-pick *vt* trier sur le volet *fig*.

cherry-picking *n liter* cueillette *f* des cerises ■ *fig* tri *m* sur le volet.

cherry red *n* rouge *m* cerise.
◆ **cherry-red** *adj* (rouge) cerise *(inv)*.

cherry tomato *n* tomate *f* cerise.

cherub [ˈtʃerəb] (*pl* **cherubs** OR *pl* **cherubim** [-bɪm]) *n* ART chérubin *m* ■ *fig* chérubin *m*, petit ange *m*.

cherubic [tʃeˈru:bɪk] *adj* [face] de chérubin ■ [child, look, smile] angélique.

Ches. *written abbr of* **Cheshire**.

Cheshire cat *n* : **to grin like a ~** avoir un sourire jusqu'aux oreilles.

chess [tʃes] *n (U)* échecs *mpl* ■ **~ player** joueur *m*, - euse *f* d'échecs.

chessboard [ˈtʃesbɔ:d] *n* échiquier *m*.

chessman [ˈtʃesmæn] (*pl* **chessmen** [-men]) *n* pion *m*, pièce *f (de jeu d'échecs)*.

chest [tʃest] ◇ *n* **1.** ANAT poitrine *f* ■ **to have a weak ~** être faible des bronches ➤ **to get sthg off one's ~** dire ce qu'on a sur le cœur **2.** [box] coffre *m*, caisse *f*.
◇ *comp* **1.** [cold, measurement, voice, pain] de poitrine ■ **~ infection** infection *f* des voies respiratoires ■ **a ~ X-ray** une radio des poumons ➤ **~ expander** extenseur *m (pour développer les pectoraux)* **2.** : **~ freezer** congélateur-bahut *m*.

chestnut [ˈtʃesnʌt] ◇ *n* **1.** [tree] châtaignier *m* ■ [fruit] châtaigne *f* **2.** [colour] châtain *m* **3.** [horse] alezan *m*, - e *f* **4.** *inf* [joke] : **old ~** plaisanterie *f* rebattue OR éculée.
◇ *comp* **1.** [blossom, wood] de châtaignier ■ [stuffing] aux marrons ■ **~ tree** châtaignier *m* **2.** [colour, hair] châtain ■ [horse] alezan ■ **~ brown** châtain *(inv)*.

chest of drawers *n* commode *f*.

chesty [ˈtʃestɪ] (*comp* **chestier**, *superl* **chestiest**) *adj* [cough] de poitrine.

cheval glass [ʃəˈvælglɑ:s] *n* psyché *f (glace)*.

chevron [ˈʃevrən] *n* ARCHIT, HERALD & MIL chevron *m*.

chew [tʃu:] ◇ *vt* mâcher, mastiquer ➤ **to ~ the cud** *liter* & *fig* ruminer ■ **to ~ the fat with sb** *inf* tailler une bavette avec qqn.
◇ *n* **1.** [act] mâchement *m*, mastication *f* **2.** [piece of tobacco] chique *f* **3.** [sweet] bonbon *m*.
◆ **chew on** *vt insep* **1.** [food] mâcher, mastiquer ■ [bone] ronger ■ [tobacco] chiquer **2.** *inf* [problem, question] ruminer, retourner dans sa tête.
◆ **chew over** *vt sep inf* ruminer, retourner dans sa tête.
◆ **chew up** *vt sep* **1.** [food] mâchonner, mastiquer **2.** [damage] abîmer à force de ronger.

chewing gum [ˈtʃu:ɪŋ-] *n* chewing-gum *m*.

chewy [ˈtʃu:ɪ] (*comp* **chewier**, *superl* **chewiest**) *adj* caoutchouteux.

Cheyenne [ʃaɪˈen] (*pl inv* OR *pl* **Cheyennes**) ◇ *n* Cheyenne *mf*.
◇ *adj* cheyenne.

chiaroscuro [kɪˌɑ:rəˈskʊərəʊ] (*pl* **chiaroscuros**) *n* clair-obscur *m*.

chic [ʃi:k] ◇ *adj* chic, élégant.
◇ *n* chic *m*, élégance *f*.

chicane [ʃɪˈkeɪn] *n* **1.** GAMES [in bridge] main *f* à sans atout **2.** [barrier] chicane *f*.

chicanery [ʃɪ'keɪnərɪ] (*pl* **chicaneries**) *n* [trickery] ruse *f*, fourberie *f* ▪ [legal trickery] chicane *f*.

Chicano [tʃɪ'kɑːnəʊ] (*pl* **Chicanos**) *n* Chicano *mf (Américain d'origine mexicaine)*.

chick [tʃɪk] *n* **1.** [baby bird - gen] oisillon *m* ; [- of chicken] poussin *m* **2.** *inf* [woman] poupée *f*.

chicken ['tʃɪkɪn] ◇ *n* **1.** [bird] poulet *m* ▪ [young] poussin *m* ▪ **she's no (spring) ~** *inf* elle n'est plus toute jeune ▪ **which came first, the ~ or the egg?** allez savoir quelle est la cause et quel est l'effet, l'œuf ou la poule? ▪ **it's a ~-and-egg situation** *inf* c'est le problème de l'œuf et de la poule, on ne sait pas lequel est à l'origine de l'autre **2.** *inf* [coward] poule *f* mouillée, froussard *m*, - e *f*.
◇ *comp* [dish, liver, stew] de poulet ▪ [sandwich] au poulet ▪ **~ breast** blanc *m* (de poulet) ▪ **~ leg** cuisse *f* (de poulet).
◇ *adj inf* [cowardly] froussard.
◆ **chicken out** *vi insep inf* se dégonfler ▪ **he ~ed out of the race** il s'est dégonflé et n'a pas pris part à la course.

chickenfeed ['tʃɪkɪnfiːd] *n (U)* **1.** *liter* nourriture *f* pour volaille **2.** *inf fig* **he earns ~** il gagne des cacahuètes.

chickenpox ['tʃɪkɪnpɒks] *n (U)* varicelle *f*.

chicken wire *n* grillage *m*.

chickpea ['tʃɪkpiː] *n* pois *m* chiche.

chicory ['tʃɪkərɪ] (*pl* **chicories**) *n* [for salad] endive *f* ▪ [for coffee] chicorée *f*.

chide [tʃaɪd] (*pret* **chided** *OR* **chid** [tʃɪd], *pp* **chid** [tʃɪd] *OR* **chidden** ['tʃɪdn]) *vt fml* gronder, réprimander.

chief [tʃiːf] ◇ *n* **1.** [leader] chef *m* ▪ **~ of police** ≃ préfet *m* de police ▪ **~ of staff** MIL chef *m* d'état-major ; *US* [at White House] secrétaire *m* général de la Maison Blanche **2.** *inf* [boss] boss *m* **3.** HERALD chef *m*.
◇ *adj* **1.** [most important] principal, premier **2.** [head] premier, en chef ▪ **Chief Constable** *en Grande-Bretagne, chef de la police d'un comté ou d'une région* ▪ ≃ commissaire *m* divisionnaire ▪ **~ executive** ADMIN directeur *m*, - trice *f* ▪ **the Chief Executive** *US* POL le président des États-Unis, le chef de l'exécutif ▪ **~ executive officer** COMM & INDUST président-directeur général *m* ▪ **~ inspector** [gen] inspecteur *m* principal, inspectrice *f* principale, inspecteur *m*, - trice *f* en chef ; *UK* [of police] ≃ commissaire *m* de police ; *UK* SCH ≃ inspecteur *m* général ≃ inspectrice *f* générale ▪ **~ justice** président *m* de la Haute Cour de justice ; *US* juge *m* à la Cour suprême ▪ **~ master sergeant** *US* MIL major *m* ▪ **~ petty officer** NAUT ≃ maître *m* ▪ **~ superintendent** *UK* [in police] ≃ commissaire *m* principal ▪ **~ technician** *UK* [in Air Force] officier *m* technicien ▪ **~ warrant officer** MIL adjudant *m* chef ▪ **Chief Whip** *responsable du maintien de la discipline à l'intérieur d'un parti à la Chambre des communes*.
◆ **in chief** *adv phr* principalement, surtout.

chiefly ['tʃiːflɪ] *adv* principalement, surtout.

chieftain ['tʃiːftən] *n* chef *m (de tribu)*.

chiffon ['ʃɪfɒn] ◇ *n* mousseline *f* de soie.
◇ *adj* **1.** [dress, scarf] en mousseline (de soie) **2.** CULIN à la mousse.

chignon ['ʃiːnjɒn] *n* chignon *m*.

chihuahua [tʃɪ'wɑːwə] *n* chihuahua *m*.

chilblain ['tʃɪlbleɪn] *n* engelure *f*.

child [tʃaɪld] ◇ *n* (*pl* **children** ['tʃɪldrən]) **1.** [boy or girl] enfant *mf* ▪ **while still a ~** tout enfant ▪ **don't be such a ~!** ne fais pas l'enfant! ▪ **to be with ~** *arch* & *lit* attendre un enfant, être enceinte **2.** *lit* [result] fruit *m*.
◇ *comp* [psychiatry, psychology] de l'enfant, infantile ▪ [psychologist] pour enfants ▪ **~ abuse** [sexual] sévices *mpl* sexuels exercés sur un enfant ; [physical] mauvais traitement *m* infligé à un enfant ▪ **she was a ~ bride** elle s'était mariée toute jeune ▪ **~ guidance** psycho-pédagogie *f* pour enfants caractériels ▪ **~ labour** travail *m* des enfants ▪ **it's ~'s play for** *OR* **to him** *inf* c'est un jeu d'enfant pour lui ▪ **~ pornography** pornographie *f* pédophile ▪ **~ prodigy** enfant *mf* prodige ▪ **~ psychiatrist** pédopsychiatre *mf* ▪ **~ seat** siège-auto *m* ▪ **~ welfare** protection *f* de l'enfance.

childbearing ['tʃaɪld,beərɪŋ] ◇ *n* grossesse *f*.
◇ *adj* [complications, problems] de grossesse ▪ **of ~ age** en âge d'avoir des enfants.

child benefit *n (U)* allocation *f* familiale *OR* allocations *fpl* familiales (pour un enfant) *(en Grande-Bretagne)*.

childbirth ['tʃaɪldbɜːθ] *n (U)* accouchement *m* ▪ **in ~** en couches.

child care *n* **1.** *UK* ADMIN protection *f* de l'enfance **2.** *US* [day care] : **~ center** crèche *f*, garderie *f*.

child-friendly *adj* [area, city] aménagé pour les enfants ▪ [house, furniture] conçu pour les enfants.

childhood ['tʃaɪldhʊd] *n* enfance *f*.

childish ['tʃaɪldɪʃ] *adj* **1.** [face, fears, voice] d'enfant **2.** [immature] enfantin, puéril ▪ **don't be so ~** ne fais pas l'enfant.

childishly ['tʃaɪldɪʃlɪ] *adv* comme un enfant, en enfant.

childless ['tʃaɪldlɪs] *adj* sans enfants.

childlike ['tʃaɪldlaɪk] *adj* d'enfant.

Childline ['tʃaɪld,laɪn] *pr n numéro de téléphone mis à la disposition des enfants maltraités*, ≃ SOS enfants battus.

childminder ['tʃaɪld,maɪndəʳ] *n UK* [for very young children] nourrice *f* ▪ [for older children] assistante *f* maternelle.

childproof ['tʃaɪldpruːf] *adj* : **~ lock** serrure *f* de sécurité pour enfants.

children ['tʃɪldrən] *pl* ▷ **child**.

Children In Need *pr n association caritative britannique de soutien aux enfants du monde entier*.

children's home *n* foyer *m* d'enfants.

Child Support Agency *pr n en Grande-Bretagne, organisme gouvernemental qui décide du montant des pensions alimentaires et les prélève au besoin*.

Chile ['tʃɪlɪ] *pr n* Chili *m* ▪ **in ~** au Chili.

Chilean ['tʃɪlɪən] ◇ *n* Chilien *m*, - enne *f*.
◇ *adj* chilien ▪ **the ~ embassy** l'ambassade *f* du Chili.

chili ['tʃɪlɪ] *n* & *comp* = **chilli**.

chill [tʃɪl] ◇ *vt* **1.** [make cold - food, wine] mettre au frais ; [- champagne] frapper ; [- glass, person] glacer ▪ **~ed white wine** vin blanc frais ▪ **to be ~ed to the bone/to the marrow** être glacé jusqu'aux os/jusqu'à la moelle **2.** *fig* [enthusiasm] refroidir **3.** TECH [metal] tremper.
◇ *vi* se refroidir, rafraîchir, = **chill out**.
◇ *n* **1.** [coldness] fraîcheur *f*, froideur *f* ▪ **there's a ~ in the air** il fait assez frais *OR* un peu froid ▪ **his remark cast a ~ over the meeting** *fig* son observation a jeté un froid dans l'assemblée ▪ **I sensed a certain ~ in his welcome** *fig* j'ai senti une certaine froideur dans son accueil **2.** [feeling of fear] frisson *m* ▪ **the story sent ~s down her spine** l'histoire lui a fait froid dans le dos **3.** [illness] coup *m* de froid, refroidissement *m* ▪ **to catch a ~** attraper *OR* prendre froid.
◇ *adj* [air, weather] frais, fraîche *f*, froid ▪ [glance, response] froid, glacial.
◆ **chill out** *vi insep inf* décompresser ▪ **~ out!** du calme!

chilli ['tʃɪlɪ] ◇ *n* [spice] *sorte de piment* ▪ [dish] chili *m*.
◇ *comp* : **~ powder** chili *m* ▪ **~ sauce** sauce *f* aux tomates et piments.

chilli con carne [,tʃɪlɪkɒn'kɑːnɪ] *n* chili *m* con carne.

chilling ['tʃɪlɪŋ] *adj* [wind] frais, fraîche *f*, froid ▪ *fig* [look, smile] froid, glacial ▪ [news, story, thought] qui donne des frissons.

chilly ['tʃɪlɪ] (*comp* **chillier**, *superl* **chilliest**) *adj* **1.** [air, room] (très) frais, fraîche *f*, froid ▪ **I feel ~** j'ai froid **2.** *fig* [greeting, look] froid, glacial.

chime [tʃaɪm] ◇ *n* [bell] carillon *m*.

<> *vi* **1.** [bell, voices] carillonner ▪ [clock] sonner **2.** *inf* [agree] s'accorder ▪ **his view ~s with mine** il est d'accord avec moi.
<> *vt* sonner ▪ **the clock ~d 6** l'horloge a sonné 6 h.
◆ **chimes** *npl* [for door] carillon *m*, sonnette *f*.
◆ **chime in** *vi insep inf* [say] intervenir ▪ **all the children ~d in** il a rejoint la majorité.

chimera [kaɪ'mɪərə] *n* MYTH & *fig* chimère *f*.

chimney ['tʃɪmnɪ] *n* **1.** [in building] cheminée *f* **2.** [of lamp] verre *m* **3.** GEOL cheminée *f*.

chimneybreast ['tʃɪmnɪbrest] *n UK* manteau *m (de cheminée)*.

chimneypiece ['tʃɪmnɪpi:s] *n UK* dessus *m OR* tablette *f* de cheminée.

chimneypot ['tʃɪmnɪpɒt] *n* tuyau *m* de cheminée.

chimneystack ['tʃɪmnɪstæk] *n* [of one chimney] tuyau *m* de cheminée ▪ [group of chimneys] souche *f* de cheminée.

chimneysweep ['tʃɪmnɪswi:p] *n* ramoneur *m*.

chimp [,tʃɪmp] *inf*, **chimpanzee** [,tʃɪmpən'zi:] *n* chimpanzé *m*.

chin [tʃɪn] (*pret & pp* **chinned**, *cont* **chinning**) *n* menton *m* ▪ **(keep your) ~ up!** courage! ▪ **he took the news on the ~** *inf* il a encaissé la nouvelle (sans broncher).

china ['tʃaɪnə] <> *n* **1.** [material] porcelaine *f* ▪ **a piece of ~** une porcelaine **2.** [porcelain objects] porcelaine *f* ▪ [porcelain dishes] porcelaine *f*, vaisselle *f* (de porcelaine) ▪ [crockery] vaisselle *f*.
<> *comp* [cup, plate] de *OR* en porcelaine ▪ [shop] de porcelaine.

China ['tʃaɪnə] *pr n* Chine *f* ▪ **in ~** en Chine ▶ **the People's Republic of ~** la République populaire de Chine.

china clay *n* kaolin *m*.

Chinaman ['tʃaɪnəmən] (*pl* **Chinamen** [-mən]) *n dated* Chinois *m*.

China Sea *pr n* : **the ~** la mer de Chine.

China tea *n* thé *m* de Chine.

Chinatown ['tʃaɪnətaʊn] *n* le quartier chinois.

chinchilla [tʃɪn'tʃɪlə] <> *n* chinchilla *m*.
<> *comp* [coat, wrap] de chinchilla.

Chinese [,tʃaɪ'ni:z] (*pl inv*) <> *n* **1.** [person] Chinois *m*, - e *f* **2.** LING chinois *m* **3.** *UK inf* [meal] repas *m* chinois.
<> *adj* chinois ▪ **the ~ embassy** l'ambassade de Chine.

Chinese cabbage *n* chou *m* chinois.

Chinese lantern *n* lanterne *f* vénitienne.

Chinese leaves *npl* bettes *fpl*.

Chinese puzzle *n* casse-tête *m inv* chinois.

chink [tʃɪŋk] <> *n* **1.** [hole] fente *f*, fissure *f* ▪ [of light] rayon *m* ▶ **we found a ~ in her armour** nous avons trouvé son point faible *OR* sensible **2.** [sound] tintement *m (de pièces de monnaie, de verres)*.
<> *vi* [jingle] tinter.
<> *vt* **1.** [jingle] faire tinter **2.** *US* [cracks] boucher les fentes dans.

Chink▲ [tʃɪnk] *n terme raciste désignant un Chinois*, ≃ Chinetoque *inf mf*.

chinless ['tʃɪnlɪs] *adj* [with receding chin] au menton fuyant ▪ *fig* [cowardly] mou *(before vowel or silent 'h' mol)*, molle *f*, sans caractère ▪ **a ~ wonder** *UK inf fig* une chiffe molle.

Chinook [tʃɪ'nu:k] (*pl inv OR pl* **Chinooks**) <> *n* [person] Chinook *mf*.
<> *adj* chinook *(inv)*.

chinos ['tʃi:nəʊz] *npl* chinos *m*.

chinstrap ['tʃɪnstræp] *n* jugulaire *f (de casque)*.

chintzy ['tʃɪntsɪ] (*comp* **chintzier**, *superl* **chintziest**) *adj* **1.** *UK* [decor] *typique des intérieurs anglais coquets abondamment ornés de tissus imprimés* **2.** *US* [stingy - person] mesquin ; [- amount] misérable, insuffisant ▪ [thing] de mauvaise qualité.

chin-up *n* traction *f* (à la barre fixe).

chinwag ['tʃɪnwæg] *n inf* causette *f* ▪ **to have a ~ with sb** tailler une bavette avec qqn.

chip [tʃɪp] <> *n* **1.** [piece] éclat *m* ▪ [of wood] copeau *m*, éclat *m* ▪ **she's a ~ off the old block** *inf* elle est bien la fille de son père/de sa mère ▪ **to have a ~ on one's shoulder** *inf* en vouloir à tout le monde **2.** [flaw - in dish, glass] ébréchure *f* ; [- in chair, wardrobe] écornure *f* ▪ **this glass has a ~ (in it)** ce verre est ébréché **3.** CULIN *UK* [French fry] (pomme de terre *f*) frite *f* ▪ *US* [crisp] chips *f inv* **4.** GAMES [counter] jeton *m*, fiche *f* ▪ **to cash in one's ~s** *liter* se faire payer ; *inf fig* inf casser sa pipe ▪ **when the ~s are down** *inf* dans les moments difficiles ▪ **to have had one's ~s** *UK inf* être fichu *OR* cuit **5.** COMPUT puce *f* **6.** [in golf] coup *m* coché.
<> *vt* (*pret & pp* **chipped**, *cont* **chipping**) **1.** [dish, glass] ébrécher ▪ [furniture] écorner ▪ [paint] écailler **2.** [cut into pieces] piler **3.** [shape by cutting] tailler **4.** *UK* CULIN couper en lamelles **5.** [in golf, football] : **to ~ the ball** cocher.
<> *vi* (*pret & pp* **chipped**, *cont* **chipping**) [dish, glass] s'ébrécher ▪ [furniture] s'écorner ▪ [paint] s'écailler.
◆ **chip away at** *vt insep* : **to ~ away at sthg** décaper qqch.
◆ **chip in** *inf* <> *vi insep* **1.** [contribute] contribuer ▪ **we all chipped in with £5** nous avons tous donné 5 livres **2.** [speak] mettre son grain de sel ▪ **he chipped in with a suggestion** il est intervenu pour faire une suggestion.
<> *vt insep* **1.** [contribute] contribuer, donner **2.** [say] dire.
◆ **chip off** *vt sep* enlever.

chip-and-pin *n UK* [payment system] paiement *m* par carte à puce.

chip-based *adj* COMPUT à puce.

chipboard ['tʃɪpbɔ:d] *n (U) UK* (panneau *m* d')aggloméré *m*, panneau *m* de particules.

chipmunk ['tʃɪpmʌŋk] *n* tamia *m*, suisse *m Canada*.

chipolata [,tʃɪpə'lɑ:tə] *n* chipolata *f*.

chip pan *n* friteuse *f*.

chipped [tʃɪpt] *adj* **1.** [dish, glass] ébréché ▪ [furniture] écorné ▪ [paint] écaillé **2.** *UK* CULIN & *fml* **~ potatoes** (pommes de terre *fpl*) frites *fpl*.

chipper ['tʃɪpər] *adj inf* **1.** [lively] vif, fringant **2.** [smartly dressed] chic, élégant.

chippie ['tʃɪpɪ] *n* = **chippy**.

chippings ['tʃɪpɪŋz] *npl* [gen] éclats *mpl*, fragments *mpl* ▪ [of wood] copeaux *mpl*, éclats *mpl* ▪ [in roadwork] gravillons *mpl* ▪ **'slow, loose ~'** 'attention gravillons'.

chippy ['tʃɪpɪ] (*pl* **chippies**) *n* **1.** *UK inf* = **chip shop** **2.** *inf UK & New Zealand* [carpenter] charpentier *m*.

chip shop *n UK boutique où l'on vend du "fish and chips"*.

chiromancer ['kaɪərəʊmænsər] *n* chiromancien *m*, - enne *f*.

chiromancy ['kaɪərəʊmænsɪ] *n* chiromancie *f*.

chiropodist [kɪ'rɒpədɪst] *n* pédicure *mf*.

chiropody [kɪ'rɒpədɪ] *n (U)* [treatment] soins *mpl* du pied ▪ [science] podologie *f*.

chiropractor ['kaɪrə,præktər] *n* chiropracteur *m*, chiropracticien *m*, - enne *f*.

chirp [tʃɜ:p] <> *vi* [bird] pépier, gazouiller ▪ [insect] chanter, striduler ▪ [person] parler d'une voix flûtée.
<> *n* [of bird] pépiement *m*, gazouillement *m* ▪ [of insect] chant *m*, stridulation *f*.

chirpy ['tʃɜ:pɪ] (*comp* **chirpier**, *superl* **chirpiest**) *adj inf* [person] gai, plein d'entrain ▪ [mood, voice] gai, enjoué.

chirrup ['tʃɪrəp] <> *vi* [bird] pépier, gazouiller ▪ [insect] chanter, striduler ▪ [person] parler d'une voix flûtée.
<> *n* [of bird] pépiement *m*, gazouillement *m* ▪ [of insect] chant *m*, stridulation *f*.

chisel ['tʃɪzl] <> *n* [gen] ciseau *m* ▪ [for engraving] burin *m*.

<> *vt* (*UK pret & pp* **chiselled**, *cont* **chiselling**) (*US pret & pp* **chiseled**, *cont* **chiseling**) **1.** [carve] ciseler ■ **chiselled features** *fig* traits burinés **2.** [engrave - form, name] graver au burin ; [- plate] buriner **3.** [cheat] : **to ~ sb out of sthg** *inf* carotter qqch à qqn.

chit [tʃɪt] *n* [memo, note] note *f* ■ [voucher] bon *m* ■ [receipt] reçu *m*, récépissé *m*.

chitchat ['tʃɪttʃæt] <> *n (U)* bavardage *m*, papotage *m*.
<> *vi* bavarder, papoter.

chitlings ['tʃɪtlɪŋz], **chitterlings** ['tʃɪtəlɪŋz] *npl* tripes *fpl*.

chitty ['tʃɪtɪ] (*pl* **chitties**) *n UK* note *f*.

chivalrous ['ʃɪvlrəs] *adj* **1.** [courteous] chevaleresque, courtois ■ [gallant] galant **2.** [exploit, tournament] chevaleresque.

chivalrously ['ʃɪvlrəslɪ] *adv* [courteously] de façon chevaleresque, courtoisement ■ [gallantly] galamment.

chivalry ['ʃɪvlrɪ] *n* **1.** [courtesy] conduite *f* chevaleresque, courtoisie *f* ■ [gallantry] galanterie *f* ■ **the age of ~ is not dead** *hum* la galanterie existe encore **2.** [knights, system] chevalerie *f*.

chives [tʃaɪvz] *npl* ciboulette *f*, civette *f*.

chiv(v)y ['tʃɪvɪ] (*pret & pp* **chivvied** *OR* **chivied**) *vt* **1.** *inf* [nag] harceler ■ **to ~ sb into doing sthg** harceler qqn jusqu'à ce qu'il fasse qqch **2.** [hunt - game] chasser ; [- criminal] pourchasser.
◆ **chivvy up** *vt sep inf* faire activer.

chloride ['klɔːraɪd] *n* chlorure *m*.

chlorinate ['klɔːrɪneɪt] *vt* [water] javelliser ■ CHEM chlorurer, chlorer.

chlorination [ˌklɔːrɪn'eɪʃn] *n* [of water] javellisation *f*, chloration *f* ■ CHEM chloration *f*.

chlorine ['klɔːriːn] <> *n* CHEM chlore *m*.
<> *comp* : **~ bleach** eau *f* de Javel.

chlorofluorocarbon ['klɔːrəˌflɔːrəʊ'kɑːbən] *n* chlorofluorocarbone *m*.

chloroform ['klɒrəfɔːm] <> *n* chloroforme *m*.
<> *vt* chloroformer.

chlorophyll *UK*, **chlorophyl** *US* ['klɒrəfɪl] *n* chlorophylle *f*.

choc [tʃɒk] *n inf* chocolat *m*.

choc-ice *n UK* ≃ Esquimau® *m*.

chock [tʃɒk] <> *n* [for door, wheel] cale *f* ■ [for barrel] cale *f*, chantier *m* ■ NAUT chantier *m*, cale *f*.
<> *vt* [barrel, door, wheel] caler ■ NAUT mettre sur un chantier *OR* sur cales.

chock-a-block, chock-full *adj inf* [room, theatre] plein à craquer ■ [container] bourré, plein à ras bord ■ **the town is ~ with tourists** la ville est archipleine de touristes.

chocoholic ['tʃɒkəˌhɒlɪk] *n inf* accro *mf* du chocolat, fondu *m*, - e *f* de chocolat.

chocolate ['tʃɒkələt] <> *n* [drink, sweet] chocolat *m*.
<> *comp* [biscuit, cake] au chocolat, chocolaté ■ **~ chip cookie** biscuit *m* avec des perles de chocolat.
<> *adj* chocolat *(inv)* ■ **~ brown** (couleur *f*) chocolat *(inv)*.

chocolate-box *adj inf* **a ~ landscape** un paysage très carte postale.

choice [tʃɔɪs] <> *n* **1.** [act of choosing] choix *m* ■ **to make a ~** faire un choix ■ **to have first ~** pouvoir choisir en premier ■ **it's your ~** c'est à vous de choisir *OR* décider ■ **by** *OR* **from ~** de *OR* par préférence ■ **the profession of her ~** la profession de son choix **2.** [option] choix *m*, option *f* ■ **you have no ~** vous n'avez pas le choix ■ **I had no ~ but to leave** je ne pouvais que partir **3.** [selection] choix *m*, assortiment *m* ■ **a wide ~ of goods** un grand choix de marchandises **4.** [thing, person chosen] choix *m* ■ **he would be a good ~ for president** il ferait un bon président ■ **you made the right/wrong ~** vous avez fait le bon/mauvais choix.
<> *adj* **1.** [fruit, meat] de choix, de première qualité **2.** [well-chosen - phrase, words] bien choisi **3.** [coarse - language] grossier.

choir ['kwaɪəʳ] <> *n* **1.** [group of singers] chœur *m*, chorale *f* ■ [in church] chœur *m*, maîtrise *f* ■ **we sing in the ~** [gen] nous faisons partie du chœur *OR* de la chorale ; [in church] nous faisons partie du chœur, nous chantons dans la maîtrise **2.** ARCHIT chœur *m* **3.** [group of instruments] chœur *m*.
<> *comp* : **~ practice** répétition *f* de la chorale.

choirboy ['kwaɪəbɔɪ] *n* jeune choriste *m*.

choirmaster ['kwaɪəˌmɑːstəʳ] *n* [gen] chef *m* de chœur ■ [in church] maître *m* de chapelle.

choir school *n* maîtrise *f*.

choirstall ['kwaɪəstɔːl] *n* stalle *f* du chœur.

choke [tʃəʊk] <> *vi* étouffer, s'étouffer, s'étrangler ■ **to ~ on sthg** s'étouffer *OR* s'étrangler en avalant qqch de travers ■ **to ~ to death** mourir étouffé ■ **to ~ with rage** s'étouffer *OR* s'étrangler de rage.
<> *vt* **1.** [asphyxiate] étrangler, étouffer ■ **in a voice ~d with emotion** d'une voix étranglée par l'émotion **2.** [strangle] étrangler **3.** [clog] boucher, obstruer ■ **~d with traffic** embouteillé, bouché ■ **~d with weeds** étouffé par les mauvaises herbes **4.** TECH [engine, fire] étouffer.
<> *n* **1.** AUT starter *m* ■ TECH [in pipe] buse *f* **2.** [of artichoke] foin *m*.
◆ **choke back, choke down** *vt sep* [anger] refouler, étouffer ■ [tears] refouler, contenir ■ [complaint, cry] retenir.
◆ **choke off** *vt sep* [objection, opposition] étouffer (dans l'œuf) ■ [discussion] empêcher.
◆ **choke up** *vt sep* **1.** [road] boucher, embouteiller **2.** *inf* [emotionally] émouvoir, toucher profondément.

choked [tʃəʊkt] *adj* **1.** [cry, voice] étranglé **2.** *UK inf* [person - moved] secoué ; [- sad] peiné, attristé ; [- annoyed] énervé, fâché.

choker ['tʃəʊkəʳ] *n* [necklace] collier *m* (court) ■ [neckband] tour *m* de cou.

choking ['tʃəʊkɪŋ] *n* étouffement *m*, suffocation *f*.

cholera ['kɒlərə] *n* choléra *m*.

cholesterol [kə'lestərɒl] *n* cholestérol *m*.

chomp ['tʃɒmp] *inf* <> *vi & vt* mastiquer bruyamment.
<> *n* mastication *f* bruyante.

chong-sam [tʃɑŋ'sæm] *n* robe *f* chinoise *(fendue sur les côtés)*.

choose [tʃuːz] (*pret* **chose** [tʃəʊz], *pp* **chosen** ['tʃəʊzn]) <> *vt* **1.** [select] choisir, prendre ■ **~ your words carefully** pesez bien vos mots ■ **there's little** *OR* **not much to ~ between the two parties** les deux partis se valent **2.** [elect] élire **3.** [decide] décider, juger bon ■ **I didn't ~ to invite her** [invited unwillingly] je l'ai invitée contre mon gré.
<> *vi* choisir ■ **do as you ~** faites comme bon vous semble *OR* comme vous l'entendez *OR* comme vous voulez ■ **there's not a lot to ~ from** il n'y a pas beaucoup de choix.

choos(e)y ['tʃuːzɪ] (*comp* **choosier**, *superl* **choosiest**) *adj inf* difficile ■ **she's very ~ about what she eats** elle ne mange pas n'importe quoi, elle est très difficile sur la nourriture.

chop [tʃɒp] <> *vt* (*pret & pp* **chopped**, *cont* **chopping**) **1.** [cut - gen] couper ; [- wood] couper ■ CULIN hacher **2.** [hit] donner un coup à, frapper **3.** *inf* [reduce - budget, funding] réduire, diminuer ; [- project] mettre au rancart **4.** SPORT [ball] couper.
<> *vi* (*pret & pp* **chopped**, *cont* **chopping**) [change direction] varier ■ **to ~ and change** changer constamment d'avis.
<> *n* **1.** [blow - with axe] coup *m* de hache ; [- with hand] coup *m* ■ **to get** *OR* **to be given the ~** *UK inf* [employee] être viré ; [project] être mis au rancart ■ **the welfare programmes are for the ~** *UK inf* les programmes d'assistance sociale vont être supprimés **2.** CULIN [of meat] côtelette *f* **3.** GOLF coup *m* piqué ■ TENNIS volée *f* coupée *OR* arrêtée.

◆ **chops** *npl* [jowls - of person] joue *f* ; [- of animal] bajoues *fpl* ■ **to lick one's ~s** se pourlécher les babines.
◆ **chop down** *vt sep* abattre.
◆ **chop off** *vt sep* trancher, couper ■ **they chopped off the king's head** ils ont coupé la tête au roi.
◆ **chop up** *vt sep* couper en morceaux, hacher.

chop-chop *inf* ◇ *adv* rapidement, vite.
◇ *interj* : **~!** allez, et que ça saute!

Chopin ['ʃɒpæn] *pr n* Chopin.

chopper ['tʃɒpəʳ] *n* **1.** *UK* [axe] petite hache *f* ■ CULIN [cleaver] couperet *m*, hachoir *m* **2.** *inf* [helicopter] hélico *m* **3.** *inf* [motorcycle] chopper *m* ■ [bicycle] vélo *m (à haut guidon).*

chopping board ['tʃɒpɪŋ-] *n* planche *f* à découper.

choppy ['tʃɒpɪ] (*comp* **choppier**, *superl* **choppiest**) *adj* **1.** [lake, sea] un peu agité ■ [waves] clapotant **2.** [wind] variable.

chopstick ['tʃɒpstɪk] *n* baguette *f (pour manger).*

chopsuey [,tʃɒp'su:ɪ] *n* chop suey *m*.

choral ['kɔ:rəl] ◇ *adj* choral.
◇ *n* = **chorale**.

chorale [kɒ'rɑ:l] *n* **1.** [hymn] chœur *m*, choral *m* **2.** *US* [choir] chœur *m*, chorale *f*.

chord [kɔ:d] *n* **1.** ANAT & GEOM corde *f* **2.** MUS [group of notes] accord *m* ■ **to strike** *OR* **to touch a ~** toucher la corde sensible.

chore [tʃɔ:ʳ] *n* [task - routine] travail *m* de routine ; [- unpleasant] corvée *f* ■ **household ~s** travaux *mpl* ménagers ■ **I have to do the ~s** *US* il faut que je fasse le ménage.

choreograph ['kɒrɪəgrɑ:f] *vt* [ballet, dance] chorégraphier, faire la chorégraphie de ■ *fig* [meeting, party] organiser.

choreographer [,kɒrɪ'ɒgrəfəʳ] *n* chorégraphe *mf*.

choreography [,kɒrɪ'ɒgrəfɪ] *n* chorégraphie *f*.

chorister ['kɒrɪstəʳ] *n* choriste *mf*.

chortle ['tʃɔ:tl] ◇ *vi* glousser.
◇ *n* gloussement *m*, petit rire *m*.

chorus ['kɔ:rəs] ◇ *n* **1.** [choir] chœur *m*, chorale *f* **2.** [piece of music] chœur *m*, choral *m* **3.** [refrain] refrain *m* ■ **we all joined in (on) the ~** nous avons tous repris le refrain (en chœur) **4.** THEAT [dancers, singers] troupe *f* ■ [speakers] chœur *m* **5.** [of complaints, groans] concert *m*.
◇ *vt* [song] chanter en chœur ■ [poem] réciter en chœur ■ [approval, discontent] dire *OR* exprimer en chœur.

chorus girl *n* girl *f*.

chorus line *n* troupe *f*.

chose [tʃəʊz] *pt* ▷ **choose**.

chosen ['tʃəʊzn] ◇ *pp* ▷ **choose**.
◇ *adj* choisi ■ **she told only a ~ few** elle ne s'est confiée qu'à quelques privilégiés ■ **the ~ people** les élus *mpl*.
◇ *npl* : **the ~** les élus *mpl*.

choux pastry [ʃu:-] *n (U)* pâte *f* à choux.

chow [tʃaʊ] *n* **1.** [dog] chow-chow *m* **2.** *inf* [food] bouffe *f*.

chowder ['tʃaʊdəʳ] *n potage épais contenant du poisson ou des fruits de mer.*

Christ [kraɪst] ◇ *pr n* le Christ, Jésus-Christ *m* ■ **the ~ child** l'enfant *m* Jésus.
◇ *interj* : **~!**△ Bon Dieu (de Bon Dieu)!△.

christen ['krɪsn] *vt* **1.** [gen] appeler, nommer ■ [nickname] baptiser, surnommer ■ NAUT & RELIG baptiser ■ **she was ~ed Victoria but is known as Vicky** son nom de baptême est Victoria mais tout le monde l'appelle Vicky ■ **he was ~ed after his grandfather** on lui avait donné le nom de son grand-père **2.** *inf* [use for first time] étrenner.

Christendom ['krɪsndəm] *n* chrétienté *f*.

christening ['krɪsnɪŋ] *n* baptême *m*.

Christian ['krɪstʃən] ◇ *n* chrétien *m*, - enne *f*.
◇ *adj liter* chrétien ■ *fig* [charitable] charitable, bon.

Christianity [,krɪstɪ'ænətɪ] *n* [religion] christianisme *m*.

Christian name *n* nom *m* de baptême, prénom *m*.

Christian Science *n* la Science chrétienne.

Christian Scientist *n* scientiste chrétien *m*, scientiste chrétienne *f*.

Christlike ['kraɪstlaɪk] *adj* semblable *OR* qui ressemble au Christ.

Christmas ['krɪsməs] ◇ *n* Noël *m* ■ **at ~** à Noël ■ **for ~** pour Noël ■ **Merry ~!** joyeux Noël!
◇ *comp* [party, present, dinner] de Noël ■ **~ cracker** *papillote contenant un pétard et une surprise traditionnelle au moment des fêtes.*

Christmas box *n* *UK* étrennes *fpl (offertes à Noël).*

Christmas cake *n* gâteau *m* de Noël *(cake décoré au sucre glace).*

Christmas card *n* carte *f* de Noël.

Christmas carol *n* chant *m* de Noël, noël *m* ■ RELIG cantique *m* de Noël.

Christmas club *n caisse de contributions pour les cadeaux de Noël.*

Christmas Day *n* le jour de Noël.

Christmas Eve *n* la veille de Noël.

Christmas Island *pr n* l'île *f* Christmas ■ **in** *OR* **on ~** à l'île Christmas.

Christmas pudding *n* *UK* pudding *m*, plum-pudding *m*.

Christmas stocking *n chaussette que les enfants suspendent à la cheminée pour que le père Noël y dépose les cadeaux.*

Christmassy ['krɪsməsɪ] *adj* qui rappelle la fête de Noël ■ **the town looks so ~** la ville a un tel air de fête.

Christmastime ['krɪsməstaɪm] *n* la période de Noël *OR* des fêtes (de fin d'année).

Christmas tree *n* sapin *m* *OR* arbre *m* de Noël.

Christopher ['krɪstəfəʳ] *pr n* : **Saint ~** saint Christophe.

chromatic [krə'mætɪk] *adj* chromatique ■ **~ printing** TYPO impression *f* polychrome.

chromatography [,krəʊmə'tɒgrəfɪ] *n* chromatographie *f*.

chrome [krəʊm] ◇ *n* chrome *m*.
◇ *adj* [fittings, taps] chromé.

chrome green *n* vert *m* de chrome.

chrome steel *n* acier *m* chromé, chromé *m*.

chrome yellow *n* jaune *m* de chrome.

chromium ['krəʊmɪəm] *n* chrome *m*.

chromium-plated [-'pleɪtɪd] *adj* chromé.

chromium-plating [-'pleɪtɪŋ] *n* chromage *m*.

chromolithograph [,krəʊməʊ'lɪθəgrɑ:f] *n* chromolithographie *f*.

chromosome ['krəʊməsəʊm] *n* chromosome *m*.

chromosome number *n* nombre *m* chromosomique.

chronic ['krɒnɪk] *adj* **1.** [long-lasting - illness, unemployment] chronique **2.** [habitual - smoker, gambler] invétéré **3.** [serious - problem, situation] difficile, grave **4.** *UK inf* [very bad] atroce, affreux.

chronically ['krɒnɪklɪ] *adv* **1.** [habitually] chroniquement **2.** [severely] gravement, sérieusement.

chronicle ['krɒnɪkl] ◇ *n* chronique *f* ■ **their holiday was a ~ of misadventures** leurs vacances furent une succession de mésaventures.
◇ *vt* faire la chronique de, raconter.

◆ **Chronicles** *n* : **the (Book of) Chronicles** le livre des Chroniques.

chronicler ['krɒnɪkləʳ] *n* chroniqueur *m*, - euse *f*.

chronograph ['krɒnəgrɑ:f] *n* chronographe *m*.

chronological [,krɒnə'lɒdʒɪkl] *adj* chronologique ■ **in ~ order** par ordre *OR* dans un ordre chronologique.

chronologically [,krɒnə'lɒdʒɪklɪ] *adv* chronologiquement, par ordre chronologique.

chronology [krə'nɒlədʒɪ] *n* chronologie *f*.

chronometer [krə'nɒmɪtəʳ] *n* chronomètre *m*.

chrysalid ['krɪsəlɪd] (*pl* **chrysalides** [-'sælɪdi:z]) *n* chrysalide *f*.

chrysalis ['krɪsəlɪs] (*pl* **chrysalises** [-si:z]) *n* chrysalide *f*.

chrysanthemum [krɪ'sænθəməm] *n* chrysanthème *m*.

chub [tʃʌb] (*pl inv OR pl* **chubs**) *n* chevesne *m*, chevaine *m*.

chubbiness ['tʃʌbɪnɪs] *n* rondeur *f*.

Chubb lock® [tʃʌb-] *n type de serrure réputé incrochetable*.

chubby ['tʃʌbɪ] (*comp* **chubbier**, *superl* **chubbiest**) *adj* [fingers, person] potelé ■ [face] joufflu ■ **~-cheeked** joufflu.

chuck [tʃʌk] ◇ *vt* **1.** *inf* [toss] jeter, lancer ■ **they ~ed him off the bus** ils l'ont vidé du bus **2.** *inf* [give up - activity, job] laisser tomber, lâcher **3.** *inf* [jilt - boyfriend, girlfriend] plaquer.
◇ *n UK* **1.** TECH mandrin *m* **2.** = **chuck steak**.
◆ **chuck away** *vt sep inf* [old clothing, papers] balancer ■ [chance, opportunity] laisser passer ■ [money] jeter par les fenêtres.
◆ **chuck in** *vt sep UK inf* [give up - activity, job] lâcher ; [- attempt] renoncer à.
◆ **chuck out** *vt sep inf* [old clothing, papers] balancer ■ [person] vider, sortir ■ **he ~ed the troublemakers out** il a flanqué les provocateurs à la porte.

chucker-out [,tʃʌkər-] *n UK inf* videur *m*.

chuckle ['tʃʌkl] ◇ *vi* glousser, rire ■ **to ~ with delight** rire avec jubilation.
◇ *n* gloussement *m*, petit rire *m* ■ **they had a good ~ over her mishap** sa mésaventure les a bien fait rire.

chuck steak *n* morceau *m* de bœuf dans le paleron.

chuck wagon *n* cantine *f* ambulante *(pour les cowboys)*.

chuffed [tʃʌft] *adj UK inf* vachement *OR* super content, ravi ■ **to be ~ about** *OR* **at sthg** être ravi de qqch.

chug [tʃʌg] ◇ *vi* **1.** [make noise - engine, car, train] s'essouffler, haleter **2.** [move] avancer en soufflant *OR* en haletant.
◇ *n* [of engine, car, train] halètement *m*.

chukka, chukker ['tʃʌkə] *n* [in polo] période *f* de jeu *(de sept minutes et demie)*.

chum [tʃʌm] *n inf* copain *m*, copine *f*.

chummy ['tʃʌmɪ] (*comp* **chummier**, *superl* **chummiest**) *adj inf* amical ■ **to be ~ with sb** être copain/copine avec qqn.

chump [tʃʌmp] *n inf dated* **1.** [dolt - boy] ballot *m* ; [- girl] gourde *f* **2.** *UK* [head] boule *f*.

chump chop *n UK* côte *f (d'agneau)*.

chunk [tʃʌŋk] *n* [of meat, wood] gros morceau *m* ■ [of budget, time] grande partie *f*.

chunky ['tʃʌŋkɪ] (*comp* **chunkier**, *superl* **chunkiest**) *adj* **1.** [person - stocky] trapu ; [- chubby] potelé, enrobé ■ [food, stew] avec des morceaux **2.** *UK* [clothing, sweater] de grosse laine ■ [jewellery] gros, grosse *f*.

Chunnel ['tʃʌnl] *n UK inf* **the ~** *terme familier désignant le tunnel sous la Manche*.

chunter ['tʃʌntəʳ] *vi UK dial* râler, rouspéter.

church [tʃɜ:tʃ] ◇ *n* **1.** [building - gen] église *f* ; [- Protestant] église *f*, temple *m* **2.** [services - Protestant] office *m* ; [- Catholic] messe *f* ■ **to go to ~** [Protestants] aller au temple *OR* à l'office ; [Catholics] aller à la messe *OR* à l'église ■ **do you go to ~?** êtes-vous pratiquant? **3.** *(U)* [clergy] : **the ~** les ordres *mpl* ■ **to go into the ~** entrer dans les ordres.
◇ *vt UK* [gen] faire assister à la messe ■ [woman after childbirth] faire assister à la messe de relevailles.
◆ **Church** *n* [institution] : **the Church** l'Église *f* ➲ **Church of Christ, Scientist** Église de la Science chrétienne ■ **Church of England** Église anglicane ■ **Church of France/of Scotland** Église de France/d'Écosse ■ **Church of Rome** Église catholique.

THE CHURCH OF ENGLAND

L'Église d'Angleterre (de confession anglicane) est l'Église officielle de la Grande-Bretagne ; son chef laïc est le souverain, son chef spirituel, l'archevêque de Cantorbéry.

churchgoer ['tʃɜ:tʃ,gəʊəʳ] *n* pratiquant *m*, - e *f*.

church hall *n* salle *f* paroissiale.

churchman ['tʃɜ:tʃmən] (*pl* **churchmen** [-mən]) *n* [clergyman] ecclésiastique *m* ■ [churchgoer] pratiquant *m*.

church school *n UK* école *f* religieuse *OR* confessionnelle.

churchwarden [,tʃɜ:tʃ'wɔ:dn] *n* bedeau *m*, marguillier *m*.

churchwoman ['tʃɜ:tʃ,wʊmən] (*pl* **churchwomen** [-,wɪmɪn]) *n* pratiquante *f*.

churchy ['tʃɜ:tʃɪ] (*comp* **churchier**, *superl* **churchiest**) *adj* **1.** [atmosphere, song] qui rappelle l'église **2.** *pej* [person] bigot.

churchyard ['tʃɜ:tʃjɑ:d] *n* [grounds] terrain *m* autour de l'église ■ [graveyard] cimetière *m (autour d'une église)*.

churl [tʃɜ:l] *n lit* [ill-bred person] rustre *m*, malotru *m* ■ [surly person] ronchon *m*.

churlish ['tʃɜ:lɪʃ] *adj* [rude] fruste, grossier ■ [bad-tempered - person] qui a mauvais caractère, revêche ; [- attitude, behaviour] revêche, désagréable ■ **it would be ~ not to acknowledge the invitation** ce serait grossier *OR* impoli de ne pas répondre à l'invitation.

churn [tʃɜ:n] ◇ *vt* **1.** [cream] baratter **2.** [mud] remuer ■ [water] faire bouillonner.
◇ *vi* [sea, water] bouillonner ■ **the thought made my stomach ~** j'ai eu l'estomac tout retourné à cette idée.
◇ *n* **1.** [for butter] baratte *f* **2.** *UK* [milk can] bidon *m*.
◆ **churn out** *vt sep inf* **1.** [produce rapidly - gen] produire rapidement ; [- novels, reports] pondre à la chaîne *OR* en série **2.** [produce mechanically] débiter.
◆ **churn up** *vt sep* [mud] remuer ■ [sea, water] faire bouillonner.

churning ['tʃɜ:nɪŋ] *n* [act] barattage *m*.

chute [ʃu:t] *n* **1.** [for parcels] glissière *f* **2.** [for sledding, in swimming pool] toboggan *m* **3.** [in river] rapide *m* **4.** *inf* [parachute] parachute *m*.

chutney ['tʃʌtnɪ] *n* chutney *m (condiment à base de fruits)*.

chutzpah ['hʊtspə] *n (esp) US inf* culot *m*.

CIA (*abbrev of* **Central Intelligence Agency**) *pr n* CIA *f*.

ciabatta [tʃə'bɑ:tə] *n* ciabatta *m*.

ciborium [sɪ'bɔ:rɪəm] *n* [canopy] ciborium *m*.

cicada [sɪ'kɑ:də] (*pl* **cicadas** *OR pl* **cicadae** [-di:]) *n* cigale *f*.

Cicero ['sɪsə,rəʊ] *pr n* Cicéron.

Ciceronian [,sɪsə'rəʊnɪən] *adj* cicéronien.

CID (*abbrev of* **Criminal Investigation Department**) *pr n police judiciaire britannique*, ≃ PJ.

cider ['saɪdəʳ] ◇ *n* cidre *m*.
◇ *comp* : **~ press** pressoir *m* à cidre ■ **~ vinegar** vinaigre *m* de cidre.

cider apple *n* pomme *f* à cidre.

cif, CIF (*abbrev of* **cost, insurance and freight**) *adj & adv* CAF, caf.

cig [sɪg] *n inf* clope *m ou f*, sèche *f*.

cigar [sɪ'gɑ:ʳ] ◇ *n* cigare *m*.

◇ *comp* [box, case, tobacco] à cigares ■ [ash, smoke] de cigare ■ **~ holder** fume-cigare *m inv* ■ **~ lighter** allume-cigare *m inv*.

cigaret [ˌsɪgəˈret] *n* & *comp US* = **cigarette**.

cigarette [ˌsɪgəˈret] ◇ *n* cigarette *f*.
◇ *comp* [ash, burn, smoke] de cigarette ■ [packet, smoke] de cigarettes ■ [paper, tobacco] à cigarettes ■ **~ case** étui *m* à cigarettes, porte-cigarettes *m inv*.

cigarette card *n image offerte autrefois avec chaque paquet de cigarettes.*

cigarette end *n* mégot *m*.

cigarette holder *n* fume-cigarette *m inv*.

cigarette lighter *n* briquet *m*.

cigarillo [ˌsɪgəˈrɪləʊ] (*pl* **cigarillos**) *n* petit cigare *m*, cigarillo *m*.

ciggie [ˈsɪgɪ] *n* ***inf*** clope *m ou f*, sèche *f*.

CIM (*abbrev of* **computer-integrated manufacturing**) *n* FAO *f*.

cinch [sɪntʃ] *n* ***inf*** **it's a ~** [certainty] c'est du tout cuit ; [easy to do] c'est du gâteau.

cinder [ˈsɪndəʳ] *n* cendre *f* ■ **~s** [in fireplace] cendres ; [from furnace, volcano] scories *fpl* ■ **burnt to a ~** réduit en cendres.

cinder block *n US* parpaing *m*.

Cinderella [ˌsɪndəˈrelə] ◇ *pr n* Cendrillon.
◇ *n* ***fig*** parent *m* pauvre.

cinder track *n* (piste *f*) cendrée *f*.

cinecamera [ˈsɪnɪˌkæmərə] *n UK* caméra *f*.

cine-film [ˈsɪnɪ-] *n UK* film *m*.

cinema [ˈsɪnəmə] *n* [building] *UK* cinéma *m* ■ [industry] (industrie *f* du) cinéma *m*.

cinemagoer [ˈsɪnɪməˌgəʊəʳ] *n* personne *f* qui fréquente les cinémas.

Cinemascope® [ˈsɪnəməskəʊp] *n* Cinémascope® *m*.

cinematic [ˌsɪnɪˈmætɪk] *adj* cinématique.

cinematograph [ˌsɪnəˈmætəgrɑːf] *n UK* cinématographe *m*.

cinematography [ˌsɪnəməˈtɒgrəfɪ] *n UK* cinématographie *f*.

cine-projector [ˈsɪnɪ-] *n UK* projecteur *m* de cinéma.

cineraria [ˌsɪnəˈreərɪə] ◇ *pl* ▷ **cinerarium**.
◇ *n* BOT cinéraire *f*.

cinerarium [ˌsɪnəˈreərɪəm] (*pl* **cineraria** [ˌsɪnəˈreərɪə]) *n* cinéraire *m*.

cinnamon [ˈsɪnəmən] ◇ *n* **1.** [spice] cannelle *f* **2.** [colour] cannelle *f*.
◇ *comp* [flavour, tea] à la cannelle.
◇ *adj* cannelle *(inv)*.

Cinque Ports [ˈsɪŋkpɔːts] *pr npl* Cinq ports *mpl (ancienne confédération réunissant les cinq ports de la côte sud-est de l'Angleterre)*.

cipher [ˈsaɪfəʳ] ◇ *n* **1.** [code] chiffre *m*, code *m* secret **2.** [monogram] chiffre *m*, monogramme *m* **3.** [Arabic numeral] chiffre *m* **4.** ***lit*** [zero] zéro *m* ■ **they're mere ~s** ***fig*** ce sont des moins que rien.
◇ *vt* **1.** [encode] crypter, chiffrer, coder **2.** MATHS chiffrer.

circa [ˈsɜːkə] *prep* circa, vers.

circadian [sɜːˈkeɪdɪən] *adj* circadien.

circle [ˈsɜːkl] ◇ *n* **1.** [gen - GEOM] cercle *m* ■ [around eyes] cerne *m* ■ **he had us going** *OR* **running round in ~s trying to find the information** il nous a fait tourner en rond à chercher les renseignements ■ **to come full ~** revenir au point de départ, boucler la boucle **2.** [group of people] cercle *m*, groupe *m* ■ **she has a wide ~ of friends** elle a beaucoup d'amis *OR* un grand cercle d'amis ■ **in artistic/political ~s** dans les milieux artistiques/politiques **3.** THEAT balcon *m*.
◇ *vt* **1.** [draw circle round] entourer (d'un cercle), encercler **2.** [move round] tourner autour de ■ **the moon ~s the earth** la lune est en orbite autour *OR* tourne autour de la terre **3.** [surround] encercler, entourer.
◇ *vi* **1.** [bird, plane] faire *OR* décrire des cercles **2.** [planet] tourner.

circuit [ˈsɜːkɪt] *n* **1.** [series of events, places] circuit *m* ■ **the tennis ~** le circuit des matches de tennis **2.** [periodical journey] tournée *f* ■ LAW tournée *f (d'un juge d'assises)* **3.** [journey around] circuit *m*, tour *m* ■ **we made a ~ of the grounds** nous avons fait le tour des terrains ■ **the Earth's ~ around the Sun** l'orbite de la terre autour du soleil **4.** ELEC circuit *m* **5.** SPORT [track] circuit *m*, parcours *m*.

circuit board *n* plaquette *f* (de circuits imprimés).

circuit breaker *n* ELEC disjoncteur *m*.

circuit judge *n juge itinérant.*

circuitous [səˈkjuːɪtəs] *adj* [route] qui fait un détour, détourné ■ [journey] compliqué ■ ***fig*** [reasoning, thinking] contourné, compliqué.

circuitry [ˈsɜːkɪtrɪ] *n* système *m* de circuits.

circuit training *n* SPORT préparation *f OR* entraînement *m (en accomplissant plusieurs sortes d'exercices)*.

circular [ˈsɜːkjʊləʳ] ◇ *adj* **1.** [movement, shape, ticket] circulaire ● **~ letter** *OR* **memo** circulaire *f* ■ **~ saw** scie *f* circulaire **2.** [reasoning] faux, fausse *f*, mal fondé ■ **~ argument** pétition *f* de principe.
◇ *n* **1.** [letter, memo] circulaire *f* **2.** [advertisement] prospectus *m*.

circularity [ˌsɜːkjʊˈlærətɪ] *n* **1.** [of movement, shape] forme *f* circulaire **2.** [of argument, reasoning] circularité *f*.

circularize, *UK* ise [ˈsɜːkjʊləraɪz] *vt* [send letters to] envoyer des circulaires à ■ [send advertising to] envoyer des prospectus à.

circulate [ˈsɜːkjʊleɪt] ◇ *vt* [book, bottle] faire circuler ■ [document - from person to person] faire circuler ; [- in mass mailing] diffuser ■ [news, rumour] propager.
◇ *vi* circuler.

circulating library *n* bibliothèque *f* de prêt.

circulation [ˌsɜːkjʊˈleɪʃn] *n* **1.** [gen - FIN] circulation *f* ■ **to be in ~** [book, money] être en circulation ; [person] être dans le circuit ■ **she's out of ~ at the moment** elle a disparu de la circulation pour l'instant **2.** [of magazine, newspaper] tirage *m* ■ **the Times has a ~ of 200,000** le Times tire à 200 000 exemplaires **3.** ANAT & BOT circulation *f* ■ **to have good/poor ~** avoir une bonne/une mauvaise circulation **4.** [of traffic] circulation *f*.

circulatory [ˌsɜːkjʊˈleɪtərɪ] *adj* circulatoire.

circumcise [ˈsɜːkəmsaɪz] *vt* circoncire.

circumcision [ˌsɜːkəmˈsɪʒn] *n* [act] circoncision *f* ■ [religious rite] (fête *f* de la) circoncision *f*.

circumference [səˈkʌmfərəns] *n* circonférence *f*.

circumflex [ˈsɜːkəmfleks] ◇ *n* accent *m* circonflexe.
◇ *adj* circonflexe.

circumlocution [ˌsɜːkəmləˈkjuːʃn] *n* circonlocution *f*.

circumlocutory [ˌsɜːkəmˈlɒkjʊtərɪ] *adj* ***fml*** qui procède par circonlocutions.

circumnavigate [ˌsɜːkəmˈnævɪgeɪt] *vt* [iceberg, island] contourner *(en bateau)* ■ **to ~ the world** faire le tour du monde en bateau, naviguer autour du globe.

circumnavigation [ˈsɜːkəmˌnævɪˈgeɪʃn] *n* circumnavigation *f*.

circumscribe [ˈsɜːkəmskraɪb] *vt* **1.** [restrict] circonscrire, limiter **2.** GEOM circonscrire.

circumscription [ˌsɜːkəm'skrɪpʃn] *n* circonscription *f.*

circumspect ['sɜːkəmspekt] *adj* circonspect.

circumspection [ˌsɜːkəm'spekʃn] *n* circonspection *f.*

circumstance ['sɜːkəmstəns] *n* **1.** *(U)* [events] : **force of ~** contrainte *f* *OR* force *f* des circonstances ▪ **I am a victim of ~** je suis victime des circonstances **2.** *fml (U)* [ceremony] : **pomp and ~** grand apparat *m*, pompe *f* *fml.*
◆ **circumstances** *npl* **1.** [conditions] circonstance *f*, situation *f* ▪ **in** *OR* **under these ~s** dans les circonstances actuelles, vu la situation actuelle *OR* l'état actuel des choses ▪ **in** *OR* **under normal ~s** en temps normal ▪ **under no ~s** en aucun cas ▪ **under similar ~s** en pareil cas **2.** [facts] circonstance *f*, détail *m* ▪ **you have to take into account the ~s** il faut tenir compte des circonstances.

circumstantial [ˌsɜːkəm'stænʃl] *adj* **1.** [incidental] accidentel, fortuit ▪ LAW [evidence] indirect **2.** *fml* [description, report] circonstancié, détaillé.

circumstantiate [ˌsɜːkəm'stænʃɪeɪt] *vt* [event, report] donner des détails circonstanciés sur ▪ LAW [evidence] confirmer en donnant des détails sur.

circumvent [ˌsɜːkəm'vent] *vt* **1.** [law, rule] tourner, contourner **2.** [outwit - person] circonvenir *fml*, manipuler ; [- plan] faire échouer **3.** [enemy] encercler, entourer.

circumvention [ˌsɜːkəm'venʃn] *n* [of law, rule] fait *m* de tourner *OR* contourner.

circus ['sɜːkəs] ◇ *n* **1.** [gen - ANTIQ] cirque *m* **2.** *UK* [roundabout] rond-point *m.*
◇ *comp* [act, clown, company, tent] de cirque.

cirrhosis [sɪ'rəʊsɪs] *n (U)* cirrhose *f.*

cirrocumulus [ˌsɪrəʊ'kjuːmjʊləs] (*pl* **cirrocumuli** [-laɪ]) *n* cirrocumulus *m.*

cirrostratus [ˌsɪrəʊ'strɑːtəs] (*pl* **cirrostrati** [-taɪ]) *n* cirrostratus *m.*

cirrus ['sɪrəs] (*pl* **cirri** [-raɪ]) *n* **1.** [cloud] cirrus *m* **2.** BOT vrille *f.*

CIS (*abbrev of* **Commonwealth of Independent States**) *pr n* CEI *f* ▪ **in the ~** dans la CEI.

cissy ['sɪsɪ] *n* & *adj* = **sissy**.

Cistercian [sɪ'stɜːʃn] ◇ *n* cistercien *m*, -enne *f.*
◇ *adj* cistercien ▪ **the ~ Order** l'ordre *m* de Cîteaux.

cistern ['sɪstən] *n* [tank] citerne *f* ▪ [for toilet] réservoir *m* de chasse d'eau.

citadel ['sɪtədəl] *n* *liter* & *fig* citadelle *f.*

citation [saɪ'teɪʃn] *n* citation *f.*

cite [saɪt] *vt* **1.** [quote] citer ▪ **he ~d it as an example** il l'a cité en exemple **2.** [commend] citer ▪ **she was ~d for bravery** elle a été citée pour sa bravoure **3.** LAW citer ▪ **they were ~d to appear as witnesses** ils étaient cités comme témoins.

citizen ['sɪtɪzn] *n* **1.** [of nation, state] citoyen *m*, -enne *f* ▪ ADMIN [national] ressortissant *m*, - e *f* ▪ **to become a French ~** prendre la nationalité française **2.** [of town] habitant *m*, - e *f* **3.** [civilian] civil *m*, - e *f* *(opposé à militaire)* ◐ **~'s arrest** *arrestation par un citoyen d'une personne soupçonnée d'avoir commis un délit.*

Citizens' Advice Bureau *pr n en Grande-Bretagne, bureau où les citoyens peuvent obtenir des conseils d'ordre juridique, social, etc.*

Citizens' Band *n fréquence (de radio) réservée au public* ▪ **~ radio** CB *f* ▪ **~ user** cibiste *mf.*

Citizen's Charter *n programme lancé par le gouvernement britannique en 1991 et qui vise à améliorer la qualité des services publics.*

citizenship ['sɪtɪznʃɪp] *n* citoyenneté *f*, nationalité *f* ▪ **~ papers** déclaration *f* de naturalisation.

citric ['sɪtrɪk] *adj* citrique ▪ **~ acid** acide *m* citrique.

citrus ['sɪtrəs] *adj* : **~ fruit** *OR* **fruits** agrumes *mpl.*

city ['sɪtɪ] ◇ *n* (*pl* **cities**) [town] (grande) ville *f* ▪ **the whole ~ turned out** toute la ville était présente, tous les habitants de la ville étaient présents.
◇ *comp* **1.** [lights, limits, streets] de la ville ▪ [officers, police, services] municipal ▪ **~ life** vie *f* en ville, vie citadine ◐ **~ fathers** édiles *mpl* locaux ▪ **'City Lights'** ***Chaplin*** 'les Lumières de la ville' **2.** *UK* PRESS [news, page, press] financier.
◆ **City** *pr n* [of London] *centre d'affaires de Londres* ▪ **the City** la City (de Londres) ▪ **he's something in the City** il travaille à la City (de Londres).

THE CITY

La City, quartier financier de Londres, est une circonscription administrative autonome de la capitale, dont le conseil siège au Guildhall. Elle est dotée de sa propre police et de son propre maire. La City est ausi connue sous son surnom *the Square Mile* (bien qu'elle couvre une superficie plus étendue). Le terme *the City* est souvent employé pour désigner le monde britannique de la finance.

City and Guilds *n diplôme britannique d'enseignement technique.*

city centre *n* centre *m* de la ville, centre-ville *m.*

city desk *n* PRESS *UK* service *m* financier ▪ *US* service *m* des nouvelles locales.

city-dweller *n* citadin *m*, - e *f.*

city editor *n* PRESS *UK* rédacteur *m* en chef pour les nouvelles financières ▪ *US* rédacteur *m* en chef pour les nouvelles locales.

city hall *n* **1.** [building] mairie *f*, hôtel *m* de ville **2.** *US* [municipal government] administration *f* (municipale).

city planner *n* urbaniste *mf.*

cityscape ['sɪtɪskeɪp] *n* paysage *m* urbain.

city slicker *n* *inf pej* *citadin sophistiqué.*

city-state *n* ANTIQ cité *f.*

city technology college *n* = **CTC**.

civet ['sɪvɪt] *n* [mammal, secretion] civette *f.*

civic ['sɪvɪk] *adj* [authority, building] municipal ▪ [duty, right] civique ▪ **~ event** événement *m* officiel local.

civics ['sɪvɪks] *n (U)* SCOL instruction *f* civique.

civil ['sɪvl] *adj* **1.** [of community] civil ▪ **~ disturbance** émeute *f* ▪ **~ strife** conflit *m* interne *OR* intestin *lit* ▪ **~ wedding** *OR* **marriage** mariage *m* civil **2.** [non-military] civil **3.** [polite] poli, courtois, civil *fml* ▪ **she was very ~ to me** elle s'est montrée très aimable avec moi ▪ **keep a ~ tongue in your head!** restez poli!

Civil Aviation Authority *pr n* *UK* *organisme de contrôle des compagnies aériennes.*

civil defence *n* protection *f* civile.

civil disobedience *n* résistance *f* passive (à la loi).

civil engineer *n* ingénieur *m* des travaux publics.

civil engineering *n* génie *m* civil.

civilian [sɪ'vɪljən] ◇ *adj* civil *(opposé à militaire)* ▪ **in ~ life** dans le civil.
◇ *n* civil *m*, - e *f* *(opposé à militaire).*

civility [sɪ'vɪlətɪ] (*pl* **civilities**) *n* **1.** [quality] courtoisie *f*, civilité *f* **2.** [act] civilité *f*, politesse *f.*

civilization [ˌsɪvɪlaɪ'zeɪʃn] *n* civilisation *f.*

civilize, *UK* **ise** ['sɪvɪlaɪz] *vt* civiliser.

civilized ['sɪvɪlaɪzd] *adj* [person, society] civilisé.

civil law *n* droit *m* civil.

civil liberties *n* libertés *fpl* civiques.

Civil List *n* liste *f* civile *(allouée à la famille royale britannique).*

civil partnership *n loi britannique qui garantit aux couples homosexuels les mêmes droits qu'aux couples mariés en matière de succession, de retraite, et pour les questions de garde et d'éducation des enfants.*

civil rights *npl* droits *mpl* civils *OR* civiques ■ **the ~ movement** la lutte pour les droits civils *OR* civiques.

civil servant *n* fonctionnaire *mf*.

civil service *n* fonction *f* publique, administration *f*.

civil war *n* guerre *f* civile ■ **the American Civil War** la guerre de Sécession ■ **the English Civil War** la guerre civile anglaise.

CIVIL WAR

Déclenchée par l'élection d'Abraham Lincoln, attisée par les différences sociales et économiques, la guerre civile opposa, de 1861 à 1865, le Sud, esclavagiste (les *Confederates*), au Nord, abolitionniste (les *Unionists*). Le conflit se termina par la victoire des fédéraux, dont les troupes étaient supérieures en nombre et en moyens.

THE ENGLISH CIVIL WAR

Guerre entre les partisans du Parlement et les royalistes, qui eut lieu de 1642 à 1646 et généra de nombreuses émeutes de 1646 à 1648. La victoire fut remportée par l'armée de Cromwell, qui fit exécuter le roi Charles Ier en 1649.

civvy ['sɪvɪ] ***UK inf*** ◇ *n* (*pl* **civvies**) [civilian] civil *m*, - e *f* (*opposé à militaire*).
◇ *adj* civil.
◆ **civvies** *npl* [dress] vêtements *mpl* civils ■ **in civvies** (habillé) en civil.

CJD *n* = **Creutzfeldt-Jakob disease**.

cl (*written abbrev of* **centilitre**) cl.

clad [klæd] ◇ *pp* ▻ **clothe**.
◇ *adj* ***lit*** vêtu.
◇ *vt* TECH revêtir.

cladding ['klædɪŋ] *n* TECH revêtement *m*, parement *m*.

claim [kleɪm] ◇ *vt* **1.** [assert, maintain] prétendre, déclarer ■ **it is ~ed that...** on dit *OR* prétend que... ■ **to ~ to be sthg** se faire passer pour qqch, prétendre être qqch
2. [assert one's right to] revendiquer, réclamer ■ [responsibility, right] revendiquer ■ **he ~s all the credit** il s'attribue tout le mérite ■ **to ~ damages/one's due** réclamer des dommages et intérêts/son dû
3. [apply for - money] demander ; [- expenses] demander le remboursement de
4. [call for - attention] réclamer, demander ; [- respect, sympathy] solliciter
5. [take] : **the storm ~ed five lives** *OR* **five victims** l'orage a fait cinq victimes.
◇ *vi* : **to ~ for** *OR* **on sthg** [insurance] demander le paiement de qqch ; [travel expenses] demander le remboursement de qqch.
◇ *n* **1.** [assertion] affirmation *f*, prétention *f* ■ **I make no ~s to understand why** je ne prétends pas comprendre pourquoi
2. [right] droit *m*, titre *m* ■ [by trade unions] demande *f* d'augmentation, revendication *f* salariale ■ **his only ~ to fame is that he once appeared on TV** c'est à une apparition à la télévision qu'il doit d'être célèbre
3. [demand] demande *f* ■ **he has no ~s on me** je ne lui suis redevable de rien ■ **he made too many ~s on their generosity** il a abusé de leur générosité ■ **she has many ~s on her time** elle est très prise ■ **to lay ~ to sthg** prétendre à qqch, revendiquer son droit à qqch ■ **we put in a ~ for better working conditions** nous avons demandé de meilleures conditions de travail ■ **pay ~** demande *f* d'augmentation (de salaire)
4. [in insurance] demande *f* d'indemnité, déclaration *f* de sinistre ■ **to put in a ~ for sthg** demander une indemnité pour qqch, faire une déclaration de sinistre pour qqch ■ **the company pays 65% of all ~s** la société satisfait 65 % de toutes les demandes de dédommagement ■ **~ form** [for insurance] formulaire *m* de déclaration de sinistre ; [for expenses] note *f* de frais
5. [piece of land] concession *f*.

claimant ['kleɪmənt] *n* **1.** ADMIN demandeur *m*, demanderesse *f* ■ LAW demandeur *m*, demanderesse *f*, requérant *m*, - e *f* **2.** [to throne] prétendant *m*, - e *f*.

clairvoyant [kleə'vɔɪənt] ◇ *n* voyant *m*, - e *f*, extralucide *mf*.
◇ *adj* doué de seconde vue.

clam [klæm] ◇ *n* palourde *f*, clam *m*.
◇ *vi* ***US*** **to go clamming** aller ramasser des clams.
◆ **clam up** *vi insep* ***inf*** refuser de parler.

clambake ['klæmbeɪk] *n* ***US*** **1.** ***liter*** *repas de fruits de mer sur la plage* **2.** ***fig*** grande fête *f*.

clamber ['klæmbəʳ] ◇ *vi* grimper (en s'aidant des mains) ■ **to ~ aboard a train** se hisser à bord d'un train ■ **he ~ed over the rocks** il a escaladé les rochers.
◇ *n* escalade *f*.

clam chowder *n potage épais aux palourdes*.

clammy ['klæmɪ] (*comp* **clammier**, *superl* **clammiest**) *adj* [hands, skin] moite (et froid) ■ [weather] humide, lourd ■ [walls] suintant, humide.

clamor ***US*** *vi* & *n* = **clamour**.

clamorous ['klæmərəs] *adj* ***fml*** **1.** [noisy] bruyant **2.** [demands] insistant.

clamour ***UK***, **clamor** ***US*** ['klæməʳ] ◇ *vi* vociférer, crier ■ **to ~ for sthg** demander *OR* réclamer qqch à grands cris *OR* à cor et à cri.
◇ *n* **1.** [noise] clameur *f*, vociférations *fpl*, cri *m*, cris *mpl* **2.** [demand] revendication *f* bruyante.

clamp [klæmp] ◇ *n* **1.** [fastener] pince *f* ■ MED clamp *m* ■ TECH crampon *m* ■ [on worktable] valet *m* (d'établi) **2.** TECH [for joint] serre-joint *m inv*, serre-joints *m inv* **3.** NAUT serre-câbles *m inv* **4.** AGRIC *tas (de navets, de pommes de terre) couvert de paille* **5.** [of bricks] tas *m*, pile *f* **6.** AUT = **wheelclamp**.
◇ *vt* **1.** [fasten] attacher, fixer ■ TECH serrer, cramponner ■ **to ~ sthg to sthg** fixer qqch sur qqch (à l'aide d'une pince) **2.** [vehicle] mettre un sabot à.
◆ **clamp down** *vi insep* donner un coup de frein ■ **to ~ down on** [expenses, inflation] mettre un frein à ; [crime, demonstrations] stopper ; [information] censurer ; [the press] bâillonner ; [person] serrer la vis à.

clampdown ['klæmpdaʊn] *n* mesures *fpl* répressives, répression *f* ■ **a ~ on crime** un plan de lutte contre la criminalité ■ **a ~ on demonstrations** une interdiction de manifester.

clan [klæn] *n* clan *m*.

clandestine [klæn'destɪn] *adj* clandestin.

clang [klæŋ] ◇ *vi* retentir *OR* résonner (d'un bruit métallique) ■ **the gate ~ed shut** le portail s'est fermé avec un bruit métallique.
◇ *vt* faire retentir *OR* résonner.
◇ *n* bruit *m* métallique.

clanger ['klæŋəʳ] *n* ***UK inf*** gaffe *f* ■ **to drop a ~** faire une gaffe.

clank [klæŋk] ◇ *n* cliquetis *m*, bruit *m* sec et métallique.
◇ *vi* cliqueter, faire un bruit sec.
◇ *vt* faire cliqueter.

clansman ['klænzmən] (*pl* **clansmen** [-mən]) *n* membre *m* d'un clan.

clanswoman ['klænz,wʊmən] (*pl* **clanswomen** [-,wɪmɪn]) *n* membre *m* d'un clan.

clap [klæp] ◇ *vt* (*pret & pp* **clapped**, *cont* **clapping**) **1.** : **to ~ one's hands** [to get attention, to mark rhythm] frapper dans ses mains, taper des mains ; [to applaud] applaudir **2.** [pat] taper, frapper **3.** [put] mettre, poser ■ **she clapped her hand to her forehead** elle s'est frappé le front ■ **the minute she clapped eyes on him** ***inf*** dès qu'elle eut posé les yeux sur lui.
◇ *vi* (*pret & pp* **clapped**, *cont* **clapping**) [in applause] applaudir ■ [to get attention, to mark rhythm] frapper dans ses mains.
◇ *n* **1.** [sound - gen] claquement *m* ; [- of hands] battement *m* ; [- of applause] applaudissements *mpl* ■ **let's give them a ~!** on les applaudit (bien fort)! ■ **~ of thunder** coup *m* de tonnerre **2.** [pat] tape *f* ■ **she gave him a ~ on the back** elle lui a donné une tape dans le dos **3.** △ [VD] chaude-pisse△ *f*.

clapboard ['klæpbɔːd] *n* bardeau *m*.

Clapham ['klæpəm] *pr n* : **the man on the ~ omnibus** Monsieur Tout-le-Monde.

clapped-out [klæpt-] *adj UK inf* [machine] fichu ▪ [person] crevé.

clapper ['klæpəʳ] *n* [of bell] battant *m*.
◆ **clappers** *npl UK inf* **to go** *OR* **to move like the ~s** aller à toute vitesse ▪ **he ran like the ~s** il a couru à toutes jambes, il a pris ses jambes à son cou.

clapperboard ['klæpəbɔ:d] *n* CIN claquette *f*, claquoir *m*, clap *m*.

clapping ['klæpɪŋ] *n (U)* [for attention, to music] battements *mpl* de mains ▪ [applause] applaudissements *mpl*.

claptrap ['klæptræp] *n (U) inf* [nonsense] âneries *fpl*, bêtises *fpl*.

claret ['klærət] ◇ *n UK* (vin *m* de) Bordeaux *m* (rouge).
◇ *adj* bordeaux *(inv)*.

clarification [,klærɪfɪ'keɪʃn] *n* **1.** [explanation] clarification *f*, éclaircissement *m* **2.** [of butter] clarification *f* ▪ [of wine] collage *m*.

clarify ['klærɪfaɪ] (*pret & pp* **clarified**) ◇ *vt* **1.** [explain] clarifier, éclaircir **2.** [butter] clarifier ▪ [wine] coller.
◇ *vi* **1.** [matter, situation] s'éclaircir **2.** [butter] se clarifier.

clarinet [,klærə'net] *n* clarinette *f*.

clarinet(t)ist [,klærə'netɪst] *n* clarinettiste *mf*.

clarion call *n* appel *m* de clairon ▪ **a ~ to action** un appel à l'action.

clarity ['klærətɪ] *n* **1.** [of explanation, of text] clarté *f*, précision *f* ▪ **~ of mind** lucidité *f*, clarté d'esprit **2.** [of liquid] clarté *f*.

clash [klæʃ] ◇ *n* **1.** [sound - gen] choc *m* métallique, fracas *m* ; [- of cymbals] retentissement *m* **2.** [between people - fight] affrontement *m*, bagarre *f* ; [- disagreement] dispute *f*, différend *m* **3.** [incompatibility - of ideas, opinions] incompatibilité *f* ; [- of interests] conflit *m* ; [- of colours] discordance *f* **4.** [of appointments, events] coïncidence *f* fâcheuse.
◇ *vi* **1.** [metallic objects] s'entrechoquer, se heurter ▪ [cymbals] résonner **2.** [people - fight] se battre ; [- disagree] se heurter ▪ **to ~ with sb over sthg** avoir un différend avec qqn à propos de qqch **3.** [be incompatible - ideas, opinions] se heurter, être incompatible *OR* en contradiction ; [- interests] se heurter, être en conflit ; [- colours] jurer, détonner ▪ **that shirt ~es with your trousers** cette chemise jure avec ton pantalon **4.** [appointments, events] tomber en même temps.
◇ *vt* [metallic objects] heurter *OR* entrechoquer bruyamment ▪ [cymbals] faire résonner.

clasp [klɑ:sp] ◇ *vt* [hold] serrer, étreindre ▪ [grasp] saisir ▪ **to ~ sb/sthg in one's arms** serrer qqn/qqch dans ses bras.
◇ *vi* s'attacher, se fermer.
◇ *n* **1.** [fastening - of dress, necklace] fermoir *m* ; [- of belt] boucle *f* **2.** [hold] prise *f*, étreinte *f* ▪ **hand ~** poignée *f* de mains.

clasp knife *n* couteau *m* pliant.

class [klɑ:s] ◇ *n* **1.** [category, division] classe *f*, catégorie *f* ▪ **~ A eggs** œufs de catégorie A ▪ **he's just not in the same ~ as his brother** il n'arrive pas à la cheville de son frère ▪ **to be in a ~ by oneself** *OR* **in a ~ of one's own** être unique, former une classe à part **2.** BIOL, BOT, SOCIOL & ZOOL classe *f* **3.** SCH & UNIV [group of students] classe *f* ▪ [course] cours *m*, classe *f* ▪ **the ~ of 1972** *US* la promotion de 1972 **4.** *UK* UNIV [grade] : **first ~ honours** licence *f* avec mention très bien **5.** *inf* [elegance] classe *f* ▪ **to have ~** avoir de la classe.
◇ *vt* classer, classifier.

class action *n US* : **~ suit** recours *m* collectif en justice.

class-conscious *adj* [person - aware] conscient des distinctions sociales ; [- snobbish] snob ▪ [attitude, manners] snob.

classic ['klæsɪk] ◇ *adj liter & fig* classique.
◇ *n* **1.** [gen] classique *m* **2.** [in horse racing, cycling] classique *f* **3.** SCH & UNIV : **the ~s** les lettres classiques *fpl*.

classical ['klæsɪkl] *adj* **1.** [gen] classique ▪ **~ music** musique *f* classique **2.** SCH & UNIV : **~ education** études *fpl* de lettres classiques ▪ **~ scholar** humaniste *mf*.

classically ['klæsɪklɪ] *adv* classiquement, de façon classique ▪ **a ~ trained musician** un musicien de formation classique.

classic car *n* voiture *f* ancienne.

classicism ['klæsɪsɪzm] *n* classicisme *m*.

classicist ['klæsɪsɪst] *n* **1.** [scholar] humaniste *mf* **2.** ART & LIT classique *m*.

classics ['klæsɪks] *n (U)* ≃ les lettres classiques *fpl*.

classifiable ['klæsɪfaɪəbl] *adj* qui peut être classifié, classable.

classification [,klæsɪfɪ'keɪʃn] *n* classification *f*.

classified ['klæsɪfaɪd] ◇ *adj* **1.** [arranged] classifié, classé ▪ **~ ad** *OR* **advertisement** petite annonce *f* **2.** [secret] (classé) secret.
◇ *n* petite annonce *f*.

classifier ['klæsɪfaɪəʳ] *n* classeur *m*.

classify ['klæsɪfaɪ] *vt* ranger.

classless ['klɑ:slɪs] *adj* [society] sans classes ▪ [person, accent] qui n'appartient à aucune classe (sociale).

classmate ['klɑ:smeɪt] *n* camarade *mf* de classe.

classroom ['klɑ:srʊm] *n* (salle *f* de) classe *f*.

classroom assistant *n* SCOL aide-éducateur *m*, - rice *f*.

class struggle *n* lutte *f* des classes.

class war(fare) *n* lutte *f* des classes.

classy ['klɑ:sɪ] (*comp* **classier**, *superl* **classiest**) *adj inf* [hotel, restaurant] chic *(inv)*, de luxe *(inv)*, classe *(inv)* ▪ [person] chic *(inv)*, qui a de la classe, classe *(inv)*.

clatter ['klætəʳ] ◇ *n* [rattle] cliquetis *m* ▪ [commotion] fracas *m* ▪ **the ~ of dishes** le bruit d'assiettes entrechoquées.
◇ *vt* heurter *OR* entrechoquer bruyamment.
◇ *vi* [typewriter] cliqueter ▪ [dishes] s'entrechoquer bruyamment ▪ [falling object] faire du bruit.

Claudius ['klɔ:dɪəs] *pr n* [emperor] Claude.

clausal ['klɔ:zl] *adj* **1.** GRAM propositionnel **2.** LAW relatif aux clauses.

clause [klɔ:z] *n* **1.** GRAM proposition *f* **2.** LAW clause *f*, disposition *f*.

claustrophobia [,klɔ:strə'fəʊbjə] *n* claustrophobie *f*.

claustrophobic [,klɔ:strə'fəʊbɪk] *adj* [person] claustrophobe ▪ [feeling] de claustrophobie ▪ [place, situation] où l'on se sent claustrophobe.

clavichord ['klævɪkɔ:d] *n* clavicorde *m*.

clavicle ['klævɪkl] *n* clavicule *f*.

claw [klɔ:] ◇ *n* **1.** [of bird, cat, dog] griffe *f* ▪ [of bird of prey] serre *f* ▪ [of crab, lobster] pince *f* ▪ *inf* [hand] *inf* patte *f* ▪ **to draw in/to show one's ~s** *liter & fig* rentrer/sortir ses griffes ▪ **to get one's ~s into sb** *inf* mettre le grappin sur qqn **2.** TECH [of hammer] pied-de-biche *m*.
◇ *vt* [scratch] griffer ▪ [grip] agripper *OR* serrer (avec ses griffes) ▪ [tear] déchirer (avec ses griffes) ▪ **he ~ed his way to the top** *fig* il a travaillé dur pour arriver en haut de l'échelle.
◆ **claw back** *vt sep* récupérer.

claw hammer *n* marteau *m* à pied-de-biche, marteau *m* fendu.

clay [kleɪ] ◇ *n* [gen] argile *f*, (terre *f*) glaise *f* ▪ [for pottery] argile *f*.
◇ *comp* [brick, pot] en argile, en terre ▪ **~ court** SPORT court *m* en terre battue.

claymore ['kleɪmɔ:ʳ] *n* claymore *f*.

clay pigeon *n* **1.** *liter* pigeon *m* d'argile *OR* de ball-trap ▪ **~ shooting** ball-trap *m* **2.** *US inf fig* [sitting duck] cible *f* facile.

clay pipe *n* pipe *f* en terre.

clean [kli:n] ◇ *adj* **1.** [free from dirt - hands, shirt, room] propre, net ; [- animal, person] propre ; [- piece of paper] vierge, blanc,

blanche *f* ▪ **my hands are ~** *liter* j'ai les mains propres, mes mains sont propres ; *fig* j'ai la conscience nette *OR* tranquille ▪ **he made a ~ breast of it** il a dit tout ce qu'il avait sur la conscience, il a déchargé sa conscience ▪ **to make a ~ sweep** faire table rase
2. [free from impurities - air] pur, frais, fraîche *f* ; [- water] pur, clair ; [- sound] net, clair
3. [morally pure - conscience] net, tranquille ; [- joke] qui n'a rien de choquant ▪ **~ living** une vie saine
4. [honourable - fight] loyal ; [- reputation] net, sans tache ▪ **he's got a ~ driving licence** il n'a jamais eu de contraventions graves ▪ **to have a ~ record** avoir un casier (judiciaire) vierge
5. [smooth - curve, line] bien dessiné, net ; [- shape] fin, élégant ; [- cut] net, franc, franche *f* ▪ **to make a ~ break** couper net ▪ **we made a ~ break with the past** nous avons rompu avec le passé, nous avons tourné la page
6. [throw] adroit, habile
7. *inf* **I'm ~** [innocent] je n'ai rien à me reprocher, je n'ai rien fait ; [without incriminating material] je n'ai rien sur moi ; [unarmed] je n'ai pas d'arme, je ne suis pas armé
8. [not radioactive] non radioactif.
◇ *vt* **1.** [room, cooker] nettoyer ▪ [clothing] laver ▪ **I ~ed the mud from my shoes** j'ai enlevé la boue de mes chaussures ▪ **to ~ one's teeth** se laver *OR* se brosser les dents ▪ **to ~ the windows** faire les vitres *OR* les carreaux
2. [chicken, fish] vider.
◇ *vi* **1.** [person] nettoyer ▪ **she spends her day ~ing** elle passe sa journée à faire le ménage
2. [carpet, paintbrush] se nettoyer ▪ **this cooker ~s easily** ce four est facile à nettoyer *OR* se nettoie facilement.
◇ *adv inf* **1.** [completely] carrément ▪ **the handle broke ~ off** l'anse a cassé net ▪ **he cut ~ through the bone** il a coupé l'os de part en part ▪ **we ~ forgot about the appointment** nous avions complètement oublié le rendez-vous
2. *phr* **to come ~ about sthg** révéler qqch.
◇ *n* nettoyage *m* ▪ **the carpet needs a good ~** la moquette a grand besoin d'être nettoyée.
◆ **clean off** *vt sep* **1.** [mud, stain] enlever
2. [sofa, table] débarrasser.
◆ **clean out** *vt sep* **1.** [tidy] nettoyer à fond ▪ [empty] vider
2. *inf* [person] nettoyer, plumer ▪ [house] vider.
◆ **clean up** ◇ *vt sep* **1.** [make clean] nettoyer à fond ▪ **~ this mess up!** nettoyez-moi ce fouillis!
2. [make orderly - cupboard, room] ranger ; [- affairs, papers] ranger, mettre de l'ordre dans ▪ **the police intend to ~ up the city** la police a l'intention d'épurer *OR* de nettoyer cette ville.
◇ *vi insep* **1.** [tidy room] nettoyer ▪ [tidy cupboard, desk] ranger ▪ [wash oneself] faire un brin de toilette
2. *inf* [make profit] gagner gros ▪ **we ~ed up on the deal** nous avons touché un gros paquet sur cette affaire, cette affaire nous a rapporté gros.

clean-cut *adj* **1.** [lines] net ▪ [shape] bien délimité, net **2.** [person] propre (sur soi), soigné.

cleaner ['kli:nər] *n* **1.** [cleaning lady] femme *f* de ménage ▪ [man] (ouvrier *m*) nettoyeur *m* **2.** [product - gen] produit *m* d'entretien ; [- stain remover] détachant *m* ▪ [device] appareil *m* de nettoyage **3.** [dry cleaner] teinturier *m*, - ère *f* ▶ **to take sb to the ~s** *inf* nettoyer *OR* plumer qqn.

cleaning ['kli:nɪŋ] *n* **1.** [activity - gen] nettoyage *m* ; [- household] ménage *m* ▪ **to do the ~** faire le ménage **2.** [clothes] vêtements *mpl* à faire nettoyer.

cleaning lady, cleaning woman *n* femme *f* de ménage.

cleanliness ['klenlɪnɪs] *n* propreté *f* ▪ **~ is next to godliness** *prov* la propreté du corps s'apparente à celle de l'âme.

clean-living *adj* qui mène une vie saine.

cleanly[1] ['kli:nlɪ] *adv* **1.** [smoothly] net ▪ **she cut it ~ in two** elle l'a coupé en deux parties égales **2.** [fight, play] loyalement.

cleanly[2] ['klenlɪ] (*comp* **cleanlier**, *superl* **cleanliest**) *adj* propre.

cleanness ['kli:nnɪs] *n* propreté *f*.

cleanout ['kli:naʊt] *n* = **cleanup**.

cleanse [klenz] *vt* **1.** [clean - gen] nettoyer ; [- with water] laver ▪ MED [blood] dépurer ▪ [wound] nettoyer **2.** *fig* [purify] purifier ▪ **to ~ sb of their sins** laver qqn de ses péchés.

cleanser ['klenzər] *n* **1.** [detergent] détergent *m*, détersif *m* **2.** [for skin] (lait *m*) démaquillant *m*.

clean-shaven *adj* [face, man] rasé de près.

cleansing ['klenzɪŋ] ◇ *n* nettoyage *m*.
◇ *adj* [lotion] démaquillant ▪ [power, property] de nettoyage.

cleanup ['kli:nʌp] *n* nettoyage *m* à fond ▪ **to give sthg a ~** nettoyer qqch à fond.

clear [klɪər] ◇ *adj* **1.** [transparent - glass, plastic] transparent ; [- water] clair, limpide ; [- river] limpide, transparent ; [- air] pur ▪ **~ honey** miel liquide ▪ **~ soup** [plain stock] bouillon *m* ; [with meat] consommé *m*
2. [cloudless - sky] clair, dégagé ; [- weather] clair, beau *(before vowel or silent 'h'* **bel***)*, belle *f* ▪ **on a ~ day** par temps clair ▶ **as ~ as day** clair comme le jour *OR* comme de l'eau de roche
3. [not dull - colour] vif ; [- light] éclatant, radieux ▪ [untainted - complexion, skin] clair, frais, fraîche *f*
4. [distinct - outline] net, clair ; [- photograph] net ; [- sound] clair, distinct ; [- voice] clair, argentin ▪ **make sure your writing is ~** efforcez-vous d'écrire distinctement *OR* proprement ▪ **the lyrics are not very ~** je ne distingue pas très bien les paroles de la chanson ▶ **the sound was as ~ as a bell** on entendait un son aussi clair que celui d'une cloche
5. [not confused - mind] pénétrant, lucide ; [- thinking, argument, style] clair ; [- explanation, report] clair, intelligible ; [- instructions] clair, explicite ; [- message] en clair ▪ **I want to keep a ~ head** je veux rester lucide *OR* garder tous mes esprits ▪ **he is quite ~ about what has to be done** il sait parfaitement ce qu'il y a à faire ▪ **now let's get this ~ – I want no nonsense** comprenons-nous bien *OR* soyons clairs – je ne supporterai pas de sottises
6. [obvious, unmistakable] évident, clair ▪ **it is a ~ case of favouritism** c'est manifestement du favoritisme, c'est un cas de favoritisme manifeste ▪ **it's ~ that he's lying** il est évident *OR* clair qu'il ment ▪ **he was unable to make his meaning ~** il n'arrivait pas à s'expliquer ▪ **she made it quite ~ to them what she wanted** elle leur a bien fait comprendre ce qu'elle voulait ▪ **it is important to make ~ exactly what our aims are** il est important de bien préciser quels sont nos objectifs ▪ **do I make myself ~?** est-ce que je me fais bien comprendre?, est-ce que c'est bien clair? ▶ **as ~ as mud** *hum* clair comme l'encre
7. [free from doubt, certain] certain ▪ **I want to be ~ in my mind about it** je veux en avoir le cœur net
8. [unqualified] net, sensible ▪ **it's a ~ improvement over the other** c'est nettement mieux que l'autre, il y a un net progrès par rapport à l'autre ▪ **they won by a ~ majority** ils ont gagné avec une large majorité
9. [unobstructed, free - floor, path] libre, dégagé ; [- route] sans obstacles, sans danger ; [- view] dégagé ▪ **the roads are ~ of snow** les routes sont déblayées *OR* déneigées ▪ **~ of obstacles** sans obstacles ▪ **to be ~ of sthg** être débarrassé de qqch ▪ **we're ~ of the traffic** nous sommes sortis des encombrements ▪ **once the plane was ~ of the trees** une fois que l'avion eut franchi les arbres ▪ **can you see your way ~ to lending me £5?** *fig* auriez-vous la possibilité de me prêter 5 livres?
10. [free from guilt] : **is your conscience ~?** as-tu la conscience tranquille?
11. [of time] libre ▪ **his schedule is ~** il n'a rien de prévu sur son emploi du temps ▪ **we have four ~ days to finish** nous avons quatre jours pleins *OR* entiers pour finir
12. [net - money, wages] net ▪ **a ~ profit** un bénéfice net ▪ **a ~ loss** une perte sèche ▪ **~ of taxes** net d'impôts
13. LING antérieur.
◇ *adv* **1.** [distinctly] distinctement, nettement ▪ **reading you loud and ~** RADIO je te reçois cinq sur cinq
2. [out of the way] : **when we got ~ of the town** quand nous nous sommes éloignés de la ville ▪ **we pulled him ~ of the wrecked car/of the water** nous l'avons sorti de la carcasse de la voiture/de l'eau ▪ **stand ~!** écartez-vous! ▪ **stand ~ of the entrance!** dégagez l'entrée!
3. [all the way] entièrement, complètement ▪ **the thieves got ~ away** les voleurs ont disparu sans laisser de trace.

◇ *n phr* : **to be in the ~** [out of danger] être hors de danger ; [out of trouble] être tiré d'affaire ; [free of blame] être blanc comme neige ; [above suspicion] être au-dessus de tout soupçon ; [no longer suspected] être blanchi (de tout soupçon) ; SPORT être démarqué.
◇ *vt* **1.** [remove - object] débarrasser, enlever ; [- obstacle] écarter ; [- weeds] arracher, enlever ▪ **she ~ed the plates from the table** elle a débarrassé la table
2. [remove obstruction from - gen] débarrasser ; [- entrance, road] dégager, déblayer ; [- forest, land] défricher ; [- pipe] déboucher ▪ **it's your turn to ~ the table** c'est à ton tour de débarrasser la table *OR* de desservir ▪ **to ~ one's throat** s'éclaircir la gorge *OR* la voix ▪ **~ the room!** évacuez la salle! ▪ **the judge ~ed the court** le juge a fait évacuer la salle ▪ **the police ~ed the way for the procession** la police a ouvert un passage au cortège ▪ **the talks ~ed the way for a ceasefire** *fig* les pourparlers ont préparé le terrain *OR* ont ouvert la voie pour un cessez-le-feu ➲ **to ~ the ground** *liter* & *fig* déblayer le terrain ▪ **to ~ the decks** [prepare for action] se mettre en branle-bas de combat ; [make space] faire de la place, faire le ménage
3. [clarify - liquid] clarifier ; [- wine] coller, clarifier ; [- skin] purifier ; [- complexion] éclaircir ▪ **his apology ~ed the air** *fig* ses excuses ont détendu l'atmosphère ▪ **I went for a walk to ~ my head** [from hangover] j'ai fait un tour pour m'éclaircir les idées ; [from confusion] j'ai fait un tour pour me rafraîchir les idées *OR* pour me remettre les idées en place
4. [authorize] autoriser, approuver ▪ **you'll have to ~ it with the boss** il faut demander l'autorisation *OR* l'accord *OR* le feu vert du patron
5. [vindicate, find innocent] innocenter, disculper ▪ **to ~ sb of a charge** disculper qqn d'une accusation ▪ **the court ~ed him of all blame** la cour l'a totalement disculpé *OR* innocenté ▪ **give him a chance to ~ himself** donnez-lui la possibilité de se justifier *OR* de prouver son innocence ▪ **to ~ one's name** se justifier, défendre son honneur
6. [avoid touching] franchir ▪ [obstacle] éviter ▪ **the horse ~ed the fence with ease** le cheval a sauté sans peine par-dessus *OR* a franchi sans peine la barrière ▪ **hang the curtains so that they just ~ the floor** accrochez les rideaux de façon à ce qu'ils touchent à peine le parquet
7. [make a profit of] : **she ~ed 10% on the deal** l'affaire lui a rapporté 10 % net *OR* 10 % tous frais payés
8. [dispatch - work] finir, terminer ▪ COMM [- stock] liquider ▪ **he ~ed the backlog of work** il a rattrapé le travail en retard
9. [settle - account] liquider, solder ; [- cheque] compenser ; [- debt] s'acquitter de ; [- dues] acquitter
10. [subj: customs officer - goods] dédouaner ; [- ship] expédier
11. [pass through] : **to ~ customs** [person] passer la douane ; [shipment] être dédouané ▪ **the bill ~ed the Senate** le projet de loi a été voté par le Sénat
12. MED [blood] dépurer, purifier ▪ [bowels] purger, dégager
13. SPORT : **to ~ the ball** dégager le ballon
14. TECH [decode] déchiffrer.
◇ *vi* **1.** [weather] s'éclaircir, se lever ▪ [sky] se dégager ▪ [fog] se lever, se dissiper
2. [liquid] s'éclaircir ▪ [skin] devenir plus sain ▪ [complexion] s'éclaircir ▪ [expression] s'éclairer
3. [cheque] : **it takes three days for the cheque to ~** il y a trois jours de délai d'encaissement
4. [obtain clearance] recevoir l'autorisation.
◆ **clear away** ◇ *vt sep* [remove] enlever, ôter ▪ **we ~ed away the dishes** nous avons débarrassé (la table) *OR* desservi.
◇ *vi insep* **1.** [tidy up] débarrasser, desservir
2. [disappear - fog, mist] se dissiper.
◆ **clear off** ◇ *vi insep inf* filer ▪ **~ off!** fiche le camp!
◇ *vt sep* [get rid of - debt] s'acquitter de ▪ COMM [- stock] liquider.
◆ **clear out** ◇ *vt sep* **1.** [tidy] nettoyer, ranger ▪ [empty - cupboard] vider ; [- room] débarrasser
2. [throw out - rubbish, old clothes] jeter ▪ **he ~ed everything out of the house** il a fait le vide dans la maison ▪ **to ~ everyone out of a room** faire évacuer une pièce
3. *inf* [leave without money] nettoyer, plumer
4. *inf* [goods, stock] épuiser.
◇ *vi insep inf* filer ▪ **~ out (of here)!** dégage!, fiche le camp!
◆ **clear up** ◇ *vt sep* **1.** [settle - problem] résoudre ; [- misunderstanding] dissiper ; [- mystery] éclaircir, résoudre ▪ **let's ~ this matter up** tirons cette affaire au clair
2. [tidy up] ranger, faire du rangement dans.
◇ *vi insep* **1.** [weather] s'éclaircir, se lever ▪ [fog, mist] se dissiper, se lever ▪ **it's ~ing up** le temps se lève
2. [illness] : **his cold is ~ing up** sa grippe tire à sa fin
3. [tidy up] ranger, faire le ménage ▪ **I'm fed up with ~ing up after you** j'en ai assez de faire le ménage derrière toi.

clearance ['klɪərəns] *n* **1.** [removal - of buildings, litter] enlèvement *m* ; [- of obstacles] déblaiement *m* ; [- of people] évacuation *f* ▪ COMM [- of merchandise] liquidation *f* ▪ **land ~** déblaiement *OR* dégagement *m* du terrain **2.** [space] jeu *m*, dégagement *m* ▪ **there was a 10-centimetre ~ between the lorry and the bridge** il y avait un espace de 10 centimètres entre le camion et le pont ▪ **how much ~ is there?** que reste-t-il comme place? **3.** [permission] autorisation *f*, permis *m* ▪ [from customs] dédouanement *m* ▪ **they sent the order to headquarters for ~** ils ont envoyé la commande au siège pour contrôle **4.** BANK [of cheque] compensation *f* **5.** SPORT dégagement *m*.

clearance sale *n* liquidation *f*, soldes *mpl*.

clear-cut *adj* **1.** [lines, shape] nettement défini, net **2.** [decision, situation] clair ▪ [difference] clair, net ▪ [opinion, plan] bien défini, précis.

clear-headed *adj* [person] lucide, perspicace ▪ [decision] lucide, rationnel.

clearing ['klɪərɪŋ] *n* **1.** [in forest] clairière *f* ▪ [in clouds] éclaircie *f* **2.** [of land] défrichement *m* ▪ [of passage] dégagement *m*, déblaiement *m* ▪ [of pipe] débouchage *m* **3.** [removal - of objects] enlèvement *m* ; [- of people] évacuation *f* **4.** [of name, reputation] réhabilitation *f* ▪ LAW [of accused] disculpation *f* **5.** BANK [of cheque] compensation *f* ▪ [of account] liquidation *f*, solde *m* **6.** [of debt] acquittement *m*.

clearing bank *n UK* banque *f* de dépôt.

clearing house *n* **1.** BANK chambre *f* de compensation **2.** [for information, materials] bureau *m* central.

clearing-up *n* nettoyage *m*.

clearly ['klɪəlɪ] *adv* **1.** [distinctly - see, understand] clairement, bien ; [- hear, speak] distinctement ; [- describe, explain] clairement, précisément ; [- think] clairement, lucidement **2.** [obviously] manifestement, à l'évidence ▪ **they ~ didn't expect us** il était clair *OR* évident qu'ils ne nous attendaient pas.

clearness ['klɪənɪs] *n* **1.** [of air, glass] transparence *f* ▪ [of water] limpidité *f* **2.** [of speech, thought] clarté *f*, précision *f*.

clearout ['klɪəraʊt] *n UK inf* rangement *m*.

clearway ['klɪəweɪ] *n UK* AUT route *f* à stationnement interdit.

cleat [kli:t] *n* **1.** [on shoe] clou *m* **2.** [block of wood] tasseau *m* ▪ NAUT taquet *m*.

cleavage ['kli:vɪdʒ] *n* **1.** [of woman] décolleté *m* **2.** BIOL [of cell] division *f* ▪ CHEM & GEOL clivage *m*.

cleave [kli:v] (*pret* **cleaved** *OR* **clove** [kləʊv] *arch OR* **cleft** [kleft], *pp* **cleaved** *OR* **cloven** ['kləʊvn] *arch OR* **cleft** [kleft]) *vt* **1.** *lit* [split] fendre ▪ *fig* diviser, séparer **2.** BIOL [cell] diviser ▪ GEOL [mineral] cliver.
◆ **cleave through** *vt insep* : **to ~ through the waves** fendre les vagues.
◆ **cleave to** (*pret* **cleaved** *OR* **clove** *arch OR* **cleft**, *pp* **cleaved** *OR* **clove**) *vt insep* se cramponner à, s'accrocher à.

cleaver ['kli:vəʳ] *n* couperet *m*.

clef [klef] *n* MUS clef *f*, clé *f*.

cleft [kleft] ◇ *pt* & *pp arch* ▻ **cleave**.
◇ *adj* [split - gen] fendu ▪ [branch] fourchu ▪ **to be in a ~ stick** *UK inf* être *OR* se trouver entre le marteau et l'enclume.
◇ *n* [opening - gen] fissure *f* ; [- in rock] fissure *f*, crevasse *f*.

cleft palate *n* palais *m* fendu.

clematis ['klemətɪs] *n* clématite *f*.

clemency ['klemənsɪ] *n* **1.** [mercy] clémence *f*, magnanimité *f* **2.** [of weather] douceur *f*, clémence *f*.

clement ['klemənt] *adj* **1.** [person] clément, magnanime **2.** [weather] doux, douce *f*, clément.

clementine ['kleməntaɪn] *n* clémentine *f*.

clench [klentʃ] ◇ *vt* [fist, jaw, buttocks] serrer ■ [grasp firmly] empoigner, agripper ■ [hold tightly] serrer.
◇ *n* **1.** [grip] prise *f*, étreinte *f* **2.** TECH [clamp] crampon *m*.

Cleopatra [kliːə'pætrə] *pr n* Cléopâtre ■ **~'s Needle** l'obélisque *m* de Cléopâtre.

clergy ['klɜːdʒɪ] *n* (membres *mpl* du) clergé *m*.

clergyman ['klɜːdʒɪmən] (*pl* **clergymen** [-mən]) *n* [gen] ecclésiastique *m* ■ [Catholic] curé *m*, prêtre *m* ■ [Protestant] pasteur *m*.

clergywoman ['klɜːdʒɪˌwʊmən] (*pl* **clergywomen** [-ˌwɪmɪn]) *n* (femme *f*) pasteur *m*.

cleric ['klerɪk] *n* ecclésiastique *m*.

clerical ['klerɪkl] *adj* **1.** [office - staff, work] de bureau ; [- position] de commis ■ **to do ~ work** travailler dans un bureau ■ **~ error** [in document] faute *f* de copiste ; [in accounting] erreur *f* d'écriture **2.** RELIG clérical, du clergé ■ **~ collar** col *m* de pasteur.

clericalism ['klerɪkəlɪzm] *n* cléricalisme *m*.

clerk [*UK* klɑːk, *US* klɜːrk] ◇ *n* **1.** [in office] employé *m*, - e *f* (de bureau), commis *m* ■ [in bank] employé *m*, - e *f* de banque ■ **~ of works** *UK* CONSTR conducteur *m* de travaux **2.** LAW clerc *m* ■ **Clerk of the Court** greffier *m* (du tribunal) **3.** *US* [sales person] vendeur *m*, - euse *f* **4.** *US* [receptionist] réceptionniste *mf* **5.** RELIG : **~ in holy orders** ecclésiastique *m*.
◇ *vi US* [as assistant] : **to ~ for sb** être assistant de qqn.

clever ['klevəʳ] *adj* **1.** [intelligent] intelligent, astucieux **2.** [skilful - person] adroit, habile ; [- work] bien fait ■ **to be ~ with one's hands** être adroit *OR* habile de ses mains ■ **to be ~ at sthg/at doing sthg** être doué pour qqch/pour faire qqch ■ **to be ~ at maths** être fort en maths **3.** [cunning] malin, - igne *f*, astucieux ■ *pej* rusé **4.** [ingenious - book] intelligemment *OR* bien écrit, ingénieux ; [- film] ingénieux, intelligent ; [- idea, plan] ingénieux, astucieux ; [- story] fin, astucieux ■ **there's a ~ way of getting around the problem** il y a une astuce pour contourner le problème.

clever-clever *adj UK inf* trop malin, - igne *f*.

clever Dick *n UK inf* petit malin *m*.

cleverly ['klevəlɪ] *adv* [intelligently] intelligemment, astucieusement ■ [skilfully] adroitement, habilement ■ [cunningly] avec ruse ■ [ingeniously] ingénieusement.

cleverness ['klevənɪs] *n* [intelligence] intelligence *f*, astuce *f* ■ [skilfulness] habileté *f*, adresse *f* ■ [cunning] ruse *f* ■ [ingenuity] ingéniosité *f*.

cliché [*UK* 'kliːʃeɪ, *US* kliː'ʃeɪ] *n* **1.** [idea] cliché *m* ■ [phrase] cliché *m*, lieu commun *m*, banalité *f* **2.** TYPO cliché *m*.

clichéd [*UK* 'kliːʃeɪd, *US* kliː'ʃeɪd] *adj* banal ■ **a ~ phrase** un cliché, une banalité, un lieu commun.

click [klɪk] ◇ *n* **1.** [sound] petit bruit *m* sec ■ [of tongue] claquement *m* ■ LING clic *m*, click *m* **2.** [of ratchet, wheel] cliquet *m*.
◇ *vt* **1.** [fingers, tongue] faire claquer ■ **he ~ed his heels (together)** il a claqué les talons **2.** COMPUT cliquer sur.
◇ *vi* **1.** [make sound] faire un bruit sec ■ **the lock ~ed into place** la serrure s'est enclenchée avec un déclic **2.** *inf* [become clear] : **it suddenly ~ed** tout à coup ça a fait "tilt" **3.** *inf* [be a success] bien marcher ■ [get on well] : **they ~ed from the beginning** ils se sont bien entendus dès le début, ça a tout de suite collé entre eux **4.** COMPUT cliquer ■ **to ~ on sthg** cliquer sur qqch.

clicking ['klɪkɪŋ] *n* cliquetis *m*.

client ['klaɪənt] *n* [gen - COMPUT] client *m*, - e *f*.

clientele [ˌkliːɒn'tel] *n* COMM clientèle *f* ■ THEAT clientèle, public *m* (habituel).

client-server COMPUT ◇ *n* client-serveur *m*.
◇ *comp* : **~ database** base de données client-serveur.

cliff [klɪf] *n* escarpement *m* ■ [on coast] falaise *f* ■ [in mountaineering] à-pic *m inv*.

cliffhanger ['klɪfˌhæŋəʳ] *n inf* [situation in film, story] situation *f* à suspense ■ [moment of suspense] moment *m* d'angoisse ■ **the election was a real ~** le résultat des élections est resté incertain jusqu'au dernier moment.

climactic [klaɪ'mæktɪk] *adj* à son apogée, à son point culminant.

climate ['klaɪmɪt] *n* METEOR climat *m* ■ *fig* climat *m*, ambiance *f* ■ **the ~ of opinion** (les courants *mpl* de) l'opinion *f* ■ **the economic ~** la conjoncture économique.

climate change *n* changement *m* climatique.

climatic [klaɪ'mætɪk] *adj* climatique.

climax ['klaɪmæks] ◇ *n* **1.** [culmination] apogée *m*, point *m* culminant ■ **this brought matters to a ~** ceci a porté l'affaire à son point culminant ■ **as the battle reached its ~** lorsque la bataille fut à son paroxysme ■ **he worked up to the ~ of his story** il amena le récit à son point culminant **2.** [sexual] orgasme *m* **3.** [in rhetoric] gradation *f*.
◇ *vi* **1.** [film, story] atteindre le *OR* son point culminant **2.** [sexually] atteindre l'orgasme.

climb [klaɪm] ◇ *vi* **1.** [road, sun] monter ■ [plane] monter, prendre de l'altitude ■ [prices] monter, augmenter ■ [plant] grimper **2.** [person] grimper ■ **I ~ed into bed/into the boat** j'ai grimpé dans mon lit/à bord du bateau ■ **to ~ over an obstacle** escalader un obstacle ■ **he ~ed (up) out of the hole/through the opening** il s'est hissé hors du trou/par l'ouverture ■ **to ~ to power** se hisser au pouvoir **3.** SPORT faire de l'escalade ■ [on rocks] varapper ■ **to go ~ing** faire de l'escalade.
◇ *vt* **1.** [ascend - stairs, steps] monter, grimper ; [- hill] escalader, grimper ; [- mountain] gravir, faire l'ascension de ; [- cliff, wall] escalader ; [- ladder, tree] monter sur ; [- rope] monter à **2.** SPORT [rockface] escalader, grimper sur.
◇ *n* **1.** [of hill, slope] montée *f*, côte *f* ■ [in mountaineering] ascension *f*, escalade *f* ■ **it's quite a ~** ça monte dur ■ **it was an easy ~ to the top (of the hill)** ça montait en pente douce jusqu'au sommet (de la colline) ■ **there were several steep ~s along the route** il y avait plusieurs bonnes côtes sur le trajet **2.** [of plane] montée *f*, ascension *f*.
◆ **climb down** *vi insep* **1.** [descend] descendre ■ [in mountaineering] descendre, effectuer une descente **2.** [back down] en rabattre, céder.

climb-down *n* dérobade *f*, reculade *f*.

climber ['klaɪməʳ] *n* **1.** [person] grimpeur *m*, - euse *f* ■ [mountaineer] alpiniste *mf* ■ [rock climber] varappeur *m*, - euse *f* **2.** [plant] plante *f* grimpante **3.** [bird] grimpeur *m*.

climbing ['klaɪmɪŋ] ◇ *n* **1.** [action] montée *f* ■ **the ~ of Everest** l'escalade de l'Everest **2.** [mountaineering] alpinisme *m* ■ [rock climbing] varappe *f*, escalade *f*.
◇ *adj* [bird] grimpeur ■ [plant] grimpant ■ [plane, star] ascendant.

climbing frame *n UK* cage *f* à poules *(jeu)*.

climes [klaɪmz] *npl lit* régions *fpl*, contrées *fpl* ■ **he's gone to sunnier ~** il est allé sous des climats plus souriants.

clinch [klɪntʃ] ◇ *vt* **1.** [settle - deal] conclure ; [- argument] régler, résoudre ; [- agreement] sceller ■ **the ~ing argument** l'argument décisif **2.** TECH [nail] river ■ NAUT étalinguer.
◇ *vi* BOX combattre corps à corps.
◇ *n* **1.** TECH rivetage *m* ■ NAUT étalingure *f* **2.** BOX corps à corps *m* **3.** *inf* [embrace] étreinte *f*, enlacement *m*.

clincher ['klɪntʃəʳ] *n inf* argument *m* irréfutable, argument *m* massue.

cline [klaɪn] *n* cline *m*.

cling [klɪŋ] (*pret & pp* **clung** [klʌŋ]) *vi* **1.** [hold on tightly] s'accrocher, se cramponner ■ **they clung to one another** ils se sont enlacés, ils se sont cramponnés l'un à l'autre ■ *fig* **to ~ to a hope/to a belief/to the past** se raccrocher à à un espoir/une croyance/au passé ■ **we can't afford to ~ to the past** il est dangereux de se raccrocher au passé **2.** [stick] adhérer, coller ▪ **a dress that ~s to the body** une robe très près du corps *OR* très ajustée **3.** [smell] persister.

clingfilm ['klɪŋfɪlm] *n UK* film *m* alimentaire transparent.

clinging ['klɪŋɪŋ] *adj* [clothing] collant, qui moule le corps ▪ *pej* [person] importun ▪ **~ vine** *US inf fig* pot *m* de colle.

clingy ['klɪŋɪ] (*comp* **clingier**, *superl* **clingiest**) *adj* [clothing] moulant ▪ *pej* [person] importun.

clinic ['klɪnɪk] *n* **1.** [part of hospital] service *m* ▪ **eye ~** clinique *f* ophtalmologique **2.** [treatment session] consultation *f* ▪ **the doctor holds his ~ twice a week** le docteur consulte deux fois par semaine **3.** *UK* [private hospital] clinique *f* **4.** [consultant's teaching session] clinique *f* **5.** [health centre] centre *m* médico-social *OR* d'hygiène sociale **6.** *UK* [of MP] permanence *f*.

clinical ['klɪnɪkl] *adj* **1.** MED [lecture, tests] clinique **2.** *fig* [attitude] froid, aseptisé.

clinically ['klɪnɪklɪ] *adv* **1.** MED cliniquement **2.** *fig* [act, speak] objectivement, froidement.

clinical psychologist *n* spécialiste *mf* en psychologie clinique.

clinical psychology *n* psychologie *f* clinique.

clinical thermometer *n* thermomètre *m* médical.

clinician [klɪ'nɪʃn] *n* clinicien *m*, - enne *f*.

clink [klɪŋk] ◇ *vt* faire tinter *OR* résonner ▪ **they ~ed (their) glasses (together)** ils ont trinqué.
◇ *vi* tinter, résonner.
◇ *n* **1.** [sound] tintement *m* (de verres) **2.** *inf* [jail] *inf* prison *f*, taule *f*.

clinker ['klɪŋkəʳ] *n* **1.** *(U)* [ash] mâchefer *m*, scories *fpl* **2.** [brick] brique *f* vitrifiée **3.** *US inf* [mistake] gaffe *f* ▪ MUS couac *m* **4.** *US inf* [film, play] bide *m*.

clip [klɪp] ◇ *vt* (*pret & pp* **clipped**, *cont* **clipping**) **1.** [cut] couper (avec des ciseaux), rogner ▪ [hedge] tailler ▪ [animal] tondre ▪ **~ the coupon out of the magazine** découpez le bon dans le magazine ▪ **I clipped five seconds off my personal best** j'ai amélioré mon record de cinq secondes ▪ **to ~ a bird's wings** rogner les ailes d'un oiseau ⊳ **to ~ sb's wings** laisser moins de liberté à qqn **2.** *UK* [ticket] poinçonner **3.** [attach] attacher ▪ [papers] attacher (avec un trombone) ▪ [brooch] fixer **4.** *inf* [hit] frapper, cogner ▪ **to ~ sb round the ear** flanquer une taloche à qqn ▪ **I clipped the gate as I drove in** j'ai cogné *OR* heurté la barrière en rentrant la voiture.
◇ *n* **1.** [snip] petit coup *m* de ciseaux **2.** [excerpt - CIN], RADIO & TV court extrait *m* ▪ *US* [from newspaper] coupure *f* **3.** [clasp] pince *f* ▪ [for paper] trombone *m*, pince *f* ▪ [for pipe] collier *m*, bague *f* **4.** [for bullets] chargeur *m* **5.** [brooch] clip *m* ▪ [for hair] barrette *f* ▪ [for tie] fixe-cravate *m* **6.** *inf* [blow] gifle *f*, taloche *f* ▪ **he got a ~ round the ear** il s'est pris une taloche ▪ **at one ~** *US fig* d'un seul coup.
◆ **clip on** ◇ *vt sep* [document] attacher (avec un trombone) ▪ [brooch, earrings] mettre.
◇ *vi* s'attacher *OR* se fixer avec une pince.

clipboard ['klɪpbɔːd] *n* **1.** [writing board] écritoire *f* à pince, clipboard *m* **2.** COMPUT bloc-notes *m*.

clip-clop [-klɒp] ◇ *n* & *onom* clip-clop *m*.
◇ *vi* (*pret & pp* **clip-clopped**, *cont* **clip-clopping**) faire clip-clop.

clip joint△ *n boîte de nuit où l'on pratique des prix excessifs.*

clip-on *adj* amovible ▪ **~ earrings** clips *mpl (d'oreilles)*.
◆ **clip-ons** *npl* **1.** [glasses] *verres teintés amovibles* **2.** [earrings] clips *mpl (d'oreilles)*.

clipped [klɪpt] *adj* **1.** [speech, style] heurté, saccadé **2.** [hair] bien entretenu.

clipper ['klɪpəʳ] *n* **1.** [ship] clipper *m* **2.** [horse] cheval *m* qui court vite.
◆ **clippers** *npl* [for nails] pince *f* à ongles ▪ [for hair] tondeuse *f* ▪ [for hedge] sécateur *m* à haie.

clipping ['klɪpɪŋ] *n* [small piece] petit bout *m*, rognure *f* ▪ [from newspaper] coupure *f* (de presse) ▪ **grass ~s** herbe coupée.

clique [kliːk] *n pej* clique *f*, coterie *f*.

cliquey ['kliːkɪ], **cliquish** ['kliːkɪʃ] *adj pej* exclusif, qui a l'esprit de clan.

clitic ['klɪtɪk] *adj* [enclitic] enclitique ▪ [proclitic] proclitique.

clitoral ['klɪtərəl] *adj* clitoridien.

clitoris ['klɪtərɪs] *n* clitoris *m*.

cloak [kləʊk] ◇ *n* [cape] grande cape *f* ▪ **under the ~ of darkness** *fig* à la faveur de l'obscurité ▪ **as a ~ for his illegal activities** pour cacher *OR* masquer ses activités illégales.
◇ *vt* **1.** *liter* revêtir d'un manteau **2.** *fig* masquer, cacher ▪ **~ed with** *OR* **in secrecy/mystery** empreint de secret/mystère.

cloak-and-dagger *adj* : **a ~ story** un roman d'espionnage.

cloakroom ['kləʊkrʊm] *n* **1.** [for coats] vestiaire *m* **2.** *UK euph* [toilet - public] toilettes *fpl* ; [- in home] cabinets *mpl*.

clobber ['klɒbəʳ] *inf* ◇ *vt* [hit] tabasser ▪ *fig* [defeat] battre à plate couture.
◇ *n UK (U)* effets *mpl*, barda *m*.

cloche [klɒʃ] *n* **1.** : **~ (hat)** chapeau *m* cloche, cloche *f* **2.** AGRIC cloche *f*.

clock [klɒk] ◇ *n* **1.** [gen] horloge *f* ▪ [small] pendule *f* ▪ **to put a ~ back/forward** retarder/avancer une horloge ▮ *fig* **you can't turn the ~ back** ce qui est fait est fait ▪ **this law will put the ~ back a hundred years** cette loi va nous ramener cent ans en arrière ▪ **they worked against** *OR* **to beat the ~** ils ont travaillé dur pour finir à temps ▪ **a jump-off against the ~** EQUIT un barrage contre la montre ▪ **we worked round the ~** nous avons travaillé 24 heures d'affilée ▪ **to sleep the ~ round** faire le tour du cadran **2.** [taximeter] compteur *m*, taximètre *m* **3.** *inf* AUT [mileometer] ≃ compteur *m* kilométrique ▪ **a car with 30,000 miles on the ~** *inf* une voiture qui a 30 000 miles au compteur **4.** COMPUT horloge *f*.
◇ *vt* **1.** [measure time] enregistrer ▪ **winds ~ed at 50 miles per hour** des vents qui ont atteint 50 miles à l'heure ▮ SPORT [runner] chronométrer ▪ **she's ~ed five minutes for the mile** elle court le mile en cinq minutes **2.** △ *UK* [hit] flanquer un marron à.
◆ **clock in** *vi insep* pointer (à l'arrivée).
◆ **clock off** *vi insep* pointer (à la sortie), dépointer.
◆ **clock on** *vt insep* = **clock in**.
◆ **clock out** *vt insep* = **clock off**.
◆ **clock up** *vt sep* [work] effectuer, accomplir ▪ [victory] remporter ▪ **she ~ed up 300 miles** AUT elle a fait 300 miles au compteur.

clockmaker ['klɒk,meɪkəʳ] *n* horloger *m*, - ère *f*.

clock radio *n* radio-réveil *m*.

clock tower *n* tour *f* (de l'horloge).

clockwise ['klɒkwaɪz] ◇ *adv* dans le sens des aiguilles d'une montre.
◇ *adj* : **in a ~ direction** dans le sens des aiguilles d'une montre.

clockwork ['klɒkwɜːk] ◇ *n* [of clock, watch] mouvement *m* (d'horloge) ▪ [of toy] mécanisme *m*, rouages *mpl* ▪ **to go** *OR* **to run like ~** marcher comme sur des roulettes.
◇ *adj* mécanique ▪ **'A Clockwork Orange'** ***Burgess, Kubrick*** 'Orange mécanique'.

clod [klɒd] *n* **1.** [of earth] motte *f* (de terre) **2.** *inf* [idiot] imbécile *m*, crétin *m*.

clodhopper ['klɒd,hɒpəʳ] *n* **1.** *inf* [clumsy person] balourd *m*, - e *f* **2.** *hum* [shoe] godillot *m*.

clog [klɒg] ◇ *vt* (*pret & pp* **clogged**, *cont* **clogging**) **1.** [pipe] boucher, encrasser ▪ [street] boucher, bloquer ▪ [wheel] bloquer **2.** *fig* [hinder] entraver, gêner.
◇ *vi* (*pret & pp* **clogged**, *cont* **clogging**) se boucher.
◇ *n* [wooden] sabot *m* ▪ [leather] sabot *m*.

◆ **clog up** ◇ *vt sep* = **clog** *(vt).*
◇ *vi insep* = **clog** *(vi).*

cloister ['klɔɪstəʳ] ◇ *n* cloître *m.*
◇ *vt* RELIG cloîtrer ▪ *fig* éloigner *OR* isoler (du monde).

cloistered ['klɔɪstəd] *adj fig* [life] de reclus.

clone [kləʊn] ◇ *n* clone *m.*
◇ *vt* cloner.

cloning ['kləʊnɪŋ] *n* clonage *m.*

clonk [klɒŋk] ◇ *vi* faire un bruit sourd.
◇ *vt inf* cogner, frapper.
◇ *n* bruit *m* sourd.

close[1] [kləʊs] (*comp* **closer**, *superl* **closest**) ◇ *adj* **1.** [near in space or time] : **the library is ~ to the school** la bibliothèque est près de l'école ▪ **in ~ proximity to sthg** dans le voisinage immédiat de *OR* tout près de qqch ▪ **they're very ~ in age** ils ont presque le même âge ▪ **his death brought the war closer to home** c'est avec sa mort que nous avons vraiment pris conscience de la guerre ▪ **we are ~ to an agreement** nous sommes presque arrivés à un accord ▪ **at ~ range** à bout portant ▪ **to be ~ at** *OR* **to hand** [shop, cinema etc] être tout près ; [book, pencil etc] être à portée de main ▪ **to be ~ to tears** être au bord des larmes ▪ **I came ~ to thumping him one** *inf* j'ai bien failli lui en coller une ▪ **he keeps things ~ to his chest** il ne fait guère de confidences ▪ **to see sthg at ~ quarters** voir qqch de près ▪ **to give sb a ~ shave** *liter* raser qqn de près ▪ **that was a ~ shave** *OR* **thing** *OR US* **call!** *inf* on l'a échappé belle!, on a eu chaud!
2. [in relationship] proche ▪ **they're very ~ (friends)** ils sont très proches ▪ **a ~ relative** un parent proche ▪ **I'm very ~ to my sister** je suis très proche de ma sœur ▪ **he has ~ ties with Israel** il a des rapports étroits avec Israël ▪ **sources ~ to the royal family** des sources proches de la famille royale ▪ **a subject ~ to my heart** un sujet qui me tient à cœur
3. [continuous] : **they stay in ~ contact** ils restent en contact en permanence
4. [in competition, race etc] serré ▪ **it was a ~ contest** ce fut une lutte serrée
5. [thorough, careful] attentif, rigoureux ▪ **have a ~ look at these figures** examinez ces chiffres de près ▪ **upon ~ examination** après un examen détaillé *OR* minutieux ▪ **keep a ~ eye on the kids** surveillez les enfants de près
6. [roughly similar] proche ▪ **he bears a ~ resemblance to his father** il ressemble beaucoup à son père ▪ **it's the closest thing we've got to an operating theatre** voilà à quoi se réduit notre salle d'opération
7. [compact - handwriting, print] serré ; [- grain] dense, compact
8. *UK* [stuffy - room] mal aéré, qui manque de ventilation *OR* d'air ▪ **it's terribly ~ today** il fait très lourd aujourd'hui
9. [secretive] renfermé, peu communicatif ▪ **he's very ~ about his private life** il est très discret sur sa vie privée
10. *inf* [stingy] avare, pingre
11. LING [vowel] fermé.
◇ *adv* **1.** [near] près ▪ **don't come too ~** n'approche pas *OR* ne t'approche pas trop ▪ **I live ~ to the river** j'habite près de la rivière ▪ **did you win? – no, we didn't even come ~** avez-vous gagné? – non, loin de là ▪ **she lives ~ by** elle habite tout près ▪ **I looked at it ~ to** *OR* **up** je l'ai regardé de près ▪ **~ together** serrés les uns contre les autres ▪ **sit closer together!** serrez-vous!
2. [tight] étroitement, de près ▪ **he held me ~** il m'a serré dans ses bras.
◇ *n* **1.** [field] clos *m*
2. *UK* [street] impasse *f*
3. *UK* [of cathedral] enceinte *f.*
◆ **close on** *prep phr* : **it's ~ on 9 o'clock** il est presque 9 h.
◆ **close to** *prep phr* [almost, nearly] presque.

close[2] [kləʊz] ◇ *vt* **1.** [shut - door, window, shop, book] fermer ▪ *fig* **to ~ one's eyes to sthg** fermer les yeux sur qqch ▪ **to ~ one's mind to sthg** refuser de penser à qqch ▪ **she ~d her mind to anything new** elle s'est fermée à tout ce qui était neuf
2. [opening, bottle] fermer, boucher ▪ **we must ~ the gap between the rich and the poor** *fig* nous devons combler le fossé entre riches et pauvres
3. [block - border, road] fermer
4. [shut down - factory] fermer
5. [conclude] clore, mettre fin à ▪ **she ~d the conference with a rallying call to the party faithful** elle termina la conférence en lançant un appel de solidarité aux fidèles du parti ▪ **the subject is now ~d** l'affaire est close
6. COMPUT fermer, quitter ▪ **to ~ (a window)** fermer (une fenêtre) ▪ **to ~ (a software)** quitter (une application)
7. COMM & FIN [account] arrêter, clore
8. [settle - deal] conclure
9. [move closer together] serrer, rapprocher ▪ **the party ~d ranks behind their leader** *fig* le parti a serré les rangs derrière le leader.
◇ *vi* **1.** [shut - gate, window] fermer, se fermer ; [- shop] fermer ; [- cinema, theatre] faire relâche ▪ **this window doesn't ~ properly** cette fenêtre ne ferme pas bien *OR* ferme mal ▪ **the door ~d quietly behind them** la porte s'est refermée sans bruit derrière eux
2. [wound, opening] se refermer ▪ **the gap was closing fast** l'écart diminuait rapidement
3. [cover, surround] : **the waves ~d over him** les vagues se refermèrent sur lui ▪ **my fingers ~d around the gun** mes doigts se resserrèrent sur le revolver
4. [meeting] se terminer, prendre fin ▪ [speaker] terminer, finir
5. ST. EX : **the share index ~d two points down** l'indice (boursier) a clôturé en baisse de deux points.
◇ *n* fin *f*, conclusion *f* ▪ [of day] tombée *f* ▪ **the year drew to a ~** l'année s'acheva ▪ **it's time to draw the meeting to a ~** il est temps de mettre fin à cette réunion.
◆ **close down** ◇ *vi insep* **1.** [business, factory] fermer
2. *UK* RADIO & TV terminer les émissions.
◇ *vt sep* [business, factory] fermer.
◆ **close in** *vi insep* **1.** [approach] approcher, se rapprocher ▪ [encircle] cerner de près ▪ **to ~ in on** *OR* **upon** se rapprocher de
2. [evening, night] approcher, descendre ▪ [day] raccourcir ▪ [darkness, fog] descendre ▪ **darkness ~d in on us** la nuit nous enveloppa.
◆ **close off** *vt sep* isoler, fermer ▪ **the area was ~d off to the public** le quartier était fermé au public.
◆ **close on** *vt insep* se rapprocher de.
◆ **close out** *vt sep US* liquider *(avant fermeture).*
◆ **close up** ◇ *vt sep* fermer ▪ [opening, pipe] obturer, boucher ▪ [wound] refermer, recoudre.
◇ *vi insep* [wound] se refermer.
◆ **close with** *vt insep* **1.** [finalize deal with] conclure un marché avec
2. *lit* [fight with] engager la lutte *OR* le combat avec.

close-cropped [,kləʊs'krɒpt] *adj* [hair] (coupé) ras ▪ [grass] ras.

closed [kləʊzd] *adj* **1.** [shut - shop, museum etc] fermé ; [- eyes] fermé, clos ; [- opening, pipe] obturé, bouché ; [- road] barré ; [- economy, mind] fermé ▪ **'road ~ to traffic'** 'route interdite à la circulation' ▪ **'~ on Tuesdays'** 'fermé le mardi' ; THEAT 'relâche le mardi' ▪ **we found the door ~** *fig* nous avons trouvé porte close ◗ **in ~ session** LAW à huis clos ▪ **to do sthg behind ~ doors** faire qqch en cachette ▪ **economics is a ~ book to me** je ne comprends rien à l'économie **2.** [restricted] exclusif ▪ **a ~ society** un cercle fermé **3.** LING [sound, syllable] fermé **4.** ELEC [circuit, switch] fermé.

closed circuit television *n* télévision *f* en circuit fermé.

closedown ['kləʊzdaʊn] *n* **1.** [of shop] fermeture *f* (définitive) **2.** *UK* RADIO & TV fin *f* des émissions.

closed shop *n* **1.** [practice] monopole *m* d'embauche **2.** [establishment] *entreprise dans laquelle le monopole d'embauche est pratiqué.*

closefisted [,kləʊs'fɪstɪd] *adj* avare, pingre.

close-fitting [kləʊs-] *adj* ajusté, près du corps.

close-knit [kləʊs-] *adj fig* [community, family] très uni.

closely ['kləʊslɪ] *adv* **1.** [near] de près ▪ [tightly] en serrant fort ▪ **I held her ~** je l'ai serrée fort *OR* (tout) contre moi **2.** [carefully - watch] de près ; [- study] minutieusement, de près ; [- listen] attentivement **3.** [directly] : **he's ~ related to him**

il est l'un de ses proches parents ■ ~ **connected with sthg** étroitement lié à qqch **4.** [evenly] : ~ **contested elections** élections très serrées *OR* très disputées.

closeness ['kləʊsnɪs] *n* **1.** [nearness] proximité *f* **2.** [intimacy - of relationship, friendship, family] intimité *f* **3.** [compactness - of weave] texture *f OR* contexture *f* serrée ; [- of print] resserrement *m (des caractères)*.

closeout ['kləʊzaʊt] *n US* liquidation *f*.

close-range [kləʊs-] *adj* à courte portée.

close-run ['kləʊs-] *adj* = **close** *(adj, sense 4)*.

close season [kləʊs-] *n UK* HUNT fermeture *f* de la chasse ■ FISHING fermeture de la pêche ■ FTBL intersaison *f*.

close-set [kləʊs-] *adj* rapproché.

close-shaven [kləʊs-] *adj* rasé de près.

closet ['klɒzɪt] ◇ *n* **1.** [cupboard] placard *m*, armoire *f* ■ [for hanging clothes] penderie *f* ■ *fig* **to come out of the** ~ *inf* [gen] sortir de l'anonymat ; [homosexual] ne plus cacher son homosexualité **2.** [small room] cabinet *m*.
◇ *comp* secret, - ète *f* ■ **she's a ~ gambler** elle n'ose pas avouer qu'elle joue.
◇ *vt* enfermer *(pour discuter)* ■ **to be ~ed with sb** être en tête à tête avec qqn.

close-up [kləʊs-] ◇ *n* [photograph] gros plan *m* ■ [programme] portrait *m*, portrait-interview *m* ■ **in ~** en gros plan.
◇ *adj* [shot, photograph, picture] en gros plan ■ **a ~ lens** une bonnette.

closing ['kləʊzɪŋ] ◇ *n* [of shop] fermeture *f* ■ [of meeting] clôture *f* ■ ST. EX clôture *f*.
◇ *adj* **1.** [concluding] final, dernier ■ ~ **remarks** observations finales ■ ~ **speech** discours *m* de clôture **2.** [last] de fermeture ■ ~ **date** [for applications] date *f* limite de dépôt ; [for project] date *f* de réalisation *(d'une opération)* **3.** ST. EX : ~ **price** cours *m* à la clôture.

closing time *n* heure *f* de fermeture.

closure ['kləʊʒə^r] *n* **1.** [gen] fermeture *f* ■ [of factory, shop] fermeture *f* définitive **2.** [of meeting] clôture *f* ■ **to move the ~** [in Parliament] demander la clôture ■ ~ **rule** POL *règle du Sénat américain limitant le temps de parole* **3.** [for container] fermeture *f* **4.** LING fermeture *f (d'une voyelle)*.

clot [klɒt] ◇ *vt* (*pret & pp* **clotted**, *cont* **clotting**) cailler, coaguler.
◇ *vi* (*pret & pp* **clotted**, *cont* **clotting**) (se) cailler, (se) coaguler.
◇ *n* **1.** [of blood] caillot *m* ■ [of milk] caillot *m*, grumeau *m* ■ **a ~ on the lung/on the brain** une embolie pulmonaire/cérébrale **2.** *UK inf* [fool] cruche *f*.

cloth [klɒθ] ◇ *n* **1.** [material] tissu *m*, étoffe *f* ■ NAUT [sail] toile *f*, voile *f* ■ [for bookbinding] toile *f* **2.** [for cleaning] chiffon *m*, linge *m* ■ [tablecloth] nappe *f* **3.** [clergy] : **man of the ~** membre *m* du clergé.
◇ *comp* [clothing] de *OR* en tissu, de *OR* en étoffe.

clothbound ['klɒθbaʊnd] *adj* [book] relié toile.

cloth cap *n* casquette *f (symbole de la classe ouvrière britannique)*.

clothe [kləʊð] (*pret & pp* **clothed** *lit OR* **clad** [klæd]) *vt* habiller, vêtir ■ *fig* revêtir, couvrir.

cloth-eared *adj UK inf* dur de la feuille, sourdingue.

clothes [kləʊðz] *npl* **1.** [garments] vêtements *mpl*, habits *mpl* ■ **to put one's ~ on** s'habiller ■ **to take one's ~ off** se déshabiller **2.** *UK* [bedclothes] draps *mpl*.

clothes basket *n* panier *m* à linge.

clothes brush *n* brosse *f* à habits.

clothes hanger *n* cintre *m*.

clotheshorse ['kləʊðzhɔːs] (*pl* [-hɔːsɪz]) *n* **1.** [for laundry] séchoir *m* à linge **2.** *fig* [model] mannequin *m* ■ **she's such a ~** *pej* elle ne pense qu'à ses toilettes.

clothesline ['kləʊðzlaɪn] *n* corde *f* à linge.

clothes peg *UK*, **clothespin** ['kləʊðzpɪn] *US n* pince *f* à linge.

clothespole ['kləʊðzpəʊl], **clothesprop** ['kləʊðzprɒp] *n* support *m* pour corde à linge.

clothier ['kləʊðɪə^r] *n* [cloth dealer, maker] drapier *m* ■ [clothes seller] marchand *m* de vêtements *OR* de confection.

clothing ['kləʊðɪŋ] ◇ *n (U)* **1.** [garments] vêtements *mpl*, habits *mpl* ■ **an article of ~** un vêtement **2.** [act of dressing] habillage *m* ■ [providing with garments] habillement *m* ■ RELIG [of monk, nun] prise *f* d'habit.
◇ *comp* [industry, trade] du vêtement, de l'habillement ■ [shop] de vêtements ■ ~ **allowance** indemnité *f* vestimentaire.

clotted cream ['klɒtɪd-] *n crème fraîche très épaisse typique du sud-ouest de l'Angleterre*.

cloud [klaʊd] ◇ *n* **1.** METEOR nuage *m*, nuée *f lit* ■ **he resigned under a ~** [of suspicion] en butte aux soupçons, il a dû démissionner ; [in disgrace] tombé en disgrâce, il a dû démissionner ■ **to be on ~ nine** être aux anges *OR* au septième ciel ■ **to come down from the ~s** revenir sur terre ■ **to have one's head in the ~s** être dans les nuages *OR* la lune ■ **every ~ has a silver lining** *prov* à quelque chose malheur est bon *prov* **2.** [of dust, smoke] nuage *m* ■ [of gas] nappe *f* ■ [of insects] nuée *f* **3.** [haze - on mirror] buée *f* ; [- in liquid] nuage *m* ; [- in marble] tache *f* noire.
◇ *vt* **1.** [make hazy - mirror] embuer ; [- liquid] rendre trouble ■ **a ~ed sky** un ciel couvert *OR* nuageux **2.** [confuse] obscurcir ■ **don't ~ the issue** ne brouillez pas les cartes **3.** [spoil - career, future] assombrir ; [- reputation] ternir.
◇ *vi* **1.** [sky] se couvrir (de nuages), s'obscurcir **2.** [face] s'assombrir.
◆ **cloud over** *vi insep* = **cloud** *(vi)*.

cloudbase ['klaʊdbeɪs] *n* plafond *m* de nuages.

cloudburst ['klaʊdbɜːst] *n* grosse averse *f*.

cloud-cuckoo-land *n UK inf* : **they are living in ~** ils n'ont pas les pieds sur terre.

clouded ['klaʊdɪd] *adj* **1.** = **cloudy** *(sense 1)* **2.** *fig* [expression] sombre, attristé ■ [reputation] terni ■ [judgement] altéré.

cloudless ['klaʊdlɪs] *adj* [sky] sans nuages ■ *fig* [days, future] sans nuages, serein.

cloudy ['klaʊdɪ] (*comp* **cloudier**, *superl* **cloudiest**) *adj* **1.** METEOR nuageux, couvert ■ **it will be ~ today** le temps sera couvert aujourd'hui **2.** [liquid] trouble ■ [mirror] embué ■ [gem] taché, nuageux **3.** *fig* [confused] obscur, nébuleux ■ [gloomy] sombre, attristé.

clout [klaʊt] *inf* ◇ *n* **1.** [blow] coup *m* ■ [with fist] coup *m* de poing **2.** *fig* [influence] influence *f*, poids *m* ■ **to have** *OR* **to carry a lot of ~** avoir le bras long.
◇ *vt* frapper, cogner ■ [with fist] donner un coup de poing à, filer une taloche à.

clove [kləʊv] ◇ *pt* ▷ **cleave**.
◇ *n* **1.** [spice] clou *m* de girofle ■ [tree] giroflier *m* **2.** [of garlic] gousse *f*.

clove hitch *n* demi-clef *f*.

cloven ['kləʊvn] ◇ *pp* ▷ **cleave**.
◇ *adj* fendu, fourchu.

cloven-footed, cloven-hoofed [-huːft] *adj* [animal] aux sabots fendus ■ [devil] aux pieds fourchus.

clover ['kləʊvə^r] *n* trèfle *m* ■ **to be in ~** *fig* être comme un coq en pâte.

cloverleaf ['kləʊvəliːf] (*pl* **cloverleaves** [-liːvz]) *n* BOT feuille *f* de trèfle.

clown [klaʊn] ◇ *n* [entertainer] clown *m* ■ *fig* [fool] pitre *m*, imbécile *mf*.
◇ *vi* [joke] faire le clown ■ [act foolishly] faire le pitre *OR* l'imbécile.
◆ **clown about** *UK*, **clown around** *vi insep* = **clown** *(vi)*.

clownery ['klaʊnərɪ], **clowning** ['klaʊnɪŋ] *n (U)* clowneries *fpl*, pitreries *fpl*.

cloy [klɔɪ] *vt liter & fig* écœurer.

cloying ['klɔɪɪŋ] *adj* écœurant.

cloze test [kləʊz-] *n* ≃ exercice *m* à trous.

club [klʌb] ◇ *n* **1.** [association] club *m*, cercle *m* ■ [nightclub] boîte *f* de nuit ■ **the ~ scene** *milieux branchés fréquentant les boîtes de nuit* ■ **a tennis ~** un club de tennis ■ **join the ~!** *hum* bienvenue au club!, vous n'êtes pas le seul! ■ **she's in the ~** *UK inf euph* elle a un polichinelle dans le tiroir **2.** [weapon] matraque *f*, massue *f* **3.** [golf club] club *m* (de golf) **4.** CARDS trèfle *m*.
◇ *vt* (*pret & pp* **clubbed**, *cont* **clubbing**) matraquer, frapper avec une massue ■ **he was clubbed to death** il a été matraqué à mort.
◆ **club together** *vi insep* [share cost] se cotiser.

CLUB

Les « clubs » britanniques, aussi appelés *gentlemen's clubs*, sont des lieux de rencontre et de détente très sélectifs, traditionnellement fermés aux femmes ; ils jouaient autrefois un rôle important dans la vie sociale des milieux aisés en Grande-Bretagne.

club car *n US* RAIL wagon-restaurant *m*.

club class *n* classe *f* club.

clubfoot [,klʌb'fʊt] (*pl* **clubfeet** [-'fi:t]) *n* pied *m* bot.

clubhouse ['klʌbhaʊs] (*pl* [-haʊzɪz]) *n* club *m*.

clubland ['klʌblənd] *n UK* [nightclubs] *quartier des boîtes de nuit*.

clubroom ['klʌbrʊm] *n* salle *f* de club *OR* de réunion.

club sandwich *n US* sandwich *m* mixte *(à trois étages)*.

cluck [klʌk] ◇ *vi* [hen, person] glousser ■ **she ~ed in disapproval** elle a claqué sa langue de désapprobation.
◇ *n* **1.** [of hen] gloussement *m* ■ [of person - in pleasure] gloussement *m* ; [- in disapproval] claquement *m* de langue **2.** *inf* [fool] idiot *m*, - e *f*.

clue [klu:] *n* [gen] indice *m*, indication *f* ■ [in crosswords] définition *f* ■ **give me a ~** mettez-moi sur la piste ■ **where's John? – I haven't a ~!** où est John? – je n'en ai pas la moindre idée *OR* je n'en ai aucune idée! ■ **he's useless at cooking, he hasn't got a ~!** il est nul en cuisine, il n'y connaît absolument rien!

clued-up [klu:d-] *adj inf* informé.

clueless ['klu:lɪs] *adj UK inf pej* qui ne sait rien de rien.

clump [klʌmp] ◇ *n* **1.** [cluster - of bushes] massif *m* ; [- of trees] bouquet *m* ; [- of hair, grass] touffe *f* **2.** [mass - of earth] motte *f* **3.** [sound] bruit *m* sourd.
◇ *vi* [walk] : **to ~ (about** *OR* **around)** marcher d'un pas lourd.
◇ *vt* [gather] : **to ~ together** grouper.

clumsily ['klʌmzɪlɪ] *adv* [awkwardly] maladroitement ■ [tactlessly] sans tact.

clumsiness ['klʌmzɪnɪs] *n* **1.** [lack of coordination] maladresse *f*, gaucherie *f* **2.** [awkwardness - of tool] caractère *m* peu pratique ; [- of design] lourdeur *f* **3.** [tactlessness] gaucherie *f*, manque *m* de tact.

clumsy ['klʌmzɪ] *adj* **1.** [uncoordinated - person] maladroit, gauche **2.** [awkward - tool] peu commode *OR* pratique ; [- design] lourd, disgracieux ; [- painting] maladroit ; [- style] lourd, maladroit **3.** [tactless] gauche, malhabile ■ **he made a ~ apology** il s'est excusé de façon gauche.

clung [klʌŋ] *pt & pp* ▷ **cling**.

clunk [klʌŋk] ◇ *n* [sound] bruit *m* sourd.
◇ *vi* faire un bruit sourd.

clunker ['klʌŋkər] *n US inf* [car] tas *m* de ferraille.

cluster ['klʌstər] ◇ *n* **1.** [of fruit] grappe *f* ■ [of dates] régime *m* ■ [of flowers] touffe *f* ■ [of trees] bouquet *m* ■ [of stars] amas *m* ■ [of diamonds] entourage *m* **2.** [group - of houses] groupe *m* ; [- of people] rassemblement *m*, groupe *m* ; [- of bees] essaim *m* **3.** LING groupe *m*, agglomérat *m*.
◇ *vi* **1.** [people] se grouper **2.** [things] former un groupe ■ **pretty cottages ~ed around the church** l'église était entourée de petites maisons coquettes.

cluster bomb *n* bombe *f* à fragmentation.

clutch [klʌtʃ] ◇ *vt* **1.** [hold tightly] serrer fortement, étreindre **2.** [seize] empoigner, se saisir de.
◇ *vi* : **to ~ at sthg** *liter* se cramponner à qqch, s'agripper à qqch ; *fig* se cramponner à qqch, se raccrocher à qqch.
◇ *n* **1.** [grasp] étreinte *f*, prise *f* **2.** AUT [mechanism] embrayage *m* ■ [pedal] pédale *f* d'embrayage ■ **to let in the ~** embrayer ■ **to let out the ~** débrayer **3.** [cluster of eggs] couvée *f* ■ *fig* série *f*, ensemble *m* **4.** *US inf* [crisis] crise *f* **5.** *US* [bag] pochette *f* *(sac à main)*.
◆ **clutches** *npl fig* [control] influence *f* ■ **to have sb in one's ~es** tenir qqn en son pouvoir ■ **to fall into sb's ~es** tomber dans les griffes de qqn.

clutch bag *n* [handbag] pochette *f* *(sac à main)*.

clutter ['klʌtər] ◇ *n* **1.** [mess] désordre *m* **2.** [disordered objects] désordre *m*, fouillis *m*.
◇ *vt* : **~ (up)** [room] mettre en désordre ■ **a desk ~ed with papers** un bureau encombré de papiers ■ **his mind was ~ed with useless facts** son esprit était encombré d'informations inutiles.

cm (*written abbrev of* **centimetre**) cm.

CND (*abbrev of* **Campaign for Nuclear Disarmament**) *pr n en Grande-Bretagne, mouvement pour le désarmement nucléaire*.

CNG [si:en'dʒi:] (*abbrev of* **compressed natural gas**) *n* GNC.

Cnut [kə'nju:t] *pr n* = **Canute**.

co- [kəʊ] *in cpds* co- ■ **~worker** collègue *mf* ■ **he's her ~star** il partage l'affiche avec elle.

c/o (*written abbrev of* **care of**) a/s.

Co. [kəʊ] **1.** (*written abbrev of* **company**) Cie **2.** *written abbr of* **county**.

coach [kəʊtʃ] ◇ *n* **1.** [tutor] répétiteur *m*, - trice *f* ■ SPORT [trainer] entraîneur *m*, - euse *f* ■ [ski instructor] moniteur *m*, - trice *f* **2.** [bus] car *m*, autocar *m* ■ *UK* RAIL voiture *f*, wagon *m* ■ [carriage] carrosse *m* ■ **(stage) ~** diligence *f*, coche *m*.
◇ *comp* [driver] de car ■ [tour, trip] en car.
◇ *vt* [tutor] donner des leçons particulières à ■ SPORT entraîner ■ **to ~ sb in maths/in English** donner des leçons de math/d'anglais à qqn ■ **they employed a tutor to ~ him for the exam** ils ont fait appel à un professeur particulier pour le préparer à l'examen.
◇ *vi* [tutor] donner des leçons particulières ■ SPORT être entraîneur.

coach-and-four *n* carrosse *m* à quatre chevaux.

coach class *n US* classe *f* économique.

coach house *n* remise *f* *(pour carrosse ou voiture)*.

coaching ['kəʊtʃɪŋ] *n* **1.** SCH leçons *fpl* particulières **2.** SPORT entraînement *m*.

coachload ['kəʊtʃləʊd] *n* : **a ~ of tourists** un autocar *OR* car plein de touristes.

coachman ['kəʊtʃmən] (*pl* **coachmen** [-mən]) *n* cocher *m*.

coach party *n esp UK* excursion *f* en car.

coach station *n UK* gare *f* routière.

coachwork ['kəʊtʃwɜ:k] *n* carrosserie *f*.

coagulant [kəʊ'ægjʊlənt] *n* coagulant *m*.

coagulate [kəʊ'ægjʊleɪt] ◇ *vi* (se) coaguler.
◇ *vt* coaguler.

coagulation [kəʊ,ægjʊ'leɪʃn] *n* coagulation *f*.

coal [kəʊl] ◇ *n* **1.** [gen] charbon *m* ■ **a piece** *OR* **lump of ~** un morceau de charbon ➤ **he was treading on hot ~s** il était sur des charbons ardents **2.** INDUST houille *f*.

◇ *comp* [bunker, cellar, chute] à charbon ▪ [depot, fire] de charbon ▪ **~ industry** industrie *f* houillère.
◇ *vt* [supply with coal] fournir *OR* ravitailler en charbon ▪ NAUT charbonner.
◇ *vi* NAUT charbonner.

coal-burning *adj* à charbon, qui marche au charbon.

coaldust ['kəʊldʌst] *n* poussier *m* *OR* poussière *f* de charbon.

coalesce [,kəʊə'les] *vi* s'unir (en un groupe), se fondre (ensemble).

coalface ['kəʊlfeɪs] *n* front *m* de taille.

coalfield ['kəʊlfi:ld] *n* bassin *m* houiller, gisement *m* de houille.

coal-fired *adj* à charbon, qui marche au charbon.

coalfish ['kəʊlfɪʃ] (*pl inv OR pl* **coalfishes**) *n* lieu *m* noir, colin *m*.

coal gas *n* gaz *m* de houille.

coalition [,kəʊə'lɪʃn] *n* coalition *f* ▪ **~ government** gouvernement *m* de coalition.

coalman ['kəʊlmæn] (*pl* **coalmen** [-men]) *n* charbonnier *m*, marchand *m* de charbon.

coal merchant *n* = **coalman**.

coalmine ['kəʊlmaɪn] *n* mine *f* de charbon, houillère *f*.

coalminer ['kəʊl,maɪnə^r] *n* mineur *m*.

coalmining ['kəʊl,maɪnɪŋ] *n* charbonnage *m*.

coal scuttle *n* seau *m* à charbon.

coal tar *n* coaltar *m*, goudron *m* de houille.

coal tit *n* mésange *f* noire.

coarse [kɔ:s] *adj* **1.** [rough in texture] gros, grosse *f*, grossier ▪ [skin] rude ▪ [hair] épais, - aisse *f* ▪ [salt] gros, grosse *f* ▪ **~ cloth** drap grossier **2.** [vulgar - person, behaviour, remark, joke] grossier, vulgaire ; [- laugh] gros, grosse *f*, gras, grasse *f* ; [- accent] commun, vulgaire **3.** [inferior - food, drink] ordinaire, commun.

coarse fishing *n* pêche *f* à la ligne en eau douce.

coarse-grained *adj* à gros grain.

coarsely ['kɔ:slɪ] *adv* **1.** [roughly] grossièrement ▪ **~ woven** de texture grossière **2.** [uncouthly - speak] vulgairement, grossièrement ; [- laugh] grassement ▪ [vulgarly] indécemment, crûment.

coarsen ['kɔ:sn] ◇ *vi* **1.** [texture] devenir rude *OR* grossier **2.** [person] devenir grossier *OR* vulgaire ▪ [features] s'épaissir.
◇ *vt* **1.** [texture] rendre rude *OR* grossier **2.** [person, speech] rendre grossier *OR* vulgaire ▪ [features] épaissir.

coarseness ['kɔ:snɪs] *n* **1.** [of texture] rudesse *f* **2.** [uncouthness] manque *m* de savoir-vivre ▪ [vulgarity] grossièreté *f*, vulgarité *f*.

coast [kəʊst] ◇ *n* côte *f* ▪ **off the ~ of Ireland** au large des côtes irlandaises ▪ **broadcast from ~ to ~** diffusé dans tout le pays ➊ **the ~ is clear** *inf* la voie est libre.
◇ *vi* [vehicle] avancer en roue libre ▪ NAUT caboter ▪ **he ~ed through the exam** *inf fig* il a eu l'examen les doigts dans le nez.

coastal ['kəʊstl] *adj* littoral, côtier ▪ **~ waters** eaux *fpl* littorales.

coaster ['kəʊstə^r] *n* **1.** [protective mat - for glass] dessous *m* de verre ; [- for bottle] dessous *m* de bouteille ▪ [stand, tray] présentoir *m* à bouteilles **2.** NAUT [ship] caboteur *m* **3.** *US* = **roller coaster**.

coastguard ['kəʊstgɑ:d] *n* **1.** [organization] ≃ gendarmerie *f* maritime **2.** *UK* [person] membre *m* de la gendarmerie maritime ▪ HIST garde-côte *m*.

coastline ['kəʊstlaɪn] *n* littoral *m*.

coast-to-coast *adj* [walk, route, race] d'un bout du pays à l'autre ▪ [TV channel, network] national.

coat [kəʊt] ◇ *n* **1.** [overcoat] manteau *m* ▪ [man's overcoat] manteau *m*, pardessus *m* ▪ [jacket] veste *f* ▪ **~ of mail** cotte *f* de mailles ‖ HERALD : **~ of arms** blason *m*, armoiries *fpl* **2.** [of animal] pelage *m*, poil *m* ▪ [of horse] robe *f* **3.** [covering - of dust, paint] couche *f*.
◇ *vt* **1.** [cover] couvrir, revêtir ▪ [with paint, varnish] enduire ▪ **the shelves were ~ed with dust** les étagères étaient recouvertes de poussière **2.** CULIN : **to ~ sthg with flour/sugar** saupoudrer qqch de farine/de sucre ▪ **to ~ sthg with chocolate** enrober qqch de chocolat ▪ **to ~ sthg with egg** dorer qqch à l'œuf.

coat hanger *n* cintre *m*.

coating ['kəʊtɪŋ] *n* couche *f* ▪ [on pan] revêtement *m*.

coatrack ['kəʊtræk], **coatstand** ['kəʊtstænd] *n* portemanteau *m*.

coat tails *npl* queue *f* de pie *(costume)* ▪ **to ride on sb's ~** profiter de l'influence *OR* de la position de qqn ▪ **she hangs on his ~** elle est pendue à ses basques.

coauthor [kəʊ'ɔ:θə^r] *n* coauteur *m*.

coax [kəʊks] *vt* cajoler, enjôler ▪ **he ~ed us into going** à force de nous cajoler, il nous a persuadés d'y aller ▪ **he ~ed the box open with a screwdriver** il est parvenu à ouvrir la boîte en faisant levier avec un tournevis.

coaxial [,kəʊ'æksɪəl] *adj* coaxial ▪ **~ cable** COMPUT câble *m* coaxial.

coaxing ['kəʊksɪŋ] ◇ *n (U)* cajolerie *f*, cajoleries *fpl* ▪ **after a lot of ~, he agreed** il s'est fait prier avant d'accepter.
◇ *adj* enjôleur, cajoleur.

cob [kɒb] *n* **1.** [horse] cob *m* **2.** [swan] cygne *m* mâle **3.** [of corn] épi *m* **4.** [of coal] briquette *f* de charbon ▪ [of bread] pain *m* **5.** *UK* [nut] noisette *f* **6.** CONSTR torchis *m*, pisé *m*.

cobalt ['kəʊbɔ:lt] *n* cobalt *m*.

cobble ['kɒbl] ◇ *n* [stone] pavé *m*.
◇ *vt* paver.
⬥ **cobble together** *vt sep* bricoler, concocter.

cobbled ['kɒbld] *adj* pavé.

cobbler ['kɒblə^r] *n* [shoemender] cordonnier *m*.
⬥ **cobblers**△ *npl* *UK* : **that's a load of ~s!** *fig* c'est de la connerie!△.

cobblestone ['kɒblstəʊn] *n* pavé *m (rond)*.

cobnut ['kɒbnʌt] *n* noisette *f*, aveline *f*.

cobra ['kəʊbrə] *n* cobra *m*.

cobweb ['kɒbweb] *n* toile *f* d'araignée ▪ **I'm going for a walk to clear away the ~ s** *OR* **to blow the ~s away** *fig* je vais faire un tour pour me rafraîchir les idées.

Coca-Cola® *n* Coca® *m*, Coca-Cola® *m*.

cocaine [kəʊ'keɪn] ◇ *n* cocaïne *f*.
◇ *comp* : **~ addict** *OR* **freak** *inf* cocaïnomane *mf* ▪ **~ addiction** cocaïnomanie *f*.

cochineal ['kɒtʃɪni:l] *n* [insect] cochenille *f* ▪ [dye] carmin *m*, cochenille *f* des teinturiers.

cock [kɒk] ◇ *n* **1.** [rooster] coq *m* ▪ [male bird] (oiseau *m*) mâle *m* **2.** [tap] robinet *m* **3.** [of gun] chien *m* ▪ **at full ~** armé **4.** ▲ [penis] bitte *f*△, bite△ *f* **5.** [tilt] inclinaison *f*, aspect *m* penché **6.** AGRIC [of hay] meulon *m*.
◇ *vt* **1.** [gun] armer **2.** [raise] : **the dog ~ed its ears** le chien a dressé les oreilles ▪ **she ~ed an ear towards the door** *fig* elle a tendu une oreille du côté de la porte ▪ **the dog ~ed its leg** le chien a levé la patte ➊ **to ~ a snook** *OR* **snoot at sb** *UK inf* faire un pied de nez à qqn **3.** [head, hat] pencher, incliner ▪ [thumb] tendre **4.** [hay] mettre en meulons.
⬥ **cock up**△ *UK* ◇ *vt sep* saloper△, faire foirer△.
◇ *vi insep* : **he's ~ed up again** il a encore tout fait foirer△.

cockade [kɒ'keɪd] *n* cocarde *f*.

cock-a-doodle-doo [,kɒkədu:dl'du:] *n* & *onom* cocorico.

cock-a-hoop *adj inf* fier comme Artaban.

cock-and-bull story *n* histoire *f* à dormir debout.

cockatoo [,kɒkə'tu:] *n* cacatoès *m*.

cockcrow ['kɒkkrəʊ] *n* aube *f*.

cocked hat *n* tricorne *m* ▪ **to knock sthg into a ~** surpasser qqch.

cockerel ['kɒkrəl] *n* jeune coq *m*.

cocker spaniel ['kɒkəʳ-] *n* cocker *m*.

cockeyed ['kɒkaɪd] *adj* *inf* **1.** [cross-eyed] qui louche **2.** [crooked] de travers **3.** [absurd - idea, plan] absurde ; [- story] qui ne tient pas debout.

cockfight ['kɒkfaɪt] *n* combat *m* de coqs.

cockiness ['kɒkɪnɪs] *n* impertinence *f*.

cockle ['kɒkl] <> *n* **1.** [shellfish] coque *f* **2.** [in cloth] faux pli *m* ▪ [in paper] froissure *f*, pliure *f*.
<> *vt* [paper] froisser ▪ [cloth] chiffonner.
<> *vi* [paper] se froisser ▪ [cloth] se chiffonner.

Cockney ['kɒknɪ] <> *n* **1.** [person] cockney *mf (Londonien né dans le "East End")* **2.** LING cockney *m*.
<> *adj* cockney.

cockpit ['kɒkpɪt] *n* **1.** [of plane] cabine *f* de pilotage, cockpit *m* ▪ [of racing car] poste *m* du pilote ▪ [of yacht] cockpit *m* **2.** [in cockfighting] arène *f* ▪ *fig* arènes *fpl*.

cockroach ['kɒkrəʊtʃ] *n* cafard *m*, blatte *f*.

cockscomb ['kɒkskəʊm] *n* **1.** [of rooster] crête *f* **2.** BOT crête-de-coq *f*.

cock sparrow *n* moineau *m* mâle.

cocksure [,kɒk'ʃɔ:ʳ] *adj* *pej* suffisant.

cocktail ['kɒkteɪl] *n* [mixed drink] cocktail *m (boisson)* ▪ [gen - mixture of things] mélange *m*, cocktail *m*.

cocktail bar *n* bar *m (dans un hôtel, un aéroport)*.

cocktail dress *n* robe *f* de cocktail.

cocktail lounge *n* bar *m (dans un hôtel, un aéroport)*.

cocktail party *n* cocktail *m (fête)*.

cocktail shaker *n* shaker *m*.

cocktail stick *n* pique *f* à apéritif.

cockteaser▲ ['kɒk,ti:zəʳ] *n* *pej* allumeuse *f*.

cock-up△ *n* *UK* : **it was a ~** ça a foiré△ ▪ **he made a ~ of his exam** il s'est planté à l'examen△.

cocky ['kɒkɪ] (*comp* **cockier**, *superl* **cockiest**) *adj* *inf* suffisant, qui a du toupet.

cocoa ['kəʊkəʊ] *n* **1.** [powder, drink] cacao *m* **2.** [colour] marron *m* clair.

cocoa bean *n* graine *f* de cacao.

cocoa butter *n* beurre *m* de cacao.

coconut ['kəʊkənʌt] *n* noix *f* de coco ▪ **~ milk** lait *m* de coco.

coconut matting *n* tapis *m* en fibres de noix de coco.

coconut oil *n* huile *f* de coco.

coconut palm *n* cocotier *m*.

coconut shy *n* jeu *m* de massacre *liter*.

cocoon [kə'ku:n] <> *n* cocon *m* ▪ *fig* **wrapped in a ~ of blankets** emmitouflé dans des couvertures.
<> *vt* [wrap] envelopper avec soin ▪ [overprotect - child] couver.

cocooned [kə'ku:nd] *adj* enfermé, cloîtré.

cod [kɒd] (*pl inv* OR *pl* **cods**) *n* [fish] morue *f* ▪ CULIN : **dried ~** merluche *f*, morue.

Cod [kɒd] *pr n* : **Cape ~** cap *m* Cod.

COD (*abbrev of* **cash on delivery**) (*abbrev of* **collect on delivery**) *adv* *US* : **to send sthg ~** envoyer qqch contre remboursement.

coda ['kəʊdə] *n* *lit* & MUS coda *f*.

coddle ['kɒdl] *vt* **1.** [pamper - child] dorloter, choyer **2.** CULIN (faire) cuire à feu doux ▪ **a ~d egg** un œuf à la coque.

code [kəʊd] <> *n* **1.** [cipher] code *m*, chiffre *m* ▪ BIOL & COMPUT code *m* ▪ **a message in ~** un message chiffré OR codé **2.** [statement of rules] code *m* ▪ **~ of conduct/of honour** code de conduite/de l'honneur ▪ **~ of ethics** [gen] sens *m* des valeurs morales, moralité *f* ; [professional] déontologie *f* ▪ **~ of practice** [gen] déontologie *f* ; [rules] règlements *mpl* et usages *mpl* **3.** [postcode] code *m* postal **4.** [dialling code] code *m*, indicatif *m*.
<> *vt* [message] coder, chiffrer.

codeine ['kəʊdi:n] *n* codéine *f*.

code name *n* nom *m* de code.

code-named *adj* qui porte le nom de code de.

codeword ['kəʊdwɜ:d] *n* [password] mot *m* de passe ▪ [name] mot *m* codé.

codex ['kəʊdeks] (*pl* **codices** [-dɪsi:z]) *n* volume *m* de manuscrits anciens.

codger ['kɒdʒəʳ] *n* *inf* bonhomme *m* ▪ **he's a bad-tempered old ~** c'est un vieux bonhomme bourru.

codices [-dɪsi:z] *pl* ▷ **codex**.

codicil ['kɒdɪsɪl] *n* codicille *m*.

codify ['kəʊdɪfaɪ] (*pret* & *pp* **codified**) *vt* codifier.

coding ['kəʊdɪŋ] *n* [of message] chiffrage *m* ▪ COMPUT codage *m* ▪ **~ line** ligne *f* de programmation ▪ **~ sequence** séquence *f* programmée.

cod-liver oil *n* huile *f* de foie de morue.

codpiece ['kɒdpi:s] *n* *dated* braguette *f*.

codswallop ['kɒdz,wɒləp] *n* *(U)* *UK* *inf* bêtises *fpl*, âneries *fpl*.

co-ed [-'ed] <> *adj* = **coeducational**.
<> *n* **1.** *US* [female student] *étudiante d'un établissement mixte* **2.** *UK* (*abbrev of* **coeducational school**) école *f* mixte.

co-edition *n* coédition *f*.

co-editor *n* coéditeur *m*.

coeducation [,kəʊedʒʊ'keɪʃn] *n* éducation *f* mixte.

coeducational [,kəʊedʒʊ'keɪʃənl] *adj* mixte.

coefficient [,kəʊɪ'fɪʃnt] *n* coefficient *m*.

coeliac *UK*, **celiac** *US* ['si:lɪæk] *adj* cœliaque.

coerce [kəʊ'ɜ:s] *vt* contraindre, forcer ▪ **we ~d them into confessing** nous les avons contraints à avouer.

coercion [kəʊ'ɜ:ʃn] *n* *(U)* coercition *f*, contrainte *f*.

coexist [,kəʊɪg'zɪst] *vi* coexister.

coexistence [,kəʊɪg'zɪstəns] *n* coexistence *f*.

coexistent [,kəʊɪg'zɪstənt] *adj* coexistant.

coextensive [,kəʊɪk'stensɪv] *adj* *fml* : **~ with** [in space] de même étendue que ; [in time] de même durée que.

C of E (*abbrev of* **Church of England**) <> *pr n* Église *f* anglicane.
<> *adj* anglican.

coffee ['kɒfɪ] <> *n* **1.** [drink] café *m* ▪ **we talked over ~** nous avons bavardé en prenant un café ▪ **black ~** café noir ▪ **white ~** *UK*, **~ with cream** OR **milk** *US* [gen] café au lait ; [in café] café crème, crème *m* **2.** [colour] café au lait *((inv))*.
<> *comp* [filter, jar, service] à café ▪ [ice cream, icing] au café ▪ **~ cake** *UK* moka *m* ; *US* gâteau *m (que l'on sert avec le café)* ▪ **~ cream** [chocolate] chocolat *m* fourré au café ▪ **~ grounds** marc *m* de café.

coffee bar *n* *UK* café *m*, caféteria *f*.

coffee bean *n* grain *m* de café.

coffee break *n* pause-café *f*.

coffee cup *n* tasse *f* à café.

coffee grinder *n* moulin *m* à café.

coffee house *n* café *m*.

coffee klatch [-klætʃ] *n* US *inf* **he's probably in the ~** il est sans doute en train de prendre un café et de papoter avec les autres.

coffee machine *n* [gen] cafetière *f* ▪ [in café] percolateur *m*.

coffee mill *n* moulin *m* à café.

coffee morning *n* UK *rencontre amicale autour d'un café, destinée souvent à réunir de l'argent au profit d'œuvres de bienfaisance*.

coffeepot ['kɒfɪpɒt] *n* cafetière *f*.

coffee shop *n* ≃ café-restaurant *m*.

coffee spoon *n* cuillère *f* OR cuiller *f* à café, petite cuillère *f* OR cuiller *f* ▪ [smaller] cuillère *f* OR cuiller *f* à moka.

coffee table *n* table *f* basse.

coffee-table book *n* ≃ beau livre *m (destiné à être feuilleté plutôt que véritablement lu)*.

coffee tree *n* caféier *m*.

coffer ['kɒfəʳ] *n* **1.** [strongbox] coffre *m*, caisse *f* **2.** [watertight chamber] caisson *m* **3.** ARCHIT caisson *m (de plafond)*.
◆ **coffers** *npl* [funds - of nation] coffres *mpl* ; [- of organization] caisses *fpl*, coffres *mpl* ▪ **the Government hasn't got much left in the ~ s** le gouvernement n'a plus grand-chose dans ses coffres.

cofferdam ['kɒfədæm] *n* batardeau *m*.

coffin ['kɒfɪn] *n* **1.** [box] cercueil *m*, bière *f* **2.** [of hoof] cavité *f* du sabot.

coffin nail *n inf hum* [cigarette] cigarette *f*.

C of I (*abbrev of* **Church of Ireland**) *pr n* Église *f* d'Irlande.

C of S (*abbrev of* **Church of Scotland**) *pr n* Église *f* d'Écosse.

cog [kɒg] *n* [gearwheel] roue *f* dentée ▪ [tooth] dent *f (d'engrenage)* ▪ **you're only a (small) ~ in the machine** OR **the wheel** *fig* vous n'êtes qu'un simple rouage (dans OR de la machine).

cogency ['kəʊdʒənsɪ] *n* force *f*, puissance *f*.

cogent ['kəʊdʒənt] *adj fml* [argument, reasons - convincing] convaincant, puissant ; [- pertinent] pertinent ; [- compelling] irrésistible.

cogitate ['kɒdʒɪteɪt] *vi fml* méditer, réfléchir.

cogitation [ˌkɒdʒɪ'teɪʃn] *n* réflexion *f*, méditation *f* ▪ *hum* cogitations *fpl*.

cognac ['kɒnjæk] *n* cognac *m*.

cognate ['kɒgneɪt] ◇ *n* **1.** LING mot *m* apparenté **2.** LAW [person] parent *m* proche, cognat *m* LAW.
◇ *adj* LING apparenté, de même origine ▪ LAW parent.

cognition [kɒg'nɪʃn] *n* [gen] connaissance *f* ▪ PHILOS cognition *f*.

cognitive ['kɒgnɪtɪv] *adj* cognitif.

cognizance, isance ['kɒgnɪzəns] *n* **1.** *fml* [knowledge] connaissance *f* ▪ **to take ~ of sthg** prendre connaissance de qqch **2.** *fml* [range, scope] compétence *f* **3.** HERALD [badge] emblème *m*.

cognizant, isant ['kɒgnɪzənt] *adj* **1.** *fml* [aware] ayant connaissance, conscient **2.** LAW compétent.

cognoscenti [ˌkɒnjə'ʃenti:] *npl* connaisseurs *mpl*.

cogwheel ['kɒgwi:l] *n* roue *f* dentée.

cohabit [ˌkəʊ'hæbɪt] *vi* cohabiter.

cohabitation [ˌkəʊhæbɪ'teɪʃn] *n* cohabitation *f*.

cohabitee [kəʊˌhæbɪ'ti:] *n* concubin *m*, - e *f*, partenaire *mf* en union libre.

cohere [kəʊ'hɪəʳ] *vi* **1.** [stick together] adhérer, coller **2.** [be logically consistent] être cohérent ▪ [reasoning, argument] (se) tenir.

coherence [kəʊ'hɪərəns] *n* **1.** [cohesion] adhérence *f* **2.** [logical consistency] cohérence *f*.

coherent [kəʊ'hɪərənt] *adj* [logical - person, structure] cohérent, logique ; [- story, speech] facile à suivre OR comprendre.

coherently [kəʊ'hɪərəntlɪ] *adv* de façon cohérente.

cohesion [kəʊ'hi:ʒn] *n* cohésion *f*.

cohesive [kəʊ'hi:sɪv] *adj* cohésif.

cohort ['kəʊhɔ:t] *n* **1.** [group, band] cohorte *f* **2.** MIL cohorte *f* **3.** [companion] comparse *mf*, compère *m* **4.** BIOL ordre *m*.

COHSE ['kəʊzɪ] (*abbrev of* **Confederation of Health Service Employees**) *pr n ancien syndicat des employés des services de santé en Grande-Bretagne*.

COI (*abbrev of* **Central Office of Information**) *pr n service public d'information en Grande-Bretagne*.

coiffure [kwɑ:'fjʊəʳ] *n fml* coiffure *f*.

coil [kɔɪl] ◇ *n* **1.** [spiral - of rope, wire] rouleau *m* ▪ [- of hair] rouleau *m* ▪ [in bun] chignon *m* **2.** [single loop - of rope, wire] tour *m* ; [- of hair] boucle *f* ; [- of smoke, snake] anneau *m* **3.** ELEC & TECH bobine *f* **4.** MED [for contraception] stérilet *m*.
◇ *vt* **1.** [rope] enrouler ▪ [hair] enrouler, torsader ▪ **the snake ~ed itself up** le serpent s'est lové OR enroulé **2.** ELEC bobiner.
◇ *vi* **1.** [river, smoke, procession] onduler, serpenter **2.** [rope] s'enrouler ▪ [snake] se lover, s'enrouler.
◆ **coil up** *vt sep* [rope, hose] enrouler.

coiled [kɔɪld] *adj* [rope] enroulé, en spirale ▪ [spring] en spirale ▪ [snake] lové.

coin [kɔɪn] ◇ *n* **1.** [item of metal currency] pièce *f* (de monnaie) ▪ **a pound ~** une pièce d'une livre ▶ **that's the other side of the ~** c'est le revers de la médaille **2.** *(U)* [metal currency] monnaie *f* ▶ **to pay sb back in his own ~** rendre à qqn la monnaie de sa pièce.
◇ *vt* **1.** [money] : **to ~ money** battre monnaie ▶ **she's ~ing it(in)** *inf* elle se fait du fric **2.** [word] fabriquer, inventer ▪ **to ~ a phrase** *hum* si je puis m'exprimer ainsi.

coinage ['kɔɪnɪdʒ] *n* **1.** [creation - of money] frappe *f* ▪ *fig* [- of word] invention *f* **2.** [coins] monnaie *f* ▪ [currency system] système *m* monétaire **3.** [invented word, phrase] invention *f*, création *f*.

coin-box *n* UK cabine *f* téléphonique (à pièces).

coincide [ˌkəʊɪn'saɪd] *vi* **1.** [in space, time] coïncider **2.** [correspond] coïncider, s'accorder.

coincidence [kəʊ'ɪnsɪdəns] *n* **1.** [accident] coïncidence *f*, hasard *m* **2.** [correspondence] coïncidence *f*.

coincidental [kəʊˌɪnsɪ'dentl] *adj* **1.** [accidental] de coïncidence ▪ **our meeting was entirely ~** notre rencontre était une pure coïncidence **2.** [having same position] coïncident.

coincidentally [kəʊˌɪnsɪ'dentəlɪ] *adv* par hasard.

coin-operated [-'ɒpəˌreɪtɪd] *adj* automatique.

coitus ['kəʊɪtəs] *n* coït *m*.

coke [kəʊk] *n* **1.** [fuel] coke *m* **2.** △ *drug sl* [cocaine] cocaïne *f*, coke *f*.

Coke® [kəʊk] *n* [cola] Coca® *m*.

col [kɒl] *n* col *m (d'une montagne)*.

Col. (*written abbrev of* **colonel**) Col.

cola ['kəʊlə] *n* cola *m*.

colander ['kʌləndəʳ] *n* passoire *f*.

cold [kəʊld] ◇ *adj* **1.** [body, object, food etc] froid ▪ **I'm ~** j'ai froid ▪ **her hands are ~** elle a les mains froides ▪ **eat it before it gets ~** mangez avant que cela refroidisse ▪ **the trail was ~** *fig* toute trace avait disparu ▪ **her answer was ~ comfort to us** sa réponse ne nous a pas réconfortés ▪ **is it over here? – no, you're getting ~er** [in children's game] est-ce par ici? – non, tu refroidis ▪ **she poured ~ water on our plans** *fig* sa réaction devant nos projets nous a refroidis ▶ **to be as ~ as ice** [thing] être froid comme de la glace ; [room] être glacial ; [person]

être glacé jusqu'aux os ■ **to get** *OR* **to have ~ feet** avoir la trouille ■ **~ hands, warm heart** *prov* mains froides, cœur chaud *prov*
2. [weather] froid ■ **it will be ~ today** il va faire froid aujourd'hui ■ **it's freezing ~** il fait un froid de loup *OR* de canard ■ **it's getting ~er** la température baisse
3. [unfeeling] froid, indifférent ■ [objective] froid, objectif ■ [unfriendly] froid, peu aimable ■ **to be ~ towards sb** se montrer froid envers qqn ■ **the play left me ~** la pièce ne m'a fait ni chaud ni froid ■ **to have a ~ heart** avoir un cœur de pierre ■ **in the ~ light of day** dans la froide lumière du jour ■ **in ~ blood** de sang-froid ■ **'In Cold Blood'** ***Capote*** 'De sang-froid'
4. [unconscious] : **she was out ~** elle était sans connaissance ■ **he knocked him (out) ~** il l'a mis KO
5. [colour] froid.
<> *n* **1.** METEOR froid *m* ■ **come in out of the ~** entrez vous mettre au chaud ➤ **to come in from the ~** rentrer en grâce ■ **the newcomer was left out in the ~** personne ne s'est occupé du nouveau venu
2. MED rhume *m* ■ **to have a ~** être enrhumé.
<> *adv* **1.** [without preparation] à froid
2. *US inf* [absolutely] : **she turned me down ~** elle m'a dit non carrément ■ **he knows his subject ~** il connait son sujet à fond.

cold-blooded *adj* **1.** [animal] à sang froid **2.** *fig* [unfeeling] insensible ■ [ruthless] sans pitié ■ **a ~ murder** un meurtre commis de sang-froid.

cold-bloodedly [-'blʌdɪdlɪ] *adv* de sang-froid.

cold calling *n* [on phone] démarchage *m* téléphonique ■ [at home] démarchage *m* à domicile.

cold cream *n* crème *f* de beauté, cold-cream *m*.

cold cuts *npl* [gen] viandes *fpl* froides ■ [on menu] assiette *f* anglaise.

cold fish *n inf* **he's a ~** *inf* c'est un pisse-froid.

cold frame *n* châssis *m* de couches *(pour plantes)*.

cold front *n* front *m* froid.

cold-hearted *adj* sans pitié, insensible.

coldly ['kəʊldlɪ] *adv* froidement, avec froideur.

coldness ['kəʊldnɪs] *n liter & fig* froideur *f*.

cold-pressed [-prest] *adj* [olive oil] pressé à froid.

cold room *n* chambre *f* froide *OR* frigorifique.

cold shoulder *n inf* **to give sb the ~** snober qqn.
◆ **cold-shoulder** *vt inf* snober.

cold snap *n* courte offensive *f* du froid.

cold sore *n* bouton *m* de fièvre.

cold storage *n* conservation *f* par le froid ■ **to put sthg into ~** [food] mettre qqch en chambre froide ; [furs] mettre qqch en garde ; *fig* mettre qqch en attente.

cold store *n* entrepôt *m* frigorifique.

Coldstream Guards ['kəʊld,stri:m-] *pr npl* : **the ~** *régiment d'infanterie de la Garde Royale britannique*.

cold sweat *n* sueur *f* froide ■ **to be in a ~ about sthg** *inf* avoir des sueurs froides au sujet de qqch.

cold turkey△ *n drug sl* [drugs withdrawal] manque *m* ■ **to go ~** être en manque.

cold war *n* guerre *f* froide.

coleslaw ['kəʊlslɔ:] *n* salade *f* de chou cru.

colic ['kɒlɪk] *n (U)* coliques *fpl*.

Coliseum [,kɒlɪ'sɪəm] *pr n* Colisée *m*.

colitis [kɒ'laɪtɪs] *n (U)* colite *f*.

collaborate [kə'læbəreɪt] *vi* collaborer ■ **she ~d with us on the project** elle a collaboré avec nous au projet.

collaboration [kə,læbə'reɪʃn] *n* collaboration *f* ■ **~ (with sb) on sthg** collaboration (avec qqn) à qqch ■ **in ~ with** en collaboration avec.

collaborative [kə'læbərətɪv] *adj* conjugué, combiné.

collaborator [kə'læbəreɪtər] *n* collaborateur *m*, - trice *f*.

collage ['kɒlɑ:ʒ] *n* **1.** ART [picture, method] collage *m* **2.** [gen - combination of things] mélange *m*.

collagen ['kɒlədʒən] *n* collagène *m*.

collapse [kə'læps] <> *vi* **1.** [building, roof] s'écrouler, s'effondrer ■ [beam] fléchir **2.** *fig* [institution] s'effondrer, s'écrouler ■ [government] tomber, chuter ■ [plan] s'écrouler ■ [market, defence] s'effondrer **3.** [person] s'écrouler, s'effondrer ■ [health] se délabrer, se dégrader ■ **he ~d and died** il a eu un malaise et il est mort ■ **he ~d onto the bed and slept for hours** il s'est écroulé sur son lit et a dormi pendant des heures ■ **to ~ with laughter** se tordre de rire **4.** [fold up] se plier.
<> *vt* [fold up - table, chair] plier.
<> *n* **1.** [of building] écroulement *m*, effondrement *m* ■ [of beam] rupture *f* **2.** *fig* [of institution, plan] effondrement *m*, écroulement *m* ■ [of government] chute *f* ■ [of market, defence] effondrement *m* **3.** [of person] écroulement *m*, effondrement *m* ■ [of health] délabrement *m* ■ [of lung] collapsus *m*.

collapsed [kə'læpst] *adj* : **to have a ~ lung** avoir fait un collapsus pulmonaire.

collapsible [kə'læpsəbl] *adj* pliant.

collar ['kɒlər] <> *n* **1.** [on clothing] col *m* ■ [detachable - for men] faux col *m* ; [- for women] col *m*, collerette *f* **2.** [for animal] collier *m* ■ [neck of animal] collier *m* ■ CULIN [beef] collier *m* ■ [mutton, veal] collet *m* **3.** TECH [on pipe] bague *f*.
<> *vt* **1.** *inf* [seize] prendre *OR* saisir au collet, colleter ■ [criminal] arrêter ■ [detain] intercepter, harponner **2.** TECH [pipe] baguer.

collarbone ['kɒləbəʊn] *n* clavicule *f*.

collar stud *n* bouton *m* de col.

collate [kə'leɪt] *vt* **1.** [information, texts] collationner **2.** RELIG nommer *(à un bénéfice ecclésiastique)*.

collateral [kɒ'lætərəl] <> *n* FIN [guarantee] nantissement *m* ■ **offered as ~** remis en nantissement.
<> *adj* **1.** [secondary] subsidiaire, accessoire ■ FIN subsidiaire ■ **~ loan** prêt *m* avec garantie ■ **~ security** nantissement *m* ■ **~ damage** MIL dommages *mpl* de guerre **2.** [parallel] parallèle ■ [fact] concomitant ■ LAW & MED collatéral.

collation [kə'leɪʃn] *n* **1.** [of text] collation *f* **2.** [light meal] collation *f*.

collator [kə'leɪtər] *n* **1.** [person] collationneur *m*, - euse *f* ■ [machine] collationneur *m* **2.** RELIG collateur *m*.

colleague ['kɒli:g] *n* [in office, school] collègue *mf* ■ [professional, doctor, lawyer] confrère *m*.

collect[1] [kə'lekt] <> *vt* **1.** [gather - objects] ramasser ; [- information, documents] recueillir, rassembler ; [- evidence] rassembler ; [- people] réunir, rassembler ; [- wealth] accumuler, amasser ■ *fig* **to ~ o.s.** [calm down] se reprendre, se calmer ; [reflect] se recueillir ■ **let me ~ my thoughts** laissez-moi réfléchir *OR* me concentrer **2.** [as hobby] collectionner, faire collection de **3.** [money] recueillir ■ [taxes, fines, dues] percevoir ■ [pension, salary] toucher **4.** *UK* [take away] ramasser ■ **the council ~s the rubbish** la commune se charge du ramassage des ordures ■ **to ~ an order** COMM retirer une commande **5.** [pick up - people] aller chercher, (passer) prendre.
<> *vi* **1.** [accumulate - people] se rassembler, se réunir ; [- things] s'accumuler, s'amasser ; [- water, dirt] s'accumuler **2.** [raise money] : **to ~ for charity** faire la quête *OR* quêter pour une œuvre de bienfaisance.
<> *adv US* : **to call ~** téléphoner en PCV.
<> *adj US* **a ~ call** un (appel en) PCV.
◆ **collect up** *vt sep* ramasser.

collect[2] ['kɒlekt] *n* [prayer] collecte *f*.

collectable [kə'lektəbl] *adj* [desirable to collectors] (très) recherché.

collected [kə'lektɪd] *adj* **1.** [composed] maître de soi, calme **2.** [complete] complet, - ète *f* ■ **the ~ works of Whitman** les œuvres complètes de Whitman.

collecting [kə'lektɪŋ] *n* collection *f*.

collection [kə'lekʃn] *n* **1.** *(U)* [collecting - objects] ramassage *m* ; [- information] rassemblement *m* ; [- wealth] accumulation *f* ; [- rent, money] encaissement *m* ; [- debts] recouvrement *m* ; [- taxes] perception *f* **2.** [things collected] collection *f* ▪ **the fashion designers' winter ~** la collection d'hiver des couturiers **3.** [picking up - of rubbish] ramassage *m* ▪ *UK* [- of mail] levée *f* ▪ **your order is ready for ~** votre commande est prête **4.** [sum of money] collecte *f*, quête *f* ▪ **to take** *OR* **to make a ~ for** faire une quête *OR* collecte pour ⊳ **~ box** [gen] caisse *f* ; [in church] tronc *m* ▪ **~ plate** [in church] corbeille *f* **5.** [group - of people, things] rassemblement *m*, groupe *m* **6.** [anthology] recueil *m*.

collective [kə'lektɪv] ◇ *adj* collectif ▪ LING : **~ noun** collectif *m*.
◇ *n* coopérative *f*.

collective bargaining *n négociations pour une convention collective.*

collective farm *n* ferme *f* collective.

collectively [kə'lektɪvlɪ] *adv* collectivement.

collectivism [kə'lektɪvɪzm] *n* collectivisme *m*.

collectivize, *UK* **ise** [kə'lektɪvaɪz] *vt* collectiviser.

collector [kə'lektər] *n* **1.** [as a hobby] collectionneur *m*, - euse *f* ▪ **~ 's item** pièce *f* de collection **2.** [of money] encaisseur *m* ▪ [of taxes] percepteur *m* ▪ [of debts] receveur *m*.

college ['kɒlɪdʒ] *n* **1.** [institution of higher education] établissement *m* d'enseignement supérieur ▪ [within university] collège *m (dans les universités traditionnelles, communauté indépendante d'enseignants et d'étudiants)* ▪ **I go to ~** je suis étudiant ▪ **~ degree** *US* diplôme *m* universitaire **2.** [for professional training] école *f* professionnelle, collège *m* technique ▪ **~ of art** école des Beaux-Arts ▪ **~ of music** conservatoire *m* de musique ⊳ **College of Education** *UK* ≃ institut *m* de formation des maîtres ▪ **College of Further Education** *UK* ≃ institut *m* d'éducation permanente **3.** [organization] société *f*, académie *f* ▪ **the College of Cardinals** le Sacré Collège ▪ **the Royal College of Physicians/Surgeons** l'Académie *f* de médecine/de chirurgie.

collegiate [kə'liːdʒɪət] *adj* [life] universitaire ▪ [university] composé de diverses facultés ▪ *Canada* [school] secondaire.

collide [kə'laɪd] *vi* **1.** [crash] entrer en collision, se heurter ▪ NAUT aborder ▪ **the bus ~d with the lorry** le bus est entré en collision avec *OR* a heurté le camion **2.** *fig* [clash] entrer en conflit, se heurter.

collie ['kɒlɪ] *n* colley *m*.

collier ['kɒlɪər] *n UK* [miner] mineur *m* ▪ [ship] charbonnier *m*.

colliery ['kɒljərɪ] (*pl* **collieries**) *n* houillère *f*, mine *f* (de charbon).

collision [kə'lɪʒn] *n* **1.** [crash] collision *f*, choc *m* ▪ RAIL collision *f*, tamponnement *m* ▪ NAUT abordage *m* ▪ **to come into ~ with sthg** entrer en collision avec *OR* tamponner qqch ▪ **the two ships came into ~** les deux navires se sont abordés ⊳ **~ damage waiver** *réduction sur le prix d'une assurance accordée aux automobilistes qui acceptent de payer les dommages dont ils sont responsables* **2.** *fig* [clash] conflit *m*, opposition *f*.

collision course *n* : **the two planes were on a ~** les deux avions risquaient d'entrer en collision ▪ **the government is on a ~ with the unions** le gouvernement va au-devant d'un conflit avec les syndicats.

collocate ◇ *vi* ['kɒləkeɪt] être cooccurrent ▪ **to ~ with sthg** être cooccurrent de qqch.
◇ *n* ['kɒləkət] cooccurrent *m*.

collocation [ˌkɒlə'keɪʃn] *n* collocation *f*.

colloquia [kə'ləʊkwɪə] *pl* ⊳ **colloquium**.

colloquial [kə'ləʊkwɪəl] *adj* [language, expression] familier, parlé ▪ [style] familier.

colloquialism [kə'ləʊkwɪəlɪzm] *n* expression *f* familière.

colloquially [kə'ləʊkwɪəlɪ] *adv* familièrement, dans la langue parlée.

colloquium [kə'ləʊkwɪəm] (*pl* **colloquiums** *OR pl* **colloquia** [kə'ləʊkwɪə]) *n* colloque *m*.

colloquy ['kɒləkwɪ] (*pl* **colloquies**) *n fml* [conversation] colloque *m*, conversation *f* ▪ [meeting] colloque *m*.

collude [kə'luːd] *vi* être de connivence *OR* de mèche ▪ **to ~ with sb (in sthg)** être de connivence avec qqn (dans *OR* pour qqch).

collusion [kə'luːʒn] *n* collusion *f* ▪ **to act in ~ with sb** agir de connivence avec qqn.

collywobbles ['kɒlɪˌwɒblz] *npl UK inf* [stomachache] mal *m* au ventre ▪ [nervousness] trouille *f*.

Colombia [kə'lɒmbɪə] *pr n* Colombie *f* ▪ **in ~** en Colombie.

Colombian [kə'lɒmbɪən] ◇ *n* Colombien *m*, - enne *f*.
◇ *adj* colombien.

colon ['kəʊlən] *n* **1.** [in punctuation] deux-points *m* **2.** ANAT côlon *m*.

colonel ['kɜːnl] *n* colonel *m*, -elle *f* ▪ **Colonel Jones** le colonel *m*, la colonelle *f* Jones.

COLONEL BLIMP

Colonel Blimp est un personnage de vieil officier, réfractaire au changement, créé par le dessinateur britannique David Low ; on l'emploie, ou simplement *Blimp*, pour désigner une personne du même tempérament.

colonial [kə'ləʊnjəl] ◇ *adj* **1.** [power, life] colonial ▪ *pej* [attitude] colonialiste **2.** *US* [design] colonial américain *(style XVIIIe aux États-Unis)* **3.** BIOL [animals, insects] qui vit en colonie.
◇ *n* colonial *m*, - e *f*.

colonialism [kə'ləʊnjəlɪzm] *n* colonialisme *m*.

colonialist [kə'ləʊnjəlɪst] ◇ *adj* colonialiste.
◇ *n* colonialiste *mf*.

colonist ['kɒlənɪst] *n* colon *m*.

colonization [ˌkɒlənaɪ'zeɪʃn] *n* colonisation *f*.

colonize, *UK* **ise** ['kɒlənaɪz] *vt* coloniser.

colonnade [ˌkɒlə'neɪd] *n* colonnade *f*.

colony ['kɒlənɪ] (*pl* **colonies**) *n* colonie *f*.

colophon ['kɒləfən] *n* **1.** [logo] logo *m*, colophon *m* **2.** [end text in book] achevé *m* d'imprimer ▪ [end text in manuscript] colophon *m*.

color *etc US n, vt, vi & comp* = **colour**.

Colorado [ˌkɒlə'rɑːdəʊ] *pr n* Colorado *m* ▪ **in ~** dans le Colorado ▪ **the ~ (River)** le Colorado.

Colorado beetle *n* doryphore *m*.

colorant ['kʌlərənt] *n* colorant *m*.

coloration [ˌkʌlə'reɪʃn] *n* [colouring] coloration *f* ▪ [choice of colours] coloris *m*.

colossal [kə'lɒsl] *adj* colossal.

Colosseum [ˌkɒlə'sɪəm] *pr n* Colisée *m*.

colossus [kə'lɒsəs] (*pl* **colossuses** *OR pl* **colossi** [-saɪ]) *n* colosse *m*.

colostomy [kə'lɒstəmɪ] (*pl* **colostomies**) *n* colostomie *f*.

colour *UK*, **color** *US* ['kʌlər] ◇ *n* **1.** [hue] couleur *f* ▪ **what ~ are his eyes?** de quelle couleur sont ses yeux? ▪ **the movie is in ~** le film est en couleur *OR* couleurs **2.** *fig* **the political ~ of a newspaper** la couleur politique d'un journal ⊳ **we've yet to see the ~ of his money** *inf* nous n'avons pas encore vu la couleur de son argent **3.** ART [shade] coloris *m*, ton *m* ▪ [paint] peinture *f* ▪ [dye] teinture *f*, matière *f* colorante **4.** [complexion] teint *m*, couleur *f (du visage)* ▪ **he changed ~** il a changé de couleur *OR* de visage ▪ **to lose one's ~** pâlir, perdre ses couleurs ▪ **to get one's ~ back** reprendre des couleurs ▪ **to have a high ~** avoir le visage rouge **5.** [race] couleur *f* ▪ **of ~** noir **6.** [interest] couleur *f* ▪ **to add ~ to a story** colorer un récit.

◇ *comp* [photography, picture, slide] en couleur, en couleurs ▪ **~ film** [for camera] pellicule *f* (en) couleur ; [movie] film *m* en couleur ▪ **~ filter** PHOT filtre *m* coloré ▪ **~ television (set)** téléviseur *m* couleur.
◇ *vt* **1.** [give colour to] colorer ▪ [with paint] peindre ▪ [with crayons] colorier ▪ **he ~ed it blue** il l'a colorié en bleu **2.** *fig* [distort - judgment] fausser ▪ [exaggerate - story, facts] exagérer.
◇ *vi* [person] rougir ▪ [things] se colorer ▪ [fruit] mûrir.
◆ **colours** *npl* **1.** [of team] *élément vestimentaire (écusson, cravate etc) décerné aux nouveaux membres d'une équipe sportive* ▪ **to get** *OR* **to win one's ~s** être sélectionné pour faire partie d'une équipe ➲ **to show one's true ~s** se montrer sous son vrai jour **2.** [of school] couleurs *fpl* **3.** MIL [flag] couleurs *fpl*, drapeau *m* ▪ NAUT couleurs *fpl*, pavillon *m* **4.** [clothes for washing] couleurs *fpl*.
◆ **colour in** *vt sep* colorier.
◆ **colour up** *vi insep* [blush] rougir.

colour bar *n UK* discrimination *f* raciale.

colour-blind *adj liter* daltonien ▪ *fig* qui ne fait pas de discrimination raciale.

colour blindness *n liter* daltonisme *m* ▪ *fig* fait *m* de ne pas faire de discrimination raciale.

colour code *n* code *m* coloré.
◆ **colour-code** *vt* : **to colour-code sthg** coder qqch avec des couleurs.

colour-coded *adj* dont la couleur correspond à un code ▪ **the wires are ~** la couleur des fils correspond à un code.

coloured *UK*, **colored** *US* ['kʌləd] *adj* **1.** [having colour] coloré ▪ [drawing] colorié ▪ [pencils] de couleur **2.** [person - gen] de couleur ; [- in South Africa] métis **3.** *fig* [distorted - judgment] faussé ▪ [exaggerated - story] exagéré.
◆ **coloureds** *npl* **1.** [clothes for washing] couleurs *fpl* **2.** ▲ [people - gen] gens *mpl* de couleur ; [- in South Africa] métis *mpl (attention: le substantif "coloureds" est considéré comme raciste)*.

-coloured *UK*, **-colored** *US in cpds* (de) couleur... ▪ **rust~** couleur de rouille.

colourfast *UK*, **colorfast** *US* ['kʌləfɑːst] *adj* grand teint, qui ne déteint pas.

colourful *UK*, **colorful** *US* ['kʌləfʊl] *adj* **1.** [brightly coloured] coloré, vif **2.** *fig* [person] original, pittoresque ▪ [story] coloré.

colourfully *UK*, **colorfully** *US* ['kʌləfʊlɪ] *adv* : **a ~ dressed woman** une femme vêtue de couleurs vives.

colouring *UK*, **coloring** *US* ['kʌlərɪŋ] ◇ *n* **1.** [act] coloration *f* ▪ [of drawing] coloriage *m* **2.** [hue] coloration *f*, coloris *m* **3.** [complexion] teint *m* **4.** *fig* [exaggeration] travestissement *m*, dénaturation *f* **5.** [for food] colorant *m*.
◇ *comp* : **~ book** album *m* à colorier *OR* de coloriages.

colourist *UK*, **colorist** *US* ['kʌlərɪst] *n* coloriste *mf*.

colourize *UK*, **colorize** *US* ['kʌləraɪz] *vt* CIN coloriser.

colourless *UK*, **colorless** *US* ['kʌləlɪs] *adj* **1.** [without colour] incolore, sans couleur **2.** *fig* [uninteresting] sans intérêt, fade.

colour scheme *n* palette *f OR* combinaison *f* de couleurs ▪ **to choose a ~** assortir les couleurs *OR* les tons.

colour supplement *n UK* supplément *m* illustré.

colposcopy ['kɒlpəˌskəʊpɪ] *n* MED colposcopie *f*.

colt [kəʊlt] *n* **1.** [horse] poulain *m* **2.** *fig* [young person] petit jeune *m* ▪ [inexperienced person] novice *m*.

Colt® [kəʊlt] *n* [revolver] colt *m*, pistolet *m* (automatique).

Columbia [kə'lʌmbɪə] *pr n* **1.** : **the District of ~** le district fédéral de Columbia **2.** : **the ~ (River)** la Columbia.

Columbia University *pr n université de la ville de New York, faisant partie de la Ivy League, célèbre pour son école de journalisme.*

columbine ['kɒləmbaɪn] *n* ancolie *f*.

Columbus [kə'lʌmbəs] *pr n* : **Christopher ~** Christophe Colomb.

Columbus Day *n aux États-Unis, jour commémorant l'arrivée de Christophe Colomb en Amérique (deuxième lundi d'octobre).*

column ['kɒləm] *n* **1.** [gen - ARCHIT] colonne *f* **2.** PRESS [section of print] colonne *f* ▪ [regular article] rubrique *f*.

column inch *n unité de mesure des espaces publicitaires équivalant à une colonne sur un pouce.*

columnist ['kɒləmnɪst] *n* chroniqueur *m*, - euse *f*, échotier *m*, - ère *f*.

coma ['kəʊmə] *n* coma *m* ▪ **in a ~** dans le coma.

Comanche [kə'mæntʃɪ] (*pl inv OR pl* **Comanches**) *n* [person] Comanche *mf* ▪ **the ~** les Comanches.

comatose ['kəʊmətəʊs] *adj* comateux ▪ **to be ~** être dans le coma.

comb [kəʊm] ◇ *n* **1.** [for hair] peigne *m* ▪ [large-toothed] démêloir *m* ▪ **to run a ~ through one's hair, to give one's hair a ~** se donner un coup de peigne, se peigner **2.** [for horses] étrille *f* **3.** TEX [for cotton, wool] peigne *m*, carde *f* ▪ ELEC balai *m* **4.** [of fowl] crête *f* ▪ [on helmet] cimier *m* **5.** [honeycomb] rayon *m* de miel.
◇ *vt* **1.** [hair] peigner ▪ **he ~ed his hair** il s'est peigné ▪ **I ~ed the girl's hair** j'ai peigné la petite fille **2.** [horse] étriller **3.** TEX peigner, carder **4.** *fig* [search] fouiller, ratisser ▪ **the police ~ed the area for clues** la police a passé le quartier au peigne fin *OR* a ratissé le quartier à la recherche d'indices.
◆ **comb out** *vt sep* **1.** [hair] démêler, peigner **2.** *fig* [remove] éliminer.

combat ['kɒmbæt] ◇ *n* combat *m* ▪ **killed/lost in ~** tué/perdu au combat.
◇ *comp* [troops, zone] de combat ▪ **on ~ duty** en service commandé ▪ **~ jacket** veste *f* de treillis.
◇ *vt* (*pret & pp* **combated**, *cont* **combating**) combattre, lutter contre.
◇ *vi* (*pret & pp* **combated**, *cont* **combating**) combattre, lutter.

combatant ['kɒmbətənt] ◇ *n* combattant *m*, - e *f*.
◇ *adj* combattant.

combat fatigue *n* psychose *f* traumatique, syndrome *m* commotionnel.

combative ['kɒmbətɪv] *adj* combatif.

combination [ˌkɒmbɪ'neɪʃn] *n* **1.** [gen - CHEM] & MATHS combinaison *f* ▪ [of circumstances] concours *m* **2.** [of lock] combinaison *f* **3.** [association, team] association *f*, coalition *f* ▪ **together they formed a winning ~** ensemble ils formaient une équipe gagnante **4.** *UK* AUT side-car *m*.
◆ **combinations** *npl UK* [underclothing] combinaison-culotte *f*.

combination lock *n* serrure *f* à combinaison.

combination skin *n* peau *f* mixte.

combination therapy *n* MED trithérapie *f*.

combine ◇ *vt* [kəm'baɪn] [gen] combiner, joindre ▪ CHEM combiner ▪ **to ~ business and** *OR* **with pleasure** joindre l'utile à l'agréable ▪ **this, ~d with her other problems, made her ill** ceci, conjugué à ses autres problèmes, l'a rendue malade ▪ **furniture combining comfort with style** meubles alliant confort et style.
◇ *vi* [kəm'baɪn] [unite] s'unir, s'associer ▪ [workers] se syndiquer ▪ POL [parties] fusionner ▪ CHEM se combiner ▪ **events ~d to leave her penniless** les événements ont concouru à la laisser sans le sou.
◇ *n* ['kɒmbaɪn] **1.** [association] association *f* ▪ FIN trust *m*, cartel *m* ▪ LAW corporation *f* **2.** AGRIC = **combine harvester**.

combined [kəm'baɪnd] *adj* combiné, conjugué ▪ **a ~ effort** un effort conjugué ▮ MIL : **~ forces** forces alliées ▪ **~ operation** [by several nations] opération alliée ; [by forces of one nation] opération interarmées.

combine harvester ['kɒmbaɪn-] *n* moissonneuse-batteuse *f*.

combining form [kəm'baɪnɪŋ-] *n* LING affixe *m*.

combo ['kɒmbəʊ] (*pl* **combos**) *n* **1.** MUS combo *m* **2.** *inf* [combination] combinaison *f*.

combustible [kəm'bʌstəbl] *adj* combustible.

combustion [kəm'bʌstʃn] *n* combustion *f*.

combustion chamber *n* chambre *f* de combustion.

combustion engine *n* moteur *m* à combustion.

come [kʌm] ◇ *vi* (*pret* **came** [keɪm], *pp* **come** [kʌm]) **1.** [move in direction of speaker] venir ■ **coming!** j'arrive! ■ **~ here** venez ici ■ **~ with me** [accompany] venez avec moi, accompagnez-moi ; [follow] suivez-moi ■ **please ~ this way** par ici *OR* suivez-moi s'il vous plaît ■ **I ~ this way every week** je passe par ici toutes les semaines ■ **~ and look, ~ look** *US* venez voir ■ **~ and get it!** *inf* à la soupe! ■ **a car came hurtling round the corner** une voiture a pris le virage à toute vitesse ▶ **to ~ and go** [gen] aller et venir ; *fig* [pains, cramps etc] être intermittent ■ **people are constantly coming and going** il y a un va-et-vient continuel ■ **fashions ~ and go** la mode change tout le temps ■ **I don't know whether I'm coming or going** *inf* je ne sais pas où j'en suis ■ **you have ~ a long way** *liter* vous êtes venu de loin ; *fig* [made progress] vous avez fait du chemin ■ **the computer industry has ~ a very long way since then** l'informatique a fait énormément de progrès depuis ce temps-là ■ **to ~ running** *liter* & *fig* arriver en courant ■ **we could see him coming a mile off** on l'a vu venir avec ses gros sabots ■ **you could see it coming** *inf* on l'a vu venir de loin, c'était prévisible ■ **everything ~s to him who waits** *prov* tout vient à point à qui sait attendre *prov*
2. [as guest, visitor] venir ■ **would you like to ~ for lunch/dinner?** voulez-vous venir déjeuner/dîner? ■ **I've got people coming** [short stay] j'ai des invités ; [long stay] il y a des gens qui viennent ■ **he couldn't have ~ at a worse time** il n'aurait pas pu tomber plus mal
3. [arrive] venir, arriver ■ **to ~ in time/late** arriver à temps/en retard ■ **we came to a small town** nous sommes arrivés dans une petite ville ■ **the time has ~ to tell the truth** le moment est venu de dire la vérité ■ **there will ~ a point when...** il viendra un moment où... ▮ [reach] : **her hair ~s (down) to her waist** ses cheveux lui arrivent à la taille
4. [occupy specific place, position] venir, se trouver ■ **the address ~s above the date** l'adresse se met au-dessus de la date ■ **my birthday ~s before yours** mon anniversaire vient avant *OR* précède le tien ■ **that speech ~s in Act 3/on page 10** on trouve ce discours dans l'acte 3/à la page 10
5. [occur, happen] arriver, se produire ■ **such an opportunity only ~s once in your life** une telle occasion ne se présente qu'une fois dans la vie ■ **he has a birthday coming** son anniversaire approche ■ **success was a long time coming** la réussite s'est fait attendre ■ **take life as it ~s** prenez la vie comme elle vient ▶ **~ what may** advienne que pourra, quoi qu'il arrive *OR* advienne
6. [occur to the mind] : **I said the first thing that came into my head** *OR* **that came to mind** j'ai dit la première chose qui m'est venue à l'esprit ■ **the answer came to her** elle a trouvé la réponse
7. [be experienced in a specified way] : **writing ~s natural** *inf OR* **naturally to her** écrire lui est facile, elle est douée pour l'écriture ■ **a house doesn't ~ cheap** une maison coûte *OR* revient cher ■ **the news came as a shock to her** la nouvelle lui a fait un choc ■ **her visit came as a surprise** sa visite nous a beaucoup surpris ▶ **he's as silly as they ~** il est sot comme pas un ■ **they don't ~ any tougher than Big Al** on ne fait pas plus fort que Big Al ■ **it'll all ~ right in the end** tout cela va finir par s'arranger
8. [be available] exister ■ **this table ~s in two sizes** cette table existe *OR* se fait en deux dimensions ■ **the dictionary ~s with a magnifying glass** le dictionnaire est livré avec une loupe
9. [become] devenir ■ **it was a dream ~ true** c'était un rêve devenu réalité ■ **to ~ unhooked** se décrocher ■ **to ~ unravelled** se défaire
10. (+ *infinitive*) [indicating gradual action] en venir à, finir par ■ **we have ~ to expect this kind of thing** nous nous attendons à ce genre de chose maintenant ▮ [indicating chance] arriver ■ **how did you ~ to lose your umbrella?** comment as-tu fait pour perdre ton parapluie? ▶ **(now that I) ~ to think of it** maintenant que j'y songe, réflexion faite
11. [be owing, payable] : **I still have £5 coming (to me)** on me doit encore 5 livres ▶ **you'll get what's coming to you** *inf* tu l'auras cherché *OR* voulu ■ **he had it coming (to him)** *inf* il ne l'a pas volé
12. △ [have orgasm] jouir
13. *phr* **how ~?** comment ça? ■ **~ again?** *inf* quoi? ■ **I haven't seen her in weeks, or her husband, ~ to that** ça fait des semaines que je ne l'ai pas vue, son mari non plus d'ailleurs ■ **if it ~s to that, I'd rather stay home** à ce moment-là *OR* à ce compte-là, je préfère rester à la maison ■ **don't ~ the innocent!** ne fais pas l'innocent! ■ **you're coming it a bit strong!** *UK* tu y vas un peu fort! ■ **don't ~ it with me!** *UK* [try to impress] n'essaie pas de m'en mettre plein la vue! ; [lord it over] pas la peine d'être si hautain avec moi! ■ **to ~ : the days to ~** les prochains jours, les jours qui viennent ■ **the battle to ~** la bataille qui va avoir lieu ■ **in times to ~** à l'avenir ■ **for some time to ~** pendant quelque temps.
◇ *prep* [by] : **~ tomorrow/Tuesday you'll feel better** vous vous sentirez mieux demain/mardi ■ **I'll have been here two years ~ April** ça fera deux ans en avril que je suis là.
◇ *interj* : **~, ~!, ~ now!** allons!, voyons!
◇ *n*▲ foutre△ *m*.

◆ **come about** *vi insep* [occur] arriver, se produire ■ **how could such a mistake ~ about?** comment une telle erreur a-t-elle pu se produire? ■ **the discovery of penicillin came about quite by accident** la pénicilline a été découverte tout à fait par hasard.

◆ **come across** ◇ *vi insep* **1.** [walk, travel across - field, street] traverser ■ **as we stood talking she came across to join us** pendant que nous discutions, elle est venue se joindre à nous
2. [create specified impression] donner l'impression de ■ [communicate effectively] : **he never ~s across as well on film as in the theatre** il passe mieux au théâtre qu'à l'écran ■ **the author's message ~s across well** le message de l'auteur passe bien ■ **her disdain for his work came across** le mépris qu'elle avait pour son travail transparaissait.
◇ *vt insep* [person] rencontrer par hasard, tomber sur ■ [thing] trouver par hasard, tomber sur ■ **she reads everything she ~s across** elle lit tout ce qui lui tombe sous la main.

◆ **come across with**△ *vt insep* [give - information] donner, fournir ; [- help] offrir ; [- money] raquer△, se fendre de△.

◆ **come after** *vt insep* [pursue] poursuivre.

◆ **come along** *vi insep* **1.** [encouraging, urging] : **~ along, drink your medicine!** allez, prends *OR* bois ton médicament!
2. [accompany] venir, accompagner ■ **she asked me to ~ along (with them)** elle m'a invité à aller avec eux *OR* à les accompagner
3. [occur, happen] arriver, se présenter ■ **don't accept the first job that ~s along** ne prenez pas le premier travail qui se présente ■ **he married the first woman that came along** il a épousé la première venue
4. [progress] avancer, faire des progrès ■ [grow] pousser ■ **the patient is coming along well** le patient se remet bien ■ **how's your computer class coming along?** comment va ton cours d'informatique?

◆ **come apart** *vi insep* [object - come to pieces] se démonter ; [- break] se casser ■ [project, policy] échouer ■ **the book came apart in my hands** le livre est tombé en morceaux quand je l'ai pris ■ **under pressure he came apart** *fig* sous la pression il a craqué.

◆ **come around** *vt insep* = **come round**.

◆ **come at** *vt insep* [attack] attaquer, se jeter sur ■ **questions came at me from all sides** *fig* j'ai été assailli de questions.

◆ **come away** *vi insep* **1.** [leave] partir, s'en aller ■ **~ away from that door!** écartez-vous de cette porte! ■ **he asked her to ~ away with him** [elope] il lui a demandé de s'enfuir avec lui ; *UK* [go on holiday] il lui a demandé de partir avec lui
2. [separate] partir, se détacher ■ **the page came away in my hands** la page m'est restée dans les mains.

◆ **come back** *vi insep* **1.** [return] revenir ■ **to ~ back home** rentrer (à la maison) ▮ *fig* **the colour came back to her cheeks** elle reprit des couleurs ■ **to ~ back to what we were saying** pour en revenir à ce que nous disions
2. [to memory] : **it's all coming back to me** tout cela me revient (à l'esprit *OR* à la mémoire)
3. [reply] répondre ■ *US* [retort] rétorquer, répliquer

4. [recover] remonter ▪ **they came back from 3-0 down** ils ont remonté de 3 à 0 ▮ [make comeback] faire un come-back
5. [become fashionable again] revenir à la mode.

◆ **come before** *vt insep* LAW [person] comparaître devant ▪ [case] être entendu par.

◆ **come between** *vt insep* brouiller, éloigner ▪ **he came between her and her friend** il l'a brouillée avec son amie, il l'a éloignée de son amie.

◆ **come by** <> *vi insep* [stop by] passer, venir.
<> *vt insep* [acquire - work, money] obtenir, se procurer ; [- idea] se faire ▪ **jobs are hard to ~ by** il est difficile de trouver du travail.

◆ **come down** <> *vt insep* [descend - ladder, stairs] descendre ; [- mountain] descendre, faire la descente de.
<> *vi insep* **1.** [descend - plane, person] descendre ▪ **~ down from that tree!** descends de cet arbre! ➋ **he's ~ down in the world** il a déchu
2. [fall] tomber ▪ **rain was coming down in sheets** il pleuvait des cordes ▪ **the ceiling came down** le plafond s'est effondré
3. [reach] descendre
4. [decrease] baisser
5. [be passed down] être transmis (de père en fils) ▪ **this custom ~s down from the Romans** cette coutume nous vient des Romains
6. [reach a decision] se prononcer ▪ **the majority came down in favour of/against abortion** la majorité s'est prononcée en faveur de/contre l'avortement
7. [be demolished] être démoli *OR* abattu.

◆ **come down on** *vt insep* [rebuke] s'en prendre à ▪ **the boss really came down hard on him** le patron lui a passé un de ces savons.

◆ **come down to** *vt insep* [amount] se réduire à, se résumer à ▪ **it all ~s down to what you want to do** tout cela dépend de ce que vous souhaitez faire ▪ **it all ~s down to the same thing** tout cela revient au même ▪ **that's what his argument ~s down to** voici à quoi se réduit son raisonnement.

◆ **come down with** *vt insep* [become ill] attraper.

◆ **come forward** *vi insep* [present oneself] se présenter ▪ **more women are coming forward as candidates** davantage de femmes présentent leur candidature.

◆ **come forward with** *vt insep* [offer] : **the townspeople came forward with supplies** les habitants de la ville ont offert des provisions ▪ **he came forward with a new proposal** il a fait une nouvelle proposition ▪ **to ~ forward with evidence** LAW présenter des preuves.

◆ **come from** *vt insep* venir de ▪ **she ~s from China** [Chinese person] elle vient *OR* elle est originaire de Chine ▪ **this passage ~s from one of his novels** ce passage est extrait *OR* provient d'un de ses romans ▪ **that's surprising coming from him** c'est étonnant de sa part ➋ **I'm not sure where he's coming from**△ je ne sais pas très bien ce qui le motive.

◆ **come in** *vi insep* **1.** [enter] entrer ▪ **~ in!** entrez! ▮ [come inside] rentrer
2. [plane, train] arriver
3. [in competition] arriver
4. [be received - money, contributions] rentrer ▪ **there isn't enough money coming in to cover expenditure** l'argent qui rentre ne suffit pas à couvrir les dépenses ▪ **how much do you have coming in every week?** combien touchez-vous *OR* encaissez-vous chaque semaine? ▮ PRESS [news, report] être reçu ▪ **news is just coming in of a riot in Red Square** on nous annonce à l'instant des émeutes sur la place Rouge
5. RADIO & TV [begin to speak] parler ▪ **~ in car number 1 over** j'appelle voiture 1, à vous
6. [become seasonable] être de saison ▪ **when do endives ~ in?** quand commence la saison des endives? ▮ [become fashionable] entrer en vogue
7. [prove to be] : **to ~ in handy** *OR* **useful** [tool, gadget] être utile *OR* commode ; [contribution] arriver à point
8. [be involved] être impliqué ▪ [participate] participer, intervenir ▪ **where do I ~ in?** quel est mon rôle là-dedans? ▪ **this is where the law ~s in** c'est là que la loi intervient ▪ **he should ~ in on the deal** il devrait participer à l'opération
9. [tide] monter.

◆ **come in for** *vt insep* [be object of - criticism] être l'objet de, subir ; [- blame] supporter ; [- abuse, reproach] subir.

◆ **come into** *vt insep* **1.** [inherit] hériter de ▪ [acquire] entrer en possession de ▪ **they came into a fortune** [received] ils ont reçu une fortune ; [won] ils ont gagné une fortune ; [inherited] ils ont hérité d'une fortune
2. [play a role in] jouer un rôle.

◆ **come of** *vt insep* résulter de ▪ **no good will ~ from** *OR* **of it** ça ne mènera à rien de bon, il n'en résultera rien de bon ▪ **let me know what ~s of the meeting** faites-moi savoir ce qui ressortira de la réunion ▪ **that's what ~s from listening to you!** voilà ce qui arrive quand on vous écoute!

◆ **come off** <> *vt insep* **1.** [fall off - subj: rider] tomber de ; [- subj: button] se détacher de, se découdre de ; [- subj: handle, label] se détacher de ▪ [be removed - stain, mark] partir de, s'enlever de
2. [stop taking - drug, medicine] arrêter de prendre ; [- drink] arrêter de boire
3. FTBL [leave] sortir de
4. *phr* **oh, ~ off it!** *inf* allez, arrête ton char!
<> *vi insep* **1.** [rider] tomber ▪ [handle] se détacher ▪ [stains] partir, s'enlever ▪ [tape, wallpaper] se détacher, se décoller ▪ [button] se détacher, se découdre ▪ **the handle came off in his hand** la poignée lui est restée dans la main
2. FTBL [leave the field] sortir
3. [fare, manage] s'en sortir, se tirer de ▪ **you came off well in the competition** tu t'en es bien tiré au concours ▪ **to ~ off best** gagner
4. *inf* [happen] avoir lieu, se passer ▪ **my trip to China didn't ~ off** mon voyage en Chine n'a pas eu lieu ▮ [be carried through] se réaliser ▪ [succeed] réussir
5. CIN & THEAT [film, play] fermer
6. △ [have orgasm] décharger△.

◆ **come on** <> *vi insep* **1.** [follow] suivre ▪ **I'll ~ on after (you)** je vous suivrai
2. *(in imperative)* [hurry] : **~ on!** allez! ▪ **~ on in/up!** entre/monte donc!
3. [progress] avancer, faire des progrès ▪ [grow] pousser, venir bien ▪ **how is your work coming on?** où en est votre travail?
4. [begin - illness] se déclarer ; [- storm] survenir, éclater ; [- season] arriver ▪ **as night came on** quand la nuit a commencé à tomber ▪ **I feel a headache/cold coming on** je sens un mal de tête qui commence/que je m'enrhume
5. [start functioning - electricity, gas, heater, lights, radio] s'allumer ; [- motor] se mettre en marche ; [- utilities at main] être mis en service ▪ **has the water ~ on?** y a-t-il de l'eau?
6. [behave, act] : **don't ~ on all macho with me!** ne joue pas les machos avec moi! ▪ **you came on a bit strong** *inf* tu y es allé un peu fort
7. THEAT [actor] entrer en scène ▪ [play] être joué *OR* représenté.
<> *vt insep* = **come upon**.

◆ **come on to** *vt insep* **1.** [proceed to consider] aborder, passer à
2. △ *US* [flirt with] draguer.

◆ **come out** *vi insep* **1.** [exit] sortir ▪ **as we came out of the theatre** au moment où nous sommes sortis du théâtre ▮ [socially] sortir ▪ **would you like to ~ out with me tonight?** est-ce que tu veux sortir avec moi ce soir? ➋ **if he'd only ~ out of himself** *OR* **out of his shell** *fig* si seulement il sortait de sa coquille
2. [make appearance - stars, sun] paraître, se montrer ; [- flowers] sortir, éclore ▪ *fig* [- book] paraître, être publié ; [- film] paraître, sortir ; [- new product] sortir ▪ **I didn't mean it the way it came out** ce n'est pas ce que je voulais dire
3. [be revealed - news, secret] être divulgué *OR* révélé ; [- facts, truth] émerger, se faire jour
4. [colour - fade] passer, se faner ; [- run] déteindre ▪ [stain] s'enlever, partir
5. [declare oneself publicly] se déclarer ▪ **the governor came out against/for abortion** le gouverneur s'est prononcé (ouvertement) contre/pour l'avortement ➋ **to ~ out (of the closet)** *inf* ne plus cacher son homosexualité
6. *UK* [on strike] se mettre en *OR* faire grève
7. [emerge, finish up] se tirer d'affaire, s'en sortir ▪ **everything will ~ out fine** tout va s'arranger ▮ [in competition] se classer ▪ **I came out top in maths** j'étais premier en maths ▪ **to ~ out on top** gagner
8. [go into society] faire ses débuts *OR* débuter dans le monde

9. PHOT : **the pictures came out well/badly** les photos étaient très bonnes/n'ont rien donné ■ **the house didn't ~ out well** la maison n'est pas très bien sur les photos.

◆ **come out at** *vt insep* [amount to] s'élever à.

◆ **come out in** *vt insep* : **to ~ out in spots** *OR* **a rash** avoir une éruption de boutons.

◆ **come out with** *vt insep* [say] dire, sortir.

◆ **come over** ◇ *vi insep* **1.** [move, travel in direction of speaker] venir ■ **do you want to ~ over this evening?** tu veux venir à la maison ce soir? ■ **his family came over with the early settlers** sa famille est arrivée *OR* venue avec les premiers pionniers
2. [stop by] venir, passer
3. [change sides] : **they came over to our side** ils sont passés de notre côté ■ **he finally came over to their way of thinking** il a fini par se ranger à leur avis
4. [make specified impression] : **her speech came over well** son discours a fait bon effet *OR* bonne impression ■ **he came over as honest** il a donné l'impression d'être honnête
5. *inf* [feel] devenir ■ **he came over all funny** [felt ill] il s'est senti mal tout d'un coup, il a eu un malaise ; [behaved oddly] il est devenu tout bizarre.
◇ *vt insep* affecter, envahir ■ **a feeling of fear came over him** il a été saisi de peur, la peur s'est emparée de lui ■ **what has ~ over him?** qu'est-ce qui lui prend?

◆ **come round** *vi insep* **1.** [make a detour] faire le détour ■ **we came round by the factory** nous sommes passés par *OR* nous avons fait le détour par l'usine
2. [stop by] passer, venir
3. [occur - regular event] : **don't wait for Christmas to ~ round** n'attendez pas Noël ■ **when the championships/elections ~ round** au moment des championnats/élections ■ **the summer holidays will soon be coming round again** bientôt, ce sera de nouveau les grandes vacances
4. [change mind] changer d'avis ■ **he finally came round to our way of thinking** il a fini par se ranger à notre avis ‖ [change to better mood] : **don't worry, she'll soon ~ round** ne t'en fais pas, elle sera bientôt de meilleure humeur
5. [recover consciousness] reprendre connaissance, revenir à soi ■ [get better] se remettre, se rétablir.

◆ **come through** ◇ *vi insep* **1.** [be communicated] : **his sense of conviction came through** on voyait qu'il était convaincu ■ **her enthusiasm ~s through in her letters** son enthousiasme se lit dans ses lettres ‖ TELEC & RADIO : **your call is coming through** je vous passe votre communication ■ **you're coming through loud and clear** je vous reçois cinq sur cinq
2. [be granted, approved] se réaliser ■ **did your visa ~ through?** avez-vous obtenu votre visa?
3. [survive] survivre, s'en tirer
4. *US inf* [do what is expected] : **he came through for us** il a fait ce qu'on attendait de lui ■ **they came through with the documents** ils ont fourni les documents.
◇ *vt insep* **1.** [cross] traverser ■ *fig* [penetrate] traverser
2. [survive] : **they came through the accident without a scratch** ils sont sortis de l'accident indemnes ■ **she came through the examination with flying colours** elle a réussi l'examen avec brio.

◆ **come to** ◇ *vi insep* [recover consciousness] reprendre connaissance, revenir à soi.
◇ *vt insep* **1.** [concern] : **when it ~s to physics, she's a genius** pour ce qui est de la physique, c'est un génie ■ **when it ~s to paying...** quand il faut payer...
2. [amount to] s'élever à, se monter à
3. *fig* [arrive at, reach] : **now we ~ to questions of health** nous en venons maintenant aux questions de santé ■ **to ~ to power** accéder au pouvoir ➤ **what is the world coming to?** où va le monde? ■ **I never thought it would ~ to this** je ne me doutais pas qu'on en arriverait là.

◆ **come together** *vi insep* **1.** [assemble] se réunir, se rassembler ■ [meet] se rencontrer
2. *inf* [combine successfully] : **everything came together at the final performance** tout s'est passé à merveille pour la dernière représentation.

◆ **come under** *vt insep* **1.** [be subjected to - authority, control] dépendre de ; [- influence] tomber sous, être soumis à ■ **the government is coming under pressure to lower taxes** le gouvernement subit des pressions visant à réduire les impôts
2. [be classified under] être classé sous ■ **that subject ~s under 'current events'** ce sujet est classé *OR* se trouve sous la rubrique "actualités".

◆ **come up** *vi insep* **1.** [move upwards] monter ■ [moon, sun] se lever ■ [travel in direction of speaker] : **I ~ up to town every Monday** je viens en ville tous les lundis ➤ **to ~ up for air** [diver] remonter à la surface ; *fig* [take break] faire une pause ■ **an officer who came up through the ranks** MIL un officier sorti du rang
2. [approach] s'approcher ■ **to ~ up to sb** s'approcher de qqn, venir vers qqn ■ **it's coming up to 5 o'clock** il est presque 5 h ■ **one coffee, coming up!** *inf* et un café, un!
3. [plant] sortir, germer
4. [come under consideration - matter] être soulevé, être mis sur le tapis ; [- question, problem] se poser, être soulevé ■ **she ~s up for re-election this year** son mandat prend fin cette année ■ **my contract is coming up for review** mon contrat doit être révisé ■ LAW [accused] comparaître ■ [case] être entendu ■ **her case ~s up next Wednesday** elle passe au tribunal mercredi prochain
5. [happen unexpectedly - event] survenir, surgir ; [- opportunity] se présenter ■ **she's ready for anything that might ~ up** elle est prête à faire face à toute éventualité ■ **I can't make it, something has ~ up** je ne peux pas venir, j'ai un empêchement
6. [intensify - wind] se lever ; [- light] s'allumer ; [- sound] s'intensifier
7. [be vomited] : **everything she eats ~s up (again)** elle vomit *OR* rejette tout ce qu'elle mange
8. [colour, wood etc] : **the colour ~s up well when it's cleaned** la couleur revient bien au nettoyage
9. *inf* [win] gagner ■ **did their number ~ up?** [in lottery] ont-ils gagné au loto?

◆ **come up against** *vt insep* [be confronted with] rencontrer ■ **they came up against some tough competition** ils se sont heurtés à des concurrents redoutables.

◆ **come up to** *vt insep* **1.** [reach] arriver à ■ **the mud came up to their knees** la boue leur montait *OR* arrivait jusqu'aux genoux
2. [equal] : **the play didn't ~ up to our expectations** la pièce nous a déçus.

◆ **come up with** *vt insep* [offer, propose - money, loan] fournir ■ [think of - plan, suggestion] suggérer, proposer ; [- answer] trouver ; [- excuse] trouver, inventer ■ **they came up with a wonderful idea** ils ont eu une idée géniale.

◆ **come upon** *vt insep* [find unexpectedly - person] rencontrer par hasard, tomber sur ; [- object] trouver par hasard, tomber sur.

comeback ['kʌmbæk] *n inf* **1.** [return] retour *m*, comeback *m* ■ THEAT rentrée *f* ■ **to make** *OR* **to stage a ~** faire une rentrée *OR* un comeback **2.** [retort] réplique *f*.

Comecon ['kɒmɪkɒn] (*abbrev of* **Council for Mutual Economic Aid**) *pr n* Comecon *m*.

comedian [kə'mi:djən] *n* **1.** [comic] comique *m* ■ *fig* [funny person] clown *m*, pitre *m* **2.** THEAT comédien *m*.

comedienne [kə,mi:dɪ'en] *n* **1.** [comic] actrice *f* comique **2.** THEAT [comic actress] comédienne *f*.

comedown ['kʌmdaʊn] *n inf* déchéance *f*, dégringolade *f* ■ **he finds working in sales a bit of a ~** il trouve plutôt humiliant de travailler comme vendeur.

comedy ['kɒmədɪ] (*pl* **comedies**) *n* [gen] comédie *f* ■ THEAT genre *m* comique, comédie *f* ■ **~ of manners** comédie de mœurs ■ **'The Comedy of Errors'** ***Shakespeare*** 'la Comédie des erreurs'.

come-hither *adj inf* aguichant ■ **a ~ look** un regard aguichant.

comely ['kʌmlɪ] (*comp* **comelier**, *superl* **comeliest**) *adj arch* charmant, beau (*before vowel or silent 'h'* **bel**), belle *f*.

come-on *n inf* attrape-nigaud *m* ■ **to give sb the ~** faire les yeux doux à qqn.

comer ['kʌməʳ] *n* [arrival] arrivant *m*, - e *f* ■ **open to all ~s** ouvert à tous *OR* au tout-venant.

comet ['kɒmɪt] *n* comète *f*.

come-uppance [ˌkʌm'ʌpəns] *n inf* **you'll get your ~** tu auras ce que tu mérites.

comfort ['kʌmfət] <> *n* **1.** [well-being] confort *m*, bien-être *m* ▪ **to live in ~** vivre dans l'aisance *OR* à l'aise ▪ **the explosion was too close for ~** *fig* l'explosion a eu lieu un peu trop près à mon goût **2.** *(usu pl)* [amenities] aises *fpl*, commodités *fpl* ▪ **every modern ~** tout le confort moderne **3.** [consolation] réconfort *m*, consolation *f* ▪ **to take ~ in sthg** trouver un réconfort dans qqch ▪ **she took ~ from his words** elle a trouvé un réconfort dans ses paroles ▪ **if it's any ~ to you** si cela peut vous consoler ▪ **you've been a great ~ to me** vous avez été pour moi un grand réconfort.
<> *vt* **1.** [console] consoler ▪ [relieve] soulager **2.** [cheer] réconforter, encourager.

comfortable ['kʌmftəbl] *adj* **1.** [chair, shoes, bed, room] confortable ▪ [temperature] agréable ▪ *fig* [lead, win] confortable **2.** [person] à l'aise ▪ **are you ~?** êtes-vous bien installé? ▪ **make yourself ~** [sit down] installez-vous confortablement ; [feel at ease] mettez-vous à l'aise, faites comme chez vous ▪ **I'm not very ~ about** *OR* **I don't feel ~ with the idea** l'idée m'inquiète un peu ▪ [after illness, operation, accident] : **to be ~** ne pas souffrir **3.** [financially secure] aisé, riche ▪ [easy - job] tranquille ▪ **he makes a ~ living** il gagne bien sa vie **4.** [ample] : **that leaves us a ~ margin** ça nous laisse une marge confortable.

comfortably ['kʌmftəblɪ] *adv* **1.** [in a relaxed position - sit, sleep] confortablement, agréablement **2.** [in financial comfort] à l'aise ▪ **to be ~ off** être à l'aise **3.** [easily] facilement, à l'aise ▪ **we can fit five people in the car ~** la voiture contient bien cinq personnes, on tient à l'aise à cinq dans la voiture ▪ **we should manage it ~ in two hours** deux heures suffiront largement.

comforter ['kʌmfətəʳ] *n* **1.** [person] consolateur *m*, - trice *f* **2.** *UK* [scarf] cache-nez *m* **3.** [for baby] tétine *f*, sucette *f* **4.** *US* [quilt] édredon *m*.

comforting ['kʌmfətɪŋ] <> *adj* [consoling - remark, thought] consolant, réconfortant, rassurant ▪ [encouraging] encourageant.
<> *n* [consolation] réconfort *m*, consolation *f* ▪ [encouragement] encouragement *m*.

comfort station *n US* toilettes *fpl* publiques *(sur le bord d'une route)*.

comfy ['kʌmfɪ] (*comp* **comfier**, *superl* **comfiest**) *adj inf* [chair] confortable ▪ **are you ~?** vous êtes bien installés?

comic ['kɒmɪk] <> *adj* comique, humoristique ▪ **~ relief** THEAT intervalle *m* comique ; *fig* moment *m* de détente (comique) ▪ **Comic Relief** *association caritative en Grande-Bretagne qui collecte des fonds en organisant chaque année un 'téléthon' et en vendant des petits nez rouges en plastique que les gens portent en signe de solidarité.*
<> *n* **1.** [entertainer] (acteur *m*) comique *m*, actrice *f* comique **2.** [magazine] BD *f*, bande dessinée *f*.
◆ **comics** *npl US* [in newspaper] bandes *fpl* dessinées.

comical ['kɒmɪkl] *adj* drôle, comique.

comically ['kɒmɪklɪ] *adv* drôlement, comiquement.

comic book *n* magazine *m* de bandes dessinées.

comic opera *n* opéra *m* comique.

comic strip *n* bande *f* dessinée.

coming ['kʌmɪŋ] <> *adj* **1.** [time, events] à venir, futur ▪ [in near future] prochain ▪ **this ~ Tuesday** mardi prochain ▪ **the ~ storm** l'orage qui approche **2.** *inf* [promising - person] d'avenir, qui promet.
<> *n* **1.** [gen] arrivée *f*, venue *f* ▶ **~ and going** va-et-vient *m* ▪ **~s and goings** allées *fpl* et venues **2.** RELIG avènement *m*.

coming of age *n* majorité *f*.

COMING OF AGE

À sa majorité (fixée à 18 ans), tout Britannique acquiert le droit de voter, de faire partie d'un jury, de boire de l'alcool dans les pubs. Il peut aussi se marier sans le consentement de ses parents.

coming out *n* entrée *f* dans le monde *(d'une jeune fille)*.

Comintern ['kɒmɪntɜ:n] (*abbrev of* **Communist International**) *pr n* Komintern *m*.

comma ['kɒmə] *n* GRAM & MUS virgule *f*.

command [kə'mɑ:nd] <> *n* **1.** [order] ordre *m* ▪ MIL ordre *m*, commandement *m* ▪ **they are at your ~** ils sont à vos ordres **2.** [authority] commandement *m* ▪ **who is in ~ here?** qui est-ce qui commande ici? ▪ **to be in ~ of sthg** avoir qqch sous ses ordres, être à la tête de qqch ▪ **he had/took ~ of the situation** il avait/a pris la situation en main ▪ **they are under her ~** ils sont sous ses ordres *OR* son commandement
3. [control, mastery] maîtrise *f* ▪ **he's in full ~ of his faculties** il est en pleine possession de ses moyens ▪ **she has a good ~ of two foreign languages** elle possède bien deux langues étrangères ▪ **her ~ of Spanish** sa maîtrise de l'espagnol ▪ **all the resources at my ~** toutes les ressources à ma disposition *OR* dont je dispose ▪ **I'm at your ~** je suis à votre disposition
4. MIL [group of officers] commandement *m* ▪ [troops] troupes *fpl* ▪ [area] région *f* militaire
5. COMPUT commande *f*.
<> *vt* **1.** [order] ordonner, commander ▪ **she ~ed that we leave immediately** elle nous a ordonné *OR* nous a donné l'ordre de partir immédiatement ▪ **the general ~ed his men to attack** le général a donné l'ordre à ses hommes d'attaquer
2. [have control over - army] commander ; [- emotions] maîtriser, dominer
3. [receive as due] commander, imposer ▪ **to ~ respect** inspirer le respect, en imposer ▪ **to ~ the attention of one's audience** tenir son public en haleine ▪ **the translator ~s a high fee** les services du traducteur valent cher ▪ **this painting will ~ a high price** ce tableau se vendra à un prix élevé
4. [have use of] disposer de ▪ **all the resources that the country can ~** toutes les ressources dont le pays peut disposer
5. [subj: building, statue - overlook] : **to ~ a view of** avoir vue sur, donner sur.
<> *vi* **1.** [order] commander, donner des ordres
2. [be in control] commander ▪ MIL commander, avoir le commandement.

commandant [ˌkɒmən'dænt] *n* commandant *m*.

command economy *n* économie *f* planifiée.

commandeer [ˌkɒmən'dɪəʳ] *vt* [officially] réquisitionner ▪ [usurp] accaparer.

commander [kə'mɑ:ndəʳ] *n* **1.** [person in charge] chef *m* ▪ MIL commandant *m*, -e *f* ▪ NAUT capitaine *mf* de frégate **2.** *UK* [of police] ≃ commissaire *m* divisionnaire, ≃ divisionnaire *m*.

commander-in-chief *n* commandant *m* en chef, généralissime *m*.

commanding [kə'mɑ:ndɪŋ] *adj* **1.** [in command] qui commande **2.** [overlooking - view] élevé **3.** [tone, voice] impérieux, de commandement ▪ [look] impérieux ▪ [air] imposant.

commanding officer *n* commandant *m*.

commandment [kə'mɑ:ndmənt] *n* commandement *m* ▪ **the Ten Commandments** les dix commandements, le décalogue *fml*.

commando [kə'mɑ:ndəʊ] <> *n* (*pl* **commandos** *OR pl* **commandoes**) commando *m*.
<> *comp* [raid, unit] de commando.

command performance *n représentation (d'un spectacle) à la requête d'un chef d'État.*

command post *n* poste *m* de commandement.

commemorate [kə'meməreɪt] *vt* commémorer.

commemoration [kəˌmemə'reɪʃn] *n* commémoration *f* ▪ RELIG commémoraison *f* ▪ **in ~ of** en commémoration de.

commemorative [kə'memərətɪv] *adj* commémoratif.

commence [kə'mens] *fml* <> *vi* commencer.
<> *vt* commencer ▪ **she ~d speaking at 2 p.m.** elle a commencé à parler à 2 h de l'après-midi.

commencement [kə'mensmənt] *n* **1.** *fml* [beginning] commencement *m*, début *m* ▪ LAW [of law] date *f* d'entrée en vigueur **2.** *US* UNIV remise *f* des diplômes.

Commencement Day *n jour de la remise des diplômes dans une université américaine.*

commend [kə'mend] *vt* **1.** [recommend] recommander, conseiller ▪ **the report has little to ~ it** il n'y a pas grand-chose d'intéressant dans ce rapport **2.** [praise] louer, faire l'éloge de ▪ **to ~ sb for bravery** louer qqn pour sa bravoure ▪ **you are to be ~ed for your hard work** on doit vous féliciter pour votre dur labeur **3.** [entrust] confier ▪ **to ~ sthg to sb** confier qqch à qqn, remettre qqch aux bons soins de qqn ▪ **we ~ our souls to God** RELIG nous recommandons notre âme à Dieu.

commendable [kə'mendəbl] *adj* louable.

commendably [kə'mendəblɪ] *adv* de façon louable ▪ **his speech was ~ brief** son discours avait le mérite de la brièveté.

commendation [,kɒmen'deɪʃn] *n* **1.** [praise] éloge *f*, louange *f* **2.** [recommendation] recommendation *f* **3.** [award for bravery] décoration *f*.

commensurable [kə'menʃərəbl] *adj fml* commensurable ▪ **~ with** *OR* **to sthg** commensurable avec qqch.

commensurate [kə'menʃərət] *adj fml* **1.** [of equal measure] de même mesure, commensurable ▪ **the side is ~ with the diagonal** MATHS on peut mesurer le côté en fonction de la diagonale **2.** [proportionate] proportionné ▪ **~ with** *OR* **to sthg** proportionné à qqch ▪ **the salary will be ~ with your experience** le salaire sera en fonction de votre expérience.

comment ['kɒment] <> *n* **1.** [remark] commentaire *m*, observation *f* ▪ **she let it pass without ~** elle n'a pas relevé ▪ **it's a ~ on our society** *fig* c'est une réflexion sur notre société ▪ **no ~!** je n'ai rien à dire! ▪ **(it's a) fair ~** c'est juste **2.** *(U)* [gossip, criticism] : **the decision provoked much ~** la décision a suscité de nombreux commentaires **3.** [note] commentaire *m*, annotation *f* ▪ [critical] critique *f* ▪ **teacher's ~s** SCH appréciations *fpl* du professeur.
<> *vi* **1.** [remark] faire une remarque *OR* des remarques ▪ **she ~ed on his age** elle a fait des remarques *OR* commentaires sur son âge ▪ **he ~ed that...** il a fait la remarque que... **2.** [give opinion] : **~ on the text** commentez le texte, faites le commentaire du texte.

commentary ['kɒməntrɪ] (*pl* **commentaries**) *n* **1.** [remarks] commentaire *m*, observations *fpl* **2.** RADIO & TV commentaire *m*.

commentary box *n* tribune *f* des journalistes.

commentate ['kɒmənteɪt] <> *vt* commenter.
<> *vi* faire un reportage.

commentator ['kɒmənteɪtə^r] *n* **1.** RADIO & TV reporter *m* **2.** [analyst] commentateur *m*, - trice *f*.

commerce ['kɒmɜːs] *n (U)* [trade] commerce *m*, affaires *fpl* ▪ **Secretary/Department of Commerce** *US* ministre *m* /ministère *m* du Commerce.

commercial [kə'mɜːʃl] <> *adj* **1.** [economic] commercial ▪ **~ district** quartier *m* commerçant ▪ **~ law** droit *m* commercial **2.** [profitable] commercial, marchand ▪ **~ value** valeur *f* marchande **3.** *pej* [profit-seeking - record, book, pop group] commercial **4.** TV & RADIO commercial.
<> *n* publicité *f*, spot *m* publicitaire.

commercial art *n* graphisme *m*.

commercial bank *n* banque *f* commerciale.

commercial break *n* page *f* de publicité.

commercial college *n* école *f* de commerce.

commercialism [kə'mɜːʃəlɪzm] *n* **1.** [practice of business] (pratique *f* du) commerce *m*, (pratique des) affaires *fpl* **2.** *pej* [profit-seeking] mercantilisme *m*, esprit *m* commercial ▪ [on large scale] affairisme *m*.

commercialization [kə,mɜːʃəlaɪ'zeɪʃn] *n* commercialisation *f*.

commercialize, *UK* **ise** [kə'mɜːʃəlaɪz] *vt* commercialiser.

commercially [kə'mɜːʃəlɪ] *adv* commercialement.

commercial traveller *n dated* voyageur *m* *OR* représentant *m* de commerce, VRP *m*.

commercial vehicle *n* véhicule *m* utilitaire.

commie ['kɒmɪ] *inf pej* <> *adj* coco.
<> *n* coco *mf*.

commiserate [kə'mɪzəreɪt] *vi* : **to ~ with sb** [feel sympathy] éprouver de la compassion pour qqn ; [show sympathy] témoigner de la sympathie à qqn ▪ **we ~d with him on his misfortune** nous avons compati à sa malchance.

commiseration [kə,mɪzə'reɪʃn] *n* commisération *f*.

commissar ['kɒmɪsɑː^r] *n* commissaire *m* (du peuple).

commissariat [,kɒmɪ'seərɪət] *n* **1.** POL commissariat *m* **2.** MIL [department] intendance *f* ▪ [food supply] ravitaillement *m*.

commissary ['kɒmɪsərɪ] (*pl* **commissaries**) *n* **1.** *US* MIL [shop] intendance *f* ▪ [officer] intendant *m* **2.** *US* CIN [cafeteria] restaurant *m* (du studio) **3.** RELIG délégué *m (d'un évêque)*.

commission [kə'mɪʃn] <> *n* **1.** [authority for special job] commission *f*, mission *f*, ordres *mpl*, instructions *fpl* ▪ ART commande *f* ▪ **work done on ~** travail fait sur commande **2.** [delegation of authority] délégation *f* de pouvoir *OR* d'autorité, mandat *m* ▪ [formal warrant] mandat *m*, pouvoir *m* ▪ MIL brevet *m* ▪ **to resign one's ~** démissionner **3.** [committee] commission *f*, comité *m* ▪ **~ of inquiry, fact-finding ~** commission d'enquête ▪ **Royal Commission** *UK* POL commission extra parlementaire **4.** COMM [fee] commission *f*, courtage *m* ▪ **to work on a ~ basis** travailler à la commission ▪ **I get (a) 5% ~** je reçois une commission de 5% **5.** LAW [of crime] perpétration *f* **6.** NAUT [of ship] armement *m* ▪ **to put a ship into ~** armer un navire.
<> *vt* **1.** [work of art] commander ▪ [artist] passer commande à ▪ **we ~ed the architect to design a new house** nous avons engagé un architecte pour faire les plans d'une nouvelle maison **2.** [grant authority to] donner pouvoir *OR* mission à, déléguer, charger ▪ **to ~ sb to do sthg** charger qqn de faire qqch **3.** MIL [make officer] nommer à un commandement ▪ **he was ~ed general** il a été promu au grade de *OR* nommé général **4.** [make operative] mettre en service ▪ NAUT [ship] mettre en service, armer.
◆ **in commission** *adj phr* [gen] en service ▪ NAUT [ship] en armement, en service.
◆ **out of commission** *adj phr* [gen] hors service ▪ [car] en panne ▪ NAUT [not working] hors service ▪ [in reserve] en réserve.

commissionaire [kə,mɪʃə'neə^r] *n UK* portier *m (d'un hôtel, etc)*.

commissioned officer [kə'mɪʃənd-] *n* officier *m*.

commissioner [kə'mɪʃnə^r] *n* **1.** [member of commission] membre *m* d'une commission, commissaire *mf* **2.** [of police] *UK* ≃ préfet *m* de police ▪ *US* ≃ (commissaire *mf*) divisionnaire *m* ▪ [of government department] haut fonctionnaire **3.** *US* SCH & UNIV : **~ of education** ≃ recteur *m*, ≃ doyen *m* **4.** LAW : **~ for oaths** *officier ayant qualité pour recevoir les déclarations sous serment.*

Commission for Racial Equality *pr n organisme britannique qui intervient auprès des institutions et des entreprises pour enrayer la discrimination raciale.*

commit [kə'mɪt] (*pret & pp* **committed**, *cont* **committing**) *vt* **1.** [crime] commettre, perpétrer ▪ [mistake] faire, commettre ▪ **to ~ suicide** se suicider **2.** [entrust - thing] confier, remettre ; [- person] confier ▪ **to ~ sthg to sb's care** confier qqch aux soins de qqn *OR* à la garde de qqn ▪ **he was committed to a mental hospital** il a été interné ▪ **they committed her to prison** ils l'ont incarcérée ▪ **to ~ sthg to memory** apprendre qqch par cœur ▪ **to ~ sthg to paper** coucher *OR* consigner qqch par écrit ➔ **committing magistrate** *US* LAW juge *m* d'instruction **3.** [promise] engager ▪ **to ~ o.s. to sthg/to do sthg** s'engager à qqch/à faire qqch ▪ **he refused to ~ himself** il s'est tenu sur la réserve, il a refusé de prendre parti OR de s'engager ▪ **to ~ troops (to a region)** MIL engager des troupes (dans une région) **4.** [legislative bill] renvoyer en commission.

commitment [kə'mɪtmənt] *n* **1.** [promise, loyalty] engagement *m* ▪ **to make a ~** [emotionally, intellectually] s'engager **2.** [obligation] obligations *fpl*, responsabilités *fpl* ▪ COMM & FIN engagement *m* financier ▪ **with no ~** sans obligation d'achat **3.** [of legislative bill] renvoi *m* en commission.

committal [kə'mɪtl] *n* **1.** [sending - gen] remise *f* ; [- to prison] incarcération *f*, emprisonnement *m* ; [- to mental hospital] internement *m* ; [- to grave] mise *f* en terre **2.** LAW : **~ proceedings, ~ for trial** ≃ mise *f* en accusation **3.** [of crime] perpétration *f*.

committed [kə'mɪtɪd] *adj* [writer, artist] engagé ▪ **a ~ Socialist/Christian** un socialiste/chrétien convaincu.

committee [kə'mɪtɪ] <> *n* commission *f*, comité *m* ▪ **to be OR to sit on a ~** faire partie d'une commission OR d'un comité ▪ [in government] commission *f* ▪ **Committee of Ways and Means** commission *f* du budget.
<> *comp* [meeting] de commission OR comité ▪ [member] d'une commission, d'un comité.

commode [kə'məʊd] *n* **1.** [chest of drawers] commode *f* **2.** [for chamber pot] chaise *f* percée.

commodious [kə'məʊdjəs] *adj fml* spacieux, vaste.

commodity [kə'mɒdətɪ] (*pl* **commodities**) *n* **1.** [product] marchandise *f* ▪ [consumer goods] produit *m*, article *m* ▪ [food] denrée *f* **2.** ECON [raw material] produit *m* de base, matière *f* première ▪ **the ~ OR commodities market** le marché des matières premières.

commodore ['kɒmədɔːr] *n* **1.** MIL contre-amiral *m* **2.** NAUT [of merchant ships] commodore *m* ▪ [of shipping line] doyen *m* ▪ [of yacht club] président *m*.

common ['kɒmən] <> *adj* **1.** [ordinary] commun, ordinaire ▪ [plant] commun ▪ **it's quite ~** c'est courant OR tout à fait banal ▪ **it's a ~ experience** cela arrive à beaucoup de gens OR à tout le monde ▪ **a ~ expression** une expression courante ▪ **a ~ occurrence** une chose fréquente OR qui arrive souvent ▪ **the ~ man** l'homme du peuple ▪ **the ~ parts** [in building] les parties communes ▪ **the ~ people** le peuple, les gens du commun ▪ **~ salt** sel *m* (ordinaire) ▪ **a ~ soldier** un simple soldat ▪ **it's only ~ courtesy to reply** la politesse la plus élémentaire veut qu'on réponde ➋ **to have the ~ touch** UK savoir parler aux gens simples
2. [shared, public] commun ▪ **by ~ consent** d'un commun accord ▪ **the ~ good** le bien public ➋ **~ land** terrain *m* communal OR banal ▪ **~ ground** [in interests] intérêt *m* commun ; [for discussion] terrain *m* d'entente
3. [widespread] général, universel ▪ **in ~ use** d'usage courant ▪ **it's ~ knowledge that...** tout le monde sait que..., il est de notoriété publique que... ▪ **it's ~ practice to thank your host** il est d'usage de remercier son hôte
4. *pej* [vulgar] commun, vulgaire
5. GRAM [gender] non marqué
6. MUS : **~ time OR measure** mesure *f* à quatre temps.
<> *n* [land] terrain *m* communal.
◆ **Commons** *npl* UK & *Canada* POL : **the Commons** les Communes *fpl*.
◆ **in common** *adv phr* en commun ▪ **to have sthg in ~ with sb** avoir qqch en commun avec qqn ▪ **we have nothing in ~** nous n'avons rien en commun ▪ **they have certain ideas in ~** ils partagent certaines idées.

common cold *n* rhume *m*.

common denominator *n* MATHS & *fig* dénominateur *m* commun.

Common Entrance *n* UK SCOL *examen de fin d'études primaires permettant d'entrer dans une "public school"*.

commoner ['kɒmənər] *n* [not noble] roturier *m*, - ère *f*.

common factor *n* facteur *m* commun.

common fraction *n* US fraction *f* ordinaire.

common law *n* droit *m* coutumier, common law *f*.

◆ **common-law** *adj* : **common-law wife** concubine *f* (reconnue juridiquement) ▪ **common-law marriage** mariage *m* de droit coutumier.

COMMON LAW

Ensemble des règles qui constituent la base des systèmes juridiques anglais, gallois, américain et d'autres pays du Commonwealth. À l'inverse des systèmes issus du droit romain, qui s'appuient sur des textes écrits, ces règles ne sont pas écrites et sont établies par la jurisprudence.

commonly ['kɒmənlɪ] *adv* **1.** [usually] généralement, communément ▪ **what is ~ known as...** ce que l'on appelle dans le langage courant... **2.** *pej* [vulgarly] vulgairement.

Common Market *n* : **the ~** le Marché commun.

commonness ['kɒmənnɪs] *n* **1.** [usualness] caractère *m* commun OR ordinaire **2.** [frequency] fréquence *f* **3.** [universality] généralité *f*, universalité *f* **4.** *pej* [vulgarness] vulgarité *f*.

common noun *n* nom *m* commun.

common-or-garden *adj* UK *inf* **the ~ variety** le modèle standard OR ordinaire.

commonplace ['kɒmənpleɪs] <> *adj* banal, ordinaire ▪ **compact discs have become ~** les disques compacts sont devenus courants OR sont maintenant monnaie courante.
<> *n* [thing] banalité *f* ▪ [saying] lieu *m* commun, platitude *f*.

common room *n* UK SCH & UNIV [for students] salle *f* commune ▪ [for staff] salle *f* des professeurs.

commonsense ['kɒmən,sens], **commonsensical** [,kɒmən'sensɪkl] *adj* [attitude, approach, decision] sensé, plein de bon sens.

common sense *n* bon sens *m*, sens *m* commun.

commonwealth ['kɒmənwelθ] *n* **1.** [country] pays *m* ▪ [state] État *m* ▪ [republic] république *f* **2.** [body politic] corps *m* politique.
◆ **Commonwealth** <> *n* **1.** POL : **the (British) Commonwealth (of Nations)** le Commonwealth **2.** HIST : **the Commonwealth** *période de l'histoire britannique de 1649 (mort de Charles Ier) à 1660 (rétablissement de la monarchie)*.
<> *comp* [games, nations] du Commonwealth.

Commonwealth of Independent States *pr n* : **the ~** la Communauté des États indépendants.

commotion [kə'məʊʃn] *n* **1.** [noise] brouhaha *m* ▪ **what's all the ~ (about)?** qu'est-ce que c'est que ce brouhaha OR vacarme? **2.** [disturbance] agitation *f* ▪ **what a ~!** quel cirque! **3.** [civil unrest] insurrection *f*, troubles *mpl*.

comms package [kɒmz-] *n* COMPUT logiciel *m* de communication.

communal ['kɒmjʊnl] *adj* **1.** [shared] commun **2.** [of community] communautaire, collectif.

communally ['kɒmjʊnəlɪ] *adv* collectivement, en commun.

commune <> *n* ['kɒmjuːn] **1.** [group of people] communauté *f* ▪ **to live in a ~** vivre en communauté **2.** ADMIN [district] commune *f*.
<> *vi* [kə'mjuːn] **1.** [communicate] communier ▪ **to ~ with nature** communier avec la nature **2.** RELIG communier.

communicable [kə'mjuːnɪkəbl] *adj* communicable ▪ MED [disease] contagieux, transmissible.

communicant [kə'mjuːnɪkənt] <> *n* **1.** RELIG communiant *m*, - e *f* **2.** [informant] informateur *m*, - trice *f*.
<> *adj* **1.** [communicating] qui communique, communicant **2.** RELIG pratiquant.

communicate [kə'mjuːnɪkeɪt] <> *vi* **1.** [be in touch] communiquer ▪ [contact] prendre contact, se mettre en contact ▪ **they ~ with each other by phone** ils communiquent par téléphone ▪ **I find it difficult to ~ (with others)** j'ai du mal à entrer en relation avec les autres **2.** [rooms - connect] communiquer **3.** RELIG communier, recevoir la communion.

◇ *vt* **1.** [impart - news] communiquer, transmettre ; [- feelings] communiquer, faire partager ▪ **she ~d the news to them** elle leur a fait part de la nouvelle **2.** [disease] transmettre.

communicating [kə'mju:nɪkeɪtɪŋ] *adj* [room] communicant ▪ **~ door** porte *f* de communication.

communication [kə,mju:nɪ'keɪʃn] *n* **1.** [contact] communication *f* ▪ **are you in ~ with her?** êtes-vous en contact *OR* en relation avec elle? ▪ **we broke off all ~ with him** nous avons rompu tout contact avec lui ▪ **to be in radio ~ with sb** communiquer avec qqn par radio, être en communication radio avec qqn ▮ [of thoughts, feelings] communication *f* ▪ **to be good at ~, to have good ~ skills** avoir des talents de communicateur, être un bon communicateur **2.** [message] communication *f*, message *m*.
◆ **communications** *npl* [technology] communications *fpl* ▪ [roads, telegraph lines etc] communications *fpl* ▪ MIL liaison *f*, communications *fpl*.

communication cord *n UK* sonnette *f* d'alarme *(dans les trains)*.

communications satellite *n* satellite *m* de télécommunication.

communicative [kə'mju:nɪkətɪv] *adj* **1.** [talkative] communicatif, expansif **2.** [ability, difficulty] de communication.

communicator [kə'mju:nɪkeɪtə^r] *n personne douée pour la communication* ▪ **she's a good/bad ~** elle est douée/n'est pas douée pour la communication.

communion [kə'mju:njən] *n* **1.** [sharing] communion *f* ▪ **a ~ of interests** une communauté d'intérêts **2.** RELIG [group] communion *f* ▪ [denomination] confession *f*.
◆ **Communion** *n* RELIG [sacrament] communion *f* ▪ **to give Communion** donner la communion ▪ **to take** *OR* **to receive Communion** recevoir la communion.

communiqué [kə'mju:nɪkeɪ] *n* communiqué *m*.

communism, Communism ['kɒmjʊnɪzm] *n* communisme *m*.

communist, Communist ['kɒmjʊnɪst] ◇ *n* communiste *mf*.
◇ *adj* communiste ▪ **'The Communist Manifesto'** *Marx, Engels* 'le Manifeste du parti communiste'.

community [kə'mju:nətɪ] (*pl* **communities**) *n* **1.** [group of people, animals] communauté *f*, groupement *m* ▪ RELIG communauté *f* ▪ [locality] communauté *f* ▪ **the business ~** le monde des affaires ▪ **the international ~** la communauté internationale ▶ **~ leader** *personne qui joue un rôle actif dans la vie d'une communauté* ▪ **~ policing** ≃ îlotage *m* ▪ **~ relations** relations *fpl* publiques ▪ **~ spirit** esprit *m* de groupe **2.** [sharing] propriété *f* collective ▪ LAW communauté *f* ▪ **~ of goods/interests** communauté de biens/d'intérêts.
◆ **Community** *n* : **the (European) Community** la Communauté (européenne).

community association *n en Grande-Bretagne, association socioculturelle locale*.

community care *n système britannique d'assistance sociale au niveau local*.

community centre *n* foyer *m* municipal, centre *m* social.

community charge *fml* = **poll tax**.

community chest *n US* fonds *m* commun *(à des fins sociales)*.

community college *n US* centre *m* universitaire (de premier cycle).

community home *n UK* **1.** [for deprived children] assistance *f* publique **2.** [for young offenders] centre *m* d'éducation surveillée.

community school *n UK école servant de maison de la culture*.

community service *n* ≃ travail *m* d'intérêt général.

commutable [kə'mju:təbl] *adj* [exchangeable] interchangeable, permutable ▪ LAW commuable ▪ **a death sentence ~ to life imprisonment** une peine capitale commuable en emprisonnement à perpétuité.

commutation ticket *n US* carte *f* d'abonnement.

commutator ['kɒmju:teɪtə^r] *n* commutateur *m*.

commute [kə'mju:t] ◇ *vi* faire un trajet régulier, faire la navette ▪ **I ~ from the suburbs** je viens tous les jours de banlieue.
◇ *vt* **1.** [exchange] substituer, échanger **2.** [convert] convertir ▪ **to ~ an annuity into a lump sum** FIN racheter une rente en un seul versement **3.** LAW [sentence] commuer ▪ **a sentence ~d to life imprisonment** une peine commuée en emprisonnement à vie.

commuter [kə'mju:tə^r] ◇ *n* banlieusard *m*, - e *f (qui fait un trajet journalier pour se rendre au travail)* ▪ RAIL abonné *m*, - e *f*.
◇ *comp* [line, train] de banlieue ▪ **the ~ belt** *UK* la grande banlieue.

commuting [kə'mju:tɪŋ] *n (U)* trajets *mpl* réguliers, migrations *fpl* quotidiennes *(entre le domicile, généralement en banlieue, et le lieu de travail)*.

Como ['kəʊməʊ] *pr n* Côme ▪ **Lake ~** le lac de Côme.

Comoran ['kɒmərən], **Comorian** [kə'mɒrjən] ◇ *n* Comorien *m*, - enne *f*.
◇ *adj* comorien.

Comoro Islands ['kɒmərəʊ-] *npl* : **the ~** les îles Comores ▪ **in the ~** aux îles Comores.

Comoros [kə'mɔ:rəs] *pl prn* Comores *fpl* ▪ **the ~** les Comores.

compact ◇ *adj* [kəm'pækt] **1.** [small] compact, petit ▪ [dense] dense, serré ▪ **the gadget is ~ and easy to use** ce gadget ne prend pas de place et est facile à utiliser **2.** [concise] concis, condensé.
◇ *vt* [kəm'pækt] [compress] compacter, tasser.
◇ *n* ['kɒmpækt] **1.** [for powder] poudrier *m* **2.** *US* = **compact car 3.** [agreement] convention *f*, contrat *m* ▪ [informal] accord *m*, entente *f*.

compact camera [,kɒmpækt-] *n* (appareil photo *m*) compact *m*.

compact car *n US* (voiture *f*) compacte *f*, petite voiture *f*.

compact disc [,kɒmpækt-] ◇ *n* (disque *m*) compact *m*, CD *m*.
◇ *comp* : **~ player** platine *f* CD.

compactly [kəm'pæktlɪ] *adv* **1.** [made] de manière compacte **2.** [concisely] de manière concise.

companion [kəm'pænjən] *n* **1.** [friend] compagnon *m*, compagne *f* ▪ [employee] dame *f* de compagnie ▪ **a travelling ~** un compagnon de voyage ▪ **~s in arms/distress** compagnons d'armes/d'infortune **2.** [one of pair] pendant *m* ▪ **the ~ volume** le volume qui va de pair **3.** [handbook] manuel *m* **4.** [in titles] compagnon *m* **5.** NAUT capot *m* (d'escalier).

companionable [kəm'pænjənəbl] *adj* [person] sociable, d'une compagnie agréable.

companionship [kəm'pænjənʃɪp] *n (U)* [fellowship] compagnie *f* ▪ [friendship] amitié *f*, camaraderie *f*.

companionway [kəm'pænjənweɪ] *n* NAUT escalier *m* de descente ▪ [on smaller boat] montée *f*, descente *f*.

company ['kʌmpənɪ] ◇ *n* (*pl* **companies**) **1.** [companionship] compagnie *f* ▪ **we enjoy one another's ~** nous aimons être ensemble ▪ **she's good ~** elle est d'agréable compagnie ▪ **to keep sb ~** tenir compagnie à qqn ▪ **in ~ with others** en compagnie d'autres ▪ **here's where we part ~** *liter* voilà où nos chemins se séparent ; *fig* là, je ne suis plus d'accord avec vous **2.** [companions] compagnie *f*, fréquentation *f* ▪ **she has got into** *OR* **she's keeping bad ~** elle a de mauvaises fréquentations ▪ **to be in good ~** être en bonne compagnie ▪ **if I'm wrong, I'm in good ~** *fig* si j'ai tort, je ne suis pas le seul ▶ **a man is known by the ~ he keeps** *prov* dis-moi qui tu fréquentes, je te dirai qui tu es *prov*

3. *(U)* [guests] invités *mpl*, compagnie *f* ■ **are you expecting ~?** attendez-vous de la visite?
4. [firm] société *f*, compagnie *f* ■ **Jones & Company** Jones et Compagnie
5. [group of people] compagnie *f*, assemblée *f* ■ [of actors] troupe *f*, compagnie *f* ■ MIL compagnie *f* ■ NAUT [crew] équipage *m*.
◇ *comp* [policy] d'entreprise ■ **he's a ~ man** c'est un employé dévoué ■ **~ car** voiture *f* de fonction.
◆ **Company** *pr n US inf* **the Company** la CIA.

company director *n* directeur *m*, - trice *f*.

company secretary *n* secrétaire *m* général, secrétaire *f* générale *(d'une entreprise)*.

comparable ['kɒmprəbl] *adj* comparable ■ **to be ~ to sthg** être comparable à qqch ■ **the salaries aren't at all ~** il n'y a pas de comparaison possible entre les salaires.

comparative [kəm'pærətɪv] ◇ *adj* **1.** [relative] relatif ■ **she's a ~ stranger to me** je la connais relativement peu **2.** [study] comparatif ■ [field of study] comparé ■ **~ linguistics** linguistique *f* comparée **3.** GRAM comparatif.
◇ *n* comparatif *m* ■ **in the ~** au comparatif.

comparatively [kəm'pærətɪvlɪ] *adv* **1.** [quite] relativement **2.** [study] comparativement.

compare [kəm'peəʳ] ◇ *vt* **1.** [contrast] comparer, mettre en comparaison ■ **let's ~ Fitzgerald with Hemingway** comparons Fitzgerald à *OR* avec Hemingway ■ **~d with** *OR* **to sthg** en comparaison de *OR* par comparaison avec qqch ■ **~d with the others she's brilliant** elle est brillante par rapport aux autres ➊ **to ~ notes** échanger ses impressions **2.** [liken] comparer, assimiler ■ **to ~ sthg to sthg** comparer qqch à qqch ■ **it's impossible to ~ the two systems** il n'y a pas de comparaison possible entre les deux systèmes **3.** GRAM former les degrés de comparaison de.
◇ *vi* être comparable à ■ **to ~ favourably (with sthg)** soutenir la comparaison (avec qqch) ■ **how do the two candidates ~?** quelles sont les qualités respectives des deux candidats? ■ **how do the brands ~ in (terms of) price?** les marques sont-elles comparables du point de vue prix? ■ **her cooking doesn't** *OR* **can't ~ with yours** il n'y a aucune comparaison entre sa cuisine et la tienne.
◇ *n lit*: **beauty beyond ~** beauté sans pareille.

comparison [kəm'pærɪsn] *n* **1.** [gen] comparaison *f* ■ **there's no ~** il n'y a aucune comparaison (possible) ■ **to draw** *OR* **to make a ~ between sthg and sthg** faire la comparaison de qqch avec qqch *OR* entre qqch et qqch ■ **this book stands** *OR* **bears ~ with the classics** ce livre soutient la comparaison avec les classiques **2.** GRAM comparaison *f*.
◆ **by comparison** *adv phr* par comparaison.
◆ **in comparison with** *prep phr* en comparaison de, par rapport à.
Voir module d'usage

compartment [kəm'pɑ:tmənt] *n* compartiment *m*, subdivision *f* ■ NAUT & RAIL compartiment *m*.

compartmentalize, UK ise [,kɒmpɑ:t'mentəlaɪz] *vt* compartimenter.

compass ['kʌmpəs] ◇ *n* **1.** [for direction] boussole *f* ■ NAUT compas *m* **2.** GEOM compas *m* **3.** [limits] étendue *f* ■ [range] portée *f* ■ MUS étendue *f*, portée *f* ■ **that does not lie within the ~ of this committee** ce n'est pas du ressort de ce comité.
◇ *comp* [bearing, error] du compas ■ **to take a ~ bearing** prendre un relèvement au compas.
◇ *vt* [go round] faire le tour de ■ [surround] encercler, entourer.
◆ **compasses** *npl* GEOM : **(a pair of) ~es** un compas.

compassion [kəm'pæʃn] *n* compassion *f*.

compassionate [kəm'pæʃənət] *adj* compatissant ■ **on ~ grounds** pour des raisons personnelles *OR* familiales.

compassionate leave *n* [gen - MIL] permission *f* exceptionnelle *(pour raisons personnelles)*.

compass point *n* aire *f* de vent.

compass saw *n* scie *f* à guichet.

compass window *n* fenêtre *f* en saillie ronde.

compatibility [kəm,pætə'bɪlətɪ] *n* compatibilité *f*.

compatible [kəm'pætəbl] *adj* compatible.

compatriot [kəm'pætrɪət] *n* compatriote *mf*.

compel [kəm'pel] (*pret & pp* **compelled**, *cont* **compelling**) *vt* **1.** [force] contraindre, obliger ■ **to ~ sb to do sthg** contraindre *OR* forcer qqn à faire qqch **2.** [demand] imposer, forcer ■ **the sort of woman who ~s admiration** le genre de femme qu'on ne peut s'empêcher d'admirer *OR* qui force l'admiration.

compelling [kəm'pelɪŋ] *adj* **1.** [reason, desire] convaincant, irrésistible **2.** [book, story] envoûtant.

compendious [kəm'pendɪəs] *adj fml* concis.

compendium [kəm'pendɪəm] (*pl* **compendiums** *OR pl* **compendia** [-dɪə]) *n* **1.** [summary] abrégé *m*, précis *m* **2.** UK [collection] collection *f* ■ **a ~ of games** une boîte de jeux.

compensate ['kɒmpenseɪt] ◇ *vt* **1.** [make amends to - person] dédommager, indemniser ■ **to ~ sb for sthg** [for loss] dédommager qqn de qqch ; [for injury] dédommager qqn pour qqch **2.** [offset] compenser, contrebalancer ■ TECH compenser, neutraliser.

COMPARISONS

Ils sont aussi paresseux l'un que l'autre. They're both as lazy as each other.

Ils en ont eu autant que nous. They've had as much/as many as us.

C'est comme l'an dernier. It's like last year.

Elle est plus grande/bien plus grande/encore plus grande que toi. She's taller/much taller/even taller than you.

On a mis plus de temps que prévu. It's taken us longer than we thought.

C'est mieux que l'an dernier. It's better than last year.

Il est moins en forme que ses concurrents/que l'an dernier. He's not as fit as the other competitors/as last year.

Elle court moins vite que toi. She can't run as fast as you.

Il est loin d'être aussi rapide qu'elle. He's nowhere near as fast as she is.

C'est moins bien/C'est pire que l'an dernier. It's not as good as/It's worse than last year.

Par rapport à *OU* **Comparée à Rome, Venise est une petite ville.** Compared with Rome, Venice is quite small.

À côté de Paul, il est franchement lent. Compared with Paul, he's really quite slow.

À l'inverse *OU* **À la différence de son frère, il comprend la plaisanterie.** Unlike his brother, he has a good sense of humour.

Il adore l'opéra et la peinture tandis *OU* **alors qu'elle est plutôt sportive.** He loves opera and painting whereas she is more interested in sport.

Autant son dernier spectacle était ennuyeux, autant celui-ci m'a passionnée. I loved this show, whereas I found the last one boring.

<> *vi* **1.** [make up] être une *OR* servir de compensation, compenser ▪ **she ~s for her short stature by wearing high heels** elle porte des talons hauts pour compenser sa petite taille **2.** [with money] dédommager, indemniser.

compensation [ˌkɒmpen'seɪʃn] *n* **1.** [recompense] indemnité *f*, dédommagement *m* ▪ [payment] rémunération *f* ▪ **working for oneself has its ~s** travailler à son compte a ses avantages ▪ **in ~ for** en compensation de **2.** [adaptation] compensation *f* ▪ [in weight] contrepoids *m* ▪ TECH compensation *f*, neutralisation *f*.

compensatory [ˌkɒmpen'seɪtərɪ] *adj* compensateur ▪ **~ levy** ECON [in EEC] prélèvement *m* compensatoire.

compere ['kɒmpeəʳ] *UK* <> *n* animateur *m*, - trice *f*, présentateur *m*, - trice *f*.
<> *vi* & *vt* animer, présenter.

compete [kəm'piːt] *vi* **1.** [vie] rivaliser ▪ **to ~ with sb for sthg** rivaliser avec qqn pour qqch, disputer qqch à qqn ▪ **seven candidates are competing for the position** sept candidats se disputent le poste ▪ **her cooking can't ~ with yours** *fig* sa cuisine n'a rien de commun *OR* ne peut pas rivaliser avec la vôtre **2.** COMM faire concurrence ▪ **they ~ with foreign companies for contracts** ils sont en concurrence avec des entreprises étrangères pour obtenir des contrats ▪ **we have to ~ on an international level** nous devons être à la hauteur de la concurrence sur le plan international **3.** SPORT [take part] participer ▪ [contend] concourir ▪ **to ~ against sb for sthg** concourir *OR* être en compétition avec qqn pour qqch.

competence ['kɒmpɪtəns] *n* **1.** [ability] compétence *f*, aptitude *f*, capacité *f* ▪ LING compétence *f* ▪ **sb's ~ for** *OR* **in sthg** la compétence de qqn pour *OR* en qqch, l'aptitude de qqn à *OR* pour qqch ▪ **to have the ~ to do sthg** avoir les moyens *OR* la capacité de faire qqch **2.** LAW compétence *f* ▪ **to be within the ~ of the court** être de la compétence du tribunal.

competent ['kɒmpɪtənt] *adj* **1.** [capable] compétent, capable ▪ [qualified] qualifié ▪ **is she ~ to handle the accounts?** est-elle compétente *OR* qualifiée pour tenir la comptabilité? **2.** [sufficient] suffisant **3.** LAW [witness] habile ▪ [court] compétent ▪ [evidence] admissible, recevable.

competently ['kɒmpɪtəntlɪ] *adv* **1.** [capably] avec compétence **2.** [sufficiently] suffisamment.

competing [kəm'piːtɪŋ] *adj* en concurrence.

competition [ˌkɒmpɪ'tɪʃn] *n* **1.** [rivalry] compétition *f*, rivalité *f* ▪ **~ for the position is fierce** il y a beaucoup de concurrence pour le poste, on se dispute âprement le poste ▪ **to be in ~ with sb** être en compétition *OR* concurrence avec qqn ‖ COMM concurrence *f* **2.** [opposition] concurrence *f* ▪ **what's the ~ doing?** que fait la concurrence?, que font nos rivaux *OR* concurrents? **3.** [contest] concours *m* ▪ SPORT compétition *f* ▪ [race] course *f* ▪ **beauty/fishing ~** concours de beauté/de pêche ▪ **to enter a ~** se présenter à un concours **4.** BIOL concurrence *f*.

competitive [kəm'petətɪv] *adj* **1.** [involving competition] de compétition ▪ **~ examination** concours *m* **2.** [person] qui a l'esprit de compétition **3.** [product, price] concurrentiel, compétitif ▪ **~ bidding** appel *m* d'offres.

competitively [kəm'petətɪvlɪ] *adv* avec un esprit de compétition ▪ **~ priced goods** COMM produits au prix compétitif.

competitiveness [kəm'petətɪvnɪs] *n* compétitivité *f*.

competitor [kəm'petɪtəʳ] *n* [gen - COMM] & SPORT concurrent *m*, - e *f* ▪ [participant] participant *m*, - e *f*.

compilation [ˌkɒmpɪ'leɪʃn] *n* compilation *f*.

compile [kəm'paɪl] *vt* **1.** [gather - facts, material] compiler **2.** [compose - list] dresser ; [- dictionary] composer *(par compilation)* ▪ **~d from** établi d'après **3.** COMPUT compiler.

compiler [kəm'paɪləʳ] *n* **1.** [gen] compilateur *m*, - trice *f* **2.** [of dictionary] rédacteur *m*, - trice *f* **3.** COMPUT compilateur *m*.

complacence [kəm'pleɪsns], **complacency** [kəm'pleɪsnsɪ] *n* autosatisfaction *f*.

complacent [kəm'pleɪsnt] *adj* satisfait *OR* content de soi, suffisant.

complacently [kəm'pleɪsntlɪ] *adv* [act] d'un air suffisant, avec suffisance ▪ [speak] d'un ton suffisant, avec suffisance.

complain [kəm'pleɪn] <> *vi* **1.** [grumble] se plaindre ▪ **he ~ed of a headache** il s'est plaint d'un mal de tête ▪ **how's it going? - can't ~** *inf* comment ça va? – je n'ai pas à me plaindre *OR* ça peut aller **2.** [make formal protest] formuler une plainte *OR* une réclamation, se plaindre ▪ **to ~ to sb (about sthg)** se plaindre à *OR* auprès de qqn (au sujet de qqch).
<> *vt* se plaindre ▪ **she ~ed that he was always late** elle s'est plainte qu'il était toujours en retard.

complainant [kəm'pleɪnənt] *n* demandeur *m*, demanderesse *f*.

complaint [kəm'pleɪnt] *n* **1.** [protest] plainte *f*, récrimination *f* ▪ **to make** *OR* **lodge a ~** se plaindre ‖ COMM réclamation *f* ▪ LAW plainte *f* ▪ **to lodge a ~ against sb** porter plainte contre qqn **2.** [grievance] sujet *m* *OR* motif *m* de plainte, grief *m* ▪ **I have no ~** *OR* **no cause for ~** je n'ai aucune raison de me plaindre **3.** [illness] maladie *f*, affection *f* ▪ **she has a liver ~** elle souffre du foie.
Voir module d'usage

COMPLAINTS

J'ai une réclamation à faire au sujet du réveil que vous m'avez vendu. I have a complaint about the alarm clock you sold me.

Il y a un problème avec le chauffage, il ne marche plus du tout. There's a problem with the heating. It's not working.

Je ne suis pas très content/pas content du tout du service qui nous a été fourni. I am not very happy/not at all happy with the service we have received.

J'estime que le travail a été effectué de façon déplorable. I am not at all happy with the way in which the work was done.

La façon dont on nous a traités est inadmissible. The way we have been treated is quite unacceptable.

Je pense que vous devriez me rembourser/me le remplacer. I think you should give me my money back/replace it.

Je pense être en droit d'attendre un dédommagement. I think I am well within my rights to ask for compensation.

J'exige le remboursement intégral de l'appareil photo/de mes frais. I expect the cost of the camera/my expenses to be fully reimbursed.

Je voudrais voir le directeur, s'il vous plaît. I'd like to see the manager, please.

J'aimerais que ce problème soit résolu le plus vite possible. I would be grateful if you could deal with this problem as soon as possible.

J'espère que vous ferez le nécessaire pour régler ce problème. I trust you will see to it that this problem is dealt with.

Je compte sur vous pour régler ce problème. I am relying on you to sort this problem out.

complement <> *n* ['kɒmplɪmənt] **1.** [gen - MATHS] & MUS complément *m* ▪ **with a full ~** au grand complet **2.** GRAM [of verb] complément *m* ▪ [of subject] attribut *m* **3.** [ship's crew, staff] personnel *m*, effectif *m* (complet).
<> *vt* ['kɒmplɪ,ment] compléter, être le complément de.

complementary [,kɒmplɪ'mentərɪ] *adj* [gen - MATHS] complémentaire ▪ **the two pieces are ~** les deux morceaux se complètent.

complementary medicine *n* médecine *f* douce.

complete [kəm'pli:t] <> *adj* **1.** [entire] complet, total ▪ **Christmas wouldn't be ~ without the traditional dinner** Noël ne serait pas Noël sans le repas traditionnel ▪ **the ~ works of Shakespeare** les œuvres complètes de Shakespeare **2.** [finished] achevé, terminé **3.** [as intensifier] complet, absolu ▪ **if the job is not done to your ~ satisfaction** si vous n'êtes pas entièrement satisfait du travail effectué ▪ **he's a ~ fool** c'est un crétin fini *OR* un parfait imbécile ▪ **a ~ (and utter) failure** un échec total *OR* sur toute la ligne ▪ **the project was a ~ success** le projet a pleinement réussi.
<> *vt* **1.** [make whole] compléter ▪ **to ~ her happiness** pour combler son bonheur ▪ **to ~ an order** COMM exécuter une commande **2.** [finish] achever, finir **3.** [form] remplir.
◆ **complete with** *prep phr* avec, doté *OR* pourvu de ▪ **~ with instructions** comprenant des instructions.

completely [kəm'pli:tlɪ] *adv* complètement.

completeness [kəm'pli:tnɪs] *n* état *m* complet.

completion [kəm'pli:ʃn] *n* **1.** [of work] achèvement *m* ▪ **the bridge is due for ~ in January** le pont doit être fini en janvier ▪ **near ~** près d'être achevé **2.** LAW [of sale] exécution *f* ▪ **payment on ~ of contract** paiement à l'exécution du contrat.

complex ['kɒmpleks] <> *adj* [gen - GRAM] & MATHS complexe.
<> *n* **1.** [system] complexe *m*, ensemble *m* ▪ **housing ~** grand ensemble ▪ **shopping/industrial ~** complexe commercial/industriel **2.** PSYCHOL complexe *m* ▪ **she has a ~ about her weight** elle est complexée par son poids.

complexion [kəm'plekʃn] *n* **1.** [of face] teint *m* **2.** [aspect] aspect *m* ▪ **that puts a different ~ on things** voilà qui change la situation.

complexity [kəm'pleksətɪ] *n* complexité *f*.

compliance [kəm'plaɪəns] *n* **1.** [conformity] conformité *f* **2.** [agreement] acquiescement *m* ▪ [submission] complaisance *f* **3.** TECH [flexibility] élasticité *f*.
◆ **in compliance with** *prep phr* conformément à.

compliant [kəm'plaɪənt] *adj* [subj: person] accommodant, docile ▪ [subj: object] conforme.

complicate ['kɒmplɪkeɪt] *vt* compliquer, embrouiller ▪ **why ~ things?** pourquoi se compliquer la vie?

complicated ['kɒmplɪkeɪtɪd] *adj* [complex] compliqué, complexe ▪ [muddled] embrouillé ▪ **to become** *OR* **to get ~** se compliquer.

complication [,kɒmplɪ'keɪʃn] *n* [gen - MED] complication *f*.

complicity [kəm'plɪsətɪ] *n* complicité *f* ▪ **his ~ in the murder** sa complicité dans le meurtre.

compliment <> *n* ['kɒmplɪmənt] [praise] compliment *m* ▪ **to pay sb a ~** faire *OR* adresser un compliment à qqn ▪ **she returned the ~** *iron* elle lui a retourné le compliment.
<> *vt* ['kɒmplɪment] faire des compliments à, complimenter ▪ **to ~ sb on sthg** féliciter qqn de qqch, faire des compliments à qqn sur qqch.
◆ **compliments** *npl fml* [respects] compliments *mpl*, respects *mpl* ▪ **to convey** *OR* **present one's ~s to sb** présenter ses compliments *OR* hommages à qqn *fig* ▪ **give him my ~s** faites-lui mes compliments ▪ **'~s of the season'** 'meilleurs vœux' ▪ **'with compliments'** 'avec nos compliments' ▪ **with the ~s of Mr Smith** avec les hommages *OR* compliments de M. Smith.

complimentary [,kɒmplɪ'mentərɪ] *adj* **1.** [approving] flatteur ▪ **~ remarks** compliments *mpl*, félicitations *fpl* **2.** [given free] gratuit, gracieux ▪ **~ copy** exemplaire *m* offert à titre gracieux ▪ **~ ticket** billet *m* de faveur.

compliments slip *n* papillon *m* (joint à un envoi).

comply [kəm'plaɪ] (*pret & pp* **complied**) *vi* **1.** [obey] : **to ~ with the law** se soumettre à la loi ▪ **to ~ with the rules** observer *OR* respecter les règlements ▪ **I will ~ with your wishes** je me conformerai à vos désirs ▪ **she complied with our request** elle a accédé à notre demande **2.** [machinery] être conforme ▪ **cars must ~ with existing regulations** les voitures doivent être conformes aux normes en vigueur.

component [kəm'pəʊnənt] <> *n* [gen] élément *m* ▪ ELEC composant *m* ▪ AUT & TECH pièce *f*.
<> *adj* composant, constituant ▪ **~ parts** parties *fpl* constituantes.

componential [,kɒmpə'nenʃl] *adj* componentiel.

comportment [kəm'pɔ:tmənt] *n fml* comportement *m*, conduite *f*.

compose [kəm'pəʊz] <> *vt* **1.** [make up] : **to be ~d of sthg** se composer *OR* être composé de qqch **2.** [create, write] composer ▪ **I ~d a reply to his letter** j'ai formulé une réponse à sa lettre **3.** TYPO [set] composer **4.** [make calm] : **~ yourself!** calmez-vous! ▪ **I need to ~ my thoughts** j'ai besoin de mettre de l'ordre dans mes idées **5.** [settle - quarrel] arranger, régler.
<> *vi* composer.

composed [kəm'pəʊzd] *adj* calme, posé.

composer [kəm'pəʊzər] *n* TYPO & MUS compositeur *m*, - trice *f*.

composite ['kɒmpəzɪt] <> *adj* [gen - ARCHIT] & PHOT composite ▪ BOT & MATHS composé.
<> *n* [compound] composite *m* ▪ ARCHIT (ordre *m*) composite *m* ▪ BOT composée *f*, composacée *f*.

composition [,kɒmpə'zɪʃn] *n* **1.** [gen - ART], LIT & MUS composition *f*, création *f* **2.** [thing created] composition *f*, œuvre *f* ▪ SCH [essay] dissertation *f* **3.** [constitution - parts] composition *f*, constitution *f* ; [- mixture] mélange *m*, composition *f* ▪ CONSTR stuc *m* ▪ **the chemical ~ of water** la composition chimique de l'eau **4.** LING [of sentence] construction *f* ▪ [of word] composition *f* **5.** TYPO composition *f* **6.** LAW [agreement] arrangement *m* (avec un créancier), accommodement *m*.

compositor [kəm'pɒzɪtər] *n* TYPO compositeur *m*, - trice *f*.

compos mentis [,kɒmpəs'mentɪs] *adj* sain d'esprit.

compost [*UK* 'kɒmpɒst, *US* 'kɒmpəʊst] <> *n* compost *m* ▪ **~ heap** tas *m* de compost.
<> *vt* composter (*une terre*).

composure [kəm'pəʊʒər] *n* calme *m*, sang-froid *m* ▪ **to lose one's ~** perdre son calme ▪ **she regained her ~** elle s'est calmée *OR* a retrouvé son calme.

compote ['kɒmpɒt] *n* [dessert] compote *f* ▪ *US* [dish] compotier *m*.

compound <> *adj* ['kɒmpaʊnd] **1.** [gen] composé ▪ CHEM composé, combiné ▪ MATHS complexe ▪ TECH [engine] compound (*inv*) ▪ **~ eye** BIOL œil *m* composé *OR* à facettes **2.** GRAM [sentence] complexe ▪ [tense, word] composé **3.** MUS composé.
<> *n* ['kɒmpaʊnd] **1.** [enclosed area] enceinte *f*, enclos *m* ▪ [for prisoners of war] camp *m* **2.** [mixture] composé *m*, mélange *m* ▪ CHEM composé *m* ▪ TECH compound *m* **3.** GRAM mot *m* composé.
<> *vt* [kəm'paʊnd] **1.** [combine] combiner, mélanger ▪ [form by combining] composer **2.** [make worse - difficulties, mistake] aggraver **3.** LAW [settle] régler à l'amiable ▪ **to ~ an offence** composer *OR* pactiser avec un criminel.
<> *vi* LAW composer, transiger.

compound fracture *n* fracture *f* multiple.

compound interest *n (U)* intérêts *mpl* composés.

comprehend [,kɒmprɪ'hend] <> *vt* **1.** [understand] comprendre, saisir **2.** [include] comprendre, inclure.
<> *vi* [understand] comprendre, saisir.

comprehensible [,kɒmprɪ'hensəbl] *adj* compréhensible, intelligible.

comprehension [ˌkɒmprɪ'henʃn] *n* **1.** [understanding] compréhension *f* ▪ **things that are beyond our ~** des choses qui nous dépassent **2.** SCH [exercise] exercice *m* de compréhension **3.** [inclusion] inclusion *f*.

comprehensive [ˌkɒmprɪ'hensɪv] ◇ *adj* **1.** [thorough] complet, exhaustif ▪ [detailed] détaillé, complet ▪ **~ knowledge** connaissances vastes *OR* étendues ▪ **~ measures** mesures d'ensemble ▪ **(a)~ insurance (policy)** *UK*, **~ assurance** *US* une assurance tous risques **2.** *UK* SCH : **the schools went ~** les écoles ont abandonné les critères sélectifs d'entrée ▪ **~ school** *établissement secondaire d'enseignement général*.
◇ *n UK* [school] *établissement secondaire d'enseignement général*.

comprehensively [ˌkɒmprɪ'hensɪvlɪ] *adv* [thoroughly] complètement, exhaustivement ▪ [in detail] en détail.

compress ◇ *vt* [kəm'pres] [squeeze together] comprimer ▪ *fig* [condense - ideas, facts, writing] condenser, concentrer ▪ **three centuries are ~ed into two chapters** trois siècles sont concentrés en deux chapitres.
◇ *vi* [material] se comprimer ▪ *fig* [be condensed] se condenser, se concentrer.
◇ *n* ['kɒmpres] compresse *f*.

compressed air *n* air *m* comprimé.

compression [kəm'preʃn] *n* compression *f* ▪ *fig* [condensing] réduction *f*.

compression chamber *n* chambre *f* de compression.

compressor [kəm'presəʳ] *n* ANAT & TECH compresseur *m* ▪ **~ unit** groupe *m* compresseur.

comprise [kəm'praɪz] *vt* **1.** [consist of] comprendre, consister en ▪ **the group ~s** *OR* **is ~d of four women and two men** il y a quatre femmes et deux hommes dans le groupe, le groupe est formé de quatre femmes et deux hommes **2.** [constitute] constituer ▪ **women ~ 60 % of the population** les femmes représentent 60 % de la population.

compromise ['kɒmprəmaɪz] ◇ *n* compromis *m* ▪ **to reach** *OR* **arrive at a ~** aboutir *OR* parvenir à un compromis.
◇ *comp* [decision, solution] de compromis.
◇ *vi* transiger, aboutir à *OR* accepter un compromis ▪ **to ~ with sb (on sthg)** transiger avec qqn *OR* aboutir à un compromis avec qqn (sur qqch).
◇ *vt* **1.** [principles, reputation] compromettre ▪ **don't say anything to ~ yourself** ne dites rien qui puisse vous compromettre **2.** [jeopardize] mettre en péril, risquer.

compromising ['kɒmprəmaɪzɪŋ] *adj* compromettant.

comptroller [kən'trəʊləʳ] *n* ADMIN administrateur *m*, - trice *f*, intendant *m*, - e *f* ▪ FIN contrôleur *m*, - euse *f* ▪ **Comptroller General** *US* ≃ président *m* de la Cour des comptes.

compulsion [kəm'pʌlʃn] *n* **1.** [force] contrainte *f*, coercition *f* ▪ **he is under no ~ to sell** il n'est nullement obligé de vendre, rien ne l'oblige à vendre **2.** PSYCHOL [impulse] compulsion *f*.

compulsive [kəm'pʌlsɪv] *adj* **1.** PSYCHOL [behaviour] compulsif ▪ **he's a ~ liar** il ne peut pas s'empêcher de mentir, mentir est un besoin chez lui ▪ **~ eating** boulimie *f* **2.** [reason] coercitif ▪ *fig* [absorbing] irrésistible ▪ **this TV series is ~ viewing** quand on commence à regarder ce feuilleton de télé, on ne peut plus s'en passer.

compulsively [kəm'pʌlsɪvlɪ] *adv* **1.** PSYCHOL [drink, steal, smoke] d'une façon compulsive **2.** *fig* irrésistiblement.

compulsory [kəm'pʌlsərɪ] *adj* **1.** [obligatory] obligatoire ▪ **~ liquidation** FIN liquidation *f* forcée ▪ **~ retirement** mise *f* à la retraite d'office **2.** [compelling] irrésistible ▪ [law] obligatoire.

compulsory purchase *n UK* expropriation *f* pour cause d'utilité publique ▪ **~ order** ordre *m* d'expropriation.

compunction [kəm'pʌŋkʃn] *n* [remorse] remords *m* ▪ [misgiving] scrupule *m* ▪ RELIG componction *f* ▪ **he has no ~ about stealing** il n'a aucun scrupule *OR* il n'hésite pas à voler.

computation [ˌkɒmpjuː'teɪʃn] *n* **1.** [calculation] calcul *m* **2.** [reckoning] estimation *f*.

computational [ˌkɒmpjuː'teɪʃənl] *adj* quantitatif, statistique ▪ **~ linguistics** linguistique *f* computationnelle.

compute [kəm'pjuːt] ◇ *vt* calculer.
◇ *vi* calculer ▪ **it doesn't ~** *inf* ça n'a pas de sens.

computer [kəm'pjuːtəʳ] ◇ *n* [electronic] ordinateur *m* ▪ **he's good with/he works in ~s** il est bon en/il travaille dans l'informatique.
◇ *comp* : **~ model** modèle *m* informatique ▪ **~ network** réseau *m* informatique ▪ **~ printout** sortie *f* papier.

computer-aided, computer-assisted [-ə'sɪstɪd] *adj* assisté par ordinateur.

computer-aided design *n* conception *f* assistée par ordinateur.

computer-aided engineering *n* ingénierie *f* assistée par ordinateur.

computer crime *n* fraude *f* informatique.

computer dating *n rencontres sélectionnées par ordinateur*.

computer game *n* jeu *m* électronique.

computer-generated [kəmˌpjuːtə'dʒenəreɪtɪd] *adj* généré par ordinateur.

computer graphics ◇ *npl* [function] graphiques *mpl*.
◇ *n* [field] infographie® *f*.

computer-integrated manufacturing *n* fabrication *f* assistée par ordinateur.

computerization [kəmˌpjuːtəraɪ'zeɪʃn] *n* **1.** [of system, of work] automatisation *f*, informatisation *f* **2.** [of information - inputting] saisie *f* sur ordinateur ; [- processing] traitement *m* (électronique).

computerize, *UK* **ise** [kəm'pjuːtəraɪz] *vt* [data - put on computer] saisir sur ordinateur ; [- process by computer] traiter par ordinateur ▪ [firm] informatiser.

computerized [kəm'pjuːtəraɪzd] *adj* : **~ typesetting** composition *f* par ordinateur.

computer language *n* langage *m* de programmation.

computer literacy, computer-literacy *n* compétence *f* informatique.

computer-literate *adj* ayant des compétences en informatique.

computer program *n* programme *m* informatique.

computer programmer *n* programmeur *m*, - euse *f*.

computer programming *n* programmation *f*.

computer science *n* informatique *f*.

computer scientist *n* informaticien *m*, - enne *f*.

computing [kəm'pjuːtɪŋ] *n* **1.** [use of computers] informatique *f* **2.** [calculation] calcul *m* ▪ [reckoning] estimation *f*.

comrade ['kɒmreɪd] *n* [gen - POL] camarade *mf*.

comrade-in-arms (*pl* **comrades-in-arms**) *n* compagnon *m* d'armes.

comradeship ['kɒmreɪdʃɪp] *n* camaraderie *f*.

comsat ['kɒmsæt] *n* = **communications satellite**.

con [kɒn] ◇ *vt* (*pret & pp* **conned**, *cont* **conning**) **1.** *inf* [swindle] arnaquer ▪ [trick] duper ▪ **I've been conned!** je me suis fait avoir!, on m'a eu! ▪ **he conned us into buying it** il nous a persuadés de l'acheter et nous nous sommes fait avoir **2.** NAUT [steer] gouverner, piloter.
◇ *n* **1.** *inf* [swindle] arnaque ▪ [trick] duperie *f* **2.** *inf* [convict] taulard *m* **3.** [disadvantage] contre *m*.

Con. *written abbr of* **constable**.

con artist *n inf* arnaqueur *m*.

concatenation [kɒn,kætɪ'neɪʃn] *n* [series] série *f*, chaîne *f* ▪ [of circumstances] enchaînement *m* ▪ COMPUT & LING concaténation *f*.

concave [,kɒn'keɪv] *adj* concave.

conceal [kən'si:l] *vt* [hide - object] cacher, dissimuler ; [- emotion, truth] cacher, dissimuler ; [- news] tenir secret ▪ **to ~ sthg from sb** cacher qqch à qqn.

concealed [kən'si:ld] *adj* [lighting] indirect ▪ [driveway, entrance] caché.

concealment [kən'si:lmənt] *n* [act of hiding] dissimulation *f* ▪ LAW [of criminal] recel *m* ▪ [of facts, truth] non-divulgation *f*.

concede [kən'si:d] ◇ *vt* **1.** [admit] concéder, admettre ▪ **he ~d (that) he was wrong** il a admis *OR* reconnu qu'il avait tort ▪ **to ~ defeat** s'avouer vaincu **2.** [give up] concéder, accorder ▪ SPORT concéder ▪ **they ~d a free kick/a goal** SPORT ils ont concédé un coup franc/un but **3.** [grant - privileges] concéder.
◇ *vi* céder.
Voir module d'usage

conceit [kən'si:t] *n* **1.** [vanity] vanité *f*, suffisance *f* **2.** *lit* [witty expression] trait *m* d'esprit.

conceited [kən'si:tɪd] *adj* vaniteux, suffisant.

conceivable [kən'si:vəbl] *adj* concevable, imaginable ▪ **every ~ means** tous les moyens possibles et imaginables ▪ **it's quite ~ that it was an accident** il est tout à fait concevable que ç'ait été un accident.

conceivably [kən'si:vəblɪ] *adv* : **this might ~ start a war** il est concevable que *OR* il se peut que cela déclenche une guerre ▪ **it couldn't ~ have been him** il n'est pas possible que ç'ait été lui.

conceive [kən'si:v] ◇ *vt* **1.** [idea, plan] concevoir ▪ **I can't ~ why they did it** je ne comprends vraiment pas pourquoi ils l'ont fait **2.** [child] concevoir ▪ **she ~d a passion for jazz** *fig* elle conçut une passion pour le jazz.
◇ *vi* **1.** [think] concevoir ▪ **can't you ~ of a better plan?** ne pouvez-vous rien concevoir de mieux? **2.** [become pregnant] concevoir.

concentrate ['kɒnsəntreɪt] ◇ *vi* **1.** [pay attention] se concentrer, concentrer *OR* fixer son attention ▪ **to ~ on sthg** se concentrer sur qqch ▪ **~ on your work!** appliquez-vous à votre travail! ▮ [focus] : **the government should ~ on improving the economy** le gouvernement devrait s'attacher à améliorer la situation économique ▪ **just ~ on getting the suitcases ready!** occupe-toi seulement des valises! ▪ **the speaker ~d on the Luddite movement** le conférencier a surtout traité du luddisme **2.** [gather] se concentrer, converger.
◇ *vt* **1.** [focus] concentrer ▪ **to ~ one's attention on sthg** concentrer son attention sur qqch ▪ **it ~s the mind** cela aide à se concentrer **2.** [bring together] concentrer, rassembler ▪ CHEM concentrer.
◇ *n* concentré *m*.

concentrated ['kɒnsəntreɪtɪd] *adj* **1.** [liquid] concentré **2.** [intense] intense.

concentration [,kɒnsən'treɪʃn] *n* [gen - CHEM] concentration *f* ▪ **to lose (one's) ~** perdre sa concentration.

concentration camp *n* camp *m* de concentration.

concentric [kən'sentrɪk] *adj* concentrique.

concept ['kɒnsept] *n* concept *m*.

conception [kən'sepʃn] *n* [gen - MED] conception *f* ▪ **she has no ~ of time** elle n'a aucune notion du temps.

conceptual [kən'septʃuəl] *adj* conceptuel.

conceptualize, *UK* **ise** [kən'septʃuəlaɪz] *vt* conceptualiser.

concern [kən'sɜ:n] ◇ *n* **1.** [worry] inquiétude *f*, souci *m* ▪ **there's no cause for ~** il n'y a pas de raison de s'inquiéter ▪ **she showed great ~ for their welfare** elle s'est montrée très soucieuse de leur bien-être ▪ **a look of ~** un regard inquiet ▪ **this is a matter of great ~** c'est un sujet très inquiétant ▮ [source of worry] souci *m*, préoccupation *f* ▪ **my main ~ is the price** ce qui m'inquiète surtout, c'est le prix **2.** [affair, business] affaire *f* ▪ **what ~ is it of yours?** en quoi est-ce que cela vous regarde? ▪ **it's none of my ~** cela ne me regarde pas, ce n'est pas mon affaire **3.** COMM [firm] : **a (business) ~** une affaire, une firme **4.** [share] intérêt *m*.
◇ *vt* **1.** [worry] inquiéter ▪ **they're ~ed about her** ils s'inquiètent *OR* se font du souci à son sujet ▪ **we were ~ed to learn that...** nous avons appris avec inquiétude que... ▪ **I'm only ~ed with the facts** je ne m'intéresse qu'aux faits **2.** [involve] concerner ▪ **where** *OR* **as far as the budget is ~ed** en ce qui concerne le budget ▪ **to ~ o.s. in** *OR* **with sthg** s'occuper de *OR* s'intéresser à qqch ▪ **this doesn't ~ you** cela ne vous regarde pas ▪ **as far as I'm ~ed** en ce qui me concerne, quant à moi ▪ **to whom it may ~** à qui de droit **3.** [be important to] intéresser, importer ▪ **the outcome ~s us all** les résultats nous importent à tous **4.** [subj: book, report] traiter.

concerned [kən'sɜ:nd] *adj* **1.** [worried] inquiet, - ète *f*, soucieux ▪ **we were ~ for** *OR* **about his health** nous étions inquiets pour sa santé **2.** [involved] intéressé ▪ **pass this request on to the department ~** transmettez cette demande au service compétent ▪ **notify the person ~** avisez qui de droit ▪ **the people ~** [in question] les personnes en question *OR* dont il s'agit ; [involved] les intéressés.

concerning [kən'sɜ:nɪŋ] *prep* au sujet de, à propos de ▪ **I wrote to her ~ the lease** je lui ai écrit au sujet du bail ▪ **any news ~ the accident?** y a-t-il du nouveau au sujet de *OR* concernant l'accident?

concert ◇ *n* ['kɒnsət] **1.** MUS [performance] concert *m* ▪ **Miles Davis in ~** Miles Davis en concert **2.** *UK fig* [agreement] accord *m*, entente *f*.
◇ *comp* ['kɒnsət] [hall, performer, pianist] de concert.
◇ *vt* [kən'sɜ:t] concerter, arranger.
◆ **in concert with** *prep phr UK fml* de concert avec.

concerted [kən'sɜ:tɪd] *adj* concerté ▪ **a ~ effort** un effort concerté.

concertgoer ['kɒnsət,gəʊə^r] *n* amateur *m* de concerts.

concert grand *n* piano *m* de concert.

concertina [,kɒnsə'ti:nə] ◇ *n* concertina *m*.
◇ *vi* : **the front of the car ~ed** le devant de la voiture a été télescopé.

concertmaster ['kɒnsət,mɑ:stə^r] *n US* premier violon *m*.

concerto [kən'tʃeətəʊ] (*pl* **concertos** *OR pl* **concerti** [-ti:]) *n* concerto *m*.

CONCEDING A POINT

Je dois reconnaître *OU* **admettre que vous avez raison.** I have to admit that you're right.

Effectivement, c'est une manière de voir les choses. Well, that's one way of looking at things.

Peut-être, effectivement. You may well be right.

C'est possible, oui. I suppose so.

Tu n'as pas tort. You're right there.

C'est très cher, je vous l'accorde. It's very expensive, granted.

C'est juste. You've got a point there.

concession [kən'seʃn] *n* **1.** [gen - LAW] concession *f* ■ COMM [reduction] réduction *f* ■ **to make a ~ (to sb)** faire une concession (à qqn) **2.** MIN & PETR concession *f*.

concessionary [kən'seʃnərɪ] ◇ *adj* [gen - FIN] & LAW concessionnaire ■ COMM [fare, ticket] à prix réduit.
◇ *n* (*pl* **concessionaries**) concessionnaire *mf*.

concession stand *n* US buvette *f* (*dans un cinéma, un stade, etc*).

concessive clause [kən'sesɪv-] *n* (proposition *f*) concessive *f*.

conch [kɒntʃ, kɒŋk] (*pl* **conches** OR *pl* **conchs**) *n* **1.** ZOOL [mollusc, shell] conque *f* **2.** ARCHIT (voûte *f* d')abside *f*.

conciliation [kən,sɪlɪ'eɪʃn] *n* **1.** [appeasement] apaisement *m* **2.** [reconciliation] conciliation *f* ■ INDUST médiation *f* ■ **a ~ service** un service de conciliation ■ **~ board** conseil *m* d'arbitrage.

conciliatory [kən'sɪlɪətrɪ] *adj* [manner, words] conciliant ■ [person] conciliateur, conciliant ■ LAW & POL [procedure] conciliatoire ■ **in a ~ spirit** dans un esprit de conciliation.

concise [kən'saɪs] *adj* [succinct] concis ■ [abridged] abrégé.

concisely [kən'saɪslɪ] *adv* avec concision.

conciseness [kən'saɪsnɪs], **concision** [kən'sɪʒn] *n* concision *f*.

conclave ['kɒŋkleɪv] *n* [private meeting] assemblée *f* OR réunion *f* à huis clos ■ RELIG conclave *m* ■ **in ~** en réunion privée.

conclude [kən'klu:d] ◇ *vt* **1.** [finish] conclure, terminer ■ [meeting] clore, clôturer **2.** [settle - deal, treaty] conclure **3.** [deduce] conclure, déduire ■ **may I ~ from your statement that...** dois-je inférer de votre remarque que... **4.** [decide] décider.
◇ *vi* **1.** [person] conclure ■ **to ~, I would just like to say...** en conclusion OR pour conclure, je voudrais simplement dire... **2.** [event] se terminer, s'achever.

concluding [kən'klu:dɪŋ] *adj* de conclusion, final.

conclusion [kən'klu:ʒn] *n* **1.** [end] conclusion *f*, fin *f* ■ **to bring sthg to a ~** mener qqch à sa conclusion OR à terme **2.** [decision, judgment] conclusion *f*, décision *f* ■ **we've come to the ~ that...** nous avons conclu que... ■ **it's up to you to draw your own ~s** c'est à vous d'en juger ■ **the facts lead me to the ~ that...** les faits m'amènent à conclure que... **3.** [settling - of deal, treaty] conclusion *f* **4.** PHILOS conclusion *f*.
◆ **in conclusion** *adv phr* en conclusion, pour conclure.

conclusive [kən'klu:sɪv] *adj* [decisive - proof, argument] concluant, décisif ■ [final] final.

conclusively [kən'klu:sɪvlɪ] *adv* de façon concluante OR décisive, définitivement.

concoct [kən'kɒkt] *vt* **1.** [prepare] composer, confectionner ■ **to ~ a dish** mitonner OR mijoter un plat **2.** *fig* [invent - excuse, scheme] combiner, concocter.

concoction [kən'kɒkʃn] *n* **1.** [act] confection *f*, préparation *f* **2.** [mixture] mélange *m*, mixture *f* *pej* **3.** *fig* [scheme] combinaison *f*.

concomitant [kən'kɒmɪtənt] *fml* ◇ *adj* concomitant.
◇ *n* accessoire *m*.

concord ['kɒŋkɔ:d] *n* **1.** *fml* [harmony] concorde *f*, harmonie *f* **2.** [treaty] accord *m*, entente *f* **3.** GRAM accord *m* **4.** MUS accord *m*.

concordance [kən'kɔ:dəns] *n* **1.** *fml* [agreement] accord *m* **2.** [index] index *m* ■ [of Bible, of author's works] concordance *f*.
◆ **in concordance with** *prep phr* en accord avec.

concordant [kən'kɔ:dənt] *adj* *fml* concordant, s'accordant ■ **~ with** s'accordant avec.

concourse ['kɒŋkɔ:s] *n* **1.** [of people, things] multitude *f*, rassemblement *m* ■ [crowd] foule *f* **2.** [of circumstances, events] concours *m* **3.** [meeting place] lieu *m* de rassemblement ■ [in building] hall *m* ■ US [street] boulevard *m* ■ [crossroads] carrefour *m*.

concrete ['kɒŋkri:t] ◇ *n* **1.** CONSTR béton *m* **2.** PHILOS : **the ~** le concret.
◇ *adj* **1.** [specific - advantage] concret, - ète *f*, réel ; [- example, proposal] concret, - ète *f* **2.** GRAM, MATHS & MUS concret, - ète *f* **3.** CONSTR en OR de béton ■ **the ~ jungle** la forêt de béton.
◇ *vt* bétonner.

concrete mixer *n* bétonnière *f*.

concrete noun *n* nom *m* concret.

concubine ['kɒŋkjʊbaɪn] *n* concubine *f*.

concur [kən'kɜ:ʳ] (*pret & pp* **concurred**, *cont* **concurring**) *vi* **1.** [agree] être d'accord, s'entendre ■ **to ~ with sb/sthg** être d'accord avec qqn/qqch ■ **the experts' opinions ~** les avis des experts convergent **2.** [occur together] coïncider, arriver en même temps ■ **events concurred to make it a miserable Christmas** tout a concouru à gâcher les fêtes de Noël.

concurrent [kən'kʌrənt] *adj* **1.** [simultaneous] concomitant, simultané **2.** [acting together] concerté **3.** [agreeing] concordant, d'accord **4.** MATHS & TECH [intersecting] concourant.

concurrently [kən'kʌrəntlɪ] *adv* simultanément ■ **the two sentences to run ~** LAW avec confusion des deux peines.

concuss [kən'kʌs] *vt* **1.** [injure brain] commotionner ■ **to be ~ed** être commotionné **2.** [shake] ébranler, secouer violemment.

concussion [kən'kʌʃn] *n* **1.** *(U)* [brain injury] commotion *f* cérébrale **2.** [shaking] ébranlement *m*.

condemn [kən'dem] *vt* **1.** [gen - LAW] condamner ■ **~ed to death** condamné à mort ■ **people who are ~ed to live in poverty** *fig* les gens qui sont condamnés à vivre dans la misère **2.** [disapprove of] condamner, censurer **3.** [declare unfit] condamner, déclarer inutilisable ■ [building] déclarer inhabitable, condamner **4.** US LAW [property] exproprier pour cause d'utilité publique.

condemnation [,kɒndem'neɪʃn] *n* **1.** [gen - LAW] condamnation *f* **2.** [criticism] condamnation *f*, censure *f* **3.** [of building] condamnation *f* **4.** US LAW [of property] expropriation *f* pour cause d'utilité publique.

condemnatory [kən'demnətrɪ] *adj* condamnatoire.

condemned [kən'demd] *adj* condamné ■ **the ~ man** le condamné ■ **~ cell** cellule *f* des condamnés.

condensation [,kɒnden'seɪʃn] *n* [gen - CHEM] condensation *f* ■ [on glass] buée *f*, condensation *f*.

condense [kən'dens] ◇ *vt* **1.** [make denser] condenser, concentrer ■ CHEM [gas] condenser ■ PHYS [beam] concentrer **2.** [report, book] condenser, résumer.
◇ *vi* [become liquid] se condenser ■ [become concentrated] se concentrer.

condensed [kən'denst] *adj* condensé, concentré ■ **in ~ print** TYPO en petits caractères.

condensed milk *n* lait *m* concentré.

condenser [kən'densəʳ] *n* ELEC & TECH condensateur *m* ■ CHEM [of gas] condenseur *m* ■ PHYS [of light] condensateur.

condescend [,kɒndɪ'send] *vi* **1.** [behave patronizingly] : **to ~ (to sb)** se montrer condescendant (envers qqn OR à l'égard de qqn) **2.** [lower o.s.] : **to ~ to do sthg** condescendre à OR daigner faire qqch ■ **she ~ed to speak to me** elle a condescendu à OR a daigné me parler.

condescending [,kɒndɪ'sendɪŋ] *adj* condescendant.

condescendingly [,kɒndɪ'sendɪŋlɪ] *adv* avec condescendance ■ [speak] d'un ton condescendant ■ **he treated me very ~** il m'a traité de haut, il m'a pris de très haut.

condescension [,kɒndɪ'senʃn] *n* condescendance *f*.

condiment ['kɒndɪmənt] *n* condiment *m*.

condition [kən'dɪʃn] <> *n* **1.** [state - mental, physical] état *m* ■ **you're in no ~ to drive** vous n'êtes pas en état de conduire ■ **books in good/poor ~** livres en bon/mauvais état ■ **I'm out of ~** je ne suis pas en forme ■ **in working ~** en état de marche **2.** [stipulation] condition *f* ■ **to make a ~ that** stipuler que **3.** [illness] maladie *f*, affection *f* ■ **he has a heart ~** il a une maladie du cœur **4.** *fml* [social status] situation *f*, position *f*.
<> *vt* **1.** [train] conditionner ■ PSYCHOL provoquer un réflexe conditionné chez, conditionner ■ **her upbringing ~ed her to believe in God** son éducation l'a automatiquement portée à croire en Dieu **2.** [make fit - animal, person] mettre en forme ; [- thing] mettre en bon état ■ **to ~ one's hair/skin** traiter ses cheveux/sa peau **3.** [determine] conditionner, déterminer.
◆ **conditions** *npl* [circumstances] conditions *fpl*, circonstances *fpl* ■ **living/working ~s** conditions de vie/de travail ■ **under these ~s** dans ces conditions ■ **the weather ~s** les conditions météorologiques.
◆ **on condition that** *conj phr* : **I'll tell you on ~ that you keep it secret** je vais vous le dire à condition que vous gardiez le secret ■ **he'll do it on ~ that he's well paid** il le fera à condition d'être bien payé.

conditional [kən'dɪʃənl] <> *adj* **1.** [dependent on other factors] conditionnel ■ **to be ~ on** *OR* **upon sthg** dépendre de qqch **2.** GRAM conditionnel.
<> *n* conditionnel *m* ■ **in the ~** au conditionnel.
Voir module d'usage

conditionality [kən,dɪʃə'nælətɪ] *n* conditionnalité *f*.

conditionally [kən'dɪʃnəlɪ] *adv* conditionnellement.

conditioned [kən'dɪʃnd] *adj* conditionné.

conditioner [kən'dɪʃnər] *n* [for hair] baume *m* démêlant ■ [for skin] crème *f* traitante *OR* équilibrante ■ [for fabric] assouplisseur *m*.

conditioning [kən'dɪʃnɪŋ] <> *n* [gen] conditionnement *m*.
<> *adj* traitant.

condo ['kɒndəʊ] *n* *US inf* = **condominium** *(sense 3)*.

condole [kən'dəʊl] *vi lit* exprimer ses condoléances *OR* sa sympathie.

condolence [kən'dəʊləns] *n* condoléance *f* ■ **a letter of ~** une lettre de condoléances ■ **to offer one's ~s to sb** présenter ses condoléances à qqn.

condom ['kɒndəm] *n* préservatif *m (masculin)*.

condominium [,kɒndə'mɪnɪəm] *n* **1.** [government] condominium *m* **2.** [country] condominium *m* **3.** *US* [ownership] copropriété *f* ■ [building] immeuble *m* (en copropriété) ■ [flat] appartement *m* en copropriété.

condone [kən'dəʊn] *vt* [overlook] fermer les yeux sur ■ [forgive] pardonner, excuser ■ **we cannot ~ such immoral behaviour** nous ne pouvons excuser un comportement aussi immoral.

condor ['kɒndɔːr] *n* condor *m*.

conducive [kən'djuːsɪv] *adj* favorable ■ **this weather is not ~ to study** ce temps n'incite pas à étudier.

conduct <> *n* ['kɒndʌkt] **1.** [behaviour] conduite *f*, comportement *m* ■ **her ~ towards me** son comportement envers moi *OR* à mon égard **2.** [handling - of business, negotiations] conduite *f*.
<> *vt* [kən'dʌkt] **1.** [manage, carry out - campaign] diriger, mener ; [- inquiry] conduire, mener ■ **this is not the way to ~ negotiations** ce n'est pas ainsi qu'on négocie **2.** [guide] conduire, mener ■ **the director ~ed us through the factory** le directeur nous a fait visiter l'usine **3.** [behave] : **to ~ o.s.** se conduire, se comporter **4.** MUS [musicians, music] diriger ■ **Bernstein will be ~ing (the orchestra)** l'orchestre sera (placé) sous la direction de Bernstein **5.** ELEC & PHYS [transmit] conduire, être conducteur de.

conducted tour [kən'dʌktɪd-] *n UK* [short] visite *f* guidée ■ [longer] voyage *m* organisé.

conduction [kən'dʌkʃn] *n* conduction *f*.

conductive [kən'dʌktɪv] *adj* conducteur.

conductivity [,kɒndʌk'tɪvətɪ] *n* conductivité *f*.

conductor [kən'dʌktər] *n* **1.** MUS chef *m* d'orchestre **2.** [on bus, train] receveur *m* ■ *US* [railway official] chef *m* de train **3.** ELEC & PHYS (corps *m*) conducteur *m*.

conductress [kən'dʌktrɪs] *n* contrôleuse *f*.

conduit ['kɒndɪt] *n* [for fluid] conduit *m*, canalisation *f* ■ ELEC tube *m* ■ *fig* [for money] intermédiaire *mf*.

cone [kəʊn] *n* **1.** [gen - MATHS], OPT & TECH cône *m* ■ **a traffic ~** un cône de signalisation **2.** [for ice cream] cornet *m* **3.** BOT [of pine, fir] pomme *f*, cône *m*.
◆ **cone off** *vt sep UK* mettre des cônes de signalisation sur.

coney ['kəʊni] = **cony**.

Coney Island ['kəʊnɪ-] *pr n* Coney Island *(île située au large de New York et où se trouve un grand parc d'attractions)*.

confab ['kɒnfæb] *UK inf* <> *n* causette *f*.
<> *vi* (*pret & pp* **confabbed**, *cont* **confabbing**) causer, bavarder.

confection [kən'fekʃn] *n* **1.** [act] confection *f* **2.** CULIN [sweet] sucrerie *f*, friandise *f* ■ [pastry] pâtisserie *f* ■ [cake] gâteau *m*.

confectioner [kən'fekʃnər] *n* [of sweets] confiseur *m*, - euse *f* ■ [of pastry] pâtissier *m*, - ère *f* ■ **a ~'s (shop)** [for sweets] une confiserie ; [for pastry] une pâtisserie ➲ **~'s custard** crème *f* pâtissière ■ **~'s sugar** *US* sucre *m* glace.

confectionery [kən'fekʃnərɪ] (*pl* **confectioneries**) *n* [sweets] confiserie *f* ■ [pastry] pâtisserie *f*.

confederacy [kən'fedərəsɪ] (*pl* **confederacies**) *n* **1.** [alliance] confédération *f* **2.** [conspiracy] conspiration *f*.
◆ **Confederacy** *n* HIST : **the Confederacy** les États *mpl* confédérés *(pendant la guerre de Sécession américaine)*.

confederate <> *n* [kən'fedərət] **1.** [member of confederacy] confédéré *m*, - e *f* **2.** [accomplice] complice *mf*.
<> *adj* [kən'fedərət] confédéré.
<> *vt* [kən'fedəreɪt] confédérer.
<> *vi* se confédérer.

CONDITIONAL CLAUSES

Si tu pars tout de suite, tu y seras peut-être ce soir. If you leave now, there's a chance you'll get there by tonight.

Si tu ne viens pas, préviens-moi. Let me know if you're not coming.

Qu'est-ce que tu ferais si tu gagnais au loto ? What would you do if you won the lottery?

Si j'avais su, je t'aurais prévenu. If I'd known I would have told you.

Nous partirons demain, à moins qu'il ne se mette à pleuvoir. We'll leave tomorrow, unless it starts raining.

Je le ferai à condition que tu m'aides. I'll do it if you help me.

◆ **Confederate** HIST ◇ *n* sudiste *mf (pendant la guerre de Sécession américaine)* ■ **the Confederates** les Confédérés.
◇ *adj* : **the Confederate flag** *drapeau des sudistes américains, considéré aujourd'hui comme un symbole raciste* ■ **the Confederate States** les États *mpl* confédérés *(pendant la guerre de Sécession américaine)*.

confederation [kən,fedə'reɪʃn] *n* confédération *f*.

confer [kən'fɜːʳ] *(pret & pp* **conferred**, *cont* **conferring***)* ◇ *vi* conférer, s'entretenir ■ **to ~ with sb (about sthg)** s'entretenir avec qqn (de qqch).
◇ *vt* conférer, accorder ■ **to ~ sthg on sb** conférer qqch à qqn ■ **degrees were conferred on thirty students** des diplômes ont été remis à trente étudiants.

conference ['kɒnfərəns] *n* **1.** [meeting] conférence *f* ■ [consultation] conférence *f*, consultation *f* ■ **the manager is in ~** le directeur est en conférence *OR* en réunion **2.** [convention] congrès *m*, colloque *m* ■ POL congrès *m*, assemblée *f* ■ **~ centre** [building] centre de congrès ; [town] *ville pouvant accueillir des congrès* ■ **~ hall** salle *f* de conférence **3.** *US* SPORT [association] association *f*, ligue *f*.

conference call *n* téléconférence *f*.

conferencing ['kɒnfərənsɪŋ] *n (U)* téléconférence *f*.

conferment [kən'fɜːmənt], **conferral** [kən'fɜːrəl] *n* action *f* de conférer ■ [of diploma] remise *f* (de diplôme) ■ [of favour, title] octroi *m*.

confess [kən'fes] ◇ *vt* **1.** [admit - fault, crime] avouer, confesser ■ **to ~ one's guilt** *OR* **that one is guilty** avouer sa culpabilité, s'avouer coupable ■ **I must** *OR* **I have to ~ I was wrong** je dois reconnaître *OR* admettre que j'avais tort **2.** RELIG [sins] confesser, se confesser de ■ [subj: priest] confesser.
◇ *vi* **1.** [admit] faire des aveux ■ **the thief ~ed** le voleur est passé aux aveux ■ **she ~ed to five murders** elle a avoué *OR* confessé cinq meurtres ■ **he ~ed to having lied** il a reconnu *OR* avoué avoir menti ■ **I ~ to a weakness for sweets** j'avoue *OR* je reconnais que j'ai un faible pour les sucreries **2.** RELIG se confesser.

confessant [kən'fesənt] *n* pénitent *m*, - e *f*.

confessed [kən'fest] *adj* de son propre aveu ■ **he was a ~ liar** il reconnaissait lui-même être menteur.

confession [kən'feʃn] *n* **1.** [of guilt] aveu *m*, confession *f* ■ **to make a full ~** faire des aveux complets ■ **on his own ~** de son propre aveu **2.** RELIG confession *f* ■ [sect] confession *f* ■ **she made her ~** elle s'est confessée ■ **the priest heard our ~** le prêtre nous a confessés.

confessional [kən'feʃənl] ◇ *n* confessionnal *m*.
◇ *adj* confessionnel.

confessor [kən'fesəʳ] *n* confesseur *m*.

confetti [kən'fetɪ] *n (U)* confettis *mpl*.

confidant ['kɒnfɪdænt] *n* confident *m*.

confidante [,kɒnfɪ'dænt] *n* confidente *f*.

confide [kən'faɪd] *vt* **1.** [reveal] avouer en confidence, confier ■ **to ~ a secret to sb** confier un secret à qqn ■ **I didn't ~ my thoughts to anyone** je n'ai révélé mes pensées à personne **2.** [entrust] confier.
◆ **confide in** *vt insep* **1.** [talk freely to] se confier à ■ **there's nobody I can ~ in** il n'y a personne à qui je puisse me confier **2.** [trust] avoir confiance en.

confidence ['kɒnfɪdəns] *n* **1.** [faith] confiance *f* ■ **we have ~ in her ability** nous avons confiance en ses capacités ■ **I have every ~ that you'll succeed** je suis absolument certain que vous réussirez ■ **to put one's ~ in sb/sthg** faire confiance à qqn/qqch ■ **the ~ placed in me** la confiance qui m'a été témoignée **2.** [self-assurance] confiance *f* (en soi), assurance *f* ■ **he spoke with ~** il a parlé avec assurance ■ **he lacks ~** il n'est pas très sûr de lui **3.** [certainty] confiance *f*, certitude *f* ■ **I can say with ~** je peux dire avec confiance *OR* assurance **4.** [trust] confiance *f* ■ **I was told in ~** on me l'a dit confidentiellement *OR* en confiance ■ **she told me in the strictest ~** elle me l'a dit dans la plus stricte confidence ■ **to take sb into one's ~** se confier à qqn, faire des confidences à qqn **5.** [private message] confidence *f*.

confidence man *n* escroc *m*.

confidence trick *n* escroquerie *f*, abus *m* de confiance.

confidence trickster = **confidence man**.

confident ['kɒnfɪdənt] *adj* **1.** [self-assured] sûr (de soi), assuré **2.** [certain] assuré, confiant ■ **~ of success** sûr de réussir ■ **in a ~ tone** d'un ton assuré *OR* plein d'assurance ■ **we are ~ that the plan will work** nous sommes persuadés que le projet va réussir.

confidential [,kɒnfɪ'denʃl] *adj* [private] confidentiel ■ [on envelope] confidentiel ⓒ **~ secretary** secrétaire *m* particulier, secrétaire *f* particulière.

confidentiality ['kɒnfɪ,denʃɪ'ælətɪ] *n* confidentialité *f* ■ **'all inquiries treated with complete ~'** 'les demandes de renseignements sont traitées en toute discrétion'.

confidentially [,kɒnfɪ'denʃəlɪ] *adv* confidentiellement.

confidently ['kɒnfɪdəntlɪ] *adv* **1.** [with certainty] avec confiance ■ **I can ~ predict (that)...** je peux prédire avec assurance (que)... **2.** [assuredly] avec assurance.

configuration [kən,fɪgə'reɪʃn] *n* configuration *f*.

configure [kən'fɪgə] *vt*configurer.

confine [kən'faɪn] *vt* **1.** [restrict] limiter, borner ■ **to ~ o.s. to sthg** se borner *OR* s'en tenir à qqch ■ **the report ~s itself to single women** le rapport ne traite que des femmes célibataires ■ **please ~ your remarks to the subject under consideration** veuillez vous limiter au sujet en question **2.** [shut up] confiner, enfermer ■ [imprison] incarcérer, enfermer ■ **her illness ~d her to the house/to bed** sa maladie l'a obligée à rester à la maison/à garder le lit ■ **to ~ sb to barracks** MIL consigner qqn **3.** [pregnant woman] : **to be ~d** accoucher, être en couches.

confined [kən'faɪnd] *adj* **1.** [area, atmosphere] confiné ■ **in a ~ space** dans un espace restreint *OR* réduit **2.** [shut up] renfermé ■ [imprisoned] emprisonné, incarcéré ■ **to be ~ to barracks** MIL être consigné.

confinement [kən'faɪnmənt] *n* **1.** [detention] détention *f*, réclusion *f* ■ [imprisonment] emprisonnement *m*, incarcération *f* ■ **~ to bed** alitement *m* ■ **~ to barracks** MIL consigne *f* (au quartier) ■ **six months' ~** six mois de prison **2.** [in childbirth] couches *fpl*, accouchement *m*.

confines ['kɒnfaɪnz] *npl* confins *mpl*, limites *fpl* ■ **within the ~ of the monastery** dans les limites du monastère.

confirm [kən'fɜːm] *vt* **1.** [verify] confirmer, corroborer ■ **we ~ receipt of** *OR* **that we have received your letter** nous accusons réception de votre lettre **2.** [finalize - arrangement, booking] confirmer **3.** [strengthen - position] assurer, consolider ; [- belief, doubts, resolve] fortifier, confirmer, raffermir ■ **that ~s her in her opinion** cela la confirme dans son opinion **4.** [make valid - treaty] ratifier ; [- election] valider ■ LAW entériner, homologuer **5.** RELIG confirmer.

confirmation [,kɒnfə'meɪʃn] *n* **1.** [verification] confirmation *f* ■ **the report is still awaiting ~** cette nouvelle n'a pas encore été confirmée **2.** [finalization - of arrangements] confirmation *f* **3.** [strengthening - of position] consolidation *f*, raffermissement *m* **4.** [validation] validation *f* ■ LAW entérinement *m*, homologation *f* ■ [of treaty] ratification *f* **5.** RELIG confirmation *f*.

confirmed [kən'fɜːmd] *adj* **1.** [long-established] invétéré ■ **he's a ~ bachelor** c'est un célibataire endurci **2.** RELIG confirmé.

confiscate ['kɒnfɪskeɪt] *vt* confisquer ■ **to ~ sthg from sb** confisquer qqch à qqn.

confiscation [,kɒnfɪ'skeɪʃn] *n* confiscation *f*.

conflagration [,kɒnflə'greɪʃn] *n fml* incendie *m*, sinistre *m fml*.

conflate [kən'fleɪt] *vt fml* colliger.

conflict ◇ *n* ['kɒnflɪkt] **1.** [clash] conflit *m*, lutte *f* ▪ MIL conflit *m*, guerre *f* ▪ **she often comes into ~ with her mother** elle entre souvent en conflit *OR* se heurte souvent avec sa mère ▪ **a ~ of interests** un conflit d'intérêts **2.** [disagreement] dispute *f* ▪ LAW conflit *m* ▪ **to be in ~ (with)** être en conflit (avec) ▪ **our differing beliefs brought us into ~** nos croyances divergentes nous ont opposés ▪ **there is a ~ between the two statements** les deux déclarations ne concordent pas **3.** PSYCHOL [turmoil] conflit *m*.
◇ *vi* [kən'flɪkt] **1.** [ideas, interests] s'opposer, se heurter ▪ **the research findings ~ with this view** les résultats des recherches sont en contradiction avec *OR* contredisent cette idée **2.** [fight] être en conflit *OR* en lutte.

conflicting [kən'flɪktɪŋ] *adj* [opinions] incompatible ▪ [evidence, reports] contradictoire.

confluence ['kɒnfluəns] *n* **1.** [of rivers] confluent *m* **2.** [gathering together] confluence *f* ▪ *fig* [crowd] rassemblement *m*.

conform [kən'fɔ:m] *vi* **1.** [comply - person] se conformer, s'adapter ▪ **to ~ to** *OR* **with sthg** se conformer *OR* s'adapter à qqch **2.** [action, thing] être en conformité ▪ **all cars must ~ to** *OR* **with the regulations** toute voiture doit être conforme aux normes **3.** [correspond] correspondre, répondre ▪ **she ~s to** *OR* **with my idea of a president** elle correspond *OR* répond à ma conception d'un président **4.** RELIG être conformiste.

conformation [,kɒnfɔ:'meɪʃn] *n* **1.** [configuration] conformation *f*, structure *f* **2.** [act of forming] conformation *f*.

conformism [kən'fɔ:mɪzm] *n* conformisme *m*.

conformist [kən'fɔ:mɪst] ◇ *adj* conformiste.
◇ *n* [gen - RELIG] conformiste *mf*.

conformity [kən'fɔ:mətɪ] (*pl* **conformities**) *n* **1.** [with rules, regulations] conformité *f* **2.** [in behaviour, dress etc] conformisme *m* **3.** RELIG conformisme *m*.
◆ **in conformity with** *prep phr* en accord avec, conformément à.

confound [kən'faund] *vt* **1.** [perplex] déconcerter ▪ **to be ~ed** être confondu **2.** *fml* [mix up] confondre **3.** *arch* [defeat - enemy] confondre.

confounded [kən'faundɪd] *adj inf dated* [wretched] maudit ▪ **it's a ~ nuisance!** c'est la barbe!, quelle barbe!

confront [kən'frʌnt] *vt* **1.** [face] affronter, faire face à ▪ **the obstacles ~ing us** les obstacles auxquels nous devons faire face ▪ **the headmaster ~ed him in the corridor** le directeur l'affronta dans le couloir ▪ **to be ~ed by** *OR* **with sthg** [problem, risk] se trouver en face de qqch **2.** [present] confronter ▪ **she ~ed him with the facts** elle l'a confronté avec les faits.

confrontation [,kɒnfrʌn'teɪʃn] *n* **1.** [conflict] conflit *m*, affrontement *m* ▪ **he hates ~** il a horreur des affrontements ▪ MIL affrontement *m* **2.** [act of confronting] confrontation *f*.

confrontational [,kɒnfrʌn'teɪʃənl] *adj* [situation] d'affrontement ▪ [policy] de confrontation ▪ [person] : **to be ~** aimer les conflits.

Confucian [kən'fju:ʃn] ◇ *adj* confucéen.
◇ *n* confucéen *m*, - enne *f*.

Confucius [kən'fju:ʃəs] *pr n* Confucius.

confuse [kən'fju:z] *vt* **1.** [muddle - person] embrouiller ; [- thoughts] embrouiller, brouiller ; [- memory] brouiller ▪ **don't ~ me!** ne m'embrouillez pas (les idées)! ▪ **to ~ the issue further** pour embrouiller *OR* compliquer encore plus les choses **2.** [perplex] déconcerter, rendre perplexe ▪ [fluster] troubler ▪ [embarrass] embarrasser **3.** [mix up] confondre ▪ **you're confusing me with my brother** vous me confondez avec mon frère **4.** [disconcert - opponent] confondre.

confused [kən'fju:zd] *adj* **1.** [muddled - person] désorienté ; [- sounds] confus, indistinct ; [- thoughts] confus, embrouillé ; [- memory] confus, vague ▪ **wait a minute, I'm getting ~** attends, là, je ne suis plus ▪ **very old people often get ~** les personnes très âgées ont souvent les idées confuses **2.** [flustered] troublé ▪ [embarrassed] confus **3.** [disordered] en désordre ▪ [enemy] confus.

confusing [kən'fju:zɪŋ] *adj* embrouillé, déroutant ▪ **the plot is ~** on se perd dans l'intrigue.

confusingly [kən'fju:zɪŋlɪ] *adv* de façon embrouillée.

confusion [kən'fju:ʒn] *n* **1.** [bewilderment] confusion *f* ▪ [embarrassment] déconfiture *f*, trouble *m*, embarras *m* ▪ **he stared at it in ~** il le fixa d'un regard perplexe ▪ **she's in a state of ~** elle a l'esprit troublé **2.** [mixing up] confusion *f* ▪ **to avoid ~** pour éviter toute confusion ▪ **there is some ~ as to who won** il y a incertitude sur le vainqueur **3.** [disorder] désordre *m* ▪ [of enemy] désordre *m*, désarroi *m*.

conga ['kɒŋgə] ◇ *n* conga *f*.
◇ *vi* danser la conga.

congeal [kən'dʒi:l] ◇ *vi* [thicken] prendre ▪ [oil] (se) figer ▪ [blood] (se) coaguler ▪ [milk] (se) cailler.
◇ *vt* [thicken] faire prendre ▪ [oil] (faire) figer ▪ [blood] (faire) coaguler ▪ [milk] (faire) cailler.

congenial [kən'dʒi:njəl] *adj* [pleasant] sympathique, agréable.

congenital [kən'dʒenɪtl] *adj* MED congénital, de naissance ▪ **he's a ~ liar** *fig* c'est un menteur né.

conger (eel) ['kɒŋgər-] *n* congre *m*, anguille *f* de mer.

congest [kən'dʒest] ◇ *vt* **1.** [crowd] encombrer **2.** MED [clog] congestionner.
◇ *vi* **1.** [become crowded] s'encombrer **2.** MED [become clogged] se congestionner.

congested [kən'dʒestɪd] *adj* **1.** [area, town] surpeuplé ▪ [road] encombré, embouteillé ▪ [communication lines] encombré ▪ **the roads are ~ with traffic** il y a des embouteillages *OR* des encombrements sur les routes **2.** MED [clogged] congestionné.

congestion [kən'dʒestʃn] *n* **1.** [of area] surpeuplement *m* ▪ [of road, traffic] encombrement *m*, embouteillage *m* **2.** MED [blockage] congestion *f*.

CONGRATULATIONS

(Toutes mes) félicitations ! Congratulations!

Félicitations pour votre promotion ! Congratulations on your promotion!

Laissez-moi vous féliciter (pour votre remarquable travail). Let me congratulate you (on your excellent work).

Je suis très content pour vous. I'm so happy for you.

Ça m'a fait très plaisir d'apprendre que tu avais réussi ton concours. I was so pleased to hear that you'd passed your exam.

Nous sommes ravis d'apprendre la bonne nouvelle. We were delighted to hear the good news.

C'était très réussi ta soirée. It was a wonderful party.

C'est formidable ! That's wonderful!

Bravo ! Well done!

Bien joué ! Well done!

Ça, c'est une bonne nouvelle ! That's great news!

congestion charge *n UK* taxe *f* anti-embouteillages.

conglomerate ◇ *n* [kən'glɒmərət] [gen - FIN] & GEOL conglomérat *m*.
◇ *adj* [kən'glɒmərət] congloméré, aggloméré ■ GEOL congloméré.
◇ *vt* agglomérer, conglomérer *fml*.
◇ *vi* [kən'glɒməreɪt] s'agglomérer.

conglomeration [kən,glɒmə'reɪʃn] *n* **1.** [mass] groupement *m*, rassemblement *m* ■ [of buildings] agglomération *f* **2.** [act, state] agglomération *f*, conglomération *f fml*.

Congo ['kɒŋgəʊ] *pr n* **1.** [country] : **the ~** le Congo ■ **in the ~** au Congo **2.** [river] : **the ~** le fleuve Zaïre.

Congo-Brazzaville [,kaŋgəʊ'bræzəvɪl] *pr n* Congo-Brazzaville *m*.

Congo-Kinshasa [,kaŋgəʊkɪn'ʃasə] *pr n* Congo-Kinshasa *m*.

Congolese [,kɒŋgə'li:z] ◇ *n* Congolais *m*, - e *f*.
◇ *adj* congolais.

congrats [kən'græts] *interj inf* **~!** chapeau!

congratulate [kən'grætʃʊleɪt] *vt* féliciter, complimenter ■ **her parents ~d her on passing her exams** ses parents l'ont félicitée d'avoir réussi à ses examens ■ **she ~d them on their engagement** elle leur a présenté ses félicitations à l'occasion de leurs fiançailles.

congratulation [kən,grætʃʊ'leɪʃn] *n* félicitation *f*.
◆ **congratulations** ◇ *interj* : **~s!** (toutes mes) félicitations!, je vous félicite!
◇ *npl* félicitations *fpl* ■ **~s on the new job/your engagement** félicitations pour votre nouveau poste/vos fiançailles ■ **I hear ~s are in order** il paraît qu'il faut vous féliciter.
Voir module d'usage

congratulatory [kən'grætʃʊlətrɪ] *adj* de félicitations.

congregate ['kɒŋgrɪgeɪt] *vi* se rassembler, se réunir.

congregation [,kɒŋgrɪ'geɪʃn] *n* **1.** [group] assemblée *f*, rassemblement *m* ■ RELIG [of worshippers] assemblée *f* (de fidèles), assistance *f* ■ [of priests] congrégation *f* **2.** *UK* UNIV assemblée *f* générale.

congress ['kɒŋgres] *n* **1.** [association, meeting] congrès *m* **2.** *(U) fml* [sexual intercourse] rapports *mpl* sexuels.
◆ **Congress** *n* POL Congrès *m* ■ [session] *session du Congrès américain*.

CONGRESS

Le Congrès, organe législatif américain, est constitué du Sénat et de la Chambre des représentants ; tout projet de loi doit être approuvé séparément par ces deux chambres.

congressional [kəŋ'greʃənl] *adj* [gen] d'un congrès.
◆ **Congressional** *adj* POL du Congrès ■ **Congressional district** *circonscription d'un représentant du Congrès américain* ■ **Congressional Record** *journal officiel du Congrès américain*.

congressman ['kɒŋgresmən] (*pl* **congressmen** [-mən]) *n* POL membre *m* du Congrès américain **--at-large** *représentant du Congrès américain non attaché à une circonscription électorale*.

congresswoman ['kɒŋgres,wʊmən] (*pl* **congresswomen** [-,wɪmɪn]) *n* POL membre *m* (féminin) du Congrès américain.

congruent ['kɒŋgrʊənt] *adj* **1.** *fml* [similar] conforme ■ **~ with** *OR* **to** conforme à **2.** *fml* [corresponding] en harmonie ■ [suitable] convenable ■ **to be ~ with sthg** être en harmonie avec qqch **3.** MATHS [number] congru, congruent ■ [triangle] congruent.

congruous ['kɒŋgrʊəs] *adj fml* **1.** [corresponding] qui s'accorde ■ **~ with sthg** qui s'accorde avec qqch **2.** [suitable] convenable, qui convient.

conic(al) ['kɒnɪk(l)] *adj* en forme de cône, conique.

conifer ['kɒnɪfər] *n* conifère *m*.

coniferous [kə'nɪfərəs] *adj* conifère ■ **a ~ forest** une forêt de conifères.

conjectural [kən'dʒektʃərəl] *adj* conjectural.

conjecture [kən'dʒektʃər] ◇ *n* conjecture *f* ■ **whether he knew or not is a matter for ~** savoir s'il était au courant ou pas relève de la conjecture.
◇ *vt* conjecturer, présumer.
◇ *vi* conjecturer, faire des conjectures.

conjugal ['kɒndʒʊgl] *adj* conjugal.

conjugate ◇ *vt* ['kɒndʒʊgeɪt] conjuguer.
◇ *vi* se conjuguer.
◇ *adj* ['kɒndʒʊgɪt] conjoint, uni.

conjugation [,kɒndʒʊ'geɪʃn] *n* conjugaison *f*.

conjunction [kən'dʒʌŋkʃn] *n* **1.** [combination] conjonction *f*, union *f* **2.** ASTRON & GRAM conjonction *f*.
◆ **in conjunction with** *prep phr* conjointement avec.

conjunctive [kən'dʒʌŋktɪv] *adj* [gen - ANAT] & GRAM conjonctif.

conjunctivitis [kən,dʒʌŋktɪ'vaɪtɪs] *n* conjonctivite *f* ■ **to have ~** avoir de la conjonctivite.

conjure ['kʌndʒər] ◇ *vt* **1.** [produce - gen] faire apparaître, produire ; [- by magic] faire apparaître *(par prestidigitation)* **2.** [kən'dʒʊər] *arch* [appeal to] conjurer, implorer.
◇ *vi* faire des tours de passe-passe ■ **his is a name to ~ with** *UK fig* c'est quelqu'un d'important.
◆ **conjure away** *vt sep* faire disparaître.
◆ **conjure up** *vt sep* [object, rabbit] faire apparaître, produire ■ [gods, spirits] faire apparaître, invoquer ■ [memory] évoquer, rappeler ■ [image] évoquer.

conjurer ['kʌndʒərər] *n* [magician] prestidigitateur *m*, - trice *f* ■ [sorcerer] sorcier *m*, - ère *f*.

conjuring ['kʌndʒərɪŋ] ◇ *n* prestidigitation *f*.
◇ *adj* : **~ trick** tour *m* de passe-passe *OR* de prestidigitation.

conjuror ['kʌndʒərər] = **conjurer**.

conk [kɒŋk] *inf* ◇ *vt* [hit] cogner *OR* frapper (sur la caboche).
◇ *n* **1.** [blow] gnon *m* **2.** *UK* [head] caboche *f* **3.** *UK* [nose] pif *m*.
◆ **conk out** *vi insep inf* tomber en panne.

conker ['kɒŋkər] *n UK inf* marron *m*.
◆ **conkers** *n inf (U) jeu d'enfant qui consiste à tenter de casser un marron tenu au bout d'un fil par son adversaire*.

conman ['kɒnmæn] (*pl* **conmen** [-men]) *n inf* arnaqueur *m*.

connect [kə'nekt] ◇ *vt* **1.** [join - pipes, wires] raccorder ; [- pinions, shafts, wheels] engrener, coupler ■ **to ~ sthg up to sthg** joindre *OR* relier *OR* raccorder qqch à qqch **2.** [join to supply - machine, house, telephone] brancher, raccorder ■ **to ~ sthg to sthg** raccorder qqch à qqch, brancher qqch sur qqch **3.** TELEC mettre en communication, relier ■ **to ~ sb to sb** mettre qqn en communication avec qqn ■ **I'm trying to ~ you** j'essaie d'obtenir votre communication **4.** [link - subj: path, railway, road, airline] relier ■ **to ~ with** *OR* **to** relier à **5.** [associate - person, place, event] associer, faire le rapprochement ■ **to ~ sb/sthg with sb/sthg** associer une personne/chose à une autre ■ **I'd never ~ed the two things before** je n'avais (encore) jamais fait le rapprochement entre les deux.
◇ *vi* **1.** [bus, plane, train] assurer la correspondance ■ **to ~ with** assurer la correspondance avec **2.** [blow, fist, kick] frapper.

connected [kə'nektɪd] *adj* **1.** [linked - subjects, species] connexe **2.** [coherent - speech, sentences] cohérent, suivi **3.** [associated] : **to be ~ed with** avoir un lien *OR* rapport avec **4.** [related] : **to be ~ed with** *OR* **to** être parent de.

Connecticut [kə'netɪkət] *pr n* Connecticut *m* ■ **in ~** dans le Connecticut.

connecting [kə'nektɪŋ] *adj* [cable, wire] de connexion ■ **~ rod** bielle *f* ■ **~ flight** correspondance *f* ■ **~ door** porte *f* de communication.

connection [kə'nekʃn] *n* **1.** [link between two things] lien *m*, rapport *m*, connexion *f* ■ **to make a ~ between** *OR* **to** *OR* **with sthg** faire le lien avec qqch ■ **does this have any ~ with what happened yesterday?** ceci a-t-il un rapport quelconque avec ce qui s'est passé hier? ■ **in this** *OR* **that ~** à ce propos, à ce sujet **2.** ELEC prise *f*, raccord *m* **3.** TELEC communication *f*, ligne *f* **4.** [transfer - between buses, planes, trains] correspondance *f* ▪ **to miss one's ~** rater sa correspondance **5.** [transport] liaison *f* ▪ **the town enjoys excellent road and rail ~s** la ville dispose d'excellentes liaisons routières et ferroviaires **6.** [relationship] rapport *m*, relation *f* ▪ **he has CIA ~s** il a des liens avec la CIA ▪ **family ~s** parenté *f* **7.** [colleague, business contact] relation *f* (d'affaires).

◆ **in connection with** *prep phr* à propos de.

connective [kə'nektɪv] ◇ *adj* [word, phrase] conjonctif.
◇ *n* GRAM conjonction *f*.

connect-the-dots *n (U)* US *jeu qui consiste à relier des points numérotés pour découvrir un dessin.*

connexion [kə'nekʃn] = **connection**.

conning tower ['kɒnɪŋ-] *n* [on submarine] kiosque *m* ▪ [on warship] centre *m* opérationnel.

connivance [kə'naɪvəns] *n pej* connivence *f* ▪ **with the ~ of, in ~ with** de connivence avec.

connive [kə'naɪv] *vi pej* [plot] être de connivence ▪ **they ~d together to undermine government policy** ils étaient de connivence pour déstabiliser la politique du gouvernement.

◆ **connive at** *vt insep* **1.** [ignore] fermer les yeux sur **2.** [abet] être complice de.

conniving [kə'naɪvɪŋ] *adj pej* malhonnête.

connoisseur [ˌkɒnə'sɜːʳ] *n* connaisseur *m*, - euse *f* ▪ **a ~ of fine wine/good literature** un connaisseur en vins/littérature.

connotation [ˌkɒnə'teɪʃn] *n* **1.** [association] connotation *f* ▪ **the name has ~s of quality and expertise** ce nom évoque la qualité et la compétence **2.** LING connotation *f* **3.** LOGIC implication *f*.

connote [kə'nəʊt] *vt* **1.** *fml* [imply - subj: word, phrase, name] évoquer **2.** LING connoter **3.** LOGIC impliquer.

conquer ['kɒŋkəʳ] *vt* **1.** [defeat - person, enemy] vaincre **2.** [take control of - city, nation] conquérir **3.** [master - feelings, habits] surmonter ; [- disease, disability] vaincre, surmonter **4.** [win over - sb's heart] conquérir ; [- audience, public] conquérir, subjuguer.

conqueror ['kɒŋkərəʳ] *n* conquérant *m*.

conquest ['kɒŋkwest] *n* [of land, person] conquête *f* ▪ **the ~ of space** la conquête de l'espace ❙ [land, person conquered] conquête *f* ▪ **he's her latest ~** c'est sa dernière conquête.

Conrail®, **ConRail**® ['kɒnreɪl] *pr n transport urbain newyorkais.*

Cons. *written abbr of* **Conservative**.

consanguinity [ˌkɒnsæŋ'gwɪnətɪ] *n* consanguinité *f*.

conscience ['kɒnʃəns] *n* **1.** [moral sense] conscience *f* ▪ **a matter of ~** un cas de conscience ▪ **to have a clear** OR **an easy ~** avoir la conscience tranquille ▪ **my ~ is clear** j'ai la conscience tranquille ▪ **to have a bad** OR **guilty ~** avoir mauvaise conscience ▪ **to have sthg on one's ~** avoir qqch sur la conscience ▪ **in all ~** en toute conscience **2.** *(U)* [scruples] mauvaise conscience *f*, remords *m*, scrupule *m* ▪ **to have no ~ (about doing sthg)** ne pas avoir de scrupules (à faire qqch).

conscience clause *n clause de conscience.*

conscience money *n* argent *m* restitué *(pour soulager sa conscience).*

conscience-stricken *adj* pris de remords ▪ **to be** OR **to look ~** être pris de remords, être la proie des remords.

conscientious [ˌkɒnʃɪ'enʃəs] *adj* consciencieux ▪ **she was her usual ~ self** elle était consciencieuse comme toujours.

conscientiously [ˌkɒnʃɪ'enʃəslɪ] *adv* consciencieusement.

conscientiousness [ˌkɒnʃɪ'enʃəsnɪs] *n* conscience *f*.

conscientious objector *n* objecteur *m* de conscience.

conscious ['kɒnʃəs] ◇ *adj* **1.** [aware] conscient ▪ **to be ~ of (doing) sthg** être conscient de (faire) qqch ▪ **to become ~ of sthg** prendre conscience de qqch ▪ **politically ~** politisé **2.** [awake] conscient ▪ **to become ~** reprendre connaissance **3.** [deliberate - attempt, effort] conscient ; [- cruelty, rudeness] intentionnel, délibéré **4.** [able to think - being, mind] conscient.
◇ *n* PSYCHOL **: the ~** le conscient.

-conscious *in cpds* conscient de ▪ **clothes~** qui fait attention à sa tenue ▪ **fashion~** qui suit la mode ▪ **age~** conscient de son âge ▪ **health ~** soucieux de sa santé.

consciously ['kɒnʃəslɪ] *adv* consciemment, délibérément.

consciousness ['kɒnʃəsnɪs] *n* **1.** [awareness] conscience *f* ▪ **political ~** conscience politique **2.** [mentality] conscience *f* ▪ **the national ~** la conscience nationale **3.** [state of being awake] connaissance *f* ▪ **to lose ~** perdre connaissance ▪ **to regain ~** reprendre connaissance.

consciousness raising *n* sensibilisation *f*.

◆ **consciousness-raising** *comp* [group, session] de prise de conscience.

conscript ◇ *vt* [kən'skrɪpt] [men, troops] enrôler, recruter ▪ [workers, labourers] recruter.
◇ *n* ['kɒnskrɪpt] conscrit *m*, appelé *m*.
◇ *adj* ['kɒnskrɪpt] [army] de conscrits.

conscription [kən'skrɪpʃn] *n* conscription *f*.

consecrate ['kɒnsɪkreɪt] *vt* **1.** [sanctify - church, building, place] consacrer ; [- bread and wine] consacrer ▪ **~d ground** terre *f* sainte OR bénie **2.** [ordain - bishop] consacrer, sacrer **3.** [dedicate] consacrer, dédier ▪ **to ~ one's life to sthg** consacrer sa vie à qqch **4.** [make venerable] consacrer ▪ **a custom ~d by time** une coutume consacrée par l'usage.

consecration [ˌkɒnsɪ'kreɪʃn] *n* **1.** [sanctification] consécration *f* **2.** [ordination] sacre *m* **3.** [dedication] consécration *f* **4.** [veneration] consécration *f*.

consecutive [kən'sekjʊtɪv] *adj* **1.** [successive - days, weeks] consécutif ▪ **for the third ~ day** pour le troisième jour consécutif **2.** GRAM [clause] consécutif.

consecutively [kən'sekjʊtɪvlɪ] *adv* consécutivement ▪ **for five years ~** pendant cinq années consécutives ▪ **the sentences to be served ~** LAW avec cumul de peines.

consensual [kən'sensjʊəl] *adj* LAW & MED [contract, agreement] consensuel.

consensus [kən'sensəs] ◇ *n* consensus *m* ▪ **they failed to reach a ~ (of opinion)** ils n'ont pas obtenu de consensus (d'opinion) ▪ **what is the scientific ~ on the matter?** quelle est l'opinion des scientifiques sur ce sujet?
◇ *comp* [politics] de consensus.

consent [kən'sent] ◇ *vi* consentir ▪ **to ~ to (do) sthg** consentir à (faire) qqch.
◇ *n* consentement *m*, accord *m* ▪ **he refused his ~ to a divorce** il a refusé son consentement pour le divorce ▪ **by common ~** d'un commun accord ▪ **by mutual ~** par consentement mutuel ▪ **the age of ~** l'âge *m* nubile.

consenting adult [kən'sentɪŋ-] *n* adulte *m* consentant.

consequence ['kɒnsɪkwəns] *n* **1.** [result] conséquence *f*, suite *f* ▪ **as a ~ of** à la suite de ▪ **the policy had terrible ~s for the poor** cette mesure a eu des conséquences terribles pour les pauvres ▪ **in ~ of which** par suite de quoi **2.** [importance] conséquence *f*, importance *f* ▪ **a person of no** OR **little ~** une personne sans importance ▪ **a man of ~** un homme important ▪ **it's of no ~** c'est sans conséquence, cela n'a pas d'importance.

◆ **consequences** ◇ *npl* conséquences *fpl* ▪ **to take** OR **to suffer the ~s** accepter OR subir les conséquences ▪ **to face the ~s** faire face aux conséquences.
◇ *n (U)* UK GAMES ≃ cadavres *mpl* exquis.

◆ **in consequence** *adv phr* par conséquent.

consequent ['kɒnsɪkwənt] *adj fml* consécutif ▪ **~ on** OR **upon** [resulting from] résultant de ; [following] consécutif à.

consequential [ˌkɒnsɪ'kwenʃl] *adj fml* **1.** = **consequent** **2.** [important - decision] de conséquence, conséquent.

consequently ['kɒnsɪkwəntlɪ] *adv* par conséquent, donc.

conservation [ˌkɒnsə'veɪʃn] *n* **1.** [of works of art] préservation *f* **2.** [of natural resources] préservation *f* ■ **nature ~** défense *f* de l'environnement **3.** PHYS conservation *f*.

conservation area *n* zone *f* protégée.

conservationist [ˌkɒnsə'veɪʃənɪst] *n* défenseur *m* de l'environnement.

conservatism [kən'sɜːvətɪzm] *n* **1.** POL = **Conservatism** **2.** [traditionalism] conservatisme *m*.
◆ **Conservatism** *n* [policy of Conservative Party] conservatisme *m*.

conservative [kən'sɜːvətɪv] ◇ *n* [traditionalist] traditionaliste *mf*, conformiste *mf*.
◇ *adj* **1.** [traditionalist - views] conformiste **2.** [conventional - suit, clothes] classique **3.** [modest - estimate] prudent **4.** PHYS conservateur.
◆ **Conservative** POL ◇ *n* conservateur *m*, - trice *f*.
◇ *adj* [policy, government, MP] conservateur.

conservatively [kən'sɜːvətɪvlɪ] *adv* [dress] de façon conventionnelle.

Conservative Party *pr n* : **the ~** le parti conservateur.

conservatoire [kən'sɜːvətwɑːʳ] *n* conservatoire *m*.

conservator [kən'sɜːvətəʳ] *n* gardien *m*, - enne *f*.

conservatory [kən'sɜːvətrɪ] (*pl* **conservatories**) *n* **1.** [greenhouse] jardin *m* d'hiver **2.** = **conservatoire**.

conserve ◇ *vt* [kən'sɜːv] **1.** [save - energy, resources, battery] économiser ■ **to ~ one's strength** ménager ses forces **2.** *lit* [preserve - privilege, freedom] protéger, préserver.
◇ *n* ['kɒnsɜːv, kən'sɜːv] confiture *f* ■ **strawberry ~** confiture de fraises.

consider [kən'sɪdəʳ] ◇ *vt* **1.** [believe] considérer, estimer, penser ■ **I've always ~ed her (as** *OR* **to be) a good friend** je l'ai toujours considérée comme une bonne amie ■ **she ~s it wrong to say such things** elle pense qu'il est mauvais de dire de telles choses ■ **I ~ myself lucky** je m'estime heureux **2.** [ponder - problem, offer, possibility] considérer, examiner ; [- issue, question] réfléchir à ■ **have you ever ~ed becoming an actress?** avez-vous jamais songé à devenir actrice? ■ **I'll ~ it** je verrai, je réfléchirai **3.** [bear in mind - points, facts] prendre en considération ; [- costs, difficulties, dangers] tenir compte de ■ **we got off lightly, when you ~ what might have happened** nous nous en sommes bien tirés, quand on pense à ce qui aurait pu arriver ■ **all things ~ed** tout bien considéré **4.** [show regard for - feelings, wishes] tenir compte de ■ **he has a wife and family to ~** il a une femme et une famille à prendre en considération **5.** [discuss - report, case] examiner, considérer ■ **she's being ~ed for the post of manager** on pense à elle pour le poste de directeur **6.** [contemplate - picture, scene] examiner, observer.
◇ *vi* réfléchir.

considerable [kən'sɪdrəbl] *adj* considérable ■ **she showed ~ courage** elle a fait preuve de beaucoup de courage ■ **a ~ number** un nombre considérable ■ **to a ~ extent** dans une (très) large mesure.

considerably [kən'sɪdrəblɪ] *adv* considérablement.

considerate [kən'sɪdərət] *adj* [person] prévenant, plein d'égards, aimable ■ **that's very ~ of you** c'est très aimable à vous ■ **he's always so ~ of** *OR* **towards others** il est toujours si prévenant envers les autres.

considerately [kən'sɪdərətlɪ] *adv* avec des égards.

consideration [kənˌsɪdə'reɪʃn] *n* **1.** [thought] considération *f* ■ **the matter needs careful ~** le sujet demande une attention particulière ■ **to take sthg into ~** prendre qqch en considération ■ **taking everything into ~** tout bien considéré ■ **after due ~** après mûre réflexion **2.** [factor] considération *f*, préoccupation *f* **3.** [thoughtfulness] égard *m* ■ **to show ~ for sb/sb's feelings** ménager qqn/la sensibilité de qqn ■ **have you no ~ for other people?** n'as-tu donc aucun égard pour les autres? ■ **she remained silent out of ~ for his family** elle se tut par égard pour sa famille **4.** [discussion] étude *f* ■ **the matter is under ~** l'affaire est à l'étude **5.** [importance] : **of no ~** sans importance **6.** *fml* [payment] rémunération *f*, finance *f*.

considered [kən'sɪdəd] *adj* **1.** [reasoned - opinion, manner] bien pesé, mûrement réfléchi ■ **it's my ~ opinion that...** après mûre réflexion, je pense que... **2.** *fml* [respected - artist, writer] considéré, respecté.

considering [kən'sɪdərɪŋ] ◇ *conj* étant donné que, vu que ■ **~ she'd never played the part before, she did very well** pour quelqu'un qui n'avait jamais tenu ce rôle, elle s'est très bien débrouillée.
◇ *prep* étant donné, vu ■ **~ how hard he tried, he did rather poorly** vu tout le mal qu'il s'est donné, c'était plutôt médiocre.
◇ *adv inf* tout compte fait, finalement ■ **she writes quite well, ~** elle écrit assez bien, finalement.

consign [kən'saɪn] *vt* **1.** [send - goods] envoyer, expédier **2.** [relegate - thing] reléguer ■ **I ~ed his last letter to the rubbish bin** sa dernière lettre s'est retrouvée à la poubelle **3.** [entrust - person] confier ■ **to ~ sb to sb** confier qqn à *OR* aux soins de qqn.

consignee [ˌkɒnsaɪ'niː] *n* consignataire *mf*.

consigner [kən'saɪnəʳ] = **consignor**.

consignment [ˌkən'saɪnmənt] *n* **1.** [despatch] envoi *m*, expédition *f* ■ **goods for ~** marchandise *f* à expédier ■ **~ note** bordereau *m* d'expédition **2.** [batch of goods] arrivage *m*, lot *m*.

consignor [kən'saɪnəʳ] *n* expéditeur *m*, - trice *f*.

consist [kən'sɪst] ◆ **consist of** *vt insep* consister en, se composer de ■ **the panel ~s of five senior lecturers** le jury se compose de cinq maîtres de conférence ■ **the book ~s largely of photos of his family** le livre est constitué surtout de photos de sa famille.
◆ **consist in** *vt insep fml* : **to ~ in (doing) sthg** consister à faire qqch *OR* dans qqch ■ **the book's success ~s largely in its simplicity** le succès du livre réside en grande partie dans sa simplicité.

consistence [kən'sɪstəns], **consistency** [kən'sɪstənsɪ] (*pl* **consistences** *OR pl* **consistencies**) *n* **1.** [texture] consistance *f* **2.** [coherence - of behaviour, argument etc] cohérence *f*, logique *f*.

consistent [kən'sɪstənt] *adj* **1.** [constant - opponent, loyalty] constant **2.** [steady - growth, improvement] constant **3.** [idea, argument, account] cohérent ■ **his story is not ~ with the known facts** son histoire ne correspond pas aux faits.

consistently [kən'sɪstəntlɪ] *adv* régulièrement, constamment ■ **they have won ~ throughout the season** ils ont gagné tout au long de la saison.

consolation [ˌkɒnsə'leɪʃn] *n* consolation *f*, réconfort *m* ■ **if it's any ~, the same thing happened to me** si cela peut te consoler, il m'est arrivé la même chose ■ **she sought ~ in music** elle cherchait le réconfort dans la musique ■ **her children were a great ~ to her** ses enfants étaient une grande consolation pour elle.

consolation prize *n liter & fig* prix *m* de consolation.

console ◇ *vt* [kən'səʊl] consoler ■ **to ~ sb for sthg (with** *OR* **by)** consoler qqn de qqch (avec *OR* en).
◇ *n* ['kɒnsəʊl] **1.** [control panel] console *f*, pupitre *m* **2.** [cabinet] meuble *m (pour téléviseur, chaîne hi-fi)* **3.** MUS [on organ] console *f* **4.** ARCHIT console *f*.

consolidate [kən'sɒlɪdeɪt] *vt* **1.** [reinforce - forces, power] consolider ; [- knowledge] consolider, renforcer **2.** [combine - companies, states] réunir, fusionner ; [- funds, loans] consolider.

consolidated [kən'sɒlɪdeɪtɪd] *adj* [annuity, loan, loss] consolidé ■ [in name of company] *désigne une société née de la fusion de deux entreprises* ■ **~ accounts** états *mpl* financiers consolidés.

consolidation [kən,sɒlɪ'deɪʃn] *n* **1.** [reinforcement - of power] consolidation *f* ; [- of knowledge] consolidation *f*, renforcement *m* **2.** [amalgamation - of companies] fusion *f* ; [- of funds, loans] consolidation *f*.

consoling [kən'səʊlɪŋ] *adj* [idea, thought] réconfortant.

consols ['kɒnsəlz] *npl* *UK* fonds *mpl* consolidés.

consonance ['kɒnsənəns] *n* **1.** *fml* [of ideas] accord *m* **2.** LIT & MUS consonance *f*.

consonant ['kɒnsənənt] ◇ *n* consonne *f*.
◇ *adj fml* en accord.

consonantal [,kɒnsə'næntl] *adj* consonantique.

consonant shift *n* mutation *f* des consonnes.

consort ◇ *n* ['kɒnsɔ:t] **1.** [spouse] époux *m*, épouse *f* ▪ [of monarch] consort *m* **2.** [ship] escorteur *m*.
◇ *vi* [kən'sɔ:t] : **to ~ with sb** fréquenter qqn, frayer avec qqn.

consortium [kən'sɔ:tjəm] (*pl* **consortiums** *OR pl* **consortia** [-tjə]) *n* consortium *m*.

conspicuous [kən'spɪkjʊəs] *adj* **1.** [visible - behaviour, hat, person] voyant ▪ **he felt ~ in his new hat** il avait l'impression que son nouveau chapeau ne passait pas inaperçu ▪ **to make o.s. ~** se faire remarquer **2.** [obvious - failure, lack] manifeste, évident ; [- bravery, gallantry] insigne ▪ **to be ~ by one's absence** briller par son absence.

conspicuous consumption *n* consommation *f* ostentatoire *OR* de prestige.

conspicuously [kən'spɪkjʊəslɪ] *adv* **1.** [visibly - dressed] de façon à se faire remarquer **2.** [obviously - successful] de façon remarquable *OR* évidente.

conspiracy [kən'spɪrəsɪ] ◇ *n* (*pl* **conspiracies**) [plotting] conspiration *f*, complot *m* ▪ [plot] complot *m* ▪ **a ~ of silence** une conspiration du silence.
◇ *comp* : **~ theory** thèse *f* du complot.

conspirator [kən'spɪrətə^r] *n* conspirateur *m*, - trice *f*, comploteur *m*, - euse *f*, conjuré *m*, - e *f*.

conspiratorial [kən,spɪrə'tɔ:rɪəl] *adj* [smile, whisper, wink] de conspirateur ▪ [group] de conspirateurs.

conspiratorially [kən,spɪrə'tɔ:rɪəlɪ] *adv* [smile, whisper, wink] d'un air de conspiration.

conspire [kən'spaɪə^r] *vi* **1.** [plot] conspirer ▪ **to ~ (with sb) to do sthg** comploter *OR* s'entendre (avec qqn) pour faire qqch ▪ **to ~ against sb** conspirer contre qqn **2.** [combine - events, the elements] concourir, se conjurer ▪ **to ~ to do sthg** concourir à faire qqch ▪ **to ~ against sthg** se conjurer contre qqch.

constable ['kʌnstəbl] *n* agent *m*, gendarme *m*, sergent *m* ▪ **Constable Jenkins** Sergent Jenkins ▪ **police ~** agent *m* de police.

constabulary [kən'stæbjʊlərɪ] ◇ *n* (*pl* **constabularies**) : **the ~** la police, la gendarmerie.
◇ *adj* [duties] de policier.

Constance ['kɒnstəns] *pr n* : **Lake ~** le lac de Constance.

constancy ['kɒnstənsɪ] *n* **1.** [steadfastness] constance *f* ▪ [of feelings] constance *f*, fidélité *f* **2.** [stability - of temperature, light] constance *f*.

constant ['kɒnstənt] ◇ *adj* **1.** [continuous - interruptions, noise, pain] constant, continuel, perpétuel ▪ **the entrance is in ~ use** il y a un mouvement continuel à l'entrée **2.** [unchanging - pressure, temperature] constant **3.** [faithful - affection, friend] fidèle, loyal.
◇ *n* [gen - MATHS] constante *f*.

Constantine ['kɒnstəntaɪn] *pr n* **1.** [emperor] Constantin **2.** GEOG Constantine.

constantly ['kɒnstəntlɪ] *adv* constamment, sans cesse.

constellation [,kɒnstə'leɪʃn] *n* **1.** [of stars] constellation *f* **2.** *fig* [of celebrities] constellation *f*.

consternation [,kɒnstə'neɪʃn] *n* consternation *f* ▪ **I watched in ~** je regardais avec consternation ▪ **the prospect filled me with ~** cette perspective m'a plongé dans la consternation.

constipated ['kɒnstɪpeɪtɪd] *adj* constipé.

constipation [,kɒnstɪ'peɪʃn] *n* constipation *f*.

constituency [kən'stɪtjʊənsɪ] ◇ *n* (*pl* **constituencies**) [area] circonscription *f* électorale ▪ [people] électeurs *mpl*.
◇ *comp* [meeting, organization] local.

constituent [kən'stɪtjʊənt] ◇ *adj* **1.** [component - part, element] constituant, composant **2.** POL [assembly, power] constituant.
◇ *n* **1.** [voter] électeur *m*, - trice *f* **2.** [element] élément *m* constitutif.

constitute ['kɒnstɪtju:t] *vt* **1.** [represent] constituer ▪ **what ~s a state of emergency?** qu'est-ce que c'est qu'un état d'urgence? ▪ **they ~ a threat to the government** ils représentent une menace pour le gouvernement **2.** [make up] constituer **3.** [set up - committee] constituer **4.** [appoint - chairman] désigner.

constitution [,kɒnstɪ'tju:ʃn] *n* **1.** POL [statute] constitution *f* ▪ **the (United States) Constitution** *US* POL la Constitution ▪ **the Constitution State** le Connecticut **2.** [health] constitution *f* ▪ **to have a strong/weak ~** avoir une constitution robuste/chétive **3.** [structure] composition *f*.

CONSTITUTION

La Constitution britannique, à la différence de la Constitution américaine ou française (qui repose sur un texte écrit et définitif), n'est pas un document en soi, mais le résultat de la succession des lois dans le temps, fonctionnant sur le principe de la jurisprudence.

constitutional [,kɒnstɪ'tju:ʃənl] *adj* **1.** POL constitutionnel ▪ **~ monarchy** monarchie constitutionnelle **2.** [official - head, privilege] constitutionnel **3.** [inherent - weakness] constitutionnel.

constitutional law *n* droit *m* constitutionnel.

constitutionally [,kɒnstɪ'tju:ʃnəlɪ] *adv* **1.** POL [act] constitutionnellement **2.** [strong, weak] de *OR* par nature.

constitutive [kən'stɪtjʊtɪv] *adj* **1.** [body, organization] constitutif **2.** = **constituent** *(sense 1)*.

constrain [kən'streɪn] *vt fml* **1.** [force] contraindre, forcer ▪ **to ~ sb to do sthg** contraindre qqn à faire qqch **2.** [limit - feelings, freedom] contraindre, restreindre.

constrained [kən'streɪnd] *adj* **1.** [inhibited] contraint ▪ **to feel ~ to do sthg** se sentir contraint *OR* obligé de faire qqch ▪ **he felt ~ by his clothes** il se sentait à l'étroit dans ses vêtements **2.** [tense - manner, speech] contraint ; [- atmosphere, smile] contraint, gêné.

constraint [kən'streɪnt] *n* **1.** [restriction] contrainte *f* ▪ **there are certain ~s on their activities** ils subissent certaines contraintes dans leurs activités **2.** [pressure] contrainte *f* ▪ **to do sthg under ~** agir *OR* faire qqch sous la contrainte.

constrict [kən'strɪkt] *vt* **1.** [make narrower - blood vessels, throat] resserrer, serrer **2.** [hamper - breathing, movement] gêner.

constricted [kən'strɪktɪd] *adj* [breathing, movement] gêné, restreint ▪ **to feel ~ by sthg** *liter & fig* se sentir limité par qqch.

constricting [kən'strɪktɪŋ] *adj* [clothes] étroit ▪ *fig* [beliefs, ideology] limité.

constriction [kən'strɪkʃn] *n* **1.** [in chest, throat] constriction *f* **2.** [restriction] restriction *f*.

construct ◇ *vt* [kən'strʌkt] **1.** [build - bridge, dam, house, road] construire ; [- nest, raft] construire, bâtir ▪ **to ~ sthg (out) of sthg** construire qqch à partir de qqch **2.** [formulate - sentence, play] construire, composer ; [- system, theory] bâtir.
◇ *n* ['kɒnstrʌkt] *fml* construction *f*.

construction [kən'strʌkʃn] <> *n* **1.** [act of building - road, bridge, house] construction *f* ; [- machine] construction *f*, réalisation *f* ; [- system, theory] construction *f*, élaboration *f* ▪ **under ~** en construction ▪ **to work in ~** travailler dans le bâtiment **2.** [structure] construction *f*, édifice *m*, bâtiment *m* ▪ **a building of simple/solid ~** un bâtiment de construction simple/solidement construit **3.** [interpretation] interprétation *f* ▪ **to put a wrong ~ on sb's words** mal interpréter les paroles de qqn **4.** GRAM construction *f* **5.** GEOM construction *f*.
<> *comp* [site, work] de construction ▪ [worker] du bâtiment ▪ **the ~ industry** le bâtiment.

constructive [kən'strʌktɪv] *adj* [criticism, remark] constructif.

constructive dismissal *n* démission *f* provoquée *(sous la pression de la direction)*.

constructively [kən'strʌktɪvlɪ] *adv* de manière constructive.

constructivism [kən'strʌktɪvɪzm] *n* ART & PHILOS constructivisme *m*.

constructor [kən'strʌktəʳ] *n* [of building, road, machine] constructeur *m* ▪ [of system, theory] créateur *m*.

construe [kən'stru:] *vt* **1.** [interpret, understand - attitude, statement] interpréter, expliquer ▪ *dated* [Greek, Latin] expliquer **2.** [parse - Greek or Latin text] analyser, décomposer.

consul ['kɒnsəl] *n* consul *m*, -e *f*.

consular ['kɒnsjʊləʳ] *adj* consulaire.

consulate ['kɒnsjʊlət] *n* consulat *m*.

consult [kən'sʌlt] <> *vt* **1.** [ask - doctor, expert] consulter ▪ **to ~ sb about sthg** consulter qqn sur OR au sujet de qqch **2.** [consider - person's feelings] prendre en considération **3.** [refer to - book, map, watch] consulter.
<> *vi* consulter, être en consultation ▪ **to ~ together over sthg** se consulter sur OR au sujet de qqch ▪ **to ~ with sb** conférer avec qqn.

consultancy [kən'sʌltənsɪ] (*pl* **consultancies**) *n* **1.** [company] cabinet *m* d'expert-conseil **2.** [advice] assistance *f* technique ▪ **~ fee** frais *mpl* de consultation **3.** [hospital post] poste *m* de médecin OR chirurgien consultant.

consultant [kən'sʌltənt] <> *n* **1.** [doctor - specialist] médecin *mf* spécialiste, consultant *m* ; [- in charge of department] consultant *m* **2.** [expert] expert-conseil *m*, consultant *m*.
<> *comp* [engineer] conseil *(inv)* ▪ MED consultant.

consultation [ˌkɒnsəl'teɪʃn] *n* **1.** [discussion] consultation *f*, délibération *f* ▪ **a matter for ~** un sujet à débattre ▪ **in ~ with** en consultation OR en concertation avec ▪ **to hold ~s about sthg** avoir des consultations sur qqch **2.** [reference] consultation *f* ▪ **the dictionary is designed for easy ~** le dictionnaire a été conçu pour être consulté facilement.

consultative [kən'sʌltətɪv] *adj* consultatif.

consulting [kən'sʌltɪŋ] *adj* [engineer] conseil *(inv)*.

consulting room *n* cabinet *m* de consultation.

consumable [kən'sju:məbl] *adj* [substance - by fire] consumable ▪ [foodstuffs] consommable, de consommation.
◆ **consumables** *npl* [food] denrées *fpl* alimentaires, comestibles *mpl* ▪ [hardware] consommables *mpl*.

consume [kən'sju:m] *vt* **1.** [eat or drink] consommer **2.** [use up - energy, fuel] consommer ; [- time] dépenser **3.** [burn up - subj: fire, flames] consumer ▪ **the city was ~d by fire** la ville a brûlé ▪ **to be ~d with hatred/jealousy** *fig* être dévoré par la haine/jalousie.

consumer [kən'sju:məʳ] <> *n* **1.** [purchaser] consommateur *m*, - trice *f* **2.** [user] consommateur *m*, - trice *f* ▪ **gas/electricity ~** abonné *m* au gaz/à l'électricité.
<> *comp* [advice, protection] du consommateur, des consommateurs ▪ **~ credit** crédit *m* à la consommation ▪ **~ durables** biens *mpl* ▪ **~ goods** biens *mpl* de consommation ▪ **~ research** étude *f* de marché ▪ **~ spending** dépenses *fpl* de consommation.

consumerism [kən'sju:mərɪzm] *n* **1.** [consumer protection] consumérisme *m* **2.** *pej* [consumption] consommation *f* à outrance.

Consumers' Association *pr n association britannique des consommateurs.*

consumer society *n* société *f* de consommation.

consuming [kən'sju:mɪŋ] *adj* [desire, interest] dévorant.

consummate <> *adj* [kən'sʌmət] *fml* **1.** [very skilful - artist, musician] consommé, accompli **2.** [utter - coward, fool, liar, snob] accompli, parfait, fini.
<> *vt* ['kɒnsəmeɪt] [love, marriage] consommer.

consummation [ˌkɒnsə'meɪʃn] *n* **1.** [of marriage] consommation *f* **2.** [culmination - of career, life's work] couronnement *m* **3.** [achievement - of ambitions, desires] achèvement *m*.

consumption [kən'sʌmpʃn] *n* **1.** [eating, drinking] consommation *f* ▪ **unfit for human ~** non comestible ▪ **his words were not intended for public ~** *fig* ses paroles n'étaient pas destinées au public **2.** [purchasing] consommation *f* **3.** [using up, amount used - of gas, energy, oil] consommation *f*, dépense *f* **4.** *dated* [tuberculosis] consomption *f* (pulmonaire), phtisie *f*.

consumptive [kən'sʌmptɪv] <> *adj* [disease, illness] consomptif, destructif.
<> *n* phtisique *mf*, tuberculeux *m*, - euse *f*.

cont. *written abbr of* **continued**.

contact ['kɒntækt] <> *n* **1.** [communication] contact *m*, rapport *m* ▪ **we don't have much ~ with our neighbours** nous n'avons pas beaucoup de contacts avec nos voisins ▪ **to be in ~ with sb** être en contact OR en rapport avec qqn ▪ **to come into ~ with sb** entrer OR se mettre en contact OR en rapport avec qqn ▪ **to make ~ with sb** prendre contact avec qqn **2.** [touch] contact *m* ▪ **always keep one foot in ~ with the ground** gardez toujours un pied au sol ▪ **eye ~** contact visuel **3.** [person] relation *f* ▪ **she has some useful business ~s** elle a quelques bons contacts (professionnels) **4.** ELEC [connector] contact *m* ▪ [connection] contact *m* ▪ **to make/break (the) ~** mettre/couper le contact **5.** MED *personne ayant approché un malade contagieux* **6.** = **contact print 7.** *inf* = **contact lens**.
<> *comp* : **shall I give you a ~ address/number?** voulez-vous que je vous donne l'adresse/le numéro où vous pouvez me joindre OR me contacter? ▪ **~ sport** sport *m* de contact.
<> *vt* prendre contact avec, contacter.

contactable [kɒn'tæktəbl] *adj* que l'on peut joindre OR contacter, joignable ▪ **I'm ~ at this number** on peut me contacter OR m'appeler à ce numéro.

contact breaker *n* rupteur *m*, levier *m* de rupture.

contact lens *n* verre *m* OR lentille *f* de contact.

contact print *n* épreuve *f* par contact.

contact sport *n* sport *m* de contact.

contagion [kən'teɪdʒn] *n* **1.** [contamination] contagion *f* **2.** [disease] contagion *f*, maladie *f* contagieuse.

contagious [kən'teɪdʒəs] *adj* *liter* & *fig* contagieux.

contain [kən'teɪn] *vt* **1.** [hold - subj: bag, house, city] contenir **2.** [include - subj: pill, substance] contenir ; [- subj: book, speech] contenir, comporter ▪ **her story does ~ some truth** il y a du vrai dans son histoire **3.** [restrain - feelings] contenir, cacher ▪ **I could barely ~ myself** j'avais du mal à me contenir **4.** [curb - enemy, growth, riot] contenir, maîtriser **5.** [hold back - fire] circonscrire ; [- flood waters] contenir, endiguer **6.** [limit - damage] limiter **7.** MATHS être divisible par.

contained [kən'teɪnd] *adj* [person] maître de soi.

container [kən'teɪnəʳ] <> *n* **1.** [bottle, box, tin etc] récipient *m*, boîte *f* **2.** [for transporting cargo] conteneur *m*, container *m*.
<> *comp* [port, ship, terminal] porte-conteneurs ▪ [dock, line, transport] pour porte-conteneurs.

containerize, UK ise [kən'teɪnəraɪz] *vt* [cargo] conteneuriser ▪ [port] convertir à la conteneurisation.

containment [kən'teɪnmənt] *n* **1.** POL endiguement *m*, freinage *m*, retenue *f* **2.** PHYS confinement *m*.

contaminate [kən'tæmɪneɪt] *vt* **1.** [pollute - food, river, water] contaminer ■ *fig* [corrupt] contaminer, souiller **2.** [irradiate - land, person, soil] contaminer.

contaminated [kən'tæmɪneɪtɪd] *adj* **1.** [polluted - food, river, water] contaminé ; [- air] contaminé, vicié ■ *fig* [corrupted] contaminé, corrompu **2.** [irradiated - land, person, soil] contaminé.

contamination [kən,tæmɪ'neɪʃn] *n* **1.** [pollution - of food, river, water] contamination *f* ■ *fig* contamination *f*, corruption *f* **2.** [irradiation - of land, person, soil] contamination *f*.

cont'd, contd *written abbr of* **continued**.

contemplate ['kɒntempleɪt] ◇ *vt* **1.** [ponder] considérer, réfléchir sur **2.** [consider] considérer, envisager ■ **to ~ doing sthg** envisager de *OR* songer à faire qqch **3.** [observe] contempler.
◇ *vi* **1.** [ponder] méditer, se recueillir **2.** [consider] réfléchir.

contemplation [,kɒntem'pleɪʃn] *n* **1.** [thought] réflexion *f* ■ **deep in ~** en pleine réflexion **2.** [observation] contemplation *f* **3.** [meditation] contemplation *f*, recueillement *m*, méditation *f*.

contemplative [kən'templətɪv] ◇ *adj* [look, mood] songeur, pensif ■ [life] contemplatif ■ RELIG [order, prayer] contemplatif.
◇ *n* contemplatif *m*, - ive *f*.

contemporaneous [kən,tempə'reɪnjəs] *adj fml* contemporain ■ **to be ~ (with sb/sthg)** être contemporain (de qqn/qqch).

contemporaneously [kən,tempə'reɪnjəslɪ] *adv fml* [exist, live] à la même époque.

contemporary [kən'tempərərɪ] ◇ *adj* **1.** [modern - art, writer] contemporain, d'aujourd'hui ; [- design, style] moderne **2.** [of the same period - account, report] contemporain ■ **he was ~ with Thackeray** il vivait à la même époque que *OR* il était contemporain de Thackeray.
◇ *n* (*pl* **contemporaries**) contemporain *m*, - e *f* ■ **he was a ~ of mine at university** nous étions ensemble *OR* en même temps à l'université.

contempt [kən'tempt] *n* **1.** [scorn] mépris *m* ■ **to feel ~ for sb/sthg, to hold sb/sthg in ~** mépriser qqn/qqch, avoir du mépris pour qqn/qqch ■ **to be beneath ~** être tout ce qu'il y a de plus méprisable **2.** LAW outrage *m* ■ **to charge sb with ~ (of court)** accuser qqn d'outrage (à magistrat *OR* à la Cour).

contemptible [kən'temptəbl] *adj* [action, attitude, person] méprisable.

contemptuous [kən'temptʃʊəs] *adj fml* [look, manner, remark] dédaigneux, méprisant ■ **to be ~ of sb/sthg** dédaigner qqn/qqch, faire peu de cas de qqn/qqch.

contemptuously [kən'temptʃʊəslɪ] *adv* [laugh, reject, smile] avec mépris, avec dédain.

contend [kən'tend] ◇ *vi* **1.** [deal] : **this is just one of the difficulties we have to ~ with** ce n'est que l'une des difficultés auxquelles nous devons faire face ■ **if you do that again, you'll have me to ~ with** si tu recommences, tu auras affaire à moi **2.** [compete] combattre, lutter ■ **to ~ with sb for** *OR* **over sthg** disputer *OR* contester qqch à qqn.
◇ *vt fml* **to ~ that...** soutenir que ...

contender [kən'tendəʳ] *n* [in fight] adversaire *mf* ■ [in race] concurrent *m*, - e *f* ■ [for title] prétendant *m*, - e *f* ■ [for political office] candidat *m*, - e *f*.

contending [kən'tendɪŋ] *adj* opposé.

content ◇ *n* ['kɒntent] **1.** [amount contained] teneur *f* ■ **with a high iron ~** avec une forte teneur en fer, riche en fer **2.** [substance - of book, film, speech] contenu *m* ■ [meaning] teneur *f*, fond *m* ■ **his films are all style and no ~** dans ses films, il y a la forme mais pas le fond **3.** [kən'tent] [satisfaction] contentement *m*, satisfaction *f*.
◇ *adj* [kən'tent] content, satisfait ■ **to be ~ to do sthg** ne pas demander mieux que de faire qqch ■ **he seems quite ~ with his lot in life** il semble assez content de son sort.
◇ *vt* [kən'tent] : **to ~ oneself with (doing) sthg** se contenter de *OR* se borner à (faire) qqch ■ **my reply seemed to ~ them** ils semblaient satisfaits de ma réponse.
◆ **contents** *npl* **1.** [of bag, bottle, house etc] contenu *m* **2.** [of book, letter] contenu *m* ■ **the ~s (list), the list of ~s** la table des matières.

contented [kən'tentɪd] *adj* [person] content, satisfait ■ [smile] de contentement, de satisfaction.

contentedly [kən'tentɪdlɪ] *adv* avec contentement.

contention [kən'tenʃn] *n* **1.** *fml* [belief] affirmation *f* ■ **it is my ~ that...** je soutiens que ... **2.** [disagreement] dispute *f* ■ **his morals are not in ~** sa moralité n'est pas ici mise en doute **3.** *phr* **to be in ~ for sthg** être en compétition pour qqch.

contentious [kən'tenʃəs] *adj* **1.** [controversial - issue, subject] contesté, litigieux **2.** [argumentative - family, group, person] querelleur, chicanier **3.** LAW contentieux.

contentment [kən'tentmənt] *n* contentement *m*, satisfaction *f*.

content word ['kɒntent-] *n* LING mot *m* à contenu lexical.

contest ◇ *n* ['kɒntest] **1.** [competition] concours *m* ■ **beauty ~** concours *m* de beauté **2.** [struggle] combat *m*, lutte *f* ■ **a ~ for/between** un combat pour/entre **3.** SPORT rencontre *f* ■ [boxing] combat *m*, rencontre *f* ■ **a ~ with/between** un combat contre/entre.
◇ *vt* [kən'test] **1.** [dispute - idea, statement] contester, discuter ■ **to ~ a will** contester un testament **2.** POL [fight for - election, seat] disputer ■ SPORT [- match, title] disputer ■ **a keenly ~ed game** une partie disputée avec acharnement.

contestant [kən'testənt] *n* concurrent *m*, - e *f*, adversaire *mf*.

contestation [,kɒntes'teɪʃn] *n* contestation *f*.

context ['kɒntekst] *n* contexte *m* ■ **in ~** dans son contexte ■ **her comments had been taken out of ~** ses commentaires avaient été retirés de leur contexte.

context-sensitive *adj* COMPUT contextuel.

contextual [kɒn'tekstjʊəl] *adj* [criticism] contextuel.

contextualize, *UK* **ise** [kɒn'tekstjʊəlaɪz] *vt* [events, facts] contextualiser, remettre dans son contexte.

contiguous [kən'tɪgjʊəs] *adj fml* contigu(ë) ■ **to be ~ to** *OR* **with sthg** être contigu à qqch.

continence ['kɒntɪnəns] *n* **1.** MED continence *f* **2.** *fml* [chastity] continence *f*, chasteté *f*.

continent ['kɒntɪnənt] ◇ *n* GEOG continent *m*.
◇ *adj* **1.** MED continent, qui n'est pas incontinent **2.** *fml* [chaste] continent, chaste.
◆ **Continent** *n UK* : **the Continent** l'Europe *f* continentale ■ **on the Continent** en Europe (continentale), outre-Manche.

continental [,kɒntɪ'nentl] ◇ *adj* **1.** [European] d'outre-Manche, européen, d'Europe continentale **2.** GEOG [crust, divide] continental ■ **~ Latin America** l'Amérique *f* latine continentale ■ **~ United States** *US désigne les 48 États des États-Unis qui forment un bloc géographique (excluant Hawaii et l'Alaska).*
◇ *n UK* continental *m*, - e *f*, habitant *m*, - e *f* de l'Europe continentale.

continental breakfast *n* petit déjeuner *m* à la française.

CONTINENTAL BREAKFAST

Ce terme désigne un petit déjeuner léger, par opposition au breakfast anglais traditionnel, beaucoup plus copieux et comportant un plat chaud.

continental drift *n* dérive *f* des continents.

continental quilt *n* couette *f*, duvet *m*.

continental shelf *n* plateau *m* continental.

contingency [kən'tɪndʒənsɪ] ◇ *n* (*pl* **contingencies**) *fml* **1.** [possibility] éventualité *f*, contingence *f* ▪ **to provide for all contingencies** parer à toute éventualité **2.** [chance] événement *m* inattendu ▪ [uncertainty] (cas *m*) imprévu *m*, éventualité *f* **3.** [in statistics] contingence *f*.
◇ *comp* [fund] de prévoyance ▪ [plan] d'urgence ▪ [table, coefficient] des imprévus.
◆ **contingencies** *npl* FIN frais *mpl* divers.

contingency fee *n* LAW *aux États-Unis, principe permettant à un avocat de recevoir une part des sommes attribuées à son client si ce dernier gagne son procès.*

contingent [kən'tɪndʒənt] ◇ *adj fml* **1.** [dependent] contingent ▪ **to be ~ on** *OR* **upon sthg** dépendre de qqch **2.** [accidental] accidentel, fortuit **3.** [uncertain] éventuel.
◇ *n* **1.** MIL contingent *m* **2.** [representative group] groupe *m* représentatif.

continual [kən'tɪnjʊəl] *adj* **1.** [continuous - pain, pleasure, struggle] continuel **2.** [repeated - nagging, warnings] incessant, continuel.

continually [kən'tɪnjʊəlɪ] *adv* **1.** [continuously - change, evolve] continuellement **2.** [repeatedly - complain, nag, warn] sans cesse.

continuance [kən'tɪnjʊəns] *n* **1.** [continuation] continuation *f*, persistance *f*, durée *f* **2.** *US* LAW ajournement *m* (*d'un procès*).

continuation [kən,tɪnjʊ'eɪʃn] *n* **1.** [sequel] continuation *f*, suite *f* **2.** [resumption] reprise *f* **3.** [prolongation] prolongement *m*, suite *f*.

continue [kən'tɪnju:] ◇ *vi* **1.** [carry on] continuer ▪ **to ~ to do sthg** *OR* **doing sthg** continuer à faire qqch ▪ **we ~d on our way** nous avons poursuivi notre chemin, nous nous sommes remis en route ▪ **to ~ with a treatment** continuer un traitement **2.** [begin again] reprendre.
◇ *vt* **1.** [carry on - education] poursuivre, continuer ; [- tradition] perpétuer, continuer ; [- treatment] continuer **2.** [resume - conversation, performance, talks] reprendre, continuer ▪ **"furthermore", he ~d...** "de plus", continua-t-il... ▪ **to be ~d** à suivre ▪ **~d on the next page** suite à la page suivante.

continuity [,kɒntɪ'nju:ətɪ] ◇ *n* (*pl* **continuities**) **1.** [cohesion] continuité *f* **2.** CIN & TV continuité *f*.
◇ *comp* [department, studio] pour raccords.

continuity girl *n* scripte *f*.

continuous [kən'tɪnjʊəs] *adj* **1.** [uninterrupted - noise, process] continu, ininterrompu ▪ **~ assessment** contrôle *m* continu ▪ **~ performances** CIN spectacle *m* permanent ▪ **~ stationery** papier *m* en continu **2.** [unbroken - line] continu **3.** GRAM [tense] continu.

continuously [kən'tɪnjʊəslɪ] *adv* continuellement, sans arrêt.

continuum [kən'tɪnjʊəm] (*pl* **continuums** *OR pl* **continua** [-njʊə]) *n* continuum *m*.

contort [kən'tɔ:t] *vt* [body, features] tordre.

contorted [kən'tɔ:tɪd] *adj* [body, features] tordu, crispé.

contortion [kən'tɔ:ʃn] *n* [of body, features] contorsion *f*, convulsion *f*, crispation *f* ▪ **mental ~s** *fig* contorsions *OR* acrobaties *fpl* mentales.

contortionist [kən'tɔ:ʃənɪst] *n* contorsionniste *mf*, homme *m* caoutchouc.

contour ['kɒn,tʊəʳ] ◇ *n* **1.** [line] contour *m* **2.** = **contour line 3.** [shape - of body, car] contour *m*.
◇ *vt* **1.** [map] tracer les courbes de niveaux sur **2.** [shape - dress, car] tracer les contours de.

contour line *n* courbe *f* de niveau.

contour map *n* carte *f* topographique.

Contra ['kɒntrə] *pr n* [Nicaraguan] contra *mf*.

contraband ['kɒntrəbænd] ◇ *n (U)* **1.** [smuggling] contrebande *f* **2.** [smuggled goods] (marchandises *fpl* de) contrebande *f*.
◇ *adj* [activities, goods] de contrebande.

contraception [,kɒntrə'sepʃn] *n* contraception *f*.

contraceptive [,kɒntrə'septɪv] ◇ *n* contraceptif *m* ▪ **~ pill** pilule *f* contraceptive.
◇ *adj* [device, method] contraceptif.

contract ◇ *n* ['kɒntrækt] [agreement] contrat *m*, convention *f* ▪ [document] contrat *m* ▪ **to be under ~** être sous contrat, avoir un contrat ▪ **to put work out to ~** sous-traiter du travail ▪ **to put out a ~ on sb** *inf* mettre la tête de qqn à prix ➲ **marriage ~** contrat de mariage ▪ **~ of employment** contrat de travail.
◇ *comp* [work] à forfait, contractuel ▪ **~ killer** tueur *m* à gages.
◇ *vt* [kən'trækt] **1.** *fml* [agree] : **to ~ (with sb) to do sthg** s'engager par contrat à faire qqch **2.** *fml* [agree to - alliance, marriage] contracter **3.** [acquire - disease, illness, debt] contracter **4.** [make shorter - vowel, word] contracter **5.** [make tense - muscle] contracter.
◇ *vi* se contracter.
◆ **contract in** *vi insep* [kən'trækt] *UK* s'engager (par contrat préalable).
◆ **contract out** ◇ *vt sep* [work] sous-traiter.
◇ *vi insep UK* : **to ~ out of sthg** cesser de cotiser à qqch.

contract bridge *n* bridge *m* contrat.

contraction [kən'trækʃn] *n* **1.** [shrinkage - of metal] contraction *f* **2.** [short form of word] contraction *f*, forme *f* contractée **3.** [of muscle - esp in childbirth] contraction *f*.

contractor [kən'træktəʳ] *n* [worker] entrepreneur *m*.

contractual [kən'træktʃʊəl] *adj* [agreement, obligation] contractuel.

contractually [kən'træktʃʊəlɪ] *adv* [binding] par contrat.

contradict [,kɒntrə'dɪkt] *vt* **1.** [challenge - person, statement] contredire **2.** [conflict with - subj: facts, stories] contredire.

contradiction [,kɒntrə'dɪkʃn] *n* **1.** [inconsistency] contradiction *f* ▪ **in ~ with** en désaccord avec **2.** [conflicting statement] démenti *m*, contradiction *f* ▪ **a ~ in terms** une contradiction dans les termes.

contradictory [,kɒntrə'dɪktərɪ] *adj* [statements, stories] contradictoire, opposé ▪ [person] qui a l'esprit de contradiction.

contradistinction [,kɒntrədɪ'stɪŋkʃn] *n fml* opposition *f*, contraste *m*.

contraflow ['kɒntrəfləʊ] *UK* ◇ *n* circulation *f* à contre-courant.
◇ *comp* [system] de circulation *f* à contre-courant.

contraindication ['kɒntrə,ɪndɪ'keɪʃn] *n fml* contre-indication *f*.

contralto [kən'træltəʊ] ◇ *n* (*pl* **contraltos**) [voice] contralto *m* ▪ [singer] contralto *mf*.
◇ *adj* [part, voice] de contralto.

contraption [kən'træpʃn] *n* engin *m*, truc *m*.

contrariness [kən'treərɪnɪs] *n* [obstinacy] esprit *m* de contradiction.

contrary ['kɒntrərɪ] *adj* **1.** [opposed - attitudes, ideas, opinions] contraire, en opposition ▪ **~ to nature** contre nature **2.** [kən'treərɪ] [obstinate - attitude, person] contrariant **3.** *fml* [winds] contraire.
◆ **contrary to** *prep phr* contrairement à ▪ **~ to popular belief** contrairement à ce que l'on croit généralement.
◆ **on the contrary** *adv phr* au contraire.
◆ **to the contrary** *adv phr* : **the meeting will be at six, unless you hear to the ~** la réunion sera à six heures, sauf contrordre *OR* avis contraire.

contrast ◇ *vt* [kən'trɑ:st] contraster, mettre en contraste ▪ **to ~ sb/sthg with, to ~ sb/sthg to** mettre en contraste qqn/qqch avec.

<> *vi* [kən'trɑ:st] contraster, trancher ▪ **to ~ with sthg** contraster avec qqch.
<> *n* ['kɒntrɑ:st] **1.** [difference] contraste *m* ▪ [person, thing] contraste *m* ▪ **there is a marked ~ between his public and his private life** il y a un contraste frappant entre sa vie d'homme public et sa vie privée ▪ **life in Africa was a complete ~ to life in Europe** la vie en Afrique présentait un contraste total avec la vie en Europe ▪ **her response was in stark ~ to the government's** sa réponse était en contraste absolu avec celle du gouvernement **2.** ART & TV contraste *m*.
◆ **by contrast, in contrast** *adv phr* par contraste.
◆ **in contrast with, in contrast to** *prep phr* par opposition à, par contraste avec.

contrasting [kən'trɑ:stɪŋ], **contrastive** [kən'trɑ:stɪv] *adj* [attitudes, lifestyles, responses] qui fait contraste ▪ [colours] opposé, contrasté.

contravene [ˌkɒntrə'vi:n] *vt* [infringe - law, rule] transgresser, enfreindre, violer.

contravention [ˌkɒntrə'venʃn] *n* infraction *f*, violation *f* ▪ **in ~ of the law** en infraction par rapport à la loi.

contribute [kən'trɪbju:t] <> *vt* [give - money] donner ; [- article, poem] écrire ; [- ideas] apporter ▪ **they ~d their ideas and enthusiasm to the project** ils ont apporté leurs idées et leur enthousiasme au projet.
<> *vi* **1.** [donate money] contribuer **2.** [give] donner ▪ **she still has a lot to ~ to her family** elle a encore beaucoup à apporter à sa famille **3.** [influence] : **to ~ to sthg** contribuer à qqch **4.** [journalist, author] : **to ~ to** écrire pour.

contributing [kən'trɪbju:tɪ] *adj* : **to be a ~ factor in** *OR* **to** contribuer à.

contribution [ˌkɒntrɪ'bju:ʃn] *n* **1.** [of money, goods] contribution *f*, cotisation *f* ▪ [of ideas, enthusiasm] apport *m* ▪ **he made a valuable ~ to the project** il a apporté une collaboration précieuse au projet **2.** [article] article *m (écrit pour un journal)*.

contributor [kən'trɪbjutəʳ] *n* **1.** [of money, goods] donateur *m*, - trice *f* **2.** [to magazine] collaborateur *m*, - trice *f* **3.** [factor] facteur *m*.

contributory [kən'trɪbjutərɪ] <> *adj* [cause, factor] contribuant, qui contribue ▪ **~ pension scheme** régime *m* de retraite *(avec participation de l'assuré)*.
<> *n (pl* **contributories***)* FIN *actionnaire qui doit contribuer au paiement des dettes.*

contrite ['kɒntraɪt] *adj* [face, look] contrit, repentant.

contrition [kən'trɪʃn] *n* contrition *f*, pénitence *f*.

contrivance [kən'traɪvəns] *n* **1.** [contraption] dispositif *m*, mécanisme *m* **2.** [stratagem] manigance *f*.

contrive [kən'traɪv] <> *vt* **1.** [engineer - meeting] combiner **2.** [invent - device, machine] inventer, imaginer.
<> *vi* : **to ~ to do sthg** trouver le moyen de faire qqch ▪ **she ~d to confuse matters still further** elle a réussi à embrouiller encore plus les choses.

contrived [kən'traɪvd] *adj* **1.** [deliberate] délibéré, arrangé **2.** [artificial] forcé, peu naturel.

control [kən'trəʊl] <> *n* **1.** [of country, organization] direction *f* ▪ [of car, machine] contrôle *m* ▪ [of one's life] maîtrise *f* ▪ [of oneself] maîtrise *f* (de soi) ▪ SPORT [of ball] contrôle *m* ▪ **to have ~ of** *OR* **over sb** avoir de l'autorité sur qqn ▪ **to have ~ of** *OR* **over sthg** avoir le contrôle de qqch ▪ **to gain ~ of sthg** prendre le contrôle de qqch ▪ **to be in ~ of sthg** être maître de qqch ▪ **to lose ~ of sthg** [of car] perdre le contrôle de qqch ; [of situation] ne plus être maître de qqch ▪ **under ~ : the situation is under ~** nous maîtrisons la situation ▪ **everything's under ~** tout va bien, aucun problème, tout est au point ▪ **to keep sthg under ~** maîtriser qqch ▪ **dogs must be kept under ~** les chiens doivent être tenus en laisse ▪ **beyond** *OR* **outside one's ~** indépendant de sa volonté ▪ **out of ~ : the fire was out of ~** on n'arrivait pas à maîtriser l'incendie ▪ **the crowd got out of ~** la foule s'est déchaînée ▪ **her children are completely out of ~** ses enfants sont intenables
2. [check] contrôle *m*
3. [device] : **volume ~** réglage *m* du volume ▪ **~s** [on car, aircraft, machine] commandes *fpl* ▪ **the pilot was at the ~s/took over the ~s** le pilote était aux commandes/a pris les commandes
4. [in experiment] témoin *m*
5. [checkpoint - at border] douane *f* ; [- in car rally] contrôle *m* ▪ **passport and custom ~s** formalités *fpl* de douane
6. [restraint] contrôle *m* ▪ **price/wage ~s** contrôle des prix/des salaires.
<> *comp* [button, knob, switch] de commande, de réglage.
<> *vt* **1.** [run - government, organization] diriger
2. [regulate - machine, system] régler ; [- animal, pupil] tenir, se faire obéir de ; [- crowd] contenir ; [- traffic] régler
3. [curb - inflation, prices, spending, fire] maîtriser ; [- disease] enrayer, juguler ; [- activities, emotions] maîtriser ; [- imports] limiter ▪ **try to ~ yourself** essaie de te contrôler *OR* maîtriser
4. [verify - accounts] contrôler ; [- experiment] vérifier.

control code *n* COMPUT code *m* de commande.

control column *n* manche *m* à balai.

control experiment *n* cas *m* témoin.

control group *n* groupe *m* témoin.

control key *n* touche *f* "control".

controllable [kən'trəʊləbl] *adj* [animal, person, crowd] discipliné ▪ [emotions, situation] maîtrisable ▪ [expenditure, inflation] contrôlable.

controlled [kən'trəʊld] *adj* **1.** [emotions, voice] contenu ▪ [person] calme **2.** ECON : **~ economy** économie *f* dirigée *OR* planifiée **3.** [directed] : **~ explosion** neutralisation *f (d'un explosif)* ▪ **the bomb was let off in a ~ explosion** la bombe a été neutralisée.

controller [kən'trəʊləʳ] *n* **1.** [person in charge] responsable *m* **2.** [accountant] contrôleur *m*.

controlling [kən'trəʊlɪŋ] *adj* [factor] déterminant.

controlling interest *n* participation *f* majoritaire.

control panel *n* tableau *m* de bord.

control rod *n* NUCL PHYS barre *f* de commande.

control room *n* salle *f* des commandes, centre *m* de contrôle.

control tower *n* tour *f* de contrôle.

controversial [ˌkɒntrə'vɜ:ʃl] *adj* [book, film, issue, subject] controversé ▪ [decision, speech] sujet à controverse ▪ [person] controversé.

controversy ['kɒntrəvɜ:sɪ, *UK* kən'trɒvəsɪ] *n* controverse *f*, polémique *f* ▪ **her speech caused a lot of ~** son discours a provoqué beaucoup de controverses.

contumacy ['kɒntjʊməsɪ] *n* **1.** *lit* [disobedience] insubordination *f* **2.** LAW contumace *f*.

contumely ['kɒntju:mlɪ] *n lit* [language] insolence *f* ▪ [insult] offense *f*.

contusion [kən'tju:ʒn] *n fml* contusion *f*.

conundrum [kə'nʌndrəm] *n* **1.** [riddle] devinette *f*, énigme *f* **2.** [problem] énigme *f*.

conurbation [ˌkɒnɜ:'beɪʃn] *n* conurbation *f*.

convalesce [ˌkɒnvə'les] *vi* se remettre *(d'une maladie)* ▪ **she's convalescing (from a bad bout of flu)** elle se remet (d'une mauvaise grippe).

convalescence [ˌkɒnvə'lesns] *n* [return to health] rétablissement *m* ▪ [period of recovery] convalescence *f*.

convalescent [ˌkɒnvə'lesnt] <> *n* convalescent *m*, - e *f*.
<> *adj* : **~ home** maison *f* de convalescence *OR* de repos.

convection [kən'vekʃn] <> *n* GEOL, METEOR & PHYS convection *f*.

<> *comp* [heater, heating] à convection ■ [current] de convection.

convector (heater) [kən'vektər-] *n* radiateur *m* à convection, convecteur *m*.

convene [kən'vi:n] <> *vt* [conference, meeting] convoquer.
<> *vi* [board, jury, members] se réunir.

convener [kən'vi:nər] *n* **1.** *UK* [in trade union] *secrétaire des délégués syndicaux* **2.** [of meeting] président *m*, - e *f*.

convenience [kən'vi:njəns] *n* **1.** [ease of use] commodité *f* ■ [benefit] avantage *m* ■ **for ~** *OR* **for ~'s sake** par commodité ■ **at your earliest ~** *fml* dans les meilleurs délais ■ **at your ~** quand cela vous conviendra **2.** [facility] commodités *fpl*, confort *m* ■ **the house has every modern ~** la maison a tout le confort moderne **3.** *UK fml* & *euph* [lavatory] toilettes *fpl* ■ **public ~s** toilettes publiques.

convenience food *n* aliment *m* prêt à consommer, plat *m* cuisiné.

convenience store *n US supérette de quartier qui reste ouverte tard le soir.*

convenient [kən'vi:njənt] *adj* **1.** [suitable] commode ■ **when would be ~ for you?** quand cela vous arrangerait-il? **2.** [handy] pratique ■ **the house is very ~ for local shops and schools** la maison est très bien située pour les magasins et les écoles **3.** [nearby] : **I grabbed a ~ chair and sat down** j'ai saisi la chaise la plus proche et me suis assis.

conveniently [kən'vi:njəntlɪ] *adv* : **the cottage is ~ situated for the beach** le cottage est bien situé pour la plage ■ **they very ~ forgot to enclose the cheque** comme par hasard, ils ont oublié de joindre le chèque.

convening [kən'vi:nɪŋ] <> *adj* [authority, country] habilité à convoquer, hôte.
<> *n* convocation *f*.

convent ['kɒnvənt] <> *n* **1.** RELIG couvent *m* ■ **to enter a ~** entrer au couvent **2.** [convent school] institution *f* religieuse.
<> *comp* [education, school] religieux ■ **she was ~-educated** elle a fait ses études dans une institution religieuse.

convention [kən'venʃn] *n* **1.** *(U)* [custom] usage *m*, convenances *fpl* ■ **to defy ~** braver les usages **2.** [agreement] convention *f* ■ **to sign a ~ on sthg** signer une convention sur qqch **3.** [meeting] convention *f* **4.** [accepted usage] convention *f*.

CONVENTION

Aux États-Unis, les *conventions* sont d'immenses rassemblements politiques, au cours desquels les partis nationaux choisissent leurs candidats et définissent leurs objectifs.

conventional [kən'venʃənl] *adj* **1.** [behaviour, ideas] conventionnel ■ [person] conformiste ■ **~ wisdom** sagesse *f* populaire ■ **~ wisdom has it that...** d'aucuns disent que... **2.** [medicine, methods, art] classique, traditionnel **3.** [nonnuclear] conventionnel.

conventionally [kən'venʃnəlɪ] *adv* de façon conventionnelle.

convention centre *n* palais *m* des congrès.

converge [kən'vɜ:dʒ] *vi* **1.** [merge - paths, lines] converger ; [- groups, ideas, tendencies] converger **2.** [groups, people] se rassembler ■ **thousands of fans ~d on the stadium** des milliers de fans se sont rassemblés sur le stade **3.** MATHS converger.

convergence [kən'vɜ:dʒəns] *n* [of paths, ideas] convergence *f*.

convergence criteria *npl* critères *mpl* de convergence.

convergent [kən'vɜ:dʒənt] *adj* **1.** [paths, tendencies] convergent **2.** MATHS convergent.

conversant [kən'vɜ:sənt] *adj fml* qui est au courant, qui connaît ■ **we were expected to be fully ~ with colloquial French** nous étions censés avoir une connaissance parfaite du français familier.

conversation [,kɒnvə'seɪʃn] *n* conversation *f* ■ **we had a long ~ about fishing** nous avons eu une longue conversation sur la pêche ■ **she was deep in ~ with my sister** elle était en grande conversation avec ma sœur ■ **to get into ~ with sb** engager la conversation avec qqn ■ **to make ~** faire la conversation ▶ **that's a~ stopper!** ça jette toujours un froid dans la conversation!

conversational [,kɒnvə'seɪʃənl] *adj* [tone, voice] de la conversation ■ **~ Spanish** espagnol courant.

conversationalist [,kɒnvə'seɪʃnəlɪst] *n* causeur *m*, - euse *f* ■ **he's a brilliant ~** il brille dans la conversation.

conversationally [,kɒnvə'seɪʃnəlɪ] *adv* [mention, say] sur le ton de la conversation.

conversation piece *n* **1.** [unusual object] curiosité *f* **2.** [play] *pièce au dialogue brillant*.

converse <> *vi* [kən'vɜ:s] *fml* converser ■ **to ~ with sb** s'entretenir avec qqn.
<> *adj* ['kɒnvɜ:s] [opinion, statement] contraire.
<> *n* ['kɒnvɜ:s] **1.** [gen] contraire *m*, inverse *m* **2.** MATHS & PHILOS inverse *m* **3.** *fml* & *lit* conversation *f*, entretien *m*.

conversely [kən'vɜ:slɪ] *adv* inversement, réciproquement ■ **~, people who save more spend less** inversement les gens qui économisent dépensent moins.

conversion [kən'vɜ:ʃn] *n* **1.** [process] conversion *f*, transformation *f* **2.** MATHS conversion *f* **3.** [change of beliefs] conversion *f* **4.** RUGBY transformation *f* **5.** [converted building] *appartement aménagé dans un ancien hôtel particulier, entrepôt, atelier etc* **6.** LAW conversion *f*.

conversion table *n* table *f* de conversion.

convert <> *vt* [kən'vɜ:t] **1.** [building, car] aménager, convertir ■ [machine] transformer ■ **to ~ sthg to** *OR* **into sthg** transformer *OR* convertir qqch en qqch **2.** MATHS convertir ■ **to ~ pesetas into pounds** [as calculation] convertir des pesetas en livres ; [by exchanging money] changer des pesetas en livres **3.** RELIG convertir ■ **to ~ sb to sthg** convertir qqn à qqch **4.** RUGBY transformer **5.** LAW convertir **6.** FIN [bond] convertir.
<> *vi* [kən'vɜ:t] **1.** [vehicle, machine] se convertir **2.** [in rugby] se transformer.
<> *n* ['kɒnvɜ:t] converti *m*, -e *f* ■ **she's a ~ to Catholicism** c'est une catholique convertie.

converted [kən'vɜ:tɪd] *adj* [factory, farmhouse, school] aménagé, transformé.

converter [kən'vɜ:tər] *n* METALL & PHYS convertisseur *m* ■ RADIO modulateur *m* de fréquence ■ COMPUT convertisseur *m*.

convertible [kən'vɜ:təbl] <> *adj* [currency] convertible ■ [car, machine, couch] convertible.
<> *n* AUT décapotable *f*.

convertor [kən'vɜ:tər] = **converter**.

convex [kɒn'veks] *adj* [lens, surface] convexe.

convey [kən'veɪ] *vt* **1.** *fml* [transport] transporter **2.** [communicate] transmettre ■ **I tried to ~ to him the importance of the decision** j'ai essayé de lui faire comprendre l'importance de la décision ■ **no words can ~ my gratitude** aucun mot ne peut traduire ma gratitude **3.** LAW transférer.

conveyance [kən'veɪəns] *n* **1.** [transport] transport *m* **2.** *dated* [vehicle] véhicule *m* **3.** LAW [transfer of property] cession *f*, transfert *m* ■ [document] acte *m* de cession.

conveyancing [kən'veɪənsɪŋ] *n UK* LAW procédure *f* translative (de propriété).

conveyor [kən'veɪər] *n* **1.** [transporter] transporteur *m* **2.** = **conveyor belt**.

conveyor belt *n* tapis *m* roulant.

convict <> *vt* [kən'vɪkt] déclarer *OR* reconnaître coupable ■ **to ~ sb of** *OR* **for sthg** déclarer *OR* reconnaître qqn coupable de qqch.
<> *n* ['kɒnvɪkt] détenu *m*, - e *f*.
<> *vi* rendre un verdict de culpabilité.

convicted [kən'vɪktɪd] *adj* [criminal] reconnu coupable.

conviction [kən'vɪkʃn] *n* **1.** [belief] conviction *f* **2.** [certainty] certitude *f*, conviction *f* ■ **I suppose so, I said without much ~** je suppose, dis-je sans grande conviction **3.** [plausibility] : **the theory carries little ~** la théorie est peu convaincante **4.** LAW condamnation *f* ■ **she has several previous ~s** elle a déjà été condamnée plusieurs fois.

convince [kən'vɪns] *vt* convaincre, persuader ■ **to ~ sb of sthg** convaincre *OR* persuader qqn de qqch ■ **to ~ sb to do sthg** convaincre *OR* persuader qqn de faire qqch.

convinced [kən'vɪnst] *adj* convaincu ■ **to be ~ of sthg** être convaincu de qqch.

convincing [kən'vɪnsɪŋ] *adj* [argument, person] convaincant ■ [victory, win] décisif, éclatant.

convincingly [kən'vɪnsɪŋlɪ] *adv* [argue, speak, pretend] de façon convaincante ■ [beat, win] de façon éclatante.

convivial [kən'vɪvɪəl] *adj* [atmosphere, lunch] convivial, joyeux ■ [manner, person] joyeux, plein d'entrain.

convocation [ˌkɒnvə'keɪʃn] *n* **1.** [summoning] convocation *f* **2.** [meeting] assemblée *f* ■ RELIG synode *m*.

convoke [kən'vəʊk] *vt* [assembly, meeting] convoquer.

convoluted ['kɒnvəlu:tɪd] *adj* [shape] convoluté ■ [prose, reasoning, sentence] alambiqué.

convolvulus [kən'vɒlvjʊləs] (*pl* **convolvuluses** *OR pl* **convolvuli** [-laɪ]) *n* liseron *m*.

convoy ['kɒnvɔɪ] ◇ *n* convoi *m* ■ **to travel in ~** voyager en convoi.
◇ *vt* convoyer, escorter.

convulsant [kən'vʌlsənt] ◇ *adj* [drug] convulsivant.
◇ *n* convulsivant *m*.

convulse [kən'vʌls] *vi* [face, lungs, muscle] se convulser, se contracter, se crisper.

convulsed [kən'vʌlst] *adj* : **he was ~ with pain** il se tordait de douleur ■ **the audience were ~ with laughter** l'auditoire se tordait de rire.

convulsion [kən'vʌlʃn] *n* **1.** MED convulsion *f* ■ **to have ~s** avoir des convulsions **2.** [revolution, war] bouleversement *m* ■ [earthquake] secousse *f*.

convulsive [kən'vʌlsɪv] *adj* convulsif.

cony ['kəʊnɪ] (*pl* **conies**) *n* [rabbit] lapin *m* ■ [rabbit fur] lapin *m*.

coo [ku:] ◇ *n* (*pl* **coos**) roucoulement *m*.
◇ *vi* [pigeon] roucouler ■ [baby, person] babiller, gazouiller.
◇ *interj inf* **~!** ça alors!

cooee, cooey ['ku:ɪ] *interj inf* **~!** coucou!

cooing ['ku:ɪŋ] *n* [of pigeon] roucoulement *m* ■ [of baby, person] gazouillement *m*.

cook [kʊk] ◇ *n* cuisinier *m*, - ère *f* ▶ **too many ~s spoil the broth** *prov* trop de cuisinières gâtent la sauce.
◇ *vt* **1.** [food, meal] cuisiner, cuire ■ **to ~ sb's goose** *inf* mettre qqn dans le pétrin **2.** *UK inf* [fiddle - accounts, books] truquer.
◇ *vi* [person] cuisiner ■ [food] cuire ■ **it ~s in five minutes** ça cuit en cinq minutes ▶ **what's ~ing?** *inf* qu'est-ce qui se mijote?
◆ **cook up** *vt sep inf* [plan] mijoter ■ [excuse, story] inventer.

cookbook ['kʊkˌbʊk] *n* livre *m* de cuisine.

cooked [kʊkt] *adj* [food, meal] cuit ■ **~ breakfast** *UK* petit déjeuner *m* anglais.

cooker ['kʊkər] *n UK* [stove] cuisinière *f*.

cookery ['kʊkərɪ] *n* cuisine *f*.

cookery book *n UK* livre *m* de cuisine.

cookie ['kʊkɪ] *n* **1.** *US* biscuit *m* **2.** *phr* **that's the way the ~ crumbles!** c'est la vie! **3.** COMPUT cookie *m*, mouchard *m*.

cooking ['kʊkɪŋ] ◇ *n* [activity] cuisine *f* ■ [food] cuisine *f* ■ **~ time** temps *m* de cuisson.
◇ *comp* [oil, sherry] de cuisine ■ [apple] à cuire.

cookout ['kʊkaʊt] *n US* barbecue *m*.

cool [ku:l] ◇ *adj* **1.** [in temperature - breeze, room, weather] frais, fraîche *f* ; [- drink, water] rafraîchissant, frais, fraîche *f* ; [- clothes, material] léger ■ **keep in a ~ place** conservez dans un endroit frais **2.** [of colour - blue, green] clair **3.** [calm - person, manner, voice] calme ■ **keep ~!** *inf* du calme! ■ **a ~ customer** *inf* une personne effrontée *OR* qui a du culot ▶ **to be** *OR* **to look as ~ as a cucumber** garder son sang-froid *OR* calme **4.** [unfriendly - person, greeting, welcome] froid **5.** *inf* [of sum of money] coquet, rondelet ■ **she earned a ~ half million** elle a gagné un petit demi-million **6.** *inf* [great] génial, super.
◇ *n* **1.** [coolness] fraîcheur *f* **2.** [calm] calme *m*, sang-froid *m* ■ **to keep/to lose one's ~** *inf* garder/perdre son calme.
◇ *vt* [air, liquid, room] rafraîchir, refroidir ■ [brow, feet] rafraîchir ■ **to ~ one's heels** faire le pied de grue ■ **~ it!** du calme!
◇ *vi* [food, liquid] (se) refroidir ■ [enthusiasm, passion, temper] s'apaiser, se calmer.
◆ **cool down** ◇ *vi insep* **1.** [machine] se refroidir ■ *fig* [situation] se détendre **2.** [person] se calmer.
◇ *vt sep* [person] calmer ■ [situation] calmer, détendre.
◆ **cool off** *vi insep* [person - become calmer] se calmer.

coolant ['ku:lənt] *n* (fluide *m*) caloporteur *m*.

coolbox ['ku:lbɒks] *n* glacière *f*.

cooler ['ku:lər] *n* **1.** [for food] glacière *f* **2.** *inf* [prison] taule *f* **3.** [drink] rafraîchissement *m*.

cool-headed *adj* calme, imperturbable.

cooling ['ku:lɪŋ] *n* [in temperature] rafraîchissement *m*, refroidissement *m* ■ [in relationships] refroidissement *m*.

cooling-off period *n* **1.** [in dispute] moment *m* de répit **2.** [after purchase] délai *m* de réflexion.

cooling system *n* système *m* de refroidissement.

cooling tower *n* refroidisseur *m*.

cool jazz *n* MUS cool *m*.

coolly ['ku:lɪ] *adv* **1.** [calmly - react, respond] calmement **2.** [without enthusiasm - greet, welcome] froidement **3.** [impertinently - behave, say] avec impertinence.

coolness ['ku:lnɪs] *n* **1.** [in temperature - of air, water, weather] fraîcheur *f* ; [- of clothes] légèreté *f* **2.** [calmness] calme *m*, sang-froid *m* **3.** [lack of enthusiasm] flegme *m* **4.** [impertinence] culot *m*, toupet *m*.

coon [ku:n] *n* **1.** *inf* = **raccoon 2.** ▲ *terme raciste désignant un Noir*, ≃ nègre *m*, ≃ négresse *f*.

coop [ku:p] *n* poulailler *m*.
◆ **coop up** *vt sep* [animal, person, prisoner] enfermer ■ **I've been ~ed up at home all day** j'ai été cloîtré chez moi toute la journée.

co-op ['kəʊˌɒp] (*abbrev of* **co-operative society**) *n* coopérative *f*, coop *f*.
◆ **Co-op** *pr n UK* : **the Co-op** la Coop.

cooper ['ku:pər] *n* tonnelier *m*.

cooperate [kəʊ'ɒpəreɪt] *vi* **1.** [work together] collaborer, coopérer ■ **to ~ with sb** collaborer avec qqn **2.** [be willing to help] se montrer coopératif.

cooperation [kəʊˌɒpə'reɪʃn] *n* **1.** [collaboration] coopération *f*, concours *m* ■ **in ~ with** *OR* **with the ~ of sb** avec la coopération *OR* le concours de qqn **2.** [willingness to help] coopération *f*.

cooperative [kəʊ'ɒpərətɪv] ◇ *adj* **1.** [joint - activity, work] coopératif **2.** [helpful - attitude, person] coopératif.
◇ *n* coopérative *f*.

co-opt *vt* coopter, admettre ■ **to be ~ed into** *OR* **onto sthg** être coopté à qqch.

coordinate ◇ *vt* [kəʊ'ɔ:dɪneɪt] coordonner.
◇ *n* [kəʊ'ɔ:dɪnət] MATHS coordonnée *f*.
◇ *adj* [kəʊ'ɔ:dɪnət] GRAM & MATHS coordonné ■ **~ clause** proposition *f* coordonnée ■ **~ geometry** géométrie *f* analytique.
◆ **coordinates** *npl* coordonnés *mpl*.

coordinating [kəʊ'ɔ:dɪneɪtɪŋ] *adj* [body, officer] de coordination ■ **~ conjunction** conjonction *f* de coordination.

coordination [kəʊˌɔ:dɪ'neɪʃn] *n* coordination *f*.

coordinator [kəʊ'ɔ:dɪneɪtəʳ] *n* coordinateur *m*, coordonnateur *m*.

coot [ku:t] *n* [bird] foulque *f*.

co-owner *n* copropriétaire *mf*.

co-ownership *n* copropriété *f*.

cop [kɒp] *inf* ◇ *n* **1.** [policeman] flic *mf* ■ **to play ~s and robbers** jouer aux gendarmes et aux voleurs **2.** *UK* [arrest] arrestation *f* ■ **it's a fair ~!** je suis fait! **3.** *UK phr* **it's not much ~** ça ne vaut pas grand-chose, c'est pas terrible.
◇ *vt* (*pret & pp* **copped**, *cont* **copping**) attraper, empoigner ■ **you'll ~ it if he finds out!** qu'est-ce que tu vas prendre s'il s'en rend compte!
◆ **cop out** *vi insep inf* se défiler ■ **to ~ out of sthg** réussir à échapper à qqch.

copartner [,kəʊ'pɑ:tnəʳ] *n* coassocié *m*, - e *f*.

cope [kəʊp] ◇ *vi* [person] se débrouiller, s'en sortir ■ [business, machine, system] supporter ■ **I can't ~ anymore** je n'en peux plus ■ **to ~ with : we ~ with more than 5,000 visitors a week** nous recevons plus de 5 000 visiteurs par semaine ■ **the system can't ~ with this volume of work** le système ne peut pas supporter ce volume de travail ■ **I'll just have to ~ with the problems as they arise** il faudra que je m'occupe des problèmes au fur et à mesure qu'ils se présenteront.
◇ *n* RELIG chape *f*.
◇ *vt* [provide with coping - wall] chaperonner.

Copenhagen [,kəʊpən'heɪgən] *pr n* Copenhague.

Copernicus [kə'pɜ:nɪkəs] *pr n* Copernic.

copier ['kɒpɪəʳ] *n* photocopieuse *f*, copieur *m*.

copilot ['kəʊ,paɪlət] *n* copilote *mf*.

coping ['kəʊpɪŋ] *n* chaperon *m*.

copious ['kəʊpjəs] *adj* [amount, food] copieux ■ [sunshine] abondant ■ [notes] abondant.

copiously ['kəʊpjəslɪ] *adv* [cry, produce, write] en abondance, abondamment.

cop-out *n inf* dérobade *f*.

copper ['kɒpəʳ] ◇ *n* **1.** [colour, metal] cuivre *m* **2.** *inf* [coins] monnaie *f* **3.** *inf* [policeman] flic *m* **4.** [container] lessiveuse *f*.
◇ *comp* [coin, kettle, wire] en cuivre.
◇ *adj* [colour, hair] cuivré.

copper beech *n* hêtre *m* pourpre.

copper-bottomed [-'bɒtəmd] *adj liter* [saucepan] à fond de cuivre ■ *fig* [deal] en béton.

copperplate ['kɒpəpleɪt] ◇ *n* **1.** [plate] cuivre *m* **2.** [print] planche *f* (de cuivre) **3.** [handwriting] écriture *f* moulée.
◇ *comp* [handwriting] moulé.

coppersmith ['kɒpəsmɪθ] *n* chaudronnier *m*, - ère *f*.

coppice ['kɒpɪs] *n* taillis *m*.

coproduce [,kəʊprə'dju:s] *vt* [film, play] coproduire.

coproduction [,kəʊprə'dʌkʃn] *n* coproduction *f*.

copse [kɒps] *n* taillis *m*.

Copt [kɒpt] *n* Copte *mf*.

Coptic ['kɒptɪk] ◇ *adj* copte.
◇ *n* copte *m*.

copula ['kɒpjʊlə] (*pl* **copulas** *OR pl* **copulae** [-li:]) *n* copule *f*.

copulate ['kɒpjʊleɪt] *vi* copuler.

copulation [,kɒpjʊ'leɪʃn] *n* copulation *f*.

copy ['kɒpɪ] ◇ *n* (*pl* **copies**) **1.** [duplicate - of painting] copie *f*, reproduction *f* ; [- of document, photograph] copie *f* **2.** [of book, magazine, record] exemplaire *m* **3.** *(U)* [written material] copie *f* ■ [in advertisement] texte *m* **4.** *(U)* PRESS copie *f* ■ **his story made good ~** son histoire a fait un bon papier.
◇ *vt* (*pret & pp* **copied**) **1.** [write out - letter, notes] copier ■ **to ~ sthg down/out** noter/copier qqch **2.** [imitate - person, movements, gestures] copier, imiter ; [- style, system] copier **3.** [cheat] copier **4.** [photocopy] photocopier.
◇ *vi* (*pret & pp* **copied**) [cheat] copier ■ **no ~ing!** on ne copie pas!

copybook ['kɒpɪbʊk] ◇ *n* cahier *m*.
◇ *adj* [sentiments] commun.

copycat ['kɒpɪkæt] ◇ *n inf* copieur *m*, - euse *f*.
◇ *comp* [killings, murder] inspiré par un autre.

copy-edit *vt* [article, book] rédiger.

copy editor *n* secrétaire *mf* de rédaction.

copy in *vt insep* mettre (qn) en copie ■ **to copy sb in (on sth)** mettre qn en copie (de qch).

copyist ['kɒpɪɪst] *n* copiste *mf*.

copy-protected [-prə'tektɪd] *adj* COMPUT protégé (contre la copie).

copyread ['kɒpɪri:d] (*pret & pp* [-red]) *US* = **subedit**.

copyreader ['kɒpɪ,ri:dəʳ] *US* = **subeditor**.

copyright ['kɒpɪraɪt] ◇ *n* copyright *m*, droit *m* d'auteur ■ **she has ~ on the book** elle a des droits d'auteur sur le livre ■ **out of ~** dans le domaine public.
◇ *vt* obtenir les droits exclusifs *OR* le copyright.
◇ *adj* de copyright.

copy typist *n* dactylographe *mf*.

copywriter ['kɒpɪ,raɪtəʳ] *n* rédacteur *m*, - trice *f* publicitaire.

copywriting ['kɒpɪ,raɪtɪŋ] *n* rédaction *f* publicitaire.

coquetry ['kəʊkɪtrɪ, 'kɒkɪtrɪ] (*pl* **coquetries**) *n* coquetterie *f*.

coquette [kəʊ'ket, kɒ'ket] *n* coquette *f*.

coquettish [kəʊ'ketɪʃ, kɒ'ketɪʃ] *adj* [behaviour, look, woman] coquet, provoquant.

cor [kɔ:ʳ] *interj UK inf* **~ (blimey)!** ça alors!

coracle ['kɒrəkl] *n* coracle *m*.

coral ['kɒrəl] ◇ *n* corail *m*.
◇ *comp* [earrings, necklace] de corail ■ [island] coralien.
◇ *adj* [pink, red, lipstick] corail ■ *lit* [lips] de corail.

coral reef *n* récif *m* de corail.

corbel ['kɔ:bəl] *n* corbeau *m*.

cord [kɔ:d] ◇ *n* **1.** [string] cordon *m* **2.** [cable] câble *m* **3.** [corduroy] velours *m* côtelé.
◇ *comp* [skirt, trousers] en velours côtelé.
◇ *vt* corder.
◆ **cords** *npl inf* **(a pair of) ~** un pantalon *m* en velours côtelé.

cordial ['kɔ:djəl] ◇ *adj* **1.** [warm - greeting, welcome] chaleureux **2.** [strong - hatred] cordial ■ **to have a ~ dislike for sb** détester qqn cordialement.
◇ *n* [drink] cordial *m*.

cordially ['kɔ:dɪəlɪ] *adv* [greet, detest etc] cordialement ■ **~ yours** *US* [at end of letter] salutations amicales.

cordite ['kɔ:daɪt] *n* cordite *f*.

cordless ['kɔ:dlɪs] *adj* [telephone] sans fil.

Cordoba ['kɔ:dəbə] *pr n* Cordoue.

cordon ['kɔ:dn] ◇ *n* **1.** [barrier] cordon *m* ■ **police ~** cordon de police ■ **the police put a ~ round the building** la police a encerclé le bâtiment **2.** HORT cordon *m* **3.** [decoration] cordon *m*.
◇ *vt* = **cordon off**.
◆ **cordon off** *vt sep* barrer, interdire l'accès à, isoler.

cordon bleu [-blɜ:] ◇ *adj* de cordon bleu ■ **a ~ cook** un cordon bleu.
◇ *n* : **she's a ~** c'est un cordon bleu.

corduroy ['kɔ:dərɔɪ] ◇ *n* velours *m* côtelé ■ **(a pair of) ~s** (un) pantalon *m* de *OR* en velours côtelé.
◇ *adj* de velours côtelé.

corduroy road *n route pratiquée en terrain marécageux grâce à des rondins de bois.*

core [kɔ:ʳ] ◇ *n* [of apple, pear] trognon *m*, cœur *m* ■ [of magnet, earth, organization] noyau *m* ■ [of electric cable] âme *f*, noyau *m* ■ [of nuclear reactor] cœur *m* ■ [of argument] essen-

tiel *m*, centre *m* ■ **to be French/a socialist to the ~** *fig* être français/socialiste jusqu'à la mœlle ■ **rotten to the ~** *fig* pourri jusqu'à l'os.
<> *comp* : **~ business** activité *f* principale ■ **~ curriculum** SCH tronc *m* commun ■ **~ memory** COMPUT mémoire *f* à tores (magnétiques) ■ **~ sample** GEOL carotte *f* ■ **~ subject** SCH matière *f* principale ■ **~ time** [in flexitime] plage *f* fixe ■ **~ vocabulary** LING vocabulaire *m* de base.
<> *vt* [apple, pear] enlever le trognon de.

core dump *n* COMPUT vidage *m* de mémoire.

corer ['kɔ:rəʳ] *n* : **apple ~** vide-pomme *m inv*.

co-respondent [ˌkəʊrɪ'spɒndənt] <> *adj* [shoes] bicolore *(style années quarante)*.
<> *n* LAW [in divorce suit] codéfendeur *m*, - eresse *f*.

Corfu [kɔ:'fu:] *pr n* Corfou ■ **in ~** à Corfou.

corgi ['kɔ:gɪ] *n* corgi *m*.

coriander [ˌkɒrɪ'ændəʳ] *n* coriandre *f*.

Corinth ['kɒrɪnθ] *pr n* Corinthe.

Corinthian [kə'rɪnθɪən] <> *n* Corinthien *m*, - enne *f*.
<> *adj* corinthien.

Coriolanus [ˌkɒrɪə'leɪnəs] *pr n* Coriolan.

cork [kɔ:k] <> *n* **1.** [substance] liège *m* **2.** [stopper] bouchon *m* ■ **he took** *OR* **pulled the ~ out of the bottle** il a débouché la bouteille ▶ **put a ~ in it!** *inf* la ferme! **3.** FISHING [float] flotteur *m*, bouchon *m*.
<> *comp* [tile, bathmat etc] de *OR* en liège.
<> *vt* **1.** [seal - bottle] boucher **2.** [blacken] : **to ~ one's face** se noircir le visage avec un bouchon brûlé.

corkage ['kɔ:kɪdʒ] *n (U) droit de débouchage sur un vin qui a été apporté par des consommateurs.*

corked [kɔ:kt] *adj* [wine] qui sent le bouchon.

corker ['kɔ:kəʳ] *n UK inf dated* **he's/a real ~** [good-looking] c'est un beau gars/un beau brin de fille ■ **it's a ~** [car, bike etc] c'est un (vrai) bijou.

corkscrew ['kɔ:kskru:] <> *n* tire-bouchon *m*.
<> *comp* : **~ curl** tire-bouchon *m*.
<> *vi* [staircase] tourner en vrille ■ [plane] vriller.

cork-tipped [-tɪpt] *adj* [cigarette] (à bout) filtre.

corm [kɔ:m] *n* bulbe *m*.

cormorant ['kɔ:mərənt] *n* cormoran *m*.

corn [kɔ:n] <> *n* **1.** [cereal] *UK* blé *m* ■ *US* maïs *m* ■ **~ on the cob** épi *m* de maïs ▶ **the Corn Laws** *UK* HIST les lois *fpl* sur le blé **2.** *inf (U)* [banality] banalité *f* ■ [sentimentality] sentimentalité *f* bébête **3.** [on foot] cor *m* ■ **to tread on sb's ~s** *UK inf* [upset] toucher qqn à l'endroit sensible ; [trespass] marcher sur les plates-bandes de qqn.
<> *comp* : **~ plaster** pansement *m* (pour cors).

THE CORN LAWS

Mesure protectionniste prise par le Parlement britannique en 1815 pour pallier l'effet des mauvaises récoltes en augmentant le prix du grain importé. Très impopulaires, ces lois provoquèrent la naissance de la *Anti-Corn Law League*, mouvement défendant la liberté de commerce. Ces lois furent abrogées en 1846.

Corn *written abbr of* **Cornwall**.

corn bread *n* pain *m* à la farine de maïs.

corncrake ['kɔ:nkreɪk] *n* râle *m* des genêts.

corn dolly *n objet décoratif en paille tressée.*

cornea ['kɔ:nɪə] *n* cornée *f*.

corneal ['kɔ:nɪəl] *adj* cornéen.

corned beef [kɔ:nd-] *n* corned beef *m*.

cornelian [kɔ:'ni:lɪən] *n* cornaline *f*.

Cornell [kɒ:'nel] *pr n université dans l'État de New York faisant partie de la Ivy League.*

corner ['kɔ:nəʳ] <> *n* **1.** [of page, painting, table etc] coin *m* ■ **to turn down the ~ of a page** faire une corne à une page **2.** [inside room, house etc] coin *m* ▶ **to fight one's ~** *UK* [argue one's case] défendre sa position **3.** [of street] coin *m* ■ [bend in the road] tournant *m*, virage *m* ■ **on** *OR* **at the ~** au coin ■ **the house on** *OR* **at the ~** la maison qui fait l'angle ■ **at the ~ of Regent Street and Oxford Street** à l'intersection *OR* à l'angle de Regent Street et d'Oxford Street ■ **he/the car took the ~ at high speed** il/la voiture a pris le tournant à toute allure ■ **to overtake on a ~** doubler dans un virage ■ **it's just around** *OR UK* **round the ~** [house, shop etc] c'est à deux pas d'ici ; *fig* [Christmas, economic recovery etc] c'est tout proche ■ **you never know what's round the ~** *fig* on ne sait jamais ce qui peut arriver ■ **to turn the ~** [car] prendre le tournant ; *fig* [patient] passer le moment *OR* stade critique ; [business, economy, relationship] passer un cap critique ■ **to cut the ~** [in car, on bike] couper le virage, prendre le virage à la corde ; [on foot] couper au plus court, prendre le plus court **4.** [of eye] coin *m* ■ [of mouth] coin *m*, commissure *f* ■ **to look at sb/sthg out of the ~ of one's eye** regarder qqn/qqch du coin de l'œil **5.** *inf* [difficulty] situation *f* difficile, mauvaise passe *f* ■ **to drive sb into a tight ~** acculer qqn, mettre qqn dans une situation difficile **6.** [remote place] coin *m* ■ **the four ~s of the earth** les quatre coins de la terre **7.** FTBL corner *m* **8.** COMM : **to make** *OR* **to have a ~ in sthg** avoir le monopole de qqch, accaparer qqch.
<> *comp* [cupboard, table etc] d'angle.
<> *vt* **1.** [animal, prey etc] coincer, acculer **2.** COMM accaparer ■ **to ~ the market in sthg** accaparer le marché de qqch.
<> *vi* AUT prendre un virage ■ **the car ~s well** la voiture tient bien la route dans les virages.

cornered ['kɔ:nəd] *adj* [animal, prey] acculé, coincé ■ **we've got him ~** on l'a acculé *OR* coincé.

corner flag *n* SPORT drapeau *m* de corner.

cornering ['kɔ:nərɪŋ] *n UK* **1.** AUT [of driver] façon *f* de prendre les virages ■ [of car] stabilité *f* dans les virages **2.** COMM accaparement *m*.

corner kick *n* FTBL corner *m*.

corner post *n* FTBL piquet *m* de corner.

corner shop *n UK* magasin *m* du coin.

cornerstone ['kɔ:nəstəʊn] *n* pierre *f* d'angle *OR* angulaire ■ *fig* pierre *f* angulaire, fondement *m*.

corner store *US* = **corner shop**.

cornet ['kɔ:nɪt] *n* **1.** MUS [instrument] cornet *m* à pistons **2.** *UK* **(ice-cream) ~** cornet *m* (de glace).

corn exchange *n* halle *f* au blé.

cornfield ['kɔ:nfi:ld] *n UK* champ *m* de blé ■ *US* champ *m* de maïs.

cornflakes ['kɔ:nfleɪks] *npl* cornflakes *mpl*, pétales *mpl OR* flocons *mpl* de maïs.

cornflour ['kɔ:nflaʊəʳ] *n UK* fécule *f* de maïs.

cornflower ['kɔ:nflaʊəʳ] <> *n* [plant] bleuet *m*, bluet *m*, barbeau *m* ■ [colour] bleu *m* centaurée.
<> *adj* : **~ (blue)** bleu centaurée.

cornice ['kɔ:nɪs] *n* ARCHIT corniche *f* ■ [snow] corniche *f*.

Cornish ['kɔ:nɪʃ] <> *npl* [people] : **the ~** les Cornouaillais *mpl*.
<> *n* LING cornouaillais *m*.
<> *adj* cornouaillais.

Cornishman ['kɔ:nɪʃmən] (*pl* **Cornishmen** [-mən]) *n* Cornouaillais *m*.

Cornish pasty *n UK* CULIN *chausson à la viande et aux légumes.*

Cornishwoman ['kɔ:nɪʃˌwʊmən] (*pl* **Cornishwomen** [-ˌwɪmɪn]) *n* Cornouaillaise *f*.

corn meal *n* farine *f* de maïs.

corn oil *n* huile *f* de maïs.

corn poppy *n* coquelicot *m*.

cornstarch ['kɔ:nstɑ:tʃ] *US* = **cornflour**.

cornucopia [ˌkɔ:njʊ'kəʊpjə] *n* MYTH & *fig* corne *f* d'abondance.

Cornwall ['kɔ:nwɔ:l] *pr n* Cornouailles *f* ▪ **in ~** en Cornouailles.

corn whiskey *n* whisky *m* de maïs.

corny ['kɔ:nɪ] (*comp* **cornier**, *superl* **corniest**) *adj* [trite] bateau, banal ▪ [sentimental] sentimental, à l'eau de rose ▪ **he's so ~** il est vraiment lourd *fig*.

corolla [kə'rɒlə] *n* BOT corolle *f*.

corollary [kə'rɒlərɪ] (*pl* **corollaries**) *n fml* corollaire *m*.

corona [kə'rəʊnə] (*pl* **coronas** *OR pl* **coronae** [-ni:]) *n* **1.** ANAT, ASTRON, BOT & PHYS couronne *f* **2.** ARCHIT larmier *m* **3.** [cigar] corona *m*.

coronary ['kɒrənrɪ] MED ◇ *adj* coronaire ▪ **the country has a high incidence of ~ heart disease** il y a de nombreux cas de maladies coronariennes dans ce pays.
◇ *n* infarctus *m* du myocarde.

coronary care unit *n* MED unité *f* de soins coronariens.

coronary thrombosis *n* MED infarctus *m* du myocarde, thrombose *f* coronarienne.

coronation [,kɒrə'neɪʃn] ◇ *n* [of monarch] couronnement *m*, sacre *m*.
◇ *comp* [robes, day] du couronnement, du sacre ▪ **'Coronation Street'** *feuilleton télévisé britannique*.

CORONATION STREET

Ce feuilleton télévisé, le plus ancien des *soap operas* encore à l'écran, évoque la vie quotidienne de plusieurs familles ouvrières vivant dans une rue d'une ville du nord de l'Angleterre.

coroner ['kɒrənəʳ] *n* LAW coroner *m* ▪ **~'s inquest** enquête *f* judiciaire *(menée par le coroner)*.

coronet ['kɒrənɪt] *n* [of prince, duke] couronne *f* ▪ [for woman] diadème *m*.

Corp. 1. (*written abbrev of* **corporation**) Cie **2.** *written abbr of* **corporal**.

corpora ['kɔ:pərə] *pl* ▻ **corpus**.

corporal ['kɔ:pərəl] ◇ *n* MIL caporal-chef *m*, caporale-chef *f*.
◇ *adj* corporel ▪ **~ punishment** châtiment *m* corporel.

corporate ['kɔ:pərət] *adj* **1.** LAW : **~ body** *OR* **institution** personne *f* morale **2.** [of a specific company] d'une société, de la société ▪ [of companies in general] d'entreprise ▪ [taxation] sur les sociétés ▪ **to make one's way up the ~ ladder** faire carrière dans l'entreprise ▪ **he's a good ~ man** il est dévoué à l'entreprise ▪ **the restaurant is hoping for good ~ business** le restaurant espère attirer une nombreuse clientèle d'affaires ▪ **~ culture** culture *f* d'entreprise ▪ **we have a number of ~ customers** certains de nos clients sont des entreprises ▪ **~ entertainment** divertissement *m* fourni par la société ➊ **~ hospitality** *réceptions, déjeuners, billets de spectacles etc offerts par une entreprise à ses clients* ▪ **~ identity** image *f* de marque ▪ **~ law** droit *m* des sociétés *OR* des entreprises ▪ **~ lawyer** juriste *m* spécialisé en droit des sociétés ▪ **~ name** raison *f* sociale ▪ **~ sponsorship** sponsoring *m*, parrainage *m* d'entreprises ▪ **~ structure** structure *f* de l'entreprise **3.** [collective - decision, responsibility] collectif.

corporately ['kɔ:pərətlɪ] *adv* **1.** [as a corporation] : **I don't think we should involve ourselves ~** je ne pense pas que nous devrions nous impliquer en tant que société **2.** [as a group] collectivement.

corporate tax *US* = **corporation tax**.

corporation [,kɔ:pə'reɪʃn] ◇ *n* **1.** [company] compagnie *f*, société *f* ▪ LAW personne *f* morale **2.** *UK* [municipal authorities] municipalité *f* **3.** *inf* [paunch] bedaine *f*, brioche *f*.
◇ *comp UK* [bus, worker] municipal, de la ville.

corporation tax *n UK* impôt *m* sur les sociétés.

corporatism ['kɔ:pərətɪzm] *n* corporatisme *m*.

corporeal [kɔ:'pɔ:rɪəl] *adj* corporel, matériel.

corps [kɔ:ʳ] (*pl inv*) *n* **1.** MIL corps *m* ▪ MIL & ADMIN service *m* ▪ **medical/intelligence ~** service de santé/de renseignements ▪ **pay ~** service de la solde **2.** [trained team of people] corps *m* ▪ **~ de ballet** corps de ballet.

corpse [kɔ:ps] *n* cadavre *m*, corps *m*.

corpulence ['kɔ:pjʊləns] *n* corpulence *f*, embonpoint *m*.

corpulent ['kɔ:pjʊlənt] *adj* corpulent.

corpus ['kɔ:pəs] (*pl* **corpuses** *OR pl* **corpora** ['kɔ:pərə]) *n* **1.** [collection of writings - by author] recueil *m* ; [- on specific subject] corpus *m* **2.** [main body] corpus *m*.

Corpus Christi [,kɔ:pəs'krɪstɪ] *n* la Fête-Dieu.

corpuscle ['kɔ:pʌsl] *n* PHYSIOL corpuscule *m* ▪ **red/white blood ~s** globules *mpl* rouges/blancs.

corral [kɒ'rɑ:l] *US* ◇ *n* corral *m*.
◇ *vt* (*pret & pp* **corralled**, *cont* **corralling**) [cattle, horses] enfermer dans un corral ▪ *fig* encercler.

correct [kə'rekt] ◇ *adj* **1.** [right - answer, spelling etc] correct ▪ **do you have the ~ time?** avez-vous l'heure exacte? ▪ **that is ~** c'est exact ▪ **to prove (to be) ~** s'avérer juste ▪ **~ to four decimal places** exact à quatre chiffres après la virgule ▪ **am I ~ in thinking that...?** ai-je raison de penser que...? ▪ **she was quite ~ in her assumptions** ses suppositions étaient parfaitement justes **2.** [suitable, proper - behaviour, manners etc] correct, convenable, bienséant ; [- person] correct, convenable ▪ **the ~ thing for him to do in the circumstances is to resign** dans ces circonstances la bienséance veut qu'il démissionne ▪ **the ~ procedure** la procédure d'usage.
◇ *vt* **1.** [rectify - mistake, spelling etc] corriger, rectifier ; [- squint, bad posture, imbalance] corriger ; [- situation] rectifier **2.** [indicate error - to person] corriger, reprendre ; [- in exam, proofs etc] corriger ▪ **to ~ sb on** *OR* **about sthg** corriger *OR* reprendre qqn sur qqch ▪ **to ~ sb's French** corriger le français de qqn, reprendre qqn sur son français ▪ **~ me if I'm wrong, but...** corrigez-moi si je me trompe, mais... ▪ **I stand ~ed** je reconnais mon erreur ▪ **to ~ o.s.** se reprendre, se corriger.
Voir module d'usage

CORRECTING SOMEONE

Je crois que ce n'est pas tout à fait ça. I don't think that's quite right.

En fait, ce n'est pas tout à fait exact. Actually, that's not strictly true.

Vous croyez ? Moi je dirais plutôt que... Do you think so? I'd say...

Tu es sûr que ça se dit/s'écrit comme ça ? Are you sure that's how you say/spell it?

Ah non, je n'ai pas dit ça ! I didn't say that at all!

Si je peux me permettre, je pense que ce n'est pas tout à fait ça. With all due respect, I don't think that's quite right.

Vous vous trompez, il n'a rien à voir là-dedans. You're wrong, this has nothing to do with him.

Non, c'est faux. No, that's wrong.

Ce n'est pas ça du tout. That's totally wrong.

Tu as mal interprété ce que j'ai dit. You misunderstood what I said.

correction [kə'rekʃn] *n* **1.** [of exam paper, homework, proofs etc] correction *f* ■ [of error] correction *f*, rectification *f* **2.** [in essay, school work, proofs etc] correction *f* ■ **to make ~s** faire des corrections ■ **to make ~s to sthg** apporter des corrections à qqch **3.** *arch* [punishment] correction *f*, punition *f*, châtiment *m*.

correction fluid *n* liquide *m* correcteur.

correction tape *n* [for typewriter] ruban *m* correcteur.

corrective [kə'rektɪv] ◇ *adj* [action, measure] rectificatif, correctif ■ [exercises, treatment] correctif.
◇ *n* correctif *m* ■ MED [for teeth] appareil *m* dentaire ■ [for deformed limb] appareil *m* orthopédique ■ **a ~ to sthg** un correctif de qqch.

correctly [kə'rektlɪ] *adv* **1.** [in the right way - answer, pronounce] correctement ■ **he ~ predicted that...** il a prédit avec raison que... ■ **the XYZ, more ~ known as...** XYZ, ou selon son appellation plus correcte... **2.** [properly - behave, dress, speak] correctement.

correctness [kə'rektnɪs] *n* **1.** [of answer, prediction etc] exactitude *f*, justesse *f* **2.** [of behaviour, dress etc] correction *f*.

Correggio [kɒ'redʒjəʊ] *pr n* le Corrège.

correlate ['kɒrəleɪt] ◇ *vi* : **to ~ (with sthg)** [gen] être en corrélation *OR* rapport (avec qqch), correspondre (à qqch) ; [in statistics] être en corrélation (avec qqch).
◇ *vt* [gen] mettre en corrélation *OR* en rapport, faire correspondre ■ [in statistics] corréler ■ **to ~ sthg with sthg** [gen] mettre qqch en corrélation *OR* rapport avec qqch ; [in statistics] corréler qqch avec qqch ■ **these two trends are closely ~d** ces deux tendances sont en rapport étroit.

correlation [,kɒrə'leɪʃn] *n* corrélation *f*.

correspond [,kɒrɪ'spɒnd] *vi* **1.** [tally - dates, statements] correspondre ■ **to ~ with sthg** correspondre à qqch **2.** [be equivalent] correspondre, équivaloir ■ **this animal ~s roughly with *OR* to our own domestic cat** cet animal correspond à peu près à notre *OR* est à peu près l'équivalent de notre chat domestique **3.** [exchange letters] correspondre ■ **we have been ~ing (with each other) for years** cela fait des années que nous correspondons.

correspondence [,kɒrɪ'spɒndəns] ◇ *n* **1.** [relationship, similarity] correspondance *f*, rapport *m*, relation *f* **2.** [letter-writing] correspondance *f* ■ **to be in ~ with sb** être en correspondance avec qqn ■ **to enter into (a) ~ with sb** établir une *OR* entrer en correspondance avec qqn ■ **no ~ will be entered into** [in competition] il ne sera répondu à aucun courrier **3.** [letters] correspondance *f*, courrier *m* ■ **to read/to do one's ~** lire/faire son courrier *OR* sa correspondance.
◇ *comp* [course] par correspondance ■ [school] d'enseignement par correspondance ■ **~ column** PRESS courrier *m* des lecteurs.

correspondent [,kɒrɪ'spɒndənt] ◇ *n* **1.** PRESS, RADIO & TV [reporter] correspondant *m*, - e *f* ■ **special ~** envoyé *m* spécial, envoyée *f* spéciale ■ **sports ~** correspondant sportif ■ **war/environment ~** correspondant de guerre/pour les questions d'environnement ■ **our Moscow ~** notre correspondant à Moscou **2.** [letter-writer] correspondant *m*, - e *f*.
◇ *adj* = **corresponding**.

corresponding [,kɒrɪ'spɒndɪŋ] *adj* correspondant.

correspondingly [,kɒrɪ'spɒndɪŋlɪ] *adv* **1.** [proportionally] proportionnellement **2.** [related to this, in line with this] : **the translation should be ~ informal in register** la traduction devrait être d'un niveau de familiarité correspondant ■ **we got a lot of negative press and our election results were ~ poor** nous avons eu beaucoup de commentaires négatifs dans la presse, ce qui nous a valu de mauvais résultats aux élections.

corridor ['kɒrɪdɔːʳ] *n* [in building] corridor *m*, couloir *m* ■ [in train] couloir *m* ■ **the ~s of power** *fig* les allées du pouvoir ; [behind the scenes] les coulisses du pouvoir.

corroborate [kə'rɒbəreɪt] *vt* [statement, view etc] confirmer, corroborer *lit* ■ **for lack of corroborating evidence** faute de preuves à l'appui.

corroboration [kə,rɒbə'reɪʃn] *n* confirmation *f*, corroboration *f lit* ■ **to provide ~ of sthg** confirmer *OR* corroborer qqch ■ **evidence produced in ~ of sb's testimony** des preuves fournies à l'appui du témoignage de qqn.

corroborative [kə'rɒbərətɪv] *adj* [evidence, statement] à l'appui.

corrode [kə'rəʊd] ◇ *vt* [subj: acid, rust] corroder, ronger ■ *fig* [happiness] entamer, miner.
◇ *vi* [due to acid, rust] se corroder ■ [due to rust] se rouiller.

corrosion [kə'rəʊʒn] *n* [of metal] corrosion *f*.

corrosive [kə'rəʊsɪv] ◇ *adj* corrosif ■ **the ~ effects of long-term unemployment** les effets destructeurs du chômage de longue durée.
◇ *n* corrosif *m*.

corrugated ['kɒrəgeɪtɪd] *adj* [cardboard, paper] ondulé ■ **~ iron** tôle *f* ondulée.

corrupt [kə'rʌpt] ◇ *adj* **1.** [dishonest - person, society] corrompu ■ **~ practices** pratiques *fpl* malhonnêtes **2.** [depraved, immoral] dépravé, corrompu **3.** [containing alterations - text] altéré **4.** COMPUT [containing errors - disk, file] altéré.
◇ *vt* **1.** [make dishonest] corrompre ■ **~ed by power** corrompu par le pouvoir **2.** [deprave, debase - person, society] dépraver, corrompre ; [- language] corrompre ■ **the ~ing influence of television** l'influence corruptrice de la télévision **3.** [alter - text] altérer, corrompre **4.** COMPUT altérer.

corruptible [kə'rʌptəbl] *adj* corruptible.

corruption [kə'rʌpʃn] *n* **1.** [of official, politician etc - action, state] corruption *f* **2.** [depravity, debasement - action, state] dépravation *f*, corruption *f* ■ **the ~ of minors** LAW le détournement de mineurs **3.** [of text - action] altération *f*, corruption *f* ; [- state] version *f* corrompue ■ [of word - action] corruption *f* ; [- state] forme *f* corrompue **4.** COMPUT altération *f*.

corruptly [kə'rʌptlɪ] *adv* **1.** [dishonestly] de manière corrompue **2.** [in a depraved way] d'une manière dépravée *OR* corrompue.

corsage [kɔː'sɑːʒ] *n* [flowers] *petit bouquet de fleurs (à accrocher au corsage ou au poignet)* ■ [bodice] corsage *m*.

corset ['kɔːsɪt] *n* corset *m*.

Corsica ['kɔːsɪkə] *pr n* Corse *f* ■ **in ~** en Corse.

Corsican ['kɔːsɪkən] ◇ *n* **1.** [person] Corse *mf* **2.** LING corse *m*.
◇ *adj* corse.

cortège [kɔː'teɪʒ] *n* cortège *m*.

cortex ['kɔːteks] (*pl* **cortices** [-tɪsiːz]) *n* ANAT & BOT cortex *m*.

cortical ['kɔːtɪkl] *adj* cortical.

cortisone ['kɔːtɪzəʊn] ◇ *n* cortisone *f*.
◇ *comp* : **~ injection** piqûre *f* de cortisone.

coruscate ['kɒrəskeɪt] *vi fml* briller, scintiller.

coruscating ['kɒrəskeɪtɪŋ] *adj fml* brillant, scintillant ■ *fig* [wit] brillant, étincelant.

corvette ['kɔːvet] *n* NAUT corvette *f*.

cos[1] [kɒz] ◇ *conj inf* = **because**.
◇ *n* = **cosine**.

cos[2] [kɒs] *n UK* **~ (lettuce)** (laitue *f*) romaine *f*.

C.O.S. (*written abbrev of* **Cash on shipment**) *paiement à l'expédition*.

cosh [kɒʃ] ◇ *n* gourdin *m*, matraque *f*.
◇ *vt* assommer, matraquer.

cosignatory [,kəʊ'sɪgnətrɪ] (*pl* **cosignatories**) *n fml* cosignataire *mf*.

cosily *UK*, **cozily** *US* ['kəʊzɪlɪ] *adv* [furnished] confortablement.

cosine ['kəʊsaɪn] *n* MATHS cosinus *m*.

cosmetic [kɒz'metɪk] ◇ *adj* [preparation] cosmétique ■ *fig* [superficial - change, measure] superficiel, symbolique ■ **it's purely ~** c'est purement symbolique, c'est uniquement pour la forme ▶ **to have ~ surgery** se faire faire de la chirurgie esthétique.
◇ *n* cosmétique *m*, produit *m* de beauté ■ **the ~s industry/counter** l'industrie/le rayon des cosmétiques ■ **she's in ~s** elle est dans les cosmétiques.

cosmic ['kɒzmɪk] *adj* cosmique ■ **of ~ proportions** *fig* aux proportions gigantesques.

cosmology [kɒz'mɒlədʒɪ] *n* cosmologie *f*.

cosmonaut ['kɒzmənɔːt] *n* cosmonaute *mf*.

cosmopolitan [kɒzmə'pɒlɪtn] ◇ *adj* [city, person, restaurant etc] cosmopolite.
◇ *n* cosmopolite *mf*.

cosmos ['kɒzmɒs] *n* cosmos *m* ■ *fig* univers *m*.

cosset ['kɒsɪt] *vt* [person] dorloter, choyer, câliner ■ **to ~ o.s.** se dorloter.

cost [kɒst] ◇ *vt* **1.** (*pret & pp* **cost**) coûter ■ **how much** *OR* **what does it ~?** combien ça coûte? ■ **how much is it going to ~ me?** combien est-ce que ça va me coûter?, à combien est-ce que ça va me revenir? ■ **it ~ me £200** cela m'est revenu à *OR* m'a coûté 200 livres ■ **did it ~ much?** est-ce que cela a coûté cher? ■ **it ~s nothing to join** l'inscription est gratuite ■ **it didn't ~ me a penny** ça ne m'a rien coûté du tout, ça ne m'a pas coûté un sou ■ **it'll ~ you!** *inf* [purchase] tu vas le sentir passer! ; [help, favour] ce ne sera pas gratuit! ■ **electricity ~s money, you know!** l'électricité, ce n'est pas gratuit! ■ **it ~ her a lot of time and effort** cela lui a demandé beaucoup de temps et d'efforts ■ **it ~ him his job** cela lui a coûté son travail, cela lui a fait perdre son travail ■ **drinking and driving ~s lives** la conduite en état d'ivresse coûte des vies humaines ■ **it doesn't ~ anything to be polite** ça ne coûte rien d'être poli ■ **it must have ~ him to say sorry** cela a dû lui coûter de s'excuser ■ **whatever it ~s** [purchase] quel qu'en soit le prix ■ **whatever it ~s, I'm not going to give up** quoi qu'il m'en coûte, je n'abandonnerai pas ▶ **to ~ an arm and a leg** *inf*, **to ~ the earth** coûter les yeux de la tête *OR* la peau des fesses **2.** (*pret & pp* **costed**) [work out price of - trip] évaluer le coût de ; [- job, repairs] établir un devis pour ■ **to ~ a product** COMM établir le prix de revient d'un produit ■ **a carefully ~ed budget** un budget calculé avec soin.
◇ *n* **1.** [amount charged or paid] coût *m* ■ **the car was repaired at a ~ of £50** la réparation de la voiture a coûté 50 livres ■ **the ~ of petrol has gone up** le prix de l'essence a augmenté ■ **think of the ~ (involved)!** imagine un peu le prix que ça coûte! ■ **to bear the ~ of sthg** payer qqch ; [with difficulty] faire face aux frais *OR* aux dépenses de qqch ■ **to buy/to sell sthg at ~** [cost price] acheter/vendre qqch au prix coûtant ■ **at no extra ~** sans frais supplémentaires ■ **the firm cut its ~s by 30%** l'entreprise a réduit ses frais de 30 % ▶ **~, insurance and freight** COMM coût, assurance et fret **2.** *fig* prix *m* ■ **whatever the ~** à tout prix, à n'importe quel prix ■ **whatever the ~ to his health** quoi qu'il en coûte à sa santé, quel qu'en soit le prix pour sa santé ■ **at the ~ of her job/reputation/marriage** au prix de son travail/sa réputation/son mariage ■ **to find out** *OR* **to learn** *OR* **to discover to one's ~** apprendre *OR* découvrir à ses dépens ■ **as I know to my ~** comme j'en ai fait la dure expérience ■ **to count the ~ of sthg** faire le bilan de qqch ■ **no-one stopped to count the ~** [in advance] personne n'a pensé au prix à payer ■ **the ~ in human life** le prix en vies humaines.
◇ *comp* [analysis] de coût.
◆ **costs** *npl* LAW frais *mpl* (d'instance) et dépens *mpl* ■ **to be awarded ~s** se voir accorder des frais et dépens ■ **to be ordered to pay ~s** être condamné aux dépens.
◆ **at all costs** *adv phr* à tout prix.
◆ **at any cost** *adv phr* en aucun cas ■ **he should not be approached at any ~** en aucun cas il ne doit être approché.
◆ **cost out** *vt sep* = **cost** *(sense 2)*.

Costa Brava [ˌkɒstə'brɑːvə] *pr n* Costa Brava *f*.

cost accounting *n* comptabilité *f* analytique *OR* d'exploitation.

Costa del Sol [ˌkɒstədel'sɒl] *pr n* Costa del Sol *f*.

co-star CIN & TV ◇ *n* [of actor, actress] partenaire *mf*.
◇ *vi* (*pret & pp* **co-starred**, *cont* **co-starring**) [in film] être l'une des vedettes principales ■ **to ~ with sb** partager la vedette *OR* l'affiche avec qqn.
◇ *vt* (*pret & pp* **co-starred**, *cont* **co-starring**) : **the film ~s Joe Smith and Mary Brown** le film met en scène Joe Smith et Mary Brown dans les rôles principaux *OR* vedettes ■ **co-starring...** [in credits] avec...

Costa Rica [ˌkɒstə'riːkə] *pr n* Costa Rica *m* ■ **in ~** au Costa Rica.

Costa Rican [ˌkɒstə'riːkən] ◇ *n* Costaricien *m*, - enne *f*.
◇ *adj* costaricien.

cost-benefit analysis *n* analyse *f* des coûts et rendements.

cost-conscious *adj* : **to be ~** contrôler ses dépenses ■ **in these ~ days** par les temps qui courent où tout le monde fait attention à *OR* surveille ses dépenses.

cost-cutting ◇ *n* compression *f* *OR* réduction *f* des coûts.
◇ *adj* de compression *OR* de réduction des coûts.

cost-effective *adj* rentable.

cost-effectiveness *n* rentabilité *f*.

costermonger ['kɒstəˌmʌŋgəʳ] *n UK* marchand *m*, - e *f* de quatre-saisons.

costing ['kɒstɪŋ] *n* [of product] estimation *f* du prix de revient ■ [of job, repairs] établissement *m* d'un devis ■ **based on detailed ~s** basé sur des calculs détaillés.

costly ['kɒstlɪ] (*comp* **costlier**, *superl* **costliest**) *adj* **1.** [expensive] coûteux, cher ■ **this may be a ~ mistake** cette erreur pourrait me/vous *etc* coûter cher **2.** [of high quality] somptueux, riche.

cost of living ◇ *n* coût *m* de la vie.
◇ *comp* : **~ allowance** indemnité *f* de vie chère ■ **~ increase** *OR* **adjustment** [in salary] augmentation *f* de salaire indexée sur le coût de la vie ■ **~ index** indice *m* du coût de la vie.

cost-plus *adj* : **on a ~ basis** sur la base du prix de revient majoré.

cost price *n* prix *m* coûtant *OR* de revient ■ **to buy/to sell sthg at ~** acheter/vendre qqch à prix coûtant.

costume ['kɒstjuːm] ◇ *n* **1.** CIN, THEAT & TV costume *m* ■ **to be (dressed) in ~** porter un costume (de scène) ■ **~s by...** [in credits] costumes réalisés par... **2.** [fancy dress] costume *m*, déguisement *m* ■ **to be (dressed) in ~** être costumé *OR* déguisé **3.** [traditional dress] : **national ~** costume *m* national ■ **to wear national ~** porter le costume national **4.** [for swimming] maillot *m* de bain.
◇ *comp* : **~ ball** *OR* **party** bal *m* costumé ■ **~ designer** costumier *m*, - ère *f* ■ **~ drama** *OR* **piece** *OR* **play** pièce *f* en costumes d'époque.
◇ *vt* [film, play] réaliser les costumes pour.

costume jewellery *n (U)* bijoux *mpl* fantaisie ■ **a piece of ~** un bijou fantaisie.

costumier [kɒ'stjuːmɪəʳ], **costumer** ['kɒstjuːməʳ] *n* costumier *m*, - ère *f*.

cosy *UK*, **cozy** *US* ['kəʊzɪ] (*UK comp* **cosier**, *superl* **cosiest**) (*US comp* **cozier**, *superl* **coziest**) ◇ *adj* **1.** [warm, snug - flat, room, atmosphere] douillet, confortable ■ **it's nice and ~ in here** on est bien ici ■ **to feel ~** se sentir bien à l'aise ■ **isn't this ~?** on n'est pas bien ici? **2.** [intimate - chat, evening etc] intime ; [- novel] à l'atmosphère douce ■ **they've got a very ~ relationship** *pej* ils sont très copain-copain.
◇ *n* [for tea-pot] couvre-théière *m* ■ [for egg] couvre-œuf *m*.
◆ **cosy up to** *vt insep inf* se mettre dans les petits papiers de ■ **he's always ~ing up to the boss** il essaie tout le temps de se mettre dans les petits papiers du patron.

cot [kɒt] *n UK* [for baby] lit *m* d'enfant ■ *US* [camp bed] lit *m* de camp.

cotangent [kəʊ'tændʒənt] *n* MATHS cotangente *f*.

cot death *n UK* mort *f* subite du nourrisson.

cote [kəʊt] *n* [for doves] colombier *m*, pigeonnier *m* ■ [for sheep] abri *m*, bergerie *f*.

coterie ['kəʊtərɪ] *n* cercle *m*, cénacle *m* ■ *pej* coterie *f*, clique *f*.

Cotswolds ['kɒtswəʊldz] *pr npl* : **the ~** *région touristique du sud-ouest de l'Angleterre, connue pour ses pittoresques villages en pierre.*

cottage ['kɒtɪdʒ] *n* **1.** [in country] petite maison *f* (à la campagne), cottage *m* ■ **thatched ~** chaumière *f* **2.** *US* [holiday home] maison *f* de campagne.

cottage cheese *n* fromage *m* blanc (égoutté), cottage cheese *m*.

cottage industry *n* industrie *f* familiale *OR* artisanale.

cottage loaf *n UK miche de pain en forme de brioche.*

cottage pie *n UK* hachis *m* parmentier.

cottaging△ ['kɒtɪdʒɪŋ] *n (U) UK rencontres homosexuelles dans les toilettes publiques.*

cotter ['kɒtər] *n* MECH [wedge] goupille *f* ■ **~ (pin)** clavette *f*.

cotton ['kɒtn] <> *n* **1.** [material, plant] coton *m* ■ **to pick ~** cueillir le coton ■ **is this dress ~?** [made of cotton] cette robe est-elle en coton? **2.** *UK* [thread for sewing] fil *m*.
<> *comp* [garment] en coton ■ [industry, trade] du coton ■ [culture, field, grower, plantation] de coton ■ **~ picker** [person] cueilleur *m*, - euse *f* de coton.
◆ **cotton on** *vi insep inf* piger ■ **to ~ on to sthg** piger qqch.
◆ **cotton to** *vt insep US inf* [like - person] être attiré par ; [- idea, plan, suggestion] approuver.

cotton batting *US* = **cotton wool** *(n)*.

Cotton Belt *n* GEOG *région du coton dans le sud des États-Unis.*

cotton bud *n UK* coton-tige *m*.

cotton candy *n US* barbe *f* à papa.

cotton mill *n* filature *f* de coton.

cotton-picking△ *adj US* sale, sacré.

cotton swab *n US* = **cotton bud**.

cottontail ['kɒtnteɪl] *n* lapin *m* (de garenne).

cotton wool *UK* <> *n* coton *m* hydrophile, ouate *f* ■ **my legs feel like ~** *inf* j'ai les jambes en coton ■ **to wrap sb in ~** être aux petits soins pour qqn.
<> *comp* : **~ balls** boules *fpl* de coton ■ **~ pads** rondelles *fpl* de coton *OR* d'ouate.

cotyledon [ˌkɒtɪ'liːdən] *n* BOT cotylédon *m*.

couch [kaʊtʃ] <> *n* [sofa] canapé *m*, divan *m*, sofa *m* ■ [in psychiatrist's office] divan *m*.
<> *vt* formuler ■ **to be ~ed in very polite terms/in jargon** [letter, document] être formulé en termes très polis/en jargon.

couchette [kuː'ʃet] *n* RAIL couchette *f*.

couch potato *n inf pej* **he's a ~** il passe son temps affalé devant la télé.

cougar ['kuːgər] *n* couguar *m*, cougouar *m*, puma *m*.

cough [kɒf] <> *n* toux *f* ■ **you want to get that ~ seen to** avec cette toux, tu devrais te faire examiner ■ **I can't get rid of this ~** cette toux ne me passe pas ■ **to have a ~** tousser ■ **she gave a loud ~** elle a toussé fort ■ **smoker's ~** toux de fumeur.
<> *comp* [medicine, sweets] pour *OR* contre la toux, antitussif *spec*.
<> *vi* tousser ■ **the engine ~ed into life** *fig* le moteur a toussé puis s'est mis en marche.
<> *vt* [blood] cracher ■ **the old car ~ed its way down the street** *fig* la vieille voiture a descendu la rue en faisant des ratés.
◆ **cough out** *vt sep* **1.** cracher (en toussant) ■ **you sound as if you're ~ing your insides out** on dirait que tu es en train de cracher tes poumons **2.** [words] dire en toussant.
◆ **cough up** <> *vt sep* **1.** [blood] cracher (en toussant) **2.** *inf* [money] cracher, raquer.
<> *vi insep inf* [pay up] banquer, raquer.

cough drop *n* pastille *f* contre la toux *OR* antitussive.

coughing ['kɒfɪŋ] *n* toux *f* ■ **your ~ woke me up** tu m'as réveillé en toussant ■ **fit of ~, ~ fit** quinte *f* de toux.

cough mixture *n* sirop *m* antitussif *OR* contre la toux.

cough sweet = **cough drop**.

could [kʊd] *modal vb* **1.** [be able to] : **I'd come if I ~** je viendrais si je (le) pouvais ■ **she ~ no longer walk** elle ne pouvait plus marcher ■ **they ~n't very well refuse** il leur aurait été difficile de refuser ■ **five years ago I ~ run a mile in four minutes but I can't anymore** il y a cinq ans, je courais un mile en quatre minutes mais je ne pourrais plus maintenant ■ **she ~ have had the job if she'd wanted it** elle aurait pu obtenir cet emploi si elle l'avait voulu
2. [with verbs of perception or understanding] : **he ~ see her talking to her boss** il la voyait qui parlait avec son patron ■ **I ~ see his point of view** je comprenais son point de vue
3. [indicating ability or skill] : **she ~ read and write** elle savait lire et écrire ■ **she ~ speak three languages** elle parlait trois langues
4. [in polite requests] : **~ I borrow your sweater?** est-ce que je pourrais t'emprunter ton pull? ■ **~ you help me please?** pourriez-vous *OR* est-ce que vous pourriez m'aider, s'il vous plaît?
5. [indicating supposition or speculation] : **they ~ give up at any time** ils pourraient abandonner n'importe quand ■ **~ he be lying?** se pourrait-il qu'il mente? ■ **they ~ have changed their plans** ils ont peut-être changé leurs plans ‖ [indicating possibility] : **you ~ have told me the truth** tu aurais pu me dire la vérité ■ **what ~ I have done with the keys?** qu'est-ce que j'ai bien pu faire des clés? ■ **I ~ kill him!** je pourrais le tuer! ■ **he ~ have jumped for joy** il en aurait presque sauté de joie ➋ **I'm as happy as ~ be** je suis on ne peut plus heureux
6. [indicating unwillingness] : **I ~n't just leave him there, could I?** je ne pouvais vraiment pas le laisser là ■ **I ~n't possibly do it before tomorrow** je ne pourrai vraiment pas le faire avant demain
7. [in polite suggestions] : **you ~ always complain to the director** tu pourrais toujours te plaindre au directeur ■ **~n't we at least talk about it?** est-ce que nous ne pourrions pas au moins en discuter?
8. [introducing comments or opinions] : **if I ~ just intervene here** est-ce que je peux me permettre d'intervenir ici? ■ **you ~ argue it's a waste of resources** tu pourrais argumenter que c'est un gaspillage de ressources
9. [indicating surprise or disbelief] : **the house ~n't have been THAT expensive** la maison n'a pas dû coûter si cher que ça ■ **how ~ you say that?** comment avez-vous pu dire ça *OR* une chose pareille? ■ **who on earth ~ that be?** qui diable cela peut-il bien être?
10. [inviting agreement] : **he left and you ~n't blame him** il est parti et on ne peut pas lui en vouloir.

couldn't ['kʊdnt] = **could not**.

couldn't-care-less *adj inf* [attitude] je-m'en-foutiste.

could've ['kʊdəv] = **could have**.

coulis ['kuːlɪ] *n* coulis *m*.

council ['kaʊnsl] <> *n* **1.** [group of people] conseil *m* **2.** *UK* [elected local body] conseil *m* ■ **to be on the ~** être au conseil ➋ **county** *OR* ***Scotland*** **regional ~** conseil *m* régional **3.** [meeting] conseil *m* ■ **to hold a ~ of war** tenir un conseil de guerre.
<> *comp* **1.** [meeting] du conseil **2.** *UK* [election, service, worker] municipal ■ [leader, meeting] du conseil municipal ■ **~ estate** cité *f* ■ **to live on a ~ estate** habiter dans une cité ■ **~ flat/house** ≃ habitation *f* à loyer modéré ■ ≃ HLM *m ou f* ■ **~ housing** ≃ habitations *fpl* à loyer modéré ■ ≃ HLM *fpl OR mpl* ■ **~ tenants** *locataires d'un appartement ou d'une maison appartenant à la municipalité.*

councillor *UK*, **councilor** *US* ['kaʊnsələr] *n* conseiller *m*, - ère *f* ■ **Councillor (John) Murray** Monsieur le Conseiller Murray ■ **town/county ~** conseiller municipal/régional.

councilman ['kaʊnslmæn] (*pl* **councilmen** [-men]) *n US* conseiller *m*.

Council of Europe *n* Conseil *m* de l'Europe.

councilor *US* = councillor.

council tax *n (U)* impôts *mpl* locaux *(en Grande-Bretagne)*.

councilwoman ['kaʊnsl,wʊmən] (*pl* **councilwomen** [-,wɪmɪn]) *n US* conseillère *f*.

counsel ['kaʊnsəl] ◇ *n* **1.** *fml* [advice] conseil *m* ▪ **to keep one's own ~** garder ses opinions *OR* intentions pour soi **2.** LAW avocat *m*, - e *f (qui plaide dans une cour)* ▪ **~ for the defence/prosecution** avocat de la défense/du ministère public ▶ **King's ~, Queen's ~** *UK membre supérieur du barreau*.
◇ *vt* (*UK pret & pp* **counselled**, *cont* **counselling**) (*US pret & pp* **counseled**, *cont* **counseling**) **1.** *fml* conseiller ▪ **to ~ sb to do sthg** conseiller à qqn de faire qqch ▪ **to ~ caution** recommander la prudence **2.** [in therapy] conseiller.

counselling *UK*, **counseling** *US* ['kaʊnsəlɪŋ] *n* [psychological] assistance *f*, conseils *mpl* ▪ **to seek ~** se faire conseiller, prendre conseil ▪ **she does ~ at the university** elle est conseillère auprès des étudiants à l'université.

counsellor *UK*, **counselor** *US* ['kaʊnsələr] *n* **1.** [in therapy] conseiller *m*, - ère *f* **2.** *US* LAW avocat *m*, - e *f* ▪ **that's enough, ~!** cela suffit, maître!

count [kaʊnt] ◇ *n* **1.** compte *m* ▪ [of ballot papers] décompte *m* ▪ **it took three/several ~s** il a fallu faire trois/plusieurs fois le compte, il a fallu compter trois/plusieurs fois ▪ **to have a second ~** refaire le compte, recompter ▪ **to lose ~** perdre le compte ▪ **I've lost ~ of the number of times he's been late** je ne compte plus le nombre de fois où il est arrivé en retard ▪ **to keep ~ (of sthg)** tenir le compte (de qqch) ▪ **at the last ~** [gen] la dernière fois qu'on a compté ; ADMIN [of people] au dernier recensement ▪ **on the ~ of three, begin** à trois, vous commencez
2. [in boxing] : **to take the ~** être mis K-O ▶ **to be out for the ~** [boxer, person in brawl] être K-O ; [fast asleep] dormir comme une souche
3. LAW chef *m* d'accusation ▪ **guilty on three ~s of murder** coupable de meurtre sur trois chefs d'accusation ▪ *fig* **the argument is flawed on both ~s** l'argumentation est défectueuse sur les deux points ▪ **I'm annoyed with you on a number of ~s** je suis fâché contre toi pour un certain nombre de raisons *OR* à plus d'un titre
4. MED taux *m* ▪ **blood (cell) ~** numération *f* globulaire
5. [nobleman] comte *m*.
◇ *vt* **1.** [add up - gen] compter ; [- votes] compter, décompter ▶ **to ~ sheep** *fig* [when sleepless] compter les moutons ▪ **to ~ the pennies** faire attention à ses sous ▪ **they can be ~ed on the fingers of one hand** on peut les compter sur les doigts de la main ▪ **~ your blessings** pense à tout ce que tu as pour être heureux ▪ **don't ~ your chickens (before they're hatched)** *prov* il ne faut pas vendre la peau de l'ours (avant de l'avoir tué) *prov*
2. [include] compter ▪ **not ~ing public holidays** sans compter les jours fériés
3. [consider] considérer, estimer ▪ **do you ~ her as a friend?** la considères-tu comme une amie? ▪ **student grants are not ~ed as taxable income** les bourses d'études ne sont pas considérées comme revenu imposable ▪ **~ yourself lucky (that...)** estime-toi heureux (que...)
◇ *vi* **1.** [add up] compter ▪ **to ~ to twenty/fifty/a hundred** compter jusqu'à vingt/cinquante/cent ▪ **to ~ on one's fingers** compter sur ses doigts ▪ **~ing from tomorrow** à partir de demain
2. [be considered, qualify] compter ▪ **two children ~ as one adult** deux enfants comptent pour un adulte ▪ **unemployment benefit ~s as taxable income** les allocations (de) chômage comptent comme revenu imposable ▪ **this exam ~s towards the final mark** cet examen compte dans la note finale ▪ **that/he doesn't ~** ça/il ne compte pas ▪ **his record ~ed in his favour/against him** son casier judiciaire a joué en sa faveur/l'a desservi
3. [be important] compter ▪ **experience ~s more than qualifications** l'expérience compte davantage que les diplômes ▪ **he ~s for nothing** il n'est pas important, il ne compte pas ▪ **a private education doesn't ~ for much now** avoir reçu une éducation privée n'est plus un grand avantage de nos jours.

◆ **count down** *vi insep* faire le compte à rebours.

◆ **count in** *vt sep* [include] compter, inclure ▪ **to ~ sb in on sthg** inclure *OR* compter qqn dans qqch ▪ **~ me in** compte sur moi, je suis partant.

◆ **count on** *vt insep* **1.** [rely on] compter sur ▪ **we're ~ing on you** nous comptons sur toi ▪ **I wouldn't ~ on him turning up, if I were you** si j'étais vous, je ne m'attendrais pas à ce qu'il vienne ▪ **I wouldn't ~ on it** je n'y compterais pas
2. [expect] compter ▪ **I wasn't ~ing on getting here so early** je ne comptais pas arriver si tôt ▪ **I wasn't ~ing on my husband being here** je ne comptais *OR* pensais pas que mon mari serait ici.

◆ **count out** *vt sep* **1.** [money, objects] compter
2. [exclude] : **(you can) ~ me out** ne compte surtout pas sur moi
3. [in boxing] : **to be ~ed out** être déclaré K-O.

◆ **count up** ◇ *vt sep* compter, additionner ▪ **when you ~ it all up** *fig* en fin de compte.
◇ *vi insep* compter, additionner.

countable ['kaʊntəbl] *adj* GRAM [noun] comptable.

countdown ['kaʊntdaʊn] *n* ASTRONAUT compte *m* à rebours ▪ **the ~ to the wedding/Christmas has begun** *fig* la date du mariage/de Noël se rapproche.

countenance ['kaʊntənəns] ◇ *n* **1.** *fml & lit* [face] visage *m* ▪ [facial expression] expression *f*, mine *f* **2.** *fml* [support, approval] : **to give** *OR* **to lend ~ to sthg** approuver qqch.
◇ *vt fml* [support, approve of - terrorism, violence, lying] approuver ; [- idea, proposal] approuver, accepter ▪ **the government will never ~ (doing) a deal with the terrorists** le gouvernement n'approuvera *OR* n'acceptera jamais l'idée d'un marché avec les terroristes.

counter ['kaʊntər] ◇ *n* **1.** [in shop] comptoir *m* ▪ **ask at the ~** [in bank, post office] demandez au guichet ▶ **it's available over the ~** [medication] on peut l'acheter sans ordonnance ▪ **to sell sthg under the ~** *UK inf* vendre qqch en douce *OR* sous le manteau **2.** [device] compteur *m* **3.** [in board game] jeton *m* ▪ **bargaining ~** *UK fig* monnaie *f* d'échange.
◇ *comp* : **~ staff** [in bank, post office] employés *mpl* du guichet, guichetiers *mpl*.
◇ *vt* [respond to - increase in crime, proposal] contrecarrer ; [- accusation, criticism] contrer ; [- threat] contrer ▪ **he ~ed that the project...** il a contré *OR* riposté en disant que le projet...
◇ *vi* [in boxing] contrer ▪ **then he ~ed with his left** puis il a contré du gauche *OR* fait un contre du gauche ▪ **she ~ed with a suggestion that/by asking whether...** elle a riposté en suggérant que/en demandant si...
◇ *adv* : **to go** *OR* **to run ~ to sthg** aller à l'encontre de qqch ▪ **to act ~ to sb's advice/wishes** agir à l'encontre des conseils/des souhaits de qqn.

counteract [,kaʊntə'rækt] *vt* [person] contrebalancer l'influence de ▪ [influence] contrebalancer ▪ [effects of drug, taste of sthg] neutraliser ▪ [rising crime] lutter contre.

counterattack [,kaʊntərə'tæk] ◇ *n* MIL & SPORT contre-attaque *f*, contre-offensive *f* ▪ *fig* [in business, election etc] contre-offensive *f*.
◇ *vi* MIL & SPORT contre-attaquer ▪ *fig* riposter, contrer.

counterbalance [,kaʊntə'bæləns] ◇ *n* contrepoids *m*.
◇ *vt* contrebalancer, faire contrepoids à ▪ *fig* contrebalancer, compenser.

counterbid ['kaʊntəbɪd] *n* FIN [during takeover] contre-OPA *f inv*.

counterblast ['kaʊntəblɑ:st] *n inf* riposte *f*.

counterclaim ['kaʊntəkleɪm] *n* LAW demande *f* reconventionnelle.

counterclockwise [,kaʊntə'klɒkwaɪz] *adj & adv US* dans le sens inverse *OR* contraire des aiguilles d'une montre.

counterculture ['kaʊntə,kʌltʃər] *n* contre-culture *f*.

counterespionage [,kaʊntər'espɪənɑ:ʒ] *n* contre-espionnage *m*.

counterfeit ['kaʊntəfɪt] ◇ *n* [banknote, document] faux *m*, contrefaçon *f* ▪ [piece of jewellery] faux *m*.

◇ *adj* [banknote, document] faux, fausse *f* ■ [piece of jewellery] contrefait ■ *fig* [sympathy, affection] feint.
◇ *vt* [banknote, passport, document, piece of jewellery] contrefaire ■ *fig* [sympathy, affection] feindre.

counterfeiter ['kaʊntəfɪtəʳ] *n* [of banknote] faux-monnayeur *m* ■ [of document, jewellery] faussaire *m*.

counterfoil ['kaʊntəfɔɪl] *n UK* [of cheque, ticket] talon *m*.

counterinsurgency [ˌkaʊntərɪn'sɜːdʒənsɪ] ◇ *n* contre-insurrection *f*.
◇ *adj* [activities, tactics etc] de contre-insurrection.

counterintelligence [ˌkaʊntərɪn'telɪdʒəns] *n* contre-espionnage *m* ■ [information] renseignements *mpl* (provenant du contre-espionnage).

countermand [ˌkaʊntə'mɑːnd] *vt* [order] annuler.

countermeasure [ˌkaʊntə'meʒəʳ] *n* contre-mesure *f*.

countermove ['kaʊntəmuːv] *n* contre-mesure *f*.

counteroffensive [ˌkaʊntərə'fensɪv] *n MIL* contre-offensive *f*.

counteroffer [ˌkaʊntər'ɒfəʳ] *n* offre *f* ■ [higher] surenchère *f*.

counterpane ['kaʊntəpeɪn] *n UK* dessus-de-lit *m inv*, couvre-lit *m*.

counterpart ['kaʊntəpɑːt] *n* homologue *mf* ■ [thing] équivalent *m*.

counterpoint ['kaʊntəpɔɪnt] *n MUS* contrepoint *m*.

counterpoise ['kaʊntəpɔɪz] ◇ *n* contrepoids *m* ■ **to be in ~** *fig* être en équilibre.
◇ *vt* = **counterbalance**.

counterproductive [ˌkaʊntəprə'dʌktɪv] *adj* qui va à l'encontre du but recherché, qui a des effets contraires, contre-productif.

Counter-Reformation *n HIST* contre-réforme *f*.

counter-revolution *n* contre-révolution *f*.

counter-revolutionary ◇ *n* contre-révolutionnaire *mf*.
◇ *adj* contre-révolutionnaire.

countersign ['kaʊntəsaɪn] *vt* contresigner.

countersunk [-sʌŋk] *adj* [screw] noyé ■ [hole] fraisé.

countertenor [ˌkaʊntə'tenəʳ] *n MUS* [singer] haute-contre *m* ■ [voice] haute-contre *f*.

countertop ['kaʊntəˌtɒp] *n US* plan *m* de travail.

countervailing ['kaʊntəveɪlɪŋ] *adj* compensatoire, compensateur.

counterweight ['kaʊntəweɪt] *n* contrepoids *m*.

countess ['kaʊntɪs] *n* comtesse *f*.

counting ['kaʊntɪŋ] *n* calcul *m*.

countless ['kaʊntlɪs] *adj* [deaths, reasons] innombrable ■ [difficulties, opportunities] innombrable, sans nombre ■ **~ letters/people** un nombre incalculable de lettres/personnes ■ **I've told you ~ times not to do that** je t'ai répété des centaines de fois de ne pas faire ça.

count noun *n GRAM* nom *m* comptable.

countrified ['kʌntrɪfaɪd] *adj* **1.** *pej* campagnard, provincial **2.** [rural] : **it's quite ~ round here** c'est vraiment la campagne ici.

country ['kʌntrɪ] ◇ *n* (*pl* **countries**) **1.** [land, nation] pays *m* ■ [homeland] patrie *f* ■ **to fight/to die for one's ~** se battre/mourir pour sa patrie ▶ **my ~ right or wrong** *expression typique du patriotisme instinctif* ■ **to go to the ~** *UK* appeler le pays aux urnes **2.** [as opposed to the city] campagne *f* ■ **to live in the ~** vivre à la campagne ■ **to travel across ~** [in car, on bike] prendre *OR* emprunter les petites routes (de campagne) ; [on foot] aller à travers champs **3.** [area of land, region] région *f* ■ **we passed through some beautiful ~** nous avons traversé de beaux paysages ■ **this is good farming ~** c'est une bonne région agricole ■ **Wordsworth/Constable ~** le pays de Wordsworth/Constable ■ **this is bear ~** il y a beaucoup d'ours par ici **4.** *MUS* = **country and western**.
◇ *comp* [house, road, town, bus] de campagne ■ [people] de la campagne ■ [life] à la campagne ■ **~ boy** gars *m OR* homme *m* de la campagne ■ **~ music** musique *f* country ■ **'The Country Wife'** ***Wycherly*** 'la Provinciale'.

country and western *MUS* ◇ *n* musique *f* country.
◇ *comp* [band, music, singer] country ■ [fan] de country.

country bumpkin *n inf pej* péquenaud *m*, - e *f*, plouc *mf*.

country club *n club sportif ou de loisirs situé à la campagne.*

country dance *n* danse *f* folklorique.

country dancing *n* danse *f* folklorique ■ **to go ~** aller danser des danses folkloriques.

country-dweller *n* campagnard *m*, - e *f*, habitant *m*, - e *f* de la campagne.

country house *n grande maison de campagne, souvent historique.*

countryman ['kʌntrɪmən] (*pl* **countrymen** [-mən]) *n* **1.** [who lives in the country] campagnard *m*, habitant *m* de la campagne **2.** [compatriot] compatriote *m*.

country park *n UK* parc *m* naturel.

country seat *n* [of noble family] manoir *m*.

countryside ['kʌntrɪsaɪd] *n* campagne *f* ■ [scenery] paysage *m* ■ **in the ~** à la campagne ■ **there is some magnificent ~ around here** il y a des paysages magnifiques par ici.

countrywoman ['kʌntrɪˌwʊmən] (*pl* **countrywomen** [-ˌwɪmɪn]) *n* **1.** [who lives in the country] campagnarde *f*, habitante *f* de la campagne **2.** [compatriot] compatriote *f*.

county ['kaʊntɪ] ◇ *n* (*pl* **counties**) comté *m*.
◇ *comp* [councillor, boundary] de comté ■ **~ cricket** *UK grands matchs de cricket disputés par les équipes du comté.*
◇ *adj UK pej* **the horse sale was full of ~ types** le marché aux chevaux grouillait de petits hoberaux.

county council *n UK* ≃ conseil *m* général.

county court *n* [in England] tribunal *m* d'instance.

County Hall *n UK* hôtel *m* du comté, siège *m* du conseil de comté.

county town *n* [in England] chef-lieu *m* de comté.

coup [kuː] *n* **1.** [feat] (beau) coup *m* ■ **to pull off a ~** réussir un beau coup **2.** [overthrow of government] coup *m* d'État.

coupé ['kuːpeɪ] *n AUT* coupé *m*.

couple ['kʌpl] ◇ *n* **1.** [pair] couple *m* ■ **they make a lovely ~** ils forment un beau couple ■ **the happy ~** les jeunes mariés ■ **they go everywhere as a ~** ils vont partout ensemble *OR* en couple **2.** [as quantifier] : **a ~** [a few] quelques-uns, quelques-unes ■ **a ~ of** [a few] quelques ; [two] deux ■ **he's a ~ years older** *US* il a deux ou trois ans de plus.
◇ *vi* [animals, birds, humans] s'accoupler.
◇ *vt* **1.** [horse] atteler ■ *RAIL* atteler, accrocher **2.** *fig* [studies] associer, suivre en parallèle ■ **to ~ sthg with sthg** associer qqch à qqch ■ **her name has been ~d with his** [romantically] son nom a été uni au sien ■ **~d with** [accompanied by] associé à ■ **~d with that,...** en plus de cela,..., venant s'ajouter à cela,...

couplet ['kʌplɪt] *n* distique *m*.

coupling ['kʌplɪŋ] *n* **1.** [mating - of animals, birds, humans] accouplement *m* **2.** [connecting device] accouplement *m* ■ *RAIL* attelage *m*.

coupon ['kuːpɒn] *n* [voucher, form] coupon *m* ■ **(money-off) ~** coupon de réduction.

courage ['kʌrɪdʒ] *n* courage *m* ■ **to have the ~ to do sthg** avoir le courage de faire qqch ■ **a woman of great ~** une femme d'un grand courage, une femme très courageuse ■ **to take one's ~ in both hands** prendre son courage à deux mains ■ **to**

take ~ from the fact that... être encouragé par le fait que... ■ to have the ~ of one's convictions avoir le courage de ses opinions.

courageous [kə'reɪdʒəs] *adj* courageux.

courageously [kə'reɪdʒəslɪ] *adv* courageusement.

courgette [kɔ:'ʒet] *n UK* courgette *f*.

courier ['kʊrɪəʳ] *n* **1.** [messenger] courrier *m*, messager *m* ■ [company] messagerie *f* ■ to send sthg by ~ envoyer qqch par courrier **2.** [on journey] accompagnateur *m*, - trice *f*.

course [kɔ:s] <> *n* **1.** [path, route - of ship, plane] route *f* ; [- of river] cours *m* ■ what is our ~? quelle est notre route? ■ to change ~ [ship, plane, company] changer de cap *OR* de direction ; *fig* [argument, discussion] changer de direction, dévier ■ to be on ~ [ship, plane] suivre le cap fixé, *fig* être en bonne voie ■ the company is on ~ to achieve a record profit *fig* la société est bien partie pour atteindre des bénéfices record ■ to be off ~ [ship, plane] dévier de son cap ■ you're a long way off ~ [walking, driving] vous n'êtes pas du tout dans la bonne direction *OR* sur la bonne route ; [with project, workflow] vous êtes en mauvaise voie ■ to set a ~ for Marseilles [ship, plane] mettre le cap sur Marseille
2. *fig* [approach] : ~ (of action) ligne *f* (de conduite) ■ what other ~ is open to us? quelle autre solution avons-nous? ■ your best ~ of action is to sue la meilleure chose que vous ayez à faire est d'intenter un procès
3. [development, progress - of history, war] cours *m* ■ the law must take its ~ la loi doit suivre son cours ■ the illness takes *OR* runs its ~ la maladie suit son cours ⊃ you will forget him in the ~ of time tu finiras par l'oublier ■ in the normal *OR* ordinary ~ of events normalement, en temps normal
4. SCH & UNIV enseignement *m*, cours *mpl* ■ it's a five-year ~ c'est un enseignement sur cinq ans ■ we offer ~s in a number of subjects nous offrons *OR* proposons des enseignements *OR* des cours dans plusieurs domaines ■ I'm taking *OR* doing a computer ~ je suis des cours *OR* un stage d'informatique ■ what are the other people on the ~ like? comment sont les autres personnes qui suivent les cours?
5. MED : a ~ of injections une série de piqûres ■ a ~ of pills un traitement à base de comprimés ■ ~ of treatment [for an illness] traitement *m*
6. [in meal] plat *m* ■ first ~ entrée *f* ■ there's a cheese ~ as well il y a aussi du fromage
7. [for golf] terrain *m* ■ [for horse-racing] champ *m* de courses ■ to stay the ~ tenir le coup
8. [of bricks] assise *f*.
<> *vi* **1.** [flow] : tears ~d down his cheeks les larmes ruisselaient sur ses joues ■ I could feel the blood coursing through my veins je sentais le sang bouillonner dans mes veines
2. [hunt rabbits, hares] chasser le lièvre.
◆ **in the course of** *prep phr* au cours de ■ in the ~ of the next few weeks dans le courant des semaines qui viennent.
◆ **of course** *adv phr* bien sûr ■ of ~ I believe you/she loves you bien sûr que je te crois/qu'elle t'aime ■ no-one believed me, of ~ évidemment *OR* bien sûr, personne ne m'a cru ■ I'll tell you of ~ il va de soi que je vous le dirai ■ was there much damage? – of ~! y a-t-il eu beaucoup de dégâts? – tu parles! ■ of ~ not! bien sûr que non!

-course *in cpds* : a three/five~ meal un repas comprenant trois/cinq plats ■ she served a four~ dinner elle a servi quatre plats au dîner.

'course *adv inf* = of course.

coursebook ['kɔ:sbʊk] *n* livre *m* de classe.

coursework ['kɔ:swɜ:k] *n* travail *m* de l'année *(qui permet d'exercer le contrôle continu)*.

court [kɔ:t] <> *n* **1.** LAW [institution] cour *f*, tribunal *m* ■ [court room, people in room] cour *f* ■ silence in ~! silence dans la salle! ■ to appear in ~ [accused, witness] comparaître au tribunal ■ to come before a ~ comparaître devant un tribunal ■ to take sb to ~ poursuivre qqn en justice, intenter un procès contre qqn ■ to go to ~ faire appel à la justice, aller en justice ■ to go to ~ over sthg faire appel à la justice pour régler qqch ■ to settle sthg out of ~ régler qqch à l'amiable ■ it won't stand up in ~ *OR* in a ~ of law cela n'aura aucun poids au tribunal ■ to put *OR* to rule sthg out of ~ *fig* exclure qqch **2.** [of monarch - people] cour *f* ; [- building] palais *m* ■ to be presented at ~ *UK* être introduit à la cour ■ to hold ~ *fig* avoir une cour d'adorateurs **3.** SPORT [tennis, badminton] court *m*, terrain *m* ■ [squash] court *m* ■ to come on ~ entrer sur le court *OR* terrain ■ on ~ and off, on and off ~ sur le court et dans la vie **4.** [courtyard] cour *f*.
<> *comp* **1.** LAW : ~ reporter chroniqueur *m* judiciaire ■ ~ usher huissier *m* de justice **2.** [royal] : ~ jester bouffon *m* de cour ■ it is said in ~ circles that... on dit à la cour que...
<> *vt* **1.** *liter & dated* faire la cour à, courtiser **2.** *fig* [voters] courtiser, chercher à séduire ■ to ~ popularity chercher à se rendre populaire ■ to ~ sb's approval/support chercher à gagner l'approbation/le soutien de qqn ■ to ~ danger/disaster aller au devant du danger/désastre.
<> *vi dated* [one person] fréquenter ■ [two people] se fréquenter.

court case *n* procès *m*, affaire *f*.

court circular *n rubrique d'un journal indiquant les engagements officiels de la famille royale.*

courteous ['kɜ:tjəs] *adj* [person, gesture, treatment] courtois.

courteously ['kɜ:tjəslɪ] *adv* [speak, reply etc] avec courtoisie, courtoisement.

courtesan [,kɔ:tɪ'zæn] *n* courtisane *f*.

courtesy ['kɜ:tɪsɪ] <> *n* (*pl* **courtesies**) **1.** [politeness] courtoisie *f* ■ at least have the ~ to apologize aie au moins la courtoisie de t'excuser ■ it would only have been common ~ to apologize la moindre des courtoisies *OR* politesses aurait été de s'excuser ■ do her the ~ of hearing what she has to say aie l'obligeance d'écouter ce qu'elle a à dire **2.** [polite action, remark] politesse *f* ■ after a brief exchange of courtesies après un bref échange de politesses ■ to show sb every ~ faire montre d'une extrême courtoisie envers qqn.
<> *comp* [call, visit] de politesse ■ to pay a ~ call on sb faire une visite de politesse à qqn ■ ~ coach *OR* shuttle [at airport] navette *f* gratuite ■ ~ car voiture *f* de courtoisie *(voiture mise à la disposition d'un client)* ■ ~ light AUT plafonnier *m*.
◆ **(by) courtesy of** *prep phr* avec l'aimable autorisation de ■ the following footage is brought to you ~ of French TV la séquence qui suit vous est présentée avec l'aimable permission *OR* autorisation de la télévision française.

courthouse ['kɔ:thaʊs] (*pl* [-haʊzɪz]) *n US* palais *m* de justice, tribunal *m*.

courtier ['kɔ:tjəʳ] *n* courtisan *m*.

courting ['kɔ:tɪŋ] *dated adj* : ~ couple couple *m* d'amoureux.

courtly ['kɔ:tlɪ] *adj* [person, manners] plein de style et de courtoisie ■ ~ love HIST amour *m* courtois.

court-martial MIL <> *n* (*pl* **courts-martial**) tribunal *m* militaire ■ to be tried by ~ être jugé par un tribunal militaire.
<> *vt* (*UK*, *pret & pp* **court-martialled**, *cont* **court-martialling**, *US pret & pp* **court-martialed**, *cont* **court-martialing**) faire comparaître devant un tribunal militaire ■ he was court-martialled il est passé au tribunal militaire.

Court of Appeal *pr n* cour *f* d'appel.

court of appeals *n US* cour *f* d'appel.

court of inquiry *n UK* [body of people] commission *f* d'enquête ■ [investigation] enquête *f*.

court order *n* ordonnance *f* du tribunal.

courtroom ['kɔ:trʊm] *n* salle *f* d'audience.

courtship ['kɔ:tʃɪp] <> *n* **1.** [of couple] : their ~ lasted six years ils se sont fréquentés pendant six ans **2.** [of animals] période *f* nuptiale, période *f* des amours.
<> *adj* [dance, display, ritual] nuptial.

court shoe *n UK* escarpin *m*.

courtyard ['kɔ:tjɑ:d] *n* [of building] cour *f*.

cousin ['kʌzn] *n* cousin *m*, - e *f* ■ our American ~s *fig* nos cousins américains.

couture [ku:'tʊəʳ] *n* couture *f*.

couturier [ku:'tʊərɪeɪ] *n* couturier *m*, - ère *f*.

cove [kəʊv] *n* [bay] crique *f*.

coven ['kʌvən] *n* ordre *m* OR réunion *f* de sorcières.

covenant ['kʌvənənt] ◇ *n* **1.** [promise of money] convention *f*, engagement *m* ■ **(deed of) ~** contrat *m* **2.** [agreement] engagement *m*.
◇ *vt* [promise payment of] s'engager (par contrat) à payer.
◇ *vi* : **to ~ for a sum** s'engager (par contrat) à payer une somme.

Covent Garden ['kɒvənt-] *pr n* Covent Garden.

COVENT GARDEN

Covent Garden, halle de l'ancien marché aux fruits, aux légumes et aux fleurs du centre de Londres, est aujourd'hui une galerie marchande à la mode ; elle désigne aussi, par extension, la Royal Opera House, située près de l'ancien marché.

Coventry ['kɒvəntrɪ] *pr n* : **to send sb to ~** *UK* mettre qqn en quarantaine *fig*.

cover ['kʌvər] ◇ *n* **1.** [material - for bed] couverture *f* ; [- for cushion, typewriter] housse *f*
2. [lid] couvercle *m*
3. [of book, magazine] couverture *f* ■ **to read a book (from) ~ to ~** lire un livre de la première à la dernière page OR d'un bout à l'autre
4. [shelter, protection] abri *m* ■ [for birds, animals] couvert *m* ■ **to take ~** se mettre à l'abri ■ **to take ~ from the rain** s'abriter de la pluie ■ **that tree will provide ~** cet arbre va nous permettre de nous abriter OR nous offrir un abri ■ **air ~** MIL couverture *f* aérienne ■ **to keep sthg under ~** garder qqch à l'abri ■ **to do sthg under ~ of darkness** faire qqch à la faveur de la nuit ■ **they escaped under ~ of the riot/noise** ils ont profité de l'émeute/du bruit pour s'échapper ■ **to work under ~** travailler clandestinement ➲ **to break ~** [animal, person in hiding] sortir à découvert
5. [in insurance] couverture *f* ■ **to have ~ against sthg** être couvert OR assuré contre qqch ■ **I've taken out ~ for medical costs** j'ai pris une assurance pour les frais médicaux
6. [disguise, front - for criminal enterprise] couverture *f* ; [- for spy] fausse identité *f*, identité *f* d'emprunt ■ **your ~ has been blown** *inf* vous avez été démasqué ■ **it's just a ~ for her shyness** c'est juste pour cacher OR masquer sa timidité
7. [during a person's absence] remplacement *m* ■ **to provide ~ for sb** remplacer qqn
8. MUS [new version of song] reprise *f*
9. [in restaurant] couvert *m*
10. [envelope] enveloppe *f* ■ **under plain/separate ~** sous pli discret/séparé ➲ **~ letter** *US* lettre *f* explicative OR de couverture ■ **first-day ~** [for philatelist] émission *f* du premier jour, enveloppe *f* premier jour.
◇ *vt* **1.** [in order to protect] couvrir ■ [in order to hide] cacher, dissimuler ■ [cushion, chair, settee] recouvrir ■ **to ~ sthg with a sheet/blanket** recouvrir qqch d'un drap/d'une couverture ■ **to ~ one's eyes/ears** se couvrir les yeux/les oreilles ■ **to ~ one's shyness/nervousness** dissimuler OR masquer sa timidité/nervosité
2. [coat - subj: dust, snow] recouvrir ■ **to be ~ed in dust/snow** être recouvert de poussière/neige ■ **his face was ~ed in spots** son visage était couvert de boutons ■ **you're ~ing everything in dust/paint** tu mets de la poussière/peinture partout ■ **to ~ o.s. in glory** *fig* se couvrir de gloire
3. [extend over, occupy - subj: city, desert etc] couvrir une surface de ■ **water ~s most of the earth's surface** l'eau recouvre la plus grande partie de la surface de la terre ■ **his interests ~ a wide field** il a des intérêts très variés ■ **does this translation ~ the figurative meaning of the word?** cette traduction recouvre-t-elle bien le sens figuré du mot?
4. [travel over] parcourir, couvrir ■ **we've ~ed every square inch of the park looking for it** nous avons ratissé chaque centimètre carré du parc pour essayer de le retrouver
5. [deal with] traiter ■ **there's one point we haven't ~ed** il y a un point que nous n'avons pas traité OR vu ■ **the law doesn't ~ that kind of situation** la loi ne prévoit pas ce genre de situation
6. PRESS, RADIO & TV [report on] couvrir, faire la couverture de
7. [subj: salesman, representative] couvrir
8. [be enough money for - damage, expenses] couvrir ; [- meal] suffire à payer ■ **£30 should ~ it** 30 livres devraient suffire ■ **to ~ one's costs** [company] rentrer dans ses frais
9. [insure] couvrir, garantir ■ **to be ~ed against** OR **for sthg** être couvert OR assuré contre qqch
10. [with gun - colleague] couvrir ■ **I've got you ~ed** [to criminal] j'ai mon arme braquée sur toi
11. [monitor permanently - exit, port etc] avoir sous surveillance
12. SPORT marquer
13. MUS [song] faire une reprise de
14. [subj: male animal] couvrir, s'accoupler avec.
◇ *vi* : **to ~ for sb** [replace] remplacer qqn.

◆ **cover up** ◇ *vt sep* **1.** [hide, conceal] cacher, dissimuler ■ [in order to protect] recouvrir ■ *pej* [involvement, report etc] dissimuler, garder secret ■ [affair] étouffer ■ **they ~ed up the body with a sheet** ils ont recouvert le cadavre d'un drap
2. [in order to keep warm] couvrir.
◇ *vi insep* [hide something] : **to ~ up for sb** servir de couverture à qqn, couvrir qqn ■ **they're ~ing up for each other** ils se couvrent l'un l'autre.

coverage ['kʌvərɪdʒ] *n* **1.** *(U)* PRESS, RADIO & TV reportage *m* ■ **his ~ of the coup** le reportage qu'il a fait du coup d'État ■ **royal weddings always get a lot of ~** les mariages de la famille royale bénéficient toujours d'une importante couverture médiatique ■ **the author's ~ of the years 1789 to 1815 is sketchy** l'auteur traite les années 1789-1815 de manière sommaire ■ **radio/television ~ of the tournament** la retransmission radiophonique/télévisée du tournoi **2.** [in insurance] couverture *f*.

coveralls ['kʌvərɔːlz] *npl US* bleu *m* OR bleus *mpl* (de travail).

cover charge *n* [in restaurant] couvert *m*.

cover girl *n* cover-girl *f*.

covering ['kʌvərɪŋ] ◇ *n* [of snow, dust] couche *f*.
◇ *adj* : **~ fire** MIL tir *m* de couverture ■ **~ letter** *UK* lettre *f* explicative OR de couverture.

cover note *n UK* attestation *f* provisoire.

cover price *n* [of magazine] prix *m*.

cover story *n* article *m* principal (faisant la couverture).

covert ['kʌvət] ◇ *adj* [operation, payments, contacts] secret, - ète *f* ■ [threats] voilé ■ [glance, look] furtif ■ **she had a ~ dislike of him** sans le laisser paraître, elle ne pouvait pas le souffrir.
◇ *n* [hiding place for animals] fourré *m*, couvert *m*.

covertly ['kʌvətlɪ] *adv* [sold, paid] secrètement ■ [threaten] de manière voilée ■ [signal] furtivement.

cover-up *n* : **the government has been accused of a ~** le gouvernement a été accusé d'avoir étouffé l'affaire ■ **it's a ~** c'est un complot.

cover version *n* MUS [of song] reprise *f*.

covet ['kʌvɪt] *vt* [crave, long for] convoiter ■ [wish for] avoir très envie de ■ **the much ~ed prix Goncourt** le prix Goncourt, objet de tant de convoitise.

covetous ['kʌvɪtəs] *adj* [person] avide ■ [look] de convoitise.

covetously ['kʌvɪtəslɪ] *adv* avec convoitise.

covetousness ['kʌvɪtəsnɪs] *n* convoitise *f*, avidité *f*.

covey ['kʌvɪ] *n* compagnie *f* OR vol *m* de perdrix.

cow [kaʊ] ◇ *n* **1.** [farm animal] vache *f* ■ **we'll be here until the ~s come home!** *fig* on y sera encore dans dix ans! ■ **I could eat chocolate ice cream until the ~s come home** de la glace au chocolat, je pourrais en manger des kilos et des kilos **2.** [female elephant] éléphant *m* femelle, éléphante *f* ■ [female seal] phoque *m* femelle ■ [female whale] baleine *f* femelle **3.** △ *UK pej* [woman] conasse *f* ■ **you silly ~!** espèce d'abrutie!
◇ *vt* effrayer, intimider.

coward ['kaʊəd] *n* lâche *mf*, poltron *m*, - onne *f* ■ **don't be such a ~** ne sois pas aussi lâche ■ **I'm an awful ~ when it comes to physical pain** j'ai très peur de OR je redoute beaucoup la douleur physique.

cowardice ['kauədɪs] *n* lâcheté *f* ▪ **moral ~** manque *m* de force morale.

cowardliness ['kauədlɪnɪs] *n* lâcheté *f*.

cowardly ['kauədlɪ] *adj* lâche.

cowbell ['kaubel] *n* clochette *f*, sonnaille *f*.

cowboy ['kaubɔɪ] <> *n* **1.** [in American West] cow-boy *m* ▪ **to play ~s and Indians** jouer aux cow-boys et aux Indiens **2.** *inf pej* petit rigolo *m* ▪ **some ~ builder/plumber** un petit rigolo d'entrepreneur/de plombier, un soi-disant entrepreneur/plombier.
<> *comp* de cow-boy ▪ **~ boots** bottes *fpl* de cow-boy, santiags *fpl* ▪ **~ film** *OR* **movie** film *m* de cow-boys.

cowcatcher ['kau,kætʃər] *n* US RAIL, UK AUTO chasse-pierres *m inv*.

cower ['kauər] *vi* [person] se recroqueviller ▪ [animal] se tapir ▪ **I ~ed** *OR* **was ~ing in my seat** j'étais recroquevillé sur ma chaise ▪ **she ~ed away from him** tremblante de peur, elle s'est écartée de lui ▪ **he stood ~ing before the boss** il tremblait devant le patron.

cowgirl ['kaugɜ:l] *n* fille *f* de l'ouest.

cowherd ['kauhɜ:d] *n* vacher *m*, bouvier *m*.

cowhide ['kauhaɪd] *n* peau *f* de vache ▪ [leather] cuir *m* *OR* peau *f* de vache.

cowl [kaul] *n* **1.** [of chimney] capuchon *m* **2.** [of monk] capuchon *m* **3.** [on sweater, dress] : **~ neck** *OR* **neckline** col *m* boule.

cowlick ['kau,lɪk] *n* US mèche *f* rebelle.

cowman ['kaumən] (*pl* **cowmen** [-mən]) *n* vacher *m*, bouvier *m*.

co-worker *n* collègue *mf*.

cowpat ['kaupæt] *n* bouse *f* de vache.

cowrie, cowry ['kaurɪ] (*pl* **cowries**) *n* [shell] cauri *m*.

cowshed ['kauʃed] *n* étable *f*.

cowslip ['kauslɪp] *n* BOT primevère *f*, coucou *m*.

cox [kɒks] <> *n* [of rowing team] barreur *m*, - euse *f*.
<> *vt* barrer.
<> *vi* barrer ▪ **he has ~ed for Cambridge** il a été barreur dans l'équipe de Cambridge.

coxswain ['kɒksən] *n* [of rowing team] barreur *m*, - euse *f* ▪ [of lifeboat] timonier *m*, homme *m* de barre.

coy [kɔɪ] *adj* **1.** [shy - person] qui fait le/la timide ; [- answer, smile] faussement timide **2.** [provocative, playful] coquet **3.** [evasive] évasif.

coyly ['kɔɪlɪ] *adv* [timidly] avec une timidité affectée *OR* feinte ▪ [provocatively] coquettement.

coyness ['kɔɪnɪs] *n* [timidness] timidité *f* affectée *OR* feinte ▪ [provocativeness] coquetteries *fpl*.

coyote [kɔɪ'əutɪ] *n* coyote *m*.

cozy US = **cosy**.

cp. (*written abbrev of* **compare**) cf.

c/p (*written abbrev of* **carriage paid**) pp.

CP (*abbrev of* **Communist Party**) *pr n* PC *m*.

CPA *n* US = **certified public accountant**.

CPI (*abbrev of* **Consumer Price Index**) *n* IPC *m*.

Cpl. *written abbr of* **corporal**.

CP/M (*abbrev of* **control program for microcomputers**) *n* CP/M *m*.

cps (*written abbrev of* **characters per second**) cps.

CPS (*abbrev of* **Crown Prosecution Service**) *n* ≃ ministère *m* publique.

CPSA (*abbrev of* **Civil and Public Services Association**) *pr n* *syndicat de la fonction publique*.

CPU (*abbrev of* **central processing unit**) *n* unité *f* centrale (de traitement).

cr. 1. *written abbr of* **credit 2.** *written abbr of* **creditor**.

crab [kræb] <> *n* **1.** ZOOL crabe *m* **2.** : **to catch a ~** [above surface of water] donner un coup d'aviron dans le vide ; [below surface of water] engager la rame trop profond **3.** ASTRON : **the Crab** le Cancer.
<> *vi* (*pret & pp* **crabbed**, *cont* **crabbing**) [grumble] maugréer, rouspéter.
◆ **crabs** *npl* MED morpions *mpl*.

crab apple *n* [fruit] pomme *f* sauvage ▪ **~ (tree)** pommier *m* sauvage.

crabby ['kræbɪ] (*comp* **crabbier**, *superl* **crabbiest**) *adj* *inf* grognon, ronchon.

crack [kræk] <> *n* **1.** [in cup, glass, egg] fêlure *f* ▪ [in ceiling, wall] lézarde *f*, fissure *f* ▪ [in ground] crevasse *f* ▪ [in varnish, enamel] craquelure *f* ▪ [in skin] gerçure *f*, crevasse *f* ▪ [in bone] fêlure *f* ▪ *fig* [fault - in policy, argument etc] fissure *f*, faiblesse *f* ▪ **did you know there was a ~ in this glass?** avais-tu remarqué que ce verre était fêlé? ▪ **the ~s are beginning to show in their marriage** *fig* leur mariage commence à donner des signes de délabrement
2. [small opening or gap - in floorboards, door etc] fente *f* ; [- in wall] fissure *f* ▪ **there were some ~s in the wall** le mur était fissuré
3. [noise] craquement *m* ▪ [of thunder] coup *m*
4. [blow - on head, knee etc] coup *m* ▪ **I gave myself a ~ on the head** je me suis cogné la tête
5. *inf* [attempt] tentative *f* ▪ **I'll have a ~ (at it), I'll give it a ~** je vais tenter le coup, je vais essayer (un coup) ▪ **do you want another ~ (at it)?** tu veux réessayer?, tu veux retenter le coup? ➊ **to give sb a fair ~ of the whip** donner toutes ses chances *OR* sa chance à qqn
6. [joke, witticism] blague *f*, plaisanterie *f*
7. [drug] crack *m* ▪ **~ baby** *bébé né dépendant du crack*
8. *phr* **at the ~ of dawn** au point du jour ▪ **I've been up since the ~ of dawn** je suis debout *OR* levé depuis l'aube.
<> *adj* [regiment, team etc] d'élite ▪ **one of their ~ players** un de leurs meilleurs joueurs ▪ **~ shot** tireur *m*, - euse *f* d'élite.
<> *vt* **1.** [damage - cup, glass, egg] fêler ; [- ice] fendre ; [- ceiling, wall] lézarder, fissurer ; [- ground] crevasser ; [- varnish, enamel] craqueler ; [- skin] gercer, crevasser ; [- bone] fêler
2. [open - eggs, nuts] casser ▪ **to ~ a safe** fracturer un coffre-fort ▪ **to ~ (open) a bottle** *inf* ouvrir *OR* déboucher une bouteille ▪ **she never ~ed a smile the entire evening** *inf* elle n'a pas souri une seule fois de la soirée
3. [bang, hit - head, knee] : **to ~ one's head/knee on sthg** se cogner la tête/le genou contre qqch
4. [make noise with - whip] faire claquer ; [- knuckles] faire craquer ▪ **to ~ the whip** faire le gendarme
5. *inf phr* **to ~ a joke** sortir une blague
6. [solve] : **to ~ a code** déchiffrer un code ▪ **the police think they have ~ed the case** la police pense qu'elle a résolu l'affaire ▪ **I think we've ~ed it** je pense que nous y sommes arrivés
7. CHEM craquer.
<> *vi* **1.** [cup, glass, ice] se fissurer, se fêler ▪ [ceiling, wall] se lézarder, se fissurer ▪ [ground] se crevasser ▪ [varnish, enamel] se craqueler ▪ [skin] se gercer, se crevasser ▪ [bone] se fêler
2. [make noise - whip] claquer ; [- twigs] craquer ▪ **a rifle ~ed and he dropped to the ground** un coup de fusil a retenti et il s'est effondré
3. [give way, collapse - through nervous exhaustion] s'effondrer, craquer ; [- under questioning, surveillance] craquer ▪ **their marriage ~ed under the strain** leur mariage s'est détérioré sous l'effet du stress ▪ **his voice ~ed with emotion** sa voix se brisa sous le coup de l'émotion
4. *inf phr* **to get ~ing** [start work] s'y mettre, se mettre au boulot ; [get ready, get going] se mettre en route ▪ **I'll get ~ing on dinner/cleaning the windows** je vais me mettre à préparer le dîner/nettoyer les vitres ▪ **get ~ing!, let's get ~ing!** au boulot!
◆ **crack down** *vi insep* sévir ▪ **to ~ down on sthg/sb** sévir contre qqch/qqn.
◆ **crack open** *vt sep* [eggs, nuts] casser ▪ *inf* [bottle] *inf* ouvrir, déboucher.

◆ **crack up** ◇ *vi insep* **1.** [ice] se fissurer ■ [paint, enamel, make-up] se craqueler ■ [ground] se crevasser ■ [skin] se gercer, se crevasser
2. *inf* [through nervous exhaustion] s'effondrer, craquer ■ **I must be ~ing up** [going mad] je débloque
3. *inf* [with laughter] se tordre de rire
4. *US inf* [vehicle] s'écraser.
◇ *vt sep* **1.** [make laugh] faire se tordre de rire
2. *(always passive)* [say good things about] : **he's not what he's ~ed up to be** il n'est pas aussi fantastique qu'on le dit *OR* prétend ■ **the play is everything it's ~ed up to be** la pièce a toutes les qualités qu'on lui vante
3. *US inf* [car, motorbike] bousiller.

crackbrained ['krækbreɪnd] *adj inf* débile, dingue.

crackdown ['krækdaʊn] *n* : **we're going to have a ~ on petty theft** on va sévir contre les petits larcins ■ **the annual Christmas ~ on drunk driving** les mesures répressives prises tous les ans à Noël contre la conduite en état d'ivresse.

cracked [krækt] *adj* **1.** [damaged - cup, glass] fêlé ; [- ice] fendu ; [- ceiling, wall] lézardé ; [- ground] crevassé ; [- varnish] craquelé ; [- skin] gercé, crevassé **2.** *inf* [mad - person] fêlé, taré.

cracker ['krækəʳ] *n* **1.** [savoury biscuit] biscuit *m* salé, cracker *m* **2.** *UK* [for pulling] *papillotte contenant un pétard et une surprise, traditionnelle au moment des fêtes* **3.** [firework] pétard *m* **4.** *inf* [good-looking person] canon *m* **5.** *inf* [something excellent of its kind] : **that was a ~ of a goal** c'était un but sensass.

CRACKER

En Grande-Bretagne, les *crackers* sont des décorations de Noël, posées sur les tables, en forme de gros bonbon enveloppé et contenant un jouet, une blague et un chapeau en papier. On se met à deux pour les ouvrir, chacun tirant à une extrémité, jusqu'à ce que le papier se déchire et fasse exploser un petit pétard.

crackers ['krækəz] *adj inf* cinglé, fêlé, taré ■ **to drive sb ~** faire tourner qqn en bourrique.

cracking ['krækɪŋ] ◇ *adj* **1.** [excellent] génial, épatant **2.** [fast] : **to keep up a ~ pace** aller à fond de train.
◇ *adv UK inf dated* **~ good** [match, meal] de première.
◇ *n* CHEM craquage *m* ■ **~ plant** usine *f* de craquage.

crackle ['krækl] ◇ *vi* [paper, dry leaves] craquer ■ [fire] crépiter, craquer ■ [radio] grésiller ■ **to ~ with energy** *fig* pétiller d'énergie.
◇ *vt* [glaze] craqueler.
◇ *n* [of paper, twigs] craquement *m* ■ [of fire] crépitement *m*, craquement *m* ■ [of radio] grésillement *m* ■ [on telephone] friture *f* ■ [of machine-gun fire] crépitement *m*.

crackling ['kræklɪŋ] *n* **1.** CULIN couenne *f* rôtie **2.** [noise] = **crackle**.

crackly ['kræklɪ] (*comp* **cracklier**, *superl* **crackliest**) *adj* : **the line is a bit ~** [on phone] il y a de la friture sur la ligne ■ **the radio's a bit ~** la radio grésille un peu.

cracknel ['kræknl] *n* [biscuit] craquelin *m* ■ [filling for chocolate] nougatine *f*.

crackpot ['krækpɒt] *inf* ◇ *n* [person] tordu *m*, - e *f*, cinglé *m*, - e *f*.
◇ *adj* [idea, scheme] tordu ■ [person] tordu, cinglé.

crack-up *n inf* **1.** [of person] dépression *f* (nerveuse) **2.** [of country, economy] effondrement *m*.

Cracow ['krækaʊ] *pr n* Cracovie.

cradle ['kreɪdl] ◇ *n* **1.** [for baby] berceau *m* ■ *fig* berceau *m* ■ **from the ~ to the grave** du berceau au tombeau ■ **to rob the ~** *US hum* les prendre au berceau *OR* biberon **2.** [frame - for painter, window cleaner] pont *m* volant, échafaudage *m* volant ; [- in hospital bed] arceau *m* **3.** TELEC support *m* (du combiné).
◇ *vt* [hold carefully - baby, kitten] tenir tendrement (dans ses bras) ; [- delicate object] tenir précieusement *OR* délicatement (dans ses bras).

cradle-snatcher *n UK inf* **~!** tu les prends au berceau!

cradle-song *n* berceuse *f*.

craft [krɑːft] ◇ *n* **1.** [of artist, artisan] art *m*, métier *m* ■ **to do ~s at school** faire des travaux manuels à l'école **2.** [guile, cunning] ruse *f* ■ **to obtain sthg by ~** obtenir qqch par la ruse **3.** (*pl* craft) [boat, ship] bateau *m* ■ [aircraft] avion *m* ■ [spacecraft] engin *m OR* vaisseau *m* spatial ■ **all the small ~ in the harbour** tous les petits bateaux *OR* toutes les embarcations dans le port.
◇ *comp* : **~ (s) fair** foire *f* d'artisanat ■ **~ guild** corporation *f* artisanale *OR* d'artisans.
◇ *vt (usu passive)* travailler ■ **a hand ~ed table** une table travaillée à la main ■ **a beautifully ~ed film** *fig* un film magnifiquement travaillé.

craftily ['krɑːftɪlɪ] *adv* astucieusement ■ **to behave ~** agir astucieusement *OR* habilement ; *pej* agir avec ruse.

craftiness ['krɑːftɪnɪs] *n* habileté *f* ■ *pej* ruse *f*, roublardise *f*.

craftsman ['krɑːftsmən] (*pl* **craftsmen** [-mən]) *n* artisan *m*, homme *m* de métier ■ [writer, actor] homme *m* de métier.

craftsmanship ['krɑːftsmənʃɪp] *n* connaissance *f* d'un *OR* du métier ■ **a fine example of ~** un bel ouvrage, un vrai travail d'artiste ■ **the ~ is superb** cela a été superbement travaillé.

crafty ['krɑːftɪ] (*comp* **craftier**, *superl* **craftiest**) *adj* [person, idea, scheme] malin, - igne *f*, astucieux ■ *pej* [person] rusé, roublard ■ [idea, scheme] rusé ■ **you ~ old devil!** espèce de vieux renard!

crag [kræg] *n* [steep rock] rocher *m* escarpé *OR* à pic.

craggy ['krægɪ] (*comp* **craggier**, *superl* **craggiest**) *adj* [hill] escarpé, à pic ■ *fig* [features] anguleux, taillé à la serpe.

cram [kræm] (*pret & pp* **crammed**, *cont* **cramming**) ◇ *vt* **1.** [objects] fourrer ■ [people] entasser ■ **to ~ sthg into a drawer** fourrer qqch dans un tiroir ■ **to ~ clothes into a suitcase** bourrer des vêtements dans une valise, bourrer une valise de vêtements ■ **could you ~ one more person in?** y aurait-il encore une petite place? ■ **to ~ food into one's mouth** se bourrer de nourriture, se gaver ■ **I crammed a lot of quotations into my essay** j'ai bourré ma dissertation de citations ■ **we crammed a lot into one day** on en a fait beaucoup en une seule journée **2.** *inf* SCH [facts] apprendre à toute vitesse ■ [students] faire bachoter.
◇ *vi* **1.** *inf* [study hard] bachoter **2.** [into small space] : **we all crammed into his office** nous nous sommes tous entassés dans son bureau.

crammed ['kræmd] *adj* [full - bus, train, room, suitcase] bourré, bondé ■ **to be ~ with people** être bondé ■ **to be ~ with sthg** être plein à craquer *OR* bourré de qqch ■ **the encyclopedia is ~ with useful information** l'encyclopédie regorge d'informations utiles.

cramming ['kræmɪŋ] *n inf* [intensive learning] bachotage *m* ■ [intensive teaching] bourrage *m* de crâne.

cramp [kræmp] ◇ *n* **1.** *(U)* [muscle pain] crampe *f* ■ **to have ~** *OR US* **a ~** avoir une crampe ■ **I've got ~ in my leg** j'ai une crampe à la jambe ■ **to have stomach ~, to have ~s** *US* avoir des crampes d'estomac ➲ **writer's ~** crampe *f* des écrivains **2.** [in carpentry] serre-joint *m*.
◇ *vt* **1.** [hamper - person] gêner ; [- project] entraver, contrarier ■ **to ~ sb's style** *inf* faire perdre tous ses moyens à qqn, priver qqn de ses moyens **2.** [secure with a cramp] maintenir à l'aide d'un serre-joint.

cramped [kræmpt] *adj* **1.** [room, flat] exigu, - ë *f* ■ **they live in very ~ conditions** ils vivent très à l'étroit ■ **we're a bit ~ for space** nous sommes un peu à l'étroit **2.** [position] inconfortable **3.** [handwriting] en pattes de mouche, serré.

crampon ['kræmpən] *n* crampon *m* (à glace).

cranberry ['krænbərɪ] ◇ *n* (*pl* **cranberries**) airelle *f*.
◇ *comp* : **~ sauce** sauce *f* aux airelles.

crane [kreɪn] ◇ *n* **1.** ORNITH grue *f* **2.** TECH & CIN grue *f*.
◇ *comp* : **~ driver** *OR* **operator** grutier *m*.
◇ *vt* : **to ~ one's neck** tendre le cou.

◇ *vi* : **to ~ (forward)** tendre le cou.

crane fly *n* tipule *f* des prés *OR* des prairies.

crania ['kreɪnjə] *pl* ▷ **cranium**.

cranial ['kreɪnjəl] *adj* crânien.

cranium ['kreɪnjəm] (*pl* **craniums** *OR pl* **crania** ['kreɪnjə]) *n* [skull - gen] crâne *m* ; [- enclosing brain] boîte *f* crânienne.

crank [kræŋk] ◇ *n* **1.** *inf* [eccentric] excentrique *mf* ■ **a religious ~** un/une fanatique ■ **she's a bit of a ~** elle est un peu excentrique, c'est un cas **2.** *US inf* [bad-tempered person] grognon *m*, - onne *f* **3.** MECH : **~ (handle)** manivelle *f*.
◇ *vt* [engine] démarrer à la manivelle ■ [gramophone] remonter à la manivelle.
◆ **crank out** *vt sep US inf* [books, plays etc] produire en quantités industrielles.
◆ **crank up** *vt sep inf* **1.** = **crank** *(vt)* **2.** *fig* [increase] augmenter.

crankshaft ['kræŋkʃɑ:ft] *n* vilebrequin *m*.

cranky ['kræŋkɪ] (*comp* **crankier**, *superl* **crankiest**) *adj inf* **1.** [eccentric - person, behaviour, ideas] bizarre **2.** [bad-tempered] grognon **3.** [unreliable - machine] capricieux.

cranny ['krænɪ] (*pl* **crannies**) *n* fente *f*.

crap [kræp] ◇ *n (U)* **1.** ▲ [faeces] merde△ *f* ■ **to have a ~** chier▲ **2.** △ *fig* [nonsense] conneries△ *fpl* ■ **to talk ~** raconter *OR* dire des conneries△ ■ **don't give me that ~!** arrête de me raconter des conneries!△ **3.** △ *fig* [rubbish] merde△ *f* ■ **get all this ~ off the table** enlève tout ce bordel△ *OR* toute cette merde△ de la table ■ **he writes absolute ~** ce qu'il écrit c'est de la merde△ **4.** *US* [dice game] *jeu de dés similaire au quatre-cent-vingt-et-un et où on parie sur le résultat* ■ **~ game** partie *f* de dés.
◇ *vi*▲ (*pret & pp* **crapped**, *cont* **crapping**) [defecate] chier▲.
◇ *adj*△ *UK* [of very poor quality] de merde△, merdique△.
◆ **craps** *n US* : **to shoot ~** [play game] jouer aux dés, faire une partie de dés ; [throw dice] lancer les dés.

crappy△ ['kræpɪ] (*comp* **crappier**, *superl* **crappiest**) *adj* [programme, book etc] de merde△, merdique△, à la con△ ■ [remark, action] dégueulasse.

crash [kræʃ] ◇ *n* **1.** [accident] accident *m* ■ **car/plane/train ~** accident de voiture/d'avion/ferroviaire ■ **to have a ~** avoir un accident ■ **to be (involved) in a ~** [person] avoir un accident ■ **the car looks as though it has been in a ~** la voiture semble avoir été accidentée
2. [loud noise] fracas *m* ■ **a ~ of thunder** un coup de tonnerre ■ **there was a loud ~ as the plate hit the ground** cela a fait un bruit fracassant quand l'assiette est tombée par terre
3. FIN [slump] krach *m*, débâcle *f*
4. COMPUT panne *f*.
◇ *comp* [diet, programme] intensif, de choc.
◇ *adv* : **he ran ~ into a wall** il est rentré en plein dans le mur ■ **it went ~** ça a fait boum.
◇ *interj* boum.
◇ *vi* **1.** [car, train] avoir un accident ■ [plane, pilot] s'écraser, se crasher ■ [driver] avoir un accident ■ **we're going to ~** [plane] on va s'écraser ; [car] on va lui rentrer dedans/rentrer dans le mur *etc* ; [train] on va avoir un accident ■ **the cars ~ed (head on)** les voitures se sont embouties *OR* percutées (par l'avant) ■ **to ~ into sthg** percuter qqch ■ **the car ~ed through the fence** la voiture est passée à travers la clôture ■ **to ~ into sb** [subj: person] rentrer dans qqn
2. [make loud noise - thunder] retentir ■ **what are you ~ing about at this hour for?** pourquoi fais-tu autant de vacarme *OR* boucan à cette heure? ■ **the elephants ~ed through the undergrowth** les éléphants ont traversé le sous-bois dans un vacarme terrible
3. [fall, hit with loud noise or violently] : **the tree came ~ing down** l'arbre est tombé avec fracas ■ **her world came ~ing down (about) her** *OR* **her ears** tout son monde s'est écroulé ■ **the vase ~ed to the ground** le vase s'est écrasé au sol
4. ST. EX s'effondrer
5. COMPUT tomber en panne
6. △ [sleep] dormir ■ [fall asleep] s'endormir ■ **can I ~ at your place?** je peux dormir chez toi? ■ **I need somewhere to ~ for the next week** j'ai besoin d'un endroit où crécher△ la semaine prochaine.
◇ *vt* **1.** [vehicle] : **to ~ a car** avoir un accident avec une voiture ; [on purpose] démolir une voiture ■ **to ~ a plane** s'écraser en avion ■ **he ~ed the car through the fence/shop-window** il a traversé la clôture/la vitrine avec la voiture ■ **she ~ed the car into a wall** elle est rentrée dans *OR* a percuté un mur (avec la voiture)
2. *inf* [attend without invitation] : **to ~ a party** entrer dans une fête sans y être invité
3. COMPUT planter *inf*.
◆ **crash out**△ *vi insep* [fall asleep] s'endormir ■ [spend the night, sleep] roupiller ■ **I found him ~ed out in the corner** je l'ai trouvé endormi *OR* qui roupillait dans le coin.

crash barrier *n* glissière *f* de sécurité.

crash course *n* cours *m* intensif ■ **a ~ in French** un cours intensif de français.

crash-dive *vi* [submarine] plonger ■ [plane] faire un plongeon.

crash helmet *n* casque *m* (de protection).

crashing ['kræʃɪŋ] *adj UK inf* : **he's a ~ bore** c'est un raseur de première.

crash-land ◇ *vi* [aircraft] faire un atterrissage forcé, atterrir en catastrophe.
◇ *vt* [aircraft] poser *OR* faire atterrir en catastrophe.

crash landing *n* atterrissage *m* forcé *OR* en catastrophe.

crash pad△ *n* piaule△ *f* de dépannage ■ **he let me use this place as a ~** il m'a laissé crécher chez lui pour me dépanner△.

crass [kræs] *adj* [comment, person] lourd ■ [behaviour, stupidity] grossier ■ [ignorance] grossier, crasse.

crassly ['kræslɪ] *adv* [behave, comment] lourdement.

crassness ['kræsnɪs] *n* [of comment, person] lourdeur *f*, manque *m* de finesse ■ **the ~ of his behaviour** son manque de finesse.

crate [kreɪt] ◇ *n* **1.** [for storage, transport] caisse *f* ■ [for fruit, vegetables] cageot *m*, cagette *f* ■ [for bottles] caisse *f* **2.** *UK inf* [old car] caisse *f* ■ [plane] coucou *m*.
◇ *vt* [furniture, bottles] mettre dans une caisse *OR* en caisses ■ [fruit, vegetables] mettre dans un cageot *OR* en cageots.

crater ['kreɪtər] *n* [of volcano, moon etc] cratère *m* ■ **bomb ~** entonnoir *m* ■ **shell ~** entonnoir, trou *m* d'obus.

cravat [krə'væt] *n UK* foulard *m*.

crave [kreɪv] *vt* **1.** [long for - cigarette, drink] avoir terriblement envie de ; [- affection, love] avoir soif *OR* terriblement besoin de ; [- stardom] avoir soif de ; [- luxury, wealth] avoir soif *OR* être avide de ■ [in medical, psychological context] éprouver un besoin impérieux de **2.** *fml* [beg] implorer ■ **to ~ sb's indulgence** faire appel à l'indulgence de qqn.
◆ **crave for** *vt insep* = **crave** *(vt sense 1)*.

craven ['kreɪvn] *adj fml* [person, attitude] lâche, veule.

craving ['kreɪvɪŋ] *n* [longing] envie *f* impérieuse *OR* irrésistible ■ [physiological need] besoin *m* impérieux ■ **to have a ~ for sthg** [chocolate, sweets, cigarette] avoir terriblement envie de qqch ; [subj: alcoholic, drug addict] avoir un besoin impérieux de qqch.

craw [krɔ:] *n* [of bird] jabot *m* ■ [of animal] estomac *m* ■ **it sticks in my ~** *inf* cela me reste en travers de la gorge, j'ai du mal à l'avaler.

crawfish ['krɔ:fɪʃ] = **crayfish**.

crawl [krɔ:l] ◇ *n* **1.** [person] : **it involved a laborious ~ through the undergrowth** il a fallu ramper tant bien que mal à travers le sous-bois **2.** [vehicle] ralenti *m* ■ **to move at a ~** avancer au ralenti *OR* au pas **3.** SPORT crawl *m* ■ **to do the ~** nager le crawl.

◇ *vi* **1.** [move on all fours - person] ramper ; [- baby] marcher à quatre pattes ■ **he ~ed out of/into bed** il se traîna hors du/au lit ■ **to ~ on one's hands and knees** marcher *OR* se traîner à quatre pattes ■ **she ~ed under the desk** elle s'est mise à quatre pattes sous le bureau ■ **what are you ~ing about on the floor for?** qu'est-ce que tu fais à quatre pattes? **2.** [move slowly - traffic, train] avancer au ralenti *OR* au pas ; [- insect, snake] ramper ■ **the train ~ed out of the station** le train est sorti de la gare au ralenti *OR* au pas ■ **there's a caterpillar ~ing up your arm** il y a une chenille qui te grimpe sur le bras **3.** [be infested] : **to be ~ing with** être infesté de, grouiller de ■ **the streets were ~ing with police/tourists** *inf fig* les rues grouillaient de policiers/touristes **4.** [come out in goose pimples] : **to make sb's flesh ~** donner la chair de poule à qqn ■ **just the thought of it makes my skin ~** j'ai la chair de poule rien que d'y penser **5.** *inf* [grovel] : **to ~ to sb** ramper *OR* s'aplatir devant qqn, lécher les bottes de qqn ■ **he'll come ~ing back** il reviendra te supplier à genoux.

crawler ['krɔ:ləʳ] *n* **1.** *inf pej* [groveller] lèche-bottes *mf* **2.** *UK* AUT : **~ lane** file *f OR* voie *f* pour véhicules lents.
◆ **crawlers** *npl* [for baby] grenouillère *f*.

crawling ['krɔ:lɪŋ] ◇ *adj* **1.** *inf pej* [grovelling] rampant, de lèche-bottes **2.** [on all fours] : **she's reached the ~ stage** [baby] elle commence à marcher à quatre pattes.
◇ *n inf pej* [grovelling] : **if there's one thing I hate, it's ~ to the teacher** s'il y a bien quelque chose que je déteste, c'est qu'on lèche les bottes du prof.

crayfish ['kreɪfɪʃ] (*pl inv OR pl* **crayfishes**) *n* écrevisse *f*.

crayon ['kreɪɒn] ◇ *n* [coloured pencil] crayon *m* de couleur ■ **eye/lip ~** crayon pour les yeux/à lèvres ■ **wax ~** crayon gras.
◇ *vt* [draw] dessiner avec des crayons de couleurs ■ [colour] colorier (avec des crayons).

craze [kreɪz] ◇ *n* engouement *m*, folie *f* ■ **it's the latest ~** c'est la dernière folie *OR* lubie ■ **the latest dance/music ~** la nouvelle danse/musique à la mode ■ **a ~ for sthg** un engouement pour qqch.
◇ *vt* **1.** [send mad] rendre fou **2.** [damage - ceramics] craqueler ; [- windscreen, glass] étoiler.
◇ *vi* [ceramics] se craqueler ■ [windscreen, glass] s'étoiler.

crazed [kreɪzd] *adj* **1.** [mad - look, expression] fou *(before vowel or silent 'h'* **fol***)*, folle *f* ■ **~ with fear/grief** fou de peur/douleur **2.** [ceramics] craquelé.

-crazed *in cpds* rendu fou par ■ **drug~** rendu fou par la drogue ■ **power~ dictators** des dictateurs fous de pouvoir ■ **he was half~ with fear** il était à moitié fou de peur.

crazily ['kreɪzɪlɪ] *adv* [behave] comme un fou.

craziness ['kreɪzɪnɪs] *n* folie *f*.

crazy ['kreɪzɪ] (*comp* **crazier**, *superl* **craziest**) *adj* **1.** [insane - person, dream] fou *(before vowel or silent'h'* **fol***)*, folle *f* ■ **that's a ~ idea!, that's ~!** c'est de la folie! ■ **that's the craziest thing I've ever heard** c'est la chose la plus insensée que j'aie jamais entendue ■ **to drive** *OR* **to send sb ~** rendre qqn fou ■ **he went ~** [insane] il est devenu fou ; [angry] il est devenu fou (de colère *OR* de rage) ■ **the fans went ~** *inf* les fans ne se sont plus sentis ■ **power ~** avide de pouvoir ■ **you must be ~!** mais tu es fou! ■ **like ~** [work, drive, run, spend money] comme un fou **2.** *inf* [very fond] : **to be ~ about** être fou *OR* dingue de ■ **I'm not ~ about the idea** l'idée ne m'emballe pas vraiment ■ **he's football ~** c'est un fana *OR* un cinglé de foot **3.** [strange, fantastic] bizarre, fou *(before vowel or silent 'h'* **fol***)*, folle *f*.

crazy golf *n* minigolf *m*.

crazy paving *n UK dallage irrégulier en pierres plates.*

CRB [,si:ɑ:'bi:] (*abbrev of* **Criminal Records Bureau**) *n Organisme chargé de vérifier le casier judiciaire de personnels sensibles.*

CRE (*abbrev of* **Commission for Racial Equality**) *pr n* : **the ~** *commission contre la discrimination raciale.*

creak [kri:k] ◇ *vi* [chair, floorboard, person's joints] craquer ■ [door hinge] grincer ■ [shoes] crisser ■ **to ~ with age** *fig* donner des signes de vieillesse.
◇ *n* [of chair, floorboard, person's joints] craquement *m* ■ [of door hinge] grincement *m* ■ [of shoes] crissement *m* ■ **to give a ~** craquer, grincer, crisser.

creaking ['kri:kɪŋ] ◇ *adj* = **creaky**.
◇ *n* [of chair, floorboard, person's joints] craquement *m* ■ [of door hinge] grincement *m* ■ [of shoes] crissement *m*.

creaky ['kri:kɪ] (*comp* **creakier**, *superl* **creakiest**) *adj* [chair, floorboard, person's joints] qui craque ■ [door hinge] grinçant ■ [shoes] qui crisse ■ **a ~ noise** un craquement, un grincement, un crissement.

cream [kri:m] ◇ *n* **1.** crème *f* ■ **strawberries and ~** des fraises à la crème ■ **~ of tomato soup** velouté *m* de tomates **2.** [filling for biscuits, chocolates] crème *f* ■ **vanilla ~** [biscuit] biscuit *m* fourré à la vanille ; [dessert] crème *f* à la vanille **3.** [mixture] mélange *m* crémeux **4.** *fig* [best, pick] crème *f* ■ **the ~ of society** la crème *OR* le gratin de la société ■ **they were the ~ of their year at university** ils formaient l'élite de leur promotion à l'université ➤ **the ~ of the crop** le dessus du panier **5.** [for face, shoes etc] crème *f* **6.** [colour] crème *m*.
◇ *comp* [cake, bun] à la crème ■ [jug] à crème ■ **~-coloured** crème ■ **~ sherry** sherry *m OR* xérès *m* doux.
◇ *adj* crème.
◇ *vt* **1.** [skim - milk] écrémer **2.** CULIN [beat] écraser, travailler ■ **~ the butter and sugar** travailler le beurre et le sucre en crème ■ **~ed potatoes** purée *f* de pommes de terre **3.** [hands, face] mettre de la crème sur **4.** [add cream to - coffee] mettre de la crème dans **5.** *US inf* [beat up] casser la figure à ■ [defeat] battre à plate couture, mettre la pâtée à.
◆ **cream off** *vt sep fig* **to ~ off the best students** sélectionner les meilleurs étudiants ■ **they have ~ed off the elite** ils se sont accaparé l'élite.

cream cheese *n* fromage *m* frais.

cream cracker *n UK* biscuit *m* sec.

creamer ['kri:məʳ] *n* **1.** [machine] écrémeuse *f* **2.** [for coffee] succédané *m* de crème **3.** *US* [jug] pot *m* à crème.

cream puff *n* chou *m* à la crème.

cream soda *n boisson gazeuse aromatisée à la vanille.*

cream tea *n UK goûter composé de thé et de scones servis avec de la confiture et de la crème.*

creamy ['kri:mɪ] (*comp* **creamier**, *superl* **creamiest**) *adj* **1.** [containing cream - coffee, sauce] à la crème ; [- milk] qui contient de la crème ■ **it's too ~** il y a trop de crème **2.** [smooth - drink, sauce etc] crémeux ; [- complexion, voice] velouté **3.** [colour] : **~ white** blanc cassé.

crease [kri:s] ◇ *n* **1.** [in material, paper - made on purpose] pli *m* ; [- accidental] faux pli *m* ■ [in skin, on face] pli *m* ■ **to put a ~ in a pair of trousers** faire le pli d'un pantalon ■ **in order to get rid of the ~s** [in shirt, blouse etc] pour le/la défroisser **2.** [in cricket] limite *f* du batteur.
◇ *vt* **1.** [on purpose] faire les plis de ■ [accidentally] froisser, chiffonner ■ **this shirt is all ~d** cette chemise est toute froissée **2.** *inf* [amuse] : **this one'll ~ you** celle-là va te faire mourir de rire.
◇ *vi* [clothes] se froisser, se chiffonner ■ **his face ~d with laughter** son visage s'est plissé de rire.
◆ **crease up** *inf* ◇ *vi insep* se tordre de rire.
◇ *vt sep* faire mourir *OR* se tordre de rire.

creased [kri:st] *adj* **1.** [fabric] froissé **2.** [face] plissé.

crease-resistant *adj* infroissable.

create [kri:'eɪt] ◇ *vt* **1.** [employment, problem, the world] créer ■ [fuss, noise, impression, draught] faire ■ **to ~ a stir** *OR* **a sensation** faire sensation ■ **to ~ a disturbance** LAW porter atteinte à l'ordre public **2.** [appoint] : **he was ~d (a) baron** il a été fait baron.
◇ *vi* **1.** [be creative] créer **2.** *UK inf* [cause a fuss] faire des histoires.

creation [kriː'eɪʃn] *n* **1.** [process of creating] création *f* ▪ **the Creation** BIBLE la Création ▪ **the most beautiful woman in all ~** *OR* **the whole of ~** *fig* la plus belle femme de la terre **2.** [something created] création *f*.

creative [kriː'eɪtɪv] *adj* [person, mind, skill] créatif ▪ *hum & pej* (trop) libre ▪ **the ~ instinct** l'instinct *m* de création ▪ **to encourage sb to be ~** encourager la créativité chez qqn ▪ **we need some ~ thinking** nous avons besoin d'idées originales ➔ **~ writing** techniques *fpl* de l'écriture.

creatively [kriː'eɪtɪvlɪ] *adv* de manière créative ▪ **you're not thinking very ~ about your future** tu n'as pas d'idées très originales pour ton avenir.

creativeness [kriː'eɪtɪvnɪs], **creativity** [,kriːeɪ'tɪvətɪ] *n* créativité *f*.

creator [kriː'eɪtər] *n* créateur *m*, -trice *f* ▪ **the Creator** le Créateur.

creature ['kriːtʃər] *n* **1.** [person] créature *f* ▪ [animal] bête *f* ▪ **dumb ~s** les bêtes ▪ **poor ~!** [person, animal] le/la pauvre! ▪ **he's a ~ of habit** il est esclave de ses habitudes **2.** *lit & pej* [dependent person] créature *f*.

creature comforts *npl* confort *m* matériel ▪ **I like my ~** j'aime *OR* je suis attaché à mon (petit) confort.

crèche [kreʃ] *n UK* crèche *f*, garderie *f*.

credence ['kriːdns] *n* croyance *f*, foi *f* ▪ **to give** *OR* **to attach ~ to sthg** ajouter foi à qqch ▪ **to give** *OR* **to lend ~ to sthg** rendre qqch crédible.

credentials [krɪ'denʃlz] *npl* **1.** [references] références *fpl* **2.** [identity papers] papiers *mpl* d'identité ▪ **to ask to see sb's ~** demander ses papiers (d'identité) à qqn, demander une pièce d'identité à qqn **3.** [of diplomat] lettres *fpl* de créance.

credibility [,kredə'bɪlətɪ] ◇ *n* **1.** [trustworthiness] crédibilité *f* ▪ **the party has lost ~ with the electorate** le parti a perdu de sa crédibilité auprès de l'électorat **2.** [belief] : **it's beyond ~** c'est invraisemblable, c'est difficile à croire.
◇ *comp* : **~ rating** crédibilité *f* ▪ **he has a ~ problem** il manque de crédibilité.

credibility gap *n* manque *m* de crédibilité.

credible ['kredəbl] *adj* [person] crédible ▪ [evidence, statement] crédible, plausible ▪ **I don't find his reassurances very ~** j'ai du mal à croire ce qu'il dit pour me rassurer.

credibly ['kredəblɪ] *adv* [argue] de manière crédible.

credit ['kredɪt] ◇ *n* **1.** FIN crédit *m* ▪ **to be in ~** [person] avoir de l'argent sur son compte ; [account] être approvisionné ▪ **he has £50 to his ~** il a 50 livres sur son compte ▪ **to enter** *OR* **to place a sum to sb's ~** créditer le compte de qqn d'une somme ▮ [loan] : **to give sb ~, to give ~ to sb** [bank] accorder un découvert à qqn ; [shop, pub] faire crédit à qqn ▪ **'we do not give ~'** 'la maison ne fait pas crédit' ▪ **to sell/to buy/to live on ~** vendre/acheter/vivre à crédit ▪ **interest-free ~** crédit gratuit ▪ **line of ~** *US* limite *f OR* plafond *m* de crédit ▪ **her ~ is good** elle a une bonne réputation de solvabilité ; *fig* [trustworthy] elle est digne de confiance
2. [merit, honour] mérite *m* ▪ **all the ~ should go to the team** tout le mérite doit revenir à l'équipe ▪ **to take the ~ for sthg/doing sthg** s'attribuer le mérite de qqch/d'avoir fait qqch ▪ **I can't take all the ~ for it** tout le mérite ne me revient pas ▪ **to give sb the ~ for sthg/doing sthg** attribuer à qqn le mérite de qqch/d'avoir fait qqch ▪ **give her ~ for what she has achieved** reconnais ce qu'elle a accompli ▪ **nobody emerged with any ~ except him** c'est le seul qui s'en soit sorti à son honneur ▪ **it must be said to his ~ that...** il faut dire en sa faveur que... ▪ **to her ~ she did finish the exam** il faut lui accorder qu'elle a fini l'examen ▪ **she has five novels to her ~** elle a cinq romans à son actif ▪ **to be a ~ to one's family/school, to do one's family/school ~** faire honneur à sa famille/son école, être l'honneur de sa famille/son école ▪ **it does you ~ that you gave the money back** c'est tout à votre honneur d'avoir rendu l'argent ▪ **give me SOME~!** je ne suis quand même pas si bête! ▪ **~ where ~ is due** il faut reconnaître ce qui est
3. [credence] croyance *f* ▪ **to give ~ to sb/sthg** ajouter foi à qqn/qqch ▪ **the theory is gaining ~** cette théorie est de plus en plus acceptée ▪ **he's cleverer than I gave him ~ for** il est plus intelligent que je le pensais *OR* supposais ▪ **I gave you ~ for more sense** je vous supposais plus de bon sens
4. UNIV unité *f* de valeur, UV *f*.
◇ *comp* [boom, control] du crédit ▪ [sales] à crédit ▪ [balance] créditeur ▪ **~ entry** écriture *f* au crédit ▪ **~ side** crédit *m*, avoir *m* ▪ **on the ~ side, the proposed changes will cut costs** *fig* les changements projetés auront l'avantage de réduire les coûts ▪ **to run a ~ check on sb** [to ensure enough money in account] vérifier la solvabilité de qqn, vérifier que le compte de qqn est approvisionné ; [to ensure no record of bad debts] vérifier le passé bancaire de qqn ➔ **~ agency** *UK OR* **bureau** *US établissement chargé de vérifier le passé bancaire de personnes ou d'entreprises sollicitant un crédit* ▪ **~ broker** courtier *m* en crédits *OR* en prêts ▪ **~ note** avis *m* de crédit.
◇ *vt* **1.** FIN [account] créditer ▪ **to ~ an account with £200, to ~ £200 to an account** créditer un compte de 200 livres
2. [accord] : **to ~ sb with intelligence/tact/sense** supposer de l'intelligence/du tact/du bon sens à qqn ▪ **~ me with a bit more intelligence!** tu serais gentil de ne pas sous-estimer mon intelligence! ▪ **he is ~ed with the discovery of DNA** on lui attribue la découverte de l'ADN
3. [believe] croire ▪ **you wouldn't ~ some of the things he's done** tu n'en reviendrais pas si tu savais les choses qu'il a faites ▪ **I could hardly ~ it** j'avais du mal à le croire.
◆ **credits** *npl* CIN & TV générique *m*.

creditable ['kredɪtəbl] *adj* honorable, estimable.

creditably ['kredɪtəblɪ] *adv* honorablement.

credit account *n* **1.** BANK compte *m* créditeur **2.** *UK* [with shop] compte *m* client.

credit card ◇ *n* carte *f* de crédit ▪ **to pay by ~** payer avec une *OR* régler par carte de crédit.
◇ *comp* : **~ fraud** usage *m* frauduleux de cartes de crédit ▪ **~ number** numéro *m* de carte de crédit ▪ **~ transactions** transactions *fpl* effectuées par carte de crédit.

credit facilities *npl* facilités *fpl* de crédit.

credit limit *n* limite *f OR* plafond *m* de crédit.

credit line *n* **1.** *UK* [loan] autorisation *f* de crédit **2.** *US* = **credit limit**.

credit note *n UK* [in business] facture *f OR* note *f* d'avoir ▪ [in shop] avoir *m*.

creditor ['kredɪtər] *n* créancier *m*, - ère *f*.

credit rating *n* degré *m* de solvabilité.

credit squeeze *n* restriction *f OR* encadrement *m* du crédit.

credit terms *npl* modalités *fpl* de crédit.

credit transfer *n* virement *m*, transfert *m* (de compte à compte).

creditworthiness ['kredɪt,wɜːðɪnɪs] *n* solvabilité *f*.

creditworthy ['kredɪt,wɜːðɪ] *adj* solvable.

credo ['kreɪdəʊ] *n* credo *m inv*.

credulity [krɪ'djuːlətɪ] *n* crédulité *f*.

credulous ['kredjʊləs] *adj* crédule, naïf.

credulously ['kredjʊləslɪ] *adv* naïvement.

creed [kriːd] *n* [religious] credo *m*, croyance *f* ▪ [political] credo *m* ▪ **people of every colour and ~** des gens de toutes races et de toutes croyances ▪ **the Creed** RELIG le Credo.

creek [kriːk] *n UK* [of sea] crique *f*, anse *f* ▪ *US* [stream] ruisseau *m* ▪ [river] rivière *f* ▪ **to be up the ~** *inf* être dans de beaux draps *OR* dans le pétrin ▪ **to be up shit ~ (without a paddle)**△ être dans la merde (jusqu'au cou)△.

creep [kriːp] ◇ *n inf* [unpleasant person] sale type *m*, rat *m* ▪ [weak, pathetic person] pauvre type *m*.
◇ *vi* (*pret & pp* **crept** [krept]) **1.** [person, animal] se glisser ▪ **to ~ into a room** entrer sans bruit *OR* se glisser dans une pièce ▪ **I crept upstairs** je suis monté sans bruit ▪ **to ~ into bed** se glisser dans le lit ▪ **I was ~ing about so as not to waken you** je ne faisais pas de bruit pour ne pas te réveiller ▪ **I can hear**

somebody ~ing about downstairs j'entends quelqu'un bouger en bas ■ the dog crept under the chair le chien s'est tapi sous la chaise ■ the shadows crept across the lawn l'ombre a peu à peu envahi la pelouse ■ the hours crept slowly by les heures se sont écoulées lentement **2.** [plant - along the ground] ramper ; [- upwards] grimper **3.** *phr* to make sb's flesh ~ donner la chair de poule à qqn, faire froid dans le dos à qqn.

◆ **creeps** *npl inf* he gives me the ~s [is frightening] il me fait froid dans le dos, il me donne la chair de poule ; [is unpleasant] il me dégoûte *OR* répugne.

◆ **creep in** *vi insep* [person] entrer sans bruit ■ *fig* [mistakes] se glisser ■ [doubts, fears] s'insinuer ■ the use of the word as a verb is beginning to ~ in l'usage de ce mot en tant que verbe commence à se répandre *OR* gagner du terrain.

◆ **creep out** *vi insep* sortir sans bruit.

◆ **creep up** *vi insep* **1.** [approach] s'approcher sans bruit ■ to ~ up to sthg s'approcher sans bruit de qqch **2.** [increase - water, prices] monter lentement ; [- sales] monter *OR* progresser lentement.

◆ **creep up on** *vt insep* **1.** [in order to attack, surprise] s'approcher discrètement de, s'approcher à pas de loup de ■ don't ~ up on me like that! ne t'approche pas de moi sans faire de bruit comme ça! ■ old age crept up on me je suis devenu vieux sans m'en rendre compte **2.** [catch up with - in competition, business etc] rattraper peu à peu ■ the deadline is ~ing up on us la date limite se rapproche.

creeper ['kri:pəʳ] *n* **1.** [plant] plante *f* grimpante **2.** *UK inf* [shoe] chaussure *f* à semelles de crêpe.

creeping ['kri:pɪŋ] *adj* **1.** [plant - upwards] grimpant ; [- along the ground] rampant **2.** [insect] rampant **3.** *fig* [inflation] rampant ■ [change] graduel ■ ~ paralysis paralysie *f* progressive.

creepy ['kri:pɪ] (*comp* creepier, *superl* creepiest) *adj inf* qui donne la chair de poule.

creepy-crawly [-'krɔ:lɪ] (*pl* creepy-crawlies) *inf n UK* petite bestiole *f*.

cremate [krɪ'meɪt] *vt* incinérer.

cremation [krɪ'meɪʃn] *n* incinération *f*, crémation *f*.

crematorium [ˌkremə'tɔ:rɪəm] (*pl* crematoria [-rɪə] *OR pl* crematoriums) *n* [establishment] crématorium *m* ■ [furnace] four *m* crématoire.

crematory ['kremətrɪ] (*pl* crematories) *US* = crematorium.

crème de la crème ['kremdəlæ'krem] *n* : the ~ le gratin, le dessus du panier.

crenellated *UK*, **crenelated** *US* ['krenəleɪtɪd] *adj* crénelé, à créneaux.

crenellation *UK*, **crenelation** *US* [ˌkrenə'leɪʃn] *n (usu pl)* créneau *m*.

Creole ['kri:əʊl] ◇ *n* **1.** LING créole *m* **2.** [person] créole *mf*.
◇ *adj* créole.

creosote ['krɪəsəʊt] ◇ *n* créosote *f*.
◇ *vt* traiter à la créosote.

crepe [kreɪp] ◇ *n* **1.** [fabric] crêpe *m* **2.** = crepe rubber **3.** = crepe paper **4.** [pancake] crêpe *f*.
◇ *comp* [skirt, blouse etc] de *OR* en crêpe.

crepe bandage *n* bande *f* Velpeau®.

crepe paper *n* papier *m* crépon.

crepe rubber *n* crêpe *m*.

crepe(-soled) shoes [-səʊld-] *npl* chaussures *fpl* à semelles de crêpe.

crept [krept] *pt & pp* ▷ creep.

Cres. *written abbr of* Crescent.

crescendo [krɪ'ʃendəʊ] ◇ *n* (*pl* crescendos *OR pl* crescendoes) *fig* & MUS crescendo *m*.
◇ *vi* [gen] augmenter ■ MUS faire un crescendo.
◇ *adv* MUS crescendo, en augmentant.

crescent ['kresnt] ◇ *n* **1.** [shape] croissant *m* **2.** *UK* [street] rue *f* (en arc de cercle).
◇ *adj* [shaped] en (forme de) croissant ■ ~ moon croissant *m* de lune.

cress [kres] *n* cresson *m*.

crest [krest] *n* **1.** [peak - of hill, wave] crête *f* ; [- of ridge] arête *f* ; [- of road] haut *m OR* sommet *m* de côte ■ she's (riding) on the ~ of a wave just now *fig* tout lui réussit *OR* elle a le vent en poupe en ce moment **2.** [on bird, lizard] crête *f* ■ [on helmet] cimier *m* **3.** [coat of arms] timbre *m* ■ [emblem] armoiries *fpl*.

crested ['krestɪd] *adj* **1.** [animal] orné d'une crête ■ [bird] huppé **2.** [with emblem] armorié.

crestfallen ['krestˌfɔ:ln] *adj* découragé, déconfit.

Cretan ['kri:tn] ◇ *n* Crétois *m*, - e *f*.
◇ *adj* crétois.

Crete [kri:t] *pr n* Crète *f* ■ in ~ en Crète.

cretin ['kretɪn] *n* **1.** MED crétin *m*, - e *f* **2.** *inf* [idiot] crétin *m*, - e *f*, imbécile *mf*.

cretinous ['kretɪnəs] *adj* MED & *fig* crétin.

Creutzfeld-Jacob disease ['krɔɪtsfeld 'jækɒb-] *n* maladie *f* de Creutzfeld-Jacob.

crevasse [krɪ'væs] *n* crevasse *f*.

crevice ['krevɪs] *n* fissure *f*, fente *f*.

crew [kru:] ◇ *pt UK* ▷ crow.
◇ *n* **1.** [gen - CIN] équipe *f* ■ [on plane, ship] équipage *m* **2.** *inf* [crowd, gang] bande *f*, équipe *f*.
◇ *comp* : ~ member membre *mf* d'équipage.
◇ *vi* : to ~ for sb être l'équipier de qqn.
◇ *vt* armer (*d'un équipage*).

crew cut *n* coupe *f* de cheveux en brosse.

crewman ['kru:mən] (*pl* crewmen [-mən]) *n* membre *m* de l'équipage.

crew-neck(ed) *adj* : a ~ sweater un pull ras le *OR* du cou.

crew neck *n* col *m* ras le *OR* du cou, ras-le-cou *m*.

crib [krɪb] ◇ *n* **1.** (*esp*) *US* [cot] lit *m* d'enfant **2.** [bin] grenier *m* (à blé) ■ [stall] stalle *f* **3.** [manger] mangeoire *f*, râtelier *m* ■ RELIG crèche *f* **4.** *inf* [plagiarism] plagiat *m* ■ *UK* SCH [list of answers] antisèche *mf* **5.** = cribbage.
◇ *vt* (*pret & pp* cribbed, *cont* cribbing) **1.** *inf* [plagiarize] plagier, copier ■ he cribbed the answers from his friend SCH il a copié les réponses sur son ami, il a pompé sur son ami **2.** [line with planks] consolider avec des planches ■ TECH boiser.
◇ *vi* (*pret & pp* cribbed, *cont* cribbing) copier ■ the author had cribbed from Shaw l'auteur avait plagié Shaw ■ don't ~ off me! SCH ne copie pas sur moi!

cribbage ['krɪbɪdʒ] *n (U) jeu de cartes où les points sont marqués sur une planche de bois.*

crib death *n US* mort *f* subite (du nourrisson).

crick [krɪk] ◇ *n* : to have a ~ in the neck avoir un torticolis.
◇ *vt* : she ~ed her neck elle a attrapé un torticolis.

cricket ['krɪkɪt] ◇ *n* **1.** [insect] grillon *m* **2.** [game] cricket *m* ■ that's not ~ *UK inf* ça ne se fait pas, ce n'est pas fair-play.
◇ *comp* [ball, bat, ground, match] de cricket.

cricketer ['krɪkɪtəʳ] *n* joueur *m*, - euse *f* de cricket.

cried [kraɪd] *pt & pp* ▷ cry.

crier ['kraɪəʳ] *n* crieur *m*, - euse *f* ■ [in court] huissier *m*.

crikey ['kraɪkɪ] *interj UK inf dated* mince alors.

crime [kraɪm] *n* **1.** [gen] crime *m* ■ ~ is on the decline il y a une baisse de la criminalité ■ a life of ~ une vie de criminel ■ ~ doesn't pay le crime ne paie pas ■ a minor *OR* petty ~ un délit mineur ■ it's a ~ that she died so young *fig* c'est vraiment injuste qu'elle soit morte si jeune ➊ ~ prevention lutte *f* contre la criminalité ■ ~ reporter journaliste *mf* qui couvre les affaires criminelles ■ crimes against humanity crimes contre l'humanités ■ ~ wave vague *f* de criminalité ■ ~ writer auteur *m* de romans noirs ■ 'Crime and Punishment' *Dostoievsky* 'Crime et châtiment' **2.** MIL manquement *m* à la discipline, infraction *f*.

Crimea [kraɪ'mɪə] *pr n* : **the ~** la Crimée ▪ **in the ~** en Crimée.

Crimean [kraɪ'mɪən] ◇ *n* Criméen *m*, - enne *f*.
◇ *adj* criméen ▪ **the ~ (War)** la guerre de Crimée.

criminal ['krɪmɪnl] ◇ *n* criminel *m*, - elle *f*.
◇ *adj* criminel ▪ **to take ~ proceedings against sb** LAW poursuivre qqn au pénal ▪ **it's ~ the way he treats her** *fig* il ne devrait pas avoir le droit de la traiter comme ça ▶ **the Criminal Investigation Department** *UK* = **CID** ▪ **the Criminal Records Office** *UK* l'identité *f* judiciaire.

criminal assault *n* agression *f* criminelle, voie *f* de fait.

criminal court *n* cour *f* d'assises.

criminal damage *n délit consistant à causer volontairement des dégâts matériels.*

criminality [,krɪmɪ'nælətɪ] *n* criminalité *f*.

criminalize, *UK* **ise** ['krɪmɪnəlaɪz] *vt* criminaliser.

criminal law *n* droit *m* pénal *OR* criminel.

criminal lawyer *n* avocat *m*, - e *f* au criminel, pénaliste *mf*.

criminally ['krɪmɪnəlɪ] *adv* criminellement ▪ **he's been ~ negligent** sa négligence est criminelle.

criminal offence *n* délit *m* ▪ **drunk driving is a ~** la conduite en état d'ivresse est un crime puni par la loi.

criminal record *n* casier *m* judiciaire ▪ **she hasn't got a ~** son casier judiciaire est vierge, elle n'a pas de casier judiciaire.

Criminal Records Bureau *n Organisme chargé de vérifier le casier judiciaire de personnels sensibles.*

criminology [,krɪmɪ'nɒlədʒɪ] *n* criminologie *f*.

crimp [krɪmp] ◇ *vt* **1.** [hair] crêper, friser ▪ [pie crust] pincer ▪ [metal] onduler **2.** *inf* TECH [pinch together] pincer, sertir.
◇ *n* **1.** [wave in hair] cran *m*, ondulation *f* ▪ [fold in metal] ondulation *f* **2.** TEX pli *m*.

crimson ['krɪmzn] ◇ *adj* cramoisi.
◇ *n* cramoisi *m*.

cringe [krɪndʒ] *vi* **1.** [shrink back] avoir un mouvement de recul, reculer ▪ [cower] se recroqueviller ▪ **to ~ in terror** reculer de peur ▪ **to ~ with embarrassment** être mort de honte ▪ **I ~ at the very thought** j'ai envie de rentrer sous terre rien que d'y penser **2.** [be servile] ramper.

cringeworthy ['krɪndʒ,wɜːðɪ] *adj inf* hérissant, qui hérisse.

cringing ['krɪndʒɪŋ] *adj* [fearful] craintif ▪ [servile] servile, obséquieux.

crinkle ['krɪŋkl] ◇ *vt* froisser, chiffonner.
◇ *vi* se froisser, se chiffonner.
◇ *n* **1.** [wrinkle] fronce *f*, pli *m* ▪ [on face] ride *f* **2.** [noise] froissement *m*.

crinkle-cut *adj* [crisps, chips] dentelé.

crinkly ['krɪŋklɪ] (*comp* **crinklier**, *superl* **crinkliest**) *adj* [material, paper] gaufré ▪ [hair] crépu, crêpelé.

crinoline ['krɪnəliːn] *n* crinoline *f*.

cripple ['krɪpl] ◇ *vt* **1.** [person] estropier **2.** *fig* [damage - industry, system] paralyser ; [- plane, ship] désemparer.
◇ *n* **1.** *dated* & *offens* [lame person] estropié *m*, - e *f* ▪ [invalid] invalide *mf* ▪ [maimed person] mutilé *m*, - e *f* **2.** *fig* **an emotional ~** un caractériel *m*, une caractérielle *f*.

crippled ['krɪpld] *adj* **1.** [person] : **to be ~ with rheumatism** être perclus de rhumatismes **2.** *fig* [industry, country] paralysé ▪ [plane, ship] accidenté.

crippling ['krɪplɪŋ] *adj* **1.** [disease] invalidant **2.** *fig* [strikes] paralysant ▪ [prices, taxes] écrasant.

crisis ['kraɪsɪs] (*pl* **crises** [-siːz]) *n* crise *f* ▪ **things have come to a ~** la situation est à un point critique ▪ **the oil ~** le choc pétrolier ▪ **a ~ of confidence** une crise de confiance ▪ **~ management** gestion *f* des crises ▪ **~ point** point *m* critique.

crisis centre *n* [for disasters] cellule *f* de crise ▪ [for personal help] centre *m* d'aide ▪ [for battered women] association *f* d'aide d'urgence.

crisp [krɪsp] ◇ *adj* **1.** [crunchy - vegetable] croquant ; [- cracker] croquant, croustillant ; [- bread] croustillant ; [- snow] craquant **2.** [fresh - clothing] pimpant ; [- linen] apprêté ; [- paper] craquant, raide **3.** [air, weather] vif, tonifiant **4.** [concise - style] précis, clair et net **5.** [brusque] tranchant, brusque ▪ [manner] brusque ▪ [tone] acerbe.
◇ *n* : **(potato) ~s** *UK* (pommes *fpl*) chips *fpl* ▪ **burnt to a ~** carbonisé.
◇ *vt* faire chauffer pour rendre croustillant.

crispbread ['krɪspbred] *n* biscuit *m* scandinave.

crisply ['krɪsplɪ] *adv* **1.** [succinctly] avec concision **2.** [sharply] d'un ton acerbe *OR* cassant.

crispness ['krɪspnɪs] *n* **1.** [of food, paper] craquant *m* ▪ [of clothing, sheets, weather] fraîcheur *f* **2.** [of reasoning] clarté *f*, rigueur *f* **3.** [of style] précision *f* **4.** [brusqueness] tranchant *m*, brusquerie *f*.

crispy ['krɪspɪ] (*comp* **crispier**, *superl* **crispiest**) *adj* [vegetables] croquant ▪ [biscuits] croquant, croustillant ▪ [bacon] croustillant.

crisscross ['krɪskrɒs] ◇ *vt* entrecroiser ▪ **footpaths ~ed the hillside** des chemins s'entrecroisaient sur le flanc de la colline.
◇ *vi* s'entrecroiser.
◇ *adj* [lines] entrecroisé ▪ [in disorder] enchevêtré ▪ **in a ~ pattern** en croisillons.
◇ *n* entrecroisement *m*.
◇ *adv* en réseau.

criterion [kraɪ'tɪərɪən] (*pl* **criteria** [-rɪə]) *n* critère *m*.

critic ['krɪtɪk] *n* [reviewer] critique *m* ▪ [fault-finder] critique *m*, détracteur *m*, - trice *f* ▪ **film/art/theatre ~** critique *m* de cinéma/d'art/de théâtre.

critical ['krɪtɪkl] *adj* **1.** [crucial] critique, crucial ▪ [situation] critique ▪ **he's in a ~ condition** *OR* **on the ~ list** il est dans un état critique ▪ **the ~ path** [gen - COMPUT] le chemin critique ▮ PHYS critique **2.** [analytical] critique ▪ [disparaging] critique, négatif ▪ **he's very ~ of others** il critique beaucoup les autres, il est très critique vis-à-vis des autres **3.** ART, LIT & MUS [analysis, edition] critique ▪ [essay, study] critique, de critique ▪ [from the critics] des critiques ▪ **the play met with ~ acclaim** la pièce fut applaudie par la critique.

critically ['krɪtɪklɪ] *adj* **1.** [analytically] d'un œil critique, en critique ▪ [disparagingly] sévèrement **2.** [seriously] gravement ▪ **she is ~ ill** elle est gravement malade, elle est dans un état critique.

critical mass *n* masse *f* critique.

criticism ['krɪtɪsɪzm] *n* critique *f* ▪ **to come in for ~** se faire *OR* se voir critiquer ▪ **literary ~** la critique littéraire.

criticize, *UK* **ise** ['krɪtɪsaɪz] *vt* **1.** [find fault with] critiquer, réprouver **2.** [analyse] critiquer, faire la critique de.

critique [krɪ'tiːk] ◇ *n* critique *f* (argumentée, raisonnée).
◇ *vt* faire une critique de.

critter ['krɪtər] *n US inf* [creature] créature *f* ▪ [animal] bête *f*, bestiole *f*.

croak [krəʊk] ◇ *vi* **1.** [frog] coasser ▪ [crow] croasser **2.** [person] parler d'une voix rauque ▪ [grumble] ronchonner **3.** *inf* [die] crever.
◇ *vt* [utter] dire d'une voix rauque *OR* éraillée.
◇ *n* [of frog] coassement *m* ▪ [of crow] croassement *m* ▪ [of person] ton *m* rauque.

croaking ['krəʊkɪŋ] *n* [of frog] coassement *m* ▪ [of crow] croassement *m*.

croaky ['krəʊkɪ] *adj* enroué.

Croat ['krəʊæt] = **Croatian** *(n)*.

Croatia [krəʊ'eɪʃə] *pr n* Croatie *f* ▪ **in ~** en Croatie.

Croatian [krəʊ'eɪʃn] ◇ *n* **1.** [person] Croate *mf* **2.** LING croate *m*.
◇ *adj* croate.

crochet ['krəʊʃeɪ] ◇ *n* : **~ (work)** (travail *m* au) crochet *m*.
◇ *vt* faire au crochet.
◇ *vi* faire du crochet.

crock [krɒk] *n* **1.** [jar, pot] cruche *f*, pot *m* de terre ▪ [broken earthenware] morceau *m* de faïence, tesson *m* **2.** *UK inf* **old ~** [car] tacot *m*, guimbarde *f* ; [person] croulant *m*.

crockery ['krɒkərɪ] *n* [pottery] poterie *f*, faïence *f* ▪ [plates, cups, bowls etc] vaisselle *f*.

crocodile ['krɒkədaɪl] *n* **1.** [reptile] crocodile *m* **2.** *UK* SCH cortège *m* en rangs *(par deux)*.

crocodile clip *n* pince *f* crocodile.

crocodile tears *npl* larmes *fpl* de crocodile.

crocus ['krəʊkəs] *n* crocus *m*.

Croesus ['kri:səs] *pr n* Crésus ▪ **as rich as ~** riche comme Crésus.

croft [krɒft] *n UK* petite ferme *f*.

crofter ['krɒftər] *n UK* [farmer] petit fermier *m*.

crofting ['krɒftɪŋ] *n* (exploitation *f* en) affermage *m*.

crone [krəʊn] *n inf* vieille bique *f*.

crony ['krəʊnɪ] (*pl* **cronies**) *n inf* pote *m*, copine *f*.

cronyism ['krəʊnɪɪzm] *n* copinage *m*.

crook [krʊk] ◇ *n* **1.** *inf* [thief] escroc *m*, filou *m* **2.** [bend - in road] courbe *f*, coude *m* ; [- in river] coude *m*, détour *m* ; [- in arm] coude *m* ; [- in leg] flexion *f* **3.** [staff - of shepherd] houlette *f* ; [- of bishop] crosse *f*.
◇ *vt* [finger] courber, recourber ▪ [arm] plier.

crooked ['krʊkɪd] ◇ *adj* **1.** [not straight, bent - stick] courbé, crochu ; [- path] tortueux ; [- person] courbé ▪ **a ~ smile** un sourire grimaçant **2.** *inf* [dishonest] malhonnête.
◇ *adv* de travers.

croon [kru:n] *vi* & *vt* **1.** [sing softly] fredonner, chantonner ▪ [professionally] chanter *(en crooner)* **2.** [speak softly, sentimentally] susurrer.

crooner ['kru:nər] *n* crooner *m*, chanteur *m* de charme.

crop [krɒp] ◇ *n* **1.** [produce] produit *m* agricole, culture *f* ▪ **food ~s** cultures vivrières | [harvest] récolte *f* ▪ [of fruit] récolte *f*, cueillette *f* ▪ [of grain] moisson *f* **2.** *fig* fournée *f* ▪ **what do you think of this year's ~ of students?** que pensez-vous des étudiants de cette année? **3.** [of whip] manche *m* ▪ [riding whip] cravache *f* **4.** [of bird] jabot *m* **5.** [haircut - for man] coupe *f* rase *OR* courte ; [- for woman] coupe courte *OR* à la garçonne ▪ **the barber gave me a (close) ~** le coiffeur m'a coupé les cheveux ras.
◇ *vt* (*pret* & *pp* **cropped**, *cont* **cropping**) **1.** [cut - hedge] tailler, tondre ; [- hair] tondre ; [- tail] écourter ▪ PHOT recadrer **2.** [subj: animal] brouter, paître **3.** [farm] cultiver ▪ [harvest] récolter.
◇ *vi* (*pret* & *pp* **cropped**, *cont* **cropping**) [land, vegetables] donner *OR* fournir une récolte.
◆ **crop up** *vi insep inf* survenir, se présenter ▪ **his name cropped up in the conversation** son nom a surgi dans la conversation ▪ **we'll deal with anything that ~s up while you're away** on s'occupera de tout pendant votre absence.

crop dusting = **crop spraying**.

cropper ['krɒpər] *n UK inf phr* **to come a ~** [fall] se casser la figure ; [fail] se planter.

crop rotation *n* assolement *m*, rotation *f* des cultures.

crop spraying *n* pulvérisation *f* des cultures.

croquet ['krəʊkeɪ] ◇ *n* croquet *m*.
◇ *comp* [hoop, lawn, mallet] de croquet.

croquette [krɒ'ket] *n* croquette *f* ▪ **potato ~** croquette de pomme de terre.

crosier ['krəʊʒjər] *n* crosse *f (d'évêque)*.

cross [krɒs] ◇ *n* **1.** [mark, symbol] croix *f* ▪ **he signed with a ~** il a signé d'une croix ▶ **the Iron Cross** la Croix de fer **2.** RELIG croix *f* ▪ **the Cross** la Croix | *fig* [burden] croix *f* ▪ **we each have our ~ to bear** chacun a *OR* porte sa croix **3.** [hybrid] hybride *m* ▪ **a ~ between a horse and a donkey** un croisement *m* d'un cheval et d'une ânesse ▪ **the novel is a ~ between a thriller and a comedy** *fig* ce roman est un mélange de policier et de comédie **4.** SEW : **on the ~** en biais.
◇ *vt* **1.** [go across - road, room, sea] traverser ; [- bridge, river] traverser, passer ; [- fence, threshold] franchir ▪ **the bridge ~es the river at Orléans** le pont franchit *OR* enjambe le fleuve à Orléans ▪ **it ~ed my mind that...** j'ai pensé *OR* l'idée m'a effleuré que... ▶ **to ~ the floor (of the House)** *UK* POL changer de parti politique ▪ **I'll ~ that bridge when I come to it** je m'occuperai de ce problème en temps voulu **2.** [place one across the other] croiser ▪ **to ~ one's arms/one's legs** croiser les bras/les jambes ▶ **~ your fingers** *OR* **keep your fingers ~ed for me** pense à moi et croise les doigts ▪ **to ~ swords with sb** croiser le fer avec qqn ▪ **~ my palm (with silver)!** donnez-moi une petite pièce! **3.** [mark with cross] faire une croix ▪ **to ~ o.s.** RELIG faire le signe de (la) croix, se signer ▪ **~ your "t"s** barrez *OR* mettez des barres à vos "t" ▪ **to ~ a cheque** *UK* barrer un chèque ▶ **~ my heart and hope to die** *inf* croix de bois croix de fer, si je mens je vais en enfer **4.** [animals, plants] croiser **5.** [oppose] contrarier, contrecarrer ▪ **~ed in love** malheureux en amour **6.** TELEC : **we've got a ~ed line** il y a des interférences sur la ligne.
◇ *vi* **1.** [go across] traverser ▪ **she ~ed (over) to the other side of the road** elle a traversé la route ▪ **they ~ed from Dover to Boulogne** ils ont fait la traversée de Douvres à Boulogne **2.** [intersect - lines, paths, roads] se croiser, se rencontrer ▪ **our letters ~ed in the post** nos lettres se sont croisées.
◇ *adj* **1.** [angry] de mauvaise humeur, en colère ▪ **she's ~ with me** elle est fâchée contre moi ▪ **he makes me so ~!** qu'est-ce qu'il peut m'agacer! ▪ **I never heard her utter a ~ word** elle ne dit jamais un mot plus haut que l'autre ▶ **to be as ~ as a bear** *inf* être dans une colère noire **2.** [diagonal] diagonal ▪ **~ member** CONSTR traverse *f*, entremise *f*.
◆ **cross off** *vt sep* [item] barrer, rayer ▪ [person] radier ▪ **to ~ sb off the list** radier qqn.
◆ **cross out** *vt sep* barrer, rayer.

crossbar ['krɒsbɑ:r] *n* [on bike] barre *f* ▪ [on goalposts] barre *f* traversale.

crossbeam ['krɒsbi:m] *n* traverse *f*, sommier *m*.

crossbench ['krɒsbentʃ] *n (usu pl)* *UK* POL *banc où s'assoient les députés non inscrits à un parti* ▪ **on the ~es** du côté des non-inscrits.

crossbencher [ˌkrɒs'bentʃər] *n UK* POL *au Parlement britannique, membre non inscrit, assis sur les bancs transversaux.*

crossbones ['krɒsbəʊnz] *npl* os *mpl* en croix *OR* de mort.

crossbow ['krɒsbəʊ] *n* arbalète *f*.

crossbred ['krɒsbred] ◇ *adj* hybride, métis.
◇ *n* hybride *m*, métis *m*, - isse *f*.

crossbreed ['krɒsbri:d] ◇ *vt* (*pret* & *pp* **crossbred** ['krɒsbred]) croiser.
◇ *n* [animal, plant] hybride *m*, métis *m*, - isse *f* ▪ *pej* [person] métis *m*, - isse *f*, sang-mêlé *mf*.

cross-Channel *adj UK* [ferry, route] qui traverse la Manche.

cross-check ◇ *vt* contrôler (par contre-épreuve *OR* par recoupement).
◇ *vi* vérifier par recoupement.
◇ *n* contre-épreuve *f*, recoupement *m*.

cross-country ◇ *n* cross-country *m*, cross *m*.

◇ *adj* : **~ runner** coureur *m*, - euse *f* de cross ▪ **~ skiing** ski *m* de fond.
◇ *adv* à travers champs.

cross-cultural *adj* interculturel.

cross-current *n* contre-courant *m*.

cross-dressing *n* travestisme *m*, transvestisme *m*.

crossed [krɒst] *adj* croisé ▪ **~ cheque** chèque *m* barré ▪ **~ line** TELEC ligne *f* embrouillée.

cross-examination *n* contre-interrogatoire *m*.

cross-examine *vt* [gen] soumettre à un interrogatoire serré ▪ LAW faire subir un contre-interrogatoire à.

cross-eyed *adj* qui louche.

cross-fertilization *n* croisement *m* ▪ *fig* osmose *f*.

cross-fertilize, *UK* **ise** *vt* croiser.

crossfire ['krɒs,faɪəʳ] *n* feux *mpl* croisés ▪ **to be caught in the ~** *liter & fig* être pris entre deux feux.

cross hairs *npl fils croisés d'une lunette qui déterminent la ligne de visée.*

crossheaded ['krɒshedɪd] *adj* [screwdriver] cruciforme.

cross-index ◇ *vi* renvoyer à.
◇ *vt* établir les renvois de.
◇ *n* renvoi *m*, référence *f*.

crossing ['krɒsɪŋ] *n* **1.** [intersection] croisement *m* ▪ [of roads] croisement *m*, carrefour *m* **2.** [sea journey] traversée *f* **3.** [inter-breeding] croisement *m*.

cross-legged [krɒs'legɪd] *adv* en tailleur.

crossly ['krɒslɪ] *adv* avec mauvaise humeur.

crossover ['krɒs,əʊvəʳ] ◇ *n* **1.** [of roads] (croisement *m* par) pont *m* routier ▪ [for pedestrians] passage *m* clouté ▪ RAIL voie *f* de croisement **2.** BIOL croisement *m*.
◇ *adj* MUS [style] hybride.

cross-party *adj* POL : **~ agreement** accord *m* entre partis.

crosspatch ['krɒspætʃ] *n inf* grincheux *m*, - euse *f*.

crosspiece ['krɒspi:s] *n* traverse *f*.

crossply ['krɒsplaɪ] *adj* [tyre] à carcasse biaise *OR* croisée.

cross-purposes *npl* : **to be at ~ with sb** [misunderstand] comprendre qqn de travers ; [oppose] être en désaccord avec qqn ▪ **they were talking at ~** leur conversation tournait autour d'un quiproquo.

cross-question = **cross-examine**.

cross-refer ◇ *vi* : **to ~ to sthg** renvoyer à qqch.
◇ *vt* renvoyer.

cross-reference *n* renvoi *m*, référence *f*.

crossroads ['krɒsrəʊdz] (*pl inv*) *n* croisement *m*, carrefour *m* ▪ **her career is at a ~** sa carrière va maintenant prendre un tournant décisif.

cross-section *n* **1.** [gen - BIOL] coupe *f* transversale **2.** [sample - of population] échantillon *m*.

cross-stitch ◇ *n* point *m* de croix.
◇ *vt* coudre au point de croix.

cross street *n US* rue *f* transversale.

crosstie ['krɒstaɪ] *n US* traverse *f (de voie ferrée)*.

crosswalk ['krɒswɔ:k] *n US* passage *m* clouté.

crossways ['krɒsweɪz] (*pl inv*) ◇ *n US* = **crossroads**.
◇ *adj & adv* = **crosswise**.

crosswind ['krɒswɪnd] *n* vent *m* de travers.

crosswise ['krɒswaɪz] *adj & adv* [shaped like cross] en croix ▪ [across] en travers ▪ [diagonally] en travers, en diagonale.

crossword (puzzle) ['krɒswɜ:d-] *n* mots *mpl* croisés.

crotch [krɒtʃ] *n* [of tree] fourche *f* ▪ [of trousers] entre-jambes *m*.

crotchet ['krɒtʃɪt] *n UK* noire *f*.

crotchety ['krɒtʃɪtɪ] *adj inf* grognon, bougon.

crouch [kraʊtʃ] ◇ *vi* : **to ~ (down)** [person] s'accroupir, se tapir ; [animal] s'accroupir, se ramasser.
◇ *n* [posture] accroupissement *m* ▪ [act] action *f* de se ramasser.

croup [kru:p] *n* **1.** [of animal] croupe *f* **2.** MED croup *m*.

croupier ['kru:pɪəʳ] *n* croupier *m*, -ère *f*.

crouton ['kru:tɒn] *n* croûton *m*.

crow [krəʊ] ◇ *n* **1.** ORNITH corbeau *m* ▪ [smaller] corneille *f* ▪ **it's 3 miles as the ~ flies** c'est à 3 miles à vol d'oiseau ▪ **he had to eat ~** *US inf* il a dû admettre qu'il avait tort **2.** [sound of cock] chant *m* du coq, cocorico *m* **3.** [of baby] gazouillis *m*.
◇ *vi* (*UK pret* **crowed** *OR* **crew** [kru:]) (*US pret* **crowed**) **1.** [cock] chanter **2.** [baby] gazouiller **3.** [boast] se vanter ▪ **to ~ over sthg** se vanter de qqch.

crowbar ['krəʊbɑ:ʳ] *n* (pince *f* à) levier *m*.

crowd [kraʊd] ◇ *n* **1.** [throng] foule *f*, masse *f* ▪ **there was quite a ~ at the match** il y avait beaucoup de monde au match ▪ **she stands out in a ~** elle se distingue de la masse **2.** *inf* [social group] bande *f* ▪ **to be in with the wrong ~** avoir de mauvaises fréquentations **3.** *fig & pej* [people as a whole] : **the ~** la foule, la masse du peuple ▪ **she always goes with** *OR* **follows the ~** elle suit toujours le mouvement.
◇ *vi* se presser ▪ **to ~ round sb/sthg** se presser autour de qqn/qqch ▪ **they ~ed round to read the poster** ils se sont attroupés pour lire l'affiche ▪ **the reporters ~ed into the room** les journalistes se sont entassés dans la pièce.
◇ *vt* **1.** [cram] serrer, entasser ▪ **people ~ed the streets/the shops** des gens se pressaient dans les rues/les magasins ▪ **the park was ~ed with sunbathers** le parc était plein de gens qui prenaient des bains de soleil **2.** *inf* [jostle] bousculer.

◆ **crowd in** *vi insep* **1.** [enter] entrer en foule, affluer **2.** *fig* [flood in] : **to ~ in on sb** submerger qqn.

◆ **crowd out** ◇ *vi insep* sortir en foule.
◇ *vt sep* : **independent traders are being ~ed out by bigger stores** les petits commerçants sont étouffés par les grands magasins.

crowded ['kraʊdɪd] *adj* **1.** [busy - room, building, bus etc] bondé, plein ; [- street] plein (de monde) ; [- town] encombré (de monde), surpeuplé ▪ **a room ~ with furniture/with people** une pièce encombrée de meubles/pleine de monde ▪ **he has a ~ schedule** son emploi du temps est surchargé **2.** [overpopulated] surpeuplé.

crowdpuller ['kraʊd,pʊləʳ] *n UK inf* **his play is a real ~** sa pièce attire les foules.

crown [kraʊn] ◇ *n* **1.** [headdress] couronne *f* ▪ **to succeed to the ~** accéder à la couronne ▪ **~ of thorns** couronne d'épines **2.** [regal power] couronne *f*, pouvoir *m* royal **3.** [award] prix *m* ▪ **she won the Wimbledon ~ for the second year running** elle a remporté le tournoi de Wimbledon pour la seconde année consécutive **4.** [top - of head] sommet *m* de la tête ; [- of hat] fond *m* ; [- of hill, tree] sommet *m*, cime *f* ; [- of roof] faîte *m* ; [- of road] milieu *m* ; [- of tooth] couronne *f* ▪ ARCHIT [- of arch] clef *f* **5.** [coin] couronne *f* **6.** [outstanding achievement] couronnement *m* **7.** [paper size] couronne *f* **8.** [of anchor] diamant *m*.
◇ *vt* **1.** [confer a title on] couronner, sacrer ▪ **she was ~ed queen/champion** elle fut couronnée reine/championne **2.** [top] couronner ▪ **to ~ a tooth** couronner une dent ▪ **and to ~ it all, it started to rain** *fig* et pour couronner le tout, il s'est mis à pleuvoir **3.** [in draughts] damer **4.** *inf* [hit] flanquer un coup (sur la tête) à.

◆ **Crown** *n* : **the Crown** la Couronne, l'État *m* (monarchique) ▪ **counsel for the Crown** *UK* LAW conseiller *m* juridique de la Couronne ▪ **Crown witness** *UK* LAW témoin *m* à charge.

crown cap *n UK* capsule *f* (de bouteille).

crown colony *n UK* colonie *f* de la Couronne.

crown court *n* ≃ Cour *f* d'assises *(en Angleterre et au Pays de Galles)*.

crowning ['kraʊnɪŋ] ◇ *n* couronnement *m*.

◇ *adj fig* suprême ▪ ~ **glory** [hair] *hum* chevelure *f* ▪ **the ~ glory** *OR* **moment of her career** le plus grand triomphe de sa carrière.

crown jewels *npl* joyaux *mpl* de la Couronne.

crown land *n* terres *fpl* domaniales.

crown prince *n* prince *m* héritier.

crown princess *n* [heir to throne] princesse *f* héritière ▪ [wife of crown prince] princesse *f* royale.

crow's feet *npl* [wrinkles] pattes *fpl* d'oie *(rides)*.

crow's nest *n* NAUT nid *m* de pie.

crozier ['krəʊʒjəʳ] = **crosier**.

CRT [siːɑː'tiː] (*abbrev of* **cathode ray tube**) *n* tube *m* cathodique.

cruces ['kruːsiːz] *pl* ▷ **crux**.

crucial ['kruːʃl] *adj* **1.** [critical] critique, crucial ▪ MED & PHILOS crucial **2.** △ [excellent] d'enfer△.

crucially ['kruːʃəlɪ] *adv* fondamentalement.

crucible ['kruːsɪbl] *n* [vessel] creuset *m* ▪ *fig* [test] (dure) épreuve *f* ▪ **'The Crucible'** ***Miller*** 'les Sorcières de Salem'.

crucifix ['kruːsɪfɪks] *n* christ *m*, crucifix *m* ▪ **(roadside) ~** calvaire *m*.

crucifixion [ˌkruːsɪ'fɪkʃn] *n* crucifiement *m*.
◆ **Crucifixion** *n* : **the Crucifixion** RELIG la crucifixion, la mise en croix.

crucify ['kruːsɪfaɪ] (*pret & pp* **crucified**) *vt* **1.** [execute] crucifier, mettre en croix **2.** *fig* [treat harshly] mettre au pilori ▪ **my mum will ~ us if she finds out!** ma mère va nous étriper si elle découvre ça!

crude [kruːd] ◇ *adj* **1.** [vulgar - person, behaviour] vulgaire, grossier ; [- manners] fruste, grossier ▪ **a ~ remark** une grossièreté **2.** [raw] brut ▪ [sugar] non raffiné **3.** [unsophisticated - tool] grossier, rudimentaire ; [- piece of work] mal fini, sommaire ; [- drawing] grossier ▪ **it was a ~ attempt at self-promotion** c'était une tentative grossière pour se mettre en avant **4.** [stark - colour, light] cru, vif.
◇ *n* = **crude oil**.

crudely ['kruːdlɪ] *adv* **1.** [vulgarly] grossièrement ▪ [bluntly] crûment, brutalement **2.** [unsophisticatedly] grossièrement, sommairement ▪ **a ~ built hut** une cabane grossière.

crudeness ['kruːdnɪs] = **crudity**.

crude oil *n* (pétrole *m*) brut *m*.

crudity ['kruːdɪtɪ] *n* **1.** [vulgarity] grossièreté *f* **2.** [rawness - of material] état *m* brut **3.** [lack of sophistication - of tool] caractère *m* rudimentaire ; [- of drawing, work] manque *m* de fini, caractère *m* sommaire.

cruel [krʊəl] *adj* **1.** [unkind] cruel ▪ **to be ~ to sb** être cruel envers qqn ➲ **you've got to be ~ to be kind** qui aime bien châtie bien *prov* **2.** [painful] douloureux, cruel ▪ **it was a ~ disappointment** ce fut une cruelle déception.

cruelly ['krʊəlɪ] *adv* cruellement ▪ **she was ~ deprived of victory** elle a été rattrapée sur la ligne d'arrivée.

cruelty ['krʊəltɪ] (*pl* **cruelties**) *n* **1.** [gen] cruauté *f* ▪ **~ to animals** la cruauté envers les animaux **2.** LAW sévices *mpl* ▪ **divorce on the grounds of ~** divorce pour sévices **3.** [cruel act] cruauté *f*.

cruet ['kruːɪt] *n* **1.** [for oil, vinegar] petit flacon *m* **2.** [set of condiments] service *m* à condiments **3.** RELIG burette *f*.

Cruft's [krʌfts] *pr n le plus important concours canin de Grande-Bretagne, qui se tient chaque année à Londres.*

cruise [kruːz] ◇ *n* **1.** [sea trip] croisière *f* ▪ **they went on a ~** ils sont partis en *OR* ont fait une croisière **2.** = **cruise missile**.
◇ *vi* **1.** [ship] croiser ▪ [tourists] être en croisière **2.** [car] rouler ▪ [plane] voler ▪ **I ~d through the exam** j'ai trouvé l'examen très facile ▪ [police car, taxi] marauder, être en maraude ▪ **cruising speed** AERON & AUT vitesse *f OR* régime *m* de croisière **3.** *inf* [for sexual partner] draguer.
◇ *vt* **1.** [ocean] croiser dans **2.** *inf* [sexual partner] draguer.

cruise control *n* AUT régulateur *m* d'allure.

cruise missile *n* missile *m* de croisière.

cruiser ['kruːzəʳ] *n* **1.** [warship] croiseur *m* ▪ [pleasure boat] yacht *m* de croisière **2.** *US* [police patrol car] voiture *f* de police (en patrouille).

cruiserweight ['kruːzəweɪt] *n* poids *m* mi-lourd.

cruller ['krʌləʳ] *n US* beignet *m*.

crumb [krʌm] *n* **1.** [of bread] miette *f* ▪ [inside loaf] mie *f* ▪ *fig* [small piece] miette *f*, brin *m* ▪ **a few ~s of information** les bribes d'information ▪ **the news from the hospital didn't offer any ~s of comfort/hope** les nouvelles de l'hôpital n'apportèrent pas le moindre réconfort/espoir **2.** *US inf* [person] nul *m*, nulle *f*.

crumble ['krʌmbl] ◇ *vt* [bread, stock cube] émietter ▪ [earth, plaster] effriter.
◇ *vi* [bread] s'émietter ▪ [plaster] s'effriter ▪ [building] tomber en ruines, se désagréger ▪ [earth, stone] s'ébouler ▪ *fig* [hopes, society] s'effondrer, s'écrouler ▪ **his world was crumbling around him** *fig* tout son petit monde s'écroulait *OR* s'effondrait.
◇ *n* crumble *m (dessert composé d'une couche de compote de fruits recouverte de pâte sablée).*

crumbly ['krʌmblɪ] (*comp* **crumblier**, *superl* **crumbliest**) *adj* friable.

crumbs [krʌmz] *interj UK inf dated* mince, zut.

crummy ['krʌmɪ] (*comp* **crummier**, *superl* **crummiest**) *adj inf* [bad] minable, nul.

crumpet ['krʌmpɪt] *n UK* **1.** [cake] *galette épaisse qu'on mange chaude et beurrée* **2.** △ [women] nanas *fpl*, pépées *fpl*.

crumple ['krʌmpl] ◇ *vt* froisser, friper ▪ **to ~ a piece of paper (up) into a ball** chiffonner un papier.
◇ *vi* **1.** [crease] se froisser, se chiffonner **2.** [collapse] s'effondrer, s'écrouler ▪ **his face ~d and tears came to his eyes** *fig* son visage se contracta et ses yeux se remplirent de larmes.

crunch [krʌntʃ] ◇ *vi* **1.** [gravel, snow] craquer, crisser **2.** [chew] croquer ▪ **to ~ on sthg** croquer qqch.
◇ *vt* **1.** [chew] croquer **2.** [crush underfoot] faire craquer *OR* crisser, écraser **3.** [process - data, numbers] traiter.
◇ *n* **1.** [sound - of teeth] coup *m* de dents ; [- of food] craquement *m* ; [- of gravel, snow] craquement *m*, crissement *m* **2.** *inf* [critical moment] moment *m* critique ▪ **when it comes to the ~** dans une situation critique, au moment crucial.
◇ *adj inf* critique, décisif.
◆ **crunch up** *vt sep* broyer.

crunchy ['krʌntʃɪ] (*comp* **crunchier**, *superl* **crunchiest**) *adj* [food] croquant ▪ [snow, gravel] qui craque *OR* crisse.

crusade [kruː'seɪd] ◇ *n fig* & HIST croisade *f*.
◇ *vi* HIST partir en croisade, être à la croisade ▪ *fig* faire une croisade ▪ **to ~ for/against sthg** mener une croisade pour/contre qqch.

crusader [kruː'seɪdəʳ] *n* HIST croisé *m* ▪ *fig* champion *m*, - onne *f*, militant *m*, - e *f*.

crush [krʌʃ] ◇ *vt* **1.** [smash - gen] écraser, broyer ▪ **~ed ice** glace *f* pilée ▪ **they were ~ed to death** ils sont morts écrasés **2.** [crease] froisser, chiffonner ▪ **~ed velvet** velours *m* frappé **3.** [defeat - enemy] écraser ▪ [suppress - revolt] écraser, réprimer ▪ *fig* [- hopes] écraser ▪ **she felt ~ed by the news** elle a été accablée *OR* atterrée par la nouvelle **4.** [squash, press] serrer ▪ **we were ~ed in the race for the door** nous avons été écrasés dans la ruée vers la porte.
◇ *vi* **1.** [throng] se serrer, s'écraser ▪ **we all ~ed into the lift** nous nous sommes tous entassés dans l'ascenseur **2.** [crease] se froisser.

◇ *n* **1.** [crowd] foule *f*, cohue *f* ■ **in the ~ to enter the stadium** dans la bousculade pour entrer dans le stade **2.** *inf* [infatuation] béguin *m* ■ **to have a ~ on sb** en pincer pour qqn **3.** *UK* [drink] jus *m* de fruit ■ **lemon ~** citron *m* pressé.

crush barrier *n* barrière *f* de sécurité.

crushing ['krʌʃɪŋ] *adj* [defeat] écrasant ■ [remark] cinglant, percutant.

crust [krʌst] ◇ *n* **1.** [of bread, pie] croûte *f* ■ [of snow, ice] couche *f* ■ **a ~ of bread** un croûton, une croûte ■ **the earth's ~** GEOL la croûte *OR* l'écorce terrestre ▶ **to earn a ~** gagner sa croûte **2.** [on wound] croûte *f*, escarre *f* **3.** [on wine] dépôt *m*.
◇ *vt* couvrir d'une croûte.
◇ *vi* former une croûte.

crustacean [krʌ'steɪʃn] ◇ *adj* crustacé.
◇ *n* crustacé *m*.

crusty ['krʌstɪ] (*comp* **crustier**, *superl* **crustiest**) ◇ *adj* **1.** [bread] croustillant **2.** [bad-tempered - person] hargneux, bourru ; [- remark] brusque, sec, sèche *f*.
◇ *n UK inf* jeune *mf* crado.

crutch [krʌtʃ] *n* **1.** [support] support *m*, soutien *m* ■ [for walking] béquille *f* ■ ARCHIT étançon *m* ■ NAUT support *m* ■ **she uses ~es** elle marche avec des béquilles **2.** *fig* soutien *m* **3.** *UK* = **crotch**.

crux [krʌks] (*pl* **cruxes** *OR pl* **cruces** ['kru:si:z]) *n* **1.** [vital point] point *m* crucial *OR* capital ■ [of problem] cœur *m* ■ **the ~ of the matter** le nœud de l'affaire **2.** [in climbing] passage-clef *m*.

cry [kraɪ] ◇ *vi* (*pret & pp* **cried**) **1.** [weep] pleurer ■ **she cried in** *OR* **with frustration** elle pleurait d'impuissance ■ **we laughed until we cried** nous avons pleuré de rire *OR* avons ri aux larmes ■ **to ~ loudly/bitterly** pleurer à chaudes larmes/amèrement ▶ **it's no use ~ing over spilt milk** *prov* ce qui est fait est fait **2.** [call out] crier, pousser un cri ■ **to ~ (out) in pain** pousser un cri de douleur ■ **to ~ for help** crier au secours ▶ **to ~ for the moon** demander la lune *OR* l'impossible **3.** [bird, animal] pousser un cri *OR* des cris ■ [hounds] donner de la voix, aboyer.
◇ *vt* (*pret & pp* **cried**) **1.** [weep] pleurer ■ **she cried herself to sleep** elle s'est endormie en pleurant ■ **he cried tears of joy** il versa des larmes de joie ■ **he was ~ing his heart** *OR* **eyes out** il pleurait toutes les larmes de son corps **2.** [shout] crier ■ **"look", she cried** "regardez", s'écria-t-elle ■ **he cried quits** *OR* **mercy** il s'est avoué vaincu ▶ **to ~ wolf** crier au loup.
◇ *n* (*pl* **cries**) **1.** [exclamation] cri *m* ■ **he heard a ~ for help** il a entendu crier au secours ■ **there have been cries for lower taxes** *fig* on a réclamé une baisse des impôts ■ **to be in full ~** crier à tue-tête **2.** [of birds, animals] cri *m* ■ [of hounds] aboiements *mpl*, voix *f* **3.** [weep] : **to have a good ~** pleurer un bon coup.
◆ **cry down** *vt sep* décrier.
◆ **cry off** *vi insep* [from meeting] se décommander ■ [from promise] se rétracter, se dédire.
◆ **cry out** ◇ *vi insep* pousser un cri ■ **I cried out to them** je les ai appelés ■ **to ~ out against** *fig* protester contre ■ **to ~ out for sthg** demander *OR* réclamer qqch ■ **the system is ~ing out for revision** *OR* **to be revised** *fig* le système a grand besoin d'être révisé ▶ **for ~ing out loud!** *inf* bon sang!
◇ *vt sep* s'écrier ■ **"listen", she cried out** "écoutez", s'écria-t-elle.

crybaby ['kraɪ,beɪbɪ] (*pl* **crybabies**) *n inf* pleurnichard *m*, - e *f*.

crying ['kraɪɪŋ] ◇ *adj* **1.** [person] qui pleure, pleurant **2.** *inf* [as intensifier] criant, flagrant ■ **it's a ~ shame** c'est un scandale.
◇ *n (U)* **1.** [shouting] cri *m*, cris *mpl* **2.** [weeping] pleurs *mpl*.

cryogenic [,kraɪə'dʒenɪk] *adj* cryogène.

cryogenics [,kraɪə'dʒenɪks] *n (sg)* cryogénie *f*, cryologie *f*.

cryonics [kraɪ'ɒnɪks] *n (U)* cryogénisation *f*.

cryosurgery [,kraɪəʊ'sɜ:dʒərɪ] *n* cryo-chirurgie *f*.

crypt [krɪpt] *n* crypte *f*.

cryptic ['krɪptɪk] *adj* [secret] secret, - ète *f* ■ [obscure] énigmatique, sibyllin ■ **~ crossword** *mot-croisé dont les définitions sont des énigmes qu'il faut résoudre*.

cryptically ['krɪptɪklɪ] *adv* [secretly] secrètement ■ [obscurely] énigmatiquement.

crypto- ['krɪptəʊ] *in cpds* crypto- ■ **~fascist** cryptofasciste *mf*.

cryptographer [krɪp'tɒgrəfəʳ] *n* cryptographe *mf*.

cryptography [krɪp'tɒgrəfɪ], **cryptology** [krɪp'tɒlədʒɪ] *n* cryptographie *f*.

crystal ['krɪstl] ◇ *n* **1.** [gen - MINER] cristal *m* **2.** [chip] cristal *m* ■ **salt/snow ~s** cristaux de sel/de neige **3.** *US* [of watch] verre *m* (de montre) **4.** ELECTRON galène *f*.
◇ *adj* [vase, glass, water] de cristal.

crystal ball *n* boule *f* de cristal.

crystal clear *adj* clair comme le jour *OR* comme de l'eau de roche ■ [voice] cristalline.

crystal-gazing *n (U)* [in ball] (art *m* de la) voyance *f* ■ *fig* prédictions *fpl*, prophéties *fpl*.

crystalline ['krɪstəlaɪn] *n* cristallin.

crystallization [,krɪstəlaɪ'zeɪʃn] *n* [gen - SCI] cristallisation *f*.

crystallize, *UK* ise ['krɪstəlaɪz] ◇ *vi liter & fig* se cristalliser.
◇ *vt* cristalliser ■ [sugar] (faire) candir ■ **~d fruit** fruits *mpl* confits.

crystal set *n* poste *m* à galène.

CSE (*abbrev of* **Certificate of Secondary Education**) *n ancien brevet de l'enseignement secondaire en Grande-Bretagne, aujourd'hui remplacé par le GCSE*.

CSEU (*abbrev of* **Confederation of Shipbuilding and Engineering Unions**) *pr n confédération britannique des syndicats de la construction navale et de la mécanique*.

CS gas *n UK* gaz *m* CS *OR* lacrymogène.

CST *n* = **Central Standard Time**.

CSU (*abbrev of* **Civil Service Union**) *pr n syndicat de la fonction publique*.

ct *written abbr of* **carat**.

CT *written abbr of* **Connecticut**.

CTC (*abbrev of* **city technology college**) *n collège technique britannique, généralement établi dans des quartiers défavorisés*.

cu. *written abbr of* **cubic**.

cub [kʌb] *n* **1.** [animal] petit *m*, - e *f* **2.** *inf* [youngster] : **young ~** jeune blanc-bec *m* **3.** [scout] louveteau *m (scout)*.

Cuba ['kju:bə] *pr n* Cuba ■ **in ~** à Cuba.

Cuban ['kju:bən] ◇ *n* Cubain *m*, - e *f*.
◇ *adj* cubain ■ **~ heel** talon *m* cubain ■ **the ~ missile crisis** la crise de Cuba *(conflit américano-soviétique dû à la présence de missiles soviétiques à Cuba (1962))*.

cubbyhole ['kʌbɪhəʊl] *n* **1.** [cupboard] débarras *m*, remise *f* ■ [small room] cagibi *m*, réduit *m* **2.** [in desk] case *f* ■ AUT videpoches *m*.

cube [kju:b] ◇ *n* [gen - MATHS] cube *m*.
◇ *vt* **1.** [cut into cubes] couper en cubes *OR* en dés **2.** MATHS cuber ■ TECH [measure] cuber ■ **3 ~d is 27** 3 cubés/au cube fait 27.

cube root *n* racine *f* cubique.

cubic ['kju:bɪk] *adj* [shape, volume] cubique ■ [measurement] cube ■ **~ equation** MATHS équation *f* du troisième degré ■ **~ metre** mètre *m* cube.

cubicle ['kju:bɪkl] *n* [in dormitory, hospital ward] alcôve *f*, box *m* ■ [in swimming baths, public toilets] cabine *f*.

cubism, Cubism ['kju:bɪzm] *n* cubisme *m*.

cubist, Cubist ['kju:bɪst] ◇ *adj* cubiste.
◇ *n* cubiste *mf*.

cubit ['kju:bɪt] *n* [measurement] coudée *f (unité de mesure)*.

cub master *n* chef *m (des scouts)*.

cub mistress *n* cheftaine *f (des scouts)*.

cub reporter *n* jeune journaliste *mf*.

cub scout, Cub Scout *n* louveteau *m (scout)*.

cuckold ['kʌkəʊld] ◇ *n* (mari *m*) cocu *m*.
◇ *vt* faire cocu, cocufier.

cuckoo ['kʊku:] ◇ *n* (*pl* **cuckoos**) ORNITH [bird, sound] coucou *m*.
◇ *adj inf* [mad] loufoque, toqué.

cuckoo clock *n* coucou *m (pendule)*.

cuckoopint ['kʊku:paɪnt] *n* pied-de-veau *m*.

cucumber ['kju:kʌmbəʳ] *n* concombre *m*.

cud [kʌd] *n* bol *m* alimentaire *(d'un ruminant)*.

cuddle ['kʌdl] ◇ *vi* se faire un câlin, se câliner.
◇ *vt* câliner, caresser ■ [child] bercer *(dans ses bras)*.
◇ *n* câlin *m*, caresse *f*, caresses *fpl* ■ **they were having a ~** ils se faisaient un câlin ■ **she gave the child a ~** elle a fait un câlin à l'enfant.
➡ **cuddle up** *vi insep* se blottir, se pelotonner ■ **she ~d up close to him** elle se blottit contre lui.

cuddly ['kʌdlɪ] (*comp* **cuddlier**, *superl* **cuddliest**) *adj* [child, animal] câlin.

cuddly toy *n* peluche *f*.

cudgel ['kʌdʒəl] ◇ *n* gourdin *m*, trique *f* ■ **to take up the ~s for sb** *OR* **on behalf of sb** prendre fait et cause pour qqn.
◇ *vt* (*UK pret & pp* **cudgelled**, *cont* **cudgelling**, *US pret & pp* **cudgeled**, *cont* **cudgeling**) battre à coups de gourdin.

cue [kju:] ◇ *n* **1.** CIN & THEAT [verbal] réplique *f* ■ [action] signal *m* ■ MUS signal *m* d'entrée ■ **to give sb their ~** donner la réplique à qqn ■ **he took his ~** il a entamé sa réplique ■ **her yawn was our ~ to leave** nous avons compris qu'il fallait partir quand elle s'est mise à bâiller **2.** *fig* [signal] signal *m* ■ **on ~** au bon moment ■ **to take one's ~ from sb** prendre exemple sur qqn **3.** [for snooker etc] queue *f (de billard)* **4.** [of hair] queue *f (de cheval)*.
◇ *vi* [in snooker, pool] queuter.
◇ *vt* [prompt] donner le signal à ■ THEAT donner la réplique à.
➡ **cue in** *vt sep* [gen - RADIO] & TV donner le signal à ■ THEAT donner la réplique à.

cue ball *n* bille *f* de joueur.

cuff [kʌf] ◇ *n* **1.** [of sleeve] poignet *m*, manchette *f* ■ [of glove] poignet *m* ■ [of coat] parement *m* ■ *US* [of trousers] revers *m* ■ **off the ~** à l'improviste ■ **she was speaking off the ~** elle improvisait son discours, elle faisait un discours improvisé **2.** [blow] gifle *f*, claque *f*.
◇ *vt* **1.** [hit] gifler, donner une gifle *OR* une claque à **2.** *inf* [handcuff] mettre *OR* passer les menottes à **3.** *US* [trousers] faire un revers à.
➡ **cuffs** *npl inf* [handcuffs] menottes *fpl*.

cuff link *n* bouton *m* de manchette.

cu.in. *written abbr of* **cubic inch(es)**.

cuisine [kwɪ'zi:n] *n* cuisine *f*.

cul-de-sac ['kʌldəsæk] *n* cul-de-sac *m*, impasse *f* ■ **'cul-de-sac'** 'voie sans issue'.

culinary ['kʌlɪnərɪ] *adj* culinaire.

cull [kʌl] ◇ *vt* **1.** [sample] sélectionner **2.** [remove from herd] éliminer, supprimer ■ [slaughter - seals] abattre, massacrer **3.** [gather - flowers, fruit] cueillir.
◇ *n* **1.** [slaughter] massacre *m* **2.** [animal] animal *m* à éliminer.

Culloden Moor [kə'lɒdn'mɔ:ʳ] *pr n bataille à l'issue de laquelle, en 1746, les partisans écossais de Charles-Édouard Stuart furent vaincus par l'armée anglaise.*

culminate ['kʌlmɪneɪt] *vi* ASTRON culminer.
➡ **culminate in** *vt insep* : **the demonstration ~d in a riot** la manifestation s'est terminée en émeute.

culmination [,kʌlmɪ'neɪʃn] *n* **1.** [climax - of career] apogée *m* ; [- of efforts] maximum *m* ; [- of disagreement] point *m* culminant **2.** ASTRON culmination *f*.

culottes [kju:'lɒts] *npl* jupe-culotte *f*.

culpable ['kʌlpəbl] *adj fml* coupable ■ LAW : **~ homicide** homicide *m* volontaire.

culprit ['kʌlprɪt] *n* coupable *mf*.

cult [kʌlt] ◇ *n fig* & RELIG culte *m* ■ **personality ~** culte *m* de la personnalité.
◇ *comp* [book, film] culte ■ **~ figure** idole *f* ■ **the film has a ~ following** c'est un film culte.

cultivate ['kʌltɪveɪt] *vt* **1.** [land] cultiver, exploiter ■ [crop] cultiver **2.** *fig* [idea, person] cultiver ■ **reading is the best way to ~ the mind** la lecture est le meilleur moyen de se cultiver (l'esprit).

cultivated ['kʌltɪveɪtɪd] *adj* [land] cultivé, exploité ■ [person] cultivé ■ [voice] distingué.

cultivation [,kʌltɪ'veɪʃn] *n* **1.** [of land, crops] culture *f* ■ **fields under ~** cultures *fpl* **2.** *fig* [of taste] éducation *f* ■ [of relations] entretien *m*.

cultivator ['kʌltɪveɪtəʳ] *n* [person] cultivateur *m*, - trice *f* ■ [tool] cultivateur *m* ■ [power-driven] motoculteur *m*.

cultural ['kʌltʃərəl] *adj* **1.** [events, background] culturel ■ **~ integration** acculturation *f* ■ **a ~ desert** *fig* un désert culturel **2.** AGRIC de culture, cultural.

culturally ['kʌltʃərəlɪ] *adv* culturellement.

Cultural Revolution *n* : **the ~** la Révolution culturelle.

culture ['kʌltʃəʳ] ◇ *n* **1.** [civilization, learning] culture *f* ■ **a man of ~** un homme cultivé *OR* qui a de la culture **2.** AGRIC [of land, crops] culture *f* ■ [of animals] élevage *m* ■ [of fowl] aviculture *f* **3.** BIOL culture *f*.
◇ *vt* [plants] cultiver ■ [animals] élever ■ [bacteria] faire une culture de.

cultured ['kʌltʃəd] *adj* **1.** [refined - person] cultivé, lettré **2.** [grown artificially] cultivé ■ **~ pearls** perles *fpl* de culture.

culture gap *n* fossé *m* culturel.

culture medium *n* milieu *m* de culture.

culture shock *n* choc *m* culturel.

culture vulture *n inf hum* fana *mf* de culture, culturophage *mf*.

cum [kʌm] *prep* avec ■ **a kitchen-~-dining area** une cuisine *f* avec coin-repas ■ **he's a teacher-~-philosopher** il est philosophe aussi bien qu'enseignant.

cumbersome ['kʌmbəsəm] *adj* [bulky] encombrant, embarrassant ■ *fig* [process, system, style] lourd, pesant.

cumin ['kʌmɪn] *n* cumin *m*.

cummerbund ['kʌməbʌnd] *n* large ceinture *f (de smoking)*.

cumulative ['kju:mjʊlətɪv] *adj* cumulatif ■ **~ evidence** LAW preuve *f* par accumulation de témoignages ■ **~ interest** FIN intérêts *mpl* cumulatifs ■ **~ voting** POL vote *m* plural.

cumuli ['kju:mjʊlaɪ] *pl* ▷ **cumulus**.

cumulonimbus [,kju:mjʊləʊ'nɪmbəs] (*pl* **cumulonimbi** [-baɪ] *OR pl* **cumulonimbuses**) *n* cumulo-nimbus *m*.

cumulus ['kju:mjʊləs] (*pl* **cumuli** ['kju:mjʊlaɪ]) *n* cumulus *m*.

cuneiform ['kju:nɪɪfɔ:m] ◇ *adj* cunéiforme.
◇ *n* écriture *f* cunéiforme.

cunnilingus [,kʌnɪ'lɪŋgəs] *n* cunnilingus *m*.

cunning ['kʌnɪŋ] ◇ *adj* **1.** [shrewd] astucieux, malin, - igne *f* ■ *pej* rusé, fourbe ■ **he's as ~ as a fox** il est rusé comme un renard **2.** [skilful] habile, astucieux **3.** *US* [cute] mignon, charmant.
◇ *n* **1.** [guile] finesse *f*, astuce *f* ■ *pej* ruse *f*, fourberie *f* **2.** [skill] habileté *f*, adresse *f*.

cunningly ['kʌnɪŋlɪ] *adv* **1.** [shrewdly] astucieusement, finement ▪ *pej* avec ruse *OR* fourberie **2.** [skilfully] habilement, astucieusement.

cunt▲ [kʌnt] *n* **1.** [vagina] con▲ *m*, chatte▲ *f* **2.** [man] enculé▲ *m* ▪ [woman] salope▲ *f*.

cup [kʌp] ◇ *n* **1.** [for drinking, cupful] tasse *f* ▪ RELIG calice *m* ▪ **a ~ of coffee** une tasse de café ▶ **my ~ runneth over** *lit* mon bonheur est complet *OR* parfait ▪ **he drained the ~ of sorrow** *lit* il a bu la coupe jusqu'à la lie ▪ **jazz isn't everyone's ~ of tea** *inf* tout le monde n'aime pas le jazz
2. SPORT [trophy, competition] coupe *f*
3. [shape - of plant] corolle *f* ; [- of bone] cavité *f* articulaire, glène *f* ; [- of bra] bonnet *m*
4. [punch] boisson *f* alcoolisée ▪ **champagne ~** punch *m* au champagne ▪ **fruit ~** cocktail *m* aux fruits *(pouvant contenir de l'alcool)*
5. TECH godet *m*, cuvette *f*
6. *US* [in golf] trou *m*.
◇ *comp* **1.** SPORT [winners, holders, match] de coupe
2. [handle] de tasse ▪ [rack] pour tasses.
◇ *vt* (*pret & pp* **cupped**, *cont* **cupping**) [hands] mettre en coupe ▪ [hold] : **to ~ one's hands around sthg** mettre ses mains autour de qqch ▪ **he cupped a hand to his ear** il mit sa main derrière son oreille ▪ **she cupped her hands around her mouth and shouted** elle mit ses mains en porte-voix et cria ▪ **he sat with his chin cupped in his hand** il était assis, le menton dans le creux de sa main.

cupboard ['kʌbəd] *n* [on wall] placard *m* ▪ [free-standing - for dishes, pans] buffet *m*, placard *m* ; [- for clothes] placard *m*, armoire *f* ▪ **the ~ is bare** *fig* il n'y a rien à se mettre sous la dent.

cupboard love *n UK* amour *m* intéressé.

cup cake *n* [cake] petit gâteau *m*.

cup final *n* finale *f* de la coupe ▪ **the Cup Final** *UK* la finale de la Coupe de Football.

cup finalist *n* finaliste *mf* de la coupe.

cupful ['kʌpfʊl] *n* tasse *f*.

Cupid ['kju:pɪd] *pr n* MYTH Cupidon *m* ▪ **to play ~** *fig* jouer les entremetteurs *mpl*, - euses *f*.
◆ **cupid** *n* ART [cherub] chérubin *m*, amour *m*.

cupidity [kju:'pɪdɪtɪ] *n* cupidité *f*.

cupola ['kju:pələ] *n* **1.** ARCHIT [ceiling, roof] coupole *f*, dôme *m* ▪ [tower] belvédère *m* **2.** METALL [furnace] cubilot *m*.

cuppa ['kʌpə] *n UK inf* tasse *f* de thé.

cup tie *n* match *m* de coupe.

cup-tied *adj* [player] disqualifié pour un match de coupe.

cur [kɜ:ʳ] *n* **1.** [dog] (chien *m*) bâtard *m*, sale chien *m* **2.** [person] malotru *m*, - e *f*, roquet *m*.

curable ['kjʊərəbl] *adj* guérissable, curable.

curate ['kjʊərət] *n* vicaire *m (de l'Église anglicane)*.

curate's egg *n UK* **it's a bit of a ~** il y a du bon et du mauvais.

curative ['kjʊərətɪv] *adj* curatif.

curator [,kjʊə'reɪtəʳ] *n* **1.** [of museum] conservateur *m*, - trice *f* **2.** *Scotland* [guardian] curateur *m*, - trice *f*.

curb [kɜ:b] ◇ *n* **1.** [restraint] frein *m* ▪ **a ~ on trade** une restriction au commerce **2.** [on harness] : **~ (bit)** mors *m* ▪ **~ (chain)** gourmette *f* ▪ **~ reins** rênes *fpl* de filet **3.** [of well] margelle *f* **4.** *US* = **kerb**.
◇ *vt* **1.** [restrain - emotion] refréner, maîtriser ; [- expenses] restreindre, mettre un frein à ; [- child] modérer, freiner ▪ **~ your tongue!** mesure tes paroles! **2.** [horse] mettre un mors à **3.** *US* **'~ your dog'** 'votre chien doit faire ses besoins dans le caniveau'.

curbstone ['kɜ:bstəʊn] *US* = **kerbstone**.

curd [kɜ:d] *n (usu pl)* [of milk] caillot *m*, grumeau *m* ▪ **~s** lait *m* caillé, caillebotte *f* ▪ **~s and whey** lait caillé sucré.

curd cheese *n* fromage *m* blanc battu.

curdle ['kɜ:dl] ◇ *vi* [milk] cailler ▪ [sauce] tourner ▪ [mayonnaise] tomber ▪ **his screams made my blood ~** *fig* ses cris m'ont glacé le sang.
◇ *vt* [milk] cailler ▪ [sauce] faire tourner ▪ [mayonnaise] faire tomber ▪ **the thought's enough to ~ your blood** *fig* c'est une idée à vous glacer le sang.

cure [kjʊəʳ] ◇ *vt* **1.** [disease, person] guérir ▪ *fig* [problem] éliminer, remédier à ▪ **he was ~d of cancer** il a été guéri du cancer ▪ **his experiences in politics ~d him of all his illusions** *fig* son expérience de la politique lui a fait perdre toutes ses illusions ▶ **what can't be ~d must be endured** *prov* il faut faire avec **2.** [tobacco, meat, fish - gen] traiter ; [- with salt] saler ; [- by smoking] fumer ; [- by drying] sécher.
◇ *n* **1.** [remedy] remède *m*, cure *f* ▪ **a ~ for the common cold** un remède contre le rhume de cerveau ▪ **there's no known ~** on ne connaît pas de remède ▪ **to take** *OR* **to follow a ~** faire une cure ▪ **a ~ for all ills** *fig* la panacée **2.** [recovery] guérison *f* ▪ **to be beyond** *OR* **past ~** [person] être incurable ; *fig* [problem, situation] être irrémédiable **3.** RELIG : **the ~ of souls** la charge d'âmes.

cure-all *n* panacée *f*.

curfew ['kɜ:fju:] *n* couvre-feu *m* ▪ **the authorities imposed a/lifted the ~** les autorités ont imposé/levé le couvre-feu.

curio ['kjʊərɪəʊ] (*pl* **curios**) *n* curiosité *f*, bibelot *m*.

curiosity [,kjʊərɪ'ɒsətɪ] (*pl* **curiosities**) *n* **1.** [interest] curiosité *f* ▪ **out of ~** par curiosité ▶ **~ killed the cat** *prov* la curiosité est un vilain défaut *prov* **2.** [novelty - object] curiosité *f* ; [- person] bête *f* curieuse.

curious ['kjʊərɪəs] *adj* **1.** [inquisitive] curieux ▪ **I'm ~ to see/know** je suis curieux de voir/savoir **2.** [strange] curieux, singulier.

curiously ['kjʊərɪəslɪ] *adv* **1.** [inquisitively] avec curiosité **2.** [strangely] curieusement, singulièrement ▪ **~ enough** chose bizarre *OR* curieuse.

curl [kɜ:l] ◇ *vi* **1.** [hair] friser ▪ [loosely] boucler **2.** [paper, leaf] se recroqueviller, se racornir ▪ [lip] se retrousser **3.** [road] serpenter ▪ [smoke] monter en spirale **4.** SPORT jouer au curling.
◇ *vt* **1.** [hair] friser ▪ [loosely] (faire) boucler **2.** [paper] enrouler ▪ [ribbon] faire boucler ▪ [lip] retrousser ▪ **he ~ed his lip in scorn** il a fait une moue de mépris.
◇ *n* **1.** [of hair] boucle *f* (de cheveux) **2.** [spiral] courbe *f* ▪ [of smoke] spirale *f* ▪ [of wave] ondulation *f* ▪ **with a scornful ~ of the lip** *fig* avec une moue méprisante.
◆ **curl up** ◇ *vi insep* **1.** [leaf, paper] s'enrouler, se recroqueviller ▪ [bread] se racornir **2.** [person] se pelotonner ▪ [cat] se mettre en boule, se pelotonner ▪ [dog] se coucher en rond ▪ **the cat was sleeping ~ed up in a ball** le chat dormait roulé en boule ▪ **I just wanted to ~ up and die** *fig* [in shame] j'aurais voulu rentrer sous terre.
◇ *vt sep* enrouler ▪ **to ~ o.s. up** [person] se pelotonner ; [cat] se mettre en boule, se pelotonner ; [dog] se coucher en rond.

curler ['kɜ:ləʳ] *n* **1.** [for hair] bigoudi *m*, rouleau *m* **2.** SPORT joueur *m*, - euse *f* de curling.

curlew ['kɜ:lju:] *n* courlis *m*.

curlicue ['kɜ:lɪkju:] *n* [in design, handwriting] enjolivure *f* ▪ [in skating] figure *f* (compliquée).

curling ['kɜ:lɪŋ] *n* SPORT curling *m*.

curling iron, curling tongs *(npl)* *n* fer *m* à friser.

curly ['kɜ:lɪ] (*comp* **curlier**, *superl* **curliest**) *adj* [hair - tight] frisé ; [- loose] bouclé ▪ **~ lettuce** (laitue *f*) frisée *f*.

curly kale *n* chou *m* frisé.

currant ['kʌrənt] *n* **1.** BOT [fruit] groseille *f* ▪ **~ bush** groseiller *m* **2.** [dried grape] raisin *m* de Corinthe.

currant bun *n* petit pain *m* aux raisins.

currency ['kʌrənsɪ] (*pl* **currencies**) *n* **1.** ECON & FIN monnaie *f*, devise *f* ▪ **he has no Spanish ~** il n'a pas d'argent espagnol ▪ **this coin is no longer legal ~** cette pièce n'a plus cours (légal)

OR n'est plus en circulation ■ ~ **unit** unité *f* monétaire **2.** *fig* [prevalence] cours *m*, circulation *f* ■ **the theory has gained ~** cette théorie s'est répandue.

current ['kʌrənt] <> *n* [gen - ELEC] courant *m* ■ *fig* [trend] cours *m*, tendance *f* ■ **to go against the ~** *liter* remonter le courant ; *fig* aller à contre-courant ■ **to go with the ~** *liter* & *fig* suivre le courant.
<> *adj* **1.** [widespread] courant, commun ■ **the ~ theory** la théorie actuelle ■ **it's in ~ use** c'est d'usage courant ■ **words that are in ~ use** des mots courants OR qui s'emploient couramment **2.** [most recent - fashion, trend] actuel ; [- price] courant ■ **the ~ issue of this magazine** le dernier numéro de cette revue ■ **the ~ month** le mois courant OR en cours ■ **the ~ exhibition at the Louvre** l'exposition qui a lieu en ce moment au Louvre ■ **his ~ girlfriend** la fille avec qui il est en ce moment, sa copine du moment ■ **the ~ rate of exchange** FIN le cours actuel du change.

current account *n UK* compte *m* courant.

current affairs <> *npl* l'actualité *f*, les questions *fpl* d'actualité.
<> *comp* [programme, magazine] d'actualités.

current assets *npl* actif *m* de roulement.

current liabilities *npl* passif *m* exigible à court terme.

currently ['kʌrəntlɪ] *adv* actuellement, à présent.

curricular [kə'rɪkjələr] *adj* au programme.

curriculum [kə'rɪkjələm] (*pl* **curricula** [-lə] OR *pl* **curriculums**) *n* programme *m* d'enseignement ■ **the maths ~** le programme de maths.

curriculum vitae [-'vi:taɪ] (*pl* **curricula vitae**) *n UK* curriculum *m* (vitae).

curried ['kʌrɪd] *adj* au curry OR cari ■ **~ eggs** des œufs au curry OR à l'indienne.

curry ['kʌrɪ] <> *n* (*pl* **curries**) CULIN curry *m*, cari *m* ■ **chicken ~** curry de poulet.
<> *vt* (*pret* & *pp* **curried**) **1.** CULIN accommoder au curry **2.** [horse] étriller ■ [leather] corroyer ■ **he's trying to ~ favour with the boss** il cherche à se faire bien voir du patron.

currycomb ['kʌrɪkəum] *n* étrille *f*.

curry powder *n* curry *m*, cari *m*.

curse [kɜ:s] <> *n* **1.** [evil spell] malédiction *f* ■ **to call down** OR **to put a ~ on sb** maudire qqn ■ **the town is under a ~** la ville est sous le coup d'une malédiction **2.** [swearword] juron *m*, imprécation *f* ■ **~s!** *inf* zut!, mince alors! **3.** *fig* [bane] fléau *m*, calamité *f* **4.** *inf euph* [menstruation] : **the ~** les règles *fpl*.
<> *vt* **1.** [damn] maudire ■ **~ him!** maudit soit-il! **2.** [swear at] injurier **3.** [afflict] affliger ■ **he's ~d with a bad temper** il est affligé d'un mauvais caractère.
<> *vi* [swear] jurer, blasphémer.

cursed ['kɜ:sɪd] *adj* maudit.

cursive ['kɜ:sɪv] <> *adj* cursif.
<> *n* (écriture *f*) cursive *f*.

cursor ['kɜ:sər] *n* curseur *m*.

cursory ['kɜ:sərɪ] *adj* [superficial] superficiel ■ [hasty] hâtif ■ **she gave the painting only a ~ glance** elle n'a jeté qu'un bref coup d'œil au tableau.

curt [kɜ:t] *adj* [person, reply, manner] brusque, sec, sèche *f*.

curtail [kɜ:'teɪl] *vt* **1.** [cut short - story, visit, studies] écourter **2.** [reduce - expenses] réduire, rogner ; [- power, freedom] limiter, réduire.

curtailment [kɜ:'teɪlmənt] *n* **1.** [of studies, visit] raccourcissement *m* **2.** [of expenses] réduction *f* ■ [of power, freedom] limitation *f*, réduction *f*.

curtain ['kɜ:tn] <> *n* **1.** [gen - THEAT] rideau *m* ■ *fig* rideau *m*, voile *m* ▶ **if she finds out, it's ~s for us** *inf* si elle apprend ça, on est fichus **2.** THEAT [for actor] rappel *m* ■ **the singer took four ~s** le chanteur a été rappelé quatre fois.
<> *vt* garnir de rideaux.
◆ **curtain off** *vt sep* séparer par un rideau.

curtain call *n* rappel *m* ■ **she took four ~s** elle a été rappelée quatre fois.

curtain hook *n* crochet *m* de rideau.

curtain rail *n* tringle *f* à rideau OR à rideaux.

curtain raiser *n* THEAT lever *m* de rideau ■ *fig* événement *m* avant-coureur, prélude *m*.

curtain ring *n* anneau *m* de rideau.

curtain rod = **curtain rail**.

curtly ['kɜ:tlɪ] *adv* [bluntly - say, reply] avec brusquerie, sèchement, sans ménagement.

curtness ['kɜ:tnɪs] *n* [bluntness - of tone, reply, manner, person] brusquerie *f*, sécheresse *f*.

curtsey, curtsy ['kɜ:tsɪ] <> *n* (*pl* **curtseys** OR *pl* **curtsies**) révérence *f* ■ **she made** OR **gave a ~** elle a fait une révérence.
<> *vi* (*pret* & *pp* **curtseyed** OR **curtsied**) faire une révérence.

curvaceous [kɜ:'veɪʃəs] *adj hum* bien fait.

curvature ['kɜ:vətjər] *n* [gen] courbure *f* ■ **the ~ of space** la courbure de l'espace ‖ MED déviation *f* ■ **~ of the spine** [abnormal] déviation de la colonne vertébrale, scoliose *f*.

curve [kɜ:v] <> *n* **1.** [gen] courbe *f* ■ [in road] tournant *m*, virage *m* ■ ARCHIT [of arch] voussure *f* ■ [of beam] cambrure *f* ■ **a woman's ~s** les rondeurs *fpl* d'une femme **2.** MATHS courbe *f* **3.** *US* SPORT balle *f* coupée ■ **to throw sb a ~** *fig* prendre qqn de court.
<> *vi* [gen] se courber ■ [road] être en courbe, faire une courbe ■ **the path ~d round to the left** le chemin tournait vers la gauche.
<> *vt* [gen] courber ■ TECH cintrer.

curveball ['kɜ:vbɔ:l] *n fig* ▶ **to throw a ~ at sb, to throw sb a ~** prendre qn au dépourvu.

curved [kɜ:vd] *adj* [gen] courbe ■ [edge] arrondi ■ [road] en courbe ■ [convex] convexe ■ TECH cintré.

curvilinear [,kɜ:vɪ'lɪnɪər] *adj* curviligne.

curvy ['kɜ:vɪ] (*comp* **curvier**, *superl* **curviest**) *adj* **1.** [road, line] sinueux **2.** *inf* [woman] bien fait.

cushion ['kuʃn] <> *n* **1.** [pillow] coussin *m* ■ *fig* tampon *m* ■ **a ~ of air** *fig* un coussin d'air **2.** [in snooker, billiards etc] bande *f*.
<> *vt* **1.** [sofa] mettre des coussins à ■ [seat] rembourrer ■ TECH matelasser **2.** *fig* [shock, blow] amortir ■ **to ~ a fall** amortir une chute *fig* **to ~ the blow** dire, faire qqch pour rendre une mauvaise nouvelle moins pénible.

cushy ['kuʃɪ] (*comp* **cushier**, *superl* **cushiest**) *adj inf* peinard, pépère ■ **a ~ job** une bonne planque.

cusp [kʌsp] *n* ANAT & BOT cuspide *f* ■ ASTRON [of moon] cuspide *f* ■ ASTROL corne *f*.

cuspidor ['kʌspɪdɔ:r] *n US* crachoir *m*.

cuss [kʌs] *inf* <> *vi* jurer, blasphémer.
<> *vt* injurier.
<> *n* **1.** [oath] juron *m* **2.** [person] type *m pej*.
◆ **cuss out** *vt sep inf US* **to ~ sb out** traiter qqn de tous les noms.

cussed ['kʌsɪd] *adj inf* **1.** [obstinate] têtu, entêté **2.** [cursed] sacré.

custard ['kʌstəd] *n* **1.** [sauce] *crème sucrée épaisse servie chaude ou froide*, ≃ crème *f* anglaise **2.** [dessert] crème *f* renversée, flan *m*.

custard apple *n* anone *f*.

custard cream *n* biscuit *m* fourré à la vanille.

custard pie *n* tarte *f* à la crème.

custard powder *n* ≃ crème *f* anglaise instantanée.

custard tart = **custard pie**.

Custer ['kʌstər] *pr n* Custer ■ **~'s Last Stand** *expression désignant la bataille de Little Bighorn*.

custodial [kʌ'stəudjəl] *adj* **1.** LAW de prison ■ **~ sentence** peine *f* de prison **2.** [guarding] : **~ staff** personnel *m* de surveillance.

custodian [kʌ'stəudjən] *n* **1.** [of building] gardien *m*, - enne *f* ■ [of museum] conservateur *m*, - trice *f* ■ [of prisoner] gardien *m*, - enne *f*, surveillant *m*, - e *f* **2.** *fig* [of morals, tradition] gardien *m*, - enne *f*, protecteur *m*, - trice *f*.

custodianship [kʌ'stəudjənʃɪp] *n* **1.** [guarding] surveillance *f* **2.** *UK* LAW *garde d'un enfant à long terme sans obligation d'adoption.*

custody ['kʌstədɪ] (*pl* **custodies**) *n* **1.** [care] garde *f* ■ **the son is in the ~ of his mother** le fils est sous la garde de sa mère ■ **to be given** *OR* **awarded ~ of a child** LAW obtenir la garde d'un enfant ■ **in safe ~** sous bonne garde **2.** [detention] garde *f* à vue ■ [imprisonment] emprisonnement *m* ■ [before trial] détention *f* préventive ■ **the police held her in ~** la police l'a mise en garde à vue ■ **he was taken into (police) ~** il a été mis en état d'arrestation.

custom ['kʌstəm] *n* **1.** [tradition] coutume *f*, usage *m* ■ **it is the ~ to eat fish on Friday** l'usage veut qu'on mange du poisson le vendredi ■ **as ~ has it** selon la coutume *OR* les us et coutumes **2.** COMM [trade] clientèle *f* ■ **they have a lot of foreign ~** ils ont beaucoup de clients étrangers ■ **I'll take my ~ elsewhere** je vais me fournir ailleurs **3.** LAW coutume *f*, droit *m* coutumier.

customary ['kʌstəmrɪ] *adj fml* **1.** [traditional] coutumier, habituel ■ [usual] habituel ■ **as is ~** comme le veut l'usage ■ **it is ~ to tip taxi drivers** l'usage *OR* la coutume veut que l'on donne un pourboire aux chauffeurs de taxi **2.** LAW coutumier.

custom-built *adj* (fait) sur commande.

customer ['kʌstəməʳ] *n* **1.** [client] client *m*, - e *f* **2.** *inf* [character] type *m* *pej* ■ **she's a cool ~** elle en prend à son aise.

customer services *npl* service *m* (à la) clientèle.

customize, *UK* **ise** ['kʌstəmaɪz] *vt* [make to order] faire *OR* fabriquer *OR* construire sur commande ■ [personalize] personnaliser ■ **~d software** COMPUT logiciel *m* sur mesure.

custom-made *adj* [clothing] (fait) sur mesure ■ [other articles] (fait) sur commande.

customs ['kʌstəmz] *npl* **1.** [authorities, checkpoint] douane *f* ■ **to clear** *OR* **go through ~** passer la douane ⊳ **Customs and Excise** *UK* ≃ la Régie **2.** [duty] droits *mpl* de douane.

customs duty *n* droit *m* *OR* droits *mpl* de douane.

customs house *n* (poste *m* *OR* bureau *m* de) douane *f*.

customs officer *n* douanier *m*, - ère *f*.

customs union *n* union *f* douanière.

cut [kʌt] ◇ *vt* (*pret & pp* **cut**, *cont* **cutting**) **1.** [incise, slash, sever] couper ■ **~ the box open with the knife** ouvrez la boîte avec le couteau ■ **he fell and ~ his knee (open)** il s'est ouvert le genou en tombant ■ **she ~ her hand** elle s'est coupé la main *OR* à la main ■ **he ~ his wrists** il s'est ouvert *OR* taillé les veines ■ **they ~ his throat** ils lui ont coupé la gorge, ils l'ont égorgé ■ **they ~ the prisoners free** *OR* **loose** ils ont détaché les prisonniers ▌*fig* **the atmosphere was so tense, you could ~ it with a knife** l'atmosphère était extrêmement tendue
2. [divide into parts] couper, découper ■ [meat] découper ■ [slice] découper en tranches ■ **she ~ articles from the paper** elle découpait des articles dans le journal ■ **~ the cake in half/in three pieces** coupez le gâteau en deux/en trois ■ **the enemy ~ the army to pieces** *fig* l'ennemi a taillé l'armée en pièces ■ **the critics ~ the play to pieces** *fig* les critiques ont esquinté la pièce
3. [trim - grass, lawn] tondre ; [- bush, tree] tailler ■ [reap - crop] couper, faucher ■ **I ~ my nails/my hair** je me suis coupé les ongles/les cheveux ■ **you've had your hair ~** vous vous êtes fait couper les cheveux
4. [shape - dress, suit] couper ; [- diamond, glass, key] tailler ; [- screw] fileter ■ [dig - channel, tunnel] creuser, percer ■ [engrave] graver ■ [sculpt] sculpter ■ **steps had been ~ in the rock** on avait taillé des marches dans le rocher ⊳ **you must ~ your coat according to your cloth** il ne faut pas vivre au-dessus de ses moyens
5. [cross, traverse] couper, croiser ■ MATHS couper ■ **where the path ~s the road** à l'endroit où le chemin coupe la route
6. [interrupt] interrompre, couper ■ **to ~ sb short** couper la parole à qqn ■ **we had to ~ our visit short** nous avons dû écourter notre visite ■ **his career was tragically ~ short by illness** sa carrière a été tragiquement interrompue par la maladie ⊳ **to ~ a long story short, I left** bref *OR* en deux mots, je suis parti
7. [stop] arrêter, cesser ■ **he ~ working weekends** il a arrêté de travailler le weekend
8. [switch off] couper ■ **he ~ the engine** il a coupé *OR* arrêté le moteur
9. [reduce] réduire, diminuer ■ **to ~ prices** casser les prix ■ **the athlete ~ 5 seconds off the world record** *OR* **~ the world record by 5 seconds** l'athlète a amélioré le record mondial de 5 secondes
10. [edit out] faire des coupures dans, réduire ■ **the censors ~ all scenes of violence** la censure a coupé *OR* supprimé toutes les scènes de violence
11. [hurt feelings of] blesser profondément
12. *inf* [ignore, snub] : **they ~ me (dead) in the street** dans la rue ils ont fait comme s'ils ne me voyaient pas
13. *inf* [absent oneself from - meeting, appointment etc] manquer (volontairement), sauter ■ **I had to ~ lunch in order to get there on time** j'ai dû me passer de déjeuner pour arriver à l'heure ■ **to ~ class** *OR* **school** sécher les cours
14. [tooth] percer ■ **a pianist who ~ her teeth on Bach** *inf fig* une pianiste qui s'est fait la main sur du Bach
15. [dilute] couper
16. [record, track] graver, faire
17. [pack of cards] couper
18. CIN [film] monter
19. MED [incise] inciser ■ VET [castrate] châtrer
20. SPORT [ball] couper
21. *phr* **to ~ the ground from under sb's feet** couper l'herbe sous le pied de qqn ■ **he couldn't ~ the mustard** *US* il n'était pas à la hauteur ■ **to ~ sthg fine** compter un peu juste, ne pas se laisser de marge ■ **that argument ~s no ice with me** *inf* cet argument ne m'impressionne pas ■ **to ~ one's losses** sauver les meubles ■ **to ~ a caper** *OR* **capers** [skip] faire des cabrioles, gambader ; [fool around] faire l'idiot ■ **to ~ a corner** AUT prendre un virage à la corde, couper un virage ; *fig* sauter des étapes.
◇ *vi* (*pret & pp* **cut**, *cont* **cutting**) **1.** [incise, slash] couper, trancher ■ **~ around the edge** découpez *OR* coupez en suivant le bord ■ **she ~ into the bread** elle a entamé le pain ■ **the rope ~ into my wrists** la corde m'a coupé *OR* cisaillé les poignets ■ **he ~ through all the red tape** *fig* il s'est dispensé de toutes les formalités administratives ■ **the yacht ~ through the waves** *fig* le yacht fendait les vagues ■ **the boat ~ loose** NAUT le bateau a rompu les amarres ■ **to ~ loose** *fig* se libérer ⊳ **to ~ and run** se sauver, filer ■ **that argument ~s both** *OR* **two ways** c'est un argument à double tranchant
2. COMPUT couper
3. [cloth, paper] se couper ■ **the cake will ~ into six pieces** ce gâteau peut se couper en six
4. [hurtfully] faire mal
5. [take shorter route] couper, passer ■ **we ~ across the fields** nous avons coupé par les champs
6. [cross] traverser, couper ■ MATHS [lines] se couper ■ **this path ~s across** *OR* **through the swamp** ce sentier traverse *OR* coupe à travers le marécage
7. [in cards] couper
8. CIN & TV [stop filming] couper ■ [change scenes] : **the film ~s straight from the love scene to the funeral** l'image passe directement de la scène d'amour à l'enterrement.
◇ *n* **1.** [slit] coupure *f* ■ [deeper] entaille *f* ■ [wound] balafre *f* ■ MED incision *f* ■ **she had a nasty ~ on her leg from the fall** elle s'était fait une vilaine entaille à la jambe en tombant ⊳ **to be a ~ above the rest** être nettement mieux que les autres *OR* le reste
2. [act of cutting] coupure *f*, entaille *f* ■ **to make a ~ in sthg** [with knife, scissors etc] faire une entaille dans qqch
3. [blow, stroke] coup *m* ■ **a knife/sword ~** un coup de couteau/d'épée

4. [meat - piece] morceau *m* ; [- slice] tranche *f* ▪ **a ~ off the joint** CULIN un morceau de rôti
5. [reduction - in price, taxes] réduction *f*, diminution *f* ; [- in staff] compression *f* ▪ **a ~ in government spending** une réduction OR diminution des dépenses publiques ▪ **the ~s in the Health Service** la réduction OR diminution du budget de la Sécurité sociale ▪ **the ~s** FIN les compressions *fpl* budgétaires
6. [deletion] coupure *f* ▪ **they made several ~s in the film** ils ont fait plusieurs coupures dans le film
7. [gibe, nasty remark] trait *m*, coup *m*
8. [shape, style - of clothes, hair] coupe *f* ; [- of jewel] taille *f*
9. *inf* [portion, share] part *f* ▪ **what's his ~ (of the profits)?** à combien s'élève sa part?
10. *US inf* [absence] absence *f*
11. [in cards] coupe *f*
12. *inf* [on record] plage *f*
13. CIN & TV coupe *f*
14. SPORT [backspin] effet *m*.
◇ *adj* **1.** [hand, flowers] coupé ▪ [tobacco] découpé
2. [reduced] réduit ▪ **to sell sthg at ~ prices** vendre qqch au rabais
3. [shaped - clothing] coupé ▪ [faceted - gem] taillé ▪ **a well-~ suit** un costume bien coupé OR de bonne coupe.
◆ **cut across** *vt insep* **1.** [cross, traverse] traverser, couper à travers ▪ **they ~ across country** ils ont coupé à travers champs
2. [go beyond] surpasser, transcender ▪ **the issue ~s across party lines** la question déborde le clivage des partis
3. [contradict] contredire, aller à l'encontre de.
◆ **cut along** *vi insep UK inf* filer.
◆ **cut away** *vt sep* [remove] enlever OR ôter (en coupant) ▪ [branch] élaguer, émonder.
◆ **cut back** ◇ *vi insep* **1.** [return] rebrousser chemin, revenir sur ses pas
2. CIN revenir en arrière.
◇ *vt sep* **1.** [reduce] réduire, diminuer
2. [prune, trim] tailler ▪ [shrub, tree] élaguer, tailler.
◆ **cut back on** *vt insep* réduire.
◆ **cut down** *vt sep* **1.** [tree] couper, abattre ▪ [person - in battle] abattre
2. [make smaller - article, speech] couper, tronquer ; [- clothing] rendre plus petit ▶ **to ~ sb down to size** remettre qqn à sa place
3. [curtail] réduire, diminuer ▪ [expenses] réduire, rogner ▪ **he ~ his smoking down to 10 a day** il ne fume plus que 10 cigarettes par jour.
◆ **cut down on** *vt insep* réduire ▪ **I'm going to ~ down on drinking/smoking** je vais boire/fumer moins.
◆ **cut in** ◇ *vi insep* **1.** [interrupt] interrompre ▪ **she ~ in on their conversation** elle est intervenue dans leur conversation ▪ **the new store is cutting in on our business** *fig* le nouveau magasin nous fait perdre de la clientèle
2. AUT faire une queue de poisson ▪ **the taxi ~ in on them** le taxi leur a fait une queue de poisson.
◇ *vt sep* [include] : **we should ~ him in on the deal** nous devrions l'intéresser à l'affaire.
◆ **cut off** *vt sep* **1.** [hair, piece of meat, bread] couper ▪ [arm, leg] amputer, couper ▪ **they ~ off the king's head** ils ont décapité le roi ▶ **he was ~ off in his prime** il a été emporté à la fleur de l'âge ▪ **she ~ off her nose to spite her face** elle l'a fait par esprit de contradiction
2. [interrupt - speaker] interrompre, couper
3. [disconnect, discontinue] couper ▪ **they ~ off his allowance** ils lui ont coupé les vivres ▪ **I was ~ off** TELEC j'ai été coupé
4. [separate, isolate] isoler ▪ **the house was ~ off by snow drifts** la maison était isolée par des congères ▪ **he ~ himself off from his family** il a rompu avec sa famille
5. [bar passage of] couper la route à ▪ **the police ~ off the thief** la police a barré le passage au voleur.
◆ **cut out** ◇ *vt sep* **1.** [make by cutting - coat, dress] couper, tailler ; [- statue] sculpter, tailler ▪ **a valley ~ out by the river** une vallée creusée par le fleuve ▶ **I'm not ~ out for living abroad** je ne suis pas fait pour vivre à l'étranger ▪ **he's not ~ out to be a politician** il n'a pas l'étoffe d'un homme politique ▪ **you have your work ~ out for you** vous avez du pain sur la planche OR de quoi vous occuper
2. [remove by cutting - article, picture] découper ▪ **advertisements ~ out from OR of the paper** des annonces découpées dans le journal
3. [eliminate] supprimer ▪ [stop] arrêter ▪ **they ~ out all references to the president** ils ont supprimé toute référence au président ▪ **he ~ out smoking** il a arrêté de fumer ▶ **~ it out!** *inf* ça suffit!, ça va comme ça!
4. *inf* [rival] supplanter
5. [deprive] priver ▪ **his father ~ him out of his will** son père l'a rayé de son testament
6. PHOT & TYPO détourer.
◇ *vi insep* [machine - stop operating] caler ; [- switch off] s'éteindre.
◆ **cut up** ◇ *vt sep* **1.** [food, wood] couper ▪ [meat - carve] découper ; [- chop up] hacher
2. *inf (usu passive) inf* [affect deeply] : **she's really ~ up about her dog's death** la mort de son chien a été un coup pour elle.
◇ *vi insep inf* **1.** *UK phr* **to ~ up rough** se mettre en rogne OR en boule
2. *US* [fool around] faire le pitre.

cut-and-dried *adj inf* **a ~ formula** une formule toute faite ▪ **it's all ~** [prearranged] tout est déjà décidé ; [inevitable] il n'y a rien à (y) faire.

cut-and-paste *vt & vi* couper-coller.

cut and thrust *n* : **the ~ of parliamentary debate** les joutes oratoires des débats parlementaires ▪ **it's ~** la lutte est acharnée.

cutaway ['kʌtəweɪ] *n* **1.** [coat] jaquette *f (d'homme)* **2.** [drawing, model] écorché *m* **3.** CIN changement *m* de plan.

cutback ['kʌtbæk] *n* **1.** [reduction - in costs] réduction *f*, diminution *f* ; [- in staff] compression *f* ▪ **a ~ in production** une réduction de production **2.** *US* CIN retour *m* en arrière, flashback *m*.

cute [kju:t] *adj inf* **1.** [pretty] mignon ▪ *pej* affecté **2.** [clever] malin, - igne *f* ▪ **don't get ~ with me** *pej* ne fais pas le malin avec moi.

cut glass *n* cristal *m* taillé.
◆ **cut-glass** *adj* : **a cut-glass vase** un vase *m* en cristal taillé ▪ **a cut-glass accent** *UK fig* un accent distingué.

cuticle ['kju:tɪkl] *n* **1.** [skin] épiderme *m* ▪ [on nails] petites peaux *fpl*, envie *f* **2.** BOT cuticule *f*.

cutlass ['kʌtləs] *n* coutelas *m*.

cutlery ['kʌtlərɪ] *n (U)* **1.** [eating utensils] couverts *mpl* **2.** [knives, trade] coutellerie *f*.

cutlet ['kʌtlɪt] *n* **1.** [gen] côtelette *f* ▪ [of veal] escalope *f* **2.** *UK* [croquette] croquette *f* ▪ **vegetable ~s** croquettes de légumes.

cutoff ['kʌtɒf] *n* **1.** [stopping point] arrêt *m* ▪ **$100 is our ~ (point)** nous nous arrêtons à 100 dollars ▪ **~ switch** TECH interrupteur *m* **2.** *US* [shortcut] raccourci *m*.
◆ **cutoffs** *npl* : **(a pair of) ~s** *un jean coupé pour en faire un short.*

cutout ['kʌtaʊt] *n* **1.** [figure] découpage *m* ▪ **cardboard ~s** découpages *mpl* en carton **2.** ELEC disjoncteur *m*, coupe-circuit *m* ▪ AUT échappement *m* libre.

cut-price ◇ *adj* [articles] à prix réduit, au rabais ▪ [shop] à prix réduits ▪ [manufacturer] qui vend à prix réduits.
◇ *adv* à prix réduit.

cut-rate *adj* en promotion, à prix réduit.

cutter ['kʌtəʳ] *n* **1.** [person - of clothes] coupeur *m*, - euse *f* ; [- of jewels] tailleur *m* ; [- of film] monteur *m*, - euse *f* **2.** [tool] coupoir *m* **3.** [sailing boat] cotre *m*, cutter *m* ▪ [motorboat] vedette *f* ▪ [of coastguard] garde-côte *m* ▪ [warship] canot *m*.

cutthroat ['kʌtθrəʊt] ◇ *n* **1.** [murderer] assassin *m* **2.** [razor] : **~ (razor)** rasoir *m* à main.
◇ *adj* féroce ▪ [competition] acharné ▪ [prices] très compétitif ▪ **lexicography is a ~ business** le milieu de la lexicographie est un panier de crabes.

cutting ['kʌtɪŋ] ◇ *n* **1.** [act] coupe *f* ▪ [of jewel, stone] taille *f* ▪ [of film] montage *m* ▪ [of trees] coupe *f*, abattage *m* **2.** [piece - of cloth] coupon *m* ; [- from newspaper] coupure *f* ▪ AGRIC [of shrub, vine] marcotte *f* ▪ HORT [of plant] bouture *f* **3.** [for railway, road] tranchée *f*.
◇ *adj* **1.** [tool] tranchant, coupant ▪ **~ edge** *liter* tranchant *m* ▪ **to be at the ~ edge of technological progress** *fig* être à la pointe du progrès en technologie **2.** [wind] glacial, cinglant ▪ [rain] cinglant **3.** [hurtful - remark] mordant, tranchant ; [- word] cinglant, blessant.

cuttingly ['kʌtɪŋlɪ] *adv* méchamment.

cuttlebone ['kʌtlbəʊn] *n* os *m* de seiche.

cuttlefish ['kʌtlfɪʃ] (*pl inv*) *n* seiche *f*.

cutup ['kʌtʌp] *n* *US inf* farceur *m*, rigolo *m*, - ote *f*.

CV *n* (*abbrev of* **curriculum vitae**) *UK* CV *m*.

CVS (*abbrev of* **chorionic villus sampling**) *n* prélèvement *m* des villosités choriales.

c.w.o., CWO (*written abbrev of* **cash with order**) payable à la commande.

cwt. *written abbr of* **hundredweight**.

cyan ['saɪən] ◇ *adj* cyan.
◇ *n* cyan *m*.

cyanide ['saɪənaɪd] *n* cyanure *m*.

cybercafé ['saɪbə,kæfeɪ] *n* cybercafé *m*.

cybercrime ['saɪbəkraɪm] *n* cybercriminalité *f*.

cyberculture ['saɪbə,kʌltʃəʳ] *n* cyberculture *f*.

cyberlaw ['saɪbə,lɔː] *n* droit *m* de l'Internet.

cyberlawyer ['saɪbə,lɔːjəʳ] *n* spécialiste *mf* du droit de l'Internet.

cybernaut ['saɪbə,nɔːt] *n* cybernaute *mf*.

cybernetics [,saɪbə'netɪks] *n (U)* cybernétique *f*.

cyberpet ['saɪbə,pet] *n* animal *m* virtuel.

cyberpunk ['saɪbə,pʌnk] *n* cyberpunk *m*.

cybersex ['saɪbə,seks] *n* cybersexe *m*.

cyberspace ['saɪbəspeɪs] *n* espace *m* virtuel, cyberespace *m*.

cybersurfer ['saɪbə,sɜːfəʳ] *n* cybernaute *mf*.

cyberworld ['saɪbə,wɜːld] *n* cybermonde *m*.

cyborg ['saɪbɔːg] *n* cyborg *m*.

cyclamen ['sɪkləmən] (*pl inv*) *n* cyclamen *m*.

cycle ['saɪkl] ◇ *n* **1.** [gen - COMPUT], ELEC & LIT cycle *m* **2.** [bicycle] bicyclette *f*, vélo *m* ▪ [tricycle] tricycle *m* ▪ [motorcycle] motocyclette *f*, moto *f*.
◇ *comp* [path, track] cyclable ▪ **~ racing track** vélodrome *m* ▪ **~ rack** [on pavement] râtelier *m* à bicyclettes *OR* à vélos ; [on car] porte-vélos *m (inv)*.
◇ *vi* faire de la bicyclette *OR* du vélo ▪ **she ~d into town everyday** elle allait en ville à bicyclette *OR* à vélo chaque jour.

cyclic(al) ['saɪklɪk(l)] *adj* cyclique.

cycling ['saɪklɪŋ] ◇ *n* cyclisme *m* ▪ **I go ~ every weekend** [gen] je fais du vélo tous les week-ends ; SPORT tous les week-ends, je fais du cyclisme.
◇ *comp* [magazine, shoes, shorts] de cyclisme ▪ **a ~ tour** un circuit à bicyclette *OR* à vélo ▪ **we went on a ~ holiday** nous avons fait du cyclotourisme.

cyclist ['saɪklɪst] *n* cycliste *mf*.

cyclo-cross ['saɪkləʊkrɒs] *n* cyclo-cross *m*.

cyclone ['saɪkləʊn] *n* cyclone *m*.

cyclops ['saɪklɒps] *n* cyclope *m*.
◆ **Cyclops** *n* : **(the) ~** le Cyclope.

cyclostyle ['saɪkləʊstaɪl] ◇ *n* machine *f* à polycopier.
◇ *vt* polycopier.

cyclotron ['saɪklətrɒn] *n* cyclotron *m*.

cygnet ['sɪgnɪt] *n* jeune cygne *m*.

cylinder ['sɪlɪndəʳ] *n* **1.** AUT, MATHS & TECH cylindre *m* ▪ **four ~ engine** moteur *m* à quatre cylindres ▪ **oxygen/gas ~** bouteille *f* d'oxygène/de gaz **2.** [of typewriter] rouleau *m* ▪ [of gun] barillet *m*.

cylinder block *n* bloc-cylindres *m*.

cylinder head *n* culasse *f (d'un moteur)*.

cylindrical [sɪ'lɪndrɪkl] *adj* cylindrique.

cymbal ['sɪmbl] *n* cymbale *f*.

cynic ['sɪnɪk] ◇ *adj* [gen - PHILOS] cynique.
◇ *n* cynique *mf*.

cynical ['sɪnɪkl] *adj* [gen - PHILOS] cynique.

cynically ['sɪnɪklɪ] *adv* cyniquement, avec cynisme.

cynicism ['sɪnɪsɪzm] *n* [gen - PHILOS] cynisme *m* ▪ **~s** remarques *fpl* cyniques.

CYO (*abbrev of* **Catholic Youth Organization**) *pr n* *association de jeunes catholiques aux États-Unis.*

cypher ['saɪfəʳ] = **cipher**.

cypress ['saɪprəs] *n* cyprès *m*.

Cypriot ['sɪprɪət] ◇ *n* Chypriote *mf*, Cypriote *mf* ▪ **Greek ~** Chypriote grec *m*, Chypriote grecque *f* ▪ **Turkish ~** Chypriote turc *m*, Chypriote turque *f*.
◇ *adj* chypriote, cypriote.

Cyprus ['saɪprəs] *pr n* Chypre ▪ **in ~** à Chypre.

Cyrillic [sɪ'rɪlɪk] ◇ *adj* cyrillique.
◇ *n* alphabet *m* cyrillique.

cyst [sɪst] *n* **1.** MED kyste *m* **2.** BIOL sac *m* (membraneux).

cystic fibrosis ['sɪstɪk-] *n* mucoviscidose *f*.

cystitis [sɪs'taɪtɪs] *n* cystite *f*.

cytology [saɪ'tɒlədʒɪ] *n* cytologie *f*.

cytoplasm ['saɪtəʊ,plæzm] *n* cytoplasme *m*.

CZ *pr n* = **Canal Zone**.

czar [zɑːʳ] *n* **1.** [monarch] tsar *m* **2.** [top person] éminence *f* grise, ponte *m* ▪ **the government's drug(s) ~** le 'Monsieur drogue' du gouvernement.

czarevitch ['zɑːrəvɪtʃ] *n* tsarévitch *m*.

czarina [zɑː'riːnə] *n* tsarine *f*.

czarism ['zɑːrɪzm] *n* tsarisme *m*.

czarist ['zɑːrɪst] ◇ *adj* tsariste.
◇ *n* tsariste *mf*.

Czech [tʃek] ◇ *n* **1.** [person] Tchèque *mf* **2.** LING tchèque *m*.
◇ *adj* tchèque.

Czechoslovak [,tʃekə'sləʊvæk] = **Czechoslovakian**.

Czechoslovakia [,tʃekəslə'vækɪə] *pr n* Tchécoslovaquie *f* ▪ **in ~** en Tchécoslovaquie.

Czechoslovakian [,tʃekəslə'vækɪən] ◇ *n* Tchécoslovaque *mf*.
◇ *adj* tchécoslovaque.

Czech Republic *pr n* : ▪ **the ~ Republic** la République tchèque.

d (*pl* **d's** *OR pl* **ds**)**, D** (*pl* **D's** *OR pl* **Ds**) [diː] *n* [letter] d *m*, D *m* ▪ **D for dog** *OR* **David** ≃ D comme Désirée ▪ **in 3-D** en trois dimensions, en 3-D, *see also* **f**.

d 1. (*written abbrev of* **penny**) *symbole du penny anglais jusqu'en 1971* **2.** (*written abbrev of* **died**) ▪ **d 1913** mort en 1913.

D ◇ *n* **1.** MUS ré *m* **2.** SCH & UNIV [grade] *note inférieure à la moyenne (7 sur 20)*.
◇ *US written abbr of* **democrat(ic)**.

3-D [ˌθriːˈdiː] = **three-D**.

DA (*abbrev of* **District Attorney**) *n US* ≃ Procureur *m* de la République.

dab [dæb] (*pret & pp* **dabbed**, *cont* **dabbing**) ◇ *n* **1.** [small amount] : **a ~** un petit peu **2.** [fish] limande *f*.
◇ *vt* **1.** [touch lightly] tamponner ▪ **she dabbed her eyes** elle s'est tamponné *OR* essuyé les yeux **2.** [daub] : **he dabbed the canvas with paint** il posait la peinture sur la toile par petites touches.
◆ **dab on** *vt sep* appliquer par petites touches.

dabble [ˈdæbl] ◇ *vt* mouiller ▪ **they ~d their feet in the water** ils trempaient les pieds dans l'eau.
◇ *vi fig* **she ~s in politics** elle fait un peu de politique.

dabbler [ˈdæblər] *n* dilettante *mf*.

dab hand *n UK inf* **to be a ~ at sthg** être doué en *OR* pour qqch ▪ **to be a ~ at doing sthg** être doué pour faire qqch.

dace [deɪs] *n* dard *m*, vandoise *f*.

dachshund [ˈdækshʊnd] *n* teckel *m*.

Dacia [ˈdeɪʃɪə] *n* Dacie *f*.

Dacron® [ˈdækrɒn] *n* Dacron® *m*, ≃ Tergal® *m*.

dactyl [ˈdæktɪl] *n* dactyle *m*.

dad [dæd] *n inf* [father] papa *m* ▪ [old man] pépé *m*.

Dada [ˈdɑːdɑː] ◇ *n* dada *m*.
◇ *adj* dada (*inv*), dadaïste.

Dadaist [ˈdɑːdɑːɪst] ◇ *adj* dadaïste.
◇ *n* dadaïste *mf*.

daddy [ˈdædɪ] (*pl* **daddies**) *n inf* papa *m* ▪ **the ~ of them all** *US* le meilleur de tous.

daddy longlegs [-ˈlɒŋlegz] *n UK* [cranefly] tipule *f* ▪ *US* [harvestman] faucheur *m*, faucheux *m*.

dado [ˈdeɪdəʊ] (*pl* **dadoes**) *n* [of wall] lambris *m* d'appui ▪ ARCHIT [of pedestal] dé *m*.

Daedalus [ˈdaɪdələs] *pr n* MYTH Dédale.

daffodil [ˈdæfədɪl] *n* jonquille *f* ▪ **~ yellow** jaune *m* d'or.

DAFFODIL

La jonquille est le symbole du pays de Galles.

daft [dɑːft] *inf* ◇ *adj UK* [foolish] idiot, bête ▪ **don't be ~!** (ne) fais pas l'idiot!
◇ *adv* : **don't talk ~** ne dites pas de bêtises.

dagger [ˈdægər] *n* **1.** [weapon] poignard *m* ▪ [smaller] dague *f* ▪ **to be at ~s drawn with sb** être à couteaux tirés avec qqn ▪ **to shoot** *US OR* **to look ~s at sb** foudroyer qqn du regard **2.** TYPO croix *f*.

dago▲ [ˈdeɪgəʊ] (*pl* **dagos** *OR pl* **dagoes**) *n terme injurieux désignant une personne d'origine espagnole, italienne ou portugaise*.

daguerreotype [dəˈgerətaɪp] *n* daguerréotype *m*.

dahlia [ˈdeɪljə] *n* dahlia *m*.

daily [ˈdeɪlɪ] (*pl* **dailies**) ◇ *adj* **1.** [routine, task] quotidien, de tous les jours ▪ [output, wage] journalier ▪ **a ~ paper** un quotidien ▪ **to be paid on a ~ basis** être payé à la journée ▪ **(to earn) one's ~ bread** (gagner) son pain quotidien ▪ **the ~ routine** *OR* **grind** *inf* le train-train quotidien ➊ **she has a ~ help** *UK* elle a une femme de ménage **2.** PRESS : **the Daily Express** *quotidien britannique populaire conservateur* ▪ **the Daily Mail** *quotidien britannique populaire du centre droit* ▪ **the Daily Mirror** *quotidien britannique populaire du centre gauche* ▪ **the Daily Sport** *quotidien britannique à sensation* ▪ **the Daily Star** *quotidien britannique à sensation de droite* ▪ **the Daily Telegraph** *quotidien britannique de qualité, de tendance conservatrice*, *see also* **broadsheet, tabloid**.
◇ *adv* tous les jours, quotidiennement ▪ **twice ~** deux fois par jour.
◇ *n* **1.** [newspaper] quotidien *m* **2.** *UK inf* [cleaner] femme *f* de ménage.

daintily [ˈdeɪntɪlɪ] *adv* **1.** [eat, hold] délicatement ▪ [walk] avec grâce **2.** [dress] coquettement.

daintiness [ˈdeɪntɪnɪs] *n* **1.** [of manner] délicatesse *f*, raffinement *m* **2.** [of dress] coquetterie *f*.

dainty [ˈdeɪntɪ] (*comp* **daintier**, *superl* **daintiest**, *pl* **dainties**) ◇ *adj* **1.** [small] menu, petit ▪ [delicate] délicat **2.** [food] de choix, délicat.
◇ *n* [food] mets *m* délicat ▪ [sweet] friandise *f*.

daiquiri [ˈdaɪkɪrɪ] *n* daiquiri *m*.

dairy [ˈdeərɪ] (*pl* **dairies**) ◇ *n* AGRIC [building on farm] laiterie *f* ▪ [shop] crémerie *f*, laiterie *f*.
◇ *comp* [cow, farm, products] laitier ▪ [butter, cream] fermier ▪ **~ cattle** vaches *fpl* laitières ▪ **~ farmer** producteur *m* de lait *OR* laitier ▪ **~ farming** industrie *f* laitière.

dairymaid ['deərɪmeɪd] *n* fille *f* de laiterie.

dairyman ['deərɪmən] (*pl* **dairymen** [-mən]) *n* [on farm] employé *m* de laiterie ▪ [in shop] crémier *m*, laitier *m*.

dais ['deɪɪs] *n* estrade *f*.

daisy ['deɪzɪ] (*pl* **daisies**) *n* marguerite *f* ▪ [smaller] pâquerette *f*.

daisy chain *n* guirlande *f* de pâquerettes.

daisywheel ['deɪzɪwi:l] *n* marguerite *f* ▪ **~ printer** imprimante *f* à marguerite.

Dakar ['dækɑ:] *pr n* Dakar.

Dakota [də'kəʊtə] *pr n* Dakota *m* ▪ **in ~** dans le Dakota.

Dalai Lama [ˌdælaɪ'lɑ:mə] *pr n* dalaï-lama *m*.

dale [deɪl] *n* vallée *f*, vallon *m*.

dally ['dælɪ] (*pret & pp* **dallied**) *vi* **1.** [dawdle] lanterner ▪ **to ~ over sthg** lanterner sur *OR* dans qqch **2.** [toy - with idea] badiner, caresser ; [- with affections] jouer.

Dalmatian [dæl'meɪʃn] *n* [dog] dalmatien *m*, - enne *f*.

daltonism ['dɔ:ltəˌnɪzm] *n* daltonisme *m*.

dam [dæm] (*pret & pp* **dammed**, *cont* **damming**) ◇ *n* **1.** [barrier] barrage *m* (de retenue) **2.** [reservoir] réservoir *m* **3.** [animal] mère *f*.
◇ *vt* construire un barrage sur ▪ **plans to ~ the Seine** projet de construction d'un barrage pour contenir les eaux de la Seine.
◆ **dam up** *vt sep* **1.** *liter* construire un barrage sur **2.** *fig* [feelings] refouler, ravaler ▪ [words] endiguer.

damage ['dæmɪdʒ] ◇ *n* **1.** *(U)* [harm] dommage *m*, dommages *mpl* ▪ [visible effects] dégâts *mpl*, dommages *mpl* ▪ [to ship, shipment] avarie *f*, avaries *fpl* ▪ **~ to property** dégâts *mpl* matériels ▪ **~ limitation** effort *m* pour limiter les dégâts **2.** *fig* tort *m*, préjudice *m* ▪ **the scandal has done the government serious ~** le scandale a fait énormément de tort *OR* a énormément porté préjudice au gouvernement ▪ **the ~ is done** le mal est fait ▪ **what's the ~?** *inf hum* ça fait combien?
◇ *vt* [harm - crop, object] endommager, causer des dégâts à ; [- food] abîmer, gâter ; [- eyes, health] abîmer ; [- ship, shipment] avarier ; [- reputation] porter atteinte à, nuire à ; [- cause] faire du tort à, porter préjudice à.
◆ **damages** *npl* LAW dommages *mpl* et intérêts *mpl* ▪ **to award ~s to sb for sthg** accorder des dommages et intérêts à qqn pour qqch ▪ **liable for ~s** civilement responsable ▪ **war ~s** dommages *mpl OR* indemnités *fpl* de guerre.

damaging ['dæmɪdʒɪŋ] *adj* dommageable, nuisible ▪ LAW préjudiciable ▪ **psychologically ~** dommageable sur le plan psychologique.

Damascus [də'mæskəs] *pr n* Damas.

damask ['dæməsk] ◇ *n* **1.** [silk] damas *m*, soie *f* damassée ▪ [linen] damassé *m* **2.** [steel] (acier *m*) damasquiné *m* **3.** [colour] vieux rose *m*.
◇ *adj* [cloth] damassé.

damask rose *n* rose *f* de Damas.

dame [deɪm] *n* **1.** *arch & lit* [noble] dame *f* ▪ **Dame Fortune** Dame Fortune ▪ **(pantomime) ~** *UK* THEAT *rôle travesti outré et ridicule dans la pantomime anglaise* **2.** *UK* [title] : **Dame** *titre donné à une femme ayant reçu certaines distinctions honorifiques.*

dammit ['dæmɪt] *interj inf* mince ▪ **as near as ~** *UK* à un cheveu près.

damn [dæm] ◇ *interj inf* : **~!** mince!
◇ *n inf* : **I don't give a ~ about the money** je me fiche pas mal de l'argent.
◇ *vt* **1.** RELIG damner **2.** [condemn] condamner ▪ **they ~ed him with faint praise** ils l'ont éreinté sous couleur d'éloge **3.** *inf phr* **~ you!** va te faire voir!△ ▪ **well I'll be ~ed!** ça, c'est le comble! ▪ **I'll be ~ed if I'll apologize!** m'excuser? plutôt mourir!△.
◇ *adj inf* fichu, sacré ▪ **you ~ fool!** espèce d'idiot! ▪ **he's a ~ nuisance** il est vraiment casse-pied△.
◇ *adv inf* **1.** [as intensifier] très ▪ **he knows ~ well what I mean** il sait exactement *OR* très bien ce que je veux dire **2.** *UK phr* **~ all** que dalle△.

damnable ['dæmnəbl] *adj* **1.** RELIG damnable **2.** *inf dated* [awful] exécrable, odieux.

damnation [dæm'neɪʃn] ◇ *n* damnation *f*.
◇ *interj inf* : **~!** enfer et damnation! *hum*.

damned [dæmd] ◇ *adj* **1.** RELIG damné, maudit **2.** *inf* = **damn**.
◇ *adv inf* rudement, vachement△ ▪ **do what you ~ well like!** fais ce que tu veux, je m'en fiche.
◇ *npl* RELIG & *lit* **the ~** les damnés *mpl*.

damnedest ['dæmdəst] *inf* ◇ *n* [utmost] : **he did his ~ to ruin the party** il a vraiment fait tout ce qu'il pouvait pour gâcher la soirée.
◇ *adj US* incroyable.

damn-fool *adj inf* crétin, idiot.

damning ['dæmɪŋ] *adj* [evidence, statement] accablant.

Damocles ['dæməˌkli:z] *pr n* Damoclès ▪ **the sword of ~** l'épée *f* de Damoclès.

damp [dæmp] ◇ *adj* [air, clothes, heat] humide ▪ [skin] moite.
◇ *n* **1.** [moisture] humidité *f* **2.** MIN [air] mofette *f* ▪ [gas] grisou *m*.
◇ *vt* **1.** [wet] humecter **2.** [stifle - sounds] amortir, étouffer ▪ MUS étouffer ▪ *fig* [spirits] décourager, refroidir **3.** [fire] couvrir **4.** TECH amortir.
◆ **damp down** *vt sep* [fire] couvrir ▪ *fig* [enthusiasm] refroidir ▪ [crisis] atténuer, rendre moins violent.

damp course ['dæmpkɔ:s] *n* couche *f* d'étanchéité.

dampen ['dæmpən] *vt* **1.** [wet] humecter **2.** [ardour, courage] refroidir ▪ **don't ~ their spirits** ne les découragez pas.

damper ['dæmpəʳ] *n* **1.** [in furnace] registre *m* **2.** *fig* douche *f* froide ▪ **the news put a ~ on the party/his enthusiasm** la nouvelle a jeté un froid sur la fête/a refroidi son enthousiasme **3.** AUT, ELEC & TECH amortisseur *m* ▪ MUS étouffoir *m* **4.** [for linen, stamps] mouilleur *m*.

damping ['dæmpɪŋ] *n* **1.** [wetting] mouillage *m* **2.** AUT, ELEC & TECH amortissement *m*.

dampness ['dæmpnɪs] *n* humidité *f* ▪ [of skin] moiteur *f*.

damp-proof *adj* protégé contre l'humidité, hydrofuge ▪ **~ course** CONSTR couche *f* d'étanchéité.

damp squib *n UK inf* déception *f*.

damsel ['dæmzl] *n arch & lit* damoiselle *f* ▪ **a ~ in distress** *hum* une demoiselle en détresse.

damson ['dæmzn] ◇ *n* [tree] prunier *m* de Damas ▪ [fruit] prune *f* de Damas.
◇ *comp* [jam, wine] de prunes (de Damas).

dan [dæn] *n* [in judo] dan *m*.

dance [dɑ:ns] ◇ *n* **1.** danse *f* ▪ **may I have the next ~?** voulez-vous m'accorder la prochaine danse? ▶ **~ of death** danse macabre ▪ **to lead sb a (merry *OR* pretty) ~** [exasperate] donner du fil à retordre à qqn ; [deceive] faire marcher qqn ; [in romantic context] mener qqn en bateau **2.** [piece of music] morceau *m* (de musique) **3.** [art] danse *f* **4.** [social occasion] soirée *f* dansante ▪ [larger] bal *m*.
◇ *comp* [class, school, step, studio] de danse ▪ **~ band** orchestre *m* de bal ▪ **~ floor** piste *f* de danse ▪ **~ hall** salle *f* de bal ▪ **~ music** musique *f* dansante.
◇ *vi* [person] danser ▪ *fig* [leaves, light, words] danser ▪ [eyes] scintiller ▪ **to ~ with sb** danser avec qqn ▪ **to ask sb to ~** inviter qqn à danser ▪ **it's not the type of music you can ~ to** ce n'est pas le genre de musique sur lequel on peut danser ▪ **to ~ with joy** sauter de joie ▪ **she ~d along the street** elle descendit la rue d'un pas joyeux ▶ **to ~ to sb's tune** obéir à qqn au doigt et à l'œil.

◇ *vt* [waltz, polka] danser ▪ **to ~ a step** faire *OR* exécuter un pas de danse ▪ **to ~ a baby on one's knee** faire sauter un bébé sur ses genoux ➤ **to ~ attendance on sb** *UK* s'empresser auprès de qqn.

dancer ['dɑːnsəʳ] *n* danseur *m*, - euse *f*.

dancing ['dɑːnsɪŋ] ◇ *n* danse *f* ▪ **to go ~** aller danser.
◇ *comp* [class, teacher] de danse ▪ **~ partner** cavalier *m*, - ère *f*.
◇ *adj* [eyes] scintillant.

dancing girl *n* danseuse *f*.

dancing shoe *n* [for dance] chaussure *f* de bal ▪ [for ballet] chausson *m* de danse.

D and C (*abbrev of* **dilation and curettage**) *n* MED (dilation *f* et) curetage *m*.

dandelion ['dændɪlaɪən] *n* pissenlit *m*, dent-de-lion *f*.

dander *dated* ['dændəʳ] *n inf* **to get one's/sb's ~ up** se mettre/mettre qqn en rogne.

dandified ['dændɪfaɪd] *adj* [person] à l'allure de dandy ▪ [appearance] de dandy.

dandruff ['dændrʌf] *n (U)* pellicules *fpl* ▪ **to have ~** avoir des pellicules ▪ **~ shampoo** shampooing *m* antipelliculaire.

dandy ['dændɪ] (*pl* **dandies**) ◇ *n* dandy *m*.
◇ *adj US inf* extra, épatant ▪ **that's just ~!** *iron* c'est vraiment génial!

Dane [deɪn] *n* Danois *m*, - e *f*.

danger ['deɪndʒəʳ] ◇ *n* danger *m* ▪ **is there any ~ of fire?** y a-t-il un danger *OR* risque d'incendie? ▪ **'~, keep out!'** 'danger, entrée interdite!' ▪ **to be out of/in ~** être hors de/en danger ▪ **he was in no ~** il n'était pas en danger, il ne courait aucun danger ▪ **to be in ~ of doing sthg** courir le risque *OR* risquer de faire qqch ▪ **to be a ~ to sb/sthg** être un danger pour qqn/qqch ▪ **it's a ~ to my health** c'est dangereux pour ma santé ▪ **there is no ~ of that happening** il n'y a pas de danger *OR* de risque que cela se produise ▪ **no ~** *inf* pas de danger.
◇ *comp* : **~ area** *OR* **zone** zone *f* dangereuse ▪ **to be on the ~ list** MED être dans un état critique ▪ **to be off the ~ list** être hors de danger ▪ **~ money** prime *f* de risque ▪ **~ point** cote *f* d'alerte ▪ **~ signal** RAIL signal *m* d'arrêt ; *fig* signal *m* d'alerte *OR* d'alarme.

dangerous ['deɪndʒərəs] *adj* [job, sport, criminal, animal] dangereux ▪ MED [illness] dangereux, grave ▪ [operation] délicat, périlleux ▪ [assumption] risqué ▪ **to be on ~ ground** *fig* être sur un terrain glissant ▪ **~ driving** conduite *f* dangereuse.

dangerously ['deɪndʒərəslɪ] *adv* dangereusement ▪ [ill] gravement ▪ **to live ~** vivre dangereusement ▪ **you're coming ~ close to being fired** continue comme ça et tu es viré ▪ **this firm is ~ close to collapse/bankruptcy** cette entreprise est au bord de l'effondrement/la faillite.

dangle ['dæŋgl] ◇ *vt* [legs, arms, hands] laisser pendre ▪ [object on chain, string] balancer ▪ **to ~ sthg in front of sb** balancer qqch devant qqn ; *fig* faire miroiter qqch aux yeux de qqn.
◇ *vi* [legs, arms, hands] pendre ▪ [keys, earrings] se balancer ▪ **the climber was dangling at the end of the rope** l'alpiniste se balançait *OR* était suspendu au bout de la corde ▪ **to keep sb dangling** *fig* laisser qqn dans le vague.

Danish ['deɪnɪʃ] ◇ *n* **1.** LING danois *m* **2.** [pastry] = **danish pastry**.
◇ *npl* : **the ~** les Danois *mpl*.
◇ *adj* [person, food, Parliament, countryside] danois ▪ [king] du Danemark ▪ [ambassador, embassy, representative] danois, du Danemark ▪ [dictionary, teacher] de danois ▪ **the ~ people** les Danois *mpl*.

Danish blue *n* [cheese] bleu *m* du Danemark.

Danish pastry *n* CULIN *sorte de pâtisserie fourrée.*

dank [dæŋk] *adj* humide et froid.

Dante ['dæntɪ] *pr n* Dante.

Danube ['dænjuːb] *pr n* : **the ~** le Danube ▪ **'The Blue ~'** *Strauss* 'le Beau Danube bleu'.

Daphne ['dæfnɪ] *pr n* MYTH Daphné.

dapper ['dæpəʳ] *adj* propre sur soi, soigné.

dapple ['dæpl] *vt* tacheter.

dappled ['dæpld] *adj* [animal] tacheté.

dapple-grey ◇ *adj* gris pommelé.
◇ *n* [colour] gris *m* pommelé ▪ [horse] cheval *m*, jument *f* gris pommelé.

Darby and Joan [ˌdɑːbɪən'dʒəʊn] *n couple uni de personnes âgées* ▪ **~ club** club *m* du troisième âge *(en Grande-Bretagne).*

dare [deəʳ] ◇ *modal vb* [venture] oser ▪ **to ~ (to) do sthg** oser faire qqch ▪ **she didn't ~ (to)** *OR* **~d not say a word** elle n'a pas osé dire un mot ▪ **don't you ~ tell me what to do!** ne t'avise surtout pas de me dire ce que j'ai à faire! ▪ **don't you ~!** je te le déconseille! ➤ **~ I say it** si j'ose m'exprimer ainsi ▪ **I ~ say you're hungry after your journey** je suppose que vous êtes affamés après ce voyage ▪ **he was most apologetic – I ~ say!** il s'est confondu en excuses – j'imagine!
◇ *vt* **1.** [challenge] défier ▪ **to ~ sb to do sthg** défier qqn de faire qqch ▪ **I ~ you!** chiche! **2.** *lit* [death, dishonour] braver, défier ▪ [displeasure] braver.
◇ *n* [challenge] défi *m* ▪ **to do sthg for a ~** faire qqch par défi.

daredevil ['deəˌdevl] ◇ *n* casse-cou *m inv*.
◇ *adj* casse-cou.

daren't [deənt] = **dare not**.

daresay [ˌdeə'seɪ] *vi UK* **I ~** [probably, I suppose] j'imagine, je suppose ▪ **she's telling the truth – I ~ (she is)** elle dit la vérité – je veux bien le croire.

daring ['deərɪŋ] ◇ *n* [of person] audace *f*, hardiesse *f* ▪ [of feat] hardiesse *f*.
◇ *adj* [audacious] audacieux, hardi ▪ [provocative] audacieux, provocant.

daringly ['deərɪŋlɪ] *adv* audacieusement, hardiment ▪ **a ~ low neckline** un décolleté audacieux *OR* provocant.

dark [dɑːk] ◇ *n* noir *m* ▪ **to see in the ~** voir dans le noir ▪ **before/after ~** avant/après la tombée de la nuit ➤ **in the ~ : I can't work in the ~!** je ne peux pas travailler sans savoir où je vais! ▪ **to keep sb in the ~ about sthg** maintenir qqn dans l'ignorance à propos de qqch.
◇ *adj* **1.** [without light - night, room, street] sombre ▪ *fig* [thoughts] sombre ▪ [ideas] noir ▪ **it's very ~ in here** il fait très sombre ici ▪ **it's getting ~** il commence à faire nuit, la nuit tombe ▪ **it's getting ~er** il fait de plus en plus nuit ▪ **it gets ~ early** il fait nuit de bonne heure ▪ **to get ~** [sky] s'assombrir ▪ **the ~ days of the war** la sombre période de la guerre ▪ **to look on the ~ side** voir tout en noir ➤ **~ satanic mills** *citation d'un hymne religieux utilisée pour évoquer le paysage industriel du nord de l'Angleterre* **2.** [colour] foncé ▪ [dress, suit] sombre ▪ **~ chocolate** chocolat *m* noir **3.** [hair, eyes] foncé ▪ [skin, complexion] foncé, brun ▪ **a ~ man** un brun ▪ **a ~ woman** une brune ▪ **to be ~** être brun ▪ **to have ~ hair** avoir les cheveux bruns, être brun ▪ **to get ~er** [hair] foncer **4.** [hidden, mysterious] mystérieux, secret, - ète *f* ▪ [secret] bien gardé ▪ [hint] mystérieux, énigmatique ▪ **the ~ side of the moon** la face cachée de la lune ▪ **to keep sthg ~** tenir qqch secret ▪ **you kept that very ~!** tu nous avais caché ça! **5.** [sinister] noir ▪ **there's a ~ side to her** elle a un côté désagréable ▪ **a ~ chapter in the country's history** un chapitre peu glorieux de l'histoire du pays.

Dark Ages *npl* HIST Haut Moyen Âge *m* ▪ **he's still in the ~** *fig* il est resté au Moyen Âge.

darken ['dɑːkn] ◇ *vt* [sky] assombrir ▪ [colour] foncer ▪ **a ~ed room** une pièce sombre ➤ **never ~ my door again!** ne viens plus jamais frapper à ma porte!
◇ *vi* [sky, room] s'assombrir, s'obscurcir ▪ [hair, wood] foncer ▪ [face] s'assombrir ▪ [painting] s'obscurcir.

dark glasses *npl* lunettes *fpl* noires.

dark horse *n* **1.** [secretive person] : **to be a ~** être très secret ▪ **you're a ~!** tu nous en caches des choses! **2.** [competitor, horse] participant *m* inconnu ▪ *US* POL candidat *m* surprise.

darkish ['dɑːkɪʃ] *adj* [colour, sky, wood] plutôt *OR* assez sombre ▪ [hair, skin] plutôt brun *OR* foncé ▪ [person] plutôt brun.

darkly ['dɑːklɪ] *adv* [hint] énigmatiquement ▪ [say] sur un ton sinistre.

darkness ['dɑːknɪs] *n* **1.** [of night, room, street] obscurité *f* ▪ **to be in ~** être plongé dans l'obscurité **2.** [of hair, skin] couleur *f* foncée.

darkroom ['dɑːkrʊm] *n* PHOT chambre *f* noire.

dark-skinned *adj* à la peau foncée.

darling ['dɑːlɪŋ] <> *n* **1.** [term of affection] chéri *m*, - e *f* ▪ **yes ~?** oui (mon) chéri? ▪ **she's a ~** c'est un amour ▪ **he was an absolute ~ about it** il a été absolument charmant ▪ **be a ~ and...** sois gentil *OR* un amour... **2.** [favourite - of teacher, parents] favori *m*, - ite *f*, chouchou *m*, - oute *f* ; [- of media] coqueluche *f*.
<> *adj* [beloved] chéri ▪ [delightful] charmant, adorable.

darn [dɑːn] <> *n* **1.** SEW reprise *f* ▪ **there was a ~ in the elbow of his sweater** son pull était reprisé au coude **2.** *inf phr* **I couldn't** *OR* **I don't give a ~** je m'en fiche.
<> *vt* **1.** SEW repriser, raccommoder **2.** *inf* [damn] : **~ it!** bon sang! ▪ **~ that cat/man!** encore ce chat/bonhomme de malheur!
<> *interj inf* bon sang.
<> *adj inf* de malheur.
<> *adv inf* vachement ▪ **it's too ~ late** bon sang, il est trop tard ▪ **don't be so ~ stupid!** ce que tu peux être bête!

darned [dɑːnd] *US inf* = **darn** *(adj, adv)*.

darning ['dɑːnɪŋ] *adj* [action] reprise *f*, raccommodage *m* ▪ [items to be darned] linge *m* à repriser *OR* raccommoder.

darning needle *n* aiguille *f* à repriser.

dart [dɑːt] <> *n* **1.** SPORT fléchette *f* ▪ [weapon] flèche *f* ▪ **to play ~s** jouer aux fléchettes **2.** SEW pince *f* **3.** [sudden movement] : **to make a ~ for the door/telephone** se précipiter vers la porte/sur le téléphone ▪ **to make a ~ at sb/sthg** se précipiter sur qqn/qqch.
<> *vt* [glance, look - quickly] lancer, jeter ; [- angrily] darder ▪ [rays] lancer ▪ [stronger] darder.
<> *vi* : **to ~ away** *OR* **off** partir en *OR* comme une flèche ▪ **to ~ for the door/telephone** se précipiter vers la porte/sur le téléphone ▪ **to ~ at sthg/sb** se précipiter sur qqch/qqn.

dartboard ['dɑːtbɔːd] *n* cible *f* (de jeu de fléchettes).

Darwinian [dɑː'wɪnɪən] *adj* [of Darwin - theory] darwinien ▪ [in favour of Darwinism - thinker] darwiniste.

Darwinism ['dɑːwɪnɪzm] *n* darwinisme *m*.

dash [dæʃ] <> *n* **1.** [quick movement] mouvement *m* précipité ▪ **to make a ~ for freedom** s'enfuir vers la liberté ▪ **to make a ~ for it** [rush] se précipiter ; [escape] s'enfuir, s'échapper ▪ **it was a headlong ~ to the station** ça n'a été qu'une course effrénée jusqu'à la gare
2. *US* SPORT sprint *m*
3. [small amount - of water, soda] goutte *f*, trait *m* ; [- of cream, milk] nuage *m* ; [- of lemon juice, vinegar] filet *m* ; [- of salt, pepper] soupçon *m* ; [- of colour, humour] pointe *f*
4. [punctuation mark] tiret *m* ▪ [in Morse code] trait *m*
5. [style] panache *m* ▪ **to cut a ~** faire de l'effet
6. = **dashboard**.
<> *vt* **1.** [throw] jeter (avec violence) ▪ **several boats were ~ed against the cliffs** plusieurs bateaux ont été projetés *OR* précipités contre les falaises ▪ **to ~ sb's hopes** *fig* réduire les espoirs de qqn à néant ▪ **to ~ sb's spirits** *fig* démoraliser *OR* abattre qqn
2. *inf* [damn] : **~ it!** *dated* bon sang! ▪ **I'll be ~ed!** ça alors!, oh, la vache!
<> *vi* **1.** [rush] se précipiter ▪ **I must ~** *UK* je dois filer ▪ **I'll just ~ out to the post-office/library** *UK* je vais juste faire un saut à la poste/bibliothèque ▪ **~ upstairs and fetch it, will you?** *UK* monte vite le chercher, s'il te plaît ▪ **the dog ~ed across the road in front of us** le chien a traversé la route à toute vitesse devant nous
2. [waves] se jeter.
<> *interj UK dated* **~!** bon sang!

◆ **dash off** <> *vi insep* partir en flèche.
<> *vt sep* [letter, memo] écrire en vitesse ▪ [drawing] faire en vitesse.

dashboard ['dæʃbɔːd] *n* AUT tableau *m* de bord.

dashed [dæʃt] *UK dated* <> *adj* de malheur.
<> *adv* vachement.

dashing ['dæʃɪŋ] *adj* pimpant, fringant.

dastardly ['dæstədlɪ] *adj lit* [deed, person] odieux, infâme.

DAT [dæt] (*abbrev of* **digital audio tape**) *n* DAT *m*.

data ['deɪtə] *(pl of datum usu with sing vb)* <> *n* informations *fpl*, données *fpl* ▪ COMPUT données *fpl* ▪ **a piece of ~** une donnée, une information ; COMPUT une donnée.
<> *comp* COMPUT [entry, retrieval, security, input] de données.

data bank *n* COMPUT banque *f* de données.

database ['deɪtəbeɪs] <> *n* COMPUT base *f* de données ▪ **~ management** gestion *f* de base de données ▪ **~ management system** système *m* de gestion de base de données.
<> *vt* mettre sous forme de base de données.

data capture *n* COMPUT saisie *f* de données.

dataglove ['deɪtəglʌv] *n* gant *m* de données.

data processing <> *n* traitement *m* de l'information.
<> *comp* [department, service] de traitement des données *OR* de l'information, informatique.

data protection *n* protection *f* de l'information.

Data Protection Act *n* loi *f* sur la protection de l'information *(en Grande-Bretagne)*.

date [deɪt] <> *n* **1.** [of letter, day of the week] date *f* ▪ **what's the ~ today?, what's today's ~?** quelle est la date aujourd'hui?, le combien sommes-nous aujourd'hui? ▪ **today's ~ is the 20th January** nous sommes le 20 janvier ▪ **what's the ~ of the coin/building?** de quelle année est cette pièce/ce bâtiment? ▪ **would you be free on that ~?** est-ce que vous seriez libre ce jour-là *OR* à cette date? ▪ **at a later** *OR* **some future ~** plus tard, ultérieurement *fml* ▪ **of an earlier/a later ~** plus ancien/récent ▪ **to set a ~** fixer une date ; [engaged couple] fixer la date de son mariage ▪ **to put a ~ to sthg** [remember when it happened] se souvenir de la date de qqch ; [estimate when built, established etc] attribuer une date à qqch, dater qqch ➲ **~ of birth** date de naissance **2.** [meeting] rendez-vous *m* ▪ **let's make a ~ for lunch** prenons rendez-vous pour déjeuner ensemble ▪ **to go out on a ~** sortir en compagnie de quelqu'un ▪ **her parents don't let her go out on ~s** ses parents ne la laissent pas sortir avec des garçons **3.** [person] ami *m*, - e *f* ▪ **who's your ~ tonight?** avec qui sors-tu ce soir? **4.** [fruit] datte *f*.
<> *vt* **1.** [write date on - cheque, letter, memo] dater ▪ **a fax ~d May 6th** un fax daté du 6 mai **2.** [attribute date to - building, settlement etc] dater ▪ **gosh, that ~s him!** eh bien, ça montre qu'il n'est plus tout jeune *OR* ça ne le rajeunit pas! **3.** *US* [go out with] sortir avec.
<> *vi* **1.** [clothes, style] se démoder ▪ [novel] vieillir **2.** *US* [go out on dates] sortir avec des garçons/filles ▪ **how long have you two been dating?** ça fait combien de temps que vous sortez ensemble *OR* que vous vous voyez?

◆ **out of date** *adj phr* : **to be out of ~** [dress, style, concept, slang] être démodé *OR* dépassé ; [magazine, newspaper] être vieux ; [dictionary] ne pas être à jour *OR* à la page ; [passport, season ticket etc] être périmé ▪ **it's the kind of dress that will never go out of ~** c'est le genre de robe indémodable *OR* qui ne se démodera jamais.

◆ **to date** *adv phr* à ce jour.

◆ **up to date** *adj phr* : **to be up to ~** [dress, style, person] être à la mode *OR* à la page ; [newspaper, magazine] être du jour/de la semaine etc ; [dictionary] être à la page *OR* à jour ; [passport] être valide *OR* valable ; [list] être à jour ▪ **to keep up to ~ with the news/scientific developments** se tenir au courant de l'actualité/des progrès de la science ▪ **to keep sb up to ~ on sthg** tenir qqn au courant de qqch ▪ **to bring sb up to ~ on sthg** mettre qqn au courant de qqch.

◆ **date back to, date from** *vt insep* dater de.

DATE

En anglais américain parlé, l'article défini n'est pas utilisé devant les dates. On dira : ***December ninth*** (américain) ou ***the ninth*** (britannique). Pour les dates en chiffres, les Américains donnent le mois, le jour, l'année (5.17.07), alors que les Britanniques commencent par le jour, puis le mois et l'année (17.5.07).

datebook ['deɪtbʊk] *n* US agenda *m*.

dated ['deɪtɪd] *adj* [clothes, style] démodé ■ [novel, term, expression, concept] vieilli.

dateline ['deɪt,laɪn] *n* **1.** PRESS date *f* de rédaction **2.** = **International Date Line**.

date palm *n* palmier *m* dattier.

date rape *n viol commis par une personne connue de la victime.*

datestamp ['deɪtstæmp] ◇ *n* tampon *m* dateur ■ [used for cancelling] oblitérateur *m*, timbre *m* à date ■ [postmark] cachet *m* de la poste.
◇ *vt* [book] tamponner, mettre le cachet de la date sur ■ [letter] oblitérer.

dating ['deɪtɪŋ] *n* [of building, artefact etc] datation *f*.

dative ['deɪtɪv] ◇ *n* datif *m* ■ **in the ~** au datif.
◇ *adj* datif.

datum ['deɪtəm] (*pl* **data**) *n fml* donnée *f*.

daub [dɔ:b] ◇ *n* **1.** [of paint] tache *f*, barbouillage *m* ■ [done on purpose] barbouillage *m* **2.** *pej* [painting] croûte *f* **3.** [for walls] enduit *m*.
◇ *vt* enduire ■ [with mud] couvrir ■ **a wall ~ed with slogans** un mur couvert de slogans.
◇ *vi pej* [paint badly] peinturlurer, barbouiller.

daughter ['dɔ:tər] *n* fille *f*.

daughter board *n* COMPUT carte *f* fille.

daughter-in-law *n* bru *f*, belle-fille *f*.

daughterly ['dɔ:təlɪ] *adj* filial.

Daughters of the American Revolution *pr npl organisme à tendance nationaliste et conservatrice regroupant des femmes descendant des patriotes de la guerre d'Indépendance aux États-Unis.*

daunt [dɔ:nt] *vt* intimider ■ **nothing ~ed** nullement découragé.

daunting ['dɔ:ntɪŋ] *adj* [task, question] intimidant.

dauntless ['dɔ:ntlɪs] *adj* déterminé.

dauphine ['dɔ:fi:n] *n* HIST dauphine *f*.

davenport ['dævnpɔ:t] *n* UK [desk] secrétaire *m*.

David ['deɪvɪd] *pr n* David.

Davy Crockett ['deɪvɪ'krɒkɪt] *pr n pionnier américain rendu célèbre par sa participation héroïque à la bataille de Fort Alamo. Il est toujours représenté portant une toque ornée d'une queue de raton laveur.*

Davy Jones ['deɪvɪ,dʒəʊnz] *n* : **in ~'s locker** [person, ship] au fond de la mer.

Davy lamp *n* lampe *f* de sécurité de mineur.

dawdle ['dɔ:dl] *vi pej* traîner, lambiner, traînasser ■ **to ~ over sthg** traînasser OR traîner en faisant qqch.

dawdler ['dɔ:dlər] *n* lambin *m*, - e *f*, traînard *m*, - e *f*.

dawdling ['dɔ:dlɪŋ] ◇ *n* : **stop all this ~!** arrête de traînasser!
◇ *adj* traînard.

dawn [dɔ:n] ◇ *n* **1.** *liter* aube *f* ■ **at ~** à l'aube ■ **from ~ till dusk** du matin au soir ■ **at the crack of ~** au point du jour ■ **(just) as ~ was breaking** alors que l'aube pointait ■ **to watch the ~** regarder le jour se lever **2.** *fig* [of civilization, era] aube *f* ■ [of hope] naissance *f*, éclosion *f* ■ **since the ~ of time** depuis la nuit des temps.
◇ *vi* **1.** [day] se lever **2.** *fig* [new era, hope] naître ■ **the truth ~ed on** OR **upon him** la vérité lui apparut ■ **it suddenly ~ed on her that...** il lui est soudain apparu que...

dawn chorus *n* chant *m* des oiseaux à l'aube.

dawning ['dɔ:nɪŋ] ◇ *adj* naissant.
◇ *n* = **dawn** *(sens 2)*.

dawn raid *n* descente *f* à l'aube ■ [by police] descente *f* OR rafle *f* à l'aube ■ ST. EX attaque *f* à l'ouverture.

day [deɪ] ◇ *n* **1.** [period of twenty-four hours] jour *m*, journée *f* ■ **it's a nice** OR **fine ~** c'est une belle journée, il fait beau aujourd'hui ■ **on a clear ~** par temps clair ■ **a summer's/winter's ~** un jour d'été/d'hiver ■ **we went to the country for the ~** nous sommes allés passer la journée à la campagne ■ **what ~ is it (today)?** quel jour sommes-nous (aujourd'hui)? ■ **(on) that ~** ce jour-là ■ **(on) the ~ (that** OR **when) she was born** le jour où elle est née ■ **the ~ after, (on) the next** OR **following ~** le lendemain, le jour suivant ■ **the ~ after the party** le lendemain de OR le jour d'après la fête ■ **the ~ after tomorrow** après-demain ■ **the ~ before, (on) the previous ~** la veille, le jour d'avant ■ **the ~ before yesterday** avant-hier ■ **in four ~s, in four ~s' time** dans quatre jours ▌[in greetings] : **good ~!** bonjour! ■ **have a nice ~!** bonne journée! ➊ **Day of Judgment** RELIG (jour du) jugement dernier ■ **the Day of Atonement** RELIG Jour *m* du Grand Pardon ■ **dish of the ~** plat *m* du jour ■ **any ~ now** d'un jour à l'autre ■ **~ after ~, ~ in ~ out** jour après jour ■ **for ~s on end** OR **at a time** pendant des jours et des jours ■ **from ~ to ~** de jour en jour ■ **to live from ~ to ~** vivre au jour le jour ■ **from one ~ to the next** d'un jour à l'autre ■ **from that ~ on** OR **onwards** à partir de ce jour-là ■ **from that ~ to this** depuis ce jour-là ■ **to the ~ I die** OR **my dying ~** jusqu'à mon dernier jour ■ **I'd rather work in Madrid any ~ (of the week)** je préférerais largement OR de loin travailler à Madrid ■ **from Day One** depuis le premier jour ■ **she's seventy if she's a ~** elle a au moins soixante-dix ans ■ **it's been one of those ~s!** tu parles d'une journée! ■ **let's make a ~ of it** passons-y la journée ■ **you've made my ~!** rien ne saurait me faire plus plaisir! ■ **it's not my (lucky) ~** ce n'est pas mon jour (de chance) ■ **that'll be the ~!** *inf* [it's highly unlikely] il n'y a pas de danger que ça arrive de sitôt!
2. [hours of daylight] jour *m*, journée *f* ■ **in the cold light of ~** à la froide lumière du jour ■ **all ~ (long)** toute la journée ■ **we haven't got all ~** nous n'avons pas que ça à faire ■ **to travel during the** OR **by ~** voyager pendant la journée OR de jour ■ **~ and night, night and ~** jour et nuit, nuit et jour
3. [working hours] journée *f* ■ **to work a seven-hour ~** travailler sept heures par jour, faire des journées de sept heures ➊ **~ off** jour *m* de congé ■ **let's call it a ~** [stop work] arrêtons-nous pour aujourd'hui ; [end relationship] finissons-en ■ **it's all in a ~'s work!** ça fait partie du travail!
4. *(often pl)* [lifetime, era] époque *f* ■ **in the ~s of King Arthur, in King Arthur's ~** du temps du Roi Arthur ■ **in ~s to come** à l'avenir ■ **in ~s gone by** par le passé ■ **in the good old ~s** dans le temps ■ **in my/our ~** de mon/notre temps ■ **in his younger ~s** dans son jeune temps, dans sa jeunesse ■ **the happiest/worst ~s of my life** les plus beaux/les pires jours de ma vie ■ **during the early ~s of the strike/my childhood** au tout début de la grève/de mon enfance ➊ **her ~ will come** son heure viendra ■ **he's had his ~** il a eu son heure ■ **he's/this chair has seen better ~s** il/cette chaise a connu des jours meilleurs ■ **those were the ~s** c'était le bon temps
5. [battle, game] : **to win** OR **to carry the ~** l'emporter.
◇ *comp* : **~ labourer** journalier *m*, - ère *f* ■ **~ pass** [for skiing] forfait *m* journalier ■ **~ work** travail *m* de jour.

◆ **days** *adv* : **to work ~** travailler de jour.

◆ **in this day and age** *adv phr* de nos jours, aujourd'hui.

◆ **in those days** *adv phr* à l'époque.

◆ **one day** *adv phr* un jour.

◆ **one of these days** *adv phr* un de ces jours.

◆ **some day** *adv phr* un jour.

◆ **the other day** *adv phr* l'autre jour.

◆ **these days** *adv phr* : **what are you up to these ~s?** qu'est-ce que tu fais de beau ces temps-ci? ■ **honestly, teenagers these ~s!** vraiment, les adolescents d'aujourd'hui!

◆ **to the day** *adv phr* jour pour jour.

◆ **to this day** *adv phr* à ce jour, aujourd'hui encore.

day bed *n* lit *m* de repos.

daybook ['deɪbʊk] *n* main *f* courante, journal *m*.

dayboy ['deɪbɔɪ] *n UK* SCH demi-pensionnaire *m*.

daybreak ['deɪbreɪk] *n* point *m* du jour ■ **at ~** au point du jour.

day care *n* [for elderly, disabled] service *m* d'accueil de jour ■ [for children] service *m* de garderie.
◆ **day-care** *adj* [facilities - for elderly, disabled] d'accueil de jour ; [- for children] de garderie ■ **~ centre** *centre d'animation et d'aide sociale ;* *US* [for children] garderie *f*.

day centre *n centre d'animation et d'aide sociale.*

daydream ['deɪdriːm] ◇ *n* rêverie *f* ■ *pej* rêvasserie *f* ■ **to be in the middle of a ~** être en pleine rêverie.
◇ *vi* rêver ■ *pej* rêvasser ■ **to ~ about sthg** rêver *OR* rêvasser à qqch.

daydreamer ['deɪdriːməʳ] *n* rêveur *m*, - euse *f*.

daydreaming ['deɪdriːmɪŋ] *n (U)* rêveries *fpl*, rêvasseries *fpl*.

daygirl ['deɪgɜːl] *n UK* SCH demi-pensionnaire *f*.

Day-Glo® ['deɪgləʊ] ◇ *n* tissu *m* fluorescent.
◇ *adj* fluorescent.

daylight ['deɪlaɪt] *n* **1.** [dawn] = **daybreak** **2.** [light of day] jour *m*, lumière *f* du jour ■ **it was still ~** il faisait encore jour ■ **in ~** de jour ■ **in broad ~** en plein jour ■ **to begin to see ~** *fig* [approach end of task] commencer à voir le bout (du tunnel) ➤ **to beat** *OR* **to thrash** *OR* **to knock the living ~s out of sb** *inf* tabasser qqn ■ **to scare** *OR* **to frighten the living ~s out of sb** *inf* flanquer une trouille bleue à qqn.

daylight robbery *n inf* **it's ~** c'est du vol pur et simple.

daylight saving (time) *n* heure *f* d'été.

day nursery *n* garderie *f*.

day-old *adj* [chick, baby] d'un jour.

day pupil *n* SCH (élève *mf*) externe *mf*.

day release *n UK* formation *f* continue en alternance.

day return *n UK* RAIL aller-retour *m* valable pour la journée.

day room *n* salle *f* commune.

day school *n* externat *m*.

day shift *n* [period worked] service *m* de jour ■ [workers] équipe *f* de jour ■ **to work the ~** travailler de jour, être (dans l'équipe) de jour.

daytime ['deɪtaɪm] ◇ *n* journée *f* ■ **in the ~** le jour, pendant la journée.
◇ *adj* de jour.

day-to-day *adj* [life, running of business] quotidien ■ [chores, tasks] journalier, quotidien ■ **to lead a ~ existence** vivre au jour le jour ; [with difficulty] vivre péniblement jour après jour.

day trip *n* excursion *f*.

day tripper *n* excursionniste *mf*.

daze [deɪz] ◇ *n* [caused by blow] étourdissement *m* ■ [caused by emotional shock, surprise] ahurissement *m* ■ [caused by medication] abrutissement *m* ■ **to be in a ~** [because of blow] être étourdi ; [because of emotional shock, surprise] être abasourdi *OR* ahuri ; [because of medication] être abruti.
◇ *vt* [subj: blow] étourdir ■ [subj: emotional shock, surprise] abasourdir, ahurir ■ [subj: medication] abrutir.

dazed [deɪzd] *adj* [by blow] étourdi ■ [by emotional shock, surprise] abasourdi, ahuri ■ [by medication] abruti.

dazzle ['dæzl] *vt liter & fig* éblouir.

dazzling ['dæzlɪŋ] *adj* éblouissant.

dazzlingly ['dæzlɪŋlɪ] *adv* : **~ beautiful** d'une beauté éblouissante.

DBE (*abbrev of* **Dame Commander of the Order of the British Empire**) *n distinction honorifique britannique pour les femmes.*

DBMS (*abbrev of* **database management system**) *n* SGBD *m*.

DBS (*abbrev of* **direct broadcasting by satellite**) *n* télédiffusion *f* directe par satellite.

DC *n* **1.** = **direct current** **2.** = **District of Columbia**.

dd. *written abbr of* **delivered**.

DD (*abbrev of* **Doctor of Divinity**) *n (titulaire d'un) doctorat en théologie.*

D/D *written abbr of* **direct debit**.

D-day *n* le jour J.

DDS (*abbrev of* **Doctor of Dental Science**) *n (titulaire d'un) doctorat en dentisterie.*

DDT (*abbrev of* **dichlorodiphenyltrichloroethane**) *n* DDT *m*.

DE *written abbr of* **Delaware**.

DEA (*abbrev of* **Drug Enforcement Agency**) *pr n agence américaine de lutte contre la drogue.*

deacon ['diːkn] *n* RELIG diacre *m*.

deaconess [ˌdiːkə'nes] *n* RELIG diaconesse *f*.

deactivate [diː'æktɪˌveɪt] *vt* désamorcer.

dead [ded] ◇ *adj* **1.** [not alive - person, animal, plant] mort ; [- flower] fané ■ **~ man** mort *m* ■ **~ woman** morte *f* ■ **the ~ woman's husband** le mari de la défunte ■ **to be ~ on arrival** être mort *OR* décédé à l'arrivée à l'hôpital ■ **~ or alive** mort ou vif ■ **more ~ than alive** plus mort que vif ■ **half ~ with hunger/exhaustion/fear** à demi mort de faim/d'épuisement/de peur ■ **~ and buried** *liter & fig* mort et enterré ■ **stone ~** raide mort ■ **to drop (down)** *OR* **to fall down ~** tomber mort ■ **to shoot sb ~** tuer qqn (avec une arme à feu), abattre qqn ■ **to leave sb for ~** laisser qqn pour mort ■ **you're ~ if he finds out** *inf fig* c'en est fini de toi s'il l'apprend ➤ **drop ~!** *inf* va te faire voir! ■ **~ as a doornail** *OR* **a dodo** *inf* on ne peut plus mort ■ **over my ~ body** *inf* je ne permettrai pas cela de mon vivant, moi vivant c'est hors de question ■ **I wouldn't be seen ~ with him** *inf* plutôt mourir que de me montrer en sa compagnie ■ **~ men tell no tales** *prov* les morts ne parlent pas
2. [lacking in sensation - fingers, toes etc] engourdi ■ **to go ~** s'engourdir ■ **he is ~ to reason** il ne veut pas entendre raison ➤ **she's ~ from the neck up** *inf* elle n'a rien dans la tête ■ **to be ~ to the world** *inf* dormir d'un sommeil de plomb
3. [not alight - fire] mort, éteint ; [- coals] éteint ; [- match] usé
4. [lacking activity - town] mort ; [- business, market] très calme
5. [language] mort
6. SPORT [out of play - ball] hors jeu *(inv)*
7. ELEC [battery] mort, à plat ■ TELEC [phone, line] coupé ■ **the line went ~** la ligne a été coupée
8. [dull - colour] terne, fade ; [- sound] sourd
9. *inf* [tired out] mort, crevé
10. [complete, exact] : **~ calm** NAUT calme *m* plat ■ **~ silence** silence *m* complet *OR* de mort ■ **on a ~ level with sthg** exactement au même niveau que qqch ■ **in ~ earnest** [be] très sérieux ; [speak] très sérieusement ■ **~ cert** *UK inf* [in race, competition] valeur *f* sûre ■ **she fell to the floor in a ~ faint** elle tomba à terre, inconsciente ■ **~ loss** *UK* COMM perte *f* sèche ■ **to be a ~ loss** *UK inf* [person, thing] être complètement nul.
◇ *adv* **1.** [precisely] : **~ ahead** tout droit ■ **~ in the middle** juste au milieu, au beau milieu ■ **to be ~ level (with sthg)** *UK* être exactement au même niveau (que qqch) ■ **~ on time** *UK* juste à l'heure ■ **~ on target** *UK* [hit sthg] en plein dans le mille ■ **you're ~ right** *UK inf* tu as entièrement raison
2. *inf* [very] super ■ **~ drunk** ivre mort
3. [completely] : **the sea was ~ calm** la mer était parfaitement calme ■ **to be ~ against sthg/sb** être absolument contre qqch/qqn
4. : **'~ slow'** AUT 'au pas'
5. *phr* **to play ~** faire le mort ■ **to stop ~** s'arrêter net ■ **to stop sb ~** arrêter qqn net.
◇ *npl* : **the ~** les morts ■ **to rise from the ~** RELIG ressusciter d'entre les morts.
◇ *n* [depth] : **in the ~ of winter** au cœur de l'hiver ■ **in the** *OR* **at ~ of night** au milieu *OR* au plus profond de la nuit.

deadbeat ['dedbi:t] *n inf* bon à rien *m*, bonne à rien *f* ▪ [tramp] épave *f*, loque *f*.

dead beat *adj fig* crevé, mort.

dead duck *n fig* [plan, proposal - which will fail] désastre *m* assuré, plan *m* foireux ; [- which has failed] désastre *m*, fiasco *m* ▪ **he's a ~** c'en est fini de lui.

deaden ['dedn] *vt* [sound] assourdir ▪ [sense, nerve, hunger pangs] calmer ▪ [pain] endormir, calmer ▪ [blow] amortir.

dead end *n* cul *m* de sac, voie *f* sans issue, impasse *f* ▪ **it's a ~** [job] il n'y a aucune perspective d'avenir ; [line of investigation, research] cela ne mènera *OR* conduira à rien ▪ **to come to** *OR* **to reach a ~** *fig* aboutir à une impasse.
◆ **dead-end** *adj* [street] sans issue ▪ **a dead-end job** *fig* un travail qui n'offre aucune perspective d'avenir.

deadening ['dednɪŋ] *adj* [boredom, task] abrutissant.

dead hand *n* **1.** [influence] mainmise *f*, emprise *f* **2.** LAW mainmorte *f*.

deadhead ['dedhed] <> *n* **1.** *inf* [dull person] nullité *f* **2.** [person using free ticket - in theatre] spectateur *m*, - trice *f* ayant un billet de faveur ; [- on train] voyageur *m*, - euse *f* muni(e) d'un billet gratuit **3.** *US* [empty vehicle] *train, avion, camion etc circulant à vide*.
<> *vt* [flowers] enlever les fleurs fanées de.
<> *vi US* [train] circuler à vide.

dead heat *n course dont les vainqueurs sont déclarés ex aequo* ▪ [horse race] dead-heat *m*.

dead letter *n* **1.** [letter that cannot be delivered] lettre *f* non distribuée, (lettre *f* passée au) rebut *m* **2.** [law, rule] loi *f* *OR* règle *f* caduque *OR* tombée en désuétude ▪ **it's a ~** *fig* c'est mort et enterré.

dead-letter box, dead-letter drop *n* cachette *f*.

deadline ['dedlaɪn] *n* [day] date *f* limite ▪ [hour] heure *f* limite ▪ **Monday is the absolute ~** c'est pour lundi dernier délai *OR* dernière limite ▪ **to meet/to miss a ~** respecter/laisser passer une date limite ▪ **I'm working to a ~** j'ai un délai à respecter.

deadliness ['dedlɪnɪs] *n* [of poison, snake] caractère *m* mortel ▪ [of weapon] caractère *m* meurtrier.

deadlock ['dedlɒk] *n* impasse *f* ▪ **to reach (a) ~** arriver à une impasse ▪ **to break the ~** [negotiators] sortir de l'impasse ; [concession] apporter une solution à l'impasse.

deadlocked ['dedlɒkt] *adj* : **to be ~** être dans une impasse.

deadly ['dedlɪ] (*comp* **deadlier**, *superl* **deadliest**) <> *adj* **1.** [lethal - poison, blow] mortel ; [- snake] au venin mortel ; [- weapon] meurtrier ▪ *fig* [hatred] mortel ▪ [silence, pallor] de mort, mortel ▪ **they are ~ enemies** *fig* ce sont des ennemis mortels ⊙ **the seven ~ sins** les sept péchés capitaux **2.** [precise] : **his aim is ~** il a un tir excellent ▪ **with ~ accuracy** avec une extrême précision **3.** [extreme] : **in ~ earnest** [say] avec le plus grand sérieux **4.** *inf* [boring] mortel, barbant.
<> *adv* extrêmement, terriblement ▪ **it was ~ boring** c'était mortellement ennuyeux.

deadly nightshade *n* BOT belladone *f*.

deadpan ['dedpæn] <> *adj* [face, expression] impassible ▪ [humour] pince-sans-rire *(inv)*.
<> *adv* d'un air impassible.

dead ringer *n inf* sosie *m* ▪ **to be a ~ for sb** être le sosie de qqn.

Dead Sea *pr n* : **the ~** la mer Morte.

dead set *adj* : **to be ~ on doing sthg** être fermement décidé à faire qqch ▪ **to be ~ on sthg** tenir absolument *OR* à tout prix à qqch ▪ **to be ~ against sthg/sb** être résolument opposé à qqch/qqn.

dead weight *n liter & fig* poids *m* mort.

dead wood *UK*, **deadwood** ['dedwʊd] *n* [trees, branches] bois *m* mort ▪ *fig* [people] personnel *m* inutile.

deaf [def] <> *adj* sourd ▪ **~ in one ear** sourd d'une oreille ▪ **to turn a ~ ear to sthg/sb** *fig* faire la sourde oreille à qqch/qqn ▪ **our complaints fell on ~ ears** *fig* nos protestations n'ont pas été entendues ⊙ **(as) ~ as a post** sourd comme un pot ▪ **there are none so ~ as those who will not hear** *prov* il n'est pire sourd que celui qui ne veut entendre *prov*.
<> *npl* : **the ~** les sourds *mpl*.

deaf-aid *n* appareil *m* acoustique.

deaf-and-dumb <> *adj* sourd-muet *(attention: le terme 'deaf-and-dumb' est considéré comme injurieux)*.
<> *n* sourd-muet *m*, sourde-muette *f*.

deafen ['defn] *vt liter* rendre sourd ▪ *fig* casser les oreilles à.

deafening ['defnɪŋ] *adj* [music, noise, roar] assourdissant ▪ [applause] retentissant ▪ **the silence was ~** *hum* il y avait un grand silence *OR* un silence impressionnant.

deafeningly ['defnɪŋlɪ] *adv* : **~ loud** assourdissant.

deaf-mute = **deaf-and-dumb**.

deafness ['defnɪs] *n* surdité *f*.

deal [di:l] (*pret & pp* **dealt** [delt]) <> *n* **1.** [agreement] affaire *f*, marché *m* ▪ ST. EX opération *f*, transaction *f* ▪ **business ~** affaire, marché, transaction ▪ **to do** *OR* **to make a ~ with sb** conclure une affaire *OR* un marché avec qqn ▪ **the ~ is off** l'affaire est annulée, le marché est rompu ▪ **the government does not do ~s with terrorists** le gouvernement ne traite pas avec les terroristes ▪ **no ~s!** pas de marchandage! ▪ **no ~!** je ne marche pas! ▪ **it's a ~!** marché conclu! ▪ **you've got (yourself) a ~!** *inf* ça marche!, ça roule! ▪ **that wasn't the ~** ce n'est pas ce qui était convenu ▪ **to get a good ~** faire une bonne affaire
2. [treatment] : **to give sb a fair ~** traiter loyalement avec qqn ▪ **the government promised (to give) teachers a better ~** le gouvernement a promis d'améliorer la condition des enseignants ⊙ **the New Deal** le New Deal, la Nouvelle Donne
3. CARDS donne *f*, distribution *f* ▪ **it's my ~** c'est à moi de donner
4. [quantity] : **a (good) ~ of, a great ~ of** [money, time etc] beaucoup de ▪ **he thinks a good/great ~ of her** il l'estime beaucoup/énormément ▪ **I didn't enjoy it a great ~** je n'ai pas trop *OR* pas tellement aimé ▪ **I didn't do a great ~ last night** je n'ai pas fait grand-chose hier soir ▪ **big ~!** *inf iron* tu parles d'un coup!, la belle affaire! ▪ **he made a big ~ out of it** *inf* il en a fait tout un plat *OR* tout un cinéma ▪ **what's the big ~?** *inf* et alors?, et puis quoi?
5. [timber] planche *f*.
<> *vt* **1.** CARDS donner, distribuer
2. [strike] : **to ~ sb a blow** assener un coup à qqn ▪ **to ~ sthg a blow, to ~ a blow to sthg** *fig* porter un coup à qqch
3. [drugs] revendre.
<> *vi* **1.** CARDS distribuer les cartes
2. COMM négocier, traiter ▪ **to ~ on the Stock Exchange** faire des opérations *OR* des transactions en bourse ▪ **to ~ in death/human misery** *fig* être un marchand de mort/de misère humaine
3. *inf* [in drugs] revendre de la drogue.
◆ **deal in** *vt sep* CARDS [player] donner *OR* distribuer des cartes à, servir ▪ **~ me in** *fig* tu peux compter sur moi.
◆ **deal out** *vt sep* [cards, gifts] donner, distribuer ▪ [justice] rendre ▪ [punishment] distribuer ▪ **~ me out** *fig* ne compte pas sur moi.
◆ **deal with** *vt insep* **1.** [handle - problem, situation, query, complaint] traiter ; [- customer, member of the public] traiter avec ; [- difficult situation, child] s'occuper de ▪ **a difficult child to ~ with** un enfant difficile ▪ **I can't ~ with all the work I've got** je ne me sors pas de tout le travail que j'ai ▪ **the management dealt with the situation promptly** la direction a réagi immédiatement ▪ **the culprits were dealt with severely** les coupables ont été sévèrement punis ▪ **that's that dealt with** voilà qui est fait
2. [do business with] traiter *OR* négocier avec
3. [be concerned with] traiter de ▪ **in my lecture, I shall ~ with...** dans mon cours, je traiterai de...

dealer ['di:ləʳ] *n* **1.** COMM marchand *m*, - e *f*, négociant *m*, - e *f* ▪ ST. EX marchand *m*, -e *f* de titres ▪ AUT concessionnaire *mf* **2.** [in drugs] dealer *m* **3.** CARDS donneur *m*, - euse *f*.

dealership ['di:ləʃɪp] *n* AUT & COMM concession *f*.

dealing ['di:lɪŋ] *n* **1.** *(U)* ST. EX opérations *fpl*, transactions *fpl* ▪ [trading] commerce *m* **2.** *(U)* [of cards] donne *f*, distribution *f* **3.** : **~s** [business] affaires *fpl*, transactions *fpl* ; [personal] relations *fpl* ▪ **to have ~s with sb** [in business] traiter avec qqn, avoir affaire à qqn ; [personal] avoir affaire à qqn **4.** [in drugs] trafic *m* de drogue.

dealt [delt] *pt & pp* ▻ **deal**.

dean [di:n] *n* UNIV & RELIG doyen *m*, - enne *f*.

deanery ['di:nərɪ] *n* RELIG doyenné *m* ▪ UNIV résidence *f* du doyen.

dear [dɪəʳ] <> *adj* **1.** [loved] cher ▪ [precious] cher, précieux ▪ [appealing] adorable, charmant ▪ **he is a ~ friend of mine** c'est un ami très cher ▪ **she's such a ~ girl** elle est tellement gentille ▪ **Margaret ~est** ma chère Margaret ▪ **he/the memory is very ~ to me** il/ce souvenir m'est très cher ▪ **to hold sb/sthg ~** *lit* chérir qqn/qqch ▪ **to run for ~ life** courir à toute vitesse ▪ **to hang on for ~ life** s'accrocher désespérément ; MED s'accrocher à la vie ▪ **my ~ fellow** mon cher ami ▪ **my ~ Mrs Stevens** chère madame Stevens ▪ **what a ~ little child/cottage/frock!** quel enfant/quel cottage/quelle robe adorable! **2.** [in letter] : **Dear Sir** Monsieur ▪ **Dear Sir or Madam** Madame, Monsieur ▪ **Dear Mrs Baker** Madame ; [less formal] Chère Madame ; [informal] Chère Madame Baker ▪ **Dear Mum and Dad** Chers Maman et Papa ▪ **My ~ Clare** Ma chère Clare ▪ **Dearest Richard** Très cher Richard **3.** [expensive - item, shop] cher ; [- price] haut, élevé ▪ **things are getting ~er** *esp UK* la vie augmente.
<> *interj* : **~!, ~!~!, ~ me!, oh ~!** [surprise] oh mon Dieu! ; [regret] oh là là! ▪ **oh ~!** [worry] mon Dieu!
<> *n* : **my ~** [to child, spouse, lover] mon chéri, ma chérie ; [to friend] mon cher, ma chère ▪ **my ~est** mon chéri, ma chérie ▪ **she's such a ~** elle est tellement gentille ▪ **I gave the old ~ my seat** *UK inf* j'ai laissé ma place à la vieille dame ▪ **be a ~ and answer the phone, answer the phone, there's a ~** sois gentil *OR* un amour, réponds au téléphone.
<> *adv* [sell, pay, cost] cher *(adv)*.

dear Abby [-'æbɪ] *n US la rubrique courrier du cœur.*

dearie ['dɪərɪ] *inf* <> *n* chéri *m*, - e *f*.
<> *interj* : **(oh) ~ me!** oh mon Dieu!

Dear John (letter) *n inf* lettre *f* de rupture.

dearly ['dɪəlɪ] *adv* **1.** [very much] beaucoup, énormément ▪ **~ beloved son of...** [on gravestone] fils bien-aimé de... **2.** [at high cost] : **to pay ~ for sthg** payer cher qqch.

dearth [dɜ:θ] *n* pénurie *f*.

death [deθ] *n* mort *f* ▪ LAW décès *m* ▪ **their ~s were caused by smoke inhalation** leur mort a été causée *OR* provoquée par l'inhalation de fumée ▪ **a ~ in the family** un décès dans la famille ▪ **to fall/to jump to one's ~** se tuer en tombant/se jetant dans le vide ▪ **to freeze/to starve to ~** mourir de froid/de faim ▪ **to be beaten to ~** être battu à mort ▪ **to be burnt to ~** mourir brûlé ▪ **to bleed to ~** perdre tout son sang ▪ **to fight to the ~** se battre à mort ▪ **to meet one's ~** trouver la mort ▪ **to meet an early ~** mourir jeune ▪ **condemned to** *OR* **under sentence of ~** condamné à mort ▪ **to sentence/to put sb to ~** condamner/mettre qqn à mort ▪ **to smoke/to drink o.s. to ~** se tuer à force de fumer/boire ▪ **till ~ do us part** jusqu'à ce que la mort nous sépare ▪ **this means the ~ of the steel industry** cela sonne le glas de la sidérurgie ▪ **it's been done to ~** *fig* [play, subject for novel etc] ça a été fait et refait ▪ **to discuss sthg to ~** *fig* discuter de qqch jusqu'à l'épuisement du sujet ▪ **to look like ~ (warmed up)** *inf* avoir une mine de déterré ▪ **to feel like ~ (warmed up)** *inf* être en piteux état ▪ **to catch one's ~ (of cold)** *inf* attraper la mort *OR* la crève ▪ **to be in at the ~** *fig* être présent à la fin ▪ **to die a horrible ~** avoir une mort atroce ▪ **to be sick** *OR* **tired to ~ of** *inf* en avoir ras le bol de ▪ **to be bored to ~** *inf* s'ennuyer à mourir ▪ **to be worried/scared to ~** *inf* être mort d'inquiétude/de frousse ▪ **you'll be the ~ of me** *inf* [with amusement] tu me feras mourir (de rire) ; [with irritation] tu es tuant ▪ **that job will be the ~ of her** ce travail la tuera ➋ **to be at ~'s door** [patient] être à l'article de la mort ▪ **to die a thousand ~s** [worry about somebody] mourir d'inquiétude ; [worry about oneself] être mort de peur ; [be embarrassed] mourir de honte ▪ **to die a ~** *inf* [actor, film] faire un bide ; [joke] tomber à plat ; [idea, plan, hope] tomber à l'eau ▪ **~ by misadventure** mort accidentelle ▪ **to hang** *OR* **to hold** *OR* **to cling on like grim ~** s'accrocher désespérément ▪ **'Death in the Afternoon'** *Hemingway* 'Mort dans l'après-midi' ▪ **'Death of a Salesman'** *Miller* 'Mort d'un commis voyageur'.

deathbed ['deθbed] <> *n* lit *m* de mort ▪ **on one's ~** sur son lit de mort.
<> *adj* [confession] fait à l'article de la mort ▪ [repentance] exprimé à l'article de la mort ▪ **the ~ scene** THEAT la scène du lit de mort.

deathblow ['deθbləʊ] *n fig* coup *m* fatal *OR* mortel ▪ **to be the ~ for sthg** porter un coup fatal *OR* mortel à qqch.

death camp *n* camp *m* de la mort.

death certificate *n* acte *m OR* certificat *m* de décès.

death-dealing *adj* mortel, fatal.

death duty *n* droits *mpl* de succession.

death knell *n* glas *m* ▪ **to sound the ~ for** *OR* **of sthg** *fig* sonner le glas de qqch.

deathless ['deθlɪs] *adj* immortel ▪ *hum* [prose] inimitable.

deathly ['deθlɪ] <> *adj* [silence, pallor] de mort, mortel.
<> *adv* : **~ pale** pâle comme la mort ▪ **~ cold** glacial ▪ **the house was ~ quiet** [silent] la maison était plongée dans un profond silence ; [sinister] la maison était plongée dans un silence de mort.

death mask *n* masque *m* mortuaire.

death penalty *n* peine *f* de mort, peine *f* capitale.

death rate *n* taux *m* de mortalité.

death rattle *n* râle *m* d'agonie.

death row *n* quartier *m* des condamnés à mort ▪ **he's been on ~ for ten years** cela fait dix ans qu'il est au quartier des condamnés à mort.

death sentence *n* condamnation *f* à mort.

death squad *n* escadron *m* de la mort.

death tax *US* = **death duty**.

death throes [-,θrəʊz] *npl* agonie *f* ▪ [painful] affres *fpl* de la mort ▪ *fig* agonie *f* ▪ **to be in one's ~** agoniser, être agonisant ; [suffering] connaître les affres de la mort ▪ **to be in its ~** *fig* [project, business etc] agoniser, être agonisant.

death toll *n* nombre *m* de morts ▪ **the ~ stands at 567** il y a 567 morts, le bilan est de 567 morts.

death trap *n* : **the building is a ~** l'édifice est extrêmement dangereux.

Death Valley *pr n* la Vallée de la Mort.

death warrant *n* ordre *m* d'exécution ▪ **to sign one's own ~** *fig* signer son propre arrêt de mort.

deathwatch beetle *n* grande *OR* grosse vrillette *f*, horloger *m* de la mort.

death wish *n* PSYCHOL désir *m* de mort ▪ **he seems to have a ~** *fig* il faut croire qu'il est suicidaire.

deb [deb] *inf* = **debutante**.

debacle [deɪ'bɑ:kl] *n* débâcle *f*.

debar [di:'bɑ:ʳ] (*pret & pp* **debarred**, *cont* **debarring**) *vt* interdire à ▪ **to ~ sb from sthg/doing sthg** interdire qqch à qqn/à qqn de faire qqch.

debase [dɪ'beɪs] *vt* [degrade - person, sport] avilir, abaisser ; [- quality of object] dégrader, altérer ; [- currency] altérer ▪ *fig* dévaloriser.

debasement [dɪ'beɪsmənt] *n* [of person, sport] avilissement *m*, abaissement *m* ▪ [of quality of object] dégradation *f*, altération *f* ▪ [of currency] altération *f* ▪ *fig* dévalorisation *f*.

debatable [dɪ'beɪtəbl] *adj* discutable, contestable ▪ **it is ~ whether...** on peut se demander si..., on peut se poser la question de savoir si..

debate [dɪ'beɪt] ◇ *vt* [one person] se demander ■ [two or more people] débattre, discuter ■ **a much ~d question** une question très débattue.
◇ *vi* discuter ■ **to ~ (with o.s.) whether to do sthg or not** se demander si on doit faire qqch.
◇ *n* [gen] discussion *f* ■ [organized] débat *m* ■ **to have** *OR* **to hold a ~ about** *OR* **on sthg** tenir un débat *OR* avoir une discussion sur *OR* à propos de qqch ■ **there's been a lot of ~ about it** cela a été très *OR* longuement débattu ■ **the subject under ~** le sujet des débats ■ **open to ~** discutable, contestable ■ **after much** *OR* **lengthy ~** [between two or more people] après de longs débats ; [with oneself] après de longs débats intérieurs ■ **to be the subject of ~** faire le thème de débats.

debater [dɪ'beɪtəʳ] *n* débatteur *m* ■ **to be a skilled ~** exceller dans les débats.

debating [dɪ'beɪtɪŋ] ◇ *n* art *m* du débat.
◇ *comp* : **~ society** société *f* de débats contradictoires.

debauch [dɪ'bɔːtʃ] *vt* débaucher ■ *arch* & *lit* [woman] séduire.

debauched [dɪ'bɔːtʃt] *adj* débauché.

debauchee [dɪbɔː'tʃiː] *n* débauché *m*, - e *f*.

debauchery [dɪ'bɔːtʃərɪ] *n* débauche *f*.

debenture [dɪ'bentʃəʳ] FIN ◇ *n* obligation *f*.
◇ *comp* : **~ bond** titre *m* d'obligation.

debilitate [dɪ'bɪlɪteɪt] *vt* débiliter.

debilitating [dɪ'bɪlɪteɪtɪŋ] *adj* [illness] débilitant ■ [climate] anémiant.

debility [dɪ'bɪlətɪ] *n* débilité *f*.

debit ['debɪt] FIN ◇ *n* débit *m* ■ **your account is in ~** *UK* votre compte est déficitaire *OR* débiteur.
◇ *comp* [balance, account] débiteur ■ **~ entry** écriture *f* au débit ■ **~ note** note *f* de débit ■ **~ side** débit *m* ■ **on the ~ side, it means we won't see her** *fig* l'inconvénient, c'est que nous ne la verrons pas.
◇ *vt* [account] débiter ■ [person] porter au débit de qqn ■ **to ~ £50 from sb's account, to ~ sb's account with £50** débiter 50 livres du compte de qqn, débiter le compte de qqn de 50 livres.

debit card *n* carte *f* de paiement à débit immédiat.

debonair [ˌdebə'neəʳ] *adj* d'une élégance nonchalante.

debrief [ˌdiː'briːf] *vt* faire faire un compte rendu verbal de mission à, débriefer.

debriefing [ˌdiː'briːfɪŋ] ◇ *n* compte rendu *m* verbal de mission.
◇ *comp* : **~ officer** officier *m* chargé de recevoir le compte rendu verbal des pilotes ■ **~ room** salle *f* de compte rendu de mission.

debris ['deɪbriː] *n (U)* débris *mpl*.

debt [det] ◇ *n* [gen] dette *f* ■ ADMIN créance *f* ■ **to be in ~, to have ~s** avoir des dettes, être endetté ■ **to get** *OR* **to run into ~** s'endetter ■ **to get out of ~** s'acquitter de ses dettes ■ **to pay one's ~s** régler ses dettes ■ **he has paid his ~ to society** il s'est acquitté de sa dette envers la société ■ **to be in ~ to sb** être endetté auprès de qqn ; *fig* avoir une dette envers qqn, être redevable à qqn ▶ **bad ~** mauvaise créance ■ **outstanding ~** dette *OR* créance à recouvrer.
◇ *comp* [rescheduling, servicing] de la dette ■ **~ collector** agent *m* de recouvrement ■ **~ collection agency** bureau *m* de recouvrement *OR* récupération des créances.

debtor ['detəʳ] *n* débiteur *m*, - trice *f* ■ **~ nations** pays *mpl* débiteurs.

debt-ridden *adj* criblé de dettes.

debug [ˌdiː'bʌg] (*pret & pp* **debugged**, *cont* **debugging**) *vt* **1.** COMPUT [program] déboguer ■ [machine] mettre au point **2.** [remove hidden microphones from] débarrasser des micros (cachés) **3.** [remove insects from] débarrasser des insectes, désinsectiser.

debugger [ˌdiː'bʌgəʳ] *n* COMPUT débogueur *m*.

debugging [ˌdiː'bʌgɪŋ] ◇ *n* **1.** COMPUT [of program] débogage *m* ■ [of machine] mise *f* au point **2.** [removal of microphones] élimination *f* des micros (cachés) **3.** [removal of insects] désinsectisation *f*.
◇ *comp* **1.** COMPUT de débogage **2.** [to remove microphones - operation] d'élimination des micros (cachés) ; [- team] chargé d'éliminer les micros (cachés) ; [- expert] dans l'élimination de micros (cachés) **3.** [to remove insects] de désinsectisation.

debunk [ˌdiː'bʌŋk] *vt inf* [ridicule] tourner en ridicule ■ [show to be false] discréditer.

debut ['deɪbjuː] (*pret & pp* **debut'd**) ◇ *n* début *m* ■ **to make one's ~** faire ses débuts.
◇ *vi* débuter.

debutante ['debjʊtɑːnt] *n* débutante *f*.

Dec. (*written abbrev of* **December**) déc.

decade ['dekeɪd] *n* **1.** [ten years] décennie *f* ■ **over a ~ ago** il y a plus de dix ans **2.** RELIG dizaine *f*.

decadence ['dekədəns] *n* décadence *f*.

decadent ['dekədənt] ◇ *adj* décadent.
◇ *n* **1.** personne *f* décadente **2.** ART décadent *m*, - e *f*.

decaf(f) ['diːkæf] *n inf* [coffee] déca *m*.

decaffeinated [dɪ'kæfɪneɪtɪd] *adj* décaféiné.

decagon ['dekəgən] *n* décagone *m*.

decagramme *UK*, **decagram** *US* ['dekəgræm] *n* décagramme *m*.

decal ['diːkæl] *n inf* décalcomanie *f*.

decalcify [ˌdiː'kælsɪfaɪ] *vt* décalcifier.

decalitre *UK*, **decaliter** *US* ['dekəˌliːtəʳ] *n* décalitre *m*.

decametre *UK*, **decameter** *US* ['dekəˌmiːtəʳ] *n* décamètre *m*.

decamp [dɪ'kæmp] *vi* **1.** MIL lever le camp **2.** *inf* [abscond] décamper, ficher le camp.

decant [dɪ'kænt] *vt* décanter.

decanter [dɪ'kæntəʳ] *n* carafe *f*.

decapitate [dɪ'kæpɪteɪt] *vt* décapiter.

decapitation [dɪˌkæpɪ'teɪʃn] *n* décapitation *f*.

decathlete [dɪ'kæθliːt] *n* décathlonien *m*, - enne *f*.

decathlon [dɪ'kæθlɒn] *n* décathlon *m*.

decay [dɪ'keɪ] ◇ *vi* **1.** [rot - food, wood, flowers] pourrir ; [- meat] s'avarier, pourrir ; [- corpse] se décomposer ; [- tooth] se carier ; [- building] se délabrer ; [- stone] s'effriter, se désagréger ■ *fig* [- beauty, civilization, faculties] décliner **2.** PHYS dépérir, se dégrader, se désintégrer.
◇ *vt* [wood] pourrir ■ [stone] désagréger ■ [tooth] carier.
◇ *n* **1.** [of food, wood, flowers] pourrissement *m* ■ [of corpse] décomposition *f* ■ [of building] délabrement *m* ■ [of stone] effritement *m*, désagrégation *f* ■ *fig* [of beauty, faculties] délabrement *m* ■ [of civilization] déclin *m* ■ **to fall into ~** *liter* & *fig* se délabrer ■ **moral ~** déchéance *f* morale ▶ **tooth ~** *(U)* caries *fpl* **2.** PHYS désintégration *f*, dégradation *f*.

decayed [dɪ'keɪd] *adj* [food, wood, flowers] pourri ■ [meat] avarié, pourri ■ [corpse] décomposé ■ [tooth] carié ■ [building] délabré, en ruines ■ [stone] effrité, désagrégé ■ *fig* [beauty] fané ■ [civilization] délabré, en ruines.

decaying [dɪ'keɪɪŋ] *adj* [food, wood, flowers] pourrissant ■ [meat] en train de s'avarier ■ [corpse] en décomposition ■ [tooth] en train de se carier ■ [building] qui se délabre ■ [stone] en désagrégation ■ *fig* [beauty] qui se fane ■ [civilization] sur le déclin.

decease [dɪ'siːs] ◇ *n* décès *m*.
◇ *vi* décéder.

deceased [dɪ'siːst] (*pl inv*) ◇ *adj* décédé, défunt.
◇ *n* : **the ~** le défunt, la défunte.

deceit [dɪ'siːt] *n* **1.** [quality] duplicité *f* **2.** [trick] supercherie *f*, tromperie *f* **3.** LAW fraude *f* ■ **by ~** frauduleusement.

deceitful [dɪ'si:tfʊl] *adj* trompeur ▪ [behaviour] trompeur, sournois.

deceitfully [dɪ'si:tfʊlɪ] *adv* trompeusement, avec duplicité.

deceive [dɪ'si:v] *vt* tromper ▪ **to ~ sb into doing sthg** amener qqn à faire qqch en le trompant ▪ **she ~d me into believing that...** elle m'a fait croire que... ▪ **to ~ o.s.** se mentir à soi-même ▪ **unless my eyes ~ me** à moins que mes yeux ne me jouent des tours *OR* que ma vue ne me joue des tours.

deceiver [dɪ'si:vər] *n* trompeur *m*, - euse *f*.

decelerate [,di:'seləreɪt] *vi* & *vt* ralentir.

deceleration ['di:,selə'reɪʃn] *n* ralentissement *m*.

December [dɪ'sembər] *n* décembre, *see also* **February**.

decency ['di:snsɪ] (*pl* **decencies**) *n* décence *f* ▪ **for ~'s sake** pour respecter les convenances ▪ **an offence against public ~** *UK* un outrage à la pudeur ▪ **to have the (common) ~ to do sthg** avoir la décence de faire qqch ▪ **to observe the decencies** observer les convenances.

decent ['di:snt] *adj* **1.** [proper, morally correct] décent, convenable ▪ **to do the ~ thing** se comporter *OR* agir dans les règles ; [marry woman one has made pregnant] faire son devoir, réparer ▪ **are you ~?** [dressed] es-tu visible? **2.** [satisfactory, reasonable - housing, wage] décent, convenable ; [- price] convenable, raisonnable ▪ **a ~ night's sleep** une bonne nuit de sommeil ▪ **the rooms are a ~ size** les pièces sont de bonne taille ▪ **to speak ~ French** parler assez bien *OR* parler convenablement le français **3.** *inf* [kind, good] bien, sympa ▪ **that's very ~ of you** c'est très sympa de ta part.

decently ['di:sntlɪ] *adv* **1.** [properly] décemment, convenablement **2.** [reasonably] : **the job pays ~** le travail paie raisonnablement bien.

decentralization [di:,sentrəlaɪ'zeɪʃn] *n* décentralisation *f*.

decentralize [,di:'sentrəlaɪz] *vt* décentraliser.

deception [dɪ'sepʃn] *n* **1.** [act of deceiving] tromperie *f*, duperie *f* LAW : **by ~** en usant de tromperie **2.** [trick] subterfuge *m*, tromperie *f* **3.** [state of being deceived] duperie *f*.

deceptive [dɪ'septɪv] *adj* trompeur ▪ **appearances can be ~** il ne faut pas se fier aux apparences, les apparences sont trompeuses.

deceptively [dɪ'septɪvlɪ] *adv* : **it looks ~ easy/near** cela donne l'illusion d'être facile/tout près, on a l'impression que c'est facile/tout près ▪ **he has a ~ calm exterior** il a une apparence calme qui n'est qu'illusoire.

decibel ['desɪbel] *n* décibel *m*.

decide [dɪ'saɪd] <> *vt* **1.** [resolve] décider ▪ **to ~ to do sthg** décider de faire qqch ▪ **it was ~d to alter our strategy** il a été décidé que nous devions modifier notre stratégie ▪ **the weather hasn't ~d what it's doing yet** le temps n'arrive pas à se décider **2.** [determine - outcome, sb's fate, career] décider de, déterminer ; [- person] décider ▪ **that was what ~d me to leave him** c'est ce qui m'a décidé à le quitter **3.** [settle - debate, war] décider de l'issue de.
<> *vi* **1.** [make up one's mind] décider, se décider ▪ **I can't ~** je n'arrive pas à me décider ▪ **you ~** c'est toi qui décides ▪ **to ~ against/in favour of doing sthg** décider de ne pas/de faire qqch ▪ **to ~ in favour of sb/sthg** LAW décider en faveur de qqn/qqch ▪ **to ~ against sb/sthg** LAW décider contre qqn/qqch ▪ **you'll have to ~ between me and him** il va falloir choisir entre moi et lui **2.** [determine] : **but circumstances ~d otherwise** mais les circonstances en ont décidé autrement.
◆ **decide on** *vt insep* décider de, se décider pour ▪ **what plan of action have you ~d on?** pour quel plan d'action vous êtes-vous décidé?, quel plan d'action avez-vous décidé de suivre?

decided [dɪ'saɪdɪd] *adj* **1.** [distinct - improvement, difference] net, incontestable ; [- success] éclatant **2.** [resolute - person, look] décidé, résolu ; [- opinion, stance] ferme ; [- effort] résolu ; [- refusal] ferme, catégorique.

decidedly [dɪ'saɪdɪdlɪ] *adv* **1.** [distinctly - better, different] vraiment ▪ **I feel ~ unwell today** je ne me sens vraiment pas bien aujourd'hui **2.** [resolutely] résolument, fermement.

decider [dɪ'saɪdər] *n* [goal] but *m* décisif ▪ [point] point *m* décisif ▪ [match] match *m* décisif, rencontre *f* décisive ▪ [factor] facteur *m* décisif.

deciding [dɪ'saɪdɪŋ] *adj* décisif, déterminant ▪ **the chairperson has the ~ vote** la voix du président est prépondérante.

deciduous [dɪ'sɪdjʊəs] *adj* [tree] à feuilles caduques ▪ [leaves, antlers] caduc.

decilitre *UK*, **deciliter** *US* ['desɪ,li:tər] *n* décilitre *m*.

decimal ['desɪml] <> *adj* décimal ▪ **to go ~** adopter le système décimal.
<> *n* chiffre *m* décimal.

decimal currency *n* monnaie *f* décimale.

decimal fraction = **decimal** *(n)*.

decimalization [,desɪməlaɪ'zeɪʃn] *n* décimalisation *f*.

decimal place *n* décimale *f* ▪ **correct to four ~s** exact jusqu'à la quatrième décimale *OR* jusqu'au quatrième chiffre après la virgule *OR* au dix millième près.

decimal point *n* virgule *f*.

decimal system *n* système *m* décimal.

decimate ['desɪmeɪt] *vt* décimer.

decimetre *UK*, **decimeter** *US* ['desɪ,mi:tər] *n* décimètre *m*.

decipher [dɪ'saɪfər] *vt* [code, handwriting] déchiffrer.

decipherable [dɪ'saɪfərəbl] *adj* déchiffrable.

decision [dɪ'sɪʒn] <> *n* **1.** décision *f* ▪ **to make** *OR* **to take a ~** prendre une décision, se décider ; LAW & ADMIN prendre une décision ▪ **to come to** *OR* **to arrive at** *OR* **to reach a ~** parvenir à une décision ▪ **to make the right/wrong ~** faire le bon/mauvais choix ▪ **it's your ~** c'est toi qui décides ▪ **is that your ~?** ta décision est prise? ▪ **the referee's ~ is final** la décision de l'arbitre est irrévocable *OR* sans appel **2.** *fml* [decisiveness] résolution *f*, fermeté *f* **3.** [decision-making] : **it's a matter for personal ~** c'est une affaire de choix personnel.
<> *comp* COMPUT : **~ table** table *f* de décision.

decision-maker *n* décideur *m*, - euse *f*, décisionnaire *mf*.

decision-making *n* prise *f* de décision.

decisive [dɪ'saɪsɪv] *adj* **1.** [manner, person] décidé, résolu ▪ **be ~!** montre-toi décidé *OR* résolu! **2.** [factor, argument] décisif, déterminant.

decisively [dɪ'saɪsɪvlɪ] *adv* **1.** [resolutely] résolument, sans hésitation **2.** [conclusively] de manière décisive.

decisiveness [dɪ'saɪsɪvnɪs] *n* **1.** [of person] décision *f* **2.** [of battle] caractère *m* décisif *OR* déterminant.

deck [dek] <> *n* **1.** NAUT pont *m* ▪ **on ~** sur le pont ▪ **below ~** *OR* **~s** sous le pont ▪ **to clear the ~s** *fig* mettre de l'ordre avant de passer à l'action **2.** [of plane, bus] étage *m* ▪ **top** *OR* **upper ~** [of bus] impériale *f* **3.** *US* CARDS jeu *m* de cartes **4.** [in hi-fi system] platine *f* **5.** *US* [of house] ponton *m*.
<> *comp* NAUT [officer, cabin, crane] de pont ▪ **~ cargo** pontée *f*.
<> *vt* = **deck out**.
◆ **deck out** *vt sep* parer, orner ▪ **to ~ o.s. out in one's best clothes** se mettre sur son trente et un.

deckchair ['dektʃeər] *n* chaise *f* longue, transat *m*.

deckhand ['dekhænd] *n* matelot *m*.

deckhouse ['dekhaʊs] (*pl* [-haʊzɪz]) *n* rouf *m*.

deckle ['dekl] *n* cadre *m* volant *(utilisé dans la fabrication artisanale du papier)*.

deck shoe *n* chaussure *f* bateau.

declaim [dɪ'kleɪm] <> *vi* déclamer ▪ **to ~ against sthg** récriminer *OR* se récrier contre qqch.
<> *vt* déclamer.

declamation [ˌdekləˈmeɪʃn] *n* déclamation *f*.

declamatory [dɪˈklæmətrɪ] *adj* [style] déclamatoire.

declaration [ˌdekləˈreɪʃn] *n* **1.** [gen] déclaration *f* ■ **to make a ~ that...** déclarer que... ■ **customs ~** déclaration en douane **2.** CARDS annonce *f*.

Declaration of Independence *n* : **the ~** *US* HIST la Déclaration d'indépendance (américaine).

THE DECLARATION OF INDEPENDENCE

Document rédigé par Thomas Jefferson et proclamant, le 4 juillet 1776, l'indépendance des 13 colonies de la Nouvelle-Angleterre. Cette déclaration est considérée comme l'acte de naissance des États-Unis d'Amérique.

declarative [dɪˈklærətɪv] *adj* déclaratif.

declaratory [dɪˈklærətrɪ] *adj* LAW déclaratoire.

declare [dɪˈkleəʳ] ◇ *vt* **1.** [proclaim - independence, war etc] déclarer ■ **have you anything to ~?** [at customs] avez-vous quelque chose à déclarer? **2.** [announce] déclarer ■ **to ~ o.s.** [proclaim one's love] se déclarer ; POL se présenter, présenter sa candidature **3.** CARDS : **to ~ one's hand** annoncer son jeu.
◇ *vi* **1.** : **to ~ for/against** faire une déclaration en faveur de/contre ■ **well, I (do) ~!** eh bien ça alors! **2.** CARDS faire l'annonce, annoncer ■ [in cricket] déclarer la tournée terminée *(avant sa fin normale)*.

declared [dɪˈkleəd] *adj* [intention, opponent] déclaré, ouvert.

declassified [ˌdi:ˈklæsɪfaɪd] *adj* [information] déclassé.

declassify [ˌdi:ˈklæsɪfaɪ] (*pret & pp* **declassified**) *vt* [information] déclasser.

declension [dɪˈklenʃn] *n* GRAM déclinaison *f*.

declination [ˌdeklɪˈneɪʃn] *n* ASTRON déclinaison *f*.

decline [dɪˈklaɪn] ◇ *n* [decrease - in prices, standards, crime, profits] baisse *f* ■ *fig* [of civilization] déclin *m* ■ **to be in ~** être en déclin ■ **to be on the ~** [prices, sales] être en baisse ; [civilization, influence] être sur le déclin ■ **to fall into a ~** *dated* [person] dépérir ➊ **'Decline and Fall'** ***Waugh*** 'Grandeur et décadence'.
◇ *vt* **1.** [refuse - invitation, honour, offer of help] décliner, refuser ; [- food, drink] refuser ; [- responsibility] décliner ■ **to ~ to do sthg** refuser de faire qqch **2.** GRAM décliner.
◇ *vi* **1.** [decrease, diminish - empire, health] décliner ; [- prices, sales, population] baisser, être en baisse, diminuer ; [- influence, enthusiasm, fame] baisser, diminuer ■ **to ~ in importance/value/significance** perdre de son importance/de sa valeur/de sa signification **2.** [refuse] refuser **3.** [slope downwards] être en pente, descendre **4.** GRAM se décliner.

declining [dɪˈklaɪnɪŋ] *adj* [health, industry, market] sur le déclin ■ **he is in ~ health** sa santé décline *OR* faiblit.

declutch [dɪˈklʌtʃ] *vi* AUT débrayer.

decode [ˌdi:ˈkəʊd] *vt* décoder, déchiffrer ■ COMPUT & TV décoder.

decoder [ˌdi:ˈkəʊdəʳ] *n* décodeur *m*.

decoding [ˌdi:ˈkəʊdɪŋ] *n* décodage *m*.

decoke [ˌdi:ˈkəʊk] *UK* AUT ◇ *vt* décalaminer.
◇ *n* décalaminage *m*.

décolleté [deɪˈkɒlteɪ] ◇ *adj* décolleté.
◇ *n* décolleté *m*.

decolonization [di:ˌkɒlənaɪˈzeɪʃn] *n* décolonisation *f*.

decommission [ˌdi:kəˈmɪʃn] *vt* **1.** [shut down - nuclear power station] déclasser **2.** MIL [remove from active service - warship, aircraft, weapon] mettre hors service.

decompose [ˌdi:kəmˈpəʊz] ◇ *vi* se décomposer.
◇ *vt* CHEM & PHYS décomposer.

decomposition [ˌdi:kɒmpəˈzɪʃn] *n* [gen - CHEM & PHYS] décomposition *f*.

decompress [ˌdi:kəmˈpres] *vt* [gas, air] décomprimer ■ [diver] faire passer en chambre de décompression.

decompression [ˌdi:kəmˈpreʃn] *n* décompression *f*.

decompression chamber *n* chambre *f* de décompression.

decompression sickness *n* maladie *f* des caissons.

decongestant [ˌdi:kənˈdʒestənt] MED ◇ *n* décongestif *m*.
◇ *adj* décongestif.

deconstruct [ˌdi:kənˈstrʌkt] *vt* déconstruire.

deconstruction [ˌdi:kənˈstrʌkʃn] *n* déconstruction *f*.

decontaminate [ˌdi:kənˈtæmɪneɪt] *vt* décontaminer.

decontamination [ˈdi:kənˌtæmɪˈneɪʃn] ◇ *n* décontamination *f*.
◇ *comp* [equipment, team] de décontamination ■ [expert] en décontamination.

decontrol [ˌdi:kənˈtrəʊl] ◇ *vt* lever le contrôle gouvernemental sur ■ **to ~ prices** libérer les prix.
◇ *n* [of prices] libération *f*.

decontrolled road [ˌdi:kənˈtrəʊld-] *n* route *f* sans limitation de vitesse.

decor [ˈdeɪkɔ:ʳ] *n* décor *m*.

decorate [ˈdekəreɪt] ◇ *vt* **1.** [house, room - paint] peindre ; [- wallpaper] tapisser, décorer **2.** [dress, hat] garnir, orner ■ [cake, tree, street] décorer **3.** [give medal to] décorer, médailler ■ **to be ~d for bravery** être décoré pour son courage.
◇ *vi* [paint] peindre ■ [wallpaper] tapisser.

decorating [ˈdekəreɪtɪŋ] *n* **1.** [of house, room] décoration *f* ■ **painting and ~** *UK* peinture *f* et décoration **2.** [of dress, hat] garnissage *m*, ornementation *f* ■ [of cake, tree, street] décoration *f*.

decoration [ˌdekəˈreɪʃn] *n* **1.** [action - of house, street, cake, tree] décoration *f* ; [- of dress, hat] ornementation *f* **2.** [ornament - for house, street, cake, tree] décoration *f* ; [- for dress, hat] garniture *f*, ornements *mpl* ■ **Christmas ~s** décorations de Noël **3.** [medal] décoration *f*, médaille *f*.

Decoration Day *n fête nationale américaine en souvenir des soldats morts à la guerre; appelée aussi 'Memorial Day' (dernier lundi de mai)*.

decorative [ˈdekərətɪv] *adj* décoratif, ornemental.

decorator [ˈdekəreɪtəʳ] *n* décorateur *m*, - trice *f*.

decorous [ˈdekərəs] *adj fml* [behaviour] bienséant, séant, convenable ■ [person] convenable, comme il faut.

decorum [dɪˈkɔ:rəm] *n* bienséance *f*, décorum *m* ■ **to have a sense of ~** avoir le sens des convenances.

decoy ◇ *n* [ˈdi:kɔɪ] **1.** [for catching birds - live bird] appeau *m*, chanterelle *f* ; [- artificial device] leurre *m* **2.** *fig* [person] appât *m* ■ [message, tactic] piège *m*.
◇ *comp* : **~ duck** [live] appeau *m*, chanterelle *f* ; [wooden] leurre *m*.
◇ *vt* [dɪˈkɔɪ] [bird - using live bird] attirer à l'appeau *OR* à la chanterelle ; [- using artificial means] attirer au leurre ■ [person] appâter, attirer ■ **they ~ed him into leaving his house** ils l'ont appâté *OR* attiré hors de chez lui.

decrease ◇ *vi* [dɪˈkri:s] [number, enthusiasm, population, speed] décroître, diminuer ■ [value, price] diminuer, baisser ■ [in knitting] diminuer, faire des diminutions.
◇ *vt* [dɪˈkri:s] réduire, diminuer.
◇ *n* [ˈdi:kri:s] [in size] réduction *f*, diminution *f* ■ [in popularity] baisse *f* ■ [in price] réduction *f*, baisse *f* ■ **a ~ in numbers** une baisse des effectifs ■ **to be on the ~** être en diminution *OR* en baisse.

decreasing [di:ˈkri:sɪŋ] *adj* [amount, energy, population] décroissant ■ [price, value, popularity] en baisse ■ **a ~ number of students are going into industry** de moins en moins d'étudiants se dirigent vers l'industrie.

decreasingly [di:ˈkri:sɪŋlɪ] *adv* de moins en moins.

decree [dɪ'kriː] ◇ *n* POL décret *m*, arrêté *m* ▪ RELIG décret *m* ▪ LAW jugement *m*, arrêt *m* ▪ **by royal ~** par décret du roi/de la reine.
◇ *vt* décréter ▪ POL décréter, arrêter ▪ RELIG décréter ▪ LAW ordonner (par jugement).

decree absolute *n* LAW jugement *m* définitif (de divorce).

decree nisi [-'naɪsaɪ] *n* LAW jugement *m* provisoire (de divorce).

decrepit [dɪ'krepɪt] *adj* [building, furniture] délabré ▪ [person, animal] décrépit.

decrepitude [dɪ'krepɪtjuːd] *n* décrépitude *f*.

decriminalization [diːˌkrɪmɪnəlaɪ'zeɪʃn] *n* dépénalisation *f*.

decriminalize [diː'krɪmɪnəˌlaɪz] *vt* dépénaliser.

decry [dɪ'kraɪ] (*pret & pp* **decried**) *vt* décrier, dénigrer.

decrypt [diː'krɪpt] *vt* décrypter.

dedicate ['dedɪkeɪt] *vt* **1.** [devote] consacrer ▪ **to ~ o.s. to sb/sthg** se consacrer à qqn/qqch **2.** [book, record etc] dédier **3.** [consecrate - church, shrine] consacrer.

dedicated ['dedɪkeɪtɪd] *adj* **1.** [devoted] dévoué ▪ **to be ~ to one's work** être dévoué à son travail ▪ **she is ~ to her family/to helping the poor** elle se dévoue pour sa famille/pour aider les pauvres ▪ **he is ~** il se donne à fond **2.** COMPUT dédié ▪ **~ word processor** machine *f* exclusivement destinée au traitement de texte.

dedication [ˌdedɪ'keɪʃn] *n* **1.** [devotion] dévouement *m* ▪ **~ is what is needed** il est essentiel de pouvoir tout donner **2.** [in book, on photograph etc] dédicace *f* ▪ **I've got a few ~s to play** [records] j'ai quelques dédicaces à passer **3.** [of church, shrine] consécration *f*.

deduce [dɪ'djuːs] *vt* déduire ▪ **to ~ sthg from sthg** déduire qqch de qqch ▪ **I ~d that she was lying** j'en ai déduit qu'elle mentait.

deducible [dɪ'djuːsəbl] *adj* qui peut se déduire.

deduct [dɪ'dʌkt] *vt* déduire, retrancher ▪ [tax] prélever ▪ **to ~ £10 from the price** déduire *OR* retrancher 10 livres du prix ▪ **to be ~ed at source** [tax] être prélevé à la source ▪ **after ~ing expenses** après déduction des frais.

deductible [dɪ'dʌktəbl] *adj* déductible.

deduction [dɪ'dʌkʃn] *n* **1.** [inference] déduction *f* ▪ **by (a process of) ~** par déduction **2.** [subtraction] déduction *f* ▶ **tax ~s** prélèvements *mpl* fiscaux.

deductive [dɪ'dʌktɪv] *adj* déductif.

deed [diːd] ◇ *n* **1.** [action] action *f* ▪ **in word and ~** en parole et en fait *OR* action ▪ **brave ~** acte *m* de bravoure ▪ **to do one's good ~ for the day** faire sa bonne action *OR* sa BA de la journée **2.** LAW acte *m* notarié ▪ **~ of covenant** contrat *m* ▪ **mortgage ~** contrat *m* d'hypothèque ▪ **title ~** titre *m* de propriété.
◇ *vt* US LAW transférer par acte notarié.

deed poll *n* LAW contrat *m* unilatéral LAW : **to change one's name by ~** changer de nom par contrat unilatéral, changer de nom officiellement.

deejay ['diːdʒeɪ] *n inf* DJ *mf*.

deem [diːm] *vt fml* juger, considérer, estimer ▪ **it was ~ed necessary/advisable to call an enquiry** on a jugé qu'il était nécessaire/opportun d'ordonner une enquête ▪ **he ~ed it a great honour** il considéra cela comme un grand honneur, il estima que c'était un grand honneur.

de-emphasize [diː'emfəsaɪz] *vt* [need, claim, feature] moins insister sur, se montrer moins insistant sur.

deep [diːp] ◇ *adj* **1.** [going far down - water, hole, wound etc] profond ▪ **~ snow lay round about** une épaisse couche de neige recouvrait les alentours ▪ **the water/hole is five metres ~** l'eau/le trou a cinq mètres de profondeur ▪ **the road was a foot ~ in snow** la route était sous *OR* recouverte de 30 centimètres de neige ▪ **a hole ten feet ~** un trou de trois mètres de profondeur ▪ **the ~ blue sea** le vaste océan ▪ **to be in a ~ sleep** être profondément endormi ▪ **~ in thought/study** plongé dans ses pensées/l'étude ▪ **~ in debt** criblé de dettes ▪ **a ~ breath** une inspiration profonde ▪ **take a ~ breath and just do it** *fig* respire un bon coup et vas-y ▪ **~ breathing** [action, noise] respiration *f* profonde ; [exercices] exercices *mpl* respiratoires ▪ **we're in ~ trouble** nous sommes dans de sales draps ▪ **the ~ end** [of swimming pool] le grand bain ▶ **to plunge** *OR* **to jump in at the ~ end** y aller carrément ▪ **to be in ~ water** être dans le pétrin, avoir des problèmes ▪ **to go off the ~ end** *inf* [lose one's temper] piquer une crise *OR* une colère ; [panic] perdre tous ses moyens, paniquer à mort ▪ **to be thrown in at the ~ end** *fig* être mis dans le bain tout de suite **2.** [going far back - forest, cupboard, serve] profond ▪ **~ in the forest** au (fin) fond de la forêt ▪ **the crowd stood 15 ~** la foule se tenait sur 15 rangées ▶ **the Deep South** [of the USA] le Sud profond ▪ **~ space** profondeurs *fpl* de l'espace
3. [strong - feelings] profond ▪ **with ~est sympathy** avec mes plus sincères condoléances
4. [profound - thinker] profond
5. [mysterious, difficult to understand - book] profond ▪ **a ~ dark secret** un sinistre secret ▪ **he's a ~ one** on ne peut jamais savoir ce qu'il pense
6. [dark - colour] profond ▪ **to be in ~ mourning** être en grand deuil
7. [low - sound, note] grave ; [- voice] grave, profond.
◇ *adv* profondément ▪ **they went ~ into the forest** ils se sont enfoncés dans la forêt ▪ **the snow lay ~ on the ground** il y avait une épaisse couche de neige sur le sol ▪ **he looked ~ into her eyes** [romantically] il a plongé ses yeux dans les siens ; [probingly] il l'a regardée intensément dans les yeux ▪ **to go** *OR* **to run ~** [emotions] être profond ▪ **~ down she knew she was right** au fond *OR* dans son for intérieur elle savait qu'elle avait raison ▪ **he thrust his hands ~ into his pockets** il plongea les mains au fond de ses poches ▪ **~ into the night** tard dans la nuit ▪ **don't go in too ~** [in water] n'allez pas où c'est profond, n'allez pas trop loin ▪ **don't get in too ~** [involved] ne t'implique pas trop.
◇ *n lit* **1.** [ocean] : **the ~** l'océan *m*
2. [depth] : **in the ~ of winter** au plus profond *OR* au cœur de l'hiver.

-deep *in cpds* : **she was knee/waist ~ in water** elle avait de l'eau jusqu'aux genoux/jusqu'à la taille ▪ **the water is only ankle~** l'eau ne monte *OR* n'arrive qu'aux chevilles.

deepen ['diːpn] ◇ *vt* [hole, river bed, knowledge] approfondir ▪ [mystery] épaissir ▪ [love, friendship] faire grandir, intensifier ▪ [sound, voice] rendre plus grave ▪ [colour] rendre plus profond, intensifier.
◇ *vi* [sea, river] devenir plus profond ▪ [silence, mystery] s'épaissir ▪ [crisis] s'aggraver, s'intensifier ▪ [knowledge] s'approfondir ▪ [love, friendship] s'intensifier, grandir ▪ [colour] devenir plus profond, s'intensifier ▪ [sound] devenir plus grave.

deepening ['diːpnɪŋ] ◇ *adj* [silence, shadows, emotion] de plus en plus profond ▪ [crisis] qui s'aggrave *OR* s'intensifie ▪ [love, friendship] de plus en plus profond.
◇ *n* [of hole, channel] approfondissement *m* ▪ [of silence, love] intensification *f*.

deep-fat fryer *n* friteuse *f*.

deep freeze *n* [in home, shop] congélateur *m* ▪ [industrial] surgélateur *m*.
◆ **deep-freeze** *vt* [at home] congeler ▪ [industrially] surgeler.

deep-fried *adj* frit.

deep-frozen *adj* [at home] congelé ▪ [industrially] surgelé.

deep-fry *vt* faire frire.

deep-heat treatment *n* MED thermothérapie *f*.

deeply ['diːplɪ] *adv* **1.** [dig, breathe, sleep, admire, regret, think] profondément ▪ [drink] à grands traits **2.** [offended, relieved, grateful, religious] profondément, extrêmement.

deepness ['diːpnɪs] *n* [of ocean, voice, writer, remark] profondeur *f* ▪ [of note, sound] gravité *f*.

deep-rooted *adj* [tree] dont les racines sont profondes ■ *fig* [ideas, belief, prejudice] profondément ancré *OR* enraciné ■ [feeling] profond.

deep-sea *adj* [creatures, exploration] des grands fonds ■ **~ diver** plongeur *m* sous-marin, plongeuse *f* sous-marine ■ **~ diving** plongée *f* sous-marine ■ **~ fisherman** pêcheur *m* hauturier *OR* en haute mer ■ **~ fishing** pêche *f* hauturière *OR* en haute mer.

deep-seated [-'si:tɪd] *adj* [sorrow, dislike] profond ■ [idea, belief, complex, prejudice] profondément ancré *OR* enraciné.

deep-set *adj* enfoncé.

deep-throated [-'θrəʊtɪd] *adj* [cough, laugh, roar] caverneux.

deer [dɪəʳ] (*pl inv*) <> *n* cerf *m*, biche *f*.
<> *comp* [hunter, park] de cerf *OR* cerfs ■ **'The Deer Hunter'** *Cimino* 'Voyage au bout de l'enfer'.

deerhound ['dɪəhaʊnd] *n* limier *m*.

deerskin ['dɪəskɪn] *n* peau *f* de daim.

deerstalker ['dɪə,stɔ:kəʳ] *n* **1.** [hunter] chasseur *m*, - euse *f* de cerf **2.** [hat] chapeau *m* à la Sherlock Holmes.

de-escalate [,di:'eskəleɪt] <> *vt* [crisis] désamorcer ■ [tension] faire baisser.
<> *vi* [crisis] se désamorcer ■ [tension] baisser.

deface [dɪ'feɪs] *vt* [statue, painting - with paint, aerosol spray] barbouiller ; [- by writing slogans] dégrader par des inscriptions ■ [book] abîmer *OR* endommager par des gribouillages *OR* des inscriptions.

de facto [deɪ'fæktəʊ] *adv* & *adj* de facto, de fait.

defalcation [,di:fæl'keɪʃn] *n* détournement *m* de fonds.

defamation [,defə'meɪʃn] *n* diffamation *f* ■ **to sue sb for ~ of character** poursuivre qqn en justice pour diffamation.

defamatory [dɪ'fæmətrɪ] *adj* diffamatoire.

defame [dɪ'feɪm] *vt* diffamer, calomnier.

default [dɪ'fɔ:lt] <> *n* **1.** LAW [non-appearance - in civil court] défaut *m*, non-comparution *f* ; [- in criminal court] contumace *f* ■ **judgement by ~** jugement *m* par défaut *OR* contumace **2.** *fml* [absence] : **in ~ of** à défaut de **3.** COMPUT sélection *f* par défaut ■ **drive C is the ~** C est l'unité de disque par défaut **4.** FIN défaut *m* de paiement, manquement *m* à payer.
<> *comp* COMPUT [drive, font, setting, value] par défaut.
<> *vi* **1.** LAW manquer à comparaître, faire défaut **2.** FIN manquer *OR* faillir à ses engagements ■ **to ~ on a payment** ne pas honorer un paiement **3.** SPORT [win, lose] déclarer forfait **4.** COMPUT prendre une sélection par défaut ■ **the computer automatically ~s to drive C** l'ordinateur sélectionne l'unité de disque C par défaut.
◆ **by default** *adv phr* **1.** [lack of action] : **you are responsible by ~** tu es responsable pour n'avoir rien fait **2.** SPORT par forfait **3.** COMPUT par défaut.

defaulter [dɪ'fɔ:ltəʳ] *n* **1.** LAW inculpé *m*, - e *f* contumace *OR* défaillant(e) *OR* par défaut, témoin *m* défaillant **2.** FIN & ST. EX débiteur *m* défaillant, débitrice *f* défaillante **3.** *UK* MIL & NAUT soldat *m* *OR* marin *m* qui a transgressé la discipline.

defeat [dɪ'fi:t] <> *n* [of army, opposition] défaite *f* ■ [of project, bill] échec *m* ■ **to suffer a ~** connaître une défaite, échouer ■ **to admit ~** s'avouer vaincu.
<> *vt* [army, adversary] vaincre ■ [team, government] battre ■ [attempts, project, bill] faire échouer ■ **we were ~ed by the weather** nous avons échoué à cause du temps ■ **that ~s the object** ça n'avance à rien.

defeatism [dɪ'fi:tɪzm] *n* défaitisme *m*.

defeatist [dɪ'fi:tɪst] <> *adj* défaitiste.
<> *n* défaitiste *mf*.

defecate ['defəkeɪt] *vi* déféquer.

defecation [,defə'keɪʃn] *n* défécation *f*.

defect <> *n* ['di:fekt] défaut *m* ■ **physical ~** malformation *f* ■ **hearing/speech ~** défaut de l'ouïe/de prononciation.
<> *vi* [dɪ'fekt] POL [to another country] passer à l'étranger ■ [to another party] quitter son parti pour un autre ■ **to ~ to the West** passer à l'Ouest.

defection [dɪ'fekʃn] *n* [to another country] passage *m* à un pays ennemi ■ [to another party] passage *m* à un parti adverse ■ **the country was shocked by his ~** le pays a été choqué quand il est passé à l'étranger.

defective [dɪ'fektɪv] <> *adj* **1.** [machine, reasoning] défectueux ■ [hearing, sight, organ] déficient ■ *dated* **to be mentally ~** souffrir de débilité mentale **2.** GRAM & *dated* défectif.
<> *n* : **mental ~** débile *m* mental, débile *f* mentale.

defector [dɪ'fektəʳ] *n* POL & *fig* transfuge *mf*.

defence *etc* *UK*, **defense** *US* [dɪ'fens] <> *n* **1.** [protection] défense *f* ■ **to carry a weapon for ~** porter une arme pour se défendre ■ **to come to sb's ~** venir à la défense de qqn ■ **to act/to speak in ~ of sthg** [following attack] agir/parler en défense de qqch ; [in support of] agir/parler en faveur de qqch ■ **to speak in ~ of sb, to speak in sb's ~** [following attack] parler en défense de qqn ; [in support of] parler en faveur de qqn ➲ **Ministry of Defence** *UK*, **Department of Defense** *US* ≃ ministère *m* de la Défense ■ **Secretary of State for Defence** *UK*, **Secretary of Defense** *US* ≃ ministre *m* de la Défense
2. [thing providing protection] protection *f*, défense *f* ■ [argument] défense *f* ■ **~s** [weapons] moyens *mpl* de défense ; [fortifications] défenses, fortifications *fpl* ■ **to use sthg as a ~ against sthg** se servir de qqch comme défense *OR* protection contre qqch, se servir de qqch pour se défendre *OR* se protéger de qqch ■ **the body's natural ~s against infection** les défenses naturelles de l'organisme contre l'infection
3. LAW défense *f* ■ **the ~** [lawyers] la défense ■ **witness for the ~** témoin *m* à décharge, témoin de la défense ■ **the case for the ~** la défense ■ **to conduct one's own ~** assurer sa propre défense ■ **it must be said in her ~ that...** il faut dire à sa décharge *OR* pour sa défense que...
4. SPORT défense *f*.
<> *comp* **1.** MIL [forces] de défense ■ [cuts, minister, spending] de la défense
2. LAW [lawyer] de la défense ■ [witness] à décharge.

defenceless *UK*, **defenseless** *US* [dɪ'fenslɪs] *adj* sans défense, vulnérable.

defence mechanism *n* mécanisme *m* de défense.

defend [dɪ'fend] *vt* **1.** [protect] défendre ■ [justify] justifier ■ **to ~ sthg/sb from** *OR* **against attack** défendre qqch/qqn contre une attaque ■ **to ~ o.s.** se défendre **2.** SPORT [goalmouth, title] défendre **3.** LAW défendre.

defendant [dɪ'fendənt] *n* LAW [in civil court] défendeur *m*, - eresse *f* ■ [in criminal court] inculpé *m*, - e *f* ■ [accused of serious crimes] accusé *m*, - e *f*.

defender [dɪ'fendəʳ] *n* **1.** [of a cause, rights etc] défenseur *m*, avocat *m*, - e *f* ■ **Defender of the Faith** Défenseur de la foi **2.** SPORT [player] défenseur *m* ■ [of title, record] détenteur *m*, - trice *f* **3.** *US* LAW : **public ~** avocat *m* commis d'office.

defending [dɪ'fendɪŋ] *adj* **1.** SPORT [champion] en titre **2.** LAW de la défense.

defenestration [,di:fenɪ'streɪʃn] *n* défenestration *f*.

defense *etc* *US* = **defence**.

defensible [dɪ'fensəbl] *adj* [idea, opinion etc] défendable.

defensive [dɪ'fensɪv] <> *adj* [strategy, weapon, game etc] défensif ■ **she's very ~ about it** elle est très susceptible quand on parle de cela.
<> *n* MIL & *fig* défensive *f* ■ **to be on the ~** être *OR* se tenir sur la défensive ■ **to go on the ~** se mettre sur la défensive.

defensively [dɪ'fensɪvlɪ] *adv* : **they played very ~** SPORT ils ont eu un jeu très défensif ■ **"it's not my fault," she said, ~** "ce n'est pas de ma faute", dit-elle, sur la défensive.

defer [dɪ'fɜ:ʳ] (*pret* & *pp* **deferred**, *cont* **deferring**) <> *vt* [decision, meeting] remettre, reporter ■ [payment, business, judgment] différer, retarder ■ **to ~ sentencing** LAW suspendre le prononcé du jugement.

◇ *vi* [give way] : **to ~ to sb** s'en remettre à qqn ■ **to ~ to sb's judgment/knowledge** s'en remettre au jugement/aux connaissances de qqn.

deference ['defərəns] *n* déférence *f*, égard *m*, considération *f* ■ **out of** *OR* **in ~ to sb/sb's wishes** par égard *OR* considération pour qqn/les souhaits de qqn ■ **to treat sb with ~, to pay** *OR* **to show ~ to sb** traiter qqn avec déférence *OR* égards.

deferential [ˌdefə'renʃl] *adj* déférent, révérencieux ■ **to be ~ to sb** faire montre de déférence *OR* d'égards envers qqn.

deferment [dɪ'fɜːmənt], **deferral** [dɪ'fɜːrəl] *n* [of decision, meeting, payment, sentence] report *m*, ajournement *m* ■ **to apply for ~** MIL demander à être réformé.

deferred [dɪ'fɜːd] *adj* [gen] ajourné, retardé ■ [payment, shares] différé ■ [annuity] à paiement différé, à jouissance différée ■ **~ sentence** LAW jugement *m* dont le prononcé est suspendu, jugement ajourné.

defiance [dɪ'faɪəns] *n* défi *m* ■ **your ~ of my orders meant that people's lives were put at risk** en défiant mes ordres vous avez mis la vie d'autrui en danger ■ **gesture/act of ~** geste *m* /acte *m* de défi.
◆ **in defiance of** *prep phr* : **in ~ of sb/sthg** au mépris de qqn/qqch.

defiant [dɪ'faɪənt] *adj* [gesture, remark, look] de défi ■ [person, reply] provocateur.

defiantly [dɪ'faɪəntlɪ] *adv* [act] avec une attitude de défi ■ [reply, look at] d'un air de défi.

defibrillation [diːˌfaɪbrɪ'leɪʃn] *n* MED défibrillation *f*.

defibrillator [diː'fɪbrɪleɪtəʳ] *n* MED défibrillateur *m*.

deficiency [dɪ'fɪʃnsɪ] (*pl* **deficiencies**) *n* **1.** MED [shortage] carence *f* ■ **a ~ in** *OR* **of calcium, a calcium ~** une carence en calcium ■ **mental ~** déficience *f* mentale **2.** [flaw - in character, system] défaut *m*.

deficient [dɪ'fɪʃnt] *adj* **1.** [insufficient] insuffisant ■ **to be ~ in sthg** manquer de qqch **2.** [defective] défectueux.

deficit ['defɪsɪt] *n* FIN & COMM déficit *m* ■ **to be in ~** être en déficit, être déficitaire ■ **budget ~** déficit budgétaire.

defile ◇ *vt* [dɪ'faɪl] [grave, memory] profaner.
◇ *vi* [dɪ'faɪl] MIL défiler.
◇ *n* ['diːfaɪl] [valley, passage] défilé *m*.

defilement [dɪ'faɪlmənt] *n* [of grave, memory] profanation *f*.

definable [dɪ'faɪnəbl] *adj* définissable.

define [dɪ'faɪn] *vt* **1.** [term, word] définir ■ [boundary, role, subject] définir, délimiter ■ [concept, idea, feeling] définir, préciser ■ **he ~s politics as being the art of the possible** il définit la politique comme l'art du possible **2.** [object, shape] définir ■ **the figures in the painting are not clearly ~d** les formes humaines du tableau ne sont pas bien définies.

defining [dɪ'faɪnɪŋ] *adj* restrictif.

definite ['defɪnɪt] *adj* **1.** [precise, clear] précis ■ [advantage, improvement, opinion] net ■ [orders, proof] formel ■ [price] fixe ■ **the boss was very ~ about the need for punctuality** le patron a été très ferme en ce qui concerne la ponctualité **2.** [certain] certain, sûr ■ **I've heard rumours of a merger, but nothing ~** j'ai entendu dire qu'il allait y avoir une fusion, mais rien de sûr pour l'instant.

definite article *n* article *m* défini.

definitely ['defɪnɪtlɪ] *adv* certainement, sans aucun doute ■ **she's ~ leaving, but I don't know when** je sais qu'elle part, mais je ne sais pas quand ■ **are you ~ giving up your flat?** allez-vous vraiment quitter votre appartement? ■ **that's ~ not the man I saw** je suis sûr que ce n'est pas l'homme que j'ai vu ■ **are you going to the show? – ~!** est-ce que tu vas au spectacle? – absolument!

definition [defɪ'nɪʃn] *n* **1.** [of term, word] définition *f* ■ [of duties, territory] définition, délimitation *f* ■ **by ~** par définition **2.** [of photograph, sound] netteté *f* ■ TV définition *f*.

definitive [dɪ'fɪnɪtɪv] *adj* **1.** [conclusive] définitif ■ [battle, victory] définitif, décisif ■ [result] définitif, qui fait autorité **2.** [authoritative] : **the ~ book on the subject** le livre qui fait autorité *OR* décisif en la matière.

definitively [dɪ'fɪnɪtɪvlɪ] *adv* définitivement.

deflate [dɪ'fleɪt] ◇ *vt* **1.** [balloon, tyre] dégonfler ■ *fig* [person] démonter **2.** ECON [prices] faire baisser, faire tomber ■ **the measure is intended to ~ the economy** cette mesure est destinée à faire de la déflation.
◇ *vi* [balloon, tyre] se dégonfler.

deflation [dɪ'fleɪʃn] *n* **1.** [of balloon, tyre] dégonflement *m* **2.** ECON & GEOG déflation *f* **3.** [anti-climax] abattement *m*.

deflationary [dɪ'fleɪʃnərɪ] *adj* déflationniste.

deflect [dɪ'flekt] ◇ *vt* faire dévier ■ *fig* [attention, criticism] détourner ■ **he would not be ~ed from his purpose** rien ne l'aurait détourné de son but.
◇ *vi* dévier ■ [magnetic needle] décliner.

deflection [dɪ'flekʃn] *n* déviation *f* ■ [of magnetic needle] déclinaison *f* ■ PHYS déflexion *f*.

deflower [ˌdiː'flaʊəʳ] *vt* **1.** *lit* [woman] déflorer **2.** BOT défleurir.

defog [ˌdiː'fɒg] *vt* *US* AUT désembuer.

defogger [ˌdiː'fɒgəʳ] *n* *US* AUT dispositif *m* anti-buée *(inv)*.

defoliant [ˌdiː'fəʊlɪənt] *n* défoliant *m*.

defoliate [ˌdiː'fəʊlɪeɪt] *vt* défolier.

deforest [ˌdiː'fɒrɪst] *vt* déboiser.

deforestation [diːˌfɒrɪ'steɪʃn] *n* déboisement *m*, déforestation *f*.

deform [di'fɔːm] *vt* déformer ■ *fig* [distort, ruin] défigurer.

deformation [ˌdiːfɔː'meɪʃn] *n* déformation *f*.

deformed [dɪ'fɔːmd] *adj* difforme.

deformity [dɪ'fɔːmətɪ] *n* difformité *f*.

Defra ['defrə] (*abbrev of* **Department for Environment, Food & Rural Affairs**) *n* ADMIN ministère *m* de l'Agriculture britannique *m*.

defragment [ˌdiːfræg'ment] *vt* COMPUT défragmenter.

defraud [dɪ'frɔːd] *vt* [the state] frauder ■ [company, person] escroquer, frustrer *spec* ■ **he ~ed the government of £15,000 in unemployment benefits** il a frauduleusement perçu 15 000 livres d'allocations chômage.

defray [dɪ'freɪ] *vt* *fml* rembourser, prendre en charge ■ **we will ~ the cost of your air fare** nous vous rembourserons le prix de votre billet d'avion.

defrock [ˌdiː'frɒk] *vt* défroquer.

defrost [ˌdiː'frɒst] ◇ *vt* **1.** [food] décongeler ■ [refrigerator] dégivrer **2.** *US* [demist] désembuer ■ [de-ice] dégivrer.
◇ *vi* [food] se décongeler ■ [refrigerator] se dégivrer.

deft [deft] *adj* adroit, habile ■ [fingers] habile.

deftly ['deftlɪ] *adv* adroitement, habilement.

defunct [dɪ'fʌŋkt] *adj* défunt.

defuse [ˌdiː'fjuːz] *vt* *liter* & *fig* désamorcer.

defy [dɪ'faɪ] (*pret* & *pp* **defied**) *vt* **1.** [disobey] s'opposer à ■ [law, rule] braver ■ **the union defied the court order** le syndicat n'a pas tenu compte de la décision judiciaire **2.** [challenge, dare] défier ■ **she defied him to justify his claims** elle l'a défié *OR* mis au défi de justifier ses revendications ■ **a death-~ing feat** un exploit téméraire **3.** *fig* [make impossible] défier ■ **his behaviour defies explanation** son comportement défie toute explication.

degeneracy [dɪ'dʒenərəsɪ] *n* [process] dégénérescence *f* ■ [state] décadence *f*, corruption *f*.

degenerate ◇ *vi* [dɪ'dʒenəreɪt] dégénérer ■ **the discussion ~d into an argument** *fig* la discussion dégénéra en dispute.
◇ *adj* [dɪ'dʒenərət] *lit* dégénéré ■ [person] dépravé.

◇ n [dɪ'dʒenərət] *lit* [person] dépravé *m*, - e *f*.

degeneration [dɪ,dʒenə'reɪʃn] *n* [process, state] dégénérescence *f*.

degenerative [dɪ'dʒenərətɪv] *adj* dégénératif.

degradation [,degrə'deɪʃn] *n* **1.** [deterioration] dégradation *f* ▪ ECOL dégradation *f* **2.** [corruption, debasement] avilissement *m*, dégradation *f* ▪ [poverty] misère *f* abjecte.

degrade [dɪ'greɪd] *vt* **1.** [deteriorate] dégrader **2.** [debase] avilir, dégrader ▪ **I refuse to ~ myself (by) playing these silly games** je refuse de m'abaisser à ces jeux idiots.

degrading [dɪ'greɪdɪŋ] *adj* avilissant, dégradant.

degree [dɪ'gri:] *n* **1.** [unit of measurement] degré *m* ▪ **the temperature is 28 ~s in New York** la température est de 28 degrés à New York ▪ **he had to work in 32 ~s of heat** il a dû travailler par une chaleur de 32 degrés ▪ **it's three ~s outside** il fait trois degrés dehors ▪ **Paris is about two ~s east of Greenwich** GEOG Paris est environ à deux degrés de longitude est de Greenwich ▪ **a 90 ~ angle** GEOM un angle de 90 degrés
2. [extent, amount] : **there was a certain ~ of mistrust between them** il y avait un certain degré de méfiance entre eux ▪ **the Prime Minister does accept criticism to a ~** le Premier ministre accepte les critiques, mais jusqu'à un certain point ▪ **there are varying ~s of opposition to the new law** il y a une opposition plus ou moins forte à la nouvelle loi ▪ **his allergy affected him to such a ~ that he had to stop working** son allergie était un tel handicap pour lui qu'il a dû s'arrêter de travailler
3. [stage, step] degré *m* ▪ **a ~ of precision never before thought possible** un niveau de précision jusqu'à présent considéré comme inaccessible
4. [academic qualification] diplôme *m* universitaire ▪ **she has a ~ in economics** elle est diplômée en sciences économiques ▪ **he's taking** *OR* **doing a ~ in biology** il fait une licence de biologie
5. GRAM & MUS degré *m*
6. *arch* & *lit* [rank, status] rang *m*
7. *US* LAW : **murder in the first ~** homicide *m* volontaire.
◆ **by degrees** *adv phr* par degrés, au fur et à mesure.
◆ **to a degree** *adv phr* **1.** [to an extent] jusqu'à un certain point ▪ **the Prime Minister does accept criticism to a ~** le Premier ministre accepte les critiques, mais jusqu'à un certain point
2. [very much] extrêmement.

-degree *in cpds* : **first/second/third~ burns** brûlures *fpl* au premier/deuxième/troisième degré ▪ **first~ murder** *US* LAW ≃ homicide *m* volontaire.

dehumanize, ise [di:'hju:mənaɪz] *vt* déshumaniser.

dehumidify [,di:hju:'mɪdɪfaɪ] *vt* déshumidifier.

dehydrate [,di:haɪ'dreɪt] *vt* déshydrater.

dehydration [,di:haɪ'dreɪʃn] *n* déshydratation *f*.

de-ice [di:'aɪs] *vt* dégivrer.

de-icer [di:'aɪsər] *n* dégivreur *m*.

deictic ['daɪktɪk] *adj* déictique.

deification [,di:ɪfɪ'keɪʃn] *n* déification *f*.

deify ['di:ɪfaɪ] *vt* déifier.

deign [deɪn] *vt* daigner ▪ **he didn't ~ to reply** *fml* & *hum* il n'a pas daigné répondre.

deindustrialization, isation ['di:ɪn,dʌstrɪəlaɪ'zeɪʃn] *n* désindustrialisation *f*.

deism ['di:ɪzm] *n* déisme *m*.

deist ['di:ɪst] *n* déiste *mf*.

deity ['di:ɪtɪ] (*pl* **deities**) *n* **1.** MYTH dieu *m*, déesse *f*, divinité *f* **2.** RELIG : **the Deity** Dieu *m*, la Divinité.

déjà vu [,deʒɑ:'vu:] *n* déjà-vu *m inv*.

dejected [dɪ'dʒektɪd] *adj* abattu, découragé.

dejectedly [dɪ'dʒektɪdlɪ] *adv* [speak] d'un ton abattu ▪ [look] d'un air abattu.

dejection [dɪ'dʒekʃn] *n* abattement *m*, découragement *m*.

Del (*written abbrev of* **delete**) [on keyboard] Suppr.

Del. *written abbr of* **Delaware**.

Delaware ['deləweər] *pr n* Delaware *m* ▪ **in ~** dans le Delaware.

delay [dɪ'leɪ] ◇ *vt* **1.** [cause to be late] retarder ▪ [person] retarder, retenir ▪ **the flight was ~ed (for) three hours** le vol a été retardé de trois heures **2.** [postpone, defer] reporter, remettre ▪ **she ~ed handing in her resignation** elle a tardé à donner sa démission ▪ **the poison had a ~ed effect** le poison a agi avec retard.
◇ *vi* tarder ▪ **don't ~, write off today for your free sample** demandez aujourd'hui même votre échantillon gratuit.
◇ *n* **1.** [lateness] retard *m* ▪ **there are long ~s on the M25** *UK* la circulation est très ralentie *OR* est très perturbée sur la M25 ▪ **there's a three to four hour ~ on all international flights** il y a trois à quatre heures de retard sur tous les vols internationaux **2.** [waiting period] : **without ~** sans tarder *OR* délai ▪ **there's no time for ~** il n'y a pas de temps à perdre.

delayed-action [dɪ'leɪd-] *adj* [fuse, shutter] à retardement.

delaying [dɪ'leɪɪŋ] *adj* dilatoire ▪ **~ tactics** *OR* **action** manœuvres *fpl* dilatoires.

delectable [dɪ'lektəbl] *adj* délectable.

delectation [,di:lek'teɪʃn] *n* *lit* & *hum* délectation *f* ▪ **for your ~** pour votre plus grand plaisir.

delegate ◇ *n* ['delɪgət] délégué *m*, - e *f*.
◇ *vt* ['delɪgeɪt] déléguer ▪ **the parents ~d Mrs Parker to represent them at the meeting** les parents déléguèrent *OR* designèrent Mme Parker pour les représenter à la réunion.
◇ *vi* ['delɪgeɪt] déléguer.

delegation [,delɪ'geɪʃn] *n* **1.** [group of delegates] délégation *f* **2.** [of duties, power] délégation *f*.

delete [dɪ'li:t] *vt* supprimer ▪ [erase - COMPUT] effacer ▪ [cross out] barrer, biffer.

delete key *n* COMPUT touche *f* effacer.

deleterious [,delɪ'tɪərɪəs] *adj fml* [effect] nuisible ▪ [influence, substance] nuisible, délétère.

deletion [dɪ'li:ʃn] *n* suppression *f*.

Delhi belly *n inf hum* tourista *f*.

deli ['delɪ] *n inf* = **delicatessen**.

deliberate ◇ *adj* [dɪ'lɪbərət] **1.** [intentional] délibéré, volontaire, voulu ▪ **it was a ~ attempt to embarrass the minister** cela visait délibérément à embarrasser le ministre **2.** [unhurried, careful] mesuré, posé.
◇ *vi* [dɪ'lɪbəreɪt] délibérer ▪ **to ~ on** *OR* **upon sthg** délibérer sur qqch ▪ **they ~d whether or not to expel him** ils ont délibéré pour savoir s'ils allaient l'expulser.
◇ *vt* [dɪ'lɪbəreɪt] délibérer sur.

deliberately [dɪ'lɪbərətlɪ] *adv* **1.** [intentionally] volontairement ▪ **I didn't hurt him ~** je n'ai pas fait exprès de le blesser ▪ **you have ~ lied to the court** vous avez menti délibérément *OR* sciemment à la cour **2.** [carefully] de façon mesurée, avec mesure ▪ [walk] d'un pas ferme.

deliberation [dɪ,lɪbə'reɪʃn] *n* **1.** [consideration, reflection] délibération *f*, réflexion *f* ▪ **after much ~ we have decided to accept your application** après délibération *OR* mûre réflexion, nous avons décidé d'accepter votre demande **2.** [care, caution] attention *f*, soin *m*.
◆ **deliberations** *npl* délibérations *fpl*.

deliberative [dɪ'lɪbərətɪv] *adj* [group, assembly] délibérant.

delicacy ['delɪkəsɪ] (*pl* **delicacies**) *n* **1.** [refinement] délicatesse *f*, finesse *f* ▪ [fragility, frailty] délicatesse *f*, fragilité *f* ▪ [difficulty] délicatesse *f* ▪ [tact] délicatesse *f* ▪ **it's a matter of great ~** c'est une affaire très délicate **2.** [fine food] mets *m* délicat.

delicate ['delɪkət] *adj* **1.** [fingers, lace, china] délicat, fin **2.** [child, health] délicat, fragile **3.** [situation, question] délicat, difficile **4.** [smell, colour] délicat **5.** [instrument] sensible.

delicately ['delɪkətlɪ] *adv* délicatement, avec délicatesse.

delicatessen [ˌdelɪkə'tesn] *n* **1.** *UK* [fine foods shop] épicerie fine *f* **2.** *US* [food shop] ≃ traiteur *m* ▪ [restaurant] ≃ restaurant *m*.

delicious [dɪ'lɪʃəs] *adj* délicieux.

deliciously [dɪ'lɪʃəslɪ] *adv* délicieusement.

delight [dɪ'laɪt] <> *vi* : **she ~s in irritating people** elle prend plaisir *OR* se complaît à énerver les gens ▪ **she ~s in her grandchildren** elle adore ses petits-enfants.
<> *vt* ravir, réjouir ▪ **her show has ~ed audiences everywhere** son spectacle a partout conquis *OR* ravi le public.
<> *n* [pleasure] joie *f*, (grand) plaisir *m* ▪ **she listened with ~** elle écoutait avec délectation ▪ **to the ~ of the audience** à la plus grande joie *OR* pour le plus grand plaisir de l'auditoire ▪ **her brother took (great) ~ in teasing her** son frère prenait (un malin) plaisir à la taquiner ▪ **the ~s of gardening** les charmes *mpl OR* délices *fpl* du jardinage ▪ **the child was a ~ to teach** c'était un plaisir d'enseigner à cet enfant.

delighted [dɪ'laɪtɪd] *adj* ravi ▪ **I'm ~ to see you again** je suis ravi de vous revoir ▪ **we are ~ that you were able to accept our invitation** nous sommes ravis que vous ayez pu accepter notre invitation ▪ **I was ~ at the news** la nouvelle m'a fait très plaisir ▪ **to be ~ with sthg** être ravi de qqch ▪ **could you come to dinner on Saturday? – I'd be ~** pourriez-vous venir dîner samedi? – avec (grand) plaisir.

delightedly [dɪ'laɪtɪdlɪ] *adv* avec joie, joyeusement.

delightful [dɪ'laɪtfʊl] *adj* [person, place] charmant ▪ [book, experience, film] merveilleux ▪ **she looked ~ in her new dress** sa nouvelle robe lui allait à ravir.

delightfully [dɪ'laɪtfʊlɪ] *adv* [dance, perform, sing] merveilleusement, à ravir.

Delilah [dɪ'laɪlə] *pr n* Dalila.

delimit [di:'lɪmɪt] *vt fml* délimiter.

delimitation [di:ˌlɪmɪ'teɪʃn] *n* délimitation *f*.

delineate [dɪ'lɪnɪeɪt] *vt fml* **1.** [outline, sketch] tracer **2.** *fig* [define, describe] définir, décrire.

delineation [dɪˌlɪnɪ'eɪʃn] *n* **1.** [sketch] tracé *m* **2.** [definition] définition *f*, description *f*.

delinquency [dɪ'lɪŋkwənsɪ] (*pl* **delinquencies**) *n* **1.** [criminal behaviour] délinquance *f* **2.** [negligence] faute *f*.

delinquent [dɪ'lɪŋkwənt] <> *adj* **1.** [law-breaking] délinquant ▪ [negligent] fautif **2.** FIN [overdue] impayé.
<> *n* **1.** [law-breaker] délinquant *m*, - e *f* **2.** [bad debtor] mauvais payeur *m*.

delirious [dɪ'lɪrɪəs] *adj* **1.** MED en délire ▪ **the fever made him ~** la fièvre l'a fait délirer ▪ **to become ~** se mettre à délirer, être pris de délire **2.** *fig* [excited, wild] délirant, en délire ▪ **he was ~ with joy** il était délirant de joie.

deliriously [dɪ'lɪrɪəslɪ] *adv* de façon délirante, frénétiquement ▪ **~ happy** follement heureux.

delirium [dɪ'lɪrɪəm] *n* **1.** MED délire *m* **2.** *fig* [state of excitement] délire *m*.

delirium tremens [-'tri:menz] *n* delirium tremens *m*.

deliver [dɪ'lɪvəʳ] <> *vt* **1.** [carry, transport] remettre ▪ COMM livrer ▪ **what time is the post** *OR* **mail ~ed?** le courrier est distribué à quelle heure? ➊ **can he ~ the goods?** *inf* est-ce qu'il peut tenir parole? **2.** *fml* & *lit* [save, rescue] délivrer ▪ **~ us from evil** BIBLE délivre-nous du mal **3.** MED : **to ~ a baby** faire un accouchement ▪ **he ~ed the mare of her foal** il aida la jument à mettre bas **4.** [pronounce, utter] : **to ~ a sermon/speech** prononcer un sermon/discours ▪ **to ~ o.s. of an opinion** *fml* faire part de *OR* émettre son opinion ▪ **the jury ~ed a verdict of not guilty** LAW le jury a rendu un verdict de non-culpabilité **5.** *US* POL : **can he ~ the Black vote?** est-ce qu'il peut nous assurer les voix des Noirs? **6.** [strike] : **to ~ a blow (to the head/stomach)** porter *OR lit* asséner un coup (à la tête/à l'estomac).
<> *vi* **1.** [make delivery] livrer **2.** *inf* [do as promised] tenir parole, tenir bon.

⇝ **deliver over** *vt sep* remettre ▪ **he ~ed himself over to the police** il s'est livré *OR* rendu à la police.

⇝ **deliver up** *vt sep* [fugitive, town] livrer.

deliverance [dɪ'lɪvərəns] *n* **1.** *fml* & *lit* [release, rescue] délivrance *f* **2.** [pronouncement] déclaration *f* ▪ LAW prononcé *m*.

deliverer [dɪ'lɪvərəʳ] *n* **1.** *fml* & *lit* [saviour] sauveur *m* **2.** COMM livreur *m*.

delivery [dɪ'lɪvərɪ] (*pl* **deliveries**) <> *n* **1.** COMM livraison *f* ▪ **to take ~ of sthg** prendre livraison de qqch ▪ **'allow two weeks for ~'** 'délai de livraison: deux semaines' ▪ **payment on ~** règlement *m OR* paiement *m* à la livraison **2.** [transfer, handing over] remise *f* **3.** MED accouchement *m* **4.** [manner of speaking] débit *m*, élocution *f* **5.** *fml* & *lit* [release, rescue] délivrance *f*.
<> *comp* **1.** COMM [note, truck, van, service] de livraison ▪ **~ boy** livreur *m* **2.** MED : **the ~ room** la salle de travail *OR* d'accouchement.

deliveryman [dɪ'lɪvərɪmæn] (*pl* **deliverymen** [-men]) *n* livreur *m*.

dell [del] *n* vallon *m*.

delouse [ˌdi:'laʊs] *vt* [animal, person] épouiller ▪ [clothing, furniture] enlever les poux de.

Delphi ['delfaɪ] *pr n* Delphes.

Delphic ['delfɪk] *adj* delphique, de Delphes ▪ *fig* [obscure] obscur.

delphinium [del'fɪnɪəm] (*pl* **delphiniums** *OR pl* **delphinia** [-nɪə]) *n* delphinium *m*.

delta ['deltə] <> *n* delta *m*.
<> *comp* en delta.

Delta Force *pr n force militaire américaine spécialisée notamment dans les opérations de sauvetage.*

delta wing *n* aile *f* (en) delta.

delude [dɪ'lu:d] *vt* tromper, duper ▪ **he ~d investors into thinking that the company was doing well** il a fait croire aux investisseurs que la société se portait bien ▪ **let's not ~ ourselves about his motives** ne nous leurrons pas sur ses motivations.

deluded [dɪ'lu:dɪd] *adj* **1.** [mistaken, foolish] : **a poor ~ young man** un pauvre jeune homme qu'on a trompé *OR* induit en erreur **2.** PSYCHOL sujet à des délires.

deluge ['delju:dʒ] <> *n liter* & *fig* déluge *m*.
<> *vt* inonder ▪ **we have been ~d with letters** nous avons été submergés *OR* inondés de lettres.

delusion [dɪ'lu:ʒn] *n* **1.** [illusion, mistaken idea] illusion *f* ▪ **she's under the ~ that her illness isn't serious** elle s'imagine à tort que sa maladie n'est pas grave **2.** PSYCHOL délire *m* ▪ **he has ~s of grandeur** *fig* il est sujet au délire de grandeur.

delusive [dɪ'lu:sɪv] *adj* trompeur, illusoire.

delusory [dɪ'lu:sərɪ] = **delusive**.

deluxe [də'lʌks] *adj* de luxe.

delve [delv] *vi* **1.** [investigate] fouiller ▪ **she preferred not to ~ too deeply into the past** elle préférait ne pas fouiller trop profondément (dans) le passé **2.** [search] : **he ~d into the bag** il a fouillé dans le sac **3.** [dig, burrow] creuser ▪ [animal] fouiller.

Dem. *written abbr of* **Democrat(ic)**.

demagnetize, ise [ˌdi:'mægnɪtaɪz] *vt* démagnétiser.

demagog ['deməgɒg] *US* = **demagogue**.

demagogic [ˌdemə'gɒgɪk] *adj* démagogique.

demagogue ['deməgɒg] *n* démagogue *mf*.

demagoguery [ˌdemə'gɒgərɪ] *n* démagogie *f*.

demagogy ['deməgɒgɪ] *n* démagogie *f*.

demand [dɪ'mɑ:nd] <> *vt* **1.** [ask forcefully] exiger ▪ [money] réclamer ▪ **the terrorists ~ed to be flown to Tehran** les terroristes exigeaient d'être emmenés en avion à Téhéran ▪ **pressure groups are ~ing that fuller information be released** les groupes de pression exigent la publication de plus amples

informations ■ **to ~ one's rights** revendiquer ses droits ■ **she ~ed nothing of** *OR* **from her children** elle n'exigeait rien de ses enfants **2.** [require, necessitate] exiger, réclamer ■ **he doesn't have the imagination ~ed of a good writer** il n'a pas l'imagination que l'on attend d'un bon écrivain.
<> *n* **1.** [obligation, requirement] exigence *f* ■ **to make ~s on sb** exiger beaucoup de qqn ■ **his work makes great ~s on his time** son travail lui prend beaucoup de temps ■ **there are many ~s on her at work** elle est très prise au travail **2.** [firm request] : **wage ~s** revendications *fpl* salariales ■ **there have been many ~s for the minister's resignation** beaucoup de voix se sont élevées pour exiger la démission du ministre **3.** ECON & COMM demande *f* ■ **due to public ~** à la demande du public ■ **there is not much ~ for books on the subject** les livres sur ce sujet ne sont pas très demandés ■ **qualified maths teachers are in increasing ~** les professeurs de mathématiques diplômés sont de plus en plus demandés.
◆ **on demand** *adv phr* sur demande ■ **she's in favour of abortion on ~** elle est pour l'avortement libre.

demand deposit *n UK* épargne *f* disponible sur demande.

demanding [dɪ'mɑːndɪŋ] *adj* [person] exigeant ■ [job, profession] difficile, astreignant ■ **the work is not physically ~** ce travail ne demande pas beaucoup de force physique.

demarcate ['diːmɑːkeɪt] *vt fml* délimiter.

demarcation [ˌdiːmɑː'keɪʃn] *n* **1.** [boundary, border] démarcation *f* **2.** INDUST attributions *fpl* ■ **~ dispute** conflit *m* d'attributions.

dematerialize, ise [diːmə'tɪərɪəlaɪz] *vi* se volatiliser.

demean [dɪ'miːn] *vt fml* avilir, rabaisser ■ **she wouldn't ~ herself by marrying him** elle refusait de se rabaisser en l'épousant ■ **your behaviour ~s the office you hold** votre comportement déshonore la charge que vous occupez.

demeaning [dɪ'miːnɪŋ] *adj* avilissant, déshonorant.

demeanour *UK*, **demeanor** *US* [dɪ'miːnəʳ] *n fml* [behaviour] comportement *m* ■ [manner] allure *f*, maintien *m*.

demented [dɪ'mentɪd] *adj* MED dément ■ *fig* fou *(before vowel or silent 'h' fol)*, folle *f*.

dementia [dɪ'menʃə] *n* démence *f*.

dementia praecox [-'priːkɒks] *n dated* démence *f* précoce.

demerara [ˌdemə'reərə] *n* : **~ sugar** cassonade *f*.

demerger [ˌdiː'mɜːdʒəʳ] *n* scission *f*.

demerit [diː'merɪt] *n* **1.** *fml* [flaw] démérite *m*, faute *f* **2.** *US* SCH & MIL blâme *m*.

demesne [dɪ'meɪn] *n* **1.** [land] domaine *m* **2.** LAW : **land held in ~** terrain possédé en toute propriété.

demigod ['demɪgɒd] *n* demi-dieu *m*.

demijohn ['demɪdʒɒn] *n* dame-jeanne *f*, bonbonne *f*.

demilitarize, ise [ˌdiː'mɪlɪtəraɪz] *vt* démilitariser ■ **a ~d zone** une zone démilitarisée.

demimonde [ˌdemɪ'mɒnd] *n* demi-monde *m*.

demise [dɪ'maɪz] <> *n* **1.** *arch* & *lit* [death] mort *f*, disparition *f* ■ [end] fin *f*, mort *f* **2.** LAW [transfer] cession *f* **3.** HIST : **the ~ of the Crown** la transmission de la Couronne.
<> *vt* **1.** LAW [lease] louer à bail ■ [bequeath] léguer **2.** HIST [transfer] transmettre.

demisemiquaver ['demɪsemɪˌkweɪvəʳ] *n UK* triple croche *f*.

demist [ˌdiː'mɪst] *vt UK* désembuer.

demister [ˌdiː'mɪstəʳ] *n UK* dispositif *m* antibuée.

demitasse ['demɪtæs] *n* [cup] tasse *f* à café ■ [coffee] café *m* serré, express *m inv*.

demo ['deməʊ] (*pl* **demos**) (*abbrev of* **demonstration**) *n inf* manif *f*.

demob [ˌdiː'mɒb] (*pret & pp* **demobbed**, *cont* **demobbing**) *UK inf* <> *vt* démobiliser.
<> *n* **1.** [demobilization] démobilisation *f* **2.** [soldier] soldat *m* démobilisé.
<> *comp* : **~ suit** ≃ tenue *f* civile.

demobilization [diːˌməʊbɪlaɪ'zeɪʃn] *n* démobilisation *f*.

demobilize, ise [ˌdiː'məʊbɪlaɪz] *vt* démobiliser.

democracy [dɪ'mɒkrəsɪ] (*pl* **democracies**) *n* démocratie *f*.

democrat ['deməkræt] *n* démocrate *mf*.
◆ **Democrat** *n* [in US] démocrate *mf*.

democratic [ˌdemə'krætɪk] *adj* [country, organization, principle] démocratique ■ [person] démocrate ■ **the Democratic Party** le parti démocrate (américain).

democratically [ˌdemə'krætɪklɪ] *adv* démocratiquement.

Democratic Republic of Congo *n* République *f* démocratique du Congo.

democratize, ise [dɪ'mɒkrətaɪz] <> *vt* démocratiser.
<> *vi* se démocratiser.

Democritus [dɪ'mɒkrɪtəs] *pr n* Démocrite.

demodulate [ˌdiː'mɒdjʊleɪt] *vt* démoduler.

demographic [ˌdemə'græfɪk] *adj* démographique.

demography [dɪ'mɒgrəfɪ] *n* démographie *f*.

demolish [dɪ'mɒlɪʃ] *vt* **1.** *liter* & *fig* [destroy] démolir **2.** *inf* [devour] dévorer.

demolition [ˌdemə'lɪʃn] *n liter* & *fig* démolition *f*.
◆ **demolitions** *npl* MIL explosifs *mpl* ■ **a ~s expert** *UK* un expert en explosifs.

demon ['diːmən] *n* **1.** [devil, evil spirit] démon *m* **2.** *fig* diable *m* ■ **she works like a ~** c'est un bourreau de travail.

demonic [diː'mɒnɪk] *adj* diabolique.

demonology [ˌdiːmə'nɒlədʒɪ] *n* démonologie *f*.

demonstrable [dɪ'mɒnstrəbl] *adj* démontrable.

demonstrably [dɪ'mɒnstrəblɪ] *adv* manifestement.

demonstrate ['demənstreɪt] <> *vt* **1.** [prove, establish] démontrer **2.** [appliance, machine] faire une démonstration de ■ **he ~d how to use a sewing machine** il a montré comment se servir d'une machine à coudre **3.** [ability, quality] faire preuve de.
<> *vi* POL manifester ■ **to ~ against sthg** manifester contre qqch.

demonstration [ˌdemən'streɪʃn] <> *n* **1.** [proof] démonstration *f* **2.** COMM & INDUST démonstration *f* ■ **the salesman gave a ~ of the word processor** le vendeur a fait une démonstration du traitement de texte **3.** POL [protest] manifestation *f* ■ **to hold a ~** faire une manifestation **4.** [of emotion] démonstration *f*, manifestation *f* **5.** MIL démonstration *f*.
<> *comp* [car, copy, lesson, model] de démonstration.

demonstrative [dɪ'mɒnstrətɪv] <> *adj* démonstratif.
<> *n* démonstratif *m*.

demonstrator ['demənstreɪtəʳ] *n* **1.** COMM & INDUST [person] démonstrateur *m*, - trice *f* **2.** POL [protester] manifestant *m*, - e *f* **3.** *UK* UNIV ≃ préparateur *m*, - trice *f* **4.** *US* COMM [appliance, machine] modèle *m* de démonstration.

demoralization [dɪˌmɒrəlaɪ'zeɪʃn] *n* démoralisation *f*.

demoralize, ise [dɪ'mɒrəlaɪz] *vt* démoraliser.

demoralized [dɪ'mɒrəlaɪzd] *adj* démoralisé ■ **to become ~** perdre courage *OR* le moral.

demoralizing [dɪ'mɒrəlaɪzɪŋ] *adj* démoralisant.

Demosthenes [dɪ'mɒsθəniːz] *pr n* Démosthène.

demote [ˌdiː'məʊt] *vt* rétrograder.

demotic [dɪ'mɒtɪk] <> *adj* **1.** [of the people] populaire **2.** LING démotique.
<> *n* [ancient Egyptian] démotique *m*.
◆ **Demotic** *n* grec *m* démotique.

demotion [ˌdiːˈməʊʃn] *n* rétrogradation *f*.

demotivate [ˌdiːˈməʊtɪveɪt] *vt* démotiver.

demount [ˌdiːˈmaʊnt] *vt* démonter.

demur [dɪˈmɜːr] (*pret & pp* **demurred**, *cont* **demurring**) ◇ *vi* **1.** *fml* soulever une objection ▪ **he demurred at the idea of accepting a reward** il s'est opposé à l'idée de recevoir une récompense **2.** LAW opposer une exception.
◇ *n* objection *f* ▪ **without ~** sans sourciller OR faire d'objection.

demure [dɪˈmjʊər] *adj* **1.** [modest] modeste, pudique ▪ [well-behaved] sage ▪ [reserved] retenu **2.** *pej* [coy] d'une modestie affectée.

demurely [dɪˈmjʊəlɪ] *adv* **1.** [modestly] modestement ▪ [reservedly] avec retenue **2.** *pej* [coyly] avec une modestie affectée.

demystification [ˈdiːˌmɪstɪfɪˈkeɪʃn] *n* démystification *f*.

demystify [ˌdiːˈmɪstɪfaɪ] (*pret & pp* **demystified**) *vt* démystifier.

demythologize, ise [ˌdiːmɪˈθɒlədʒaɪz] *vt* démythifier.

den [den] *n* **1.** ZOOL repaire *m*, tanière *f* ▪ *fig* [hideout] repaire *m*, nid *m* ▪ **a ~ of thieves** un nid de brigands ▪ **a ~ of iniquity** un lieu de perdition **2.** [room, study] ≃ bureau *m*, ≃ cabinet *m* de travail.

denationalization [ˈdiːˌnæʃnəlaɪˈzeɪʃn] *n* dénationalisation *f*.

denationalize, ise [ˌdiːˈnæʃnəlaɪz] *vt* dénationaliser.

denature [ˌdiːˈneɪtʃər] *vt* dénaturer.

deniable [dɪˈnaɪəbl] *adj* niable.

denial [dɪˈnaɪəl] *n* **1.** [of story, rumour] démenti *m* ▪ [of wrongdoing] dénégation *f* ▪ [of request, right] refus *m* ▪ **in ~** en déni ▪ **~ of justice** LAW déni *m* de justice **2.** [disavowal, repudiation] reniement *m* **3.** [abstinence] abnégation *f* **4.** PSYCHOL dénégation *f*.

denier [ˈdenɪər, dəˈnɪər] *n* **1.** *UK* [measure] denier *m* ▪ **15 ~ stockings** bas *m* de 15 deniers **2.** [coin] denier *m*.

denigrate [ˈdenɪɡreɪt] *vt* dénigrer.

denigration [ˌdenɪˈɡreɪʃn] *n* dénigrement *m*.

denigrator [ˈdenɪɡreɪtər] *n* dénigreur *m*, - euse *f*.

denim [ˈdenɪm] ◇ *n* TEX (toile *f* de) jean *m*, denim *m*.
◇ *comp* [jacket] en jean.
◆ **denims** *npl* blue-jean *m*, jean *m*.

denizen [ˈdenɪzn] *n* **1.** *lit & hum* [inhabitant] habitant *m*, - e *f*, hôte *mf lit* ▪ [regular visitor] habitué *m*, - e *f* **2.** *UK* [permanent resident] ≃ résident *m*, - e *f* **3.** [non-native plant] plante *f* allogène ▪ [non-native animal] animal *m* allogène.

Denmark [ˈdenmɑːk] *pr n* Danemark *m* ▪ **in ~** au Danemark.

denominate [dɪˈnɒmɪneɪt] *vt* dénommer.

denomination [dɪˌnɒmɪˈneɪʃn] *n* **1.** FIN valeur *f* ▪ **small/large ~ notes** petites/grosses coupures **2.** RELIG confession *f*, culte *m* **3.** *fml* [designation, specification] dénomination *f*.

denominational [dɪˌnɒmɪˈneɪʃənl] *adj* : **a ~ school** une école confessionnelle.

denominative [dɪˈnɒmɪnətɪv] ◇ *adj* dénominatif.
◇ *n* dénominatif *m*.

denominator [dɪˈnɒmɪneɪtər] *n* dénominateur *m*.

denotation [ˌdiːnəʊˈteɪʃn] *n (U)* [indication] dénotation *f* ▪ [representation, symbol] signes *mpl*, symboles *mpl* ▪ [specific meaning] signification *f*.

denotative [dɪˈnəʊtətɪv] *adj* dénotatif.

denote [dɪˈnəʊt] *vt* [indicate] dénoter ▪ [represent] signifier.

denounce [dɪˈnaʊns] *vt* dénoncer ▪ **the union's president ~d the practice as unjust** le président du syndicat a dénoncé cette pratique comme étant injuste.

denouncement [dɪˈnaʊnsmənt] *n* dénonciation *f*.

denouncer [dɪˈnaʊnsər] *n* dénonciateur *m*, - trice *f*.

dense [dens] *adj* **1.** [thick] dense ▪ [fog, smoke] épais, - aisse *f* ▪ [undergrowth, vegetation] dense, dru *lit* ▪ PHOT opaque **2.** [prose] dense, ramassé **3.** *inf* [stupid] bouché, obtus.

densely [ˈdenslɪ] *adv* : **a ~ populated area** une région très peuplée OR à forte densité de population ▪ **a ~ wooded valley** une vallée très boisée.

denseness [ˈdensnɪs] *n* **1.** [thickness] densité *f* **2.** *inf* [stupidity] stupidité *f*.

density [ˈdensətɪ] *n* densité *f*.

dent [dent] ◇ *n* **1.** [in metal] bosse *f* ▪ [in bed, pillow] creux *m* ▪ **he made a ~ in his car** il a cabossé sa voiture ▪ **the car has a ~ in the bumper** la voiture a le pare-chocs cabossé **2.** *fig* [reduction] : **to make a ~ in one's savings** faire un trou dans ses économies.
◇ *vt* [metal] cabosser, bosseler ▪ *fig* [pride] froisser ▪ [confidence] entamer.

dental [ˈdentl] ◇ *adj* **1.** MED dentaire **2.** LING dental.
◇ *n* dentale *f*.

dental floss *n* fil *m* dentaire.

dental hygienist *n* ≃ assistant *m*, - e *f*, de dentiste *(qui s'occupe du détartrage etc)*.

dental plate *n* dentier *m*.

dental surgeon *n UK* chirurgien-dentiste *m*.

dental surgery *n* **1.** [activity] chirurgie *f* dentaire **2.** *UK* [office] cabinet *m* dentaire.

dental technician *n* prothésiste *mf* (dentaire).

dental treatment *n* traitement *m* dentaire.

dented [ˈdentɪd] *adj* [metal] cabossé.

dentifrice [ˈdentɪfrɪs] *n* [paste] pâte *f* dentifrice ▪ [powder] poudre *f* dentifrice.

dentine [ˈdentiːn], **dentin** [ˈdentɪn] *US n* dentine *f*.

dentist [ˈdentɪst] *n* dentiste *mf* ▪ **the ~'s surgery** *UK* OR **office** *US* le cabinet dentaire ▪ **to go to the ~'s** aller chez le dentiste.

dentistry [ˈdentɪstrɪ] *n* dentisterie *f*.

dentition [denˈtɪʃn] *n* dentition *f*.

denture [ˈdentʃər] *n* [artificial tooth] prothèse *f* dentaire.
◆ **dentures** *npl* dentier *m*.

denuclearize, ise [ˌdiːˈnjuːklɪəraɪz] *vt* dénucléariser.

denude [dɪˈnjuːd] *vt* dénuder.

denunciation [dɪˌnʌnsɪˈeɪʃn] *n* dénonciation *f*.

deny [dɪˈnaɪ] (*pret & pp* **denied**) *vt* **1.** [declare untrue] nier ▪ [report, rumour] démentir ▪ **the prisoner denied having conspired** OR **conspiring against the government** le prisonnier nia avoir conspiré contre le gouvernement ▪ **he denied that he had been involved** il nia avoir été impliqué ▪ **there's no ~ing that we have a problem** il est indéniable que nous avons un problème **2.** [refuse] refuser, dénier *lit* ▪ **in many countries people are denied even basic human rights** dans beaucoup de pays les gens sont privés des droits les plus fondamentaux **3.** [deprive] priver ▪ **she thought that by ~ing herself she could help others** elle pensait qu'en se privant elle pourrait aider les autres **4.** *arch & lit* [disavow, repudiate] renier.

deodorant [diːˈəʊdərənt] *n* déodorant *m*.

deodorize, ise [diːˈəʊdəraɪz] *vt* désodoriser.

deontology [ˌdiːɒnˈtɒlədʒɪ] *n* déontologie *f*.

deoxidize, ise [diːˈɒksɪdaɪz] *vt* désoxyder.

deoxyribonucleic [ˈdiːɒksɪˌraɪbəʊnjuːˈkliːɪk] *adj* : **~ acid** acide *m* désoxyribonucléique.

depart [dɪˈpɑːt] ◇ *vi fml* **1.** [leave] partir ▪ **the train now ~ing from platform two is the express to Liverpool** le train en par-

tance au quai numéro deux est l'express de Liverpool **2.** [deviate, vary] s'écarter ▪ to ~ from tradition s'écarter de la tradition.
◇ *vt* quitter ▪ to ~ this life *euph* quitter ce monde.

departed [dɪ'pɑːtɪd] *euph* & *fml* ◇ *adj* [dead] défunt, disparu.
◇ *n* : the ~ le défunt, la défunte, le disparu, la disparue.

department [dɪ'pɑːtmənt] *n* **1.** ADMIN [division] département *m* ▪ [ministry] ministère *m* ➤ the Department of State *US* le Département d'État, ≃ le ministère des Affaires étrangères ▪ the Department for *UK* OR of *US* Education ≃ (le ministère de) l'Éducation nationale ▪ the Department of Trade and Industry *UK* ≃ le ministère de l'Industrie et du Commerce ▪ Department of Trade *US* ministère du Commerce **2.** INDUST service *m* ▪ the sales/personnel ~ le service commercial/du personnel **3.** [field, responsibility] domaine *m* ▪ recruiting staff is not my ~ le recrutement du personnel n'est pas mon domaine OR de mon ressort ▪ cooking's not really my ~ *fig* la cuisine n'est pas vraiment mon domaine OR ma spécialité **4.** COMM rayon *m* ▪ the toy ~ le rayon des jouets **5.** SCH département *m*, section *f* ▪ UNIV département, UFR *f* **6.** GEOG département *m*.

departmental [ˌdiːpɑːt'mentl] *adj* **1.** ADMIN du département ▪ INDUST du service ▪ COMM du rayon **2.** GEOG du département, départemental.

department store *n* grand magasin *m*.

departure [dɪ'pɑːtʃəʳ] ◇ *n* **1.** [leaving] départ *m* ▪ the crew were preparing for ~ l'équipage se préparait au départ **2.** [variation, deviation] modification *f* ▪ a ~ from standard company policy une entorse à la politique habituelle de l'entreprise **3.** [orientation] orientation *f* ▪ farming was an entirely new ~ for him l'agriculture était une voie OR orientation tout à fait nouvelle pour lui.
◇ *comp* [gate] d'embarquement ▪ [time] de départ ▪ ~ lounge salle *f* d'embarquement.

depend [dɪ'pend] ◆ **depend on, depend upon** *vt insep* **1.** [be determined by] dépendre de ▪ the outcome of the war will ~ on OR upon a number of factors l'issue de la guerre dépendra d'un certain nombre de facteurs ▪ his job ~s on his OR him getting the contract il ne gardera son emploi que s'il obtient le contrat ▪ survival ~ed on their finding enough water pour survivre, il leur fallait trouver suffisamment d'eau ▪ are we going out? – it (all) ~s est-ce qu'on sort? – ça dépend **2.** [rely on] dépendre de ▪ the firm ~s heavily on orders from abroad l'entreprise dépend beaucoup des commandes de l'étranger ▪ she ~s on the money her children give her l'argent qu'elle reçoit de ses enfants est sa seule ressource **3.** [trust, be sure of] compter sur ▪ he's a friend you can ~ on c'est un ami sur qui vous pouvez compter.
◆ **depending on** *prep phr* selon.

dependability [dɪˌpendə'bɪlətɪ] *n* fiabilité *f*.

dependable [dɪ'pendəbl] *adj* [machine] fiable ▪ [person] fiable, sérieux ▪ [organization, shop] sérieux.

dependant [dɪ'pendənt] *n* ADMIN personne *f* à charge.

dependence [dɪ'pendəns] *n* dépendance *f* ▪ the government hopes to reduce our ~ on oil le gouvernement espère diminuer notre dépendance vis-à-vis du pétrole.

dependency [dɪ'pendənsɪ] (*pl* dependencies) *n* dépendance *f*.

dependent [dɪ'pendənt] ◇ *adj* **1.** [person] dépendant ▪ he became increasingly ~ on his children il devenait de plus en plus dépendant de ses enfants ▪ she's financially ~ on her parents elle dépend financièrement OR elle est à la charge de ses parents ▪ he has two ~ children ADMIN il a deux enfants à charge ▪ she's heavily ~ on sleeping pills elle ne peut se passer de somnifères **2.** [contingent] : the prosperity of his business was ~ on the continuation of the war la prospérité de son entreprise dépendait OR était tributaire de la poursuite de la guerre **3.** GRAM [clause] subordonné **4.** MATHS [variable] dépendant.
◇ *n* GRAM subordonnée *f*.

depersonalize, ise [ˌdiː'pɜːsnəlaɪz] *vt* dépersonnaliser.

depict [dɪ'pɪkt] *vt* **1.** [describe] dépeindre ▪ Shakespeare ~s Richard III as cruel and calculating Shakespeare dépeint Richard III comme un homme cruel et calculateur **2.** [paint, draw] représenter.

depiction [dɪ'pɪkʃn] *n* **1.** [description] description *f* **2.** [picture] représentation *f*.

depilatory [dɪ'pɪlətrɪ] (*pl* depilatories) ◇ *adj* épilatoire, dépilatoire.
◇ *n* épilatoire *m*, dépilatoire *m*.

deplane [ˌdiː'pleɪn] *vi* descendre d'avion.

deplete [dɪ'pliːt] *vt* **1.** [reduce] diminuer, réduire ▪ the illness ~d her strength la maladie amoindrissait ses forces ▪ our stocks have become ~d nos stocks ont beaucoup diminué **2.** [impoverish, exhaust] épuiser ▪ the stream is ~d of fish la rivière est beaucoup moins poissonneuse qu'avant.

depletion [dɪ'pliːʃn] *n* **1.** [reduction] diminution *f*, réduction *f* **2.** [exhaustion] épuisement *m* ▪ [of soil] appauvrissement *m*.

deplorable [dɪ'plɔːrəbl] *adj* déplorable, lamentable.

deplorably [dɪ'plɔːrəblɪ] *adv* d'une manière déplorable, lamentablement.

deplore [dɪ'plɔːʳ] *vt* **1.** [regret] déplorer, regretter **2.** [condemn, disapprove of] désapprouver, condamner.

deploy [dɪ'plɔɪ] ◇ *vt* déployer.
◇ *vi* se déployer.

deployment [dɪ'plɔɪmənt] *n* déploiement *m*.

depoliticize, ise [ˌdiːpə'lɪtɪsaɪz] *vt* dépolitiser.

deponent [dɪ'pəʊnənt] ◇ *n* **1.** GRAM déponent *m* **2.** LAW déposant *m*, - e *f*.
◇ *adj* déponent.

depopulate [ˌdiː'pɒpjʊleɪt] *vt* dépeupler.

depopulated [ˌdiː'pɒpjʊleɪtɪd] *adj* dépeuplé.

depopulation [diːˌpɒpjʊ'leɪʃn] *n* dépeuplement *m*.

deport [dɪ'pɔːt] *vt* **1.** [expel] expulser ▪ HIST [to colonies, camp] déporter ▪ they were ~ed to Mexico ils furent expulsés vers le Mexique **2.** *fml* [behave] : to ~ o.s. se comporter, se conduire.

deportation [ˌdiːpɔː'teɪʃn] *n* expulsion *f* ▪ HIST [to colonies, camp] déportation *f* ▪ ~ order arrêt *m* d'expulsion.

deportee [ˌdiːpɔː'tiː] *n* expulsé *m*, - e *f* ▪ HIST [prisoner] déporté *m*, - e *f*.

deportment [dɪ'pɔːtmənt] *n* *fml* & *dated* [behaviour] comportement *m* ▪ [carriage, posture] maintien *m*.

depose [dɪ'pəʊz] ◇ *vt* **1.** [remove] destituer ▪ [sovereign] déposer, destituer **2.** LAW déposer.
◇ *vi* faire une déposition.

deposit [dɪ'pɒzɪt] ◇ *vt* **1.** [leave, place] déposer **2.** [subj: liquid, river] déposer **3.** BANK déposer, remettre ▪ I'd like to ~ £500 j'aimerais faire un versement de 500 livres **4.** [pay] verser **5.** *US* [insert] mettre ▪ please ~ one dollar for your call veuillez introduire un dollar pour votre appel.
◇ *vi* GEOL se déposer.
◇ *n* **1.** BANK dépôt *m* ▪ to make a ~ of £200 faire un versement de 200 livres ▪ on ~ en dépôt **2.** FIN & COMM [down payment] acompte *m*, arrhes *fpl* ▪ she put down a ~ on a house elle a versé un acompte OR a fait un premier versement pour une maison ▪ a £50 ~ 50 livres d'acompte OR d'arrhes **3.** [guarantee against loss or damage] caution *f* ▪ [on a bottle] consigne *f* ▪ is there a ~ on the bottle? est-ce que la bouteille est consignée? **4.** *UK* POL cautionnement *m* **5.** MINER gisement *m* **6.** [sediment, silt] dépôt *m* ▪ [in wine] dépôt *m*.

deposit account *n* *UK* compte *m* sur livret.

deposition [ˌdepə'zɪʃn] *n* **1.** LAW déposition *f* **2.** MINER dépôt *m* **3.** [removal of leader] déposition *f*.

depositor [də'pɒzɪtəʳ] *n* déposant *m*, - e *f*.

depot *n* ['depəʊ] **1.** [warehouse] dépôt *m* ▪ *UK* [garage] dépôt *m*, garage *m* **2.** *UK* MIL ≃ caserne *f* **3.** ['di:pəʊ] *US* [station] gare *f* ▪ **bus ~** gare routière.

depravation [ˌdeprəˈveɪʃn] *n* dépravation *f*.

deprave [dɪˈpreɪv] *vt* dépraver.

depraved [dɪˈpreɪvd] *adj* dépravé, perverti.

depravity [dɪˈprævətɪ] (*pl* **depravities**) *n* dépravation *f*, corruption *f*.

deprecate [ˈdeprɪkeɪt] *vt* **1.** *fml* [disapprove of, deplore] désapprouver **2.** [denigrate, disparage] dénigrer.

deprecating [ˈdeprɪkeɪtɪŋ] = **deprecatory**.

deprecatory [ˈdeprɪkətrɪ] *adj* **1.** [disapproving] désapprobateur ▪ [derogatory] dénigrant **2.** [apologetic] navré.

depreciate [dɪˈpri:ʃɪeɪt] <> *vt* **1.** FIN [devalue] déprécier, dévaloriser **2.** [denigrate] dénigrer, déprécier.
<> *vi* se déprécier, se dévaloriser.

depreciation [dɪˌpri:ʃɪˈeɪʃn] *n* **1.** FIN dépréciation *f*, dévalorisation *f* **2.** [disparagement] dénigrement *m*, dépréciation *f*.

depress [dɪˈpres] *vt* **1.** [deject, sadden] déprimer **2.** ECON [reduce] (faire) baisser **3.** *fml* [push down on] appuyer sur.

depressant [dɪˈpresənt] MED <> *adj* dépresseur.
<> *n* dépresseur *m*.

depressed [dɪˈprest] *adj* **1.** [melancholy] déprimé, abattu ▪ MED déprimé ▪ **you mustn't get ~ about your exam results** tu ne dois pas te laisser abattre *OR* perdre le moral à cause de tes résultats d'examen ▪ **visiting her grandparents made her feel ~** le fait de rendre visite à ses grands-parents la déprimait *OR* lui donnait le cafard **2.** ECON [area, industry] en déclin, touché par la crise, déprimé ▪ [prices, profits, wages] en baisse **3.** [sunken, hollow] creux.

depressing [dɪˈpresɪŋ] *adj* déprimant ▪ [idea, place] triste, sinistre.

depressingly [dɪˈpresɪŋlɪ] *adv* [say, speak] d'un ton abattu ▪ **unemployment is ~ high** le taux de chômage est déprimant.

depression [dɪˈpreʃn] *n* **1.** [melancholy] dépression *f* ▪ MED dépression *f* (nerveuse) ▪ **she suffers from ~** elle fait de la dépression **2.** ECON [slump] dépression *f*, crise *f* économique ▪ **the country's economy is in a state of ~** l'économie du pays est en crise ➊ **the Great Depression** *US* HIST la grande dépression **3.** [hollow, indentation] creux *m* ▪ GEOG dépression *f* **4.** METEOR dépression *f*.

THE GREAT DEPRESSION

On appelle ainsi la plus grave crise économique qui ébranla les États-Unis. Elle dura de 1929 (date du krach de Wall Street) au début des années 40 et plongea le pays dans le chômage et la misère.

depressive [dɪˈpresɪv] <> *adj* dépressif.
<> *n* dépressif *m*, -ive *f*.

depressurize, ise [ˌdi:ˈpreʃəraɪz] *vt* dépressuriser.

deprivation [ˌdeprɪˈveɪʃn] *n* (*U*) privation *f*.

deprive [dɪˈpraɪv] *vt* priver ▪ **to ~ sb of sthg** priver qqn de qqch ▪ **he was ~d of his rank** il fut déchu de son grade ▪ **she ~s herself of nothing** elle ne se prive de rien ▪ **the legitimate heir was ~d of his inheritance** l'héritier légitime fut frustré *OR* dépossédé de son héritage.

deprived [dɪˈpraɪvd] *adj* [area, child] défavorisé ▪ **the boy is emotionally ~** le garçon souffre d'une carence affective.

dept. *written abbr of* **department**.

depth [depθ] *n* **1.** [distance downwards] profondeur *f* ▪ **the wreck was located at a ~ of 200 metres** l'épave a été repérée à 200 mètres de profondeur *OR* par 200 mètres de fond ▪ **the canal is about 12 metres in ~** le canal a environ 12 mètres de profondeur ▪ **this submarine could dive to a ~ of 500 feet** ce sous-marin pouvait descendre jusqu'à une profondeur de 500 pieds **2.** [in deep water] : **she swam too far and got out of her ~** elle a nagé trop loin et a perdu pied ➊ **to be out of one's ~** *liter* ne plus avoir pied ; *fig* perdre pied **3.** PHOT : **~ of field/focus** profondeur *f* de champ/foyer **4.** [of a voice, sound] registre *m* grave **5.** [extent, intensity] profondeur *f* ▪ [of colour] intensité *f* ▪ **we must study the proposal in ~** nous devons étudier à fond *OR* en profondeur cette proposition.
◆ **depths** *npl* : **the ocean ~s** les grands fonds *mpl* ▪ **the ~s of the earth** les profondeurs *fpl OR* entrailles *fpl* de la terre ▮ *fig* **she's in the ~s of despair** elle touche le fond du désespoir ▪ **in the ~s of winter** au cœur de l'hiver.

depth charge *n* grenade *f* sous-marine.

deputation [ˌdepjʊˈteɪʃn] *n* députation *f*, délégation *f*.

deputize, ise [ˈdepjʊtaɪz] <> *vt* députer.
<> *vi* : **to ~ for sb** représenter qqn.

deputy [ˈdepjʊtɪ] (*pl* **deputies**) <> *n* **1.** [assistant] adjoint *m*, - e *f* **2.** [substitute] remplaçant *m*, - e *f* ▪ **to act as sb's ~** remplacer qqn, agir en tant qu'adjoint **3.** POL [elected representative] député *m* **4.** *US* [law enforcement agent] shérif *m* adjoint.
<> *comp* : **~ chairman** vice-président *m* ▪ **~ head teacher, ~ head** *inf* directeur *m* adjoint, directrice *f* adjointe ▪ **~ manager** directeur *m* adjoint.

derail [dɪˈreɪl] <> *vt* faire dérailler.
<> *vi* dérailler.

derailleur [dɪˈreɪljəʳ] *n UK* dérailleur *m*.

derailment [dɪˈreɪlmənt] *n* déraillement *m*.

derange [dɪˈreɪndʒ] *vt* **1.** [disarrange, disorder] déranger **2.** [drive insane] rendre fou.

deranged [dɪˈreɪndʒd] *adj* dérangé, déséquilibré ▪ **it's the work of a ~ mind** c'est l'œuvre d'un esprit dérangé *OR* détraqué.

derangement [dɪˈreɪndʒmənt] *n* **1.** [disorder, disarray] désordre *m* **2.** [mental illness] démence *f*.

derby [*UK* ˈdɑ:bɪ, *US* ˈdɜ:bɪ] *n* **1.** [match] : **a local ~** un derby **2.** *US* [race] derby *m*.

deregulate [ˌdi:ˈregjʊleɪt] *vt* **1.** ECON [prices, wages] libérer, déréguler **2.** [relax restrictions on] assouplir les règlements de, déréglementer.

deregulation [ˌdi:regjʊˈleɪʃn] *n* **1.** ECON [of prices, wages] libération *f*, dérégulation *f* **2.** [relaxation of restrictions] assouplissement *m* des règlements, déréglementation *f*.

derelict [ˈderəlɪkt] <> *adj* **1.** [abandoned] abandonné, délaissé ▪ **a ~ old building** un vieux bâtiment à l'abandon **2.** [negligent, neglectful] négligent.
<> *n* **1.** [vagrant] clochard *m*, - e *f*, vagabond *m*, - e *f* **2.** NAUT navire *m* abandonné.

dereliction [ˌderəˈlɪkʃn] *n* **1.** [abandonment] abandon *m* **2.** *UK* [negligence] négligence *f* ▪ **~ of duty** manquement *m* au devoir.

derestrict [ˌdi:rɪˈstrɪkt] *vt UK* **to ~ a road** supprimer une limitation de vitesse sur une route.

deride [dɪˈraɪd] *vt* tourner en dérision, railler.

derision [dɪˈrɪʒn] *n* dérision *f*.

derisive [dɪˈraɪsɪv] *adj* moqueur.

derisively [dɪˈraɪsɪvlɪ] *adv* avec dérision ▪ [say, speak] d'un ton moqueur.

derisory [dəˈraɪzərɪ] *adj* **1.** [ridiculous] dérisoire **2.** [mocking, scornful] moqueur.

derivation [ˌderɪˈveɪʃn] *n* dérivation *f*.

derivative [dɪˈrɪvətɪv] <> *adj* **1.** [gen] dérivé **2.** *pej* peu original, banal.
<> *n* [gen] dérivé *m* ▪ MATHS dérivée *f*.

derive [dɪˈraɪv] <> *vt* **1.** [gain, obtain] : **she ~s great pleasure from her garden** elle tire beaucoup de plaisir de son jardin ▪ **the young man ~d little benefit from his expensive education** le

jeune homme n'a guère tiré profit de ses études coûteuses ■ **to ~ courage/strength from** trouver du courage/des forces dans **2.** [deduce] dériver de.
<> *vi* : **to ~ from** provenir de ■ **the word "coward" ~s originally from French** LING le mot "coward" vient du français.

dermabrasion ['dɜːmə,breɪʒn] *n* dermabrasion *f*.

dermatitis [,dɜːmə'taɪtɪs] *n (U)* dermite *f*, dermatite *f*.

dermatologist [,dɜːmə'tɒlədʒɪst] *n* dermatologiste *mf*, dermatologue *mf*.

dermatology [,dɜːmə'tɒlədʒɪ] *n* dermatologie *f*.

derogate ['derəgeɪt] <> *vt fml* [disparage] dénigrer, déprécier.
<> *vi* : **to ~ from** porter atteinte à.

derogation [,derə'geɪʃn] *n* dépréciation *f*.

derogatorily [dɪ'rɒgətrəlɪ] *adv* de façon péjorative.

derogatory [dɪ'rɒgətrɪ] *adj* [comment, remark] désobligeant, critique ■ [word] péjoratif.

derrick ['derɪk] *n UK* [crane] mât *m* de charge ■ PETR derrick *m*.

derring-do [,derɪŋ'duː] *n lit & hum* bravoure *f* ■ **deeds of ~** prouesses *fpl*.

derv [dɜːv] *n UK* gas-oil *m*.

dervish ['dɜːvɪʃ] *n* derviche *m* ■ **a whirling ~** un derviche tourneur.

DES (*abbrev of* **Department of Education and Science**) *pr n ancien ministère britannique de l'Éducation et de la Recherche scientifique*.

desalinate [,diː'sælɪneɪt] *vt* dessaler.

desalination [diː,sælɪ'neɪʃn] <> *n* dessalement *m*.
<> *comp* [plant] de dessalement.

descale [,diː'skeɪl] *vt* détartrer.

descant ['deskænt] <> *n* déchant *m*.
<> *comp* : **~ recorder** flûte *f* à bec soprano.
<> *vi* **1.** MUS déchanter **2.** *lit & pej* [comment, ramble] discourir, pérorer *pej*.

descend [dɪ'send] *vi* **1.** *fml* [go, move down] descendre **2.** [fall] tomber, s'abattre ■ **a thick blanket of fog ~ed on the valley** une couche épaisse de brouillard tomba sur la vallée ■ **despair ~ed upon the families of the missing men** *fig* le désespoir gagna *OR* envahit les familles des disparus **3.** [pass on by ancestry] descendre ■ [pass on by inheritance] revenir ■ **dogs and wolves probably ~ from a common ancestor** les chiens et les loups descendent probablement d'un ancêtre commun ■ **Lord Grey's title ~ed to his grandson** le titre de Lord Grey est revenu à son petit-fils **4.** [attack, invade] : **my in-laws ~ed on us last weekend** *hum* ma belle-famille a débarqué chez nous le week-end dernier **5.** [sink, stoop] s'abaisser, descendre ■ **you don't want to ~ to their level** tu ne vas quand même pas te rabaisser à leur niveau.

descendant [dɪ'sendənt] *n* descendant *m*, - e *f*.

descended [dɪ'sendɪd] *adj* : **she is ~ from the Russian aristocracy** elle descend *OR* est issue de l'aristocratie russe ■ **man is ~ from the apes** l'homme descend du singe.

descender [dɪ'sendəʳ] *n* jambage *m*.

descending [dɪ'sendɪŋ] *adj* descendant ■ **in ~ order of importance** par ordre décroissant d'importance.

descent [dɪ'sent] *n* **1.** [move downward] descente *f* ■ **the aircraft made a sudden ~** l'avion a fait une descente subite ■ **the stream makes a gentle ~** le lit du ruisseau est en pente douce **2.** *fig & lit* [decline] chute *f* **3.** [origin] origine *f* ■ **of Irish ~** d'origine irlandaise **4.** [succession, transmission] transmission *f* **5.** [invasion] descente *f* ■ **we're braced for the ~ on the town of thousands of football fans** nous sommes prêts pour la venue des milliers de fans de football qui vont s'abattre sur la ville.

describe [dɪ'skraɪb] *vt* **1.** [recount, represent] décrire ■ **how would you ~ yourself?** comment vous décririez-vous? ■ **witnesses ~d the man as tall and dark-haired** des témoins ont décrit l'homme comme étant grand et brun ■ **she ~d her attacker to the police** elle a fait une description *OR* un portrait de son agresseur à la police **2.** [characterize] définir, qualifier ■ **the general ~d himself as a simple man** le général s'est défini comme un homme simple ■ **the Chancellor's methods have been ~ed as unorthodox** on a qualifié les méthodes du Chancelier de pas très orthodoxes **3.** [outline, draw] décrire.

description [dɪ'skrɪpʃn] *n* **1.** [account, representation] description *f* ■ [physical] portrait *m* ■ ADMIN signalement *m* ■ **the brochure gives a detailed ~ of the hotel** la brochure donne une description détaillée de l'hôtel ■ **a man answering the police ~** un homme correspondant au signalement donné par la police ■ **her father was angry beyond ~** son père était dans une colère indescriptible **2.** [kind] sorte *f*, genre *m* ■ **the police seized weapons of every ~** la police a saisi toutes sortes d'armes ■ **we were unable to find a vehicle of any ~** nous étions incapables de trouver un quelconque véhicule.

descriptive [dɪ'skrɪptɪv] *adj* descriptif.

descriptive linguistics *n* linguistique *f* descriptive.

descriptivism [dɪ'skrɪptɪvɪzm] *n* descriptivisme *m*.

descry [dɪ'skraɪ] (*pret & pp* **descried**) *vt lit* apercevoir, distinguer.

desecrate ['desɪkreɪt] *vt* profaner.

desecration [,desɪ'kreɪʃn] *n* profanation *f*.

desegregate [,diː'segrɪgeɪt] *vt* abolir la ségrégation raciale dans ■ **~d schools** écoles qui ne sont plus soumises à la ségrégation raciale.

desegregation [,diːsegrɪ'geɪʃn] *n* déségrégation *f*.

deselect [,diːsɪ'lekt] *vt UK* POL ne pas réinvestir *(un candidat)*.

desensitize, ise [,diː'sensɪtaɪz] *vt* désensibiliser.

desert[1] ['dezət] <> *n* [wilderness] désert *m*.
<> *comp* [area, plant, sand] désertique.

desert[2] [dɪ'zɜːt] <> *vt* [person] abandonner, délaisser *lit* ■ [place] abandonner, déserter ■ [organization, principle] déserter ■ **his wits ~ed him** *fig* il a perdu son sang-froid.
<> *vi* MIL déserter ■ **one of the officers ~ed to the enemy** un des officiers est passé à l'ennemi.

desert boots *npl chaussures en daim à lacets*.

deserted [dɪ'zɜːtɪd] *adj* désert.

deserter [dɪ'zɜːtəʳ] *n* déserteur *m*.

desertification [dɪ,zɜːtɪfɪ'keɪʃn] *n* désertification *f*.

desertion [dɪ'zɜːʃn] *n* MIL désertion *f* ■ LAW [of spouse] abandon *m* (du domicile conjugal) ■ [of cause, organization] défection *f*, désertion *f*.

desert island ['dezət-] *n* île *f* déserte.

desert rat ['dezət-] *n* **1.** ZOOL gerboise *f* **2.** *UK* MIL *soldat britannique combattant en Afrique du Nord (pendant la Seconde Guerre mondiale)*.

deserts [dɪ'zɜːts] *npl* [reward] : **to get one's just ~** avoir ce que l'on mérite.

deserve [dɪ'zɜːv] <> *vt* mériter ■ **the book, though controversial, didn't ~ to be banned** le livre, bien que controversé, ne méritait pas d'être interdit *OR* qu'on l'interdise ■ **she ~s wider recognition** elle mérite d'être plus largement reconnue ■ **she's taking a much ~d holiday** elle prend des vacances bien méritées ■ **frankly, they ~ each other** franchement ils se valent l'un l'autre *OR* ils sont dignes l'un de l'autre.
<> *vi* mériter ■ **to ~ well of sthg** *fml* bien mériter de qqch.

deservedly [dɪ'zɜːvɪdlɪ] *adv* à juste titre, à bon droit ■ **Mozart has been described as a genius, and ~ so** on a décrit Mozart comme un génie, à juste titre.

deserving [dɪ'zɜ:vɪŋ] *adj* [person] méritant ■ [cause, organization] méritoire ■ **a musician ~ of greater recognition** *fml* un musicien qui mérite d'être davantage reconnu du public.

deshabille ['dezæbi:l] *n* : **in ~** en déshabillé, en négligé.

desiccated ['desɪkeɪtɪd] *adj* **1.** [dehydrated] : **~ coconut** noix *f* de coco séchée **2.** [dull - style] aride ; [- person] desséché.

desideratum [dɪ,zɪdə'rɑ:təm] (*pl* **desiderata** [-tə]) *n (usu pl)* desideratum *m*.

design [dɪ'zaɪn] <> *n* **1.** [drawing, sketch] dessin *m* ■ INDUST dessin *m*, plan *m* ■ ARCHIT plan *m*, projet *m* ■ TEX modèle *m* ■ [of book] maquette *f* ■ **the ~ for the new museum has been severely criticized** les projets OR plans du nouveau musée ont été sévèrement critiqués **2.** INDUST [composition, structure - of car, computer etc] conception *f* ■ **the problems were all due to poor ~** tous les problèmes viennent de ce que la conception est mauvaise **3.** [subject for study] design *m* ■ **book ~** conception *f* graphique ■ **fashion ~** stylisme *m* ■ **industrial ~** dessin *m* industriel **4.** [pattern] motif *m* **5.** [purpose, intent] dessein *m* ■ **to do sthg by ~** faire qqch à dessein OR exprès ■ **to have ~s on sb/sthg** avoir des vues sur qqn/qqch.
<> *comp* [course] de dessin ■ **~ award** prix *m* du meilleur design ■ **~ department** bureau *m* d'études ■ **~ engineer** ingénieur *m* d'études ■ **~ studio** cabinet *m* de design.
<> *vt* [plan] concevoir ■ [on paper] dessiner ■ ARCHIT faire les plans de ■ TEX concevoir, créer ■ **the system is ~ed to favour the landowners** le système est conçu pour OR vise à favoriser les propriétaires terriens ■ **it's specially ~ed for very low temperatures** c'est spécialement conçu pour les très basses températures ■ **she ~s jewellery** elle dessine des bijoux.

designate <> *vt* ['dezɪgneɪt] *fml* **1.** [appoint, name] désigner, nommer ■ **he has been ~d as the new Foreign Minister** il a été désigné pour être le nouveau ministre des Affaires étrangères ■ **the theatre should rightfully be ~d a national monument** il serait légitime que le théâtre soit classé monument historique **2.** [indicate, signify] indiquer, montrer.
<> *adj* ['dezɪgnət] désigné.

designation [,dezɪg'neɪʃn] *n* désignation *f*.

designer [dɪ'zaɪnə^r] <> *n* ART & INDUST dessinateur *m*, - trice *f* ■ TEX modéliste *mf*, styliste *mf* ■ CIN & THEAT décorateur *m*, - trice *f* ■ [of high fashion clothes] couturier *m*, - ère *f* ■ [of books, magazines] maquettiste *mf* ■ [of furniture] designer *m*.
<> *comp* [jeans] haute couture ■ [glasses, handbag] de marque ■ [furniture] design.

designer drug *n* drogue *f* de synthèse.

designer stubble *n hum* barbe *f* de deux jours.

designing [dɪ'zaɪnɪŋ] <> *adj* [cunning] rusé ■ [scheming] intrigant.
<> *n* [design work] conception *f*, dessin *m*, design *m*.

desirability [dɪ,zaɪərə'bɪlətɪ] *n (U)* **1.** [benefits] intérêt *m*, avantage *m*, opportunité *f* ■ **no one questions the ~ of lowering interest rates** personne ne conteste les avantages d'une baisse des taux d'intérêts **2.** [attractiveness] charmes *mpl*, attraits *mpl*.

desirable [dɪ'zaɪərəbl] *adj* **1.** [advisable] souhaitable, désirable *fml* **2.** [attractive] à désirer, tentant ■ **a ~ residence** une belle propriété **3.** [sexually appealing] désirable, séduisant.

desire [dɪ'zaɪə^r] <> *n* **1.** [wish] désir *m*, envie *f* ■ **she had no ~ to go back** elle n'avait aucune envie d'y retourner **2.** [sexual attraction] désir *m*.
<> *vt* **1.** [want, wish] désirer ■ **the Prince ~s that you should be his guest tonight** *fml* le Prince désire que vous soyez son invité ce soir ■ **the agreement left much** OR **a great deal** OR **a lot to be ~d** l'accord laissait beaucoup à désirer ■ **his words had the ~d effect** ses paroles eurent l'effet désiré OR escompté **2.** [want sexually] désirer.

desirous [dɪ'zaɪərəs] *adj fml* désireux ■ **he was ~ of re-establishing friendly relations** il était désireux de rétablir des relations amicales.

desist [dɪ'zɪst] *vi fml* cesser ■ **he was asked to ~ from his political activities** on lui a demandé de cesser ses activités politiques.

desk [desk] <> *n* **1.** [in home, office] bureau *m* ■ [with folding top] secrétaire *m* ■ SCH [for pupil] pupitre *m* ■ [for teacher] bureau *m* **2.** [reception counter] réception *f* ■ [cashier] caisse *f* **3.** PRESS [section] service *m* ■ **the sports ~** le service des informations sportives.
<> *comp* [diary, job, lamp] de bureau ■ **~ blotter** *UK* sous-main *m inv* ■ **~ tidy** porte-crayon *m*.

deskbound ['deskbaʊnd] *adj* sédentaire ■ **she hates being ~** elle déteste faire un travail sédentaire.

desk clerk *n US* réceptionniste *mf*.

desk editor *n* rédacteur *m*, - trice *f*.

deskill [,di:'skɪl] *vt* déqualifier.

desktop ['desktɒp] <> *n* ordinateur *m* de bureau.
<> *adj* [computer, model] de bureau.

desktop publishing *n* publication *f* assistée par ordinateur, microédition *f*.

desolate <> *adj* ['desələt] **1.** [area, place - empty] désert ; [- barren, lifeless] désolé ■ *fig* [gloomy, bleak] morne, sombre **2.** [person - sorrowful] consterné, abattu ; [- friendless] délaissé.
<> *vt* ['desəleɪt] **1.** [area, place - devastate] dévaster, saccager ; [- depopulate] dépeupler **2.** [person] désoler, navrer ■ **he was ~d at** OR **by the loss of his job** il était désolé OR navré d'avoir perdu son emploi.

desolation [,desə'leɪʃn] *n* **1.** [barrenness, emptiness] caractère *m* désert, désolation *f* ■ [devastation, ruin] dévastation *f*, ravages *mpl* **2.** [despair, sorrow] désolation *f*, consternation *f* ■ [loneliness] solitude *f*.

despair [dɪ'speə^r] <> *n* **1.** [hopelessness] désespoir *m* ■ **in ~, she took her own life** de désespoir elle a mis fin à ses jours ■ **the people are in ~ at** OR **over the prospect of war** les gens sont désespérés à cause des perspectives de guerre ■ **their son drove them to ~** leur fils les désespérait OR les réduisait au désespoir **2.** [cause of distress] désespoir *m* ■ **William was the ~ of his teachers** William faisait OR était le désespoir de tous ses professeurs.
<> *vi* désespérer ■ **she began to ~ of ever finding her brother alive** elle commençait à désespérer de retrouver un jour son frère vivant ■ **he ~ed at the thought of all the work he had to do** il était désespéré à l'idée de tout le travail qu'il avait à faire.

despairing [dɪ'speərɪŋ] *adj* [cry, look] de désespoir, désespéré ■ [person] abattu, consterné.

despairingly [dɪ'speərɪŋlɪ] *adv* [look, speak] avec désespoir.

despatch [dɪ'spætʃ] = **dispatch**.

desperado [,despə'rɑ:dəʊ] (*pl* **desperadoes** OR *pl* **desperados**) *n lit* & *hum* desperado *m*, hors-la-loi *m inv*.

desperate ['desprət] *adj* **1.** [hopeless, serious] désespéré ■ **the refugees are in ~ need of help** les réfugiés ont désespérément besoin d'assistance **2.** [reckless] désespéré ■ **he died in a ~ attempt to escape** il est mort en essayant désespérément de s'évader ■ **I'm afraid she'll do something ~** j'ai bien peur qu'elle ne tente un acte désespéré ■ **a ~ criminal/man** un criminel/homme prêt à tout **3.** [intent, eager] : **to be ~ for money** avoir un besoin urgent d'argent ■ **she was ~ to leave home** elle voulait à tout prix partir de chez elle ■ **I'm ~ to go to the loo** *inf*, **I'm ~** *inf hum* je ne tiens plus, ça urge^△.

desperately ['desprətlɪ] *adv* **1.** [hopelessly, seriously] désespérément ■ **their country is ~ poor** leur pays est d'une pauvreté désespérante ■ **they're ~ in love** ils s'aiment éperdument **2.** [recklessly] désespérément ■ **the soldiers fought ~** les soldats se battaient désespérément OR avec acharnement **3.** [as intensifier] terriblement ■ **he ~ wanted to become an actor** il voulait à tout prix devenir acteur.

desperation [,despə'reɪʃn] *n* désespoir *m* ■ **he agreed in ~** en désespoir de cause, il a accepté.

despicable [dɪ'spɪkəbl] *adj* [person] méprisable, détestable ▪ [action, behaviour] méprisable, ignoble.

despicably [dɪ'spɪkəblɪ] *adv* [behave] bassement, d'une façon indigne.

despise [dɪ'spaɪz] *vt* [feel contempt for] mépriser ▪ **he ~d himself for his cowardice** il se méprisait d'avoir été lâche.

despite [dɪ'spaɪt] *prep* malgré, en dépit de ▪ **~ having a degree she's still unemployed** bien que diplômée *OR* malgré son diplôme, elle est toujours au chômage ▪ **he laughed ~ himself** il n'a pas pu s'empêcher de rire.

despoil [dɪ'spɔɪl] *vt fml & lit* [person] spolier, dépouiller ▪ [land, town] piller.

despondence [dɪ'spɒndəns], **despondency** [dɪ'spɒndənsɪ] *n* abattement *m*, consternation *f*.

despondent [dɪ'spɒndənt] *adj* abattu, consterné.

despondently [dɪ'spɒndəntlɪ] *adv* d'un air consterné ▪ [say, speak] d'un ton consterné.

despot ['despɒt] *n* despote *m*.

despotic [de'spɒtɪk] *adj* despotique.

despotism ['despətɪzm] *n* despotisme *m*.

des res [dez rez] *n UK hum* [flat] appartement *m* de standing ▪ [house] belle maison *f*.

dessert [dɪ'zɜ:t] <> *n* dessert *m* ▪ **what's for ~?** qu'est-ce qu'il y a comme dessert?
<> *comp* [dish, plate] à dessert ▪ **a ~ apple** une pomme à couteau ▪ **a ~ wine** un vin de dessert.

dessertspoon [dɪ'zɜ:tspu:n] *n* cuiller *f* à dessert.

dessertspoonful [dɪ'zɜ:tspu:n,fʊl] *n* cuillerée *f* à dessert.

destabilization [di:,steɪbɪlaɪ'zeɪʃn] *n* déstabilisation *f*.

destabilize, ise [,di:'steɪbɪlaɪz] *vt* déstabiliser.

destination [,destɪ'neɪʃn] *n* destination *f*.

destined ['destɪnd] *adj* **1.** [intended] : **she felt she was ~ for an acting career** elle sentait qu'elle était destinée à une carrière d'actrice ▪ **she was ~ for greater things** elle était promise à un plus grand avenir ▪ **their plan was ~ to fail** *OR* **for failure** leur projet était voué à l'échec ▪ **she was ~ never to have children** le destin a voulu qu'elle n'ait jamais d'enfant **2.** [bound] : **the flight was ~ for Sydney** le vol était à destination de Sydney.

destiny ['destɪnɪ] *n* [fate] destin *m* ▪ [personal fate] destinée *f*, destin *m* ▪ **she felt it was her ~ to become a writer** elle avait le sentiment que c'était son destin de devenir écrivain.

destitute ['destɪtju:t] <> *adj* **1.** [extremely poor] dans la misère, sans ressources ▪ **the drought has left many farmers ~** la sécheresse a réduit beaucoup d'agriculteurs à la misère **2.** *fml* [lacking] : **~ of** dépourvu de.
<> *npl* : **the ~** les indigents *mpl OR* démunis *mpl*.

destitution [,destɪ'tju:ʃn] *n* misère *f*, indigence *f*.

de-stress [di:'stres] *n* dé-stresser *inf*.

destroy [dɪ'strɔɪ] *vt* **1.** [demolish, wreck] détruire ▪ **they threaten to ~ our democratic way of life** ils menacent d'anéantir *OR* de détruire nos institutions démocratiques **2.** [ruin, spoil - efforts, hope, love] anéantir, briser ; [- career, friendship, marriage] briser ; [- health] ruiner ▪ **his wartime experiences ~ed his faith in humanity** ses expériences de guerre ont brisé sa foi en l'humanité ▪ **to ~ sb's life** briser la vie de qqn **3.** [kill - farm animal] abattre ; [- pet] supprimer, (faire) piquer ▪ **we had to have the dog ~ed** nous avons dû faire piquer le chien.

destroyer [dɪ'strɔɪəʳ] *n* **1.** MIL destroyer *m*, contre-torpilleur *m* **2.** [person] destructeur *m*, - trice *f*.

destruct [dɪ'strʌkt] <> *vt* détruire.
<> *vi* se détruire.
<> *n* destruction *f*.
<> *comp* [button, mechanism] de destruction.

destructible [dɪ'strʌktəbl] *adj* destructible.

destruction [dɪ'strʌkʃn] *n* **1.** [demolition, devastation] destruction *f* ▪ **a nuclear war would result in total ~** une guerre nucléaire mènerait à une destruction totale **2.** [elimination - of evidence] suppression *f* ; [- of life, hope] anéantissement *m* **3.** *fig* [ruin] ruine *f*.

destructive [dɪ'strʌktɪv] *adj* destructeur ▪ **the ~ power of a bomb** le pouvoir destructif d'une bombe ▪ **she's a ~ child** c'est une enfant qui aime casser.

destructively [dɪ'strʌktɪvlɪ] *adv* de façon destructrice.

destructiveness [dɪ'strʌktɪvnɪs] *n* [of bomb, weapon] capacité *f* destructrice ▪ [of criticism] caractère *m* destructeur ▪ [of person] penchant *m* destructeur.

desultory ['desəltrɪ] *adj fml* [conversation] décousu, sans suite ▪ [attempt] peu suivi, peu soutenu, sans suite ▪ **he made only a ~ attempt to learn Italian** il n'a pas vraiment fait d'efforts pour apprendre l'italien.

Det. *written abbr of* **detective**.

detach [dɪ'tætʃ] *vt* **1.** [handle, hood] détacher **2.** [person] : **to ~ o.s.** se détacher, prendre du recul ▪ **he can't ~ himself sufficiently from the conflict** il n'a pas assez de recul par rapport au conflit **3.** MIL [troops] envoyer en détachement.

detachable [dɪ'tætʃəbl] *adj* [collar, lining] amovible.

detached [dɪ'tætʃt] *adj* **1.** [separate] détaché, séparé ▪ **~ house** *UK* maison *f* individuelle, pavillon *m* **2.** [objective] objectif ▪ [unemotional] détaché.

detachment [dɪ'tætʃmənt] *n* **1.** [separation] séparation *f* **2.** [indifference] détachement *m* ▪ [objectivity] objectivité *f* **3.** MIL détachement *m*.

detail [*UK* 'di:teɪl, *US* dɪ'teɪl] <> *n* **1.** [item, element] détail *m* ▪ **there's no need to go into ~** *OR* **~s** ça ne sert à rien d'entrer dans les détails ▪ **the author recounts his childhood in great ~** l'auteur raconte son enfance dans les moindres détails ▪ **attention to ~ is important** il faut être minutieux *OR* méticuleux ▪ **that's a mere ~!** ce n'est qu'un détail! **2.** MIL détachement *m*.
<> *vt* **1.** [enumerate, specify] raconter en détail, détailler, énumérer ▪ **operating instructions are fully ~ed in the booklet** le mode d'emploi détaillé se trouve dans le livret **2.** MIL détacher, affecter.
◆ **details** *npl* [particulars] renseignements *mpl*, précisions *fpl* ▪ [name, address etc] coordonnées *fpl*.

detailed [*UK* 'di:teɪld, *US* dɪ'teɪld] *adj* détaillé.

detain [dɪ'teɪn] *vt* **1.** *fml* [delay] retenir **2.** LAW [keep in custody] retenir, garder à vue ▪ **to ~ sb for questioning** mettre *OR* placer qqn en garde à vue.

detainee [,di:teɪ'ni:] *n* détenu *m*, - e *f*.

detect [dɪ'tekt] *vt* déceler, discerner, distinguer, découvrir ▪ MIL & MIN détecter ▪ MED dépister ▪ **the aircraft cannot be ~ed by radar** l'avion ne peut pas être détecté *OR* repéré par radar ▪ **do I ~ a certain lack of enthusiasm on your part?** je crois déceler un certain manque d'enthousiasme de ta part.

detectable [dɪ'tektəbl] *adj* MIL & MIN détectable ▪ [illness] que l'on peut dépister.

detection [dɪ'tekʃn] <> *n* **1.** [discovery] découverte *f* ▪ MIL & MIN détection *f* ▪ MED dépistage *m* ▪ **athletes who have used banned drugs have so far escaped ~** on n'a pas encore repéré les athlètes qui se sont dopés avec des substances interdites **2.** [investigation] recherche *f* ▪ **crime ~** la recherche des criminels ▪ **the killer escaped ~** le tueur échappa aux recherches.
<> *adj* [device] de détection ▪ MED de dépistage.

detective [dɪ'tektɪv] <> *n* [on a police force] ≃ inspecteur *m*, - trice *f* de police ▪ [private] détective *m*.
<> *comp* [film, novel, story] policier.

detective constable *n UK* ≃ inspecteur *m*, - trice *f* de police.

detective inspector *n UK* ≃ inspecteur de police principal *m*, inspectrice de police principale *f*.

detective sergeant *n UK* ≃ inspecteur *m*, - trice *f* de police.

detector [dɪ'tektər] *n* détecteur *m*.

detector van *n UK voiture-radar utilisée pour la détection des postes de télévision non déclarés.*

detention [dɪ'tenʃn] *n* **1.** [captivity] détention *f* ■ **in ~** [gen] en détention ; MIL aux arrêts **2.** SCH retenue *f*, consigne *f* ■ **to put sb in ~** consigner qqn, mettre qqn en retenue.

deter [dɪ'tɜːr] (*pret & pp* **deterred**, *cont* **deterring**) *vt* **1.** [discourage - person] dissuader ■ **to ~ sb from doing sthg** dissuader qqn de faire qqch ■ **he was not to be deterred from his purpose** il n'allait pas se laisser détourner de son but **2.** [prevent - attack] prévenir.

detergent [dɪ'tɜːdʒənt] ◇ *n* détergent *m*, détersif *m* ■ *US* [washing powder] lessive *f*.
◇ *adj* détersif, détergent.

deteriorate [dɪ'tɪərɪəreɪt] *vi* se détériorer.

deterioration [dɪˌtɪərɪə'reɪʃn] *n* détérioration *f* ■ [in health, relations] dégradation *f*, détérioration *f*.

determination [dɪˌtɜːmɪ'neɪʃn] *n* **1.** [resolve] détermination *f*, résolution *f* ■ **she showed a dogged ~ to find her natural mother** elle était plus que déterminée *OR* résolue à retrouver sa vraie mère **2.** [establishment, fixing - of prices, wages etc] détermination *f*, fixation *f* ; [- of boundaries] délimitation *f*, établissement *m*.

determinative [dɪ'tɜːmɪnətɪv] ◇ *adj* déterminant ■ GRAM déterminatif.
◇ *n* élément *m* déterminant ■ GRAM déterminant *m*, déterminatif *m*.

determine [dɪ'tɜːmɪn] *vt* **1.** [control, govern] déterminer, décider de **2.** [establish, find out] déterminer, établir **3.** [settle - date, price] déterminer, fixer ; [- boundary] délimiter, établir **4.** *lit* [resolve] : **she ~d to prove her innocence** elle a décidé de *OR* s'est résolue à prouver son innocence.

determined [dɪ'tɜːmɪnd] *adj* **1.** [decided, resolved] déterminé, décidé ■ **to be ~ to do sthg** être déterminé *OR* résolu à faire qqch ■ **she was ~ (that) her son would go to university** elle était bien décidée *OR* déterminée à ce que son fils fasse des études supérieures ■ **he's a very ~ young man** c'est un jeune homme très décidé *OR* qui a de la suite dans les idées **2.** [resolute] : **they made ~ efforts to find all survivors** ils ont fait tout ce qu'ils ont pu pour retrouver tous les survivants.

determiner [dɪ'tɜːmɪnər] *n* déterminant *m*.

determining [dɪ'tɜːmɪnɪŋ] *adj* déterminant.

determinism [dɪ'tɜːmɪnɪzm] *n* déterminisme *m*.

determinist [dɪ'tɜːmɪnɪst] ◇ *adj* déterministe.
◇ *n* déterministe *mf*.

deterministic [dɪˌtɜːmɪ'nɪstɪk] = **determinist** *(adj)*.

deterrence [dɪ'terəns] *n* [gen] dissuasion *f* ■ MIL force *f* de dissuasion.

deterrent [dɪ'terənt] ◇ *n* **1.** [gen] agent *m* de dissuasion ■ **fear acted as a strong ~** la peur a eu un très grand effet de dissuasion **2.** MIL arme *f* de dissuasion.
◇ *adj* dissuasif, de dissuasion.

detest [dɪ'test] *vt* détester ■ **I ~ housework** j'ai horreur de *OR* je déteste faire le ménage.

detestable [dɪ'testəbl] *adj* détestable, exécrable.

detestation [ˌdiːte'steɪʃn] *n* haine *f*, horreur *f*.

dethrone [dɪ'θrəʊn] *vt* détrôner, déposer.

detonate ['detəneɪt] ◇ *vt* faire détoner *OR* exploser.
◇ *vi* détoner, exploser.

detonation [ˌdetə'neɪʃn] *n* détonation *f*, explosion *f*.

detonator ['detəneɪtər] *n* détonateur *m*, amorce *f* ■ RAIL pétard *m*.

detour ['diːˌtʊər] ◇ *n* [in road, stream] détour *m* ■ [for traffic] déviation *f*.
◇ *vi* faire un détour.
◇ *vt* (faire) dévier.

detox ['diːtɒks] *n inf* désintoxication *f* ■ **~ centre** centre *m* de désintoxication.

detoxicate [ˌdiː'tɒksɪkeɪt] *vt* **1.** [person] désintoxiquer **2.** [poison] détoxiquer.

detoxication ['diːˌtɒksɪ'keɪʃn] *n* **1.** [of person] désintoxication *f* **2.** [of poison] détoxication *f*.

detoxification [diːˌtɒksɪfɪ'keɪʃn] *n* [of person] désintoxication *f*.

detoxify [ˌdiː'tɒksɪfaɪ] (*pret & pp* **detoxified**) *vt* [person] désintoxiquer.

detract [dɪ'trækt] *vi* : **to ~ from sthg** diminuer qqch ■ **the criticism in no way ~s from her achievements** la critique ne réduit en rien la portée de *OR* n'enlève rien à ce qu'elle a accompli.

detraction [dɪ'trækʃn] *n* critique *f*, dénigrement *m*.

detractor [dɪ'træktər] *n* détracteur *m*, - trice *f*.

detriment ['detrɪmənt] *n* : **to his ~** à son détriment *OR* préjudice ■ **to the ~ of his work** aux dépens de son travail.

detrimental [ˌdetrɪ'mentl] *adj* : **~ to** [health, reputation] nuisible à, préjudiciable à ■ **~ to** [interests] qui nuit à, qui cause un préjudice à ■ **pollution has a ~ effect on** *OR* **is ~ to plant life** la pollution nuit à la flore.

detritus [dɪ'traɪtəs] *n (U) fml* [debris] détritus *m* ■ GEOL roches *fpl* détritiques, pierrailles *fpl*.

detumescence [ˌdiːtjuː'mesəns] *n* détumescence *f*.

deuce [djuːs] *n* **1.** [on card, dice] deux *m* **2.** TENNIS égalité *f* **3.** *inf dated* [as expletive] : **where the ~ is it?** où diable peut-il bien être? ■ **how the ~ should I know?** comment voulez-vous que je sache?

deuterium [djuː'tɪərɪəm] *n* deutérium *m*.

Deuteronomy [ˌdjuːtə'rɒnəmɪ] *pr n* Deutéronome.

devaluation [ˌdiːvæljʊ'eɪʃn] *n* dévaluation *f*.

devalue [ˌdiː'væljuː] *vt* dévaluer.

devastate ['devəsteɪt] *vt* **1.** [country, town] dévaster, ravager ■ [enemy] anéantir **2.** [overwhelm] foudroyer, accabler, anéantir ■ **he was ~d by his mother's death** la mort de sa mère l'a complètement anéanti.

devastated ['devəsteɪtɪd] *adj* **1.** [area, city] dévasté **2.** [person] accablé.

devastating ['devəsteɪtɪŋ] *adj* **1.** [disastrous - passion, storm] dévastateur, ravageur ; [- news] accablant ; [- argument, effect] accablant, écrasant **2.** [highly effective - person, charm] irrésistible.

devastatingly ['devəsteɪtɪŋlɪ] *adv* de manière dévastatrice ■ [as intensifier] : **~ beautiful** d'une beauté irrésistible.

devastation [ˌdevə'steɪʃn] *n* [disaster] dévastation *f*.

develop [dɪ'veləp] ◇ *vi* **1.** [evolve - country, person] se développer, évoluer ; [- feeling] se former, grandir ; [- plot] se développer, se dérouler ■ **to ~ into sthg** devenir qqch **2.** [become apparent - disease] se manifester, se déclarer ; [- talent, trend] se manifester ; [- event] se produire **3.** PHOT se développer.
◇ *vt* **1.** [form - body, mind] développer, former ; [- story] développer ; [- feeling] former **2.** [expand - business, market] développer ; [- idea, argument] développer, expliquer (en détail), exposer (en détail) **3.** [improve - skill] développer, travailler ; [- machine, process] mettre au point **4.** [acquire - disease] contracter ; [- cold, tic] attraper ; [- symptoms] présenter ■ **she ~ed a habit of biting her nails** elle a pris l'habitude de se ronger les ongles ■ **I've ~ed a taste for jazz** je me suis mis à aimer le

jazz **5.** [land, resources] exploiter, mettre en valeur, aménager ■ **the site is to be ~ed** on va construire sur ce terrain, on va aménager le site **6.** MATHS, MUS & PHOT développer.

developed [dɪ'veləpt] *adj* [film] développé ■ [land] mis en valeur, aménagé ■ [country] développé.

developer [dɪ'veləpəʳ] *n* **1.** [of land] promoteur *m* (de construction) **2.** [person] : **to be a late ~** se développer sur le tard **3.** PHOT révélateur *m*, développateur *m*.

developing [dɪ'veləpɪŋ] ◇ *adj* [crisis, storm] qui se prépare, qui s'annonce ■ [industry] en expansion.
◇ *n* PHOT développement *m* ■ **'~ and printing'** travaux photographiques, développement et tirage ▶ **~ bath** (bain *m*) révélateur *m* ■ **~ tank** cuve *f* à développement.

developing country, developing nation *n* pays *m* OR nation *f* en voie de développement.

development [dɪ'veləpmənt] *n* **1.** [of body, person, mind] développement *m*, formation *f* ■ [of ideas, language] développement *m*, évolution *f* ■ [of argument, theme] développement *m*, exposé *m* ■ [of plot, situation] déroulement *m*, développement *m* ■ [of business] développement *m*, expansion *f* ■ [of invention, process] mise *f* au point ■ [of region] mise *f* en valeur, exploitation *f* ▶ **~ grant** subvention *f* pour le développement **2.** [incident] fait *m* nouveau ■ **we're awaiting further ~s** nous attendons la suite des événements OR les derniers développements ■ **a surprise ~** un rebondissement ■ **there has been an unexpected ~** l'affaire a pris une tournure inattendue ■ **there are no new ~s** il n'y a rien de nouveau **3.** [tract of land] : **housing ~** cité *f* (ouvrière) **4.** MATHS, MUS & PHOT développement *m*.

developmental [dɪ,veləp'mentl] *adj* de développement.

development area *n zone économiquement sinistrée bénéficiant d'aides publiques en vue de sa reconversion.*

development system *n système informatique conçu pour le développement de logiciels.*

deviance ['di:vjəns], **deviancy** ['di:vjənsɪ] *n* [gen - PSYCHOL] déviance *f* ■ **~ from the norm** écart *m* par rapport à la norme.

deviant ['di:vjənt] ◇ *adj* **1.** [behaviour] déviant, qui s'écarte de la norme ■ [growth] anormal ■ **sexually ~** perverti **2.** LING déviant.
◇ *n* déviant *m*, - e *f* ■ **sexual ~** pervers *m*, - e *f*.

deviate ['di:vɪeɪt] *vi* **1.** [differ] dévier, s'écarter ■ **those who ~ from the norm** ceux qui s'écartent de la norme **2.** [plane, ship] dévier, dériver ■ [missile] dévier.

deviation [,di:vɪ'eɪʃn] *n* **1.** [from custom, principle] déviation *f* ■ [from social norm] déviance *f* ■ **there must be no ~ from the party line** on ne doit en aucun cas s'écarter de la ligne du parti **2.** [in statistics] écart *m* **3.** [of plane, ship] déviation *f*, dérive *f* ■ [of missile] déviation *f*, dérivation *f* **4.** MATHS, MED & PHILOS déviation *f*.

deviationist [,di:vɪ'eɪʃənɪst] ◇ *adj* déviationniste.
◇ *n* déviationniste *mf*.

device [dɪ'vaɪs] *n* **1.** [gadget] appareil *m*, engin *m*, mécanisme *m* ▶ **nuclear ~** engin nucléaire **2.** [scheme] ruse *f*, stratagème *m* ■ **it was just a ~ to get attention** ce n'était qu'une ruse pour OR c'était juste un moyen de se faire remarquer ▶ **to leave sb to their own ~s** laisser qqn se débrouiller (tout seul) **3.** *lit* [figure of speech] formule *f* **4.** HERALD devis *m*, emblème *m*.

devil ['devl] (*UK pret & pp* **devilled**, *cont* **devilling**) (*US pret & pp* **deviled**, *cont* **deviling**) ◇ *n* **1.** [demon] diable *m*, démon *m* ■ **the Devil** RELIG le Diable, Satan *m* ■ **~ worship** culte *m* du diable ■ **~-worshipper** adorateur *m*, - trice *f* du diable ■ **go to the ~!** *inf dated* va te faire voir!, va au diable! ▶ **to play ~'s advocate** se faire l'avocat du diable
2. *inf fig* [person] : **you little ~!** petit monstre! ■ **you lucky ~!** veinard! ■ **poor ~!** pauvre diable! ▶ **go on, be a ~!** *hum* allez, laisse-toi faire OR tenter !
3. *inf* [as intensifier] : **what the ~ are you doing?** mais enfin, qu'est-ce que tu fabriques? ■ **how the ~ should I know?** comment voulez-vous que je sache? ■ **I had a ~ of a time getting here** j'ai eu un mal fou OR un mal de chien à arriver jusqu'ici ■ **there'll be the ~ to pay when your father finds out** ça va barder quand ton père apprendra ça ■ **we had the ~ of a job** OR **the ~'s own job finding the house** on a eu un mal fou à trouver la maison ▶ **between the ~ and the deep blue sea** entre l'enclume et le marteau ■ **to give the ~ his due...** en toute honnêteté, il faut dire que..., rendons OR rendons-lui justice... ■ **he has the luck of the ~** OR **the ~'s own luck** il a une veine de pendu OR de cocu ■ **speak** OR **talk of the ~ (and he appears)!** quand on parle du loup (on en voit la queue)! ■ **better the ~ you know than the ~ you don't** *prov* on sait ce qu'on perd, on ne sait pas ce qu'on trouve ■ **the ~ finds** OR **makes work for idle hands** *prov* l'oisiveté est (la) mère de tous les vices *prov* ■ **let the ~ take the hindmost** *prov* chacun pour soi et Dieu pour tous *prov*
4. [brazier] brasero *m*
5. [ghostwriter] nègre *m (d'un écrivain)* ■ LAW [assistant] avocat *m* stagiaire ■ **printer's ~** TYPO apprenti *m* imprimeur.
◇ *vt* **1.** CULIN accommoder à la moutarde et au poivre ■ **devilled egg** œuf *m* à la diable
2. *US inf* [harass] harceler.
◇ *vi UK* : **to ~ for sb** [author] servir de nègre à qqn ; [lawyer] être avocat stagiaire auprès de qqn ; [printer] être apprenti imprimeur chez qqn.

devilfish ['devlfɪʃ] *n* mante *f*.

devilish ['devlɪʃ] *adj* **1.** [fiendish] diabolique, infernal ■ [mischievous] espiègle **2.** *inf dated* [extreme] sacré, satané.

devilishly ['devlɪʃlɪ] *adv* **1.** [fiendishly] diaboliquement ■ [mischievously] par espièglerie **2.** *inf dated* [as intensifier] rudement, sacrément.

devil-may-care *adj* [careless] insouciant ■ [reckless] cassecou.

devilment ['devlmənt] *n* [mischief] espièglerie *f* ■ [malice] méchanceté *f*, malice *f*.

devilry ['devlrɪ] *n (U)* **1.** [mischief] espièglerie *f* ■ [recklessness] témérité *f* **2.** [black magic] magie *f* noire, maléfices *mpl*.

devious ['di:vjəs] *adj* **1.** [cunning - person] retors, sournois ; [- means, method] détourné ; [- mind] tortueux ■ **she can be very ~** elle fait parfois les choses en dessous OR en sousmain **2.** [winding - route] sinueux.

deviously ['di:vjəslɪ] *adv* sournoisement.

deviousness ['di:vjəsnɪs] *n* [of person] sournoiserie *f* ■ [of plan] complexité *f*.

devise [dɪ'vaɪz] ◇ *vt* **1.** [plan] imaginer, inventer, concevoir, élaborer ■ [plot] combiner, manigancer ■ **a scheme of my own devising** un plan de mon invention **2.** LAW [property] léguer.
◇ *n* legs *m* (de biens immobiliers).

deviser [dɪ'vaɪzəʳ] *n* [of plan] inventeur *m*, - trice *f* ■ [of scheme] auteur *m*.

devitalize, ise [,di:'vaɪtəlaɪz] *vt* affaiblir.

devocalize, ise [,di:'vəʊkəlaɪz] *vt* assourdir.

devoid [dɪ'vɔɪd] *adj* : **~ of** dépourvu de, dénué de.

devolution [,di:və'lu:ʃn] *n* **1.** [of duty, power] délégation *f* ■ LAW [of property] transmission *f*, dévolution *f* **2.** POL décentralisation *f* **3.** BIOL dégénérescence *f*.

devolutionist [,di:və'lu:ʃnɪst] ◇ *adj* décentralisateur.
◇ *n* partisan *m* de la décentralisation.

devolve [dɪ'vɒlv] ◇ *vi* **1.** [duty, job] incomber ■ [by chance] incomber, échoir ■ **the responsibility ~s on** OR **upon him** la responsabilité lui incombe OR lui échoit **2.** LAW [estate] passer.
◇ *vt* déléguer ■ **to ~ sthg on** OR **upon** OR **to sb** déléguer qqch à qqn, charger qqn de qqch.

devote [dɪ'vəʊt] *vt* consacrer ■ **to ~ o.s. to** [study, work] se consacrer OR s'adonner à ; [a cause] se vouer OR se consacrer à ; [pleasure] se livrer à.

devoted [dɪ'vəʊtɪd] *adj* [friend, servant, service] dévoué, fidèle ■ [admirer] fervent ■ **I'm ~ to my children** je ferais tout pour mes enfants.

devotedly [dɪ'vəʊtɪdlɪ] *adv* avec dévouement.

devotee [ˌdevə'ti:] *n* [of opera, sport etc] passionné *m*, - e *f* ■ [of doctrine] adepte *mf*, partisan *m*, - e *f* ■ [of religion] adepte *mf*.

devotion [dɪ'vəʊʃn] *n* **1.** [to person] dévouement *m*, attachement *m* ■ [to cause] dévouement *m* ■ **he showed great ~ to duty** il a prouvé son sens du devoir **2.** RELIG dévotion *f*, piété *f*.
◆ **devotions** *npl* dévotions *fpl*, prières *fpl*.

devotional [dɪ'vəʊʃənl] <> *adj* [book, work] de dévotion OR piété ■ [attitude] de prière, pieux.
<> *n* service *m* (religieux).

devour [dɪ'vaʊəʳ] *vt* **1.** [food] dévorer, engloutir ■ *fig* [book] dévorer ■ **he ~ed her with his eyes** il l'a dévorée des yeux **2.** [subj: fire] dévorer, consumer ■ **~ed by hatred** *fig* dévoré de haine.

devouring [dɪ'vaʊərɪŋ] *adj* [hunger, jealousy] dévorant ■ [interest] ardent ■ [need] urgent.

devout [dɪ'vaʊt] *adj* [person] pieux, dévot ■ [hope, prayer] fervent.

devoutly [dɪ'vaʊtlɪ] *adv* **1.** [pray] avec dévotion, dévotement **2.** *fml* [earnestly] sincèrement.

dew [dju:] *n* rosée *f*.

dewdrop ['dju:drɒp] *n* goutte *f* de rosée.

dewlap ['dju:læp] *n* fanon *m*.

dewy ['dju:ɪ] (*comp* **dewier**, *superl* **dewiest**) *adj* couvert OR humide de rosée.

dewy-eyed *adj* [innocent] innocent ■ [trusting] naïf, ingénu.

Dexedrine® ['deksɪdri:n] *n* Dexédrine® *f*.

dexterity [dek'sterətɪ] *n* adresse *f*, dextérité *f*.

dexterous ['dekstrəs] *adj* [person] adroit, habile ■ [movement] adroit, habile, agile.

dextrose ['dekstrəʊs] *n* dextrose *m*.

dextrous *etc* ['dekstrəs] = **dexterous**.

DFE *pr n* = **Department for Education**.

DG *n* = **director-general**.

dhal [dɑ:l] *n* CULIN *plat à base de lentilles et d'épices*.

DHSS *pr n* UK (*abbrev of* **Department of Health and Social Security**) *ancien nom du ministère britannique de la santé et de la Sécurité sociale*.

DHTML [ˌdi:eɪtʃti:em'el] (*abbrev of* **Dynamic Hypertext Markup Language**) *n* COMPUT DHTML *m*.

diabetes [ˌdaɪə'bi:ti:z] *n* diabète *m*.

diabetic [ˌdaɪə'betɪk] <> *adj* diabétique.
<> *n* diabétique *mf*.

diabolic [ˌdaɪə'bɒlɪk] *adj* [action, plan] diabolique, infernal ■ [look, smile] diabolique, satanique.

diabolical [ˌdaɪə'bɒlɪkl] *adj* **1.** = **diabolic 2.** *inf* [terrible] atroce, épouvantable, infernal ■ **I think it's a ~ liberty** il faut un toupet monstre OR un sacré culot pour faire une chose pareille.

diabolically [ˌdaɪə'bɒlɪklɪ] *adv* **1.** [fiendishly] diaboliquement, de manière diabolique **2.** UK *inf* [as intensifier] vachement, rudement, sacrément.

diachronic [ˌdaɪə'krɒnɪk] *adj* diachronique.

diacritic [ˌdaɪə'krɪtɪk] <> *adj* diacritique.
<> *n* signe *m* diacritique.

diadem ['daɪədem] *n* diadème *m*.

diaeresis [daɪ'erɪsɪs] (*pl* **diaereses** [-ˌsi:z]) = **dieresis**.

diagnosable [ˌdaɪəg'nəʊzəbl] *adj* susceptible d'être diagnostiqué, décelable.

diagnose ['daɪəgnəʊz] *vt* [illness] diagnostiquer ■ **they ~d her illness as cancer** ils ont diagnostiqué un cancer ‖ *fig* [fault, problem] déceler, discerner.

diagnosis [ˌdaɪəg'nəʊsɪs] (*pl* **diagnoses** [-si:z]) *n* MED & *fig* diagnostic *m* ■ BIOL & BOT diagnose *f*.

diagnostic [ˌdaɪəg'nɒstɪk] *adj* diagnostique.

diagnostician [ˌdaɪəgnɒs'tɪʃn] *n* diagnostiqueur *m*.

diagnostics [ˌdaɪəg'nɒstɪks] *n (U)* COMPUT & MED diagnostic *m*.

diagonal [daɪ'ægənl] <> *adj* diagonal.
<> *n* diagonale *f*.

diagonally [daɪ'ægənəlɪ] *adv* en diagonale, diagonalement, obliquement ■ **we cut ~ across the field** nous avons traversé le champ en diagonale OR en biais ■ **his desk is ~ across from mine** son bureau est diagonalement opposé au mien ■ **a ribbon worn ~ across the chest** un ruban porté en écharpe sur la poitrine.

diagram ['daɪəgræm] (UK *pret & pp* **diagrammed**, *cont* **diagramming**) (US *pret & pp* **diagramed** OR **diagrammed**, *cont* **diagraming** OR **diagramming**) <> *n* [gen] diagramme *m*, schéma *m* ■ MATHS diagramme *m*, figure *f*.
<> *vt* donner une représentation graphique de.

diagrammatic [ˌdaɪəgrə'mætɪk] *adj* schématique.

dial ['daɪəl] (UK *pret & pp* **dialled**, *cont* **dialling**) (US *pret & pp* **dialed**, *cont* **dialing**) <> *n* [of clock, telephone] cadran *m* ■ [of radio, TV] bouton *m* (de réglage).
<> *vt* [number] faire, composer ■ **to ~ Spain direct** appeler l'Espagne par l'automatique ■ **~ the operator** appelez l'opératrice ▶ **~-a-joke/disc** la plaisanterie/le disque du jour par téléphone.

DIAL-A-...

Ce préfixe introduit le nom de certains services téléphoniques : *dial-a-wake-up* (réveil), *dial-a-date* (rencontres), *dial-a-prayer* (prières préenregistrées), etc.

dial. *written abbr of* **dialect**.

dialect ['daɪəlekt] *n* [regional] dialecte *m*, parler *m* ■ [local, rural] patois *m*.

dialectal [ˌdaɪə'lektl] *adj* dialectal, de dialecte.

dialectic [ˌdaɪə'lektɪk] <> *adj* dialectique.
<> *n* dialectique *f*.

dialectical [ˌdaɪə'lektɪkl] *adj* dialectique.

dialectical materialism *n* matérialisme *m* dialectique.

dialectology [ˌdaɪəlek'tɒlədʒɪ] *n* dialectologie *f*.

dialling code ['daɪəlɪŋ-] *n* UK indicatif *m*.

dialling tone UK ['daɪəlɪŋ-], **dial tone** US *n* tonalité *f*.

dialogue UK, **dialog** US ['daɪəlɒg] *n* dialogue *m*.

dialogue box UK, **dialog box** US *n* COMPUT boîte *f* de dialogue.

dial tone US = **dialling tone**.

dialysis [daɪ'ælɪsɪs] (*pl* **dialyses** [-si:z]) *n* dialyse *f* ■ **~ machine** dialyseur *m*.

diamanté [dɪə'mɒnteɪ] *n* tissu *m* diamanté.

diamantine [ˌdaɪə'mæntaɪn] *adj* diamantin.

diameter [daɪ'æmɪtəʳ] *n* **1.** [gen - GEOM] diamètre *m* ■ **the tree is two metres in ~** l'arbre fait deux mètres de diamètre **2.** [of microscope] unité *f* de grossissement.

diametric(al) [ˌdaɪə'metrɪk(l)] *adj* GEOM & *fig* diamétral.

diametrically [ˌdaɪə'metrɪklɪ] *adv* GEOM & *fig* diamétralement ■ **~ opposed** diamétralement opposé.

diamond ['daɪəmənd] ◇ *n* **1.** [gem] diamant *m* ■ **he's a ~ in the rough** *esp US* il a un cœur d'or sous ses dehors frustes **2.** [shape] losange *m* **3.** CARDS carreau *m* **4.** [in baseball] terrain *m* (de baseball).
◇ *comp* **1.** [brooch, ring etc] de diamant *OR* diamants ■ **~ necklace** collier *m OR* rivière *f* de diamants **2.** [mine] de diamant *OR* diamants ■ **~ drill** foreuse *f* à pointe de diamant ■ **~ merchant** diamantaire *m*.

diamond jubilee *n* (célébration *f* du) soixantième anniversaire *m*.

diamond wedding *n* noces *fpl* de diamant.

Diana [daɪ'ænə] *pr n* MYTH Diane.

diaper ['daɪəpəʳ] *n* **1.** *US* [nappy] couche *f (de bébé)* **2.** [fabric] damassé *m*.

diaphanous [daɪ'æfənəs] *adj* diaphane.

diaphragm ['daɪəfræm] *n* diaphragme *m*.

diarist ['daɪərɪst] *n* [private] auteur *m* d'un journal intime ■ [of public affairs] chroniqueur *m*.

diarrhoea *UK*, **diarrhea** *US* [,daɪə'rɪə] *n* diarrhée *f* ■ **to have ~** avoir la diarrhée.

diary ['daɪərɪ] (*pl* **diaries**) *n* **1.** [personal] journal *m* (intime) ■ **to keep a ~** tenir un journal **2.** *UK* [for business] agenda *m*.

diaspora [daɪ'æspərə] *n* HIST & *fig* diaspora *f*.

diatribe ['daɪətraɪb] *n* diatribe *f*.

dib [dɪb] (*pret & pp* **dibbed**, *cont* **dibbing**) *vi* pêcher à la ligne flottante.

dibber ['dɪbəʳ] *UK* = **dibble** *(n)*.

dibble ['dɪbl] ◇ *n* plantoir *m*.
◇ *vt* [plant] repiquer au plantoir.

dibs [dɪbz] *npl* **1.** [jacks] osselets *mpl* **2.** *inf* [claim] : **to have ~ on sthg** avoir des droits sur qqch.

dice [daɪs] (*pl inv*) ◇ *n* **1.** [game] dé *m* ■ **to play ~** jouer aux dés ▶ **no ~!** *US inf* des clous! **2.** CULIN dé *m*, cube *m*.
◇ *vt* CULIN couper en dés *OR* en cubes.
◇ *vi* jouer aux dés ■ **to ~ with death** jouer avec sa vie.

dicey ['daɪsɪ] (*comp* **dicier**, *superl* **diciest**) *adj inf* risqué, dangereux, délicat.

dichotomy [daɪ'kɒtəmɪ] (*pl* **dichotomies**) *n* dichotomie *f*.

dick [dɪk] *n* **1.** ▲ [penis] queue▲ *f* **2.** △ *UK* [idiot] con△ *m*.

dickens ['dɪkɪnz] *n inf* **what the ~ are you doing?** mais qu'est-ce que tu fabriques? ■ **we had a ~ of a job getting a babysitter** ça a été la galère *OR* la croix et la bannière pour trouver une baby-sitter.

Dickensian [dɪ'kenzɪən] *adj* à la Dickens.

dickey ['dɪkɪ] *n* **1.** [shirt] faux plastron *m* (de chemise) **2.** *UK* [in carriage] siège *m* du cocher ■ AUT spider *m*, strapontin *m* **3.** *UK inf* [bow tie] : **~ (bow)** nœud *m* pap.

dickhead△ ['dɪkhed] *n* con△ *m*.

Dick Turpin [-'tɜ:pɪn] *pr n bandit de grand chemin anglais devenu héros populaire.*

dicky ['dɪkɪ] (*pl* **dickies**, *comp* **dickier**, *superl* **dickiest**) ◇ *n* = **dickey**.
◇ *adj inf UK inf* [ladder] peu solide, branlant ■ [heart] qui flanche ■ [situation] peu sûr.

dickybird ['dɪkɪbɜ:d] *n inf* petit oiseau *m*.

dicta ['dɪktə] *pl* ▷ **dictum**.

Dictaphone® ['dɪktəfəʊn] *n* Dictaphone® *m*, machine *f* à dicter.

dictate ◇ *vt* [dɪk'teɪt] **1.** [letter] dicter ■ **to ~ sthg to sb** dicter qqch à qqn **2.** [determine - terms, conditions] dicter, imposer ■ **he ~s how we run the business** c'est lui qui décide de la marche de l'entreprise ■ **our budget will ~ the type of computer we buy** le type d'ordinateur que nous achèterons dépendra de notre budget.
◇ *vi* [dɪk'teɪt] [give dictation] dicter.
◇ *n* ['dɪkteɪt] **1.** [order] ordre *m* **2.** *(usu pl)* [principle] précepte *m* ■ **the ~s of conscience/reason** la voix de la conscience/raison.
◆ **dictate to** *vt insep* donner des ordres à ■ **I won't be ~d to** je n'ai pas d'ordres à recevoir!

dictation [dɪk'teɪʃn] *n* [of letter, story] dictée *f* ■ **to take ~** écrire sous la dictée ■ **French ~** dictée de français.

dictator [dɪk'teɪtəʳ] *n* dictateur *m*.

dictatorial [,dɪktə'tɔ:rɪəl] *adj* dictatorial.

dictatorially [,dɪktə'tɔ:rɪəlɪ] *adv* dictatorialement, en dictateur.

dictatorship [dɪk'teɪtəʃɪp] *n* dictature *f*.

diction ['dɪkʃn] *n* **1.** [pronunciation] diction *f*, élocution *f* **2.** [phrasing] style *m*, langage *m*.

dictionary ['dɪkʃənrɪ] (*pl* **dictionaries**) *n* dictionnaire *m*.

dictum ['dɪktəm] (*pl* **dicta** ['dɪktə] *OR pl* **dictums**) *n fml* **1.** [statement] affirmation *f* ■ LAW remarque *f* superfétatoire **2.** [maxim] dicton *m*, maxime *f*.

did [dɪd] *pt* ▷ **do**.

didactic [dɪ'dæktɪk] *adj* didactique.

didactically [dɪ'dæktɪklɪ] *adv* didactiquement.

diddle ['dɪdl] *vt UK inf* duper, rouler ■ **to ~ sb out of sthg** carotter qqch à qqn.

diddums ['dɪdəmz] *n inf* pauvre petit.

didn't ['dɪdnt] = **did not**.

didst [dɪdst] *vb (2nd pers sg) arch* ▷ **did**.

die [daɪ] ◇ *vi* **1.** [person] mourir, décéder ■ **she's dying** elle est mourante *OR* à l'agonie ■ **she ~d of cancer** elle est morte du *OR* d'un cancer ■ **thousands are dying of hunger** des milliers de gens meurent de faim ■ **to ~ a hero** mourir en héros ■ **he left us to ~** il nous a abandonnés à la mort ■ *fig* **to ~ laughing** *inf* mourir de rire ■ **I nearly ~d** *inf*, **I could have ~d** *inf* [from fear] j'étais mort de trouille ; [from embarrassment] j'aurais voulu rentrer sous terre, je ne savais plus où me mettre ▶ **to ~ with one's boots on** *OR* **in harness** mourir debout *OR* en pleine activité ■ **never say ~!** il ne faut jamais désespérer! **2.** [animal, plant] mourir **3.** [engine] caler, s'arrêter **4.** [fire, love, memory] s'éteindre, mourir ■ [tradition] s'éteindre, disparaître, mourir ■ [smile] disparaître, s'évanouir ■ **old habits ~ hard** les mauvaises habitudes ne se perdent pas facilement ■ **her secret ~d with her** elle a emporté son secret dans la tombe **5.** *inf* [want very much] : **to be dying for sthg** avoir une envie folle de qqch ■ **to be dying to do sthg** mourir d'envie de faire qqch.
◇ *vt* : **to ~ a natural/violent death** mourir de sa belle mort/de mort violente.
◇ *n* **1.** (*pl* dice [daɪs]) GAMES dé *m* (à jouer) ■ **the ~ is cast** *fig* les dés sont jetés **2.** (*pl* dies) ARCHIT [dado] dé *m (d'un piédestal)* ■ TECH [stamp] matrice *f* ■ [in minting] coin *m* ■ **as straight as a ~** franc comme l'or.
◆ **die away** *vi insep* s'affaiblir, s'éteindre, mourir.
◆ **die back** *vi insep* [plant] dépérir.
◆ **die down** *vi insep* **1.** [wind] tomber, se calmer ■ [fire - in chimney] baisser ; [- in building, forest] s'apaiser, diminuer ■ [noise] diminuer ■ [anger, protest] se calmer, s'apaiser **2.** [plant] se flétrir, perdre ses feuilles et sa tige.
◆ **die off** *vi insep* mourir les uns après les autres.
◆ **die out** *vi insep* [family, tribe, tradition] disparaître, s'éteindre ■ [fire] s'éteindre ■ **the panda is in danger of dying out** le panda est menacé d'extinction.

die-cast ◇ *vt* mouler sous pression *OR* en matrice.
◇ *adj* moulé sous pression *OR* en matrice.

die-casting *n* moulage *m* en matrice.

diehard ['daɪhɑ:d] ◇ *n* conservateur *m*, - trice *f*, réactionnaire *mf* ■ **the party ~s** les durs du parti.
◇ *adj* intransigeant ■ POL réactionnaire ■ **a ~ liberal** un libéral pur et dur.

dieresis [daɪ'erɪsɪs] (*pl* **diereses** [-si:z]) *n* [sound] diérèse *f* ▪ [sign] tréma *m*.

diesel ['di:zl] *n* [vehicle] diesel *m* ▪ [fuel] gas-oil *m*, gazole *m*.

diesel-electric ◇ *adj* diesel-électrique.
◇ *n* diesel-électrique *m*.

diesel engine *n* AUT moteur *m* diesel ▪ RAIL motrice *f*.

diesel fuel, diesel oil *n* gas-oil *m*, gazole *m*.

diesel train *n* autorail *m*.

diet ['daɪət] ◇ *n* **1.** [regular food] alimentation *f*, nourriture *f* ▪ **they live on a ~ of rice and fish** ils se nourrissent de riz et de poisson **2.** [restricted or special food] régime *m* ▪ **to be on a ~** être au régime ▪ **to go on a ~** faire *OR* suivre un régime ▪ **a low-fat ~** un régime à faible teneur en matières grasses **3.** [assembly] diète *f*.
◇ *comp* [drink, food] de régime, basses calories ▪ **~ pill** coupe-faim *m inv*.
◇ *vi* suivre un régime.

dietary ['daɪətrɪ] (*pl* **dietaries**) ◇ *adj* [supplement] alimentaire ▪ [of special food] de régime, diététique ▪ **~ fibre** cellulose *f* végétale.
◇ *n* régime *m* alimentaire *(d'un malade, d'une prison)*.

dietetic [,daɪə'tetɪk] *adj* diététique.

dietetics [,daɪə'tetɪks] *n (U)* diététique *f*.

dietician [,daɪə'tɪʃn] *n* diététicien *m*, - enne *f*.

differ ['dɪfər] *vi* **1.** [vary] différer, être différent ▪ **in what way does this text ~ from the first?** en quoi ce texte diffère-t-il du premier? ▪ **the two approaches ~ quite considerably** les deux approches n'ont pas grand-chose à voir l'une avec l'autre ▪ **the houses ~ in size and design** les maisons diffèrent par leurs dimensions et leur conception **2.** [disagree] être en désaccord, ne pas être d'accord.

difference ['dɪfrəns] *n* **1.** [dissimilarity] différence *f* ▪ [in age, size, weight] écart *m*, différence *f* ▪ **there are many ~s between the two cultures** les deux cultures sont très différentes l'une de l'autre ▪ **I can't tell the ~ between the two** je ne vois pas la différence entre les deux ▪ **there's a ~ in height of six inches** il y a une différence de hauteur de quinze centimètres ▪ **it makes no ~, it doesn't make the slightest ~** ça n'a aucune importance, ça revient au même, ça ne change absolument rien ▪ **it makes no ~ to me (one way or the other)** (d'une manière ou d'une autre), cela m'est (parfaitement) égal ▪ **does it make any ~ whether he comes or not?** est-ce que ça change quelque chose qu'il vienne ou pas? ▪ **that makes all the ~** voilà qui change tout ▪ **a house with a ~** une maison pas comme les autres **2.** [disagreement] différend *m* ▪ **we have our ~s** nous ne sommes pas toujours d'accord ▪ **a ~ of opinion** une différence *OR* divergence d'opinion **3.** [in numbers, quantity] différence *f*.

different ['dɪfrənt] *adj* **1.** [not identical] différent, autre ▪ **~ from *OR* to *OR esp US* than** différent de ▪ **it's very ~ from any other city I've visited** ça ne ressemble en rien aux autres villes que j'ai visitées ▪ **you look ~ today** tu n'es pas comme d'habitude aujourd'hui ▪ **he put on a ~ shirt** il a mis une autre chemise ▪ **she's a ~ person since their wedding** elle a beaucoup changé depuis leur mariage ▪ **I feel like a ~ person since my holiday** j'ai l'impression d'avoir fait peau neuve depuis mes vacances ▪ **what's ~ about it?** qu'est-ce qu'il y a de différent *OR* de changé? ▪ **I now see things in a ~ light** je vois désormais les choses sous un autre jour *OR* angle ▪ **that's quite a ~ matter** ça, c'est une autre affaire *OR* histoire **2.** [various] divers, différents, plusieurs ▪ **she visited ~ schools** elle a visité diverses *OR* différentes écoles **3.** [unusual] singulier ▪ **I'm looking for something ~** je cherche quelque chose d'original *OR* qui sorte de l'ordinaire ▪ **she always has to be ~** elle veut toujours se singulariser, elle ne peut jamais faire comme tout le monde ▪ **I've been out with a lot of men before, but he's ~** je suis sortie avec beaucoup d'hommes, mais celui-là n'est pas comme les autres.

differential [,dɪfə'renʃl] ◇ *adj* **1.** MATHS différentiel **2.** AUT différentiel *m* ▪ **~ housing** boîtier *m* de différentiel.
◇ *n* **1.** [in salary] écart *m* salarial **2.** MATHS différentielle *f* **3.** = **differential gear**.

differential calculus *n* calcul *m* différentiel.

differential coefficient *n* dérivée *f*.

differential equation *n* équation *f* différentielle.

differential gear *n* différentiel *m*.

differentiate [,dɪfə'renʃɪeɪt] ◇ *vt* **1.** [distinguish] différencier, distinguer ▪ **what ~s this product from its competitors?** qu'est-ce qui différencie *OR* distingue ce produit de ses concurrents? **2.** MATHS différencier, calculer la différentielle de.
◇ *vi* faire la différence *OR* distinction ▪ **I'm unable to ~ between the two** je ne vois pas de différence entre les deux.

differentiation [,dɪfərenʃɪ'eɪʃn] *n* [gen] différenciation *f* ▪ MATHS différentiation *f*.

differently ['dɪfrəntlɪ] *adv* différemment, autrement ▪ **I do it ~ from *OR (esp) US* than you** je le fais différemment de *OR* autrement que vous, je ne fais pas ça comme vous.

differently abled *adj* [in politically correct language] handicapé.

difficult ['dɪfɪkəlt] *adj* **1.** [problem, task] difficile, dur, ardu ▪ [book, question] difficile ▪ **he's had a ~ life** il a eu une vie difficile ▪ **I find it ~ to believe she's gone** j'ai du mal à *OR* il m'est difficile de croire qu'elle est partie ▪ **the most ~ part is over** le plus difficile *OR* le plus dur est fait **2.** [awkward] difficile, peu commode ▪ **don't be so ~!** ne fais pas le difficile!, ne fais pas la fine bouche! ▪ **he's ~ to get along with** il n'est pas commode, il a un caractère difficile ▪ **we could make life/things very ~ for you** on pourrait sérieusement vous compliquer la vie/les choses.

difficulty ['dɪfɪkəltɪ] (*pl* **difficulties**) *n* **1.** *(U)* [trouble] difficulté *f*, difficultés *fpl* ▪ **to have *OR* experience ~ (in) doing sthg** avoir du mal *OR* de la peine *OR* des difficultés à faire qqch ▪ **with ~** avec difficulté *OR* peine ▪ **without ~** sans difficulté *OR* peine **2.** [obstacle, problem] difficulté *f*, problème *m* ▪ **the main ~ is getting the staff** le plus difficile, c'est de trouver le personnel ▮ [predicament] difficulté *f*, embarras *m* ▪ **to get into difficulties** être *OR* se trouver en difficulté ▪ **to be in financial difficulties** avoir des ennuis d'argent, être dans l'embarras.

diffidence ['dɪfɪdəns] *n* manque *m* d'assurance *OR* de confiance en soi, timidité *f*.

diffident ['dɪfɪdənt] *adj* [person] qui manque de confiance en soi *OR* d'assurance ▪ [remark, smile] timide ▪ [tone] hésitant.

diffidently ['dɪfɪdəntlɪ] *adv* avec timidité *OR* embarras, de façon embarrassée.

diffract [dɪ'frækt] *vt* diffracter.

diffraction [dɪ'frækʃn] *n* diffraction *f*.

diffuse ◇ *vt* [dɪ'fju:z] diffuser, répandre.
◇ *vi* [dɪ'fju:z] se diffuser, se répandre.
◇ *adj* [dɪ'fju:s] **1.** [light] diffus ▪ [thought] diffus, vague **2.** [wordy] diffus, prolixe.

diffused [dɪ'fju:zd] *adj* diffus.

diffuser [dɪ'fju:zər] *n* [gen - ELEC] diffuseur *m*.

diffusion [dɪ'fju:ʒn] *n* **1.** [of light, news] diffusion *f* **2.** [of style] prolixité *f*.

dig [dɪg] (*pret & pp* **dug** [dʌg], *cont* **digging**) ◇ *vt* **1.** [in ground - hole] creuser ; [- tunnel] creuser, percer ▪ [with spade] bêcher ▪ **he dug his way under the fence** il s'est creusé un passage sous la clôture ▪ **to ~ potatoes** arracher des pommes de terre ➊ **to ~ one's own grave** creuser sa propre tombe **2.** [jab] enfoncer ▪ **she dug me in the ribs (with her elbow)** elle m'a donné un coup de coude dans les côtes **3.** △ *dated* [understand] piger ▪ [appreciate, like] aimer ▪ [look at] viser ▪ **~ that music!** écoute-moi (un peu) cette musique!
◇ *vi* **1.** [person] creuser ▪ [animal] fouiller, fouir ▪ **to ~ for gold** creuser pour trouver de l'or ▪ **he spends hours digging about in old junk shops** *fig* il passe des heures à fouiller dans les magasins de brocante **2.** △ *dated* [understand] piger.

◇ *n* **1.** [in ground] coup *m* de bêche **2.** archaeology fouilles *fpl* ▪ **to go on a ~** faire des fouilles **3.** [jab] coup *m* ▪ **to give sb a ~ in the ribs** donner un coup de coude dans les côtes de qqn **4.** *inf* [snide remark] coup *m* de patte ▪ **that was a ~ at you** c'était une pierre dans votre jardin.

◆ **dig in** ◇ *vi insep* **1.** MIL [dig trenches] se retrancher ▪ *fig* tenir bon **2.** *inf* [eat] commencer à manger ▪ **~ in!** allez-y, mangez!, attaquez!

◇ *vt sep* **1.** [mix with ground] enterrer **2.** [jab] enfoncer ▶ **to ~ in one's heels** se braquer, se buter ▪ **to ~ o.s. in** *liter* se retrancher ; *fig* camper sur ses positions.

◆ **dig into** *vt insep* **1.** [delve into] fouiller dans ▪ **don't ~ into your savings** *fig* n'entame pas tes économies, ne pioche pas dans tes économies **2.** [jab] : **your elbow is digging into me** ton coude me rentre dans les côtes.

◆ **dig out** *vt sep* **1.** [remove] extraire ▪ [from ground] déterrer ▪ **they had to ~ the car out of the snow** il a fallu qu'ils dégagent la voiture de la neige (à la pelle) **2.** *inf* [find] dénicher.

◆ **dig up** *vt sep* **1.** [ground - gen] retourner ; [- with spade] bêcher **2.** [plant] arracher **3.** [unearth] déterrer ▪ *inf fig* [find] *inf* dénicher ▪ **where did you ~ him up?** où est-ce que tu l'as pêché *OR* dégoté?

digest ◇ *vt* [dɪ'dʒest] **1.** [food] digérer **2.** [idea] assimiler, digérer **3.** [classify] classer ▪ [sum up] résumer.

◇ *vi* [dɪ'dʒest] digérer.

◇ *n* ['daɪdʒest] **1.** [of book, facts] résumé *m* ▪ **in ~ form** en abrégé **2.** LAW digeste *m* **3.** [magazine] digest *m*.

digestible [dɪ'dʒestəbl] *adj liter & fig* digeste, facile à digérer.

digestion [dɪ'dʒestʃn] *n* digestion *f*.

digestive [dɪ'dʒestɪv] ◇ *adj* digestif ▪ **~ troubles** troubles *mpl* de la digestion ▶ **~ biscuit** *UK sorte de sablé* ▪ **~ system** système *m* digestif.

◇ *n* [drink] digestif *m* ▪ *UK* [biscuit] *sorte de sablé*.

digger ['dɪgəʳ] *n* **1.** [miner] mineur *m* ▪ *UK inf* CONSTR terrassier *m* **2.** [machine] excavatrice *f*, pelleteuse *f*.

diggings ['dɪgɪŋz] *npl* **1.** archaeology fouilles *fpl* **2.** MIN [dirt] terrassement *m* ▪ [pit] creusement *m*, excavation *f* ▪ [of gold] placer *m* **3.** *UK inf dated* = **digs**.

digibox ['dɪdʒɪbɒks] *n UK* [TV] décodeur *m* numérique.

digit ['dɪdʒɪt] *n* **1.** [number] chiffre *m* ▪ **three-~ number** nombre à trois chiffres **2.** [finger] doigt *m* ▪ [toe] orteil *m* **3.** ASTRON doigt *m*.

digital ['dɪdʒɪtl] *adj* **1.** ANAT digital **2.** [clock, watch] à affichage numérique ▪ [display] numérique ▪ COMPUT numérique.

digital audio tape = **DAT**.

digital camera *n* appareil photo *m* numérique.

digital computer *n* calculateur *m* numérique.

digitalis [ˌdɪdʒɪ'teɪlɪs] *n* BOT digitale *f* ▪ PHARM digitaline *f*.

digital radio *n* radio *f* numérique.

digital recording *n* enregistrement *m* numérique.

digital television, digital TV *n* télévision *f* numérique.

digitization [ˌdɪdʒɪtaɪ'zeɪʃn] *n* numérisation *f*.

digitize, ise ['dɪdʒɪtaɪz] *vt* numériser.

dignified ['dɪgnɪfaɪd] *adj* [person] plein de dignité, digne ▪ [silence] digne ▪ **he behaved in a very ~ manner** il s'est comporté avec beaucoup de dignité.

dignify ['dɪgnɪfaɪ] (*pret & pp* **dignified**) *vt* donner de la dignité à ▪ **I refuse to even ~ that question with an answer** cette question n'est même pas digne de réponse *OR* ne mérite même pas une réponse.

dignitary ['dɪgnɪtrɪ] (*pl* **dignitaries**) *n* dignitaire *m*.

dignity ['dɪgnətɪ] (*pl* **dignities**) *n* **1.** [importance, poise] dignité *f* ▪ **it would be beneath my ~ to accept** accepter serait indigne de moi *OR* serait m'abaisser ▪ **she considered it beneath her ~** elle s'estimait au-dessus de ça ▪ **to stand on one's ~** se draper dans sa dignité **2.** [rank] dignité *f*, haut rang *m* ▪ [title] titre *m*, dignité *f*.

digress [daɪ'gres] *vi* s'éloigner, s'écarter ▪ **but I ~** mais je m'égare, revenons à nos moutons.

digression [daɪ'greʃn] *n* digression *f*.

digressive [daɪ'gresɪv] *adj* qui s'écarte *OR* s'éloigne du sujet.

digs [dɪgz] *npl inf* piaule *f* ▪ **I'm in ~ in Wimbledon** je crèche *OR* j'ai une piaule à Wimbledon.

dike [daɪk] = **dyke**.

diktat ['dɪktæt] *n* **1.** POL [decree] diktat *m* **2.** [statement] affirmation *f* catégorique.

dilapidated [dɪ'læpɪdeɪtɪd] *adj* [house] délabré ▪ [car] déglingué ▪ **in a ~ state** dans un état de délabrement *OR* de dégradation avancé.

dilapidation [dɪˌlæpɪ'deɪʃn] *n* [of building] délabrement *m*, dégradation *f*.

dilate [daɪ'leɪt] ◇ *vi* **1.** [physically] se dilater **2.** *fml* [talk] : **to ~ on *OR* upon a topic** s'étendre sur un sujet.

◇ *vt* dilater.

dilation [daɪ'leɪʃn] *n* **1.** [gen - MED] dilatation *f* ▪ **~ and curettage** (dilatation et) curetage *m* **2.** *fml* [talk] exposition *f* en détail.

dilator [daɪ'leɪtəʳ] *n* [instrument] dilatateur *m* ▪ [muscle] muscle *m* dilatateur.

dilatory ['dɪlətrɪ] *adj fml* [action, method] dilatoire ▪ [person] lent.

dildo ['dɪldəʊ] (*pl* **dildos**) *n* godemiché *m*.

dilemma [dɪ'lemə] *n* dilemme *m* ▪ **to be in a ~** être pris dans un dilemme ▪ **her decision leaves me in something of a ~** sa décision me pose un cruel dilemme.

dilettante [ˌdɪlɪ'tæntɪ] (*pl* **dilettantes** *OR pl* **dilettanti** [-tɪ])

◇ *n* dilettante *mf*.

◇ *adj* dilettante.

dilettantism [ˌdɪlɪ'tæntɪzm] *n* dilettantisme *m*.

diligence ['dɪlɪdʒəns] *n* **1.** [effort] assiduité *f*, application *f*, zèle *m* **2.** [carriage] diligence *f*.

diligent ['dɪlɪdʒənt] *adj* [person] assidu, appliqué ▪ [work] appliqué, diligent.

diligently ['dɪlɪdʒəntlɪ] *adv* avec assiduité *OR* soin *OR* application, assidûment.

dill [dɪl] *n* aneth *m*.

dill pickle *n* cornichon *m* à l'aneth.

dilly-dally ['dɪlɪdælɪ] (*pret & pp* **dilly-dallied**) *vi inf* [dawdle] lanterner, lambiner ▪ [hesitate] hésiter, tergiverser.

dilute [daɪ'lu:t] ◇ *vt* **1.** [liquid] diluer, étendre ▪ [milk, wine] mouiller, couper d'eau ▪ [sauce] délayer, allonger ▪ [colour] délayer ▪ **'~ to taste'** 'diluer selon votre goût' **2.** PHARM diluer **3.** *fig* [weaken] diluer, édulcorer ▪ **~d socialism** socialisme affadi *OR* édulcoré.

◇ *adj* [liquid] dilué, coupé *OR* étendu (d'eau) ▪ [colour] délayé, adouci ▪ *fig* dilué, édulcoré.

dilution [daɪ'lu:ʃn] *n* [act, product] dilution *f* ▪ [of milk, wine] coupage *m*, mouillage *m* ▪ *fig* édulcoration *f*.

dim [dɪm] (*pret & pp* **dimmed**, *cont* **dimming**) ◇ *adj* **1.** [light] faible, pâle ▪ [lamp] faible ▪ [room] sombre ▪ [colour] terne, sans éclat ▪ **to grow ~** [light] baisser ; [room] devenir sombre ; [colour] devenir terne **2.** [indistinct - shape] vague, imprécis ; [- sight] faible, trouble ; [- sound] vague, indistinct ▪ **she has only a ~ memory of it** elle n'en a qu'un vague souvenir ▪ **in the ~ and distant past** *hum* au temps jadis **3.** [gloomy] sombre, morne ▪ **to take a ~ view of sthg** *inf* ne pas beaucoup apprécier qqch, voir qqch d'un mauvais œil **4.** *inf* [stupid] gourde.

◇ *vt* **1.** [light] baisser ▪ **~ your headlights** *US* AUT mettez-vous en codes **2.** [beauty, colour, hope, metal] ternir ▪ [memory] estomper, effacer ▪ [mind, senses] affaiblir, troubler ▪ [sound] affaiblir ▪ [sight] baisser, troubler ▪ **his eyes were dimmed with tears** ses yeux étaient voilés de larmes.
◇ *vi* [light] baisser, s'affaiblir ▪ [beauty, glory, hope] se ternir ▪ [colour] devenir terne *OR* mat ▪ [memory] s'estomper, s'effacer ▪ [sound] s'affaiblir ▪ [sight] baisser, se troubler.
◆ **dim out** *vt sep US* plonger dans un black-out partiel.

dime [daɪm] *n US* pièce *f* de dix cents ▪ **guys like that are a ~ a dozen** *inf* des types comme lui, on en trouve à la pelle ▪ **it's not worth a ~** *OR* **one thin ~** *inf* ça ne vaut pas un clou.

dimension [daɪ'menʃn] *n* **1.** [measurement, size] dimension *f* ▪ ARCHIT & GEOM dimension *f*, cote *f* ▪ MATHS & PHYS dimension *f* **2.** *fig* [scope] étendue *f* ▪ [aspect] dimension *f*.
◆ **dimensions** *npl* TECH [of bulky object] encombrement *m*.

-dimensional [dɪ'menʃənl] *in cpds* : **two/four~** à deux/quatre dimensions.

dime store *n US* supérette *f* de quartier.

diminish [dɪ'mɪnɪʃ] ◇ *vt* **1.** [number] diminuer, réduire ▪ [effect, power] diminuer, amoindrir ▪ [value] réduire **2.** [person] déprécier, rabaisser **3.** ARCHIT [column] amincir, diminuer ▪ MUS diminuer.
◇ *vi* diminuer, se réduire.

diminished [dɪ'mɪnɪʃt] *adj* **1.** [number, power, speed] diminué, amoindri ▪ [reputation] diminué, terni ▪ [value] réduit ▪ **~ responsibility** LAW responsabilité *f* atténuée **2.** MUS diminué.

diminishing [dɪ'mɪnɪʃɪŋ] ◇ *adj* [influence, number, speed] décroissant, qui va en diminuant ▪ [price, quality] qui baisse, en baisse ▪ **the law of ~ returns** la loi des rendements décroissants.
◇ *n* diminution *f*, baisse *f*.

diminuendo [dɪˌmɪnjʊ'endəʊ] (*pl* **diminuendos**) ◇ *n* diminuendo *m*.
◇ *adv* diminuendo.

diminution [ˌdɪmɪ'njuːʃn] *n* **1.** [in number, value] diminution *f*, baisse *f* ▪ [in speed] réduction *f* ▪ [in intensity, importance, strength] diminution *f*, affaiblissement *m* ▪ [in temperature] baisse *f*, abaissement *m* ▪ [in authority, price] baisse *f* ▪ **there has been no ~ in** *OR* **of our enthusiasm** notre enthousiasme n'a en rien faibli **2.** MUS diminution *f*.

diminutive [dɪ'mɪnjʊtɪv] ◇ *adj* [tiny] minuscule, tout petit ▪ LING diminutif.
◇ *n* diminutif *m*.

dimly ['dɪmlɪ] *adv* [shine] faiblement, sans éclat ▪ [see] indistinctement, à peine ▪ [remember] vaguement, à peine ▪ **the room was ~ lit** la pièce était mal *OR* faiblement éclairée.

dimmer ['dɪmər] *n* **1.** [on lamp] rhéostat *m* *OR* variateur *m* (de lumière) **2.** *US* AUT [switch] basculeur *m* (de phares).
◆ **dimmers** *npl* [headlights] phares *mpl* code ▪ [parking lights] feux *mpl* de position.

dimmer switch *n* variateur *m* (de lumière).

dimness ['dɪmnɪs] *n* **1.** [of light, sight] affaiblissement *m* ▪ [of room] obscurité *f* ▪ [of colour, metal] aspect *m* terne ▪ [of memory, shape] imprécision *f* **2.** *inf* [stupidity] sottise *f*.

dimple ['dɪmpl] ◇ *n* [in cheek, chin] fossette *f* ▪ [in surface of ground, water] ride *f*, ondulation *f*.
◇ *vi* [cheek] former *OR* creuser des fossettes ▪ [surface of ground] onduler, former des rides ▪ [surface of water] onduler, se rider.

dimpled ['dɪmpld] *adj* [cheek, chin] à fossettes ▪ [arm, knee] potelé ▪ [surface] ridé, ondulé.

dimwit ['dɪmwɪt] *n inf* crétin *m*, - e *f*.

dim-witted *adj inf* crétin, gourde.

din [dɪn] (*pret & pp* **dinned**, *cont* **dinning**) ◇ *n* [of people] tapage *m*, tumulte *m* ▪ [in classroom] chahut *m* ▪ [of industry, traffic] vacarme *m* ▪ **they were kicking up** *inf OR* **making a real ~** ils faisaient un boucan d'enfer *OR* monstre.
◇ *vt* : **to ~ sthg into sb** *inf* faire (bien) comprendre qqch à qqn, faire entrer qqch dans la tête à qqn.

DIN [dɪn] *n* **1.** (*abbrev of* **Deutsche Industrie Norm**) (indice *m*) DIN *f* **2.** PHOT DIN *f*.

dindins ['dɪndɪnz] *n baby* dîner *m*.

dine [daɪn] ◇ *vi* dîner ▪ **to ~ off** *OR* **on sthg** dîner de qqch.
◇ *vt* offrir à dîner à.
◆ **dine out** *vi insep* dîner dehors *OR* en ville ▪ **I ~d out on that story for weeks** *fig* ça m'a fait une bonne histoire à raconter pendant des semaines.

diner ['daɪnər] *n* **1.** [person] dîneur *m*, - euse *f* **2.** RAIL wagon-restaurant *m* ▪ *US* petit restaurant *m* sans façon.

dinette [daɪ'net] *n* coin-repas *m*.

ding [dɪŋ] ◇ *vi* tinter.
◇ *vt* = **din**.
◇ *n* tintement *m*.

ding-a-ling ['dɪŋəˌlɪŋ] *n* [ring] dring dring *m*, tintement *m*.

dingbat ['dɪŋbæt] *inf n* **1.** *US* [thing] truc *m*, machin *m* **2.** [fool] crétin *m*, - e *f*, gourde *f*.

dingdong [ˌdɪŋ'dɒŋ] ◇ *n* **1.** [sound] ding dong *m* **2.** *UK inf* [quarrel] dispute *f* ▪ [fight] bagarre *f*.
◇ *adj inf* [argument, fight] acharné ▪ [race] très disputé.

dinger ['dɪŋər] *n US inf* [person] imbécile *mf*.

dinghy ['dɪŋgɪ] (*pl* **dinghies**) *n* [rowing boat] petit canot *m*, youyou *m* ▪ [sailboat] dériveur *m* ▪ [rubber] canot *m* pneumatique, dinghy *m*.

dinginess ['dɪndʒɪnɪs] *n* [shabbiness] aspect *m* miteux *OR* douteux ▪ [drabness] couleur *f* terne.

dingle ['dɪŋgl] *n* vallon *m* boisé.

dingo ['dɪŋgəʊ] (*pl* **dingoes**) *n* dingo *m*.

dingy ['dɪndʒɪ] (*comp* **dingier**, *superl* **dingiest**) *adj* [shabby] miteux ▪ [dirty] douteux ▪ [colour] terne.

dining car ['daɪnɪŋ-] *n* wagon-restaurant *m*.

dining hall ['daɪnɪŋ-] *n* réfectoire *m*, salle *f* à manger.

dining room ['daɪnɪŋ-] ◇ *n* salle *f* à manger.
◇ *comp* [curtains, furniture] de (la) salle à manger ▪ **~ suite** salle *f* à manger *(meubles)*.

dining table ['daɪnɪŋ-] *n* table *f* de salle à manger.

dinkie ['dɪŋkɪ] (*abbrev of* **double income no kids**) *n inf personne mariée aisée et sans enfants*.

dinky ['dɪŋkɪ] (*comp* **dinkier**, *superl* **dinkiest**) *adj* **1.** *UK inf* [small, neat] mignon, coquet **2.** *US pej* [insignificant] de rien du tout.

dinner ['dɪnər] ◇ *n* [evening meal - early] dîner *m* ; [- very late] souper *m* ▪ *dial* [lunch] déjeuner *m* ▪ **to be at ~** être en train de dîner ▪ **she's having guests to ~** elle a des invités à dîner ▪ **they went out to ~** [in restaurant] ils ont dîné au restaurant *OR* en ville ; [at friends] ils ont dîné chez des amis ▪ **did you give the cat its ~?** avez-vous donné à manger au chat? ▪ **a formal ~** un grand dîner *OR* dîner officiel ▶ **I've played more cup matches in my time than you've had hot ~s** *UK inf* j'ai joué plus de matchs de coupe dans ma vie que tu n'en joueras jamais.
◇ *comp* [fork, knife] de table ▪ **she rang the ~ bell** elle a sonné pour annoncer le dîner ▪ **~ duty** SCH service *m* de réfectoire ▪ **~ hour** [at work] heure *f* du déjeuner ; [at school] pause *f* de midi ▪ **~ plate** (grande) assiette *f*.

dinner dance *n* dîner *m* dansant.

dinner jacket *n* smoking *m*.

dinner lady *n UK employée d'une cantine scolaire*.

dinner party *n* dîner *m (sur invitation)* ▪ **we're having** *OR* **giving a ~** nous avons du monde à dîner, nous donnons un dîner.

dinner service *n* service *m* de table.

dinner table *n* table *f* de salle à manger ▪ **at** *OR* **over the ~** pendant le dîner, au dîner.

dinnertime ['dɪnətaɪm] *n* heure *f* du dîner.

dinnerware ['dɪnəweəʳ] *n US* vaisselle *f*.

dinosaur ['daɪnəsɔːʳ] *n* dinosaure *m* ▪ **the institute's become a bit of a ~** *fig* l'institut est le survivant d'une époque révolue *OR* a fait son temps.

dint [dɪnt] = **dent**.
◆ **by dint of** *prep phr* à force de.

diocesan [daɪ'ɒsɪsn] <> *adj* diocésain.
<> *n* (évêque *m*) diocésain *m*.

diocese ['daɪəsɪs] *n* diocèse *m*.

diode ['daɪəʊd] *n* diode *f*.

Diogenes [daɪ'ɒdʒɪniːz] *pr n* Diogène.

Dionysiac [ˌdaɪə'nɪzɪæk], **Dionysian** [ˌdaɪə'nɪzɪən] *adj* dionysiaque.

Dionysus [ˌdaɪə'naɪsəs] *pr n* Dionysos.

diorama [ˌdaɪə'rɑːmə] *n* diorama *m*.

dioxide [daɪ'ɒksaɪd] *n* dioxyde *m*.

dioxin [daɪ'ɒksɪn] *n* dioxine *f*.

dip [dɪp] (*pret & pp* **dipped**, *cont* **dipping**) <> *vi* **1.** [incline - ground] descendre, s'incliner ; [- road] descendre, plonger ; [- head] pencher, s'incliner **2.** [drop - sun] baisser, descendre à l'horizon ; [- price] diminuer, baisser ; [- temperature] baisser ; [- plane] piquer ; [- boat] tanguer, piquer.
<> *vt* **1.** [immerse] tremper, plonger ▪ TECH tremper ▪ [clean] décaper ▪ [dye] teindre ▪ [sheep] laver **2.** [plunge] plonger **3.** *UK* AUT : **to ~ one's headlights** se mettre en codes ▪ **dipped headlights** codes *mpl*, feux *mpl* de croisement.
<> *n* **1.** *inf* [swim] baignade *f*, bain *m (en mer, en piscine)* ▪ **to go for a ~** aller se baigner, aller faire trempette ▪ **a brief ~ into Homer** *fig* un survol rapide d'Homère **2.** [liquid] bain *m* ▪ [for sheep] bain *m* parasiticide **3.** [slope - in ground] déclivité *f* ; [- in road] descente *f* ▪ GEOL pendage *m* ▪ **angle of ~** PHYS inclinaison *f* magnétique **4.** [bob] inclinaison *f* ▪ [of head] hochement *m* **5.** [drop - in temperature] baisse *f* ; [- in price] fléchissement *m*, baisse *f* **6.** CULIN *pâte ou mousse (à tartiner) servie avec du pain ou des biscuits salés* ▪ **avocado ~** mousse *f* à l'avocat.
◆ **dip into** *vt insep* **1.** [dabble] : **I've only really dipped into Shakespeare** j'ai seulement survolé *OR* feuilleté Shakespeare **2.** [draw upon] puiser dans.

Dip. *written abbr of* **diploma**.

DipEd [dɪp'ed] (*abbrev of* **Diploma in Education**) *n UK* ≃ CAPES *m*.

diphtheria [dɪf'θɪərɪə] *n* diphtérie *f* ▪ **~ vaccine** vaccin *m* antidiphtérique.

diphthong ['dɪfθɒŋ] *n* diphtongue *f*.

diploma [dɪ'pləʊmə] *n* diplôme *m* ▪ **she has a ~ in business studies** elle est diplômée de *OR* en commerce ▪ **teaching ~** diplôme d'enseignement.

diplomacy [dɪ'pləʊməsɪ] *n* POL & *fig* diplomatie *f*.

diplomat ['dɪpləmæt] *n* POL & *fig* diplomate *mf*.

diplomatic [ˌdɪplə'mætɪk] *adj* **1.** POL diplomatique **2.** *fig* [person] diplomate ▪ [action, remark] diplomatique ▪ **you have to be ~ when dealing with these people** il faut faire preuve de tact *OR* user de diplomatie pour traiter avec ces gens-là.

diplomatically [ˌdɪplə'mætɪklɪ] *adv* POL diplomatiquement ▪ *fig* avec diplomatie, diplomatiquement.

diplomatic bag *UK*, **diplomatic pouch** *US n* valise *f* diplomatique.

diplomatic corps *n* corps *m* diplomatique.

diplomatic immunity *n* immunité *f* diplomatique ▪ **to claim ~** faire valoir l'immunité diplomatique.

Diplomatic Service *n* : **the ~** la diplomatie, le service diplomatique.

diplomatist [dɪ'pləʊmətɪst] = **diplomat**.

dipper ['dɪpəʳ] *n* **1.** [ladle] louche *f* **2.** [of machine] godet *m* (de pelleteuse) ▪ [for lake, river] benne *f* (de drague), hotte *f* à draguer **3.** *UK* AUT basculeur *m* (de phares) **4.** ORNITH cincle *m* (plongeur).

dippy ['dɪpɪ] (*comp* **dippier**, *superl* **dippiest**) *adj inf* écervelé.

dipso△ ['dɪpsəʊ] *n* alcoolo *mf*.

dipsomania [ˌdɪpsə'meɪnjə] *n* dipsomanie *f*.

dipsomaniac [ˌdɪpsə'meɪnɪæk] <> *adj* dipsomane.
<> *n* dipsomane *mf*.

dipstick ['dɪpstɪk] *n* **1.** AUT jauge *f* (de niveau d'huile) **2.** *inf* [idiot] empoté *m*, - e *f*.

dipswitch ['dɪpswɪtʃ] *n UK* basculeur *m* (des phares).

dire ['daɪəʳ] *adj* **1.** [fearful] affreux, terrible ▪ [ominous] sinistre ▪ **~ warnings** avertissements sinistres **2.** [very bad] : **the film was pretty ~** le film était vraiment mauvais **3.** [extreme] extrême ▪ **he's in ~ need of sleep** il a absolument besoin de sommeil ➊ **to be in ~ straits** être dans une mauvaise passe *OR* aux abois.

direct [dɪ'rekt] <> *vt* **1.** [supervise - business] diriger, gérer, mener ; [- office, work] diriger ; [- movements] guider ; [- traffic] régler
2. CIN, RADIO & TV [film, programme] réaliser ▪ [actors] diriger ▪ THEAT [play] mettre en scène
3. [address] adresser ▪ **the accusation was ~ed at him** l'accusation le visait ▪ **he ~ed my attention to the map** il a attiré mon attention sur la carte ▪ **we should ~ all our efforts towards improving our education service** nous devrions consacrer tous nos efforts à améliorer notre système scolaire
4. [point] diriger ▪ **can you ~ me to the train station?** pourriez-vous m'indiquer le chemin de la gare?
5. [instruct] ordonner ▪ **I did as I was ~ed** j'ai fait comme on m'avait dit *OR* comme on m'en avait donné l'ordre ▪ **'take as ~ed'** 'se conformer à la prescription du médecin'
6. LAW : **to ~ the jury** instruire le jury ▪ **the judge ~ed the jury to bring in a verdict of guilty** le juge incita le jury à rendre un verdict de culpabilité ➊ **~ed verdict** *US verdict rendu par le jury sur la recommandation du juge*
7. *US* MUS diriger.
<> *vi* **1.** [command] diriger, commander
2. *US* MUS diriger
3. THEAT mettre en scène.
<> *adj* **1.** [straight] direct ▪ **~ flight/route** vol *m* /chemin *m* direct ➊ **~ memory access** COMPUT accès *m* direct à la mémoire ▪ **~ tax** impôt *m* direct ▪ **~ taxation** imposition *f* directe
2. MIL : **~ hit** coup *m* au but ▪ **the missile made a ~ hit** le missile a atteint son objectif
3. [immediate - cause, effect] direct, immédiat ▪ **he's a ~ descendant of the King** il descend du roi en ligne directe ▪ **'keep out of ~ sunlight'** 'évitez l'exposition directe au soleil'
4. [frank] franc, franche *f*, direct ▪ [denial, refusal] catégorique, absolu ▪ **she asked some very ~ questions** elle a posé des questions parfois très directes
5. [exact] exact, précis ▪ **~ quotation** citation exacte ▪ **it's the ~ opposite of what I said** c'est exactement le contraire de ce que j'ai dit
6. ASTRON, GRAM & LOGIC direct ▪ **~ question** GRAM question *f* au style direct.
<> *adv* directement.

direct access *n* accès *m* direct.

direct action *n* action *f* directe.

direct current *n* courant *m* continu.

direct debit *n* prélèvement *m* automatique.

direct dialling *n* automatique *m*.

direct discourse *US* = **direct speech**.

direct-grant school *n UK établissement scolaire privé subventionné par l'État si l'établissement accepte un certain nombre d'élèves qui ne paient pas*.

direction [dɪ'rekʃn] *n* **1.** [way] direction *f*, sens *m* ▪ **in every ~** dans toutes les directions, en tous sens, dans tous les sens

■ **in the ~ of Chicago** dans la *OR* en direction de Chicago ■ **a step in the right ~** *fig* un pas dans la bonne voie *OR* direction ■ **she lacks ~** *fig* elle ne sait pas très bien où elle va **2.** [control] direction *f* **3.** CIN, RADIO & TV réalisation *f* ■ THEAT mise *f* en scène.
◆ **directions** *npl* indications *fpl*, instructions *fpl*, mode *m* d'emploi ■ **to give sb ~** indiquer le chemin à qqn ■ **I asked for ~s to the station** j'ai demandé le chemin de la gare ▶ **stage ~s** THEAT indications scéniques.

directional [dɪ'rekʃənl] *adj* [gen - ELECTRON] directionnel.

direction finder *n* radiogoniomètre *m*.

directive [dɪ'rektɪv] <> *n* directive *f*, instruction *f*.
<> *adj* directeur.

directly [dɪ'rektlɪ] <> *adv* **1.** [straight] directement ■ **to be ~ descended from sb** descendre en droite ligne *OR* en ligne directe de qqn **2.** [promptly] immédiatement ■ **~ after lunch** tout de suite après le déjeuner ■ **~ before the film** juste avant le film ■ **I'll be there ~** j'arrive tout de suite **3.** [frankly] franchement **4.** [exactly] exactement ■ **~ opposite the station** juste en face de la gare.
<> *conj UK* aussitôt que, dès que.

direct mail *n* publipostage *m*.

directness [dɪ'rektnɪs] *n* **1.** [of person, reply] franchise *f* ■ [of remark] absence *f* d'ambiguïté **2.** [of attack] caractère *m* direct.

direct object *n* complément *m* (d'objet) direct.

director [dɪ'rektər] *n* **1.** [person - of business] directeur *m*, -trice *f*, chef *m* ; [- of organization] directeur *m*, -trice *f* ■ **Director of Education** *UK* ≃ recteur *m*, -trice *f* d'académie ■ **Director of Public Prosecutions** *UK* LAW ≃ procureur *mf* de la République ■ **~ of studies** UNIV directeur *m*, -trice *f* d'études *OR* de travaux **2.** *US* MUS chef *m* d'orchestre **3.** CIN, RADIO & TV réalisateur *m*, -trice *f* ■ THEAT metteur *m* en scène **4.** [device] guide *m*.

directorate [dɪ'rektərət] *n* **1.** [board] conseil *m* d'administration **2.** [position] direction *f*, poste *m* de directeur.

director-general *n* directeur *m* général.

directorial [ˌdaɪrek'tɔːrɪəl] *adj* de mise en scène.

director's chair *n* régisseur *m*.

directorship [dɪ'rektəʃɪp] *n* direction *f*, poste *m* *OR* fonctions *fpl* de directeur.

directory [dɪ'rektərɪ] (*pl* **directories**) <> *n* **1.** [of addresses] répertoire *m* (d'adresses) ■ TELEC annuaire *m* (des téléphones), bottin *m* ■ COMPUT répertoire *m* ■ **street ~** répertoire des rues ■ **commercial ~** annuaire du commerce **2.** [of instructions] mode *m* d'emploi ■ RELIG directoire *m*.
<> *adj* directeur.
◆ **Directory** *n* HIST : **the Directory** le Directoire.

directory enquiries *UK*, **directory assistance** *US* *n* (service *m* des) renseignements *mpl* téléphoniques.

direct rule *n contrôle direct du maintien de l'ordre par le gouvernement britannique en Irlande du Nord, depuis 1972.*

direct speech *n UK* discours *m* *OR* style *m* direct.

dirge [dɜːdʒ] *n* hymne *m* *OR* chant *m* funèbre ■ *fig* chant *m* lugubre.

dirigible ['dɪrɪdʒəbl] <> *adj* dirigeable.
<> *n* dirigeable *m*.

dirt [dɜːt] *n (U)* **1.** [grime] saleté *f*, crasse *f* ■ [mud] boue *f* ■ [excrement] crotte *f*, ordure *f* ■ **this dress really shows the ~** cette robe fait vite sale *OR* est très salissante **2.** [soil] terre *f* ▶ **to be as common as ~** [person] avoir mauvais genre ■ **to treat sb like ~** traiter qqn comme un chien **3.** [obscenity] obscénité *f* **4.** *inf* [scandal] ragots *mpl*, cancans *mpl* ■ **to dig up some ~ on sb** dénicher des ragots **5.** INDUST [in material, solution] impuretés *fpl*, corps *mpl* étrangers ■ [in machine] encrassement *m*.

dirt-cheap *inf* <> *adv* pour rien ■ **I bought it ~** je l'ai payé trois fois rien.
<> *adj* très bon marché.

dirt farmer *n* petit fermier *m*.

dirtiness ['dɜːtɪnɪs] *n* malpropreté *f*.

dirt track *n* [gen] piste *f* ■ SPORT (piste) cendrée *f* ■ **~ racing** courses *fpl* sur cendrée.

dirty ['dɜːtɪ] (*comp* **dirtier**, *superl* **dirtiest**, *pret & pp* **dirtied**) <> *adj* **1.** [not clean - clothes, hands, person] sale, malpropre, crasseux ; [- machine] encrassé ; [- wound] infecté ■ [muddy] plein de boue, crotté ■ **don't get ~!** ne vous salissez pas! ■ **he got his shirt ~** il a sali sa chemise ■ **this rug gets ~ easily** ce tapis est salissant
2. [colour] sale
3. [nasty] sale ■ **politics is a ~ business** il est difficile de garder les mains propres quand on fait de la politique ■ **a ~ campaign** une campagne sordide ■ **that's a ~ lie** ce n'est absolument pas vrai ■ **~ money** argent sale *OR* mal acquis ■ **he's a ~ fighter** il se bat en traître ▶ **to give sb a ~ look** regarder qqn de travers *OR* d'un sale œil ■ **that's ~ pool!** *US* c'est un tour de cochon! ■ **you ~ rat!** *inf* espèce de salaud!
4. [weather] sale, vilain
5. [obscene] grossier, obscène ■ **to have a ~ mind** avoir l'esprit mal tourné ▶ **~ magazines** revues *fpl* pornographiques ■ **a ~ old man** *inf* un vieux cochon *OR* vicelard ■ **a ~ joke/story** une blague/histoire cochonne ■ **a ~ word** une grossièreté, un gros mot
6. *inf* [sexy] : **a ~ weekend** un week-end coquin.
<> *adv inf* **1.** [fight, play] déloyalement ■ [talk] grossièrement **2.** *UK* [as intensifier] vachement ■ **a ~ great skyscraper** un gratte-ciel énorme.
<> *vt* [soil] salir ■ [machine] encrasser ■ **to ~ one's hands** *liter & fig* se salir les mains.
<> *n UK* : **to do the ~ on sb** *inf* jouer un sale tour *OR* faire une vacherie à qqn.

dirty bomb *n* bombe *f* sale.

dirty-minded *adj* qui a l'esprit mal tourné.

dirty trick *n* [malicious act] sale tour *m* ■ **to play a ~ on sb** jouer un sale tour *OR* un tour de cochon à qqn.
◆ **dirty tricks** *npl* : **they've been up to their ~s again** ils ont encore fait des leurs ■ **~s campaign** POL *manœuvres déloyales visant à discréditer un adversaire politique.*

dirty work *n (U)* **1.** [unpleasant work] travail *m* salissant ■ **he wants someone else to do his ~** il veut que quelqu'un d'autre se salisse les mains à sa place **2.** *inf* [dishonest work] magouille *f*.

disability [ˌdɪsə'bɪlətɪ] (*pl* **disabilities**) *n* **1.** [state - physical] incapacité *f*, invalidité *f* **2.** [handicap] infirmité *f* ■ ADMIN handicap *m* ■ **people with disabilities** les handicapés.

disability clause *n clause d'une police d'assurance-vie permettant à l'assuré de cesser tout paiement et de recevoir une pension en cas d'invalidité.*

disability pension *n* pension *f* d'invalidité.

disable [dɪs'eɪbl] *vt* **1.** [accident, illness] rendre infirme ■ [maim] mutiler, estropier ■ **a disabling disease** une maladie invalidante **2.** [machine] mettre hors service ■ [ship] faire subir une avarie à, désemparer ■ [gun, tank] mettre hors d'action ■ [army, battalion] mettre hors de combat **3.** LAW : **to ~ sb from doing sthg** rendre qqn inhabile à faire qqch ; [pronounce] prononcer qqn inhabile à faire qqch.

disabled [dɪs'eɪbld] <> *adj* **1.** [handicapped] infirme ADMIN handicapé ■ [maimed] mutilé, estropié ■ **~ ex-servicemen** invalides *mpl* *OR* mutilés *mpl* de guerre **2.** MIL mis hors de combat **3.** [machine] hors service ■ [ship] avarié, désemparé ■ [propeller] immobilisé **4.** LAW : **to be ~ from doing sthg** être incapable de *OR* inhabile à faire qqch.
<> *npl* : **the ~** [handicapped] les handicapés *mpl* ; [maimed] les mutilés *mpl* *OR* estropiés *mpl*.

disablement [dɪs'eɪblmənt] *n* invalidité *f*, infirmité *f* ■ **~ benefit** allocation *f* d'invalidité ■ **~ insurance** assurance *f* invalidité ■ **~ pension** pension *f* d'invalidité.

disabuse [ˌdɪsə'bjuːz] *vt* détromper, ôter ses illusions à.

disadvantage [ˌdɪsəd'vɑːntɪdʒ] <> *n* **1.** [condition] désavantage *m*, inconvénient *m* ■ **to be at a ~** être désavantagé *OR* dans une position désavantageuse ■ **to put sb at a ~**

désavantager *OR* défavoriser qqn ■ **the situation works** *OR* **is to her ~** la situation est un handicap *OR* un désavantage pour elle **2.** COMM [loss] perte *f.*
◇ *vt* désavantager, défavoriser.

disadvantaged [ˌdɪsəd'vɑ:ntɪdʒd] ◇ *adj* [gen] défavorisé ■ [economically] déshérité ■ **socially ~** défavorisé sur le plan social.
◇ *npl* **: the ~** les défavorisés *mpl.*

disadvantageous [ˌdɪsædvɑ:n'teɪdʒəs] *adj* désavantageux, défavorable ■ **to be ~ to sb** être désavantageux *OR* défavorable à qqn.

disaffected [ˌdɪsə'fektɪd] *adj* [discontented] hostile, mécontent ■ [disloyal] rebelle ■ **~ youth** jeunesse révoltée.

disaffection [ˌdɪsə'fekʃn] *n* désaffection *f*, détachement *m*.

disagree [ˌdɪsə'gri:] *vi* **1.** [person, people] ne pas être d'accord, être en désaccord ■ **to ~ with sb about** *OR* **on sthg** ne pas être d'accord avec *OR* ne pas être du même avis que qqn sur qqch ■ **I ~ with everything they've done** je suis contre *OR* je désapprouve tout ce qu'ils ont fait ■ **we ~ on everything** [differ] nous ne sommes jamais d'accord **2.** [figures, records] ne pas concorder **3.** [food, weather] ne pas convenir ■ **spicy food ~s with him** les plats épicés ne lui réussissent pas, il digère mal les plats épicés.

disagreeable [ˌdɪsə'grɪəbl] *adj* [person, remark] désagréable, désobligeant ■ [experience, job] désagréable, pénible ■ [smell] désagréable, déplaisant.

disagreeably [ˌdɪsə'grɪəblɪ] *adv* désagréablement, d'une façon désagréable *OR* désobligeante.

disagreement [ˌdɪsə'gri:mənt] *n* **1.** [of opinions, records] désaccord *m*, conflit *m* ■ **they are in ~ about** *OR* **on what action to take** ils ne sont pas d'accord sur les mesures à prendre **2.** [quarrel] différend *m*, querelle *f* ■ **they've had a ~ over** *OR* **about money** ils se sont disputés à propos d'argent, ils ont eu une querelle d'argent.
Voir module d'usage

disallow [ˌdɪsə'laʊ] *vt* [argument, opinion] rejeter ■ SPORT refuser ■ LAW débouter, rejeter.

disappear [ˌdɪsə'pɪər] *vi* **1.** [vanish - person, snow] disparaître ; [- object] disparaître, s'égarer ■ LING s'amuïr ■ **she ~ed from sight** on l'a perdue de vue ■ **he ~ed into the crowd** il s'est perdu dans la foule ■ **to make sthg ~** [gen] faire disparaître qqch ; [magician] escamoter qqch ■ **Michael did his usual ~ing act** *inf* Michael a encore joué la fille de l'air **2.** [cease to exist - pain, tribe] disparaître ; [- problem] disparaître, s'aplanir ; [- memory] s'effacer, s'estomper ; [- tradition] disparaître, tomber en désuétude ■ **as a species, the turtle is fast ~ing** les tortues sont une espèce en voie de disparition.

disappearance [ˌdɪsə'pɪərəns] *n* [gen] disparition *f* ■ LING amuïssement *m*.

disappoint [ˌdɪsə'pɔɪnt] *vt* **1.** [person] décevoir, désappointer ■ **you promised to come, so don't ~ him** vous avez promis de venir, alors ne lui faites pas faux bond **2.** [hope] décevoir ■ [plan] contrarier, contrecarrer.

disappointed [ˌdɪsə'pɔɪntɪd] *adj* **1.** [person] déçu, désappointé ■ **I'm very ~ in him** il m'a beaucoup déçu ■ **I was ~ to hear you won't be coming** j'ai été déçu d'apprendre que vous ne viendrez pas ■ **are you ~ at** *OR* **with the results?** les résultats vous ont-ils déçu?, avez-vous été déçu par les résultats? ■ **to be ~ in love** être malheureux en amour **2.** [ambition, hope] déçu ■ [plan] contrarié, contrecarré.

disappointing [ˌdɪsə'pɔɪntɪŋ] *adj* décevant ■ **how ~!** quelle déception!, comme c'est décevant!

disappointingly [ˌdɪsə'pɔɪntɪŋlɪ] *adv* **: ~ low grades** des notes d'une faiblesse décourageante *OR* décevante ■ **he did ~ badly in the exam** ses résultats à l'examen ont été très décevants.

disappointment [ˌdɪsə'pɔɪntmənt] *n* **1.** [state] déception *f*, désappointement *m*, déconvenue *f* ■ **to her great ~ she failed** à sa grande déception *OR* déconvenue, elle a échoué **2.** [letdown] déception *f*, désillusion *f* ■ **she has suffered many ~s** elle a essuyé bien des déboires ■ **he has been a great ~ to me** il m'a beaucoup déçu.

disapprobation [ˌdɪsæprə'beɪʃn] *n fml* désapprobation *f* ■ [strong] réprobation *f.*

disapproval [ˌdɪsə'pru:vl] *n* désapprobation *f* ■ [strong] réprobation *f* ■ **to shake one's head in ~** faire un signe désapprobateur de la tête ■ **she showed/expressed her ~ of his decision** elle a montré/exprimé sa désapprobation à l'égard de sa décision.
Voir module d'usage

disapprove [ˌdɪsə'pru:v] ◇ *vi* désapprouver ■ **to ~ of sthg** désapprouver qqch ■ **your mother ~s of your going** votre mère n'est pas d'accord pour que vous y alliez ■ **he ~s of everything I do** il trouve à redire à tout ce que je fais ■ **her father ~s of me** son père ne me trouve pas à son goût.
◇ *vt* désapprouver.

disapproving [ˌdɪsə'pru:vɪŋ] *adj* désapprobateur, de désapprobation ■ **don't look so ~** ne prends pas cet air désapprobateur.

disapprovingly [ˌdɪsə'pru:vɪŋlɪ] *adv* [look] d'un air désapprobateur ■ [speak] d'un ton désapprobateur, avec désapprobation.

disarm [dɪs'ɑ:m] ◇ *vt* **1.** [country, enemy, critic] désarmer **2.** [charm] désarmer, toucher.
◇ *vi* désarmer.

disarmament [dɪs'ɑ:məmənt] ◇ *n* désarmement *m*.
◇ *comp* [conference, negotiations, talks] sur le désarmement.

disarming [dɪs'ɑ:mɪŋ] ◇ *adj* désarmant, touchant.
◇ *n* désarmement *m*.

disarmingly [dɪs'ɑ:mɪŋlɪ] *adv* de façon désarmante ■ **~ honest/friendly** d'une honnêteté/amabilité désarmante.

DISAGREEMENT

Je ne suis absolument pas *OU* **pas du tout d'accord.** I totally disagree.

Je ne suis pas de cet *OU* **votre avis.** I don't agree with you.

Désolé *OU* **Je regrette, mais je ne suis pas d'accord.** I'm sorry, but I don't agree.

Je ne suis pas convaincu du tout. I'm not at all convinced.

Oui, mais cela ne veut pas dire pour autant que... Yes, but that doesn't mean to say that...

Peut-être, mais il n'en est pas moins vrai que... Maybe, but it's nonetheless true that...

Je ne pense pas qu'il s'agisse de ça. I don't think that's what it's about.

Je ne partage pas votre opinion. I do not share your view.

disarrange [ˌdɪsəˈreɪndʒ] *vt* [order, room] déranger, mettre en désordre ■ [plans] déranger, bouleverser ■ [hair] défaire.

disarray [ˌdɪsəˈreɪ] *n* [of person] confusion *f*, désordre *m* ■ [of clothing] désordre *m* ■ **the group was thrown into ~** la confusion *OR* le désordre régnait dans le groupe ■ **the enemy was in ~** l'ennemi était en déroute ■ **the party is in complete ~** le parti est en plein désarroi ■ **her thoughts were in ~** ses pensées étaient très confuses.

disassemble [ˌdɪsəˈsembl] *vt* démonter, désassembler.

disassociate *etc* [ˌdɪsəˈsəʊʃɪeɪt] = **dissociate**.

disaster [dɪˈzɑːstəʳ] ◇ *n* **1.** [misfortune] désastre *m*, catastrophe *f* ■ [natural] catastrophe *f*, sinistre *m* ■ **air ~** catastrophe aérienne ■ **at the scene of the ~** sur les lieux de la catastrophe *OR* du sinistre ■ **the town has suffered one ~ after another** la ville a subi désastre après désastre ■ **the project is heading for ~** le projet est voué à l'échec *OR* à la catastrophe ■ **she's heading for *OR* courting ~** elle court à sa perte *OR* à la catastrophe **2.** *fig* **as a manager, he's a ~!** en tant que directeur, ce n'est pas une réussite! ■ **my hair's a ~ this morning!** mes cheveux sont dans un état épouvantable ce matin!
◇ *comp* [fund] d'aide aux sinistrés ■ [area] sinistré ■ **~ movie** film *m* catastrophe.

disaster area *n liter* région *f* sinistrée ■ *fig* champ *m* de bataille ■ **your sister's a walking ~!** ta sœur est une vraie catastrophe ambulante!

disastrous [dɪˈzɑːstrəs] *adj* désastreux, catastrophique.

disastrously [dɪˈzɑːstrəslɪ] *adv* désastreusement.

disavow [ˌdɪsəˈvaʊ] *vt fml* [child, opinion] désavouer ■ [responsibility, faith] renier.

disavowal [ˌdɪsəˈvaʊəl] *n fml* [of child, opinion] désaveu *m* ■ [of responsibility, faith] reniement *m*.

disband [dɪsˈbænd] ◇ *vt* [army, club] disperser ■ [organization] disperser, dissoudre.
◇ *vi* [army] se disperser ■ [organization] se dissoudre.

disbandment [dɪsˈbændmənt] *n* [of army, club] dispersion *f* ■ [of organization] dissolution *f*.

disbar [dɪsˈbɑːʳ] (*pret & pp* **disbarred**, *cont* **disbarring**) *vt* LAW rayer du barreau *OR* du tableau de l'ordre *(des avocats)*.

disbelief [ˌdɪsbɪˈliːf] *n* incrédulité *f* ■ **she looked at him in ~** elle l'a regardé avec incrédulité.

disbelieve [ˌdɪsbɪˈliːv] ◇ *vt* [person] ne pas croire ■ [news, story] ne pas croire à.
◇ *vi* RELIG ne pas croire.

disbelieving [ˌdɪsbɪˈliːvɪŋ] *adj* incrédule.

disburse [dɪsˈbɜːs] *vt* débourser.

disc [dɪsk] *n* **1.** [flat circular object] disque *m* **2.** [record] disque *m* **3.** ANAT disque *m* (invertébral) **4.** [identity tag] plaque *f* d'identité ■ **parking ~** AUT disque *m* de stationnement.

discard ◇ *vt* [dɪˈskɑːd] **1.** [get rid of] se débarrasser de, mettre au rebut ■ [idea, system] renoncer, abandonner **2.** CARDS se défausser de, défausser ■ [in cribbage] écarter.
◇ *vi* [dɪˈskɑːd] CARDS se défausser ■ [in cribbage] écarter.
◇ *n* [ˈdɪskɑːd] **1.** COMM & INDUST [reject] pièce *f* de rebut **2.** CARDS défausse *f* ■ [in cribbage] écart *m*.

discarded [dɪˈskɑːdɪd] *adj* [small object] jeté ■ [larger] abandonné.

disc brake *n* frein *m* à disque.

discern [dɪˈsɜːn] *vt* [see] discerner, distinguer ■ [understand] discerner.

discernible [dɪˈsɜːnəbl] *adj* [visible] visible ■ [detectable] discernable, perceptible.

discernibly [dɪˈsɜːnəblɪ] *adv* [visibly] visiblement ■ [perceptibly] perceptiblement, sensiblement.

discerning [dɪˈsɜːnɪŋ] *adj* [person] judicieux, sagace ■ [taste] fin, délicat ■ [look] perspicace.

discernment [dɪˈsɜːnmənt] *n* discernement *m*.

discharge ◇ *vt* [ˈdɪstʃɑːdʒ] **1.** [release - patient] laisser sortir, libérer ; [- prisoner] libérer, mettre en liberté ■ **he was ~d yesterday** il est sorti hier ■ **the patient ~d herself** la malade a signé une décharge et est partie **2.** [dismiss - employee] renvoyer, congédier ; [- official] destituer ■ LAW [jury] dessaisir ■ [accused] acquitter, relaxer ■ MIL [from service] renvoyer à la vie civile ■ [from active duty] démobiliser ■ [for lack of fitness] réformer ■ **~d bankrupt** failli *m* réhabilité **3.** [unload - cargo] décharger ; [- passengers] débarquer **4.** [emit - liquid] dégorger, déverser ; [- gas] dégager, émettre ■ ELEC décharger ■ **the wound was discharging pus** MED la blessure suppurait **5.** [perform - duty] remplir, s'acquitter de ; [- function] remplir **6.** [debt] acquitter, régler **7.** [gun] décharger, tirer ■ [arrow] décocher.
◇ *vi* [ˈdɪstʃɑːdʒ] **1.** [ship] décharger **2.** [wound] suinter **3.** ELEC être en décharge.
◇ *n* [dɪsˈtʃɑːdʒ] **1.** [release - of patient] sortie *f* ■ [of prisoner] libération *f*, mise *f* en liberté **2.** [dismissal - of employee] renvoi *m* ; [- of soldier] libération *f* ■ [after active duty] démobilisation *f* ■ LAW [acquittal] acquittement *m* **3.** [of cargo] déchargement *m* **4.** [emission] émission *f* ■ [of liquid] écoulement *m* ■ MED [of wound] suintement *m* ■ [vaginal] pertes *fpl* (blanches) ■ [of pus] suppuration *f* ■ ELEC décharge *f* **5.** [of duty] accomplissement *m* **6.** [of debt] acquittement *m* **7.** [of gun] décharge *f*.

disc harrow *n* pulvériseur *m*.

disciple [dɪˈsaɪpl] *n* [gen - RELIG] disciple *m*.

disciplinarian [ˌdɪsɪplɪˈneərɪən] ◇ *n* partisan *m* de la manière forte.
◇ *adj* disciplinaire.

disciplinary [ˈdɪsɪplɪnərɪ] *adj* **1.** [corrective - measure] disciplinaire ■ [committee] de discipline **2.** [relating to field] relatif à une discipline.

discipline [ˈdɪsɪplɪn] ◇ *n* **1.** [training, control] discipline *f* **2.** [area of study] discipline *f*, matière *f*.
◇ *vt* **1.** [train - person] discipliner ; [- mind] discipliner, former **2.** [punish] punir.

disciplined [ˈdɪsɪplɪnd] *adj* discipliné.

DISAPPROVAL

Je désapprouve totalement son attitude. I don't approve of his attitude at all.

Ça ne me plaît pas qu'il fréquente ces gens. I don't like him mixing with those people.

Elle a eu tort de lui parler comme ça. She had no right to speak to him like that.

Ce ne sont pas des façons de faire. That's no way to behave.

Mais qu'est-ce qui lui a pris de lui dire ça ? What on earth made him say that to her?

Je ne peux pas dire que j'approuve entièrement son attitude. I can't say that I entirely approve of his attitude.

Je ne sais pas si elle a bien fait de lui en parler. I'm not sure she did the right thing by telling him.

C'est inadmissible ! It's just not on!

disc jockey *n* animateur *m*, - trice *f (de radio ou de discothèque)*, disc-jockey *m*.

disclaim [dɪs'kleɪm] *vt* **1.** [deny - responsibility] rejeter, décliner ; [- knowledge] nier ; [- news, remark] démentir ; [- paternity] désavouer **2.** LAW se désister de, renoncer à.

disclaimer [dɪs'kleɪməʳ] *n* **1.** [denial] démenti *m*, désaveu *m* **2.** LAW désistement *m*, renonciation *f*.

disclose [dɪs'kləʊz] *vt* **1.** [reveal - secret] divulguer, dévoiler ; [- news] divulguer ; [- feelings] révéler **2.** [uncover] exposer, montrer.

disclosure [dɪs'kləʊʒəʳ] *n* **1.** [revelation] divulgation *f*, révélation *f* **2.** [fact revealed] révélation *f*.

disco ['dɪskəʊ] (*pl* **discos**) <> *n* discothèque *f*, boîte *f*.
<> *comp* [dancing, music] disco.

discography [dɪs'kɒgrəfɪ] *n* discographie *f*.

discolor *US* = **discolour**.

discoloration [dɪsˌkʌlə'reɪʃn] *n* [fading] décoloration *f* ■ [yellowing] jaunissement *m* ■ [dulling] ternissement *m*.

discolour *UK*, **discolor** *US* [dɪs'kʌləʳ] <> *vt* [change colour of, fade] décolorer ■ [turn yellow] jaunir.
<> *vi* [change colour, fade] se décolorer ■ [turn yellow] jaunir.

discoloured *UK*, **discolored** *US* [dɪs'kʌləd] *adj* [faded] décoloré ■ [yellowed] jauni.

discomfit [dɪs'kʌmfɪt] *vt fml* **1.** [confuse, embarrass] déconcerter, gêner **2.** [thwart - plan, project] contrecarrer, contrarier.

discomfiture [dɪs'kʌmfɪtʃəʳ] *n fml* [embarrassment] embarras *m*, gêne *f*.

discomfort [dɪs'kʌmfət] <> *n* **1.** [pain] malaise *m* ■ [unease] gêne *f* ■ **she's in some ~** elle a assez mal ■ **you may experience some ~** il se peut que vous ressentiez une gêne ■ **her letter caused him some ~** sa lettre l'a mis un peu mal à l'aise **2.** [cause of pain, unease] incommodité *f*, inconfort *m*.
<> *vt* incommoder, gêner.

disconcert [ˌdɪskən'sɜːt] *vt* **1.** [fluster] déconcerter, dérouter **2.** [upset] troubler, gêner.

disconcerting [ˌdɪskən'sɜːtɪŋ] *adj* **1.** [unnerving] déconcertant, déroutant **2.** [upsetting] gênant.

disconcertingly [ˌdɪskən'sɜːtɪŋlɪ] *adv* de façon déconcertante OR déroutante.

disconnect [ˌdɪskə'nekt] *vt* **1.** [detach] détacher, séparer ■ [plug, pipe, radio, TV] débrancher ■ RAIL [carriages] décrocher **2.** [gas, electricity, telephone, water] couper.

disconnected [ˌdɪskə'nektɪd] *adj* **1.** [remarks, thoughts] décousu, sans suite ■ [facts] sans rapport **2.** [detached - wire, plug etc] détaché ; [- telephone] déconnecté.

disconsolate [dɪs'kɒnsələt] *adj* triste, inconsolable.

disconsolately [dɪs'kɒnsələtlɪ] *adv* tristement, inconsolablement.

discontent [ˌdɪskən'tent] <> *n* **1.** [dissatisfaction] mécontentement *m* ■ **a cause of ~** grief *m* **2.** [person] mécontent *m*, - e *f*.
<> *adj* mécontent.
<> *vt* mécontenter.

discontented [ˌdɪskən'tentɪd] *adj* mécontent.

discontinue [ˌdɪskən'tɪnjuː] *vt* **1.** [gen] cesser, interrompre ■ COMM & INDUST [production] abandonner ■ [product] interrompre ■ [publication] interrompre la publication de ■ **this item/model has been ~d** cet article/ce modèle ne se fait plus ■ **~d line** fin *f* de série **2.** LAW [action, suit] abandonner.

discontinuous [ˌdɪskən'tɪnjʊəs] *adj* [gen - LING] & MATHS discontinu.

discord ['dɪskɔːd] *n* **1.** *(U)* [conflict] désaccord *m*, discorde *f* ■ **civil ~** dissensions *fpl* sociales **2.** MUS dissonance *f*.

discordant [dɪ'skɔːdənt] *adj* **1.** [opinions] incompatible, opposé ■ [colours, sounds] discordant **2.** MUS dissonant.

discotheque ['dɪskəʊtek] *n* discothèque *f (pour danser)*.

discount <> *n* ['dɪskaʊnt] **1.** COMM [price reduction] remise *f*, rabais *m* ■ **I bought it at a ~** je l'ai acheté au rabais ■ **she got a ~** on lui a fait une remise ■ **the store is currently offering a 5% ~ on radios** le magasin fait (une réduction de) 5% sur les radios en ce moment **2.** FIN [deduction] escompte *m* ■ **'~ for cash'** 'escompte au comptant' ■ **shares offered at a ~** des actions offertes en dessous du pair.
<> *vt* ['dɪskaʊnt, dɪs'kaʊnt] **1.** [disregard] ne pas tenir compte de ■ **they did not ~ the possibility** ils n'ont pas écarté cette possibilité **2.** COMM [article] faire une remise OR un rabais sur **3.** FIN [sum of money] faire une remise de, escompter ■ [bill, banknote] prendre à l'escompte, escompter.

discount store *n* solderie *f*.

discourage [dɪ'skʌrɪdʒ] *vt* **1.** [dishearten] décourager ■ **to become ~d** se laisser décourager **2.** [dissuade] décourager, dissuader ■ **to ~ sb from doing sthg** dissuader qqn de faire qqch ■ **a type of diet which should be ~d** un type de régime qui devrait être déconseillé.

discouraged [dɪs'kʌrɪdʒd] *adj* découragé ■ **don't be ~** ne te laisse pas abattre OR décourager.

discouragement [dɪ'skʌrɪdʒmənt] *n* **1.** [attempt to discourage] : **I met with ~ on all sides** tout le monde a essayé de me décourager ■ **my plans met with ~** on a essayé de me dissuader de poursuivre mes projets **2.** [deterrent] : **the metal shutters act as a ~ to vandals** les rideaux métalliques servent à décourager les vandales.

discouraging [dɪ'skʌrɪdʒɪŋ] *adj* décourageant.

discourse <> *n* ['dɪskɔːs] **1.** *fml* [sermon] discours *m* ■ [dissertation] discours *m*, traité *m* ■ **'Discourse on Method'** ***Descartes*** 'Discours de la méthode' **2.** LING discours *m* **3.** *(U)* *lit* [conversation] conversation *f*, débat *m*.
<> *vi* [dɪ'skɔːs] **1.** *fml* [speak] : **to ~ on** OR **upon sthg** traiter de OR parler de qqch **2.** *lit* [converse] s'entretenir.

discourse analysis *n* LING analyse *f* du discours.

discourteous [dɪs'kɜːtjəs] *adj* discourtois, impoli ■ **to be ~ to** OR **towards sb** être discourtois OR impoli avec OR envers qqn.

discourtesy [dɪs'kɜːtɪsɪ] (*pl* **discourtesies**) *n* manque *m* de courtoisie, impolitesse *f* ■ **to treat sb with ~** manquer de courtoisie envers qqn.

discover [dɪ'skʌvəʳ] *vt* **1.** [country, answer, reason] découvrir ■ **I finally ~ed my glasses in my desk** j'ai fini par trouver mes lunettes dans mon bureau **2.** [realize] se rendre compte ■ **when did you ~ that your wallet had been stolen?** quand vous êtes-vous rendu compte qu'on vous avait volé votre portefeuille? **3.** [actor, singer etc] découvrir.

discoverer [dɪ'skʌvərəʳ] *n* découvreur *m* ■ **the ~ of penicillin** la personne qui a découvert la pénicilline.

discovery [dɪ'skʌvərɪ] (*pl* **discoveries**) *n* **1.** [act, event] découverte *f* **2.** [actor, singer, place, thing] découverte *f* **3.** LAW [of documents] divulgation *f*.

discredit [dɪs'kredɪt] <> *vt* **1.** [person] discréditer **2.** [report, theory - cast doubt on] discréditer, mettre en doute ; [- show to be false] montrer l'inexactitude de.
<> *n* [loss of good reputation] discrédit *m* ■ **to bring ~ on** OR **upon** jeter le discrédit sur ■ **it is very much to his ~** ce n'est pas du tout à son honneur.

discredited [dɪs'kredɪtɪd] *adj* discrédité.

discreet [dɪ'skriːt] *adj* discret, - ète *f* ■ **to follow sb at a ~ distance** suivre qqn à une distance respectueuse.

discreetly [dɪ'skriːtlɪ] *adv* discrètement, de manière discrète.

discrepancy [dɪ'skrepənsɪ] (*pl* **discrepancies**) *n* [in figures] contradiction *f* ▪ [in statements] contradiction *f*, désaccord *m*, divergence *f* ▪ **there's a ~ between these reports** ces rapports se contredisent OR divergent (sur un point).

discrete [dɪ'skri:t] *adj* [gen - TECH] & MATHS discret, - ète *f*.

discretion [dɪ'skreʃn] *n* **1.** [tact, prudence] discrétion *f* ▪ **to be the soul of ~** être la discrétion même ▪ **~ is the better part of valour** *prov* prudence est mère de sûreté *prov* **2.** [judgment, taste] jugement *m* ▪ **use your own ~** jugez par vous-même ▪ **a woman of ~** une femme de raison ▪ **at the manager's ~** à la discrétion du directeur ▪ **the committee has ~ to award more than one prize** à la discrétion du comité, plus d'un prix peut être accordé.

discretionary [dɪ'skreʃnərɪ] *adj* discrétionnaire.

discriminate [dɪ'skrɪmɪneɪt] ◇ *vi* **1.** [on grounds of race, sex etc] : **to ~ in favour of** favoriser ▪ **she was ~d against** elle faisait l'objet OR était victime de discriminations **2.** [distinguish] établir OR faire une distinction, faire une différence ▪ **to ~ between right and wrong** distinguer le bien du mal.
◇ *vt* distinguer ▪ **to ~ right from wrong** distinguer le bien du mal.

discriminating [dɪ'skrɪmɪneɪtɪŋ] *adj* **1.** [showing discernment] judicieux ▪ [in matters of taste] qui a un goût sûr ▪ **the company was very ~ in its choice of employees** l'entreprise était très sélective dans le choix de ses employés ▪ **a car for the ~ motorist** une voiture pour l'automobiliste averti **2.** [tax, tariff] différentiel.

discrimination [dɪˌskrɪmɪ'neɪʃn] *n* **1.** [on grounds of race, sex etc] discrimination *f* **2.** [good judgment] discernement *m* ▪ [in matters of taste] goût *m* ▪ **he is a man of great ~** c'est un homme qui a énormément de goût **3.** [ability to distinguish] : **powers of ~** capacités *fpl* de distinction, discernement *m*.

discriminatory [dɪ'skrɪmɪnətrɪ] *adj* [treatment, proposals] discriminatoire ▪ **the company is being ~** la société pratique la discrimination.

discursive [dɪ'skɜ:sɪv] *adj fml* [essay, report, person etc] discursif.

discus ['dɪskəs] (*pl* **discuses** OR *pl* **disci** [-kaɪ]) *n* SPORT disque *m* ▪ **~ thrower** lanceur *m*, -euse *f* de disque ▪ [in antiquity] discobole *m*.

discuss [dɪ'skʌs] *vt* [talk about - problem, price, subject etc] discuter de, parler de ; [- person] parler de ▪ [debate] discuter de ▪ [examine - subj: author, book, report etc] examiner, parler de, traiter de ▪ **I'll ~ it with you later** nous en parlerons OR discuterons plus tard ▪ **it is being ~ed** c'est en cours de discussion.

discussion [dɪ'skʌʃn] *n* [talk] discussion *f* ▪ [debate] débat *m* ▪ [examination - by author in report] traitement *m* ; [- of report] examen *m* ▪ **the report contained a ~ of the recent findings** le rapport parlait OR traitait des découvertes récentes ▪ **there's been a lot of ~ about it** on en a beaucoup parlé ; [in parliament, on board etc] cela a été beaucoup débattu ; [in press, in media] cela a été largement traité ▪ **to come up for ~** [report, proposal etc] être discuté ▪ **it is still under ~** c'est encore en cours de discussion.

disdain [dɪs'deɪn] ◇ *vt fml* dédaigner.
◇ *n* dédain *m*, mépris *m* ▪ **with** OR **in ~** avec dédain, dédaigneusement ▪ **a look of ~** un regard dédaigneux.

disdainful [dɪs'deɪnfʊl] *adj* dédaigneux ▪ **to be ~ of sb/sthg** se montrer dédaigneux envers qqn/qqch, dédaigner qqn/qqch.

disease [dɪ'zi:z] *n* **1.** BOT, MED & VET maladie *f* ▪ **he's suffering from a kidney ~** il a une maladie des reins, il est malade des reins ▪ **to combat ~** combattre la maladie ➲ **heart ~** maladie cardiaque OR du cœur **2.** *fig* mal *m*, maladie *f*.

diseased [dɪ'zi:zd] *adj* BOT, MED & VET malade ▪ *fig* [mind] malade, dérangé ▪ [imagination] malade.

disembark [ˌdɪsɪm'bɑ:k] ◇ *vi* débarquer ▪ **to ~ from the ferry** débarquer du ferry.
◇ *vt* [passengers, cargo] débarquer.

disembarkation [ˌdɪsembɑ:'keɪʃn], **disembarkment** [ˌdɪsɪm'bɑ:kmənt] *n* [of passengers, cargo] débarquement *m*.

disembodied [ˌdɪsɪm'bɒdɪd] *adj* [voice, spirit] désincarné.

disembowel [ˌdɪsɪm'baʊəl] *vt* éviscérer, éventrer.

disenchanted [ˌdɪsɪn'tʃɑ:ntɪd] *adj* désillusionné ▪ **to be ~ with sb/sthg** avoir perdu ses illusions sur qqn/qqch, être désillusionné par qqn/qqch ▪ **to become ~ with sb/sthg** perdre ses illusions sur qqn/qqch.

disenchantment [ˌdɪsɪn'tʃɑ:ntmənt] *n* désillusion *f* ▪ **~ with the government has been growing** de plus en plus de gens sont déçus par le gouvernement.

disenfranchise [ˌdɪsɪn'fræntʃaɪz] *vt* priver du droit de vote.

disengage [ˌdɪsɪn'geɪdʒ] ◇ *vt* **1.** MECH désenclencher ▪ [lever, catch] dégager ▪ AUT [handbrake] desserrer ▪ **to ~ the clutch** AUT débrayer **2.** [release] dégager **3.** MIL : **the order came through to ~ the troops** l'ordre arriva de cesser le combat.
◇ *vi* **1.** MIL cesser le combat **2.** MECH se désenclencher.

disengagement [ˌdɪsɪn'geɪdʒmənt] *n* **1.** [from political group, organization] désengagement *m* **2.** MIL cessez-le-feu *m inv*.

disentangle [ˌdɪsɪn'tæŋgl] *vt* [string, plot, mystery] démêler ▪ **I tried to ~ myself from the net** j'ai essayé de me dépêtrer du filet ▪ **to ~ o.s. from a difficult situation** se sortir à grand-peine d'une situation difficile.

disfavour UK, **disfavor** US [dɪs'feɪvər] *n* désapprobation *f*, défaveur *f* ▪ **to fall into ~ with sb** tomber en défaveur auprès de qqn.

disfigure [dɪs'fɪgər] *vt* défigurer.

disfigured [dɪs'fɪgəd] *adj* défiguré.

disfigurement [dɪs'fɪgəmənt] *n* défigurement *m*.

disgorge [dɪs'gɔ:dʒ] ◇ *vt* **1.** [food] régurgiter, rendre ▪ *fig* [contents, passengers, pollutants] déverser ▪ **chimneys disgorging smoke** des cheminées crachant de la fumée **2.** [give unwillingly - information] donner avec répugnance OR à contrecœur.
◇ *vi* [river] se jeter, se dégorger.

disgrace [dɪs'greɪs] ◇ *n* **1.** [dishonour] disgrâce *f* ▪ **it will bring ~ on** OR **to the family** cela fera tomber la famille dans la disgrâce, cela déshonorera la famille ▪ **there's no ~ in not knowing** il n'y a pas de honte à ne pas savoir **2.** [disapproval] : **to be in ~ (with sb)** être en disgrâce (auprès de qqn) **3.** [shameful example or thing] honte *f* ▪ **it's a ~** c'est une honte, c'est honteux ▪ **look at you, you're a ~!** regarde-toi, tu fais honte (à voir)! ▪ **look at you, your hair's a ~** regarde-toi, tu es coiffé n'importe comment ▪ **you're a ~ to your family** tu déshonores ta famille, tu es la honte de ta famille.
◇ *vt* **1.** [bring shame on] faire honte à, couvrir de honte, déshonorer ▪ **to ~ o.s.** se couvrir de honte **2.** *(usu passive)* [discredit] disgracier.

disgraceful [dɪs'greɪsfʊl] *adj* [behaviour] honteux, scandaleux ▪ *inf* [hat, jacket etc] *inf* miteux ▪ **look at you, you're ~!** regarde-toi, tu fais honte (à voir)! ▪ **it's ~** c'est honteux.

disgracefully [dɪs'greɪsfʊlɪ] *adv* honteusement.

disgruntled [dɪs'grʌntld] *adj* mécontent.

disguise [dɪs'gaɪz] ◇ *n* déguisement *m* ▪ **in ~** déguisé ▪ **to put on a ~** se déguiser ▪ **to be a master of ~** être un roi du déguisement.
◇ *vt* **1.** [voice, handwriting, person] déguiser ▪ **to be ~d as sb/sthg** être déguisé en qqn/qqch **2.** [feelings, disappointment etc] dissimuler, masquer ▪ [truth, facts] dissimuler, cacher ▪ [unsightly feature] cacher ▪ [bad taste of food, cough mixture etc] couvrir ▪ **there's no disguising the fact that business is bad** on ne peut pas cacher le fait que les affaires vont mal.

disgust [dɪs'gʌst] ◇ *n* [sick feeling] dégoût *m*, aversion *f*, répugnance *f* ▪ [displeasure] écœurement *m*, dégoût *m* ▪ **to be filled with ~ by sthg** être écœuré par qqch ▪ **in order to express**

our ~ with the decision pour montrer que nous sommes écœurés par cette décision ▪ I resigned in ~ dégoûté OR écœuré, j'ai démissionné.
◇ vt [sicken] dégoûter ▪ [displease] écœurer ▪ I am ~ed with him/this government/his behaviour il/ce gouvernement/son comportement m'écœure ▪ I was ~ed by the accounts of torture [sickened] les récits de torture m'ont écœuré OR m'ont donné la nausée ▪ I am ~ed with OR at my own stupidity [displeased] je m'en veux d'être aussi stupide.

disgusted [dɪs'gʌstɪd] *adj* [displeased] écœuré ▪ [sick] écœuré, dégoûté.

disgusting [dɪs'gʌstɪŋ] *adj* [sickening - person, behaviour, smell] écœurant, dégoûtant ; [- habit, language] dégoûtant ▪ [very bad] écœurant, déplorable ▪ how ~! c'est écœurant!, c'est dégoûtant!

disgustingly [dɪs'gʌstɪŋlɪ] *adv*: a ~ bad meal un repas épouvantable ▪ she is ~ clever/successful *inf* elle est intelligente/elle réussit au point que c'en est écœurant.

dish [dɪʃ] ◇ *n* **1.** [plate] assiette *f* ▪ the ~es la vaisselle ▪ to wash OR to do the ~es faire la vaisselle ▪ to wash ~es [in restaurant] faire la plonge **2.** [food] plat *m* **3.** [amount of food] plat *m* **4.** *inf* [good-looking man or woman] canon *m* **5.** [of telescope] miroir *m* concave *(de télescope)*.
◇ *vt inf* **1.** *UK* [chances, hopes] ruiner **2.** *phr* to ~ the dirt [gossip] faire des commérages.
◆ **dish out** ◇ *vt sep* **1.** [food] servir **2.** *inf fig* [money, leaflets etc] distribuer ▪ [advice] prodiguer ▪ you can ~ it out but you can't take it [criticism] tu es bon pour critiquer mais pour ce qui est d'accepter la critique, c'est un autre problème!
◇ *vi insep* [serve food] faire le service.
◆ **dish up** ◇ *vt sep* [food] servir OR verser OR mettre dans un plat ▪ *inf* [arguments, excuses etc] *inf* ressortir.
◇ *vi insep* [serve food] servir.

dish aerial *n UK* TV antenne *f* parabolique.

disharmony [,dɪs'hɑːmənɪ] *n* manque *m* d'harmonie.

dishcloth ['dɪʃklɒθ] *n* torchon *m* (à vaisselle).

dishearten [dɪs'hɑːtn] *vt* décourager, abattre, démoraliser ▪ don't get ~ed ne te décourage pas, ne te laisse pas abattre.

disheartened [dɪs'hɑːtnd] *adj* découragé.

disheartening [dɪs'hɑːtnɪŋ] *adj* décourageant.

dished [dɪʃt] *adj* [angled] non parallèle ▪ [convex] lenticulaire.

dishevelled *UK*, **disheveled** *US* [dɪ'ʃevld] *adj* [hair] ébouriffé, dépeigné ▪ [clothes] débraillé, en désordre ▪ [person, appearance] débraillé.

dishful ['dɪʃfʊl] *n* [of food] plat *m*.

dish mop *n* lavette *f*.

dishonest [dɪs'ɒnɪst] *adj* malhonnête ▪ you're being ~ not telling him how you feel c'est malhonnête de ne pas lui dire ce que tu ressens.

dishonestly [dɪs'ɒnɪstlɪ] *adv* de manière malhonnête, malhonnêtement.

dishonesty [dɪs'ɒnɪstɪ] *n* malhonnêteté *f*.

dishonour *UK*, **dishonor** *US* [dɪs'ɒnər] ◇ *n* déshonneur *m* ▪ to bring ~ on sb/one's country déshonorer qqn/son pays.
◇ *vt* **1.** [family, country, profession etc] déshonorer **2.** FIN [cheque] refuser d'honorer.

dishonourable *UK*, **dishonorable** *US* [dɪs'ɒnrəbl] *adj* [conduct] déshonorant ▪ he was given a ~ discharge MIL il a été renvoyé pour manquement à l'honneur.

dishpan ['dɪʃpæn] *n US* bassine *f*.

dish rack *n* égouttoir *m* (à vaisselle).

dishrag ['dɪʃræg] = **dishcloth**.

dish soap *n US* liquide *m* vaisselle.

dishtowel ['dɪʃtaʊəl] *US* = **tea towel**.

dishwasher ['dɪʃ,wɒʃər] *n* [machine] lave-vaisselle *m* ▪ [person] plongeur *m*, -euse *f*.

dishwater ['dɪʃ,wɔːtər] *n* eau *f* de vaisselle ▪ this coffee is like ~! c'est du jus de chaussettes, ce café!

dishy ['dɪʃɪ] (*comp* **dishier**, *superl* **dishiest**) *adj UK inf* séduisant, sexy.

disillusion [,dɪsɪ'luːʒn] ◇ *vt* faire perdre ses illusions à, désillusionner.
◇ *n* = **disillusionment**.

disillusioned [,dɪsɪ'luːʒnd] *adj* désillusionné, désabusé ▪ to be ~ with sb/sthg avoir perdu ses illusions sur qqn/qqch.

disillusionment [,dɪsɪ'luːʒnmənt] *n* désillusion *f*, désabusement *m*.

disincentive [,dɪsɪn'sentɪv] *n* : taxes are a ~ to expansion les impôts découragent l'expansion ▪ are social security payments a ~ to work? est-ce que les prestations sociales dissuadent les gens de travailler?

disinclination [,dɪsɪnklɪ'neɪʃn] *n* [of person] peu *m* d'inclination ▪ her ~ to believe him sa tendance à ne pas le croire ▪ the West's ~ to go on lending le peu d'enthousiasme dont fait preuve l'Occident pour continuer à prêter de l'argent.

disinclined [,dɪsɪn'klaɪnd] *adj* : to be ~ to do sthg être peu disposé OR enclin à faire qqch.

disinfect [,dɪsɪn'fekt] *vt* désinfecter.

disinfectant [,dɪsɪn'fektənt] *n* désinfectant *m*.

disinfection [,dɪsɪn'fekʃn] *n* désinfection *f*.

disinformation [,dɪsɪnfə'meɪʃn] *n* désinformation *f*.

disingenuous [,dɪsɪn'dʒenjʊəs] *adj* peu sincère.

disingenuously [,dɪsɪn'dʒenjʊəslɪ] *adv* avec peu de sincérité.

disingenuousness [,dɪsɪn'dʒenjʊəsnɪs] *n* manque *m* de sincérité.

disinherit [,dɪsɪn'herɪt] *vt* déshériter.

disinherited [,dɪsɪn'herɪtɪd] *adj* déshérité.

disintegrate [dɪs'ɪntɪgreɪt] *vi* [stone, wet paper] se désagréger ▪ [plane, rocket] se désintégrer ▪ *fig* [coalition, the family] se désagréger.

disintegration [dɪs,ɪntɪ'greɪʃn] *n* [of stone, wet paper] désagrégation *f* ▪ [of plane, rocket] désintégration *f* ▪ *fig* [of coalition, the family] désagrégation *f*.

disinter [,dɪsɪn'tɜːr] (*pret & pp* **disinterred**, *cont* **disinterring**) *vt* [body] déterrer, exhumer.

disinterest [,dɪs'ɪntərest] *n* **1.** [objectivity] : his ~ was the reason we chose him on l'a choisi parce qu'il n'avait aucun intérêt dans l'affaire **2.** [lack of interest] manque *m* d'intérêt.

disinterested [,dɪs'ɪntrəstɪd] *adj* **1.** [objective] désintéressé **2.** *inf* [uninterested] indifférent.

disinvest [,dɪsɪn'vest] *vi* désinvestir.

disjointed [dɪs'dʒɔɪntɪd] *adj* [conversation, film, speech] décousu, incohérent.

disjunctive [dɪs'dʒʌŋktɪv] *adj* GRAM disjonctif.

disk [dɪsk] *n* **1.** COMPUT [hard] disque *m* ▪ [soft] disquette *f* ▪ on ~ sur disque, sur disquette ▪ to write sthg to ~ sauvegarder qqch sur disque OR disquette **2.** *US* = **disc**.

disk crash *n* COMPUT atterrissage *m* de tête.

disk drive *n* COMPUT lecteur *m* de disquettes.

diskette [dɪs'ket] *n* COMPUT disquette *f*.

diskette drive *US* = **disk drive**.

disk operating system *n* COMPUT système *m* d'exploitation de disques.

dislike [dɪs'laɪk] <> *vt* ne pas aimer ▪ **I ~ flying** je n'aime pas prendre l'avion ▪ **why do you ~ him so much?** pourquoi le détestes-tu autant? ▪ **he is much ~d** il est loin d'être apprécié ▪ **I don't ~ him** je n'ai rien contre lui.
<> *n* [for sb] aversion *f*, antipathie *f* ▪ [for sthg] aversion *f* ▪ **to have a ~ for** *OR* **of sthg** détester qqch ▪ **to take a ~ to sb/sthg** prendre qqn/qqch en grippe.
Voir module d'usage

dislocate ['dɪsləkeɪt] *vt* **1.** [shoulder, knee etc - subj: person] se démettre, se déboîter, se luxer ; [- subj: accident, fall] démettre, déboîter, luxer ▪ **he has ~d his shoulder** il s'est démis *OR* déboîté *OR* luxé l'épaule ▪ **a ~d shoulder** une épaule démise *OR* déboîtée *OR* luxée **2.** [disrupt - plans] désorganiser, perturber.

dislocation [ˌdɪslə'keɪʃn] *n* **1.** [of shoulder, knee etc] luxation *f*, déboîtement *m* **2.** [disruption - of plans] perturbation *f*.

dislodge [dɪs'lɒdʒ] *vt* [fish bone, piece of apple etc] dégager ▪ [large rock] déplacer ▪ *fig* [enemy, prey] déloger ▪ [leader, title holder] prendre la place de.

disloyal [ˌdɪs'lɔɪəl] *adj* déloyal ▪ **to be ~ to sb/sthg** être déloyal envers qqn/qqch.

disloyalty [ˌdɪs'lɔɪəltɪ] *n* déloyauté *f* ▪ **an act of ~** un acte déloyal.

dismal ['dɪzml] *adj* [day, weather] horrible ▪ [streets, countryside] lugubre ▪ [song] mélancolique, triste ▪ *fig* [result, performance] lamentable ▪ [future, prospect] sombre ▪ **what are you looking so ~ about?** pourquoi as-tu l'air aussi lugubre? ▪ **to be a ~ failure** [person] être un zéro sur toute la ligne ; [film, project] échouer lamentablement.

dismally ['dɪzməlɪ] *adv* lugubrement ▪ [fail] lamentablement.

dismantle [dɪs'mæntl] <> *vt* [object, scenery, exhibition] démonter ▪ *fig* [system, arrangement] démanteler.
<> *vi* se démonter.

dismantling [dɪs'mæntlɪŋ] *n* [of object, scenery] démontage *m* ▪ *fig* [of system, reforms] démantèlement *m*.

dismay [dɪs'meɪ] <> *n* consternation *f* ▪ [stronger] désarroi *m* ▪ **in** *OR* **with ~** avec consternation *OR* désarroi ▪ **to be filled with ~ by sthg** être consterné par *OR* rempli de désarroi à cause de qqch ▪ **(much) to my ~** à ma grande consternation, à mon grand désarroi.
<> *vt* consterner ▪ [stronger] emplir de désarroi, effondrer.

dismayed [dɪs'meɪd] *adj* consterné, effondré.

dismember [dɪs'membəʳ] *vt* démembrer.

dismiss [dɪs'mɪs] <> *vt* **1.** [from job - employee] licencier, congédier, renvoyer ; [- magistrate, official] destituer, révoquer, relever de ses fonctions
2. [not take seriously - proposal] rejeter ; [- objection, warning] ne pas tenir compte de, ne pas prendre au sérieux ; [- problem] écarter, refuser de considérer ▪ **he ~ed him as a crank** il a déclaré que c'était un excentrique à ne pas prendre au sérieux ▪ **police ~ed the warning as a hoax** la police n'a pas tenu compte de l'avertissement et l'a pris pour une mauvaise plaisanterie
3. [send away] congédier ▪ *fig* [thought, possibility] écarter ▪ [memory] effacer ▪ [suggestion, idea] rejeter ▪ SCH [class] laisser partir ▪ **~ him from your thoughts** chasse-le de tes pensées ▪ **class ~ed!** vous pouvez sortir! ▪ **~ed!** MIL rompez!
4. LAW [hung jury] dissoudre ▪ **to ~ a charge** [judge] rendre une ordonnance de non-lieu ▪ **all charges against her have been ~ed** toutes les accusations qui pesaient sur elle ont été levées ▪ **the judge ~ed the case** le juge a rendu une fin de non-recevoir ▪ **case ~ed!** affaire classée!
5. [in cricket - batsman, team] éliminer.
<> *vi* : **~!** MIL rompez (les rangs)!

dismissal [dɪs'mɪsl] *n* **1.** [from work - of employee] licenciement *m*, renvoi *m* ; [- of magistrate, official] destitution *f*, révocation *f* **2.** [of proposal] rejet *m* **3.** LAW : **the judge's ~ of the case met with widespread approval** la fin de non-recevoir rendue par le juge a été accueillie avec satisfaction ▪ **the ~ of the charges against you** le non-lieu qui a été prononcé en votre faveur.

dismissive [dɪs'mɪsɪv] *adj* [tone of voice, gesture] dédaigneux ▪ **to be ~ of sb/sthg** ne faire aucun cas de qqn/qqch ▪ **you're always so ~ of my efforts** tu fais toujours si peu de cas de mes efforts.

dismissively [dɪs'mɪsɪvlɪ] *adv* [offhandedly] d'un ton dédaigneux ▪ [in final tone of voice] d'un ton sans appel.

dismount [ˌdɪs'maʊnt] <> *vi* descendre ▪ **she ~ed from her horse/bike** elle est descendue de son cheval/vélo.
<> *vt* **1.** [cause to fall - from horse] désarçonner, démonter ; [- from bicycle, motorcycle] faire tomber **2.** [gun, device] démonter.

disobedience [ˌdɪsə'bi:djəns] *n* désobéissance *f* ▪ **she was punished for (her) ~** elle a été punie pour avoir désobéi.

disobedient [ˌdɪsə'bi:djənt] *adj* désobéissant ▪ **don't be ~ to your father!** ne désobéis pas à ton père!

disobediently [ˌdɪsə'bi:djəntlɪ] *adv* de manière désobéissante.

disobey [ˌdɪsə'beɪ] *vt* désobéir à.

disobliging [ˌdɪsə'blaɪdʒɪŋ] *adj fml* **1.** [unhelpful] : **I'm sorry to be ~** je suis désolé de ne pouvoir vous rendre service **2.** [unpleasant] désobligeant.

disorder [dɪs'ɔ:dəʳ] <> *n* **1.** [untidiness - of house, room, desk] désordre *m* ▪ **to be in (a state of) ~** être en désordre ▪ **his financial affairs were in total ~** le désordre le plus total régnait dans ses finances ▪ **the meeting broke up in ~** la réunion s'est achevée dans le désordre *OR* la confusion **2.** [unrest] trouble *m* ▪ **public ~** atteinte *f* à *OR* trouble *m* de l'ordre public **3.** MED trouble *m*, troubles *mpl* ▪ **nervous/blood ~** troubles nerveux/de la circulation.
<> *vt* [make untidy - files, papers] mettre en désordre.

DISLIKE

Je déteste le foot/conduire la nuit. I hate football/driving at night.

Je ne supporte pas le mensonge/qu'on me parle comme ça. I can't stand lies/I will not be spoken to like that.

Ça m'agace qu'elle s'invite sans prévenir. It annoys me the way she comes round without any warning.

Il me tape sur les nerfs *OU* **le système** *inf.* He gets on my nerves.

Je ne peux pas le voir (en peinture) *OU* **le supporter** *inf.* I can't stand him.

Je ne l'aime pas trop. I don't really like him/her/it.

Je ne suis pas très branché sport *inf.* I'm not really into sport.

Les jeux vidéo, c'est pas vraiment mon truc *inf.* Video games aren't really my thing.

Les films de science-fiction, ce n'est pas ma tasse de thé. Science fiction films aren't really my cup of tea.

Ses tableaux ne m'emballent pas (tellement) *inf.* I don't think much of his paintings.

disordered [dɪs'ɔ:dəd] *adj* [room] en désordre.

disorderly [dɪs'ɔ:dəlɪ] *adj* **1.** [untidy - room, house] en désordre, désordonné **2.** [unruly - crowd, mob] désordonné, agité ; [- conduct] désordonné ; [- meeting, demonstration] désordonné, confus.

disorganization [dɪs,ɔ:gənaɪ'zeɪʃn] *n* désorganisation *f*.

disorganized [dɪs'ɔ:gənaɪzd] *adj* désorganisé.

disorient [dɪs'ɔ:rɪənt], **disorientate** *UK* [dɪs'ɔ:rɪənteɪt] *vt* désorienter ■ **to be ~ed** être désorienté ■ **it's easy to become ~ed** c'est facile de perdre son sens de l'orientation ; *fig* on a vite fait d'être désorienté.

disorientation [dɪs,ɔ:rɪən'teɪʃn] *n* désorientation *f*.

disown [dɪs'əʊn] *vt* [child, opinion, statement] renier, désavouer ■ [country] renier.

disparage [dɪ'spærɪdʒ] *vt* dénigrer, décrier.

disparaging [dɪ'spærɪdʒɪŋ] *adj* [person, newspaper report - about person] désobligeant ; [- about proposals, ideas] critique ■ **to make ~ remarks about sb** faire des remarques désobligeantes à propos de *OR* sur qqn ■ **the critics were very ~ about his latest play** les critiques ont beaucoup dénigré sa dernière pièce.

disparagingly [dɪ'spærɪdʒɪŋlɪ] *adv* [say, look at] d'un air désobligeant.

disparate ['dɪspərət] *adj fml* disparate.

disparity [dɪ'spærətɪ] (*pl* **disparities**) *n* [in ages] disparité *f* ■ [in report, statement] contradiction *f*.

dispassionate [dɪ'spæʃnət] *adj* [objective - person, report, analysis etc] impartial, objectif ■ **to be ~** rester objectif *OR* impartial.

dispassionately [dɪ'spæʃnətlɪ] *adv* [unemotionally] sans émotion, calmement ■ [objectively] objectivement, impartialement.

dispatch [dɪ'spætʃ] <> *vt* **1.** [send - letter, merchandise, telegram] envoyer, expédier ; [- messenger] envoyer, dépêcher ; [- troops, envoy] envoyer **2.** [complete - task, work] expédier, en finir avec **3.** *euph* [kill - person] tuer **4.** *inf* [food] s'envoyer.
<> *n* **1.** [of letter, merchandise, telegram] envoi *m*, expédition *f* ■ [of messenger, troops, envoy] envoi *m* **2.** MIL & PRESS [report] dépêche *f* ■ **to be mentioned in ~es** MIL être cité à l'ordre du jour **3.** [swiftness] promptitude *f*.
<> *comp* : **~ clerk** expéditionnaire *mf*.

dispatch box *n* **1.** [for documents] boîte *f* à documents **2.** *UK* POL : **the ~** *tribune d'où parlent les membres du gouvernement et leurs homologues du cabinet fantôme.*

dispatch rider *n* estafette *f*.

dispel [dɪ'spel] (*pret & pp* **dispelled**, *cont* **dispelling**) *vt* [clouds, mist - subj: sun] dissiper ; [- subj: wind] chasser ■ [doubts, fears, anxiety] dissiper.

dispensable [dɪ'spensəbl] *adj* dont on peut se passer, superflu ■ **the rest of the employees were ~** les autres employés n'étaient pas indispensables.

dispensary [dɪ'spensərɪ] (*pl* **dispensaries**) *n* pharmacie *f* ■ [for free distribution of medicine] dispensaire *m*.

dispensation [,dɪspen'seɪʃn] *n* **1.** [handing out] distribution *f* **2.** [administration - of charity, justice] exercice *m* **3.** ADMIN, LAW & RELIG [exemption] dispense *f* ■ **to receive ~ from military service** être exempté du service militaire ■ **special ~** permission *f* exceptionnelle **4.** POL & RELIG [system] régime *m*.

dispense [dɪ'spens] *vt* **1.** [subj: person, machine] distribuer **2.** [administer - justice, charity] exercer **3.** PHARM préparer **4.** *fml* [exempt] dispenser ■ **to ~ sb from (doing)sthg** dispenser qqn de (faire) qqch.
◆ **dispense with** *vt insep* [do without] se passer de ■ [get rid of] se débarrasser de ■ **to ~ with the formalities** couper court aux *OR* se dispenser des formalités ■ **to ~ with the need for sthg** rendre qqch superflu.

dispenser [dɪ'spensər] *n* **1.** PHARM pharmacien *m*, - enne *f* **2.** [machine] distributeur *m*.

dispensing [dɪ'spensɪŋ] *adj* *UK* **~ chemist** [person] préparateur *m*, - trice *f* en pharmacie ; [establishment] pharmacie *f* ■ **~ optician** opticien *m*.

dispersal [dɪ'spɜ:sl] *n* [of crowd, seeds] dispersion *f* ■ [of gas - disappearance] dissipation *f* ; [- spread] dispersion *f* ■ [of light - by prism] dispersion *f*, décomposition *f*.

dispersant [dɪ'spɜ:sənt] *n* CHEM dispersant *m*.

disperse [dɪ'spɜ:s] <> *vt* **1.** [crowd, seeds] disperser ■ [clouds, mist - subj: sun] dissiper ; [- subj: wind] chasser ■ [gas, chemical - cause to spread] propager ; [- cause to vanish] disperser ■ **a prism ~s light** un prisme disperse *OR* décompose la lumière **2.** [place at intervals] répartir ■ **policemen were ~d along the length of the road** des agents de police étaient répartis *OR* disséminés le long de la route.
<> *vi* [crowds, seeds] se disperser ■ [clouds, mist, smoke - with sun] se dissiper ; [- with wind] être chassé ■ [gas, chemicals - spread] se propager ; [- vanish] se dissiper ■ [light - with prism] se décomposer.

dispersion [dɪ'spɜ:ʃn] *n* **1.** = **dispersal** **2.** RELIG : **the Dispersion** la Diaspora.

dispirited [dɪ'spɪrɪtɪd] *adj* abattu.

dispiriting [dɪ'spɪrɪtɪŋ] *adj* décourageant.

displace [dɪs'pleɪs] *vt* **1.** [refugees, population] déplacer **2.** [supplant] supplanter, remplacer **3.** CHEM & PHYS [water, air etc] déplacer.

displaced [dɪs'pleɪst] *adj* : **~ person** ADMIN & POL personne *f* déplacée.

displacement [dɪs'pleɪsmənt] *n* **1.** [of people, bone] déplacement *m* **2.** [supplanting] remplacement *m* **3.** NAUT déplacement *m* **4.** PSYCHOL déplacement *m*.

displacement activity *n* PSYCHOL déplacement *m*.

displacement ton *n* NAUT tonne *f*.

display [dɪ'spleɪ] <> *vt* **1.** [gifts, medals, ornaments etc] exposer ■ *pej* exhiber ■ [items in exhibition] mettre en exposition, exposer ■ COMM [goods for sale] mettre en étalage, exposer
2. [notice, poster, exam results] afficher
3. [courage, determination, skill] faire preuve de, montrer ■ [anger, affection, friendship, interest] manifester ■ **to ~ one's ignorance/talent** faire la preuve de son ignorance/talent
4. PRESS & TYPO mettre en vedette
5. COMPUT [subj: screen] afficher ■ [subj: user] visualiser.
<> *vi* [birds, fish etc] faire la parade.
<> *n* **1.** [of gifts, medals, ornaments] exposition *f* ■ COMM [of goods, merchandise] mise *f* en étalage ■ [goods, merchandise] étalage *m*, exposition *f* ■ **to be on ~** être exposé ■ **to put sthg on ~** exposer qqch ■ **to be on public ~** être présenté au public ■ **'for ~ (only)'** [on book] 'exemplaire de démonstration'
2. [of poster, notice etc] affichage *m* ■ **the exam results were on ~** les résultats des examens étaient affichés
3. [of affection, friendship, interest, anger] manifestation *f* ■ [of courage, determination, ignorance etc] démonstration *f* ■ **an air ~** un meeting aérien ■ **a military ~** une parade militaire ■ **a fireworks ~** un feu d'artifice ■ **I have never seen such a ~ of incompetence** je n'ai jamais vu un tel déploiement *OR* étalage d'incompétence ■ **to make a great ~ of sthg** faire parade de qqch
4. COMPUT [screen, device] écran *m* ■ [visual information] affichage *m*, visualisation *f* ■ [of calculator] viseur *m*
5. [by birds, fish] parade *f*.
<> *comp* : **~ advertisement** encadré *m* ■ **~ advertising** publicité *f* par affichage ■ **~ cabinet** *OR* **case** [in shop] étalage *m*, vitrine *f* ; [in home] vitrine *f* ■ **~ copy** [of book] exemplaire *m* de démonstration ■ **~ rack** *OR* **unit** présentoir *m* ■ **~ unit** COMPUT unité *f* de visualisation *OR* d'affichage ■ **~ window** [of calculator] viseur *m*.

displease [dɪs'pli:z] *vt* mécontenter.

displeased [dɪs'pli:zd] *adj* mécontent ■ **to be ~ with** *OR* **at** être mécontent de.

displeasure [dɪs'pleʒər] *n* mécontentement *m*.

disport [dɪ'spɔ:t] *vt fml* **to ~ o.s.** s'ébattre, folâtrer.

disposable [dɪ'spəʊzəbl] ◇ *adj* **1.** [throwaway - lighter, nappy, cup] jetable ; [- bottle] non consigné ; [- wrapping] perdu **2.** [available - money] disponible ▪ **~ income** FIN revenus *mpl* disponibles (après impôts).
◇ *n* **1.** [nappy] couche *f* jetable **2.** [lighter] briquet *m* jetable.

disposal [dɪ'spəʊzl] *n* **1.** [taking away] enlèvement *m* ▪ [of rubbish, by authority] enlèvement *m*, ramassage *m* ▪ [sale] vente *f* ▪ LAW [of property] cession *f* ▪ **she left no instructions for the ~of her property** elle n'a laissé aucune instruction quant à ce qui devait être fait de ses biens ▪ **an ingenious method for the ~ of the body** une idée ingénieuse pour se débarrasser du corps ▶ **waste** *OR* **refuse ~** traitement *m* des ordures **2.** [resolution - of problem, question] résolution *f* ; [- of business] exécution *f*, expédition *f* **3.** *US* [disposal unit] broyeur *m* d'ordures *(dans un évier)* **4.** [availability] **: to be at sb's ~** être à la disposition de qqn ▪ **to have sthg at one's ~** avoir qqch à sa disposition ▪ **to put sthg/sb at sb's ~** mettre qqch/qqn à la disposition de qqn **5.** *fml* [arrangement] disposition *f*, arrangement *m* ▪ [of troops] déploiement *m*.

dispose [dɪ'spəʊz] *vt* **1.** *fml* [arrange - ornaments, books] disposer, arranger ; [- troops, forces] déployer **2.** [incline] **: his moving testimonial ~d the jury to leniency** son témoignage émouvant a disposé le jury à l'indulgence.
➡ **dispose of** *vt insep* **1.** [get rid of - waste, rubbish, problem] se débarrasser de ▪ [by taking away - refuse] enlever, ramasser ▪ [by selling] vendre ▪ [by throwing away] jeter ▪ [workers] congédier, renvoyer ▪ **I can ~ of this old table for you** je peux te débarrasser de cette vieille table **2.** [deal with - problem, question] résoudre, régler ; [- task, matter under discussion] expédier, régler ; [- food] s'envoyer **3.** [have at one's disposal] disposer de, avoir à sa disposition **4.** *inf* [kill - person, animal] liquider ▪ *fig* [team, competitor] se débarrasser de.

disposed [dɪ'spəʊzd] *adj* **: to be ~ to do sthg** être disposé à faire qqch ▪ **to be well/ill ~ towards sb** être bien/mal disposé envers qqn.

disposition [ˌdɪspə'zɪʃn] *n* **1.** [temperament, nature] naturel *m* ▪ **to have** *OR* **to be of a cheerful ~** être d'un naturel enjoué **2.** *fml* [arrangement - of troops, buildings] disposition *f* ; [- of ornaments] disposition *f*, arrangement *m* **3.** [inclination, tendency] disposition *f*.

dispossess [ˌdɪspə'zes] *vt* déposséder ▪ LAW exproprier.

dispossessed [ˌdɪspə'zest] ◇ *npl* **: the ~** les dépossédés *mpl*.
◇ *adj* dépossédé.

disproportion [ˌdɪsprə'pɔ:ʃn] *n* disproportion *f*.

disproportionate [ˌdɪsprə'pɔ:ʃnət] *adj* [excessive] disproportionné ▪ **to be ~ to sthg** être disproportionné à *OR* avec qqch ▪ **we spent a ~ amount of time on it** on a passé plus de temps dessus que cela ne le méritait.

disproportionately [ˌdɪsprə'pɔ:ʃnətlɪ] *adv* d'une façon disproportionnée ▪ **a ~ large sum** une somme disproportionnée.

disprove [ˌdɪs'pru:v] (*pp* **disproved** *OR* **disproven** [-'pru:vn]) *vt* [theory] prouver la fausseté de ▪ **you can't ~ it** tu ne peux pas prouver que ce n'est pas vrai.

disputable [dɪ'spju:təbl] *adj* discutable, contestable.

dispute [dɪ'spju:t] ◇ *vt* **1.** [question - claim, theory, statement etc] contester, mettre en doute ▪ LAW [will] contester ▪ **I would ~ that** je ne suis pas d'accord
2. [debate - subject, motion] discuter, débattre
3. [fight for - territory, championship, title] disputer.
◇ *vi* [argue] se disputer ▪ [debate] discuter, débattre ▪ **to ~ over** *OR* **about sthg** débattre qqch *OR* de qqch.
◇ *n* **1.** [debate] discussion *f*, débat *m* ▪ **there's some ~ about the veracity of his statement** la véracité de sa déclaration fait l'objet de discussions *OR* est sujette à controverse ▪ **your honesty is not in ~** votre honnêteté n'est pas mise en doute *OR* contestée ▪ **the matter is beyond (all) ~** la question est tout à fait incontestable ▪ **open to ~** contestable **2.** [argument - between individuals] dispute *f*, différend *m* ; [- between management and workers] conflit *m* ▪ LAW litige *m* ▪ **these are the main areas of ~** ce sont là les questions les plus conflictuelles *OR* litigieuses ▪ **to be in ~ with sb over sthg** être en conflit avec qqn sur qqch ▪ **to be in ~** [proposals, territory, ownership] faire l'objet d'un conflit ▪ **a border ~** un litige portant sur une question de frontière.

disputed [dɪ'spju:tɪd] *adj* **1.** [decision, fact, claim] contesté **2.** [fought over] **: this is a much ~ territory** ce territoire fait l'objet de beaucoup de conflits.

disqualification [dɪsˌkwɒlɪfɪ'keɪʃn] *n* [from standing for election] exclusion *f* ▪ [from sporting event] disqualification *f* ▪ [from exam] exclusion *f* ▪ LAW [of witness] inhabilité *f*, incapacité *f* ▪ [of testimony] exclusion *f* ▪ **your ~ from driving will last for four years** vous aurez un retrait de permis (de conduire) de quatre ans.

disqualify [ˌdɪs'kwɒlɪfaɪ] (*pret & pp* **disqualified**) *vt* exclure ▪ SPORT disqualifier ▪ SCH exclure ▪ LAW [witness] rendre inhabile *OR* incapable ▪ [testimony] exclure ▪ [juror] empêcher de faire partie du jury ▪ **to ~ sb from driving** retirer son permis (de conduire) *OR* infliger un retrait de permis (de conduire) à qqn ▪ **he's been disqualified for speeding** AUT on lui a retiré son permis *OR* il a eu un retrait de permis pour excès de vitesse.

disquiet [dɪs'kwaɪət] *fml* ◇ *n* inquiétude *f*.
◇ *vt* inquiéter, troubler ▪ **to be ~ed by sthg** être inquiet *OR* s'inquiéter de qqch.

disquieting [dɪs'kwaɪətɪŋ] *adj fml* inquiétant, troublant.

disregard [ˌdɪsrɪ'gɑ:d] ◇ *vt* [person, order, law, rules] ne tenir aucun compte de ▪ [sb's feelings, instructions, remark, warning] ne tenir aucun compte de, négliger ▪ [danger] ne tenir aucun compte de, ignorer.
◇ *n* [for person, feelings] manque *m* de considération ▪ [of order, warning, danger etc] mépris *m* ▪ **with complete ~ for her own safety** au mépris total de sa vie.

disrepair [ˌdɪsrɪ'peəʳ] *n* [of building] mauvais état *m*, délabrement *m* ▪ [of road] mauvais état *m* ▪ **in (a state of) ~** en mauvais état ▪ **to fall into ~** [building] se délabrer ; [road] se dégrader, s'abîmer.

disreputable [dɪs'repjʊtəbl] *adj* [dishonourable - behaviour] honteux ▪ [not respectable - person] de mauvaise réputation, louche ; [- area, club] mal famé, de mauvaise réputation ▪ *hum* [- clothing] miteux.

disreputably [dɪs'repjʊtəblɪ] *adv* [behave] d'une manière honteuse.

disrepute [ˌdɪsrɪ'pju:t] *n* discrédit *m* ▪ **to bring sthg into ~** discréditer qqch ▪ **to fall into ~** [acquire bad reputation] tomber en discrédit ; [become unpopular] tomber en défaveur.

disrespect [ˌdɪsrɪ'spekt] *n* irrespect *m*, irrévérence *f* ▪ **she has a healthy ~ for authority** elle porte un irrespect *OR* une irrévérence salutaire à toute forme d'autorité ▪ **I meant no ~ (to your family)** je ne voulais pas me montrer irrespectueux *OR* irrévérencieux (envers votre famille) ▪ **to show ~ towards sb/sthg** manquer de respect à qqn/qqch ▪ **to treat sb/sthg with ~** traiter qqn/qqch irrespectueusement.

disrespectful [ˌdɪsrɪ'spektfʊl] *adj* irrespectueux, irrévérencieux ▪ **to be ~ to sb** manquer de respect à qqn.

disrobe [ˌdɪs'rəʊb] *fml* ◇ *vi* [judge, priest] enlever sa robe ▪ [undress] se déshabiller.
◇ *vt* [judge, priest] aider à enlever sa robe ▪ [undress] déshabiller.

disrupt [dɪs'rʌpt] *vt* [lesson, meeting, train service] perturber ▪ [conversation] interrompre ▪ [plans] déranger, perturber.

disruption [dɪs'rʌpʃn] *n* [of lesson, meeting, train service, plans] perturbation *f* ▪ [of conversation] interruption *f*.

disruptive [dɪs'rʌptɪv] *adj* [factor, person, behaviour] perturbateur.

diss [dɪs] *vt*△ **to ~ sb** se foutre de qn.

dissatisfaction [ˈdɪsˌsætɪsˈfækʃn] *n* mécontentement *m* ■ **there is growing ~ with his policies** le mécontentement grandit à l'égard de sa politique.

dissatisfied [ˌdɪsˈsætɪsfaɪd] *adj* mécontent ■ **to be ~ with sb/sthg** être mécontent de qqn/qqch.

dissect [dɪˈsekt] *vt* [animal, plant] disséquer ■ *fig* [argument, theory] disséquer ■ [book, report] éplucher.

dissection [dɪˈsekʃn] *n* [of body] dissection *f* ■ *fig* [of argument, theory] dissection *f* ■ [of book, report] épluchage *m*.

dissemble [dɪˈsembl] *lit* ◇ *vi* dissimuler.
◇ *vt* [feelings, motives] dissimuler.

disseminate [dɪˈsemɪneɪt] *vt* [knowledge, ideas] disséminer, propager ■ [information, news] diffuser, propager.

dissemination [dɪˌsemɪˈneɪʃn] *n* [of knowledge, of ideas] propagation *f*, dissémination *f* ■ [of information] diffusion *f*, propagation *f*.

dissension [dɪˈsenʃn] *n* dissension *f*, discorde *f*.

dissent [dɪˈsent] ◇ *vi* **1.** [person] différer ■ [opinion] diverger ■ **to ~ from an opinion** être en désaccord avec une opinion **2.** RELIG être dissident *OR* en dissidence.
◇ *n* **1.** *(U)* [gen] opinion *f* divergente ■ **to voice** *OR* **to express one's ~** exprimer son désaccord **2.** RELIG dissidence *f* **3.** *US* LAW avis *m* contraire *(d'un juge)*.

dissenter [dɪˈsentəʳ] *n* **1.** [gen] dissident *m*, - e *f* **2.** RELIG : **Dissenter** *dissident de l'Église anglicane*.

dissenting [dɪˈsentɪŋ] *adj* [opinion] divergent ■ **mine was the only ~ voice** j'étais le seul à ne pas être d'accord.

dissertation [ˌdɪsəˈteɪʃn] *n* **1.** UNIV *UK* mémoire *m* ■ *US* thèse *f* **2.** *fml* [essay] dissertation *f* ■ [speech] exposé *m*.

disservice [ˌdɪsˈsɜːvɪs] *n* mauvais service *m* ■ **to do sb a ~** faire du tort à qqn, rendre un mauvais service à qqn ■ **to do o.s. a ~** se faire du tort.

dissidence [ˈdɪsɪdəns] *n* [disagreement] désaccord *m* ■ POL dissidence *f*.

dissident [ˈdɪsɪdənt] ◇ *n* dissident *m*, - e *f*.
◇ *adj* dissident.

dissimilar [ˌdɪˈsɪmɪləʳ] *adj* différent ■ **they are not ~** ils se ressemblent ■ **the situation now is not ~ to what was going on 20 years ago** la situation actuelle n'est pas sans rappeler ce qui s'est passé il y a 20 ans.

dissimilarity [ˌdɪsɪmɪˈlærətɪ] (*pl* **dissimilarities**) *n* différence *f*.

dissimulate [dɪˈsɪmjʊleɪt] *fml* ◇ *vt* dissimuler, cacher.
◇ *vi* dissimuler.

dissimulation [dɪˌsɪmjʊˈleɪʃn] *n fml* dissimulation *f*.

dissipate [ˈdɪsɪpeɪt] ◇ *vt* [disperse - cloud, fears] dissiper ■ [waste - fortune] dilapider, gaspiller ; [- energies] disperser, gaspiller ■ PHYS [heat, energy] dissiper.
◇ *vi* [cloud, crowd] se disperser ■ [fears, hopes] s'évanouir ■ PHYS [energy] se dissiper.

dissipated [ˈdɪsɪpeɪtɪd] *adj* [person] débauché ■ [habit, life] de débauche ■ [society] décadent.

dissipation [ˌdɪsɪˈpeɪʃn] *n* **1.** [of cloud, fears, hopes etc] dissipation *f* ■ [of fortune] dilapidation *f* ■ [of energies] dispersion *f*, gaspillage *m* ■ PHYS [of energy, heat] dissipation *f* **2.** [debauchery] débauche *f*.

dissociate [dɪˈsəʊʃɪeɪt] ◇ *vt* **1.** [gen] dissocier, séparer ■ **to ~ o.s. from sthg** se dissocier *OR* désolidariser de qqch **2.** CHEM dissocier.
◇ *vi* CHEM [subj: chemist] opérer une dissociation ■ [subj: molecules] se dissocier.

dissolute [ˈdɪsəluːt] *adj* [person] débauché ■ [life] de débauche, dissolu *lit*.

dissoluteness [ˈdɪsəluːtnɪs] *n* débauche *f*.

dissolution [ˌdɪsəˈluːʃn] *n* **1.** [gen] dissolution *f* **2.** *US* LAW [divorce] divorce *m*.

dissolvable [dɪˈzɒlvəbl] *adj* soluble.

dissolve [dɪˈzɒlv] ◇ *vt* **1.** [salt, sugar] dissoudre **2.** [empire, marriage, Parliament] dissoudre.
◇ *vi* **1.** [salt, sugar] se dissoudre ■ *fig* [fear, hopes] s'évanouir, s'envoler ■ [apparition] s'évanouir ■ [crowd] se disperser ■ [clouds] disparaître ■ **to ~ into tears** fondre en larmes ■ **to ~ into laughter** être pris de rire **2.** [marriage, Parliament] être dissout ■ [empire] se dissoudre **3.** CIN & TV faire un fondu enchaîné.
◇ *n* CIN & TV fondu enchaîné *m*.

dissonance [ˈdɪsənəns] *n* MUS dissonance *f* ■ *fig* discordance *f*.

dissonant [ˈdɪsənənt] *adj* MUS dissonant ■ *fig* [colours, opinions] discordant.

dissuade [dɪˈsweɪd] *vt* [person] dissuader ■ **to ~ sb from doing sthg** dissuader qqn de faire qqch ■ **to ~ sb from sthg** détourner qqn de qqch.

dissuasive [dɪˈsweɪsɪv] *adj* [person, effect] dissuasif.

distaff [ˈdɪstɑːf] *n* [for spinning] quenouille *f* ■ **on the ~ side** *fig* du côté maternel.

distance [ˈdɪstəns] ◇ *n* **1.** [between two places] distance *f* ■ **at a ~ of 50 metres** à (une distance de) 50 mètres ■ **within walking/cycling ~ from the station** à quelques minutes de marche/en vélo de la gare ■ **is it within walking ~?** peut-on y aller à pied? ■ **it's some** *OR* **quite a** *OR* **a good ~ from here** c'est assez loin d'ici ■ **a short ~ away** tout près ■ **it's no ~ (at all)** c'est tout près *OR* à deux pas ■ **we covered the ~ in ten hours** nous avons fait le trajet en dix heures ■ **to keep at a safe ~ (from)** se tenir à une distance prudente (de) ■ *fig* **to keep sb at a ~** tenir qqn à distance (respectueuse) ■ **to keep one's ~ (from sb)** garder ses distances (par rapport à qqn) ➊ **to go the ~** [boxer, political campaigner] tenir la distance ■ **the fight went the ~** le combat est allé jusqu'à la limite
2. [distant point, place] : **to see/to hear sthg in the ~** voir/entendre qqch au loin ■ **in the middle ~** au second plan ■ **to see sthg from a ~** voir qqch de loin ■ **you can't see it from** *OR* **at this ~** on ne peut pas le voir à cette distance ■ **to admire sb from** *OR* **at a ~** *fig* admirer qqn de loin
3. [separation in time] : **at a ~ of 200 years, it's very difficult to know** 200 ans plus tard, il est très difficile de savoir
4. *fig* [gap] : **there's a great ~ between us** il y a un grand fossé entre nous
5. [aloofness, reserve] froideur *f*.
◇ *comp* : **~ learning** *OR* **teaching** enseignement *m* à distance ■ **~ race** SPORT épreuve *f* de fond ■ **~ runner** SPORT coureur *m*, - euse *f* de fond.
◇ *vt* distancer ■ **to ~ o.s. (from sb/sthg)** *fig* prendre ses distances (par rapport à qqn/qqch).

distant [ˈdɪstənt] ◇ *adj* **1.** [faraway - country, galaxy, place] lointain, éloigné ■ **the ~ sound of the sea** le bruit de la mer au loin **2.** [in past - times] lointain, reculé ; [- memory] lointain ■ **in the (dim and) ~ past** il y a bien *OR* très longtemps, dans le temps **3.** [in future - prospect] lointain ■ **in the ~ future** dans un avenir lointain ■ **in the not too ~ future** dans un avenir proche, prochainement **4.** [relation] éloigné ■ [resemblance] vague **5.** [remote - person, look] distant ■ [aloof] froid.
◇ *adv* : **three miles ~ from here** à trois miles d'ici ■ **not far ~** pas très loin.

distantly [ˈdɪstəntlɪ] *adv* **1.** [in the distance] au loin **2.** [resemble] vaguement ■ **to be ~ related** [people] avoir un lien de parenté éloigné ; [ideas, concepts etc] avoir un rapport éloigné **3.** [speak, behave, look] froidement, d'un air distant *OR* froid.

distaste [dɪsˈteɪst] *n* dégoût *m*, répugnance *f*.

distasteful [dɪsˈteɪstfʊl] *adj* [unpleasant - task] désagréable ■ [in bad taste - joke, remark etc] de mauvais goût ■ **to be ~ to sb** déplaire à qqn.

distastefully [dɪsˈteɪstfʊlɪ] *adv* [with repugnance - look] d'un air dégoûté ■ [with bad taste - presented, portrayed] avec mauvais goût.

Dist. Atty *written abbr of* **district attorney**.

distemper [dɪ'stempəʳ] ◇ *n* **1.** [paint] détrempe *f* **2.** VET maladie *f* de Carré.
◇ *vt* peindre à la *OR* en détrempe.

distend [dɪ'stend] ◇ *vt* gonfler.
◇ *vi* [stomach] se ballonner, se gonfler ▪ [sails] se gonfler.

distended [dɪ'stendɪd] *adj* gonflé ▪ [stomach] gonflé, ballonné.

distil *UK*, **distill** *US* [dɪ'stɪl] (*pret & pp* **distilled**, *cont* **distilling**) ◇ *vt liter & fig* distiller.
◇ *vi* se distiller.

distillation [ˌdɪstɪ'leɪʃn] *n liter & fig* distillation *f*.

distiller [dɪ'stɪləʳ] *n* distillateur *m*.

distillery [dɪ'stɪlərɪ] (*pl* **distilleries**) *n* distillerie *f*.

distinct [dɪ'stɪŋkt] *adj* **1.** [different] distinct ▪ **to be ~ from** se distinguer de ▪ **the two poems are quite ~ from each other** les deux poèmes sont tout à fait différents l'un de l'autre **2.** [clear - memory] clair, net ; [- voice, announcement] distinct **3.** [decided, evident - accent] prononcé ; [- preference] marqué ; [- lack of respect, interest] évident ; [- likeness] clair, net, prononcé ; [- advantage, improvement] net ▪ **she had a ~ feeling that something would go wrong** elle avait le sentiment très net que quelque chose allait mal tourner ▪ **I have the ~ impression you're trying to avoid me** j'ai la nette impression que tu essaies de m'éviter ▪ **there's a ~ smell of smoke in here** cela sent vraiment la fumée ici ▪ **a ~ possibility** une forte possibilité.
◆ **as distinct from** *prep phr* par opposition à.

distinction [dɪ'stɪŋkʃn] *n* **1.** [difference] distinction *f* ▪ **to make** *OR* **to draw a ~ between two things** faire *OR* établir une distinction entre deux choses **2.** [excellence] distinction *f* ▪ **a writer/artist of great ~** un écrivain/artiste très réputé ▪ **to win** *OR* **to gain ~ (as)** se distinguer (en tant que) ▪ **she has the ~ of being the only woman to become Prime Minister** elle se distingue pour être la seule femme à avoir été nommée Premier ministre **3.** SCH & UNIV [mark] mention *f* ▪ **he got a ~ in maths** il a été reçu en maths avec mention **4.** [honour, award] honneur *m*.

distinctive [dɪ'stɪŋktɪv] *adj* [colour, feature] distinctif ▪ **her car is quite ~** sa voiture se remarque facilement.

distinctively [dɪ'stɪŋktɪvlɪ] *adv* [coloured] de manière distinctive.

distinctly [dɪ'stɪŋktlɪ] *adv* **1.** [clearly - speak, hear] distinctement, clairement ▪ [remember] clairement ▪ **I ~ told you not to do that** je t'ai bien dit de ne pas faire cela **2.** [very] vraiment, franchement.

distinguish [dɪ'stɪŋgwɪʃ] ◇ *vt* **1.** [set apart] distinguer ▪ **to ~ o.s.** se distinguer ▪ **to ~ sthg from sthg** distinguer qqch de qqch **2.** [tell apart] distinguer **3.** [discern] distinguer.
◇ *vi* faire *OR* établir une distinction ▪ **to ~ between two things/people** faire la distinction entre deux choses/personnes.

distinguishable [dɪ'stɪŋgwɪʃəbl] *adj* **1.** [visible] visible **2.** [recognizable] reconnaissable ▪ **to be easily ~ from** se distinguer facilement de, être facile à distinguer de ▪ **the male is ~ by his red legs** le mâle est reconnaissable à *OR* se distingue par ses pattes rouges.

distinguished [dɪ'stɪŋgwɪʃt] *adj* **1.** [eminent] distingué **2.** [refined - manners, voice] distingué ▪ **~-looking** distingué.

distinguishing [dɪ'stɪŋgwɪʃɪŋ] *adj* [feature, mark, characteristic etc] distinctif ▪ **~ features** [on passport] signes *mpl* particuliers.

distort [dɪ'stɔːt] ◇ *vt* **1.** [face, image, structure etc] déformer ▪ *fig* [facts, truth] déformer, dénaturer ▪ [judgment] fausser **2.** ELECTRON, RADIO & TV déformer.
◇ *vi* [face, structure, sound] se déformer.

distorted [dɪ'stɔːtɪd] *adj* [face, limbs] déformé ▪ *fig* [facts, truth, account] déformé, dénaturé ▪ [view of life] déformé, faussé ▪ [judgment] faussé.

distortion [dɪ'stɔːʃn] *n* **1.** *liter & fig* déformation *f* **2.** ELECTRON & RADIO distorsion *f* ▪ TV déformation *f*.

distract [dɪ'strækt] *vt* **1.** [break concentration of] distraire ▪ [disturb] déranger ▪ **to ~ sb from his/her objective** détourner qqn de son but ▪ **to ~ sb** *OR* **sb's attention** [accidentally] distraire l'attention de qqn ; [on purpose] détourner l'attention de qqn **2.** [amuse] distraire.

distracted [dɪ'stræktɪd] *adj* **1.** [with thoughts elsewhere] distrait **2.** [upset] affolé, bouleversé ▪ **~ with worry/with grief** fou d'inquiétude/de chagrin.

distracting [dɪ'stræktɪŋ] *adj* **1.** [disruptive] gênant ▪ **I find it ~** ça m'empêche de me concentrer ▪ **it's very ~ having so many people in the office** c'est très difficile de se concentrer (sur son travail) avec autant de gens dans le bureau **2.** [amusing] distrayant.

distraction [dɪ'strækʃn] *n* **1.** [interruption - of attention, from objective] distraction *f* ▪ **taking on another job now would just be an unwelcome ~ for us** entreprendre un nouveau travail maintenant nous détournerait de notre objet **2.** [amusement] distraction *f* **3.** [anxiety] affolement *m* ▪ [absent-mindedness] distraction *f* **4.** [madness] affolement *m* ▪ **to drive sb to ~** rendre qqn fou ▪ **to love sb to ~** aimer qqn éperdument *OR* à la folie.

distraught [dɪ'strɔːt] *adj* [with worry] angoissé, fou d'angoisse ▪ [after death] fou *OR* éperdu de douleur, désespéré ▪ **to be ~ with grief** être fou de douleur.

distress [dɪ'stres] ◇ *n* **1.** [suffering - mental] angoisse *f* ; [- physical] souffrance *f* ▪ [hardship] détresse *f* ▪ **to cause sb ~** causer du tourment à qqn ▪ **to be in ~** [horse, athlete] souffrir ; [mentally] être angoissé ; [ship] être en détresse *OR* perdition ; [aircraft] être en détresse ▪ **to be in financial ~** avoir de sérieux problèmes financiers **2.** LAW saisie *f*.
◇ *vt* **1.** [upset] faire de la peine à, tourmenter ▪ **he was ~ed by the animal's suffering** les souffrances de la bête lui faisaient de la peine **2.** [furniture] vieillir.

distressed [dɪ'strest] *adj* **1.** [mentally] tourmenté ▪ [very sorry] affligé ▪ [physically] souffrant ▪ [financially] dans le besoin ▪ **to be ~ by** *OR* **about sthg** être affligé par qqch ▪ **they are in ~ circumstances** *euph* ils sont dans le besoin **2.** [furniture, leather, clothing] vieilli.

distressing [dɪ'stresɪŋ] *adj* pénible.

distress signal *n* signal *m* de détresse.

distribute [dɪ'strɪbjuːt] *vt* **1.** [hand out - money, leaflets, gifts etc] distribuer **2.** [share out, allocate - wealth, weight] répartir ; [- paint] répandre **3.** CIN & COMM [supply] distribuer.

distribution [ˌdɪstrɪ'bjuːʃn] ◇ *n* **1.** [of leaflets, money etc] distribution *f* **2.** CIN & COMM [delivery, supply] distribution *f* ▪ **to have a wide ~** COMM être largement distribué ▪ [of books] diffusion *f* **3.** [of wealth] répartition *f*, distribution *f* ▪ [of load] répartition *f*.
◇ *comp* COMM [channel, network] de distribution ▪ **~ rights** CIN droits *mpl* de distribution.

distributor [dɪ'strɪbjʊtəʳ] *n* **1.** CIN & COMM distributeur *m* **2.** AUT distributeur *m* ▪ **~ cap** tête *f* de Delco® *OR* d'allumeur.

district ['dɪstrɪkt] ◇ *n* [of country] région *f* ▪ [of town] quartier *m* ▪ [administrative area - of country] district *m* ; [- of city] arrondissement *m* ▪ [surrounding area] région *f* ▪ **the District of Columbia** le district fédéral de Columbia.
◇ *comp* : **~ manager** COMM directeur *m* régional, directrice *f* régionale.

district attorney *n* [in US] procureur *mf* de la République.

district council *n* [in UK] conseil *m* municipal.

district court *n* [in US] ≃ tribunal *m* d'instance (fédéral).

district nurse *n UK* infirmière *f* visiteuse.

distrust [dɪs'trʌst] ◇ *vt* se méfier de.

◇ *n* méfiance *f* ■ **my ~ of her** la méfiance que j'éprouve pour elle *OR* à son égard ■ **to have a deep ~ of sb/sthg** éprouver une profonde méfiance à l'égard de qqn/qqch.

distrustful [dɪs'trʌstfʊl] *adj* méfiant ■ **to be deeply ~ of** éprouver une extrême méfiance pour *OR* à l'égard de.

disturb [dɪ'stɜ:b] *vt* **1.** [interrupt - person] déranger ; [- silence, sleep] troubler ■ **'(please) do not ~'** '(prière de) ne pas déranger' ■ **to ~ the peace** LAW troubler l'ordre public **2.** [distress, upset] troubler, perturber ■ [alarm] inquiéter **3.** [alter condition of - water] troubler ; [- mud, sediment] agiter, remuer ; [- papers] déranger.

disturbance [dɪ'stɜ:bəns] *n* **1.** [interruption, disruption] dérangement *m* **2.** POL : **~s** [unrest] troubles *mpl*, émeute *f* **3.** [noise] bruit *m*, vacarme *m* ■ **to cause a ~** LAW troubler l'ordre public ■ **you're creating a ~** vous dérangez tout le monde ■ **police were called to a ~ in the early hours of the morning** la police a été appelée au petit matin pour mettre fin à un tapage nocturne **4.** [distress, alarm] trouble *m*, perturbation *f*.

disturbed [dɪ'stɜ:bd] *adj* **1.** [distressed, upset] troublé, perturbé ■ [alarmed] inquiet, - ète *f* ■ **to be ~ at** *OR* **by sthg** être troublé par *OR* perturbé par *OR* inquiet de qqch ■ **mentally ~** mentalement dérangé **2.** [interrupted - sleep] troublé.

disturbing [dɪ'stɜ:bɪŋ] *adj* [alarming] inquiétant ■ [distressing, upsetting] troublant, perturbant ■ **some viewers may find the programme ~** cette émission pourrait troubler *OR* perturber certains spectateurs.

disturbingly [dɪ'stɜ:bɪŋlɪ] *adv* : **the level of pollution is ~ high** la pollution a atteint un niveau inquiétant.

disunited [,dɪsju:'naɪtɪd] *adj* désuni.

disunity [,dɪs'ju:nətɪ] *n* désunion *f*.

disuse [,dɪs'ju:s] *n* : **to fall into ~** [word, custom, law] tomber en désuétude.

disused [,dɪs'ju:zd] *adj* [building, mine] abandonné, désaffecté.

ditch [dɪtʃ] ◇ *n* [by roadside] fossé *m* ■ [for irrigation, drainage] rigole *f* ■ **he drove the car into the ~** il est tombé dans le fossé avec la voiture.
◇ *vt inf* **1.** *inf* [abandon - car] abandonner ; [- plan, idea] abandonner, laisser tomber ; [- boyfriend, girlfriend] plaquer, laisser tomber ■ [throw out] se débarrasser de **2.** AERON : **to ~ a plane** faire un amerrissage forcé.
◇ *vi* **1.** AERON faire un amerrissage forcé **2.** AGRIC creuser un fossé.

ditchwater ['dɪtʃ,wɔ:tər] *n phr* **to be as dull as ~** *inf* être ennuyeux comme la pluie.

dither ['dɪðər] *inf* ◇ *vi* [be indecisive] hésiter, se tâter ■ **stop ~ing (about)** [decide] décide-toi ; [make a start] arrête de tourner en rond.
◇ *n* : **to be in a ~** hésiter, se tâter ■ **he was in** *OR* **all of a ~ about his exams** il était dans tous ses états à cause de ses examens.

ditherer ['dɪðərər] *n inf* **he's such a terrible ~** il est toujours à hésiter sur tout.

dithery ['dɪðərɪ] *adj inf* **1.** [indecisive] hésitant, indécis **2.** [agitated] nerveux, agité.

ditsy ['dɪtsɪ] (*comp* **ditsier**, *superl* **ditsiest**) *adj US inf* écervelé.

ditto ['dɪtəʊ] ◇ *adv inf* **I feel like a drink** - **~** j'ai bien envie de prendre un verre - idem ■ **I don't like her** - **~** je ne l'aime pas - moi non plus.
◇ *comp* : **~ mark** guillemets *mpl* itératifs, signes *mpl* d'itération.

ditty ['dɪtɪ] (*pl* **ditties**) *n hum* chanson *f*.

diuretic [,daɪjʊ'retɪk] ◇ *adj* diurétique.
◇ *n* diurétique *m*.

diva ['di:və] *n* diva *f*.

divan [dɪ'væn] *n* [couch] divan *m* ■ **~ (bed)** divan-lit *m*.

dive [daɪv] (*UK pret & pp* **dived**) (*US pret* **dove** [dəʊv] *OR* **dived**, *pp* **dived**) ◇ *vi* **1.** [person, bird, submarine] plonger ■ [aircraft] plonger, piquer, descendre en piqué ■ **to ~ for clams/pearls** pêcher la palourde/des perles *(en plongée)* ■ **she ~d off the side of the boat** elle a plongé depuis le bord du bateau **2.** [as sport] faire de la plongée **3.** *inf* [rush] : **they ~d for the exit** ils se sont précipités *OR* ils ont foncé vers la sortie ■ **she ~d out of sight** elle s'est cachée précipitamment ■ **to ~ under the table** plonger *OR* se jeter sous la table.
◇ *n* **1.** [of swimmer, bird, submarine] plongeon *m* ■ [by aircraft] piqué *m* ■ **to go into a ~** [aircraft] plonger, piquer, descendre en piqué **2.** *inf* [sudden movement] : **to make a ~ for the exit** se précipiter vers la sortie ■ **to make a ~ for shelter** se précipiter pour se mettre à l'abri **3.** *inf pej* [bar, café etc] bouge *m*.

◆ **dive in** *vi insep* **1.** [swimmer] plonger **2.** *inf* **~ in!** [eat] attaquez!

dive-bomb *vt* [subj: plane] bombarder *OR* attaquer en piqué ■ [subj: bird] attaquer en piqué.

diver ['daɪvər] *n* **1.** [from diving board, underwater] plongeur *m*, - euse *f* ■ [deep-sea] scaphandrier *m* ■ **pearl/clam ~** pêcheur *m*, - euse *f* de perles/de palourdes *(en plongée)* **2.** [bird] plongeur *m*.

diverge [daɪ'vɜ:dʒ] *vi* [paths] se séparer, diverger ■ *fig* [opinions] diverger.

divergence [daɪ'vɜ:dʒəns] *n* [of paths] séparation *f*, divergence *f* ■ *fig* [of opinions] divergence *f*.

divergent [daɪ'vɜ:dʒənt] *adj* [opinions] divergent.

diverse [daɪ'vɜ:s] *adj* divers.

diversification [daɪ,vɜ:sɪfɪ'keɪʃn] *n* diversification *f* ■ **the company's recent ~ into cosmetics** la diversification qu'a récemment entreprise la société en pénétrant le marché des cosmétiques.

diversify [daɪ'vɜ:sɪfaɪ] (*pret & pp* **diversified**) ◇ *vi* [company] se diversifier ■ **to ~ into a new market** se diversifier en pénétrant un nouveau marché ■ **to ~ into a new product** se diversifier en fabriquant un nouveau produit.
◇ *vt* diversifier.

diversion [daɪ'vɜ:ʃn] *n* **1.** [of traffic] déviation *f* ■ [of river] dérivation *f*, détournement *m* **2.** [distraction] diversion *f* ■ **to create a ~** [distract attention] faire (une) diversion ; MIL opérer une diversion **3.** [amusement] distraction *f*.

diversionary [daɪ'vɜ:ʃnrɪ] *adj* [remark, proposal] destiné à faire diversion ■ **~ tactics** tactique *f* de diversion.

diversity [daɪ'vɜ:sətɪ] *n* diversité *f*.

divert [daɪ'vɜ:t] *vt* **1.** [reroute - traffic] dévier ; [- train, plane, ship] dévier (la route de) ; [- river, attention, conversation, blow] détourner ■ **the plane was ~ed to London** l'avion a été dévié *OR* détourné sur Londres **2.** [money] transférer ■ [illegally] détourner **3.** [amuse] distraire.

diverting [daɪ'vɜ:tɪŋ] *adj* divertissant.

divest [daɪ'vest] *vt fml* **1.** [take away from] priver ■ **to ~ sb of sthg** priver qqn de qqch **2.** [rid] : **to ~ o.s. of** [opinion, belief] se défaire de ; [coat] enlever ; [luggage] se débarrasser de.

divestiture [daɪ'vestɪtʃər] *n US* désinvestissement *m*.

divestment [daɪ'vestmənt] *n US* désinvestissement *m*.

divide [dɪ'vaɪd] ◇ *vt* **1.** [split up - territory, property, work] diviser ■ [share out] partager, répartir ■ **to ~ sthg in** *OR* **into two** couper *OR* diviser qqch en deux ■ **she ~d the cake equally among the children** elle a partagé le gâteau en parts égales entre les enfants ■ **they ~d the work between them** ils se sont partagé *OR* réparti le travail ■ **he ~s his time between the office and home** il partage son temps entre le bureau et la maison **2.** [separate] séparer ■ **the Berlin Wall used to ~ East and West** le mur de Berlin séparait l'Est de l'Ouest **3.** MATHS diviser ■ **to ~ 10 by 2** diviser 10 par 2 **4.** [disunite - family, party] diviser **5.** *UK* POL : **to ~ the House** faire voter la Chambre.
◇ *vi* **1.** [cells, group of people, novel] se diviser ■ **a policy of ~ and rule** POL une politique consistant à diviser pour régner ■ **the class ~d into groups** la classe s'est divisée *OR* répartie en

groupes **2.** [river, road] se séparer **3.** MATHS diviser ▪ **we're learning to ~** nous apprenons à faire des divisions ▪ **10 ~s by 2** 10 est divisible par 2, 10 est un multiple de 2 **4.** *UK* POL : **the House ~d on the question** la Chambre a voté sur la question.
◇ *n* **1.** [gap] fossé *m* ▪ **the North-South ~** la division Nord-Sud **2.** *US* GEOG [watershed] ligne *f* de partage des eaux ▪ **the Great** *OR* **Continental Divide** ligne de partage des eaux des Rocheuses ▪ **to cross the Great Divide** [die] passer de vie à trépas.
◆ **divide off** *vt sep* séparer ▪ **to ~ sthg off from sthg** séparer qqch de qqch.
◆ **divide out** *vt sep* partager, répartir ▪ **to ~ sthg out between** *OR* **among people** partager qqch entre des gens.
◆ **divide up** ◇ *vi insep* = **divide** *(vi sense 1)*.
◇ *vt sep* = **divide** *(vt sense 1)*.

divided [dɪ'vaɪdɪd] *adj* **1.** [property, territory] divisé ▪ BOT découpé ▪ **~ highway** *US* route *f* à quatre voies ▪ **~ skirt** jupe-culotte *f* **2.** [disunited - family, party] divisé ▪ **opinion is ~ on the matter** les avis sont partagés sur ce problème ▪ **to have ~ loyalties** être déchiré.

dividend ['dɪvɪdend] *n* FIN & MATHS dividende *m* ▪ **to pay a ~** FIN [company] verser un dividende ; [shares] rapporter un dividende ▪ **to pay ~s** *fig* porter ses fruits.

divider [dɪ'vaɪdəʳ] *n* [in room] meuble *m* de séparation.
◆ **dividers** *npl* MATHS : **(a pair of) ~s** un compas à pointes sèches.

dividing [dɪ'vaɪdɪŋ] *adj* [fence, wall] de séparation ▪ **~ line** *liter* limite *f* ; *fig* distinction *f*.

divination [,dɪvɪ'neɪʃn] *n* divination *f*.

divine [dɪ'vaɪn] ◇ *adj* **1.** RELIG divin ▪ **the ~ right of kings** HIST la monarchie de droit divin ▪ **'The Divine Comedy'** *Dante* 'la Divine Comédie' **2.** *inf* [delightful] divin.
◇ *n* [priest] théologien *m*.
◇ *vt* **1.** *lit* [foretell - the future] présager, prédire **2.** *lit* [conjecture, guess] deviner **3.** *lit* [perceive by intuition] pressentir **4.** [locate - water, metal] détecter *OR* découvrir par la radiesthésie.
◇ *vi* : **to ~ for water** détecter *OR* découvrir de l'eau par la radiesthésie.

divinely [dɪ'vaɪnlɪ] *adv* divinement.

diving ['daɪvɪŋ] *n* [underwater] plongée *f* sous-marine ▪ [from board] plongeon *m*.

diving bell *n* cloche *f* à plongeur *OR* de plongée.

diving board *n* plongeoir *m*.

diving suit *n* scaphandre *m*.

divining rod [dɪ'vaɪnɪŋ-] *n* baguette *f* de sourcier.

divinity [dɪ'vɪnətɪ] (*pl* **divinities**) ◇ *n* **1.** [quality, state] divinité *f* **2.** [god, goddess] divinité *f* ▪ **the Divinity** la Divinité **3.** [theology] théologie *f* ▪ SCH instruction *f* religieuse ▪ **Faculty/Doctor of Divinity** faculté *f* de/docteur *m* en théologie.
◇ *comp* : **~ student** étudiant *m*, -e *f* en théologie.

divisible [dɪ'vɪzəbl] *adj* divisible ▪ **~ by** divisible par.

division [dɪ'vɪʒn] *n* **1.** [act, state] division *f* ▪ [sharing out] partage *m* ▪ **the ~ of labour** la division du travail **2.** [section - of company, organization] division *f* ; [- of scale, thermometer] graduation *f* ▪ [compartment - in box, bag] compartiment *m* **3.** BIOL, MIL & SPORT division *f* **4.** MATHS division *f* **5.** [that which separates] division *f* ▪ [dividing line] division *f*, scission *f* ▪ [in room] cloison *f* ▪ **class ~s** divisions entre les classes, divisions sociales **6.** [dissension] division *f* **7.** *UK* POL *vote officiel à la Chambre des communes (pour lequel les députés se répartissent dans les deux "division lobbies")* ▪ **to call for a ~ on sthg** demander que qqch soit soumis à un vote.

divisional [dɪ'vɪʒənl] *adj* de la division, de division ▪ **the ~ manager** le directeur de la division ▪ **there were six ~ managers there** il y avait six directeurs de division.

division sign *n* MATHS symbole *m* de division.

divisive [dɪ'vaɪsɪv] *adj* [policy, issue] qui crée des divisions.

divisiveness [dɪ'vaɪsɪvnɪs] *n* : **the ~ of this policy is evident to everyone** il apparaît clairement à tout le monde que cette politique crée des *OR* est source de divisions.

divisor [dɪ'vaɪzəʳ] *n* MATHS diviseur *m*.

divorce [dɪ'vɔːs] ◇ *n* **1.** LAW divorce *m* ▪ **I want a ~** je veux divorcer, je veux le divorce ▪ **he asked his wife for a ~** il a demandé à sa femme de divorcer, il a demandé le divorce à sa femme ▪ **her first marriage ended in ~** son premier mariage s'est soldé par un divorce ▪ **to file** *OR* **to sue for (a) ~** demander le divorce ▪ **to get** *OR* **to obtain a ~** obtenir le divorce ▪ **Mary's getting a ~ from John** Mary divorce d'avec John ▪ **they're getting a ~** ils divorcent **2.** *fig* séparation *f*, divorce *m*.
◇ *comp* [case, proceedings] de divorce ▪ **~ court** *chambre spécialisée dans les affaires familiales au tribunal de grande instance* ▪ **~ lawyer** avocat *m* spécialisé dans les affaires *OR* cas de divorce.
◇ *vt* **1.** LAW [subj: husband, wife] divorcer d'avec ▪ [subj: judge] prononcer le divorce de ▪ **they got ~d a few years ago** ils ont divorcé il y a quelques années **2.** *fig* séparer ▪ **to ~ sthg from sthg** séparer qqch de qqch.
◇ *vi* divorcer.

divorcé [dɪ'vɔːseɪ] *n* divorcé *m*.

divorced [dɪ'vɔːst] *adj* **1.** LAW divorcé ▪ **a ~ woman** une (femme) divorcée **2.** *fig* **to be ~ from reality** [person] être coupé de la réalité, ne pas avoir les pieds sur terre ; [suggestion, plan] être irréaliste.

divorcée [dɪvɔː'siː] *n* divorcée *f*.

divot ['dɪvət] *n* motte *f* de terre.

divulge [daɪ'vʌldʒ] *vt* divulguer, révéler.

Dixie ['dɪksɪ] *pr n* *US* *inf* le Sud *(terme désignant le sud-est des États-Unis, particulièrement les anciens États esclavagistes)*.

DIY *n* & *comp* = **do-it-yourself**.

dizzily ['dɪzɪlɪ] *adv* **1.** [walk] avec une sensation de vertige **2.** [behave] étourdiment.

dizziness ['dɪzɪnɪs] *n (U)* vertiges *mpl*.

dizzy ['dɪzɪ] (*comp* **dizzier**, *superl* **dizziest**) *adj* **1.** [giddy] : **to feel ~** avoir le vertige, avoir la tête qui tourne ▪ **it makes me (feel) ~** cela me donne le vertige ▪ **~ spell** *OR* **turn** éblouissement *m* **2.** [height, speed] vertigineux ▪ **the ~ heights of fame** les sommets grisants de la célébrité *OR* gloire **3.** *inf* [scatterbrained] étourdi.

DJ *n* **1.** (*abbrev of* **disk jockey**) DJ *m* **2.** (*abbrev of* **dinner jacket**) smoking *m*.

Djerba ['dʒɜːbə] *pr n* Djerba ▪ **in ~** à Djerba.

Djibouti [dʒɪ'buːtɪ] *pr n* (République *f* de)Djibouti ▪ **in ~** à Djibouti.

Djibouti City *pr n* Djibouti ▪ **in ~** à Djibouti.

dl (*written abbrev of* **decilitre**) dl.

DLit(t) [diː'lɪt] *n* **1.** (*abbrev of* **Doctor of Literature**) docteur *m* ès lettres **2.** (*abbrev of* **Doctor of Letters**) docteur *m* ès lettres.

dm (*written abbrev of* **decimetre**) dm.

DM (*written abbrev of* **Deutsche Mark**) DM.

DMA *n* = **direct memory access**.

DMus [,diː'mjuːz] (*abbrev of* **Doctor of Music**) *n* docteur *m* en musique.

DNA (*abbrev of* **deoxyribonucleic acid**) *n* ADN *m* ▪ **~ profiling** séquençage *m* de l'ADN.

DNS [,diːen'es] (*abbrev of* **Domain Name System**) *n* COMPUT DNS.

do[1] [duː] (*pres (3rd sing)* **does** [dʌz], *pret* **did** [dɪd], *pp* **done** [dʌn], *cont* **doing** ['duːɪŋ]), *(negative forms* **do not** *frequently shortened to* **don't** [dəʊnt], **does not** *frequently shortened to* doesn't ['dʌznt], **did not** *frequently shortened to* **didn't** [dɪdnt]*)* ◇ *aux vb* **1.** [in questions] : **do you know her?** est-ce que tu la connais?, la connais-tu? ▪ [in exclamations] : **do I know London!** si je connais Londres? ▪ **boy, do I hate paperwork!** nom d'un chien, qu'est-ce que je peux avoir horreur des paperasses!

2. [in tag questions] : **he takes you out a lot, doesn't he?** il te sort souvent, n'est-ce pas *or* hein? ■ **he doesn't take you out very often, does he?** il ne te sort pas souvent, n'est-ce pas *or* hein? ■ **so you want to be an actress, do you?** alors tu veux devenir actrice? ■ **you didn't sign it, did you?** [disbelief, horror] tu ne l'as pas signé, quand même? ■ **look, we don't want any trouble, do we?** [encouraging, threatening] écoute, nous ne voulons pas d'histoires, hein?
3. [with the negative] : **I don't believe you** je ne te crois pas
4. [for emphasis] : **do you mind if I smoke? – yes I DO mind** cela vous dérange-t-il que je fume? – justement, oui, ça me dérange ■ **I DID tell you** [refuting sb's denial] mais si, je te l'ai dit, bien sûr que je te l'ai dit ; [emphasizing earlier warning] je te l'avais bien dit ■ **if you DO decide to buy it** si tu décides finalement de l'acheter ■ **DO sit down** asseyez-vous donc ■ **DO let us know how your mother is** surtout dites-nous comment va votre mère ■ **DO stop crying** mais arrête de pleurer, enfin
5. [elliptically] : **you know as much as/more than I do** tu en sais autant que/plus que moi ■ **so do I/does she** moi/elle aussi ■ **neither do I/does she** moi/elle non plus ■ **I'll talk to her about it – please do/don't!** je lui en parlerai – oh, oui/non s'il vous plaît! ■ **don't, you'll make me blush!** arrête, tu vas me faire rougir! ■ **will you tell her? – I may do** (le) lui diras-tu? – peut-être ■ **I may come to Paris next month – let me know if you do** il se peut que je vienne à Paris le mois prochain – préviens-moi si tu viens ■ **you said eight o'clock – oh, so I did** tu as dit huit heures – oh, c'est vrai ■ **I liked her – you didn't!** [surprised] elle m'a plu – non! vraiment? ■ **I wear a toupee – you do?** [astonished] je porte une perruque – vraiment? *or* non! *or* pas possible! ‖ [asserting opposites] : **yes it does – no it doesn't** mais si – mais non ■ **you know her, I don't** tu la connais, moi pas ■ **you don't know her – I do!** tu ne la connais pas – si (je la connais)! ▶ **I do** [marriage service] ≃ oui
6. [in sentences beginning with adverbial phrase] : **not only did you lie...** non seulement tu as menti... ■ **little did I realize...** j'étais bien loin de m'imaginer...

◇ *vt* **1.** [be busy or occupied with] faire ■ **what are you doing?** qu'est-ce que tu fais?, que fais-tu?, qu'es-tu en train de faire? ■ **what do you do for a living?** qu'est-ce que vous faites dans la vie? ■ **what are these files doing here?** qu'est-ce que ces dossiers font ici? ■ **somebody DO something!** que quelqu'un fasse quelque chose! ‖ [carry out - task, work] faire ■ **he did a good job** il a fait du bon travail ■ **what do I have to do to make you understand?** mais qu'est-ce que je dois faire pour que tu comprennes? ■ **to do sthg about sthg/sb : what are you going to do about the noise?** qu'est-ce que tu vas faire au sujet du bruit? ■ **to do sthg for sb/sthg : what can I do for you?** que puis-je (faire) pour vous? ■ **the doctors can't do anything more for him** la médecine ne peut plus rien pour lui ■ **that dress really does something/nothing for you** cette robe te va vraiment très bien/ne te va vraiment pas du tout ■ **what do you do for entertainment?** quelles sont vos distractions?, comment est-ce que vous vous distrayez? ■ **to do sthg to sb/sthg : who did this to you?** qui est-ce qui t'a fait ça? ■ **what have you done to your hair?** qu'est-ce que tu as fait à tes cheveux? ■ **I hate what your job is doing to you** je n'aime pas du tout l'effet que ton travail a sur toi ▶ **that does it!** cette fois c'en est trop! ■ **that's done it, the battery's flat** et voilà, la batterie est à plat
2. [produce, provide - copy, report] faire ■ **I don't do portraits** je ne fais pas les portraits ■ **the pub does a good lunch** *UK* on sert un bon déjeuner dans ce pub ■ **could you do me a quick translation of this?** pourriez-vous me traduire ceci rapidement? ■ **do you do day trips to France?** [to travel agent] est-ce que vous avez des excursions d'une journée en France?
3. [work on, attend to] s'occuper de ■ **he's doing your car now** il est en train de s'occuper de votre voiture ■ **to do the garden** s'occuper du jardin
4. [clean, tidy - room, cupboard] faire ■ [decorate - room] faire la décoration de ■ **to do one's teeth** se brosser les dents ■ [arrange - flowers] arranger
5. SCH & UNIV [subject] étudier ■ *UK* [course] suivre ■ **to do medicine/law** étudier la médecine/le droit, faire sa médecine/son droit
6. [solve - sums, crossword, equation] faire
7. AUT & TRANSP [speed, distance] faire ■ **the car will do over 100** la voiture peut faire du 160
8. CIN, THEAT & TV [produce - play, film] faire ■ [appear in] être dans ■ [play part of] faire ■ MUS [perform] jouer
9. CULIN [cook] faire ■ [prepare - vegetables, salad] préparer ■ **how would you like your steak done?** comment voulez-vous votre steak?
10. *inf* [spend time - working, in prison] faire
11. [be enough or suitable for] suffire ■ **will £10 do you?** 10 livres, ça te suffira? ■ **those shoes will have to do the children for another year** les enfants devront encore faire un an avec ces chaussures
12. [finish] : **well that's that done, thank goodness** bon, voilà qui est fait, dieu merci ■ **have you done eating/crying?** tu as fini de manger/pleurer? ■ **done!** [in bargain] marché conclu!
13. [imitate] imiter, faire
14. *UK inf* [arrest] : **she was done for speeding** elle s'est fait pincer pour excès de vitesse ■ **we could do you for dangerous driving** nous pourrions vous arrêter pour conduite dangereuse
15. *inf* [rob, burgle - bank, shop] cambrioler, se faire
16. *inf* [cheat] rouler, avoir ■ **you've been done** tu t'es fait rouler *or* avoir
17. *inf* [visit] faire ■ **to do the sights** faire le tour des sites touristiques
18. △ [take] : **to do drugs** se camer△
19. *UK inf* [beat up] s'occuper de qqn, en mettre une à qqn.

◇ *vi* **1.** [perform - in exam, competition etc] s'en tirer, s'en sortir ■ **the company's not doing too badly** l'entreprise ne se débrouille pas trop mal ■ **try to do better in future** essaie de mieux faire à l'avenir ■ **how are we doing with the corrections?** [checking progress] où en sommes-nous avec les corrections? ■ **well done!** bien joué!, bravo!
2. [referring to health] : **how is she doing, doctor?** comment va-t-elle, docteur? ■ **mother and baby are both doing well** la maman et le bébé se portent tous les deux à merveille ▶ **how do you do?** [on being introduced] enchanté, ravi
3. [act, behave] faire ■ **do as you're told!** fais ce qu'on te dit! ▶ **you would do well to listen to your mother** tu ferais bien d'écouter ta mère ■ **to do well by sb** bien traiter qqn ■ **to be/to feel hard done by** *UK* être/se sentir lésé ■ **do as you would be done by** *prov* traite les autres comme tu voudrais être traité
4. [be enough] suffire ■ **will £20 do?** 20 livres, ça ira *or* suffira?
5. [be suitable] aller ■ **that will do (nicely)** ça ira *or* conviendra parfaitement, cela fera très bien l'affaire ■ **this won't do** ça ne peut pas continuer comme ça ■ **it wouldn't do to be late** ce ne serait pas bien d'arriver en retard
6. *(always in continuous form)* [happen] : **is there anything doing at the club tonight?** est-ce qu'il y a quelque chose au club ce soir? ■ **there's nothing doing here at weekends** il n'y a rien à faire ici le week-end ▶ **nothing doing** *inf* [rejection, refusal] rien à faire
7. *(always in perfect tense)* [finish] : **have you done?** tu as fini?
8. [be connected with] : **it has to do with your missing car** c'est au sujet de votre voiture volée ■ **that's got nothing to do with it!** [is irrelevant] cela n'a rien à voir! ■ **I want nothing to do with it/you** je ne veux rien avoir à faire là-dedans/avec toi ■ **it's nothing to do with me** je n'y suis pour rien ■ **we don't have much to do with the people next door** nous n'avons pas beaucoup de contacts avec les gens d'à côté ■ **what I said to him has got nothing to do with you** [it's none of your business] ce que je lui ai dit ne te regarde pas ; [it's not about you] ce que je lui ai dit n'a rien à voir avec toi ■ **that has a lot to do with it** cela joue un rôle très important ■ **he is** *or* **has something to do with printing** il est dans l'imprimerie
9. *UK inf* [work as cleaner] faire le ménage.

◇ *n* **1.** [tip] : **the do's and don'ts of car maintenance** les choses à faire et à ne pas faire dans l'entretien des voitures
2. *inf* [party, celebration] fête *f*.

◆ **do away with** *vt insep* **1.** [abolish - institution, rule, restriction] abolir ■ [get rid of - object] se débarrasser de
2. [kill] se débarrasser de, faire disparaître.

◆ **do down** *vt sep UK inf* **1.** [criticize, disparage] rabaisser, médire sur, dire du mal de ■ **to do o.s. down** se rabaisser
2. [cheat] avoir, rouler.

◆ **do for**△ *vt insep* **1.** *UK* [murder] zigouiller ■ [cause death of] tuer
2. [ruin - object, engine] bousiller ■ [cause failure of - plan] ruiner ; [- company] couler ■ **I'm done for** je suis cuit ■ **the project is done for** le projet est tombé à l'eau *or* foutu

3. *UK* [exhaust] tuer, crever ▪ **shopping always does for me** je suis toujours crevé après les courses ▪ **I'm done for** je suis mort *OR* crevé.

◆ **do in**△ *vt sep* **1.** [murder, kill] zigouiller, buter, butter **2.** [exhaust] = **do for** *(sense 3)* **3.** [injure] : **to do one's back/one's knee in** se bousiller le dos/le genou.

◆ **do out** *vt sep UK inf* [clean thoroughly] nettoyer à fond ▪ [decorate] refaire.

◆ **do out of** *vt sep inf* [money, job] faire perdre.

◆ **do over** *vt sep* **1.** [room] refaire **2.** *US* [do again] refaire **3.** *inf* [beat up] casser la gueule *OR* la tête à **4.** *inf* [burgle, rob - house, bank etc] cambrioler.

◆ **do up** ◇ *vt sep* **1.** [fasten - dress, jacket] fermer ; [- zip] fermer, remonter ; [- buttons] boutonner ; [- shoelaces] attacher ▪ **do me up will you?** tu peux fermer ma robe? **2.** [wrap, bundle up] emballer ▪ **envelopes done up in bundles of 20** des enveloppes en paquets de 20 **3.** *inf* [renovate - house, cottage etc] refaire, retaper ▪ [old dress, hat] arranger ▪ [make more glamorous] : **to do o.s. up** se faire beau/belle.
◇ *vi insep* [skirt, dress] se fermer ▪ [zip] se fermer, se remonter ▪ [buttons] se fermer, se boutonner.

◆ **do with** *vt insep* **1.** *inf UK (after 'could') inf* [need, want] avoir besoin de ▪ **I could have done with some help** j'aurais eu bien besoin d'aide ▪ **I could do with a drink** je prendrais bien un verre, j'ai bien envie de prendre un verre **2.** *inf UK (after 'can't') inf* [tolerate] supporter ▪ **I can't do** *OR* **be doing with all this noise** je ne supporte pas ce vacarme **3.** *(after 'what')* [act with regard to] faire de ▪ **they don't know what to do with themselves** ils ne savent pas comment s'occuper ▪ **what do you want me to do with this?** que veux-tu que je fasse de ça? **4.** *(always with pp)* [finish with] finir avec ▪ **can I borrow the ashtray if you've done with it?** puis-je emprunter le cendrier si tu n'en as plus besoin?

◆ **do without** ◇ *vi insep* faire sans.
◇ *vt insep* se passer de ▪ **I could have done without this long wait** j'aurais bien pu me passer de cette longue attente.

do² [dəʊ] *n* MUS do *m*.

do. *(written abbrev of* **ditto***) adv* do.

DOA *adj UK* = **dead on arrival**.

doable ['du:əbl] *adj inf* faisable.

d.o.b., DOB *written abbr of* **date of birth**.

Doberman (pinscher) ['dəʊbəmən('pɪnʃəʳ)] *n* doberman *m*.

doc [dɒk] *n inf* [doctor] toubib *m* ▪ **morning, ~** bonjour docteur.

docile [*UK* 'dəʊsaɪl, *US* 'dɒsəl] *adj* docile.

docility [də'sɪlətɪ] *n* docilité *f*.

dock [dɒk] ◇ *vi* [ship] se mettre à quai ▪ [spacecraft] s'amarrer.
◇ *vt* **1.** [ship] mettre à quai ▪ [spacecraft] amarrer **2.** [money] : **to ~ sb's pay/pocket money** faire une retenue sur la paye/réduire l'argent de poche de qqn ▪ **you'll be ~ed £20** on retiendra 20 livres sur votre salaire **3.** [animal's tail] couper.
◇ *n* **1.** NAUT dock *m*, docks *mpl* ▪ **the ~s** les docks ▪ **to be in dry ~** [ship] être en cale sèche ▪ **to be in ~** *fig* [car, plane] être en réparation **2.** LAW banc *m* des accusés ▪ **the prisoner in the ~** l'accusé ▪ **to be in the ~** *fig* être sur la sellette **3.** BOT patience *f*.
◇ *comp* [manager] des docks ▪ **~ worker** *UK* docker *m* ▪ **~ strike** grève *f* des dockers.

docker ['dɒkəʳ] *n UK* docker *m*.

docket ['dɒkɪt] ◇ *n* **1.** *UK* [on file, package] fiche *f* (de renseignements) **2.** LAW *US* liste *f* des affaires en instance ▪ *UK* compte-rendu *m* des jugements.
◇ *vt* **1.** [parcel, file] mettre une fiche (indiquant le contenu) sur **2.** LAW [make summary of] résumer ▪ [register] enregistrer.

docking ['dɒkɪŋ] *n* [of ship] mise *f* à quai ▪ [of spacecraft] amarrage *m* ▪ **~ manoeuvre** accostage *m*.

dockland ['dɒklənd] *n* quartier *m* des docks.

◆ **Docklands** *pr n quartier d'affaires très moderne à Londres sur les bords de la Tamise.*

dockside ['dɒksaɪd] *n* : **on the ~** sur le quai.

dockyard ['dɒkjɑ:d] *n* chantier *m* naval *OR* de constructions navales ▪ **naval ~** arsenal *m* maritime *OR* de la marine.

doctor ['dɒktəʳ] ◇ *n* **1.** MED docteur *m*, médecin *mf* ▪ **dear Doctor Cameron** [in letter] docteur ▪ **I've an appointment with Doctor Cameron** j'ai rendez-vous avec le docteur Cameron ▪ **thank you, ~** merci, docteur ▪ **he/she is a ~** il/elle est docteur *OR* médecin ▪ **to go to the ~** *OR* **~'s** aller chez le docteur *OR* médecin ▪ **you should see a ~** tu devrais consulter un docteur *OR* médecin ▪ **to be under the ~** *inf* être sous traitement médical ▪ **woman ~** *UK*, **female ~** *US* médecin *f*, femme *f* médecin ▪ **army ~** médecin militaire ➲ **~'s line** *OR* **note** certificat *m* médical ▪ **that's just what the ~ ordered!** *inf* c'est exactement ce qu'il me faut *OR* fallait! ▪ **'Doctor Zhivago'** ***Pasternak, Lean*** 'le Docteur Jivago' ▪ **'Doctor Faustus'** ***Mann*** 'le Docteur Faustus' ▪ ***Marlowe*** 'la Tragique Histoire du docteur Faustus' **2.** UNIV docteur *mf* ▪ **Doctor of Science** docteur ès *OR* en sciences.
◇ *vt* **1.** [tamper with - results, figures] falsifier, trafiquer ; [- wine] frelater ▪ **we'll need to ~ the figures a little** il va falloir un peu arranger ces chiffres **2.** [drug - drink, food] mettre de la drogue dans ; [- racehorse] doper **3.** *UK* [castrate, sterilize - cat, dog] châtrer **4.** [treat] soigner.

doctoral ['dɒktərəl] *adj* [thesis, degree] de doctorat.

doctorate ['dɒktərət] *n* doctorat *m* ▪ **to have/to do a ~in sthg** avoir/faire un doctorat en qqch.

doctrinaire [,dɒktrɪ'neəʳ] *adj* doctrinaire.

doctrinal [dɒk'traɪnl] *adj* doctrinal.

doctrine ['dɒktrɪn] *n* doctrine *f*.

docudrama [,dɒkjʊ'drɑ:mə] *n* TV docudrame *m*.

document ◇ *n* ['dɒkjʊmənt] document *m* ▪ LAW acte *m* ▪ **to draw up a ~** rédiger un document ▪ **may I have a look at your travel ~s, sir?** pourrais-je voir votre titre de transport, monsieur? ▪ **the ~s in the case** LAW le dossier de l'affaire.
◇ *vt* ['dɒkjʊment] **1.** [write about in detail] décrire (de façon détaillée) ▪ [record on film - subj: film] montrer (en détail), présenter (de façon détaillée) ; [- subj: photographer] faire un reportage sur ▪ **the book ~s life in the 1920s** le livre décrit la vie dans les années 20 ▪ **it is well ~ed** c'est bien documenté ▪ **the first ~ed case of smallpox** le premier cas de variole qu'on ait enregistré **2.** [support - with evidence or proof] fournir des preuves à l'appui de, attester ; [- with citations, references] documenter.

documentary [,dɒkjʊ'mentərɪ] *(pl* **documentaries***)* ◇ *adj* **1.** LAW [consisting of documents] : **~ evidence** preuve *f* littérale ▪ **~ credit** crédit *m* documentaire **2.** [factual - film, programme] documentaire.
◇ *n* CIN & TV documentaire *m*.

documentation [,dɒkjʊmen'teɪʃn] *n* documentation *f*.

document case *n* porte-documents *m inv*.

DOD *pr n US* = **Department of Defense**.

dodderer ['dɒdərəʳ] *n inf pej* croulant *m*, - e *f*, gâteux *m*, - euse *f*.

doddering ['dɒdərɪŋ] *adj inf* [walk] hésitant, chancelant ▪ *pej* [elderly person] gâteux.

doddery ['dɒdərɪ] *adj inf* [walk] hésitant ▪ **I still feel a bit ~** [after illness] je me sens encore un peu faible *OR* flagada.

doddle ['dɒdl] *n UK inf* **it's a ~** c'est simple comme bonjour, c'est du gâteau.

dodecagon [dəʊ'dekəgən] *n* dodécagone *m*.

dodge [dɒdʒ] ◇ *n* **1.** [evasive movement] écart *m* ▪ [by footballer, boxer] esquive *f* **2.** *UK inf* [trick] truc *m*, combine *f*.
◇ *vi* [make evasive movement] s'écarter vivement ▪ [footballer, boxer] faire une esquive ▪ **he ~d into the doorway** il s'est esquivé *OR* il a disparu dans l'entrée ▪ **to ~ out of the way** s'écarter vivement ▪ **to ~ out of doing sthg** *fig* se défiler pour ne pas faire qqch.

<> *vt* [blow] esquiver ▪ [falling rock, ball] éviter ▪ [bullets] passer entre, éviter ▪ [pursuer, police] échapper à ▪ [creditor, landlord etc] éviter ▪ [question] éluder ▪ **he has ~d the taxman** *OR* **paying tax all his life** il a échappé au fisc toute sa vie ▪ **to ~ the issue** éluder *OR* esquiver le problème.

Dodgem® ['dɒdʒəm] *n UK* auto *f* tamponneuse ▪ **to have a ride on the ~s** faire un tour d'autos tamponneuses.

dodger ['dɒdʒəʳ] *n inf* [workshy] tire-au-flanc *m inv* ▪ [dishonest] combinard *m*, -e *f*, roublard *m*, -e *f* ▪ **fare ~** resquilleur *m*, -euse *f*.

dodgy ['dɒdʒɪ] (*comp* **dodgier**, *superl* **dodgiest**) *adj UK inf* **1.** [risky, dangerous - plan, idea] risqué ▪ **the brakes are really ~** les freins sont très douteux ▪ **the weather looks pretty ~** [unreliable] le temps a l'air plutôt douteux *OR* menaçant **2.** [dishonest - person] roublard, combinard ; [- scheme] douteux, suspect.

dodo ['dəʊdəʊ] (*pl* **dodos** *OR pl* **dodoes**) *n* **1.** [extinct bird] dronte *m*, dodo *m* **2.** *inf* [fool] andouille *f*.

doe [dəʊ] *n* [deer] biche *f* ▪ [rabbit] lapine *f* ▪ [hare] hase *f* ▪ [rat] rate *f*, ratte *f*.

DoE (*abbrev of* **Department of the Environment**) *pr n ministère britannique de l'Environnement.*

DOE (*abbrev of* **Department of Energy**) *pr n ministère américain de l'Énergie.*

doer ['du:əʳ] *n* : **she is more (of) a ~ than a talker** elle préfère l'action à la parole.

does [dʌz] ▭> **do** *(vb)*.

doesn't ['dʌznt] = **does not**, *see also* **do**[1].

doff [dɒf] *vt* [hat] ôter.

dog [dɒg] (*pret & pp* **dogged**, *cont* **dogging**) <> *n* **1.** chien *m* ▪ **'beware of the ~'** 'attention, chien méchant' ▪ **to follow sb about like a ~** suivre qqn comme un petit chien ➊ **this is a real ~'s dinner** *OR* **breakfast** [mess] *UK* c'est un vrai torchon *OR* gâchis ▪ **to be dressed** *OR* **done up like a ~'s dinner** *UK inf* [gaudy, showy] être habillé de façon extravagante ▪ **to lead sb a ~'s life** mener la vie dure à qqn ▪ **it's a ~'s life being a traffic warden** c'est une vie de chien que d'être contractuel ▪ **a ~ in the manger** un empêcheur de danser *OR* tourner en rond ▪ **I'm going to see a man about a ~** *inf façon humoristique d'éviter de dire où l'on va* ▪ **it's(a case of)~ eat ~** c'est la loi de la jungle ▪ **every ~ has its** *OR* **his day** *prov* tout le monde a son heure de gloire ▪ **give a ~ a bad name (and hang him)** *prov* qui veut noyer son chien l'accuse de la rage *prov* ▪ **let sleeping ~s lie** *prov* n'éveillez pas le chat qui dort *prov* ▪ **you can't teach an old ~ new tricks** *prov* les vieilles habitudes ont la vie dure ▪ **the ~s** *UK inf* SPORT les courses de lévriers ▪ **this country's going to the ~s** *inf* le pays va à sa ruine
2. [male fox, wolf etc] mâle *m*
3. *inf* [person] : **you lucky ~!** sacré veinard! ▪ **dirty ~** sale type *m* ▪ **there's life in the old ~ yet!** je ne suis/ce n'est pas encore un vieux croulant!
4. △ *pej* [ugly woman] cageot△ *m*, boudin△ *m*
5. *US inf* [hopeless - product, company] catastrophe *f* ; [- thing] : **it's a ~** c'est nul
6. [firedog] chenet *m*
7. TECH [pawl] cliquet *m* ▪ [cramp] crampon *m*
8. *US* [hot dog] hot dog *m*.
<> *comp* [breeder, breeding] de chiens ▪ [bowl, basket, food] pour chien ▪ **~ fox** renard *m* mâle ▪ **~ racing** courses *fpl* de lévriers ▪ **~ track** cynodrome *m*.
<> *vt* **1.** [follow closely] suivre de près ▪ **to ~ sb's footsteps** ne pas lâcher qqn d'une semelle
2. [plague] : **to be dogged by bad health/problems** ne pas arrêter d'avoir des ennuis de santé/des problèmes ▪ **the team has been dogged by injury** l'équipe n'a pas arrêté d'avoir des blessés ▪ **she is dogged by misfortune** *OR* **bad luck** elle est poursuivie par la malchance.

dog biscuit *n* biscuit *m* pour chien.

dog-catcher *n* employé *m*, -e *f* de la fourrière.

dog collar *n* [for dog] collier *m* pour *OR* de chien ▪ *hum* [of clergyman] col *m* d'ecclésiastique.

dog days *npl* canicule *f*.

dog-eared *adj* [page] corné ▪ [book] aux pages cornées.

dog-eat-dog *adj* [business] impitoyable, sans pitié.

dog-end *n inf* [of cigarette] mégot *m*.

dogfight ['dɒgfaɪt] *n* [between dogs] combat *m* de chiens ▪ MIL [between aircraft] combat *m* rapproché.

dogfish ['dɒgfɪʃ] *n* roussette *f*, chien *m* de mer.

dogged ['dɒgɪd] *adj* [courage, perseverance] tenace ▪ [person, character] tenace, déterminé, persévérant ▪ [refusal] obstiné.

doggedly ['dɒgɪdlɪ] *adv* [fight, persist] avec ténacité *OR* persévérance ▪ [refuse] obstinément.

doggedness ['dɒgɪdnɪs] *n* [of person] ténacité *f*, persévérance *f* ▪ [of courage] ténacité *f*.

doggerel ['dɒgərəl] <> *n* poésie *f* burlesque.
<> *adj* [rhyme, verse] burlesque.

doggie ['dɒgɪ] = **doggy**.

doggone ['dɑ:gɑ:n] *US inf* <> *interj* : **~ (it)!** zut!, nom d'une pipe!
<> *adj* = **doggoned**.

doggoned ['dɑ:gɑ:nd] *adj US inf* fichu ▪ **it's a ~ shame!** c'est vraiment honteux!

doggy ['dɒgɪ] (*pl* **doggies**) *inf* <> *n baby* toutou *m* ▪ **~-fashion**△ : **~-style** en levrette△.
<> *adj* [smell] de chien ▪ **he's a ~ person** il adore les chiens.

doggy bag *n sachet (ou boîte) que l'on propose aux clients dans les restaurants pour qu'ils emportent ce qu'ils n'ont pas consommé.*

doggy paddle <> *n* nage *f* du petit chien.
<> *vi* faire la nage du petit chien.

dog handler *n* maître-chien *m*.

doghouse ['dɒghaʊs] (*pl* [-haʊzɪz]) *n* **1.** *US* [kennel] chenil *m*, niche *f* **2.** *inf phr* **to be in the ~ (with sb)** ne pas être en odeur de sainteté *OR* être en disgrâce (auprès de qqn).

dog Latin *n* latin *m* de cuisine.

dogleg ['dɒgleg] <> *n* [in pipe, road] coude *m*.
<> *vi* [pipe, road] faire un coude.
<> *adj* [pipe, road] qui fait un coude.

dog licence *n UK permis de posséder un chien.*

doglike ['dɒglaɪk] *adj* [devotion] aveugle.

dogma ['dɒgmə] *n* dogme *m*.

dogmatic [dɒg'mætɪk] *adj* dogmatique ▪ **to be ~ about sthg** être dogmatique au sujet de qqch.

dogmatism ['dɒgmətɪzm] *n* dogmatisme *m*.

dogmatist ['dɒgmətɪst] *n* personne *f* dogmatique.

do-gooder [-'gʊdəʳ] *n pej* âme *f* charitable, bonne âme *f*.

dog paddle = **doggy paddle**.

dog rose *n* églantine *f*.

dogsbody ['dɒgz,bɒdɪ] (*pl* **dogsbodies**) *n UK inf* bonne *f* à tout faire ▪ **I'm not your ~** je ne suis pas ton chien *OR* ta bonne.

dog show *n* exposition *f* canine.

dogsled ['dɒgsled] *n* luge *f* tirée par des chiens.

dog's-tooth check *n UK* pied-de-poule *m*.

dog-tired *adj inf* épuisé.

dogwarden ['dɒgwɔ:dn] *n employé municipal chargé de recueillir les chiens errants.*

doh [dəʊ] *n* MUS do *m*.

doily ['dɔɪlɪ] (*pl* **doilies**) *n* napperon *m*.

doing ['du:ɪŋ] *n* [work, activity] : **it's all your ~** tout cela, c'est de ta faute ■ **is this your ~?** [have you done this?] c'est toi qui as fait cela? ; [are you behind this?] c'est toi qui es derrière cela? ■ **it's none of my ~** je n'y suis pour rien ■ **that'll take some ~** cela ne va pas être facile.

doings ['du:ɪŋz] *n* ***UK inf*** [thing] machin *m*, truc *m*.

do-it-yourself ◇ *n* bricolage *m*.
◇ *comp* [manual, shop] de bricolage ■ **a ~ enthusiast** un bricoleur ■ **a ~ kit** des éléments en kit.

doldrums ['dɒldrəmz] *npl* **1.** GEOG [zone] zones *fpl* des calmes équatoriaux, pot au noir *m* ■ [weather] calme *m* équatorial **2.** ***phr*** **to be in the ~** [person] avoir le cafard, broyer du noir ; [activity, trade] être en plein marasme.

dole [dəʊl] *n (U)* ***UK inf*** **~ (money)** (indemnités *fpl* de) chômage *m* ■ **how much is the ~ nowadays?** combien est-ce qu'on touche au chômage maintenant? ■ **to be/to go on the ~** être/s'inscrire au chômage ■ **the ~ queues are getting longer** de plus en plus de gens pointent au chômage.
◆ **dole out** *vt sep* [distribute] distribuer ■ [in small amounts] distribuer au compte-gouttes.

doleful ['dəʊlfʊl] *adj* [mournful - look, voice] malheureux ; [- person, song] triste.

doll [dɒl] *n* **1.** [for child] poupée *f* ■ [for ventriloquist] marionnette *f* de ventriloque ■ **to play with ~s** jouer à la poupée ■ **~'s pram** poussette *f* de poupée ▶ **~'s house** ***UK***, **~ house** ***US liter*** & ***fig*** maison *f* de poupée **2.** ***inf*** [girl] nana *f*, souris *f* ■ [attractive girl] poupée *f* **3.** ***inf*** [dear person] amour *m* ■ **you're a ~** tu es un amour **4.** ***US inf*** [nice person] : **he's a real ~** il est vraiment adorable.
◆ **doll up** *vt sep* : **to get ~ed up, to ~ o.s. up** se faire beau/belle, se pomponner.

dollar ['dɒlər] ◇ *n* [currency] dollar *m* ■ **you can bet your bottom ~** *OR* **~s to doughnuts that he'll be there** tu peux être sûr qu'il sera là ■ **I feel like a million ~s** je me sens merveilleusement bien ■ **you look like a million ~s in that dress** ***inf*** tu es magnifique avec cette robe ■ **that's the sixty-four thousand ~ question** c'est la question à mille francs.
◇ *comp* : **~ bill** billet *m* d'un dollar ■ **~ diplomacy** diplomatie *f* du dollar ■ **~ sign** (signe *m* du) dollar *m*.

dollarization [dɒlərаɪ'zeɪʃn] *n* dollarisation *f* ***inf.***

dollop ['dɒləp] ***inf*** ◇ *n* [of mashed potatoes, cream etc] (bonne) cuillerée *f* ■ [of mud, plaster, clay] (petit) tas *m* ■ [of butter, margarine] (gros *OR* bon)morceau *m*.
◇ *vt* : **to ~ food out onto plates** balancer de la nourriture dans des assiettes.

dolly ['dɒlɪ] (*pret & pp* **dollied**, *pl* **dollies**) ◇ *n* **1.** ***inf*** [for child] = **doll** *(sense 1)* **2.** CIN & TV [for camera] chariot *m* **3.** [in cricket] prise *f* au vol facile ■ [in tennis] coup *m* facile.
◇ *vt* CIN & TV : **to ~ a camera in/out** faire un travelling avant/arrière.

dolly bird *n* ***UK inf dated*** poupée *f (femme)*.

dolly mixtures *npl* ***UK*** [sweets] petits bonbons *mpl* assortis.

dolmen ['dɒlmən] *n* archaeology dolmen *m*.

dolomite ['dɒləmaɪt] *n* dolomie *f*, dolomite *f*.

Dolomites ['dɒləmaɪts] *pr npl* : **the ~** les Dolomites *fpl*, les Alpes *fpl* dolomitiques.

dolphin ['dɒlfɪn] *n* dauphin *m* ■ **~-friendly** [tuna] *pêché sans dommages pour les dauphins.*

dolt [dəʊlt] *n* [stupid person] lourdaud *m*, gourde *f*.

domain [də'meɪn] *n* **1.** [territory, sphere of interest] domaine *m* ■ **that's your ~** ***fig*** c'est ton domaine ■ **to be in the public ~** [information] être dans le domaine public **2.** MATHS, COMPUT & SCI domaine *m*.

domain name *n* COMPUT nom *m* de domaine.

dome [dəʊm] *n* **1.** ARCHIT dôme *m*, coupole *f* **2.** [of head] calotte *f* ■ [of hill] dôme *m* ■ [of heavens, sky] voûte *f* ■ **the ~ of his bald head** le sommet de son crâne chauve.

domed [dəʊmd] *adj* [building] à coupole, à dôme ■ [roof] en forme de dôme *OR* de coupole ■ [forehead] bombé.

Domesday Book ['du:mzdeɪ-] *pr n* : **the ~** *recueil cadastral établi à la fin du XIe siècle à l'initiative de Guillaume le Conquérant afin de permettre l'évaluation des droits fiscaux sur les terres d'Angleterre.*

domestic [də'mestɪk] ◇ *adj* **1.** [household - duty, chore] ménager ■ **a ~ servant** un domestique ■ **to be in ~ service** être employé de maison ■ **~ staff** employés *mpl* de maison, domestiques *mpl* ■ **a ~ help** une aide ménagère ■ **'for ~ use only'** 'réservé à l'usage domestique' ■ **~ appliance/product** appareil *m* /produit *m* ménager ▶ **~ science** ***UK*** SCH & ***dated*** enseignement *m* ménager **2.** [of the family - duties, problems] familial ; [- life] familial, de famille ■ **they lived in ~ bliss for many years** ça a été un ménage très heureux pendant de nombreuses années ■ **a minor ~ crisis** un petit problème à la maison ■ **a ~ sort of person** [woman] une femme d'intérieur ; [man] un homme d'intérieur **3.** [not foreign - affairs, flight, trade, policy] intérieur ; [- currency, economy, news, produce] national **4.** [not wild - animal] domestique.
◇ *n* ***fml UK*** domestique *mf* ■ ***US*** femme *f* de ménage.

domestically [də'mestɪklɪ] *adv* ECON & POL : **to be produced ~** être produit à l'intérieur du pays *OR* au niveau national.

domesticate [də'mestɪkeɪt] *vt* [animal] domestiquer, apprivoiser ■ ***hum*** [person] habituer aux tâches ménagères.

domesticated [də'mestɪkeɪtɪd] *adj* [animal] domestiqué, apprivoisé ■ **she's very ~** c'est une vraie femme d'intérieur.

domestication [də,mestɪ'keɪʃn] *n* [of animal] domestication *f*, apprivoisement *m*.

domesticity [,dəʊme'stɪsətɪ] *n* [home life] vie *f* de famille.

domicile ['dɒmɪsaɪl] ADMIN, FIN & LAW ◇ *n* domicile *m*.
◇ *vt* domicilier ■ **~d at** domicilié à.

domiciliary [,dɒmɪ'sɪljərɪ] *adj* ADMIN [visit] domiciliaire ■ [care, services] à domicile.

dominance ['dɒmɪnəns] *n* **1.** [ascendancy - of race, person, football team etc] prédominance *f* ; [- of animal, gene] dominance *f* **2.** [importance] importance *f*.

dominant ['dɒmɪnənt] ◇ *adj* **1.** dominant ■ [nation, political party, team etc] prédominant ■ [person, personality] dominateur ■ [building, geographical feature - most elevated] dominant ; [- most striking] le plus frappant **2.** MUS de dominante.
◇ *n* MUS dominante *f* ■ SCI dominance *f*.

dominate ['dɒmɪneɪt] ◇ *vt* dominer ■ **to be ~d by sb** être dominé par qqn.
◇ *vi* dominer.

dominating ['dɒmɪneɪtɪŋ] *adj* dominateur.

domination [,dɒmɪ'neɪʃn] *n* domination *f* ■ [of organization] contrôle *m* ■ [of conversation] monopolisation *f* ■ **Spain was under Roman ~ at the time** à cette époque, l'Espagne était sous la domination romaine.

domineer [,dɒmɪ'nɪər] *vi* se montrer autoritaire ■ **to ~ over sb** se montrer autoritaire avec qqn.

domineering [,dɒmɪ'nɪərɪŋ] *adj* autoritaire.

Dominica [də'mɪnɪkə] *pr n* Dominique *f* ■ **in ~** à la Dominique.

Dominican [də'mɪnɪkən] ◇ *n* **1.** [person from the Dominican Republic] Dominicain *m*, - e *f* **2.** [person from Dominica] Dominiquais *m*, - e *f* **3.** RELIG dominicain *m*, - e *f*.
◇ *adj* **1.** [from the Dominican Republic] dominicain **2.** [from Dominica] dominiquais **3.** RELIG dominicain.

Dominican Republic *pr n* : **the ~** la République Dominicaine ■ **in the ~** en République Dominicaine.

dominion [də'mɪnjən] *n* **1.** [rule, authority] domination *f*, empire *m* ■ **to have ~ over a country** avoir un pays sous sa domination **2.** [territory] territoire *m* ■ [in British Commonwealth] dominion *m*.

domino ['dɒmɪnəʊ] (*pl* **dominoes**) ◇ *n* **1.** domino *m* ▪ **to play ~es** jouer aux dominos **2.** [cloak, mask] domino *m*.
◇ *comp* : **~ effect** effet *m* d'entraînement ▪ **~ theory** théorie *f* des dominos.

don [dɒn] (*pret & pp* **donned**, *cont* **donning**) ◇ *vt fml* [put on] mettre.
◇ *n* **1.** *UK* UNIV *professeur d'université (en particulier à Oxford et Cambridge)* **2.** [Spanish title] don *m* **3.** *US* chef *m* de la Mafia.

Donald Duck ['dɒnld-] *pr n* Donald.

donate [də'neɪt] ◇ *vt* [money, goods] faire un don de ▪ [specific amount] faire (un) don de ▪ **to ~ blood** donner son *OR* du sang.
◇ *vi* [give money, goods] faire un don, faire des dons.

donation [də'neɪʃn] *n* [action] don *m*, donation *f* ▪ [money, goods or blood given] don *m* ▪ **to make a ~ to a charity** faire un don *OR* une donation à une œuvre (de charité).

done [dʌn] ◇ *pp* ▷ **do.**
◇ *adj* **1.** [finished] fini ▪ **are you ~ yet?** tu as enfin fini? ▪ **to get sthg ~** [completed] finir qqch **2.** [cooked - food] cuit **3.** *inf* [exhausted] crevé, claqué **4.** *inf* [used up] : **that's the milk ~** il n'y a plus de lait **5.** [fitting] : **it's not the ~ thing, it's not ~** ça ne se fait pas.

dong [dɒŋ] *n* **1.** [noise of bell] ding-dong *m* **2.** ▲ [penis] queue▲ *f*, bite△ *f*.

dongle ['dɒŋgl] *n* COMPUT boîtier *m* de sécurité, clé *f* gigogne.

Don Juan [-'dʒu:ən] *n liter & fig* don Juan *m* ▪ **he's a bit of a ~** il est un peu du genre don Juan ➊ **'Don Juan'** *Byron* 'Don Juan'.

donkey ['dɒŋkɪ] *n* âne *m*, ânesse *f* ▪ **I haven't seen her for ~'s years** *inf* je ne l'ai pas vue depuis une éternité.

donkey jacket *n UK veste longue en tissu épais, généralement bleu foncé.*

donkeywork ['dɒŋkɪwɜ:k] *n (U) inf* **to do the ~** [drudgery] faire le sale boulot ; [difficult part] faire le gros du travail.

donnish ['dɒnɪʃ] *adj UK* [person] érudit, savant ▪ [look, speech] d'érudit, cultivé ▪ *pej* pédant.

donor ['dəʊnəʳ] *n* **1.** [gen - LAW] donateur *m*, - trice *f* **2.** MED [of blood, organ] donneur *m*, - euse *f*.

donor card *n* carte *f* de don d'organe.

don't [dəʊnt] ◇ *vb* = **do not**.
◇ *n (usu pl)* chose *f* à ne pas faire.

don't know *n* [on survey] sans opinion *mf inv* ▪ [voter] indécis *m*, - e *f*.

donut ['dəʊnʌt] *US* = **doughnut**.

doodah ['du:dɑ:] *n inf* truc *m*, bidule *m*.

doodle ['du:dl] ◇ *vi & vt* gribouiller, griffonner.
◇ *n* gribouillage *m*, griffonnage *m*.

doodlebug ['du:dlbʌg] *n inf* [bomb] V1 *m*, bombe *f* volante.

doohickey ['du:ˌhɪkɪ] *n US inf* truc *m*, machin *m*.

doolally [ˌdu:'lælɪ] *adj inf* timbré.

doom [du:m] ◇ *n (U)* [terrible fate] destin *m* (malheureux), sort *m* (tragique) ▪ [ruin] perte *f*, ruine *f* ▪ [death] mort *f* ▪ **to meet one's ~** trouver la mort ▪ **thousands were sent to their ~** on envoya des milliers de gens à la mort.
◇ *vt* condamner.

doomed [du:md] *adj* condamné ▪ **to be ~ (to failure)** être voué à l'échec ▪ **she is ~ to a life of poverty** elle est condamnée à une vie de misère.

doom-laden *adj* de mauvais augure, sinistre.

Doomsday ['du:mzdeɪ] *n* jour *m* du Jugement dernier ▪ **till ~** *inf* jusqu'à la fin du monde *OR* des temps.

Doomsday Book = **Domesday Book**.

door [dɔ:ʳ] *n* **1.** [of building, room] porte *f* ▪ **she walked through the ~** elle franchit la porte ▪ **they shut the ~ in my face** ils m'ont fermé la porte au nez ▪ **he lives two ~s down** il habite deux portes plus loin ▪ **I found the ~ closed** j'ai trouvé porte close ▪ **out of ~s** dehors, en plein air ▪ **to go from ~ to ~** aller de porte en porte ▪ **can someone answer the ~?** est-ce que quelqu'un peut aller ouvrir? ▪ **I'll see you to the ~** je vous reconduis jusqu'à la porte ▪ **'tickets available at the ~'** THEAT 'billets en vente à l'entrée' ▪ **the agreement leaves the ~ open for further discussion** l'accord laisse la porte ouverte à des discussions ultérieures ▪ **the discovery opens the ~ to medical advances** la découverte ouvre la voie à des progrès médicaux ▪ **having a famous name certainly helps to open ~s** avoir un nom célèbre permet sans aucun doute de voir s'ouvrir des portes ▪ **to lay sthg at sb's ~** imputer qqch à qqn, reprocher qqch à qqn ▪ **she closed** *OR* **shut the ~ on any further negotiations** elle a rendu toute nouvelle négociation impossible ▪ **to show sb the ~** *liter & fig* montrer la porte à qqn **2.** [of car] porte *f*, portière *f* ▪ [of train] portière *f*.

doorbell ['dɔ:bel] *n* sonnette *f* ▪ **the ~ rang** on sonna à la porte.

door chain *n* chaînette *f* de sûreté.

do-or-die *adj* [chance, effort] désespéré, ultime ▪ [attitude, person] jusqu'au-boutiste.

doorframe ['dɔ:freɪm] *n* chambranle *m*, châssis *m* de porte.

door handle *n* poignée *f* de porte ▪ AUT poignée *f* de portière.

doorjamb ['dɔ:dʒæm] *n* montant *m* de porte, jambage *m*.

doorkeeper ['dɔ:ˌki:pəʳ] *n* [at hotel] portier *m* ▪ [at apartment building] concierge *mf*.

doorknob ['dɔ:nɒb] *n* poignée *f* de porte.

doorknocker ['dɔ:ˌnɒkəʳ] *n* heurtoir *m*, marteau *m (de porte)*.

doorman ['dɔ:mən] (*pl* **doormen** [-mən]) *n* [at hotel] portier *m* ▪ [at apartment building] concierge *m*.

doormat ['dɔ:mæt] *n liter* paillasson *m*, essuie-pieds *m (inv)* ▪ *fig* [person] chiffe *f* molle ▪ **to treat sb like a ~** traiter qqn comme un moins que rien.

doornail ['dɔ:neɪl] *n* clou *m* de porte.

doorpost ['dɔ:pəʊst] *n* montant *m* de porte, jambage *m*.

doorstep ['dɔ:step] ◇ *n* **1.** [step] pas *m* de la porte, seuil *m* de porte ▪ **leave the milk on the ~** laissez le lait devant la porte ▪ **don't leave him standing on the ~, ask him to come in!** ne le laisse pas à la porte, fais-le entrer! ▪ **they're building a huge factory practically on my ~** ils construisent une immense usine presque à ma porte **2.** *UK hum* [piece of bread] grosse tranche *f* de pain.
◇ *adj UK* **~ salesman** vendeur *m* à domicile, démarcheur *m* ▪ **~ selling** vente *f* à domicile, porte-à-porte *m inv*, démarchage *m*.

doorstepping ['dɔ:stepɪŋ] *UK* ◇ *n* [by politician] démarchage *m* électoral ▪ [by journalists] *pratique journalistique qui consiste à harceler les gens jusque chez eux.*
◇ *adj* [politician] *qui fait du démarchage électoral* ▪ [journalist] *qui harcèle les gens jusque chez eux.*

doorstop ['dɔ:stɒp] *n* butoir *m* de porte.

door-to-door ◇ *adj* : **~ salesman** vendeur *m* à domicile, démarcheur *m* ▪ **~ selling** vente *f* à domicile, porte-à-porte *m inv* ▪ **~ service** service *m* à domicile.
◇ *adv* : **a 2-hour trip ~** un trajet de 2 heures de porte à porte.

doorway ['dɔ:weɪ] *n* porte *f* ▪ **standing in the ~** debout dans l'embrasure de la porte.

dope [dəʊp] ◇ *n* **1.** *inf (U) inf* [illegal drug] drogue *f*, dope *f* **2.** [for athlete, horse] dopant *m* **3.** *inf* [idiot] crétin *m*, - e *f*, andouille *f* **4.** *inf (U) inf dated* [news] tuyau *m*, renseignement *m* **5.** [varnish] enduit *m* ▪ AUT, CHEM & TECH dopant *m* **6.** [for dynamite] absorbant *m*.

◇ *comp inf* [drugs] : **~ addict** toxicomane *mf*, drogué *m*, - e *f* ■ **~ dealer** *OR* **pusher** dealer *m* ■ **~ test** test *m* antidoping.
◇ *vt* **1.** [drug - horse, person] doper ; [- drink, food] mettre une drogue *OR* un dopant dans ■ **she was all ~d up** *inf* elle planait complètement **2.** AUT, CHEM & TECH doper.

dopey ['dəʊpɪ] (*comp* **dopier**, *superl* **dopiest**) = **dopy**.

doppelgänger ['dɒpl,gæŋəʳ] *n* double *m (d'une personne vivante)*, sosie *m*.

dopy ['dəʊpɪ] (*comp* **dopier**, *superl* **dopiest**) *adj* **1.** [drugged] drogué, dopé ■ [sleepy] (à moitié) endormi **2.** *inf* [silly] idiot, abruti.

Dorian ['dɔːrɪən] ◇ *n* Dorien *m*, - enne *f*.
◇ *adj* LING & MUS dorien.

Doric ['dɒrɪk] ◇ *adj* dorique.
◇ *n* dorique *m*.

dorm [dɔːm] *n inf* = **dormitory**.

dormant ['dɔːmənt] *adj* **1.** [idea, passion] qui sommeille ■ [energy, reserves] inexploité ■ [disease] à l'état latent ■ [law] inappliqué ■ **to lie ~** sommeiller **2.** [animal] endormi ■ [plant] dormant **3.** [volcano] en repos, en sommeil **4.** HERALD dormant.

dormer ['dɔːməʳ] *n* : **~ (window)** lucarne *f*.

dormice ['dɔːmaɪs] *pl* ▷ **dormouse**.

dormitory ['dɔːmətrɪ] (*pl* **dormitories**) ◇ *n* [room] dortoir *m* ■ *US* UNIV résidence *f* universitaire.
◇ *comp UK* **~ town** ville-dortoir *f*.

Dormobile® ['dɔːmə,biːl] *n UK* camping-car *m*.

dormouse ['dɔːmaʊs] (*pl* **dormice** ['dɔːmaɪs]) *n* loir *m*.

Dors *written abbr of* **Dorset**.

dorsal ['dɔːsl] ◇ *adj* ANAT, LING & ZOOL dorsal.
◇ *n* dorsale *f*.

dorsal fin *n* nageoire *f* dorsale.

dory ['dɔːrɪ] (*pl* **dories**) *n* **1.** [salt-water fish] saint-pierre *m inv*, dorée *f* ■ [freshwater fish] dorée *f* **2.** *US* [boat] doris *m*.

DOS [dɒs] (*abbrev of* **disk operating system**) *n* DOS *m*.

dosage ['dəʊsɪdʒ] *n* [giving of dose] dosage *m* ■ [amount] dose *f* ■ [directions on bottle] posologie *f*.

dose [dəʊs] ◇ *n* **1.** [amount] dose *f* ■ **she took her daily ~ of medicine** elle a pris son médicament quotidien ■ **in small/large ~ s** à faible/haute dose ■ **I can only take him in small ~s** je ne peux le supporter qu'à petites doses **2.** [of illness] attaque *f* ■ **a bad ~ of flu** une mauvaise grippe **3.** △ [venereal disease] bléno△ *f*.
◇ *vt* **1.** [subj: pharmacist] doser **2.** [person] administrer un médicament à ■ **she ~d herself (up) with pills** elle s'est bourrée de médicaments.

dosh△ [dɒʃ] *n UK* fric *m*.

do-si-do [,dəʊsɪ'dəʊ] *n figure de quadrille où les danseurs sont dos à dos.*

doss△ [dɒs] *UK* ◇ *n* **1.** [bed] lit *m*, pieu *m* **2.** [nap] somme *m*, roupillon *m* **3.** [easy thing] : **it was a real ~** c'était fastoche.
◇ *vi* coucher, roupiller.
◆ **doss around**△ *vi insep* glander.
◆ **doss down**△ *vi insep* coucher, crécher.

dosser△ ['dɒsəʳ] *n UK* [person] sans-abri *mf inv*, clochard *m*, - e *f* ■ [house] foyer *m* de sans-abri.

dosshouse ['dɒshaʊs] (*pl* [-haʊzɪz]) *n UK inf* foyer *m* de sans-abri.

dossier ['dɒsɪeɪ] *n* dossier *m*, documents *mpl*.

Dostoievsky [,dɒstɔɪ'efskɪ] *pr n* Dostoïevski.

dot [dɒt] (*pret & pp* **dotted**, *cont* **dotting**) ◇ *n* [gen - MUS] point *m* ■ [on material] pois *m* ■ **~, ~, ~** [in punctuation] points de suspension ■ **~s and dashes** [Morse code] points et traits *mpl*.
◇ *vt* **1.** [mark] marquer avec des points, pointiller ■ [an 'i'] mettre un point sur ■ **to ~ one's i's and cross one's t's** *fig* mettre les points sur les i **2.** [spot] parsemer ■ **the lake was dotted with boats** des bateaux étaient dispersés sur le lac ■ **~ the surface with butter** CULIN mettez des morceaux de beurre sur le dessus.
◆ **on the dot** *adv phr* : **at 3 o'clock on the ~** à 3 h pile *OR* tapantes ■ **he always pays right on the ~** il paye toujours recta.

dotage ['dəʊtɪdʒ] *n* gâtisme *m* ■ **to be in one's ~** être gâteux, être retombé en enfance.

dote [dəʊt] *vi* : **to ~ on sb** être fou de qqn, aimer qqn à la folie.

dotcom [dɒt'kɒm] *adj* COMPUT qui a trait à la netéconomie.

doth [(*weak form* [dəθ], *strong form* [dʌθ])] *arch vb (3rd pers sg)* ▷ **do** *(vb)*.

doting ['dəʊtɪŋ] *adj* : **he has a ~ mother** sa mère l'aime à la folie.

dot-matrix printer *n* imprimante *f* matricielle.

dotted ['dɒtɪd] *adj* **1.** [shirt, tie] à pois **2.** : **~ line** ligne *f* en pointillés ; AUT ligne *f* discontinue ■ **tear along the ~ line** détachez suivant le pointillé **3.** MUS : **~ note** note *f* pointée ■ **~ rhythm** notes *fpl* pointées.

dotty ['dɒtɪ] (*comp* **dottier**, *superl* **dottiest**) *adj UK inf* [crazy] fou *(before vowel or silent 'h' fol)*, folle *f*, dingue ■ **he's absolutely ~ about her** il est fou d'elle ■ **he's ~ about steam trains** c'est un fana *OR* un mordu des trains à vapeur.

Douay Bible ['daʊeɪ-] *n* Bible *f* de Douai.

double ['dʌbl] ◇ *adj* **1.** [twice as large - quantity, portion] double
2. [line, row] double ■ **~ doors, a ~ door** une porte à deux battants ‖ [with figures, letters] deux fois ■ **~ five two one** [figure] deux fois cinq deux un ; [phone number] cinquante-cinq, vingt et un ■ **"letter" is spelt with a ~ "t"** "lettre" s'écrit avec deux "t" ■ **to throw a ~ six/three** faire un double six/trois ■ **to be into ~ figures** dépasser la dizaine
3. [folded in two] en double, replié ■ **~ thickness** double épaisseur
4. [for two people] pour *OR* à deux personnes
5. [dual - purpose, advantage] double ■ [ambiguous] double, ambigu, - uë *f* ■ **a word with a ~ meaning** un mot à double sens.
◇ *predet* [twice] deux fois plus ■ **she earns ~ my salary** elle gagne deux fois plus que moi *OR* le double de moi.
◇ *n* **1.** [twice the amount] double *m* ■ [of alcohol] double *m* ■ **he charged us ~** il nous a fait payer le double ⊙ **at** *OR* **on the ~** au pas de course ■ **on the ~!** *liter & fig* magnez-vous! ■ **~ or quits** quitte ou double
2. [duplicate] double *m*, réplique *f* ■ [of person] double *m*, sosie *m* ■ CIN & TV [stand-in] doublure *f* ■ THEAT [actor with two parts] acteur *m*, - trice *f* qui tient deux rôles
3. [turn] demi-tour *m*.
◇ *adv* [in two] en deux ■ [two of the same] : **to see ~** voir double.
◇ *vt* **1.** [increase] doubler
2. [fold] plier en deux, replier
3. CIN & TV doubler.
◇ *vi* **1.** [increase] doubler
2. [turn] tourner, faire un crochet
3. [serve two purposes] : **the dining room ~s as a study** la salle à manger sert également de bureau.
◆ **double back** ◇ *vi insep* [animal, person, road] tourner brusquement ■ **the path ~s back on itself** le sentier te ramène sur tes pas.
◇ *vt sep* [sheet] mettre en double.
◆ **double for** *vt insep* CIN & THEAT doubler.
◆ **double over** = **double up** *(vi sense 1)*.
◆ **double up** ◇ *vi insep* **1.** [bend over] se plier, se courber ■ **he ~d up in pain** il se plia en deux de douleur ■ **to ~ up with laughter** se tordre de rire
2. [share] partager ■ **there weren't enough rooms so we ~d up** il n'y avait pas assez de place, alors nous nous sommes mis à deux par chambre.
◇ *vt sep* plier en deux, replier.

double act *n* duo *m* comique.

double-acting *adj* à double effet.

double agent *n* agent *m* double.

double bar *n* double barre *f*.

double-barrelled *UK*, **double-barreled** *US* [-'bærəld] *adj* **1.** [gun] à deux coups ▪ *fig* [question, remark] équivoque **2.** *UK* [name] ≃ à particule.

double bass [-beɪs] *n* contrebasse *f*.

double bassoon *n* contrebasson *m*.

double bed *n* grand lit *m*, lit *m* à deux places.

double bill *n* double programme *m*.

double bind *n* PSYCHOL double contrainte *f* ▪ **to be caught in a ~** se trouver dans une situation insoluble, être dans une impasse.

double-blind *adj* [experiment, test] en double aveugle ▪ [method] à double insu, à double anonymat.

double-breasted [-'brestɪd] *adj* croisé.

double-check *vi* & *vt* revérifier.
◆ **double check** *n* revérification *f*.

double chin *n* double menton *m*.

double click, double-click *n* COMPUT double-clic *m*.
◆ **double click** ◇ *vi* faire un double-clic, cliquer deux fois.
◇ *vt* double-cliquer ▪ **to double-click on sth** double-cliquer sur.

double cream *n* *UK* crème *f* fraîche épaisse.

double-cross *vt* trahir, doubler.
◆ **double cross** *n* trahison *f*, traîtrise *f*.

double-crosser [-'krɒsəʳ] *n* traître *m*, -esse *f*, faux jeton *m*.

double dagger *n* TYPO diésis *m*.

double date *n* *US* sortie *f* à quatre *(deux couples)*.
◆ **double-date** *vi* *US* sortir à quatre *(deux couples)*.

double-dealing ◇ *n (U)* fourberie *f*, double jeu *m*.
◇ *adj* fourbe, faux comme un jeton.

double-decker [-'dekəʳ] *n* **1.** *UK* [bus] autobus *m* à impériale **2.** *inf* [sandwich] club sandwich *m*.

double-declutch *vi* *UK* faire un double débrayage.

double-density *adj* [disk] double densité.

double-dutch *n* *UK* *inf* charabia *m*, baragouin *m* ▪ **it's all ~ to me!** c'est de l'hébreu pour moi!

double-edged *adj* [blade, knife, sword] à double tranchant, à deux tranchants ▪ *fig* [compliment, remark] à double tranchant.

double entendre [,du:blɑ̃'tɑ̃dr] *n* mot *m* *OR* expression *f* à double sens.

double entry *n* comptabilité *f* en partie double ▪ **~ bookkeeping** digraphie *f*, comptabilité en partie double.

double exposure *n* surimpression *f*.

double fault *n* double faute *f*.

double feature *n* *séance de cinéma où sont projetés deux longs métrages.*

double first *n* *UK* ≃ mention *f* très bien *(dans deux disciplines à la fois).*

double flat *n* double bémol *m*.

double-glaze *vt* *UK* isoler *(par système de double vitrage)* ▪ **to ~ a window** poser un double vitrage.

double-glazing *UK* ◇ *n (U)* double vitrage *m*.
◇ *comp* [salesman] de double vitrage.

double helix *n* double hélice *f*.

double indemnity *n* *US* indemnité *f* double.

double-jointed *adj* désarticulé.

double knitting *n* *laine assez épaisse utilisée en tricot.*

double-lock *vt* fermer à double tour.

double negative *n* double négation *f*.

double-park ◇ *vi* stationner en double file.
◇ *vt* garer en double file.

double parking *n* stationnement *m* en double file.

double pneumonia *n* pneumonie *f* double.

double-quick *adj* très rapide ▪ **in ~ time** [move] au pas de course *OR* de gymnastique ; [finish, work] en vitesse, en moins de rien.

double room *n* chambre *f* pour deux personnes.

doubles ['dʌblz] *(pl inv)* *n* double *m* ▪ **to play ~** jouer un double ▪ **a ~ player** un joueur de double ▪ **ladies'/men's ~** double dames/messieurs.

double sharp *n* double dièse *m*.

double-sided *adj* [disk] double face.

double spacing *n* double interligne *m* ▪ **in ~** à double interligne.

double standard *n* : **to have ~s** faire deux poids, deux mesures.

double stopping *n* double-corde *f*.

doublet ['dʌblɪt] *n* **1.** [jacket] pourpoint *m*, justaucorps *m* **2.** [of words] doublet *m*.

double take *n* *inf* **to do a ~** marquer un temps d'arrêt *(par surprise).*

double-talk *n (U)* *inf* [ambiguous] *propos ambigus et contournés* ▪ [gibberish] charabia *m*.

doublethink ['dʌbl,θɪŋk] *n (U)* *raisonnement de mauvaise foi qui contient des contradictions flagrantes* ▪ **it's another case of ~** c'est encore un raisonnement pervers.

double time *n* **1.** [pay] salaire *m* double ▪ **I get ~ on Sundays** je suis payé le double le dimanche **2.** MIL pas *m* redoublé **3.** MUS mesure *f* double.

double-tongue *vi* MUS faire des doubles coups de langue *(sur un instrument à vent).*

double vision *n* double vision *f*.

double whammy [-'wæmɪ] *n* *inf* double malédiction *f*.

doubling ['dʌblɪŋ] *n* [of letter, number] redoublement *m*, doublement *m*.

doubloon [dʌ'blu:n] *n* doublon *m*.

doubly ['dʌblɪ] *adv* [twice as much] doublement, deux fois plus ▪ [in two ways] doublement ▪ **she's ~ careful now** elle redouble de prudence maintenant.

doubt [daʊt] ◇ *n* **1.** [uncertainty - about fact] doute *m*, incertitude *f* ▪ **there is now considerable ~ about the convictions** on a maintenant de sérieux doutes au sujet des condamnations ▪ **beyond all reasonable ~** à n'en pas douter, sans le moindre doute ▪ **to cast ~ on sthg** mettre en doute *OR* jeter le doute sur qqch ▪ **the report casts ~ on the police evidence** les auteurs du rapport émettent des doutes sur les preuves fournies par la police ▪ **her honesty is in ~** *OR* **open to ~** [generally] on a des doutes sur son honnêteté, son honnêteté est sujette à caution ; [this time] son honnêteté est mise en doute ▪ **the future of the company is in some ~** l'avenir de l'entreprise est incertain ▪ **if** *OR* **when in ~** s'il y a un doute, en cas de doute ▪ **when in ~, do nothing** dans le doute, abstiens-toi *prov* ▪ **there is some ~ as to whether they paid** on n'est pas certain qu'ils aient payé ▪ **there is no ~ about it** cela ne fait pas de doute ▪ **there's no ~ (but) that it will be a difficult journey** il n'y a pas de doute que le voyage sera pénible ▪ **no ~** sans doute ▪ **he'll no ~ be late** il sera sûrement en retard ▪ **without (any) ~** sans aucun *OR* le moindre doute **2.** [feeling of distrust] doute *m* ▪ **I have my ~s about him** j'ai des doutes sur lui *OR* à son sujet ▪ **she has her ~s (about) whether it's true** elle doute que cela soit vrai ▪ **I have no ~ *OR* ~s about it** je n'en doute pas.
◇ *vt* **1.** [consider unlikely] : **I ~ (whether) she'll be there** je doute qu'elle soit là ▪ **she'll be there – I don't ~ it** elle sera là – je n'en doute pas *OR* j'en suis certain ▪ **I ~ it** j'en doute ▪ **I ~ if it makes**

him happy je doute que cela le rende heureux **2.** [distrust] douter de ▪ **there was no ~ing their sincerity** on ne pouvait pas mettre en doute leur sincérité.
◇ *vi* douter, avoir des doutes.

doubter ['daʊtəʳ] *n* incrédule *mf*, sceptique *mf*.

doubtful ['daʊtfʊl] *adj* **1.** [unlikely] improbable, douteux **2.** [uncertain - person] incertain, indécis ▪ **I'm ~ about his chances** je doute de *OR* j'ai des doutes sur ses chances ▪ **we're ~ about accepting** nous hésitons à accepter ▪ **it's ~ whether they're really serious** il est douteux qu'ils soient vraiment sérieux, on ne sait pas s'ils sont vraiment sérieux **3.** [questionable - answer, results] douteux, discutable **4.** [dubious - person] louche, suspect ; [- affair] douteux, louche ▪ **a joke in ~ taste** une plaisanterie d'un goût douteux.

doubtfully ['daʊtfʊlɪ] *adv* [uncertainly] avec doute, d'un air de doute ▪ [indecisively] avec hésitation, de façon indécise.

doubtfulness ['daʊtfʊlnɪs] *n* **1.** [uncertainty] incertitude *f* ▪ [hesitation] indécision *f* **2.** [dubiousness] caractère *m* équivoque *OR* douteux.

doubting ['daʊtɪŋ] *adj* sceptique, incrédule.

doubting Thomas *n* Thomas *m* l'incrédule ▪ **don't be such a ~** ne fais pas l'incrédule, ne fais pas comme saint Thomas.

doubtless ['daʊtlɪs] *adv* [certainly] sans aucun *OR* le moindre doute ▪ [probably] (très) probablement.

douche [du:ʃ] ◇ *n* MED lavage *m* interne, douche *f* ▪ [instrument] poire *f* à injections.
◇ *vt* doucher.

dough [dəʊ] *n* **1.** CULIN pâte *f* ▪ **bread ~** pâte à pain **2.** *inf* [money] blé *m*.

doughnut ['dəʊnʌt] *n* beignet *m*.

doughty ['daʊtɪ] (*comp* **doughtier**, *superl* **doughtiest**) *adj lit* vaillant.

dour [dʊəʳ] *adj* [sullen] renfrogné ▪ [stern] austère, dur ▪ [stubborn] buté.

dourly ['dʊəlɪ] *adv* [look] d'un air dur *OR* renfrogné ▪ [say] d'un ton dur *OR* maussade.

douse [daʊs] *vt* **1.** [fire] éteindre **2.** [drench] tremper, inonder.

dove[1] [dʌv] *n* ORNITH & POL colombe *f*.

dove[2] [dəʊv] *US pt* ▷ **dive**.

dovecot(e) ['dʌvkɒt] *n* colombier *m*, pigeonnier *m*.

Dover ['dəʊvəʳ] *pr n* Douvres ▪ **the Strait of ~** le pas de Calais.

Dover sole *n* ZOOL sole *f*.

dovetail ['dʌvteɪl] ◇ *vt* TECH assembler à queue d'aronde ▪ [fit] faire concorder, raccorder ▪ **he managed to ~ his plans with hers** il s'est débrouillé pour accorder *OR* faire concorder ses projets avec les siens.
◇ *vi* **1.** TECH se raccorder **2.** [combine] bien cadrer, concorder ▪ **the two projects ~ nicely** les deux projets se rejoignent parfaitement.
◇ *n* TECH queue-d'aronde *f* ▪ **a ~ joint** un assemblage à queue-d'aronde.

dowager ['daʊədʒəʳ] *n* douairière *f* ▪ **the ~ duchess** la duchesse douairière.

dowdy ['daʊdɪ] (*comp* **dowdier**, *superl* **dowdiest**) *adj* [person] sans chic, inélégant ▪ [dress] peu flatteur, sans chic.

dowel(l)ing ['daʊəlɪŋ] *n* **1.** [act] assemblage *m* à goujons, goujonnage *m* **2.** [wood] tourillon *m*.

Dow-Jones [,daʊ'dʒəʊnz] *pr n* : **the ~ (average** *OR* **index)** l'indice *m* Dow Jones.

down[1] [daʊn] ◇ *prep* **1.** [towards lower level of] : **a line ~ the middle of the page** une ligne verticale au milieu de la page ▪ **to go ~ the steps/the escalator/the mountain** descendre l'escalier/l'escalier mécanique/la montagne ▪ **tears ran ~ her face** des larmes coulaient le long de son visage ▮ [into] : **to go ~ the plughole** passer par le trou (de l'évier/de la baignoire *etc*) ▪ **the rabbit disappeared back ~ its hole** le lapin a redisparu dans son trou
2. [at lower level of] en bas de ▪ **it's ~ the stairs** c'est en bas de l'escalier ▪ **to work ~ a mine** travailler au fond d'une mine ▪ **they live ~ the street** ils habitent plus loin *OR* plus bas dans la rue
3. [along] le long de ▪ **he walked ~ the street** il a descendu la rue
4. [through] à travers ▪ **~ (through) the ages** à travers les âges
5. *UK inf* [to] à ▪ **they went ~ the shops** ils sont partis faire des courses.
◇ *adv* **1.** [downwards] vers le bas, en bas ▪ **~!** [to dog] couché!, bas les pattes! ▪ **~ and ~** de plus en plus bas
2. [on lower level] en bas ▪ **~ at the bottom of the hill/page** en bas de la colline/de la page ▪ **she lives three floors ~** elle habite trois étages plus bas ▪ **the blinds are ~** les stores sont baissés ▮ [downstairs] : **I'll be ~ in a minute** je descends dans un instant ▮ [on the ground or floor] à terre
3. [facing downwards] vers le bas, dessous
4. [reduced, lower] : **prices are ~** les prix ont baissé ▪ **the pound is ~ two cents against the dollar** FIN la livre a baissé de deux cents par rapport au dollar ▮ [below expected, desired level] : **the tyres are ~** [underinflated] les pneus sont dégonflés ; [flat] les pneus sont à plat ▪ **the cashier is £10 ~** il manque 10 livres au caissier ▪ **we were two goals ~ at half-time** FTBL on avait deux buts de retard à la mi-temps
5. [on paper] : **get it ~ in writing** *OR* **on paper** mettez-le par écrit ▪ **it's ~ in my diary/on the calendar** c'est dans mon agenda/sur le calendrier ▪ **he's ~ to speak at the conference** il est inscrit en tant qu'intervenant à la conférence
6. [from city, the north] : **we're going ~ south** nous descendons vers le sud ▪ *UK* UNIV : **she came ~ from Oxford** [on vacation] elle est descendue d'Oxford ; [graduated] elle est sortie d'Oxford
7. [out of action - machine, computer] en panne ▪ **the wires are ~** les lignes sont coupées
8. [paid] : **he paid** *OR* **put £5 ~** [whole amount] il a payé 5 livres comptant ; [as deposit] il a versé (un acompte de) 5 livres ➊ **5 ~ and 3 to go** ça fait 5, il en reste 3
9. [ill] : **he's (gone) ~ with flu** il est au lit avec la grippe
10. *phr* **to be ~ on sb** *inf* être monté contre qqn ▪ **~ with the system!** à bas le système!
◇ *adj* **1.** [depressed] déprimé, malheureux ▪ **to feel ~** avoir le cafard
2. [elevator] qui descend.
◇ *vt* **1.** [knock down - opponent] mettre à terre ; [- object, target] faire tomber ▪ **the pilot ~ed two enemy aircraft** le pilote a descendu deux avions ennemis
2. [drink] descendre ▪ [eat] avaler.
◇ *n* **1.** [setback] revers *m*, bas *m*
2. *phr* **to have a ~ on sb** *inf* avoir une dent contre qqn.

◆ **down for** *prep phr* : **she's ~ for physics** elle est inscrite au cours de physique ▪ **the meeting is ~ for today** la réunion est prévue pour aujourd'hui.

◆ **down to** *prep phr* **1.** [through to and including] jusqu'à ▪ **she sold everything right ~ to the house** elle a tout vendu, y compris la maison ▪ **from the Middle Ages ~ to the present** du *OR* depuis le Moyen Âge jusqu'à nos jours
2. [reduced to] : **I'm ~ to my last pound** il ne me reste qu'une livre ▪ **the team was ~ to 10 men** l'équipe était réduite à 10 hommes
3. [indicating responsibility] : **it's ~ to you now** c'est à toi de jouer maintenant *fig*.

down[2] [daʊn] *n* **1.** [on bird, person, plant, fruit] duvet *m* **2.** [hill] colline *f* dénudée ▪ [sand dune] dune *f*.

down-and-out ◇ *adj* indigent, sans ressources ▪ **'Down and Out in Paris and London'** *Orwell* 'Dans la dèche à Paris et à Londres'.
◇ *n* clochard *m*, - e *f* ▪ **the ~** *OR* **~s** les sans-abri *(mpl)*.

down-at-heel *adj* [shabby] miteux ▪ [shoe] éculé.

downbeat ['daʊnbi:t] ◇ *n* MUS temps *m* frappé.
◇ *adj inf* **1.** [gloomy - person] abattu, triste ; [- story] pessimiste **2.** [relaxed - person] décontracté, flegmatique ; [- situation] décontracté.

downcast [ˈdaʊnkɑːst] ◇ *adj* **1.** [dejected] abattu, démoralisé **2.** [eyes, look] baissé.
◇ *n* MIN puits *m* d'aérage.

downer [ˈdaʊnəʳ] *n* **1.** *inf* [experience] expérience *f* déprimante ▪ **to be on a ~** faire de la déprime, être déprimé **2.** △ [drug] tranquillisant *m*, sédatif *m*.

downfall [ˈdaʊnfɔːl] *n* **1.** [of person, institution] chute *f*, ruine *f* ▪ [of dream, hopes] effondrement *m* ▪ **drink was his ~** la boisson l'a perdu **2.** [of rain, snow] chute *f*.

downgrade [ˈdaʊngreɪd] *vt* **1.** [job] dévaloriser, déclasser ▪ [person] rétrograder ▪ [hotel] déclasser **2.** [belittle] rabaisser.

downhearted [ˌdaʊnˈhɑːtɪd] *adj* abattu, découragé.

downhill [ˌdaʊnˈhɪl] ◇ *adv* : **to go ~** [car, road] descendre, aller en descendant ; [business] péricliter ; *fig* se dégrader ▪ **her health went rapidly ~** sa santé déclina OR baissa rapidement.
◇ *adj* **1.** [road] en pente, incliné ▪ [walk] en descente ▪ *fig* **when you get to 40, it's ~ all the way** passé la quarantaine, vous ne faites plus que décliner ▪ **it should all be ~ from now on** maintenant ça devrait aller comme sur des roulettes **2.** [in skiing] : **~ skiing** ski *m* alpin ▪ **~ race** descente *f* ▪ **~ racer** OR **skier** descendeur *m*, - euse *f*.
◇ *n* [of road] descente *f* ▪ [in skiing] descente *f*.

Downing Street [ˈdaʊnɪŋ-] *pr n* Downing Street *(rue de Londres où se trouve la résidence officielle du Premier ministre britannique)*.

DOWNING STREET

C'est à Downing Street, à Londres, que se trouvent les résidences officielles du Premier ministre (au n°10) et du chancelier de l'Échiquier (au n°11). Tony Blair est le premier chef d'État à avoir choisi de résider au n° 11 pour des raisons de confort familial. Par extension, le nom de la rue est employé pour désigner le Premier ministre et ses fonctions.

Downing Street Declaration *pr n déclaration commune anglo-irlandaise qui, en 1993, a relancé le processus de paix en Irlande du Nord.*

down-in-the-mouth *adj* : **to be ~** être abattu.

download [ˌdaʊnˈləʊd] *vt* COMPUT télécharger.

downloadable [ˌdaʊnˈləʊdəbl] *adj* COMPUT téléchargeable.

downloading [ˌdaʊnˈləʊdɪŋ] *n* COMPUT téléchargement *m*.

down-market *adj* [product] bas de gamme ▪ [book] grande diffusion *(inv)* ▪ **it's a rather ~ area** ce n'est pas un quartier très chic.

down payment *n* acompte *m* ▪ **to make a ~ on sthg** verser un acompte pour qqch.

downpipe [ˈdaʊnpaɪp] *n* UK (tuyau *m* de) descente *f*.

downplay [ˈdaʊnpleɪ] *vt* [event, person] minimiser l'importance de ▪ [situation] dédramatiser.

downpour [ˈdaʊnpɔːʳ] *n* averse *f*, déluge *m*.

downright [ˈdaʊnraɪt] ◇ *adj* **1.** [lie] effronté, flagrant ▪ [refusal] catégorique ▪ **~ stupidity** bêtise crasse **2.** [of person, speech] franc, franche *f*, direct.
◇ *adv* [as intensifier] franchement, carrément.

downriver [ˌdaʊnˈrɪvəʳ] ◇ *adj* (situé) en aval.
◇ *adv* [move] vers l'aval ▪ [live] en aval.

downs [daʊnz] *npl* UK **the ~** les Downs *fpl*.

downshift [ˌdaʊnˈʃɪft] *vi* US rétrograder.

downside [ˈdaʊnsaɪd] *n* **1.** [underside] dessous *m* ▪ **~ up** US sens dessous dessus **2.** [trend] : **prices have tended to be on the ~** la tendance des prix est plutôt à la baisse **3.** [disadvantage] inconvénient *m*.

downsize [ˈdaʊnsaɪz] *vt* **1.** [company] réduire les effectifs de **2.** COMPUT [application] réduire l'échelle de.

downsizing [ˈdaʊnsaɪzɪŋ] *n* INDUST réduction *f* des effectifs ▪ COMPUT réduction *f* d'échelle.

downspout [ˈdaʊnspaʊt] *n* US (tuyau *m* de) descente *f*.

Down's syndrome [daʊnz-] *n* trisomie 21 *f* ▪ **~ baby** bébé *m* trisomique.

downstage [ˌdaʊnˈsteɪdʒ] ◇ *adj* du devant de la scène.
◇ *adv* vers le devant de la scène.
◇ *n* avant-scène *f*.

downstairs [ˌdaʊnˈsteəz] ◇ *adv* **1.** [gen] en bas (de l'escalier) ▪ **to come** OR **to go ~** descendre (les escaliers) ▪ **she ran ~** elle a descendu l'escalier OR elle est descendue en courant ▪ **he fell ~** il a dégringolé l'escalier **2.** [on lower floor] à l'étage en dessous OR inférieur ▪ [on ground floor] au rez-de-chaussée ▪ **the family ~** la famille du dessous.
◇ *adj* **1.** [gen] en bas ▪ **I'm using the ~ phone** j'utilise le téléphone d'en bas **2.** [of lower floor] de l'étage au-dessous OR inférieur ▪ [of ground floor] du rez-de-chaussée.
◇ *n* rez-de-chaussée *m inv*.

downstream [ˌdaʊnˈstriːm] ◇ *adv* **1.** [live] en aval ▪ [move] vers l'aval ▪ **the boat drifted ~** le bateau était poussé par le courant **2.** ECON en aval.
◇ *adj* **1.** [gen] (situé) en aval **2.** ECON en aval.

downstroke [ˈdaʊnstrəʊk] *n* [of piston] course *f* descendante ▪ [in handwriting] plein *m*.

downswing [ˈdaʊnswɪŋ] *n* **1.** [trend] tendance *f* à la baisse, baisse *f* **2.** GOLF mouvement *m* descendant.

downtime [ˈdaʊntaɪm] *n (U)* période *f* de non-fonctionnement *(d'une machine, d'une usine)*.

down-to-earth *adj* terre à terre *(inv)*, réaliste ▪ **she's very ~** elle a les pieds sur terre.

downtown [ˌdaʊnˈtaʊn] US ◇ *n* centre-ville *m*.
◇ *adj* : **~ New York** le centre OR centre-ville de New York.
◇ *adv* en ville.

downtrodden [ˈdaʊnˌtrɒdn] *adj* **1.** [person] opprimé **2.** [grass] piétiné.

downturn [ˈdaʊntɜːn] *n* baisse *f*.

down under UK *adv inf* **to go/to live ~** [to Australia] aller/vivre en Australie ; [to New Zealand] aller/vivre en Nouvelle-Zélande ; [gen] aller/vivre aux antipodes.

downward [ˈdaʊnwəd] ◇ *adj* [movement] vers le bas ▪ *fig* **a ~ trend** une tendance à la baisse ▪ **the economy is on a ~ path** l'économie est sur une mauvaise pente.
◇ *adv* = **downwards**.

downwards [ˈdaʊnwədz] *adv* vers le bas, de haut en bas ▪ **she put the letter face ~** elle a posé la lettre à l'envers ▪ **the road drops sharply ~** la route descend brusquement ▮ *fig* **everyone from the president ~** tout le monde depuis le président jusqu'en bas de la hiérarchie ▪ **we will have to revise our estimates ~** il faudra que nous revoyions nos estimations à la baisse.

downwind [ˌdaʊnˈwɪnd] *adj & adv* sous le vent ▪ **to be ~ of sthg** être sous le vent de qqch.

downy [ˈdaʊnɪ] (*comp* **downier**, *superl* **downiest**) *adj* **1.** [leaf, skin] couvert de duvet, duveté ▪ [fruit] duveté, velouté **2.** [fluffy] duveteux **3.** [filled with down] garni de duvet.

dowry [ˈdaʊərɪ] (*pl* **dowries**) *n* dot *f*.

dowse [daʊz] ◇ *vi* [for water, for minerals] faire de la radiesthésie, prospecter à la baguette.
◇ *vt* = **douse**.

dowsing [ˈdaʊzɪŋ] *n* radiesthésie *f*.

dowsing rod *n* baguette *f* (de sourcier).

doxology [dɒkˈsɒlədʒɪ] *n* doxologie *f*.

doyen [ˈdɔɪən] *n* doyen *m* (d'âge).

doyenne [ˈdɔɪen] *n* doyenne *f* (d'âge).

doz. (*written abbrev of* **dozen**) douz.

doze [dəʊz] ◇ *vi* sommeiller.
◇ *n* somme *m*.

◆ **doze off** *vi insep* s'assoupir.

dozen ['dʌzn] *n* douzaine *f* ■ **a ~ eggs** une douzaine d'œufs ■ **30 pence a ~** 30 pence la douzaine ■ **half a ~** une demi-douzaine ■ **have some more, there are ~s of them** reprenez-en, il y en a beaucoup OR des tas ■ **I've told you a ~ times** je te l'ai dit vingt fois.

dozy ['dəʊzɪ] (*comp* **dozier**, *superl* **doziest**) *adj* **1.** [drowsy] à moitié endormi, assoupi **2.** *inf* [stupid] lent, engourdi.

DP *n* **1. = data processing 2. = disabled person**.

DPh (*written abbrev of* **Doctor of Philosophy**) = **PhD**.

DPhil [ˌdiː'fɪl] = **PhD**.

DPP *pr n* = **Director of Public Prosecutions**.

dr *written abbr of* **debtor**.

Dr 1. (*written abbrev of* **Doctor**) ■ **~ Jones** [on envelope] Dr Jones ■ **Dear ~ Jones** [in letter] Monsieur, Madame ; [less formal] Cher Monsieur, Chère Madame ; [if acquainted] Cher Docteur **2.** *written abbr of* **drive**.

drab [dræb] (*comp* **drabber**, *superl* **drabbest**) *adj* **1.** [colour] terne, fade ■ [surroundings] morne, triste **2.** [shabby] miteux.

drabness ['dræbnɪs] *n* [of colour] caractère *m* OR aspect *m* terne, fadeur *f* ■ [of surroundings] caractère *m* OR aspect *m* morne, tristesse *f*, grisaille *f*.

drachma ['drækmə] (*pl* **drachmas** OR *pl* **drachmae** [-miː]) *n* **1.** [currency] drachme *f* **2.** [gen - PHARM] drachme *m*.

draconian [drə'kəʊnjən] *adj* draconien.

draft [drɑːft] ◇ *n* **1.** [of letter] brouillon *m* ■ [of novel, speech] premier jet *m*, ébauche *f* ■ [of plan] avant-projet *m* ■ **this is only the first ~** ceci n'est qu'une ébauche ■ **~ quality** COMPUT qualité *f* brouillon **2.** COMM & FIN traite *f*, effet *m* **3.** MIL [detachment] détachement *m* **4.** US MIL conscription *f* ■ **he left in order to avoid the ~** il est parti pour éviter de faire son service **5.** US = **draught**.

◇ *vt* **1.** [draw up - first version] faire le brouillon de, rédiger ; [- diagram] dresser ; [- plan] esquisser, dresser ■ LAW [contract, will] rédiger, dresser ■ [bill] préparer **2.** [gen - MIL] détacher, désigner ■ **to ~ sb to sthg/to do sthg** détacher qqn à qqch/pour faire qqch **3.** US MIL [enlist] appeler (sous les drapeaux), incorporer.

◇ *comp* [version] préliminaire ■ **~ letter** [gen] brouillon *m* de lettre ; [formal] projet *m* de lettre ■ **~ treaty** projet *m* de convention.

draft card *n* US ordre *m* d'incorporation.

draft dodger *n* US MIL réfractaire *m*.

draftee [ˌdrɑːf'tiː] *n* US recrue *f*.

draft resister *n* US MIL réfractaire *m*.

draftsman *etc* (*pl* **draftsmen**) US = **draughtsman**.

drafty (*comp* **draftier**, *superl* **draftiest** *etc*) US = **draughty**.

drag [dræg] (*pret & pp* **dragged**, *cont* **dragging**) ◇ *vt* **1.** [pull] traîner, tirer ■ **to ~ sthg on** OR **along the ground** traîner qqch par terre ■ **to ~ one's feet** traîner les pieds ■ **don't ~ me into this!** ne me mêlez pas à vos histoires! ■ **I had to ~ the truth out of her** il m'a fallu lui arracher la vérité ■ **to ~ anchor** NAUT chasser sur ses ancres ➊ **the government has been accused of dragging its feet** OR **heels over the issue** on a accusé le gouvernement de montrer peu d'empressement à s'occuper de la question ■ **to ~ sb's name through the mud** traîner qqn dans la boue **2.** [search] draguer ■ **they dragged the lake for the body** ils ont dragué le lac à la recherche du corps **3.** COMPUT faire glisser.

◇ *vi* **1.** [trail] traîner (par terre) ■ [anchor] chasser **2.** [hang behind] traîner, rester à l'arrière **3.** [search] draguer **4.** [go on and on] traîner, s'éterniser **5.** AUT [brakes] frotter, gripper, se gripper.

◇ *n* **1.** [pull] tirage *m* ■ AERON, AUT & NAUT résistance *f*, traînée *f* **2.** [dredge] drague *f* ■ [sledge] traîneau *m* ■ AGRIC [harrow] herse *f* ■ NAUT araignée *f* **3.** [brake] sabot *m* OR patin *m* de frein **4.** [handicap] entrave *f*, frein *m* ■ **unemployment is a ~ on the economy** le chômage est un frein pour l'économie **5.** *inf* [bore] : **he's a real ~!** c'est un vrai casse-pieds! ■ **what a ~!** quelle barbe!, c'est la barbe! **6.** *inf* [puff on cigarette] bouffée *f*, taffe *f* ■ **I had a ~ on** OR **of his cigarette** j'ai tiré une bouffée de sa cigarette **7.** *inf* [women's clothing] : **in ~** en travesti **8.** US *inf* [street] : **the main ~** la rue principale.

◇ *comp inf* [disco, show] de travestis ■ **~ artist** transformiste *m*.

◆ **drag along** *vt sep* [chair, toy] tirer, traîner ■ [person] traîner, entraîner ■ **to ~ o.s. along** se traîner.

◆ **drag apart** *vt sep* séparer de force.

◆ **drag away** *vt sep* emmener de force ■ **I couldn't ~ him away from his work** je ne pouvais pas l'arracher à son travail.

◆ **drag down** *vt sep* **1.** [lower] entraîner (en bas) ■ **being rude only ~s you down to his level** être grossier ne fait que vous rabaisser à son niveau **2.** [weaken] affaiblir ■ [depress] déprimer, décourager.

◆ **drag in** *vt sep* apporter (de force) ■ **he insisted on dragging in the issue of housing** il voulait à tout prix mettre la question du logement sur le tapis.

◆ **drag on** ◇ *vi insep* se prolonger, s'éterniser ■ **don't let the matter ~ on** ne laissez pas traîner l'affaire.

◇ *vt insep* : **to ~ on a cigarette** tirer sur une cigarette.

◆ **drag out** *vt sep* [prolong] faire traîner.

◆ **drag up** *vt sep* **1.** [affair, story] remettre sur le tapis, ressortir **2.** UK *inf* [child] élever à la diable OR tant bien que mal.

draggy ['drægɪ] (*comp* **draggier**, *superl* **draggiest**) *adj* UK *inf* [boring] ennuyeux, assommant ■ [listless] mou (*before vowel or silent 'h' mol*), molle *f*, avachi.

draglift ['dræglɪft] *n* tire-fesses *m inv*.

dragnet ['drægnet] *n* **1.** [for fish] seine *f*, drège *f* ■ [for game] tirasse *f* **2.** [for criminals] rafle *f*.

dragon ['drægən] *n* MYTH & ZOOL & *fig* dragon *m*.

dragonfly ['drægənflaɪ] (*pl* **dragonflies**) *n* libellule *f*.

dragoon [drə'guːn] ◇ *n* dragon *m*.

◇ *vt* [force] contraindre, forcer ■ **he ~ed us into going** il nous a contraints à y aller.

drag queen *n inf* travelo[△] *m*.

drag racing *n* course *f* de dragsters.

dragrope ['drægrəʊp] *n* AERON guiderope *m*.

dragster ['drægstəʳ] *n* voiture *f* à moteur gonflé, dragster *m*.

drain [dreɪn] ◇ *n* **1.** [in house] canalisation *f* OR tuyau *m* d'évacuation ■ [of dishwasher] tuyau *m* de vidange ■ [outside house] puisard *m* ■ [sewer] égout *m* ■ [grid in street] bouche *f* d'égout ■ **all our plans went down the ~** tous nos projets sont tombés à l'eau ■ **to laugh like a ~** rire comme une baleine **2.** AGRIC & MED drain *m* **3.** [depletion] perte *f*, épuisement *m* ■ **a ~ on resources** une ponction sur les ressources.

◇ *vt* **1.** [dry - dishes, vegetables] égoutter ; [- land] drainer, assécher ; [- reservoir] vider, mettre à sec ; [- mine] drainer ; [- oil tank] vider, vidanger ■ AGRIC & MED drainer ■ **she ~ed her glass** elle a vidé son verre OR a tout bu jusqu'à la dernière goutte ■ **~ed weight** COMM poids *m* net égoutté **2.** [deplete] épuiser ■ **to ~ sb of his/her strength** épuiser qqn ■ **the war ~ed the country of its resources** la guerre a saigné le pays.

◇ *vi* **1.** [colour] disparaître ■ [blood] s'écouler ■ **the colour ~ed from her face** son visage a blêmi **2.** [dishes, vegetables] s'égoutter ■ **leave the dishes to ~** laisse égoutter la vaisselle.

◆ **drain away** ◇ *vi insep* [liquid] s'écouler ■ [hope, strength] s'épuiser.

◇ *vt sep* faire écouler.

◆ **drain off** ◇ *vt sep* **1.** [liquid] faire écouler ■ [dishes, vegetables] égoutter **2.** AGRIC & MED drainer.

◇ *vi insep* s'écouler.

drainage ['dreɪnɪdʒ] *n (U)* **1.** [process] drainage *m*, assèchement *m* **2.** [system - in house] système *m* d'évacuation des eaux ; [- in town] système *m* d'égouts ; [- of land] système *m* de drainage ■ GEOL système *m* hydrographique **3.** [sewage] eaux *fpl* usées, vidanges *fpl*.

drainboard ['dreɪnbɔːrd] US = **draining board**.

drained [dreɪnd] *adj* épuisé, éreinté.

drainer ['dreɪnəʳ] = **draining board**.

draining ['dreɪnɪŋ] *adj* [person, task] épuisant.

draining board *n* égouttoir *m*.

drainpipe ['dreɪnpaɪp] *n* [from roof] (tuyau *m* de) descente *f* ▪ [from sink] tuyau *m* d'écoulement ▪ AGRIC [on land] drain *m*.

drainpipe trousers *npl UK* pantalon-cigarette *m*.

drake [dreɪk] *n* canard *m* (mâle).

Dralon® ['dreɪlɒn] *n* Dralon® *m*.

dram [dræm] *n* **1.** [gen - PHARM] drachme *m* **2.** *inf* [drop] goutte *f* ▪ **a ~ (of whisky)** un petit verre (de whisky).

drama ['drɑːmə] *n* **1.** [theatre] théâtre *m* ▪ **she teaches ~** elle enseigne l'art dramatique ▪ **Spanish ~** le théâtre espagnol ▪ **~ critic** critique *mf* de théâtre ▪ **~ school** école *f* de théâtre **2.** [play] pièce *f* (de théâtre), drame *m* **3.** [situation] drame *m* **4.** [excitement] drame *m*.

dramatic [drə'mætɪk] *adj* **1.** LIT, MUS & THEAT dramatique ▪ **the ~ works of Racine** le théâtre de Racine **2.** [effect, entry] théâtral, dramatique ▪ [change] remarquable, spectaculaire.

dramatically [drə'mætɪklɪ] *adv* **1.** LIT, MUS & THEAT du point de vue théâtral **2.** [act, speak] de manière dramatique, dramatiquement ▪ [change] de manière remarquable *OR* spectaculaire.

dramatics [drə'mætɪks] <> *n (U)* THEAT art *m* dramatique, dramaturgie *f*.
<> *npl fig* [behaviour] comédie *f*, cirque *m*.

dramatis personae [ˌdrɑːmətɪspɜː'səʊnaɪ] *npl* personnages *mpl (d'une pièce ou d'un roman)*.

dramatist ['dræmətɪst] *n* auteur *m* dramatique, dramaturge *m*.

dramatization [ˌdræmətaɪ'zeɪʃn] *n* **1.** [for theatre] adaptation *f* pour la scène ▪ [for film] adaptation *f* pour l'écran ▪ [for television] adaptation *f* pour la télévision **2.** [exaggeration] dramatisation *f*.

dramatize, ise ['dræmətaɪz] <> *vt* **1.** [for theatre] adapter pour la scène ▪ [for film] adapter pour l'écran ▪ [for television] adapter pour la télévision **2.** [exaggerate] faire un drame de, dramatiser ▪ [make dramatic] rendre dramatique.
<> *vi* dramatiser.

drank [dræŋk] *pt* ▷ **drink**.

drape [dreɪp] <> *n* [way something hangs] drapé *m*.
<> *vt* **1.** [adorn - person, window] draper ; [- altar, room] tendre ▪ **the stage was ~d with** *OR* **in black** la scène était tendue de noir **2.** [hang] étendre ▪ **she ~d a leg over the chair arm** elle a étendu sa jambe sur l'accoudoir.
◆ **drapes** *npl UK* [drapery] tentures *fpl* ▪ *US* [curtains] rideaux *mpl*.

draper ['dreɪpəʳ] *n UK* marchand *m*, - e *f* de tissus.

drapery ['dreɪpərɪ] (*pl* **draperies**) *n* **1.** *(U)* [material] étoffes *fpl* ▪ [arrangement of material] draperie *f* **2.** *(usu pl)* [hangings] tentures *fpl* ▪ [curtains] rideaux *mpl*.

drastic ['dræstɪk] *adj* [measures] sévère, draconien ▪ [change, effect] radical ▪ [remedy] énergique ▪ **~ cutbacks** ECON coupes *fpl* sombres ▪ **to take ~ steps** trancher dans le vif, prendre des mesures draconiennes *OR* énergiques.

drastically ['dræstɪklɪ] *adv* radicalement ▪ [cut, reduce] radicalement, sévèrement.

drat [dræt] *interj inf* **~!** diable!, bon sang!

dratted ['drætɪd] *adj inf* sacré.

draught *UK*, **draft** *US* [drɑːft] <> *n* **1.** [breeze] courant *m* d'air **2.** [in fireplace] tirage *m* **3.** [drink - swallow] trait *m*, gorgée *f* ▪ **in one ~** d'un seul trait *OR* coup **4.** [medicine] potion *f*, breuvage *m* **5. : on ~** [beer] à la pression **6.** GAMES dame *f* **7.** [pulling] traction *f*, tirage *m* ▪ NAUT [of ship] tirant *m* (d'eau).
<> *adj* [horse] de trait.

draught beer *n* bière *f* pression.

draughtboard ['drɑːftbɔːd] *n UK* GAMES damier *m*.

draught excluder [-ɪk'skluːdəʳ] *n UK* bourrelet *m* (de porte).

draught-proof <> *vt* calfeutrer.
<> *adj* calfeutré.

draught-proofing [-ˌpruːfɪŋ] *n* calfeutrage *m*.

draughts [drɑːfts] *n UK* GAMES (jeu *m* de) dames *fpl* ▪ **a game of ~** un jeu de dames.

draughtsman *UK* (*pl* **draughtsmen** [-mən]), **draftsman** *US* (*pl* **draughtsmen** [-mən]) ['drɑːftsmən] *n* [artist] dessinateur *m*, - trice *f* ▪ ARCHIT & INDUST dessinateur *m* industriel, dessinatrice *f* industrielle.

draughtsmanship *UK*, **draftsmanship** *US* ['drɑːftsmənʃɪp] *n* [of artist] talent *m* de dessinateur, coup *m* de crayon ▪ [of work] art *m* du dessin.

draughty *UK*, **drafty** *US* ['drɑːftɪ] (*UK comp* **draughtier**, *superl* **draughtiest**) (*US comp* **draftier**, *superl* **draftiest**) *adj* [house, room] plein de courants d'air ▪ [street, corner] exposé à tous les vents *OR* aux quatre vents.

draw [drɔː] (*pret* **drew** [druː], *pp* **drawn** [drɔːn]) <> *vt* **1.** [pull] tirer ▪ **to ~ the curtains** [open] tirer *OR* ouvrir les rideaux ; [shut] tirer *OR* fermer les rideaux ▪ **I drew my coat closer around me** je me suis enveloppé dans mon manteau ▪ **to ~ a bow** [in archery] tirer à l'arc
2. [haul, pull behind - car] tirer, traîner, remorquer ; [- trailer] remorquer ▪ **a carriage drawn by two horses** un équipage attelé à *OR* tiré par deux chevaux
3. [take out] tirer, retirer ▪ [remove] retirer, enlever ▪ [tooth] arracher, extraire ▪ **he drew his knife from** *OR* **out of his pocket** il a tiré son couteau de sa poche ▪ **the thief drew a gun on us** le voleur a sorti un pistolet et l'a braqué sur nous ▪ **to ~ a sword** dégainer une épée
4. [lead] conduire, entraîner ▪ *fig* **I was drawn into the controversy** j'ai été mêlé à *OR* entraîné dans la dispute ▪ **the senator refused to be drawn** [refused to answer] le sénateur refusa de répondre ; [refused to be provoked] le sénateur refusa de réagir ▪ **to ~ a meeting to a close** mettre fin à une réunion
5. [attract, elicit] attirer ▪ **to be drawn to sb** être attiré par qqn ▪ **to ~ sb's attention to sthg** faire remarquer qqch à qqn ▪ **to ~ the enemy's fire** *fig* attirer le feu de l'ennemi sur soi
6. [take from source] tirer, puiser ▪ **to ~ water from a well** puiser de l'eau dans un puits ▪ **to ~ (out) money from the bank** retirer de l'argent à la banque ▪ **the university ~s its students from all social backgrounds** l'université recrute ses étudiants dans toutes les couches sociales ▪ **her performance drew an ovation from the audience** son interprétation lui a valu l'ovation du public ▪ **his confession drew tears from his mother** son aveu a arraché des larmes à sa mère ▪ **I ~ comfort from the fact that he didn't suffer** je me console en me disant qu'il n'a pas souffert ▪ **to ~ trumps** CARDS faire tomber les atouts
7. [breathe in] **: we barely had time to ~ (a) breath** nous avons à peine eu le temps de souffler
8. [choose at random] tirer ▪ **to ~ lots** tirer au sort
9. [earn - amount, salary] gagner, toucher ; [- pension] toucher ▪ FIN [- interest] rapporter
10. [sketch] dessiner ▪ [line, triangle] tracer ▪ [map] faire ▪ **to ~ a picture of sb** faire le portrait de qqn ▪ **she drew a vivid picture of village life** *fig* elle (nous) a fait une description vivante de la vie de village ▪ **the author has drawn his characters well** *fig* l'auteur a bien dépeint ses personnages ◗ **to ~ the line at sthg** ne pas admettre qqch, se refuser à qqch ▪ **you have to ~ the line somewhere** il faut fixer des limites, il y a des limites
11. [formulate - comparison, parallel, distinction] établir, faire ; [- conclusion] tirer
12. FIN **: to ~ a cheque on one's account** tirer un chèque sur son compte
13. [disembowel] vider
14. SPORT [tie] **: the game was drawn** SPORT ils ont fait match nul ; CARDS ils ont fait partie nulle
15. HUNT [game] débusquer ▪ [covert] battre.
<> *vi* **1.** [move] **: the crowd drew to one side** la foule s'est rangée sur le côté *OR* s'est écartée ▪ **the bus drew into the coach station** l'autocar est arrivé *OR* entré dans la gare routière ▪ **to ~ ahead of sb** prendre de l'avance sur qqn ▪ **to ~ to a halt** s'arrêter ▪ **they drew level with** *OR* **alongside the window** ils sont

arrivés à la hauteur de la fenêtre ▪ **they drew nearer to us** ils se sont approchés un peu plus de nous ▪ **to ~ to an end** *OR* **to a close** tirer *OR* toucher à sa fin
2. [pull out gun] tirer ▪ **the policeman drew and fired** le policier a dégainé *OR* sorti son pistolet et a tiré
3. [choose at random] tirer au hasard ▪ **they drew for partners** ils ont tiré au sort leurs partenaires
4. [sketch] dessiner
5. [fireplace, pipe] tirer ▪ [pump, vacuum cleaner] aspirer
6. [tea] infuser
7. [be equal - two competitors] être ex aequo *(inv)* ; [- two teams] faire match nul ▪ **Italy drew against Spain** l'Italie et l'Espagne ont fait match nul ▪ **the two contestants drew for third prize** les deux concurrents ont remporté le troisième prix ex aequo *OR* sont arrivés troisièmes ex aequo.
◇ *n* **1.** [act of pulling] : **to be quick on the ~** *liter* dégainer vite, avoir la détente rapide ; *fig* avoir de la repartie ▪ **to beat sb to the ~** *liter* dégainer plus vite que qqn ; *fig* devancer qqn
2. [card] carte *f* tirée ▪ **it's your ~** c'est à vous de tirer une carte
3. [raffle, lottery] loterie *f*, tombola *f* ▪ **the ~ will take place tonight** le tirage aura lieu ce soir
4. [attraction] attraction *f*
5. GAMES partie *f* nulle ▪ SPORT match *m* nul ▪ **the chess tournament ended in a ~** le tournoi d'échecs s'est terminé par une partie nulle
6. *US* [gully] ravine *f* ▪ [drain] rigole *f*.
◆ **draw apart** ◇ *vi insep* se séparer.
◇ *vt sep* prendre à l'écart.
◆ **draw aside** ◇ *vi insep* s'écarter, se ranger.
◇ *vt sep* [person] prendre *OR* tirer à l'écart ▪ [thing] écarter.
◆ **draw away** *vi insep* **1.** [move away - person] s'éloigner, s'écarter ; [- vehicle] s'éloigner, démarrer
2. [move ahead] prendre de l'avance.
◆ **draw back** ◇ *vi insep* **1.** [move backwards] reculer, se reculer, avoir un mouvement de recul ▪ **the child drew back in fear** l'enfant a reculé de peur
2. [avoid commitment] se retirer.
◇ *vt sep* [person] faire reculer ▪ [one's hand, thing] retirer.
◆ **draw down** *vt sep* **1.** [lower - blinds] baisser, descendre
2. [provoke] attirer ▪ **their policy drew down a storm of protest** leur politique a soulevé une vague de protestations.
◆ **draw in** ◇ *vi insep* **1.** [move] : **the train drew in** le train est entré en gare ▪ **the bus drew in to the kerb** [pulled over] le bus s'est rapproché du trottoir ; [stopped] le bus s'est arrêté le long du trottoir
2. [day, evening] diminuer, raccourcir ▪ **the nights are ~ing in** les nuits raccourcissent *OR* diminuent.
◇ *vt sep* **1.** [pull in] rentrer ▪ **to ~ in the reins** tirer sur les rênes, serrer la bride
2. [involve] impliquer, mêler ▪ **he drew me into the conversation** il m'a mêlé à la conversation ▪ **I got drawn into the project** je me suis laissé impliquer dans le projet ▪ **he listened to the debate but refused to be drawn in** il a écouté le débat mais a refusé d'y participer *OR* de s'y joindre
3. [attract] attirer ▪ **the film is ~ing in huge crowds** le film fait de grosses recettes
4. [sketch] ébaucher
5. [air] aspirer, respirer ▪ **to ~ in a deep breath** respirer profondément.
◆ **draw off** *vt sep* **1.** *UK* [remove - clothing] enlever, ôter ; [- gloves] retirer, ôter
2. [liquid] tirer.
◆ **draw on** ◇ *vt sep UK* **1.** [put on - gloves, trousers, socks] enfiler
2. [entice, encourage] encourager, entraîner.
◇ *vt insep* **1.** [as source] faire appel à ▪ **I drew on my own experiences for the novel** je me suis inspiré *OR* servi de mes propres expériences pour mon roman ▪ **I had to ~ on my savings** j'ai dû prendre *OR* tirer sur mes économies
2. [suck] tirer sur ▪ **to ~ on a pipe** tirer sur une pipe.
◇ *vi insep* [time - come near] approcher ; [- get late] avancer.
◆ **draw out** ◇ *vt sep* **1.** [remove] sortir, retirer, tirer ▪ [money] retirer
2. [extend - sound, visit] prolonger ; [- meeting, speech] prolonger, faire traîner ▪ TECH [- metal] étirer ; [- wire] tréfiler
3. [cause to speak freely] faire parler
4. [information, secret] soutirer ▪ **to ~ sthg out of sb** soutirer qqch de qqn.
◇ *vi insep* [vehicle] sortir, s'éloigner.
◆ **draw up** ◇ *vt sep* **1.** *UK* [pull up] tirer ▪ **she drew herself up (to her full height)** elle s'est redressée (de toute sa hauteur)
2. *UK* [move closer - chair] approcher ▪ MIL [- troops] aligner, ranger ▪ **~ your chair up to the table** approche ta chaise de la table
3. [formulate - document] dresser, rédiger ; [- bill, list] dresser, établir ; [- plan] préparer, établir.
◇ *vi insep UK* **1.** [move] se diriger ▪ **the other boat drew up alongside us** l'autre bateau est arrivé à notre hauteur *OR* à côté de nous
2. [stop - vehicle] s'arrêter, stopper ; [- person] s'arrêter.
◆ **draw upon** *vt insep* : **they had to ~ upon their emergency funds** ils ont dû tirer sur *OR* prendre sur leur caisse de réserve ▪ **you have to ~ upon your previous experience** il faut faire appel à votre expérience antérieure.

drawback ['drɔːbæk] *n* inconvénient *m*, désavantage *m* ▪ **there are ~s to the scheme** ce projet présente des inconvénients ▪ **the main ~ to the plan is its cost** le principal inconvénient du projet est son coût.

drawbridge ['drɔːbrɪdʒ] *n* pont-levis *m*, pont *m* basculant *OR* à bascule.

drawee [drɔː'iː] *n* tiré *m*.

drawer *n* **1.** [drɔːʳ] [in chest, desk] tiroir *m* **2.** ['drɔːəʳ] [of cheque] tireur *m*.

drawers [drɔːz] *npl* ***dated*** & ***hum*** [for men] caleçon *m* ▪ [for women] culotte *f*.

drawing ['drɔːɪŋ] ◇ *n* **1.** ART dessin *m* **2.** METALL [shaping, tapering] étirage *m*.
◇ *comp* [paper, table] à dessin ▪ [lesson, teacher] de dessin ▪ **~ pen** tire-ligne *m*.

drawing board *n* planche *f* à dessin ▪ **it's back to the ~** il faudra tout recommencer.

drawing pin *n UK* punaise *f (à papier)*.

drawing room *n* **1.** [living room] salon *m* ▪ [reception room] salle *f OR* salon *m* de réception **2.** *US* RAIL compartiment *m* privé.

drawl [drɔːl] ◇ *n* débit *m* traînant, voix *f* traînante ▪ **a Southern ~** un accent du Sud.
◇ *vi* parler d'une voix traînante.
◇ *vt* dire d'une voix traînante.

drawn [drɔːn] ◇ *pp* ▻ **draw**.
◇ *adj* **1.** [blind, curtain] fermé, tiré **2.** [face, features] tiré ▪ **he looked tired and ~** il avait l'air fatigué et avait les traits tirés **3.** [game] nul **4.** CULIN : **~ butter** beurre fondu.

drawn-out *adj* prolongé, qui traîne ▪ **a long ~ dispute** un conflit qui traîne en longueur *OR* qui n'en finit pas.

drawstring ['drɔːstrɪŋ] *n* cordon *m*.

dread [dred] ◇ *n* terreur *f*, effroi *m* ▪ **she lives in ~ of her ex-husband** elle vit dans la crainte de son ex-mari.
◇ *vt* craindre, redouter ▪ **I ~ to think of what might happen** je n'ose pas imaginer ce qui pourrait arriver.
◇ *adj* redoutable, effrayant.

dreaded ['dredɪd] *adj* redoutable, terrible ***hum*** & ***liter***.

dreadful ['dredfʊl] *adj* **1.** [terrible - crime, pain] affreux, épouvantable ; [- enemy, weapon] redoutable ▪ **how ~!** quelle horreur! **2.** [unpleasant] atroce, affreux ▪ **they said some ~ things about her** ils ont raconté des horreurs sur son compte ▪ **I feel ~** [ill] je ne me sens pas du tout bien ; [embarrassed] je suis vraiment gêné **3.** [as intensifier] : **he's a ~ bore!** c'est un casse-pieds insupportable!, c'est un horrible casse-pieds! ▪ **what a ~ waste!** quel affreux gaspillage!

dreadfully ['dredfʊlɪ] *adv* **1.** [very] terriblement ▪ **I'm ~ sorry** je regrette infiniment *OR* énormément **2.** [badly] affreusement ▪ **the children behaved ~** les enfants se sont affreusement mal comportés.

dreadlocks ['dredlɒks] *npl coiffure des rastas.*

dreadnought ['drednɔːt] *n* cuirassé *m*.

dream [driːm] (*pret & pp* **dreamt** [dremt] *OR* **dreamed**) ◇ *vi* **1.** [in sleep] rêver ■ **to ~ about sb** rêver de qqn ■ **it can't be true, I must be ~ing** ce n'est pas vrai, je rêve
2. [daydream] rêvasser, rêver ■ **he's always ~ing** il est toujours dans la lune ■ **for years she'd dreamt of having a cottage in the country** elle a, durant des années, rêvé d'avoir un cottage à la campagne ■ **~ on!** *inf* on peut toujours rêver!
3. [imagine] : **to ~ of doing sthg** songer à faire qqch ■ **nobody dreamt of suspecting her** personne n'a songé à *OR* il n'est venu à l'idée de personne de la soupçonner.
◇ *vt* **1.** [in sleep] rêver ■ **he dreamt a ~** il a fait un rêve ■ **you must have dreamt it** vous avez dû le rêver
2. [daydream] rêvasser ■ **to ~ idle ~s** se nourrir d'illusions, rêver creux
3. [imagine] songer, imaginer.
◇ *n* **1.** [during sleep] rêve *m* ■ **I had a ~ about my mother last night** j'ai rêvé de ma mère la nuit dernière ■ **to see sthg in a ~** voir qqch en rêve ■ **the child had a bad ~** l'enfant a fait un mauvais rêve *OR* un cauchemar ■ **the meeting was like a bad ~** la réunion était un cauchemar ■ **sweet ~s!** faites de beaux rêves!
2. [wish, fantasy] rêve *m*, désir *m* ■ **the woman of his ~s** la femme de ses rêves ■ **her ~ was to become a pilot** elle rêvait de devenir pilote ■ **a job beyond my wildest ~s** un travail comme je n'ai jamais osé imaginer *OR* qui dépasse tous mes rêves ■ **even in her wildest ~s she never thought she'd win first prize** même dans ses rêves les plus fous, elle n'avait jamais pensé remporter le premier prix ■ **in your ~s!** *inf* tu peux toujours rêver! ■ **the American ~** le rêve américain ■ **the holiday was like a ~ come true** les vacances étaient comme un rêve devenu réalité
3. [marvel] merveille *f* ■ **my interview went like a ~** mon entretien s'est passé à merveille ■ **a ~ of a house** *inf* une maison de rêve
4. [daydream] rêverie *f*, rêve *m* ■ **he's always in a ~** il est toujours dans les nuages *OR* en train de rêver.
◇ *comp* [car, person, house] de rêve ■ **a ~ world** [ideal] un monde utopique ; [imaginary] un monde imaginaire ■ **she lives in a ~ world** elle vit dans les nuages ■ **the ~ ticket** POL [policies] le programme utopique *OR* à faire rêver ; [candidates] le couple idéal ■ **~ sequence** CIN séquence *f* onirique.
◆ **dream up** *vt sep* imaginer, inventer, concocter ■ **where did you ~ that up?** où es-tu allé pêcher ça?

"I HAVE A DREAM"

Ce célèbre discours de Martin Luther King Jr. a été prononcé à Washington le 28 août 1963 à l'occasion d'un immense rassemblement de partisans des droits civiques aux États-Unis. Le pasteur, commençant par ces mots, y évoque l'espoir de voir un jour toutes les communautés de son pays vivre en harmonie.

dreamboat ['driːmbəʊt] *n inf dated* homme *m*, femme *f* de rêve.

dreamer ['driːmər] *n liter* rêveur *m*, - euse *f* ■ [idealist] rêveur *m*, - euse *f*, utopiste *mf* ■ *pej* songe-creux *m inv*.

dreamily ['driːmɪlɪ] *adv* [act] d'un air rêveur *OR* songeur ■ [speak] d'un ton rêveur *OR* songeur ■ [absent-mindedly] d'un air absent.

dreamland ['driːmlænd] *n* pays *m* imaginaire *OR* des rêves *OR* des songes ■ **she's in ~** elle est au pays des rêves.

dreamless ['driːmlɪs] *adj* sans rêves.

dreamlike ['driːmlaɪk] *adj* irréel, onirique.

dreamt [dremt] *pt & pp* ▷ **dream**.

dreamy ['driːmɪ] (*comp* **dreamier**, *superl* **dreamiest**) *adj* **1.** [vague - person] rêveur, songeur ; [- expression] rêveur ■ [absent-minded] rêveur, distrait **2.** [impractical - person] utopique, rêveur ; [- idea] chimérique, utopique **3.** [music, voice] langoureux **4.** *inf* [wonderful] magnifique, ravissant.

drearily ['drɪərəlɪ] *adv* tristement.

dreariness ['drɪərɪnɪs] *n* [of surroundings] aspect *m* morne *OR* terne, monotonie *f* ■ [of life] monotonie *f*, tristesse *f*.

dreary ['drɪərɪ] (*comp* **drearier**, *superl* **dreariest**) *adj* [surroundings] morne, triste ■ [life] morne, monotone ■ [work, job] monotone, ennuyeux ■ [person] ennuyeux (comme la pluie) ■ [weather] maussade, morne.

dredge [dredʒ] ◇ *vt* **1.** [river] draguer **2.** CULIN [with flour, sugar] saupoudrer ■ [with breadcrumbs] paner.
◇ *n* NAUT drague *f*.
◆ **dredge up** *vt sep liter* draguer ■ *fig* [scandal, unpleasant news] déterrer, ressortir.

dredger ['dredʒər] *n* **1.** NAUT [ship] dragueur *m* ■ [machine] drague *f* **2.** CULIN saupoudreuse *f*, saupoudroir *m*.

dregs [dregz] *npl liter & fig* lie *f* ■ **the ~ of society** la lie *OR* les bas-fonds de la société.

drench [drentʃ] ◇ *vt* **1.** [soak] tremper, mouiller ■ **by the time we got home we were absolutely ~ed** le temps d'arriver à la maison, nous étions complètement trempés ■ **she had ~ed herself with perfume** *fig* elle s'était aspergée de parfum **2.** VET donner *OR* faire avaler un médicament à.
◇ *n* VET (dose *f* de) médicament *m*.

drenching ['drentʃɪŋ] ◇ *n* trempage *m*.
◇ *adj* : **~ rain** pluie *f* battante *OR* diluvienne.

Dresden ['drezdən] ◇ *pr n* [city] Dresde.
◇ *n* [china] porcelaine *f* de Saxe, saxe *m*.

dress [dres] ◇ *n* **1.** [frock] robe *f* **2.** [clothing] habillement *m*, tenue *f* **3.** [style of dress] tenue *f*, toilette *f* ■ **formal/informal ~** tenue de cérémonie/de ville.
◇ *vt* **1.** [clothe] habiller ■ **she ~ed herself** *OR* **got ~ed** elle s'est habillée **2.** [arrange] orner, parer ■ [groom - horse] panser ; [- hair] coiffer ; [- shop window] faire la vitrine de ; [- ship] pavoiser **3.** [wound] panser ■ **he ~ed my wound** il a fait mon pansement **4.** CULIN [salad] assaisonner, garnir ■ [meat, fish] parer ■ **~ed chicken** poulet *m* prêt à cuire **5.** [treat - cloth, skins] préparer, apprêter ; [- leather] corroyer ; [- stone] tailler, dresser ; [- metal] polir ; [- timber] dégrossir **6.** [bush, tree] tailler ■ [woods] dégrossir **7.** AGRIC [field] façonner **8.** MIL [troops] aligner ■ **to ~ ranks** se mettre en rangs **9.** [neuter - animal] dresser.
◇ *vi* **1.** [get dressed, wear clothes] s'habiller ■ **to ~ for dinner** [gen] se mettre en tenue de soirée ; [men] se mettre en smoking ; [women] se mettre en robe du soir ■ **do we have to ~ for dinner?** est-ce qu'il faut s'habiller pour le dîner? **2.** MIL [soldiers] s'aligner.
◆ **dress down** *UK* ◇ *vi insep* s'habiller simplement.
◇ *vt sep inf* [scold] passer un savon à.
◆ **dress up** ◇ *vi insep* **1.** [put on best clothes] s'habiller, se mettre sur son trente et un ■ **he was all ~ed up** il était tout endimanché **2.** [put on disguise] se déguiser, se costumer ■ **she ~ed up as a clown** elle s'est déguisée en clown.
◇ *vt sep* **1.** [put on best clothes] habiller **2.** [disguise] déguiser ■ **his mother had ~ed him up as a soldier** sa mère l'avait déguisé en soldat **3.** [smarten] rendre plus habillé **4.** [embellish] orner ■ **you could ~ up the outfit with a nice scarf** tu pourrais rendre la tenue plus habillée avec un joli foulard ■ **it's the same old clichés ~ed up as new ideas** c'est toujours les mêmes clichés, mais présentés comme des idées novatrices.

dressage ['dresɑːʒ] *n* EQUIT dressage *m*.

dress circle *n* premier balcon *m*, corbeille *f*.

dress designer *n* modéliste *mf*, dessinateur *m*, - trice *f* de mode ■ [famous] couturier *m*.

dressed [drest] *adj* habillé ■ **a well-~/smartly-~ man** un homme bien habillé/élégant ■ **~ in blue chiffon** vêtu de mousseline de soie bleue ■ **she was not appropriately ~ for the country/for gardening** elle n'avait pas la tenue appropriée *OR* qui convenait pour la campagne/pour jardiner ■ **she was ~ as a man** elle était habillée en homme ▶ **she was ~ to kill** *inf* elle avait un look d'enfer.

dresser ['dresər] *n* **1.** [person] : **he's a smart/sloppy ~** il s'habille avec beaucoup de goût/avec négligence **2.** THEAT habilleur *m*, - euse *f* **3.** [tool - for wood] raboteuse *f* ; [- for stone] rabotin *m* **4.** [for dishes] buffet *m*, dressoir *m* **5.** *US* [for clothing] commode *f*.

dressing ['dresɪŋ] *n* **1.** [act of getting dressed] habillement *m*, habillage *m* **2.** CULIN [sauce] sauce *f*, assaisonnement *m* ▪ *US* [stuffing] farce *f* ▪ **an oil and vinegar ~** une vinaigrette **3.** [for wound] pansement *m* **4.** AGRIC [fertilizer] engrais *m* **5.** [for cloth, leather] apprêt *m*.

dressing-down *n UK inf* réprimande *f*, semonce *f* ▪ **to give sb a ~** passer un savon à qqn.

dressing gown *n* robe *f* de chambre, peignoir *m*.

dressing room *n* [at home] dressing-room *m*, dressing *m*, vestiaire *m* ▪ [at gymnasium, sports ground] vestiaire *m* ▪ THEAT loge *f* (d'acteur) ▪ *US* [in shop] cabine *f* d'essayage.

dressing table *n* coiffeuse *f*, (table *f* de) toilette *f*.

dressing-up *n* [children's game] déguisement *m*.

dressmaker ['dres,meɪkəʳ] *n* couturière *f* ▪ [famous] couturier *m*.

dressmaking ['dres,meɪkɪŋ] *n* couture *f*, confection *f* des robes.

dress rehearsal *n* THEAT (répétition *f*) générale *f* ▪ *fig* [practice] répétition *f* générale.

dress sense *n* : **to have good ~** savoir s'habiller ▪ **she's got no ~** elle ne sait pas s'habiller.

dress shirt *n* chemise *f* de soirée.

dress uniform *n* tenue *f* de cérémonie.

dressy ['dresɪ] (*comp* **dressier**, *superl* **dressiest**) *adj* [clothes] (qui fait) habillé, élégant ▪ [person] élégant, chic ▪ [event] habillé.

drew [dru:] *pt* ▻ **draw**.

drib [drɪb] *n phr* : **in ~s and drabs** petit à petit.

dribble ['drɪbl] ◇ *vi* **1.** [trickle] couler lentement, tomber goutte à goutte ▪ **the strikers slowly ~d back to work** *fig* les grévistes reprenaient le travail par petits groupes **2.** [baby] baver **3.** SPORT dribbler.
◇ *vt* **1.** [trickle] laisser couler OR tomber lentement **2.** SPORT [ball, puck] dribbler.
◇ *n* **1.** [trickle] filet *m* **2.** *fig* [small amount] : **a ~ of** un petit peu de **3.** SPORT dribble *m*.

dried [draɪd] *adj* [fruit] sec, sèche *f* ▪ [meat] séché ▪ [milk, eggs] déshydraté.

dried-up *adj* [apple, person] ratatiné, desséché ▪ [talent, well] tari ▪ [beauty, love] fané.

drier ['draɪəʳ] ◇ *compar* ▻ **dry**.
◇ *n* [for clothes] séchoir *m* (à linge) ▪ [for hair - hand-held] séchoir *m* (à cheveux), sèche-cheveux *m inv* ; [- helmet] casque *m* (sèche-cheveux).

driest ['draɪɪst] *superl* ▻ **dry**.

drift [drɪft] ◇ *vi* **1.** [float - on water] aller à la dérive, dériver ; [- in current, wind] être emporté ▪ AERON dériver ▪ **the clouds ~ed** les nuages étaient poussés par le vent **2.** [sand, snow] s'amonceler, s'entasser **3.** [move aimlessly] marcher nonchalamment ▪ **people began to ~ away/in/out** les gens commençaient à s'en aller/entrer/sortir d'un pas nonchalant ▮ *fig* **the conversation ~ed from one topic to another** la conversation passait d'un sujet à un autre ▪ **he just ~s along** il flâne simplement ▪ **to ~ apart** [friends] se perdre de vue ; [couple] se séparer petit à petit ▪ **he ~ed into a life of crime** il s'est laissé entraîner dans la criminalité **4.** ELECTRON se décaler.
◇ *vt* **1.** [subj: current] entraîner, charrier ▪ [subj: wind] emporter, pousser **2.** [sand, snow] amonceler, entasser.
◇ *n* **1.** [flow] mouvement *m*, force *f* ▪ [of air, water] poussée *f* ▪ **the ~ of the tide** [speed] la vitesse de la marée ; [direction] le sens de la marée ➊ **the North Atlantic Drift** GEOG le courant nord-atlantique **2.** [of leaves, sand] amoncellement *m*, entassement *m* ▪ [of fallen snow] amoncellement *m*, congère *f* ▪ [of falling snow] rafale *f*, bourrasque *f* ▪ [of clouds] traînée *f* ▪ [of dust, mist] nuage *m* ▪ GEOL [deposits] apports *mpl* **3.** [of plane, ship] dérivation *f* ▪ [of missile] déviation *f* ▪ [deviation from course] dérive *f* ▪ **continental ~** dérive des continents **4.** ELECTRON déviation *f* **5.** [trend] tendance *f* **6.** [meaning] sens *m*, portée *f* ▪ **do you get my ~?** voyez-vous où je veux en venir? **7.** LING évolution *f* (*d'une langue*) **8.** MIN galerie *f* chassante.
◆ **drift off** *vi insep* [fall asleep] s'assoupir.

drifter ['drɪftəʳ] *n* **1.** [person] *personne qui n'a pas de but dans la vie* ▪ **he's a bit of a ~** il n'arrive pas à se fixer, il ne sait pas ce qu'il veut **2.** [boat] drifter *m*, dériveur *m*.

drift ice *n (U)* glaces *fpl* flottantes OR en dérive.

drift net *n* filet *m* dérivant.

driftwood ['drɪftwʊd] *n (U)* bois *mpl* flottants.

drill [drɪl] ◇ *n* **1.** [manual] porte-foret *m* ▪ [electric] perceuse *f* ▪ [of dentist] fraise *f* (*de dentiste*), roulette *f* ▪ [for oil well] trépan *m* ▪ [pneumatic] marteau *m* piqueur ▪ MIN perforatrice *f* **2.** [bit] : **~ (bit)** foret *m*, mèche *f* **3.** [exercise] exercice *m* ▪ MIL manœuvre *f*, drill *m* ▪ **I know the ~** *UK inf fig* je sais ce qu'il faut faire, je connais la marche à suivre **4.** TEX treillis *m*, coutil *m* **5.** AGRIC [machine] semoir *m* ▪ [furrow] sillon *m*.
◇ *vt* **1.** [metal, wood] forer, percer ▪ [hole] percer ▪ [dentist] fraiser ▪ **to ~ an oil well** forer un puits de pétrole **2.** *inf* SPORT [ball] : **he ~ed the ball into the back of the net** il envoya la balle droit au fond du filet **3.** [train] faire faire des exercices à ▪ **I ~ed him as to what to say** je lui ai fait la leçon sur ce qu'il fallait dire ▮ MIL faire faire l'exercice à ▪ **the troops are well ~ed** les troupes sont bien entraînées **4.** [seeds] semer en sillon ▪ [field] tracer des sillons dans.
◇ *vi* **1.** [bore] forer ▪ **they are ~ing for oil** ils forent OR effectuent des forages pour trouver du pétrole **2.** [train] faire de l'exercice, s'entraîner ▪ MIL être à l'exercice, manœuvrer.
◆ **drill into** *vt sep* faire comprendre, enfoncer dans la tête ▪ **it was ~ed into them from an early age not to accept lifts from strangers** depuis leur plus jeune âge, on leur avait enfoncé dans la tête qu'il ne fallait pas accepter de monter en voiture avec des inconnus.

drilling ['drɪlɪŋ] *n (U)* [in metal, wood] forage *m*, perçage *m* ▪ [by dentist] fraisage *m* ▪ **~ for oil** forage pétrolier.

drilling platform *n* plate-forme *f* (de forage).

drilling rig *n* **1.** [on land] derrick *m*, tour *f* de forage **2.** [at sea] = **drilling platform**.

drill sergeant *n* sergent *m* instructeur.

drily ['draɪlɪ] *adv* [wryly] d'un air pince-sans-rire ▪ [coldly] sèchement, d'un ton sec.

drink [drɪŋk] (*pret* **drank** [dræŋk], *pp* **drunk** [drʌŋk]) ◇ *vt* boire, prendre ▪ **would you like something to ~?** voulez-vous boire quelque chose? ▪ **the water is not fit to ~** l'eau n'est pas potable ▪ **this coffee isn't fit to ~** ce café est imbuvable ▪ **red Burgundy is best drunk at room temperature** le bourgogne rouge est meilleur bu chambré ▪ **to ~ one's fill** boire à sa soif ▪ **to ~ sb's health, to ~ a toast to sb** boire à la santé de qqn ▪ **he drank himself into a stupor** il s'est soûlé jusqu'à l'hébétude ▪ **he's ~ing himself to death** l'alcool le tue peu à peu ➊ **to ~ sb under the table** faire rouler qqn sous la table.
◇ *vi* boire ▪ **she drank out of** OR **from the bottle** elle a bu à la bouteille ▪ **I only ~ socially** je ne bois jamais seul ▪ **'don't ~ and drive'** 'boire ou conduire, il faut choisir' ➊ **he ~s like a fish** il boit comme un trou.
◇ *n* **1.** [nonalcoholic] boisson *f* ▪ **may I have a ~?** puis-je boire quelque chose? ▪ **a ~ of water** un verre d'eau ▪ **give the children a ~** donnez à boire aux enfants ▪ **there's plenty of food and ~** il y a tout ce qu'on veut à boire et à manger
2. [alcoholic] verre *m* ▪ [before dinner] apéritif *m* ▪ [after dinner] digestif *m* ▪ **we invited them in for a ~** nous les avons invités à prendre un verre ▪ **he likes** OR **enjoys a ~** il aime bien boire un verre ▪ **~s are on the house!** la maison offre à boire! ▪ **he'd had one ~ too many** il avait bu un verre de trop, il avait un verre dans le nez
3. [mouthful] gorgée *f*
4. [alcohol] la boisson, l'alcool *m* ▪ **she's taken to ~** elle s'adonne à la boisson, elle boit ▪ **to be the worse for ~** être en état d'ébriété ▪ **to drive under the influence of ~** conduire en état d'ivresse OR d'ébriété ▪ **to smell of ~** sentir l'alcool
5. *UK inf* [sea] flotte *f*.
◇ *comp* : **he has a ~ problem** il boit trop, il s'adonne à la boisson.

◆ **drink away** *vt sep* [troubles] noyer ■ [fortune] boire.
◆ **drink down** *vt sep* avaler *OR* boire d'un trait.
◆ **drink in** *vt sep* [story, words] boire ■ [atmosphere, surroundings] s'imprégner de.
◆ **drink to** *vt insep* boire à, porter un toast à ■ **I'll ~ to that!** je suis pour!
◆ **drink up** ◇ *vt sep* boire (jusqu'à la dernière goutte), finir.
◇ *vi insep* vider son verre ■ **~ up!** finissez vos verres!

drinkable ['drɪŋkəbl] *adj* [safe to drink] potable ■ [tasty] buvable.

drink-driving *n* conduite *f* en état d'ivresse.

drinker ['drɪŋkəʳ] *n* buveur *m*, - euse *f* ■ **he's a hard** *OR* **heavy ~** il boit sec *OR* beaucoup.

drinking ['drɪŋkɪŋ] ◇ *n* fait *m* de boire ■ **heavy ~** ivrognerie *f* ■ **I'm not used to ~** je n'ai pas l'habitude de boire ■ **his ~ is becoming a problem** le fait qu'il boive devient un problème.
◇ *comp* [man] qui boit ■ [habits] de buveur ■ [bout, companion, session] de beuverie.

drinking chocolate *n* chocolat *m* à boire ■ [powder] chocolat *m* en poudre ■ [hot drink] chocolat *m* chaud.

drinking fountain *n* [in street] fontaine *f* publique ■ [in corridor, public conveniences] jet *m* d'eau potable.

drinking song *n* chanson *f* à boire.

drinking-up time *n UK moment où les clients doivent finir leur verre avant la fermeture du bar.*

drinking water *n* eau *f* potable.

drinks machine, drink machine *n US* distributeur *m* de boissons.

drip [drɪp] (*pret & pp* **dripped**, *cont* **dripping**) ◇ *vi* **1.** [liquid] tomber goutte à goutte, dégoutter ■ **the rain is dripping down my neck** la pluie me dégouline dans le cou ■ **I was dripping with sweat** j'étais en nage ■ **dripping with sentimentality** *fig* dégoulinant de sentimentalité **2.** [tap] fuir, goutter ■ [nose] couler ■ [washing] s'égoutter ■ [walls] suinter ■ [hair, trees] dégoutter, ruisseler.
◇ *vt* laisser tomber goutte à goutte ■ **you're dripping coffee everywhere** tu mets du café partout.
◇ *n* **1.** [falling drops - from tap, gutter, ceiling] égouttement *m*, dégoulinement *m* **2.** [sound - from trees, roofs] bruit *m* de l'eau qui goutte ; [- from tap] bruit d'un robinet qui fuit *OR* goutte **3.** [drop] goutte *f* **4.** *inf pej* [person] nouille *f*, lavette *f* **5.** MED [device] goutte-à-goutte *m inv* ■ [solution] perfusion *f* ■ **she's on a ~** elle est sous perfusion **6.** ARCHIT larmier *m*.

drip-dry ◇ *adj* qui ne nécessite aucun repassage.
◇ *vi* s'égoutter.
◇ *vt* (faire) égoutter.

drip-feed ◇ *n* [device] goutte-à-goutte *m inv* ■ [solution] perfusion *f*.
◇ *vt* alimenter par perfusion.

dripping ['drɪpɪŋ] ◇ *n* **1.** CULIN [of meat] graisse *f (de rôti)* **2.** [of liquid] égouttement *m*, égouttage *m*.
◇ *adj* **1.** [tap] qui fuit *OR* goutte ■ **~ with blood/with sweat** ruisselant de sang/de sueur **2.** [very wet] trempé.

drippy ['drɪpɪ] (*comp* **drippier**, *superl* **drippiest**) *adj* **1.** *inf pej* [person] mou *(before vowel or silent 'h'* **mol***)*, molle *f* **2.** [tap] qui fuit *OR* goutte.

drive [draɪv] (*pret* **drove** [drəʊv], *pp* **driven** ['drɪvn]) ◇ *vt* **1.** [bus, car, train] conduire ■ [racing car] piloter ■ **I ~ a Volvo** j'ai une Volvo ■ **he ~s a taxi/lorry** il est chauffeur de taxi/camionneur ■ **she ~s racing cars** elle est pilote de course ■ **he drove her into town** il l'a conduite *OR* emmenée en voiture en ville ■ **she drove the car into a tree** elle a heurté un arbre avec la voiture
2. [chase] chasser, pousser ■ **to ~ sb out of the house/of the country** chasser qqn de la maison/du pays ■ **we drove the cattle back into the shed** nous avons fait rentrer le bétail dans l'étable ■ **the waves drove the ship against the rocks** les vagues ont jeté le navire contre les rochers ■ **the strong winds had driven the ship off course** les vents forts avaient dévié le navire de sa route ‖ *fig* **her words drove all worries from his mind** ses paroles lui ont fait complètement oublier ses soucis ■ **they have driven us into a corner** ils nous ont mis au pied du mur
3. [work] : **it doesn't pay to ~ your workers too hard** on ne gagne rien à surmener ses employés ■ **he ~s himself too hard** il exige trop de lui-même
4. [force] pousser, inciter ■ **he was driven to it** on lui a forcé la main ■ **driven by jealousy, he killed her** il l'a tuée sous l'emprise de la jalousie ■ **the situation is driving me to despair/distraction** la situation me pousse au désespoir/me rend fou ■ **to ~ sb crazy** *OR* **mad** *OR* **up the wall** *inf* rendre qqn fou ■ **his performance drove the audience wild** *inf* son spectacle a mis le public en délire
5. [hammer] : **to ~ a nail home** enfoncer un clou ‖ *fig* **to ~ a point home** faire admettre son point de vue ■ **to ~ a hard bargain** avoir toujours le dernier mot en affaires, être dur en affaires
6. [bore - hole] percer ; [- tunnel] percer, creuser
7. [operate - machine] faire fonctionner ■ MECH entraîner ■ **driven by electricity** marchant à l'électricité ■ **the pinion is driven in rotation** le pignon est actionné par rotation
8. SPORT : **to ~ a ball** exécuter un drive ; [in golf] driver
9. HUNT [game] rabattre ■ [area] battre.
◇ *vi* **1.** [operate a vehicle] conduire ■ [travel in vehicle] aller en voiture ■ **do you** *OR* **can you ~?** savez-vous conduire? ■ **I was driving at 100 mph** je roulais à 160 km/h ■ **we drove home/down to the coast** nous sommes rentrés/descendus sur la côte en voiture ■ **they drove all night** ils ont roulé toute la nuit ■ **are you walking or driving?** êtes-vous à pied ou en voiture? ■ **~ on the right** roulez à droite, tenez votre droite
2. [car] rouler
3. [dash] se ruer ■ **rain was driving against the window** la pluie fouettait les vitres.
◇ *n* **1.** AUT [trip] promenade *f OR* trajet *m* (en voiture) ■ **we went for a ~** nous avons fait une promenade *OR* un tour en voiture ■ **it's an hour's ~ from here** c'est à une heure d'ici en voiture
2. [road - public] avenue *f*, rue *f* ; [- private] voie *f* privée *(menant à une habitation)* ■ [in street names] allée *f*
3. [energy] dynamisme *m*, énergie *f* ■ **we need someone with ~** il nous faut quelqu'un de dynamique *OR* d'entreprenant
4. [urge] besoin *m*, instinct *m*
5. [campaign] campagne *f* ■ **the company is having a sales ~** la compagnie fait une campagne de vente
6. *UK* [for bridge, whist] tournoi *m*
7. SPORT [in cricket, tennis] coup *m* droit ■ [in golf] drive *m* ■ [in football] tir *m*, shoot *m*
8. [of animals] rassemblement *m* ■ [in hunting] battue *f*
9. TECH [power transmission] transmission *f*, commande *f* ■ AUT : **four-wheel ~** quatre roues motrices *f inv*, quatre-quatre *m inv OR f inv*
10. COMPUT [for disk] unité *f OR* lecteur *m* de disquettes ■ [for tape] dérouleur *m*
11. MIL poussée *f*, offensive *f*.
◇ *comp* TECH [mechanism, device] d'entraînement, d'actionnement, de transmission.
◆ **drive along** ◇ *vi insep* [car] rouler, circuler ■ [person] rouler, conduire.
◇ *vt sep* [subj: river, wind] pousser, chasser.
◆ **drive at** *vt insep* vouloir dire ■ **she didn't understand what he was driving at** elle ne comprenait pas où il voulait en venir.
◆ **drive away** ◇ *vi insep* [person] s'en aller *OR* partir (en voiture) ■ [car] démarrer.
◇ *vt sep* [car] démarrer ■ [person] *liter* emmener en voiture ■ *fig* repousser, écarter ■ [animal] chasser, éloigner.
◆ **drive back** ◇ *vi insep* [person] rentrer en voiture ■ [car] retourner.
◇ *vt sep* **1.** [person] ramener *OR* reconduire en voiture ■ [car] reculer
2. [repel] repousser, refouler ■ **fear drove them back** la peur leur a fait rebrousser chemin.
◆ **drive in** ◇ *vi insep* [person] entrer (en voiture) ■ [car] entrer.
◇ *vt sep* [nail, stake] enfoncer ■ [screw] visser ■ [rivet] poser.

◆ **drive off** ◇ *vi insep* **1.** [leave - person] s'en aller *OR* s'éloigner en voiture ; [- car] démarrer **2.** GOLF driver.
◇ *vt sep* [frighten away] éloigner, chasser.
◆ **drive on** ◇ *vi insep* [continue trip] poursuivre sa route ■ [after stopping] reprendre la route.
◇ *vt sep* [push] pousser, inciter.
◆ **drive out** ◇ *vi insep* [person] sortir (en voiture) ■ [car] sortir.
◇ *vt sep* [person] chasser, faire sortir ■ [thought] chasser ■ **to ~ out evil spirits** [from a place] chasser les mauvais esprits ; [from a person] chasser le mauvais œil.
◆ **drive over** ◇ *vi insep* venir *OR* aller en voiture.
◇ *vt insep* [crush] écraser.
◇ *vt sep* conduire *OR* emmener en voiture.
◆ **drive up** *vi insep* [person] arriver (en voiture) ■ [car] arriver.

drive-by *adj* : **~ shooting** *fusillade exécutée d'un véhicule en marche.*

drive-in ◇ *n* [cinema] drive-in *m inv*, ciné-parc *m offic* ■ [restaurant, bank etc] *désigne tout commerce où l'on est servi dans sa voiture.*
◇ *adj* où l'on reste dans sa voiture.

drivel ['drɪvl] (*UK pret & pp* **drivelled**, *cont* **drivelling**) (*US pret & pp* **driveled**, *cont* **driveling**) ◇ *n (U)* **1.** [nonsense] bêtises *fpl*, radotage *m* ■ **you're talking ~!** tu racontes n'importe quoi! **2.** [saliva] bave *f*.
◇ *vi* **1.** [speak foolishly] dire des bêtises, radoter ■ **what's he drivelling on about?** qu'est-ce qu'il radote? **2.** [dribble] baver.

driven ['drɪvn] ◇ *pp* ⊳ **drive.**
◇ *adj* TECH : **a ~ shaft** un arbre mené *OR* récepteur.

-driven *in cpds* **1.** MECH (fonctionnant) à ■ **electricity/steam~ engine** machine électrique/à vapeur **2.** *fig* déterminé par ■ **market/consumer~** déterminé par les contraintes du marché/les exigences du consommateur **3.** COMPUT contrôlé par ■ **menu~** contrôlé par menu.

driver ['draɪvər] *n* **1.** [of car] conducteur *m*, - trice *f* ■ [of bus, taxi, lorry] chauffeur *m*, conducteur *m*, - trice *f* ■ [of racing car] pilote *m* ■ [of train] mécanicien *m*, conducteur *m*, - trice *f* ■ [of cart] charretier *m*, - ère *f* ■ SPORT [of horse-drawn vehicle] driver *m* ■ **she's a good ~** elle conduit bien ■ **car ~s** automobilistes *mpl* ■ **the ~'s seat** la place du conducteur **2.** [of animals] conducteur *m*, - trice *f* **3.** [golf club] driver *m* **4.** COMPUT pilote *m*.

driver's license *n US* permis *m* de conduire.

drive shaft *n* arbre *m* de transmission.

drive-through ◇ *adj* où l'on reste dans sa voiture.
◇ *n* drive-in *m inv*, ciné-parc *m offic.*

driveway ['draɪvweɪ] *n* voie *f* privée *(menant à une habitation).*

driving ['draɪvɪŋ] ◇ *adj* **1.** [rain] battant **2.** [powerful] fort ■ [ambition] ferme.
◇ *n* conduite *f* ■ **her ~ is good** elle conduit bien ■ **I like ~** j'aime conduire ■ **bad ~** conduite imprudente ■ **~ under the influence** *OR* **~ while intoxicated** *US* conduite en état d'ivresse.

driving force *n* MECH force *f* motrice ■ **she's the ~ behind the project** *fig* c'est elle le moteur du projet.

driving instructor *n* moniteur *m*, - trice *f* de conduite *OR* d'auto-école.

driving lesson *n* leçon *f* de conduite.

driving licence *n UK* permis *m* de conduire.

driving school *n* auto-école *f*.

driving seat *n* place *f* du conducteur ■ **she's in the ~** *fig* c'est elle qui mène l'affaire *OR* qui tient les rênes.

driving shaft *n* arbre *m* moteur.

driving test *n* examen *m* du permis de conduire ■ **I passed my ~ today/in 1972** j'ai eu mon permis aujourd'hui/en 1972 ■ **he failed his ~** il a raté son permis.

drizzle ['drɪzl] ◇ *n* bruine *f*, crachin *m*.
◇ *vi* bruiner, crachiner.

drizzly ['drɪzlɪ] *adj* de bruine *OR* crachin, bruineux.

droll [drəʊl] *adj* [comical] drôle, comique ■ [odd] curieux, drôle.

dromedary ['drɒmədərɪ] (*pl* **dromedaries**) *n* dromadaire *m*.

drone [drəʊn] ◇ *n* **1.** [sound - of bee] bourdonnement *m* ; [- of engine] ronronnement *m* ■ [louder] vrombissement *m* **2.** [male bee] abeille *f* mâle, faux-bourdon *m* ■ *pej* [person] fainéant *m*, - e *f* **3.** MUS bourdon *m* **4.** [plane] avion *m* téléguidé, drone *m*.
◇ *vi* [bee] bourdonner ■ [engine] ronronner ■ [loudly] vrombir ■ **to ~ on** [person] parler d'un ton monotone.

drool [dru:l] *vi* baver ■ **to ~ over sthg** *fig* baver d'admiration *OR* s'extasier devant qqch.

droop [dru:p] ◇ *vi* [head] pencher ■ [eyelids] s'abaisser ■ [body] s'affaisser ■ [shoulders] tomber ■ [flowers] commencer à baisser la tête *OR* à se faner ■ **her spirits ~ed** elle s'est démoralisée.
◇ *n* [of eyelids] abaissement *m* ■ [of head] attitude *f* penchée ■ [of body, shoulders] affaissement *m* ■ [of spirits] langueur *f*, abattement *m*.

drooping ['dru:pɪŋ] *adj* [eyelids] abaissé ■ [flowers] qui commence à se faner.

droopy ['dru:pɪ] (*comp* **droopier**, *superl* **droopiest**) *adj* [moustache, shoulders] qui tombe ■ [flowers] qui commence à se faner.

drop [drɒp] (*pret & pp* **dropped**, *cont* **dropping**) ◇ *vt* **1.** [let fall - accidentally] laisser tomber ; [- liquid] laisser tomber goutte à goutte ; [- trousers] laisser tomber ; [- bomb] lancer, lâcher ; [- stitch] sauter, laisser tomber ■ [release] lâcher ■ **~ it!** [to dog] lâche ça! ■ **they dropped soldiers/supplies by parachute** ils ont parachuté des soldats/du ravitaillement ■ **to ~ a curtsy** faire une révérence ■ **to ~ anchor** NAUT mouiller, jeter l'ancre ▌SPORT : **to ~ a goal** [in rugby] marquer un drop ■ **she dropped the ball over the net** [in tennis] elle a placé un amorti juste derrière le filet ➊ **to ~ a brick** *inf OR* **a clanger** *UK inf* faire une gaffe
2. [lower - voice] baisser ; [- speed] réduire ; [- hem] ressortir
3. [deliver] déposer ■ **could you ~ me at the corner please?** pouvez-vous me déposer au coin s'il vous plaît?
4. [abandon - friend] laisser tomber, lâcher ; [- discussion, work] abandonner, laisser tomber ■ **I've dropped the idea of going** j'ai renoncé à y aller ■ **let's ~ the subject** ne parlons plus de cela, parlons d'autre chose ■ **just ~ it!** laissez tomber!, assez!
5. [utter - remark] laisser échapper ■ **to ~ a hint about sthg** faire allusion à qqch ■ **he dropped me a hint that she wanted to come** il m'a fait comprendre qu'elle voulait venir ■ **she let (it) ~ that she had been there** [accidentally] elle a laissé échapper qu'elle y était allée ; [deliberately] elle a fait comprendre qu'elle y était allée
6. [send - letter, note] écrire, envoyer ■ **I'll ~ you a line next week** je t'enverrai un petit mot la semaine prochaine ■ **I'll ~ it in the post** *OR* **mail** je la mettrai à la poste
7. [omit - when speaking] ne pas prononcer ; [- when writing] omettre ; [- intentionally] supprimer ■ **he ~s his h's** il n'aspire pas les h ■ **let's ~ the formalities, shall we?** oublions les formalités, d'accord? ■ **to ~ a player from a team** SPORT écarter un joueur d'une équipe
8. *UK* [lose] perdre ■ **they dropped one game** SPORT ils ont perdu un match
9. *inf* [knock down - with punch] sonner ; [- with shot] descendre.
◇ *vi* **1.** [fall - object] tomber, retomber ; [- liquid] tomber goutte à goutte ; [- ground] s'abaisser ■ **the road ~s into the valley** la route plonge vers la vallée ■ **the curtain dropped** THEAT le rideau tomba
2. [sink down - person] se laisser tomber, tomber ■ [collapse] s'écrouler, s'affaisser ■ **she dropped to her knees** elle est tombée à genoux ■ **I'm ready to ~** [from fatigue] je tombe de fatigue, je ne tiens plus sur mes jambes ; [from sleepiness] je tombe de sommeil ■ **he'll work until he ~s** il va travailler jusqu'à épuisement ■ **she dropped dead** elle est tombée

raide morte ■ ~ **dead!** *inf* va te faire voir! ■ **I find that I ~ back into the local dialect when I go home** je réalise que je retombe dans le dialecte quand je rentre chez moi ■ **the team dropped to third place** l'équipe est descendue à la troisième position
3. [decrease - price, speed] baisser, diminuer ; [- temperature] baisser ; [- wind] se calmer, tomber ; [- voice] baisser
4. [end] cesser ■ **there the matter dropped** l'affaire en est restée là
5. [give birth - subj: animals] mettre bas.
◇ *n* **1.** [of liquid] goutte *f* ■ **~ by ~** goutte à goutte ■ **he's had a ~ too much (to drink)** *inf* il a bu un verre de trop ▶ **it's just a ~ in the ocean** ce n'est qu'une goutte d'eau dans la mer
2. [decrease - in price] baisse *f*, chute *f* ; [- in temperature] baisse *f* ; [- in voltage] chute *f* ■ **a ~ in prices** une baisse *OR* une chute des prix
3. [fall] chute *f* ■ [in parachuting] saut *m* (en parachute) ■ **it was a long ~ from the top of the wall** ça faisait haut depuis le haut du mur ▶ **at the ~ of a hat** sans hésiter, à tout moment
4. [vertical distance] hauteur *f* de chute ■ [slope] descente *f* brusque ■ [abyss] à-pic *m inv*, précipice *m* ■ [in climbing] vide *m* ■ **a sudden ~ in the ground level** une soudaine dénivellation ■ **it's a 50 m ~ from the cliff to the sea** il y a (un dénivelé de) *OR* une hauteur de 50 m entre le haut de la falaise et la mer ▶ **to have the ~ on sb** *US* avoir l'avantage sur qqn
5. [earring] pendant *m*, pendeloque *f* ■ [on necklace] pendentif *m* ■ [on chandelier] pendeloque *f*
6. [sweet] bonbon *m*, pastille *f*
7. [delivery] livraison *f* ■ [from plane] parachutage *m*, droppage *m* ■ **to make a ~** déposer un colis
8. [hiding place] cachette *f*, dépôt *m* (clandestin)
9. [place to leave sthg] lieu *m* de dépôt ■ **a mail ~** *un lieu de dépôt pour le courrier*.
◆ **drops** *npl* MED gouttes *fpl*.
◆ **drop away** *vi insep* **1.** [interest, support] diminuer, baisser
2. [land] s'abaisser.
◆ **drop back** *vi insep* retourner en arrière, se laisser devancer *OR* distancer.
◆ **drop by** *vi insep* passer.
◆ **drop down** *vi insep* [person] tomber (par terre) ■ [table leaf] se rabattre.
◆ **drop in** ◇ *vi insep* passer ■ **to ~ in on sb** passer voir qqn.
◇ *vt sep* [deliver] déposer.
◆ **drop off** ◇ *vt sep* [person] déposer ■ [package, thing] déposer, laisser.
◇ *vi insep* **1.** [fall asleep] s'endormir ■ [have a nap] faire un (petit) somme
2. [decrease] diminuer, baisser
3. [fall off] tomber.
◆ **drop out** *vi insep* **1.** [fall out] tomber
2. [withdraw] renoncer ■ **she dropped out of the race** elle s'est retirée de la course ■ **he dropped out of school** il a abandonné ses études ■ [from society] vivre en marge de la société.
◆ **drop round** *UK* ◇ *vi insep* = **drop in**.
◇ *vt sep* [deliver] déposer.

drop-dead *inf adv* vachement ■ **he's ~ gorgeous** il est craquant.

drop-down *adj* COMPUT [menu] déroulant.

drop front *adj* [bureau] à abattant.

drop goal *n* drop-goal *m*, drop *m*.

drop handlebars *npl* guidon *m* renversé.

drop-in centre *n UK* centre *m* d'assistance sociale *(où l'on peut aller sans rendez-vous)*.

drop kick *n* coup *m* de pied tombé.

drop-leaf *adj* : **a ~ table** une table à abattants *OR* à volets.

droplet ['drɒplɪt] *n* gouttelette *f*.

drop-off *n* **1.** [decrease] baisse *f*, diminution *f* ■ **a ~ in sales** une baisse des ventes **2.** *US* [descent] à-pic *m inv* ■ **there's a sharp ~ in the road** la rue descend en pente très raide.

dropout ['drɒpaʊt] *n inf* [from society] marginal *m*, - e *f* ■ [from studies] étudiant *m*, - e *f* qui abandonne ses études ■ **he's a high school ~** *US* il a quitté le lycée avant le bac.

drop-out *n* RUGBY renvoi *m* aux 22 mètres.

dropper ['drɒpər] *n* compte-gouttes *m inv*.

droppings ['drɒpɪŋz] *npl* [of animal] crottes *fpl* ■ [of bird] fiente *f*.

drop shot *n* amorti *m*.

dropsy ['drɒpsɪ] *n* hydropisie *f*.

dross [drɒs] *n (U)* **1.** METALL scories *fpl*, crasse *f* ■ INDUST [of minerals] schlamm *m* **2.** [waste] déchets *mpl*, impuretés *fpl* ■ **they chose all the nice things and we were left with the ~** *fig* ils ont choisi tout ce qu'il y avait de joli et nous ont laissé le rebut.

drought [draʊt] *n* **1.** [no rain] sécheresse *f* **2.** [shortage] disette *f*, manque *m*.

drove [drəʊv] ◇ *pt* ▷ **drive**.
◇ *n* **1.** [of animals] troupeau *m* en marche ■ [of people] foule *f*, multitude *f* ■ **every summer the tourists come in ~s** chaque été les touristes arrivent en foule **2.** [chisel] boucharde *f*.
◇ *vt* **1.** [animals] chasser, conduire **2.** [stone] boucharder.

drover ['drəʊvər] *n* toucheur *m* de bestiaux.

drown [draʊn] ◇ *vt* **1.** [person, animal] noyer ■ **to be ~ed** se noyer ; [in battle, disaster etc] mourir noyé ■ **to ~ o.s.** se noyer **2.** [field, village] noyer ■ **don't ~ it!** [my drink] ne mets pas trop d'eau! ▶ **to ~ one's sorrows** noyer son chagrin (dans la boisson) **3.** [make inaudible] noyer, couvrir ■ **his voice was ~ed (out) by the music** sa voix était couverte par la musique.
◇ *vi* se noyer ■ [in battle, disaster etc] mourir noyé.
◆ **drown out** *vt sep* = **drown** *(sense 3)*.

drowned [draʊnd] *adj* noyé.

drowning ['draʊnɪŋ] ◇ *adj* : **the ~ woman was saved just in time** la noyée a été sauvée de justesse ▶ **a ~ man will clutch at a straw** *prov* dans une situation désespérée on se raccroche à un rien.
◇ *n* noyade *f* ■ **to save sb from ~** sauver qqn de la noyade ■ **he died of ~** il est mort noyé.

drowse [draʊz] *vi* somnoler.
◆ **drowse off** *vi insep* s'assoupir.

drowsily ['draʊzɪlɪ] *adv* d'un air somnolent.

drowsiness ['draʊzɪnɪs] *n (U)* somnolence *f* ■ **'may cause ~'** 'peut provoquer des somnolences'.

drowsy ['draʊzɪ] (*comp* **drowsier**, *superl* **drowsiest**) *adj* [person, voice] somnolent, engourdi ■ [place] endormi ■ **to feel ~** être tout endormi ■ **to make sb feel ~** [atmosphere] engourdir qqn ; [drug] endormir qqn, provoquer des somnolences chez qqn.

drubbing ['drʌbɪŋ] *n* [thorough defeat] volée *f* de coups ■ **to give sb a real ~** donner une correction à qqn.

drudge [drʌdʒ] ◇ *n* **1.** [person] bête *f* de somme **2.** [work] besogne *f*.
◇ *vi* besogner, peiner.

drudgery ['drʌdʒərɪ] *n (U)* travail *m* de bête de somme.

drug [drʌg] (*pret & pp* **drugged**, *cont* **drugging**) ◇ *n* **1.** [medication] médicament *m* ■ **to be on ~s** prendre des médicaments ■ **to be put on ~s by the doctor** se voir prescrire des médicaments par le médecin **2.** [illegal substance] drogue *f* ■ LAW stupéfiant *m* ■ **to be on ~s** se droguer ■ **to take ~s** se droguer ; [athlete] se doper ■ **to do** *inf OR* **to use ~s** se droguer ▶ **a ~ on the market** un produit invendable *OR* qui ne se vend pas.
◇ *comp* [abuse, dealing, trafficking] de drogue ■ **~-related** [crime, offence] lié à la drogue ■ **~ baron** gros bonnet *m* de la drogue ■ **to be arrested on ~s charges** [possession] être arrêté pour détention de drogue *OR* de stupéfiants ; [trafficking] être arrêté pour trafic de drogue ■ **~ courier** passeur *m*, - euse *f* de drogue ■ **~ czar** responsable *m* de la lutte contre la drogue ■ **~ habit** accoutumance *f* à la drogue ■ **~ money** argent *m* de la drogue ■ **~ prevention** prévention *f* de la toxicomanie ■ **Drug Squad** [police] brigade *f* des stupéfiants ■ **~ taker** [addict] drogué *m*, - e *f* ; [athlete] consommateur *m*, - trice *f* de produits

dopants ■ ~ **taking** dopage *m* ■ **~s test** [of athlete, horse] contrôle *m* antidopage ■ ~ **traffic** trafic *m* de drogue *OR* stupéfiants ■ ~ **user** drogué *m*, - e *f*.
◇ *vt* droguer ■ [athlete, horse] doper ■ **to be drugged with sleep** *fig* être engourdi de sommeil.

drug addict *n* drogué *m*, - e *f*, toxicomane *mf*.

drug addiction *n* toxicomanie *f*.

druggist ['drʌgɪst] *n US* [person] pharmacien *m*, - enne *f* ■ [shop] : ~, **~'s** pharmacie *f*.

drug-peddler, drug-pusher *n* dealer *m*.

drugstore ['drʌgstɔːʳ] *n US* drugstore *m*.

druid ['druːɪd] *n* druide *m*, - esse *f*.

drum [drʌm] (*pret & pp* **drummed**, *cont* **drumming**) ◇ *n* **1.** [instrument - gen] tambour *m* ; [- African] tam-tam *m* ■ **to play (the) ~s** jouer de la batterie ■ **to beat** *OR* **to bang a ~** taper *OR* frapper sur un tambour ▶ **to beat the ~ for sb/sthg** faire de la publicité pour qqn/qqch **2.** [for fuel] fût *m*, bidon *m* ■ [for rope] cylindre *m* ■ COMPUT [cylinder] tambour *m* ■ **(concrete) mixing~** tambour *m* mélangeur (de béton) **3.** ANAT [eardrum] tympan *m* **4.** [noise - of rain, fingers] tambourinement *m*.
◇ *vi* **1.** MUS [on drum kit] jouer de la batterie ■ [on one drum] jouer du tambour **2.** [rain, fingers] tambouriner.
◇ *vt* [on instrument] tambouriner ■ **to ~ one's fingers on the table** tambouriner de ses doigts sur la table.
➡ **drum in** *vt sep* insister lourdement sur.
➡ **drum into** *vt sep* : **to ~ sthg into sb** enfoncer qqch dans la tête de qqn ■ **~ it into her that...** mets-lui bien dans la tête que...
➡ **drum out** *vt sep* expulser ■ **he was drummed out of the club/the army** il a été expulsé du club/de l'armée.
➡ **drum up** *vt insep* [customers, support] attirer, rechercher ■ [supporters] battre le rappel de ■ [enthusiasm] chercher à susciter.

drumbeat ['drʌmbiːt] *n* battement *m* de tambour.

drum brake *n* AUT frein *m* à tambour.

drumfire ['drʌmfaɪəʳ] *n* MIL tir *m* de barrage, feu *m* roulant.

drumhead ['drʌmhed] *n* MUS peau *f* de tambour ■ ~ **court-martial** MIL conseil *m* de guerre.

drum kit *n* batterie *f*.

drum machine *n* boîte *f* à rythmes.

drum major *n* MIL tambour-major *m*.

drum majorette *n esp US* chef-majorette *f*.

drummer ['drʌməʳ] *n* [in band] batteur *m* ■ [tribal] joueur *m* de tambour ■ MIL tambour *m*.

drumming ['drʌmɪŋ] *n (U)* [sound - of one drum] son *m* du tambour ; [- of set of drums] son *m* de la batterie ; [- of fingers, rain, in the ears] tambourinement *m*, tambourinage *m* ; [- of woodpecker] tambourinement *m*, tambourinage *m* ■ **some really great ~** un jeu de batterie superbe.

drum roll *n* roulement *m* de tambour.

drumstick ['drʌmstɪk] *n* **1.** MUS baguette *f* **2.** CULIN pilon *m*.

drunk [drʌŋk] ◇ *pp* ⊳ **drink**.
◇ *adj* **1.** *liter* soûl, saoul, ivre ■ **to get ~ (on beer/on wine)** se soûler (à la bière/au vin) ■ **to get sb ~** soûler qqn ■ **~ and disorderly** LAW en état d'ivresse publique ■ **dead** *OR* **blind ~** *inf* ivre mort ▶ **as ~ as a lord** soûl comme une grive **2.** *fig* ~ **with power/success** ivre de pouvoir/succès.
◇ *n* [habitual] ivrogne *mf* ■ [on one occasion] homme *m* soûl *OR* ivre, femme *f* soûle *OR* ivre.

drunkard ['drʌŋkəd] *n* ivrogne *mf*.

drunk-driving = **drink-driving**.

drunken ['drʌŋkn] *adj* [person] ivre ■ [laughter, sleep] d'ivrogne ■ [evening, party] très arrosé ■ ~ **brawl** querelle *f* d'ivrognes ■ ~ **orgy** beuverie *f*, soûlerie *f*.

drunkenly ['drʌŋkənlɪ] *adv* [speak, sing, shout etc] comme un ivrogne.

drunkenness ['drʌŋkənnɪs] *n* [state] ivresse *f* ■ [habit] ivrognerie *f*.

Drury Lane ['drʊərɪ-] *pr n nom courant du Théâtre Royal de Londres.*

DRURY LANE

Fondé en 1663, Drury Lane est le plus ancien théâtre londonien encore en activité. Il est notamment connu pour ses comédies musicales.

Drusean, Druzean ['druːzɪən] *adj* druze.

dry [draɪ] ◇ *adj* (*comp* **drier**, *superl* **driest**) **1.** [climate, season, clothing, skin] sec, sèche *f* ■ ~ **spell** période *f* sèche ■ **to go** *OR* **to run ~** [well, river] s'assécher, se tarir ■ **to keep sthg ~** garder qqch au sec ■ **her mouth had gone** *OR* **turned ~ with fear** elle avait la bouche sèche de peur ■ **to be ~** [be thirsty] mourir de soif *fig*, avoir soif ; [cow] être tarie *OR* sèche ▶ **to be (as) ~ as a bone, to be bone ~** [washing, earth etc] être très sec ■ **there wasn't a ~ eye in the house** *hum* tout le monde pleurait **2.** [vermouth, wine] sec, sèche *f* ■ [champagne] brut ■ **medium ~** [wine] demi-sec **3.** [where alcohol is banned] où l'alcool est prohibé ■ [where alcohol is not sold] où on ne vend pas d'alcool ■ [person] : ~ **state** *US État ayant adopté les lois de la prohibition* **4.** [boring - book, lecture] aride ■ ~ **as dust** ennuyeux comme la pluie **5.** [wit, sense of humour] caustique, mordant **6.** *UK inf* POL [hardline] ultraconservateur.
◇ *n* **1.** [with towel, cloth] : **to give sthg a ~** essuyer qqch ■ **give your hair a ~** sèche tes cheveux **2.** [dry place] : **come into the ~** viens te mettre au sec **3.** *UK inf* POL [hardliner] ultraconservateur *m*, - trice *f*.
◇ *vt* (*pret & pp* **dried**) [hair, clothes, fruit, leaves] (faire) sécher ■ [dishes] essuyer ■ **to ~ one's eyes** se sécher les yeux, sécher ses yeux.
◇ *vi* (*pret & pp* **dried**) **1.** [clothes, hair, fruit, leaves] sécher ■ **you wash, I'll ~** tu laves et moi j'essuie **2.** [cow] se tarir.
➡ **dry off** ◇ *vi insep* [clothes, person] = **dry out** *(sense 1)*.
◇ *vt sep* sécher ■ **to ~ o.s. off** se sécher.
➡ **dry out** ◇ *vi insep* **1.** [clothes] sécher ■ [person] se sécher **2.** [alcoholic] se désintoxiquer.
◇ *vt sep* [alcoholic] désintoxiquer.
➡ **dry up** *vi insep* **1.** [well, river] s'assécher, se tarir ■ [puddle, street] sécher ■ [inspiration] se tarir ■ [cow] se tarir **2.** [dry the dishes] essuyer la vaisselle **3.** *inf* [be lost for words - actor, speaker] sécher ■ **~ up, will you?** ferme-la *OR* boucle-la, tu veux?

dryad ['draɪəd] (*pl* **dryads** *OR pl* **dryades** [-diːz]) *n* MYTH dryade *f*.

dry battery = **dry cell**.

dry cell *n* pile *f* sèche.

dry-clean *vt* nettoyer à sec ■ **to take sthg to be ~ed** emmener qqch au nettoyage (à sec) *OR* chez le teinturier *OR* à la teinturerie ■ **'~ only'** 'nettoyage à sec'.

dry cleaner *n* [person] teinturier *m*, - ère *f* ■ **~'s** [shop] teinturerie *f* ■ **to be in** *OR* **at the ~ 's** être chez le teinturier *OR* à la teinturerie.

dry-cleaning *n (U)* **1.** [action] nettoyage *m* à sec **2.** [clothes - being cleaned] vêtements *mpl* laissés au nettoyage (à sec) *OR* chez le teinturier *OR* à la teinturerie ; [- to be cleaned] vêtements à emmener au nettoyage (à sec) *OR* chez le teinturier *OR* à la teinturerie.

dry dock *n* cale *f* sèche ■ **in ~** en cale sèche.

dryer ['draɪəʳ] = **drier**.

dry ginger *n boisson gazeuse au gingembre.*

dry goods *npl US* tissus et articles de bonneterie *mpl*.

dry ice *n* neige *f* carbonique.

drying ['draɪɪŋ] ◇ *n* [of clothes, hair] séchage *m* ■ [of skin, flowers, wood] dessèchement *m* ■ [with a cloth] essuyage *m*.
◇ *adj* [wind] desséchant.

drying cupboard *n* armoire *f* sèche-linge.

drying up *n UK* [of dishes] : **to do the ~** essuyer la vaisselle.

drying-up cloth *n* torchon *m* (à vaisselle), essuie-verres *m inv*.

dry land *n* terre *f* ferme.

dryly ['draɪlɪ] = **drily**.

dry martini *n* martini dry *m*.

dry measure *n unité de mesure des matières sèches.*

dryness ['draɪnɪs] *n* **1.** [of region, weather, skin] sécheresse *f* **2.** [of wit, humour] mordant *m*, causticité *f*.

dry-roasted *adj* [peanuts] grillé à sec.

dry rot *n (U)* [in wood] moisissure *f* sèche ■ [in potatoes] pourriture *f* sèche.

dry run *n* **1.** [trial, practice] coup *m* d'essai, test *m* ■ **to have a ~** faire un essai **2.** MIL entraînement *m* avec tir à blanc.

dry ski slope *n* piste *f* de ski artificielle.

dry-stone *adj* [wall] en pierres sèches.

drysuit ['draɪsu:t] *n* combinaison de plongée (étanche) *f*.

DSc (*abbrev of* **Doctor of Science**) *n (titulaire d'un) doctorat en sciences.*

DSS (*abbrev of* **Department of Social Security**) *pr n ministère britannique de la Sécurité sociale.*

DST *n* = **daylight saving time**.

DT *n* = **data transmission**.

DTI (*abbrev of* **Department of Trade and Industry**) *pr n ministère britannique du Commerce et de l'Industrie.*

DTp (*abbrev of* **Department of Transports**) *pr n* **UK** ≃ ministère *m* des Transports.

DTP (*abbrev of* **desktop publishing**) *n* PAO *f*.

DT's [ˌdi:'ti:z] (*abbrev of* **delirium tremens**) *npl* ***inf*** **to have the ~** avoir une crise de delirium tremens.

dual ['dju:əl] *adj* [purpose, nationality] double ■ **with the ~ aim of reducing inflation and stimulating demand** dans le but à la fois de réduire l'inflation et de stimuler la demande ■ **to have a ~ personality** souffrir d'un dédoublement de la personnalité ➤ **~ controls** AERON & AUT double commande *f*.

dual carriageway *n* **UK** AUT route *f* à quatre voies.

dual-control *adj* [car, plane] à double commande.

dualism ['dju:əlɪzm] *n* PHILOS & RELIG dualisme *m*.

duality [dju:'ælətɪ] *n* dualité *f*.

dual-purpose *adj* à double fonction.

dub [dʌb] (*pret & pp* **dubbed**, *cont* **dubbing**) *vt* **1.** [nickname] surnommer **2.** CIN & TV [add soundtrack, voice] sonoriser ■ [in foreign language] doubler ■ **dubbed into French** doublé en français **3.** ***lit & arch*** armer chevalier.

Dubai [ˌdu:'baɪ] *pr n* Dubayy ■ **in ~** à Dubayy.

dubbin ['dʌbɪn] *n* graisse *f* à chaussures, dégras *m*.

dubbing ['dʌbɪŋ] *n* CIN & TV [addition of soundtrack] sonorisation *f* ■ [in a foreign language] doublage *m*.

dubious ['dju:bjəs] *adj* **1.** [unsure - reply, voice] dubitatif ; [- expression] dubitatif, d'incertitude ; [- outcome, value] incertain ■ **I'm rather ~ about the whole thing** j'ai des doutes sur toute cette affaire ■ **I'm a bit ~ about whether it will work** je ne suis pas très sûr que ça marche **2.** [suspect - person, nature, reputation, decision] douteux ■ **of ~ character** douteux ■ **a ~ distinction** OR **honour** un triste honneur.

dubiously ['dju:bjəslɪ] *adv* **1.** [doubtfully] d'un air de doute **2.** [in suspect manner] d'une manière douteuse.

Dublin ['dʌblɪn] *pr n* Dublin.

Dublin Bay prawn *n* grosse crevette *f*.

Dubliner ['dʌblɪnəʳ] *n* Dublinois *m*, - e *f* ■ **'Dubliners'** ***Joyce*** 'Gens de Dublin'.

ducal ['dju:kl] *adj* ducal.

duchess ['dʌtʃɪs] *n* duchesse *f*.

duchy ['dʌtʃɪ] (*pl* **duchies**) *n* duché *m*.

duck [dʌk] ◇ *n* **1.** [bird] canard *m* ■ **to take to sthg like a ~ to water** [become good at sthg very quickly] se mettre à qqch très rapidement ; [develop a liking for sthg] mordre à qqch **2.** [in cricket] score *m* nul ■ **to break one's ~** marquer son premier point **3.** MIL véhicule *m* amphibie **4.** [material] coutil *m*.
◇ *vt* **1.** [dodge - blow] esquiver ■ **to ~ one's head (out of the way)** baisser vivement la tête **2.** [submerge in water] faire boire la tasse à **3.** [evade - responsibility, question] se dérober à, esquiver.
◇ *vi* **1.** [drop down quickly] se baisser vivement ■ [in boxing] esquiver un coup ■ **to ~ behind a hedge** se cacher derrière une haie **2.** [move quickly] : **to ~ out of a room** s'esquiver d'une pièce **3.** ***inf*** [avoid] se défiler ■ **to ~ out of doing sthg** se défiler pour ne pas faire qqch.

duckbilled platypus [ˌdʌkbɪld'plætɪpəs] *n* ornithorynque *m*.

duckboards ['dʌkbɔ:dz] *npl* caillebotis *m*.

ducking ['dʌkɪŋ] *n* : **he got a ~** on lui a fait boire la tasse.

duckling ['dʌklɪŋ] *n* caneton *m* ■ [female] canette *f* ■ [older] canardeau *m*.

duckpond ['dʌkpɒnd] *n* mare *f* aux canards.

ducks [dʌks] ◇ *n* ***inf*** **UK** ***inf*** = **ducky** *(n)*.
◇ *npl* [trousers] pantalon *m* de coutil.

ducks and drakes *n* **UK** [game] : **to play ~** ***liter*** faire des ricochets ■ **to play ~ with sthg** gaspiller qqch.

duckweed ['dʌkwi:d] *n* lentille *f* d'eau.

ducky ['dʌkɪ] ***inf*** ◇ *n* **UK** [term of endearment] mon canard.
◇ *adj* **US** **1.** [perfect] impec **2.** [cute] joli.

duct [dʌkt] *n* [for gas, liquid, electricity] conduite *f*, canalisation *f* ■ ANAT conduit *m*, canal *m* ■ BOT vaisseau *m* ■ **tear/hepatic ~** canal *m* lacrymal/hépatique.

ductile ['dʌktaɪl] *adj* [metal, plastic] ductile ■ ***fig*** [person] malléable, influençable.

dud [dʌd] ***inf*** ◇ *adj* [false - coin, note] faux, fausse *f* ■ [useless - drill, video] qui ne marche pas ; [- shell, bomb] qui a raté ; [- idea] débile.
◇ *n* [person] nullité *f*, tache *f* ■ [cheque] chèque *m* en bois ■ [coin] fausse pièce *f* de monnaie ■ [note] faux billet *m* ■ [shell] obus *m* qui a raté OR qui n'a pas explosé ■ **it's a ~** [firework] ça a raté, ce n'est pas parti.

dude [dju:d] *n* **US** ***inf*** [man] type *m*, mec *m*.

dude ranch *n* **US** *ranch qui propose des activités touristiques.*

dudgeon ['dʌdʒən] *n* : **in high ~** ***fml*** très en colère, fort indigné.

due [dju:] ◇ *n* [what one deserves] : **but then, to give him his ~,...** mais pour lui rendre justice...
◇ *adj* **1.** [owed, payable - amount, balance, money] dû ■ **when's the next instalment ~?** quand le prochain versement doit-il être fait? ■ **he's ~ some money from me** je lui dois de l'argent ■ **repayment ~ on December 1st** remboursement à effectuer le 1er décembre ■ **to fall ~** [bill] arriver à échéance ■ **~ date** [of bill, payment] échéance *f* ■ **to be ~ an apology** avoir droit à des excuses ■ **to be ~ a bit of luck/some good weather** mériter un peu de chance/du beau temps ■ **I'm ~ (for) a rise** [I will receive one] je vais être augmenté, je vais recevoir une augmentation ; [I deserve one] je suis en droit d'attendre une augmentation ■ **(to give) credit where credit's ~** pour dire ce qui est, pour être juste
2. [expected] : **we're ~ round there at 7.30** on nous attend à 7 h 30, nous devons y être à 7 h 30 ■ **to be ~ to do sthg** devoir faire qqch ■ **the train is ~ (in)** OR **to arrive now** le train devrait arriver d'un instant à l'autre ■ **her baby is** OR **she's ~ any day now** elle doit accoucher d'un jour à l'autre
3. [proper] : **to give sthg ~ consideration** accorder mûre réflexion à qqch ■ **to fail to exercise ~ care and attention** ne pas prêter l'attention nécessaire ■ **to give sb ~ warning** prévenir qqn suffisamment tôt ■ **~ process of law** garantie suffisante

du droit ▶ **in ~ course** *OR* **time** [at the proper time] en temps voulu ; [in the natural course of events] à un certain moment ; [at a later stage, eventually] plus tard ■ **to treat sb with ~ respect** traiter qqn avec le respect qui lui est dû ■ **with (all) ~ respect...** avec tout le respect que je vous dois..., sauf votre respect...
◇ *adv* [east, west etc] plein.
◆ **dues** *npl* droits *mpl* ■ **to pay one's ~** *fig* faire sa part.
◆ **due to** *prep phr* **1.** [owing to] à cause de, en raison de ■ **~ to bad weather they arrived late** ils sont arrivés en retard à cause du mauvais temps
2. [because of] grâce à ■ **it's all ~ to you** c'est grâce à toi ■ **her success was ~ in (large) part to hard work** elle doit sa réussite en grande partie à son travail acharné ■ **our late arrival was ~ to the bad weather** notre retard était dû au mauvais temps.

duel ['dju:əl] (*UK pret & pp* **duelled**, *cont* **duelling**) (*US pret & pp* **dueled**, *cont* **dueling**) ◇ *n* duel *m* ■ **to fight a ~** se battre en duel.
◇ *vi* se battre en duel.

duelling *UK*, **dueling** *US* ['dju:əlɪŋ] *adj* : **~ pistols** pistolets *mpl* de duel.

duellist *UK*, **duelist** *US* ['dju:əlɪst] *n* duelliste *mf*.

duet [dju:'et] *n* duo *m* ■ **to sing/to play a ~** chanter/jouer en duo.

duff [dʌf] ◇ *adj inf UK* [useless] qui ne marche pas ■ [idea] débile.
◇ *n* CULIN *variante du plum-pudding.*
◆ **duff up** *vt sep UK inf* [beat up] tabasser, démolir.

duffel ['dʌfl] *n* **1.** [fabric] tissu *m* de laine **2.** *US* = **duffel bag**.

duffel bag *n* sac *m* marin.

duffel coat *n* duffel-coat *m*, duffle-coat *m*.

duffer ['dʌfəʳ] *n UK inf* **1.** [useless person] gourde *f* ■ SCH nullité *f*, cancre *m* ■ **to be a ~ at sthg** être nul en qqch **2.** [old man] vieux bonhomme *m*.

duffle ['dʌfl] = **duffel**.

dug [dʌg] ◇ *pt & pp* ▷ **dig**.
◇ *n* mamelle *f* ■ [of cow, goat] pis *m*.

dugout ['dʌgaʊt] *n* **1.** MIL tranchée-abri *f* ■ SPORT banc *m* abri de touche **2.** [canoe] canoë *m* creusé dans un tronc.

duke [dju:k] *n* duc *m*.

dukedom ['dju:kdəm] *n* [territory] duché *m* ■ [title] titre *m* de duc.

Duke of Edinburgh's Award Scheme *pr n* : **the ~** ≃ la bourse du duc d'Édimbourg.

DUKE OF EDINBURGH'S AWARD SCHEME

Cette bourse récompense des projets d'intérêt collectif ou personnel réalisés par des jeunes de 14 à 23 ans. Réputés pour leur grande difficulté, ces projets font parfois l'objet de comparaisons humoristiques : *I should get a Duke of Edinburgh award for sitting through that film!*

dukes [dju:ks] *npl inf* [fists] poings *mpl* ■ **to put up one's ~** se mettre en garde.

dulcet ['dʌlsɪt] *adj lit* doux, douce *f*, suave ■ **her ~ tones** ses intonations douces ; *hum* sa douce voix.

dulcimer ['dʌlsɪməʳ] *n* MUS dulcimer *m*, tympanon *m*.

dull [dʌl] ◇ *adj* **1.** [slow-witted - person] peu intelligent ; [- reflexes] ralenti ■ **to grow ~** [intellectual capacities] s'affaiblir, décliner **2.** [boring - book, person, lecture] ennuyeux, assommant ■ **there's never a ~ moment with him around** on ne s'ennuie jamais avec lui **3.** [not bright - colour] terne, fade ; [- light, eyes] terne ; [- weather, sky] sombre, maussade **4.** [not sharp - blade] émoussé ; [- pain] sourd ; [- sound] sourd, étouffé **5.** [listless - person] abattu.
◇ *vt* [sound] assourdir ■ [colour, metal] ternir ■ [blade, pleasure, senses, impression] émousser ■ [grief] endormir.
◇ *vi* [colour] se ternir, perdre son éclat ■ [pleasure] s'émousser ■ [pain] s'atténuer ■ [eyes] s'assombrir, perdre son éclat ■ [mind] s'affaiblir, décliner.

dullness ['dʌlnɪs] *n* **1.** [slow-wittedness] lenteur *f OR* lourdeur *f* d'esprit **2.** [tedium - of book, speech] caractère *m* ennuyeux **3.** [dimness - of light] faiblesse *f* ; [- of weather] caractère *m* maussade **4.** [of sound, pain] caractère *m* sourd ■ [of blade] manque *m* de tranchant **5.** [listlessness] apathie *f*.

dully ['dʌlɪ] *adv* **1.** [listlessly] d'un air déprimé **2.** [tediously] de manière ennuyeuse **3.** [dimly] faiblement **4.** [not sharply] sourdement.

duly ['dju:lɪ] *adv* **1.** [properly] comme il convient ■ [in accordance with the rules] dans les règles, dûment **2.** [as expected - arrive, call] comme prévu ■ **I was ~ surprised** comme de bien entendu, j'ai été surpris.

dumb [dʌm] *adj* **1.** [unable or unwilling to speak] muet ■ **to be struck ~ (with fear/surprise)** rester muet (de peur/surprise) ■ **~ animal** bête *f*, animal *m* **2.** *inf* [stupid] bête ■ **don't act ~ with me** ne joue pas les imbéciles avec moi ■ **~ blonde** *pej* blonde *f* évaporée.
◆ **dumb down** *vt insep* [society, television programme] niveler par le bas.

dumbbell ['dʌmbel] *n* SPORT haltère *m*.

dumbfound [dʌm'faʊnd] *vt* abasourdir, interloquer.

dumbfounded [dʌm'faʊndɪd] *adj* [person] muet de stupeur, abasourdi, interloqué ■ [silence] stupéfait ■ **to be ~ at** *OR* **by sthg** être abasourdi *OR* interloqué par qqch.

dumbing down ['dʌmɪŋ-] *n* nivellement *m* par le bas.

dumbo ['dʌmbəʊ] *n inf* [fool] abruti *m*, - e *f*.

dumb show *n pantomime faisant partie d'une pièce de théâtre.*

dumbstruck ['dʌmstrʌk] = **dumbfounded**.

dumb waiter *n UK* [lift] monte-plats *m inv* ■ [trolley] table *f* roulante ■ [revolving tray] plateau *m* tournant.

dumdum ['dʌmdʌm] *n* **1.** MIL [bullet] balle *f* dum-dum **2.** *inf* [fool] imbécile *mf*.

dummy ['dʌmɪ] (*pl* **dummies**) ◇ *n* **1.** [in shop window, for dressmaking] mannequin *m* ■ [of ventriloquist] marionnette *f* ■ FIN [representative] prête-nom *m*, homme *m* de paille **2.** [fake object] objet *m* factice ■ [book, model for display] maquette *f* **3.** *UK* [for baby] tétine *f* **4.** [in bridge - cards] main *f* du mort ; [- player] mort *m* **5.** *pej* [mute] muet *m*, - ette *f* **6.** *inf* [fool] imbécile *mf* **7.** SPORT feinte *f* ■ **to sell sb a ~** feinter qqn.
◇ *adj* [fake] factice ■ **~ buyer** FIN acheteur *m* prête-nom.
◇ *vi & vt* SPORT feinter.

dummy run *n* [trial] essai *m* ■ AERON & MIL attaque *f* simulée *OR* d'entraînement.

dump [dʌmp] ◇ *vt* **1.** [rubbish, waste] déverser, déposer ■ [sand, gravel] déverser ■ [car, corpse] abandonner ■ [oil - subj: ship] vidanger ■ **to ~ waste at sea** rejeter *OR* immerger des déchets dans la mer ■ **he just ~ed me off at the motorway exit** il m'a déposé à la sortie de l'autoroute **2.** *inf* [get rid of - boyfriend, girlfriend] plaquer ; [- member of government, board] se débarrasser de ■ **to ~ sb/sthg on sb** *inf* laisser qqn/qqch sur les bras de qqn **3.** [set down - bags, shopping, suitcase] poser **4.** COMM vendre en dumping **5.** COMPUT [memory] vider.
◇ *n* **1.** [rubbish heap] tas *m* d'ordures ■ [place] décharge *f*, dépôt *m* d'ordures **2.** MIL dépôt *m* **3.** *inf pej* [town, village] trou *m* ■ [messy room, flat] dépotoir *m* ■ **it's a real ~ here** [town] c'est vraiment mortel ici **4.** COMPUT [of memory] vidage *m*.
◇ *vi* chier▲ ■ *inf* ■ **to dump on sb** mettre qn dans la merde▲.

dumper truck ['dʌmpə-] = **dump truck**.

dumping ['dʌmpɪŋ] *n* **1.** [of rubbish, waste] dépôt *m OR* décharge *f* d'ordures *OR* de déchets ■ [of toxic or nuclear waste - at sea] déversement *m OR* immersion *f* de déchets ; [- underground] entreposage *m* sous terre de déchets ■ [of oil from ship] vidange *f* ■ **'no ~'** 'dépôt d'ordures interdit', 'décharge interdite' **2.** COMM dumping *m* **3.** COMPUT [of memory] vidage *m*.

dumping ground *n* [for rubbish] décharge *f*, dépôt *m* d'ordures ■ *fig* [for inferior goods] dépotoir *m*.

dumpling ['dʌmplɪŋ] *n* **1.** CULIN [savoury] boulette *f* de pâte, knödel *m* ■ *Scotland* [sweet] *variante du plum-pudding* **2.** *inf* [plump person] boulot *m*, - otte *f*.

dumps [dʌmps] *npl inf* **to be down in the ~** avoir le cafard *OR* bourdon.

dump truck *n* dumper *m*, tombereau *m*.

dumpy ['dʌmpɪ] *adj inf* [person] courtaud ■ [bottle] pansu.

dun [dʌn] (*pret & pp* **dunned**, *cont* **dunning**) <> *adj* brun gris *(inv)*.
<> *n* [colour] brun *m* gris ■ [horse] cheval *m* louvet ■ [mare] jument *f* louvette.
<> *vt* COMM presser, harceler.

dunce [dʌns] *n* âne *m*, cancre *m*.

dunce cap, dunce's cap *n* bonnet *m* d'âne.

Dundee cake [dʌn'diː-] *n cake épicé aux fruits secs, décoré avec des amandes.*

dunderhead ['dʌndəhed] *n* âne *m*.

dune [djuːn] *n* dune *f*.

dung [dʌŋ] *n (U)* crotte *f* ■ [of cow] bouse *f* ■ [of horse] crottin *m* ■ [of wild animal] fumées *fpl* ■ [manure] fumier *m*.

dungarees [ˌdʌŋgə'riːz] *npl UK* salopette *f* ■ *US* [overalls] bleu *m* de travail ■ **a pair of ~** *UK* une salopette ; *US* un bleu de travail.

dung beetle, dung chafer *n* bousier *m*.

dungeon ['dʌndʒən] *n* [in castle] cachot *m* souterrain ■ [tower] donjon *m*.

dunghill ['dʌŋhɪl] *n* gros tas *m* de fumier.

dunk [dʌŋk] <> *vt* **1.** [dip] tremper **2.** SPORT : **to ~ the ball** faire un lancer coulé.
<> *n* [basketball] dunk *m*, lancer *m* coulé.

Dunkirk [dʌn'kɜːk] *pr n* **1.** GEOG Dunkerque **2.** HIST *l'évacuation des troupes alliées de Dunkerque, en mai-juin 1940.*

dunno [də'nəʊ] *inf* = **I don't know**.

dunnock ['dʌnək] *n* accenteur *m* mouchet.

duo ['djuːəʊ] *n* MUS & THEAT duo *m* ■ [couple] couple *m*.

duodecimal [ˌdjuːəʊ'desɪml] *adj* duodécimal.

duodenal [ˌdjuːəʊ'diːnl] *adj* duodénal ■ **~ ulcer** ulcère *m* duodénal.

duodenum [ˌdjuːəʊ'diːnəm] (*pl* **duodenums** *OR pl* **duodena** [-nə]) *n* duodénum *m*.

dupe [djuːp] <> *vt* duper, leurrer ■ **to ~ sb into doing sthg** duper *OR* leurrer qqn pour qu'il/elle fasse qqch.
<> *n* dupe *f*.

duplex ['djuːpleks] <> *adj* **1.** [double, twofold] double ■ **~ apartment** (appartement *m* en) duplex *m* **2.** ELEC & TELEC duplex.
<> *n* [apartment] (appartement *m* en) duplex *m* ■ *US* [house] *maison convertie en deux appartements.*

duplicate <> *vt* ['djuːplɪkeɪt] **1.** [document] dupliquer, faire un double *OR* des doubles de ■ [key] faire un double *OR* des doubles de **2.** [repeat - work] refaire ; [- feat] reproduire.
<> *n* ['djuːplɪkət] [of document, key] double *m* ■ ADMIN & LAW duplicata *m*, copie *f* conforme ■ **in ~** en double, en deux exemplaires.
<> *adj* ['djuːplɪkət] [key, document] en double ■ [receipt, certificate] en duplicata.

duplicating machine ['djuːplɪkeɪtɪŋ-] *n* duplicateur *m*.

duplication [ˌdjuːplɪ'keɪʃn] *n* **1.** [on machine] reproduction *f* ■ [result] double *m* **2.** [repetition - of work, efforts] répétition *f*.

duplicity [djuː'plɪsətɪ] *n* fausseté *f*, duplicité *f*.

durability [ˌdjʊərə'bɪlətɪ] *n* [of construction, relationship, peace] caractère *m* durable, durabilité *f* ■ [of fabric] résistance *f* ■ [of politician, athlete] longévité *f*.

durable ['djʊərəbl] *adj* [construction, friendship, peace] durable ■ [fabric, metal] résistant ■ [politician, athlete] qui jouit d'une grande longévité ■ COMM : **~ goods** biens *mpl* durables *OR* non périssables.

duration [djʊ'reɪʃn] *n* durée *f* ■ **of short ~** de courte durée ■ **for the ~ of the summer holiday** pendant toute la durée des grandes vacances ■ **are you here for the ~?** êtes-vous ici jusqu'à la fin?

duress [djʊ'res] *n* contrainte *f* ■ **under ~** sous la contrainte.

Durex® ['djʊəreks] *n* **1.** *UK* [condom] préservatif *m* **2.** *Australia* Scotch® *m (ruban adhésif)*.

during ['djʊərɪŋ] *prep* pendant ■ **they met ~ the war** ils se sont rencontrés pendant la guerre | [in the course of] au cours de.

durst [dɜːst] *arch & lit pt* ▷ **dare**.

durum (wheat) ['djʊərəm-] *n* blé *m* dur.

dusk [dʌsk] *n* crépuscule *m* ■ **at ~** au crépuscule.

dusky ['dʌskɪ] (*comp* **duskier**, *superl* **duskiest**) *adj* **1.** [light] crépusculaire ■ [colour] sombre, foncé ■ [room] sombre **2.** [skin] mat.

dust [dʌst] <> *n* **1.** *(U)* [on furniture, of gold, coal] poussière *f* ■ **a speck of ~** une poussière, un grain de poussière ■ **thick ~ covered the furniture** une poussière épaisse couvrait les meubles ■ **to gather ~** [ornaments] amasser la poussière ; [plans, proposals] rester en plan ▶ **to allow the ~ to** *OR* **to let the ~ settle** *fig* attendre que les choses se calment ■ **to trample sb in the ~** *fig* fouler qqn aux pieds ■ **to kick up** *OR* **to raise a ~** *inf* faire tout un cinéma *OR* foin ■ **to throw ~ in sb's eyes** tromper qqn ■ **we won't see him for ~** [he'll leave] il partira en moins de temps qu'il n'en faut pour le dire **2.** [action] : **to give sthg a ~** épousseter qqch **3.** [earthly remains] poussière *f*.
<> *vt* **1.** [furniture, room] épousseter **2.** [with powder, flour] saupoudrer ■ **to ~ a field with insecticide** répandre de l'insecticide sur un champ.
◆ **dust down** *vt sep* [with brush] brosser ■ [with hand] épousseter.
◆ **dust off** *vt sep* [dust, crumbs, dandruff] nettoyer, enlever ■ *fig* [skill] se remettre à ■ [speech, lecture notes] ressortir.

dust bag *n* [for vacuum cleaner] sac *m* à poussière.

dust-bath *n* : **to take a ~** [bird] prendre un bain de poussière.

dustbin ['dʌstbɪn] *n UK* poubelle *f* ■ **~ lid** couvercle *m* de poubelle ■ **~ liner** sac-poubelle *m*.

dustbin man *UK* = **dustman**.

dust bowl *n* GEOG zone *f* semi-désertique ■ [in US] : **the Dust Bowl** le Dust Bowl.

THE DUST BOWL

Nom d'une région des Grandes Plaines aux États-Unis où sévissaient, dans les années 30, de redoutables tempêtes de poussière provoquées par la sécheresse et l'érosion. Le changement de climat ajouté à la dépression des années trente poussa des milliers de paysans à émigrer vers la Californie. C'est ce thème qu'on retrouve dans le roman de J. Steinbeck « les Raisins de la colère ».

dustcart ['dʌstkɑːt] *n UK* camion *m* des éboueurs.

dustcloth ['dʌstklɒθ] *US* = **duster** *(sense 1)*.

dustcloud ['dʌstklaʊd] *n* nuage *m* de poussière.

dust coat *n* cache-poussière *m inv*.

dust cover *n* **1.** = **dust jacket 2.** [for machine] housse *f* de rangement ■ [for furniture] housse *f* de protection.

duster ['dʌstər] *n* **1.** [cloth] chiffon *m* (à poussière) ■ [for blackboard] tampon *m* effaceur **2.** *US* [garment - for doing housework] blouse *f*, tablier *m* ; [- for driving] cache-poussière *m inv*

3. [lightweight coat] manteau *m* léger **4.** AGRIC poudreuse *f* ■ [aircraft] *avion servant à répandre de l'insecticide sur les champs.*

dust-free *adj* [environment] protégé de la poussière.

dustiness ['dʌstɪnɪs] *n* état *m* poussiéreux.

dusting ['dʌstɪŋ] *n* **1.** [of room, furniture] époussetage *m*, dépoussiérage *m* ■ **to do the ~** épousseter, enlever *OR* faire la poussière **2.** [with sugar, insecticide] saupoudrage *m*.

dusting powder *n* talc *m*.

dust jacket *n* [for book] jaquette *f*.

dustman ['dʌstmən] (*pl* **dustmen** [-mən]) *n UK* éboueur *m*.

dustpan ['dʌstpæn] *n* pelle *f* à poussière.

dustproof ['dʌstpru:f] *adj* imperméable *OR* étanche à la poussière.

dust sheet *n UK* housse *f* de protection.

dust storm *n* tempête *f* de poussière.

dust trap *n* nid *m* à poussière.

dust-up *n inf* accrochage *m*, prise *f* de bec.

dusty ['dʌstɪ] (*comp* **dustier**, *superl* **dustiest**) *adj* **1.** [room, furniture, road] poussiéreux ■ **to get ~** s'empoussiérer, se couvrir de poussière **2.** [colour] cendré **3.** *inf dated* & *phr* **to get a ~ answer** se faire envoyer balader *OR* paître, se faire recevoir.

Dutch [dʌtʃ] ◇ *npl* : **the ~** les Hollandais *mpl*, les Néerlandais *mpl*.
◇ *n* LING néerlandais *m*.
◇ *adj* [cheese] de Hollande ■ [bulbs, city] hollandais ■ [embassy, government etc] néerlandais ■ [dictionary, teacher] de néerlandais.
◇ *adv* : **to go ~ (with sb)** *inf* [share cost equally] partager les frais (avec qqn).

Dutch auction *n* vente *f* à la baisse.

Dutch barn *n UK* hangar *m* à armature métallique.

Dutch cap *n* diaphragme *m* (*contraceptif*).

Dutch courage *n inf courage trouvé dans la boisson* ■ **I need some ~** il faut que je boive un verre pour me donner du courage.

Dutch door *n US* porte *f* à deux vantaux.

Dutch elm disease *n* (*U*) maladie *f* des ormes.

Dutchman ['dʌtʃmən] (*pl* **Dutchmen** [-mən]) *n* Hollandais *m*, Néerlandais *m* ■ **(then) I'm a ~!** *fig* je mange mon chapeau!

Dutch uncle *n* : **to talk (to sb) like a ~** faire la morale (à qqn).

Dutchwoman ['dʌtʃ,wʊmən] (*pl* **Dutchwomen** [-,wɪmɪn]) *n* Hollandaise *f*, Néerlandaise *f*.

dutiable ['dju:tjəbl] *adj* taxable.

dutiful ['dju:tɪfʊl] *adj* [child] obéissant, respectueux ■ [husband, wife] qui remplit ses devoirs conjugaux ■ [worker, employee] consciencieux.

dutifully ['dju:tɪflɪ] *adv* consciencieusement.

duty ['dju:tɪ] *n* **1.** [moral or legal obligation] devoir *m* ■ **to do one's ~ (by sb)** faire son devoir (envers qqn) ■ **to fail in one's ~** manquer à son devoir ■ **it is my painful ~ to inform you that...** j'ai la douloureuse tâche de vous informer que... ■ **to make it one's ~ to do sthg** se faire un devoir de faire qqch ■ **~ calls** *hum* le devoir m'appelle ■ **to do sthg out of a sense of ~** faire qqch par sens du devoir **2.** (*usu pl*) [responsibility] fonction *f* ■ **to take up one's duties** entrer en fonction ■ **in the course of one's duties** dans l'exercice de ses fonctions ■ **public duties** responsabilités *fpl* publiques *OR* envers la communauté **3.** *phr* **on ~** [soldier, doctor] de garde ; [policeman] de service ■ **to go on/off ~** [soldier] prendre/laisser la garde ; [doctor] prendre la/cesser d'être de garde ; [policeman] prendre/quitter son service ■ **to do ~ for sb** remplacer qqn ■ **to do ~ for sthg** *fig* faire office de qqch ▶ **active ~** *US* MIL service *m* actif **4.** [tax] taxe *f*, droit *m*.

duty-bound *adj* tenu (par son devoir).

duty doctor *n* médecin *m* de garde.

duty-free ◇ *adj* [goods] hors taxe, en franchise ■ [shop] hors taxe ■ **my ~ allowance** les marchandises hors taxe auxquelles j'ai droit.
◇ *adv* hors taxe, en franchise.
◇ *n* marchandises *fpl* hors taxe *OR* en franchise.

duty officer *n* officier *m* de service.

duty roster, duty rota *n* tableau *m* de service.

duvet ['du:veɪ] *n* couette *f* ■ **~ cover** housse *f* de couette.

DVD (*abbrev of* **digital versatile OR video disc**) *n* DVD *m*.

DVD player *n* lecteur *m* de DVD.

DVD-ROM (*abbrev of* **digital versatile OR video disc read only memory**) *n* DVD-ROM *m*.

DVLC (*abbrev of* **Driver and Vehicle Licensing Centre**) *pr n service des immatriculations et des permis de conduire en Grande-Bretagne.*

DVM (*abbrev of* **Doctor of Veterinary Medicine**) *n docteur vétérinaire.*

dwarf [dwɔ:f] (*pl* **dwarfs** *OR pl* **dwarves** [dwɔ:vz]) ◇ *n* **1.** [person] nain *m*, - e *f* **2.** [tree] arbre *m* nain **3.** MYTH nain *m*, - e *f*.
◇ *adj* [plant, animal] nain.
◇ *vt* **1.** *fig* [in size] écraser ■ [in ability] éclipser **2.** [make small - tree] rabougrir.

dwarf star *n* ASTRON étoile *f* naine, naine *f*.

dweeb [dwi:b] *n US inf* crétin *m*, - e *f*.

dwell [dwel] (*pret & pp* **dwelt** [dwelt] *OR* **dwelled**) *vi lit* résider, demeurer.
➠ **dwell on, dwell upon** *vt insep* [the past - think about] penser sans cesse à ; [- talk about] parler sans cesse de ■ [problem, fact, detail] s'attarder sur ■ **don't ~ on it** [in thought] n'y pense pas trop.

-dweller ['dwelə^r] *in cpds* habitant *m*, - e *f* ■ **city~** citadin *m*, - e *f* ■ **cave~** troglodyte *mf*.

dwelling ['dwelɪŋ] *n hum & lit* résidence *f*.

dwelling house *n* LAW maison *f* d'habitation.

dwelt [dwelt] *pt & pp* ▷ **dwell**.

dwindle ['dwɪndl] *vi* [hopes, savings, population] se réduire, diminuer ■ **the island's population has ~d to 120** la population de l'île est descendue à 120 habitants ■ **to ~ (away) to nothing** se réduire à rien.

dwindling ['dwɪndlɪŋ] ◇ *n* [of savings, hopes] diminution *f* ■ [of population, membership] baisse *f*, diminution *f*.
◇ *adj* [population, audience] en baisse, décroissant ■ [savings, hopes] décroissant.

dye [daɪ] ◇ *n* [substance] teinture *f* ■ [colour] teinte *f*, couleur *f* ■ **the ~ will run in the wash** la couleur partira au lavage.
◇ *vt* [fabric, hair] teindre ■ **to ~ sthg yellow/green** teindre qqch en jaune/en vert ■ **~d blond hair** les cheveux teints en blond.
◇ *vi* [fabric] se teindre.

dyed-in-the-wool [daɪd-] *adj* bon teint (*inv*).

dyer ['daɪə^r] *n* teinturier *m*, - ère *f*.

dyestuff ['daɪstʌf] *n* teinture *f*, colorant *m*.

dying ['daɪɪŋ] ◇ *adj* **1.** [person, animal] mourant ■ *lit* agonisant ■ [tree, forest] mourant ■ [species] en voie de disparition ■ **the ~ man** le mourant ■ **her ~ words** les mots qu'elle a prononcés en mourant, ses derniers mots ■ **to** *OR* **till my ~ day** jusqu'à ma mort, jusqu'à mon dernier jour ■ **men like him are a ~ breed** des hommes comme lui, on n'en fait plus **2.** *fig* [art, craft] en train de disparaître ■ [industry] agonisant, en train de disparaître.
◇ *n* [death] mort *f*.
◇ *npl* : **the ~** les mourants *mpl*, les agonisants *mpl*.

dyke [daɪk] *n* **1.** [against flooding] digue *f* ■ [for carrying water away] fossé *m* ■ *Scotland* [wall] mur *m* **2.** △ [lesbian] gouine△ *f*.

dynamic [daɪ'næmɪk] <> *adj* **1.** [person] dynamique **2.** TECH dynamique.
<> *n* dynamique *f*.

dynamically [daɪ'næmɪklɪ] *adv* dynamiquement.

dynamics [daɪ'næmɪks] <> *npl* [of a situation, group] dynamique *f*.
<> *n (U)* TECH dynamique *f*.

dynamism ['daɪnəmɪzm] *n* [of person] dynamisme *m*.

dynamite ['daɪnəmaɪt] <> *n* [explosive] dynamite *f* ▪ **a stick of ~** un bâton de dynamite ▪ **this story is ~!** *fig* cette histoire, c'est de la dynamite!
<> *vt* [blow up] dynamiter.

dynamo ['daɪnəməʊ] *n* TECH dynamo *f* ▪ **a human ~** *fig* une boule d'énergie.

dynastic [dɪ'næstɪk] *adj* dynastique.

dynasty [*UK* 'dɪnəstɪ, *US* 'daɪnəstɪ] *n* dynastie *f* ▪ **the Romanov/Bourbon ~** la dynastie des Romanov/des Bourbon.

dysentery ['dɪsntrɪ] *n (U)* MED dysenterie *f*.

dysfunction [dɪs'fʌŋkʃn] *n* MED dysfonction *f*, dysfonctionnement *m*.

dysfunctional [dɪs'fʌŋkʃənl] *adj* dysfonctionnel (*f* le).

dyslexia [dɪs'leksɪə] *n* dyslexie *f*.

dyslexic [dɪs'leksɪk] <> *adj* dyslexique.
<> *n* dyslexique *mf*.

dysmenorrhoea *UK*, **dysmenorrhea** *US* [ˌdɪsmenə'rɪə] *n (U)* MED dysménorrhée *f*.

dyspepsia [dɪs'pepsɪə] *n (U)* MED dyspepsie *f*.

dyspeptic [dɪs'peptɪk] <> *adj* **1.** MED dyspeptique, dyspepsique **2.** *fig* [irritable] irritable.
<> *n* MED dyspeptique *mf*, dyspepsique *mf*.

dystrophy ['dɪstrəfɪ] *n* MED dystrophie *f*.

E

e (*pl* **e's** *OR pl* **es**)**, E** (*pl* **E's** *OR pl* **Es**) [i:] *n* [letter] e *m*, E *m*, *see also* **f**.

E ◇ *n* **1.** MUS mi *m* ▪ **in E flat** en mi bémol **2.** △ ***drug sl*** (*abbrev of* **ecstasy**) [drug] ecstasy *m* ▪ [pill] comprimé *m* d'ecstasy.
◇ (*written abbrev of* **East**) E.

ea. (*written abbrev of* **each**) : **£3.00 ~** 3 livres pièce.

e-account *n* compte *m* en banque en ligne.

each [i:tʃ] ◇ *det* chaque ▪ **~ day** chaque jour, tous les jours ▪ **~ (and every) one of us/you/them** chacun/chacune d'entre nous/vous/eux (sans exception).
◇ *pron* [every one] chacun, chacune ▪ **~ of his six children** chacun de ses six enfants ▪ **a number of suggestions, ~ more crazy than the last** un certain nombre de suggestions toutes plus folles les unes que les autres ▪ **or would you like some of ~?** ou bien voudriez-vous un peu de chaque? ▶ **to ~ his own, ~ to his own** à chacun ses goûts.
◇ *adv* [apiece] : **we have a book/a room ~** nous avons chacun un livre/une pièce ▪ **the tickets cost £20 ~** les billets coûtent 20 livres chacun.
◆ **each other** *pron phr* : **to hate ~ other** se détester (l'un l'autre) ; [more than two people] se détester (les uns les autres) ▪ **do you two know ~ other?** est-ce que vous vous connaissez? ▪ **the two sisters wear ~ other's clothes** les deux sœurs échangent leurs vêtements ▪ **they walked towards ~ other** ils ont marché l'un vers l'autre ▪ **we get on ~ other's nerves** nous nous portons mutuellement sur les nerfs ▪ **we get on very well with ~ other's parents** nous nous entendons très bien avec les parents l'un de l'autre.

each way ◇ *adj* : **~ bet** pari sur un cheval gagnant, premier ou placé.
◇ *adv* [in betting] placé ▪ **to put money ~ on a horse** jouer un cheval placé.

eager [ˈi:gəʳ] *adj* [impatient, keen] impatient ▪ [learner, helper] enthousiaste, fervent ▪ [crowd, face, look] passionné, enfiévré ▪ **to be ~ to do sthg** [impatient] avoir hâte de faire qqch ; [very willing] faire preuve d'enthousiasme *OR* de ferveur pour faire qqch ▪ **I am ~ to help in any way I can** je tiens absolument à apporter mon aide ▪ **to be ~ to please** avoir envie de faire plaisir ▪ **to be ~ for affection/for success** être avide d'affection/de succès ▪ **he's ~ for me to see his work** il a très envie que je voie son travail.

eager beaver *n* ***inf*** travailleur *m* acharné, travailleuse *f* acharnée, mordu *m*, - e *f* du travail.

eagerly [ˈi:gəlɪ] *adv* [wait] impatiemment ▪ [help] avec empressement ▪ [say, look at] avec passion *OR* enthousiasme.

eagerness [ˈi:gənɪs] *n* [to know, see, find out] impatience *f* ▪ [to help] empressement *m* ▪ [in eyes, voice] excitation *f*, enthousiasme *m* ▪ **his ~ to please** sa volonté de plaire.

eagle [ˈi:gl] *n* **1.** [bird] aigle *m* ▪ **to have an ~ eye** avoir un œil d'aigle **2.** [standard, seal] aigle *f* **3.** [lectern] aigle *m* **4.** GOLF eagle *m*.

eagle-eyed ◇ *adj* aux yeux d'aigle.
◇ *adv* [watch] avec une grande attention.

eagle owl *n* grand duc *m*.

eaglet [ˈi:glɪt] *n* aiglon *m*, - onne *f*.

Ealing comedy [ˈi:lɪŋ-] *n genre de film comique britannique produit dans les studios d'Ealing (Londres) vers 1950.*

E and OE (*written abbrev of* **errors and omissions excepted**) ***UK*** s e & o.

ear [ɪəʳ] *n* **1.** [of person, animal] oreille *f* ▪ **to have a good ~** avoir de l'oreille ▪ **to have an ~ for music** avoir l'oreille musicale ▪ **to keep an ~** *OR* **one's ~s open** ouvrir les oreilles, tendre l'oreille ▪ **it has reached my ~s that...** j'ai entendu dire que... ▪ **he closed his ~s to her request for help** elle lui a demandé de l'aide mais il a fait la sourde oreille ▪ **I've heard that until it's coming out of my ~ s** ***inf*** je l'ai tellement entendu que ça me sort par les oreilles ▪ **to have the ~ of sb** [have influence with] avoir l'oreille de qqn ▪ **to be grinning from ~ to ~** sourire jusqu'aux oreilles ▶ **~ infection** otite *f* ▪ **~, nose and throat department** service *m* d'oto-rhino-laryngologie ▪ **~, nose and throat specialist** oto-rhino *mf*, oto-rhino-laryngologiste *mf* ▪ **to be all ~s** ***inf*** être tout oreilles *OR* tout ouïe ▪ **to be out on one's ~** ***inf*** [from job, school] être viré ▪ **he's out on his ~** [been dismissed] il s'est fait virer ; [from family home] il s'est fait flanquer dehors ▪ **to be up to one's ~s in work** *OR* **in it** ***inf*** être débordé (de travail) ▪ **it just goes in one ~ and out the other** ça entre par une oreille et ça ressort par l'autre ▪ **to keep one's ~ to the ground** ouvrir l'oreille, être à l'écoute ▪ **my ~s are burning!** j'ai les oreilles qui (me) sifflent! ▪ **to play by ~** MUS jouer à l'oreille ▪ **to play it by ~** improviser **2.** [of grain] épi *m*.

earache [ˈɪəreɪk] *n* mal *m* d'oreille ▪ **to have ~** ***UK OR*** **an ~** ***US*** avoir mal aux oreilles.

ear buds *npl* oreillettes *fpl*.

eardrops [ˈɪədrɒps] *npl* gouttes *fpl* pour les oreilles.

eardrum [ˈɪədrʌm] *n* tympan *m*.

-eared [ɪəd] *in cpds* : **long/short~** à oreilles *fpl* longues/courtes ▪ **pointy~** ***inf*** aux oreilles en pointe.

earful [ˈɪəfʊl] *n* : **to get an ~ of water** prendre de l'eau plein l'oreille ▶ **to give sb an ~** ***inf*** [tell off] passer un savon à qqn ▪ **to give sb an ~ about sthg** ***US*** [say a lot to] raconter qqch à qqn en long, en large et en travers.

earhole [ˈɪəhəʊl] *n* ***UK inf*** [ear] esgourde *f*.

earl [ɜ:l] *n* comte *m*.

earldom ['ɜ:ldəm] *n* [title] titre *m* de comte ▪ [estates, land] comté *m*.

earlier ['ɜ:lɪə] *compar* ▻ **early**.

earliest ['ɜ:lɪəst] *superl* ▻ **early**.

earlobe ['ɪələʊb] *n* lobe *m* de l'oreille.

Earls Court [ɜ:lz-] *pr n grand centre d'exposition à Londres.*

early ['ɜ:lɪ] (*comp* **earlier**, *superl* **earliest**) ◇ *adj* **1.** [morning] matinal ▪ **I had an ~ breakfast** j'ai déjeuné de bonne heure ▪ **to get off to an ~ start** partir de bonne heure ▪ **the ~ shuttle to London** le premier avion pour Londres ▪ **it's too ~ to get up** il est trop tôt pour se lever ▪ **to be an ~ riser** être matinal *OR* un lève-tôt
2. [belonging to the beginning of a period of time - machine, film, poem] premier ; [- Edwardian, Victorian etc] du début de l'époque ▪ **in the ~ afternoon/spring/fifties** au début de l'après-midi/du printemps/des années cinquante ▪ **when was that? – ~ September** quand était-ce? – début septembre ▪ **it's ~ days yet** *UK* [difficult to be definite] il est trop tôt pour se prononcer ; [might yet be worse, better] il est encore tôt ▪ **from the earliest times** depuis le début des temps ▪ **I need an ~ night** je dois me coucher de bonne heure ▪ **it's too ~ to tell** il est trop tôt pour se prononcer, on ne peut encore rien dire ▪ **the earliest human artefacts** les premiers objets fabriqués par l'homme ▪ **the ~ Roman Empire** l'Empire romain naissant ▪ **~ music** [baroque] musique *f* ancienne ▪ **an ~ Picasso** une des premières œuvres de Picasso ▪ **he's in his ~ twenties** il a une vingtaine d'années ▪ **from an ~ age** dès l'enfance ▪ **at an ~ age** de bonne heure, très jeune ▪ **~ reports from the front indicate that...** les premières nouvelles du front semblent indiquer que... ▪ **in the ~ stages of the project** dans une phase initiale du projet
3. [ahead of time] : **to be ~** [person, train, flight, winter] être en avance ▪ **let's have an ~ lunch** déjeunons de bonne heure ▪ **you're too ~** vous arrivez trop tôt, vous êtes en avance ▪ **Easter is ~ this year** Pâques est de bonne heure cette année
4. [relating to the future - reply] prochain ▪ **at your earliest convenience** COMM dans les meilleurs délais ▪ **what is your earliest possible delivery date?** quelle est votre première possibilité de livraison?
◇ *adv* **1.** [in the morning - rise, leave] tôt, de bonne heure ▪ **let's set off as ~ as we can** mettons-nous en route le plus tôt possible ▪ **how ~ should I get there?** à quelle heure dois-je y être?
2. [at the beginning of a period of time] : **~ in the evening/in the afternoon** tôt le soir/(dans) l'après-midi ▪ **~ in the year/winter** au début de l'année/de l'hiver ▪ **I can't make it earlier than 2.30** je ne peux pas avant 14 h 30 ▪ **what's the earliest you can make it?** [be here] quand pouvez-vous être ici? ➊ **~ on** tôt ▪ **earlier on** plus tôt
3. [ahead of schedule] en avance ▪ [earlier than usual] de bonne heure ▪ **shop/post ~ for Christmas** faites vos achats/postez votre courrier à l'avance pour Noël
4. [relating to the future] : **at the earliest** au plus tôt ▪ **we can't deliver earlier than Friday** nous ne pouvons pas livrer avant vendredi.

early American *n style de mobilier et d'architecture du début du XIXe siècle.*

early bird *n* : **to be an ~** *inf* être matinal ➊ **it's the ~ that catches the worm** *prov* [it's good to get up early] le monde appartient à ceux qui se lèvent tôt *prov* ; [it's good to arrive early] les premiers arrivés sont les mieux servis.

early closing *n UK* COMM *jour où l'on ferme tôt.*

Early Learning Centre *n UK* magasin *m* de jouets d'éveil.

early-warning *adj* : **~ system** système *m* de préalerte.

earmark ['ɪəmɑ:k] ◇ *vt* réserver ▪ [money] affecter, assigner ▪ **this land is ~ed for development** ce terrain est réservé *OR* assigné à l'aménagement.
◇ *n* marque *f* à l'oreille.

earmuffs ['ɪəmʌfs] *npl* protège-oreille *m*.

earn [ɜ:n] ◇ *vt* **1.** [money] gagner ▪ [interest] rapporter ▪ **to ~ a living** gagner sa vie ➊ **~ed income** revenu *m* salarial, revenus *mpl* salariaux **2.** [respect, punishment - subj: activities] valoir ; [- subj: person] mériter ▪ **it ~ed him ten years in prison** cela lui a valu dix ans de prison.
◇ *vi* [person] gagner de l'argent ▪ [investment] rapporter ▪ **~ing capacity** [of person] potentiel *m* de revenu ; [of firm] rentabilité *f*.

earner ['ɜ:nə^r] *n* **1.** [person] salarié *m*, - e *f* ▪ **she's the main ~ in the family** c'est elle qui fait vivre la famille **2.** *UK inf* [source of income] : **it's a nice little ~** [business, shop etc] c'est une bonne petite affaire.

earnest ['ɜ:nɪst] *adj* **1.** [person, expression, tone] sérieux **2.** [hope, request] ardent, fervent ▪ [endeavour] fervent ▪ [desire] profond.
◆ **in earnest** ◇ *adv phr* [seriously] sérieusement, sincèrement ▪ [in a determined way] sérieusement ▪ **it's raining in ~ now** il pleut pour de bon cette fois.
◇ *adj phr* : **to be in ~** être sérieux.

earnestly ['ɜ:nɪstlɪ] *adv* [behave] sérieusement ▪ [study, work] sérieusement, avec ardeur ▪ [speak, nod, look at] gravement ▪ **we ~ hope that...** nous espérons sincèrement que...

earnestness ['ɜ:nɪstnɪs] *n* sérieux *m*, gravité *f*.

earnings ['ɜ:nɪŋz] *npl* [of person, business] revenus *mpl* ▪ **to live off immoral ~** gagner sa vie par des procédés immoraux.

earnings-related *adj* proportionnel au revenu.

earphones ['ɪəfəʊnz] *npl* écouteurs *mpl*, casque *m*.

earpiece ['ɪəpi:s] *n* [of telephone receiver, personal stereo] écouteur *m*.

ear piercing *n (U)* : **'ear piercing'** 'ici, on perce les oreilles'.
◆ **ear-piercing** *adj* [noise] perçant, strident.

earplugs ['ɪəplʌgz] *npl* [for sleeping] boules *fpl* Quiès® ▪ [for protection against water, noise] protège-tympans *mpl*.

earring ['ɪərɪŋ] *n* boucle *f* d'oreille.

earshot ['ɪəʃɒt] *n* : **out of/within ~** hors de/à portée de voix.

ear-splitting *adj* [noise] assourdissant.

earth [ɜ:θ] ◇ *n* **1.** [the world, the planet] terre *f* ▪ **the planet Earth** la planète Terre ▪ **on ~** sur terre ➊ **why/how/who on ~ ?** pourquoi/comment/qui diable? ▪ **there's nothing on ~ I'd like better** il n'y a rien au monde dont j'aie plus envie ▪ **to cost the ~** *inf* coûter les yeux de la tête *OR* la peau des fesses ▪ **to promise (sb) the ~** promettre la lune (à qqn), promettre monts et merveilles (à qqn)
2. [ground] terre *f* ▪ **to fall to ~** tomber par terre ➊ **to bring sb down to ~ (with a bump)** ramener qqn sur terre (brutalement) ▪ **to come back down to ~ again** revenir *OR* redescendre sur terre
3. [soil] terre *f*
4. *UK* ELEC [connection, terminal] terre *f* ▪ **~ lead** conducteur *m* de terre
5. [of fox] terrier *m*, tanière *f* ▪ **to run a fox to ~** chasser un renard jusqu'à son terrier *OR* sa tanière ▪ **to run sb/sthg to ~** [find] dénicher qqn/qqch ▪ **to go to ~** *liter* & *fig* aller se terrer.
◇ *vt UK* ELEC mettre à la terre.

earthbound ['ɜ:θbaʊnd] *adj* **1.** [insects] non volant **2.** [spaceship] progressant en direction de la terre ▪ [journey] en direction de la terre **3.** [unimaginative] terre à terre.

earth closet *n* fosse *f* d'aisance.

earthen ['ɜ:θn] *adj* [dish] en *OR* de terre (cuite) ▪ [floor] en terre.

earthenware ['ɜ:θnweə^r] ◇ *n* [pottery] poterie *f* ▪ [glazed] faïence *f*.
◇ *adj* en *OR* de terre (cuite), en *OR* de faïence.

earthiness ['ɜ:θɪnɪs] *n* **1.** [of humour] truculence *f* ▪ [of person, character] nature *f* directe **2.** [of food] goût *m* de terre.

earthling ['ɜ:θlɪŋ] *n* terrien *m*, - enne *f*.

earthly ['ɜ:θlɪ] ◇ *adj* **1.** [worldly] terrestre ▪ **~ possessions** biens *mpl* matériels **2.** *inf* [possible] : **there's no ~ reason why I should believe you** je n'ai absolument aucune raison de te croire.
◇ *n UK inf* [chance] : **he doesn't have an ~ of passing the exam** il n'a aucune chance de réussir à l'examen.

earth mother *n* **1.** MYTH déesse *f* de la Terre **2.** *inf fig* mère *f* nourricière.

earthquake ['ɜ:θkweɪk] *n* tremblement *m* de terre.

earth sciences *npl* sciences *fpl* de la terre.

earth-shaking [-,ʃeɪkɪŋ], **earth-shattering** *adj inf* fracassant, extraordinaire.

earth tremor *n* secousse *f* sismique.

earthward ['ɜ:θwəd] ◇ *adj* [journey] en direction de la Terre.
◇ *adv* en direction de la Terre.

earthwards ['ɜ:θwədz] *adv* en direction de la Terre.

earthwork(s) ['ɜ:θwɜ:k(s)] *npl* CONSTR terrassement *m* ▪ ARCHEOL & MIL fortification *f* en terre.

earthworm ['ɜ:θwɜ:m] *n* ver *m* de terre, lombric *m*.

earthy ['ɜ:θɪ] *adj* **1.** [taste, smell] de terre **2.** [humour] truculent ▪ [person, character] direct.

ear trumpet *n* cornet *m* acoustique.

earwax ['ɪəwæks] *n* cire *f (sécrétée par les oreilles)*, cérumen *m*.

earwig ['ɪəwɪg] *n* perce-oreille *m*.

ease [i:z] ◇ *n* **1.** [comfort] aise *f* ▪ **to be** *OR* **to feel at ~** être *OR* se sentir à l'aise ▪ **to be** *OR* **to feel ill at ~** être *OR* se sentir mal à l'aise ▪ **to set sb's mind at ~** tranquilliser qqn ▪ **to put sb at (his** *OR* **her) ~** mettre qqn à l'aise ▪ **(stand) at ~!** MIL repos! **2.** [facility] facilité *f* ▪ [of movements] aisance *f* ▪ **to do sthg with ~** faire qqch facilement *OR* aisément ▪ **~ of access** facilité d'accès **3.** [affluence] : **to live a life of ~** avoir la belle vie, mener une vie facile.
◇ *vt* **1.** [alleviate - anxiety, worry] calmer ; [- pain] calmer, soulager ; [- pressure, tension] relâcher ; [- traffic flow] rendre plus fluide ; [- sb's workload] alléger ▪ **to ~ sb's mind** rassurer qqn ▪ **to ~ sb of their anxiety/pain** calmer l'inquiétude/la douleur de qqn **2.** [move gently] : **to ~ o.s. into a chair** s'installer délicatement dans un fauteuil ▪ **she ~d the rucksack from her back** elle fit glisser le sac à dos de ses épaules ▪ **they ~d him out of the car** ils l'ont aidé à sortir de la voiture ▪ **to ~ sthg out** faire sortir qqch délicatement ▪ **to ~ sb out** [from position, job] pousser qqn vers la sortie *fig* ▪ **he ~d himself through the gap in the hedge** il s'est glissé *OR* faufilé à travers le trou dans la haie.
◇ *vi* [pain] se calmer, s'adoucir ▪ [situation, tension, rain] se calmer ▪ **the awkwardness between them ~d** le malaise qu'il y avait entre eux s'est dissipé.
◆ **ease back** *vt sep* [throttle, lever] tirer doucement.
◆ **ease off** ◇ *vt sep* [lid, bandage] enlever délicatement.
◇ *vi insep* [rain] se calmer ▪ [business] ralentir ▪ [traffic] diminuer ▪ [tension] se relâcher ▪ **work has ~d off** il y a moins de travail.
◆ **ease up** *vi insep* [slow down - in car] ralentir ▪ [rain] se calmer ▪ [business, work] ralentir ▪ [traffic] diminuer ▪ **to ~ up on sb/sthg** y aller doucement avec qqn/qqch.

easel ['i:zl] *n* chevalet *m*.

easily ['i:zɪlɪ] *adv* **1.** [without difficulty] facilement ▪ **that's ~ said/done** c'est facile à dire/faire ▪ **she is ~ pleased** elle n'est pas difficile **2.** [undoubtedly] sans aucun doute ▪ **she's ~ the best** c'est de loin la meilleure ▪ **it's ~ two hours from here** c'est facilement à deux heures d'ici **3.** [very possibly] : **he could ~ change his mind** il pourrait bien changer d'avis **4.** [in a relaxed manner - talk] de manière décontractée ; [- smile, answer] d'un air décontracté.

easing ['i:zɪŋ] *n* [of discomfort] soulagement *m* ▪ [of tension] relâchement *m*.

east [i:st] ◇ *n* est *m* ▪ **the East** [the Orient] l'Orient *m* ; [Eastern Europe] l'Est *m* ; [in US] l'Est *m (États situés à l'est du Mississippi)* ▪ **East-West relations** relations *fpl* Est-Ouest ▪ **on the ~ of the island** à l'est de l'île ▪ **to the ~ of the mainland** à l'est *OR* au large de la côte est du continent ▪ **the wind is (coming) from the ~** le vent vient de l'est.
◇ *adj* [coast, shore, face of mountain] est, oriental ▪ [wind] d'est ▪ **to live in ~ London** habiter dans l'est de Londres.
◇ *adv* [go, look, travel] en direction de l'est, vers l'est ▪ [sail] cap sur l'est ▪ **further ~** plus à l'est ▪ **~ of** à l'est de ▪ **~ by north/south** est quart nord/sud ▪ **back ~** *US inf* dans l'est *(des États-Unis)*.

East Africa *pr n* Afrique *f* orientale.

East African ◇ *adj* d'Afrique orientale.
◇ *n* Africain *m*, - e *f* de l'est.

eastbound ['i:stbaʊnd] *adj* [traffic, train] en direction de l'est.

East End *n* [of city] quartiers *mpl* est ▪ **the ~** *quartier industriel de Londres, connu pour ses docks et, autrefois, pour sa pauvreté.*

Easter ['i:stəʳ] ◇ *n* Pâques *fpl* ▪ **Happy ~!** joyeuses Pâques! ▪ **last/next ~** à Pâques l'année dernière/l'année prochaine.
◇ *comp* [holiday, Sunday, weekend] de Pâques ▪ [week] de Pâques, pascal ▪ [celebrations] pascal ▪ **~ Day** (jour *m* de) Pâques.

Easter bunny *n* [gen] lapin *m* de Pâques ▪ [in the US] *personnage imaginaire qui distribue des friandises aux enfants.*

Easter egg *n* œuf *m* de Pâques.

Easter Island *pr n* l'île *f* de Pâques ▪ **in** *OR* **on ~** à l'île de Pâques.

easterly ['i:stəlɪ] ◇ *adj* [in the east] situé à l'est ▪ [from the east] d'est ▪ [to the east] vers l'est, en direction de l'est.
◇ *n* vent *m* d'est.

eastern ['i:stən] *adj* [Europe] de l'Est ▪ [France, Scotland etc] de l'Est ▪ [region, seaboard] est, oriental ▪ [culture, philosophy] oriental ▪ **~ hemisphere** hémisphère *m* oriental ▪ **the Eastern Bloc** le bloc de l'Est.

Eastern Daylight Time *n* heure *f* d'été de New York.

Easterner ['i:stənəʳ] *n* **1.** [in US] *personne qui vient de l'est des États-Unis* **2.** [oriental] Oriental *m*, - e *f*.

Eastern European Time *n* heure *f* d'Europe orientale.

easternmost ['i:stənməʊst] *adj* situé le plus à l'est.

Eastern Standard Time *n* heure *f* d'hiver de New York.

Easter Rising *pr n* HIST : **the ~** *insurrection irlandaise contre la Grande-Bretagne en 1916.*

Eastertide ['i:stətaɪd] *n lit* (saison *f* de) Pâques *fpl*.

east-facing *adj* exposé *OR* donnant à l'est.

East German ◇ *adj* est-allemand, d'Allemagne de l'Est.
◇ *n* Allemand *m*, - e *f* de l'Est.

East Germany *pr n* : **(former) ~** (l'ex-)Allemagne *f* de l'Est ▪ **in ~** en Allemagne de l'Est.

East Indies *pr npl* HIST : **the ~** les Indes orientales.

east-northeast ◇ *n* est-nord-est *m*.
◇ *adj* [direction] est-nord-est ▪ [wind] d'est-nord-est.
◇ *adv* en direction de l'est-nord-est ▪ [blow] d'est-nord-est.

East Side *pr n* : **the ~** l'East Side *m (quartier situé à l'est de Manhattan)*.

east-southeast ◇ *n* est-sud-est *m*.
◇ *adj* [direction] est-sud-est ▪ [wind] d'est-sud-est.
◇ *adv* en direction de l'est-sud-est ▪ [blow] d'est-sud-est.

eastward ['i:stwəd] ◇ *adj* est.
◇ *adv* = **eastwards**.

eastwards ['i:stwədz] *adv* en direction de l'est, vers l'est ▪ **facing ~** [building] exposé *OR* donnant à l'est ▪ **to sail ~** naviguer cap sur l'est.

easy ['i:zɪ] (*comp* **easier**, *superl* **easiest**) <> *adj* **1.** [not difficult] facile ▪ **it's ~ to see why/that...** on voit bien pourquoi/que... ▪ **it's ~ to say that...** c'est facile de dire que... ▪ **she is (an) ~ (person) to please** c'est facile de lui faire plaisir ▪ **it's an ~ mistake to make** c'est une erreur qui est facile à faire ▪ **in ~ stages** [travel] par petites étapes ; [learn] sans peine ▪ **within ~ reach of** près de ▪ **the ~ way out** *OR* **option** la solution facile *OR* de facilité ▪ **~ to get on with** facile à vivre ▪ **to have an ~ time (of it)** [a good life] avoir la belle vie *OR* la vie facile ▪ **it's ~ money** *inf* c'est de l'argent gagné facilement *OR* sans se fatiguer ▪ **to come in an ~ first** [in a race] gagner haut la main ▶ **~ game** *OR* **meat** *inf* bonne poire *f* ▪ **as ~ as pie** *OR* **ABC** *inf* simple comme bonjour *OR* tout ▪ **to be on ~ street** *inf* rouler sur l'or
2. [at peace] : **to feel ~ in one's mind** être tranquille, avoir l'esprit tranquille
3. [easygoing - person, atmosphere] décontracté ; [- disposition, nature] facile ; [- manner] décontracté, naturel ; [- style] coulant, facile ▪ **I'm ~** *inf* [I don't mind] ça m'est égal ▪ **to be on ~ terms with sb** avoir des rapports plutôt amicaux avec qqn ▪ **on ~ terms** COMM avec facilités de paiement
4. [sexually] : **a woman of ~ virtue** *lit* une femme de petite vertu *OR* aux mœurs légères ▪ **she's an ~ lay**△ *pej* elle couche avec tout le monde, c'est une Marie-couche-toi-là
5. [pleasant] : **to be ~ on the eye** [film, painting] être agréable à regarder ; [person] être un plaisir pour les yeux ▪ **to be ~ on the ear** [music] être agréable à écouter
6. ST. EX [market] calme.
<> *adv* [in a relaxed or sparing way] doucement ▪ **to go ~** y aller doucement ▪ **to go ~ on** *OR* **with sb** y aller doucement avec qqn ▪ **to go ~ on** *OR* **with sthg** y aller doucement avec *OR* sur qqch ▪ **he's got it ~** *inf* [has an easy life] il se la coule douce, il a la belle vie ▪ **take it ~!** [gen] doucement! ; *US* [on parting] bon courage! ▪ **to take things** *OR* **it** *OR* **life ~** [relax] se reposer ▪ **~ now!** *inf*, **~ does it!** *inf* doucement! ▪ **to sleep ~ in one's bed** dormir sur ses deux oreilles ▪ **stand ~!** MIL repos! ▪ **easier said than done** plus facile à dire qu'à faire.

easy chair *n* fauteuil *m*.

easy-clean *adj* [garment, surface] facile à nettoyer, d'entretien facile.

easygoing [i:zɪgəʊɪŋ] *adj* [person] décontracté, facile à vivre ▪ [lifestyle] décontracté.

easy listening *n* MUS variété *f*.

easy-peasy *n* fastoche *inf hum*, facile.

easy-to-use *adj* facile à utiliser.

eat [i:t] (*pret* **ate** [et, eɪt], *pp* **eaten** ['i:tn]) <> *vt* manger ▪ **to ~ (one's) breakfast/lunch/dinner** prendre son petit déjeuner/déjeuner/dîner ▪ **it looks good enough to ~!** on en mangerait! ▪ **he/she looks good enough to ~** il est beau/elle est belle à croquer ▶ **I'll ~ my hat if he gets elected** s'il est élu, je veux bien être pendu ▪ **he ~s people like you for breakfast** il ne fait qu'une bouchée des gens comme toi ▪ **to ~ one's words** ravaler ses mots ▪ **they ate us out of house and home** ils ont dévalisé notre frigo ▪ **what's ~ing you?** *inf* qu'est-ce que tu as?
<> *vi* manger ▪ **let's ~** à table ▪ **to ~ for two** [pregnant woman] manger pour deux ▶ **he's got her ~ing out of his hand** elle lui mangerait dans la main.
◆ **eats** *npl inf* bouffe *f*.
◆ **eat away** <> *vt sep* [subj: waves] ronger ▪ [subj: mice] ronger ▪ [subj: acid, rust] ronger, corroder ▪ *fig* [confidence] miner ▪ [support, capital, resources] entamer.
<> *vi insep* [person] manger.
◆ **eat away at** *vt insep* = **eat away** *(vt sep)*.
◆ **eat in** *vi insep* manger chez soi *OR* à la maison.
◆ **eat into** *vt insep* **1.** [destroy] attaquer **2.** [use up - savings] entamer ; [- time] empiéter sur.
◆ **eat out** <> *vi insep* sortir déjeuner *OR* dîner, aller au restaurant.
<> *vt sep* : **to ~ one's heart out** se morfondre ▪ **~ your heart out!** dommage pour toi!
◆ **eat up** <> *vi insep* manger.
<> *vt sep* [food] terminer, finir ▪ *fig* [electricity, gas, petrol] consommer beaucoup de ▪ **to ~ up the miles** dévorer *OR* avaler les kilomètres ▪ **to be eaten up with** [jealousy, hate, ambition] être rongé *OR* dévoré par.

eatable ['i:təbl] *adj* [fit to eat] mangeable ▪ [edible] comestible.

eaten ['i:tn] *pp* ▷ **eat**.

eater ['i:tər] *n* **1.** [person] mangeur *m*, - euse *f* ▪ **to be a messy ~** manger salement **2.** *UK inf* [apple] pomme *f* à couteau.

eatery ['i:tərɪ] (*pl* **eateries**) *n inf* café-restaurant *m*.

eating ['i:tɪŋ] <> *n* : **~ is one of his favourite pastimes** manger constitue un de ses passe-temps favoris.
<> *adj* **1.** [for eating] : **~ apple/pear** pomme *f* /poire *f* à couteau ▪ **~ place** *OR* **house** restaurant *m* **2.** [of eating] : **~ habits** habitudes *fpl* alimentaires ▪ **~ disorder** trouble *m* du comportement alimentaire.

eau de Cologne [,əʊdəkə'ləʊn] *n* eau *f* de Cologne.

eaves ['i:vz] *npl* avant-toit *m*, corniche *f*.

eavesdrop ['i:vzdrɒp] (*pret & pp* **eavesdropped**, *cont* **eavesdropping**) *vi* écouter de manière indiscrète, espionner ▪ **to ~ on sb's conversation** espionner la conversation de qqn.

e-banking *n* services *mpl* bancaires en ligne.

ebb [eb] <> *n* [of tide] reflux *m* ▪ [of public opinion] variations *fpl* ▪ **~ and flow** flux *m* et reflux ▪ **to be at a low ~** [person] ne pas avoir le moral ; [patient, enthusiasm, spirits] être bien bas ; [business] aller mal, être *OR* tourner au ralenti ; [finances, relations] aller mal.
<> *vi* **1.** [tide] baisser, descendre ▪ **to ~ and flow** monter et baisser *OR* descendre **2.** *fig* = **ebb away**.
◆ **ebb away** *vi insep* [confidence, enthusiasm, strength etc] baisser peu à peu ▪ [completely] disparaître.

ebb tide *n* marée *f* descendante.

Ebola [ɪ'bələ] *n* MED (virus *m*) Ebola *m*.

ebony ['ebənɪ] <> *n* [tree] ébénier *m* ▪ [wood] ébène *m*.
<> *adj* [chair, table etc] en ébène ▪ *fig* [eyes, hair] d'ébène.

EBRD (*abbrev of* **European Bank of Reconstruction and Development**) *pr n* BERD *f*.

ebullience [ɪ'bʊljəns] *n* exubérance *f*.

ebullient [ɪ'bʊljənt] *adj* exubérant.

e-business *n (U)* commerce *m* en ligne.

EC (*abbrev of* **European Community**) <> *n* CE *f*.
<> *comp* [ruling, states, membership] de la CE.

e-cash ['i:-] *n* argent *m* électronique.

ECB (*abbrev of* **European Central Bank**) *n* BCE *f*.

eccentric [ɪk'sentrɪk] <> *adj* **1.** [person, clothes, behaviour] excentrique **2.** ASTRON, MATHS & TECH excentrique, excentré.
<> *n* **1.** [person] excentrique *mf* **2.** TECH excentrique *m*.

eccentrically [ɪk'sentrɪklɪ] *adv* **1.** [dress, talk] de manière excentrique **2.** ASTRON, MATHS & TECH excentriquement.

eccentricity [,eksen'trɪsətɪ] (*pl* **eccentricities**) *n* excentricité *f*.

Eccles cake ['eklz-] *n petit gâteau rond en pâte feuilletée fourré de fruits secs.*

Ecclesiastes [ɪ,kli:zɪ'æsti:z] *pr n* BIBLE : **(the book of) ~** l'Ecclésiaste *m*.

ecclesiastical [ɪ,kli:zɪ'æstɪkl] *adj* [robes, traditions, calendar] ecclésiastique ▪ [history] de l'Église ▪ [music] d'église.

ECG *n* **1.** (*abbrev of* **electrocardiogram**) ECG *m* **2.** (*abbrev of* **electrocardiograph**) ECG *m*.

echelon ['eʃəlɒn] *n* **1.** [level] échelon *m* **2.** MIL échelon *m*.

echinoderm [ɪ'kaɪnəʊdɜ:m] *n* échinoderme *m*.

echo ['ekəʊ] (*pl* **echoes**) <> *n* écho *m* ▪ **~es of Kafka** *fig* des éléments qui rappellent *OR* évoquent Kafka.
<> *vt* [sound] répéter ▪ *fig* [colour, theme] reprendre, rappeler ▪ [architecture, style] rappeler, évoquer ▪ **to ~ sb's opinions** [person] se faire l'écho des opinions de qqn ; [editorial] reprendre les opinions de qqn.

<> *vi* [noise, voice, music] résonner ■ [place] faire écho, résonner ■ **the corridor ~ed with shouts/footsteps** des cris/bruits de pas résonnèrent dans le couloir, le couloir résonna de cris/ bruits de pas.

echo chamber *n* chambre *f* de réverbération.

echo sounder *n* échosondeur *m*.

eclampsia [ɪ'klæmpsɪə] *n* MED éclampsie *f*.

eclectic [ɪ'klektɪk] <> *n* éclectique *mf*.
<> *adj* éclectique.

eclecticism [ɪ'klektɪsɪzm] *n* éclectisme *m*.

eclipse [ɪ'klɪps] ASTRON & *fig* <> *n* éclipse *f* ■ **an ~ of the sun/moon** une éclipse de soleil/lune ■ **to be in ~** être éclipsé ■ **to go into ~** [sun, moon] s'éclipser.
<> *vt* éclipser.

ecliptic [ɪ'klɪptɪk] ASTRON <> *n* écliptique *m*.
<> *adj* écliptique.

ECM US (*abbrev of* **European Common Market**) *n Marché commun européen.*

eco- ['iːkəʊ] (*abbrev of* **ecology or ecological**) *prefix* éco-.

eco-friendly [ˌiːkəʊ-] *adj* qui respecte l'environnement.

E-coli [ˌiː'kəʊlaɪ] *n* MED E-coli *m*, bactérie *f* Escherischia coli.

ecological [ˌiːkə'lɒdʒɪkl] *adj* écologique.

ecologically [ˌiːkə'lɒdʒɪklɪ] *adv* écologiquement ■ **~ (speaking)** du point de vue de l'écologie ■ **~ harmful/sound** qui est nuisible à/qui respecte l'environnement.

ecologist [ɪ'kɒlədʒɪst] *n* écologiste *mf*.

ecology [ɪ'kɒlədʒɪ] *n* écologie *f*.

e-commerce [ˌiː-] *n* commerce *m* électronique, cybercommerce *m*.

econometrics [ɪˌkɒnə'metrɪks] *n (U)* économétrie *f*.

economic [ˌiːkə'nɒmɪk] *adj* **1.** ECON [climate, growth, system, indicator] économique ■ **~ migrant** OR **refugee** *émigré qui a quitté son pays pour des raisons économiques* ■ **~ performance** [of a country] résultats *mpl* économiques **2.** [profitable] rentable ■ **it isn't ~, it doesn't make ~ sense** ce n'est pas rentable OR avantageux.

economical [ˌiːkə'nɒmɪkl] *adj* [person] économe ■ [machine, method, approach] économique ■ **it's more ~ to buy in bulk** c'est plus économique OR avantageux d'acheter par grandes quantités ■ **to be ~ to run** [car, heating] être économique ■ **to be ~ with sthg** économiser qqch ■ **to be ~ with the truth** *euph* dire la vérité avec parcimonie ■ **~ use of language** emploi sobre du langage.

economically [ˌiːkə'nɒmɪklɪ] *adv* **1.** ECON économiquement **2.** [live] de manière économe ■ [write] avec sobriété ■ [use] de manière économe, avec parcimonie.

Economic and Monetary Union *n* Union *f* économique et monétaire.

economics [ˌiːkə'nɒmɪks] <> *n (U)* [science] économie *f* (politique), sciences *fpl* économiques.
<> *npl* [financial aspects] aspect *m* économique.

economist [ɪ'kɒnəmɪst] *n* économiste *mf* ■ **the Economist** PRESS *hebdomadaire britannique politique, économique et financier.*

economize [ɪ'kɒnəmaɪz] *vi* économiser, faire des économies ■ **to ~ on sthg** économiser sur qqch.

economy [ɪ'kɒnəmɪ] (*pl* **economies**) <> *n* **1.** [system] économie *f* **2.** [saving] économie *f* ■ **with ~ of effort** sans effort inutile ■ **~ of language** sobriété *f* de langage ➊ **economies of scale** économies d'échelle ■ **false ~** fausse économie.
<> *comp* [pack] économique ■ **~ car** *aux États-Unis, voiture de taille moyenne, consommant peu par rapport aux "grosses américaines"* ■ **~ class** classe *f* touriste ■ **~ drive** politique *f* de réduction des dépenses.
<> *adv* [fly, travel] en classe touriste.

economy-class syndrome *n* syndrome *m* de la classe économique.

economy-size(d) *adj* [pack, jar] taille économique *(inv)*.

ecosystem ['iːkəʊˌsɪstəm] *n* écosystème *m*.

ecotax ['iːkəʊtæks] *n* écotaxe *f*.

ecoterrorist ['iːkəʊˌterərɪst] *n* écoterroriste *mf*.

eco-tourism ['iːkəʊ-] *n* éco-tourisme *m*, tourisme *m* vert.

ecotype ['iːkəʊtaɪp] *n* écotype *m*.

eco-warrior ['iːkəʊ-] *n* éco-guerrier *m*, - ère *f*.

ecstasy ['ekstəsɪ] (*pl* **ecstasies**) *n* **1.** extase *f*, ravissement *m* ■ **to be in/to go into ecstasies** être/tomber en extase **2.** [drug] ecstasy *f*.

ecstatic [ek'stætɪk] *adj* ravi ■ **to be ~ about sthg/sb** [in admiration] être en extase devant qqch/qqn ; [with joy] être ravi de qqch/qqn ■ **I'm not ~ about it** cela ne m'enchante pas.

ecstatically [ek'stætɪklɪ] *adv* avec extase ■ **to be ~ happy** être dans un bonheur extatique.

ECT *n* = **electroconvulsive therapy**.

ectomorph ['ektəʊmɔːf] *n* ectomorphe *mf*.

ectopic [ek'tɒpɪk] *adj* : **~ pregnancy** grossesse *f* extra-utérine OR ectopique.

ectoplasm ['ektəplæzm] *n* ectoplasme *m*.

ECU ['ekjuː] (*abbrev of* **European Currency Unit**) *n* ECU *m*, écu *m*.

Ecuador ['ekwədɔːr] *pr n* Équateur *m* ■ **in ~** en Équateur.

Ecuadoran [ˌekwə'dɔːrən], **Ecuadorian** [ˌekwə'dɔːrɪən]
<> *n* Équatorien *m*, - enne *f*.
<> *adj* équatorien.

ecumenical [iːkjʊ'menɪkl] *adj* œcuménique.

ecumenism [iː'kjuːmənɪzm], **ecumenicism** [ˌiːkjuː'menɪsɪzm] *n* œcuménisme *m*.

eczema [ɪg'ziːmə] *n* MED eczéma *m* ■ **to have ~** avoir de l'eczéma.

ed. <> **1.** (*written abbrev of* **edited**) sous la dir. de, coll **2.** (*written abbrev of* **edition**) éd., édit.
<> *n* (*abbrev of* **editor**) éd., édit.

Edam ['iːdæm] *n* édam *m*.

eddy ['edɪ] (*pl* **eddies**) <> *n* tourbillon *m*.
<> *vi* tourbillonner.

edelweiss ['eɪdlvaɪs] *n* edelweiss *m*, immortelle *f* des neiges.

edema US = **oedema**.

Eden ['iːdn] *pr n* BIBLE Éden *m* ■ *fig* éden *m* ■ **'East of ~'** *Steinbeck, Kazan* 'À l'est d'Éden'.

edge [edʒ] <> *n* **1.** [of blade] fil *m*, tranchant *m* ■ **to put an ~ on** [knife, blade] aiguiser, affiler, affûter ■ **to take the ~ off** [blade] émousser ■ **the sandwich took the ~ off my hunger** ce sandwich a calmé ma faim ■ **to have the ~ on** [be better than] avoir légèrement le dessus OR l'avantage sur ; [have an advantage over] avoir l'avantage sur ■ **the performance lacked ~** le spectacle manquait de ressort OR d'énergie **2.** [outer limit - of table, cliff, road] bord *m* ; [- of page] bord *m*, marge *f* ; [- of forest] lisière *f*, orée *f* ; [- of coin, book] tranche *f* ; [- of ski] carre *f* ■ **at** OR **by the water's ~** au bord de l'eau ■ **to stand sthg on its ~** [coin, book] mettre qqch sur la tranche ; [brick, stone] poser OR mettre qqch de OR sur chant ■ **to be on the ~ of** [war, disaster, madness] être au bord de ■ **this film will have you on the ~ of your seat** *fig* ce film est d'un suspense à vous faire frémir ■ **to be close to the ~** *liter* être près du bord ; *fig* être au bord du précipice ■ **to push sb over the ~** *fig* faire craquer qqn ■ **to live on the ~** prendre des risques.
<> *vt* **1.** [give a border to] border ■ **to ~ sthg with sthg** border qqch de qqch **2.** [sharpen] aiguiser, affiler, affûter **3.** [in skiing] : **to ~ one's skis** planter ses carres **4.** [move gradually] : **to**

~ one's way avancer *OR* progresser lentement ■ **to ~ one's chair nearer sb/sthg** approcher peu à peu sa chaise de qqn/qqch.

<> *vi* avancer *OR* progresser lentement ■ **to ~ through the crowd** se frayer un chemin à travers la foule ■ **to ~ past sb/sthg** se faufiler à côté de qqn/qqch ■ **the car ~d forward/backward** la voiture avança/recula doucement.

◆ **on edge** *adj & adv phr* : **to be on ~** être énervé *OR* sur les nerfs ■ **to set sb's teeth on ~** faire grincer les dents à qqn ■ **to set sb's nerves on ~** mettre les nerfs de qqn à fleur de peau.

◆ **edge out** <> *vt sep* : **to ~ sb out of a job** pousser qqn vers la sortie en douceur.

<> *vi insep* sortir lentement ■ **to ~ out of a room** se glisser hors d'une pièce.

◆ **edge up** <> *vt sep* : **to ~ prices up** faire monter les prix doucement.

<> *vi insep* **1.** [prices] monter doucement **2.** [approach slowly] : **to ~ up to sb/sthg** s'avancer lentement vers qqn/qqch.

edge tool *n* outil *m* tranchant.

edgewise ['edʒwaɪz], **edgeways** ['edʒweɪz] *adv* de côté ■ **I couldn't get a word in ~** je n'ai pas pu placer un mot.

edginess ['edʒɪnɪs] *n* nervosité *f*.

edging ['edʒɪŋ] *n* [border - on dress, of flowers etc] bordure *f* ■ **~ shears** cisailles *fpl* à gazon.

edgy ['edʒɪ] (*comp* **edgier**, *superl* **edgiest**) *adj* nerveux, sur les nerfs.

edible ['edɪbl] *adj* [mushroom, berry] comestible ■ **is it ~?** c'est bon à manger?

edict ['i:dɪkt] *n* POL décret *m* ■ *fig* ordre *m* ■ **the Edict of Nantes** HIST l'édit *m* de Nantes.

edification [,edɪfɪ'keɪʃn] *n fml* édification *f*, instruction *f*.

edifice ['edɪfɪs] *n liter & fig* édifice *m*.

edify ['edɪfaɪ] (*pret & pp* **edified**) *vt fml* édifier.

edifying ['edɪfaɪɪŋ] *adj fml* édifiant.

Edinburgh ['edɪnbrə] *pr n* Édimbourg ■ **the ~ Festival** le Festival d'Édimbourg.

EDINBURGH FESTIVAL

Le Festival international d'Édimbourg, créé en 1947, est aujourd'hui l'un des plus grands festivals de théâtre et de musique du monde ; il a lieu chaque année d'août à septembre. Le festival *off* (*fringe*) est une grande rencontre du théâtre expérimental.

edit ['edɪt] <> *n* [of text] révision *f*, correction *f*.

<> *vt* **1.** [correct - article, book] corriger, réviser ■ COMPUT [- file] éditer ■ [prepare for release - book, article] éditer, préparer pour la publication ; [- film, TV programme, tape] monter ■ **the footnotes were ~ed from the book** les notes ont été coupées dans le *OR* retranchées du livre **2.** [be in charge of - review, newspaper] diriger la rédaction de.

◆ **edit down** *vt sep* raccourcir.

◆ **edit out** *vt sep* couper, supprimer.

editing ['edɪtɪŋ] *n* [of newspaper, magazine] rédaction *f* ■ [initial corrections] révision *f*, correction *f* ■ [in preparation for publication] édition *f*, préparation *f* à la publication ■ [of film, tape] montage *m* ■ COMPUT [of file] édition *f*.

edition [ɪ'dɪʃn] *n* [of book, newspaper] édition *f* ■ **first ~** première édition ■ **revised/limited ~** édition revue et corrigée/à tirage limité.

editor ['edɪtər] *n* **1.** [of newspaper, review] rédacteur *m*, - trice *f* en chef ■ [of author] éditeur *m*, - trice *f* ■ [of dictionary] rédacteur *m*, - trice *f* ■ [of book, article - who makes corrections] correcteur *m*, - trice *f* ; [- who writes] rédacteur *m*, - trice *f* ■ [of film] monteur *m*, - euse *f* ■ **political ~** PRESS rédacteur *m*, - trice *f* politique ■ **~'s note** PRESS note *f* de la rédaction **2.** COMPUT éditeur *m*.

editorial [,edɪ'tɔ:rɪəl] <> *adj* PRESS [decision, comment] de la rédaction ■ [job, problems, skills] de rédaction, rédactionnel ■ **~ freedom** [in publishing] liberté *f* de publier ; [of columnist] liberté *f* d'expression ■ **~ changes** corrections *fpl*.

<> *n* PRESS éditorial *m*.

editorially [,edɪ'tɔ:rɪəlɪ] *adv* du point de vue de la rédaction.

editor-in-chief *n* rédacteur *m*, - trice *f* en chef.

editorship ['edɪtəʃɪp] *n* rédaction *f* ■ **during her ~** quand elle dirigeait la rédaction.

EDP *n* = **electronic data processing**.

EDT *n* = **Eastern Daylight Time**.

educable ['edʒʊkəbl] *adj fml* éducable.

educate ['edʒʊkeɪt] *vt* [pupil] instruire, donner une éducation à ■ [mind, tastes, palate] éduquer, former ■ [customers, public] éduquer ■ **she was ~d in Edinburgh/at Birmingham University** elle a fait sa scolarité à Édimbourg/ses études à l'université de Birmingham.

educated ['edʒʊkeɪtɪd] *adj* [person] instruit ■ [voice] distingué ■ **to make an ~ guess** faire une supposition bien informée.

education [,edʒʊ'keɪʃn] <> *n* éducation *f* ■ [teaching] enseignement *m* ■ **a classical/scientific ~** une formation classique/scientifique ■ **the ~ of poor countries in modern farming techniques** la formation des pays pauvres aux techniques agricoles modernes ■ **she completed her ~ in Italy** elle a terminé ses études en Italie ■ **standards of ~** niveau *m* scolaire ■ **it was an ~** cela m'a beaucoup appris ; *hum* c'était très édifiant ➔ **adult** *OR* **continuing ~** éducation *f* pour adultes, formation *f* continue ■ **further ~** *enseignement postscolaire, mais non universitaire* ■ **higher** *OR* **university ~** enseignement *m* supérieur *OR* universitaire ■ **Minister of** *OR* **Secretary of State for Education** *UK* ministre *m* de l'Éducation ■ **physical ~** éducation *f* physique ■ **primary/secondary ~** (enseignement *m*) primaire *m* /secondaire *m* ■ **tertiary ~** enseignement *m* supérieur.

<> *comp* [costs, budget] de l'éducation ■ **Education Act** ≃ réforme *f* (de l'Éducation) ■ **~ correspondent** PRESS correspondant chargé, correspondante chargée des problèmes d'enseignement ■ **the ~ system** le système éducatif ■ **(local) ~ authority** *UK* ≃ académie *f* régionale.

educational [,edʒʊ'keɪʃənl] *adj* [programme, system] éducatif ■ [establishment] d'éducation, d'enseignement ■ [books, publisher] scolaire ■ [method, film, visit, TV] éducatif, pédagogique ■ **they talked about rising/falling ~ standards** ils ont évoqué la hausse/baisse du niveau scolaire ■ **~ qualifications** qualifications *fpl*, diplômes *mpl* ■ **it was very ~** c'était très instructif ; *hum* c'était très édifiant ➔ **~ age** niveau *m* scolaire ■ **~ psychologist** psychopédagogue *mf*.

educationalist [,edʒʊ'keɪʃnəlɪst] *n* pédagogue *mf*.

educationally [,edʒʊ'keɪʃnəlɪ] *adv* d'un point de vue éducatif ■ **~ deprived child** *enfant qui n'a pas suivi une scolarité normale* ■ **~ subnormal** *dated* en retard sur le plan scolaire.

educative ['edʒʊkətɪv] *adj* éducatif.

educator ['edʒʊkeɪtər] *n esp US* éducateur *m*, - trice *f*.

Edward ['edwəd] *pr n* : **~ the Confessor** Édouard le Confesseur.

Edwardian [ed'wɔ:dɪən] *adj* [architecture, design] édouardien, de style Édouard VII, (des années) 1900 ■ [society, gentleman] de l'époque d'Édouard VII, des années 1900 ■ **~ style** style *m* Édouard VII ■ **the ~ era** ≃ la Belle Époque.

EEA (*abbrev of* **European Economic Area**) *n* EEE *m*.

EEC (*abbrev of* **European Economic Community**) *pr n* CEE *f*.

EEG *n* **1.** (*abbrev of* **electroencephalogram**) EEG *m* **2.** (*abbrev of* **electroencephalograph**) EEG *m*.

eek [i:k] *interj inf* hi.

eel [iːl] *n* anguille *f* ■ **to be as slippery as an ~** glisser comme une anguille.

e'en [iːn] *lit* = **even** *(adv)*.

EENT *(abbrev of* **eye, ear, nose and throat***)* *n* ophtalmologie *f* et ORL *f*.

EEOC *(abbrev of* **Equal Employment Opportunity Commission***)* *pr n Commission pour l'égalité des chances d'emploi aux États-Unis.*

e'er [eəʳ] *lit* = **ever** *(adv)*.

eerie ['ɪərɪ] *(comp* **eerier**, *superl* **eeriest***)* *adj* [house, silence, sound] inquiétant, sinistre ■ **it gave me an ~ feeling** ça m'a fait froid dans le dos.

eerily ['ɪərəlɪ] *adv* sinistrement, d'une manière sinistre ■ **it was ~ quiet in the house** un calme inquiétant régnait dans la maison.

eery ['ɪərɪ] *(comp* **eerier**, *superl* **eeriest***)* = **eerie**.

EET *n* = **Eastern European Time**.

eew [iːw] *excl US* beurk *inf*.

eff△ [ef] *vi UK euph* **to ~ and blind** jurer à tout va.
◆ **eff off**△ *vi insep UK* **~ off!** va te faire voir!△.

efface [ɪ'feɪs] *vt liter & fig* effacer ■ **to ~ o.s.** s'effacer.

effect [ɪ'fekt] ◇ *n* **1.** [of action, law] effet *m* ■ [of chemical, drug, weather] effet *m*, action *f* ■ **to have an ~ on** avoir *OR* produire un effet sur ■ **the ~ of the law will be to...** la loi aura pour effet de... ■ **the ~ of all this is that...** tout cela a pour résultat que... ■ **with ~ from January 1st** *UK* à partir *OR* à compter du 1er janvier ■ **with immediate ~** à compter d'aujourd'hui ■ **to no** *OR* **little ~** en vain ■ **to use** *OR* **to put sthg to good ~** [technique, talent] utiliser qqch avec succès ; [money, inheritance] faire bon usage de qqch ■ **to put** *OR* **to bring** *OR* **to carry into ~** [law] mettre en pratique ■ **to come into** *OR* **to take ~** [law] entrer en vigueur ■ **to take ~** [drug] (commencer à) faire effet **2.** [meaning] sens *m* ■ **to this** *OR* **that ~** dans ce sens ■ **a telegram/an announcement to the ~ that...** un télégramme/une annonce disant que... ■ **or words to that ~** ou quelque chose dans le genre **3.** [impression] effet *m* ■ **(just) for ~** (juste) pour faire de l'effet **4.** THEAT : **stage ~s** effets *mpl* de scène.
◇ *vt fml* [reform] effectuer ■ [sale, purchase] réaliser, effectuer ■ [improvement] apporter ■ [cure, rescue, reconciliation] mener à bien ■ **to ~ entry** LAW entrer.
◆ **effects** *npl fml* **household ~s** articles *mpl* ménagers ■ **personal ~s** effets *mpl* personnels.
◆ **in effect** ◇ *adj phr* [law, system] en vigueur.
◇ *adv phr* [in fact] en fait, en réalité.

effective [ɪ'fektɪv] *adj* **1.** [which works well - measure, treatment, advertising etc] efficace ; [- worker, manager] efficace ; [- argument] qui porte ; [- service, system] qui fonctionne bien ; [- disguise] réussi **2.** ADMIN & FIN : **~ as from January 1st** [law] en vigueur *OR* applicable à compter du 1er janvier ■ **to become ~** entrer en vigueur **3.** [actual] véritable ■ **~ income** revenu *m* réel **4.** [creating effect - colour, illustration] qui fait de l'effet.

effectively [ɪ'fektɪvlɪ] *adv* **1.** [efficiently - work, run, manage] efficacement **2.** [successfully] avec succès **3.** [in fact] en réalité, en fait **4.** [impressively] d'une manière impressionnante.

effectiveness [ɪ'fektɪvnɪs] *n* **1.** [efficiency - of treatment, advertising] efficacité *f* ; [- of undertaking, attempt] succès *m* **2.** [effect - of entrance, gesture, colour] effet *m* ■ **to improve the ~ of your backhand** pour améliorer votre revers.

effectual [ɪ'fektʃʊəl] *adj fml* [action, plan, law] efficace.

effectuate [ɪ'fektjʊeɪt] *vt fml* effectuer, réaliser.

effeminacy [ɪ'femɪnəsɪ] *n* [of man] caractère *m* efféminé.

effeminate [ɪ'femɪnət] *adj* [man, voice] efféminé.

effervesce [ˌefə'ves] *vi* [liquid] être en effervescence ■ [wine] pétiller ■ [gas] s'échapper (d'un liquide) par effervescence ■ *fig* [person] déborder de vie.

effervescence [ˌefə'vesəns] *n* [of liquid] effervescence *f* ■ [of wine] pétillement *m* ■ *fig* [of person] vitalité *f*, pétulance *f* ■ [of personality] pétulance *f*.

effervescent [ˌefə'vesənt] *adj* [liquid] effervescent ■ [wine] pétillant ■ *fig* [person] débordant de vie, pétulant ■ [personality] pétulant.

effete [ɪ'fiːt] *adj fml* [weak - person] mou *(before vowel or silent 'h' mol)*, molle *f* ; [- civilization, society] affaibli ■ [decadent] décadent.

efficacious [efɪ'keɪʃəs] *adj fml* efficace.

efficacy ['efɪkəsɪ] *n fml* efficacité *f*.

efficiency [ɪ'fɪʃənsɪ] *n* [of person, company, method] efficacité *f* ■ [of machine - in operation] fonctionnement *m* ; [- in output] rendement *m*.

efficiency expert *n* expert *m* en organisation.

efficient [ɪ'fɪʃənt] *adj* [person, staff, method, company] efficace ■ [piece of work] bien fait ■ [machine - in operation] qui fonctionne bien ; [- in output] qui a un bon rendement.

efficiently [ɪ'fɪʃəntlɪ] *adv* [work - person] efficacement ■ **the machine works ~** [functions well] la machine fonctionne bien ; [has high output] la machine a un bon rendement.

effigy ['efɪdʒɪ] *(pl* **effigies***)* *n* effigie *f* ■ **to burn sb in ~** brûler qqn en effigie.

effing ['efɪŋ] △ *UK* ◇ *adj* de merde△.
◇ *adv* foutrement△.
◇ *n* : **there was a lot of ~ and blinding** on a eu droit à un chapelet de jurons.

effluent ['eflʊənt] *n* **1.** [waste] effluent *m* **2.** [stream] effluent *m*.

effluvium [ɪ'fluːvjəm] *(pl* **effluviums** *OR pl* **effluvia** [-vjə]*)* *n fml* émanation *f* pestilentielle.

effort ['efət] *n* **1.** [physical or mental exertion] effort *m* ■ **without much ~** sans trop d'effort *OR* de peine ■ **your ~s on our behalf** les efforts que vous avez faits pour nous ■ **it was an ~ for me to stay awake** j'avais du mal à rester éveillé ; [stronger] rester éveillé me coûtait ■ **put some ~ into it!** fais un effort! ■ **I put a lot of ~ into that project** je me suis donné beaucoup de mal *OR* de peine pour ce projet ■ **in an ~ to do sthg** dans le but de faire qqch ■ **to make no ~ to do sthg** ne pas essayer de faire qqch ■ **to make every ~ to do sthg** faire tout son possible pour faire qqch ■ **it's not worth the ~** ça ne vaut pas la peine de se fatiguer **2.** [attempt] essai *m*, tentative *f* ■ **it's only my first ~** ce n'est que la première fois que j'essaie ■ **it was a good ~** pour un essai, c'était bien.

effortless ['efətlɪs] *adj* [win] facile ■ [style, movement] aisé.

effortlessly ['efətlɪslɪ] *adv* facilement, sans effort *OR* peine.

effrontery [ɪ'frʌntərɪ] *n* effronterie *f*.

effulgent [ɪ'fʌldʒənt] *adj lit* rayonnant.

effusion [ɪ'fjuːʒn] *n lit* **1.** [of words] effusion *f* **2.** [of liquid] écoulement *m* ■ [of blood] hémorragie *f*.

effusive [ɪ'fjuːsɪv] *adj* [person] expansif ■ [welcome, thanks] chaleureux ■ *pej* exagéré.

effusively [ɪ'fjuːsɪvlɪ] *adv* avec effusion ■ *pej* avec une effusion exagérée.

EFL *(abbrev of* **English as a foreign language***)* *n anglais langue étrangère.*

EFTA ['eftə] *(abbrev of* **European Free Trade Association***)* *pr n* AELE *f*, AEL-E *f*.

EFTPOS ['eftpɒs] *(abbrev of* **electronic funds transfer at point of sale***)* *n transfert électronique de fonds au point de vente.*

EFTS [efts] *(abbrev of* **electronic funds transfer system***)* *n système électronique de transfert de fonds.*

e.g. *(abbrev of* **exempli gratia***)* *adv* par exemple.

egad [iː'gæd] *interj arch* sacredieu.

egalitarian [ɪˌgælɪ'teərɪən] ◇ *n* égalitariste *mf*.

◇ *adj* égalitaire.

egalitarianism [ɪˌgælɪ'teərɪənɪzm] *n* égalitarisme *m*.

egg [eg] *n* **1.** CULIN œuf *m* ■ **~s and bacon** œufs au bacon ■ **fried ~** œuf sur le plat ■ **hard-boiled ~** œuf dur ■ **soft-boiled ~** œuf à la coque ■ **~ white/yolk** blanc *m* /jaune *m* d'œuf ■ **~s Benedict** *œufs pochés à la béchamel* ■ **to be left with** *OR* **to get ~ on one's face** avoir l'air ridicule **2.** [of bird, insect, fish] œuf *m* ■ [of woman] ovule *m* ■ **to lay an ~** [bird] pondre un œuf ; *US*△ [person, performer] être nul ; *US*△ [play, film etc] faire un bide ■ **to put all one's ~s in one basket** mettre tous ses œufs dans le même panier **3.** *UK dated* [person] : **he's/she's a good ~** c'est un brave garçon/une brave fille ■ **a bad ~** un sale individu.
◆ **egg on** *vt sep* encourager, inciter ■ **to ~ sb on to do sthg** encourager *OR* inciter qqn à faire qqch.

egg-and-spoon race *n jeu consistant à courir en tenant un œuf dans une cuillère.*

eggbox ['egbɒks] *n* boîte *f* à œufs.

eggcup ['egkʌp] *n* coquetier *m*.

egg custard *n* CULIN ≃ crème *f* anglaise.

egghead ['eghed] *n inf* intello *mf*.

eggnog [eg'nɒg] *n boisson composée d'œufs, de lait, de sucre, d'épices, de brandy, de rhum, etc.*

eggplant ['egplɑ:nt] *n US* aubergine *f*.

egg-shaped *adj* en forme d'œuf, ovoïde.

eggshell ['egʃel] ◇ *n* **1.** coquille *f* d'œuf **2.** [colour] coquille *f* d'œuf.
◇ *adj* [finish, paint] coquille d'œuf *(inv)*.

egg timer *n* sablier *m*.

egg whisk *n* CULIN fouet *m*.

eglantine ['eglǝntaɪn] *n* BOT [bush] églantier *m* ■ [flower] églantine *f*.

ego ['i:gǝʊ] *n* [self-esteem] amour-propre *m* ■ PSYCHOL ego *m inv*, moi *m inv* ■ **to have an enormous ~** être imbu de soi-même ■ **it's just your ~ that's hurt** tu es seulement blessé dans ton amour-propre.

egocentric [ˌi:gǝʊ'sentrɪk] *adj* égocentrique.

egocentricity [ˌi:gǝʊsen'trɪsǝtɪ], **egocentrism** [ˌi:gǝʊ'sentrɪzm] *n* égocentrisme *m*.

egoism ['i:gǝʊɪzm] *n* [selfishness] égoïsme *m*.

egoist ['i:gǝʊɪst] *n* égoïste *mf*.

egoistic [ˌi:gǝʊ'ɪstɪk] *adj* égoïste.

egoistically [ˌi:gǝʊ'ɪstɪklɪ] *adv* égoïstement.

egomania [ˌi:gǝʊ'meɪnjǝ] *n* égocentrisme *m* extrême.

egomaniac [ˌi:gǝʊ'meɪnɪæk] *n* égocentrique *mf*.

egotism ['i:gǝtɪzm] *n* égocentrisme *m*, égotisme *m*.

egotist ['i:gǝtɪst] *n* égocentrique *mf*, égotiste *mf*.

egotistic(al) [ˌi:gǝ'tɪstɪk(l)] *adj* égocentrique, égotiste.

egotistically [ˌi:gǝ'tɪstɪklɪ] *adv* de manière égocentrique *OR* égotiste.

ego trip *n inf* **she's just on an ~** c'est par vanité qu'elle le fait.
◆ **ego-trip** *vi inf* **you're just ego-tripping** tu fais ça par vanité.

egregious [ɪ'gri:dʒǝs] *adj fml* [blatant - error, mistake] monumental, énorme ; [- lie] énorme ; [- cowardice, incompetence] extrême.

egret ['i:grɪt] *n* [bird] aigrette *f*.

Egypt ['i:dʒɪpt] *pr n* Égypte *f* ■ **in ~** en Égypte.

Egyptian [ɪ'dʒɪpʃn] ◇ *n* **1.** [person] Égyptien *m*, - enne *f* **2.** LING égyptien *m*.
◇ *adj* égyptien.

eh [eɪ] *interj* **1.** [what did you say?] : **~?** hein? **2.** [seeking agreement] : **~?** hein? **3.** [in astonishment] : **~?** quoi? **4.** [in doubt, hesitation] heu.

eider ['aɪdǝʳ] *n* [bird] eider *m*.

eiderdown ['aɪdǝdaʊn] *n* **1.** [feathers] duvet *m* d'eider **2.** [for bed] édredon *m*.

eider duck = **eider**.

Eiffel ['aɪfl] *pr n* : **the ~ Tower** la tour Eiffel.

eight [eɪt] ◇ *n* **1.** [number, numeral] huit *m* ■ **to live at number ~** habiter au huit ● **to have had one over the ~** *UK dated* avoir bu plus que son compte **2.** [in rowing] huit *m*.
◇ *adj* huit ■ **to work an ~-hour day** travailler huit heures par jour, faire des journées de huit heures, *see also* **five**.
◇ *pron* huit.

eight ball *n US* [ball] bille *f* numéro huit ■ [game] *variante du billard* ■ **to be right behind the ~** *inf fig* être en mauvaise posture.

eighteen [ˌeɪ'ti:n] ◇ *pron* dix-huit, *see also* **fifteen**.
◇ *adj* dix-huit, *see also* **fifteen**.
◇ *n* dix-huit *m*.

eighteenth [ˌeɪ'ti:nθ] ◇ *adj* dix-huitième, *see also* **fifteenth**.
◇ *n* [in series] dix-huitième *mf* ■ [fraction] dix-huitième *m*, *see also* **fifteenth**.

eighth [eɪtθ] ◇ *adj* huitième, *see also* **fifth**.
◇ *n* [in series] huitième *mf* ■ [fraction] huitième *m*.
◇ *adv* **1.** [in contest] en huitième position, à la huitième place **2.** [on list] huitièmement, *see also* **fifth**.

eighth note *n US* MUS croche *f*.

eight hundred number *n US* numéro *m* vert.

eightieth ['eɪtɪɪθ] ◇ *adj* quatre-vingtième, *see also* **fiftieth**.
◇ *n* [in series] quatre-vingtième *mf* ■ [fraction] quatre-vingtième *m*, *see also* **fiftieth**.

Eights Week [eɪts-] *n semaine de la course d'avirons aux universités de Cambridge et d'Oxford.*

eighty ['eɪtɪ] ◇ *pron* quatre-vingt.
◇ *adj* quatre-vingts ■ **~ one** quatre-vingt-un ■ **~ first** quatre-vingt-unième ■ **page ~** page quatre-vingt ■ **~ million** quatre-vingts millions.
◇ *n* quatre-vingt *m*, *see also* **fifty**.

Eire ['eǝrǝ] *pr n* Eire *f*.

EIS (*abbrev of* **Educational Institute of Scotland**) *pr n syndicat écossais d'enseignants.*

eisteddfod [aɪ'stedfɒd] *n festival annuel de musique, littérature et théâtre au pays de Galles.*

either [*esp UK* 'aɪðǝʳ, *esp US* 'i:ðǝʳ] ◇ *det* **1.** [one or the other] l'un ou l'autre, l'une ou l'autre *f* ■ **if you don't agree with ~ suggestion...** si vous n'approuvez ni l'une ni l'autre *OR* aucune de ces suggestions... ■ **you can take ~ route** tu peux prendre l'un ou l'autre de ces chemins ■ **~ bus will get you there** les deux bus y vont ■ **he can write with ~ hand** il peut écrire avec la main droite ou avec la main gauche **2.** [each] chaque ■ **there were candles at ~ end of the table** il y avait des bougies aux deux bouts *OR* à chaque bout de la table.
◇ *pron* [one or the other] l'un ou l'autre, l'une ou l'autre *f* ■ **I don't like ~ of them** je ne les aime ni l'un ni l'autre ■ **if ~ of you two makes the slightest noise** si l'un de vous deux fait le moindre bruit ■ **which would you like? – ~** lequel voudriez-vous? – n'importe lequel.
◇ *adv* non plus ■ **we can't hear anything ~** nous n'entendons rien non plus ■ [emphatic use] : **and don't take too long about it ~!** et ne traîne pas, surtout! ■ **he had a suggestion to make and not such a silly one ~** il avait une suggestion à faire et qui n'était pas bête en plus.
◆ **either... or** *conj phr* ou... ou, soit... soit ■ [with negative] ni... ni ■ **~ you stop complaining or I go home!** ou tu arrêtes de te plaindre, ou je rentre chez moi ■ **they're ~ very rich or very stupid** ils sont soit très riches soit très bêtes ■ **I've not met ~ him or his brother** je n'ai rencontré ni lui ni son frère.
◆ **either way** *adv phr* **1.** [in either case] dans les deux cas ■ **~ way I lose** dans les deux cas je suis perdant ■ **you can do it ~ way** tu peux le faire d'une façon comme de l'autre ■ **it's fine by me ~ way** n'importe *OR* ça m'est égal **2.** [more or less]

en plus ou en moins ■ **a few days ~ way could make all the difference** quelques jours en plus ou en moins pourraient changer tout **3.** [indicating advantage] : **it could go ~ way** on ne peut rien prévoir ■ **the match could have gone ~ way** le match était ouvert.

either-or *adj* : **it's an ~ situation** il n'y a que deux solutions possibles.

ejaculate [ɪ'dʒækjʊleɪt] ◇ *vi* **1.** PHYSIOL éjaculer **2.** *fml* [call out] s'écrier, s'exclamer.
◇ *vt* **1.** PHYSIOL éjaculer **2.** *fml* [utter] lancer, pousser.

ejaculation [ɪˌdʒækjʊ'leɪʃn] *n* **1.** PHYSIOL éjaculation *f* **2.** *fml* [exclamation] exclamation *f*.

eject [ɪ'dʒekt] ◇ *vt* **1.** [troublemaker] expulser **2.** [cartridge, pilot] éjecter ■ [lava] projeter.
◇ *vi* [pilot] s'éjecter.

ejection [ɪ'dʒekʃn] *n* **1.** [of troublemaker] expulsion *f* **2.** [of cartridge, pilot] éjection *f* ■ [of lava] projection *f*.

ejection seat = **ejector seat**.

ejector [ɪ'dʒektəʳ] *n* [on gun] éjecteur *m*.

ejector seat *n* siège *m* éjectable.

eke [iːk] ◆ **eke out** *vt sep* **1.** [make last] faire durer **2.** [scrape] : **to ~ out a living** gagner tout juste sa vie **3.** [by adding something] augmenter.

EKG (*abbrev of* **electrocardiogram**) *n* *US* ECG *m*.

el [el] (*abbrev of* **elevated railroad**) *n* *US* métro *m* aérien *(à Chicago)*.

elaborate ◇ *adj* [ɪ'læbrət] [system, preparations] élaboré ■ [style, costume] recherché, travaillé ■ [pattern] compliqué ■ [details] minutieux ■ [map, plans] détaillé ■ **in ~ detail** de manière très détaillée ■ **the whole thing was an ~ joke** c'était une vaste plaisanterie.
◇ *vt* [ɪ'læbəreɪt] [work out in detail - plan, scheme etc] élaborer ■ [describe in detail] décrire en détail.
◇ *vi* [ɪ'læbəreɪt] [go into detail] donner des détails.
◆ **elaborate on** *vt insep* [idea, statement] développer.

elaborately [ɪ'læbərətlɪ] *adv* [decorated, designed etc] minutieusement, avec recherche ■ [planned] minutieusement ■ [packaged] de manière élaborée.

elaboration [ɪˌlæbə'reɪʃn] *n* [working out - of scheme, plan] élaboration *f* ■ [details] exposé *m* minutieux.

élan [eɪ'læn] *n* vigueur *f*, énergie *f*.

eland ['iːlənd] *n* éland *m*.

elapse [ɪ'læps] *vi* s'écouler, passer.

elastic [ɪ'læstɪk] ◇ *adj* **1.** [material] élastique ■ **~ stockings** bas *mpl* anti-varices **2.** *fig* [timetable, arrangements, concept] souple ■ [word, moral principles] élastique, souple ■ [working hours] élastique **3.** *lit* [step] élastique.
◇ *n* **1.** [material] élastique *m* **2.** *US* [rubber band] élastique *m*, caoutchouc *m*.

elasticated [ɪ'læstɪkeɪtɪd] *adj* [stockings, waist] élastique.

elastic band *n* *UK* élastique *m*.

elasticity [ˌelæ'stɪsətɪ] *n* élasticité *f*.

Elastoplast® [ɪ'læstəplɑːst] *n* *UK* pansement *m* adhésif.

elated [ɪ'leɪtɪd] *adj* fou de joie, exultant, euphorique.

elation [ɪ'leɪʃn] *n* allégresse *f*, exultation *f*, euphorie *f*.

Elba ['elbə] *pr n* l'île *f* d'Elbe ■ **on ~** sur l'île d'Elbe.

Elbe [elb] *pr n* : **the (River) ~** l'Elbe *m*.

elbow ['elbəʊ] ◇ *n* [of arm, jacket, pipe, river] coude *m* ■ **with his ~s on the bar** les coudes sur le bar, accoudé au bar ● **to give sb the ~** *UK inf* [employee] virer qqn ; [boyfriend, girlfriend] larguer *OR* jeter qqn ; [tenant] mettre qqn à la porte ■ **to lift the ~** *UK inf* picoler, lever le coude.
◇ *vt* [hit] donner un coup de coude à ■ [push] pousser du coude ■ **he just ~ed me aside** il m'a écarté du coude.
◆ **elbow out** *vt sep* [from job] se débarrasser de.

elbow grease *n inf* huile *f* de coude.

elbowroom ['elbəʊrʊm] *n* : **I don't have enough ~** je n'ai pas assez de place (pour me retourner) ; *fig* je n'ai pas suffisamment de liberté d'action.

elder ['eldəʳ] ◇ *adj* [brother, sister] aîné ■ **Pitt the Elder** le Premier Pitt ■ **Brueghel the Elder** Bruegel l'ancien.
◇ *n* **1.** [of two children] aîné *m*, - e *f* **2.** [of tribe, the Church] ancien *m* **3.** [senior] : **you should respect your ~s (and betters)** vous devez le respect à vos aînés **4.** BOT sureau *m*.

elderberry ['eldəˌberɪ] *n* baie *f* de sureau ■ **~ wine** vin *m* de sureau.

elderflower ['eldəˌflaʊəʳ] *n* fleur *f* de sureau.

elderly ['eldəlɪ] ◇ *adj* âgé ■ **my ~ uncle** mon vieil oncle.
◇ *npl* : **the ~** les personnes *fpl* âgées.

elder statesman *n* [gen] vétéran *m* ■ [politician] vétéran *m* de la politique.

eldest ['eldɪst] ◇ *adj* aîné.
◇ *n* aîné *m*, - e *f*.

Eleanor ['elɪnəʳ] *pr n* : **~ of Aquitaine** Aliénor *OR* Éléonore d'Aquitaine.

elect [ɪ'lekt] ◇ *vt* **1.** [by voting] élire ■ **to ~ sb President** élire qqn président ■ **to ~ sb to office** élire qqn **2.** *fml* [choose] choisir ■ **to ~ to do sthg** choisir de faire qqch.
◇ *adj* : **the President ~** le président élu.
◇ *npl* RELIG : **the ~** les élus *mpl*.

elected [ɪ'lektɪd] *adj* élu ■ **as an ~ official of the society** en tant que représentant élu de la société.

election [ɪ'lekʃn] ◇ *n* élection *f* ■ **to stand for ~** se présenter aux élections.
◇ *comp* [day, results] des élections ■ [agent, campaign, speech] électoral.

MID-TERM ELECTIONS

Les élections de mi-mandat aux États-Unis ont lieu exactement deux ans après les présidentielles, le premier mardi de novembre. Sont en jeu tous les sièges de la Chambre des Représentants, un tiers de ceux du Sénat, et la plupart des postes de gouverneur dans les états individuels. Les électeurs en profitent souvent pour faire un pied de nez au Président en exercice ; si son parti perd la majorité au Congrès, le Président peut devenir un *lame duck* (canard boiteux) qui n'arrive pas à faire adopter ses projets de loi.

electioneer [ɪlekʃə'nɪəʳ] *vi* participer à la campagne électorale ■ *pej* faire de la propagande électorale.

electioneering [ɪˌlekʃə'nɪərɪŋ] ◇ *n* campagne *f* électorale ■ *pej* propagande *f* électorale.
◇ *adj* [speech, campaign] électoral ■ *pej* propagandiste.

elective [ɪ'lektɪv] ◇ *adj* **1.** [with power to elect - assembly] électoral **2.** [chosen - official, post] électif **3.** [optional - course, subject] optionnel, facultatif ■ **~ surgery** chirurgie *f* de confort.
◇ *n* *US* SCH & UNIV [subject] cours *m* optionnel *OR* facultatif.

elector [ɪ'lektəʳ] *n* **1.** électeur *m*, - trice *f* **2.** HIST : **the Elector** l'Électeur.

electoral [ɪ'lektərəl] *adj* électoral ■ **~ college** collège *m* électoral *(qui élit le président des États-Unis)* ■ **on the ~ roll** *OR* **register** sur la liste électorale.

electorate [ɪ'lektərət] *n* électorat *m*.

Electra [ɪ'lektrə] *pr n* Électre.

Electra complex *n* PSYCHOL complexe *m* d'Électre.

electric [ɪ'lektrɪk] ◇ *adj* [cooker, cable, current, motor, musical instrument] électrique ■ *fig* [atmosphere] chargé d'électricité ■ [effect] électrisant ■ **~ blanket** couverture *f* chauffante ■ **~ fire** *OR* **heater** appareil *m* de chauffage électrique ■ **~ guitar** guitare *f* électrique ■ **~ light** [individual appliance] lumière *f* électrique ; [lighting] éclairage *m* *OR* lumière *f* électrique.
◇ *n* *UK inf* électricité *f*.

◆ **electrics** *npl UK* installation *f* électrique.

electrical [ɪ'lektrɪkl] *adj* [appliance] électrique ▪ [failure, fault] au niveau de l'installation électrique ▪ **~ engineer** ingénieur *m* électricien ▪ **~ engineering** électrotechnique *f*.

electrically [ɪ'lektrɪklɪ] *adv* électriquement ▪ **~ operated** [machine] fonctionnant à l'électricité ; [windows] à commande électrique.

electrical shock *US* = **electric shock**.

electric blue ◇ *n* bleu *m* électrique.
◇ *adj* bleu électrique.

electric chair *n* chaise *f* électrique ▪ **to go to the ~** être envoyé à la chaise électrique.

electric eel *n* anguille *f* électrique.

electric eye *n* œil *m* électrique.

electric fence *n* clôture *f* électrique.

electric field *n* champ *m* électrique.

electrician [ˌɪlek'trɪʃn] *n* électricien *m*, - enne *f*.

electricity [ˌɪlek'trɪsətɪ] ◇ *n* électricité *f* ▪ **to turn** *OR* **to switch the ~ off** couper le courant ▪ **to turn** *OR* **to switch the ~ on** mettre le courant.
◇ *comp* : **~ bill** note *f* d'électricité ▪ **~ board** *UK* agence *f* régionale de distribution de l'électricité ▪ **~ supply** alimentation *f* en électricité.

electric shock *UK*, **electrical shock** *US n* décharge *f* électrique ▪ **to get an ~** prendre une décharge (électrique), prendre le courant ● **~ treatment** traitement *m* par électrochocs.

electric storm *n* orage *m*.

electrification [ɪˌlektrɪfɪ'keɪʃn] *n* électrification *f*.

electrify [ɪ'lektrɪfaɪ] *vt* [railway line] électrifier ▪ *fig* [audience] électriser.

electrifying [ɪ'lektrɪfaɪɪŋ] *adj fig* électrisant.

electrocardiogram [ɪˌlektrəʊ'kɑːdɪəgræm] *n* électrocardiogramme *m*.

electrocardiograph [ɪˌlektrəʊ'kɑːdɪəgrɑːf] *n* électrocardiographe *m*.

electroconvulsive [ɪˌlektrəʊkən'vʌlsɪv] *adj* : **~ therapy** thérapie *f* par électrochocs.

electrocute [ɪ'lektrəkjuːt] *vt* électrocuter ▪ **you'll ~ yourself** [give yourself a shock] tu vas prendre une décharge.

electrode [ɪ'lektrəʊd] *n* électrode *f*.

electroencephalogram [ɪˌlektrəʊen'sefələgræm] *n* électro-encéphalogramme *m*.

electroencephalograph [ɪˌlektrəʊen'sefələgrɑːf] *n* électro-encéphalographe *m*.

electrolysis [ˌɪlek'trɒləsɪs] *n* électrolyse *f*.

electrolyte [ɪ'lektrəʊlaɪt] *n* électrolyte *m*.

electromagnet [ɪˌlektrəʊ'mægnɪt] *n* électro-aimant *m*.

electromagnetic [ɪˌlektrəʊmæg'netɪk] *adj* électromagnétique.

electromotive [ɪˌlektrəʊ'məʊtɪv] *adj* électromoteur.

electron [ɪ'lektrɒn] *n* électron *m*.

electron gun *n* canon *m* électronique *OR* à électrons.

electronic [ˌɪlek'trɒnɪk] *adj* électronique ▪ **~ banking** opérations *fpl* bancaires électroniques ▪ **~ cash** *OR* **money** argent *m* virtuel *OR* électronique ▪ **~ data processing** traitement *m* électronique de données ▪ **~ mail** courrier *m* électronique, messagerie *f* électronique ▪ **~ office** bureau *m* informatisé ▪ **~ organizer** agenda *m* électronique ▪ **~ publishing** édition *f* électronique ▪ **~ purse** porte-monnaie *m* électronique ▪ **~ transfer of funds** transfert *m* de fonds électronique.

◆ **electronics** ◇ *n (U)* électronique *f*.
◇ *npl* composants *mpl* électroniques.
◇ *comp* : **~s engineer** ingénieur *m* électronicien, électronicien *m*, - enne *f* ▪ **~s industry** industrie *f* électronique.

electronically [ˌɪlek'trɒnɪklɪ] *adv* électroniquement ▪ [operated] par voie électronique.

electronic mailbox *n* boîte *f* à lettres électronique.

electronic tag *n* bracelet *m* électronique.

electronic tagging *n (U)* placement *m* sous surveillance électronique.

electron microscope *n* microscope *m* électronique.

electron telescope *n* télescope *m* électronique.

electroplate [ɪ'lektrəʊpleɪt] ◇ *vt* plaquer par galvanoplastie ▪ [with gold] dorer par galvanoplastie ▪ [with silver] argenter par galvanoplastie.
◇ *n (U)* articles *mpl* plaqués (par galvanoplastie) ▪ [with silver] articles *mpl* argentés.

electroshock [ɪ'lektrəʊʃɒk] *n* électrochoc *m* ▪ **~ therapy** thérapie *f* par électrochocs.

electrostatic [ɪˌlektrəʊ'stætɪk] *adj* électrostatique.

electrostatics [ɪˌlektrəʊ'stætɪks] *n (U)* électrostatique *f*.

electrotherapy [ɪˌlektrəʊ'θerəpɪ] *n* électrothérapie *f*.

elegance ['elɪgəns] *n* élégance *f*.

elegant ['elɪgənt] *adj* [person, style, solution] élégant ▪ [building, furniture] aux lignes élégantes.

elegantly ['elɪgəntlɪ] *adv* élégamment.

elegiac [elɪ'dʒaɪək] ◇ *adj* élégiaque.
◇ *n* élégie *f*.

elegy ['elɪdʒɪ] (*pl* **elegies**) *n* élégie *f*.

element ['elɪmənt] *n* **1.** [water, air etc] élément *m* ▪ **to be exposed to/to brave the ~ s** être exposé aux/affronter les éléments ▪ **to be in one's ~** *fig* être dans son élément **2.** [in kettle, electric heater] résistance *f* **3.** [small amount - of danger, truth, the unknown] part *f* ▪ **the ~ of surprise** l'élément de *OR* le facteur surprise **4.** *(usu pl)* [rudiment] rudiment *m* **5.** [in society, group] élément *m* ▪ **the hooligan ~** l'élément hooligan de la société ▪ **a disruptive ~** [in class] un élément perturbateur.

elemental [ˌelɪ'mentl] *adj* **1.** [basic] fondamental, de base **2.** [relating to the elements] propre aux éléments ▪ **the ~ force of the storm** la force des éléments déchaînés dans la tempête **3.** CHEM élémentaire.

elementary [ˌelɪ'mentərɪ] *adj* élémentaire ▪ **~, my dear Watson!** élémentaire, mon cher Watson! ● **~ school/education** école *f* /enseignement *m* primaire ▪ **~ particle** particule *f* élémentaire.

elephant ['elɪfənt] *n* éléphant *m* ▪ **African/Indian ~** éléphant d'Afrique/d'Asie.

elephantiasis [ˌelɪfən'taɪəsɪs] *n* éléphantiasis *m*.

elephantine [ˌelɪ'fæntaɪn] *adj* [proportions, size] éléphantesque ▪ [gait] lourd, pesant ▪ [movement] gauche, maladroit.

elephant seal *n* éléphant *m* de mer.

elevate ['elɪveɪt] *vt* [raise - in height, rank etc] élever ▪ **to ~ sb to the rank of general** élever qqn au rang de général.

elevated ['elɪveɪtɪd] *adj* **1.** [height, position, rank] haut, élevé ▪ [thoughts] noble, élevé ▪ [style] élevé, soutenu **2.** [raised - road] surélevé ▪ **~ railway** *OR* **railroad** *US* métro *m* aérien.

elevation [ˌelɪ'veɪʃn] *n* **1.** [of roof, in rank] élévation *f* ▪ RELIG [of host] élévation *f* ▪ [of style, language] caractère *m* élevé *OR* soutenu **2.** [height] : **~ above sea-level** élévation *f* par rapport au niveau de la mer **3.** [hill] élévation *f*, hauteur *f* **4.** [of canon] hausse *f* **5.** ARCHIT élévation *f*.

elevator ['elɪveɪtə^r] *n* **1.** *US* [lift] ascenseur *m* **2.** [for grain] élévateur *m*.

eleven [ɪ'levn] ◇ *pron* onze, *see also* **five**.
◇ *adj* onze, *see also* **five**.

<> *n* onze *m* ■ SPORT équipe *f* ■ FTBL onze *m*, équipe *f*.

eleven-plus *n UK* SCH & *dated examen de sélection pour l'entrée dans le secondaire en Grande-Bretagne.*

elevenses [ɪ'levnzɪz] *n UK boisson ou en-cas pour la pause de onze heures.*

eleventh [ɪ'levnθ] <> *adj* onzième, *see also* **fifth**.
<> *n* [in series] onze *mf* ■ [fraction] onzième *m*, *see also* **fifth**.

eleventh hour *n* : **at the ~** à la dernière minute.
◆ **eleventh-hour** *adj* de dernière minute.

elf [elf] (*pl* **elves** [elvz]) *n* elfe *m*.

elfin ['elfɪn] *adj fig* [face, features] délicat.

elfish ['elfɪʃ] = **elfin**.

Elgin Marbles ['elgɪn-] *npl* : **the ~** les frises *fpl* du Parthénon *(exposées au British Museum).*

elicit [ɪ'lɪsɪt] *vt* [information, explanation, response] obtenir ■ [facts, truth] découvrir, mettre au jour ■ **to ~ sthg from sb** tirer qqch de qqn.

elide [ɪ'laɪd] *vt* élider.

eligibility [,elɪdʒə'bɪlətɪ] *n* [to vote] éligibilité *f* ■ [for a job] admissibilité *f*.

eligible ['elɪdʒəbl] *adj* [to vote] éligible ■ [for a job] admissible ■ [for promotion] pouvant bénéficier d'une promotion ■ [for marriage] mariable ■ **to be ~ for a pension/a tax rebate** avoir droit à une retraite/un dégrèvement fiscal ■ **an ~ bachelor** un bon *OR* beau parti.

Elijah [ɪ'laɪdʒə] *pr n* Élie.

eliminate [ɪ'lɪmɪneɪt] *vt* [competitor, alternative] éliminer ■ [stain, mark] enlever, faire disparaître ■ [item from diet] supprimer, éliminer ■ [possibility] écarter, éliminer ■ [kill] éliminer, supprimer ■ MATHS & PHYSIOL éliminer ■ **to ~ hunger and poverty from the world** éliminer *OR* supprimer la faim et la pauvreté dans le monde.

elimination [ɪ,lɪmɪ'neɪʃn] *n* élimination *f* ■ **by (a process of) ~** par élimination.

Elisha [ɪ'laɪʃə] *pr n* Élisée.

elision [ɪ'lɪʒn] *n* élision *f*.

elite [ɪ'li:t], **élite** [eɪ'li:t] <> *n* élite *f*.
<> *adj* d'élite.

elitism [ɪ'li:tɪzm] *n* élitisme *m*.

elitist [ɪ'li:tɪst] <> *n* élitiste *mf*.
<> *adj* élitiste.

elixir [ɪ'lɪksəʳ] *n* élixir *m* ■ **~ of life** élixir *m* de vie.

Elizabeth [ɪ'lɪzəbəθ] *pr n* : **Queen ~** la reine Élisabeth.

Elizabethan [ɪ,lɪzə'bi:θn] <> *adj* élisabéthain.
<> *n* Élisabéthain *m*, - e *f*.

elk [elk] (*pl inv OR pl* **elks**) *n* élan *m* ■ **American ~** wapiti *m*.

ellipse [ɪ'lɪps] *n* MATHS ellipse *f*.

ellipsis [ɪ'lɪpsɪs] (*pl* **ellipses** [-si:z]) *n* GRAM ellipse *f*.

elliptic [ɪ'lɪptɪk] *adj* elliptique.

elliptically [ɪ'lɪptɪklɪ] *adv* de manière elliptique, par ellipse.

Ellis Island ['elɪs-] *pr n* Ellis Island *(dans la première moitié du XX*[e] *siècle, lieu de débarquement des immigrés, situé au large de New York).*

elm [elm] *n* orme *m*.

elocution [,elə'kju:ʃn] *n* élocution *f*, diction *f*.

elongate ['i:lɒŋgeɪt] <> *vt* allonger ■ [line] prolonger.
<> *vi* s'allonger, s'étendre.

elongated ['i:lɒŋgeɪtɪd] *adj* [in space] allongé ■ [in time] prolongé.

elongation [,i:lɒŋ'geɪʃn] *n* allongement *m* ■ [of line] prolongement *m*.

elope [ɪ'ləʊp] *vi* s'enfuir pour se marier ■ **to ~ with sb** s'enfuir avec qqn pour l'épouser.

elopement [ɪ'ləʊpmənt] *n* fugue *f* amoureuse *(en vue d'un mariage).*

eloquence ['eləkwəns] *n* éloquence *f*.

eloquent ['eləkwənt] *adj* éloquent.

eloquently ['eləkwəntlɪ] *adv* éloquemment, avec éloquence.

El Salvador [el'sælvədɔ:ʳ] *pr n* Salvador *m* ■ **in ~** au Salvador.

else [els] *adv* **1.** [after indefinite pronoun] d'autre ■ **anybody** *OR* **anyone ~** [at all] n'importe qui d'autre ; [in addition] quelqu'un d'autre ■ **he's no cleverer than anybody ~** il n'est pas plus intelligent qu'un autre ■ **anything ~** [at all] n'importe quoi d'autre ; [in addition] quelque chose d'autre ■ **would you like** *OR* **will there be anything ~?** [in shop] vous fallait-il autre chose? ; [in restaurant] désirez-vous autre chose? ■ **I couldn't do anything ~ but** *OR* **except apologize** je ne pouvais (rien faire d'autre) que m'excuser ■ **anywhere ~** ailleurs ■ **I haven't got anywhere ~** *OR* **I've got nowhere ~ to go** je n'ai nulle part ailleurs où aller ■ **everybody ~** tous les autres ■ **everything ~** tout le reste ■ **everywhere ~** partout ailleurs ■ **and much ~ (besides)** et beaucoup de choses encore ■ **nobody** *OR* **no one ~** personne d'autre ■ **we're alive, nothing ~ matters** nous sommes vivants, c'est tout ce qui compte ■ **there's nothing ~ for it** il n'y a rien d'autre à faire ■ **somebody** *OR* **someone ~** quelqu'un d'autre ■ **something ~** autre chose, quelque chose d'autre ■ **somewhere** *OR* *US* **someplace ~** ailleurs, autre part ▶ **if all ~ fails** en dernier recours ■ **it'll teach him a lesson, if nothing ~** au moins, ça lui servira de leçon ■ **he's/she's/it's something ~!** *inf* il est/elle est/c'est incroyable! **2.** *(after interrogative pronoun)* [in addition] d'autre ■ **what/who ~?** quoi/qui d'autre? ▮ [otherwise] autrement ■ **how/why ~ would I do it?** comment/pourquoi le ferais-je sinon? ■ **where ~ would he be?** où peut-il être à part là?

elsewhere [els'weəʳ] *adv* ailleurs ■ **~ in France** ailleurs en France.

ELT (*abbrev of* **English language teaching**) *n enseignement de l'anglais.*

elucidate [ɪ'lu:sɪdeɪt] <> *vt* [point, question] élucider, expliciter ■ [reasons] expliquer.
<> *vi* expliquer, être plus clair.

elucidation [ɪ,lu:sɪ'deɪʃn] *n* [of point, question] élucidation *f*, éclaircissement *m* ■ [of reasons] explication *f*.

elude [ɪ'lu:d] *vt* [enemy, pursuers] échapper à ■ [question] éluder ■ [blow] esquiver ■ [sb's gaze] éviter, fuir ■ [obligation, responsibility] se dérober à, se soustraire à ■ [justice] se soustraire à ■ **his name/that word ~s me** son nom/ce mot m'échappe ■ **to ~ sb's grasp** échapper à (l'emprise de) qqn ■ **success has always ~d him** la réussite lui a toujours échappé.

elusive [ɪ'lu:sɪv] *adj* [enemy, prey, happiness, thought] insaisissable ■ [word, concept] difficile à définir ■ [answer] élusif, évasif ■ **she's being rather ~** [difficult to find] elle se fait plutôt discrète ces derniers temps ; [vague] elle se montre assez évasive.

elusively [ɪ'lu:sɪvlɪ] *adv* [answer] de manière élusive ■ [move] de manière insaisissable.

elves [elvz] *pl* ▷ **elf**.

Elysium [ɪ'lɪzɪəm] *n* MYTH Élysée *m*.

em [em] *n* TYPO cadratin *m*.

'em [əm] *inf* = **them**.

emaciated [ɪ'meɪʃɪeɪtɪd] *adj* émacié, décharné.

emaciation [ɪ,meɪsɪ'eɪʃn] *n* émaciation *f*.

e-mail *n* adresse *f* électronique *inf*.

E-mail, e-mail ['i:meɪl] (*abbrev of* **electronic mail**) <> *n* courrier *m* électronique, e-mail *m*.
<> *vt* [message] envoyer par courrier électronique *OR* e-mail ■ [person] envoyer un courrier électronique *OR* e-mail à.

◇ *comp* : **~ address** adresse *f* électronique.

emanate [ˈemәneɪt] ◇ *vi* : **to ~ from** émaner de.
◇ *vt* [love, affection] exsuder, rayonner de ■ [concern] respirer.

emanation [ˌemәˈneɪʃn] *n* émanation *f.*

emancipate [ɪˈmænsɪpeɪt] *vt* [women] émanciper ■ [slaves] affranchir.

emancipated [ɪˈmænsɪpeɪtɪd] *adj* émancipé.

emancipation [ɪˌmænsɪˈpeɪʃn] *n* émancipation *f* ■ **the Emancipation Proclamation** *US* HIST la proclamation d'émancipation.

THE EMANCIPATION PROCLAMATION

Discours du président Abraham Lincoln, en 1863, déclarant les esclaves de la Confédération (États sudistes) libres. Bien qu'elle soit restée sans effet pratique (ces États échappaient au contrôle fédéral), cette proclamation représente, pour les Américains, l'officialisation de l'émancipation des esclaves.

emasculate [ɪˈmæskjʊleɪt] *vt* [castrate] émasculer ■ *fig* émasculer, affaiblir.

emasculation [ɪˌmæskjʊˈleɪʃn] *n* [castration] émasculation *f* ■ *fig* émasculation *f*, affaiblissement *m.*

embalm [ɪmˈbɑːm] *vt* embaumer.

embalmer [ɪmˈbɑːmәʳ] *n* embaumeur *m*, thanatopracteur *m.*

embalming [ɪmˈbɑːmɪŋ] *n* embaumement *m* ■ **~ fluid** fluide *m* de thanatopraxie.

embankment [ɪmˈbæŋkmәnt] *n* [of concrete] quai *m* ■ [of earth] berge *f* ■ [to contain river] digue *f* ■ [along railway, road] talus *m.*

embargo [emˈbɑːgәʊ] (*pl* **embargoes**) ◇ *n* **1.** COMM & POL embargo *m* ■ **to put** *OR* **to place** *OR* **to lay an ~ on sthg** mettre l'embargo sur qqch ■ **to lift/to break an ~** lever/enfreindre un embargo ■ **there is still an ~ on arms, arms are still under an ~** les armes sont encore sous embargo ■ **oil/arms ~** embargo pétrolier/sur les armes **2.** *fig* [on spending] interdiction *f* ■ **to put an ~ on sthg** interdire *OR* bannir qqch.
◇ *vt* COMM & POL mettre l'embargo sur ■ *fig* interdire.

embark [ɪmˈbɑːk] ◇ *vt* [passengers, cargo] embarquer.
◇ *vi* embarquer, monter à bord.
◆ **embark on, embark upon** *vt insep* [journey, career] commencer, entreprendre ■ [explanation, venture] se lancer dans.

embarkation [ˌembɑːˈkeɪʃn], **embarkment** [ɪmˈbɑːkmәnt] *n* [of passengers, cargo] embarquement *m* ■ **~ papers** *OR* **card** carte *f* d'embarquement.

embarrass [ɪmˈbærәs] *vt* embarrasser, gêner ■ **to ~ the government** mettre le gouvernement dans l'embarras.

embarrassed [ɪmˈbærәst] *adj* embarrassé ■ **to feel ~ (about sthg)** être embarrassé *OR* se sentir gêné (à propos de qqch) ■ **to be (financially) ~** être gêné, avoir des problèmes d'argent.

embarrassing [ɪmˈbærәsɪŋ] *adj* [experience, person] embarrassant, gênant ■ [situation] embarrassant, délicat ■ **this is rather ~ but...** cela me gêne beaucoup mais...

embarrassingly [ɪmˈbærәsɪŋlɪ] *adv* de manière embarrassante ■ **it was ~ obvious** c'était évident au point d'en être embarrassant.

embarrassment [ɪmˈbærәsmәnt] *n* embarras *m*, gêne *f* ■ **(much) to my ~** à mon grand embarras ■ **to cause sb ~** mettre qqn dans l'embarras ■ **to be in a state of financial ~** avoir des problèmes *OR* embarras financiers ■ **to be an ~** *OR* **a source of ~ to sb** être une source d'embarras pour qqn, faire honte à qqn.

embassy [ˈembәsɪ] (*pl* **embassies**) *n* ambassade *f* ■ **the British/French Embassy** l'ambassade de Grande-Bretagne/France.

embattled [ɪmˈbætld] *adj* [army] engagé dans la bataille ■ [town] ravagé par les combats ■ *fig* en difficulté, aux prises avec des difficultés.

embed [ɪmˈbed] (*pret & pp* **embedded**, *cont* **embedding**) *vt* [in wood] enfoncer ■ [in rock] sceller ■ [in cement] sceller, noyer ■ [jewels] enchâsser, incruster.

embedded [ɪmˈbedɪd] *adj* [in wood] enfoncé ■ [in rock] scellé ■ [in cement] scellé, noyé ■ [jewels] enchâssé, incrusté ▶ **~ command** COMPUT commande *f* intégrée ■ **~ clause** GRAM proposition *f* enchâssée.

embedding [ɪmˈbedɪŋ] *n* [in wood] enfoncement *m* ■ [in rock, cement] scellement *m* ■ GRAM enchâssement *m.*

embellish [ɪmˈbelɪʃ] *vt* [garment, building] embellir, décorer, orner ■ [account, story etc] enjoliver, embellir.

embellishment [ɪmˈbelɪʃmәnt] *n* [of building] embellissement *m* ■ [of garment] décoration *f* ■ [of account, story etc] enjolivement *m*, embellissement *m* ■ [in handwriting] fioritures *fpl.*

ember [ˈembәʳ] *n* charbon *m* ardent, morceau *m* de braise ■ **~s** braise *f.*

embezzle [ɪmˈbezl] ◇ *vt* [money] détourner, escroquer ■ **to ~ money from sb** escroquer de l'argent à qqn.
◇ *vi* : **to ~ from a company** détourner les fonds d'une société.

embezzlement [ɪmˈbezlmәnt] *n* [of funds] détournement *m* ■ **to be convicted of ~** être reconnu coupable de détournement de fonds.

embezzler [ɪmˈbezlәʳ] *n* escroc *m*, fraudeur *m*, - euse *f.*

embitter [ɪmˈbɪtәʳ] *vt* [person] remplir d'amertume, aigrir ■ [relations] altérer, détériorer.

embittered [ɪmˈbɪtәd] *adj* aigri.

emblazon [ɪmˈbleɪzn] *vt* blasonner.

emblazoned [ɪmˈbleɪznd] *adj* : **the shield is ~ with dragons** le bouclier porte des dragons.

emblem [ˈemblәm] *n* emblème *m.*

emblematic [ˌemblәˈmætɪk] *adj* emblématique.

embodiment [ɪmˈbɒdɪmәnt] *n* **1.** [epitome] incarnation *f*, personnification *f* ■ **to be the ~ of goodness/evil** [person] être la bonté même/le mal incarné **2.** [inclusion] intégration *f*, incorporation *f.*

embody [ɪmˈbɒdɪ] (*pret & pp* **embodied**) *vt* **1.** [epitomize - subj: person] incarner ; [- subj: action] exprimer **2.** [include] inclure, intégrer.

embolden [ɪmˈbәʊldәn] *vt fml* enhardir ■ **to feel ~ed to do sthg** se sentir le courage de faire qqch.

embolism [ˈembәlɪzm] *n* MED embolie *f.*

emboss [ɪmˈbɒs] *vt* [metal] repousser, estamper ■ [leather] estamper, gaufrer ■ [cloth, paper] gaufrer.

embossed [ɪmˈbɒst] *adj* [metal] repoussé ■ [leather] gaufré ■ [cloth, wallpaper] gaufré, à motifs en relief.

embouchure [ˌɑːmbuːˈʃʊәʳ] *n* MUS embouchure *f.*

embrace [ɪmˈbreɪs] ◇ *vt* **1.** [friend, child] étreindre ■ [lover] étreindre, enlacer ■ [official, visitor, statesman] donner l'accolade à **2.** [include] regrouper, comprendre, embrasser **3.** [adopt - religion, cause] embrasser ; [- opportunity] saisir.
◇ *vi* [friends] s'étreindre ■ [lovers] s'étreindre, s'enlacer ■ [statesmen] se donner l'accolade.
◇ *n* [of friend, child] étreinte *f* ■ [of lover] étreinte *f*, enlacement *m* ■ [of official visitor, statesman] accolade *f* ■ **to hold** *OR* **to clasp sb in an ~** étreindre qqn.

embrocation [ˌembrәˈkeɪʃn] *n* embrocation *f.*

embroider [ɪmˈbrɔɪdәʳ] ◇ *vt* [garment, cloth] broder ■ *fig* [story, truth] embellir, enjoliver.
◇ *vi* [with needle] broder ■ *fig* [embellish] broder, enjoliver.

embroidered [ɪmˈbrɔɪdәd] *adj* [garment, cloth] brodé.

embroidery [ɪm'brɔɪdərɪ] (*pl* **embroideries**) ◇ *n* [on garment, cloth] broderie *f* ■ *fig* [of story, truth] enjolivement *m*, embellissement *m*.
◇ *comp* [frame, silk, thread] à broder.

embroil [ɪm'brɔɪl] *vt* mêler, impliquer ■ **to get ~ed in sthg** se retrouver mêlé à qqch.

embryo ['embrɪəʊ] (*pl* **embryos**) *n* BIOL & *fig* embryon *m* ■ **in ~** [foetus, idea] à l'état embryonnaire.

embryology [,embrɪ'ɒlədʒɪ] *n* embryologie *f*.

embryonic [,embrɪ'ɒnɪk] *adj* BIOL embryonnaire ■ *fig* à l'état embryonnaire.

emcee [,em'si:] *inf* ◇ *n* = **master of ceremonies**.
◇ *vt* animer.

emend [i:'mend] *vt* corriger.

emendation [,i:men'deɪʃn] *n fml* correction *f*.

emerald ['emərəld] ◇ *n* **1.** [gem stone] émeraude *f* **2.** [colour] : **~ (green)** (vert *m*) émeraude *m*.
◇ *comp* [brooch, ring] en émeraude.

Emerald Isle *pr n lit* Île *f* d'Émeraude.

emerge [ɪ'mɜ:dʒ] *vi* [person, animal] sortir ■ [sun] sortir, émerger ■ [truth, difficulty] émerger, apparaître ■ **to ~ from hiding** sortir de sa cachette ■ **to ~ as favourite** apparaître comme le favori ■ **it later ~d that...** il est apparu par la suite que...

emergence [ɪ'mɜ:dʒəns] *n* émergence *f*.

emergency [ɪ'mɜ:dʒənsɪ] (*pl* **emergencies**) ◇ *n* **1.** (cas *m* d')urgence *f* ■ **this is an ~!** c'est une urgence! ■ **in case of ~, in an ~** en cas d'urgence ■ **to be prepared for any ~** être prêt à toutes les éventualités **2.** MED [department] (service *m* des) urgences *fpl*.
◇ *comp* [measures, procedure, meeting] d'urgence ■ **~ brake** frein *m* de secours ; *US* frein *m* à main ■ **~ case** MED urgence *f* ■ **'~ exit'** 'sortie *f* de secours' ■ **~ food aid** aide *f* alimentaire d'urgence ■ **~ landing** AERON atterrissage *m* forcé ■ **~ operation** MED opération *f* à chaud ■ **~ patient** urgence *f* ■ **~ powers** pouvoirs *mpl* extraordinaires ■ **~ rations** vivres *mpl* de secours *OR* de réserve ■ **~ room** *US* salle *f* des urgences ■ **~ service** AUT service *m* de dépannage ; MED service *m* des urgences ■ **~ services** services *mpl* d'urgence ■ **~ stop** AUT arrêt *m* d'urgence ■ **~ supply** réserve *f* ■ **~ tank** AERON réservoir *m* auxiliaire ■ **'for ~ use only'** 'à n'utiliser qu'en cas d'urgence' ■ **~ ward** *UK* MED salle *f* des urgences.

emergent [ɪ'mɜ:dʒənt] *adj* [theory, nation] naissant.

emeritus [ɪ'merɪtəs] *adj* UNIV honoraire.

emery ['emərɪ] *n* émeri *m*.

emery board *n* lime *f* à ongles.

emery paper *n* papier *m* (d')émeri.

emetic [ɪ'metɪk] ◇ *adj* émétique.
◇ *n* émétique *m*, vomitif *m*.

emigrant ['emɪgrənt] ◇ *n* émigrant *m*, - e *f* ■ [when established abroad] émigré *m*, - e *f*.
◇ *comp* [worker, population] émigré.

emigrate ['emɪgreɪt] *vi* émigrer.

emigration [,emɪ'greɪʃn] *n* émigration *f*.

émigré ['emɪgreɪ] *n* émigré *m*.

eminence ['emɪnəns] *n* **1.** [prominence] rang *m* éminent **2.** [high ground] éminence *f*, hauteur *f*.
◆ **Eminence** *n* RELIG [title] Éminence *f* ■ **Your/His Eminence** Votre/Son Éminence.

eminent ['emɪnənt] *adj* [distinguished] éminent ■ [conspicuous] éminent, remarquable, insigne.

eminently ['emɪnəntlɪ] *adv* éminemment ■ **~ suitable** qui convient parfaitement.

emir [e'mɪə^r] *n* émir *m*.

emirate ['emərət] *n* émirat *m*.

emissary ['emɪsərɪ] (*pl* **emissaries**) *n* émissaire *m*.

emission [ɪ'mɪʃn] *n* émission *f*.

emit [ɪ'mɪt] (*pret & pp* **emitted**, *cont* **emitting**) *vt* [sound, radiation, light] émettre ■ [heat] dégager, émettre ■ [gas] dégager ■ [sparks, cry] lancer.

Emmental, Emmenthal ['emən,tɑ:l] *n* Emmental *m*.

Emmy ['emɪ] *n* : **~ (award)** *distinction récompensant les meilleures émissions télévisées américaines de l'année.*

emollient [ɪ'mɒlɪənt] ◇ *adj* émollient ■ *fig* adoucissant, calmant.
◇ *n* émollient *m*.

emolument [ɪ'mɒljʊmənt] *n fml (usu pl)* **~s** émoluments *mpl*, rémunération *f*.

emote [ɪ'məʊt] *vi* [on stage] faire dans le genre tragique ■ [in life] avoir un comportement théâtral.

emoticon [ɪ'məʊtɪkɒn] *n* émoticon *m*, souriant *m*.

emotion [ɪ'məʊʃn] *n* [particular feeling] sentiment *m* ■ [faculty] émotion *f* ■ **to show no ~** ne laisser paraître aucune émotion ■ **to express one's ~s** exprimer ses sentiments ■ **full of ~** ému.

emotional [ɪ'məʊʃənl] *adj* **1.** [stress] émotionnel ■ [life, problems] affectif **2.** [person - easily moved] sensible, qui s'émeut facilement ; [- stronger] émotif ■ [appealing to the emotions - plea, speech, music] émouvant ■ [charged with emotion - issue] passionné, brûlant ; [- reunion, scene] chargé d'émotion ■ [governed by emotions - person] passionné, ardent ; [- reaction, state] émotionnel ■ **why do you always have to get so ~ ?** pourquoi faut-il toujours que tu te mettes dans de tels états? ■ **~ blackmail** chantage *m* affectif.

emotional intelligence *adj* intelligence *f* émotionnelle.

emotionally [ɪ'məʊʃnəlɪ] *adv* [react, speak] avec émotion ■ **to feel ~ exhausted** *OR* **drained** se sentir vidé (sur le plan émotionnel) ■ **to be ~ disturbed** souffrir de troubles affectifs ■ **to be ~ involved with sb** avoir des liens affectifs avec qqn.

emotionless [ɪ'məʊʃnlɪs] *adj* [person, face, eyes] impassible ■ [style] froid.

emotive [ɪ'məʊtɪv] *adj* [issue] sensible ■ [word, phrase] à forte teneur émotionnelle.

empanel [ɪm'pænl] (*UK pret & pp* **empanelled**, *cont* **empanelling** *US*, *pret & pp* **empaneled**, *cont* **empaneling**) *vt* [jury] constituer ■ [juror] inscrire sur la liste *OR* le tableau du jury.

empathize ['empəθaɪz] *vi* : **to ~ with sb** s'identifier à qqn.

empathy ['empəθɪ] *n* [affinity - gen] affinité *f*, affinités *fpl*, sympathie *f* ■ PHILOS & PSYCHOL empathie *f* ■ [power, ability] capacité *f* à s'identifier à autrui ■ **the ~ between them** les affinités qui existent entre eux.

emperor ['empərə^r] *n* empereur *m* ■ **'The Emperor's New Clothes'** ***Andersen*** 'les Nouveaux Habits de l'empereur'.

emperor moth *n* saturnie *f*, paon de nuit *m*.

emperor penguin *n* manchot *m* empereur.

emphasis ['emfəsɪs] (*pl* **emphases** [-si:z]) *n* **1.** [importance] accent *m* ■ **to place** *OR* **to lay** *OR* **to put ~ on sthg** mettre l'accent sur qqch ■ **there is too much ~ on materialism in our society** on accorde trop d'importance aux choses matérielles dans notre société ■ **the ~ now is on winning votes** ce qui est important maintenant c'est de gagner des voix **2.** LING [stress] accent *m*.

emphasize ['emfəsaɪz] *vt* **1.** [detail, need, importance] insister sur ■ **I can't ~ this strongly enough** je n'insisterai jamais assez sur cela **2.** [physical feature] accentuer ■ **to ~ the waist** [dress] marquer *OR* accentuer la taille **3.** LING [syllable] accentuer ■ [word] accentuer, appuyer sur.

emphatic [ɪm'fætɪk] *adj* [gesture, refusal] emphatique ■ [speaker, manner] énergique, vigoureux ■ LING emphatique ■ **to be ~ in one's denials** nier avec emphase.

emphatically [ɪm'fætɪklɪ] *adv* **1.** [forcefully] emphatiquement, avec emphase ■ [deny] avec emphase **2.** [definitely] clairement ■ **I most ~ do not agree with you** je ne suis absolument pas d'accord avec vous.

emphysema [,emfɪ'si:mə] *n* emphysème *m*.

empire ['empaɪəʳ] *n* empire *m*.
◆ **Empire** *comp* [costume, furniture, style] Empire.

empire-builder *n fig* bâtisseur *m* d'empires.

empire-building *n* : **there's too much ~ going on** on joue trop les bâtisseurs d'empires.

Empire State *n* : **the ~** l'État *m* de New York.

empirical [ɪm'pɪrɪkl] *adj* empirique.

empirically [ɪm'pɪrɪklɪ] *adv* empiriquement.

empiricism [ɪm'pɪrɪsɪzm] *n* empirisme *m*.

empiricist [ɪm'pɪrɪsɪst] *n* empiriste *mf*.

emplacement [ɪm'pleɪsmənt] *n* MIL [of canon] emplacement *m*.

employ [ɪm'plɔɪ] ◇ *vt* **1.** [give work to] employer ■ **they ~ 245 staff** ils ont 245 employés ■ **he has been ~ed with the firm for twenty years** il travaille pour cette entreprise depuis vingt ans **2.** [use - means, method, word] employer, utiliser ; [- skill, diplomacy] faire usage de, employer ; [- force] employer, avoir recours à **3.** [occupy] : **to ~ oneself/to be ~ed in doing sthg** s'occuper/être occupé à faire qqch ■ **you'd be better ~ed doing your homework** tu ferais mieux de faire tes devoirs.
◇ *n fml* service *m* ■ **to be in sb's ~** travailler pour qqn, être au service de qqn.

employable [ɪm'plɔɪəbl] *adj* [person] susceptible d'être employé ■ [method] utilisable ■ **a good education makes you more ~** une bonne formation donne plus de chances de trouver du travail.

employed [ɪm'plɔɪd] ◇ *adj* employé ■ **I am not ~ at the moment** je n'ai pas de travail en ce moment.
◇ *npl* personnes *fpl* qui ont un emploi ■ **employers and ~** patronat *m* et salariat *m*.

employee [ɪm'plɔɪi:] *n* employé *m*, - e *f*, salarié *m*, - e *f* ■ **management and ~s** la direction et les employés *OR* le personnel ; [in negotiations] les partenaires *mpl* sociaux ■ **~'s contribution** *OR* **share** [to benefits] cotisation *f* ouvrière.

employer [ɪm'plɔɪəʳ] *n* employeur *m*, patron *m* ■ ADMIN employeur *m* ■ **who is your ~?** pour qui travaillez-vous? ■ **~s** [as a body] patronat *m* ■ **~'s contribution** *OR* **share** [to employee benefits] cotisation *f* patronale.

employment [ɪm'plɔɪmənt] *n* **1.** [work] emploi *m* ■ **to be in ~** avoir un emploi *OR* du travail ■ **full ~** plein emploi ■ **conditions of ~** conditions *fpl* de travail ■ **to look for** *OR* **to seek ~** chercher du travail *OR* un emploi, être demandeur d'emploi ■ **(the) ~ figures** les chiffres de l'emploi ▶ **Department of Employment** *US OR dated UK*, **Employment Department** ≃ ministère *m* du Travail ■ **Secretary (of State) for** *OR* **Minister of Employment** *UK*, **Secretary for Employment** *US* ≃ ministre *m* du Travail **2.** [recruitment] embauche *f* ■ [providing work] emploi *m* **3.** [use - of method, word] emploi *m* ; [- of force, skill] usage *m*, emploi *m*.

employment agency, employment bureau *n* agence *f OR* bureau *m* de placement.

employment exchange, employment office *n UK dated* ≃ ANPE *f*.

employment tribunal *n* LAW conseil *m* de prud'hommes.

emporium [em'pɔ:rɪəm] (*pl* **emporiums** *OR pl* **emporia** [-rɪə]) *n* grand magasin *m*.

empower [ɪm'paʊəʳ] *vt fml* habiliter, autoriser ■ **to ~ sb to do sthg** habiliter *OR* autoriser qqn à faire qqch.

empowering [ɪm'paʊərɪŋ] *adj* qui donne un sentiment de pouvoir.

empowerment [ɪm'paʊəmənt] *n* : **the ~ of women/of ethnic minorities** la plus grande autonomie des femmes/des minorités ethniques.

empress ['emprɪs] *n* impératrice *f*.

emptiness ['emptɪnɪs] *n* vide *m* ■ **a feeling of ~** un sentiment de vide.

empty ['emptɪ] (*pl* **empties**, *comp* **emptier**, *superl* **emptiest**) ◇ *adj* [glass, room, box etc] vide ■ [city, street] désert ■ [cinema] désert, vide ■ [job, post] vacant, à pourvoir ■ *fig* [words, talk] creux ■ [promise] en l'air, vain ■ [gesture] dénué de sens ■ [threat] en l'air ■ **~ of meaning** vide *OR* dénué de sens ■ **my stomach is ~** [I'm hungry] j'ai un creux (à l'estomac) ■ **to do sthg on an ~ stomach** faire qqch à jeun ■ **to feel ~** [drained of emotion] se sentir vidé (sur le plan émotionnel) ▶ **~ vessels make the most sound** *prov* moins on en sait, plus on parle.
◇ *n inf* [bottle] bouteille *f* vide ■ [glass] verre *m* vide.
◇ *vt* [glass, pocket, room] vider ■ [car, lorry] décharger.
◇ *vi* [building, street, container] se vider ■ [water] s'écouler ■ **to ~ into the sea** [river] se jeter dans la mer.
◆ **empty out** ◇ *vt sep* vider.
◇ *vi insep* [tank, container] se vider ■ [water, liquid] s'écouler.

empty-handed [-'hændɪd] *adj* les mains vides ■ **to return ~** rentrer bredouille *OR* les mains vides.

empty-headed *adj* écervelé, sans cervelle.

EMS (*abbrev of* **European Monetary System**) *pr n* SME *m*.

EMT (*abbrev of* **emergency medical technician**) *n technicien médical des services d'urgence.*

emu ['i:mju:] *n* émeu *m*.

EMU (*abbrev of* **Economic and Monetary Union**) *n* UEM *f*.

emulate ['emjʊleɪt] *vt* [person, action] imiter ■ COMPUT émuler.

emulation [,emjʊ'leɪʃn] *n* [gen - COMPUT] émulation *f*.

emulator ['emjʊleɪtəʳ] *n* COMPUT émulateur *m*.

emulsifier [ɪ'mʌlsɪfaɪəʳ] *n* émulsifiant *m*.

emulsify [ɪ'mʌlsɪfaɪ] *vt* émulsionner, émulsifier.

emulsion [ɪ'mʌlʃn] ◇ *n* **1.** CHEM & PHOT émulsion *f* **2.** [paint] (peinture *f*) émulsion *f*.
◇ *vt* appliquer de la peinture émulsion sur.

emulsion paint = **emulsion** (*n sense 2*).

en [en] *n* TYPO demi-cadratin *m*.

enable [ɪ'neɪbl] *vt* : **to ~ sb to do sthg** permettre à qqn de faire qqch ; LAW habiliter *OR* autoriser qqn à faire qqch.

enabling [ɪ'neɪblɪŋ] *adj* LAW habilitant.

enact [ɪ'nækt] *vt* **1.** LAW [bill, law] promulguer **2.** [scene, play] jouer ■ **to be ~ed** *fig* se dérouler.

enactment [ɪ'næktmənt] *n* **1.** LAW [of bill, law etc] promulgation *f* **2.** [of play] représentation *f*.

enamel [ɪ'næml] (*UK pret & pp* **enamelled**, *cont* **enamelling**) (*US pret & pp* **enameled**, *cont* **enameling**) ◇ *n* **1.** ART [on clay, glass etc] émail *m* **2.** [paint] peinture *f* laquée *OR* vernie **3.** [on teeth] émail *m*.
◇ *comp* [mug, saucepan] en émail, émaillé ■ **~ paint** peinture *f* laquée *OR* vernie ■ **~ painting** peinture *f* sur émail.
◇ *vt* émailler.

enamelled *UK*, **enameled** *US* [ɪ'næmld] *adj* [mug, saucepan] émaillé, en émail.

enamelling *UK*, **enameling** *US* [ɪ'næməlɪŋ] *n* émaillage *m*.

enamelware [ɪ'næmlweəʳ] *n* ustensiles *mpl* en émail.

enamoured *UK*, **enamored** *US* [ɪ'næməd] *adj* : **to be ~ of** *lit* [person] être amoureux *OR* épris de ; [job, flat] être enchanté *OR* ravi de ■ **he wasn't exactly ~ of our proposal** notre proposition ne l'enchantait guère.

en bloc [ɑ̃'blɒk] *adv* en bloc.

enc. 1. (*written abbrev of* **enclosure**) PJ **2.** *written abbr of* **enclosed**.

encamp [ɪn'kæmp] ◇ *vi* camper.

◇ *vt* faire camper ■ **to be ~ed** camper.

encampment [ɪn'kæmpmənt] *n* campement *m*.

encapsulate [ɪn'kæpsjʊleɪt] *vt* PHARM mettre en capsule ■ *fig* résumer.

encase [ɪn'keɪs] *vt* recouvrir, entourer.

encash [ɪn'kæʃ] *vt* *UK* encaisser.

encashment [ɪn'kæʃmənt] *n* *UK* encaissement *m*.

encephalitis [,ensefə'laɪtɪs] *n* encéphalite *f*.

encephalogram [en'sefələgræm] *n* encéphalogramme *m*.

enchant [ɪn'tʃɑ:nt] *vt* **1.** [delight] enchanter, ravir **2.** [put spell on] enchanter, ensorceler.

enchanted [ɪn'tʃɑ:ntɪd] *adj* enchanté.

enchanting [ɪn'tʃɑ:ntɪŋ] *adj* charmant.

enchantingly [ɪn'tʃɑ:ntɪŋlɪ] *adv* [sing, play] merveilleusement bien ■ **~ pretty** ravissant.

enchantment [ɪn'tʃɑ:ntmənt] *n* **1.** [delight] enchantement *m*, ravissement *m* ■ **to fill sb with ~** enchanter *OR* ravir qqn ■ **the Land of Enchantment** le Nouveau Mexique **2.** [casting of spell] enchantement *m*, ensorcellement *m*.

enchantress [ɪn'tʃɑ:ntrɪs] *n* enchanteresse *f*.

enchilada [,entʃɪ'lɑ:də] *n* *plat mexicain consistant en une galette de maïs frite, farcie à la viande et servie avec une sauce piquante.*

encircle [ɪn'sɜ:kl] *vt* entourer ■ MIL & HUNT encercler, cerner.

encircling [ɪn'sɜ:klɪŋ] ◇ *n* encerclement *m*.
◇ *adj* MIL : **~ movement** manœuvre *f* d'encerclement.

encl. = **enc.**

enclave ['enkleɪv] *n* enclave *f*.

enclose [ɪn'kləʊz] *vt* **1.** [surround - with wall] entourer, ceinturer ; [- with fence] clôturer **2.** [in letter] joindre ■ **to ~ sthg with a letter** joindre qqch à une lettre.

enclosed [ɪn'kləʊzd] *adj* **1.** [area] clos ■ **~ order** RELIG ordre *m* claustral **2.** COMM [cheque] ci-joint, ci-inclus ■ **please find ~ my CV** veuillez trouver ci-joint *OR* ci-inclus mon CV.

enclosure [ɪn'kləʊʒəʳ] *n* **1.** [enclosed area] enclos *m*, enceinte *f* ■ **public ~** [at sports ground, racecourse] pelouse *f* **2.** [with letter] pièce *f* jointe *OR* annexée *OR* incluse **3.** [action] action *f* de clôturer **4.** *UK* HIST enclosure *f*.

encode [en'kəʊd] *vt* coder, chiffrer ■ COMPUT encoder.

encoder [en'kəʊdəʳ] *n* [gen - COMPUT] encodeur *m*.

encoding [en'kəʊdɪŋ] *n* codage *m* ■ COMPUT encodage *m*.

encompass [ɪn'kʌmpəs] *vt* **1.** [include] englober, comprendre, regrouper **2.** *fml* [surround] entourer, encercler.

encore ['ɒŋkɔ:ʳ] ◇ *interj* : **~!, ~!** bis!, bis!
◇ *n* bis *m* ■ **to call for an ~** bisser ■ **to give an ~** [performer] donner un bis ■ **how many ~s were there?** combien de rappels y a-t-il eu?
◇ *vt* [singer, performer] rappeler, bisser ■ [song] bisser.

encounter [ɪn'kaʊntəʳ] ◇ *vt* [person, enemy] rencontrer ■ [difficulty, resistance, danger] rencontrer, se heurter à.
◇ *n* [gen - MIL] rencontre *f*.

encounter group *n* *séance de psychothérapie de groupe.*

encourage [ɪn'kʌrɪdʒ] *vt* [person] encourager, inciter ■ [project, research, attitude] encourager ■ **to ~ sb to do sthg** encourager *OR* inciter qqn à faire qqch ■ **to ~ sb in his/her belief that...** renforcer qqn dans sa conviction que..., conforter qqn dans son idée que...

encouragement [ɪn'kʌrɪdʒmənt] *n* encouragement *m* ■ **to give sb ~, to give ~ to sb** donner des encouragements à *OR* encourager qqn ■ **shouts/words of ~** cris/mots d'encouragement.

encouraging [ɪn'kʌrɪdʒɪŋ] *adj* encourageant ■ [smile, words] d'encouragement.

encouragingly [ɪn'kʌrɪdʒɪŋlɪ] *adv* [smile, speak] de manière encourageante.

encroach [ɪn'krəʊtʃ] ◆ **encroach on, encroach upon** *vi insep* : **the sea is gradually ~ing on the land** la mer gagne progressivement du terrain ■ **the new buildings are ~ing on the countryside** les nouveaux bâtiments envahissent la campagne ■ **to ~ on sb's territory** *fig* marcher *OR* empiéter sur les plates-bandes de qqn.

encroachment [ɪn'krəʊtʃmənt] *n* [on freedom, property, time] empiétement *m* ■ [by sea, river] envahissement *m*, ingression *f* *spec* ■ [buildings] envahissement.

encrust [ɪn'krʌst] *vt* [with jewels] incruster ■ [with mud, snow, ice] couvrir ■ **to be ~ed with sthg** être incrusté *OR* couvert *OR* recouvert de qqch.

encrustation [ɪn,krʌst'eɪʃn] *n* incrustation *f*.

encrypt [en'krɪpt] *vt* coder, chiffrer ■ COMPUT crypter.

encryption [en'krɪpʃn] *n* COMPUT cryptage *m*, cryptologie *f*.

encumber [ɪn'kʌmbəʳ] *vt* *fml* [person, room] encombrer, embarrasser ■ **~ed estate** LAW [with debts] propriété *f* grevée de dettes ; [with mortgage] propriété *f* hypothéquée.

encumbrance [ɪn'kʌmbrəns] *n* *fml* [burden] charge *f*, fardeau *m* ■ LAW charge *f* hypothécaire.

encyclical [ɪn'sɪklɪkl] RELIG ◇ *adj* encyclique.
◇ *n* encyclique *f*.

encyclopaedia *etc* [ɪn,saɪklə'pi:djə] = **encyclopedia**.

encyclopedia [ɪn,saɪklə'pi:djə] *n* encyclopédie *f*.

encyclopedic [ɪn,saɪkləʊ'pi:dɪk] *adj* encyclopédique.

end [end] ◇ *n* **1.** [furthermost part, tip, edge] bout *m* ■ **at the ~ of the garden** au bout *OR* fond du jardin ■ **at either ~ of the political spectrum** aux deux extrémités de l'éventail politique ■ **third from the ~** troisième en partant de la fin ■ **the deep/shallow ~** le grand/petit bain ■ **to change ~s** SPORT changer de côté ▌ [area, aspect] côté *m* ■ **the marketing/manufacturing ~ of the operation** le côté marketing/fabrication de l'opération, tout ce qui est marketing/fabrication ▶ **this is the ~ of the road** *OR* **line** c'est fini ■ **to go to the ~s of the earth** aller jusqu'au bout du monde ■ **to keep one's ~ of the bargain** tenir parole ■ **to keep one's ~ up** tenir bon ■ **he doesn't know** *OR* **can't tell one ~ of a word processor from the other** il ne sait même pas à quoi ressemble un traitement de texte ■ **to make (both) ~s meet** [financially] joindre les deux bouts
2. [conclusion, finish] fin *f* ■ **from beginning to ~** du début à la fin, de bout en bout ■ **to be at an ~** être terminé *OR* fini ■ **my patience is at** *OR* **has come to an ~** ma patience est à bout ■ **to bring sthg to an ~** [meeting] clore qqch ; [situation] mettre fin à qqch ; [speech] achever qqch ■ **to come to an ~** s'achever, prendre fin ■ **to draw to an ~** arriver *OR* toucher à sa fin ■ **to put an ~ to sthg** mettre fin à qqch ■ **we want an ~ to the war** nous voulons que cette guerre cesse *OR* prenne fin ■ **and that was the ~ of that** et ça s'est terminé comme ça ▶ **he's/you're the ~!** *inf* [impossible] il est/tu es incroyable! ; [extremely funny] il est/tu es trop (drôle) ! ■ **~ of story!** *inf* [stop arguing] plus de discussions! ; [I don't want to talk about it] un point, c'est tout! ■ **it's not the ~ of the world** *inf* ce n'est pas la fin du monde ■ **we'll never hear the ~ of it** on n'a pas fini d'en entendre parler ■ **is there no ~ to his talents?** a-t-il donc tous les talents?, n'y a-t-il pas de limite à ses talents?
3. [aim] but *m*, fin *f* ■ **to achieve** *OR* **to attain one's ~** atteindre son but ■ **with this ~ in view** *OR* **mind, to this ~** dans ce but, à cette fin ▶ **an ~ in itself** une fin en soi ■ **the ~ justifies the means** la fin justifie les moyens
4. [remnant - of cloth, rope] bout *m* ; [- of loaf] croûton *m*
5. *euph* & *lit* [death] mort *f* ■ **I was with him at the ~** j'étais auprès de lui dans ses derniers moments.
◇ *comp* [house, seat, table] du bout.
◇ *vt* [speech, novel] terminer, conclure ■ [meeting, discussion] clore ■ [day] terminer, finir ■ [war, speculation, relationship]

mettre fin OR un terme à ■ [work] terminer, finir, achever ■ **the war to ~ all wars** la dernière de toutes les guerres ➋ **he decided to ~ it all** [life, relationship] il décida d'en finir.
◇ *vi* [story, film] finir, se terminer, s'achever ■ [path, road etc] se terminer, s'arrêter ■ [season, holiday] se terminer, toucher à sa fin ■ **how** OR **where will it all ~?** comment tout cela finira-t-il OR se terminera-t-il? ■ **where does society ~ and the individual begin?** où s'arrête la société et où commence l'individu? ■ **the discussion ~ed in an argument** la discussion s'est terminée en dispute ■ **to ~ in failure/divorce** se solder par un échec/un divorce ■ **the word ~s in -ed** le mot se termine par OR en -ed ➋ **it'll ~ in tears** ça va mal finir.
◆ **at the end of the day** *adv phr liter* à la fin de la journée ■ *fig* au bout du compte, en fin de compte.
◆ **end on** *adv phr* par le bout.
◆ **end to end** *adv phr* **1.** [with ends adjacent] bout à bout **2.** = **from end to end**.
◆ **from end to end** *adv phr* d'un bout à l'autre.
◆ **in the end** *adv phr* finalement ■ **we got there in the ~** finalement nous y sommes arrivés, nous avons fini par y arriver.
◆ **no end** *adv phr inf* **it upset her/cheered her up no ~** ça l'a bouleversée/ravie à un point (inimaginable).
◆ **no end of** *det phr inf* **it'll do you no ~ of good** cela vous fera un bien fou ■ **to have no ~ of trouble doing sthg** avoir énormément de mal OR un mal fou OR un mal de chien à faire qqch ■ **we met no ~ of interesting people** on a rencontré des tas de gens intéressants.
◆ **on end** *adv phr* **1.** [upright] debout ■ **her hair was standing on ~** elle avait les cheveux dressés sur la tête **2.** [in succession] entier ■ **for hours/days on ~** pendant des heures entières/des jours entiers.
◆ **end off** *vt sep* terminer.
◆ **end up** *vi insep* finir ■ **they ~ed up in Manchester** ils se sont retrouvés à Manchester ■ **to ~ up in hospital/in prison** finir à l'hôpital/en prison ■ **to ~ up doing sthg** finir par faire qqch ■ **I wonder what he'll ~ up as/how he'll ~ up** je me demande ce qu'il deviendra/comment il finira.

end-all ▻ **be-all**.

endanger [ɪn'deɪndʒəʳ] *vt* [life, country] mettre en danger ■ [health, reputation, future, chances] compromettre.

endangered species [ɪn'deɪndʒəd-] *n* espèce *f* en voie de disparition.

endear [ɪn'dɪəʳ] *vt* faire aimer ■ **what ~s him to me** ce qui le rend cher à mes yeux ■ **to ~ o.s. to sb** se faire aimer de qqn ■ **the Chancellor's decision did not ~ him to the voters** la décision du chancelier ne lui a pas gagné la faveur des électeurs.

endearing [ɪn'dɪərɪŋ] *adj* [personality, person] attachant ■ [smile] engageant.

endearingly [ɪn'dɪərɪŋlɪ] *adv* de manière attachante ■ [smile] de manière engageante.

endearment [ɪn'dɪəmənt] *n* : **~s, words of ~** mots *mpl* tendres ■ **term of ~** terme *m* affectueux.

endeavour *UK*, **endeavor** *US* [ɪn'devəʳ] *fml* ◇ *n* effort *m* ■ **to make every ~ to obtain sthg** faire tout son possible pour obtenir qqch ■ **to use one's best ~s to do sthg** employer tous ses efforts à faire qqch ■ **a new field of human ~** une nouvelle perspective pour l'homme.
◇ *vi* : **to ~ to do sthg** s'efforcer OR essayer de faire qqch.

endemic [en'demɪk] MED ◇ *adj* endémique.
◇ *n* endémie *f*.

endgame ['endgeɪm] *n* CHESS fin *f* de partie ■ **'Endgame'** ***Beckett*** 'Fin de partie'.

ending ['endɪŋ] *n* **1.** [of story, book] fin *f* ■ **a story with a happy/sad ~** une histoire qui finit bien/mal **2.** LING terminaison *f*.

endive ['endaɪv] *n* **1.** [curly-leaved] (chicorée *f*) frisée *f* **2.** *esp US* [chicory] endive *f*.

endless ['endlɪs] *adj* **1.** [speech, road, job] interminable, sans fin ■ [patience] sans bornes, infini ■ [resources] inépuisable, infini **2.** TECH [belt, screw] sans fin.

endlessly ['endlɪslɪ] *adv* [speak] continuellement, sans cesse ■ [extend] à perte de vue, interminablement ■ **to be ~ patient/generous** être d'une patience/générosité sans bornes.

endmost ['endməʊst] *adj* du bout.

endocarp ['endə phˋₒ₋'kɑ:p] *n* endocarpe *m*.

endocrine ['endəʊkraɪn] *adj* PHYSIOL [disorders, system] endocrinien ■ **~ gland** glande *f* endocrine.

endocrinology [,endəʊkraɪ'nɒlədʒɪ] *n* MED endocrinologie *f*.

endorphin [en'dɔ:fɪn] *n* MED endorphine *f*.

endorse [ɪn'dɔ:s] *vt* **1.** [cheque] endosser ■ [document - sign] apposer sa signature sur ; [- annotate] apposer une remarque sur **2.** *UK* LAW : **to ~ a driving licence** faire état d'une infraction sur un permis de conduire **3.** [approve - action, decision] approuver ; [- opinion] soutenir, adhérer à ; [- appeal, candidature] appuyer ■ **sportswear ~d by top athletes** vêtements de sport adoptés par les athlètes de haut niveau.

endorsement [ɪn'dɔ:smənt] *n* **1.** [of cheque] endossement *m* ■ [of document - signature] signature *f* ; [- annotation] remarque *f* **2.** *UK* LAW [on driving licence] *infraction dont il est fait état sur le permis de conduire* **3.** [approval - of action, decision] approbation *f* ; [- of claim, candidature] appui *m* ■ **it was the ultimate ~ of his ideas** ce fut la reconnaissance ultime OR la consécration de sa théorie.

endoscope ['endəskəʊp] *n* MED endoscope *m*.

endoscopy [en'dɒskəpɪ] *n* MED endoscopie *f*.

endow [ɪn'daʊ] *vt* **1.** [institution] doter ■ [university chair, hospital ward] fonder ■ **to ~ a hospice with £1 million** doter un hospice d'un million de livres **2.** *(usu passive)* **to be ~ed with sthg** être doté de qqch.

endowment [ɪn'daʊmənt] *n* **1.** [action, money] dotation *f* **2.** *(usu pl)* *fml* [talent, gift] don *m*, talent *m*.

endowment assurance, endowment insurance *n* assurance *f* à capital différé.

endowment mortgage *n hypothèque garantie par une assurance-vie*.

endowment policy *n* assurance *f* mixte.

endpaper ['end,peɪpə] *n* garde *f*, page *f* de garde.

end product *n* INDUST & COMM produit *m* final ■ *fig* résultat *m*.

end result *n* résultat *m* final.

endurable [ɪn'djʊərəbl] *adj* supportable, endurable.

endurance [ɪn'djʊərəns] ◇ *n* endurance *f* ■ **powers of ~** endurance ■ **it is beyond ~** c'est insupportable.
◇ *comp* : **~ test** épreuve *f* d'endurance.

endure [ɪn'djʊəʳ] ◇ *vt* [bear - hardship] endurer, subir ; [- pain] endurer ; [- person, stupidity, laziness] supporter, souffrir.
◇ *vi fml* [relationship, ceasefire, fame] durer ■ [memory] rester.

enduring [ɪn'djʊərɪŋ] *adj* [friendship, fame, peace] durable ■ [democracy, dictatorship] qui dure ■ [epidemic, suffering] tenace ■ [actor, politician] qui jouit d'une grande longévité *(en tant qu'acteur, homme politique, etc.)*

end user *n* [gen - COMPUT] utilisateur *m* final.

endways ['endweɪz] *adv* : **put it ~ on** mets-le en long ■ **put them ~ on** mets-les bout à bout.

enema ['enɪmə] *n* [act] lavement *m* ■ [liquid] produit *m* à lavement.

enemy ['enɪmɪ] (*pl* **enemies**) ◇ *n* **1.** ennemi *m*, - e *f* ■ **to make enemies** se faire des ennemis ■ **I made an ~ of her** je m'en suis fait une ennemie ■ **to be one's own worst ~** se nuire à soi-même **2.** MIL : **the ~ was** OR **were advancing** l'ennemi avançait ■ **boredom is the ~** voilà l'ennemi.

◇ *comp* [forces, attack, missile, country] ennemi ■ [advance, strategy] de l'ennemi ■ **~ alien** ressortissant *m*, - e *f* d'un pays ennemi ■ **~ fire** feu *m* de l'ennemi ■ **~-occupied territory** territoire *m* occupé par l'ennemi.

energetic [ˌenəˈdʒetɪk] *adj* [person, measures] énergique ■ [music] vif, rapide ■ [campaigner, supporter] enthousiaste ■ **to feel ~** se sentir d'attaque *OR* en forme ■ **do you feel ~ enough for a game of tennis?** te sens-tu d'attaque pour une partie de tennis?

energetically [ˌenəˈdʒetɪklɪ] *adv* énergiquement.

energize [ˈenədʒaɪz] *vt* [person] donner de l'énergie à, stimuler ■ ELEC exciter, envoyer de l'électricité dans.

energy [ˈenədʒɪ] ◇ *n* (*pl* **energies**) **1.** [vitality] énergie *f* ■ **to be/to feel full of ~** être/se sentir plein d'énergie ■ **to have no ~** se sentir sans énergie ■ **she didn't have the ~ for an argument** elle n'avait pas assez d'énergie pour se disputer ■ **glucose is full of ~** le glucose est très énergétique **2.** [effort] énergie *f* ■ **to devote** *OR* **to apply (all) one's ~** *OR* **energies to sthg** consacrer toute son énergie *OR* toutes ses énergies à qqch **3.** PHYS énergie *f* **4.** [power] énergie *f* ■ **to save** *OR* **to conserve ~** faire des économies d'énergie ➔ **Minister of** *OR* **Secretary (of State) for Energy** ministre *m* de l'Énergie.
◇ *comp* [conservation, consumption] d'énergie ■ [supplies, programme, level] énergétique ■ **~ crisis** crise *f* énergétique *OR* de l'énergie.

enervate [ˈenəveɪt] *vt* amollir, débiliter.

enervating [ˈenəveɪtɪŋ] *adj* amollissant, débilitant.

enfeeble [ɪnˈfiːbl] *vt* affaiblir.

enfold [ɪnˈfəʊld] *vt* [embrace] étreindre ■ **to ~ sb in one's arms** étreindre qqn, entourer qqn de ses bras.

enforce [ɪnˈfɔːs] *vt* [policy, decision] mettre en œuvre, appliquer ■ [law] mettre en vigueur ■ [subj: police] faire exécuter ■ [one's rights] faire valoir ■ [one's will, discipline] faire respecter ■ [contract] faire exécuter ■ **to ~ obedience** se faire obéir.

enforceable [ɪnˈfɔːsəbl] *adj* exécutoire.

enforced [ɪnˈfɔːst] *adj* forcé.

enforcement [ɪnˈfɔːsmənt] *n* [of law] application *f* ■ [of contract] exécution *f*.

enfranchise [ɪnˈfræntʃaɪz] *vt* [give vote to - women, workers] accorder le droit de vote à ■ [emancipate - slaves] affranchir.

engage [ɪnˈgeɪdʒ] ◇ *vt* **1.** [occupy, involve] : **to ~ sb in conversation** [talk to] discuter avec qqn ; [begin talking to] engager la conversation avec qqn **2.** *fml* [employ - staff] engager ; [- lawyer] engager les services de **3.** *fml* [attract, draw - interest, attention] attirer ; [- sympathy] susciter **4.** AUT & TECH engager ■ **to ~ the clutch** embrayer **5.** MIL : **to ~ the enemy** engager (le combat avec) l'ennemi.
◇ *vi* **1.** [take part] : **to ~ in** prendre part à ■ **to ~ in conversation** discuter **2.** MIL : **to ~ in battle with the enemy** engager le combat avec l'ennemi **3.** AUT & TECH s'engager ■ [cogs] s'engrener ■ [machine part] s'enclencher **4.** *fml* [promise] : **to ~ to do sthg** s'engager à faire qqch.

engaged [ɪnˈgeɪdʒd] *adj* **1.** [of couple] fiancé ■ **to be ~ to be married** être fiancé ■ **to get ~** se fiancer ■ **the ~ couple** les fiancés *mpl* **2.** [busy, occupied] occupé ■ **I'm otherwise ~** je suis déjà pris ■ **to be ~ in discussions with sb** être engagé dans des discussions avec qqn ■ **to be ~ in a conversation** être en pleine discussion **3.** *UK* [telephone] occupé ■ **I got the ~ tone** ça sonnait occupé **4.** [toilet] occupé.

engagement [ɪnˈgeɪdʒmənt] *n* **1.** [betrothal] fiançailles *fpl* **2.** [appointment] rendez-vous *m* ■ **he couldn't come, owing to a prior** *OR* **previous ~** il n'a pas pu venir car il était déjà pris **3.** MIL engagement *m* **4.** AUT & TECH engagement *m* **5.** [recruitment] engagement *m*, embauche *f* **6.** *fml* [promise, duty] obligation *f*, engagement *m* **7.** [for actor, performer] engagement *m*, contrat *m*.

engagement ring *n* bague *f* de fiançailles.

engaging [ɪnˈgeɪdʒɪŋ] *adj* [smile, manner, tone] engageant ■ [person, personality] aimable, attachant.

engender [ɪnˈdʒendəʳ] *vt* engendrer, créer ■ **to ~ sthg in sb** engendrer qqch chez qqn.

engine [ˈendʒɪn] ◇ *n* [in car, plane] moteur *m* ■ [in ship] machine *f* ■ **(railway) ~** *UK* locomotive *f* ■ **to sit with one's back to the ~** être assis dans le sens opposé à *OR* inverse de la marche ■ **to sit facing the ~** être assis dans le sens de la marche.
◇ *comp* [failure, trouble] de moteur *OR* machine ■ **~ block** AUT bloc-moteur *m* ■ **~ oil** AUT huile *f* à *OR* de moteur.

engine driver *n UK* RAIL mécanicien *m*, conducteur *m*.

engineer [ˌendʒɪˈnɪəʳ] ◇ *n* **1.** [for roads, machines, bridges] ingénieur *m* ■ [repairer] dépanneur *m*, réparateur *m* ■ [technician] technicien *m*, - enne *f* ■ MIL soldat *m* du génie ■ NAUT mécanicien *m* ■ **aircraft ~** AERON mécanicien *m* de piste *OR* d'avion ■ **flight ~** AERON ingénieur *m* de vol, mécanicien *m* naviguant ■ **the Royal Engineers** MIL le génie *(britannique)* **2.** *US* RAIL = **engine driver 3.** *fig* [of plot, scheme etc] instigateur *m*, - trice *f*, artisan *m*.
◇ *vt* **1.** [road, bridge, car] concevoir **2.** *pej* [bring about - event, situation] manigancer **3.** [work - goal, victory] amener.

engineering [ˌendʒɪˈnɪərɪŋ] ◇ *n* ingénierie *f*, engineering *m* ■ **to study ~** faire des études d'ingénieur ■ **an incredible feat of ~** une merveille de la technique.
◇ *comp* : **~ department** service *m* technique ■ **~ and design department** bureau *m* d'études ■ **~ firm** entreprise *f* de construction mécanique ■ **~ work** [on railway line] travail *m* d'ingénierie.

engine room *n* NAUT salle *f* des machines.

engine shed *n* RAIL dépôt *m*.

England [ˈɪŋglənd] *pr n* Angleterre *f* ■ **to live in ~** habiter l'Angleterre *OR* en Angleterre ■ **to go to ~** aller en Angleterre ■ **the ~ team** SPORT l'équipe d'Angleterre.

English [ˈɪŋglɪʃ] ◇ *adj* anglais ■ [history, embassy] d'Angleterre ■ [dictionary, teacher] d'anglais.
◇ *n* LING anglais *m* ■ **to study ~** étudier *OR* apprendre l'anglais ■ **she speaks excellent ~** elle parle très bien (l')anglais ■ **we spoke (in) ~ to each other** nous nous sommes parlé en anglais ■ **that's not good ~** ce n'est pas du bon anglais ■ **in plain** *OR* **simple ~** clairement ➔ **~ as a Foreign Language** anglais langue étrangère ■ **~ Language Teaching** enseignement *m* de l'anglais ■ **the King's** *OR* **Queen's ~** l'anglais correct ■ **~ as a Second Language** anglais deuxième langue.
◇ *npl* : **the ~** les Anglais *mpl*.

English breakfast *n* petit déjeuner *m* anglais *OR* à l'anglaise, breakfast *m*.

ENGLISH BREAKFAST

Le petit déjeuner traditionnel anglais se compose d'un plat chaud (œufs au bacon, saucisses, etc.), de céréales ou de porridge, et de toasts, le tout accompagné de café ou de thé ; il est aujourd'hui souvent remplacé par une collation plus légère.

English Channel *pr n* : **the ~** la Manche.

English Heritage *pr n organisme britannique de protection du patrimoine historique*.

English horn *n US* cor *m* anglais.

Englishman [ˈɪŋglɪʃmən] (*pl* **Englishmen** [-mən]) *n* Anglais *m* ■ **an ~'s home is his castle** *prov* charbonnier est maître dans sa maison *prov*.

English muffin *n US sorte de gaufre*.

English rose *n* femme *f* au charme anglais, beauté *f* britannique.

English speaker *n* [as native speaker] anglophone *mf* ■ [as non-native speaker] personne *f* parlant anglais.

English-speaking *adj* [as native language] anglophone ■ [as learned language] parlant anglais.

Englishwoman [ˈɪŋglɪʃˌwʊmən] (*pl* **Englishwomen** [-ˌwɪmɪn]) *n* Anglaise *f*.

engrave [ɪn'greɪv] *vt* graver ■ **~d on** *OR* **in her memory** gravé dans sa mémoire.

engraver [ɪn'greɪvəʳ] *n* graveur *m*.

engraving [ɪn'greɪvɪŋ] *n* gravure *f*.

engross [ɪn'grəʊs] *vt* [absorb] absorber.

engrossed [ɪn'grəʊst] *adj* : **to be ~ in sthg** être absorbé par qqch ■ **to be ~ in a book** être absorbé *OR* plongé dans un livre ■ **I was so ~ in what I was doing** j'étais tellement absorbé par ce que je faisais.

engrossing [ɪn'grəʊsɪŋ] *adj* absorbant.

engulf [ɪn'gʌlf] *vt* engloutir ■ **to be ~ed by the sea/in flames** être englouti par la mer/les flammes.

enhance [ɪn'hɑ:ns] *vt* [quality, reputation, performance] améliorer ■ [value, chances, prestige] augmenter, accroître ■ [taste, beauty] rehausser, mettre en valeur.

enhanced [ɪn'hɑ:nst] *adj* [reputation, quality, performance] amélioré, meilleur ■ [prestige - value, chances] augmenté, accru ; [- taste, beauty] rehaussé, mis en valeur.

-enhanced *in cpds* : **computer~** [graphics] optimisé par ordinateur ■ **protein~** enrichi en protéines.

enhancement [ɪn'hɑ:nsmənt] *n* [of quality, reputation, performance] amélioration *f* ■ [of value, chances, prestige] augmentation *f*, accroissement *m* ■ [of taste, beauty] rehaussement *m*, mise *f* en valeur.

enigma [ɪ'nɪgmə] *n* énigme *f*.

enigmatic [,enɪg'mætɪk] *adj* énigmatique.

enigmatically [,enɪg'mætɪklɪ] *adv* [smile, speak] d'un air énigmatique ■ [worded] d'une manière énigmatique.

enjoin [ɪn'dʒɔɪn] *vt fml* **1.** [urge strongly] : **to ~ sb to do sthg** [urge] exhorter qqn à faire qqch, recommander fortement *OR* vivement à qqn de faire qqch ; [command] enjoindre *OR* ordonner à qqn de faire qqch ■ **to ~ sthg on sb** enjoindre qqch à qqn **2.** *US* [forbid] interdire à.

enjoy [ɪn'dʒɔɪ] <> *vt* **1.** [like - in general] aimer ; [- on particular occasion] apprécier ■ **to ~ sthg/doing sthg** aimer qqch/faire qqch ■ **to ~ life** aimer la vie ■ **I don't ~ being made fun of** je n'aime pas qu'on se moque de moi ■ **~ your meal!** bon appétit! ■ **did you ~ your meal, sir?** avez-vous bien mangé, monsieur? ■ **I ~ed that** [book, film] cela m'a plu ; [meal] je me suis régalé ■ **I thoroughly ~ed the weekend/party** j'ai passé un excellent week-end/une excellente soirée ■ **I'm really ~ing this fine weather** quel plaisir, ce beau temps ■ **to ~ o.s.** s'amuser ■ **~ yourselves!** amusez-vous bien! ■ **did you ~ yourself?** alors, c'était bien? **2.** [possess - rights, respect, privilege, income, good health] jouir de ■ [profits] bénéficier de.
<> *vi* : **~!** *US* [enjoy yourself] amusez-vous bien! ; [in restaurant] bon appétit!

enjoyable [ɪn'dʒɔɪəbl] *adj* [book, film, day] agréable ■ [match, contest] beau *(before vowel or silent 'h'* **bel**), belle *f* ■ [meal] excellent.

enjoyably [ɪn'dʒɔɪəblɪ] *adv* de manière agréable.

enjoyment [ɪn'dʒɔɪmənt] *n* **1.** [pleasure] plaisir *m* ■ **to get ~ from sthg/doing sthg** tirer du plaisir de qqch/à faire qqch ■ **to get ~ out of life** jouir de la vie **2.** [of privileges, rights etc] jouissance *f*.

enlarge [ɪn'lɑ:dʒ] <> *vt* **1.** [expand - territory, house, business] agrandir ; [- field of knowledge, group of friends] étendre, élargir ; [- hole] agrandir, élargir ; [- pores] dilater ■ MED [- organ] hypertrophier ■ **~d edition** édition *f* augmentée **2.** PHOT agrandir.
<> *vi* [gen] s'agrandir, se développer ■ [pores] se dilater ■ MED [organ] s'hypertrophier.
◆ **enlarge on, enlarge upon** *vt insep* [elaborate on] s'étendre sur, donner des détails sur.

enlargement [ɪn'lɑ:dʒmənt] *n* **1.** [of territory, house, business] agrandissement *m* ■ [of group of friends, field of knowledge] élargissement *m* ■ [of hole] agrandissement *m*, élargissement *m* ■ [of pore] dilatation *f* ■ MED [of organ] hypertrophie *f* **2.** PHOT agrandissement *m*.

enlighten [ɪn'laɪtn] *vt* éclairer ■ **to ~ sb about sthg/as to why...** éclairer qqn sur qqch/sur la raison pour laquelle...

enlightened [ɪn'laɪtnd] *adj* [person, view, policy] éclairé ■ **~ self-interest** magnanimité *f* intéressée.

enlightening [ɪn'laɪtnɪŋ] *adj* [book, experience] instructif ■ **the film was very ~ about the subject** le film en apprenait beaucoup sur le sujet.

enlightenment [ɪn'laɪtnmənt] *n* [explanation, information] éclaircissements *mpl* ■ [state] édification *f*, instruction *f*.
◆ **Enlightenment** *n* HIST : **the (Age of) Enlightenment** le Siècle des lumières.

enlist [ɪn'lɪst] *vt* **1.** MIL enrôler **2.** [help, support etc] mobiliser, faire appel à.

enlisted [ɪn'lɪstɪd] *adj US* **~ man** (simple) soldat *m*.

enlistment [ɪn'lɪstmənt] *n* MIL enrôlement *m*, engagement *m*.

enliven [ɪn'laɪvn] *vt* [conversation, party] animer.

en masse [ɑ̃'mæs] *adv* en masse, massivement.

enmesh [ɪn'meʃ] *vt liter* prendre dans un filet ■ *fig* mêler ■ **to become** *OR* **get ~ ed in sthg** s'empêtrer dans qqch.

enmity ['enmətɪ] (*pl* **enmities**) *n fml* inimitié *f*, hostilité *f* ■ **~ for/towards sb** inimitié pour/envers qqn.

ennoble [ɪ'nəʊbl] *vt* [confer title upon] anoblir ■ *fig* [exalt, dignify] ennoblir, grandir.

enology *etc* [i:'nɒlədʒɪ] *US* = **oenology**.

enormity [ɪ'nɔ:mətɪ] (*pl* **enormities**) *n* **1.** [of action, crime] énormité *f* **2.** *fml* [atrocity] atrocité *f* ■ [crime] crime *m* très grave **3.** [great size] énormité *f* ■ **they were aware of the ~ of the task ahead of them** ils se rendaient compte de l'énormité de la tâche qui les attendait.

enormous [ɪ'nɔ:məs] *adj* **1.** [very large - thing] énorme ; [- amount, number] énorme, colossal ■ **~ amounts of food** une quantité énorme *OR* énormément de vivres ■ **an ~ number of cars** une énorme quantité de voitures **2.** [as intensifier] énorme, grand ■ **it has given me ~ pleasure** cela m'a fait énormément plaisir.

enormously [ɪ'nɔ:məslɪ] *adv* énormément, extrêmement ■ **demand has increased ~** la demande a énormément augmenté ■ **it was ~ successful** ce fut extrêmement réussi.

enough [ɪ'nʌf] <> *det* assez de ■ **~ money** assez *OR* suffisamment d'argent ■ **you've had more than ~ wine** tu as bu plus qu'assez de vin ■ **the report is proof ~** le rapport est une preuve suffisante ■ **she's not fool ~ to believe that!** elle n'est pas assez bête pour le croire!
<> *pron* : **do you need some money? – I've got ~** avez-vous besoin d'argent? – j'en ai assez *OR* suffisamment ■ **we earn ~ to live on** nous gagnons de quoi vivre ■ **more than ~** plus qu'il n'en faut ▶ **~ is ~!** ça suffit comme ça!, trop c'est trop! ■ **~ said!** *inf* je vois! ■ **that's ~!** ça suffit! ■ **it's ~ to drive you mad** c'est à vous rendre fou ■ **I can't get ~ of his films** je ne me lasse jamais de ses films ■ **to have had ~ (of sthg)** en avoir assez de qqch.
<> *adv* **1.** [sufficiently] assez, suffisamment ■ **he's old ~ to understand** il est assez grand pour comprendre ■ **it's a good ~ reason** c'est une raison suffisante ■ **you know well ~ what I mean** vous savez très bien ce que je veux dire **2.** [fairly] assez ■ **she's honest ~** elle est assez honnête **3.** [with adverb] : **oddly** *OR* **strangely ~, nobody knows her** chose curieuse, personne ne la connaît.

en passant [ɑ̃'pæsɑ̃] *adv* en passant.

enquire [ɪn'kwaɪəʳ] = **inquire**.

enquiry [ɪn'kwaɪərɪ] (*pl* **enquiries**) *n* **1.** [request for information] demande *f* (de renseignements) ■ **we have received hundreds of enquiries** nous avons reçu des centaines de demandes de renseignements ▪ **to make enquiries about sthg** se renseigner sur qqch **2.** [investigation] enquête *f* ▪ **upon further ~** après vérification.

◆ **enquiries** *npl* [information desk, department] renseignements *mpl.*

enquiry desk, enquiry office *n* accueil *m.*

enrage [ɪn'reɪdʒ] *vt* rendre furieux, mettre en rage.

enraged [ɪn'reɪdʒd] *adj* [person] furieux ▪ [animal] enragé ▪ **he was ~ to discover that...** il enrageait de découvrir que...

enrapture [ɪn'ræptʃəʳ] *vt* enchanter, ravir ▪ **we were ~d by the beauty of the island** nous étions en extase devant la beauté de l'île.

enrich [ɪn'rɪtʃ] *vt* [mind, person, life] enrichir ▪ [soil] fertiliser, amender ▪ PHYS enrichir ▪ **breakfast cereals ~ed with vitamins** céréales enrichies en vitamines.

enriching [ɪn'rɪtʃɪŋ] *adj* enrichissant.

enrichment [ɪn'rɪtʃmənt] *n* [of mind, person, life] enrichissement *m* ▪ [of soil] fertilisation *f*, amendement *m* ▪ PHYS enrichissement *m.*

enrol *UK*, **enroll** *US* [ɪn'rəʊl] (*pret & pp* **enrolled**, *cont* **enrolling**) ◇ *vt* **1.** [student] inscrire, immatriculer ▪ [member] inscrire ▪ MIL [recruit] enrôler, recruter **2.** *US* POL [prepare] dresser, rédiger ▪ [register] enregistrer ▪ **~ed bill** projet *m* de loi enregistré.

◇ *vi* [student] s'inscrire ▪ MIL s'engager, s'enrôler ▪ **to ~ on** *OR* **for a course** s'inscrire à un cours.

enrolment *UK*, **enrollment** *US* [ɪn'rəʊlmənt] *n* [registration - of members] inscription *f* ; [- of students] inscription *f*, immatriculation *f* ; [- of workers] embauche *f* ▪ MIL enrôlement *m*, recrutement *m* ▪ **a school with an ~ of 300 students** une école avec un effectif de 300 élèves.

ensconce [ɪn'skɒns] *vt fml & hum* installer ▪ **she ~d herself/was ~d in the armchair** elle se cala/était bien calée dans le fauteuil.

ensemble [ɒn'sɒmbl] *n* [gen - MUS] ensemble *m.*

enshrine [ɪn'ʃraɪn] *vt liter* enchâsser ▪ *fig* [cherish] conserver pieusement *OR* religieusement ▪ **our fundamental rights are ~d in the constitution** nos droits fondamentaux font partie intégrante de la constitution.

ensign ['ensaɪn] *n* **1.** [flag] drapeau *m*, enseigne *f* ▪ NAUT pavillon *m* **2.** [symbol] insigne *m*, emblème *m* **3.** *UK* MIL (officier *m*) porte-étendard *m* **4.** *US* NAUT enseigne *m* de vaisseau de deuxième classe.

enslave [ɪn'sleɪv] *vt liter* réduire en esclavage, asservir ▪ *fig* asservir, captiver.

enslavement [ɪn'sleɪvmənt] *n liter* asservissement *m* ▪ *fig* sujétion *f*, asservissement *m.*

ensnare [ɪn'sneəʳ] *vt liter & fig* prendre au piège ▪ **~d by her charms** séduit par ses charmes.

ensue [ɪn'sjuː] *vi* s'ensuivre, résulter ▪ **the problems that have ~d from government cutbacks** les problèmes qui ont résulté des restrictions gouvernementales.

ensuing [ɪn'sjuːɪŋ] *adj* [action, event] qui s'ensuit ▪ [month, year] suivant.

en suite [,ɒn'swiːt] *adj & adv* : **with ~ bathroom, with bathroom ~** avec salle de bain particulière.

ensure [ɪn'ʃʊəʳ] *vt* **1.** [guarantee] assurer, garantir ▪ **I did everything I could to ~ that he would succeed** *OR* **to ~ his success** j'ai fait tout ce que j'ai pu pour m'assurer qu'il réussirait *OR* pour assurer son succès **2.** [protect] protéger, assurer.

ENT (*abbrev of* **ear, nose & throat**) ◇ *n* ORL *f.*

◇ *adj* ORL.

entail [ɪn'teɪl] *vt* **1.** [imply - consequence, expense] entraîner ; [- difficulty, risk] comporter ; [- delay, expense] occasionner ▪ LOGIC entraîner ▪ **starting a new job often ~s a lot of work** prendre un nouveau poste exige souvent *OR* nécessite souvent beaucoup de travail **2.** LAW : **to ~ an estate** substituer un héritage ▪ **an ~ed estate** un bien grevé.

entangle [ɪn'tæŋgl] *vt* **1.** [ensnare] empêtrer, enchevêtrer ▪ **to become** *OR* **get ~d in sthg** s'empêtrer dans qqch **2.** [snarl - hair] emmêler ; [- threads] emmêler, embrouiller **3.** *fig* [involve] entraîner, impliquer ▪ **she got ~d in the dispute** elle s'est retrouvée impliquée dans la dispute.

entanglement [ɪn'tæŋglmənt] *n* **1.** [in net, undergrowth] enchevêtrement *m* **2.** [of hair, thread] emmêlement *m* **3.** *fig* [involvement] implication *f* ▪ **emotional ~s** complications *fpl* sentimentales.

entente [ɒn'tɒnt] *n* entente *f.*

enter ['entəʳ] ◇ *vt* **1.** [go into - room] entrer dans ; [- building] entrer dans, pénétrer dans ▪ **the ship ~ed the harbour** le navire est entré au *OR* dans le port ▪ **where the bullet ~ed the body** l'endroit où la balle a pénétré le corps ▪ **the war ~ed a new phase** la guerre est entrée dans une phase nouvelle ▪ **the thought never ~ed my head** l'idée ne m'est jamais venue à l'esprit **2.** [join - university] s'inscrire à, se faire inscrire à ; [- profession] entrer dans ; [- army] s'engager *OR* entrer dans ; [- politics] se lancer dans ▪ **to ~ the church** entrer dans les ordres **3.** [register] inscrire ▪ **the school ~ed the pupils for the exam/in the competition** l'école a présenté les élèves à l'examen/au concours ▪ **to ~ a horse for a race** engager *OR* inscrire un cheval dans une course **4.** [record - on list] inscrire ; [- in book] noter ▪ COMPUT [data] entrer, introduire ▪ **he ~ed the figures in the ledger** il a porté les chiffres sur le livre de comptes **5.** [submit] présenter ▪ **to ~ a protest** protester officiellement ▪ **to ~ an appeal** LAW interjeter appel.

◇ *vi* **1.** [come in] entrer ▪ **~ Juliet** THEAT entre Juliette **2.** [register] s'inscrire ▪ **she ~ed for the race/for the exam** elle s'est inscrite pour la course/à l'examen.

◆ **enter into** *vt insep* **1.** [begin - explanation] se lancer dans ; [- conversation, relations] entrer en ; [- negotiations] entamer **2.** [become involved in] : **to ~ into an agreement with sb** conclure un accord avec qqn ▪ **I ~ed into the spirit of the game** *fig* je suis entré dans le jeu **3.** [affect] entrer dans ▪ **my feelings don't ~ into my decision** mes sentiments n'ont rien à voir avec *OR* ne sont pour rien dans ma décision.

◆ **enter up** *vt sep* [amount] inscrire, porter.

◆ **enter upon** *vt insep* **1.** [career] débuter *OR* entrer dans ▪ [negotiations] entamer ▪ [policy] commencer **2.** LAW [inheritance] prendre possession de.

enteritis [,entə'raɪtɪs] *n (U)* entérite *f.*

enter key *n* COMPUT (touche *f*) entrée *f*, retour *m* chariot.

enterprise ['entəpraɪz] *n* **1.** [business, project] entreprise *f* **2.** [initiative] initiative *f*, esprit *m* entreprenant *OR* d'initiative.

enterprise culture *n expression évoquant le libéralisme et l'esprit d'entreprise de la société britannique des années 80.*

enterprise zone *n UK zone d'encouragement à l'implantation d'entreprises dans les régions économiquement défavorisées.*

enterprising ['entəpraɪzɪŋ] *adj* [person] entreprenant, plein d'initiative ▪ [project] audacieux, hardi.

entertain [,entə'teɪn] ◇ *vt* **1.** [amuse] amuser, divertir ▪ **I ~ed them with a story** je leur ai raconté une histoire pour les distraire *OR* amuser **2.** [show hospitality towards] recevoir ▪ **he ~ed them to dinner** [at restaurant] il leur a offert le dîner ; [at home] il les a reçus à dîner **3.** [idea] considérer, penser à ▪ [hope] caresser, nourrir ▪ [doubt] entretenir ▪ [suggestion] admettre ▪ **I refused to ~ such a suggestion** j'ai refusé d'admettre pareille suggestion.

◇ *vi* recevoir ▪ **we ~ quite often** nous recevons (du monde) assez souvent.

entertainer [,entə'teɪnəʳ] *n* [comedian] comique *m*, amuseur *m*, - euse *f* ▪ [in music hall] artiste *mf* (de music-hall), fantaisiste *mf* ▪ **a well-known television ~** un artiste de télévision bien connu.

entertaining [,entə'teɪnɪŋ] ◇ *n* : **she enjoys ~** elle aime bien recevoir ▪ **they do a lot of business ~** ils donnent pas mal de réceptions d'affaires.

◇ *adj* amusant, divertissant.

entertainment [ˌentəˈteɪnmənt] *n* **1.** [amusement] amusement *m*, divertissement *m* ■ **this film is** *OR* **provides good family ~** ce film est un bon divertissement familial ▶ **~ allowance** frais *mpl* de représentation **2.** [performance] spectacle *m*, attraction *f* ■ **musical ~s will be provided** des attractions musicales sont prévues.

enthral *UK*, **enthrall** *US* [ɪnˈθrɔːl] (*pret & pp* **enthralled**, *cont* **enthralling**) *vt* [fascinate] captiver, passionner ■ **she was ~ed by the idea** elle était séduite par l'idée.

enthralling [ɪnˈθrɔːlɪŋ] *adj* [book, film] captivant, passionnant ■ [beauty, charm] séduisant.

enthrone [ɪnˈθrəʊn] *vt* [monarch] mettre sur le trône, introniser ■ [bishop] introniser.

enthronement [ɪnˈθrəʊnmənt] *n* intronisation *f*.

enthuse [ɪnˈθjuːz] ◇ *vi* s'enthousiasmer ■ **she ~d over the plan** elle parlait du projet avec beaucoup d'enthousiasme.
◇ *vt* enthousiasmer, emballer.

enthusiasm [ɪnˈθjuːzɪæzm] *n* **1.** [interest] enthousiasme *m* ■ **the discovery has aroused** *OR* **stirred up considerable ~ among historians** la découverte a suscité un grand enthousiasme chez les historiens **2.** [hobby] passion *f*.

enthusiast [ɪnˈθjuːzɪæst] *n* enthousiaste *mf*, fervent *m*, - e *f* ■ **football ~s** passionnés *mpl* de football.

enthusiastic [ɪnˌθjuːzɪˈæstɪk] *adj* [person, response] enthousiaste ■ [shout, applause] enthousiaste, d'enthousiasme ■ **they gave me an ~ welcome** ils m'ont accueilli chaleureusement ■ **she's very ~ about the project** elle est très enthousiaste à l'idée de ce projet ■ **to be ~ about a suggestion** accueillir une proposition avec enthousiasme.

enthusiastically [ɪnˌθjuːzɪˈæstɪklɪ] *adv* [receive] avec enthousiasme ■ [speak, support] avec enthousiasme *OR* ferveur ■ [work] avec zèle.

entice [ɪnˈtaɪs] *vt* attirer, séduire ■ **to ~ sb away from sthg** éloigner qqn de qqch ■ **I managed to ~ him away from the television** j'ai réussi à l'arracher à la télévision ■ **~d by their offer** alléché *OR* attiré par leur proposition.

enticement [ɪnˈtaɪsmənt] *n* **1.** [attraction] attrait *m*, appât *m* **2.** [act] séduction *f*.

enticing [ɪnˈtaɪsɪŋ] *adj* [offer] attrayant, séduisant ■ [person] séduisant ■ [food] alléchant, appétissant.

enticingly [ɪnˈtaɪsɪŋlɪ] *adv* de façon séduisante ■ **delicious smells wafted ~ from the kitchen** de délicieuses odeurs de cuisine mettaient l'eau à la bouche.

entire [ɪnˈtaɪəʳ] *adj* **1.** [whole] entier, tout ■ **my ~ life** toute ma vie, ma vie entière ■ **the ~ world** le monde entier **2.** [total] entier, complet, - ète *f* ■ [absolute] total, absolu ■ **she has my ~ support** elle peut compter sur mon soutien sans réserve **3.** [intact] entier, intact.

entirely [ɪnˈtaɪəlɪ] *adv* entièrement, totalement ■ **I agree with you ~** je suis entièrement d'accord avec vous ■ **that's ~ unnecessary** c'est absolument inutile.

entirety [ɪnˈtaɪrətɪ] (*pl* **entireties**) *n* **1.** [completeness] intégralité *f* ■ **in its ~** en (son) entier, intégralement **2.** [total] totalité *f*.

entitle [ɪnˈtaɪtl] *vt* **1.** [give right to] autoriser ■ **the results ~ them to believe that...** les résultats les autorisent à croire que... ■ **his disability ~s him to a pension** son infirmité lui donne droit à une pension ■ **to be ~d to do sthg** [by status] avoir qualité pour *OR* être habilité à faire qqch ; [by rules] avoir le droit *OR* être en droit de faire qqch ■ **you're ~d to your own opinion but...** vous avez le droit d'avoir votre avis mais... ■ **you're quite ~d to say that...** vous pouvez dire à juste titre que... ■ **to be ~d to vote** avoir le droit de vote ‖ LAW habiliter ■ **to be ~d to act** être habilité à agir **2.** [film, painting etc] intituler ■ **the book is ~d...** le livre s'intitule... **3.** [bestow title on] donner un titre à.

entitlement [ɪnˈtaɪtlmənt] *n* droit *m* ■ **~ to social security** droit à la sécurité sociale.

entity [ˈentətɪ] (*pl* **entities**) *n* entité *f* ■ **legal ~** personne *f* morale.

entomb [ɪnˈtuːm] *vt liter* mettre au tombeau, ensevelir ■ *fig* ensevelir.

entomological [ˌentəməˈlɒdʒɪkl] *adj* entomologique.

entomologist [ˌentəˈmɒlədʒɪst] *n* entomologiste *mf*.

entomology [ˌentəˈmɒlədʒɪ] *n* entomologie *f*.

entourage [ˌɒntʊˈrɑːʒ] *n* entourage *m*.

entrails [ˈentreɪlz] *npl liter & fig* entrailles *fpl*.

entrain [ɪnˈtreɪn] ◇ *vi fml* monter dans un train.
◇ *vt* **1.** *fml* [person] embarquer dans un train **2.** [subj: liquid, gas] entraîner.

entrance[1] [ˈentrəns] ◇ *n* **1.** [means of entry] entrée *f* ■ [large] portail *m* ■ [foyer] entrée *f*, vestibule *m* ■ **the ~ to the store** l'entrée du magasin **2.** [arrival] entrée *f* ■ **to make an ~** [gen] faire une entrée ; THEAT entrer en scène **3.** [admission] admission *f* ■ **to gain ~ to** [club, profession, college etc] être admis à **4.** [access] accès *m*, admission *f* ■ **the police gained ~ to the building from the back** la police a accédé au bâtiment par derrière.
◇ *comp* [card, ticket] d'entrée, d'admission ■ **~ examination** [for school] examen *m* d'entrée ; [for job] concours *m* de recrutement ■ **~ requirements** qualifications *fpl* exigées à l'entrée.

entrance[2] [ɪnˈtrɑːns] *vt* **1.** [hypnotize] hypnotiser, faire entrer en transe **2.** *fig* [delight] ravir, enchanter ■ **she was ~d by the beauty of the place** elle était en extase devant la beauté de l'endroit.

entrance fee [ˈentrəns-] *n* [to exhibition, fair etc] droit *m* d'entrée ■ *UK* [to club, organization etc] droit *m OR* frais *mpl* d'inscription.

entrance hall [ˈentrəns-] *n* [in house] vestibule *m* ■ [in hotel] hall *m*.

entrance ramp [ˈentrəns-] *n US* bretelle *f* d'accès.

entrancing [ɪnˈtrɑːnsɪŋ] *adj* enchanteur, ravissant.

entrancingly [ɪnˈtrɑːnsɪŋlɪ] *adv* [smile] de façon ravissante *OR* séduisante ■ [dance, sing] à ravir.

entrant [ˈentrənt] *n* **1.** [in exam] candidat *m*, - e *f* ■ [in race] concurrent *m*, - e *f*, participant *m*, - e *f* ■ **all ~s for the exam/competition** tous les candidats à l'examen/participants à la compétition **2.** [to profession, society] débutant *m*, - e *f* ■ **a training course for (new) ~s to the profession** un cours de formation pour ceux qui débutent dans la profession.

entrap [ɪnˈtræp] (*pret & pp* **entrapped**, *cont* **entrapping**) *vt fml* prendre au piège.

entrapment [ɪnˈtræpmənt] *n incitation au délit par un policier afin de justifier une arrestation.*

entreat [ɪnˈtriːt] *vt fml* implorer, supplier ■ **to ~ sb to do sthg** supplier qqn de faire qqch ■ **I ~ you to help me** je vous supplie de m'aider.

entreaty [ɪnˈtriːtɪ] (*pl* **entreaties**) *n fml* supplication *f*, prière *f* ■ **a look of ~** un regard suppliant.

entrée [ˈɒntreɪ] *n* **1.** [right of entry] entrée *f* **2.** CULIN [course preceding main dish] entrée *f* ■ *US* [main dish] plat *m* principal *OR* de résistance.

entrench [ɪnˈtrentʃ] *vt* MIL retrancher.

entrenched [ɪnˈtrentʃt] *adj* **1.** MIL retranché **2.** *fig* [person] inflexible, inébranlable ■ [idea] arrêté ■ [power, tradition] implanté ■ **attitudes that are firmly ~ in our society** des attitudes qui sont fermement ancrées dans notre société.

entrepreneur [ˌɒntrəprəˈnɜːʳ] *n* entrepreneur *m (homme d'affaires)*.

entrepreneurial [ˌɒntrəprəˈnɜːrɪəl] *adj* [spirit, attitude] d'entrepreneur ■ [society, person] qui a l'esprit d'entreprise ■ [skills] d'entrepreneur.

entropy [ˈentrəpɪ] *n* entropie *f*.

entrust [ɪn'trʌst] *vt* confier ▪ **to ~ sthg to sb** confier qqch à qqn ▪ **to ~ sb with a job** charger qqn d'une tâche, confier une tâche à qqn.

entry ['entrɪ] (*pl* **entries**) <> *n* **1.** [way in] entrée *f* ▪ [larger] portail *m* **2.** [act] entrée *f* ▪ **to make an ~** [gen] faire une entrée ; THEAT entrer en scène **3.** [admission] entrée *f*, accès *m* ▪ **this ticket gives you free ~ to the exhibition** ce billet te donne le droit d'entrer gratuitement à l'exposition ▪ **she was refused ~ to the country** on lui a refusé l'entrée dans le pays ▪ **'no ~'** [on door] 'défense d'entrer', 'entrée interdite' ; [in street] 'sens interdit' **4.** [in dictionary] entrée *f* ▪ [in diary] notation *f* ▪ [in encyclopedia] article *m* ▪ [on list] inscription *f* ▪ COMPUT [of data] entrée (des données) ▪ [in account book, ledger] écriture *f* ▪ **an ~ in the log** NAUT un élément du journal de bord **5.** [competitor] inscription *f* ▪ [item submitted for competition] participant *m*, - e *f*, concurrent *m*, - e *f* **6.** *(U)* [number of entrants] taux *m* de participation ▪ **the ~ is down this year** [in competition] le taux de participation est en baisse cette année ; [in exam] les candidats sont moins nombreux cette année ; [at school, university] le nombre d'inscriptions a baissé cette année.
<> *comp* [fee, form] d'inscription.

entryism ['entrɪɪzm] *n* POL entrisme *m*, noyautage *m*.

Entryphone® ['entrɪ,fəʊn] *n* Interphone® *m (à l'entrée d'un immeuble ou de bureaux)*.

entryway ['entrɪ,weɪ] *n* US entrée *f* ▪ [larger] portail *m* ▪ [foyer] foyer *m*, vestibule *m*.

entwine [ɪn'twaɪn] *vt* entrelacer ▪ **the ivy had become ~d** OR **had ~d itself around the trellis** le lierre s'était entortillé autour du treillis.

E number *n* UK *inf* additif *m* code E.

enumerate [ɪ'nju:məreɪt] *vt* énumérer, dénombrer.

enumeration [ɪ,nju:mə'reɪʃn] *n* énumération *f*, dénombrement *m*.

enunciate [ɪ'nʌnsɪeɪt] <> *vt* **1.** [articulate] articuler, prononcer **2.** *fml* [formulate - idea, theory, policy] énoncer, exprimer.
<> *vi* articuler.

enunciation [ɪ,nʌnsɪ'eɪʃn] *n* **1.** [of sound, word] articulation *f*, prononciation *f* **2.** *fml* [of theory] énonciation *f*, exposition *f* ▪ [of problem] énoncé *m*.

enuresis [,enjʊə'ri:sɪs] *n* énurésie *f*.

envelop [ɪn'veləp] *vt* envelopper ▪ **~ed in mystery** entouré OR voilé de mystère ▪ **~ed in mist** voilé de brume.

envelope ['envələʊp] *n* **1.** [for letter] enveloppe *f* ▪ **put the letter in an ~** mettez la lettre sous enveloppe ▪ **in a sealed ~** sous pli cacheté ▪ **they came in the same ~** ils sont arrivés dans le même pli **2.** BIOL enveloppe *f*, tunique *f* ▪ MATHS enveloppe *f* ▪ ELECTRON enveloppe *f* **3.** [of balloon] enveloppe *f*.

enviable ['envɪəbl] *adj* enviable.

envious ['envɪəs] *adj* [person] envieux, jaloux ▪ [look, tone] envieux, d'envie ▪ **she's ~ of their new house** elle est envieuse de leur nouvelle maison ▪ **I am very ~ of you!** comme je t'envie!

enviously ['envɪəslɪ] *adv* avec envie.

environment [ɪn'vaɪərənmənt] *n* **1.** ECOL & POL [nature] environnement *m* ▪ **the Secretary of State for the Environment** ≃ le ministre de l'Environnement **2.** [surroundings - physical] cadre *m*, milieu *m* ; [- social] milieu *m*, environnement *m* ; [- psychological] milieu *m*, ambiance *f* ▪ BIOL, BOT & GEOG milieu *m* ▪ LING & COMPUT environnement *m* ▪ **the novel examines the effect of ~ on character** le roman étudie les effets du milieu ambiant sur le caractère ▪ **a pleasant working ~** des conditions de travail agréables.

environmental [ɪn,vaɪərən'mentl] *adj* **1.** ECOL & POL écologique ➤ **Environmental Protection Agency** US Agence *f* pour la protection de l'environnement ▪ **~ science/studies** science *f* /études *fpl* de l'environnement **2.** [of surroundings] du milieu.

Environmental Heath Officer *n* UK inspecteur *m* sanitaire.

environmentalism [ɪn,vaɪərən'mentəlɪzm] *n* **1.** ECOL étude *f* de l'environnement **2.** PSYCHOL environnementalisme *m*.

environmentalist [ɪn,vaɪərən'mentəlɪst] *n* **1.** ECOL écologiste *mf* **2.** PSYCHOL environnementaliste *mf*.

environmentally [ɪn,vaɪərən'mentəlɪ] *adv* ECOL écologiquement.

environment-friendly, environmentally friendly *adj* [policy] respectueux de l'environnement ▪ [product] non polluant.

environs [ɪn'vaɪərənz] *npl fml* environs *mpl*, alentours *mpl*.

envisage [ɪn'vɪzɪdʒ] *vt* [imagine] envisager ▪ [predict] prévoir ▪ **I don't ~ (that there will be) any difficulty** je n'envisage pas (qu'il puisse y avoir) la moindre difficulté.

envision [ɪn'vɪʒn] US = **envisage**.

envoy ['envɔɪ] *n* **1.** [emissary] envoyé *m*, - e *f*, représentant *m*, - e *f* ▪ **~ (extraordinary)** POL ministre *m* plénipotentiaire **2.** LIT envoi *m*.

envy ['envɪ] (*pl* **envies**, *pret & pp* **envied**) <> *n* **1.** [jealousy] envie *f*, jalousie *f* ▪ **out of ~** par envie OR jalousie ▪ **filled with ~** dévoré de jalousie **2.** [object of jealousy] objet *m* d'envie ▪ **she was the ~ of all her friends** elle excitait OR faisait l'envie de tous ses amis.
<> *vt* envier ▪ **I do ~ her** je l'envie vraiment ▪ **I ~ him his success** je lui envie son succès.

enzyme ['enzaɪm] *n* enzyme *f*.

EOC *pr n* = **Equal Opportunities Commission**.

Eocene ['i:əʊsi:n] *adj* éocène.

eolith ['i:əʊlɪθ] *n* éolithe *m*.

eon ['i:ən] US = **aeon**.

eosin(e) ['i:əʊsɪn] *n* éosine *f*.

Eozoic [,i:əʊ'zəʊɪk] *adj* précambrien.

EP (*abbrev of* **extended play**) *n* **1.** super 45 tours *m*, EP *m* **2.** = **European Plan**.

EPA *pr n* = **Environmental Protection Agency**.

epaulette UK, **epaulet** US [,epə'let] *n* [gen - MIL] épaulette *f*.

ephemera [ɪ'femərə] (*pl* **ephemeras** OR *pl* **ephemerae** [-,ri:]) *n* **1.** ZOOL éphémère *m* **2.** [short-lived thing] chose *f* éphémère.

ephemeral [ɪ'femərəl] *adj* [short-lived] éphémère, fugitif ▪ ZOOL éphémère.

epic ['epɪk] <> *adj* **1.** [impressive] héroïque, épique ▪ *hum* épique, homérique **2.** LIT épique.
<> *n* **1.** LIT épopée *f*, poème *m* OR récit *m* épique **2.** [film] film *m* à grand spectacle.

epicarp ['epɪ,kɑ:p] *n* épicarpe *m*.

epicene ['epɪsi:n] *adj* **1.** [hermaphrodite] hermaphrodite ▪ [sexless] asexué **2.** [effeminate] efféminé **3.** GRAM épicène.

epicentre UK, **epicenter** US ['epɪsentəʳ] *n* épicentre *m*.

epicure ['epɪ,kjʊəʳ] *n lit* gourmet *m*, gastronome *mf*.

epicurean [,epɪkjʊə'ri:ən] <> *adj* [gen] épicurien.
<> *n* **1.** [gen] épicurien *m*, - enne *f* **2.** [gourmet] gourmet *m*, gastronome *mf*.
◆ **Epicurean** PHILOS <> *adj* épicurien.
<> *n* épicurien *m*, - enne *f*.

epicyclic [,epɪ'saɪklɪk] *adj* épicycloïdal.

epidemic [,epɪ'demɪk] *liter & fig* <> *n* épidémie *f*.
<> *adj* épidémique ▪ **of ~ proportions** qui prend les proportions d'une épidémie.

epidemiology ['epɪ,di:mɪ'ɒlədʒɪ] *n* épidémiologie *f*.

epidermis [,epɪ'dɜ:mɪs] *n* épiderme *m*.

epidiascope [,epɪ'daɪəskəʊp] *n* épidiascope *m*.

epidural [ˌepɪ'djʊərəl] ◇ *adj* épidural.
◇ *n* anesthésie *f* épidurale, péridurale *f*.

epifocal [ˌepɪ'fəʊkl] *adj* épicentral.

epigenesis [ˌepɪ'dʒenɪsɪs] *n* BIOL épigenèse *f* ■ GEOL épigénie *f*.

epiglottis [ˌepɪ'glɒtɪs] (*pl* **epiglottises** *OR pl* **epiglotides** [-tɪˌdiːz]) *n* épiglotte *f*.

epigram ['epɪgræm] *n* épigramme *f*.

epigrammatic [ˌepɪgrə'mætɪk] *adj* épigrammatique.

epigraph ['epɪgrɑːf] *n* épigraphe *f*.

epilepsy ['epɪlepsɪ] *n* épilepsie *f*.

epileptic [ˌepɪ'leptɪk] ◇ *adj* épileptique ■ **an ~ fit** une crise d'épilepsie.
◇ *n* épileptique *mf*.

epilog *US*, **epilogue** ['epɪlɒg] *n* épilogue *m*.

epinephrine [ˌepɪ'nefrɪn] *n US* adrénaline *f*.

Epiphany [ɪ'pɪfənɪ] *n* Épiphanie *f*, fête *f* des rois.

episcopal [ɪ'pɪskəpl] *adj* épiscopal.

Episcopal Church *n* : **the ~** l'Église *f* épiscopale.

episcopalian [ɪˌpɪskəʊ'peɪljən] ◇ *adj* épiscopal, épiscopalien.
◇ *n* épiscopalien *m*, - enne *f*.

episcopate [ɪ'pɪskəpət] *n* épiscopat *m*.

episcope ['epɪskəʊp] *n UK* épiscope *m*.

episiotomy [ɪˌpɪzɪ'ɒtəmɪ] (*pl* **episiotomies**) *n* épisiotomie *f*.

episode ['epɪsəʊd] *n* [period, event] épisode *m* ■ [part of story] épisode *m*.

episodic [ˌepɪ'sɒdɪk] *adj* épisodique.

epistemology [eˌpɪstiː'mɒlədʒɪ] *n* épistémologie *f*.

epistle [ɪ'pɪsl] *n* **1.** *fml* & *hum* [letter] lettre *f*, épître *f hum* ■ ADMIN courrier *m* **2.** LIT épître *f*.
◆ **Epistle** *n* BIBLE : **the Epistle to the Romans** l'Épître *f* aux Romains.

epistolary [ɪ'pɪstələrɪ] *adj fml* épistolaire.

epitaph ['epɪtɑːf] *n* épitaphe *f*.

epithet ['epɪθet] *n* épithète *f*.

epitome [ɪ'pɪtəmɪ] *n* **1.** [typical example] modèle *m*, type *m OR* exemple *m* même ■ **she's the ~ of generosity** elle est l'exemple même de la générosité *OR* la générosité même **2.** [of book] abrégé *m*, résumé *m*.

epitomize, ise [ɪ'pɪtəmaɪz] *vt* **1.** [typify] personnifier, incarner ■ **this latest announcement ~s the government's attitude towards education** cette dernière déclaration est caractéristique de l'attitude du gouvernement concernant l'éducation **2.** [book] abréger, résumer.

EPNS (*abbrev of* **electroplated nickel silver**) *n* rudz *m*.

epoch ['iːpɒk] *n* époque *f* ■ **the discovery marked a new ~ in the history of science** cette découverte a fait date dans l'histoire de la science.

epoch-making *adj* qui fait époque, qui fait date.

eponym ['epəʊnɪm] *n* éponyme *m*.

eponymous [ɪ'pɒnɪməs] *adj* du même nom, éponyme.

epoxy [ɪ'pɒksɪ] (*pl* **epoxies**) ◇ *adj* CHEM [function, group] époxy *(inv)*.
◇ *n* époxyde *m*.

EPROM ['iːprɒm] (*abbrev of* **erasable programmable read only memory**) *n* mémoire *f* morte effaçable.

Epsom salts ['epsəm] *npl* sel *m* d'Epsom, epsomite *f*.

EQ [iː'kjuː] (*abbrev of* **emotional intelligence quotient**) *n* QE *m*, quotient *m* émotionnel.

equable ['ekwəbl] *adj* [character, person] égal, placide ■ [climate] égal, constant.

equably ['ekwəblɪ] *adv* tranquillement, placidement.

equal ['iːkwəl] (*UK pret & pp* **equalled**, *cont* **equalling**) (*US pret & pp* **equaled**, *cont* **equaling**) ◇ *adj* **1.** [of same size, amount, degree, type] égal ■ **~ in number** égal en nombre ■ **~ in size to an orange** d'une taille égale à une orange ■ **to be ~ to sthg** égaler qqch ■ **mix ~ parts of sand and cement** mélangez du sable et du ciment en parts égales ■ **she speaks French and German with ~ ease** elle parle français et allemand avec la même facilité ■ **to be on an ~ footing with sb** être sur un pied d'égalité avec qqn ■ **to meet/to talk to sb on ~ terms** rencontrer qqn/parler à qqn d'égal à égal ■ **other** *OR* **all things being ~** toutes choses égales par ailleurs ◉ **~ ops** *inf*, **~ opportunities** chances *fpl* égales, égalité *f* des chances ■ **~ opportunity employer** *entreprise s'engageant à respecter la législation sur la non-discrimination dans l'emploi* ■ **~ pay for ~ work** à travail égal salaire égal ■ **~ rights** égalité des droits ■ **Equal Rights Amendment** = **ERA** ■ **~ time** RADIO & TV droit *m* de réponse **2.** [adequate] : **~ to** : **he proved ~ to the task** il s'est montré à la hauteur de la tâche ■ **to feel ~ to doing sthg** se sentir le courage de faire qqch.
◇ *n* égal *m*, - e *f*, pair *m* ■ **to talk to sb as an ~** parler à qqn d'égal à égal ■ **we worked together as ~s** nous avons travaillé ensemble sur un pied d'égalité ■ **he has no ~** il est hors pair, il n'a pas son pareil.
◇ *vt* **1.** [gen - MATHS] égaler ■ **2 and 2 ~ (s) 4** 2 et 2 égalent *OR* font 4 ■ **let x ~ y** si x égale y **2.** [match] égaler ■ **there is nothing to ~ it** il n'y a rien de comparable *OR* de tel ■ **his arrogance is only equalled by his vulgarity** son arrogance n'a d'égale que sa vulgarité.

equality [iː'kwɒlətɪ] (*pl* **equalities**) *n* égalité *f* ■ **~ of opportunity** égalité des chances ■ **the Equality State** le Wyoming.

equalization [ˌiːkwəlaɪ'zeɪʃn] *n* [gen] égalisation *f* ■ ELECTRON régularisation *f* ■ FIN péréquation *f*.

equalize, ise ['iːkwəlaɪz] ◇ *vt* [chances] égaliser ■ [taxes, wealth] faire la péréquation de.
◇ *vi* SPORT égaliser.

equalizer ['iːkwəlaɪzər] *n* **1.** SPORT but *m OR* point *m* égalisateur **2.** ELECTRON égaliseur *m*.

equally ['iːkwəlɪ] *adv* **1.** [evenly] également ■ **divided ~** divisé en parts *OR* parties égales **2.** [to same degree] également, aussi ■ **~ well** tout aussi bien ■ **~ talented students** élèves également *OR* pareillement doués **3.** [by the same token] : **efficiency is important, but ~ we must consider the welfare of the staff** l'efficacité, c'est important, mais nous devons tout autant considérer le bien-être du personnel.

Equal Opportunities Commission *pr n* commission *f* pour l'égalité des chances *(en Grande-Bretagne)*.

equal sign, equals sign *n* signe *m* d'égalité *OR* d'équivalence.

equanimity [ˌekwə'nɪmətɪ] *n fml* sérénité *f*, équanimité *f lit*.

equatable [ɪ'kweɪtəbl] *adj* comparable, assimilable.

equate [ɪ'kweɪt] *vt* **1.** [regard as equivalent] assimiler, mettre sur le même pied ■ **some people wrongly ~ culture with elitism** certaines personnes assimilent à tort culture et élitisme **2.** [make equal] égaler, égaliser ■ **our aim is to ~ exports and imports** notre but est d'amener au même niveau les exportations et les importations ■ **to ~ sthg to sthg** MATHS mettre qqch en équation avec qqch.

equation [ɪ'kweɪʒn] *n* **1.** *fml* [association] assimilation *f* **2.** *fml* [equalization] égalisation *f* **3.** CHEM & MATHS équation *f*.

equator [ɪ'kweɪtər] *n* équateur *m* ■ **at** *OR* **on the ~** sous *OR* à l'équateur.

equatorial [ˌekwə'tɔːrɪəl] *adj* équatorial.

Equatorial Guinea *pr n* Guinée-Équatoriale *f* ■ **in ~** en Guinée-Équatoriale.

equerry ['ekwərɪ] (*pl* **equerries**) *n UK* [of household] intendant *m*, - e *f (de la maison du roi, de la reine)* ■ [of stable] écuyer *m*, - ère *f*.

equestrian [ɪ'kwestrɪən] ◇ *adj* [event] hippique ■ [skills] équestre ■ [statue] équestre ■ [equipment, clothing] d'équitation.
◇ *n* [rider] cavalier *m*, - ère *f* ■ [in circus - MIL] écuyer *m*, - ère *f*.

equestrianism [ɪ'kwestrɪənɪzm] *n* équitation *f*, hippisme *m*.

equidistant [,i:kwɪ'dɪstənt] *adj* équidistant, à distance égale.

equilateral [,i:kwɪ'lætərəl] *adj* équilatéral ■ **~ triangle** triangle *m* équilatéral.

equilibrium [,i:kwɪ'lɪbrɪəm] *n* équilibre *m* ■ **in ~** en équilibre ■ **she lost her ~** elle a perdu l'équilibre.

equine ['ekwaɪn] *adj* [disease, family] équin ■ [profile] chevalin.

equinox ['i:kwɪnɒks] *n* équinoxe *m* ■ **spring** *OR* **vernal ~** équinoxe de printemps, point *m* vernal.

equip [ɪ'kwɪp] (*pret & pp* **equipped**, *cont* **equipping**) *vt* **1.** [fit out - factory] équiper, outiller ; [- laboratory, kitchen] installer, équiper ; [- army, ship] équiper ■ **the hospital is not equipped to perform heart surgery** l'hôpital n'est pas équipé pour pratiquer la chirurgie du cœur **2.** *fig* [prepare] : **to be well-equipped to do sthg** avoir tout ce qu'il faut pour faire qqch ■ **it won't ~ her for life's hardships** cela ne la préparera pas à affronter les épreuves de la vie ■ **he is ill-equipped to handle the situation** il est mal armé pour faire face à la situation **3.** [supply - person] équiper, pourvoir ; [- army, machine, factory] équiper, munir ■ **the fighter plane is equipped with the latest technology** l'avion de combat est doté des équipements les plus modernes ■ **she equipped herself for the hike with a tent and a sleeping bag** elle s'est munie pour la randonnée d'une tente et d'un sac de couchage ■ **if your computer is equipped with a hard disk** si votre ordinateur est pourvu d'un disque dur.

equipage ['ekwɪpɪdʒ] *n* [carriage - MIL] équipage *m*.

equipment [ɪ'kwɪpmənt] *n (U)* **1.** [gen] équipement *m* ■ [in laboratory, office, school] matériel *m* ■ MIL & SPORT équipement *m*, matériel *m* ■ **camping ~** matériel de camping ■ **electrical ~** appareillage *m* électrique ■ **kitchen ~** ustensiles *mpl* de cuisine **2.** [act] équipement *m*.

equitable ['ekwɪtəbl] *adj* équitable, juste.

equitably ['ekwɪtəblɪ] *adv* équitablement, avec justice.

equity ['ekwətɪ] (*pl* **equities**) *n* **1.** [fairness] équité *f* **2.** LAW [system] équité *f* ■ [right] droit *m* équitable **3.** FIN [market value] fonds *mpl OR* capitaux *mpl* propres ■ [share] action *f* ordinaire.

◆ **Equity** *pr n principal syndicat britannique des gens du spectacle.*

equivalence [ɪ'kwɪvələns] *n* équivalence *f*.

equivalent [ɪ'kwɪvələnt] ◇ *adj* équivalent ■ **to be ~ to sthg** être équivalent à qqch, équivaloir à qqch.
◇ *n* équivalent *m* ■ **the French ~ for** *OR* **of "pound"** l'équivalent français du mot " pound " ■ **it costs the ~ of £5 per week** cela coûte l'équivalent de 5 livres par semaine.

equivocal [ɪ'kwɪvəkl] *adj* **1.** [ambiguous - words, attitude] ambigu, - uë *f*, équivoque **2.** [dubious - behaviour, person] suspect, douteux ; [- outcome] incertain, douteux.

equivocally [ɪ'kwɪvəklɪ] *adv* **1.** [ambiguously] de manière équivoque *OR* ambiguë **2.** [dubiously] de manière douteuse.

equivocate [ɪ'kwɪvəkeɪt] *vi fml* user d'équivoques *OR* de faux-fuyants, équivoquer *lit*.

equivocation [ɪ,kwɪvə'keɪʃn] *n (U) fml* [words] paroles *fpl* équivoques ■ [prevarication] tergiversation *f*.

er [3:ʳ] *interj* heu.

ER (*written abbrev of* **Elizabeth Regina**) *emblème de la reine Élisabeth.*

era ['ɪərə] *n* [gen] époque *f* ■ GEOL & HIST ère *f* ■ **her election marked a new ~ in politics** son élection a marqué un tournant dans la vie politique.

ERA ['ɪərə] (*abbrev of* **Equal Rights Amendment**) *n projet de loi américain rejeté en 1982 qui posait comme principe l'égalité des individus quels que soient leur sexe, leur religion ou leur race.*

eradicate [ɪ'rædɪkeɪt] *vt* [disease] éradiquer, faire disparaître ■ [poverty, problem] faire disparaître, supprimer ■ [abuse, crime] extirper, supprimer ■ [practice] bannir, mettre fin à ■ [weeds] détruire.

eradication [ɪ,rædɪ'keɪʃn] *n* [of disease] éradication *f* ■ [of poverty, problem] suppression *f* ■ [of abuse, crime] extirpation *f*, suppression *f* ■ [of practice] fin *f* ■ [of weeds] destruction *f*.

erase [ɪ'reɪz] ◇ *vt* [writing] effacer, gratter ■ [with rubber] gommer ■ *fig* & COMPUT effacer.
◇ *vi* s'effacer.

erase head *n* tête *f* d'effacement.

eraser [ɪ'reɪzəʳ] *n* gomme *f*.

erasing [ɪ'reɪzɪŋ] *n* effacement *m*.

Erasmus [ɪ'ræzməs] *pr n* Érasme.

erasure [ɪ'reɪʒəʳ] *n* **1.** [act] effacement *m*, grattage *m* **2.** [mark] rature *f*, grattage *m*.

ere [eəʳ] ◇ *prep lit* avant ■ **~ long** sous peu ■ **~ now, ~ this** déjà, auparavant.
◇ *conj arch & lit* avant que.

erect [ɪ'rekt] ◇ *adj* **1.** [upright] droit ■ [standing] debout ■ **she holds herself very ~** elle se tient bien droite **2.** PHYSIOL [penis, nipples] dur.
◇ *vt* **1.** [build - building, wall] bâtir, construire ; [- statue, temple] ériger, élever ; [- equipment] installer ; [- roadblock, tent] dresser **2.** *fig* [system] édifier ■ [obstacle] élever.

erectile [ɪ'rektaɪl] *adj* érectile.

erection [ɪ'rekʃn] *n* **1.** [of building, wall] construction *f* ■ [of statue, temple] érection *f* ■ [of equipment] installation *f* ■ [of roadblock, tent] dressage *m* ■ *fig* [of system, obstacle] édification *f* **2.** [building] bâtiment *m*, construction *f* **3.** PHYSIOL érection *f* ■ **to have** *OR* **to get an ~** avoir une érection.

erector [ɪ'rektəʳ] *n* **1.** [muscle] érecteur *m* **2.** [builder] constructeur *m*, - trice *f* ■ **~ set** *US* jeu *m* de construction.

ergative ['3:gətɪv] ◇ *adj* ergatif.
◇ *n* ergatif *m*.

ergo ['3:gəʊ] *adv fml & hum* donc, par conséquent.

ergonomic [,3:gəʊ'nɒmɪk] *adj* ergonomique.

ergonomically [,3:gəʊ'nɒmɪkəlɪ] *adv* du point de vue ergonomique.

ergonomics [,3:gə'nɒmɪks] *n (U)* ergonomie *f*.

Erie ['ɪərɪ] *pr n* : **Lake ~** le lac Érié.

ERISA [ə'ri:sə] (*abbrev of* **Employee Retirement Income Security Act**) *n loi américaine sur les pensions de retraite.*

Eritrea [,erɪ'treɪə] *pr n* Érythrée *f* ■ **in ~** en Érythrée.

Eritrean [,erɪ'treɪən] ◇ *n* Érythréen *m*, - enne *f*.
◇ *adj* érythréen.

ERM (*abbrev of* **exchange rate mechanism**) *n* mécanisme *m* de change (du SME).

ermine ['3:mɪn] *n* [fur, robe, stoat] hermine *f*.

Ernie ['3:nɪ] (*abbrev of* **Electronic Random Number Indicator Equipment**) *n en Grande-Bretagne, ordinateur qui sert au tirage des numéros gagnants des bons à lots.*

erode [ɪ'rəʊd] ◇ *vt* [subj: water, wind] éroder, ronger ■ [subj: acid, rust] ronger, corroder ■ *fig* [courage, power] ronger, miner ■ **the rock face had been ~d away** la paroi du rocher avait été érodée.
◇ *vi* [rock, soil] s'éroder.

erogenous [ɪ'rɒdʒɪnəs] *adj* érogène ■ **~ zone** zone *f* érogène.

Eros ['ɪərɒs] *pr n* **1.** MYTH Éros **2.** *UK surnom donné au monument en l'honneur du comte de Shaftesbury, à Piccadilly Circus.*

erosion [ɪ'rəʊʒn] *n* [of soil, rock] érosion *f* ■ [of metal] corrosion *f* ■ *fig* [of courage, power] érosion *f*, corrosion *f*.

erotic [ɪ'rɒtɪk] *adj* érotique.

erotica [ɪ'rɒtɪkə] *npl* ART art *m* érotique ■ LIT littérature *f* érotique.

erotically [ɪ'rɒtɪklɪ] *adv* érotiquement.

eroticism [ɪ'rɒtɪsɪzm] *n* érotisme *m*.

err [ɜːʳ] *vi fml* **1.** [make mistake] se tromper ■ **I ~ed on the side of caution** j'ai péché par excès de prudence ▶ **to ~ is human (to forgive divine)** *prov* l'erreur est humaine (le pardon divin) **2.** [sin] pécher, commettre une faute.

errand ['erənd] *n* commission *f*, course *f* ■ **to go on** *OR* **to do** *OR* **to run an ~ (for sb)** faire une course (pour qqn) ■ **an ~ of mercy** mission de charité.

errand boy *n* garçon *m* de courses.

errant ['erənt] *adj* **1.** [wayward] dévoyé **2.** [roaming] errant.

errata [e'rɑːtə] ◇ *pl* ▷ **erratum**.
◇ *npl* [list] errata *m inv*.

erratic [ɪ'rætɪk] *adj* **1.** [irregular - results] irrégulier ; [- performance] irrégulier, inégal ; [- person] fantasque, excentrique ; [- mood] changeant ; [- movement, course] mal assuré ■ **he is a bit ~** on ne sait jamais comment il va réagir **2.** GEOL & MED erratique.

erratically [ɪ'rætɪklɪ] *adv* [act, behave] de manière fantasque *OR* capricieuse ■ [move, work] irrégulièrement, par à-coups ■ **he drives ~** il conduit de façon déconcertante.

erratum [e'rɑːtəm] (*pl* **errata** [e'rɑːtə]) *n* erratum *m*.

erroneous [ɪ'rəʊnjəs] *adj* erroné, inexact.

erroneously [ɪ'rəʊnjəslɪ] *adv* erronément, à tort.

error ['erəʳ] *n* **1.** [mistake] erreur *f*, faute *f* ■ **to make** *OR* **to commit an ~** faire (une) erreur ■ **~s and omissions excepted** COMM sauf erreur ou omission **2.** MATHS [mistake] faute *f* ■ [deviation] écart *m* **3.** [mistakenness] erreur *f* ■ **it was done in ~** cela a été fait par erreur *OR* méprise ■ **I've seen the ~ of my ways** je suis revenu de mes erreurs.

error message *n* message *m* d'erreur.

ersatz ['eəzæts] ◇ *adj* : **this is ~ coffee** c'est de l'ersatz *OR* du succédané de café.
◇ *n* ersatz *m*, succédané *m*.

erstwhile ['ɜːstwaɪl] *lit & hum* ◇ *adj* d'autrefois.
◇ *adv* autrefois, jadis.

erudite ['eruːdaɪt] *adj* [book, person] érudit, savant ■ [word] savant.

erudition [ˌeruː'dɪʃn] *n* érudition *f*.

erupt [ɪ'rʌpt] *vi* **1.** [volcano - start] entrer en éruption ; [- continue] faire éruption ■ **an ~ing volcano** un volcan en éruption **2.** [pimples] sortir, apparaître ■ [tooth] percer ■ **her face ~ed in spots** elle a eu une éruption de boutons sur le visage **3.** *fig* [fire, laughter, war] éclater ■ [anger] exploser ■ **the city ~ed into violence** il y eut une explosion de violence dans la ville.

eruption [ɪ'rʌpʃn] *n* **1.** [of volcano] éruption *f* **2.** [of pimples] éruption *f*, poussée *f* ■ [of teeth] percée *f* **3.** *fig* [of laughter] éclat *m*, éruption *f* ■ [of anger] accès *m*, éruption *f* ■ [of violence] explosion *f*, accès *m*.

erysipelas [ˌerɪ'sɪpɪləs] *n* érysipèle *m*, érésipèle *m*.

ESA (*abbrev of* **European Space Agency**) *pr n* ESA *f*, ASE *f*.

escalate ['eskəleɪt] ◇ *vi* [fighting, war] s'intensifier ■ [prices] monter en flèche.
◇ *vt* [fighting] intensifier ■ [problem] aggraver ■ [prices] faire grimper.

escalation [ˌeskə'leɪʃn] *n* [of fighting, war] escalade *f*, intensification *f* ■ [of prices] escalade *f*, montée *f* en flèche.

escalator ['eskəleɪtəʳ] *n* escalier *m* roulant *OR* mécanique, escalator *m*.

escalator clause *n* clause *f* d'indexation *OR* de révision.

escalope ['eskəˌlɒp] *n* escalope *f*.

escapade [ˌeskə'peɪd] *n* [adventure] équipée *f* ■ [scrape] fredaine *f*, escapade *f* ■ [prank] frasque *f*.

escape [ɪ'skeɪp] ◇ *vi* **1.** [get away - person, animal] échapper, s'échapper ; [- prisoner] s'évader ■ **they ~d from the enemy/from the hands of their kidnappers** ils ont échappé à l'ennemi/des mains de leurs ravisseurs ■ **the thieves ~d after a police chase** les voleurs ont pris la fuite après avoir été poursuivis par la police ■ **she ~d from the camp** elle s'est échappée du camp ■ **he ~d to Italy** il s'est enfui en Italie **2.** [gas, liquid, steam] s'échapper, fuir **3.** [survive, avoid injury] s'en tirer, en réchapper ■ **she ~d uninjured** elle s'en est tirée sans aucun mal ■ **he ~d with a reprimand** il en a été quitte pour une réprimande.
◇ *vt* **1.** [avoid] échapper à ■ **to ~ doing sthg** éviter de faire qqch ■ **I narrowly ~d being killed** j'ai failli *OR* manqué me faire tuer ■ **he ~d detection** il ne s'est pas fait repérer ■ **there's no escaping the fact that...** il n'y a pas moyen d'échapper au fait que... **2.** [elude notice, memory of] échapper à ■ **her name ~s me** son nom m'échappe ■ **her blunder ~d notice** sa gaffe est passée inaperçue.
◇ *n* **1.** [of person] fuite *f*, évasion *f* ■ [of prisoner] évasion *f* ■ [of animal] fuite *f* ■ **I made my ~** je me suis échappé *OR* évadé ■ **he had a narrow ~** *fig* [from danger] il l'a échappé belle, il a eu chaud ; [from illness] il revient de loin **2.** [diversion] évasion *f* ■ **an ~ from reality** une évasion hors de la réalité **3.** [of gas, liquid] fuite *f* ■ [of exhaust fumes, steam] échappement *m*.
◇ *comp* [plot, route] d'évasion ■ [device] de sortie, de secours ■ **~ key** COMPUT touche *f* d'échappement.

escape clause *n* clause *f* échappatoire.

escaped [ɪ'skeɪpt] *adj* échappé ■ **an ~ prisoner** un évadé.

escapee [ɪˌskeɪ'piː] *n* évadé *m*, - e *f*.

escape hatch *n* trappe *f* de secours.

escape mechanism *n liter* mécanisme *m* de secours ■ PSYCHOL fuite *f* (devant la réalité).

escapement [ɪ'skeɪpmənt] *n* [of clock, piano] échappement *m* ■ MECH échappement *m*.

escape road *n* talus *m* de protection.

escape valve *n* soupape *f* d'échappement.

escape velocity *n* vitesse *f* de libération.

escapism [ɪ'skeɪpɪzm] *n* évasion *f* hors de la réalité, fuite *f* devant la réalité.

escapist [ɪ'skeɪpɪst] ◇ *n* personne *f* cherchant à s'évader du réel.
◇ *adj* d'évasion.

escapologist [ˌeskə'pɒlədʒɪst] *n virtuose de l'évasion dans les spectacles de magie.*

escarpment [ɪ'skɑːpmənt] *n* escarpement *m*.

eschatology [ˌeskə'tɒlədʒɪ] *n* eschatologie *f*.

eschew [ɪs'tʃuː] *vt fml* [duty, work, activity] éviter ■ [alcohol] s'abstenir de ■ [publicity, temptation, involvement] fuir.

escort ◇ *n* ['eskɔːt] **1.** [guard] escorte *f*, cortège *m* ■ MIL & NAUT escorte *f* ■ **under the ~ of** sous l'escorte de ■ **they were given a police ~** on leur a donné une escorte de police **2.** [consort - male] cavalier *m* ; [- female] hôtesse *f*.
◇ *comp* ['eskɔːt] d'escorte ■ **an ~ vessel** un bâtiment d'escorte, un (vaisseau) escorteur.
◇ *vt* [ɪ'skɔːt] *fml* accompagner, escorter ■ [police - MIL] escorter ■ **they ~ed him in/out** ils l'ont fait entrer/sortir sous escorte.

escort agency *n* service *m* *OR* bureau *m* d'hôtesses.

escrow ['eskrəʊ] *n* LAW dépôt *m* fiduciaire *OR* conditionnel ■ **in ~** en dépôt fiduciaire, en main tierce.

escutcheon [ɪ'skʌtʃn] *n* **1.** [shield] écu *m*, écusson *m* **2.** [on door, handle, light switch] écusson *m*.

ESE *written abbr of* **east-southeast**.

ESF [iːes'ef] (*abbrev of* **European Social Fund**) *n* FSE *m*.

e-shopping *n* achats *mpl* en ligne.

Eskimo ['eskɪməʊ] (*pl inv OR pl* **Eskimos**) ◇ *n* **1.** [person] Esquimau *m*, Esquimaude *f* **2.** LING esquimau *m*.
◇ *adj* esquimau.

ESKIMO

Aux États-Unis et au Canada, le terme *Eskimo* est souvent considéré comme dénigrant car il se traduit par « mangeur de viande crue » ; on lui préfère *Inuit*.

ESL (*abbrev of* **English as a Second Language**) *n anglais langue seconde.*

esophagus [iː'sɒfəgəs] (*pl* **esophagi** [-gaɪ]) *US* = **oesophagus**.

esoteric [,esə'terɪk] *adj* [obscure] ésotérique ■ [private] secret, - ète *f*.

esp. *written abbr of* **especially**.

ESP *n* **1.** (*abbrev of* **extrasensory perception**) perception *f* extrasensorielle **2.** (*abbrev of* **English for special purposes**) *anglais spécialisé.*

espadrille [,espə'drɪl] *n* espadrille *f*.

especial [ɪ'speʃl] *adj fml* [notable] particulier, exceptionnel ■ [specific] particulier.

especially [ɪ'speʃəlɪ] *adv* **1.** [to a particular degree] particulièrement, spécialement ■ [particularly] en particulier, surtout ■ **I can't mention it, ~ since** *OR* **as I'm not supposed to know anything about it** je ne peux pas en parler d'autant que *OR* surtout que je ne suis pas censé savoir quoi que ce soit à ce sujet ■ **you ~ ought to know better!** vous devriez le savoir mieux que personne! ■ **be ~ careful with this one** faites particulièrement attention à celui-ci **2.** [for a particular purpose] exprès ■ **he went ~ to meet her** il est allé exprès pour la rencontrer.

Esperanto [,espə'ræntəʊ] ◇ *n* espéranto *m*.
◇ *adj* en espéranto.

espionage ['espɪə,nɑːʒ] *n* espionnage *m*.

esplanade [,esplə'neɪd] *n* esplanade *f*.

espousal [ɪ'spaʊzl] *n fml* [of belief, cause] adoption *f*.

espouse [ɪ'spaʊz] *vt fml* [belief, cause] épouser, adopter.

espresso [e'spresəʊ] (*pl* **espressos**) *n* (café *m*) express *m* ■ **~ machine** machine *f* à express.

espy [ɪ'spaɪ] (*pret & pp* **espied**) *vt lit* apercevoir, distinguer.

Esq. (*written abbrev of* **esquire**) ■ **James Roberts, ~** M. James Roberts.

esquire [ɪ'skwaɪəʳ] *n UK* **1.** = **Esq 2.** HIST écuyer *m*.

essay ◇ *n* ['eseɪ] **1.** LIT essai *m* ■ SCH composition *f*, dissertation *f* ■ UNIV dissertation *f* ■ **'An Essay on Man'** ***Pope*** 'Essai sur l'homme' **2.** *fml* [attempt] essai *m*, tentative *f*.
◇ *vt* [e'seɪ] *fml* **1.** [try] essayer, tenter **2.** [test] mettre à l'épreuve.

essayist ['eseɪɪst] *n* essayiste *mf*.

essence ['esns] *n* **1.** [gen] essence *f*, essentiel *m* ■ **the ~ of her speech was that...** l'essentiel de son discours tenait en ceci que... ■ **time is of the ~** il est essentiel de faire vite, la vitesse s'impose **2.** PHILOS essence *f*, nature *f* ■ RELIG essence *f* **3.** CHEM essence *f* **4.** CULIN extrait *m*.

◆ **in essence** *adv phr* essentiellement, surtout.

essential [ɪ'senʃl] ◇ *adj* **1.** [vital - action, equipment, services] essentiel, indispensable ; [- point, role] essentiel, capital ; [- question] essentiel, fondamental ■ **it is ~ to know whether...** il est essentiel *OR* il importe de savoir si... ■ **the ~ thing is to relax** l'essentiel est de rester calme ■ **a balanced diet is ~ for good health** un régime équilibré est essentiel pour être en bonne santé ■ **~ goods** biens *m* de première nécessité **2.** [basic] essentiel, fondamental ■ **the ~ goodness of man** la bonté essentielle de l'homme ■ **~ oils** huiles *fpl* essentielles.
◇ *n* objet *m* indispensable ■ **the ~s** l'essentiel ■ **we can only afford to buy the ~s** nous n'avons les moyens d'acheter que l'essentiel ■ **the ~s of astronomy** les rudiments *mpl* de l'astronomie ■ **in (all) ~s** essentiellement.

essentially [ɪ'senʃəlɪ] *adv* [fundamentally] essentiellement, fondamentalement ■ [mainly] essentiellement, principalement ■ **it's ~ a question of taste** c'est avant tout une question de goût.

est. 1. *written abbr of* **established 2.** *written abbr of* **estimated**.

EST *n* = **Eastern Standard Time**.

establish [ɪ'stæblɪʃ] *vt* **1.** [create, set up - business] fonder, créer ; [- government] constituer, établir ; [- society, system] constituer ; [- factory] établir, monter ; [- contact] établir ; [- relations] établir, nouer ; [- custom, law] instaurer ; [- precedent] créer ; [- order, peace] faire régner **2.** [confirm - authority, power] affermir ; [- reputation] établir ■ **she has already ~ed her reputation as a physicist** elle s'est déjà fait une réputation de physicienne ■ **he ~ed himself as a computer consultant** il s'est établi conseiller en informatique **3.** [prove - identity, truth] établir ; [- cause, nature] déterminer, établir ; [- guilt, need] établir, prouver ; [- innocence] établir, démontrer ■ **it has been ~ed that there is no case against the defendant** il a été démontré qu'il n'y a pas lieu de poursuivre l'accusé.

established [ɪ'stæblɪʃt] *adj* **1.** [existing, solid - order, system] établi ; [- government] établi, au pouvoir ; [- business] établi, solide ; [- law] établi, en vigueur ; [- tradition] établi, enraciné ; [- reputation] établi, bien assis ■ **~ in 1890** COMM maison fondée en 1890 ■ **the ~ Church** l'Église *f* officielle **2.** [proven - fact] acquis, reconnu ; [- truth] établi, démontré.

establishment [ɪ'stæblɪʃmənt] *n* **1.** [of business] fondation *f*, création *f* ■ [of government] constitution *f* ■ [of society, system] constitution *f*, création *f* ■ [of law] instauration *f* **2.** [institution] établissement *m* ■ **a business ~** un établissement commercial, une firme **3.** [staff] personnel *m* ■ MIL & NAUT effectif *m*.

◆ **Establishment** *n* [ruling powers] : **the Establishment** les pouvoirs *mpl* établis, l'ordre *m* établi, l'establishment *m* ■ **the financial Establishment** ceux qui comptent dans le monde financier.

estate [ɪ'steɪt] *n* **1.** [land] propriété *f*, domaine *m* ■ **her country ~** ses terres *fpl* **2.** *UK* [development - housing] lotissement *m*, cité *f* ; [- trading] zone *f* commerciale **3.** LAW [property] biens *mpl*, fortune *f* ■ [of deceased] succession *f* ■ **she left a large ~** elle a laissé une grosse fortune (en héritage) **4.** *fml* [state, position] état *m*, rang *m* ■ **men of low/high ~** les hommes d'humble condition/de haut rang.

estate agency *n UK* agence *f* immobilière.

estate agent *n UK* **1.** [salesperson] agent *m* immobilier **2.** [manager] intendant *m*, régisseur *m*.

estate car *n UK* break *m*.

estate duty *n UK* droits *mpl* de succession.

estd., est'd. *written abbr of* **established**.

esteem [ɪ'stiːm] ◇ *vt* **1.** [respect - person] avoir de l'estime pour, estimer ; [- quality] estimer, apprécier **2.** *fml* [consider] estimer, considérer ■ **I ~ it a great honour** je m'estime très honoré.
◇ *n* estime *f*, considération *f* ■ **to hold sb/sthg in high ~** tenir qqn/qqch en haute estime.

esteemed [ɪ'stiːmd] *adj fml* estimé ■ **our ~ president** notre (très) estimé président.

esthete *etc* ['iːsθiːt] *US* = **aesthete**.

estimate ◇ *n* ['estɪmət] **1.** [evaluation] évaluation *f*, estimation *f* ■ **give me an ~ of how much you think it will cost** donnez-moi une idée du prix que cela coûtera, à votre avis ■ **at a rough ~** approximativement ■ **these figures are only a rough ~** ces chiffres ne sont que très approximatifs ■ **at the lowest ~ it will take five years** il faudra cinq ans au bas mot **2.** COMM [quote] devis *m* ■ **get several ~s before deciding who to employ** faites faire plusieurs devis avant de décider quelle entreprise choisir.
◇ *vt* ['estɪmeɪt] **1.** [calculate - cost, number] estimer, évaluer ; [- distance, speed] estimer, apprécier ■ **the cost was ~d at £2,000** le coût était évalué à 2 000 livres ■ **I ~ (that) it will take at least five years** à mon avis cela prendra au moins cinq ans, j'estime que cela prendra au moins cinq ans **2.** [judge] estimer, juger ■ **I don't ~ him very highly** je n'ai guère d'estime pour lui.

estimated [ˈestɪmeɪtɪd] *adj* estimé ■ **an ~ 50,000 people attended the demonstration** environ 50 000 personnes auraient manifesté ▶ **~d time of arrival/of departure** heure probable d'arrivée/de départ.

estimation [ˌestɪˈmeɪʃn] *n* **1.** [calculation] estimation *f*, évaluation *f* **2.** [judgment] jugement *m*, opinion *f* ■ **in my ~** à mon avis, selon moi **3.** [esteem] estime *f*, considération *f* ■ **he went down/up in my ~** il a baissé/monté dans mon estime.

Estonia [eˈstəʊnjə] *pr n* Estonie *f* ■ **in ~** en Estonie.

Estonian [eˈstəʊnjən] <> *n* **1.** [person] Estonien *m*, - enne *f* **2.** LING estonien *m*.
<> *adj* estonien.

estrange [ɪˈstreɪndʒ] *vt* aliéner, éloigner.

estranged [ɪˈstreɪndʒd] *adj* [couple] séparé ■ **to become ~ from sb** se brouiller avec OR se détacher de qqn ■ **her ~ husband** son mari, dont elle est séparée.

estrogen *US* = **oestrogen**.

estrus *US* = **oestrus**.

estuary [ˈestjʊərɪ] (*pl* **estuaries**) *n* estuaire *m*.

ET (*abbrev of* **Employment Training**) *n programme gouvernemental en faveur des chômeurs de longue durée en Grande-Bretagne.*

ETA (*abbrev of* **estimated time of arrival**) *n* HPA.

e-tailer *n* détaillant *m* en ligne.

et al. [ˌetˈæl] (*abbrev of* **et alii**) *adv phr* et al.

etc. (*written abbrev of* **et cetera**) etc.

et cetera [ɪtˈsetərə] <> *adv* et cetera, et cætera.
<> *n* : **the ~s** les et cætera *mpl*.

etch [etʃ] *vi* & *vt* graver ■ ART & TYPO graver à l'eau-forte ■ **~ed on my memory** *fig* gravé dans ma mémoire.

etching [ˈetʃɪŋ] *n* **1.** [print] (gravure *f* à l')eau-forte *f* **2.** [technique] gravure *f* à l'eau-forte.

ETD (*abbrev of* **estimated time of departure**) *n* HPD *f*.

eternal [ɪˈtɜːnl] <> *adj* **1.** [gen - PHILOS] & RELIG éternel **2.** [perpetual] continuel, perpétuel ■ [arguments, problems] éternel ■ [discussion, wrangling] continuel, sempiternel *pej* ■ **he's an ~ student** c'est l'étudiant éternel ■ **to my ~ shame** à ma grande honte.
<> *n* : **the Eternal** l'Éternel *m*.

eternally [ɪˈtɜːnəlɪ] *adv* **1.** [forever] éternellement ■ **I shall be ~ grateful** je serai infiniment reconnaissant **2.** *pej* [perpetually] perpétuellement, continuellement.

eternal triangle *n* : **the ~** l'éternel trio *m* (*femme, mari, amant*).

eternity [ɪˈtɜːnətɪ] (*pl* **eternities**) *n* *liter* & *fig* éternité *f* ■ **it seemed like an ~** on aurait dit une éternité ▶ **'From Here to Eternity'** *Jones, Zinnemann* 'Tant qu'il y aura des hommes'.

ethanol [ˈeθənɒl] *n* alcool *m* éthylique, éthanol *m*.

ether [ˈiːθəʳ] *n* **1.** CHEM & PHYS éther *m* **2.** *lit* & MYTH [sky] : **the ~** l'éther *m*, la voûte céleste ■ **over** OR **through the ~** RADIO sur les ondes.

ethereal [ɪˈθɪərɪəl] *adj* [fragile] éthéré, délicat ■ [spiritual] éthéré, noble.

ethic [ˈeθɪk] <> *n* éthique *f*, morale *f*.
<> *adj* moral, éthique *fml*.

ethical [ˈeθɪkl] *adj* moral, éthique *fml* ■ **an ~ code** un code déontologique.

ethics [ˈeθɪks] <> *n (U)* [study] éthique *f*, morale *f*.
<> *npl* [principles] morale *f* ■ [morality] moralité *f* ■ **professional ~** déontologie *f* ▶ **medical ~** code *m* déontologique OR de déontologie.

Ethiopia [ˌiːθɪˈəʊpjə] *pr n* Éthiopie *f* ■ **in ~** en Éthiopie.

Ethiopian [ˌiːθɪˈəʊpjən] <> *n* **1.** [person] Éthiopien *m*, - enne *f* **2.** LING éthiopien *m*.
<> *adj* éthiopien.

ethnic [ˈeθnɪk] <> *adj* **1.** [of race] ethnique ■ **~ cleansing** purification *f* ethnique ■ **~ group** ethnie *f* **2.** [traditional] folklorique, traditionnel.
<> *n US* membre *m* d'une minorité ethnique.

ethnically [ˈeθnɪklɪ] *adv* du point de vue ethnique, ethniquement.

ethnicity [ˈeθnɪsɪtɪ] *n* appartenance *f* ethnique.

ethnic minority *n* minorité *f* ethnique.

ethnocentric [ˌeθnəʊˈsentrɪk] *adj* ethnocentrique.

ethnocentrism [ˌeθnəʊˈsentrɪzm] *n* ethnocentrisme *m*.

ethnographer [eθˈnɒgrəfəʳ] *n* ethnographe *mf*.

ethnography [eθˈnɒgrəfɪ] *n* ethnographie *f*.

ethnology [eθˈnɒlədʒɪ] *n* ethnologie *f*.

ethos [ˈiːθɒs] *n* éthos *m*.

ethyl [ˈeθɪl, ˈiːθaɪl] *n* éthyle *m* ■ **~ acetate** acétate *m* d'éthyle.

etiquette [ˈetɪket] *n (U)* [code of practice] étiquette *f* ■ [customs] bon usage *m*, convenances *fpl* ■ **according to ~** selon l'usage ■ **courtroom ~** cérémonial *m* de cour ■ **that's not professional ~** c'est contraire à la déontologie OR aux usages de la profession.

Etna [ˈetnə] *pr n* : **(Mount) ~** l'Etna *m*.

Eton [ˈiːtn] *pr n* : **~ (College)** l'école d'Eton.

ETON

> Eton, l'une des plus anciennes et des plus célèbres *public schools*, est fréquentée essentiellement par les enfants de la grande bourgeoisie et de l'aristocratie britanniques. Plusieurs anciens Premiers ministres et membres de la famille royale y ont fait leurs études.

Etonian [iːˈtəʊnjən] *n* élève *m* de l'école d'Eton.

e-trade *n (U)* commerce *m* en ligne.

etymological [ˌetɪməˈlɒdʒɪkl] *adj* étymologique.

etymologist [ˌetɪˈmɒlədʒɪst] *n* étymologiste *mf*.

etymology [ˌetɪˈmɒlədʒɪ] *n* étymologie *f*.

EU *pr n* = **European Union**.

eucalyptus [ˌjuːkəˈlɪptəs] (*pl* **eucalyptuses** OR *pl* **eucalypti** [-taɪ]) *n* eucalyptus *m*.

Eucharist [ˈjuːkərɪst] *n* Eucharistie *f*.

Euclidian [juːˈklɪdɪən] *adj* euclidien ■ **~ geometry** la géométrie euclidienne.

eugenic [juːˈdʒenɪk] *adj* eugénique.
◆ **eugenics** *n (U)* eugénique *f*, eugénisme *m*.

eulogistic [ˌjuːləˈdʒɪstɪk] *adj* très élogieux, louangeur.

eulogize, ise [ˈjuːlədʒaɪz] *vt* faire l'éloge OR le panégyrique de.

eulogy [ˈjuːlədʒɪ] (*pl* **eulogies**) *n* **1.** [commendation] panégyrique *m* **2.** [funeral oration] oraison *f* OR éloge *m* funèbre.

Eumenides [juːˈmenɪˌdiːz] *npl* : **the ~** les Euménides.

eunuch [ˈjuːnək] *n* eunuque *m*.

euphemism [ˈjuːfəmɪzm] *n* euphémisme *m*.

euphemistic [ˌjuːfəˈmɪstɪk] *adj* euphémique.

euphemistically [ˌjuːfəˈmɪstɪklɪ] *adv* par euphémisme, euphémiquement *fml*.

euphonium [juːˈfəʊnjəm] *n* euphonium *m*.

euphony [ˈjuːfənɪ] *n* euphonie *f*.

euphoria [juːˈfɔːrɪə] *n* euphorie *f*.

euphoric [juːˈfɒrɪk] *adj* euphorique.

Eurasia [jʊəˈreɪʒjə] *pr n* Eurasie *f*.

Eurasian [jʊəˈreɪʒjən] <> *n* Eurasien *m*, - enne *f*.
<> *adj* [person] eurasien ■ [continent] eurasiatique.

Euratom [jʊərˈætəm] (*abbrev of* **European Atomic Energy Community**) *pr n* CEEA *f*.

eureka [jʊəˈriːkə] *interj* : **~!** eurêka!

eurhythmics [ju:'rɪðmɪks] *n (U)* gymnastique *f* rythmique.

Euripedes [jʊə'rɪpɪˌdi:z] *pr n* Euripide.

euro ['jʊərəʊ] *n* [currency] euro *m*.

Euro- *in cpds* euro-.

Eurobabble ['jʊərəʊˌbæbl] *n* jargon *m* des eurocrates.

Eurobank ['jʊərəʊˌbæŋk] *n* eurobanque *f*.

Eurobond ['jʊərəʊˌbɒnd] *n* euro-obligation *f*.

Eurocentric ['jʊərəʊˌsentrɪk] *adj* européocentrique.

Eurocheque ['jʊərəʊˌtʃek] *n* eurochèque *m*.

Eurocrat ['jʊərəʊˌkræt] *n* eurocrate *mf*.

Eurocurrency ['jʊərəʊˌkʌrənsɪ] *n* eurodevise *f*, euromonnaie *f*.

Eurodollar ['jʊərəʊˌdɒlə^r] *n* eurodollar *m*.

Euro-election *n* : **the ~s** les élections *fpl* européennes.

Euro-MP (*abbrev of* **European Member of Parliament**) ['jʊərəʊ-] *n* député *m* OR parlementaire *m* européen, eurodéputé *m*.

Europa [jʊ'rəʊpə] *pr n* MYTH Europe.

Europe ['jʊərəp] *pr n* Europe *f* ■ **in ~** en Europe.

European [ˌjʊərə'pi:ən] <> *n* [inhabitant of Europe] Européen *m*, - enne *f* ■ [pro-Europe] partisan *m* de l'Europe unie, Européen *m*, - enne *f*.
<> *adj* européen ■ **we must adopt a more ~ outlook** nous devons adopter un point de vue plus européen OR plus ouvert sur l'Europe ➲ **the Single ~ Market** le Marché unique (européen) ■ **~ plan** *US* [in hotel] chambre *f* sans pension.

European Bank of Reconstruction and Development *pr n* : **the ~** la Banque européenne de reconstruction et de développement.

European Central Bank *pr n* Banque *f* centrale européenne.

European Commission *pr n* Commission *f* des communautés européennes.

European Community *pr n* Communauté *f* européenne.

European Council *pr n* Conseil *m* européen.

European Court of Human Rights *pr n* : **the ~** la Cour européenne des droits de l'homme.

European Court of Justice *pr n* : **the ~** la Cour européenne de justice.

European Currency Unit *n* Unité *f* monétaire européenne.

European Economic Area *pr n* Espace *m* économique européen.

European Economic Community *pr n* Communauté *f* économique européenne.

European Free Trade Association *pr n* Association *f* européenne de libre-échange.

Europeanism [ˌjʊərə'pi:ənɪzm] *n* européanisme *m*.

Europeanize, ise [ˌjʊərə'pi:ənaɪz] *vt* européaniser.

European Monetary System *pr n* : **the ~** le Système monétaire européen.

European Parliament *pr n* Parlement *m* européen.

European Union *pr n* Union *f* européenne.

Europe-wide *adj* [reforms, policy, tax rate] européen.

Europhile ['jʊərəʊˌfaɪl] *n* partisan *m* de l'Europe unie.

Eurosceptic ['jʊərəʊˌskeptɪk] *n* eurosceptique *mf*.

Eurospeak ['jʊərəʊspi:k] *n* jargon *m* communautaire.

Eurostar® ['jʊərəʊstɑ:^r] *pr n* Eurostar®.

Eurotunnel® ['jʊərəʊˌtʌnl] *pr n* Eurotunnel *m*.

Eurovision® ['jʊərəʊˌvɪʒn] *n* Eurovision® *f* ■ **the ~ Song Contest** le concours Eurovision de la chanson.

euro-zone *n* zone *f* euro.

Eustachian tube [ju:'steɪʃən-] *n* trompe *f* d'Eustache.

euthanasia [ˌju:θə'neɪzjə] *n* euthanasie *f*.

evacuate [ɪ'vækjʊeɪt] *vt* [gen - PHYSIOL] évacuer.

evacuation [ɪˌvækjʊ'eɪʃn] *n* [gen - PHYSIOL] évacuation *f*.

evacuee [ɪˌvækju:'i:] *n* évacué *m*, - e *f*.

evade [ɪ'veɪd] *vt* **1.** [escape from - pursuers] échapper à ; [- punishment] échapper à, se soustraire à **2.** [avoid - responsibility] éviter, esquiver ; [- question] esquiver, éluder ; [- eyes, glance] éviter ■ **to ~ paying taxes** frauder le fisc ■ **to ~ military service** se dérober à ses obligations militaires.

evaluate [ɪ'væljʊeɪt] *vt* **1.** [value] évaluer, déterminer le montant de **2.** [assess - situation, success, work] évaluer, former un jugement sur la valeur de ; [- evidence, reasons] peser, évaluer.

evaluation [ɪˌvæljʊ'eɪʃn] *n* **1.** [of damages, worth] évaluation *f* **2.** [of situation, work] évaluation *f*, jugement *m* ■ [of evidence, reasons] évaluation *f*.

evanescent [ˌi:və'nesnt] *adj fml* & *lit* évanescent, fugitif.

evangelical [ˌi:væn'dʒelɪkl] <> *adj* évangélique.
<> *n* évangélique *m*.

evangelicalism [ˌi:væn'dʒelɪkəlɪzm] *n* évangélisme *m*.

evangelism [ɪ'vændʒəlɪzm] *n* évangélisme *m*.

evangelist [ɪ'vændʒəlɪst] *n* **1.** BIBLE : **Evangelist** évangéliste *m* **2.** [preacher] évangélisateur *m*, - trice *f* **3.** *fig* [zealous advocate] prêcheur *m*, - euse *f*.

evangelize, ise [ɪ'vændʒəlaɪz] <> *vt* évangéliser, prêcher l'Évangile à.
<> *vi* RELIG prêcher l'Évangile.

evaporate [ɪ'væpəreɪt] <> *vi* [liquid] s'évaporer ■ *fig* [hopes, doubts] s'envoler, se volatiliser.
<> *vt* faire évaporer.

evaporated milk [ɪ'væpəreɪtɪd-] *n* lait *m* condensé.

evaporation [ɪˌvæpə'reɪʃn] *n* évaporation *f*.

evasion [ɪ'veɪʒn] *n* **1.** [avoidance] fuite *f*, évasion *f* ■ [of duty] dérobade *f* ■ **~ of a responsibility** dérobade devant une responsabilité **2.** [deception, trickery] détour *m*, faux-fuyant *m*, échappatoire *f* ■ **to answer without ~** répondre sans détours OR sans biaiser.

evasive [ɪ'veɪsɪv] *adj* évasif ■ **to take ~ action** [gen] louvoyer ; MIL effectuer une manœuvre dilatoire.

evasively [ɪ'veɪsɪvlɪ] *adv* évasivement ■ **he replied ~** il a répondu en termes évasifs.

evasiveness [ɪ'veɪsɪvnɪs] *n* caractère *m* évasif.

eve [i:v] *n* veille *f* ■ RELIG vigile *f* ■ **on the ~ of the election** à la veille des élections.

Eve [i:v] *pr n* Ève.

even[1] ['i:vn] <> *adj* **1.** [level] plat, plan ■ [smooth] uni ■ **to make sthg ~** égaliser OR aplanir qqch ■ **it's ~ with the desk** c'est au même niveau que le bureau **2.** [steady - breathing, temperature] égal ; [- rate, rhythm] régulier **3.** [equal - distribution, spread] égal ■ **the score is** OR **the scores are ~** ils sont à égalité ■ **it's an ~ game** la partie est égale ■ **now we're ~** nous voilà quittes, nous sommes quittes maintenant ■ **there's an ~ chance he'll lose** il y a une chance sur deux qu'il perde ➲ **to bet ~ money** [gen] donner chances égales ; [in betting] parier le même enjeu ■ **to get ~ with sb** se venger de qqn **4.** [calm - temper] égal ; [- voice] égal, calme **5.** [number] pair.
<> *adv* **1.** [indicating surprise] même ■ **he ~ works on Sundays** il travaille même le dimanche ■ **she's ~ forgotten his name** elle a oublié jusqu'à son nom ■ **not ~** même pas **2.** (*with comparative*) [still] encore ■ **~ better** encore mieux ■ **~ less** encore moins **3.** [qualifying] : **he seemed indifferent, ~ hostile** il avait l'air indifférent, hostile même.
<> *vt* égaliser, aplanir.
<> *vi* s'égaliser, s'aplanir.

◆ **even as** *conj phr* **1.** *fml* [at the very moment that] au moment même où ■ **~ as we speak** au moment même où nous parlons **2.** *lit & arch* [just as] comme.
◆ **even if** *conj phr* même si ■ **~ if I say so myself** sans fausse modestie.
◆ **even now** *adv phr* **1.** [despite what happened before] même maintenant **2.** *lit* [at this very moment] en ce moment même.
◆ **even so** *adv phr* [nevertheless] quand même, pourtant ■ **yes, but ~ so** oui, mais quand même.
◆ **even then** *adv phr* **1.** [in that case also] quand même ■ **but ~ then we wouldn't be able to afford it** mais nous ne pourrions quand même pas nous le permettre **2.** [at that time also] même à ce moment-là.
◆ **even though** *conj phr* : **~ though she explained it in detail** bien qu'elle l'ait expliqué en détail.
◆ **even with** *prep phr* même avec, malgré.
◆ **even out** ◇ *vt sep* [surface] égaliser, aplanir ■ [prices] égaliser ■ [supply] répartir *OR* distribuer plus également.
◇ *vi insep* [road] s'égaliser, s'aplanir ■ [prices] s'égaliser ■ [supply] être réparti plus également.
◆ **even up** *vt sep* égaliser ■ **to ~ things up** rétablir l'équilibre.

even[2] ['i:vn] *n arch & lit* [evening] soir *m*.

even-handed *adj* équitable, impartial.

evening ['i:vnɪŋ] ◇ *n* **1.** [part of day] soir *m* ■ **(good) ~!** bonsoir! ■ **in the ~** le soir ■ **it is 8 o'clock in the ~** il est 8 h du soir ■ **I'm hardly ever at home ~s** *US OR* **in the ~** *UK* je suis rarement chez moi le soir ■ **this ~** ce soir ■ **that ~** ce soir-là ■ **tomorrow ~** demain soir ■ **on the ~ of the next day, on the following ~** le lendemain soir, le soir suivant ■ **on the ~ of the fifteenth** le quinze au soir ■ **on the ~ of her departure** le soir de son départ ■ **one fine spring ~** (par) un beau soir de printemps ■ **every Friday ~** tous les vendredis soir *OR* soirs ■ **the long winter ~s** les longues soirées *OR* veillées d'hiver ■ **I work ~s** je travaille le soir ■ **in the ~ of her life** *fig* au soir *OR* au déclin de sa vie **2.** [length of time] soirée *f* ■ **we spent the ~ playing cards** nous avons passé la soirée à jouer aux cartes **3.** [entertainment] soirée *f* ■ **a musical ~** une soirée musicale.
◇ *comp* [newspaper, train] du soir ■ **the ~ performance starts at 7.30** en soirée la représentation débute à 19 h 30 ■ **~ prayers/service** RELIG office *m* /service *m* du soir ■ **an ~ match** SPORT une nocturne ➊ **the Evening Standard** PRESS *quotidien populaire londonien de tendance conservatrice, see also* **tabloid**.

evening class *n* cours *m* du soir.

evening dress *n* [for men] tenue *f* de soirée, habit *m* ■ [for women] robe *f* du soir ■ **in ~** [man] en tenue de soirée ; [woman] en robe du soir, en toilette de soirée.

evening star *n* étoile *f* du berger.

evening wear *n (U)* = **evening dress**.

evenly ['i:vnlɪ] *adv* **1.** [breathe, move] régulièrement ■ [talk] calmement, posément **2.** [equally - divide] également, de façon égale ; [- spread] de façon égale, régulièrement ■ **they are ~ matched** ils sont de force égale.

evenness ['i:vnnɪs] *n* **1.** [of surface] égalité *f*, caractère *m* lisse **2.** [of competition, movement] régularité *f*.

evens *UK* ['i:vənz], **even odds** *US* ◇ *npl* : **to lay ~** donner à égalité.
◇ *comp* : **~ favorite** favori *m*, - ite *f* à égalité.

evensong ['i:vnsɒŋ] *n* [Anglican] office *m* du soir ■ [Roman Catholic] vêpres *fpl*.

event [ɪ'vent] *n* **1.** [happening] événement *m* ■ **the course of ~s** la suite des événements, le déroulement des faits ■ **in the course of ~s** par la suite, au cours des événements ■ **in the normal course of ~s** normalement ■ **I realized after the ~** j'ai réalisé après coup ■ **the party was quite an ~** la soirée était un véritable événement **2.** [organized activity] manifestation *f* ■ **the society organizes a number of social ~s** l'association organise un certain nombre de soirées *OR* de rencontres **3.** SPORT [meeting] manifestation *f* ■ [competition] épreuve *f* ■ [in horseracing] course *f* ■ **field ~s** épreuves d'athlétisme ■ **track ~s** épreuves sur piste.
◆ **at all events, in any event** *adv phr* en tout cas, de toute façon.
◆ **in either event** *adv phr* dans l'un ou l'autre cas.
◆ **in the event** *adv phr* en fait, en l'occurence.
◆ **in the event of** *prep phr* : **in the ~ of rain** en cas de pluie ■ **in the ~ of her refusing** au cas où *OR* dans le cas où elle refuserait.
◆ **in the event that** *conj phr* au cas où ■ **in the unlikely ~ that he comes** au cas *OR* dans le cas fort improbable où il viendrait.

even-tempered *adj* d'humeur égale.

eventful [ɪ'ventfʊl] *adj* **1.** [busy - day, holiday, life] mouvementé, fertile en événements **2.** [important] mémorable, très important.

eventide ['i:vntaɪd] *n lit* soir *m*, tombée *f* du jour.

eventing [ɪ'ventɪŋ] *n participation à toutes les épreuves d'un concours hippique.*

eventual [ɪ'ventʃʊəl] *adj* [final] final, ultime ■ [resulting] qui s'ensuit ■ **bad management led to the ~ collapse of the company** une mauvaise gestion a finalement provoqué la faillite de l'entreprise.

eventuality [ɪˌventʃʊ'ælətɪ] (*pl* **eventualities**) *n* éventualité *f*.

eventually [ɪ'ventʃʊəlɪ] *adv* finalement, en fin de compte ■ **I'll get around to it ~** je le ferai un jour ou l'autre ■ **she ~ became a lawyer** elle a fini par devenir avocat ■ **~, I decided to give up** pour finir *OR* en fin de compte, j'ai décidé d'abandonner, j'ai finalement décidé d'abandonner.

ever ['evər] *adv* **1.** [always] toujours ■ **~ hopeful/the pessimist, he...** toujours plein d'espoir/pessimiste, il... ■ **yours ~, ~ yours** [in letter] amicalement vôtre
2. [at any time] jamais ■ **do you ~ meet him?** est-ce qu'il vous arrive (jamais) de le rencontrer? ■ **all they ~ do is work** ils ne font que travailler ■ **he hardly** *OR* **scarcely ~ smokes** il ne fume presque jamais ▌[with comparatives] : **lovelier/more slowly than ~** plus joli/plus lentement que jamais ■ **he's as sarcastic as ~** il est toujours aussi sarcastique ▌[with superlatives] : **the first/biggest ~** le tout premier/plus grand qu'on ait jamais vu ■ **the worst earthquake ~** le pire tremblement de terre qu'on ait jamais connu
3. *inf* [in exclamations] : **do you enjoy dancing? – do I ~!** *US* aimez-vous danser? – et comment! ■ **well, did you ~!** ça, par exemple!
4. [as intensifier] : **as soon as ~ she comes** aussitôt *OR* dès qu'elle sera là ■ **before ~ they** *OR* **before they ~ set out** avant même qu'ils partent ▌[in questions] : **how ~ did you manage that?** comment donc y êtes-vous parvenu? ■ **where ~ can it be?** où diable peut-il être? ■ **why ~ not?** mais enfin, pourquoi pas?
◆ **ever after** *adv phr* pour toujours ■ **they lived happily ~ after** ils vécurent heureux jusqu'à la fin de leurs jours.
◆ **ever so** *adv phr* **1.** *inf* [extremely] vraiment ■ **she's ~ so clever** elle est vraiment intelligente ■ **~ so slightly off-centre** un tout petit peu décentré ■ **thanks ~ so much** merci vraiment
2. *fml* [however] : **no teacher, be he ~ so patient...** aucun enseignant, aussi patient soit-il...
◆ **ever such** *det phr inf* vraiment ■ **they've got ~ such pretty curtains in the shop** ils ont vraiment de jolis rideaux dans ce magasin.

Everest ['evərɪst] *pr n* : **(Mount) ~** le mont Everest, l'Everest *m*.

evergreen ['evəgri:n] ◇ *n* **1.** [tree] arbre *m* à feuilles persistantes ■ **the Evergreen State** l'Etat de Washington ▌[conifer] conifère *m* ■ [bush] arbuste *m* à feuilles persistantes **2.** *fig* [song, story] chanson *f OR* histoire *f* qui ne vieillit jamais.
◇ *adj* **1.** [bush, tree] à feuilles persistantes **2.** *fig* [song, story] qui ne vieillit pas.

everlasting [ˌevə'lɑ:stɪŋ] *adj* **1.** [eternal - hope, mercy] éternel, infini ; [- fame] éternel, immortel ; [- God, life] éternel **2.** [incessant] perpétuel, éternel.

everlastingly [ˌevə'lɑ:stɪŋlɪ] *adv* **1.** [eternally] éternellement **2.** [incessantly] sans cesse, perpétuellement.

evermore [ˌevə'mɔ:r] *adv* toujours ■ **for ~** pour toujours, à jamais.

every ['evrɪ] *det* **1.** [each] tout, chaque ■ **~ room has a view of the sea** les chambres ont toutes vue *OR* toutes les chambres ont vue sur la mer ■ **not ~ room is as big as this** toutes les chambres ne sont pas aussi grandes que celle-ci ■ **he drank ~ drop** il a bu jusqu'à la dernière goutte ■ **~ one of these apples** chacune de *OR* toutes ces pommes ■ **~ one of them arrived late** ils sont tous arrivés en retard ■ **~ (single) one of these pencils is broken** tous ces crayons (sans exception) sont cassés ■ **~ (single) person in the room** tous ceux qui étaient dans la pièce (sans exception) ■ **~ day** tous les jours, chaque jour ■ **~ time I go out** chaque fois que je sors ■ **of ~ age/~ sort/~colour** de tout âge/toute sorte/toutes les couleurs ▶ **~ little helps** *prov* les petits ruisseaux font les grandes rivières *prov* **2.** [with units of time, measurement etc] tout ■ **~ two days, ~ second day, ~ other day** tous les deux jours, un jour sur deux ■ **once ~ month** une fois par mois ■ **~ third man** un homme sur trois ■ **three women out of** *OR* **in ~ ten, three out of ~ ten women** trois femmes sur dix ■ **~ other Sunday** un dimanche sur deux **3.** [indicating confidence, optimism] tout ■ **I have ~ confidence that...** je ne doute pas un instant que... ■ **you have ~ reason to be happy** vous avez toutes les raisons *OR* tout lieu d'être heureux ■ **we wish you ~ success** nous vous souhaitons très bonne chance **4.** [with possessive adj] chacun, moindre ■ **his ~ action bears witness to it** chacun de ses gestes *OR* tout ce qu'il fait en témoigne ■ **her ~ wish** son moindre désir, tous ses désirs.

◆ **every now and again, every once in a while, every so often** *adv phr* de temps en temps, de temps à autre.

◆ **every which way** *adv phr* *US* [everywhere] partout ■ [from all sides] de toutes parts ■ **he came home with his hair ~ which way** il est rentré les cheveux en bataille.

everybody ['evrɪ,bɒdɪ] = **everyone**.

everyday ['evrɪdeɪ] *adj* **1.** [daily] de tous les jours, quotidien ■ **~ life** la vie de tous les jours **2.** [ordinary] banal, ordinaire ■ **an ~ expression** une expression courante ■ **in ~ use** d'usage courant.

Everyman ['evrɪmæn] *n* l'homme *m* de la rue.

everyone ['evrɪwʌn] *pron* tout le monde, chacun ■ **as ~ knows** comme chacun *OR* tout le monde le sait ■ **~ else** tous les autres ■ **in a small town where ~ knows ~ (else)** dans une petite ville où tout le monde se connaît ▶ **~ who was anyone was there** tous les gens qui comptent étaient là.

everyplace ['evrɪ,pleɪs] *adv US* = **everywhere**.

everything ['evrɪθɪŋ] *pron* **1.** [all things] tout ■ **~ he says** tout ce qu'il dit ■ **they sell ~** ils vendent de tout ■ **she means ~ to me** elle est tout pour moi, je ne vis que pour elle ▶ **a party with clowns, cakes and ~** *inf* une fête avec des clowns, des gâteaux et tout **2.** [the most important thing] l'essentiel *m* ■ **winning is ~** l'essentiel, c'est de gagner ■ **money isn't ~** il n'y a pas que l'argent qui compte.

everywhere ['evrɪweər] ◇ *adv* partout ■ **~ she went** partout où elle allait ▶ **the card indexes were ~** *inf* [in complete disorder] les cartes étaient rangées n'importe comment.
◇ *pron inf* tout ■ **~'s in such a mess** tout est sens dessus dessous.

evict [ɪ'vɪkt] *vt* **1.** [person] expulser, chasser **2.** [property] récupérer par moyens juridiques.

eviction [ɪ'vɪkʃn] *n* expulsion *f* ■ **an ~ notice** un mandat d'expulsion.

evidence ['evɪdəns] ◇ *n* **1.** [proof] preuve *f* ■ [testimony] témoignage *m* ■ **on the ~ of eye witnesses** à en croire les témoins **2.** LAW [proof] preuve *f* ■ [testimony] témoignage *m* ■ **to give ~ against/for sb** témoigner contre/en faveur de qqn ■ **the ~ is against him** les preuves pèsent contre lui ▶ **to turn King's** *OR* **Queen's ~** *UK*, **to turn State's ~** *US* témoigner contre ses complices **3.** [indication] signe *m*, marque *f* ■ **to show ~ of** laisser voir ■ **to be in ~** [person] : **his daughter was nowhere in ~** sa fille n'était pas là *OR* n'était pas présente ■ **a politician very much in ~ these days** un homme politique très en vue ces temps-ci.
◇ *vt fml* manifester, montrer.

evident ['evɪdənt] *adj* évident, manifeste ■ **with ~ pleasure** avec un plaisir manifeste ■ **it is ~ from the way she talks** cela se voit à sa manière de parler ■ **it is quite ~ that he's not interested** on voit bien qu'il ne s'y intéresse pas, il ne s'y intéresse pas, c'est évident ■ **he's lying, that's ~** il ment, c'est évident.

evidently ['evɪdəntlɪ] *adv* **1.** [apparently] apparemment ■ **did he refuse ? – ~ not** a-t-il refusé? – non apparemment *OR* à ce qu'il paraît ■ **unemployment is ~ rising again** de toute évidence le chômage est à nouveau en hausse **2.** [clearly] de toute évidence, manifestement ■ **he was ~ in pain** il était évident *OR* clair qu'il souffrait.

evil ['i:vl] (*UK comp* **eviller**, *superl* **evillest**) (*US comp* **eviler**, *superl* **evilest**) ◇ *adj* **1.** [wicked - person] malveillant, méchant ; [- deed, plan, reputation] mauvais ; [- influence] néfaste ; [- doctrine, spell, spirit] malfaisant ■ **she has an ~ temper** elle a un sale caractère *OR* un caractère de chien ▶ **the Evil One** le Malin **2.** [smell, taste] infect, infâme.
◇ *n* mal *m* ■ **to speak ~ of sb** dire du mal de qqn ■ **social ~s** plaies sociales, maux sociaux ■ **pollution is one of the ~s of our era** la pollution est un fléau de notre époque ■ **it's the lesser ~** *OR* **of two ~s** c'est le moindre mal.

evildoer [,i:vl'du:ər] *n* méchant *m*, - e *f*, scélérat *m*, - e *f*.

evil eye *n* : **the ~** le mauvais œil ■ **to give sb the ~** jeter le mauvais œil à qqn.

evil-looking *adj* [person] qui a l'air mauvais ■ [weapon] menaçant.

evil-minded *adj* malveillant, mal intentionné.

evil-smelling *adj* nauséabond.

evince [ɪ'vɪns] *vt fml* [show - interest, surprise] manifester, montrer ; [- quality] faire preuve de, manifester.

eviscerate [ɪ'vɪsəreɪt] *vt* éventrer, étriper ■ MED éviscérer.

evocation [,evəʊ'keɪʃn] *n* évocation *f*.

evocative [ɪ'vɒkətɪv] *adj* **1.** [picture, scent] évocateur **2.** [magic] évocatoire.

evoke [ɪ'vəʊk] *vt* **1.** [summon up - memory, spirit] évoquer **2.** [elicit - admiration] susciter ; [- response, smile] susciter, provoquer.

evolution [,i:və'lu:ʃn] *n* **1.** [of language, situation] évolution *f* ■ [of art, society, technology] développement *m*, évolution *f* ■ [of events] développement *m*, déroulement *m* **2.** BIOL, BOT & ZOOL évolution *f* **3.** [of dancers, troops] évolution *f* **4.** MATHS extraction *f* (de la racine).

evolutionary [,i:və'lu:ʃnərɪ] *adj* évolutionniste.

evolutionist [,i:və'lu:ʃənɪst] ◇ *adj* évolutionniste.
◇ *n* évolutionniste *mf*.

evolve [ɪ'vɒlv] ◇ *vi* évoluer, se développer ■ BIOL, BOT & ZOOL évoluer ■ **to ~ from sthg** se développer à partir de qqch.
◇ *vt* [system, theory] développer, élaborer.

ewe [ju:] *n* brebis *f* ■ **a ~ lamb** une agnelle.

ewer ['ju:ər] *n* aiguière *f*.

ex [eks] ◇ *prep* **1.** COMM départ, sortie ■ **price ~ works** prix *m* départ *OR* sortie usine **2.** FIN sans.
◇ *n inf* [gen] ex *mf* ■ [husband] ex-mari *m* ■ [wife] ex-femme *f* ■ **my ~** [girlfriend] mon ancienne petite amie ; [boyfriend] mon ancien petit ami.

ex- *in cpds* ex-, ancien ■ **his ~wife** son ex-femme ■ **the ~president** l'ancien président, l'ex-président.

exacerbate [ɪg'zæsəbeɪt] *vt fml* **1.** [make worse] exacerber, aggraver **2.** [annoy] énerver, exaspérer.

exact [ɪg'zækt] ◇ *adj* **1.** [accurate, correct] exact, juste ■ **it's an ~ copy** [picture] c'est fidèle à l'original ; [document] c'est une copie conforme *OR* textuelle ■ **she told me the ~ opposite** elle m'a dit exactement le contraire ■ **those were her ~ words** ce furent ses propres paroles, voilà ce qu'elle a dit textuellement **2.** [precise - amount, idea, value] exact, précis ; [- directions, place, time] précis ■ **is it 5 o'clock? – 5:03 to be ~** est-il 5 h? – 5 h 03 plus exactement *OR* précisément ■ **I'm 35 and 2 days to be ~** j'ai exactement 35 ans et 2 jours ■ **she likes music, or**

to be ~, classical music elle aime la musique, ou plus précisément la musique classique ■ **can you be more ~?** pouvez-vous préciser? **3.** [meticulous - work] rigoureux, précis ; [- mind] rigoureux ; [- science] exact ; [- instrument] de précision.
◇ *vt* **1.** [demand - money] extorquer **2.** [insist upon] exiger.

exacting [ɪg'zæktɪŋ] *adj* [person] exigeant ■ [activity, job] astreignant, exigeant.

exaction [ɪg'zækʃn] *n* **1.** [act] exaction *f*, extorsion *f* **2.** [money] paiement *m*.

exactitude [ɪg'zæktɪtju:d] *n* exactitude *f*.

exactly [ɪg'zæktlɪ] *adv* **1.** [accurately] précisément, avec précision ■ **the computer can reproduce this sound ~** l'ordinateur peut reproduire exactement ce son **2.** [entirely, precisely] exactement, justement ■ **I don't remember ~** je ne me rappelle pas au juste ■ **it's ~ the same thing** c'est exactement la même chose ■ **it's ~ 5 o'clock** il est 5 h juste ■ **it's been six months ~** cela fait six mois jour pour jour.

exactness [ɪg'zæktnɪs] *n* exactitude *f*, soin *m*.

exaggerate [ɪg'zædʒəreɪt] ◇ *vi* exagérer.
◇ *vt* **1.** [overstate - quality, situation, size] exagérer ; [- facts] amplifier ; [- importance] s'exagérer ■ **he is exaggerating the seriousness of the problem** il s'exagère la gravité du problème **2.** [emphasize] accentuer ■ **she ~s her weakness to gain sympathy** elle se prétend plus faible qu'elle ne l'est réellement pour s'attirer la compassion.

exaggerated [ɪg'zædʒəreɪtɪd] *adj* **1.** [number, story] exagéré ■ [fashion, style] outré ■ **to have an ~ opinion of o.s.** *OR* **of one's own worth** avoir une trop haute opinion de soi-même **2.** MED exagéré.

exaggeratedly [ɪg'zædʒəreɪtɪdlɪ] *adv* d'une manière exagérée, exagérément.

exaggeration [ɪg,zædʒə'reɪʃn] *n* exagération *f*.

exalt [ɪg'zɔ:lt] *vt* **1.** [praise highly] exalter, chanter les louanges de **2.** [in rank] élever (à un rang plus important).

exaltation [,egzɔ:l'teɪʃn] *n (U)* **1.** [praise] louange *f*, louanges *fpl*, exaltation *f* **2.** [elation] exultation *f*, exaltation *f*.

exalted [ɪg'zɔ:ltɪd] *adj* **1.** [prominent - person] de haut rang, haut placé ; [- position, rank] élevé **2.** [elated] exalté.

exam [ɪ,'zæm] (*abbrev of* **examination**) ◇ *n* : **to sit** *OR* **to take an ~** passer un examen ■ **to pass/to fail an ~** réussir à/échouer à un examen.
◇ *comp* d'examen ■ **~ board** commission *f* d'examen ■ **~ nerves** trac *m* des examens ■ **~ paper** [set of questions] sujet *m* d'examen ; [written answer] copie *f* (d'examen).

examination [ɪg,zæmɪ'neɪʃn] ◇ *n* **1.** [of records, proposal etc] examen *m* ■ [of building - by official] inspection *f* ; [- by potential buyer] visite *f* ■ **it doesn't stand up to ~** [argument, theory] cela ne résiste pas à l'examen ; [alibi] cela ne tient pas ■ **to carry out** *OR* **to make an ~ of sthg** procéder à l'examen de qqch ■ **on ~** après examen ■ **the proposal is still under ~** la proposition est encore à l'étude **2.** MED examen *m* médical ■ [at school, work] visite *f* médicale ■ [regular] bilan *m* de santé ■ **I'm just going in for an ~** j'y vais juste pour passer un examen médical **3.** *fml* & SCH & UNIV examen *m* **4.** LAW [of witness] audition *f* ■ [of suspect] interrogatoire *m*.
◇ *comp* [question, results] d'examen ■ **~ board** commission *f* d'examen ■ **~ paper** [set of questions] sujet *m* d'examen ; [written answer] copie *f* (d'examen).

examine [ɪg'zæmɪn] *vt* **1.** [records, proposal etc] examiner, étudier ■ [building] inspecter ■ **the weapon is being ~d for fingerprints** on est en train d'examiner l'arme pour voir si elle porte des empreintes digitales **2.** MED examiner **3.** SCH & UNIV faire passer un examen à ■ **you'll be ~d in French/in all six subjects/on your knowledge of the subject** vous aurez à passer un examen de français/dans ces six matières/pour évaluer vos connaissances sur le sujet **4.** LAW [witness] entendre ■ [suspect] interroger.

examinee [ɪg,zæmɪ'ni:] *n* candidat *m*, - e *f (à un examen)*.

examiner [ɪg'zæmɪnəʳ] *n* [in school, driving test] examinateur *m*, - trice *f* ■ **the ~s** SCH & UNIV les examinateurs, le jury.

examining body [ɪg'zæmɪnɪŋ-] *n* jury *m* d'examen.

examining magistrate *n UK* LAW juge *m* d'instruction.

example [ɪg'zɑ:mpl] *n* **1.** [illustration] exemple *m* ■ **to mention just a few ~s** pour ne citer que quelques exemples ■ **this is an excellent ~ of what I meant** ceci illustre parfaitement ce que je voulais dire **2.** [person or action to be imitated] exemple *m*, modèle *m* ■ **you're an ~ to us all** vous êtes un modèle pour nous tous ■ **to follow sb's ~** suivre l'exemple de qqn ■ **following France's ~, Britain has introduced sanctions** à l'exemple *OR* à l'instar de la France, la Grande-Bretagne a pris des sanctions ■ **to set an ~** montrer l'exemple ■ **to set a good/bad ~** montrer le bon/mauvais exemple ■ **to hold sb up as an ~** citer qqn en exemple **3.** [sample, specimen] exemple *m*, spécimen *m* ■ [of work] échantillon *m* **4.** [warning] exemple *m* ■ **let this be an ~ to you** que ça te serve d'exemple ■ **to make an ~ of sb** faire un exemple du cas de qqn.
➡ **for example** *adv phr* par exemple.

exasperate [ɪg'zæspəreɪt] *vt* [irritate] exaspérer ■ **her father was so ~d with her that he lost his temper** elle a tellement exaspéré son père que celui-ci s'est mis en colère.

exasperating [ɪg'zæspəreɪtɪŋ] *adj* exaspérant.

exasperatingly [ɪg'zæspəreɪtɪŋlɪ] *adv* : **the service is ~ slow in this restaurant** le service est d'une lenteur exaspérante *OR* désespérante dans ce restaurant.

exasperation [ɪg,zæspə'reɪʃn] *n* [irritation, frustration] exaspération *f* ■ **to look at sb in ~** regarder qqn avec exaspération *OR* un air exaspéré ■ **she was nearly weeping with** *OR* **from ~** elle pleurait presque d'exaspération.

excavate ['ekskəveɪt] *vt* **1.** [hole, trench] creuser, excaver **2.** archaeology [temple, building] mettre au jour ■ **to ~ a site** faire des fouilles sur un site.

excavation [,ekskə'veɪʃn] *n* **1.** [of hole, trench] excavation *f*, creusement *m* **2.** archaeology [of temple, building] mise *f* au jour ■ **the ~s at Knossos** les fouilles *fpl* de Knossos.

excavator ['ekskə,veɪtəʳ] *n* **1.** [machine] excavateur *m*, excavatrice *f* **2.** [archaeologist] personne qui conduit des fouilles.

exceed [ɪk'si:d] *vt* **1.** [be more than] dépasser, excéder ■ **her salary ~s mine by £5,000 a year** son salaire annuel dépasse le mien de 5 000 livres **2.** [go beyond - expectations, fears] dépasser ; [- budget] excéder, déborder ■ **to ~ one's authority** outrepasser ses pouvoirs ■ **to ~ the speed limit** dépasser la limite de vitesse, faire un excès de vitesse ■ **'do not ~ the stated dose'** 'ne pas dépasser la dose prescrite'.

exceedingly [ɪk'si:dɪŋlɪ] *adv* [extremely] extrêmement.

excel [ɪk'sel] (*pret & pp* **excelled**) ◇ *vi* exceller ■ **to ~ at** *OR* **in music** exceller en musique ■ **I've never excelled at games** je n'ai jamais été très fort en sport.
◇ *vt* surpasser ■ **to ~ o.s.** *liter* & *iron* se surpasser.

excellence ['eksələns] *n* [high quality] qualité *f* excellente ■ [commercially] excellence *f* ■ **a prize for general ~** SCH un prix d'excellence ■ **to strive for ~** s'efforcer d'atteindre une qualité excellente ■ **awards for ~** prix d'excellence ➤ **centre of ~** centre *m* d'excellence.

Excellency ['eksələnsɪ] (*pl* **Excellencies**) *n* Excellence *f* ■ **Your/His ~** Votre/Son Excellence.

excellent ['eksələnt] *adj* excellent ■ [weather] magnifique ■ **~!** formidable!, parfait!

excellently ['eksələntlɪ] *adv* de façon excellente, superbement ■ **it was ~ done** cela a été fait de main de maître.

except [ɪk'sept] ◇ *prep* [apart from] à part, excepté, sauf ■ **~ weekends** à part *OR* excepté *OR* sauf le week-end ■ **I know nothing about it ~ what he told me** je ne sais rien d'autre que ce qu'il m'a raconté ■ **I remember nothing ~ that I was scared** je ne me souviens de rien sauf que *OR* excepté que j'avais peur.
◇ *conj* **1.** [apart from] : **I'll do anything ~ sell the car** je ferai tout sauf vendre la voiture ■ **~ if** sauf *OR* à part si **2.** [only] seule-

ment, mais ■ **we would stay longer ~ (that) we have no more money** nous resterions bien plus longtemps, mais *OR* seulement nous n'avons plus d'argent.
<> *vt* [exclude] excepter, exclure ■ **all countries, France ~ed** tous les pays, la France exceptée *OR* à l'exception de la France ■ **present company ~ed** à l'exception des personnes présentes, les personnes présentes exceptées.
◆ **except for** *prep phr* sauf, à part ■ **the office will be empty over Christmas ~ for the boss and me** il n'y aura que le patron et moi au bureau au moment de Noël ■ **he would have got away with it ~ for that one mistake** sans cette erreur il s'en serait tiré.

excepting [ɪk'septɪŋ] <> *prep* à part, excepté, sauf ■ **not ~......** y compris.
<> *conj arch* = **unless.**

exception [ɪk'sepʃn] *n* **1.** [deviation, exemption] exception *f* ■ **the ~ proves the rule** l'exception confirme la règle ■ **I'll make an ~ this time/in your case** je ferai une exception cette fois/dans votre cas ■ **but she's an ~** mais elle n'est pas comme les autres ■ **with the ~ of Daniel** à l'exception de Daniel ■ **and you're no ~** et cela te concerne aussi **2.** *phr* **to take ~ to sthg** s'offenser *OR* s'offusquer de qqch, être outré par qqch ■ **he takes ~ to being kept waiting** il n'aime pas du tout qu'on le fasse attendre.

exceptionable [ɪk'sepʃnəbl] *adj* [objectionable] offensant, outrageant.

exceptional [ɪk'sepʃənl] *adj* exceptionnel ■ **in ~ circumstances** dans des circonstances exceptionnelles.

exceptionally [ɪk'sepʃnəlɪ] *adv* exceptionnellement ■ **that's ~ kind of you** c'est extrêmement gentil de votre part ■ **she's an ~ bright child** c'est une enfant d'une intelligence exceptionnelle.

excerpt ['eksɜ:pt] *n* [extract] extrait *m* ■ **an ~ from sthg** un extrait de qqch.

excess <> *n* [ɪk'ses] **1.** [unreasonable amount] excès *m* ■ **an ~ of salt/fat in the diet** un excès de sel/de graisses dans l'alimentation **2.** [difference between two amounts] supplément *m*, surplus *m* ■ [in insurance] franchise *f* **3.** [over-indulgence] excès *m* ■ **a life of ~** une vie d'excès **4.** *(usu pl)* [unacceptable action] excès *m*, abus *m* ■ **the ~es of the occupying troops** les excès *OR* abus commis par les soldats pendant l'occupation.
<> *adj* ['ekses] [extra] en trop, excédentaire.
◆ **in excess of** *prep phr* [a stated percentage, weight] au-dessus de ■ **she earns in ~ of £25,000 a year** elle gagne plus de 25 000 livres par an.
◆ **to excess** *adv phr*: **to carry sthg to ~** pousser qqch trop loin ■ **he does** *OR* **carries it to ~** il exagère, il dépasse les bornes ■ **to eat/to drink to ~** manger/boire à l'excès.

excess baggage ['ekses-] *n (U)* [on plane] excédent *m* de bagages.

excess fare ['ekses-] *n UK* supplément *m* de prix.

excessive [ɪk'sesɪv] *adj* [unreasonable] excessif ■ [demand] excessif, démesuré.

excessively [ɪk'sesɪvlɪ] *adv* excessivement.

exchange [ɪks'tʃeɪndʒ] <> *vt* **1.** [give and receive - gifts, letters, blows] échanger ■ **shots were ~d** il y a eu un échange de coups de feu ■ **to ~ sthg with sb** échanger qqch avec qqn ■ **to ~ places with sb** changer de place avec qqn ■ **we ~d addresses** nous avons échangé nos adresses
2. [give in return for sthg else] échanger ■ **to ~ sthg for sthg** échanger qqch contre qqch.
<> *n* **1.** [of prisoners, ideas] échange *m* ➲ **~ of contracts** échange *m* de contrats à la signature ■ **fair ~ is no robbery** *UK prov* donnant donnant ■ **Exchange and Mart** *hebdomadaire britannique de petites annonces*
2. [discussion] échange *m* ■ **a heated ~** un échange enflammé **3.** [cultural, educational] échange *m* ■ **as part of an ~** dans le cadre d'un échange ➲ **~ student** *étudiant qui prend part à un échange avec l'étranger* ■ **the Spanish students are here on an ~ visit** les étudiants espagnols sont en visite ici dans le cadre d'un échange
4. TELEC central *m* téléphonique
5. FIN change *m* ■ **foreign ~ office** bureau *m* de change ■ **~ control** contrôle *m* des changes
6. = **stock exchange.**
◆ **in exchange** *adv phr* en échange.
◆ **in exchange for** *prep phr* en échange de ■ **in ~ for helping with the housework she was given food and lodging** elle aidait aux travaux ménagers et en échange *OR* en contrepartie elle était nourrie et logée.

exchangeable [ɪks'tʃeɪndʒəbl] *adj* échangeable, qui peut être échangé ■ **goods are ~ only when accompanied by a valid receipt** les articles ne peuvent être échangés que s'ils sont accompagnés du ticket de caisse.

exchange rate *n* taux *m* de change.

Exchange Rate Mechanism *pr n* mécanisme *m* (des taux) de change (du SME).

exchequer [ɪks'tʃekəʳ] *n* [finances] finances *fpl.*
◆ **Exchequer** *n* POL [department] : **the ~** le ministère des Finances *(en Grande-Bretagne).*

excise[1] ['eksaɪz] *n* **1.** [tax] taxe *f*, contribution *f* indirecte **2.** *UK* [government office] régie *f*, service *m* des contributions indirectes.

excise[2] [ek'saɪz] *vt* **1.** *fml* [remove from a text] retrancher **2.** MED exciser.

excise duty ['eksaɪz-] *n* [taxation] contribution *f* indirecte.

exciseman ['eksaɪzmæn] *(pl* **excisemen** [-men]) *n UK* employé *m* de la régie *OR* des contributions indirectes.

excitability [ɪk,saɪtə'bɪlətɪ] *n* nervosité *f*, émotivité *f*.

excitable [ɪk'saɪtəbl] *adj* excitable, nerveux.

excitation [,eksɪ'teɪʃn] *n* **1.** [process, state] excitation *f* **2.** TECH excitation *f*.

excite [ɪk'saɪt] *vt* **1.** [agitate] exciter, énerver ■ **the doctor said you weren't to ~ yourself** le docteur a dit qu'il ne te fallait pas d'excitation *OR* qu'il ne fallait pas que tu t'énerves **2.** [fill with enthusiasm] enthousiasmer ■ **I'm very ~d by this latest development** ce fait nouveau me remplit d'enthousiasme **3.** [sexually] exciter **4.** [arouse - interest, curiosity] exciter, soulever, éveiller **5.** PHYSIOL exciter.

excited [ɪk'saɪtɪd] *adj* **1.** [enthusiastic, eager] excité ■ **to be ~ about** *OR* **at sthg** être excité par qqch ■ **the children were ~ at the prospect of going to the seaside** les enfants étaient tout excités à l'idée d'aller au bord de la mer ■ **you must be very ~ at being chosen to play for your country** vous devez être fou de joie d'avoir été choisi pour jouer pour votre pays ■ **don't get too ~** ne t'excite *OR* t'emballe pas trop **2.** [agitated] : **don't go getting ~, don't get ~** ne va pas t'énerver **3.** [sexually] excité **4.** PHYS excité.

excitedly [ɪk'saɪtɪdlɪ] *adv* [behave, watch] avec agitation ■ [say] sur un ton animé ■ [wait] fébrilement.

excitement [ɪk'saɪtmənt] *n* **1.** [enthusiasm] excitation *f*, animation *f*, enthousiasme *m* ■ **in her ~ at the news she knocked over a vase** les nouvelles l'ont mise dans un tel état d'excitation *OR* d'enthousiasme qu'elle a renversé un vase **2.** [agitation] excitation *f*, agitation *f* ■ **the ~ would kill her** une telle émotion lui serait fatale ■ **I've had quite enough ~ for one day** j'ai eu assez de sensations fortes pour une seule journée **3.** [sexual] excitation *f* **4.** [exciting events] animation *f* ■ **there should be plenty of ~ in today's match** le match d'aujourd'hui devrait être très animé ■ **all the ~ seemed to have gone out of their marriage** leur mariage semblait maintenant totalement dénué de passion ■ **what's all the ~ about?** mais que se passe-t-il?

exciting [ɪk'saɪtɪŋ] *adj* **1.** [day, life, events, match] passionnant, palpitant ■ [prospect] palpitant ■ [person, novel, restaurant] formidable ■ [news] sensationnel ■ **we've had an ~ time (of it) recently** ces derniers temps ont été mouvementés ■ **it was ~ to think that we'd soon be in New York** c'était excitant de penser que nous serions bientôt à New York **2.** [sexually] excitant.

excl. (*written abbrev of* **excluding**) : **~ taxes** HT.

exclaim [ɪk'skleɪm] <> *vi* s'exclamer.

<> *vt* : **"but why?", he ~ed** "mais pourquoi?", s'exclama-t-il.

exclamation [,eksklə'meɪʃn] *n* exclamation *f*.

exclamation mark *UK*, **exclamation point** *US* *n* point *m* d'exclamation.

exclamatory [ɪk'sklæmətrɪ] *adj* exclamatif.

exclude [ɪk'sklu:d] *vt* **1.** [bar] exclure ▪ **to ~ sb from sthg** exclure qqn de qqch ▪ **I felt that I was being ~d from the conversation** je sentais qu'on m'excluait de la conversation **2.** [not take into consideration] exclure ▪ **to ~ sthg/sb from sthg** exclure qqch/qqn de qqch ▪ **submarine-launched missiles were ~d from the arms talks** les missiles sous-marins n'entraient pas dans le cadre des négociations sur les armements.

excluding [ɪk'sklu:dɪŋ] *prep* à l'exclusion *OR* l'exception de, sauf, à part ▪ **not ~......** y compris.

exclusion [ɪk'sklu:ʒn] *n* **1.** [barring] exclusion *f* ▪ **the ~ of sb from a society/conversation** l'exclusion de qqn d'une société/conversation **2.** [omission] exclusion *f* ▪ **the ~ of sthg/sb from sthg** l'exclusion de qqch/qqn de qqch ▪ **to the ~ of everything** *OR* **all else** à l'exclusion de toute autre chose.

exclusion clause *n* clause *f* d'exclusion.

exclusive [ɪk'sklu:sɪv] <> *adj* **1.** [select - restaurant, neighbourhood] chic ; [- club] fermé **2.** [deal] exclusif ▪ **to have an ~ contract with a company** avoir un contrat exclusif avec une société ▪ **~ to** réservé (exclusivement) à **3.** [excluding taxes, charges etc] : **~ of VAT** TVA non comprise ▪ **a single room is £30 a night, ~** une chambre pour une personne coûte 30 livres la nuit, hors taxe ▪ **the rent is £100 a week ~** le loyer est de 100 livres par semaine sans les charges **4.** [excluding time] : **from the 14th to the 19th October, ~** du 14 au 19 octobre exclu **5.** [incompatible] exclusif ▪ **they are mutually ~** [propositions] l'une exclut l'autre, elles sont incompatibles **6.** [sole] unique ▪ **their ~ concern** leur seul souci ▪ **the ~ use of gold** l'emploi exclusif d'or.
<> *n* PRESS exclusivité *f* ▪ [interview] interview *f* exclusive.

exclusively [ɪk'sklu:sɪvlɪ] *adv* [only] exclusivement ▪ **published ~ in the "Times"** publié en exclusivité dans le "Times".

exclusiveness [ɪk'sklu:sɪvnɪs], **exclusivity** [,eksklu:'sɪvətɪ] *n* **1.** [of restaurant, address, district] chic *m* **2.** [of contract] nature *f* exclusive.

excommunicate [,ekskə'mju:nɪkeɪt] *vt* RELIG excommunier.

excommunication ['ekskə,mju:nɪ'keɪʃn] *n* RELIG excommunication *f*.

excoriate [eks'kɔ:rɪeɪt] *vt fml* [censure, reprimand] condamner.

excrement ['ekskrɪmənt] *n (U) fml* excréments *mpl*.

excreta [ɪk'skri:tə] *npl fml* excréments *mpl*.

excrete [ɪk'skri:t] *vt* excréter.

excretion [ɪk'skri:ʃn] *n* **1.** [action] excrétion *f* **2.** [substance] sécrétion *f*.

excruciating [ɪk'skru:ʃɪeɪtɪŋ] *adj* **1.** [extremely painful] extrêmement douloureux, atroce **2.** *inf* [extremely bad] atroce, abominable ▪ **it was ~** [embarrassing] c'était affreux ; [boring] c'était atroce.

excruciatingly [ɪk'skru:ʃɪeɪtɪŋlɪ] *adv* [painful, boring] atrocement, affreusement.

exculpate ['ekskʌlpeɪt] *vt fml* disculper ▪ **to ~ sb from sthg** disculper qqn de qqch.

excursion [ɪk'skɜ:ʃn] *n* **1.** [organized trip] excursion *f* **2.** [short local journey] expédition *f* **3.** [into a different field] incursion *f* ▪ **after a brief ~ into politics** après une brève incursion dans la politique.

excursion ticket *n UK* RAIL billet *m* circulaire *(bénéficiant de tarifs réduits)*.

excusable [ɪk'skju:zəbl] *adj* excusable, pardonnable.

excuse <> *n* [ɪk'skju:s] **1.** [explanation, justification] excuse *f* ▪ **her ~ for not coming** son excuse pour n'être pas venue ▪ **to give sthg as one's ~** donner qqch comme excuse ▪ **that's no ~** ce n'est pas une excuse *OR* une raison ▪ **there's no ~ for that kind of behaviour** ce genre de comportement est sans excuse *OR* inexcusable ▪ **I don't want (to hear) any ~s!** je ne veux pas d'excuse! ▪ **you'd better have a good ~!** tu as intérêt à avoir une bonne excuse! ▪ **~s, ~s!** des excuses, toujours des excuses! ▪ **he's always finding ~s for them/for their behaviour** il est tout le temps en train de leur trouver des excuses/d'excuser leur comportement ▪ **I'm not making ~s for them** je ne les excuse pas ▪ **to make one's ~s** s'excuser, présenter ses excuses ▪ **ignorance is no ~** l'ignorance n'excuse pas tout ▪ **by way of (an) ~** en guise d'excuse
2. [example] : **a poor ~ for a father** un père lamentable ▪ **this is a poor ~ for a bus service** ce service d'autobus est lamentable **3.** [pretext] excuse *f*, prétexte *m* ▪ **an ~ to do** *OR* **for doing sthg** une excuse *OR* un prétexte pour faire qqch ▪ **any ~ for a drink!** toutes les excuses sont bonnes pour boire un verre!
<> *vt* [ɪk'skju:z] **1.** [justify - bad behaviour] excuser ▪ **he tried to ~ himself by saying that...** il a essayé de se justifier en disant que...
2. [forgive - bad behaviour, person] excuser, pardonner ▪ **you can ~ that in someone of his age** c'est pardonnable chez quelqu'un de son âge ▪ **I'll ~ your lateness (just) this once** je te pardonne ton retard pour cette fois ▪ **now, if you will ~ me** maintenant, si vous voulez bien m'excuser ▪ **one could be ~d for thinking that he was much younger** on dirait *OR* croirait qu'il est beaucoup plus jeune ▪ **~ my interrupting, but...** excusez-moi *OR* pardon de vous interrompre, mais... ▪ **~ me** [to get past] pardon ; [as interruption, to attract sb's attention] pardon, excusez-moi ; *US* [as apology] pardon, excusez-moi ▪ **~ me for asking!** oh, ça va, je ne faisais que demander!, ce n'était qu'une question! ▪ **well, ~ me for mentioning it!** oh, ça va, je n'en parlerai plus! ▪ **to ~ o.s.** s'excuser
3. [exempt] dispenser ▪ **to ~ sb from sthg** dispenser qqn de qqch ▪ **to ~ sb from doing sthg** dispenser qqn de faire qqch
4. [allow to go] excuser ▪ **please may I be ~d?** [to go to lavatory] puis-je sortir, s'il vous plaît? ; [from table] puis-je sortir de table, s'il vous plaît?

excuse-me [ɪk'skju:z-] *n danse pendant laquelle on peut prendre le ou la partenaire de quelqu'un d'autre.*

ex-directory *UK* <> *adj* sur la liste rouge ▪ **an ~ number** un numéro ne figurant pas dans l'annuaire *OR* figurant sur la liste rouge.
<> *adv* : **to go ~** se mettre sur la liste rouge.

exec. [ɪg'zek] *n* = **executive**.

execrable ['eksɪkrəbl] *adj fml* exécrable.

execrate ['eksɪkreɪt] *vt fml* **1.** [loathe] exécrer **2.** [denounce] condamner, s'élever contre.

executant [ɪg'zekjʊtənt] *n* **1.** *fml* [of an order] exécutant *m*, - e *f* **2.** MUS exécutant *m*, - e *f*.

execute ['eksɪkju:t] *vt* **1.** [put to death] exécuter ▪ **~d for murder/treason** exécuté pour meurtre/trahison **2.** *fml* [carry out] exécuter **3.** LAW [will, sentence, law] exécuter **4.** COMPUT exécuter.

execution [,eksɪ'kju:ʃn] *n* **1.** [of person] exécution *f* **2.** *fml* [of order, plan, drawing] exécution *f* ▪ **to put sthg into ~** mettre qqch à exécution **3.** LAW [of will, sentence, law] exécution *f* **4.** COMPUT exécution *f*.

executioner [,eksɪ'kju:ʃnər] *n* bourreau *m*.

executive [ɪg'zekjʊtɪv] <> *n* **1.** [person] cadre *mf* ▪ **a business ~** un cadre commercial **2.** [body] corps *m* exécutif ▪ POL [branch of government] exécutif *m*.
<> *adj* **1.** [dining room, washroom etc] des cadres, de la direction ▪ [suite, chair] de cadre, spécial cadre ▪ **~ model** *OR* **version** [of car] modèle *m* grand luxe ⊙ **~ briefcase** attaché-case *m* ▪ **~ toys** gadgets *mpl* pour cadres **2.** [function, role] exécutif ▪ **an ~ officer in the civil service** un cadre de l'administration ▪ **he's not good at making ~ decisions** il n'est pas doué pour prendre des décisions importantes ▪ **we need an ~ decision** il faut trancher ⊙ **~ director** cadre *m* supérieur ▪ **~ producer** producteur *m* délégué.

executor [ɪg'zekjʊtər] *n* LAW [of will] exécuteur *m*, - trice *f* testamentaire.

exegesis [,eksɪ'dʒi:sɪs] *n* exégèse *f*.

exemplary [ɪg'zemplərɪ] *adj* **1.** [very good - behaviour, pupil] exemplaire **2.** [serving as a warning] exemplaire ▪ **~ damages** LAW dommages-intérêts *mpl* exemplaires *OR* à titre exemplaire.

exemplification [ɪg,zemplɪfɪ'keɪʃn] *n* illustration *f*, illustrations *fpl*, exemplification *f*.

exemplify [ɪg'zemplɪfaɪ] *vt* **1.** [give example of] illustrer, exemplifier **2.** [be example of] illustrer.

exempt [ɪg'zempt] <> *adj* exempt ▪ **to be ~ from sthg** être exempt de qqch.
<> *vt* [gen] exempter ▪ [from tax] exonérer ▪ **to ~ sb/sthg from sthg** exempter qqn/qqch de qqch.

exemption [ɪg'zempʃn] *n* [action, state] exemption *f* ▪ **tax ~** exonération *f* fiscale.

exercise ['eksəsaɪz] <> *n* **1.** [physical] exercice *m* ▪ **~ is good for you** l'exercice est bon pour la santé ▪ **it's good ~** c'est un bon exercice ▪ **the doctor has told him to take more ~** le docteur lui a dit de faire plus d'exercice
2. [mental, in education] exercice *m* ▪ **piano ~s** exercices de piano
3. [use] exercice *m* ▪ **in the ~ of one's duties** dans l'exercice de ses fonctions ▪ **by the ~ of a little imagination** en usant d'un peu d'imagination, avec un peu d'imagination
4. MIL exercice *m* ▪ **they're on ~s** ils sont à l'exercice
5. [activity, operation] : **it was an interesting ~** cela a été une expérience intéressante ▪ **this is more than just a PR ~** ce n'est pas seulement de la poudre aux yeux ▪ **it was a pointless ~** cela n'a servi absolument à rien
6. *US* [ceremony] cérémonie *f* ▪ **graduation ~s** cérémonie de remise des diplômes.
<> *vt* **1.** [body, muscle] exercer, faire travailler ▪ [dog, horse] donner de l'exercice à ▪ **if you were to ~ your brain on the problem** si tu faisais travailler tes méninges pour régler ce problème
2. [troops] entraîner
3. [use, put into practice - right, option, authority] exercer
4. *fml* [preoccupy] préoccuper.
<> *vi* **1.** [take exercise] faire de l'exercice
2. [train] s'exercer, s'entraîner.

exercise bike *n* vélo *m* d'appartement.

exercise book *n* **1.** [for writing in] cahier *m* d'exercices **2.** [containing exercises] livre *m* d'exercices.

exerciser ['eksəsaɪzə^r] *n* [piece of equipment] appareil *m* de gymnastique ▪ [bike] vélo *m* d'appartement.

exercise yard *n* [in prison] cour *f*, préau *m*.

exert [ɪg'zɜ:t] *vt* **1.** [pressure, force] exercer ▪ **they were willing to ~ their influence on behalf of our campaign** ils étaient d'accord pour mettre leur influence au service de notre campagne **2.** : **to ~ o.s.** [make effort] se donner de la peine *OR* du mal ▪ **don't ~ yourself!** *iron* ne te donne pas trop de mal, surtout!

exertion [ɪg'zɜ:ʃn] *n* **1.** [of force] exercice *m* ▪ **the ~ of pressure on sb/sthg** la pression exercée sur qqn/qqch **2.** [effort] effort *m* ▪ **by one's own ~s** par ses propres moyens.

exeunt ['eksɪʌnt] *vi* THEAT [in stage directions] : **~ the Queen and her attendants** la reine et sa suite sortent.

exfoliate [eks'fəʊlɪeɪt] <> *vi* s'exfolier.
<> *vt* exfolier.

ex gratia [eks'greɪʃə] *adj* : **~ payment** paiement *m* à titre gracieux.

exhalation [,eksə'leɪʃn] *n* **1.** [breathing out - of air] expiration *f* ; [- of smoke, fumes] exhalation *f* **2.** [air breathed out] air *m* expiré, souffle *m*, exhalaison *f*.

exhale [eks'heɪl] <> *vt* [air] expirer ▪ [gas, fumes] exhaler.
<> *vi* [breathe out] expirer.

exhaust [ɪg'zɔ:st] <> *n* **1.** [on vehicle - system] échappement *m* ; [- pipe] pot *m* *OR* tuyau *m* d'échappement **2.** *(U)* [fumes] gaz *mpl* d'échappement.
<> *vt* **1.** [use up - supplies, possibilities] épuiser ▪ **you're ~ing my patience** tu mets ma patience à bout **2.** [tire out] épuiser, exténuer.

exhausted [ɪg'zɔ:stɪd] *adj* **1.** [person, smile] épuisé, exténué **2.** [used up - mine, land] épuisé ▪ **my patience is ~** je suis à bout de patience.

exhausting [ɪg'zɔ:stɪŋ] *adj* [job, climb, climate] épuisant, exténuant, éreintant ▪ [person] fatigant, excédant.

exhaustion [ɪg'zɔ:stʃn] *n* **1.** [tiredness] épuisement *m*, éreintement *m*, grande fatigue *f* ▪ **to be suffering from ~** être dans un état d'épuisement **2.** [of supplies, topic] épuisement *m*.

exhaustive [ɪg'zɔ:stɪv] *adj* [analysis, treatment] exhaustif ▪ [investigation, enquiry] approfondi, poussé ▪ **the list is not ~** cette liste n'est pas exhaustive.

exhaustively [ɪg'zɔ:stɪvlɪ] *adv* exhaustivement.

exhaust pipe *n* *UK* pot *m* *OR* tuyau *m* d'échappement.

exhaust system *n* AUT échappement *m*.

exhibit [ɪg'zɪbɪt] <> *vt* **1.** [subj: artist] exposer ▪ [subj: companies] présenter **2.** [show, display - ID card, passport] montrer **3.** [manifest - courage, self-control] montrer, manifester.
<> *vi* [painter, company] exposer.
<> *n* **1.** [in an exhibition] objet *m* (exposé) ▪ **one of the most interesting ~s at the fair** l'une des pièces les plus intéressantes en exposition à la foire **2.** LAW pièce *f* à conviction **3.** *US* [exhibition] exposition *f*.

exhibition [,eksɪ'bɪʃn] *n* **1.** [of paintings, products] exposition *f* ▪ [of film] présentation *f* ▪ **the Klee ~** l'exposition Klee ⊳ **~ centre** centre *m* d'exposition **2.** [of bad manners, ingenuity] démonstration *f* ▪ **to make an ~ of o.s.** se donner en spectacle **3.** *UK* UNIV bourse *f* d'études.

exhibitioner [,eksɪ'bɪʃnə^r] *n* *UK* UNIV boursier *m*, - ère *f*.

exhibitionism [,eksɪ'bɪʃnɪzm] *n* **1.** [gen] besoin *m* *OR* volonté *f* de se faire remarquer **2.** PSYCHOL exhibitionnisme *m*.

exhibitionist [,eksɪ'bɪʃnɪst] *n* **1.** [gen] *personne qui cherche toujours à se faire remarquer* ▪ **he's a terrible ~** il faut toujours qu'il cherche à se faire remarquer **2.** PSYCHOL exhibitionniste *mf*.

exhibition match *n* match-exhibition *m*.

exhibitor [ɪg'zɪbɪtə^r] *n* [at gallery, trade fair] exposant *m*.

exhilarate [ɪg'zɪləreɪt] *vt* exalter, griser.

exhilarated [ɪg'zɪləreɪtɪd] *adj* [mood, laugh] exalté.

exhilarating [ɪg'zɪləreɪtɪŋ] *adj* exaltant, grisant.

exhilaration [ɪg,zɪlə'reɪʃn] *n* exaltation *f*, griserie *f*.

exhort [ɪg'zɔ:t] *vt* *fml* exhorter ▪ **to ~ sb to do sthg** exhorter qqn à faire qqch.

exhortation [,egzɔ:'teɪʃn] *n* *fml* [act, words] exhortation *f*.

exhumation [,ekshju:'meɪʃn] *n* *fml* exhumation *f*.

exhume [eks'hju:m] *vt* *fml* exhumer.

ex-husband *n* ex-mari *m*.

exigency ['eksɪdʒənsɪ] (*pl* **exigencies**), **exigence** ['eksɪdʒəns] *n* *fml* **1.** *(usu pl)* [demand] exigence *f* **2.** [urgent situation] situation *f* urgente **3.** [urgency] urgence *f*.

exigent ['eksɪdʒənt] *adj* *fml* **1.** [urgent] urgent, pressant **2.** [demanding, exacting] exigeant.

exile ['eksaɪl] <> *n* **1.** [banishment] exil *m* ▪ **his self-imposed ~** son exil volontaire ▪ **to live in ~** vivre en exil ▪ **to send sb into ~** envoyer qqn en exil ▪ **to go into ~** partir en exil **2.** [person] exilé *m*, - e *f* ▪ **tax ~** *personne qui s'expatrie pour échapper au fisc*.
<> *vt* exiler, expatrier ▪ **he was ~d from his native Poland** il a été exilé *OR* expatrié de sa Pologne natale.

exiled ['eksaɪld] *adj* exilé ▪ **the ~ government** le gouvernement en exil.

exist [ɪg'zɪst] *vi* exister ▪ **do ghosts ~?** les fantômes existent-ils? ▪ **that's not living, that's just ~ing!** je n'appelle pas ça vivre, j'appelle ça subsister *OR* survivre ▪ **can life ~ under these**

conditions? la vie est-elle possible dans ces conditions? ▪ **he earns enough to ~ on** il gagne suffisamment pour vivre ▪ **we can't ~ without oxygen** nous ne pouvons pas vivre sans oxygène.

existence [ɪg'zɪstəns] *n* **1.** [being] existence *f* ▪ **the continued ~ of life on this planet/of these old-fashioned procedures** la survivance de la vie sur la planète/de ces procédures arriérées ▪ **to come into ~** [species] apparaître ; [the earth] se former ; [law, institution] naître, être créé ▪ **the oldest steam engine still in ~** la plus vieille machine à vapeur encore existante ▪ **the only whale left in ~** la dernière baleine encore en vie ▪ **to go out of ~** cesser d'exister **2.** [life] existence *f* ▪ **to lead a pleasant/wretched ~** mener une existence agréable/misérable.

existent [ɪg'zɪstənt] *adj* existant.

existential [,egzɪ'stenʃl] *adj* existentiel.

existentialism [,egzɪ'stenʃəlɪzm] *n* existentialisme *m*.

existentialist [,egzɪ'stenʃəlɪst] <> *n* existentialiste *mf*.
<> *adj* existentialiste.

existing [ɪg'zɪstɪŋ] *adj* actuel.

exit ['eksɪt] <> *n* **1.** [way out - from room, motorway] sortie *f* ▪ **'~ only'** 'réservé à la sortie' **2.** THEAT sortie *f*, exit *m inv* ▪ [act of going out - from a room] sortie *f* ▪ **to make one's ~** THEAT & *fig* faire sa sortie **3.** COMPUT sortie *f*.
<> *vi* **1.** THEAT sortir ▪ **~ Anne** [as stage direction] exit Anne, Anne sort **2.** [go out, leave] sortir ▪ [bullet] ressortir **3.** COMPUT sortir.
<> *vt* COMPUT sortir de ▪ [leave] quitter, sortir de.

exit poll *UK*, **exit survey** ['-sɜːveɪ] *US n sondage réalisé auprès des votants à la sortie du bureau de vote*.

exit visa *n* visa *m* de sortie.

exodus ['eksədəs] *n* exode *m* ▪ **there was a general ~ to the bar** il y a eu un mouvement de masse en direction du bar.
◆ **Exodus** *n* **1.** [book] : **(the Book of) Exodus** (l')Exode **2.** [journey] exode *m*.

ex officio [eksə'fɪʃɪəʊ] <> *adj* [member] de droit.
<> *adv* [act, decide etc] de droit.

exonerate [ɪg'zɒnəreɪt] *vt* disculper, innocenter.

exoneration [ɪg,zɒnə'reɪʃn] *n* disculpation *f*.

exorbitant [ɪg'zɔːbɪtənt] *adj* [price, demands, claims] exorbitant, démesuré, excessif.

exorbitantly [ɪg'zɔːbɪtəntlɪ] *adv* [priced] excessivement, démesurément.

exorcism ['eksɔːsɪzm] *n* exorcisme *m* ▪ **to carry out** *OR* **to perform an ~** pratiquer un exorcisme.

exorcist ['eksɔːsɪst] *n* exorciste *mf*.

exorcize, ise ['eksɔːsaɪz] *vt* [evil spirits, place] exorciser.

exotic [ɪg'zɒtɪk] *adj* exotique ▪ **an ~-sounding name** un nom à consonance exotique.

exotica [ɪg'zɒtɪkə] *npl* objets *mpl* exotiques.

exotically [ɪg'zɒtɪklɪ] *adv* [dressed, decorated] avec exotisme ▪ **~ perfumed** [flower] aux senteurs exotiques ; [person] au parfum exotique.

exoticism [ɪg'zɒtɪsɪzm] *n* exotisme *m*.

expand [ɪk'spænd] <> *vt* **1.** [empire, army, staff] agrandir ▪ [company, business] agrandir, développer ▪ [chest, muscles, ideas] développer ▪ [knowledge, influence] élargir, étendre ▪ COMPUT [memory] étendre ▪ [gas, metal] dilater ▪ **to ~ a company into a multinational** agrandir une société pour en faire une multinationale **2.** MATHS [equation] développer.
<> *vi* **1.** [empire, army, staff] s'agrandir ▪ [company, business] s'agrandir, se développer ▪ [chest, muscles, market] se développer ▪ [knowledge, influence] s'étendre, s'élargir ▪ [gas, metal] se dilater ▪ [volume of traffic] augmenter ▪ [in business] se développer, s'agrandir ▪ **we are looking to ~ into the cosmetics industry** nous envisageons de nous diversifier en nous lançant dans l'industrie des cosmétiques **2.** [on an idea] s'étendre.

◆ **expand on** *vt insep* développer ▪ **in the next chapter I shall ~ further on these ideas** je développerai ces idées *OR* je m'étendrai davantage sur ces idées au chapitre suivant.

expandable [ɪk'spændɪbl] *adj* [gas, material] expansible ▪ [idea, theory] qui peut être développé ▪ [basic set] qui peut être complété ▪ COMPUT [memory] extensible.

expanded [ɪk'spændɪd] *adj* [metal, gas] expansé.

expanding [ɪk'spændɪŋ] *adj* **1.** [company, empire, gas, metal] en expansion ▪ [influence] grandissant ▪ [industry, market] en expansion, qui se développe ▪ **the ~ universe theory** la théorie de l'expansion de l'univers **2.** [extendable] : **~ suitcase/briefcase** valise/serviette extensible.

expanse [ɪk'spæns] *n* étendue *f* ▪ **the vast ~ of the plain** l'immensité de la plaine ▪ **she was showing a large ~ of thigh** on lui voyait une bonne partie des cuisses.

expansion [ɪk'spænʃn] *n* [of empire] expansion *f*, élargissement *m* ▪ [of army, staff] augmentation *f*, accroissement *m* ▪ [of chest, muscles, ideas] développement *m* ▪ [of knowledge, influence] élargissement *m* ▪ [of gas, metal] expansion *f*, dilatation *f* ▪ COMPUT [of memory] extension *f* ▪ [of business] développement *m*, agrandissement *m*, extension *f*.

expansion card *n* COMPUT carte *f* d'extension.

expansionism [ɪk'spænʃənɪzm] *n* expansionnisme *m*.

expansionist [ɪk'spænʃənɪst] <> *adj* expansionniste.
<> *n* expansionniste *mf*.

expansion slot *n* COMPUT emplacement *m OR* logement *m* pour carte d'extension.

expansive [ɪk'spænsɪv] *adj* **1.** [person, mood, gesture] expansif **2.** PHYS [gas] expansible, dilatable.

expansively [ɪk'spænsɪvlɪ] *adv* [talk, gesture] de manière expansive.

expansiveness [ɪk'spænsɪvnɪs] *n* [of person] expansivité *f*.

expat [,eks'pæt] (*abbrev of* **expatriate**) *inf* <> *n* expatrié *m*, - e *f*.
<> *adj* [Briton, American] expatrié ▪ [bar, community] des expatriés.

expatiate [eks'peɪʃɪeɪt] *vi fml* s'étendre, discourir ▪ **to ~ on sthg** s'étendre *OR* discourir sur qqch.

expatriate <> *n* [eks'pætrɪət] expatrié *m*, - e *f*.
<> *adj* [eks'pætrɪət] [Briton, American etc] expatrié ▪ [bar, community] des expatriés.
<> *vt* [eks'pætrɪeɪt] expatrier, exiler.

expect [ɪk'spekt] <> *vt* **1.** [anticipate] s'attendre à ▪ **we ~ed that it would be much bigger** nous nous attendions à ce qu'il soit beaucoup plus gros, nous pensions qu'il allait être beaucoup plus gros ▪ **we ~ed you to bring your own** nous pensions que vous alliez apporter le vôtre ▪ **to ~ sb to do sthg** s'attendre à ce que qqn fasse qqch ▪ **she knew more Russian than I ~ed her to** elle était meilleure en russe que je ne m'y attendais ▪ **to ~ the worst** s'attendre au pire ▪ **I ~ed as much!** je m'en doutais!, c'est bien ce que je pensais! ▪ **it was better/worse than I ~ed** c'était mieux/pire que je ne m'y attendais ▪ **she is as well as can be ~ed** elle va aussi bien que sa condition le permet ▪ **I had ~ed better of** *OR* **from you** je n'aurais pas cru ça de vous ▪ **what can you ~ from a government like that?** que voulez-vous, avec un gouvernement pareil! ▪ **as might have been ~ed, as was to be ~ed** comme on pouvait s'y attendre
2. [count on] : **we're ~ing you to help us** nous comptons sur votre aide ▪ **don't ~ me to be there!** ne t'attends pas à ce que j'y sois!
3. [demand] : **to ~ sb to do sthg** demander à qqn de faire qqch ▪ **I ~ something to be done** j'exige qu'on fasse quelque chose à ce sujet ▪ **you ~ too much of him** tu lui en demandes trop ▪ **it's no less than I would have ~ed from my own family** je ne me serais pas attendu à moins de la part de ma propre famille ▪ **I'm ~ed to write all his speeches** je suis censé *OR* supposé rédiger tous ses discours
4. [suppose, imagine] imaginer, penser, supposer ▪ **I ~ so** je pense, j'imagine ▪ **I don't ~ so** je ne pense pas, j'imagine que

non ■ **I ~ you're right** tu dois avoir raison ■ **I ~ you'll be wanting something to drink** vous boirez bien quelque chose ; [grudgingly] j'imagine que vous voulez quelque chose à boire **5.** [baby] attendre
6. [await] attendre ■ **I'm ~ing friends for dinner** j'attends des amis à dîner ■ **(at) what time should we ~ you then?** à quelle heure devons-nous vous attendre alors?
<> *vi* : **to be ~ing** [be pregnant] être enceinte, attendre un enfant.

expectancy [ɪk'spektənsɪ], **expectance** [ɪk'spektəns] *n* [anticipation] : **the look of ~ on his face** l'attente qui se lisait sur son visage ■ **in a tone of eager ~** sur un ton plein d'espérance *OR* d'espoir.

expectant [ɪk'spektənt] *adj* **1.** [anticipating] : **with an ~ look in his eye** avec dans son regard l'air d'attendre quelque chose ■ **in an ~ tone of voice** la voix chargée d'espoir **2.** [pregnant] : **~ mother** future maman *f*.

expectantly [ɪk'spektəntlɪ] *adv* [enquire, glance] avec l'air d'attendre quelque chose ■ [wait] impatiemment.

expectation [,ekspek'teɪʃn] *n* **1.** *(U)* [anticipation] : **with eager ~** avec l'air d'espérer quelque chose ■ **in ~ of** dans l'attente de ■ **we live in ~** nous vivons dans l'attente *OR* l'expectative **2.** *(usu pl)* [sthg expected] attente *f* ■ **my ~s for its success were not that high** je n'espérais pas vraiment que ça réussirait ■ **this merely confirms our worst ~s** cela ne fait que confirmer nos prévisions les plus noires ■ **contrary to ~s** contrairement à *OR* contre toute attente ■ **to exceed sb's ~s** dépasser l'attente *OR* les espérances de qqn ■ **(not) to come up to ~s** (ne pas) être à la hauteur des espérances ■ **to have high ~s of sb/sthg** attendre beaucoup de qqn/qqch ■ **we have certain ~s of our employees** [requirements] nous avons certaines exigences envers nos employés ■ **to have great ~s** [prospects] avoir de grandes espérances ■ **what are your ~s?** [for salary, job prospects] quelles sont vos conditions *OR* exigences? ➊ **'Great Expectations'** *Dickens* 'les Grandes Espérances'.

expected [ɪk'spektɪd] *adj* attendu.

expectorant [ɪk'spektərənt] *n* expectorant *m*.

expediency [ɪk'spi:djənsɪ] (*pl* **expediencies**), **expedience** [ɪk'spi:djəns] *n* [advisability - of measure, policy etc] opportunité *f* ■ [self-interest] opportunisme *m*.

expedient [ɪk'spi:djənt] <> *adj* [advisable] indiqué, convenable, opportun ■ [involving self-interest] commode.
<> *n* expédient *m*.

expedite ['ekspɪdaɪt] *vt fml* [work, legal process] hâter, activer, accélérer ■ [completion of contract, deal] hâter ■ **to ~ matters** accélérer *OR* activer les choses.

expedition [,ekspɪ'dɪʃn] *n* [scientific, of explorers, to shops etc] expédition *f* ■ **to go on an ~** aller *OR* partir en expédition, aller faire une expédition.

expeditionary [,ekspɪ'dɪʃnərɪ] *adj* MIL : **~ mission** mission *f* d'expédition ■ **~ force** force *f* expéditionnaire.

expeditious [,ekspɪ'dɪʃəs] *adj fml* diligent.

expel [ɪk'spel] *vt* **1.** [from school] renvoyer ■ [from country, club] expulser **2.** [gas, liquid] expulser.

expend [ɪk'spend] *vt* **1.** [time, energy] consacrer ■ [resources] utiliser, employer ■ **to ~ time/energy on sthg** consacrer du temps/de l'énergie à qqch **2.** [use up] épuiser.

expendability [ɪk,spendə'bɪlətɪ] *n* [of people, workforce, equipment] superfluité *f* ■ [of troops, spies] caractère *m* sacrifiable.

expendable [ɪk'spendəbl] *adj* [person, workforce, object] superflu ■ [troops, spies] qui peut être sacrifié ■ **he thinks people are ~** il pense qu'il peut se débarrasser des gens comme bon lui semble.

expenditure [ɪk'spendɪtʃəʳ] *n* **1.** [act of spending] dépense *f* **2.** *(U)* [money spent] dépenses *fpl* ■ **~ on sthg** dépenses en qqch ■ **arms/defence ~** dépenses en armes/liées à la défense.

expense [ɪk'spens] *n* **1.** [cost] coût *m* ■ **anything we can do to offset the ~** tout ce que nous pouvons faire pour compenser le coût *OR* les coûts *OR* les frais ■ **if it can really be done with such little ~** si cela peut vraiment se faire à si peu de frais ■ **the huge ~ of moving house** le coût énorme qu'entraîne un déménagement ■ **to go to considerable ~ to do sthg** faire beaucoup de frais pour faire qqch ■ **don't go to any ~ over it** ne vous mettez pas en frais pour cela ■ **they had gone to the ~ of hiring a firm of caterers** ils s'étaient mis en frais et avaient engagé des traiteurs ■ **no ~ was spared** on n'a pas regardé à la dépense ■ **I'll do it at my own ~** je le ferai à mes frais **2.** [expensiveness] cherté *f*, coût *m* élevé **3.** *fig* **a joke at somebody else's ~** une plaisanterie aux dépens de quelqu'un d'autre ■ **at the ~ of sthg** aux dépens de qqch ■ **to succeed at other people's ~** réussir aux dépens des autres **4.** COMM : **no, that's my ~** non, c'est sur mon compte.
◆ **expenses** *npl* frais *mpl* ■ **it's on ~s** c'est l'entreprise qui paie, cela passe dans les notes de frais ■ **to live on ~s** vivre sur ses notes de frais, vivre aux frais de son entreprise ■ **to put sthg on ~s** mettre qqch dans les notes de frais ■ **to get ~s** [be paid expenses] être indemnisé de ses frais ■ **travelling ~s** frais de déplacement ■ **all ~s paid** tous frais payés.

expense account <> *n* indemnité *f OR* allocation *f* pour frais professionnels ■ **to put sthg on the ~** mettre qqch dans les (notes de) frais.
<> *comp* : **an ~ dinner** un dîner passé dans les notes de frais.

expenses-paid *adj* [trip, holiday] tous frais payés.

expensive [ɪk'spensɪv] *adj* cher ■ **it's an ~ hobby** c'est un passe-temps coûteux *OR* qui coûte cher ■ **the central heating became too ~ to run** le chauffage central a commencé à revenir trop cher ■ **to have ~ tastes** avoir des goûts de luxe ■ **it's an ~ place to live** la vie y est chère ■ **that could be an ~ mistake** *liter & fig* c'est une erreur qui pourrait coûter cher.

expensively [ɪk'pensɪvlɪ] *adv* à grands frais.

expensiveness [ɪk'spensɪvnɪs] *n* cherté *f*.

experience [ɪk'spɪərɪəns] <> *n* **1.** [in life, in a subject] expérience *f* ■ **I had no previous ~** je n'avais aucune expérience préalable ■ **do you have any ~ of working with animals?** avez-vous déjà travaillé avec des animaux? ■ **she has considerable management ~** elle a une expérience considérable de *OR* dans la gestion ■ **~ shows *OR* proves that...** l'expérience démontre *OR* montre *OR* prouve que... ■ **I know from ~ that he's not to be trusted** je sais par expérience qu'il ne faut pas lui faire confiance ■ **to know from bitter ~** savoir pour en avoir fait la cruelle expérience ■ **to speak from ~** parler en connaissance de cause ■ **in *OR* from my (own) ~, (speaking) from personal ~** d'après mon expérience personnelle ■ **my ~ has been *OR* it has been my ~ that...** d'après mon expérience... ■ **has that been your ~?** [do you agree?] avez-vous remarqué la même chose? ■ **to put sthg down to ~** tirer un enseignement *OR* une leçon de qqch ■ **it's all good ~** [as consolation] à quelque chose malheur est bon **2.** [event] expérience *f* ■ **I had so many exciting ~s** j'ai vécu tant d'aventures passionnantes ■ **after this stressful ~** après ce stress ■ **how did you enjoy the American ~?** comment as-tu trouvé l'Amérique? ■ **my first ~ of French cooking/of a real Scottish New Year** la première fois que j'ai goûté à la cuisine française/que j'ai assisté à un vrai réveillon écossais.
<> *vt* **1.** [undergo - hunger, hardship, recession] connaître ■ **to ~ military combat** faire l'expérience du combat militaire ■ **he ~d great difficulty in opening the door** il a eu beaucoup de mal à ouvrir la porte **2.** [feel - thrill, emotion, despair] sentir, ressentir ■ **he is experiencing a great deal of anxiety at the moment** il est très angoissé en ce moment **3.** [have personal knowledge of] : **come and ~ Manhattan** venez découvrir Manhattan ■ **if you've never ~d French cooking** si vous n'avez jamais goûté à la cuisine française ■ **to ~ a real Scottish New Year** assister à un vrai réveillon écossais.

experienced [ɪk'spɪərɪənst] *adj* expérimenté ■ **we're looking for someone a bit more ~** nous recherchons quelqu'un qui ait un peu plus d'expérience ■ **to be ~ in sthg** avoir l'expérience de qqch ■ **to be ~ at doing sthg** avoir l'habitude de faire qqch.

experiential [ɪkspɪərɪ'enʃəl] *adj fml &* PHILOS empirique, expérientiel.

experiment [ɪk'sperɪmənt] <> *n liter & fig* expérience *f* ■ **to carry out *OR* to conduct an ~** réaliser *OR* effectuer une expé-

rience ▪ **an ~ in sthg** une expérience de qqch ▪ **~s on animals** des expériences sur les animaux ▪ **as an** *OR* **by way of ~** à titre d'expérience.
<> *vi* faire une expérience *OR* des expériences ▪ **to ~ with a new technique** expérimenter une nouvelle technique ▪ **to ~ with drugs** essayer la drogue ▪ **to ~ on animals** faire des expériences sur les animaux.

experimental [ɪk,sperɪ'mentl] *adj* expérimental.

experimentally [ɪk,sperɪ'mentəlɪ] *adv* [by experimenting] expérimentalement ▪ [as an experiment] à titre expérimental.

experimentation [ɪk,sperɪmen'teɪʃn] *n* expérimentation *f*.

experimenter [ɪk'sperɪmentəʳ] *n* expérimentateur *m*, -trice *f*.

expert ['ekspɜ:t] <> *n* expert *m*, -e *f*, spécialiste *mf* ▪ **to be an ~ on one's subject/in one's field** être un expert dans sa matière/dans son domaine ▪ **he's an ~ at archery** c'est un expert au tir à l'arc ▪ **to look at sthg with the eye of an ~** regarder qqch avec l'œil d'un expert ▪ **I'm no ~, but...** je ne suis pas expert *OR* spécialiste en la matière, mais...
<> *adj* [person] expert ▪ [advice, opinion] autorisé, d'expert ▪ **to be ~ at doing sthg** être expert à faire qqch ▪ **to be ~ at sthg** être expert en qqch ▪ **to run** *OR* **to cast an ~ eye over sthg** jeter un œil expert sur qqch ▪ **~ testimony** LAW témoignage *m* d'expert ▪ **~ panel** commission *f* d'experts.

expertise [,ekspɜ:'ti:z] *n* compétence *f* d'expert, savoir-faire *m* ▪ **to do sthg with great ~** faire qqch avec beaucoup de compétence.

expertly ['ekspɜ:tlɪ] *adv* d'une manière experte, expertement.

expert system *n* COMPUT système *m* expert.

expert witness *n* LAW expert *m (appelé comme témoin)*.

expiate ['ekspɪeɪt] *vt fml* expier.

expiation [,ekspɪ'eɪʃn] *n fml* expiation *f* ▪ **in ~ of one's sins** en expiation de ses péchés.

expire [ɪk'spaɪəʳ] *vi* **1.** [contract, lease, visa etc] expirer, arriver à terme **2.** [exhale] expirer **3.** *arch* & *lit* [die] expirer.

expiry [ɪk'spaɪərɪ] *n* [of contract, lease, visa etc] expiration *f*, échéance *f*.

expiry date *n* [of contract, lease, visa etc] date *f* d'expiration *OR* d'échéance.

explain [ɪk'spleɪn] <> *vt* **1.** [clarify] expliquer ▪ **he ~ed to us how the machine worked** il nous a expliqué comment la machine marchait ▪ **to ~ sthg in full** expliquer qqch en détail ▪ **that is easily ~ed, that is easy to ~** c'est facile à expliquer, cela s'explique facilement **2.** [account for] expliquer ▪ **she's got a cold which ~s** *OR* **will ~ why she's off work today** elle a un rhume, ce qui explique pourquoi elle ne travaille pas aujourd'hui ▪ **to ~ o.s.** s'expliquer.
<> *vi* [clarify] expliquer ▪ **I don't understand, you'll need to ~** je ne comprends pas, il va falloir que tu m'expliques ▪ **you've got a bit of** *OR* **a little** *OR* **some ~ing to do** il va falloir que tu t'expliques.
◆ **explain away** *vt sep* [justify, excuse] justifier.

explainable [ɪk'spleɪnəbl] *adj* [explicable] : **it's easily ~** cela s'explique facilement, c'est facilement explicable.

explanation [,eksplə'neɪʃn] *n* **1.** [clarification] explication *f* ▪ **the instructions for this new video need a bit of ~** les instructions de ce nouveau magnétoscope nécessitent des explications ▪ **to give** *OR* **to offer an ~ for sthg** donner une explication à qqch ▪ **to find an ~ for sthg** trouver une explication à qqch **2.** [justification] explication *f* ▪ **you'd better have a good ~!** j'espère que tu as une bonne excuse *OR* une explication valable!
Voir module d'usage

explanatory [ɪk'splænətrɪ] *adj* explicatif.

expletive [ɪk'spli:tɪv] <> *n* **1.** [swearword] juron *m* ▪ **a stream** *OR* **string of ~s** un chapelet de jurons **2.** GRAM explétif *m*.
<> *adj* GRAM explétif.

explicable [ɪk'splɪkəbl] *adj* explicable.

explicate ['eksplɪkeɪt] *vt fml* éclaircir, clarifier.

explicit [ɪk'splɪsɪt] *adj* [denial, meaning, support] explicite ▪ **~ sex and violence on the television** le sexe et la violence montrés ouvertement à la télévision ▪ **sexually ~** cru.

explicitly [ɪk'splɪsɪtlɪ] *adv* explicitement.

explode [ɪk'spləʊd] <> *vt* [detonate] faire exploser *OR* sauter ▪ *fig* [theory, myth etc] détruire, anéantir.
<> *vi* [bomb, mine etc] exploser, sauter ▪ *fig* **to ~ with laughter** éclater de rire ▪ **to ~ with anger** exploser de colère ▪ **the game ~d into life** le match s'est animé d'un seul coup.

exploded [ɪk'spləʊdɪd] *adj* **1.** [bomb, mine etc] qu'on a fait exploser ▪ *fig* [theory, myth etc] détruit, anéanti **2.** [view, diagram] éclaté.

exploit <> *n* ['eksplɔɪt] exploit *m*.
<> *vt* [ɪk'splɔɪt] **1.** [workers] exploiter **2.** [natural resources] exploiter.

exploitation [,eksplɔɪ'teɪʃn] *n* [of workers, of natural resources] exploitation *f*.

exploitative [ɪk'splɔɪtətɪv] *adj* [practices] relevant de l'exploitation ▪ **the company's ~ attitude towards the workforce** la manière dont l'entreprise exploite la main-d'œuvre.

exploiter [ɪk'splɔɪtəʳ] *n* **1.** [of workers] exploiteur *m*, - euse *f* **2.** [of natural resources] exploitant *m*, - e *f*.

exploration [,eksplə'reɪʃn] *n* **1.** [of place, problem] exploration *f* **2.** MED exploration *f*.

exploratory [ɪk'splɒrətrɪ] *adj* [journey] d'exploration ▪ [talks, discussions] exploratoire ▪ **~ drilling** forage *m* d'exploration ▪ **~ surgery** chirurgie *f* exploratrice.

explore [ɪk'splɔ:ʳ] <> *vt* **1.** [country] explorer ▪ [town] découvrir **2.** [issue, possibility, problem] explorer, examiner ▪ **to ~**

EXPLANATIONS

Asking for explanations

Qu'est-ce que tu veux dire, exactement ? What do you mean exactly?
C'est-à-dire ? Meaning?
Pourriez-vous être plus précis ? Could you be a little more specific?
Qu'entendez-vous par là ? What do you mean by that?
Qu'est-ce que tu veux dire au juste ? What do you mean exactly?
Comment ça ? How do you mean?

Giving explanations

Je veux/voulais dire que... I mean/meant that...
Je vais tâcher d'être plus clair... Let me try to explain a little more clearly...
Je m'explique :... Let me explain:...
Ce que j'essaie de dire, c'est... What I'm trying to say is...

every avenue *fig* explorer toutes les voies *OR* solutions possibles ■ **to ~ the ground** *fig* tâter le terrain **3.** MED explorer, sonder.

◇ *vi* faire une exploration ■ **let's go exploring** [in the woods, countryside etc] partons en exploration ; [in a city] allons découvrir la ville.

explorer [ɪk'splɔːrəʳ] *n* **1.** [person] explorateur *m*, - trice *f* **2.** [instrument] sonde *f*.

explosion [ɪk'spləʊʒn] *n* **1.** [of bomb, gas] explosion *f* ■ **an ~ ripped through the building** une explosion a ébranlé le bâtiment ▮ *fig* **there was an ~ of laughter from the dining room** une explosion *OR* une tempête de rires est arrivée de la salle à manger **2.** [act of exploding] explosion *f*.

explosive [ɪk'spləʊsɪv] ◇ *adj* **1.** explosif ■ [gas] explosible ■ **~ device** dispositif *m* explosif ■ **~ situation** *fig* situation *f* explosive **2.** LING explosif.

◇ *n* **1.** [in bomb] explosif *m* ■ **high ~** explosif puissant **2.** LING explosive *f*.

exponent [ɪk'spəʊnənt] *n* **1.** [of idea, theory] apôtre *m*, avocat *m*, - e *f* ■ [of skill] représentant *m*, - e *f* ■ **he is a leading ~ of this theory** il est l'un des plus fervents apôtres de cette théorie **2.** MATHS exposant *m*.

exponential [ˌekspə'nenʃl] *adj* exponentiel.

exponentially [ˌekspə'nenʃəlɪ] *adv* de manière exponentielle.

export ◇ *n* ['ekspɔːt] **1.** [action] exportation *f* **2.** [product] exportation *f*.

◇ *comp* [duty, licence, trade] d'exportation ■ **~ drive** campagne *f* visant à stimuler l'exportation ■ **~-driven** [expansion, recovery] basé *OR* centré sur les exportations ■ **~ earnings** revenus *mpl OR* recettes *fpl* de l'exportation ■ **~ reject** produit *m* impropre à l'exportation.

◇ *vt* [ɪk'spɔːt] **1.** *liter* & *fig* exporter ■ **to ~ goods to other countries** exporter des marchandises vers d'autres pays **2.** COMPUT exporter.

◇ *vi* [ɪk'spɔːt] exporter ■ **~ing company** société exportatrice.

exportation [ˌekspɔː'teɪʃn] *n fml* exportation *f*.

exporter [ek'spɔːtəʳ] *n* exportateur *m*, - trice *f*.

expose [ɪk'spəʊz] *vt* **1.** [uncover] découvrir ■ PHOT exposer ■ **to ~ sb/sthg to sthg** exposer qqn/qqch à qqch ■ **he was ~d to German from the age of five** il a été au contact de l'allemand depuis l'âge de cinq ans ■ **to ~ o.s.** [exhibitionist] s'exhiber ■ **to ~ o.s. to sthg** [to criticism, ridicule, risk] s'exposer à qqch **2.** [reveal, unmask - plot] découvrir ; [- spy] découvrir, démasquer.

exposé [eks'pəʊzeɪ] *n* PRESS révélations *fpl*.

exposed [ɪk'spəʊzd] *adj* [location, house, position etc] exposé ■ TECH [parts, gears] apparent, à découvert ■ ARCHIT [beam] apparent ■ **the troops are in an ~ position** les soldats sont à découvert ■ **in an ~ position** *fig* dans une position précaire.

exposition [ˌekspə'zɪʃn] *n* **1.** [explanation] exposé *m* **2.** [exhibition] exposition *f*.

expostulate [ɪk'spɒstʃʊleɪt] *vi fml* récriminer ■ **to ~ with sb about sthg** récriminer contre qqn à propos de qqch.

exposure [ɪk'spəʊʒəʳ] *n* **1.** [to harm, radiation] exposition *f* ■ **~ to danger is something he encounters daily** il est quotidiennement exposé au danger **2.** [to cold] : **to suffer from (the effects of) ~** souffrir des effets d'une exposition au froid ■ **to die of ~** mourir de froid **3.** [unmasking, revealing - of crime, scandal] révélation *f*, divulgation *f* **4.** PHOT pose *f* ■ **a film with 24 ~s** une pellicule de 24 poses ➊ **~ time** temps *m* de pose ■ **~ counter** compteur *m* de prises de vue **5.** [position of house] exposition *f* ■ **the building has a southern ~** le bâtiment est exposé au sud **6.** [media coverage] couverture *f* ■ **pop stars suffer from too much media ~** les stars de la musique pop sont l'objet d'une attention excessive des média.

expound [ɪk'spaʊnd] *vt* exposer.

express [ɪk'spres] ◇ *n* **1.** [train] express *m* ■ **to travel by ~** voyager en express **2.** [system of delivery] exprès *m* ■ **the Express** PRESS *nom abrégé du "Daily Express"*.

◇ *adj* **1.** [clear - instructions, purpose] clair ■ **with the ~ intention of...** avec la claire intention de... **2.** [fast - delivery, messenger] express ■ **~ company** entreprise *f* de livraison exprès ■ **~ train** train *m* express, express *m*.

◇ *adv* [send] en exprès.

◇ *vt* **1.** [voice, convey] exprimer ■ **to ~ an interest in (doing) sthg** manifester de l'intérêt pour (faire) qqch ■ **she ~es her feelings by painting** elle exprime ses sentiments par *OR* à travers la peinture ■ **to ~ o.s.** s'exprimer ■ **to ~ o.s. through sthg** s'exprimer par *OR* à travers qqch **2.** [render in a different form] exprimer ■ **to ~ sthg as a fraction** MATHS exprimer qqch sous la forme d'une fraction **3.** *fml* [juice] extraire, exprimer ■ [milk] tirer **4.** [send] envoyer en exprès.

expression [ɪk'spreʃn] *n* **1.** [of feelings, thoughts, friendship] expression *f* ■ **we'd like you to have it as an ~ of our gratitude** nous vous l'offrons en témoignage de notre reconnaissance ■ **to give ~ to sthg** exprimer qqch ■ **her feelings found ~ in music** ses sentiments trouvèrent leur expression dans la musique ■ **freedom of ~** liberté *f* d'expression **2.** [feeling - in art, music] expression *f* ■ **he puts a lot of ~ into what he plays** il met beaucoup d'expression dans ce qu'il joue **3.** [phrase] expression *f* ■ **set** *OR* **fixed ~** LING expression *OR* locution *f* figée *OR* toute faite **4.** [facial] expression *f* ■ **I could tell by her ~** je voyais bien à son expression.

expressionism [ɪk'spreʃənɪzm] *n* ART expressionnisme *m*.

expressionist [ɪk'spreʃənɪst] ART ◇ *adj* expressionniste.

◇ *n* expressionniste *mf*.

expressionistic [ɪkˌspreʃə'nɪstɪk] *adj* ART expressionniste.

expressionless [ɪk'spreʃənlɪs] *adj* [face, person] inexpressif, sans expression ■ [voice] inexpressif, éteint, terne.

expressive [ɪk'spresɪv] *adj* [face, gesture, smile] expressif ■ **to be ~ of sthg** être indicatif de qqch.

expressively [ɪk'spresɪvlɪ] *adv* [gesture, smile] avec expression.

expressiveness [ɪk'spresɪvnɪs] *n* [of face, gesture, smile] expressivité *f*.

expressly [ɪk'spreslɪ] *adv* expressément ■ **I ~ forbid you to leave** je vous interdis formellement de partir.

expressway [ɪk'spresweɪ] *n* *US* autoroute *f*.

expropriate [eks'prəʊprɪeɪt] *vt* exproprier.

expulsion [ɪk'spʌlʃn] *n* **1.** [from party, country] expulsion *f* ■ [from school] renvoi *m* **2.** [of breath] expulsion *f*.

expunge [ɪk'spʌndʒ] *vt fml* [delete] supprimer, effacer ■ [from memory] effacer.

expurgate ['ekspəgeɪt] *vt* [book, play] expurger.

exquisite [ɪk'skwɪzɪt] *adj* **1.** [food, beauty, manners] exquis ■ [jewellery, craftsmanship] raffiné **2.** [intense - pleasure, pain, thrill] intense.

exquisitely [ɪk'skwɪzɪtlɪ] *adv* **1.** [superbly] de façon exquise, exquisément *lit* **2.** [intensely] intensément.

ex-serviceman (*pl* **ex-servicemen**) *n* retraité *m* de l'armée.

ex-servicewoman (*pl* **ex-servicewomen**) *n* retraitée *f* de l'armée.

ext. (*written abbrev of* **extension**) : **~ 4174** p. 4174.

extant [ek'stænt] *adj fml* encore existant.

extemporaneous [ɪkˌstempə'reɪnjəs], **extemporary** [ɪk'stempərərɪ] *adj* improvisé, impromptu.

extempore [ɪk'stempərɪ] ◇ *adj* improvisé, impromptu.

◇ *adv* [speak] impromptu.

extemporize [ɪk'stempəraɪz] ◇ *vt* [speech, piece of music] improviser.

◇ *vi* [speaker, musician] improviser.

extend [ɪk'stend] ◇ *vt* **1.** [stretch out - arm, leg] étendre, allonger ; [- wings] ouvrir, déployer ; [- aerial] déplier, déployer ■ **to ~ one's hand to sb** tendre la main à qqn **2.** [in length, duration - guarantee, visa, news programme] prolonger ; [- road, runway] prolonger, allonger ■ **they ~ed his visa by six months** on

a prolongé son visa de six mois **3.** [make larger, widen - frontiers, law, enquiry, search] étendre ; [- building] agrandir ; [- vocabulary] enrichir, élargir ■ **the company decided to ~ its activities into the export market** la société a décidé d'étendre ses activités au marché de l'exportation **4.** [offer - friendship, hospitality] offrir ; [- thanks, condolences, congratulations] présenter ; [- credit] accorder ■ **to ~ an invitation to sb** faire une invitation à qqn ■ **to ~ a welcome to sb** souhaiter la bienvenue à qqn **5.** [stretch - horse, person] pousser au bout de ses capacités *OR* à son maximum.
◇ *vi* **1.** [protrude - wall, cliff] avancer, former une avancée **2.** [stretch - country, forest, hills etc] s'étendre ■ *fig* **the parliamentary recess ~s into October** les vacances parlementaires se prolongent jusqu'en octobre ■ **the laughter ~ed to the others in the room** le rire a gagné le reste de la salle ■ **the legislation does not ~ to single mothers** la législation ne concerne pas les mères célibataires.

extendable [ɪk'stendəbl] *adj* **1.** [in space] : **~ aerial** antenne *f* télescopique ■ **~ ladder** échelle *f* à coulisse **2.** [in time - contract, visa] renouvelable.

extended [ɪk'stendɪd] *adj* **1.** [in time - contract, visit] prolongé ■ **to be on ~ leave** être en arrêt prolongé ■ **owing to the ~ news bulletin** en raison de la prolongation du bulletin d'informations ▶ **~ coverage** [on radio, TV] *informations détaillées sur un événement* **2.** [larger, wider - frontiers, enquiry, search] étendu ■ **~ coverage** [in insurance] couverture *f* multirisque **3.** [in space] étendu, allongé ■ [building] agrandi.

extended family *n* : **the ~** la famille élargie.

extended-play *adj* [record] double.

extending [ɪk'stendɪŋ] ◇ *adj* [table] à rallonge *OR* rallonges ■ [ladder] à coulisse.
◇ *n* **1.** [of arm, leg, freedom] extension *f* **2.** [of contract, visa, road] prolongation *f*.

extension [ɪk'stenʃn] *n* **1.** [of arm, legislation, frontiers] extension *f* **2.** [of house, building] : **to build an ~ onto** agrandir ■ **do you like the new ~?** [to the house] la nouvelle partie de la maison vous plaît-elle? ; [of library, museum etc] la nouvelle aile vous plaît-elle? **3.** [of contract, visa, time period] prolongation *f* ■ **to ask for/to get an ~** [to pay, hand in work] demander/obtenir un délai ■ **the bar's been granted an ~** le bar a obtenu une prolongation de ses heures d'ouverture **4.** [telephone - in office building] poste *m* ; [- in house] poste *m* supplémentaire ■ **can I have ~ 946?** pouvez-vous me passer le poste 946? **5.** ELEC prolongateur *m*, rallonge *f*.
◆ **by extension** *adv phr* par extension.

extension cord *US n* = **extension lead**.

extension course *n* cours *m* de formation permanente.

extension ladder *n* échelle *f* à coulisse.

extension lead *n UK* prolongateur *m*, rallonge *f*.

extensive [ɪk'stensɪv] *adj* [desert, powers, knowledge] étendu ■ [damage] important, considérable ■ [tests, research, investigation] approfondi ■ AGRIC extensif ■ **the issue has been given ~ coverage in the media** ce problème a été largement traité dans les médias ■ **to make ~ use of sthg** beaucoup utiliser qqch, faire un usage considérable de qqch.

extensively [ɪk'stensɪvlɪ] *adv* [damaged, altered, revised] considérablement ■ [quote] abondamment ■ [travel, read] beaucoup ■ [discuss] en profondeur ■ **to use sthg ~** beaucoup utiliser qqch, faire un usage considérable de qqch.

extent [ɪk'stent] *n* **1.** [size, range - of ground, damage, knowledge] étendue *f* ; [- of debts] importance *f* ■ **trees ran along the entire ~ of the boulevard** des arbres longeaient le boulevard sur toute sa longueur **2.** [degree] mesure *f*, degré *m* ■ **these figures show the ~ to which tourism has been affected** ces chiffres montrent à quel point le tourisme a été affecté ■ **to what ~?** dans quelle mesure? ■ **to that ~** sur ce point, à cet égard ■ **to the ~ that..., to such an ~ that...** à tel point que...
◆ **to a large extent, to a great extent** *adv phr* dans une grande mesure, à un haut point *OR* degré.
◆ **to an extent, to some extent,, to a certain extent** *adv phr* dans une certaine mesure, jusqu'à un certain point *OR* degré.

extenuating [ɪk'stenjʊeɪtɪŋ] *adj* : **~ circumstances** circonstances *fpl* atténuantes.

exterior [ɪk'stɪərɪəʳ] ◇ *adj* extérieur ■ **~ angle** MATHS angle externe ■ **~ to** extérieur à.
◇ *n* [of house, building] extérieur *m* ■ [of person] apparence *f*, dehors *m*.

exteriorize [ɪk'stɪərɪəraɪz] *vt* extérioriser.

exterminate [ɪk'stɜːmɪneɪt] *vt* [pests] exterminer ■ [race, people] exterminer, anéantir.

extermination [ɪkˌstɜːmɪ'neɪʃn] *n* [of pests] extermination *f* ■ [of race, people] extermination *f*, anéantissement *m*.

exterminator [ɪk'stɜːmɪneɪtəʳ] *n* [person - gen] exterminateur *m*, - trice *f* ; [- of rats, mice] dératiseur *m* ■ [poison] mort-aux-rats *f inv*.

external [ɪk'stɜːnl] ◇ *adj* [events, relations, trade, wall] extérieur ■ **~ ear** oreille *f* externe ■ **'for ~ use only'** PHARM 'à usage externe uniquement' ■ **~ pressure** [on person] pression *f* de l'extérieur ; [on device] pression *f* extérieure *OR* du dehors ■ **~ examiner** UNIV examinateur *m*, - trice *f* venant de l'extérieur ■ **~ device** COMPUT dispositif *m* externe, périphérique *m*.
◇ *n (usu pl)* **he judges people by ~s** il juge les gens sur leur apparence.

externalize, ise [ɪk'stɜːnəlaɪz] *vt* extérioriser.

externally [ɪk'stɜːnəlɪ] *adv* à l'extérieur ■ **'to be used ~'** PHARM 'à usage externe'.

extinct [ɪk'stɪŋkt] *adj* [species, race] disparu ■ **~ volcano** volcan *m* éteint ■ **the horse and plough are nearly ~** le cheval et la charrue sont en voie d'extinction ■ **to become ~** [species, tradition] s'éteindre, disparaître ; [method] disparaître.

extinction [ɪk'stɪŋkʃn] *n* [of race, species] extinction *f*, disparition *f* ■ [of fire] extinction *f* ■ **to hunt an animal to ~** chasser un animal jusqu'à extinction de l'espèce.

extinguish [ɪk'stɪŋgwɪʃ] *vt* [fire, candle etc] éteindre ■ *fig* [memory] effacer.

extinguisher [ɪk'stɪŋgwɪʃəʳ] *n* extincteur *m*.

extirpate ['ekstəpeɪt] *vt fml* extirper.

extn. = **ext.**

extol, extoll *US* [ɪk'stəʊl] (*pret & pp* **extolled**, *cont* **extolling**) *vt fml* [person] chanter les louanges de ■ [system, virtues, merits] vanter.

extort [ɪk'stɔːt] *vt* [money] extorquer, soutirer ■ [confession, promise] extorquer, arracher ■ **to ~ money from sb** extorquer *OR* soutirer de l'argent à qqn.

extortion [ɪk'stɔːʃn] *n* [of money, promise, confession] extorsion *f*.

extortionate [ɪk'stɔːʃnət] *adj* [price, demand] exorbitant, démesuré ■ **that's ~!** [very expensive] c'est exorbitant *OR* du vol!

extortionately [ɪk'stɔːʃnətlɪ] *adv* démesurément, excessivement.

extra ['ekstrə] ◇ *adj* **1.** [additional] supplémentaire ■ **I put an ~ jumper on** j'ai mis un pull en plus ■ **he made an ~ effort to get there on time** il a redoublé d'efforts pour y arriver à l'heure ■ **as an ~ precaution** pour plus de précaution ■ **an ~ helping of cake** une autre part de gâteau ■ **no ~ charge/cost** aucun supplément de prix/frais supplémentaire ■ **service/VAT is ~** le service/la TVA est en supplément ■ **~ pay** supplément de salaire ■ **she asked for an ~ £2** elle a demandé 2 livres de plus ■ **at no ~ charge** sans supplément de prix ▶ **~ time** [to pay, finish etc] délai *m* ; SPORT prolongations *fpl* ■ **the game has gone into ~ time** les joueurs sont en train de jouer les prolongations **2.** [spare] en plus.
◇ *adv* **1.** [extremely - polite, kind] extrêmement ; [- strong, white] super- ■ **to work ~ hard** travailler d'arrache-pied ■ **~ dry** [wine] très sec ; [champagne, vermouth] extra-dry *(inv)* ■ **~ fine** [flour, sugar] extrafin, surfin **2.** [in addition] plus, davantage ■ **to pay ~ for a double room** payer plus *OR* un supplément pour une chambre double.

◇ *n* **1.** [addition] supplément *m* ▪ **the paper comes with a business ~** le journal est vendu avec un supplément affaires ▪ **a car with many ~s** une voiture avec de nombreux accessoires en option **2.** [in film] figurant *m*, - e *f* **3.** [additional charge] supplément *m* **4.** [luxury] : **little ~s** petits extras *mpl* OR luxes *mpl*.

extra- *in cpds* extra- ▪ **~large** grande taille ▪ **~special** ultra-spécial ▪ **you'll have to take ~special care over it** il faudra que tu y fasses super attention.

extract ◇ *vt* [ɪk'strækt] **1.** [take out - juice, oil, bullet] extraire ; [- tooth] arracher, extraire ; [- cork] ôter, enlever ▪ **to ~ a quotation from a passage** extraire OR tirer une citation d'un passage **2.** [obtain - information] soutirer, arracher ; [- money] soutirer ▪ **to ~ a confession from sb** soutirer OR arracher un aveu à qqn.
◇ *n* ['ekstrækt] **1.** [from book, piece of music] extrait *m* **2.** [substance] extrait *m* ▪ PHARM extrait *m*, essence *f* ▪ **beef/malt/vegetable ~** extrait de bœuf/de malt/de légumes.

extraction [ɪk'strækʃn] *n* **1.** [removal - of juice, oil, bullet] extraction *f* ; [- of tooth] extraction *f*, arrachage *m* **2.** [descent] extraction *f* ▪ **of noble/humble ~** de noble/modeste extraction ▪ **he is of Scottish ~** il est d'origine écossaise.

extractor [ɪk'stræktəʳ] *n* [machine, tool] extracteur *m* ▪ [fan] ventilateur *m*, aérateur *m* ▪ **juice ~** UK presse-fruits *m inv*.

extractor fan *n* ventilateur *m*, aérateur *m*.

extractor hood *n* [on stove] hotte *f* aspirante.

extracurricular [ˌekstrəkə'rɪkjʊləʳ] *adj* SCH hors programme, extrascolaire ▪ UNIV hors programme ▪ **~ activities** activités *fpl* extrascolaires.

extraditable ['ekstrəˌdaɪtəbl] *adj* passible d'extradition.

extradite ['ekstrədaɪt] *vt* [send back] extrader ▪ [procure extradition of] obtenir l'extradition de.

extradition [ˌekstrə'dɪʃn] ◇ *n* extradition *f*.
◇ *comp* [order, treaty] d'extradition.

extramarital [ˌekstrə'mærɪtl] *adj* extraconjugal ▪ **~ sex** rapports *mpl* extraconjugaux.

extramural [ˌekstrə'mjʊərəl] *adj* **1.** UNIV [course, studies, activities] : **Department of Extramural Studies** ≃ Institut *m* d'éducation permanente **2.** [district] extra-muros.

extraneous [ɪk'streɪnjəs] *adj* **1.** [irrelevant - idea, point, consideration, issue] étranger, extérieur ▪ **to be ~ to sthg** [idea, point, issue] être étranger à qqch ; [detail] être sans rapport avec qqch **2.** [from outside - noise, force] extérieur.

extraordinarily [ɪk'strɔːdnrəlɪ] *adv* **1.** [as intensifier] extraordinairement, incroyablement **2.** [unusually] extraordinairement, d'une manière inhabituelle.

extraordinary [ɪk'strɔːdnrɪ] *adj* **1.** [remarkable] extraordinaire ▪ **(why,) that's** OR **how ~!** c'est extraordinaire OR incroyable! **2.** [surprising, unusual - story] inouï, invraisemblable ; [- house] curieux, singulier ; [- appearance, outfit] insolite, singulier ; [- event] invraisemblable ; [- behaviour, speech] étonnant, surprenant **3.** [additional - meeting, session] extraordinaire.

extrapolate [ɪk'stræpəleɪt] ◇ *vt* [infer from facts] déduire par extrapolation ▪ MATHS établir par extrapolation ▪ **if we ~ these figures** [use them as a basis] si nous extrapolons à partir de ces chiffres.
◇ *vi* extrapoler ▪ **to ~ from sthg** extrapoler à partir de qqch.

extrapolation [ɪkˌstræpə'leɪʃn] *n* extrapolation *f*.

extrasensory [ˌekstrə'sensərɪ] *adj* extrasensoriel ▪ **~ perception** perception *f* extrasensorielle.

extraterrestrial [ˌekstrətə'restrɪəl] ◇ *adj* extraterrestre.
◇ *n* extraterrestre *mf*.

extraterritorial ['ekstrəˌterɪ'tɔːrɪəl] *adj* [possessions] situé hors du territoire national ▪ [rights] d'exterritorialité, d'extra-territorialité.

extravagance [ɪk'strævəgəns] *n* **1.** [wasteful spending] dépenses *fpl* extravagantes ▪ **a piece of ~** une folie **2.** [extravagant purchase] folie *f*.

extravagant [ɪk'strævəgənt] *adj* **1.** [wasteful, profligate - person] dépensier, prodigue ; [- tastes] coûteux, de luxe ▪ **I think you're being a bit ~, having the central heating on all the time** je trouve que c'est du gaspillage de laisser le chauffage central allumé en permanence comme tu le fais ▪ **to be ~ with one's money** être gaspilleur OR dépensier, gaspiller son argent **2.** [exaggerated - idea, opinion] extravagant ; [- claim, behaviour, prices] extravagant, excessif ▪ **to make ~ claims** avoir des prétentions exagérées OR excessives.

extravagantly [ɪk'strævəgəntlɪ] *adv* **1.** [wastefully] : **to live ~** vivre sur un grand pied ▪ **an ~ furnished room** une pièce meublée à grands frais OR luxueusement meublée **2.** [exaggeratedly - behave, act, talk] de manière extravagante ; [- praise] avec excès ▪ **~ worded claims** des affirmations exagérées OR excessives.

extravaganza [ɪkˌstrævə'gænzə] *n* [lavish performance] œuvre *f* à grand spectacle.

extreme [ɪk'striːm] ◇ *adj* **1.** [heat, pain, views, measures] extrême ▪ **they live in ~ poverty** ils vivent dans une misère extrême ▪ **to be in ~ pain** souffrir terriblement OR atrocement ▪ **the ~ left wing of the party** l'aile d'extrême gauche du parti ▪ **~ old age** grand âge *m* ➔ **~ sports** sports *mpl* extrêmes **2.** [furthest away] extrême ▪ **at the ~ end of the platform** à l'extrémité du quai ▪ **on the ~ right of the screen** à l'extrême droite de l'écran ▪ **they are ~ opposites of the political spectrum** ils sont aux deux extrémités de l'éventail politique.
◇ *n* extrême *m* ▪ **~s of temperature** extrêmes de température ▪ **to go to ~s** exagérer ▪ **to take** OR **to carry sthg to ~s, to go to ~s with sthg** pousser qqch à l'extrême ▪ **to be driven to ~s** être poussé à bout ▪ **to go from one ~ to the other** aller OR passer d'un extrême à l'autre.
◆ **in the extreme** *adv phr* à l'extrême ▪ **polite/careful in the ~** poli/soigneux à l'extrême.

extremely [ɪk'striːmlɪ] *adv* [as intensifier] extrêmement.

extreme unction *n* RELIG extrême-onction *f*.

extremis [ɪk'striːmɪs] ◆ **in extremis** *adv phr* en dernier recours, au pire.

extremism [ɪk'striːmɪzm] *n* POL extrémisme *m*.

extremist [ɪk'striːmɪst] ◇ *adj* extrémiste.
◇ *n* extrémiste *mf*.

extremity [ɪk'stremətɪ] (*pl* **extremities**) *n* **1.** [furthermost tip] extrémité *f* ▪ **at the southernmost ~ of the peninsula** à l'extrémité sud de la péninsule **2.** *(usu pl)* [hand, foot] : **the extremities** les extrémités *fpl* **3.** [extreme nature - of belief, view etc] extrémité *f* **4.** [adversity, danger] extrémité *f* ▪ **to help sb in their ~** aider qqn dans son malheur **5.** *(usu pl)* [extreme measure] extrémité *f* ▪ **to drive sb to extremities** pousser OR conduire qqn à des extrêmes.

extricate ['ekstrɪkeɪt] *vt* [thing] extirper, dégager ▪ [person] dégager ▪ **to ~ o.s. from a tricky situation** se sortir OR se tirer d'une situation délicate.

extrinsic [ek'strɪnsɪk] *adj* extrinsèque.

extrovert ['ekstrəvɜːt] PSYCHOL ◇ *adj* extraverti, extroverti.
◇ *n* extraverti *m*, - e *f*, extroverti *m*, - e *f*.

extrude [ɪk'struːd] ◇ *vt* **1.** TECH [metals, plastics] extruder **2.** *fml* [force out - lava] extruder.
◇ *vi* [protrude] déborder, s'avancer.

extruded [ɪk'struːdɪd] *adj* extrudé.

extrusion [ɪk'struːʒn] *n* **1.** TECH [of metal, plastic] extrusion *f* **2.** *fml* [action] extraction *f* **3.** [protrusion] extrusion *f*.

exuberance [ɪg'zjuːbərəns] *n* **1.** [of person, writing] exubérance *f* **2.** [of vegetation] exubérance *f*.

exuberant [ɪg'zjuːbərənt] *adj* **1.** [person, mood, style] exubérant **2.** [vegetation] exubérant.

exuberantly [ɪg'zjuːbərəntlɪ] *adv* avec exubérance.

exude [ɪg'zjuːd] ◇ *vi* [liquid, sap, blood etc] exsuder.
◇ *vt* [blood, sap] exsuder ▪ *fig* [confidence, love] déborder de.

exult [ɪg'zʌlt] *vi* [rejoice] exulter, jubiler ■ [triumph] exulter ■ **to ~ at** *OR* **in one's success** [rejoice] se réjouir de son succès ■ **to ~ over defeated opponents** [triumph] exulter de la défaite de ses adversaires.

exultant [ɪg'zʌltənt] *adj* [feeling, shout, look] d'exultation ■ [mood, crowd] jubilant ■ **to be** *OR* **to feel ~** exulter.

exultantly [ɪg'zʌltəntlɪ] *adv* avec exultation.

exultation [,egzʌl'teɪʃn] *n* exultation *f*.

ex-wife *n* ex-femme *f*.

eye [aɪ] (*cont* **eyeing** *OR* **eying**) ◇ *n* **1.** [organ] œil *m* ■ **to have green ~s** avoir les yeux verts ■ **a girl with green ~s** une fille aux yeux verts ■ **before your very ~s!** sous vos yeux! ■ **look me in the ~ and say that** regarde-moi bien dans les yeux et dis-le moi ■ **I saw it with my own ~s** je l'ai vu de mes yeux vu *OR* de mes propres yeux ■ **with one's ~s closed/open** les yeux fermés/ouverts ■ **she can't keep her ~s open** *fig* elle dort debout ➊ **I could do it with my ~s closed** je pourrais le faire les yeux fermés ■ **he went into it with his ~s open** il s'y est lancé en toute connaissance de cause
2. [gaze] regard *m* ■ **the film looks at the world through the ~s of a child** dans ce film, on voit le monde à travers les yeux d'un enfant ■ **with a critical ~** d'un œil critique ■ **I couldn't believe my ~s** je n'en croyais pas mes yeux ■ **he couldn't take his ~s off her** il ne pouvait pas la quitter des yeux
3. MIL : **~s left/right!** tête à gauche/à droite! ■ **~s front!** fixe!
4. SEW [of needle] chas *m*, œil *m* ■ [eyelet] œillet *m*
5. [of potato, twig] œil *m*
6. [of storm] œil *m*, centre *m*
7. [photocell] œil *m* électrique
8. *phr* **we can't close** *OR* **shut our ~s to the problem** on ne peut pas fermer les yeux sur ce problème ■ **the incident opened his ~s to the truth about her** l'incident lui ouvrit les yeux sur ce qu'elle était vraiment ■ **for your ~s only** ultra-confidentiel ■ **she has a good ~ for detail** elle a l'œil pour ce qui est des détails ■ **to get one's ~ in** *UK* prendre ses repères ■ **he only has ~s for her** il n'a d'yeux que pour elle ■ **the boss has his ~ on Smith for the job** le patron a Smith en vue pour le poste ■ **she has her ~ on the mayor's position** elle vise la mairie ■ **he always has an ~ for** *OR* **to the main chance** il ne perd jamais de vue ses propres intérêts ■ **in my/her ~s** à mes/ses yeux ■ **in the ~s of the law** aux yeux *OR* au regard de la loi ■ **to run** *OR* **to cast one's ~ over sthg** jeter un coup d'œil à qqch ■ **to try to catch sb's ~** essayer d'attirer le regard de qqn ■ **keep your ~ on the ball** fixez *OR* regardez bien la balle ■ **could you keep your ~ on the children/the house?** pourriez-vous surveiller les enfants/la maison? ■ **keep an ~ on the situation** suivez de près la situation ■ **to keep one's ~ open for sthg** être attentif à qqch ■ **keep your ~s open** *OR* **an ~ out for a filling station** essayez de repérer une station service ■ **the children were all ~s** les enfants n'en perdaient pas une miette ■ **an ~ for an ~ (and a tooth for a tooth)** œil pour œil, (dent pour dent) ■ **his ~s are too big for his stomach** il a les yeux plus grands que le ventre ■ **to give sb the ~** *inf* [flirt] faire de l'œil à qqn ; [give signal] faire signe à qqn (d'un clin d'œil) ■ **he has ~s in the back of his head** il a des yeux derrière la tête ■ **I've never clapped** *inf OR* **set** *OR* **laid ~s on her** je ne l'ai jamais vue de ma vie ■ **keep your ~s skinned** *inf OR* **peeled** *inf* **for trouble** *inf* restez vigilant ■ **to make ~s at sb** faire de l'œil à qqn ■ **my ~!** *inf* mon œil! ■ **she and I don't see ~ to ~** [disagree] elle ne voit pas les choses du même œil que moi, elle n'est pas de mon avis ; [dislike one another] elle et moi, nous ne nous entendons pas ■ **that's one in the ~ for him!** *inf* ça lui fera les pieds! ■ **there's more to this than meets the ~** [suspicious] on ne connaît pas les dessous de l'affaire ; [difficult] c'est moins simple que cela n'en a l'air ■ **there's more to her than meets the ~** elle gagne à être connue ■ **we're up to our ~s in it!** [overworked] on a du travail jusque là! ; [in deep trouble] on est dans les ennuis jusqu'au cou!
◇ *comp* [hospital, specialist] des yeux ■ **~ bank** banque *f* des yeux.
◇ *vt* regarder, mesurer du regard ■ **the child ~d the man warily** l'enfant dévisagea l'homme avec circonspection.
◆ **with an eye to** *prep phr* : **with an ~ to sthg/to doing sthg** en vue de qqch/de faire qqch ■ **with an ~ to the future** en vue *OR* en prévision de l'avenir.
◆ **eye up**[△] *vt sep* reluquer.

eyeball ['aɪbɔːl] ◇ *n* globe *m* oculaire ■ **drugged (up) to the ~s** *fig* drogué à mort ■ **~ to ~ (with)** nez à nez (avec).
◇ *vt inf* regarder fixement, reluquer.

eyeball-to-eyeball *adj inf* nez à nez ■ **an ~ confrontation** une confrontation entre quatre yeux *OR* quat'z'yeux, un face-à-face *(inv)*.

eyebath ['aɪbɑːθ] *n UK* MED œillère *f*.

eyebrow ['aɪbraʊ] *n* sourcil *m* ■ **to raise one's ~s** lever les sourcils ■ **her behaviour raised a few ~s** *fig* son comportement en a fait tiquer quelques-uns.

eyebrow pencil *n* crayon *m* à sourcils.

eye candy *n (U) inf* tape *m* à l'oeil *hum & pej*.

eye-catching *adj* [colour, dress] qui attire l'œil ■ [poster, title] accrocheur, tapageur.

eye contact *n* croisement *m* des regards ■ **to establish ~ (with sb)** croiser le regard (de qqn) ■ **to maintain ~ (with sb)** regarder (qqn) dans les yeux.

-eyed [aɪd] *in cpds* aux yeux... ■ **blue~** aux yeux bleus ■ **she stared at him, wide~** elle le regardait, les yeux écarquillés ■ **one~** borgne, qui n'a qu'un œil.

eye drops *npl* gouttes *fpl* (pour les yeux).

eyeful ['aɪfʊl] *n* **1.** *inf* [look] regard *m* ■ **get an ~ of that!** visez un peu ça! **2.** *inf* [woman] belle fille *f*.

eyeglass ['aɪglɑːs] *n* [monocle] monocle *m*.
◆ **eyeglasses** *npl US* [spectacles] lunettes *fpl*.

eyehole ['aɪhəʊl] *n* **1.** [peephole - in mask] trou *m* pour les yeux ; [- in door, wall] judas *m* **2.** [eyelet] œillet *m* **3.** *inf* [eye socket] orbite *f*.

eyelash ['aɪlæʃ] *n* cil *m*.

eyelet ['aɪlɪt] *n* **1.** [gen - SEW] œillet *m* **2.** [peephole - in mask] trou *m* pour les yeux ; [- in door, wall] judas *m*.

eye level *adj* qui est au niveau des yeux ■ **eye-level grill** gril *m* surélevé.

eyelid ['aɪlɪd] *n* paupière *f*.

eyeliner ['aɪ,laɪnər] *n* eye-liner *m*.

eye makeup *n* maquillage *m* pour les yeux ■ **~ remover** démaquillant *m* pour les yeux.

eye-opener *n inf* **1.** [surprise] révélation *f*, surprise *f* ■ **her behaviour was a real ~ for him** son comportement lui a ouvert les yeux **2.** *US* [drink] *petit verre pris au réveil*.

eyepatch ['aɪpætʃ] *n* [after operation] cache *m*, pansement *m* *(sur l'œil)* ■ [permanent] bandeau *m*.

eyepiece ['aɪpiːs] *n* oculaire *m*.

eyeshade ['aɪʃeɪd] *n* visière *f*.

eye shadow *n* fard *m* à paupières.

eyesight ['aɪsaɪt] *n* vue *f* ■ **do you have good ~?** avez-vous une bonne vue *OR* de bons yeux? ■ **his ~ is failing** sa vue baisse ■ **to lose one's ~** perdre la vue.

eye socket *n* orbite *f*.

eyesore ['aɪsɔːr] *n* abomination *f*, horreur *f*.

eyestrain ['aɪstreɪn] *n* fatigue *f* des yeux ■ **computer screens can cause ~** les ordinateurs fatiguent les yeux ■ **to suffer from ~** avoir la vue fatiguée.

eyetooth ['aɪtuːθ] (*pl* **eyeteeth** [-tiːθ]) *n* canine *f* supérieure ■ **I'd give my eyeteeth for a bike like that** *inf* je donnerais n'importe quoi pour avoir un vélo comme ça.

eyewash ['aɪwɒʃ] *n* MED collyre *m* ■ **that's a load of ~!** *UK inf fig* [nonsense] c'est de la foutaise! ; [boasting] ce n'est que de la frime!

eyewitness [,aɪ'wɪtnɪs] ◇ *n* témoin *m* oculaire.
◇ *comp* [account, description] d'un témoin oculaire.

eyrie ['ɪərɪ] *n* aire *f (d'aigle)*.

Ezekiel [ɪ'zɪkɪəl] *pr n* Ézéchiel.

e-zine ['iːziːn] *n* magazine *m* électronique.

F

f (*pl* **f's** *OR pl* **fs**), **F** (*pl* **F's** *OR pl* **Fs**) [ef] <> *n* [letter] f *m*, F *m* ▪ **f for Freddie** ≃ F comme François ▪ **the F word** *UK euph le mot "fuck"*, ≃ le mot de Cambronne.
<> **1.** *written abbr of* **fathom** **2.** *written abbr of* **female** **3.** (*written abbrev of* **feminine**) f, fém.

f 1. (*written abbrev of* **function of**) MATHS f de **2.** (*written abbrev of* **forte**) MUS f.

F <> *n* **1.** MUS fa *m* ▪ **a concerto in F** un concerto en fa **2.** SCH [grade] : **to get an F** échouer.
<> **1.** (*written abbrev of* **Fahrenheit**) F **2.** (*written abbrev of* **franc**) F.

fa [fɑː] = **fah**.

FA (*abbrev of* **Football Association**) *pr n* : **the ~** *la Fédération britannique de football* ▪ **the ~ cup** *championnat de football dont la finale se joue à Cardiff.*

fab [fæb] *adj inf* super.

Fabian ['feɪbjən] <> *adj* temporisateur.
<> *n* Fabien *m*, - enne *f*.

Fabian Society *pr n* : **the ~** *groupe socialiste de la fin du XIXe siècle en Grande-Bretagne.*

THE FABIAN SOCIETY

Organisation fondée en 1883, au moment de l'émergence du socialisme en Grande-Bretagne. Composée en grande partie d'intellectuels, elle visait à accomplir un « changement progressif et pacifique » de la société capitaliste. Elle est aujourd'hui toujours en activité.

fable ['feɪbl] *n* **1.** [legend] fable *f*, légende *f* ▪ LIT fable **2.** [false account] fable *f*.

fabled ['feɪbld] *adj* [famous] légendaire, célèbre ▪ [fictitious] légendaire, fabuleux.

fabric ['fæbrɪk] *n* **1.** [cloth] tissu *m*, étoffe *f* **2.** [framework, structure] structure *f* ▪ **the ~ of society** *fig* la structure de la société.

fabricate ['fæbrɪkeɪt] *vt* **1.** [make] fabriquer **2.** [story] inventer, fabriquer ▪ [document] faire un faux, contrefaire.

fabrication [,fæbrɪ'keɪʃn] *n* **1.** *fml* [manufacture] fabrication *f*, production *f* **2.** [falsehood] fabrication *f* ▪ **it's pure ~** c'est de la pure invention.

fabric conditioner *n* assouplissant *m* (textile).

fabulist ['fæbjʊlɪst] *n lit* [storyteller] fabuliste *mf* ▪ [liar] fabulateur *m*, - trice *f*, menteur *m*, - euse *f*.

fabulous ['fæbjʊləs] *adj* **1.** [astounding] fabuleux, incroyable **2.** *inf* [good] génial, super **3.** [fictitious] fabuleux, légendaire.

fabulously ['fæbjʊləslɪ] *adv* fabuleusement.

facade, façade [fə'sɑːd] *n* ARCHIT & *fig* façade *f*.

face [feɪs] <> *n* **1.** ANAT visage *m*, figure *f* ▪ **I know that ~** je connais cette tête-là, cette tête me dit quelque chose ▪ **she was lying ~ down** *OR* **downwards** elle était étendue à plat ventre *OR* face contre terre ▪ **she was lying ~ up** *OR* **upwards** elle était étendue sur le dos ▪ **he told her to her ~ what he thought of her** il lui a dit en face *OR* sans ambages ce qu'il pensait d'elle ▪ **to look sb in the ~** *liter* regarder qqn en face *OR* dans les yeux ▪ **I'll never be able to look him in the ~ again** *fig* je n'oserai plus jamais le regarder en face ▶ **to put on one's ~** *inf* [woman] se maquiller ▪ **in your face** *inf* provocant
2. [expression] mine *f*, expression *f* ▪ **to make** *OR* **to pull a ~ at sb** faire une grimace à qqn ▪ **to pull a funny ~** faire des simagrées, faire le singe ▶ **she put on a brave** *OR* **bold ~** elle a fait bon visage *OR* bonne contenance ▪ **put a good** *OR* **brave ~ on it** vous n'avez qu'à faire contre mauvaise fortune bon cœur
3. [appearance] apparence *f*, aspect *m* ▪ **it changed the ~ of the town** cela a changé la physionomie de la ville ▪ **this is the ugly ~ of capitalism** voici l'autre visage *OR* le mauvais côté du capitalisme
4. [front - of building] façade *f*, devant *m* ; [- of cliff] paroi *f* ▪ [of mountain] face *f*
5. [of clock] cadran *m* ▪ [of coin] face *f* ▪ [of page] recto *m* ▪ [of playing card] face *f*, dessous *m* ▪ [of the earth] surface *f* ▪ **it fell ~ down/up** [gen] c'est tombé du mauvais/bon côté ; [card, coin] c'est tombé face en dessous/en dessus ▪ **she has vanished off the ~ of the earth** *fig* elle a complètement disparu de la circulation
6. *UK inf* [impudence] culot *m*, toupet *m*
7. MIN front *m* de taille
8. TYPO [typeface] œil *m* ▪ [fount] fonte *f*
9. *phr* **she laughed/shut the door in his ~** elle lui a ri/fermé la porte au nez ▪ **to lose/to save ~** perdre/sauver la face ▪ **he set his ~ against our marriage** il s'est élevé contre notre mariage ▪ **he won't show his ~ here again!** il ne risque pas de remettre les pieds ici! ▪ **her plans blew up in her ~** tous ses projets se sont retournés contre elle.
<> *comp* [cream] pour le visage.
<> *vt* **1.** [turn towards] faire face à ▪ **~ the wall** tournez-vous vers le mur
2. [be turned towards] faire face à, être en face de ▪ **he ~d the blackboard** il était face au *OR* faisait face au tableau ▪ **she was facing him** elle était en face de lui ▪ **facing one another** l'un en face de l'autre, en vis-à-vis ▪ **a room facing the courtyard** une chambre sur cour *OR* donnant sur la cour ▪ **the house ~s south** la maison est orientée *OR* exposée au sud ▪ **facing page 9** en regard *OR* en face de la page 9
3. [confront] faire face *OR* front à, affronter ▪ **to be ~d with sthg** être obligé de faire face à *OR* être confronté à qqch ▪ **I was ~d with having to pay for the damage** j'ai été obligé *OR* dans l'obligation de payer les dégâts ▪ **~d with the evidence** devant l'évidence, confronté à l'évidence ▶ **we'll just have to ~ the music** *inf* il va falloir affronter la tempête *OR* faire front

4. [deal with] faire face à ■ **I can't ~ telling her** je n'ai pas le courage de le lui dire ■ **we must ~ facts** il faut voir les choses comme elles sont ■ **let's ~ it, we're lost** admettons-le, nous sommes perdus
5. [risk - disaster] être menacé de ; [- defeat, fine, prison] encourir, risquer ■ **~d with eviction, he paid his rent** face à *OR* devant la perspective d'une expulsion, il a payé son loyer
6. [subj: problem, situation] se présenter à ■ **the problem facing us** le problème qui se pose (à nous) *OR* devant lequel on se trouve ■ **the difficulties facing the EC** les difficultés que rencontre la CEE *OR* auxquelles la CEE doit faire face
7. [cover] revêtir de.
◇ *vi* **1.** [turn] se tourner ■ [be turned] être tourné ■ **she was facing towards the camera** elle était tournée vers *OR* elle faisait face à l'appareil photo ▌MIL : **right ~!** *US* à droite, droite! ■ **about ~!** *US* demi-tour!
2. [house, window] être orienté ■ [look over] faire face à, donner sur ■ **the terrace ~s towards the mountain** la terrasse donne sur la montagne ■ **facing forwards** [in bus, train] dans le sens de la marche ■ **facing backwards** dans le mauvais sens.
◆ **in the face of** *prep phr* : **she succeeded in the ~ of fierce opposition** elle a réussi malgré une opposition farouche ■ **in the ~ of adversity** face à l'adversité.
◆ **on the face of it** *adv phr* à première vue.
◆ **face down** *vt sep* tenir tête (à).
◆ **face out** *vt sep UK* surmonter.
◆ **face up to** *vt insep* faire face à, affronter ■ **he won't ~ up to the fact that he's getting older** il ne veut pas admettre qu'il vieillit.

facecloth ['feɪsklɒθ] *UK* = **face flannel**.

-faced [feɪst] *in cpds* au visage... ■ **round~** au visage rond ■ **white~** blême.

face flannel *n UK* ≃ gant *m* de toilette.

faceless ['feɪslɪs] *adj* anonyme.

face-lift *n* **1.** [surgery] lifting *m* ■ **to have a ~** se faire faire un lifting **2.** *inf* [renovation] restauration *f* ■ **the school has had a ~** l'école a fait peau neuve.

face mask *n* [cosmetic] masque *m* de beauté ■ SPORT masque *m*.

face-off *n* SPORT remise *f* en jeu ■ *fig* confrontation *f*.

face pack *n* masque *m* de beauté.

face powder *n* poudre *f* de riz.

facer ['feɪsər] *n US inf* [problem] os *m*, tuile *f*.

face-saver *n* quelque chose qui sauve la face ■ **the new legislation is just a ~** le gouvernement passe ces nouvelles lois simplement pour sauver la face.

face-saving *adj* qui sauve la face.

facet ['fæsɪt] *n* **1.** ANAT, ARCHIT & ENTOM [gen] facette *f* **2.** [aspect] aspect *m*, facette *f*.

faceted ['fæsɪtɪd] *adj* à facettes.

facetious [fə'siːʃəs] *adj* [person] facétieux, moqueur ■ [remark] facétieux, comique.

facetiously [fə'siːʃəslɪ] *adv* de manière facétieuse, facétieusement.

face to face *adv* face à face ■ **it brought us ~ with the problem** cela nous a mis directement devant le problème.
◆ **face-to-face** *adj* [discussion, confrontation] face à face ■ **a face-to-face meeting** un face-à-face.

face towel *n* serviette *f* de toilette.

face value *n* FIN valeur *f* nominale ■ **I took her remark at ~** *fig* j'ai pris sa remarque au pied de la lettre *OR* pour argent comptant.

facia ['feɪʃə] = **fascia**.

facial ['feɪʃl] ◇ *adj* facial ■ **~ hair** poils *mpl* du visage ■ **to remove ~ hair** enlever les poils disgracieux (du visage) ■ **~ scrub** lotion *f* exfoliante pour le visage.
◇ *n* soin *m* du visage ■ **to have a ~** se faire faire un soin du visage.

facially ['feɪʃəlɪ] *adv* de visage.

facies ['feɪʃiːz] (*pl inv*) *n* faciès *m*.

facile [*UK* 'fæsaɪl, *US* 'fæsl] *adj* [solution, victory] facile ■ [remark, reasoning] facile, creux ■ [style] facile, coulant ■ [person] superficiel, complaisant.

facilitate [fə'sɪlɪteɪt] *vt* faciliter.

facilitator [fə'sɪlɪteɪtər] *n* SOCIOL animateur *m*, - trice *f* de groupe.

facility [fə'sɪlətɪ] (*pl* **facilities**) *n* **1.** [ease] facilité *f* ■ **with great ~** avec beaucoup de facilité **2.** [skill] facilité *f*, aptitude *f* ■ **to have a ~ for** *OR* **with languages** avoir beaucoup de facilité pour les langues **3.** *(usu pl)* [equipment] équipement *m* ■ [means] moyen *m* ■ **there are facilities for cooking** il y a la possibilité de *OR* il y a ce qu'il faut pour faire la cuisine ■ **we don't have the facilities to hold a conference here** nous ne sommes pas équipés pour organiser une conférence ici ■ **washing facilities** installations sanitaires ■ **sports facilities** équipements sportifs ■ **transport facilities** moyens de transport ■ **the facilities** *euph* les toilettes *fpl* **4.** [building] installation *f* **5.** [device] mécanisme *m* ■ COMPUT fonction *f* ■ **the clock also has a radio ~** ce réveil fait aussi radio **6.** [service] service *m* ■ **we offer easy credit facilities** nous offrons des facilités de paiement *OR* crédit ■ **an overdraft ~** *UK* une autorisation de découvert.

facing ['feɪsɪŋ] *n* CONSTR revêtement *m* ■ SEW revers *m*.

-facing *in cpds* orienté vers... ■ **north~** orienté *OR* exposé au nord.

facsimile [fæk'sɪmɪlɪ] *n* fac-similé *m* ■ **in ~** en fac-similé.

facsimile machine *n fml* télécopieur *m*.

fact [fækt] *n* **1.** [true item of data] fait *m* ■ **it's a (well-known) ~ that...** tout le monde sait (bien) que... ■ **let's get the ~s straight** mettons les choses au clair ■ **ten ~s about whales** dix choses à savoir sur les baleines ■ **I'll give you all the ~s and figures** je vous donnerai tous les détails voulus ▌[known circumstance] : **the ~ that he left is in itself incriminating** le fait qu'il soit parti est compromettant en soi ■ **he broke his promise, there's no getting away from the ~** disons les choses comme elles sont, il n'a pas tenu sa promesse ▶ **I know for a ~ that they're friends** je sais pertinemment qu'ils sont amis ■ **I know it for a ~** je le sais de source sûre, c'est un fait certain ■ **to teach sb the ~s of life** [sex] apprendre à qqn comment les enfants viennent au monde ; [hard reality] apprendre à qqn la réalité des choses, mettre qqn devant la réalité de la vie ■ **there's something strange going on, (and) that's a ~** il se passe quelque chose de bizarre, c'est sûr ■ **is that a ~?** c'est pas vrai? **2.** *(U)* [reality] faits *mpl*, réalité *f* ■ **based on ~** [argument] basé sur des faits ; [book, film] basé sur des faits réels ■ **~ and fiction** le réel et l'imaginaire ▶ **the ~ (of the matter) is that I forgot all about it** la vérité, c'est que j'ai complètement oublié ■ **the ~ remains he's my brother** il n'en est pas moins mon frère.
◆ **in fact** *adv phr* **1.** [giving extra information] : **he asked us, in ~ ordered us, to be quiet** il nous a demandé, ou plutôt ordonné, de nous taire **2.** [correcting] en fait ■ **he claims to be a writer, but in (actual) ~ he's a journalist** il prétend être écrivain mais en fait c'est un journaliste **3.** [emphasizing, reinforcing] : **did she in ~ say when she was going to arrive?** est-ce qu'elle a dit quand elle arriverait en fait?

fact-finding *adj* d'information ■ **a ~ mission** une mission d'information.

faction ['fækʃn] *n* **1.** [group] faction *f* **2.** [strife] dissension *f*, discorde *f* **3.** [book, programme] docudrame *m*.

factional ['fækʃənl] *adj* de faction ■ **~ strife** luttes *fpl* intestines.

factious ['fækʃəs] *adj* factieux.

factitious [fæk'tɪʃəs] *adj lit* factice, artificiel.

factor ['fæktər] *n* **1.** [element] facteur *m*, élément *m* ■ **age is an important ~** l'âge joue un rôle important ■ **the safety ~** le

facteur de sécurité ■ **the chill ~** le coefficient de froid ■ **~ 6** [in suntan cream] indice *m* 6 **2.** BIOL & MATHS facteur *m* **3.** [agent] agent *m*.
◆ **factor in** *vt sep* [add to calculation] inclure.

factorage ['fæktərɪdʒ] *n* courtage *m*, commission *f*.

factorial [fæk'tɔ:rɪəl] ◇ *adj* factoriel.
◇ *n* factorielle *f*.

factoring ['fæktərɪŋ] *n* affacturage *m*.

factorize, ise ['fæktəraɪz] *vt* mettre en facteurs.

factory ['fæktərɪ] (*pl* **factories**) ◇ *n* usine *f* ■ [smaller] fabrique *f* ■ **a car ~** une usine d'automobiles ■ **a porcelain ~** une manufacture de porcelaine.
◇ *comp* [chimney, worker] d'usine ■ **~ inspector** inspecteur *m*, - trice *f* du travail ■ **on the ~ floor** dans les ateliers, parmi les ouvriers.

factory farm *n* ferme *f* industrielle.

factory farming *n* élevage *m* industriel.

factory ship *n* navire-usine *m*.

factotum [fæk'təʊtəm] *n* factotum *m*.

fact sheet *n* prospectus *m*, brochure *f*.

factual ['fæktʃʊəl] *adj* [account, speech] factuel, basé sur les *OR* des faits ■ [event] réel.

factually ['fæktʃʊəlɪ] *adv* en se tenant aux faits ■ **~ inaccurate** inexact dans les faits.

facultative ['fækltətɪv] *adj* **1.** [optional] facultatif **2.** PHILOS casuel, contingent.

faculty ['fækltɪ] (*pl* **faculties**) ◇ *n* **1.** [mental] faculté *f* ■ **she's in full command of her faculties** elle a toutes ses facultés ■ **his critical faculties** son sens critique **2.** UNIV [section] faculté *f* ■ *US* [staff] corps *m* enseignant ■ **the Faculty of Arts/of Medicine** la faculté de lettres/de médecine.
◇ *comp* [member, staff] de faculté.

fad [fæd] *n inf* [craze] mode *f*, vogue *f* ■ [personal] lubie *f*, (petite) manie *f*.

fade [feɪd] ◇ *vi* **1.** [colour] pâlir, passer ■ [material] se décolorer, passer ■ [light] baisser, diminuer ■ **guaranteed not to ~** TEX garanti bon teint **2.** [wither - flower] se faner, se flétrir ■ *fig* [- beauty] se faner **3.** [disappear - figure] disparaître ; [- memory, sight] baisser ; [- thing remembered, writing] s'effacer ; [- sound] baisser, s'éteindre ; [- anger, interest] diminuer ; [- hope, smile] s'éteindre ■ **to ~ from sight** disparaître aux regards ■ **the sound keeps fading** RADIO & TV il y a du fading, le son s'en va **4.** *lit* [die] dépérir, s'éteindre ■ **he's fading fast** il dépérit à vue d'œil.
◇ *vt* **1.** [discolour - material] décolorer ; [- colour] faner **2.** [reduce] baisser ■ CIN & TV faire disparaître en fondu.
◆ **fade away** *vi insep* [gen] disparaître ■ [memory, sight] baisser ■ [thing remembered, writing] s'effacer ■ [sound] s'éteindre ■ [anger, interest] diminuer ■ [hope, smile] s'éteindre.
◆ **fade in** ◇ *vt sep* CIN & TV faire apparaître en fondu ■ RADIO monter.
◇ *vi insep* CIN & TV apparaître en fondu.
◆ **fade out** ◇ *vi insep* **1.** [sound] disparaître, s'éteindre ■ *fig* [interest] diminuer, tomber ■ [fashion] passer **2.** CIN & TV disparaître en fondu ■ RADIO être coupé par un fondu sonore.
◇ *vt sep* CIN & TV faire disparaître en fondu ■ RADIO couper par un fondu sonore.

fade-away *n* CIN fondu *m* en fermeture ■ TV disparition *f* graduelle ■ RADIO évanouissement *m*, fading *m*.

faded ['feɪdɪd] *adj* [material] décoloré, déteint ■ [jeans] délavé ■ [flower] fané, flétri ■ [beauty] défraîchi, fané.

fade-in *n* CIN fondu *m* en ouverture ■ TV apparition *f* graduelle ■ RADIO fondu *m* sonore.

fade-out *n* CIN fondu *m* en fermeture ■ TV disparition *f* graduelle ■ RADIO fondu *m* sonore.

faecal *UK*, **fecal** *US* ['fi:kl] *adj* fécal.

faeces *UK*, **feces** *US* ['fi:si:z] *npl* fèces *fpl*.

Faeroe ['feərəʊ] *pr n* : **the ~ Islands, the ~ s** les îles Féroé *fpl* ■ **in the ~ Islands** aux îles Féroé.

Faeroese [,feərəʊ'i:z] (*pl inv*) ◇ *n* [person] Féroïen *m*, - enne *f*, Féringien *m*, - enne *f*.
◇ *adj* féroïen, féringien.

faff [fæf] *UK inf* ◇ *vi* faire la mouche du coche ■ **stop ~ing (about *OR* around)!** arrêtez de tourner en rond!
◇ *n* [panic] panique *f* ■ [effort] : **it's too much of a ~** c'est trop compliqué.

fag [fæg] (*pret & pp* **fagged**, *cont* **fagging**) ◇ *n* **1.** *UK inf* [cigarette] clope *m ou f* **2.** △ *US pej* [homosexual] pédé△ *m* **3.** *UK inf* [task] corvée *f*, barbe *f* **4.** *UK* [at school] *jeune élève d'une "public school" assujetti à un élève de dernière année.*
◇ *vi UK* [at school] : **to ~ for sb** faire les corvées de qqn.

fag end *n UK inf* [remainder] reste *m* ■ [of cloth] bout *m* ■ [of conversation] dernières bribes *fpl* ■ [cigarette] mégot *m*.

fagged [fægd] *adj UK inf* **1.** [exhausted] : **~ (out)** crevé, claqué **2.** [bothered] : **I can't be ~** j'ai trop la flemme.

faggot ['fægət] *n* **1.** *UK* [of sticks] fagot *m* **2.** *UK* CULIN boulette *f* de viande **3.** △ *US pej* [homosexual] pédé△ *m*, tapette△ *f*.

fag hag△ *n US* : **she's a ~** elle a beaucoup d'amis homos.

fagot ['fægət] *US* = **faggot** *(sense 1)*.

fah [fɑ:] *n* fa *m*.

Fahrenheit ['færənhaɪt] *adj* Fahrenheit *(inv)* ■ **the ~ scale** l'échelle *f* Fahrenheit ■ **it's 6° Centigrade – what's that in ~?** il fait 6° Centigrade – ça fait combien en Fahrenheit?

fail [feɪl] ◇ *vi* **1.** [not succeed - attempt, plan] échouer, ne pas réussir ; [- negotiations] échouer, ne pas aboutir ; [- person] échouer ■ **he ~ed (in his efforts) to convince us** il n'a pas réussi *OR* il n'est pas arrivé à nous convaincre ■ **her attempt was bound to ~** sa tentative était vouée à l'échec ■ **to ~ by three votes/five minutes** échouer à trois voix près/cinq minutes près ■ **it never ~s** ça ne rate jamais ■ **if all else ~s** en désespoir de cause
2. SCH & UNIV échouer, être recalé ■ **I ~ed in maths** j'ai été collé *OR* recalé en maths
3. [stop working] tomber en panne, céder ■ [brakes] lâcher ■ **his heart ~ed** son cœur s'est arrêté ■ **the power ~ed** il y a eu une panne d'électricité
4. [grow weak - eyesight, health, memory] baisser, faiblir ; [- person, voice] s'affaiblir ; [- light] baisser
5. [be insufficient] manquer, faire défaut ■ **their crops ~ed because of the drought** ils ont perdu les récoltes à cause de la sécheresse ■ **she ~ed in her duty** elle a manqué *OR* failli à son devoir
6. [go bankrupt] faire faillite.
◇ *vt* **1.** [not succeed in] échouer à, ne pas réussir à ■ **he ~ed his driving test** il n'a pas eu son permis ‖ SCH & UNIV [exam] échouer à, être recalé à ■ [candidate] refuser, recaler ■ **he ~ed the exam/history** il a échoué à l'examen/en histoire
2. [let down] décevoir, laisser tomber ■ **my memory ~s me** la mémoire me fait défaut, ma mémoire me trahit ■ **her courage ~ed her** le courage lui a fait défaut *OR* lui a manqué ■ **words ~ me** je ne sais pas quoi dire
3. [neglect] manquer, négliger ■ **he ~ed to mention he was married** il a omis de signaler qu'il était marié ■ **they never ~ to call** ils ne manquent jamais d'appeler ■ **he ~ed to keep his word** il a manqué à sa parole ■ **I ~ to see how I can help** je ne vois pas comment je peux aider ■ **such success never ~s to arouse jealousy** une telle réussite ne va jamais sans provoquer des jalousies ■ **to ~ to appear** LAW faire défaut.
◇ *n* SCH & UNIV échec *m* ■ **out of a class of 25, I had 23 passes and 2 ~s** sur une classe de 25, 23 ont été reçus et 2 ont été recalés.
◆ **without fail** *adv phr* [for certain] sans faute, à coup sûr ■ [always] inévitablement, immanquablement.

failed [feɪld] *adj* qui n'a pas réussi, raté ■ **she's a ~ artist** c'est une artiste manquée.

failing ['feɪlɪŋ] ◇ *n* défaut *m*.

◇ *prep* à défaut de ■ **~ this** à défaut ■ **~ which** faute *OR* à défaut de quoi.
◇ *adj* [health] défaillant ■ [business] qui fait faillite ■ [marriage] qui va à la dérive ■ *US* [student] faible, mauvais.

fail-safe *adj* [device, machine] à sûreté intégrée ■ [plan] infaillible.

failure ['feɪljəʳ] *n* **1.** [lack of success] échec *m*, insuccès *m* ■ **to end in ~** se terminer par un échec **2.** SCH & UNIV échec *m* ■ **~ in an exam/in maths** échec à un examen/en maths **3.** [fiasco] échec *m*, fiasco *m* ■ [of plan] échec *m*, avortement *m* ■ **the play was a dismal ~** la pièce a été *OR* a fait un four noir **4.** [person] raté *m*, - e *f* ■ **I feel a complete ~** je me sens vraiment nulle, j'ai l'impression d'être complètement nulle ■ **I'm a complete ~ at maths** je suis totalement nul en maths **5.** [breakdown] panne *f* ■ **a power ~** une panne d'électricité **6.** [lack] manque *m* ■ **crop ~** perte *f* des récoltes **7.** [non-performance] manquement *m*, défaut *m* ■ **the press criticized the government's ~ to act** la presse a critiqué l'immobilisme du gouvernement ■ **~ to observe the rules will result in a fine** le manquement au règlement est passible d'une amende ■ **~ to appear** LAW défaut *m* de comparution **8.** [bankruptcy] faillite *f*.

faint [feɪnt] ◇ *adj* **1.** [slight - breeze, feeling, sound, smell] faible, léger ; [- idea] flou, vague ; [- breathing, light] faible ; [- voice] faible, éteint ■ **he hasn't the ~est chance of winning** il n'a pas la moindre chance de gagner ■ **I haven't the ~est idea** je n'en ai pas la moindre idée ■ **her cries grew ~er** ses cris s'estompaient *OR* diminuaient **2.** [colour] pâle, délavé **3.** [half-hearted] faible, sans conviction ■ **a ~ smile** [feeble] un vague sourire ; [sad] un pauvre *OR* triste sourire ■ **~ praise** éloges *mpl* tièdes **4.** [dizzy] prêt à s'évanouir, défaillant ■ **to feel ~** se sentir mal, être pris d'un malaise ■ **he was ~ with exhaustion** la tête lui tournait de fatigue **5.** *phr* **~ heart never won fair lady** *UK prov* la pusillanimité n'a jamais conquis de cœur féminin.
◇ *vi* s'évanouir ■ **he ~ed from the pain** il s'est évanoui de douleur ■ **a ~ing fit** un évanouissement ■ **to be ~ing from** *OR* **with hunger** défaillir de faim ■ **I almost ~ed when they told me I'd got the job** *fig* j'ai failli m'évanouir quand on m'a dit que j'avais le poste.
◇ *n* évanouissement *m*, syncope *f* ■ **she fell to the floor in a (dead) ~** elle s'est évanouie *OR* est tombée en syncope.

faint-hearted ◇ *adj* [person] timoré, pusillanime ■ [attempt] timide, sans conviction.
◇ *npl* : **not for the ~** à déconseiller à ceux qui ont le cœur mal accroché.

faintly ['feɪntlɪ] *adv* **1.** [breathe, shine] faiblement ■ [mark, write] légèrement ■ [say, speak] d'une voix éteinte, faiblement **2.** [slightly] légèrement, vaguement ■ **~ absurd/ridiculous** quelque peu absurde/ridicule.

faintness ['feɪntnɪs] *n* **1.** [of light, sound, voice] faiblesse *f* ■ [of image, writing] manque *m* de clarté **2.** [dizziness] malaise *m*, défaillance *f*.

fair [feəʳ] ◇ *adj* **1.** [just - person, decision] juste, équitable ; [- contest, match, player] loyal, correct ; [- deal, exchange] équitable, honnête ; [- price] correct, convenable ; [- criticism, profit] justifié, mérité ■ **it's not ~ to the others** ce n'est pas juste *OR* honnête vis-à-vis des autres ■ **that's a ~ point** c'est une remarque pertinente ■ **to be ~ (to them), they did contribute their time** rendons-leur cette justice, ils ont donné de leur temps ■ **it's only ~ to let him speak** ce n'est que justice de le laisser parler ■ **as is only ~** ce n'est que justice, comme de juste ■ **I gave him ~ warning** je l'ai prévenu à temps ■ **he got his ~ share of the property** il a eu tous les biens qui lui revenaient (de droit) ■ **she's had more than her ~ share of problems** elle a largement eu sa part de problèmes ▶ **to have a ~ crack of the whip** *UK* ne pas être désavantagé par rapport aux autres ■ **the boss gave her a ~ go** *US inf OR* **a ~ shake (of the dice)** *inf OR* **a ~ deal** le patron l'a traitée équitablement *OR* a été fair-play *(inv)* avec elle ■ **it's all ~ and above board, it's all ~ and square** tout est régulier *OR* correct ■ **all's ~ in love and war** tous les moyens sont bons ■ **by ~ means or foul** par tous les moyens, d'une manière ou d'une autre ■ **~ enough!** très bien!, d'accord! ■ **~'s ~, it's her turn now** il faut être juste, c'est son tour maintenant
2. [light - hair] blond ; [- skin] clair, blanc, blanche *f*
3. *lit* [lovely] beau *(before vowel or silent 'h' **bel**)*, belle *f*
4. [weather] beau *(before vowel or silent 'h' **bel**)*, belle *f* ■ [tide, wind] favorable, propice ■ **the wind's set ~ for France** le temps est au beau fixe sur la France
5. [adequate] passable, assez bon ■ **you have a ~ chance of winning** vous avez des chances de gagner ■ **a ~ standard** un assez bon niveau ▶ **~ to middling** passable, pas mal
6. [substantial] considérable ■ **she reads a ~ amount** elle lit pas mal ■ **I have a ~ idea (of) why** je crois bien savoir pourquoi ■ **at a ~ pace** à une bonne allure
7. *UK inf* [real] véritable ■ **I had a ~ old time getting here** j'ai eu pas mal de difficultés à arriver jusqu'ici.
◇ *adv* **1.** [act] équitablement, loyalement ■ **to play ~** jouer franc jeu ▶ **he told us ~ and square** il nous l'a dit sans détours *OR* carrément
2. *UK inf dial* [completely] tout à fait, vraiment ■ **you ~ scared me to death** tu m'as vraiment fait une peur atroce.
◇ *n* **1.** [entertainment] foire *f*, fête *f* foraine ■ [for charity] kermesse *f*, fête *f*
2. COMM foire *f* ■ **the Book Fair** la Foire du livre ; [in Paris] le Salon du livre.

fair copy *n UK* copie *f* au propre *OR* au net ■ **I made a ~ of the report** j'ai recopié le rapport au propre.

fair game *n* proie *f* idéale ■ **after such behaviour he was ~ for an attack** *fig* après s'être comporté de cette façon, il méritait bien qu'on s'en prenne à lui.

fairground ['feəgraʊnd] *n* champ *m* de foire ■ **~ attraction** *OR* **ride** attraction *f (de fête foraine)*.

fair-haired *adj* [blond] blond, aux cheveux blonds ■ **the ~ girl** la blonde ▶ **the boss's ~ boy** *US inf* le favori *OR* le chouchou du patron.

fairing ['feərɪŋ] *n* [on vehicle] carénage *m*.

Fair Isle, Fairisle ['feəraɪl] ◇ *adj* tricoté avec des motifs de couleurs vives.
◇ *pr n* GEOG Fair Isle *(dans les îles Shetland)*.
◇ *n* [sweater] *pull avec des motifs de couleurs vives*.

fairly ['feəlɪ] *adv* **1.** [justly - treat] équitablement, avec justice ; [- compare, judge] impartialement, avec impartialité **2.** [honestly] honnêtement, loyalement ■ **~ priced goods** articles à un prix honnête *OR* raisonnable **3.** [moderately] assez, passablement ■ **a ~ good book** un assez bon livre ■ **he works ~ hard** il travaille plutôt dur **4.** *UK* [positively] absolument, vraiment ■ **he was ~ beside himself with worry** il était dans tous ses états.

fair-minded *adj* équitable, impartial.

fairness ['feənɪs] *n* **1.** [justice] justice *f*, honnêteté *f* ■ **in all ~** en toute justice ■ **in ~** *OR* **out of ~ to you** pour être juste envers *OR* avec vous **2.** [of hair] blondeur *f*, blond *m* ■ [of skin] blancheur *f*.

fair play *n* fair-play *m inv*, franc-jeu *m offic*.

fair sex *n* : **the ~** le beau sexe.

fair-sized *adj* assez grand.

fair-skinned *adj* blanc, blanche *f*, de peau.

fair trade *n* commerce *m* équitable.

fairway ['feəweɪ] *n* **1.** [in golf] fairway *m* **2.** NAUT chenal *m*, passe *f*.

fair-weather *adj* [clothing, vessel] qui convient seulement au beau temps ■ **a ~ friend** un ami des beaux *OR* bons jours.

fairy ['feərɪ] (*pl* **fairies**) ◇ *n* **1.** [sprite] fée *f* ■ **the bad ~** la fée Carabosse **2.** △ *pej* [homosexual] pédé△ *m*, tapette△ *f*.
◇ *adj* [enchanted] magique ■ [fairylike] féerique, de fée.

fairy godmother *n* LIT & *fig* bonne fée *f*.

fairyland ['feərɪlænd] *n* LIT royaume *m* des fées, féerie *f* ■ *fig* féerie *f*.

fairy lights *npl* guirlande *f* électrique.

fairy queen *n* reine *f* des fées.

fairy story *n* LIT conte *m* de fées ▪ [untruth] histoire *f* à dormir debout.

fairy tale *n* LIT conte *m* de fées ▪ [untruth] histoire *f* invraisemblable *OR* à dormir debout.
◆ **fairy-tale** *adj* : **a fairy-tale ending** une fin digne d'un conte de fées.

fait accompli [ˌfeɪtəˈkɒmplɪ] *n* fait *m* accompli.

faith [feɪθ] *n* **1.** [trust] confiance *f* ▪ **I have ~ in him** je lui fais confiance ▪ **she has lost (all) ~ in the doctors** elle n'a plus aucune confiance dans les médecins ▪ **to put one's ~ in sthg** mettres ses espoirs dans qqch **2.** RELIG [belief] foi *f* ▪ **~ in God** foi en Dieu **3.** [particular religion] foi *f*, religion *f* **4.** [honesty] : **he did it in good ~** il l'a fait en toute bonne foi ▪ **he acted in bad ~** il a agi de mauvaise foi **5.** [loyalty] fidélité *f* ▪ **you must keep ~ with the movement** il faut tenir vos engagements envers le mouvement ▪ **to break ~ with sb** manquer à sa parole envers qqn.

faithful [ˈfeɪθfʊl] ◇ *adj* **1.** [believer, friend, lover] fidèle ▪ **~ to sb/sthg** fidèle à qqn/qqch **2.** [reliable] sûr, solide **3.** [accurate - account, translation] fidèle, exact ; [- copy] conforme.
◇ *npl* : **the ~** [supporters] les fidèles *mpl* ; RELIG les fidèles *OR* croyants *mpl*.

faithfully [ˈfeɪθfʊlɪ] *adv* **1.** [loyally] fidèlement, loyalement ▪ **she promised ~ to come** elle a donné sa parole qu'elle viendrait ▪ **yours ~** [in letter] veuillez agréer mes salutations distinguées **2.** [accurately] exactement, fidèlement.

faithfulness [ˈfeɪθfʊlnɪs] *n* **1.** [loyalty] fidélité *f*, loyauté *f* **2.** [of report, translation] fidélité *f*, exactitude *f* ▪ [of copy] conformité *f*.

faith healer *n* guérisseur *m*, - euse *f*.

faith healing *n* guérison *f* par la foi.

faithless [ˈfeɪθlɪs] *adj* **1.** [dishonest, unreliable] déloyal, perfide **2.** RELIG infidèle, non-croyant.

faith school *n* *UK* SCH école *f* confessionnelle.

fake [feɪk] ◇ *vt* **1.** [make - document, painting] faire un faux de, contrefaire ; [- style, furniture] imiter **2.** [alter - document] falsifier, maquiller ; [- account] falsifier ; [- election, interview, photograph] truquer **3.** [simulate] feindre ▪ **he ~d a headache/sadness** il a fait semblant d'avoir mal à la tête/d'être triste ▪ **to ~ a pass** SPORT feinter la passe **4.** [ad-lib] improviser.
◇ *vi* faire semblant ▪ SPORT feinter.
◇ *n* **1.** [thing] article *m* *OR* objet *m* truqué ▪ [antique, painting] faux *m* **2.** [person] imposteur *m* ▪ **she's a ~** elle n'est pas ce qu'elle prétend être.
◇ *adj* [antique, painting] faux, fausse *f* ▪ [account, document] falsifié, faux, fausse *f* ▪ [elections, interview, photograph] truqué.

Falangist [fæˈlændʒɪst] ◇ *adj* phalangiste.
◇ *n* phalangiste *mf*.

falcon [ˈfɔːlkən] *n* faucon *m*.

falconer [ˈfɔːlkənəʳ] *n* fauconnier *m*.

falconry [ˈfɔːlkənrɪ] *n* fauconnerie *f*.

falderol [ˈfældɪˌrɒl] = **folderol**.

Falkland [ˈfɔːklənd] *pr n* : **the ~ Islands, the ~ s** les (îles *fpl*) Falkland *fpl*, les (îles *fpl*) Malouines *fpl* ▪ **in the ~ Islands** aux îles Falkland, aux Malouines ▪ **the Falklands War** la guerre des Malouines.

THE FALKLANDS WAR

Conflit armé qui opposa, en 1982, l'Argentine au Royaume-Uni, à la suite de l'attaque par la junte militaire argentine d'une colonie britannique, les îles Malouines. L'armée argentine se rendit deux mois plus tard. Cette victoire, très populaire en Angleterre, renforça, à l'époque, de manière significative la cote de popularité du Premier ministre, Margaret Thatcher.

fall [fɔːl] (*pret* **fell** [fel], *pp* **fallen** [ˈfɔːln]) ◇ *vi* **1.** [barrier, cup, napkin, person] tomber ▪ **the napkin fell to the floor** la serviette est tombée par terre ▪ **she fell off the stool/out of the window** elle est tombée du tabouret/par la fenêtre ▪ **he fell over the pile of books** il est tombé en butant contre le tas de livres ▪ **just let your arms ~ to your sides** laissez simplement vos bras pendre *OR* tomber sur les côtés ▪ **he fell in a heap on the floor** il s'est affaissé *OR* il est tombé comme une masse ▪ **he fell full length** il est tombé de tout son long ▪ **the crowd fell on** *OR* **to their knees** la foule est tombée à genoux ▪ **the book fell open at page 20** le livre s'est ouvert à la page 20 ➋ **to ~ on one's feet** *liter* & *fig* retomber sur ses pieds ▪ **I fell flat on my face** *liter* je suis tombé à plat ventre *OR* face contre terre ; *inf fig* je me suis planté ▪ **he fell flat on his ass**△ *US liter* & *fig* il s'est cassé la gueule ▪ **his only joke fell flat** la seule plaisanterie qu'il a faite est tombée à plat ▪ **to ~ to bits** *OR* **to pieces** tomber en morceaux ▪ **all her good intentions fell by the wayside** toutes ses bonnes intentions sont tombées à l'eau ▪ **the job fell short of her expectations** le poste ne répondait pas à ses attentes
2. [move deliberately] se laisser tomber ▪ **I fell into the armchair** je me suis laissé tomber dans le fauteuil ▪ **they fell into one another's arms** ils sont tombés dans les bras l'un de l'autre
3. [bridge, building] s'écrouler, s'effondrer
4. [err, go astray] s'écarter du droit chemin ▪ RELIG [sin] pécher ▪ **to ~ from grace** RELIG perdre la grâce ; *fig* tomber en disgrâce
5. [ground] descendre, aller en pente
6. [government] tomber, être renversé ▪ [city, country] tomber ▪ **Constantinople fell to the Turks** Constantinople est tombée aux mains des Turcs
7. [darkness, light, night, rain, snow] tomber ▪ **as night fell** à la tombée de la nuit ▪ **the tree's shadow fell across the lawn** l'arbre projetait son ombre sur la pelouse
8. [land - eyes, blow, weapon] tomber ▪ **my eyes fell on the letter** mon regard est tombé sur la lettre
9. [face, spirits] s'assombrir ▪ **my spirits fell** j'ai perdu le moral
10. [hang down] tomber, descendre ▪ **the curtains ~ right to the floor** les rideaux tombent *OR* descendent jusqu'au sol
11. [decrease in level, value - price, temperature] baisser, tomber ▪ **their voices fell to a whisper** ils se sont mis à chuchoter
12. [issue forth] tomber, s'échapper ▪ **the tears started to ~** il/elle se mit à pleurer
13. [occur] tomber ▪ **May Day ~s on a Tuesday this year** le Premier Mai tombe un mardi cette année ▪ **the accent ~s on the third syllable** l'accent tombe sur la troisième syllabe
14. [descend] : **a great sadness fell over the town** une grande tristesse s'abattit sur la ville
15. [become] : **to ~ asleep** s'endormir ▪ **the bill ~s due on the 6th** la facture arrive à échéance le 6 ▪ **to ~ ill** *OR* **sick** tomber malade ▪ **to ~ in love (with sb)** tomber amoureux (de qqn) ▪ **to ~ silent** se taire ▪ **it ~s vacant in February** [job] il se trouvera vacant au mois de février ; [apartment] il se trouvera libre *OR* il se libérera au mois de février ▪ **to ~ victim to sthg** être victime de qqch
16. [die] mourir ▪ **the young men who fell in battle** les jeunes tombés au champ d'honneur
17. [be classified] : **the athletes ~ into two categories** les sportifs se divisent en deux catégories ▪ **that ~s outside my area of responsibility** cela ne relève pas de ma responsabilité
18. [inheritance] : **the fortune fell to his niece** c'est sa nièce qui a hérité de sa fortune
19. SPORT [in cricket] : **two English wickets fell on the first day** deux batteurs anglais ont été éliminés le premier jour.
◇ *n* **1.** [tumble] chute *f* ▪ **have you had a ~?** êtes-vous tombé?, avez-vous fait une chute? ▪ **a ~ from a horse** une chute de cheval ➋ **the ~ of night** *lit* la tombée de la nuit ▪ **the Fall (of Man)** RELIG la chute (de l'homme) ▪ **to be heading** *OR* **riding for a ~** courir à l'échec
2. [of rain, snow] chute *f* ▪ **there was a heavy ~ of snow overnight** il y a eu de fortes chutes de neige dans la nuit
3. [collapse - of building, wall] chute *f*, effondrement *m* ; [- of dirt, rock] éboulement *m*, chute *f* ; [- of city, country] chute *f*, capitulation *f* ; [- of regime] chute *f*, renversement *m*
4. [decrease - in price, temperature] baisse *f* ; [- in currency] dépréciation *f*, baisse *f* ▪ [more marked] chute *f*
5. [drape] : **the ~ of her gown** le drapé de sa robe, la façon dont tombe sa robe
6. [slope] pente *f*, inclinaison *f*
7. *US* [autumn] automne *m* ▪ **in the ~** en automne
8. SPORT [in judo] chute *f* ▪ [in wrestling] chute *f*.
◇ *adj* *US* [colours] automnal.
◆ **falls** *npl* [waterfall] cascade *f*, chute *f* d'eau ▪ **Niagara Falls** les chutes du Niagara.

◆ **fall about** *vi insep UK inf* se tordre de rire ▪ **they fell about (laughing)** ils se tordaient de rire.
◆ **fall apart** *vi insep* **1.** [book, furniture] tomber en morceaux ▪ *fig* [nation] se désagréger ▪ [conference] échouer ▪ [system] s'écrouler, s'effondrer ▪ **her plans fell apart at the seams** ses projets sont tombés à l'eau ▪ **their marriage is ~ing apart** leur mariage est en train de se briser *OR* va à vau-l'eau
2. [person] s'effondrer ▪ **he more or less fell apart after his wife's death** il a plus ou moins craqué après la mort de sa femme.
◆ **fall away** *vi insep* **1.** [paint, plaster] s'écailler
2. [diminish in size - attendance, figures] diminuer ; [- fears] se dissiper, fondre
3. [defect] déserter ▪ **support for his policies is beginning to ~ away** dans la politique qu'il mène il commence à perdre ses appuis
4. [land, slope] s'affaisser.
◆ **fall back** *vi insep* **1.** [retreat, recede] reculer, se retirer ▪ MIL se replier, battre en retraite
2. [lag, trail] se laisser distancer, être à la traîne.
◆ **fall back on** *vt insep* : **to ~ back on sthg** avoir recours à qqch ▪ **it's good to have sthg to ~ back on** [skill] c'est bien de pouvoir se raccrocher à qqch ; [money] il vaut mieux avoir d'autres ressources.
◆ **fall behind** ◇ *vi insep* se laisser distancer, être à la traîne ▪ SPORT se laisser distancer ▪ [in cycling] décrocher ▪ **we can't ~ behind in** *OR* **with the rent** nous ne pouvons pas être en retard pour le loyer.
◇ *vt insep* prendre du retard sur.
◆ **fall down** *vi insep* [book, person, picture] tomber (par terre) ▪ [bridge, building] s'effondrer, s'écrouler ▪ [argument, comparison] s'écrouler, s'effondrer.
◆ **fall down on** *vt insep* : **to ~ down on sthg** échouer à qqch ▪ **he's been ~ing down on the job lately** il n'était pas *OR* ne s'est pas montré à la hauteur dernièrement.
◆ **fall for** *vt insep inf* **1.** [become infatuated with] tomber amoureux de ▪ **they really fell for Spain in a big way** ils ont vraiment été emballés par l'Espagne
2. [be deceived by] se laisser prendre par ▪ **they actually fell for it!** ils ont vraiment mordu!, ils se sont vraiment fait avoir!
◆ **fall in** *vi insep* **1.** [tumble] tomber ▪ **you'll ~ in!** tu vas tomber dedans!
2. [roof] s'effondrer, s'écrouler ▪ **then the roof fell in** *fig* puis tout s'est écroulé
3. [line up] se mettre en rang, s'aligner ▪ MIL [troops] former les rangs ▪ [one soldier] rentrer dans les rangs ▪ **~ in!** à vos rangs!
◆ **fall in with** *vt insep* **1.** [frequent] : **to ~ in with sb** se mettre à fréquenter qqn
2. [agree with] : **I'll ~ in with whatever you decide to do** *UK* je me rangerai à ce que tu décideras.
◆ **fall into** *vt insep* **1.** [tumble into] tomber dans ▪ **to ~ into sb's clutches** *OR* **sb's hands** tomber dans les griffes de qqn, tomber entre les mains de qqn ▪ **the pieces began to ~ into place** *fig* les éléments ont commencé à se mettre en place
2. [begin] : **she fell into conversation with the stranger** elle s'est mise à discuter avec l'étranger.
◆ **fall off** *vi insep* **1.** [drop off] tomber ▪ [in mountain climbing] dévisser ▪ **she fell off the bicycle/horse** elle est tombée du vélo/de cheval
2. [diminish - attendance, exports, numbers, sales] diminuer, baisser ; [- enthusiasm, production] baisser, tomber ; [- population, rate] baisser, décroître ; [- interest, zeal] se relâcher.
◆ **fall on** *vt insep* **1.** [drop on] tomber sur ▪ **something fell on my head** j'ai reçu quelque chose sur la tête
2. [attack] attaquer, se jeter sur ▪ **the guerrillas fell on the unsuspecting troops** MIL les guérilleros ont fondu sur *OR* attaqué les troupes sans qu'elles s'y attendent
3. [meet with] tomber sur, trouver ▪ **they fell on hard times** ils sont tombés dans la misère, ils ont subi des revers de fortune
4. [responsibility] revenir à, incomber à.
◆ **fall out** *vi insep* **1.** [drop out] tomber ▪ **the keys must have fallen out of my pocket** les clés ont dû tomber de ma poche
2. [quarrel] se brouiller, se disputer ▪ **she's fallen out with her boyfriend** elle est *OR* s'est brouillée avec son petit ami
3. [happen] se passer, advenir
4. MIL rompre les rangs ▪ **~ out!** rompez!
◆ **fall over** *vi insep* **1.** [lose balance] tomber (par terre)
2. *inf phr* **the men were ~ing over each other to help her** les hommes ne savaient pas quoi inventer pour l'aider.
◆ **fall through** *vi insep* échouer ▪ **the deal fell through** l'affaire n'a pas abouti.
◆ **fall to** ◇ *vt insep* **1.** *UK* [begin] se mettre à ▪ **we fell to work** nous nous sommes mis à l'œuvre
2. [devolve upon] appartenir à, incomber à ▪ **the task that ~s to us is not an easy one** la tâche qui nous incombe *OR* revient n'est pas facile ▪ **it fell to her to break the news to him** ce fut à elle de lui annoncer la nouvelle.
◇ *vi insep* [eat] : **he brought in the food and they fell to** il a apporté à manger et ils se sont jetés dessus.
◆ **fall upon** *vt insep* **1.** [attack] attaquer, se jeter sur ▪ **the army fell upon the enemy** MIL l'armée s'est abattue *OR* a fondu sur l'ennemi
2. [meet with] tomber sur, trouver ▪ **the family fell upon hard times** la famille a subi des revers de fortune.

fallacious [fəˈleɪʃəs] *adj* [statement] fallacieux, faux, fausse *f* ▪ [hope] faux, fausse *f*, illusoire.

fallacy [ˈfæləsɪ] (*pl* **fallacies**) *n* [misconception] erreur *f*, idée *f* fausse ▪ [false reasoning] mauvais raisonnement *m*, sophisme *m* ▪ LOGIC sophisme *m*.

fallback [ˈfɔːlbæk] *n* **1.** [retreat] retraite *f*, recul *m* **2.** [reserve] réserve *f* ▪ **what's our ~ position?** sur quoi est-ce qu'on peut se rabattre?

fallen [ˈfɔːln] ◇ *pp* ▷ **fall**.
◇ *adj* **1.** [gen] tombé ▪ [hero, soldier] tombé, mort ▪ [leaf] mort **2.** [immoral] perdu ▪ [angel, woman] déchu.
◇ *npl* : **the ~** ceux qui sont morts à la guerre.

fallen arches *npl* MED affaissement *m* de la voûte plantaire.

fall guy *n inf* [dupe] pigeon *m* ▪ [scapegoat] bouc *m* émissaire.

fallibility [ˌfæləˈbɪlətɪ] *n* faillibilité *f*.

fallible [ˈfæləbl] *adj* faillible ▪ **everyone is ~** tout le monde peut se tromper.

falling [ˈfɔːlɪŋ] *adj* [gen] qui tombe ▪ [population] décroissant ▪ [prices, value] en baisse.

falling-off *n* réduction *f*, diminution *f* ▪ **a gradual ~ of interest/of support** une baisse progressive d'intérêt/de soutien.

falling star *n* étoile *f* filante.

Fallopian tube [fəˈləʊpɪən-] *n* trompe *f* utérine *OR* de Fallope.

fallout [ˈfɔːlaʊt] *n (U)* [radioactive] retombées *fpl* (radioactives) ▪ *inf fig* inf [consequences] retombées *fpl*, répercussions *fpl* ▪ **~ shelter** abri *m* antiatomique.

fallow [ˈfæləʊ] ◇ *adj* **1.** AGRIC [field, land] en jachère, en friche ▪ **to lie ~** être en jachère ▮ *fig* [period] non productif **2.** [colour] fauve.
◇ *n* jachère *f*, friche *f*.

fallow deer *n* daim *m*.

Falls Road *pr n rue du quartier catholique de Belfast qui a souvent été le théâtre d'affrontements violents.*

false [fɔːls] ◇ *adj* **1.** [wrong] faux, fausse *f* ▪ [untrue] erroné, inexact ▶ **~ dawn** lueurs annonciatrices de l'aube ▪ **don't make any ~ moves** ne faites pas de faux pas ▪ **~ pride** vanité *f* ▪ **~ start** faux départ *m* **2.** [fake] faux, fausse *f* ▪ [artificial] artificiel ▪ **a ~ bottom** un double fond ▪ **a suitcase with a ~ bottom** une valise à double fond ▪ **~ eyelashes** faux cils *mpl* **3.** [deceptive] faux, fausse *f*, mensonger ▪ LAW : **under ~ pretences** par des moyens frauduleux ▪ **you've got me here under ~ pretences** *fig* tu m'as bien piégé ▪ **to bear ~ witness** porter un faux témoignage **4.** [insincere] perfide, fourbe ▪ [disloyal] déloyal ▪ **a ~ friend** un ami déloyal ; LING un faux ami ▶ **~ modesty** fausse modestie *f*.
◇ *adv* faux ▪ **to play sb ~** trahir qqn.

false alarm *n* fausse alerte *f*.

falsehood ['fɔːlshʊd] *n fml* **1.** [lie] mensonge *m* **2.** [lying] faux *m* **3.** [falseness] fausseté *f*.

falsely ['fɔːlslɪ] *adv* [claim, state] faussement ■ [accuse, judge] à tort, injustement ■ [interpret] mal ■ [act] déloyalement.

falseness ['fɔːlsnɪs] *n* **1.** [of belief, statement] fausseté *f* **2.** [of friend, lover] infidélité *f* **3.** [insincerity] fausseté *f*, manque *m* de sincérité.

false teeth *npl* dentier *m*.

falsetto [fɔː'setəʊ] (*pl* **falsettos**) ◇ *n* fausset *m*.
◇ *adj* de fausset, de tête.

falsies ['fɔːlsɪz] *npl inf* soutien-gorge *m* rembourré.

falsification [,fɔːlsɪfɪ'keɪʃn] *n* falsification *f*.

falsify ['fɔːlsɪfaɪ] (*pret & pp* **falsified**) *vt* **1.** [document] falsifier ■ [evidence] maquiller ■ [accounts, figures] truquer **2.** [misrepresent] déformer, dénaturer **3.** [disprove] réfuter.

falsity ['fɔːlsətɪ] (*pl* **falsities**) *n* **1.** [falseness] fausseté *f*, erreur *f* **2.** [lie] mensonge *m*.

falter ['fɔːltəʳ] ◇ *vi* **1.** [waver] vaciller, chanceler ■ [courage, memory] faiblir **2.** [stumble] chanceler, tituber **3.** [in speech] hésiter, parler d'une voix mal assurée.
◇ *vt* balbutier, bredouiller.

faltering ['fɔːltərɪŋ] *adj* [attempt] timide, hésitant ■ [voice] hésitant ■ [steps] chancelant, mal assuré ■ [courage, memory] défaillant.

fame [feɪm] *n* célébrité *f*, renommée *f* ■ **the film brought her ~ and fortune** le film l'a rendue riche et célèbre ■ **to rise to ~** se faire un nom ■ **Mick Jagger of Rolling Stones ~** Mick Jagger, le chanteur du célèbre groupe The Rolling Stones.

famed [feɪmd] *adj* célèbre, renommé ■ **~ for his generosity** connu OR célèbre pour sa générosité.

familial [fə'mɪlɪəl] *adj* familial.

familiar [fə'mɪljəʳ] ◇ *adj* **1.** [well-known] familier ■ **his name is ~** j'ai déjà entendu son nom (quelque part), son nom me dit quelque chose ■ **she's a ~ sight about town** tout le monde la connaît de vue en ville ■ **there's something ~ about the place** il me semble connaître cet endroit ■ **a ~ feeling** un sentiment bien connu ■ **it's a ~ story** c'est toujours la même histoire ■ **we're on ~ territory** *fig* nous voilà en terrain de connaissance
2. [acquainted] : **to be ~ with sthg** bien connaître qqch ■ **she's ~ with the situation** elle est au courant OR au fait de la situation ■ **to become ~ with sthg** se familiariser avec qqch
3. [informal] familier, intime ■ **to be on ~ terms with sb** entretenir des rapports amicaux avec qqn
4. *pej* [presumptuous - socially] familier ; [- sexually] trop entreprenant ■ **don't let him get too ~ (with you)** ne le laissez pas devenir trop entreprenant.
◇ *n* **1.** [friend] familier *m*, ami *m*, - e *f*
2. [spirit] démon *m* familier.

familiarity [fə,mɪlɪ'ærətɪ] (*pl* **familiarities**) *n* **1.** [of face, place] caractère *m* familier **2.** [with book, rules, language] connaissance *f* ■ **her ~ with his work** sa connaissance de ses œuvres ▶ **~ breeds contempt** *prov* la familiarité engendre le mépris **3.** [intimacy] familiarité *f*, intimité *f* **4.** (*usu pl*) *pej* [undue intimacy] familiarité *f*, privauté *f*.

familiarization [fə,mɪljəraɪ'zeɪʃn] *n* familiarisation *f*.

familiarize, ise [fə'mɪljəraɪz] *vt* **1.** [inform] familiariser ■ **to ~ o.s. with sthg** se familiariser avec qqch **2.** [make widely known] répandre, vulgariser.

familiarly [fə'mɪljəlɪ] *adv* familièrement.

family ['fæmlɪ] (*pl* **families**) ◇ *n* [gen - BIOL], BOT & LING famille *f* ■ **have you any ~?** [relatives] avez-vous de la famille? ; [children] avez-vous des enfants? ■ **a large ~** une famille nombreuse ■ **to start a ~** avoir un (premier) enfant ■ **she's (just like) one of the ~** elle fait (tout à fait) partie OR elle est (tout à fait) de la famille ■ **his musical talent runs in the ~** il tient son talent musical de la famille.
◇ *comp* [life] familial, de famille ■ [car, friend] de la famille ■ [dinner, likeness, quarrel] de famille ■ [business, programme] familial ■ **~ room** [in hotel] chambre *f* familiale ■ **a ~-size** OR **~-sized jar of jam** [in pub] un pot de confiture familial ▶ **~ circle** cercle *m* de (la) famille ■ **~ doctor** docteur *m* de famille ■ **~ law** droit *m* de la famille ■ **~ practice** US médecine *f* générale ■ **~ practitioner** US médecin *m* de famille, (médecin) généraliste *m* ■ **to be in the ~ way** *inf dated & euph* être enceinte, attendre un enfant.

family allowance *n* UK allocations *fpl* familiales (*aujourd'hui "child benefit"*).

family court *n* US *tribunal pour toute affaire concernant des enfants.*

family credit *n prestation complémentaire pour familles à faibles revenus ayant au moins un enfant.*

Family Division *n* UK LAW *division du "High Court" s'occupant des affaires matrimoniales.*

family income supplement *n* ≃ complément *m* familial (*aujourd'hui "family credit"*).

family man *n* : **he's a ~** il aime la vie de famille, c'est un bon père de famille.

family name *n* nom *m* de famille.

family planning *n* planning *m* familial ■ **a ~ clinic** un centre de planning familial.

family tree *n* arbre *m* généalogique.

famine ['fæmɪn] *n* famine *f*.

famished ['fæmɪʃt] *adj* affamé ■ **I'm ~!** *inf* je meurs de faim!, j'ai une faim de loup!

famous ['feɪməs] *adj* **1.** [renowned] célèbre, renommé ■ **the stately home is ~ for its gardens** le château est connu OR célèbre pour ses jardins ▶ **the Famous Five** LIT le Club des Cinq ■ **~ last words!** c'est ce que tu crois! **2.** *dated* [first-rate] fameux, formidable.

famously ['feɪməslɪ] *adv inf* fameusement (bien), rudement bien ■ **they get on ~** ils s'entendent à merveille OR comme larrons en foire.

fan [fæn] (*pret & pp* **fanned**, *cont* **fanning**) ◇ *n* **1.** [supporter] enthousiaste *mf*, passionné *m*, - e *f* ■ [of celebrity] fan *mf* ■ SPORT supporteur *m*, - trice *f* ■ **she's a chess/jazz ~** elle se passionne pour les échecs/le jazz ■ **I'm not one of her ~s, I'm not a great ~ of hers** je suis loin d'être un de ses admirateurs **2.** [ventilator - mechanical] ventilateur *m* ; [- hand-held] éventail *m* ■ **shaped like a ~** en éventail **3.** AGRIC [machine] tarare *m* ■ [basket] van *m*.
◇ *vt* **1.** [face, person] éventer ■ **to ~ o.s.** s'éventer **2.** [fire] attiser, souffler sur ■ **to ~ the flames** *fig* jeter de l'huile sur le feu **3.** = **fan out**.
◇ *vi* s'étaler (en éventail).
➡ **fan out** ◇ *vi insep* [spread out] s'étaler (en éventail) ■ [army, search party] se déployer.
◇ *vt sep* étaler (en éventail).

fanatic [fə'nætɪk] ◇ *adj* fanatique.
◇ *n* fanatique *mf*.

fanatical [fə'nætɪkl] *adj* fanatique.

fanatically [fə'nætɪkəlɪ] *adv* fanatiquement.

fanaticism [fə'nætɪsɪzm] *n* fanatisme *m*.

fan belt *n* courroie *f* de ventilateur.

fanciable ['fænsɪəbl] *adj* UK *inf* plutôt bien, pas mal du tout.

fancied ['fænsɪd] *adj* **1.** [imagined] imaginaire **2.** SPORT [favoured] coté, en vogue.

fancier ['fænsɪəʳ] *n* **1.** [fan] amateur *m*, - trice *f* **2.** [breeder] éleveur *m*, - euse *f*.

fanciful ['fænsɪfʊl] *adj* **1.** [imaginary] imaginaire **2.** [imaginative] imaginatif, plein d'imagination **3.** [whimsical - person] capricieux, fantaisiste ; [- notion] fantasque, excentrique ; [- clothing] extravagant.

fancifully ['fænsɪfʊlɪ] *adv* **1.** [draw, write] avec imagination **2.** [act] capricieusement ■ [dress] d'une façon extravagante *OR* fantaisiste.

fancily ['fænsɪlɪ] *adv* d'une façon recherchée *OR* raffinée.

fanciness ['fænsɪnɪs] *n* caractère *m* raffiné.

fan club *n* cercle *m OR* club *m* de fans ■ **her ~ is here** *fig* ses admirateurs sont là.

fancy ['fænsɪ] (*comp* **fancier**, *superl* **fanciest**, *pl* **fancies**, *pret & pp* **fancied**) <> *adj* **1.** [elaborate - clothes] recherché, raffiné ; [- style] recherché, travaillé ; [- excuse] recherché, compliqué ■ **~ cakes** pâtisseries *fpl* **2.** [high-quality] de qualité supérieure, de luxe **3.** *pej* [overrated - price] exorbitant ; [- talk, words] extravagant ■ **with all her ~ ways** avec ses grands airs.
<> *n* **1.** [whim] caprice *m*, fantaisie *f* ■ **as the ~ takes him** comme ça lui chante ■ **it's just a passing ~** ce n'est qu'une lubie **2.** *UK* [liking] goût *m*, penchant *m* ■ **to take a ~ to sb** se prendre d'affection pour qqn ■ **the dress took** *OR* **caught her ~** la robe lui a fait envie *OR* lui a tapé dans l'œil ▶ **the idea tickled my ~** *inf* l'idée m'a séduit **3.** [imagination] imagination *f*, fantaisie *f* **4.** [notion] idée *f* fantasque, fantasme *m* ■ **I have a ~ that...** j'ai idée que...
<> *vt* **1.** *UK inf* [want] avoir envie de ■ [like] aimer ■ **do you ~ a cup of tea?** ça te dirait une tasse de thé? ■ **I don't ~ travelling** je n'ai pas envie *OR* cela ne me dit rien de voyager ■ **I don't ~ your chances of getting that job** j'imagine mal que vous obteniez ce travail ■ **to fancy sb** s'enticher de qqn ■ **she really fancies herself** elle ne se prend vraiment pas pour rien ■ **which horse do you ~?** SPORT à votre avis, quel sera le cheval gagnant?, quel cheval donnez-vous gagnant? **2.** *inf* [imagine] imaginer, s'imaginer ■ **she fancies herself as an intellectual** elle se prend pour une intellectuelle ■ **~ meeting you here!** tiens! je ne m'attendais pas à vous voir ici! ■ **~ her coming!** qui aurait cru qu'elle allait venir! ▶ **~ that!** tiens! voyez-vous cela! **3.** *lit* [believe] croire, se figurer ■ **he fancies he knows everything** il se figure tout savoir.

fancy dress *n UK* déguisement *m*, costume *m* ■ **in ~** déguisé ■ **a ~ ball** un bal masqué *OR* costumé ■ **~ party** fête *f* déguisée.

fancy-free *adj* sans souci.

fancy goods *npl* nouveautés *fpl*, articles *mpl* de fantaisie.

fancy man *n inf pej* jules *m*.

fancy woman *n inf pej* maîtresse *f*, petite amie *f*.

fanfare ['fænfeəʳ] *n* MUS fanfare *f* ■ *fig* [ostentation] : **with much ~** avec des roulements de tambour, avec éclat.

fang [fæŋ] *n* [of snake] crochet *m* ■ [of wolf, vampire] croc *m*, canine *f*.

fan heater *n* radiateur *m* soufflant.

fanlight ['fænlaɪt] *n* imposte *f* (semi-circulaire).

fan mail *n* courrier *m* des admirateurs.

fanny ['fænɪ] (*pl* **fannies**) *n* **1.** ▲ *UK* [female genitals] chatte△ *f* **2.** *US inf* [buttocks] fesses *fpl*.

fanny adams *n UK inf* **(sweet) ~** que dalle.

fanny pack *n US* banane *f (sac)*.

fantasia [fæn'teɪzjə] *n* LIT & MUS fantaisie *f*.

fantasize, ise ['fæntəsaɪz] *vi* fantasmer, se livrer à des fantasmes ■ **she ~d about becoming rich and famous** elle rêvait de devenir riche et célèbre.

fantastic [fæn'tæstɪk] *adj* **1.** *inf* [wonderful] fantastique, sensationnel **2.** *inf* [very great - success] inouï, fabuleux ; [- amount, rate] phénoménal, faramineux **3.** [preposterous, strange - idea, plan, story] fantastique, bizarre.

fantastically [fæn'tæstɪklɪ] *adv* fantastiquement, extraordinairement ■ **it's ~ expensive** c'est incroyablement *OR* terriblement cher.

fantasy ['fæntəsɪ] (*pl* **fantasies**) *n* **1.** [dream] fantasme *m* ■ PSYCHOL fantasme *m* ■ [notion] idée *f* fantasque **2.** [imagination] imagination *f*, fantaisie *f* ■ **to live in a ~ world** vivre dans un monde à soi **3.** LIT & MUS fantaisie *f*.

fanzine ['fænzi:n] *n* revue *f* spécialisée, fanzine *m*.

fao (*written abbrev of* **for the attention of**) à l'attention de.

FAO (*abbrev of* **Food and Agriculture Organization**) *pr n* FAO *f*.

FAQ [fak, ˌefeɪ'kju:] (*abbrev of* **frequently asked questions**) *n* COMPUT foire *f* aux questions, FAQ *f*.

far [fɑ:ʳ] (*comp* **farther** ['fɑ:ðəʳ] *OR* **further** ['fɜ:ðəʳ], *superl* **farthest** ['fɑ:ðɪst] *OR* **furthest** ['fɜ:ðɪst]) <> *adv* **1.** [distant in space] loin ■ **how ~ is it to town?** combien y a-t-il jusqu'à la ville? ■ **how ~ is he going?** jusqu'où va-t-il? ■ **have you come ~?** êtes-vous venu de loin? ■ **he went as ~ north as Alaska** il est allé au nord jusqu'en Alaska ■ **~ away** *OR* **off in the distance** au loin, dans le lointain ■ **~ beyond** bien au-delà ■ **~ out at sea** en pleine mer ‖ *fig* **his thoughts are ~ away** son esprit est ailleurs ■ **his work is ~ above the others'** son travail est de loin supérieur à celui des autres ■ **that's ~ beyond me** [physically] c'est bien au-dessus de mes forces ; [intellectually] ça me dépasse ■ **how ~ can you trust him?** jusqu'à quel point peut-on lui faire confiance? ■ **how ~ have you got with the translation?** où en es-tu de la traduction? ▶ **~ and wide** de tous côtés ■ **they came from ~ and wide** ils sont venus de partout ■ **~ be it from me to interfere!** loin de moi l'idée d'intervenir! ■ **to be ~ out** *UK*, **to be ~ off** *US* [person] se tromper complètement ; [report, survey] être complètement erroné ; [guess] être loin du compte ■ **he's not ~ off** *OR* **wrong** il n'a pas tout à fait tort ■ **have you got ~ to go?** *liter* avez-vous encore beaucoup de chemin à faire? ; *fig* êtes-vous loin du but?
2. [distant in time] loin ■ **as ~ back as 1800** déjà en 1800, dès 1800 ■ **as ~ back as I can remember** aussi loin que je m'en souvienne ■ **she worked ~ into the night** elle a travaillé très avant *OR* jusque tard dans la nuit ■ **he's not ~ off sixty** il n'a pas loin de la soixantaine
3. *(with compar)* [much] beaucoup, bien ■ **she is ~ more intelligent than I am** elle est bien *OR* beaucoup plus intelligente que moi
4. *phr* **to go ~** [person, idea] aller loin, faire son chemin ■ **this has gone ~ enough** trop, c'est trop ■ **his policy doesn't go ~ enough** sa politique ne va pas assez loin ■ **I would even go so ~ as to say...** j'irais même jusqu'à dire..., je dirais même... ■ **to go too ~** [exaggerate] dépasser les bornes, exagérer ‖ [make progress] : **she's gone too ~ to back out** elle s'est trop engagée pour reculer ‖ [money] : **£5 doesn't go ~ nowadays** on ne va pas loin avec 5 livres de nos jours.
<> *adj* **1.** [distant] lointain, éloigné ■ [remote] éloigné ■ **it's a ~ cry from what she expected** ce n'est pas du tout *OR* c'est loin de ce qu'elle attendait
2. [more distant] autre, plus éloigné ■ **on the ~ side** de l'autre côté ■ **the ~ end of** l'autre bout de, l'extrémité de ■ **at the ~ end of the room** au fond de la salle
3. [extreme] extrême ■ **the ~ left/right** POL l'extrême gauche *f* /droite *f*.

◆ **as far as** <> *prep phr* jusqu'à ■ **I'll walk with you as ~ as the end of the lane** je vais vous accompagner jusqu'au bout du chemin.
<> *conj phr* **1.** [distance] : **as ~ as the eye can see** à perte de vue ▶ **that's fine as ~ as it goes** c'est très bien, jusqu'à un certain point
2. [to the extent that] autant que ■ **as ~ as possible** autant que possible, dans la mesure du possible ■ **as ~ as I can** dans la mesure de mon possible ■ **as ~ as I know** (pour) autant que je sache ■ **as ~ as she's/I'm concerned** en ce qui la/me concerne, pour sa/ma part ■ **as ~ as money goes** *OR* **is concerned** pour ce qui est de l'argent.

◆ **by far** *adv phr* de loin, de beaucoup ■ **she's by ~ the cleverest** *OR* **the cleverest by ~** c'est de loin *OR* de beaucoup la plus intelligente.

◆ **far and away** *adv phr* de loin.

◆ **far from** <> *adv phr* [not at all] loin de ■ **I'm ~ from approving all he does** je suis loin d'approuver tout ce qu'il fait ▶ **he's not rich, ~ from it** il n'est pas riche, loin de là *OR* tant s'en faut.
<> *prep phr* [rather than] loin de ■ **~ from being generous, he is rather stingy** loin d'être généreux, il est plutôt radin.

◆ **in so far as** *conj phr* dans la mesure où.

◆ **so far** *adv phr* jusqu'ici, jusqu'à présent ■ **so ~ this month** depuis le début du mois ▶ **so ~ so good** jusqu'ici ça va.

◆ **so far as** *conj phr* = **as far as** *(sense 2)*.

faraway ['fɑːrəweɪ] *adj* [distant] lointain, éloigné ■ [isolated] éloigné ■ [sound, voice] lointain ■ [look] absent ■ **her eyes had a ~ look** son regard était perdu dans le vague.

farce [fɑːs] *n* **1.** THEAT & *fig* farce *f* ■ **this law is a ~** cette loi est grotesque OR dérisoire **2.** CULIN farce *f*.

farcical ['fɑːsɪkl] *adj* risible, ridicule ■ **the election was completely ~** l'élection était grotesque OR était une pure comédie.

fare [feəʳ] ◇ *n* **1.** [charge - for bus, underground] prix *m* du billet OR ticket ; [- for boat, plane, train] prix *m* du billet ; [- in taxi] prix *m* de la course ■ **what is the ~?** [gen] combien coûte le billet? ; [in taxi] combien je vous dois? ■ **~s are going up** les tarifs des transports augmentent ■ **have you got the ~?** avez-vous de quoi payer le billet? ■ **(any more) ~s, please!** [in bus, train] qui n'a pas son ticket? **2.** [passenger] voyageur *m*, - euse *f* ■ [in taxi] client *m*, - e *f* **3.** [food] nourriture *f*, chère *f* ■ **hospital ~** régime *m* d'hôpital.
◇ *comp* : **~ dodger** resquilleur *m*, - euse *f*.
◇ *vi* : **how did you ~ at the booking office?** comment ça s'est passé au bureau de réservation?

Far East *pr n* : **the ~** l'Extrême-Orient *m*.

Far Eastern *adj* extrême-oriental.

fare stage *n* UK [of bus] section *f*.

fare-thee-well *n* US *inf* **to a ~** à la perfection.

farewell [ˌfeə'wel] ◇ *n* adieu *m* ■ **to bid sb ~** dire adieu à qqn ➲ **'A Farewell to Arms'** ***Hemingway*** 'l'Adieu aux armes'.
◇ *comp* [dinner, party] d'adieu.

far-fetched [-'fetʃt] *adj* bizarre, farfelu ■ **a ~ alibi** un alibi tiré par les cheveux ■ **a ~ story** une histoire à dormir debout.

far-flung *adj* [widespread] étendu, vaste ■ [far] lointain.

farinaceous [ˌfærɪ'neɪʃəs] *adj* farinacé.

farm [fɑːm] ◇ *n* ferme *f*, exploitation *f* (agricole) ■ **to work on a ~** travailler dans une ferme.
◇ *comp* [equipment] agricole ■ **~ labourer** OR **worker** ouvrier *m*, - ère *f* agricole ■ **~ produce** produits *mpl* agricoles OR de ferme ■ **~ shop** *magasin qui vend des produits de la ferme.*
◇ *vt* [land] cultiver, exploiter ■ [animals] élever.
◇ *vi* être fermier, être cultivateur.
➡ **farm out** *vt sep* **1.** [shop] mettre en gérance ■ [work] donner OR confier à un sous-traitant ■ **she ~s some work out to local people** elle cède du travail à des sous-traitants locaux **2.** [child] : **she ~s her children out on an aunt** elle confie (la garde de) ses enfants à une tante.

farmer ['fɑːməʳ] *n* [of land] fermier *m*, - ère *f*, agriculteur *m*, - trice *f* ■ [of animals] éleveur *m*, - euse *f*.

farmhand ['fɑːmhænd] *n* ouvrier *m*, - ère *f* agricole.

farmhouse ['fɑːmhaʊs] (*pl* [-haʊzɪz]) *n* (maison *f* de) ferme *f*.

farming ['fɑːmɪŋ] ◇ *n* agriculture *f* ■ **fish/mink ~** élevage *m* de poisson/vison ■ **fruit/vegetable ~** culture *f* fruitière/ maraîchère.
◇ *comp* [methods] de culture, cultural ■ [equipment, machines] agricole ■ [community, region] rural.

farmland ['fɑːmlænd] *n (U)* terre *f* arable, terres *fpl* arables.

farmstead ['fɑːmsted] *n* ferme *f (et ses dépendances)*.

farmyard ['fɑːmjɑːd] *n* cour *f* de ferme.

Far North *pr n* : **the ~** le Grand Nord.

Faroes Isles [ˌfeərəʊ'iːz-], **Faroes** *npl* îles *fpl* Féroé.

Faroese ◇ *adj* féroïen.
◇ *n* **1.** GEOG Féroïen *m*, - ne *f* **2.** LING féroïen *m*.

far-off *adj* [place, time] lointain, éloigné.

far-out *adj inf* **1.** [odd] bizarre, farfelu ■ [avant-garde] d'avant-garde **2.** [excellent] génial, super.

farrago [fə'rɑːgəʊ] (*pl* **farragoes**) *n pej* amas *m* ■ **a ~ of lies** un fatras de mensonges.

far-reaching [-'riːtʃɪŋ] *adj* d'une grande portée ■ **to have ~ consequences** avoir des conséquences considérables OR d'une portée considérable.

farrier ['færɪəʳ] *n* UK [blacksmith] maréchal-ferrant *m* [vet].

farrow ['færəʊ] ◇ *vi* & *vt* mettre bas.
◇ *n* portée *f* (de cochons).

Farsi [ˌfɑː'siː] *n* farsi *m*.

farsighted [ˌfɑː'saɪtɪd] *adj* **1.** [shrewd - person] prévoyant, perspicace ; [- action] prévoyant ■ [decision] pris avec clairvoyance **2.** US MED hypermétrope.

farsightedness [ˌfɑː'saɪtɪdnɪs] *n* **1.** [of person] prévoyance *f*, perspicacité *f* ■ [of act, decision] clairvoyance *f* **2.** US MED hypermétropie *f*, presbytie *f*.

fart△ [fɑːt] ◇ *n* **1.** [gas] pet△ *m* **2.** [person] birbe *m* ■ **he's a boring old ~** il est rasoir, c'est un raseur.
◇ *vi* péter△.
➡ **fart about**△ UK, **fart around**△ *vi insep* gaspiller OR perdre son temps, glander.

farther ['fɑːðəʳ] *(compar of far)* ◇ *adv* **1.** [more distant] plus loin ■ **how much ~ is it?** c'est encore à combien? ■ **have we much ~ to go?** avons-nous encore beaucoup de chemin à faire? ■ **~ ahead** loin devant ■ **~ along the corridor** plus loin dans le couloir ■ **~ away, ~ off** plus éloigné, plus loin ■ **to move ~ and ~ away** s'éloigner de plus en plus ■ **~ back** plus (loin) en arrière ■ **move ~ back** reculez (-vous) ■ **~ back than 1900** avant 1900 ■ **~ down/up** plus bas/haut ■ **~ on** OR **forward** plus loin **2.** [in addition] en plus, de plus.
◇ *adj* plus éloigné, plus lointain ■ **the ~ end of the tunnel** l'autre bout du tunnel.

farthermost ['fɑːðəˌməʊst] *adj* plus lointain, plus éloigné.

farthest ['fɑːðɪst] *(superl of far)* ◇ *adj* le plus lointain, le plus éloigné ■ **in the ~ depths of Africa** au fin fond de l'Afrique.
◇ *adv* le plus loin ■ **it's 3 km at the ~** il y a 3 km au plus OR au maximum ■ **the ~ removed** le plus éloigné.

farthing ['fɑːðɪŋ] *n pièce de monnaie qui valait le quart d'un ancien penny.*

fas, FAS (*abbrev of* **free alongside ship**) *adj* & *adv* UK FLB.

fascia ['feɪʃə] (*pl* **fasciae** [-ʃiː]) *n* **1.** [on building] panneau *m* **2.** UK [dashboard] tableau *m* de bord **3.** ['fæʃɪə] ANAT fascia *m* **4.** [mobile phone] coque *f*.

fascinate ['fæsɪneɪt] *vt* **1.** [delight] fasciner, captiver ■ **she was ~d by** OR **with his story** elle était fascinée par son histoire **2.** [prey] fasciner.

fascinating ['fæsɪneɪtɪŋ] *adj* [country, idea, person] fascinant, captivant ■ [book, speaker, speech] fascinant, passionnant.

fascinatingly ['fæsɪneɪtɪŋlɪ] *adv* d'une façon fascinante OR passionnante.

fascination [ˌfæsɪ'neɪʃn] *n* fascination *f*, attrait *m* ■ **her ~ with the Orient** la fascination qu'exerce sur elle l'Orient ■ **it holds a ~ for him** ça le fascine.

fascism ['fæʃɪzm] *n* fascisme *m*.

fascist ['fæʃɪst] ◇ *adj* fasciste.
◇ *n* fasciste *mf*.

fascistic [fə'ʃɪstɪk] *adj* fasciste.

fashion ['fæʃn] ◇ *n* **1.** [current style] mode *f* ■ **in ~** à la mode, en vogue ■ **to come back into ~** revenir à la mode ■ **big weddings are no longer in ~** ça ne se fait plus, les grands mariages ■ **she dresses in the latest ~** elle s'habille à la dernière mode ■ **the Paris ~s** les collections (de mode) parisiennes ■ **to set the ~** donner le ton, lancer la mode ■ **out of ~** démodé, passé de mode ■ **to go out of ~** se démoder **2.** [manner] façon *f*, manière *f* ■ **in an orderly ~** d'une façon méthodique, méthodi-

quement ■ **after the ~ of Shakespeare** à la manière de Shakespeare ■ **after a ~** tant bien que mal ■ **he can paint after a ~** il peint à sa manière.
◇ *comp* [editor, magazine, photographer] de mode ■ [industry] de la mode ■ **~ designer** modéliste *mf* ■ **the great ~ designers** les grands couturiers ■ **~ house** maison *f* de (haute) couture ■ **~ model** mannequin *m* ■ **~ show** présentation *f* des modèles *OR* des collections, défilé *m* de mode.
◇ *vt* [gen] fabriquer, modeler ■ [carving, sculpture] façonner ■ [dress] confectionner ■ *fig* [character, person] former, façonner ■ **to ~ sthg out of clay** façonner qqch en argile.

-fashion *in cpds* : **he wore his scarf pirate~** il portait son foulard comme les pirates.

fashionable ['fæʃnəbl] *adj* [clothing] à la mode ■ [café, neighbourhood] chic, à la mode ■ [subject, writer] à la mode, en vogue ■ **a café ~ with writers** un café fréquenté par des écrivains ■ **it is no longer ~ to eat red meat** cela ne se fait plus de manger de la viande rouge.

fashionably ['fæʃnəblɪ] *adv* élégamment, à la mode ■ **her hair is ~ short** elle a les cheveux coupés court selon la mode.

fashion-conscious *adj* qui suit la mode.

fashionista [fæʃn'i:stə] *n* modeux *m*, - euse *f*.

fashion victim *n hum* victime *f* de la mode.

fast [fɑ:st] ◇ *adj* **1.** [quick] rapide ■ **she's a ~ runner** elle court vite ▶ **~ bowler** [in cricket] lanceur *m* rapide ■ **~ train** rapide *m* ■ **to pull a ~ one on sb** *inf* jouer un mauvais tour à qqn ■ **he's a ~ worker** *liter* il va vite en besogne ; *fig* il ne perd pas de temps
2. [clock] en avance ■ **my watch is (three minutes) ~** ma montre avance (de trois minutes)
3. [secure - knot, rope] solide ; [- door, window] bien fermé ; [- grip] ferme, solide ; [- friend] sûr, fidèle ■ **to make a boat ~** amarrer un bateau
4. [colour] bon teint *(inv)*, grand teint *(inv)* ■ **the colour is not ~** la couleur déteint *OR* s'en va
5. [wild] libertin ■ **~ living** vie dissolue *OR* de dissipation.
◇ *adv* **1.** [quickly] vite, rapidement ■ **how ~ is the car going?** à quelle vitesse roule la voiture? ■ **he needs help ~** il lui faut de l'aide de toute urgence ■ **she ran off as ~ as her legs would carry her** elle s'est sauvée à toutes jambes, elle a pris ses jambes à son cou ■ **the insults came ~ and furious** les insultes volaient *OR* pleuvaient dru ■ **not so ~!** doucement!, pas si vite!
2. [ahead of correct time] en avance ■ **my watch is running ~** ma montre avance
3. [securely] ferme, solidement ■ **shut ~** bien fermé ■ **to hold ~ (on) to sthg** tenir fermement qqch ■ **they held ~ despite the threats** *fig* ils ont tenu bon malgré les menaces
4. [soundly] profondément ■ **to be ~ asleep** dormir à poings fermés *OR* profondément.
◇ *n* jeûne *m* ■ **a ~ day** RELIG un jour maigre *OR* de jeûne.
◇ *vi* [gen] jeûner, rester à jeun ■ RELIG jeûner, faire maigre.

fastback ['fɑ:stbæk] *n* voiture *f* deux-volumes, voiture *f* à hayon arrière.

fast breeder reactor *n* surrégénérateur *m*, surgénérateur *m*.

fasten ['fɑ:sn] ◇ *vt* **1.** [attach] attacher ■ [close] fermer ■ **to ~ sthg with glue/nails/string to sthg** coller/clouer/lier qqch à qqch ■ **~ your seatbelts** attachez votre ceinture ■ **he ~ed the two ends together** il a attaché les deux bouts ensemble *OR* l'un à l'autre **2.** [attention, eyes] fixer ■ **he ~ed his eyes on the door** il a fixé la porte des yeux *OR* a fixé son regard sur la porte **3.** [ascribe - guilt, responsibility] attribuer ; [- crime] imputer ■ **to ~ sthg on sb** attribuer qqch à qqn.
◇ *vi* [bra, dress] s'attacher ■ [bag, door, window] se fermer.
◆ **fasten down** *vt sep* [flap, shutter] fermer ■ [envelope, sticker] coller.
◆ **fasten on** *vt sep* [belt, holster] fixer.
◆ **fasten onto** *vt insep* **1.** [seize upon] saisir ■ **to ~ onto an idea** se mettre une idée en tête **2.** [grip] se cramponner à, s'accrocher à ■ **he ~ed onto our group** *fig* il s'est attaché à notre groupe.
◆ **fasten up** *vt sep* fermer, attacher.
◆ **fasten upon** *vt insep* **1.** [gaze at] fixer ■ **her eyes ~ed upon the letter** elle fixait la lettre du regard *OR* des yeux **2.** [seize upon] saisir ■ **she ~ed upon the idea of escaping** elle s'est mis en tête de s'échapper *OR* de s'évader.

fastener ['fɑ:snəʳ], **fastening** ['fɑ:snɪŋ] *n* [gen] attache *f* ■ [on box, door] fermeture *f* ■ [on bag, necklace] fermoir *m* ■ [on clothing] fermeture *f* ■ [button] bouton *m* ■ [hook] agrafe *f* ■ [press stud] pression *f*, bouton-pression *m* ■ [zip] fermeture *f* Éclair® ■ **what kind of ~ is it?** comment cela se ferme-t-il *OR* s'attache-t-il?

fast food *n* fast-food *m*, prêt-à-manger *m offic*.
◆ **fast-food** *comp* [chain, place, restaurant] de restauration rapide, de fast-food ■ **fast-food restaurants** des fast-foods *mpl*.

fast-forward ◇ *vi* se dérouler en avance rapide.
◇ *vt* : **to ~ a tape** faire avancer *OR* défiler une cassette.
◇ *comp* : **~ button** touche *f* d'avance rapide.

fastidious [fə'stɪdɪəs] *adj* **1.** [fussy about details] tatillon, pointilleux ■ [meticulous - person] méticuleux, minutieux ; [- work] minutieux ■ **he is ~ about the way he dresses** il est d'une coquetterie méticuleuse **2.** [fussy about cleanliness] méticuleux, maniaque.

fastidiously [fə'stɪdɪəslɪ] *adv* **1.** [meticulously] méticuleusement, minutieusement **2.** [fussily] : **he ~ examined the fork** il examina la fourchette avec un soin maniaque.

fast lane *n* [in the UK] voie *f* de droite ■ [on the continent, in the US etc] voie *f* de gauche ■ **life in the ~** *fig* vie *f* excitante.

fast-moving *adj* [film] plein d'action ■ **~ events** des évènements rapides.

fastness ['fɑ:stnɪs] *n* **1.** [secureness] solidité *f* **2.** [of colour] solidité *f*, résistance *f* **3.** [stronghold] place *f* forte, repaire *m*.

fast-track *adj* : **~ executives** *des cadres qui gravissent rapidement les échelons.*

fat [fæt] (*comp* **fatter**, *superl* **fattest**, *pret & pp* **fatted**, *cont* **fatting**) ◇ *adj* **1.** [heavy, overweight - person] gros, grosse *f*, gras, grasse *f* ; [- cheeks, limb] gros, grosse *f* ; [- face] joufflu ■ **to get *OR* to grow ~** grossir, engraisser ■ **they had grown ~ on their investments** *fig* ils s'étaient enrichis *OR* engraissés grâce à leurs investissements ▶ **he's a ~ cat** *inf* [rich] c'est un richard ; [important] c'est une huile
2. [meat] gras, grasse *f*
3. [thick, hefty] gros, grosse *f* ■ **he made a ~ profit** *inf* il a fait de gros bénéfices
4. [productive - year] gras, grasse *f*, prospère ; [- land, soil] fertile, riche
5. *inf phr* **get this into your ~ head** mets-toi ça dans la tête une fois pour toutes ■ **I reckon you'll get it back – ~ chance!** je pense qu'on te le rendra – tu parles ! ■ **~ chance you have of winning!** comme si tu avais la moindre chance de gagner! ■ **a ~ lot of good it did him!** ça l'a bien avancé!, le voilà bien avancé!
◇ *n* **1.** [gen - ANAT] graisse *f*
2. CULIN [on raw meat] graisse *f*, gras *m* ■ [on cooked meat] gras *m* ■ [as cooking medium] matière *f* grasse ■ [as part of controlled diet] lipide *m* ■ **we are trying to eat less ~** nous nous efforçons de manger moins de matières grasses *OR* corps gras ■ **margarine low in ~** margarine pauvre en matières grasses *OR* allégée ■ **pork ~** saindoux *m* ■ **~ content** (teneur *f* en) matières *fpl* grasses ▶ **the ~ is in the fire** *inf* ça va chauffer ■ **to live off the ~ of the land** vivre comme un coq en pâte.
◇ *vt* engraisser ■ **to kill the fatted calf** *fig* tuer le veau gras.

fatal ['feɪtl] *adj* **1.** [deadly - disease, injury] mortel ; [- blow] fatal, mortel ; [- result] fatal **2.** [ruinous - action, consequences] désastreux, catastrophique ; [- influence] néfaste, pernicieux ; [- mistake] fatal, grave ■ **such a decision would be ~ to our plans** une décision de ce type porterait un coup fatal *OR* le coup de grâce à nos projets **3.** [crucial] fatal, fatidique.

fatalism ['feɪtəlɪzm] *n* fatalisme *m*.

fatalist ['feɪtəlɪst] ◇ *adj* fataliste.
◇ *n* fataliste *mf*.

fatalistic [,feɪtə'lɪstɪk] *adj* fataliste.

fatality [fə'tælətɪ] (*pl* **fatalities**) *n* **1.** [accident] accident *m* mortel ▪ [person killed] mort *m*, - e *f* **2.** *fml* [destiny] fatalité *f*.

fatally ['feɪtəlɪ] *adv* **1.** [mortally] mortellement ▪ **~ ill** condamné, perdu **2.** [inevitably] fatalement ▪ **the plan was ~ flawed** le projet était fatalement OR forcément imparfait.

fate [feɪt] *n* **1.** [destiny] destin *m*, sort *m* ▪ **what does ~ have in store for them?** qu'est-ce que le destin OR le sort leur réserve? **2.** [of person, thing] sort *m* ▪ **to meet one's ~** trouver la mort ▪ **the new project met with a similar ~** le nouveau projet a connu un destin semblable ▪ **a ~ worse than death** *fig* un sort pire que la mort.
◆ **Fates** *pr npl* : **the ~** les Parques *fpl*.

fated ['feɪtɪd] *adj* **1.** [destined] destiné ▪ **they seem ~ to be unhappy** ils semblent destinés OR condamnés à être malheureux **2.** [doomed] voué au malheur.

fateful ['feɪtfʊl] *adj* **1.** [decisive - day, decision] fatal, décisif ▪ [disastrous] désastreux, catastrophique **2.** [prophetic] fatidique.

fat-free *adj* sans matières grasses, sans corps gras.

fathead ['fæthed] *n dated inf* imbécile *mf*.

father ['fɑːðər] ◇ *n* **1.** [male parent] père *m* ▪ **he's like a ~ to me** il est comme un père pour moi ▪ **on my ~'s side** du côté de mon père ► **like ~, like son** *prov* tel père, tel fils *prov*, bon chien chasse de race *prov* **2.** *(usu pl)* [ancestor] ancêtre *m*, père *m* **3.** [founder, leader] père *m*, fondateur *m* ▪ **founding ~** père *m* fondateur.
◇ *vt* **1.** [child] engendrer ▪ *fig* [idea, science] concevoir, inventer **2.** [impose] attribuer ▪ **to ~ sthg on sb** attribuer qqch à qqn.
◆ **Father** *n* RELIG **1.** [priest] père *m* ▪ **Father Brown** le (révérend) père Brown ▪ **yes, Father** oui, mon père **2.** [God] : **the Father, the Son and the Holy Ghost** le Père, le Fils et le Saint Esprit ▪ **Our Father who art in Heaven** Notre Père qui êtes aux cieux **3.** POL : **the Father of the House** *titre traditionnel donné au doyen (par l'ancienneté) des parlementaires britanniques*.

Father Christmas *pr n* UK le Père Noël.

father confessor *n* directeur *m* de conscience, père *m* spirituel.

father figure *n* personne *f* qui joue le rôle du père ▪ **he was a ~ for all the employees** le personnel le considérait un peu comme un père.

fatherhood ['fɑːðəhʊd] *n* paternité *f*.

father-in-law *n* beau-père *m*.

fatherland ['fɑːðəlænd] *n* patrie *f*, mère *f* patrie.

fatherly ['fɑːðəlɪ] *adj* paternel.

Father's Day *n* fête *f* des pères.

Father Time *n* : **(Old) ~** le Temps.

fathom ['fæðəm] (*pl inv* OR *pl* **fathoms**) ◇ *n* brasse *f (unité de mesure)*.
◇ *vt* **1.** [measure depth of] sonder **2.** *inf* [understand] sonder, pénétrer ▪ **I just can't ~ it** je n'y comprends rien.

fatigue [fə'tiːg] ◇ *n* **1.** [exhaustion] fatigue *f*, épuisement *m* **2.** TECH [in material] fatigue *f* ▪ **metal ~** fatigue du métal **3.** MIL [chore] corvée *f* ▪ **I'm on ~s** je suis de corvée.
◇ *comp* **1.** MIL [shirt, trousers] de corvée ▪ **~ duty** corvée *f* ▪ **a ~ party** une corvée **2.** TECH [limit] de fatigue.
◇ *vt* **1.** *fml* [person] fatiguer, épuiser **2.** TECH [material] fatiguer.
◆ **fatigues** *npl* MIL [clothing] treillis *m*, tenue *f* de corvée.

fatless ['fætlɪs] *adj* sans matières grasses.

fatness ['fætnɪs] *n* **1.** [of person] embonpoint *m*, corpulence *f* **2.** [of meat] teneur *f* en graisse.

fatso ['fætsəʊ] (*pl* **fatsoes**) *n inf pej* gros lard *m*.

fatten ['fætn] ◇ *vt* [animal, person] engraisser ▪ [ducks, geese] gaver.
◇ *vi* [animals] engraisser ▪ [person] engraisser, prendre de l'embonpoint.
◆ **fatten up** *vt sep* [person] engraisser, faire grossir ▪ AGRIC [animal] mettre à l'engrais.

fattening ['fætnɪŋ] ◇ *adj* qui fait grossir.
◇ *n* [of animals] engraissement *m* ▪ [of ducks, geese] gavage *m*.

fatty ['fætɪ] (*comp* **fattier**, *superl* **fattiest**, *pl* **fatties**) ◇ *adj* **1.** [food] gras, grasse *f* **2.** [tissue] adipeux ▪ **~ degeneration** MED dégénérescence *f* graisseuse.
◇ *n inf pej* gros *m* (bonhomme *m*), grosse *f* (bonne femme *f*).

fatty acid *n* acide *m* gras.

fatuous ['fætjʊəs] *adj* [person, remark] sot, sotte *f*, niais ▪ [look, smile] niais, béat.

fatuously ['fætjʊəslɪ] *adv* [say] sottement, niaisement ▪ [smile] niaisement, béatement.

fatwa ['fætwə] *n* RELIG fatwa *f*.

faucet ['fɔːsɪt] *n* US robinet *m*.

fault ['fɔːlt] ◇ *n* **1.** *(U)* [blame, responsibility] faute *f* ▪ **it's not my ~** ce n'est pas de ma faute ▪ **whose ~ is it?** à qui la faute?, qui est fautif? ▪ **it's nobody's ~ but your own** vous n'avez à vous en prendre qu'à vous-même ▪ **to be at ~** être fautif OR coupable ▪ **the judge found him to be at ~** le juge lui a donné tort **2.** [mistake] erreur *f* ▪ **a ~ in the addition** une erreur d'addition **3.** [flaw - in person] défaut *m* ; [- in machine] défaut *m*, anomalie *f* ▪ **an electrical ~** un défaut électrique ▪ **a mechanical ~** une défaillance mécanique ► **honest to a ~** honnête à l'excès ▪ **to find ~ with sthg** trouver à redire à qqch, critiquer qqch ▪ **to find ~ with sb** critiquer qqn ▪ **she finds ~ with everything** elle trouve toujours à redire **4.** GEOL faille *f* **5.** TENNIS faute *f*.
◇ *vt* critiquer ▪ **to ~ sthg/sb** trouver des défauts à qqch/chez qqn ▪ **you can't ~ her on her work** il n'y a rien à redire à son travail, vous ne pouvez pas prendre son travail en défaut ▪ **I can't ~ her logic** je ne trouve aucune faille à sa logique.
◇ *vi* [make mistake] commettre une faute.

faultfinding ['fɔːlt,faɪndɪŋ] *pej* ◇ *n (U)* critiques *fpl*.
◇ *adj* chicanier, grincheux.

faultless ['fɔːltlɪs] *adj* [performance, work] impeccable, irréprochable ▪ [behaviour, person] irréprochable ▪ [logic, reasoning] sans faille.

fault line *n* GEOL ligne *f* de faille.

faulty ['fɔːltɪ] (*comp* **faultier**, *superl* **faultiest**) *adj* [machine] défectueux ▪ [work] défectueux, mal fait ▪ [reasoning] défectueux, erroné ▪ **the wiring is ~** il y a un défaut dans l'installation électrique.

faun [fɔːn] *n* faune *m*.

fauna ['fɔːnə] (*pl* **faunas** OR *pl* **faunae** [-niː]) *n* faune *f*.

Faunus ['fɔːnəs] *pr n* Faune.

Faustian ['faʊstɪən] *adj* faustien.

Fauvism ['fəʊvɪzm] *n* fauvisme *m*.

faux pas [,fəʊ'pɑː] (*pl inv* [,fəʊ'pɑː]) *n* bévue *f*, gaffe *f*.

fave [feɪv] *adj inf* préféré.

favor *etc* US = **favour**.

favorite *etc* US = **favourite**.

favour UK, **favor** US ['feɪvər] ◇ *n* **1.** [approval] faveur *f*, approbation *f* ▪ **to be in ~** [person] être bien en cour, être bien vu ; [artist, fashion] être à la mode OR en vogue ▪ **to be out of ~** [person] être mal en cour, ne pas être bien vu ; [artist, book] ne pas être à la mode OR en vo gue ; [fashion] être démodé OR dépassé ▪ **he speaks in their ~** il parle en leur faveur ▪ **to fall out of ~ with sb** perdre les bonnes grâces de qqn ▪ **to find ~ with sb** trouver grâce aux yeux de qqn, gagner l'approbation de qqn ▪ **to be in ~ of sthg** être partisan de qqch, être pour qqch ▪ **to be in ~ of doing sthg** être d'avis de OR être pour faire qqch
2. [act of goodwill] service *m*, faveur *f* ▪ **will you do me a ~** OR **do a ~ for me?** voulez-vous me rendre (un) service? ▪ **may I ask a ~ of you** OR **ask you a ~?** puis-je vous demander un service? ▪ **do me a ~ and play somewhere else** soyez gentil, allez jouer ailleurs ► **are you going to buy it? – do me a ~!** *inf* tu vas l'acheter? – je t'en prie!
3. [advantage] : **everything is in our ~** tout joue en notre faveur, nous avons tout pour nous ▪ **the odds are in his ~** il est (donné)

favori ▪ **the magistrates decided in his ~** les juges lui ont donné raison *OR* gain de cause ▪ **he dropped the idea in ~ of our suggestion** il a laissé tomber l'idée au profit de notre suggestion
4. [partiality] faveur *f*, partialité *f*
5. HIST [badge] faveur *f*
6. *lit* **a woman's ~s** les faveurs d'une femme
7. [gift] petit cadeau *m (offert aux invités lors d'une fête)*
8. *UK arch* & COMM [letter] communication *f*.
<> *vt* **1.** [prefer] préférer ▪ [show preference for] montrer une préférence pour
2. [support - suggestion, team] être partisan de, être pour ; [- candidate, project] favoriser, appuyer ; [- theory] soutenir
3. [benefit] favoriser, faciliter ▪ **circumstances that would ~ a June election** des circonstances (qui seraient) favorables à une élection en juin
4. [honour] favoriser, gratifier ▪ **she ~ed him with a smile** elle l'a gratifié d'un sourire ▪ **he ~ed us with his company** il nous a fait l'honneur de se joindre à nous
5. [resemble] ressembler à.

favourable *UK*, **favorable** *US* ['feɪvrəbl] *adj* [answer, comparison, impression] favorable ▪ [time, terms] bon, avantageux ▪ [weather, wind] propice ▪ **in a ~ light** sous un jour favorable ▪ **to be ~ to an idea** approuver une idée.

favourably *UK*, **favorably** *US* ['feɪvrəblɪ] *adv* [compare, react] favorablement ▪ [consider] d'un bon œil ▪ **to be ~ disposed to** *OR* **towards sthg** voir qqch d'un bon œil ▪ **to be ~ disposed to** *OR* **towards sb** être bien disposé envers qqn ▪ **she speaks very ~ of you** elle parle de vous en très bons termes.

favoured *UK*, **favored** *US* ['feɪvəd] *adj* favorisé ▪ **the ~ few** les privilégiés *mpl*.

favourite *UK*, **favorite** *US* ['feɪvrɪt] <> *adj* favori, préféré ▪ **he's not one of my ~ people** je ne le porte pas dans mon cœur.
<> *n* **1.** [gen] favori *m*, - ite *f*, préféré *m*, - e *f* ▪ **that book is one of my ~s** c'est un de mes livres préférés ▪ **let's listen to some old ~s** écoutons de vieilles chansons à succès **2.** SPORT favori *m* **3.** COMPUT favori *m*, signet *m*.

favouritism *UK*, **favoritism** *US* ['feɪvrɪtɪzm] *n* favoritisme *m*.

fawn [fɔːn] <> *n* **1.** [animal] faon *m* **2.** [colour] fauve *m*.
<> *adj* (de couleur) fauve.
<> *vi* : **to ~ on sb** [person] ramper devant qqn, passer de la pommade à qqn ; [dog] faire la fête à qqn.

fawning ['fɔːnɪŋ] *adj* [attitude, person] flagorneur, servile ▪ [dog] trop affectueux *OR* démonstratif.

fax [fæks] <> *n* [machine] fax *m*, télécopieur *m offic* ▪ [document] fax *m*, télécopie *f offic* ▪ **by ~** par télécopie.
<> *vt* faxer, envoyer par télécopie *OR* par télécopieur ▪ **~ me (through) the information** faxez-moi l'information.

fax machine *n* fax *m*, télécopieur *m offic*.

fax message *n* fax *m*, télécopie *f offic*.

fax modem *n* modem *m* fax.

fax number *n* numéro *m* de fax.

faze [feɪz] *vt inf* déconcerter, dérouter.

FBI (*abbrev of* **Federal Bureau of Investigation**) *pr n* : **the ~** le FBI.

FC *written abbr of* **Football Club**.

FCO *pr n* = **Foreign and Commonwealth Office**.

FDA *pr n* = **Food and Drug Administration**.

FDD [,efdiː'diː] (*abbrev of* **floppy disk drive**) *n* COMPUT lecteur *m* de disquettes.

fealty ['fiːəltɪ] (*pl* **fealties**) *n* HIST fidélité *f*, allégeance *f*.

fear [fɪəʳ] <> *n* **1.** [dread] crainte *f*, peur *f* ▪ **have no ~** ne craignez rien, soyez sans crainte ▪ **he expressed his ~s about their future** il a exprimé son inquiétude en ce qui concerne leur avenir ▪ **my one ~ is that he will hurt himself** je n'ai qu'une crainte, c'est qu'il se blesse ▪ **there are ~s that he has escaped** on craint fort qu'il ne se soit échappé ▪ **to be** *OR* **to go in ~ for** *OR* **of one's life** craindre pour sa vie ▪ **she lives in a state of constant ~** elle vit dans la peur ▪ **for ~ of what people would think** par peur du qu'en-dira-t-on ▪ **for ~ that she might find out** de peur qu'elle ne l'apprenne ◗ **without ~ or favour** impartialement ▪ **(a) ~ of heights** (le) vertige
2. [awe] crainte *f*, respect *m* ▪ **I put the ~ of God into him** *inf* [scared] je lui ai fait une peur bleue ; [scolded] je lui ai passé un savon
3. [risk] risque *m*, danger *m* ▪ **there is no ~ of her leaving** elle ne risque pas de partir, il est peu probable qu'elle parte ◗ **will you tell him? – no ~!** *inf* lui direz-vous? – pas de danger *OR* pas question !
<> *vt* **1.** [be afraid of] craindre, avoir peur de ▪ **to ~ the worst** craindre le pire ▪ **he is a man to be ~ed** c'est un homme redoutable ▪ **I ~ he's in danger** je crains *OR* j'ai peur qu'il ne soit en danger ▪ **it is to be ~ed that...** *fml* il est à craindre que... ▪ **never ~, ~ not** ne craignez rien, soyez tranquille
2. *fml* [be sorry] regretter ▪ **I ~ it's too late** je crois bien qu'il est trop tard
3. [revere - God] révérer, craindre.
<> *vi* : **I ~ for my children** je crains *OR* je tremble pour mes enfants ▪ **he ~s for his life** il craint pour sa vie.
Voir module d'usage

fearful ['fɪəfʊl] *adj* **1.** [very bad] épouvantable, affreux **2.** *inf dated* [as intensifier] affreux **3.** [afraid] peureux, craintif ▪ **she is ~ of angering him** elle craint de le mettre en colère.

fearfully ['fɪəfʊlɪ] *adv* **1.** [look, say] peureusement, craintivement **2.** *inf dated* [as intensifier] affreusement, horriblement.

fearless ['fɪəlɪs] *adj* intrépide, sans peur.

fearlessly ['fɪəlɪslɪ] *adv* avec intrépidité.

fearlessness ['fɪəlɪsnɪs] *n* audace *f*, absence *f* de peur.

fearsome ['fɪəsəm] *adj* **1.** [frightening] redoutable, effroyable **2.** *lit* [afraid] peureux, craintif ▪ [timid] extrêmement timide.

FEAR

J'ai peur des araignées. I'm scared of spiders.

J'ai peur dans le noir/de tomber. I'm afraid of the dark/of falling.

J'ai peur qu'il se perde. I'm worried that he'll get lost.

J'étais mort de peur. *inf* I was petrified.

J'ai une peur bleue des serpents. I'm terrified of snakes.

Je m'inquiète pour lui/pour sa santé. I'm worried about him/about his health.

Il se fait beaucoup de souci pour son fils. He's very worried about his son.

Je suis paniqué à l'idée de lui annoncer la nouvelle. I dread telling him the news.

Je crains qu'il ne fasse pas beau pour le pique-nique. I'm worried that it won't be nice for the picnic.

J'appréhende sa réaction. I'm worried about how he'll react.

Je redoute la fin des vacances. I'm dreading the end of the holidays.

feasibility [,fi:zə'bɪlətɪ] *n* : **to show the ~ of a plan** démontrer qu'un plan est réalisable *OR* faisable ■ **the ~ of doing sthg** la possibilité de faire qqch.

feasibility study *n* étude *f* de faisabilité.

feasible ['fi:zəbl] *adj* [plan, suggestion] faisable, réalisable.

feast [fi:st] ◇ *n* **1.** [large meal] festin *m* ■ **midnight ~** festin *m* nocturne ■ **a ~ for the eyes** *fig* un régal *OR* une fête pour les yeux ■ **a ~ of music/poetry** *fig* une véritable fête de la musique/poésie **2.** RELIG fête *f*.
◇ *comp* : **~ day** (jour *m* de) fête *f*.
◇ *vi* festoyer ■ **to ~ on** *OR* **off sthg** se régaler de qqch.
◇ *vt* **1.** *fig* **to ~ o.s. on sthg** se régaler de qqch ■ **to ~ one's eyes on sthg** repaître ses yeux de qqch *lit*, se délecter à la vue de qqch **2.** [give feast to] donner un banquet en l'honneur de.

feasting ['fi:stɪŋ] *n* festin *m*.

feat [fi:t] *n* exploit *m*, prouesse *f* ■ **a ~ of courage** un acte courageux ■ **a ~ of engineering** une (véritable) prouesse technique, un chef-d'œuvre de la technique.

feather ['feðər] ◇ *n* [of bird] plume *f* ■ [on tail, wing] penne *f* ■ [of arrow] penne *f* ■ **as light as a ~** léger comme une plume ■ **to show the white ~** manquer de courage ■ **that's a ~ in his cap** il peut en être fier ■ **you could have knocked me down with a ~** les bras m'en sont tombés.
◇ *comp* [mattress] de plume ■ [headdress] de plumes.
◇ *vt* **1.** [put feathers on - arrow] empenner ■ **to ~ one's (own) nest** *pej* faire son beurre **2.** AERON [propeller] mettre en drapeau.
◇ *vi* [in rowing] plumer.

featherbed ['feðəbed] (*pret & pp* **featherbedded**, *cont* **featherbedding**) *vt pej* [industry, business] protéger (excessivement).

feather bed *n* lit *m* de plumes.

featherbedding ['feðəbedɪŋ] *n pej* protection *f* excessive.

feather boa *n* boa *m* de plumes.

featherbrained ['feðəbreɪnd] *adj inf* étourdi, tête en l'air.

feather duster *n* plumeau *m*.

feathered ['feðəd] *adj* [headdress] de plumes ■ **our ~ friends** *hum* nos amis les oiseaux.

featherweight ['feðəweɪt] ◇ *n* **1.** [boxer, category] poids plume *m inv* **2.** *fig* [person of little importance] poids plume *m inv* ■ **he's a (political/literary) ~** il n'a pas beaucoup de poids (sur le plan politique/littéraire).
◇ *adj* [contest, championship] poids plume ■ [champion] de la catégorie *OR* des poids plume.

feathery ['feðərɪ] *adj* **1.** [bird] à plumes **2.** *fig* [light and soft - snowflake] doux et léger comme la plume.

feature ['fi:tʃər] ◇ *n* **1.** [facial] trait *m* ■ **a woman with delicate ~s** une femme aux traits fins **2.** [characteristic - of style, landscape, play etc] caractéristique *f*, particularité *f* ; [- of personality] trait *m*, caractéristique *f* ; [- of car, machine, house, room] caractéristique *f* ■ **the most interesting ~ of the exhibition** l'élément *OR* l'aspect le plus intéressant de l'exposition ■ **seafood is a special ~ of the menu** les fruits de mer sont l'un des points forts du menu ■ **to make a ~ of sthg** mettre qqch en valeur ■ **the novel has just one redeeming ~** le roman est sauvé par un seul élément **3.** RADIO & TV reportage *m* ■ PRESS [special] article *m* de fond ■ [regular] chronique *f* **4.** CIN film *m*, long métrage *m* ■ **double-~ (programme)** programme *m* proposant deux films.
◇ *vt* **1.** CIN [star - actor, actress] avoir pour vedette ■ **also featuring Mark Williams** avec Mark Williams **2.** PRESS [display prominently] : **the story/the picture is ~d on the front page** le récit/la photo est en première page **3.** COMM [promote] promouvoir, mettre en promotion **4.** [subj: car, appliance] comporter, être équipé *OR* doté de ■ [subj: house, room] comporter.
◇ *vi* **1.** CIN figurer, jouer **2.** [appear, figure] figurer ■ **the millionaire ~d prominently in the scandal** le millionnaire était très impliqué dans le scandale.

feature article *n* PRESS article *m* de fond.

feature film *n* CIN long métrage *m*.

feature-length *adj* CIN : **a ~ film** un long métrage ■ **a ~ cartoon** un film d'animation.

featureless ['fi:tʃəlɪs] *adj* [desert, city etc] sans traits distinctifs *OR* marquants.

features editor *n journaliste responsable d'une rubrique.*

feature story = **feature article**.

feature writer *n* PRESS journaliste *mf*.

Feb. (*written abbrev of* **February**) févr.

febrile ['fi:braɪl] *adj lit* fébrile, fiévreux.

February ['februərɪ] ◇ *n* février *m* ■ **I don't like ~** je n'aime pas le mois de février ■ **this has been the wettest ~ on record** cela a été le mois de février le plus pluvieux qu'on ait jamais vu ■ **in ~** en février, au mois de février ■ **in the month of ~** au mois de février ■ **~ first/ninth** *US*, **the first/ninth of ~, ~ the first/ninth** le premier/neuf février ■ **during (the month of) ~** pendant le mois de février ■ **last/next ~** en février dernier/prochain ■ **at the beginning/end of ~** au début/à la fin février ■ **in the middle of ~** au milieu du mois de février, à la mi-février ■ **early/late in ~, in early/late ~** au début/à la fin du mois de février ■ **every** *OR* **each ~** tous les ans en février.
◇ *comp* [weather] de février, du mois de février.

fecal *US* = **faecal**.

feces *US* = **faeces**.

feckless ['feklɪs] *adj* [ineffectual] incapable, qui manque d'efficacité ■ [irresponsible] irresponsable.

fecklessness ['feklɪsnɪs] *n* [ineffectuality] manque *m* d'efficacité ■ [irresponsibility] irresponsabilité *f*.

fecund ['fi:kənd] *adj lit* **1.** *liter* [woman, female animal] fécond **2.** *fig* [author] fécond ■ [imagination] fécond, fertile.

fecundity [fɪ'kʌndətɪ] *n lit* **1.** *liter* [of woman, female animal] fécondité *f* **2.** *fig* [of author] fécondité *f* ■ [of imagination] fécondité *f*, fertilité *f*.

fed [fed] ◇ *pt & pp* ▷ **feed**.
◇ *n inf US* agent *m* (du bureau) fédéral *OR* du FBI.

Fed [fed] ◇ *pr n* **1.** = **Federal Reserve Board 2.** = **Federal Reserve System**.
◇ **1.** *written abbr of* **federal 2.** *written abbr of* **federation**.

federal ['fedrəl] ◇ *adj* **1.** [republic, system] fédéral ● **the Federal Bureau of Investigation** = **FBI** ■ **the Federal Republic of Germany** la République fédérale d'Allemagne ■ **the Federal Reserve Board** *organe de contrôle de la banque centrale américaine* ■ **the Federal Reserve System** *système bancaire fédéral américain* ■ **the Federal Trade Commission** *l'une des deux autorités fédérales chargées du respect de la loi antitrust aux États-Unis* **2.** [responsibility, funding] du gouvernement fédéral ■ [taxes] fédéral.
◇ *n US* HIST nordiste *m*, fédéral *m*.

federalism ['fedrəlɪzm] *n* fédéralisme *m*.

federalist ['fedrəlɪst] ◇ *adj* fédéraliste.
◇ *n* fédéraliste *mf*.

federalize ['fedrəlaɪz] ◇ *vt* fédéraliser.
◇ *vi* se fédéraliser.

federally ['fedrəlɪ] *adv* : **to be ~ funded** être financé par le gouvernement fédéral.

federate ◇ *vt* ['fedəreɪt] fédérer.
◇ *vi* ['fedəreɪt] se fédérer.
◇ *adj* ['fedərət] fédéré.

federation [,fedə'reɪʃn] *n* fédération *f*.

fedora [fɪ'dɔ:rə] *n* [hat] chapeau *m* mou.

fed up *adj inf* **to be ~** en avoir marre, en avoir ras le bol ■ **she's ~ with him** elle en a marre de lui ■ **to be ~ (to the back teeth) with sb/with sthg/with doing sthg** en avoir (vraiment) marre *OR* ras le bol de qqn /de qqch/de faire qqch.

fee [fi:] *n* **1.** [for doctor, lawyer] honoraires *mpl* **2.** [for speaker, performer] cachet *m* ■ [retainer - for company director] jetons *mpl* de présence *(d'un administrateur)* ■ [for private tutor] appointements *mpl* ■ [for translator] tarif *m* ■ [for agency] commission *f* ■ **for a small ~** contre une somme modique.

feeble ['fi:bəl] *adj* **1.** [lacking strength] faible **2.** [lacking conviction, force - attempt, excuse] piètre ; [- argument] léger ; [- smile] timide **3.** [silly - joke] qui manque de finesse, bête.

feeble-minded *adj* faible d'esprit.

feebly ['fi:blɪ] *adv* [say, shine] faiblement ■ [smile] timidement ■ [suggest] sans (grande) conviction.

feed [fi:d] (*pret & pp* **fed** [fed]) ◇ *vt* **1.** [provide food for - person, family] nourrir ; [- country] approvisionner ; [- army] ravitailler ■ **there are ten mouths to ~** il y a dix bouches à nourrir **2.** [give food to - person, animal] donner à manger à ■ [subj: bird] donner la becquée à ■ [breastfeed] allaiter ■ [bottlefeed] donner le biberon à ■ [fertilize - plant, soil, lawn etc] nourrir ■ **to ~ sthg to sb, to ~ sb sthg** donner qqch à manger à qqn ■ **'please do not ~ the animals'** 'prière de ne pas donner à manger aux animaux' **3.** *fig* [supply - fire, furnace] alimenter ; [- lake, river] se jeter dans ; [- imagination, hope, rumour] alimenter, nourrir ■ **to ~ a parking meter** mettre des pièces dans un parcmètre **4.** [transmit] : **the results are fed to the departments concerned** les résultats sont transmis aux services concernés ■ **to ~ information to sb, to ~ sb information** donner des informations à qqn ; [in order to mislead] donner de fausses informations à qqn *(afin de le tromper)* ▶ **to ~ sb a line** *inf* faire avaler une histoire à qqn **5.** TECH [introduce - liquid] faire passer ; [- solid] faire avancer ■ [insert - paper, wire etc] introduire ■ **to ~ data into a computer** entrer des données dans un ordinateur **6.** THEAT [give cue to] donner la réplique à **7.** SPORT passer la balle à, servir.

◇ *vi* [person, animal] manger ■ [baby - gen] manger ; [- breastfeed] téter ■ **to ~ on demand** [nursing mother] donner la tétée chaque fois que le bébé le réclame *OR* à la demande.

◇ *n* **1.** [foodstuff for animal] nourriture *f* ■ [hay, oats etc] fourrage *m* **2.** [meal for baby - breast milk] tétée *f* ; [- bottled milk] biberon *m* **3.** *inf* [meal] repas *m* **4.** TECH [introduction - of liquid] alimentation *f* ; [- of solid] avancement *m* ■ [device] dispositif *m* d'alimentation *OR* d'avancement ■ **~ pump** pompe *f* d'alimentation *OR* de circulation **5.** *inf* THEAT [cue] réplique *f* ■ [comedian's partner] faire-valoir *m*.

◆ **feed back** *vt sep* [information, results] renvoyer.

◆ **feed in** *vt sep* [paper, wire] introduire ■ COMPUT [data] entrer.

◆ **feed on** *vt insep* se nourrir de ■ *fig* se repaître de.

◆ **feed up** *vt sep* [animal] engraisser ■ [goose] gaver ■ **he needs ~ing up** [person] il a besoin d'engraisser un peu.

feedback ['fi:dbæk] *n* **1.** ELECTRON rétroaction *f* ■ [in microphone] effet *m* Larsen ■ COMPUT réaction *f*, rétroaction *f*, retour *m OR* remontée *f* de l'information ■ **positive/negative ~** ELECTRON réactions positives/négatives **2.** *(U)* [information] réactions *fpl*, échos *mpl* ■ **we haven't had much ~ from them** nous n'avons pas eu beaucoup de réactions *OR* d'échos de leur part ■ **we welcome ~ from customers** nous sommes toujours heureux d'avoir les impressions *OR* les réactions de nos clients.

feeder ['fi:dər] ◇ *n* **1.** [person] mangeur *m* **2.** [child's bottle] biberon *m* **3.** [feeding device - for cattle] nourrisseur *m*, mangeoire *f* automatique ; [- for poultry] mangeoire *f* automatique ; [- for machine] chargeur *m* **4.** [river] affluent *m* ■ [road] voie *f OR* bretelle *f* de raccordement ■ [air route] ligne *f* régionale de rabattement *(regroupant les passagers vers un aéroport principal)* **5.** ELEC câble *m OR* ligne *f* d'alimentation.

◇ *comp* : **~ primary school** *école primaire fournissant des élèves à un collège* ■ **~ road** voie *f OR* bretelle *f* de raccordement ■ **~ route** [in air transport] ligne *f* régionale de rabattement *(regroupant les passagers vers un aéroport principal)*.

feeding ['fi:dɪŋ] ◇ *n* [of person, baby, animal, machine] alimentation *f*.

◇ *comp* : **~ bottle** biberon *m* ■ **~ cup** MED canard *m* ■ **to be in a ~ frenzy** [sharks] être rendu fou *OR* frénétique par la présence de nourriture ■ **~ ground** *OR* **grounds** *lieux où viennent se nourrir des animaux* ■ **~ time** [for child, animal] heure *f* des repas ■ **it's like ~ time at the zoo** *hum* on dirait le moment du repas dans un zoo.

feeding frenzy *n* frénésie *f* alimentaire.

feed pipe *n* tuyau *m* d'alimentation.

feedstuff ['fi:dstʌf] *n* nourriture *f OR* aliments *mpl* pour animaux.

feel [fi:l] (*pret & pp* **felt** [felt]) ◇ *vi (with complement)* **1.** [physically] : **to ~ hot/cold/hungry/thirsty** avoir chaud/froid/faim/soif ■ **my hands/feet ~ cold** j'ai froid aux mains/pieds ■ **to ~ good/old/full of energy** se sentir bien/vieux/plein d'énergie ■ **I felt really bad about it** j'étais dans mes petits souliers ■ **to ~ as though** *OR* **as if** *OR* **like** *inf* croire que, avoir l'impression que ▶ **he's not ~ing himself today** il n'est pas en forme aujourd'hui ■ **you'll soon be ~ing (more) yourself** *OR* **your old self again** tu iras bientôt mieux, tu seras bientôt remis ■ **you're as old as you ~** on a l'âge que l'on veut bien avoir **2.** [emotionally] : **to ~ glad/sad/undecided** être heureux/triste/indécis ■ **to ~ (like) a fool** se sentir bête ■ **to ~ (like) a failure** avoir l'impression d'être un raté ■ **I know how you ~** je sais ce que tu ressens ■ **if that's how you ~...** si c'est comme ça que tu vois les choses... ■ **how do you ~ about him/the plan?** qu'est-ce que tu penses de lui/ce projet?, comment le trouves-tu/trouves-tu ce projet? ■ **she ~s very strongly about it** elle a une position très arrêtée là-dessus ■ **how do you ~ about him coming to stay with us for a few months?** qu'est-ce que ça te ferait s'il venait habiter chez nous pendant quelques mois? **3.** [in impersonal constructions] : **it ~s good to be alive/home** c'est bon d'être en vie/chez soi ■ **it ~s strange to be back** ça fait drôle d'être de retour ■ **does that ~ better?** est-ce que c'est mieux comme ça? ■ **it ~s all wrong for me to be doing this** ça me gêne de faire ça ■ **it ~s like spring** ça sent le printemps ■ **what does it ~ like** *OR* **how does it ~ to be Prime Minister?** quelle impression ça fait d'être Premier ministre? **4.** [give specified sensation] : **to ~ hard/soft/smooth/rough** être dur/doux/lisse/rêche (au toucher) ■ **the room felt hot/stuffy** il faisait chaud/l'atmosphère était étouffante dans la pièce ■ **your forehead ~s hot** ton front est brûlant ■ **your neck ~s swollen** on dirait que ton cou est enflé **5.** [be capable of sensation] sentir **6.** [grope] = **feel about** **7.** *phr* **to ~ like** [want, have wish for] avoir envie de ■ **do you ~ like going out tonight?** ça te dit de sortir ce soir?

◇ *vt* **1.** [touch] toucher ■ [explore] tâter, palper ■ **~ the quality of this cloth** apprécie la qualité de ce tissu ▶ **to ~ one's way** avancer à tâtons ; [in new job, difficult situation etc] avancer avec précaution ■ **to ~ one's way into/out of/up** entrer/sortir/monter à tâtons ■ **I'm still ~ing my way** je suis en train de m'habituer tout doucement **2.** [be aware of - wind, sunshine, atmosphere, tension] sentir ; [- pain] sentir, ressentir ■ [be sensitive to - cold, beauty] être sensible à ■ **I could ~ myself blushing** je me sentais rougir ■ **~ the weight of it!** soupèse-moi ça! ■ **he felt the full force of the blow** il a reçu le coup de plein fouet ▶ **I can ~ it in my bones** j'en ai le pressentiment **3.** [experience - sadness, happiness, joy, relief] ressentir, éprouver ■ [to be affected by - sb's absence, death] être affecté par ■ **to ~ fear/regret** avoir peur/des regrets ■ **to ~ the effects of sthg** ressentir les effets de qqch **4.** [think] penser, estimer ■ **I ~ it is my duty to tell you** j'estime qu'il est de mon devoir de te le dire ■ **she ~s very strongly that...** elle est tout à fait convaincue que... ■ **I can't help ~ing that...** je ne peux pas m'empêcher de penser que... ■ **I ~ that things have changed between us** j'ai l'impression que les choses ont changé entre nous ■ **you mustn't ~ you have to do it** il ne faut pas que tu te sentes obligé de le faire.

◇ *n* **1.** [tactile quality, sensation] : **this garment has a really nice ~ to it** ce vêtement est vraiment agréable au toucher ■ **I like the ~ of cotton next to** *OR* **against my skin** j'aime bien le contact du coton sur ma peau **2.** [act of feeling, touching] : **to have a ~ of sthg** toucher qqch **3.** [knack] : **to get the ~ of sthg** s'habituer à qqch ■ **to have a real ~ for translation/music** avoir la traduction/la musique dans la peau **4.** [atmosphere] atmosphère *f* ■ **the room has a nice homely ~ (to it)** on se sent vraiment bien dans cette pièce ■ **his music has a really Latin ~ (to it)** il y a vraiment une influence latine dans sa musique.

◆ **feel about** *vi insep* [in drawer, pocket] fouiller ▪ **to ~ about in the dark for sthg** chercher qqch à tâtons dans le noir, tâtonner dans le noir pour trouver qqch.

◆ **feel for** *vt insep* **1.** [sympathize with] : **I ~ for you** je compatis ; *hum* comme je te plains! ▪ **that poor woman, I ~ for her** la pauvre, ça me fait de la peine pour elle
2. [in drawer, handbag, pocket] chercher.

◆ **feel up to** *vt insep* : **to ~ up to (doing) sthg** [feel like] se sentir le courage de faire qqch ; [feel physically strong enough] se sentir la force de faire qqch ; [feel qualified, competent] se sentir capable *OR* à même de faire qqch ▪ **I don't really ~ up to it** [feel strong enough] je ne m'en sens pas la force.

feeler ['fi:ləʳ] *n* [of insect] antenne *f* ▪ [of snail] corne *f* ▪ [of octopus] tentacule *m* ▪ **to put out ~s** *fig* tâter le terrain.

feelgood ['fi:lgʊd] *adj* : **it's a real ~ film** c'est un film qui donne la pêche ▪ **the ~ factor** l'optimisme *m* ambiant.

feeling ['fi:lɪŋ] ◇ *n* **1.** [sensation] sensation *f* ▪ **she gets a tingling ~ in her fingers** elle a une sensation de fourmillement dans les doigts ▪ **there's a ~ of spring in the air** ça sent le printemps ▪ **a ~ of unease came over her** elle a commencé à se sentir mal à l'aise
2. [opinion] avis *m*, opinion *f* ▪ **she has very strong ~s about it** elle a des opinions très arrêtées là-dessus ▪ **what is your ~ about...?** que pensez-vous de...? ▪ **the ~ I have is that...** à mon avis... ▪ **the general ~ is that..., there is a general ~ that...** l'opinion générale est que...
3. [awareness - relating to the future] pressentiment *m* ; [- caused by external factors] impression *f* ▪ **I had a ~ he would write** j'avais le pressentiment qu'il allait écrire ▪ **I had a ~ you'd say that** j'étais sûr que tu allais dire ça ▪ **I have a nasty ~ that...** j'ai le mauvais pressentiment que... ▪ **I have the ~ you're trying to avoid me** j'ai l'impression que tu essaies de m'éviter
4. [sensitivity, understanding] émotion *f*, sensibilité *f* ▪ **a writer/a person of great ~** un écrivain/une personne d'une grande sensibilité ▪ **to play the piano/to sing with ~** jouer du piano/chanter avec cœur *OR* sentiment ▪ **to have a ~ for poetry/music** être sensible à *OR* apprécier la poésie/la musique ▪ **you have no ~ for other people** les autres te sont indifférents
5. *(often pl)* [emotion] sentiment *m* ▪ **to have mixed ~s about sb/sthg** avoir des sentiments mitigés à l'égard de qqn/qqch ▪ **~s are running high** les passions sont déchaînées ▪ **to hurt sb's ~s** blesser qqn ▪ **bad** *OR* **ill ~** hostilité *f* ▪ **I know the ~** je sais ce que c'est ▪ **the ~ is mutual** c'est réciproque ▪ **to say sthg with ~** dire qqch avec émotion ● **no hard ~s?** sans rancune?
◇ *adj* [person, look] sympathique.

fee-paying *adj* [school] privé ▪ **~ students** *étudiants qui paient tous les droits d'inscription.*

feet [fi:t] *pl* ▻ **foot**.

feign [feɪn] *vt* [surprise, innocence] feindre ▪ [madness, death] simuler ▪ **to ~ sleep** faire semblant *OR* mine de dormir ▪ **to ~ illness/interest** faire semblant *OR* mine d'être malade/intéressé.

feint [feɪnt] MIL & SPORT ◇ *n* feinte *f*.
◇ *vi* faire une feinte.

feint-ruled *adj* [paper] à réglure légère.

feisty ['faɪstɪ] (*comp* **feistier**, *superl* **feistiest**) *adj inf* [lively] plein d'entrain ▪ [combative] qui a du cran.

felicitous [fɪ'lɪsɪtəs] *adj fml* **1.** [happy] heureux **2.** [word] bien trouvé, heureux ▪ [colour combination] heureux.

felicity [fɪ'lɪsətɪ] *n fml* **1.** [happiness] félicité *f* **2.** [aptness - of word, term] à-propos *m*, justesse *f*.

feline ['fi:laɪn] ◇ *adj* [grace] félin ▪ [characteristic] du chat.
◇ *n* félin *m*.

fell [fel] ◇ *pt* ▻ **fall**.
◇ *vt* [tree] abattre, couper ▪ *fig* [opponent] abattre, terrasser.
◇ *n* **1.** *UK* GEOG montagne *f*, colline *f* ▪ **the ~s** [high moorland] les landes *fpl* des plateaux **2.** [hide, pelt] fourrure *f*, peau *f*.
◇ *comp* : **~ walking** randonnée *f* en basse montagne ▪ **~ running** course *f* en basse montagne.
◇ *adj* **1.** *arch* & *lit* [fierce - person] féroce, cruel ▪ [deadly - disease] cruel **2.** *phr* **in** *OR* **at one ~ swoop** d'un seul coup.

fella ['felə] *n inf* [man] mec *m*, type *m*, *see also* **fellow** *(sense 1)*.

fellatio [fe'leɪʃɪəʊ] *n* fellation *f*.

feller ['feləʳ] *UK inf* = **fellow** *(n sense 1)*.

fellow ['feləʊ] ◇ *n* **1.** *inf dated* [man] gars *m*, type *m* ▪ **a good ~** un type *OR* gars bien ▪ **an old ~** un vieux bonhomme ▪ **the poor ~'s just lost his job** le pauvre vient juste de perdre son travail ▪ **my dear ~** mon cher ami **2.** *lit* [comrade] ami *m*, - e *f*, camarade *mf* ▪ [other human being] semblable *mf* ▪ [person in same profession] confrère *m*, consœur *f* ▪ **~s in misfortune** compagnons *mpl* d'infortune **3.** UNIV [professor] professeur *m* *(faisant également partie du conseil d'administration)* ▪ [postgraduate student] étudiant *m*, - e *f* de troisième cycle *(souvent chargé de cours)* ▪ **research ~** chercheur *m*, - euse *f* dans une université **4.** [of society] membre *m*.
◇ *adj* : **~ prisoner/student** camarade *mf* de prison/d'études ▪ **~ passenger/sufferer/soldier** compagnon *m* de voyage/d'infortune/d'armes ▪ **~ being** *OR* **creature** semblable *mf*, pareil *m*, - eille *f* ▪ **one's ~ man** son semblable ▪ **~ worker** [in office] collègue *mf* (de travail) ; [in factory] camarade *mf* (de travail), compagnon *m* de travail ▪ **~ citizen** concitoyen *m*, - enne *f* ▪ **~ countryman/countrywoman** compatriote *mf* ▪ **~ traveller** [companion on journey] compagnon *m* de voyage *OR* de route ; POL communisant *m* (*f* e) ▪ **an opportunity to meet your ~ translators** une occasion de rencontrer vos confrères traducteurs.

fellow feeling *n* sympathie *f*.

fellowship ['feləʊʃɪp] *n* **1.** [friendship] camaraderie *f* ▪ [company] compagnie *f* **2.** [organization] association *f*, société *f* ▪ RELIG confrérie *f* **3.** UNIV [scholarship] bourse *f* d'études de l'enseignement supérieur ▪ [position] poste *m* de chercheur.

felon ['felən] *n* LAW criminel *m*, - elle *f*.

felony ['felənɪ] *n* LAW crime *m*.

felt [felt] ◇ *pt* & *pp* ▻ **feel**.
◇ *n* TEX feutre *m* ▪ **roofing ~** feutre *m* bitumé.
◇ *comp* de *OR* en feutre ▪ **~ pen** feutre *m*.

felt-tip (pen) *n* (stylo *m*) feutre *m*.

fem [fem] = **feminine**.

female ['fi:meɪl] ◇ *adj* **1.** [animal, plant, egg] femelle ▪ [sex, quality, voice, employee] féminin ▪ [vote] des femmes ▪ [equality] de la femme, des femmes ▪ **~ doctor** femme médecin ▪ **~ company** la compagnie féminine *OR* des femmes ▪ **male and ~ clients** des clients et des clientes ▪ **there are not enough ~ politicians** il n'y a pas assez de femmes sur la scène politique **2.** TECH femelle.
◇ *n* [animal, plant] femelle *f* ▪ **the ~ of the species** la femelle ▮ *offens* gonzesse *f*.

female condom *n* préservatif *m* féminin.

female impersonator *n* travesti *m (dans un spectacle)*.

feminine ['femɪnɪn] ◇ *adj* **1.** [dress, woman, hands etc] féminin ▪ **the bedroom is very ~** c'est une vraie chambre de femme ▪ **this flat needs the ~ touch** cet appartement a besoin de la présence d'une femme **2.** GRAM [ending, form] féminin.
◇ *n* GRAM féminin *m* ▪ **in the ~** au féminin.

femininity [,femɪ'nɪnətɪ] *n* féminité *f*.

feminism ['femɪnɪzm] *n* féminisme *m*.

feminist ['femɪnɪst] ◇ *adj* féministe.
◇ *n* féministe *mf*.

femur ['fi:məʳ] *n* ANAT fémur *m*.

fen [fen] *n* marais *m*, marécage *m* ▪ **the Fens** *région de plaines anciennement marécageuses dans le sud-est de l'Angleterre.*

fence [fens] ◇ *n* **1.** [gen] barrière *f* ▪ [completely enclosing] barrière *f*, clôture *f* ▪ [high and wooden] palissade *f* ▪ **electric/barbed-wire ~** clôture électrique/en fil barbelé ● **to be on the other side of the ~** être de l'autre côté de la barricade ▪ **to**

mend one's ~s with sb [fans, electorate] se refaire une réputation auprès *OR* regagner les faveurs de qqn ; [friends, colleagues] se réconcilier avec qqn ▪ **to sit on the ~** ne pas se prononcer, rester neutre ▪ **stop sitting on** *OR* **come down off the ~** prononce-toi **2.** [in show-jumping] obstacle *m* **3.** △ [of stolen goods] receleur *m*, - euse *f* **4.** TECH protection *f*.
<> *comp* : ~ **post** piquet *m* de clôture.
<> *vt* **1.** [land] clôturer, *see also* **fence in 2.** △ [stolen goods] receler.
<> *vi* **1.** SPORT faire de l'escrime **2.** [evade question] se dérober ▪ [joust verbally] s'affronter verbalement **3.** △ [handle stolen goods] faire du recel.
◆ **fence in** *vt sep* **1.** [garden] clôturer **2.** *fig* [restrict - person] enfermer, étouffer.
◆ **fence off** *vt sep* séparer à l'aide d'une clôture.

fencer ['fensəʳ] *n* SPORT escrimeur *m*, - euse *f*.

fencing ['fensɪŋ] <> *n* **1.** SPORT escrime *f* **2.** [fences] clôture *f*, barrière *f* ▪ [material] matériaux *mpl* pour clôture **3.** △ [handling stolen goods] recel *m*.
<> *comp* [lesson, match] d'escrime.

fend [fend] *vi* : **to ~ for o.s.** se débrouiller tout seul ; [financially] s'assumer, subvenir à ses besoins.
◆ **fend off** *vt sep* [blow] parer ▪ [attack, attacker] repousser ▪ *fig* [question] éluder, se dérober à ▪ [person at door, on telephone] éconduire.

fender ['fendəʳ] *n* **1.** [for fireplace] garde-feu *m inv* **2.** NAUT défense *f* **3.** *US* [on car] aile *f* ▪ [on bicycle] garde-boue *m inv* ▪ [on train, tram - shock absorber] pare-chocs *m inv* ; [- for clearing track] chasse-pierres *m inv*.

fennel ['fenl] *n* fenouil *m*.

fenugreek ['fenjʊˌgri:k] *n* fenugrec *m*.

feral ['fɪərəl] *adj* [cat, goat, sheep] devenu sauvage.

ferment <> *vt* [fə'ment] faire fermenter ▪ **to ~ trouble** *fig* fomenter des troubles.
<> *vi* [fə'ment] fermenter.
<> *n* ['fɜ:ment] **1.** [agent] ferment *m* ▪ [fermentation] fermentation *f* **2.** *fig* [unrest] agitation *f* ▪ **to be in (a state of) ~** être en effervescence.

fermentation [ˌfɜ:mən'teɪʃn] *n* fermentation *f*.

fermented [fə'mentɪd] *adj* fermenté.

fern [fɜ:n] *n* fougère *f*.

ferocious [fə'rəʊʃəs] *adj* [animal, appetite, criticism, fighting] féroce ▪ [weapon] meurtrier ▪ [competition] acharné ▪ [heat] terrible, intense ▪ [climate] rude.

ferociously [fə'rəʊʃəslɪ] *adv* [bark, criticize, attack] avec férocité, férocement ▪ [look at sb] d'un œil féroce ▪ **this business is ~ competitive** ce secteur est caractérisé par une concurrence acharnée.

ferociousness [fə'rəʊʃəsnɪs], **ferocity** [fə'rɒsətɪ] *n* [of person, animal, attack, criticism] férocité *f* ▪ [of climate] rudesse *f* ▪ [of heat] intensité *f*, caractère *m* torride.

ferret ['ferɪt] <> *n* furet *m*.
<> *vi* **1.** [hunt with ferrets] chasser au furet ▪ **to go ~ing** aller à la chasse au furet **2.** *fig* = **ferret about**, = **ferret around**.
◆ **ferret about** *UK*, **ferret around** *vi insep* [in pocket, drawer] fouiller ▪ [in room] fouiller, fureter ▪ **to ~ about for information** fureter dans le but de trouver des renseignements.
◆ **ferret out** *vt sep* [information, truth] dénicher.

Ferris wheel ['ferɪs-] *n* grande roue *f*.

ferrous ['ferəs] *adj* ferreux.

ferrule ['feru:l] *n* [of umbrella, walking stick] virole *f*.

ferry ['ferɪ] <> *n* (*pl* **ferries**) [large] ferry *m* ▪ [small] bac *m* ▪ **to take the ~** prendre le ferry *OR* le bac ▪ **a ~ crossing** une traversée en ferry *OR* bac ▪ **~ service** ligne *f* de ferry ▪ **~ terminal** gare *f* maritime ▪ **passenger ~** ferry *m* pour passagers piétons ▪ **car ~** car-ferry *m*.
<> *vt* (*pret & pp* **ferried**) **1.** [by large boat - subj: company] transporter en ferry ▪ [by small boat - subj: company] faire traverser en bac ; [- subj: boat] transporter **2.** *fig* [by vehicle - goods] transporter ; [- people] conduire ▪ **he spends most of his time ~ing the kids around** il passe la majeure partie de son temps à conduire les enfants à droite et à gauche.

ferryboat ['ferɪbəʊt] *n* ferry *m*.

ferryman ['ferɪmən] (*pl* **ferrymen** [-mən]) *n* passeur *m*.

fertile ['fɜ:taɪl] *adj* [land, soil] fertile ▪ [person, couple, animal] fécond ▪ *fig* [imagination] fertile, fécond ▪ **a ~ egg** un œuf fécondé ▪ **to fall on ~ ground** *fig* trouver un terrain propice.

fertility [fɜ:'tɪlətɪ] <> *n* [of land, soil] fertilité *f* ▪ [of person, animal] fécondité *f* ▪ *fig* [of imagination] fertilité *f*, fécondité *f*.
<> *comp* [rate] de fécondité ▪ [rite, symbol] de fertilité ▪ **~ clinic** centre *m* de traitement de la stérilité ▪ **~ drug** médicament *m* pour le traitement de la stérilité.

fertilization [ˌfɜ:tɪlaɪ'zeɪʃn] *n* **1.** BIOL [of egg] fécondation *f* **2.** AGRIC [of soil] fertilisation *f*.

fertilize, ise ['fɜ:tɪlaɪz] *vt* **1.** BIOL [animal, plant, egg] féconder **2.** AGRIC [land, soil] fertiliser.

fertilizer ['fɜ:tɪlaɪzəʳ] *n* AGRIC engrais *m*.

ferule ['feru:l] = **ferrule**.

fervent ['fɜ:vənt] *adj* [desire, supporter etc] fervent, ardent ▪ **he is a ~ believer in reincarnation** il croit ardemment à la réincarnation.

fervently ['fɜ:vəntlɪ] *adv* [beg, desire, speak etc] avec ferveur ▪ [believe] ardemment.

fervour *UK*, **fervor** *US* ['fɜ:vəʳ] *n* ferveur *f*.

fess up *vi insep inf* cracher le morceau.

fester ['festəʳ] *vi* **1.** [wound] suppurer ▪ *fig* [memory, resentment] s'aigrir **2.** *UK inf* [do nothing] buller.

festering ['festrɪŋ] *adj* [wound] suppurant.

festival ['festəvl] *n* [of music, film etc] festival *m* ▪ RELIG fête *f* ▪ **street ~** festival de rue.

festive ['festɪv] *adj* [atmosphere] de fête ▪ **the ~ season** la période des fêtes ▪ **to be in ~ mood** [person] se sentir d'une humeur de fête ▪ **the village is in ~ mood** une ambiance de fête règne dans le village ▪ **to look ~** [place] être décoré comme pour une fête.

festivity [fes'tɪvətɪ] (*pl* **festivities**) *n* [merriness] fête *f*.
◆ **festivities** *npl* festivités *fpl* ▪ **the Christmas festivities** les fêtes *fpl* de Noël.

festoon [fe'stu:n] <> *n* feston *m*, guirlande *f*.
<> *vt* orner de festons, festonner ▪ **to be ~ed in sthg** *fig* [draped with] être couvert de qqch.

festoon blind *n* store *m* autrichien.

feta ['fetə] *n* : **~ (cheese)** feta *f*.

fetal *US* = **foetal**.

fetch [fetʃ] <> *vt* **1.** [go to get] aller chercher ▪ [come to get] venir chercher ▪ **to ~ sb from the station/from school** aller chercher qqn à la gare/à l'école ▪ **go/run and ~ him** va/va vite le chercher ▪ **to ~ sb in** faire rentrer qqn ▪ **to ~ sthg in** rentrer qqch ▪ **she ~ed him down from upstairs** elle est montée le chercher **2.** [generate - response, laugh] susciter ▪ **it ~ed no response** cela n'a suscité *OR* soulevé aucune réaction **3.** [be sold for - money] rapporter ; [- price] atteindre ▪ **it should ~ you £8,000** cela devrait vous rapporter 8 000 livres, vous devriez en tirer 8 000 livres ▪ **the painting ~ed £8,000** le tableau a atteint la somme de 8 000 livres **4.** *fml* [utter - sigh, groan] pousser **5.** *inf* [deal - blow] : **he ~ed him one with his right fist** il lui a flanqué *OR* envoyé un droit.
<> *vi* aller chercher ▪ **~!** [to dog] va chercher! ▪ **to ~ and carry for sb** faire le grouillot pour qqn, être le grouillot de qqn.
◆ **fetch up** *inf* <> *vi insep* **1.** [end up] se retrouver ▪ **to ~ up in hospital/in a ditch** se retrouver à l'hôpital/dans un fossé **2.** [vomit] rendre.
<> *vt sep* [vomit] rendre.

fetching ['fetʃɪŋ] *adj* [smile, person, look] séduisant ▪ [hat, dress] seyant.

fetchingly ['fetʃɪŋlɪ] *adv* [smile] d'un air séduisant ■ **with his hat balanced ~ on his head** avec son chapeau élégamment posé sur la tête.

fête [feɪt] <> *n* fête *f*, kermesse *f* ■ **village ~** fête de village.
<> *vt* fêter.

FÊTE

En Grande-Bretagne, les *village fêtes* sont des fêtes de village, avec des ventes de produits artisanaux, des manifestations sportives et des jeux pour enfants ; elles sont souvent destinées à réunir des fonds pour des œuvres de charité.

fetid ['fetɪd] *adj* fétide.

fetish ['fetɪʃ] *n* PSYCHOL & RELIG fétiche *m* ■ **to have a ~ for sthg** être un fétichiste de qqch ■ **to have a ~ for** *OR* **to make a ~ of sthg** être obsédé par qqch, être un maniaque de qqch.

fetishism ['fetɪʃɪzm] *n* PSYCHOL & RELIG fétichisme *m* ■ **food ~** obsession *f* pour la nourriture.

fetishist ['fetɪʃɪst] *n* PSYCHOL & RELIG fétichiste *mf* ■ **food ~** personne *f* obsédée par la nourriture.

fetishistic [,fetɪ'ʃɪstɪk] *adj* PSYCHOL fétichiste.

fetlock ['fetlɒk] *n* [of horse - part of leg] partie *f* postérieure du pied ; [- joint] boulet *m* ; [- hair] fanon *m*.

fetter ['fetəʳ] *vt* [slave, prisoner] enchaîner ■ [horse] entraver ■ *fig* entraver.
◆ **fetters** *npl* [of prisoner] fers *mpl*, chaînes *fpl* ■ [of horse] entraves *fpl* ■ *fig* [of marriage, job] chaînes *fpl*, sujétions *fpl* ■ **in ~s** [prisoner] enchaîné ; *fig* entravé ■ **to put sb in ~s** mettre qqn aux fers ; *fig* entraver qqn.

fettle ['fetl] *n inf* **to be in fine** *OR* **good ~** aller bien.

fetus *US* = **foetus**.

feud [fju:d] <> *n* [between people, families] querelle *f* ■ [more aggressive - between families] vendetta *f* ■ **a bloody ~** une vendetta ■ **to have a ~ with sb** être à couteaux tirés avec qqn.
<> *vi* se quereller, se disputer ■ **to ~ with sb (over sthg)** se quereller *OR* se disputer avec qqn (pour qqch).

feudal ['fju:dl] *adj* [society, system] féodal ■ *pej* [extremely old-fashioned] moyenâgeux.

feudalism ['fju:dəlɪzm] *n* féodalisme *m*.

feuding ['fju:dɪŋ] *n (U)* querelle *f*, querelles *fpl* ■ [more aggressive] vendetta *f*.

fever ['fi:vəʳ] *n* **1.** MED [illness] fièvre *f* ■ **to have a ~** [high temperature] avoir de la température *OR* de la fièvre ■ **to have a high ~** avoir beaucoup de température *OR* de fièvre **2.** *fig* excitation *f* fébrile ■ **a ~ of anticipation** une attente fièvreuse *OR* fébrile ■ **football/election/gold ~** fièvre *f* du football/des élections/de l'or ■ **gambling ~** démon *m* du jeu ■ **to be in a ~ about sthg** [nervous, excited] être tout excité à cause de qqch.

fevered ['fi:vəd] *adj* [brow] fiévreux ■ *fig* [imagination] enfiévré.

feverish ['fi:vərɪʃ] *adj* MED fiévreux ■ *fig* [activity, atmosphere] fébrile.

fever pitch *n fig* **things are at ~ here** l'excitation ici est à son comble ■ **excitement is rising to ~** l'excitation est de plus en plus fébrile.

few [fju:] <> *det* **1.** [not many] peu de ■ **so/too ~ books to read** si/trop peu de livres à lire ■ **there are four books too ~** il manque quatre livres ■ **with ~ exceptions** à peu d'exceptions près, sauf de rares exceptions ■ *(with def art, poss adj etc)* **on the ~ occasions that I have met him** les rares fois où je l'ai rencontré ■ **her ~ remaining possessions** le peu de biens qui lui restaient ■ **these ~ precious souvenirs** ces quelques précieux souvenirs ➊ **visitors are ~ and far between** les visiteurs sont rares **2.** [indicating an unspecified or approximate number] **: the first ~ copies** les deux ou trois premiers exemplaires ■ **in the past/next ~ days** pendant les deux ou trois derniers/prochains jours ■ **he's been living in London for the past ~ years** ça fait quelques années qu'il habite à Londres ■ **these past ~ weeks have been wonderful** ces dernières semaines ont été merveilleuses.
<> *pron* [not many] **: how many of them are there? – very ~** combien sont-ils? – très peu nombreux ■ **I didn't realize how ~ there were** je ne m'étais pas rendu compte qu'ils étaient aussi peu nombreux ■ **~ could have predicted the outcome** peu de personnes *OR* rares sont ceux qui auraient pu prévoir le résultat ■ **the ~ who knew her** les quelques personnes qui la connaissaient ➊ **the chosen ~** les heureux élus.
◆ **a few** <> *det phr* quelques ■ **he has a ~ more friends than I have** il a un peu plus d'amis que moi ■ **a ~ more days/months/years** quelques jours/mois/années de plus.
<> *pron phr* quelques-uns, quelques-unes *f* ■ **we need a ~ more/less** il nous en faut un peu plus/moins ■ **a ~ of you** quelques-uns d'entre vous ➊ **he's had a ~ (too many)** *inf* [drinks] il a bu un coup (de trop) ■ **to name but a ~** pour n'en citer que quelques-uns ■ **not a ~** pas peu.
◆ **a good few, quite a few** <> *det phr* un assez grand nombre de ■ **there were a good ~** *OR* **quite a ~ mistakes in it** il y avait un assez grand nombre de *OR* pas mal de fautes dedans.
<> *pron phr* un assez grand nombre ■ **quite a ~ of us/of the books** un assez grand nombre d'entre nous/de livres.

fewer ['fju:əʳ] *(compar of few)* <> *det* moins de ■ **there have been ~ accidents than last year** il y a eu moins d'accidents que l'an dernier ■ **~ and ~ people** de moins en moins de gens ■ **the ~ people turn up the better** moins il y aura de monde et mieux ce sera ➊ **no ~ than** pas moins de.
<> *pron* moins ■ **there are ~ of you than I thought** vous êtes moins nombreux que je ne le pensais ■ **the ~ the better** moins il y en a mieux c'est ■ **how many days are you going to spend there? – the ~ the better** combien de jours vas-tu passer là-bas? – le moins possible.

fewest ['fju:ɪst] *(superl of few)* <> *adj* le moins de ■ **the ~ mistakes possible** le moins d'erreurs possible ■ **this is the part where the ~ people live** c'est la région la moins peuplée.
<> *pron* **: I had the ~** c'est moi qui en ai eu le moins.

fey [feɪ] *adj* [whimsical - person, behaviour] bizarre.

fez [fez] *n* fez *m*.

fiancé [fɪ'ɒnseɪ] *n* fiancé *m*.

fiancée [fɪ'ɒnseɪ] *n* fiancée *f*.

fiasco [fɪ'æskəʊ] (*pl* **fiascos** *OR pl* **fiascoes**) *n* fiasco *m* ■ **it was a ~** ça a été un véritable fiasco.

fiat ['faɪæt] *n* [decree] décret *m*.

fib [fɪb] *inf* <> *n* petit mensonge *m* ■ **to tell ~s** raconter des histoires.
<> *vi* raconter des histoires.

fibber ['fɪbəʳ] *n inf* menteur *m*, - euse *f*.

fibre *UK*, **fiber** *US* ['faɪbəʳ] *n* **1.** [of cloth, wood] fibre *f* ■ **moral ~** *fig* force *f* morale ■ **to love sb/sthg with every ~ of one's being** *fig* aimer qqn/qqch de tout son être **2.** *(U)* [in diet] fibres *fpl* ■ **high-~ diet** régime *m* *OR* alimentation *f* riche en fibres.

fibreboard *UK*, **fiberboard** *US* ['faɪbəbɔ:d] *n* panneau *m* de fibres.

fibreglass *UK*, **fiberglass** *US* ['faɪbəglɑ:s] <> *n* fibre *f* de verre.
<> *comp* [boat, hull etc] en fibre de verre.

fibre optic <> *n* **: ~s** fibre *f* optique, fibres *fpl* optiques.
<> *adj* [cable] en fibres optiques.

fibrillation [,faɪbrɪ'leɪʃn] *n* fibrillation *f*.

fibroid ['faɪbrɔɪd] <> *adj* [tissue] fibreux ■ **~ tumour** fibrome *m*.
<> *n* [tumour] fibrome *m*.

fibrositis [,faɪbrə'saɪtɪs] *n (U)* fibrosite *f*.

fibrous ['faɪbrəs] *adj* fibreux.

fibula ['fɪbjʊlə] (*pl* **fibulas** *OR pl* **fibulae** [-li:]) *n* ANAT péroné *m*.

fickle ['fɪkl] *adj* [friend, fan] inconstant ■ [weather] changeant, incertain ■ [lover] inconstant, volage.

fiction ['fɪkʃn] ◇ *n* **1.** *(U)* LIT ouvrages *mpl* *OR* œuvres *fpl* de fiction ■ **a work** *OR* **piece of ~** un ouvrage *OR* une œuvre de fiction **2.** [invention] fiction *f* ■ **we'll have to keep up the ~ a little longer** il nous faudra continuer encore un peu à faire semblant.
◇ *comp* : **~ writer** auteur *m* d'ouvrages de fiction.

fictional ['fɪkʃənl] *adj* fictif ■ **a well-known ~ character** un célèbre personnage de la littérature.

fictitious [fɪk'tɪʃəs] *adj* [imaginary, invented] fictif.

fiddle ['fɪdl] ◇ *n* **1.** MUS [instrument] violon *m* ■ **to be as fit as a ~** être en pleine forme, être frais comme un gardon ■ **to play second ~ to sb** jouer les seconds violons *OR* rôles auprès de qqn **2.** *inf* [swindle] truc *m*, combine *f* ■ **to work a ~** *UK* combiner quelque chose ■ **to be on the ~** traficoter.
◇ *vi* **1.** [be restless] : **stop fiddling!** tiens-toi tranquille!, arrête de remuer! ■ **to ~ with sthg** [aimlessly, nervously] jouer avec qqch ; [interfere with] jouer avec *OR* tripoter qqch **2.** [tinker] bricoler ■ **he ~d with the knobs on the television** il a tourné les boutons de la télé dans tous les sens **3.** MUS jouer du violon ■ **to ~ while Rome burns** s'occuper de futilités alors qu'il est urgent d'agir **4.** *inf* [cheat] trafiquer.
◇ *vt* **1.** *inf* [falsify - results, financial accounts] truquer, falsifier ; [- election] truquer ■ **he ~d it so that he got the results he wanted** il a trafiqué pour obtenir les résultats qu'il voulait **2.** *inf* [gain dishonestly - money, time off] carotter **3.** *inf* [swindle - person] : **he ~d me out of £20** il m'a refait de 20 livres **4.** [play - tune] jouer au violon.
◆ **fiddle about** *UK*, **fiddle around** *vi insep* **1.** [fidget] jouer **2.** *inf* [mess about] bricoler ■ [loaf about, waste time] traînasser.

fiddler ['fɪdlə^r] *n inf* **1.** MUS joueur *m*, - euse *f* de violon, violoniste *mf* **2.** [swindler] arnaqueur *m*, - euse *f*.

fiddlesticks ['fɪdlstɪks] *interj inf dated* [in disagreement] balivernes *fpl*, sornettes *fpl* ■ [in annoyance] bon sang de bonsoir.

fiddling ['fɪdlɪŋ] ◇ *adj* [trivial - job] futile, insignifiant.
◇ *n* **1.** [fidgeting] : **stop your ~ !** arrête de gigoter! **2.** *inf* [swindling] trafic *m*, falsification *f*.

fiddly ['fɪdlɪ] *adj inf* [awkward - job, task] délicat, minutieux ; [- small object] difficile à manier, difficile à tenir entre les doigts ■ **it's a bit ~** ça demande de la minutie.

fidelity [fɪ'delətɪ] *n* **1.** [of people] fidélité *f* **2.** [of translation] fidélité *f* **3.** ELECTRON fidélité *f*.

fidget ['fɪdʒɪt] *inf* ◇ *vi* [be restless] avoir la bougeotte, gigoter ■ **stop ~ing!** arrête de gigoter! ■ **to ~ with sthg** jouer avec qqch, tripoter qqch.
◇ *n* **1.** [restless person] : **she's such a ~** elle ne tient pas en place, elle gigote tout le temps **2.** *phr* **to have** *OR* **to get the ~s** [be restless, nervous] ne pas tenir en place.

fidgety ['fɪdʒɪtɪ] *adj inf* qui ne tient pas en place.

Fido ['faɪdəʊ] *pr n nom typique pour un chien*, ≃ Médor.

fief [fi:f] *n* HIST & *fig* fief *m*.

fiefdom ['fi:fdəm] *n* HIST & *fig* fief *m*.

field [fi:ld] ◇ *n* **1.** AGRIC champ *m* ■ **to work in the ~s** travailler dans les *OR* aux champs
2. SPORT [pitch] terrain *m* ■ **the ~** [in baseball] les défenseurs *mpl* ■ **Smith is way ahead of the (rest of the) ~** Smith est loin devant *OR* devance largement les autres ■ **there's a very strong ~ for the 100 metres** il y a une très belle brochette de concurrents *OR* participants au départ du 100 mètres ◆ **sports** *OR* **games ~** terrain de sport ■ **to take the ~** entrer sur le terrain ■ **to lead the ~** [in race] mener la course, être en tête ; *fig* [in sales, area of study] être en tête ; [subj: theory] faire autorité ■ **to play the ~** *inf* [romantically] jouer sur plusieurs tableaux
3. [of oil, minerals etc] gisement *m*
4. MIL : **~ (of battle)** champ *m* de bataille ■ **bravery in the ~** bravoure sur le champ de bataille ■ **to hold the ~** ne pas lâcher de terrain, tenir
5. [sphere of activity, knowledge] domaine *m* ■ **in the political ~, in the ~ of politics** dans le domaine politique ■ **what's your ~?, what ~ are you in?** quel est ton domaine?
6. [practice rather than theory] terrain *m* ■ **to work/to study in the ~** travailler/étudier sur le terrain
7. PHYS & OPT champ *m* ■ **~ of vision** champ visuel *OR* de vision ■ MIL : **~ of fire** champ *m* de tir
8. COMPUT champ *m*
9. HERALD [on coat of arms, coin] champ *m* ■ [on flag] fond *m*.
◇ *vt* **1.** [team] présenter ■ [player] faire jouer ■ MIL [men, hardware] réunir ■ POL [candidate] présenter
2. [in cricket, baseball - ball] arrêter (et renvoyer) ■ **to ~ a question** *fig* savoir répondre à une question.
◇ *vi* [in cricket, baseball] être en défense, tenir le champ.

field ambulance *n* MIL ambulance *f*.

field artillery *n* MIL artillerie *f* de campagne.

field day *n* SCH journée *f* en plein air ■ MIL jour *m* des grandes manœuvres ■ **to have a ~** *inf fig* s'en donner à cœur joie ; [do good business] faire recette.

fielder ['fi:ldə^r] *n* [in cricket, baseball] joueur *m* de l'équipe défendante *OR* champ.

field events *npl* SPORT concours *mpl (d'athlétisme)*.

field glasses *npl* jumelles *fpl*.

field gun *n* MIL canon *m*.

field hockey *n US* hockey *m* (sur gazon).

field hospital *n* MIL antenne *f* chirurgicale, hôpital *m* de campagne.

field marshal *n* MIL maréchal *m*.

fieldmouse ['fi:ldmaʊs] (*pl* **fieldmice** [-maɪs]) *n* mulot *m*.

field officer *n* MIL officier *m* supérieur.

field sports *npl la chasse et la pêche*.

field study *n* étude *f* sur le terrain.

field test *n* essai *m* sur le terrain.
◆ **field-test** *vt* [machine] soumettre à des essais sur le terrain.

field trials *npl* [for machine] essais *mpl* sur le terrain.

field trip *n* SCH & UNIV voyage *m* d'études ■ [of one afternoon, one day] sortie *f* d'études.

fieldwork ['fi:ldwɜ:k] *n (U)* travaux *mpl* sur le terrain ■ [research] recherches *fpl* sur le terrain.

field worker *n* [social worker] travailleur *m* social, travailleuse *f* sociale ■ [researcher] chercheur *m*, - euse *f* de terrain.

fiend [fi:nd] *n* **1.** [demon] démon *m*, diable *m* ■ [evil person] monstre *m* **2.** *inf* [fanatic, freak] mordu *m*, - e *f*, fana *mf* ■ **tennis ~** fana *OR* mordu de tennis ■ **sex ~** satyre *m* ; [in newspaper headline] maniaque *m* sexuel.

fiendish ['fi:ndɪʃ] *adj* **1.** [fierce - cruelty, look] diabolique, démoniaque **2.** *inf* [plan, cunning] diabolique ■ [very difficult - problem] abominable, atroce.

fiendishly ['fi:ndɪʃlɪ] *adv* **1.** [cruelly] diaboliquement **2.** *inf* [extremely] : **~ difficult** abominablement *OR* atrocement difficile.

fierce [fɪəs] *adj* **1.** [animal, person, look, words] féroce **2.** [heat, sun] torride ■ [competition, fighting, loyalty, resistance] acharné ■ [battle, criticism, desire, hatred, temper] féroce.

fiercely ['fɪəslɪ] *adv* **1.** *liter* férocement ■ **to look ~ at sb** regarder qqn d'un air féroce **2.** *fig* [argue, attack, criticize, fight] violemment ■ [resist] avec acharnement ■ [independent] farouchement ■ **it is a ~ competitive business** c'est un secteur où la concurrence est acharnée ■ **to be ~ loyal to sb** faire preuve d'une loyauté à toute épreuve *OR* farouche envers qqn.

fierceness ['fɪəsnɪs] *n* **1.** [of animal, look, person] férocité *f* **2.** [of desire] violence *f* ■ [of sun] ardeur *f* ■ [of resistance] acharnement *m* ■ [of criticism] férocité *f*.

fiery ['faɪərɪ] *adj* [heat, sun, coals] ardent ■ [speech] violent, fougueux ■ [temper] fougueux ■ [sky, sunset] embrasé ■ [curry] très épicé ■ **~ red hair** cheveux d'un roux flamboyant ◆ **the ~ cross** *US* la croix en flammes *(symbole du Ku Klux Klan)*.

fiesta [fɪ'estə] *n* fiesta *f*.

FIFA ['fi:fə] (*abbrev of* **Fédération Internationale de Football Association**) *pr n* FIFA *f*.

fife [faɪf] *n* MUS fifre *m*.

fifteen [fɪf'ti:n] ◇ *det* quinze ■ **about ~ people** une quinzaine de personnes ■ **to be ~** avoir quinze ans.
◇ *n* **1.** [numeral] quinze *m inv* ■ **about ~** une quinzaine **2.** [in rugby] quinze *m* ■ **the opposing ~** l'équipe rivale.
◇ *pron* quinze ■ **~ is not enough** quinze, ce n'est pas assez.

fifteenth [fɪf'ti:nθ] ◇ *det* quinzième ■ **Louis the Fifteenth** Louis Quinze.
◇ *n* [fraction] quinzième *m* ■ [in series] quinzième *mf*.

fifth [fɪfθ] ◇ *det* cinquième ■ **a ~ part** un cinquième ■ **on the ~ day of the month** le cinq du mois ■ **in ~ place** à la cinquième place ■ **~ from the end/right** cinquième en partant de la fin/droite ■ **on the ~ floor** *UK* au cinquième étage ; *US* au quatrième étage ■ **~ gear** AUT cinquième vitesse ■ **~ form** *UK* SCH ≃ classe de seconde ▶ **to feel like a ~ wheel** avoir l'impression d'être la cinquième roue du carrosse ■ **Fifth Amendment** Cinquième Amendement *m (de la Constitution des États-Unis, permettant à un accusé de ne pas répondre à une question risquant de jouer en sa défaveur)* ■ **Fifth Avenue** la cinquième avenue ■ **the Fifth Republic** la Cinquième *OR* Ve République ■ **George the Fifth** Georges Cinq.
◇ *n* **1.** [day of month] cinq *m inv* ■ **the ~, on the ~** le cinq ■ **July ~** *US*, **the ~ of July, July the ~** le cinq juillet ▶ **the ~ of November** *jour anniversaire de la conspiration des poudres aussi appelé Guy Fawkes' Day* ■ [fraction] cinquième *m* ■ [in series] cinquième *mf* **2.** MUS quinte *f* **3.** *US* [Fifth Amendment] : **I'll take the Fifth** *US expression utilisée par une personne appréhendée pour invoquer le Cinquième Amendement.*

fifth column *n* cinquième colonne *f*.

fifth-generation *adj* COMPUT de cinquième génération.

fifthly ['fɪfθlɪ] *adv* cinquièmement.

fiftieth ['fɪftɪəθ] ◇ *adj* cinquantième.
◇ *n* [fraction] cinquantième *m* ■ [in series] cinquantième *mf*.

fifty ['fɪftɪ] ◇ *det* cinquante ■ **about ~ people** une cinquantaine de personnes.
◇ *n* **1.** [numeral] cinquante *m inv* ■ **about ~** une cinquantaine ■ **to be ~** avoir cinquante ans ■ **the fifties** les années cinquante ■ **in the early/late fifties** au début/à la fin des années cinquante ■ **she is in her fifties** elle a dans les cinquante ans ■ **to be in one's early/late fifties** avoir une petite cinquantaine/la cinquantaine bien sonnée ■ **he must be close to** *OR* **getting on for ~** il doit approcher de la cinquantaine ■ **to do ~** AUT ≃ faire du quatre-vingts **2.** *US* [money] billet *m* de cinquante (dollars).
◇ *comp* : **~-one** cinquante et un ■ **~-two/-three** cinquante-deux/-trois ■ **~-first** cinquante et unième ■ **~-second** cinquante-deuxième ■ **there were ~-odd people at the party** il y avait une cinquantaine de personnes à la soirée.
◇ *pron* cinquante ■ **there are ~ (of them)** il y en a cinquante.

fifty-fifty ◇ *adj* : **on a ~ basis** moitié-moitié, fifty-fifty ■ **his chances of winning/surviving are ~** il a une chance sur deux de gagner/de s'en tirer.
◇ *adv* moitié-moitié, fifty-fifty ■ **to go ~ (with sb on sthg)** faire moitié-moitié *OR* fifty-fifty (avec qqn pour qqch).

fig [fɪg] *n* [fruit] figue *f* ■ **~ (tree)** figuier *m* ■ **it's not worth a ~** *inf* ça ne vaut pas un radis ■ **I don't give** *OR* **care a ~ what she thinks** je me contrefiche de ce qu'elle pense.

fight [faɪt] (*pret & pp* **fought** [fɔ:t]) ◇ *n* **1.** [physical] bagarre *f* ■ [verbal] dispute *f* ■ [of army, boxer] combat *m*, affrontement *m* ■ [against disease, poverty etc] lutte *f*, combat *m* ■ **do you want a ~?** tu veux te battre? ■ **to have** *OR* **to get into a ~ with sb** [physical] se battre avec qqn ; [verbal] se disputer avec qqn ■ **you've been in a ~ again** tu t'es encore battu *OR* bagarré ■ **to pick a ~ (with sb)** chercher la bagarre (avec qqn) ■ **a ~ to the death** une lutte à mort ■ **are you going to the ~?** [boxing match] est-ce que tu vas voir le combat? ■ **to put up a (good) ~** (bien) se défendre ■ **to give in without (putting up) a ~** capituler sans (opposer de) résistance ■ **he realized he would have a ~ on his hands** il s'est rendu compte qu'il allait devoir lutter **2.** [fighting spirit] combativité *f* ■ **there's not much ~ left in him** il a perdu beaucoup de sa combativité.
◇ *vi* [physically - person, soldier] se battre ; [- boxer] combattre ; [- two boxers] s'affronter ■ [verbally] se disputer ■ [against disease, injustice etc] lutter ■ **to ~ to the death/the last** se battre à mort/jusqu'à la fin ■ **he fought in the war** il a fait la guerre ■ **they were always ~ing over** *OR* **about money** ils se disputaient toujours pour des problèmes d'argent ■ **the children were ~ing over the last biscuit** les enfants se disputaient (pour avoir) le dernier biscuit ■ **to ~ for one's rights/to clear one's name** lutter pour ses droits/pour prouver son innocence ■ **they fought for the leadership of the party** ils se sont disputé la direction du parti ■ **he fought for breath** il se débattait *OR* il luttait pour respirer ■ **to ~ for one's life** [ill person] lutter contre la mort ; *fig* [in race, competition] se battre avec la dernière énergie, se démener ▶ **to go down ~ing** se battre jusqu'au bout ■ **to ~ shy of doing sthg** tout faire pour éviter de faire qqch.
◇ *vt* [person, animal] se battre contre ■ [boxer] combattre (contre), se battre contre ■ [disease, terrorism, fire etc] lutter contre, combattre ■ **to ~ a duel** se battre en duel ■ **to ~ a battle** livrer (une) bataille ■ **I'm not going to ~ your battles for you** *fig* c'est à toi de te débrouiller ■ **to ~ a court case** [subj: lawyer] défendre une cause ; [subj: plaintiff, defendant] être en procès ■ **to ~ an election** [politician] se présenter à une élection ■ **to ~ an election campaign** *UK* mener une campagne électorale ■ **I'll ~ you for it** on réglera ça par une bagarre ■ **to ~ a losing battle (against sthg)** livrer une bataille perdue d'avance (contre qqch) ■ **she fought the urge to laugh** elle essayait de réprimer une forte envie de rire ■ **don't ~ it** [pain, emotion] n'essaie pas de lutter ■ **you've got to ~ it** il faut que tu te battes ■ **to ~ sb/a newspaper in court** emmener qqn/un journal devant les tribunaux, faire un procès à qqn/à un journal ■ **to ~ one's way through the crowd/the undergrowth** se frayer un passage à travers la foule/les broussailles ■ **to ~ one's way to the top of one's profession** se battre pour atteindre le sommet de sa profession ■ **he fought his way back to power** c'est en luttant qu'il est revenu au pouvoir.

◆ **fight back** ◇ *vi insep* [in physical or verbal dispute] se défendre, riposter ■ [in boxing, football match] se reprendre ■ [in race] revenir.
◇ *vt sep* [tears] refouler ■ [despair, fear, laughter] réprimer.

◆ **fight off** *vt sep* [attack, enemy, advances] repousser ■ [sleep] combattre ■ [disease] résister à ■ **she has to ~ men off** [has a lot of admirers] elle a des admirateurs à la pelle *OR* à ne plus savoir qu'en faire.

◆ **fight on** *vi insep* continuer le combat.

◆ **fight out** *vt sep* : **just leave them to ~ it out** laisse-les se bagarrer et régler cela entre eux.

fightback ['faɪtbæk] *n* reprise *f*.

fighter ['faɪtə[r]] ◇ *n* **1.** [person who fights] combattant *m*, - e *f* ■ [boxer] boxeur *m* ■ **he's a ~** *fig* c'est un battant **2.** [plane] avion *m* de chasse, chasseur *m*.
◇ *comp* [pilot] de chasseur, d'avion de chasse ■ [squadron] de chasseurs, d'avions de chasse ■ [plane] de chasse.

fighter-bomber *n* MIL chasseur *m* bombardier.

fighting ['faɪtɪŋ] ◇ *n (U)* [physical] bagarre *f*, bagarres *fpl* ■ [verbal] dispute *f*, disputes *fpl*, bagarre *f*, bagarres *fpl* ■ MIL combat *m*, combats *mpl* ■ **~ broke out between police and fans** une bagarre s'est déclenchée entre la police et les fans ■ **~ is not allowed in the playground** il est interdit de se bagarrer dans la cour.
◇ *comp* [forces, unit] de combat ■ **~ cock** coq *m* de combat ■ **~ men** MIL combattants *mpl* ■ **to be in with** *OR* **to have a ~ chance** avoir de bonnes chances ■ **to be ~ fit** être dans une forme éblouissante, avoir la forme olympique ■ **~ spirit** esprit *m* combatif ■ **that's ~ talk!** c'est un langage offensif!

fig leaf *n* BOT feuille *f* de figuier ■ [on statue, in painting] feuille *f* de vigne ■ *fig* camouflage *m*.

figment ['fɪgmənt] *n* : **a ~ of the imagination** un produit *OR* une création de l'imagination.

figurative ['fɪgərətɪv] *adj* **1.** [language, meaning] figuré **2.** ART figuratif.

figuratively ['fɪgərətɪvlɪ] *adv* au (sens) figuré.

figure [*UK* 'fɪgəʳ, *US* 'fɪgjər] ◇ *n* **1.** [number, symbol] chiffre *m* ■ [amount] somme *f* ■ **six-~ number** nombre de six chiffres ■ **his salary is in** *OR* **runs to six ~s** ≃ il gagne plus d'un million de francs ■ **in round ~s** en chiffres ronds ■ **to be in double ~s** [inflation, unemployment] dépasser la barre *OR* le seuil des 10 % ■ **to put a ~ on sthg** [give cost] évaluer le coût de *OR* chiffrer qqch ■ **I couldn't put a ~ on the number of people there** je ne pourrais pas dire combien de personnes il y avait ■ **she's good at ~s** elle est bonne en calcul ■ **name your ~** [to purchaser, seller] quel est votre prix?
2. [human shape] ligne *f* ■ **she has a good ~** elle a une jolie silhouette, elle est bien faite ■ **to look after one's ~** faire attention à sa ligne ■ **to keep/to lose one's ~** garder/perdre la ligne ▶ **a fine ~ of a woman/man** une femme/un homme qui a de l'allure ■ **to cut a fine ~** avoir beaucoup d'allure ■ **to cut a sorry ~** faire piètre figure
3. [human outline] silhouette *f* ■ **a ~ appeared on the horizon** une silhouette est apparue à l'horizon
4. [character in novel, film etc] personnage *m* ■ **the group of ~s on the left** le groupe de personnes à gauche ▶ **key ~** personnage *m* central ■ **~ of fun** objet *m* de risée
5. [in geometry, skating, dancing] figure *f* ■ **~ of eight** *UK*, **~ eight** *US* huit *m*
6. [illustration, diagram] figure *f*
7. [rhetorical] : **~ of speech** figure *f* de rhétorique ■ **it was just a ~ of speech** ce n'était qu'une façon de parler
8. [statuette] figurine *f*.
◇ *vi* **1.** [appear] figurer, apparaître ■ **where do I ~ in all this?** quelle est ma place dans tout cela? ■ **guilt ~s quite a lot in his novels** la culpabilité a *OR* tient une place relativement importante dans ses romans ■ **she ~d prominently in the scandal** elle a été très impliquée dans le scandale
2. *inf* [make sense] sembler logique *OR* normal ■ **that ~s!** [I'm not surprised] tu m'étonnes! ; [that makes sense] c'est logique ■ **it just doesn't ~** *US* ça n'a pas de sens ▶ **go ~!** *inf* qui aurait imaginé ça?
◇ *vt* **1.** *inf* [reckon] penser ■ **we ~d something like that must have happened** nous pensions *OR* nous nous doutions bien que quelque chose de ce genre était arrivé
2. *US inf* = **figure out** *(sense 1)*
3. [decorate - silk] brocher ■ **~d velvet** *UK* velours *m* figuré
4. MUS chiffrer.
◆ **figure in** *vt sep* [in calculations] inclure.
◆ **figure on** *vt insep inf* [plan on] compter.
◆ **figure out** *vt sep* **1.** [understand - person] arriver à comprendre ■ **we couldn't ~ it out** nous n'arrivions pas à comprendre *OR* saisir
2. [work out - sum, cost etc] calculer ■ **~ it out for yourself** réfléchis donc un peu ■ **she still hasn't ~d out how to do it** elle n'a toujours pas trouvé comment faire.

figurehead ['fɪgəhed] *n* NAUT figure *f* de proue ■ *fig* [of organization, society] représentant *m* nominal, représentante *f* nominale ■ *pej* homme *m* de paille.

figure-hugging [-ˌhʌgɪŋ] *adj* [dress] moulant.

figure skating ◇ *n* patinage *m* artistique.
◇ *comp* [champion, championship] de patinage artistique.

figurine [*UK* 'fɪgəri:n, *US* ˌfɪgjə'ri:n] *n* figurine *f*.

Fiji ['fi:dʒi:] *pr n* Fidji ■ **in ~** à Fidji ■ **the ~ Islands** les îles *fpl* Fidji ■ **in the ~ Islands** aux îles Fidji.

Fijian [ˌfi:'dʒi:ən] ◇ *n* [person] Fidjien *m*, - enne *f*.
◇ *adj* fidjien.

filament ['fɪləmənt] *n* BOT & ELEC filament *m*.

filch [fɪltʃ] *vt inf* [steal] piquer.

file [faɪl] ◇ *n* **1.** [folder] chemise *f* ■ [box] classeur *m*
2. [dossier, documents] dossier *m* ■ [series or system of files] fichier *m* ■ **to have/to keep sthg on ~** avoir/garder qqch dans ses dossiers ■ **it's on ~** c'est dans les dossiers, c'est classé ■ **we have placed your CV on ~** *OR* **in our ~s** nous avons classé votre CV dans nos dossiers ■ **to have/to keep a ~ on** avoir/garder un dossier sur ■ **to open/to close a ~ on** ouvrir/fermer un dossier sur ■ **the police have closed their ~ on the case** la police a classé l'affaire
3. COMPUT fichier *m* ■ **data on ~** données *fpl* sur fichier ■ **data ~** fichier de données
4. [row, line] file *f* ■ **in single** *OR* **Indian ~** en *OR* à la file indienne
5. [for metal, fingernails] lime *f*.
◇ *comp* : **~ copy** copie *f* à classer ■ **~ name** COMPUT nom *m* de fichier.
◇ *vt* **1.** [documents, information] classer ■ **to be ~d under a letter/subject** être classé sous une lettre/dans une catégorie
2. LAW : **to ~ a suit against sb** intenter un procès à qqn ■ **to ~ a complaint (with the police/the manager)** déposer une plainte(au commissariat/auprès du directeur) ■ **to ~ a claim** déposer une demande ■ **to ~ a claim for damages** intenter un procès en dommages-intérêts ■ **to ~ a petition in bankruptcy** déposer son bilan
3. [metal] limer ■ **to ~ one's fingernails** se limer les ongles ■ **to ~ through sthg** limer qqch.
◇ *vi* **1.** [classify documents, information] faire du classement
2. [walk one behind the other] : **they ~d up the hill** ils ont monté la colline en file (indienne) *OR* les uns derrière les autres ■ **the troops ~d past the general** les troupes ont défilé devant le général ■ **they all ~d in/out** ils sont tous entrés/sortis à la file.
◆ **file away** *vt sep* **1.** [documents] classer
2. [rough edges] polir à la lime ■ [excess material] enlever à la lime.
◆ **file down** *vt sep* [metal, fingernails, rough surface] polir à la lime.
◆ **file for** *vt insep* : **to ~ for divorce** demander le divorce ■ **to ~ fot bankrupcy** déposer son bilan.

file cabinet *n US* classeur *m*.

file clerk *n US* documentaliste *mf*.

file management *n* COMPUT gestion *f* de fichiers.

file manager *n* COMPUT gestionnaire *m* de fichiers.

file server *n* COMPUT serveur *m* de fichiers.

filet *US* = **fillet**.

filial ['fɪljəl] *adj* [devotion, respect] filial.

filibuster ['fɪlɪbʌstəʳ] POL ◇ *n* obstruction *f* (parlementaire).
◇ *vi* faire de l'obstruction ■ **~ing tactics** tactiques obstructionnistes.
◇ *vt* [legislation] faire obstruction à.

filibustering ['fɪlɪbʌstərɪŋ] *n* POL obstructionnisme *m*.

filigree ['fɪlɪgri:] ◇ *n* filigrane *m*.
◇ *adj* en *OR* de filigrane.

filing ['faɪlɪŋ] *n* **1.** [of documents] classement *m* ■ **I still have a lot of ~ to do** j'ai encore beaucoup de choses à classer **2.** LAW [of complaint, claim] dépôt *m*.

filing cabinet *n* classeur *m*.

filing clerk *n* documentaliste *mf*.

filings ['faɪlɪŋz] *npl* [of metal] limaille *f*.

Filipino [ˌfɪlɪ'pi:nəʊ] (*pl* **Filipinos**) ◇ *n* [person] Philippin *m*.
◇ *adj* philippin.

fill [fɪl] ◇ *n* : **to eat one's ~** manger à sa faim, se rassasier ■ **to drink one's ~** boire tout son soûl ▶ **I've had my ~ of it/her** *inf* j'en ai assez/assez d'elle.
◇ *vt* **1.** [cup, glass, bottle] remplir ■ [room, streets - subj: people, smoke, laughter] envahir ■ [chocolates] fourrer ■ [cake, pie] garnir ■ [vegetables] farcir ■ [pipe] bourrer ■ **to ~ a page with writing** remplir une page d'écriture ■ **wind ~ed the sails** le vent a gonflé les voiles ■ **she ~ed his head with nonsense** elle lui a bourré le crâne de bêtises ■ **to be ~ed with people** [room, street] être plein *OR* rempli de gens ■ **to be ~ed with horror/admiration** être rempli d'horreur/d'admiration ■ **it ~ed me with sorrow** cela m'a profondément peiné
2. [plug - hole] boucher ; [- tooth] plomber ■ **to have a tooth ~ed** se faire plomber une dent ■ **the product ~ed a gap in the market** le produit a comblé un vide sur le marché ▶ **...or I'll ~ you full of lead!** [shoot]...ou je te farcis le crâne de plomb!
3. [position, vacancy - subj: employee] occuper ; [- subj: employer] pourvoir ■ **to ~ the office of president** remplir les fonctions de président ■ **the post has been ~ed** le poste a été pris *OR* pourvu
4. [occupy - time] occuper
5. [meet - requirement] répondre à

6. [supply] : to ~ an order [in bar, restaurant] apporter ce qui a été commandé ; [for stationery, equipment etc] livrer une commande.

◇ *vi* [room, bath, bus] se remplir ■ [sail] se gonfler ■ **her eyes ~ed with tears** ses yeux se sont remplis de larmes.

◆ **fill in** ◇ *vi insep* faire un remplacement ■ **to ~ in for sb** remplacer qqn.

◇ *vt sep* **1.** [hole, window, door] boucher ■ **he ~ed it in in green** [outline] il l'a colorié *OR* rempli en vert
2. [complete - form, questionnaire] compléter, remplir ■ [insert - name, missing word] insérer
3. [bring up to date] mettre au courant ■ **to ~ sb in on sthg** mettre qqn au courant de qqch
4. [use - time] occuper ■ **he's just ~ing in time** il fait ça pour s'occuper *OR* pour occuper son temps.

◆ **fill out** ◇ *vi insep* **1.** [cheeks] se remplir ■ [person] s'étoffer
2. [sails] se gonfler.
◇ *vt sep* **1.** [complete - form] remplir
2. [pad out - essay, speech] étoffer.

◆ **fill up** ◇ *vi insep* se remplir ■ **to ~ up with petrol** faire le plein d'essence ■ **don't ~ up on biscuits, you two!** ne vous gavez pas de biscuits, vous deux!
◇ *vt sep* **1.** [make full] remplir ■ [person with food] rassasier ■ **he ~ed the car up** il a fait le plein (d'essence)
2. [use - day, time] occuper
3. = **fill out** *(vt sep sense 1)*.

filler ['fɪlər] *n* **1.** [for holes, cracks] mastic *m* ■ [for cavity, open space] matière *f* de remplissage **2.** [funnel] entonnoir *m* **3.** [in quilt, bean bag etc] matière *f* de rembourrage ■ [in cigar] tripe *f* **4.** PRESS & TV bouche-trou *m* **5.** LING : ~ **(word)** mot *m* de remplissage.

filler cap *n* bouchon *m* du réservoir d'essence.

fillet ['fɪlɪt] ◇ *n* CULIN filet *m* ■ **two pieces of ~ steak** deux biftecks dans le filet ■ **~ steak is expensive** le filet de bœuf est cher.
◇ *vt* [meat, fish - prepare] préparer ■ [cut into fillets - fish] faire des filets dans, lever les filets de ; [- meat] faire des steaks dans ■ **~ed sole** filets *mpl* de sole.

filling ['fɪlɪŋ] ◇ *adj* [foodstuff] bourratif ■ **it was very ~** cela m'a rassasié.
◇ *n* **1.** [in tooth] plombage *m* ■ **I had to have a ~** il a fallu qu'on me fasse un plombage **2.** CULIN [for cake, pie - sweet] garniture *f* ■ [for vegetables, poultry - savoury] farce *f* ■ **they all have different ~s** [chocolates] ils sont tous fourrés différemment.

filling station *n* station-service *f*, station *f* d'essence.

fillip ['fɪlɪp] *n* coup *m* de fouet ■ **to give sb/sthg a ~** donner un coup de fouet à qqn/qqch.

filly ['fɪlɪ] *(pl* **fillies***)* *n* **1.** [horse] pouliche *f* **2.** *inf dated* [girl] fille *f*.

film [fɪlm] ◇ *n* **1.** [thin layer - of oil, mist, dust] film *m*, pellicule *f* ■ **plastic ~** film plastique **2.** PHOT pellicule *f* ■ **a roll of ~** une pellicule **3.** CIN film *m* ■ **the ~ of the book** le film tiré du livre ■ **full-length/short-length ~** (film) long/court métrage *m* ■ **to shoot** *OR* **to make a ~ (about sthg)** tourner *OR* faire un film (sur qqch) ■ **to be in ~s** faire du cinéma.
◇ *comp* [critic, star, producer] de cinéma ■ [clip, premiere] d'un film ■ [sequence] de film ■ [archives, award, rights] cinématographique ■ **~ buff** *inf* cinéphile *mf* ■ **the ~ crew** les techniciens du film ■ **a ~ crew** une équipe de cinéma ■ **~ director** metteur *m* en scène ■ **the ~ industry** l'industrie *f* cinématographique *OR* du cinéma ■ **~ maker** cinéaste *mf* ■ **~ set** plateau *m* de tournage ■ **~ speed** PHOT sensibilité *f* d'une pellicule ■ **~ strip** bande *f* (de film) fixe ■ **~ studio** studio *m* (de cinéma).
◇ *vt* [event, people] filmer ■ CIN [scene] filmer, tourner.
◇ *vi* **1.** [record] filmer ■ CIN tourner ■ **they started ~ing at 7a.m.** ils ont commencé à tourner *OR* le tournage a commencé à 7 h **2.** = **film over**.

◆ **film over** *vi insep* s'embuer, se voiler.

filmgoer ['fɪlm,gəʊər] *n* amateur *m* de cinéma, cinéphile *mf* ■ **she is a regular ~** elle va régulièrement au cinéma.

filmic ['fɪlmɪk] *adj fml* cinématographique.

filming ['fɪlmɪŋ] *n* CIN tournage *m*.

film noir *n* CIN film *m* noir.

filmset ['fɪlmset] *vt UK* photocomposer.

filmsetter ['fɪlm,setər] *n UK* [machine] photocomposeuse *f* ■ [person] photocompositeur *m*.

filmsetting ['fɪlm,setɪŋ] *n UK* photocomposition *f*.

filmy ['fɪlmɪ] *adj* [material] léger, vaporeux, aérien.

filo ['fi:ləʊ] *n* CULIN : **~ (pastry)** *pâte feuilletée très fine utilisée dans les pâtisseries moyen-orientales*.

Filofax® ['faɪləʊfæks] *n* agenda *m* modulaire.

filter ['fɪltər] ◇ *n* **1.** CHEM, MECH & PHOT filtre *m* **2.** *UK* AUT flèche *f* lumineuse *(autorisant le dégagement des voitures à droite ou à gauche)*.
◇ *comp* : **~ coffee** café *m* filtre ■ **~ lane** *UK* AUT voie *f* de dégagement ■ **~ paper** papier *m* filtre.
◇ *vt* [coffee, oil, water etc] filtrer.
◇ *vi* **1.** [liquid, light] filtrer **2.** *UK* AUT suivre la voie de dégagement ■ **the cars ~ed to the left** les voitures ont suivi la voie de dégagement vers la gauche.

◆ **filter in** *vi insep* [light, sound, information, news] filtrer ■ [people] entrer petit à petit.

◆ **filter out** ◇ *vt sep* [sediment, impurities] éliminer par filtrage *OR* filtration.
◇ *vi insep* [people] sortir petit à petit.

◆ **filter through** *vi insep liter & fig* filtrer.

filter tip *n* [tip] (bout *m*) filtre *m* ■ [cigarette] cigarette *f* (bout) filtre.

filter-tipped *adj* [cigarette] (bout) filtre.

filth [fɪlθ] *n (U)* **1.** [on skin, clothes] crasse *f* ■ [in street] saleté *f* **2.** [obscene books, films etc] ordures *fpl*, obscénités *fpl* ■ [obscene words, jokes] grossièretés *fpl*, obscénités *fpl* ■ **it's sheer ~** [film, book] c'est un recueil d'ordures *OR* d'obscénités **3.** △ *UK* **the ~** [police] les flics *mpl*.

filthy ['fɪlθɪ] *(comp* **filthier**, *superl* **filthiest***)* ◇ *adj* **1.** [dirty] dégoûtant, crasseux **2.** [obscene, smutty - language, talk, jokes] grossier, obscène, ordurier ; [- person] grossier, dégoûtant ; [- film, book, photograph] obscène, dégoûtant ; [- habit] dégoûtant ■ **to have a ~ mind** avoir l'esprit mal tourné **3.** *inf* [nasty - temper, day] atroce, abominable ; [- trick] vicieux, méchant ; [- look] méchant ; [- weather] sale ■ **he's in a ~ mood** il est de sale humeur, il est d'une humeur massacrante.
◇ *adv* : **to be ~ rich** *inf* être plein aux as.

filtrate ['fɪltreɪt] *n* filtrat *m*.

filtration [fɪl'treɪʃn] *n* filtrage *m*, filtration *f*.

filtration plant *n* station *f* d'épuration.

Fimbra ['fɪmbrə] *(abbrev of* **Financial Intermediaries, Managers and Brokers Regulatory Association***)* *pr n organisme britannique contrôlant les activités des courtiers d'assurances*.

fin [fɪn] *n* **1.** [of fish] nageoire *f* ■ [of shark] aileron *m* ■ [of boat] dérive *f* **2.** [of aircraft, spacecraft] empennage *m* ■ [of rocket, bomb] ailette *f* **3.** AUT [of radiator] ailette *f*.

final ['faɪnl] ◇ *adj* **1.** [last] dernier ■ **~ demand** dernier rappel *m* ■ **the ~ irony** le comble de l'ironie ■ **a ~-year student** UNIV un étudiant en *OR* de dernière année **2.** [definitive] définitif ■ [score] final ■ **that's my ~ offer** c'est ma dernière offre ■ **I'm not moving, and that's ~!** je ne bouge pas, un point c'est tout! ■ **the referee's decision is ~** la décision de l'arbitre est sans appel ■ **is that your ~ answer?** c'est ta réponse définitive? ■ **nothing's ~ yet** il n'y a encore rien de définitif, rien n'est encore arrêté **3.** PHILOS [cause] final ■ GRAM [clause] de but, final.
◇ *n* **1.** SPORT finale *f* ■ **to get to the ~** *OR* **~s** arriver en finale **2.** PRESS dernière édition *f* ■ **late ~** dernière édition du soir.

◆ **finals** *npl* UNIV examens *mpl* de dernière année.

finale [fɪ'nɑ:lɪ] *n* MUS finale *m* ■ *fig* final *m*, finale *m*.

finalist ['faɪnəlɪst] *n* [in competition] finaliste *mf*.

finality [faɪ'nælətɪ] *n* [of decision, death] irrévocabilité *f*, caractère *m* définitif ■ **there was a note of ~ in his voice** il y avait quelque chose d'irrévocable dans sa voix.

finalization [ˌfaɪnəlaɪˈzeɪʃn] *n* [of details, plans, arrangements] mise *f* au point ▪ [of deal, agreement] conclusion *f*.

finalize, ise [ˈfaɪnəlaɪz] *vt* [details, plans] mettre au point ▪ [deal, decision, agreement] mener à bonne fin ▪ [preparations] mettre la dernière main *OR* touche à, mettre la touche finale à ▪ [date] arrêter ▪ **nothing has been ~d yet** rien n'a encore été décidé *OR* arrêté.

finally [ˈfaɪnəlɪ] *adv* **1.** [eventually] finalement, enfin ▪ **she ~ agreed to come** elle a fini par accepter de venir ▪ **~!** enfin! **2.** [lastly] enfin ▪ **and, ~, I would like to say...** et pour finir je voudrais dire que... **3.** [irrevocably] définitivement ▪ **no, she said ~** non, dit-elle fermement.

finance ◇ *n* [ˈfaɪnæns] *(U)* [money management] finance *f* ▪ [financing] financement *m* ▪ **in the world of French ~** dans le monde français de la finance ▶ **high ~** la haute finance ▪ **Minister/Ministry of Finance** ministre *m* /ministère *m* des Finances.

◇ *vt* [faɪˈnæns] financer ▪ [project, enterprise] financer, trouver les fonds pour.

◆ **finances** *npl* finances *fpl*, fonds *mpl* ▪ **my ~s are a bit low just now** je ne suis pas très en fonds en ce moment.

finance company *n* établissement *m* de crédit.

finance director *n* directeur *m* financier.

financial [faɪˈnænʃl] *adj* financier ▪ **but does it make ~ sense?** mais est-ce que c'est avantageux *OR* intéressant du point de vue financier? ▪ **~ adviser** conseiller *m* financier ▪ **~ backer** bailleur *m* de fonds ▪ **~ controller** contrôleur *m* financier ▪ **~ director** directeur *m* financier ▪ **~ services** services *mpl* financiers.

financially [faɪˈnænʃəlɪ] *adv* financièrement ▪ **are they ~ sound?** est-ce qu'ils ont une bonne assise financière?

Financial Times *pr n* : **the ~** *quotidien britannique d'information financière.*

FINANCIAL TIMES

Le *Financial Times* est un quotidien britannique de qualité, spécialisé dans l'actualité financière et économique; il est reconnaissable à la couleur saumon de son papier. Il existe une édition internationale, diffusée notamment en Allemagne et en France.

financial year *n UK* [gen] année *f* fiscale ▪ [of company] exercice *m* financier ▪ ADMIN année *f* budgétaire.

FINANCIAL YEAR

En Grande-Bretagne, pour les impôts sur le revenu, l'année fiscale commence le 6 avril pour les particuliers et le 1er avril pour les organismes publics.

financier [fɪˈnænsɪəʳ] *n* financier *m*.

finch [fɪntʃ] *n* fringillidé *m spec* ▪ [goldfinch] chardonneret *m* ▪ [chaffinch] pinson *m* ▪ [bullfinch] bouvreuil *m*.

find [faɪnd] (*pret & pp* **found** [faʊnd]) ◇ *vt* **1.** [by searching] trouver ▪ [lost thing, person] retrouver ▪ **the police could ~ no reason** *OR* **explanation for his disappearance** la police n'arrivait pas à expliquer sa disparition ▪ **I can't ~ my place** [in book] je ne sais plus où j'en suis ▪ **my wallet/he was nowhere to be found** mon portefeuille/il était introuvable ▮ [look for, fetch] chercher ▪ **go and ~ me a pair of scissors** va me chercher une paire de ciseaux ▶ **to ~ one's feet** [in new job, situation] prendre ses repères ▪ **I'm still ~ing my feet** je ne suis pas encore complètement dans le bain ▪ **she couldn't ~ it in her heart** *OR* **herself to say no** elle n'a pas eu le cœur de dire non ▪ **to ~ one's way** trouver son chemin ▪ **I'll ~ my own way out** je trouverai la sortie tout seul ▪ **somehow, the book had found its way into my room** sans que je sache comment, le livre s'était retrouvé dans ma chambre
2. [come across by chance] trouver ▪ **we left everything as we found it** nous avons tout laissé dans l'état où nous l'avions trouvé ▪ **the complete list is to be found on page 18** la liste complète se trouve page 18 ▪ **I found her waiting outside** je l'ai trouvée qui attendait dehors ▪ **to ~ happiness/peace** trouver le bonheur/la paix ▶ **I take people as I ~ them** je prends les gens comme ils sont
3. [expressing an opinion, personal view] trouver ▪ **I ~ her very pretty** je la trouve très jolie ▪ **she ~s it very difficult/impossible to talk about it** il lui est très difficile/impossible d'en parler ▪ **he ~s it very hard/impossible to make friends** il a beaucoup de mal à/il n'arrive pas à se faire des amis ▶ **Rovers have been found wanting** *OR* **lacking in defence** les Rovers ont fait preuve de faiblesse au niveau de la défense
4. [discover, learn] constater ▪ **they came back to ~ the house had been burgled** à leur retour, ils ont constaté que la maison avait été cambriolée ▪ **I think you'll ~ I'm right** je pense que tu t'apercevras que j'ai raison
5. LAW : **to ~ sb guilty/innocent** déclarer qqn coupable/non coupable ▪ **how do you ~ the accused?** déclarez-vous l'accusé coupable ou non coupable?
6. [reflexive use] : **to ~ o.s.** : **I woke up to ~ myself on a ship** je me suis réveillé sur un bateau ▪ **I ~/found myself in an impossible situation** je me trouve/me suis retrouvé dans une situation impossible ▪ **she found herself forced to retaliate** elle s'est trouvée dans l'obligation de riposter.

◇ *vi* LAW : **to ~ for/against the plaintiff** prononcer en faveur de l'accusation/de la défense.

◇ *n* [object] trouvaille *f* ▪ [person] merveille *f*.

◆ **find out** ◇ *vi insep* **1.** [investigate, make enquiries] se renseigner ▪ **to ~ out about sthg** se renseigner sur qqch
2. [learn, discover] : **his wife/his boss found out** sa femme/son chef a tout découvert ▪ **his wife found out about his affair** sa femme a découvert qu'il avait une liaison ▪ **what if the police ~ out?** et si la police l'apprend? ▪ **I didn't ~ out about it in time** je ne l'ai pas su à temps.

◇ *vt sep* **1.** [learn, discover - truth, real identity] découvrir ; [- answer, phone number] trouver ; [- by making enquiries, reading instructions] se renseigner sur ▪ **what have you found out about him/it?** qu'est-ce que tu as découvert sur lui/là-dessus? ▪ **can you ~ out the date of the meeting for me?** est-ce que tu peux te renseigner sur la date de la réunion? ▪ **when I found out the date of the meeting** quand j'ai appris la date de la réunion ▪ **I found out where he'd put it** j'ai trouvé où il l'avait mis
2. [catch being dishonest] prendre ▪ [show to be a fraud] prendre en défaut ▪ **make sure you don't get found out** veille à ne pas te faire prendre ▪ **you've been found out** tu as été découvert.

finder [ˈfaɪndəʳ] *n* **1.** [of lost object] : **it becomes the property of the ~** celui/celle qui l'a trouvé en devient propriétaire ▶ **~s keepers (losers weepers)** celui qui le trouve le garde **2.** [of camera] viseur *m*.

finding [ˈfaɪndɪŋ] *n* **1.** [discovery, conclusion] : **~s** conclusions *fpl*, résultats *mpl* **2.** LAW verdict *m*.

fine [faɪn] (*comp* **finer**, *superl* **finest**) ◇ *adj* **1.** [of high quality - meal, speech, view] excellent ▪ [beautiful and elegant - clothes, house] beau *(before vowel or silent 'h'* **bel***)*, belle *f* ; [- fabric] précieux ▪ **this is very ~ workmanship** c'est un travail d'une grande qualité ▪ **she is a very ~ athlete** c'est une excellente athlète ▪ **she is a ~ lady** [admirable character] c'est une femme admirable ; [elegant] c'est une femme élégante ▪ **to appeal to sb's finer feelings** faire appel aux nobles sentiments de qqn ▪ **a ~ example** un bel exemple ▪ **of the finest quality** de première qualité ▪ **made from the finest barley** fabriqué à base d'orge de la meilleure qualité ▪ **her finest hour was winning the gold** elle a eu son heure de gloire quand elle a remporté la médaille d'or
2. [very thin - hair, nib, thread] fin ▪ **it's a ~ line** la différence *OR* la distinction est infime *OR* très subtile
3. [not coarse - powder, grain, drizzle] fin ; [- features, skin] fin, délicat ▪ **to chop** *OR* **to cut sthg (up) ~** hacher qqch menu ▶ **to cut it ~** calculer juste
4. [good, OK] : **how are you? – ~, thanks** comment ça va? – bien, merci ▪ **more coffee? – no thanks, I'm ~** encore du café? – non, ça va, merci ▪ **the tent's ~ for two, but too small for three** la tente convient pour deux personnes, mais elle est trop petite pour trois ▪ **I'll be back in about an hour or so – ~** je serai de retour d'ici environ une heure – d'accord *OR* entendu *OR* très bien ▪ **I was a bit worried about the new job, but it turned out ~ in the end** j'étais un peu inquiet à propos de mon nouveau travail mais ça s'est finalement bien passé ▪ **that's ~ by** *OR* **with me** ça me va ▪ **that's all very ~, but what about me?** tout ça c'est bien joli, mais moi qu'est-ce que je deviens dans l'affaire?

5. [well] : **that looks ~ to me** cela m'a l'air d'aller ■ **he looks ~ now** [in health] il a l'air de bien aller maintenant ■ **you look just ~, it's a very nice dress** tu es très bien, c'est une très jolie robe ■ **that sounds ~** [suggestion, idea] très bien, parfait ; [way of playing music] cela rend très bien
6. *UK* [weather] beau ■ **a ~ day** une belle journée ■ **there will be ~ weather** *OR* **it will be ~ in all parts of the country** il fera beau *OR* il y aura du beau temps dans tout le pays ■ **I hope it keeps ~ for you** j'espère que tu auras du beau temps ■ **one of these ~ days** un de ces jours ■ **one ~ day** un beau jour
7. [subtle - distinction, language] subtil ■ [precise - calculations] minutieux, précis ■ **~ detail** petit détail *m* ● **not to put too ~ a point on it** pour parler carrément
8. *inf iron* [awful, terrible] : **that's a ~ thing to say!** c'est charmant de dire ça! ■ **look at you, you're in a ~ state!** non mais tu t'es vu, ah tu es dans un bel état! ■ **you picked a ~ time to leave me/tell me!** tu as bien choisi ton moment pour me quitter/me le dire! ■ **you're a ~ one to talk!** ça te va bien de dire ça!, tu peux parler! ■ **here's another ~ mess you've got me into!** tu m'as encore mis dans un beau pétrin! ■ **a ~ friend you are!** eh bien, tu fais un bon copain/une bonne copine! ■ **this is a ~ time to come in/get up!** c'est à cette heure-ci que tu rentres/te lèves?
◇ *adv* [well] bien ■ **yes, that suits me ~** oui, cela me va très bien ■ **the baby is doing ~** le bébé va très bien.
◇ *n* [punishment] amende *f*, contravention *f* ■ **to impose a ~ on sb** infliger une amende à qqn ■ **a parking ~** une contravention *OR* amende pour stationnement interdit.
◇ *vt* [order to pay] condamner à une amende, donner une contravention à ■ **she was ~d heavily** elle a été condamnée à une lourde amende *OR* contravention ■ **she was ~d for speeding** elle a reçu une contravention pour excès de vitesse ■ **they ~d her £25 for illegal parking** ils lui ont donné *OR* elle a eu une amende *OR* contravention de 25 livres pour stationnement illégal.

fine art *n (U)* beaux-arts *mpl* ● **he's got it down to a ~** *inf* il est expert en la matière.

fine-drawn *adj fig* [distinction] subtil ■ [features] fin.

fine-grained *adj* [wood] à fibres fines, à fil fin ■ **~ leather** cuir *m* à grain peu apparent.

finely ['faɪnlɪ] *adv* **1.** [grated, ground, sliced] finement ■ **~ chopped** haché menu, finement haché ■ **~ powdered** en poudre fine **2.** [delicately, subtly - tuned] avec précision ■ **the situation is very ~ balanced** la situation est caractérisée par un équilibre précaire **3.** [carved, sewn etc] délicatement.

fineness ['faɪnnɪs] *n* **1.** [of clothes, manners] raffinement *m* ■ [of work of art, features, handwriting] finesse *f* **2.** [of sand, sugar etc] finesse *f* **3.** [purity - of metal] pureté *f* **4.** [thinness - of thread, hair, nib] finesse *f* ■ *fig* [of detail, distinction] subtilité *f*.

finery ['faɪnərɪ] *n (U)* parure *f* ■ **the princess in all her ~** la princesse dans *OR* parée de ses plus beaux atours ■ **to be dressed in all one's ~** porter sa tenue d'apparat.

finesse [fɪ'nes] ◇ *n* **1.** [skill] finesse *f* **2.** CARDS impasse *f*.
◇ *vi* CARDS : **to ~ against a card** faire l'impasse à une carte.
◇ *vt* CARDS : **to ~ a card** faire l'impasse en jouant une carte.

fine-tooth(ed) comb *n* peigne *m* fin ■ **to go through sthg with a ~** *fig* passer qqch au peigne fin.

fine-tune *vt* [machine, engine, radio] régler avec précision ■ *fig* [plan] peaufiner ■ [economy] *régler grâce à des mesures fiscales et monétaires.*

fine-tuning [-'tju:nɪŋ] *n* [of machine, engine, radio] réglage *m* fin ■ *fig* [of plan] peaufinage *m* ■ [of economy] *réglage obtenu par des mesures fiscales et monétaires.*

finger ['fɪŋgə^r] ◇ *n* **1.** ANAT doigt *m* ■ **to wear a ring on one's ~** porter une bague au doigt ■ **she ran her ~s through his hair** elle a passé ses doigts *OR* sa main dans ses cheveux ■ **to lick one's ~s** se lécher les doigts ■ **a ~'s breadth** un doigt ■ **to point a ~ at sb/sthg** montrer qqn/qqch du doigt ● **to twist sb round one's little ~** faire ce qu'on veut de qqn ■ **to be all ~s and thumbs** avoir des mains de beurre, avoir deux mains gauches ■ **get** *OR* **pull your ~ out!**△ *UK* remue-toi! ■ **to have a ~ in every pie** jouer sur tous les tableaux ■ **if you lay a ~ on her** si tu touches à un seul de ses cheveux ■ **to keep one's ~s crossed** croiser les doigts *(pour souhaiter bonne chance)* ■ **to point the ~ (of suspicion) at sb** diriger les soupçons sur qqn ■ **the ~ of suspicion points at the accountant** les soupçons pèsent sur le comptable ■ **to put the ~ on sb** *inf* [inform against] balancer *OR* donner qqn ■ **to put one's ~ on sthg** [identify] mettre le doigt sur qqch ■ **something has changed but I can't put my ~ on it** il y a quelque chose de changé mais je n'arrive pas à dire ce que c'est ■ **to have one's ~ on the pulse** [person] être très au fait de ce qui se passe ; [magazine, TV programme] être à la pointe de l'actualité ■ **to put two ~s up at sb** *UK inf*, **to give sb the ~** *US inf* ≃ faire un bras d'honneur à qqn ■ **success/happiness/the suspect slipped through his ~s** le succès/le bonheur/le suspect lui a glissé entre les doigts ■ **to work one's ~s to the bone** s'épuiser à la tâche ■ **you never lift** *OR* **raise a ~ to help** tu ne lèves jamais le petit doigt pour aider **2.** [of glove] doigt *m* **3.** [of alcohol] doigt *m* ■ [of land] bande *f* ■ **to cut a cake into ~s** couper un gâteau en petits morceaux rectangulaires.
◇ *comp* : **~ exercises** MUS exercices *mpl* de doigté ■ **~ puppet** marionnette *f* à doigt.
◇ *vt* **1.** [feel] tâter du doigt ■ *pej* tripoter **2.** MUS doigter, indiquer le doigté de **3.** △ [inform on] balancer, donner.

fingerboard ['fɪŋgəbɔ:d] *n* MUS touche *f*.

finger bowl *n* rince-doigts *m inv*.

finger buffet *n buffet où sont servis des petits sandwiches, des petits fours et des légumes crus.*

fingered ['fɪŋgəd] *adj* **1.** [dirty, soiled] qui a été tripoté **2.** MUS doigté.

finger food *n* [savoury] amuse-gueules *mpl* ■ [sweet] petits-fours *mpl*.

fingering ['fɪŋgərɪŋ] *n* **1.** MUS [technique, numerals] doigté *m* **2.** *pej* [touching] tripotage *m* **3.** [knitting wool] laine *f* fine à tricoter.

fingerless ['fɪŋgələs] *adj* : **~ glove** mitaine *f*.

fingermark ['fɪŋgəmɑ:k] *n* trace *f OR* marque *f* de doigt.

fingernail ['fɪŋgəneɪl] *n* ongle *m* (de la main) ■ **to hang on by one's ~s** *liter* se retenir du bout des doigts ; *fig* se raccrocher comme on peut.

finger paint *n* peinture *f* pour peindre avec les doigts.

fingerprint ['fɪŋgəprɪnt] ◇ *n* empreinte *f* digitale ■ **five different sets of ~s** cinq empreintes digitales différentes ■ **his ~s are all over it** *liter* c'est couvert de ses empreintes digitales ; *fig* tout indique que c'est lui ■ **to take sb's ~s** prendre les empreintes digitales de qqn ● **genetic ~** empreinte *OR* code *m* génétique.
◇ *comp* : **~ expert** spécialiste *mf* en empreintes digitales *OR* en dactyloscopie.
◇ *vt* [person] prendre les empreintes digitales de ■ [object, weapon] relever les empreintes digitales sur ■ **to ~ sb genetically** identifier l'empreinte *OR* le code génétique de qqn.

fingerprinting ['fɪŋgə,prɪntɪŋ] *n (U)* [of person] prise *f* d'empreintes digitales ■ [of object] relevé *m* d'empreintes digitales ■ **DNA** *OR* **genetic ~** identification *f* de l'empreinte *OR* du code génétique.

fingerstall ['fɪŋgəstɔ:l] *n* doigtier *m*.

fingertip ['fɪŋgətɪp] ◇ *n* bout *m* du doigt ■ **he rolled a cigarette between his ~s** il s'est roulé une cigarette entre les doigts ● **to be Irish to one's ~s** être irlandais jusqu'au bout des ongles ■ **to have information at one's ~s** [be conversant with] connaître des informations sur le bout des doigts ; [readily available] avoir des informations à portée de main.
◇ *comp* : **~ controls** commandes *fpl* à touches.

finicky ['fɪnɪkɪ] *adj* **1.** [person] pointilleux, tatillon *pej* ■ [habit] tatillon ■ **to be ~ about sthg** être pointilleux *OR pej* tatillon sur qqch **2.** [job, task] minutieux.

finish ['fɪnɪʃ] ◇ *n* **1.** [end, closing stage - of life, game etc] fin *f* ; [- of race] arrivée *f* ■ **a close ~** [in race] une arrivée serrée *OR* dans un mouchoir ● **to fight to the ~** se battre jusqu'au bout ■ **it was a fight to the ~** la partie fut serrée ■ **to be in at the ~** voir la fin **2.** [created with paint, varnish, veneer] finitions *fpl* ■ **stained with a walnut ~** teinté imitation noyer

3. [quality of workmanship, presentation etc] finition *f* ▪ **his prose/acting lacks ~** sa prose/son jeu manque de poli **4.** SPORT [of athlete] finish *m* **5.** [shot at goal] but *m*.
◇ *vt* **1.** [end, complete - work, meal, school] finir, terminer, achever ; [- race] finir, terminer ▪ [consume - supplies, food, drink] finir, terminer ▪ **to ~ doing sthg** finir *OR* terminer de faire qqch ▪ **when do you ~ work?** [time] à quelle heure est-ce que tu finis? ; [date] quand *OR* à quelle date finis-tu? ▪ **to be in a hurry to get sthg ~ed** être pressé de finir *OR* terminer qqch **2.** [ruin - sb's career] mettre un terme à ; [- sb's chances] détruire, anéantir **3.** [exhaust] achever, tuer **4.** [put finish on - wood, garment] finir, mettre les finitions à.
◇ *vi* [come to an end - concert, film etc] (se) finir, se terminer, s'achever ▪ [complete activity - person] finir, terminer ▪ **to ~ by doing sthg** finir *OR* terminer en faisant qqch ▪ **please let me ~** [speaking] s'il te plaît, laisse-moi finir *OR* terminer ▪ **to ~ first/third** [in race] arriver premier/troisième ▪ **where did he ~?** [in race] en quelle position est-il arrivé *OR* a-t-il fini? ▪ **the runner ~ed strongly/well** [in race] le coureur a fini fort/a bien fini.
◆ **finish off** ◇ *vi insep* [in speech, meal] finir, terminer ▪ **they ~ed off with a coffee/by singing the national anthem** ils ont terminé par un café/en chantant l'hymne national.
◇ *vt sep* **1.** [complete - work, letter] finir, terminer, achever ; [- passing move in sport] terminer, finir, conclure **2.** [consume - drink] finir, terminer **3.** [kill - person, wounded animal] achever ▪ *fig* [exhaust - person] achever, tuer ▪ **fierce competition ~ed the industry off** *fig* une concurrence féroce a eu raison de cette industrie.
◆ **finish up** ◇ *vi insep* [end up] finir ▪ **to ~ up in jail/hospital** finir en prison/à l'hôpital ▪ **they ~ed up arguing** ils ont fini par se disputer ▪ **she ~ed up a nervous wreck** à la fin c'était une vraie boule de nerfs, elle a fini à bout de nerfs.
◇ *vt sep* [meal, food, drink] finir, terminer.
◆ **finish with** *vt insep* **1.** [have no further use for] ne plus avoir besoin de ▪ **I haven't ~ed with it yet** j'en ai encore besoin **2.** [want no more contact with] en finir avec ▪ **I've ~ed with journalism for good** j'en ai fini à jamais avec le journalisme, moi et le journalisme, c'est fini **3.** [end relationship] rompre avec **4.** [stop punishing] régler son compte à ▪ **just wait till I ~ with him** attends que je lui règle son compte, attends que j'en aie fini avec lui.

finished ['fɪnɪʃt] *adj* **1.** fini ▪ *fig* [performance] parfaitement exécuté ▪ [appearance] raffiné ▪ **it's beautifully ~** les finitions sont magnifiques, c'est magnifiquement fini **2.** *inf* [exhausted] mort, crevé **3.** [ruined - career] fini, terminé ▪ **he's ~ as a politician** sa carrière d'homme politique est terminée *OR* finie, il est fini en tant qu'homme politique ▪ **you're ~** c'est fini *OR* terminé pour vous **4.** [completed - work, job] fini, terminé, achevé ▪ [consumed - wine, cake] fini ▪ **the butter is ~** il n'y a plus de beurre ▪ **the plumber was ~ by 4 p.m.** le plombier avait terminé *OR* fini à 16 h ➤ **~ product** *OR* **article** produit *m* fini **5.** [over] fini ▪ **I'm ~ with him/my boyfriend** lui/mon petit ami et moi, c'est fini ▪ **I'm ~ with politics/journalism** la politique/le journalisme et moi, c'est fini, j'en ai fini avec la politique/le journalisme.

finisher ['fɪnɪʃəʳ] *n* **1.** SPORT finisseur *m*, - euse *f* ▪ FTBL marqueur *m* ▪ **he's a fast ~** [athlete] il finit vite, il est rapide au finish **2.** [thorough person] **: he's not a ~** il ne finit jamais complètement son travail **3.** INDUST finisseur *m*, - euse *f*.

finishing line ['fɪnɪʃɪŋ-] *n UK* SPORT ligne *f* d'arrivée.

finishing school *n école privée de jeunes filles surtout axée sur l'enseignement des bonnes manières.*

finishing touch *n* **: to put the ~es to sthg** mettre la dernière touche *OR* la dernière main à qqch.

finish line *US* = **finishing line**.

finite ['faɪnaɪt] *adj* limité ▪ PHILOS & MATHS [number, universe] fini ▪ GRAM [verb] à aspect fini.

fink [fɪŋk] *US inf n* [strikebreaker] jaune *m* ▪ [informer] mouchard *m*, - e *f* ▪ [to police] indic *m*, balance *f* ▪ [nasty person] salaud *m*, salope *f*.
◆ **fink out** *vi insep US inf* [withdraw - from undertaking] laisser tomber, se dégonfler ; [- from promise] ne pas tenir parole ▪ **to ~ out of doing sthg** laisser tomber *OR* se dégonfler et ne pas faire qqch.

Finland ['fɪnlənd] *pr n* Finlande *f* ▪ **in ~** en Finlande.

Finn [fɪn] *n* **1.** [inhabitant of Finland] Finlandais *m*, - e *f* **2.** HIST Finnois *m*, - e *f*.

Finnish ['fɪnɪʃ] ◇ *n* LING finnois *m*.
◇ *adj* **1.** [gen] finlandais **2.** HIST finnois.

fiord [fjɔːd] ◇ *n* LING finnois *m*.
◇ *adj* **1.** [gen] finlandais **2.** HIST finnois.

fiord [fjɔːd] *n* fjord *m*.

fir [fɜːʳ] ◇ *n* [tree, wood] sapin *m*.
◇ *comp* **: ~ cone** *UK* pomme *f* de pin ▪ **~ tree** sapin *m*.

fire ['faɪəʳ] ◇ *n* **1.** [destructive] incendie *m* ▪ **~!** au feu! ▪ **to catch ~** prendre feu ▪ **to set ~ to sthg, to set sthg on ~** mettre le feu à qqch ▪ **to cause** *OR* **to start a ~** [person, faulty wiring] provoquer un incendie ▪ **that's how ~s start** c'est comme ça qu'on met le feu ▪ **on ~** en feu ▪ **the building/village was set on ~** le bâtiment/village a été incendié ▪ **my throat's on ~** *fig* j'ai la gorge en feu ▪ **his forehead/he is on ~** *fig* [because of fever] son front/il est brûlant ➤ **forest ~** incendie *OR* feu *m* de forêt ▪ **to play with ~** jouer avec le feu ▪ **fight ~ with ~** combattre le mal par le mal ▪ **he would go through ~ and water for her** il se jetterait au feu pour elle ▪ **this novel is not going to set the world** *OR* **the Thames** *UK* **on ~** *inf* ce roman ne casse pas des briques ▪ **the Great Fire of London** le grand incendie de Londres *(qui, en 1666, détruisit les trois quarts de la ville, et notamment la cathédrale Saint-Paul)*
2. [in hearth, campsite] feu *m* ▪ **to lay a ~** préparer un feu ▪ **to light** *OR* **to make a ~** allumer un feu, faire du feu ➤ **open ~** feu de cheminée ▪ **wood/coal ~** feu de bois/de charbon
3. [element] feu *m*
4. MIL feu *m* ▪ **to open/to cease ~** ouvrir/cesser le feu ▪ **to open ~ on sb** ouvrir le feu *OR* tirer sur qqn ▪ **to draw the enemy's ~** faire diversion en attirant le feu de l'ennemi ▪ **to return (sb's) ~** riposter (au tir de qqn) ▪ **hold your ~** [don't shoot] ne tirez pas ; [stop shooting] cessez le feu ➤ **to come under ~** *liter* essuyer le feu de l'ennemi ; *fig* être vivement critiqué *OR* attaqué ▪ **between two ~s** entre deux feux
5. *UK* [heater] appareil *m* de chauffage ▪ **to turn the ~ on/off** allumer/éteindre le chauffage
6. [passion, ardour] flamme *f* ▪ **the ~ of youth** la fougue de la jeunesse.
◇ *comp* **: ~ appliance** *UK* camion *m* de pompiers ▪ **~ prevention** mesures *fpl* de sécurité contre l'incendie ▪ **~ prevention officer** *personne chargée des mesures de sécurité contre l'incendie* ▪ **~ regulations** consignes *fpl* en cas d'incendie.
◇ *vt* **1.** [shot, bullet] tirer ▪ [gun, cannon, torpedo] décharger ▪ [arrow] décocher ▪ **without a shot being ~d** sans un seul coup de feu ▪ **to ~ questions at sb** *fig* bombarder qqn de questions
2. [inspire - person, an audience, supporters, the imagination] enflammer ▪ **to ~ sb with enthusiasm/desire** remplir qqn d'enthousiasme/de désir
3. [in kiln] cuire
4. [power, fuel - furnace] chauffer
5. *inf* [dismiss] virer.
◇ *vi* **1.** [shoot - person] tirer, faire feu ▪ **the rifle failed to ~** le coup n'est pas parti ▪ **~!** MIL feu! ▪ **to ~ at** *OR* **on sb** tirer sur qqn
2. [engine] tourner ▪ [spark plug] s'allumer ▪ [pin on print head] se déclencher ▪ **the engine is only firing on two cylinders** le moteur ne tourne que sur deux cylindres ➤ **to ~ on all cylinders** *liter* & *fig* marcher à pleins tubes.
◆ **fire away** *vi insep inf* [go ahead] **: ~ away!** allez-y!
◆ **fire off** *vt sep* [round of ammunition] tirer ▪ *fig* [facts, figures] balancer ▪ **to ~ off questions at sb** bombarder qqn de questions.

fire alarm *n* alarme *f* d'incendie.

fire-and-brimstone *adj* [preacher, sermon] menaçant des feux de l'enfer.

firearm ['faɪərɑːm] *n* arme *f* à feu ▪ **~s offence** LAW délit *m* lié à la détention d'armes à feu.

fireball ['faɪəbɔːl] *n* boule *f* de feu.

firebomb ['faɪəbɒm] ◇ *n* bombe *f* incendiaire.
◇ *vt* [building] attaquer à la bombe incendiaire.

firebrand ['faɪəbrænd] *n fig* exalté *m*, - e *f*.

fire brigade *n* brigade *f* des pompiers *OR* sapeurs-pompiers ▪ **have you called the ~?** as-tu appelé les pompiers?

fire chief *n* capitaine *m* des pompiers *OR* sapeurs-pompiers.

firecracker ['faɪə,krækəʳ] *n* pétard *m*.

fire curtain *n* THEAT rideau *m* de fer.

-fired ['faɪəd] *in cpds* chauffé à ▪ **oil~/gas~ central heating** chauffage central au mazout/gaz.

fire-damaged *adj* endommagé par le feu.

firedamp ['faɪədæmp] *n* MIN grisou *m*.

fire department *US* = **fire brigade**.

fire door *n* porte *f* coupe-feu.

fire drill *n* exercice *m* de sécurité *(en cas d'incendie)*.

fire-eater *n* [in circus] cracheur *m* de feu ▪ *fig* personne *f* belliqueuse, bagarreur *m*, - euse *f*.

fire engine *n* voiture *f* de pompiers.

fire escape *n* escalier *m* de secours *OR* d'incendie.

fire exit *n* sortie *f* de secours.

fire extinguisher *n* extincteur *m*.

firefight ['faɪəfaɪt] *n* bataille *f* armée.

fire fighter *n* pompier *m*, sapeur-pompier *m* (volontaire).

fire-fighting ◇ *n* lutte *f* contre les incendies.
◇ *comp* [equipment, techniques] de lutte contre les incendies.

firefly ['faɪəflaɪ] (*pl* **fireflies**) *n* luciole *f*.

fireguard ['faɪəgɑːd] *n* [for open fire] garde-feu *m*.

fire hazard *n* : **all those empty boxes are a ~** toutes ces boîtes vides constituent *OR* représentent un risque d'incendie.

fire hose *n* tuyau *m* de pompe à incendie.

firehouse ['faɪəhaʊs] *n US* caserne *f* de pompiers.

fire hydrant *n* bouche *f* d'incendie.

firelight ['faɪəlaɪt] *n* lueur *f OR* lumière *f* du feu.

firelighter ['faɪəlaɪtəʳ] *n* allume-feu *m*.

fireman ['faɪəmən] (*pl* **firemen** [-mən]) *n* **1.** pompier *m*, sapeur-pompier *m* **2.** RAIL chauffeur *m* de locomotive.

fire marshal *US* = **fire chief**.

fireplace ['faɪəpleɪs] *n* cheminée *f*.

fire plug *n US* [fire hydrant] bouche *f* d'incendie.

firepower ['faɪə,paʊəʳ] *n* puissance *f* de feu.

fireproof ['faɪəpruːf] ◇ *adj* [door, safe] à l'épreuve du feu ▪ [clothing, toys] ininflammable ▪ [dish] allant au feu.
◇ *vt* ignifuger, rendre ininflammable.

fire-raising [-'reɪzɪŋ] *n* pyromanie *f*.

fire screen *n* écran *m* de cheminée.

fire service = **fire brigade**.

fireside ['faɪəsaɪd] *n* coin *m* du feu ▪ **sitting by the ~** assis au coin du feu ▪ **~ chat** [by politician] causerie *f* au coin du feu.

fire station *n* caserne *f* de pompiers.

firetrap ['faɪətræp] *n* : **there are too many of these ~s** il y a trop de bâtiments qui sont de véritables pièges en cas d'incendie.

fire truck *n US* voiture *f* de pompiers.

fire walker *n personne en transe qui marche sur des braises.*

firewall ['faɪəwɔːl] *n* COMPUT pare-feu *m*.

fire warden *n* [in forest] guetteur *m* d'incendie.

firewood ['faɪəwʊd] *n* bois *m* à brûler ▪ [for use in home] bois *m* de chauffage.

firework ['faɪəwɜːk] *n* pièce *f* d'artifice ▪ **~** *OR* **~s display** feu *m* d'artifice ▪ **there were ~s at the meeting** *inf fig* il y a eu des étincelles à la réunion.

firing ['faɪərɪŋ] ◇ *n* **1.** *(U)* MIL tir *m* ▪ **~ has been heavy** de nombreux coups de feu ont été tirés **2.** [of piece of pottery] cuisson *f*, cuite *f* **3.** *inf* [dismissal] renvoi *m* **4.** AUT [of engine, sparkplug] allumage *m*.
◇ *comp* : **~ order** *OR* **sequence** AUT [of engine] ordre *m* d'allumage ▪ **~ pin** percuteur *m* ▪ **~ practice** exercice *m* de tir ▪ **~ range** champ *m* de tir.

firing line *n* MIL ligne *f* de tir ▪ **to be in the ~** *fig* être dans la ligne de tir.

firing squad *n* peloton *m* d'exécution ▪ **to be executed by ~** passer devant le peloton d'exécution.

firm [fɜːm] ◇ *n* [company] entreprise *f* ▪ [of solicitors] étude *f* ▪ [of lawyers, barristers, consultants] cabinet *m*.
◇ *adj* **1.** [solid, hard - flesh, fruit, mattress etc] ferme ▪ **on ~ ground** *liter* sur la terre ferme ; *fig* sur un terrain solide **2.** [stable, secure - basis] solide ; [- foundations] stable ▪ COMM & FIN [currency, market etc] stable **3.** [strong - handshake, grip, leadership] ferme ▪ **to have a ~ hold** *OR* **grasp** *OR* **grip of sthg** tenir qqch fermement **4.** [unshakeable, definite - belief, evidence, friendship] solide ; [- view, opinion] déterminé, arrêté ; [- intention, voice, agreement, offer] ferme ; [- date] définitif ▪ **they are ~ friends** ce sont de bons amis ▪ **she gave a ~ denial** elle a nié fermement ▪ **I am a ~ believer in women's equality** je crois fermement à l'égalité de la femme ▪ **to be ~ with a child/dog** être ferme avec un enfant/chien.
◇ *adv* : **to stand ~ on sthg** ne pas céder sur qqch ▪ **he stands ~ on this issue** il a une position bien arrêtée sur le sujet.
◇ *vt* : **to ~ the soil** tasser le sol.
◇ *vi* = **firm up** *(vi insep)*.
◆ **firm up** ◇ *vt sep* [make firm - muscles, prices] raffermir ▪ **to ~ up an agreement** régler les derniers détails d'un accord.
◇ *vi insep* [muscles, prices] se raffermir.

firmament ['fɜːməmənt] *n arch & lit* [sky] firmament *m*.

firmly ['fɜːmlɪ] *adv* **1.** [securely - hold, grasp sthg] fermement ; [- closed, secured] bien ▪ **to keep one's feet ~ on the ground** *fig* bien garder les pieds sur terre, rester fermement ancré dans la réalité **2.** [say, deny, refuse, deal with] fermement, avec fermeté.

firmness ['fɜːmnɪs] *n* **1.** [hardness - of flesh, fruit, mattress] fermeté *f* **2.** [stability - of basis] solidité *f* ; [- of foundations] stabilité *f* ▪ COMM & FIN [of currency, market, prices] stabilité *f* **3.** [strength - of grip, character, belief] fermeté *f* **4.** [of voice, denial, refusal] fermeté *f*.

firmware ['fɜːmweəʳ] *n* COMPUT microprogramme *m*.

first [fɜːst] ◇ *det* **1.** [in series] premier ▪ **the ~ six months** les six premiers mois ▪ **Louis the First** Louis Premier *OR* Ier ▪ **I'm ~** je suis *OR* c'est moi le premier ▪ **she's in ~ place** [in race] elle est en tête ▪ **to win ~ prize** gagner le premier prix ▪ **the First State** le Delaware ▶ **~ floor** *UK* premier étage *m* ; *US* rez-de-chaussée *m* ▪ **put the car into ~ gear** passe la première (vitesse) ▪ **~ year** *UK* UNIV première année *f* ; SCH sixième *f* ▪ **I learned of her resignation at ~ hand** c'est elle-même qui m'a appris sa démission ▪ **I don't know the ~ thing about cars** je n'y connais absolument rien en voitures ▪ **I'll pick you up ~ thing (in the morning)** je passerai te chercher demain matin à la première heure ▪ **I'm not at my best ~ thing in the morning** je ne suis pas au mieux de ma forme très tôt le matin ▪ **there's a ~ time for everything** il y a un début à tout
2. [immediately] tout de suite ▪ **~ thing after lunch** tout de suite après le déjeuner
3. [most important - duty, concern] premier ▪ **the ~ priority** la priorité des priorités ▶ **~ things ~!** prenons les choses dans l'ordre!
◇ *adv* **1.** [before the others - arrive, leave, speak] le premier, la première, en premier ▪ **I saw it ~!** c'est moi qui l'ai vu le premier *OR* en premier! ▪ **you go ~** vas-y en premier ▪ **women and children ~** les femmes et les enfants d'abord ▶ **to come ~** [in race] arriver premier ; [in exam] avoir la première place, être premier ▪ **her career comes ~** sa carrière passe d'abord *OR* avant tout ▪ **to put one's family ~** faire passer sa famille d'abord *OR* avant tout ▪ **~ come ~ served** *prov* les premiers arrivés sont les premiers servis
2. [firstly, before anything else] d'abord ▪ **~, I want to say thank you** tout d'abord, je voudrais vous remercier, je voudrais

d'abord vous remercier ■ **what should I do ~?** qu'est-ce que je dois faire en premier? ■ **I'm a mother ~ and a wife second** je suis une mère avant d'être une épouse
3. [for the first time] pour la première fois ■ **we ~ met in London** nous nous sommes rencontrés à Londres ▌ [initially] au début ■ **when I ~ knew him** quand je l'ai connu
4. [sooner, rather] : **I'd die ~** plutôt mourir.
◇ *n* **1.** [before all others] : **the ~** le premier, la première *f* ■ **he was among the ~ to realise** il a été parmi les premiers à s'en rendre compte ■ **he came in an easy ~** [in race] il est arrivé premier haut la main, *see also* **fifth**
2. [achievement] première *f* ■ **that's a notable ~ for France** c'est une grande première pour la France
3. [first time] : **the ~ we heard/knew of it was when...** nous en avons entendu parler pour la première fois/l'avons appris quand... ■ **it's the ~ I've heard of it!** première nouvelle!
4. *UK* UNIV : **he got a ~ in economics** ≃ il a eu mention très bien en économie
5. AUT première *f*.
◆ **at first** *adv phr* au début.
◆ **first and foremost** *adv phr* d'abord et surtout.
◆ **first and last** *adv phr* avant tout.
◆ **first of all** *adv phr* tout d'abord, pour commencer.
◆ **first off** *adv phr inf* pour commencer.
◆ **from first to last** *adv phr* du début à la fin.
◆ **from the (very) first** *adv phr* dès le début.
◆ **in the first instance** *adv phr* d'abord.
◆ **in the first place** *adv phr* **1.** [referring to a past action] d'abord ■ **why did you do it in the ~ place?** et puis d'abord, pourquoi as-tu fait cela?
2. [introducing an argument] d'abord.

first aid ◇ *n (U)* [technique] secourisme *m* ■ [attention] premiers soins *mpl* ■ **does anyone know any ~?** quelqu'un s'y connaît-il en secourisme? ■ **to give/to receive ~** donner/recevoir les premiers soins.
◇ *comp* [class, manual] de secourisme ■ **~ kit** *OR* **box** trousse *f* à pharmacie ■ **~ post** *OR* **station** *UK* poste *m* de secours.

First Amendment *n US* **the ~** le Premier Amendement *(de la Constitution des États-Unis garantissant les libertés individuelles du citoyen américain, notamment la liberté d'expression).*

first-born ◇ *adj* premier-né.
◇ *n* premier-né *m*, première-née *f*.

first class *n* **1.** [on train, plane] première classe *f* **2.** [for letter, parcel] tarif *m* normal.
◆ **first-class** ◇ *adj* **1.** [seat] en première classe ■ [compartment, ticket] de première classe **2.** [letter, stamp] au tarif normal **3.** *UK* UNIV : **to graduate with first-class honours** obtenir son diplôme avec mention très bien **4.** [excellent] = **first-rate**.
◇ *adv* [travel] en première classe ■ [send letter] au tarif normal.

first cousin *n* cousin *m* germain, cousine *f* germaine.

first-day cover *n* [for stamp collector] émission *f* premier jour.

first-degree *adj* **1.** MED [burn] au premier degré **2.** LAW [in US] : **~ murder** meurtre *m* avec préméditation.

first-ever *n inf* tout premier *m*, toute première *f*.

first-foot *vt Scotland* **to ~ sb** *être le premier à rendre visite à qqn pour lui souhaiter la bonne année la nuit de la Saint-Sylvestre.*

first form *n UK* SCH sixième *f*.

first-former *n UK* SCH élève *mf* de sixième.

first-generation *adj* de première génération.

firsthand [fɜːst'hænd] ◇ *adj* [knowledge, information, news] de première main ■ **I know from ~ experience what it is like to be poor** je sais d'expérience ce que c'est que d'être pauvre.
◇ *adv* [hear of sthg] de première main.

first lady *n* [in US] *femme du président des États-Unis* ■ **the ~ of rock/of the detective novel** *fig* la grande dame du rock/du roman policier.

first language *n* langue *f* maternelle.

first lieutenant *n* NAUT lieutenant *m* de vaisseau ■ *US* MIL & AERON lieutenant *m*.

firstly ['fɜːstlɪ] *adv* premièrement.

first mate *n* NAUT second *m*.

first name *n* prénom *m* ■ **to be on ~ terms with sb** appeler qqn par son prénom ■ **we're on ~ terms** ≃ on se tutoie.

first night THEAT ◇ *n* première *f*.
◇ *comp* : **~ nerves** trac *m (du soir de la première).*

first offender *n* délinquant *m*, - e *f* primaire.

first officer = **first mate**.

first-past-the-post *adj UK* POL [system] majoritaire à un tour.

first person *n* GRAM première personne *f* ■ **in the ~** à la première personne.
◆ **first-person** *adj* GRAM [pronoun] de la première personne ■ **a first-person narrative** un récit à la première personne.

first principle *n* principe *m* fondamental *OR* de base.

first-rate *adj* [excellent - wine, meal, restaurant] de première qualité, excellent ; [- idea, performance, student] excellent ■ **that's absolutely ~!** *UK* [idea, news etc] c'est formidable!

first refusal *n* préférence *f* ■ **to give sb ~ on sthg** donner la préférence à qqn pour qqch.

first-strike *adj* MIL [missile] de première frappe ■ **a ~ capability** une force de frappe importante (permettant d'attaquer en premier).

first-time *adj* : **~ (house) buyer** personne *f* devenant propriétaire pour la première fois ■ **~ visitors to the country** les personnes visitant le pays pour la première fois.

first violin *n* MUS [person, instrument] premier violon *m*.

firth [fɜːθ] *n Scotland* estuaire *m*.

fiscal ['fɪskl] ◇ *adj* [measures, policy etc] fiscal ■ **~ year** *US* [gen] année *f* fiscale ; [of company] exercice *m* financier ; ADMIN année *f* budgétaire.
◇ *n Scotland* LAW : **procurator ~** ≃ procureur *m* de la République.

FISCAL YEAR

Aux États-Unis, l'année fiscale correspond à l'année civile pour les particuliers et elle commence le 1er octobre pour le gouvernement.

fish [fɪʃ] (*pl inv OR pl* **fishes**) ◇ *n* poisson *m* ■ **to catch a ~** pêcher un poisson ➊ **~ and chips** poisson frit avec des frites ■ **he's a queer ~** *inf* c'est un drôle de type ■ **to feel like a ~ out of water** ne pas se sentir dans son élément ■ **to drink like a ~** *inf* boire comme un trou ■ **there are plenty more ~ in the sea** un de perdu, dix de retrouvés ■ **to have other ~ to fry** avoir d'autres chats à fouetter ■ **to be a big ~ in a little pond** être le premier dans son village ■ **to be a little ~ in a big pond** être perdu dans la masse ■ **neither ~ nor fowl** ni chair ni poisson.
◇ *comp* [course, restaurant] de poisson.
◇ *vi* **1.** SPORT pêcher ■ **to go ~ing** aller à la pêche ■ **to ~ in troubled waters** *fig* pêcher en eau trouble **2.** [search, seek] : **he ~ed around for his pen under the papers** il a fouillé sous ses papiers pour trouver son crayon ■ **to ~ for information** essayer de soutirer des informations ■ **to ~ for compliments** rechercher les compliments.
◇ *vt* [river, lake etc] pêcher dans.
◆ **fish out** *vt sep* [from water] repêcher ■ **he ~ed out his wallet** *fig* il a sorti son portefeuille ; [with difficulty] il a extrait son portefeuille.
◆ **fish up** *vt sep* [from water] repêcher ■ **where did you ~ that up from?** *inf* [object] où est-ce que tu as été dénicher ça? ; [idea] où est-ce que tu as été pêcher ça?

fish-and-chip shop *n UK magasin vendant du poisson frit et des frites.*

fishbone ['fɪʃbəʊn] *n* arête *f* de poisson.

fishbowl ['fɪʃbəʊl] *n* bocal *m* à poissons.

fishcake ['fɪʃkeɪk] *n* CULIN croquette *f* de poisson.

fisher ['fɪʃəʳ] *n* **1.** *arch* [fisherman] pêcheur *m* **2.** [bird, animal] pêcheur *m*.

fisherman ['fɪʃəmən] (*pl* **fishermen** [-mən]) *n* pêcheur *m*.

fishery ['fɪʃərɪ] (*pl* **fisheries**) *n* [fishing ground] pêcherie *f* ■ [fishing industry] industrie *f* de la pêche.

fish-eye lens *n* PHOT fish-eye *m*.

fish farm *n* établissement *m* piscicole.

fish farming *n* pisciculture *f*.

fish finger *n* CULIN bâtonnet *m* de poisson pané.

fish hook *n* hameçon *m*.

fishing ['fɪʃɪŋ] ◇ *n* pêche *f* ■ **trout/salmon ~** pêche à la truite/au saumon ■ **there is some good ~ to be had along this river** il y a de bons coins de pêche dans cette rivière ■ **'no ~'** 'pêche interdite'.
◇ *comp* [vessel, permit, port, tackle] de pêche ■ [season] de la pêche ■ [village, party] de pêcheurs.

fishing boat *n* bateau *m* de pêche.

fishing ground *n* zone *f* de pêche.

fishing line *n* ligne *f* de pêche.

fishing net *n* filet *m* de pêche.

fishing rod *n* canne *f* à pêche, gaule *f*.

fish market *n* marché *m* au poisson.

fishmonger ['fɪʃˌmʌŋgəʳ] *n* *UK* poissonnier *m*, - ère *f* ■ **to go to the ~'s** aller à la poissonnerie *OR* chez le poissonnier.

fishnet ['fɪʃnet] ◇ *n* *US* [for catching fish] filet *m* (de pêche).
◇ *adj* : **~ stockings/tights** bas *mpl* /collants *mpl* résille.

fish paste *n* pâte *f* de poisson.

fishpond ['fɪʃpɒnd] *n* étang *m* (à poissons).

fish slice *n* pelle *f* à poisson.

fish stick *US* = **fish finger**.

fish tank *n* [in house] aquarium *m* ■ [on fish farm] vivier *m*.

fishwife ['fɪʃwaɪf] (*pl* **fishwives** [-waɪvz]) *n* poissonnière *f*, marchande *f* de poisson ■ **she's a real ~** *fig* elle a un langage de charretier, elle parle comme un charretier.

fishy ['fɪʃɪ] (*comp* **fishier**, *superl* **fishiest**) *adj* **1.** [smell] de poisson **2.** *inf* [suspicious] louche.

fissile ['fɪsaɪl] *adj* fissible.

fission ['fɪʃn] *n* PHYS fission *f* ■ BIOL scissiparité *f*.

fissionable ['fɪʃnəbl] *adj* PHYS fissible.

fission bomb *n* bombe *f* atomique.

fissure ['fɪʃəʳ] ◇ *n* [crevice, crack] fissure *f* ■ *fig* fissure *f*, brèche *f*.
◇ *vi* se fissurer, se fendre.

fist [fɪst] *n* poing *m* ■ **to clench one's ~s** serrer les poings ■ **he shook his ~ at me** il m'a menacé du poing ■ **to put one's ~s up** se mettre en garde ■ **make a ~** serrez le poing.

fistfight ['fɪstfaɪt] *n* bagarre *f* aux poings ■ **to have a ~ with sb** se battre aux poings contre qqn.

fisticuffs ['fɪstɪkʌfs] *n (U)* *hum* bagarre *f*.

fit [fɪt] (*comp* **fitter**, *superl* **fittest** *UK*, *pret & pp* **fitted**) (*US pret & pp* **fit**, *cont* **fitting**) ◇ *adj* **1.** [suitable] convenable ■ **that dress isn't ~ to wear** cette robe n'est pas mettable ■ **~ to eat** [edible] mangeable ; [not poisonous] comestible ■ **~ to drink** [water] potable ■ **this coffee is not ~ to drink** ce café est imbuvable ■ **a meal ~ for a king** un repas digne d'un roi ■ **she's not ~ to look after children** elle ne devrait pas avoir le droit de s'occuper d'enfants ■ **she's not a ~ mother** c'est une mère indigne ■ **I'm not ~ to be seen** je ne suis pas présentable ■ **these programmes aren't ~ for children** ce ne sont pas des programmes pour les enfants ■ **that's all he's ~ for** c'est tout ce qu'il mérite ■ **to think** *OR* **to see ~ to do sthg** trouver *OR* juger bon de faire qqch ■ **do as you see** *OR* **think ~** fais comme tu penses *OR* juges bon
2. *inf* [ready] : **to be ~ to drop** être mort de fatigue ■ **I feel ~ to burst** je me sens prêt à éclater ■ **to laugh ~ to burst** être plié en deux de rire ▶ **I was ~ to be tied** *US* [extremely angry] j'étais furieux
3. [healthy] en forme ■ **to get ~** *UK* retrouver la forme ■ **to keep** *OR* **to stay ~** entretenir sa forme ■ **the patient is not ~ enough to be discharged** le patient n'est pas en état de quitter l'hôpital ■ **it's a case of the survival of the fittest** ce sont les plus forts qui survivent ▶ **to be as ~ as a fiddle** se porter comme un charme.
◇ *n* **1.** [size] : **it's a perfect ~** [item of clothing] cela me/vous *etc* va à merveille ; [fridge, stove, piece of furniture] cela s'adapte parfaitement ; [two interlocking pieces] cela s'emboîte bien ■ **it's not a very good ~** [too large] c'est trop grand ; [too tight] c'est trop juste ■ **tight/loose/comfortable ~** [item of clothing] coupe *f* ajustée/ample/confortable ■ **these trousers are a bit of a tight ~** ce pantalon est un peu juste ■ **it was a bit of a tight ~** [in room, car] on était un peu à l'étroit ; [parking car] il n'y avait pas beaucoup de place
2. MED [of apoplexy, epilepsy, hysterics] crise *f* ■ **~ of coughing, coughing ~** quinte *f* de toux ■ **~ of crying** crise de larmes ▶ **to have a ~** MED avoir une crise ■ **she'll have a ~ when she finds out** *fig* elle va faire une crise quand elle le saura ■ **to throw a ~** *inf* piquer une crise ■ **he nearly threw a ~ when he heard the news** il a failli exploser quand il a appris la nouvelle
3. [outburst - of anger] mouvement *m*, accès *m*, moment *m* ; [- of depression] crise *f* ; [- of pique, generosity] moment *m* ■ **he did it in a ~ of rage** il a fait cela dans un mouvement de rage ■ **he had us all in ~s** il nous a fait hurler *OR* mourir de rire ■ **to get a ~ of the giggles** être pris d'un *OR* piquer un fou rire ▶ **to work by** *OR* **in ~s and starts** travailler par à-coups.
◇ *vt* **1.** [be of the correct size for] : **those trousers ~ you better than the other ones** ce pantalon te va mieux que l'autre ■ **none of the keys fitted the lock** aucune des clés n'entrait dans la serrure ■ **the nut doesn't ~ the bolt** l'écrou n'est pas de la même taille que le boulon ■ **the lid doesn't ~ the pot very well** ce couvercle n'est pas très bien adapté à la casserole
2. [correspond to, match - description] correspondre à ■ **to make the punishment ~ the crime** adapter le châtiment au crime ■ **the music fitted the occasion** la musique était de circonstance ▶ **to ~ the bill** faire l'affaire
3. [make suitable for] : **what do you think ~s you for the job?** en quoi estimez-vous correspondre au profil de l'emploi?
4. [install - lock, door, window etc] installer ; [- carpet] poser ■ **to ~ a key in a lock** engager *OR* mettre une clé dans une serrure ■ **I've got special tyres fitted** *UK* je me suis fait mettre des pneus spéciaux
5. [attach, fix on] fixer ■ **then you ~ the parts together** puis vous assemblez les différentes pièces
6. [equip] équiper ■ **to ~ sthg with sthg** équiper qqch de qqch ■ **she has been fitted with a new hip replacement** elle s'est fait mettre une nouvelle hanche artificielle
7. [take measurements of - person] : **to be fitted for a new suit** faire un essayage pour un nouveau costume
8. [adjust - idea, theory] adapter ■ **I'll ~ the dress on you** j'essaierai la robe sur vous.
◇ *vi* **1.** [be of the correct size] : **the dress doesn't ~** la robe ne lui/me *etc* va pas ■ **this lid/key doesn't ~** ce couvercle/cette clé n'est pas le bon/la bonne ■ **the key won't ~ in the lock** la clé n'entre pas dans la serrure ■ **do these pieces ~ together?** est-ce que ces morceaux vont ensemble? ■ **it won't ~** cela n'ira pas ■ **we won't all ~ round one table** nous ne tiendrons pas tous autour d'une table ■ **cut the pieces to ~** couper les morceaux aux mesures adéquates
2. [correspond, match - description] correspondre ■ **it all ~s** tout concorde ■ **to ~ with sthg** correspondre à qqch ▶ **my face didn't ~** *inf* je n'avais pas le profil de l'emploi.

◆ **fit in** ◇ *vi insep* **1.** [go in space available] tenir ■ **we won't all ~ in** nous ne tiendrons pas tous ■ **that piece ~s in here** [jigsaw] ce morceau va là
2. [in company, group etc] s'intégrer ■ **I feel that I don't ~ in** j'ai l'impression de ne pas être à ma place ■ **to ~ in with** [statement] correspondre à ; [plans, arrangements] cadrer avec ; [colour scheme] s'accorder avec ■ **she doesn't ~ in easily with other people** elle a du mal à s'entendre avec les autres ■ **I think you should ~ in with what I want to do** je pense que tu devrais t'adapter à ce que je veux faire.

<> *vt sep* **1.** [install] installer
2. [find room for - clothes in suitcase] faire entrer ■ **can you ~ one more in?** [in car] peux-tu prendre une personne de plus? ■ **how on earth are you going to ~ everyone in?** [in room, car etc] comment diable vas-tu réussir à faire tenir tout le monde?
3. [find time for - patient] prendre ; [- friend] trouver du temps pour ■ **could you ~ in this translation by the end of the week?** est-ce que vous pourriez faire cette traduction d'ici la fin de la semaine? ■ **could you ~ in lunch this week?** [with me] est-ce que tu seras libre pour déjeuner avec moi cette semaine?

◆ **fit into** <> *vt insep* [furniture into room, clothes into suitcase etc] entrer dans, tenir dans ■ [people into room, car] tenir dans ■ [piece into another] s'emboîter dans.
<> *vt sep* : **to ~ sthg into sthg** faire entrer OR tenir qqch dans qqch ■ **he ~s a lot into one day** il en fait beaucoup en une journée.

◆ **fit on** <> *vi insep* : **this lid won't ~ on** ce couvercle ne va pas ■ **where does this part ~ on?** où va cette pièce?
<> *vt sep* [attach] mettre.

◆ **fit out** *vt sep* [ship] armer ■ [person - with equipment] équiper ■ **to ~ a child out with new clothes** renouveler la garde-robe d'un enfant.

◆ **fit up** *vt sep* **1.** [equip - house, car] équiper ; [- person] munir ■ **to ~ sb/sthg up with sthg** munir qqn/équiper qqch de qqch
2. △ *UK crime sl* monter un coup contre ■ **I've been fitted up** c'est un coup monté.

fitful ['fɪtfʊl] *adj* [sleep] intermittent ■ **attendance has been ~** les gens ne sont pas venus régulièrement.

fitfully ['fɪtfʊlɪ] *adv* [work] par à-coups ■ [attend] irrégulièrement ■ [sleep] de manière intermittente.

fitment ['fɪtmənt] *n UK* [in bathroom, kitchen etc] élément *m* démontable.

fitness ['fɪtnɪs] <> *n* **1.** [health] forme *f* physique **2.** [suitability - of person for job] aptitude *f* ■ **your ~ as a mother is not in question** vos compétences de mère ne sont pas en cause.
<> *comp* : **~ centre** *UK* club *m* de mise en forme ■ **~ freak** *inf* fana *mf* d'exercice physique ■ **~ training** entraînement *m* physique.

fitted ['fɪtəd] *adj* **1.** [jacket] ajusté **2.** *UK* [made to measure] : **the house has ~ carpets in every room** il y a de la moquette dans toutes les pièces de la maison ■ **~ sheet** drap-housse *m* **3.** *UK* [built-in - cupboard] encastré ■ **~ kitchen** cuisine *f* encastrée **4.** [suited] : **to be ~ for sthg/doing sthg** être apte à qqch/à faire qqch.

fitter ['fɪtər] *n* **1.** [of machine] monteur *m*, - euse *f* ■ [of carpet] poseur *m*, - euse *f* **2.** [of clothes] essayeur *m*, - euse *f*.

fitting ['fɪtɪŋ] <> *adj* [suitable - conclusion, remark] approprié ; [- tribute] adéquat ■ [socially correct] convenable.
<> *n* **1.** [trying on - of clothes] essayage *m* **2.** *UK* [of shoe] : **have you got it in a wider/narrower ~?** l'avez-vous en plus large/plus étroit?
<> *comp* : **~ room** salon *m* OR salle *f* d'essayage ; [cubicle] cabine *f* d'essayage.

◆ **fittings** *npl UK* : **bathroom ~s** éléments *mpl* de salle de bains ■ **electrical ~s** appareillage *m* électrique.

-fitting *in cpds* : **close~**, **tight~** [item of clothing] moulant ; [screwtop lid] qui ferme bien ; [lid of saucepan] adapté ■ **loose~** [item of clothing] ample.

fittingly ['fɪtɪŋlɪ] *adv* [dressed] convenablement ■ **~, the government has agreed to ratify the treaty** comme il le fallait, le gouvernement a accepté de ratifier le traité.

fit-up *n*△ *UK crime sl* coup *m* monté.

five [faɪv] <> *n* [number, numeral, playing card] cinq *m* ■ **~ times table** table *f* des cinq ■ **I'm waiting for a number ~ (bus)** j'attends le (bus numéro) cinq ■ **to be ~** [image] avoir cinq ans ■ **it's ~ to/past ~** il est cinq heures moins cinq/cinq heures cinq ■ **to get ~ out of ten** avoir cinq sur dix ■ **a table for ~** une table pour cinq (personnes).
<> *det* cinq ■ **trains leave at ~ minutes to the hour** le train part toutes les heures à moins cinq ■ **to be ~ years old** avoir cinq ans.
<> *pron* cinq ■ **there are ~ (of them)** [people] ils sont cinq ; [objects] il y en a cinq ■ **give me ~!**△ tope là! *(pour conclure un marché, dire bonjour ou manifester son approbation).*

◆ **fives** *n sorte de squash où l'on utilise ses mains ou des battes en guise de raquettes.*

five and dime *n US* bazar *m*, supérette *f*.

five-a-side *UK* SPORT <> *n* football *m* à dix.
<> *comp* : **~ football** football *m* à dix.

fivefold ['faɪvfəʊld] <> *adj* [increase] au quintuple.
<> *adv* par cinq, au quintuple.

five-o'clock shadow *n* barbe *f* d'un jour, barbe *f* naissante ■ **he's always got ~** il a toujours l'air mal rasé.

fiver ['faɪvər] *n inf* [five pounds] billet *m* de cinq livres ■ [five dollars] billet *m* de cinq dollars.

five-star *adj* [hotel] cinq étoiles.

five-year *adj* [plan] quinquennal.

fix [fɪks] <> *vt* **1.** [fasten in position - mirror, sign] fixer ■ [attention, gaze] fixer ■ [sthg in mind] inscrire, graver ■ **to ~ the blame on sb** attribuer OR imputer la faute à qqn ■ **to ~ one's hopes on sthg/sb** mettre tous ses espoirs en qqch/qqn
2. [set - date, price, rate, limit] fixer ; [- meeting place] convenir de ■ **nothing has been ~ed yet** rien n'a encore été fixé ■ **have you (got) anything ~ed for Friday?** as-tu quelque chose de prévu pour vendredi?
3. [arrange, sort out] s'occuper de ■ **I'll ~ it** je vais m'en occuper ■ **try to ~ it so you don't have to stay overnight** essaye de t'arranger pour que tu ne sois pas obligé de passer la nuit là-bas ■ **I'll ~ it with your teacher** j'arrangerai cela avec ton professeur
4. *inf* [settle a score with] s'occuper de, régler son compte à ■ **that'll ~ him** ça devrait lui régler son compte
5. *US inf* [prepare - meal, drink] préparer ■ **can I ~ you a drink?** puis-je te servir un verre?
6. *inf* [adjust - make-up, tie] arranger ■ **to ~ one's hair** se coiffer ; [redo] se recoiffer
7. [mend, repair - car, puncture etc] réparer
8. *inf* [race, fight, election, result] truquer ■ [interview] arranger ■ [jury, official, security guard etc - bribe] acheter
9. AERON & NAUT [position] déterminer
10. CHEM [nitrogen] fixer
11. ART & PHOT [drawing, photo] fixer.
<> *n* **1.** *inf* [tight spot, predicament] pétrin *m* ■ **to be in a ~** être dans une mauvaise passe ■ **to get into/out of a ~** se mettre dans une/sortir d'une mauvaise passe
2. △ *drug sl* dose *f*, fix *m*
3. AERON & NAUT : **to get a ~ on** [ship] déterminer la position de ; *fig* [get clear idea of] se faire une idée de
4. *inf* [unfair arrangement] : **the result was a ~** le résultat avait été truqué.

◆ **fix on** <> *vt sep* [attach] fixer.
<> *vt insep* [decide on - date, candidate] choisir.

◆ **fix up** <> *vt sep* **1.** [install, erect] mettre en place, installer
2. *inf* [arrange - date, meeting] fixer ; [- deal, holiday] organiser, mettre au point ■ **~ me up with an appointment with the dentist** prends-moi un rendez-vous chez le dentiste ■ **he'll try to ~ something up for us** il va essayer de nous arranger quelque chose ■ **have you got anything ~ed up for this evening?** as-tu quelque chose de prévu pour ce soir? ■ **I've managed to ~ him up with some work** j'ai réussi à lui trouver du travail ■ **you can stay here until you get ~ed up (with a place to stay)** tu peux loger ici jusqu'à ce que tu trouves un endroit où habiter ■ **to ~ sb up with a date** trouver un/une partenaire à qqn
3. [room] refaire ■ [flat, house] refaire, retaper ■ **we could always ~ the smallest bedroom up as a study** on pourrait toujours transformer la plus petite chambre en bureau.
<> *vi insep* s'arranger pour que.

fixated [fɪk'seɪtɪd] *adj* fixé ■ **to be ~ on sthg** être fixé sur qqch.

fixation [fɪk'seɪʃn] *n* **1.** PSYCHOL fixation *f* ■ **to have a ~ about sthg** faire une fixation sur qqch **2.** CHEM fixation *f*.

fixative ['fɪksətɪv] *n* PHOT fixateur *m* ■ ART fixatif *m*.

fixed [fɪkst] *adj* **1.** [immovable - glare] fixe ; [- idea] arrêté ; [- smile] figé ■ **the seats are ~ to the floor** les sièges sont fixés au sol **2.** [set, unchangeable - price, rate, plans] fixe ■ **people on ~ incomes** des gens disposant de revenus fixes ■ **of no ~ abode** LAW sans domicile fixe ■ **~ assets** FIN immobilisations *fpl* ■ **~ capital** FIN capitaux *mpl* immobilisés ■ **~ costs** FIN coûts *mpl* fixes ■ **~ disk** COMPUT disque *m* non amovible ■ **~-rate mortgage** emprunt *m* immobilier à intérêt fixe **3.** *inf* [placed] : **how are you ~ for time/money?** [how much] combien de temps/d'argent as-tu? ; [is it sufficient] as-tu suffisamment de temps/d'argent?

fixedly ['fɪksɪdlɪ] *adv* [stare] fixement.

fixer ['fɪksəʳ] *n* **1.** *inf* [person] combinard *m*, - e *f* **2.** PHOT fixateur *m* **3.** [adhesive] adhésif *m*.

fixing bath *n* [container] cuvette *f* de fixage ■ [solution] bain *m* de fixage.

fixings ['fɪksɪŋz] *npl* *US* CULIN accompagnement *m*.

fixture ['fɪkstʃəʳ] ◇ *n* **1.** [in building] installation *f* fixe ■ **she's become a ~ here** *fig* elle fait partie des meubles à présent ▶ **bathroom ~s** installations *fpl* sanitaires ■ **'~s and fittings £2000'** 'reprise 2 000 livres' **2.** SPORT rencontre *f*.
◇ *comp* : **~ list** SPORT calendrier *m*.

fizz [fɪz] ◇ *vi* [drink] pétiller ■ [firework] crépiter.
◇ *n* **1.** [of drink] pétillement *m* ■ **the champagne has lost its ~** le champagne est éventé **2.** [sound] sifflement *m* **3.** *inf* [soft drink] boisson *f* gazeuse ■ *UK* [champagne] champagne *m*.

fizziness ['fɪzɪnɪs] *n* [of drink] pétillement *m*.

fizzle ['fɪzl] *vi* [drink] pétiller ■ [fire, firework] crépiter.
► **fizzle out** *vi insep fig* [interest, enthusiasm] tomber ■ [plan, project] tomber à l'eau ■ [book, film, party, strike etc] tourner *OR* partir en eau de boudin ■ [career] tourner court.

fizzy ['fɪzɪ] (*comp* **fizzier**, *superl* **fizziest**) *adj* [soft drink] gazeux ■ [wine] pétillant, mousseux.

fjord [fjɔːd] = **fiord**.

FL *written abbr of* **Florida**.

flab [flæb] *n inf* [of person] graisse *f*, lard *m* ■ [in text] délayage *m*, verbiage *m* ■ **to fight the ~** essayer de perdre sa graisse.

flabbergasted ['flæbəgaːstɪd] *adj inf* sidéré ■ **I was ~ at** *OR* **by the news** j'ai été sidéré par la nouvelle, la nouvelle m'a sidéré.

flabby ['flæbɪ] (*comp* **flabbier**, *superl* **flabbiest**) *adj inf* [arms, stomach] flasque, mou *(before vowel or silent 'h' mol)*, molle *f* ■ [person] empâté ■ *fig* [argument, speech] qui manque de concision.

flaccid ['flæsɪd] *adj* flasque.

flack [flæk] *US inf* ◇ *n* [press agent] attaché *m*, - e *f* de presse.
◇ *vi* : **to ~ for sb** être l'attaché de presse de qqn.

flag [flæg] (*pret & pp* **flagged**, *cont* **flagging**) ◇ *n* **1.** [emblem of country, signal] drapeau *m* ■ [for celebration] banderole *f*, fanion *m* ■ NAUT pavillon *m* ■ **all the ~s are out in the city** la ville est pavoisée ▶ **~ of convenience** NAUT pavillon de complaisance ■ **yellow ~** NAUT pavillon de quarantaine ■ **to fly the ~** défendre les couleurs de son pays ■ **to go down with all ~s flying** NAUT couler pavillon haut ; *fig* échouer la tête haute ■ **to keep the ~ flying** faire front ■ **to put out the ~s for sb** organiser une fête en l'honneur de qqn ■ **to show the ~** *fig* faire acte de présence **2.** [for charity] *badge ou autocollant que l'on obtient lorsque l'on verse de l'argent à une œuvre de charité* **3.** [in taxi] : **the ~ was down/up** le taxi était pris/libre **4.** COMPUT drapeau *m*, fanion *m* **5.** [paving stone] dalle *f* **6.** BOT iris *m*.
◇ *vt* **1.** [put marker on - page of book] marquer ■ **to ~ an error** COMPUT indiquer *OR* signaler une erreur par un drapeau *OR* un fanion **2.** [floor] daller.
◇ *vi* [strength] faiblir ■ [energy, enthusiasm, interest, spirits] faiblir, tomber ■ [efforts] se relâcher ■ [conversation] tomber, s'épuiser ■ **I'm flagging** [becoming physically or mentally tired] je fatigue ; [unable to eat any more] je commence à être rassasié, je cale.
► **flag down** *vt sep* [taxi, bus, motorist etc] faire signe de s'arrêter à.
► **flag up** *vt sep* [identify] marquer.

flag day *n* **1.** [in UK] *jour de quête d'une œuvre de charité* **2.** [in US] : **Flag Day** le 14 juin *(fête nationale des États-Unis)*.

FLAG DAY

En Grande-Bretagne, les *flag days* ont lieu en général le samedi. On fait appel à la générosité des particuliers qui, en contrepartie de leur dons pour des œuvres de bienfaisance, reçoivent un insigne ou un badge. Aux États-Unis, *Flag Day* commémore l'adoption le 14 juin 1777 de ***Stars and Stripes***, l'actuel drapeau américain.

flagellate ['flædʒəleɪt] ◇ *vt fml* flageller ■ *fig* fustiger.
◇ *adj* BIOL & BOT flagellé.
◇ *n* BIOL & BOT flagellé *m*.

flagellation [ˌflædʒɪ'leɪʃn] *n* flagellation *f*.

flagged [flægd] *adj* dallé.

flagging ['flægɪŋ] *adj* [enthusiasm, spirits] qui baisse ■ [conversation] qui tombe *OR* s'épuise.

flagon ['flægən] *n* [jug] cruche *f* ■ [bottle] bouteille *f*.

flagpole ['flægpəʊl] *n* mât *m* ■ **let's run it up the ~ (and see who salutes)** *inf fig* soumettons-le et voyons les réactions.

flagrant ['fleɪgrənt] *adj* [injustice, lie, abuse] flagrant ■ **a ~ disregard for the safety of others** un mépris flagrant *OR* évident pour la sécurité d'autrui.

flagrante delicto [flə'græntɪdɪ'lɪktəʊ] *adv phr* : **to be caught in ~** être surpris en flagrant délit.

flagrantly ['fleɪgrəntlɪ] *adv* [abuse, disregard, defy etc] d'une manière flagrante.

flagship ['flægʃɪp] ◇ *n* NAUT vaisseau *m OR* bâtiment *m* amiral ■ *fig* [product] tête *f* de gamme.
◇ *comp* : **~ restaurant/store** restaurant *m* /magasin *m* principal.

flagstaff ['flægstaːf] = **flagpole**.

flagstone ['flægstəʊn] = **flag** *(n sense 5)*.

flag-waving *n (U) inf fig* discours *mpl* cocardiers.

flail [fleɪl] ◇ *n* AGRIC fléau *m*.
◇ *vt* AGRIC battre au fléau ■ [arms] agiter.
◇ *vi* [person, limbs] s'agiter violemment.
► **flail about** ◇ *vi insep* [person, limbs] s'agiter dans tous les sens.
◇ *vt sep* [arms, legs] battre.

flair [fleəʳ] *n* **1.** [stylishness] style *m* **2.** [gift] don *m* ■ **to have a ~ for sthg** avoir un don pour qqch.

flak [flæk] ◇ *n* **1.** [gunfire] tir *m* antiaérien *OR* de DCA **2.** *inf (U) inf fig* [criticism] critiques *fpl* ■ **I took a lot of ~ over it** on m'a beaucoup critiqué pour cela.
◇ *comp* : **~ jacket** gilet *m* pare-balles.

flake [fleɪk] ◇ *n* **1.** [of snow] flocon *m* ■ [of metal] paillette *f* ■ [of skin] peau *f* morte ■ [of paint] écaille *f* **2.** *US inf* [person] barjo *mf*.
◇ *vi* [plaster] s'effriter, s'écailler ■ [paint] s'écailler ■ [skin] peler ■ [fish] s'émietter.
◇ *vt* CULIN [fish] émietter ■ **~d almonds** amandes *fpl* effilées.
► **flake off** *vi insep* = **flake** *(vi)*.
► **flake out** *vi insep inf* s'écrouler ■ [fall asleep] s'endormir.

flaky ['fleɪkɪ] (*comp* **flakier**, *superl* **flakiest**) *adj* **1.** [paint, rock] effrité ■ **~ pastry** CULIN pâte *f* feuilletée **2.** *US inf* [person] barjo ■ [idea] loufoque.

flambé ['flɑ̃be] (*pret & pp* **flambéed**, *cont* **flambéing**) ◇ *vt* flamber.
◇ *adj* flambé.

flamboyance [flæm'bɔɪəns] *n* [of style, dress, behaviour etc] extravagance *f*.

flamboyant [flæm'bɔɪənt] *adj* [behaviour, lifestyle, personality] extravagant ■ [colour] éclatant ■ [clothes] aux couleurs éclatantes ■ *pej* voyant ■ ARCHIT flamboyant.

flamboyantly [flæm'bɔɪəntlɪ] *adv* de manière extravagante.

flame [fleɪm] <> *n* **1.** [of fire, candle] flamme *f* ▪ **to be in ~s** [building, car] être en flammes ▪ **to burst into ~s** prendre feu, s'enflammer ▪ **to go up in ~s** s'embraser ➲ **to be shot down in ~s** *liter* & *fig* être descendu en flammes **2.** *lit* [of passion, desire] flamme *f*.
<> *vi fig* [face, cheeks] s'empourprer ▪ [passion, anger] brûler.
<> *vt* **1.** CULIN flamber **2.** [via e-mail] descendre, injurier.
◆ **flame up** *vi insep* [fire] s'embraser ▪ *fig* [person] s'enflammer.

flamenco [flə'meŋkəʊ] <> *n* flamenco *m*.
<> *comp* [dancer] de flamenco ▪ **~ music** flamenco *m*.

flameproof ['fleɪmpru:f] *adj* [clothing] ininflammable, à l'épreuve des flammes ▪ [dish] allant au feu.

flamethrower ['fleɪmθrəʊə^r] *n* lance-flammes *m inv*.

flaming ['fleɪmɪŋ] <> *n* [via e-mail] échange *m* OR envoi *m* de propos injurieux.
<> *adj* **1.** [sun, sky] embrasé ▪ [fire] flamboyant **2.** *UK inf* [extremely angry] : **to be in a ~ temper** être d'une humeur massacrante, être furax ▪ **we had a ~ row about it** nous avons eu une belle engueulade là-dessus **3.** *inf* [as intensifier] fichu ▪ **you ~ idiot!** espèce d'abruti!
<> *adv UK inf* [as intensifier] fichtrement ▪ **don't be so ~ stupid!** ne sois donc pas aussi bête!

flamingo [flə'mɪŋgəʊ] *n* flamant *m* rose.

flammable ['flæməbl] *adj* [material, substance] inflammable.

flan [flæn] CULIN <> *n* tarte *f* ▪ [savoury] quiche *f*.
<> *comp* : **~ case** fond *m* de tarte.

Flanders ['flɑ:ndəz] *pr n* Flandre *f*, Flandres *fpl* ▪ **in ~** dans les Flandres, en Flandre.

flange [flændʒ] <> *n* [on pipe] bride *f*, collerette *f* ▪ RAIL [on rail] patin *m*.
<> *comp* : **~ girder** poutre *f* en I.

flanged [flændʒd] *adj* [with flanges] à brides ▪ [attached by flanges] fixé par brides.

flank [flæŋk] <> *n* flanc *m* ➲ **~ of beef** CULIN flanchet *m*.
<> *vt* **1.** [be on either side of] encadrer ▪ **~ed by his wife and son** entouré de sa femme et de son fils **2.** MIL flanquer.

flanker ['flæŋkə^r] *n* RUGBY avant-aile *m*, flanqueur *m*.

flannel ['flænl] (*UK pret & pp* **flannelled**, *cont* **flannelling** *US*, *pret & pp* **flanneled**, *cont* **flanneling**) <> *n* **1.** TEX flanelle *f* **2.** *UK* [for washing] ≃ gant *m* de toilette **3.** *(U) UK inf* [empty words] baratin *m*, blabla *m*, blablabla *m*.
<> *comp* TEX [nightgown, sheet, trousers, suit] en OR de flanelle.
<> *vi UK inf* [use empty words] faire du baratin OR du blabla OR du blablabla.
◆ **flannels** *npl* pantalon *m* en OR de flanelle.

flannelette [flænə'let] TEX <> *n* pilou *m*.
<> *comp* [nightgown, sheet] en OR de pilou.

flap [flæp] (*pret & pp* **flapped**, *cont* **flapping**) <> *n* **1.** [of sails] claquement *m* ▪ [of wings] battement *m* **2.** [of counter, desk - hinged] abattant *m* ; [- sliding] rallonge *f* ▪ [of pocket, tent, envelope] rabat *m* ▪ [in floor, door] trappe *f* ▪ [of aircraft] volet *m* (hypersustentateur) ▪ **a ~ of skin** un morceau de peau décollée **3.** *inf* [panic] panique *f* ▪ **to be in a ~** être dans tous ses états, être paniqué ▪ **to get into a ~** paniquer.
<> *vi* **1.** [wings] battre ▪ [sails, shutters, washing, curtains] claquer **2.** *inf* [panic] paniquer, s'affoler.
<> *vt* : **the bird flapped its wings** l'oiseau a battu des ailes ▪ **he was flapping his arms about to keep warm** il agitait ses bras pour se tenir chaud.

flapjack ['flæpdʒæk] *n* CULIN [in UK] biscuit *m* à l'avoine ▪ [in US] *petite crêpe épaisse*.

flapper ['flæpə^r] *n jeune fille dans le vent (dans les années 20)*.

flare [fleə^r] <> *n* **1.** [bright flame - of fire, match] flamboiement *m* **2.** [signal] signal *m* lumineux ▪ [rocket] fusée *f* éclairante **3.** [in clothes] évasement *m*.
<> *vi* **1.** [flame, match] flamboyer **2.** [tempers] s'échauffer ▪ **tempers ~d** les esprits se sont échauffés **3.** [nostrils] frémir **4.** [clothes] s'évaser.
<> *vt* [clothes] évaser.
◆ **flares** *npl* : **(a pair of) ~s** un pantalon à pattes d'éléphant.
◆ **flare up** *vi insep* [fire] s'embraser ▪ *fig* [dispute, quarrel, violence] éclater ▪ [disease, epidemic, crisis] apparaître, se déclarer ▪ [person] s'emporter.

flared [fleəd] *adj* [trousers] à pattes d'éléphant ▪ [dress] évasé ▪ [skirt] évasé, à godets.

flare gun *n* pistolet *m* de détresse, lance-fusées *m inv*.

flare-up *n* [of fire, light] flamboiement *m* ▪ *fig* [of anger, violence] explosion *f* ▪ [of tension] montée *f* ▪ [of disease, epidemic] apparition *f* ▪ [quarrel] dispute *f* ▪ **renewed ~** [of anger, violence] reprise *f*, nouvelle explosion ; [of tension] remontée *f* ; [of disease, epidemic] réapparition *f*.

flash [flæʃ] <> *n* **1.** [of light, diamond] éclat *m* ▪ [of metal] reflet *m*, éclat *m* ▪ **we saw a ~ of light in the distance** nous avons vu l'éclat d'une lumière au loin ▪ **~ of wit/humour** pointe *f* d'esprit/d'humour ▪ **~ of inspiration** éclair *m* de génie ▪ **in a ~** [very quickly] en un éclair, en un clin d'œil ▪ **it came to me in a ~** cela m'est venu d'un seul coup ➲ **~ of lightning** éclair *m* ▪ **a ~ in the pan** un feu de paille ▪ **(as) quick as a ~** aussi rapide que l'éclair, rapide comme l'éclair
2. [of news] flash *m* (d'information)
3. MIL [on uniform] écusson *m*
4. [of colour] tache *f*
5. PHOT flash *m* ▪ **are you going to use a ~ for this one?** est-ce que tu vas la prendre au flash, celle-ci?
6. *US inf* [flashlight] torche *f*.
<> *vi* **1.** [light, torch, sign] clignoter ▪ [diamond] briller, lancer des éclats ▪ **lightning ~ed directly overhead** il y a eu des éclairs juste au-dessus ▪ **her eyes ~ed** ses yeux ont lancé des éclairs ▪ **to ~ at sb** AUT faire un appel de phares à qqn
2. [move fast] filer comme l'éclair, aller à la vitesse de l'éclair ▪ **to ~ past** OR **by** [time] passer à toute vitesse ▪ **the thought ~ed through** OR **across her mind that...** la pensée que... lui a traversé l'esprit ▪ **information ~ed onto** OR **up on the screen** des informations sont apparues sur l'écran ▪ **my life ~ed before me** ma vie a défilé devant mes yeux
3. *UK inf* [expose o.s.] s'exhiber.
<> *vt* **1.** [torch - turn on and off] faire clignoter ▪ **to ~ a light in sb's face** OR **eyes** diriger une lumière dans les yeux de qqn ▪ **to ~ (one's headlights at) sb** AUT faire un appel de phares à qqn ▪ **to ~ a smile at sb** *fig* lancer OR adresser un sourire à qqn **2.** [give brief glimpse of - passport, photograph etc] montrer rapidement ▪ **to ~ one's money around** [to impress] dépenser son argent avec ostentation ; [be indiscreet] montrer son argent **3.** [news, information] diffuser ▪ **to ~ a message up on the screen** faire apparaître un message sur l'écran.
<> *adj inf* **1.** *pej* = **flashy**
2. [expensive - looking] chic.
◆ **flash back** *vi insep* [in novel, film etc] : **to ~ back to sthg** revenir en arrière sur OR faire un flash-back sur qqch.

flashback ['flæʃbæk] *n* [in novel, film, etc] flash-back *m inv*, retour *m* en arrière ▪ **a ~ to the war** un flash-back sur la guerre ▪ **I had a ~ to when I was a child** mon enfance m'est revenue à l'esprit.

flashbulb ['flæʃbʌlb] *n* PHOT ampoule *f* de flash.

flash card *n* SCH *carte portant un mot, une image etc utilisée dans l'enseignement comme aide à l'apprentissage*.

flashcube ['flæʃkju:b] *n* PHOT cube *m* de flash.

flasher ['flæʃə^r] *n* **1.** AUT [indicator] clignotant *m* **2.** *inf* [person] exhibitionniste *mf*.

flash flood *n* crue *f* subite.

flash gun *n* PHOT flash *m*.

flashily ['flæʃɪlɪ] *adv inf pej* d'une manière tapageuse OR tape-à-l'œil, tapageusement.

flashing ['flæʃɪŋ] <> *adj* [indicator, light, torch] clignotant ▪ **with ~ eyes, she stormed out** elle sortit brutalement, les yeux ardents (de colère) ➲ **~ light** [on police car] gyrophare *m*.
<> *n* **1.** *inf* [indecent exposure] exhibitionnisme *m* **2.** *(U)* [on roof] raccord *m*.

flashlight ['flæʃlaɪt] *n* **1.** PHOT ampoule *f* de flash **2.** *esp US* [torch] torche *f* électrique, lampe *f* électrique *OR* de poche **3.** [flashing signal] fanal *m*.

flash photography *n* photographie *f* au flash.

flashpoint ['flɒʃpɔɪnt] *n* **1.** CHEM point *m* d'éclair **2.** *fig* [trouble spot] poudrière *f* ▪ **the situation has reached ~** *fig* la situation est explosive *OR* sur le point d'exploser.

flashy ['flæʃɪ] *adj inf pej* [person, car, clothes, taste] tapageur, tape-à-l'œil *(inv)* ▪ [colour] voyant, criard.

flask [flɑːsk] *n* PHARM fiole *f* ▪ CHEM ballon *m* ▪ [for water, wine] gourde *f* ▪ **(vacuum** *OR* **Thermos®)~** (bouteille *f*) Thermos® *f*.

flat [flæt] ◇ *adj* **1.** [countryside, feet, stomach] plat ▪ [surface] plan ▪ [roof] plat, en terrasse ▪ [nose] épaté, camus ▪ [tyre - deflated] à plat, dégonflé ; [- punctured] crevé ▪ [ball, balloon] dégonflé ▪ **it folds up ~** c'est pliable ▪ **he was lying ~ on his back** il était allongé à plat sur le dos ▪ **to be ~ on one's back** *fig* [with illness] être alité ▪ **lay the book ~ on the desk** pose le livre à plat sur le bureau ▪ **to fall ~ on one's back** tomber sur le dos ▪ **to fall ~** [joke] tomber à plat ▶ **to fall ~ on one's face** *liter* tomber la tête la première ; *fig* se casser le nez **2.** [soft drink, beer, champagne] éventé ▪ **to go ~** [beer, soft drink] s'éventer, perdre ses bulles ▮ *fig* [monotonous - style, voice] monotone, terne ▪ [without emotion - voice] éteint ▪ [stock market, business] au point mort ▪ [social life] peu animé ▪ **to feel ~** *fig* se sentir vidé *OR* à plat **3.** [battery] à plat **4.** MUS en dessous du ton ▪ **to be ~** [singer] chanter en dessous du ton ; [instrumentalist] jouer en dessous du ton ▪ **E ~** mi bémol **5.** [categorical - refusal, denial] catégorique ▪ **to give a ~ refusal** refuser catégoriquement **6.** COMM [rate, fare, fee] fixe.
◇ *adv* **1.** [categorically] catégoriquement ▪ **she turned me down ~** elle m'a opposé un refus catégorique **2.** [exactly] : **in thirty seconds ~** en trente secondes pile **3.** MUS en dessous du ton **4.** *inf phr* **~ broke** *inf* complètement fauché.
◇ *n* **1.** *UK* [in house] appartement *m* ▪ **(block of) ~s** immeuble *m* (d'habitation) **2.** [of hand, blade] plat *m* **3.** [in horse racing] : **the ~** [races] le plat ; [season] la saison des courses de plat **4.** MUS bémol *m* **5.** *inf* [puncture] crevaison *f* ▪ [punctured tyre] pneu *m* crevé ▪ [deflated tyre] pneu *m* à plat ▪ **we had a ~** [puncture] nous avons crevé **6.** THEAT ferme *f*.
◆ **flats** *npl* GEOG : **salt ~s** marais *mpl* salants.
◆ **flat out** *adv phr* : **to work ~ out** travailler d'arrache-pied ▪ **to be ~ out** [exhausted] être à plat, être vidé ; [drunk] être fin saoul ; [knocked out] être K-O ▪ **to be going ~ out** [car] être à sa vitesse maximum ; [driver, runner, horse] être au maximum *OR* à fond.

flat cap *n* casquette *f*.

flat-chested [-'tʃestɪd] *adj* : **to be ~** ne pas avoir de poitrine ; *pej* être plat comme une planche à pain *OR* une limande.

flatfish ['flætfɪʃ] *n* poisson *m* plat.

flat-footed *adj* **1.** MED aux pieds plats **2.** *inf* [clumsy] empoté ▪ [tactless] maladroit, lourdaud **3.** *inf* [off guard] : **to catch sb ~** *inf* prendre qqn par surprise.

flat-hunt *vi (usu in progressive) UK* chercher un appartement.

flatland ['flætlænd] *n* plaine *f*.

flatlet ['flætlɪt] *n UK* studio *m*.

flatly ['flætlɪ] *adv* **1.** [categorically - deny, refuse] catégoriquement **2.** [without emotion - say, speak] d'une voix éteinte ▪ [monotonously] avec monotonie.

flatmate ['flætmeɪt] *n UK personne avec qui on partage un appartement* ▪ **she and I were ~s in London** elle et moi partagions un appartement à Londres.

flat racing *n* [in horse racing - races] plat *m* ; [- season] saison *f* des courses de plat.

flat-screen *adj* TV & COMPUT à écran plat.

flat season *n* [in horse racing] saison *f* des courses de plat.

flatten ['flætn] ◇ *vt* **1.** [path, road, ground] aplanir ▪ [dough, metal] aplatir ▪ [animal, person - subj: vehicle] écraser ▪ [house, village - subj: bulldozer, earthquake] raser ▪ [crop - subj: wind, storm] écraser, aplatir ▪ [piece of paper] étaler ▪ **to ~ o.s. against a wall** se plaquer *OR* se coller contre un mur **2.** *inf* [defeat thoroughly] écraser, battre à plate couture **3.** *inf* [knock to the ground] démolir **4.** *inf* [subdue - person] clouer le bec à **5.** MUS [note] baisser d'un demi-ton, bémoliser.
◇ *vi* = **flatten out**.
◆ **flatten out** ◇ *vi insep* **1.** [countryside, hills] s'aplanir **2.** AERON [plane] se redresser ▪ [pilot] redresser l'appareil.
◇ *vt sep* [piece of paper] étaler à plat ▪ [bump, path, road] aplanir.

flatter ['flætəʳ] ◇ *vt* [subj: person] flatter ▪ [subj: dress, photo, colour] avantager ▪ **don't ~ yourself!, you ~ yourself!** non mais tu rêves! ▪ **he ~s himself (that) he's a good singer** il a la prétention d'être un bon chanteur.
◇ *vi* flatter.

flatterer ['flætərəʳ] *n* flatteur *m*, -euse *f*.

flattering ['flætərɪŋ] *adj* [remark, person, offer] flatteur ▪ [picture, colour] avantageux, flatteur ▪ [dress] seyant.

flattery ['flætərɪ] *n (U)* flatterie *f* ▪ **~ will get you nowhere** la flatterie ne vous mènera nulle part, vous n'obtiendrez rien par la flatterie.

flattie ['flætɪ] *n* chaussure *f* plate.

flat top *n* [haircut] brosse *f*.

flatulence ['flætjʊləns] *n* flatulence *f*.

flatulent ['flætjʊlənt] *adj* flatulent.

flatware ['flætweəʳ] *n (U) US* [cutlery] couverts *mpl* ▪ [serving dishes] plats *mpl* ▪ [plates] assiettes *fpl*.

flatworm ['flæt,wɜːm] *n* plathelminthe *m*, ver *m* plat.

flaunt [flɔːnt] *vt* [wealth, beauty] étaler, faire étalage de ▪ [car, jewellery] faire parade de, exhiber ▪ **to ~ o.s.** s'afficher ▪ **if you've got it, ~ it** si tu as ce qu'il faut, ne t'en cache pas.

flautist ['flɔːtɪst] *n UK* MUS flûtiste *mf*.

flavor *etc US* = **flavour**.

flavour *UK*, **flavor** *US* ['fleɪvəʳ] ◇ *n* [of food, drink] goût *m* ▪ [of ice-cream, tea] parfum *m* ▪ **chocolate/coffee ~ ice-cream** glace au chocolat/au café ▪ **it's got quite a spicy ~** c'est assez épicé ▪ **it gives the film a South American ~** *fig* cela donne une note sud-américaine au film ▶ **to be ~ of the month** [in vogue] être au goût du jour ▪ **you're not exactly ~ of the month at the moment** *inf* tu n'es pas comme qui dirait en odeur de sainteté en ce moment, tu n'as pas vraiment la cote en ce moment.
◇ *comp* : **~ enhancers** agents *mpl* de sapidité.
◇ *vt* [with spices, herbs] assaisonner ▪ [with fruit, alcohol] parfumer.

-flavoured ['fleɪvəd] *in cpds* : **chocolate~** au chocolat ▪ **vanilla~** à la vanille.

flavouring *UK*, **flavoring** *US* ['fleɪvərɪŋ] *n* CULIN [savoury] assaisonnement *m* ▪ [sweet] parfum *m*, arôme *m* ▪ **'no artificial ~s'** [on tin, package] 'sans arômes artificiels'.

flavourless *UK*, **flavorless** *US* ['fleɪvəlɪs] *adj* sans goût, insipide.

flaw [flɔː] ◇ *n* [in material, plan, character] défaut *m* ▪ LAW vice *m* de forme.
◇ *vt* [object] endommager ▪ [sb's character, beauty] altérer.

flawed [flɔːd] *adj* imparfait ▪ **the argument is, however, ~** cette argumentation a cependant un défaut *OR* des défauts.

flawless ['flɔːlɪs] *adj* parfait.

flax [flæks] *n* lin *m*.

flaxen ['flæksn] *adj* [hair] blond pâle *OR* filasse.

flay [fleɪ] *vt* [animal] dépouiller, écorcher ▪ [person] fouetter ▪ *fig* [criticize] éreinter ▪ **to ~ sb alive** faire la peau à qqn.

flea [fliː] ◇ *n* puce *f* ▪ **to have ~s** avoir des puces ▶ **to send sb off with a ~ in his/her ear** *inf* [dismiss] envoyer balader qqn ; [scold] passer un savon à qqn.
◇ *comp* : **~ circus** cirque *m* de puces savantes.

fleabite ['fliːbaɪt] *n* piqûre *f OR* morsure *f* de puce ▪ *fig* [trifle] broutille *f*.

flea-bitten *adj* couvert de puces ■ *fig* [shabby] miteux.

flea collar *n* collier *m* anti-puces.

flea market *n* marché *m* aux puces.

fleapit ['fli:pɪt] *n inf* cinéma *m* OR théâtre *m* miteux ■ **the local ~** *hum* le cinéma du coin.

fleck [flek] ◇ *n* [of colour] moucheture *f*, tacheture *f* ■ [of sunlight] moucheture *f* ■ [of dust] particule *f*.
◇ *vt* [with colour] moucheter, tacheter ■ [with sunlight] moucheter ■ **hair ~ed with grey** cheveux *mpl* grisonnants.

fled [fled] *pt* & *pp* ▷ **flee**.

fledged [fledʒd] *adj* [bird] emplumé, ▷ **fully fledged**.

fledgeling ['fledʒlɪŋ] ◇ *n* **1.** [young bird] oisillon *m* **2.** *fig* novice *mf*, débutant *m*, - e *f*.
◇ *comp* [company, industry, political party etc] naissant.

flee [fli:] (*pret* & *pp* **fled** [fled]) ◇ *vi* s'enfuir, fuir ■ **to ~ from sb/sthg** fuir qqn/qqch ■ **to ~ from a house/country** s'enfuir d'une maison/d'un pays.
◇ *vt* [person, danger, temptation] fuir ■ [country, town] s'enfuir de.

fleece [fli:s] ◇ *n* **1.** [of sheep] toison *f* ■ **the Golden Fleece** MYTH la Toison d'or **2.** TEX peau *f* de mouton, laine *f* polaire, polaire *f*.
◇ *comp* [lining] en peau de mouton ■ **~-lined** [coat, jacket, gloves] doublé en peau de mouton.
◇ *vt* **1.** *inf* [cheat] escroquer **2.** [shear - sheep] tondre.

fleecy ['fli:sɪ] *adj* [material] laineux ■ [clouds] cotonneux.

fleet [fli:t] ◇ *n* **1.** NAUT flotte *f* ■ [smaller] flottille *f* **2.** [of buses, taxis] parc *m* ■ **a ~ of ambulances took the injured to hospital** plusieurs ambulances ont transporté les blessés à l'hôpital ▶ **car ~** parc *m* automobile.
◇ *adj lit* rapide ■ **~ of foot** aux pieds ailés.

fleet admiral *n* NAUT ≃ amiral *m* de France.

Fleet Air Arm *pr n* : **the ~** *l'aéronavale britannique*.

fleeting ['fli:tɪŋ] *adj* [memory] fugace ■ [beauty, pleasure] passager ■ **to catch a ~ glimpse of** apercevoir, entrevoir.

fleetingly ['fli:tɪŋlɪ] *adv* [glimpse] rapidement.

Fleet Street [fli:t-] *pr n rue de Londres, dont le nom sert à désigner les grands journaux britanniques.*

FLEET STREET

Cette rue de la City est traditionnellement associée à la presse. Même si, aujourd'hui, de nombreux journaux se sont établis dans d'autres quartiers de Londres, notamment les Docklands, *Fleet Street* continue à désigner le monde du journalisme.

Fleming ['flemɪŋ] *n* Flamand *m*, - e *f*.

Flemish ['flemɪʃ] ◇ *n* LING flamand *m*.
◇ *npl* : **the ~** les Flamands *mpl*.
◇ *adj* flamand.

flesh [fleʃ] *n* **1.** [of person, animal, fruit] chair *f* ■ **she looks better on TV than she does in the ~** elle est plus jolie à la télé qu'en chair et en os ▶ **I'm only ~ and blood, you know** je suis comme tout le monde, tu sais ■ **it's more than ~ and blood can bear** OR **stand** c'est plus que ce que la nature humaine peut endurer ■ **she's my own ~ and blood** c'est ma chair et mon sang ■ **to press the ~** *inf* [politicians, royalty etc] serrer des mains **2.** RELIG chair *f* ■ **pleasures/sins of the ~** plaisirs de la/péchés de chair ■ **the spirit is willing but the ~ is weak** l'esprit est prompt mais la chair est faible ■ **to go the way of all ~** retourner à la OR redevenir poussière **3.** [colour] couleur *f* chair.
◆ **flesh out** ◇ *vt sep* [essay, report etc] étoffer.
◇ *vi insep* [person] s'étoffer, prendre de la carrure.

flesh-coloured *adj* [tights] couleur chair.

fleshpots ['fleʃpɒts] *npl hum* & *pej* lieux *mpl* de plaisir.

flesh wound *n* blessure *f* superficielle OR légère.

fleshy ['fleʃɪ] (*comp* **fleshier**, *superl* **fleshiest**) *adj* [person] bien en chair ■ [part of the body, fruit, leaf] charnu.

flew [flu:] *pt* ▷ **fly**.

flex [fleks] ◇ *vt* [one's arms, knees] fléchir ■ **to ~ one's muscles** *liter* bander OR faire jouer ses muscles ; *fig* faire étalage de sa force.
◇ *n* [wire] fil *m* ■ [heavy-duty] câble *m*.

flexibility [ˌfleksə'bɪlətɪ] *n* [of object] flexibilité *f*, souplesse *f* ■ *fig* [of plan, approach] flexibilité *f* ■ [of person's character] souplesse *f* ■ **he has always shown a lot of ~** [in timing, arrangements] il s'est toujours montré très disponible OR arrangeant.

flexible ['fleksəbl] *adj* flexible, souple ■ *fig* [approach, plans, timetable etc] flexible ■ [person's character] souple ■ [as regards timing, arrangements] arrangeant ■ **~ working hours** horaires *mpl* (de travail) à la carte OR flexibles ■ **~ response** MIL riposte *f* graduée.

flexitime ['fleksɪtaɪm] *n (U)* horaires *m* à la carte OR flexibles ■ **to be on** OR **to work ~** avoir des horaires à la carte.

flick [flɪk] ◇ *n* [with finger] chiquenaude *f* ■ [with wrist] petit OR léger mouvement *m* ■ [with tail, whip, duster] petit OR léger coup *m* ■ **at the ~ of a switch** en appuyant simplement sur un interrupteur.
◇ *vt* [switch] appuyer sur ■ **don't ~ your ash on the floor** ne mets pas tes cendres par terre ■ **she ~ed the ash off the table** [with duster] d'un coup de chiffon, elle a enlevé la cendre de la table ; [with finger] d'une chiquenaude, elle a enlevé la cendre de la table.
◆ **flicks** *npl inf dated* **the ~s** le ciné, le cinoche.
◆ **flick over** *vt sep* [pages of book, newspaper etc] tourner rapidement.
◆ **flick through** *vt insep* [book, newspaper] feuilleter ■ **to ~ through the channels** TV passer rapidement d'une chaîne à une autre.

flicker ['flɪkəʳ] ◇ *vi* [flame, light] vaciller, trembler ■ [eyelids, TV screen] trembler ■ **the candle was ~ing** la flamme de la bougie vacillait.
◇ *n* [of flame, light] vacillement *m*, tremblement *m* ■ [of eyelids, TV screen] tremblement *m*.

flick knife *n* (couteau *m* à) cran *m* d'arrêt.

flier ['flaɪəʳ] *n* **1.** AERON [pilot] aviateur *m*, - trice *f* ■ **she's a frequent ~** elle prend souvent l'avion **2.** ORNITH : **the heron is an ungainly ~** le héron a un vol peu élégant **3.** *inf* SPORT [start to race] départ *m* lancé ■ [false start] faux départ *m* ■ **to get a ~** [good start] partir comme un boulet de canon **4.** *inf* [fall] vol *m* plané **5.** [leaflet] prospectus *m*.

flies [flaɪz] *npl* **1.** = **fly** *(sense 2)* **2.** THEAT dessus *mpl*, cintres *mpl*.

flight [flaɪt] *n* **1.** [flying] vol *m* ■ **capable of ~** capable de voler ■ **to be in ~** être en vol
2. [journey - of bird, spacecraft, plane, missile] vol *m* ■ **manned ~** [of spacecraft] vol habité
3. AERON [journey in plane - by passenger] voyage *m* ; [- by pilot] vol *m* ■ [plane itself] vol *m* ■ **how was your ~?** as-tu fait bon voyage? ■ **~ BA 314 to Paris** le vol BA 314 à destination de Paris ■ **when is the next ~ to Newcastle?** à quelle heure part le prochain vol pour OR à destination de Newcastle? ■ **all ~s out of Gatwick** tous les vols en provenance de Gatwick
4. [group of birds] vol *m*, volée *f* ■ [group of aircraft] flotte *f* aérienne
5. [fleeing] fuite *f* ■ **to take ~** prendre la fuite ■ **to put sb/the enemy to ~** mettre qqn/l'ennemi en fuite ▶ **the Flight into Egypt** la fuite en Égypte
6. [of stairs] : **~ (of) stairs** OR **steps** escalier *m* ■ **it's another three ~s up** c'est trois étages plus haut ■ **a short ~ of steps** quelques marches
7. *fig* **a ~ of the imagination** une envolée de l'imagination ■ **it was just a ~ of fancy** ce n'était qu'une idée folle
8. [on arrow, dart] penne *f*, empennage *m*
9. *phr* **to be in the first** OR **top ~** faire partie de l'élite.

flight attendant *n* [male] steward *m* ■ [female] hôtesse *f* de l'air ■ **one of our ~s** un des membres de l'équipage.

flight control *n* [place] contrôle *m* aérien ■ [people] contrôleurs *mpl* aériens.

flight crew *n* équipage *m (d'un avion)*.

flight deck *n* [of aircraft] poste *m* OR cabine *f* de pilotage, habitacle *m* ■ [of aircraft carrier] pont *m* d'envol.

flightless ['flaɪtlɪs] *adj* [bird] coureur.

flight lieutenant *n capitaine de l'armée de l'air britannique.*

flight number *n* numéro *m* de vol.

flight path *n* trajectoire *f* de vol.

flight plan *n* plan *m* de vol.

flight recorder *n* enregistreur *m* de vol.

flight sergeant *n sergent-chef de l'armée de l'air britannique.*

flight simulator *n* simulateur *m* de vol.

flighty ['flaɪtɪ] (*comp* **flightier**, *superl* **flightiest**) *adj* inconstant ■ [in romantic relationships] volage, inconstant.

flimsily ['flɪmzɪlɪ] *adv* [built, constructed] d'une manière peu solide, peu solidement.

flimsy ['flɪmzɪ] (*comp* **flimsier**, *superl* **flimsiest**) ◇ *adj* **1.** [material] fin, léger ■ [clothes, shoes] léger ■ [sthg built] peu solide ■ [paper] peu résistant, fragile ■ [toys, books] fragile **2.** [argument, case, excuse etc] léger.
◇ *n* [paper] papier *m* pelure ■ [with typing on it] double *m* sur pelure.

flinch [flɪntʃ] *vi* **1.** [wince, with pain] tressaillir ■ **without ~ing** sans broncher **2.** [shy away] : **to ~ from one's duty/obligations** reculer devant son devoir/ses obligations.

fling [flɪŋ] (*pret & pp* **flung** [flʌŋ]) ◇ *vt* lancer, jeter ■ **to ~ one's arms around sb's neck** jeter ses bras autour du cou de qqn ■ **he flung himself into an armchair** il s'est jeté dans un fauteuil ■ **I flung a few things into a suitcase** j'ai fourré quelques affaires dans une valise ■ **he flung himself off the top of the cliff** il s'est jeté du haut de la falaise ■ **with his coat casually flung over his shoulders** avec son manteau négligemment jeté sur ses épaules ■ **she flung the windows wide open** elle ouvrit les fenêtres en grand ■ **to ~ sthg in sb's face** *fig* envoyer qqch à la figure de qqn.
◇ *n* **1.** *inf* [attempt, try] : **to have a ~ at sthg** essayer de faire qqch **2.** [wild behaviour] : **youth must have its ~** il faut que jeunesse se passe ■ **to have a ~ with sb** *inf* [affair] avoir une aventure avec qqn **3.** [dance] *danse traditionnelle écossaise.*
◆ **fling about** *vt sep* [objects] lancer ■ **he flung his arms about wildly** [fighting] il se démenait violemment ; [gesticulating] il gesticulait violemment.
◆ **fling away** *vt sep* [discard] jeter (de côté).
◆ **fling back** *vt sep* [ball] renvoyer ■ [curtains] ouvrir brusquement ■ **she flung back her head** elle a rejeté sa tête en arrière.
◆ **fling off** *vt sep* [coat, dress] jeter.
◆ **fling out** *vt sep* [object] jeter, balancer ■ [person] mettre à la porte, jeter dehors.
◆ **fling up** *vt sep* [throw - in air] jeter en l'air ; [- to sb in higher position] lancer, envoyer ■ **he flung up his hands in horror** horrifié, il leva les bras au ciel.

flint [flɪnt] ◇ *n* [substance] silex *m* ■ [for cigarette lighter] pierre *f* à briquet.
◇ *comp* [tools, axe] en silex.

flintlock ['flɪntlɒk] *n* [rifle] mousquet *m* ■ [pistol] pistolet *m* à fusil.

flinty ['flɪntɪ] (*comp* **flintier**, *superl* **flintiest**) *adj* [rocks, soil] siliceux ■ *fig* [heart] de pierre.

flip [flɪp] (*pret & pp* **flipped**, *cont* **flipping**) ◇ *n* **1.** [little push, flick] petit coup *m* **2.** [turning movement] demi-tour *m (sur soi-même)* ■ [somersault - in diving] saut *m* périlleux ; [- in gymnastics] flip-flap *m* **3.** : **to have a (quick) ~ through a magazine** feuilleter un magazine **4.** [drink] *boisson alcoolisée à l'œuf.*
◇ *vt* **1.** [move with a flick] donner un petit coup sec à ■ **he flipped the packet shut** d'un petit coup sec, il a refermé le paquet **2.** [throw] envoyer, balancer ■ **to ~ a coin (for sthg)** décider (qqch) à pile ou face **3.** *phr* **to ~ one's lid** *inf* = **flip** *(vi sense 2).*
◇ *vi inf* **1.** [become ecstatic] être emballé, flasher ■ **to ~ over sthg** être emballé par qqch, flasher sur qqch **2.** [get angry] exploser, piquer une crise ■ [go mad] devenir dingue, perdre la boule ■ [under effects of stress] craquer.
◇ *adj inf* [flippant] désinvolte.
◇ *interj inf* mince, zut.
◆ **flip out** *vi insep inf* [get angry] exploser, piquer une crise ■ [become ecstatic] être emballé, flasher.
◆ **flip over** ◇ *vt sep* [turn over - stone, person] retourner ; [- page] tourner.
◇ *vi insep* [turn over - plane, boat, fish] se retourner ; [- page] tourner tout seul.
◆ **flip through** *vt insep* [magazine] feuilleter.

flip chart *n* tableau *m* à feuilles.

flip-flop ◇ *n* **1.** [sandal] tong *f* **2.** ELECTRON bascule *f* **3.** *US inf* [in attitude, policy] volte-face *f inv*, revirement *m* ■ **to do a ~** faire volte-face, retourner sa veste.
◇ *vi inf US inf* faire volte-face, retourner sa veste.

flippant ['flɪpənt] *adj* désinvolte ■ **he was just being ~** il ne parlait pas sérieusement.

flippantly ['flɪpəntlɪ] *adv* avec désinvolture.

flipper ['flɪpər] *n* **1.** [for swimming] palme *f* **2.** [of seal, penguin] nageoire *f.*

flip phone *n* téléphone *m* à clapet.

flipping ['flɪpɪŋ] *UK inf* ◇ *adj* [as intensifier] fichu ■ **you ~ idiot!** espèce d'idiot!
◇ *adv* [as intensifier] fichtrement ■ **not ~ likely!** il n'y a pas de risque!

flip side *n inf* [of record] face *f* B ■ *fig* [disadvantage] inconvénient *m.*

flip-top *adj* [mobile phone] à clapet.

flip top *n* [of packet] couvercle *m* à rabat.

flirt [flɜːt] ◇ *vi* **1.** [sexually] flirter ■ **he ~s with everybody** il flirte avec tout le monde **2.** *fig* **to ~ with danger/death** frayer avec le danger/la mort ■ **to ~ with an idea** jouer avec une idée.
◇ *n* **1.** [person] charmeur *m*, - euse *f* ■ **he's just a ~** il fait du charme à tout le monde, c'est un charmeur **2.** [act] badinage *m* amoureux.

flirtation [flɜː'teɪʃn] *n* badinage *m* amoureux ■ **his ~ with danger/the idea ended in disaster** *fig* il a frayé avec le danger/joué avec cette idée et cela a tourné au désastre.

flirtatious [flɜː'teɪʃəs] *adj* charmeur.

flit [flɪt] (*pret & pp* **flitted**, *cont* **flitting**) ◇ *vi* **1.** [bird, bat etc] voleter ■ [person] : **people were constantly flitting in and out of his office** les gens n'arrêtaient pas d'entrer et de sortir de son bureau ■ **to ~ from one subject to another** sauter d'un sujet à un autre, passer du coq à l'âne **2.** *UK dial* [move house] déménager.
◇ *n UK dial* déménagement *m.*

flitting ['flɪtɪŋ] *n UK dial* déménagement *m.*

float [fləʊt] ◇ *n* **1.** [for fishing line] bouchon *m*, flotteur *m* ■ [on raft, seaplane, fishing net, in carburettor, toilet cistern] flotteur *m* ■ [for swimming] planche *f* **2.** [vehicle - in parade, carnival] char *m* ; [- for milk delivery] voiture *f* du livreur de lait **3.** [cash advance] avance *f* ■ [business loan] prêt *m* de lancement ■ [money in cash register] encaisse *f* **4.** [drink] *soda avec une boule de glace.*
◇ *vi* **1.** [on water] flotter ■ [be afloat - boat] flotter, être à flot ■ **the raft/log ~ed down the river** le radeau/le tronc d'arbre a descendu la rivière au fil de l'eau ■ **the bottle ~ed out to sea** la bouteille a été emportée vers le large ■ **we ~ed downstream** [in boat] le courant nous a portés **2.** [in the air - balloon, piece of paper] voltiger ; [- mist, clouds] flotter ; [- ghost, apparition] flotter, planer ■ **music/the sound of laughter ~ed in through the open window** de la musique est entrée/des bruits de rires sont entrés par la fenêtre ouverte **3.** [currency] flotter.
◇ *vt* **1.** [put on water - ship, raft, platform] mettre à flot ; [- paper ship, toy] faire flotter ■ **the timber is then ~ed downstream to the mill** le bois est ensuite flotté jusqu'à l'usine située en aval **2.** [launch - company] lancer, créer ■ FIN [bonds, share issue] émettre **3.** FIN [currency] faire flotter **4.** *fig* [idea] lancer, proposer ■ [plan] proposer.

▸ **float about** *UK*, **float around** *vi insep* ***inf*** [rumours] courir ▪ [unoccupied person] traîner.
▸ **float off** ◇ *vt sep* [free - boat] remettre à flot.
◇ *vi insep* **1.** [be carried away - log, ship etc] partir *OR* être emporté au fil de l'eau ▪ [in the air - balloon, piece of paper] s'envoler **2.** ***fig*** [person] s'envoler, disparaître.

floatation [fləʊ'teɪʃn] = **flotation**.

floater ['fləʊtəʳ] *n* ***US*** [floating voter] (électeur *m*) indécis *m*, électrice *f* indécise.

floating ['fləʊtɪŋ] ◇ *adj* **1.** [on water] flottant ▪ **~ crane** ponton-grue *m* **2.** [not fixed] : **he has led a sort of ~ existence** il a mené une vie assez vagabonde ▶ **~ population** [within country] population *f* migrante ▪ **~ voters** (électeurs *mpl*) indécis *mpl* **3.** FIN [currency, exchange rate] flottant ▪ [capital] disponible **4.** COMPUT [accent] flottant ▪ **~ point** virgule *f* flottante.
◇ *n* **1.** [putting on the water] mise *f* à flot ▪ [getting afloat again] remise *f* à flot **2.** [of new company] lancement *m*, création *f* **3.** [of currency] flottement *m* **4.** [of new idea, plan] proposition *f*.

flock [flɒk] ◇ *n* [of sheep] troupeau *m* ▪ [of birds] vol *m*, volée *f* ▪ [of people] ***inf*** foule *f* ▪ RELIG ouailles *fpl* ▪ TEX bourre *f* ▶ **~ wallpaper** papier *m* tontisse.
◇ *vi* aller *OR* venir en foule *OR* en masse, affluer ▪ **the people ~ed around him** les gens se sont massés *OR* attroupés autour de lui.
▸ **flock together** *vi insep* [sheep] se regrouper, s'attrouper.

floe [fləʊ] = **ice floe**.

flog [flɒg] (*pret & pp* **flogged**, *cont* **flogging**) *vt* **1.** [beat] fouetter ▪ **we're just flogging a dead horse** ***inf*** nous nous dépensons en pure perte, nous nous acharnons inutilement ▪ **to ~ an idea/a joke to death** ***inf*** accommoder une idée/blague à toutes les sauces **2.** ***UK inf*** [sell] vendre.
▸ **flog off** *vt sep* ***UK inf*** [sell off] bazarder.

flogging ['flɒgɪŋ] *n* [beating] flagellation *f* ▪ LAW supplice *m* du fouet *OR* de la flagellation.

flood [flʌd] ◇ *n* **1.** ***liter*** inondation *f* ▪ **the Flood** le déluge ▪ **to be in ~** [river] être en crue **2.** ***fig*** [of applications, letters, offers] déluge *m* ▪ [of light] flot *m* ▪ **to be in ~s of tears** pleurer à chaudes larmes **3.** = **flood tide 4.** = **floodlight**.
◇ *vt* **1.** [unintentionally] inonder ▪ [deliberately] inonder, noyer **2.** AUT [carburettor] noyer **3.** [river - subj: rain] faire déborder **4.** *(usu passive)* ***fig*** [person - with letters, replies] inonder, submerger ▪ **to be ~ed with applications/letters** être submergé de demandes/lettres ▪ **to be ~ed in light** [room, valley] être inondé de lumière **5.** COMM : **to ~ the market** inonder le marché.
◇ *vi* **1.** [river] être en crue, déborder **2.** [land, area] être inondé **3.** ***fig*** [move in large quantities] : **refugees are still ~ing across the border** les réfugiés continuent à passer la frontière en foule *OR* en masse ▪ **light was ~ing through the window** la lumière entrait à flots par la fenêtre.
▸ **flood back** *vi insep* [people] revenir en foule *OR* en masse ▪ [strength, memories] revenir à flots, affluer ▪ **suddenly it all came ~ing back to me** soudain tous mes souvenirs ont reflué en masse.
▸ **flood in** *vi insep* [people] entrer en foule *OR* en masse, affluer ▪ [applications, letters] affluer ▪ [light, sunshine] entrer à flots.
▸ **flood out** ◇ *vt sep* inonder ▪ **hundreds of families have been ~ed out** [from homes] l'inondation a forcé des centaines de familles à quitter leurs maisons.
◇ *vi insep* [people] sortir en foule *OR* en masse ▪ [words] sortir à flots ▪ [ideas] se bousculer, affluer.

flood barrier *n* digue *f* de retenue.

flood-damaged *adj* abîmé *OR* endommagé par les eaux.

floodgate ['flʌdgeɪt] *n* vanne *f*, porte *f* d'écluse ▪ **to open the ~s** ***fig*** **: the new law will open the ~s to all kinds of fraudulent practices** cette nouvelle loi est la porte ouverte à toutes sortes de pratiques frauduleuses.

flooding ['flʌdɪŋ] *n (U)* inondation *f* ▪ [of submarine's tanks] remplissage *m* ▪ **~ is a major problem** les inondations sont un grand problème.

floodlight ['flʌdlaɪt] (*pret & pp* **floodlit** [-lɪt] *OR* **floodlighted**) ◇ *n* [lamp] projecteur *m* ▪ [light] lumière *f* des projecteurs ▪ **to play under ~s** jouer à la lumière des projecteurs.
◇ *vt* [football pitch, stage] éclairer (aux projecteurs) ▪ [building] illuminer *f*.

floodlit ['flʌdlɪt] *adj* [match, stage] éclairé (aux projecteurs) ▪ [building] illuminé.

floodplain ['flʌdpleɪn] *n* lit *m* majeur.

flood tide *n* marée *f* montante.

floor [flɔːʳ] ◇ *n* **1.** [ground - gen] sol *m* ; [- wooden] plancher *m*, parquet *m* ; [- tiled] carrelage *m* ▪ **to put sthg/to sit on the ~** poser qqch/s'asseoir par terre ▪ **the forest ~** le sol de la forêt, la couverture ***spec*** ▶ **to wipe the ~ with sb** ***inf*** [in match, fight] battre qqn à plate couture, réduire qqn en miettes ; [in argument] descendre qqn
2. [bottom part - of lift, cage] plancher *m* ; [- of sea, ocean] fond *m*
3. [storey] étage *m* ▪ **on the second ~** ***UK*** au deuxième étage ; ***US*** au premier étage
4. [for dancing] piste *f* (de danse) ▪ **to take the ~** aller sur la piste (de danse)
5. [in parliament, assembly etc] enceinte *f* ▪ [of stock exchange] parquet *m* ▪ **the ~ of the House** ≃ l'hémicycle *m* ▪ **to have/to take the ~** [speaker] avoir/prendre la parole ▪ **questions from the ~** questions du public ▶ **to cross the ~** [in parliament] changer de parti.
◇ *vt* **1.** [building, house] faire le sol de ▪ [with linoleum] poser le revêtement de sol dans ▪ [with parquet] poser le parquet *OR* plancher dans, parqueter ▪ [with tiles] poser le carrelage dans, carreler
2. ***inf*** [opponent] terrasser
3. ***inf*** [puzzle, baffle] dérouter ▪ [surprise, amaze] abasourdir.

floor area *n* [of room, office] surface *f*.

floorboard ['flɔːbɔːd] *n* lame *f* (de parquet) ▪ **to take the ~s up** enlever les lames du parquet.

floor cloth *n* serpillière *f* ▪ [old rag] chiffon *m*.

floor covering *n* [linoleum, fitted carpet] revêtement *m* de sol ▪ [rug] tapis *m*.

floor exercise *n* [in gymnastics] exercice *m* au sol.

flooring ['flɔːrɪŋ] *n (U)* **1.** [act] : **the ~ has still to be done** il reste encore le plancher à faire **2.** [material] revêtement *m* de sol ▪ **~ tiles** carreaux *mpl*.

floor lamp *n* ***US*** lampadaire *m*.

floor leader *n* POL *chef de file d'un parti siégeant au Sénat ou à la Chambre des représentants aux États-Unis.*

floor manager *n* **1.** [in department store] chef *m* de rayon **2.** TV régisseur *m*, - euse *f* de plateau.

floor-mounted [-'maʊntɪd] *adj* [gear lever] au plancher.

floor plan *n* plan *m*.

floor polish *n* encaustique *f*, cire *f*.

floor polisher *n* [machine] cireuse *f*.

floor show *n* spectacle *m* de cabaret.

floorspace ['flɔːspeɪs] *n* espace *m*.

floor tile *n* carreau *m*.

floorwalker ['flɔː,wɔːkəʳ] *n* ≃ chef *m* de rayon.

floozie, floozy ['fluːzɪ] (*pl* **floozies**) *n* ***inf*** traînée *f*.

flop [flɒp] (*pret & pp* **flopped**, *cont* **flopping**) ◇ *vi* **1.** [fall slackly - head, arm etc] tomber ; [- person] s'affaler, s'effondrer **2.** ***inf*** [attempt, idea, recipe] louper ▪ [fail - play, film] faire un four *OR* un bide ; [- actor] faire un bide.
◇ *n* ***inf*** [failure] fiasco *m*, bide *m* ▪ **this cake is a ~** ce gâteau est complètement loupé ▪ **he was a ~ as Othello** il était complètement nul dans le rôle d'Othello *OR* en Othello.

flophouse ['flɒphaʊs] (*pl* [-haʊzɪz]) *n* ***US inf*** asile *m* de nuit.

floppy ['flɒpɪ] (*comp* **floppier**, *superl* **floppiest**) ◇ *adj* [ears, tail, plant] pendant ▪ [collar, brim of hat] mou *(before vowel or silent 'h'* **mol**), molle *f* ▪ [trousers, sweater] flottant, large.
◇ *n* COMPUT disquette *f*.

floppy disk *n* COMPUT disquette *f*.

flora ['flɔːrə] *npl* flore *f*.
◆ **Flora** *pr n* MYTH Flore.

floral ['flɔːrəl] *adj* [arrangement, display] floral ▪ [pattern, fabric, dress] à fleurs, fleuri.

floral tribute *n* [gen] bouquet *m* OR gerbe *f* de fleurs ▪ [funeral wreath] couronne *f* de fleurs.

floret ['flɔːrɪt] *n* fleuron *m*.

florid ['flɒrɪd] *adj* **1.** [complexion] coloré **2.** [style, architecture] chargé ▪ [music] qui comporte trop de fioritures.

Florida ['flɒrɪdə] *pr n* Floride *f* ▪ **in ~** en Floride.

florin ['flɒrɪn] *n* [British, Dutch] florin *m*.

florist ['flɒrɪst] *n* fleuriste *mf* ▪ **~'s (shop)** fleuriste *m*.

floss [flɒs] ◇ *n* **1.** [for embroidery] fil *m* de schappe OR de bourrette **2.** [for teeth] fil *m* OR soie *f* dentaire.
◇ *vt* [teeth] nettoyer au fil OR à la soie dentaire.

flotation [fləʊ'teɪʃn] *n* **1.** [of ship - putting into water] mise *f* à flot ; [- off sandbank] remise *f* à flot ▪ [of logs] flottage *m* ▪ **~ rings** flotteurs *mpl* ▪ **~ tank** caisson *m* étanche **2.** [of new company] lancement *m*, création *f* ▪ FIN [of loan by means of share issues] émission *f* d'actions *(permettant de financer la création d'une entreprise)*.

flotilla [flə'tɪlə] *n* flottille *f*.

flotsam ['flɒtsəm] *n (U)* morceaux *mpl* d'épave ▪ **~ and jetsam** morceaux d'épave et détritus *mpl* ▪ **the ~ and jetsam of society** *fig* les laissés-pour-compte *mpl* de la société.

flounce [flaʊns] ◇ *n* [in garment] volant *m*.
◇ *vi* : **to ~ into/out of a room** entrer dans une/sortir d'une pièce de façon très théâtrale.

flounced [flaʊnst] *adj* [skirt] à volants.

flounder ['flaʊndəʳ] ◇ *vi* **1.** [in water, mud] patauger péniblement **2.** [in speech, lecture etc] perdre pied, s'empêtrer ▪ **somehow he ~ed through his speech** il est allé tant bien que mal jusqu'à la fin de son discours.
◇ *n* [fish] flet *m*.

flour ['flaʊəʳ] ◇ *n* farine *f*.
◇ *vt* saupoudrer de farine, fariner.

flourish ['flʌrɪʃ] ◇ *vi* [business, economy, plant] prospérer ▪ [arts, literature etc] fleurir, s'épanouir ▪ [in health] être en pleine forme OR santé.
◇ *vt* [wave, brandish - sword, diploma] brandir.
◇ *n* **1.** [in lettering, design] ornement *m*, fioriture *f* ▪ [in signature] paraphe *m*, parafe *m* **2.** [wave] grand geste *m* de la main ▪ **with a ~ of his sword** en faisant un moulinet avec son épée **3.** [in musical or written style] fioriture *f* ▪ **a little literary ~** un petit effet de style.

flourishing ['flʌrɪʃɪŋ] *adj* [business, trade] florissant, prospère ▪ [trader] prospère ▪ [in health] en pleine forme OR santé ▪ [plant] qui prospère.

flourmill ['flaʊəmɪl] *n* minoterie *f*.

floury ['flaʊərɪ] *adj* **1.** [covered in flour - hands] enfariné ; [- clothes] couvert de farine **2.** [potatoes] farineux.

flout [flaʊt] *vt* [orders, instructions] passer outre à ▪ [tradition, convention] se moquer de ▪ [laws of physics] défier.

flow [fləʊ] ◇ *vi* **1.** [liquid] couler ▪ [electric current, air] circuler ▪ **the river ~s into the sea** la rivière se jette dans la mer ▪ **I let the waves ~ over me** j'ai laissé les vagues glisser sur moi ▪ **blood was still ~ing from the wound** le sang continuait à couler OR s'écouler de la blessure ▪ **I let the sound of the music just ~ over me** *fig* j'ai laissé la musique m'envahir **2.** [traffic, crowd] circuler, s'écouler ▪ **new measures designed to enable the traffic to ~ more freely** de nouvelles mesures destinées à rendre la circulation plus fluide **3.** [hair, dress] flotter **4.** [prose, style, novel] couler ▪ [work, project] avancer, progresser **5.** [appear in abundance] : **the whisky ~ed freely** le whisky a coulé à flots ▪ **ideas ~ed fast and furious** les idées fusaient de tous côtés **6.** [tide] monter **7.** [emanate] provenir.
◇ *n* **1.** [of liquid] circulation *f* ▪ [of river] écoulement *m* ▪ [of lava] coulée *f* ▪ [of tears] ruissellement *m* **2.** [amount - of traffic, people, information, work] flux *m* ▪ [movement - of work] acheminement *m* ; [- of information] circulation *f* ▪ **there is normally a very heavy ~ of traffic here** il y a généralement beaucoup de circulation OR une circulation intense par ici **3.** [of dress, cape] drapé *m* **4.** [of prose, novel, piece of music] flot *m* ▪ **to be in full ~** [orator] être en plein discours ▪ **there's no stopping him once he's in full ~** il n'y a pas moyen de l'arrêter quand il est lancé **5.** [of the tide] flux *m*.
◆ **flow in** *vi insep* [water, liquid] entrer, s'écouler ▪ [contributions, messages of sympathy, people] affluer.
◆ **flow out** *vi insep* [water, liquid] sortir, s'écouler ▪ [people, crowds] s'écouler.

flowchart ['fləʊtʃɑːt] *n* organigramme *m*, graphique *m* d'évolution.

flower ['flaʊəʳ] ◇ *n* **1.** BOT fleur *f* ▪ **to be in ~** être en fleur OR fleurs ▪ **to come into ~** fleurir **2.** *fig* **the ~ of the youth of Athens/of the army** *lit* la fine fleur de la jeunesse athénienne/de l'armée ▪ **in the full ~ of youth** dans la fleur de la jeunesse **3.** CHEM : **~s of sulphur** fleur *f* de soufre.
◇ *vi* **1.** [plant, tree] fleurir **2.** *lit* [artistic movement, genre] fleurir, s'épanouir.

flower arrangement *n* art *m* floral ▪ [actual arrangement] composition *f* florale.

flower arranging [-ə'reɪndʒɪŋ] *n (U)* art *m* floral.

flowerbed ['flaʊəbed] *n* parterre *m* de fleurs.

flower child *n* hippy *mf*, hippie *mf (surtout des années soixante)*.

flower girl *n* **1.** [selling flowers] marchande *f* de fleurs **2.** *US & Scotland* [at wedding] *petite fille qui porte des fleurs dans un mariage*, ≃ demoiselle *f* d'honneur.

flowering ['flaʊərɪŋ] ◇ *n* **1.** [of plant, tree] floraison *f* **2.** [of artistic movement, talents] épanouissement *m*.
◇ *adj* [plant, tree - which flowers] à fleurs ; [- which is in flower] en fleurs ▪ **~ cherry** cerisier *m* à fleurs.

flower people *n* hippies *mpl (surtout des années soixante)*.

flowerpot ['flaʊəpɒt] *n* pot *m* de fleurs.

flower power *n pacifisme prôné par les hippies, surtout dans les années soixante*.

flower-seller *n* vendeur *m*, - euse *f* de fleurs.

flower shop *n* fleuriste *m*, boutique *f* de fleurs.

flower show *n* exposition *f* de fleurs ▪ [outdoors, on a large scale] floralies *fpl*.

flowery ['flaʊərɪ] *adj* **1.** [fields, perfume] fleuri ▪ [smell] de fleurs ▪ [pattern, dress, carpet] à fleurs **2.** [language, compliments] fleuri.

flowing ['fləʊɪŋ] *adj* [style, prose] fluide ▪ [beard, hair, robes] flottant ▪ [movement] fluide, coulant.

flown [fləʊn] *pp* ▷ **fly**.

fl. oz. *written abbr of* **fluid ounce**.

flu [fluː] *n* grippe *f* ▪ **to have ~** *UK*, **to have the ~** avoir la grippe, être grippé.

flub *inf vt* rater, louper.

fluctuate ['flʌktʃʊeɪt] *vi* [rate, temperature, results etc] fluctuer ▪ [interest, enthusiasm, support] être fluctuant OR variable ▪ [person - in enthusiasm, opinions etc] être fluctuant OR changeant ▪ **our production ~s from week to week** notre production est fluctuante OR varie d'une semaine sur l'autre.

fluctuating ['flʌktʃʊeɪtɪŋ] *adj* [rate, figures, prices etc] fluctuant ▪ [enthusiasm, support etc] fluctuant, variable ▪ [needs, opinions etc] fluctuant, changeant.

fluctuation [,flʌktʃʊ'eɪʃn] *n* fluctuation *f*.

flue [fluː] *n* [chimney] conduit *m* ▪ [for stove, boiler] tuyau *m* ▪ MUS [of organ] tuyau *m*.

fluency ['fluːənsɪ] *n* **1.** [in speaking, writing] facilité *f*, aisance *f* **2.** [in a foreign language] : **~ in French is desirable** la connaissance du français parlé est souhaitable ■ **I doubt whether I'll ever achieve complete ~** je doute d'arriver un jour à parler couramment **3.** SPORT [of play, strokes] facilité *f*, aisance *f*.

fluent ['flu:ənt] *adj* **1.** [prose, style] fluide ■ **he's a ~ speaker** il s'exprime aisément *OR* avec facilité **2.** [in a foreign language] : **to be ~ in French, to speak ~ French** parler couramment (le) français ■ **he replied in ~ Urdu** il a répondu dans un ourdou aisé *OR* coulant **3.** SPORT [play, strokes] facile, aisé.

fluently ['flu:əntlɪ] *adv* **1.** [speak, write] avec facilité *OR* aisance **2.** [speak a foreign language] couramment **3.** SPORT [play] avec facilité *OR* aisance.

fluff [flʌf] ◇ *n (U)* [on baby animal, baby's head] duvet *m* ■ [from pillow, material etc] peluches *fpl* ■ [collected dust] moutons *mpl* ■ **a bit of ~** des peluches ■ *inf UK dated* [pretty girl] une minette, une nana.
◇ *vt UK inf* [lines, entrance] rater, louper.
◆ **fluff up** *vt sep* [feathers] hérisser, ébouriffer ■ [pillows, cushions] secouer.

fluffy ['flʌfɪ] (*comp* **fluffier**, *superl* **fluffiest**) *adj* **1.** [material, sweater] pelucheux ■ [chick, kitten, hair] duveteux ■ [mousse, sponge] léger ■ [clouds] cotonneux ■ **~ toy** *UK* (jouet *m* en) peluche *f* **2.** [covered in fluff, dust] couvert de moutons.

flugelhorn ['flu:gəlhɔ:n] *n* bugle *m*.

fluid ['flu:ɪd] ◇ *adj* **1.** [substance] fluide, liquide **2.** [flowing - style, play, match] fluide **3.** [liable to change - situation] indécis, indéterminé ; [- plans] indéterminé.
◇ *n* fluide *m*, liquide *m* ■ **body ~s** sécrétions *fpl* corporelles ■ **to be on ~s** [patient] ne prendre que des liquides.

fluidity [flu:'ɪdətɪ] *n* **1.** [of substance] fluidité *f* **2.** [of style, play] fluidité *f* **3.** [liability to change - of situation, plans] indétermination *f*.

fluid ounce *n UK* ≃ 0,028 litre ■ *US* ≃ 0,03 litre.

fluke [flu:k] ◇ *n* **1.** *inf* [piece of good luck] coup *m* de bol *OR* pot ■ [coincidence] hasard *m* ■ **by (a) sheer ~** [coincidence] par un pur hasard **2.** [on anchor] patte *f*, bras *m* ■ [on whale's tail] lobe *m* de la nageoire caudale **3.** [flounder] flet *m* ■ [flatworm] douve *f*.
◇ *comp* [shot, discovery] heureux ■ **it was a ~ discovery** cela a été découvert par hasard.

fluky ['flu:kɪ] *adj inf* [lucky - shot, guess] heureux ; **what a ~ goal!** quel coup de bol, ce but!

flummery ['flʌmərɪ] *n (U) inf* [flattering nonsense] baratin *m*.

flummox ['flʌməks] *vt* déconcerter, dérouter.

flummoxed ['flʌməkst] *adj* : **I was completely ~** ça m'a complètement démonté.

flung [flʌŋ] *pt* & *pp* ▷ **fling**.

flunk [flʌŋk] *US inf* ◇ *vi* [in exam, course] se planter.
◇ *vt* [subj: student - French, maths] se planter en ; [- exam] se planter à.
◆ **flunk out** *US inf* ◇ *vi insep* [from college, university] se faire virer *(à cause de la médiocrité de ses résultats)*.
◇ *n* raté *m*, - e *f*.

flunk(e)y ['flʌŋkɪ] (*pl* **flunkies** *OR pl* **flunkeys**) *n* [manservant] laquais *m* ■ *pej* [assistant] larbin *m*.

fluorescence [flʊə'resəns] *n* fluorescence *f*.

fluorescent [flʊə'resənt] *adj* [lighting, paint] fluorescent ■ **~ tube** tube *m* fluorescent.

fluoridation [ˌflʊərɪ'deɪʃn] *n* fluoration *f*, fluoruration *f*.

fluoride ['flʊəraɪd] *n* fluorure *m* ■ **~ toothpaste** dentifrice *m* au fluor.

fluorine ['flʊəri:n] *n* fluor *m*.

flurried ['flʌrɪd] *adj* paniqué ■ **to get ~** perdre la tête, paniquer.

flurry ['flʌrɪ] ◇ *n* (*pl* **flurries**) **1.** [of snow, wind] rafale *f* **2.** *fig* **a ~ of activity** un branle-bas de combat ■ **to be in a ~ of excitement** être tout excité.
◇ *vt* (*pret* & *pp* **flurried**, *cont* **flurrying**) *(usu passive)* agiter, troubler.

flush [flʌʃ] ◇ *n* **1.** [facial redness] rougeur *f* ■ **to bring a ~ to sb's cheeks** [compliment, crude joke] faire rougir qqn ; [wine] mettre le feu aux joues à qqn ➤ **hot ~es** MED bouffées *fpl* de chaleur **2.** [of beauty, youth] éclat *m* ■ **in the full ~ of youth** dans tout l'éclat de la jeunesse ■ **in the first ~ of victory/success** dans l'ivresse de la victoire/du succès **3.** [on toilet - device] chasse *f* (d'eau) ■ **to pull/push the ~** tirer la chasse (d'eau) **4.** [in card games] flush *m*.
◇ *vi* **1.** [face, person] rougir **2.** [toilet] : **it's not ~ing properly** la chasse d'eau ne marche pas bien ■ **the toilet ~es automatically** la chasse d'eau fonctionne automatiquement.
◇ *vt* **1.** [cheeks, face] empourprer **2.** [with water] : **to ~ the toilet** tirer la chasse (d'eau) ■ **you ~ it by pushing this button/pulling this chain** pour actionner la chasse d'eau, appuyez sur le bouton/tirez sur la chaîne ■ **to ~ sthg down the toilet/sink** jeter qqch dans les toilettes/l'évier **3.** HUNT lever, faire sortir.
◇ *adj* **1.** [level] au même niveau ■ **~ with the side of the cupboard** dans l'alignement du placard ■ **~ with the ground** au niveau du sol, à ras de terre **2.** *inf* [with money] en fonds **3.** TYPO justifié.
◇ *adv* **1.** [fit, be positioned] : **this piece has to fit ~ into the frame** ce morceau doit être de niveau avec la charpente **2.** TYPO : **set ~ left/right** justifié à gauche/droite.
◆ **flush away** *vt sep* [in toilet] jeter dans les toilettes ■ [in sink] jeter dans l'évier.
◆ **flush out** *vt sep* **1.** [clean out - container, sink etc] nettoyer à grande eau ; [- dirt, waste] faire partir **2.** HUNT [animal] faire sortir, lever ■ *fig* [person] faire sortir ■ [truth] faire éclater.

flushed [flʌʃt] *adj* **1.** [person] rouge ■ [cheeks] rouge, en feu ■ **he was looking rather ~** il était plutôt rouge **2.** *fig* **~ with success** enivré *OR* grisé par le succès.

fluster ['flʌstəʳ] ◇ *vt* [make agitated, nervous] troubler, rendre nerveux.
◇ *n* : **to be in a ~** être troublé *OR* nerveux ■ **to get into a ~** se troubler, devenir nerveux.

flustered ['flʌstəd] *adj* troublé ■ **you're looking a bit ~** tu as l'air un peu agité ■ **to get ~** se troubler, devenir nerveux.

flute [flu:t] *n* **1.** MUS flûte *f* **2.** ARCHIT [groove on column] cannelure *f* **3.** [glass] flûte *f*.

fluted ['flu:tɪd] *adj* ARCHIT cannelé.

fluting ['flu:tɪŋ] *n* ARCHIT cannelures *fpl*.

flutist ['flu:tɪst] *US* = **flautist**.

flutter ['flʌtəʳ] ◇ *vi* **1.** [wings] battre ■ [flag] flotter ■ [washing] flotter, voler ■ [heart] palpiter ■ [pulse] battre irrégulièrement **2.** [butterfly, bird] voleter, voltiger ■ [leaf, paper] voltiger ■ **a butterfly ~ed in through the window** un papillon est entré par la fenêtre en voletant *OR* voltigeant.
◇ *vt* [fan, piece of paper] agiter ■ [wings] battre ■ **to ~ one's eyelashes at sb** aguicher qqn en battant des cils.
◇ *n* **1.** [of heart] battement *m* irrégulier, pulsation *f* irrégulière ■ [of pulse] battement *m* irrégulier ■ MED palpitation *f* ■ [of wings] battement *m* **2.** *inf* [nervous state] : **to be all in** *OR* **of a ~** être dans tous ses états **3.** AERON oscillation *f* **4.** *UK inf* [gamble] pari *m* ■ **I have the odd little ~ from time to time** [on horse] je fais un petit pari *OR* je parie de petites sommes de temps en temps ■ **to have a ~ on the Stock Exchange** tenter sa chance à la Bourse.

fluvial ['flu:vjəl] *adj fml* fluvial.

flux [flʌks] *n (U)* **1.** [constant change] : **to be in a state of constant ~** [universe] être en perpétuel devenir ; [government, private life etc] être en proie à des changements permanents **2.** MED flux *m* **3.** METALL fondant *m*.

fly [flaɪ] (*pl* **flies**, *pret* **flew** [flu:], *pp* **flown** [fləʊn]) ◇ *n* **1.** ENTOM & FISHING mouche *f* ■ **they're dropping like flies** *inf* [dying, fainting] ils tombent comme des mouches ■ **the ~ in the ointment** [person] l'empêcheur *m* de tourner en rond ; [problem] l'os *m* ■ **there are no flies on him** *inf* il n'est pas fou ■ **he wouldn't hurt a ~** il ne ferait pas de mal à une mouche ■ **I wouldn't mind being a ~ on the wall** *inf* j'aimerais bien être une petite souris ■ **to live on the ~** *US inf* vivre à cent à l'heure
2. *(often pl)* [on trousers] braguette *f*
3. [entrance to tent] rabat *m*
4. = **flysheet**

5. = **flywheel**
6. [in aeroplane] : **to go for a ~** faire un tour en avion
7. *UK inf phr* **to do sthg on the ~** [craftily, secretively] faire qqch en douce.
◇ *vi* **1.** [bird, insect, plane, pilot] voler ■ [passenger] prendre l'avion ■ [arrow, bullet, missile] voler, filer ■ **the first plane to ~ faster than the speed of sound** le premier avion à dépasser la vitesse du son ■ **it flies well** [plane] il se pilote bien ■ **he flies to Paris about twice a month** [passenger] il va à Paris en avion environ deux fois par mois ■ **soon we'll be ~ing over Manchester** nous allons bientôt survoler Manchester ■ **which airline did you ~ with?** avec quelle compagnie aérienne as-tu voyagé? ■ **the trapeze artist flew through the air** le trapéziste a voltigé ▶ **the bird had already flown** *fig* l'oiseau s'était envolé
2. [move quickly - person] filer ; [- time] passer à toute vitesse ■ [shoot into air - sparks, dust, shavings] voler ■ **I really must ~!** *inf* il faut vraiment que je file *OR* que je me sauve! ■ **he came ~ing round the corner** il a débouché du coin comme un bolide ■ **the past two years have just flown** les deux dernières années ont passé à toute vitesse *OR* se sont envolées ■ **time flies!, doesn't time ~!** comme le temps passe! ■ **the door flew open and there stood...** la porte s'est ouverte brusquement sur... ■ **to ~ into a rage** *OR* **temper** s'emporter, sortir de ses gonds ■ **to knock** *OR* **to send sb ~ing** envoyer qqn rouler à terre ■ **to knock** *OR* **to send sthg ~ing** envoyer qqch voler ■ **his hat went ~ing across the room** son chapeau a volé *OR* voltigé à travers la pièce
3. [kite] voler ■ [flag] être déployé ■ [in wind - flag, coat] flotter ; [- hair] voler
4. *phr* **to let ~** [physically] envoyer *OR* décocher un coup ; [verbally] s'emporter ■ **she then let ~ with a string of accusations** elle a alors lancé un flot d'accusations ■ **to (let) ~ at sb** [physically] sauter *OR* se jeter sur qqn ; [verbally] s'en prendre violemment à qqn ■ **to ~ in the face of sthg** [reason, evidence, logic] défier qqch.
◇ *vt* **1.** [plane, helicopter - subj: pilot] piloter ■ **to ~ Concorde** [pilot] piloter le Concorde ; [passenger] prendre le Concorde, voyager en Concorde
2. [passengers, people, goods] transporter en avion ■ [route - subj: pilot, passenger] emprunter ■ [airline] voyager avec ■ [distance - subj: passenger, pilot, plane] parcourir ■ [combat mission] effectuer ■ **to ~ the Atlantic** [pilot, passenger] traverser l'Atlantique en avion ; [plane] traverser l'Atlantique
3. [flag - subj: ship] arborer ■ [kite] faire voler
4. [flee from - the country] fuir ■ **to ~ the nest** [baby bird] quitter le nid ; *fig* quitter le foyer familial.
◇ *adj UK inf dated* [sharp] malin, - igne *f*, rusé.
◆ **fly about** *vi insep* [bird, insect] voleter, voltiger ■ [plane, pilot] voler dans les parages, survoler les parages.
◆ **fly away** *vi insep* [bird, insect, plane] s'envoler.
◆ **fly back** ◇ *vi insep* [bird, insect] revenir ■ [plane] revenir ■ [passenger] rentrer en avion.
◇ *vt sep* [person, passengers - to an area] emmener en avion ; [- from an area] ramener en avion ; [- to own country] rapatrier en avion.
◆ **fly by** *vi insep* [time] passer à toute vitesse.
◆ **fly in** ◇ *vi insep* **1.** [person] arriver en avion ■ [plane] arriver
2. [bird, insect] entrer.
◇ *vt sep* [troops, reinforcements, food] envoyer en avion ■ [subj: pilot - to an area] emmener ; [- from an area] amener.
◆ **fly off** ◇ *vi insep* **1.** [bird, insect] s'envoler ■ [plane] décoller ■ [person] partir en avion ■ **she's always ~ing off somewhere** elle est toujours entre deux avions
2. [hat, lid] s'envoler ■ [button] sauter.
◇ *vt sep* **1.** [from oil rig, island] évacuer en avion *OR* hélicoptère
2. [transport by plane - to an area] emmener en avion ; [- from an area] amener en avion.
◆ **fly out** ◇ *vi insep* **1.** [person] partir (en avion), prendre l'avion ■ [plane] s'envoler ■ **I'll ~ out to join you next Monday** je prendrai l'avion pour te rejoindre lundi prochain ■ **we flew out but we're going back by boat** nous avons fait l'aller en avion mais nous rentrons en bateau
2. [come out suddenly - from box, pocket] s'échapper.
◇ *vt sep* [person, supplies - to an area] envoyer par avion ; [- from an area] évacuer par avion.
◆ **fly past** *vi insep* **1.** [plane, bird] passer ■ [plane - as part of display, ceremony] défiler
2. [time, days] passer à toute vitesse.

flyaway ['flaɪə,weɪ] *adj* **1.** [hair] fin, difficile **2.** [person] frivole, étourdi ■ [idea] frivole.

flyblown ['flaɪbləʊn] *adj liter* couvert *OR* plein de chiures de mouches ■ [meat] avarié ■ *fig* très défraîchi.

flyby ['flaɪ,baɪ] (*pl* **flybys**) *n* **1.** [of spacecraft] *passage d'un avion ou d'un engin spatial à proximité d'un objectif* **2.** *US* = **flypast**.

fly-by-night *inf* ◇ *adj* **1.** [unreliable] peu fiable, sur qui on ne peut pas compter ■ [firm, operation] véreux, louche **2.** [passing] éphémère.
◇ *n* **1.** [person - irresponsible] écervelé *m*, - e *f* ; [- in debt] débiteur *m*, - trice *f* qui décampe en douce **2.** [nightclubber] fêtard *m*, - e *f*, couche-tard *mf*.

flycatcher ['flaɪ,kætʃə^r] *n* gobe-mouches *m inv*.

fly-drive *adj* : **a ~ holiday package** une formule avion plus voiture.

flyer ['flaɪə^r] = **flier**.

fly-fishing *n* pêche *f* à la mouche.

fly half *n* RUGBY demi *m* d'ouverture.

flying ['flaɪɪŋ] ◇ *n* [piloting plane] pilotage *m* ■ [travelling by plane] voyage *m* en avion ■ **I love ~** [as traveller] j'adore prendre l'avion ■ **to be afraid of ~** avoir peur de prendre l'avion ■ **he goes ~ at the weekends** le week-end, il fait de l'aviation.
◇ *adj* **1.** [animal, insect] volant ■ **~ machine** machine *f* volante **2.** [school] d'aviation ■ [staff] navigant ■ **~ lessons** leçons *fpl* de pilotage (aérien) ■ **~ time** heures *fpl* *OR* temps *m* de vol **3.** [fast] rapide ■ **she took a ~ leap over the fence** elle a sauté par-dessus la barrière.

flying boat *n* hydravion *m*.

flying bomb *n* bombe *f* volante.

flying buttress *n* arc-boutant *m*.

flying colours *npl* : **to pass with ~** réussir brillamment.

flying doctor *n* médecin *m* volant.

Flying Dutchman *n* : **the ~** [legend] le Hollandais volant ■ **'The Flying Dutchman'** *Wagner* 'le Vaisseau fantôme'.

flying fish *n* poisson *m* volant, exocet *m*.

flying fox *n* roussette *f*.

flying officer *n* lieutenant *m*, -e *f* de l'armée de l'air.

flying picket *n* piquet *m* de grève volant.

flying saucer *n* soucoupe *f* volante.

Flying Squad *pr n* : **the ~** *brigade de détectives britanniques spécialisés dans la grande criminalité*.

flying start *n* SPORT départ *m* lancé ■ **the runner got off to a ~** le coureur est parti comme une flèche ▌ *fig* **the campaign got off to a ~** la campagne a démarré sur les chapeaux de roues.

flying visit *n* visite *f* éclair.

fly kick *n* coup *m* de pied à suivre.

flyleaf ['flaɪli:f] (*pl* **flyleaves** [-li:vz]) *n* page *f* de garde.

fly-on-the-wall *adj* [documentary] pris sur le vif.

flyover ['flaɪ,əʊvə^r] *n* **1.** *UK* AUT pont *m* routier **2.** *US* = **flypast**.

flypaper ['flaɪ,peɪpə^r] *n* papier *m* tue-mouches.

flypast ['flaɪ,pɑ:st] *n UK* défilé *m* aérien.

flyposting ['flaɪ,pəʊstɪŋ] *n* affichage *m* illégal.

fly rod *n* canne *f* à mouche.

flyscreen ['flaɪskri:n] *n* moustiquaire *f*.

flysheet ['flaɪʃi:t] *n* **1.** [on tent] auvent *m* **2.** [circular] feuille *f* volante ■ [instructions] mode *m* d'emploi.

flyspecked ['flaɪspekt] *adj* sali par les mouches.

fly spray *n* bombe *f* insecticide.

flyswat ['flaɪswɒt], **flyswatter** ['flaɪ,swɒtəʳ] *n* tapette *f (pour tuer les mouches).*

fly-tipping *n* dépôt *m* d'ordures illégal.

flytrap ['flaɪtræp] *n* [plant] dionée *f*, tue-mouches *m inv* ■ [device] attrape-mouches *m inv.*

flyweight ['flaɪweɪt] ◇ *n* poids *m* mouche.
◇ *adj* de poids mouche.

flywheel ['flaɪwi:l] *n* TECH volant *m.*

FM *n* **1.** (*abbrev of* **frequency modulation**) FM *f* ■ **~ radio** (radio *f*) FM ■ **broadcast on ~ only** diffusion en FM seulement **2.** = **field marshal.**

FMD [,efem'di:] (*abbrev of* **foot and mouth disease**) *n* fièvre *f* aphteuse.

FO *n* **1.** = **field officer 2.** *UK* = **Foreign Office.**

foal [fəʊl] ◇ *n* [of horse] poulain *m* ■ [of donkey] ânon *m* ■ **the mare is in ~** la jument est pleine.
◇ *vi* mettre bas, pouliner.

foam [fəʊm] ◇ *n* [gen] mousse *f* ■ [of mouth, sea] écume *f* ■ [in fire-fighting] mousse *f* (carbonique) ■ **~ bath** bain *m* moussant.
◇ *vi* [soapy water] mousser, faire de la mousse ■ [sea] écumer, moutonner ■ **to ~ at the mouth** [animal] baver, écumer ; [person] baver, avoir l'écume aux lèvres ■ **she was practically ~ing at the mouth** *fig* elle écumait de rage.

foam-backed *adj* avec envers de mousse.

foaming ['fəʊmɪŋ] = **foamy.**

foam rubber *n* caoutchouc *m* Mousse®.

foamy ['fəʊmɪ] (*comp* **foamier**, *superl* **foamiest**) *adj* [liquid] mousseux ■ [sea] écumeux.

fob[1] [fɒb] (*pret & pp* **fobbed**, *cont* **fobbing**) *n* [pocket] gousset *m* ■ [chain] chaîne *f* (de gousset).
◆ **fob off** *vt sep* se débarrasser de ■ **he fobbed her off with promises** il s'est débarrassé d'elle avec de belles promesses ■ **don't try to ~ that rubbish off on me!** n'essayez pas de me refiler cette camelote!

fob[2], **FOB** (*abbrev of* **free on board**) *adj & adv* FOB.

fob watch *n* montre *f* de gousset.

focaccia [,fə'kætʃjə] *n* focacce *f (sorte de pain italien).*

focal ['fəʊkl] *adj* focal.

focal length *n* distance *f* focale, focale *f.*

focal plane *n* **1.** OPT plan *m* focal **2.** PHOT : **~ shutter** obturateur *m* focal *OR* à rideau.

focal point *n* OPT foyer *m* ■ *fig* [of room] point *m* de convergence ■ **the ~ of the debate** le point central du débat.

foci ['fəʊsaɪ] *pl* ▷ **focus.**

fo'c'sle ['fəʊksl] = **forecastle.**

focus ['fəʊkəs] ◇ *n* (*pl* **focuses** *OR pl* **foci** ['fəʊsaɪ]) **1.** OPT foyer *m* ■ **the picture is in/out of ~** l'image est nette/floue, l'image est/n'est pas au point ■ **bring the image into ~** fais la mise au point, mets l'image au point **2.** [centre - of interest] point *m* central ; [- of trouble] foyer *m*, siège *m* ■ **taxes are currently the ~ of attention** en ce moment, les impôts sont au centre des préoccupations ■ **let's try and get the problem into ~** essayons de préciser le problème **3.** MED siège *m*, foyer *m*.
◇ *vt* (*pret & pp* **focussed**, *cont* **focussing**) **1.** OPT mettre au point ■ **to ~ a camera (on sthg)** faire la mise au point d'un appareil photo (sur qqch) **2.** [eyes] fixer ■ **all eyes were focussed on him** tous les regards étaient rivés sur lui **3.** [direct - heat, light] faire converger ; [- beam, ray] diriger ■ *fig* [attention] concentrer.
◇ *vi* (*pret & pp* **focussed**, *cont* **focussing**) **1.** OPT mettre au point **2.** [eyes] se fixer, accommoder *spec* ■ **to ~ on sthg** [eyes] se fixer sur qqch ; [person] fixer le regard sur qqch ■ **I can't ~ properly** je vois trouble, je n'arrive pas à accommoder **3.** [converge - light, rays] converger ■ *fig* [- attention] se concentrer ■ **the debate focussed on unemployment** le débat était centré sur le problème du chômage ■ **his speech focussed on the role of the media** son discours a porté principalement sur le rôle des médias.

focussed ['fəʊkəst] *adj* : **she's very ~** elle sait où elle va.

fodder ['fɒdəʳ] *n (U)* [feed] fourrage *m* ■ *fig & pej* [material] substance *f*, matière *f.*

foe [fəʊ] *n lit & fml* ennemi *m*, - e *f*, adversaire *mf.*

foetal *UK*, **fetal** *US* ['fi:tl] *adj* fœtal ■ **in the ~ position** en position fœtale, dans la position du fœtus.

foetus *UK*, **fetus** *US* ['fi:təs] *n* fœtus *m.*

fog [fɒg] (*pret & pp* **fogged**, *cont* **fogging**) ◇ *n* **1.** [mist] brouillard *m*, brume *f* **2.** *fig* [mental] brouillard *m*, confusion *f* **3.** PHOT voile *f.*
◇ *vt* **1.** [glass, mirror] embuer ■ PHOT [film] voiler **2.** [confuse] embrouiller.
◇ *vi* : **to ~ (over** *OR* **up)** [glass, mirror] s'embuer ; PHOT [film] se voiler.

fog bank *n* banc *m* de brume.

fogbound ['fɒgbaʊnd] *adj* pris dans le brouillard *OR* la brume.

fogey ['fəʊgɪ] *n inf* schnock *m* ■ **he's a bit of an old ~** il est un peu vieux jeu.

fogged [fɒgd] *adj* PHOT voilé.

foggiest ['fɒgɪəst] ◇ *n inf* **I haven't the ~** je n'ai aucune idée, je n'en ai pas la moindre idée.
◇ *adj* ▷ **foggy.**

foggy ['fɒgɪ] (*comp* **foggier**, *superl* **foggiest**) *adj* **1.** [misty] brumeux ■ **it's ~** il y a du brouillard *OR* de la brume ■ **it's getting ~** le brouillard commence à tomber ■ **on a ~ day** par un jour de brouillard **2.** *phr* **I haven't the foggiest idea** *OR* **notion** je n'ai aucune idée, je n'en ai pas la moindre idée **3.** PHOT [film] voilé.

foghorn ['fɒghɔ:n] *n* corne *f OR* sirène *f* de brume ■ **a voice like a ~** une voix tonitruante *OR* de stentor.

fog lamp *UK*, **fog light** *US n* feu *m* de brouillard.

foible ['fɔɪbl] *n* [quirk] marotte *f*, manie *f* ■ [weakness] faiblesse *f.*

foil [fɔɪl] ◇ *n* **1.** [metal sheet] feuille *f OR* lame *f* de métal ■ **(silver) ~** CULIN (papier *m*) aluminium *m*, papier *m* alu ■ **cooked in ~** en papillote **2.** [complement] repoussoir *m* ■ [person] faire-valoir *m inv* ■ **he's the perfect ~ to his wife** il sert de faire-valoir à sa femme **3.** [sword] fleuret *m.*
◇ *vt* [thwart - attempt] déjouer ; [- plan, plot] contrecarrer.

foist [fɔɪst] ◆ **foist on** *vt sep* **1.** [pass on] : **you're not ~ing (off) your old rubbish on** *OR* **onto me** il n'est pas question que j'hérite de ta vieille camelote **2.** [impose on] : **she ~ed her ideas on us** elle nous a imposé ses idées ■ **he ~ed himself on us for the weekend** il s'est imposé *OR* invité pour le week-end.

fold [fəʊld] ◇ *vt* [bend] plier ■ **~ the blanket in two** pliez la couverture en deux ■ **she sat with her legs ~ed under her** elle s'assit les jambes repliées sous elle ■ **he ~ed his arms** il s'est croisé les bras ■ **she sat with her hands ~ed in her lap** elle était assise, les mains jointes sur les genoux ■ **the bird ~ed its wings** l'oiseau replia ses ailes ■ **he ~ed her in his arms** il l'a serrée dans ses bras, il l'a enlacée.
◇ *vi* **1.** [bed, chair] se plier, se replier **2.** *inf* [fail - business] faire faillite, fermer (ses portes) ; [- newspaper] disparaître, cesser de paraître ; [- play] être retiré de l'affiche ■ **the bakery ~ed last year** le boulanger a mis la clef sous la porte l'année dernière.
◇ *n* **1.** [crease] pli *m* **2.** [enclosure] parc *m* à moutons ■ [flock] troupeau *m* **3.** *fig* [group] : **to return to the ~** rentrer au bercail **4.** GEOL pli *m.*
◆ **fold away** ◇ *vt sep* plier et ranger.
◇ *vi insep* se plier, se replier.
◆ **fold down** ◇ *vt sep* [sheet] replier, rabattre ■ [chair, table] plier ■ **he ~ed down a corner of the page** il a corné la page.
◇ *vi insep* se rabattre, se replier.
◆ **fold in** *vt sep* CULIN incorporer.

◆ **fold over** ◇ *vt sep* [newspaper] plier, replier ▪ [sheet] replier, rabattre.
◇ *vi insep* se rabattre, se replier.
◆ **fold up** ◇ *vt sep* plier, replier.
◇ *vi insep* **1.** [chair, table] se plier, se replier **2.** = **fold** *(vi sense 2).*

-fold *in cpds* : **a ten~ increase** une multiplication par dix ▪ **your investment should multiply six~** votre investissement devrait vous rapporter six fois plus.

foldaway ['fəʊldə,weɪ] *adj* pliant.

folder ['fəʊldəʳ] *n* **1.** [cover] chemise *f* ▪ [binder] classeur *m* ▪ [for drawings] carton *m* ▪ **where's the ~ on the new project?** où est le dossier sur le nouveau projet? **2.** [circular] dépliant *m*, brochure *f* **3.** TYPO [machine] plieuse *f* **4.** COMPUT dossier *m*, répertoire *m*.

folderol ['fɒldərɒl] *n lit* **1.** *(U)* [nonsense] absurdités *fpl*, sottises *fpl* **2.** [trifle] bibelot *m*, babiole *f*.

folding ['fəʊldɪŋ] *adj* pliant ▪ **~ chair** [without arms] chaise *f* pliante ; [with arms] fauteuil *m* pliant ▪ **~ door** porte *f* (en) accordéon ▪ **~ seat** *OR* **stool** [gen] pliant *m* ; AUT & THEAT strapontin *m*.

foldout ['fəʊldaʊt] *n* encart *m*.

foliage ['fəʊlɪɪdʒ] *n* feuillage *m* ▪ **~ plant** plante *f* verte.

foliation [,fəʊlɪ'eɪʃn] *n* **1.** [of book] foliotage *m* **2.** [of metal] battage *m* ▪ [of mirror] étamage *m* **3.** BOT foliation *f*, feuillaison *f* ▪ GEOL foliation *f* **4.** [decoration] rinceaux *mpl*.

folic acid ['fəʊlɪk-] *n* acide *m* folique.

folio ['fəʊlɪəʊ] *(pl* **folios***) n* **1.** [of paper] folio *m*, feuillet *m* **2.** [book] (livre *m*) in-folio *m inv*.

folk [fəʊk] ◇ *npl* **1.** [people] gens *mpl* ▶ **city/country ~** les gens *mpl* de la ville/de la campagne **2.** [race, tribe] race *f*, peuple *m*.
◇ *n* MUS [traditional] musique *f* folklorique ▪ [contemporary] musique *f* folk, folk *m*.
◇ *adj* : **~ dance** *OR* **dancing** danse *f* folklorique ▪ **~ wisdom** la sagesse populaire.
◆ **folks** *npl inf* **1.** *esp US* [family] famille *f*, parents *mpl* ▪ **my ~s are from Chicago** ma famille est de Chicago **2.** [people] : **the old ~s** les vieux *mpl* ▪ **the young ~s** les jeunes *mpl* ▪ **hi ~s!** bonjour tout le monde!

folk etymology *n* étymologie *f* populaire.

folklore ['fəʊklɔːʳ] *n* folklore *m*.

folk medicine *n (U)* remèdes *mpl* de bonne femme.

folk memory *n* tradition *f* populaire.

folk music *n* [traditional] musique *f* folklorique ▪ [contemporary] musique *f* folk, folk *m*.

folk rock *n* folk-rock *m*.

folk singer *n* [traditional] chanteur *m*, - euse *f* de chansons folkloriques ▪ [contemporary] chanteur *m*, - euse *f* folk.

folk song *n* [traditional] chanson *f* *OR* chant *m* folklorique ▪ [contemporary] chanson *f* folk.

folksy ['fəʊksɪ] *(comp* **folksier**, *superl* **folksiest***) adj inf* **1.** *US* [friendly] sympa **2.** [casual - person] sans façon ; [- speech] populaire **3.** [dress, manners, town] typique ▪ [story] populaire.

follicle ['fɒlɪkl] *n* follicule *m*.

follow ['fɒləʊ] ◇ *vt* **1.** [come after] suivre ▪ [in procession] aller *OR* venir à la suite de, suivre ▪ **~ me** suivez-moi ▪ **he left, ~ed by his brother** il est parti, suivi de son frère ▪ **to ~ sb in/out** entrer/sortir à la suite de qqn ▪ **his eyes ~ed her everywhere** il la suivait partout du regard *OR* des yeux ▪ **his talk will be ~ed by a discussion** son exposé sera suivi d'une discussion ▪ **he ~ed his father into politics** il est entré en politique sur les traces de son père ▪ **she'll be a hard act** *inf* *OR* **hard person to ~** il sera difficile de lui succéder ▪ **to ~ suit** [in cards] fournir ▪ **she sat down and I ~ed suit** *fig* elle s'est assise, et j'en ai fait autant *OR* j'ai fait de même ▶ **just ~ your nose** [walk] continuez tout droit ; [act] suivez votre instinct
2. [pursue] suivre, poursuivre ▪ [suspect] filer ▪ **he ~ed them to Rome** il les a suivis *OR* il a suivi leurs traces jusqu'à Rome ▪ **~ that car!** suivez cette voiture! ▪ **I'm being ~ed** on me suit ▪ **we're continuing to ~ this line of enquiry** nous continuons l'enquête dans la même direction
3. [go along] suivre, longer ▪ **~ the path** suivez le chemin
4. [conform to - diet, instructions, rules] suivre ; [- orders] exécuter ; [- fashion] suivre, se conformer à ; [- sb's advice, example] suivre
5. [understand] suivre, comprendre
6. [watch] suivre *OR* regarder attentivement ▪ [listen] suivre *OR* écouter attentivement ▪ **to ~ a score** suivre une partition
7. [take an interest in] suivre, se tenir au courant de ▪ **have you been ~ing that nature series on TV?** avez-vous suivi ces émissions sur la nature à la télé?
8. [accept - ideas] suivre ; [- leader] appuyer, être partisan de ; [- cause, party] être partisan de, être pour
9. [practice - profession] exercer, suivre ; [- career] poursuivre ; [- religion] pratiquer ; [- method] employer, suivre.
◇ *vi* **1.** [come after] suivre ▪ **he answered as ~s** il a répondu comme suit ▪ **my theory is as ~s** ma théorie est la suivante ▪ **his sister ~ed hard on his heels** sa sœur le suivait de près *OR* était sur ses talons ▪ **revolution ~ed hard on the heels of the elections** la révolution suivit de très près *OR* immédiatement les élections ▪ **to ~ in sb's footsteps** *liter & fig* suivre les traces de qqn
2. [ensue] s'ensuivre, résulter ▪ **it doesn't necessarily ~ that he'll die** cela ne veut pas forcément dire qu'il va mourir ▪ **that doesn't ~** ce n'est pas forcément *OR* nécessairement vrai
3. [understand] suivre, comprendre
4. [imitate] suivre, faire de même ▪ **Paris sets the trend and the world ~s** Paris donne le ton et le reste du monde suit.
◆ **follow on** *vi insep* **1.** [come after] suivre
2. [in cricket] *reprendre la garde du guichet au début de la seconde partie faute d'avoir marqué le nombre de points requis.*
◆ **follow through** ◇ *vt sep* [idea, plan] poursuivre jusqu'au bout *OR* jusqu'à sa conclusion.
◇ *vi insep* [in ball games] accompagner son coup *OR* sa balle ▪ [in billiards] faire *OR* jouer un coulé.
◆ **follow up** ◇ *vt sep* **1.** [pursue - advantage, success] exploiter, tirer parti de ; [- offer] donner suite à
2. [maintain contact] suivre ▪ [subj: doctor] suivre, surveiller
3. [continue, supplement] faire suivre, compléter ▪ **~ up your initial phone call with a letter** confirmez votre coup de téléphone par écrit ▪ **I ~ed up your suggestion for a research project** j'ai repris votre suggestion pour un projet de recherche.
◇ *vi insep* exploiter un avantage, tirer parti d'un avantage.

follower ['fɒləʊəʳ] *n* **1.** [disciple] disciple *m*, partisan *m*, - e *f* ▪ **a ~ of fashion** quelqu'un qui suit la mode **2.** [supporter] partisan *m*, fan *mf* **3.** [attendant] domestique *mf* ▪ **the king and his ~s** le roi et sa suite.

following ['fɒləʊɪŋ] ◇ *adj* **1.** [next] suivant ▪ **the ~ day** le jour suivant, le lendemain ▪ **the ~ names** les noms suivants, les noms que voici **2.** [wind] arrière *(inv)*.
◇ *prep* après, suite à ▪ **~ your letter** COMM suite à *OR* en réponse à votre lettre.
◇ *n* **1.** [supporters] partisans *mpl*, disciples *mpl* ▪ [entourage] suite *f* ▪ **she has a large ~** elle a de nombreux partisans *OR* fidèles **2.** [about to be mentioned] : **he said the ~** il a dit ceci ▪ **her reasons are the ~** ses raisons sont les suivantes.

follow-my-leader *n UK jeu où tout le monde doit imiter tous les mouvements d'un joueur désigné.*

follow-on *n* [in cricket] *reprise de la garde du guichet par une équipe au début de la deuxième partie faute d'avoir marqué assez de points.*

follow-the-leader *US* = **follow-my-leader**.

follow-through *n* **1.** [of plan] suite *f*, continuation *f* **2.** [in ball games] accompagnement *m (d'un coup)* ▪ [in billiards] coulé *m*.

follow-up ◇ *n* **1.** [to event, programme] suite *f* ▪ [on case, file] suivi *m* ▪ MED [appointment] visite *f* *OR* examen *m* de contrôle ▪ **this meeting is a ~ to the one held in May** cette réunion est la suite de celle tenue en mai **2.** [bill, letter] rappel *m*.

◇ *adj* [action, survey, work] complémentaire ■ **a ~ visit** une visite de contrôle ■ **a ~ letter/phone call** une lettre/un coup de téléphone de rappel *OR* de relance ■ **~ care** MED soins *mpl* post-hospitaliers.

folly ['fɒlɪ] (*pl* **follies**) *n* **1.** *(U) fml* [foolishness] folie *f*, sottise *f* ■ **it would be ~ to continue** ce serait folie de continuer **2.** [building - ARCHIT] folie *f*.
◆ **follies** *npl* THEAT folies *fpl*.

foment [fəʊ'ment] *vt* MED & *fig* fomenter.

fond [fɒnd] *adj* **1.** [to appreciate] : **to be ~ of sb** aimer beaucoup qqn, avoir de l'affection pour qqn ■ **to be ~ of sthg** aimer beaucoup qqch, être amateur de qqch ■ **he's ~ of reading** il aime lire ■ [loving - friend, wife] affectueux, tendre ; [- parent] indulgent, bon ; [- look] tendre ■ **with ~est love** affectueusement **2.** [hope] fervent ■ [ambition, wish] cher **3.** *lit* [foolish] naïf.

fondant ['fɒndənt] *n* fondant *m*.

fondle ['fɒndl] *vt* caresser.

fondly ['fɒndlɪ] *adv* **1.** [lovingly] tendrement, affectueusement **2.** [foolishly] naïvement.

fondness ['fɒndnɪs] *n* [for person] affection *f*, tendresse *f* ■ [for things] prédilection *f*, penchant *m* ■ **~ for sb** affection pour *OR* envers qqn ■ **to have a ~ for drink** avoir un penchant pour la boisson.

fondue ['fɒndu:] *n* fondue *f* ■ **~ set** service *m* à fondue.

font [fɒnt] *n* **1.** RELIG fonts *mpl* baptismaux **2.** TYPO fonte *f* ■ COMPUT police *f*.

fontanelle *UK*, **fontanel** *US* [ˌfɒntə'nel] *n* fontanelle *f*.

food [fu:d] ◇ *n* **1.** *(U)* [nourishment] nourriture *f*, vivres *mpl* ■ **is there any ~?** y a-t-il de quoi manger? ■ **do you have enough ~ for everyone?** avez-vous assez à manger *OR* assez de nourriture pour tout le monde? ■ **they like spicy ~** ils aiment la cuisine épicée ■ **we need to buy some ~** il faut qu'on achète à manger *OR* qu'on fasse des provisions ■ **the ~ here is especially good** dans ce restaurant la cuisine est particulièrement bonne ■ **he's off his ~** il n'a pas d'appétit, il a perdu l'appétit ■ **~ for babies/for pets** aliments *mpl* pour bébés/pour animaux **2.** *fig* [material] matière *f* ■ **the accident gave her much ~ for thought** l'accident l'a fait beaucoup réfléchir **3.** HORT engrais *m*.
◇ *comp* [industry, product] alimentaire ■ [crop] vivrier ■ **~ hall** [in shop] rayon *m* d'alimentation ■ **~ processing** [preparation] traitement *m* industriel des aliments ; [industry] industrie *f* alimentaire ■ **~ stamp** *US* bon *m* alimentaire *(accordé aux personnes sans ressources)* ■ **~ value** valeur *f* nutritive ■ **Food and Agriculture Organization** Organisation *f* des Nations Unies pour l'alimentation et l'agriculture ■ **Food and Drug Administration** *US organisme officiel chargé de contrôler la qualité des aliments et de délivrer les autorisations de mise sur le marché pour les produits pharmaceutiques.*

food chain *n* chaîne *f* alimentaire.

food court *n partie d'un centre commercial où se trouvent les restaurants.*

foodie ['fu:dɪ] *n inf* fin gourmet *m*.

food mixer *n* mixeur *m*.

food parcel *n* colis *m* de vivres.

food poisoning *n* intoxication *f* alimentaire.

food processor *n* robot *m* ménager *OR* de cuisine.

foodstuff ['fu:dstʌf] *n* aliment *m*.

fool [fu:l] ◇ *n* **1.** [idiot] idiot *m*, - e *f*, imbécile *mf* ■ **you stupid ~!** espèce d'imbécile *OR* d'abruti ! ■ **what a ~ I am!** suis-je idiot *OR* bête! ■ **don't be a ~!** ne fais pas l'idiot! ■ **she was a ~ to go** elle a été idiote d'y aller ■ **I felt such a ~** je me suis senti bête ■ **he's no ~** *OR* **nobody's ~** il n'est pas bête, il n'est pas né d'hier ■ **to make a ~ of sb** [ridicule] ridiculiser qqn, se payer la tête de qqn ; [trick] duper qqn ■ **she doesn't want to make a ~ of herself** elle ne veut pas passer pour une imbécile *OR* se ridiculiser ● **more ~ you!** tu n'as qu'à t'en prendre à toi-même! ■ **there's no ~ like an old ~** il n'y a pire imbécile qu'un vieil imbécile ■ **a ~ and his money are soon parted** *prov* aux idiots l'argent brûle les doigts *prov* **2.** [jester] bouffon *m*, fou *m* **3.** CULIN *sorte de mousse aux fruits* ■ **raspberry ~** mousse *f* aux framboises.
◇ *vt* [deceive] duper, berner ■ **(I) ~ed you!** je t'ai eu! ■ **your excuses don't ~ me** vos excuses ne prennent pas avec moi ■ **he ~ed me into believing it** il a réussi à me le faire croire.
◇ *vi* **1.** [joke] faire l'imbécile *OR* le pitre ■ **I'm only ~ing** je ne fais que plaisanter, c'est pour rire ■ **stop ~ing!** arrête de faire l'imbécile! **2.** [mess with] : **to ~ with** [drugs] toucher à ; [machine] tripoter ■ **you'd better not ~ with him** on ne plaisante pas avec lui.
◇ *adj US inf* idiot, sot ■ **that's just the kind of ~ thing he'd do** c'est tout à fait le genre de bêtise *OR* d'ânerie qu'il ferait ■ **that ~ son of yours** ton imbécile de fils ■ **he was ~ enough to agree** il a été assez bête pour accepter, il a fait la bêtise d'accepter.
◆ **fool about** *UK*, **fool around** *vi insep* **1.** [joke] faire l'imbécile *OR* le pitre ■ **I'm only ~ing around** je ne fais que plaisanter, c'est pour rire **2.** [waste time] perdre du temps ■ **stop ~ing around and get up!** arrête de traîner et lève-toi! **3.** [mess with] : **to ~ around with** [drugs] toucher à ■ **stop ~ing around with that computer!** arrête de jouer avec *OR* tripoter cet ordinateur! **4.** *inf* [have sex] avoir *OR* se payer des aventures ■ **he's been ~ing around with a married woman** il batifole avec une femme mariée.

foolery ['fu:lərɪ] (*pl* **fooleries**) *n* [behaviour] bouffonnerie *f*, pitrerie *f*, pitreries *fpl*.

foolhardy ['fu:lˌhɑ:dɪ] *adj* [act, person] téméraire, imprudent ■ [remark] imprudent.

foolish ['fu:lɪʃ] *adj* **1.** [unwise] insensé, imprudent ■ **it would be ~ to leave now** ce serait de la folie de partir maintenant ■ **I was ~ enough to believe her** j'ai été assez bête pour la croire ■ **don't do anything ~** ne faites pas de bêtises **2.** [ridiculous] ridicule, bête ■ **the question made him look ~** la question l'a ridiculisé.

foolishly ['fu:lɪʃlɪ] *adv* [stupidly] bêtement, sottement ■ [unwisely] imprudemment ■ **~, I believed him** comme un idiot *OR* un imbécile je l'ai cru.

foolishness ['fu:lɪʃnɪs] *n* bêtise *f*, sottise *f*.

foolproof ['fu:lpru:f] *adj* [machine] indéréglable ■ [plan] infaillible, à toute épreuve.

foolscap ['fu:lzkæp] ◇ *n* ≃ papier *m* ministre.
◇ *comp* [paper, size] ministre *(inv)* ■ **~ envelope** enveloppe *f* longue ■ **~ pad** bloc *m* de papier ministre.

foot [fʊt] (*pl* **feet** [fi:t]) ◇ *n* **1.** [of person, cow, horse, pig] pied *m* ■ [of bird, cat, dog] patte *f* ■ **I came on ~** je suis venu à pied ■ **to be on one's feet** [standing] être *OR* se tenir debout ; [after illness] être sur pied *OR* rétabli *OR* remis ■ **on your feet!** debout! ■ **the speech brought the audience to its feet** l'auditoire s'est levé pour applaudir le discours ■ **to get *OR* to rise to one's feet** se mettre debout, se lever ■ **put your feet up** reposez-vous un peu ■ **to set ~ on land** poser le pied sur la terre ferme ■ **I've never set ~ in her house** je n'ai jamais mis les pieds dans sa maison ■ **we got the project back on its feet** *fig* on a relancé le projet ■ **it's slippery under ~** c'est glissant par terre ■ **the children are always under my feet** les enfants sont toujours dans mes jambes ● **~ passenger** piéton *m (passager sans véhicule)*
2. *phr* **feet first** *inf* les pieds devant ■ **to run *OR* to rush sb off their feet** accabler qqn de travail, ne pas laisser à qqn le temps de souffler ■ **I've been rushed off my feet all day** je n'ai pas arrêté de toute la journée ■ **he claims he's divorced – divorced, my ~!** *inf* il prétend être divorcé – divorcé, mon œil ! ■ **to fall *OR* to land on one's feet** retomber sur ses pieds ■ **to find one's feet** s'adapter ■ **to get a ~ in the door** poser des jalons, établir le contact ■ **to have a ~ in the door** être dans la place ■ **well at least it's a ~ in the door** au moins, c'est un premier pas *OR* contact ■ **to have a ~ in both camps** avoir un pied dans chaque camp ■ **to have one ~ in the grave** *inf* [person] avoir un pied dans la tombe ; [business] être moribond ■ **to have one's *OR* both feet (firmly) on the ground** avoir les pieds sur terre ■ **to have two left feet** *inf* être pataud *OR* empoté ■ **to have feet of clay** avoir un point faible *OR* vulnérable, avoir une faiblesse de caractère ■ **to put one's best ~ forward** [hurry] se dépêcher, presser le pas ; [do one's best] faire de son mieux ■ **to put one's ~ down** faire acte d'autorité ; AUT accé-

lérer ■ **to put one's ~ in it** *UK inf* *OR* **in one's mouth** *inf* mettre les pieds dans le plat ■ **she didn't put a ~ wrong** *UK* elle n'a pas commis la moindre erreur ■ **to get** *OR* **to start off on the right/wrong ~** être bien/mal parti ■ **the boot** *UK* *OR* **shoe** *US* **is on the other ~** les rôles sont inversés
3. [of chair, glass, lamp] pied *m*
4. [lower end - of bed, stocking] pied *m* ; [- of table] bout *m* ; [- of cliff, mountain, hill] pied *m* ; [- of page, stairs] bas *m* ■ **at the ~ of the page** au bas *OR* en bas de la page ■ **at the ~ of the stairs** en bas de l'escalier
5. [measurement] pied *m* (anglais) ■ **a 40-~ fall, a fall of 40 feet** une chute de 40 pieds ▶ **to feel ten feet tall** *inf* être aux anges *OR* au septième ciel
6. LIT pied *m*
7. *UK* MIL infanterie *f*.
<> *vt* [pay] : **to ~ the bill** *inf* payer (l'addition) ■ **who's going to ~ the bill?** qui va régler la douloureuse?

footage ['fʊtɪdʒ] *n (U)* **1.** [length] longueur *f* en pieds **2.** CIN [length] métrage *m* ■ [material filmed] séquences *fpl* ■ **the film contains previously unseen ~ of the war** le film contient des séquences inédites sur la guerre.

foot-and-mouth disease *n* fièvre *f* aphteuse.

football ['fʊtbɔːl] <> *n* **1.** *UK* football *m* ■ *US* football américain **2.** [ball] ballon *m* (de football), balle *f* ■ **the abortion issue has become a political ~** *fig* les partis politiques se renvoient la balle à propos de l'avortement.
<> *comp* [match, team] de football ■ [season] du football ■ **~ club** *UK* club *m* de football ■ **~ field** *US*, **~ pitch** *UK* terrain *m* de football ■ **~ game** *US* match *m* de football américain ■ **~ ground** *UK* terrain *m* de football ■ **~ hooligans** hooligans *mpl* ■ **~ fan** fan *mf* de foot ■ **the Football League** *association réunissant les clubs de football professionnels en Angleterre, excepté ceux qui jouent en première division* ■ **~ supporter** supporter *m* (de football).

football coupon *n* *UK* grille *f* de Loto sportif.

footballer ['fʊtbɔːləʳ] *n* *UK* joueur *m*, - euse *f* de football, footballeur *m*, - euse *f* ■ *US* joueur *m*, - euse *f* de football américain.

football pools *npl* *UK* pronostics *mpl (sur les matchs de football)* ■ **to do the ~** parier sur les matchs de football ■ **he won £20 on the ~** il a gagné 20 livres en pariant sur les matchs de football.

footbath ['fʊtbɑːθ] (*pl* [-bɑːðz]) *n* bain *m* de pieds.

footbrake ['fʊtbreɪk] *n* frein *m* à pied.

footbridge ['fʊtbrɪdʒ] *n* passerelle *f*.

footer ['fʊtəʳ] *n* COMPUT titre *m* en bas de page.

-footer *in cpds* : **the boat is a 15~** le bateau mesure 15 pieds *OR* environ 4,50 mètres.

footfall ['fʊtfɔːl] *n* bruit *m* de pas.

foot fault *n* TENNIS faute *f* de pied.

foothills ['fʊthɪlz] *npl* contreforts *mpl*.

foothold ['fʊthəʊld] *n* *liter* prise *f* de pied ■ *fig* position *f* avantageuse ■ **to gain** *OR* **to get a ~** *liter & fig* prendre pied ■ **to get** *OR* **to secure a ~ in a market** COMM prendre pied sur un marché.

footing ['fʊtɪŋ] *n* **1.** [balance] prise *f* de pied ■ **to get one's ~** prendre pied ■ **to keep/to lose one's ~** garder/perdre l'équilibre **2.** [position] : **to be on an equal ~** être sur un pied d'égalité ■ **let's try to keep things on a friendly ~** essayons de rester en bons termes.

footle ['fuːtl] ◆ **footle about** *UK*, **footle around** *vi insep inf* **1.** [potter] passer son temps à des futilités **2.** [talk nonsense] dire des bêtises, radoter.

footless ['fʊtlɪs] *adj* [tights] sans pieds.

footlights ['fʊtlaɪts] *npl* *liter* rampe ■ *fig* [the stage] le théâtre, les planches *fpl*.

footling ['fuːtlɪŋ] *adj inf* [trivial] insignifiant, futile.

footloose ['fʊtluːs] *adj* : **~ and fancy-free** libre comme l'air.

footman ['fʊtmən] (*pl* **footmen** [-mən]) *n* valet *m* de pied.

footmark ['fʊtmɑːk] *n* *UK* empreinte *f* (de pied).

footmen [-mən] *pl* ▻ **footman**.

footnote ['fʊtnəʊt] <> *n* [on page] note *f* en bas de page ■ [in speech] remarque *f* supplémentaire ■ **he was doomed to become just a ~ in the history of events** *fig* il était destiné à rester en marge de l'histoire des événements *OR* à ne jouer qu'un rôle secondaire dans l'histoire des événements.
<> *vt* annoter, mettre des notes de bas de page.

footpad ['fʊtpæd] *n* **1.** *arch* [thief] voleur *m* **2.** TECH [of spacecraft] semelle *f*.

footpath ['fʊtpɑːθ] (*pl* [-pɑːðz]) *n* [path] sentier *m* ■ [paved] trottoir *m*.

footplate ['fʊtpleɪt] *n* *UK* plate-forme *f (d'une locomotive)*.

footplateman ['fʊtpleɪtmən] (*pl* **footplatemen** [-mən]) *n* *UK* agent *m* de conduite.

footprint ['fʊtprɪnt] *n* **1.** [of foot] empreinte *f* (de pied) **2.** [of satellite] empreinte *f* **3.** COMPUT encombrement *m*.

footrest ['fʊtrest] *n* [gen] repose-pieds *m* ■ [stool] tabouret *m*.

footsie ['fʊtsɪ] *n inf* **to play ~ with sb** *UK* faire du pied à qqn ; *US* être le complice de qqn.

Footsie ['fʊtsɪ] *pr n inf* *nom familier de l'indice boursier du Financial Times.*

footslog ['fʊtslɒg] (*pret & pp* **footslogged**, *cont* **footslogging**) *vi inf* marcher (d'un pas lourd).

foot soldier *n* fantassin *m*.

footsore ['fʊtsɔːʳ] *adj* : **I was tired and ~** j'étais fatigué et j'avais mal aux pieds.

footstep ['fʊtstep] *n* [action] pas *m* ■ [sound] bruit *m* de pas.

footstool ['fʊtstuːl] *n* tabouret *m*.

footwear ['fʊtweəʳ] *n (U)* chaussures *fpl*.

footwork ['fʊtwɜːk] *n* **1.** SPORT jeu *m* de jambes ■ **it took some fancy ~ to avoid legal action** *fig* il a fallu manœuvrer adroitement pour éviter un procès **2.** [walking] marche *f* ■ **the job entails a lot of ~** le travail oblige à beaucoup marcher.

fop [fɒp] *n* dandy *m*.

foppish ['fɒpɪʃ] *adj* [man] dandy ■ [dress] de dandy ■ [manner] de dandy.

for [fɔːʳ] <> *prep*

A.

1. [expressing purpose or function] pour ■ **we were in Vienna ~ a holiday/~ work** nous étions à Vienne en vacances/pour le travail ■ **what ~?** pourquoi? ■ **I don't know what she said that ~** je ne sais pas pourquoi elle a dit ça ■ **what's this knob ~?** à quoi sert ce bouton? ■ **it's ~ adjusting the volume** ça sert à régler le volume ■ **'not suitable ~ freezing'** 'ne pas congeler'
2. [in order to obtain] pour ■ **write ~ a free catalogue** demandez votre catalogue gratuit *(par écrit)* ■ **~ further information write to...** pour de plus amples renseignements, écrivez à...
3. [indicating recipient or beneficiary] pour, à l'intention de ■ **these flowers are ~ her** ces fleurs sont pour elle ■ **I've got some news ~ you** j'ai une nouvelle à vous annoncer ■ **he left a note ~ them** il leur a laissé un mot, il a laissé un mot à leur intention ■ **'parking ~ customers only'** 'parking réservé à la clientèle' ■ **he often cooks ~ himself** il se fait souvent la cuisine ■ **see ~ yourself!** voyez par vous-même!
4. [indicating direction, destination] pour, dans la direction de ■ **they left ~ Spain** ils sont partis pour l'Espagne ■ **before leaving ~ the office** avant de partir au bureau ■ **she ran ~ the door** elle s'est précipitée vers la porte en courant ■ **he made ~ home** il a pris la direction de la maison ■ **the ship made ~ port** le navire a mis le cap sur le port
5. [available for] à ■ **'~ sale'** 'à vendre' ■ **these books are ~ reference only** ces livres sont à consulter sur place

B.

1. [indicating span of time - past, future] pour, pendant ; [- action uncompleted] depuis ■ **they're going away ~ the weekend** ils partent pour le week-end ■ **they will be gone ~ some time** ils

seront absents (pendant *OR* pour) quelque temps ▪ **I lived there ~ one month** j'y ai vécu pendant un mois ▪ **I've lived here ~ two years** j'habite ici depuis deux ans ▪ **you haven't been here ~ a long time** il y a *OR* voilà *OR* ça fait longtemps que vous n'êtes pas venu ▪ **we've known them ~ years** nous les connaissons depuis des années, il y a des années que nous les connaissons ▪ **she won't be able to go out ~ another day or two** elle devra rester sans sortir pendant encore un jour ou deux ▪ **can you stay ~ a while?** pouvez-vous rester un moment?
2. [indicating a specific occasion or time] pour ▪ **I went home ~ Christmas** je suis rentré chez moi pour Noël ▪ **it's time ~ bed** c'est l'heure de se coucher *OR* d'aller au lit
3. [indicating distance] pendant ▪ **you could see ~ miles around** on voyait à des kilomètres à la ronde ▪ **we walked ~ several miles** nous avons marché pendant plusieurs kilomètres
4. [indicating amount] : **they paid him £100 ~ his services** ils lui ont donné 100 livres pour ses services ▪ **it's £2 ~ a ticket** c'est 2 livres le billet ▪ **he's selling it ~ £200** il le vend 200 livres ▪ **I wrote a cheque ~ £15** j'ai fait un chèque de 15 livres

C.
1. [indicating exchange, equivalence] : **do you have change ~ a pound?** vous avez la monnaie d'une livre? ▪ **he exchanged the bike ~ another model** il a échangé le vélo contre *OR* pour un autre modèle ▪ **"salvia" is the Latin term ~ "sage"** "salvia" veut dire "sauge" en latin ▪ **what's the Spanish ~ "good"?** comment dit-on "bon" en espagnol? ▪ **F ~ François** F comme François ▪ **what's the M ~?** qu'est-ce que le M veut dire? ▪ **he has cereal ~ breakfast** il prend des céréales au petit déjeuner ▪ **I ~ one don't care** pour ma part, je m'en fiche
2. [indicating ratio] pour ▪ **there's one woman applicant ~ every five men** sur six postulants il y a une femme et cinq hommes ▪ **~ every honest politician there are a hundred dishonest ones** pour un homme politique honnête, il y en a cent qui sont malhonnêtes
3. [on behalf of] pour ▪ **I'm speaking ~ all parents** je parle pour *OR* au nom de tous les parents ▪ **I'll go to the meeting ~ you** j'irai à la réunion à votre place ▪ **the representative ~ the union** le représentant du syndicat
4. [in favour of] pour ▪ **~ or against** pour ou contre ▪ **who's ~ a drink?** qui veut boire un verre?
5. [because of] pour, en raison de ▪ **candidates were selected ~ their ability** les candidats ont été retenus en raison de leurs compétences ▪ **she couldn't sleep ~ the pain** la douleur l'empêchait de dormir ▪ **he couldn't speak ~ laughing** il ne pouvait pas parler tellement il riait ▪ **you'll feel better ~ a rest** vous vous sentirez mieux quand vous vous serez reposé ▪ **if it weren't ~ you, I'd leave** sans vous, je partirais
6. [indicating cause, reason] de ▪ **the reason ~ his leaving** la raison de son départ ▪ **she apologized ~ being late** elle s'est excusée d'être en retard
7. [concerning, as regards] pour ▪ **so much ~ that** voilà qui est classé ▪ **it may be true ~ all I know** c'est peut-être vrai, je n'en sais rien ▪ **I'm very happy ~ her** je suis très heureux pour elle
8. [given normal expectations] pour ▪ **it's warm ~ March** il fait bon pour un mois de mars
9. [in phrase with infinitive verbs] : **it's not ~ him to decide** il ne lui appartient pas *OR* ce n'est pas à lui de décider ▪ **it was difficult ~ her to apologize** il lui était difficile de s'excuser ▪ **this job is too complicated ~ us to finish today** ce travail est trop compliqué pour que nous le finissions aujourd'hui ▪ **there is still time ~ her to finish** elle a encore le temps de finir ▪ **~ us to arrive on time we'd better leave now** si nous voulons être à l'heure, il vaut mieux partir maintenant ▪ **the easiest thing would be ~ you to lead the way** le plus facile serait que vous nous montriez le chemin

D.
phr **oh ~ a holiday!** ah, si je pouvais être en vacances! ▪ **you'll be (in) ~ it if your mother sees you!** *inf* ça va être ta fête si ta mère te voit! ▪ **there's nothing ~ it but to pay him** il n'y a qu'à *OR* il ne nous reste qu'à le payer ▪ **that's the postal service ~ you!** ça c'est bien la poste!
◇ *conj fml* car, parce que.
◆ **for all** ◇ *prep phr* malgré ▪ **~ all their efforts** malgré tous leurs efforts.
◇ *conj phr* : **~ all she may say** quoi qu'elle en dise ▮ [as far as] : **~ all I know** autant que je sache ▪ **~ all the good it does** pour tout l'effet que ça fait.
◆ **for all that** ◇ *adv phr* pour autant, malgré tout.
◇ *conj phr fml* [although] : **~ all that he tried to persuade me** malgré tous ses efforts pour me persuader.
◆ **for ever** *adv phr* [last, continue] pour toujours ▪ [leave] pour toujours, sans retour ▪ **~ ever and a day** jusqu'à la fin des temps ▪ **~ ever and ever** à tout jamais, éternellement ▪ **~ ever and ever, amen** pour les siècles des siècles, amen.

fora ['fɔ:rə] *pl* ▻ **forum**.

forage ['fɒrɪdʒ] ◇ *n* **1.** [search] fouille *f* ▪ [food] fourrage *m* **2.** MIL [raid] raid *m*, incursion *f*.
◇ *vi* **1.** [search] fourrager, fouiller ▪ **to ~ for sthg** fouiller pour trouver qqch **2.** MIL [raid] faire un raid *OR* une incursion.
◇ *vt* **1.** [obtain] trouver en fourrageant **2.** [feed] donner du fourrage à, donner à manger à.

forage cap *n* calot *m*.

forasmuch as [fərəz'mʌtʃ-] *conj arch & lit* vu que.

foray ['fɒreɪ] ◇ *n* MIL [raid] raid *m*, incursion *f* ▪ [excursion] incursion *f* ▪ **he made a ~ into politics** il a fait une incursion dans la politique.
◇ *vi* faire un raid *OR* une incursion.

forbad(e) [fə'bæd] *pt* ▻ **forbid**.

forbear [fɔ:'beəʳ] (*pret* **forbore** [-'bɔ:ʳ], *pp* **forborne** [-'bɔ:n]) *fml* ◇ *vi* [abstain] s'abstenir ▪ **to ~ from doing** *OR* **to do sthg** se garder *OR* s'abstenir de faire qqch.
◇ *vt* renoncer à, se priver de.
◇ *n* = **forebear**.

forbearance [fɔ:'beərəns] *n* **1.** [patience] patience *f*, tolérance *f* **2.** [restraint] abstention *f*.

forbearing [fɔ:'beərɪŋ] *adj* patient.

forbid [fə'bɪd] (*pret* **forbad** *OR* **forbade** [fə'bæd], *pp* **forbidden** [-'bɪdn]) *vt* **1.** [not allow] interdire, défendre ▪ **to ~ sb alcohol** interdire l'alcool à qqn ▪ **to ~ sb to do sthg** défendre *OR* interdire à qqn de faire qqch ▪ **students are forbidden to talk during exams** les étudiants n'ont pas le droit de parler pendant les examens ▪ **it is strictly forbidden to smoke** il est formellement interdit de fumer **2.** [prevent] empêcher ▪ **God ~!** pourvu que non! ▪ **Heaven ~ (that) all her family should come too!** pourvu qu'elle ne vienne pas avec toute sa famille!

forbidden [-'bɪdn] ◇ *pp* ▻ **forbid**.
◇ *adj* interdit, défendu.

forbidden fruit *n* fruit *m* défendu.

forbidding [fə'bɪdɪŋ] *adj* [building, look, sky] menaçant ▪ [person] sévère, menaçant.

forbore [-'bɔ:ʳ] *pt* ▻ **forbear**.

forborne [-'bɔ:n] *pp* ▻ **forbear**.

force [fɔ:s] ◇ *vt* **1.** [compel] forcer, obliger ▪ **to ~ sb to do sthg** contraindre *OR* forcer qqn à faire qqch ▪ **don't ~ yourself!** *hum* ne te force surtout pas! ▸ **to ~ sb's hand** forcer la main à qqn
2. [wrest] arracher, extorquer ▪ **I ~d a confession from** *OR* **out of him** je lui ai arraché une confession
3. [impose] imposer ▪ **to ~ sthg on** *OR* **upon sb** imposer qqch à qqn ▪ **to ~ o.s. on sb** imposer sa présence à qqn ▪ **he ~d himself** *OR* **his attentions on her** il l'a poursuivie de ses assiduités
4. [push] : **to ~ one's way into a building** entrer *OR* pénétrer de force dans un immeuble ▪ **I ~d my way through the crowd** je me suis frayé un chemin *OR* passage à travers la foule ▪ **don't ~ it** ne force pas ▪ **the car ~d us off the road** la voiture nous a forcés à quitter la route ▸ **to ~ sb into a corner** *liter* pousser qqn dans un coin ; *fig* mettre qqn au pied du mur
5. [break open] forcer ▪ **to ~ open a door/lock** forcer une porte/une serrure
6. [answer, smile] forcer ▪ **she managed to ~ a smile** elle eut un sourire forcé
7. [hurry] forcer, hâter ▪ **to ~ flowers/plants** forcer des fleurs/des plantes ▪ **we ~d the pace** nous avons forcé l'allure *OR* le pas
8. [strain - metaphor, voice] forcer ; [- word] forcer le sens de.

◇ *n* **1.** [power] force *f*, puissance *f* ■ **television could be a ~ for good** la télévision pourrait avoir une bonne influence ■ **France is a ~ to be reckoned with** la France est une puissance *OR* force avec laquelle il faut compter
2. [strength] force *f* ■ [violence] force *f*, violence *f* ■ **they used ~ to control the crowd** ils ont employé la force pour contrôler la foule ■ **I hit it with as much ~ as I could muster** je l'ai frappé aussi fort que j'ai pu
3. [of argument, word] force *f*, poids *m*
4. *phr* **~ of circumstances** force *f* des choses ■ **by** *OR* **from ~ of habit** par la force de l'habitude ■ **by sheer ~** de vive force ■ **she managed it through sheer ~ of will** elle y est arrivée uniquement à force de volonté ■ **the law comes into ~ this year** la loi entre en vigueur cette année
5. PHYS force *f* ■ **the ~ of gravity** la pesanteur
6. [of people] force *f* ■ **the allied ~s** les armées *fpl* alliées, les alliés *mpl* ■ **the (armed) ~s** les forces armées ■ **the (police) ~** les forces de police.

◆ **in force** ◇ *adj phr* en application, en vigueur ■ **the rules now in ~** le règlement en vigueur.
◇ *adv phr* en force ■ **the students were there in ~** les étudiants étaient venus en force *OR* en grand nombre ■ **in full ~** au grand complet.

◆ **force back** *vt sep* **1.** [push back] repousser, refouler ■ MIL faire reculer
2. [repress] réprimer ■ **I ~d back my tears** j'ai refoulé mes larmes.

◆ **force down** *vt sep* **1.** [push down] faire descendre (de force) ■ **he ~d down the lid of the box** il a fermé la boîte en forçant ■ **to ~ down prices** faire baisser les prix
2. [plane] forcer à atterrir
3. [food] se forcer à manger *OR* à avaler ■ **more cake? – I expect I could ~ down another slice** *hum* encore un peu de gâteau? – ma foi, je suis sûr que j'ai encore un peu de place pour un autre petit morceau.

◆ **force out** *vt sep* **1.** [push out] faire sortir (de force) ■ **the opposition ~d him out** *fig* l'opposition l'a poussé dehors
2. [remark] : **he ~d out an apology** il s'est excusé du bout des lèvres.

◆ **force up** *vt sep* faire monter (de force).

forced [fɔːst] *adj* **1.** [compulsory] forcé ■ **~ labour** travail *m* forcé ■ **a ~ landing** un atterrissage forcé ■ **~ march** MIL marche *f* forcée **2.** [smile] forcé, artificiel ■ **he gave a ~ laugh** il a ri du bout des lèvres **3.** [plant] forcé.

force-feed *vt* nourrir de force ■ [livestock] gaver.

forceful ['fɔːsfʊl] *adj* [person] énergique, fort ■ [argument, style] puissant ■ [impression] puissant.

forcefully ['fɔːsfʊlɪ] *adv* avec force, avec vigueur.

forcefulness ['fɔːsfʊlnɪs] *n* vigueur *f*.

forcemeat ['fɔːsmiːt] *n* farce *f*.

forceps ['fɔːseps] *npl* : **(a pair of) ~** un forceps ■ **~ delivery** accouchement *m* au forceps.

forcible ['fɔːsəbl] *adj* **1.** [by force] de *OR* par force ■ **~ entry** LAW effraction *f* **2.** [powerful - argument, style] puissant ; [- personality] puissant, fort ; [- speaker] puissant **3.** [emphatic - opinion] catégorique ; [- wish] vif.

forcibly ['fɔːsəblɪ] *adv* **1.** [by force] de force, par la force ■ **they were ~ removed from the house** on les a fait sortir de force de la maison **2.** [argue, speak] énergiquement, avec vigueur *OR* force **3.** [recommend, remind] fortement.

forcing house *n* forcerie *f*, serre *f* chaude.

ford [fɔːd] ◇ *n* gué *m*.
◇ *vt* passer *OR* traverser à gué.

fore [fɔːʳ] ◇ *adj* **1.** [front] à l'avant, antérieur ■ **the ~ and hind legs** les pattes de devant et de derrière **2.** NAUT à l'avant.
◇ *n* NAUT avant *m*, devant *m* ■ *fig* **to come to the ~** [person] percer, commencer à être connu ; [courage] se manifester, se révéler ■ **the revolt brought these issues to the ~** la révolte a mis ces problèmes en évidence, la révolte a attiré l'attention sur ces problèmes.
◇ *adv* NAUT à l'avant ■ **~ and aft** de l'avant à l'arrière.
◇ *interj* [in golf] : **~!** attention!, gare!

fore-and-aft *adj* NAUT aurique.

forearm ◇ *n* ['fɔːr,ɑːm] avant-bras *m*.
◇ *vt* [fɔːr'ɑːm] prémunir.

forebear ['fɔːbeəʳ] *n* ancêtre *m* ■ **our ~s** nos aïeux *mpl*.

forebode [fɔː'bəʊd] *vt fml* augurer.

foreboding [fɔː'bəʊdɪŋ] *n* [feeling] pressentiment *m*, prémonition *f* ■ [omen] présage *m*, augure *m* ■ **she had a ~ that things would go seriously wrong** elle a eu le pressentiment que les choses allaient très mal tourner ■ **her laughter filled me with ~** ses rires m'ont rendu très appréhensif.

forecast ['fɔːkɑːst] (*pret & pp* **forecast** *OR* **forecasted**) ◇ *vt* [gen - METEOR] prévoir ■ [in betting] pronostiquer.
◇ *n* **1.** [gen - METEOR] prévision *f* ■ **economic ~** prévisions économiques ■ **the weather ~** le bulletin météorologique, la météo **2.** [in betting] pronostic *m*.

forecaster ['fɔːkɑːstəʳ] *n* pronostiqueur *m*, -euse *f* ■ **weather ~** météorologiste *mf*, météorologue *mf*.

forecastle ['fəʊksl] *n* NAUT gaillard *m* d'avant ■ [in merchant navy] poste *m* d'équipage.

foreclose [fɔː'kləʊz] ◇ *vt* [mortgage] saisir.
◇ *vi* saisir le bien hypothéqué ■ **to ~ on sb** saisir les biens de qqn ■ **to ~ on a mortgage** saisir un bien hypothéqué.

foreclosure [fɔː'kləʊʒəʳ] *n* forclusion *f*.

forecourt ['fɔːkɔːt] *n* avant-cour *f*, cour *f* de devant ■ [of petrol station] devant *m* ■ **~ prices** prix à la pompe.

forefather ['fɔː,fɑːðəʳ] *n* ancêtre *m* ■ **our ~s** nos aïeux *mpl*.

forefinger ['fɔː,fɪŋgəʳ] *n* index *m*.

forefront ['fɔːfrʌnt] *n* premier rang *m* ■ **to be at** *OR* **in the ~ of sthg** [country, firm] être au premier rang de qqch ; [person] être une sommité dans qqch.

foregather [fɔː'gæðəʳ] = **forgather**.

forego [fɔː'gəʊ] (*pret* **forewent** [-'went], *pp* **foregone** [-'gɒn]) = **forgo**.

foregone [-'gɒn] *pp* ▷ **forego**.

foregone conclusion ['fɔːgɒn-] *n* issue *f* certaine *OR* prévisible ■ **it was a ~** c'était gagné d'avance.

foreground ['fɔːgraʊnd] ◇ *n* [gen - ART] & PHOT premier plan ■ **in the ~** au premier plan.
◇ *vt* privilégier.

forehand ['fɔːhænd] ◇ *n* **1.** SPORT coup *m* droit **2.** [of horse] avant-main *m*.
◇ *adj* : **~ volley** volée *f* de face.

forehead ['fɔːhed] *n* front *m*.

foreign ['fɒrən] *adj* **1.** [country, language, person] étranger ■ [aid, visit - to country] à l'étranger ; [- from country] de l'étranger ■ [products] de l'étranger ■ [trade] extérieur ■ **students from ~ countries** des étudiants venant de l'étranger ■ **~ relations** relations avec l'étranger ● **~ affairs** affaires *fpl* étrangères ■ **~ agent** [spy] agent *m* étranger ; COMM représentant *m*, -e *f* à l'étranger ■ **~ competition** concurrence *f* étrangère ■ **~ correspondent** correspondant *m*, -e *f* à l'étranger ■ **~ currency** *OR* **exchange** devises *fpl* étrangères ■ **~ exchange market** marché *m* des changes ■ **~ investment** investissement *m* étranger ■ **~ minister** ministre *m* des Affaires étrangères ■ **~ policy** politique *f* étrangère *OR* extérieure **2.** [alien] étranger ■ **such thinking is ~ to them** un tel raisonnement leur est étranger ■ **a ~ body, ~ matter** un corps étranger.

foreigner ['fɒrənəʳ] *n* étranger *m*, -ère *f*.

Foreign Legion *n* : **the ~** la Légion (étrangère).

Foreign Office *n* : **the Foreign (and Commonwealth) Office** *le ministère britannique des Affaires étrangères*.

Foreign Secretary, Foreign and Commonwealth Secretary *n* : **the ~** *le ministre britannique des Affaires étrangères*.

foreign service *n* US service *m* diplomatique.

foreknowledge [,fɔː'nɒlɪdʒ] *n fml* connaissance *f* anticipée, prescience *f* ■ **I had no ~ of her plans** je ne savais pas à l'avance quels étaient ses projets.

foreleg ['fɔ:leg] *n* [of horse] jambe *f* de devant *OR* antérieure ■ [of dog, cat] patte *f* de devant *OR* antérieure.

forelock ['fɔ:lɒk] *n* [of person] mèche *f*, toupet *m* ■ [of horse] toupet *m* ■ **to touch** *OR* **to tug one's ~** *liter* saluer en portant la main au front ; *fig* faire des courbettes.

foreman ['fɔ:mən] (*pl* **foremen** [-mən]) *n* INDUST contremaître *m*, chef *m* d'équipe ■ LAW président *m*, - e *f*.

foremast ['fɔ:mɑ:st] *n* mât *m* de misaine.

foremost ['fɔ:məʊst] <> *adj* [first - in position] le plus en avant ; [- in importance] principal, le plus important.
<> *adv* en avant.

forename ['fɔ:neɪm] *n UK* prénom *m*.

forensic [fə'rensɪk] *adj* **1.** [chemistry] légal ■ [expert] légiste ■ **~ department** département de médecine légale ■ **~ evidence** expertise médico-légale ■ **~ medicine** *OR* **science** médecine *f* légale ■ **~ scientist** médecin *m* légiste **2.** [skill, term] du barreau.

foreplay ['fɔ:pleɪ] *n (U)* préliminaires *mpl*.

forerunner ['fɔ:,rʌnəʳ] *n* [precursor] précurseur *m* ■ [omen] présage *m*, signe *m* avant-coureur.

foresee [fɔ:'si:] (*pret* **foresaw** [-'sɔ:], *pp* **foreseen** [-'si:n]) *vt* prévoir, présager.

foreseeable [fɔ:'si:əbl] *adj* prévisible ■ **in the ~ future** dans un avenir prévisible.

foreseen [-'si:n] *pp* ▷ **foresee**.

foreshadow [fɔ:'ʃædəʊ] *vt* présager, annoncer ■ **her first novel ~ed this masterpiece** son premier roman a laissé prévoir ce chef-d'œuvre.

foreshorten [fɔ:'ʃɔ:tn] *vt* ART faire un raccourci de ■ PHOT [horizontally] réduire ■ [vertically] écraser.

foreshortened [fɔ:'ʃɔ:tnd] *adj* réduit.

foreshortening [fɔ:'ʃɔ:tnɪŋ] *n* ART raccourci *m* ■ PHOT [horizontal] réduction *f* ■ [vertical] écrasement *m*.

foresight ['fɔ:saɪt] *n* prévoyance *f* ■ **lack of ~** imprévoyance *f*.

foreskin ['fɔ:skɪn] *n* prépuce *m*.

forest ['fɒrɪst] *n* forêt *f* ■ **a ~ of hands** *fig* une multitude de mains.

forestall [fɔ:'stɔ:l] *vt* **1.** [prevent] empêcher, retenir **2.** [anticipate - desire, possibility] anticiper, prévenir ; [- person] devancer, prendre les devants sur.

forester ['fɒrɪstəʳ] *n* forestier *m*, - ère *f*.

forest ranger *n US* garde *m* forestier.

forestry ['fɒrɪstrɪ] *n* sylviculture *f* ■ **the Forestry Commission** *organisme britannique de gestion des forêts domaniales*, ≃ les eaux et forêts *fpl*.

foretaste ['fɔ:teɪst] *n* avant-goût *m*.

foretell [fɔ:'tel] (*pret & pp* **foretold** [-'təʊld]) *vt* prédire.

forethought ['fɔ:θɔ:t] *n* [premeditation] préméditation *f* ■ [foresight] prévoyance *f*.

foretold [-'təʊld] *pt & pp* ▷ **foretell**.

forever [fə'revəʳ] *adv* **1.** [eternally] (pour) toujours, éternellement ■ **it won't last ~** ça ne durera pas toujours ■ **Europe ~!** vive l'Europe! **2.** [incessantly] toujours, sans cesse ■ **he's ~ finding fault** il trouve toujours à redire **3.** [for good] pour toujours ■ **dinosaurs have vanished ~** les dinosaures ont disparu pour toujours **4.** *inf* [a long time] très longtemps ■ **it'll take ~!** ça va prendre des lustres! ■ **he took ~ to get ready** il a mis des heures à se préparer ■ **we can't wait ~** nous ne pouvons pas attendre jusqu'à la saint-glinglin.

forevermore [fə,revə'mɔ:] *adv* pour toujours, à jamais.

forewarn [fɔ:'wɔ:n] *vt* prévenir, avertir ▶ **~ed is forearmed** *prov* un homme averti en vaut deux *prov*.

forewent [-'went] *pt* ▷ **forego**.

foreword ['fɔ:wɜ:d] *n* avant-propos *m*, préface *f*.

forfeit ['fɔ:fɪt] <> *vt* **1.** [lose] perdre ■ [give up] renoncer à, abandonner **2.** LAW [lose] perdre (par confiscation) ■ [confiscate] confisquer.
<> *n* **1.** [penalty] prix *m*, peine *f* ■ COMM [sum] amende *f*, dédit *m* **2.** LAW [loss] perte *f* (par confiscation) **3.** [game] : **to play ~s** jouer aux gages ■ **to pay a ~** avoir un gage.
<> *adj fml* [subject to confiscation] susceptible d'être confisqué ■ [confiscated] confisqué ■ **her life could be ~** *fig* elle pourrait le payer de sa vie.

forfeiture ['fɔ:fɪtʃəʳ] *n* **1.** LAW [loss] perte *f* par confiscation ■ *fig* [surrender] renonciation *f* ■ **~ of rights** renonciation aux droits **2.** [penalty] prix *m*, peine *f* ■ COMM [sum] amende *f*, dédit *m*.

forgather [fɔ:'gæðəʳ] *vi fml* se réunir, s'assembler.

forgave [fə'geɪv] *pt* ▷ **forgive**.

forge [fɔ:dʒ] <> *vt* **1.** [metal, sword] forger ■ **to ~ an alliance/a friendship** *fig* sceller une alliance/une amitié **2.** [counterfeit - money, signature] contrefaire ; [- picture] faire un faux de, contrefaire ; [- document] faire un faux de ■ **a ~d passport** un faux passeport ■ **a ~d £20 note** un faux billet de 20 livres.
<> *vi* [go forward] avancer ■ **to ~ into the lead** prendre la tête.
<> *n* [machine, place] forge *f*.
◆ **forge ahead** *vi insep* prendre de l'avance ■ *fig* faire son chemin, réussir, prospérer.

forger ['fɔ:dʒəʳ] *n* [gen] faussaire *mf* ■ [of money] faux-monnayeur *m*, faussaire *mf*.

forgery ['fɔ:dʒərɪ] (*pl* **forgeries**) *n* **1.** [of money, picture, signature] contrefaçon *f* ■ [of document] falsification *f* ■ **to prosecute sb for ~** poursuivre qqn pour faux (et usage de faux) **2.** [object] faux *m*.

forget [fə'get] (*pret* **forgot** [-'gɒt], *pp* **forgotten** [-'gɒtn]) <> *vt* **1.** [be unable to recall] oublier ■ **I'll never ~ seeing him play Lear** je ne l'oublierai jamais *OR* je le reverrai toujours dans le rôle de Lear ■ **I forgot (that) you had a sister** j'avais oublié que tu avais une sœur ■ **she's forgotten how to swim** elle ne sait plus (comment) nager ■ **I never ~ a face** j'ai la mémoire des visages ■ **she'll never let him ~ his mistake** elle n'est pas près de lui pardonner son erreur ■ [not think about] oublier ■ **I forgot the time** j'ai oublié l'heure ■ **to ~ o.s.** s'oublier ■ **he was so overwhelmed by emotion that he quite forgot himself** il était tellement ému qu'il perdit toute retenue ■ **it's my idea and don't you ~ it!** c'est moi qui ai eu cette idée, tâchez de ne pas l'oublier! ■ **such things are best forgotten** il vaut mieux ne pas penser à de telles choses ■ **that never-to-be-forgotten day** ce jour inoubliable *OR* mémorable **2.** [neglect, overlook] oublier, omettre ■ **she forgot to mention that she was married** elle a oublié *OR* a omis de dire qu'elle était mariée ■ **not forgetting...** sans oublier... ■ **~ it!** *inf* [in reply to thanks] il n'y a pas de quoi! ; [in reply to apology] ce n'est pas grave!, ne vous en faites pas! ; [in irritation] laissez tomber! ; [in reply to question] cela n'a aucune importance!, peu importe! **3.** [leave behind] oublier, laisser **4.** [give up - idea, plan] abandonner, renoncer à.
<> *vi* : **to ~ about sb/sthg** oublier qqn/qqch ■ **sorry, I completely forgot about it** désolé, j'avais complètement oublié ■ **he agreed to ~ about the outburst** il a accepté de fermer les yeux sur l'incartade.

forgetful [fə'getfʊl] *adj* [absent-minded] distrait ■ [careless] négligent, étourdi ■ **to be ~ of sthg** *fml* être oublieux de qqch.

forgetfulness [fə'getfʊlnɪs] *n* [absent-mindedness] manque *m* de mémoire ■ [carelessness] négligence *f*, étourderie *f*.

forget-me-not *n* myosotis *m*.

forgettable [fə'getəbl] *adj* qui ne présente pas d'intérêt.

forgivable [fə'gɪvəbl] *adj* pardonnable.

forgivably [fə'gɪvəblɪ] *adv* : **she was, quite ~, rather annoyed with him!** elle était plutôt en colère contre lui, et on la comprend!

forgive [fə'gɪv] (*pret* **forgave** [fə'geɪv], *pp* **forgiven** [-'gɪvn]) *vt* **1.** [pardon] pardonner ■ **to ~ sb (for) sthg** pardonner qqch à qqn ■ **he asked me to ~ him** il m'a demandé pardon ■ **can you ever ~ me?** pourras-tu jamais me pardonner?

■ **one might be forgiven for thinking that...** on pourrait penser que... ■ ~ **and forget** pardonner et oublier **2.** [debt, payment] : **to ~ (sb) a debt** faire grâce (à qqn) d'une dette.

forgiveable [fəˈgɪvəbl] = **forgivable**.

forgiveness [fəˈgɪvnɪs] *n* **1.** [pardon] pardon *m* ■ **to ask sb's ~** demander pardon à qqn **2.** [tolerance] indulgence *f*, clémence *f*.

forgiving [fəˈgɪvɪŋ] *adj* indulgent, clément.

forgo [fɔːˈgəʊ] (*pret* **forwent** [-ˈwent], *pp* **forgone** [-ˈgɒn]) *vt* renoncer à, se priver de.

forgot [-ˈgɒt] *pt* ▻ **forget**.

forgotten [-ˈgɒtn] *pp* ▻ **forget**.

fork [fɔːk] ◇ *n* **1.** [for eating] fourchette *f* **2.** AGRIC fourche *f* **3.** [junction - in road, railway] bifurcation *f*, embranchement *m* ■ **take the right ~** tournez *OR* prenez à droite à l'embranchement **4.** [on bicycle, motorbike] fourche *f*.
◇ *vt* **1.** AGRIC fourcher **2.** [food] prendre avec une fourchette.
◇ *vi* **1.** [river, road] bifurquer, fourcher ■ **the road ~s at Newton** la route fait une fourche à Newton **2.** [car, person] bifurquer, tourner.
◆ **fork out** *inf* ◇ *vt sep* [money] allonger, cracher.
◇ *vi insep* casquer△.

forked [fɔːkt] *adj* [tongue] fourchu ■ [river, road] à bifurcation.

forked lightning *n* éclair *m* en zigzags.

forklift [ˈfɔːklɪft] *n* : **~ (truck)** chariot *m* élévateur.

forlorn [fəˈlɔːn] *adj* **1.** [wretched] triste, malheureux ■ **a ~ cry** un cri de désespoir **2.** [lonely - person] abandonné, délaissé ; [- place] désolé, désert **3.** [desperate] désespéré ■ **I went there in the ~ hope that she'd see me** j'y suis allé en espérant contre tout espoir qu'elle accepterait de me voir.

form [fɔːm] ◇ *n* **1.** [shape] forme *f* ■ **in the ~ of a heart** en forme de cœur ■ **her plan began to take ~** son projet a commencé à prendre tournure *OR* forme
2. [body, figure] forme *f*, silhouette *f*
3. [aspect, mode] forme *f* ■ **it's written in the ~ of a letter** c'est écrit sous forme de lettre ■ **the Devil appeared in the ~ of a goat** le diable apparut sous la forme d'une chèvre ■ **the same product in a new ~** le même produit présenté différemment ■ **what ~ should my questions take?** comment devrais-je formuler mes questions? ■ **the interview took the ~ of an informal chat** l'entrevue prit la forme d'une discussion informelle ■ **her anxiety showed itself in the ~ of anger** son inquiétude se manifesta par de la colère
4. [kind, type] forme *f*, sorte *f* ■ **we studied three different ~s of government** nous avons examiné trois systèmes de gouvernement *OR* trois régimes différents ■ **all ~s of sugar** le sucre sous toutes ses formes ■ **she sent some flowers as a ~ of thanks** elle a envoyé des fleurs en guise de remerciements
5. [document] formulaire *m* ■ [for bank, telegram] formule *f* ■ **to fill in** *OR* **out a ~** remplir un formulaire ● **printed ~** imprimé *m*
6. [condition] forme *f*, condition *f* ■ **John was on** *UK OR* **in good ~ at lunch** John était en forme *OR* plein d'entrain pendant le déjeuner ■ **he's off ~** *UK OR* **out of ~** il n'est pas en forme ■ **I'm on** *UK OR* **in top ~** je suis en pleine forme ■ **to study the ~** [in horse racing] examiner le tableau des performances des chevaux
7. [gen - ART], LIT & MUS forme *f* ■ **~ and content** la forme et le fond ■ **her ideas lack ~** ses idées sont confuses
8. [standard practice] forme *f*, règle *f* ■ **to do sthg as a matter of ~** faire qqch pour la forme ■ **what's the usual ~ in these cases?** que fait-on d'habitude *OR* quelle est la marche à suivre dans ces cas-là?
9. *dated* [etiquette] forme *f*, formalité *f* ■ **it's bad ~** cela ne se fait pas ■ **it's good ~** c'est de bon ton, cela se fait
10. [formula] forme *f*, formule *f* ■ **~ of address** formule de politesse ■ **the correct ~ of address for a senator** la manière correcte de s'adresser à un sénateur
11. [mould] forme *f*, moule *m*
12. GRAM & LING forme *f* ■ **the masculine ~** la forme du masculin, le masculin
13. PHILOS [structure] forme *f* ■ [essence] essence *f*
14. *UK* SCH [class] classe *f* ■ **she's in the first ~** ≃ elle est en sixième
15. *UK* [bench] banc *m*
16. *UK inf* [criminal record] casier *m* (judiciaire).
◇ *comp UK* SCH : **~ master, ~ mistress, ~ teacher** professeur *m* principal.
◇ *vt* **1.** [shape] former, construire ■ [character, mind] former, façonner ■ [sentence] construire ■ **he ~ed the model out of** *OR* **from clay** il a sculpté *OR* façonné le modèle dans l'argile ■ **~ the dough into a ball** pétrissez la pâte en forme de boule
2. [take the shape of] former, faire ■ **~ a queue** *UK OR* **line** *US* **please** faites la queue, s'il vous plaît
3. [develop - opinion] se former, se faire ; [- plan] concevoir, élaborer ; [- habit] contracter ■ **he's wary of ~ing friendships** il hésite à nouer des amitiés ■ **to ~ an impression** avoir une impression
4. [organize - association, club] créer, fonder ; [- committee, government] former ■ COMM [- company] fonder, créer
5. [constitute] composer, former ■ **to ~ the basis of sthg** constituer la base de *OR* servir de base à qqch ■ **to ~ a part of sthg** faire partie de qqch
6. GRAM former.
◇ *vi* **1.** [materialize] se former, prendre forme ■ **doubts began to ~ in his mind** des doutes commencèrent à prendre forme dans son esprit, il commença à avoir des doutes
2. [take shape] se former ■ **we ~ed into groups** nous nous sommes mis en groupes, nous avons formé des groupes.
◆ **form up** *vi insep UK* se mettre en ligne, s'aligner.

formal [ˈfɔːml] ◇ *adj* **1.** [conventional - function] officiel, solennel ; [- greeting] solennel, cérémonieux ■ **a ~ dance** un grand bal ■ **a ~ dinner** un dîner officiel ■ **~ dress** [for ceremony] tenue *f* de cérémonie ; [for evening] tenue *f* de soirée
2. [official - announcement, approval] officiel ; [- order] formel, explicite ■ **~ agreement/contract** accord *m* /contrat *m* en bonne et due forme ■ **she had no ~ education** elle n'a jamais fait d'études ■ **we gave him a ~ warning** nous l'avons averti officiellement *OR* dans les règles
3. [correct - person] solennel ; [- behaviour, style] soigné, solennel, guindé *pej* ■ **don't be so ~** ne sois pas si sérieux, sois un peu plus détendu ■ **in ~ language** dans un style soigné *OR* soutenu ■ **"vous" is the ~ form** "vous" est la formule de politesse
4. [ordered] formaliste, méthodique
5. [nominal] de forme ■ **she is the ~ head of State** c'est elle le chef d'État officiel
6. GRAM & LING formaliste, formel
7. PHILOS formel.
◇ *n US* **1.** [dance] bal *m*
2. [suit] habit *m* de soirée.

formaldehyde [fɔːˈmældɪhaɪd] *n* formaldéhyde *m*.

formalism [ˈfɔːməlɪzm] *n* formalisme *m*.

formalist [ˈfɔːməlɪst] ◇ *adj* formaliste.
◇ *n* formaliste *mf*.

formality [fɔːˈmælətɪ] (*pl* **formalities**) *n* **1.** [ceremoniousness] cérémonie *f* ■ [solemnity] solennité *f*, gravité *f* ■ [stiffness] froideur *f* ■ [convention] formalité *f* **2.** [procedure] formalité *f* ■ **it's a mere ~** c'est une simple formalité.

formalize, ise [ˈfɔːməlaɪz] *vt* formaliser.

formally [ˈfɔːməlɪ] *adv* **1.** [conventionally] solennellement, cérémonieusement ■ **~ dressed** [for ceremony] en tenue de cérémonie ; [for evening] en tenue de soirée **2.** [officially] officiellement, dans les règles ■ **an agreement was ~ drawn up** un accord a été rédigé en bonne et due forme **3.** [speak] de façon soignée ■ [behave] de façon solennelle *OR* guindée *pej* **4.** [study, research] de façon méthodique ■ [arrange] de façon régulière **5.** [nominally] pour la forme.

format [ˈfɔːmæt] (*cont* **formatting**, *pret* & *pp* **formatted**) ◇ *n* **1.** [size] format *m* **2.** [layout] présentation *f* ■ **the TV news now has a new ~** le journal télévisé a adopté une nouvelle présentation **3.** COMPUT format *m*.
◇ *vt* **1.** [layout] composer la présentation de **2.** COMPUT formater.

formation [fɔːˈmeɪʃn] *n* **1.** [establishment - of club] création *f*, fondation *f* ; [- of committee, company] formation *f*, fondation *f* ; [- of government] formation *f* **2.** [development - of character, person] formation *f* ; [- of idea] développement *m*, élaboration *f* ;

[- of plan] élaboration *f*, mise *f* en place **3.** BOT, GEOL & MED formation *f* **4.** [arrangement] formation *f*, disposition *f* ▪ MIL [unit] formation *f*, dispositif *m* ▪ **battle ~** formation de combat ▪ **in close ~** en ordre serré.

formative ['fɔːmətɪv] ◇ *adj* formateur ▪ **the ~ years** les années *fpl* formatrices.
◇ *n* formant *m*, élément *m* formateur.

formatting ['fɔːmætɪŋ] *n* COMPUT formatage *m*.

-formed [fɔːmd] *in cpds* formé.

former ['fɔːmər] ◇ *adj* **1.** [time] passé ▪ **in ~ times** *OR* **days** autrefois, dans le passé **2.** [earlier, previous] ancien, précédent ▪ **my ~ boss** mon ancien patron ▪ **my ~ wife** mon ex-femme ▪ **in a ~ life** dans une vie antérieure ▪ **he's only a shadow of his ~ self** il n'est plus que l'ombre de lui-même **3.** [first] premier ▪ **I prefer the ~ idea to the latter** je préfère la première idée à la dernière.
◇ *n* **1.** [first] premier *m*, - ère *f*, celui-là *m*, celle-là *f* ▪ **of the two methods I prefer the ~** des deux méthodes je préfère la première **2.** TECH gabarit *m*.

-former *in cpds UK* élève de ▪ **first~** ≃ élève *mf* de sixième.

formerly ['fɔːməlɪ] *adv* autrefois, jadis.

form feed *n* COMPUT avancement *m* du papier.

Formica® [fɔː'maɪkə] *n* Formica® *m*, plastique *m* laminé.

formidable ['fɔːmɪdəbl] *adj* **1.** [inspiring fear] redoutable, terrible ▪ [inspiring respect] remarquable ▪ **a ~ intellect** un esprit brillant **2.** [difficult] ardu ▪ **a ~ problem** un problème difficile.

formidably ['fɔːmɪdəblɪ] *adv* redoutablement, terriblement.

formless ['fɔːmlɪs] *adj* [shape] informe ▪ [fear, idea] vague.

formula ['fɔːmjʊlə] *n* **1.** (*pl* formulas *OR pl* formulae [-liː]) [gen - CHEM] & MATHS formule *f* ▪ **a ~ for happiness** une recette qui assure le bonheur **2.** (*pl* formulas) [expression] formule *f* **3.** (*pl* formulas) [for baby] ≃ bouillie *f (pour bébé)* **4.** (*pl inv*) AUT formule *f* ▪ **~ 1 (racing)** la formule 1.

formulaic [,fɔːmjʊ'leɪɪk] *adj* : **~ expression** formule *f*.

formulate ['fɔːmjʊleɪt] *vt* **1.** [express] formuler **2.** [plan] élaborer.

formulation [,fɔːmjʊ'leɪʃn] *n* **1.** [of idea] formulation *f*, expression *f* **2.** [of plan] élaboration *f*.

fornicate ['fɔːnɪkeɪt] *vi fml* forniquer.

fornication [,fɔːnɪ'keɪʃn] *n fml* fornication *f*.

forsake [fə'seɪk] (*pret* **forsook** [-'sʊk], *pp* **forsaken** [-'seɪkn]) *vt fml* **1.** [abandon - family, spouse] abandonner ; [- friend] délaisser ; [- place] quitter ▪ **her customary patience forsook her** sa patience habituelle lui fit défaut **2.** [give up] renoncer à.

forsaken [-'seɪkn] ◇ *pp* ▷ **forsake**.
◇ *adj lit* [person] abandonné ▪ [place] abandonné, désert.

forsook [-'sʊk] *pt* ▷ **forsake**.

forsooth [fə'suːθ] *arch* ◇ *adv* à vrai dire, en vérité.
◇ *interj* ma foi, par exemple.

forswear [fɔː'sweər] (*pret* **forswore** [-'swɔːr], *pp* **forsworn** [-'swɔːn]) *fml* ◇ *vt* **1.** [renounce] abjurer **2.** [deny] désavouer ▪ **to ~ o.s.** se parjurer.
◇ *vi* se parjurer.

forsythia [fɔː'saɪθjə] *n* forsythia *m*.

fort [fɔːt] *n* fort *m* ▪ [smaller] fortin *m* ▪ **to hold the ~** *UK*, **to hold down the ~** *US* assurer la permanence.

forte[1] ['fɔːteɪ] *n* [strong point] fort *m* ▪ **patience is hardly his ~** la patience n'est pas vraiment son (point) fort.

forte[2] ['fɔːtɪ] ◇ *adj* & *adv* MUS forte.
◇ *n* forte *m*.

forth [fɔːθ] *adv lit* **1.** [out, forward] en avant ▪ **to go** *OR* **to set ~** se mettre en route ▪ **to bring ~** produire ▪ **to send ~** envoyer **2.** [forwards in time] : **from this moment ~** dorénavant, désormais ▪ **from this day ~** à partir d'aujourd'hui *OR* de ce jour.

Forth Bridge *pr n* : **the ~** *pont ferroviaire construit au XIX*^e^ *siècle sur l'estuaire de la Forth, en Écosse.*

forthcoming [fɔːθ'kʌmɪŋ] *adj* **1.** [imminent - event] à venir ; [- book] à paraître ; [- film] qui va sortir prochainement ▪ **the ~ elections** les prochaines élections ▪ **'~ attractions'** 'prochainement' **2.** [made available] : **no answer was ~** il n'y a eu aucune réponse ▪ **the funds were not ~** les fonds n'ont pas été débloqués **3.** [verbally] : **he wasn't very ~** il n'a pas été très bavard.

forthright ['fɔːθraɪt] *adj* [person, remark] franc, franche *f*, direct ▪ **he's a ~ critic of the government** il critique le gouvernement ouvertement.

forthwith [,fɔːθ'wɪθ] *adv fml* incontinent *lit*, sur-le-champ.

fortieth ['fɔːtɪɪθ] ◇ *n* **1.** [ordinal] quarantième *m*, *see also* **fifth** **2.** [fraction] quarantième *m*.
◇ *det* quarantième, *see also* **fifth**.

fortification [,fɔːtɪfɪ'keɪʃn] *n* fortification *f*.

fortified ['fɔːtɪfaɪd] *adj* fortifié.

fortified wine *n UK* vin *m* de liqueur, vin *m* doux naturel.

fortify ['fɔːtɪfaɪ] (*pret* & *pp* **fortified**) *vt* **1.** [place] fortifier, armer ▪ *fig* [person] réconforter **2.** [wine] augmenter la teneur en alcool, alcooliser ▪ [food] renforcer en vitamines.

fortitude ['fɔːtɪtjuːd] *n* courage *m*, force *f* morale.

Fort Knox [-nɒks] *pr n fort militaire dans le Kentucky contenant les réserves d'or des États-Unis.*

fortnight ['fɔːtnaɪt] *n UK* quinzaine *f*, quinze jours *mpl* ▪ **for a ~** pour quinze jours ▪ **a ~ ago** il y a quinze jours ▪ **a ~ tomorrow** demain en quinze ▪ **a ~'s holiday** quinze jours de vacances ▪ **it's been postponed for a ~** cela a été remis à quinzaine.

fortnightly ['fɔːt,naɪtlɪ] (*pl* **fortnightlies**) *UK* ◇ *adj* bimensuel.
◇ *adv* tous les quinze jours.
◇ *n* bimensuel *m*.

Fortnum and Mason ['fɒːtnʌm-] *pr n grand magasin londonien réputé pour ses produits de luxe.*

fortress ['fɔːtrɪs] *n* [fort] fort *m* ▪ [prison] forteresse *f* ▪ [castle] château *m* fort ▪ [place, town] place *f* forte.

fortuitous [fɔː'tjuːɪtəs] *adj* fortuit, imprévu.

Fortuna [fɔː'tjuːnə] *pr n* Fortune.

fortunate ['fɔːtʃnət] ◇ *adj* [person] heureux, chanceux ▪ [choice, meeting] heureux, propice ▪ **you are ~** vous avez de la chance ▪ **I was ~ enough to get the job** j'ai eu la chance d'obtenir le travail ▪ **he is ~ in his friends** il a de bons amis ▪ **how ~!** quelle chance!
◇ *npl* : **the less ~** les déshérités *mpl*.

fortunately ['fɔːtʃnətlɪ] *adv* heureusement, par bonheur.

fortune ['fɔːtʃuːn] *n* **1.** [wealth] fortune *f* ▪ **he came to London to make his ~** il est venu à Londres pour faire fortune ▪ **she makes a ~** elle gagne beaucoup d'argent ▪ **to come into a ~** hériter d'une fortune, faire un gros héritage ▪ **to cost/to pay/to spend a (small) ~** coûter/payer/dépenser une (petite) fortune **2.** [future] destin *m* ▪ **to tell sb's ~** dire la bonne aventure à qqn **3.** [chance, fate] sort *m*, fortune *f* ▪ **the novel traces its hero's changing ~s** le roman retrace les tribulations de son héros ▪ **the ~s of war** les hasards de la guerre **4.** [luck] fortune *f*, chance *f* ▪ **he had the good ~ to win** il a eu la chance de gagner ▪ **by good ~** par chance, par bonheur.

fortune cookie *n US biscuit chinois dans lequel est caché un horoscope.*

Fortune Five Hundred *npl les 500 plus grosses entreprises américaines (dont la liste est établie, chaque année, par le magazine Fortune).*

fortune-hunter *n pej* [man] coureur *m* de dot ▪ [woman] aventurière *f*, femme *f* intéressée.

fortune-teller *n* [gen] diseur *m*, - euse *f* de bonne aventure ▪ [with cards] tireur *m*, - euse *f* de cartes.

fortune-telling *n* [gen] *fait de dire la bonne aventure* ■ [with cards] cartomancie *f*.

forty ['fɔːtɪ] (*pl* **forties**) ◇ *det* quarante *(inv)*.
◇ *n* quarante *m* ■ **about ~** environ quarante, une quarantaine ■ **the lower ~-eight** *US* les quarante-huit États américains *(à part l'Alaska et Hawaï)*, *see also* **fifty**.

forty-five *n* **1.** [record] quarante-cinq tours *m* **2.** *US* [pistol] quarante-cinq *m*.

forty winks *npl inf* petit somme *m*.

forum ['fɔːrəm] (*pl* **forums** *OR pl* **fora** ['fɔːrə]) *n* [gen] *fig* forum *m*, tribune *f* ■ HIST forum *m*.

forward ['fɔːwəd] ◇ *adj* **1.** [towards front - movement] en avant, vers l'avant ; [- position] avant ■ **the seat is too far ~** le siège est trop avancé *OR* en avant ■ **~ line** SPORT ligne *f* des avants **2.** [advanced] : **the project is no further ~** le projet n'a pas avancé ■ **~ planning** planification *f* à long terme **3.** [brash] effronté, impertinent **4.** [buying, delivery] à terme.
◇ *adv* **1.** [in space] en avant ■ NAUT à l'avant ■ **to move ~** avancer ■ **he reached ~** il a tendu le bras en avant ■ **three witnesses came ~** *fig* trois témoins se sont présentés ■ **clocks go ~ one hour at midnight** il faut avancer les pendules d'une heure à minuit **2.** *fml* [in time] : **from this moment ~** à partir de maintenant ■ **from this day ~** désormais, dorénavant.
◇ *vt* **1.** [send on] faire suivre ■ COMM expédier, envoyer ■ **'please ~'** 'faire suivre SVP, prière de faire suivre' **2.** [advance, promote] avancer, favoriser.
◇ *n* SPORT avant *m*.

forwarding ['fɔːwədɪŋ] *n* [sending] expédition *f*, envoi *m*.

forwarding address ['fɔːwədɪŋ-] *n* adresse *f* pour faire suivre le courrier ■ COMM adresse *f* pour l'expédition ■ **he left no ~** il est parti sans laisser d'adresse.

forwarding agent ['fɔːwədɪŋ-] *n* transitaire *mf*.

forward-looking *adj* [person] tourné vers *OR* ouvert sur l'avenir ■ [plans] tourné vers l'avenir *OR* le progrès ■ [company, policy] qui va de l'avant, dynamique, entreprenant.

forwardness ['fɔːwədnɪs] *n* **1.** [presumption] effronterie *f*, impertinence *f* ■ [eagerness] empressement *m* **2.** *UK* [of child, season] précocité *f* ■ [of project] état *m* avancé.

forward pass *n* en-avant *m inv*, passe *f* en avant.

forward roll *n* cabriole *f*, culbute *f*.

forwards ['fɔːwədz] *adv* = **forward**.

forward slash *n* COMPUT barre *f* oblique.

forwent [-'went] *pt* ▷ **forgo**.

Fosbury flop ['fɒzbərɪ-] *n* fosbury(-flop) *m*.

Fosse Way [fɒs-] *pr n* : **the ~** *voie romaine entre Lincoln et Exeter en Angleterre*.

fossil ['fɒsl] ◇ *n* fossile *m*.
◇ *adj* fossilisé.

fossil fuel *n* combustible *m* fossile.

fossilized ['fɒsɪlaɪzd] *adj* **1.** *liter* fossilisé **2.** *fig* fossilisé, figé ■ LING figé.

foster ['fɒstəʳ] ◇ *vt* **1.** *UK* LAW [subj: family, person] accueillir ■ [subj: authorities, court] placer ■ **the children were ~ed (out) at an early age** les enfants ont été placés dans une famille tout jeunes **2.** [idea, hope] nourrir, entretenir **3.** [promote] favoriser, encourager.
◇ *adj* : **~ child** enfant *m* placé dans une famille d'accueil ■ **~ home** *OR* **parents** famille *f* d'accueil ■ **~ mother/father** mère *f* /père *m* de la famille d'accueil.

fostering ['fɒstərɪŋ] *n* LAW accueil *m (d'un enfant)*.

fought [fɔːt] *pt & pp* ▷ **fight**.

foul [faʊl] ◇ *adj* **1.** [food, taste] infect ■ [smell] infect, fétide ■ [breath] fétide ■ **to smell ~** puer ■ **to taste ~** avoir un goût infect **2.** [filthy - linen] sale, souillé ; [- place] immonde, crasseux ; [- air] vicié, pollué ; [- water] croupi **3.** *inf* [horrible - weather] pourri ; [- person] infect, ignoble ■ **I've had a ~ day** j'ai eu une sale journée ■ **she's in a ~ mood** elle est d'une humeur massacrante ■ **he has a ~ temper** il a un sale caractère *OR* un caractère de chien **4.** [language] grossier, ordurier ■ **he has a ~ mouth** il est très grossier **5.** *lit* [vile] vil ■ [unfair] déloyal **6.** [clogged] obstrué, encrassé **7.** *phr* **to fall** *OR* **to run ~ of sb** se brouiller avec qqn ■ **they fell ~ of the law** ils ont eu des démêlés avec la justice.
◇ *n* SPORT [in boxing] coup *m* bas ■ [in football, baseball etc] faute *f*.
◇ *vt* **1.** [dirty] salir ■ [air, water] polluer, infecter ■ [subj: dog] salir, souiller **2.** [clog] obstruer, encrasser ■ [entangle] embrouiller, emmêler ■ [nets] se prendre dans **3.** [collide with] entrer en collision avec **4.** SPORT commettre une faute contre **5.** *fig* [reputation] salir.
◇ *vi* **1.** [tangle] s'emmêler, s'embrouiller **2.** SPORT commettre une faute.
◆ **foul up** *vt sep* **1.** [contaminate] polluer ■ [clog] obstruer, encrasser **2.** *inf* [bungle] ficher en l'air, flanquer par terre.

foul-mouthed *adj* au langage grossier.

foul play *n* SPORT jeu *m* irrégulier *OR* déloyal ■ [in cards, games] tricherie *f* ■ **the police suspect ~** *fig* la police croit qu'il y a eu meurtre *OR* croit au meurtre.

foul-smelling [-'smelɪŋ] *adj* puant, fétide.

foul-up *n inf* [mix-up] cafouillage *m* ■ [mechanical difficulty] problème *m OR* difficulté *f* mécanique.

found [faʊnd] ◇ *pt & pp* ▷ **find**.
◇ *adj dated* **1.** [furnished] équipé **2.** *phr* **all ~** *UK* tout compris.
◇ *vt* **1.** [establish - organization, town] fonder, créer ; [- business] fonder, établir **2.** [base] fonder, baser ■ **to be ~ed on** être fondé sur **3.** [cast] fondre.

foundation [faʊn'deɪʃn] *n* **1.** [of business, town] fondation *f*, création *f* **2.** [institution] fondation *f*, institution *f* dotée ■ [endowment] dotation *f*, fondation *f* **3.** [basis] base *f*, fondement *m* ■ **his work laid the ~** *OR* **~s of modern science** son œuvre a jeté les bases de la science moderne ■ **the rumour is entirely without ~** la rumeur est dénuée de tout fondement **4.** [make-up] fond *m* de teint **5.** *US* [of building] fondations *fpl*.
◆ **foundations** *npl* CONSTR fondations *fpl* ■ **to lay the ~s** poser les fondations.

foundation course *n* cours *m* introductif.

foundation cream *n* fond *m* de teint.

foundation garment *n* [girdle] gaine *f*, combiné *m* ■ [bra] soutien-gorge *m*.

foundation hospital *n UK hôpital faisant partie du système de sécurité sociale britannique, mais géré par une équipe privée*.

foundation stone *n* pierre *f* commémorative ■ **to lay the ~** poser la première pierre.

founder ['faʊndəʳ] ◇ *n* fondateur *m*, - trice *f* ■ **~ member** *UK* membre *m* fondateur.
◇ *vi* **1.** [ship] sombrer, chavirer **2.** *fig* [fail] s'effondrer, s'écrouler ■ **the project ~ed for lack of financial support** le projet s'est effondré faute de soutien financier **3.** [horse - in mud] s'embourber ; [- go lame] se mettre à boîter.

founding ['faʊndɪŋ] ◇ *n* [of business, organization, town] fondation *f*, création *f*.
◇ *adj* fondateur.

founding father *n* père *m* fondateur.

Founding Fathers *pr npl* : **the ~** *les "pères fondateurs" des États-Unis (Washington, Jefferson, Franklin)*.

foundling ['faʊndlɪŋ] *n fml* enfant *mf* trouvé ■ **~ hospital** hospice *m* pour enfants trouvés.

foundry ['faʊndrɪ] (*pl* **foundries**) *n* [place] fonderie *f* ■ [of articles] fonderie *f*, fonte *f* ■ [articles] fonte *f*.

fount [faʊnt] *n* **1.** *UK* TYPO fonte *f* **2.** *lit* [spring] source *f* ■ **a ~ of knowledge** un puits de science.

fountain ['faʊntɪn] *n* **1.** [natural] fontaine *f*, source *f* ■ [manmade] jet *m* d'eau ■ **drinking ~** [in street] fontaine publique ; [in building] fontaine d'eau potable **2.** *fig* source *f*.

fountainhead ['faʊntɪnhed] *n* [spring] source *f* ■ *fig* [source] source *f*, origine *f*.

fountain pen *n* stylo *m* à encre.

four [fɔːʳ] ◇ *n* **1.** [number] quatre *m* ■ **on all ~s** à quatre pattes, *see also* **five** **2.** [in rowing] quatre *m*.

◇ *det* quatre.

four-by-four *n* AUT 4 x 4 *m*.

four-colour *adj* quadrichrome ▪ **~ printing process** TYPO quadrichromie *f*.

four-door *adj* à quatre portes.

four-engined *adj* à quatre moteurs.

four-eyes *n inf* binoclard *m*, - e *f*.

fourfold ['fɔː,fəʊld] ◇ *adv* au quadruple.
◇ *adj* quadruple.

four-four *n* quatre-quatre *m* ▪ **in ~ (time)** à quatre-quatre.

four-handed *adj* à quatre mains.

four-leaf clover, four-leaved clover *n* trèfle *m* à quatre feuilles.

four-legged [-'legɪd] *adj* quadrupède, à quatre pattes ▪ **our ~ friends** *hum* nos compagnons à quatre pattes.

four-letter word *n* gros mot *m*, obscénité *f*.

four-ply *adj* [wool] à quatre fils ▪ [wood] contreplaqué *(à quatre plis)*.

four-poster (bed) *n* lit *m* à baldaquin *OR* à colonnes.

fourscore [,fɔː'skɔːʳ] *arch* ◇ *adj* quatre-vingts ▪ **~ years and ten** quatre-vingt-dix ans.
◇ *n* quatre-vingts *m*.

foursome ['fɔːsəm] *n* **1.** [people] groupe *m* de quatre personnes ▪ [two couples] deux couples *mpl* ▪ **we went as a ~** nous y sommes allés à quatre **2.** [game] partie *f* à quatre ▪ **will you make up a ~ for bridge?** voulez-vous faire le quatrième au bridge?

foursquare [,fɔː'skweəʳ] ◇ *adj* **1.** [square] carré **2.** [position, style] solide ▪ [approach, decision] ferme, inébranlable **3.** [forthright] franc, franche *f*.
◇ *adv* [solidly] fermement.

four-star *adj* [gen - MIL] à quatre étoiles ▪ **~ hotel** hôtel *m* quatre étoiles *OR* de première catégorie ▪ **~ petrol** *UK* super *m*, supercarburant *m*.

four-stroke ◇ *adj* à quatre temps.
◇ *n* moteur *m* à quatre temps.

fourteen [,fɔː'tiːn] ◇ *det* quatorze, *see also* **five**.
◇ *n* quatorze *m*, *see also* **five**.

fourteenth [,fɔː'tiːnθ] ◇ *n* **1.** [ordinal] quatorzième *mf* **2.** [fraction] quatorzième *m*.
◇ *det* quatorzième ▪ **Louis the Fourteenth** Louis Quatorze, *see also* **fifth**.
◇ *adv* quatorzièmement ▪ **he came ~ in the marathon** il est arrivé en quatorzième position *OR* quatorzième dans le marathon.

fourth [fɔːθ] ◇ *n* **1.** [ordinal] quatrième *mf* ▪ **the Fourth of July** le quatre juillet *(fête nationale de l'Indépendance aux États-Unis)*, *see also* **fifth 2.** [fraction] quart *m* **3.** MUS quarte *f*.
◇ *det* quatrième ▪ **~-class mail** *US* paquet-poste *m* ordinaire ▪ **the ~ finger** l'annulaire *m* ▪ **to go** *OR* **to change into ~ (gear)** AUT passer en quatrième, *see also* **fifth**.
◇ *adv* quatrièmement ▪ **she finished ~ in the race** elle a fini la course à la quatrième place.

fourth estate *n* : **the ~** le quatrième pouvoir, la presse.

fourthly ['fɔːθlɪ] *adv* quatrièmement, en quatrième lieu.

Fourth World *pr n* : **the ~** le quart-monde.

four-wheel *vi US* faire du quatre-quatre.

four-wheel drive *n* propulsion *f* à quatre roues motrices ▪ **with ~** à quatre roues motrices.

fowl [faʊl] *(pl inv OR pl* **fowls***)* *n* [for eating - collectively] volaille *f* ; [- one bird] volaille *f*, volatile *m*.

fox [fɒks] *(pl inv OR pl* **foxes***)* ◇ *n* [animal, fur] renard *m* ▪ **he's a sly old ~** *fig* c'est un vieux renard ▪ **~ cub** renardeau *m* ▪ **as sly as a ~** rusé comme un renard.
◇ *vt* **1.** [outwit] duper, berner **2.** [baffle] souffler.

foxed [fɒkst] *adj* [paper] marqué *OR* taché de rousseurs.

foxglove ['fɒksglʌv] *n* digitale *f* (pourprée).

foxhole ['fɒkshəʊl] *n* **1.** [of fox] terrier *m* de renard, renardière *f* **2.** MIL gourbi *m*.

foxhound ['fɒkshaʊnd] *n* fox-hound *m*.

foxhunt ['fɒkshʌnt] *n* chasse *f* au renard.

foxhunter ['fɒks,hʌntəʳ] *n* chasseur *m*, - euse *f* de renard.

foxhunting ['fɒks,hʌntɪŋ] *n* chasse *f* au renard ▪ **to go ~** aller chasser le renard *OR* à la chasse au renard.

foxtrot ['fɒkstrɒt] ◇ *n* fox-trot *m*.
◇ *vi* danser le fox-trot.

foxy ['fɒksɪ] *(comp* **foxier**, *superl* **foxiest***)* *adj* **1.** [wily] rusé, malin, - igne *f* **2.** [colour] roux, rousse *f* **3.** *US inf dated* [sexy] sexy *(inv)*.

foyer ['fɔɪeɪ] *n* **1.** [of cinema, hotel] hall *m*, vestibule *m* ▪ [of theatre] foyer *m* **2.** *US* [of house] entrée *f*, vestibule *m*.

FPA *(abbrev of* **Family Planning Association***)* *pr n association pour le planning familial*.

fracas [*UK* 'frækɑː, *US* 'freɪkæs] *(UKpl inv* [-kaːz]*)* *(USpl* **fracases** [-kəsɪz]*)* *n* [brawl] rixe *f*, bagarre *f* ▪ [noise] fracas *m*.

fraction ['frækʃn] *n* **1.** MATHS fraction *f* **2.** *fig* [bit] fraction *f*, petite partie *f* ▪ **at a ~ of the cost** pour une fraction du prix ▪ **for a ~ of a second** pendant une fraction de seconde ▪ **move back just a ~** reculez un tout petit peu.

fractional ['frækʃənl] *adj* **1.** MATHS fractionnaire **2.** *fig* [tiny] tout petit, infime ▪ **~ part** fraction *f*.

fractional distillation *n* distillation *f* fractionnée.

fractionally ['frækʃnəlɪ] *adv* **1.** [slightly] un tout petit peu **2.** CHEM par fractionnement.

fractious ['frækʃəs] *adj fml* **1.** [unruly] indiscipliné, turbulent **2.** [irritable - child] grognon, pleurnicheur ; [- adult] irascible, revêche.

fracture ['fræktʃəʳ] ◇ *n* fracture *f*.
◇ *vt* [break] fracturer ▪ **he ~d his arm** il s'est fracturé le bras ▪ **their withdrawal ~d the alliance** *fig* leur retrait brisa l'alliance.
◇ *vi* [break] se fracturer.

fragile [*UK* 'frædʒaɪl, *US* 'frædʒl] *adj* **1.** [china, glass] fragile ▪ *fig* [peace, happiness] précaire, fragile **2.** [person] fragile, frêle ▪ **I'm feeling a bit ~ today** je ne suis pas dans mon assiette ce matin.

fragility [frə'dʒɪlətɪ] *n* fragilité *f*.

fragment ◇ *n* ['frægmənt] [of china, text] fragment *m*, morceau *m* ▪ [of bomb] éclat *m* ▪ *fig* [of conversation] bribe *f* ▪ **the report contains not a ~ of truth** le rapport ne contient pas un atome *OR* une once de vérité.
◇ *vt* [fræg'ment] [break] fragmenter, briser ▪ [divide] fragmenter, morceler.
◇ *vi* [fræg'ment] se fragmenter.

fragmentary ['frægməntrɪ] *adj* fragmentaire.

fragmentation [,frægmen'teɪʃn] *n* [breaking] fragmentation *f* ▪ [division] fragmentation *f*, morcellement *m* ▪ **~ bomb** bombe *f* à fragmentation ▪ **~ grenade** grenade *f* offensive.

fragmented [fræg'mentɪd] *adj* fragmentaire, morcelé.

fragrance ['freɪgrəns] *n* parfum *m*.

fragrant ['freɪgrənt] *adj* parfumé.

frail [freɪl] *adj* **1.** [object] fragile ▪ [person] fragile, frêle ▪ [health] délicat, fragile ▪ **she's rather ~** elle a une petite santé **2.** [happiness, hope] fragile, éphémère.

frailty ['freɪltɪ] *(pl* **frailties***)* *n* [of health, hope, person] fragilité *f* ▪ [of character] faiblesse *f*.

frame [freɪm] ◇ *n* **1.** [border - gen] cadre *m* ; [- of canvas, picture etc] cadre *m*, encadrement *m* ; [- of window] cadre *m*, châssis *m* ; [- of door] encadrement *m* ; [- for spectacles] monture *f* ▪ **glasses with red ~s** des lunettes avec une monture rouge **2.** [support, structure - gén] cadre *m* ; [- of bicycle] cadre *m* ; [- of car] châssis *m* ; [- of lampshade, racket, tent] arma-

ture *f* ; [- of machine] bâti *m* ; [- for walking] déambulateur *m* ■ CONSTR charpente *f* ■ TEX métier *m* **3.** [body] charpente *f* ■ **the wrestler heaved his massive ~ up from the floor** le lutteur releva sa masse imposante **4.** [setting, background] cadre *m* ■ [area, scope] cadre *m* **5.** PHOT image *f* ■ CIN image *f*, photogramme *m* ■ TV trame *f*.
◇ *vt* **1.** [enclose, encase] encadrer **2.** *fml* [design, draft] élaborer ■ [formulate, express] formuler **3.** *inf* [incriminate falsely] : **to ~ sb** monter un (mauvais) coup contre qqn ■ **I've been ~d** j'ai été victime d'un coup monté.

frame of mind *n* état *m* d'esprit ■ **I'm not in the right ~ for celebrating** je ne suis pas d'humeur à faire la fête.

frame of reference *n* système *m* de référence.

frame rucksack *UK*, **frame backpack** *US n* sac *m* à dos à armature.

frame-up *n inf* coup *m* monté.

framework ['freɪmwɜ:k] *n* **1.** [structure] cadre *m*, structure *f* ■ CONSTR charpente *f* ■ TECH bâti *m* **2.** *fig* cadre *m* ■ **the bill seeks to provide a legal ~ for divorce** le projet de loi vise à instaurer un cadre juridique pour les procédures de divorce.

framing ['freɪmɪŋ] *n* encadrement *m*.

franc [fræŋk] *n* franc *m*.

France [frɑ:ns] *pr n* France *f* ■ **in ~** en France.

franchise ['fræntʃaɪz] ◇ *n* **1.** POL suffrage *m*, droit *m* de vote **2.** COMM & LAW franchise *f*.
◇ *vt* accorder une franchise à.

franchising ['fræntʃaɪzɪŋ] *n* franchisage *m*.

Francis ['frɑ:nsɪs] *pr n* : **Saint ~ (of Assisi)** saint François (d'Assise).

Franciscan [fræn'sɪskən] ◇ *adj* franciscain.
◇ *n* franciscain *m*, - e *f*.

Franco- ['fræŋkəʊ] *in cpds* franco-.

Francophile ['fræŋkəfaɪl] ◇ *adj* francophile.
◇ *n* francophile *mf*.

Francophobe ['fræŋkəfəʊb] ◇ *adj* francophobe.
◇ *n* francophobe *mf*.

Francophone ['fræŋkəfəʊn] ◇ *adj* francophone.
◇ *n* francophone *mf*.

Franglais ['frɒŋgleɪ] *n* franglais *m*.

frank [fræŋk] ◇ *adj* franc, franche *f* ■ **I'll be ~ with you** je vais vous parler franchement *OR* être franc avec vous ■ **to be (perfectly) ~** franchement *OR* sincèrement.
◇ *vt UK* affranchir.
◇ *n UK* **1.** [on letter] affranchissement *m* **2.** *US inf* [sausage] saucisse *f* (de Francfort) ■ [hot dog] hot-dog *m*.

Frank [fræŋk] *n* HIST Franc *m*, Franque *f*.

Frankenstein ['fræŋkənstaɪn] *pr n* Frankenstein.

Frankfurt ['fræŋkfət] *pr n* : **~ (am Main)** Francfort (-sur-le-Main).

frankfurter ['fræŋkfɜ:tə^r] *n* saucisse *f* de Francfort.

frankincense ['fræŋkɪnsens] *n* encens *m*.

franking machine ['fræŋkɪŋ-] *n* machine *f* à affranchir.

Frankish ['fræŋkɪʃ] ◇ *adj* franc, franque *f*.
◇ *n* francique *m*.

frankly ['fræŋklɪ] *adv* franchement, sincèrement ■ **can I speak ~?** puis-je parler franchement *OR* en toute franchise?

frankness ['fræŋknɪs] *n* franchise *f* ■ **I admire his ~** j'admire sa franchise *OR* son franc-parler.

frantic ['fræntɪk] *adj* **1.** [distraught, wild] éperdu, affolé ■ **she was ~ with worry** elle était folle d'inquiétude **2.** [very busy] : **a scene of ~ activity** une scène d'activité frénétique ■ **things are pretty ~ at the office** *inf* il y a un travail fou au bureau.

frantically ['fræntɪklɪ] *adv* désespérément ■ **she worked ~ to finish the dress** elle travailla comme une forcenée pour terminer la robe ■ **the shop is ~ busy just before Christmas** il y a un monde fou au magasin juste avant Noël.

frappe [*UK* 'fræpeɪ, *US* fræ'peɪ] *n* [drink] milk-shake *m (épais)*.

fraternal [frə'tɜ:nl] *adj* fraternel ■ **~ twins** des faux jumeaux.

fraternally [frə'tɜ:nəlɪ] *adv* fraternellement.

fraternity [frə'tɜ:nətɪ] (*pl* **fraternities**) *n* **1.** [friendship] fraternité *f* **2.** [association] confrérie *f* ■ **the medical ~** la confrérie des médecins **3.** *US* UNIV *association d'étudiants très sélective.*

fraternity pin *n US* UNIV insigne *m* de confrérie.

fraternization [,frætənaɪ'zeɪʃn] *n* fraternisation *f*.

fraternize, ise ['frætənaɪz] *vi* fraterniser.

fratricidal [,frætrɪ'saɪdl] *adj* fratricide.

fratricide ['frætrɪsaɪd] *n* fratricide *mf*.

fraud [frɔ:d] *n* **1.** LAW fraude *f* ■ FIN escroquerie *f* ■ **tax ~** fraude fiscale ■ **he obtained the painting by ~** il a eu le tableau en fraude **2.** [dishonest person] imposteur *m* **3.** [product, work] supercherie *f*.

Fraud Squad *n UK* **the ~** *section de la police britannique spécialisée dans les fraudes des entreprises.*

fraudulence ['frɔ:djʊləns] *n* caractère *m* frauduleux.

fraudulent ['frɔ:djʊlənt] *adj* frauduleux ■ LAW fraudatoire.

fraudulently ['frɔ:djʊləntlɪ] *adv* frauduleusement.

fraught [frɔ:t] *adj* **1.** [filled] chargé, lourd ■ **~ with danger** rempli de dangers **2.** *UK inf* [tense] tendu ■ **I'm feeling a bit ~** je me sens un peu angoissé *OR* tendu ■ **things got rather ~ at work today** l'atmosphère était plutôt tendue au bureau aujourd'hui ■ **I've had a particularly ~ week** j'ai eu une semaine particulièrement stressante.

fray [freɪ] ◇ *vt (usu passive)* **1.** [clothing, fabric, rope] effilocher **2.** [nerves] mettre à vif ■ **her nerves were ~ed** elle avait les nerfs à vif.
◇ *vi* **1.** [clothing, fabric, rope] s'effilocher ■ **her dress is ~ing at the hem** l'ourlet de sa robe s'effiloche **2.** *fig* **tempers began to ~** les gens commençaient à s'énerver *OR* perdre patience.
◇ *n* : **the ~** la mêlée ■ **to enter** *OR* **to join the ~** se jeter dans la mêlée.

frayed [freɪd] *adj* **1.** [garment] élimé **2.** *fig* **tempers were increasingly ~** les gens étaient de plus en plus irritables.

frazzle ['fræzl] *inf* ◇ *vt* [exhaust] tuer, crever.
◇ *n* : **worn to a ~** crevé ■ **burnt to a ~** carbonisé, calciné.

frazzled ['fræzld] *adj inf* [exhausted] crevé.

FRB (*abbrev of* **Federal Reserve Board**) *pr n organe de contrôle de la Banque centrale américaine.*

FRCP (*abbrev of* **Fellow of the Royal College of Physicians**) *n membre du RCP.*

FRCS (*abbrev of* **Fellow of the Royal College of Surgeons**) *n membre du RCS.*

freak [fri:k] ◇ *n* **1.** [abnormal event] caprice *m* de la nature ■ [abnormal person] phénomène *m* de foire ■ [eccentric person] phénomène *m*, farfelu *m*, - e *f* ■ **by a ~ of nature** par un caprice de la nature ➜ **~ show** exhibition *f* de monstres *(à la foire)* **2.** *inf* [fanatic] fana *mf* **3.** △ [hippie] hippie *mf* **4.** *lit* [caprice] foucade *f*.
◇ *adj* [accident, storm] insolite, anormal ■ **~ weather conditions** des conditions atmosphériques anormales.
◇ *vi*△ = **freak out** *(vi insep)*.
➜ **freak out**△ ◇ *vi insep* **1.** [on drugs] flipper△ **2.** [lose control of one's emotions] perdre les pédales.
◇ *vt sep* **1.** [cause to hallucinate] faire flipper△ **2.** [upset emotionally] déboussoler.

freakish ['fri:kɪʃ] *adj* **1.** [abnormal, strange] étrange, insolite **2.** *lit* [capricious, changeable] changeant.

freaky ['fri:kɪ] *adj inf* bizarre, insolite.

freckle ['frekl] ◇ *n* tache *f* de rousseur *OR* son.
◇ *vt* marquer de taches de rousseur.
◇ *vi* se couvrir de taches de rousseur.

freckled ['frekld] *adj* taché de son, marqué de taches de rousseur ■ **a ~ face/nose** un visage/nez couvert de taches de rousseur.

Frederick ['fredrɪk] *pr n* : **~ the Great** Frédéric le Grand.

free [fri:] ◇ *adj* **1.** [unconfined, unrestricted - person, animal, passage, way] libre ■ **the hostage managed to get ~** l'otage a réussi à se libérer ■ **to cut sb ~** délivrer qqn en coupant ses liens ■ **to let sb go ~** relâcher qqn, remettre qqn en liberté ■ **to set ~** [prisoner, animal] remettre en liberté ; [slave] affranchir ; [hostage] libérer ■ **you are ~ to leave** vous êtes libre de partir ■ **you are ~ to refuse** libre à vous de refuser ■ **feel ~ to visit us any time** ne vous gênez pas pour nous rendre visite quand vous voulez ■ **can I use the phone? – yes, feel ~** puis-je téléphoner? – mais certainement ▶ **~ pardon** LAW grâce *f*
2. [unattached] libre, sans attaches ■ **grab the ~ end of the rope** attrape le bout libre de la corde
3. [democratic] libre ■ **it's a ~ country!** on est en démocratie!
4. [at no cost] gratuit ■ **~ admission** entrée *f* gratuite *OR* libre ▶ **there's no such thing as a ~ lunch** les gens sont tous intéressés
5. [not in use, unoccupied] libre ■ **she doesn't have a ~ moment** elle n'a pas un moment de libre ■ **could you let us know when you're ~?** pourriez-vous nous faire savoir quand vous êtes libre *OR* disponible? ■ **what do you do in your ~ time?** que faites-vous pendant vos loisirs? ■ **she has very little ~ time** elle a peu de temps libre
6. [unhampered] : **the jury was not entirely ~ of** *OR* **from prejudice** les jurés n'étaient pas entièrement sans préjugés *OR* parti pris ■ **to be ~ from pain** ne plus souffrir ■ **an operation ~ from pain** une opération indolore ■ **I just want to be ~ of him!** je veux être débarrassé de lui! ■ **they're trying to keep Antarctica ~ from pollution** ils essaient de préserver l'Antarctique de la pollution ▶ **~ and easy** désinvolte, décontracté ■ **~ love** amour *m* libre
7. [generous] : **she's very ~ with her criticism** elle ne ménage pas ses critiques
8. [disrespectful] trop familier ■ **he's a bit ~ in his manners for my liking** il est un peu trop sans gêne à mon goût
9. CHEM libre, non combiné ■ **~ nitrogen** azote *m* à l'état libre.
◇ *adv* **1.** [at no cost] gratuitement ■ **they will deliver ~ of charge** ils livreront gratuitement ■ **children travel (for) ~** les enfants voyagent gratuitement
2. [without restraint] librement ■ **to make ~ with sthg** se servir de qqch sans se gêner.
◇ *vt* **1.** [release - gen] libérer ; [- prisoner] libérer, relâcher ; [- tied-up animal] détacher ; [- caged animal] libérer ; [- slave] affranchir ■ **giving up work has ~d me to get on with my painting** arrêter de travailler m'a permis de continuer à peindre ■ COMM [prices, trade] libérer ■ [funds] débloquer
2. [disengage, disentangle] dégager ■ **she tried to ~ herself from his grasp** elle essaya de se libérer *OR* dégager de son étreinte ■ **he cannot ~ himself of guilt** *fig* il ne peut pas se débarrasser d'un sentiment de culpabilité
3. [unblock - pipe] déboucher ; [- passage] libérer.

-free *in cpds* : **additive~** sans additifs ■ **salt~** sans sel ■ **trouble~** sans ennuis *OR* problèmes.

free agent *n* personne *f* libre *OR* indépendante ■ **I'm a ~** je ne dépends de personne.

free association *n* association *f* libre.

freebie, freebee ['fri:bɪ] *inf n* cadeau *m*.

freeboard ['fri:bɔ:d] *n* franc-bord *m*.

freeborn ['fri:bɔ:n] *adj* né libre.

freedom ['fri:dəm] *n* liberté *f* ■ **the journalists were given complete ~ to talk to dissidents** les journalistes ont pu parler aux dissidents en toute liberté ■ **~ of speech/association** liberté d'expression/de réunion ■ **~ of information** liberté d'information ■ **~ of worship** liberté du culte ■ **~ from persecution** le droit de vivre sans persécution ■ **she had the ~ of the whole house** elle avait la maison à son entière disposition ▶ **to be given** *OR* **granted the ~ of the city** être nommé citoyen d'honneur de la ville.

freedom fighter *n* combattant *m*, - e *f* de la liberté.

free enterprise *n* libre entreprise *f*.

free-fall *n* chute *f* libre.

free-floating *adj* en mouvement libre.

Freefone® ['fri:fəʊn] *n UK appel gratuit*, ≃ numéro *m* vert ■ **call ~ 800** appelez le numéro vert 800.

free-for-all *n* mêlée *f* générale.

free gift *n* COMM cadeau.

free hand *n* liberté *f* d'action ■ **to give sb a ~ to do sthg** donner carte blanche à qqn pour faire qqch.
➜ **freehand** *adj* & *adv* à main levée.

freehold ['fri:həʊld] ◇ *n* ≃ propriété *f* foncière inaliénable.
◇ *adv* : **to buy/to sell sthg ~** acheter/vendre qqch en propriété inaliénable.
◇ *adj* : **~ property** propriété *f* inaliénable.

freeholder ['fri:həʊldər] *n* ≃ propriétaire *m* foncier, ≃ propriétaire *f* foncière *(à perpétuité)*.

free house *n UK pub libre de ses approvisionnements (et non lié à une brasserie particulière)*.

freeing ['fri:ɪŋ] *n* [of prisoner] libération *f*, délivrance *f* ■ [of slave] affranchissement *m*.

free kick *n* coup *m* franc.

freelance ['fri:lɑ:ns] ◇ *n* travailleur *m* indépendant, travailleuse *f* indépendante, free-lance *mf inv* ■ [journalist, writer] pigiste *mf*.
◇ *adj* indépendant, free-lance.
◇ *adv* en free-lance, en indépendant.
◇ *vi* travailler en free-lance *OR* indépendant.

freelancer ['fri:lɑ:nsər] *n* travailleur *m* indépendant, travailleuse *f* indépendante, free-lance *mf inv*.

freeload ['fri:ləʊd] *vi inf* vivre aux crochets des autres.

freeloader ['fri:ləʊdər] *n inf* pique-assiette *mf*, parasite *mf*.

freely ['fri:lɪ] *adv* **1.** [without constraint] librement ■ **she made her confession ~** elle a avoué de son plein gré ■ **traffic is moving ~ again** la circulation est redevenue fluide ■ **the book is now ~ available** on peut se procurer le livre facilement maintenant **2.** [liberally - spend] largement ; [- perspire, weep] abondamment.

freeman ['fri:mən] (*pl* **freemen** [-mən]) *n* HIST homme *m* libre ■ [citizen] citoyen *m* ■ **he's a ~ of the city** il est citoyen d'honneur de la ville.

free-market *adj* : **~ economy** économie *f* de marché.

free-marketeer [-ˌmɑ:kə'tɪər] *n* libéral *m*, - e *f*, partisan *m* de l'économie de marché.

freemason, Freemason ['fri:ˌmeɪsn] *n* franc-maçon *m*.

freemasonry, Freemasonry ['fri:ˌmeɪsnrɪ] *n* franc-maçonnerie *f*.

free on board *adj* & *adv* franco à bord.

free port *n* port *m* franc.

Freepost® ['fri:pəʊst] *n UK* port *m* payé.

free-range *adj* [chicken] fermier ■ **~ eggs** œufs *mpl* de poules élevées en plein air.

freesheet ['fri:ʃi:t] *n* publication *f* gratuite.

freesia ['fri:zjə] *n* freesia *m*.

free speech *n* liberté *f* de parole *OR* d'expression.

free spirit *n* non-conformiste *mf*.

free-standing *adj* isolé ■ GRAM indépendant.

freestyle ['fri:staɪl] *n* [in swimming] nage *f* libre ■ [in skiing] ski *m* artistique *OR* acrobatique ■ [in wrestling] lutte *f* libre.

freethinker [ˌfri:'θɪŋkər] *n* libre-penseur *m*.

free trade *n* libre-échange *m*.

free verse *n* vers *m* libre.

free vote *n* vote *m* libre.

freeware ['fri:weər] *n* COMPUT logiciel *m* public, logiciel *m* libre.

freeway ['fri:weɪ] *n* US autoroute *f*.

freewheel [,fri:'wi:l] <> *n* [on bicycle] roue *f* libre.
<> *vi* **1.** [cyclist] être en roue libre **2.** [motorist] rouler au point mort.

freewheeling [,fri:'wi:lɪŋ] *adj inf* désinvolte, sans-gêne *(inv)*.

free will *n* libre arbitre *m* ▪ **to do sthg of one's own ~** faire qqch de son plein gré.

freeze [fri:z] *(pret* **froze** [frəʊz], *pp* **frozen** ['frəʊzn]) <> *vi* **1.** [earth, pipes, water] geler ▪ [food] se congeler ▪ **to ~ to death** mourir de froid **2.** *fig* [stop moving] : **(everybody) ~!** que personne ne bouge! ▪ **she froze (in her tracks)** elle est restée figée sur place ▪ **her blood froze** son sang se figea *OR* se glaça dans ses veines **3.** COMPUT se bloquer.
<> *vt* **1.** [water] geler, congeler ▪ [food] congeler ▪ [at very low temperatures] surgeler ▪ MED [blood, human tissue] congeler **2.** ECON & FIN [assets] geler ▪ [prices, wages] bloquer **3.** CIN : **~ it!** arrêtez l'image!
<> *n* METEOR gel *m* ▪ ECON & FIN gel *m*, blocage *m* ▪ **we're in for another big ~** METEOR il va y avoir une période de très grand froid ◐ **pay ~** gel *OR* blocage des salaires.
◆ **freeze out** *vt sep inf* exclure.
◆ **freeze over** *vi insep* geler.
◆ **freeze up** <> *vi* se bloquer.
<> *vi insep* **1.** [turn to ice] geler **2.** *inf* [become immobilized] rester pétrifié.

freeze-dried *adj* lyophilisé.

freeze-dry *vt* lyophiliser.

freeze-frame *n* arrêt *m* sur image.

freezer ['fri:zər] *n* congélateur *m* ▪ [in refrigerator] freezer *m* ▪ **~ compartment** compartiment *m* congélateur *(d'un réfrigérateur)*.

freezing ['fri:zɪŋ] <> *adj* METEOR glacial ▪ [person] gelé, glacé ▪ **~ rain** neige *f* fondue ▪ **it's ~ in this room!** on gèle dans cette pièce! ▪ **your hands are ~** vous avez les mains gelées *OR* glacées.
<> *n* : **it's two degrees above/below ~** il fait deux degrés au-dessus/au-dessous de zéro.
<> *adv* : **a ~ cold day** une journée glaciale ▪ **it's ~ cold outside** il fait un froid glacial dehors.

freezing point *n* point *m* de congélation.

freight [freɪt] <> *n* **1.** [goods] fret *m* **2.** [transport] : **to send goods by ~** envoyer des marchandises en régime ordinaire ▪ **air ~** fret *m* par avion.
<> *comp* [transport] de fret ▪ **~ charges** frais *mpl* de port.
<> *vt* transporter.

freightage ['freɪtɪdʒ] *n* fret *m*.

freight car *n* US wagon *m* de marchandises, fourgon *m*.

freighter ['freɪtər] *n* NAUT navire *m* de charge ▪ AERON avion-cargo *m*, avion *m* de fret.

Freightliner® ['freɪt,laɪnər] *n* train *m* de transport de conteneurs.

freight train *n* US train *m* de marchandises.

French [frentʃ] <> *npl* [people] : **the ~** les Français.
<> *n* LING français *m* ▪ **pardon my ~** *hum* passez-moi l'expression.
<> *adj* [person, cooking, customs] français ▪ [ambassador, embassy, king] de France ▪ **'The French Lieutenant's Woman' Fowles** 'Sarah et le lieutenant français'.

French bean *n* haricot *m* vert.

French bread *n* baguette *f*.

French Canadian <> *adj* canadien français.
<> *n* **1.** [person] Canadien *m* français, Canadienne *f* française **2.** LING français *m* canadien.

French curve *n* pistolet *m* (de dessinateur).

French door = **French window**.

French dressing *n* [in UK] vinaigrette *f* ▪ [in US] *sauce de salade à base de mayonnaise et de ketchup*.

French fried potatoes *npl* pommes *fpl* frites.

French fries *npl* frites *fpl*.

French horn *n* cor *m* d'harmonie.

Frenchie ['frentʃɪ] *inf* <> *adj* français.
<> *n* Français *m*, - e *f*.

French kiss <> *n* baiser *m* profond.
<> *vt* embrasser sur la bouche *(avec la langue)*.
<> *vi* s'embrasser sur la bouche *(avec la langue)*.

French knickers *npl* ≃ caleçon *m (culotte pour femme)*.

French leave *n* : **to take ~** *inf UK dated* filer à l'anglaise.

French letter *n UK dated* [condom] capote *f* anglaise.

French loaf *n* baguette *f*.

Frenchman ['frentʃmən] *(pl* **Frenchmen** [-mən]) *n* Français *m*.

French polish *n UK* vernis *m* (à l'alcool).
◆ **French-polish** *vt UK* vernir (à l'alcool).

French Riviera *pr n* : **the ~** la Côte d'Azur.

French-speaking *adj* francophone.

French stick *n UK* baguette *f*.

French toast *n* [in UK] *pain grillé d'un seul côté* ▪ [in US] pain *m* perdu.

French Triangle *pr n* : **the ~** *région du sud des États-Unis comprise entre La Nouvelle-Orléans, Alexandria et Cameron*.

French window *n UK* porte-fenêtre *f*.

Frenchwoman ['frentʃ,wʊmən] *(pl* **Frenchwomen** [-,wɪmɪn]) *n* Française *f*.

Frenchy ['frentʃɪ] *(pl* **Frenchies**) *inf* = **Frenchie**.

frenetic [frə'netɪk] *adj* frénétique.

frenetically [frə'netɪklɪ] *adv* frénétiquement.

frenzied ['frenzɪd] *adj* [activity] frénétique, forcené ▪ [crowd] déchaîné ▪ [person] forcené, déchaîné.

frenzy ['frenzɪ] *n* **1.** [fury, passion] frénésie *f* ▪ **to work o.s. (up) into a ~ (over sthg)** se mettre dans une colère noire **2.** [fit, outburst] accès *m*, crise *f*.

frequency ['fri:kwənsɪ] *n* fréquence *f*.

frequency distribution *n* distribution *f* des fréquences.

frequency modulation *n* modulation *f* de fréquence.

frequent <> *adj* ['fri:kwənt] fréquent ▪ **a ~ visitor** un habitué.
<> *vt* [frɪ'kwent] *lit* fréquenter.

frequentative [frɪ'kwentətɪv] *adj* LING fréquentatif.

frequently ['fri:kwəntlɪ] *adv* fréquemment, souvent.

fresco ['freskəʊ] *(pl* **frescoes** *OR pl* **frescos**) *n* fresque *f*.

fresh [freʃ] <> *adj* **1.** [recently made or produced] frais, fraîche *f* ▪ **the vegetables are ~ from the garden** les légumes viennent directement du jardin ▪ **~ from** *OR* **out of university** (tout) frais émoulu de l'université **2.** [idea, problem] nouveau *(before vowel or silent 'h'* **nouvel***)*, nouvelle *f*, original ▪ [news, paint] frais, fraîche *f* ▪ [impression] frais, fraîche *f* ▪ **I need some ~ air** j'ai besoin de prendre l'air ▪ **they have agreed to ~ talks** ils ont accepté de reprendre leurs négociations ▪ **to make a ~ start** prendre un nouveau départ ▪ **he put on a ~ shirt** il mit une chemise propre ▪ **start on a ~ page** prenez une nouvelle page **3.** [not salt - water] doux, douce *f* **4.** [rested] frais, fraîche *f* ◐ **as ~ as a daisy** frais comme une rose **5.** [clean] frais, fraîche *f*, pur **6.** [bright] : **~ colours** des couleurs fraîches **7.** METEOR [gen] frais, fraîche *f* ▪ [on Beaufort scale] : **~ breeze** bonne brise *f* ▪ **~ gale** coup *m* de vent **8.** [refreshing - taste] rafraîchissant **9.** *US inf* [impudent] insolent ▪ [child] mal élevé ▪ **don't you get ~ with me, young man!** pas d'insolence avec moi, jeune homme! **10.** *US inf* [sexually forward] effronté.
<> *adv* fraîchement ▪ **~ cut flowers** des fleurs fraîchement cueillies ▪ **to be ~ out of sthg** *inf* être à court de *OR* manquer de qqch.

freshen ['freʃn] ◇ *vt* rafraîchir.
◇ *vi* NAUT [wind] fraîchir.
◆ **freshen up** ◇ *vi insep* faire un brin de toilette.
◇ *vt sep* **1.** [person] faire un brin de toilette à **2.** [house, room] donner un petit coup de peinture à **3.** [drink] : **let me ~ up your drink** laisse-moi te resservir à boire.

fresher ['freʃəʳ] *n inf* UNIV bizut *m*, bizuth *m*, étudiant *m*, -e *f* de première année.

freshly ['freʃlɪ] *adv* récemment ■ **~ made coffee** du café qui vient d'être fait ■ **~ squeezed orange juice** jus *m* d'oranges pressées ■ **the grave had been ~ dug** la fosse avait été fraîchement creusée.

freshman ['freʃmən] (*pl* **freshmen** [-mən]) *US* = **fresher**.

freshness ['freʃnɪs] *n* fraîcheur *f*.

freshwater ['freʃ,wɔ:təʳ] *adj* : **~ fish** poisson *m* d'eau douce.

fret [fret] (*pret & pp* **fretted**, *cont* **fretting**) ◇ *vi* [worry] tracasser ■ **to ~ about** *OR* **over sb** se faire du souci pour qqn ■ **the small boy was fretting for his mother** le petit garçon réclamait sa mère en pleurant.
◇ *vt* **1.** [worry] : **to ~ one's life away** passer sa vie à se tourmenter *OR* à se faire du mauvais sang **2.** [erode, wear down] ronger **3.** [decorate - metal, wood] chantourner.
◇ *n* **1.** *inf* [state] : **to get in a ~ about sthg** se faire du mauvais sang *OR* se ronger les sangs à propos de qqch **2.** [on a guitar] touchette *f*, frette *f*.

fretful ['fretfʊl] *adj* [anxious] soucieux ■ [irritable, complaining] grincheux, maussade ■ **a ~ child** un enfant grognon ■ **the baby's ~ crying** les pleurnichements du bébé.

fretfully ['fretfʊlɪ] *adv* [anxiously - ask, say] avec inquiétude.

fretsaw ['fretsɔ:] *n* scie *f* à chantourner.

fretwork ['fretwɜ:k] *n* chantournement *m*.

Freudian ['frɔɪdɪən] ◇ *adj* freudien.
◇ *n* disciple *mf* de Freud.

Freudian slip *n* lapsus *m*.

FRG (*abbrev of* **Federal Republic of Germany**) *pr n* RFA *f*.

Fri. (*written abbrev of* **Friday**) ven.

friable ['fraɪəbl] *adj* friable.

friar ['fraɪəʳ] *n* frère *m*, moine *m*.

friary ['fraɪərɪ] (*pl* **friaries**) *n* monastère *m*.

fricassee ['frɪkəsi:] ◇ *n* fricassée *f*.
◇ *vt* fricasser.

fricative ['frɪkətɪv] ◇ *adj* constrictif, fricatif.
◇ *n* constrictive *f*, fricative *f*.

friction ['frɪkʃn] *n* **1.** PHYS friction *f* **2.** [discord] friction *f*, conflit *m* ■ **it's an issue that often causes ~ between neighbours** c'est un problème qui est souvent cause de frictions entre voisins.

frictionless ['frɪkʃənlɪs] *adj* sans friction.

Friday ['fraɪdeɪ] *n* vendredi *m* ■ **it's ~ today** nous sommes *OR* on est vendredi aujourd'hui ■ **I'll see you (on) ~** je te verrai vendredi ■ **he leaves on ~, he leaves ~** *US* il part vendredi ■ **the cleaning woman comes on ~s** la femme de ménage vient le vendredi ■ **I work ~s** je travaille le vendredi ■ **there's a market each ~** *OR* **every ~** il y a un marché tous les vendredis *OR* chaque vendredi ■ **every other ~, every second ~** un vendredi sur deux ■ **we arrive on the ~ and leave on the Sunday** nous arrivons le vendredi et repartons le dimanche ■ **the programme's usually shown on a ~** généralement cette émission passe le vendredi ■ **the following ~** le vendredi suivant ■ **she saw the doctor last ~** elle a vu le médecin vendredi dernier ■ **I have an appointment next ~** j'ai un rendez-vous vendredi prochain ■ **the ~ after next** vendredi en huit ■ **the ~ before last** l'autre vendredi ■ **a week from ~, a week on ~** *UK*, **~ week** *UK* vendredi en huit ■ **a fortnight on ~, ~ fortnight** *UK* vendredi en quinze ■ **a week/fortnight ago ~** il y a eu huit/quinze jours vendredi ■ **~ morning** vendredi matin ■ **~ afternoon** vendredi après-midi ■ **~ evening** vendredi soir ■ **we're going out (on) ~ night** nous sortons vendredi soir ■ **she spent ~ night at her friend's house** elle a passé la nuit de vendredi chez son amie ■ **~ 26 February** vendredi 26 février ■ **they were married on ~ June 12th** ils se sont mariés le vendredi 12 juin ■ **~ the thirteenth** vendredi treize.

fridge [frɪdʒ] *n UK* réfrigérateur *m* ■ **~ magnet** magnet *m*.

fridge-freezer *n* réfrigérateur-congélateur *m*.

fried [fraɪd] *adj* frit ■ **~ eggs** œufs *mpl* poêlés *OR* sur le plat ■ **~ food** friture *f* ■ **~ potatoes** pommes *fpl* frites ■ **(special) ~ rice** riz *m* cantonais.

friend [frend] *n* **1.** [gen] ami *m*, -e *f* ■ **his school ~s** ses camarades d'école ■ **Bill's a good ~ of mine** Bill est un grand ami à moi ■ **we're just good ~s** nous sommes bons amis sans plus ■ **she's someone I used to be ~s with** nous avons été amies ■ **to make ~s** se faire des amis ■ **he tried to make ~s with her brother** il essaya d'être ami avec son frère ■ **shall we be ~s?** on est amis? ; [after a quarrel] on fait la paix? ■ **she's no ~ of mine** elle ne fait pas partie de mes amis ■ **I tell you this as a ~** je vous dis ça en ami ▶ **she has ~s in high places** elle a des amis en haut lieu *OR* bien placés ■ **Friends of the Earth** les Amis de la Terre ■ **the (Society of) Friends** RELIG la Société des Amis, les Quakers ■ **a ~ in need is a ~ indeed** *prov* c'est dans le besoin qu'on reconnaît ses vrais amis **2.** [colleague] collègue *mf* ■ **~s, we are gathered here tonight...** chers amis *OR* collègues, nous sommes réunis ici ce soir.. **3.** [patron] mécène *m*, ami *m*, -e *f*.

friendless ['frendlɪs] *adj* sans amis.

friendliness ['frendlɪnɪs] *n* gentillesse *f*.

friendly ['frendlɪ] (*comp* **friendlier**, *superl* **friendliest**) ◇ *adj* **1.** [person] aimable, gentil ■ [animal] gentil ■ [advice, game, smile] amical ■ **to be ~ to** *OR* **towards sb** être gentil *OR* aimable avec qqn ■ **a ~ welcome** *OR* **reception** un accueil chaleureux **2.** [close, intimate] ami ■ [allied] ami ■ **Anne is still on ~ terms with her brother** Anne est toujours en bons termes avec son frère ■ **a ~ nation** un pays ami ■ **don't let him get too ~** *inf* garde tes distances avec lui ▶ **~ fire** MIL feu *m* allié.
◇ *n* [match] match *m* amical.

friendly society *n UK* société *f* mutuelle *OR* de secours mutuels.

friendship ['frendʃɪp] *n* amitié *f* ■ **to form a ~ with sb** se lier d'amitié avec qqn, nouer une amitié avec qqn ■ **to strike up a ~ with sb** lier amitié avec qqn.

frier ['fraɪəʳ] = **fryer**.

Friesian ['fri:ʒən] *n* : **~ (cow)** frisonne *f*.

frieze [fri:z] *n* **1.** ARCHIT frise *f* **2.** TEX ratine *f*.

frigate ['frɪgət] *n* frégate *f*.

frigging△ ['frɪgɪŋ] *adj* : **move your ~ car!** enlève-moi cette foutue bagnole!△.

fright [fraɪt] *n* **1.** [sudden fear] frayeur *f*, peur *f* ■ **to take ~ at sthg** avoir peur de qqch ■ **to give sb a ~** faire une frayeur à qqn ■ **you gave me a terrible ~!** vous m'avez fait une de ces frayeurs! ■ **I got the ~ of my life when he said that** j'ai eu la peur de ma vie quand il a dit ça **2.** *inf* [mess] : **you look an absolute ~** tu fais vraiment peur à voir.

frighten ['fraɪtn] *vt* effrayer, faire peur à ■ **to ~ sb out of doing sthg** dissuader qqn de faire qqch en lui faisant peur ■ **to ~ sb into doing sthg** obliger qqn à faire qqch en lui faisant peur ■ **to ~ sb to death** *OR* **out of their wits, to ~ the life out of sb** faire une peur bleue à qqn.
◆ **frighten away** *vt sep* faire fuir (par la peur) ■ [animal] effaroucher ■ **the burglars were ~ed away by the police siren** effrayés par la sirène de police, les cambrioleurs ont pris la fuite.
◆ **frighten off** *vt sep* **1.** [cause to flee] faire fuir ■ [animal] effaroucher **2.** [intimidate] chasser, faire peur à, faire fuir.

frightened ['fraɪtnd] *adj* effrayé ■ **to be ~ of sthg** avoir peur de qqch ■ **I was too ~ to speak** je n'arrivais pas à parler tellement j'avais peur ■ **there's nothing to be ~ of** il n'y a rien à craindre ■ **he looked ~** il avait l'air d'avoir peur ■ **~ faces/children** des visages/des enfants apeurés.

frightener ['fraɪtnəʳ] *n phr*: **to put the ~s on sb**△ filer la trouille à qqn.

frightening ['fraɪtnɪŋ] *adj* effrayant ■ **the consequences are too ~ to contemplate** on n'ose pas imaginer les conséquences ■ **it's ~ to think what might have happened** ça fait peur de penser à ce qui aurait pu arriver.

frighteningly ['fraɪtnɪŋlɪ] *adv* à faire peur ■ **the story was ~ true to life** l'histoire était d'un réalisme effrayant.

frightful ['fraɪtfʊl] *adj* **1.** [horrible] affreux, horrible **2.** *UK inf* [unpleasant] : **we had a ~ time parking the car** on a eu un mal fou à garer la voiture ■ **he's a ~ bore** [as intensifier] il est horriblement *OR* affreusement casse-pieds.

frightfully ['fraɪtfʊlɪ] *adv UK dated*: **he's a ~ good dancer** il danse remarquablement bien ■ **I'm ~ sorry** je suis absolument désolé.

frigid ['frɪdʒɪd] *adj* **1.** [very cold] glacial, glacé ■ GEOG & METEOR glacial **2.** [sexually] frigide.

frigidity [frɪ'dʒɪdətɪ] *n* **1.** [coldness] froideur *f* **2.** PSYCHOL frigidité *f*.

frijoles [frɪ'həʊlɪz] *npl purée de haricots rouges frits.*

frill [frɪl] *n* TEX ruche *f*, volant *m* ■ CULIN papillote *f* ■ ORNITH collerette *f*.
◆ **frills** *npl* [ornamentation, luxuries] : **without ~s** sans façon ■ **a cheap, basic package holiday with no ~s** des vacances organisées simples et pas chères.

frilly ['frɪlɪ] *adj* **1.** TEX orné de fanfreluches **2.** [style] affecté, apprêté.

fringe [frɪndʒ] <> *n* **1.** [decorative edge] frange *f* **2.** [of hair] frange *f* **3.** [periphery] périphérie *f*, frange *f* ■ **on the ~** *OR* **~s of** *liter* en bordure de ; *fig* en marge de ◗ **~ group** frange *f* **4.** THEAT : **the Fringe (festival)** *UK* le festival off.
<> *vt* franger ■ **the path was ~d with rosebushes** le sentier était bordé de rosiers.

fringe benefit *n* avantage *m* annexe *OR* en nature.

fringe theatre *n UK* théâtre *m* d'avant-garde *OR* expérimental.

frippery ['frɪpərɪ] (*pl* **fripperies**) *n* **1.** [showy objects] colifichets *mpl*, babioles *fpl* ■ [on clothing] fanfreluches *fpl* **2.** [ostentation] mignardises *fpl*, chichi *m*.

Frisbee® ['frɪzbɪ] *n* Frisbee® *m inv*.

Frisian ['fri:ʒən] <> *n* **1.** [person] Frison *m*, - onne *f* **2.** LING frison *m*.
<> *adj* frison.

Frisian Islands *pr npl* : **the ~** l'archipel *m* frison.

frisk [frɪsk] <> *vi* [play] gambader.
<> *vt* [search] fouiller.
<> *n* [search] fouille *f*.

frisky ['frɪskɪ] (*comp* **friskier**, *superl* **friskiest**) *adj* [animal] fringant ■ [person] gaillard.

fritillary [frɪ'tɪlərɪ] *n* fritillaire *f*.

fritter ['frɪtəʳ] <> *n* CULIN beignet *m* ■ **banana ~s** beignets *mpl* de banane.
<> *vt* = **fritter away**.
◆ **fritter away** *vt sep* gaspiller.

frivolity [frɪ'vɒlətɪ] (*pl* **frivolities**) *n* frivolité *f*.

frivolous ['frɪvələs] *adj* frivole.

frizz [frɪz] <> *n* : **she had a ~ of blond hair** elle avait des cheveux blonds tout frisés.
<> *vt* faire friser.
<> *vi* friser.

frizzly ['frɪzlɪ] (*comp* **frizzlier**, *superl* **frizzliest**), **frizzy** ['frɪzɪ] (*comp* **frizzier**, *superl* **frizziest**) *adj* crépu.

fro [frəʊ] **to and fro**.

frock [frɒk] *n* [dress] robe *f* ■ RELIG froc *m*.

frock coat *n* redingote *f*.

frog [frɒg] *n* **1.** ZOOL grenouille *f* ■ **~'s legs** CULIN cuisses *fpl* de grenouille ■ **to have a ~ in one's throat** *inf* avoir un chat dans la gorge **2.** [on uniform] brandebourg *m* ■ [on women's clothing] soutache *f*.
◆ **Frog**△ *n UK* [French person] *terme injurieux désignant un Français.*

Froggy△ ['frɒgɪ] *n UK terme injurieux désignant un Français.*

frogman ['frɒgmən] (*pl* **frogmen** [-mən]) *n* homme-grenouille *m*.

frogmarch ['frɒgmɑ:tʃ] *vt UK porter par les bras et les jambes, le visage vers le sol* ■ **the protesters were ~ed to a police van** les manifestants furent entraînés jusqu'au fourgon de police ■ **they ~ed us out of the building** [moved forcibly] ils nous ont délogés du bâtiment sans ménagement.

frogspawn ['frɒgspɔ:n] *n* frai *m* de grenouilles.

fro-ing ['frəʊɪŋ] **to-ing and fro-ing**.

frolic ['frɒlɪk] (*pret & pp* **frolicked**, *cont* **frolicking**) <> *vi* s'ébattre, gambader.
<> *n* [run] gambades *fpl*, ébats *mpl* ■ [game] jeu *m* ■ **we let the dogs have a ~ in the park** on a laissé les chiens s'ébattre dans le parc.

from [(*weak form* [frəm], *strong form* [frɒm])] *prep* **1.** [indicating starting point - in space] de ; [- in time] de, à partir de, depuis ; [- in price, quantity] à partir de ■ **where's your friend ~?** d'où est *OR* vient votre ami? ■ **I've just come back ~ there** j'en reviens ■ **there are no direct flights ~ Hobart** il n'y a pas de vol direct à partir d'Hobart ■ **the 11:10 ~ Cambridge** le train de 11 h 10 en provenance de Cambridge ■ **~ now on** désormais, dorénavant ■ **~ the age of four** à partir de quatre ans ■ **she was unhappy ~ her first day at boarding school** elle a été malheureuse dès son premier jour à l'internat ■ **a week ~ today** dans huit jours ■ **we've got food left over ~ last night** nous avons des restes d'hier soir ■ **knives ~ £2 each** des couteaux à partir de 2 livres la pièce ■ **6 ~ 14 is 8** 6 ôté de 14 donne 8
2. [indicating origin, source] de ■ **who's the letter ~?** de qui est la lettre? ■ **he got the idea ~ a book he read** il a trouvé l'idée dans un livre qu'il a lu ■ **you can get a money order ~ the post office** vous pouvez avoir un mandat à la poste ■ **I bought my piano ~ a neighbour** j'ai acheté mon piano à un voisin ■ **you mustn't borrow money ~ them** vous ne devez pas leur emprunter de l'argent ■ **I heard about it ~ the landlady** c'est la propriétaire qui m'en a parlé ■ **he translates ~ English into French** il traduit d'anglais en français ■ **she's been away ~ work for a week** ça fait une semaine qu'elle n'est pas allée au travail
3. [off, out of] : **she took a book ~ the shelf** elle a pris un livre sur l'étagère ■ **he drank straight ~ the bottle** il a bu à même la bouteille ■ **he took a beer ~ the fridge** il a pris une bière dans le frigo
4. [indicating position, location] de ■ **you get a great view ~ the bridge** on a une très belle vue du pont
5. [indicating cause, reason] : **you can get sick ~ drinking the water** vous pouvez tomber malade en buvant l'eau ■ **his back hurt ~ lifting heavy boxes** il avait mal au dos après avoir soulevé des gros cartons ■ **I guessed she was Australian ~ the way she spoke** j'ai deviné qu'elle était australienne à sa façon de parler ■ **he died ~ grief** il est mort de chagrin
6. [using] : **Calvados is made ~ apples** le calvados est fait avec des pommes ■ **she played the piece ~ memory** elle joua le morceau de mémoire ■ **I speak ~ personal experience** je sais de quoi je parle
7. [judging by] d'après ■ **~ the way she talks you'd think she were the boss** à l'entendre, on croirait que c'est elle le patron ■ **~ what I gather...** d'après ce que j'ai cru comprendre...
8. [in comparisons] de ■ **it's no different ~ riding a bike** c'est comme faire du vélo ■ **how do you tell one ~ the other?** comment les reconnais-tu l'un de l'autre?
9. [indicating prevention, protection] de ■ **we sheltered ~ the rain in a cave** nous nous sommes abrités de la pluie dans une caverne.

frond [frɒnd] *n* fronde *f* ■ [on palm tree] feuille *f*.

front [frʌnt] <> *n* **1.** [forward part] devant *m* ■ [of vehicle] avant *m* ■ [of queue] début *m* ■ [of stage] devant *m* ■ [of building]

façade *f* ■ **I'll be at the ~ of the train** je serai en tête de *OR* à l'avant du train ■ **he sat up ~ near the driver** il s'est assis à l'avant près du conducteur ■ **our seats were at the ~ of the theatre** nous avions des places aux premiers rangs (du théâtre) ■ **come to the ~ of the class** venez devant ■ **the Times' theatre critic is out ~ tonight** le critique dramatique du Times est dans la salle ce soir ■ **she wrote her name on the ~ of the envelope** elle écrivit son nom sur le devant de l'enveloppe ■ **he got wine down his ~ OR the ~ of his shirt** du vin a été renversé sur le devant de sa chemise
2. [seashore] bord *m* de mer, front *m* de mer ■ **the hotel is on the ~** l'hôtel est au bord de la *OR* sur le front de mer ■ **a walk along OR on the ~** une promenade au bord de la mer
3. MIL front *m* ■ **on the Eastern/Western ~** sur le front Est/Ouest ■ *fig* **the Prime Minister is being attacked on all ~s** on s'en prend au Premier ministre de tous côtés ● **'All Quiet on the Western Front'** ***Remarque*** 'À l'Ouest, rien de nouveau'
4. [joint effort] front *m* ■ **to present a united ~ (on sthg)** faire front commun (devant qqch)
5. [appearance] façade *f* ■ **to put on a bold OR brave ~** faire preuve de courage
6. [cover] façade *f*, couverture *f* ■ **the shop is just a ~ for a drugs ring** le magasin n'est qu'une couverture pour des trafiquants de drogue
7. METEOR front *m*
8. ARCHIT façade *f*
9. *phr* **up ~** *inf* d'avance ■ **they want £5,000 up ~** ils veulent 5 000 livres d'avance.
◇ *adj* **1.** [in a forward position] de devant ■ **~ seat/wheel** AUT siège *m* /roue *f* avant ■ **the ~ page** PRESS la première page ■ **his picture is on the ~ page** sa photo est en première page ■ **I'll be in the ~ end of the train** je serai en tête de *OR* à l'avant du train ■ **his name is on the ~ cover** son nom est en couverture ■ **a ~ view** une vue de face
2. [bogus, fake] de façade
3. LING : **a ~ vowel** une voyelle avant *OR* antérieure.
◇ *adv* par devant ■ **eyes ~!** MIL fixe!
◇ *vi* **1.** *UK* [face] : **the hotel ~s onto the beach** l'hôtel donne sur la plage
2. [cover] : **the newspaper ~ed for a terrorist organization** le journal servait de façade à une organisation terroriste.
◇ *vt* **1.** [stand before] : **lush gardens ~ed the building** il y avait des jardins luxuriants devant le bâtiment
2. CONSTR : **the house was ~ed with stone** la maison avait une façade en pierre
3. [lead] être à la tête de, diriger ■ TV [present] présenter.
◆ **in front** *adv phr* [in theatre, vehicle] à l'avant ■ [ahead, leading] en avant ■ **there was a very tall man in the row in ~** il y avait un très grand homme assis devant moi ■ **the women walked in ~ and the children behind** les femmes marchaient devant et les enfants derrière ■ **to be in ~** SPORT être en tête *OR* premier.
◆ **in front of** *prep phr* devant ■ **he was right in ~ of me** il était juste devant moi.

frontage ['frʌntɪdʒ] *n* **1.** [wall] façade *f* ■ [shopfront] devanture *f* **2.** [land] terrain *m* en bordure.

frontage road *n US* contre-allée *f*.

frontal ['frʌntl] ◇ *adj* MIL [assault, attack] de front ■ ANAT & MED frontal ■ **~ system** METEOR système *m* de fronts.
◇ *n* RELIG parement *m*.

frontbench [ˌfrʌnt'bentʃ] *n UK* POL [members of the government] ministres *mpl* ■ [members of the opposition] ministres *mpl* du cabinet fantôme ■ **the ~es** [in Parliament] *à la Chambre des communes, bancs situés à droite et à gauche du Président et occupés respectivement par les ministres du gouvernement en exercice et ceux du gouvernement fantôme.*

frontbencher [ˌfrʌnt'bentʃəʳ] *n UK* POL [member of the government] ministre *m* ■ [member of the opposition] membre *m* du cabinet fantôme.

front desk *n* réception *f*.

front door *n* [of house] porte *f* d'entrée ■ [of vehicle] portière *f* avant.

frontier [*UK* 'frʌnˌtɪəʳ, *US* frʌn'tɪər] ◇ *n* **1.** *liter* & *fig* [border] frontière *f* ■ **the ~s of science** les frontières *OR* limites de la science **2.** *US* **the ~** la Frontière *(nom donné à la limite des terres habitées par les colons pendant la colonisation de l'Amérique du Nord)* ■ **the Last Frontier** l'Alaska *m*.
◇ *comp* **1.** [dispute] de frontière ■ [post] frontière **2.** *US* [spirit] de pionnier ■ **a ~ town** *une bourgade d'une région limitrophe du pays.*

frontiersman [*UK* 'frʌntɪəzmən, *US* frʌn'tɪrzmən] (*pl* **frontiersmen** [-mən]) *n* pionnier *m*.

frontispiece ['frʌntɪspiːs] *n* frontispice *m*.

front line *n* : **the ~** MIL la première ligne ■ **she is in the ~ in the fight against drug abuse** *fig* elle joue un rôle important dans la lutte contre la toxicomanie.
◆ **front-line** *adj* **1.** MIL [soldiers, troops] en première ligne ■ [ambulance] de zone de combat **2.** POL : **the ~ states** les États *mpl* limitrophes **3.** *US* SPORT : **~ player** avant *m*.

front-loading *adj* [washing machine] à chargement frontal.

front man *n* **1.** [representative, spokesman] porte-parole *m inv*, représentant *m* **2.** *pej* [figurehead] prête-nom *m* **3.** TV [presenter] présentateur *m*.

front of house *n* THEAT *partie d'un théâtre où peuvent circuler les spectateurs.*

front-page, front page *adj* [article, story] de première page ■ **it wasn't exactly ~ news** ça n'a pas fait la une des journaux.

front-page *n* COMPUT page *f* d'accueil.

front room *n* [at front of house] *pièce qui donne sur le devant de la maison* ■ [sitting room] salon *m*.

front-runner *n* favori *m*, - e *f*.

frontwards ['frʌntwədz] *adv* en avant, vers l'avant.

front-wheel drive *n* traction *f* avant.

frost [frɒst] ◇ *n* **1.** [freezing weather] gel *m*, gelée *f* ■ **there was a ~ last night** il a gelé hier soir **2.** [frozen dew] givre *m*, gelée *f* blanche ■ **the grass was covered in ~** le gazon était couvert de givre **3.** *inf* [cold manner] froideur *f*.
◇ *vt* **1.** [freeze] geler ■ [cover with frost] givrer ■ **the rim of the glass was ~ed with sugar** le bord du verre avait été givré avec du sucre **2.** *US* [cake] glacer **3.** TECH [glass pane] dépolir.
◇ *vi* [freeze] geler ■ [become covered with frost] se givrer.
◆ **frost over, frost up** ◇ *vi insep* se givrer.
◇ *vt sep* givrer.

frostbite ['frɒstbaɪt] *n (U)* gelure *f* ■ **he got ~ in his toes** il a eu les orteils gelés.

frostbitten ['frɒstˌbɪtn] *adj* [hands, nose] gelé ■ [plant] gelé, grillé par le gel.

frosted ['frɒstɪd] *adj* **1.** [frozen] gelé ■ [covered with frost] givré **2.** [pane of glass] dépoli **3.** *US* [cake] glacé **4.** [lipstick, nail varnish] nacré **5.** [hair] grisonnant.

frostily ['frɒstɪlɪ] *adv* de manière glaciale, froidement.

frosting ['frɒstɪŋ] *n US* glaçage *m*, glace *f*.

frosty ['frɒstɪ] (*comp* **frostier**, *superl* **frostiest**) *adj* **1.** [weather, air] glacial ■ **we had several ~ nights** il a gelé plusieurs nuits **2.** [ground, window] couvert de givre **3.** [answer, manner] glacial, froid.

froth [frɒθ] ◇ *n (U)* **1.** [foam] écume *f*, mousse *f* ■ [on beer] mousse *f* ■ [on lips] écume *f* **2.** [trivialities, empty talk] futilités *fpl*.
◇ *vi* [liquid] écumer, mousser ■ [beer, soap] mousser ■ **to ~ at the mouth** écumer, baver.
◇ *vt* faire mousser.

frothy ['frɒθɪ] (*comp* **frothier**, *superl* **frothiest**) *adj* **1.** [liquid] mousseux, écumeux ■ [beer] mousseux ■ [sea] écumeux **2.** [entertainment, literature] creux **3.** [dress, lace] léger, vaporeux.

frown [fraʊn] ◇ *vi* froncer les sourcils, se renfrogner ■ **she ~ed at my remark** mon observation lui a fait froncer les sourcils ■ **to ~ at sb** regarder qqn de travers, faire les gros yeux à qqn.

◇ *n* froncement *m* de sourcils ■ **he gave a ~** il fronça les sourcils.
◇ *comp* : **~ lines** rides *fpl* intersourcilières.
◆ **frown on, frown upon** *vt insep* désapprouver ■ **such behaviour is rather ~ed upon** ce type de comportement n'est pas vu d'un très bon œil.

frowsty ['fraʊstɪ] (*comp* **frowstier**, *superl* **frowstiest**) *adj* qui sent le renfermé.

froze [frəʊz] *pt* ▷ **freeze**.

frozen ['frəʊzn] ◇ *pp* ▷ **freeze**.
◇ *adj* **1.** [ground, lake, pipes] gelé ■ [person] gelé, glacé ■ **the lake is ~ solid** le lac est complètement gelé ■ **my hands are ~** j'ai les mains gelées *OR* glacées ■ **I'm ~ stiff** je suis gelé jusqu'à la moelle (des os) ▶ **~ food** [in refrigerator] aliments *mpl* congelés ; [industrially frozen] surgelés *mpl* ■ **~ food compartment** congélateur *m* **2.** [prices, salaries] bloqué ■ FIN [assets, credit] gelé, bloqué **3.** MED : **~ shoulder** épaule *f* ankylosée.

FRS ◇ *n* (*abbrev of* **Fellow of the Royal Society**) ≃ membre *m* de l'Académie des sciences.
◇ *pr n* = **Federal Reserve System**.

fructify ['frʌktɪfaɪ] (*pret & pp* **fructified**) *fml* ◇ *vi* fructifier.
◇ *vt* faire fructifier.

frugal ['fru:gl] *adj* **1.** [person] économe, frugal ■ [life] frugal, simple ■ **she's very ~ with her money** elle est près de ses sous **2.** [meal] frugal.

frugality [fru:'gælətɪ] *n* **1.** [of person] parcimonie *f*, frugalité *f* ■ [of life] frugalité *f*, simplicité *f* **2.** [of meal] frugalité *f*.

frugally ['fru:gəlɪ] *adv* [live] simplement, frugalement ■ [distribute, give] parcimonieusement.

fruit [fru:t] (*pl* **fruits**) ◇ *n* **1.** (*pl inv*) *liter* fruit *m* ■ **to eat ~** manger des fruits ■ **a piece of ~** un fruit ■ **would you like ~ or cheese?** voulez-vous un fruit ou du fromage? ■ **a tree in ~** un arbre qui porte des fruits ■ *fig* fruit *m* ■ **the ~ of her womb** le fruit de ses entrailles ■ **their plans have never borne fruit** leurs projets ne se sont jamais réalisés **2.** *UK inf dated* [term of address] : **old ~** mon vieux **3.** △ *US pej* [homosexual] pédé△ *m*, tante△ *f*.
◇ *comp* [basket, knife] à fruits ■ [diet, farm, stall] fruitier ■ **~ dish** [individual] coupe *f*, coupelle *f* ; [large] coupe *f* à fruits, compotier *m* ■ **~ farmer** arboriculteur *m* (fruitier) ■ **~ farming** arboriculture *f* (fruitière) ■ **~ juice/salad** jus *m* /salade *f* de fruits ■ **~ tree** arbre *m* fruitier.
◇ *vi* BOT donner.

fruit bat *n* chauve-souris *f* frugivore.

fruit cake *n* **1.** [cake] cake *m* **2.** *inf* [lunatic] cinglé *m*, - e *f*.

fruit cocktail *n* macédoine *f* de fruits.

fruit drop *n* bonbon *m* aux fruits.

fruiterer ['fru:tərəʳ] *n UK* marchand *m*, - e *f* de fruits, fruitier *m*, - ère *f*.

fruit fly *n* mouche *f* du vinaigre, drosophile *f*.

fruitful ['fru:tful] *adj* **1.** [discussion, suggestion] fructueux, utile ■ [attempt, collaboration] fructueux **2.** [soil] fertile, fécond ■ [plant, tree] fécond, productif.

fruitfully ['fru:tfulɪ] *adv* fructueusement.

fruit gum *n UK* boule *f* de gomme.

fruition [fru:'ɪʃn] *n fml* réalisation *f* ■ **to come to ~** se réaliser ■ **to bring sthg to ~** réaliser qqch, concrétiser qqch.

fruitless ['fru:tlɪs] *adj* **1.** [discussion, effort] vain, sans résultat **2.** [plant, tree] stérile, infécond ■ [soil] stérile.

fruitlessly ['fru:tlɪslɪ] *adv* en vain, vainement.

fruit machine *n UK* machine *f* à sous.

fruity ['fru:tɪ] (*comp* **fruitier**, *superl* **fruitiest**) *adj* **1.** [flavour, sauce] fruité, de fruit ■ [perfume, wine] fruité **2.** [voice] étoffé, timbré **3.** *inf* [joke, story] corsé, salé.

frump [frʌmp] *n* femme *f* mal habillée.

frumpish ['frʌmpɪʃ], **frumpy** ['frʌmpɪ] *adj* mal habillé ■ **she wears rather ~ clothes** elle s'habille plutôt mal.

frustrate [frʌ'streɪt] *vt* [person] frustrer, agacer, contrarier ■ [efforts, plans] contrecarrer, faire échouer, contrarier ■ [plot] déjouer, faire échouer ■ **all our efforts to contact her were ~** tous nos efforts pour la contacter ont été vains *OR* ont échoué ■ **the prisoner was ~d in his attempt to escape** le prisonnier a raté sa tentative d'évasion.

frustrated [frʌ'streɪtɪd] *adj* **1.** [annoyed] frustré, agacé ■ [disappointed] frustré, déçu ■ [sexually] frustré ■ **a ~ poet** un poète manqué **2.** [attempt, effort] vain.

frustrating [frʌ'streɪtɪŋ] *adj* agaçant, frustrant, pénible.

frustration [frʌ'streɪʃn] *n* [gen - PSYCHOL] frustration *f* ■ **it's one of the ~s of the job** c'est un des aspects frustrants du travail.

fry [fraɪ] (*pret & pp* **fried**, *pl* **fries**) ◇ *vt* CULIN faire frire, frire ■ **he fried himself an egg** il s'est fait un œuf sur le plat ▶ **go ~ an egg!** *US inf* va te faire cuire un œuf!
◇ *vi* [food] frire ■ *fig* [person] griller.
◇ *n (U)* ZOOL [fish] fretin *m* ■ [frogs] têtards *mpl*.
◆ **fries** *npl US* = **french fries**.
◆ **fry up** *vt sep* faire frire, frire.

fryer ['fraɪəʳ] *n* **1.** [pan] poêle *f* (à frire) ■ [for deep-fat frying] friteuse *f* **2.** [chicken] poulet *m* à frire.

frying ['fraɪɪŋ] *n* friture *f*.

frying pan *UK*, **fry pan** *US n* poêle *f* (à frire) ■ **to jump out of the ~ into the fire** tomber de Charybde en Scylla, changer un cheval borgne pour un cheval aveugle.

fry-up *n UK inf plat constitué de plusieurs aliments frits ensemble.*

FSA [,efes'eɪ] (*abbrev of* **food standards agency**) *n agence pour la sécurité alimentaire.*

f-stop *n* ouverture *f* (du diaphragme).

ft **1.** *written abbr of* **foot** **2.** *written abbr of* **fort**.

FT *pr n* = **Financial Times**.

FTC *pr n* = **Federal Trade Commission**.

FT Index (*abbrev of* **Financial Times Industrial Ordinary Share Index**) *n UK* indice *m* du "Financial Times" *(moyenne quotidienne des principales valeurs boursières britanniques)*.

FTP [,efti:'pi:] (*abbrev of* **file transfer protocol**) *n* FTP *m*.

fuchsia ['fju:ʃə] *n* [colour] fuchsia *m* ■ BOT fuchsia *m*.

fuck▲ [fʌk] ◇ *vt* baiser▲ ■ **~ you!, go ~ yourself!** va te faire enculer *OR* foutre!▲ ■ **~ it!** putain de merde!▲ ■ **~ me!** putain!△.
◇ *vi* baiser▲ ■ **don't ~ with me!** *fig* essaie pas de te foutre de ma gueule!
◇ *n* **1.** [act] baise▲ *f* **2.** [sexual partner] : **he's a good ~** il baise bien▲ **3.** *US* [idiot] : **you stupid ~!** espèce de connard!△ **4.** *phr* **I don't give a ~** j'en ai rien à branler△ **5.** [as intensifier] : **what the ~ do you expect?** mais qu'est-ce que tu veux, putain de merde?▲.
◇ *interj* putain de merde!▲.
◆ **fuck about▲** *UK*, **fuck around▲** ◇ *vi insep* déconner△.
◇ *vt sep* faire chier▲.
◆ **fuck off▲** *vi insep* foutre le camp△ ■ **~ off!** va te faire enculer *OR* foutre!▲.
◆ **fuck up▲** ◇ *vt sep* [plan, project] foutre la merde dans△ ■ [person] foutre dans la merde△ ■ **he's really ~ed up emotionally** il est complètement paumé.
◇ *vi insep* merder△.

fucker▲ ['fʌkəʳ] *n* : **you stupid ~!** mais qu'est-ce que tu peux être con!△.

fucking▲ ['fʌkɪŋ] ◇ *adj* : **I'm fed up with this ~ car!** j'en ai plein le cul de cette putain de bagnole!▲ ■ **you ~ idiot!** pauvre con!▲ ■ **~ hell!** putain de merde!▲.
◇ *adv* : **he's ~ stupid!** tu parles d'un con!▲ ■ **it was a ~ awful day!** tu parles d'une putain de journée!▲.

fuddled ['fʌdld] *adj* [ideas, mind] embrouillé, confus ▪ [person - confused] confus ; [- tipsy] gris, éméché.

fuddy-duddy ['fʌdɪ,dʌdɪ] (*pl* **fuddy-duddies**) *n inf* vieux schnock *m*, vieille schnoque *f*.

fudge [fʌdʒ] <> *n* **1.** *(U)* [sweet] caramel *m* ▪ **a piece of ~** un caramel **2.** *(U)* [nonsense] balivernes *fpl*, âneries *fpl* **3.** *(U)* [dodging] faux-fuyant *m*, échappatoire *f* **4.** TYPO [stop press box] emplacement *m* de la dernière heure ▪ [stop press news] (insertion *f* de) dernière heure *f*, dernières nouvelles *fpl*.
<> *vi* [evade, hedge] esquiver le problème ▪ **the President ~d on the budget issue** le président a esquivé les questions sur le budget.
<> *vt* **1.** [make up - excuse] inventer ; [- story] monter ; [- figures, results] truquer **2.** [avoid, dodge] esquiver.

fuel [fjʊəl] (*UK pret & pp* **fuelled**, *cont* **fuelling**) (*US pret & pp* **fueled**, *cont* **fueling**) <> *n* **1.** [gen - AERON] combustible *m* ▪ [coal] charbon *m* ▪ [oil] mazout *m*, fuel *m*, fioul *m* ▪ [wood] bois *m* ▪ AUT carburant *m* ▪ **coal is not a very efficient ~** le charbon n'est pas une source d'énergie très efficace ➡ **nuclear ~** combustible *m* nucléaire **2.** *fig* **to add ~ to the flames** jeter de l'huile sur le feu ▪ **his words were merely ~ to her anger** ses paroles n'ont fait qu'attiser *OR* qu'aviver sa colère.
<> *comp* [bill, costs] de chauffage ▪ **~ injector** injecteur *m* de carburant ▪ **~ tank** [in home] cuve *f* à mazout ; [in car] réservoir *m* de carburant *OR* d'essence ; [in ship] soute *f* à mazout *OR* à fuel.
<> *vt* **1.** [furnace] alimenter (en combustible) ▪ [car, plane, ship] approvisionner en carburant **2.** *fig* [controversy] aviver ▪ **his words only fuelled their anger/their suspicions** ses paroles n'ont servi qu'à aviver leur colère/leurs soupçons.

fuel cell *n* élément *m* de conversion.

fuel-efficient *adj* économique, qui ne consomme pas beaucoup.

fuel injection *n* injection *f* (de carburant).

fuel oil *n* mazout *m*, fuel *m*, fioul *m*.

fug [fʌg] *n UK* renfermé *m*.

fugitive ['fju:dʒətɪv] <> *n* [escapee] fugitif *m*, - ive *f*, évadé *m*, - e *f* ▪ [refugee] réfugié *m*, - e *f* ▪ **she's a ~ from justice** elle fuit la justice, elle est recherchée par la justice.
<> *adj* **1.** [debtor, slave] fugitif **2.** *lit* [beauty, happiness] éphémère, passager ▪ [impression, thought, vision] fugitif, passager.

fugue [fju:g] *n* MUS & PSYCHOL fugue *f*.

Fuji ['fu:dʒɪ] *pr n* : **Mount ~** le Fuji-Yama.

Fulbright Scholarship ['fʊlbraɪt-] *n aux États-Unis, bourse destinée à favoriser les échanges entre étudiants et professeurs d'universités de différents pays.*

fulcrum ['fʊlkrəm] (*pl* **fulcrums** *OR pl* **fulcra** [-krə]) *n* [pivot] pivot *m*, point *m* d'appui ▪ *fig* [prop, support] point *m* d'appui.

fulfil *UK*, **fulfill** *US* [fʊl'fɪl] (*pret & pp* **fulfilled**, *cont* **fulfilling**) *vt* **1.** [carry out - ambition, dream, plan] réaliser ; [- prophecy, task] accomplir, réaliser ; [- promise] tenir ; [- duty, obligation] remplir, s'acquitter de **2.** [satisfy - condition] remplir ; [- norm, regulation] répondre à, obéir à ; [- desire, need] satisfaire, répondre à ; [- prayer, wish] exaucer ▪ **it's important to feel fulfilled** il est important de se réaliser (dans la vie) **3.** [complete, finish - prison sentence] achever, terminer **4.** COMM [order] exécuter ▪ [contract] remplir, respecter.

fulfilled [fʊl'fɪld] *adj* [life] épanoui, heureux ▪ [person] épanoui, comblé.

fulfilling [fʊl'fɪlɪŋ] *adj* extrêmement satisfaisant.

fulfilment *UK*, **fulfillment** *US* [fʊl'fɪlmənt] *n* **1.** [of ambition, dream, wish] réalisation *f* ▪ [of desire] satisfaction *f* ▪ [of plan, condition, contract] exécution *f* ▪ [of duty, prophecy] accomplissement *m* ▪ [of prayer] exaucement *m* **2.** [satisfaction] (sentiment *m* de) contentement *m OR* satisfaction *f* ▪ **she gets a sense** *OR* **feeling of ~ from her work** son travail la comble **3.** [of prison sentence] achèvement *m*, fin *f* **4.** COMM [of order] exécution *f*.

full [fʊl] <> *adj* **1.** [completely filled] plein, rempli ▪ **will you open the door for me, my hands are ~** vous voulez bien m'ouvrir la porte, j'ai les mains occupées ▪ **don't talk with your mouth ~** ne parle pas la bouche pleine ▪ **you shouldn't go swimming on a ~ stomach** tu ne devrais pas nager après avoir mangé ▪ **I've got a ~ week ahead of me** j'ai une semaine chargée devant moi
2. *fig* **(to be) ~ of** [filled with] (être) plein de ▪ **the children were ~ of excitement** les enfants étaient très excités ▪ **her parents were ~ of hope** ses parents étaient remplis d'espoir ▪ **her letters are ~ of spelling mistakes** ses lettres sont truffées de fautes d'orthographe ▪ **~ of energy** *OR* **of life** plein de vie ▪ **to be ~ of o.s.** être plein de soi-même *OR* imbu de sa personne ▪ **he's ~ of his own importance** il est pénétré de sa propre importance ▪ **they/the papers were ~ of news about China** ils/les journaux ne parlaient que de la Chine ➡ **to be ~ of it** *inf OR* **~ of shit** ▲ brasser du vent
3. [crowded - room, theatre] comble, plein ; [- hotel, restaurant, train] complet, - ète *f* ▪ **the hotel was ~ (up)** l'hôtel était complet
4. [satiated] rassasié, repu ▪ **I'm ~ (up)!** *UK* je n'en peux plus!
5. [complete, whole] tout, complet, - ète *f* ▪ **she listened to him for three ~ hours** elle l'a écouté pendant trois heures entières ▪ **the house is a ~ 10 miles from town** la maison est à 15 bons kilomètres *OR* est au moins à 15 kilomètres de la ville ▪ **~ fare** [for adult] plein tarif ; [for child] une place entière ▪ **he rose to his ~ height** il s'est dressé de toute sa hauteur ▪ **to fall ~ length** tomber de tout son long ▪ **he leads a very ~ life** il a une vie bien remplie ▪ **I don't want a ~ meal** je ne veux pas un repas entier ▪ **give him your ~ name and address** donnez-lui vos nom, prénom et adresse ▪ **in ~ uniform** en grande tenue ▪ **in ~ view of the cameras/of the teacher** devant les caméras/le professeur ➡ **~ marks : to get ~ marks** avoir vingt sur vingt ▪ **~ marks for observation!** bravo, vous êtes très observateur!
6. [maximum] plein ▪ **make ~ use of this opportunity** mettez bien cette occasion à profit, tirez bien profit de cette occasion ▪ **they had the music on ~ volume** ils avaient mis la musique à fond ▪ **peonies in ~ bloom** des pivoines épanouies ▪ **the trees are in ~ bloom** les arbres sont en fleurs ▪ **it was going ~ blast** [heating] ça chauffait au maximum ; [radio, TV] ça marchait à pleins tubes ; [car] ça roulait à toute allure ▪ **the orchestra was at ~ strength** l'orchestre était au grand complet ▪ **~ employment** ECON plein emploi *m* ▪ **she caught the ~ force of the blow** elle a reçu le coup de plein fouet
7. [detailed] détaillé ▪ **I didn't get the ~ story** je n'ai pas entendu tous les détails de l'histoire ▪ **I asked for ~ information** j'ai demandé des renseignements complets
8. [plump - face] plein, rond ; [- figure] rondelet, replet, - ète *f* ; [- lips] charnu ▪ **dresses designed to flatter the ~er figure** des robes qui mettent en valeur les silhouettes épanouies
9. [ample, wide - clothes] large, ample
10. [sound] timbré ▪ [voice] étoffé, timbré
11. [flavour] parfumé ▪ [wine] robuste, qui a du corps
12. [brother, sister] germain
13. *UK* MIL : **~ colonel** colonel *m* ▪ **~ general** ≃ général *m* à cinq étoiles.
<> *adv* **1.** [entirely, completely] complètement, entièrement ▪ **I turned the heat ~ on** *UK OR* **on ~** j'ai mis le chauffage à fond ▪ **he put the radio ~ on** *UK* il a mis la radio à fond
2. [directly, exactly] carrément ▪ **the blow caught her ~ in the face** elle a reçu le coup en pleine figure
3. *phr* **you know ~ well I'm right** tu sais très bien *OR* parfaitement que j'ai raison ▪ **~ out** *UK* à toute vitesse, à pleins gaz.
◆ **in full** *adv phr* intégralement ▪ **she paid in ~** elle a tout payé ▪ **they refunded my money in ~** ils m'ont entièrement remboursé ▪ **write out your name in ~** écrivez votre nom en toutes lettres ▪ **they published the book in ~** ils ont publié le texte intégral *OR* dans son intégralité.
◆ **to the full** *adv phr* au plus haut degré, au plus haut point ▪ **enjoy life to the ~** *UK* profitez de la vie au maximum.

fullback ['fʊlbæk] *n* arrière *m*.

full-blooded [-'blʌdɪd] *adj* **1.** [hearty - person] vigoureux, robuste ; [- effort] vigoureux, puissant ; [- argument] violent **2.** [purebred] de pure race, pur sang.

full-blown *adj* **1.** [flower] épanoui **2.** *fig* [complete] à part entière ▪ **a ~ doctor** *UK* un médecin diplômé ▪ **~ war** la guerre totale ■ **the discussion developed into a ~ argument** la discussion a dégénéré en véritable dispute **3.** MED : ~ **AIDS** *UK* sida *m* avéré.

full board *n* pension *f* complète.

full-bodied [-'bɒdɪd] *adj* [wine] qui a du corps, corsé.

full cream milk *n UK* lait *m* entier.

full dress *n* [evening clothes] tenue *f* de soirée ■ [uniform] grande tenue *f*.

◆ **full-dress** *adj* : **full-dress uniform** tenue *f* de cérémonie, grande tenue *f* ■ **full-dress rehearsal** THEAT répétition *f* générale.

fuller's earth ['fʊləz-] *n* terre *f* à foulon.

full-face(d) *adj* **1.** [person] au visage rond **2.** [photograph] de face **3.** TYPO gras, grasse *f*.

full-fashioned *US* = **fully-fashioned**.

full-fledged *US* = **fully-fledged**.

full frontal *n photographie montrant une personne nue de face.*

◆ **full-frontal** *adj* : **full-frontal photograph** nu *m* de face *(photographie)* ■ **full-frontal nudity** [in show] nu *m* intégral.

full-grown *adj* adulte.

full house *n* **1.** CARDS full *m* **2.** THEAT salle *f* comble ■ **to play to a ~** jouer à guichets fermés.

full-length <> *adj* [mirror, portrait] en pied ■ [curtain, dress] long, longue *f* ■ **a ~ film** un long métrage.

<> *adv* : **he was stretched out ~ on the floor** il était étendu de tout son long par terre.

full monty [-'mɒntɪ] *n inf* : **the ~** la totale.

full moon *n* pleine lune *f*.

fullness ['fʊlnɪs] *n* **1.** [state] état *m* plein, plénitude *f* ■ MED [of stomach] plénitude *f* ■ **in the ~ of time** avec le temps **2.** [of details, information] abondance *f* **3.** [of face, figure] rondeur *f* ■ **the ~ of his lips** ses lèvres charnues **4.** [of skirt, sound, voice] ampleur *f*.

full-on *adj inf* [documentary, film - hard-hitting] dur ; [- sexually explicit] cru ■ **he's ~** [gen] il en fait trop ; [making sexual advances] il est entreprenant.

full-page *adj* pleine page ■ **~ advertisement** annonce *f* pleine page.

full professor *n US* professeur *m* d'université *(titulaire d'une chaire)*.

full-scale *adj* **1.** [model, plan] grandeur nature *(inv)* **2.** [all-out - strike, war] total ; [- attack, investigation] de grande envergure ■ **the factory starts ~ production this week** l'usine commence à tourner à plein rendement cette semaine ■ **~ fighting** MIL bataille *f* rangée.

full score *n* partition *f*.

full-size(d) *adj* [animal, plant] adulte ■ [drawing, model] grandeur nature *(inv)* ■ **~ car** *US* grosse voiture *f*.

full stop *n UK* **1.** [pause] arrêt *m* complet ■ **the whole airport came to a ~** toute activité a cessé dans l'aéroport **2.** GRAM point *m* ■ **I won't do it, ~!** je ne le ferai pas, un point c'est tout!

full-throated [-'θrəʊtɪd] *adj* à pleine gorge.

full time *n* [of working week] temps *m* complet ■ SPORT fin *f* de match.

◆ **full-time** <> *adj* **1.** [job] à plein temps ■ **it's a full-time job taking care of a baby!** ça prend beaucoup de temps de s'occuper d'un bébé! **2.** SPORT : **full-time score** score *m* final.

<> *adv* à plein temps, à temps plein.

full-timer *n personne qui travaille à plein temps.*

fully ['fʊlɪ] *adv* **1.** [totally - automatic, dressed, satisfied, trained] complètement, entièrement ■ **I ~ understand** je comprends très bien *OR* parfaitement **2.** [thoroughly - answer, examine, explain] à fond, dans le détail **3.** [at least] au moins, bien ■ **it was ~ two hours before he arrived** au moins deux heures ont passé avant qu'il n'arrive.

fully-fashioned *UK*, **full-fashioned** *US* [-'fæʃnd] *adj* moulant.

fully-fledged *UK*, **full-fledged** *US adj* **1.** [bird] qui a toutes ses plumes **2.** *fig* à part entière ■ **a ~ doctor** un médecin diplômé ■ **a ~ atheist** un athée pur et dur.

fulmar ['fʊlmər] *n* fulmar *m*.

fulminate ['fʌlmɪneɪt] <> *vi fml* fulminer, pester ■ **the preacher ~d against the abuse of drugs** le pasteur fulminait contre l'abus de stupéfiants.

<> *n* fulminate *m*.

fulsome ['fʊlsəm] *adj* [apology, thanks] excessif, exagéré ■ [welcome] plein d'effusions ■ [compliments, praise] dithyrambique.

fumble ['fʌmbl] <> *vi* [grope - in the dark] tâtonner ; [- in pocket, purse] fouiller ■ **he ~d (about *OR* around)in the dark for the light switch** il a cherché l'interrupteur à tâtons dans l'obscurité.

<> *vt* **1.** [handle awkwardly] manier gauchement *OR* maladroitement ■ **he ~d his lines** il récita son texte en bafouillant **2.** SPORT [miss - catch] attraper *OR* arrêter maladroitement.

<> *n* **1.** [grope] tâtonnements *mpl* **2.** SPORT [bad catch] prise *f* de balle maladroite.

fume [fju:m] <> *n (usu pl)* **~s** [gen] exhalaisons *fpl*, émanations *fpl* ; [of gas, liquid] vapeurs *fpl* ■ **factory ~s** fumées *fpl* d'usine.

<> *vi* **1.** [gas] émettre *OR* exhaler des vapeurs ■ [liquid] fumer **2.** [person] rager ■ **the boss is fuming** le patron est furieux.

<> *vt* **1.** [treat with fumes] fumer, fumiger **2.** [rage] : **"this is your fault", she ~d** "c'est de ta faute", dit-elle d'un ton rageur.

fume cupboard *n* sorbonne *f* (de laboratoire).

fumigate ['fju:mɪgeɪt] *vi* & *vt* désinfecter par fumigation, fumiger *fml*.

fun [fʌn] <> *n* **1.** [amusement] amusement *m* ■ [pleasure] plaisir *m* ■ **to have ~** s'amuser ■ **have ~!** amusez-vous bien! ■ **what ~!** ce que c'est drôle *OR* amusant! ■ **skiing is good *OR* great ~** c'est très amusant de faire du ski ■ **her brother is a lot of ~** son frère est très drôle ■ **the children got a lot of ~ out of the bicycle** les enfants se sont bien amusés avec le vélo ■ **I'm learning Chinese for ~ *OR* for the ~ of it** j'apprends le chinois pour mon plaisir ■ **he only went for the ~ of it** il n'y est allé que pour s'amuser ■ **just for the ~ of it he pretended to be the boss** histoire de rire, il a fait semblant d'être le patron ■ **his sister spoiled the ~** sa sœur a joué les trouble-fête *OR* les rabat-joie ■ **having to wear a crash helmet takes all the ~ out of motorcycling** devoir porter un casque gâche tout le plaisir qu'on a à faire de la moto ■ **her boyfriend walked in and that's when the ~ began** *iron* son copain est entré et c'est là qu'on a commencé à rire ■ **the president has become a figure of ~** le président est devenu la risée de tous ■ **to make ~ of *OR* to poke ~ at sb** se moquer de qqn ▶ **~ and games : we'll have a children's party with lots of ~ and games** on va organiser une fête pour les enfants avec des tas de jeux *OR* divertissements ■ **I've had enough of your ~ and games** [foolish behaviour] j'en ai assez de tes blagues *OR* farces ■ **there'll be some ~ and games if his wife finds out** [trouble] ça va mal aller si sa femme l'apprend **2.** [playfulness] enjouement *m*, gaieté *f* ■ **to be full of ~** être plein d'entrain *OR* très gai ■ **he said it in ~** il l'a dit pour rire *OR* en plaisantant.

<> *adj inf* rigolo, marrant ■ **he's a ~ guy *OR* person** il est rigolo *OR* marrant.

funboard ['fʌnbɔ:d] *n* funboard *m*.

function ['fʌŋkʃn] <> *vi* fonctionner, marcher ■ **this room ~s as a study** cette pièce sert de bureau *OR* fait fonction de bureau.

<> *n* **1.** [role - of machine, organ] fonction *f* ; [- of person] fonction *f*, charge *f* ■ **it is the ~ of a lawyer to provide sound legal advice** l'avocat a pour fonction *OR* tâche de donner de bons conseils juridiques **2.** [working] fonctionnement *m* **3.** [ceremony] cérémonie *f* ■ [reception] réception *f* ■ [meeting] réunion *f* **4.** [gen - LING] & MATHS fonction *f* **5.** COMPUT fonction *f*.

functional ['fʌŋkʃnəl] *adj* **1.** [gen - MATHS] & PSYCHOL fonctionnel ■ **~ illiterate** *personne qui, sans être tout à fait anal-*

phabète, est incapable de raisonner et n'a aucun sens pratique **2.** [in working order] : **the machine is no longer ~** la machine ne marche plus *OR* ne fonctionne plus.

functionalism ['fʌŋkʃnəlɪzm] *n* fonctionnalisme *m*.

functionality [fʌŋkʃ'næləti] *n* fonctionnalité *f*.

functionary ['fʌŋkʃnəri] (*pl* **functionaries**) *n* [employee] employé *m*, - e *f (dans une administration)* ■ [civil servant] fonctionnaire *mf*.

function key *n* COMPUT touche *f* de fonction.

function room *n* salle *f* de réception.

function word *n* mot *m* fonctionnel.

fund [fʌnd] ◇ *n* **1.** [reserve of money] fonds *m*, caisse *f* ■ **they've set up a ~ for the earthquake victims** ils ont ouvert une souscription en faveur des victimes du séisme **2.** *fig* fond *m*, réserve *f* ■ **a ~ of knowledge** un trésor de connaissances.
◇ *vt* **1.** [provide money for] financer **2.** FIN [debt] consolider.
◆ **funds** *npl* [cash resources] fonds *mpl* ■ **secret ~s** une caisse noire ■ **to be in/out of ~ s** être/ne pas être en fonds ■ **I'm a bit short of ~s** je n'ai pas beaucoup d'argent ■ **insufficient ~s** [in banking] défaut *m* de provision.

fundamental [,fʌndə'mentl] ◇ *adj* **1.** [basic - concept, rule, principle] fondamental, de base ; [- difference, quality] fondamental, essentiel ; [- change, mistake] fondamental ■ **a knowledge of economics is ~ to a proper understanding of this problem** il est essentiel *OR* fondamental d'avoir des connaissances en économie pour bien comprendre ce problème **2.** [central] fondamental, principal ■ **it's of ~ importance** c'est d'une importance capitale **3.** MUS fondamental.
◇ *n* **1.** *(usu pl)* **the ~s of chemistry** les principes *mpl* de base de la chimie ■ **when it comes to the ~s** quand on en vient à l'essentiel **2.** MUS fondamentale *f*.

fundamentalism [,fʌndə'mentəlɪzm] *n* [gen - RELIG] fondamentalisme *m* ■ [Muslim] intégrisme *m*.

fundamentalist [,fʌndə'mentəlɪst] ◇ *adj* [gen - RELIG] fondamentaliste ■ [Muslim] intégriste.
◇ *n* [gen - RELIG] fondamentaliste *mf* ■ [Muslim] intégriste *mf*.

fundamentally [,fʌndə'mentəlɪ] *adv* **1.** [at bottom] fondamentalement, essentiellement ■ **she seems hard but ~ she's good-hearted** elle a l'air dure, mais au fond elle a bon cœur **2.** [completely] : **I disagree ~ with his policies** je suis radicalement *OR* fondamentalement opposé à sa politique.

fundamental particle *n* particule *f* élémentaire.

fundholder ['fʌndhəʊldəʳ] *n cabinet médical ayant obtenu le droit de gérer son propre budget auprès du système de sécurité sociale britannique.*

funding ['fʌndɪŋ] *n (U)* fonds *mpl*, financement *m*.

fundraiser ['fʌnd,reɪzəʳ] *n* [person] collecteur *m*, - trice *f* de fonds ■ [event] *projet organisé pour collecter des fonds.*

fund-raising [-,reɪzɪŋ] ◇ *n* collecte *f* de fonds.
◇ *adj* [dinner, project, sale] organisé pour collecter des fonds.

funeral ['fju:nərəl] ◇ *n* **1.** [service] enterrement *m*, obsèques *fpl* ■ [more formal] funérailles *fpl* ■ [in announcement] obsèques *fpl* ■ [burial] enterrement *m* ▸ **it's** *OR* **that's your ~!** *inf* débrouille-toi!, c'est ton affaire! **2.** [procession - on foot] cortège *m* funèbre ; [- in cars] convoi *m* mortuaire.
◇ *adj* funèbre.

funeral director *n* entrepreneur *m* de pompes funèbres.

funeral home *US* = **funeral parlour**.

funeral march *n* marche *f* funèbre.

funeral parlour *n* entreprise *f* de pompes funèbres.

funeral pyre *n* bûcher *m* (funéraire).

funeral service *n* service *m OR* office *m* funèbre.

funereal [fju:'nɪərɪəl] *adj* [atmosphere, expression] funèbre, lugubre ■ [voice] sépulcral, lugubre ■ [pace] lent, mesuré.

funfair ['fʌnfeəʳ] *n* fête *f* foraine.

fungal ['fʌŋgl] *adj* fongique.

fungi ['fʌŋgaɪ] *pl* ▷ **fungus**.

fungicide ['fʌndʒɪsaɪd] *n* fongicide *m*.

fungoid ['fʌŋgɔɪd] *adj* fongique.

fungus ['fʌŋgəs] (*pl* **fungi** ['fʌŋgaɪ]) ◇ *n* BOT champignon *m* ■ [mould] moisissure *f* ■ MED fongus *m*.
◇ *comp* : **~ infection** fongus *m*.

funicular [fju:'nɪkjʊləʳ] ◇ *adj* funiculaire ■ **~ railway** funiculaire *m*.
◇ *n* funiculaire *m*.

funk [fʌŋk] ◇ *n* **1.** MUS musique *f* funk, funk *m inv* **2.** *inf dated* [fear] trouille *f*, frousse *f* ■ [depression] découragement *m* ■ **to be in a blue ~** avoir une peur bleue **3.** *dated* [coward] froussard *m*, - e *f*.
◇ *vt* **1.** [be afraid of] ne pas avoir le courage de ■ **she had her chance and she ~ed it** elle a eu sa chance mais elle s'est dégonflée **2.** *(usu passive)* [make afraid] ficher la frousse à.
◇ *adj* funky *(inv)*.

funky ['fʌŋkɪ] (*comp* **funkier**, *superl* **funkiest**) *adj inf* **1.** *esp US* [excellent] super ■ [fashionable] branché, dans le vent **2.** MUS funky *(inv)*.

fun-loving *adj* qui aime s'amuser *OR* rire.

funnel ['fʌnl] (*UK pret & pp* **funnelled**, *cont* **funnelling**) (*US pret & pp* **funneled**, *cont* **funneling**) ◇ *n* **1.** [utensil] entonnoir *m* **2.** [smokestack] cheminée *f*.
◇ *vt* [liquid] (faire) passer dans un entonnoir ■ [crowd, funds] canaliser.
◇ *vi* : **the crowd funnelled out of the gates** la foule s'est écoulée par les grilles.

funnies ['fʌnɪz] *npl* : **the ~** les bandes *fpl* dessinées *(dans un journal)*.

funnily ['fʌnɪlɪ] *adv* **1.** [oddly] curieusement, bizarrement ■ **~ enough, I was just thinking of you** c'est drôle *OR* chose curieuse, je pensais justement à toi **2.** [in a funny manner] drôlement, comiquement.

funny ['fʌnɪ] (*pl* **funnies**) ◇ *adj* **1.** [amusing] amusant, drôle, comique ■ **it's not ~** ce n'est pas drôle ■ **she didn't see the ~ side of it** elle n'a pas vu le côté comique de la situation ■ **he's trying to be ~** il cherche à faire de l'esprit ■ **was it ~ ha-ha or ~ peculiar?** *inf* c'était drôle-rigolo ou drôle-bizarre? **2.** [odd] bizarre, curieux, drôle ■ **she has some ~ ideas about work** elle a de drôles d'idées sur le travail ■ **the wine tastes ~** le vin a un drôle de goût ■ **I think it's ~ that he should turn up now** je trouve (ça) bizarre qu'il arrive maintenant ■ **the ~ thing (about it) is that she claimed she was away** ce qu'il y a de bizarre *OR* de curieux c'est qu'elle ait prétendu ne pas être là ■ **she's ~ that way** *inf* elle est comme ça ■ **that's ~, I thought I heard the phone ring** c'est curieux *OR* drôle, j'ai cru entendre le téléphone ■ **the whole conversation left me with a ~ feeling** la conversation m'a fait un drôle d'effet ■ **I've got a ~ feeling that's not the last we've seen of her** j'ai comme l'impression qu'on va la revoir ■ **I feel a bit ~** *inf* [odd] je me sens tout drôle *OR* tout chose ; [ill] je ne suis pas dans mon assiette, je suis un peu patraque **3.** [dubious, suspicious] louche ■ **there's some ~ business** *inf OR* **there's something ~ going on** il se passe quelque chose de louche *OR* de pas très catholique ■ **there's something ~ about her wanting to see him** ça me paraît louche qu'elle veuille le voir **4.** *UK inf* [mad] fou *(before vowel or silent 'h'* **fol**), folle *f* ■ **he went ~ in the head** il a perdu la tête.
◇ *n inf* [joke] blague *f* ■ **to pull a ~ on sb** *US* jouer un tour à qqn, faire une farce à qqn.
◇ *adv inf* [walk, talk] bizarrement.

funny bone *n inf* ANAT petit juif *m*.

funny farm *n inf* maison *f* de fous.

fun run *n* course *f* à pied pour amateurs.

fur [fɜ:ʳ] (*pret & pp* **furred**, *cont* **furring**) ◇ *n* **1.** [on animal] poil *m*, pelage *m*, fourrure *f* ■ **her remark made the ~ fly** *OR* **set the ~ flying** *inf* ça a fait du grabuge quand elle a dit ça **2.** [coat, pelt] fourrure *f* **3.** [in kettle, pipe] incrustation *f*, (dépôt *m* de) tartre *m* **4.** MED [on tongue] enduit *m*.

◇ *vt* **1.** [person] habiller de fourrures **2.** [kettle, pipe] entartrer, incruster **3.** MED [tongue] empâter.
◇ *vi* : **to ~ (up)** [kettle, pipe] s'entartrer, s'incruster.

furbelow ['fɜ:bɪləʊ] *n* falbala *m pej.*

furbish ['fɜ:bɪʃ] *vt* [polish] fourbir, astiquer ■ [renovate] remettre à neuf.

fur coat *n* (manteau *m* de) fourrure *f.*

furious ['fjʊərɪəs] *adj* **1.** [angry] furieux ■ **she was ~ with me for being late** elle m'en voulait de mon retard ■ **he was ~ when he saw the car** il s'est mis en colère quand il a vu la voiture ■ **a ~ look** un regard furibond **2.** [raging, violent - sea, storm] déchaîné ; [- effort, struggle] acharné ; [- pace, speed] fou *(before vowel or silent 'h'* **fol***)*, folle *f.*

furiously ['fjʊərɪəslɪ] *adv* **1.** [answer, look] furieusement **2.** [fight, work] avec acharnement ■ [drive, run] à une allure folle.

furled [fɜ:ld] *adj* [umbrella, flag] roulé ■ [sail] serré.

furlong ['fɜ:lɒŋ] *n* furlong *m (= 201,17 mètres).*

furlough ['fɜ:ləʊ] ◇ *n* **1.** MIL [leave of absence] permission *f*, congé *m* ■ **to be on ~** être en permission **2.** *US* [laying off] *f* à pied provisoire.
◇ *vt* **1.** MIL [grant leave of absence] accorder une permission à **2.** *US* [lay off] mettre à pied provisoirement.

furnace ['fɜ:nɪs] *n* [for central heating] chaudière *f* ■ INDUST fourneau *m*, four *m* ■ **the office was like a ~** *fig* le bureau était une vraie fournaise.

furnish ['fɜ:nɪʃ] *vt* **1.** [supply - food, provisions] fournir ; [- information, reason] fournir, donner ■ **they ~ed us with the translation** il nous ont donné la traduction **2.** [house, room] meubler ■ **a comfortably ~ed house** une maison confortablement aménagée.

furnished ['fɜ:nɪʃt] *adj* [room, apartment] meublé.

furnishings ['fɜ:nɪʃɪŋz] *npl* **1.** [furniture] meubles *mpl*, mobilier *m*, ameublement *m* **2.** *US* [clothing] habits *mpl*, vêtements *mpl* ■ [accessories] accessoires *mpl.*

furniture ['fɜ:nɪtʃəʳ] ◇ *n (U)* **1.** [for house] meubles *mpl*, mobilier *m*, ameublement *m* ■ **a piece of ~** un meuble ■ **he treats me as if I were part of the ~** pour lui, je fais partie des meubles **2.** NAUT & TYPO garniture *f* **3.** [accessories] : **street ~** mobilier *m* urbain ■ **door ~** *éléments décoratifs pour portes d'entrée.*
◇ *comp* [shop, store] d'ameublement, de meubles ■ **~ van** camion *m* de déménagement ■ **~ polish** encaustique *f*, cire *f.*

furore [fjʊ'rɔ:rɪ] *UK*, **furor** ['fjʊrəʳ] *US n* scandale *m*, tumulte *m* ■ **to cause** *OR* **to create a ~** faire un scandale.

furred [fɜ:d] *adj* [kettle, pipe] entartré ■ [tongue] pâteux, chargé.

furrier ['fʌrɪəʳ] *n* fourreur *m.*

furrow ['fʌrəʊ] ◇ *n* [in field] sillon *m* ■ [in garden] rayon *m*, sillon *m* ■ [on forehead] ride *f*, sillon *m* ■ [on sea] sillage *m.*
◇ *vt* **1.** [soil, surface] sillonner **2.** [brow] rider.
◇ *vi* se plisser.

furrowed ['fʌrəʊd] *adj* ridé, sillonné de rides ■ **he looked up with ~ed brow** il a levé les yeux en plissant le front.

furry ['fɜ:rɪ] *(comp* **furrier**, *superl* **furriest***) adj* **1.** [animal] à poils ■ [fabric] qui ressemble à de la fourrure ■ [toy] en peluche **2.** [kettle, pipe] entartré ■ [tongue] pâteux, chargé.

further ['fɜ:ðəʳ] ◇ *adv (compar of far)* **1.** [at a greater distance in space, time] plus loin ■ **~ to the south** plus au sud ■ **she's never been ~ north than Leicester** elle n'est jamais allée plus au nord que Leicester ■ **how much ~ is it?** c'est encore loin? ■ **he got ~ and ~ away from the shore** il a continué à s'éloigner de la rive ■ **she moved ~ back** elle a reculé encore plus ■ **~ back than 1960** avant 1960 ■ **~ forward, ~ on** plus en avant, plus loin ■ **she's ~ on than the rest of the students** *fig* elle est en avance sur les autres étudiants ■ **I've got no ~ with finding a nanny** mes recherches pour trouver une nourrice n'ont pas beaucoup avancé ■ **nothing could be ~ from the truth** rien n'est moins vrai ■ **nothing could be ~ from my mind** j'étais bien loin de penser à ça
2. [more] plus, davantage ■ **I have nothing ~ to say** je n'ai rien à ajouter, je n'ai rien d'autre *OR* rien de plus à dire ■ **don't try my patience any ~** ne pousse pas ma patience à bout, n'abuse pas de ma patience ■ **the police want to question him ~** la police veut encore l'interroger ■ **I want nothing ~ to do with him** je ne veux plus avoir affaire à lui ■ **until you hear ~** jusqu'à nouvel avis
3. [to a greater degree] : **her arrival only complicated things ~** son arrivée n'a fait que compliquer les choses ■ **play was ~ interrupted by rain** le jeu fut à nouveau interrompu par la pluie
4. *fml* [moreover] de plus, en outre
5. *phr* **I would go even ~ and say he's a genius** j'irais même jusqu'à dire que c'est un génie ■ **we need to go ~ into the matter** il faut approfondir davantage la question ■ **I'll go no ~** [move] je n'irai pas plus loin ; [say nothing more] je vais en rester là ■ **this information must go no ~** cette information doit rester entre nous *OR* ne doit pas être divulguée.
◇ *adj (compar of far)* **1.** [more distant] plus éloigné, plus lointain
2. [additional - comments, negotiations] additionnel, autre ; [- information, news] supplémentaire, complémentaire ■ **do you have any ~ questions?** avez-vous d'autres questions à poser? ■ **I need a ~ nine hundred pounds** j'ai encore besoin de neuf cents livres ■ **upon ~ consideration** à la réflexion, après plus ample réflexion ■ **I have no ~ use for it** je ne m'en sers plus, je n'en ai plus besoin *OR* l'usage ■ **for ~ information, phone this number** pour tout renseignement complémentaire, appelez ce numéro ■ **without ~ delay** sans autre délai, sans plus attendre ■ **until ~ notice** jusqu'à nouvel ordre ► **without ~ ado** sans plus de cérémonie.
◇ *vt* [cause, one's interests] avancer, servir, favoriser ■ [career] servir, favoriser ■ [chances] augmenter.
◆ **further to** *prep phr fml* suite à ■ **~ to your letter of July 12** suite à votre lettre du 12 juillet.

furtherance ['fɜ:ðərəns] *n fml* **in (the) ~ of their policy** pour servir leur politique.

further education ◇ *n UK* enseignement *m* postscolaire.
◇ *comp* [class, college] d'éducation permanente.

furthermore [ˌfɜ:ðə'mɔ:ʳ] *adv* en outre, par ailleurs.

furthermost ['fɜ:ðəməʊst] *adj lit* le plus éloigné, le plus lointain.

furthest ['fɜ:ðɪst] *(superl of far)* ◇ *adv* le plus loin ■ **her house is the ~ away** sa maison est la plus éloignée.
◇ *adj* le plus lointain, le plus éloigné ■ **it's 10 miles at the ~** il y a 16 kilomètres au plus *OR* au maximum.

furtive ['fɜ:tɪv] *adj* [behaviour, look] furtif ■ [person] sournois.

fury ['fjʊərɪ] *(pl* **furies***) n* **1.** [anger] fureur *f*, furie *f* ■ **to be in a ~** être dans une colère noire *OR* en furie **2.** [violence - of storm, wind] violence *f* ; [- of fight, struggle] acharnement *m* ■ **to work like ~** *UK* travailler d'arrache-pied *OR* avec acharnement ■ **to run like ~** *UK* courir ventre à terre **3.** [frenzy] frénésie *f* ■ **a ~ of activity** une période d'activité débordante.
◆ **Furies** *npl* MYTH : **the Furies** les Furies *fpl*, les Érynies *fpl.*

furze [fɜ:z] *n (U)* ajoncs *mpl.*

fuse, fuze [fju:z] ◇ *vi* **1.** [melt] fondre ■ [melt together] fusionner **2.** [join] s'unifier, fusionner **3.** *UK* ELEC : **the lights/the appliance ~d** les plombs ont sauté.
◇ *vt* **1.** [melt] fondre ■ [melt together] fondre, mettre en fusion **2.** [unite] fusionner, unifier, amalgamer ■ **an attempt to ~ traditional and modern methods** une tentative pour associer les méthodes modernes et traditionnelles **3.** *UK* ELEC : **to ~ the lights** faire sauter les plombs **4.** [explosive] amorcer.
◇ *n* **1.** ELEC plomb *m*, fusible *m* ■ **the ~ keeps blowing** les plombs n'arrêtent pas de sauter ‖ *fig* **to blow a ~** *inf* se mettre dans une colère noire, exploser **2.** [of explosive] amorce *f*, détonateur *m* ■ MIN cordeau *m* ■ **to have a short ~** *inf* être soupe au lait, se mettre facilement en rogne.

fuse box *n* boite *f* à fusibles, coupe-circuit *m inv* ■ AUT porte-fusible *m.*

fused [fjuːzd] *adj* [kettle, plug] avec fusible incorporé.

fuselage [ˈfjuːzəlɑːʒ] *n* fuselage *m*.

fuse wire *n* fusible *m*.

fusilier [ˌfjuːzəˈlɪəʳ] *n* fusilier *m*.

fusillade [ˌfjuːzəˈleɪd] *n* fusillade *f*.

fusion [ˈfjuːʒn] *n* METALL fonte *f*, fusion *f* ▪ PHYS fusion *f* ▪ *fig* [of ideas, parties] fusion *f*, fusionnement *m*.

fusion bomb *n* bombe *f* thermonucléaire *OR* à hydrogène.

fusion reactor *n* réacteur *m* nucléaire.

fuss [fʌs] ◇ *n* **1.** *(U)* [bother] histoires *fpl* ▪ **what a lot of ~ about nothing!** que d'histoires pour rien! ▪ **after a great deal of ~ she accepted** après avoir fait toutes sortes de manières, elle a accepté **2.** [state of agitation] panique *f* ▪ **don't get into a ~ over it!** ne t'affole pas pour ça! **3.** *phr* **to kick up** *inf OR* **to make a ~ about** *OR* **over sthg** faire des histoires *OR* tout un plat au sujet de qqch ▪ **people are making a ~ about the new road** les gens protestent contre la nouvelle route ▪ **you should have made a ~ about it** tu n'aurais pas dû laisser passer ça ▪ **to make a ~ of** *OR* **over sb** être aux petits soins pour qqn ▪ **he likes to be made a ~ over** il aime bien qu'on fasse grand cas de lui.
◇ *vi* [become agitated] s'agiter ▪ [worry] s'inquiéter, se tracasser ▪ [rush around] s'affairer ▪ **she kept ~ing with her hair** elle n'arrêtait pas de tripoter ses cheveux ▪ **to ~ over sb** être aux petits soins pour qqn ▪ **stop ~ing over me!** laisse-moi tranquille! ▪ **don't ~, we'll be on time** ne t'en fais pas, on sera à l'heure.
◇ *vt* **1.** *esp US* agacer, embêter **2.** *UK inf phr* **do you want meat or fish? – I'm not ~ed** veux-tu de la viande ou du poisson? – ça m'est égal ▪ **I don't think he's particularly ~ed whether we go or not** je crois que cela lui est égal qu'on y aille ou pas.
◆ **fuss about** *UK*, **fuss around** *vi insep* [rush around] s'affairer.

fussbudget [ˈfʌsˌbʌdʒət] *US* = **fusspot**.

fussily [ˈfʌsɪlɪ] *adv* **1.** [fastidiously] de façon méticuleuse *OR* tatillonne ▪ [nervously] avec anxiété **2.** [over-ornate] de façon tarabiscotée.

fussiness [ˈfʌsɪnɪs] *n* **1.** [fastidiousness] côté *m* tatillon **2.** [ornateness - of decoration] tarabiscotage *m*.

fusspot [ˈfʌspɒt] *n inf* **1.** [worrier] anxieux *m*, - euse *f* ▪ **don't be such a ~** arrête de te faire du mauvais sang **2.** [fastidious person] tatillon *m*, - onne *f* ▪ **she's such a ~!** qu'est-ce qu'elle peut être difficile!

fussy [ˈfʌsɪ] (*comp* **fussier**, *superl* **fussiest**) *adj* **1.** [fastidious] tatillon, pointilleux ▪ **he's ~ about his food/about what he wears** il fait très attention à ce qu'il mange/à ce qu'il porte ▪ **where shall we go? – I'm not ~** où est-ce qu'on va? – ça m'est égal **2.** [over-ornate - decoration] trop chargé, tarabiscoté ; [- style] ampoulé, qui manque de simplicité.

fustian [ˈfʌstɪən] *n* [fabric] futaine *f* ▪ *fig & lit* [bombast] grandiloquence *f*.

fusty [ˈfʌstɪ] (*comp* **fustier**, *superl* **fustiest**) *adj* [room] qui sent le renfermé ▪ [smell] de renfermé, de moisi ▪ *fig* [idea, outlook] vieux jeu.

futile [*UK* ˈfjuːtaɪl, *US* ˈfuːtl] *adj* [action, effort] vain ▪ [remark, question] futile, vain ▪ [idea] futile, creux ▪ **it's ~ trying to reason with him** il est inutile d'essayer de lui faire entendre raison.

futility [fjuːˈtɪlətɪ] (*pl* **futilities**) *n* [of action, effort] futilité *f*, inutilité *f* ▪ [of remark, question] inanité *f* ▪ [of gesture] futilité *f*.

futon [ˈfuːtɒn] *n* futon *m*.

future [ˈfjuːtʃəʳ] ◇ *n* **1.** [time ahead] avenir *m* ▪ **in (the) ~** à l'avenir ▪ **sometime in the near ~** *OR* **in the not so distant ~** [gen] bientôt ; [more formal] dans un avenir proche ▪ **in the distant ~** dans un avenir lointain ▪ **young people today don't have much of a ~** les jeunes d'aujourd'hui n'ont pas beaucoup d'avenir ▪ **he has a great ~ ahead of him as an actor** c'est un comédien plein d'avenir ▪ **I'll have to see what the ~ holds** *OR* **has in store** on verra ce que l'avenir me réserve **2.** GRAM futur *m*.
◇ *adj* **1.** futur ▪ **at a ~ date** à une date ultérieure ▪ **I kept it for ~ reference** je l'ai conservé comme document **2.** COMM [delivery, estate] à terme.
◆ **in future** *adv phr* à l'avenir ▪ **I shan't offer my advice in ~!** je ne donnerai plus de conseils désormais!

future perfect *n* futur *m* antérieur.

futures [ˈfjuːtʃəz] *npl* ST. EX marchandises *fpl* achetées à terme ▪ **the ~ market** le marché à terme ▪ **sugar ~** sucre *m* (acheté) à terme.

future tense *n* future *m*.

futurism [ˈfjuːtʃərɪzm] *n* futurisme *m*.

futurist [ˈfjuːtʃərɪst] ◇ *adj* futuriste.
◇ *n* futuriste *mf*.

futuristic [ˌfjuːtʃəˈrɪstɪk] *adj* futuriste.

futurology [ˌfjuːtʃəˈrɒlədʒɪ] *n* futurologie *f*, prospective *f*.

fuze [fjuːz] *US* = **fuse** *(n)*.

fuzz [fʌz] ◇ *n (U)* **1.** [down - on peach] duvet *m* ; [- on body] duvet *m*, poils *mpl* fins ; [- on head] duvet *m*, cheveux *mpl* fins **2.** [frizzy hair] cheveux *mpl* crépus *OR* frisottants **3.** [on blanket, sweater] peluches *fpl* **4.** △ [police] : **the ~** les flics *mpl* **5.** *US* [lint] peluches *fpl*.
◇ *vt* **1.** [hair] frisotter **2.** [image, sight] rendre flou.
◇ *vi* **1.** [hair] frisotter **2.** [image, sight] devenir flou **3.** [blanket, sweater] pelucher.

fuzzy [ˈfʌzɪ] (*comp* **fuzzier**, *superl* **fuzziest**) *adj* **1.** [cloth, garment] peluché, pelucheux **2.** [image, picture] flou **3.** [confused - ideas] confus ▪ **my head feels a bit ~ today** j'ai un peu la tête qui tourne aujourd'hui **4.** [hair] crépu, frisottant.

fuzzy logic *n* logique *f* floue.

fwd. *written abbr of* **forward**.

f-word *n euph* **the ~** le mot 'fuck'.

fwy *written abbr of* **freeway**.

FX *npl* CIN [special effects] effets *mpl* spéciaux.

FY *n* = **fiscal year**.

FYI (*abbrev of* **for your information**) *adv* pour information.

G

g 1. (*written abbrev of* **gram**) g
2. (*written abbrev of* **gravity**) g.

g (*pl* **g's** *OR pl* **gs**)**, G** (*pl* **G's** *OR pl* **Gs**) [dʒiː] *n* [letter] g *m*, G *m*, *see also* **F**.

G ◇ *n* **1.** MUS [note] sol *m* **2.** *inf* (*abbrev of* **grand**) *UK* mille livres *fpl*, *US* mille dollars *mpl*.
◇ **1.** (*written abbrev of* **good**) B **2.** *US* CIN (*written abbrev of* **general (audience)**) *tous publics*.

GA *written abbr of* **Georgia**.

gab [gæb] (*pret & pp* **gabbed**, *cont* **gabbing**) *inf* ◇ *n (U)* [chatter] parlotte *f*, parlote *f*.
◇ *vi* papoter.

gabardine [ˌgæbəˈdiːn] = **gaberdine**.

gabble [ˈgæbl] ◇ *vi* **1.** [idly] faire la parlote, papoter **2.** [inarticulately] bredouiller, balbutier.
◇ *vt* bredouiller, bafouiller ▪ **she ~d (out) her story** elle a raconté son histoire en bredouillant.
◇ *n* baragouin *m*, flot *m* de paroles ▪ **a ~ of voices** un bruit confus de conversations ▪ **to talk at a ~** parler vite *OR* avec volubilité, jacasser.

gabbler [ˈgæblər] *n* bavard *m*, - e *f*.

gabby [ˈgæbɪ] (*comp* **gabbier**, *superl* **gabbiest**) *adj inf* bavard.

gaberdine [ˌgæbəˈdiːn] ◇ *n* gabardine *f*.
◇ *comp* : **~ raincoat** gabardine *f*.

gable [ˈgeɪbl] *n* [wall] pignon *m* ▪ [over arch, door etc] gâble *m*, gable *m*.

gabled [ˈgeɪbld] *adj* [house] à pignon *OR* pignons ▪ [wall] en pignon ▪ [roof] sur pignon *OR* pignons ▪ [arch] à gâble.

gable-end *n* pignon *m*.

Gabon [gæˈbɒn] *pr n* Gabon *m* ▪ **in ~** au Gabon.

Gabonese [ˌgæbɒˈniːz] ◇ *n* Gabonais *m*, - e *f*.
◇ *npl* : **the ~** les Gabonais.
◇ *adj* gabonais.

gad [gæd] (*pret & pp* **gadded**, *cont* **gadding**) ◇ *vi* : **to ~ about** vadrouiller.
◇ *vt* MIN casser au coin *OR* au picot.
◇ *n* **1.** MIN [chisel] coin *m* ▪ [pick] picot *m* **2.** [goad] aiguillon *m*.

gadabout [ˈgædəbaʊt] *n UK inf* vadrouilleur *m*, - euse *f*.

gadfly [ˈgædflaɪ] (*pl* **gadflies**) *n* **1.** [insect] taon *m* **2.** [annoying person] enquiquineur *m*, - euse *f*, casse-pieds *mf inv*.

gadget [ˈgædʒɪt] *n* gadget *m*.

gadgetry [ˈgædʒɪtrɪ] *n (U)* gadgets *mpl*.

Gael [geɪl] *n* : **the ~s** les Gaëls *mpl*.

Gaelic [ˈgeɪlɪk] ◇ *adj* gaélique.
◇ *n* LING gaélique *m*.

gaff [gæf] ◇ *n* **1.** [fishhook] gaffe *f* **2.** NAUT [spar] corne *f* **3.** *inf UK (U)* [nonsense] foutaise *f*, foutaises *fpl* **4.** *phr* **to blow the ~** *inf* vendre la mèche ▪ **to blow the ~ on sb** vendre qqn.
◇ *vt* [fish] gaffer.

gaffe [gæf] *n* [blunder] bévue *f* ▪ **a social ~** un faux pas, un impair.

gaffer [ˈgæfər] *n inf* **1.** *UK* [boss] : **the ~** le patron, le chef **2.** [old man] vieux *m*.

gag [gæg] (*pret & pp* **gagged**, *cont* **gagging**) ◇ *n* **1.** [over mouth] bâillon *m* ▪ **they want to put a ~ on the press** *fig* ils veulent bâillonner la presse **2.** *inf* [joke] gag *m* **3.** MED ouvre-bouche *m*.
◇ *vt* [silence] bâillonner ▪ *fig* bâillonner, museler.
◇ *vi* **1.** [retch] avoir un haut-le-cœur ▪ **he gagged on a fishbone** il a failli s'étrangler avec une arête de poisson **2.** *inf* [joke] blaguer, rigoler **3.** THEAT faire des improvisations comiques.

gaga [ˈgɑːgɑː] *adj inf* [senile, crazy] gaga ▪ **he's absolutely ~ about her** il est complètement fou d'elle.

gage [geɪdʒ] ◇ *n* **1.** *US* = **gauge 2.** [pledge] gage *m* **3.** [challenge] défi *m* **4.** *arch* [glove] gant *m*.
◇ *vt arch* [pledge, wager] gager.

gaggle [ˈgægl] ◇ *n liter & fig* troupeau *m*.
◇ *vi* cacarder.

gag resolution, gag rule *n US* règle *f* du bâillon (*procédure parlementaire permettant de limiter le temps de parole et d'éviter l'obstruction systématique*).

gaiety [ˈgeɪətɪ] (*pl* **gaieties**) *n* gaieté *f*.

gaily [ˈgeɪlɪ] *adv* **1.** [brightly] gaiement ▪ **~ coloured clothes** des vêtements aux couleurs vives **2.** [casually] tranquillement.

gain [geɪn] ◇ *n* **1.** [profit] gain *m*, profit *m*, bénéfice *m* ▪ *fig* avantage *m* ▪ **to do sthg for personal ~** faire qqch par intérêt ▪ **their loss is our ~** ce n'est pas perdu pour tout le monde
2. [acquisition] gain *m* ▪ **there were large Conservative ~s** le parti conservateur a gagné de nombreux sièges
3. [increase] augmentation *f* ▪ **a ~ in speed/weight** une augmentation de vitesse/poids
4. ELECTRON gain *m*.
◇ *vt* **1.** [earn, win, obtain] gagner ▪ **what would we (have to) ~ by joining?** quel intérêt avons-nous à adhérer? ▪ **to ~ friends (by doing sthg)** se faire des amis (en faisant qqch) ▪ **they managed to ~ entry to the building** ils ont réussi à s'introduire dans le bâtiment ▪ **he managed to ~ a hearing** il a réussi à se faire écouter
2. [increase] gagner ▪ **the share index has ~ed two points** l'indice des actions a gagné deux points

3. [obtain more] gagner, obtenir ▪ **to ~ weight/speed** prendre du poids/de la vitesse ▪ **to ~ experience** acquérir de l'expérience ▪ **to ~ ground** gagner du terrain ▪ **to ~ time** gagner du temps
4. [subj: clock, watch] avancer de ▪ **my watch ~s ten minutes a day** ma montre avance de dix minutes par jour
5. *lit* [reach] atteindre, gagner.
◇ *vi* **1.** [profit] profiter, gagner ▪ **who stands to ~ by this deal?** qui y gagne dans cette affaire?
2. [clock] avancer.
◆ **gain on** *vt insep* [catch up] rattraper.

gainful ['geɪnfʊl] *adj fml* **1.** [profitable] profitable, rémunérateur **2.** [paid] rémunéré ▪ **~ employment** un emploi rémunéré.

gainfully ['geɪnfʊlɪ] *adv fml* de façon profitable, avantageusement ▪ **to be ~ employed** avoir un emploi rémunéré.

gainsay [,geɪn'seɪ] (*pret & pp* **gainsaid** [-'sed]) *vt fml* [deny] nier ▪ [contradict] contredire ▪ **there's no ~ing her skill as an artist** on ne peut pas nier son talent artistique.

gainst [geɪnst], **'gainst** [genst] *lit* = **against** *(prep)*.

gait [geɪt] *n* démarche *f*, allure *f* ▪ **to walk with an unsteady ~** marcher d'un pas chancelant.

gaiters ['geɪtəz] *npl* guêtres *fpl*.

gal [gæl] *n* **1.** *inf* [girl] fille *f* **2.** PHYS [unit of acceleration] gal *m*.

gal. *written abbr of* **gallon**.

gala ['gɑːlə] ◇ *n* **1.** [festivity] gala *m* **2.** *UK* SPORT réunion *f* sportive ▪ **swimming ~** concours *m* de natation.
◇ *comp* [dress, day, evening] de gala ▪ **a ~ occasion** une grande occasion.

galactic [gə'læktɪk] *adj* galactique.

Galapagos Islands [gə'læpəgəs-] *pr npl* : **the ~** les (îles *fpl*) Galapagos *fpl*.

Galatian [gə'leɪʃjən] *n* : **the Epistle of Paul to the ~ s** l'Épître de saint Paul aux Galates.

galaxy ['gæləksɪ] (*pl* **galaxies**) *n* **1.** ASTRON galaxie *f* ▪ **the Galaxy** la Voie lactée **2.** [gathering] constellation *f*, pléiade *f*.

gale [geɪl] *n* **1.** [wind] coup *m* de vent, grand vent *m* ▪ **a force 9 ~** un vent de force 9 ▪ **it's blowing a ~ outside!** quel vent! ➲ **~ warning** avis *m* de coup de vent **2.** [outburst] éclat *m* ▪ **~s of laughter** des éclats de rire.

gale force *n* force *f* 8 à 9 ▪ **gale-force winds** coups *mpl* de vent.

Galicia [gə'lɪʃɪə] *pr n* **1.** [Central Europe] Galicie *f* **2.** [Spain] Galice *f*.

Galician [gə'lɪʃɪən] ◇ *adj* galicien.
◇ *n* **1.** [person] Galicien *m*, - enne *f* **2.** LING galicien *m*.

Galilean [,gælɪ'liːən] ◇ *adj* galiléen.
◇ *n* Galiléen *m*, - enne *f*.

Galilee ['gælɪliː] *pr n* Galilée *f* ▪ **in ~** en Galilée ▪ **the Sea of ~** le lac de Tibériade, la mer de Galilée.

Galileo [,gælɪ'leɪəʊ] *pr n* Galilée.

gall [gɔːl] ◇ *n* **1.** ANAT [human] bile *f* ▪ [animal] fiel *m* **2.** [bitterness] fiel *m*, amertume *f* **3.** [nerve] culot *m* ▪ **he had the ~ to say it was my fault!** il a eu le culot de dire que c'était de ma faute! **4.** BOT galle *f* **5.** MED & VET écorchure *f*, excoriation *f*.
◇ *comp* : **~ duct** ANAT voie *f* biliaire.
◇ *vt* **1.** [annoy] énerver ▪ **it ~ed him to have to admit he was wrong** ça l'a énervé de devoir reconnaître qu'il avait tort **2.** MED & VET excorier.

gall. *written abbr of* **gallon**.

gallant ['gælənt] ◇ *adj* **1.** [brave] courageux, vaillant ▪ **~ deeds** des actions d'éclat, des prouesses **2.** *(also* [gə'lænt]*)* [chivalrous] galant **3.** *lit* [noble] noble ▪ [splendid] superbe, splendide.
◇ *n lit* galant *m*.

gallantly ['gæləntlɪ] *adv* **1.** [bravely] courageusement, vaillamment **2.** [chivalrously] galamment.

gallantry ['gæləntrɪ] (*pl* **gallantries**) *n* **1.** [bravery] courage *m*, vaillance *f* **2.** [brave deed] prouesse *f*, action *f* d'éclat **3.** [chivalry, amorousness] galanterie *f*.

gall bladder *n* vésicule *f* biliaire.

galleon ['gælɪən] *n* galion *m*.

galleria [gælə'rɪə] *n* puits *m (aménagé dans un grand magasin à plusieurs étages)*.

gallery ['gælərɪ] (*pl* **galleries**) ◇ *n* **1.** [of art] musée *m* (des beaux-arts) ▪ **private ~** galerie *f* **2.** [balcony] galerie *f* ▪ [for spectators] tribune *f* ▪ **the press ~** la tribune de la presse **3.** [covered passageway] galerie *f* **4.** THEAT [upper balcony] dernier balcon *m* ▪ [audience] galerie *f* ▪ **to play to the ~** *fig* poser pour la galerie **5.** [tunnel] galerie *f* **6.** GOLF [spectators] public *m*.
◇ *comp* : **~ forest** forêt-galerie *f*, galerie *f* forestière.

galley ['gælɪ] ◇ *n* **1.** [ship] galère *f* ▪ [ship's kitchen] cambuse *f* ▪ [aircraft kitchen] office *m ou f* **2.** TYPO [container] galée *f* ▪ [proof] placard *m*.
◇ *comp* : **~ kitchen** kitchenette *f*, cuisinette *f offic.*

galley proof *n* TYPO (épreuve *f* en) placard *m*.

galley slave *n* galérien *m*.

Gallic ['gælɪk] *adj* **1.** [French] français ▪ **~ charm** charme *m* latin **2.** [of Gaul] gaulois ▪ **the ~ Wars** la guerre des Gaules.

gallicism ['gælɪsɪzm] *n* gallicisme *m*.

gallicize, ise ['gælɪsaɪz] *vt* franciser.

galling ['gɔːlɪŋ] *adj* [annoying] irritant ▪ [humiliating] humiliant, vexant.

gallivant [,gælɪ'vænt] *vi hum* : **to ~ about** *OR* **around** se balader ▪ **he's off ~ing around Europe** il se balade quelque part en Europe.

gallon ['gælən] *n* gallon *m*.

gallop ['gæləp] ◇ *vi* galoper ▪ **to ~ away** *OR* **off** partir au galop ▪ **he came ~ing down the stairs** *fig* il a descendu l'escalier au galop.
◇ *vt* faire galoper.
◇ *n* galop *m* ▪ **the pony broke into a ~** le poney a pris le galop ▪ **to do sthg at a ~** *fig* faire qqch à toute vitesse.
◆ **gallop through** *vt insep* faire à toute vitesse ▪ **I positively ~ed through the book** j'ai vraiment lu ce livre à toute allure.

galloping ['gæləpɪŋ] *adj* [horse] au galop ▪ *fig* galopant.

Gallo-Roman [,gæləʊ'rəʊmən] ◇ *adj* [dialects] gallo-roman ▪ [civilization, remains] gallo-romain.
◇ *n* LING gallo-roman *m*.

gallows ['gæləʊz] (*pl inv*) *n* potence *f*, gibet *m*.

gallows humour *n UK* humour *m* noir.

gallows tree = **gallows**.

gallstone ['gɔːlstəʊn] *n* calcul *m* biliaire.

Gallup Poll ['gæləp-] *n* sondage *m* (d'opinion) *(réalisé par l'institut Gallup)*.

galore [gə'lɔːʳ] *adv* en abondance ▪ **we've got food ~** nous avons de la nourriture en abondance.

galoshes [gə'lɒʃɪz] *npl* caoutchoucs *mpl (pour protéger les chaussures)*.

galumph [gə'lʌmf] *vi inf* courir lourdement *OR* comme un pachyderme ▪ **he came ~ing down the stairs** il a descendu l'escalier avec la légèreté d'un éléphant *OR* d'un hippopotame.

galvanic [gæl'vænɪk] *adj* **1.** ELEC galvanique **2.** [convulsive] convulsif **3.** [stimulating] galvanisant.

galvanism ['gælvənɪzm] *n* galvanisme *m*.

galvanize, ise ['gælvənaɪz] *vt* MED & METALL & *fig* galvaniser ▪ **it ~d the team into action** ça a poussé l'équipe à agir.

galvanometer [ˌgælvəˈnɒmɪtəʳ] *n* galvanomètre *m*.

Gambia [ˈgæmbɪə] *pr n* : **(the) ~** (la) Gambie ■ **in (the) ~** en Gambie.

Gambian [ˈgæmbɪən] ◇ *n* Gambien *m*, - enne *f*.
◇ *adj* gambien.

gambit [ˈgæmbɪt] *n* [chess] gambit *m*.

gamble [ˈgæmbl] ◇ *vi* jouer ■ **to ~ on the stock exchange** jouer à la Bourse, boursicoter.
◇ *vt* parier, miser.
◇ *n* **1.** [wager] pari *m* ■ **I like an occasional ~ on the horses** j'aime bien jouer aux courses de temps en temps **2.** [risk] coup *m* de poker ■ **it's a ~ we have to take** c'est un risque qu'il faut prendre ■ **it's a bit of a ~ whether it'll work or not** nous n'avons aucun moyen de savoir si ça marchera.
◆ **gamble away** *vt sep* perdre au jeu.
◆ **gamble on** *vt insep* miser OR tabler OR compter sur ■ **we'd ~d on having fine weather** on avait misé sur le beau temps.

gambler [ˈgæmbləʳ] *n* joueur *m*, - euse *f*.

gambling [ˈgæmblɪŋ] ◇ *n (U)* jeu *m*, jeux *mpl* d'argent ■ **~ debts** dettes *fpl* de jeu.
◇ *adj* joueur ■ **I'm not a ~ man but I would guess that they will accept the offer** je ne suis pas homme à parier mais je crois qu'ils vont accepter la proposition.

gambling house, gambling parlor *US n* maison *f* de jeu.

gambol [ˈgæmbl] (*UK pret & pp* **gambolled**, *cont* **gambolling**) (*US pret & pp* **gamboled**, *cont* **gamboling**) ◇ *vi* gambader, cabrioler.
◇ *n* gambade *f*, cabriole *f*.

game [geɪm] ◇ *n* **1.** [gen] jeu *m* ■ **card/party ~s** jeux de cartes/de société ■ **a ~ of chance/of skill** un jeu de hasard/d'adresse ■ **ball ~s are forbidden** il est interdit de jouer au ballon ■ **she plays a good ~ of chess** c'est une bonne joueuse d'échecs, elle joue bien aux échecs ■ **I'm off my ~ today** je joue mal aujourd'hui ■ **it put me right off my ~** ça m'a complètement déconcentré ■ **to play sb's ~** entrer dans le jeu de qqn ▶ **the ~ is not worth the candle** *UK* le jeu n'en vaut pas la chandelle
2. [contest] partie *f* ■ [esp professional] match *m* ■ **do you fancy a ~ of chess?** ça te dit de faire une partie d'échecs?
3. [division of match - in tennis, bridge] jeu *m* ■ **~, set and match** jeu, set et match
4. [playing equipment, set] jeu *m*
5. *inf* [scheme, trick] ruse *f*, stratagème *m* ■ **what's your (little) ~?** qu'est-ce que tu manigances?, à quel jeu joues-tu? ▶ **to play a double ~** jouer un double jeu ■ **to beat sb at his/her own game** battre qqn sur son propre terrain ■ **the ~'s up!** tout est perdu! ■ **two can play at that ~!** moi aussi je peux jouer à ce petit jeu-là ■ **to give the ~ away** vendre la mèche ■ **that gave the ~ away** c'est comme ça qu'on a découvert le pot aux roses
6. *inf* [undertaking, operation] : **at this stage in the ~** à ce stade des opérations ▶ **to be ahead of the ~** mener le jeu *fig*
7. [activity] travail *m* ■ **I'm new to this ~** je suis novice en la matière ■ **when you've been in this ~ as long as I have, you'll understand** quand tu auras fait ça aussi longtemps que moi, tu comprendras
8. CULIN & HUNT gibier *m*
9. *phr* **to be on the ~**[△] *UK* faire le tapin[△].
◇ *comp* de chasse ■ **~ laws** réglementation *f* de la chasse.
◇ *adj* **1.** [plucky] courageux, brave
2. [willing] prêt, partant ■ **they're ~ for anything** ils sont toujours partants
3. *UK* [lame] estropié.
◇ *vi fml* [gamble] jouer (de l'argent).
◆ **games** *npl* [international] jeux *mpl* ■ *UK* SCH sport *m*.

game bird *n* : **~s** gibier *m* à plumes.

game fish *n* poisson *m* noble *(saumon, brochet)*.

game-fishing *n* pêche *f (au saumon, à la truite, au brochet)*.

game fowl = **game bird**.

gamekeeper [ˈgeɪmˌkiːpəʳ] *n* garde-chasse *m*.

gamelan orchestra [ˈgæmɪlæn -], *n* gamelan *m*.

gamely [ˈgeɪmlɪ] *adv* courageusement, vaillamment.

game park *n* [in Africa] réserve *f*.

game pie *n* tourte *f* au gibier, ≃ pâté *m* en croûte.

game plan *n* stratégie *f*, plan *m* d'attaque.

game point *n* balle *f* de jeu.

game reserve *n* réserve *f (pour animaux sauvages)*.

games console *n* console *f* de jeu.

game show *n* jeu *m* télévisé.

gamesmanship [ˈgeɪmzmənʃɪp] *n art de gagner (aux jeux) en déconcertant son adversaire.*

gamete [ˈgæmiːt] *n* gamète *m*.

game theory *n* théorie *f* des jeux.

game warden *n* **1.** [gamekeeper] garde-chasse *m* **2.** [in safari park] garde *m* (d'une réserve).

gamey [geɪmɪ] (*comp* **gamier**, *superl* **gamiest**) = **gamy**.

gamine [ˈgæmiːn] *UK* ◇ *n* [impish girl] jeune fille *f* espiègle ■ [tomboy] garçon *m* manqué.
◇ *adj* gamin ■ **a ~ haircut** une coupe à la garçonne.

gaming [ˈgeɪmɪŋ] *n (U)* **1.** jeux *mpl* informatiques **2.** *fml* = **gambling** *(n)*.

gaming laws *npl lois réglementant les jeux de hasard.*

gaming table *n* table *f* de jeu.

gamma [ˈgæmə] *n* gamma *m*.

gamma ray *n* rayon *m* gamma.

gammon [ˈgæmən] *n UK* [cut] jambon *m* ■ [meat] jambon *m* fumé.

gammon steak *n UK (épaisse) tranche de jambon fumé.*

gammy [ˈgæmɪ] (*comp* **gammier**, *superl* **gammiest**) *adj UK inf* estropié ■ **to have a ~ leg** avoir une jambe estropiée, avoir une patte folle.

gamut [ˈgæmət] *n* MUS & *fig* gamme *f* ■ **to run the (whole) ~ of sthg** passer par toute la gamme de qqch.

gamy [ˈgeɪmɪ] (*comp* **gamier**, *superl* **gamiest**) *adj* [meat] faisandé.

gander [ˈgændəʳ] *n* **1.** [goose] jars *m* **2.** *UK inf* [simpleton] nigaud *m*, - e *f*, andouille *f* **3.** *UK inf* [look] : **to have** OR **to take a ~ at sthg** jeter un coup d'œil sur qqch.

gang [gæŋ] ◇ *n* **1.** [gen] bande *f* ■ [of criminals] gang *m* **2.** [of workmen] équipe *f* ■ [of convicts] convoi *m* **3.** TECH [of tools] série *f*.
◇ *vt* TECH [tools, instruments] coupler.
◆ **gang up** *vi insep* se mettre à plusieurs ■ **to ~ up against** OR **on sb** se liguer contre qqn.

gang-bang[▲] *n* viol *m* collectif.

ganger [ˈgæŋəʳ] *n UK* [foreman] contremaître *m*, chef *m* d'équipe.

Ganges [ˈgændʒiːz] *pr n* : **the (River) ~** le Gange.

gangland [ˈgæŋlænd] ◇ *n* le milieu.
◇ *comp* : **a ~ killing** un règlement de comptes *(dans le milieu)*.

ganglia [ˈgæŋglɪə] *pl* ▷ **ganglion**.

gangling [ˈgæŋglɪŋ] *adj* dégingandé.

ganglion [ˈgæŋglɪən] (*pl* **ganglia** [ˈgæŋglɪə]) *n* **1.** ANAT ganglion *m* **2.** [centre, focus] centre *m*, foyer *m*.

gangly [ˈgæŋlɪ] = **gangling**.

gangplank [ˈgæŋplæŋk] *n* passerelle *f* (d'embarquement).

gangrene [ˈgæŋgriːn] ◇ *n* MED & *fig* gangrène *f*.
◇ *vi* se gangrener.

gangrenous ['gæŋgrɪnəs] *adj* gangreneux ■ **the wound went ~** la blessure s'est gangrenée.

gang show *n spectacle de variétés organisé par les scouts.*

gangster ['gæŋstəʳ] ◇ *n* gangster *m*.
◇ *comp* [film, story] de gangsters.

gangster capitalism *n* capitalisme *m* sauvage.

gangway ['gæŋweɪ] ◇ *n* **1.** NAUT = **gangplank 2.** [passage] passage *m* ■ *UK* [in theatre] allée *f*.
◇ *interj* : ~! dégagez le passage!

gannet ['gænɪt] *n* **1.** ORNITH fou *m* de Bassan **2.** *UK inf* [greedy person] glouton *m*, - onne *f*.

gantry ['gæntrɪ] (*pl* **gantries**) *n* [for crane] portique *m* ■ **(launching) ~** ASTRON portique (de lancement) ■ **(signal) ~** RAIL portique (à signaux).

gantry crane *n* grue *f* (à) portique.

Ganymede ['gænɪmi:d] *pr n* Ganymède.

GAO (*abbrev of* **General Accounting Office**) *pr n Cour des comptes américaine.*

gaol *etc* [dʒeɪl] *UK* = **jail**.

gap [gæp] *n* **1.** [hole, breach] trou *m*, brèche *f* ■ **the sun shone through a ~ in the clouds** le soleil perça à travers les nuages **2.** [space between objects] espace *m* ■ [narrower] interstice *m*, jour *m* ■ **he has a ~ between his front teeth** il a les dents de devant écartées ■ **I could see through a ~ in the curtains** je voyais par la fente entre les rideaux **3.** [blank] blanc *m* **4.** [in time] intervalle *m* ■ **she returned to work after a ~ of six years** elle s'est remise à travailler après une interruption de six ans **5.** [lack] vide *m* ■ **to bridge** *OR* **to fill a ~** combler un vide ■ **a ~ in the market** un créneau sur le marché **6.** [omission] lacune *f* ■ **there are several ~s in his story** il y a plusieurs trous dans son histoire **7.** [silence] pause *f*, silence *m* **8.** [disparity] écart *m*, inégalité *f* **9.** [mountain pass] col *m*.

gape [geɪp] ◇ *vi* **1.** [stare] regarder bouche bée ■ **what are you gaping at?** qu'est-ce que tu regardes avec cet air bête? **2.** [open one's mouth wide] ouvrir la bouche toute grande **3.** [be open] être béant, béer *lit*.
◇ *n* [stare] regard *m* ébahi.

gaping ['geɪpɪŋ] *adj* **1.** [staring] bouche bée *(inv)* **2.** [wide open] béant.

gappy ['gæpɪ] (*comp* **gappier**, *superl* **gappiest**) *adj* **1.** [account, knowledge] plein de lacunes **2.** : **~ teeth** des dents écartées.

gap-toothed *adj* [with spaces between teeth] aux dents écartées ■ [with missing teeth] à qui il manque des dents.

gap year *n* SCH & UNIV *année d'interruption volontaire des études, avant l'entrée à l'université.*

garage ◇ *n* [*UK* 'gærɑ:ʒ, 'gærɪdʒ, *US* gə'rɑ:ʒ] **1.** [for cars] garage *m* **2.** MUS garage *m*.
◇ *vt* [*UK* 'gærɑ:ʒ, *US* gə'rɑ:ʒ] mettre au garage.

garage mechanic *n* garagiste *mf*, mécanicien *m*, - enne *f*.

garage sale *n vente d'occasion chez un particulier*, ≃ vide-grenier *m*.

garb [gɑ:b] *lit* ◇ *n* costume *m*, mise *f* ■ **she was in gipsy ~** elle était en costume de gitane, elle était déguisée en gitane.
◇ *vt* vêtir.

garbage ['gɑ:bɪdʒ] *n (U)* **1.** *US* [waste matter] ordures *fpl*, détritus *mpl* ■ **throw it in the ~** jette-le à la poubelle **2.** *inf* [nonsense] bêtises *fpl*, âneries *fpl* ■ **you're talking ~!** tu racontes des bêtises! ■ **this newspaper is ~!** ce journal est nul! **3.** COMPUT données *fpl* erronées ■ **~ in, ~ out** la qualité des résultats est fonction de la qualité des données à l'entrée.

garbage can *n US* poubelle *f*.

garbage chute *n US* vide-ordures *m inv*.

garbage collector *n US* éboueur *m*.

garbage disposal unit *n US* broyeur *m* d'ordures.

garbage dump *n US* décharge *f*.

garbage man *US* = **garbage collector**.

garbage truck *n US* camion *m* des éboueurs.

garbanzo [gɑ:'bɑ:nzəʊ] (*pl* **garbanzos**) *n US* : **~(bean)** pois *m* chiche.

garble ['gɑ:bl] *vt* [involuntarily - story, message] embrouiller ; [- quotation] déformer ■ [deliberately - facts] dénaturer, déformer.

garbled ['gɑ:bld] *adj* [story, message, explanation - involuntarily] embrouillé, confus ; [- deliberately] dénaturé, déformé.

garda ['gɑ:də] (*pl* **gardai** [-di:]) *n* policier *m (en République d'Irlande).*

Garda ['gɑ:də] *pr n* : **Lake ~** le lac de Garde.

garden ['gɑ:dn] ◇ *n* jardin *m* ■ **to do the ~** jardiner, faire du jardinage ■ **vegetable ~** (jardin *m*) potager *m* ➡ **the Garden of Eden** le jardin *m* d'Éden, l'Éden *m* ■ **the Garden of England** *surnom du comté de Kent, célèbre pour ses vergers et ses champs de houblon* ■ **everything in the ~ is rosy** *OR* **lovely** tout va bien ■ **the Garden State** le New Jersey.
◇ *comp* : **~ path** allée *f (dans un jardin)* ■ **~ produce** produits *mpl* maraîchers ■ **~ shears** cisaille *f OR* cisailles *fpl* de jardin ■ **~ shed** resserre *f* ■ **~ tools** outils *mpl* de jardinage ■ **~ wall** mur *m* du jardin.
◇ *vi* jardiner, faire du jardinage.
➡ **gardens** *npl* [park] jardin *m* public.

garden centre *n* jardinerie *f*.

gardener ['gɑ:dnəʳ] *n* jardinier *m*, - ère *f*.

garden flat *n* rez-de-jardin *m inv*.

garden gnome *n* gnome *m* (décoratif).

gardenia [gɑ:'di:njə] *n* gardénia *m*.

gardening ['gɑ:dnɪŋ] ◇ *n* jardinage *m*.
◇ *comp* [book, programme] de *OR* sur le jardinage ■ [gloves] de jardinage.

garden party *n UK* garden-party *f*.

garden suburb *n* banlieue *f* verte.

garden-variety *adj US* ordinaire.

gargantuan [gɑ:'gæntjʊən] *adj* gargantuesque.

gargle ['gɑ:gl] ◇ *vi* se gargariser, faire des gargarismes.
◇ *n* gargarisme *m*.

gargoyle ['gɑ:gɔɪl] *n* gargouille *f*.

garibaldi [,gærɪ'bɔ:ldɪ] *n UK biscuit aux raisins secs.*

garish ['geərɪʃ] *adj* [colour] voyant, criard ■ [clothes] voyant, tapageur ■ [light] cru, aveuglant.

garishly ['geərɪʃlɪ] *adv* : **~ dressed** vêtu de manière tapageuse.

garishness ['geərɪʃnɪs] *n* [of appearance] tape-à-l'œil *m inv* ■ [of colour] crudité *f*, violence *f*.

garland ['gɑ:lənd] ◇ *n* **1.** [on head] couronne *f* de fleurs ■ [round neck] guirlande *f OR* collier *m* de fleurs ■ [hung on wall] guirlande *f* **2.** LIT [of poems] guirlande *f*, florilège *m*.
◇ *vt* [decorate] décorer avec des guirlandes, enguirlander ■ [crown] couronner de fleurs.

garlic ['gɑ:lɪk] *n* ail *m* ■ **~ bread** *pain beurré frotté d'ail et servi chaud* ■ **~ butter** beurre *m* d'ail ■ **~ salt** sel *m* d'ail ■ **~ sausage** saucisson *m* à l'ail.

garlicky ['gɑ:lɪkɪ] *adj* [taste] d'ail ■ [breath] qui sent l'ail.

garlic press *n* presse-ail *m inv*.

garment ['gɑ:mənt] *n* vêtement *m* ■ **the ~ industry** la confection.

garner ['gɑ:nəʳ] ◇ *n lit* grenier *m* (à grain), grange *f*.
◇ *vt* [grain] rentrer, engranger ■ *fig* [information] glaner, grappiller ■ [compliments] recueillir.
➡ **garner in, garner up** *vt sep* engranger.

garnet ['gɑːnɪt] ◇ *n* [stone, colour] grenat *m*.
◇ *adj* **1.** [in colour] grenat *(inv)* **2.** [jewellery] de OR en grenat.

garnish ['gɑːnɪʃ] ◇ *vt* CULIN garnir ■ [decorate] embellir ■ **~ed with parsley** garni de persil.
◇ *n* garniture *f*.

garnishing ['gɑːnɪʃɪŋ] *n* CULIN garniture *f* ■ *fig* embellissement *m*.

garnishment ['gɑːnɪʃmənt] *n* **1.** LAW saisie-arrêt *f* **2.** CULIN garniture *f*.

garotte [gə'rɒt] = **garrot(t)e**.

garret ['gærət] *n* [room] mansarde *f* ■ **to live in a ~** habiter une chambre sous les combles.

garrison ['gærɪsn] ◇ *n* garnison *f*.
◇ *vt* **1.** [troops] mettre en garnison **2.** [town] placer une garnison dans.

garrison town *n* ville *f* de garnison.

garrison troops *npl* (troupes *fpl* de) garnison *f*.

garrot(t)e [gə'rɒt] ◇ *n* **1.** [execution] (supplice *m* du) garrot *m* **2.** [collar] garrot *m*.
◇ *vt* garrotter.

garrulous ['gærələs] *adj* **1.** [person] loquace, bavard **2.** [style] prolixe, verbeux.

garter ['gɑːtəʳ] *n* **1.** *UK* [for stockings] jarretière *f* ■ [for socks] fixe-chaussette *m* ■ **Knight of the Garter** chevalier *m* de l'ordre de la Jarretière **2.** *US* [suspender] jarretelle *f*.

garter belt *n US* porte-jarretelles *m inv*.

garter stitch *n* point *m* mousse.

gas [gæs] (*pl* **gasses**) ◇ *n* **1.** [domestic] gaz *m* ■ **to turn on/off the ~** allumer/éteindre le gaz **2.** CHEM gaz *m* **3.** MIN grisou *m* **4.** MED gaz *m* anesthésique OR anesthésiant ■ **to have ~** subir une anesthésie gazeuse OR par inhalation ■ **the dentist gave me ~** le dentiste m'a endormi au gaz **5.** *US* AUT essence *f* ■ **step on** OR **hit the ~!** *inf liter* appuie sur le champignon! ; *fig* grouille!, grouille-toi! **6.** *US inf* [amusement] : **the party was a real ~** on s'est bien marrés OR on a bien rigolé à la soirée **7.** *UK inf* [chatter] bavardage *m* **8.** *(U) US* [in stomach] gaz *mpl*.
◇ *vt* **1.** [poison] asphyxier OR intoxiquer au gaz ■ **to ~ o.s.** [poison] s'asphyxier au gaz ; [suicide] se suicider au gaz **2.** MIL gazer.
◇ *vi* **1.** *inf* [chatter] bavarder, jacasser **2.** CHEM dégager des gaz.
◇ *comp* [company, industry] du gaz ■ [engine, boiler] à gaz ■ **~ central heating** chauffage *m* central au gaz ■ **~ pedal** *US* accélérateur *m*.
➡ **gas up** *US* ◇ *vt sep* : **to ~ the automobile up** faire le plein d'essence.
◇ *vi insep* faire le plein d'essence.

gasbag ['gæsbæg] *n UK inf pej* moulin *m* à paroles, pie *f*.

gas burner *n* brûleur *m*.

gas chamber *n* chambre *f* à gaz.

Gascon ['gæskən] ◇ *n* [person] Gascon *m*, - onne *f*.
◇ *adj* gascon.

Gascony ['gæskənɪ] *pr n* Gascogne *f*.

gas cooker *n UK* cuisinière *f* à gaz, gazinière *f*.

gaseous ['gæsjəs, 'geɪzjəs] *adj* PHYS gazeux.

gas fire *n UK* (appareil *m* de) chauffage *m* au gaz.

gas-fired *adj UK* **~ central heating** chauffage *m* central au gaz.

gas fitter *n* installateur *m* d'appareils à gaz.

gas guzzler *n inf* AUT voiture *f* qui consomme beaucoup.

gash [gæʃ] ◇ *vt* **1.** [knee, hand] entailler ■ [face] balafrer, taillader ■ **she fell and ~ed her knee** elle est tombée et s'est entaillé OR ouvert le genou **2.** [material] déchirer, lacérer.
◇ *n* **1.** [on knee, hand] entaille *f* ■ [on face] balafre *f*, estafilade *f* **2.** [in material] (grande) déchirure *f*, déchiqueture *f*.
◇ *adj*[△] [surplus] superflu, en trop.

gas heater *n* [radiator] radiateur *m* à gaz ■ [for water] chauffe-eau *m inv* à gaz.

gasholder ['gæs,həʊldəʳ] *n* gazomètre *m*.

gas jet *n* brûleur *m*.

gasket ['gæskɪt] *n* **1.** MECH joint *m* (d'étanchéité) ■ **(cylinder) head ~** AUT joint *m* de culasse **2.** NAUT raban *m* de ferlage.

gaslight ['gæslaɪt] *n* **1.** [lamp] lampe *f* à gaz, appareil *m* d'éclairage à gaz ■ [in street] bec *m* de gaz **2.** [light produced] lumière *f* produite par du gaz ■ **by ~** à la lumière d'une lampe à gaz.

gas lighter *n* [for cooker] allume-gaz *m* ■ [for cigarettes] briquet *m* à gaz.

gaslit ['gæslɪt] *adj* éclairé au gaz.

gas main *n* conduite *f* de gaz.

gasman ['gæsmæn] (*pl* **gasmen** [-men]) *n* employé *m* du gaz.

gas mantle *n* manchon *m* à incandescence.

gas mask *n* masque *m* à gaz.

gas meter *n* compteur *m* à gaz.

gas oil *n* gas-oil *m*, gazole *m*.

gasoline ['gæsəliːn] *n US* AUT essence *f*.

gasometer [gæ'sɒmɪtəʳ] *n* gazomètre *m*.

gas oven *n* [domestic] four *m* à gaz ■ [cremation chamber] four *m* crématoire.

gasp [gɑːsp] ◇ *vi* **1.** [be short of breath] haleter, souffler ■ **to ~ for breath** OR **for air** haleter, suffoquer **2.** [in shock, surprise] avoir le souffle coupé ■ **to ~ in** OR **with amazement** avoir le souffle coupé par la surprise **3.** *UK inf fig* **I'm ~ing for a cigarette** je meurs d'envie de fumer une cigarette ■ **I'm ~ing (for a drink)** je meurs de soif.
◇ *vt* : **"what?" he ~ed** "quoi?", dit-il d'une voix pantelante.
◇ *n* halètement *m* ■ **she gave** OR **she let out a ~ of surprise** elle a eu un hoquet de surprise ■ **to give a ~ of horror** avoir le souffle coupé par l'horreur ■ **to the last ~** jusqu'au dernier souffle.

gas pipe *n* tuyau *m* à gaz.

gas ring *n* [part of cooker] brûleur *m* ■ [small cooker] réchaud *m* à gaz.

gas station *n US* poste *m* d'essence, station-service *f*.

gas stove *n UK* [in kitchen] cuisinière *f* à gaz, gazinière *f* ■ [for camping] réchaud *m* à gaz.

gassy ['gæsɪ] (*comp* **gassier**, *superl* **gassiest**) *adj* **1.** CHEM gazeux **2.** [drink] gazeux **3.** *inf* [person] bavard **4.** MIN grisouteux.

gas tank *n* **1.** [domestic] cuve *f* à gaz **2.** *US* AUT réservoir *m* à essence.

gas tap *n* [on cooker] bouton *m* de cuisinière à gaz ■ [at mains] robinet *m* de gaz.

gasteropod ['gæstrəpɒd] = **gastropod**.

gastrectomy [gæs'trektəmɪ] (*pl* **gastrectomies**) *n* gastrectomie *f*.

gastric ['gæstrɪk] *adj* gastrique.

gastric flu *n (U)* grippe *f* intestinale OR gastro-intestinale.

gastric ulcer *n* ulcère *m* de l'estomac, gastrite *f* ulcéreuse.

gastritis [gæs'traɪtɪs] *n (U)* gastrite *f*.

gastroenteritis [,gæstrəʊ,entə'raɪtɪs] *n (U)* gastro-entérite *f*.

gastronome ['gæstrənəʊm] *n* gastronome *mf*.

gastronomic [,gæstrə'nɒmɪk] *adj* gastronomique.

gastronomy [gæs'trɒnəmɪ] *n* gastronomie *f*.

gastropub ['gæstrəʊpʌb] *n UK* pub *m* gastronomique.

gas turbine *n* turbine *f* à gaz.

gasworks ['gæswɜːks] *npl* usine *f* à gaz.

gate [geɪt] ◇ *n* **1.** [into garden] porte *f* ■ [into driveway, field] barrière *f* ■ [bigger - of mansion] portail *m* ; [- into courtyard] porte *f* cochère ■ [low] portillon *m* ■ [wrought iron] grille *f* ■ **the main ~** la porte *OR* l'entrée principale ■ **the ~s of heaven/hell** les portes du paradis/de l'enfer ■ **to pay at the ~** [for match] payer à l'entrée ▶ **to give sb the ~** *US inf* flanquer qqn à la porte ■ **'The Gates of Hell'** ***Rodin*** 'la Porte de l'enfer' **2.** [at airport] porte *f* ■ **proceed to ~ 22** embarquement porte 22 **3.** [on ski slope] porte *f* **4.** [on canal] : **lock ~s** écluse *f*, portes *fpl* d'écluse **5.** SPORT [spectators] nombre *m* de spectateurs (admis) ■ [money] recette *f*, entrées *fpl* ■ **there was a good/poor ~** il y a eu beaucoup/peu de spectateurs **6.** ELECTRON gâchette *f* **7.** PHOT fenêtre *f* **8.** [in horse racing] starting-gate *f*.
◇ *vt UK* SCH consigner, mettre en retenue.

gateau ['gætəʊ] (*pl* **gateaux** [-təʊz]) *n* gros gâteau *m (décoré et fourré à la crème)*.

gatecrash ['geɪtkræʃ] *inf* ◇ *vi* [at party] s'inviter, jouer les pique-assiette ■ [at paying event] resquiller.
◇ *vt* : **to ~ a party** aller à une fête sans invitation.

gatecrasher ['geɪtkræʃər] *n inf* [at party] pique-assiette *mf* ■ [at paying event] resquilleur *m*, - euse *f*.

gated community ['geɪtɪd-] *n* zone *f* résidentielle clôturée.

gatehouse ['geɪthaʊs] (*pl* [-haʊzɪz]) *n* [of estate] loge *f* du portier ■ [of castle] corps *m* de garde.

gatekeeper ['geɪt,ki:pər] *n* portier *m*, - ère *f* ■ RAIL garde-barrière *mf*.

gate-leg table, gate-legged table *n* table *f* pliante.

gate money *n* recette *f*, montant *m* des entrées.

gatepost ['geɪtpəʊst] *n* montant *m* de barrière *OR* de porte ■ **between you, me and the ~** *UK inf* soit dit entre nous.

gateway ['geɪtweɪ] *n* porte *f*, entrée *f* ■ *fig* porte *f* ■ **Istanbul, ~ to the East** Istanbul, la porte de l'Orient.

gather ['gæðər] ◇ *vt* **1.** [pick, collect - mushrooms, wood] ramasser ; [- flowers, fruit] cueillir **2.** [bring together - information] recueillir ; [- taxes] percevoir, recouvrer ; [- belongings] ramasser ■ **to ~ a crowd** attirer une foule de gens **3.** [gain] prendre ■ **to ~ strength** prendre des forces ■ **to ~ speed** prendre de la vitesse **4.** [prepare] : **to ~ one's thoughts** se concentrer ■ **to ~ one's wits** rassembler ses esprits **5.** [embrace] serrer ■ **he ~ed the children to him** il serra les enfants dans ses bras *OR* sur son cœur **6.** [clothes] ramasser ■ **she ~ed her skirts about her** elle ramassa ses jupes **7.** [deduce] déduire, comprendre ■ **I ~ he isn't coming then** j'en déduis qu'il ne vient pas, donc il ne vient pas ■ **as far as I can ~** d'après ce que j'ai cru comprendre **8.** SEW froncer ■ **the dress is ~ed at the waist** la robe est froncée à la taille **9.** TYPO [signatures] assembler **10.** *phr* **to ~ dust** ramasser la poussière.
◇ *vi* **1.** [people] se regrouper, se rassembler ■ [crowd] se former ■ [troops] se masser **2.** [clouds] s'amonceler ■ [darkness] s'épaissir ■ [storm] menacer, se préparer **3.** MED [abscess] mûrir ■ [pus] se former.
◆ **gathers** *npl* SEW fronces *fpl*.
◆ **gather in** *vt sep* **1.** [harvest] rentrer ■ [wheat] récolter ■ [money, taxes] recouvrer ■ [books, exam papers] ramasser **2.** SEW : **~ed in at the waist** froncé à la taille.
◆ **gather round** *vi insep* se regrouper, se rassembler ■ **~ round and listen** approchez(-vous) et écoutez.
◆ **gather together** ◇ *vi insep* se regrouper, se rassembler.
◇ *vt sep* [people] rassembler, réunir ■ [books, belongings] rassembler, ramasser.
◆ **gather up** *vt sep* **1.** [objects, belongings] ramasser **2.** [skirts] ramasser, retrousser ■ [hair] ramasser, relever ■ **her hair was ~ed up into a bun** ses cheveux étaient ramassés *OR* relevés en chignon.

gathering ['gæðərɪŋ] ◇ *n* **1.** [group] assemblée *f*, réunion *f* **2.** [accumulation] accumulation *f* ■ [of clouds] amoncellement *m* **3.** [bringing together - of people] rassemblement *m* ; [- of objects] accumulation *f*, amoncellement *m* **4.** [harvesting] récolte *f* ■ [picking] cueillette *f* **5.** [increase - in speed, force] accroissement *m* **6.** *(U)* SEW froncis *m*, fronces *fpl* **7.** *(U)* MED [abscess] abcès *m*.
◇ *adj lit* **the ~ storm** l'orage qui se prépare *OR* qui menace.

GATT [gæt] (*abbrev of* **General Agreement on Tariffs and Trade**) *pr n* GATT *m*.

gauche [gəʊʃ] *adj* gauche, maladroit.

gaudily ['gɔ:dɪlɪ] *adv* [dress] de manière voyante, tapageusement ■ [decorate] de couleurs criardes.

gaudy ['gɔ:dɪ] (*comp* **gaudier**, *superl* **gaudiest**) *adj* [dress] voyant ■ [colour] voyant, criard ■ [display] tapageur.

gauge *UK*, **gage** *US* [geɪdʒ] ◇ *n* **1.** [instrument] jauge *f*, indicateur *m* **2.** [standard measurement] calibre *m*, gabarit *m* ■ [diameter - of wire, cylinder, gun] calibre *m* **3.** RAIL [of track] écartement *m* ■ AUT [of wheels] écartement *m* **4.** TECH [of steel] jauge *f* **5.** CIN [of film] pas *m* **6.** *fig* **the survey provides a ~ of current trends** le sondage permet d'évaluer les tendances actuelles.
◇ *vt* **1.** [measure, calculate] mesurer, jauger ■ **she tried to ~ how much it would cost her** elle a essayé d'évaluer combien ça lui coûterait **2.** [predict] prévoir **3.** [standardize] normaliser.

Gaul [gɔ:l] ◇ *pr n* GEOG Gaule *f*.
◇ *n* [person] Gaulois *m*, - e *f*.

Gaullism ['gəʊlɪzm] *n* POL Gaullisme *m*.

Gaullist ['gəʊlɪst] POL ◇ *adj* Gaulliste.
◇ *n* Gaulliste *mf*.

gaunt [gɔ:nt] *adj* **1.** [emaciated - face] creux, émacié ; [- body] décharné, émacié **2.** [desolate - landscape] morne, lugubre, désolé ; [- building] lugubre, désert.

gauntlet ['gɔ:ntlɪt] *n* [medieval glove] gantelet *m* ■ [for motorcyclist, fencer] gant *m* (à crispin *OR* à manchette) ■ **to throw down/to take up the ~** jeter/relever le gant ■ **to run the ~** *liter* passer par les baguettes ; *fig* se faire fustiger ■ **to run the ~ of an angry mob** se forcer *OR* se frayer un passage à travers une foule hostile.

gauze [gɔ:z] *n* gaze *f*.

gave [geɪv] *pt* ▷ **give**.

gavel ['gævl] *n* marteau *m (de magistrat etc)*.

gavotte [gə'vɒt] *n* gavotte *f*.

gawk [gɔ:k] *inf* ◇ *vi* être *OR* rester bouche bée ■ **to ~ at sb** regarder qqn bouche bée.
◇ *n* [person] godiche *f*, grand dadais *m*.

gawkish ['gɔ:kɪʃ] *adj* gauche, emprunté.

gawky ['gɔ:kɪ] (*comp* **gawkier**, *superl* **gawkiest**) *adj inf* gauche, emprunté.

gawp [gɔ:p] *vi UK inf* rester bouche bée ■ **don't just stand there ~ing!** ne reste pas là à bayer aux corneilles *OR* à rêvasser!

gay [geɪ] ◇ *adj* **1.** [homosexual] gay, homosexuel ■ **~ rights** les droits *mpl* des homosexuels **2.** [cheerful, lively - appearance, party, atmosphere] gai, joyeux ; [- laughter] enjoué, joyeux ; [- music, rhythm] gai, entraînant, allègre ■ **with ~ abandon** avec insouciance **3.** [bright - colours, lights] gai, vif, éclatant.
◇ *n* homosexuel *m*, gay *m*.

Gay Lib *n* = **Gay Liberation Movement**.

Gay Liberation Movement *n* : **the ~** le mouvement de libération des homosexuels.

Gaza Strip ['gɑ:zə] *pr n* : **the ~** la bande de Gaza.

gaze [geɪz] ◇ *vi* : **to ~ at sthg** regarder qqch fixement *OR* longuement ■ **to ~ into space** avoir le regard perdu dans le vague, regarder dans le vide.
◇ *n* regard *m* fixe.
◆ **gaze about** *UK*, **gaze around** *vi insep* regarder autour de soi.

gazebo [gə'zi:bəʊ] (*pl* **gazebos**) *n* belvédère *m*.

gazelle [gə'zel] (*pl inv OR pl* **gazelles**) *n* gazelle *f*.

gazette [gə'zet] <> *n* [newspaper] journal *m* ▪ [official publication] journal *m* officiel.
<> *vt UK* publier *OR* faire paraître au journal officiel.

gazetteer [,gæzɪ'tɪər] *n* index *m OR* nomenclature *f* géographique.

gazump [gə'zʌmp] *UK inf* <> *vt augmenter le prix d'une maison après une promesse de vente orale* ▪ **we've been ~ed** la maison nous est passée sous le nez.
<> *vi rompre une promesse de vente (d'une maison) à la suite d'une surenchère.*

GB[1], Gb [dʒi:'bi:] (*abbrev of* **gigabyte**) *n* gigabyte *m*.

GB[2] (*abbrev of* **Great Britain**) *pr n* G-B *f*.

GBH *n* = **grievous bodily harm**.

GCE (*abbrev of* **General Certificate of Education**) *n certificat de fin d'études secondaires en deux étapes (O-level et A-level) dont la première est aujourd'hui remplacée par le GCSE.*

GCH *UK written abbr of* **gas central heating**.

GCHQ (*abbrev of* **Government Communications Headquarters**) *pr n centre d'interception des télécommunications étrangères en Grande-Bretagne.*

GCSE (*abbrev of* **General Certificate of Secondary Education**) *n premier examen de fin de scolarité en Grande-Bretagne.*

GCSE

Examen sanctionnant la fin de la première partie de l'enseignement secondaire. Chaque élève présente les matières de son choix (généralement entre 5 et 10) selon un système d'unités de valeur. Le nombre d'unités et les notes obtenues déterminent le passage dans la classe supérieure. Après cet examen, les élèves peuvent choisir d'arrêter leurs études ou de préparer les *A-levels*.

Gdns. *written abbr of* **Gardens**.

GDP (*abbrev of* **gross domestic product**) *n UK* PIB *m*.

GDR (*abbrev of* **German Democratic Republic**) *pr n* RDA *f*.

gear [gɪər] <> *n* **1.** *(U)* [accessories, equipment - for photography, camping] équipement *m*, matériel *m* ; [- for manual work] outils *mpl*, matériel *m* ; [- for household] ustensiles *mpl* ▪ **he brought along all his skiing ~** il a apporté tout son équipement *OR* toutes ses affaires de ski **2.** *(U)* [personal belongings] effets *mpl* personnels, affaires *fpl* ▪ [luggage] bagages *mpl* **3.** *(U)* [clothes] vêtements *mpl*, tenue *f* ▪ **she was in her jogging/swimming ~** elle était en (tenue de) jogging/en maillot de bain **4.** *inf (U) UK inf* [fashionable clothes] fringues *fpl* **5.** *(U)* [apparatus] mécanisme *m*, dispositif *m* **6.** [in car, on bicycle] vitesse *f* ▪ **to change ~** changer de vitesse ▪ **put the car in ~** passez une vitesse ▪ **to be in first/second ~** être en première/seconde ▪ **'use *OR* engage low ~'** 'utiliser le frein moteur, rétrograder' ▪ **I'm back in ~ again now** *fig* c'est reparti pour moi maintenant **7.** MECH [cogwheel] roue *f* dentée, pignon *m* ▪ [system of cogs] engrenage *m*.
<> *vt* **1.** [adapt] adapter ▪ **the government's policies were not ~ed to cope with an economic recession** la politique mise en place par le gouvernement n'était pas prévue pour faire face à une récession économique ▪ **the city's hospitals were not ~ed to cater for such an emergency** les hôpitaux de la ville n'étaient pas équipés pour répondre à une telle situation d'urgence **2.** AUT & TECH engrener.
◆ **gear up** *vt sep* [prepare] : **to be ~ed up** être paré *OR* fin prêt ▪ **she'd ~ed herself up to meet them** elle s'était mise en condition pour les rencontrer.

gearbox ['gɪəbɒks] *n* boîte *f* de vitesses.

gear change *n* changement *m* de vitesse.

gearing ['gɪərɪŋ] *n* **1.** MECH engrenage *m* **2.** *UK* FIN effet *m* de levier.

gearknob ['gɪənɒb] *n* AUT boule *f* du levier de vitesse.

gear lever *UK*, **gear shift** *US n* levier *m* de vitesse.

gear stick *n* levier *m* de changement de vitesse.

gee [dʒi:] *interj US inf* **~!** ça alors! ▪ **~ whiz!** super!, génial!

gee-gee ['dʒi:dʒi:] *n UK baby* dada *m*.

geek [gi:k] *n inf* débile *mf* ▪ **computer ~** fada *mf OR* dingue *mf* d'informatique.

geese [gi:s] *pl* ▷ **goose**.

gee up <> *interj* hue!
<> *vt sep inf UK inf* faire avancer.

geezer ['gi:zər] *n UK inf* bonhomme *m*, coco *m*.

Geiger counter ['gaɪgər-] *n* compteur *m* Geiger.

geisha (girl) ['geɪʃə-] *n* geisha *f*.

gel[1] [dʒel] (*pret & pp* **gelled**, *cont* **gelling**) <> *n* **1.** CHEM [gen] gel *m* **2.** THEAT filtre *m* coloré.
<> *vi* **1.** [idea, plan - take shape] prendre forme *OR* tournure, se cristalliser **2.** [jellify] se gélifier.

gel[2] [gel] *UK hum* = **girl**.

gelatin ['dʒelətɪn], **gelatine** [,dʒelə'ti:n] *n* **1.** [substance] gélatine *f* **2.** THEAT filtre *m* coloré.

gelatinous [dʒə'lætɪnəs] *adj* gélatineux.

geld [geld] *vt* [bull] châtrer ▪ [horse] hongrer.

gelding ['geldɪŋ] *n* (cheval *m*) hongre *m*.

gelignite ['dʒelɪgnaɪt] *n* gélignite *f*.

gem [dʒem] <> *n* **1.** [precious stone] gemme *f*, pierre *f* précieuse ▪ [semiprecious stone] gemme *f*, pierre *f* fine ▪ **the Gem State** l'Idaho *m* **2.** [masterpiece] joyau *m*, bijou *m*, merveille *f* ▪ **that antique table is a real ~** cette table d'époque est une vraie merveille **3.** [person] : **you're a ~!** tu es un ange! ▪ **our baby-sitter is a real ~** notre baby-sitter est une perle **4.** [in printing] diamant *m*.
<> *vt* orner, parer.

Gemini ['dʒemɪnaɪ] *pr n* ASTROL & ASTRON Gémeaux *mpl* ▪ **he's a ~** il est Gémeaux.

gemstone ['dʒemstəʊn] *n* [precious] gemme *f*, pierre *f* précieuse ▪ [semiprecious] gemme *f*, pierre *f* fine.

gen [dʒen] (*pret & pp* **genned**, *cont* **genning**) *n (U) UK inf* tuyaux *mpl*, renseignements *mpl*.
◆ **gen up** *UK inf* <> *vi insep* se rencarder ▪ **to ~ up on** se rencarder sur.
<> *vt sep* rencarder, mettre au parfum.

gen. (*written abbrev of* **general, generally**) gén.

Gen. (*written abbrev of* **general**) Gal.

gender ['dʒendər] *n* **1.** GRAM genre *m* **2.** [sex] sexe *m* ▪ **~ studies** *à l'université, matière qui formule une critique des rôles de l'homme et de la femme tels qu'ils sont établis par la société.*

gender-bender△ *n* travelo *m*.

gene [dʒi:n] *n* gène *m*.

genealogical [,dʒi:njə'lɒdʒɪkl] *adj* généalogique.

genealogical tree *n* arbre *m* généalogique.

genealogist [,dʒi:nɪ'ælədʒɪst] *n* généalogiste *mf*.

genealogy [,dʒi:nɪ'ælədʒɪ] *n* généalogie *f*.

gene pool *n* patrimoine *m OR* bagage *m* héréditaire.

genera ['dʒenərə] *pl* ▷ **genus**.

general ['dʒenərəl] <> *adj* **1.** [common] général ▪ **as a ~ rule** en règle générale, en général ▪ **in ~ terms** en termes généraux ▪ **in the ~ interest** dans l'intérêt de tous ▪ **there was a ~ movement to leave the room** la plupart des gens se sont levés pour sortir
2. [approximate] général ▪ **a ~ resemblance** une vague ressemblance ▪ **to go in the ~ direction of sthg** se diriger plus ou moins vers qqch
3. [widespread] général, répandu ▪ **to be in ~ use** être d'usage courant *OR* répandu ▪ **this word is no longer in ~ use** ce mot est tombé en désuétude ▪ **there is ~ agreement on the matter** il y a consensus sur la question
4. [overall - outline, plan, impression] d'ensemble ▪ **the ~ effect is quite pleasing** le résultat général est assez agréable ▪ **I get the ~ idea** je vois en gros
5. [ordinary] : **this book is for the ~ reader** ce livre est destiné au lecteur moyen ▪ **the ~ public** le grand public *m*.

◇ *n* **1.** [in reasoning] : **to go from the ~ to the particular** aller du général au particulier
2. MIL général *m*, -e *f*
3. [domestic servant] bonne *f* à tout faire.
◆ **in general** *adv phr* en général.

General Agreement on Tariffs and Trade *pr n* Accord *m* général sur les tarifs douaniers et le commerce.

general assembly *n* assemblée *f* générale.

general degree *n* UNIV licence *f* comportant plusieurs matières.

general delivery *n US* poste *f* restante.

general election *n* élections *fpl* législatives.

general headquarters *n* (grand) quartier *m* général.

general hospital *n* centre *m* hospitalier.

generalist ['dʒenərəlɪst] *n* non-spécialiste *mf*, généraliste *mf*.

generality [ˌdʒenə'rælətɪ] (*pl* **generalities**) *n* **1.** [generalization] généralité *f* ▪ **in the ~** en règle générale **2.** *fml* [majority] plupart *f*.

generalization [ˌdʒenərəlaɪ'zeɪʃn] *n* **1.** [general comment] généralisation *f* **2.** [spread] généralisation *f*.

generalize, ise ['dʒenərəlaɪz] ◇ *vt* généraliser.
◇ *vi* **1.** [person] généraliser **2.** MED [disease] se généraliser.

generalized ['dʒenərəlaɪzd] *adj* **1.** [involving many] généralisé **2.** [non-specific] général.

general knowledge *n* culture *f* générale.

generally ['dʒenərəlɪ] *adv* **1.** [usually] en général, d'habitude **2.** [in a general way] en général, de façon générale ▪ **~ speaking** en général, en règle générale **3.** [by most] dans l'ensemble ▪ **it is ~ agreed that it cannot be done** on s'accorde en général à penser que c'est infaisable.

general manager *n* directeur *m* général, directrice *f* générale.

general meeting *n* assemblée *f* générale.

General Post Office = **GPO**.

general practice *n* médecine *f* générale.

general practitioner *n* médecin *m* généraliste, omnipraticien *m*, - enne *f*.

general-purpose *adj* polyvalent.

general staff *n* état-major *m*.

general store *n* bazar *m*.

general strike *n* grève *f* générale ▪ **the General Strike** *la grève de mai 1926 en Grande-Bretagne, lancée par les syndicats par solidarité avec les mineurs.*

General Studies *npl* SCH ≃ cours *m* de culture générale.

General Synod *pr n le Synode général de l'Église anglicane.*

generate ['dʒenəreɪt] *vt* **1.** [produce - electricity, power] produire, générer ▪ *fig* [- emotion] susciter, donner naissance à **2.** LING & COMPUT générer.

generating station *n* centrale *f* électrique.

generation [ˌdʒenə'reɪʃn] *n* **1.** [age group] génération *f* ▪ **the rising ~** la jeune OR nouvelle génération **2.** [by birth] : **she is second ~ Irish** elle est née de parents irlandais ▪ **third ~ black Britons** les noirs britanniques de la troisième génération **3.** [period of time] génération *f* ▪ **the house has been in the family for three ~s** la maison est dans la famille depuis trois générations ▪ **traditions that have been practised for ~s** des traditions en vigueur depuis des générations **4.** [model - of machine] génération *f* **5.** *(U)* [of electricity] génération *f*, production *f* ▪ LING génération *f*.

generation gap *n* écart *m* entre les générations ▪ [conflict] conflit *m* des générations.

generative ['dʒenərətɪv] *adj* génératif.

generative grammar *n* grammaire *f* générative.

generator ['dʒenəreɪtər] *n* **1.** [electric] générateur *m*, groupe *m* électrogène ▪ [of steam] générateur *m*, chaudière *f* (à vapeur) ▪ [of gas] gazogène *m* **2.** [person] générateur *m*, - trice *f*.

generic [dʒɪ'nerɪk] *adj* générique.

generically [dʒɪ'nerɪklɪ] *adv* génériquement.

generosity [ˌdʒenə'rɒsətɪ] *n* générosité *f*.

generous ['dʒenərəs] *adj* **1.** [with money, gifts] généreux ▪ **he was very ~ in his praise** il ne tarissait pas d'éloges **2.** [in value - gift] généreux ▪ [in quantity - sum, salary] généreux, élevé **3.** [copious] copieux, abondant ▪ [large] bon, abondant ▪ **food and drink were in ~ supply** il y avait à boire et à manger en abondance **4.** *UK* [strong - wine] généreux **5.** [physically - size] généreux, ample.

generously ['dʒenərəslɪ] *adv* **1.** [unsparingly] généreusement, avec générosité **2.** [with magnanimity - agree, offer] généreusement ; [- forgive] généreusement, avec magnanimité **3.** [copiously] : **a plate of fish and chips ~ sprinkled with salt and vinegar** une assiette de "fish and chips" généreusement salée et vinaigrée ▪ **the soup was rather ~ salted** [oversalted] la soupe était très généreusement salée **4.** [in size] amplement ▪ **to be ~ built** *euph* avoir des formes généreuses.

genesis ['dʒenəsɪs] (*pl* **geneses** [-siːz]) *n* genèse *f*, origine *f*.
◆ **Genesis** *n* BIBLE la Genèse.

genetic [dʒɪ'netɪk] *adj* génétique.

genetically [dʒɪ'netɪklɪ] *adv* génétiquement ▪ **~ modified** génétiquement modifié ▪ **~ modified organism** organisme *m* génétiquement modifié.

genetic code *n* code *m* génétique.

genetic engineering *n* génie *m* génétique.

genetic fingerprinting *n* empreinte *f* génétique.

geneticist [dʒɪ'netɪsɪst] *n* généticien *m*, - enne *f*.

genetics [dʒɪ'netɪks] *n (U)* génétique *f*.

Geneva [dʒɪ'niːvə] *pr n* Genève ▪ **Lake ~** le lac Léman.

Geneva Convention *pr n* : **the ~** la Convention de Genève.

Genevan [dʒɪ'niːvn], **Genevese** [ˌdʒenɪ'viːz] (*pl* **Genevese**) ◇ *n* Genevois *m*, - e *f*.
◇ *adj* genevois.

genial ['dʒiːnjəl] *adj* **1.** [friendly - person] aimable, affable ; [- expression, voice] cordial, chaleureux ; [- face] jovial **2.** *lit* [clement - weather] clément.

geniality [ˌdʒiːnɪ'ælətɪ] *n* **1.** [of person, expression] cordialité *f*, amabilité *f* **2.** *lit* [of weather] clémence *f*.

genially ['dʒiːnjəlɪ] *adv* cordialement, chaleureusement.

genie ['dʒiːnɪ] (*pl* **genii** [-nɪaɪ]) *n* génie *m*, djinn *m*.

genii [-nɪaɪ] *pl* ▷ **genie**, ▷ **genius**.

genital ['dʒenɪtl] *adj* génital.
◆ **genitals** *npl* organes *mpl* génitaux.

genitalia [ˌdʒenɪ'teɪlɪə] *npl* organes *mpl* génitaux, parties *fpl* génitales.

genitive ['dʒenɪtɪv] ◇ *n* génitif *m* ▪ **in the ~** au génitif.
◇ *adj* du génitif ▪ **the ~ case** le génitif.

genito-urinary [ˌdʒenɪtəʊ'jʊərɪnərɪ] *adj* génito-urinaire ▪ **the ~ tract** l'appareil *m* génito-urinaire.

genius ['dʒiːnjəs] (*pl* **geniuses** [-nɪaɪ]) *n* **1.** [person] génie *m* ▪ **she's a ~ at music** c'est un génie en musique **2.** [special ability] génie *m* ▪ **a work/writer of ~** une œuvre/un écrivain de génie ▪ **to have a ~ for sthg** avoir le génie de qqch ▪ **her ~ lies in her power to evoke atmosphere** son génie, c'est de savoir recréer une atmosphère **3.** [special character - of system, idea] génie *m* (particulier), esprit *m* **4.** (*pl* genii) [spirit, demon] génie *m*.

Genoa ['dʒenəʊə] *pr n* Gênes.

genocide ['dʒenəsaɪd] *n* génocide *m*.

genome ['dʒi:nəʊm] *n* génome *m*.

genomics [dʒɪ'nəʊmɪks] *n (sg)* génomique.

genotype ['dʒenəʊtaɪp] *n* génotype *m*.

genre ['ʒɑ̃rə] <> *n* genre *m*.
<> *comp* : **~ painting** peinture *f* de genre.

gent [dʒent] (*abbrev of* **gentleman**) *n* *esp* **UK** *inf* monsieur *m* ■ **~s' outfitters** magasin *m* de confection *OR* d'habillement pour hommes.
◆ **gents** *n inf* **the ~s** les toilettes *fpl* (pour hommes).

genteel [dʒen'ti:l] *adj* **1.** [refined] comme il faut, distingué ■ **to live in ~ poverty** vivre dans une misère respectable *OR* une misère qui s'efforce de sauver les apparences **2.** [affected - speech] maniéré, affecté ; [- manner] affecté ; [- language] précieux.

gentian ['dʒenʃɪən] *n* gentiane *f*.

Gentile ['dʒentaɪl] <> *n* **HIST** gentil *m*.
<> *adj* **HIST** des gentils.

gentility [dʒen'tɪlətɪ] *n* **1.** [good breeding] distinction *f* **2.** [gentry] petite noblesse *f* **3.** *(U)* [affected politeness] manières *fpl* affectées.

gentle ['dʒentl] <> *adj* **1.** [mild - person, smile, voice] doux, douce *f* ; [- landscape] agréable ■ **a ~ soul** une bonne âme, une âme charitable ◐ **the ~ sex** le sexe faible ■ **as ~ as a lamb** doux comme un agneau **2.** [light - knock, push, breeze] léger ; [- rain] fin, léger ; [- exercise] modéré **3.** [discreet - rebuke, reminder] discret, - ète *f* ■ **the ~ art of persuasion** *hum* l'art subtil de la persuasion ■ **to try ~ persuasion on sb** essayer de convaincre qqn par la douceur ■ **we gave him a ~ hint** nous l'avons discrètement mis sur la voie **4.** [gradual - slope, climb] doux, douce *f* ■ **a ~ transition** une transition progressive *OR* sans heurts **5.** *arch* [noble] noble, de bonne naissance.
<> *vt* [animal] apaiser, calmer.
<> *n* [maggot] asticot *m*.

gentlefolk ['dʒentlfəʊk] *npl arch* personnes *fpl* de bonne famille *OR* de la petite noblesse.

gentleman ['dʒentlmən] (*pl* **gentlemen** [-mən]) *n* **1.** [man] monsieur *m* ■ **show the ~ in** faites entrer monsieur **2.** [well-bred man] homme *m* du monde, gentleman *m* ■ **to act like a ~** agir en gentleman ■ **a born ~** un gentleman né ◐ **'Gentlemen Prefer Blondes'** ***Hawks*** 'les Hommes préfèrent les blondes' **3.** [man of substance] rentier *m* ■ [at court] gentilhomme *m*.

gentleman farmer *n* gentleman-farmer *m*.

gentleman-in-waiting *n* **UK** gentilhomme *m* (au service du roi).

gentlemanly ['dʒentlmənlɪ] *adj* [person] bien élevé ■ [appearance, behaviour] distingué ■ [status] noble ■ **to behave in a ~ way** agir en gentleman.

gentleman's gentleman *n* **UK** *domestique personnel d'un gentleman.*

gentlemen [-mən] *pl* ▷ **gentleman.**

gentlemen's agreement *n* gentleman's agreement *m*, accord *m* reposant sur l'honneur.

gentleness ['dʒentlnɪs] *n* douceur *f*, légèreté *f*.

gentlewoman ['dʒentl,wʊmən] (*pl* **gentlewomen** [-,wɪmɪn]) *n* **1.** [of noble birth] dame *f* **2.** [refined] femme *f* du monde **3.** [lady-in-waiting] dame *f* d'honneur *OR* de compagnie.

gently ['dʒentlɪ] *adv* **1.** [mildly - speak, smile] avec douceur **2.** [discreetly - remind, reprimand, suggest] discrètement ■ **he broke the news to her as ~ as possible** il fit de son mieux pour lui annoncer la nouvelle avec tact *OR* ménagement **3.** [lightly] : **the rain was falling ~** la pluie tombait doucement **4.** [gradually] doucement, progressivement ■ **~ rolling hills** des collines qui ondoient (doucement) **5.** [slowly - move, heat] doucement ■ **a ~ flowing river** une rivière qui coule paisiblement ◐ **~ does it!** doucement!

gentrification [,dʒentrɪfɪ'keɪʃn] *n* embourgeoisement *m*.

gentrify ['dʒentrɪfaɪ] (*pret & pp* **gentrified**) *vt* [suburb] embourgeoiser, rendre chic *OR* élégant ■ **the area has been gentrified** le quartier est devenu chic.

gentry ['dʒentrɪ] (*pl* **gentries**) *n* petite noblesse *f*.

genuflect ['dʒenju:flekt] *vi* faire une génuflexion.

genuflection, genuflexion [,dʒenju:'flekʃn] *n* génuflexion *f*.

genuine ['dʒenjʊɪn] *adj* **1.** [authentic - antique] authentique ; [- gold, mahogany] véritable, vrai ■ **he's the ~ article** *fig* c'est un vrai de vrai **2.** [sincere - person] naturel, franc, franche *f* ; [- emotion] sincère, vrai ; [- smile, laugh] vrai, franc, franche *f* ■ **it is my ~ belief that he is innocent** je suis intimement persuadé de son innocence **3.** [real - mistake] fait de bonne foi **4.** [not impersonated - repairman, official] vrai, véritable **5.** [serious - buyer] sérieux ■ **'~ enquiries only'** [in advert] 'pas sérieux s'abstenir'.

genuinely ['dʒenjʊɪnlɪ] *adv* [truly] authentiquement ■ [sincerely] sincèrement, véritablement.

genus ['dʒi:nəs] (*pl* **genera** ['dʒenərə]) *n* **BIOL** genre *m*.

geocentric [,dʒi:əʊ'sentrɪk] *adj* géocentrique.

geodesic [,dʒi:əʊ'desɪk] *adj* géodésique.

geodesic dome *n* dôme *m* géodésique.

geographer [dʒɪ'ɒgrəfər] *n* géographe *mf*.

geographical [dʒɪə'græfɪkl] *adj* géographique.

geographically [dʒɪə'græfɪklɪ] *adv* géographiquement.

geography [dʒɪ'ɒgrəfɪ] (*pl* **geographies**) *n* **1.** [science] géographie *f* **2.** [layout] : **I don't know the ~ of the building** je ne connais pas le plan du bâtiment.

geological [,dʒɪə'lɒdʒɪkl] *adj* géologique.

geologist [dʒɪ'ɒlədʒɪst] *n* géologue *mf*.

geology [dʒɪ'ɒlədʒɪ] *n* géologie *f*.

geomagnetic [,dʒi:əʊmæg'netɪk] *adj* géomagnétique.

geometer [dʒɪ'ɒmɪtər] *n* géomètre *mf*.

geometric [,dʒɪə'metrɪk] *adj* géométrique.

geometrical [,dʒɪə'metrɪkl] *adj* géométrique.

geometrically [,dʒɪə'metrɪklɪ] *adv* géométriquement.

geometrician [,dʒɪəʊmə'trɪʃn] *n* géomètre *mf*.

geometric progression *n* progression *f* géométrique.

geometry [dʒɪ'ɒmətrɪ] *n* géométrie *f*.

geomorphology [,dʒi:əʊmɔ:'fɒlədʒɪ] *n* géomorphologie *f*.

geophysical [,dʒi:əʊ'fɪzɪkl] *adj* géophysique.

geophysics [,dʒi:əʊ'fɪzɪks] *n (U)* géophysique *f*.

geopolitical [,dʒi:əʊpə'lɪtɪkl] *adj* géopolitique.

geopolitics [,dʒi:əʊ'pɒlətɪks] *n (U)* géopolitique *f*.

Geordie ['dʒɔ:dɪ] **UK** *n* **1.** [person] *surnom des habitants de Tyneside, dans le Nord-Est de l'Angleterre* **2.** [dialect] *dialecte parlé par les habitants de Tyneside.*

George ['dʒɔ:dʒ] *pr n* : **Saint ~** saint Georges ■ **King ~ V** le roi George V ◐ **by ~!** *inf dated* sapristi!

George Cross *n décoration britannique décernée aux civils pour des actes de bravoure.*

georgette [dʒɔ:'dʒet] *n* crêpe *m* georgette.

Georgia ['dʒɔ:dʒjə] *pr n* [in US, CIS] Géorgie *f* ■ **in ~** en Géorgie.

Georgian ['dʒɔ:dʒjən] <> *n* **1.** [inhabitant of Georgia] Géorgien *m*, - enne *f* **2.** **LING** géorgien *m*.
<> *adj* **1.** [of Georgia] géorgien **2.** **HIST** géorgien *(du règne des rois George I-IV 1714-1830)* **3.** **LIT** : **~ poetry** poésie *f* géorgienne *(poésie britannique des années 1912-1922).*

geoscience [ˌdʒiːəʊ'saɪəns] *n* **1.** [particular] science *f* de la terre **2.** *(U)* [collectively] sciences *fpl* de la terre.

geothermal [ˌdʒiːəʊ'θɜːml], **geothermic** [ˌdʒiːəʊ'θɜːmɪk] *adj* géothermique.

geranium [dʒɪ'reɪnjəm] ◇ *n* géranium *m*.
◇ *adj* rouge géranium *(inv)*, incarnat.

gerbil ['dʒɜːbɪl] *n* gerbille *f*.

geriatric [ˌdʒerɪ'ætrɪk] ◇ *adj* MED gériatrique ■ **~ hospital** hospice *m* ■ **~ medicine** gériatrie *f* ■ **~ nurse** infirmier *m* (spécialisé), infirmière *f* (spécialisée) en gériatrie ■ **~ ward** service *m* de gériatrie.
◇ *n* **1.** [patient] malade *mf* en gériatrie **2.** *pej* vieux *m*, vieille *f*.

geriatrician [ˌdʒerɪə'trɪʃn] *n* gériatre *mf*.

geriatrics [ˌdʒerɪ'ætrɪks] *n (U)* gériatrie *f*.

germ [dʒɜːm] *n* **1.** [microbe] microbe *m*, germe *m* **2.** BIOL germe *m* **3.** *fig* germe *m*, ferment *m* ■ **the ~ of an idea** le germe d'une idée.

German ['dʒɜːmən] ◇ *n* **1.** [person] Allemand *m*, - e *f* **2.** LING allemand *m*.
◇ *adj* allemand.

German Democratic Republic *pr n* : **the ~** la République démocratique allemande, la RDA.

germane [dʒɜː'meɪn] *adj fml* pertinent ■ **~ to** en rapport avec.

Germanic [dʒɜː'mænɪk] ◇ *adj* germanique.
◇ *n* LING germanique *m*.

German measles *n (U)* rubéole *f*.

German shepherd (dog) *n* berger *m* allemand.

Germany ['dʒɜːmənɪ] *pr n* Allemagne *f* ■ **in ~** en Allemagne.

germ-free *adj* stérilisé, aseptisé.

germicide ['dʒɜːmɪsaɪd] *n* bactéricide *m*.

germinal ['dʒɜːmɪnl] *adj* **1.** BIOL germinal **2.** *fig & fml* embryonnaire.

germinate ['dʒɜːmɪneɪt] ◇ *vi* **1.** BIOL germer **2.** *fig* [originate] germer, prendre naissance.
◇ *vt* **1.** BIOL faire germer **2.** *fig* faire germer, donner naissance à.

germination [ˌdʒɜːmɪ'neɪʃn] *n* germination *f*.

germ warfare *n* guerre *f* bactériologique.

Gerona [dʒə'rəʊnə] *pr n* Gérone.

Geronimo *pr n nom d'un célèbre chef apache (traditionnellement, les parachutistes américains crient son nom en sautant dans le vide).*

gerontocracy [ˌdʒerɒn'tɒkrəsɪ] (*pl* **gerontocracies**) *n* gérontocratie *f*.

gerontology [ˌdʒerɒn'tɒlədʒɪ] *n* gérontologie *f*.

gerrymandering ['dʒerɪmændərɪŋ] *n pej* charcutage *m* électoral.

gerund ['dʒerənd] *n* gérondif *m*.

gerundive [dʒɪ'rʌndɪv] ◇ *n* adjectif *m* verbal.
◇ *adj* du gérondif.

gestalt psychology *n* gestaltisme *m*, théorie *f* de la forme.

Gestapo [ge'stɑːpəʊ] *pr n* Gestapo *f*.

gestate [dʒe'steɪt] ◇ *vi* être en gestation ■ *fig* mûrir.
◇ *vt* **1.** BIOL [young] porter **2.** *fig* [idea, plan] laisser mûrir.

gestation [dʒe'steɪʃn] *n* gestation *f* ■ **~ period** période *f* de gestation.

gesticulate [dʒe'stɪkjʊleɪt] ◇ *vi* gesticuler.
◇ *vt* [answer, meaning] mimer.

gesticulation [dʒeˌstɪkjʊ'leɪʃn] *n* gesticulation *f*.

gesture ['dʒestʃər] ◇ *n* **1.** [expressive movement] geste *m* ■ **a ~ of acknowledgment** un signe de reconnaissance **2.** [sign, token] geste *m* ■ **as a ~ of friendship** en signe OR en témoignage d'amitié ■ **it was a nice ~** c'était une gentille attention.
◇ *vi* : **to ~ with one's hands/head** faire un signe de la main/de la tête ■ **he ~d to me to stand up** il m'a fait signe de me lever ■ **she ~d towards the pile of books** elle désigna OR montra la pile de livres d'un geste.
◇ *vt* mimer.

gesundheit [gə'zʊnthaɪt] *interj US* à vos/tes souhaits.

get [get] (*UK pret & pp* **got** [gɒt], *cont* **getting** [getɪŋ]) (*US pret* **got** [gɒt], *pp* **gotten** [gɒtn], *cont* **getting** [getɪŋ])
◇ *vt*

A.

1. [receive - gift, letter, phone call] recevoir, avoir ; [- benefits, pension] recevoir, toucher ■ MED [- treatment] suivre ■ **I ~ "The Times" at home** je reçois le "Times" à la maison ■ **the living room ~s a lot of sun** le salon est très ensoleillé ■ **I rang but I got no answer** [at door] j'ai sonné mais je n'ai pas obtenu OR eu de réponse ; [on phone] j'ai appelé sans obtenir de réponse ■ **he got 5 years for smuggling** il a écopé de OR il a pris 5 ans (de prison) pour contrebande ▶ **you're really going to ~ it!** *inf* qu'est-ce que tu vas prendre OR écoper!
2. [obtain - gen] avoir, trouver, obtenir ; [- through effort] se procurer, obtenir ; [- licence, loan, permission] obtenir ; [- diploma, grades] avoir, obtenir ■ **they got him a job** ils lui ont trouvé du travail ■ **I got the job!** ils m'ont embauché! ■ **can you ~ them the report?** pouvez-vous leur procurer le rapport? ■ **the town ~s its water from the reservoir** la ville reçoit son eau du réservoir ■ **I'm going out to ~ a breath of fresh air** je sors prendre l'air ■ **I'm going to ~ something to drink/eat** [fetch] je vais chercher quelque chose à boire/manger ; [consume] je vais boire/manger quelque chose ■ **can I ~ a coffee?** *US* je pourrais avoir un café, s'il vous plaît? ■ **~ yourself a good lawyer** trouvez-vous un bon avocat ■ **to ~ sb to o.s.** avoir qqn pour soi tout seul ■ **~ plenty of exercise** faites plein d'exercice ■ **~ plenty of sleep** dormez beaucoup ■ **I got a lot from** OR **out of my trip to China** mon voyage en Chine m'a beaucoup apporté ■ **he didn't ~ a chance to introduce himself** il n'a pas eu l'occasion de se présenter
3. [inherit - characteristic] tenir ■ **she ~s her shyness from her father** elle tient sa timidité de son père
4. [obtain in exchange] recevoir ■ **they got a lot of money for their flat** la vente de leur appartement leur a rapporté beaucoup d'argent ■ **they got a good price for the painting** le tableau s'est vendu à un bon prix ■ **you don't ~ something for nothing** on n'a rien pour rien
5. [offer as gift] offrir, donner ■ **I don't know what to ~ Jill for her birthday** je ne sais pas quoi acheter à Jill pour son anniversaire
6. [buy] acheter, prendre
7. [learn - information, news] recevoir, apprendre ■ **we turned on the radio to ~ the news** nous avons allumé la radio pour écouter les informations
8. [reach by calculation or experimentation - answer, solution] trouver ; [- result] obtenir
9. [earn, win - salary] recevoir, gagner, toucher ; [- prize] gagner ; [- reputation] se faire ■ **someone's trying to ~ your attention** [calling] quelqu'un vous appelle ; [waving] quelqu'un vous fait signe
10. [bring, fetch] (aller) chercher ■ **~ me my coat** va me chercher OR apporte-moi mon manteau ■ **we had to ~ a doctor** nous avons dû faire venir un médecin ■ **what can I ~ you to drink?** qu'est-ce que je vous sers à boire? ■ **they sent him to ~ help** ils l'ont envoyé chercher de l'aide
11. [catch - ball] attraper ; [- bus, train] prendre, attraper
12. [capture] attraper, prendre ■ [seize] prendre, saisir ■ **(I've) got you!** je te tiens!
13. [book, reserve] réserver, retenir
14. [answer - door, telephone] répondre ■ **the doorbell's ringing – I'll ~ it!** quelqu'un sonne à la porte – j'y vais!

B.

1. [become ill with] attraper ■ **he got a chill** il a pris OR attrapé froid ■ **I ~ a headache when I drink red wine** le vin rouge me donne mal à la tête ▶ **to ~ it bad for sb** *inf* avoir quelqu'un dans la peau

2. [experience, feel - shock] recevoir, ressentir, avoir ; [- fun, pain, surprise] avoir ■ **I ~ the impression he doesn't like me** j'ai l'impression que je ne lui plais pas ■ **to ~ a thrill out of (doing) sthg** prendre plaisir à (faire) qqch ■ **to ~ religion** *inf* devenir croyant
3. [encounter] : **you ~ some odd people on these tours** il y a de drôles de gens dans ces voyages organisés

C.
1. *(with adj or past participle)* [cause to be] : **she managed to ~ the window closed/open** elle a réussi à fermer/ouvrir la fenêtre ■ **don't ~ your feet wet!** ne te mouille pas les pieds! ■ **~ the suitcases ready** préparez les bagages ■ **let me ~ this clear** que ce soit bien clair ■ **to ~ things under control** prendre les choses en main ■ **he likes his bath as hot as he can ~ it** il aime que son bain soit aussi chaud que possible ■ **he got himself nominated president** il s'est fait nommer président ■ **don't ~ yourself all worked up** ne t'en fais pas
2. *(with infinitive)* [cause to do or carry out] : **we couldn't ~ her to leave** on n'a pas pu la faire partir ■ **~ him to move the car** demande-lui de déplacer la voiture ■ **I got it to work** *OR* **working** j'ai réussi à le faire marcher ■ **he got the other members to agree** il a réussi à obtenir l'accord des autres membres ■ **I can always ~ someone else to do it** je peux toujours le faire faire par quelqu'un d'autre ■ **I got her to talk about life in China** je lui ai demandé de parler de la vie en Chine ■ **they can't ~ the landlord to fix the roof** ils n'arrivent pas à obtenir du propriétaire qu'il fasse réparer le toit
3. *(with past participle)* [cause to be done or carried out] : **to ~ sthg done/repaired** faire faire/réparer qqch ■ **to ~ one's hair cut** se faire couper les cheveux ■ **it's impossible to ~ anything done around here** [by oneself] il est impossible de faire quoi que ce soit ici ; [by someone else] il est impossible d'obtenir quoi que ce soit ici
4. [cause to come, go, move] : **how are you going to ~ this package to them?** comment allez-vous leur faire parvenir ce paquet? ■ **they eventually got all the boxes downstairs/upstairs** ils ont fini par descendre/monter toutes leurs boîtes ■ **~ him away from me** débarrassez-moi de lui ■ **his friends managed to ~ him home** ses amis ont réussi à le ramener (à la maison) ■ **he can't ~ the kids to bed** il n'arrive pas à mettre les enfants au lit ■ **I can't ~ my boots off/on** je n'arrive pas à enlever/mettre mes bottes ■ **that won't ~ you very far!** ça ne te servira pas à grand-chose!, tu ne seras pas beaucoup plus avancé!

D.
1. [prepare - meal, drink] préparer
2. [hear correctly] entendre, saisir ■ **I didn't ~ his name** je n'ai pas saisi son nom
3. [establish telephone contact with] : **I got her father on the phone** j'ai parlé à son père *OR* j'ai eu son père au téléphone ■ **~ me extension 3500** passez-moi *OR* donnez-moi le poste 3500
4. *inf* [understand] comprendre, saisir ■ **I don't ~ it, I don't ~ the point** je ne comprends *OR* ne saisis pas, je n'y suis pas du tout ■ **don't ~ me wrong** comprenez-moi bien ■ **I don't ~ the joke** je ne vois pas ce qui est (si) drôle ■ **(I've) got it!** ça y est!, j'y suis!
5. [take note of] remarquer ■ **did you ~ his address?** lui avez-vous demandé son adresse?
6. △ [look at] viser ■ **~ him! who does he think he is?** vise un peu ce mec, mais pour qui il se prend? ■ **~ (a load of) that!** vise un peu ça!

E.
1. *inf* [hit] atteindre ■ [hit and kill] tuer ■ **she got him in the face with a pie** elle lui a jeté une tarte à la crème à la figure
2. *inf* [harm, punish] : **everyone's out to ~ me** tout le monde est après moi
3. *inf* [take vengeance on] se venger de ■ **we'll ~ you for this!** on te revaudra ça!
4. *inf* [affect physically] : **the pain ~s me in the back** j'ai des douleurs dans le dos ‖ [affect emotionally] émouvoir ■ **that song really ~s me** cette chanson me fait vraiment quelque chose
5. *inf* [baffle, puzzle] : **you've got me there** alors là, aucune idée
6. *inf* [irritate] énerver, agacer
7. *US* [learn] apprendre
8. RADIO & TV [signal, station] capter, recevoir
9. *phr* **he got his in Vietnam** *inf* il est mort au Viêt-nam.

◇ *vi*

A.
1. [become] devenir ■ **I'm getting hungry/thirsty** je commence à avoir faim/soif ■ **~ dressed!** habille-toi! ■ **to ~ fat** grossir ■ **to ~ married** se marier ■ **to ~ divorced** divorcer ■ **don't ~ lost!** ne vous perdez pas! ■ **how did that vase ~ broken?** comment se fait-il que ce vase soit cassé? ■ **to ~ used to (doing) sthg** s'habituer à (faire) qqch ■ **will you ~ with it!** *inf* mais réveille-toi un peu!
2. [used to form passive] : **to ~ elected** se faire élire, être élu ■ **suppose he ~s killed** et s'il se fait tuer? ■ **I'm always getting invited to parties** on m'invite toujours à des soirées
3. *(with present participle)* [start] commencer à, se mettre à ■ **let's ~ going** *OR* **moving!** [let's leave] allons-y! ; [let's hurry] dépêchons(-nous)!, grouillons-nous! ; [let's start to work] au travail! ■ **I'll ~ going on that right away** je m'y mets tout de suite ■ **I can't seem to ~ going today** je n'arrive pas à m'activer aujourd'hui ■ **we got talking about racism** nous en sommes venus à parler de racisme ■ **he got to thinking about it** il s'est mis à réfléchir à la question

B.
1. [go] aller, se rendre ■ [arrive] arriver ■ **when did you ~ home?** quand es-tu rentré? ■ **how do you ~ to the museum?** comment est-ce qu'on fait pour aller au musée? ■ **how did you ~ here?** comment es-tu venu? ■ **how did that bicycle ~ here?** comment se fait-il que ce vélo se trouve ici? ■ **he got as far as buying the tickets** il est allé jusqu'à acheter les billets ■ **I'd hoped things wouldn't ~ this far** j'avais espéré qu'on n'en arriverait pas là ■ **now you're getting somewhere!** enfin tu avances! ■ **I'm not getting anywhere** *OR* **I'm getting nowhere (fast)** *inf* **with this project** je fais du sur place avec ce projet ■ **she won't ~ anywhere** *OR* **she'll ~ nowhere if she's rude to people** elle n'arrivera à rien en étant grossière avec les gens ■ **where's your sister got to?** où est passée ta sœur?
2. [move in specified direction] : **to ~ into bed** se coucher ■ **~ in** *OR* **into the car!** monte dans la voiture! ■ **~ over here!** viens ici!
3. *(with infinitive)* [start] commencer à, se mettre à ■ **to ~ to know sb** apprendre à connaître qqn ■ **you'll ~ to like it in the end** ça finira par te plaire ■ **his father got to hear of the rumours** son père a fini par entendre les rumeurs ■ **they got to talking about the past** ils en sont venus *OR* ils se sont mis à parler du passé
4. [become] devenir ■ **it's getting to be impossible to find a flat** ça devient impossible de trouver un appartement
5. [manage] réussir à ■ **we never got to see that film** nous n'avons jamais réussi à *OR* nous ne sommes jamais arrivés à voir ce film
6. *inf* [be allowed to] : **I never ~ to drive** on ne me laisse jamais conduire
7. *US inf* [leave] se tirer ■ **~!** fous le camp!△, tire-toi!

◆ **get about** *vi insep* **1.** [be up and about, move around] se déplacer ■ **she ~s about on crutches/in a wheelchair** elle se déplace avec des béquilles/en chaise roulante **2.** [travel] voyager **3.** [be socially active] : **she certainly ~s about** elle connaît beaucoup de monde **4.** [story, rumour] se répandre, circuler.

◆ **get across** ◇ *vi insep* pénétrer, passer ■ **the river was flooded but we managed to ~ across** la rivière était en crue mais nous avons réussi à traverser.
◇ *vt sep* communiquer ■ **I can't seem to ~ the idea across to them** je n'arrive pas à leur faire comprendre ça ■ **he managed to ~ his point across** il a réussi à faire passer son message.

◆ **get after** *vt insep* poursuivre.

◆ **get ahead** *vi insep* [succeed] réussir, arriver ■ **to ~ ahead in life** *OR* **in the world** réussir dans la vie.

◆ **get along** *vi insep* **1.** [fare, manage] aller ■ **how are you getting along?** comment vas-tu?, comment ça va? ■ **she's getting along well in her new job** elle se débrouille bien dans son nouveau travail ■ **we can ~ along without him** nous pouvons nous passer de lui *OR* nous débrouiller sans lui **2.** [advance, progress] avancer, progresser **3.** [be on good terms] s'entendre ■ **she's easy to ~ along with** elle est facile à vivre **4.** [move away] s'en aller, partir ■ [go] aller, se rendre ▶ **~ along with you!** *UK* [leave] va-t-en!, fiche le camp! ; [I don't believe you] *inf* à d'autres!

◆ **get around** ◇ *vt insep* [obstacle, problem] contourner ■ [law, rule] tourner.
◇ *vi insep* = **get about**.

◆ **get around to** *vt insep* : **she won't ~ around to reading it before tomorrow** elle n'arrivera pas à (trouver le temps de) le lire avant demain ▪ **he finally got around to fixing the radiator** il a fini par *OR* il est finalement arrivé à réparer le radiateur.

◆ **get at** *vt insep* **1.** [reach - object, shelf] atteindre ; [- place] parvenir à, atteindre ▪ **I've put the pills where the children can't ~ at them** j'ai mis les pilules là où les enfants ne peuvent pas les prendre **2.** [discover] trouver ▪ **to ~ at the truth** connaître la vérité **3.** [mean, intend] entendre ▪ **I see what you're getting at** je vois où vous voulez en venir **4.** *inf* [criticize] s'en prendre à, s'attaquer à **5.** *inf* [bribe, influence] acheter, suborner.

◆ **get away** *vi insep* **1.** [leave] s'en aller, partir ▪ **she has to ~ away from home/her parents** il faut qu'elle parte de chez elle/s'éloigne de ses parents ▪ **to ~ away from the daily grind** échapper au train-train quotidien ▪ **~ away from it all, come to Florida!** quittez tout, venez en Floride! ▪ **she's gone off for a couple of weeks to ~ away from it all** elle est partie quelques semaines loin de tout **2.** [move away] s'éloigner ▪ **~ away from me!** fichez-moi le camp! **3.** [escape] s'échapper, se sauver ▪ **the thief got away with all the jewels** le voleur est parti *OR* s'est sauvé avec tous les bijoux ⊳ **there's no getting away from** *OR* **you can't ~ away from the fact that the other solution would have been cheaper** on ne peut pas nier (le fait) que l'autre solution aurait coûté moins cher ▪ **you can't ~ away from it, there's no getting away from it** c'est comme ça, on n'y peut rien **4.** *UK phr* **~ away (with you)!** *inf* à d'autres!

◆ **get away with** *vt insep* : **he got away with cheating on his taxes** personne ne s'est aperçu qu'il avait fraudé le fisc ▪ **I can't believe you got away with it!** je n'arrive pas à croire que personne ne t'ait rien dit!

◆ **get back** <> *vi insep* **1.** [move backwards] reculer **2.** [return] revenir, retourner ▪ **I can't wait to ~ back home** je suis impatient de rentrer (à la maison) ▪ **~ back in bed!** va te recoucher!, retourne au lit! ▪ **I got back in the car/on the bus** je suis remonté dans la voiture/dans le bus ▪ **to ~ back to sleep** se rendormir ▪ **to ~ back to work** [after break] se remettre au travail ; [after holiday, illness] reprendre le travail ▪ **things eventually got back to normal** les choses ont peu à peu repris leur cours (normal) ▪ **getting** *OR* **to ~ back to the point** pour en revenir au sujet qui nous préoccupe ▪ **I'll ~ back to you on that** [call back] je vous rappelle pour vous dire ce qu'il en est ; [discuss again] nous reparlerons de cela plus tard **3.** [return to political power] revenir ▪ **do you think the Democrats will ~ back in?** croyez-vous que le parti démocrate reviendra au pouvoir?

<> *vt sep* **1.** [recover - something lost or lent] récupérer ; [- force, strength] reprendre, récupérer ; [- health, motivation] retrouver ▪ **he got his job back** il a été repris ▪ **you'll have to ~ your money back from the shop** il faut que vous vous fassiez rembourser par le magasin **2.** [return] rendre **3.** [return to original place] remettre, replacer ▪ **he managed to ~ the children back to bed** il a réussi à remettre les enfants au lit **4.** *phr* **to ~ one's own back (on sb)** *inf* se venger (de qqn).

◆ **get back at** *vt insep* se venger de.

◆ **get behind** *vi insep* [gen] rester à l'arrière, se laisser distancer ▪ SPORT se laisser distancer ▪ *fig* **he got behind with his work** il a pris du retard dans son travail ▪ **we mustn't ~ behind with the rent** il ne faut pas qu'on soit en retard pour le loyer.

◆ **get by** *vi insep* **1.** [pass] passer **2.** [be acceptable] passer, être acceptable **3.** [manage, survive] se débrouiller, s'en sortir ▪ **how do you ~ by on that salary?** comment tu te débrouilles *OR* tu t'en sors avec un salaire comme ça?

◆ **get down** <> *vi insep* descendre ▪ **~ down off that chair!** descends de cette chaise! ▪ **they got down on their knees** ils se sont mis à genoux ▪ **~ down!** [hide] couchez-vous! ; [to dog] bas les pattes!

<> *vt sep* **1.** [write down] noter **2.** [depress] déprimer, démoraliser ▪ **don't let it ~ you down** ne te laisse pas abattre **3.** [swallow] avaler, faire descendre.

◆ **get down to** *vt insep* se mettre à ▪ **it's not so difficult once you ~ down to it** ce n'est pas si difficile une fois qu'on s'y met ▪ **it's hard getting down to work after the weekend** c'est difficile de reprendre le travail après le week-end.

◆ **get in** <> *vi insep* **1.** [into building] entrer ▪ **the thief got in through the window** le cambrioleur est entré par la fenêtre ‖ [into vehicule] : **a car pulled up and she got in** une voiture s'est arrêtée et elle est montée dedans **2.** [return home] rentrer **3.** [arrive] arriver ▪ **what time does your plane ~ in?** à quelle heure ton avion arrive-t-il? **4.** [be admitted - to club] se faire admettre ; [- to school, university] entrer, être admis *OR* reçu ▪ **he applied to Oxford but he didn't ~ in** il voulait entrer à Oxford mais il n'a pas pu **5.** [be elected - person] être élu ; [- party] accéder au pouvoir **6.** *inf* [become involved] participer ▪ **she got in at the beginning** elle est arrivée au début **7.** [interject] glisser.

<> *vt sep* **1.** [fit in] : **I hope to ~ in a bit of reading on holiday** j'espère pouvoir lire *OR* que je trouverai le temps de lire pendant mes vacances **2.** [collect, gather - crops] rentrer, engranger ; [- debts] recouvrer ; [- taxes] percevoir **3.** [lay in] : **I must ~ in some more coal** je dois faire une provision de charbon ▪ **to ~ in supplies** s'approvisionner **4.** [call in - doctor, plumber] faire venir **5.** [hand in, submit] rendre, remettre **6.** [cause to be admitted - to club, university] faire admettre *OR* accepter ▪ [cause to be elected] faire élire **7.** [plant - seeds] planter, semer ; [- bulbs, plants] planter **8.** *UK inf* [pay for drinks] payer, offrir.

<> *vt insep* [building] entrer dans ▪ [vehicle] monter dans ▪ **he had just got in the door when the phone rang** il venait juste d'arriver *OR* d'entrer quand le téléphone a sonné.

◆ **get in on** <> *vt insep* : **to ~ in on a deal** prendre part à un marché ▪ **to ~ in on the fun** se mettre de la partie.

<> *vt sep* faire participer à ▪ **he got me in on the deal** il m'a intéressé à l'affaire.

◆ **get into** <> *vt insep* **1.** [arrive in] arriver à ▪ **the train got into the station at 3 o'clock** le train est entré en gare à 3 h **2.** [put on - dress, shirt, shoes] mettre ; [- trousers, stockings] enfiler, mettre ; [- coat] endosser ▪ **can you still ~ into your jeans?** est-ce que tu rentres encore dans ton jean? **3.** [be admitted to - club, school, university] entrer dans ▪ **to ~ into office** être élu **4.** [become involved in] : **he wants to ~ into politics** il veut se lancer dans la politique ▪ **they got into a conversation about South Africa** ils se sont mis à parler de l'Afrique du Sud ▪ **we got into a fight over who had to do the dishes** nous nous sommes disputés pour savoir qui devait faire la vaisselle ▪ **this is not the moment to ~ into that** ce n'est pas le moment de parler de ça **5.** *inf* [take up] s'intéresser à ▪ **he got into Eastern religions** il a commencé à s'intéresser aux religions orientales **6.** [become accustomed to] : **he soon got into her way of doing things** il s'est vite fait *OR* s'est vite mis à sa façon de faire les choses **7.** [experience a specified condition or state] : **to ~ into debt** s'endetter ▪ **he got into a real mess** il s'est mis dans un vrai pétrin ▪ **the children were always getting into mischief** les enfants passaient leur temps à faire des bêtises ▪ **I got into a real state about the test** j'étais dans tous mes états à cause du test ▪ **she got into trouble with the teacher** elle a eu des ennuis avec le professeur **8.** [cause to act strangely] prendre ▪ **what's got into you?** qu'est-ce qui te prend?, quelle mouche te pique? ▪ **I wonder what got into him to make him act like that** je me demande ce qui l'a poussé à réagir comme ça.

<> *vt sep* **1.** [cause to be admitted to - club] faire entrer à ; [- school, university] faire entrer dans ▪ **the president got his son into Harvard** le président a fait entrer *OR* accepter *OR* admettre son fils à Harvard **2.** [cause to be in a specified condition or state] mettre ▪ **she got herself into a terrible state** elle s'est mis dans tous ses états ▪ **he got them into a lot of trouble** il leur a attiré de gros ennuis **3.** [involve in] impliquer dans, entraîner dans ▪ **you're the one who got us into this** c'est toi qui nous as embarqués dans cette histoire **4.** *inf* [make interested in] faire découvrir ▪ [accustom to] habituer à, faire prendre l'habitude de **5.** *phr* **when will you ~ it into your thick head that I don't want to go?** *inf* quand est-ce que tu vas enfin comprendre que je ne veux pas y aller?

◆ **get in with** *vt insep* s'insinuer dans les bonnes grâces de, se faire bien voir de.

◆ **get off** <> *vi insep* **1.** [leave bus, train etc] descendre ⊳ **I told him where to ~ off!** *inf* je l'ai envoyé sur les roses!, je l'ai envoyé promener! ▪ **where do you ~ off telling me what to do?** *US inf* qu'est-ce qui te prend de me dicter ce que je dois faire? **2.** [depart - person] s'en aller, partir ; [- car] démarrer ; [- plane] décoller ; [- letter, parcel] partir ▪ **the project got off to a bad/good start** *fig* le projet a pris un mauvais/bon départ **3.** [leave work] finir, s'en aller ▪ [take time off] se libérer ▪ **can you ~ off early tomorrow?** peux-tu quitter le travail de bonne heure demain? **4.** [escape punishment] s'en sortir, s'en tirer, en être quitte ▪ **the students got off with a fine/warning** les étudiants en ont été quittes pour une amende/un avertissement **5.** [go to sleep] s'endormir.

<> *vt insep* **1.** [leave - bus, train etc] descendre de ▪ **he got off his horse** il est descendu de cheval ▶ **if only the boss would ~ off my back** si seulement le patron me fichait la paix **2.** [depart from] partir de, décamper de ▪ **~ off my property** fichez le camp de chez moi ▪ **we got off the road to let the ambulance pass** nous sommes sortis de la route pour laisser passer l'ambulance **3.** [escape from] se libérer de ▪ [avoid] échapper à ▪ **how did you ~ off doing the housework?** comment as-tu fait pour échapper au ménage?

<> *vt sep* **1.** [cause to leave, climb down] faire descendre ▪ **the conductor got the passengers off the train** le conducteur a fait descendre les passagers du train ▪ **try to ~ her mind off her troubles** *fig* essaie de lui changer les idées **2.** [send] envoyer, faire partir ▪ **I want to ~ this letter off** je veux expédier cette lettre *OR* mettre cette lettre à la poste **3.** [remove - clothing, lid] enlever, ôter ; [- stains] faire partir *OR* disparaître, enlever ▪ **~ your hands off me!** ne me touche pas! ▪ **he'd like to ~ that house off his hands** *fig* il aimerait bien se débarrasser de cette maison **4.** [free from punishment] tirer d'affaire ▪ [in court] faire acquitter ▪ **he'll need a good lawyer to ~ him off** il lui faudra un bon avocat pour se tirer d'affaire **5.** [put to sleep] endormir.

◆ **get off on** *vt insep inf* [sexually] : **he ~s off on pornographic films** il prend son pied en regardant des films porno ▮ *fig* **I really ~ off on jazz!** j'adore le jazz!

◆ **get off with** *vt insep UK inf* draguer ▪ **did you ~ off with anyone last night?** est-ce que tu as fait des rencontres hier soir?

◆ **get on** <> *vi insep* **1.** [bus, plane, train] monter ▪ [ship] monter à bord **2.** [fare, manage] : **how's your husband getting on?** comment va votre mari? ▪ **how did he ~ on at the interview?** comment s'est passé son entretien?, comment ça a marché pour son entretien? **3.** [make progress] avancer, progresser ▪ **John is getting on very well in maths** John se débrouille très bien en maths **4.** [succeed] réussir, arriver ▪ **to ~ on in life** *OR* **in the world** faire son chemin *OR* réussir dans la vie **5.** [continue] continuer ▪ **we must be getting on** il faut que nous partions ▪ **~ on with your work!** allez! au travail! ▪ **they got on with the job** ils se sont remis au travail **6.** [be on good terms] s'entendre ▪ **my mother and I ~ on well** je m'entends bien avec ma mère ▪ **to be difficult/easy to ~ on with** être difficile/facile à vivre **7.** [grow late - time] : **time's getting on** il se fait tard ▪ **it was getting on in the evening, the evening was getting on** la soirée tirait à sa fin **8.** [grow old - person] se faire vieux ▪ **she's getting on (in years)** elle commence à se faire vieille **9.** *phr* **~ on with it!** [continue speaking] continuez! ; [continue working] allez! au travail! ; [hurry up] mais dépêchez-vous enfin!

<> *vt insep* [bus, train] monter dans ▪ [plane] monter dans, monter à bord de ▪ [ship] monter à bord de ▪ [bed, horse, table, bike] monter sur ▪ **~ on your feet** levez-vous, mettez-vous debout ▪ **it took the patient a while to ~ (back) on his feet** *fig* le patient a mis longtemps à se remettre sur pied.

<> *vt sep* **1.** [help onto - bus, train] faire monter dans ; [- bed, bike, horse, table] faire monter sur ▪ **they got him on his feet** ils l'ont mis debout ▪ **the doctor got her on her feet** *fig* le médecin l'a remise sur pied **2.** [coat, gloves, shoes] mettre, enfiler ▪ [lid] mettre.

◆ **get on for** *vt insep* : **the president is getting on for sixty** le président approche la soixantaine *OR* a presque soixante ans ▪ **it's getting on for midnight** il est presque minuit, il n'est pas loin de minuit ▪ **it's getting on for three weeks since we saw her** ça va faire bientôt trois semaines que nous ne l'avons pas vue ▪ **there were getting on for ten thousand demonstrators** il n'y avait pas loin *OR* il y avait près de dix mille manifestants.

◆ **get onto** <> *vt insep* **1.** = **get on** *(vt insep)* **2.** [turn attention to] : **to ~ onto a subject** *OR* **onto a topic** aborder un sujet ▪ **I'll ~ right onto it!** je vais m'y mettre tout de suite! **3.** [contact] prendre contact avec, se mettre en rapport avec ▪ [speak to] parler à ▪ [call] téléphoner à, donner un coup de fil à **4.** *inf* [become aware of] découvrir **5.** [nag, rebuke] harceler ▪ **his father is always getting onto him to find a job** son père est toujours à le harceler pour qu'il trouve du travail **6.** [be elected to] : **he got onto the school board** il a été élu au conseil d'administration de l'école.

<> *vt sep* **1.** = **get on** *(vt sep sense 1)* **2.** [cause to talk about] faire parler de, amener à parler de.

◆ **get out** <> *vi insep* **1.** [leave - of building, room] sortir ; [- of car, train] descendre ; [- organization, town] quitter ▪ **to ~ out of bed** se lever, sortir de son lit ▪ **you'd better ~ out of here** tu ferais bien de partir *OR* sortir ▶ **~ out of here!** [leave] sortez d'ici! ; *US inf* [I don't believe it] *inf* mon œil! ▪ **to ~ out while the going is good** partir au bon moment **2.** [go out] sortir **3.** [information, news] se répandre, s'ébruiter ▪ **the secret got out** le secret a été éventé **4.** [escape] s'échapper ▪ **he was lucky to ~ out alive** il a eu de la chance de s'en sortir vivant.

<> *vt sep* **1.** [champagne, furniture] sortir ▪ [person] (faire) sortir **2.** [produce, publish - book] publier, sortir ; [- list] établir, dresser **3.** [speak with difficulty] prononcer, sortir ▪ **I could barely ~ a word out** c'est à peine si je pouvais dire *OR* prononcer *OR* sortir un mot ▶ **to ~ out from under** *inf* s'en sortir, s'en tirer.

◆ **get out of** <> *vt insep* **1.** [avoid] éviter, échapper à ▪ [obligation] se dérober *OR* se soustraire à ▪ **he tried to ~ out of helping me** il a essayé de se débrouiller pour ne pas devoir m'aider ▪ **we have to go, there's no getting out of it** il faut qu'on y aille, il n'y a rien à faire *OR* il n'y a pas moyen d'y échapper **2.** [escape from] : **to ~ out of trouble** se tirer d'affaire ▪ **how can I ~ out of this mess?** comment puis-je me tirer de ce pétrin?

<> *vt sep* **1.** [take out of] sortir de ▪ **how many books did you ~ out of the library?** combien de livres as-tu emprunté à *OR* sorti de la bibliothèque? **2.** [help to avoid] : **the lawyer got his client out of jail** l'avocat a fait sortir son client de prison ▪ **the phone call got her out of having to talk to me** *fig* le coup de fil lui a évité d'avoir à me parler ▪ **he'll never ~ himself out of this one!** il ne s'en sortira jamais! ▪ **my confession got him out of trouble** ma confession l'a tiré d'affaire **3.** [extract - cork] sortir de ; [- nail, splinter] enlever de ; [- stain] faire partir de, enlever de ▪ **the police got a confession/the truth out of him** la police lui a arraché une confession/la vérité ▪ **we got the money out of him** nous avons réussi à obtenir l'argent de lui ▪ **I can't ~ anything out of him** je ne peux rien tirer de lui **4.** [gain from] gagner, retirer ▪ **to ~ a lot out of sthg** tirer (un) grand profit de qqch ▪ **I didn't ~ much out of that class** ce cours ne m'a pas apporté grand-chose, je n'ai pas retiré grand-chose de ce cours.

◆ **get over** <> *vt insep* **1.** [cross - river, street] traverser, franchir ; [- fence, wall] franchir, passer par-dessus **2.** [recover from - illness] se remettre de, guérir de ; [- accident] se remettre de ; [- loss] se remettre de, se consoler de ▪ **I'll never ~ over her** je ne l'oublierai jamais ▪ **we couldn't ~ over our surprise** nous n'arrivions pas à nous remettre de notre surprise ▪ **I can't ~ over it!** je n'en reviens pas! ▪ **he couldn't ~ over the fact that she had come back** il n'en revenait pas qu'elle soit revenue ▪ **he'll ~ over it!** il n'en mourra pas! **3.** [master, overcome - obstacle] surmonter ; [- difficulty] surmonter, venir à bout de ▪ **they soon got over their shyness** ils ont vite oublié *OR* surmonté leur timidité.

<> *vt sep* **1.** [cause to cross] faire traverser, faire passer **2.** [communicate - idea, message] faire passer.

<> *vi insep* **1.** [cross] traverser **2.** [idea, message] passer.

◆ **get over with** *vt insep* [finish with] en finir avec ▪ **let's ~ it over (with)** finissons-en.

◆ **get round** <> *vt insep* = **get around**.

<> *vt sep* = **get around**.

<> *vi insep* = **get about**.

◆ **get round to** = **get around to**.

◆ **get through** <> *vi insep* **1.** [reach destination] parvenir ▪ **the letter got through to her** la lettre lui est parvenue ▪ **the message didn't ~ through** le message n'est pas arrivé ▪ **despite the crowds, I managed to ~ through** malgré la foule, j'ai réussi à passer **2.** [candidate, student - succeed] réussir ; [- in exam] être reçu, réussir ▪ **the team got through to the final** l'équipe s'est classée pour la finale **3.** [bill, motion] passer, être adopté *OR* voté **4.** [make oneself understood] se faire comprendre **5.** [contact] contacter ▪ TELEC obtenir la communication ▪ **I can't ~ through to his office** je n'arrive pas à avoir son bureau **6.** *US* [finish] finir, terminer.

<> *vt insep* **1.** [come through - hole, window] passer par ; [- crowd] se frayer un chemin à travers *OR* dans ; [- military lines] percer, franchir **2.** [survive - storm, winter] survivre à ; [- difficulty] se sortir de, se tirer de ▪ **he got through it alive** il s'en est sorti (vivant) **3.** [complete, finish - book] finir, terminer ; [- job, project]

achever, venir à bout de ▪ **I got through an enormous amount of work** j'ai abattu beaucoup de travail **4.** [consume, use up] consommer, utiliser ▪ **they got through their monthly salary in one week** en une semaine ils avaient dépensé tout leur salaire du mois **5.** [endure, pass - time] faire passer ▪ **how will I~ through this without you?** comment pourrai-je vivre cette épreuve sans toi? **6.** [exam] réussir, être reçu à **7.** [subj: bill, motion] passer ▪ **the bill got through both Houses** le projet de loi a été adopté par les deux Chambres.
◇ *vt sep* **1.** [transmit - message] faire passer, transmettre, faire parvenir **2.** [make understood] : **when will you ~ it through your thick head that I don't want to go?** *inf* quand est-ce que tu vas enfin comprendre que je ne veux pas y aller? **3.** [bill, motion] faire adopter, faire passer ▪ **the party got the bill through the Senate** le parti a fait voter *OR* adopter le projet de loi par le Sénat.

◆ **get through with** *vt insep* terminer, finir.

◆ **get together** ◇ *vi insep* **1.** [meet] se réunir, se rassembler ▪ **can we ~ together after the meeting?** on peut se retrouver après la réunion? **2.** [reach an agreement] se mettre d'accord.
◇ *vt sep* [people] réunir, rassembler ▪ [things] rassembler, ramasser ▪ [thoughts] rassembler ▪ **to ~ one's act together** *inf* se secouer.

◆ **get to** *vt insep* **1.** [reach] arriver à ▪ **where have you got to in the book?** où en es-tu dans le livre? ▪ **it got to the point where he couldn't walk another step** il en est arrivé au point de ne plus pouvoir faire un pas **2.** [deal with] s'occuper de ▪ **I'll ~ to you in a minute** je suis à toi *OR* je m'occupe de toi dans quelques secondes **3.** *inf* [have an effect on] : **that music really ~s to me** [moves me] cette musique me touche vraiment ; [annoys me] cette musique me tape sur le système ▪ **don't let it ~ to you!** ne t'énerve pas pour ça! **4.** *US inf* **they got to the witness** [bribed] ils ont acheté le témoin ; [killed] ils ont descendu le témoin.

◆ **get up** ◇ *vi insep* **1.** [arise from bed] se lever ▪ **~ up!** sors du lit!, debout!, lève-toi! **2.** [rise to one's feet] se lever, se mettre debout ▪ **to ~ up from the table** se lever *OR* sortir de table ▪ **~ up off the floor!** relève-toi! ▪ **please don't bother getting up** restez assis, je vous prie **3.** [climb up] monter ▪ **they got up on the roof** ils sont montés sur le toit **4.** [subj: wind] se lever.
◇ *vt insep* [stairs] monter ▪ [ladder, tree] monter à ▪ [hill] gravir.
◇ *vt sep* **1.** [cause to rise to feet] faire lever ▪ [awaken] réveiller **2.** [generate, work up] : **to ~ up speed** gagner de la vitesse ▪ **to ~ one's courage up** rassembler son courage ▪ **I can't ~ up any enthusiasm for the job** je n'arrive pas à éprouver aucun enthousiasme pour ce travail **3.** *inf* [organize - entertainment, party] organiser, monter ; [- petition] organiser ; [- play] monter ; [- excuse, story] fabriquer, forger **4.** [dress up] habiller ▪ [in costume] déguiser **5.** *inf* [study - subject] travailler, bûcher ; [- notes, speech] préparer.

◆ **get up to** *vt insep* faire ▪ **he ~s up to all kinds of mischief** il fait des tas de bêtises.

getaway ['getəweɪ] ◇ *n* **1.** [escape] fuite *f* ▪ **to make one's ~** s'enfuir, filer ▪ **they made a quick ~** ils ont vite filé **2.** AUT [start] démarrage *m* ▪ [in racing] départ *m*.
◇ *adj* : **a ~ car/vehicle** une voiture/un véhicule de fuyard.

Gethsemane [geθ'semənɪ] *pr n* Gethsémani.

get-rich-quick *adj inf* **a ~ scheme** un projet pour faire fortune rapidement.

get-together *n* [meeting] (petite) réunion *f* ▪ [party] (petite) fête *f*.

Gettysburg Address ['getɪzbɜ:g-] *pr n* : **the ~** *discours prononcé par Abraham Lincoln pendant la guerre de Sécession.*

THE GETTYSBURG ADDRESS

Ce discours, prononcé le 19 novembre 1863 par Lincoln après la défaite des confédérés, appelle à la volonté de construire une nation libre, dirigée « par le peuple, pour le peuple » (*a government of the people, by the people, for the people*) ; cette formule est souvent utilisée comme définition de la démocratie.

getup ['getʌp] *n inf* **1.** [outfit] accoutrement *m* ▪ [disguise] déguisement *m* **2.** [of book, product] présentation *f*.

get-up-and-go *n inf* allant *m*, dynamisme *m* ▪ **to have plenty of ~** avoir beaucoup d'allant, être très dynamique.

get-well card *n carte de vœux pour un bon rétablissement.*

geyser [*UK* 'gi:zəʳ, *US* 'gaɪzər] *n* **1.** GEOL geyser *m* **2.** *UK* [domestic] chauffe-eau *m inv* (à gaz).

Ghana ['gɑ:nə] *pr n* Ghana *m* ▪ **in ~** au Ghana.

Ghanaian [gɑ:'neɪən], **Ghanian** ['gɑ:nɪən] ◇ *n* Ghanéen *m*, - enne *f*.
◇ *adj* ghanéen.

ghastly ['gɑ:stlɪ] (*comp* **ghastlier**, *superl* **ghastliest**) *adj* **1.** *inf* [very bad] affreux, épouvantable, atroce ▪ **there's been a ~ mistake** une terrible erreur a été commise ▪ **you look ~!** vous avez l'air d'un déterré! **2.** [frightening, unnatural] horrible, effrayant.

Ghent [gent] *pr n* Gand.

gherkin ['gɜ:kɪn] *n* cornichon *m*.

ghetto ['getəʊ] (*pl* **ghettos** *OR pl* **ghettoes**) *n* ghetto *m*.

ghetto blaster [-,blɑ:stəʳ] *n inf grand radiocassette portatif.*

ghettoization [getəʊaɪ'zeɪʃn] *n* ghettoïsation *f*.

ghost [gəʊst] ◇ *n* **1.** [phantom] revenant *m*, fantôme *m*, spectre *m* ▪ **you look as if you've just seen a ~!** on dirait que vous venez de voir un fantôme! **2.** [shadow, hint] ombre *f* ▪ **you don't have the ~ of a chance** vous n'avez pas la moindre chance *OR* l'ombre d'une chance **3.** TV image *f* secondaire *OR* résiduelle **4.** *phr* **to give up the ~** rendre l'âme **5.** [writer] nègre *m*.
◇ *vt* : **to ~ a book for an author** servir de nègre à l'auteur d'un livre.
◇ *adj* [story, film] de revenants, de fantômes ▪ **a ~ ship/train** un vaisseau/un train fantôme.

ghostly ['gəʊstlɪ] (*comp* **ghostlier**, *superl* **ghostliest**) *adj* spectral, fantomatique ▪ **a ~ figure** une véritable apparition ▪ **a ~ silence** un silence de mort.

ghost town *n* ville *f* fantôme.

ghostwrite ['gəʊstraɪt] (*pret* **ghostwrote** [-rəʊt], *pp* **ghostwritten** [-,rɪtn]) ◇ *vt* écrire *OR* rédiger (comme nègre) ▪ **I'm sure his books are ghostwritten** je suis sûr qu'il n'a écrit aucun des livres publiés sous son nom.
◇ *vi* : **to ~ for sb** servir de nègre à qqn.

ghostwriter ['gəʊst,raɪtəʳ] *n* nègre *m*.

ghoul [gu:l] *n* **1.** [evil spirit] goule *f* **2.** [macabre person] amateur *mf* de macabre.

ghoulish ['gu:lɪʃ] *adj* **1.** [ghostly] de goule, vampirique **2.** [person, humour] morbide, macabre.

GHQ (*abbrev of* **general headquarters**) *n* GQG *m*.

GHz (*abbrev of* **gigahertz**) *n* GHz *m*.

GI [1] (*abbrev of* **Government Issue**) ◇ *n* [soldier] GI *m*, soldat *m* américain.
◇ *comp* : **~ bride** épouse *f* (étrangère) d'un GI.

GI [2] (*abbrev of* **glycaemic index**) *n* IG *m*.

giant ['dʒaɪənt] ◇ *n* **1.** [in size] géant *m*, - e *f* **2.** *fig* **a literary ~** un géant de la littérature ▪ **an industrial ~** un magnat de l'industrie.
◇ *adj* géant, gigantesque ▪ **with ~ footsteps** à pas de géant.

giantess ['dʒaɪəntes] *n* géante *f*.

giantkiller ['dʒaɪənt,kɪləʳ] *n* SPORT *petite équipe victorieuse d'une équipe plus forte.*

giant panda *n* panda *m* géant.

giant sequoia *n* séquoia *m* géant.

giant-size(d) *adj* [pack] géant.

giant star *n* étoile *f* géante.

gibber ['dʒɪbəʳ] *vi* [person] bredouiller, bafouiller ▪ **to ~ with fear** bafouiller de peur.

gibbering ['dʒɪbərɪŋ] *adj* : **I was a ~ wreck!** j'étais dans un de ces états! ▪ **he's a ~ idiot** *inf* c'est un sacré imbécile.

gibberish ['dʒɪbərɪʃ] *n* baragouin *m*, charabia *m* ▪ **this instruction leaflet is a load of ~** *inf* ce mode d'emploi, c'est du vrai charabia.

gibbet ['dʒɪbɪt] <> *n* potence *f*, gibet *m*.
<> *vt* [hang] pendre.

gibbon ['gɪbən] *n* gibbon *m*.

gibbous ['gɪbəs] *adj* ASTRON gibbeux.

gibe [dʒaɪb] <> *vt* [taunt] railler, se moquer de.
<> *vi* : **to ~ at sb** railler qqn, se moquer de qqn.
<> *n* [remark] raillerie *f*, moquerie *f*.

giblets ['dʒɪblɪts] *npl* abats *mpl* de volaille.

Gibraltar [dʒɪ'brɔːltəʳ] *pr n* Gibraltar ▪ **in ~** à Gibraltar ▪ **the Strait of ~** le détroit de Gibraltar.

Gibraltarian [,dʒɪbrɔːl'teərɪən] <> *adj* & *n* gibraltarien (*f* ne).
<> *n* Gibraltarien *m*, - ne *f*.

giddily ['gɪdɪlɪ] *adv* **1.** [dizzily] vertigineusement **2.** [frivolously] à la légère, avec insouciance.

giddiness ['gɪdɪnɪs] *n (U)* **1.** [dizziness] vertiges *mpl*, étourdissements *mpl* **2.** [frivolousness] légèreté *f*, étourderie *f*.

giddy ['gɪdɪ] (*comp* **giddier**, *superl* **giddiest**) *adj* **1.** [dizzy - person] : **to be** *OR* **to feel ~** [afraid of height] avoir le vertige, être pris de vertige ; [unwell] avoir un étourdissement ▪ **I feel ~ just watching them** j'ai la tête qui tourne *OR* le vertige rien que de les regarder **2.** [lofty] vertigineux, qui donne le vertige ▪ **the ~ heights of success** les hautes cimes de la réussite **3.** [frivolous - person, behaviour] frivole, écervelé ▪ **a ~ round of parties and social events** un tourbillon de soirées et de sorties mondaines ➊ **my ~ aunt!** *inf UK dated* *inf* oh la la!

giddy up *interj* [to horse] : **~!** hue!

gift [gɪft] <> *n* **1.** [present - personal] cadeau *m* ; [- official] don *m* ▪ **to make sb a ~ of sthg** offrir qqch à qqn, faire cadeau de qqch à qqn ▪ **is it a ~?** c'est pour offrir? ▪ **he thinks he's God's ~ to mankind** *inf* **/to women** *inf* il se prend pour le Messie/pour Don Juan ▪ **the ~ of friendship/of tears** *lit* le don de l'amitié/des larmes **2.** [talent] don *m* ▪ **he has a great ~ for telling jokes** il n'a pas son pareil pour raconter des plaisanteries ▪ **she has a ~ for music** elle a un don *OR* elle est douée pour la musique ➊ **to have the ~ of the gab** *inf* avoir la langue bien pendue, avoir du bagou(t) **3.** *inf* [bargain] affaire *f* ▪ **at £5, it's a ~** 5 livres, c'est donné **4.** *inf* [easy thing] : **that exam question was a ~** ce sujet d'examen, c'était du gâteau **5.** [donation] don *m*, donation *f* ▪ **as a ~** LAW à titre d'avantage *OR* gracieux ▪ **the posts abroad are in the ~ of the French department** l'attribution des postes à l'étranger relève du département de français **6.** RELIG : **the ~ of faith** la grâce de la foi ▪ **the ~ of tongues** le don des langues.
<> *vt US fml* donner, faire don de ▪ **'~ed by Mr Evans'** [on plaque] 'don de M. Evans'.

GIFT [gɪft] (*abbrev of* **gamete in fallopian transfer**) *n* FIVETE *f*.

gift certificate *US* = **gift token**.

gift coupon *n* bon *m* de réduction, point-cadeau *m*.

gifted ['gɪftɪd] *adj* [person] doué ▪ [performance] talentueux ▪ **highly ~ children** des enfants surdoués ▪ **she's ~ with a fantastic memory** elle a une mémoire fantastique.

gift horse *n phr* **don't** *OR* **never look a ~ in the mouth** *prov* à cheval donné on ne regarde pas la bouche *prov*.

gift shop *n* boutique *f* de cadeaux.

gift token *n* bon *m* d'achat.

gift voucher *UK* **1.** = **gift token 2.** = **gift coupon**.

gift-wrap *vt* faire un paquet cadeau de.

gift wrapping *n* papier-cadeau *m*.

gig [gɪg] *n* **1.** [carriage] cabriolet *m* **2.** [boat] yole *f*, guigue *f* **3.** *inf* [concert] concert *m (de rock, de jazz)*.

gigabyte ['gɪgəbaɪt] *n* gigaoctet *m*.

gigahertz ['gɪgəhɜːts] *n* gigahertz *m*.

gigantic [dʒaɪ'gæntɪk] *adj* géant, gigantesque.

giggle ['gɪgl] <> *vi* [stupidly] rire bêtement, ricaner ▪ [nervously] rire nerveusement ▪ **they couldn't stop giggling** ils ne pouvaient pas se retenir de glousser *OR* de pouffer.
<> *n* [uncontrollable] fou rire *m* ▪ [nervous] petit rire *m* nerveux ▪ [stupid] ricanement *m* ▪ **to have a fit of the ~s** avoir le fou rire.

giggling ['gɪglɪŋ] <> *adj* = **giggly**.
<> *n (U)* fou rire *m*.

giggly ['gɪglɪ] *adj* qui rit bêtement.

GIGO ['gaɪgəʊ] *n* = **garbage in, garbage out**.

gigolo ['ʒɪgələʊ] (*pl* **gigolos**) *n* gigolo *m*.

gigot ['dʒɪgət] *n* gigot *m*.

GI Joe *n surnom collectif des soldats américains, notamment pendant la Deuxième Guerre mondiale.*

gild [gɪld] (*pret* **gilded**, *pp* **gilded** *OR* **gilt** [gɪlt]) <> *n* = **guild**.
<> *vt* dorer ▪ **it would be ~ing the lily** ce serait du peaufinage.

gilded ['gɪldɪd] *adj* doré ▪ **~ youth** *fig* jeunesse *f* dorée.

gilding ['gɪldɪŋ] *n* dorure *f*.

gill[1] [dʒɪl] *n* [measure] quart *m* de pinte.

gill[2] [gɪl] *n* **1.** [of mushroom] lamelle *f* **2.** *UK dial* [ravine] ravin *m* ▪ [stream] ruisseau *m (de montagne)*.
◆ **gills** *npl* [of fish] ouïes *fpl*, branchies *fpl* ▪ **to be/to go green around the ~s** [from shock] être/devenir vert (de peur) ; [from illness] avoir mauvaise mine.

gilt [gɪlt] <> *pp* ▷ **gild**.
<> *adj* doré.
<> *n* **1.** [gilding] dorure *f* ▪ **to take the ~ off the gingerbread** *UK* gâcher le plaisir **2.** [security] valeur *f* de tout repos.

gilt-edged [-edʒd] *adj* **1.** ST. EX [securities] de père de famille, sans risque **2.** [page] doré sur tranche.

gimcrack ['dʒɪmkræk] *adj* [jewellery] en toc ▪ [ornament, car] de pacotille ▪ [theory, idea] bidon.

gimlet ['gɪmlət] *n* [tool] vrille *f*.

gimlet-eyed *adj* à l'œil perçant, aux yeux perçants.

gimme ['gɪmɪ] *inf* = **give me**.

gimmick ['gɪmɪk] *n* **1.** [sales trick] truc *m*, astuce *f* ▪ [in politics] astuce *f*, gadget *m* ▪ **advertising ~** trouvaille *f* publicitaire ▪ **it's just a sales ~** c'est un truc pour faire vendre **2.** [gadget, device] gadget *m*.

gimmickry ['gɪmɪkrɪ] *n (U) inf* truquage *m*, astuces *fpl*.

gimmicky ['gɪmɪkɪ] *adj inf* qui relève du procédé.

gimp [gɪmp] *n US inf* **1.** *pej* [person] gogol△ *mf* **2.** [object] scoubidou *m*.

gin [dʒɪn] (*pret* & *pp* **ginned**, *cont* **ginning**) <> *n* **1.** [drink] gin *m* ▪ **~ and tonic** gin-tonic *m* ▪ **~ and it** *UK* martini-gin *m* **2.** [trap] piège *m* **3.** INDUST [machine] égreneuse *f* (de coton).
<> *vt* attraper, piéger.

ginger ['dʒɪndʒəʳ] <> *n* **1.** [spice] gingembre *m* ▪ **crystallized ~** gingembre confit ▪ **ground ~** gingembre en poudre ▪ **root** *OR* **fresh ~** gingembre en racine *OR* frais **2.** *inf fig* entrain *m*, allant *m*, dynamisme *m* **3.** [colour] brun roux *m*.
<> *adj* [hair] roux, rousse *f*, rouquin ▪ [cat] roux, rousse *f*.
◆ **Ginger** *pr n inf* [nickname] Poil de Carotte.
◆ **ginger up** *vt sep* [activity, group, meeting] animer ▪ [speech, story] relever, pimenter, égayer.

ginger ale *n boisson gazeuse aux extraits de gingembre.*

ginger beer *n boisson légèrement alcoolisée obtenue par la fermentation de gingembre.*

gingerbread ['dʒɪndʒəbred] <> *n* pain *m* d'épices ■ **~ man** sujet *m* en pain d'épices.
<> *adj* [ornament, style] tarabiscoté.

ginger group *n dans une organisation politique ou autre, faction dynamique cherchant à faire bouger les choses en incitant à l'action.*

ginger-haired *adj* roux, rousse *f*.

gingerly ['dʒɪndʒəlɪ] <> *adv* [cautiously] avec circonspection, précautionneusement ■ [delicately] délicatement.
<> *adj* [cautious] circonspect, prudent ■ [delicate] délicat.

ginger nut *n* biscuit *m* au gingembre.

ginger snap = **ginger nut**.

gingery ['dʒɪndʒərɪ] *adj* **1.** [taste] de gingembre ■ [colour] roux, rousse *f* **2.** *fig* [full of vigour] animé ■ [biting] acerbe.

gingham ['gɪŋəm] *n* (toile *f* de) vichy *m*.

gingivitis [,dʒɪndʒɪ'vaɪtɪs] *n (U)* MED gingivite *f*.

gin mill *US* = **gin palace**.

ginormous [,dʒaɪ'nɔ:məs] *adj inf* gigantesque.

gin palace *n UK* tripot *m*.

gin rummy *n* gin-rummy *m*, gin-rami *m*.

ginseng ['dʒɪnseŋ] *n* ginseng *m*.

gippy ['dʒɪpɪ] *adj UK inf* **to have a ~ tummy** avoir la courante.

gipsy ['dʒɪpsɪ] (*pl* **gipsies**) <> *n* gitan *m*, - e *f*, bohémien *m*, - enne *f* ■ *fig* [wanderer] vagabond *m*, - e *f*.
<> *adj* [camp] de gitans ■ [dance, music] gitan ■ **~ caravan** roulotte *f*.

gipsy moth *n* zigzag *m*, bombyx *m* disparate.

giraffe [dʒɪ'rɑ:f] *n* girafe *f* ■ **a young** *OR* **baby ~** un girafeau, un girafon.

gird [gɜ:d] (*pret & pp* **girded** *OR* **girt** [gɜ:t]) *vt lit* **1.** [waist] ceindre ■ **to ~ (up) one's loins** se préparer à l'action **2.** [clothe] : **to ~ with** revêtir de.
◆ **gird on** *vt sep arch & lit* **to ~ on one's sword** ceindre l'épée.

girder ['gɜ:dər] *n* poutre *f* (métallique), fer *m* profilé ■ [light] poutrelle *f*.

girdle ['gɜ:dl] <> *n* **1.** [corset] gaine *f* **2.** *lit* [belt] ceinture *f* **3.** [in tree] incision *f* annulaire.
<> *vt* **1.** *lit* **to ~ sthg with sthg** ceindre qqch de qqch **2.** [tree] baguer.

girl [gɜ:l] *n* **1.** [child] (petite) fille *f* ■ **a little ~** une fillette, une petite fille **2.** [daughter] fille *f* ■ **the Murphy ~** la fille des Murphy **3.** [young woman] (jeune) fille *f* ■ **come in, ~s!** entrez, mesdemoiselles! ■ **she's having an evening with the ~s** elle passe la soirée dehors avec les filles ■ **he married a French ~** il a épousé une Française **4.** *inf* [girlfriend] (petite) amie *f*, copine *f* **5.** SCH [pupil] élève *f* **6.** [employee] (jeune) employée *f* ■ [maid] bonne *f* ■ [in shop] vendeuse *f* ■ [in factory] ouvrière *f*.

girl Friday *n employée de bureau affectée à des tâches diverses.*

girlfriend ['gɜ:lfrend] *n* [of boy] copine *f*, (petite) amie *f* ■ *US* [of girl] copine *f*, amie *f*.

Girl Guide *UK*, **Girl Scout** *US n* éclaireuse *f*.

girlhood ['gɜ:lhʊd] *n* [as child] enfance *f* ■ [as adolescent] adolescence *f*.

girlie ['gɜ:lɪ] *adj inf* **~ magazine** magazine *m* masculin, revue *f* érotique.

girlish ['gɜ:lɪʃ] *adj* [appearance, smile, voice] de fillette, de petite fille ■ *pej* [boy] efféminé.

Girl Scout *US* = **Girl Guide**.

giro ['dʒaɪrəʊ] *n* **1.** [system] *système de virement interbancaire introduit par la Poste britannique* ■ **(bank) ~** virement *m* bancaire ■ **~ cheque** chèque *m* postal ■ **National Giro** ≃ Comptes Chèques Postaux **2.** *inf* [for unemployed] chèque *m* d'allocation de chômage.

Girobank ['dzaɪrəʊbæŋk] *pr n service bancaire de la Poste britannique.*

girt [gɜ:t] *pt & pp* ▷ **gird**.

girth [gɜ:θ] <> *n* **1.** [circumference] circonférence *f*, tour *m* **2.** [stoutness] corpulence *f*, embonpoint *m* **3.** [of saddle] sangle *f*.
<> *vt* [horse] sangler.

gist [dʒɪst] *n* essentiel *m* ■ **give me the ~ of the discussion** expliquez-moi les grandes lignes du débat.

git△ [gɪt] *n UK* connard△ *m*, connasse△ *f*.

give [gɪv] (*pret* **gave** [geɪv], *pp* **given** ['gɪvn]) <> *vt*

A.

1. [hand over] donner ■ [as gift] donner, offrir ■ **I gave him the book, I gave the book to him** je lui ai donné le livre ■ **the family gave the paintings to the museum** la famille a fait don des tableaux au musée ■ **I ~ you the newlyweds!** [in toast] je lève mon verre au bonheur des nouveaux mariés! ■ **I gave him my coat to hold** je lui ai confié mon manteau ■ **she gave them her trust** elle leur a fait confiance, elle leur a donné sa confiance ➊ **to ~ as good as one gets** rendre coup pour coup ■ **~ it all you've got!** *inf* mets-y le paquet! ■ **I'll ~ you something to cry about!** *inf* je vais te donner une bonne raison de pleurer, moi!
2. [grant - right, permission, importance etc] donner ■ **~ the matter your full attention** prêtez une attention toute particulière à cette affaire ■ **the court gave her custody of the child** LAW la cour lui a accordé la garde de l'enfant ■ **she hasn't given her approval yet** elle n'a pas encore donné son consentement
3. [provide with - drink, food] donner, offrir ; [- lessons, classes, advice] donner ; [- help] prêter ■ **the children can wash up, it will ~ them something to do** les enfants peuvent faire la vaisselle, ça les occupera ■ **to ~ sb/sthg one's support** soutenir qqn/qqch ■ **do you ~ a discount?** faites-vous des tarifs préférentiels? ■ **~ me time to think** donnez-moi *OR* laissez-moi le temps de réfléchir ■ **just ~ me time!** sois patient! ➊ **~ me jazz any day!** *inf* à mon avis rien ne vaut le jazz!

B.

1. [confer - award] conférer ■ **they gave her an honorary degree** ils lui ont conféré un diplôme honorifique
2. [dedicate] donner, consacrer ■ **she gave all she had to the cause** elle s'est entièrement consacrée à cette cause ■ **he gave his life to save the child** il est mort *OR* il a donné sa vie pour sauver l'enfant
3. [in exchange] donner ■ [pay] payer ■ **I gave him my sweater in exchange for his gloves** je lui ai échangé mon pull contre ses gants
4. [transmit] donner, passer ■ **I hope I don't ~ you my cold** j'espère que je ne vais pas te passer mon rhume

C.

1. [cause] donner, causer ■ [headache] donner ■ [pleasure, surprise, shock] faire ■ **the walk gave him an appetite** la promenade l'a mis en appétit *OR* lui a ouvert l'appétit
2. [impose - task] imposer ; [- punishment] infliger ■ **to ~ sb a black mark** infliger un blâme à qqn ■ **he was given (a sentence of) 15 years** LAW il a été condamné à 15 ans de prison
3. [announce - verdict, judgment] : **the court ~s its decision today** la cour prononce *OR* rend l'arrêt aujourd'hui ■ **the court gave the case against/for the management** la cour a décidé contre/en faveur de la direction
4. [communicate - impression, order, signal] donner ; [- address, information] donner, fournir ; [- news, decision] annoncer ■ **to ~ sb a message** communiquer un message à qqn ■ **she gave her age as 45** elle a déclaré avoir 45 ans ■ **you gave me to believe he was trustworthy** vous m'avez laissé entendre qu'on pouvait lui faire confiance ■ **I was given to understand she was ill** on m'a donné à croire qu'elle était malade
5. [suggest, propose - explanation, reason] donner, avancer ; [- hint] donner ■ **don't ~ me any nonsense about missing your train!** ne me raconte pas que tu as raté ton train! ■ **don't ~ me that (rubbish)!** *inf* ne me raconte pas d'histoires!
6. [admit, concede] reconnaître, accorder ■ **she's certainly intelligent, I'll ~ you that** elle est très intelligente, ça, je te l'accorde

D.

1. [utter - sound] rendre, émettre ; [- answer] donner, faire ; [- cry, sigh] pousser ■ **he gave a laugh** il a laissé échapper un rire ■ **~ us a song** chantez-nous quelque chose
2. [make - action, gesture] faire ■ **she gave them an odd look** elle leur a jeté *OR* lancé un regard curieux ■ **~ me a kiss** [gen] fais-moi la bise ; [lover] embrasse-moi ■ **she gave him a slap** elle lui a donné une claque ■ **he gave an embarrassed smile** il a eu un sourire gêné
3. [perform in public - concert] donner ; [- lecture, speech] faire ; [- interview] accorder ■ **that evening she gave the performance of a lifetime** ce soir-là elle était au sommet de son art
4. [hold - lunch, party, supper] donner, organiser ■ **they gave a dinner for the professor** ils ont donné un dîner en l'honneur du professeur
5. [estimate the duration of] donner, estimer ■ **I ~ him one week at most** je lui donne une semaine (au) maximum
6. MATHS [produce] donner, faire ■ **17 minus 4 ~s 13** 17 moins 4 font *OR* égalent 13
7. *phr* **to ~ way** [ground] s'affaisser ; [bridge, building, ceiling] s'effondrer, s'affaisser ; [ladder, rope] céder, (se) casser ■ **her legs gave way (beneath her)** ses jambes se sont dérobées sous elle ■ **his health finally gave way** sa santé a fini par se détériorer *OR* se gâter ■ **it's easier to ~ way to his demands than to argue** il est plus commode de céder à ses exigences que de lui résister ■ **I gave way to tears/to anger** je me suis laissé aller à pleurer/emporter par la colère ■ **he gave way to despair** il s'est abandonné au désespoir ■ **the fields gave way to factories** les champs ont fait place aux usines ■ **his joy gave way to sorrow** sa joie a fait place à la peine ■ **'~ way to pedestrians'** 'priorité aux piétons' ■ **'~ way'** 'cédez le passage'.

◇ *vi* **1.** [contribute] donner ■ **please ~ generously** nous nous en remettons à votre générosité **2.** [collapse, yield - ground, wall] s'affaisser ■ **something's got to ~** quelque chose va lâcher ; [- cloth, elastic] se relâcher ; [- person] céder **3.** *US inf* [talk] : **now ~!** accouche!^△^, vide ton sac! **4.** *US inf* **what ~s?** qu'est-ce qui se passe?

◇ *n* [of metal, wood] élasticité *f*, souplesse *f* ■ **there's not enough ~ in this sweater** ce pull n'est pas assez ample.

◆ **give or take** *prep phr* à... près ■ **~ or take a few days** à quelques jours près.

◆ **give away** *vt sep* **1.** [hand over] donner ■ [as gift] donner, faire cadeau de ■ [prize] distribuer ■ **it's so cheap they're practically giving it away** c'est tellement bon marché, c'est comme s'ils en faisaient cadeau **2.** [bride] conduire à l'autel **3.** [throw away - chance, opportunity] gâcher, gaspiller **4.** [reveal - information] révéler ; [- secret] révéler, trahir ■ **he didn't ~ anything away** il n'a rien dit **5.** [betray] trahir ■ **her accent gave her away** son accent l'a trahie.

◆ **give back** *vt sep* **1.** [return] rendre ■ [property, stolen object] restituer ■ **the store gave him his money back** le magasin l'a remboursé **2.** [reflect - image, light] refléter, renvoyer ■ [sound] renvoyer.

◆ **give in** ◇ *vi insep* [relent, yield] céder ■ **to ~ in to sthg/sb** céder à qqch/qqn.

◇ *vt sep* [hand in - book, exam paper] rendre ; [- found object, parcel] remettre ; [- application, name] donner.

◆ **give off** *vt sep* **1.** [emit, produce - gas, smell] émettre **2.** BOT [shoots] former.

◆ **give onto** *vt insep* donner sur.

◆ **give out** ◇ *vt sep* **1.** [hand out] distribuer **2.** [emit] émettre, faire entendre **3.** [make known] annoncer, faire savoir.

◇ *vi insep* **1.** [fail - machine] tomber en panne ; [- brakes] lâcher ; [- heart] flancher ■ **the old car finally gave out** la vieille voiture a fini par rendre l'âme *hum* **2.** [run out] s'épuiser, manquer ■ **her strength was giving out** elle était à bout de forces, elle n'en pouvait plus ■ **his mother's patience gave out** sa mère a perdu patience ■ **my luck gave out** la chance m'a abandonné.

◆ **give over** ◇ *vt sep* **1.** [entrust] donner, confier **2.** [set aside for] donner, consacrer ■ ADMIN affecter ■ **the land was given over to agriculture** la terre a été consacrée à l'agriculture.

◇ *vt insep UK inf* cesser de, arrêter de.

◇ *vi insep UK inf* cesser, arrêter ■ **~ over!** assez!, arrête!

◆ **give up** ◇ *vt sep* **1.** [renounce - habit] renoncer à, abandonner ; [- friend] abandonner, délaisser ; [- chair, place] céder ; [- activity] cesser ■ **she'll never ~ him up** elle ne renoncera jamais à lui ■ **he's given up smoking** il a arrêté de fumer, il a renoncé au tabac ■ **I haven't given up the idea of going to China** je n'ai pas renoncé à l'idée d'aller en Chine ■ **don't ~ up hope** ne perdez pas espoir ■ **he was ready to ~ up his life for his country** il était prêt à mourir pour la patrie ■ **we gave her brother up for dead** nous avons conclu que son frère était mort ■ **to ~ up the throne** renoncer au trône **2.** [resign from - job] quitter ; [- position] démissionner de ■ **they gave up the restaurant business** ils se sont retirés de la restauration **3.** [hand over - keys] rendre, remettre ; [- prisoner] livrer ; [- responsibility] se démettre de ■ **the murderer gave himself up (to the police)** le meurtrier s'est rendu *OR* livré (à la police).

◇ *vi insep* : **I ~ up** [in game, project] je renonce ; [in guessing game] je donne ma langue au chat ■ **we can't ~ up now!** on ne va pas laisser tomber maintenant.

◆ **give up on** *vt insep* : **to ~ up on sb** [stop waiting for] renoncer à attendre qqn ; [stop expecting sthg from] ne plus rien attendre de qqn ■ **I ~ up on him, he won't even try** j'abandonne, il ne fait pas le moindre effort.

◆ **give up to** *vt sep* : **to ~ o.s. up to sthg** se livrer à qqch ■ **he gave his life up to caring for the elderly** il a consacré sa vie à soigner les personnes âgées.

give-and-take *n* **1.** [compromise] concessions *fpl* (mutuelles) ■ **in a relationship there has to be some ~** pour fonder une relation, il faut que chacun fasse des concessions *OR* que chacun y mette du sien **2.** [in conversation] échange.

giveaway ['gɪvə,weɪ] ◇ *n* **1.** [free gift] cadeau *m* ■ COMM prime *f*, cadeau *m* publicitaire **2.** *US* RADIO & TV jeu *m* (doté de prix) **3.** *inf* [revelation] révélation *f* (involontaire) ■ **her guilty expression was a dead ~** son air coupable l'a trahie ■ **the fact that he knew her name was a ~** le fait qu'il sache son nom était révélateur *OR* en disait long.

◇ *adj* **1.** [free] gratuit ■ [price] dérisoire **2.** *US* **~ program** RADIO jeu *m* radiophonique ; TV jeu *m* télévisé **3.** *inf* [revealing] révélateur.

given ['gɪvn] ◇ *pp* ▷ **give**.

◇ *adj* **1.** [specified] donné ■ [precise] déterminé ■ **at a ~ moment** à un moment donné **2.** [prone] : **to be ~ to sthg** avoir une tendance à qqch ■ **to be ~ to doing sthg** être enclin à faire qqch ■ **I'm not ~ to telling lies** je n'ai pas l'habitude de mentir ■ [on official statement] : **~ in Melbourne on the sixth day of March** fait à Melbourne le six mars.

◇ *prep* **1.** [considering] étant donné ■ **~ the rectangle ABCD** MATHS soit le rectangle ABCD **2.** *phr* **~ the chance** *OR* **opportunity** si l'occasion se présentait.

◆ **given that** *conj phr* étant donné que.

given name *n US* prénom *m*.

giver ['gɪvəʳ] *n* donateur *m*, - trice *f*.

gizmo ['gɪzməʊ] (*pl* **gizmos**) *n US* gadget *m*, truc *m*.

gizzard ['gɪzəd] *n* gésier *m* ■ **it sticks in my ~** *fig* ça me reste en travers de la gorge.

glacé ['glæseɪ] *adj* **1.** [cherries] glacé, confit ■ **~ icing** glaçage *m* *(d'un gâteau)* **2.** [leather, silk] glacé.

glacial ['gleɪsjəl] *adj* **1.** [weather, wind] glacial **2.** [politeness, atmosphere] glacial **3.** GEOL glaciaire **4.** CHEM cristallisé, en cristaux.

glaciation [,gleɪsɪ'eɪʃn] *n* glaciation *f*.

glacier ['glæsjəʳ] *n* glacier *m*.

glaciology [,glæsɪ'ɒlədʒɪ] *n* glaciologie *f*.

glad [glæd] ◇ *adj* **1.** [person] heureux, content ■ **(I'm) ~ you came** (je suis) heureux *OR* bien content que tu sois venu ■ **he's decided not to go – I'm ~ about that** il a décidé de ne pas partir – tant mieux ■ **I was ~ to hear the news** j'étais ravi d'apprendre la nouvelle ■ **I'd be only too ~ to help** je ne demanderais pas mieux que d'aider ■ **could you do me a favour? – I'd be ~ to** pourriez-vous me rendre service? – avec plaisir *OR* volontiers ■ **I was ~ of your help** votre aide a été la bienvenue **2.** *lit* [news, occasion] joyeux, heureux ■ [laughter] de bonheur ■ [shout] joyeux **3.** *phr* **to give sb the ~ eye** faire les yeux doux à qqn, faire de l'œil à qqn.

◇ *n inf* = **gladiolus**.

gladden ['glædn] *vt* [person] rendre heureux, réjouir ■ [heart] réjouir.

glade [gleɪd] *n lit* clairière *f*.

glad-hand ['glædhænd] *vt inf pej* accueillir avec de grandes démonstrations d'amitié.

gladiator ['glædɪeɪtəʳ] *n* gladiateur *m*.

gladiatorial [,glædɪə'tɔːrɪəl] *adj* de gladiateurs.

gladiolus [,glædɪ'əʊləs] (*pl* **gladioli** [-laɪ] *OR pl* **gladioluses**) *n* glaïeul *m*.

gladly ['glædlɪ] *adv* avec plaisir, avec joie, de bon cœur.

gladness ['glædnɪs] *n* contentement *m*, joie *f*.

glad rags *npl inf* vêtements *mpl* chic ■ **to put on one's ~** se mettre sur son trente et un, se saper.

gladsome ['glædsəm] *adj arch & lit* joyeux, gai.

Gladstone bag ['glædstən-] *n sacoche de voyage en cuir*.

glam [glæm] (*pret & pp* **glammed**, *cont* **glamming**) *UK inf*
◇ *adj* = **glamorous**.
◇ *n* = **glamour**.
◆ **glam up** *vt sep inf* **1.** [person] : **to get glammed up** [with clothes] mettre ses belles fringues, se saper ; [with make-up] se faire une beauté, se faire toute belle **2.** [building] retaper ■ [town] embellir.

glamor *US* = **glamour**.

glamorize, ise ['glæməraɪz] *vt* idéaliser, montrer *OR* présenter sous un jour séduisant ■ **the film ~s peasant life** le film idéalise la vie des paysans.

glamorous ['glæmərəs] *adj* **1.** [alluring - person] séduisant, éblouissant ■ **a ~ actress** une actrice éblouissante *OR* resplendissante **2.** [exciting - lifestyle] brillant ; [- career] brillant, prestigieux ; [- show] splendide ; [- place] chic.

glamorously ['glæmərəslɪ] *adv* brillamment, de manière éblouissante.

glamour *UK*, **glamor** *US* ['glæməʳ] ◇ *n* **1.** [allure - of person] charme *m*, fascination *f* ; [- of appearance, dress] élégance *f*, chic *m* **2.** [excitement - of lifestyle, show] éclat *m*, prestige *m* ■ **there isn't much ~ in my job** mon travail n'a rien de bien excitant *OR* passionnant.
◇ *comp* de charme ■ **~ boy** *inf* beau gosse *m* ■ **~ girl** *inf* pin-up *f inv* ; [model] mannequin *m*.

glamourize, ise ['glæməraɪz] = **glamorize**.

glamourous ['glæmərəs] = **glamorous**.

glance [glɑːns] ◇ *vi* **1.** [look] : **to ~ at sb** *OR* **sthg** jeter un coup d'œil (rapide) à qqn *OR* sur qqch **2.** [read quickly] : **she ~d through** *OR* **over the letter** elle parcourut rapidement la lettre ■ **to ~ through a book** feuilleter un livre **3.** [look in given direction] : **he ~d back** *OR* **behind** il a jeté un coup d'œil en arrière ■ **they ~d towards the door** leurs regards se sont tournés vers la porte **4.** [gleam] étinceler.
◇ *n* **1.** [look] coup *m* d'œil, regard *m* ■ **to have** *OR* **to take a ~ at** jeter un coup d'œil sur ■ **at first ~** au premier coup d'œil, à première vue ■ **I could tell** *OR* **see at a ~** je m'en suis aperçu tout de suite ■ **she walked away without a backward ~** elle est partie sans se retourner ■ **to give sb a sidelong ~** lancer un regard oblique à qqn **2.** [gleam] lueur *f*, éclat *m* ■ [in water] reflet *m*.
◆ **glance away** *vi insep* détourner les yeux.
◆ **glance off** ◇ *vi insep* [arrow, bullet] ricocher, faire ricochet ■ [sword, spear] être dévié, ricocher ■ **the arrow hit a tree and ~d off** la flèche a ricoché sur un arbre.
◇ *vt insep* : **to ~ off sthg** [subj: arrow, bullet] ricocher sur qqch ; [subj: sword, spear] dévier sur qqch.
◆ **glance up** *vi insep* **1.** [look upwards] regarder en l'air *OR* vers le haut **2.** [from book] lever les yeux.

glancing ['glɑːnsɪŋ] *adj* **1.** [blow] : **he struck me a ~ blow** il m'asséna un coup oblique **2.** [gleaming - sunlight] étincelant **3.** [indirect - allusion] indirect, fortuit.

gland [glænd] *n* **1.** PHYSIOL glande *f* **2.** MECH presse-étoupe *m inv*.

glanders ['glændəz] *n (U)* VET morve *f*.

glandular ['glændjʊləʳ] *adj* glandulaire, glanduleux.

glandular fever *n (U)* mononucléose *f* (infectieuse).

glans [glænz] (*pl* **glandes** ['glændiːz]) *n* ANAT gland *m*.

glare [gleəʳ] ◇ *vi* **1.** [sun, light] briller d'un éclat éblouissant ■ **the sun ~d down on them** un soleil de plomb les aveuglait **2.** [person] : **to ~ at sb** regarder qqn avec colère ■ **they ~d at each other** ils échangèrent un regard menaçant.
◇ *n* **1.** [light] lumière *f* éblouissante *OR* aveuglante ■ [of sun] éclat *m* ■ **he stood in the ~ of the headlights** il était pris dans la lumière (aveuglante) des phares **2.** [of publicity] feux *mpl* ■ **politicians lead their lives in the (full) ~ of publicity** la vie des hommes politiques est toujours sous les feux des projecteurs **3.** [of anger] regard *m* furieux ■ [of contempt] regard *m* méprisant.

glare ice *n US* verglas *m*.

glaring ['gleərɪŋ] *adj* **1.** [dazzling - light] éblouissant, éclatant ; [- car headlights] éblouissant ; [- sun] aveuglant **2.** [bright - colour] vif ■ *pej* criard, voyant **3.** [angry] furieux **4.** [obvious - error] qui saute aux yeux, qui crève les yeux, patent ; [- injustice, lie] flagrant, criant ■ **a ~ abuse of public funds** un détournement manifeste des fonds publics.

glaringly ['gleərɪŋlɪ] *adv* : **it's ~ obvious** ça crève les yeux.

glasnost ['glæznɒst] *n* glasnost *f*.

glass [glɑːs] ◇ *n* **1.** [substance] verre *m* ■ **made of ~** en verre ■ **a pane of ~** un carreau, une vitre ■ **these plants are grown under ~** ces plantes sont cultivées en serre **2.** [vessel, contents] verre *m* ■ **a ~ of champagne** une coupe de champagne ■ **to raise one's ~ to sb** [in toast] lever son verre à qqn **3.** [in shop, museum] vitrine *f* ■ **displayed under ~** exposé en vitrine **4.** [glassware] verrerie *f* **5.** [telescope] longue-vue *f* **6.** [barometer] baromètre *m*.
◇ *comp* [ornament, bottle] en verre ■ [door] vitré ■ [industry] du verre.
◇ *vt* [bookcase, porch] vitrer ■ [photograph] mettre sous verre.
◆ **glasses** *npl* **1.** [spectacles] lunettes *fpl* ■ **to wear ~es** porter des lunettes ■ **~es case** étui *m* à lunettes **2.** [binoculars] jumelles *fpl*.

glassblower ['glɑːs,bləʊəʳ] *n* souffleur *m (de verre)*.

glassblowing ['glɑːs,bləʊɪŋ] *n* soufflage *m (du verre)*.

glass case *n* [for display] vitrine *f*.

glass ceiling *n terme désignant le "plafond" qui empêche la progression dans la hiérarchie*.

glasscutter ['glɑːs,kʌtəʳ] *n* **1.** [person] vitrier *m* **2.** [implement] coupe-verre *m inv*, diamant *m*.

glass eye *n* œil *m* de verre.

glass fibre ◇ *n* fibre *m* de verre.
◇ *adj* en fibre de verre.

glassful ['glɑːsfʊl] *n* (plein) verre *m*.

glasshouse ['glɑːshaʊs] (*pl* [-haʊzɪz]) *n* **1.** *UK* [greenhouse] serre *f* **2.** △ *UK mil sl* [prison] prison *f* militaire, trou *m*.

glassily ['glɑːsɪlɪ] *adv* d'un œil vitreux *OR* terne.

glasspaper ['glɑːs,peɪpəʳ] ◇ *n* papier *m* de verre.
◇ *vt* poncer au papier de verre.

glassware ['glɑːsweəʳ] *n* [glass objects] verrerie *f* ■ [tumblers] verrerie *f*, gobeleterie *f*.

glass wool *n* laine *f* de verre.

glasswork ['glɑːswɜːk] *n* [gen] verrerie ■ [making windows] vitrerie *f*.

glassworks ['glɑːswɜːks] (*pl inv*) *n* verrerie *f (usine)*.

glassy ['glɑːsɪ] (*comp* **glassier**, *superl* **glassiest**) *adj* **1.** [eye, expression] vitreux, terne **2.** [smooth - surface] uni, lisse ■ **a ~ sea** une mer d'huile.

glassy-eyed *adj* à l'œil terne *OR* vitreux ■ **to be ~** avoir le regard vitreux *OR* terne.

Glaswegian [glæz'wi:dʒjən] <> *n* [inhabitant] habitant *m*, -e *f* de Glasgow ▪ [by birth] natif *m*, -ive *f* de Glasgow ▪ [dialect] dialecte *m* de Glasgow.
<> *adj* de Glasgow.

glaucoma [glɔː'kəʊmə] *n (U)* glaucome *m*.

glaze [gleɪz] <> *vt* **1.** [floor, tiles] vitrifier ▪ [pottery, china] vernisser ▪ [leather, silk] glacer **2.** [photo, painting] glacer **3.** CULIN glacer **4.** [window] vitrer.
<> *n* **1.** [on pottery] vernis *m* ▪ [on floor, tiles] vernis *m*, enduit *m* vitrifié ▪ [on cotton, silk] glacé *m* **2.** [on painting, on paper, photo] glacé *m*, glacis *m* **3.** CULIN glace *f* **4.** *US* [ice] verglas *m*.
◆ **glaze over** *vi insep* : **his eyes ~d over** ses yeux sont devenus vitreux.

glazed [gleɪzd] *adj* **1.** [floor, tiles] vitrifié ▪ [pottery] vernissé, émaillé ▪ [leather, silk] glacé **2.** [photo, painting] glacé **3.** CULIN glacé **4.** [window] vitré ▪ [picture] sous verre **5.** [eyes] vitreux, terne ▪ **there was a ~ look in her eyes** elle avait le regard vitreux *OR* absent.

glazier ['gleɪzjəʳ] *n* vitrier *m*.

glazing ['gleɪzɪŋ] *n* **1.** [of pottery] vernissage *m* ▪ [of floor, tiles] vitrification *f* ▪ [of leather, silk] glaçage *m* **2.** CULIN [process] glaçage *m* ▪ [substance] glace *f*.

GLC (*abbrev of* **Greater London Council**) *pr n ancien organe administratif du grand Londres*.

gleam [gli:m] <> *vi* **1.** [metal, polished surface] luire, reluire ▪ [stronger] briller ▪ [cat's eyes] luire ▪ [water] miroiter **2.** *fig* **her eyes ~ed with anticipation/mischief** ses yeux brillaient d'espoir/de malice.
<> *n* **1.** [on surface] lueur *f*, miroitement *m* **2.** *fig* lueur *f* ▪ **a ~ of hope** une lueur d'espoir.

gleaming ['gli:mɪŋ] *adj* [metal] luisant, brillant ▪ [furniture] reluisant ▪ [kitchen] étincelant.

glean [gli:n] *vt* **1.** [collect - information, news] glaner, grappiller **2.** AGRIC glaner.

gleaner ['gli:nəʳ] *n* glaneur *m*, -euse *f*.

gleanings ['gli:nɪŋz] *npl* **1.** [information] bribes *fpl* de renseignements (glanées çà et là) **2.** AGRIC glanure *f*, glanures *fpl*.

glee [gli:] *n* **1.** [joy] joie *f*, allégresse *f* ▪ **to jump up and down with ~** sauter de joie **2.** MUS chant *m* a capella *(à plusieurs voix)*.

glee club *n US* chorale *f*.

gleeful ['gli:fʊl] *adj* joyeux, radieux.

gleefully ['gli:fʊlɪ] *adv* joyeusement, avec allégresse *OR* joie.

glen [glen] *n* vallon *m*, vallée *f* étroite et encaissée *(en Écosse ou en Irlande)*.

glib [glɪb] *adj* [answer, excuse] (trop) facile, désinvolte ▪ [lie] éhonté, désinvolte ▪ **he's rather too ~** il parle trop facilement, il est trop volubile.

glibly ['glɪblɪ] *adv* [talk, argue, reply] avec aisance, facilement ▪ [lie] avec désinvolture, sans sourciller.

glibness ['glɪbnɪs] *n* **1.** [of person] facilité *f* de parole **2.** [of argument, excuse] facilité *f*, désinvolture *f*.

glide [glaɪd] <> *vi* **1.** [gen] glisser ▪ [person] : **to ~ in/out** [noiselessly] entrer/sortir sans bruit ; [gracefully] entrer/sortir avec grâce ; [stealthily] entrer/sortir furtivement ▪ **the clouds ~d across the sky** les nuages passaient dans le ciel ▪ **the boat ~d silently down the river** le bateau glissait sans bruit sur la rivière *OR* descendait la rivière sans bruit ▪ **the actress ~d majestically into the room** la comédienne entra dans la salle d'un pas majestueux **2.** *fig* [time, weeks] : **to ~ by** s'écouler **3.** AERON planer ▪ **to go gliding** faire du vol à voile **4.** [in skating, skiing] glisser.
<> *vt* (faire) glisser.
<> *n* **1.** [gen] glissement *m* **2.** DANCE glissade *f* **3.** MUS port *m* de voix **4.** AERON vol *m* plané **5.** LING [in diphthong] glissement *m* ▪ [between two vowels] semi-voyelle *f* de transition.

glider ['glaɪdəʳ] *n* **1.** AERON planeur *m* **2.** *US* [swing] balançoire *f*.

gliding ['glaɪdɪŋ] *n* AERON vol *m* à voile.

glimmer ['glɪməʳ] <> *vi* [moonlight, candle] jeter une faible lueur, luire faiblement.
<> *n* **1.** [of light] (faible) lueur *f* **2.** *fig* **a ~ of hope/interest** une (faible) lueur d'espoir/d'intérêt ▪ **he showed not the faintest ~ of intelligence** il n'y avait pas la moindre étincelle d'intelligence chez lui *OR* dans son regard.

glimpse [glɪmps] <> *vt* entrevoir, entrapercevoir.
<> *n* : **to catch a ~ of sthg** entrevoir *OR* entrapercevoir qqch.

glint [glɪnt] <> *vi* **1.** [knife] étinceler, miroiter ▪ [water] miroiter **2.** *fig* [eyes] étinceler.
<> *n* **1.** [of light] reflet *m*, miroitement *m* **2.** *fig* **there was a strange ~ in his eye** il y avait une lueur étrange dans son regard.

glissade [glɪ'sɑ:d] <> *vi* **1.** [in climbing] glisser, descendre en ramasse **2.** DANCE faire une glissade.
<> *n* glissade *f*.

glissando [glɪ'sændəʊ] (*pl* **glissandos** *OR pl* **glissandi** [-di:]) *n* glissando *m*.

glisten ['glɪsn] *vi* [wet or damp surface] luire, miroiter ▪ **his eyes ~ed with tears** des larmes brillaient dans ses yeux.

glistening ['glɪsnɪŋ] *adj* luisant.

glitch [glɪtʃ] *n inf* [in plan] pépin *m* ▪ [in machine] *signal indiquant une baisse de tension du courant*.

glitter ['glɪtəʳ] <> *vi* **1.** [bright object] étinceler, scintiller, miroiter ▪ [jewel] chatoyer, étinceler ▪ [metal] reluire ▪ **her fingers ~ed with jewels** ses doigts brillaient de l'éclat des bijoux ◗ **all that ~s is not gold** *prov* tout ce qui brille n'est pas or *prov* **2.** [eyes] briller.
<> *n* **1.** [of object] scintillement *m* **2.** [of glamour] éclat *m*, splendeur *f* **3.** [decoration, make-up] paillettes *fpl*.

glitterati [,glɪtə'rɑ:ti:] *npl inf* **the ~** *hum* le beau monde *m inv*.

glittering ['glɪtərɪŋ] *adj* **1.** [jewels] scintillant, étincelant, brillant **2.** [glamorous] éclatant, resplendissant.

glittery ['glɪtərɪ] *adj* **1.** [light] scintillant, brillant **2.** *pej* [jewellery] clinquant ▪ [make-up, décor] voyant, tape-à-l'œil.

glitz [glɪts] *n inf* tape-à-l'œil *m*, clinquant *m* ▪ **Hollywood ~** le clinquant de Hollywood.

glitzy ['glɪtsɪ] (*comp* **glitzier**, *superl* **glitziest**) *adj inf* tape-à-l'œil *(inv)*.

gloaming ['gləʊmɪŋ] *n Scotland lit* crépuscule *m*.

gloat [gləʊt] <> *vi* exulter, se délecter, jubiler ▪ **to ~ over sthg** se réjouir de qqch.
<> *n* exultation *f*, jubilation *f* ▪ **to have a ~** exulter.

gloating ['gləʊtɪŋ] *adj* [smile, look] triomphant.

global ['gləʊbl] *adj* **1.** [world-wide] mondial, planétaire ▪ **~ warming** réchauffement *m* de la planète **2.** [overall - system, view] global.

globalism ['gləʊbəlɪzm] *n* mondialisme *m*.

globalization, isation [,gləʊbəlaɪ'zeɪʃn] *n* mondialisation *f*.

globalize, ise ['gləʊbəlaɪz] *vt* **1.** [make world-wide] rendre mondial ▪ **a ~d conflict** un conflit mondial **2.** [generalize] globaliser.

globally ['gləʊbəlɪ] *adv* **1.** [world-wide] mondialement, à l'échelle planétaire **2.** [generally] globalement.

global village *n* village *m* planétaire.

globe [gləʊb] *n* **1.** GEOG globe *m* (terrestre), terre *f* ▪ **all over the ~** [surface] sur toute la surface du globe ; [in all parts] dans le monde entier **2.** [model] globe *m*, mappemonde *f* **3.** [spherical object] globe *m*, sphère *f* ▪ [as lampshade] globe ▪ [as goldfish bowl] bocal *m* ▪ [of eye] globe.

globe artichoke *n* artichaut *m*.

globetrotter ['gləʊb,trɒtə^r] *n* globe-trotteur *m*, globe-trotteuse *f*.

globetrotting ['gləʊb,trɒtɪŋ] *n (U)* voyages *mpl* aux quatre coins du monde.

globular ['glɒbjʊlə^r] *adj* globulaire, globuleux.

globule ['glɒbju:l] *n* globule *m*.

glockenspiel ['glɒkənʃpi:l] *n* glockenspiel *m*.

gloom [glu:m] ◇ *n (U)* **1.** [darkness] obscurité *f*, ténèbres *fpl* **2.** [despondency] tristesse *f*, mélancolie *f* ■ **the news filled me with ~** la nouvelle me plongea dans la consternation ■ **the news is all ~ and doom these days** les nouvelles sont des plus sombres ces temps-ci.
◇ *vi* [person] être mélancolique, broyer du noir.

gloomily ['glu:mɪlɪ] *adv* sombrement, mélancoliquement, tristement.

gloomy ['glu:mɪ] (*comp* **gloomier**, *superl* **gloomiest**) *adj* **1.** [person - depressed] triste, mélancolique ; [- morose] sombre, lugubre ■ **to feel ~** broyer du noir, avoir le cafard ■ **don't look so ~** ne prends pas cet air malheureux **2.** [pessimistic - outlook] sombre ; [- news] triste ■ **she always takes a ~ view of things** elle voit toujours tout en noir ■ **the future looks ~** l'avenir se présente sous des couleurs sombres **3.** [sky] obscur, sombre ■ [weather] morne, triste ■ **to become ~** s'assombrir **4.** [place, landscape] morne, lugubre.

glorification [,glɔ:rɪfɪ'keɪʃn] *n* glorification *f*.

glorified ['glɔ:rɪfaɪd] *adj* : **he's called an engineer but he's really just a ~ mechanic** on a beau l'appeler ingénieur, il n'est que mécanicien, il n'a d'ingénieur que le nom, en réalité c'est un mécanicien ■ **they call it a health club but it's just a ~ swimming pool** en fait de centre de remise en forme, il ne s'agit que d'une vulgaire piscine.

glorify ['glɔ:rɪfaɪ] (*pret & pp* **glorified**) *vt* **1.** RELIG glorifier, rendre gloire à **2.** [praise - hero, writer] exalter ■ **the film glorifies war** le film fait l'apologie de *OR* magnifie la guerre.

glorious ['glɔ:rɪəs] *adj* **1.** [illustrious - reign, saint, victory] glorieux ; [- hero] glorieux, illustre ; [- deed] glorieux, éclatant ■ **the Glorious Twelfth** [in Ireland] *célébration de la victoire des Protestants sur les Catholiques (le 12 juillet 1690) en Irlande ;* [in UK] *date d'ouverture de la chasse à la grouse (le 12 août)* **2.** [wonderful - view, place] merveilleux, splendide ; [- weather, day] splendide, superbe, magnifique ; [- colours] superbe ; [- holiday, party] merveilleux, sensationnel.

gloriously ['glɔ:rɪəslɪ] *adv* glorieusement.

Glorious Revolution *pr n* : **the ~** *UK* HIST la Glorieuse Révolution.

THE GLORIOUS REVOLUTION

Désapprouvant la politique religieuse menée par le roi catholique Jacques II, ses adversaires protestants firent appel à Guillaume d'Orange pour le renverser, en 1688. Jacques II s'enfuit en France et le Parlement proclama son abdication et couronna sa fille Mary, conjointement à Guillaume, en 1689. Cette révolution aboutit à instaurer en Angleterre une monarchie constitutionnelle.

glory ['glɔ:rɪ] *n* (*pl* **glories**) **1.** [honour, fame] gloire *f* ■ [magnificence] magnificence *f*, éclat *m* ■ **to be covered in ~** être couvert de gloire ■ **to have one's moment of ~** avoir son heure de gloire **2.** [splendour] gloire *f*, splendeur *f* ■ **in all her ~** dans toute sa splendeur *OR* gloire **3.** [masterpiece] gloire *f*, joyau *m* ■ **the palace is one of the greatest glories of the age** le palais est un des joyaux *OR* des chefs-d'œuvre de cette époque **4.** RELIG : **to give ~ to God** rendre gloire à Dieu ■ **~ be!** *inf* mon Dieu! **5.** *euph* [death] : **to go to ~** passer de vie à trépas **6.** *US* **Old Glory** *le drapeau américain*.
◆ **glory in** *vt insep* (*pret & pp* **gloried**) : **to ~ in (doing) sthg** se glorifier de *OR* s'enorgueillir de (faire) qqch ■ **she was ~ing in her new-found freedom** elle jouissait de *OR* elle savourait sa nouvelle liberté ■ **he glories in the title of King of Hollywood** il se donne le titre ronflant de roi d'Hollywood.

glory hole *n* **1.** *UK inf* [cupboard] débarras *m* ■ [untidy place] capharnaüm *m* **2.** NAUT [locker] petit placard *m* ■ [storeroom] soute *f*.

Glos *written abbr of* **Gloucestershire**.

gloss [glɒs] ◇ *n* **1.** [sheen] lustre *m*, brillant *m*, éclat *m* ■ [on paper, photo] glacé *m*, brillant *m* ■ [on furniture] vernis *m* **2.** [appearance] apparence *f*, vernis *m* ■ **a ~ of politeness/respectability** un vernis de politesse/de respectabilité **3.** [charm] charme *m*, attrait *m* ■ **to take the ~ off sthg** gâcher *OR* gâter qqch **4.** [annotation, paraphrase] glose *f*, commentaire *m* **5.** = **gloss paint**.
◇ *vt* **1.** [paper] satiner, glacer ■ [metal] faire briller, lustrer **2.** [explain, paraphrase] gloser.
◆ **gloss over** *vt insep* **1.** [minimize - failure, fault, mistake] glisser sur, passer sur, atténuer **2.** [hide - truth, facts] dissimuler, passer sous silence.

glossary ['glɒsərɪ] (*pl* **glossaries**) *n* glossaire *m*.

gloss paint *n* peinture *f* brillante.

glossy ['glɒsɪ] (*comp* **glossier**, *superl* **glossiest**, *pl* **glossies**) ◇ *adj* **1.** [shiny - fur] lustré, luisant ; [- hair] brillant ; [- leather, satin] lustré, luisant, glacé ; [- leaves] luisant ■ [surface - polished] brillant, poli ; [- painted] brillant, laqué **2.** *fig* [display, presentation, spectacle] brillant, scintillant, clinquant *pej* **3.** [photo] glacé, sur papier glacé ■ [paper] glacé.
◇ *n inf* = **glossy magazine**.

glossy magazine *n* magazine *m (sur papier glacé)*.

glottal ['glɒtl] *adj* **1.** ANAT glottique **2.** LING glottal ■ **~ stop** coup *m* de glotte.

glottis ['glɒtɪs] *n* glotte *f*.

glove [glʌv] ◇ *n* gant *m* ▶ **it fits like a ~** ça me/te/lui *etc* va comme un gant ■ **once the campaign started the ~s were off!** une fois la campagne partie, plus question de prendre des gants *OR* tous les coups étaient permis!
◇ *comp* à gants, de gants ■ **~ factory** ganterie *f (usine)* ■ **~ maker** gantier *m*, - ère *f* ■ **~ shop** ganterie *f (magasin)*.

glove compartment *n* AUT boîte *f* à gants.

gloved [glʌvd] *adj* ganté.

glove puppet *n* marionnette *f (à gaine)*.

glover ['glʌvə^r] *n* gantier *m*, - ère *f*.

glow [gləʊ] ◇ *vi* **1.** [embers, heated metal] rougeoyer ■ [sky, sunset] s'embraser, flamboyer ■ [jewel] briller, rutiler **2.** [person] rayonner ■ [eyes] briller, flamboyer ■ **to ~ with pleasure** rayonner de plaisir.
◇ *n* **1.** [of fire, embers] rougeoiement *m* ■ [of heated metal] lueur *f* ■ [of sky, sunset] embrasement *m*, flamboiement *m* ■ [of sun] feux *mpl* ■ [of colours, jewel] éclat *m* ■ **it gives off a blue ~** cela émet une lumière bleue **2.** [of health, beauty] éclat *m* ■ **the compliments brought a ~ to her cheeks** les compliments la faisaient rougir de plaisir **3.** [pleasure] plaisir *m*.

glower ['glaʊə^r] *vi* avoir l'air furieux, lancer des regards furieux ■ **to ~ at sb** [angrily] lancer à qqn un regard noir ; [threateningly] jeter à qqn un regard menaçant.

glowering ['glaʊərɪŋ] *adj* [expression] mauvais, méchant, hostile ■ [person] à l'air mauvais *OR* méchant.

glowing ['gləʊɪŋ] *adj* **1.** [fire, embers] rougeoyant ■ [heated metal] incandescent ■ [sky, sunset] radieux, flamboyant ■ [jewel] brillant **2.** [complexion] éclatant ■ [eyes] brillant, flamboyant ■ **~ with health** rayonnant *OR* florissant (de santé) **3.** [laudatory] élogieux, dithyrambique ■ **he spoke of you in ~ terms** il a chanté tes louanges ■ **to paint sthg in ~ colours** présenter qqch sous un jour favorable.

glowingly ['gləʊɪŋlɪ] *adv* : **to speak ~ of sb/sthg** parler de qqn/qqch en termes enthousiastes *OR* chaleureux.

glow-worm *n* ver *m* luisant.

glucose ['glu:kəʊs] *n* glucose *m*.

glue [glu:] ◇ *vt* **1.** [stick] coller ■ **to ~ sthg to/onto sthg** coller qqch à/sur qqch ■ **you'll have to ~ it (back) together again** il faudra le recoller ■ **can't you ~ it down?** vous ne pouvez pas le

faire tenir avec de la colle? **2.** *fig* coller ▪ **to be ~d to the spot** être *OR* rester cloué sur place ▪ **he kept his eyes ~d on the ball** il garda les yeux rivés sur la balle ▪ **they're always ~d to the TV screen** ils sont en permanence plantés devant la télé.
◇ *n* colle *f*.

glue-sniffer [-ˌsnɪfəʳ] *n* : **to be a ~** inhaler *OR* sniffer (de la colle).

glue-sniffing [-ˌsnɪfɪŋ] *n* inhalation *f* de colle.

gluey ['glu:ɪ] *adj* collant, gluant.

glum [glʌm] *adj* triste, morose ▪ **to be** *OR* **to feel ~** avoir le cafard, broyer du noir ▪ **don't look so ~!** ne fais pas cette tête-là!, ne sois pas si triste!

glumly ['glʌmlɪ] *adv* tristement, avec morosité.

glut [glʌt] (*pret & pp* **glutted**, *cont* **glutting**) ◇ *vt* **1.** [with food] : **to ~ o.s. with** *OR* **on sthg** se gorger *OR* se gaver de qqch ▪ **to be glutted with television** *fig* être saturé de télévision **2.** [saturate - market] saturer, inonder, surcharger ▪ **the growers glutted the market with tomatoes** les producteurs de tomates ont saturé le marché.
◇ *n* excès *m*, surabondance *f*, surplus *m* ▪ **there's a ~ of fruit on the market** il y a surabondance de fruits sur le marché.

glutamate ['glu:təmeɪt] *n* glutamate *m*.

glutamine ['glu:təmi:n] *n* glutamine *f*.

gluten ['glu:tən] *n* gluten *m*.

gluten-free *adj* sans gluten.

glutinous ['glu:tɪnəs] *adj* glutineux.

glutton ['glʌtn] *n* glouton *m*, - onne *f*, goulu *m*, - e *f* ▪ **to be a ~ for punishment** *fig* être un peu masochiste.

gluttonous ['glʌtənəs] *adj* glouton, goulu.

gluttony ['glʌtənɪ] *n* gloutonnerie *f*, goinfrerie *f*.

glycerin ['glɪsərɪn], **glycerine** ['glɪsəri:n] *n* glycérine *f*.

glycerol ['glɪsərɒl] *n* glycérol *m*.

gm (*written abbrev of* **gram**) g.

GM [dʒi:'em] (*abbrev of* **genetically modified**) *adj* génétiquement modifié (*f* e) ▪ **GM foods/ products** aliments/produits génétiquement modifiés.

GMAT (*abbrev of* **Graduate Management Admissions Test**) *n test d'admission dans le 2ᵉ cycle de l'enseignement supérieur aux États-Unis.*

GMB (*abbrev of* **General, Municipal, Boilermakers and Allied Trades Union**) *pr n important syndicat britannique.*

GMO (*abbrev of* **genetically modified organism**) *n* OGM *m*.

GMT (*abbrev of* **Greenwich Mean Time**) *n* GMT *m*.

gnarl [nɑ:l] *n* BOT nœud *m*.

gnarled [nɑ:ld] *adj* **1.** [tree, fingers] noueux **2.** [character] grincheux, hargneux.

gnash [næʃ] ◇ *vt* : **to ~ one's teeth** grincer des dents ▪ **there was much wailing and ~ing of teeth** il y a eu des pleurs et des grincements de dents.
◇ *n* grincement *m* (de dents).

gnat [næt] *n* moustique *m*.

gnaw [nɔ:] ◇ *vt* [bone] ronger ▪ **to ~ one's fingernails** se ronger les ongles ▪ **the rats have ~ed their way into the cupboard** les rats ont fini par percer un trou dans le placard.
◇ *vi* : **to ~ (away) at sthg** ronger qqch ▪ **to ~ through sthg** ronger qqch jusqu'à le percer ▪ **guilt and sorrow ~ed at his heart** *fig* la culpabilité et le chagrin lui rongeaient le cœur ▪ **hunger ~ed at him** *fig* il était tenaillé par la faim.
◆ **gnaw away** *vt sep* **1.** [animal] ronger **2.** [erode] ronger, miner.
◆ **gnaw off** *vt sep* : **to ~ sthg off** ronger qqch jusqu'à le détacher.

gnawing ['nɔ:ɪŋ] *adj* **1.** [pain] lancinant, tenaillant ▪ [hunger] tenaillant **2.** [anxiety, doubt] tenaillant, torturant.

gnome [nəʊm] *n* **1.** MYTH gnome *m* ▪ **the ~s of Zurich** *pej* les grands banquiers *OR* financiers suisses **2.** [aphorism] aphorisme *m*.

gnostic, Gnostic ['nɒstɪk] ◇ *adj* gnostique.
◇ *n* gnostique *mf*.

GNP (*abbrev of* **gross national product**) *n* PNB *m*.

gnu [nu:] *n* gnou *m*.

GNVQ (*abbrev of* **General National Vocational Qualification**) *n diplôme sanctionnant deux années d'études professionnelles à la fin du secondaire,* ≃ baccalauréat *m* professionnel.

go[1] [gəʊ] *n* [game] go *m*.

go[2] [gəʊ] (*pres (3rd pres sing)* **goes** [gəʊz], *pret* **went** [went], *pp* **gone** [gɒn], *pl* **goes** [gəʊz]) ◇ *vi*

A.

1. [move, travel - person] aller ; [- vehicle] aller, rouler ▪ **I want to go home** je veux rentrer ▪ **there goes the train!** voilà le train (qui passe)! ▪ **the bus goes by way of** *OR* **through Dover** le bus passe par Douvres ▪ **the truck was going at 150 kilometres an hour** le camion roulait à *OR* faisait 150 kilomètres à l'heure ▪ **where do we go from here?** *liter* où va-t-on maintenant? ; *fig* qu'est-ce qu'on fait maintenant? ▪ **to go to the doctor** aller voir *OR* aller chez le médecin ▪ **he went straight to the director** il est allé directement voir *OR* trouver le directeur ▪ **to go to sb for advice** aller demander conseil à qqn ▪ **let the children go first** laissez les enfants passer devant, laissez passer les enfants d'abord ▪ **I'll go next** c'est à moi après ▪ **here we go again!** ça y est, ça recommence! ▪ **there he goes!** le voilà! ▪ **there he goes again!** [there he is again] le revoilà! ; [he's doing it again] ça y est, il est reparti!
2. [engage in a specified activity] aller ▪ **to go shopping** aller faire des courses ▪ **let's go for a walk/bike ride/swim** allons nous promener/faire un tour à vélo/nous baigner ▪ **go and buy the paper** *UK*, **go buy the paper** *US* va acheter le journal ▪ **don't go and tell him!, don't go telling him!** ne va pas le lui dire!, ne le lui dis pas! ▪ **he's gone and locked us out!** il nous a enfermés dehors!
3. [proceed to specified limit] aller ▪ **he'll go as high as £300** il ira jusqu'à 300 livres ▪ **the temperature went as high as 36° C** la température est montée jusqu'à 36° C ▪ **now you've gone too far!** là tu as dépassé les bornes! ▪ **her attitude went beyond mere impertinence** son comportement était plus qu'impertinent
4. [depart, leave] s'en aller, partir ▪ **I must be going** il faut que je m'en aille *OR* que je parte ▪ **get going!** *inf* vas-y!, file! ▪ **either he goes or I go** l'un de nous deux doit partir
5. [indicating regular attendance] aller, assister ▪ **to go to church/school** aller à l'église/l'école ▪ **to go to work** [to one's place of work] aller au travail
6. [indicating direction or route] aller, mener ▪ **that road goes to the market square** cette route va *OR* mène à la place du marché

B.

1. [be or remain in specified state] être ▪ **to go barefoot/naked** se promener pieds nus/tout nu ▪ **to go armed** porter une arme ▪ **the job went unfilled** le poste est resté vacant ▪ **to go unnoticed** passer inaperçu
2. [become] devenir ▪ **my father is going grey** mon père grisonne ▪ **she went white with rage** elle a blêmi de colère ▪ **have you gone mad?** tu es devenu fou?
3. [stop working - engine] tomber en panne ; [- fuse] sauter ; [- bulb, lamp] sauter, griller ▪ **the battery's going** la pile commence à être usée
4. [wear out] s'user ▪ [split] craquer ▪ **his trousers are going at the knees** son pantalon s'use aux genoux
5. [deteriorate, fail - health] se détériorer ; [- hearing, sight] baisser ▪ **all his strength went and he fell to the floor** il a perdu toutes ses forces et il est tombé par terre ▪ **his voice is going** il devient aphone ▪ **her mind has started to go** elle n'a plus toute sa tête *OR* toutes ses facultés

C.

1. [begin an activity] commencer ▪ **what are we waiting for? let's go!** qu'est-ce qu'on attend? allons-y! ▪ **here goes!** *inf inf*, **here we go!** allez! on y va! ▪ **go!** partez! ▪ **you'd better get going on** *OR* **with that report!** tu ferais bien de te mettre à *OR* de

t'attaquer à ce rapport! ▪ **it won't be so hard once you get going** ça ne sera pas si difficile une fois que tu seras lancé ▪ **go to it!** *inf inf* [get to work] au boulot! ; [in encouragement] allez-y! **2.** [expressing intention] : **to be going to do sthg** [be about to] aller faire qqch, être sur le point de faire qqch ; [intend to] avoir l'intention de faire qqch ▪ **I was going to visit her yesterday but her mother arrived** j'avais l'intention de *OR* j'allais lui rendre visite hier mais sa mère est arrivée
3. [expressing future] : **are you going to be at home tonight?** est-ce que vous serez chez vous ce soir? ▪ **she's going to be a doctor** elle va être médecin
4. [function - clock, machine] marcher, fonctionner ▪ [start functioning] démarrer ▪ **the car won't go** la voiture ne veut pas démarrer ▪ **he had the television and the radio going** il avait mis la télévision et la radio en marche ▪ **the washing machine is still going** la machine à laver tourne encore, la lessive n'est pas terminée ▪ **to get sthg going** [car, machine] mettre qqch en marche ; [business, project] lancer qqch ▪ **her daughter kept the business going** sa fille a continué à faire marcher l'affaire ▪ **to keep a conversation/fire going** entretenir une conversation/un feu
5. [sound - alarm clock, bell] sonner ; [- alarm, siren] retentir
6. [make movement] : **she went like this with her eyebrows** elle a fait comme ça avec ses sourcils
7. [appear] : **to go on radio/television** passer à la radio/à la télévision

D.

1. [disappear] disparaître ▪ **all the sugar's gone** il n'y a plus de sucre ▪ **all our money has gone** [spent] nous avons dépensé tout notre argent ; [lost] nous avons perdu tout notre argent ; [stolen] on a volé tout notre argent ▪ **I don't know where the money goes these days** l'argent disparaît à une vitesse incroyable ces temps-ci ▪ **gone are the days when he took her dancing** elle est bien loin, l'époque où il l'emmenait danser
2. [be eliminated] : **the last paragraph must go** il faut supprimer le dernier paragraphe ▪ **I've decided that car has to go** j'ai décidé de me débarrasser de cette voiture
3. *euph* [die] disparaître, s'éteindre ▪ **after I go...** quand je ne serai plus là...

E.

1. [extend, reach] aller, s'étendre ▪ **the path goes right down to the beach** le chemin descend jusqu'à la mer ‖ *fig* **money doesn't go very far these days** l'argent part vite à notre époque ▪ **their difference of opinion goes deeper than I thought** leur différend est plus profond que je ne pensais
2. [belong] aller, se mettre, se ranger ▪ **where do the towels go?** où est-ce qu'on met les serviettes?
3. [be contained in, fit] aller ▪ **the piano barely goes through the door** le piano entre *OR* passe de justesse par la porte ▪ **this belt just goes round my waist** cette ceinture est juste assez longue pour faire le tour de ma taille ▪ **the lid goes on easily enough** le couvercle se met assez facilement
4. [develop, turn out] se passer ▪ **I'll see how things go** je vais voir comment ça se passe ▪ **the negotiations are going well** les négociations sont en bonne voie ▪ **the vote went against them/in their favour** le vote leur a été défavorable/favorable ▪ **there's no doubt as to which way the decision will go** on sait ce qui sera décidé ▪ **everything went wrong** ça a mal tourné ▪ **how's it going?** *inf*, **how are things going?** (comment) ça va? ➊ **the way things are going, we might both be out of a job soon** au train où vont *OR* vu comment vont les choses, nous allons bientôt nous retrouver tous les deux au chômage
5. [time - elapse] s'écouler, passer ; [- last] durer ▪ **the journey went quickly** je n'ai pas vu le temps passer pendant le voyage ▪ **how's the time going?** combien de temps reste-t-il?

F.

1. [be accepted] : **whatever the boss says goes** c'est le patron qui fait la loi
2. [be valid, hold true] s'appliquer ▪ **that goes for us too** [that applies to us] ça s'applique à nous aussi ; [we agree with that] nous sommes aussi de cet avis
3. [be expressed, run - report, story] : **the story** *OR* **rumour goes that she left him** le bruit court qu'elle l'a quitté ▪ **so the story goes** du moins c'est ce que l'on dit *OR* d'après les on-dit ▪ **how does the story go?** comment c'est cette histoire? ▪ **I forget how the poem goes now** j'ai oublié le poème maintenant ▪ **her theory goes something like this** sa théorie est plus ou moins la suivante
4. [be identified as] : **to go by** *OR* **under the name of** répondre au nom de ▪ **he now goes by** *OR* **under another name** il se fait appeler autrement maintenant
5. [be sold] se vendre ▪ **the necklace went for £350** le collier s'est vendu 350 livres ▪ **going, going, gone!** une fois, deux fois, adjugé!

G.

1. [be given - award, prize] aller, être donné ; [- inheritance, property] passer ▪ **credit should go to the teachers** le mérite en revient aux enseignants
2. [be spent] : **a small portion of the budget went on education** une petite part du budget a été consacrée *OR* est allée à l'éducation ▪ **all his money goes on drink** tout son argent part dans la boisson
3. [contribute] contribuer, servir ▪ **all that just goes to prove my point** tout ça confirme bien ce que j'ai dit ▪ **it has all the qualities that go to make a good film** ça a toutes les qualités d'un bon film
4. [have recourse] avoir recours, recourir ▪ **to go to arbitration** recourir à l'arbitrage

H.

1. [be compatible - colours, flavours] aller ensemble ▪ **orange and mauve don't really go** l'orange et le mauve ne vont pas vraiment ensemble
2. [be available] : **let me know if you hear of any jobs going** faites-moi savoir si vous entendez parler d'un emploi ▪ **are there any flats going for rent in this building?** y a-t-il des appartements à louer dans cet immeuble?
3. [endure] supporter, tenir le coup ▪ **we can't go much longer without water** nous ne pourrons pas tenir beaucoup plus longtemps si nous n'avons pas d'eau
4. *euph* [go to the toilet] : **we'll only stop if you're really desperate to go** on ne s'arrête que si tu ne tiens vraiment plus
5. MATHS : **5 into 60 goes 12** 60 divisé par 5 égale 12 ▪ **6 into 5 won't go** 5 n'est pas divisible par 6
6. *phr* **she isn't bad, as teachers go** elle n'est pas mal comme enseignante ▪ **as houses go, it's pretty cheap** ce n'est pas cher pour une maison ▪ **there goes my chance of winning a prize** je peux abandonner tout espoir de gagner un prix ▪ **there you go again, always blaming other people** ça y est, toujours à rejeter la responsabilité sur les autres! ▪ **there you go!** [here you are] tiens! ; [I told you so] voilà!

◇ *vt* **1.** [follow, proceed along] aller, suivre ▪ **if we go this way, we'll get there much more quickly** si nous passons par là, nous arriverons bien plus vite **2.** [travel] faire, voyager ▪ **we've only gone 5 kilometres** nous n'avons fait que 5 kilomètres **3.** [say] faire ▪ [make specified noise] faire ▪ **the gun went bang** et pan! le coup est parti ▪ **then he goes "hand it over"** *inf* puis il fait "donne-le-moi".

◇ *n* **1.** *UK* [attempt, try] coup *m*, essai *m* ▪ **to have a go at sthg/doing sthg** essayer qqch/de faire qqch ▪ **he had another go** il a fait une nouvelle tentative, il a ressayé ▪ **let's have a go!** essayons! ▪ **have another go!** encore un coup! ▪ **she passed her exams first go** elle a eu ses examens du premier coup **2.** *UK* GAMES [turn] tour *m* ▪ **it's your go** c'est ton tour *OR* c'est à toi (de jouer) **3.** *inf* [energy, vitality] dynamisme *m*, entrain *m* ▪ **to be full of go** avoir plein d'énergie, être très dynamique **4.** *inf* [success] succès *m*, réussite *f* ▪ **he's made a go of the business** il a réussi à faire marcher l'affaire ➊ **I tried to persuade her but it was no go** j'ai essayé de la convaincre mais il n'y avait rien à faire **5.** *inf phr* **to have a go at sb** [physically] rentrer dans qqn ; [verbally] passer un savon à qqn ▪ **they had a real go at one another!** qu'est-ce qu'ils se sont mis! ▪ **to have a go** *UK* [tackle a criminal] : **police have warned the public not to have a go, the fugitive may be armed** la police a prévenu la population de ne pas s'en prendre au fugitif car il pourrait être armé ▪ **it's all go** ça n'arrête pas! ▪ **all systems go!** c'est parti!

➡ **going on** *adv phr* : **he must be going on fifty** il doit approcher la *OR* aller sur la cinquantaine ▪ **it was going on (for) midnight by the time we finished** quand on a terminé il était près de minuit.

➡ **on the go** *adj & phr inf* **1.** [busy] : **I've been on the go all day** je n'ai pas arrêté de toute la journée **2.** [in hand] : **I have several projects on the go at present** j'ai plusieurs projets en route en ce moment.

◆ **to go** ◇ *adv phr* à faire ▪ **there are only three weeks/five miles to go** il ne reste plus que trois semaines/cinq miles ▪ **five done, three to go** cinq de faits, trois à faire.

◇ *adj phr esp US* **two hamburgers to go** deux hamburgers à emporter!

◆ **go about** *vt insep* **1.** [get on with] s'occuper de ▪ **to go about one's business** vaquer à ses occupations **2.** [set about] se mettre à ▪ **she showed me how to go about it** elle m'a montré comment faire *OR* comment m'y prendre.

◆ **go about with** *vt insep* [frequent] : **her son goes about with an older crowd** son fils fréquente des gens plus âgés que lui ▪ **he's going about with Mary these days** il sort avec Mary en ce moment.

◆ **go across** ◇ *vt insep* traverser.

◇ *vi insep* traverser ▪ **your brother has just gone across to the shop** ton frère est allé faire un saut au magasin en face.

◆ **go after** *vt insep* **1.** [follow] suivre **2.** [pursue, seek - criminal] poursuivre ; [- prey] chasser ; [- job, prize] essayer d'obtenir ▪ **he goes after all the women** il court après toutes les femmes.

◆ **go against** *vt insep* **1.** [disregard] aller contre, aller à l'encontre de ▪ **she went against my advice** elle n'a pas suivi mon conseil **2.** [conflict with] contredire ▪ **the decision went against public opinion** la décision est allée à l'encontre de *OR* a heurté l'opinion publique ▪ **it goes against my principles** c'est contre mes principes **3.** [be unfavourable to - subj: luck, situation] être contraire à ; [- subj: opinion] être défavorable à ; [- subj: behaviour, evidence] nuire à, être préjudiciable à ▪ **the verdict went against the defendant** le verdict a été défavorable à l'accusé *OR* a été prononcé contre l'accusé ▪ **if luck should go against him** si la chance lui était contraire.

◆ **go ahead** *vi insep* **1.** [precede] passer devant ▪ **he went (on) ahead of us** il est parti avant nous **2.** [proceed] aller de l'avant ▪ **go ahead! tell me!** vas-y! dis-le-moi! ▪ **the mayor allowed the demonstrations to go ahead** le maire a permis aux manifestations d'avoir lieu **3.** [advance, progress] progresser, faire des progrès.

◆ **go along** *vi insep* **1.** [move from one place to another] aller, avancer ▪ **we can talk it over as we go along** nous pouvons en discuter en chemin *OR* en cours de route ▶ **I just make it up as I go along** j'invente au fur et à mesure **2.** [progress] se dérouler, se passer ▪ **things were going along nicely** tout allait *OR* se passait bien.

◆ **go along with** *vt insep* [decision, order] accepter, s'incliner devant ▪ [rule] observer, respecter ▪ **I can't go along with you on that** je ne suis pas d'accord avec vous là-dessus ▪ **he went along with his father's wishes** il s'est conformé aux *OR* a respecté les désirs de son père.

◆ **go around** *vi insep* **1.** [habitually] passer son temps à ▪ **he goes around in black leather** il se promène toujours en *OR* il est toujours habillé en cuir noir **2.** [document, illness] circuler ▪ [gossip, rumour] courir, circuler **3.** [be long enough for] : **will that belt go around your waist?** est-ce que cette ceinture sera assez grande pour toi?

◆ **go around with** = go about with.

◆ **go at** *vt insep inf* [attack - food] attaquer, se jeter sur ; [- job, task] s'attaquer à ▪ **they were still going at it the next day** ils y étaient encore le lendemain.

◆ **go away** *vi insep* partir, s'en aller ▪ **go away!** va-t-en! ▪ **I'm going away for a few days** je pars pour quelques jours.

◆ **go back** *vi insep* **1.** [return] revenir, retourner ▪ **she went back to bed** elle est retournée au lit, elle s'est recouchée ▪ **to go back to sleep** se rendormir ▪ **they went back home** ils sont rentrés (chez eux *OR* à la maison) ▪ **to go back to work** [continue task] se remettre au travail ; [return to place of work] retourner travailler ; [return to employment] reprendre le travail ▪ **to go back on one's steps** rebrousser chemin, revenir sur ses pas ▪ **we went back to the beginning** nous avons recommencé ▪ **the clocks go back one hour today** on retarde les pendules d'une heure aujourd'hui **2.** [retreat] reculer **3.** [revert] revenir ▪ **we went back to the old system** nous sommes revenus à l'ancien système ▪ **he went back to his old habits** il a repris ses anciennes habitudes ▪ **men are going back to wearing their hair long** les hommes reviennent aux cheveux longs *OR* se laissent à nouveau pousser les cheveux **4.** [in time] remonter ▪ **our records go back to 1850** nos archives remontent à 1850 ▪ **we go back a long way, Sam and me** *inf* ça remonte à loin, Sam et moi **5.** [extend, reach] s'étendre ▪ **the garden goes back 150 metres** le jardin s'étend sur 150 mètres.

◆ **go back on** *vt insep* [fail to keep - agreement] rompre, violer ; [- promise] manquer à, revenir sur.

◆ **go before** ◇ *vi insep* [precede] passer devant ▪ [happen before] précéder ▪ **the election was like nothing that had gone before** l'élection ne ressemblait en rien aux précédentes.

◇ *vt insep* **1.** [precede] précéder ▪ **we are indebted to those who have gone before us** nous devons beaucoup à ceux qui nous ont précédés **2.** [appear before] : **your suggestion will go before the committee** votre suggestion sera soumise au comité ▪ **to go before a judge/jury** passer devant un juge/un jury ▪ **the matter went before the court** l'affaire est allée devant les tribunaux.

◆ **go below** *vi insep* NAUT descendre dans l'entrepont.

◆ **go by** ◇ *vi insep* [pass - car, person] passer ; [- time] passer, s'écouler ▪ **as the years go by** avec les années, à mesure que les années passent ▪ **in days** *OR* **in times** *OR* **in years gone by** autrefois, jadis.

◇ *vt insep* **1.** [act in accordance with, be guided by] suivre, se baser sur ▪ **don't go by the map** ne vous fiez pas à la carte ▪ **he goes by the rules** il suit le règlement **2.** [judge by] juger d'après ▪ **going by her accent, I'd say she's from New York** si j'en juge d'après son accent, je dirais qu'elle vient de New York.

◆ **go down** ◇ *vi insep* **1.** [descend, move to lower level] descendre ▪ [from a vertical position] : **he went down on all fours** *OR* **on his hands and knees** il s'est mis à quatre pattes **2.** [proceed, travel] aller **3.** [set - moon, sun] se coucher, tomber **4.** [sink - ship] couler, sombrer ; [- person] couler, disparaître (sous l'eau) **5.** [decrease, decline - level, price, quality] baisser ; [- amount, numbers] diminuer ; [- rate, temperature] baisser, s'abaisser ; [- fever] baisser, tomber ; [- tide] descendre ▪ **the dollar is going down in value** le dollar perd de sa valeur, le dollar baisse ▪ **eggs are going down (in price)** le prix des œufs baisse ▪ **he's gone down in my estimation** il a baissé dans mon estime ▪ **the neighbourhood's really gone down since then** le quartier ne s'est vraiment pas arrangé depuis **6.** [become less swollen - swelling] désenfler, dégonfler ; [- balloon, tyre] se dégonfler **7.** [food, medicine] descendre ▪ **this wine goes down very smoothly** ce vin se laisse boire (comme du petit lait) **8.** [produce specified reaction] être reçu ▪ **a cup of coffee would go down nicely** une tasse de café serait la bienvenue ▪ **his speech went down badly/well** son discours a été mal/bien reçu ▪ **how will the proposal go down with the students?** comment les étudiants vont-ils prendre la proposition? ▪ **that kind of talk doesn't go down well with me** je n'apprécie pas du tout ce genre de propos **9.** [lose] être battu ▪ **Mexico went down to Germany** le Mexique s'est incliné devant l'Allemagne ▪ **Madrid went down to Milan by three points** Milan a battu Madrid de trois points **10.** [be relegated] descendre ▪ **our team has gone down to the second division** notre équipe est descendue en deuxième division **11.** [be noted, recorded] être noté ▪ [in writing] être pris *OR* couché par écrit ▪ **this day will go down in history** ce jour restera une date historique ▪ **she will go down in history as a woman of great courage** elle entrera dans l'histoire grâce à son grand courage **12.** [reach as far as] descendre, s'étendre ▪ **this path goes down to the beach** ce sentier va *OR* descend à la plage **13.** [continue as far as] aller, continuer ▪ **go down to the end of the street** allez *OR* continuez jusqu'en bas de la rue **14.** *UK* UNIV entrer dans la période des vacances **15.** [in bridge] chuter **16.** COMPUT tomber en panne **17.** MUS [lower pitch] descendre **18.** △ *UK* [be sent to prison] : **he went down for three years** il a écopé de trois ans **19.** *inf* [happen] se passer.

◇ *vt insep* descendre de ▪ **my food went down the wrong way** j'ai avalé de travers ▪ **to go down a class** *UK* SCH descendre d'une classe.

◆ **go down on**▲ *vt insep* sucer▲.

◆ **go down with** *vt insep* tomber malade de ▪ **he went down with pneumonia** il a attrapé une pneumonie.

◆ **go for** *vt insep* **1.** [fetch] aller chercher ▪ **he went for a doctor** il est allé *OR* parti chercher un médecin **2.** [try to obtain] essayer d'obtenir, viser ▪ **go for it!** *inf inf* vas-y! ▪ **I'd go for it if I were you!** à ta place, je n'hésiterais pas! **3.** [attack - physically] tomber sur, s'élancer sur ; [- verbally] s'en prendre à ▪ **dogs usually go for the throat** en général, les chiens attaquent à la gorge ■ **they went for each other** [physically] ils se sont jetés l'un sur l'autre ; [verbally] ils s'en sont pris l'un à l'autre **4.** *inf* [like] aimer, adorer ■ **I don't really go for that idea** l'idée ne me dit pas grand-chose **5.** [choose, prefer] choisir, préférer **6.** [apply to, concern] concerner, s'appliquer à ■ **pollution is a real problem in Paris – that goes for Rome too** la pollution pose un énorme problème à Paris – c'est la même chose à Rome ■ **and the same goes for me** et moi aussi **7.** [have as result] servir à ■ **his twenty years of service went for nothing** ses vingt ans de service n'ont servi à rien **8.** [be to the advantage of] : **she has a lot going for her** elle a beaucoup d'atouts ■ **that idea hasn't got much going for it frankly** cette idée n'est franchement pas très convaincante.

◆ **go forth** *vi insep arch* & *lit* [leave] sortir ■ **the army went forth into battle** l'armée s'est mise en route pour la bataille ■ **go forth and multiply** BIBLE croissez et multipliez-vous.

◆ **go in** *vi insep* **1.** [enter] entrer, rentrer **2.** [disappear - moon, sun] se cacher.

◆ **go in for** *vt insep* **1.** [engage in - activity, hobby, sport] pratiquer, faire ; [- occupation] se consacrer à ; [- politics] s'occuper de, faire ■ **she went in for company law** elle s'est lancée dans le droit commercial ■ **he thought about going in for teaching** il a pensé devenir enseignant **2.** *inf* [be interested in] s'intéresser à ■ [like] aimer ■ **I don't go in much for opera** je n'aime pas trop l'opéra, l'opéra ne me dit rien **3.** [take part in - competition, race] prendre part à ; [- examination] se présenter à **4.** [apply for - job, position] poser sa candidature à, postuler.

◆ **go into** *vt insep* **1.** [enter - building, house] entrer dans ; [- activity, profession] entrer à *OR* dans ; [- politics, business] se lancer dans ■ **to go into the army** [as profession] devenir militaire de carrière ; [as conscript] partir au service ■ **he went into medicine** il a choisi la médecine **2.** [be invested - subj: effort, money, time] : **a lot of care had gone into making her feel at home** on s'était donné beaucoup de peine pour la mettre à l'aise ■ **two months of research went into our report** nous avons mis *OR* investi deux mois de recherche dans notre rapport **3.** [embark on - action] commencer à ; [- explanation, speech] se lancer *OR* s'embarquer dans, (se mettre à) donner ; [- problem] aborder ■ **the car went into a skid** la voiture a commencé à déraper **4.** [examine, investigate] examiner, étudier **5.** [explain in depth] entrer dans ■ **I won't go into details** je ne vais pas entrer dans les détails ■ **let's not go into that** ne parlons pas de ça **6.** [begin to wear] se mettre à porter ■ **to go into mourning** prendre le deuil **7.** [hit, run into] entrer dans ■ **a car went into him** une voiture lui est rentrée dedans.

◆ **go off** ◇ *vi insep* **1.** [leave] partir, s'en aller ■ **she went off to work** elle est partie travailler **2.** [stop operating - light, radio] s'éteindre ; [- heating] s'éteindre, s'arrêter ; [- pain] partir, s'arrêter ■ **the electricity went off** l'électricité a été coupée **3.** [become activated - bomb] exploser ; [- gun] partir ; [- alarm] sonner ■ **to go off into fits of laughter** *fig* être pris d'un fou rire **4.** [have specified outcome] se passer ■ **the interview went off badly/well** l'entretien s'est mal/bien passé **5.** [fall asleep] s'endormir **6.** *UK* [deteriorate - food] s'avarier, se gâter ; [- milk] tourner ; [- butter] rancir ■ **the play goes off in the second half** la pièce se gâte pendant la seconde partie.

◇ *vt insep inf UK inf* [stop liking] perdre le goût de ■ **he's gone off jazz/smoking** il n'aime plus le jazz/fumer, le jazz/fumer ne l'intéresse plus.

◆ **go off with** *vt insep* **1.** [leave with] partir avec **2.** [make off with] partir avec ■ **someone has gone off with his keys** quelqu'un est parti avec ses clés.

◆ **go on** ◇ *vi insep* **1.** [move, proceed] aller ■ [without stopping] poursuivre son chemin ■ [after stopping] repartir, se remettre en route ■ **you go on, I'll catch up** allez-y, je vous rattraperai (en chemin) ■ **they went on without us** ils sont partis sans nous **2.** [continue action] continuer ■ **she went on (with her) reading** elle a continué à *OR* de lire ■ **you can't go on being a student for ever!** tu ne peux pas être étudiant toute ta vie! ■ **go on, ask her** vas-y, demande-lui ■ **their affair has been going on for years** leur liaison dure depuis des années ■ **the party went on into the small hours** la soirée s'est prolongée jusqu'à très tôt le matin ⊙ **go on (with you)!** *UK inf* allons, arrête de me faire marcher! ■ **they have enough (work) to be going on with** ils ont du pain sur la planche *OR* de quoi faire pour le moment ■ **here's £25 to be going on with** voilà 25 livres pour te dépanner **3.** [proceed to another action] : **he went on to explain why** il a ensuite expliqué pourquoi ■ **she went on to become a doctor** elle est ensuite devenue médecin **4.** [be placed, fit] aller ■ **the lid goes on this way** le couvercle se met comme ça **5.** [happen, take place] se passer ■ **what's going on here?** qu'est-ce qui se passe ici? ■ **a lot of cheating goes on during the exams** on triche beaucoup pendant les examens ■ **several conversations were going on at once** il y avait plusieurs conversations à la fois ■ **while the war was going on** pendant la guerre **6.** [elapse] passer, s'écouler ■ **as time goes on** avec le temps, à mesure que le temps passe **7.** *inf* [chatter, talk] parler, jacasser ■ **she does go on!** elle n'arrête pas de parler!, c'est un vrai moulin à paroles! ■ **to go on about sthg : he goes on and on about politics** il parle politique sans cesse ■ **don't go on about it!** ça va, on a compris! ■ **I don't want to go on about it, but...** je ne voudrais pas avoir l'air d'insister, mais... **8.** *inf* [act, behave] se conduire, se comporter ■ **what a way to go on!** en voilà des manières! **9.** [start operating - light, radio, television] s'allumer ; [- heating, motor, power] s'allumer, se mettre en marche **10.** SPORT [player] prendre sa place, entrer en jeu **11.** THEAT [actor] entrer en scène.

◇ *vt insep* **1.** [be guided by] se laisser guider par, se fonder *OR* se baser sur ■ **the detective didn't have much to go on** le détective n'avait pas grand-chose sur quoi s'appuyer *OR* qui puisse le guider **2.** *UK inf (usu neg)* [appreciate, like] aimer.

◆ **go on at** *vt insep inf* [criticize] critiquer ■ [nag] s'en prendre à ■ **he's always going on at his wife about money** il est toujours sur le dos de sa femme avec les questions d'argent ■ **I went on at my mother to go and see the doctor** j'ai embêté ma mère pour qu'elle aille voir le médecin ■ **don't go on at me!** laisse-moi tranquille!

◆ **go out** *vi insep* **1.** [leave] sortir ■ **to go out to dinner** sortir dîner ■ **she goes out to work** elle travaille en dehors de la maison *OR* hors de chez elle ■ **he went out of her life** il est sorti de sa vie **2.** [travel] partir ■ [emigrate] émigrer ■ **they went out to Africa** [travelled] ils sont partis en Afrique ; [emigrated] ils sont partis vivre *OR* ils ont émigré en Afrique **3.** [date] sortir ■ **to go out with sb** sortir avec qqn **4.** [fire, light] s'éteindre **5.** [disappear] disparaître ■ **the spring went out of his step** il a perdu sa démarche légère **6.** [cease to be fashionable] passer de mode, se démoder ■ **to go out of style/fashion** ne plus être le bon style/à la mode **7.** [tide] descendre, se retirer **8.** *fig* [set out] : **we have to go out and do something about this** il faut que nous prenions des mesures *OR* que nous fassions quelque chose **9.** [be published - brochure, pamphlet] être distribué ■ [be broadcast - radio or television programme] être diffusé **10.** [feelings, sympathies] aller ■ **our thoughts go out to all those who suffer** nos pensées vont vers tous ceux qui souffrent ■ **my heart goes out to her** je suis de tout cœur avec elle dans son chagrin **11.** *phr* **to go all out** *inf* : **she went all out to help us** elle a fait tout son possible pour nous aider.

◆ **go over** ◇ *vi insep* **1.** [move overhead] passer ■ **I just saw a plane go over** je viens de voir passer un avion **2.** [move in particular direction] aller ■ [cross] traverser ■ **I went over to see her** je suis allé la voir ■ [capsize - boat] chavirer, capoter **3.** [change, switch] changer ■ **I've gone over to another brand of washing powder** je viens de changer de marque de lessive ■ **when will we go over to the metric system?** quand est-ce qu'on va passer au système métrique? **4.** [change allegiance] passer, se joindre ■ **he's gone over to the Socialists** il est passé dans le camp des socialistes **5.** [be received] passer ■ **the speech went over badly/well** le discours a mal/bien passé.

◇ *vt insep* **1.** [move, travel over] passer par-dessus ■ **we went over a bump** on a pris une bosse **2.** [examine - argument, problem] examiner, considérer ; [- accounts, report] examiner, vérifier **3.** [repeat] répéter ■ [review - notes, speech] réviser, revoir ; [- facts] récapituler, revoir ■ SCH réviser ■ **she went over the interview in her mind** elle a repassé l'entretien dans son esprit ■ **let's go over it again** reprenons, récapitulons **4.** TV & RADIO : **let's go over now to our Birmingham studios** passons l'antenne à notre studio de Birmingham ■ **we're going over live now to Paris** nous allons maintenant à Paris où nous sommes en direct.

◆ **go past** *vt insep* [move in front of] passer devant ■ [move beyond] dépasser.

◆ **go round** *vi insep* **1.** [be enough] : **is there enough cake to go round?** est-ce qu'il y a assez de gâteau pour tout le monde? **2.** [visit] aller ■ **we went round to his house** nous sommes allés chez lui **3.** [be continuously present - idea, tune] : **that**

song keeps going round in my head j'ai cette chanson dans la tête **4.** [spin - wheel] tourner ▪ **my head's going round** *fig* j'ai la tête qui tourne.

◆ **go through** ◇ *vt insep* **1.** [crowd, tunnel] traverser ▪ **a shiver went through her** *fig* un frisson l'a parcourue *OR* traversée **2.** [endure, experience] subir, souffrir ▪ **he's going through hell** c'est l'enfer pour lui ▪ **we all have to go through it sometime** on doit tous y passer un jour ou l'autre ▪ **we've gone through a lot together** nous avons vécu beaucoup de choses ensemble **3.** [consume, use up - supplies] épuiser ; [- money] dépenser ▪ [wear out] user ▪ **how many assistants has he gone through now?** *hum* combien d'assistants a-t-il déjà eus? **4.** [examine - accounts, document] examiner, vérifier ; [- list, proposal] éplucher ; [- mail] dépouiller ; [- drawer, pockets] fouiller (dans) ; [- files] chercher dans ▪ [sort] trier ▪ **did customs go through your suitcase?** est-ce qu'ils ont fouillé votre valise à la douane? **5.** [subj: bill, law] être voté ▪ **the bill went through Parliament last week** le projet de loi a été voté la semaine dernière au Parlement **6.** [carry out, perform - movement, work] faire ; [- formalities] remplir, accomplir ▪ **we had to go through the whole business of applying for a visa** nous avons dû nous farcir toutes les démarches pour obtenir un visa **7.** [participate in - course of study] étudier ; [- ceremony] participer à **8.** [practise - lesson, poem] réciter ▪ THEAT [- role, scene] répéter ▪ **let's go through it again from the beginning** reprenons dès le début.

◇ *vi insep* [offer, proposal] être accepté ▪ [business deal] être conclu, se faire ▪ [bill, law] passer, être voté ▪ **the adoption finally went through** l'adoption s'est faite finalement.

◆ **go through with** *vt insep* : **to go through with sthg** aller jusqu'au bout de qqch, exécuter qqch ▪ **they went through with their threat** ils ont exécuté leur menace.

◆ **go together** *vi insep* **1.** [colours, flavours] aller bien ensemble ▪ [characteristics, ideas] aller de pair **2.** *US* [people] sortir ensemble.

◆ **go towards** *vt insep* **1.** [move towards] aller vers **2.** [effort, money] être consacré à ▪ **all her energy went towards fighting illiteracy** elle a dépensé toute son énergie à combattre l'analphabétisme.

◆ **go under** ◇ *vi insep* **1.** [go down - ship] couler, sombrer ; [- person] couler, disparaître (sous l'eau) **2.** *fig* [fail - business] couler, faire faillite ; [- project] couler, échouer ; [- person] échouer, sombrer.

◇ *vt insep* passer par-dessous.

◆ **go up** ◇ *vi insep* **1.** [ascend, climb - person] monter, aller en haut ; [- lift] monter ▪ **I'm going up to bed** je monte me coucher ▪ **have you ever gone up in an aeroplane?** êtes-vous déjà monté en avion? **2.** [reach as far as] aller, s'étendre ▪ **the road goes up to the house** la route mène *OR* va à la maison **3.** [increase - amount, numbers] augmenter, croître ; [- price] monter, augmenter ; [- temperature] monter, s'élever ▪ **rents are going up** les loyers sont en hausse **4.** [sudden noise] s'élever **5.** [appear - notices, posters] apparaître ▪ [be built] être construit ▪ **new buildings are going up all over town** de nouveaux immeubles surgissent dans toute la ville **6.** [explode, be destroyed] sauter, exploser **7.** MUS [raise pitch] monter **8.** THEAT [curtain] se lever ▪ **before the curtain goes up** avant le lever du rideau **9.** △ *US* [be sent to prison] : **he went up for murder** il a fait de la taule pour meurtre△ **10.** SPORT [be promoted] : **they look set to go up to the First Division** ils ont l'air prêts à entrer en première division.

◇ *vt insep* monter ▪ **to go up a hill/ladder** monter une colline/sur une échelle ▪ **to go up a class** *UK* SCH monter d'une classe.

◆ **go with** *vt insep* **1.** [accompany, escort] accompagner, aller avec ▪ *fig* **to go with the crowd** suivre la foule *OR* le mouvement ▪ **you have to go with the times** il faut vivre avec son temps **2.** [be compatible - colours, flavours] aller avec ▪ **that hat doesn't go with your suit** ce chapeau ne va pas avec ton ensemble ▪ **a white Burgundy goes well with snails** le bourgogne blanc se marie bien *OR* va bien avec les escargots **3.** [be part of] aller avec ▪ **the sense of satisfaction that goes with having done a good job** le sentiment de satisfaction qu'apporte le travail bien fait **4.** *inf* [spend time with] sortir avec ▪ *euph* [have sex with] : **he's been going with other women** il a été avec d'autres femmes.

◆ **go without** ◇ *vt insep* se passer de, se priver de ▪ **he went without sleep** *OR* **without sleeping for two days** il n'a pas dormi pendant deux jours.

◇ *vi insep* s'en passer ▪ **we'll just have to go without** il faudra s'en passer, c'est tout!

goad [gəʊd] ◇ *n* aiguillon *m*.

◇ *vt* **1.** [cattle] aiguillonner, piquer **2.** [person] harceler, provoquer ▪ **stop ~ing the poor child!** cesse de houspiller ce petit! ▪ **to ~ sb into doing sthg** pousser qqn à faire qqch, harceler qqn jusqu'à ce qu'il fasse qqch.

◆ **goad on** *vt sep* aiguillonner ▪ **she was ~ed on by the prospect of wealth and power** elle était stimulée par la perspective des richesses et du pouvoir.

go-ahead ◇ *n* feu *m* vert ▪ **to give sb the ~ to do sthg** donner le feu vert à qqn pour (faire) qqch.

◇ *adj* [dynamic - person] dynamique, entreprenant, qui va de l'avant ; [- attitude, business] dynamique.

goal [gəʊl] ◇ *n* **1.** [aim] but *m*, objectif *m* ▪ **what's your ~ in life?** quel est ton but *OR* quelle est ton ambition dans la vie? ▪ **to achieve** *OR* **attain one's ~** atteindre *OR* réaliser son but **2.** SPORT but *m* ▪ **to score a ~** marquer un but ▪ **who plays in** *OR* **keeps ~ for Liverpool?** qui est gardien de but dans l'équipe de Liverpool? ▪ **~!** but!

◇ *comp* de but.

goal area *n* (zone *f* des) six mètres *mpl*.

goal average *n* goal-average *m*.

goal difference *n* différence *f* de buts.

goalie ['gəʊlɪ] *n inf* SPORT goal *m*, gardien *m* (de but).

goalkeeper ['gəʊl,kiːpər] *n* gardien *m* (de but), goal *m*.

goalkeeping ['gəʊl,kiːpɪŋ] *n* jeu *m* du gardien de but ▪ **we saw some great ~ on both sides** les deux gardiens de but ont très bien joué.

goal kick *n* coup *m* de pied de but, dégagement *m* aux six mètres.

goalless ['gəʊllɪs] *adj* : **a ~ draw** un match sans but marqué *OR* zéro à zéro.

goal line *n* ligne *f* de but.

goalminder ['gəʊl,maɪndər] *n* [ice hockey] gardien *m* (de but).

goalmouth ['gəʊl,maʊθ] (*pl* [-,maʊðz]) *n* : **in the ~** directement devant le but ▪ **a ~ scuffle** un cafouillage devant le but.

goalpost ['gəʊlpəʊst] *n* poteau *m* (de but) ▪ **to move** *OR* **shift the ~s** *fig* changer les règles du jeu.

goalscorer ['gəʊl,skɔːrər] *n* buteur *m*.

goat [gəʊt] *n* **1.** ZOOL chèvre *f* **2.** *inf* [lecher] : **old ~** vieux satyre *m* **3.** *inf dated* [foolish person] andouille *f* **4.** *phr* **to get sb's ~** *inf* taper sur les nerfs *OR* le système à qqn ▪ **it gets my ~** ça me tape sur les nerfs.

goatee [gəʊ'tiː] *n* barbiche *f*, bouc *m*.

goatherd ['gəʊthɜːd] *n* chevrier *m*, - ère *f*.

goatskin ['gəʊtskɪn] *n* **1.** [hide] peau *f* de chèvre **2.** [container] outre *f* (en peau de chèvre).

gob [gɒb] (*pret & pp* **gobbed**, *cont* **gobbing**) ◇ *n* **1.** △ *UK* [mouth] gueule△ *f* **2.** *inf* [lump - of mud, clay] motte *f* ; [- of spittle] crachat *m*, mollard△ *m*.

◇ *vi*△ [spit] mollarder△.

gobbet ['gɒbɪt] *n inf* morceau *m*.

gobble ['gɒbl] ◇ *vi* [turkey] glouglouter.

◇ *vt inf* [eat greedily] enfourner, engloutir ▪ **he ~d (down** *OR* **up) his lunch** il a englouti son déjeuner à toute vitesse ▪ **don't ~ your food!** ne mange pas si vite!

◇ *n* glouglou *m*.

gobbledegook, gobbledygook ['gɒbldɪguːk] *n inf* charabia *m*.

gobbler ['gɒblər] *n inf* [male turkey] dindon *m*.

go-between *n* intermédiaire *mf*.

Gobi ['gəʊbɪ] *pr n* : **the ~ Desert** le désert de Gobi.

goblet ['gɒblɪt] *n* coupe *f*, verre *m* à pied ■ HIST gobelet *m*.

goblin ['gɒblɪn] *n* esprit *m* maléfique, lutin *m*.

gobsmacked ['gɒbsmækt] *adj inf* **I was ~** j'en suis resté baba.

gobstopper ['gɒb,stɒpəʳ] *n UK gros bonbon rond qui change de couleur à mesure qu'on le suce.*

goby ['gəʊbɪ] (*pl* **gobies**) *n* gobie *m*.

go-cart *n* **1.** = go-kart **2.** *US* [toy wagon] chariot *m*.

god [gɒd] *n* dieu *m* ■ **the ~ of War** le dieu de la Guerre.
◆ **God** *n* **1.** RELIG Dieu *m* ■ **God the Father, the Son and the Holy Ghost** Dieu le Père, le Fils, le Saint-Esprit ⊳ **the God slot** *inf inf expression humoristique désignant les émissions religieuses à la télévision* **2.** [in interjections and expressions] : **God bless you!** Dieu vous bénisse! ■ **thank God!** *inf inf* heureusement! ; *lit* grâce à Dieu!, Dieu soit loué! ■ **thank God you didn't tell him** *inf* heureusement que tu ne lui as rien dit ■ **(my** *OR* **by) God!** *inf* mon Dieu! ■ **for God's sake, don't tell him !** *inf inf* surtout ne lui dis rien ■ **God knows why/how** Dieu sait pourquoi/comment ■ **God (only) knows** Dieu seul le sait ■ **God willing** s'il plaît à Dieu.
◆ **gods** *npl UK inf* THEAT : **the ~s** *inf* le poulailler.

god-awful△ *adj* atroce, affreux.

godchild ['gɒdtʃaɪld] (*pl* **godchildren** [-,tʃɪldrən]) *n* filleul *m*, - e *f*.

goddam(n)△ ['gɒdæm] *US* <> *interj* : **~!** zut!
<> *n* : **he doesn't care** *OR* **give a ~** il s'en fout△.
<> *adj* sacré, fichu ■ **you ~ fool!** pauvre imbécile!
<> *adv* vachement.

goddamned△ ['gɒdæmd] = **goddam(n)** *(adj, adv)*.

goddaughter ['gɒd,dɔːtəʳ] *n* filleule *f*.

goddess ['gɒdɪs] *n* déesse *f*.

godfather ['gɒd,fɑːðəʳ] *n* parrain *m*.

god-fearing *adj* croyant, pieux.

godforsaken ['gɒdfə,seɪkn] *adj* paumé.

godhead ['gɒdhed] *n* divinité *f* ■ **the ~** Dieu.

godless ['gɒdlɪs] *adj* irréligieux, impie.

godlike ['gɒdlaɪk] *adj* divin, céleste.

godliness ['gɒdlɪnɪs] *n* sainteté *f* (de l'âme), dévotion *f*.

godly ['gɒdlɪ] *adj* **1.** [pious] pieux **2.** [divine] divin.

godmother ['gɒd,mʌðəʳ] *n* marraine *f*.

godparent ['gɒd,peərənt] *n* parrain *m*, marraine *f*.

godsend ['gɒdsend] *n* aubaine *f*, bénédiction *f*.

godson ['gɒdsʌn] *n* filleul *m*.

godsquad ['gɒdskwɒd] *n inf pej* **the ~** les soldats de Dieu.

goer ['gəʊəʳ] *n UK inf* **1.** [fast person, vehicle, animal] fonceur *m*, - euse *f* **2.** [sexually active person] : **he's/she's a real ~** il/elle n'y va pas par quatre chemins *(pour séduire qqn)*.

goes [gəʊz] ⊳ **go** *(vb)*.

gofer ['gəʊfəʳ] *n inf* [office employee] *personne qui fait les menues tâches dans un bureau.*

go-getter [-'getəʳ] *n inf* fonceur *m*, - euse *f*, battant *m*, - e *f*.

goggle ['gɒgl] <> *vi* ouvrir de grands yeux *OR* des yeux ronds ■ **to ~ at sb/sthg** regarder qqn/qqch avec des yeux ronds.
<> *adj* : **to have ~ eyes** avoir les yeux saillants *OR* exorbités *OR* globuleux.
◆ **goggles** *npl* **1.** [protective] lunettes *fpl* (de protection) ■ [for motorcyclist] lunettes *fpl* (de motocycliste) ■ [for diver] lunettes *fpl* de plongée ■ [for swimmer] lunettes *fpl* **2.** *inf* [glasses] bésicles *fpl*.

goggle box *n UK inf hum* télé *f*.

goggle-eyed *adj* les yeux saillants *OR* exorbités *OR* globuleux ■ **to stare ~** regarder en écarquillant les yeux.

goggly ['gɒglɪ] = **goggle** *(adj)*.

go-go dancer *n* danseur *m* de go-go.

going ['gəʊɪŋ] <> *n* **1.** [leaving] départ *m* **2.** [progress] progrès *m* ■ **we made good ~ on the return journey** on est allés vite pour le retour ■ **that's pretty good ~!** c'est plutôt rapide! ■ **it was slow ~, but we got the work done** il nous a fallu du temps, mais on a réussi à finir le travail **3.** [condition of ground] état *m* du terrain ■ **it's rough** *OR* **heavy ~ on these mountain roads** c'est dur de rouler sur ces routes de montagne ■ **this novel is heavy ~** *fig* ce roman ne se lit pas facilement ■ **he left while the ~ was good** *fig* il est parti au bon moment.
<> *adj* **1.** [profitable] : **her company is a ~ concern** son entreprise est en pleine activité **2.** [current] actuel ■ **she's getting the ~ rate for the job** elle touche le tarif en vigueur *OR* normal pour ce genre de travail ■ **the best computer/novelist ~** le meilleur ordinateur/romancier du moment.

going-over (*pl* **goings-over**) *n inf* **1.** [checkup] révision *f*, vérification *f* ■ [cleanup] nettoyage *m* ■ **the house needs a good ~** il faudrait nettoyer la maison à fond **2.** *fig* **to give sb a (good) ~** [scolding] passer un savon à qqn ; [beating] passer qqn à tabac.

goings-on *npl inf* **1.** *pej* [behaviour] conduite *f*, activités *fpl* ■ **there are some funny ~ in that house** il s'en passe de drôles dans cette maison **2.** [events] événements *mpl*.

goitre *UK*, **goiter** *US* ['gɔɪtəʳ] *n* goitre *m*.

go-kart *n* kart *m*.

Golan Heights ['gəʊ,læn-] *pr npl* : **the ~** le plateau du Golan.

gold [gəʊld] <> *n* **1.** [metal, colour] or *m* ■ **1,000 French francs in ~** 1 000 francs français en or ⊳ **to be as good as ~** être sage comme une image ■ **he has a heart of ~** il a un cœur d'or ■ **to be worth its weight in ~** valoir son pesant d'or **2.** [gold medal] médaille *f* d'or ■ **to go for ~** viser la médaille d'or.
<> *adj* **1.** [made of gold - coin, ingot, medal] d'or ; [- tooth, watch] en or **2.** [gold-coloured] or *(inv)*, doré.

gold braid *n* galon *m* d'or.

gold bullion *n* or *m* en barre *OR* en lingots ■ **~ standard** étalon-or-lingot *m*.

Gold Coast *pr n* **1.** HIST : **the ~** la Côte-de-l'Or **2.** *US* [expensive area] beaux quartiers *mpl*.

gold-digger *n* chercheur *m* d'or ■ *fig* aventurier *m*, - ère *f*.

gold dust *n* poudre *f* d'or ■ **jobs are like ~ around here** *fig* le travail est rare *OR* ne court pas les rues par ici.

golden ['gəʊldən] *adj* **1.** *liter & fig* [made of gold] en or, d'or ■ [opinion] favorable ■ **a ~ opportunity** une occasion en or ■ **the Golden State** la Californie **2.** [colour] doré, (couleur) d'or **3.** *inf* [very successful] : **~ boy/girl** enfant *mf* prodige.

Golden Age *n* : **the ~** l'âge *m* d'or.

golden calf *n* veau *m* d'or.

Golden Delicious (*pl inv*) *n* golden *f*.

golden eagle *n* aigle *m* royal.

Golden Fleece *n* : **the ~** la Toison d'or.

golden handcuffs *npl inf* primes *fpl (versées à un cadre à intervalles réguliers pour le dissuader de partir)*.

golden handshake *n inf* gratification *f* de fin de service.

golden hello *n inf* gratification *f* de début de service.

golden jubilee *n* (fête *f* du) cinquantième anniversaire *m*.

golden mean *n* : **the ~** le juste milieu.

golden oldie *n inf* vieux tube *m*.

golden pheasant *n* faisan *m* doré.

golden retriever *n* golden retriever *m*.

golden rule *n* règle *f* d'or.

golden section *n* section *f* d'or *OR* dorée.

golden share *n* participation *f* majoritaire *(souvent détenue par le gouvernement britannique dans les entreprises privatisées)*.

golden syrup *n UK* mélasse *f* raffinée.

golden wedding *n* noces *fpl* d'or.

gold fever *n* fièvre *f* de l'or.

goldfield ['gəʊldfi:ld] *n* terrain *m* aurifère.

gold filling *n* obturation *f OR* incrustation *f* en or.

goldfinch ['gəʊldfɪntʃ] *n* chardonneret *m*.

goldfish ['gəʊldfɪʃ] *n* **1.** [as pet] poisson *m* rouge **2.** ZOOL cyprin *m* doré.

goldfish bowl *n* bocal *m* (à poissons rouges) ■ **it's like living in a ~** *fig* on se croirait dans un aquarium.

gold leaf *n* feuille *f* d'or.

gold medal *n* médaille *f* d'or.

goldmine ['gəʊldmaɪn] *n liter & fig* mine *f* d'or.

gold plate *n* **1.** [utensils] orfèvrerie *f*, vaisselle *f* d'or **2.** [plating] plaque *f* d'or.

gold-plated *adj* plaqué or.

gold-rimmed *adj* : **~ spectacles** lunettes *fpl* à montures en or.

gold rush *n* ruée *f* vers l'or ■ **the Gold Rush** *US* HIST la ruée vers l'or.

THE GOLD RUSH

Mouvement de migration de grande ampleur qui, en 1848, à la suite de la découverte de gisements d'or en Californie, déplaça des milliers d'Américains vers la côte Ouest. Un an plus tard, seuls 80 000 d'entre eux avaient atteint leur but, après avoir échappé à la maladie et aux dangers du voyage.

goldsmith ['gəʊldsmɪθ] *n* orfèvre *m*.

gold standard *n* étalon-or *m*.

golf [gɒlf] ◇ *n* golf *m*.
◇ *comp* : **~ bag** sac *m* de golf ■ **~ cart** caddie *m* (de golf).
◇ *vi* jouer au golf.

golf ball *n* **1.** SPORT balle *f* de golf **2.** [for typewriter] boule *f*.

golf club *n* **1.** [stick] club *m OR* crosse *f OR* canne *f* de golf **2.** [building, association] club *m* de golf.

golf course *n* (terrain *m* de) golf *m*.

golfer ['gɒlfə^r] *n* joueur *m*, -euse *f* de golf, golfeur *m*, -euse *f*.

golfing ['gɒlfɪŋ] *n* golf *m (activité)*.

golliwog ['gɒlɪwɒg] *n poupée de chiffon, au visage noir et aux cheveux hérissés.*

golly ['gɒlɪ] (*pl* **gollies**) *inf* ◇ *n UK* = **golliwog**.
◇ *interj dated* **(good) ~!** ciel!, mince (alors) !, flûte!

gollywog ['gɒlɪwɒg] = **golliwog**.

goloshes [gə'lɒʃɪz] = **galoshes**.

gonad ['gəʊnæd] *n* gonade *f*.

gondola ['gɒndələ] *n* **1.** [boat] gondole *f* **2.** [on airship or balloon, for window cleaner] nacelle *f* **3.** [in supermarket] gondole *f* **4.** [ski lift] cabine *f* (de téléphérique).

gondolier [,gɒndə'lɪə^r] *n* gondolier *m*.

gone [gɒn] ◇ *pp* ▷ **go**.
◇ *adj* **1.** [past] passé, révolu ■ **those days are ~ now** c'est bien fini tout ça ■ **~ is the time when...** le temps n'est plus où... **2.** [away] : **be ~ with you!** disparaissez de ma vue! ▶ **'Gone with the Wind'** ***Mitchell*** 'Autant en emporte le vent' **3.** *inf* [high, drunk] parti **4.** *inf* [pregnant] : **she is 4 months ~** elle est enceinte de 4 mois **5.** *inf* [infatuated] : **to be ~ on sb/sthg** être (complètement) toqué de qqn/qqch **6.** *euph* [dead] mort **7.** *phr* **to be far ~** *inf* [weak] être bien faible ; [drunk] être bien parti.
◇ *prep UK* : **it's ~ 11** il est 11 h passées *OR* plus de 11 h.

goner ['gɒnə^r] *n inf* **to be a ~** être fichu *OR* cuit.

gong [gɒŋ] *n* **1.** [instrument] gong *m* **2.** *UK inf hum* [medal] médaille *f*.

gonna ['gɒnə] *esp US inf* = **going to**.

gonorrhoea *UK*, **gonorrhea** *US* [,gɒnə'rɪə] *n* blennorragie *f*.

gonzo ['gɒnzəʊ] *adj US inf* [style] particulier, bizarre ■ [person] barge.

goo [gu:] *n inf* **1.** [sticky stuff] matière *f* poisseuse **2.** *fig & pej* sentimentalisme *m*.

good [gʊd] (*comp* **better** ['betə^r], *superl* **best** [best]) ◇ *adj*

A.

1. [enjoyable, pleasant - book, feeling, holiday] bon, agréable ; [- weather] beau *(before vowel or silent 'h' bel)*, belle *f* ■ **we're ~ friends** nous sommes très amis ■ **we're just ~ friends** on est des amis, c'est tout ■ **they had a ~ time** ils se sont bien amusés ■ **~ to eat/to hear** bon à manger/à entendre ■ **it's ~ to be home** ça fait du bien *OR* ça fait plaisir de rentrer chez soi ■ **it's ~ to be alive** il fait bon vivre ■ [agreeable] bon ■ **wait until he's in a ~ mood** attendez qu'il soit de bonne humeur ■ **to feel ~** être en forme ■ **he doesn't feel ~ about leaving her alone** [worried] ça le gêne de la laisser seule ; [ashamed] il a honte de la laisser seule ▶ **it's too ~ to be true** c'est trop beau pour être vrai *OR* pour y croire ■ **the ~ life** la belle vie ■ **she's never had it so ~!** elle n'a jamais eu la vie si belle! ■ **have a ~ day!** bonne journée! ■ **you can have too much of a ~ thing** on se lasse de tout, même du meilleur

2. [high quality - clothing, dishes] bon, de bonne qualité ; [- painting, film] bon ; [- food] bon ■ **he speaks ~ English** il parle bien anglais ■ **she put her ~ shoes on** elle a mis ses belles chaussures ■ **this house is ~ enough for me** cette maison me suffit ■ **this work isn't ~ enough** ce travail laisse beaucoup à désirer ■ **nothing is too ~ for her family** rien n'est trop beau pour sa famille

3. [competent, skilful] bon, compétent ■ **she's a ~ listener** c'est quelqu'un qui sait écouter ■ **to be ~ at sthg** être doué pour *OR* bon en qqch ■ **he's ~ with children** il sait s'y prendre avec les enfants ■ **to be ~ with one's hands** être habile *OR* adroit de ses mains ■ **they're not ~ enough to direct the others** ils ne sont pas à la hauteur pour diriger les autres ■ **you're as ~ as he is** tu le vaux bien, tu vaux autant que lui ■ **the ~ gardening guide** le guide du bon jardinier

4. [useful] bon ■ **to be ~ for nothing** être bon à rien ■ **this product is also ~ for cleaning windows** ce produit est bien aussi pour nettoyer les vitres

B.

1. [kind] bon, gentil ■ [loyal, true] bon, véritable ■ [moral, virtuous] bon ■ **she's a ~ person** c'est quelqu'un de bien ■ **he's a ~ sort** c'est un brave type ■ **you're too ~ for him** tu mérites mieux que lui ■ **to lead a ~ life** [comfortable] avoir une belle vie ; [moral] mener une vie vertueuse *OR* exemplaire ■ **they've always been ~ to me** ils ont toujours été gentils avec moi ■ **it's ~ of you to come** c'est aimable *OR* gentil à vous d'être venu ■ **would you be ~ enough to reply by return of post?** voudriez-vous avoir l'obligeance de répondre par retour du courrier?

2. [well-behaved] sage ■ **be ~!** sois sage! ■ **be a ~ boy and fetch Mummy's bag** sois mignon, va chercher le sac de maman ■ **~ dog!** t'es un gentil chien, toi!

C.

1. [desirable, positive] bon, souhaitable ■ [cause] bon ■ **she had the ~ fortune to arrive just then** elle a eu la chance d'arriver juste à ce moment-là ■ **it's a ~ job** *OR* **~ thing he decided not to go** c'est une chance qu'il ait décidé de *OR* heureusement qu'il a décidé de ne pas y aller ■ **all ~ wishes for the New Year** tous nos meilleurs vœux pour le nouvel an

2. [favourable - contract, deal] avantageux, favorable ; [- opportunity, sign] bon, favorable ■ **to buy sthg at a ~ price** acheter qqch bon marché *OR* à un prix avantageux ■ **she's in a ~ position to help us** elle est bien placée pour nous aider ■ **he put in a ~ word for me with the boss** il a glissé un mot en ma faveur au patron

3. [convenient, suitable - place, time] bon, propice ; [- choice] bon, convenable ■ **this is as ~ a time as any** autant le faire maintenant ■ **it's as ~ a way as any to do it** c'est une façon comme une autre de le faire

4. [beneficial] bon, bienfaisant ■ **whisky is ~ for a cold** le whisky est bon pour les rhumes ■ **it's ~ for him to spend time outdoors** ça lui fait du bien *OR* c'est bon pour lui de passer du temps dehors ■ **he works more than is ~ for him** il travaille plus qu'il ne faudrait *OR* devrait ■ **if you know what's ~ for you, you'll listen** *fig* si tu as le moindre bon sens, tu m'écouteras

D.

1. [sound, strong] bon, valide ■ **my eyesight/hearing is ~** j'ai une bonne vue/l'ouïe fine
2. [attractive - appearance] bon, beau *(before vowel or silent 'h'* **bel***)*, belle *f* ; [- features, legs] beau *(before vowel or silent 'h'* **bel***)*, belle *f*, joli ■ **you're looking ~!** [healthy] tu as bonne mine! ; [well-dressed] tu es très bien! ■ **that colour looks ~ on him** cette couleur lui va bien ■ **he has a ~ figure** il est bien fait
3. [valid, well-founded] bon, valable ■ **she had a ~ excuse/reason for not going** elle avait une bonne excuse pour/une bonne raison de ne pas y aller
4. [reliable, trustworthy - brand, car] bon, sûr ■ COMM & FIN [- cheque] bon ; [- investment, securities] sûr ; [- debt] bon, certain ■ **this coat is ~ for another year** ce manteau fera encore un an ■ **he's always ~ for a laugh** *inf inf* il sait toujours faire rire ■ **they are** *OR* **their credit is ~ for £500** on peut leur faire crédit jusqu'à 500 livres
5. [honourable, reputable] bon, estimé ■ **to protect their ~ name** pour défendre leur réputation ■ **she's from a ~ family** elle est de bonne famille

E.

1. [ample, considerable] bon, considérable ■ **a ~ amount** *OR* **deal of money** beaucoup d'argent ■ **a ~-sized room** une assez grande pièce ■ **take ~ care of your mother** prends bien soin de ta mère ■ **to make ~ money** bien gagner sa vie ■ **a ~ thirty years ago** il y a bien trente ans ■ **the trip will take you a ~ two hours** il vous faudra deux bonnes heures pour faire le voyage ■ **there's a ~ risk of it happening** il y a de grands risques que ça arrive
2. [proper, thorough] bon, grand ■ **I gave the house a ~ cleaning** j'ai fait le ménage à fond ■ **have a ~ cry** pleure un bon coup ■ **we had a ~ laugh** on a bien ri ■ **I managed to get a ~ look at his face** j'ai pu bien regarder son visage ■ **take a ~ look at her** regardez-la bien ▶ **~ and** *inf inf* **: we were ~ and mad** on était carrément furax ■ **she'll call when she's ~ and ready** elle appellera quand elle le voudra bien
3. [acceptable] bon, convenable ■ **we made the trip in ~ time** le voyage n'a pas été trop long ■ **that's all very ~** *OR* **all well and ~ but...** c'est bien joli *OR* bien beau tout ça mais...
4. [indicating approval] bon, très bien ■ **she left him – ~!** elle l'a quitté – tant mieux! ■ **~, that's settled** bon *OR* bien, voilà une affaire réglée ▶ **that's a ~ one!** *inf inf* [joke] elle est (bien) bonne, celle-là! ; *iron* [far-fetched story] à d'autres! ■ **~ on you!** *inf OR* **for you** bravo!, très bien!

◇ *adv* **1.** [as intensifier] bien, bon ■ **a ~ hard bed** un lit bien dur ■ **the two friends had a ~ long chat** les deux amis ont longuement bavardé ■ **we took a ~ long walk** nous avons fait une bonne *OR* une grande promenade **2.** *inf (non standard)* [well] bien ■ **their team beat us ~ and proper** leur équipe nous a battus à plate couture *OR* à plates coutures **3.** *phr* **to make ~** [succeed] réussir ; [reform] changer de conduite, se refaire une vie ■ **the prisoner made ~ his escape** le prisonnier est parvenu à s'échapper *OR* a réussi son évasion ■ **they made ~ their promise** ils ont tenu parole *OR* ont respecté leur promesse ■ **to make sthg ~** [mistake] remédier à qqch ; [damages, injustice] réparer qqch ; [losses] compenser qqch ; [deficit] combler qqch ; [wall, surface] apporter des finitions à qqch ■ **we'll make ~ any expenses you incur** nous vous rembourserons toute dépense ■ **to make ~ on sthg** *US* honorer qqch.

◇ *n* **1.** [morality, virtue] bien *m* ■ **that organization is a power for ~** cet organisme exerce une influence salutaire ■ **she recognized the ~ in him** elle a vu ce qu'il y avait de bon en lui ■ **to be up to no ~** préparer un mauvais coup ■ **their daughter came to no ~** leur fille a mal tourné **2.** [use] **: this book isn't much ~ to me** ce livre ne me sert pas à grand-chose ■ **if it's any ~ to him** si ça peut lui être utile *OR* lui rendre service ■ **I was never any ~ at mathematics** je n'ai jamais été doué pour les maths, je n'ai jamais été bon *OR* fort en maths ■ **he'd be no ~ as a teacher** il ne ferait pas un bon professeur ■ **what's the ~?** à quoi bon? ■ **what ~ would it do to leave now?** à quoi bon partir maintenant? ■ **a fat lot of ~ that did you!** *inf* te voilà bien avancé maintenant! ■ **it's no ~, I give up** ça ne sert à rien, j'abandonne ■ **it's no ~ worrying about it** ça ne sert à rien de *OR* ce n'est pas la peine de *OR* inutile de vous inquiéter ■ **I might as well talk to the wall for all the ~ it does** je ferais aussi bien de parler au mur, pour tout l'effet que ça fait **3.** [benefit, welfare] bien *m* ■ **a holiday will do her ~** des vacances lui feront du bien ■ **she resigned for the ~ of her health** elle a démissionné pour des raisons de santé ■ **it does my heart ~ to see you so happy** ça me réchauffe le cœur de vous voir si heureux ■ **the common ~** l'intérêt *m* commun.

◇ *npl* [people] **: the ~** les bons *mpl*, les gens *mpl* de bien ■ **only the ~ die young** ce sont toujours les meilleurs qui partent les premiers ▶ **'the Good, the Bad and the Ugly'** ***Leone*** 'le Bon, la bête et le truand'.

◆ **as good as** *adv phr* pour ainsi dire, à peu de choses près ■ **he's as ~ as dead** c'est comme s'il était mort ■ **it's as ~ as new** c'est comme neuf ■ **they as ~ as called us cowards** ils n'ont pas dit qu'on était des lâches mais c'était tout comme.

◆ **for good** *adv phr* pour de bon ■ **they finally settled down for ~** ils se sont enfin fixés définitivement ■ **for ~ and all** une (bonne) fois pour toutes, pour de bon.

◆ **to the good** *adv phr* **: that's all to the ~** tant mieux ■ **he finished up the card game £15 to the ~** il a fait 15 livres de bénéfice *OR* il a gagné 15 livres aux cartes.

Good Book *n* **: the ~** la Bible.

goodbye [,gʊd'baɪ] ◇ *interj* **: ~!** au revoir! ■ **~ for now** à bientôt, à la prochaine.
◇ *n* adieu *m*, au revoir *m* ■ **I hate ~s** j'ai horreur des adieux ■ **to say ~ to sb** dire au revoir *OR* faire ses adieux à qqn, prendre congé de qqn ■ **if you fail these exams, you can say ~ to a career as a doctor** *fig* si tu rates ces examens, tu peux dire adieu à ta carrière de médecin ▶ **'Goodbye to Berlin'** ***Isherwood*** 'Adieux à Berlin'.
Voir module d'usage

good day *interj* **1.** *UK dated US* [greeting] bonjour **2.** *UK dated* [goodbye] adieu.

good evening *interj* **: ~!** [greeting or saying goodbye] bonsoir!

good-for-nothing ◇ *adj* bon *OR* propre à rien ■ **he's a ~ layabout!** c'est un bon à rien et un fainéant!
◇ *n* vaurien *m*, - enne *f*, propre-à-rien *mf*.

GOODBYES

Au revoir, madame/Juliette. Goodbye, Mrs X/ Juliette.
Au revoir, et merci encore ! Goodbye, and thanks again!
Au revoir, et bon voyage. Goodbye, and have a safe journey.
Bonsoir ! Mes amitiés à Robert. Good night! Give my love to Robert.
À bientôt. See you soon *OR* Speak to you soon.
À tout à l'heure. See you later.
Bonne continuation ! All the best!
À la prochaine ! *inf* See you!
Salut ! *inf* Bye!
Bonne journée/soirée ! Have a nice day/evening!

Good Friday *n* le Vendredi saint.

Good Friday Agreement *pr n* accord *m* de paix d'Ulster.

good-hearted *adj* [person] bon, généreux ▪ [action] fait avec les meilleures intentions.

good-humoured *adj* [person] qui a bon caractère ▪ [generally] bon enfant *(inv)* ▪ [on one occasion] de bonne humeur ▪ [discussion] amical ▪ [joke, remark] sans malice.

goodie ['gʊdɪ] *inf* = **goody**.

good-looker *n inf* [man] bel homme *m* ▪ [younger] beau garçon *m* ▪ [woman] belle femme *f* ▪ [younger] belle fille *f*.

good-looking *adj* [person] beau *(before vowel or silent 'h' bel)*, belle *f*.

good looks *npl* [attractive appearance] beauté *f*.

goodly ['gʊdlɪ] *adj* **1.** *arch* [amount, size] considérable, important **2.** *arch* & *lit* [attractive] charmant, gracieux.

good morning *interj* : **~!** [greeting] bonjour! ; [goodbye] au revoir!, bonne journée!

good-natured *adj* [person] facile à vivre, qui a un bon naturel ▪ [face, smile] bon enfant *(inv)* ▪ [remark] sans malice.

goodness ['gʊdnɪs] *n* **1.** [of person] bonté *f*, bienveillance *f*, bienfaisance *f* ▪ [of thing] (bonne) qualité *f*, excellence *f*, perfection *f* **2.** [nourishment] valeur *f* nutritive ▪ **there's a lot of ~ in fresh vegetables** les légumes frais sont pleins de bonnes choses **3.** *inf* [in interjections] : **(my) ~!** mon Dieu! ▪ **for ~' sake** pour l'amour de Dieu, par pitié ▪ **~ knows!** Dieu seul le sait! ▪ **~ knows why** Dieu sait pourquoi ▪ **I wish to ~ he would shut up!** si seulement il pouvait se taire!

good night ◇ *interj* : **~ !** [when leaving] bonsoir! ; [when going to bed] bonne nuit!
◇ *n* : **they said ~ and left** ils ont dit bonsoir et sont partis.
◇ *comp* : **give your mother a ~ kiss** embrasse ta mère *(pour lui dire bonsoir)*.

goods [gʊdz] *npl* **1.** [possessions] biens *mpl* ▪ **he gave up all his worldly ~** il a renoncé à tous ses biens matériels ⊙ **~ and chattels** biens et effets *mpl* **2.** COMM marchandises *fpl*, articles *mpl* ▪ **leather ~** articles de cuir, maroquinerie *f* ⊙ **to come up with** *OR* **deliver the ~** *inf* tenir parole ▪ **have you got the ~?** *inf* vous avez ce qu'il faut? **3.** *US inf* [information] renseignements *mpl*.

good Samaritan *n* bon Samaritain *m*, bonne Samaritaine *f* ▪ **she's a real ~** elle a tout du bon Samaritain ▪ **the ~ laws** *US* LAW *lois qui protègent un sauveteur de toutes poursuites éventuelles engagées par le blessé*.
◆ **Good Samaritan** *n* BIBLE : **the Good Samaritan** le bon Samaritain.

Good Shepherd *n* : **the ~** le bon Pasteur.

goods train *n* train *m* de marchandises.

goods wagon *n* wagon *m* de marchandises.

goods yard *n* dépôt *m* de marchandises.

good-tempered *adj* [person] qui a bon caractère, d'humeur égale.

good-time girl *n inf pej* fille *f* qui ne pense qu'à se donner du bon temps, noceuse *f*.

goodwill [,gʊd'wɪl] ◇ *n* **1.** [benevolence] bienveillance *f* ▪ **to show ~ towards sb** faire preuve de bienveillance à l'égard de qqn **2.** [willingness] bonne volonté *f* ▪ **there needs to be ~ on both sides** il faut que chacun fasse preuve de bonne volonté *OR* y mette du sien **3.** COMM clientèle *f*, (biens *mpl*) incorporels *mpl*.
◇ *comp* d'amitié, de bienveillance ▪ **a ~ mission** *OR* **visit** une visite d'amitié.

goody ['gʊdɪ] *(pl* **goodies***)* *inf* ◇ *interj* : **~!** génial!, chouette!, chic!
◇ *n (usu pl)* **1.** [good thing] bonne chose *f* ▪ [sweet] bonbon *m*, friandise *f* ▪ **her latest film's a ~** son dernier film est un régal **2.** [good person] bon *m* ▪ **the goodies and the baddies** les bons et les méchants.

goody-goody *(pl* **goody-goodies***)* *inf pej* ◇ *adj* : **he's too ~** il est trop parfait.
◇ *n* âme *f* charitable *hum*, modèle *m* de vertu *hum*.

gooey ['gu:ɪ] *adj inf* **1.** [substance] gluant, visqueux, poisseux ▪ [sweets] qui colle aux dents **2.** [sentimental] sentimental ▪ **she goes all ~ over babies** elle devient gâteuse quand elle voit un bébé.

goof [gu:f] *inf* ◇ *n* **1.** [fool] imbécile *mf*, andouille *f* **2.** [blunder] gaffe *f*.
◇ *vi* [blunder] faire une gaffe.
◆ **goof off** *vi insep US inf* [waste time] flemmarder ▪ [malinger] tirer au flanc.
◆ **goof up** *vt sep inf* bousiller, saloper.

goofy ['gu:fɪ] *(comp* **goofier**, *superl* **goofiest***)* *adj inf* **1.** [stupid] dingo **2.** *UK* [teeth] en avant.

googly ['gu:glɪ] *n* [in cricket] balle *f* déviée ▪ **the boss bowled us a ~** *fig* le patron nous a joué un sale tour.

goolies△ ['gu:lɪ] *npl* roupettes *fpl*.

goon [gu:n] *n inf* **1.** [fool] abruti *m*, - e *f* **2.** *US* [hired thug] casseur *m (au service de quelqu'un)* ▪ **~ squad** [strike-breakers] milice *f* patronale.

goose [gu:s] *(pl* **geese** [gi:s]*)* ◇ *n* **1.** [bird] oie *f* ▪ **~ egg** *inf US* zéro *m* ▪ **to kill the ~ that lays the golden egg** tuer la poule aux œufs d'or **2.** *inf* [fool] : **don't be such a ~!** ne sois pas si bête!
◇ *vt US inf* [prod] : **to ~ sb** *donner un petit coup sur les fesses de quelqu'un pour le faire sursauter*.

gooseberry ['gʊzbərɪ] *n* **1.** BOT groseille *f* à maquereau **2.** [unwanted person] : **to play ~** tenir la chandelle.

gooseberry bush *n* groseillier *m*.

goose bumps *esp US inf* = **goose pimples**.

goose fat *n* graisse *f* d'oie.

gooseflesh ['gu:sfleʃ] *n (U)* = **goose pimples**.

goose pimples *npl UK* la chair de poule ▪ **to get** *OR* **to come out in ~** avoir la chair de poule.

goosestep ['gu:s,step] *(pret & pp* **goosestepped**, *cont* **goosestepping***)* ◇ *n* pas *m* de l'oie.
◇ *vi* faire le pas de l'oie.

GOP *(abbrev of* **Grand Old Party***)* *pr n le parti républicain aux États-Unis*.

gopher ['gəʊfər] *n* **1.** COMPUT gopher *m* **2.** [rodent] gaufre *m*, gauphre *m* **3.** [squirrel] spermophile *m* **4.** [tortoise] *espèce de tortues qui s'enfouissent dans le sol* **5.** *inf* = **gofer**.

gorblimey [gɔ:'blaɪmɪ] *UK inf interj* : **~!** mon Dieu!, mince!

Gordian knot ['gɔ:djən-] *n* nœud *m* gordien ▪ **to cut the ~** couper *OR* trancher le nœud gordien.

gore [gɔ:r] ◇ *n* **1.** [blood] sang *m* (coagulé) ▪ **his films are always full of blood and ~** il y a beaucoup de sang dans ses films **2.** SEW godet *m* ▪ NAUT pointe *f* (de voile) ▪ [land] langue *f* de terre.
◇ *vt* **1.** [wound] blesser à coups de cornes, encorner ▪ **he was ~d to death** il a été tué d'un coup de corne **2.** NAUT [sail] mettre une pointe à.

gored [gɔ:d] *adj* [skirt] à godets.

gorge [gɔ:dʒ] ◇ *n* GEOG défilé *m*, gorge *f*.
◇ *vt* : **to ~ o.s. (on sthg)** se gaver *OR* se gorger *OR* se bourrer (de qqch).

gorgeous ['gɔ:dʒəs] *adj* **1.** *inf* [wonderful - person, weather] magnifique, splendide, superbe ; [- flat, clothing] magnifique, très beau ; [- food, meal] délicieux **2.** [magnificent - fabric, clothing] somptueux.

Gorgon ['gɔ:gən] *pr n* MYTH : **the ~s** les Gorgones *fpl*.

gorilla [gə'rɪlə] *n* **1.** ZOOL gorille *m* **2.** *inf* [thug] voyou *m* ■ [bodyguard] gorille *m*.

Gorky ['gɔ:kɪ] *pr n* : **Maxim** ~ Maxime Gorki.

gormless ['gɔ:mlɪs] *adj* **UK** *inf* [person, expression] stupide, abruti.

gorse [gɔ:s] *n (U)* ajoncs *mpl* ■ **a ~ bush** un ajonc.

gory ['gɔ:rɪ] (*comp* **gorier**, *superl* **goriest**) *adj* [battle, scene, sight, death] sanglant ■ **spare me all the ~ details** *hum* épargne-moi les détails.

gosh [gɒʃ] *interj inf* ~! oh dis donc!, ça alors!, hé ben!

goshawk ['gɒshɔ:k] *n* autour *m*.

gosling ['gɒzlɪŋ] *n* oison *m*.

go-slow *n* **UK** grève *f* du zèle, grève *f* perlée.

gospel ['gɒspl] ◇ *n* **1.** *fig* **to take sthg as ~** prendre qqch pour parole d'évangile **2.** MUS gospel *m*.
◇ *comp* **1.** *fig* **the ~ truth** la vérité vraie **2.** MUS : **~ music** gospel *m*.
◆ **Gospel** ◇ *n* BIBLE : **the Gospel** l'Évangile *m* ■ **the Gospel according to St Mark** l'Évangile selon saint Marc.
◇ *comp* : **Gospel book** évangéliaire *m*.

gospeller *UK*, **gospeler** *US* ['gɒspələʳ] *n* évangéliste *m*.

gossamer ['gɒsəməʳ] ◇ *n (U)* [cobweb] fils *mpl* de la vierge, filandres *fpl* ■ [gauze] gaze *f* ■ [light cloth] étoffe *f* transparente.
◇ *comp* arachnéen, très léger, très fin.

gossip ['gɒsɪp] ◇ *n* **1.** *(U)* [casual chat] bavardage *m*, papotage *m* ■ *pej* [rumour] commérage *m*, ragots *mpl*, racontars *mpl* ■ [in newspaper] potins *mpl* ■ **to have a good ~** bien papoter ■ **have you heard the latest (bit of) ~?** vous connaissez la dernière (nouvelle) ? **2.** *pej* [person] bavard *m*, - e *f*, pie *f*, commère *f* ■ **he's such a ~!** quelle commère!
◇ *vi* bavarder, papoter ■ [maliciously] faire des commérages, dire du mal des gens ■ **people are always ~ing about their neighbours** les gens ont toujours des ragots à raconter sur leurs voisins.

gossip column *n* échos *mpl*.

gossip columnist *n* échotier *m*, - ère *f*.

gossiping ['gɒsɪpɪŋ] ◇ *adj* bavard ■ *pej* cancanier.
◇ *n (U)* bavardage *m*, papotage *m* ■ *pej* commérage *m*.

gossip writer = **gossip columnist**.

gossipy ['gɒsɪpɪ] *adj inf* [person] bavard ■ [letter] plein de bavardages ■ *pej* cancanier ■ [style] anecdotique.

got [gɒt] *pt & pp* ▷ **get**.

gotcha ['gɒtʃə] *interj inf* **1.** [I understand] : **~!** pigé! **2.** [cry of success] : **~!** ça y est (je l'ai)! ; [cry when catching sb] je te tiens!

Goth [gɒθ] *n* : **the ~s** les Goths *mpl*.

Gothic ['gɒθɪk] ◇ *adj* [gen - ARCHIT] & PRINT gothique ■ **~ novel** roman *m* gothique.
◇ *n* ARCHIT [gen] gothique *m* ■ LING gotique *m*, gothique *m*.

GOTHIC NOVEL

Genre littéraire, en vogue en Grande-Bretagne dans la seconde moitié du XVIIIᵉ siècle, caractérisé par des ambiances fantastiques, des événements mystérieux et violents, des atmosphères de ruine et de déclin.

gotta ['gɒtə] *US inf* = **have got a**, = **have got to**.

gotten ['gɒtn] *US & Scotland pp* ▷ **get**.

gouache [gʊ'ɑ:ʃ] *n* gouache *f*.

gouge [gaʊdʒ] ◇ *n* gouge *f*.
◇ *vt* [with gouge] gouger ■ **to ~ a hole** [intentionally] creuser un trou ; [accidentally] faire un trou.
◆ **gouge out** *vt sep* [with gouge] gouger, creuser (à la gouge) ■ [with thumb] évider, creuser ■ **to ~ sb's eyes out** crever les yeux à qqn.

goulash ['gu:læʃ] *n* goulache *m*, goulasch *m*.

gourd [gʊəd] *n* [plant] gourde *f*, cucurbitacée *f* ■ [fruit] gourde *f*, calebasse *f* ■ [container] gourde *f*, calebasse *f*.

gourmand ['gʊəmənd] *n* [glutton] gourmand *m*, - e *f* ■ [gourmet] gourmet *m*.

gourmet ['gʊəmeɪ] ◇ *n* gourmet *m*, gastronome *mf*.
◇ *comp* [meal, restaurant] gastronomique.

gout [gaʊt] *n (U)* MED goutte *f*.

gov [gʌv] *inf* = **governor** *(sense 2)*.

govern ['gʌvən] ◇ *vt* **1.** [country] gouverner, régner sur ■ [city, region, bank etc] gouverner ■ [affairs] administrer, gérer ■ [company, organization] diriger, gérer **2.** [determine - behaviour, choice, events, speed] déterminer **3.** [restrain - passions] maîtriser, dominer **4.** GRAM [case, mood] gouverner, régir **5.** TECH régler.
◇ *vi* COMM & POL gouverner, commander, diriger.

governance ['gʌvnəns] *n fml* gouvernement *m*, régime *m*.

governess ['gʌvənɪs] *n* gouvernante *f*.

governing ['gʌvənɪŋ] *adj* **1.** COMM & POL gouvernant, dirigeant ■ **the ~ party** le parti au pouvoir ■ **~ body** conseil *m* d'administration **2.** [factor] dominant ■ **the ~ principle** le principe directeur.

government ['gʌvnmənt] ◇ *n* **1.** [process of governing - country] gouvernement *m*, direction *f* ; [- company] administration *f*, gestion *f* ; [- affairs] conduite *f* **2.** POL [governing authority] gouvernement *m* ■ [type of authority] gouvernement *m*, régime *m* ■ [the State] gouvernement *m*, État *m* ■ **to form a ~** constituer OR former un gouvernement ■ **the Socialists have joined the coalition ~** les socialistes sont entrés dans le gouvernement de coalition ■ **democratic ~** la démocratie.
◇ *comp* [measure, policy] gouvernemental, du gouvernement ■ [borrowing, expenditure] de l'État, public ■ [minister, department] du gouvernement ■ **a ~-funded project** un projet subventionné par l'État ➜ **~ bonds** obligations *fpl* d'État, bons *mpl* du Trésor ■ **~ health warning** *avertissement officiel contre les dangers du tabac figurant sur les paquets de cigarettes et dans les publicités pour le tabac* ■ **'The Government Inspector'** *Gogol* 'le Revizor'.

governmental [,gʌvn'mentl] *adj* gouvernemental, du gouvernement.

Government House *n* **UK** palais *m* du gouverneur.

government issue *n* émission *f* d'État OR par le gouvernement ■ **~ uniform** uniforme *m* fourni par l'État.

governor ['gʌvənəʳ] *n* **1.** [of bank, country] gouverneur *m*, -e *f* ■ **UK** [of prison] directeur *m*, - trice *f* ■ **UK** [of school] membre *m* du conseil d'établissement ■ **State ~** *US* gouverneur *m*, -e *f* d'État **2.** **UK** *inf* [employer] patron *m*, boss *m* **3.** TECH régulateur *m*.

governor-general, Governor-General (*pl* **governor-generals**) *n* gouverneur *m*, -e *f* général(e).

governor-generalship *n* poste *m* de gouverneur général.

governorship ['gʌvənəʃɪp] *n* fonctions *fpl* de gouverneur.

govt (*written abbrev of* **government**) gvt.

gown [gaʊn] *n* **1.** [gen] robe *f* **2.** SCH & UNIV toge *f*.

goy [gɔɪ] (*pl* **goys** OR *pl* **goyim** ['gɔɪɪm]) *n* goy *mf*, goï *mf*.

GP (*abbrev of* **general practitioner**) *n* (médecin *m*) généraliste *m*.

GPMU (*abbrev of* **Graphical, Paper and Media Union**) *pr n* *syndicat britannique des ouvriers du livre*.

GPO (*abbrev of* **General Post Office**) *pr n* **1.** [in Britain] : **the ~** *titre officiel de la Poste britannique avant 1969* **2.** [in US] : **the ~** *les services postaux américains*.

GPS [,dʒi:pi:'es] (*abbrev of* **Global Positioning System**) *n* GPS *m*.

gr. *written abbr of* **gross**.

grab [græb] (*pret & pp* **grabbed**, *cont* **grabbing**) ◇ *vt* **1.** [object] saisir, s'emparer de ■ [person] attraper ■ **he grabbed the book out of my hand** il m'a arraché le livre des mains ■ **she**

grabbed my arm elle m'a attrapé par le bras **2.** *fig* [opportunity] saisir ▪ [attention] retenir ▪ [power] prendre ▪ [land] s'emparer de ▪ [quick meal] avaler, prendre (en vitesse) ▪ [taxi] prendre ▪ **I'll ~ a sandwich and work through the lunch hour** je vais me prendre un sandwich en vitesse et je travaillerai pendant l'heure du déjeuner **3.** *inf phr* **how does that ~ you?** qu'est-ce que tu en dis? ▪ **the film didn't really ~ me** le film ne m'a pas vraiment emballé.
◇ *vi* : **to ~ at sb/sthg** essayer d'agripper qqn/qqch ▪ **I grabbed at the chance** *fig* j'ai sauté sur l'occasion.
◇ *n* **1.** [movement] mouvement *m* vif ▪ [sudden theft] vol *m* (à l'arraché) ▪ **to make a ~ at** *OR* **for sthg** essayer de saisir *OR* faire un mouvement vif pour saisir qqch ➜ **to be up for ~s** *inf* être disponible **2.** *UK* TECH benne *f* preneuse.

grabby ['græbɪ] *adj inf pej* radin, pingre.

grace [greɪs] ◇ *n* **1.** [physical] grâce *f* ▪ [decency, politeness, tact] tact *m* ▪ **social ~s** bonnes manières *fpl* ▪ **to do sthg with good/bad ~** faire qqch de bonne/mauvaise grâce ▪ **at least he had the (good) ~ to apologize** il a au moins eu la décence de s'excuser **2.** RELIG grâce *f* ➜ **to fall from ~** RELIG perdre la grâce ; *fig* tomber en disgrâce ▪ **there but for the ~ of God (go I)** ça aurait très bien pu m'arriver aussi **3.** [amnesty] grâce *f* ▪ [respite] grâce *f*, répit *m* ▪ **we have two days' ~** nous disposons de deux jours de répit ▪ **days of ~** COMM jours *mpl* de grâce **4.** [prayer] : **to say ~** [before meals] dire le bénédicité ; [after meals] dire les grâces **5.** *phr* **to be in sb's good/bad ~s** être bien/mal vu par qqn.
◇ *vt* **1.** [honour] honorer ▪ **she ~d us with her presence** *hum* elle nous a honorés de sa présence **2.** *fml* & *lit* [adorn] orner, embellir ▪ **some exquisite watercolours ~d the walls** les murs étaient ornés de très jolies aquarelles.
◆ **Grace** *n* [term of address] : **Your Grace** [to Archbishop] Monseigneur *OR* (Votre) Excellence (l'Archevêque) ; [to Duke] Monsieur le duc ; [to Duchess] Madame la duchesse.
◆ **Graces** *npl* MYTH : **the three Graces** les trois Grâces *fpl*.

grace-and-favour *adj* *UK* : **~ residence** *logement appartenant à la Couronne et prêté à une personne que le souverain souhaite honorer.*

graceful ['greɪsfʊl] *adj* [person, movement] gracieux ▪ [language, style, apology] élégant.

gracefully ['greɪsfʊlɪ] *adv* [dance, move] avec grâce, gracieusement ▪ [apologize] avec élégance.

graceless ['greɪslɪs] *adj* [behaviour, person, movement] gauche.

grace note *n* note *f* d'agrément, ornement *m*.

gracious ['greɪʃəs] ◇ *adj* **1.** [generous, kind - gesture, smile] gracieux, bienveillant ; [- action] généreux ▪ **to be ~ to** *OR* **towards sb** faire preuve de bienveillance envers qqn ▪ **Your Gracious Majesty** Votre gracieuse Majesté **2.** [luxurious] : **~ living** la vie facile.
◇ *interj* : **(good** *OR* **goodness) ~ (me)!** mon Dieu!

graciously ['greɪʃəslɪ] *adv* [smile] gracieusement ▪ [accept, agree, allow] avec bonne grâce ▪ *fml* gracieusement ▪ RELIG miséricordieusement.

graciousness ['greɪʃəsnɪs] *n* [of person] bienveillance *f*, générosité *f*, gentillesse *f* ▪ [of action] grâce *f*, élégance *f* ▪ [of lifestyle, surroundings] élégance *f*, raffinement *m* ▪ RELIG miséricorde *f*, clémence *f*.

grad [græd] *n inf* = **graduate**.

gradable ['greɪdəbl] *adj* **1.** [capable of being graded] qui peut être classé **2.** LING comparatif.

gradate [grə'deɪt] ◇ *vt* graduer.
◇ *vi* être gradué.

gradation [grə'deɪʃn] *n* gradation *f*, progression *f*, échelonnement *m* ▪ [stage] gradation *f*, degré *m*, palier *m* ▪ LING alternance *f* (vocalique), apophonie *f*.

grade [greɪd] ◇ *n* **1.** [level] degré *m*, niveau *m* ▪ [on scale] échelon *m*, grade *m* ▪ [on salary scale] indice *m* **2.** MIL grade *m*, rang *m*, échelon *m* ▪ [in hierarchy] échelon *m*, catégorie *f* **3.** [quality - of product] qualité *f*, catégorie *f* ; [- of petrol] grade *m* ▪ [size of products] calibre *m* ▪ **grade A potatoes** pommes de terre de qualité A **4.** *US* SCH [mark] note *f* ▪ [year] année *f*, classe *f* ▪ **a ~ A student** un excellent élève ▪ **he's in fifth ~** ≃ il est en CM2 **5.** *US* = **grade school 6.** MATHS grade *m* **7.** *US* [gradient] déclivité *f*, pente *f* ▪ RAIL rampe *f* **8.** *phr* **to make the ~** être à la hauteur.
◇ *vt* **1.** [classify - by quality] classer ; [- by size] calibrer ▪ [arrange in order] classer ▪ **to ~ food/questions** classer de la nourriture/des questions **2.** SCH [mark] noter **3.** [cross - livestock] améliorer par sélection **4.** [level] niveler ▪ **to ~ the ground** niveler le terrain.

grade crossing *n US* RAIL passage *m* à niveau.

grader ['greɪdə^r] *n* **1.** *US* SCH [marker of exams] correcteur *m*, - trice *f* ▪ [member of a grade] : **fourth ~** élève *mf* de 4e année *(CM1)* **2.** TECH grader *m*, niveleuse *f*.

grade school *n US* école *f* primaire.

gradient ['greɪdjənt] *n* **1.** *UK* [road] déclivité *f*, pente *f*, inclinaison *f* ▪ RAIL rampe *f*, pente *f*, inclinaison *f* ▪ **a steep ~** une ligne à forte pente ▪ **a ~ of three in ten** *OR* **30%** une pente de 30% **2.** METEOR & PHYS gradient *m*.

gradient post *n* RAIL indicateur *m* de pente.

grading ['greɪdɪŋ] *n* [classification] classification *f* ▪ [by size] calibration *f* ▪ SCH notation *f*.

gradual ['grædʒʊəl] ◇ *adj* [change, improvement] graduel, progressif ▪ [slope] doux, douce *f*.
◇ *n* RELIG graduel *m*.

gradualism ['grædʒʊəlɪzm] *n* gradualisme *m* ▪ POL réformisme *m*.

gradually ['grædʒʊəlɪ] *adv* progressivement, petit à petit, peu à peu.

gradualness ['grædʒʊəlnɪs] *n* progressivité *f*.

graduand ['grædʒʊənd] *n UK* UNIV candidat *m*, - e *f*, postulant *m*, - e *f*, prétendant *m*, - e *f*.

graduate ◇ *n* ['grædʒʊət] **1.** UNIV licencié *m*, - e *f*, diplômé *m*, - e *f* ▪ *US* SCH bachelier *m*, - ère *f* ▪ **she's an Oxford ~** *OR* **a ~ of Oxford** elle a fait ses études à Oxford **2.** *US* [container] récipient *m* gradué.
◇ *adj* UNIV diplômé, licencié ▪ **~ school** *US école où l'on poursuit ses études après la licence* ▪ **~ student** étudiant de deuxième/troisième cycle.
◇ *vi* ['grædjʊeɪt] **1.** UNIV ≃ obtenir son diplôme/sa licence ▪ *US* SCH ≃ obtenir le *OR* être reçu au baccalauréat ▪ **she ~d from the Sorbonne** elle a un diplôme de la Sorbonne ▪ **he ~d in linguistics** il a une licence de linguistique **2.** [gain promotion] être promu, passer ▪ **I've ~d from cheap plonk to good wines** *inf fig* je suis passé du gros rouge aux bons vins.
◇ *vt* ['grædjʊeɪt] **1.** [calibrate] graduer **2.** [change, improvement] graduer **3.** *US* SCH & UNIV conférer *OR* accorder un diplôme à.

graduated ['grædjʊeɪtɪd] *adj* [tax] progressif ▪ [measuring container, exercise, thermometer] gradué ▪ [colours] dégradé.

graduation [,grædʒʊ'eɪʃn] ◇ *n* **1.** [gen] graduation *f* **2.** UNIV *US* SCH [ceremony] (cérémonie *f* de) remise *f* des diplômes.
◇ *comp* : **~ day** jour *m* de la remise des diplômes.

Graeco- [,gri:kəʊ] *in cpds* gréco- ▪ **~Roman** gréco-romain.

graffiti [grə'fi:tɪ] *n (U)* graffiti *mpl*.

graft [grɑ:ft] ◇ *n* **1.** HORT greffe *f*, greffon *m* ▪ MED greffe *f* **2.** *inf (U)* [corruption] magouilles *fpl* **3.** *inf (U) UK inf* [hard work] travail *m* pénible.
◇ *vt* **1.** HORT & MED greffer ▪ **they ~ed a piece of skin onto his face** ils lui ont greffé un bout de peau sur le visage **2.** [obtain by corruption] obtenir par la corruption.
◇ *vi* **1.** [be involved in bribery] donner *OR* recevoir des pots-de-vin **2.** HORT & MED : **pears ~ fairly easily** les poires se greffent assez facilement **3.** *UK inf* [work hard] bosser dur.

grafter ['grɑ:ftə^r] *n* **1.** BOT [instrument] greffoir *m* **2.** *inf* [hard worker] bourreau *m* de travail **3.** *inf* [corrupt person] corrupteur *m*, escroc *m* ▪ [corrupt official] fonctionnaire *m* corrompu, concussionnaire *m*.

graham flour ['greɪəm-] *n* ***US*** farine *f* brute.

Grail [greɪl] *n* Graal *m*.

grain [greɪn] ◇ *n* **1.** *(U)* [seeds of rice, wheat] grain *m* ■ [cereal] céréales *fpl* ■ ***US*** blé *m* **2.** [single] grain *m* ■ [particle] grain *m* **3.** ***fig*** [of madness, sense, truth etc] grain *m*, brin *m* ■ **a few ~s of comfort** une petite consolation **4.** [in leather, stone, wood etc] grain *m* ■ PHOT grain *m* ■ **I'll help you, but it goes against the ~** je vous aiderai, mais ce n'est pas de bon cœur **5.** ***UK*** [weight] ≃ grain *m (poids)*.
◇ *vt* **1.** [salt] cristalliser **2.** [leather, paper] greneler ■ [to paint to imitate wood] veiner.
◇ *vi* se cristalliser.

grain alcohol *n* alcool *m* de grains.

grain elevator *n* silo *m* à céréales.

grainy ['greɪnɪ] (*comp* **grainier**, *superl* **grainiest**) *adj* [surface, texture - of wood] veineux ; [- of stone] grenu, granuleux ; [- of leather, paper] grenu, grené ■ PHOT qui a du grain.

gram [græm] *n* **1.** [metric unit] gramme *m* **2.** BOT [plant] pois *m* ■ [seed] pois *m*, graine *f* de pois.

grammar ['græməʳ] *n* **1.** LING grammaire *f* ■ **that's not very good ~** ce n'est pas très correct du point de vue grammatical **2.** [book] grammaire *f*.

grammar checker *n* COMPUT vérificateur *m* grammatical.

grammarian [grə'meərɪən] *n* grammairien *m*, - enne *f*.

grammar school *n* [in UK] *type d'école secondaire* ■ [in US] *école primaire*.

GRAMMAR SCHOOL

En Grande-Bretagne, ces écoles secondaires peuvent recevoir le soutien de l'État, mais elles demeurent indépendantes. L'enseignement qui y est dispensé est de haut niveau, traditionnel et prépare aux études supérieures ; on y entre sur concours ou sur dossier. Les élèves des ***grammar schools*** représentent moins de cinq pour cent de l'ensemble des élèves britanniques.

grammatical [grə'mætɪkl] *adj* grammatical.

grammaticality [grə,mætɪ'kælətɪ] *n* grammaticalité *f*.

grammatically [grə'mætɪklɪ] *adv* grammaticalement, du point de vue grammatical.

gramme [græm] = **gram** *(sense 1)*.

Grammy ['græmɪ] *n* : **~ (award)** *distinction récompensant les meilleures œuvres musicales américaines de l'année (classique exclu)*.

gramophone ['græməfəun] ***UK dated*** ◇ *n* gramophone *m*, phonographe *m*.
◇ *comp* : **~ needle** aiguille *f* de phonographe ***OR*** de gramophone ■ **~ record** disque *m*.

gramps [græmps] *n* ***inf*** papy *m*, pépé *m*.

grampus ['græmpəs] *n* épaulard *m*, orque *f*.

gran [græn] *n* ***UK inf*** mamie *f*, mémé *f*.

Granada [grə'nɑ:də] *pr n* Grenade.

granary ['grænərɪ] ◇ *n* grenier *m* à blé, silo *m* (à céréales).
◇ *comp* : **~ bread**, **~ loaf** pain *m* aux céréales.

grand [grænd] ◇ *adj* **1.** [impressive - house] magnifique ; [- style] grand, noble ; [- music, occasion] grand ■ [pretentious, self-important] suffisant, prétentieux ■ [dignified, majestic] majestueux, digne ■ **to do sthg in ~ style** faire qqch en grande pompe ■ **she likes to do things on a ~ scale** elle aime faire les choses en grand **2.** ***UK dated*** & ***dial*** [wonderful] super **3.** ***phr*** **that comes to a ~ total of £536** ça fait en tout 536 livres.
◇ *n* ***UK inf*** mille livres *fpl* ■ ***US*** mille dollars *mpl*.

grandad ['grændæd] *n* ***inf*** pépé *m*, papy *m*.

grandaddy ['grændædɪ] *n* ***inf*** **1.** = **grandad** **2.** [most ancient] ancêtre *m* ■ **it's the ~ of them all** c'est leur ancêtre à tous.

Grand Canyon *pr n* : **the ~** le Grand Canyon ■ **the Grand Canyon State** l'Arizona *m*.

grandchild ['grændtʃaɪld] (*pl* **grandchildren** [-,tʃɪldrən]) *n* petit-fils *m*, petite-fille *f* ■ **she has six grandchildren** elle a six petits-enfants.

granddad ['grændæd] ***inf*** = **grandad**.

granddaddy ['grændædɪ] ***inf*** = **grandaddy**.

granddaughter ['græn,dɔ:təʳ] *n* petite-fille *f*.

grand duchess *n* grande-duchesse *f*.

grand duchy *n* grand-duché *m*.

grand duke *n* grand-duc *m*.

grandee [græn'di:] *n* grand *m* d'Espagne.

grandeur ['grændʒəʳ] *n* [of person] grandeur *f*, noblesse *f* ■ [of building, scenery] splendeur *f*, magnificence *f* ■ **an air of ~** un air de grandeur.

grandfather ['grænd,fɑ:ðəʳ] *n* grand-père *m*.

grandfather clock *n* horloge *f* (de parquet).

grand finale *n* apothéose *f*.

grandiloquence [græn'dɪləkwəns] *n* ***fml*** grandiloquence *f*.

grandiloquent [græn'dɪləkwənt] *adj* ***fml*** grandiloquent.

grandiose ['grændɪəuz] *adj* ***pej*** [building, style, plan] grandiose.

grand jury *n* [in US] jury *m* d'accusation.

grand larceny *n* ***US*** vol *m* qualifié.

grandly ['grændlɪ] *adv* [behave, say] avec grandeur ■ [live] avec faste ■ [dress] avec panache.

grandma ['grænmɑ:] *n* ***inf*** grand-mère *f*, mémé *f*, mamie *f*.

grandmama ['grænmə,mɑ:] *n* ***inf*** grand-mère *f*.

grandmaster ['grænd,mɑ:stəʳ] *n* [of chess] grand maître *m*.

Grand Master *n* [of masonic lodge] Grand Maître *m*.

grandmother ['græn,mʌðəʳ] *n* grand-mère *f*.

Grand National *pr n* : **the ~** *la plus importante course d'obstacles de Grande-Bretagne, qui se déroule à Aintree, dans la banlieue de Liverpool*.

grandnephew ['græn,nefju:] *n* petit-neveu *m*.

grandness ['grændnɪs] *n* [of behaviour] grandeur *f*, noblesse *f* ■ [of lifestyle] faste *m* ■ [of appearance] panache *m*.

grandniece ['grænni:s] *n* petite-nièce *f*.

Grand Old Party *pr n* ***US*** POL : **the ~** le parti républicain.

grand opera *n* grand opéra *m*.

grandpa ['grænpɑ:] ***inf*** = **grandad**.

grandpapa ['grænpə,pɑ:] *n* ***inf*** grand-père *m*.

grandparent ['græn,peərənt] *n* : **my ~s** mes grands-parents *mpl*.

grand piano *n* piano *m* à queue.

grand prix [,grɒn'pri:] (*pl* **grands prix** [,grɒn'pri:]) ◇ *n* grand prix *m*.
◇ *comp* : **~ racing** course *f* de grand prix.

grand slam *n* grand chelem *m*.

grandson ['grænsʌn] *n* petit-fils *m*.

grandstand ['grændstænd] ◇ *n* tribune *f*.
◇ *vi* ***US*** faire l'intéressant.

grandstand view *n* : **to have a ~ (of sthg)** être aux premières loges (pour voir qqch).

grand tour *n* : **she did *OR* went on a ~ of Italy** elle a visité toute l'Italie ➊ **the Grand Tour** le tour d'Europe.

grange [greɪndʒ] *n* **1.** ***UK*** [country house] manoir *m* ■ [farmhouse] ferme *f* **2.** ***US*** [farm] ferme *f* **3.** ***arch*** [granary] grenier *m* à blé, grange *f*.

granite ['grænɪt] <> *n* granit *m*, granite *m* ▪ **the Granite State** le New Hampshire.
<> *comp* de granit *OR* granite.

granny, grannie ['grænɪ] *n inf* mamie *f*, mémé *f*.

granny bond *n UK type d'obligation visant le marché des retraités.*

granny dumping *n abandon d'une personne âgée qu'on a à charge.*

granny flat *n UK* appartement *m* indépendant *(dans une maison).*

granny knot *n* nœud *m* de vache.

Granny Smith *n* granny-smith *f inv*.

granola [grə'nəʊlə] *n US* muesli *m*.

grant [grɑːnt] <> *vt* **1.** [permission, wish] accorder ▪ [request] accorder, accéder à ▪ [goal, point - SPORT] accorder ▪ [credit, loan, pension] accorder ▪ [charter, favour, privilege, right] accorder, octroyer, concéder ▪ [property] céder ▪ **to ~ sb permission to do sthg** accorder à qqn l'autorisation de faire qqch ▪ **to ~ sb their request** accéder à la requête de qqn **2.** [accept as true] accorder, admettre, concéder ▪ **I'll ~ you that point** je vous concède ce point ▪ **~ed, he's not very intelligent, but...** d'accord, il n'est pas très intelligent, mais... ▪ **~ed!** d'accord!, soit! **3.** *phr* **to take sthg for ~ed** considérer que qqch va de soi, tenir qqch pour certain *OR* établi ▪ **you seem to take it for ~ed he'll agree** vous semblez convaincu qu'il sera d'accord ▪ **to take sb for ~ed** ne plus faire cas de qqn ▪ **he takes her for ~ed** il la traite comme si elle n'existait pas ▪ **you take me too much for ~ed** vous ne vous rendez pas compte de tout ce que je fais pour vous.
<> *n* **1.** [money given] subvention *f*, allocation *f* ▪ [to student] bourse *f* **2.** [transfer - of property] cession *f* ; [- of land] concession *f* ▪ [permission] octroi *m* ▪ **~ of probate** validation *f OR* homologation *f* d'un testament.

grant-maintained *adj* subventionné *(par l'État)* ▪ **~ school** école privée *f* subventionnée *(acceptant en échange un droit de regard de l'État sur la gestion de ses affaires).*

grantor [grɑːn'tɔːr] *n* cédant *m*, - e *f*, donateur *m*, - trice *f*.

granular ['grænjʊlər] *adj* [surface] granuleux, granulaire ▪ [structure] grenu.

granulate ['grænjʊleɪt] *vt* [lead, powder, tin] granuler ▪ [salt, sugar] grener, grainer ▪ [surface] grener, greneler, rendre grenu.

granulated sugar ['grænjʊleɪtɪd-] *n* sucre *m* semoule.

granule ['grænjuːl] *n* granule *m*.

grape [greɪp] *n* **1.** [fruit] grain *m* de raisin ▪ **black/white ~s** du raisin noir/blanc ➋ **~ harvest** *OR* **picking** vendanges *fpl* ▪ **~ juice** jus *m* de raisin ▪ **'The Grapes of Wrath'** *Steinbeck* 'les Raisins de la colère' **2.** *(U)* = **grapeshot**.

grapefruit ['greɪpfruːt] *n* pamplemousse *m f*.

grape hyacinth *n* muscari *m*.

grapeshot ['greɪpʃɒt] *n* mitraille *f*.

grapevine ['greɪpvaɪn] *n* vigne *f* ▪ **to hear sthg through** *OR* **on the ~** entendre dire qqch.

graph [grɑːf] <> *n* **1.** [diagram] graphique *m*, courbe *f* **2.** LING graphie *f*.
<> *vt* mettre en graphique, tracer.

grapheme ['græfiːm] *n* LING graphème *m*.

graphic ['græfɪk] *adj* **1.** MATHS graphique **2.** [vivid] imagé.
◆ **graphics** <> *n (U)* [drawing] art *m* graphique.
<> *npl* MATHS (utilisation *f* des) graphiques *mpl* ▪ [drawings] représentations *fpl* graphiques ▪ COMPUT infographie *f*.

graphically ['græfɪklɪ] *adv* **1.** MATHS graphiquement **2.** [vividly] de façon très imagée.

graphic artist *n* graphiste *mf*.

graphic arts *npl* arts *mpl* graphiques.

graphic design *n* conception *f* graphique.

graphic designer *n* graphiste *mf*, maquettiste *mf*.

graphic equalizer *n* égaliseur *m* graphique.

graphic novel *n* bande *f* dessinée.

graphics card ['græfɪks-] *n* COMPUT carte *f* graphique.

graphite ['græfaɪt] <> *n* graphite *m*, mine *f* de plomb.
<> *adj* en graphite.

graphologist [græ'fɒlədʒɪst] *n* graphologue *mf*.

graphology [græ'fɒlədʒɪ] *n* graphologie *f*.

graph paper *n* papier *m* quadrillé ▪ [in millimetres] papier *m* millimétré.

grapnel ['græpnl] *n* grappin *m*.

grapple ['græpl] <> *n* TECH grappin *m*.
<> *vt* **1.** TECH saisir avec un grappin **2.** *US* [person] : **to ~ sb** saisir qqn contre soi.
<> *vi* **1.** [physically] : **to ~ with sb** en venir aux mains avec qqn **2.** *fig* **to ~ with a problem** être aux prises avec un problème.

grappling iron ['græplɪŋ-] = **grapnel**.

grasp [grɑːsp] <> *vt* **1.** [physically] saisir ▪ **to ~ (hold of) sthg** saisir qqch ▪ [opportunity] saisir ▪ [power] se saisir de, s'emparer de **2.** [understand] saisir, comprendre ▪ **I didn't quite ~ what she meant** je n'ai pas bien compris *OR* saisi ce qu'elle a voulu dire.
<> *n* **1.** [grip] (forte) poigne *f* ▪ [action of holding] prise *f*, étreinte *f* ▪ **to have sb in one's ~** *fig* avoir *OR* tenir qqn en son pouvoir ▪ **to have sthg in one's ~** avoir prise sur qqch **2.** *fig* [reach] portée *f* ▪ **within/beyond sb's ~** à la portée/hors de (la) portée de qqn **3.** [understanding] compréhension *f* ▪ **she has a thorough ~ of the subject** elle a une connaissance approfondie de la question **4.** [handle] poignée *f*.
◆ **grasp at** *vt insep* [attempt to seize] chercher à saisir, essayer de saisir ▪ [accept eagerly] saisir ▪ **to ~ at an opportunity** sauter sur *OR* saisir l'occasion.

grasping ['grɑːspɪŋ] *adj* avare, avide.

grass [grɑːs] <> *n* **1.** [gen] herbe *f* ▪ [lawn] pelouse *f*, gazon *m* ▪ **'keep off the ~'** 'défense de marcher sur la pelouse', 'pelouse interdite' ➋ **to put out to ~ : to put cattle/sheep out to ~** mettre le bétail/les moutons au pré ▪ **to put sb out to ~** mettre qqn au repos ▪ **he doesn't let the ~ grow under his feet** il ne perd pas de temps ▪ **the ~ is always greener (on the other side of the fence)** *prov* on n'est jamais content de son sort, on jalouse toujours le sort du voisin **2.** BOT : **~es** graminées *fpl* **3.** △ [marijuana] herbe△ *f* **4.** △ *UK* [informer] mouchard *m*, indic△ *m*.
<> *vt* **1.** : **to ~ (over)** [field] enherber, mettre en pré ; [garden] gazonner, engazonner **2.** *US* [animals] mettre au vert **3.** TEX herber, blanchir au pré.
<> *vi*△ *UK* cafarder ▪ **to ~ on sb** donner *OR* vendre qqn△.

grass court *n* court *m* (en gazon).

grasshopper ['grɑːs,hɒpər] *n* sauterelle *f*, grillon *m*.

grassland ['grɑːslænd] *n* prairie *f*, pré *m*.

grass roots POL <> *npl* : **the ~** la base.
<> *comp* : **at (the) ~ level** au niveau de la base ▪ **~ opposition/support** résistance *f* /soutien *m* de la base.

grass skirt *n* pagne *m (de feuilles).*

grass snake *n* couleuvre *f*.

grassy ['grɑːsɪ] *adj* herbu, herbeux.

grate [greɪt] <> *n* [fireplace] foyer *m*, âtre *m* ▪ [for holding coal] grille *f* de foyer.
<> *vt* **1.** CULIN râper **2.** [chalk, metal] faire grincer.
<> *vi* **1.** [machine, metal] grincer ▪ **to ~ on the ears** écorcher les oreilles **2.** *fig* **the baby's crying began to ~ (on him)** les pleurs du bébé ont commencé à l'agacer ▪ **his behaviour ~s after a while** son comportement est agaçant au bout d'un moment.

grateful ['greɪtfʊl] *adj* reconnaissant ▪ **to be ~ towards** *OR* **to sb for sthg** être reconnaissant envers qqn de qqch ▪ **I would be most** *OR* **very ~ if you would help me** je vous serais très reconnaissant de m'aider ■ **with ~ thanks** avec toute ma reconnaissance, avec mes sincères remerciements ■ **be ~ for what you've got** estime-toi heureux avec ce que tu as.

gratefully ['greɪtfʊlɪ] *adv* avec reconnaissance *OR* gratitude.

grater ['greɪtəʳ] *n* râpe *f* ■ **cheese ~** râpe *f* à fromage.

gratification [ˌgrætɪfɪ'keɪʃn] *n* [state or action] satisfaction *f*, plaisir *m* ■ PSYCHOL gratification *f* ■ **I noticed to my ~ that...** à ma grande satisfaction, j'ai remarqué que...

gratify ['grætɪfaɪ] *vt* **1.** [person] faire plaisir à, être agréable à ■ **I was gratified with** *OR* **at the result** j'ai été très content *OR* satisfait du résultat **2.** [whim, wish] satisfaire.

gratifying ['grætɪfaɪɪŋ] *adj* agréable, plaisant ■ PSYCHOL gratifiant ■ **it's ~ to know that...** c'est agréable *OR* ça fait plaisir de savoir que...

grating ['greɪtɪŋ] ◇ *n* grille *f*, grillage *m*.
◇ *adj* [irritating] agaçant, irritant, énervant ■ [sound] grinçant, discordant ■ [voice] discordant.

gratis ['grætɪs] ◇ *adj* gratuit.
◇ *adv* gratuitement.

gratitude ['grætɪtju:d] *n* gratitude *f*, reconnaissance *f* ■ **to show/to express one's ~ towards sb for sthg** témoigner/exprimer sa gratitude envers qqn pour qqch.

gratuitous [grə'tju:ɪtəs] *adj* [unjustified] gratuit, sans motif, injustifié ■ **~ violence** violence *f* gratuite.

gratuitously [grə'tju:ɪtəslɪ] *adv* [without good reason] gratuitement, sans motif.

gratuity [grə'tju:ətɪ] *n* **1.** *fml* [tip] gratification *f*, pourboire *m* **2.** *UK* [payment to employee] prime *f* ■ MIL peine *f* de démobilisation.

grave¹ [greɪv] ◇ *n* [hole] fosse *f* ■ [burial place] tombe *f* ■ **from beyond the ~** d'outre-tombe ➋ **mass ~** fosse *f* commune ■ **to turn in one's ~** se retourner dans sa tombe ■ **somebody has just walked over my ~** j'ai le frisson.
◇ *adj* grave, sérieux.

grave² [grɑ:v] LING ◇ *n* : **~ (accent)** accent *m* grave.
◇ *adj* grave.

gravedigger ['greɪvˌdɪgəʳ] *n* fossoyeur *m*.

gravel ['grævl] (*UK pret & pp* **gravelled**, *cont* **gravelling**) (*US pret & pp* **graveled**, *cont* **graveling**) ◇ *n* gravier *m* ■ [finer] gravillon *m* ■ MED gravelle *f*.
◇ *comp* : **~ path** chemin *m* de gravier ■ **~ pit** gravière *f*, carrière *f* de gravier.
◇ *vt* gravillonner, répandre du gravier sur.

gravelly ['grævəlɪ] *adj* **1.** [like or containing gravel] graveleux ■ [road] de gravier ■ [riverbed] caillouteux **2.** [voice] rauque, râpeux.

gravely ['greɪvlɪ] *adv* **1.** [speak] gravement, sérieusement **2.** [as intensifier - ill] gravement ; [- wounded] grièvement.

graven ['greɪvn] *adj arch & lit* **~ on my memory** gravé dans ma mémoire.

graven image *n* RELIG idole *f*, image *f*.

grave robber [greɪv-] *n* voleur *m* de cadavres *(qui les déterre et les vend pour dissection)*.

graveside ['greɪvsaɪd] *n* : **at sb's ~** sur la tombe de qqn.

gravestone ['greɪvstəʊn] *n* pierre *f* tombale.

graveyard ['greɪvjɑ:d] *n liter & fig* cimetière *m*.

graveyard shift *n* travail *m* de nuit ■ **to be on the ~** faire partie de l'équipe de nuit.

graving dock ['greɪvɪŋ-] *n* NAUT bassin *m* de radoub.

gravitate ['grævɪteɪt] *vi* graviter ■ **many young people ~ to the big cities** beaucoup de jeunes sont attirés par les grandes villes.

gravitation [ˌgrævɪ'teɪʃn] *n* gravitation *f*.

gravitational [ˌgrævɪ'teɪʃənl] *adj* gravitationnel, de gravitation.

gravitational field *n* champ *m* de gravitation.

gravitational force *n* force *f* de gravitation *OR* gravitationnelle.

gravity ['grævətɪ] *n* **1.** [seriousness] gravité *f* ■ **I don't think you appreciate the ~ of the situation** je n'ai pas l'impression que tu te rendes compte de *OR* que tu réalises la gravité de la situation **2.** PHYS [force] pesanteur *f* ■ [phenomenon] gravitation *f* ■ **the law of ~** la loi de la pesanteur.

gravity feed *n* alimentation *f* par gravité.

gravy ['greɪvɪ] *n* **1.** CULIN sauce *f (au jus de viande)* **2.**△ *US* [easy money] bénef△ *m* ■ **it's ~** [easy] c'est du gâteau.

gravy boat *n* saucière *f*.

gravy train *n inf* assiette *f* au beurre ■ **to get on the ~** être à la recherche d'un bon filon.

gray *etc US* = **grey**.

grayling ['greɪlɪŋ] *n* [fish] ombre *m*.

graze [greɪz] ◇ *vi* [animals] brouter, paître, pâturer.
◇ *vt* **1.** [touch lightly] frôler, effleurer, raser ■ **the boat just ~d the bottom** le bateau a effleuré le fond **2.** [skin] érafler, écorcher ■ **she ~d her elbow on the wall** elle s'est écorché le coude sur le mur **3.** [animals] faire paître ■ [grass] brouter, paître ■ [field] pâturer.
◇ *n* écorchure *f*, éraflure *f* ■ **it's just a ~** c'est juste un peu écorché.

grazing ['greɪzɪŋ] *n* [grass for animals] pâturage *m* ■ [land] pâture *f*, pâturage *m*.

grease [gri:s] ◇ *n* [gen] graisse *f* ■ [lubricant - AUT] graisse *f*, lubrifiant *m* ■ [used lubricant] cambouis *m* ■ [dirt] crasse *f* ■ **to remove (the) ~ from sthg** dégraisser qqch.
◇ *vt* [gen] graisser ■ AUT graisser, lubrifier.

grease gun *n* (pistolet *m*) graisseur *m*, pompe *f* à graisse.

grease monkey *n inf* mécano *m*.

grease nipple *n* graisseur *m*.

greasepaint ['gri:speɪnt] *n* THEAT fard *m* (gras).

greaseproof ['gri:spru:f] *adj UK* imperméable à la graisse ■ **~ paper** CULIN papier *m* sulfurisé.

greaser ['gri:səʳ] *n inf* **1.** [mechanic] graisseur *m*, mécano *m* **2.** *UK* [rocker] rocker *m* **3.** ▲ *US terme injurieux désignant une personne d'origine latino-américaine.*

greasy ['gri:sɪ] *adj* **1.** [food, substance] graisseux, gras, grasse *f* ■ [tools] graisseux ■ [cosmetics, hair, hands] gras, grasse *f* ■ **the ~ pole** SPORT & *fig* le mât de cocagne **2.** [pavement, road] gras *f*, grasse *f*, glissant **3.** [clothes - dirty] crasseux, poisseux ; [- covered in grease marks] taché de graisse, plein de graisse **4.** [obsequious] obséquieux.

greasy spoon *n inf* gargote *f*.

great [greɪt] (*comp* **greater**, *superl* **greatest**) ◇ *adj* **1.** [in size, scale] grand ■ **the ~ fire of London** le grand incendie de Londres ■ **he made a ~ effort to be nice** il a fait un gros effort pour être agréable
2. [in degree] : **a ~ friend** un grand ami ■ **there's ~ ignorance about the problem** les gens ne sont pas conscients du problème ■ **she's got ~ willpower** elle est très volontaire ■ **to my ~ satisfaction** à ma grande satisfaction ■ **with ~ pleasure** avec grand plaisir ■ **to be in ~ pain** souffrir (beaucoup)
3. [in quantity] : **a ~ number of** un grand nombre de ■ **a ~ crowd** une grande *OR* grosse foule, une foule nombreuse
4. [important - person, event] grand ■ **Alfred the Great** Alfred le Grand ■ **a ~ occasion** une grande occasion
5. [main] : **the ~ hall** la grande salle, la salle principale ■ **France's ~est footballer** le plus grand footballeur français
6. *inf* [term of approval] : **she has a ~ voice** elle a une voix magnifique ■ **she's ~!** [nice person] elle est super!, je l'adore! ■ **what's that film like? – ~!** comment est ce film? – génial! ■ **it**

would be ~ to have lots of money ce serait super d'avoir beaucoup d'argent ■ **you look ~ tonight!** [appearance] tu es magnifique ce soir!
7. [keen] : **she's a ~ reader** elle adore lire, elle lit beaucoup ■ **she's a ~ one for television** elle adore la télévision
8. *inf* [good at or expert on] : **he's ~ at languages** il est très doué pour les langues ■ **she's ~ on sculpture** elle s'y connaît vraiment en sculpture
9. [in exclamations] : **Great Scott!** grands dieux!
10. ZOOL : **the ~ apes** les grands singes.
◇ *n* : **it's one of the all-time ~s** c'est un des plus grands classiques ■ **she's one of the all-time ~s** c'est une des plus grandes stars.
◇ *adv* [as intensifier] : **a ~ big fish** un énorme poisson ■ **an enormous ~ house** une maison immense.

great auk *n* grand pingouin *m*.

great-aunt *n* grand-tante *f*.

Great Barrier Reef *pr n* : **the ~** la Grande Barrière.

Great Bear *pr n* : **the ~** la Grande Ourse.

Great Bear Lake *pr n* le grand lac de l'Ours.

Great Britain *pr n* Grande-Bretagne *f* ■ **in ~** en Grande-Bretagne.

great circle *n* grand cercle *m*.

greatcoat ['greɪtkəʊt] *n* pardessus *m*, manteau *m* ■ MIL manteau *m*, capote *f*.

Great Dane *n* danois *m*.

greater ['greɪtər] *compar* ▷ **great**.

Greater London *pr n* le Grand Londres.

greatest ['greɪtɪst] *superl* ▷ **great**.

great-grandchild *n* arrière-petit-fils *m*, arrière-petite-fille *f* ■ **great-grandchildren** arrière-petits-enfants *mpl*.

great-granddaughter *n* arrière-petite-fille *f*.

great-grandfather *n* arrière-grand-père *m*.

great-grandmother *n* arrière-grand-mère *f*.

great-grandparents *npl* arrière-grands-parents *mpl*.

great-grandson *n* arrière-petit-fils *m*.

great-great-granddaughter *n* arrière-arrière-petite-fille *f*.

great-great-grandfather *n* arrière-arrière-grand-père *m*.

great-great-grandmother *n* arrière-arrière-grand-mère *f*.

great-great-grandparents *npl* arrière-arrière-grands-parents *mpl*.

great-great-grandson *n* arrière-arrière-petit-fils *m*.

Great Lakes *pr npl* : **the ~** les Grands Lacs *mpl*.

greatly ['greɪtlɪ] *adv* très, beaucoup, fortement ■ **I was ~ impressed by her work** j'ai été très impressionné par son travail, son travail m'a beaucoup impressionné ■ **~ improved** beaucoup amélioré ■ **you'll be ~ missed** vous nous manquerez beaucoup.

great-nephew *n* petit-neveu *m*.

greatness ['greɪtnɪs] *n* **1.** [size] grandeur *f*, énormité *f*, immensité *f* ■ [intensity] intensité *f* **2.** [eminence] grandeur *f*, importance *f* ■ **he never achieved ~ as an artist** il n'est jamais devenu un grand artiste.

great-niece *n* petite-nièce *f*.

Great Plains *pr npl* : **the ~** les Grandes Plaines *fpl*.

great power *n* grande puissance *f* ■ **the Great Powers** les grandes puissances.

great tit *n* mésange *f* charbonnière.

great-uncle *n* grand-oncle *m*.

Great Wall of China *pr n* : **the ~** la Grande Muraille (de Chine).

Great War *n* : **the ~** la Grande Guerre, la guerre de 14 *OR* de 14-18.

grebe [gri:b] *n* grèbe *m*.

Grecian ['gri:ʃn] ◇ *adj* grec, grecque *f*.
◇ *n* Grec *m*, Grecque *f*.

Greco ['grekəʊ] *pr n* : **El ~** le Greco.

Greco- [,gri:kəʊ] = **Graeco-**.

Greece [gri:s] *pr n* Grèce *f* ■ **in ~** en Grèce.

greed [gri:d] *n* [for fame, power, wealth] avidité *f* ■ [for food] gloutonnerie *f*.

greedily ['gri:dɪlɪ] *adv* [gen] avidement ■ [consume food] gloutonnement, voracement.

greediness ['gri:dɪnɪs] = **greed**.

greedy ['gri:dɪ] *adj* [for food] glouton, gourmand ■ [for fame, power, wealth] avide ■ **~ for money** avide d'argent.

greedy-guts *n inf* glouton *m*, - onne *f*, goinfre *mf*.

Greek [gri:k] ◇ *n* **1.** [person] Grec *m*, Grecque *f* ■ **'Zorba the ~' *Kazantzakis*** 'Alexis Zorba' **2.** LING grec *m* ■ **ancient ~** grec ancien ■ **modern ~** grec moderne ▶ **it's all ~ to me** *inf* tout ça, c'est du chinois *OR* de l'hébreu pour moi.
◇ *adj* grec, grecque *f* ■ **the ~ Islands** les îles *fpl* grecques.

Greek Orthodox ◇ *n* orthodoxe grec *m*, orthodoxe grecque *f*.
◇ *comp* : **the ~ Church** l'Église *f* orthodoxe grecque.

Greek salad *n salade composée de laitue, tomates, concombre, feta et olives noires.*

green [gri:n] ◇ *adj* **1.** [colour] vert ■ [field, valley] vert, verdoyant ■ **to go *OR* to turn ~** [tree] devenir vert, verdir ; [traffic light] passer au vert ; [person] devenir blême, blêmir ■ **to be *OR* to go ~ with envy** être vert de jalousie ▶ **as ~ as grass** vert cru ■ **~ wellies *UK inf*** *bottes en caoutchouc vertes (le terme évoque les classes bourgeoises ou aristocratiques habitant à la campagne)* **2.** [unripe fruit] vert, pas mûr ■ [undried timber] vert ■ [meat] frais, fraîche *f* ■ [bacon] non fumé **3.** [naive] naïf ■ [inexperienced] inexpérimenté **4.** [ecological] écologique, vert ■ **to go ~** virer écolo **5.** *lit* [alive] vivant, vivace.
◇ *n* **1.** [colour] vert *m* ■ **~ suits you** le vert te va bien ■ **the girl in ~** la fille en vert ■ **dressed in ~** habillé de *OR* en vert **2.** [grassy patch] pelouse *f*, gazon *m* ■ **village ~** ≃ place *f* du village ■ ≃ terrain *m* communal **3.** GOLF green *m*.
◆ **Green** *adj UK* ECON & POL vert ■ **the Green party** le parti écologiste, les Verts *mpl* ■ **Green politics** la politique des Verts.
◆ **greens** *npl* **1.** [vegetables] légumes *mpl* verts **2.** *US* [foliage] feuillage *m (dans un bouquet)*.
◆ **Greens** *npl UK* POL : **the Greens** les Verts *mpl*, les écologistes *mpl*.

greenback ['gri:nbæk] *n US inf* dollar *m*.

green bean *n* haricot *m* vert.

green belt *n* ceinture *f* verte.

Green Beret *n* marine *m* ■ **the ~s** les bérets *mpl* verts.

green card *n* **1.** [insurance] carte *f* verte *(prouvant qu'un véhicule est assuré pour un voyage à l'étranger)* **2.** [work permit] carte *f* de séjour *(temporaire, aux États-Unis)*.

green cross code *n UK* : **the ~** le code de sécurité routière *(pour apprendre aux piétons à traverser la route avec moins de risques d'accident)*.

greenery ['gri:nərɪ] *n* verdure *f*.

green-eyed *adj* aux yeux verts ■ [jealous] jaloux.

greenfield ['gri:nfi:ld] *comp* : **~ site** *terrain non construit à l'extérieur d'une ville.*

greenfinch ['gri:nfɪntʃ] *n* verdier *m*.

green-fingered [-'fɪŋgəd] *adj UK* qui a la main verte.

green fingers *npl UK* : **to have ~** avoir le pouce vert, avoir la main verte.

greenfly ['gri:nflaɪ] *(pl inv OR pl* **greenflies***) n* puceron *m* (vert).

greengage ['gri:ngeɪdʒ] *n* reine-claude *f*.

greengrocer ['gri:n,grəʊsəʳ] *n UK* marchand *m* de fruits et légumes ▪ **to go to the ~'s** aller chez le marchand de fruits et légumes.

Greenham Common ['gri:nəm-] *pr n village en Angleterre où ont eu lieu de nombreuses manifestations hostiles à l'armement nucléaire.*

GREENHAM COMMON

Ancienne base aérienne qui fut le siège de nombreuses manifestations antimilitaristes conduites par des féministes.

greenhorn ['gri:nhɔ:n] *n inf* blanc-bec *m*.

greenhouse ['gri:nhaʊs] (*pl* [-haʊzɪz]) ◇ *n* serre *f*.
◇ *comp* : **~ plants** plantes *fpl* de serre ▪ **~ gases** gaz *mpl* à effet de serre.

greenhouse effect *n* : **the ~** l'effet *m* de serre.

greening ['gri:nɪŋ] *n* **1.** [way of life] prise *f* de conscience écologique **2.** *(U)* POL politique *f* d'amélioration des espaces verts.

greenkeeper ['gri:n,ki:pəʳ] *n personne qui entretient les pelouses des terrains de sport.*

Greenland ['gri:nlənd] *pr n* Groenland *m* ▪ **in ~** au Groenland.

Greenlander ['gri:nləndəʳ] *n* Groenlandais *m*, - e *f*.

green light *n liter & fig* feu *m* vert ▪ **to give the ~ to sb/sthg** donner le feu vert à qqn/pour qqch ▪ **to get the ~ from sb** obtenir le feu vert de qqn.

greenness ['gri:nnɪs] *n* **1.** [colour] couleur *f* verte, vert *m* ▪ [of field, valley] verdure *f* ▪ [of fruit] verdeur *f* **2.** [of person - inexperience] inexpérience *f*, manque *m* d'expérience ; [- naivety] naïveté *f*.

green onion *n US* ciboule *f*, cive *f*.

green paper *n* POL *document formulant des propositions destinées à orienter la politique gouvernementale.*

green peas *npl* petits pois *mpl*.

green pepper *n* poivron *m* vert.

greenroom ['gri:nrʊm] *n* THEAT foyer *m* des artistes.

green salad *n* salade *f* (verte).

greenstick fracture *n* MED fracture *f* incomplète.

greenstuff ['gri:nstʌf] *n* **1.** *(U)* [vegetables] légumes *mpl* verts **2.** *US inf* [money] fric.

green tea *n* thé *m* vert.

green thumb *US* = **green fingers**.

green-thumbed [-'θʌmd] *US* = **green-fingered**.

green vegetables *npl* légumes *mpl* verts.

Greenwich Mean Time ['grenɪdʒ-] *n* heure *f* (du méridien) de Greenwich.

green woodpecker *n* pivert *m*, pic-vert *m*.

greet [gri:t] *vt* [meet, welcome] saluer, accueillir ▪ **to ~ sb/sthg with open arms** accueillir qqn/qqch les bras ouverts ▪ **the news was ~ed with a sigh of relief** les nouvelles furent accueillies avec un soupir de soulagement ▪ **a strange sound ~ed our ears** un son étrange est parvenu à nos oreilles ▪ **the sight that ~ed her (eyes) defied description** la scène qui s'offrit à ses regards défiait toute description.

greeting ['gri:tɪŋ] *n* salut *m*, salutation *f* ▪ [welcome] accueil *m*.
◆ **greetings** *npl* [good wishes] compliments *mpl*, salutations *fpl* ▪ **birthday ~s** vœux *mpl* d'anniversaire.

greetings card *UK*, **greeting card** *US n* carte *f* de vœux.

gregarious [grɪ'geərɪəs] *adj* [animal, bird] grégaire ▪ [person] sociable.

gregariousness [grɪ'geərɪəsnɪs] *n* [of animal, bird] grégarisme *m* ▪ [of person] sociabilité *f*.

Gregorian [grɪ'gɔ:rɪən] *adj* grégorien.

Gregorian calendar *n* : **the ~** le calendrier grégorien.

Gregorian chant *n* chant *m* grégorien.

gremlin ['gremlɪn] *n inf hum diablotin malfaisant que l'on dit responsable de défauts mécaniques ou d'erreurs typographiques.*

Grenada [grə'neɪdə] *pr n* Grenade *f* ▪ **in ~** à la Grenade.

grenade [grə'neɪd] *n* MIL grenade *f*.

Grenadian [grə'neɪdɪən] ◇ *n* Grenadin *m*, - e *f*.
◇ *adj* grenadin.

grenadier [,grenə'dɪəʳ] *n* [soldier] grenadier *m*.

Grenadier Guards *pr npl* : **the ~** *régiment d'infanterie de la Garde Royale britannique.*

grenadine ['grenədi:n] *n* grenadine *f*.

Gretna Green ['gretnə-] *pr n village en Écosse où autrefois on pouvait se marier sans formalités administratives.*

GRETNA GREEN

Village frontalier écossais où, jusqu'en 1940, de jeunes couples en fuite allaient se marier, échappant ainsi aux lois sur le mariage en vigueur en Angleterre.

grew [gru:] *pt* ▷ **grow**.

grey *UK*, **gray** *US* [greɪ] ◇ *adj* **1.** [colour, weather] gris ▪ **~ skies** ciel gris *OR* couvert ▪ **a cold ~ day** un jour de froid et de grisaille **2.** [hair] gris, grisonnant ▪ **to go ~** grisonner ▪ **it's enough to make your hair go** *OR* **turn ~** il y a de quoi se faire des cheveux blancs **3.** [complexion] gris, blême **4.** [life, situation] morne.
◇ *n* **1.** [colour] gris *m* **2.** [horse] (cheval *m*) gris *m*.
◇ *vi* [hair] grisonner, devenir gris.

grey area *n* zone *f* d'incertitude *OR* de flou.

greybeard *UK*, **graybeard** *US* ['greɪ,bɪəd] *n lit* vieil homme *m*.

Grey Friar *n* franciscain *m*.

grey-haired *adj* aux cheveux gris, grisonnant.

greyhound ['greɪhaʊnd] *n* lévrier *m*, levrette *f* ▪ **~ racing** course *f* de lévriers ▪ **a ~ (racing) track** un cynodrome.

Greyhound® *pr n* : **~ buses** *réseau d'autocars couvrant tous les États-Unis.*

greying *UK*, **graying** *US* ['greɪɪŋ] *adj* grisonnant.

greylag ['greɪlæg] *n* : **~ (goose)** oie *f* cendrée.

grey matter *n* matière *f* grise.

grey mullet *n* muge *m*.

greyscale *UK*, **grayscale** *US* ['greɪskeɪl] *n* COMPUT niveau *m* de gris.

grey seal *n* phoque *m* gris.

grey squirrel *n* écureuil *m* gris, petit-gris *m*.

grey whale *n* baleine *f* grise.

grey wolf *n* loup *m* (gris).

grid [grɪd] ◇ *n* **1.** [grating] grille *f* **2.** [electrode] grille *f* ▪ *UK* ELEC réseau *m* **3.** [on chart, map] grille *f* ▪ [lines on map] quadrillage *m* **4.** [in nuclear reactor] grille *f* **5.** THEAT gril *m* **6.** CULIN gril *m* **7.** *US* AUT zone quadrillée **8.** *US* SPORT = **gridiron**.
◇ *comp* : **the city was built on a ~ pattern** la ville était construite en quadrillé.

griddle ['grɪdl] ◇ *n* [iron plate] plaque *f* en fonte ▪ [on top of stove] plaque *f* chauffante.
◇ *vt* cuire sur une plaque *(à galette)*.

gridiron ['grɪd,aɪən] *n* **1.** CULIN gril *m* **2.** THEAT gril *m* **3.** *US* [game] football *m* américain ▪ [pitch] terrain *m* de football.

gridlock ['grɪdlɒk] *n* *US* [traffic jam] embouteillage *m* ▪ *fig* blocage *m*.

grid reference *n* coordonnées *fpl* de la grille.

grief [gri:f] *n* **1.** [sorrow] chagrin *m*, peine *f*, (grande) tristesse *f* ▪ **he was driven almost mad with ~** son chagrin l'a presque rendu fou **2.** *phr* **to come to ~** [person] avoir de graves ennuis ; [project, venture] échouer, tomber à l'eau **3.** [as interjection] : **good ~!** mon Dieu!, ciel!

grief-stricken *adj* accablé de chagrin *OR* de douleur, affligé.

grievance ['gri:vns] *n* **1.** [cause for complaint] grief *m*, sujet *m* de plainte ▪ [complaint] réclamation *f*, revendication *f* ▪ **the workers put forward a list of ~s** les travailleurs ont présenté un cahier de revendications ➤ **~ procedure** *procédure permettant aux salariés de faire part de leurs revendications* **2.** [grudge] : **to nurse a ~** entretenir *OR* nourrir une rancune *OR* un ressentiment **3.** [injustice] injustice *f*, tort *m* **4.** [discontent] mécontentement *m*.

grieve [gri:v] <> *vt* peiner, chagriner ▪ **it ~d me to see him so ill/unhappy** ça m'a fait de la peine de le voir si malade/si malheureux.
<> *vi* [feel grief] avoir de la peine *OR* du chagrin, être peiné ▪ **to ~ at** *OR* **over** *OR* **about sthg** avoir de la peine à cause de qqch ▮ [express grief] pleurer ▪ **to ~ for the dead** pleurer les morts.

grieving ['gri:vɪŋ] <> *adj* [person] en deuil ▪ **the ~ process** le (processus de) deuil.
<> *n* deuil *m*.

grievous ['gri:vəs] *adj* **1.** *fml* [causing pain] affreux, cruel, atroce ▪ **a ~ loss** une perte cruelle **2.** *lit* [grave, serious] grave, sérieux ▪ **he committed a ~ error** il a commis une grave erreur **3.** LAW : **~ bodily harm** coups *mpl* et blessures *fpl*.

grievously ['gri:vəslɪ] *adv* *fml* gravement, sérieusement ▪ **~ mistaken** tout à fait dans l'erreur ▪ **~ wounded** grièvement blessé.

griffin ['grɪfɪn] *n* MYTH griffon *m*.

griffon ['grɪfn] *n* MYTH & ZOOL griffon *m*.

grifter△ ['grɪftər] *n* *US* arnaqueur *m*, - euse *f*, escroc *m*.

grill [grɪl] <> *vt* **1.** CULIN (faire) griller **2.** *inf* [interrogate] cuisiner.
<> *vi* CULIN griller.
<> *n* **1.** CULIN [device] gril *m* ▪ [dish] grillade *f* ▪ **to cook sthg under the ~** faire cuire qqch au gril **2.** [grating] grille *f* **3.** AUT = **grille**.

grille [grɪl] *n* **1.** [grating] grille *f* **2.** AUT calandre *f*.

grillroom ['grɪlrʊm] *n* grill *m* *(restaurant)*.

grilse [grɪls] *n* grilse *m*.

grim [grɪm] *adj* **1.** [hard, stern] sévère ▪ [reality, necessity, truth] dur ▪ **to look ~** avoir l'air sévère ▪ **with ~ determination** avec une volonté inflexible **2.** [gloomy] sinistre, lugubre ▪ **~ prospects** de sombres perspectives ▪ **the economic situation is looking pretty ~** la situation économique n'est pas très encourageante **3.** [unpleasant] : **his new film is pretty ~** son nouveau film n'est pas terrible ▮ [unwell] patraque ▪ [depressed] déprimé, abattu ▪ **I felt pretty ~ this morning** [unwell] je ne me sentais pas bien du tout ce matin ; [depressed] je n'avais vraiment pas le moral ce matin.

grimace [grɪ'meɪs] <> *n* grimace *f*.
<> *vi* [in disgust, pain] grimacer, faire la grimace ▪ [to amuse] faire des grimaces.

grime [graɪm] *n* *(U)* crasse *f*, saleté *f*.

grimly ['grɪmlɪ] *adv* **1.** [threateningly] d'un air menaçant ▪ [unhappily] d'un air mécontent **2.** [defend, struggle] avec acharnement ▪ [hold on] inflexiblement, fermement ▪ [with determination] d'un air résolu, fermement.

grimness ['grɪmnɪs] *n* **1.** [sternness] sévérité *f*, gravité *f* **2.** [of story] côté *m* sinistre *OR* macabre ▪ [of prospects, situation] côté *m* difficile.

grimy ['graɪmɪ] *adj* sale, crasseux.

grin [grɪn] <> *n* grand sourire *m* ▪ **a broad ~** un large sourire.
<> *vi* sourire ▪ **what are you grinning at?** qu'est-ce que tu as à sourire comme ça? ➤ **we'll just have to ~ and bear it** il faudra le prendre avec le sourire.

grind [graɪnd] (*pret & pp* **ground** [graʊnd]) <> *n* **1.** *inf* [monotonous work] corvée *f* ▪ **the daily ~** le train-train quotidien **2.** *US inf* [hard worker] bûcheur *m*, - euse *f*, bosseur *m*, - euse *f*.
<> *vt* **1.** [coffee, corn, pepper] moudre ▪ [stones] concasser ▪ *US* [meat] hacher ▪ [into powder] pulvériser, réduire en poudre ▪ [crush] broyer, écraser ▪ **he ground his feet into the sand** il a enfoncé ses pieds dans le sable **2.** [rub together] écraser l'un contre l'autre ▪ **to ~ one's teeth** grincer des dents ▪ **to ~ the gears** AUT faire grincer les vitesses **3.** [polish - lenses] polir ; [- stones] polir, égriser ▪ [sharpen - knife] aiguiser *OR* affûter (à la meule) **4.** [turn handle] tourner.
<> *vi* **1.** [crush] : **this pepper mill doesn't ~ very well** ce moulin à poivre ne moud pas très bien **2.** [noisily] grincer ▪ **to ~ to a halt/to a standstill** [machine, vehicle] s'arrêter/s'immobiliser en grinçant ; [company, economy, production] s'immobiliser peu à peu, s'arrêter progressivement **3.** *US inf* [work hard] bûcher *OR* bosser (dur).

➡ **grind away** *vi insep inf* **I've been ~ing away at this essay all weekend** j'ai bûché sur cette dissertation tout le week-end.

➡ **grind down** *vt sep* **1.** *liter* pulvériser, réduire en poudre ▪ [lens] meuler **2.** *fig* [oppress] opprimer, écraser ▪ **don't let your job ~ you down** ne te laisse pas abattre par ton boulot.

➡ **grind out** *vt sep* **1.** [extinguish by grinding] : **she ground out her cigarette in the ashtray** elle a écrasé sa cigarette dans le cendrier **2.** *fig* [produce slowly] : **he was ~ing out a tune on the barrel-organ** il jouait un air sur l'orgue de Barbarie ▪ **she's just ground out another blockbuster** elle vient de pondre un nouveau best-seller.

➡ **grind up** *vt sep* pulvériser.

grinder ['graɪndər] *n* **1.** [tooth] molaire *f* **2.** [person - of minerals] broyeur *m*, - euse *f* ; [- of knives, blades etc] rémouleur *m* **3.** [machine - for crushing] moulin *m*, broyeur *m* ; [- for sharpening] affûteuse *f*, machine *f* à aiguiser.

grinding ['graɪndɪŋ] <> *n* [sound] grincement *m*.
<> *adj* **1.** [sound] : **a ~ noise** un bruit grinçant **2.** [oppressive] : **~ poverty** misère *f* écrasante.

grindstone ['graɪndstəʊn] *n* meule *f*.

gringo△ ['grɪŋgəʊ] (*pl* **gringos**) *n* *offens* gringo *m*.

grinning ['grɪnɪŋ] *adj* [face, person] souriant.

grip [grɪp] (*pret & pp* **gripped**, *cont* **gripping**) <> *n* **1.** [strong hold] prise *f*, étreinte *f* ▪ [on racket] tenue *f* ▪ [of tyres on road] adhérence *f* ▪ **to lose one's ~** lâcher prise ▪ **he tightened his ~ on the rope** il a serré la corde plus fort ▪ **to get a ~ of sthg/sb** empoigner qqch/qqn **2.** [handclasp] poigne *f* ▪ **she held his hand in a vice-like ~** elle lui serrait la main comme un étau *OR* tenait la main d'une poigne d'acier **3.** *inf* [self-control] : **he's losing his ~** il perd les pédales ▪ **get a ~ (of *OR* on yourself)!** secoue-toi un peu! **4.** [understanding] : **he has a good ~ of the subject** il connaît *OR* domine bien son sujet **5.** [handle] poignée *f* **6.** CIN & THEAT machiniste *mf* **7.** *dated* [bag] sac *m* de voyage **8.** *phr* **to come *OR* to get to ~s with a problem** s'attaquer à un problème ▪ **to come *OR* to get to ~s with the enemy** être confronté à l'ennemi, être aux prises avec l'ennemi.
<> *vt* **1.** [grasp - rope, rail] empoigner, saisir ▪ **he gripped my arm** il m'a saisi le bras **2.** [hold tightly] serrer, tenir serré ▪ **he gripped my hand** il m'a serré la main très fort **3.** [subj: tyres] adhérer ▪ **to ~ the road** [car] coller à la route **4.** [hold interest] passionner ▪ **the trial gripped the nation** le procès a passionné *OR* captivé le pays.
<> *vi* [tyres] adhérer.

gripe [graɪp] <> *n* **1.** *inf* [complaint] ronchonnements *mpl* **2.** MED = **gripes**.
<> *vi inf* [complain] ronchonner, rouspéter.

➡ **gripes** *npl* MED coliques *fpl*.

griping ['graɪpɪŋ] *n* *(U)* *inf* ronchonnements *mpl*, rouspétance *f*.

gripping ['grɪpɪŋ] *adj* [story, play] captivant, passionnant, palpitant.

grippingly ['grɪpɪŋlɪ] *adv* [written, told] de manière captivante OR passionnante.

grisly ['grɪzlɪ] *adj* épouvantable, macabre, sinistre.

grist [grɪst] *n* blé *m* (à moudre) ▪ **it's all ~ to the mill** c'est toujours ça de pris.

gristle ['grɪsl] *n (U)* [cartilage] cartilage *m*, tendons *mpl* ▪ [in meat] nerfs *mpl*.

gristly ['grɪslɪ] *adj pej* nerveux, tendineux.

grit [grɪt] (*pret & pp* **gritted**, *cont* **gritting**) ◇ *n* **1.** [gravel] gravillon *m* **2.** [sand] sable *m* **3.** [for fowl] gravier *m* **4.** [dust] poussière *f* ▪ **I have a piece of ~ in my eye** j'ai un grain de poussière dans l'œil **5.** *inf* [courage] cran *m*.
◇ *vt* **1.** [road, steps] gravillonner, répandre du gravillon sur **2.** *phr* **to ~ one's teeth** serrer les dents.

gritter ['grɪtər] *n* camion *m* de sablage.

gritting ['grɪtɪŋ] *n* [of roads] sablage *m* ▪ **~ lorry** camion *m* de sablage.

gritty ['grɪtɪ] (*comp* **grittier**, *superl* **grittiest**) *adj* **1.** [road] couvert de gravier **2.** *inf* [person] qui a du cran **3.** [play, film] naturaliste.

grizzle ['grɪzl] *vi UK inf* [cry fretfully] pleurnicher, geindre.

grizzled ['grɪzld] *adj* [person, beard] grisonnant.

grizzly ['grɪzlɪ] (*comp* **grizzlier**, *superl* **grizzliest**) ◇ *adj* [greyish] grisâtre ▪ [hair] grisonnant.
◇ *n* = **grizzly bear**.

grizzly bear *n* grizzli *m*, grizzly *m*, ours *m* brun *(des montagnes Rocheuses)*.

groan [grəʊn] ◇ *n* **1.** [of pain] gémissement *m*, plainte *f* **2.** [of disapproval] grognement *m* ▪ **he gave a ~ of annoyance** il a poussé un grognement d'exaspération **3.** [complaint] ronchonnement *m*.
◇ *vi* **1.** [in pain] gémir **2.** [in disapproval] grogner ▪ **everybody ~ed at his corny jokes** tout le monde levait les yeux au ciel quand il sortait ses plaisanteries éculées **3.** [be weighed down by] gémir ▪ **the table ~ed under the weight of the food** la table ployait sous le poids de la nourriture **4.** [complain] ronchonner.

grocer ['grəʊsər] *n* épicier *m* ▪ **at the ~'s (shop)** à l'épicerie, chez l'épicier.

grocery ['grəʊsərɪ] (*pl* **groceries**) *n* [shop] épicerie *f*.
◆ **groceries** *npl* [provisions] épicerie *f (U)*, provisions *fpl*.

grocery shop *UK*, **grocery store** *n* épicerie *f*.

grog [grɒg] *n* grog *m*.

groggily ['grɒgɪlɪ] *adv* **1.** [weakly] faiblement **2.** [unsteadily - from exhaustion, from blows] de manière chancelante OR groggy.

groggy ['grɒgɪ] (*comp* **groggier**, *superl* **groggiest**) *adj inf* **1.** [weak] faible, affaibli **2.** [unsteady - from exhaustion] groggy *(inv)*, vacillant, chancelant ; [- from blows] groggy *(inv)*, sonné.

groin [grɔɪn] *n* **1.** ANAT aine *f* **2.** *UK euph* [testicles] bourses *fpl* **3.** ARCHIT arête *f* **4.** *US* = **groyne**.

grommet ['grɒmɪt] *n* **1.** [metal eyelet] œillet *m* **2.** MECH virole *f*, rondelle *f*.

groom [gru:m] ◇ *n* **1.** [for horses] palefrenier *m*, - ère *f*, valet *m* d'écurie **2.** = **bridegroom**.
◇ *vt* **1.** [clean - horse] panser ; [- dog] toiletter ; [- subj: monkeys, cats] : **cats ~ themselves** les chats font leur toilette **2.** [prepare - candidate] préparer, former ▪ **Ray is being ~ed for an executive position** on prépare OR forme Ray pour un poste de cadre.

groomed [gru:md] *adj* soigné ▪ **to be well-~** être soigné (de sa personne).

grooming ['gru:mɪŋ] *n* **1.** [of person] toilette *f* ▪ [neat appearance] présentation *f* **2.** [of horse] pansage *m* ▪ [of dog] toilettage *m*.

groove [gru:v] ◇ *n* **1.** [for pulley, in column] cannelure *f*, gorge *f* ▪ [in folding knife] onglet *m* ▪ [in piston] gorge *f* ▪ [for sliding door] rainure *f* ▪ [on record] sillon *m* **2.** *inf* [rut] : **to get into** OR **to be stuck in a ~** s'encroûter **3.** MUS groove *m* **4.** : **to be in the ~** [be up-to-date] être branché, être dans le coup.
◇ *vt* [make a groove] canneler, rainurer, rainer.
◇ *vi inf* **1.** *US* [enjoy oneself] s'éclater **2.** [dance] danser.

groovy ['gru:vɪ] (*comp* **groovier**, *superl* **grooviest**) *inf adj* **1.** [excellent] sensationnel, sensass, super **2.** [trendy] dans le vent.

grope [grəʊp] ◇ *vi* [seek - by touch] tâtonner, aller à l'aveuglette ; [- for answer] chercher ▪ **to ~ (about** OR **around) for sthg** chercher qqch à tâtons OR à l'aveuglette.
◇ *vt* **1.** : **to ~ one's way in the dark** avancer à tâtons dans l'obscurité **2.** *inf* [sexually] tripoter, peloter.

grosgrain ['grəʊgreɪn] *n* gros-grain *m*.

gross [grəʊs] ◇ *adj* **1.** [vulgar, loutish - person] grossier, fruste ; [- joke] cru, grossier **2.** [flagrant - inefficiency] flagrant ▪ **~ injustice** injustice *f* flagrante ▪ **~ ignorance** ignorance *f* crasse **3.** [fat] obèse, énorme **4.** [overall total] brut ▪ **~ profits** bénéfices *mpl* bruts **5.** *inf* [disgusting] dégueulasse.
◇ *n* **1.** *(pl grosses)* [whole amount] : **the ~** le gros **2.** [twelve dozen] grosse *f*, douze douzaines *fpl*.
◇ *vt* COMM faire OR obtenir une recette brute de ▪ **our firm ~ed $800,000 last year** notre société a fait OR obtenu une recette brute de 800 000 dollars l'année dernière.
◆ **gross out** *vt sep US inf* dégoûter, débecter△.

gross domestic product *n* produit *m* intérieur brut.

grossly ['grəʊslɪ] *adv* **1.** [coarsely] grossièrement **2.** [as intensifier] outre mesure, excessivement ▪ **~ unfair** extrêmement injuste.

gross national product *n* produit *m* national brut.

grotesque [grəʊ'tesk] ◇ *adj* grotesque.
◇ *n* grotesque *m*.

grotesquely [grəʊ'tesklɪ] *adv* grotesquement, absurdement.

grotto ['grɒtəʊ] (*pl* **grottos** OR *pl* **grottoes**) *n* grotte *f*.

grotty ['grɒtɪ] (*comp* **grottier**, *superl* **grottiest**) *adj UK inf* **1.** [unattractive] moche ▪ [unsatisfactory] nul **2.** [unwell] : **to feel ~** ne pas se sentir bien, être mal fichu.

grouch [graʊtʃ] *inf* ◇ *vi* rouspéter, ronchonner, grogner ▪ **to ~ about sthg** rouspéter OR ronchonner après qqch, grogner contre qqch.
◇ *n* rouspéteur *m*, - euse *f*.

grouchy ['graʊtʃɪ] (*comp* **grouchier**, *superl* **grouchiest**) *adj inf* grincheux, ronchon, grognon.

ground [graʊnd] ◇ *pt & pp* ⊳ **grind**.
◇ *n* **1.** [earth] terre *f* ▪ [surface] sol *m* ▪ **at ~ level** au niveau du sol ▪ **the children sat on the ~** les enfants se sont assis par terre ▪ **drive the stakes firmly into the ~** enfoncez solidement les pieux dans le sol ▪ **above ~** en surface ▪ **below ~** sous terre ▪ **to burn sthg to the ~** réduire qqch en cendres ▪ **to fall to the ~** tomber par OR à terre ❯ **to go to ~** se terrer ▪ **to be on firm ~** être sûr de son fait ▪ **to get off the ~** *liter* [aeroplane] décoller ; *fig* [project] démarrer ▪ **it suits him down to the ~** ça lui va à merveille, ça lui convient parfaitement ▪ **to run a car into the ~** utiliser une voiture jusqu'à ce qu'elle rende l'âme ▪ **to run a company into the ~** faire couler une entreprise
2. *(U)* [land] terrain *m* ▪ [region] région *f*, coin *m*
3. *UK* [piece of land] terrain *m* ▪ [stadium] stade *m*
4. [area used for specific purpose] : **fishing ~s** zones *fpl* réservées à la pêche ▪ **training ~** terrain *m* d'entraînement OR d'exercice
5. MIL terrain *m* ▪ **to give/to lose ~** céder/perdre du terrain ▪ **to stand** OR **to hold one's ~** tenir bon ❯ **to gain ~** [in battle] gagner du terrain ; [idea, concept] faire son chemin, progresser ; [news] se répandre

6. *(U)* [area of reference] domaine *m*, champ *m* ■ **his article covers a lot of ~** dans son article, il aborde beaucoup de domaines
7. [subject] terrain *m*, sujet *m* ■ **you're on dangerous ~** vous êtes sur un terrain glissant
8. [background] fond *m*
9. [of sea] fond *m*
10. *US* ELEC terre *f*, masse *f*
11. MUS : **~ (bass)** basse *f* contrainte.
◇ *comp* au sol ■ **~ crew** personnel *m* au sol ■ **~ fire** feu *m* de broussailles ■ **~ frost** gelée *f* blanche ■ **~ staff** *personnel qui s'occupe de l'entretien d'un terrain de sport.*
◇ *vt* **1.** [base] fonder, baser ■ **my fears proved well ~ed** mes craintes se sont révélées fondées, il s'est avéré que mes craintes étaient fondées
2. [train] former ■ **the students are well ~ed in computer sciences** les étudiants ont une bonne formation *OR* de bonnes bases en informatique
3. [plane, pilot] : **to be ~ed** être interdit de vol
4. [ship] échouer
5. *US* ELEC mettre à la terre *OR* à la masse
6. *inf* [child] priver de sortie.
◇ *vi* [ship] échouer.
◇ *adj* [wheat, coffee] moulu ■ [pepper] concassé ■ [steel] meulé ■ [meat] haché.
◆ **grounds** *npl* **1.** [around house] parc *m*, domaine *m* ■ [around block of flats, hospital] terrain *m* ■ [more extensive] parc *m*
2. [reason] motif *m*, raison *f* ■ [cause] cause *f*, raison *f* ■ [basis] base *f*, raison *f* ■ [pretext] raison *f*, prétexte *m* ■ **there are ~s for suspecting arson** il y a lieu de penser qu'il s'agit d'un incendie criminel ■ **he was excused on the ~s of poor health** il a été exempté en raison de sa mauvaise santé ■ **on medical/moral ~s** pour (des) raisons médicales/morales ‖ LAW : **~s for appeal** voies *fpl* de recours ■ **~s for complaint** grief *m* ■ **~s for divorce** motif *m* de divorce
3. [of coffee] marc *m*.

> ***GROUND ZERO***
> Depuis les attentats du 11 septembre 2001, cette expression est venue s'appliquer au site de l'ancien World Trade Center sur l'île de Manhattan à New York. Elle tire son origine du jargon militaire, où elle désigne le point d'impact sur terre d'une éventuelle frappe nucléaire.

ground beef *n US* steak *m* haché.

ground-breaking *adj* révolutionnaire ■ **this is ~ technology** c'est une véritable percée technologique.

ground control *n* AERON contrôle *m* au sol.

ground cover *n* végétation *f* basse ■ **~ plant** (plante *f*) couvre-sol *m inv*.

ground floor *n* rez-de-chaussée *m*.

ground glass *n* **1.** [glass] verre *m* dépoli **2.** [as abrasive] verre *m* pilé.

ground hog *n* marmotte *f* d'Amérique ■ **Ground Hog Day** *US le 2 février, jour où les marmottes sont censées avoir fini leur hibernation.*

ground-in *adj* [dirt] incrusté.

grounding ['graʊndɪŋ] *n* **1.** [training] formation *f* ■ [knowledge] connaissances *fpl*, bases *fpl* **2.** [of argument] assise *f* **3.** *US* ELEC mise *f* à la terre *OR* à la masse **4.** NAUT échouage *m* **5.** [of balloon] atterrissage *m* **6.** [of plane] interdiction *f* de vol.

groundless ['graʊndlɪs] *adj* sans fondement, sans motif ■ **her fears proved ~** ses craintes s'avérèrent sans fondement.

ground level *n* **1.** [ground floor] rez-de-chaussée *m* **2.** [lowest level in organization] base *f*.

groundnut ['graʊndnʌt] = **peanut**.

ground plan *n* **1.** [plan of ground floor] plan *m* au sol **2.** [plan of action] plan *m* d'action.

ground rent *n* redevance *f* foncière.

ground rule *n* procédure *f*, règle *f* ■ **to lay down the ~s** établir les règles du jeu *fig*.

groundsel ['graʊnsl] *n* séneçon *m*.

groundsheet ['graʊndʃi:t] *n* tapis *m* de sol.

groundskeeper ['graʊnzki:pəʳ] *n US* préposé *m* à l'entretien d'un terrain de sport.

groundsman ['graʊndzmən] (*pl* **groundsmen** [-mən]) *n* gardien *m* de stade.

ground stroke *n* TENNIS : **to hit a ~** frapper la balle au rebond.

groundswell ['graʊndswel] *n* lame *f* de fond ■ **there was a ~ of public opinion in favour of the president** *fig* l'opinion publique a basculé massivement en faveur du président.

groundwork ['graʊndwɜ:k] *n (U)* travail *m* préparatoire, canevas *m*.

group [gru:p] ◇ *n* **1.** [of people] groupe *m* ■ POL [party] groupement *m* ■ [literary] groupe *m*, cercle *m* **2.** [of objects] groupe *m*, ensemble *m* ■ [of mountains] massif *m* **3.** [in business] groupe *m* **4.** [blood] groupe *m* **5.** MUS groupe *m* ■ **a pop/rock ~** un groupe pop/rock **6.** LING groupe *m*, syntagme *m* **7.** MIL groupe *m*.
◇ *comp* [work] de groupe ■ [action, decision] collectif.
◇ *vt* **1.** [bring together] grouper, réunir ■ [put in groups] disposer en groupes ■ **the teacher ~ed all the eight-year-olds together** l'institutrice a groupé *OR* regroupé tous les enfants de huit ans **2.** [combine] combiner.
◇ *vi* se grouper, se regrouper.

group captain *n* colonel *m*, -elle *f* de l'armée de l'air ■ **Group Captain Ross** le colonel Ross.

groupie ['gru:pɪ] *n inf* groupie *f*.

grouping ['gru:pɪŋ] *n* groupement *m*.

group practice *n* MED cabinet *m* médical.

group therapy *n* thérapie *f* de groupe.

grouse [graʊs] ◇ *n* **1.** [bird] grouse *f*, lagopède *m* d'Écosse **2.** *inf* [grumble] rouspétance *f* ■ [complaint] grief *m* ■ **to have a ~ about sthg** rouspéter contre qqch.
◇ *comp* : **~ moor** chasse *f* réservée (à la chasse à la grouse) ■ **~ shooting** chasse *f* à la grouse.
◇ *vi inf* rouspéter, râler.

grout [graʊt] ◇ *n* coulis *m* au ciment.
◇ *vt* jointoyer.

grouting ['graʊtɪŋ] *n* jointoiement *m*.

grove [grəʊv] *n* bosquet *m*.

grovel ['grɒvl] (*UK pret & pp* **grovelled**, *cont* **grovelling**) (*US pret & pp* **groveled**, *cont* **groveling**) *vi* **1.** [act humbly] ramper, s'aplatir ■ **to ~ to sb (for sthg)** s'aplatir devant qqn (pour obtenir qqch) **2.** [crawl on floor] se vautrer par terre.

groveller *UK*, **groveler** *US* ['grɒvləʳ] *n* flagorneur *m*, -euse *f fml*, lèche-bottes *mf inv*.

grovelling *UK*, **groveling** *US* ['grɒvlɪŋ] ◇ *adj* rampant, servile ■ **a ~ letter** une lettre obséquieuse ■ **a ~ apology** de viles excuses.
◇ *n (U)* flagornerie *f*.

grow [grəʊ] (*pret* **grew** [gru:], *pp* **grown** [grəʊn]) ◇ *vi* **1.** [plants] croître, pousser ■ [hair] pousser ■ [seeds] germer ■ **money doesn't ~ on trees** l'argent ne pousse pas sur les arbres
2. [person - in age, height] grandir ■ [develop] : **to ~ in wisdom/understanding** devenir plus sage/compréhensif
3. [originate] : **this custom grew from** *OR* **out of a pagan ceremony** cette coutume est née d'une *OR* a pour origine une cérémonie païenne
4. [increase] s'accroître, augmenter ■ **our love/friendship grew over the years** notre amour/amitié a grandi au fil des ans ■ **he has grown in my esteem** il a grandi *OR* est monté dans mon estime ■ **the town grew in importance** la ville a gagné en importance

5. [become] devenir ■ **to ~ bigger** grandir, s'agrandir ■ **to ~ old** devenir vieux, vieillir
6. *(with infinitive)* [come gradually] : **I've grown to respect him** j'ai appris à le respecter ■ **to ~ to like/to dislike** finir par aimer/détester.
◇ *vt* **1.** [crops, plants] cultiver
2. [beard, hair] laisser pousser ■ **he's trying to ~ a beard** il essaie de se laisser pousser la barbe
3. FIN [company] agrandir.
◆ **grow apart** *vi insep* [couple] s'éloigner l'un de l'autre.
◆ **grow away** *vi insep* : **they began to ~ away from each other** ils ont commencé à s'éloigner l'un de l'autre *fig.*
◆ **grow back** *vi insep* [hair, nail] repousser.
◆ **grow into** *vt insep* **1.** [become] devenir (en grandissant) ■ **both her sons grew into fine-looking men** ses deux fils sont devenus de beaux jeunes gens
2. [clothes] : **he'll soon ~ into those shoes** il pourra bientôt mettre ces chaussures, bientôt ces chaussures lui iront
3. [become used to] : **to ~ into a job** s'habituer à *OR* s'adapter à un travail.
◆ **grow on** *vt insep* plaire de plus en plus à ■ **it ~s on you** on s'y fait.
◆ **grow out of** *vt insep* **1.** [clothes] : **he's grown out of most of his clothes** la plupart de ses vêtements ne lui vont plus, il ne rentre plus dans la plupart de ses vêtements
2. [habit] perdre (avec le temps).
◆ **grow up** *vi insep* **1.** [person] grandir, devenir adulte ■ **what do you want to be when you ~ up?** que veux-tu faire quand tu seras grand? ■ **I hope he won't ~ up to be a liar/thief** j'espère qu'il ne sera pas un menteur/voleur plus tard ■ **~ up!** sois un peu adulte! ■ **when are you going to ~ up?** quand est-ce que tu seras un peu raisonnable? ■ **our children are ~ now** nos enfants sont grands maintenant
2. [emotions, friendship] naître, se développer.

grow bag *n sac plastique rempli d'engrais dans lequel on fait pousser une plante.*

grower ['grəʊəʳ] *n* **1.** [producer] producteur *m*, - trice *f* ■ [professional] cultivateur *m*, - trice *f* ■ [amateur gardener] amateur *m* de jardinage ■ **vegetable ~** maraîcher *m*, - ère *f* ■ **rose ~** [professional] rosiériste *mf* ; [amateur] : **he's a keen rose ~** il se passionne pour la culture des roses **2.** [plant, tree] : **a slow ~** une plante qui pousse lentement.

growing ['grəʊɪŋ] ◇ *adj* **1.** [plant] croissant, qui pousse ■ [child] grandissant, en cours de croissance ■ **a ~ child needs a well balanced diet** un enfant en pleine croissance a besoin d'une alimentation bien équilibrée **2.** [increasing - debt] qui augmente ; [- amount, number] grandissant, qui augmente ; [- friendship, impatience] grandissant ■ **~ numbers of people are out of work** de plus en plus de gens sont *OR* un nombre croissant de gens est au chômage ■ **a ~ population** une population qui s'accroît ■ **there are ~ fears of a nuclear war** on craint de plus en plus une guerre nucléaire.
◇ *comp* : **wine ~ region** région vinicole ■ **wheat/potato ~ region** région qui produit du blé/de la pomme de terre, région à blé/pommes de terre.
◇ *n* [of agricultural products] culture *f*.

growing pains *npl* **1.** [of children] douleurs *fpl* de croissance **2.** [of business, project] difficultés *fpl* de croissance, problèmes *mpl* de départ.

growing season *n* saison *f* nouvelle.

growl [graʊl] ◇ *vi* [animal] grogner, gronder ■ [person] grogner, grommeler ■ [thunder] tonner, gronder.
◇ *vt* [answer, instructions] grommeler, grogner.
◇ *n* grognement *m*, grondement *m*.

grown [grəʊn] ◇ *pp* ▷ **grow**.
◇ *adj* **1.** [person] adulte ■ **you don't expect ~ adults to behave so stupidly** on ne s'attend pas à ce que des adultes se comportent de manière si stupide ■ **he's a ~ man** il est adulte ■ **the children are fully ~ now** les enfants sont grands maintenant **2.** [garden] : **the garden is all ~ over** le jardin est tout envahi par les mauvaises herbes.

grown-up ◇ *n* adulte *mf*, grande personne *f*.
◇ *adj* adulte.

growth [grəʊθ] *n* **1.** *(U)* [development - of child, plant] croissance *f* ; [- of friendship] développement *m*, croissance *f* ; [- of organization] développement *m* ■ **intellectual/spiritual ~** développement intellectuel/spirituel **2.** *(U)* [increase - in numbers, amount] augmentation *f*, croissance *f* ; [- of market, industry] croissance *f*, expansion *f* ; [- of influence, knowledge] développement *m*, croissance *f* ■ **the experts predict a 2% ~ in tourism/imports** les experts prédisent une croissance du tourisme/des importations de 2 % ➜ **economic ~** développement *m* *OR* croissance *f* économique ■ **population ~** croissance *f* de la population **3.** [of beard, hair, weeds] pousse *f* ■ **two days' ~ of beard** une barbe de deux jours **4.** MED excroissance *f*, tumeur *f*, grosseur *f*.

growth hormone *n* hormone *f* de croissance.

growth industry *n* industrie *f* en plein essor *OR* de pointe.

growth rate *n* taux *m* de croissance.

growth shares *npl* ST. EX valeurs *fpl* de croissance.

growth stock *n* = **growth shares**.

groyne *UK*, **groin** *US* [grɔɪn] *n* brise-lames *m inv*.

GRSM (*abbrev of* **Graduate of the Royal Schools of Music**) *n diplômé du conservatoire de musique britannique.*

grub [grʌb] ◇ *vi* **1.** [animal] fouir **2.** [rummage] fouiller ■ **he grubbed around for clues** *fig* il fouinait à la recherche d'indices.
◇ *n* **1.** [insect] asticot *m* **2.** *inf* [food] bouffe *f* ■ **~** *OR* **~'s up!** à la soupe!
◆ **grub up** *vt sep* [bone] déterrer ■ [root] extirper ■ [plant] déraciner ■ [insects] déloger.

grubby ['grʌbɪ] *adj* sale, crasseux, malpropre.

grub-kick *n* [in rugby] coup *m* qui reste au sol.

grub screw *n* vis *f* noyée, vis *f* sans tête.

grudge [grʌdʒ] ◇ *n* rancune *f* ■ **to bear** *OR* **to hold a ~ against sb** en vouloir à qqn, avoir de la rancune contre qqn.
◇ *vt* = **begrudge**.

grudging ['grʌdʒɪŋ] *adj* [compliment, praise] fait *OR* donné à contrecœur ■ [agreement] réticent.

grudgingly ['grʌdʒɪŋlɪ] *adv* à contrecœur, avec réticence.

gruel [grʊəl] *n* bouillie *f* d'avoine.

gruelling *UK*, **grueling** *US* ['grʊəlɪŋ] *adj* [race] épuisant ■ [punishment] sévère ■ [experience] très difficile, très dur.

gruesome ['gru:səm] *adj* [sight] horrible ■ [discovery] macabre.

gruff [grʌf] *adj* **1.** [manner] brusque **2.** [speech, voice] bourru ■ **a ~ voice** une grosse voix.

gruffly ['grʌflɪ] *adv* **1.** [of manner] avec brusquerie **2.** [of speech, voice] : **to speak ~** parler d'un ton bourru.

gruffness ['grʌfnɪs] *n* **1.** [of manner] brusquerie *f* **2.** [of speech, voice] ton *m* bourru.

grumble ['grʌmbl] ◇ *vi* **1.** [complain] grogner, grommeler ■ **he's always grumbling about something** il rouspète constamment contre quelque chose ■ **how are you? – oh, mustn't ~!** ça va? – on fait aller! **2.** [thunder, artillery] gronder ■ **my stomach kept grumbling loudly** mon estomac n'arrêtait pas de gargouiller bruyamment.
◇ *n* **1.** [complaint] ronchonnement *m*, sujet *m* de plainte **2.** [of thunder, artillery] grondement *m*.

grumbler ['grʌmbləʳ] *n* grincheux *m*, - euse *f*.

grumbling ['grʌmblɪŋ] ◇ *adj* grincheux, grognon ■ **a ~ stomach** un estomac qui gargouille ■ **~ appendix** MED appendicite *f* chronique.
◇ *n (U)* plaintes *fpl*, protestations *fpl*.

grump [grʌmp] *n inf* bougon *m*, - onne *f*, ronchon *m*, - onne *f* ■ **to have the ~s** être de mauvais poil.

grumpily ['grʌmpɪlɪ] *adv inf* en ronchonnant, d'un ton *OR* air ronchon.

grumpiness ['grʌmpɪnɪs] *n inf* mauvaise humeur *f*, maussaderie *f*, caractère *m* désagréable.

grumpy ['grʌmpɪ] *adj inf* ronchon, bougon.

grunge *inf* [grʌndʒ] *n* **1.** *US* [dirt] crasse *f* **2.** [music, fashion] grunge *m*.

grungy ['grʌndʒɪ] *adj inf* **1.** *US* [dirty] crasseux **2.** [style, fashion] grunge *inv*.

grunt [grʌnt] ◇ *vi* grogner, pousser un grognement.
◇ *vt* [reply] grommeler, grogner.
◇ *n* [sound] grognement *m* ▪ **to give a ~** pousser un grognement.

g-spot *n* point *m* G.

G-string *n* **1.** MUS (corde *f* de) sol *m* **2.** [item of clothing] cache-sexe *m*, string *m*.

guac(h)amole [ˌgwɑːkə'məʊlɪ] *n (U)* guacamole *m*, purée *f* d'avocat.

Guadeloupe [ˌgwɑːdə'luːp] *pr n* Guadeloupe *f* ▪ **in ~** à la *OR* en Guadeloupe.

Guam [gwɑːm] *n* Guam *f*.

guano ['gwɑːnəʊ] *n* guano *m*.

guarantee [ˌgærən'tiː] ◇ *n* **1.** COMM garantie *f* ▪ **money-back ~** remboursement *m* garanti ▪ **to be under ~** être sous garantie ▪ **this cooker has a five-year ~** cette cuisinière est garantie cinq ans **2.** LAW [pledge] caution *f*, garantie *f*, gage *m* **3.** [person] garant *m*, - e *f* ▪ **to act as ~** se porter garant **4.** [firm promise] garantie *f* ▪ **what ~ do I have that you'll bring it back?** comment puis-je être sûr que vous le rapporterez? ▪ **there's no ~ it will arrive today** il n'est pas garanti *OR* dit que ça arrivera aujourd'hui.
◇ *comp* : **~ agreement** garantie *f* ▪ **~ form** formulaire *m OR* fiche *f* de garantie.
◇ *vt* **1.** [goods] garantir ▪ **the car is ~d against rust for ten years** la voiture est garantie contre la rouille pendant dix ans **2.** [loan, cheque] garantir, cautionner ▪ **to ~ sb against loss** garantir des pertes de qqn **3.** [assure] certifier, assurer ▪ **I can't ~ that everything will go to plan** je ne peux pas vous certifier *OR* garantir que tout se passera comme prévu ▪ **our success is ~d** notre succès est garanti.

guarantor [ˌgærən'tɔː'] *n* garant *m*, - e *f*, caution *f* ▪ **to stand ~ for sb** se porter garant pour qqn.

guaranty ['gærəntɪ] *n* **1.** [security] caution *f*, garantie *f* **2.** [guarantor] garant *m*, - e *f* **3.** [written guarantee] garantie *f*.

guard [gɑːd] ◇ *n* **1.** [person] gardien *m*, garde *m* ▪ [group] garde *f* ▪ **prison ~** gardien de prison ▪ **~ of honour** garde *f* d'honneur
2. [watch] garde *f* ▪ **to be on ~ (duty)** être de garde ▪ **to mount (a) ~** monter la garde ▪ **to mount ~ on *OR* over** veiller sur ▪ **the military kept ~ over the town** les militaires gardaient la ville ▪ **to stand ~** monter la garde ▪ **the changing of the ~** la relève de la garde
3. [supervision] garde *f*, surveillance *f* ▪ **to keep a prisoner under ~** garder un prisonnier sous surveillance ▪ **to put a ~ on sb/sthg** faire surveiller qqn/qqch ▪ **the prisoners were taken under ~ to the courthouse** les prisonniers furent emmenés sous escorte au palais de justice
4. [attention] garde *f* ▪ **on ~!** [in fencing] en garde! ▪ **to be on one's ~** être sur ses gardes ▪ **to catch sb off ~** prendre qqn au dépourvu ▪ **to drop *OR* to lower one's ~** relâcher sa surveillance
5. *UK* RAIL chef *m* de train
6. [protective device - on machine] dispositif *m* de sûreté *OR* de protection ; [- personal] protection *f*.
◇ *vt* **1.** [watch over - prisoner] garder
2. [defend - fort, town] garder, défendre ▪ **the house was heavily ~ed** la maison était étroitement surveillée
3. [protect - life, reputation] protéger ▪ **to ~ sb against danger** protéger qqn d'un danger ▪ **~ the letter with your life** veille bien sur cette lettre
4. GAMES garder.

◆ **Guards** *npl* MIL [regiment] Garde *f* royale *(britannique)*.

◆ **guard against** *vt insep* se protéger contre *OR* de, se prémunir contre ▪ **to ~ against doing sthg** se garder de faire qqch ▪ **how can we ~ against such accidents (happening)?** comment éviter *OR* empêcher (que) de tels accidents (arrivent) ?

guard dog *n* chien *m* de garde.

guard duty *n* : **to be on ~** être de garde *OR* de faction.

guarded ['gɑːdɪd] *adj* prudent, circonspect, réservé ▪ **to give a ~ reply** répondre avec réserve.

guardedly ['gɑːdɪdlɪ] *adv* avec réserve, prudemment.

guardhouse ['gɑːdhaʊs] (*pl* [-haʊzɪz]) *n* MIL [for guards] corps *m* de garde ▪ [for prisoners] salle *f* de garde.

guardian ['gɑːdjən] *n* **1.** [gen] gardien *m*, - enne *f* ▪ [of museum] conservateur *m*, - trice *f* **2.** LAW [of minor] tuteur *m*, - trice *f*.

Guardian *pr n* : **the ~** PRESS *quotidien britannique de qualité, plutôt de gauche* ▪ **~ reader** *lecteur du Guardian (représentatif de la gauche intellectuelle)*, *see also* **broadsheet**.

guardian angel *n* ange *m* gardien.

Guardian Angels *pr npl vigiles bénévoles dans le métro de Londres, de New York, etc.*

guardianship ['gɑːdjənʃɪp] *n* **1.** [gen] garde *f* **2.** LAW tutelle *f*.

guardrail ['gɑːdreɪl] *n* **1.** [on ship] bastingage *m*, garde-corps *m inv* **2.** RAIL contre-rail *m* **3.** *US* [on road] barrière *f* de sécurité.

guardroom ['gɑːdrʊm] *n* **1.** MIL [for guards] corps *m* de garde **2.** [for prisoners] salle *f* de garde.

guardsman ['gɑːdzmən] (*pl* [-mən]) *n* MIL *UK* soldat *m* de la garde royale ▪ *US* soldat *m* de la garde nationale.

guard's van *n UK* fourgon *m* du chef de train.

Guatemala [ˌgwɑːtə'mɑːlə] *pr n* Guatemala *m* ▪ **in ~** au Guatemala.

Guatemalan [ˌgwɑːtə'mɑːlən] ◇ *n* Guatémaltèque *mf*.
◇ *adj* guatémaltèque.

guava ['gwɑːvə] *n* [tree] goyavier *m* ▪ [fruit] goyave *f*.

gubernatorial [ˌguːbənə'tɔːrɪəl] *adj US* de *OR* du gouverneur ▪ **~ elections** élections des gouverneurs.

guer(r)illa [gə'rɪlə] ◇ *n* guérillero *m*.
◇ *comp* : **~ band *OR* group** guérilla *f*, groupe *m* de guérilleros ▪ **~ strike** grève *f* sauvage ▪ **~ warfare** guérilla *f (combat)*.

Guernsey ['gɜːnzɪ] ◇ *pr n* [island] Guernesey ▪ **in ~** à Guernesey.
◇ *n* **1.** [cow] vache *f* de Guernesey **2.** [sweater] jersey *m*, tricot *m*.

guess [ges] ◇ *n* **1.** [at facts, figures] : **to have *UK OR* to take *US* a ~ at sthg** (essayer de) deviner qqch ▪ **at a (rough) ~, I'd say 200** à vue de nez, je dirais 200 ▪ **he made a good/a wild ~** il a deviné juste/à tout hasard ▪ **I'll give you three ~es** devine un peu **2.** [hypothesis] supposition *f*, conjecture *f* ▪ **it's anybody's ~** Dieu seul le sait, impossible de prévoir ▪ **my ~ is that he won't come** à mon avis il ne viendra pas, je pense qu'il ne viendra pas ▪ **your ~ is as good as mine** tu en sais autant que moi, je n'en sais pas plus que toi.
◇ *vt* **1.** [attempt to answer] deviner ▪ **~ what!** devine un peu! ▪ **~ who!** devine qui c'est! ▪ **~ who I saw in town** devine (un peu) qui j'ai vu en ville ▪ **I ~ed as much** je m'en doutais, c'est bien ce que je pensais **2.** [imagine] croire, penser, supposer ▪ **I ~ you're right** je suppose que vous avez raison ▪ **I ~ so** je pense que oui ▪ **I ~ not** non, effectivement.
◇ *vi* deviner ▪ **to ~ at sthg** deviner qqch ▪ **(try to) ~!** devine un peu! ▪ **the police ~ed right** la police a deviné *OR* vu juste ▪ **we ~ed wrong** nous nous sommes trompés ▪ **to keep sb ~ing** laisser qqn dans le doute.

guesstimate ['gestɪmət] *n inf* calcul *m* au pifomètre.

guesswork ['geswɜ:k] *n (U)* conjecture *f*, hypothèse *f* ■ to do sthg by ~ faire qqch au hasard ■ it's pure OR sheer ~ c'est une simple hypothèse OR supposition.

guest [gest] *n* **1.** [visitor - at home] invité *m*, - e *f*, hôte *mf* ■ [at table] invité *m*, - e *f*, convive *mf* ■ ~ of honour invité d'honneur, invitée d'honneur ■ be my ~! fais donc!, je t'en prie! **2.** [in hotel] client *m*, - e *f* ■ [in boarding-house] pensionnaire *mf*.

guest book *n* livre *m* d'or.

guesthouse ['gesthaus] (*pl* [-hauzɪz]) *n* pension *f* de famille.

guest list *n* liste *f* des invités.

guestroom ['gestrum] *n* chambre *f* d'amis.

guest speaker *n* conférencier *m*, - ère *f (invité à parler par une organisation, une association)*.

guest star *n* invité-vedette *m*, invitée-vedette *f* ■ '~ Rock Hudson' 'avec la participation de Rock Hudson'.

guest worker *n* travailleur immigré *m*, travailleuse immigrée *f*.

guff [gʌf] *n (U) inf* bêtises *fpl*, idioties *fpl*.

guffaw [gʌ'fɔ:] ◇ *n* gros éclat *m* de rire.
◇ *vi* rire bruyamment, s'esclaffer.
◇ *vt* : "of course!" he ~ed "bien sûr!", s'esclaffa-t-il.

Guiana [gɪ'ɑ:nə] *pr n* Guyane *f* ■ the ~s les Guyanes ■ in ~ en Guyane ▶ French ~ Guyane française ■ Dutch ~ Guyane hollandaise.

Guianan [gɪ'ɑ:nən], **Guianese** [,gɪə'ni:z] ◇ *n* Guyanais *m*, - e *f*.
◇ *adj* guyanais.

guidance ['gaɪdəns] *n* **1.** [advice] conseils *mpl* ■ she needs ~ concerning her education elle a besoin de conseils pour son éducation **2.** [instruction] direction *f*, conduite *f* ■ [supervision] direction *f*, supervision *f* ■ he's writing the book under the ~ of his former professor il écrit ce livre sous la direction de son ancien professeur **3.** [information] information *f* ■ diagrams are given for your ~ les schémas sont donnés à titre d'information OR à titre indicatif **4.** AERON guidage *m*.

guidance counselor *n* US conseiller *m*, - ère *f* d'orientation.

guide [gaɪd] ◇ *n* **1.** [for tourists] guide *mf* ■ Gino was our ~ during our tour of Rome Gino nous servait de guide pendant notre visite de Rome **2.** [influence, direction] guide *m*, indication *f* ■ let your conscience be your ~ laissez-vous guider par votre conscience ■ to take sthg as a ~ prendre qqch comme règle de conduite **3.** [indication] indication *f*, idée *f* ■ as a rough ~ en gros, approximativement ■ are these tests a good ~ to intelligence? ces tests fournissent-ils une bonne indication de l'intelligence? ■ conversions are given as a ~ les conversions sont données à titre indicatif **4.** [manual] guide *m*, manuel *m* pratique ■ a ~ to better French un guide pour améliorer votre français ■ a ~ to France un guide de la France **5.** UK [girl scout] : (Girl) Guide éclaireuse *f* ■ she's in the Guides elle est éclaireuse **6.** [machine part] guide *m*.
◇ *vt* **1.** [show the way] guider, conduire ■ to ~ sb in/out conduire qqn jusqu'à l'entrée/la sortie **2.** [instruct] diriger, conduire **3.** [advise] conseiller, guider, orienter ■ he ~d the country through some difficult times il a su conduire le pays durant des périodes difficiles **4.** AERON guider.

guidebook ['gaɪdbuk] *n* guide *m* touristique *(manuel)*.

guided ['gaɪdɪd] *adj* guidé, sous la conduite d'un guide.

guided missile *n* missile *m* téléguidé.

guide dog *n* chien *m* d'aveugle.

guided tour *n* visite *f* guidée.

guideline ['gaɪdlaɪn] *n* **1.** [for writing] ligne *f* **2.** [hint, principle] ligne *f* directrice, directives *fpl*.

guiding ['gaɪdɪŋ] ◇ *adj* [principle] directeur ■ she gave me a ~ hand *fig* elle m'a donné un coup de main ■ he's been a ~ light in my career il m'a toujours guidé dans ma carrière ▶ ~ star guide *m*.
◇ *n* guidage *m*, conduite *f*.

guild [gɪld] *n* **1.** [professional] guilde *f*, corporation *f* **2.** [association] confrérie *f*, association *f*, club *m* ■ women's/church ~ cercle *m* féminin/paroissial.

guilder ['gɪldər] *n* florin *m* (hollandais).

guildhall ['gɪldhɔ:l] *n* palais *m* des corporations ■ The Guildhall *l'hôtel de ville de la City de Londres*.

guile [gaɪl] *n (U) fml* [trickery] fourberie *f*, tromperie *f* ■ [cunning] ruse *f*, astuce *f*.

guileless ['gaɪllɪs] *adj fml* candide, ingénu.

guillemot ['gɪlɪmɒt] (*pl inv* OR *pl* guillemots) *n* guillemot *m*.

guillotine ['gɪlə,ti:n] ◇ *n* **1.** [for executions] guillotine *f* **2.** [for paper] massicot *m* **3.** POL *procédure parlementaire consistant à fixer des délais stricts pour l'examen de chaque partie d'un projet de loi*.
◇ *vt* **1.** [person] guillotiner **2.** [paper] massicoter **3.** [discussion] clôturer.

guilt [gɪlt] *n* culpabilité *f* ■ ~ drove him to suicide un sentiment de culpabilité l'a poussé au suicide.

guilt complex *n* complexe *m* de culpabilité.

guiltily ['gɪltɪlɪ] *adv* d'un air coupable.

guiltless ['gɪltlɪs] *adj* innocent.

guilty ['gɪltɪ] (*comp* guiltier, *superl* guiltiest) *adj* LAW coupable ■ ~ of murder coupable de meurtre ■ to plead ~/not ~ plaider coupable/non coupable ■ the judge found her ~ le juge l'a déclarée coupable.

guinea ['gɪnɪ] *n* [money] guinée *f (ancienne monnaie britannique)*.

Guinea ['gɪnɪ] *pr n* Guinée *f* ■ in ~ en Guinée.

Guinea Bissau *pr n* Guinée-Bissau *f*.

guinea fowl (*pl inv*) *n* pintade *f*.

guinea hen *n* pintade *f (femelle)*.

Guinean ['gɪnɪən] ◇ *n* Guinéen *m*, - enne *f*.
◇ *adj* guinéen.

guinea pig *n* cochon *m* d'Inde, cobaye *m* ■ [used in experiments] cobaye *m* ■ to use sb as a ~ se servir de qqn comme d'un cobaye, prendre qqn comme cobaye.

guise [gaɪz] *n* **1.** [appearance] apparence *f*, aspect *m* ■ the same old policies in a new ~ la même politique sous des dehors différents ■ under OR in the ~ of sous l'apparence de **2.** *arch* [costume] costume *m*.

guitar [gɪ'tɑ:r] *n* guitare *f*.

guitarist [gɪ'tɑ:rɪst] *n* guitariste *mf*.

Gujarati [,gu:dʒə'rɑ:tɪ] *n* gujarati *m*.

gulag ['gu:læg] *n* goulag *m* ■ 'The Gulag Archipelago' *Solzhenitsyn* 'l'Archipel du goulag'.

gulch [gʌltʃ] *n* US ravin *m*.

gulf [gʌlf] ◇ *n* **1.** [bay] golfe *m* ■ the Gulf of Aden le golfe d'Aden ■ the Gulf of Bothnia le golfe de Botnie ■ the Gulf of California le golfe de Californie ■ the Gulf of Mexico le golfe du Mexique ■ the Gulf of Siam le golfe de Thaïlande **2.** [chasm] gouffre *m*, abîme *m* ■ a huge ~ has opened up between the two parties *fig* il y a désormais un énorme fossé entre les deux partis **3.** GEOG : the Gulf le golfe Persique.
◇ *comp* [country, oil] du Golfe ■ the Gulf War la guerre du Golfe ■ Gulf War Syndrome MED syndrome *m* de la guerre du Golfe.

Gulf States *pr npl* : the ~ [in US] les États du golfe du Mexique ; [round Persian Gulf] les États du Golfe.

gull [gʌl] *n* [bird] mouette *f*, goéland *m*.

gullet ['gʌlɪt] *n* [œsophagus] œsophage *m* ■ [throat] gosier *m*.

gulley ['gʌlɪ] (*pl* gulleys) = gully.

gullibility [,gʌlə'bɪlətɪ] *n* crédulité *f*, naïveté *f*.

gullible ['gʌləbl] *adj* crédule, naïf.

gull-wing *adj* AUT : ~ **door** portière *f* en papillon.

gully ['gʌlɪ] (*pl* **gullies**) *n* **1.** [valley] ravin *m* **2.** [drain] caniveau *m*, rigole *f*.

gulp [gʌlp] ◇ *vt* : **to ~ (down)** [food] engloutir ; [drink] avaler à pleine gorge ; [air] avaler.
◇ *vi* [with emotion] avoir un serrement de gorge ▪ **he ~ed in surprise** la surprise lui a serré la gorge.
◇ *n* [act of gulping] : **she swallowed it in one ~** elle l'a avalé d'un seul coup ▪ [with emotion] serrement *m* de gorge.
◆ **gulp back** *vt sep* avaler ▪ **she ~ed back her tears** elle a ravalé *OR* refoulé ses larmes.

gum [gʌm] (*pret & pp* **gummed**, *cont* **gumming**) ◇ *n* **1.** ANAT gencive *f* **2.** [chewing gum] chewing-gum *m* ▪ **to chew ~** mâcher du chewing-gum **3.** [adhesive] gomme *f*, colle *f* **4.** BOT [substance] gomme *f* **5.** *UK* = **gumdrop**.
◇ *vt* **1.** [cover with gum] gommer ▪ **gummed paper** papier gommé **2.** [stick] coller ▪ **~ down the flap** collez le rabat ▪ **~ the two edges together** collez les deux bords ensemble.
◇ *vi* BOT exsuder de la gomme.
◇ *interj UK inf dated* : **by ~!** nom d'un chien!, mince alors!
◆ **gum up** *vt sep inf* [mechanism] bousiller ▪ [plan] ficher en l'air ▪ **that's gummed up the works!** ça a tout fichu en l'air!

GUM (*abbrev of* **genito-urinary medicine**) *n* médecine *f* génito-urinaire.

gumbo ['gʌmbəʊ] (*pl* **gumbos**) *n* **1.** [dish] *soupe épaisse aux fruits de mer* **2.** *US* [okra] gombo *m*.

gumboil ['gʌmbɔɪl] *n* parulie *f*, abcès *m* gingival.

gumboot ['gʌmbu:t] *n UK* botte *f* de caoutchouc.

gumdrop ['gʌmdrɒp] *n* boule *f* de gomme.

gumption ['gʌmpʃn] *n (U) inf* **1.** *UK* [common sense] jugeote *f* ▪ **he didn't even have the ~ to call the police** il n'a même pas eu la présence d'esprit d'appeler la police **2.** [initiative] initiative *f*.

gumshield ['gʌmʃi:ld] *n* protège-dents *m inv*.

gumshoe△ ['gʌmʃu:] *US dated* ◇ *n* **1.** [shoe] caoutchouc *m* **2.** [person] détective *m* privé.
◇ *vi* aller à pas feutrés.

gum tree *n* gommier *m* ▪ **to be up a ~** *inf* être dans le pétrin.

gun [gʌn] (*pret & pp* **gunned**, *cont* **gunning**) ◇ *n* **1.** arme *f* à feu ▪ [pistol] pistolet *m* ▪ [revolver] revolver *m* ▪ [rifle] fusil *m* ▪ [cannon] canon *m* ▪ **the burglar had a ~** le cambrioleur était armé ▪ **to draw a ~ on sb** braquer une arme sur qqn ▪ **a 21-~ salute** une salve de 21 coups de canon ▪ **the ~s** MIL l'artillerie *f* ▶ **to be going great ~s** *inf* [enterprise] marcher à merveille ▪ **she's going great ~s** ça boume pour elle ▪ **the big ~s** *inf* les huiles *fpl* ▪ **to bring out one's big ~s** *inf* mettre le paquet ▪ **to jump the ~** SPORT partir avant le signal ; *fig* brûler les étapes ▪ **to stick to one's ~s** tenir bon, camper sur ses positions **2.** [hunter] fusil *m* **3.** *inf* [gunman] gangster *m* ▪ **hired ~** tueur *m* à gages **4.** [dispenser] pistolet *m* ▪ **paint ~** pistolet *m* à peinture **5.** ELECTRON canon *m*.
◇ *comp* : **~ law** loi *f* réglementant le port d'armes ▪ **~ lobby** lobby *m* favorable au port d'armes.
◇ *vt* AUT : **to ~ the engine** accélérer.
◆ **gun down** *vt sep* abattre.
◆ **gun for** *vt insep* **1.** [look for] chercher ▪ **the boss is gunning for you** le patron te cherche *OR* est après toi **2.** [try hard for] faire des pieds et des mains pour obtenir.

gunboat ['gʌnbəʊt] *n* canonnière *f*.

gunboat diplomacy *n* diplomatie *f* imposée par la force, politique *f* de la canonnière.

gun carriage *n* affût *m* de canon.

gun crew *n* servants *mpl* de pièce.

gundog ['gʌndɒg] *n* chien *m* de chasse.

gunfight ['gʌnfaɪt] *n* fusillade *f*.

gunfire ['gʌnfaɪəʳ] *n (U)* coups *mpl* de feu, fusillade *f* ▪ [of cannon] tir *m* d'artillerie.

gunge [gʌndʒ] *n (U) inf* substance *f* collante, amas *m* visqueux.

gung-ho [,gʌŋ'həʊ] *adj* tout feu tout flamme, enthousiaste.

gunk [gʌŋk] *n (U) inf* substance *f* visqueuse, amas *m* répugnant.

gun licence *n* permis *m* de port d'armes.

gunman ['gʌnmən] (*pl* **gunmen** [-mən]) *n* gangster *m* (armé) ▪ [terrorist] terroriste *m* (armé).

gun-metal grey ◇ *adj* vert-de-gris *(inv)*.
◇ *n* vert-de-gris *m inv*.

gunnel ['gʌnl] = **gunwale**.

gunner ['gʌnəʳ] *n* artilleur *m*, canonnier *m*.

gunnery ['gʌnərɪ] *n (U)* artillerie *f*.

gunnery officer *n* officier *m* d'artillerie.

gunny ['gʌnɪ] *n* toile *f* de jute (grossière).

gunplay ['gʌnpleɪ] *n US* échange *m* de coups de feu.

gunpoint ['gʌnpɔɪnt] *n* : **to have *OR* to hold sb at ~** menacer qqn d'un pistolet *OR* d'un revolver *OR* d'un fusil ▪ **a confession obtained at ~** une confession obtenue sous la menace d'un revolver.

gunpowder ['gʌn,paʊdəʳ] *n* poudre *f* à canon.

Gunpowder Plot *n* : **the ~** *UK* HIST la conspiration des poudres.

THE GUNPOWDER PLOT

Complot catholique, conduit par Guy Fawkes, le 5 novembre 1605, pour faire sauter le Parlement britannique et tuer le roi protestant Jacques Ier qui avait refusé d'instaurer la liberté de culte. Le complot fut déjoué et son instigateur exécuté. Cet événement est commémoré tous les ans par le *Guy Fawkes' Night*.

gun room *n* [in house] armurerie *f* ▪ [on warship] poste *m* des aspirants.

gunrunner ['gʌn,rʌnəʳ] *n* trafiquant *m*, - e *f* d'armes.

gunrunning ['gʌn,rʌnɪŋ] *n (U)* trafic *m* d'armes.

gunship ['gʌnʃɪp] *n* [helicopter] hélicoptère *m* armé.

gunshot ['gʌnʃɒt] *n* **1.** [shot] coup *m* de feu ▪ **a ~ wound** une blessure de *OR* par balle **2.** [range] : **to be out of/within ~** être hors de portée de/à portée de fusil.

gunslinger ['gʌn,slɪŋəʳ] *n inf* bandit *m* armé.

gunsmith ['gʌnsmɪθ] *n* armurier *m*.

gun turret *n* tourelle *f*.

gunwale ['gʌnl] *n* NAUT plat-bord *m*.

guppy ['gʌpɪ] (*pl* **guppies**) *n* ZOOL guppy *m*.

gurgle ['gɜ:gl] ◇ *vi* [liquid] glouglouter, gargouiller ▪ [stream] murmurer ▪ [person - with delight] glousser, roucouler ▪ [baby] gazouiller.
◇ *n* [of liquid] glouglou *m*, gargouillis *m* ▪ [of stream] murmure *m*, gazouillement *m* ▪ [of laughter] gloussement *m*, roucoulement *m* ▪ [of baby] gazouillis.

Gurkha ['gɜ:kə] *n* Gurkha *m*.

gurney ['gʌrnɪ] *n US* chariot *m* d'hôpital.

guru ['gʊru:] *n* gourou *m*.

gush [gʌʃ] ◇ *vi* **1.** [flow] jaillir ▪ **water ~ed forth *OR* out** l'eau jaillissait **2.** [talk effusively] parler avec animation ▪ **everyone was ~ing over the baby** tout le monde se répandait en compliments sur le bébé.
◇ *n* **1.** [of liquid, gas] jet *m*, flot *m* ▪ **a ~ of words** *fig* un flot de paroles **2.** [of emotion] vague *f*, effusion *f*.

gushing ['gʌʃɪŋ] *adj* **1.** [liquid] jaillissant, bouillonnant **2.** [person] trop exubérant ▪ **~ compliments/praise** compliments/éloges sans fin.

gushy ['gʌʃɪ] (*comp* **gushier**, *superl* **gushiest**) *adj inf pej* [person] exubérant.

gusset ['gʌsɪt] *n* **1.** SEW soufflet *m* **2.** CONSTR gousset *m*.

gust [gʌst] ◇ *n* : **a ~ (of wind)** un coup de vent, une rafale.

<> *vi* [wind] souffler en bourrasques ▪ [rain] faire des bourrasques ▪ **winds ~ing up to 50 mph were recorded** on a enregistré des pointes de vent à 80 km/h.

gusto ['gʌstəʊ] *n* délectation *f*, enthousiasme *m*.

gusty ['gʌstɪ] (*comp* **gustier**, *superl* **gustiest**) *adj* : **a ~ wind** un vent qui souffle en rafales, des rafales de vent.

gut [gʌt] <> *n* **1.** *(usu pl)* ANAT boyau *m*, intestin *m* ▪ **~s** intestins *mpl*, boyaux *mpl*, entrailles *fpl* ▪ **I've got a pain in the ~** *inf* j'ai mal au bide ➲ **~ feeling** pressentiment *m* ▪ **~ reaction** réaction *f* instinctive *OR* viscérale **2.** *inf (usu pl) inf* [of machine] intérieur *m* **3.** *(U)* [thread - for violins] corde *f* de boyau ; [- for rackets] boyau *m*.
<> *vt* **1.** [fish, poultry etc] étriper, vider **2.** [building] ne laisser que les quatre murs de **3.** [book] résumer, extraire l'essentiel de.
◆ **guts** *inf* <> *n* [glutton] morfal *m*, - e *f* ▪ **don't be such a (greedy) ~s** ne sois pas si morfal.
<> *npl phr* **to have ~s** avoir du cran *OR* du cœur au ventre ▪ **he has no ~s** il n'a rien dans le ventre ▪ **to work** *OR* **to sweat one's ~s out** se casser les reins, se tuer au travail ▪ **to hate sb's ~s** ne pas pouvoir blairer qqn ▪ **I'll have your ~s for garters** je vais faire de toi de la chair à pâté.

gutless ['gʌtlɪs] *adj inf* [cowardly] trouillard, dégonflé.

gutsy ['gʌtsɪ] (*comp* **gutsier**, *superl* **gutsiest**) *adj inf* **1.** [courageous] qui a du cran **2.** [powerful - film, language, novel] qui a du punch, musclé ▪ **a ~ singer** un chanteur qui a des tripes.

gutted△ ['gʌtɪd] *adj UK* : **to be** *OR* **to feel ~** en être malade.

gutter ['gʌtəʳ] <> *n* **1.** [on roof] gouttière *f* ▪ [in street] caniveau *m*, ruisseau *m* ▪ *fig* **to rescue sb from** *OR* **to drag sb out of the ~** tirer qqn du ruisseau ▪ **to speak the language of the ~** parler le langage des rues **2.** [ditch] rigole *f*, sillon *m (creusé par la pluie)* ▪ [in bookbinding] petits fonds *mpl*.
<> *vi* [candle flame] vaciller, trembler.

guttering ['gʌtərɪŋ] *n (U)* [of roof] gouttières *fpl*.

gutter press *n pej* presse *f* de bas étage, presse *f* à scandale.

guttersnipe ['gʌtəsnaɪp] *n pej* gosse *mf* des rues.

guttural ['gʌtərəl] <> *adj* guttural.
<> *n* LING gutturale *f*.

guv [gʌv], **guvnor** ['gʌvnəʳ] *n UK inf* **the ~** [boss] le chef, le boss ; *dated* [father] le pater, le paternel.

guy [gaɪ] *n* **1.** *inf* [man] gars *m*, type *m* ▪ **a good ~** un mec *OR* un type bien ▪ **ok ~s, let's go** allez les gars, on y va ; *US* [to both men and women] allez les copains, on y va ▪ **are you ~s ready?** vous êtes prêts, les gars? ; *US* [to both men and women] tout le monde est prêt? **2.** *UK* [for bonfire] *effigie de Guy Fawkes* **3.** [for tent] corde *f* de tente.

Guyana [gaɪ'ænə] *pr n* Guyana *m* ▪ **in ~** au Guyana.

Guyanese [,gaɪə'ni:z] *adj* guyanais.

Guy Fawkes' Night [-'fɔ:ks-] *pr n fête célébrée le 5 novembre en commémoration de la Conspiration des poudres.*

GUY FAWKES' NIGHT

Cette fête populaire a lieu chaque année le 5 novembre autour d'un feu de joie où brûle l'effigie (*the Guy*) de Guy Fawkes, instigateur de la Conspiration des poudres. Des feux d'artifice sont tirés.

guy rope = **guy** *(sense 3)*.

guzzle ['gʌzl] *inf* <> *vt* [food] bouffer, bâfrer ▪ [drink] siffler ▪ **this car really ~s petrol** *UK OR* **the gas** *US* cette voiture bouffe vraiment beaucoup (d'essence).
<> *vi* [eat] s'empiffrer, se goinfrer ▪ [drink] boire trop vite.

guzzler ['gʌzləʳ] *n inf* [person] goinfre *mf* ▪ [car] ▷ **gas guzzler**.

gym [dʒɪm] *n* [hall, building] gymnase *m* ▪ [activity] gymnastique *f*, gym *f*.

gymkhana [dʒɪm'kɑ:nə] *n* gymkhana *m*.

gymnasium [dʒɪm'neɪzjəm] (*pl* **gymnasiums** *OR pl* **gymnasia** [-zɪə]) *n* gymnase *m*.

gymnast ['dʒɪmnæst] *n* gymnaste *mf*.

gymnastic [dʒɪm'næstɪk] *adj* [exercises] de gymnastique ▪ [ability] de gymnaste.

gymnastics [dʒɪm'næstɪks] *n (U)* gymnastique *f* ▪ **mental ~** gymnastique cérébrale.

gym shoe *n* chaussure *f* de gymnastique *OR* gym.

gymslip ['dʒɪm,slɪp], **gym tunic** *n* [part of uniform] blouse *f* d'écolière.

gynaecology *etc* [,gaɪnə'kɒlədʒɪ] *UK* = **gynecology**.

gynecological [,gaɪnəkə'lɒdʒɪkl] *adj* gynécologique.

gynecologist [,gaɪnə'kɒlədʒɪst] *n* gynécologue *mf*.

gynecology [,gaɪnə'kɒlədʒɪ] *n* gynécologie *f*.

gyp [dʒɪp] (*pret & pp* **gypped**, *cont* **gypping**) *inf n UK* : **to give sb ~** [cause pain] dérouiller qqn.

gypsum ['dʒɪpsəm] *n* gypse *m*.

gypsy ['dʒɪpsɪ] (*pl* **gypsies**) = **gipsy**.

gyrate [dʒaɪ'reɪt] *vi* tournoyer.

gyration [dʒaɪ'reɪʃn] *n* giration *f*.

gyratory ['dʒaɪrətrɪ] *adj* giratoire.

gyroscope ['dʒaɪrəskəʊp] *n* gyroscope *m*.

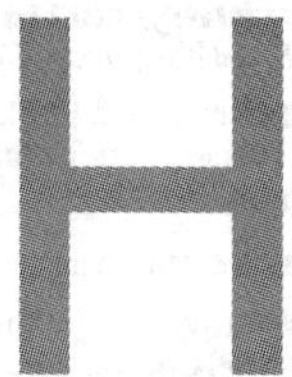

h (*pl* **h's** *OR pl* **hs**)**, H** (*pl* **H's** *OR pl* **Hs**) [eɪtʃ] *n* [letter] h *m*, H *m* ▪ **to drop one's h's** avaler ses h *(et révéler par là ses origines populaires)*, *see also* **f**.

ha [hɑː] *interj* [in triumph, sudden comprehension] ha!, ah! ▪ [in contempt] peuh!

habeas corpus [ˌheɪbjəs'kɔːpəs] *n* LAW habeas corpus *m* ▪ **to issue a writ of ~** délivrer un (acte d')habeas corpus.

THE HABEAS CORPUS ACT

Ordre écrit, datant de 1679, autorisant tout individu arrêté à demander à un juge ou à un tribunal d'examiner le caractère légal de son arrestation. Complété ultérieurement par d'autres lois (en 1816 et en 1960), cet ordre est toujours en vigueur en Grande-Bretagne et dans tous les pays soumis à la *Common Law* (Écosse exceptée). Il a également été intégré à la Constitution américaine.

haberdasher ['hæbədæʃər] *n* **1.** *UK* [draper] mercier *m*, - ère *f* **2.** *US* [shirtmaker] chemisier *m*, - ère *f*.

haberdashery ['hæbədæʃərɪ] *n* **1.** *UK* [draper's] mercerie *f* **2.** *US* [shirtmaker's] marchand *m*, - e *f* de vêtements d'hommes *(en particulier de gants et de chapeaux)*.

habit ['hæbɪt] *n* **1.** [custom] habitude *f* ▪ **to be in/to get into the ~ of doing sthg** avoir/prendre l'habitude de faire qqch ▪ **to get sb into the ~ of doing sthg** faire prendre à qqn *OR* donner à qqn l'habitude de faire qqch, habituer qqn à faire qqch ▪ **to make a ~ of sthg/of doing sthg** prendre l'habitude de qqch/de faire qqch ▪ **don't worry, I'm not going to make a ~ of it** ne t'en fais pas, cela ne deviendra pas une habitude ▪ **just don't make a ~ of it!** ne recommence pas!, que cela ne se reproduise pas! ▪ **to get out of a ~** perdre une habitude ▪ **he has a very strange ~ of pulling his ear when he talks** il a un tic très étrange consistant à se tirer l'oreille quand il parle **2.** *inf* [drug dependency] : **to have a ~** être accro[△] ▪ **to kick the ~** [drugs, tobacco] décrocher **3.** [dress - of monk, nun] habit *m* ; [- for riding] tenue *f* de cheval.

habitable ['hæbɪtəbl] *adj* habitable.

habitat ['hæbɪtæt] *n* habitat *m*.

habitation [ˌhæbɪ'teɪʃn] *n* **1.** [occupation] habitation *f* ▪ **there were signs of recent ~** l'endroit semblait avoir été habité dans un passé récent ▪ **fit/unfit for ~** habitable/inhabitable ; [from sanitary point of view] salubre/insalubre **2.** [place] habitation *f*, résidence *f*, demeure *f*.

habit-forming [-ˌfɔːmɪŋ] *adj* [drug] qui crée une accoutumance *OR* une dépendance.

habitual [hə'bɪtʃʊəl] *adj* [customary - generosity, lateness, good humour] habituel, accoutumé ; [- liar, drinker] invétéré ▪ **~ offender** LAW récidiviste *mf*.

habitually [hə'bɪtʃʊəlɪ] *adv* habituellement, ordinairement.

habituate [hə'bɪtʃʊeɪt] *vt fml* **to ~ o.s./sb to sthg** s'habituer/habituer qqn à qqch.

hack [hæk] ◇ *n* **1.** [sharp blow] coup *m* violent ▪ [kick] coup *m* de pied **2.** [cut] entaille *f* **3.** *pej* [writer] écrivaillon *m* ▪ [politician] politicard *m* **4.** [horse for riding] cheval *m* de selle ▪ [horse for hire] cheval *m* de louage ▪ [old horse, nag] rosse *f*, carne *f* **5.** [ride] : **to go for a ~** aller faire une promenade à cheval **6.** [cough] toux *f* sèche.
◇ *comp* : **~ writer** écrivaillon *m*, écrivain *m* médiocre ▪ **~ writing** travail *m* d'écrivaillon.
◇ *vt* **1.** [cut] taillader, tailler ▪ **to ~ sb/sthg to pieces** tailler qqn/qqch en pièces ; *fig* [opponent, manuscript] mettre *OR* tailler qqn/qqch en pièces ▪ **to ~ sb to death** tuer qqn à coups de couteau *OR* de hache ▪ **he ~ed his way through the jungle** il s'est taillé un passage à travers la jungle à coups de machette **2.** [kick - ball] donner un coup de pied sec dans ▪ **to ~ sb on the shins** donner un coup de pied dans les tibias à qqn **3.** COMPUT : **to ~ one's way into a system** entrer dans un système par effraction **4.** *inf phr* **I can't ~ it** [can't cope] je n'en peux plus, je craque ▪ **the new guy can't ~ it** le nouveau ne tient pas le choc.
◇ *vi* **1.** [cut] donner des coups de couteau *(de hache etc)* ▪ **to ~ (away) at sthg** taillader qqch **2.** [kick] : **to ~ at sb's shins** donner des coups de pied dans les tibias à qqn **3.** COMPUT : **to ~ into a system** entrer dans un système par effraction **4.** [on horseback] aller à cheval ▪ **to go ~ing** aller faire une promenade à cheval.
◆ **hack down** *vt sep* [tree] abattre à coups de hache ▪ [person] massacrer à coups de couteau *(de hache etc)*.
◆ **hack into** *vt sep* [body, corpse] taillader ▪ *fig* [text, article] massacrer.
◆ **hack off** *vt sep* [branch, sb's head] couper.
◆ **hack up** *vt sep* [meat, wood] tailler *OR* couper en menus morceaux ▪ [body, victim] mettre en pièces, découper en morceaux.

hacker ['hækər] *n* COMPUT [enthusiast] mordu *m*, - e *f* de l'informatique ▪ [pirate] pirate *m* informatique.

hackie ['hækɪ] *n US inf* chauffeur *m* de taxi.

hacking ['hækɪŋ] ◇ *n (U)* **1.** [in football, rugby etc] coups *mpl* de pied dans les tibias **2.** [coughing] toux *f* sèche **3.** COMPUT piratage *m (informatique)*.
◇ *adj* : **~ cough** toux *f* sèche.

hacking jacket *n* veste *f* de cheval.

hackle ['hækl] *n* [of bird] plume *f* du cou.

hackles ['hæklz] *npl* [of dog] poils *mpl* du cou ▪ **when a dog has its ~ up** quand un chien a le poil hérissé ‖ *fig* **it gets my ~ up, it makes my ~ rise** ça me hérisse.

hackney carriage ['hæknɪ-] *n* **1.** [horse-drawn] fiacre *m* **2.** *fml* [taxi] *taxi officiellement agréé.*

hackneyed ['hæknɪd] *adj* [subject] réchauffé, rebattu ■ [turn of phrase] banal, commun ■ **~ expression** cliché *m*, lieu *m* commun.

hacksaw ['hæksɔ:] *n* scie *f* à métaux.

had [(*weak form* [həd], *strong form* [hæd])] *pt* & *pp* ⇨ **have**.

haddock ['hædək] *n* aiglefin *m*, églefin *m* ■ [smoked] haddock *m*.

Hades ['heɪdi:z] *pr n* Hadès.

hadn't ['hædnt] = **had not**.

Hadrian ['heɪdrɪən] *pr n* Hadrien ■ **~'s Wall** le Mur d'Hadrien.

haematology *UK*, **hematology** *US* [ˌhi:mə'tɒlədʒɪ] *n* hématologie *f*.

haematoma *UK*, **hematoma** *US* [ˌhi:mə'təʊmə] *n* hématome *m*.

haemoglobin *UK*, **hemoglobin** *US* [ˌhi:mə'gləʊbɪn] *n* hémoglobine *f*.

haemophilia *UK*, **hemophilia** *US* [ˌhi:mə'fɪlɪə] *n* hémophilie *f*.

haemophiliac *UK*, **hemophiliac** *US* [ˌhi:mə'fɪlɪæk] *n* hémophile *mf*.

haemorrhage *UK*, **hemorrhage** *US* ['hemərɪdʒ] ◇ *n* hémorragie *f*.
◇ *vi* faire une hémorragie.

haemorrhaging *UK*, **hemorrhaging** *US* ['heməɾɪˌdʒɪŋ] *n (U)* hémorragie ■ **there's still some ~** l'hémorragie n'est pas encore arrêtée.

haemorrhoids *UK*, **hemorrhoids** *US* ['hemərɔɪdz] *npl* hémorroïdes *fpl*.

haft [hæft] *n* [of knife] manche *m* ■ [of sword] poignée *f*.

hag [hæg] *n* [witch] sorcière *f* ■ *pej* [old woman] vieille sorcière *f*, vieille chouette *f* ■ [unpleasant woman] harpie *f*.

haggard ['hægəd] *adj* [tired, worried] hâve.

haggis ['hægɪs] *n plat typique écossais fait d'une panse de brebis farcie.*

haggle ['hægl] ◇ *vi* **1.** [bargain] marchander ■ **to ~ over the price** marchander sur le prix **2.** [argue over details] chicaner, chipoter ■ **to ~ over** *OR* **about sthg** chicaner *OR* chipoter sur qqch.
◇ *n* **: after a long ~ over the price** après un long marchandage sur le prix.

haggler ['hæglər] *n* **1.** [over price] marchandeur *m*, - euse *f* **2.** [over details, wording] chicaneur *m*, - euse *f*, chipoteur *m*, - euse *f*.

haggling ['hæglɪŋ] *n (U)* **1.** [over price] marchandage *m* **2.** [about details, wording] chicanerie *f*, chipotage *m*.

hagiography [ˌhægɪ'ɒgrəfɪ] *n* hagiographie *f*.

Hague [heɪg] *pr n* **: The ~** La Haye.

hah [hɑ:] = **ha**.

ha-ha ◇ *interj* [mock amusement] ha ha ■ [representing laughter: in comic, novel] ha ha ha, hi hi hi.
◇ *n* [wall, fence] *mur ou clôture installé dans un fossé.*

hail [heɪl] ◇ *n* METEOR grêle *f* ■ *fig* [of stones] grêle *f*, pluie *f* ■ [of abuse] avalanche *f*, déluge *m* ■ [of blows] grêle *f* ■ **he died in a ~ of bullets** il est tombé sous une pluie de balles.
◇ *vi* METEOR grêler.
◇ *vt* **1.** [call to - taxi, ship, person] héler ■ **within ~ing distance** à portée de voix **2.** [greet - person] acclamer, saluer **3.** [acclaim - person, new product, invention etc] acclamer, saluer ■ **to ~ sb emperor** proclamer qqn empereur **4.** *phr* **to ~ blows on sb** faire pleuvoir les coups sur qqn.
◇ *interj arch* salut à vous *OR* toi.

◆ **hail down** ◇ *vi insep* [blows, stones etc] pleuvoir.
◇ *vt sep* **: to ~ down curses on sb** *lit* déverser un déluge de malédictions sur qqn.

◆ **hail from** *vt insep* [ship] être en provenance de ■ [person] venir de, être originaire de.

hail-fellow-well-met *adj dated* & *pej* **he's always very ~** il fait toujours montre d'une familiarité joviale.

Hail Mary *n* RELIG [prayer] Je vous salue Marie *m inv*, Ave (Maria) *m inv*.

hailstone ['heɪlstəʊn] *n* grêlon *m*.

hailstorm ['heɪlstɔ:m] *n* averse *f* de grêle.

hair [heər] ◇ *n* **1.** *(U)* [on person's head] cheveux *mpl* ■ **to have long/short ~** avoir les cheveux longs/courts ■ **to get** *OR* **to have one's ~ cut** se faire couper les cheveux ■ **to get one's ~ done** se faire coiffer ■ **I like the way you've done your ~** j'aime bien la façon dont tu t'es coiffé ■ **to wash one's ~** se laver les cheveux *OR* la tête ■ **to brush one's ~** se brosser (les cheveux) ■ **she put her ~ up** elle a relevé ses cheveux ■ **your ~ looks nice** tu es bien coiffée ■ **my ~'s a mess** je suis vraiment mal coiffé **2.** [single hair - on person's head] cheveu *m* ; [- on person's or animal's face or body] poil *m* ■ **move it a ~ over to the right** *US inf* déplace-le un chouia vers la droite
3. *(U)* [on body, face] poils *mpl* ■ [on animal] poils *mpl*
4. *phr* **it makes your ~ stand on end** [is frightening] c'est à vous faire dresser les cheveux sur la tête ■ **it would make your ~ curl** *inf* [ride, journey] c'est à vous faire dresser les cheveux sur la tête ; [prices, bad language] c'est à vous faire tomber à la renverse ; [drink] ça arrache ■ **keep your ~ on!** *UK inf* ne t'excite pas! ■ **to let one's ~ down** se laisser aller, se défouler ■ **to get in sb's ~** *inf* taper sur les nerfs de qqn ■ **keep him out of my ~** *inf* fais en sorte que je ne l'aie pas dans les jambes ■ **to have a ~ of the dog (that bit you)** *hum* reprendre un verre (pour faire passer sa gueule de bois) ■ **to split ~s** couper les cheveux en quatre, chercher la petite bête ■ **she never has a ~ out of place** [is immaculate] elle n'a jamais un cheveu de travers ■ **to win by a ~** gagner d'un cheveu *OR* d'un quart de poil ■ **she didn't turn a ~** elle n'a pas cillé ■ **this will put ~s on your chest** *inf hum* [strong drink, good steak etc] ça va te redonner du poil de la bête.
◇ *comp* **1.** [cream, conditioner, lotion] capillaire, pour les cheveux ■ **~ appointment** rendez-vous *m* chez le coiffeur ■ **~ straightener** produit *m* défrisant
2. [colour] de cheveux
3. [mattress] de crin.

hairband ['heəbænd] *n* bandeau *m*.

hairbrush ['heəbrʌʃ] *n* brosse *f* à cheveux.

hairclip ['heəklɪp] *n* barrette *f*.

hair clippers *npl* tondeuse *f* ■ **a pair of ~** une tondeuse.

haircut ['heəkʌt] *n* coupe *f* (de cheveux) ■ **I need a ~** j'ai besoin de me faire couper les cheveux ■ **to have a ~** se faire couper les cheveux ■ **to give sb a ~** couper les cheveux à qqn.

hairdo ['heədu:] *n inf* coiffure *f*.

hairdresser ['heəˌdresər] *n* [shop] salon *m* de coiffure ■ **to go to the ~'s** aller chez le coiffeur.

hairdressing ['heəˌdresɪŋ] *n* [skill] coiffure *f* ■ **~ salon** salon *m* de coiffure.

hair drier, hair dryer *n* [hand-held] sèche-cheveux *m inv*, séchoir *m* ■ [over the head] casque *m*.

-haired [heəd] *in cpds* **: long/short-~** [person] aux cheveux longs/courts ; [animal] à poil(s) long(s)/court(s) ■ **wire-~** [dog] à poil(s) dur(s).

hair follicle *n* follicule *m* pileux.

hair gel *n* gel *m* pour les cheveux.

hairgrip ['heəgrɪp] *n UK* pince *f* à cheveux.

hairless ['heəlɪs] *adj* [head] chauve, sans cheveux ■ [face] glabre ■ [body] peu poilu ■ [animal] sans poils ■ [leaf] glabre.

hairline ['heəlaɪn] <> *n* **1.** [of the hair] naissance *f* des cheveux ▪ **to have a receding ~** [above forehead] avoir le front qui se dégarnit ; [at temples] avoir les tempes qui se dégarnissent **2.** [in telescope, gun sight] fil *m*.
<> *comp* : **~ crack** fêlure *f* ▪ **~ fracture** MED fêlure *f*.

hairnet ['heənet] *n* résille *f*, filet *m* à cheveux.

hairpiece ['heəpi:s] *n* [toupee] perruque *f (pour hommes)* ▪ [extra hair] postiche *m*.

hairpin ['heəpɪn] *n* **1.** [for hair] épingle *f* à cheveux **2.** : **~ (bend)** virage *m* en épingle à cheveux.

hair-raising [-,reɪzɪŋ] *adj* [adventure, experience, story, account] à faire dresser les cheveux sur la tête, effrayant, terrifiant ▪ [prices, expenses] affolant, exorbitant.

hair remover *n* crème *f* dépilatoire.

hair restorer *n* produit *m* pour la repousse des cheveux.

hair's breadth *n* : **the truck missed us by a ~** le camion nous a manqués d'un cheveu OR de justesse ▪ **we came within a ~ of going bankrupt/of winning first prize** nous avons été à deux doigts de la faillite/de gagner le premier prix.

hair shirt *n* haire *f*, cilice *m*.

hair slide *n* barrette *f*.

hairsplitting ['heə,splɪtɪŋ] <> *adj* : **that's a ~ argument** OR **distinction** c'est de la chicanerie, c'est couper les cheveux en quatre.
<> *n (U)* chicanerie *f* ▪ **that's just ~** tu es vraiment en train de couper les cheveux en quatre.

hair spray *n* laque *f* OR spray *m* (pour les cheveux).

hairspring ['heəsprɪŋ] *n* [in clock] spiral *m (de montre)*.

hairstyle ['heəstaɪl] *n* coiffure *f*.

hairstylist ['heə,staɪlɪst] *n* styliste *mf* en coiffure.

hair trigger *n* [in firearm] détente *f* OR gâchette *f* sensible.
◆ **hair-trigger** *adj fig* **to have a hair-trigger temper** [lose one's temper easily] s'emporter facilement.

hairy ['heərɪ] (*comp* **hairier**, *superl* **hairiest**) *adj* **1.** [arms, chest] poilu, velu ▪ [person, animal] poilu ▪ [stalk of plant] velu **2.** *inf* [frightening] à faire dresser les cheveux sur la tête ▪ [difficult, daunting] qui craint ▪ **there were a few ~ moments when the brakes seemed to be failing** il y a eu des moments craignos où les freins semblaient lâcher ▪ **things are getting a bit ~ at the office** [because of workload] ça devient un peu la folie au bureau ; [because of personal or financial tension] ça commence à craindre au bureau.

Haiti ['heɪtɪ] *pr n* Haïti ▪ **in ~** à Haïti.

Haitian ['heɪʃn] <> *adj* haïtien.
<> *n* Haïtien *m*, - enne *f*.

hake [heɪk] *n* merlu *m*, colin *m*.

halal [hə'lɑ:l] <> *n* [meat] viande *f* halal.
<> *adj* halal.

halcyon ['hælsɪən] *adj* : **those ~ days** *lit* ces temps heureux.

hale [heɪl] *adj* : **~ and hearty** en pleine santé.

half [UK hɑ:f, US hæf] (*pl* **halves** [UK hɑ:vz, US hævz]) <> *n* **1.** moitié *f* ▪ [of standard measured amount] demi *m*, - e *f* ▪ [of ticket, coupon] souche *f* ▪ **to cut/to break sthg in ~** couper/casser qqch en deux ▪ **what's ~ of 13.72?** quelle est la moitié de 13,72? ▪ **two and two halves, please** [on bus, train etc] deux billets tarif normal et deux billets demi-tarif, s'il vous plaît ▪ **it cuts the journey time in ~** cela réduit de moitié la durée du voyage ▪ **three and a ~ pieces/years** trois morceaux/ans et demi ▪ **bigger by ~** UK plus grand de moitié ▪ **two halves make a whole** deux moitiés OR demis font un tout ▪ **to go halves with sb** partager avec qqn ▪ **they don't do things by halves** ils ne font pas les choses à moitié ❯ **he always was too clever by ~** UK il a toujours été un peu trop malin ▪ **that was a walk and a ~!** *inf* c'était une sacrée promenade! ▪ **and that's not the ~ of it** *inf* et ce n'est que le début ▪ **my better** OR **other ~** *hum* ma (chère) moitié ▪ **to see how the other ~ lives** *hum* voir comment on vit de l'autre côté de la barrière, voir comment vivent les autres
2. [period of sports match] mi-temps *f inv*
3. [area of football or rugby pitch] camp *m*
4. [rugby or football player] demi *m*
5. UK [half pint of beer] demi *m* (de bière).
<> *pron* : **leave ~ of it for me** laisse-m'en la moitié ▪ **~ of us were students** la moitié d'entre nous étaient des étudiants.
<> *adj* : **a ~ chicken** un demi-poulet ▪ **at ~ speed** au ralenti ▪ **to travel ~ fare** voyager à demi-tarif.
<> *predet* : **~ the time he seems to be asleep** on a l'impression qu'il est endormi la moitié du temps ▪ **he's ~ a year older than me** il a six mois de plus que moi ▪ **~ a minute!** *inf* une (petite) minute! ▪ **I'll be down in ~ a second** *inf* je descends tout de suite ▪ **I'll be there in ~ an hour** j'y serai dans une demi-heure ▪ **just ~ a cup for me** juste une demi-tasse pour moi ❯ **he's not ~ the man he used to be** il n'est plus que l'ombre de lui-même ▪ **to have ~ a mind to do sthg** *inf* avoir bien envie de faire qqch.
<> *adv* **1.** [finished, asleep, dressed] à moitié ▪ [full, empty, blind] à moitié, à demi ▪ **to be ~ full of sthg** être à moitié rempli de qqch ▪ **a strange colour, ~ green, ~ blue** une couleur bizarre, entre le vert et le bleu ▪ **to be ~ English and ~ French** être moitié anglais moitié français ▪ **I ~ think that...** je suis tenté de penser que...
2. UK *inf* [as intensifier] : **they're not ~ fit** ils sont en super-forme ▪ **it's not ~ cold today!** il fait rudement OR sacrément froid aujourd'hui! ▪ **he didn't ~ yell** il a hurlé comme un fou ▪ **did you complain? – not ~!** est-ce que vous vous êtes plaint? – et comment! OR pas qu'un peu!
3. [time] : **it's ~ past two** UK, **it's ~ two** il est deux heures et demie ▪ **~ after six** US six heures et demie
4. *phr* **to be ~ as big/fast as sb/sthg** être moitié moins grand/rapide que qqn/qqch ▪ **to earn ~ as much as sb** gagner moitié moins que qqn ▪ **to be ~ as big again (as sb/sthg)** être moitié plus grand (que qqn/qqch).

half-and-half <> *n* UK [beer] *mélange de deux bières* ▪ US [for coffee] *mélange de crème et de lait*.
<> *adv* moitié-moitié ▪ **it's ~** c'est moitié-moitié.

halfback ['hɑ:fbæk] *n* SPORT demi *m*.

half-baked [-'beɪkt] *adj inf fig* [scheme, proposal] qui ne tient pas debout ▪ [person] niais.

half-blood *n dated & offens* métis *m*, - isse *f*, *see also* **half-breed**.

half board UK <> *n* demi-pension *f*.
<> *adv* en demi-pension.

half-breed <> *n* **1.** [animal] hybride *m* ▪ [horse] cheval *m* demi-sang **2.** *dated & offens* [person] métis *m*, - isse *f*.
<> *adj* **1.** [animal] hybride ▪ [horse] demi-sang **2.** *dated & offens* [person] métis.

half-brother *n* demi-frère *m*.

half-caste *dated & offens* <> *n* [person] métis *m*, - isse *f*.
<> *adj* métis.

half-circle *n* demi-cercle *m*.

half cock *n* : **to go off at ~** [plan] avorter.

half-crazy *adj* à moitié fou.

half-cup *adj* : **~ bra** soutien-gorge *m* à balconnet.

half-day <> *n* [at school, work] demi-journée *f* ▪ **tomorrow is my ~** [work] demain c'est ma demi-journée de congé ▪ **to work ~s** faire des demi-journées.
<> *adj* : **a ~ holiday** une demi-journée de congé.

half-dead *adj* UK *inf* [very tired] à moitié mort, complètement crevé.

half-dollar *n* pièce *f* de 50 cents.

half-dozen *n* demi-douzaine *f* ▪ **a ~ eggs** une demi-douzaine d'œufs.

half-drowned [-'draʊnd] *adj* à moitié OR à demi noyé.

half-eaten *adj* à moitié mangé.

half-fill *vt* [glass] remplir à moitié OR à demi.

half-full *adj* à moitié OR à demi plein.

half-hardy *adj* BOT semi-rustique.

half-hearted *adj* [attempt, attitude] qui manque d'enthousiasme *OR* de conviction, timide, hésitant ▪ [acceptance] tiède, qui manque d'enthousiasme ▪ **he was very ~ about it** il était vraiment peu enthousiaste à ce propos.

half-heartedly [-'hɑːtɪdlɪ] *adv* [accept, agree, say] sans enthousiasme *OR* conviction, du bout des lèvres.

half-hitch *n* demi-clef *f*.

half-holiday *n* demi-journée *f* de congé.

half-hour ◇ *n* [period] demi-heure *f* ▪ **I'll wait a ~** *US* j'attendrai une demi-heure ▪ **on the ~** à la demie.
◇ *comp* : **at ~ intervals** toutes les demi-heures.

half-hourly *adj* & *adv* toutes les demi-heures.

half-joking *adj* mi-figue, mi-raisin.

half-jokingly *adv* d'un air mi-figue, mi-raisin.

half-landing *n* [on staircase] palier *m* de repos.

half-length *adj* [portrait] en buste.

half-life *n* PHYS demi-vie *f*, période *f*.

half-light *n* demi-jour *m*.

half-marathon *n* semi-marathon *m*.

half-mast *n* : **at ~** [flag] en berne ▪ *hum* [trousers] arrivant à mi-mollet.

half measure *n* demi-mesure *f*.

half-miler *n* [runner] coureur *m*, - euse *f* de demi-mile.

half-moon *n* demi-lune *f* ▪ [on fingernail] lunule *f*.

half-naked *adj* à moitié nu.

half-nelson *n* clef *f* cou côté opposé.

half-note *n US* [minim] blanche *f*.

half-open ◇ *adj* [eyes, door, window] entrouvert.
◇ *vt* [eyes, door, window] entrouvrir.

half-pay *n* demi-salaire *m* ▪ [in civil service] demi-traitement *m* ▪ MIL demi-solde *f*.

halfpenny ['heɪpnɪ] (*pl* **halfpennies**) *UK dated* ◇ *n* demi-penny *m*.
◇ *comp* d'un demi-penny.

half-pint ◇ *n* **1.** [measurement] ≃ quart *m* de litre ▪ **I'll just have a ~** [of beer] je prendrai juste un demi **2.** *inf* [small person] demi-portion *f*.
◇ *comp* : **a ~ glass** ≃ un verre de 25 cl.

half-price ◇ *n* demi-tarif *m* ▪ **reduced to ~** réduit de moitié ▪ **these goods are going at ~** ces produits sont vendus à moitié prix.
◇ *adj* [goods] à moitié prix ▪ [ticket] (à) demi-tarif.
◇ *adv* : **children get in ~** les enfants payent demi-tarif ▪ **I got it ~** [purchase] je l'ai eu à moitié prix.

half-rest *n US* MUS demi-pause *f*.

half-shut *adj* [eyes, door, window] mi-clos, à moitié fermé.

half-sister *n* demi-sœur *f*.

half-size ◇ *adj* [model] réduit de moitié.
◇ *n* [in shoes] demi-pointure *f* ▪ [in clothing] demi-taille *f*.

half-staff *US* = **half-mast**.

half-starved *adj* à moitié mort de faim, affamé.

half step *n US* MUS demi-ton *m*.

half term *n UK* SCH *congé scolaire en milieu de trimestre.*
◆ **half-term** *adj* : **half-term holiday** petites vacances *fpl*.

half-timbered [-'tɪmbəd] *adj* [house] à colombages, à pans de bois.

half-time ◇ *n* **1.** SPORT mi-temps *f inv* ▪ **at ~** à la mi-temps ▪ **that's the whistle for ~** on siffle la mi-temps **2.** [in work] mi-temps *m*.
◇ *comp* SPORT [whistle] de la mi-temps ▪ [score] à la mi-temps.

half-title *n* faux-titre *m*.

halftone ['hɑːftəʊn] *n* **1.** ART & PHOT similigravure *f* **2.** *US* MUS demi-ton *m*.

half-track *n* [vehicle] half-track *m*.

half-truth *n* demi-vérité *f*.

half-volley ◇ *n* [in tennis] demi-volée *f*.
◇ *vt* [in tennis] : **he ~ed the ball to the baseline** d'une demi-volée, il a envoyé la balle sur la ligne de fond.

halfway [hɑːf'weɪ] ◇ *adv* **1.** [between two places] à mi-chemin ▪ **it's ~ between Rennes and Cherbourg** c'est à mi-chemin entre Rennes et Cherbourg ▪ **we had got ~ to Manchester** nous étions arrivés à mi-chemin de Manchester ▪ **we had climbed ~ up the mountain** nous avions escaladé la moitié de la montagne ▪ **the path stops ~ up** le chemin s'arrête à mi-côte ▪ **the ivy reaches ~ up the wall** le lierre monte jusqu'à la moitié du mur ▪ **~ through the programme/film** à la moitié de l'émission/du film ▪ **to meet sb ~** retrouver qqn à mi-chemin ; *fig* couper la poire en deux, faire un compromis ▪ **we're almost ~ there** [in travelling, walking etc] nous sommes presque à mi-chemin, nous avons fait presque la moitié du chemin ; [in work, negotiations] nous sommes presque à mi-chemin ▪ **this will go ~ towards covering the costs** cela couvrira la moitié des dépenses **2.** *inf* [more or less] : **a ~ decent salary** un salaire à peu près décent.
◇ *comp* : **work has reached the ~ stage** le travail est à mi-chemin ▪ **at the ~ point of his career** au milieu de sa carrière ▪ **they're at the ~ mark** [in race] ils sont à mi-course ▪ **~ line** SPORT ligne *f* médiane.

halfway house *n* **1.** [on journey] (auberge *f*) relais *m* **2.** [for rehabilitation] centre *m* de réadaptation *(pour anciens détenus, malades mentaux, drogués etc)* **3.** *fig* [halfway stage] (stade *m* de) transition *f* ▪ [compromise] compromis *m*.

half-wit *n inf* imbécile.

half-witted *adj inf* [person] faible *OR* simple d'esprit ▪ [idea, suggestion, behaviour] idiot.

half-yearly ◇ *adj* semestriel.
◇ *adv* tous les six mois.

halibut ['hælɪbət] *n* flétan *m*.

halitosis [ˌhælɪ'təʊsɪs] *n (U)* mauvaise haleine *f* ▪ MED halitose *f*.

hall [hɔːl] *n* **1.** [of house] entrée *f*, vestibule *m* ▪ [of hotel, very large house] hall *m* ▪ [corridor] couloir *m* **2.** [large room] salle *f* ▪ **dining ~** SCH & UNIV réfectoire *m* ; [of stately home] salle *f* à manger ▪ **to eat in ~** *UK* UNIV manger à la cantine *OR* au restaurant universitaire **3.** [building] : **~ of residence** *UK* UNIV résidence *f* universitaire ▪ **I'm living in ~** *UK* UNIV je loge à l'université ▪ **~ of fame** *fig* panthéon *m* **4.** [mansion, large country house] château *m*, manoir *m*.

halleluja(h) [ˌhælɪ'luːjə] ◇ *interj* alléluia.
◇ *n* alléluia *m* ▪ **the Hallelujah Chorus** MUS l'Alléluia.

hallmark ['hɔːlmɑːk] ◇ *n* **1.** *liter* poinçon *m* **2.** *fig* marque *f* ▪ **to have the ~ of genius** porter la marque *OR* le sceau du génie ▪ **the ~ of any good author** ce qui caractérise tout bon auteur.
◇ *vt* [precious metals] poinçonner.

hallo [hə'ləʊ] *interj* = **hello**.

halloo [hə'luː] (*pl* **halloos**, *pret & pp* **hallooed**, *cont* **hallooing**) HUNT ◇ *interj* taïaut, tayaut.
◇ *vi* crier taïaut *OR* tayaut.
◇ *n* taïaut *m*, tayaut *m*.

hallow ['hæləʊ] *vt fml* sanctifier, consacrer ▪ **~ed be Thy name** que Ton nom soit sanctifié.

hallowed ['hæləʊd] *adj* saint, béni ▪ **~ ground** RELIG terre *f* sainte *OR* bénie ; *fig* lieu *m* de culte.

Hallowe'en [ˌhæləʊ'iːn] *pr n veille de la Toussaint, où les enfants se déguisent en fantômes et en sorcières.*

hall porter *n* [in hotel] portier *m*.

hallstand ['hɔːlstænd] *n* portemanteau *m*.

hallucinate [hə'lu:sɪneɪt] *vi* avoir des hallucinations ■ **I must be hallucinating!** je dois avoir des hallucinations!

hallucination [hə,lu:sɪ'neɪʃn] *n* hallucination *f.*

hallucinatory [hə'lu:sɪnətrɪ] *adj* hallucinatoire.

hallucinogen [hə'lu:sɪnə,dʒen] *n* hallucinogène *m.*

hallucinogenic [hə,lu:sɪnə'dʒenɪk] *adj* hallucinogène.

hallway ['hɔ:lweɪ] *n* [of house] vestibule *m*, entrée *f* ■ [corridor] couloir *m.*

halo ['heɪləʊ] (*pl* **halos** *OR pl* **haloes**) *n* [of saint] auréole *f*, nimbe *m* ■ ASTRON halo *m* ■ *fig* auréole *f.*

halogen ['hælədʒen] *n* CHEM halogène *m* ■ **~ headlights/lamps** phares *mpl* /lampes *fpl* à halogène.

halt [hɔ:lt] <> *n* **1.** [stop] halte *f* ■ **to bring to a ~** [vehicle] arrêter, immobiliser ; [horse] arrêter ; [production, project] interrompre ■ **to call a ~ to sthg** mettre fin à qqch ■ **let's call a ~ for today** arrêtons-nous pour aujourd'hui ■ **to come to a ~** [vehicle, horse] s'arrêter, s'immobiliser ■ **until the aircraft comes to a complete ~** jusqu'à l'arrêt complet de l'appareil **2.** *UK* [small railway station] halte *f.*
<> *vi* [stop] s'arrêter ■ **~! (, who goes there?)** MIL halte! (, qui va là?)
<> *vt* arrêter ■ [troops] faire faire halte à, stopper ■ [production - temporarily] interrompre, arrêter ; [- for good] arrêter définitivement.

halter ['hɔ:ltər] *n* **1.** [for horse] licou *m*, collier *m* **2.** [on women's clothing] = **halter neck**.

halter neck *n* : **a dress with a ~** une robe dos nu *OR* bain de soleil.
◆ **halter-neck** *comp* [dress] dos nu, bain de soleil.

halter top *n* bain *m* de soleil.

halting ['hɔ:ltɪŋ] *adj* [verse, style] boiteux, heurté ■ [voice, step, progress] hésitant ■ [growth] discontinu.

haltingly ['hɔ:ltɪŋlɪ] *adv* [say, speak] de façon hésitante.

halva ['hælvə], **halwa** *n (U)* halva *m.*

halve [*UK* hɑ:v, *US* hæv] *vt* **1.** [separate in two] couper *OR* diviser *OR* partager en deux **2.** [reduce by half] réduire *OR* diminuer de moitié.

halves [*UK* hɑ:vz, *US* hævz] *pl* ▷ **half.**

ham [hæm] (*pret & pp* **hammed**, *cont* **hamming**) <> *n* **1.** [meat] jambon *m* ■ **a ~** un jambon ■ **~ and eggs** œufs *mpl* au jambon ■ **~ sandwich** sandwich *m* au jambon **2.** [radio operator] radioamateur *m* ■ **~ licence** permis *m* de radioamateur **3.** [actor] cabot *m*, cabotin *m*, - e *f* **4.** [of leg] cuisse *f.*
<> *comp* : **~ acting** cabotinage *m.*
<> *vi* = **ham up**.
◆ **ham up** *vt sep* : **to ~ it up** *inf* en faire trop.

Hamburg ['hæmbɜ:g] *pr n* Hambourg.

hamburger ['hæmbɜ:gər] *n* **1.** [beefburger] hamburger *m* **2.** *US* [minced beef] viande *f* hachée.

ham-fisted [-'fɪstɪd], **ham-handed** [-'hændɪd] *adj* [person] empoté, maladroit ■ [behaviour] maladroit.

hamlet ['hæmlɪt] *n* [small village] hameau *m* ■ **'Hamlet'** *Shakespeare* 'Hamlet'.

hammam, hamam [hə'mɑ:m] *n* hammam *m.*

hammer ['hæmər] <> *n* **1.** [tool] marteau *m* ■ **(throwing the) ~** SPORT (lancer *m* du) marteau ▶ **the ~ and sickle** [flag] la faucille et le marteau ■ **to come** *OR* **to go under the ~** être vendu aux enchères ■ **to be** *OR* **to go at it ~ and tongs** [argue] se disputer comme des chiffonniers ; [in work, match] y aller à fond *OR* de bon cœur, mettre le paquet **2.** [of piano] marteau *m* ■ [of firearm] chien *m* **3.** [in ear] marteau *m.*
<> *vt* **1.** [nail, spike etc] enfoncer au marteau ■ [metal] marteler ■ **to ~ a nail into sthg** enfoncer un clou dans qqch ■ **to ~ sthg flat/straight** aplatir/redresser qqch à coups de marteau ■ **to ~ home** [nail] enfoncer à fond au marteau ; *fig* [point of view] insister lourdement sur ■ **they're always ~ing it into us that...** ils nous rabâchent sans arrêt que... **2.** *inf* [defeat] battre à plate couture ■ [criticize] descendre en flammes.
<> *vi* frapper *OR* taper au marteau ■ *fig* [heart] battre fort ■ **to ~ on the table** [with fist] taper du poing sur la table ■ **to ~ at the door** tambouriner à la porte.
◆ **hammer away** *vi insep* [with hammer] donner des coups de marteau ■ **to ~ away at sthg** taper sur qqch avec un marteau, donner des coups de marteau sur qqch ; *fig* [at agreement, contract] travailler avec acharnement à la mise au point de qqch ; [problem] travailler avec acharnement à la solution de qqch ■ **he ~ed away at the door** [with fists] il a tambouriné à la porte ■ **to ~ away at the piano/on the typewriter** marteler le piano/la machine à écrire.
◆ **hammer down** *vt sep* [nail, spike] enfoncer (au marteau) ■ [door] défoncer.
◆ **hammer in** *vt sep* [nail, spike] enfoncer (au marteau) ■ **it's no good telling him just once, you'll have to ~ it in** *fig* le lui dire une bonne fois ne suffira pas, il faudra le lui répéter sans cesse.
◆ **hammer out** *vt sep* [dent] aplatir au marteau ■ *fig* [solution, agreement] mettre au point, élaborer ■ [tune, rhythm] marteler.

hammer drill *n* perceuse *f* à percussion.

hammerhead ['hæməhed] *n* [shark] requin-marteau *m.*

hammering ['hæmərɪŋ] *n* **1.** [noise] martèlement *m* ■ *fig* [of heart] battement *m* ■ [of rain] tambourinement *m* **2.** *inf fig* [defeat] raclée *f*, pâtée *f* ■ **to give sb a ~** battre qqn à plate couture, mettre une raclée *OR* une pâtée à qqn.

hammock ['hæmək] *n* hamac *m.*

hamper ['hæmpər] <> *vt* [impede - work, movements, person] gêner ; [- project] gêner la réalisation de, entraver.
<> *n* [for picnic] panier *m* ■ [for laundry] panier *m* à linge sale ■ **a Christmas ~** un panier de friandises de Noël.

hamster ['hæmstər] *n* hamster *m.*

hamstring ['hæmstrɪŋ] (*pret & pp* **hamstrung** [-strʌŋ]) <> *n* tendon *m* ■ **to pull a ~** se claquer un tendon.
<> *vt* [cripple - animal, person] couper les tendons à ■ *fig* handicaper.

hand [hænd] <> *n* **1.** [of person] main *f* ■ **to hold sb's ~** tenir la main de qqn ■ **she's asked me to go along and hold her ~** *fig* elle m'a demandé de l'accompagner pour lui donner du courage ■ **to hold ~s** se tenir par la main ■ **to take sb's ~, to take sb by the ~** prendre qqn par la main, prendre la main de qqn ■ **to put one's ~s over one's eyes** se couvrir les yeux de ses mains ■ **to be on one's ~s and knees** être à quatre pattes ■ **to go down on one's ~s and knees** *fig* se mettre à genoux *OR* à plat ventre ■ **to be good with one's ~s** être adroit de ses mains ■ **my ~s are full** j'ai les mains occupées *OR* prises ■ **to have one's ~s full** *fig* avoir beaucoup à faire, avoir du pain sur la planche ■ **to lay one's ~s on sthg** [find] mettre la main sur qqch ■ **to get** *OR* **to lay one's ~s on sthg** [obtain] dénicher qqch ■ **just wait till I get** *OR* **lay my ~s on her!** *fig* attends un peu que je l'attrape! ■ **to lift** *OR* **to raise a ~ to sb** lever la main sur qqn ■ **~s off!** bas les pattes!, pas touche! ■ **~s off the unions/education system!** pas touche aux syndicats/au système éducatif! ■ **he can't keep his ~s to himself** il a la main baladeuse ■ **take your ~s off me!** ne me touche pas! ■ **(put your) ~s up!** les mains en l'air!, haut les mains! ■ **~s up anyone who knows the answer** SCH que ceux qui connaissent la réponse lèvent le doigt *OR* la main ■ **to tie sb's ~s** attacher les mains de qqn ■ **they tied my ~s behind my back** ils m'ont lié *OR* attaché les mains dans le dos ■ **my ~s are tied** *fig* j'ai les mains liées ■ **to sit on one's ~s** [applaud half-heartedly] applaudir sans enthousiasme ; [do nothing] ne rien faire ■ **to ask for sb's ~ in marriage** demander la main de qqn, demander qqn en mariage ■ **at ~, near** *OR* **close at ~** [about to happen] proche ; [nearby] à proximité ■ **to suffer at the ~s of sb** souffrir aux mains *OR* dans les mains de qqn ■ **to pass sthg from ~ to ~** faire passer qqch de mains en mains ■ **~ in ~** la main dans la main ■ **to go ~ in ~ (with sthg)** *fig* aller de pair (avec qqch) ▶ **to be ~ in glove with sb** travailler en étroite collaboration avec qqn ■ **to make money ~ over fist** gagner de l'argent par millions ■ **to live from ~ to mouth** arriver tout juste à joindre les deux bouts ■ **I could do it with one ~ tied behind my back** je pourrais le faire sans au-

cun effort *OR* les doigts dans le nez ■ **many ~s make light work** *prov* à beaucoup d'ouvriers la tâche devient aisée ■ **on the one ~... but on the other ~...** [used in the same sentence] d'un côté... mais de l'autre... ■ **on the other ~** [when beginning new sentence] d'un autre côté
2. [assistance] : **to give sb a ~ (with sthg)** donner un coup de main à qqn ■ **do you need a ~ (with that)?** as-tu besoin d'un coup de main?
3. [control, management] : **to need a firm ~** avoir besoin d'être sérieusement pris en main ■ **to rule with a firm ~** diriger avec de la poigne ■ **to take sb/sthg in ~** prendre qqn/qqch en main ■ **to get out of ~** [dog, child] devenir indocile ; [meeting, situation] échapper à tout contrôle ■ **the garden is getting out of ~** le jardin à l'air d'une vraie jungle ■ **to change ~s** [company, restaurant etc] changer de propriétaire ■ **it's out of my ~s** cela ne m'appartient plus, ce n'est plus ma responsabilité *OR* de mon ressort ■ **I have put the matter in the ~s of a lawyer** j'ai mis l'affaire entre les mains d'un avocat ■ **to have too much time on one's ~s** avoir trop de temps à soi ■ **to have sthg/sb on one's ~s** avoir qqch/qqn sur les bras ■ **now that that's off my ~s** à présent que je suis débarrassé de cela ■ **to fall into the wrong ~s** [information, secret etc] tomber en de mauvaises mains ■ **in the right ~s** en de bonnes mains ■ **to be in good** *OR* **safe ~s** être en de bonnes mains ■ **can I leave this in your ~s?** puis-je te demander de t'en occuper? ■ **it leaves too much power in the ~s of the police** cela laisse trop de pouvoir à la police ➲ **to give sb a free ~** donner carte blanche à qqn ■ **to take matters into one's own ~s** prendre les choses en main
4. [applause] : **to give sb a (big) ~** applaudir qqn (bien fort)
5. [influence, involvement] : **to have a ~ in sthg** avoir quelque chose à voir dans qqch ■ **I had no ~ in it** je n'avais rien à voir là-dedans, je n'y étais pour rien ■ **I see** *OR* **detect your ~ in this** j'y vois ta marque
6. [skill, ability] : **to have a light ~ with pastry** réussir une pâte légère ➲ **she can turn her ~ to anything** elle peut tout faire ■ **to keep one's ~ in** garder la main ■ **to try one's ~ at sthg** s'essayer à qqch
7. [in cards - cards held] main *f*, jeu *m* ; [- round, game] partie *f* ■ **to show** *OR* **to reveal one's ~** *fig* dévoiler son jeu ■ **to throw in one's ~** *fig* jeter l'éponge
8. [of clock] aiguille *f*
9. [handwriting] écriture *f*
10. [measurement of horse] paume *f*
11. [worker] ouvrier *m*, -ère *f* ■ [on ship] homme *m*, membre *m* de l'équipage ■ **she was lost with all ~s** [ship] il a coulé avec tous les hommes à bord *OR* tout l'équipage ■ **old ~** expert *m*, vieux *m* de la vieille ■ **to be an old ~ at sthg** avoir une vaste expérience de qqch ➲ **all ~s to the pump** *liter & fig* tout le monde à la rescousse
12. CULIN [of bananas] régime *m*.
◇ *vt* passer, donner ■ **to ~ sthg to sb** passer *OR* donner qqch à qqn ■ **you have to ~ it to her, she IS a good mother** *fig* c'est une bonne mère, il faut lui accorder cela.
◆ **by hand** *adv phr* [written] à la main ■ [made, knitted, sewn] (à la) main ■ **to wash sthg by ~** laver qqch à la main ■ **to send sthg by ~** faire porter qqch ■ **to rear an animal by ~** élever un animal au biberon.
◆ **in hand** *adv phr* **1.** [available money] disponible ■ [time] devant soi
2. [being dealt with] en cours ■ **the matter is in ~** on s'occupe de l'affaire ■ **I have the situation well in ~** j'ai la situation bien en main.
◆ **on hand** *adj phr* [person] disponible.
◆ **out of hand** *adv phr* [immediately] sur-le-champ.
◆ **to hand** *adv phr* [letter, information etc] sous la main ■ **he took the first one that came to ~** il a pris le premier qui lui est tombé sous la main.
◆ **hand back** *vt sep* [return] rapporter, rendre ■ **I now ~ you back to the studio/John Smith** RADIO & TV je rends maintenant l'antenne au studio/John Smith.
◆ **hand down** *vt sep* **1.** [pass, give from high place] passer, donner
2. [heirloom, story] transmettre ■ **the necklace/property has been ~ed down from mother to daughter for six generations** le collier s'est transmis/la propriété s'est transmise de mère en fille depuis six générations
3. LAW [decision, sentence] annoncer ■ [judgment] rendre ■ **to ~ down the budget** *US* annoncer le budget.
◆ **hand in** *vt sep* [return, surrender - book] rendre ; [- ticket] remettre ; [- exam paper] rendre, remettre ■ [something found - to authorities, police etc] déposer, remettre ■ **to ~ in one's resignation** remettre sa démission.
◆ **hand on** *vt sep* **1.** [give to someone else] passer ■ **to ~ sthg on to sb** passer qqch à qqn
2. = **hand down** *(sense 2)*.
◆ **hand out** *vt sep* [distribute] distribuer ■ **he's very good at ~ing out advice** il est très fort pour ce qui est de distribuer des conseils ■ **the French boxer ~ed out a lot of punishment** le boxeur français a frappé à coups redoublés.
◆ **hand over** ◇ *vt sep* **1.** [pass, give - object] passer, donner ■ **we now ~ you over to the weather man/Bill Smith in Moscow** RADIO & TV nous passons maintenant l'antenne à notre météorologue/Bill Smith à Moscou
2. [surrender - weapons, hostage] remettre ; [- criminal] livrer ; [- power, authority] transmettre ■ **he was ~ed over to the French police** il a été livré à la *OR* aux mains de la police française ■ **~ it over!** donne!
◇ *vi insep* : **to ~ over to** [government minister, chairman etc] passer le pouvoir à ; [in meeting] donner la parole à ■ TELEC passer *OR* donner le combiné à.
◆ **hand round** *vt sep* [distribute] distribuer.

hand- *in cpds* (à la) main ■ **~stitched** cousu main ■ **~knitted** tricoté à la main.

handbag ['hændbæg] *n* sac *m* à main.

handball *n* **1.** ['hændbɔːl] [game] handball *m* **2.** [hænd'bɔːl] FTBL main *f*.

handbasin ['hændbeɪsn] *n* lavabo *m*.

handbell ['hændbel] *n* clochette *f*.

handbill ['hændbɪl] *n UK* prospectus *m*.

handbook ['hændbʊk] *n* [for car, machine] guide *m*, manuel *m* ■ [for tourist's use] guide *m*.

handbrake ['hændbreɪk] *n UK* frein *m* à main.

handclap ['hændklæp] *n* : **to give sb the slow ~** *UK* siffler qqn.

handcrafted ['hænd,krɑːftɪd] *adj* fabriqué *OR* fait à la main.

hand cream *n* crème *f* pour les mains.

handcuff ['hændkʌf] *vt* passer les menottes à ■ **to ~ sb to sthg** attacher qqn à qqch avec des menottes ■ **he was ~ed** il avait les menottes aux poignets.

handcuffs ['hændkʌfs] *npl* menottes *fpl* ■ **to be in ~** avoir les menottes (aux mains).

hand-drier *n* sèche-mains *m inv*.

hand-drill *n* perceuse *f* à main.

-handed ['hændɪd] *in cpds* : **right~** droitier ■ **single~** tout seul ■ **empty~** les mains vides, bredouille ■ **one~ catch** interception *f* à une main.

Handel ['hændl] *pr n* Haendel.

-hander ['hændər] *in cpds* : **two-/three-~** [play] pièce *f* pour deux/trois personnes.

handfeed [hænd'fiːd] (*pret & pp* **handfed** [-'fed]) *vt* nourrir à la main.

handful ['hændfʊl] *n* **1.** [amount] poignée *f* ■ **a ~ of** *fig* [a few] quelques ■ **how many people were there? – only a ~** combien de personnes y avait-il? – seulement quelques-unes ➲ **'A Handful of Dust'** ***Waugh*** 'Une poignée de cendre' **2.** *inf* [uncontrollable person] : **to be a ~** être difficile.

hand grenade *n* grenade *f* à main.

handgrip ['hændgrɪp] *n* **1.** [on racket] grip *m* ■ [on bicycle] poignée *f* **2.** [handshake] poignée *f* de main **3.** [holdall] fourre-tout *m inv*.

handgun ['hændgʌn] *n US* revolver *m*, pistolet *m*.

hand-held *adj* [appliance] à main ■ [camera] portatif ■ **~ computer** ordinateur *m* de poche.

handheld PC *n* (ordinateur *m*) portable *m*.

handicap ['hændıkæp] (*pret & pp* **handicapped**) <> *n* **1.** [physical, mental] handicap *m* ▪ *fig* [disadvantage] handicap *m*, désavantage *m* ▪ **people with a (physical/mental) ~** les gens qui souffrent d'un handicap (physique/mental) **2.** SPORT handicap *m*.
<> *vt* **1.** *fig* handicaper, désavantager **2.** SPORT handicaper.

handicapped ['hændıkæpt] <> *adj* handicapé ▪ **to be mentally/physically ~** être handicapé mental/physique.
<> *npl* : **the ~** les handicapés *mpl*.

handicraft ['hændıkrɑ:ft] *n* **1.** [items] objets *mpl* artisanaux, artisanat *m* **2.** [skill] artisanat *m*.

handily ['hændılı] *adv* **1.** [conveniently] de façon commode *OR* pratique ▪ **the shop is ~ situated only 100 metres from the house** le magasin n'est qu'à 100 mètres de la maison, ce qui est pratique *OR* commode **2.** *US* [easily] : **to win ~** gagner haut la main.

handiwork ['hændıwɜ:k] *n (U)* [work] travail *m* manuel ▪ [result] œuvre *f* ▪ **this is YOUR~, is it?** c'est toi qui as fait ça?

handkerchief ['hæŋkətʃıf] (*pl* **handkerchiefs** *OR pl* **handkerchieves** [-tʃi:vz]) *n* mouchoir *m*.

hand-knitted *adj* tricoté main, tricoté à la main.

handle ['hændl] <> *n* **1.** [of broom, knife, screwdriver] manche *m* ▪ [of suitcase, box, drawer, door] poignée *f* ▪ [of cup] anse *f* ▪ [of saucepan] queue *f* ▪ [of stretcher] bras *m* ▪ **to fly off the ~ (at sb)** *UK inf* piquer une colère (contre qqn)
2. *inf* [name - of citizens' band user] nom *m* de code ; [- which sounds impressive] titre *m* de noblesse
3. *inf phr* **to get a ~ on sthg** piger qqch ▪ **I'll get back to you once I've got a ~ on the situation** je vous recontacterai quand j'aurai la situation en main.
<> *vt* **1.** [touch] toucher à, manipuler ▪ **'~ with care !'** 'manipuler avec précaution' ▪ **to ~ the ball** [in football] faire une main
2. [operate - ship] manœuvrer, gouverner ; [- car] conduire ; [- gun] se servir de, manier ; [- words, numbers] manier ▪ **have you any experience of handling horses?** savez-vous vous y prendre avec les chevaux?
3. [cope with - crisis, problem] traiter ; [- situation] faire face à ; [- crowd, traffic, death] supporter ▪ **you ~d that very well** tu as très bien réglé les choses ▪ **I couldn't have ~d it better myself** je n'aurais pas mieux fait ▪ **he's good at handling people** il sait s'y prendre avec les gens ▪ **leave this to me, I'LL~ him** laissemoi m'en occuper, je me charge de lui ▪ **do you think you can ~ the job?** penses-tu être capable de faire le travail? ▪ **how is she handling it?** comment s'en sort-elle? ▪ **it's nothing I can't ~** je me débrouille
4. [manage, process] s'occuper de ▪ [address - topic, subject] aborder, traiter ▪ **we're too small to ~ an order of that size** notre entreprise est trop petite pour traiter une commande de cette importance ▪ **the airport ~s two hundred planes a day** chaque jour deux cents avions passent par l'aéroport ▪ **to ~ stolen goods** receler des objets volés.
<> *vi* [car, ship] répondre.

handlebar ['hændlbɑ:ʳ] *comp* : **~ moustache** moustache *f* en guidon de vélo ▪ **~ tape** Guidoline® *f*.
◆ **handlebars** *npl* guidon *m*.

-handled ['hændld] *in cpds* [broom, screwdriver, knife] à manche de ▪ [suitcase, box, drawer, door] à poignée de ▪ **a short~ screwdriver** un tournevis à manche court.

handler ['hændləʳ] *n* [of dogs] maître-chien *m* ▪ [of baggage] bagagiste *m*.

handling ['hændlıŋ] <> *n* **1.** [of pesticides, chemicals] manipulation *f* ▪ **~ of stolen goods** recel *m* d'objets volés **2.** [of tool, weapon] maniement *m* ▪ **the size of the car makes for easy ~** la taille de la voiture permet une grande maniabilité **3.** [of situation, operation] : **my ~ of the problem** la façon dont j'ai traité le problème **4.** [of order, contract] traitement *m*, exécution *f* ▪ [of goods, baggage] manutention *f*.
<> *comp* : **~ charges** frais *mpl* de traitement ; [for physically shifting goods] frais *mpl* de manutention.

hand lotion *n* lotion *f* pour les mains.

hand luggage *n (U)* bagages *mpl* à main.

handmade [,hænd'meıd] *adj* fabriqué *OR* fait (à la) main.

handmaid(en) ['hændmeıd(n)] *n arch* servante *f*, bonne *f* ▪ *fig* bonne *f*.

hand-me-down *inf* <> *n* vêtement *m* de seconde main ▪ **this suit is a ~ from my father** ce costume appartenait à mon père.
<> *adj* [clothes] de seconde main ▪ *fig* [ideas] reçu.

handout ['hændaʊt] *n* **1.** [donation] aide *f*, don *m* ▪ **to live off ~s** vivre de dons ▪ **government ~s** subventions *fpl* gouvernementales **2.** [printed sheet or sheets] polycopié *m* ▪ **press ~** communiqué *m* pour la presse **3.** [leaflet] prospectus *m*.

handover ['hændəʊvəʳ] *n* [of power] passation *f*, transmission *f*, transfert *m* ▪ [of territory] transfert *m* ▪ [of hostage, prisoner] remise *f* ▪ [of baton] transmission *f*, passage *m*.

handpick [hænd'pık] *vt* **1.** [fruit, vegetables] cueillir à la main **2.** *fig* [people] sélectionner avec soin, trier sur le volet.

handpicked [,hænd'pıkt] *adj* [people] trié sur le volet.

handrail ['hændreıl] *n* [on bridge] rambarde *f*, garde-fou *m* ▪ NAUT rambarde *f* ▪ [of stairway - gen] rampe *f* ; [- against wall] main *f* courante.

handsaw ['hændsɔ:] *n* scie *f* à main ▪ [small] (scie *f*) égoïne *f*.

handset ['hændset] *n* TELEC combiné *m*.

handsewn [,hænd'səʊn] *adj* cousu main, cousu à la main.

hands free kit *n* kit *m* mains libres.

handshake ['hændʃeık] *n* **1.** poignée *f* de main **2.** COMPUT établissement *m* de liaison, poignée *f* de main.

hand signal *n* signal *m* de la main.

hands-off [hændz'ɒf] *adj* [policy] non interventionniste, de non-intervention ▪ [manager] non interventionniste.

handsome ['hænsəm] *adj* **1.** [good-looking - person, face, room] beau *(before vowel or silent 'h'* **bel***)*, belle *f* ; [- building, furniture] élégant ▪ **a ~ man** un bel homme ▪ **a ~ woman** une belle femme **2.** [generous - reward, compliment] beau *(before vowel or silent 'h'* **bel***)*, belle *f* ; [- conduct, treatment] généreux ; [- apology] sincère **3.** [substantial - profit, price] bon ; [- fortune] joli.

handsomely ['hænsəmlı] *adv* **1.** [beautifully] avec élégance, élégamment **2.** [generously] généreusement, avec générosité ▪ [sincerely] sincèrement **3.** [substantially] : **to win ~** gagner haut la main.

hands-on [hændz'ɒn] *adj* [training, experience] pratique ▪ [exhibition] *où le public peut toucher les objets exposés* ▪ **I go for a ~ style of management** je suis le genre de patron à contribuer concrètement au fonctionnement de mon entreprise *OR* à mettre la main à la pâte.

handstand ['hændstænd] *n* appui *m* renversé, équilibre *m* sur les mains.

handstitched [hænd'stıtʃt] *adj* cousu main.

hand-to-hand *adj & adv* au corps à corps.

hand-to-mouth <> *adj* : **to lead** *OR* **to have a ~ existence** tirer le diable par la queue.
<> *adv* : **to live ~** tirer le diable par la queue.

hand towel *n* serviette *f*, essuie-mains *m inv*.

handwash ['hændwɒʃ] <> *vt* laver à la main.
<> *n* : **to do a ~** faire une lessive à la main.

handwork ['hændwɜ:k] *n* SCH travail *m* à la main.

handwoven [,hænd'wəʊvn] *adj* tissé main.

handwriting ['hænd,raıtıŋ] *n* écriture *f* ▪ **~ expert** graphologue *mf*.

handwritten ['hænd,rıtn] *adj* manuscrit, écrit à la main.

handy ['hændı] (*comp* **handier**, *superl* **handiest**) *adj inf* **1.** [near at hand] proche ▪ **I always keep my glasses ~** je range toujours mes lunettes à portée de main ▪ **have you got a pen and pa-**

per ~? as-tu un stylo et du papier sous la main? **2.** [person - good with one's hands] adroit de ses mains ■ **he's ~ about the house** il est bricoleur ■ **she's ~ with a drill** elle sait se servir d'une perceuse ■ **he's a bit ~ with his fists** il sait se servir de ses poings **3.** [convenient, useful] commode, pratique ■ **living in the centre is ~ for work** pour le travail c'est pratique d'habiter en ville ■ **he's a ~ guy to have around** il peut rendre des tas de services ■ **a ~ piece of advice** un conseil utile ■ **to come in ~** être utile ■ **don't throw it away, it might come in ~ one day** ne le jette pas, ça pourrait servir un jour.

handyman ['hændımæn] (*pl* **handymen** [-men]) *n* [employee] homme *m* à tout faire ■ [odd job expert] bricoleur *m*.

hang [hæŋ] ◇ *vt* (*pret & pp* **hung**) **1.** [suspend - curtains, coat, decoration, picture] accrocher, suspendre ; [- door] fixer, monter ; [- art exhibition] mettre en place ; [- wallpaper] coller, poser ■ CULIN [- game, meat] faisander ■ **to ~ sthg from** *OR* **on sthg** accrocher qqch à qqch ■ **to ~ one's head (in shame)** baisser la tête (de honte) ▶ **to ~ one on sb** *US inf* [punch] balancer un coup de poing à qqn ■ **to ~ fire** [project] être en suspens ; [person] mettre les choses en suspens

2. (*usu passive*) [adorn] décorer ■ **a tree hung with lights** un arbre décoré *OR* orné de lumières

3. (*pret & pp* **hanged**) [criminal] pendre ■ **to ~ o.s.** se pendre ■ **~ed** *OR* **hung, drawn and quartered** pendu, éviscéré et écartelé ▶ **I'll be ~ed if I know** *UK inf* je veux bien être pendu si je le sais ■ **I'll be ~ed if I'm going out in that weather** *UK inf* il n'y a pas de danger que je sorte par ce temps ■ **~ it (all)!** *UK inf* ras le bol! ■ **(you) might as well be ~ed for a sheep as a lamb** *UK* quitte à être puni, autant l'être pour quelque chose qui en vaille la peine

4. *US* [turn] : **to ~ a left** prendre à gauche.

◇ *vi* (*pret & pp* **hung**) **1.** [be suspended - rope, painting, light] être accroché, être suspendu ; [- clothes on clothes line] être étendu, pendre ■ **to ~ from sthg** être accroché *OR* suspendu à qqch ■ **to ~ on sb's arm** être accroché au bras de qqn ■ **her pictures are now ~ing in several art galleries** ses tableaux sont maintenant exposés dans plusieurs galeries d'art ■ **his suit ~s well** son costume tombe bien ■ **time ~s heavy (on) my/his hands** le temps me/lui semble long ▶ **how's it ~ing?** *US inf* ça gaze?

2. [float - mist, smoke etc] flotter, être suspendu

3. COMPUT planter

4. (*pret & pp* **hanged**) [criminal] être pendu ▶ **she can go ~** *UK inf* elle peut aller se faire voir.

◇ *n inf* **1.** [knack, idea] : **to get the ~ of doing sthg** attraper le coup pour faire qqch ■ **to get the ~ of sthg** [understand] piger qqch ■ **are you getting the ~ of your new job?** est-ce que tu te fais à ton nouveau travail? ■ **you'll soon get the ~ of it** tu vas bientôt t'y faire

2. *phr* **he doesn't give a ~** *UK* [couldn't care less] il n'en a rien à taper *OR* à cirer.

◆ **hang about** *UK*, **hang around** *inf* ◇ *vi insep* **1.** [wait] attendre ■ **he kept me ~ing about** *OR* **around for half an hour** il m'a fait poireauter pendant une demi-heure ■ **I've been ~ing about** *OR* **around, waiting for her to come** je tourne en rond à l'attendre ■ **~ about, that's not what I mean!** attends *OR* doucement, ce n'est pas ce que je veux dire!

2. [be idle, waste time] traîner (à ne rien faire) ■ **we can't afford to ~ about if we want that contract** nous ne pouvons pas nous permettre de traîner si nous voulons obtenir ce contrat ■ **she doesn't ~ about** *OR* **around** [soon gets what she wants] elle ne perd pas de temps

3. [be an unwanted presence] : **Mum doesn't want me ~ing around when the guests arrive** Maman ne veut pas que je sois là quand les invités arriveront ■ **that kid's been ~ing around for the past hour** ça fait une heure que ce gamin traîne dans les parages.

◇ *vt insep* : **to ~ about** *OR* **around a place** traîner dans un endroit.

◆ **hang about with** *vt insep UK inf* traîner avec.

◆ **hang back** *vi insep* [wait behind] rester un peu plus longtemps ■ [not go forward] se tenir *OR* rester en arrière ■ **he hung back from saying what he really thought** *UK fig* il s'est retenu de dire ce qu'il pensait vraiment.

◆ **hang down** *vi insep* [light] pendre ■ [hair] descendre, tomber.

◆ **hang in** *vi insep inf* **~ in there!** tiens bon!, accroche-toi!

◆ **hang on** ◇ *vi insep* **1.** [hold tight] se tenir, s'accrocher ■ **~ on tight** tiens-toi *OR* accroche-toi bien

2. *inf* [wait] attendre ■ **~ on!** [wait] attends! ; [indicating astonishment, disagreement etc] une minute! ■ **~ on and I'll get him for you** [on phone] ne quitte pas, je te le passe

3. [hold out, survive] résister, tenir (bon) ■ **~ on in there!** *inf* [don't give up] tiens bon!, tiens le coup!

◇ *vt insep* **1.** [listen to] : **she hung on his every word** elle buvait ses paroles, elle était suspendue à ses lèvres

2. [depend on] dépendre de.

◆ **hang onto** *vt insep* **1.** [cling to] s'accrocher à

2. *inf* [keep] garder, conserver.

◆ **hang out** ◇ *vi insep* **1.** [protrude] pendre ■ **his shirt tails were ~ing out** sa chemise pendait ■ **to ~ out of the window** [flags] être déployé à la fenêtre ; [person] se pencher par la fenêtre ▶ **to let it all ~ out** *inf* [person] se relâcher complètement, se laisser aller ; [speak without restraint] se défouler

2. *inf* [frequent] traîner ■ **where does she ~ out?** quels sont les endroits qu'elle fréquente?

3. [survive, not give in] résister, tenir bon ■ **they're ~ing out for 10%** ils insistent pour obtenir 10 %.

◇ *vt sep* [washing] étendre ■ [flags] déployer.

◆ **hang out with** *vt insep inf* fréquenter.

◆ **hang over** *vt insep* être suspendu au-dessus de, planer sur ■ **a question mark ~s over his future** un point d'interrogation plane sur son avenir ■ **I can't go out with exams ~ing over me** avec les examens qui approchent, je ne peux pas sortir.

◆ **hang together** *vi insep* **1.** [be united - people] se serrer les coudes

2. [be consistent - alibi, argument, plot etc] (se) tenir ; [- different alibis, statements] concorder.

◆ **hang up** ◇ *vt sep* [coat, hat etc] accrocher ■ TELEC [receiver] raccrocher ■ **to ~ up one's dancing shoes** [retire] raccrocher ses chaussons de danse.

◇ *vi insep* **1.** TELEC raccrocher ■ **to ~ up on sb** raccrocher au nez de qqn

2. COMPUT [cease functioning] s'arrêter.

◆ **hang with** *vt insep US inf* **to ~ with sb** traîner avec qqn.

hangar ['hæŋər] *n* AERON hangar *m*.

hangdog ['hæŋdɒg] *adj* : **to have a ~ look** *OR* **expression** avoir un air penaud *OR* de chien battu.

hanger ['hæŋər] *n* [hook] portemanteau *m* ■ [coat hanger] portemanteau *m*, cintre *m* ■ [loop on garment] cordon *m* *OR* ganse *f* d'accrochage (*à l'intérieur d'un vêtement*).

hanger-on (*pl* **hangers-on**) *n pej* parasite *m*.

hang-glide *vi* faire du deltaplane.

hang-glider *n* [aircraft] deltaplane *m* ■ [person] libériste *mf*, adepte *mf* du deltaplane.

hang-gliding *n* deltaplane *m*.

hanging ['hæŋıŋ] ◇ *adj* **1.** [suspended] suspendu **2.** LAW : **~ judge** juge *m* à la main lourde ■ **~ offence** crime *m* passible de pendaison ■ **it's not a ~ offence** *fig* ce n'est pas une affaire d'État.

◇ *n* **1.** [death penalty] pendaison *f* ■ **~'s too good for him** la pendaison, c'est encore trop bon pour lui **2.** [of wallpaper] pose *f* ■ [of decorations, pictures] accrochage *m*, mise *f* en place **3.** [tapestry] : **wall ~s** tentures *fpl* (murales).

hangman ['hæŋmən] (*pl* **hangmen** [-mən]) *n* [executioner] bourreau *m* ■ **to play ~** [word game] jouer au pendu.

hang-out *n inf* **this is one of my favourite ~s** j'adore traîner dans ce coin ■ **this is one of his ~s** c'est l'un des endroits où on le trouve le plus souvent.

hangover ['hæŋ,əʊvər] *n* **1.** [from alcohol] gueule *f* de bois ■ **to have a ~** avoir la gueule de bois **2.** [relic] reste *m*, vestige *m*, survivance *f*.

hang-up *n* **1.** *inf* [complex] complexe *m*, blocage *m* ■ **she has a ~ about flying** elle a peur de prendre l'avion **2.** COMPUT blocage *m*, interruption *f*.

hank [hæŋk] *n* pelote *f*.

hanker ['hæŋkər] *vi* : **to ~ after** *OR* **for sthg** rêver de qqch, avoir énormément envie de qqch.

hankering ['hæŋkərɪŋ] *n* rêve *m*, envie *f* ■ **to have a ~ after** *OR* **for sthg** rêver de qqch, avoir énormément envie de qqch.

hankie, hanky ['hæŋkɪ] (*pl* **hankies**) *n inf* = **handkerchief**.

hanky-panky [-'pæŋkɪ] *n (U) inf* **1.** [sexual activity] galipettes *fpl* **2.** [mischief] entourloupettes *fpl*, blagues *fpl*.

Hanover ['hænəvəʳ] *pr n* Hanovre.

Hansard ['hænsɑ:d] *pr n UK* POL *compte rendu quotidien des débats de la Chambre des communes.*

hansom (cab) ['hænsəm-] *n* fiacre *m*.

Hants *written abbr of* **Hampshire**.

ha'penny ['heɪpnɪ] (*pl* **ha'pence** [-pəns]) *UK* = **halfpenny**.

haphazard [,hæp'hæzəd] *adj* mal organisé ■ **it was done in a ~ fashion** ça a été fait un peu n'importe comment ■ **the whole thing was a bit ~** c'était un peu n'importe quoi ■ **the city grew in a ~ fashion** la ville s'est agrandie au gré des circonstances.

haphazardly [,hæp'hæzədlɪ] *adv* sans organisation, n'importe comment ■ **there were objects lying ~ on the table** des choses traînaient sur la table ■ **to choose ~** choisir au petit bonheur la chance, choisir au hasard.

hapless ['hæplɪs] *adj lit* malchanceux.

happen ['hæpən] ◇ *vi* **1.** [occur] arriver, se passer, se produire ■ **what's ~ed?** qu'est-il arrivé?, que s'est-il passé? ■ **where did the accident ~?** où l'accident s'est-il produit *OR* est-il arrivé *OR* a-t-il eu lieu ? ■ **don't let it ~ again** faites en sorte que cela ne se reproduise pas ■ **as if nothing had ~ed** comme si de rien n'était ■ **whatever ~s** quoi qu'il arrive *OR* advienne ■ **as (so) often ~s** comme c'est bien souvent le cas ■ **it all ~ed so quickly** tout s'est passé si vite ■ **these things ~** ce sont des choses qui arrivent ■ **to find out what ~s next...** RADIO & TV pour connaître la suite... ■ **it's all ~ing here** ça bouge ici ■ **I wonder what has ~ed to her** [what has befallen her] je me demande ce qui a bien pu lui arriver ; [what she is doing now] je me demande ce qu'elle est devenue ■ **if anything ~s** *OR* **should ~ to me** s'il m'arrivait quelque chose ■ **it couldn't ~ to a nicer person** elle le mérite bien ■ **a funny thing ~ed to me last night** il m'est arrivé une drôle d'aventure hier soir ■ **what's ~ed to my coat?** [cannot be found] où est passé mon manteau? **2.** [chance] : **do you ~ to have his address?** auriez-vous son adresse, par hasard? ■ **it just so ~s that I do** eh bien justement, oui ■ **you wouldn't ~ to know where I could find him, would you?** vous ne sauriez pas où je pourrais le trouver? ■ **as it ~s** justement ■ **the man you're talking about ~s to be my father** il se trouve que l'homme dont vous parlez est mon père ■ **if you ~ to see him** si jamais tu le vois.
◇ *adv inf UK inf dial* [maybe] peut-être.
◆ **happen along, happen by** *vi insep inf* passer par hasard.
◆ **happen on, happen upon** *vt insep* : **I ~ed on an old friend/a good pub** je suis tombé sur un vieil ami/un bon pub.

happening ['hæpənɪŋ] ◇ *n* [occurrence] événement *m* ■ THEAT happening *m*.
◇ *adj inf* branché ■ **this is a ~ kind of place** il se passe toujours des tas de trucs ici.

happenstance ['hæpənstæns] *n US* hasard *m*.

happily ['hæpɪlɪ] *adv* **1.** [contentedly - say, smile] d'un air heureux ; [- play, chat] tranquillement ■ **I could live here very ~** je serais très heureux ici ■ **they lived ~ ever after** ≃ ils vécurent heureux et eurent beaucoup d'enfants ■ **to be ~ married** [man] être un mari comblé ; [woman] être une épouse comblée **2.** [gladly] volontiers ■ **I could quite ~ live here** je me verrais très bien vivre ici ■ **I could quite ~ strangle him** j'ai bien envie de l'étrangler **3.** [luckily] heureusement ■ **~, no-one was hurt** heureusement, il n'y a pas eu de blessés **4.** [appropriately] heureusement, avec bonheur.

happiness ['hæpɪnɪs] *n* bonheur *m* ■ **money can't buy you ~** l'argent ne fait pas le bonheur *prov*.

happy ['hæpɪ] (*comp* **happier**, *superl* **happiest**) *adj* **1.** [content] heureux ■ **to make sb ~** rendre qqn heureux ■ **I want you to be ~** je veux que tu sois heureux, je veux ton bonheur ■ **I hope you'll both be very ~** je vous souhaite beaucoup de bonheur *OR* d'être très heureux ■ **if you're ~, I'm ~** si tu es satisfait, moi aussi ■ **in happier circumstances** dans des circonstances plus heureuses ■ **those were ~ days** c'était le bon temps ■ **I'm not at all ~ about your decision** je ne suis pas du tout content de votre décision ■ **I'm still not ~ about it** je n'en suis toujours pas content ■ **that should keep the kids ~** cela devrait occuper les enfants ■ **~ ending** [in book, film] fin *f* heureuse, dénouement *m* heureux ■ **to have a ~ ending** [book, film] bien finir ■ **~ birthday** *OR* **anniversary!** joyeux anniversaire! ■ **Happy Christmas!** Joyeux Noël! ■ **Happy New Year!** Bonne Année! ⊙ **~ families** [card game] jeu *m* des sept familles ■ **to be as ~ as a lark** *UK OR* **a sandboy** *UK OR* **a clam** *US* être heureux comme tout
2. [willing] : **I'm only too ~ to help** je suis ravi de rendre service ■ **I would be ~ to do it** je le ferais volontiers ■ **we'd be ~ to put you up** nous serions heureux de vous loger, nous vous logerions volontiers ■ **I'd be ~ to live here/move to Scotland** j'aimerais bien habiter ici/aller habiter en Écosse
3. [lucky, fortunate - coincidence] heureux ■ **the ~ few** les privilégiés *mpl*
4. [apt, appropriate - turn of phrase, choice of words] heureux
5. *inf* [drunk] gris, pompette.

happy event *n* [birth] heureux événement *m*.

happy-go-lucky *adj* décontracté ■ *pej* insouciant.

happy hour *n* [in pub, bar] happy hour *f (heure, généralement en début de soirée, pendant laquelle les boissons sont moins chères).*

happy hunting ground *n* paradis *m* des Indiens ■ *fig* mine *f* d'or ■ **the market is a ~ for collectors** le marché est une vraie mine d'or pour les collectionneurs.

happy medium *n* équilibre *m*, juste milieu *m* ■ **to strike a ~** trouver un équilibre *OR* un juste milieu.

harangue [hə'ræŋ] ◇ *vt* [person, crowd etc] haranguer ■ **to ~ sb about sthg** haranguer qqn au sujet de qqch.
◇ *n* harangue *f*.

Harare [hə'rɑ:rɪ] *pr n* Harare.

harass ['hærəs] *vt* [torment] tourmenter ■ [with questions, demands] harceler ■ MIL harceler ■ **to sexually ~ an employee** harceler une employée sexuellement.

harassed ['hærəst] *adj* stressé ■ **to be sexually ~** être victime de harcèlement sexuel.

harassment ['hærəsmənt] *n* [tormenting] tracasserie *f* ■ [with questions, demands] harcèlement *m* ■ [stress] stress *m* ■ MIL harcèlement *m* ■ **police/sexual ~** harcèlement policier/sexuel.

harbinger ['hɑ:bɪndʒəʳ] *n lit* signe *m* avant-coureur ■ **a ~ of doom** [event, incident etc] un mauvais présage ; [person] un oiseau de malheur.

harbour *UK*, **harbor** *US* ['hɑ:bəʳ] ◇ *n* [for boats] port *m* ■ *fig* havre *m*.
◇ *comp* : **~ master** capitaine *m* de port.
◇ *vt* **1.** [person] abriter, héberger ■ [criminal] donner asile à, receler **2.** [grudge, suspicion] nourrir, entretenir en soi ■ **to ~ a grudge against sb** garder rancune à qqn, nourrir de la rancune envers qqn **3.** [conceal - dirt, germs] receler.

hard [hɑ:d] ◇ *adj* **1.** [not soft - substance, light, colour] dur ■ LING [consonant] dur ■ **to get** *OR* **to become ~** durcir ⊙ **~ drug** drogue *f* dure ■ **~ water** eau *f* calcaire *OR* dure ■ **a glass of wine, or would you prefer a drop of the ~ stuff?** un verre de vin, ou bien préféreriez-vous une goutte de quelque chose de plus fort? ■ **she is (as) ~ as nails** [emotionally] elle est dure, elle n'a pas de cœur ; [physically] c'est une dure à cuire ■ **rock ~, (as) ~ as rock** dur comme la pierre
2. [concrete - facts] concret, - ète *f*, tangible ; [- evidence] tangible ■ **the ~ fact is that...** le fait est que... ■ **~ news** PRESS nouvelles *fpl* sûres *OR* vérifiées
3. [difficult - question, problem etc] difficile, dur ■ **I find it ~ to understand/believe that...** je n'arrive pas à comprendre/croire que... ■ **it's ~ to say** c'est difficile à dire ■ **he's ~ to get on with** il n'est pas facile à vivre ■ **she is ~ to please** [never satisfied] elle est difficile ; [difficult to buy gifts for etc] c'est difficile

de lui faire plaisir ■ **it's ~ to beat** [value for money] pour le prix, c'est imbattable ■ **it's ~ to beat a good Bordeaux** il n'y a rien de meilleur qu'un bon bordeaux ■ **life is ~** c'est dur, la vie ■ **to fall on ~ times** [financially] connaître des temps difficiles *OR* une période de vaches maigres ; [have difficult times] connaître des temps difficiles, en voir de dures ▶ **to give sb a ~ time** en faire voir de dures à qqn ■ **you'll have a ~ time (of it) persuading him to do that** tu vas avoir du mal à le convaincre de faire cela ■ **she had a ~ time of it** [in childbirth, operation] elle a souffert ■ **to learn sthg the ~ way** [involving personal loss, suffering etc] apprendre qqch à ses dépens ; [in a difficult way] faire le rude apprentissage de qqch ■ **I learnt skiing the ~ way** j'ai appris à skier à la dure ■ **some people always have to do things the ~ way** il y a des gens qui choisissent toujours la difficulté ■ **to play ~ to get** [flirt] jouer les insaisissables ■ **'Hard Times'** ***Dickens*** 'les Temps difficiles'

4. [severe - voice, face, eyes] dur, froid ; [- climate, winter] rigoureux, rude ; [- frost] fort, rude ■ **to be ~ on sb** être dur avec qqn ■ **it was ~ on the others** ça a été dur pour les autres ■ **to be a ~ taskmaster** être dur à la tâche ■ **to take a long ~ look at sthg** examiner qqch de près ■ **the ~ left/right** POL l'extrême gauche/droite ▶ **~ cheese!** *inf UK dated* *inf*, **~ lines!** *UK inf*, **~ luck!** pas de chance!, pas de veine!, pas de bol! ■ **it will be ~ luck if he doesn't get the job** ça ne sera pas de veine *OR* de bol s'il n'obtient pas le travail ■ **he gave me some ~ luck story about having lost his investments** il a essayé de m'apitoyer en me racontant qu'il avait perdu l'argent qu'il avait investi

5. [strenuous] : **it's ~ work** c'est dur ■ **it's been a long ~ day** la journée a été longue ■ **she's ~ work** [difficult to get on with] elle n'est pas facile à vivre ; [difficult to make conversation with] elle n'est pas causante ■ **she's not afraid of ~ work** le travail ne lui fait pas peur ■ **she's a ~ worker** c'est un bourreau de travail ■ **he's a ~ drinker** c'est un gros buveur, il boit beaucoup ■ **it's ~ going making conversation with him** c'est difficile de discuter avec lui ■ **give it a good ~ shove** pousse-le un bon coup, pousse-le fort

6. TYPO [hyphen, return] imposé.

◇ *adv* **1.** [strenuously - pull, push, hit, breathe] fort ; [- work] dur ; [- run] à toutes jambes ; [- listen] attentivement ■ **to work ~ at sthg** beaucoup travailler qqch ■ **to work ~ at improving one's service/French** beaucoup travailler pour améliorer son service/français ■ **to work sb ~** faire travailler qqn dur ■ **work ~, play ~, that's what I say!** beaucoup travailler pour beaucoup s'amuser, telle est ma devise! ■ **you'll have to try ~er** il faudra que tu fasses plus d'efforts ■ **to try ~ to do sthg** essayer de son mieux de faire qqch ■ **to think ~** beaucoup réfléchir ■ **to look ~ at sb** regarder qqn bien en face ■ **to look ~ at sthg** examiner qqch ■ **as ~ as possible, as ~ as one can** [work, try] le plus qu'on peut ; [push, hit, squeeze] de toutes ses forces ■ **~ astern!** NAUT arrière, toute! ▶ **to play ~ to get** se faire désirer ■ **they're ~ at it** *UK* [working] ils sont plongés dans leur travail ; *inf* [engaged in sex] *inf* ils s'en donnent à cœur joie

2. [with difficulty] difficilement ■ **to be ~ put (to it) to do sthg** avoir du mal à faire qqch ■ **old habits die ~** les vieilles habitudes ont la vie dure

3. [harshly, severely - treat sb] durement, sévèrement ■ **he's feeling ~ done by** il a l'impression d'avoir été injustement traité ■ [heavily, strongly - rain] à verse ; [- freeze, snow] fort ■ **to be ~ hit by sthg** être durement touché par qqch ■ **she took the news/his death pretty ~** la nouvelle/sa mort l'a beaucoup éprouvée ■ **it'll go ~ with him if he keeps telling lies** ça va aller mal pour lui s'il continue à raconter des mensonges

4. [solid] : **the ground was frozen ~** le gel avait complètement durci la terre ■ **to set ~** [concrete, mortar] prendre

5. [close] : **to follow ~ on the heels of sb** être sur les talons de qqn ■ **to follow** *OR* **to come ~ on the heels of sthg** suivre qqch de très près.

◇ *n phr* **to try one's ~est** faire de son mieux.

◆ **hard by** *prep phr* près de.

hard-and-fast *adj* [rule] strict, absolu ■ [information] correct, vrai ■ **there's no ~ rule about it** il n'existe pas de règle absolue là-dessus.

hardback ['hɑːdbæk] ◇ *n* [book] livre *m* cartonné ■ **available in ~** disponible en version cartonnée.
◇ *adj* cartonné.

hardball ['hɑːdbɔːl] *n* : **to play ~** *inf fig* employer les grands moyens.

hard-bitten [-'bɪtən] *adj* endurci.

hardboard ['hɑːdbɔːd] *n* panneau *m* de fibres.

hard-boiled [-'bɔɪld] *adj* **1.** [egg] dur **2.** *inf* [person] dur.

hard case *n inf* dur *m* à cuire.

hard cash *n* (argent *m*) liquide *m*.

hard cider *n US* cidre *m*.

hard copy *n* COMPUT sortie *f* papier, tirage *m*.

hardcore ['hɑːdkɔːʳ] *n* [for roads, buildings] blocaille *f*.

hard core *n* **1.** [nucleus] noyau *m* dur **2.** MUS hard rock *m*, hard *m* **3.** [pornography] porno *m* hard.

◆ **hard-core** *adj* [belief in political system] dur ■ [believer] endurci ■ [support] ferme ■ [pornography, rock music] hard.

hard court *n UK* [for tennis] court *m* en ciment.

hardcover ['hɑːd,kʌvəʳ] = **hardback**.

hard currency *n* monnaie *f OR* devise *f* forte.

hard disk *n* COMPUT disque *m* dur.

hard-disk drive *n* COMPUT unité *f* de disque dur.

hard-earned [-'ɜːnt] *adj* [money] durement gagné ■ [victory] durement *OR* difficilement remporté ■ [reputation] durement acquis ■ [holiday, reward] bien mérité.

harden ['hɑːdn] ◇ *vt* [person - physically, emotionally] endurcir ■ [steel] tremper ■ LING [consonant] durcir ■ MED [arteries] durcir, scléroser ■ **to ~ o.s. to sthg** s'endurcir à qqch ■ **she ~ed her heart against him** elle lui a fermé son cœur.
◇ *vi* **1.** [snow, skin, steel] durcir ■ [concrete, mortar] prendre ■ MED [arteries] durcir, se scléroser ■ [person - emotionally] s'endurcir, se durcir ; [- physically] s'endurcir ■ [attitude] se durcir **2.** FIN [prices, market] s'affermir.

hardened ['hɑːdnd] *adj* [snow, skin] durci ■ [steel] trempé, durci ■ [arteries] sclérosé ■ **a ~ criminal** un criminel endurci *OR* invétéré ■ **to become ~ to sthg** se blinder contre qqch.

hardening ['hɑːdnɪŋ] *n* [of snow, skin, attitudes] durcissement *m* ■ [of steel] trempe *f* ■ [of person - physical] endurcissement *m* ; [- emotional] durcissement *m* ■ FIN [of prices] affermissement *m* ■ **~ of the arteries** MED durcissement *OR* sclérose *f* des artères.

hard-faced [-'feɪst] *adj* au visage dur.

hard-fought [-'fɔːt] *adj* [game, battle] rudement disputé.

hard hat *n* **1.** *inf* [of construction worker] casque *m* **2.** *US inf* [construction worker] ouvrier *m* du bâtiment.

◆ **hard-hat** *adj US caractéristique des attitudes conservatrices des ouvriers du bâtiment.*

hard-headed [-'hedɪd] *adj* **1.** [tough, shrewd - person] à la tête froide ; [- realism] froid, brut ; [- bargaining] dur ; [- decision] froid **2.** *US* [stubborn - person] qui a la tête dure ; [- attitude] entêté.

hard-hearted *adj* [person] insensible, dur, au cœur de pierre ■ [attitude] dur.

hard-hitting [-'hɪtɪŋ] *adj* **1.** [verbal attack] rude ■ [speech, report] implacable, sans indulgence **2.** [boxer] qui frappe dur.

hardiness ['hɑːdɪnɪs] *n* [of person] résistance *f*, robustesse *f* ■ [of plant, tree] résistance *f*.

hard labour *n (U)* travaux *mpl* forcés.

hard line *n* ligne *f* de conduite dure ■ **to take a ~ on sb/sthg** adopter une ligne de conduite dure avec qqn/sur qqch.

◆ **hard-line** *adj* [policy, doctrine] dur ■ [politician] intraitable.

hardliner [,hɑːd'laɪnəʳ] *n* partisan *m*, - e *f* de la manière forte.

hardly ['hɑːdlɪ] *adv* **1.** [barely] à peine, ne... guère ■ **he can ~ read** il sait à peine *OR* tout juste lire ■ **you can ~ move in here for furniture** c'est à peine si on peut bouger ici tellement il y a de meubles ■ **I have ~ started** je viens à peine *OR* tout juste de commencer ■ **I can ~ believe it** j'ai du mal à le croire ■ ~

anyone presque personne ▪ **I ~ ever see you these days** je ne te vois presque jamais ces temps-ci ▪ **you've ~ touched your food** tu n'as presque rien mangé ▪ **I can ~ wait to see her** je suis très impatient de la voir ▪ **~ a week goes by without a telephone call from her** il se passe rarement une semaine sans qu'elle téléphone ▪ **I need ~ say that...** ai-je besoin de vous dire que...?, je n'ai pas besoin de vous dire que... **2.** [expressing negative opinion] : **it's ~MY fault!** ce n'est quand même pas de ma faute! ▪ **it's ~ any of your business** cela ne te regarde absolument pas ▪ **this is ~ the time to be selling your house** ce n'est vraiment pas le moment de vendre votre maison ▪ **it's ~ surprising, is it?** ça n'a rien de surprenant, ce n'est guère surprenant ▪ **~!** [not in the slightest] bien au contraire!, loin de là! ▪ **she's ~ likely to agree** elle ne risque pas d'accepter ▪ **he'd ~ have said that** cela m'étonnerait qu'il ait dit cela.

hardness ['hɑːdnɪs] *n* **1.** [of snow, skin, water] dureté *f* ▪ [of steel] trempe *f*, dureté *f* **2.** [difficulty] difficulté *f* ▪ **~ of hearing** MED surdité *f* partielle **3.** [severeness - of personality] dureté *f* ; [- of heart] dureté *f*, froideur *f* **4.** [strenuousness] difficulté *f* **5.** FIN affermissement *m*.

hard-nosed *inf* [-'nəʊzd] = **hard-headed**.

hard of hearing ◇ *npl* : **the ~** les malentendants *mpl*.
◇ *adj* : **to be ~** être dur d'oreille.

hard-on▲ *n* : **to have** *OR* **to get a ~** bander△.

hard-packed [-'pækt] *adj* [snow, soil] tassé.

hard palate *n* voûte *f* du palais, palais *m* dur.

hard-pressed [-'prest], **hard-pushed** [-'pʊʃt] *adj* : **to be ~ for money/ideas/suggestions** être à court d'argent/d'idées/de suggestions ▪ **to be ~ for time** manquer de temps ▪ **to be ~ to do sthg** avoir du mal à faire qqch.

hard rock *n* hard rock *m*, hard *m*.

hard sell ◇ *n* vente *f* agressive ▪ **the salesman gave us the ~** le vendeur a essayé de nous forcer la main.
◇ *comp* : **~ approach** *OR* **tactics** méthode *f* de vente agressive.

hardship ['hɑːdʃɪp] ◇ *n* épreuves *fpl* ▪ **to suffer great ~** *OR* **~s** subir *OR* traverser de rudes épreuves.
◇ *comp* : **~ allowance** [for student] *aide accordée à un étudiant en cas de graves problèmes financiers*.

hard shoulder *n* AUT bande *f* d'arrêt d'urgence.

hardtop ['hɑːdtɒp] *n* AUT [of car] hard-top *m* ▪ [car] voiture *f* à hard-top.

hard up *adj inf* [short of money] fauché, à sec ▪ **to be ~ for ideas** manquer d'idées, être à court d'idées ▪ **you must be ~ if you're going out with him!** *fig* il faut vraiment que tu n'aies rien à te mettre sous la dent pour sortir avec lui!

hardware ['hɑːdweəʳ] ◇ *n (U)* **1.** COMM quincaillerie *f* **2.** COMPUT matériel *m*, hardware *m* **3.** MIL matériel *m* de guerre, armement *m* **4.** *inf* [guns] armes *fpl*.
◇ *comp* COMPUT [company, manufacturer] de matériel informatique ▪ [problem] de matériel *OR* hardware.

hardware shop, hardware store *n* quincaillerie *f*.

hardwearing [,hɑːd'weərɪŋ] *adj* robuste, résistant.

hard-wired [-'waɪəd] *adj* COMPUT câblé.

hard-won [-'wʌn] *adj* [victory, trophy, independence] durement gagné ▪ [reputation] durement acquis.

hardwood ['hɑːdwʊd] ◇ *n* [wood] bois *m* dur ▪ [tree] arbre *m* à feuilles caduques.
◇ *comp* [floor] en bois dur.

hardworking [,hɑːd'wɜːkɪŋ] *adj* travailleur ▪ [engine, machine, printer] robuste.

hardy ['hɑːdɪ] (*comp* **hardier**, *superl* **hardiest**) *adj* **1.** [strong - person, animal] robuste, résistant ; [- plant] résistant ▪ **~ annual** BOT plante *f* annuelle ▪ **~ perennial** BOT plante *f* vivace ; *fig* serpent *m* de mer **2.** [intrepid - explorer, pioneer] intrépide, courageux.

hare [heəʳ] (*pl inv OR pl* **hares**) ◇ *n* **1.** CULIN & ZOOL lièvre *m* ▪ **to start a ~** *UK* mettre une question sur le tapis ▪ **to run with the ~ and hunt with the hounds** jouer double jeu ▪ **'The Hare and the Tortoise'** *La Fontaine* 'le Lièvre et la tortue' **2.** SPORT [at dog race] lièvre *m* **3.** *UK* GAMES : **~ and hounds** jeu *m* de piste.
◇ *vi UK inf* : **to ~ off** filer à toutes jambes ▪ **she came haring down the stairs** elle a dévalé l'escalier à fond de train.

harebell ['heə,bel] *n* campanule *f*.

harebrained ['heə,breɪnd] *adj* [reckless, mad - person] écervelé ; [- scheme] insensé, fou *(before vowel or silent 'h' fol)*, folle *f*.

harelip [,heə'lɪp] *n* bec-de-lièvre *m*.

harem [*UK* hɑː'riːm, *US* 'hærəm] *n liter & fig* harem *m*.

hark [hɑːk] *vi lit* prêter l'oreille, ouïr ▪ **just ~ at him!** *UK inf* écoutez-le donc!
◆ **hark back to** *vt insep* [recall] revenir à ▪ **to ~ back to sthg** revenir (tout le temps) à qqch.

harken ['hɑːkn] *vi lit* prêter l'oreille.

Harlequin ['hɑːlɪkwɪn] *pr n* Arlequin.
◆ **harlequin** *adj* [costume] bigarré ▪ [dog's coat] tacheté.

Harley Street ['hɑːlɪ-] *pr n rue du centre de Londres célèbre pour ses spécialistes en médecine*.

harlot ['hɑːlət] *n arch* prostituée *f*.

harm [hɑːm] ◇ *n (U)* [physical] mal *m* ▪ [psychological] tort *m*, mal *m* ▪ **to do sb ~** faire du mal à qqn ▪ **I hope Ed won't come to (any) ~** j'espère qu'il n'arrivera rien à Ed ▪ **she has done you no ~** elle ne vous a fait aucun mal ▪ **they didn't mean any ~** ils ne voulaient pas (faire) de mal ▪ **Ted means no ~** Ted n'est pas méchant ▪ **the incident did a great deal of ~ to his reputation** cet incident a beaucoup nui à sa réputation ▪ **no ~ done** il n'y a pas de mal ▪ **there's no ~ in trying** il n'y a pas de mal à essayer, on ne perd rien à essayer ▪ **I see no ~ in their going** je ne vois pas d'inconvénient à ce qu'ils y aillent ▪ **what ~ is there in it?** qu'est-ce qu'il y a de mal (à cela)? ▪ **to do more ~ than good** faire plus de mal que de bien ▶ **out of ~'s way** [person] en sûreté, en lieu sûr ; [things] en lieu sûr.
◇ *vt* **1.** [person - physically] faire du mal à ; [- psychologically] faire du tort à, nuire à ▪ **Clive wouldn't ~ a hair on her head** Clive ne lui ferait aucun mal **2.** [surface] abîmer, endommager ▪ [crops] endommager **3.** [cause, interests] causer du tort à, être préjudiciable à ▪ [reputation] salir.

harmful ['hɑːmfʊl] *adj* **1.** [person, influence] nuisible, malfaisant **2.** [chemicals] nocif ▪ [effects] nuisible ▪ **~ to plants** nuisible pour les plantes.

harmless ['hɑːmlɪs] *adj* **1.** [person] inoffensif, qui n'est pas méchant ▪ [animal] inoffensif **2.** [joke] sans malice, anodin ▪ [pastime] innocent.

harmlessly ['hɑːmlɪslɪ] *adv* sans faire de mal, sans dommage *OR* dommages.

harmonic [hɑː'mɒnɪk] ◇ *n* MATHS & MUS harmonique *m*.
◇ *adj* [gen - MATHS] & MUS harmonique.

harmonica [hɑː'mɒnɪkə] *n* harmonica *m*.

harmonics [hɑː'mɒnɪks] *n (U)* harmoniques *mpl*.

harmonious [hɑː'məʊnjəs] *adj* harmonieux.

harmoniously [hɑː'məʊnjəslɪ] *adv* harmonieusement.

harmonist ['hɑːmənɪst] *n* harmoniste *mf*.

harmonium [hɑː'məʊnjəm] *n* harmonium *m*.

harmonization [,hɑːmənaɪ'zeɪʃn] *n* harmonisation *f*.

harmonize, ise ['hɑːmənaɪz] ◇ *vt* **1.** MUS [instrument, melody] harmoniser **2.** [colours] harmoniser, assortir **3.** [views, statements] harmoniser, faire concorder ▪ [people] concilier, amener à un accord.
◇ *vi* **1.** MUS [sing in harmony] chanter en harmonie ▪ [be harmonious] être harmonieux *OR* en harmonie ▪ [write harmony] harmoniser, faire des harmonies **2.** [colours] aller (bien) ensemble, se marier (bien) ▪ **choose colours that ~ with the background** choisissez des couleurs qui soient assorties au décor.

harmony ['hɑːmənɪ] (*pl* **harmonies**) *n* **1.** MUS harmonie *f* ▪ **to sing in ~** chanter en harmonie **2.** [agreement - of colours] harmonie *f* ; [- of temperaments] harmonie *f*, accord *m* ▪ **to live in ~ with sb** vivre en harmonie avec qqn.

harness ['hɑːnɪs] ◇ *n* **1.** [for horse, oxen] harnais *m*, harnachement *m* ▪ [for parachute, car seat] harnais *m* ▪ [for child] harnais *m* **2.** *phr* **to get** *OR* **to be back in ~** reprendre le collier.
◇ *vt* **1.** [horse] harnacher, mettre le harnais à ▪ [oxen, dogs] atteler ▪ **the pony was ~ed to the cart** le poney était attelé à la charrette **2.** *fig* [resources] exploiter, maîtriser.

harp [hɑːp] MUS ◇ *n* harpe *f*.
◇ *vi* jouer de la harpe.
◆ **harp on** *inf* ◇ *vi insep* chanter (toujours) le même refrain *OR* la même rengaine ▪ **to ~ on about sthg** rabâcher qqch, revenir sans cesse sur qqch ▪ **to ~ on at sb about sthg** rebattre les oreilles à qqn au sujet de qqch.
◇ *vt insep* : **to ~ on sthg** revenir sans cesse sur qqch, rabâcher qqch.

harpist ['hɑːpɪst] *n* harpiste *mf*.

harpoon [hɑː'puːn] ◇ *n* harpon *m*.
◇ *vt* harponner.

harpsichord ['hɑːpsɪkɔːd] *n* clavecin *m*.

harpsichordist ['hɑːpsɪˌkɔːdɪst] *n* claveciniste *mf*.

harpy ['hɑːpɪ] (*pl* **harpies**) *n fig* harpie *f*, mégère *f*.

harridan ['hærɪdn] *n* harpie *f*, vieille sorcière *f*.

harried ['hærɪd] *adj* [person] tracassé, harcelé ▪ [expression, look] tourmenté.

harrier ['hærɪəʳ] *n* **1.** [dog] harrier *m* **2.** SPORT [runner] coureur *m* (de cross) ▪ **Plymouth Harriers** l'équipe d'athlétisme de Plymouth **3.** ORNITH busard *m*.

Harris tweed® ['hærɪs-] *n* tweed *m* (des Hébrides).

Harrods ['hærədz] *pr n grand magasin de luxe à Londres.*

harrow ['hærəʊ] ◇ *n* herse *f*.
◇ *vt* **1.** AGRIC labourer à la herse **2.** *fig* torturer, déchirer le cœur à.
◆ **Harrow** *pr n prestigieuse "public school" dans la banlieue de Londres.*

harrowing ['hærəʊɪŋ] ◇ *adj* [story] poignant, navrant, angoissant ▪ [cry] déchirant ▪ [experience] pénible, angoissant ▪ **the report makes ~ reading** le rapport contient des faits pénibles à lire.
◇ *n* hersage *m*.

harrumph [hə'rʌmf] ◇ *n* & *onom bruit de désapprobation que l'on fait en se raclant la gorge.*
◇ *vi* se racler la gorge.

harry ['hærɪ] (*pret & pp* **harried**) *vt* **1.** [harass - person] harceler, tourmenter **2.** [pillage - village] dévaster, mettre à sac **3.** MIL [enemy, troops] harceler.

harsh [hɑːʃ] *adj* **1.** [cruel, severe - person] dur, sévère, cruel ; [- punishment, treatment] dur, sévère ; [- fate] cruel ; [- criticism, judgment, words] dur, sévère ▪ **to be ~ with sb** être dur envers *OR* avec qqn **2.** [conditions, weather] rude, rigoureux **3.** [bitter - struggle] âpre, acharné **4.** [cry, voice] criard, strident ▪ [tone] dur **5.** [colour, contrast] choquant ▪ [light] cru **6.** [bleak - landscape, desert] dur, austère.

harshly ['hɑːʃlɪ] *adv* **1.** [treat, punish] sévèrement, avec rigueur **2.** [answer, speak] avec rudesse *OR* dureté ▪ [judge] sévèrement, durement **3.** [cry, shout] d'un ton strident.

harshness ['hɑːʃnɪs] *n* **1.** [of person] dureté *f*, sévérité *f* ▪ [of punishment, treatment] sévérité *f* ▪ [of judgement] dureté *f*, sévérité *f* ▪ [of statement, words, tone] dureté *f* **2.** [of climate] rigueur *f*, rudesse *f* **3.** [of cry, voice] discordance *f* **4.** [of light, contrast] dureté *f*.

hart [hɑːt] (*pl inv OR pl* **harts**) *n* cerf *m*.

harum-scarum [ˌheərəm'skeərəm] *adj inf* [wild, reckless] casse-cou *(inv)*.

Harvard ['hɑːvəd] *pr n* Harvard *(prestigieuse université située à Cambridge, dans le Massachusetts, faisant partie de la Ivy League).*

harvest ['hɑːvɪst] ◇ *n* **1.** [gathering - of cereal, crops] moisson *f* ; [- of fruit, mushrooms] récolte *f*, cueillette *f* ; [- of grapes] vendange *f*, vendanges *fpl* **2.** [yield] récolte *f* **3.** *fig* [from experience, research] moisson *f*.
◇ *vt* **1.** AGRIC [cereal, crops] moissonner ▪ [fruit, mushrooms] cueillir, récolter ▪ [grapes] vendanger **2.** *fig* [benefits] moissonner ▪ [consequences] récolter.
◇ *vi* [for cereal, crops] moissonner, faire la moisson ▪ [for fruit] faire les récoltes ▪ [for grapes] vendanger.

harvester ['hɑːvɪstəʳ] *n* **1.** [machine] moissonneuse *f* **2.** [person] moissonneur *m*, - euse *f*.

harvest festival *n* fête *f* des moissons.

harvest home *n* **1.** *UK* [supper] fête *f* de la moisson **2.** [harvesting] moisson *f*.

harvest moon *n* pleine lune *f* (de l'équinoxe d'automne).

harvest mouse *n* rat *m* des moissons.

harvest supper *n en Grande-Bretagne, dîner réunissant une communauté villageoise à la fin de la moisson.*

harvest time *n* période *f* de la moisson ▪ **at ~** à la moisson.

has [(*weak form* [həz] *strong form* [hæz])] ▷ **have**.

has-been ['hæzbiːn] *n inf* has been *m inv*.

hash [hæʃ] ◇ *n* **1.** *UK inf* [muddle, mix-up] pagaille *f*, embrouillamini *m* ▪ [mess, botch] gâchis *m* ▪ **to make a ~ of sthg** bousiller qqch, ficher qqch en l'air **2.** CULIN hachis *m* **3.** *inf* [marijuana] hasch *m* **4.** *inf phr* **to fix** *OR* **to settle sb's ~** *UK dated* [in revenge, punishment] régler son compte à qqn ; [reduce to silence] clouer le bec à qqn.
◇ *vt* CULIN hacher.

hash browns *npl pommes de terre râpées et sautées (présentées parfois sous forme de galette).*

hashish ['hæʃiːʃ] *n* haschisch *m*.

hash mark *n symbole typographique ressemblant au dièse servant à indiquer un espace ou, aux États-Unis, par exemple, un numéro de téléphone.*

hash-up *n UK inf* [mess] gâchis *m*.

hasn't ['hæznt] = **has not**.

hasp [hɑːsp] ◇ *n* [for door] loquet *m*, loqueteau *m*, moraillon *m* ▪ [for jewellery, lid, clothing] fermoir *m*.
◇ *vt* [door] fermer au loquet ▪ [lid] fermer ▪ [with padlock] cadenasser.

hassle ['hæsl] *inf* ◇ *n* **1.** [difficulty, irritation] embêtement *m*, emmerdement *m* ▪ **I don't want any ~** je ne veux pas d'embêtements ▪ **it's too much ~** c'est trop compliqué ▪ **finding their house was quite a ~** trouver leur maison n'a pas été de la tarte, on a eu un mal fou à trouver leur maison **2.** [quarrel] dispute *f*, chamaillerie *f*.
◇ *vt* [annoy, nag] embêter, harceler ▪ **don't ~ me about it** ne m'embête pas avec ça ▪ **Yvonne's always hassling him to stop smoking** Yvonne est toujours après lui pour qu'il arrête de fumer.
◇ *vi* [argue] se quereller, se chamailler.

hassock ['hæsək] *n* **1.** RELIG coussin *m* d'agenouilloir **2.** [of grass] touffe *f* d'herbe **3.** *US* [pouffe] pouf *m*.

hast (*weak form* [həst], *strong form* [hæst]) *arch* & BIBLE *vb (2nd pers sing)* ▷ **have**.

haste [heɪst] *n* [speed] hâte *f* ▪ [rush] précipitation *f* ▪ **to do sthg in ~** faire qqch à la hâte, se dépêcher de faire qqch ▪ **to make ~** se hâter, se dépêcher ▪ **in my ~, I forgot my hat** dans ma hâte, j'ai oublié mon chapeau ▶ **more ~ less speed** *prov* hâtez-vous lentement.

hasten ['heɪsn] ◇ *vt* **1.** [speed up - event, decline] précipiter, hâter ▪ **stress can ~ the ageing process** le stress peut accélérer

le vieillissement **2.** [urge on - person] presser ▪ **we were ~ed along a corridor** on nous a entraînés précipitamment dans un couloir **3.** [say quickly] : **it wasn't me, I ~ed to add** ce n'était pas moi, m'empressai-je d'ajouter.
<> *vi lit* [verb of movement] : **to ~ away** partir à la hâte, se hâter de partir.

hastily ['heɪstɪlɪ] *adv* **1.** [hurriedly] précipitamment, avec précipitation, à la hâte **2.** [impetuously, rashly] hâtivement, sans réfléchir.

hasty ['heɪstɪ] *adj* **1.** [quick, hurried] précipité, à la hâte ▪ **they made a ~ departure** ils sont partis à la hâte OR précipitamment ▪ **she beat a ~ retreat** elle a rapidement battu en retraite **2.** [rash] irréfléchi, hâtif ▪ **a ~ decision** une décision prise à la hâte OR à la légère ▪ **let's not jump to any ~ conclusions** ne concluons pas à la légère OR hâtivement.

hat [hæt] *n* **1.** chapeau *m* ▪ **he always wears a ~** il porte toujours le OR un chapeau ◗ **keep this under your ~** *inf* gardez ceci pour vous, n'en soufflez mot à personne ▪ **to pass the ~ round** faire la quête ▪ **to throw one's ~ into the ring** POL se mettre sur les rangs ▪ **that's old ~** *inf* c'est dépassé ▪ **I take my ~ off to him!** chapeau! **2.** *fig* [role] rôle *m*, casquette *f* ▪ **I'm wearing three different ~s at the moment** je porte trois casquettes différentes OR j'ai trois rôles différents en ce moment.

hatband ['hæt,bænd] *n* ruban *m* de chapeau.

hatbox ['hæt,bɒks] *n* boîte *f* à chapeau.

hatch [hætʃ] <> *vt* **1.** ZOOL [eggs] faire éclore **2.** *fig* [plan, plot] tramer, manigancer **3.** ART hachurer.
<> *vi* [eggs] éclore ▪ [chicks] sortir de l'œuf.
<> *n* **1.** [hatching of egg] éclosion *f* **2.** [brood] couvée *f* **3.** NAUT écoutille *f* ▪ **to batten down the ~es** *liter* fermer les descentes ; *fig* se préparer *(pour affronter une crise)* ▪ **down the ~!** *inf* à la vôtre! **4.** [trapdoor] trappe *f* ▪ [for inspection, access] trappe, panneau *m* ▪ [in aircraft, spaceship] sas *m* ▪ [in dam, dike] vanne *f (d'écluse)* **5.** [hatchway - for service] passe-plat *m*.

hatchback ['hætʃ,bæk] *n* **1.** [door] hayon *m* **2.** [model] voiture *f* à hayon, cinq portes *f*.

hatchery ['hætʃərɪ] (*pl* **hatcheries**) *n* **1.** [for chickens, turkeys] couvoir *m* **2.** [for fish] station *f* d'alevinage.

hatchet ['hætʃɪt] *n* hachette *f*, hache *f* (à main).

hatchet-faced *adj* au visage en lame de couteau.

hatchet job *n inf* **to do a ~ on sb/sthg** démolir qqn/qqch.

hatchet man *n inf* **1.** [killer] tueur *m* à gages **2.** INDUST & POL homme *m* de main.

hatching ['hætʃɪŋ] *n* **1.** [of eggs] éclosion *f* **2.** [brood] couvée *f* **3.** *(U)* ART hachures *fpl*.

hatchway ['hætʃ,weɪ] *n* NAUT écoutille *f* ▪ [gen] trappe *f*.

hate [heɪt] <> *vt (no cont)* [gen] détester, avoir horreur de ▪ [intensely] haïr, abhorrer ▪ **she ~s having to wear school uniform** elle a horreur d'avoir à porter un uniforme scolaire ▪ **I ~ her for what she has done** je lui en veux vraiment pour ce qu'elle a fait ▪ **I ~ myself for letting them down** je m'en veux beaucoup de les avoir laissés tomber ▮ [polite use] : **I would ~ you to think I was avoiding you** je ne voudrais surtout pas vous donner l'impression que je cherchais à vous éviter ▪ **I ~ to mention it, but you still owe me £5** je suis désolé d'avoir à vous le faire remarquer, mais vous me devez toujours 5 livres.
<> *n* **1.** [emotion] haine *f* **2.** [person hated] personne *f* que l'on déteste ▪ [thing hated] chose *f* que l'on déteste.

hated ['heɪtɪd] *adj* détesté.

hateful ['heɪtfʊl] *adj* odieux, détestable, abominable.

hate mail *n* lettres *fpl* d'injures.

Hatfields and McCoys ['hætfi:ldz-] *pr npl US* : **the ~** *noms fictifs représentant des familles rivales.*

hath [hæθ] *arch* & BIBLE = **has**.

hatmaker ['hæt,meɪkəʳ] *n* [for men] chapelier *m*, - ère *f* ▪ [for women] modiste *mf*.

hatpin ['hæt,pɪn] *n* épingle *f* à chapeau.

hatred ['heɪtrɪd] *n* haine *f* ▪ **to feel ~ for sb** avoir de la haine pour qqn, haïr qqn ▪ **he had an intense ~ of the police** il avait une haine profonde de la police.

hat stand *n* portemanteau *m*.

hatter ['hætəʳ] *n* chapelier *m*, - ère *f*.

hat trick *n UK* [three goals] hat-trick *m* ▪ [three wins] trois victoires *fpl* consécutives.

haughtily ['hɔ:tɪlɪ] *adv* avec arrogance, de manière hautaine.

haughtiness ['hɔ:tɪnɪs] *n* arrogance *f*, caractère *m* hautain.

haughty ['hɔ:tɪ] (*comp* **haughtier**, *superl* **haughtiest**) *adj* hautain, arrogant.

haul [hɔ:l] <> *vt* **1.** [pull] tirer, traîner ▪ [tow] tirer, remorquer ▪ **they ~ed the boat out of the water** ils ont tiré le bateau hors de l'eau ▪ **they were ~ed in front of OR before a judge** on les traîna devant un tribunal ◗ **to ~ sb over the coals** passer un savon à qqn **2.** [transport] transporter ▪ [by truck] camionner, transporter **3.** [move with effort] hisser ▪ **he ~ed himself out of bed** il s'est péniblement sorti du lit.
<> *vi* **1.** [pull] tirer **2.** NAUT [boat] lofer.
<> *n* **1.** [catch, takings - of fisherman, customs] prise *f*, coup *m* de filet ; [- of robbers] butin *m* ▪ **the thieves have made a good ~** les voleurs ont rapporté un beau butin **2.** [pull] : **to give a ~ on a rope/fishing net** tirer sur une corde/un filet de pêche **3.** [distance] parcours *m*, trajet *m* ▪ **it was a long ~ from Madrid to Paris** la route fut longue de Madrid à Paris ▪ **long-/short-~ flights** vols *mpl* long courrier/moyen courrier **4.** [in time] : **training to be a doctor is a long ~** les études de médecine sont très longues.

➡ **haul in** *vt sep* [catch, net, rope] tirer, amener ▪ **Tom was ~ed in** *inf* **on a drink-driving charge** Tom a été épinglé pour conduite en état d'ivresse.

➡ **haul off** <> *vt sep* [take away] conduire, amener ▪ **he was ~ed off to prison** on l'a flanqué en prison.
<> *vi insep inf US inf* lever le bras OR le poing.

➡ **haul up** *vt sep* [pull up] tirer, hisser ▪ **to ~ sb up before a judge** traîner qqn devant le tribunal OR le juge.

haulage ['hɔ:lɪdʒ] <> *n (U)* **1.** [as business] transports *mpl*, transport *m* (routier) **2.** [act] transport *m* **3.** [cost] (frais *mpl* de) transport *m*.
<> *comp* [company] de transport routier, de transports routiers ▪ **~ contractor** entrepreneur *m* de transports routiers.

haulier ['hɔ:ljəʳ] *UK*, **hauler** ['hɔ:ləʳ] *US n* **1.** [business] entreprise *f* de transports routiers **2.** [owner] entrepreneur *m* de transports routiers **3.** [driver] routier *m*, -ère *f*, camionneur *m*.

haunch [hɔ:ntʃ] *n* **1.** CULIN [of venison] cuissot *m* ▪ [of beef] quartier *m* **2.** [of human] hanche *f* ▪ **to squat down on one's ~es** s'accroupir **3.** [of animal] : **~es** arrière-train *m*, derrière *m*.

haunt [hɔ:nt] <> *vt* **1.** [subj: ghost, spirit] hanter **2.** [subj: problems] hanter, tourmenter ▪ **she is ~ed by her unhappy childhood** elle est hantée OR tourmentée par son enfance malheureuse ▪ **his past continues to ~ him** son passé ne cesse de le poursuivre OR hanter **3.** *inf* [frequent - bar] hanter, fréquenter ; [- streets] hanter, traîner dans.
<> *n* **1.** [place] lieu *m* que l'on fréquente beaucoup, lieu *m* de prédilection ▪ **it's one of his favourite ~s** c'est un des endroits qu'il préfère **2.** [refuge - for animals, criminals] repaire *m*.

haunted ['hɔ:ntɪd] *adj* **1.** [house, castle] hanté **2.** [look] hagard, égaré.

haunting ['hɔ:ntɪŋ] *adj* [memory, sound] obsédant ▪ [tune] qui vous trotte dans la tête ▪ **she has a ~ beauty** elle est d'une beauté obsédante.

Havana [hə'vænə] <> *pr n* [city] la Havane.
<> *n* [cigar, tobacco] havane *m*.
<> *comp* [tobacco, cigar] de Havane.

have [hæv] (*pres* **has** *(3rd pers sing pres)* [*(weak form* [həz], *strong form* [hæz]*)*], *pret & pp* **had** [hæd]) <> *aux vb* **1.** [used to form perfect tenses] avoir, être ■ **to ~ finished** avoir fini ■ **to ~ left** être parti ■ **to ~ sat down** s'être assis ■ **has she slept?** a-t-elle dormi? ■ **~ they arrived?** sont-ils arrivés? ■ **the children will ~ gone to bed by the time we arrive** les enfants seront couchés quand nous arriverons ■ **you were silly not to ~ accepted** tu es bête de ne pas avoir accepté ■ **after** *OR* **when you ~ finished, you may leave** quand vous aurez fini, vous pourrez partir ■ **she was ashamed of having lied** elle avait honte d'avoir menti ■ **she felt she couldn't change her mind, having already agreed to go** elle sentait qu'elle ne pouvait pas changer d'avis, étant donné qu'elle avait dit être d'accord pour y aller ■ **I ~ been thinking** j'ai réfléchi ■ **I ~ known her for three years/since childhood** je la connais depuis trois ans/depuis mon enfance ■ **she claimed she hadn't heard the news** elle a prétendu ne pas avoir entendu la nouvelle ■ **we had gone to bed early** nous nous étions couchés de bonne heure ■ **when he had given his speech, I left** une fois qu'il eut terminé son discours, je partis ■ **had I known, I wouldn't ~ insisted** si j'avais su, je n'aurais pas insisté ■ **if I had known, I wouldn't ~ said anything** si j'avais su, je n'aurais rien dit ■ **they would ~ been happy if it hadn't been for the war** ils auraient vécu heureux si la guerre n'était pas survenue ■ **why don't you just leave him and ~ done with it?** pourquoi donc est-ce que vous ne le quittez pas, pour en finir? ➊ **he's had it** *inf* [is in trouble] il est fichu *OR* foutu△ ; [is worn out] il est à bout ■ **I've had it with all your complaining!** *inf* j'en ai jusque-là de tes jérémiades! ■ **this plant has had it** *inf* cette plante est fichue **2.** [elliptical uses] : **~ you ever had the measles? – yes, I ~/no, I haven't** avez-vous eu la rougeole? – oui/non ■ **she hasn't finished – yes, she has!** elle n'a pas fini – (mais) si! ■ **you've forgotten his birthday – no, I haven't!** tu as oublié son anniversaire – mais non! **3.** [in tag questions] : **you've read "Hamlet", haven't you?** vous avez lu "Hamlet", n'est-ce pas? ■ **he hasn't arrived, has he?** il n'est pas arrivé, si? ■ **so she's got a new job, has she?** elle a changé de travail alors?

◇ *vt*

A.

1. [be in possession of, own] avoir, posséder ■ **do you ~** *OR* **~ you got a car?** avez-vous une voiture? ■ **he has (got) £10 left** il lui reste 10 livres ■ **do you ~ any children? if you ~...** avez-vous des enfants? si vous en avez *OR* si oui... ■ **do we ~ any milk in the house?** est-ce qu'on a du lait *OR* est-ce qu'il y a du lait à la maison? ■ **she has a baker's shop/bookshop** elle tient une boulangerie/librairie ➊ **give it all you ~** *OR* **all you've got!** *inf* mets-y le paquet! ■ **I've got it!** ça y est, j'ai trouvé *OR* j'y suis! ■ **paper, envelopes and what ~ you** du papier, des enveloppes et je ne sais quoi encore

2. [enjoy the use of] avoir, disposer de ■ **we had a couple of hours to do our errands** nous disposions de *OR* nous avions quelques heures pour faire nos courses ■ **I don't ~ time** *OR* **I haven't got time to stop for lunch** je n'ai pas le temps de m'arrêter pour déjeuner ■ **he hasn't (got) long to live** il ne lui reste pas longtemps à vivre ■ **do you ~** *OR* **~ you (got) a minute (to spare)?** tu as une minute? ■ **such questions ~ an important place in our lives** ce genre de questions occupe une place importante dans notre vie

3. [possess as quality or attribute] avoir ■ **she has (got) red hair** elle a les cheveux roux, elle est rousse ■ **the ticket has a name on it** il y a un nom sur le billet ■ **she has what it takes** *OR* **she has it in her to succeed** elle a ce qu'il faut pour réussir ■ **you've never had it so good!** vous n'avez jamais eu la vie si belle!

4. [possess knowledge or understanding of] : **do you ~ any experience of teaching?** avez-vous déjà enseigné? ■ **she has a clear sense of what matters** elle sait très bien ce qui est important ■ **he has some Greek and Latin** il connaît un peu le grec et le latin

B.

1. [indicating experience of a specified situation] : **to ~ a dream/nightmare** faire un rêve/cauchemar ■ **I've had my appendix taken out** je me suis fait opérer de l'appendicite ■ **he had all his money stolen** il s'est fait voler *OR* on lui a volé tout son argent ■ **I love having my back rubbed** j'adore qu'on me frotte le dos ■ **they had some strange things happen to them** il leur est arrivé de drôles de choses

2. [be infected with, suffer from] avoir ■ **do you ~** *OR* **~ you got a headache?** avez-vous mal à la tête?

3. *(delexicalized use)* [perform, take part in - bath, lesson] prendre ; [- meeting] avoir ■ **we had our first argument last night** nous nous sommes disputés hier soir pour la première fois ■ **to ~ a stroll** se promener, faire un tour ■ **I want to ~ a think about it** je veux y réfléchir ■ **to ~ a party** [organize] organiser une fête ; [celebrate] faire la fête ■ **I'll ~ no part in it** je refuse de m'en mêler

4. [pass, spend] passer, avoir ■ **I had a horrible day at work** j'ai passé une journée atroce au travail ■ **~ a nice day!** bonne journée! ■ **to ~ a good time** s'amuser

5. [exhibit, show] avoir, montrer ■ **he had the nerve to refuse** il a eu le culot de refuser ■ **he didn't even ~ the decency to apologize** il n'a même pas eu la décence de s'excuser

6. [feel obligation or necessity in regard to] : **I ~ (got) a lot of work to finish** j'ai beaucoup de travail à finir ■ **he has (got) nothing to do/to read** il n'a rien à faire/à lire

C.

1. [obtain, receive] avoir, recevoir ■ **I'd like him to ~ this picture** j'aimerais lui donner cette photo ■ **we had a phone call from the mayor** nous avons reçu *OR* eu un coup de fil du maire ■ **they've still had no news of the lost plane** ils n'ont toujours pas de nouvelles de l'avion (qui a) disparu ■ **I ~ it on good authority** je le tiens de bonne source ■ **I must ~ your answer by tomorrow** il me faut votre réponse pour demain ■ **she let them ~ the wardrobe for £300** elle leur a laissé *OR* cédé l'armoire pour 300 livres ■ **there are plenty of nice flats to be had** il y a plein de jolis appartements ■ **stamps can be had at any newsagent's** on peut acheter des timbres chez le marchand de journaux ➊ **I let him ~ it** *inf* [attacked him] je lui ai réglé son compte ; [told him off] je lui ai passé un savon ■ **you had it coming!** *inf* tu ne l'as pas volé!

2. [invite] recevoir, avoir ■ **she's having some people (over) for** *OR* **to dinner** elle reçoit *OR* elle a du monde à dîner ■ **let's ~ him round for a drink** et si on l'invitait à prendre un pot?

3. [accept, take] vouloir ■ **he'd like to marry but nobody will ~ him!** il aimerait se marier mais personne ne veut de lui! ■ **do what you want, I'm having nothing more to do with your schemes** fais ce que tu veux, je ne veux plus être mêlé à tes combines

D.

1. [clutch] tenir ■ **he had (got) his assailant by the throat** il tenait son agresseur à la gorge

2. *fig* [gain control or advantage over] : **you ~ me there!** là vous me tenez! ■ **I ~ (got) you right where I want you now!** je vous tiens! ➊ **the Celtics ~ it!** SPORT les Celtics ont gagné!

3. [bewilder, perplex] : **who won? – you've got me there** qui a gagné? – là, tu me poses une colle

E.

1. [cause to be] : **the news had me worried** la nouvelle m'a inquiété ■ **I'll ~ this light fixed in a minute** j'en ai pour une minute à réparer cette lampe ■ **we'll ~ everything ready** tout sera prêt

2. *(with past participle)* [cause to be done] : **to ~ sthg done** faire faire qqch ■ **I had my hair cut** je me suis fait couper les cheveux ■ **we must ~ the curtains cleaned** nous devons faire nettoyer les rideaux *OR* donner les rideaux à nettoyer

3. *(with infinitive)* [cause to do] : **to ~ sb do sthg** faire faire qqch à qqn ■ **she had him invite all the neighbours round** elle lui a fait inviter tous les voisins ■ **he soon had them all laughing** il eut tôt fait de les faire tous rire ■ **as he would ~ us believe** comme il voudrait nous le faire croire

F.

1. [consume - food, meal] avoir, prendre ■ **we're having dinner out tonight** nous sortons dîner ce soir ■ **to ~ breakfast in bed** prendre le petit déjeuner au lit ■ **would you like to ~ coffee?** voulez-vous (prendre) un café? ■ **I had tea with her** j'ai pris le thé avec elle ■ **we stopped and had a drink** nous nous sommes arrêtés pour boire quelque chose ■ **what will you ~? – I'll ~ the lamb** [in restaurant] qu'est-ce que vous prenez? – je vais prendre de l'agneau ■ **will you ~ a cigarette?** voulez-vous une cigarette?

2. [indicating location, position] placer, mettre ■ **we'll ~ the wardrobe here and the table in there** nous mettrons l'armoire ici et la table par là ■ **I had my back to the window** je tournais le dos à la fenêtre ■ **he had his head down** il avait la tête baissée

3. [be accompanied by] : **she had her mother with her** sa mère était avec elle ▪ **I can't talk right now, I ~ someone with me** je ne peux pas parler, je ne suis pas seul *OR* je suis avec quelqu'un

4. [give birth to] : **she's had a baby** elle a eu un bébé ▪ **our dog has just had puppies** notre chien vient d'avoir des petits

5. [assert, claim] soutenir, maintenir ▪ **rumour has it that they're married** le bruit court qu'ils sont mariés ▪ **as the government would ~ it** comme dirait le gouvernement

6. *(with 'will' or 'would')* [wish for] vouloir ▪ **what would you ~ me do?** que voudriez-vous que je fasse? ▪ **I'll ~ you know I ~ a degree in French** je vous fais remarquer que j'ai une licence de français

7. *(in negative)* [allow, permit] : **I will not ~ him in my house!** il ne mettra pas les pieds chez moi! ▪ **I won't ~ it!** ça ne va pas se passer comme ça! ▪ **we can't ~ you sleeping on the floor** nous ne pouvons pas vous laisser dormir par terre

8. *inf (in passive) inf* [cheat, outwit] avoir ▪ **you've been had!** tu t'es fait avoir!

9. △ [sleep with] avoir△

G.

1. [with infinitive] [indicating obligation] : **to ~ (got) to do sthg** devoir faire qqch, être obligé de faire qqch ▪ **don't you ~ to** *OR* **haven't you got to phone the office?** est-ce que tu ne dois pas appeler le bureau? ▪ **you don't ~ to** *OR* **you haven't got to go** tu n'es pas obligé d'y aller ▪ **I hate having to get up early** j'ai horreur de devoir me lever tôt ▪ **I won't apologize – you ~ to** je ne m'excuserai pas – il le faut ▮ [expressing disbelief, dismay etc] : **you've got to be joking!** vous plaisantez!, c'est une plaisanterie! ▪ **you didn't ~ to tell your father what happened!** tu n'avais pas besoin d'aller dire à ton père ce qui s'est passé! ▪ **the train would ~ to be late today of all days!** il fallait que le train soit en retard aujourd'hui!

2. [indicating necessity] devoir ▪ **you ~ (got) to get some rest** il faut que vous vous reposiez, vous devez vous reposer ▪ **I'll ~ to think about it** il va falloir que j'y réfléchisse ▪ **some problems still ~ to be worked out** il reste encore des problèmes à résoudre ▪ **the plumbing has to be redone** la plomberie a besoin d'être refaite ▪ **you'd ~ to be deaf not to hear that noise** il faudrait être sourd pour ne pas entendre ce bruit ▪ **do you ~ to turn the music up so loud?** vous ne pourriez pas baisser un peu la musique?

3. *phr* **the book has to do with archaeology** ce livre traite de l'archéologie ▪ **their argument had to do with money** ils se disputaient à propos d'argent ▪ **this has nothing to do with you** ça ne te concerne *OR* regarde pas ▪ **I'll ~ nothing more to do with her** je ne veux plus avoir affaire à elle ▪ **they had nothing to do with her being fired** ils n'avaient rien à voir avec son licenciement.

◆ **haves** *npl* : **the ~s** les riches *mpl*, les nantis *mpl* ▪ **the ~s and the ~-nots** les riches et les pauvres, les nantis et les démunis.

◆ **have away** *vt sep UK phr* **to ~ it away with sb**△ coucher avec qqn.

◆ **have in** *vt sep* **1.** [cause to enter] faire entrer ▪ **she had him in for a chat** elle l'a fait entrer pour discuter **2.** [invite] : **to ~ friends in for a drink** inviter des amis à prendre un pot **3.** [doctor, plumber] faire venir ▪ **they've got workmen in at the moment** ils ont des ouvriers en ce moment **4.** *phr* **to ~ it in for sb** *inf* avoir une dent contre qqn.

◆ **have off** *vt sep UK phr* **to ~ it off with sb**△ coucher avec qqn.

◆ **have on** *vt sep* **1.** [wear] porter ▪ **what does she ~ on?** qu'est-ce qu'elle porte?, comment est-elle habillée? **2.** [radio, television] : **he has the radio/television on all night** sa radio/sa télévision est allumée toute la nuit **3.** [commitment, engagement] : **we ~ a lot on today** nous avons beaucoup à faire aujourd'hui **4.** *UK inf* [tease, trick] faire marcher **5.** *phr* **they ~ nothing on me** ils n'ont aucune preuve contre moi ▪ **she must ~ something on the boss** elle doit savoir quelque chose de compromettant sur le patron.

◆ **have out** *vt sep* **1.** [tooth] se faire arracher **2.** [settle] : **to ~ it out with sb** s'expliquer avec qqn.

◆ **have over** *vt sep* **1.** [invite] inviter **2.** *phr* **to ~ one over on sb** avoir le dessus sur qqn.

◆ **have up** *vt sep inf* [bring before the authorities] : **they were had up by the police for vandalism** ils ont été arrêtés pour vandalisme ▪ **he was had up (before the court) for breaking and entering** il a comparu (devant le tribunal) pour effraction.

haven ['heɪvn] *n* [refuge] abri *m*, refuge *m* ▪ **a safe ~** un abri sûr ▪ **the garden is a ~ of peace and tranquillity** *lit* le jardin est un havre de paix et de tranquillité.

have-nots *npl* : **the ~** les démunis *mpl*, les défavorisés *mpl*.

haven't ['hævnt] = **have not**.

haversack ['hævəsæk] *n* havresac *m*.

havoc ['hævək] *n (U)* ravages *mpl*, chaos *m* ▪ **to wreak ~ on sthg** ravager qqch ▪ **the strike played ~ with our plans** la grève a mis nos projets par terre.

haw [hɔ:] *n* BOT [berry] baie *f* d'aubépine, cenelle *f* ▪ [shrub] aubépine *f*.

Hawaii [hə'waɪi] *pr n* Hawaii ▪ **in ~** à Hawaii.

Hawaiian [hə'waɪɪən] <> *n* **1.** [person] Hawaïen *m*, - enne *f* **2.** LING hawaïen *m*.
<> *adj* hawaïen.

Hawaiian Standard Time *n* heure *f* de Hawaii.

hawk [hɔ:k] <> *n* **1.** [bird] faucon *m* ▪ **to watch sb/sthg like a ~** regarder qqn/qqch d'un œil perçant **2.** POL faucon *m* **3.** CONSTR taloche *f*.
<> *vi* **1.** HUNT chasser au faucon **2.** [clear throat] se racler la gorge.
<> *vt* **1.** [sell - from door to door] colporter ; [- in market, street] vendre à la criée **2.** *fig* [news, gossip] colporter **3.** [cough up] cracher.

hawker ['hɔ:kər] *n* [street vendor] marchand *m* ambulant ▪ [door-to-door] démarcheur *m*, colporteur *m* ▪ **'no ~s'** 'démarchage interdit'.

hawk-eyed *adj* **1.** [keen-sighted] au regard d'aigle **2.** *fig* [vigilant] qui a l'œil partout.

hawkish ['hɔ:kɪʃ] *adj* POL dur.

hawkmoth ['hɔ:k,mɒθ] *n* ENTOM sphinx *m*.

hawse [hɔ:z] *n* NAUT écubier *m*.

hawser ['hɔ:zər] *n* NAUT grelin *m*, aussière *f*.

hawthorn ['hɔ:θɔ:n] <> *n* aubépine *f*.
<> *comp* [hedge, berry] d'aubépine.

hay [heɪ] *n* foin *m* ▪ **to make ~** AGRIC faire les foins ▶ **to make ~ while the sun shines** *prov* battre le fer pendant qu'il est chaud *prov*.

Haydn ['haɪdn] *pr n* Haydn.

hay fever *n* rhume *m* des foins ▪ **to suffer from/to have ~** souffrir du/avoir le rhume des foins.

hayloft ['heɪ,lɒft] *n* grenier *m* à foin.

haymaker ['heɪ,meɪkər] *n* AGRIC [worker] faneur *m*, - euse *f* ▪ [machine] faneuse *f*.

haymaking ['heɪ,meɪkɪŋ] *n (U)* fenaison *f*, foins *mpl*.

hayrack ['heɪ,ræk] *n* [in barn] râtelier *m* ▪ [on cart] ridelle *f*.

hayrick ['heɪ,rɪk] *n* meule *f* de foin.

haystack ['heɪ,stæk] *n* meule *f* de foin.

haywire ['heɪ,waɪər] *adj inf* [system, person] détraqué ▪ **to go ~** [machine] débloquer, se détraquer ; [plans] mal tourner.

hazard ['hæzəd] <> *n* **1.** [danger, risk] risque *m*, danger *m* ▪ **the ~s of smoking** les dangers du tabac ▪ **a health/fire ~** un risque pour la santé/d'incendie **2.** [in golf] obstacle *m*.
<> *vt* **1.** [risk - life] risquer, hasarder ; [- reputation] risquer **2.** [venture - statement, advice, suggestion] hasarder, se risquer à faire ▪ **to ~ a guess : would you care to ~ a guess as to the weight?** voulez-vous essayer de deviner combien ça pèse? **3.** [stake, bet - fortune] risquer, miser.

◆ **hazards** *npl* AUT feux *mpl* de détresse.

hazardous ['hæzədəs] *adj* **1.** [dangerous] dangereux, risqué ■ **~ waste** déchets *mpl* dangereux **2.** [uncertain] hasardeux, incertain.

hazard warning AUT ◇ *n* signal *m* de danger.
◇ *comp* : **~ triangle** triangle *m* de présignalisation ■ **~ lights** feux *mpl* de détresse.

haze [heɪz] ◇ *n* **1.** METEOR brume *f* ■ **a heat ~** une brume de chaleur **2.** *(U)* [steam] vapeur *f*, vapeurs *fpl* ■ [smoke] nuage *m* **3.** [confusion] brouillard *m* ■ **to be in a ~** être dans le brouillard.
◇ *vt US* **1.** [harass] harceler **2.** MIL faire subir des brimades à ■ SCH bizuter.

hazel ['heɪzl] ◇ *n* noisetier *m*.
◇ *adj* [colour] noisette *(inv)*.

hazelnut ['heɪzl,nʌt] ◇ *n* [nut] noisette *f* ■ [tree] noisetier *m*.
◇ *comp* [flavour] de noisette ■ [ice cream, yoghurt] à la noisette.

haziness ['heɪzɪnɪs] *n* **1.** [of sky, weather] état *m* brumeux **2.** [of memory, thinking] flou *m*, imprécision *f* **3.** PHOT flou *m*.

hazy ['heɪzɪ] (*comp* **hazier**, *superl* **haziest**) *adj* **1.** [weather, sky] brumeux **2.** [memory] flou, vague ■ [thinking, ideas] flou, embrouillé ■ **she's rather ~ about the details of what happened** elle n'a qu'un vague souvenir de ce qui s'est passé **3.** PHOT flou **4.** [colour] pâle.

H-bomb (*abbrev of* **hydrogen bomb**) *n* bombe *f* H.

h & c *written abbr of* **hot and cold (water)**.

HDD (*abbrev of* **hard disk drive**) *n* COMPUT disque *m* dur.

HDTV (*abbrev of* **high definition television**) *n* TVHD *f*.

he [hi:] ◇ *pron* il ■ **he works in London** il travaille à Londres ■ **he and I** lui et moi ■ **there he is!** le voilà! ■ **she is older than he is** *fml* elle est plus âgée que lui ■ **that's what he thinks!** c'est ce qu'il croit!
◇ *n* [animal] mâle *m* ■ [boy] garçon *m*.

HE 1. *written abbr of* **high explosive 2.** (*written abbrev of* **His/Her Excellency**) S Exc, SE.

head [hed] (*pl* **heads**) ◇ *n* **1.** [of human, animal] tête *f* ■ **she has a lovely ~ of hair** elle a de très beaux cheveux *OR* une très belle chevelure ■ **he's already a ~ taller than his mother** il dépasse déjà sa mère d'une tête ■ **Sea Biscuit won by a ~** [in horseracing] Sea Biscuit a gagné d'une tête ■ **from ~ to toe** *OR* **foot** de la tête aux pieds ■ **she was dressed in black from ~ to foot** elle était tout en noir *OR* entièrement vêtue de noir ▶ **a ~, per ~** par tête, par personne ■ **it costs 50 francs a** *OR* **per ~** ça coûte 50 FF par tête *OR* personne ■ **to fall ~ over heels in love with sb** tomber éperdument amoureux de qqn ■ **to have one's ~ in the clouds** avoir la tête dans les nuages ■ **wine always goes to my ~** le vin me monte toujours à la tête ■ **all this praise has gone to his ~** toutes ces louanges lui ont tourné la tête ■ **to give a horse its ~** lâcher la bride à un cheval ■ **to give sb their ~** laisser agir qqn ■ **I could do it standing on my ~** c'est simple comme bonjour ■ **she's got her ~ screwed on (the right way)** elle a la tête sur les épaules ■ **she's ~ and shoulders above the rest** les autres ne lui arrivent pas à la cheville ■ **to laugh one's ~ off** rire à gorge déployée ■ **to shout** *OR* **to scream one's ~ off** crier à tue-tête ■ **~s will roll** des têtes tomberont
2. [mind, thoughts] tête *f* ■ **to take it into one's ~ to do sthg** se mettre en tête de faire qqch ■ **the idea never entered my ~** ça ne m'est jamais venu à l'esprit ■ **don't put silly ideas into his ~** ne lui mettez pas des idées stupides en tête ■ **I can't get these dates into my ~** je n'arrive pas à retenir ces dates ■ **the answer has gone right out of my ~** j'ai complètement oublié la réponse ■ **use your ~!** fais travailler tes méninges! ▶ **it's doing my ~ in!** *inf* ça me tape sur le système! ■ **I just can't get my ~ round the idea that she's gone** *inf* je n'arrive vraiment pas à me faire à l'idée qu'elle est partie ■ **to get one's ~ straight** *inf* se ressaisir
3. [aptitude] : **in my job, you need a good ~ for figures** pour faire mon métier, il faut savoir manier les chiffres ■ **she has no ~ for business** elle n'a pas le sens des affaires ■ **I've no ~ for heights** j'ai le vertige
4. [clear thinking, common sense] : **keep your ~!** gardez votre calme!, ne perdez pas la tête! ■ **to keep a cool ~** garder la tête froide ■ **you'll need a clear ~ in the morning** vous aurez besoin d'avoir l'esprit clair demain matin ▶ **he's off his ~** *UK inf* il est malade, il est pas bien
5. [intelligence, ability] tête *f* ■ **we'll have to put our ~s together and find a solution** nous devrons nous y mettre ensemble pour trouver une solution ▶ **off the top of my ~ : off the top of my ~, I'd say it would cost about £1,500** à vue de nez je dirais que ça coûte dans les 1 500 livres ■ **I don't know off the top of my ~** je ne sais pas, il faudrait que je vérifie ■ **he's talking off the top of his ~** il raconte n'importe quoi ■ **her lecture was completely over my ~** sa conférence m'a complètement dépassé ■ **to talk over sb's ~** s'exprimer de manière trop compliquée pour qqn ■ **two ~s are better than one** *prov* deux avis valent mieux qu'un
6. *inf* [headache] mal *m* de tête
7. [chief, boss - of police, government] chef *m* ; [- of school, of company] directeur *m*, - trice *f* ■ **the crowned ~s of Europe** les têtes couronnées de l'Europe
8. [authority, responsibility] : **she went over my ~ to the president** elle est allée voir le président sans me consulter ■ **they were promoted over my ~** ils ont été promus avant moi ▶ **on your (own) ~ be it!** c'est toi qui en prends la responsabilité!, à tes risques et périls!
9. [top, upper end, extremity - of racquet, pin, hammer] tête *f* ; [- of staircase] haut *m*, tête *f* ; [- of bed] chevet *m*, tête *f* ; [- of arrow] pointe *f* ; [- of page] tête *f* ; [- of letter] en-tête *m* ; [- of cane] pommeau *m* ; [- of valley] tête *f* ; [- of river] source *f* ■ **at the ~ of the procession/queue** en tête de (la) procession/de (la) queue ■ **sitting at the ~ of the table** assis au bout de la *OR* en tête de table
10. BOT & CULIN [of corn] épi *m* ■ [of garlic] tête *f*, gousse *f* ■ [of celery] pied *m* ■ [of asparagus] pointe *f*
11. [of coin] côté *m* pile ■ **~s or tails?** pile ou face? ▶ **I can't make ~ nor tail of this** pour moi ça n'a ni queue ni tête
12. (*pl inv*) [of livestock] tête *f* ■ **50 ~ of cattle** 50 têtes de bétail
13. ELECTRON [of tape recorder, VCR] tête *f*
14. [title - of chapter] tête *f*
15. [on beer] mousse *f*
16. [of drum] peau *f*
17. [of ship] proue *f*
18. MED [of abscess, spot] tête *f* ■ **to come to a ~** [abscess, spot] mûrir ; *fig* [problem] arriver au point critique ■ **his resignation brought things to a ~** sa démission a précipité les choses
19. ▲ [fellatio] : **to give sb ~** *US* tailler une pipe à qqn△
20. *US inf* [toilet] toilettes *fpl*.
◇ *comp* **1.** ANAT : **~ injuries** blessures *fpl* à la tête
2. [chief - gardener, nurse, buyer] en chef ■ **~ porter** chef-portier *m*.
◇ *vt* **1.** [command - group, organization] être à la tête de ; [- project, revolt] diriger, être à la tête de ■ [chair - discussion] mener ; [- commission] présider
2. [be first] être *OR* venir en tête de ■ **Madrid ~s the list of Europe's most interesting cities** Madrid vient *OR* s'inscrit en tête des villes les plus intéressantes d'Europe
3. [steer - vehicle] diriger ; [- person] guider, diriger
4. [provide title for] intituler ■ [be title of] être en tête de ■ **the essay is ~ed "Democracy"** l'essai s'intitule *OR* est intitulé "Démocratie"
5. FTBL : **he ~ed the ball into the goal** il a marqué de la tête
6. [plant] écimer, étêter.
◇ *vi* [car, crowd, person] aller, se diriger ■ NAUT mettre le cap sur ■ **we ~ed back to the office** nous sommes retournés au bureau.

◆ **head for** *vt insep* [car, person] se diriger vers ■ NAUT mettre le cap sur ■ **she ~ed for home** elle rentra (à la maison) ■ **he's ~ing for trouble** il va (tout droit) à la catastrophe ■ **to be ~ing for a fall** courir à l'échec ▶ **to ~ for the hills** filer.

◆ **head off** ◇ *vt sep* **1.** [divert - animal, vehicle, person] détourner de son chemin ; [- enemy] forcer à reculer ■ **she ~ed off all questions about her private life** *fig* elle a éludé toute question sur sa vie privée
2. [crisis, disaster] prévenir, éviter ■ [rebellion, revolt, unrest] éviter.
◇ *vi insep* partir.

◆ **head up** *vt sep* [be leader of] diriger.

headache ['hedeɪk] *n* **1.** [pain] mal *m* de tête ■ [migraine] migraine *f* ■ **to have a ~** [gen] avoir mal à la tête, avoir la migraine ■ **white wine gives me a ~** le vin blanc me donne mal à la tête **2.** *fig* [problem] problème *m* ■ **the trip was one big ~** le voyage a été un casse-tête du début à la fin.

headachy ['hedeɪkɪ] *adj inf* **I'm feeling a bit ~** j'ai un peu mal à la tête.

headband ['hedbænd] *n* bandeau *m*.

headboard ['hed,bɔ:d] *n* tête *f* de lit.

head boy *n UK élève chargé d'un certain nombre de responsabilités et qui représente son école aux cérémonies publiques.*

headbutt ['hedbʌt] ◇ *n* coup *m* de tête, coup *m* de boule. ◇ *vt* donner un coup de tête *OR* de boule à.

head case *n inf* dingue *mf*.

headcheese ['hed,tʃi:z] *n US* fromage *m* de tête.

head cold *n* rhume *m* de cerveau.

head count *n* vérification *f* du nombre de personnes présentes ■ **the teacher did a ~** la maîtresse a compté les élèves.

headdress ['hed,dres] *n* [gen] coiffure *f* ■ [belonging to regional costume] coiffe *f*.

-headed ['hedɪd] *in cpds* à tête... ■ **a silver~ cane** une canne à pommeau d'argent ■ **a three~ dragon** un dragon à trois têtes.

headed notepaper ['hedɪd-] *n UK* papier *m* à en-tête.

header ['hedəʳ] *n* **1.** [fall] chute *f* (la tête la première) ■ [dive] plongeon *m* (la tête la première) ■ **he took a ~ into the ditch** il est tombé la tête la première dans le fossé **2.** FTBL (coup *m* de) tête *f* ■ **he scored with a ~** il a marqué de la tête **3.** COMPUT en-tête *m* ■ **~ block** en-tête ■ **~ card** carte *f* en-tête **4.** *UK* AUT : **~ (tank)** collecteur *m* de tête **5.** CONSTR (pierre *f* en) boutisse *f*.

head first [,hed'fɜ:st] *adv* **1.** [dive, fall, jump] la tête la première ■ **he dived ~ into the pool** il a piqué une tête dans la piscine **2.** [rashly] sans réfléchir, imprudemment ■ **to jump ~ into sthg** se jeter tête baissée dans qqch.

headgear ['hed,gɪəʳ] *n (U)* coiffure *f* ■ **they were wearing some very odd ~** *hum* ils avaient tous un drôle de chapeau.

head girl *n UK élève chargée d'un certain nombre de responsabilités et qui représente son école aux cérémonies publiques.*

headhunt ['hedhʌnt] ◇ *vi* recruter des cadres (pour une entreprise).
◇ *vt* : **to be ~ed** être recruté par un chasseur de têtes.

headhunter ['hed,hʌntəʳ] *n* ANTHR & *fig* chasseur *m* de têtes.

headiness ['hedɪnɪs] *n* **1.** [of wine] bouquet *m* capiteux ■ **the ~ of sudden success** la griserie *OR* l'ivresse qu'apporte un succès imprévu **2.** [excitement] exaltation *f*, excitation *f* ■ **the ~ of the early sixties** l'euphorie du début des années 60.

heading ['hedɪŋ] *n* **1.** [title - of article, book] titre *m* ; [- of chapter] titre *m*, intitulé *m* ■ **page ~** tête *f* de page **2.** [subject] rubrique *f* ■ **their latest record comes under the ~ of jazz** leur dernier disque se trouve sous la rubrique jazz **3.** [letterhead] en-tête *m* **4.** AERON & NAUT [direction] cap *m* **5.** MIN [tunnel] galerie *f* d'avancement.

headlamp ['hedlæmp] *n* **1.** *UK* = **headlight** **2.** MIN lampe-chapeau *f*.

headland ['hedlənd] *n* promontoire *m*, cap *m*.

headless ['hedlɪs] *adj* **1.** [arrow, body, screw] sans tête ■ **he was running around like a ~ chicken** *hum* il courait dans tous les sens **2.** [company, commission] sans chef.

headlight ['hedlaɪt] *n* [on car] phare *m* ■ [on train] fanal *m*, feu *m* avant.

headline ['hedlaɪn] ◇ *n* **1.** [in newspaper] (gros) titre *m*, manchette *f* ■ **the hijacking made the ~s** le détournement a fait la une des journaux ■ **to hit the ~s** faire les gros titres **2.** RADIO & TV [news summary] grand titre *m* ■ **here are today's news ~s** voici les principaux titres de l'actualité.
◇ *vt* **1.** PRESS mettre en manchette **2.** [provide heading for] intituler **3.** *US* [have top billing in] avoir le rôle principal dans.
◇ *vi US* [have top billing] avoir le rôle principal.

headliner ['hedlaɪnəʳ] *n US* vedette *f*.

headlock ['hedlɒk] *n* cravate *f*.

headlong ['hedlɒŋ] ◇ *adv* **1.** [dive, fall] la tête la première ■ **she dived ~ into the lake** elle a piqué une tête dans le lac **2.** [rush - head down] tête baissée ; [- at great speed] à toute allure *OR* vitesse **3.** [rashly] sans réfléchir, imprudemment ■ **she rushed ~ to her downfall** elle courait tout droit à sa perte ■ **he plunged ~ into the story** il s'est lancé dans l'histoire.
◇ *adj* **1.** [dive, fall] la tête la première **2.** [impetuous - action] imprudent, impétueux.

headman ['hedmæn] (*pl* **headmen** [-men]) *n* chef *m*.

headmaster [,hed'mɑ:stəʳ] *n* SCH proviseur *m*, directeur *m*, chef *m* d'établissement.

headmistress [,hed'mɪstrɪs] *n* SCH directrice *f*, chef *m* d'établissement.

head office *n* siège *m* social, bureau *m* central.

head-on ◇ *adv* **1.** [collide, hit] de front, de plein fouet **2.** [confront, meet] de front ■ **management confronted the union ~** la direction a affronté le syndicat.
◇ *adj* **1.** [collision - of car, plane] de front, de plein fouet ; [- of ships] par l'avant **2.** [confrontation, disagreement] violent.

headphones ['hedfəunz] *npl* casque *m (à écouteurs)*.

headpiece ['hedpi:s] *n* **1.** [helmet] casque *m* **2.** TYPO vignette *f*, en-tête *m*.

headquarter [hed'kwɔ:təʳ] *vt* ■ **to be headquartered in** avoir son siège à.

headquarters [,hed'kwɔ:təz] *npl* **1.** [of bank, office] siège *m* social, bureau *m* central ■ [of army, police] quartier *m* général **2.** MIL [commanding officers] quartier *m* général.

headrest ['hedrest] *n* appuie-tête *m*, repose-tête *m*.

head restraint *n UK* appuie-tête *m*, repose-tête *m*.

headroom ['hedrum] *n* place *f*, hauteur *f* ■ **there's not much ~ in the attic** le plafond du grenier n'est pas très haut, le grenier n'est pas très haut de plafond ■ **'max ~ 10 metres'** 'hauteur limite 10 mètres'.

headscarf ['hedskɑ:f] (*pl* **headscarves** [-skɑ:vz]) *n* foulard *m*.

headset ['hedset] *n* [with microphone] casque *m (à écouteurs et à micro)* ■ *US* [headphones] casque *m (à écouteurs)*.

headship ['hedʃɪp] *n* SCH poste *m* de directeur *OR* de directrice.

headshrinker ['hed,ʃrɪŋkəʳ] *n inf* [psychiatrist] psy *mf*.

headsquare ['hedskweəʳ] *n* foulard *m*, carré *m*.

headstand ['hedstænd] *n* : **to do a ~** faire le poirier.

head start *n* **1.** [lead] avance *f* ■ **I got a ~** j'ai pris de l'avance sur les autres ■ **go on, I'll give you a ~** allez, vas-y, je te donne un peu d'avance **2.** [advantage] avantage *m* ■ **being bilingual gives her a ~ over the others** étant bilingue, elle est avantagée par rapport aux autres.

headstone ['hedstəun] *n* **1.** [of grave] pierre *f* tombale **2.** ARCHIT [keystone] clef *f* de voûte.

headstrong ['hedstrɒŋ] *adj* **1.** [wilful] têtu, entêté **2.** [rash] impétueux, imprudent.

head teacher *n* [man] proviseur *m*, directeur *m*, chef *m* d'établissement ■ [woman] proviseur *f*, directrice *f*, chef *m* d'établissement.

head-up *adj* [in aeroplane, car] : **~ display** affichage *m* tête-haute.

head waiter *n* maître *m* d'hôtel.

headwaters ['hed,wɔːtəz] *npl* sources *fpl* (d'un fleuve).

headway ['hedweɪ] *n* **1.** [progress] : **to make ~** [gen] avancer, faire des progrès ; NAUT faire route ▪ **they're making some/no ~ in their plans** leurs projets avancent/n'avancent pas **2.** [headroom] place *f*, hauteur *f* **3.** [between buses, trains] : **there is a ten-minute ~ between buses** il y a dix minutes d'attente entre les bus.

headwind ['hedwɪnd] *n* [gen - AERON] vent *m* contraire ▪ NAUT vent *m* debout.

headword ['hedwɜːd] *n* entrée *f*, adresse *f*.

heady ['hedɪ] (*comp* **headier**, *superl* **headiest**) *adj* **1.** [intoxicating - wine] capiteux, qui monte à la tête ; [- perfume] capiteux ▪ **she breathed in a ~ draught of mountain air** elle respira l'air grisant *OR* enivrant des montagnes **2.** [exciting - experience, time] excitant, passionnant ; [- atmosphere] excitant, enivrant.

heal [hiːl] <> *vt* **1.** [make healthy - person] guérir ; [- wound] guérir, cicatriser **2.** [damage, division] remédier à, réparer ▪ [disagreement] régler ▪ **I'd do anything to ~ the breach between them** je ferais n'importe quoi pour les réconcilier *OR* pour les raccommoder.
<> *vi* [person] guérir ▪ [wound] se cicatriser, se refermer ▪ [fracture] se consolider.
heal up *vi insep* [wound] se cicatriser, guérir ▪ [burn] guérir ▪ [fracture] se consolider.

healer ['hiːlə^r] *n* guérisseur *m*, - euse *f*.

healing ['hiːlɪŋ] <> *n* [of person] guérison *f* ▪ [of wound] cicatrisation *f*, guérison *f* ▪ [of fracture] consolidation *f*.
<> *adj* **1.** [remedy, treatment] curatif ▪ [ointment] cicatrisant ▪ **~ hands** mains *fpl* de guérisseur **2.** [soothing - influence] apaisant.

health [helθ] *n* **1.** [general condition] santé *f* ▪ **to be in good/poor ~** être en bonne/mauvaise santé ▪ **smoking is bad for your ~** le tabac est mauvais pour *OR* nuisible à ta santé ▪ **the economic ~ of the nation** *fig* la (bonne) santé économique de la nation ⊃ **Health and Safety Executive** ≃ inspection *f* du travail ▪ **Department of Health** ≃ ministère de la Santé **2.** [good condition] (bonne) santé *f* ▪ **she's the picture of ~** elle respire la santé **3.** [in toast] : **(to your) good ~!** à votre santé! ▪ **we drank (to) the ~ of the bride and groom** nous avons porté un toast en l'honneur des mariés.

health care *n* services *mpl* médicaux.

health centre *n* centre *m* médico-social.

health farm *n* centre *m* de remise en forme.

health food *n* aliments *mpl* diététiques *OR* biologiques ▪ **~ shop** magasin *m* de produits diététiques.

health hazard *n* risque *m* pour la santé.

healthily ['helθɪlɪ] *adv* [eat, live] sainement.

health insurance *n* assurance *f* maladie.

health risk *n* risque *m* pour la santé.

health service *n* **1.** [of firm, school] infirmerie *f* **2.** = **national health service**.

health services *npl* services *mpl* de santé.

health visitor *n* UK *infirmière visiteuse qui s'occupe surtout des enfants en bas âge, des personnes âgées etc.*

healthy ['helθɪ] (*comp* **healthier**, *superl* **healthiest**) *adj* **1.** [in good health - person] sain, en bonne santé ; [- animal, plant] en bonne santé ▪ **he's very ~** il se porte très bien, il est bien portant **2.** [showing good health - colour, skin] sain ▪ [appetite] robuste, bon **3.** [beneficial - air, climate] salubre ; [- diet, food] sain ; [- exercise] bon pour la santé, salutaire **4.** [thriving - economy] sain ; [- business] prospère, bien assis **5.** [substantial - profits] considérable ; [- sum] considérable, important ; [- difference] appréciable **6.** [sensible - attitude] sain ; [- respect] salutaire ▪ **he shows a ~ disrespect for opinion polls** il fait montre d'un dédain salutaire pour les sondages.

heap [hiːp] <> *n* **1.** [pile] tas *m*, amas *m* ▪ **her things were piled in a ~** ses affaires étaient (mises) en tas ▪ **he collapsed in a ~ on the floor** il s'écroula *OR* tomba par terre comme une masse **2.** *inf* [large quantity] tas *m*, masse *f* ▪ **you've got ~s of time** tu as largement le temps *OR* tout ton temps **3.** *inf* [old car] vieux clou *m*.
<> *vt* **1.** [collect into a pile] entasser, empiler ▪ **she ~ed roast beef onto his plate** elle l'a généreusement servi en (tranches de) rosbif **2.** *fig* [lavish] : **to ~ sthg on sb** couvrir qqn de qqch ▪ **to ~ praise on** *OR* **upon sb** couvrir *OR* combler qqn d'éloges *OR* de compliments.
heap up *vt sep* [pile - books, furniture] entasser, empiler ; [- money, riches] amasser.

heaped [hiːpt] UK, **heaping** ['hiːpɪŋ] US *adj* gros, grosse *f* ▪ **a ~ teaspoonful** une cuiller à café bombée *OR* pleine.

heaps [hiːps] *adv dated inf* drôlement ▪ **it's ~ faster to go by train** ça va drôlement plus vite en train.

hear [hɪə^r] (*pret & pp* **heard** [hɜːd]) <> *vt* **1.** [perceive with sense of hearing] entendre ▪ **can you ~ me?** m'entendez-vous (bien)? ▪ **we can't ~ you** nous ne vous entendons pas, nous n'entendons pas ce que vous dites ▪ **he could ~ someone crying** il entendait (quelqu'un) pleurer ▪ **a shout was heard** un cri se fit entendre ▪ **he was heard to observe** *OR* **remark that he was against censorship** *fml* on l'a entendu dire qu'il était opposé à la censure ▪ **I've heard it said that...** j'ai entendu dire que... ▪ **I couldn't make myself heard above the noise** je n'arrivais pas à me faire entendre dans le bruit ▪ **to ~ my sister talk you'd think we were poor** à entendre ma sœur, vous pourriez croire que nous sommes pauvres ▪ **don't believe everything you ~** n'écoutez pas tous les bruits qui courent, ne croyez pas tout ce qu'on raconte ▪ **you're ~ing things** tu t'imagines des choses ▪ **I can hardly ~ myself think** je n'arrive pas à me concentrer (tant il y a de bruit) ⊃ **let's ~ it for the Johnson sisters!** un grand bravo pour les sœurs Johnson!, et on applaudit bien fort les sœurs Johnson!
2. [listen to - music, person] écouter ; [- concert, lecture, mass] assister à, écouter ▪ **be quiet, d'you ~!** taisez-vous, vous entendez! ▪ **let's ~ what you think** dites voir *OR* un peu ce que vous pensez ▪ **so let's ~ it!** allez, dis ce que tu as à dire! ▪ **the Lord heard our prayers** le Seigneur a écouté *OR* exaucé nos prières
3. [subj: authority, official] : **the priest ~s confession on Saturdays** le prêtre confesse le samedi ▪ **the court will ~ the first witness today** LAW la cour entendra le premier témoin aujourd'hui ▪ **the case will be heard in March** l'affaire se plaidera au mois de mars
4. [understand, be told] entendre, apprendre ▪ **I ~ you're leaving** j'ai appris *OR* j'ai entendu (dire) que tu partais ▪ **I ~ you've lived in Thailand** il paraît que tu as vécu en Thaïlande ▪ **have you heard the latest?** connaissez-vous la dernière? ▪ **have you heard anything more about the accident?** avez-vous eu d'autres nouvelles de l'accident? ⊃ **have you heard the one about the Scotsman and the Irishman?** connaissez-vous l'histoire de l'Écossais et de l'Irlandais? ▪ **she's heard it all before** elle connaît la musique ▪ **I've heard good things about that school** j'ai eu des échos favorables de cette école ▪ **you haven't heard the last of this!** [gen] vous n'avez pas fini d'en entendre parler! ; [threat] vous aurez de mes nouvelles!
<> *vi* **1.** [able to perceive sound] entendre
2. [be aware of] être au courant ▪ **haven't you heard? he's dead** vous n'êtes pas au courant? il est mort
3. *phr* **~, ~!** bravo!
hear about *vt insep* **1.** [learn] entendre ▪ **have you heard about the accident?** êtes-vous au courant pour *OR* de l'accident? ▪ **yes, I heard about that** oui, je suis au courant ▪ **have you heard about the time she met Churchill?** connaissez-vous l'histoire de sa rencontre avec Churchill? ▪ **I've heard so much about you** j'ai tellement entendu parler de vous
2. [have news of] avoir *OR* recevoir des nouvelles de ▪ **I ~ about her through her sister** j'ai de ses nouvelles par sa sœur.
hear from *vt insep* **1.** [receive news of] avoir *OR* recevoir des nouvelles de ▪ **they'd be delighted to ~ from you** ils seraient ravis d'avoir de tes nouvelles ▪ **he never heard from her again** il n'a plus jamais eu de ses nouvelles ▪ **you'll be ~ing from me** [gen] je vous donnerai de mes nouvelles ; [threat] vous allez avoir de mes nouvelles, vous allez entendre parler de moi ▪ **(I am) looking forward to ~ing from you** [in letters] dans l'attente de vous lire

2. [listen to] écouter ▪ **we ~ first from one of the survivors** nous allons d'abord écouter *OR* entendre l'un des survivants.

◆ **hear of** *vt insep* **1.** [know of] entendre parler de, connaître ▪ **I've never heard of her** je ne la connais pas
2. [receive news of] entendre parler de ▪ **the whole town had heard of his success** la ville entière était au courant de son succès *OR* sa réussite ▪ **the missing boy was never heard of again** on n'a jamais retrouvé la trace du garçon qui avait disparu ▪ **who ever heard of eating pizza for breakfast!** quelle (drôle d')idée de manger de la pizza au petit déjeuner!
3. *(usu neg)* [accept, allow] : **her father won't ~ of it** son père ne veut pas en entendre parler *OR* ne veut rien savoir ▪ **may I pay for dinner? – I wouldn't ~ of it!** puis-je payer *OR* vous offrir le dîner? – (il n'en est) pas question!

◆ **hear out** *vt sep* écouter jusqu'au bout ▪ **at least ~ me out before you refuse my offer** au moins écoutez-moi jusqu'au bout avant de refuser ma proposition.

heard [hɜːd] *pt* & *pp* ⊳ **hear**.

hearer ['hɪərəʳ] *n* auditeur *m*, - trice *f*.

hearing ['hɪərɪŋ] ◇ *adj* entendant (*f* e).
◇ *n* **1.** [sense of] ouïe *f* ▪ **to have good/bad ~** entendre bien/mal ▪ **a keen sense of ~** l'oreille *f OR* l'ouïe fine ▪ **his ~ gradually deteriorated** petit à petit il est devenu dur d'oreille ▪ **cats have better ~ than humans** les chats entendent mieux *OR* ont l'ouïe plus fine que les humains **2.** [earshot] : **within ~** à portée de voix ▪ **you shouldn't have said that in** *OR* **within ~ of his mother** tu n'aurais pas dû le dire devant *OR* en présence de sa mère **3.** [act of listening] audition *f* ▪ **I didn't enjoy the symphony at (the) first ~** je n'ai pas aimé la symphonie à la première audition *OR* la première fois que je l'ai écoutée **4.** [chance to be heard] audition *f* ▪ **to give sb a fair ~** laisser parler qqn, écouter ce que qqn a à dire **5.** LAW audition *f* ▪ **the ~ of a trial** l'audience *f* ▪ **the case will come up for ~ in March** l'affaire sera entendue *OR* plaidée en mars **6.** [official meeting] séance *f*.

hearing aid *n* appareil *m* acoustique, audiophone *m*.

hearing impaired *npl* : **the ~** les malentendants *mpl*.

hearken ['hɑːkn] *vi arch* & *lit* **to ~ to** *OR* **unto sthg** écouter qqch.

hearsay ['hɪəseɪ] *n* ouï-dire *m inv*, rumeur *f* ▪ **it's only ~** ce ne sont que des rumeurs.

hearsay evidence *n* déposition *f* sur la foi d'un tiers *OR* d'autrui.

hearse [hɜːs] *n* corbillard *m*, fourgon *m* mortuaire.

heart [hɑːt] ◇ *n* **1.** ANAT [organ] cœur *m* ▪ **he has a weak ~** il est cardiaque, il a le cœur malade ▮ *fig* **her ~ leapt** son cœur bondit ▪ **her ~ sank** elle eut un serrement de cœur ▶ **he sat there, his ~ in his boots** *UK* il était là, la mort dans l'âme ▪ **she waited, her ~ in her mouth** elle attendait, son cœur battant la chamade
2. [bosom] poitrine *f* ▪ **she clutched him to her ~** elle l'a serré contre sa poitrine *OR* sur son cœur
3. [seat of feelings, love] cœur *m* ▪ **he has a ~ of gold/of stone** il a un cœur d'or/de pierre ▪ **to lose one's ~ to sb** donner son cœur à qqn, tomber amoureux de qqn ▪ **the letter was written straight from the ~** la lettre était écrite du fond du cœur ▪ **to have one's ~ set on sthg** s'être mis qqch dans la tête ▪ **he has his ~ set on winning** il veut à tout prix gagner ▪ **they have everything their ~s could desire** ils ont tout ce qu'ils peuvent désirer ▪ **my ~'s desire is to see Rome again** *lit* mon plus cher désir est *OR* ce que je désire le plus au monde c'est de revoir Rome ▪ **she hardened** *OR* **steeled her ~ against him** elle s'est endurcie contre lui ▪ **dear ~** *arch* & *hum* mon cœur, mon chéri ▶ **to wear one's ~ on one's sleeve** montrer *OR* laisser paraître ses sentiments
4. [innermost thoughts] fond *m* ▪ **in his ~ of ~s** au fond de lui-même *OR* de son cœur, en son for intérieur ▪ **there's a woman/a man after my own ~** voilà une femme/un homme selon mon cœur ▪ **I thank you from the bottom of my ~** *OR* **with all my ~** je vous remercie du fond du cœur *OR* de tout mon cœur ▪ **to take sthg to ~** prendre qqch à cœur ▪ **she opened** *OR* **poured out her ~ to me** elle m'a dévoilé son cœur
5. [disposition, humour] : **to have a change of ~** changer d'avis
6. [interest, enthusiasm] : **I worked hard but my ~ wasn't in it** j'ai beaucoup travaillé mais je n'avais pas le cœur à l'ouvrage *OR* le cœur n'y était pas ▪ **she read to her ~'s content** elle a lu tout son soûl ▪ **a subject close to one's ~** un sujet qui tient à cœur ▪ **she puts her ~** *OR* **she throws herself ~ and soul into her work** elle se donne à son travail corps et âme
7. [courage] : **to lose ~** perdre courage, se décourager ▪ **take ~!** courage! ▪ **she took ~ from the fact that others shared her experience** elle était encouragée par le fait que d'autres partageaient son expérience ▪ **to be in good ~** [person] avoir bon moral ; *UK* [land] être fécond *OR* productif
8. [compassion] cœur *m* ▪ **he has no ~** il n'a pas de cœur, il manque de cœur ▪ **she didn't have the ~ to refuse, she couldn't find it in her ~ to refuse** elle n'a pas eu le courage *OR* le cœur de refuser ▪ **can you find it in your ~ to forgive me?** est-ce que vous pourrez jamais me pardonner? ▶ **her ~'s in the right place** elle a bon cœur ▪ **have a ~!** pitié!
9. [core, vital part - of matter, topic] fond *m*, vif *m* ; [- of city, place] centre *m*, cœur *m* ▪ **the ~ of the matter** le fond du problème ▪ **the speaker went straight to the ~ of the matter** le conférencier est allé droit au cœur du sujet *OR* du problème ▪ **the law strikes at the ~ of the democratic system** la loi porte atteinte aux fondements du régime démocratique ▶ **'Heart of Darkness'** *Conrad* 'Au cœur des ténèbres' ▪ **'The Heart of the Matter'** *Greene* 'le Fond du problème'
10. [of cabbage, celery, lettuce] cœur *m* ▪ [of artichoke] cœur *m*, fond *m*
11. CARDS cœur *m* ▪ **~s are trumps** atout cœur ▪ **game of ~s** *jeu de cartes dont l'objet est de faire des plis ne comprenant ni des cœurs ni la dame de pique*
12. [shape] cœur *m*.
◇ *comp* : **~ disease** maladie *f* de cœur, maladie *f* cardiaque ▪ **~ disease is on the increase** les maladies de cœur *OR* cardiaques sont en augmentation ▪ **~ patient** cardiaque *mf* ▪ **~ surgeon** chirurgien *m* cardiologue ▪ **~ surgery** chirurgie *f* du cœur ▪ **~ trouble** *(U)* maladie *f* du cœur, troubles *mpl* cardiaques ▪ **to have** *OR* **to suffer from ~ trouble** souffrir du cœur, être cardiaque.

◆ **at heart** *adv phr* au fond ▪ **at ~ she was a good person** elle avait un bon fond ▪ **my sister's a gypsy at ~** ma sœur est une bohémienne dans l'âme ▪ **to feel sad at ~** avoir le cœur triste ▪ **to be sick at ~** avoir la mort dans l'âme ▪ **they have your welfare at ~** ils ne pensent qu'à ton bien, c'est pour ton bien qu'ils font cela.

◆ **by heart** *adv phr* par cœur ▪ **to learn/to know sthg by ~** apprendre/savoir qqch par cœur.

heartache ['hɑːteɪk] *n* chagrin *m*, peine *f* ▪ **he caused her a lot of ~** il lui a causé beaucoup de chagrin.

heart attack *n* MED crise *f* cardiaque ▪ **to have a ~** avoir une crise cardiaque, faire un infarctus ▪ **she nearly had a ~ when she heard about it** *fig* en apprenant la nouvelle, elle a failli avoir une attaque.

heartbeat ['hɑːtbiːt] *n* battement *m* de cœur, pulsation *f* ▪ **an irregular ~** un battement arythmique *OR* irrégulier ▪ **to be a ~ away from sthg** être à deux doigts de qqch.

heartbreak ['hɑːtbreɪk] *n* [grief - gen] (immense) chagrin *m*, déchirement *m* ; [- in love] chagrin *m* d'amour.

heartbreaker ['hɑːt,breɪkəʳ] *n* bourreau *m* des cœurs.

heartbreaking ['hɑːt,breɪkɪŋ] *adj* déchirant, navrant ▪ **it was ~ to see children starving** c'était à vous fendre le cœur de voir des enfants mourir de faim.

heartbroken ['hɑːt,brəʊkn] *adj* [person - gen] qui a un immense chagrin ; [- stronger] qui a le cœur brisé.

heartburn ['hɑːtbɜːn] *n (U)* brûlures *fpl* d'estomac.

heart condition *n* : **to have a ~** souffrir du cœur, être cardiaque.

hearten ['hɑːtn] *vt* encourager, donner du courage à ▪ **we were ~ed to learn of the drop in interest rates** nous avons été contents d'apprendre que les taux d'intérêt avaient baissé.

heartening ['hɑːtnɪŋ] *adj* encourageant, réconfortant ▪ **I found the news ~** la nouvelle m'a donné du courage *OR* m'a encouragé.

heart failure *n* [condition] défaillance *f* cardiaque ▪ [cessation of heartbeat] arrêt *m* du cœur.

heartfelt ['hɑ:tfelt] *adj* [apology, thanks] sincère.

hearth [hɑ:θ] *n* **1.** [of fireplace] foyer *m*, âtre *m* ▪ **a fire was burning in the ~** il y avait du feu dans la cheminée **2.** [home] foyer *m* ▪ **to leave ~ and home** quitter le foyer.

hearthrug ['hɑ:θrʌg] *n* devant *m* de foyer.

hearthstone ['hɑ:θstəʊn] *n* foyer *m*, âtre *m*.

heartily ['hɑ:tɪlɪ] *adv* **1.** [enthusiastically - joke, laugh] de tout son cœur ; [- say, thank, welcome] chaleureusement, de tout cœur ; [- eat] de bon appétit **2.** [thoroughly] : **I ~ recommend it** je vous le conseille vivement ▪ **to be ~ disgusted with sthg** être on ne peut plus dégoûté de qqch.

heartiness ['hɑ:tɪnɪs] *n* **1.** [of thanks, welcome] cordialité *f*, chaleur *f* ▪ [of agreement] sincérité *f* ▪ [of appetite] vigueur *f* ▪ [of dislike] ardeur *f* **2.** [enthusiasm] zèle *m*, empressement *m*.

heartland ['hɑ:tlænd] *n* cœur *m*, centre *m* ▪ **the ~ of France** la France profonde ▪ **the industrial ~ of Europe** le principal centre industriel de l'Europe ▪ **the Socialist ~** le fief des socialistes.

heartless ['hɑ:tlɪs] *adj* [person] sans cœur, impitoyable ▪ [laughter, treatment] cruel.

heartlessly ['hɑ:tlɪslɪ] *adv* sans pitié.

heartlessness ['hɑ:tlɪsnɪs] *n* [of person] manque *m* de cœur, caractère *m* impitoyable.

heart murmur *n* souffle *m* au cœur.

heartrending ['hɑ:t,rendɪŋ] *adj* déchirant, qui fend le cœur ▪ **~ scenes of homeless refugees** des images navrantes *OR* déchirantes de réfugiés sans abri.

heart-searching [-,sɜ:tʃɪŋ] *n* examen *m* de conscience ▪ **after much ~ she decided to leave** après s'être longuement interrogée *OR* tâtée, elle décida de partir.

heart-shaped *adj* en forme de cœur.

heartsick ['hɑ:tsɪk] *adj* découragé, démoralisé ▪ **to be ~** avoir la mort dans l'âme.

heart-stopping *adj* terrifiant.

heartstrings ['hɑ:tstrɪŋz] *npl* : **to play on** *OR* **to pull on** *OR* **to tug at sb's ~** faire vibrer *OR* toucher la corde sensible de qqn ▪ **that song always tugs at my ~** cette chanson me serre toujours le cœur.

heartthrob ['hɑ:tθrɒb] *n* coqueluche *f*, idole *f* ▪ **he's the office ~** il est la coqueluche des secrétaires.

heart-to-heart ◇ *adj & adv* à cœur ouvert *fig*.
◇ *n* conversation *f* intime *OR* à cœur ouvert ▪ **it's time we had a ~** il est temps qu'on se parle (à cœur ouvert).

heartwarming ['hɑ:t,wɔ:mɪŋ] *adj* réconfortant, qui réchauffe le cœur.

hearty ['hɑ:tɪ] ◇ *adj* (*comp* **heartier**, *superl* **heartiest**) **1.** [congratulations, welcome] cordial, chaleureux ▪ [thanks] sincère ▪ [approval, recommendation] sans réserves ▪ [laugh] gros, grosse *f*, franc, franche *f* ▪ [knock, slap] vigoureux ▪ **they're ~ eaters** ils ont un bon coup de fourchette, ce sont de gros mangeurs **2.** [person - robust] vigoureux, robuste, solide ; [- cheerful] jovial ▪ **they're a bit too ~ for my liking** ils sont un peu trop bruyants *OR* tapageurs à mon goût **3.** [meal] copieux, abondant **4.** [thorough] absolu ▪ **I have a ~ dislike of hypocrisy** j'ai horreur de l'hypocrisie.
◇ *n* (*pl* **hearties**) *arch & hum* **my hearties!** les gars!

heat [hi:t] ◇ *n* **1.** [gen - PHYSIOL] chaleur *f* ▪ [of fire, sun] ardeur *f*, chaleur *f* ▪ **you should avoid excessive ~ and cold** il faudrait que vous évitiez les trop grosses chaleurs et les trop grands froids ▪ **the radiator gives off a lot of ~** le radiateur chauffe bien ▪ **you shouldn't go out in this ~** tu ne devrais pas sortir par cette chaleur ▪ **the ~ of summer** le plus fort de l'été ▪ **in the ~ of the day** au (moment le) plus chaud de la journée ▪ **I couldn't take the ~ of the tropics** je ne pourrais pas supporter la chaleur des tropiques ▶ **if you can't stand** *OR* **take the ~, get out of the kitchen** que ceux qui ne sont pas contents s'en aillent
2. [temperature] température *f*, chaleur *f* ▪ **~ loss** perte *f* *OR* déperdition *f* de chaleur ▪ **body ~** chaleur *f* animale ‖ CULIN : **turn up the ~** mettre le feu plus fort ▪ **reduce the ~** réduire le feu *OR* la chaleur ▪ **cook at a high/low ~** faire cuire à feu vif/doux
3. [heating] chauffage *m* ▪ **the building was without ~ all week** l'immeuble est resté toute la semaine sans chauffage
4. [intensity of feeling, fervour] feu *m*, passion *f*
5. [high point of activity] fièvre *f*, feu *m* ▪ **in the ~ of argument** dans le feu de la discussion ▪ **in the ~ of the moment** dans l'agitation *OR* l'excitation du moment ▪ **in the ~ of battle** dans le feu du combat
6. *inf* [coercion, pressure] : **the mafia turned the ~ on the mayor** la mafia a fait pression sur le maire ▪ **I'm lying low until the ~ is off** je me tiens à carreau jusqu'à ce que les choses se calment
7. SPORT [round of contest] manche *f* ▪ [preliminary round] (épreuve *f*) éliminatoire *f*
8. ZOOL chaleur *f*, rut *m* ▪ **on ~** *UK*, **in ~** en chaleur, en rut.
◇ *vi* [food, liquid] chauffer ▪ [air, house, room] se réchauffer.
◇ *vt* [gen - PHYSIOL] chauffer ▪ [overheat] échauffer ▪ **wine ~s the blood** le vin échauffe le sang.
➡ **heat up** ◇ *vt sep* réchauffer.
◇ *vi insep* [food, liquid] chauffer ▪ [air, house, room] se réchauffer.

heated ['hi:tɪd] *adj* **1.** [room, swimming pool] chauffé **2.** [argument, discussion] passionné ▪ [words] vif ▪ [person] échauffé ▪ **the discussion became ~** le ton de la conversation a monté ▪ **there were a few ~ exchanges** ils échangèrent quelques propos vifs.

heatedly ['hi:tɪdlɪ] *adv* [debate, talk] avec passion ▪ [argue, deny, refuse] avec passion *OR* emportement, farouchement.

heater ['hi:tə^r] *n* **1.** [for room] appareil *m* de chauffage ▪ [for water] chauffe-eau *m inv* ▪ [for car] (appareil de) chauffage *m* **2.** △ *US* [gun] flingue *m*.

heat exhaustion *n* épuisement *m* dû à la chaleur.

heath [hi:θ] *n* **1.** [moor] lande *f* **2.** [plant] bruyère *f*.

heat haze *n* brume *f* de chaleur.

heathen ['hi:ðn] (*pl inv OR pl* **heathens**) ◇ *n* [pagan] païen *m*, - enne *f* ▪ [barbaric person] barbare *mf*.
◇ *adj* [pagan] païen ▪ [barbaric] barbare.

heather ['heðə^r] *n* bruyère *f*.

heating ['hi:tɪŋ] ◇ *n* chauffage *m*.
◇ *comp* [apparatus, appliance, system] de chauffage.

heating engineer *n* chauffagiste *m*.

heatproof ['hi:tpru:f] *adj* [gen] résistant à la chaleur ▪ [dish] qui va au four.

heat rash *n* irritation *f* *OR* inflammation *f* due à la chaleur.

heat-resistant *adj* [gen] résistant à la chaleur, thermorésistant *spec* ▪ [dish] qui va au four.

heat-seeking [-,si:kɪŋ] *adj* [missile] autoguidé par infrarouge.

heatstroke ['hi:tstrəʊk] *n (U)* coup *m* de chaleur.

heat treatment *n* traitement *m* par la chaleur, thermothérapie *f spec*.

heat wave *n* vague *f* de chaleur, canicule *f*.

heave [hi:v] (*pret & pp* **heaved**, *cont* **heaving**) ◇ *vt* **1.** [lift] lever *OR* soulever avec effort ▪ [pull] tirer fort ▪ [drag] traîner avec effort ▪ **I ~d myself out of the chair** je me suis arraché *OR* extirpé de ma chaise **2.** [throw] jeter, lancer **3.** *fig* **to ~ a sigh of relief** pousser un soupir de soulagement.
◇ *vi* **1.** [rise and fall - sea, waves, chest] se soulever ; [- ship] tanguer ▪ **his shoulders ~d with suppressed laughter** il était secoué par un rire étouffé **2.** [lift] lever, soulever ▪ [pull] tirer ▪ **~! ho! hisse!** **3.** [retch] avoir des haut-le-cœur ▪ [vomit] vomir ▪ **the sight made my stomach ~** le spectacle m'a soulevé le

cœur *OR* m'a donné des nausées **4.** (*pret & pp* **hove** [həʊv]) NAUT aller, se déplacer ▪ **to ~ into sight** *OR* **into view** NAUT & *fig* paraître *OR* poindre *lit* à l'horizon.
◇ *n* **1.** [attempt to move] : **one more ~ and we're there** encore un coup *OR* un petit effort et ça y est ▶ **to give sb the ~** *OR* **~-ho** *inf* [subj: employer] virer qqn ; [boyfriend, girlfriend] plaquer qqn **2.** [retching] haut-le-cœur *m inv*, nausée *f* ▪ [vomiting] vomissement *m*.
◆ **heaves** *npl* VET pousse *f*.
◆ **heave to** ◇ *vi insep* se mettre en panne.
◇ *vt sep* mettre en panne.

heaven ['hevn] *n* **1.** RELIG ciel *m*, paradis *m* ▪ **to go to ~** aller au ciel, aller au *OR* en paradis ▪ **in ~** au ciel, au *OR* en paradis ▪ **Our Father, who art in Heaven** notre Père qui es aux cieux **2.** *fig* **the Caribbean was like ~ on earth** les Caraïbes étaient un véritable paradis sur terre ▪ **this is sheer ~!** c'est divin *OR* merveilleux!, c'est le paradis! ‖ [emphatic uses] : **~ forbid!** pourvu que non!, j'espère bien que non! ▪ **~ help us if they catch us** que le ciel nous vienne en aide s'ils nous attrapent ▪ **~ knows I've tried!** Dieu sait si j'ai essayé! ▪ **she bought books, magazines and ~ knows what (else)** elle a acheté des livres, des revues et je ne sais *OR* Dieu sait quoi encore ▪ **what in ~'s name is that?** au nom du ciel, qu'est-ce que c'est que ça? ▪ **good ~s!** ciel!, mon dieu! ▪ **for ~'s sake!** [in annoyance] mince! ; [in pleading] pour l'amour du ciel! ▶ **it smells** *OR* **stinks to high ~ in here!** qu'est-ce que ça peut puer ici! ▪ **she's in ~ when she's with him** elle est au septième ciel *OR* aux anges quand elle est avec lui ▪ **to move ~ and earth to do sthg** remuer ciel et terre pour faire qqch.
◆ **heavens** *npl* [sky] : **the ~s** *lit* le ciel, le firmament *lit* ▪ **the ~s opened** il s'est mis à pleuvoir à torrents.

heavenly ['hevnlɪ] *adj* **1.** [of space] céleste, du ciel ▪ [holy] divin ▪ **Heavenly Father** Père *m* céleste **2.** [wonderful] divin, merveilleux.

heavenly body *n* corps *m* céleste.

heaven-sent *adj* providentiel ▪ **a ~ opportunity** une occasion providentielle *OR* qui tombe à pic.

heavenward ['hevnwəd] ◇ *adv* [ascend, point] vers le ciel ▪ [glance] au ciel.
◇ *adj* vers le ciel ▪ **with a ~ glance** [feeling] en levant les yeux au ciel.

heavenwards ['hevnwədz] *UK* = **heavenward** *(adv)*.

heavily ['hevɪlɪ] *adv* **1.** [fall, land] lourdement, pesamment ▪ [walk] d'un pas lourd *OR* pesant, lourdement ▪ **she leaned ~ on my arm** elle s'appuya de tout son poids sur mon bras ‖ *fig* **time hangs ~ on her** elle trouve le temps long, le temps lui pèse ▪ **it weighed ~ on my conscience** cela me pesait sur la conscience **2.** [laboriously - move] avec difficulté, péniblement ; [- breathe] péniblement, bruyamment **3.** [deeply - sleep] profondément ▪ **she left the room, sighing ~** en poussant un énorme *OR* gros soupir, elle a quitté la pièce **4.** [as intensifier - bet, drink, smoke] beaucoup ; [- fine, load, tax] lourdement ; [- stress] fortement, lourdement ▪ **it was raining ~** il pleuvait des cordes ▪ **it was snowing ~** il neigeait très fort *OR* dru *OR* à gros flocons ▪ **they lost ~** [team] ils se sont fait écraser ; [gamblers] ils ont perdu gros ▪ **they're ~ into yoga** *inf* ils donnent à fond dans le yoga ▪ **they're ~ dependent on foreign trade** ils sont fortement tributaires du commerce extérieur ▪ **~ populated** très peuplé, à forte densité de population.

heavily-built *adj* solidement bâti ▪ **a ~ man** un homme costaud *OR* bien charpenté.

heaviness ['hevɪnɪs] *n* **1.** [weight - of object, physique] lourdeur *f*, pesanteur *f*, poids *m* ; [- of movement, step] lourdeur, pesanteur ▪ **a feeling of ~** une lourdeur, des lourdeurs **2.** [depression] abattement *m*, découragement *m* ▪ [sadness] tristesse *f* ▪ **~ of heart** tristesse **3.** [of weather] lourdeur *f* **4.** [of humour] manque *m* de subtilité ▪ [of style] lourdeur *f* **5.** [of food] caractère *m* indigeste.

heavy ['hevɪ] ◇ *adj* (*comp* **heavier**, *superl* **heaviest**) **1.** [in weight] lourd ▪ [box, parcel] lourd, pesant ▪ **how ~ is he?** combien pèse-t-il? ▪ **it's too ~ for me to lift** je ne peux pas le soulever, c'est *OR* ça pèse trop lourd ▪ **~ machinery** matériel *m* lourd ▶ **~ goods vehicle** *UK* poids *m* lourd
2. [burdened, laden] chargé, lourd ▪ **the branches were ~ with fruit** les branches étaient chargées *OR* lourdes de fruits ▪ **her eyes were ~ with sleep** elle avait les yeux lourds de sommeil ▪ **she was ~ with child** *arch* & *lit* elle était enceinte ▪ **~ with young** ZOOL gravide, grosse
3. [in quantity - expenses, payments] important, considérable ; [- fine, losses] gros, grosse *f*, lourd ; [- taxes] lourd ; [- casualties, damages] énorme, important ; [- crop] abondant, gros, grosse *f* ; [- dew] abondant ▪ **she has a ~ cold** elle a un gros rhume, elle est fortement enrhumée ▪ **her students make ~ demands on her** ses étudiants sont très exigeants avec elle *OR* exigent beaucoup d'elle ▪ **~ rain** forte pluie ▪ **~ seas** grosse mer ▪ **~ showers** grosses *OR* fortes averses ▪ **~ snow** neige abondante, fortes chutes de neige ▪ **to be a ~ sleeper** avoir le sommeil profond *OR* lourd ▪ **~ traffic** circulation dense, grosse circulation
4. [using large quantities] : **he's a ~ drinker/smoker** il boit/fume beaucoup, c'est un grand buveur/fumeur ▪ **you've been a bit ~ on the pepper** *inf* tu as eu la main un peu lourde avec le poivre
5. [ponderous - movement] lourd ; [- step] pesant, lourd ; [- sigh] gros, grosse *f*, profond ; [- thud] gros, grosse *f* ▪ **he was dealt a ~ blow** [hit] il a reçu un coup violent ; [from fate] ça a été un rude coup *OR* un gros choc pour lui ▪ **~ breathing** [from effort, illness] respiration *f* pénible ; [from excitement] respiration *f* haletante ▪ **~ fighting is reported in the Gulf** on signale des combats acharnés dans le Golfe ▶ **~ breather** auteur *m* de coups de téléphone obscènes
6. [thick - coat, sweater] gros, grosse *f* ; [- soil] lourd, gras, grasse *f* ▪ **~ cream** *US* CULIN crème *f* fraîche épaisse
7. [person - fat] gros, grosse *f*, corpulent ; [- solid] costaud, fortement charpenté ▪ **a man of ~ build** un homme solidement bâti
8. [coarse, solid - line, lips] gros, grosse *f*, épais, épaisse *f* ▪ [thick - beard] gros, grosse *f*, fort ▪ **~ features** gros traits, traits épais *OR* lourds ▪ **~ type** TYPO caractères gras
9. [grave, serious - news] grave ; [- responsibility] lourd ; [- defeat] lourd, grave ▪ **things got a bit ~** *inf* les choses ont mal tourné
10. [depressed - mood, spirits] abattu, déprimé ▪ **with a ~ heart, ~ at heart** le cœur gros
11. [tiring - task] lourd, pénible ; [- work] pénible ; [- day, schedule, week] chargé, difficile ▪ **~ going** [in horseracing] terrain lourd ▪ *fig* **they found it ~ going** ils ont trouvé cela pénible *OR* difficile ▪ **I found his last novel very ~ going** j'ai trouvé son dernier roman très indigeste
12. [difficult to understand - not superficial] profond, compliqué, sérieux ; [- tedious] indigeste ▪ **the report makes for ~ reading** le rapport n'est pas d'une lecture facile *OR* est ardu
13. [clumsy - humour, irony] peu subtil, lourd ; [- style] lourd
14. [food, meal] lourd, indigeste ▪ [wine] corsé, lourd
15. [ominous, oppressive - air, cloud, weather] lourd ; [- sky] couvert, chargé, lourd ; [- silence] lourd, pesant, profond ; [- smell, perfume] lourd, fort ▪ **to make ~ weather of sthg** se compliquer l'existence
16. [important] important ▪ **she was getting ready for a ~ date** elle se préparait pour le rendez-vous de sa vie
17. [stress] accentué ▪ [rhythm] aux accents marqués
18. MIL : **~ artillery** artillerie *f* lourde *OR* de gros calibre
19. THEAT [part - difficult] lourd, difficile ; [- dramatic] tragique.
◇ *adv* **1.** [lie, weigh] lourd, lourdement ▪ **the lie weighed ~ on her conscience** le mensonge pesait lourd sur sa conscience
2. [harshly] : **to come on ~ with sb** être dur avec qqn.
◇ *n* (*pl* **heavies**) **1.** THEAT [serious part] rôle *m* tragique ▪ [part of villain] rôle du traître
2. *inf* [tough guy] dur *m* ▪ **he sent them round the heavies** il leur a envoyé les brutes *OR* les casseurs ▪ **don't come the ~ with me** ne joue pas au dur avec moi
3. *inf* [boxer, wrestler] (poids *m*) lourd *m*
4. MIL gros calibre *m*.

heavy-duty *adj* **1.** [clothing, furniture] résistant ▪ [cleanser, equipment] à usage industriel **2.** *inf* [serious] sérieux ▪ **we've got to do some ~ socialising** nous sommes obligés d'assister à de nombreuses réceptions.

heavy-handed *adj* **1.** [clumsy - person] maladroit ; [- style, writing] lourd **2.** [tactless - remark] qui manque de tact ; [- joke]

lourd, qui manque de subtilité ; [- compliment] lourd, (trop) appuyé **3.** [harsh - person] dur, sévère ; [- action, policy] arbitraire.

heavyhearted [ˌhevɪ'hɑ:tɪd] *adj* abattu, découragé.

heavy industry *n* industrie *f* lourde.

heavy-laden *adj* [physically] très chargé ■ [emotionally] accablé.

heavy metal *n* **1.** PHYS métal *m* lourd **2.** MUS heavy metal *m*.

heavy mob *n inf* **the ~** les casseurs *mpl*, les durs *mpl*.

heavy petting [-'petɪŋ] *n (U)* caresses *fpl* très poussées.

heavy-set *adj* [solidly built - woman] fort ; [- man] bien charpenté, costaud ■ [fat] gros, grosse *f*, corpulent.

heavy water *n* eau *f* lourde.

heavyweight ['hevɪweɪt] ◇ *n* **1.** [large person, thing] colosse *m* ■ *inf fig* [important person] personne *f* de poids *OR* d'envergure, ponte *m* ■ **a literary ~** un écrivain profond *OR* sérieux, un grand écrivain **2.** SPORT poids *m* lourd.
◇ *adj* **1.** [cloth, wool] lourd ■ [coat, sweater] gros, grosse *f* **2.** *inf fig* [important] important **3.** SPORT [championship, fight] poids lourd ■ **the ~ title** le titre (des) poids lourds.

Hebraic [hi:'breɪɪk] *adj* hébraïque.

Hebrew ['hi:bru:] ◇ *n* **1.** [person] Hébreu *m*, Israélite *mf* ■ **the ~s** les Hébreux *mpl* **2.** LING Hébreu *m*.
◇ *adj* hébreu *(m only)*, hébraïque.

Hebrides ['hebrɪdi:z] *pr npl* : **the ~** les (îles *fpl*) Hébrides ■ **in the ~** aux Hébrides.

heck [hek] *inf* ◇ *n* : **that's a ~ of a lot of money!** c'est une sacrée somme d'argent! ■ **I went just for the ~ of it** j'y suis allé, histoire de rire *OR* de rigoler ■ **oh, what the ~!** et puis flûte!
◇ *interj* zut, flûte.

heckle ['hekl] ◇ *vt* [interrupt] interrompre bruyamment ■ [shout at] interpeller, harceler.
◇ *vi* crier *(pour gêner un orateur)*.

heckler ['heklər] *n* chahuteur *m*, - euse *f*.

heckling ['heklɪŋ] ◇ *n (U)* harcèlement *m*, interpellations *fpl*.
◇ *adj* qui fait du harcèlement, qui interpelle.

hectare ['hekteər] *n* hectare *m*.

hectic ['hektɪk] *adj* **1.** [turbulent] agité, bousculé ■ [eventful] mouvementé ■ **we spent three ~ weeks preparing the play** ç'a été la course folle pendant les trois semaines où on préparait la pièce ■ **they lead a ~ life** [busy] ils mènent une vie trépidante ; [eventful] ils mènent une vie très mouvementée **2.** [flushed] fiévreux ■ MED [fever, flush] hectique.

hectolitre *UK*, **hectoliter** *US* ['hektəˌli:tər] *n* hectolitre *m*.

hector ['hektər] ◇ *vt* harceler, tyranniser.
◇ *vi* être tyrannique, être une brute.
◆ **Hector** *pr n* Hector.

hectoring ['hektərɪŋ] ◇ *n (U)* harcèlement *m*, torture *f*.
◇ *adj* [behaviour] tyrannique ■ [tone, voice] impérieux, autoritaire.

he'd [hi:d] = **he had**, = **he would**.

hedge [hedʒ] ◇ *n* **1.** [shrubs] haie *f* **2.** *fig* [protection] sauvegarde *f* ■ **a ~ against inflation** une sauvegarde *OR* une couverture contre l'inflation **3.** [statement] déclaration *f* évasive.
◇ *comp* [clippers, saw] à haie.
◇ *vt* **1.** [enclose] entourer d'une haie, enclore **2.** [guard against losing] couvrir ■ **to ~ one's bets** se couvrir.
◇ *vi* **1.** [plant] planter une haie ■ [trim] tailler une haie **2.** [in action] essayer de gagner du temps, atermoyer ■ **they are hedging slightly on the trade agreement** ils essaient de gagner du temps avant de conclure l'accord commercial ■ [in answering] éviter de répondre, répondre à côté ■ [in explaining] expliquer avec des détours **3.** [protect] se protéger.
◆ **hedge about** *UK*, **hedge around** *vt sep* entourer ■ **the offer was ~d about with conditions** *fig* l'offre était assortie de conditions.
◆ **hedge in** *vt sep* entourer d'une haie, enclore ■ **~d in by restrictions** *fig* assorti de restrictions.

+ARTICLE**hedgehog** ['hedʒhɒg] *n* hérisson *m*.

hedgehop ['hedʒhɒp] *(pret & pp* **hedgehopped**, *cont* **hedgehopping)** *vi* voler en rase-mottes, faire du rase-mottes.

hedgerow ['hedʒrəʊ] *n* haies *fpl*.

hedonism ['hi:dənɪzm] *n* hédonisme *m*.

hedonist ['hi:dənɪst] *n* hédoniste *mf*.

hedonistic [ˌhi:də'nɪstɪk] *adj* hédoniste.

HDTV *(abbrev of* **high-definition television**) *n* TVHD *f*.

heebie-jeebies [ˌhi:bɪ'dʒi:bɪz] *npl inf* **to have the ~** avoir la frousse *OR* les chocottes ■ **the film gave me the ~** [revulsion] le film m'a donné la chair de poule ; [fright] le film m'a donné la trouille *OR* la frousse ■ **he gives me the ~** il me met mal à l'aise.

heed [hi:d] ◇ *n* : **to take ~ of sthg, to pay** *OR* **to give ~ to sthg** tenir bien compte de qqch ■ **he pays little ~ to criticism** il ne se soucie guère *OR* il ne fait pas grand cas des critiques ■ **I took no ~ of her advice** je n'ai tenu aucun compte de ses conseils.
◇ *vt* **1.** [warning, words] faire bien attention à, tenir compte de, prendre garde à **2.** [person - listen to] bien écouter ; [- obey] obéir à.

heedful ['hi:dfʊl] *adj fml* attentif ■ **she's ~ of the importance of secrecy** elle est consciente qu'il est important de garder le secret.

heedless ['hi:dlɪs] *adj* : **~ of** : **~ of the danger** sans se soucier du danger ■ **~ of my warning** sans tenir compte de mon avertissement.

heedlessly ['hi:dlɪslɪ] *adv* **1.** [without thinking] sans faire attention, à la légère **2.** [inconsiderately] avec insouciance, négligemment.

hee-haw [ˌhi:'hɔ:] ◇ *n* hi-han *m*.
◇ *vi* braire, faire hi-han.
◇ *interj* hi-han.

heel [hi:l] ◇ *n* **1.** ANAT talon *m* ■ **she spun** *OR* **turned on her ~ and walked away** elle a tourné les talons ■ **under the ~ of fascism** *fig* sous le joug *OR* la botte du fascisme ⊙ **we followed hard on her ~s** [walked] nous lui emboîtâmes le pas ; [tracked] nous étions sur ses talons ■ **famine followed hard on the ~s of drought** la sécheresse fut suivie de près par la famine ■ **he brought the dog to ~** il a fait venir le chien à ses pieds ■ **to bring sb to ~** mettre qqn au pas ■ **to take to one's ~s, to show a clean pair of ~s** se sauver à toutes jambes, prendre ses jambes à son cou **2.** [of shoe] talon *m* **3.** [of glove, golf club, hand, knife, sock, tool] talon *m* **4.** [of bread] talon *m*, croûton *m* ■ [of cheese] talon *m*, croûte *f* **5.** △ *dated* [contemptible man] salaud△ *m* **6.** NAUT [of keel] talon *m* ■ [of mast] caisse *f* **7.** [incline - of ship] bande *f* ; [- of vehicle, tower] inclinaison *f*.
◇ *vt* **1.** [boot, shoe] refaire le talon de **2.** SPORT [ball] talonner.
◇ *vi* **1.** [to dog] : **~!** au pied! **2.** [ship] gîter, donner de la bande ■ [vehicle, tower] s'incliner, se pencher.
◆ **heel over** *vi insep* [ship] gîter, donner de la bande ■ [vehicle, tower] s'incliner, se pencher ■ [cyclist] se pencher.

heel bar *n* talon-minute *m*, réparations-minute *fpl*.

heels [hi:lz] = **high heels**.

hefty ['heftɪ] *(comp* **heftier**, *superl* **heftiest**) *adj inf* **1.** [package - heavy] lourd ; [- bulky] encombrant, volumineux ■ [book] épais, épaisse *f*, gros, grosse *f* ■ [person] costaud **2.** [part, profit] gros, grosse *f* ■ **a ~ sum** une jolie somme ■ **he paid a ~ price for them** il les a payés drôlement cher **3.** [blow, slap] puissant.

Hegelian [heɪ'gi:ljən] *adj* hégélien.

hegemony [hɪ'gemənɪ] *n* hégémonie *f*.

heifer ['hefər] *n* génisse *f*.

height [haɪt] *n* **1.** [tallness - of person] taille *f*, grandeur *f* ; [- of building, tree] hauteur *f* ■ **what ~ are you?** combien mesurez-vous? ▪ **I'm of average ~** je suis de taille moyenne ▪ **redwoods grow to a ~ of 100 metres** les séquoias peuvent atteindre 100 mètres (de haut) **2.** [distance above ground - of mountain, plane] altitude *f* ; [- of ceiling, river, stars] hauteur *f* ▪ **to be at a ~ of three metres above the ground** être à trois mètres au-dessus du sol ▶ **~ of land** *US* ligne *f* de partage des eaux **3.** [high position] hauteur *f* ▪ **to fall from a great ~** tomber de haut ▪ **the ~s** GEOG les hauteurs ▪ **I'm afraid of ~s** j'ai le vertige ▪ **to reach new ~s** *fig* augmenter encore ▶ **'Wuthering Heights'** ***Emily Brontë*** 'les Hauts de Hurlevent' **4.** *fig* [peak - of career, success] point *m* culminant ; [- of fortune, fame] apogée *m* ; [- of arrogance, stupidity] comble *m* ▪ **at the ~ of her powers** en pleine possession de ses moyens ▪ **at its ~ the group had 300 members** à son apogée, le groupe comprenait 300 membres ▪ **the tourist season is at its ~** la saison touristique bat son plein ▪ **at the ~ of summer** en plein été, au plus chaud de l'été ▪ **at the ~ of the battle/storm** au plus fort de la bataille/de l'orage ▪ **it's the ~ of fashion** c'est le dernier cri.

heighten ['haɪtn] ◇ *vt* **1.** [make higher - building, ceiling, shelf] relever, rehausser **2.** [increase - effect, fear, pleasure] augmenter, intensifier ; [- flavour] relever ▪ MED [fever] faire monter, aggraver ▪ **the incident has ~ed public awareness of environmental problems** l'incident a sensibilisé encore plus le public aux problèmes de l'environnement.
◇ *vi* [fear, pleasure] augmenter, monter.

heightened ['haɪtnd] *adj* **1.** [building, ceiling, shelf] relevé, rehaussé **2.** [fear, pleasure] intensifié ▪ [colour] plus vif.

Heimlich manoeuvre ['haɪmlɪk-] *n* manœuvre *f* de Heimlich.

heinous ['heɪnəs] *adj lit* & *fml* odieux, atroce.

heir [eər] *n* [gen] héritier *m* ▪ LAW héritier *m*, légataire *mf* ▪ **he is ~ to a vast fortune** il est l'héritier d'une immense fortune ▪ **the ~ to the throne** l'héritier du trône *OR* de la couronne ▶ **~ apparent** LAW héritier *m* présomptif ▪ **~ at law, rightful ~** LAW héritier légitime *OR* naturel ▪ **~ presumptive** LAW héritier présomptif *(sauf naissance d'un héritier en ligne directe)*.

heiress ['eərɪs] *n* héritière *f*.

heirloom ['eəlu:m] *n* **1.** [family property] : **(family) ~** objet *m* de famille **2.** LAW [legacy] legs *m*.

heist [haɪst] *US inf* ◇ *n* [robbery] vol *m* ▪ [in bank] braquage *m* ▪ [stolen objects] butin *m*.
◇ *vt* [steal] voler ▪ [commit armed robbery] braquer.

held [held] *pt* & *pp* ▷ **hold**.

helical ['helɪkl] *adj* hélicoïdal.

helices ['helɪsi:z] *pl* ▷ **helix**.

helicoid(al) ['helɪkɔɪd(l)] ◇ *adj* [gen] hélicoïdal ▪ GEOM hélicoïde.
◇ *n* hélicoïde *m*.

helicopter ['helɪkɒptər] ◇ *n* hélicoptère *m* ▪ **the wounded were transported by ~** les blessés ont été héliportés.
◇ *comp* [patrol, rescue] en hélicoptère ▪ [pilot] d'hélicoptère ▪ **~ transfer** *OR* **transport** héliportage *m*.
◇ *vt* transporter en hélicoptère ▪ **they managed to ~ in provisions** ils ont réussi à apporter des provisions par hélicoptère.

Helios ['hi:lɪɒs] *pr n* Hélios.

heliotrope ['heljətrəʊp] ◇ *n* **1.** BOT héliotrope *m* **2.** [colour] violet *m* clair.
◇ *adj* violet clair.

helipad ['helɪpæd] *n* héliport *m*.

heliport ['helɪpɔ:t] *n* héliport *m*.

helium ['hi:lɪəm] *n* hélium *m*.

helix ['hi:lɪks] (*pl* **helices** ['helɪsi:z] *OR pl* **helixes**) *n* **1.** ARCHIT & GEOM [spiral] hélice *f* **2.** ANAT & ZOOL hélix *m*.

hell [hel] *n* **1.** RELIG enfer *m* ▪ MYTH [underworld] les enfers ▪ **to go to ~** [Christianity] aller en enfer ; MYTH descendre aux enfers ▶ **go to ~!** *inf* va te faire voir! ▪ **to ~ with society!** *inf* au diable la société! ▪ **come ~ or high water** *inf* contre vents et marées, envers et contre tout ▪ **when ~ freezes over** à la saint-glinglin ▪ **it'll be a cold day in ~ before I apologize** je m'excuserai quand les poules auront des dents ▪ **it was a journey from ~!** *inf* ce voyage, c'était l'horreur! ▪ **all ~ broke loose** *inf* ça a bardé ▪ **to give sb ~** *inf* passer un savon *OR* faire sa fête à qqn ▪ **the damp weather plays ~ with my arthritis** *inf* ce temps humide me fait rudement souffrir de mon arthrite!, par ces temps humides, qu'est-ce que je déguste avec mon arthrite! ▪ **there'll be ~ to pay when he finds out** *inf* ça va barder *OR* chauffer quand il l'apprendra ▪ **I went along just for the ~ of it** *inf* j'y suis allé histoire de rire *OR* de rigoler ▪ **he ran off ~ for leather** *inf* il est parti ventre à terre ▪ **~'s bells!, ~'s teeth!** *inf* mince alors! **2.** [torture] enfer *m* ▪ **working there was ~ on earth** c'était l'enfer de travailler là-bas ▪ **he made her life ~** il lui a fait mener une vie infernale **3.** *inf* [used as emphasis] : **he's as happy/tired as ~** il est vachement heureux/fatigué ▪ **he's in a ~ of a mess** il est dans un sacré pétrin ▪ **a ~ of a lot of books** tout un tas *OR* un paquet de livres ▪ **we had a ~ of a good time** nous nous sommes amusés comme des fous ▪ **they had a ~ of a time getting the car started** ils en ont bavé pour faire démarrer la voiture ▪ **to run/to shout like ~** courir/crier comme un fou ▪ **I'm leaving – like (the) ~ you are!** je pars – n'y compte pas! ▪ **I just hope to ~ he leaves** j'espère de tout mon cœur qu'il partira ▪ **get the ~ out of here!** fous *OR* fous-moi le camp! ▪ **what the ~ are you doing?** qu'est-ce que tu fous? ▪ **who the ~ do you think you are?** mais tu te prends pour qui? ▪ **oh well, what the ~!** oh qu'est-ce que ça peut bien faire? ▪ **did you agree? – ~, no!** as-tu accepté? – tu plaisantes! **4.** *US inf* [high spirits] : **full of ~** plein d'entrain *OR* de vivacité **5.** *inf hum* cauchemardesque ▪ **from hell** cauchemardesque.
◄ **Hell** = **hell** *(sense 1)*.

he'll [hi:l] = **he will**.

hell-bent *adj inf* acharné ▪ **society seems ~ on self-destruction** la société semble décidée à aller tout droit à sa propre destruction.

Hellenic [he'li:nɪk] *adj* hellène, hellénique.

hellfire ['helfaɪər] ◇ *n liter* feu *m* de l'enfer ▪ *fig* [punishment] châtiment *m* divin.
◇ *comp* : **~ preacher** prédicateur *m*.
◇ *interj inf* : **~!** bon sang!, sacré nom de Dieu!

hellhole ['helhəʊl] *n inf* bouge *m*.

hellion ['heljən] *n US inf* [child] galopin *m*, polisson *m*, - onne *f* ▪ [adult] chahuteur *m*, trublion *m*.

hellish ['helɪʃ] ◇ *adj* **1.** [cruel - action, person] diabolique **2.** *inf* [dreadful] infernal ▪ **she's had a pretty ~ life** elle a eu une vie absolument infernale, sa vie a été un véritable enfer.
◇ *adv inf* = **hellishly**.

hellishly ['helɪʃlɪ] *adv UK inf* atrocement, épouvantablement.

hello [hə'ləʊ] (*pl* **hellos**) ◇ *interj* **1.** [greeting] bonjour, salut ▪ [in the evening] bonsoir ▪ [on answering telephone] allô **2.** [to attract attention] hé, ohé **3.** [in surprise] tiens.
◇ *n* [greeting] bonjour *m*, salutation *f* ▪ **he asked me to say ~ to you** il m'a demandé de vous donner le bonjour.

Hell's Angels *pr npl nom d'un groupe de motards au comportement violent.*

helluva ['heləvə] *adj inf* **he's a ~ guy** c'est un type vachement bien ▪ **I had a ~ time** [awful] je me suis emmerdé ; [wonderful] je me suis vachement marré.

helm [helm] ◇ *n* **1.** NAUT barre *f*, gouvernail *m* ▪ **to be at the ~** *liter* tenir la barre *OR* le gouvernail ; *fig* tenir la barre *OR* les rênes ▪ **to take the ~** *liter* & *fig* prendre la barre, prendre la direction des opérations ▪ **he's at the ~ of the company now** c'est lui qui dirige la société maintenant **2.** *arch* [helmet] casque *m*.
◇ *vt* NAUT gouverner, barrer ▪ *fig* diriger.

helmet ['helmɪt] *n* [gen] casque *m* ▪ [medieval] heaume *m*.

helmsman ['helmzmən] (*pl* **helmsmen** [-mən]) *n* timonier *m*, homme *m* de barre.

help [help] ◇ *vt* **1.** [assist, aid - gen] aider, venir en aide à ; [- elderly, poor, wounded] secourir, venir en aide à ■ **can I ~ you with the dishes?** puis-je t'aider à faire la vaisselle? ■ **they ~ one another take care of the children** ils s'entraident pour s'occuper des enfants ■ **we want to ~ poorer countries to ~ themselves** nous voulons aider les pays sous-développés à devenir autonomes *OR* à se prendre en main ■ **he ~ed me on/off with my coat** il m'a aidé à mettre/enlever mon manteau ■ **she ~ed the old man to his feet/across the street** elle a aidé le vieux monsieur à se lever/à traverser la rue ■ **it might ~ if you took more exercise** ça irait peut-être mieux si tu faisais un peu plus d'exercice ■ **can I ~ you?** [in shop] vous désirez? ■ **Grant Publishing, how may I ~ you?** [on telephone] ≃ les Éditions Grant, bonjour ▶ **so ~ me God!** je le jure devant Dieu! ■ **I'll get you for this, so ~ me** *inf* j'aurai ta peau, je le jure! ■ **God ~s those who ~ themselves** *prov* aide-toi, le ciel t'aidera *prov*
2. [contribute to] contribuer à ■ [encourage] encourager, favoriser ■ **the rain ~ed firefighters to bring the flames under control** la pluie a permis aux pompiers de maîtriser l'incendie
3. [remedy - situation] améliorer ; [- pain] soulager ■ **it ~ed to ease my headache** cela a soulagé mon mal de tête ■ **crying won't ~ anyone** cela ne sert à rien *OR* n'arrange rien de pleurer
4. [serve] servir ■ **I ~ed myself to the cheese** je me suis servi en fromage ■ **~ yourself!** servez-vous! ■ **he ~ed himself to the petty cash** *euph* il a pioché *OR* il s'est servi dans la caisse
5. *(with 'can', usu neg)* [avoid, refrain from] : **I can't ~ thinking that we could have done more** je ne peux pas m'empêcher de penser qu'on aurait pu faire plus ■ **we couldn't ~ laughing** *OR* **but laugh** nous ne pouvions pas nous empêcher de rire ■ **I tried not to laugh but I couldn't ~ myself** j'essayais de ne pas rire mais c'était plus fort que moi ■ **she never writes any more than she can ~** elle ne se foule pas pour écrire, elle écrit un minimum de lettres *OR* le moins possible
6. *(with 'can', usu neg)* [control] : **he can't ~ it if she doesn't like it** il n'y est pour rien *OR* ce n'est pas de sa faute si cela ne lui plaît pas ■ **she can't ~ her temper** elle ne peut rien à ses colères ■ **I can't ~ it** je n'y peux rien, ce n'est pas de ma faute ■ **it can't be ~ed** tant pis! on n'y peut rien *OR* on ne peut pas faire autrement ■ **are they coming? - not if I can ~ it!** est-ce qu'ils viennent? – pas si j'ai mon mot à dire!
◇ *vi* être utile ■ **she ~s a lot around the house** elle se rend très utile à la maison, elle rend souvent service à la maison ■ **is there anything I can do to ~?** puis-je être utile? ■ **losing your temper isn't going to ~** ça ne sert à rien de perdre ton calme ■ **every little bit ~s** les petits ruisseaux font les grandes rivières *prov*.
◇ *n* **1.** [gen] aide *f*, assistance *f* ■ [to drowning or wounded person] secours *m*, assistance *f* ■ **can I be of any ~?** puis-je faire quelque chose pour vous?, puis-je vous rendre service? ■ **he went to get ~** il est allé chercher du secours ■ **we yelled for ~** nous avons crié au secours ■ **with the ~ of a neighbour** avec l'aide d'un voisin ■ **he opened the window with the ~ of a crowbar** il a ouvert la fenêtre à l'aide d'un levier ■ **she did it without any ~** elle l'a fait toute seule ■ **she needs ~ going upstairs** il faut qu'elle se fasse aider pour *OR* elle a besoin qu'on l'aide à monter l'escalier ■ **the situation is now beyond ~** la situation est désespérée *OR* irrémédiable maintenant
2. [something that assists] aide *f*, secours *m* ■ **you've been a great ~** vous m'avez été d'un grand secours, vous m'avez beaucoup aidé
3. *(U)* *US* [employees] personnel *m*, employés *mpl* ■ **'~ wanted'** 'cherchons employés'
4. [domestic aid] femme *f* de ménage.
◇ *interj* : **~!** [in distress] au secours!, à l'aide! ; [in dismay] zut!, mince!
◆ **help along** *vt sep* [person] aider à marcher *OR* avancer ■ [plan, project] faire avancer.
◆ **help out** ◇ *vt sep* [gen] aider, venir en aide à ■ [with supplies, money] dépanner ■ **she ~s us out in the shop from time to time** elle vient nous donner un coup de main au magasin de temps en temps ■ **they ~ each other out** ils s'entraident ■ **she ~s him out with his homework** elle l'aide à faire ses devoirs.
◇ *vi insep* aider, donner un coup de main.

help desk *n* COMPUT service *m* d'assistance, support *m*.

helper ['helpəʳ] *n* **1.** [gen] aide *mf*, assistant *m*, - e *f* ■ [professional] auxiliaire *mf* **2.** *US* [home help] femme *f* de ménage.

helpful ['helpfʊl] *adj* **1.** [person] obligeant, serviable **2.** [advice, suggestion] utile ■ [gadget, information, map] utile ■ [medication] efficace, salutaire ■ **this book isn't very ~** ce livre ne sert pas à grand-chose.

helpfully ['helpfʊlɪ] *adv* avec obligeance, obligeamment.

helpfulness ['helpfʊlnɪs] *n* **1.** [of person] obligeance *f*, serviabilité *f* **2.** [of gadget, map etc] utilité *f*.

helping ['helpɪŋ] *n* portion *f* ■ **to ask for a second ~** demander à en reprendre.

helping hand *n* main *f* secourable ■ **to give** *OR* **lend (sb) a ~** donner un coup de main *OR* prêter main-forte (à qqn).

helpless ['helplɪs] *adj* **1.** [vulnerable] désarmé, sans défense **2.** [physically] faible, impotent ■ [mentally] impuissant ■ **he lay ~ on the ground** il était allongé par terre sans pouvoir bouger **3.** [powerless - person] impuissant, sans ressource ; [- anger, feeling] impuissant ; [- situation] sans recours, désespéré ■ **he was ~ to stop her leaving** il était incapable de l'empêcher de partir ■ **I feel so ~** je ne sais vraiment pas quoi faire, je me sens vraiment désarmé ■ **they were ~ with laughter** ils n'en pouvaient plus de rire, ils étaient morts de rire.

helplessly ['helplɪslɪ] *adv* **1.** [without protection] sans défense, sans ressource **2.** [unable to react] sans pouvoir réagir ■ [argue, struggle, try] en vain ■ **he looked on ~** il a regardé sans pouvoir intervenir ■ **she smiled ~** elle a eu un sourire où se lisait son impuissance ■ **they giggled ~** ils n'ont pas pu s'empêcher de glousser.

helplessness ['helplɪsnɪs] *n* **1.** [defencelessness] incapacité *f* de se défendre, vulnérabilité *f* **2.** [physical] incapacité *f*, impotence *f* ■ [mental] incapacité *f* **3.** [powerlessness - of person] impuissance *f*, manque *m* de moyens ; [- of anger, feeling] impuissance *f* ■ **a feeling of ~** un sentiment d'impuissance.

helpline ['helplaɪn] *n* service *m* d'assistance téléphonique ■ **AIDS ~** SOS SIDA.

helpmate ['helpmeɪt] *n* [companion] compagnon *m*, compagne *f* ■ [helper] aide *mf*, assistant *m*, - e *f* ■ [spouse] époux *m*, épouse *f*.

helter-skelter [ˌheltə'skeltəʳ] ◇ *adv* [run, rush] en désordre, à la débandade ■ [organize, throw] pêle-mêle, en vrac.
◇ *adj* [rush] à la débandade ■ [account, story] désordonné.
◇ *n* *UK* [ride in fairground] toboggan *m*.

Helvetia [hel'viːʃjə] *pr n* Suisse *f*, Helvétie *f*.

Helvetian [hel'viːʃjən] ◇ *n* Suisse *m*, Suissesse *f*.
◇ *adj* suisse, helvétique ■ HIST helvète.

hem [hem] (*pret & pp* **hemmed**, *cont* **hemming**) ◇ *n* **1.** [of trousers, skirt] ourlet *m* ■ [of handkerchief, sheet] bord *m*, ourlet *m* ■ **she let the ~ down on her skirt** elle a défait l'ourlet pour rallonger sa jupe **2.** [hemline] (bas *m* de l')ourlet *m* **3.** METALL ourlet *m*.
◇ *vt* ourler, faire l'ourlet de.
◇ *interj* : **~!** [to call attention] hem! ; [to indicate hesitation, pause] euh!
◇ *vi* faire hem ■ **to ~ and haw** bafouiller.
◆ **hem in** *vt sep* [house, people] entourer, encercler ■ [enemy] cerner ■ **he felt hemmed in** [in room] il faisait de la claustrophobie, il se sentait oppressé ; [in relationship] il se sentait prisonnier *OR* pris au piège ■ **hemmed in by rules** *fig* entravé par des règles *OR* règlements.

he-man ['hiːmæn] *n inf* homme *m* viril.

hematology *etc* *US* = **haematology**.

hemidemisemiquaver ['hemɪˌdemɪ'semɪˌkweɪvəʳ] *n UK* quadruple croche *f*.

hemiplegia [ˌhemɪ'pliːdʒɪə] *n* hémiplégie *f*.

hemisphere ['hemɪˌsfɪəʳ] *n* hémisphère *m*.

hemline ['hemlaɪn] *n* (bas *m* de l')ourlet *m* ■ **~s are going up** les jupes vont raccourcir.

hemlock ['hemlɒk] *n* [poison - BOT] ciguë *f*.

hemoglobin *US* = **haemoglobin**.

hemophilia *US* = **haemophilia**.

hemorrhage *US* = **haemorrhage**.

hemorrhoids *US* = **haemorrhoids**.

hemp [hemp] *n* **1.** [fibre, plant] chanvre *m* **2.** [marijuana] marijuana *f* ▪ [hash] haschisch *m*, hachisch *m*.

hemstitch ['hemstɪtʃ] ◇ *n* [stitch] jour *m*.
◇ *vt* ourler à jour.

hen [hen] *n* **1.** [chicken] poule *f* **2.** [female] femelle *f* ▪ **~ bird** oiseau *m* femelle ▪ **~ pheasant** poule *f* faisane **3.** *inf* [woman] mémère *f*.

henbane ['henbeɪn] *n* jusquiame *f* (noire), herbe *f* à poules.

hence [hens] *adv* **1.** [therefore] donc, d'où ▪ **they are cheaper and ~ more popular** ils sont moins chers et donc plus demandés **2.** *fml* [from this time] d'ici ▪ **three days ~** dans OR d'ici trois jours **3.** *fml* [from here] d'ici.

henceforward [ˌhens'fɔ:wəd], **henceforth** [ˌhens'fɔ:θ] *adv* dorénavant, désormais.

henchman ['hentʃmən] (*pl* **henchmen** [-mən]) *n* **1.** [follower] partisan *m*, adepte *m pej* ▪ [right-hand man] homme *m* de main, suppôt *m pej* **2.** [squire, page] écuyer *m*.

hen coop *n* mue *f*, cage *f* à poules.

hen house *n* poulailler *m*.

Henley ['henlɪ] *pr n ville dans le Oxfordshire* ▪ **~ Regatta** *importante épreuve internationale d'aviron.*

HENLEY REGATTA

Cette épreuve internationale d'aviron a lieu tous les ans sur la Tamise, au mois de juin. C'est une manifestation autant mondaine que sportive.

henna ['henə] ◇ *n* henné *m*.
◇ *vt* teindre au henné.

hen night, hen party *n inf* [gen] soirée entre copines ▪ [before wedding] : **she's having her ~** elle enterre sa vie de célibataire.

henpecked ['henpekt] *adj* dominé ▪ **a ~ husband** un mari dominé par sa femme.

Henry ['henrɪ] *pr n* Henri.

hepatitis [ˌhepə'taɪtɪs] *n (U)* hépatite *f* ▪ **serum ~** hépatite B OR sérique.

heptagon ['heptəgən] *n* heptagone *m*.

heptagonal [hep'tægənl] *adj* heptagonal.

heptameter [hep'tæmɪtər] *n* heptamètre *m*.

heptathlon [hep'tæθlɒn] *n* heptathlon *m*.

her [hɜ:r] ◇ *det* son *m*, sa *f*, ses *mf pl* ▪ **~ book** son livre ▪ **~ glasses** ses lunettes ▪ **~ university** son université ▪ **she has broken ~ arm** elle s'est cassé le bras.
◇ *pron* **1.** [direct object - unstressed] la, l' *(before vowel or silent 'h')* ; [- stressed] elle ▪ **I recognize ~** je la reconnais ▪ **why did you have to choose HER?** pourquoi l'as-tu choisie elle? **2.** [indirect object - unstressed] lui ; [- stressed] à elle ▪ **give ~ the money** donne-lui l'argent ▪ **he only told ~, no-one else** il ne l'a dit qu'à elle, c'est tout **3.** [after preposition] elle ▪ **I was in front of ~** j'étais devant elle **4.** [with 'to be'] : **it's ~** c'est elle **5.** *fml* [with relative pronoun] celle.

Heracles ['herəkli:z] *pr n* Héraclès.

Heraclitus [ˌherə'klaɪtəs] *pr n* Héraclite.

herald ['herəld] ◇ *vt* **1.** [announce] annoncer, proclamer ▪ **his rise to power ~ed a new era** son ascension au pouvoir a annoncé une nouvelle ère **2.** [hail] acclamer.
◇ *n* **1.** [medieval messenger] héraut *m* **2.** [forerunner] héraut *m*, avant-coureur *m*.

heraldic [he'rældɪk] *adj* héraldique.

heraldry ['herəldrɪ] *n* **1.** [system, study] héraldique *f* **2.** [coat of arms] blason *m* **3.** [pageantry] faste *m*, pompe *f* (héraldique).

herb [hɜ:b, *US* ɜ:rb] *n* **1.** BOT herbe *f* ▪ **~s** CULIN fines herbes, herbes aromatiques **2.** *inf* [marijuana] herbe *f*.

herbaceous [hɜ:'beɪʃəs, *US* ɜ:r'beɪʃəs] *adj* [plant, stem] herbacé.

herbaceous border *n* bordure *f* de plantes herbacées.

herbal ['hɜ:bl, *US* 'ɜ:rbl] ◇ *adj* aux herbes ▪ **~ medicine** [practice] phytothérapie *f* ; [medication] médicament *m* à base de plantes ▪ **~ tea** tisane *f*.
◇ *n* traité *m* sur les plantes, herbier *m arch*.

herbalist ['hɜ:bəlɪst, *US* 'ɜ:rbəlɪst] *n* herboriste *mf*.

herb garden *n* jardin *m* d'herbes aromatiques.

herbicide ['hɜ:bɪsaɪd, *US* 'ɜ:rbɪsaɪd] *n* herbicide *m*.

herbivore ['hɜ:bɪvɔ:r, *US* 'ɜ:rbɪvɔ:r] *n* herbivore *m*.

herbivorous [hɜ:'bɪvərəs, *US* ɜ:r'bɪvərəs] *adj* herbivore.

herculean, Herculean [ˌhɜ:kjʊ'li:ən] *adj* herculéen ▪ **a ~ task** un travail de Titan OR herculéen.

Hercules ['hɜ:kjʊli:z] *pr n* Hercule ▪ *fig* hercule.

herd [hɜ:d] ◇ *n* **1.** [of cattle, goats, sheep] troupeau *m* ▪ [of wild animals] troupe *f* ▪ [of horses] troupe *f*, bande *f* ▪ [of deer] harde *f* **2.** *inf* [of people] troupeau *m pej*, foule *f*.
◇ *vt* **1.** [bring together] rassembler (en troupeau) ▪ [look after] garder **2.** [drive] mener, conduire ▪ **he ~ed the students back into the classroom** il a reconduit les élèves dans la salle de cours.

➜ **herd together** ◇ *vi insep* s'assembler en troupeau, s'attrouper.
◇ *vt sep* rassembler en troupeau.

herd instinct *n* instinct *m* grégaire.

herdsman ['hɜ:dzmən] (*pl* **herdsmen** [-mən]) *n* [gen] gardien *m* de troupeau ▪ [of cattle] vacher *m*, bouvier *m* ▪ [of sheep] berger *m*.

here [hɪər] ◇ *adv* **1.** [at, in this place] : **she left ~ yesterday** elle est partie d'ici hier ▪ **is Susan ~?** est-ce que Susan est là? ▪ **he won't be ~ next week** il ne sera pas là la semaine prochaine ▪ **they're ~** [I've found them] ils sont ici ; [they've arrived] ils sont arrivés ▪ **winter is ~** c'est l'hiver, l'hiver est arrivé ▪ **the miniskirt is ~ to stay** la minijupe n'est pas près de disparaître ▪ **it is a question ~ of finances** il s'agit ici d'argent ▪ **'~ lies Tom Smith'** 'ci-gît Tom Smith' ▪ *(after preposition)* **around ~** par ici ▪ **I'm in ~** je suis là OR ici ▪ **where are you? – over ~!** où êtes-vous? – (par) ici! ➊ **I've had it up to ~** j'en ai jusque là ▪ **~ today, gone tomorrow** tout passe
2. [drawing attention to sthg] voici, voilà ▪ **~'s the key!** voilà OR voici la clef! ▪ **~ they come!** les voilà! OR voici! ▪ **~'s a man who knows what he wants** voilà un homme qui sait ce qu'il veut ➊ **~ goes** *inf*, **~ goes nothing** *US inf* allons-y! ▪ **~ we go!** [excitedly] c'est parti! ; [wearily] et voilà, c'est reparti! ▪ **~ we go again!** ça y est, c'est reparti pour un tour!
3. [emphasizing specified object, person etc] : **ask the lady ~** demandez à cette dame ici ▪ **it's this one ~ that I want** c'est celui-ci que je veux ▪ **my friend ~ saw it** mon ami (que voici) l'a vu ▪ **this ~ book you've all been talking about** *inf* ce bouquin dont vous n'arrêtez pas de parler tous
4. [at this point] maintenant ▪ [at that point] alors, à ce moment-là ▪ **~ I would like to remind you...** maintenant je voudrais vous rappeler...
5. *phr* **~'s to** [in toasts] à ▪ **~'s to us!** à nous!, à nos amours!
◇ *interj* **1.** [present] : **Alex Perrin? – ~!** Alex Perrin? – présent!
2. [giving, taking etc] : **~!** tiens!, tenez!
3. [protesting] : **~! what do you think you're doing?** hé! qu'est-ce que tu fais?

➜ **here and now** *adv phr* sur-le-champ ▪ *(as noun)* **the ~ and now** le présent.

➜ **here and there** *adv phr* ça et là ▪ **the paintwork needs retouching ~ and there** la peinture a besoin d'être refaite par endroits.

➜ **here, there and everywhere** *adv phr hum* un peu partout.

hereabouts ['hɪərə,baʊts] *UK*, **hereabout** ['hɪərə,baʊt] *US adv* par ici, près d'ici, dans les environs.

hereafter [,hɪər'ɑːftər] ◇ *n* **1.** [life after death] au-delà *m inv* ■ **in the ~** dans l'autre monde **2.** *lit* [future] avenir *m*, futur *m*. ◇ *adv* **1.** *fml* & LAW [in document] ci-après **2.** *lit* [after death] dans l'au-delà **3.** *lit* [in the future] désormais, dorénavant.

hereby [,hɪə'baɪ] *adv fml* & LAW [in statement] par la présente (déclaration) ■ [in document] par le présent (document) ■ [in letter] par la présente ■ [in act] par le présent acte, par ce geste ■ [in will] par le présent testament.

hereditament [,herɪ'dɪtəmənt] *n tout bien qui peut être transmis par héritage.*

hereditary [hɪ'redɪtrɪ] *adj* héréditaire.

heredity [hɪ'redətɪ] *n* hérédité *f*.

herein [,hɪər'ɪn] *adv fml* **1.** [in this respect] en ceci, en cela **2.** LAW [in this document] ci-inclus.

heresy ['herəsɪ] (*pl* **heresies**) *n* hérésie *f*.

heretic ['herətɪk] *n* hérétique *mf*.

hereto [,hɪə'tuː] *adv fml* à ceci, à cela ■ LAW aux présentes.

herewith [,hɪə'wɪð] *adv fml* **1.** [enclosed] ci-joint, ci-inclus ■ **I enclose ~ my curriculum vitae** veuillez trouver ci-joint mon curriculum vitae **2.** = **hereby**.

heritage ['herɪtɪdʒ] *n* héritage *m*, patrimoine *m* ■ **the national ~** le patrimoine national.

heritage centre *n* site *m* touristique *(faisant partie du patrimoine historique national)*.

hermaphrodite [hɜː'mæfrədaɪt] ◇ *adj* hermaphrodite. ◇ *n* hermaphrodite *m*.

hermeneutic(al) [,hɜːmə'njuːtɪk(l)] *adj* herméneutique.

Hermes ['hɜːmiːz] *pr n* Hermès.

hermetic [hɜː'metɪk] *adj* hermétique.

hermetically [hɜː'metɪklɪ] *adv* hermétiquement.

hermit ['hɜːmɪt] *n* [gen] ermite *m*, solitaire *m* ■ RELIG ermite *m*.

hermitage ['hɜːmɪtɪdʒ] *n* ermitage *m*.

hermit crab *n* bernard-l'ermite *m inv*, pagure *m*.

hernia ['hɜːnɪə] (*pl* **hernias** *OR pl* **herniae** [-nɪiː]) *n* hernie *f*.

hero ['hɪərəʊ] (*pl* **heroes**) *n* **1.** [person] héros *m* **2.** *US* [sandwich] *sorte de gros sandwich.*
◆ **Hero** *pr n* Héro.

Herod ['herəd] *pr n* Hérode.

Herodias [he'rəʊdɪæs] *pr n* Hérodiade.

heroic [hɪ'rəʊɪk] *adj* **1.** [act, behaviour, person] héroïque **2.** *lit* épique, héroïque.

heroically [hɪ'rəʊɪklɪ] *adv* héroïquement.

heroics [hɪ'rəʊɪks] *npl* [language] emphase *f*, déclamation *f* ■ [behaviour] affectation *f*, emphase *f*.

heroin ['herəʊɪn] ◇ *n* héroïne *f*.
◇ *comp* : **~ addict** *OR* **user** héroïnomane *mf* ■ **~ addiction** héroïnomanie *f*.

heroine ['herəʊɪn] *n* héroïne *f (femme)*.

heroism ['herəʊɪzm] *n* héroïsme *m*.

heron ['herən] (*pl inv OR pl* **herons**) *n* héron *m*.

hero worship *n* [admiration] adulation *f*, culte *m* (du héros) ■ ANTIQ culte *m* des héros.
◆ **hero-worship** *vt* aduler, idolâtrer.

herpes ['hɜːpiːz] *n (U)* herpès *m*.

herring ['herɪŋ] (*pl inv OR pl* **herrings**) ◇ *n* hareng *m*.
◇ *comp* : **~ boat** harenguier *m*.

herringbone ['herɪŋbəʊn] ◇ *n* **1.** [bone] arête *f* de hareng **2.** TEX [pattern] chevron (dessin *m* à) chevrons *mpl* ■ [fabric] tissu *m* à chevrons **3.** CONSTR appareil *m* en épi **4.** [in skiing] montée *f* en ciseaux *OR* en pas de canard.
◇ *comp* : **~ tweed** tweed *m* à chevrons.

herring gull *n* goéland *m* argenté.

hers [hɜːz] *pron* **1.** [gen] le sien *m*, la sienne *f*, les siens *mpl*, les siennes *f* ■ **this car is ~** cette voiture lui appartient *OR* est à elle ■ **~ was the best photograph** sa photographie était la meilleure ■ **~ is not an easy task** elle n'a pas la tâche facile **2.** [after preposition] : **she took his hand in ~** elle a pris sa main dans la sienne ■ **he's an old friend of ~** c'est un vieil ami à elle, c'est un de ses vieux amis ■ **no suggestion of ~ could possibly interest him** aucune suggestion venant d'elle ne risquait de l'intéresser ■ **I can't stand that boyfriend/dog of ~** je ne supporte pas son copain/chien **3.** [indicating authorship] d'elle.

herself [hɜː'self] *pron* **1.** [reflexive form] se, s' *(before vowel or silent 'h')* ■ **she bought ~ a car** elle s'est acheté une voiture ■ **she considers ~ lucky** elle considère qu'elle a de la chance **2.** [emphatic form] elle-même ■ **she built the shelves ~** elle a monté les étagères elle-même ■ **I spoke with the teacher ~** j'ai parlé au professeur en personne **3.** [with preposition] elle ■ **the old woman was talking to ~** la vieille femme parlait toute seule ■ **she did it all by ~** elle l'a fait toute seule **4.** [her usual self] : **she isn't quite ~** elle n'est pas dans son état habituel ■ **she's feeling more ~ now** elle va mieux maintenant.

Hershey bar® ['hɜːʃɪ-] *n barre de chocolat très connue aux États-Unis.*

Herts *written abbr of* **Hertfordshire**.

hertz [hɜːts] (*pl inv*) *n* hertz *m*.

he's [hiːz] = **he is**, = **he has**.

hesitance ['hezɪtəns], **hesitancy** ['hezɪtənsɪ] *n* hésitation *f*, indécision *f*.

hesitant ['hezɪtənt] *adj* **1.** [person - uncertain] hésitant, indécis ; [- cautious] réticent ■ **I'm ~ about sending her to a new school** j'hésite à l'envoyer dans une nouvelle école **2.** [attempt, speech, voice] hésitant.

hesitantly ['hezɪtəntlɪ] *adv* [act, try] avec hésitation, timidement ■ [answer, speak] d'une voix hésitante.

hesitate ['hezɪteɪt] *vi* hésiter ■ **don't ~ to call me** n'hésitez pas à m'appeler ● **he who ~s is lost** *prov* un moment d'hésitation peut coûter cher.

hesitation [,hezɪ'teɪʃn] *n* hésitation *f* ■ **she answered with some ~** elle a répondu d'une voix hésitante ■ **I would have no ~ in recommending him** je n'hésiterais pas à le recommander ■ **without a moment's ~** sans la moindre hésitation.

Hesperides [he'sperɪdiːz] *pr npl* : **the ~** les Hespérides.

hessian ['hesɪən] ◇ *n* (toile *f* de) jute *m*.
◇ *comp* [fabric, sack] de jute.

hetero ['hetərəʊ] (*pl* **heteros**) *inf* ◇ *adj* hétéro.
◇ *n* hétéro *mf*.

heterodox ['hetərədɒks] *adj* hétérodoxe.

heterogeneous [,hetərə'dʒiːnjəs] *adj* hétérogène.

heterosexual [,hetərə'sekʃʊəl] ◇ *adj* hétérosexuel.
◇ *n* hétérosexuel *m*, - elle *f*.

het up *adj inf* [angry] énervé ■ [excited] excité, agité ■ **to get all ~ (about sthg)** se mettre dans tous ses états *OR* s'énerver (pour qqch).

heuristic [hjʊə'rɪstɪk] *adj* heuristique.

hew [hjuː] (*pret* **hewed**, *pp* **hewed** *OR* **hewn** [hjuːn]) *vt* [wood] couper ■ [stone] tailler ■ [coal] abattre ■ **to ~ away** *OR* **off a branch** élaguer une branche ■ **he ~ed a statue out of the marble** il a taillé une statue dans le marbre.

hex [heks] *US* ◇ *n* **1.** [spell] sort *m*, sortilège *m* **2.** [witch] sorcière *f*.
◇ *vt* jeter un sort à.

hexadecimal (notation) [ˌheksəˈdesɪml-] *n* COMPUT codes *mpl* hexadécimaux, notation *f* hexadécimale.

hexagon [ˈheksəgən] *n* hexagone *m*.

hexagonal [hekˈsægənl] *adj* hexagonal.

hey [heɪ] *interj* : **~!** [to draw attention] hé!, ohé! ; [to show surprise] tiens! ▪ **~ presto!** [magician] passez muscade!, et hop!

heyday [ˈheɪdeɪ] *n* [of cinema, movement] âge *m* d'or, beaux jours *mpl* ▪ [of nation, organization] zénith *m*, apogée *m* ▪ **in her ~** [youth] quand elle était dans la force de l'âge ; [success] à l'apogée de sa gloire, au temps de sa splendeur.

HF (*abbrev of* **high frequency**) HF.

HGV (*abbrev of* **heavy goods vehicle**) *n* UK PL *m*.

hi [haɪ] *interj inf* **1.** [hello] salut **2.** [hey] hé, ohé.

HI *written abbr of* **Hawaii**.

hiatus [haɪˈeɪtəs] (*pl inv* OR *pl* **hiatuses**) *n* ANAT, LING & LIT hiatus *m* ▪ [in manuscript] lacune *f* ▪ [break, interruption] pause *f*, interruption *f*.

hiatus hernia *n* hernie *f* hiatale.

hibernate [ˈhaɪbəneɪt] *vi* hiberner.

hibernation [ˌhaɪbəˈneɪʃn] *n* hibernation *f*.

Hibernian [haɪˈbɜːnjən] ◇ *adj* irlandais.
◇ *n* Irlandais *m*, - e *f*.

hibiscus [hɪˈbɪskəs] *n* hibiscus *m*.

hiccough [ˈhɪkʌp], **hiccup** [ˈhɪkʌp] ◇ *n* **1.** [sound] hoquet *m* ▪ **to have (the) ~s** avoir le hoquet ▪ **it gave me the ~s** cela m'a donné le hoquet **2.** [problem] contretemps *m*.
◇ *vi* hoqueter.

hick [hɪk] US *inf* ◇ *n* péquenaud *m*, - e *f*, plouc *mf*.
◇ *adj* de péquenaud.

hickey [ˈhɪkɪ] *n* US *inf* **1.** [gadget] bidule *m* **2.** [lovebite] suçon *m*.

hickory [ˈhɪkərɪ] (*pl* **hickories**) ◇ *n* [tree] hickory *m*, noyer *m* blanc d'Amérique ▪ [wood] (bois *m* de) hickory *m*.
◇ *comp* en (bois de) hickory ▪ **~ nut** fruit *m* du hickory, noix *f* d'Amérique.

hid [hɪd] *pt* ▷ **hide**.

hidden [ˈhɪdn] ◇ *pp* ▷ **hide**.
◇ *adj* caché ▪ **~ from sight** à l'abri des regards indiscrets, caché ▪ **a village ~ away in the mountains** un village caché OR niché dans les montagnes ▪ **a ~ agenda** un plan secret ◗ **~ tax** impôt *m* indirect OR déguisé.

hide [haɪd] (*pret* **hid** [hɪd], *pp* **hidden** [ˈhɪdn]) ◇ *vt* **1.** [conceal - person, thing] cacher ; [- disappointment, dismay, fright] dissimuler ▪ **to ~ sthg from sb** [ball, letter] cacher qqch à qqn ; [emotion] dissimuler qqch à qqn ▪ **the boy hid himself behind the door** le garçon s'est caché derrière la porte ▪ **she hid her face** elle s'est caché le visage ▪ **he hid it from sight** il l'a dissimulé OR l'a dérobé aux regards ◗ **to ~ one's light under a bushel** cacher ses talents **2.** [keep secret] taire, dissimuler ▪ **to ~ the truth (from sb)** taire OR dissimuler la vérité (à qqn).
◇ *vi* se cacher ▪ **to ~ from sb** se cacher de qqn ▪ **the ambassador hid behind his diplomatic immunity** *fig* l'ambassadeur s'est réfugié derrière son immunité diplomatique.
◇ *n* **1.** UK cachette *f* ▪ [in hunting] affût *m* **2.** [animal skin - raw] peau *f* ; [- tanned] cuir *m* **3.** *inf fig* **inf** [of person] peau *f* ▪ **I'll have your ~ for that** tu vas me le payer cher ◗ **I haven't seen ~ nor hair of them** je n'ai eu aucune nouvelle d'eux.
◇ *adj* de OR en cuir.

❖ **hide away** ◇ *vi insep* se cacher ▪ **to ~ away (from sb/sthg)** se cacher (de qqn/qqch).
◇ *vt sep* cacher.

❖ **hide out** *vi insep* se tenir caché ▪ **he's hiding out from the police** il se cache de la police.

hide-and-seek *n* cache-cache *m* ▪ **to play (at) ~** jouer à cache-cache.

hideaway [ˈhaɪdəweɪ] *n* cachette *f*.

hidebound [ˈhaɪdbaʊnd] *adj* [person] obtus, borné ▪ [attitude, view] borné, rigide.

hideous [ˈhɪdɪəs] *adj* **1.** [physically ugly] hideux, affreux **2.** [ghastly - conditions, situation] atroce, abominable.

hideously [ˈhɪdɪəslɪ] *adv* **1.** [deformed, wounded] hideusement, atrocement, affreusement **2.** *fig* [as intensifier] terriblement, horriblement.

hideout [ˈhaɪdaʊt] *n* cachette *f*.

hidey-hole [ˈhaɪdɪhəʊl] *n inf* planque *f*.

hiding [ˈhaɪdɪŋ] *n* **1.** [concealment] : **to be in ~** se tenir caché ▪ **to go into ~** [criminal] se cacher, se planquer ; [spy, terrorist] entrer dans la clandestinité **2.** *inf* [thrashing] rossée *f* ▪ **to give sb a good ~** donner une bonne raclée à qqn **3.** [defeat] raclée *f*, dérouillée *f* **4.** UK *phr* **to be on a ~ to nothing** être voué à l'échec.

hiding place *n* cachette *f*.

hierarchic [ˌhaɪəˈrɑːkɪk] *adj* hiérarchique.

hierarchically [ˌhaɪəˈrɑːkɪklɪ] *adv* hiérarchiquement.

hierarchy [ˈhaɪərɑːkɪ] (*pl* **hierarchies**) *n* **1.** [organization into grades] hiérarchie *f* ▪ [of animals, plants] classification *f*, classement *m* **2.** [upper levels of authority] dirigeants *mpl*, autorités *fpl*.

hieroglyphic [ˌhaɪərəˈglɪfɪk] ◇ *adj* hiéroglyphique.
◇ *n* hiéroglyphe *m*.

hieroglyphics [ˌhaɪərəˈglɪfɪks] *npl* écriture *f* hiéroglyphique.

hi-fi [ˈhaɪfaɪ] (*abbrev of* **high fidelity**) *inf* ◇ *n* **1.** *(U)* hi-fi *f inv* **2.** [stereo system] chaîne *f* (hi-fi) ▪ [radio] radio *f* (hi-fi).
◇ *comp* [equipment, recording, system] hi-fi *(inv)* ▪ **a ~ system** une chaîne (hi-fi).

higgledy-piggledy [ˌhɪgldɪˈpɪgldɪ] *inf* ◇ *adv* pêle-mêle, en désordre.
◇ *adj* en désordre, pêle-mêle.

high [haɪ] ◇ *adj* **1.** [tall] haut ▪ **how ~ is that building?** quelle est la hauteur de ce bâtiment? ▪ **the walls are three metres ~** les murs ont OR font trois mètres de haut, les murs sont hauts de trois mètres ▪ **the building is eight storeys ~** c'est un immeuble de OR à huit étages ▪ **when I was only so ~** quand je n'étais pas plus grand que ça
2. [above ground level - river, tide] haut ; [- altitude, shelf] haut, élevé ▪ **the sun was ~ in the sky** le soleil était haut
3. [above average - number] grand, élevé ; [- speed, value] grand ; [- cost, price, rate] élevé ; [- salary] élevé, gros, grosse *f* ; [- pressure] élevé, haut ; [- polish] brillant ▪ **she suffers from ~ blood pressure** elle a de la tension ▪ **built to withstand ~ temperatures** conçu pour résister à des températures élevées ▪ **he has a ~ temperature** il a beaucoup de température OR fièvre ▪ **areas of ~ unemployment** des régions à fort taux de chômage ▪ **milk is ~ in calcium** le lait contient beaucoup de calcium ▪ **~ winds** des vents violents, de grands vents ▪ **the ~est common factor** MATHS le plus grand facteur commun
4. [better than average - quality] grand, haut ; [- standard] haut, élevé ; [- mark, score] élevé, bon ; [- reputation] bon ▪ **~-quality goods** articles de qualité supérieure OR de première qualité ▪ **to have a ~ opinion of sb** avoir une bonne OR haute opinion de qqn ▪ **she speaks of you in the ~est terms** elle dit le plus grand bien de vous ▪ **one of the ~est honours in the arts** l'un des plus grands honneurs dans le monde des arts
5. [honourable - ideal, thought] noble, élevé ; [- character] noble ▪ **a man of ~ principles** un homme qui a des principes (élevés) ▪ **he took a very ~ moral tone** il prit un ton très moralisateur
6. [of great importance or rank] haut, important ▪ **we have it on the ~est authority** nous le tenons de la source la plus sûre ▪ **to have friends in ~ places** avoir des relations haut placées, avoir le bras long
7. [sound, voice] aigu, - uë *f* ▪ MUS [note] haut
8. [at peak] : **it was ~ summer** c'était au cœur de l'été ▪ **it's ~ time we were leaving** il est grand temps qu'on parte ◗ **the High Middle Ages** le Haut Moyen Âge
9. [intensely emotional] : **resentment was ~** il y avait énormément de ressentiment ▪ **moments of ~ drama** des moments extrêmement dramatiques ▪ **~ adventure** grande aventure ▪ **~ tragedy** THEAT grande tragédie

10. *UK* [complexion] rougeaud, rubicond ■ **to have a ~ colour** être haut en couleur
11. [elaborate, formal - language, style] élevé, soutenu
12. [prominent - cheekbones] saillant
13. CARDS haut ■ **the ~est card** la carte maîtresse
14. *UK* [meat] avancé, faisandé ■ [butter, cheese] rance
15. [remote] haut ■ **High Antiquity** Haute Antiquité
16. GEOG [latitude] haut
17. [conservative] : **a ~ Tory** un tory ultra-conservateur ■ **a ~ Anglican** un anglican de tendance conservatrice
18. LING [vowel] fermé
19. [excited] excité ■ [cheerful] plein d'entrain ■ **spirits are ~ amongst the staff** la bonne humeur règne parmi le personnel
20. *inf* [drunk] parti, éméché ■ **they were feeling (as) ~ as kites** [drunk] ils étaient bien partis ; [drugged] ils planaient ; [happy] ils avaient la pêche.
◇ *adv* **1.** [at, to a height] haut, en haut ■ [at a great altitude] à haute altitude, à une altitude élevée ■ **up ~** en haut ■ **~er up** plus haut ■ **~er and ~er** de plus en plus haut ■ **she threw the ball ~ into the air** elle a lancé le ballon très haut ■ **the geese flew ~ over the fields** les oies volaient très haut au-dessus des champs ■ **the shelf was ~ above her head** l'étagère était bien au-dessus de sa tête ❙ *fig* **we looked ~ and low for him** nous l'avons cherché partout ■ **to set one's sights ~, to aim ~** viser haut ■ **they're flying ~** ils visent haut, ils voient grand ➤ **to hold one's head ~** *liter* & *fig* porter la tête haute ■ **to leave sb ~ and dry** laisser qqn en plan
2. [at, to a greater degree than normal] haut ■ **they set the price/standards too ~** ils ont fixé un prix/niveau trop élevé ■ **I turned the heating up ~** j'ai mis le chauffage à fond ■ **salaries can go as ~ as £30,000** les salaires peuvent monter jusqu'à *OR* atteindre 30 000 livres ■ **to run ~** [river] être en crue ; [sea] être houleuse *OR* grosse ■ **feelings were running ~** les esprits se sont échauffés
3. *US inf phr* **to live ~ off** *OR* **on the hog** vivre comme un roi *OR* nabab.
◇ *n* **1.** [height] haut *m* ■ **on ~** [at a height] en haut ; *fig* [in heaven] au ciel ■ **the decision came from on ~** *hum* la décision fut prononcée en haut lieu
2. [great degree or level] haut *m* ■ **to reach a new ~** atteindre un nouveau record ■ **prices are at an all-time ~** les prix ont atteint leur maximum
3. [setting - on iron, stove] : **I put the oven on ~** j'ai mis le four sur très chaud
4. AUT [fourth gear] quatrième *f* ■ [fifth gear] cinquième *f*
5. METEOR [anticyclone] anticyclone *m*
6. *inf* [state of excitement] : **she's been on a permanent ~ since he came back** elle voit tout en rose depuis son retour ■ **to be on a ~** [drunk] être (complètement) parti ; [on drugs] planer.
◆ **High** *n* RELIG : **the Most High** le Très-Haut.

-high *in cpds* à la hauteur de... ■ **shoulder~** à la hauteur de l'épaule.

high altar *n* maître-autel *m*.

high-and-mighty *adj* arrogant, impérieux ■ **to be ~** se donner de grands airs ■ **don't act so ~** ne prends pas tes airs de grand seigneur/grande dame.

highball ['haɪ,bɔːl] *US n boisson à base d'un alcool avec de l'eau et des glaçons.*

high board *n* plongeoir *m* le plus haut.

highboy ['haɪbɔɪ] *n US* commode *f* (haute).

highbrow ['haɪbraʊ] ◇ *adj* [literature, film] pour intellectuels ■ [taste] intellectuel.
◇ *n* intellectuel *m*, - elle *f*, grosse tête *f*.

high chair *n* chaise *f* haute (pour enfants).

High Church ◇ *n fraction de l'Église d'Angleterre accordant une grande importance à l'autorité du prêtre, au rituel etc.*
◇ *adj de tendance conservatrice dans l'Église anglicane.*

high-class *adj* [person] de la haute société, du grand monde ■ [flat, neighbourhood] de grand standing ■ [job, service] de premier ordre ■ [car, hotel, restaurant] de luxe ■ **a ~ prostitute** une prostituée de luxe.

high-coloured *adj* rougeaud, rubicond.

high comedy *n* THEAT comédie *f* au dialogue brillant ■ **the debate ended in scenes of ~** le débat se termina par des scènes du plus haut comique.

high command *n* haut commandement *m*.

high commissioner *n* [gen - ADMIN] haut commissaire *m*.

High Court ◇ *n* : **the ~ (of Justice)** ≃ le tribunal de grande instance *(principal tribunal civil en Angleterre et au pays de Galles)*.
◇ *comp* : **~ judge** ≃ juge *m* du tribunal de grande instance.

high-density *adj* **1.** [housing] à grande densité de population **2.** COMPUT haute densité.

higher ['haɪəʳ] ◇ *adj* **1.** [at greater height] plus haut **2.** [advanced] supérieur ■ **a sum ~ than 50** somme supérieure à 50 ■ **people in the ~ income brackets** les gens appartenant aux tranches de revenus supérieurs.
◇ *adv* plus haut.
◇ *n Scotland* = **Higher Grade**.

higher degree *n* diplôme *m* d'études supérieures.

higher education *n* enseignement *m* supérieur ■ **to go on to ~** faire des études supérieures.

Higher Grade *n Scotland* diplôme *m* de fin d'études secondaires, ≃ baccalauréat *m*.

higher mathematics *n (U)* mathématiques *fpl* supérieures.

Higher National Certificate *n brevet de technicien en Grande-Bretagne,* ≃ BTS *m*.

Higher National Diploma *n brevet de technicien supérieur en Grande-Bretagne,* ≃ DUT *m*.

higher-up *n inf* supérieur *m*, - e *f*.

high explosive *n* explosif *m* puissant.

highfalutin [,haɪfə'luːtɪn] *adj inf* affecté, prétentieux.

high fashion *n* haute couture *f*.

high fidelity *n* haute-fidélité *f*.
◆ **high-fidelity** *adj* haute-fidélité.

high finance *n* haute finance *f*.

high-five *n inf geste que font deux personnes pour se féliciter ou se dire bonjour et qui consiste à se taper dans la main.*

high-flier *n* [ambitious person] ambitieux *m*, - euse *f*, jeune loup *m* ■ [talented person] cerveau *m*.

high-flown *adj* **1.** [ideas, plans] extravagant **2.** [language] ampoulé, boursouflé ■ [style] ampoulé.

high-flyer = **high-flier**.

high-flying *adj* **1.** [aircraft] qui vole à haute altitude ■ [bird] qui vole haut **2.** [person] ambitieux ■ [behaviour, goal] extravagant.

high frequency *n* haute fréquence *f*.
◆ **high-frequency** *adj* à *OR* de haute fréquence.

Highgate ['haɪgeɪt] *pr n quartier du nord de Londres, connu pour son cimetière où repose, entre autres, Karl Marx.*

high gear *n* AUT [fourth] quatrième *f* (vitesse *f*) ■ [fifth] cinquième *f* (vitesse *f*).

High German *n* haut allemand *m*.

high-grade *adj* de haute qualité, de premier ordre ■ **~ minerals** minéraux *mpl* à haute teneur.

high-handed *adj* [overbearing] autoritaire, despotique ■ [inconsiderate] cavalier.

high-handedness [-'hændɪdnɪs] *n* [overbearing attitude - of person] caractère *m* autoritaire, despotisme *m* ; [- of behaviour] caractère *m* arbitraire ■ [lack of consideration] jugement *m* cavalier.

high-heeled [-'hiːld] *adj* à talons hauts, à hauts talons.

high heels *npl* hauts talons *mpl*.

high jinks *inf npl* chahut *m*.

high jump *n* SPORT saut *m* en hauteur ■ **you're for the ~ when he finds out!** *UK inf fig* qu'est-ce que tu vas prendre quand il l'apprendra!

high jumper *n* sauteur *m (qui fait du saut en hauteur)*.

highland ['haɪlənd] ◇ *n* région *f* montagneuse.
◇ *adj* des montagnes.
◆ **Highland** *adj* [air, scenery] des Highlands ■ [holiday] dans les Highlands.
◆ **Highlands** *npl* GEOG : **the Highlands** [of Scotland] les Highlands *fpl*.

highlander ['haɪləndər] *n* [mountain dweller] montagnard *m*, - e *f*.
◆ **Highlander** *n* habitant *m*, - e *f* des Highlands, Highlander *m*.

Highland fling *n danse des Highlands traditionnellement exécutée en solo.*

Highland games *npl* jeux *mpl* écossais.

HIGHLAND GAMES

En Écosse, fête de plein air où se déroulent simultanément des concours (danse, cornemuse) et des épreuves sportives (courses, lancer du marteau, lancer de troncs *tossing the caber*, tir à la corde *tug-of-war*, ces deux derniers étant typiquement écossais).

high-level *adj* **1.** [discussion, meeting] à un haut niveau ■ [diplomat, official] de haut niveau, de rang élevé ■ **~ officers** [of company] cadres supérieurs ; MIL officiers supérieurs **2.** COMPUT : **~ language** langage *m* évolué *OR* de haut niveau.

high life *n* : **the ~** la grande vie ■ **she has a taste for the ~** elle a des goûts de luxe.

highlight ['haɪlaɪt] ◇ *vt* **1.** [emphasize] souligner, mettre en relief **2.** [with pen] surligner ■ COMPUT mettre en surbrillance ■ **~ text** texte *m* en surbrillance **3.** ART & PHOT rehausser **4.** [hair] faire des mèches dans.
◇ *n* **1.** [major event - of news] événement *m* le plus marquant ; [- of evening, holiday] point *m* culminant, grand moment *m* **2.** [in hair - natural] reflet *m* ; [- bleached] mèche *f* **3.** ART & PHOT rehaut *m*.

highlighter (pen) ['haɪlaɪtər] *n* surligneur *m*.

highly ['haɪlɪ] *adv* **1.** [very] très, extrêmement ■ **it's ~ improbable** c'est fort peu probable **2.** [very well] très bien ■ **very ~ paid** très bien payés **3.** [favourably] : **to speak/think ~ of sb** dire/penser beaucoup de bien de qqn ■ **I ~ recommend it** je vous le conseille vivement *OR* chaudement **4.** [at an important level] haut ■ **a ~ placed source** une source haut placée ■ **a ~ placed official** [gen] un officiel de haut rang ; ADMIN un haut fonctionnaire.

highly-strung *adj* nerveux, tendu.

high mass, High Mass *n* grand-messe *f*.

high-minded *adj* de caractère noble, qui a des principes (élevés).

high-necked [-nekt] *adj* à col haut *OR* montant.

highness ['haɪnɪs] *n* [of building, wall] hauteur *f*.
◆ **Highness** *n* [title] : **His/Her Highness** son Altesse *f*.

high noon *n* plein midi *m* ■ **at ~** à midi pile ■ **'High Noon'** ***Zinnemann*** 'le Train sifflera trois fois'.

high-octane *adj liter* à haut degré d'octane ■ **~ petrol** supercarburant *m*, super *m*.

high-performance *adj* performant.

high-pitched *adj* **1.** [sound, voice] aigu, - uë *f* ■ MUS [note] haut **2.** [argument, discussion] passionné ■ [style] ampoulé ■ [excitement] intense **3.** [roof] à forte pente.

high point *n* [major event - of news] événement *m* le plus marquant ; [- of evening, holiday] point *m* culminant, grand moment *m* ; [- of film, novel] point *m* culminant ■ **the ~ of the party** le clou de la soirée.

high-powered [-'paʊəd] *adj* **1.** [engine, rifle] puissant, de forte puissance ■ [microscope] à fort grossissement **2.** [dynamic - person] dynamique, entreprenant ; [- advertising, course, method] dynamique **3.** [important] très important.

high-pressure ◇ *adj* **1.** [cylinder, gas] à haute pression ■ **~ area** METEOR anticyclone *m*, zone *f* de hautes pressions (atmosphériques) **2.** *fig* [methods, selling] agressif ■ [job, profession] stressant.
◇ *vt inf US inf* forcer la main à.

high priest *n* grand prêtre *m* ■ **the ~s of fashion** *fig* les gourous de la mode.

high priestess *n* grande prêtresse *f*.

high profile *n* : **to have a ~** être très en vue.
◆ **high-profile** *adj* [job, position] qui est très en vue ■ [campaign] qui fait beaucoup de bruit.

high-ranking *adj* de haut rang, de rang élevé ■ **a ~ official** ADMIN un haut fonctionnaire.

high-resolution *adj* à haute résolution.

high-rise *adj* [flat] qui est dans une tour ■ [skyline] composé de tours.
◆ **high rise** *n* tour *f (immeuble)*.

high-risk *adj* à haut risque, à hauts risques.

high road *n* **1.** [main road] route *f* principale, grand-route *f* **2.** *fig* [most direct route] bonne voie *f* ■ **he's on the ~ to success** il est en bonne voie de réussir.

high roller *n US inf* [spendthrift] dépensier *m*, - ère *f* ■ [gambler] flambeur *m*, - euse *f*.

high school ◇ *n* [in US] ≃ lycée *m* ■ [in UK] établissement *m* d'enseignement secondaire ■ **she's still at ~** elle est toujours scolarisée *OR* va toujours au lycée.
◇ *comp* [diploma] de fin d'études secondaires.

high seas *npl* : **on the ~** en haute *OR* pleine mer.

high season *n* haute *OR* pleine saison *f* ■ **during the ~** en haute *OR* pleine saison.
◆ **high-season** *comp* [prices] de haute saison.

high sign *n US* signe *m*.

high society *n* haute société *f*, grand monde *m*.

high-sounding *adj* [ideas] grandiloquent, extravagant ■ [language, title] grandiloquent, ronflant *pej*.

high-speed *adj* ultra-rapide ■ **~ train** train *m* à grande vitesse, TGV *m*.

high-spirited *adj* **1.** [person] plein d'entrain *OR* de vivacité ■ [activity, fun] plein d'entrain **2.** [horse] fougueux, nerveux.

high spirits *npl* pétulance *f*, vitalité *f*, entrain *m* ■ **to be in ~** avoir de l'entrain, être plein d'entrain.

high spot *n* **1.** = **high point 2.** *US* [place] endroit *m* intéressant ■ **we hit all the ~s** [tourists] nous avons vu toutes les attractions touristiques.

high street *n UK* **the ~** la grand-rue, la rue principale ■ **the ~ has been badly hit by the recession** les commerçants ont été durement touchés par la récession.
◆ **high-street** *comp UK* **the high-street banks** les grandes banques *(britanniques)* ■ **high-street shops** le petit commerce ■ **high-street fashion** prêt-à-porter *m*.

high table *n UK* [for guests of honour] table *f* d'honneur ■ SCH & UNIV table *f* des professeurs.

hightail ['haɪteɪl] *vt esp US inf* filer.

high tea *n repas léger pris en début de soirée et accompagné de thé.*

high tech *n* **1.** [technology] technologie *f* avancée *OR* de pointe **2.** [style] hi-tech *m*.
◆ **high-tech** *comp* **1.** [industry, sector] de pointe ■ [equipment] de haute technicité **2.** [furniture, style] hi-tech *(inv)*.

high-tension *adj* à haute tension.

high tide *n* **1.** [of ocean, sea] marée *f* haute ■ **at ~** à marée haute **2.** *fig* [of success] point *m* culminant.

high-tops *npl* baskets *fpl*.

high treason *n* haute trahison *f*.

high-up *inf* ◇ *n* [important person] gros bonnet *m*, huile *f* ■ [hierarchical superior] supérieur *m*, - e *f*.
◇ *adj* haut placé.

high water *n* [of ocean, sea] marée *f* haute ■ [of river] crue *f* ■ **the river is at ~** le fleuve est en crue.

high water mark *n fig* [of success] point *m* culminant.

highway ['haɪweɪ] *n* [road] route *f* ■ *US* [main road] grande route, route nationale ■ [public road] voie *f* publique ■ [interstate] autoroute *f* ■ **all the ~s and byways** tous les chemins.

Highway Code *n UK* **the ~** le code de la route.

highwayman ['haɪweɪmən] (*pl* **highwaymen** [-mən]) *n* bandit *m* de grand chemin.

highway robbery *n* banditisme *m* de grand chemin ■ **that's ~!** *inf fig* c'est du vol!

high wire *n* corde *f* raide *OR* de funambule ■ **to walk the ~** marcher sur la corde raide.

hijack ['haɪdʒæk] ◇ *vt* **1.** [plane] détourner ■ [car, train] s'emparer de, détourner **2.** [rob] voler.
◇ *n* détournement *m*.

hijacker ['haɪdʒækəʳ] *n* **1.** [of plane] pirate *m* (de l'air) ■ [of car, train] gangster *m* **2.** [robber] voleur *m*.

hijacking ['haɪdʒækɪŋ] *n* **1.** [of car, plane, train] détournement *m* **2.** [robbery] vol *m*.

hike [haɪk] ◇ *vi* faire de la marche à pied ■ **we went hiking in the mountains** nous avons fait des excursions *OR* des randonnées à pied dans les montagnes.
◇ *vt* **1.** [walk] faire à pied, marcher **2.** [price] augmenter (brusquement).
◇ *n* **1.** [gen - MIL] marche *f* à pied ■ [long walk] randonnée *f* à pied, marche *f* à pied ■ [short walk] promenade *f* ■ **it's a bit of a ~ into town** *inf* ça fait une petite trotte pour aller en ville **2.** *esp US* [increase] hausse *f*, augmentation *f*.
◆ **hike up** *vt sep* **1.** [hitch up - skirt] relever ; [- trousers] remonter **2.** [price, rent] augmenter (brusquement).

hiker ['haɪkəʳ] *n* [gen - MIL] marcheur *m*, - euse *f* ■ [in mountains, woods] randonneur *m*, - euse *f*, promeneur *m*, - euse *f*.

hiking ['haɪkɪŋ] *n (U)* [gen - MIL] marche *f* à pied ■ [in mountains, woods] randonnée *f*, trekking *m* ■ **~ boots** chaussures *fpl* de marche.

hilarious [hɪ'leərɪəs] *adj* [funny - person, joke, story] hilarant.

hilariously [hɪ'leərɪəslɪ] *adv* joyeusement, gaiement ■ **the film's ~ funny** le film est à se tordre de rire.

hilarity [hɪ'lærətɪ] *n* hilarité *f*.

Hilary term ['hɪlərɪ-] *n UK* UNIV trimestre *m* de printemps *(à Oxford)*.

hill [hɪl] *n* **1.** colline *f*, coteau *m* ■ **we walked up the ~** nous avons gravi la colline ▶ **up ~ and down dale, over ~ and dale** par monts et par vaux ■ **as old as the ~s** vieux comme le monde *OR* Mathusalem ■ **to be over the ~** *inf* commencer à se faire vieux **2.** [slope] côte *f*, pente *f* ■ **'steep ~'** [up] montée *OR* côte raide ; [down] 'descente abrupte *OR* raide' **3.** [mound - of earth] levée *f* de terre, remblai *m* ; [- of things] tas *m*, monceau *m* ■ **that car isn't worth a ~ of beans** *US inf* cette voiture ne vaut pas un clou ■ **on the Hill** *US* au parlement *(par allusion à Capitol Hill, siège du Congrès)*.

hillbilly ['hɪl,bɪlɪ] (*pl* **hillbillies**) *US* ◇ *n* montagnard *m*, - e *f* des Appalaches ■ *pej* péquenaud *m*, - e *f*, plouc *mf*.
◇ *adj* des Appalaches.

hill farmer *n* éleveur *m* de moutons dans les alpages.

hillfort ['hɪlfɔːt] *n dated ancien endroit fortifié se trouvant au sommet d'une colline* motte *f*.

hillock ['hɪlək] *n* [small hill] mamelon *m*, butte *f* ■ [artificial hill] monticule *m*, amoncellement *m*.

hillside ['hɪl,saɪd] *n* (flanc *m* de) coteau *m* ■ **vines grew on the ~** des vignes poussaient à flanc de coteau.

hill start *n* démarrage *m* en côte.

hilltop ['hɪl,tɒp] ◇ *n* sommet *m* de la colline ■ **on the ~** au sommet *OR* en haut de la colline.
◇ *adj* [village] au sommet *OR* en haut de la colline.

hilly ['hɪlɪ] (*comp* **hillier**, *superl* **hilliest**) *adj* [country, land] vallonné ■ [road] accidenté, à fortes côtes.

hilt [hɪlt] *n* [of dagger, knife] manche *m* ■ [of sword] poignée *f*, garde *f* ■ [of gun] crosse *f* ■ **(up) to the ~** au maximum ■ **to back sb up to the ~** soutenir qqn à fond.

him [hɪm] *pron* **1.** [direct object - unstressed] le, l' *(before vowel or silent 'h')* ; [- stressed] lui ■ **I recognize ~** je le reconnais ■ **why did you have to choose HIM?** pourquoi l'as-tu choisi lui? **2.** [indirect object - unstressed] lui ; [- stressed] à lui ■ **give ~ the money** donne-lui l'argent ■ **she only told ~, no one else** elle ne l'a dit qu'à lui, c'est tout **3.** [after preposition] lui ■ **I was in front of ~** j'étais devant lui **4.** [with 'to be'] : **it's ~** c'est lui ■ **if I were ~** si j'étais lui, si j'étais à sa place **5.** *fml* [with relative pronoun] celui.

Himalayan [,hɪmə'leɪən] *adj* himalayen.

Himalayas [,hɪmə'leɪəz] *pr npl* : **the ~** l'Himalaya *m* ■ **in the ~** dans l'Himalaya.

himself [hɪm'self] *pron* **1.** [reflexive form] se, s' *(before vowel or silent 'h')* ■ **he bought ~ a car** il s'est acheté une voiture ■ **he considers ~ lucky** il considère qu'il a de la chance **2.** [emphatic form] lui-même ■ **he built the shelves ~** il a monté les étagères lui-même ■ **I spoke with the teacher ~** j'ai parlé au professeur en personne **3.** [with preposition] lui ■ **the old man was talking to ~** le vieil homme parlait tout seul ■ **he did it all by ~** il l'a fait tout seul **4.** [his usual self] : **he isn't quite ~** il n'est pas dans son état habituel ■ **he's feeling more ~ now** il va mieux maintenant.

hind [haɪnd] ◇ *n* [deer] biche *f*.
◇ *adj* de derrière ■ **~ leg** patte *f* de derrière ■ **he could talk the ~ legs off a donkey** *hum* il est bavard comme une pie ■ **to get up on one's ~ legs** *hum* se mettre debout.

hinder ['hɪndəʳ] *vt* [person] gêner ■ [progress] entraver, gêner ■ **to ~ sb in his/her work** gêner qqn dans son travail ■ **to ~ sb from doing sthg** empêcher qqn de faire qqch.

Hindi ['hɪndɪ] ◇ *n* LING hindi *m*.
◇ *adj* hindi.

hindmost ['haɪndməʊst] *adj* dernier, du bout.

hindquarters ['haɪndkwɔːtəz] *npl* arrière-train *m*.

hindrance ['hɪndrəns] *n* **1.** [person, thing] obstacle *m*, entrave *f* ■ **you'll be more of a ~ than a help** tu vas gêner plus qu'autre chose **2.** *(U)* [action] : **without any ~ from the authorities** [referring to person] sans être gêné par les autorités ; [referring to project] sans être entravé par les autorités ■ **his illness has been something of a ~ to the project** sa maladie a quelque peu retardé le projet.

hindsight ['haɪndsaɪt] *n* sagesse *f* acquise après coup ■ **with the benefit** *OR* **wisdom of ~** avec du recul, après coup.

Hindu ['hɪnduː] ◇ *n* Hindou *m*, - e *f*.
◇ *adj* hindou.

Hinduism ['hɪnduːɪzm] *n* hindouisme *m*.

hinge [hɪndʒ] ◇ *n* [of door] gond *m*, charnière *f* ■ [of box] charnière *f* ■ **the door has come off its ~s** la porte est sortie de ses gonds.

◇ *vt* [door] munir de gonds *OR* charnières ▪ [box] munir de charnières.
◆ **hinge on, hinge upon** *vt insep* dépendre de ▪ **the company's future ~s on whether we get the contract** l'avenir de l'entreprise dépend de *OR* tient à *OR* repose sur ce contrat.

hinged [hɪndʒd] *adj* à charnière *OR* charnières ▪ **~ flap** [of counter] abattant *m*.

hinky ['hɪŋkɪ] *adj US inf* bizarre, louche.

hint [hɪnt] ◇ *n* **1.** [indirect suggestion] allusion *f* ▪ [clue] indice *m* ▪ **to drop a ~ (about sthg)** faire une allusion (à qqch) ▪ **you could try dropping a ~ that if his work doesn't improve...** tu pourrais essayer de lui faire comprendre que si son travail ne s'améliore pas... ▪ **he can't take a ~** il ne comprend pas les allusions ▪ **OK, I can take a ~** oh ça va, j'ai compris ▶ **I just love plain chocolate, ~, ~** j'adore le chocolat noir, si tu vois où je veux en venir **2.** [helpful suggestion, tip] conseil *m*, truc *m* **3.** [small amount, trace - of emotion] note *f* ; [- of colour] touche *f* ; [- of flavouring] soupçon *m* ▪ **there's a ~ of spring in the air** ça sent le printemps, il y a du printemps dans l'air.
◇ *vt* insinuer.
◇ *vi* : **to ~ at sthg** faire allusion à qqch ▪ **what are you ~ing at?** qu'est-ce que tu insinues? ; [in neutral sense] à quoi fais-tu allusion? ▪ **the speech seemed to ~ at the possibility of agreement being reached soon** le discours semblait laisser entendre qu'un accord pourrait être conclu prochainement.

hinterland ['hɪntəlænd] *n* arrière-pays *m*.

hip [hɪp] ◇ *n* **1.** [part of body] hanche *f* ▪ **with one's hands on one's ~s** les mains sur les hanches ▪ **to be big/small around the ~s** avoir les hanches larges/étroites ▪ **to break one's ~** se casser le col du fémur **2.** [berry] fruit *m* de l'églantier/du rosier, cynorhodon *m*, gratte-cul *m*.
◇ *comp* : **~ measurement** *OR* **size** tour *m* de hanches.
◇ *interj* : **~~, hooray!** hip hip hip, hourra!
◇ *adj inf* [fashionable] branché.

hip bath *n* bain *m* de siège.

hip flask *n* flasque *f*.

hip-hop *n* [music] hip-hop *m*.

hip joint *n* articulation *f* de la hanche.

hippie ['hɪpɪ] ◇ *n* hippie *mf*, hippy *mf*.
◇ *adj* hippie, hippy.

hippo ['hɪpəʊ] *n inf* hippopotame *m*.

Hippocrates [hɪ'pɒkrəti:z] *pr n* Hippocrate.

Hippocratic [,hɪpə'krætɪk] *adj* : **the ~ oath** le serment d'Hippocrate.

hippopotamus [,hɪpə'pɒtəməs] (*pl* **hippopotamuses** *OR pl* **hippopotami** [-maɪ]) *n* hippopotame *m*.

hippy ['hɪpɪ] (*pl* **hippies**) = **hippie**.

hip replacement *n* [operation] remplacement *m* de la hanche par une prothèse ▪ [prosthesis] prothèse *f* de la hanche.

hipsters ['hɪpstəz] *npl UK* pantalon *m* à taille basse.

hire ['haɪə^r] ◇ *n* **1.** *UK* [of car, room, suit etc] location *f* ▪ **'for ~'** 'à louer' ; [taxi] 'libre' ▪ **it's out on ~** il a été loué **2.** [cost - of car, boat etc] (prix *m* de) location *f* ; [- of worker] paye *f*.
◇ *comp* : **~ charges** (frais *mpl OR* prix *m* de) location *f*.
◇ *vt* **1.** *UK* [car, room, suit etc] louer ▪ **to ~ sthg from sb** louer qqch à qqn **2.** [staff] engager ▪ [labourer] embaucher, engager ▪ **~d killer** *OR* **assassin** tueur *m* à gages.
◇ *vi* engager du personnel, embaucher (des ouvriers) ▪ **with authority to ~ and fire** qui a pouvoir en matière d'embauche et de licenciement.
◆ **hire out** *vt sep UK* [car, room, suit etc] louer ▪ **to ~ out one's services** offrir *OR* proposer ses services ▪ **to ~ o.s. out** se faire engager ; [labourer] se faire engager *OR* embaucher.

hire car *n UK* voiture *f* de location.

hireling ['haɪəlɪŋ] *n pej* [menial] larbin *m* ▪ [illegal or immoral] mercenaire *mf*.

hire purchase *n UK* location-vente *f*, vente *f* à tempérament ▪ **to buy** *OR* **to get sthg on ~** acheter qqch en location-vente ▪ **~ agreement** contrat *m* de location ▪ **~ goods** biens achetés en location-vente *OR* à tempérament.

hiring ['haɪərɪŋ] *n* **1.** [of car] location *f* **2.** [of employee] embauche *f*.

hirsute ['hɜ:sju:t] *adj fml* poilu, velu.

his [hɪz] ◇ *det* son *m*, sa *f*, ses *mf pl* ▪ **~ table** sa table ▪ **~ glasses** ses lunettes ▪ **~ university** son université ▪ **it's his fault not mine** c'est de sa faute à lui, pas de la mienne ▪ **he has broken ~ arm** il s'est cassé le bras ▪ **with ~ hands in ~ pockets** les mains dans les poches ▪ **one has ~ pride** *US* on a sa fierté.
◇ *pron* **1.** [gen] le sien *m*, la sienne *f*, les siens *mpl*, les siennes *f* ▪ **it's ~** c'est à lui, c'est le sien ▪ **the responsibility is ~** c'est lui qui est responsable, la responsabilité lui revient ▪ **whose fault is it? – ~!** qui est le responsable? – lui! **2.** [after preposition] : **a friend of ~** un de ses amis ▪ **that dog of ~ is a nuisance** son sacré chien est vraiment embêtant ▪ **everyone wants what is ~** *fml* chacun veut ce qui lui revient.

Hispanic [hɪ'spænɪk] ◇ *n* Hispano-Américain *m*, - e *f*.
◇ *adj* hispanique.

Hispano-American [hɪ'spænəʊ-] ◇ *n* Hispano-Américain *m*, - e *f*.
◇ *adj* hispano-américain.

hiss [hɪs] ◇ *n* [of gas, steam] sifflement *m*, chuintement *m* ▪ [of person, snake] sifflement *m* ▪ [of cat] crachement *m* ▪ **he was greeted with ~es** il est arrivé sous les sifflets (du public).
◇ *vt* [say quietly] souffler ▪ [bad performer, speaker etc] siffler ▪ **the speaker was ~ed off the platform** l'orateur quitta la tribune sous les sifflets (du public).
◇ *vi* [gas, steam] siffler, chuinter ▪ [snake] siffler ▪ [cat] cracher ▪ [person - speak quietly] souffler ; [- in disapproval, anger] siffler ▪ **there was a loud ~ing noise** il y a eu un bruit ressemblant à un fort sifflement.

histamine ['hɪstəmi:n] *n* histamine *f*.

histogram ['hɪstəgræm] *n* histogramme *m*.

histology [hɪ'stɒlədʒɪ] *n* histologie *f*.

historian [hɪ'stɔ:rɪən] *n* historien *m*, - enne *f*.

historic [hɪ'stɒrɪk] *adj* **1.** [memorable - day, occasion, meeting etc] historique **2.** [of time past] révolu, passé ▪ [fear] ancestral ▪ **in ~ times** en des temps révolus ▪ **~ building** monument *m* historique.

historical [hɪ'stɒrɪkəl] *adj* historique ▪ **to be of ~ interest** présenter un intérêt historique ▶ **~ linguistics** linguistique *f* diachronique ▪ **~ present** GRAM présent *m* historique.

historically [hɪ'stɒrɪklɪ] *adv* historiquement ▪ [traditionally] traditionnellement.

historiographer [,hɪstɔ:rɪ'ɒgrəfə^r] *n* historiographe *mf*.

history ['hɪstərɪ] (*pl* **histories**) ◇ *n* **1.** *(U)* [the past] histoire *f* ▪ **ancient/modern ~** histoire ancienne/moderne ▪ **the ~ of France, French ~** l'histoire de France ▪ **to study ~** étudier l'histoire ▪ **a character in ~** un personnage historique *OR* de l'histoire ▪ **throughout ~** tout au long de l'histoire ▪ **the ~ plays of Shakespeare** les pièces historiques de Shakespeare ▪ **tell me news, not ~!** tu n'aurais pas de nouvelles un peu plus fraîches? ▪ **to make ~** entrer dans l'histoire ▪ **a day that has gone down in ~** une journée qui est entrée dans l'histoire ▶ **that's ancient ~** [forgotten, in the past] c'est de l'histoire ancienne ; [everyone knows that] c'est bien connu ▪ **the rest is ~** tout le monde connaît la suite **2.** *(U)* [development, lifespan] histoire *f* ▪ **the worst disaster in aviation ~** *OR* **in the ~ of aviation** le plus grand désastre de l'histoire de l'aviation **3.** [account] histoire *f* ▪ **Shakespeare's histories** les pièces historiques de Shakespeare **4.** *(U)* [record] : **employment ~** expérience *f* professionnelle ▪ **medical ~** antécédents *mpl* médicaux ▪ **there is a ~ of heart disease in my family** il y a des antécédents de maladie cardiaque dans ma famille **5.** COMPUT historique *m*.
◇ *comp* [book, teacher, lesson] d'histoire.

histrionic [,hɪstrɪ'ɒnɪk] *adj pej* théâtral.

histrionics [,hɪstrɪ'ɒnɪks] *npl pej* comédie *f*, simagrées *fpl*.

hit [hɪt] (*pret & pp* **hit**, *cont* **hitting**) ◇ *n* **1.** [blow] coup *m* ▪ **that was a ~ at me** *fig* ça m'était destiné, c'est moi qui étais visé
2. SPORT [in ball game] coup *m* ▪ [in shooting] tir *m* réussi ▪ [in fencing] touche *f* ▪ **to score a ~** [in shooting] faire mouche, toucher la cible ; [in fencing] faire *OR* marquer une touche ▪ **that was a ~** [in fencing] il y a eu touche ▪ **we sent the mailshot to fifty companies and got thirteen ~s** *fig* nous avons contacté cinquante entreprises par publipostage et avons eu treize réponses favorables
3. [success - record, play, book] succès *m* ; [- song] succès *m*, hit *m*, tube *m* ▪ **a ~ with the public/the critics** un succès auprès du public/des critiques ▪ **to make a ~ with sb** [person] conquérir qqn ▪ **she's a ~ with everyone** elle a conquis tout le monde
4.△ [murder] meurtre *m*, liquidation *f*
5. COMPUT visite *f*, accès *m*.
◇ *comp* : **~ record** (disque *m* à) succès *m* ▪ **~ single** *OR* **song** succès, hit *m*, tube *m*.
◇ *vt* **1.** [strike with hand, fist, stick etc - person] frapper ; [- ball] frapper *OR* taper dans ; [- nail] taper sur ▪ **to ~ sb in the face/on the head** frapper qqn au visage/sur la tête ▪ **they ~ him over the head with a base-ball bat** ils lui ont donné un coup de batte de base-ball sur la tête ▪ **to ~ a ball over the net** envoyer un ballon par-dessus le filet ▪ **to ~ sb where it hurts most** *fig* toucher qqn là où ça fait mal ➲ **to ~ a man when he's down** *liter & fig* frapper un homme quand il est à terre ▪ **to ~ the nail on the head** mettre le doigt dessus
2. [come or bring forcefully into contact with - subj: ball, stone] heurter ; [- subj: bullet, arrow] atteindre, toucher ▪ **the bullet ~ him in the shoulder** la balle l'a atteint *OR* touché à l'épaule ▪ **the windscreen was ~ by a stone** une pierre a heurté le pare-brise ▪ **he was ~ by a stone** il a reçu une pierre ▪ **the car ~ a tree** la voiture a heurté *OR* est rentrée dans un arbre ▪ **to ~ one's head/knee (against sthg)** se cogner la tête/le genou (contre qqch) ▪ **to ~ sb's head against sthg** frapper *OR* cogner la tête de qqn contre qqch ▪ **it suddenly ~ me that...** *fig* il m'est soudain venu à l'esprit que...
3. [attack - enemy] attaquer
4. [affect] toucher ▪ **the region worst ~ by the earthquake** la région la plus sévèrement touchée par le tremblement de terre ▪ **the child's death has ~ them all very hard** la mort de l'enfant les a tous durement touchés *OR* frappés ▪ **it ~s everyone in the pocket** *inf* tout le monde en subit financièrement les conséquences, tout le monde le sent passer
5. *inf* [reach] arriver à ▪ **the new model can ~ 130 mph on the straight** le nouveau modèle peut atteindre les 210 km/h ▪ **to ~ a problem** se heurter à un problème *OR* une difficulté ▪ **to ~ a note** MUS [singer] chanter une note ; [instrumentalist] jouer une note ▪ **we'll stop for dinner when we ~ town** *US* nous nous arrêterons pour dîner quand nous arriverons dans la ville ▪ **when it ~s the shops** [product] quand il sera mis en vente ▪ **you'll ~ the rush hour traffic** tu vas te retrouver en plein dans la circulation de l'heure de pointe
6. SPORT [score - runs] marquer ▪ [in fencing] toucher
7. △ [kill] descendre, liquider
8. *US inf* [borrow money from] taper ▪ **to ~ sb for $10** taper qqn de 10 dollars
9. *phr* **to ~ the books** *US inf* se mettre à étudier ▪ **to ~ the bottle** *inf* [drink] picoler ; [start to drink] se mettre à picoler ▪ **to ~ the ceiling** *OR* **roof** *inf* sortir de ses gonds, piquer une colère folle ▪ **to ~ the deck** *inf* [lie down] *inf* se mettre à terre ▪ **~ the deck!** tout le monde à terre! ; [get out of bed] debout là-dedans! ▪ **to ~ the gas** *US inf* appuyer sur le champignon ▪ **to ~ the hay** *OR* **the sack** *inf* aller se mettre au pieu, aller se pieuter ▪ **to ~ home** [remark, criticism] faire mouche ▪ **to ~ the jackpot** gagner le gros lot ▪ **to ~ the road** se mettre en route ▪ **that really ~s the spot** [food, drink] c'est juste ce dont j'avais besoin.
◇ *vi* **1.** frapper, taper ▪ **the two cars didn't actually ~** en fait les deux voitures ne se sont pas heurtées ▪ **the atoms ~ against each other** les atomes se heurtent
2. [inflation, recession etc] se faire sentir.
◆ **hit back** ◇ *vi insep* [reply forcefully, retaliate] riposter, rendre la pareille ▪ **he ~ back with accusations that they were giving bribes** il a riposté en les accusant de verser des pots-de-vin ▪ **to ~ back at sb/sthg** [in speech] répondre à qqn/qqch ▪ **our army ~ back with a missile attack** notre armée a riposté en envoyant des missiles.
◇ *vt sep* : **to ~ the ball back** renvoyer le ballon ▪ **he ~ me back** il m'a rendu mon coup.
◆ **hit off** *vt sep* **1.** [in words] décrire *OR* dépeindre à la perfection ▪ [in paint] représenter de manière très ressemblante ▪ [in mimicry] imiter à la perfection
2. *phr* **to ~ it off** [get on well] bien s'entendre ▪ **to ~ it off with sb** bien s'entendre avec qqn ▪ **we ~ it off immediately** le courant est tout de suite passé entre nous.
◆ **hit on** *vt insep* **1.** [find - solution, plan etc] trouver
2. *US inf* [try to pick up] draguer.
◆ **hit out** *vi insep* **1.** [physically - once] envoyer un coup ; [- repeatedly] envoyer des coups ▪ **he started hitting out at me** il s'est mis à envoyer des coups dans ma direction
2. [in speech, writing] : **to ~ out at** *OR* **against** s'en prendre à, attaquer.
◆ **hit upon** *vt insep* = **hit on** *(sense 1)*.

hit-and-miss = **hit-or-miss**.

hit-and-run *n* accident *m* avec délit de fuite ▪ **a child died in a ~ (accident) yesterday** un enfant est mort hier dans un accident causé par un chauffard qui a pris la fuite ▪ **~ driver** conducteur *m*, - trice *f* coupable de délit de fuite ▪ **~ attack** MIL attaque *f* éclair.

hitch [hɪtʃ] ◇ *vt* **1.** *inf* **to ~ a lift** [gen] se faire emmener en voiture ; [hitchhiker] se faire prendre en stop ▪ **can I ~ a lift, Dad?** tu m'emmènes, papa? ▪ **she has ~ed her way round Europe** elle a fait toute l'Europe en stop *OR* auto-stop **2.** [railway carriage] attacher, atteler ▪ [horse - to fence] attacher ; [- to carriage] atteler ▪ [rope] attacher, nouer **3.** *inf phr* **to get ~ed** [one person] se caser ; [couple] passer devant Monsieur le Maire.
◇ *vi* = **hitchhike**.
◇ *n* **1.** [difficulty] problème *m*, anicroche *f* ▪ **without a ~** *OR* **any ~es** sans anicroche **2.** *US inf* MIL : **he's doing a five year ~ in the navy** il s'est engagé pour cinq ans dans la marine **3.** [knot] nœud *m* **4.** [pull] : **to give sthg a ~ (up)** remonter *OR* retrousser qqch.
◆ **hitch up** *vt sep* **1.** [trousers, skirt etc] remonter, retrousser **2.** [horse, oxen etc] atteler.

hitcher ['hɪtʃəʳ] *inf* = **hitchhiker**.

hitchhike ['hɪtʃhaɪk] ◇ *vi* faire du stop *OR* de l'auto-stop ▪ **to ~ to London** aller à Londres en stop ▪ **I spent the summer hitchhiking in the South of France** j'ai passé l'été à voyager dans le sud de la France en auto-stop.
◇ *vt* : **to ~ one's way round Europe** faire l'Europe en auto-stop.

hitchhiker ['hɪtʃhaɪkəʳ] *n* auto-stoppeur *m*, - euse *f*, stoppeur *m*, - euse *f*.

hitchhiking ['hɪtʃhaɪkɪŋ], **hitching** ['hɪtʃɪŋ] *n* auto-stop *m*, stop *m*.

hi-tech, hitech ['haɪ,tek] ◇ *n* **1.** [in industry] technologie *f* de pointe **2.** [style of interior design] high-tech *m*.
◇ *adj* **1.** [equipment, industry] de pointe **2.** [design, furniture] high-tech.

hither ['hɪðəʳ] *adv arch* ici ▪ **~ and thither** *lit & hum* çà et là, de ci de là.

hitherto [,hɪðə'tuː] *adv fml* jusqu'ici, jusqu'à présent ▪ **a ~ incurable disease** une maladie jusqu'ici *OR* jusqu'à présent incurable.

hit list *n inf* liste *f* noire.

hit man *n inf* tueur *m* à gages.

hit-or-miss *adj inf* [method, approach] basé sur le hasard ▪ [work] fait n'importe comment *OR* à la va comme je te pousse ▪ **the service here is a bit ~** le service ici est fait un peu n'importe comment.

hit parade *n dated* hit-parade *m*.

hit squad *n inf* commando *m* de tueurs.

HIV (*abbrev of* **human immunodeficiency virus**) *n* VIH *m*, HIV *m* ▪ **to be ~ negative** être séronégatif ▪ **to be ~ positive** être séropositif.

hive [haɪv] ◇ *n* [for bees] ruche *f* ▪ [group of bees] essaim *m* ▪ **a ~ of industry** *OR* **activity** *fig* une vraie *OR* véritable ruche.

◇ *vt* mettre en ruche.
◇ *vi* entrer dans une ruche.
◆ **hive off** ◇ *vt sep* transférer.
◇ *vi insep inf* [go away, slip off] se tirer, se casser.

hives [haɪvz] *n (U)* MED urticaire *f*.

hiya ['haɪjə] *excl* salut *inf*.

HM (*abbrev of* **His/Her Majesty**) SM.

HMG (*abbrev of* **His/Her Majesty's Government**) *n expression utilisée sur des documents officiels en Grande-Bretagne.*

HMI (*abbrev of* **His/Her Majesty's Inspector**) *n inspecteur de l'éducation nationale en Grande-Bretagne.*

HMO (*abbrev of* **Health Maintenance Organization**) *n aux États-Unis, clinique de médecine préventive où l'on peut aller lorsqu'on a certains contrats d'assurance.*

HMS (*abbrev of* **His/Her Majesty's Ship**) *dénomination officielle précédant le nom de tous les bâtiments de guerre de la marine britannique.*

HMSO (*abbrev of* **His/Her Majesty's Stationery Office**) *pr n maison d'édition publiant les ouvrages ou documents approuvés par le Parlement, les ministères et autres organismes officiels,* ≃ l'Imprimerie nationale.

HNC *n* = **Higher National Certificate**.

HND *n* = **Higher National Diploma**.

ho [həʊ] *interj* **1.** [attracting attention] hé ho **2.** [imitating laughter] : ~~! ha ha ha!

hoard [hɔ:d] ◇ *n* [of goods] réserve *f*, provisions *fpl* ▪ [of money] trésor *m*, magot *m*.
◇ *vt* [goods] faire provision OR des réserves de, stocker ▪ [money] accumuler, thésauriser.
◇ *vi* faire des réserves, stocker.

hoarder ['hɔ:də] *n* [gen] *personne ou animal qui fait des réserves* ▪ [of money] thésauriseur *m*, - euse *f* ▪ **you're such a ~!** quel conservateur tu fais!

hoarding ['hɔ:dɪŋ] *n* **1.** *(U)* [of goods] mise *f* en réserve OR en stock ▪ [of money] thésaurisation *f*, accumulation *f* **2.** UK [fence] palissade *f* **3.** UK [billboard] panneau *m* publicitaire OR d'affichage.

hoarfrost ['hɔ:,frɒst] *n* givre *m*.

hoarse [hɔ:s] *adj* [person] enroué ▪ [voice] rauque, enroué ▪ **to shout o.s. ~** s'enrouer à force de crier.

hoarsely ['hɔ:slɪ] *adv* d'une voix rauque OR enrouée.

hoary ['hɔ:rɪ] (*comp* **hoarier**, *superl* **hoariest**) *adj* **1.** [greyish white - hair] blanc, blanche *f* ; [- person] aux cheveux blancs, chenu **2.** [old - problem, story] vieux *(before vowel or silent 'h'* **vieil**), vieille *f* ▪ **a ~ old joke** une blague usée.

hoax [həʊks] ◇ *n* canular *m* ▪ **to play a ~ on sb** jouer un tour à qqn, monter un canular à qqn ▪ **(bomb) ~** fausse alerte *f* à la bombe.
◇ *comp* : **~ (telephone) call** canular *m* téléphonique.
◇ *vt* jouer un tour à, monter un canular à.

hoaxer ['həʊksər] *n* mauvais plaisant *m*.

hob [hɒb] *n* [on stove top] plaque *f* (chauffante) ▪ [by open fire] plaque *f*.

hobble ['hɒbl] ◇ *vi* boitiller ▪ **she ~d across the street** elle a traversé la rue en boitillant.
◇ *vt* [horse] entraver.
◇ *n* **1.** [limp] boitillement *m* **2.** [for horse] entrave *f*.
◇ *comp* : **~ skirt** jupe *f* entravée.

hobby ['hɒbɪ] (*pl* **hobbies**) *n* passe-temps *m*, hobby *m*.

hobbyhorse ['hɒbɪhɔ:s] *n* **1.** [toy] cheval *m* de bois *(composé d'une tête sur un manche)* **2.** [favourite topic] sujet *m* favori, dada *m* ▪ **to get sb on his/her ~** brancher qqn sur son sujet favori OR dada.

hobbyist ['hɒbɪɪst] *n* : **a computer ~** un fana de l'informatique.

hobgoblin [hɒb'gɒblɪn] *n* diablotin *m*.

hobnail ['hɒbneɪl] *n* clou *m* à grosse tête, caboche *f* ▪ **~ boots** chaussures *fpl* ferrées.

hobnob ['hɒbnɒb] (*pret & pp* **hobnobbed**, *cont* **hobnobbing**) *vi* : **to ~ with sb** frayer avec qqn, fréquenter qqn.

hobo ['həʊbəʊ] (*pl* **hobos** OR *pl* **hoboes**) *n* US *inf* **1.** [tramp] clochard *m*, - e *f*, vagabond *m*, - e *f* **2.** [itinerant labourer] saisonnier *m*, - ère *f*.

Hobson's choice ['hɒbsnz-] *n* : **it's (a case of) ~** il n'y a pas vraiment le choix.

hock [hɒk] ◇ *n* **1.** [joint] jarret *m* **2.** [wine] vin *m* du Rhin **3.** *inf phr* **in ~** [in pawn] au clou ; [in debt] endetté.
◇ *vt* [pawn] mettre au clou.

hockey ['hɒkɪ] ◇ *n* **1.** UK hockey *m* sur gazon **2.** US hockey *m* sur glace.
◇ *comp* UK [ball, match, pitch, team] de hockey ▪ US de hockey sur glace ▪ **~ player** UK joueur *m*, - euse *f* de hockey, hockeyeur *m*, - euse *f* ; US joueur *m*, - euse *f* de hockey sur glace ▪ **~ stick** UK crosse *f* de hockey ; US crosse de hockey sur glace.

hocus-pocus [,həʊkəs'pəʊkəs] *n* **1.** [of magician] tours *mpl* de passe-passe **2.** [trickery] tricherie *f*, supercherie *f* ▪ [deceptive talk] paroles *fpl* trompeuses ▪ [deceptive action] trucage *m*, supercherie *f*.

hod [hɒd] ◇ *n* [for bricks] *ustensile utilisé par les maçons pour porter les briques* ▪ [for mortar] auge *f*, oiseau *m* ▪ [for coal] seau *m* à charbon.
◇ *comp* : **~ carrier** apprenti *m* OR aide *m* maçon.

hodgepodge ['hɒdʒpɒdʒ] US = **hotchpotch**.

hoe [həʊ] ◇ *n* houe *f*, binette *f*.
◇ *vt* biner, sarcler.

hoedown ['həʊdaʊn] *n* US bal *m* populaire.

hog [hɒg] (*pret & pp* **hogged**, *cont* **hogging**) ◇ *n* [castrated pig] cochon *m* OR porc *m* châtré ▪ US [pig] cochon *m*, porc *m* ▪ *fig* [greedy person] goinfre *mf* ▪ [dirty person] porc *m* ▪ **to go the whole ~** *inf* ne pas faire les choses à moitié ▪ **to live high on** OR **off the ~** US *inf* mener la grande vie.
◇ *vt inf* monopoliser ▪ **to ~ the limelight** accaparer OR monopoliser l'attention, se mettre en vedette ▪ **to ~ the middle of the road** prendre toute la route.

Hogmanay ['hɒgməneɪ] *n* Scotland *les fêtes de la Saint-Sylvestre en Écosse.*

hogtie ['hɒgtaɪ] *vt* US **to be ~d** être pieds et poings liés.

hogwash ['hɒgwɒʃ] *n (U)* **1.** *inf* [nonsense] bêtises *fpl*, imbécillités *fpl* **2.** [pigswill] eaux *fpl* grasses.

hogweed ['hɒgwi:d] *n* berce *f*.

hoick [hɔɪk] *vt inf* soulever ▪ **to ~ o.s. up onto a wall** se hisser sur un mur.

hoi polloi [,hɔɪpə'lɔɪ] *npl pej* **the ~** la populace.

hoist [hɔɪst] ◇ *vt* [sails, flag] hisser ▪ [load, person] lever, hisser ▪ **to be ~ with one's own petard** être pris à son propre piège.
◇ *n* **1.** [elevator] monte-charge *m* ▪ [block and tackle] palan *m* **2.** [upward push, pull] : **to give sb a ~ up** [lift] soulever qqn ; [pull] tirer qqn.

hoity-toity [,hɔɪtɪ'tɔɪtɪ] *adj inf pej* prétentieux, péteux ▪ **she's very ~** c'est une vraie bêcheuse.

hokey ['həʊkɪ] *adj* US US à l'eau de rose.

hokey cokey [-'kəʊkɪ] *n* UK *danse et chanson traditionnelles londoniennes.*

hokum ['həʊkəm] *n (U)* US *inf* [nonsense] fadaises *fpl*, foutaises *fpl* ▪ [sentimentality in play, film etc] niaiseries *fpl*, sentimentalisme *m*.

hold [həʊld] (*pret & pp* **held** [held]) ◇ *vt*

A.

1. [clasp, grasp] tenir ▪ to ~ sthg in one's hand [book, clothing, guitar] avoir qqch à la main ; [key, money] tenir qqch dans la main ▪ to ~ sthg with both hands tenir qqch à deux mains ▪ to ~ sb's hand *liter* & *fig* tenir la main à qqn ▪ to ~ hands se donner la main, se tenir (par) la main ▪ ~ my hand while we cross the street donne-moi la main pour traverser la rue ▪ to ~ sb in one's arms tenir qqn dans ses bras ▪ to ~ sb close *OR* tight serrer qqn contre soi ▪ to ~ one's nose se boucher le nez
2. [keep, sustain] : to ~ sb's attention retenir l'attention de qqn ▪ to ~ an audience tenir un auditoire ▪ to ~ one's serve [in tennis] défendre son service ▪ to ~ a seat POL [to be an MP] occuper un siège de député ; [to be re-elected] être réélu ▶ to ~ one's own tenir bon *OR* ferme ▪ she is well able to ~ her own elle sait se défendre ▪ to ~ the floor garder la parole
3. [have, possess - degree, permit, ticket] avoir, posséder ; [- job, position] avoir, occuper ▪ to ~ office [chairperson, deputy] être en fonction, remplir sa fonction ; [minister] détenir *OR* avoir un portefeuille ; [political party, president] être au pouvoir *OR* au gouvernement ▪ to ~ stock FIN détenir *OR* avoir des actions ▪ to ~ a record *liter* & *fig* détenir un record
4. [keep control or authority over] : the guerrillas held the bridge for several hours MIL les guérilleros ont tenu le pont plusieurs heures durant ▶ to ~ centre stage *fig* & THEAT occuper le centre de la scène ▪ ~ it!, ~ everything! [stop and wait] attendez! ; [stay still] arrêtez!, ne bougez plus! ▪ ~ your horses! *inf* pas si vite!
5. [reserve, set aside] retenir, réserver ▪ will the restaurant ~ the table for us? est-ce que le restaurant va nous garder la table?
6. [contain] contenir, tenir ▪ the hall ~s a maximum of 250 people la salle peut accueillir *OR* recevoir 250 personnes au maximum, il y a de la place pour 250 personnes au maximum dans cette salle ▪ to ~ one's drink bien supporter l'alcool
7. [have, exercise] exercer ▪ the subject ~s a huge fascination for some people le sujet exerce une énorme fascination sur certaines personnes
8. [have in store] réserver ▪ who knows what the future may ~? qui sait ce que nous réserve l'avenir?
9. [conserve, store] conserver, détenir ▪ COMPUT stocker ▪ the commands are held in the memory/in a temporary buffer les instructions sont gardées en mémoire/sont enregistrées dans une mémoire intermédiaire ▪ this photo ~s fond memories for me cette photo me rappelle de bons souvenirs
10. AUT : the new car ~s the road well la nouvelle voiture tient bien la route

B.

1. [maintain in position] tenir, maintenir ▪ her hair was held in place with hairpins des épingles (à cheveux) retenaient *OR* maintenaient ses cheveux ▪ ~ the picture a bit higher tenez le tableau un peu plus haut
2. [carry] tenir ▪ to ~ o.s. upright *OR* erect se tenir droit

C.

1. [confine, detain] détenir ▪ the police are ~ing him for questioning la police l'a gardé à vue pour l'interroger ▪ they're ~ing him for murder ils l'ont arrêté pour meurtre
2. [keep back, retain] retenir ▪ to ~ sthg in trust for sb tenir qqch par fidéicommis pour qqn ▪ the post office will ~ my mail for me while I'm away la poste gardera mon courrier pendant mon absence ▪ once she starts talking politics there's no ~ing her! *fig* dès qu'elle commence à parler politique, rien ne peut l'arrêter! ▪ one burger, ~ the mustard! *US* [in restaurant] un hamburger, sans moutarde!
3. [delay] : they held the plane another thirty minutes ils ont retenu l'avion au sol pendant encore trente minutes ▪ ~ all decisions on the project until I get back attendez mon retour pour prendre des décisions concernant le projet
4. [keep in check] : we have held costs to a minimum nous avons limité nos frais au minimum ▪ inflation has been held at the same level for several months le taux d'inflation est maintenu au même niveau depuis plusieurs mois ▪ they held their opponents to a goalless draw ils ont réussi à imposer le match nul

D.

1. [assert, claim] maintenir, soutenir ▪ [believe] croire, considérer ▪ the Constitution ~s that all men are free la Constitution stipule que tous les hommes sont libres ▪ he ~s strong beliefs on the subject of abortion il a de solides convictions en ce qui concerne l'avortement ▪ she ~s strong views on the subject elle a une opinion bien arrêtée sur le sujet
2. [consider, regard] tenir, considérer ▪ to ~ sb responsible for sthg tenir qqn pour responsable de qqch ▪ the president is to be held accountable for his actions le président doit répondre de ses actes ▪ to ~ sb in contempt mépriser *OR* avoir du mépris pour qqn ▪ to ~ sb in high esteem avoir beaucoup d'estime pour qqn, tenir qqn en haute estime
3. LAW [judge] juger

E.

1. [carry on, engage in - conversation, meeting] tenir ; [- party] donner ▪ [organize] organiser ▪ to ~ an election/elections procéder à une élection/à des élections ▪ the book fair is held in Frankfurt la foire du livre se tient *OR* a lieu à Francfort ▪ to ~ talks être en pourparlers
2. [continue without deviation] continuer ▪ we held our southerly course nous avons maintenu le cap au sud, nous avons continué notre route vers le sud ▪ to ~ a note MUS tenir une note
3. TELEC : will you ~ (the line)? voulez-vous patienter? ▪ ~ the line! ne quittez pas!

◇ *vi* **1.** [cling - person] se tenir, s'accrocher ▪ ~ fast!, ~ tight! accrochez-vous bien! ▪ their resolve held fast *OR* firm in the face of fierce opposition *fig* ils ont tenu bon face à une opposition acharnée ▪ [remain in place - nail, fastening] tenir bon **2.** [last - luck] durer ; [- weather] durer, se maintenir ▪ prices held at the same level as last year les prix se sont maintenus au même niveau que l'année dernière **3.** [remain valid - invitation, offer] tenir ; [- argument, theory] valoir, être valable ▪ to ~ good [invitation, offer] tenir ; [promises] tenir, valoir ; [argument, theory] rester valable ▪ the same ~s for Spain il en est de même pour l'Espagne **4.** [stay, remain] : ~ still! *inf* ne bougez pas!

◇ *n* **1.** [grasp, grip] prise *f* ▪ [in wrestling] prise *f* ▪ to catch *OR* to grab *OR* to seize *OR* to take ~ of sthg se saisir de *OR* saisir qqch ▪ grab (a) ~ of that towel tiens! prends cette serviette ▪ there was nothing for me to grab ~ of il n'y avait rien à quoi m'accrocher *OR* me cramponner ▪ get a good *OR* take a firm ~ on *OR* of the railing tenez-vous bien à la balustrade ▪ I still had ~ of his hand je le tenais toujours par la main ▪ to get ~ of sthg [find] se procurer *OR* trouver qqch ▪ where did you get ~ of that idea? où est-ce que tu es allé chercher cette idée? ▪ to get ~ of sb trouver qqn ▪ I've been trying to get ~ of you all week! je t'ai cherché toute la semaine! ▪ just wait till the newspapers get ~ of the story attendez un peu que les journaux s'emparent de la nouvelle ▪ you'd better keep ~ of the tickets tu ferais bien de garder les billets ▪ get a ~ on yourself ressaisis-toi, ne te laisse pas aller ▪ to take ~ [fire] prendre ; [idea] se répandre ▶ no ~s barred SPORT & *fig* tous les coups sont permis **2.** [controlling force or influence] prise *f*, influence *f* ▪ to have a ~ over sb avoir de l'influence sur qqn **3.** [in climbing] prise *f* **4.** [delay, pause] pause *f*, arrêt *m* ▪ the company has put a ~ on all new orders l'entreprise a suspendu *OR* gelé toutes les nouvelles commandes **5.** *US* [order to reserve] réservation *f* ▪ the association put a ~ on all the hotel rooms l'association a réservé toutes les chambres de l'hôtel **6.** [prison] prison *f* ▪ [cell] cellule *f* ▪ [fortress] place *f* forte **7.** [store - in plane] soute *f* ; [- in ship] cale *f* **8.** MUS point *m* d'orgue.

➤ **on hold** *adv phr* [gen - TELEC] en attente ▪ we've put the project on ~ nous avons mis le projet en attente ▪ the operator kept me on ~ for ten minutes le standardiste m'a mis en attente pendant dix minutes.

➤ **hold against** *vt sep* : to ~ sthg against sb en vouloir à qqn de qqch ▪ his collaboration with the enemy will be held against him sa collaboration avec l'ennemi lui sera préjudiciable.

➤ **hold back** ◇ *vt sep* **1.** [control, restrain - animal, person] retenir, tenir ; [- crowd, enemy forces] contenir ; [- anger, laughter, tears] retenir, réprimer ; [- inflation] contenir **2.** [keep - money, supplies] retenir ▪ *fig* [- information, truth] cacher, taire ▪ she's ~ing something back from me elle me cache quelque chose **3.** *US* SCH : they held her back a year ils lui ont fait redoubler une classe, ils l'ont fait redoubler **4.** [prevent progress of] empêcher de progresser ▪ his difficulties with maths are ~ing him back ses difficultés en maths l'empêchent de progresser.

◇ *vi insep* ***liter*** [stay back] rester en arrière ■ ***fig*** [refrain] se retenir ■ **he has held back from making a commitment** il s'est abstenu de s'engager ■ **the president held back before sending in the army** le président a hésité avant d'envoyer les troupes ■ **don't ~ back, tell me everything** vas-y, dis-moi tout.

◆ **hold down** *vt sep* **1.** [keep in place - paper, carpet] maintenir en place ; [- person] forcer à rester par terre, maintenir au sol **2.** [keep to limit] restreindre, limiter ■ **they're ~ing unemployment down to 4%** ils maintiennent le taux de chômage à 4 % ■ **to ~ prices down** empêcher les prix de monter, empêcher la montée des prix **3.** [employee] : **to ~ down a job** garder un emploi ■ **he's never managed to ~ down a job** il n'a jamais pu garder un emploi bien longtemps.

◆ **hold forth** *vi insep* pérorer, disserter.

◆ **hold in** *vt sep* **1.** [stomach] rentrer **2.** [emotion] retenir ■ [anger] contenir.

◆ **hold off** ◇ *vt sep* **1.** [keep at distance] tenir à distance *OR* éloigné ■ **they managed to ~ off the attack** ils ont réussi à repousser l'attaque ■ **I can't ~ the reporters off any longer** je ne peux plus faire attendre *OR* patienter les journalistes **2.** [delay, put off] remettre à plus tard ■ **he held off going to see the doctor until May** il a attendu le mois de mai pour aller voir le médecin.

◇ *vi insep* **1.** [rain] : **at least the rain held off** au moins il n'a pas plu **2.** [abstain] s'abstenir.

◆ **hold on** ◇ *vi insep* **1.** [grasp, grip] tenir bien, s'accrocher ■ **to ~ on to sthg** bien tenir qqch, s'accrocher à qqch, se cramponner à qqch **2.** [keep possession of] garder ■ **~ on to this contract for me** [keep it] garde-moi ce contrat ■ **all politicians try to ~ on to power** tous les hommes politiques essaient de rester au pouvoir **3.** [continue, persevere] tenir, tenir le coup ■ **I can't ~ on much longer** je ne peux pas tenir (le coup) beaucoup plus longtemps **4.** [wait] attendre ■ [stop] arrêter ■ **TELEC : ~ on please!** ne quittez pas! ■ **I had to ~ on for several minutes** j'ai dû patienter plusieurs minutes.

◇ *vt sep* [maintain in place] tenir *OR* maintenir en place.

◆ **hold out** ◇ *vi insep* **1.** [last - supplies, stocks] durer ■ **will the car ~ out till we get home?** la voiture tiendra-t-elle (le coup) jusqu'à ce qu'on rentre? **2.** [refuse to yield] tenir bon, tenir le coup ■ **the management held out against any suggested changes** la direction a refusé tous les changements proposés.

◇ *vt sep* [extend, offer] tendre ■ **to ~ out one's hand to sb** ***liter & fig*** tendre la main à qqn.

◇ *vt insep* [offer] offrir ■ **I can't ~ out any promise of improvement** je ne peux promettre aucune amélioration ■ **the doctors ~ out little hope for him** les médecins ont peu d'espoir pour lui.

◆ **hold out for** *vt insep* exiger ■ **the workers held out for a shorter working week** les ouvriers réclamaient une semaine de travail plus courte.

◆ **hold out on** *vt insep* ***inf*** **you're ~ing out on me!** tu me caches quelque chose!

◆ **hold over** *vt sep* **1.** [position] tenir au-dessus de ■ **they ~ the threat of redundancy over their workers** ***fig*** ils maintiennent la menace de licenciement sur leurs ouvriers **2.** [postpone] remettre, reporter ■ **we'll ~ these items over until the next meeting** on va remettre ces questions à la prochaine réunion **3.** [retain] retenir, garder ■ **they're ~ing the show over for another month** ils vont laisser le spectacle à l'affiche encore un mois.

◆ **hold to** ◇ *vt insep* [promise, tradition] s'en tenir à, rester fidèle à ■ [decision] maintenir, s'en tenir à.

◇ *vt sep* : **we held him to his promise** nous lui avons fait tenir parole ■ **if I win, I'll buy you lunch – I'll ~ you to that!** si je gagne, je t'invite à déjeuner – je te prends au mot!

◆ **hold together** *vt sep* [book, car] maintenir ■ [community, family] maintenir l'union de.

◆ **hold up** ◇ *vt sep* **1.** [lift, raise] lever, élever ■ **I held up my hand** j'ai levé la main ■ **~ the picture up to the light** tenez la photo à contre-jour ■ **she felt she would never be able to ~ her head up again** ***fig*** elle pensait qu'elle ne pourrait plus jamais marcher la tête haute **2.** [support] soutenir ■ **my trousers were held up with safety pins** mon pantalon était maintenu par des épingles de sûreté **3.** [present as example] : **they were held up as an example of efficient local government** on les présentaient comme un exemple de gouvernement local compétent ■ **to ~ sb up to ridicule** tourner qqn en ridicule **4.** [delay] retarder ■ [stop] arrêter ■ **the accident held up traffic for an hour** l'accident a bloqué la circulation pendant une heure ■ **I was held up** j'ai été retenu ■ **the project was held up for lack of funds** [before it started] le projet a été mis en attente faute de financement ; [after it started] le projet a été interrompu faute de financement **5.** [rob] faire une attaque à main armée ■ **to ~ up a bank** faire un hold-up dans une banque.

◇ *vi insep* [clothing, equipment] tenir ■ [supplies] tenir, durer ■ [weather] se maintenir ■ **the car held up well during the trip** la voiture a bien tenu le coup pendant le voyage.

◆ **hold with** *vt insep* ***UK*** [agree with] être d'accord avec ■ [approve of] approuver ■ **his mother doesn't ~ with private schools** sa mère est contre *OR* désapprouve les écoles privées.

---

holdall ['həʊldɔːl] *n* ***UK*** (sac *m*) fourre-tout *m inv.*

holder ['həʊldəʳ] *n* **1.** [for lamp, plastic cup etc] support *m* **2.** [person - of ticket] détenteur *m*, - trice *f* ; [- of passport, post, diploma] titulaire *mf* ■ SPORT [- of record, cup] détenteur *m*, - trice *f* ; [- of title] détenteur *m*, - trice *f*, tenant *m*, - e *f* ■ FIN [- of stock] porteur *m*, - euse *f*, détenteur *m*, - trice *f*.

holding ['həʊldɪŋ] ◇ *n* **1.** [of meeting] tenue *f* **2.** [in boxing] : **~ is against the rules** il est contraire au règlement de tenir son adversaire **3.** [land] propriété *f* **4.** FIN participation *f* ■ **~s** [lands] propriétés *fpl*, terres *fpl* ; [stocks] participation *f*, portefeuille *m*.

◇ *comp* : **~ company** FIN (société *f* en) holding *m* ■ **~ operation** opération *f* de maintien ■ **we were in a ~ pattern over Heathrow for two hours** AERON nous avons eu une attente de deux heures au-dessus de Heathrow.

hold-up *n* **1.** [robbery] hold-up *m*, vol *m* à main armée **2.** [delay - on road, railway track etc] ralentissement *m* ; [- in production, departure etc] retard *m*.

◆ **hold-ups** *npl* [stockings] bas *mpl* autofixants.

hole [həʊl] ◇ *n* **1.** [in the ground] trou *m* ■ [in wall, roof etc] trou *m* ■ [in clouds] éclaircie *f* ■ **his socks were full of** *OR* **in ~s** ses chaussettes étaient pleines de trous ■ **to wear a ~ in sthg** faire un trou à qqch ■ **to make a ~ in one's savings/a bottle of whisky** ***fig*** bien entamer ses économies/une bouteille de whisky ■ **money burns a ~ in my pocket** l'argent me file entre les doigts ■ **to pick ~s in an argument** trouver des failles à une argumentation ● **a ~ in the wall** un café *OR* restaurant minuscule ; [cash dispenser] un distributeur de billets ■ **I need that like a ~ in the head** ***inf*** c'est vraiment la dernière chose dont j'aie besoin ■ **you're talking through a ~ in your head** ***inf*** tu racontes n'importe quoi ■ **that's filled a ~!** ***inf*** ça m'a bien calé! **2.** ***inf pej*** [boring place] trou *m* **3.** ***inf*** [tricky situation] pétrin *m* ■ **to be in a ~** être dans le pétrin **4.** SPORT [in golf] trou *m* ■ **to get a ~ in one** faire un trou en un ■ **an 18-~ (golf) course** un parcours de 18 trous.

◇ *vt* **1.** [make hole in] trouer **2.** [in golf] : **to ~ the ball** faire le trou.

◇ *vi* **1.** [sock, stocking] se trouer **2.** [in golf] faire le trou.

◆ **hole up** ◇ *vi insep* **1.** [animal] se terrer **2.** ***inf*** [hide] se planquer.

◇ *vt sep (usu passive)* : **they're ~d up in a hotel** ils se planquent *OR* ils sont planqués dans un hôtel.

hole-and-corner *adj* ***inf*** [meeting, love affair etc] clandestin, secret, - ète *f*.

hole in the heart *n* malformation *f* du cœur ■ **a baby born with a ~** un enfant bleu.

◆ **hole-in-the-heart** *adj* [baby] bleu ■ **a hole-in-the-heart operation** une opération d'une malformation du cœur.

hole punch *n* perforatrice *f*.

holey ['həʊlɪ] *adj* troué, plein de trous.

holiday ['hɒlɪdeɪ] ◇ *n* **1.** ***UK*** [period without work] vacances *fpl* ■ **Christmas ~** vacances de Noël ■ **everyone is getting ready for the Christmas ~s** tout le monde prépare les fêtes ■ **summer ~** *OR* **~s** vacances d'été ; SCH grandes vacances ■ **on ~** en vacances ■ **to go on ~** aller *OR* partir en vacances ■ **to go on a camping ~** aller passer ses vacances en camping ■ **we went to Greece for our ~s last year** nous sommes allés passer

nos vacances en Grèce l'année dernière ▪ **to take a ~/two months' ~** prendre des vacances/deux mois de vacances ▪ **how much** *OR* **how long a ~ do you get?** combien de vacances as-tu? ▪ **~ with pay, paid ~s** congés *mpl* payés ▪ **I need** *OR* **could do with a ~** j'ai besoin de vacances ▪ **take a ~ from the housework** oublie un peu les travaux ménagers **2.** [day off] jour *m* de congé ▪ **tomorrow is a ~** demain c'est férié.
◇ *comp* [mood, feeling, destination] de vacances ▪ [pay] versé pendant les vacances ▪ **the ~ traffic** la circulation des départs en vacances ▪ **the ~ rush has started** la folie *OR* cohue des départs en vacances a commencé.
◇ *vi UK* passer les vacances.

holiday camp *n UK centre de vacances familial (avec animations et activités diverses).*

holiday home *n UK* maison *f* de vacances, résidence *f* secondaire.

holidaymaker ['hɒlɪdeɪ,meɪkəʳ] *n UK* vacancier *m*, - ère *f*.

holiday resort *n UK* lieu *m* de vacances *OR* de séjour.

holiday season *n UK* saison *f* des vacances.

holiday village *n UK* village *m* de vacances.

holier-than-thou ['həʊlɪəðən'ðaʊ] *adj pej* [attitude, tone, person] moralisateur.

holiness ['həʊlɪnɪs] *n* sainteté *f* ▪ **His/Your Holiness** Sa/Votre Sainteté.

holistic [həʊ'lɪstɪk] *adj* MED & PHILOS holistique.

Holland ['hɒlənd] *pr n* [country] Hollande *f*, Pays-Bas *mpl* ▪ **in ~** en Hollande, aux Pays-Bas.

hollandaise sauce [,hɒlən'deɪz-] *n* sauce *f* hollandaise.

holler ['hɑːlr] *inf* ◇ *vi* brailler, beugler.
◇ *vt* brailler.
◇ *n* braillement *m* ▪ **to give** *OR* **to let out a ~** brailler.
◆ **holler out** *vi insep & vt sep inf* = **holler.**

hollow ['hɒləʊ] ◇ *adj* **1.** [not solid - tree, container] creux ▪ **to have a ~ feeling in one's stomach** avoir une sensation de vide dans l'estomac ▶ **to feel ~** [hungry] avoir le ventre *OR* l'estomac creux ▪ **you must have ~ legs!** *inf* [able to eat a lot] tu dois avoir le ver solitaire! ; [able to drink a lot] qu'est-ce que tu peux boire!, tu as une sacrée descente! **2.** [sunken - eyes, cheeks] creux, cave **3.** [empty - sound] creux, caverneux ; [- laugh, laughter] faux, fausse *f*, forcé ▪ **in a ~ voice** d'une voix éteinte **4.** [worthless - promise, words] vain ▪ **it was a ~ victory for her** cette victoire lui semblait dérisoire.
◇ *adv* : **to sound ~** [tree, wall] sonner creux ; [laughter, excuse, promise] sonner faux.
◇ *n* **1.** [in tree] creux *m*, cavité *f* **2.** [in ground] enfoncement *m*, dénivellation *f* **3.** [in hand, back] creux *m*.
◇ *vt* creuser.
◆ **hollow out** *vt sep* creuser.

hollow-eyed *adj* aux yeux caves *OR* enfoncés.

hollowness ['hɒləʊnɪs] *n* **1.** [of tree] creux *m*, cavité *f* **2.** [of features] : **the ~ of his eyes** ses yeux enfoncés ▪ **the ~ of his cheeks** ses joues creuses **3.** [of sound] timbre *m* caverneux ▪ [of laughter] fausseté *f* **4.** [of promise, excuse] fausseté *f*, manque *m* de sincérité.

holly ['hɒlɪ] ◇ *n* [tree, leaves] houx *m*.
◇ *comp* : **~ berry** baie *f* de houx, cenelle *f* ▪ **~ tree** houx *m*.

hollyhock ['hɒlɪhɒk] *n* rose *f* trémière.

holocaust ['hɒləkɔːst] *n* holocauste *m* ▪ **the Holocaust** l'Holocauste.

hologram ['hɒləgræm] *n* hologramme *m*.

holograph ['hɒləgræf] ◇ *n* document *m* olographe *OR* holographe.
◇ *adj* olographe, holographe.

holography [hɒ'lɒgrəfɪ] *n* holographie *f*.

hols [hɒlz] *npl UK inf* SCH vacances *fpl*.

Holstein ['hɒlstaɪn] *n US* [cow] frisonne *f*.

holster ['həʊlstəʳ] *n* [for gun - on waist, shoulder] étui *m* de revolver ; [- on saddle] fonte *f* ▪ [for piece of equipment] étui *m*.

holy ['həʊlɪ] (*comp* **holier**, *superl* **holiest**) ◇ *adj* **1.** [sacred - bread, water] bénit ; [- place, ground, day] saint ▪ **to swear by all that is ~** jurer par tous les saints **2.** [devout] saint **3.** *inf* [as intensifier] : **that child is a ~ terror** [mischievous] cet enfant est un vrai démon ▪ **to have a ~ fear of sthg** avoir une sainte peur de qqch ▶ **~ smoke!, ~ mackerel!, ~ cow!** mince alors!, ça alors!, Seigneur!
◇ *n* : **the Holy of Holies** RELIG le saint des saints ; *hum & fig* [inner sanctum] sanctuaire *m*, antre *m* sacré ; [special place] lieu *m* saint.

Holy Bible *n* : **the ~** la Sainte Bible.

Holy City *n* : **the ~** la Ville sainte.

Holy Communion *n* la Sainte Communion ▪ **to take ~** communier, recevoir la Sainte Communion.

Holy Family *n* : **the ~** la Sainte Famille.

Holy Father *n* : **the ~** le Saint-Père.

Holy Ghost *n* : **the ~** le Saint-Esprit, l'Esprit saint.

Holy Grail *n* : **the ~** le (Saint) Graal.

Holy Joe *n inf* bigot *m*.

Holy Land *n* : **the ~** la Terre sainte.

holy matrimony *n* les liens sacrés du mariage.

holy orders *npl* ordres *mpl* ▪ **to take ~** entrer dans les ordres.

Holy Roman Empire *n* : **the ~** le Saint-Empire romain.

Holy Rood *n* : **the ~** la Sainte Croix.

Holyrood Palace ['hɒlɪruːd-] *pr n palais à Édimbourg, propriété de la famille royale.*

Holy Scripture *n* l'Écriture sainte, les Saintes Écritures.

Holy See *n* : **the ~** le Saint-Siège.

Holy Sepulchre *n* : **the ~** le Saint-Sépulcre.

Holy Spirit = **Holy Ghost.**

Holy Synod *n* : **the ~** le saint-synode.

Holy Trinity *n* : **the ~** la Sainte Trinité.

holy war *n* guerre *f* sainte.

Holy Week *n* la Semaine sainte.

Holy Writ *n* l'Écriture sainte, les Saintes Écritures.

homage ['hɒmɪdʒ] *n* hommage *m* ▪ **to pay** *OR* **to do ~ to sb, to do sb ~** rendre hommage à qqn.

homburg ['hɒmbɜːg] *n* chapeau *m* mou, feutre *m* souple.

home [həʊm] ◇ *n* **1.** [one's house] maison *f* ▪ [more subjectively] chez-soi *m inv* ▪ **a ~ from ~** un second chez-soi ▪ **I left ~ at 16** j'ai quitté la maison à 16 ans ▪ **to have a ~ of one's own** avoir un foyer *OR* un chez-soi ▪ **his ~ is in Nice** il habite Nice ▪ **New York will always be ~ for me!** c'est toujours à New York que je me sentirai chez moi! ▪ **emigrants came to make their ~s in Canada** des émigrés sont venus s'installer au Canada ▪ **to give sb a ~** recueillir qqn chez soi ▪ **they have a lovely ~!** c'est très agréable chez eux! ▶ **at ~** chez soi, à la maison ▪ **make yourself at ~** faites comme chez vous ▪ **he made himself at ~ in the chair** il s'est mis à l'aise dans le fauteuil ▪ **to be** *OR* **to feel at ~ with** se sentir à l'aise avec ▪ **I work out of** *OR* **at ~** je travaille à domicile *OR* chez moi ▪ **there's no place like ~** *prov* on n'est vraiment bien que chez soi ▪ **~ is where the heart is** *prov* où le cœur aime, là est le foyer
2. [family unit] foyer *m* ▪ ADMIN habitation *f*, logement *m* ▪ **the father left ~** le père a abandonné le foyer ▪ **are you having problems at ~?** est-ce que tu as des problèmes chez toi? ▪ **he comes from a good ~** il vient d'une famille comme il faut
3. [native land] patrie *f*, pays *m* natal ▪ **it's the same at ~** c'est la même chose chez nous *OR* dans notre pays ‖ *fig* **this discussion is getting a bit close to ~!** on aborde un sujet dangereux! ▪ **let's look at a situation closer to** *OR* **nearer ~** examinons une situation qui nous concerne plus directement ▪ **Kentucky, the ~ of bourbon** Kentucky, le pays du bourbon ▪ **the ~ of jazz** le berceau du jazz

4. BOT & ZOOL habitat *m*
5. [mental hospital] maison *f* de repos ■ [old people's home] maison *f* de retraite ■ [children's home] foyer *m* pour enfants
6. GAMES & SPORT [finishing line] arrivée *f* ■ [on board game] case *f* départ ■ [goal] but *m* ■ **they play better at ~** ils jouent mieux sur leur terrain ■ **to be at ~** to recevoir ■ **the Rams meet the Braves at ~** les Rams jouent à domicile contre les Braves.
<> *adv* **1.** [to or at one's house] chez soi, à la maison ■ **to go** *OR* **to get ~** rentrer (chez soi *OR* à la maison) ■ **to see sb ~** raccompagner qqn jusque chez lui/elle ◐ **it's nothing to write ~ about** *inf* il n'y a pas de quoi en faire un plat ■ **~ and dry** *UK*, **~ free** *US inf* sauvé
2. [from abroad] au pays natal, au pays ■ **to send sb ~** rapatrier qqn
3. [all the way] à fond ■ **to drive a nail ~** enfoncer un clou jusqu'au bout ■ **the remark really went ~** le commentaire a fait mouche ■ **to bring sthg ~ to sb** faire comprendre *OR* voir qqch à qqn.
<> *adj* **1.** [concerning family, household - life] de famille, familial ; [- for family consumption] familial, à usage familial ■ **~ comforts** confort *m* du foyer
2. [to, for house] à *OR* pour la maison ■ **~ visit/delivery** visite *f* /livraison *f* à domicile ■ **~ banking** la banque à domicile ■ **~ decorating** décoration *f* intérieure ■ **~ cleaning products** produits *mpl* ménagers
3. [national - gen] national, du pays ; [- market, policy, sales] intérieur
4. SPORT [team - national] national ; [- local] local ■ **the ~ team today is...** l'équipe qui reçoit aujourd'hui est... ■ **~ game** match *m* à domicile.
<> *vi* [person, animal] revenir *OR* rentrer chez soi ■ [pigeon] revenir au colombier.
◆ **home in on** *vt insep* **1.** [subj: missile] se diriger (automatiquement) sur *OR* vers ■ [proceed towards - goal] se diriger vers ■ *fig* mettre le cap sur
2. [direct attention to - problem, solution] mettre l'accent sur ; [- difficulty, question] viser, cerner.
◆ **home on to** = **home in on**.

home address *n* [on form] domicile *m* (permanent) ■ [not business address] adresse *f* personnelle.

home automation *n* domotique *f*.

homebound ['həʊmbaʊnd] *adj* **1.** [going home] sur le chemin du retour **2.** [confined to home] obligé de rester à la maison ■ [of sick people] qui garde la chambre.

homeboy ['həʊmbɔɪ] *n US* **he's a ~** [from our town] c'est un gars de chez nous ; [in our gang] c'est un des nôtres.

home brew *n* [beer] bière *f* faite à la maison ■ [wine] vin *m* fait à la maison.

homecoming ['həʊm,kʌmɪŋ] *n* [to family] retour *m* au foyer *OR* à la maison ■ [to country] retour *m* au pays ■ **'The Homecoming'** *Pinter* 'le Retour'.
◆ **Homecoming** *n US* SCH & UNIV *fête donnée en l'honneur de l'équipe de football d'une université ou d'une école et à laquelle sont invités les anciens élèves.*

home computer *n* ordinateur *m* personnel, micro-ordinateur *m*.

home cooking *n* cuisine *f* familiale.

Home Counties *pr npl* : **the ~** *l'ensemble des comtés limitrophes de Londres.*

home country *n* pays *m* natal ■ **the ~** le pays.

home economics, home ec *US inf n (U)* économie *f* domestique.

home front *n* **1.** [during war] arrière *m* ■ **on the ~** à l'arrière **2.** [in the home country] : **what's the news on the ~?** quelles sont les nouvelles du pays? **3.** [at home] : **how are things on the ~?** comment ça va à la maison?

home ground *n* **1.** : **to be on ~** [near home] être en pays de connaissance ; *fig* [familiar subject] être sur son terrain **2.** SPORT : **our ~** notre terrain ■ **when they play at their ~** quand ils jouent sur leur terrain, quand ils reçoivent.

homegrown [,həʊm'grəʊn] *adj* [not foreign] du pays ■ [from own garden] du jardin.

Home Guard *n* : **the ~** *les volontaires pour la défense du territoire en Grande-Bretagne en 1940-45, 1951-57.*

home help *n UK* aide *f* ménagère.

homeland ['həʊmlænd] *n* **1.** [native country] patrie *f* **2.** [South African political territory] homeland *m*.

homeless ['həʊmlɪs] <> *adj* sans foyer ■ [pet] abandonné, sans foyer.
<> *npl* : **the ~** les sans-abri *mpl*.

homelessness ['həʊmlɪsnɪs] *n* : **the problem of ~** le problème des sans-abri.

home life *n* vie *f* de famille.

home loan *n* prêt *m* immobilier.

home-loving *adj* casanier.

homely ['həʊmlɪ] (*comp* **homelier**, *superl* **homeliest**) *adj* **1.** [unpretentious] simple, modeste **2.** [kind] aimable, plein de bonté **3.** *US* [plain, unattractive - person] peu attrayant.

homemade [,həʊm'meɪd] *adj* **1.** [made at home] fait à la maison *(inv)* ■ **a ~ bomb** une bombe de fabrication artisanale **2.** [made on premises] maison *(inv)*, fait maison ■ **~ apple pie** [on menu] tarte *f* aux pommes (fait) maison.

homemaker ['həʊm,meɪkə] *n* femme *f* au foyer.

home movie *n* film *m* d'amateur.

Home Office *n* : **the ~** *le ministère britannique de l'Intérieur.*

homeopath ['həʊmɪəʊpæθ] *n* homéopathe *mf*.

homeopathic [,həʊmɪəʊ'pæθɪk] *adj* homéopathique ■ **a ~ doctor** un (médecin) homéopathe.

homeopathy [,həʊmɪ'ɒpəθɪ] *n* homéopathie *f*.

homeowner ['həʊm,əʊnəʳ] *n* propriétaire *mf*.

home page *n* COMPUT page *f* d'accueil.

Homer ['həʊməʳ] *pr n* Homère.

Homeric [həʊ'merɪk] *adj* homérique.

homeroom ['həʊm,ru:m] *n US* **1.** [place] *salle où l'on fait l'appel* **2.** [group] *élèves rassemblés pour l'appel.*

home rule *n* autonomie *f*.
◆ **Home Rule** *n mouvement pour l'autonomie de l'Irlande.*

HOME RULE

Régime d'autonomie revendiqué par l'Irlande entre 1870 et 1914. Le projet de loi fut refusé à plusieurs reprises par les Communes mais, finalement, une loi sur l'autonomie fut votée en 1914, proposant la création d'un Parlement composé de deux chambres chargées des affaires locales. La mise en vigueur de cette loi, déjà compromise par l'opposition des protestants unionistes de l'Ulster, fut reportée lorsque la Première Guerre mondiale éclata. À la suite de l'insurrection nationaliste de 1916, les partisans du *Home Rule* revendiquèrent l'autonomie totale. Après deux ans de guerre civile, l'Irlande obtint son autonomie en 1921 et devint l'État libre d'Irlande, le nord-est du pays restant lié à la Grande-Bretagne.

home run *n* **1.** [in baseball] *coup de batte qui permet au batteur de marquer un point en faisant un tour complet en une seule fois* **2.** [last leg of trip] dernière étape *f* du circuit.

Home Secretary *n* ministre *m* de l'Intérieur en Grande-Bretagne.

home shopping *n* [by telephone, computer] téléachat *m* ■ [by post] achat *m* par correspondance.

homesick ['həʊmsɪk] *adj* nostalgique ■ **to be ~** avoir le mal du pays ■ **to be ~ for sb** s'ennuyer de qqn ■ **to be ~ for sthg** avoir la nostalgie de qqch.

homesickness ['həʊm,sɪknɪs] *n* mal *m* du pays.

homespun ['həʊmspʌn] <> *adj* **1.** [wool] filé à la maison, de fabrication domestique ▪ [cloth] de homespun **2.** [simple] simple, sans recherche.
<> *n* homespun *m*.

homestead ['həʊmsted] <> *n* **1.** *US* HIST *terre dont la propriété est attribuée à un colon sous réserve qu'il y réside et l'exploite* **2.** [buildings and land] propriété *f* ▪ [farm] ferme *f* **3.** *US* [birthplace] : **he's returning to the ~** il rentre au pays.
<> *vt US* [acquire] acquérir ▪ [settle] s'installer à, coloniser.

home straight, home stretch *n* SPORT & *fig* dernière ligne *f* droite ▪ **they're on** *OR* **in the ~** ils sont dans la dernière ligne droite.

home town *n* **1.** [of birth] ville *f* natale **2.** [of upbringing] : **his ~** la ville où il a grandi.

home truth *n* vérité *f* désagréable ▪ **to tell sb a few ~s** dire ses (quatre) vérités à qqn.

homeward ['həʊmwəd] <> *adj* du retour ▪ **the ~ trip** le (voyage de) retour.
<> *adv* = **homewards**.

homeward-bound *adj* [commuters] qui rentre chez soi ▪ [ship] sur le chemin du retour ▪ **to be homeward bound** être sur le chemin du retour.

homewards ['həʊmwədz] *adv* **1.** [to house] vers la maison **2.** [to homeland] vers la patrie ▪ **to be ~ bound** prendre le chemin du retour ▪ **the plane flew ~** l'avion faisait route vers sa base.

home waters *npl* [territorial] eaux *fpl* territoriales ▪ [near home port] eaux *fpl* voisines du port d'attache.

homework ['həʊmwɜːk] <> *n (U)* SCH devoirs *mpl* (à la maison) ▪ [research] travail *m* préparatoire ▪ **the minister hadn't done his ~** le ministre n'avait pas préparé son sujet.
<> *comp* : **a ~ exercise** un devoir (à la maison).

homeworker ['həʊm,wɜːkəʳ] *n* travailleur *m*, - euse *f* à domicile.

homicidal ['hɒmɪsaɪdl] *adj* LAW homicide ▪ **a ~ maniac** un maniaque à tendances homicides *OR* meurtrières.

homicide ['hɒmɪsaɪd] *n* LAW **1.** [act] homicide *m* ▪ **accidental ~** homicide par imprudence ▪ **justifiable ~** homicide par légitime défense **2.** [person] homicide *mf*.

homily ['hɒmɪlɪ] (*pl* **homilies**) *n* **1.** RELIG homélie *f* **2.** *pej* sermon *m*, homélie *f* ▪ **to read sb a ~** sermonner qqn.

homing ['həʊmɪŋ] *adj* [pre-programmed] autoguidé ▪ [heat-seeking] à tête chercheuse ▪ **~ device** mécanisme *m* d'autoguidage ▪ **~ guidance systems** systèmes *mpl* d'autoguidage ▪ **~ missile** missile *m* à tête chercheuse.

homing pigeon *n* pigeon *m* voyageur.

hominy ['hɒmɪnɪ] *n US* bouillie *f* de semoule de maïs.

homo△ ['həʊməʊ] *pej* <> *n* pédé△ *m*, homo *mf*.
<> *adj* pédé△, homo.

homoeopath *etc* ['həʊmɪəʊpæθ] = **homeopath**.

homogeneous [,hɒmə'dʒiːnjəs] *adj* homogène.

homogenize, ise [hə'mɒdʒənaɪz] *vt* homogénéiser, homogénéifier ▪ **~d milk** lait *m* homogénéisé.

homogenous [hə'mɒdʒənɪs] = **homogeneous**.

homogeny [hə'mɒdʒənɪ] *n ressemblance due à un ancêtre génétique commun*.

homograph ['hɒməgrɑːf] *n* LING homographe *m*.

homologue ['hɒməlɒg] *n* BIOL & CHEM homologue *m*.

homonym ['hɒmənɪm] *n* homonyme *m*.

homonymy [hɒ'mɒnɪmɪ] *n* homonymie *f*.

homophobe ['həʊməʊ,fəʊb] *n* homophobe *mf*.

homophobia [,həʊməʊ'fəʊbjə] *n* homophobie *f*.

homophobic [,həʊməʊ'fəʊbɪk] *adj* homophobe.

homophone ['hɒməfəʊn] *n* LING homophone *m*.

homophony [hɒ'mɒfənɪ] (*pl* **homophonies**) *n* MUS homophonie *f*.

Homo sapiens [,həʊməʊ'sæpɪenz] *n* homo sapiens *m*.

homosexual [,hɒmə'sekʃʊəl] <> *n* homosexuel *m*, - elle *f*.
<> *adj* homosexuel.

homosexuality [,hɒmə,sekʃʊ'ælətɪ] *n* homosexualité *f*.

hon [hʌn] *n US inf* chéri *m*, - e *f*.

hon. *written abbr of* **honorary**.

Hon. *written abbr of* **honourable**.

Honduran [hɒn'djʊərən] <> *n* Hondurien *m*, - enne *f*.
<> *adj* hondurien.

Honduras [hɒn'djʊərəs] *pr n* Honduras *m*.

hone [həʊn] <> *vt* **1.** [sharpen] aiguiser, affûter, affiler ▪ [re-sharpen] repasser **2.** [refine - analysis, thought] affiner ▪ **finely ~d arguments** arguments *mpl* d'une grande finesse.
<> *n* pierre *f* à aiguiser.
◆ **hone down** *vt sep* [reduce] tailler ▪ [make slim] faire maigrir.

honest ['ɒnɪst] <> *adj* **1.** [not deceitful] honnête, probe ▪ [trustworthy] intègre ▪ **the ~ truth** la pure vérité ▪ **they are ~ workers** ce sont des ouvriers consciencieux ❯ **he's (as) ~ as the day is long** il n'y a pas plus honnête que lui **2.** [decent, upright] droit ▪ [virtuous] honnête ▪ **he's an ~ bloke** *UK inf* c'est un brave type ❯ **he's decided to make an ~ woman of her** *hum* il a décidé de régulariser sa situation **3.** [not fraudulent] honnête ▪ **an ~ day's work** une bonne journée de travail ▪ **they just want to make an ~ profit** ils ne veulent qu'un profit légitime ▪ **to earn an ~ living** gagner honnêtement sa vie **4.** [frank - face] franc, franche *f*, sincère ▪ **to be ~, I don't think it will work** à vrai dire, je ne crois pas que ça marchera ▪ **give me your ~ opinion** dites-moi sincèrement ce que vous en pensez.
<> *adv inf* : **I didn't mean it, ~!** je plaisantais, je te le jure! ▪ **~ to goodness** *OR* **to God!** parole d'honneur!

honest broker *n UK* médiateur *m*, - trice *f* neutre.

honestly ['ɒnɪstlɪ] *adv* honnêtement ▪ **quite ~, I don't see the problem** très franchement, je ne vois pas le problème ▪ **it's not my fault, ~!** ce n'est pas ma faute, je te le jure! ▪ **~, the way some people behave!** franchement *OR* vraiment, il y en a qui exagèrent!

honest-to-goodness *adj* : **a cup of ~ English tea** une tasse de bon thé anglais.

honesty ['ɒnɪstɪ] *n* **1.** [truthfulness - of person] honnêteté *f* ; [- of text, words] véracité *f*, exactitude *f* ▪ **~ is the best policy** *prov* l'honnêteté paie toujours **2.** [incorruptibility] intégrité *f* ▪ **we have never doubted his ~** nous n'avons jamais douté de son intégrité **3.** [upright conduct] droiture *f* **4.** [sincerity] sincérité *f*, franchise *f* **5.** BOT monnaie-du-pape *f*.
◆ **in all honesty** *adv phr* en toute sincérité.

honey ['hʌnɪ] (*pl* **honies**) <> *n* **1.** miel *m* ▪ **clear/wildflower ~** miel liquide/de fleurs sauvages ▮ *fig* miel *m*, douceur *f* **2.** *US inf* [sweetheart] chou *m* ▪ [addressing man] mon chéri ▪ [addressing woman] ma chérie ▪ **a ~ of a dress** une super robe.
<> *adj* miellé ▪ **~ cake** gâteau *m* d'épices au miel.

honeybee ['hʌnɪbiː] *n* abeille *f*.

honeycomb ['hʌnɪkəʊm] <> *n* **1.** [in wax] rayon *m* *OR* gâteau *m* de miel **2.** [material] structure *f* alvéolaire **3.** [pattern] nid *m* d'abeille ▪ TEX nid *m* d'abeille **4.** METALL soufflure *f*.
<> *vt* **1.** [surface] cribler **2.** [interior] miner ▪ **the hills are ~ed with secret tunnels** les collines sont truffées de passages secrets.

honeydew melon *n* melon *m* d'hiver *OR* d'Espagne.

honeyed ['hʌnɪd] *adj fig* mielleux.

honeymoon ['hʌnɪmu:n] ◇ *n* **1.** [period] lune *f* de miel ■ [trip] voyage *m* de noces ■ **they're on ~** ils sont en voyage de noces **2.** *fig* état *m* de grâce ■ **the new Prime Minister's ~ is over** l'état de grâce du nouveau Premier ministre est terminé.
◇ *comp* [couple, suite] en voyage de noces ■ **a ~ period** *fig* une lune de miel, un état de grâce.
◇ *vi* passer sa lune de miel.

honeymooner ['hʌnɪmu:nəʳ] *n* nouveau *OR* jeune marié *m*, nouvelle *OR* jeune mariée *f*.

honeypot ['hʌnɪpɒt] *n* [container] pot *m* à miel ■ **to have one's fingers in the ~** *inf* se sucrer.

honeysuckle ['hʌnɪ,sʌkl] *n* chèvrefeuille *m*.

Hong Kong [,hɒŋ'kɒŋ] *pr n* Hong Kong, Hongkong ■ **in ~** à Hongkong.

honk [hɒŋk] ◇ *vi* **1.** [car] klaxonner **2.** [goose] cacarder.
◇ *vt* : **to ~ one's horn** donner un coup de Klaxon.
◇ *n* **1.** [of car horn] coup *m* de Klaxon ■ **~, ~!** tut-tut! **2.** [of geese] cri *m* ■ **~, ~!** couin-couin!

honky-tonk ['hɒŋkɪ,tɒŋk] ◇ *n* **1.** MUS musique *f* de bastringue **2.** *US inf* [brothel] maison *f* close ■ *dated* [nightclub] beuglant△ *m* ■ [bar] bouge *m* ■ [gambling den] tripot *m*.
◇ *adj* **1.** MUS de bastringue **2.** *US* [unsavoury] louche.

honor *etc US* = **honour**.

honorary [*UK* 'ɒnərərɪ, *US* ɒnə'reərɪ] *adj* [titular position] honoraire ■ [in name only] à titre honorifique, honoraire ■ [unpaid position] à titre gracieux ■ **~ degree** grade honoris causa ■ **~ secretary** secrétaire honoraire.

honorific [,ɒnə'rɪfɪk] ◇ *adj* honorifique.
◇ *n* [general] témoignage *m* d'honneur ■ [title] titre *m* d'honneur.

honor roll *n US* tableau *m* d'honneur.

honour *UK*, **honor** *US* ['ɒnəʳ] ◇ *n* **1.** [personal integrity] honneur *m* ■ **on my ~!** parole d'honneur! ■ **he's on his ~ to behave himself** il s'est engagé sur l'honneur *OR* sur son honneur à bien se tenir ■ **it's a point of ~ (with me) to pay my debts on time** je me fais un point d'honneur de *OR* je mets un *OR* mon point d'honneur à rembourser mes dettes ▶ **(there is) ~ amongst thieves** *prov* les loups ne se mangent pas entre eux *prov*
2. [public, social regard] honneur *m* ■ **peace with ~!** la paix sans le déshonneur!
3. *fml* [pleasure] : **it is a great ~ to introduce Mr Reed** c'est un grand honneur pour moi de vous présenter Monsieur Reed ■ **may I have the ~ of your company/the next dance?** pouvez-vous me faire l'honneur de votre compagnie/de la prochaine danse? ▶ **to do the ~s** [serve drinks, food] faire le service ; [make introductions] faire les présentations (entre invités)
4. [credit] honneur *m*, crédit *m* ■ **she's an ~ to her profession** elle fait honneur à sa profession
5. [mark of respect] honneur *m* ■ **to receive sb with full ~s** recevoir qqn avec tous les honneurs ■ **Your Honour** Votre Honneur ; LAW ≃ Monsieur le Juge ■ ≃ Monsieur le Président
6. GAMES [face card] honneur *m*.
◇ *vt* **1.** [person] honorer, faire honneur à ■ **she ~ed him with her friendship** elle l'a honoré de son amitié ■ **my ~ed colleague** mon cher collègue ■ **I'm most ~ed to be here tonight** *fml* je suis très honoré d'être parmi vous ce soir
2. [fulfil the terms of] honorer ■ [observe - boycott, rule] respecter ■ **he always ~s his obligations** il honore toujours ses obligations
3. [pay - debt] honorer
4. [dance partner] saluer.
➡ **honours** *npl UK* UNIV [degree] ≃ licence *f* ■ **to take ~s in History** ≃ faire une licence d'histoire ■ **he was an ~s in university/in high school** *US* ≃ il a toujours eu mention très bien/le tableau d'honneur ■ **she got first-/second-class ~s** elle a eu sa licence avec mention très bien/mention bien.
➡ **in honour of** *prep phr* en honneur de.

honourable *UK*, **honorable** *US* ['ɒnrəbl] *adj* **1.** honorable ■ **he got an ~ discharge** il a été rendu à la vie civile **2.** [title] : **the (Right) Honourable** le (très) honorable ■ **my ~ friend the member for Calderdale** mon collègue l'honorable député du Calderdale.

HONOURABLE

Cette appellation est utilisée devant le nom de certains membres de l'aristocratie britannique : *the Honourable James Porter* ou *the Hon. James Porter*. Elle est également employée à la Chambre des communes lorsqu'un député parle d'un autre député : *the honourable member for Oxford*. Lorsqu'un député désigne un collègue du même parti, il emploie l'expression *my honourable friend* ; lorsque son interlocuteur appartient au parti opposé, le terme consacré est *the honourable gentleman ou lady*.

honourably *UK*, **honorably** *US* ['ɒnərəblɪ] *adv* honorablement.

honour bound *adj* : **to be ~ (to)** être tenu par l'honneur (à).

honours degree *n diplôme universitaire obtenu avec mention.*

honours list *n UK liste de distinctions honorifiques conférées par le monarque deux fois par an.*

Hons. *written abbr of* **honours degree**.

Hon. Sec. *written abbr of* **honorary secretary**.

hooch△ [hu:tʃ] *n US* [drink] gnôle *f*.

hood [hʊd] ◇ *n* **1.** [garment] capuchon *m* ■ [with collar] capuche *f* ■ [with eye-holes] cagoule *f* ■ UNIV épitoge *f* ■ **a rain ~** une capuche **2.** *UK* AUT [cover] capote *f* ■ *US* AUT capot *m* ■ [of pram] capote *f* ■ [for fumes, smoke] hotte *f* **3.** [of animals, plants] capuchon *m* ■ [for falcons] chaperon *m*, capuchon *m* **4.** △ *US crime sl* [gangster] gangster *m*, truand *m* **5.** *inf* = **hoodlum**.
◇ *vt* mettre le capuchon ■ [falcon] chaperonner, enchaperonner.

hooded ['hʊdɪd] *adj* [clothing] à capuchon ■ [person] encapuchonné ■ **~ eyes** *fig* yeux *mpl* tombants.

hooded crow *n* corneille *f* mantelée.

hoodie ['hʊdɪ] *n inf* **1.** [top] sweat-shirt *m* à capuche **2.** *UK* [person] *jeune qui porte un sweat-shirt à capuche.*

hoodlum ['hu:dləm] *n inf* voyou *m* ■ **a young ~** un (petit) loubar *OR* loubard, un blouson noir.

hoodoo ['hu:du:] ◇ *n US inf* [jinx] porte-malheur *mf inv*.
◇ *vt* porter la poisse *OR* la guigne à.

hoodwink ['hʊdwɪŋk] *vt* tromper, avoir ■ **he ~ed me into coming** par un tour de passe-passe il m'a fait venir.

hooey ['hu:ɪ] *n inf* foutaise *f*.

hoof [hu:f, hʊf] (*pl* **hoofs** *OR pl* **hooves** [hu:vz]) ◇ *n* sabot *m (d'animal)* ■ **on the ~** [alive] sur pied.
◇ *vt inf phr* : **to ~ it** *inf* [go on foot] aller à pinces ; [flee] se cavaler ; [dance] guincher.

hoo-ha ['hu:,hɑ:] *n inf* **1.** [noise] boucan *m*, potin *m* ■ [chaos] pagaille *f*, tohu-bohu *m* ■ [fuss] bruit *m*, histoires *fpl* **2.** *US* [party] fête *f* charivarique.

hook [hʊk] ◇ *n* **1.** [gen] crochet *m* ■ [for coats] patère *f* ■ [on clothes] agrafe *f* ■ NAUT gaffe *f* ■ **~s and eyes** agrafes (et œillets) ■ **the phone is off the ~** le téléphone est décroché ▶ **by ~ or by crook** coûte que coûte
2. [fishing] hameçon *m* ■ **he swallowed the story, ~, line and sinker** *inf* il a gobé tout le paquet
3. [in advertising] accroche *f*
4. *inf phr* **to get sb off the ~** tirer qqn d'affaire ■ **to let** *OR* **to get sb off the ~** [obligation] libérer qqn de sa responsabilité ■ **I'll let you off the ~ this time** je laisse passer cette fois-ci
5. [in golf] hook *m* ■ [in cricket] coup *m* tourné ■ **a right/left ~** [in boxing] un crochet (du) droit/gauche.
◇ *vt* **1.** [snag] accrocher ■ [seize - person, prey] attraper ; [- floating object] gaffer, crocher ■ **he ~ed his arm through hers** il lui a pris le bras
2. [loop] : **~ the rope around the tree** passez la corde autour de l'arbre ■ **she ~ed one leg round the leg of the chair** elle passa *OR* enroula une jambe autour du pied de la chaise
3. FISHING [fish] prendre ■ TECH hameçonner

4. [in golf] hooker ▪ [in boxing] donner un crochet à ▪ [in rugby] talonner *(le ballon)* ▪ [in cricket] renvoyer d'un coup tourné
5. *inf* [steal] piquer
6. *inf hum* [marry] passer la corde au cou à
7. SEW [rug] fabriquer en nouant au crochet.
◇ *vi* **1.** [fasten] s'agrafer
2. GOLF hooker.
◆ **hook on** ◇ *vi insep* s'accrocher.
◇ *vt sep* accrocher.
◆ **hook up** ◇ *vt sep* **1.** [trailer] accrocher ▪ [dress] agrafer ▪ [boat] amarrer
2. *inf* [install] installer ▪ [plug in] brancher
3. RADIO & TV faire un duplex entre
4. = **hitch up**.
◇ *vi insep* **1.** [dress] s'agrafer
2. *US inf* [meet] se rencontrer ▪ [work together] faire équipe
3. *US inf* [be in relationship] : **to ~ up with sb** sortir avec qqn
4. RADIO & TV : **to ~ up with** faire une émission en duplex avec.

hookah ['hʊkə] *n* narguilé *m*, houka *m*.

hooked [hʊkt] *adj* **1.** [hook-shaped] recourbé ▪ **a ~ nose** un nez crochu **2.** [having hooks] muni de crochets ▪ [fishing line] muni d'un hameçon **3.** *inf fig* [addicted] : **he got ~ on hard drugs** il est devenu accro aux drogues dures ▪ **she's really ~ on TV soaps** c'est une mordue des feuilletons télévisés ▪ **to get ~ on chess** devenir fana d'échecs.

hooker ['hʊkəʳ] *n* **1.** RUGBY talonneur *m* **2.** △ *US* [prostitute] pute△ *f*.

hookey, hooky ['hʊkɪ] *n US, Australia & New Zealand inf* **to play ~** sécher les cours, faire l'école buissonnière.

hook-nosed *adj* au nez recourbé *OR* crochu.

hookup ['hʊkʌp] *n inf* RADIO & TV relais *m* temporaire.

hookworm ['hʊkwɜːm] *n* ankylostome *m*.

hooligan ['huːlɪgən] *n* hooligan *m*, vandale *m*.

hooliganism ['huːlɪgənɪzm] *n* vandalisme *m*.

hoop [huːp] ◇ *n* [ring] cerceau *m*.
◇ *comp* : **~ earrings** (anneaux *mpl*) créoles *fpl*.

hoopla ['huːplɑː] *n* **1.** *UK* [funfair game] jeu *m* d'anneaux *(dans les foires)* **2.** *US inf* = **hoo-ha** *(sense 1)* **3.** *US inf* [advertising] publicité *f* tapageuse.

hoopoe ['huːpuː] *n* huppe *f*.

hooray [hʊ'reɪ] *interj* hourra, hurrah.

Hooray Henry *n UK BCBG bruyant et malappris*.

hoot [huːt] ◇ *n* **1.** [shout - of delight, pain] cri *m* ▪ [jeer] huée *f* ▪ **~s of laughter** éclats *mpl* de rire **2.** [of owl] hululement *m* **3.** AUT coup *m* de klaxon ▪ [of train] sifflement *m* ▪ [of siren] mugissement *m* **4.** *inf* [least bit] : **I don't give** *OR* **care a ~** *OR* **two ~s** je m'en fiche, mais alors complètement, je m'en contrefiche **5.** *inf* [amusing event] bonne partie *f* de rigolade ▪ **he's a real ~!** c'est un sacré rigolo!, il est tordant!
◇ *vi* **1.** *inf* [person] : **to ~ with laughter** s'esclaffer **2.** [owl] hululer **3.** AUT klaxonner ▪ [train] siffler ▪ [siren] mugir.
◆ **hoot down** *vt sep inf* [person, show] huer, conspuer.

hooter ['huːtəʳ] *n esp UK* **1.** [car horn] klaxon *m* ▪ [in factory, ship] sirène *f* **2.** [party toy] mirliton *m* **3.** *inf* [nose] pif *m*.

Hoover® ['huːvəʳ] *n* aspirateur *m*.
◆ **hoover** *vt UK* **to ~ a carpet** passer l'aspirateur sur un tapis.

hoovering ['huːvrɪŋ] *n UK* **to do the ~** passer l'aspirateur.

hooves [huːvz] *pl* ⊳ **hoof**.

hop [hɒp] (*pret & pp* **hopped**, *cont* **hopping**) ◇ *n* **1.** [jump] saut *m* à cloche-pied ▪ [in rapid series] sautillement *m* ▪ **the ~, skip** *OR* **step and jump** SPORT & *dated* le triple saut ▪ **to catch sb on the ~** *UK* prendre qqn au dépourvu **2.** AERON étape *f* ▪ **it's just a short ~ from New York to Boston by plane** Boston n'est qu'à quelques minutes d'avion de New York **3.** BOT houblon *m* ▪ **to pick ~s** cueillir le houblon.
◇ *vt inf* **1.** *phr* **~ it!** allez, dégage! **2.** *US* [bus, subway etc - legally] sauter dans ; [- illegally] prendre en resquillant.
◇ *vi* **1.** [jump] sauter ▪ [in rapid series] sautiller ▪ **to ~ on/off the bus** *inf* sauter dans le/du bus **2.** [jump on one leg] sauter à cloche-pied **3.** *inf* [travel by plane] : **we hopped across to Paris for the weekend** nous sommes allés à Paris en avion pour le week-end.
◆ **hop off** *vi insep inf* [leave] décamper.

hope [həʊp] ◇ *n* **1.** [desire, expectation] espoir *m* ▪ *fml* espérance *f* ▪ **his ~ is that...** ce qu'il espère *OR* son espoir c'est que... ▪ **in the ~ of a reward/of leaving early** dans l'espoir d'une récompense/de partir tôt ▪ **I have every ~ (that) he'll come** j'ai bon espoir qu'il viendra ▪ **there's ~ for him yet** il reste de l'espoir en ce qui le concerne ▪ **don't get your ~s up** ne comptez pas là-dessus ▪ **to give up ~ (of)** perdre l'espoir (de) ▪ **the situation is past** *OR* **beyond ~** la situation est sans espoir ▪ **she is past** *OR* **beyond all ~** *euph* [of dying person] il n'y a plus aucun espoir ▪ **to raise sb's ~s** [for first time] susciter *OR* faire naître l'espoir de qqn *OR* chez qqn ; [anew] faire renaître l'espoir de qqn ; [increase] renforcer l'espoir de qqn ▪ **don't raise his ~s too much** ne lui donne pas trop d'espoir ▪ **with high ~s** avec un grand espoir ▶ **the Cape of Good Hope** le cap de Bonne Espérance ▪ **some ~!** *inf iron* tu parles! **2.** [chance] espoir *m*, chance *f* ▪ **he's got little ~ of winning** il a peu de chances *OR* d'espoir de gagner **3.** RELIG espérance *f*.
◇ *vi* espérer ▪ **to ~ for sthg** espérer qqch ▪ **to ~ against ~** espérer contre toute attente ▪ **we just have to ~ for the best** espérons que tout finira *OR* se passera bien ▪ **you shouldn't ~ for a high return** vous ne devez pas vous attendre à un rendement élevé.
◇ *vt* espérer ▪ **hoping** *OR* **I ~ to hear from you soon** j'espère avoir de tes nouvelles bientôt ▪ **I really ~ so!** je l'espère bien! ▪ **I ~ not** j'espère que non.

hopeful ['həʊpfʊl] ◇ *adj* **1.** [full of hope] plein d'espoir ▪ **we're ~ that we'll reach an agreement** nous avons bon espoir d'aboutir à un accord ▪ **he says he'll come, but I'm not that ~** il dit qu'il viendra mais je n'y compte pas trop ▪ **I am ~ about the outcome** je suis optimiste quant au résultat **2.** [inspiring hope] encourageant, prometteur ▪ **the situation looks ~** la situation s'annonce meilleure.
◇ *n* aspirant *m*, candidat *m* ▪ **a young ~** un jeune loup.

hopefully ['həʊpfəlɪ] *adv* **1.** [smile, speak, work] avec espoir, avec optimisme **2.** [with luck] on espère que... ▪ **will you get it finished today? – ~!** est-ce que tu l'auras terminé pour aujourd'hui? – je l'espère! *OR* oui, avec un peu de chance!

hopeless ['həʊplɪs] *adj* **1.** [desperate - person] désespéré ; [- situation] désespéré, sans espoir ▪ **it's ~!** c'est impossible *OR* désespérant! **2.** [incurable - addiction, ill person] incurable ▪ **a ~ case** un cas désespéré **3.** [inveterate - drunk, liar] invétéré, incorrigible **4.** *inf* [incompetent - person] nul ; [- at job] incompétent ▪ **he's a ~ dancer** il est nul comme danseur ▪ **she's ~!** c'est un cas désespéré! ▪ **a ~ case** un bon à rien **5.** [pointless] : **it's ~ trying to explain to him** il est inutile d'essayer de lui expliquer.

hopelessly ['həʊplɪslɪ] *adv* **1.** [speak] avec désespoir **2.** [irremediably] : **they are ~ in debt/in love** ils sont complètement endettés/éperdument amoureux ▪ **by this time we were ~ late/lost** nous étions maintenant vraiment en retard/complètement perdus.

hopelessness ['həʊplɪsnɪs] *n* **1.** [despair] désespoir *m* **2.** [of position, situation] caractère *m* désespéré **3.** [pointlessness] inutilité *f*.

hopfield ['hɒpfiːld] *n* houblonnière *f*.

hopper ['hɒpəʳ] *n* **1.** [jumper] sauteur *m*, - euse *f* ▪ *Australia inf* kangourou *m* **2.** [feeder bin] trémie *f* ▪ **~ car** RAIL wagon-trémie *m*.

hopping ['hɒpɪŋ] *adv inf* [as intensifier] : **he was ~ mad** il était fou furieux.

-hopping *in cpds* : **to go island~** aller d'île en île, faire le tour des îles.

hopscotch ['hɒpskɒtʃ] *n* marelle *f*.

Horace ['hɒrɪs] *pr n* Horace.

horde [hɔːd] *n* **1.** [nomadic] horde *f* **2.** *fig* [crowd] essaim *m*, horde *f* ■ [of agitators] horde *f* ■ **the ~** *pej* la horde, la foule.

horizon [hə'raɪzn] *n* horizon *m* ■ **we saw a boat on the ~** nous vîmes un bateau à l'horizon ■ **a new star on the political ~** *fig* une nouvelle vedette à *OR* sur l'horizon politique.
◆ **horizons** *npl* [perspectives] horizons *mpl* ■ **to broaden one's ~s** élargir ses horizons.

horizontal [,hɒrɪ'zɒntl] ◇ *adj* **1.** horizontal ■ **turn the lever to the ~ position** mettez le levier à l'horizontale **2.** ADMIN & COMM [communication, integration] horizontal ■ **he asked for a ~ move** il a demandé une mutation.
◇ *n* horizontale *f*.

horizontal bar *n* SPORT barre *f* fixe.

horizontally [,hɒrɪ'zɒntəlɪ] *adv* horizontalement ■ **extend your arms ~** tendez vos bras à l'horizontale ■ **to move sb ~ (to)** ADMIN & COMM muter qqn (à).

hormonal [hɔː'məʊnl] *adj* hormonal.

hormone ['hɔːməʊn] *n* hormone *f* ■ **~ replacement therapy** traitement *m* hormonal substitutif.

Hormuz [,hɔː'muːz] *pr n* : **the Strait of ~** le détroit d'Hormuz *OR* d'Ormuz.

horn [hɔːn] ◇ *n* **1.** [gen] corne *f* ■ [pommel] pommeau *m* ■ **the ~ of plenty** la corne d'abondance ■ **the Horn of Africa** la Corne de l'Afrique, la péninsule des Somalis ■ **Cape Horn** cap *m* Horn ■ **to draw** *OR* **to pull in one's ~s** *UK* [back off] se calmer ; [spend less] restreindre son train de vie ■ **to be on the ~s of a dilemma** *UK* être pris dans un dilemme **2.** MUS cor *m* ■ **~ section** les cors *mpl* **3.** AUT klaxon *m* ■ [manual] corne *f* ■ **to sound** *OR* **to blow the ~** klaxonner, corner **4.** NAUT sirène *f* ■ **to sound** *OR* **to blow the ~** donner un coup de sirène **5.** HUNT corne *f*, cor *m*, trompe *f* **6.** *UK* CULIN cornet *m* ■ **a cream ~** *pâtisserie en forme de cornet remplie de crème*.
◇ *adj* [handle, bibelot] en corne.
◆ **horn in** *vi insep inf* [on conversation] mettre son grain de sel ■ [on a deal] s'immiscer.

hornbeam ['hɔːnbiːm] *n* charme *m*.

hornbill ['hɔːnbɪl] *n* calao *m*.

horned ['hɔːnd] *adj* cornu ■ **a two-~ rhinoceros** un rhinocéros (d'Afrique) à deux cornes.

horned owl *n* duc *m*.

hornet ['hɔːnɪt] *n* frelon *m* ■ **to stir up a ~'s nest** *fig* mettre le feu aux poudres.

hornless ['hɔːnlɪs] *adj* sans cornes.

hornpipe ['hɔːnpaɪp] *n* matelote *f (danse)*.

horn-rimmed *adj* à monture d'écaille.

horny ['hɔːnɪ] *adj* **1.** [calloused - nail, skin] calleux ■ VET encorné **2.** △ [randy] excité (sexuellement) **3.** △ [having sex appeal] sexy.

horology [hɔː'rɒlədʒɪ] *n* horlogerie *f*.

horoscope ['hɒrəskəʊp] *n* horoscope *m*.

horrendous [hɒ'rendəs] *adj* **1.** *liter* terrible **2.** *fig* [very bad] affreux, horrible.

horrendously [hɒ'rendəslɪ] *adv* horriblement.

horrible ['hɒrəbl] *adj* **1.** [horrific] horrible, affreux ■ [morally repulsive] abominable **2.** [dismaying] horrible, effroyable ■ **in a ~ mess** dans une effroyable *OR* horrible confusion ■ **I've a ~ feeling that things are going to go wrong** j'ai l'horrible pressentiment que les choses vont mal se passer **3.** [very unpleasant] horrible, atroce ■ [food] infect.

horribly ['hɒrəblɪ] *adv* **1.** [nastily] horriblement, atrocement, affreusement ■ **the story of a woman who was ~ murdered** l'histoire d'une femme qui fut assassinée de manière atroce **2.** [as intensifier] affreusement ■ **it's ~ extravagant but...** c'est de la folie douce mais... ■ **things went ~ wrong** les choses ont affreusement mal tourné.

horrid ['hɒrɪd] *adj* **1.** [unkind] méchant ■ [ugly] vilain ■ **he was ~ to me** il a été méchant avec moi **2.** = **horrible** *(sense 3)*.

horridly ['hɒrɪdlɪ] *adv* [as intensifier] atrocement, affreusement.

horrific [hɒ'rɪfɪk] *adj* **1.** *liter* horrible, terrifiant ■ *lit* horrifique **2.** *fig* [very unpleasant] horrible.

horrifically [hɒ'rɪfɪklɪ] *adv* **1.** [gruesomely] atrocement **2.** [as intensifier] : **~ expensive** affreusement cher.

horrify ['hɒrɪfaɪ] (*pret & pp* **horrified**) *vt* **1.** [terrify] horrifier **2.** [weaker use] horrifier, scandaliser.

horrifying ['hɒrɪfaɪɪŋ] *adj* **1.** [terrifying] horrifiant, terrifiant **2.** [weaker use] scandaleux.

horror ['hɒrər] *n* **1.** [feeling] horreur *f* ■ **he has a ~ of snakes** il a horreur des serpents ▌[weaker use] : **to my ~, I discovered...** c'est avec horreur que j'ai découvert... ▶ **he** *OR* **it gives me the ~s!** *UK inf* il *OR* ça me donne le frisson! ■ **~ story** *liter* histoire *f* d'horreur ■ **they told some real ~ stories about their holiday** *inf fig* ils ont raconté quelques histoires effrayantes sur leurs vacances **2.** [unpleasantness] horreur *f* **3.** *inf* [person, thing] horreur *f* ■ **~ of ~s!** l'horreur! ■ **oh, ~s!** *UK* quelle horreur!

horror film, horror movie *n* film *m* d'épouvante.

horror-stricken, horror-struck *adj* glacé *OR* frappé d'horreur.

hors d'œuvre [ɔː'dɜːvr] *n* hors-d'œuvre *m inv* ■ [cocktail snack] amuse-gueule *m* ■ **for** *OR* **as an ~, a salad** en hors-d'œuvre, une salade.

horse [hɔːs] ◇ *n* **1.** [animal] cheval *m* ■ **to ride a ~** monter à cheval ■ **he fell off his ~** il a fait une chute de cheval ■ **to play the ~s** jouer aux courses ▶ **to back the wrong ~** *fig & liter* miser sur le mauvais cheval ■ **I could eat a ~!** *inf* j'ai une faim de loup! ■ **to eat like a ~** manger comme quatre ■ **(straight) from the ~'s mouth** de source sûre ■ **to get on one's high ~** monter sur ses grands chevaux ■ **wild ~s couldn't drag it out of me** je serai muet comme une tombe **2.** [trestle] tréteau *m* ■ GYM cheval *m* d'arçons.
◇ *comp* : **~ manure** crottin *m* de cheval ; [as fertilizer] fumier *m* de cheval.
◇ *npl* MIL cavalière *f*.
◆ **horse about** *UK*, **horse around** *vi insep inf* [noisily] chahuter.

horseback ['hɔːsbæk] *n* : **on ~** à cheval.

horseback riding *n US* équitation *f*.

horsebox ['hɔːsbɒks] *n UK* [trailer] van *m* ■ [stall] box *m*.

horse brass *n* médaillon *m* de bronze *(fixé à une martingale)*.

horse butcher *n* boucher *m* hippophagique.

horse chestnut *n* [tree] marronnier *m* (d'Inde) ■ [nut] marron *m* (d'Inde).

horse-drawn *adj* tiré par des chevaux, à chevaux.

horseflesh ['hɔːsfleʃ] *n (U) inf* **1.** [horses] chevaux *mpl* ■ **he's a good judge of ~** il s'y connaît bien en chevaux **2.** = **horsemeat**.

horsefly ['hɔːsflaɪ] (*pl* **horseflies**) *n* taon *m*.

horsehair ['hɔːsheər] ◇ *n* crin *m* (de cheval).
◇ *adj* de crin (de cheval).

horseman ['hɔːsmən] (*pl* **horsemen** [-mən]) *n* **1.** [rider] cavalier *m*, écuyer *m* **2.** [breeder] éleveur *m* de chevaux.

horsemanship ['hɔːsmənʃɪp] *n* **1.** [activity] équitation *f* **2.** [skill] talent *m* de cavalier.

horsemeat ['hɔːsmiːt] *n* viande *f* de cheval.

horseplay ['hɔːspleɪ] *n (U)* chahut *m* brutal, jeux *mpl* tapageurs *OR* brutaux.

horsepower ['hɔːs,paʊər] *n* [unit] cheval-vapeur *m*, cheval *m* ■ **a 10-~ motor** un moteur de 10 chevaux ■ **it's a 4-~ car** c'est une 4 chevaux.

horse race *n* course *f* de chevaux.

horse racing *n (U)* courses *fpl* (de chevaux).

horseradish ['hɔːs,rædɪʃ] ◇ *n* BOT raifort *m*, radis *m* noir.
◇ *comp* : **~ sauce** sauce *f* au raifort.

horserider ['hɔsraɪdə] *n esp US* cavalier *m*, - ère *f*.

horse riding *n UK* équitation *f*.

horse sense *n inf* (gros) bon sens *m*.

horseshoe ['hɔːsʃuː] *n* fer *m* à cheval.

horse show *n* = **horse trials**.

horse-trading *n UK inf* négociation *f* dure ■ *pej* maquignonnage *m* ■ **after much ~ an agreement was reached** un accord a été obtenu à l'arraché.

horse trials *npl* concours *m* hippique.

horsewhip ['hɔːswɪp] (*pret & pp* **horsewhipped**, *cont* **horsewhipping**) ◇ *n* cravache *f*.
◇ *vt* cravacher ■ **I'll have him horsewhipped** je le ferai fouetter.

horsewoman ['hɔːs,wʊmən] (*pl* **horsewomen** [-,wɪmɪn]) *n* cavalière *f*, écuyère *f* ■ [sidesaddled] amazone *f*.

horsey, horsy ['hɔːsɪ] *adj inf* **1.** [horse-like] chevalin **2.** [fond of horses] féru de cheval.

horticultural [,hɔːtɪ'kʌltʃərəl] *adj* horticole ■ **~ show** exposition *f* horticole *OR* d'horticulture.

horticulturalist [,hɔːtɪ'kʌltʃərəlɪst] = **horticulturist**.

horticulture ['hɔːtɪkʌltʃəʳ] *n* horticulture *f*.

horticulturist [,hɔːtɪ'kʌltʃərɪst] *n* horticulteur *m*, - trice *f*.

hosanna [həʊ'zænə] ◇ *n* hosanna *m*.
◇ *interj* : **~!** hosanna!

hose [həʊz] ◇ *n* **1.** [tube] tuyau *m* ■ AUT Durit® *f* ■ **turn off the ~** arrêtez le jet ; TECH manche *f* à incendie ■ **garden ~** tuyau d'arrosage **2.** *(U)* [stockings] bas *mpl* ■ [tights] collant *m*, collants *mpl* ■ COMM articles *mpl* chaussants *(de bonneterie)* ■ HIST chausses *fpl* ■ [knee breeches] haut-de-chausse *m*, haut-de-chausses *m*, culotte *f* courte.
◇ *vt* [lawn] arroser au jet ■ [fire] arroser à la lance.
◆ **hose down** *vt sep* **1.** [wash] laver au jet **2.** [with fire hose] arroser à la lance.

hosepipe ['həʊzpaɪp] ◇ *n* tuyau *m*.
◇ *comp* : **a ~ ban** une interdiction d'arroser.

hosier ['həʊzɪəʳ] *n* bonnetier *m*, - ère *f*.

hosiery ['həʊzɪərɪ] *n (U)* **1.** [trade] bonneterie *f* **2.** [stockings] bas *mpl* ■ [socks] chaussettes *fpl* ■ COMM articles *mpl* chaussants *(de bonneterie)* ■ **the (women's) ~ department** le rayon des bas.

hospice ['hɒspɪs] *n* **1.** [for travellers] hospice *m* **2.** [for the terminally ill] *hôpital pour grands malades en phase terminale*.

hospitable [hɒ'spɪtəbl] *adj* hospitalier ■ **a ~ climate** *fig* un climat hospitalier.

hospitably [hɒ'spɪtəblɪ] *adv* avec hospitalité.

hospital ['hɒspɪtl] ◇ *n* hôpital *m* ■ **in ~** à l'hôpital ■ **to ~** *UK*, **to the ~** *US* à l'hôpital ■ **to go into ~** aller à l'hôpital ■ **a children's ~** un hôpital pour enfants.
◇ *comp* [centre, service, staff, treatment] hospitalier ■ [bed, ward] d'hôpital ■ **~ care** soins *mpl* hospitaliers ■ **a ~ case** un patient hospitalisé ■ **~ doctor** médecin *m* hospitalier ■ **junior ~ doctor** *UK* ≃ interne *mf* ■ **~ nurse** infirmier *m*, - ère *f (d'hôpital)* ■ **~ train** train *m* sanitaire.

hospitality [,hɒspɪ'tælətɪ] ◇ *n* hospitalité *f*.
◇ *comp* : **~ room** *OR* **suite** salon *m* de réception *(où sont offerts des rafraîchissements lors d'une conférence, d'un événement sportif etc)*.

hospitalization [,hɒspɪtəlaɪ'zeɪʃn] *n* hospitalisation *f*.

hospitalize, ise ['hɒspɪtəlaɪz] *vt* hospitaliser.

hospital ship *n* navire-hôpital *m*.

host [həʊst] ◇ *n* **1.** [person] hôte *m (qui reçoit)* ■ TV animateur *m*, - trice *f* ■ [innkeeper] aubergiste *mf* ■ **Japan will be the next ~ for the conference** c'est le Japon qui accueillera la prochaine conférence **2.** BIOL & ZOOL hôte *m* **3.** [large number] foule *f* ■ **a ~ of complaints** toute une série de plaintes **4.** *lit* & RELIG armée *f*.
◇ *adj* [cell] hôte ■ [team] qui reçoit ■ **the ~ city for the Olympic Games** la ville organisatrice des jeux Olympiques ■ **~ computer** ordinateur *m* principal ; [in network] serveur *m* ■ **~ country** pays *m* d'accueil.
◇ *vt* **1.** [TV show] animer ■ [event] organiser ■ **she adores ~ing dinner parties** elle adore recevoir à dîner **2.** COMPUT héberger.
◆ **Host** *n* RELIG : **the Host** l'hostie *f*.

hostage ['hɒstɪdʒ] *n* otage *mf* ■ **to take/to hold sb ~** prendre/garder qqn en otage ▶ **a ~ to fortune** *fig* le jouet du hasard.

hostel ['hɒstl] *n* **1.** [residence] foyer *m* **2.** *arch* auberge *f*.

hosteller *UK*, **hosteler** *US* ['hɒstələʳ] *n* [youth] ≃ ajiste *mf*.

hostelling ['hɒstəlɪŋ] *n UK* : **~ is popular with students** les étudiants aiment séjourner dans les auberges de jeunesse aux cours de leurs voyages.

hostelry ['hɒstəlrɪ] *n* hôtellerie *f* ■ *arch* hostellerie *f* ■ **the local ~** *inf hum* le bistrot du coin.

hostess ['həʊstes] *n* **1.** [at home] hôtesse *f* **2.** [in nightclub] entraîneuse *f* ■ **a ~ agency** une agence d'hôtesses **3.** [innkeeper] hôtelière *f*, aubergiste *f* **4.** = **air hostess**.

host family *n* famille *f* d'accueil.

hostile [*UK* 'hɒstaɪl, *US* 'hɒstl] ◇ *adj* hostile ■ **to be ~ to sthg** être hostile à qqch ■ **people who are ~ to change** les gens qui n'aiment pas le changement.
◇ *n inf US* ennemi *m*.

hostility [hɒ'stɪlətɪ] (*pl* **hostilities**) *n* hostilité *f* ■ **to show ~ to** *OR* **towards sb** manifester de l'hostilité *OR* faire preuve d'hostilité envers qqn ■ **the outbreak/cessation of hostilities** l'ouverture/la cessation des hostilités.

hostler ['ɒsləʳ] = **ostler**.

hot [hɒt] (*comp* **hotter**, *superl* **hottest**, *pret & pp* **hotted**, *cont* **hotting**) ◇ *adj* **1.** [high in temperature] chaud ■ **to be ~** avoir (très *OR* trop) chaud ■ **I'm getting ~** je commence à avoir chaud ■ **the water is getting ~** l'eau devient chaude ■ **how ~ should the oven be?** le four doit être à quelle température? ■ **it was ~ work** le travail donnait chaud ■ **there's ~ and cold running water** il y a l'eau courante chaude et froide ■ **we sat in the ~ sun** nous étions assis sous un soleil brûlant ■ **keep the meat ~** tenez la viande au chaud ■ **serve the soup while it's ~** servez la soupe bien chaude ■ **'~ food always available'** 'plats chauds à toute heure' ■ **you're getting ~!** *fig* [in guessing game] tu brûles! ▶ **to be** *OR* **to get (all) ~ and bothered about sthg** *inf* être dans tous ses états *OR* se faire du mauvais sang au sujet de qqch ■ **to be** *OR* **to get ~ under the collar (about sthg)** *inf* être en colère *OR* en rogne au sujet de qqch ■ **too ~ to handle** *liter* trop chaud pour le prendre *OR* saisir avec les mains ; *fig* brûlant ■ **the books were selling like ~ cakes** les livres se vendaient comme des petits pains
2. METEOR : **it's ~** il fait très chaud ■ **it's getting hotter** il commence à faire très chaud ■ **one ~ afternoon in August** (par) une chaude après-midi d'août ■ **in (the) ~ weather** pendant les chaleurs ■ **we had a ~ spell last week** c'était la canicule la semaine dernière
3. [clothing] qui tient chaud
4. [colour] chaud, vif
5. [pungent, spicy - food] épicé, piquant, relevé ; [- spice] fort ■ **a ~ curry** un curry relevé *OR* épicé
6. [fresh, recent] tout frais, toute fraîche *f* ■ **the news is ~ off the presses** ce sont des informations de toute dernière minute ■ **this book is ~ off the press** ce livre vient juste de paraître
7. [close, following closely] : **to be ~ on the trail** être sur la bonne piste ■ **the police were ~ on their heels** *OR* **on their trail** la police les talonnait *OR* était à leurs trousses ■ **he fled with the police in ~ pursuit** il s'est enfui avec la police à ses trousses
8. [fiery, vehement] violent ■ **she has a ~ temper** elle s'emporte facilement, elle est très soupe au lait
9. [intense - anger, shame] intense, profond
10. [keen] enthousiaste, passionné ■ **he's ~ on my sister** *US inf* il en pince pour ma sœur

11. *inf* [exciting] chaud ▪ **this book is ~ stuff** c'est un livre très audacieux
12. *inf* [difficult, unpleasant] chaud, difficile
13. *UK inf* [severe, stringent] sévère, dur ▪ **the police are really ~ on drunk driving** la police ne badine vraiment pas avec la conduite en état d'ivresse
14. *inf* [very good] génial, terrible ▪ [skilful] fort, calé ▪ **I don't feel so ~** je ne suis pas dans mon assiette ▪ **I'm not so ~ at maths** je ne suis pas très calé en maths ▪ **a ~ tip** un tuyau sûr *OR* increvable ▪ **a ~ favourite** SPORT un grand favori
15. *inf* [in demand, popular] très recherché ▪ **she's really ~ just now** elle a vraiment beaucoup de succès en ce moment
16. *inf* MUS : **~ jazz** (jazz *m*) hot *m*
17. *inf* [sexually attractive] : **to be ~ (stuff)** être sexy *(inv)* ▪ **he's ~** [sexually aroused] il a le feu au derrière
18. *inf* [stolen] volé
19. *UK inf* [sought by police] recherché par la police
20. ELEC [wire] sous tension
21. METALL : **~ drawing/rolling** tirage *m* /laminage *m* à chaud
22. NUCL PHYS [atom] chaud ▪ *inf* [radioactive] *inf* chaud, radioactif.
◇ *adv* : **to go ~ and cold at the thought of sthg** avoir des sueurs froides à l'idée de qqch.
◆ **hots** *npl inf* **to have the ~s for sb** craquer pour qqn.
◆ **hot up** *UK inf* ◇ *vt sep* **1.** [intensify - argument, contest] échauffer ; [- bombing, fighting] intensifier ; [- party] mettre de l'animation dans ; [- music] faire balancer, faire chauffer **2.** AUT : **to ~ up a car** gonfler le moteur d'une voiture.
◇ *vi insep* [intensify - discussion] s'échauffer ; [- fighting, situation] chauffer, s'intensifier ▪ **the price war has hotted up** les prix sont montés en flèche.

hot air *n inf* **he's full of ~** c'est une grande gueule△ ▪ **all her promises are just a lot of ~** toutes ses promesses ne sont que des paroles en l'air.

hot-air balloon *n* montgolfière *f*.

hotbed ['hɒtbed] *n* HORT couche *f* chaude, forcerie *f* ▪ *fig* pépinière *f*, foyer *m* ▪ **a ~ of crime/intrigue** un foyer de crimes/d'intrigues.

hot-blooded *adj* **1.** [person - passionate] fougueux, au sang chaud **2.** [horse - thoroughbred] de sang pur.

hotcake ['hɒtkeɪk] *n US* crêpe *f*.

hotchpotch ['hɒtʃpɒtʃ] *n UK* **1.** [jumble] fatras *m*, salmigondis *m* **2.** CULIN ≃ hochepot *m*, ≃ salmigondis *m*.

hot-cross bun *n petit pain brioché aux raisins secs et marqué d'une croix que l'on vend traditionnellement à Pâques.*

hot-desking *n* bureau *m* tournant.

hot dog ◇ *n* **1.** [sausage] hot-dog *m*, frankfurter *m* **2.** [in skiing] ski *m* acrobatique ▪ [in surfing] surf *m* acrobatique **3.** *US inf* [show-off] m'as-tu-vu *mf inv*.
◇ *vi* **1.** [in skiing] faire du ski acrobatique ▪ [in surfing] faire du surf acrobatique **2.** *US inf* [show off] crâner, poser (pour la galerie).
◇ *interj US inf* ~! génial!, super!

hotel [həʊ'tel] ◇ *n* hôtel *m* ▪ **a luxury ~** un hôtel de luxe.
◇ *comp* [prices, reservation, room] d'hôtel ▪ **~ accommodation** hébergement *m* en hôtel ▪ **~ accommodation not included** frais d'hôtel non inclus ▪ **the ~ business** l'hôtellerie *f* ▪ **~ desk** réception *f (d'un hôtel)* ▪ **the ~ industry** *OR* **trade** l'industrie *f* hôtelière.

hotelier [həʊ'telɪəʳ] *n* hôtelier *m*, - ère *f*.

hotelkeeper [həʊ'tel,ki:pəʳ] *n* hôtelier *m*, - ère *f*.

hotel management *n* **1.** [training] gestion *f* hôtelière **2.** [people] direction *f (de l'hôtel)*.

hotel manager *n* gérant *m*, - e *f* d'hôtel, directeur *m*, - trice *f* d'hôtel.

hot flush *UK*, **hot flash** *US n* bouffée *f* de chaleur.

hotfoot ['hɒt,fʊt] *inf* ◇ *adv* à toute vitesse.
◇ *vt phr* **to ~ it** galoper à toute vitesse.

hot gospeller *n prêcheur évangéliste qui harangue les foules.*

hothead ['hɒthed] *n* tête *f* brûlée, exalté *m*, - e *f*.

hotheaded [,hɒt'hedɪd] *adj* [person] impétueux, exalté ▪ [attitude] impétueux ▪ **she's very ~** c'est une exaltée *OR* une tête brûlée.

hothouse ['hɒthaʊs] (*pl* [-haʊzɪz]) ◇ *n* **1.** HORT serre *f* (chaude) **2.** *fig* [hotbed] foyer *m*.
◇ *adj* de serre (chaude) ▪ **a ~ plant** *liter & fig* une plante de serre (chaude).

hot key *n* COMPUT raccourci *m* clavier.

hot line *n* TELEC *ligne directe ouverte vingt-quatre heures sur vingt-quatre* ▪ POL téléphone *m* rouge ▪ **he has a ~ to the president** il a une ligne directe avec le président.

hotly ['hɒtlɪ] *adv* [dispute] vivement ▪ [pursue] avec acharnement ▪ [say] avec flamme ▪ **it was a ~ debated issue** c'était une question très controversée.

hot money *n (U) inf* [stolen] argent *m* volé ▪ FIN capitaux *mpl* flottants *OR* fébriles.

hot pants *npl* mini-short *m (très court et moulant)*.

hotplate ['hɒtpleɪt] *n* [on stove] plaque *f* chauffante ▪ [portable] chauffe-plats *m inv*.

hotpot ['hɒtpɒt] *n UK ragoût de viande et de pommes de terre.*

hot potato *n liter* pomme de terre *f* chaude ▪ *inf fig* *inf* sujet *m* brûlant et délicat ▪ **a political ~** un sujet brûlant *OR* une question brûlante de politique.

hot rod *n inf* AUT voiture *f* gonflée.

hot seat *n inf* **1.** [difficult situation] : **to be in the ~** être sur la sellette **2.** *US* [electric chair] chaise *f* électrique.

hotshot ['hɒtʃɒt] *inf* ◇ *n* [expert] as *m*, crack *m* ▪ [VIP] gros bonnet *m*.
◇ *adj* super ▪ **they've hired some ~ lawyer** ils ont pris un as du barreau.

hot spot *n* **1.** [dangerous area] point *m* chaud *OR* névralgique **2.** *inf* [night club] boîte *f* de nuit **3.** TECH point *m* chaud.

hot spring *n* source *f* chaude.

hot-tempered *adj* colérique, emporté ▪ **he's very ~** il est très soupe au lait.

Hottentot ['hɒtntɒt] ◇ *n* [person] Hottentot *m*, - e *f*.
◇ *adj* hottentot.

hot tub *n sorte de Jacuzzi qu'on installe dehors.*

hot water *n liter* eau *f* chaude ▪ *fig* **their latest prank got them into** *OR* **landed them in ~** leur dernière farce leur a attiré des ennuis.

hot-water bottle *n* bouillotte *f*.

houmous, houmus ['hʊməs] = **hummus**.

hound [haʊnd] ◇ *n* [dog - gen] chien *m* ; [- for hunting] chien *m* courant, chien *m* de meute ▪ **the ~s, a pack of ~s** HUNT la meute ▪ **to ride to** *OR* **to follow the ~s** HUNT chasser à courre.
◇ *vt* **1.** [give chase] traquer, pourchasser **2.** [harass] s'acharner sur, harceler ▪ **she was ~ed by reporters** elle était pourchassée *OR* harcelée par les journalistes.
◆ **hound down** *vt sep* prendre dans des rets, coincer ▪ HUNT forcer.
◆ **hound out** *vt sep* chasser de ▪ **he was ~ed out of town** il a été chassé de la ville.

houndstooth, hound's-tooth ['haʊndztu:θ] *n* TEX pied-de-poule *m*.

hour ['aʊəʳ] *n* **1.** [unit of time] heure *f* ▪ **a quarter of an ~** un quart d'heure ▪ **half an ~, a half ~** une demi-heure ▪ **an ~ and three-quarters** une heure trois quarts ▪ **at 60 km an** *OR* **per ~** à 60 km à l'heure ▪ **it's a two-~ drive/walk from here** c'est à deux heures de voiture/de marche d'ici ▪ **he gets £10 an ~** il touche 10 livres (de) l'heure ▪ **are you paid by the ~?** êtes-vous payé à l'heure? ▪ **a 35-~ week** une semaine de 35 heures

▪ **the shop is open 24 ~s a day** le magasin est ouvert 24 heures sur 24 ▪ **we arrived with ~s to spare** nous sommes arrivés avec plusieurs heures devant nous *OR* en avance de plusieurs heures ▪ **the situation is deteriorating by the ~** la situation s'aggrave d'heure en heure ▪ **it will save you ~s** cela te fera gagner des heures ▪ **we waited for ~s and ~s** on a attendu des heures ▪ **output per ~** TECH puissance *f* horaire **2.** [time of day] heure *f* ▪ **it chimes on the ~** ça sonne à l'heure juste ▪ **every ~ on the ~** toutes les heures justes ▪ **in the early** *OR* **small ~s (of the morning)** au petit matin, au petit jour ▪ **at this late ~** vu l'heure avancée **3.** *fig* [specific moment] heure *f*, moment *m* ▪ **in one's ~ of need** quand on est dans le besoin ▪ **the burning questions of the ~** l'actualité brûlante.

◆ **hours** *npl* heures *fpl* ▪ **flexible working ~s** INDUST des horaires mobiles *OR* souples ▪ **opening ~s** heures d'ouverture ▪ **you'll have to make up the ~s next week** il faudra que vous rattrapiez la semaine prochaine ▪ **do you work long ~s?** as-tu de longues journées de travail? ▪ **he keeps late ~s** c'est un couche-tard, il veille tard ▪ **to keep regular ~s** avoir une vie réglée ➋ **he was out until all ~s** il est rentré à une heure indue.

hourglass ['aʊəglɑːs] ◇ *n* sablier *m*.
◇ *adj* en forme d'amphore ▪ **an ~ figure** une taille de guêpe.

hour hand *n* petite aiguille *f*.

hour-long *adj* d'une heure.

hourly ['aʊəlɪ] ◇ *adj* **1.** [each hour - flights, trains] : **~ departures** départs toutes les heures ▪ COMM & TECH [earnings, rate] horaire **2.** [continual - anticipation] constant, perpétuel.
◇ *adv* **1.** [each hour] une fois par heure, chaque heure, toutes les heures ▪ **to be paid ~** être payé à l'heure **2.** [repeatedly] sans cesse ▪ [at any time] à tout moment.

house ◇ *n* [haʊs] (*pl* houses ['haʊzɪz]) **1.** maison *f* ▪ **at** *OR* **to his ~** chez lui ▪ **'~ for sale'** 'propriété à vendre' ▪ **a ~ of cards** un château de cartes ▪ **to clean the ~** faire le ménage ▪ **to keep ~ (for sb)** tenir la maison *OR* le ménage (de qqn) ▪ **to set up ~** monter son ménage, s'installer ▪ **they set up ~ together** ils se sont mis en ménage ➋ **we got on** *OR* **along like a ~ on fire** nous nous entendions à merveille *OR* comme larrons en foire ▪ **to set** *OR* **to put one's ~ in order** mettre de l'ordre dans ses affaires
2. COMM [establishment] maison *f (de commerce)*, compagnie *f* ▪ RELIG maison *f* religieuse ▪ *UK* SCH *au sein d'une école, répartition des élèves en groupes concurrents* ▪ **a bottle of ~ red (wine)** une bouteille de (vin) rouge de la maison *OR* de l'établissement ▪ **drinks are on the ~!** la tournée est aux frais de la maison!
3. [family line] maison *f* ▪ **the House of York** la maison de York
4. THEAT salle *f*, auditoire *m* ▪ **is there a good ~ tonight?** est-ce que la salle est pleine ce soir? ▪ **to have a full ~** jouer à guichets fermés *OR* à bureaux fermés ▪ **'~ full'** 'complet' ▪ **the second ~** *UK* la deuxième séance ➋ **to bring the ~ down** faire crouler la salle sous les applaudissements ; *fig* casser la baraque
5. : **the House** *UK* POL la Chambre ; *US* POL la Chambre des représentants ; ST. EX la Bourse
6. [in debate] : **this ~ believes...** la motion à débattre est la suivante...
7. MUS = **house music**.
◇ *vt* [haʊz] [accommodate - subj: organization, person] héberger, loger ; [- subj: building] recevoir ▪ **this wing ~s a laboratory/five families** cette aile abrite un laboratoire/cinq familles ▪ **the archives are ~d in the basement** on garde les archives dans les caves.
◇ *interj* [in bingo] : **~!** ≃ carton!

HOUSE

Dans certaines écoles en Grande-Bretagne (particulièrement dans les *grammar schools* et les *public schools*), les élèves sont répartis en groupes, qui portent chacun un nom et une couleur et développent entre eux un véritable esprit de compétition.

house arrest *n* assignation *f* à domicile *OR* à résidence ▪ **to put sb under ~** assigner qqn à domicile *OR* à résidence.

houseboat ['haʊsbəʊt] *n* house-boat *m*, péniche *f* (aménagée).

housebound ['haʊsbaʊnd] *adj* qui ne peut quitter la maison.

housebreaker ['haʊs,breɪkəʳ] *n* cambrioleur *m*, - euse *f*.

housebreaking ['haʊs,breɪkɪŋ] *n* cambriolage *m*.

housebroken ['haʊs,brəʊkn] *adj* *US* [pet] propre.

housecoat ['haʊskəʊt] *n* robe *f* d'intérieur.

house detective *n* responsable *m* de la sécurité, détective *m* de l'hôtel.

housefather ['haʊs,fɑːðəʳ] *n* responsable *m* (de groupe) *(dans un foyer)*.

housefly ['haʊsflaɪ] (*pl* **houseflies**) *n* mouche *f* (commune *OR* domestique).

houseful ['haʊsfʊl] *n* : **a ~ of guests** une pleine maisonnée d'invités ▪ **we've got a real ~ this weekend** la maison est vraiment pleine (de monde) ce week-end.

houseguest ['haʊsgest] *n* invité *m*, - e *f*.

household ['haʊshəʊld] ◇ *n* ménage *m*, (gens *mpl* de la) maison *f*, maisonnée *f* ▪ ADMIN & ECON ménage ▪ **the head of the ~** le chef de famille.
◇ *adj* [products, expenses] de ménage ▪ ADMIN & ECON des ménages ▪ **'for ~ use only'** 'à usage domestique seulement' ▪ **~ appliance** appareil *m* ménager.

householder ['haʊs,həʊldəʳ] *n* [occupant] occupant *m*, - e *f* ▪ [owner] propriétaire *mf* ▪ [tenant] locataire *mf*.

household gods *npl* HIST dieux *mpl* du foyer.

household name *n* : **we want to make our brand a ~** nous voulons que notre marque soit connue de tous ▪ **she's a ~** tout le monde la connaît *OR* sait qui elle est.

household troops *npl* garde *f* personnelle ▪ HIST garde *f* du palais ▪ [in UK] Garde *f* Royale.

household word = **household name**.

house-hunt *vi* chercher un *OR* être à la recherche d'un logement.

househunting ['haʊs,hʌntɪŋ] *n* recherche *f* d'un logement ▪ **I spent two months ~** j'ai passé deux mois à chercher un logement *OR* à la recherche d'un logement.

house husband *n* père *m* au foyer.

housekeeper ['haʊs,kiːpəʳ] *n* [institutional] économe *f*, intendante *f* ▪ [private] gouvernante *f* ▪ **she's a good/bad ~** c'est une bonne/mauvaise maîtresse de maison.

housekeeping ['haʊs,kiːpɪŋ] *n (U)* **1.** [of household - skill] économie *f* domestique ; [- work] ménage *m* ▪ **~ (money)** argent *m* du ménage **2.** [of organization] services *mpl* généraux **3.** COMPUT opérations *fpl* de nettoyage et d'entretien.

house lights *npl* THEAT lumières *fpl* *OR* éclairage *m* de la salle.

housemaid ['haʊsmeɪd] *n* bonne *f*, femme *f* de chambre.

housemaid's knee *n* MED inflammation *f* du genou.

houseman ['haʊsmən] (*pl* **housemen** [-mən]) *n* *UK* MED ≃ interne *m*.

house manager *n* THEAT directeur *m*, - trice *f* de théâtre.

house martin *n* hirondelle *f* de fenêtre.

housemaster ['haʊs,mɑːstəʳ] *n* *UK* SCH *professeur responsable d'une "house"*.

housemen [-mən] *pl* ▻ **houseman**.

housemistress ['haʊs,mɪstrɪs] *n* *UK* SCH *professeur responsable d'une "house"*.

housemother ['haʊs,mʌðəʳ] *n* responsable *f* (de groupe) *(dans un foyer)*.

house music *n* house *f* (music).

House of Commons *pr n* : **the ~** la Chambre des communes.

HOUSE OF COMMONS

La Chambre des communes est composée de 659 députés (*MPs*) élus au suffrage universel pour cinq ans, qui siègent environ 175 jours par an.

House of Lords *pr n* : **the ~** la Chambre des lords.

HOUSE OF LORDS

La Chambre des lords est composée de « lords » spirituels (hommes d'Église) et de « lords » temporels (nobles), dont la plupart sont nommés par le gouvernement. C'est la plus haute cour au Royaume-Uni (Écosse non comprise). Elle peut amender des projets de loi votés par la Chambre des communes, qui, à son tour, peut rejeter des décisions prises par la Chambre des lords. Aujourd'hui, le gouvernement travailliste essaie d'apporter des réformes majeures à cette « Deuxième Chambre », ayant déjà effectué, en 2000, une importante réduction du nombre de pairs héréditaires qui ont le droit de siéger à la Chambre.

House of Representatives *pr n* : **the ~** la Chambre des représentants *(aux États-Unis)*.

HOUSE OF REPRESENTATIVES

La Chambre des représentants constitue, avec le Sénat, l'organe législatif américain; ses membres sont élus par le peuple, proportionnellement à la population de chaque État.

house-owner *n* propriétaire *mf*.

house painter *n* peintre *m* en bâtiment.

houseparent ['haus,peərənt] *n* responsable *mf* (de groupe) *(dans un foyer)*.

house party *n* **1.** [social occasion] fête *f* de plusieurs jours *(dans une maison de campagne)* **2.** [guests] invités *mpl*.

house physician *n* [in hospital] *UK* ≃ interne *m* (en médecine) ■ [in hotel] médecin *m (attaché à un hôtel)*.

houseplant ['hausplɑ:nt] *n* plante *f* d'intérieur.

house-proud *adj* : **he's very ~** il attache beaucoup d'importance à l'aspect intérieur de sa maison, tout est toujours impeccable chez lui.

houseroom ['hausrum] *n UK* place *f (pour loger qqn ou qqch)* ■ **I wouldn't give that table ~!** je ne voudrais pas de cette table chez moi!

house-sit *vi* : **to ~ for sb** *s'occuper de la maison de qqn pendant son absence*.

Houses of Parliament *pr npl* : **the ~** le Parlement *m* (britannique).

house sparrow *n* moineau *m* domestique.

house surgeon *n UK* ≃ interne *m* (en chirurgie).

house-to-house *adj* [enquiry] de porte en porte ■ **to make a ~ search for sb/sthg** aller de porte en porte à la recherche de qqn/qqch, fouiller chaque maison à la recherche de qqn/qqch.

housetop ['haustɒp] *n* toit *m* ■ **to shout** *OR* **to proclaim sthg from the ~ s** crier qqch sur les toits.

house trailer *n US* caravane *f*.

house-train *vt* dresser à la propreté ■ **has the dog been ~ed?** est-ce que le chien est propre? ■ **he used to be really untidy, but she soon got him ~ed!** *inf hum* avant, il était très bordélique, mais elle a eu tôt fait de le dresser!

housewares ['hausweəz] *npl* articles *mpl* ménagers.

housewarming ['haus,wɔ:mɪŋ] *n* pendaison *f* de crémaillère ■ **to give** *OR* **to have a ~ (party)** pendre la crémaillère.

housewife ['hauswaɪf] (*pl* **housewives** [-waɪvz]) *n* ménagère *f* ■ [not career woman] femme *f* au foyer.

housewifely ['haus,waɪflɪ] *adj* de ménagère.

house wine *n* vin *m* de la maison.

housewives [-waɪvz] *pl* ▷ **housewife**.

housework ['hauswɜ:k] *n* (travaux *mpl* de) ménage *m* ■ **to do the ~** faire le ménage.

housing ['hauzɪŋ] ◇ *n* **1.** [accommodation] logement *m* ■ **the government has promised to provide more low-cost ~** le gouvernement a promis de fournir plus de logements à loyer modéré **2.** TECH [of mechanism] carter *m* ■ PHOT boîtier *m* ■ **wheel ~** boîte *f* de roue ■ **watch ~** boîtier de montre **3.** CONSTR encastrement *m*.

◇ *comp* : **~ shortage** crise *f* du logement ■ **the local ~ department** ≃ l'antenne logement (de la commune).

housing association *n association britannique à but non lucratif qui construit ou rénove des logements pour les louer à ses membres.*

housing benefit *n UK allocation de logement versée par l'État aux individus justifiant de revenus faibles.*

housing development *n* **1.** [estate] lotissement *m* **2.** [activity] construction *f* de logements.

housing estate *n UK* [of houses] lotissement *m* ■ [of flats] cité *f*.

housing list *n UK liste d'attente pour bénéficier d'un logement social.*

housing project *n* **1.** *US* = **housing estate 2.** [plan] plan *m* d'aménagement immobilier.

housing scheme *n* **1.** [plan] programme *m* municipal de logement **2.** [houses] = **housing estate**.

hove [həuv] *pt & pp* ▷ **heave**.

hovel ['hɒvl] *n* taudis *m*, masure *f*.

hover ['hɒvər] *vi* **1.** [in air - smoke] stagner ; [- balloon, scent] flotter ; [- insects] voltiger ; [- helicopter, hummingbird] faire du surplace **2.** [linger - person] rôder ; [- smile] flotter ; [- danger] planer ■ **the waitress ~ed over/round him** la serveuse rôdait/tournait autour de lui ■ **she was ~ing between life and death** elle restait suspendue entre la vie et la mort **3.** [hesitate] hésiter ■ **his finger ~ed over the button** son doigt hésita à appuyer sur le bouton.

hovercraft ['hɒvəkrɑ:ft] *n* aéroglisseur *m*.

hoverport ['hɒvəpɔ:t] *n* hoverport *m*.

hovertrain ['hɒvətreɪn] *n* train *m* à coussin d'air.

how [hau] ◇ *adv* **1.** [in what way] comment ■ **~ could you be so careless?** comment as-tu pu être aussi étourdi? ▶ **~ is it that...?** comment se fait-il que...? ■ **~ so?, ~ can that be?** comment cela (se fait-il)? ■ **~'s that (again)?** comment?
2. [in greetings, friendly enquiries etc] comment ■ **~ are you?** comment allez-vous? ■ **~ are things?** ça marche? ■ **~ did you like** *OR* **~ was the film?** comment as-tu trouvé le film? ■ **~ was your trip?** avez-vous fait bon voyage? ■ **~'s the water?** l'eau est bonne? ▶ **~ do you do?** bonjour!
3. [in exclamations] que, comme ■ **~ sad she is!** qu'elle est triste!, comme elle est triste! ■ **~ incredible!** c'est incroyable! ■ **~ I wish I could!** si seulement je pouvais! ▶ **~ stupid can you get!** *inf* est-il possible d'être bête à ce point-là!
4. *(with adj, adv)* [referring to measurement, rate, degree] : **~ wide is the room?** quelle est la largeur de la pièce? ■ **~ tall are you?** combien mesures-tu? ■ **~ old is she?** quel âge a-t-elle? ■ **~ well can you see it?** est-ce que tu le vois bien? ■ **~ angry is he?** il est vraiment fâché? ■ **~ fast/slowly was he walking?** à quelle vitesse marchait-il? ‖ [referring to time, distance, quantity] : **~ far is it from here to the sea?** combien y a-t-il d'ici à la mer? ■ **~ much does this bag cost?** combien coûte ce sac? ■ **~ often did he write?** est-ce qu'il écrivait souvent? ■ **~ long has he been here?** depuis quand *OR* depuis combien de temps est-il ici? ■ **~ soon can you deliver it?** à partir de quand pouvez-vous le livrer? ■ **~ late will you stay?** jusqu'à quelle heure resteras-tu?

◇ *conj* **1.** [in what way] comment ■ **he's learning ~ to read** il apprend à lire

2. [the fact that] : **I remember ~ he always used to turn up late** je me souviens qu'il était toujours en retard
3. *inf* [however] comme ▪ **arrange the furniture ~ you like** installe les meubles comme tu veux ● **did you like it? – and ~!** ça t'a plu? – et comment!
◇ *n* comment *m inv* ▪ **the ~ and the why of it don't interest me** le pourquoi et le comment ne m'intéressent pas.
◆ **how about** *adv phr inf* **~ about a beer?** et si on prenait une bière? ▪ **~ about Friday?** vendredi, ça va? ▪ **~ about you? what do you think?** et toi, qu'est-ce que tu en penses?
◆ **how come** *adv phr inf* **~ come?** comment ça se fait? ▪ **~ come you left?** comment ça se fait que tu sois parti?

howbeit [ˌhaʊ'bi:ɪt] *arch conj* bien que.

howdah ['haʊdə] *n* howdah *m*.

howdy ['haʊdɪ] *interj US inf* **~!** salut!

however [haʊ'evəʳ] ◇ *adv* **1.** [indicating contrast or contradiction] cependant, pourtant, toutefois ▪ **if, ~, you have a better suggestion...** si toutefois vous avez une meilleure suggestion (à faire)... **2.** *(with adj or adv)* [no matter how] si... que, quelque... que ▪ **~ nice he tries to be...** si gentil qu'il essaie d'être... ▪ **all contributions will be welcome, ~ small** si petites soient-elles, toutes les contributions seront les bienvenues ▪ **he'll never do it, ~ much** *OR* **hard he tries** quelque effort qu'il fasse, il n'y arrivera jamais ▪ **~ cold/hot the weather** même quand il fait très froid/chaud ▪ **~ late/early you arrive, call me** quelle que soit l'heure à laquelle tu arrives, appelle-moi **3.** *(in questions)* [emphatic use] comment ▪ **~ did he find it?** comment a-t-il bien pu le trouver?
◇ *conj* [in whatever way] de quelque manière que, comme ▪ **we can present it ~ you like** *OR* **want** on peut le présenter comme vous voulez.

howitzer ['haʊɪtsəʳ] *n* obusier *m*.

howl [haʊl] ◇ *n* **1.** [of person, animal] hurlement *m* ▪ [of child] braillement *m*, hurlement *m* ▪ [of wind] mugissement *m* ▪ **the speech was greeted with ~s of derision** le discours a été accueilli par des huées **2.** ELECTRON effet *m* Larsen.
◇ *vi* **1.** [person, animal] hurler ▪ [child] brailler ▪ [wind] mugir ▪ **to ~ with laughter** hurler de rire ▪ **to ~ in** *OR* **with rage** hurler de rage **2.** *inf* [cry] chialer ▪ [complain] gueuler.
◇ *vt* crier, hurler.
◆ **howl down** *vt sep* [speaker] : **they ~ed him down** ils l'ont réduit au silence par leurs huées.

howler ['haʊləʳ] *n inf* [blunder] gaffe *f*, bourde *f*.

howling ['haʊlɪŋ] ◇ *n* [of person, animal] hurlement *m*, hurlements *mpl* ▪ [of child] braillement *m*, braillements *mpl* ▪ [of wind] mugissement *m*, mugissements *mpl*.
◇ *adj inf* [error] énorme ▪ [success] fou.

howsoever [ˌhaʊsəʊ'evəʳ] = **however** *(adv)*.

hoy [hɔɪ] *interj UK* **~!** [to people] ohé!, hep! ; [to animals] hue!

hp, HP ◇ *n* (*abbrev of* **hire purchase**) ▪ **to buy sthg on ~** acheter qqch à crédit.
◇ (*written abbrev of* **horsepower**) CV.

HPV [eɪtʃpi:'vi] (*abbrev of* **human papilloma virus**) *n* MED PVH *m*.

HQ (*abbrev of* **headquarters**) *n* QG *m*.

hr(s) (*written abbrev of* **hour(s)**) h.

HRH (*written abbrev of* **His/Her Royal Highness**) SAR.

HRT *n* = **hormone replacement therapy**.

ht *written abbr of* **height**.

HT (*written abbrev of* **high tension**) HT.

HTML (*abbrev of* **Hypertext Markup Language**) *n* COMPUT HTML *m*.

hub [hʌb] *n* [of wheel] moyeu *m* ▪ *fig* centre *m*.

hubbub ['hʌbʌb] *n* [of voices] brouhaha *m* ▪ [uproar] vacarme *m*, tapage *m*.

hubby ['hʌbɪ] (*pl* **hubbies**) *n inf* bonhomme *m*, petit mari *m*.

hubcap ['hʌbkæp] *n* AUT enjoliveur *m* (de roue).

hubris ['hju:brɪs] *n* orgueil *m* (démesuré).

huckleberry ['hʌklbərɪ] (*pl* **huckleberries**) *n* airelle *f*, myrtille *f*.

huckster ['hʌkstəʳ] *n* **1.** [pedlar] colporteur *m*, - euse *f* **2.** *US pej* [in advertising] publicitaire *m* agressif.

huddle ['hʌdl] ◇ *n* **1.** [of people] petit groupe *m* (serré) ▪ [of objects] tas *m*, amas *m* ▪ [of roofs] enchevêtrement *m* ▪ **to go into a ~** *inf* se réunir en petit comité **2.** SPORT concentration *f* *(d'une équipe)*.
◇ *vi* **1.** [crowd together] se blottir ▪ **they ~d round the fire** ils se sont blottis autour du feu **2.** [crouch] se recroqueviller, se blottir ▪ **she was huddling under a blanket** elle se blottissait sous une couverture.
◆ **huddle together** *vi insep* se serrer *OR* se blottir les uns contre les autres ▪ [for talk] se mettre en petit groupe *OR* cercle serré.
◆ **huddle up** *vi insep* = **huddle** *(vi sense 2)*.

huddled ['hʌdld] *adj* **1.** [for shelter] blotti ▪ [curled up] pelotonné ▪ **they lay ~ under the blanket** ils étaient blottis *OR* pelotonnés les uns contre les autres sous la couverture **2.** [hunched] recroquevillé.

Hudson Bay *pr n* la baie d'Hudson.

hue [hju:] *n* **1.** [colour] teinte *f*, nuance *f* **2.** *phr* **a ~ and cry** *UK* une clameur (de haro) ▪ **to raise a ~ and a cry against sb/sthg** crier haro sur qqn/qqch.

huff [hʌf] ◇ *vi phr* **to ~ and puff** [with exertion] haleter ; [with annoyance] maugréer ▪ **they'll ~ and puff a bit but they won't stop us** *UK fig* ils protesteront, mais ils nous laisseront faire.
◇ *n inf* **to be in a ~** être froissé *OR* fâché ▪ **to take the ~** *UK* prendre la mouche, s'offusquer ▪ **he went off in a ~** il est parti froissé *OR* fâché.

huffily ['hʌfɪlɪ] *adv* [reply] d'un ton vexé *OR* fâché ▪ [behave] avec (mauvaise) humeur.

huffy ['hʌfɪ] *adj* [piqued] froissé, vexé ▪ [touchy] susceptible.

hug [hʌg] (*pret & pp* **hugged**, *cont* **hugging**) ◇ *vt* **1.** [in arms] serrer dans ses bras, étreindre ▪ **to ~ o.s. with delight (over** *OR* **about sthg)** *fig* se réjouir vivement (de qqch), jubiler **2.** *fig* [idea] tenir à, chérir **3.** [keep close to] serrer ▪ **don't ~ the kerb** AUT ne serrez pas le trottoir ▪ **to ~ the ground** AERON suivre le relief du terrain.
◇ *n* étreinte *f* ▪ **to give sb a ~** serrer qqn dans ses bras, étreindre qqn.

huge [hju:dʒ] *adj* [in size, degree] énorme, immense ▪ [in extent] vaste, immense ▪ [in volume] énorme, gigantesque.

hugely ['hju:dʒlɪ] *adv* [increase] énormément ▪ [as intensifier] énormément, extrêmement ▪ **the project has been ~ successful/expensive** le projet a été un succès complet/a coûté extrêmement cher.

Huguenot ['hju:gənəʊ] ◇ *n* Huguenot *m*, - e *f*.
◇ *adj* huguenot.

huh [hʌ] *interj* [surprise] : **~?** hein? ▪ [scepticism] : **~!** hum!

hula ['hu:lə], **hula-hula** *n* danse *f* polynésienne ▪ **a ~ skirt** une jupe en paille.

hulk [hʌlk] *n* **1.** [ship] épave *f* ▪ *pej* vieux rafiot *m* ▪ [used as prison, storehouse] ponton *m* **2.** [person, thing] mastodonte *m* ▪ **a great ~ of a man** un malabar *m*.

hulking ['hʌlkɪŋ] *adj* [person] balourd, massif ▪ [thing] gros, grosse *f*, imposant ▪ [as intensifier] : **you ~ great oaf!** espèce de malotru!

hull [hʌl] ◇ *n* **1.** [of ship] coque *f* ▪ MIL [of tank] caisse *f* **2.** [of peas, beans] cosse *f*, gousse *f* ▪ [of nut] écale *f* ▪ [of strawberry] pédoncule *m*.
◇ *vt* **1.** [peas] écosser ▪ [nuts] écaler, décortiquer ▪ [grains] décortiquer ▪ [strawberries] équeuter **2.** [ship] percer la coque de.

hullabaloo [ˌhʌləbə'lu:] *n inf* raffut *m*, chambard *m*, barouf *m* ▪ **the press made a real ~ about it** la presse en a fait tout un foin.

hullo [hə'ləʊ] *interj UK* **1.** [as greeting] : **~!** [on meeting] salut! ; [on phone] allô! **2.** [for attention] : **~!** ohé!, holà! ■ **~ there!** holà, vous! **3.** [in surprise] : **~!** tiens!

hum [hʌm] (*pret & pp* **hummed**, *cont* **humming**) ◇ *vi* **1.** [audience, bee, wires] bourdonner ■ [person] fredonner, chantonner ■ [top, fire] ronfler ■ ELECTRON ronfler ■ [air conditioner] ronronner ■ **everything was humming along nicely** *fig* tout marchait comme sur des roulettes **2.** [be lively] grouiller ■ **the airport/town was humming with activity** l'aéroport/la ville bourdonnait d'activité **3.** *UK inf* [stink] cocotter **4.** *phr* **to ~ and haw** *liter* bafouiller ; *fig* tergiverser, tourner autour du pot.
◇ *vt* [tune] fredonner, chantonner.
◇ *n* **1.** [of bees, voices] bourdonnement *m* ■ [of vehicle] vrombissement *m* ■ [of fire, top] ronflement *m* ■ ELECTRON ronflement ■ [of machine] ronronnement *m* ■ **the distant ~ of traffic** le ronronnement lointain de la circulation **2.** *UK inf* [stench] puanteur *f*, mauvaise odeur *f* ■ **there's a bit of a ~ in here!** ça cocotte là-dedans!
◇ *interj* : **~!** hem!, hum!

human ['hjuːmən] ◇ *adj* humain ■ **the ~ race** le genre humain ■ **he's only ~** personne n'est parfait ■ **the accident was caused by ~ error** l'accident était dû à une erreur *OR* défaillance humaine ➲ **'Of Human Bondage'** ***Maugham*** 'Servitude humaine'.
◇ *n* (être *m*) humain *m*.

human being *n* être *m* humain.

humane [hjuː'meɪn] *adj* [compassionate - action, person] humain, plein d'humanité ; [- treatment] humain ■ **a ~ method of killing animals** une façon humaine de tuer les animaux.

humanely [hjuː'meɪnlɪ] *adv* humainement.

human engineering *n* INDUST gestion *f* des relations humaines ■ [ergonomics] ergonomie *f*.

Human Genome Project *n* projet *m* génome humain ■ **the Human Genome Project** le projet génome humain.

human interest *n* PRESS dimension *f* humaine ■ **a ~ story** un reportage à caractère social.

humanism ['hjuːmənɪzm] *n* humanisme *m*.

humanist ['hjuːmənɪst] ◇ *n* humaniste *m*.
◇ *adj* humaniste.

humanistic [ˌhjuːmə'nɪstɪk] *adj* humaniste.

humanitarian [hjuːˌmænɪ'teərɪən] ◇ *n* humaniste *mf*.
◇ *adj* humanitaire.

humanity [hjuː'mænətɪ] *n* **1.** [mankind] humanité *f* ■ **for the good of ~** pour le bien de l'humanité **2.** [compassion] humanité *f*.
◆ **humanities** *npl* [arts] lettres *fpl* ■ [classical culture] lettres *fpl* classiques ■ **humanities students** étudiants en lettres *OR* humanités.

humanize, ise ['hjuːmənaɪz] *vt* humaniser.

humankind [ˌhjuːmən'kaɪnd] *n* l'humanité *f*, le genre humain.

humanly ['hjuːmənlɪ] *adv* humainement ■ **I'll do all that is ~ possible to help her** je ferai tout ce qui est humainement possible pour l'aider.

human nature *n* nature *f* humaine ■ **it's only ~ to be jealous** c'est normal *OR* humain d'être jaloux.

humanoid ['hjuːmənɔɪd] *n* humanoïde *mf*.

human papilloma virus *n* papillomavirus *m* humain.

human race ◇ *n* : **the ~** la race *OR* l'espèce humaine.
◇ *adj* humanoïde.

human resources *npl* ressources *fpl* humaines.

human rights *npl* droits *mpl* de l'homme ■ **a ~ organization** une organisation pour les droits de l'homme.

human shield *n* bouclier *m* humain.

human trafficking *n* trafic *m OR* traite *f* d'êtres humains.

humble ['hʌmbl] ◇ *adj* **1.** [meek] humble ■ **in my ~ opinion** à mon humble avis ■ **please accept my ~ apologies** veuillez accepter mes humbles excuses ■ **your ~ servant** [in letters] veuillez agréer, Monsieur, l'assurance de mes sentiments les plus respectueux ➲ **to eat ~ pie** faire de plates excuses, faire amende honorable ■ **to force sb to eat ~ pie** forcer qqn à se rétracter **2.** [modest] modeste ■ **she has ~ origins** elle a des origines modestes.
◇ *vt* humilier, mortifier ■ **to ~ o.s. before sb** s'humilier devant qqn ■ **it was a humbling experience** c'était une expérience humiliante.

humbly ['hʌmblɪ] *adv* **1.** [speak, ask] humblement, avec humilité **2.** [live] modestement.

humbug ['hʌmbʌg] (*pret & pp* **humbugged**, *cont* **humbugging**) ◇ *n* **1.** [person] charlatan *m*, fumiste *mf* ■ *(U)* [deception] charlatanisme *m* **2.** *(U)* [nonsense] balivernes *fpl* **3.** *UK* [sweet] berlingot *m*.
◇ *vt* tromper.

humdinger [ˌhʌm'dɪŋəʳ] *n inf* **1.** [person] : **she's a real ~!** elle est vraiment extra *OR* sensass *OR* terrible ! **2.** [thing] : **that was a ~ of a game!** quel match extraordinaire! ■ **they had a real ~ of a row!** ils se sont engueulés, quelque chose de bien!

humdrum ['hʌmdrʌm] ◇ *adj* [person, story] banal ■ [task, life] monotone, banal, routinier ■ **I'm sick of this ~ routine** j'en ai marre de ce traintrain.
◇ *n* monotonie *f*, banalité *f*.

humerus ['hjuːmərəs] (*pl* **humeri** [-raɪ]) *n* humérus *m*.

humid ['hjuːmɪd] *adj* humide.

humidifier [hjuː'mɪdɪfaɪəʳ] *n* humidificateur *m*.

humidify [hjuː'mɪdɪfaɪ] (*pret & pp* **humidified**) *vt* humidifier.

humidity [hjuː'mɪdətɪ] *n* humidité *f*.

humidor ['hjuːmɪdɔːʳ] *n* humidificateur *m*.

humiliate [hjuː'mɪlɪeɪt] *vt* humilier.

humiliating [hjuː'mɪlɪeɪtɪŋ] *adj* humiliant.

humiliatingly [hjuː'mɪlɪeɪtɪŋlɪ] *adv* d'une façon humiliante.

humiliation [hjuːˌmɪlɪ'eɪʃn] *n* humiliation *f*.

humility [hjuː'mɪlətɪ] *n* humilité *f*.

humming ['hʌmɪŋ] *n* [of bees, voices] bourdonnement *m* ■ [of air conditioner, traffic] ronronnement *m* ■ [of tune] fredonnement *m*.

hummingbird ['hʌmɪŋbɜːd] *n* oiseau-mouche *m*, colibri *m*.

hummus ['hʊmʊs] *n* houmous *m*.

humor *etc US* = **humour**.

humorist ['hjuːmərɪst] *n* humoriste *mf*.

humorous ['hjuːmərəs] *adj* [witty - remark] plein d'humour, amusant ; [- person] plein d'humour, drôle ■ **he replied in (a) ~ vein** il a répondu sur le mode humoristique.

humorously ['hjuːmərəslɪ] *adv* avec humour.

humour *UK*, **humor** *US* ['hjuːməʳ] ◇ *n* **1.** [wit, fun] humour *m* ■ **sense of ~** sens *m* de l'humour ■ **he's got no sense of ~** il n'a aucun sens de l'humour **2.** *fml* [mood] humeur *f*, disposition *f* **3.** *arch* & MED humeur *f*.
◇ *vt* [person - indulge, gratify] faire plaisir à ; [- treat tactfully] ménager ■ [whim, fantasy] se prêter à ■ **don't try to ~ me** n'essaie pas de m'amadouer.

humourless *UK*, **humorless** *US* ['hjuːməlɪs] *adj* [person] qui manque d'humour ■ [book, situation, speech] sans humour.

hump [hʌmp] ◇ *n* **1.** [on back of animal or person] bosse *f* ■ [hillock] bosse *f*, mamelon *m* ■ [bump] tas *m* ■ **we're over the ~ now** *inf* on a fait le plus dur *OR* gros maintenant **2.** *UK inf phr* **to get the ~** avoir le cafard *OR* le bourdon ■ **he gives me the ~** il me donne le cafard *OR* le bourdon.
◇ *vt* **1.** [back] arrondir, arquer **2.** *UK inf* [carry] trimbaler, trimballer **3.** △ [have sex with] baiser△.
◇ *vi*△ [have sex] baiser△.

humpback ['hʌmpbæk] *n* **1.** = **hunchback 2.** = **humpback whale**.

humpback(ed) bridge *n* pont *m* en dos d'âne.

humpbacked ['hʌmpbækt] = **hunchbacked**.

humpback whale *n* baleine *f* à bosse.

humph [mm, hʌmf] *interj* : **~!** hum!

humungous [hju:'mʌŋgəs] *adj inf* [huge] énorme ▪ [great] super, génial ▪ **the book was a ~ success** le livre a eu un méga succès.

humus ['hju:məs] *n* humus *m*.

Hun [hʌn] (*pl inv* OR *pl* **Huns**) *n* **1.** ANTIQ Hun *m* **2.**△ *dated & offens* Boche *m*.

hunch [hʌntʃ] ◇ *n* [inkling] pressentiment *m*, intuition *f* ▪ **I have a ~ we'll meet again** j'ai comme un pressentiment que nous nous reverrons ▪ **to act on a ~** suivre son instinct ▪ **it's only a ~** c'est une idée que j'ai.
◇ *vt* [back] arrondir ▪ [shoulders] voûter ▪ **don't ~ (up) your shoulders like that!** ne rentre pas la tête dans les épaules comme ça!

hunchback ['hʌntʃbæk] *n* **1.** [person] bossu *m*, - e *f* ▪ **'The Hunchback of Notre Dame'** *Hugo* 'Notre-Dame de Paris' **2.** ANAT bosse *f*.

hunchbacked ['hʌntʃbækt] *adj* bossu.

hunched [hʌntʃt] *adj* voûté ▪ **he sat ~ed in a corner** il était assis recroquevillé dans un coin ▪ **she was sitting ~ed (up) over her papers** elle était assise penchée sur ses papiers.

hundred ['hʌndrəd] ◇ *det* cent ▪ **a ~ guests** cent invités ▪ **six ~ pages** six cents pages ▪ **about a ~ metres** une centaine de mètres ▪ **one** OR **a ~ per cent** cent pour cent ▪ **I'm a ~ per cent sure** j'en suis absolument certain ▪ **to be a ~ per cent behind sb** soutenir qqn à fond ▪ **to give a** OR **one ~ per cent** se donner à fond ▪ **if I've told you once, I've told you a ~ times!** je te l'ai dit cent fois!
◇ *n* cent *m* ▪ **he has a ~ (of them)** il en a cent ▪ **one ~ and one** cent un ▪ **two ~** deux cents ▪ **two ~ and one** deux cent un ▪ **about a ~, a ~ odd** une centaine ▪ **in nineteen ~** en dix-neuf cents ▪ **in nineteen ~ and ten** en dix-neuf cent dix ▪ **I'll never forget him (even) if I live to be a ~** même si je deviens centenaire, je ne l'oublierai jamais ▪ **the theatre seats five ~** la salle contient cinq cents places (assises) ▪ **give me $500 in ~s** donnez-moi 500 dollars en billets de cent ▪ **in the seventeen ~s** au dix-septième siècle ▪ **~s of** des centaines de ▪ **I've asked you ~s of times!** je te l'ai demandé cent fois! ▪ **~s and thousands of people** des milliers de gens ▪ **they were dying in their ~s** OR **by the ~** ils mouraient par centaines.

hundredfold ['hʌndrədfəuld] ◇ *adj* centuple.
◇ *n* : **he has increased his initial investment (by) a ~** il a multiplié par cent son investissement initial.

hundreds and thousands *npl paillettes de sucre colorées servant à décorer les gâteaux.*

hundredth ['hʌndrətθ] *n* centième *mf* ▪ [fraction] centième *m*.

hundredweight ['hʌndrədweɪt] *n UK* (poids *m* de) cent douze livres *(50,8 kg)* ▪ *US* (poids *m* de) cent livres *(45,4 kg)*.

hundred-year-old *adj* centenaire.

Hundred Years' War *n* : **the ~** la guerre de Cent Ans.

hung [hʌŋ] ◇ *pt & pp* ▷ **hang**.
◇ *adj* [situation] bloqué ▪ **a ~ parliament/jury** un parlement/un jury sans majorité.

Hungarian [hʌŋ'geərɪən] ◇ *n* **1.** [person] Hongrois *m*, - e *f* **2.** LING hongrois *m*.
◇ *adj* hongrois.

Hungary ['hʌŋgərɪ] *pr n* Hongrie *f* ▪ **in ~** en Hongrie.

hunger ['hʌŋgəʳ] ◇ *n* faim *f* ▪ **a conference on world ~** une conférence sur la faim dans le monde ▪ **to satisfy one's ~ (for sthg)** satisfaire sa faim (de qqch) ▪ **he was driven by a ~ for truth/knowledge** *fig* il était poussé par une soif de vérité/de savoir.
◇ *vi fig* **to ~ after** OR **for sthg** avoir faim OR soif de qqch.

hunger march *n* marche *f* de la faim.

hunger strike *n* grève *f* de la faim ▪ **to go on (a) ~** faire la grève de la faim.

hunger striker *n* gréviste *mf* de la faim.

hung over *adj inf* **to be ~** avoir une OR la gueule de bois.

hungrily ['hʌŋgrəlɪ] *adv* [eat] voracement, avidement ▪ *fig* [read, listen] avidement.

hungry ['hʌŋgrɪ] (*comp* **hungrier**, *superl* **hungriest**) *adj* **1.** [for food] : **to be ~** avoir faim ▪ **he still felt ~** il avait encore faim ▪ **she looked tired and ~** elle avait l'air fatiguée et affamée ▪ **are you getting ~?** est-ce que tu commences à avoir faim? ▪ **to go ~** souffrir de la faim ▪ **he'd rather go ~ than cook for himself** il se passerait de manger plutôt que de faire la cuisine ▶ **this is ~ work!** ce travail donne faim! **2.** *fig* [desirous] avide ▪ **~ for affection** avide d'affection.

hung up *adj inf* coincé ▪ **to be ~ on sb/sthg** faire une fixation sur qqn/qqch ▪ **to be ~ about sthg** [personal problem] être complexé par qqch ; [sexual matters] être coincé quand il s'agit de qqch.

hunk [hʌŋk] *n* **1.** [piece] gros morceau *m* **2.** *inf* [man] beau mec *m* OR mâle *m*.

hunker ['hʌŋkəʳ] *vi US* **to ~ (down)** [crouch] s'accroupir ; [squat] s'asseoir sur ses talons, s'accroupir ; [animal] se tapir ▪ **I have to ~ down and work this term** *fig* je dois donner un bon coup de collier ce trimestre.

hunky ['hʌŋkɪ] *adj inf* **he's really ~** c'est un beau mec.

hunky-dory [,hʌŋkɪ'dɔ:rɪ] *adj inf* **to be ~** être au poil ▪ **everything is just ~!** tout baigne (dans l'huile)!

hunt [hʌnt] ◇ *vt* **1.** [for food, sport - subj: person] chasser, faire la chasse à ; [- subj: animal] chasser ▪ **they were ~ed to extinction** ils ont été chassés jusqu'à extinction de l'espèce **2.** *UK* SPORT [area] chasser dans ▪ **he ~s his horse all winter** il monte son cheval à la chasse tout l'hiver **3.** [pursue] pourchasser, poursuivre ▪ **he was being ~ed by the police** il était pourchassé OR recherché par la police **4.** [search] fouiller **5.** [drive out] chasser **6.** *phr* **to play ~ the slipper** OR **thimble** ≃ jouer à cache-tampon.
◇ *vi* **1.** [for food, sport] chasser ▪ **they ~ by night/in packs** ils chassent la nuit/en bande ▪ **to go ~ing** aller à la chasse ▪ **to ~ for sthg** [person] chasser OR faire la chasse à qqch ; [animal] chasser qqch **2.** [search] chercher (partout) ▪ **she ~ed (around** OR **about) in her bag for her keys** elle a fouillé dans son sac à la recherche de ses clefs ▪ **I've ~ed all over town for a linen jacket** j'ai parcouru OR fait toute la ville pour trouver une veste en lin **3.** TECH [gauge] osciller ▪ [engine] pomper.
◇ *n* **1.** SPORT [activity] chasse *f* ▪ [hunters] chasse *f*, chasseurs *mpl* ▪ [area] chasse *f* ▪ [fox-hunt] chasse *f* au renard ▪ **a tiger/bear ~** une chasse au tigre/à l'ours ▪ **~ ball** *bal réunissant les notables locaux amateurs de chasse* **2.** [search] chasse *f*, recherche *f* ▪ **the ~ is on for the terrorists** la chasse aux terroristes est en cours.
➤ **hunt down** *vt sep* [animal] forcer, traquer ▪ [person] traquer ▪ [thing, facts] dénicher ▪ [abuses, errors] faire la chasse à ▪ [truth] débusquer.
➤ **hunt out** *vt sep UK* dénicher, découvrir.
➤ **hunt up** *vt sep UK* [look up] rechercher.

hunted ['hʌntɪd] *adj* traqué ▪ **he has a ~ look about him** il a un air persécuté OR traqué.

hunter ['hʌntəʳ] *n* **1.** SPORT [person] chasseur *m* ▪ [horse] cheval *m* de chasse, hunter *m* ▪ [dog] chien *m* courant OR de chasse **2.** [gen] chasseur *m* ▪ [pursuer] poursuivant *m* **3.** [watch] (montre *f* à) savonnette *f*.

hunter-gatherer *n* chasseur-cueilleur *m*.

hunter-killer *adj* MIL d'attaque ▪ **a ~ submarine** un sous-marin d'attaque.

hunting ['hʌntɪŋ] ◇ *n* **1.** SPORT chasse *f* ▪ *UK* [fox-hunting] chasse *f* au renard ▪ HIST [mounted deer-hunt] chasse *f* à courre ▪ HIST [as an art] vénerie *f* **2.** [pursuit] chasse *f*, poursuite *f* ▪ **bargain ~** la chasse aux soldes.
◇ *adj* [boots, gun, knife, licence] de chasse.

hunting ground *n* SPORT & *fig* terrain *m* de chasse.

hunting horn *n* cor *m* OR trompe *f* de chasse.

hunting lodge *n* pavillon *m* de chasse.

hunting season *n* saison *f* de la chasse.

huntress ['hʌntrɪs] *n* chasseuse *f* ▪ **Diana the Huntress** *lit* Diane chasseresse.

hunt saboteur *n personne qui tente d'arrêter les parties de chasse à courre.*

huntsman ['hʌntsmən] (*pl* **huntsmen** [-mən]) *n* **1.** [hunter] chasseur *m* **2.** [master of hounds] veneur *m*.

hurdle ['hɜːdl] ◇ *n* **1.** SPORT haie *f* ▪ **the 400 metre ~s** le 400 mètres haies ▪ **she's the British ~s champion** elle est la championne britannique de course de haies ▪ **to take** OR **to clear a ~** franchir une haie **2.** *fig* obstacle *m* ▪ **the next ~ will be getting funding for the project** la prochaine difficulté sera d'obtenir des fonds pour le projet **3.** [for fences] claie *f*.
◇ *vt* [jump] sauter, franchir ▪ [overcome] franchir.
◇ *vi* SPORT faire de la course de haies.

hurdler ['hɜːdləʳ] *n* coureur *m*, - euse *f (qui fait des courses de haies).*

hurdy-gurdy ['hɜːdɪ,gɜːdɪ] *n* **1.** [barrel organ] orgue *m* de Barbarie **2.** [medieval instrument] vielle *f*.

hurl [hɜːl] *vt* **1.** [throw] lancer, jeter (avec violence) ▪ **to ~ o.s. at sb/sthg** se ruer sur qqn/qqch ▪ **he ~ed a vase at him** il lui a lancé un vase à la figure ▪ **they were ~ed to the ground** ils ont été précipités OR jetés à terre ▪ **she ~ed herself off the top of the tower** elle s'est précipitée OR jetée (du haut) de la tour ▪ **the boat was ~ed onto the rocks** le bateau a été projeté sur les rochers **2.** [yell] lancer, jeter ▪ **to ~ abuse at sb** lancer des injures à qqn, accabler qqn d'injures.

hurling ['hɜːlɪŋ] *n* SPORT *jeu irlandais voisin du hockey sur gazon.*

hurly-burly ['hɜːlɪ,bɜːlɪ] *UK* ◇ *n* tohu-bohu *m* ▪ **the ~ of city life** le tourbillon de la vie urbaine.
◇ *adj* turbulent.

Huron ['hjʊərən] *pr n* : **Lake ~** le lac Huron.

hurrah *UK* [hʊ'rɑː], **hurray** [hʊ'reɪ] ◇ *n* hourra *m*.
◇ *interj* : **~!** hourra!

hurricane ['hʌrɪkən] *n* ouragan *m* ▪ [in Caribbean] hurricane *m*.

hurricane force *n* force *f* douze (sur l'échelle Beaufort).
◆ **hurricane-force** *comp* : **hurricane-force winds** TECH des vents de force douze.

hurricane lamp *n* lampe-tempête *f*.

hurried ['hʌrɪd] *adj* [meeting, reply, gesture, trip] rapide ▪ [departure, steps] précipité ▪ [judgment, decision] hâtif ▪ [work] fait à la hâte ▪ **to have a ~ meal** manger à la hâte ▪ **I wrote a ~ note to reassure her** j'ai écrit un mot à la hâte OR un mot bref pour la rassurer.

hurriedly ['hʌrɪdlɪ] *adv* [examine] à la hâte ▪ [leave] précipitamment ▪ **she passed ~ over the unpleasant details** elle passa en vitesse sur les détails désagréables ▪ **he ~ excused himself** il s'est empressé de s'excuser.

hurry ['hʌrɪ] ◇ *n* (*pl* **hurries**) **1.** [rush] hâte *f*, précipitation *f* ▪ **to be in a ~ to do sthg** avoir hâte de faire qqch ▪ **not now, I'm in (too much of) a ~** pas maintenant, je suis (trop) pressé ▪ **he needs it in a ~** il en a besoin tout de suite ▪ **there's no big** OR **great ~** rien ne presse ▪ **there's no ~ for it** cela ne presse pas ▪ **what's the** OR **your ~ ?** qu'est-ce qui (vous) presse? ▪ **it was obviously written in a ~** de toute évidence, cela a été écrit à la hâte ▪ **he won't try that again in a ~!** *UK inf* il ne ressaiera pas de sitôt!, il n'est pas près de ressayer! **2.** [eagerness] empressement *m* ▪ **he's in no ~ to see her again** il n'est pas pressé OR il n'a aucune hâte de la revoir.
◇ *vi* (*pret & pp* **hurried**) se dépêcher, se presser, se hâter ▪ **I must** OR **I'd better ~** il faut que je me dépêche ▪ **you don't have to ~ over that report** vous pouvez prendre votre temps pour faire ce rapport ▪ **he hurried into/out of the room** il est entré dans/sorti de la pièce en toute hâte OR précipitamment ▪ **~! it's already started** dépêche-toi! c'est déjà commencé.
◇ *vt* (*pret & pp* **hurried**) **1.** [chivvy along] faire se dépêcher, presser, bousculer ▪ **don't ~ him** ne le bouscule pas ▪ **she won't be hurried, you can't ~ her** vous ne la ferez pas se dépêcher ▪ **they hurried him through customs** ils lui ont fait passer la douane à la hâte **2.** [preparations, work] activer, presser, hâter ▪ **this decision can't be hurried** cette décision exige d'être prise sans hâte **3.** [transport hastily] emmener d'urgence ▪ **aid was hurried to the stricken town** des secours ont été envoyés d'urgence à la ville sinistrée.
◆ **hurry along** ◇ *vi insep* marcher d'un pas pressé ▪ **~ along now!** pressons, pressons!
◇ *vt sep* [person] faire presser le pas à, faire se dépêcher OR s'activer ▪ [work] activer, accélérer.
◆ **hurry on** *vi insep* se dépêcher, continuer à la hâte OR en hâte ▪ **he hurried on to the next shelter** il s'est pressé de gagner l'abri suivant.
◆ **hurry up** ◇ *vi insep* se dépêcher, se presser ▪ **~ up!** dépêchez-vous!
◇ *vt sep* [person] faire se dépêcher ▪ [production, work] activer, pousser.

hurt [hɜːt] (*pret & pp* **hurt**) ◇ *vt* **1.** [cause physical pain to] faire mal à ▪ **to ~ o.s.** se faire mal ▪ **I ~ my elbow on the door** je me suis fait mal au coude contre la porte ▪ **is your back ~ing you today?** est-ce que tu as mal au dos aujourd'hui? ▪ **where does it ~ you?** où est-ce que vous avez mal?, où cela vous fait-il mal? **2.** [injure] blesser ▪ **two people were ~ in the crash** deux personnes ont été blessées dans la collision **3.** [upset] blesser, faire de la peine à ▪ **he was very ~ by your criticism** il a été très blessé par vos critiques ▪ **to ~ sb's feelings** blesser OR froisser qqn **4.** [disadvantage] nuire à ▪ **the new tax will ~ the middle classes most** ce sont les classes moyennes qui seront les plus touchées par le nouvel impôt ▪ **a bit of fresh air won't ~ you** un peu d'air frais OR de grand air ne te fera pas de mal **5.** [damage - crops, machine] abîmer, endommager ; [- eyesight] abîmer.
◇ *vi* faire mal ▪ **my head ~s** ma tête me fait mal ▪ **where does it ~?** où est-ce que vous avez mal? ▪ **he's ~ ing** *US* il a mal.
◇ *n* **1.** [physical pain] mal *m* ▪ [wound] blessure *f* **2.** [mental pain] peine *f* ▪ **he wanted to make up for the ~ he had caused them** il voulait réparer la peine qu'il leur avait faite **3.** [damage] tort *m*.
◇ *adj* **1.** [physically] blessé ▪ **he's more frightened than ~** il a eu plus de peur que de mal **2.** [offended] froissé, blessé ▪ **a ~ expression** un regard meurtri OR blessé ▪ **don't feel ~** ne le prends pas mal **3.** *US* [damaged] : **~ books** livres endommagés.

hurtful ['hɜːtfʊl] *adj* [event] préjudiciable, nuisible ▪ [memory] pénible ▪ [remark] blessant, offensant ▪ **what a ~ thing to say!** comme c'est méchant OR cruel de dire cela!

hurtle ['hɜːtl] *vi* : **to ~ along** avancer à toute vitesse OR allure ▪ **he went hurtling down the stairs** il dévala les escaliers ▪ **the motorbike came hurtling towards him** la moto fonça sur lui à toute vitesse.

husband ['hʌzbənd] ◇ *n* mari *m*, époux *m* ▪ **are they ~ and wife?** sont-ils mari et femme? ▪ **they lived (together) as ~ and wife** ils vivaient maritalement OR comme mari et femme.
◇ *vt* [resources, strength] ménager, économiser.

husbandry ['hʌzbəndrɪ] *n* **1.** AGRIC agriculture *f* ▪ [as science] agronomie *f* **2.** *fml* [thrift] économie *f*.

hush [hʌʃ] ◇ *n* silence *m*, calme *m* ▪ **a ~ fell over the room** un silence s'est installé OR s'est fait dans la salle.
◇ *interj* : **~!** [gen] silence! ; [stop talking] chut!
◇ *vt* **1.** [silence] faire taire **2.** [appease] calmer.
◇ *vi* se taire.

◆ **hush up** *vt sep* **1.** [affair] étouffer ▪ [witness] faire taire, empêcher de parler **2.** [noisy person] faire taire.

hushed [hʌʃt] *adj* [whisper, voice] étouffé ▪ [silence] profond, grand ▪ **to speak in ~ tones** parler à voix basse.

hush-hush *adj inf* secret, - ète *f*, archi-secret.

hush money *n (U) inf* pot-de-vin *m (pour acheter le silence)* ▪ **to pay sb ~** acheter le silence de qqn.

husk [hʌsk] ◇ *n* [of wheat, oats] balle *f* ▪ [of maize, rice] enveloppe *f* ▪ [of nut] écale *f*.
◇ *vt* [oats, barley] monder ▪ [maize] éplucher ▪ [rice] décortiquer ▪ [wheat] vanner ▪ [nuts] écaler.

huskily ['hʌskɪlɪ] *adv* [speak] d'une voix rauque ▪ [sing] d'une voix voilée.

husky ['hʌskɪ] ◇ *adj (comp* **huskier**, *superl* **huskiest) 1.** [of voice - hoarse] rauque, enroué ; [- breathy] voilé **2.** *inf* [burly] costaud.
◇ *n (pl* **huskies**) [dog] chien *m* esquimau OR de traîneau.

hussar [hʊ'zɑːʳ] *n* hussard *m*.

hussy ['hʌsɪ] (*pl* **hussies**) *n arch* & *hum* [shameless woman] garce *f*, gourgandine *f dated* ▪ **you brazen ~ !** espèce de garce!

hustings ['hʌstɪŋz] *npl UK* **1.** [campaign] campagne *f* électorale ▪ **to go/to be out on the ~** partir/être en campagne électorale **2.** [occasion for speeches] ≃ débat *m* public *(pendant la campagne électorale)*.

hustle ['hʌsl] ◇ *vt* **1.** [cause to move - quickly] presser ; [- roughly] bousculer, pousser ▪ **to ~ sb in/out** faire entrer/sortir qqn énergiquement ▪ **he ~d us into the president's office** il nous a pressés d'entrer chez le président ▪ **he was ~d away** OR **off by two men** il a été emmené de force par deux hommes **2.** *inf* [obtain - resourcefully] faire tout pour avoir ; [- underhandedly] magouiller pour avoir **3.** *US inf* [swindle] rouler, arnaquer ▪ **he ~d me out of $100** il m'a roulé OR arnaqué de 100 dollars ▮ [pressure] : **to ~ sb into doing sthg** forcer la main à qqn pour qu'il fasse qqch **4.** *US inf* [steal] piquer **5.** △ *US* [subj: prostitute] racoler.
◇ *vi* **1.** *UK* [shove] bousculer **2.** = **hurry 3.** *US inf* [work hard] se bagarrer(pour réussir) **4.** △ *US* [engage in suspect activity] monter des coups, trafiquer ▪ [politically] magouiller **5.** △ *US* [prostitute] faire le tapin△, tapiner△.
◇ *n* **1.** [crush] bousculade *f* **2.** [bustle] grande activité *f* ▪ **the ~ and bustle of the big city** le tourbillon d'activité des grandes villes **3.** △ *US* [swindle] arnaque *f*.
◆ **hustle up** *US inf* ◇ *vt sep* [prepare quickly] préparer en cinq sec.
◇ *vi insep* & *vt sep* = **hurry up**.

hustler ['hʌsləʳ] *n* **1.** *inf* [dynamic person] type *m* dynamique, débrouillard *m*, - e *f*, magouilleur *m*, - euse *f* **2.** *inf* [swindler] arnaqueur *m*, - euse *f* **3.** △ *US* [prostitute] putain△ *f*.

hut [hʌt] *n* [primitive dwelling] hutte *f* ▪ [shed] cabane *f*, baraque *f* ▪ [alpine] refuge *m*, chalet-refuge *m* ▪ MIL baraquement *m*.

hutch [hʌtʃ] *n* **1.** [cage] cage *f* ▪ [for rabbits] clapier *m* **2.** [chest] coffre *m* **3.** TECH [kneading trough] pétrin *m*, huche *f* **4.** MIN [wagon] wagonnet *m*, benne *f* (roulante).

hyacinth ['haɪəsɪnθ] *n* **1.** BOT jacinthe *f* **2.** [gem] hyacinthe *f* **3.** [colour] bleu jacinthe *inv*, bleu violet *inv*.

hyaena [haɪ'iːnə] = **hyena**.

hybrid ['haɪbrɪd] ◇ *n* [gen] hybride *m* ▪ [bicycle] VTC *m*.
◇ *adj* hybride.

hydra ['haɪdrə] (*pl* **hydras** OR *pl* **hydrae** [-driː]) *n fig* & ZOOL hydre *f*.
◆ **Hydra** *pr n* MYTH Hydre *f* (de Lerne).

hydrangea [haɪ'dreɪndʒə] *n* hortensia *m*.

hydrant ['haɪdrənt] *n* prise *f* d'eau.

hydrate ['haɪdreɪt] ◇ *n* hydrate *m*.
◇ *vt* hydrater.
◇ *vi* s'hydrater.

hydration [haɪ'dreɪʃn] *n* hydratation *f*.

hydraulic [haɪ'drɔːlɪk] *adj* hydraulique ▪ **~ engineer** ingénieur *m* hydraulicien, hydraulicien *m*, - enne *f*.

hydraulic brake *n* frein *m* hydraulique.

hydraulic press *n* presse *f* hydraulique.

hydraulics [haɪ'drɔːlɪks] *n (U)* hydraulique *f*.

hydraulic suspension *n* suspension *f* hydraulique.

hydro ['haɪdrəʊ] *n UK* [spa] établissement *m* thermal *(hôtel)*.

hydrocarbon [ˌhaɪdrə'kɑːbən] *n* hydrocarbure *m*.

hydrocephalic [ˌhaɪdrəsɪ'fælɪk] *adj* hydrocéphale.

hydrochloric [ˌhaɪdrə'klɒrɪk] *adj* chlorhydrique ▪ **~ acid** acide *m* chlorhydrique.

hydroelectric [ˌhaɪdrəʊɪ'lektrɪk] *adj* hydro-électrique ▪ **~ power** énergie *f* hydro-électrique.

hydroelectricity [ˌhaɪdrəʊɪlek'trɪsətɪ] *n* hydro-électricité *f*.

hydrofoil ['haɪdrəfɔɪl] *n* hydrofoil *m*, hydroptère *m*.

hydrogen ['haɪdrədʒən] *n* hydrogène *m*.

hydrogen bomb *n* bombe *f* à hydrogène.

hydrogen peroxide *n* eau *f* oxygénée.

hydrogen sulphide *n* acide *m* sulfhydrique, hydrogène *m* sulfuré.

hydrology [haɪ'drɒlədʒɪ] *n* hydrologie *f*.

hydrometer [haɪ'drɒmɪtəʳ] *n* hydromètre *m*.

hydropathy [haɪ'drɒpəθɪ] *n* hydropathie *f*.

hydrophobia [ˌhaɪdrə'fəʊbjə] *n* hydrophobie *f*.

hydroplane ['haɪdrəpleɪn] *vi* se dresser comme un hydroglisseur.

hydroponics [ˌhaɪdrə'pɒnɪks] *n (U)* culture *f* hydroponique.

hydrostatics [ˌhaɪdrə'stætɪks] *n (U)* hydrostatique *f*.

hydrotherapy [ˌhaɪdrə'θerəpɪ] *n* hydrothérapie *f*.

hyena [haɪ'iːnə] *n* hyène *f*.

hygiene ['haɪdʒiːn] *n* hygiène *f* ▪ **personal ~** hygiène personnelle OR corporelle.

hygienic [haɪ'dʒiːnɪk] *adj* hygiénique.

hygienically [haɪ'dʒiːnɪklɪ] *adv* de façon hygiénique.

hygienist [haɪ'dʒiːnɪst] *n* ≃ assistant *m* OR assistante *f* dentaire *(qui s'occupe du détartrage etc)*.

hygrometer [haɪ'grɒmɪtəʳ] *n* hygromètre *m*.

hymen ['haɪmen] *n* ANAT hymen *m*.

hymn [hɪm] ◇ *n* **1.** RELIG hymne *f*, cantique *m* **2.** [gen - song of praise] hymne *m*.
◇ *vt lit* chanter un hymne à la gloire de.

hymnal ['hɪmnəl] = **hymn book**.

hymn book *n* livre *m* de cantiques.

hype [haɪp] ◇ *n inf (U)* [publicity] battage *m* publicitaire ▪ **the film got a lot of ~** il y a eu une publicité monstre autour de ce film ▪ **it's all ~** ce n'est que du bla-bla.
◇ *vt inf* **1.** [falsify] baratiner **2.** [publicize] monter un gros coup de pub autour de ▪ **her latest novel has been heavily ~d** son dernier roman a été lancé à grand renfort de publicité.

hyped up [haɪpt-] *adj inf* speed *(inv)*, speedé.

hyper ['haɪpəʳ] *adj inf* **1.** = **hyperactive 2.** [angry] furax *(inv)*.

hyperactive [ˌhaɪpər'æktɪv] *adj* hyperactif.

hyperactivity [ˌhaɪpəræk'tɪvətɪ] *n* hyperactivité *f*.

hyperbola [haɪ'pɜːbələ] *n* MATHS hyperbole *f*.

hyperbole [haɪ'pɜːbəlɪ] *n* hyperbole *f*.

hyperbolic(al) [ˌhaɪpə'bɒlɪk(l)] *adj* hyperbolique.

hypercritical [ˌhaɪpə'krɪtɪkl] *adj* hypercritique.

hyperglycaemia *UK*, **hyperglycemia** *US* [,haɪpəglaɪ'siːmɪə] *n* hyperglycémie *f*.

hyperinflation [,haɪpərɪn'fleɪʃn] *n* hyperinflation *f*.

Hyperion [haɪ'pɪərɪən] *pr n* Hypérion.

hyperlink ['haɪpəlɪŋk] *n* COMPUT lien *m* hypertexte, hyperlien *m*.

hypermarket [,haɪpə'mɑːkɪt] *n UK* hypermarché *m*.

hyperrealism [,haɪpə'rɪəlɪzm] *n* hyperréalisme *m*.

hypersensitive [,haɪpə'sensɪtɪv] *adj* hypersensible.

hypersensitivity ['haɪpə,sensɪ'tɪvətɪ] *n* hypersensibilité *f*.

hypersonic [,haɪpə'sɒnɪk] *adj* hypersonique.

hyperspace ['haɪpəspeɪs] *n* hyperespace *m*.

hypertension [,haɪpə'tenʃn] *n* hypertension *f*.

hypertext ['haɪpətekst] *n* COMPUT & LIT hypertexte *m*.

hyperventilate [,haɪpə'ventɪleɪt] *vi* faire de l'hyperventilation *OR* de l'hyperpnée.

hyperventilation ['haɪpə,ventɪ'leɪʃn] *n* hyperventilation *f*, hyperpnée *f*.

hyphen ['haɪfn] ◇ *n* trait *m* d'union.
◇ *vt* = **hyphenate**.

hyphenate ['haɪfəneɪt] *vt* mettre un trait d'union à ■ **a ~ed word** un mot à trait d'union.

hypnosis [hɪp'nəʊsɪs] *n* hypnose *f* ■ **to be under ~** être sous hypnose, être en état hypnotique *OR* d'hypnose MED.

hypnotherapy [,hɪpnəʊ'θerəpɪ] *n* hypnothérapie *f*.

hypnotic [hɪp'nɒtɪk] ◇ *adj* hypnotique.
◇ *n* [drug] hypnotique *m* ■ [person] hypnotique *mf*.

hypnotism ['hɪpnətɪzm] *n* hypnotisme *m*.

hypnotist ['hɪpnətɪst] *n* hypnotiseur *m*, - euse *f*.

hypnotize, ise ['hɪpnətaɪz] *vt* hypnotiser.

hypoallergenic ['haɪpəʊ,ælə'dʒenɪk] *adj* hypoallergique.

hypocentre *UK*, **hypocenter** *US* ['haɪpəʊ,sentər] *n* **1.** [of earthquake] hypocentre *m* **2.** NUCL PHYS point *m* zéro.

hypochondria [,haɪpə'kɒndrɪə] *n* hypocondrie *f*.

hypochondriac [,haɪpə'kɒndrɪæk] ◇ *adj* hypocondriaque.
◇ *n* hypocondriaque *mf*, malade *mf* imaginaire.

hypocoristic [,haɪpəkɔː'rɪstɪk] *adj* LING hypocoristique.

hypocrisy [hɪ'pɒkrəsɪ] (*pl* **hypocrisies**) *n* hypocrisie *f*.

hypocrite ['hɪpəkrɪt] *n* hypocrite *mf*.

hypocritical [,hɪpə'krɪtɪkl] *adj* hypocrite ■ **it would be ~ of me to get married in church** ce serait hypocrite de ma part de me marier à l'église.

hypodermic [,haɪpə'dɜːmɪk] ◇ *adj* hypodermique ■ **~ needle** aiguille *f* hypodermique.
◇ *n* **1.** [syringe] seringue *f* hypodermique **2.** [injection] injection *f* hypodermique.

hypoglycaemia *UK*, **hypoglycemia** *US* [,haɪpəʊglaɪ'siːmɪə] *n* hypoglycémie *f*.

hypoglycaemic *UK*, **hypoglycemic** *US* [,haɪpəʊglaɪ'siːmɪk] *adj* hypoglycémiant.

hypotenuse [haɪ'pɒtənjuːz] *n* hypoténuse *f*.

hypothermia [,haɪpəʊ'θɜːmɪə] *n* hypothermie *f*.

hypothesis [haɪ'pɒθɪsɪs] (*pl* **hypotheses** [-siːz]) *n* hypothèse *f* ■ **to put forward** *OR* **to advance a ~** émettre *OR* énoncer une hypothèse ■ **this confirms my ~ that...** cela confirme mon hypothèse selon *OR* d'après laquelle...

hypothesize, ise [haɪ'pɒθɪsaɪz] ◇ *vt* supposer ■ **he ~d that she was not in fact the killer** il a formulé l'hypothèse selon laquelle ce ne serait pas elle l'assassin.
◇ *vi* faire des hypothèses *OR* des suppositions.

hypothetical [,haɪpə'θetɪkl] *adj* hypothétique ■ **it's purely ~** c'est purement hypothétique.

hypothetically [,haɪpə'θetɪklɪ] *adv* hypothétiquement.

hysterectomy [,hɪstə'rektəmɪ] (*pl* **hysterectomies**) *n* hystérectomie *f*.

hysteria [hɪs'tɪərɪə] *n* **1.** PSYCHOL hystérie *f* **2.** [hysterical behaviour] crise *f* de nerfs ■ **his voice betrayed his mounting ~** sa voix trahissait la montée d'une crise de nerfs ■ **the crowd was on the edge** *OR* **verge of ~** *fig* la foule était au bord de l'hystérie.

hysteric [hɪs'terɪk] *n* PSYCHOL hystérique *mf*.

hysterical [hɪs'terɪkl] *adj* **1.** PSYCHOL hystérique **2.** [sobs, voice] hystérique ■ [laugh] hystérique, nerveux ■ **he was ~ with grief** il était fou de chagrin **3.** [overexcited] : **it's nothing to get ~ about!** ce n'est pas la peine de faire une crise (de nerfs) ! **4.** *inf* [very funny] tordant, hilarant.

hysterically [hɪs'terɪklɪ] *adv* hystériquement ■ **it was ~ funny!** c'était super drôle!

hysterics [hɪs'terɪks] *npl* **1.** = **hysteria** *(sense 1)* **2.** [fit] (violente) crise *f* de nerfs ■ **to go into** *OR* **to have ~** avoir une (violente) crise de nerfs **3.** *inf* [laughter] crise *f* de rire ■ **to go into** *OR* **to have ~** attraper un *OR* avoir le fou rire ■ **he had me in ~** il m'a fait mourir de rire.

Hz (*written abbrev of* **hertz**) Hz.

i (*pl* **i's** *OR pl* **is**), **I** (*pl* **I's** *OR pl* **Is**) [aɪ] *n* [letter] i *m*, I *m* ▪ **I as in Ivor** ≃ I comme Irma, *see also* **F**.

I [aɪ] *pron* [gen] je, j' *(before vowel or silent 'h')* ▪ [emphatic] moi ▪ **I like skiing** j'aime skier ▪ **Ann and I have known each other for years** Ann et moi nous connaissons depuis des années ▪ **I found it, not you** c'est moi qui l'ai trouvé, pas vous.

IA *written abbr of* **Iowa**.

IAEA (*abbrev of* **International Atomic Energy Agency**) *pr n* AIEA *f*.

iambic [aɪ'æmbɪk] *adj* iambique ▪ **~ pentameter** pentamètre *m* iambique.

IBA (*abbrev of* **Independent Broadcasting Authority**) *pr n organisme d'agrément et de coordination des stations de radio et chaînes de télévision du secteur privé en Grande-Bretagne*.

Iberia [aɪ'bɪərɪə] *pr n* Ibérie *f* ▪ **in ~** en Ibérie.

Iberian [aɪ'bɪərɪən] ◇ *n* **1.** [person] Ibère *mf* **2.** LING ibère *m*.
◇ *adj* ibérique.

Iberian Peninsula *pr n* : **the ~** la péninsule Ibérique.

ibex ['aɪbeks] (*pl inv OR pl* **ibexes**) *n* bouquetin *m*.

ibid (*written abbrev of* **ibidem**) ibid.

ibis ['aɪbɪs] (*pl inv OR pl* **ibises**) *n* ibis *m*.

Ibiza [ɪ'bi:θə] *pr n* Ibiza ▪ **in ~** à Ibiza.

IBRD (*abbrev of* **International Bank for Reconstruction and Development**) *n* BIRD *f*.

i/c *written abbr of* **in charge**.

Icarus ['ɪkərəs] *pr n* Icare.

ICBM (*abbrev of* **intercontinental ballistic missile**) *n* ICBM *m*.

ice [aɪs] ◇ *n* **1.** *(U)* [frozen water] glace *f* ▪ [ice cube] glaçon *m*, glaçons *mpl* ▪ **her feet were like ~** elle avait les pieds gelés ▶ **to put sthg on ~ : the reforms have been put on ~** les réformes ont été gelées ▪ **to walk** *OR* **to be on thin ~** avancer en terrain miné **2.** [on road] verglas *m* **3.** [in ice rink] glace *f* **4.** [ice-cream] glace *f* **5.** △ *(U)* *US* [diamonds] diams△ *mpl*, cailloux△ *mpl*.
◇ *vt* **1.** [chill - drink] rafraîchir ; [- with ice cubes] mettre des glaçons dans **2.** [cake] glacer.
◇ *vi* (se) givrer.
◆ **ice over** ◇ *vi insep* [lake, river etc] geler ▪ [window, propellers] (se) givrer.
◇ *vt sep* : **to be ~d over** [lake, river etc] être gelé ; [window, propellers] être givré.
◆ **ice up** ◇ *vi insep* **1.** [lock, windscreen, propellers] (se) givrer, se couvrir de givre **2.** [road] se couvrir de verglas.
◇ *vt sep* : **to be ~d up** [lock, windscreen, propellers] être givré ; [road] être verglacé.

ice age *n* période *f* glaciaire.
◆ **ice-age** *adj* (datant) de la période glaciaire.

ice axe *n* piolet *m*.

iceberg ['aɪsbɜ:g] *n* **1.** iceberg *m* **2.** *inf* [cold person] glaçon *m*.

iceberg lettuce *n salade aux feuilles serrées et croquantes*.

ice blue ◇ *n* bleu métallique *m*.
◇ *adj* bleu métallique *(inv)*.

icebound ['aɪsbaʊnd] *adj* bloqué par les glaces.

icebox ['aɪsbɒks] *n* **1.** *UK* [freezer compartment] freezer *m* **2.** [coolbox] glacière *f* **3.** *fig* glacière *f* ▪ **their house is like an ~** c'est une vraie glacière *OR* on gèle chez eux.

icebreaker ['aɪs,breɪkər] *n* **1.** [vessel] brise-glace *m inv* **2.** [at party] façon *f* de briser la glace.

ice bucket *n* seau *m* à glace.

ice cap *n* calotte *f* glaciaire.

ice-cold *adj* [hands, drink] glacé ▪ [house, manners] glacial.

ice cream *n* glace *f* ▪ **chocolate/strawberry ~** glace au chocolat/à la fraise.

ice-cream cone, ice-cream cornet *n* cornet *m* de glace.

ice-cream parlour *n* salon *m* de dégustation de glaces.

ice-cream soda *n* soda *m* avec de la glace.

ice-cream van *n* camionnette *f* de vendeur de glaces.

ice cube *n* glaçon *m*.

iced [aɪst] *adj* **1.** [chilled - drink] glacé **2.** [decorated - cake, biscuit] glacé.

ice dancing *n* danse *f* sur glace.

icefield ['aɪsfi:ld] *n* champ *m* de glace, ice-field *m*.

ice floe *n* glace *f* flottante.

ice hockey *n* hockey *m* sur glace.

Iceland ['aɪslənd] *pr n* Islande *f* ▪ **in ~** en Islande.

Icelander ['aɪsləndər] *n* Islandais *m*, - e *f*.

Icelandic [aɪs'lændɪk] ◇ *n* islandais *m*.
◇ *adj* islandais.

ice lolly (*pl* **ice lollies**) *n* *UK* ≃ sucette *f* glacée.

ice pack *n* **1.** [pack ice] banquise *f* **2.** [ice bag] sac *m* à glaçons ▪ MED poche *f* à glace.

ice pick *n* pic *m* à glace.

ice rink *n* patinoire *f*.

ice show *n* spectacle *m* sur glace.

ice skate *n* patin *m* (à glace).
◆ **ice-skate** *vi* patiner ▪ [professionally] faire du patinage (sur glace) ▪ [for pleasure] faire du patin (à glace).

ice-skater *n* patineur *m*, - euse *f*.

ice-skating *n* patinage *m* (sur glace) ▪ **to go ~** faire du patin (à glace).

ice water *n* US eau *f* glacée.

icicle ['aɪsɪkl] *n* glaçon *m (qui pend d'une gouttière etc)*.

icily ['aɪsɪlɪ] *adv* d'une manière glaciale ▪ **to answer ~** répondre d'un ton OR sur un ton glacial.

icing ['aɪsɪŋ] *n* **1.** CULIN glaçage *m* ▪ **it's the ~ on the cake** *fig* c'est la cerise sur le gâteau **2.** [on aeroplane - process] givrage *m* ; [- ice] givre *m*.

icing sugar *n* UK sucre *m* glace.

ICJ (*abbrev of* **International Court of Justice**) *pr n* CIJ *f*.

icon ['aɪkɒn] *n* icône *f*.

iconoclast [aɪ'kɒnəklæst] *n* iconoclaste *mf*.

iconoclastic [aɪˌkɒnə'klæstɪk] *adj* iconoclaste.

iconography [ˌaɪkɒ'nɒgrəfɪ] *n* iconographie *f*.

ICR (*abbrev of* **Institute for Cancer Research**) *pr n institut américain de recherche sur le cancer*.

ICU [ˌaisi:'ju:] (*abbrev of* **intensive care unit**) *n* MED service *m* de soins intensifs.

icy ['aɪsɪ] (*comp* **icier**, *superl* **iciest**) *adj* **1.** [weather] glacial ▪ [hands] glacé ▪ [ground] gelé **2.** [covered in ice - road] verglacé ; [- window, propeller] givré, couvert de givre **3.** *fig* [reception, stare] glacial.

id [ɪd] *n* PSYCHOL ça *m*.

I'd [aɪd] = **I had**, = **I would**.

ID <> *n (U)* (*abbrev of* **identification**) papiers *mpl* ▪ **do you have any ~?** vous avez une pièce d'identité?
<> *written abbr of* **Idaho**.

Idaho ['aɪdəhəʊ] *pr n* Idaho *m* ▪ **in ~** dans l'Idaho.

ID card *n* carte *f* d'identité.

IDD (*abbrev of* **international direct dialling**) *n* indicatif *m* du pays.

idea [aɪ'dɪə] *n* **1.** [plan, suggestion, inspiration] idée *f* ▪ **what a good ~!** quelle bonne idée! ▪ **I've had an ~** j'ai une idée ▪ **it wasn't MY ~!** l'idée n'était pas de moi! ▪ **~s man** concepteur *m* ◐ **that's an ~!** ça, c'est une bonne idée! ▪ **that's the ~!** c'est ça! ▪ **what's the ~?** [showing disapproval] qu'est-ce que ça veut dire OR signifie? ▪ **the very ~!** en voilà une idée!
2. [notion] idée *f* ▪ **our ~s about the universe** notre conception de l'univers ▪ **sorry, but this is not my ~ of fun** désolé, mais je ne trouve pas ça drôle OR ça ne m'amuse pas ▪ **don't put ~s into his head** ne va pas lui fourrer OR lui mettre des idées dans la tête ▪ **it was a nice ~ to phone** c'est gentil d'avoir pensé à téléphoner ▪ **you've no ~ of the conditions in which they lived** tu ne peux pas t'imaginer les conditions dans lesquelles ils vivaient ▪ **has anyone any ~ how the accident occurred?** est-ce qu'on a une idée de la façon dont l'accident est arrivé? ▪ **I have a rough ~ of what happened** je m'imagine assez bien ce qui est arrivé ▪ **no ~!** aucune idée! ▪ **I haven't the slightest ~** je n'en ai pas la moindre idée ▪ **I've no ~ where it came from** je ne sais vraiment pas d'où ça vient ▪ **what gave him the ~ that it would be easy?** qu'est-ce qui lui a laissé croire que ce serait facile?
3. [estimate] indication *f*, idée *f* ▪ **can you give me an ~ of how much it will cost?** est-ce que vous pouvez m'indiquer à peu près combien ça va coûter?
4. [suspicion] soupçon *m*, idée *f* ▪ **she had an ~ that something was going to happen** elle se doutait que quelque chose allait arriver ▪ **I've an ~ that he'll succeed** j'ai dans l'idée qu'il finira par réussir
5. [objective, intention] but *m* ▪ **the ~ is to provide help for people in need** il s'agit d'aider ceux qui sont dans le besoin.

ideal [aɪ'dɪəl] <> *adj* idéal ▪ **that's ~!** c'est parfait! ◐ **the Ideal Home Exhibition** ≃ le salon de l'habitat.
<> *n* idéal *m*.

idealism [aɪ'dɪəlɪzm] *n* idéalisme *m*.

idealist [aɪ'dɪəlɪst] <> *n* idéaliste *mf*.
<> *adj* idéaliste.

idealistic [aɪˌdɪə'lɪstɪk] *adj* idéaliste.

idealize, ise [aɪ'dɪəlaɪz] *vt* idéaliser.

ideally [aɪ'dɪəlɪ] *adv* **1.** [perfectly] parfaitement ▪ **the shop is ~ situated** l'emplacement du magasin est idéal **2.** [in a perfect world] dans l'idéal ▪ **~, this wine should be served at room temperature** normalement OR pour bien faire, ce vin doit être servi chambré ▪ **~, I would like to work in advertising** mon rêve ce serait de travailler dans la publicité.

identical [aɪ'dentɪkl] *adj* identique ▪ **~ to** OR **with** identique à ▪ **they were wearing ~ dresses** elles portaient la même robe.

identically [aɪ'dentɪklɪ] *adv* identiquement ▪ **to be ~ dressed** être habillé exactement de la même façon.

identical twins *npl* vrais jumeaux *mpl*, vraies jumelles *fpl*.

identifiable [aɪ'dentɪfaɪəbl] *adj* identifiable.

identification [aɪˌdentɪfɪ'keɪʃn] *n* **1.** [gen] identification *f* **2.** *(U)* [identity papers] papiers *mpl* ▪ **the police asked me for ~** la police m'a demandé mes papiers OR une pièce d'identité.

identification card *n* carte *f* d'identité.

identification papers *npl* papiers *mpl* d'identité.

identification parade *n* UK séance *f* d'identification *(au cours de laquelle on demande à un témoin de reconnaître une personne)*.

identifier [aɪ'dentɪfaɪə^r] *n* COMPUT identificateur *m*, identifieur *m*.

identify [aɪ'dentɪfaɪ] (*pret & pp* **identified**) <> *vt* **1.** [recognize, name] identifier ▪ **the winner has asked not to be identified** le gagnant a tenu à garder l'anonymat **2.** [distinguish - subj: physical feature, badge etc] : **she wore a red rose to ~ herself** elle portait une rose rouge pour se faire reconnaître OR pour qu'on la reconnaisse ▪ **his accent immediately identified him to the others** les autres l'ont immédiatement reconnu à son accent **3.** [acknowledge - difficulty, issue etc] définir ▪ **the report identifies two major problems** le rapport met en lumière deux problèmes principaux **4.** [associate - people, ideas etc] : **he has long been identified with right-wing groups** il y a longtemps qu'il est assimilé OR identifié aux groupuscules de droite ▪ **to ~ o.s. with** s'identifier avec.
<> *vi* : **to ~ with** s'identifier à OR avec.

Identikit® [aɪ'dentɪkɪt] *n* : **~ (picture)** portrait-robot *m*.

identity [aɪ'dentətɪ] (*pl* **identities**) <> *n* **1.** [name, set of characteristics] identité *f* ▪ **it was a case of mistaken ~** il y a eu erreur sur la personne **2.** [sense of belonging] identité *f*.
<> *comp* [bracelet, papers] d'identité.

identity card *n* carte *f* d'identité.

identity crisis *n* crise *f* d'identité.

identity parade = **identification parade**.

identity theft *n* vol *m* d'identité.

ideogram ['ɪdɪəʊgræm], **ideograph** ['ɪdɪəʊgrɑ:f] *n* idéogramme *m*.

ideographic [ˌɪdɪəʊ'græfɪk] *adj* idéographique.

ideological [ˌaɪdɪə'lɒdʒɪkl] *adj* idéologique.

ideologically [ˌaɪdɪə'lɒdʒɪklɪ] *adv* du point de vue idéologique, idéologiquement ▪ **~ sound** [idea] défendable sur le plan idéologique ; [person] dont les idées sont défendables sur le plan idéologique.

ideologist [ˌaɪdɪ'ɒlədʒɪst] *n* idéologue *mf*.

ideologue ['aɪdɪəlɒg] *n* idéologue *mf*.

ideology [ˌaɪdɪ'ɒlədʒɪ] (*pl* **ideologies**) *n* idéologie *f*.

ides [aɪdz] *n* ides *fpl*.

idiocy ['ɪdɪəsɪ] *n* [stupidity] stupidité *f*, idiotie *f*.

idiolect ['ɪdɪəlekt] *n* idiolecte *m*.

idiom ['ɪdɪəm] *n* **1.** [expression] locution *f*, expression *f* idiomatique **2.** [language] idiome *m* **3.** [style - of music, writing etc] style *m*.

idiomatic [,ɪdɪə'mætɪk] *adj* idiomatique ■ **his Italian is fluent and ~** il parle un italien tout à fait idiomatique.

idiomatically [,ɪdɪə'mætɪklɪ] *adv* de manière idiomatique.

idiosyncrasy [,ɪdɪə'sɪŋkrəsɪ] (*pl* **idiosyncrasies**) *n* [peculiarity] particularité *f* ■ [foible] manie *f*.

idiosyncratic [,ɪdɪəsɪŋ'krætɪk] *adj* [style, behaviour] caractéristique.

idiot ['ɪdɪət] *n* **1.** [fool] idiot *m*, - e *f*, imbécile *mf* ■ **(you) stupid ~!** espèce d'idiot! ■ **don't be an ~!** ne sois pas idiot! ■ **that ~ Harry** cet imbécile de Harry **2.** PSYCHOL & *arch* idiot *m*, - e *f*.

idiot board *n inf* prompteur *m*, télésouffleur *m*.

idiotic [,ɪdɪ'ɒtɪk] *adj* idiot.

idiotically [,ɪdɪ'ɒtɪklɪ] *adv* stupidement, bêtement ■ **he behaved ~** il s'est comporté comme un imbécile.

idiot-proof *inf* ◇ *adj* COMPUT à l'épreuve de toute fausse manœuvre.
◇ *vt* rendre infaillible.

idle ['aɪdl] ◇ *adj* **1.** [person - inactive] inoccupé, désœuvré ; [- lazy] oisif, paresseux ■ **in her ~ moments** à ses moments perdus ■ **he's an ~ good-for-nothing** c'est un fainéant et un bon à rien ■ **the ~ rich** les riches désœuvrés OR oisifs **2.** [not in use - factory, equipment] arrêté, à l'arrêt ■ **to stand ~** [machine] être arrêté OR au repos ■ **to lie ~** [factory] chômer ; [money] dormir, être improductif **3.** [futile, pointless] inutile, vain ■ [empty - threat, promise etc] vain, en l'air ; [- rumour] sans fondement ■ **it would be ~ to speculate** il ne servirait à rien de se livrer à de vaines conjectures ■ [casual] : **~ gossip** ragots *mpl* ■ **out of ~ curiosity** par pure curiosité.
◇ *vi* [engine] tourner au ralenti.
◇ *vt* US [make unemployed - permanently] mettre au chômage ; [- temporarily] mettre en chômage technique.
◆ **idle away** *vt sep* : **to ~ away one's time** tuer le temps.

idleness ['aɪdlnɪs] *n* **1.** [laziness] oisiveté *f*, paresse *f* ■ [inactivity] désœuvrement *m* **2.** [futility] futilité *f*.

idler ['aɪdlər] *n* [lazy person] paresseux *m*, - euse *f*, fainéant *m*, - e *f*.

idling speed ['aɪdlɪŋ-] *n* ralenti *m*.

idly ['aɪdlɪ] *adv* **1.** [lazily] paresseusement **2.** [casually] négligemment **3.** [unresponsively] sans réagir ■ **we will not stand ~ by** nous n'allons pas rester sans réagir OR sans rien faire.

idol ['aɪdl] *n* idole *f*.

idolatrous [aɪ'dɒlətrəs] *adj* idolâtre.

idolatry [aɪ'dɒlətrɪ] *n* idolâtrie *f*.

idolize, ise ['aɪdəlaɪz] *vt* idolâtrer.

idyll ['ɪdɪl] *n* idylle *f*.

idyllic [ɪ'dɪlɪk] *adj* idyllique.

i.e. *adv* c'est-à-dire, à savoir.

if [ɪf] ◇ *conj* **1.** [supposing that] si ■ **if he comes, we'll ask him** s'il vient, on lui demandera ■ **if possible** si (c'est) possible ■ **if so** si c'est le cas ■ **if she hadn't introduced herself, I would never have recognized her** si elle ne s'était pas présentée, je ne l'aurais pas reconnue ■ **if I was older, I'd leave home** si j'étais plus âgé, je quitterais la maison ■ **if I were a millionaire, I'd buy a yacht** si j'étais millionnaire, j'achèterais un yacht ■ **would you mind if I invited Angie too?** ça te dérangerait si j'invitais aussi Angie?
2. [whenever] si ■ **if you ever come** OR **if ever you come to London, do visit us** si jamais tu passes à Londres, viens nous voir
3. [given that] si ■ **if Paul was the brains in the family, then Anne was the organizer** si Paul était le cerveau de la famille, Anne en était l'organisatrice
4. [whether] : **to ask/to know/to wonder if** demander/savoir/se demander si ■ **it doesn't matter if he comes or not** peu importe qu'il vienne ou (qu'il ne vienne) pas
5. [with verbs or adjectives expressing emotion] : **I'm sorry if I upset you** je suis désolé si je t'ai fait de la peine
6. [used to qualify a statement] : **few, if any, readers will have heard of him** peu de lecteurs auront entendu parler de lui, ou même aucun ■ **he was intelligent if a little arrogant** il était intelligent, mais quelque peu arrogant
7. [introducing comments or opinions] : **if I could just come in here...** si je puis me permettre d'intervenir... ■ **it's rather good, if I say so myself** c'est assez bon, sans fausse modestie ■ **I'll leave it there, if I may, and go on to my next point** j'en resterai là, si vous voulez bien et passerai au point suivant ■ **well, if you want my opinion** OR **if you ask me, I thought it was dreadful** eh bien, si vous voulez mon avis, c'était affreux
8. [in polite requests] si ■ **if you could all just wait in the hall, I'll be back in a second** si vous pouviez tous attendre dans l'entrée, je reviens tout de suite ■ **would you like me to wrap it for you? – if you would, please** vous voulez que je vous l'emballe? – oui, s'il vous plaît
9. [expressing surprise, indignation] tiens, ça alors ■ **well, if it isn't my old mate Jim!** tiens OR ça alors, c'est ce vieux Jim!
◇ *n* si *m* ■ **if you get the job - and it's a big if - you'll have to move to London** si tu obtiens cet emploi, et je dis bien si, tu devras aller t'installer à Londres ■ **no ifs and buts, we're going** il n'y a pas de "mais" qui tienne OR pas de discussions, on y va.
◆ **if and when** *conj phr* au cas où.
◆ **if anything** *adv phr* plutôt ■ **he doesn't look any slimmer, if anything, he's put on weight** il n'a pas l'air plus mince, il a même plutôt grossi ■ **I am, if anything, even keener to be involved** j'ai peut-être encore plus envie d'y participer.
◆ **if ever** *conj phr* : **there's a hopeless case if ever I saw one!** voilà un cas désespéré s'il en est! ■ **if ever I saw a man driven by ambition, it's him** si quelqu'un est poussé par l'ambition, c'est bien lui.
◆ **if I were you** *adv phr* à ta place ■ **if I were you I'd accept the offer** si j'étais toi OR à ta place, j'accepterais la proposition.
◆ **if not** *conj phr* sinon ■ **did you finish on time? and if not, why not?** avez-vous terminé à temps? sinon, pourquoi? ■ **hundreds, if not thousands** des centaines, voire des milliers.
◆ **if only** *conj phr* **1.** [providing a reason] au moins ■ **I think I should come along too, if only to make sure you don't get into mischief** je crois que je devrais venir aussi, ne serait-ce que pour m'assurer que vous ne faites pas de bêtises
2. [expressing a wish] si seulement ■ **if only I could drive** si seulement je savais conduire.

iffy ['ɪfɪ] (*comp* **iffier**, *superl* **iffiest**) *adj inf* [situation] incertain ■ [result] tangent ■ **it all seems a bit ~ to me** ça ne me semble pas très clair, tout ça.

igloo ['ɪglu:] *n* igloo *m*, iglou *m*.

igneous ['ɪgnɪəs] *adj* igné.

ignite [ɪg'naɪt] ◇ *vt* [set fire to] mettre le feu à, enflammer ■ [light] allumer.
◇ *vi* [catch fire] prendre feu, s'enflammer ■ [be lit] s'allumer.

ignition [ɪg'nɪʃn] *n* **1.** AUT allumage *m* ■ **to turn on/off the ~** mettre/couper le contact **2.** PHYS & CHEM ignition *f*.

ignition key *n* clef *f* de contact.

ignition switch *n* contact *m*.

ignoble [ɪg'nəubl] *adj* infâme.

ignominious [,ɪgnə'mɪnɪəs] *adj* ignominieux.

ignominiously [,ɪgnə'mɪnɪəslɪ] *adv* ignominieusement.

ignominy ['ɪgnəmɪnɪ] *n* ignominie *f*.

ignoramus [,ɪgnə'reɪməs] (*pl* **ignoramuses**) *n* ignare *mf*.

ignorance ['ɪgnərəns] *n* **1.** [lack of knowledge, awareness] ignorance *f* ■ **out of** OR **through sheer ~** par pure ignorance ■ **they kept him in ~ of his sister's existence** ils lui ont caché l'existence de sa sœur ■ **~ of the law is no excuse** nul n'est censé ignorer la loi **2.** *pej* [bad manners] grossièreté *f*.

ignorant ['ɪgnərənt] *adj* **1.** [uneducated] ignorant ■ **I'm really ~ about classical music/politics** je ne connais absolument rien à la musique classique/la politique **2.** [unaware] ignorant ■ **he was ~ of the facts** il ignorait les faits **3.** *pej* [bad-mannered] mal élevé.

ignore [ɪg'nɔːʳ] *vt* **1.** [pay no attention to - person, remark] ne pas prêter attention à, ignorer ■ **she completely ~d me** elle a fait semblant de ne pas me voir ■ **~ him and he'll go away** fais comme s'il n'était pas là et il te laissera tranquille **2.** [take no account of - warning, request etc] ne pas tenir compte de ■ **he ~d the doctor's advice and continued smoking** il n'a pas suivi les conseils de son médecin et a continué de fumer **3.** [overlook] : **they can no longer ~ what is going on here** il ne leur est plus possible d'ignorer *OR* de fermer les yeux sur ce qui se passe ici ■ **the report ~s certain crucial facts** le rapport passe sous silence des faits cruciaux.

iguana [ɪ'gwɑːnə] *n* iguane *m*.

ikon ['aɪkɒn] = **icon**.

IL *written abbr of* **Illinois**.

ileum ['ɪlɪəm] *n* iléon *m*.

Iliad ['ɪlɪəd] *pr n* : **'The ~' *Homer*** 'l'Iliade'.

ilk [ɪlk] *n* [type] : **people of that ~** ce genre de personnes ■ **books of that ~** des livres de ce genre.

ill [ɪl] ◇ *adj* **1.** [sick, unwell] malade ■ **to fall *OR* to be taken ~** tomber malade ■ **the smell makes me ~** l'odeur me rend malade **2.** *UK* [injured] : **he is critically ~ with stab wounds** il est dans un état critique après avoir reçu de nombreux coups de couteau **3.** *lit* [bad] mauvais, néfaste ■ **~ fortune** malheur *m*, malchance *f* ■ **~ deeds** méfaits *mpl* ■ **a house of ~ repute** une maison mal famée ▶ **it's an ~ wind that blows nobody any good** *prov* à quelque chose malheur est bon *prov*.
◇ *n* **1.** *lit* [evil] mal *m* ■ **to think/speak ~ of sb** penser/dire du mal de qqn ■ **for good or ~** [whatever happens] quoi qu'il arrive **2.** [difficulty, trouble] malheur *m* ■ **the nation's ~s** les malheurs du pays.
◇ *adv* **1.** [hardly] à peine, difficilement ■ **we can ~ afford these luxuries** ce sont des luxes que nous pouvons difficilement nous permettre ■ **we can ~ afford to wait** nous ne pouvons vraiment pas nous permettre d'attendre **2.** *fml* [badly] mal ■ **it ~ becomes *OR* befits you to criticize** il vous sied mal de critiquer ■ **to augur *OR* to bode ~** être de mauvais augure.

ill. (*written abbrev of* **illustration**) ill.

I'll [aɪl] = **I shall**, = **I will**.

ill-advised *adj* [remark, comment] peu judicieux, hors de propos, déplacé ■ [action] peu judicieux, déplacé ■ **he was ~ to go away** il a eu tort *OR* il a été mal avisé de partir.

ill-assorted *adj* mal assorti, disparate.

ill-at-ease *adj* gêné, mal à l'aise.

illative [ɪ'leɪtɪv] LING ◇ *adj* illatif.
◇ *n* illatif *m*.

ill-bred *adj* mal élevé.

ill-breeding *n* manque *m* de savoir-vivre.

ill-concealed *adj* mal dissimulé.

ill-conceived [-kən'siːvd] *adj* mal pensé.

ill-considered *adj* [hasty] hâtif ■ [thoughtless] irréfléchi.

ill-defined [-dɪ'faɪnd] *adj* mal défini.

ill-disposed [-dɪs'pəʊzd] *adj* mal disposé ■ **to be ~ towards sb** être mal disposé envers qqn ■ **to be ~ to do sthg** être peu enclin à faire qqch.

illegal [ɪ'liːgl] *adj* **1.** LAW illégal ■ **~ entry** violation *f* de domicile ■ **~ immigrant** immigré *m*, - e *f*, clandestin *m*, - e *f* **2.** COMPUT [character] interdit ■ [instruction] erroné.

illegality [ˌɪliː'gælətɪ] (*pl* **illegalities**) *n* illégalité *f*.

illegally [ɪ'liːgəlɪ] *adv* illégalement, d'une manière illégale ■ **to be ~ parked** être en stationnement interdit.

illegible [ɪ'ledʒəbl] *adj* illisible.

illegitimacy [ˌɪlɪ'dʒɪtɪməsɪ] *n* illégitimité *f*.

illegitimate [ˌɪlɪ'dʒɪtɪmət] ◇ *adj* **1.** [child] naturel LAW illégitime **2.** [activity] illégitime, interdit **3.** [argument] illogique.
◇ *n* enfant naturel *m*, enfant naturelle *f*.

illegitimately [ˌɪlɪ'dʒɪtɪmətlɪ] *adv* **1.** [outside marriage] hors du mariage **2.** [illegally] illégitimement.

ill-equipped *adj* **1.** [lacking equipment] mal équipé, mal préparé **2.** [lacking qualities - for job, situation] : **to be ~ (for)** ne pas être à la hauteur (de), être mal armé (pour) ■ **he felt ~ to cope with the pressures of the job** il ne se sentait pas capable d'affronter les problèmes posés par son travail.

ill-fated *adj* [action] malheureux, funeste ■ [person] qui joue de malheur, malheureux ■ [day] néfaste, de malchance ■ [journey] funeste, fatal.

ill feeling *n* ressentiment *m*, animosité *f*.

ill-founded [-'faʊndɪd] *adj* [hopes, confidence] mal fondé ■ [suspicions] sans fondement.

ill-gotten *adj* : **~ gains** biens *mpl* mal acquis.

ill health *n* mauvaise santé *f* ■ **to suffer from ~** avoir des problèmes de santé ■ **because of ~** pour des raisons de santé.

illiberal [ɪ'lɪbərəl] *adj* **1.** [bigoted, intolerant] intolérant ■ POL [regime] arbitraire, oppressif ■ [legislation] restrictif **2.** [mean] avare.

illicit [ɪ'lɪsɪt] *adj* illicite.

illicitly [ɪ'lɪsɪtlɪ] *adv* illicitement.

ill-informed *adj* [person] mal renseigné ■ [remark] inexact, faux, fausse *f*.

Illinois [ˌɪlɪ'nɔɪ] *pr n* Illinois *m* ■ **in ~** dans l'Illinois.

illiteracy [ɪ'lɪtərəsɪ] *n* illettrisme *m*, analphabétisme *m*.

illiterate [ɪ'lɪtərət] ◇ *adj* **1.** [unable to read] analphabète, illettré **2.** [uneducated] ignorant, sans éducation ■ **many young people are scientifically ~** de nombreux jeunes gens n'ont aucune formation *OR* connaissance scientifique.
◇ *n* analphabète *mf*.

ill-judged [-dʒʌdʒd] *adj* [remark, attempt] peu judicieux.

ill-mannered *adj* [person] mal élevé, impoli ■ [behaviour] grossier, impoli.

ill-natured [-neɪtʃəd] *adj* qui a mauvais caractère.

illness ['ɪlnɪs] *n* maladie *f*.

illocution [ˌɪlə'kjuːʃn] *n* illocution *f*, acte *m* illocutoire.

illocutionary [ˌɪlə'kjuːʃnrɪ] *adj* illocutoire, illocutionnaire.

illogical [ɪ'lɒdʒɪkl] *adj* illogique ■ **that's ~** ce n'est pas logique.

illogicality [ˌɪlɒdʒɪ'kælətɪ] (*pl* **illogicalities**) *n* illogisme *m*.

illogically [ɪ'lɒdʒɪklɪ] *adv* d'une manière illogique.

ill-starred [-stɑːd] *adj lit* [person] né sous une mauvaise étoile ■ [day] néfaste, funeste.

ill-suited *adj* mal assorti ■ **to be ~ for sthg** être inapte à qqch.

ill-tempered *adj* [by nature] grincheux, qui a mauvais caractère ■ [temporarily] de mauvaise humeur ■ [remark, outburst etc] plein de mauvaise humeur.

ill-timed [-'taɪmd] *adj* [arrival, visit] inopportun, intempestif, qui tombe mal ■ [remark, question] déplacé, mal à propos *(inv)* ■ **the meeting was very ~** cette réunion ne pouvait plus mal tomber.

ill-treat *vt* maltraiter.

ill-treatment *n* mauvais traitement *m*.

illuminate [ɪ'lu:mɪneɪt] <> *vt* **1.** [light up] illuminer, éclairer **2.** [make clearer] éclairer ▪ **this book ~s many difficult problems** ce livre éclaire de nombreux problèmes complexes **3.** [manuscript] enluminer.
<> *vi* s'illuminer.

illuminated [ɪ'lu:mɪneɪtɪd] *adj* **1.** [lit up - sign, notice] lumineux **2.** [decorated - manuscript] enluminé.

illuminating [ɪ'lu:mɪneɪtɪŋ] *adj* [book, speech] éclairant.

illumination [ɪ,lu:mɪ'neɪʃn] *n* **1.** [light] éclairage *m* ▪ [of building] illumination *f* **2.** [of manuscript] enluminure *f*.
◆ **illuminations** *npl* [coloured lights] illuminations *fpl*.

ill-use *lit* <> *vt* [,ɪl'ju:z] [ill-treat] maltraiter.
<> *n* [,ɪl'ju:s] [cruel treatment] mauvais traitement *m*.

illusion [ɪ'lu:ʒn] *n* **1.** [false impression] illusion *f* ▪ **mirrors give an ~ of space** les miroirs donnent une illusion d'espace **2.** [false belief] illusion *f* ▪ **to be under an ~** se faire une illusion ▪ **she has no ~s** *OR* **is under no ~s about her chances of success** elle ne se fait aucune illusion sur ses chances de succès *OR* de réussir **3.** [magic trick] illusion *f*.

illusionist [ɪ'lu:ʒənɪst] *n* [conjurer, magician] illusionniste *mf*.

illusory [ɪ'lu:sərɪ] *adj* illusoire.

illustrate ['ɪləstreɪt] *vt* **1.** [with pictures] illustrer ▪ **an ~d children's book** un livre pour enfants illustré **2.** [demonstrate] illustrer ▪ **it clearly ~s the need for improvement** cela montre bien que des améliorations sont nécessaires.

illustration [,ɪlə'streɪʃn] *n* **1.** [picture] illustration *f* **2.** [demonstration] illustration *f* ▪ **it's a clear ~ of a lack of government interest** cela illustre bien un manque d'intérêt de la part du gouvernement ▪ **by way of ~** à titre d'exemple.

illustrative ['ɪləstrətɪv] *adj* [picture, diagram] qui illustre, explicatif ▪ [action, event, fact] qui démontre, qui illustre ▪ **the demonstrations are ~ of the need for reform** les manifestations montrent que des réformes sont nécessaires ▪ **~ examples** des exemples illustratifs.

illustrator ['ɪləstreɪtə^r] *n* illustrateur *m*, - trice *f*.

illustrious [ɪ'lʌstrɪəs] *adj* illustre.

ill will *n* malveillance *f* ▪ **I bear them no ~** je ne leur garde pas rancune, je ne leur en veux pas.

ILO (*abbrev of* **International Labour Organization**) *pr n* OIT *f*.

ILWU (*abbrev of* **International Longshoremen's and Warehousemen's Union**) *pr n syndicat international de dockers et de magasiniers*.

I'm [aɪm] = **I am**.

image ['ɪmɪdʒ] *n* **1.** [mental picture] image *f* ▪ **I still have an ~ of her as a child** je la vois encore enfant ▪ **many people have the wrong ~ of her/of life in New York** beaucoup de gens se font une fausse idée d'elle/de la vie à New York **2.** [public appearance] : **(public) ~** image *f* de marque ▪ **the party tried to change its ~** le parti a essayé de changer son image de marque **3.** [likeness] image *f* ▪ **man was made in God's ~** l'homme a été créé à l'image de Dieu ▶ **you are the (very** *OR* **living) ~ of your mother** tu es tout le portrait *OR* le portrait craché de ta mère **4.** [in art] image *f* **5.** OPT & PHOT image *f*.

image-conscious *adj* soucieux de son image.

image file *n* COMPUT fichier *m* vidéo *OR* image.

image processing *n* COMPUT traitement *m* des images.

imagery ['ɪmɪdʒrɪ] *n (U)* **1.** [in literature] images *fpl* **2.** [visual images] imagerie *f*.

imaginable [ɪ'mædʒɪnəbl] *adj* imaginable ▪ **the worst thing ~ happened** ce qu'on pouvait imaginer de pire est arrivé.

imaginary [ɪ'mædʒɪnrɪ] *adj* **1.** [in one's imagination - sickness, danger] imaginaire **2.** [fictional - character] fictif.

imagination [ɪ,mædʒɪ'neɪʃn] *n* [creativity] imagination *f* ▪ [mind] : **she tends to let her ~ run away with her** elle a tendance à se laisser emporter par son imagination ▪ **it's all in her ~** elle se fait des idées ▪ **it was only my ~** c'est mon imagination qui me jouait des tours.

imaginative [ɪ'mædʒɪnətɪv] *adj* [person] imaginatif ▪ [writing, idea, plan] original.

imaginatively [ɪ'mædʒɪnətɪvlɪ] *adv* avec imagination.

imagine [ɪ'mædʒɪn] *vt* **1.** [picture - scene, person] imaginer, s'imaginer, se représenter ▪ **I'd ~d him to be a much smaller man** je l'imaginais plus petit ▪ **I can't ~ (myself) getting the job** je n'arrive pas à imaginer que je puisse être embauché ▪ **~ yourself in his situation** imaginez-vous dans sa situation, mettez-vous à sa place ▪ **you can't ~ how awful it was** vous ne pouvez pas (vous) imaginer *OR* vous figurer combien c'était horrible ▪ **(you can) ~ his delight!** vous pensez s'il était ravi! ▪ **just ~!** tu t'imagines! ▪ **you're imagining things** tu te fais des idées **2.** [suppose, think] supposer, imaginer ▪ ▪ **~ (that) you're on a beach** imagine-toi sur une plage ▪ ▪ **~ (that) you've won** imagine que tu as gagné, suppose que tu aies gagné ▪ **don't ~ I'll help you again** ne t'imagine pas que je t'aiderai encore.

imaginings [ɪ'mædʒɪnɪŋz] *npl* [fears, dreams] : **never in my worst ~ did I think it would come to this** je n'aurais jamais pensé que les choses en arriveraient là.

imam [ɪ'mɑ:m] *n* imam *m*.

imbalance [,ɪm'bæləns] <> *n* déséquilibre *m*.
<> *vt* déséquilibrer.

imbecile ['ɪmbɪsi:l] <> *n* **1.** [idiot] imbécile *mf*, idiot *m*, - e *f* ▪ **to act the ~** faire l'imbécile ▪ **you ~!** espèce d'imbécile *OR* d'idiot! **2.** PSYCHOL imbécile *mf*.
<> *adj* imbécile, idiot.

imbibe [ɪm'baɪb] *vt* **1.** *fml* & *hum* [drink] absorber **2.** *lit* [knowledge] assimiler **3.** PHYS absorber.

imbue [ɪm'bju:] *vt* : **her parents had ~d her with high ideals** ses parents lui avaient inculqué de nobles idéaux ▪ **his words were ~d with resentment** ses paroles étaient pleines de ressentiment.

IMF (*abbrev of* **International Monetary Fund**) *pr n* FMI *m*.

IMHO (*abbrev of* **in my humble opinion**) *adv inf* à mon humble avis.

imitate ['ɪmɪteɪt] *vt* imiter.

imitation [,ɪmɪ'teɪʃn] <> *n* **1.** [copy] imitation *f* ▪ **it's a cheap ~** c'est du toc ▪ **'beware of ~s'** 'méfiez-vous des contrefaçons' **2.** [act of imitating] imitation *f* ▪ **he does everything in ~ of his brother** il imite *OR* copie son frère en tout.
<> *comp* faux, fausse *f* ▪ **an ~ diamond necklace** un collier en faux diamants ▪ **~ fur** fourrure *f* synthétique ▪ **~ jewellery** bijoux *mpl* (de) fantaisie ▪ **~ leather** imitation *f* cuir, similicuir *m*.

imitative ['ɪmɪtətɪv] *adj* [behaviour, sound] imitatif ▪ [person, style] imitateur.

imitator ['ɪmɪteɪtə^r] *n* imitateur *m*, - trice *f*.

immaculate [ɪ'mækjʊlət] *adj* **1.** [clean - house, clothes] impeccable, d'une propreté irréprochable **2.** [faultless - work, behaviour etc] parfait, impeccable **3.** [morally pure] irréprochable.

Immaculate Conception *n* : **the ~** l'Immaculée Conception *f*.

immaculately [ɪ'mækjʊlətlɪ] *adv* **1.** [spotlessly - clean, tidy] impeccablement ▪ **~ dressed** tiré à quatre épingles **2.** [faultlessly - behave, perform etc] d'une manière irréprochable, impeccablement.

immanent ['ɪmənənt] *adj* immanent.

immaterial [,ɪmə'tɪərɪəl] *adj* **1.** [unimportant] sans importance ▪ **that point is ~ to what we are discussing** cela n'a rien à voir avec ce dont nous sommes en train de parler **2.** PHILOS immatériel.

immature [,ɪmə'tjʊəʳ] *adj* **1.** [childish] immature ▪ **she's very ~** elle manque vraiment de maturité **2.** BOT & ZOOL immature, jeune.

immaturity [,ɪmə'tjʊərətɪ] *n* **1.** [of person] manque *m* de maturité, immaturité *f* **2.** PSYCHOL, BOT & ZOOL immaturité *f*.

immeasurable [ɪ'meʒrəbl] *adj liter* incommensurable.

immeasurably [ɪ'meʒrəblɪ] *adv* **1.** [long, high] incommensurablement **2.** [as intensifier] infiniment.

immediacy [ɪ'mi:djəsɪ] *n* impact *m* immédiat ▪ **the ~ of the crisis** les effets immédiats de la crise.

immediate [ɪ'mi:djət] *adj* **1.** [instant] immédiat, urgent ▪ **the problem needs ~ attention** il est urgent de régler le problème ▪ **this pill gives ~ relief** ce cachet soulage instantanément, l'effet de ce cachet est instantané ▮ [close in time] immédiat ▪ **in the ~ future** dans les heures OR les jours qui viennent **2.** [nearest] immédiat, proche ▪ **my ~ relatives** mes parents les plus proches ❯ **~ constituent** LING constituant *m* immédiat **3.** [direct - cause, influence] immédiat, direct.

immediately [ɪ'mi:djətlɪ] <> *adv* **1.** [at once] tout de suite, immédiatement ▪ **I left ~ after** je suis parti tout de suite après **2.** [directly] directement **3.** [just] juste ▪ **~ above the window** juste au-dessus de la fenêtre.
<> *conj UK* dès que ▪ **let me know ~ he arrives** dès qu'il sera là, prévenez-moi.

immemorial [,ɪmɪ'mɔ:rɪəl] *adj* immémorial ▪ **since OR from time ~** de temps immémorial.

immense [ɪ'mens] *adj* immense, considérable.

immensely [ɪ'menslɪ] *adv* immensément, extrêmement.

immensity [ɪ'mensətɪ] *n* immensité *f*.

immerse [ɪ'mɜ:s] *vt* **1.** [in liquid] immerger, plonger ▪ **I'm going to ~ myself in a hot bath** je vais me plonger dans un bain chaud **2.** *fig* **I ~d myself in my work** je me suis plongé dans mon travail ▪ **they were ~d in a game of chess** ils étaient plongés dans une partie d'échecs **3.** RELIG baptiser par immersion.

immersion [ɪ'mɜ:ʃn] *n* **1.** [in liquid] immersion *f* **2.** *fig* [in reading, work] absorption *f* ▪ **~ course** stage *m* intensif **3.** ASTRON & RELIG immersion *f*.

immersion heater *n* chauffe-eau *m inv* électrique.

immigrant ['ɪmɪgrənt] <> *n* immigré *m*, - e *f*.
<> *adj* immigré ▪ **~ children** enfants d'immigrés ❯ **~ worker** travailleur *m* immigré.

immigrate ['ɪmɪgreɪt] *vi* immigrer.

immigration [,ɪmɪ'greɪʃn] <> *n* **1.** [act of immigrating] immigration *f* ❯ **the Immigration and Naturalization Service** *services américains de contrôle de l'immigration* ▪ **the Immigration Control Act** *loi de 1986 permettant aux immigrés illégaux résidant aux États-Unis depuis 1982 de recevoir un visa* **2.** [control section] : **~ (control)** services *mpl* de l'immigration ▪ **to go through ~ (control)** passer l'immigration.
<> *comp* de l'immigration ▪ **~ authorities** services *mpl* de l'immigration ▪ **~ regulations** réglementation *f* relative à l'immigration.

imminence ['ɪmɪnəns] *n* imminence *f*.

imminent ['ɪmɪnənt] *adj* imminent.

immobile [ɪ'məʊbaɪl] *adj* immobile.

immobility [,ɪmə'bɪlətɪ] *n* immobilité *f*.

immobilization [ɪ,məʊbɪlaɪ'zeɪʃn] *n* [gen - FIN] immobilisation *f*.

immobilize, ise [ɪ'məʊbɪlaɪz] *vt* [gen - FIN] immobiliser.

immobilizer [ɪ'məʊbɪlaɪzəʳ] *n* AUT système *m* antidémarrage.

immoderate [ɪ'mɒdərət] *adj* immodéré, excessif.

immodest [ɪ'mɒdɪst] *adj* **1.** [indecent] impudique **2.** [vain] prétentieux.

immodestly [ɪ'mɒdɪstlɪ] *adv* **1.** [indecently] impudiquement, de façon indécente **2.** [vainly] sans modestie ▪ **he rather ~ claims to be the best** il déclare non sans prétention qu'il est le meilleur.

immolate ['ɪməleɪt] *vt lit* immoler.

immoral [ɪ'mɒrəl] *adj* immoral.

immorality [,ɪmə'rælətɪ] *n* immoralité *f*.

immortal [ɪ'mɔ:tl] <> *adj* immortel.
<> *n* immortel *m*, - elle *f*.

immortality [,ɪmɔ:'tælətɪ] *n* immortalité *f*.

immortalize, ise [ɪ'mɔ:təlaɪz] *vt* immortaliser.

immov(e)able [ɪ'mu:vəbl] *adj* **1.** [fixed] fixe ▪ [impossible to move] impossible à déplacer ▪ **~ feast** RELIG fête *f* fixe **2.** [determined - person] inébranlable **3.** LAW : **~ property** biens *mpl* immeubles OR immobiliers.
◆ **immovables** *npl* LAW biens *mpl* immobiliers.

immune [ɪ'mju:n] *adj* **1.** MED immunisé ▪ **~ to measles** immunisé contre la rougeole ❯ **~ serum** immun-sérum *m*, antisérum *m* **2.** *fig* **~ to** [unaffected by] à l'abri de, immunisé contre ▮ [exempt] : **~ from** exempt de, exonéré de ▪ **~ from prosecution** LAW inviolable.

immune deficiency *n* immunodéficience *f*.

immune system *n* système *m* immunitaire.

immunity [ɪ'mju:nətɪ] *n* **1.** MED immunité *f*, résistance *f* ▪ **~ to OR against measles** immunité contre la rougeole **2.** [exemption] : **~ from** exonération *f* de, exemption *f* de **3.** [diplomatic, parliamentary] immunité *f* ▪ **~ from prosecution** immunité, inviolabilité *f*.

immunization [,ɪmju:naɪ'zeɪʃn] *n* immunisation *f*.

immunize, ise ['ɪmju:naɪz] *vt* immuniser, vacciner.

immunodeficiency [,ɪmju:nəʊdɪ'fɪʃənsɪ] *n* immunodéficience *f*.

immunology [,ɪmju:n'ɒlədʒɪ] *n* immunologie *f*.

immunosuppression [,ɪmju:nəʊsə'preʃn] *n* immunosuppression *f*.

immunotherapy [,ɪmju:nəʊ'θerəpɪ] *n* immunothérapie *f*.

immure [ɪ'mjʊəʳ] *vt* emmurer ▪ **to ~ o.s. in silence** *fig* se murer OR s'enfermer dans le silence.

immutability [ɪ,mu:tə'bɪlətɪ] *n* immuabilité *f*.

immutable [ɪ'mju:təbl] *adj* immuable.

imp [ɪmp] *n* [devil] lutin *m* ▪ [child] coquin *m*, - e *f*.

impact <> *n* ['ɪmpækt] **1.** *liter* impact *m* ▪ **on ~** au moment de l'impact **2.** *fig* impact *m*, impression *f* ▪ **the scandal had little ~ on the election results** le scandale a eu peu de répercussions OR d'incidence sur les résultats de l'élection ▪ **you made OR had quite an ~ on him** vous avez fait une forte impression sur lui.
<> *vt* [ɪm'pækt] **1.** [collide with] entrer en collision avec **2.** [influence] avoir un impact sur.
<> *vi* [ɪm'pækt] **1.** [affect] : **to ~ on** produire un effet sur **2.** COMPUT frapper.

impacted [ɪm'pæktɪd] *adj* [tooth] inclus ▪ [fracture] avec impaction.

impact printer *n* COMPUT imprimante *f* à impact.

impair [ɪm'peəʳ] *vt* **1.** [weaken] diminuer, affaiblir **2.** [damage] détériorer, endommager.

impaired [ɪm'peəd] *adj* **1.** [weakened] affaibli, diminué **2.** [damaged] détérioré, endommagé ▪ **~ hearing/vision** ouïe *f* /vue *f* affaiblie.

impairment [ɪm'peəmənt] *n* **1.** [weakening] affaiblissement *m*, diminution *f* **2.** [damage] détérioration *f*.

impala [ɪm'pɑ:lə] *n* impala *m*.

impale [ɪm'peɪl] *vt* empaler ▪ **to ~ o.s. on sthg** s'empaler sur qqch.

impalpable [ɪm'pælpəbl] *adj* impalpable.

impanel [ɪm'pænl] *US* = **empanel**.

impart [ɪm'pɑːt] *vt* **1.** [communicate - news, truth] apprendre **2.** [transmit - knowledge, wisdom] transmettre **3.** [give - quality, flavour] donner.

impartial [ɪm'pɑːʃl] *adj* impartial.

impartiality [ɪm,pɑːʃɪ'ælətɪ] *n* impartialité *f*.

impartially [ɪm'pɑːʃəlɪ] *adv* impartialement.

impassable [ɪm'pɑːsəbl] *adj* [road] impraticable ▪ [stream, frontier] infranchissable.

impasse [æm'pɑːs] *n* impasse *f* ▪ **the talks have reached an ~** les pourparlers sont dans une impasse ▪ **there's no way out of this ~** c'est une situation sans issue.

impassioned [ɪm'pæʃnd] *adj* passionné ▪ [plea] fervent.

impassive [ɪm'pæsɪv] *adj* impassible.

impassively [ɪm'pæsɪvlɪ] *adv* impassiblement ▪ **to look at sb/sthg ~** regarder qqn/qqch d'un air impassible.

impatience [ɪm'peɪʃns] *n* **1.** [lack of patience] impatience *f* **2.** [irritation] irritation *f* ▪ **I fully understand your ~ at the delay** je comprends parfaitement que ce retard vous irrite **3.** [intolerance] intolérance *f*.

impatient [ɪm'peɪʃnt] *adj* **1.** [eager, anxious] impatient ▪ **I'm ~ to see her again** je suis impatient de la revoir ▪ **they were ~ for the results** ils attendaient les résultats avec impatience **2.** [easily irritated] : **she's ~ with her children** elle n'a aucune patience avec ses enfants ▪ **I'm getting ~** je commence à m'impatienter *OR* à perdre patience **3.** [intolerant] intolérant ▪ **he's ~ with people who always ask the same questions** il ne supporte pas les gens qui lui posent toujours les mêmes questions.

impatiently [ɪm'peɪʃntlɪ] *adv* impatiemment, avec impatience.

impeach [ɪm'piːtʃ] *vt* **1.** [accuse] accuser, inculper **2.** ADMIN & POL [in US] entamer une procédure d'impeachment contre **3.** *UK fml* [doubt - motives, honesty] mettre en doute ; [- character] attaquer **4.** LAW : **to ~ a witness** récuser un témoin.

impeachment [ɪm'piːtʃmənt] *n* LAW [accusation] mise *f* en accusation ▪ [in US] *mise en accusation d'un élu devant le Congrès.*

impeccable [ɪm'pekəbl] *adj* impeccable, irréprochable.

impeccably [ɪm'pekəblɪ] *adv* impeccablement ▪ **~ dressed** tiré à quatre épingles.

impecunious [,ɪmpɪ'kjuːnjəs] *adj fml* nécessiteux.

impede [ɪm'piːd] *vt* **1.** [obstruct - traffic, player] gêner **2.** [hinder - progress] ralentir ; [- plan] faire obstacle à ; [- person] gêner.

impediment [ɪm'pedɪmənt] *n* **1.** [obstacle] obstacle *m* **2.** [handicap] défaut *m* (physique) **3.** LAW empêchement *m*.

impel [ɪm'pel] (*pret & pp* **impelled**, *cont* **impelling**) *vt* **1.** [urge, incite] inciter ▪ [compel] obliger, contraindre ▪ **I felt impelled to intervene** je me sentais obligé d'intervenir **2.** [propel] pousser.

impending [ɪm'pendɪŋ] *adj (before n)* imminent ▪ **the ~ arrival of all my relations** l'arrivée prochaine de ma famille au grand complet ▪ **there was an atmosphere of ~ doom** il planait une atmosphère de désastre imminent.

impenetrable [ɪm'penɪtrəbl] *adj* **1.** [wall, forest, fog] impénétrable ▪ *fig* [mystery] insondable, impénétrable **2.** [incomprehensible - jargon, system etc] incompréhensible.

impenitent [ɪm'penɪtənt] *adj* impénitent ▪ **he is still utterly ~** il n'a toujours pas le moindre remords.

imperative [ɪm'perətɪv] ◇ *adj* **1.** [essential] (absolument) essentiel, impératif ▪ **it's ~ that you reply immediately** il faut absolument que vous répondiez tout de suite **2.** [categorical - orders, voice] impérieux, impératif **3.** GRAM impératif.
◇ *n* impératif *m* ▪ **in the ~** à l'impératif.

imperatively [ɪm'perətɪvlɪ] *adv* **1.** [absolutely] impérativement **2.** [imperiously] impérieusement, impérativement.

imperceptible [,ɪmpə'septəbl] *adj* imperceptible ▪ **~ to the human eye/ear** invisible/inaudible (pour l'homme).

imperceptibly [,ɪmpə'septəblɪ] *adv* imperceptiblement.

imperfect [ɪm'pɜːfɪkt] ◇ *adj* **1.** [flawed - work, argument] imparfait ▪ [faulty - machine] défectueux ; [- goods] de second choix **2.** [incomplete] incomplet, - ète *f*, inachevé **3.** GRAM imparfait **4.** LAW inapplicable (pour vice de forme).
◇ *n* GRAM imparfait *m* ▪ **in the ~** à l'imparfait.

imperfection [,ɪmpə'fekʃn] *n* [imperfect state] imperfection *f* ▪ [fault] imperfection *f*, défaut *m*.

imperfective [,ɪmpə'fektɪv] ◇ *adj* imperfectif.
◇ *n* imperfectif *m*.

imperfectly [ɪm'pɜːfɪktlɪ] *adv* imparfaitement.

imperial [ɪm'pɪərɪəl] *adj* **1.** [in titles] impérial ▪ **His Imperial Majesty** Sa Majesté Impériale **2.** [majestic] majestueux, auguste **3.** [imperious] impérieux **4.** [size - of clothes] grande taille *(inv)* ; [- of paper] grand format *(inv) (Br = 762 mm x 559 mm, Am= 787 mm x 584 mm)* **5.** *UK* [measure] : **~ pint** pinte *f* (britannique).

Imperial College *pr n établissement relevant de l'université de Londres et spécialisé dans la recherche scientifique, la mécanique et l'informatique.*

imperialism [ɪm'pɪərɪəlɪzm] *n* impérialisme *m*.

imperialist [ɪm'pɪərɪəlɪst] ◇ *adj* impérialiste.
◇ *n* impérialiste *mf*.

imperialistic [ɪm,pɪərɪəl'ɪstɪk] *adj* impérialiste.

imperil [ɪm'perɪl] (*UK pret & pp* **imperilled**, *cont* **imperilling**) (*US pret & pp* **imperiled**, *cont* **imperiling**) *vt* mettre en péril.

imperious [ɪm'pɪərɪəs] *adj* [authoritative] impérieux, autoritaire.

imperiously [ɪm'pɪərɪəslɪ] *adv* [authoritatively] impérieusement, autoritairement.

imperishable [ɪm'perɪʃəbl] *adj* [quality, truth] impérissable ▪ [goods] non périssable.

impermanence [ɪm'pɜːmənəns] *n* fugacité *f*.

impermanent [ɪm'pɜːmənənt] *adj* fugace.

impermeable [ɪm'pɜːmɪəbl] *adj* [soil, cell, wall] imperméable ▪ [container] étanche.

impersonal [ɪm'pɜːsnl] *adj* **1.** [objective] objectif **2.** [cold] froid, impersonnel **3.** GRAM impersonnel.

impersonally [ɪm'pɜːsnəlɪ] *adv* de façon impersonnelle.

impersonate [ɪm'pɜːsəneɪt] *vt* **1.** [imitate] imiter **2.** [pretend to be] se faire passer pour.

impersonation [ɪm,pɜːsə'neɪʃn] *n* **1.** [imitation] imitation *f* **2.** [pretence of being] imposture *f*.

impersonator [ɪm'pɜːsəneɪtəʳ] *n* **1.** [mimic] imitateur *m*, - trice *f* **2.** [impostor] imposteur *m*.

impertinence [ɪm'pɜːtɪnəns] *n* impertinence *f*.

impertinent [ɪm'pɜːtɪnənt] *adj* **1.** [rude] impertinent, insolent ▪ **to be ~ to sb** être impertinent envers qqn **2.** [irrelevant] hors de propos, non pertinent.

impertinently [ɪm'pɜːtɪnəntlɪ] *adv* avec impertinence.

imperturbable [,ɪmpə'tɜːbəbl] *adj* imperturbable.

impervious [ɪm'pɜːvjəs] *adj* **1.** [unreceptive, untouched - person] imperméable, fermé ▪ **~ to criticism** imperméable à la critique ▪ **he remained ~ to our suggestions** il est resté sourd à nos propositions **2.** [resistant - material] : **~ to heat** résistant à la chaleur ▪ **~ to water** imperméable.

impetigo [,ɪmpɪ'taɪgəʊ] *n (U)* impétigo *m*.

impetuosity [ɪm,petjʊ'ɒsətɪ] *n* impétuosité *f*.

impetuous [ɪm'petʃʊəs] *adj* impétueux.

impetus ['ɪmpɪtəs] *n* **1.** [force] force *f* d'impulsion ▪ [speed] élan *m* ▪ [weight] poids *m* ▪ **to be carried by** *OR* **under one's own ~** être entraîné par son propre élan *OR* par son propre poids **2.** *fig* [incentive, drive] impulsion *f*, élan *m* ▪ **to give new ~ to sthg** donner un nouvel élan à qqch, relancer qqch.

impiety [ɪm'paɪətɪ] (*pl* **impieties**) *n* **1.** RELIG impiété *f* **2.** [disrespect] irrévérence *f*.

impinge [ɪm'pɪndʒ] *vi* **1.** [affect] : **to ~ on** *OR* **upon** affecter **2.** [encroach] : **to ~ on** *OR* **upon** empiéter sur.

impious ['ɪmpɪəs] *adj lit* impie.

impish ['ɪmpɪʃ] *adj* espiègle, taquin, malicieux.

implacable [ɪm'plækəbl] *adj* implacable.

implacably [ɪm'plækəblɪ] *adv* implacablement.

implant <> *vt* [ɪm'plɑ:nt] **1.** [instil - idea, feeling] inculquer ▪ **he tried to ~ his own beliefs in his children's minds** il a essayé d'inculquer ses propres convictions à ses enfants **2.** MED [graft] greffer ▪ [place under skin] implanter.
<> *n* ['ɪmplɑ:nt] [under skin] implant *m* ▪ [graft] greffe *f*.

implausible [ɪm'plɔ:zəbl] *adj* invraisemblable.

implement <> *n* ['ɪmplɪmənt] **1.** [tool] outil *m* ▪ **agricultural ~s** matériel *m* agricole ▪ **kitchen ~s** ustensiles *mpl* de cuisine **2.** *fig* [means] instrument *m*.
<> *vt* ['ɪmplɪment] [plan, orders] exécuter ▪ [ideas, policies] mettre en œuvre.

implementation [ˌɪmplɪmen'teɪʃn] *n* [of ideas, policies] mise *f* en œuvre ▪ [of plan, orders] exécution *f*.

implicate ['ɪmplɪkeɪt] *vt* impliquer ▪ **to be ~d in sthg** être impliqué dans qqch.

implication [ˌɪmplɪ'keɪʃn] *n* **1.** [possible repercussion] implication *f* ▪ **I don't think you understand the ~s of what you are saying** je ne suis pas sûr que vous mesuriez la portée de vos propos ▪ **the full ~s of the report are not yet clear** il est encore trop tôt pour mesurer pleinement les implications de ce rapport **2.** [suggestion] suggestion *f* ▪ [insinuation] insinuation *f* ▪ [hidden meaning] sous-entendu *m* ▪ **by ~** par voie de conséquence ▪ **the ~ was that we would be punished** tout portait à croire que nous serions punis **3.** [involvement] implication *f*.

implicit [ɪm'plɪsɪt] *adj* **1.** [implied] implicite ▪ **his feelings were ~ in his words** ses paroles laissaient deviner ses sentiments **2.** [total - confidence, obedience] total, absolu.

implicitly [ɪm'plɪsɪtlɪ] *adv* **1.** [by implication] implicitement **2.** [totally] absolument.

implied [ɪm'plaɪd] *adj* implicite, sous-entendu.

implode [ɪm'pləʊd] <> *vi* imploser.
<> *vt* LING : **~d consonant** consonne *f* implosive.

implore [ɪm'plɔ:ʳ] *vt* supplier ▪ **he ~d me to give him the money** il m'a supplié de lui donner l'argent ▪ **I ~ you!** je vous en supplie!

imploring [ɪm'plɔ:rɪŋ] *adj* suppliant.

imploringly [ɪm'plɔ:rɪŋlɪ] *adv* : **he looked at me ~** il me suppliait du regard.

implosion [ɪm'pləʊʒn] *n* implosion *f*.

implosive [ɪm'pləʊsɪv] <> *adj* implosif.
<> *n* implosive *f*.

imply [ɪm'plaɪ] (*pret & pp* **implied**) *vt* **1.** [insinuate] insinuer ▪ [give impression] laisser entendre *OR* supposer ▪ **are you ~ing that I'm mistaken?** voulez-vous insinuer que je me trompe? **2.** [presuppose] impliquer ▪ [involve] comporter.

impolite [ˌɪmpə'laɪt] *adj* impoli ▪ **to be ~ to sb** être *OR* se montrer impoli envers qqn.

impolitely [ˌɪmpə'laɪtlɪ] *adv* impoliment.

impolitic [ɪm'pɒlətɪk] *adj* peu *OR* mal avisé, maladroit.

imponderable [ɪm'pɒndrəbl] <> *adj* impondérable.
<> *n* impondérable *m*.

import <> *n* ['ɪmpɔ:t] **1.** COMM importation *f* **2.** [imported article] importation *f*, article *m* importé ▪ **the government has put a tax on ~s** le gouvernement a instauré une taxe sur les produits d'importation *OR* les produits importés **3.** *fml* [meaning] signification *f* ▪ [content] teneur *f* **4.** *fml* [importance] importance *f*.
<> *comp* [licence, surcharge] d'importation ▪ [duty] de douane, sur les importations ▪ [trade] des importations.
<> *vt* [ɪm'pɔ:t] **1.** COMM importer ▪ **lamb ~ed from New Zealand into Britain** agneau de Nouvelle-Zélande importé en Grande-Bretagne **2.** [imply] signifier.

importance [ɪm'pɔ:tns] *n* importance *f* ▪ **to be of ~** avoir de l'importance ▪ **it's of no ~ whatsoever** cela n'a aucune espèce d'importance ▪ **to give ~ to sthg** attacher de l'importance à qqch ▪ **a position of ~** un poste important.

important [ɪm'pɔ:tnt] *adj* **1.** [essential] important ▪ **it's not ~** ça n'a pas d'importance ▪ **it is ~ that you (should) get the job** il est important que vous obteniez cet emploi ▪ **it is ~ for her to know the truth** il est important pour elle de connaître *OR* il est important qu'elle connaisse la vérité ▪ **my job is ~ to me** mon travail compte beaucoup pour moi **2.** [influential] : **an ~ book/writer** un livre-clef/grand écrivain.

importantly [ɪm'pɔ:tntlɪ] *adv* d'un air important ▪ **and, more ~...** et, ce qui est plus important...

importation [ˌɪmpɔ:'teɪʃn] *n* importation *f*.

importer [ɪm'pɔ:təʳ] *n* **1.** [person] importateur *m*, - trice *f* **2.** [country] pays *m* importateur.

import-export *n* import-export *m*.

importunate [ɪm'pɔ:tjʊnət] *adj fml* [visitor, beggar] importun ▪ [demands, questions] incessant.

importune [ɪm'pɔ:tju:n] *fml vt* [gen] importuner, harceler ▪ **to ~ sb with questions** harceler *OR* presser qqn de questions.

importunity [ˌɪmpɔ:'tju:nətɪ] *n* [harassment] sollicitation *f*.

impose [ɪm'pəʊz] <> *vt* [price, tax, attitude, belief] imposer ▪ [fine, penalty] infliger ▪ **to ~ o.s. on sb** imposer sa présence à qqn.
<> *vi* s'imposer ▪ **I'm sorry to ~** je suis désolé de vous déranger ▪ **to ~ on sb** abuser de la gentillesse de qqn.

imposing [ɪm'pəʊzɪŋ] *adj* [person, building] impressionnant.

imposingly [ɪm'pəʊzɪŋlɪ] *adv* d'une manière imposante.

imposition [ˌɪmpə'zɪʃn] *n* **1.** [of tax, sanction] imposition *f* **2.** [burden] charge *f*, fardeau *m* ▪ **I don't want to be an ~ (on you)** je ne veux pas abuser de votre gentillesse *OR* de votre bonté **3.** TYPO imposition *f*.

impossibility [ɪmˌpɒsə'bɪlətɪ] (*pl* **impossibilities**) *n* impossibilité *f* ▪ **it's a physical ~ for us to arrive on time** nous sommes dans l'impossibilité matérielle d'arriver à l'heure.

impossible [ɪm'pɒsəbl] <> *adj* **1.** [not possible] impossible ▪ **it's ~ for me to leave work before 6 p.m.** il m'est impossible de quitter mon travail avant 18 h ▪ **you make it ~ for me to be civil to you** tu me mets dans l'impossibilité d'être poli envers toi ▪ **I'm afraid that's quite ~** je regrette, mais ça n'est vraiment pas possible **2.** [difficult to believe] impossible, invraisemblable ▪ **it is ~ that he should be lying** il est impossible qu'il mente **3.** [unbearable] impossible, insupportable ▪ **he made their lives ~** il leur a rendu la vie insupportable *OR* impossible.
<> *n* impossible *m* ▪ **to attempt/to ask the ~** tenter/demander l'impossible.

impossibly [ɪm'pɒsəblɪ] *adv* **1.** [extremely] extrêmement ▪ **the film is ~ long** le film n'en finit pas **2.** [unbearably] insupportablement ▪ **they behave ~** ils sont totalement insupportables.

impostor, imposter [ɪm'pɒstəʳ] *n* imposteur *m*.

imposture [ɪm'pɒstʃəʳ] *n fml* imposture *f*.

impotence ['ɪmpətəns] *n* [gen - MED] impuissance *f*.

impotent ['ɪmpətənt] *adj* **1.** [powerless] faible, impuissant **2.** [sexually] impuissant.

impound [ɪm'paʊnd] *vt* [gen] saisir ■ [car] mettre en fourrière.

impoverish [ɪm'pɒvərɪʃ] *vt* appauvrir.

impoverished [ɪm'pɒvərɪʃt] *adj* appauvri, très pauvre.

impoverishment [ɪm'pɒvərɪʃmənt] *n* appauvrissement *m*.

impracticable [ɪm'præktɪkəbl] *adj* [not feasible] irréalisable, impraticable.

impractical [ɪm'præktɪkl] *adj* [plan] irréaliste ■ [person] qui manque d'esprit pratique.

imprecation [,ɪmprɪ'keɪʃn] *n fml* imprécation *f*.

imprecise [ɪmprɪ'saɪs] *adj* imprécis.

imprecision [,ɪmprɪ'sɪʒn] *n* imprécision *f*.

impregnable [ɪm'pregnəbl] *adj* **1.** [fortress] imprenable **2.** *fig* [argument] irréfutable ■ **his position is ~** sa position est inattaquable.

impregnate ['ɪmpregneɪt] *vt* [fill] imprégner ■ **~d with** imprégné de.

impresario [,ɪmprɪ'sɑːrɪəʊ] (*pl* **impresarios**) *n* impresario *m*.

impress ◇ *vt* [ɪm'pres] **1.** [influence, affect - mind, person] faire impression sur, impressionner ■ **I was favourably ~ed by her appearance** son apparence m'a fait bonne impression **2.** : **to ~ sthg on sb** [make understand] faire comprendre qqch à qqn **3.** [print] imprimer, marquer ■ **the clay was ~ed with a design, a design was ~ed onto the clay** un motif était imprimé dans l'argile ■ **her words are ~ed on my memory** *fig* ses paroles sont gravées dans ma mémoire.
◇ *n* ['ɪmpres] empreinte *f*.

impression [ɪm'preʃn] *n* **1.** [impact - on person, mind, feelings] impression *f* ■ **he made a strong ~ on them** il leur a fait une forte impression ■ **he always tries to make an ~** il essaie toujours d'impressionner les gens ■ **my words made no ~ on him whatsoever** mes paroles n'ont eu absolument aucun effet sur lui ■ **they got a good ~ of my brother** mon frère leur a fait bonne impression **2.** [idea, thought] impression *f* ■ **it's my ~** *OR* **I have the ~ that she's rather annoyed with us** j'ai l'impression qu'elle est en colère contre nous ■ **I was under the ~ that you were unable to come** j'étais persuadé que vous ne pouviez pas venir **3.** [mark, imprint] marque *f*, empreinte *f* **4.** [printing] impression *f* ■ [edition] tirage *m* **5.** [impersonation] imitation *f* ■ **she does a very good ~ of the Queen** elle imite très bien la reine.

impressionable [ɪm'preʃnəbl] *adj* impressionnable ■ **he is at a very ~ age** il est à l'âge où on se laisse facilement impressionner.

Impressionism [ɪm'preʃənɪzm] *n* ART & LIT impressionnisme *m*.

impressionist [ɪm'preʃənɪst] *n* [entertainer] imitateur *m*, -trice *f* ■ ART & LIT impressionniste.
◆ **Impressionist** ◇ *n* impressionniste *mf*.
◇ *adj* impressionniste.

impressionistic [ɪm,preʃə'nɪstɪk] *adj* [vague] vague, imprécis.

impressive [ɪm'presɪv] *adj* impressionnant.

impressively [ɪm'presɪvlɪ] *adv* remarquablement.

imprimatur [,ɪmprɪ'meɪtər] *n* imprimatur *m inv*.

imprint ◇ *n* ['ɪmprɪnt] **1.** [mark] empreinte *f*, marque *f* ■ **the war had left its ~ on all of us** *fig* la guerre nous avait tous marqués **2.** TYPO [name] : **published under the Larousse ~** édité chez Larousse **3.** [design] logo *m*.
◇ *vt* [ɪm'prɪnt] **1.** [print] imprimer **2.** [in sand, clay, mud] imprimer **3.** *fig* [fix] implanter, graver ■ **her face was ~ed on my mind** son visage est resté gravé dans mon esprit.

imprison [ɪm'prɪzn] *vt* **1.** [put in prison] mettre en prison, incarcérer ■ **he has been ~ed several times** il a fait plusieurs séjours en prison **2.** [sentence] condamner ■ **she was ~ed for 15 years** elle a été condamnée à 15 ans de prison.

imprisonment [ɪm'prɪznmənt] *n* emprisonnement *m* ■ **to be sentenced to six months' ~** être condamné à six mois de prison.

improbability [ɪm,prɒbə'bɪlətɪ] (*pl* **improbabilities**) *n* **1.** [of event] improbabilité *f* **2.** [of story] invraisemblance *f*.

improbable [ɪm'prɒbəbl] *adj* **1.** [unlikely] improbable ■ **I think it highly ~ that he ever came here** il me paraît fort peu probable qu'il soit jamais venu ici **2.** [hard to believe] invraisemblable.

improbably [ɪm'prɒbəblɪ] *adv* invraisemblablement.

impromptu [ɪm'prɒmptjuː] ◇ *adj* impromptu, improvisé.
◇ *adv* impromptu.
◇ *n* impromptu *m*.

improper [ɪm'prɒpər] *adj* **1.** [rude, shocking - words, action] déplacé ■ **to make ~ suggestions (to sb)** faire des propositions malhonnêtes (à qqn) **2.** [unsuitable] peu convenable **3.** [dishonest] malhonnête **4.** [incorrect - method, equipment] inadapté, inadéquat.

improperly [ɪm'prɒpəlɪ] *adv* **1.** [indecently] de manière déplacée **2.** [unsuitably] : **he was ~ dressed** il n'était pas habillé comme il faut **3.** [dishonestly] malhonnêtement **4.** [incorrectly] incorrectement, de manière incorrecte.

impropriety [ɪmprə'praɪətɪ] (*pl* **improprieties**) *n* **1.** [of behaviour] inconvenance *f* ■ **to commit an ~** commettre une indélicatesse **2.** [of language] impropriété *f*.

improvable [ɪm'pruːvəbl] *adj* perfectible.

improve [ɪm'pruːv] ◇ *vt* **1.** [make better - work, facilities, result] améliorer ■ **to ~ one's chances** augmenter ses chances **2.** [increase - knowledge, productivity] accroître, augmenter **3.** [cultivate] : **to ~ one's mind** se cultiver l'esprit ■ **reading ~s the mind** on se cultive en lisant.
◇ *vi* [get better] s'améliorer ■ [increase] augmenter ■ [make progress] s'améliorer, faire des progrès ■ **business is improving** les affaires reprennent ■ **your maths has ~d** vous avez fait des progrès en maths ■ **to ~ with age/use** s'améliorer en vieillissant/à l'usage ■ **he ~s on acquaintance** il gagne à être connu.
◆ **improve on, improve upon** *vt insep* **1.** [result, work] améliorer ■ **it's difficult to see how the performance can be ~d on** il semble difficile d'améliorer cette performance **2.** [offer] : **to ~ on sb's offer** enchérir sur qqn.

improved [ɪm'pruːvd] *adj* [gen] amélioré ■ [services] amélioré, meilleur ■ [offer, performance] meilleur.

improvement [ɪm'pruːvmənt] *n* **1.** amélioration *f* ■ [in person's work, performance] progrès *m* ■ **what an ~!** c'est nettement mieux! ■ **this is a great ~ on her previous work** c'est bien mieux que ce qu'elle faisait jusqu'à présent ■ **there has been a slight ~ in his work** son travail s'est légèrement amélioré ■ **there is no ~ in the weather** le temps ne s'est pas arrangé ■ **to show some ~** [in condition] aller un peu mieux ; [in work] faire quelques progrès ■ **there's room for ~** ça pourrait être mieux **2.** [in building, road etc] rénovation *f*, aménagement *m* ■ **(home) ~s** travaux *mpl* de rénovation.

improvidence [ɪm'prɒvɪdəns] *n fml* imprévoyance *f*.

improvident [ɪm'prɒvɪdənt] *adj fml* [thriftless] dépensier ■ [heedless - person] imprévoyant ; [- life] insouciant.

improvisation [,ɪmprəvaɪ'zeɪʃn] *n* improvisation *f*.

improvise ['ɪmprəvaɪz] *vt* & *vi* improviser.

imprudence [ɪm'pruːdəns] *n* imprudence *f*.

imprudent [ɪm'pruːdənt] *adj* imprudent.

impudence ['ɪmpjʊdəns] *n* effronterie *f*, impudence *f*.

impudent ['ɪmpjʊdənt] *adj* effronté, impudent ■ **he is ~ to his teachers** il est effronté avec ses professeurs.

impudently ['ɪmpjʊdəntlɪ] *adv* effrontément, impudemment.

impugn [ɪm'pju:n] *vt fml* contester.

impulse ['ɪmpʌls] *n* **1.** [desire, instinct] impulsion *f*, besoin *m*, envie *f* ■ **to act on ~** agir par impulsion ■ **I bought it on ~** je l'ai acheté sur un coup de tête ■ **on a sudden ~, he kissed her** pris d'une envie irrésistible, il l'a embrassée **2.** *fml* [impetus] impulsion *f*, poussée *f* ■ **government grants have given an ~ to trade** les subventions gouvernementales ont relancé les affaires **3.** ELEC & PHYSIOL impulsion *f*.

impulse buy *n* achat *m* d'impulsion.

impulse buying *n (U)* achats *mpl* d'impulsion.

impulsive [ɪm'pʌlsɪv] *adj* **1.** [instinctive, spontaneous] impulsif ■ [thoughtless] irréfléchi **2.** [force] impulsif.

impulsively [ɪm'pʌlsɪvlɪ] *adv* par OR sur impulsion, impulsivement.

impulsiveness [ɪm'pʌlsɪvnɪs] *n* caractère *m* impulsif.

impunity [ɪm'pju:nətɪ] *n fml* impunité *f* ■ **to act with ~** agir en toute impunité OR impunément.

impure [ɪm'pjʊər] *adj* **1.** [unclean - air, milk] impur **2.** *lit* [sinful - thought] impur, mauvais ; [- motive] bas.

impurity [ɪm'pjʊərətɪ] (*pl* **impurities**) *n* impureté *f*.

imputation [ˌɪmpju:'teɪʃn] *n fml* **1.** [attribution] attribution *f* **2.** [accusation] imputation *f*.

impute [ɪm'pju:t] *vt fml* [attribute] imputer, attribuer.

IMRO ['ɪmrəʊ] (*abbrev of* **Investment Management Regulatory Organization**) *pr n organisme britannique contrôlant les activités de banques d'affaires et de gestionnaires de fonds de retraite.*

in [ɪn] <> *prep*

A.

1. [within a defined area or space] dans ■ **in a box** dans une boîte ■ **in the house** dans la maison ■ **in Catherine's house** chez Catherine ■ **he's still in bed/in the bath** il est encore au lit/dans son bain ■ **the light's gone in the fridge** la lumière du réfrigérateur ne marche plus
2. [within an undefined area or space] dans ■ **she trailed her hand in the water** elle laissait traîner sa main dans l'eau ■ **there's a smell of spring in the air** ça sent le printemps
3. [indicating movement] dans ■ **throw the letter in the bin** jette la lettre à la poubelle ■ **we headed in the direction of the port** nous nous sommes dirigés vers le port
4. [contained by a part of the body] dans ■ **he had a knife in his hand** il avait un couteau dans OR à la main ■ **with tears in his eyes** les larmes aux yeux
5. [on or behind a surface] dans ■ **there were deep cuts in the surface** la surface était marquée de profondes entailles ■ **who's that man in the photo?** qui est cet homme sur la photo?
6. [in a specified institution] : **she's in hospital/in prison** elle est à l'hôpital/en prison ■ **he teaches in a language school** il enseigne dans une école de langues
7. [with geographical names] : **in Paris** à Paris ■ **in France** en France ■ **in the States** aux États-Unis ■ **in Portugal** au Portugal ■ **in the Third World** dans les pays du tiers-monde
8. [wearing] en ■ **he was in a suit** il était en costume ■ **who's that woman in the hat?** qui est la femme avec le OR au chapeau?
9. [covered by] : **sardines in tomato sauce** des sardines à la sauce tomate ■ **we were up to our waists in mud** nous étions dans la boue jusqu'à la taille

B.

1. [during a specified period of time] en ■ **in 1992** en 1992 ■ **in March** en mars, au mois de mars ■ **in (the) summer/autumn/winter** en été/automne/hiver ■ **in (the) spring** au printemps ■ **he doesn't work in the afternoon/morning** il ne travaille pas l'après-midi/le matin ■ **at 5 o'clock in the afternoon/morning** à 5 h de l'après-midi/du matin ■ **in the future** un jour ■ **in the past** autrefois
2. [within a specified period of time] en ■ **he cooked the meal in ten minutes** il prépara le repas en dix minutes
3. [after a specified period of time] dans ■ **I'll be back in five minutes** je reviens dans cinq minutes, j'en ai pour cinq minutes
4. [indicating a long period of time] : **we haven't had a proper talk in ages** nous n'avons pas eu de véritable conversation depuis très longtemps ■ **I hadn't seen her in years** ça faisait des années que je ne l'avais pas vue
5. [during a specified temporary situation] : **in my absence** en OR pendant mon absence ■ **in the ensuing chaos** OR **confusion** dans la confusion qui s'ensuivit

C.

1. [indicating arrangement, shape] en ■ **stand in a ring** mettez-vous en cercle ■ **she had her hair up in a ponytail** ses cheveux étaient relevés en queue de cheval
2. [indicating form, method] : **in cash** en liquide ■ **in English/French** en anglais/français ■ **written in ink** écrit à l'encre
3. [indicating state of mind] : **she's in a bit of a state** elle est dans tous ses états ■ **to be in love** être amoureux ■ **don't keep us in suspense** ne nous tiens pas en haleine plus longtemps
4. [indicating state, situation] dans, en ■ **in the present circumstances** dans les circonstances actuelles ■ **in this weather** par OR avec ce temps ■ **in the rain/snow** sous la pluie/neige ■ **in danger/silence** en danger/silence ■ **in my presence** en ma présence
5. [referring to plants and animals] : **in blossom** en fleur OR fleurs ■ **in pup/calf/cub** plein
6. [among] chez ■ **a disease common in five-year-olds** une maladie très répandue chez les enfants de cinq ans

D.

1. [forming part of] dans ■ **in chapter six** dans le chapitre six ■ **we were standing in a queue** nous faisions la queue ■ **service is included in the charge** le service est inclus dans le prix
2. [indicating a personality trait] : **she hasn't got it in her to be nasty** elle est bien incapable de méchanceté ■ **it's the Irish in me** c'est mon côté irlandais
3. [indicating feelings about a person or thing] : **she has no confidence in him** elle n'a aucune confiance en lui ■ **they showed no interest in my work** mon travail n'a pas eu l'air de les intéresser le moins du monde
4. [according to] : **in my opinion** OR **view** à mon avis

E.

1. [indicating purpose, cause] : **he charged the door in an effort to get free** dans un effort pour se libérer, il donna un grand coup dans la porte ■ **in reply** OR **response to your letter...** en réponse à votre lettre... ■ **there's no point in complaining** il est inutile de OR ça ne sert à rien de se plaindre
2. [as a result of] en ■ **in doing so, you only encourage him** en faisant cela, vous ne faites que l'encourager
3. [as regards] : **the town has grown considerably in size** la ville s'est beaucoup agrandie ■ **a change in direction** un changement de direction ■ **he's behind in maths** il ne suit pas en maths ■ **we've found the ideal candidate in Richard** nous avons trouvé en Richard le candidat idéal
4. [indicating source of discomfort] : **I've got a pain in my arm** j'ai une douleur au OR dans le bras

F.

1. [indicating specified field, sphere of activity] dans ■ **to be in the army/navy** être dans l'armée/la marine ■ **he's in business with his sister** il dirige une entreprise avec sa sœur ■ **a degree in Italian** un diplôme d'italien
2. [indicating activity engaged in] : **our days were spent in swimming and sailing** nous passions nos journées à nager et à faire de la voile ■ **they spent hours (engaged) in complex negotiations** ils ont passé des heures en négociations difficiles ■ **you took your time in getting here!** tu en as mis du temps à venir!

G.
1. [indicating approximate number, amount] : **they came in their thousands** ils sont venus par milliers ■ **he's in his forties** il a la quarantaine
2. [in ratios] sur ■ **one child in three** un enfant sur trois ■ **a one-in-five hill** une pente de 20 %.
<> *adv*

A.
1. [into an enclosed space] à l'intérieur, dedans ■ **he jumped in** il sauta dedans
2. [indicating movement from outside to inside] : **we can't take in any more refugees** nous ne pouvons pas accueillir plus de réfugiés ■ **she's been in and out of mental hospitals all her life** elle a passé presque toute sa vie dans des hôpitaux psychiatriques
3. [at home or place of work] : **is your wife/the boss in?** est-ce que votre femme/le patron est là? ■ **it's nice to spend an evening in** c'est agréable de passer une soirée chez soi

B.
1. [indicating entry] : **to go in** entrer ■ **come in!** entrez! ■ **in we go!** on y va!
2. [indicating arrival] : **what time does your train get in?** quand est-ce que votre train arrive?
3. [towards the centre] : **the walls fell in** les murs se sont écroulés ■ **the edges bend in** le bord est recourbé
4. [towards the shore] : **the tide is in** la marée est haute

C.
1. [indicating transmission] : **entries must be in by May 1st** les bulletins doivent nous parvenir avant le 1e mai
2. [indicating participation, addition] : **we asked if we could join in** nous avons demandé si nous pouvions participer ■ **stir in the chopped onions** ajouter les oignons en lamelles

D.
1. SPORT [within area of court] : **the umpire said that the ball was in** l'arbitre a dit que la balle était bonne
2. [in cricket] à l'attaque

E.
1. POL [elected] : **he failed to get in at the last election** il n'a pas été élu aux dernières élections
2. [in fashion] à la mode

F.
phr **to be in for sthg : you're in for a bit of a disappointment** tu vas être déçu ■ **he's in for a surprise/shock** il va avoir une surprise/un choc ■ **now he's really in for it** *inf* cette fois-ci, il va y avoir droit ■ **to be in on sthg** *inf* : **he's in on the secret** il est dans le secret ■ **he's in on it** il est dans le coup ■ **to be in with sb** *inf* être en bons termes avec qqn.
<> *adj inf* **1.** [fashionable] à la mode, branché ■ **to be the in thing** être à la mode **2.** [for a select few] : **it's an in joke** c'est une plaisanterie entre nous/elles *etc.*

◆ **ins** *npl* : **the ins and outs (of a situation)** les tenants et les aboutissants (d'une situation).

◆ **in all** *adv phr* en tout ■ **there are 30 in all** il y en a 30 en tout.

◆ **in between** <> *adv phr* **1.** [in intermediate position] : **a row of bushes with little clumps of flowers in between** une rangée d'arbustes séparés par des petites touffes de fleurs ■ **she either plays very well or very badly, never in between** elle joue très bien ou très mal, jamais entre les deux **2.** [in time] entre-temps, dans l'intervalle.
<> *prep phr* entre.

◆ **in itself** *adv phr* en soi ■ **the town is not in itself beautiful but it has style** la ville n'est pas belle en soi mais elle a de l'allure ■ **this was in itself an achievement** c'était déjà un exploit en soi.

◆ **in that** *conj phr* puisque ■ **I'm not badly off in that I have a job and a flat but...** je ne peux pas me plaindre puisque j'ai un emploi et un appartement mais... ■ **we are lucky in that there are only a few of us** nous avons de la chance d'être si peu nombreux.

-in *in cpds exprime l'aspect collectif d'une activité* ■ **love-in** célébration *f* de l'amour en commun.

in. *written abbr of* **inch(es)**.

IN *written abbr of* **Indiana**.

inability [ˌɪnəˈbɪlətɪ] *n* incapacité *f* ■ **our ~ to help them** notre incapacité à les aider.

in absentia [ˌɪnæbˈsentɪə] *adv* in absentia ■ LAW par contumace.

inaccessibility [ˈɪnəkˌsesɪˈbɪlətɪ] *n* inaccessibilité *f*.

inaccessible [ˌɪnəkˈsesəbl] *adj* **1.** [impossible to reach] inaccessible ■ **the village is ~ by car** le village n'est pas accessible en voiture **2.** [unavailable - person] inaccessible, inabordable ; [- information] inaccessible **3.** [obscure - film, book, music] inaccessible, incompréhensible.

inaccuracy [ɪnˈækjʊrəsɪ] (*pl* **inaccuracies**) *n* [of translation, calculation, information] inexactitude *f* ■ [of word, expression] inexactitude *f*, impropriété *f*.

inaccurate [ɪnˈækjʊrət] *adj* [incorrect - figures] inexact ; [- term] impropre ; [- result] erroné ; [- description] inexact.

inaccurately [ɪnˈækjʊrətlɪ] *adv* inexactement ■ **the events have been ~ reported** les événements ont été présentés de façon inexacte.

inaction [ɪnˈækʃn] *n* inaction *f*.

inactivate [ɪnˈæktɪveɪt] *vt* rendre inactif, désactiver.

inactive [ɪnˈæktɪv] *adj* **1.** [person, animal - resting] inactif, peu actif ; [- not working] inactif **2.** [lazy] paresseux, oisif **3.** [inoperative - machine] au repos, à l'arrêt **4.** [dormant - volcano] qui n'est pas en activité ; [- disease, virus] inactif **5.** CHEM & PHYS inerte.

inactivity [ˌɪnækˈtɪvətɪ] *n* inactivité *f*, inaction *f*.

inadequacy [ɪnˈædɪkwəsɪ] (*pl* **inadequacies**) *n* **1.** [insufficiency - of resources, facilities] insuffisance *f* **2.** [social] incapacité *f*, inadaptation *f* ■ [sexual] impuissance *f*, incapacité *f* ■ **feelings of ~** un sentiment d'impuissance **3.** [failing] défaut *m*, faiblesse *f*.

inadequate [ɪnˈædɪkwət] *adj* **1.** [insufficient] insuffisant ■ **our resources are ~ to meet our needs** nos ressources ne correspondent pas à nos besoins **2.** [unsatisfactory] médiocre ■ **their response to the problem was ~** ils n'ont pas su trouver de réponse satisfaisante au problème **3.** [unsuitable - equipment] inadéquat ■ **our machinery is ~ for this type of work** notre outillage n'est pas adapté à ce genre de travail **4.** [incapable] incapable ■ [sexually] impuissant ■ **he's hopelessly ~ for the job** il n'est vraiment pas fait pour ce travail ■ **being unemployed often makes people feel ~** les gens au chômage se sentent souvent inutiles ■ **he's socially ~** c'est un inadapté.

inadequately [ɪnˈædɪkwətlɪ] *adv* de manière inadéquate ■ [fund, invest] insuffisamment.

inadmissible [ˌɪnədˈmɪsəbl] *adj* inacceptable ■ **~ evidence** LAW témoignage *m* irrecevable.

inadvertent [ˌɪnədˈvɜːtnt] *adj* **1.** [not deliberate] accidentel, involontaire **2.** [careless] : **an ~ error** une erreur commise par inadvertance.

inadvertently [ˌɪnədˈvɜːtəntlɪ] *adv* par mégarde OR inadvertance.

inadvisability [ˈɪnədˌvaɪzəˈbɪlətɪ] *n* inopportunité *f*.

inadvisable [ˌɪnədˈvaɪzəbl] *adj* déconseillé ■ **this plan is ~** ce projet est à déconseiller ■ **it's ~ to invest all your money in one place** il est déconseillé d'investir tout son argent dans une seule entreprise.

inalienable [ɪnˈeɪljənəbl] *adj* inaliénable.

inane [ɪˈneɪn] *adj* [person] idiot, imbécile ■ [behaviour] stupide, inepte ■ [remark] idiot, stupide, inepte.

inanely [ɪˈneɪnlɪ] *adv* de façon idiote OR stupide OR inepte.

inanimate [ɪnˈænɪmət] *adj* inanimé.

inanition [ˌɪnəˈnɪʃn] *n* **1.** [debility] inanition *f* **2.** [lethargy] léthargie *f*, torpeur *f*.

inanity [ɪ'nænətɪ] (*pl* **inanities**) *n* **1.** [stupidity] stupidité *f* **2.** [stupid remark] ineptie *f*, bêtise *f*.

inapplicable [,ɪnə'plɪkəbl] *adj* inapplicable ▪ **the rule is ~ to this case** dans ce cas, la règle ne s'applique pas.

inappropriate [,ɪnə'prəuprɪət] *adj* [unsuitable - action, remark] inopportun, mal à propos ; [- time, moment] inopportun ; [- clothing, equipment] peu approprié, inadéquat ; [- name] mal choisi ▪ **you've come at an ~ time** vous arrivez au mauvais moment, vous tombez mal.

inappropriately [,ɪnə'prəuprɪətlɪ] *adv* de manière peu convenable *OR* appropriée ▪ **she was ~ dressed** elle n'était pas vêtue pour la circonstance.

inarticulate [,ɪnɑː'tɪkjulət] *adj* **1.** [person] qui bredouille ▪ **an ~ old man** un vieil homme qui a du mal à s'exprimer ▪ **to be ~ with fear/rage** bégayer de peur/de rage ▪ **his ~ suffering** la souffrance qu'il ne pouvait exprimer **2.** [words, sounds] indistinct ▪ **~ expressions of love** des mots d'amour bredouillés **3.** ANAT & BIOL inarticulé.

inarticulately [,ɪnɑː'tɪkjulətlɪ] *adv* [express o.s.] de manière confuse *OR* peu claire ▪ [mumble] de façon indistincte, indistinctement.

inartistic [,ɪnɑː'tɪstɪk] *adj* **1.** [painting, drawing etc] dénué de toute valeur artistique **2.** [person - lacking artistic taste] sans goût artistique ; [- unskilled] sans talent.

inasmuch as [,ɪnəz'mʌtʃ-] *conj fml* [given that] étant donné que, vu que ▪ [insofar as] dans la mesure où.

inattention [,ɪnə'tenʃn] *n* manque *m* d'attention, inattention *f* ▪ **your essay shows ~ to detail** il y a beaucoup d'erreurs de détail dans votre travail.

inattentive [,ɪnə'tentɪv] *adj* **1.** [paying no attention] inattentif **2.** [neglectful] peu attentionné, négligent.

inattentively [,ɪnə'tentɪvlɪ] *adv* sans prêter *OR* faire attention.

inaudible [ɪ'nɔːdɪbl] *adj* inaudible ▪ **she spoke in an almost ~ whisper** elle s'exprimait de façon presque inaudible.

inaudibly [ɪ'nɔːdɪblɪ] *adv* indistinctement.

inaugural [ɪ'nɔːgjurəl] ◇ *adj* inaugural, d'inauguration.
◇ *n* *US* discours *m* inaugural *(d'un président des États-Unis)*.

inaugurate [ɪ'nɔːgjureɪt] *vt* **1.** [open ceremoniously] inaugurer **2.** [commence formally] inaugurer **3.** [herald - era] inaugurer **4.** [instate - official] installer (dans ses fonctions), investir ; [- king, bishop] introniser.

inauguration [ɪ,nɔːgju'reɪʃn] *n* **1.** [of building] inauguration *f*, cérémonie *f* d'ouverture ▪ [of policy, era etc] inauguration *f* **2.** [of official] investiture *f*.

Inauguration Day *n jour de l'investiture du président des États-Unis (le 20 janvier)*.

inauspicious [,ɪnɔː'spɪʃəs] *adj* défavorable, peu propice ▪ **things got off to an ~ start** les choses ont pris un mauvais départ ▪ **an ~ event** un événement de mauvais augure *OR* de sinistre présage.

inauspiciously [,ɪnɔː'spɪʃəslɪ] *adv* défavorablement ▪ **to start ~** prendre un mauvais départ.

in-between *adj* intermédiaire.

inboard ['ɪnbɔːd] *adj* NAUT : **~ motor** en-bord *m inv*.

inborn [,ɪn'bɔːn] *adj* [characteristic, quality] inné ▪ MED congénital, héréditaire.

inbound ['ɪnbaund] *adj* [flight, passenger etc] à l'arrivée.

inbox ['ɪnbɒks] *n* COMPUT boîte *f* de réception.

inbred [,ɪn'bred] *adj* **1.** [characteristic, quality] inné **2.** BIOL [trait] acquis par sélection génétique ▪ [strain] produit par le croisement d'individus consanguins ▪ [person] de parents consanguins ▪ [family, group] consanguin.

inbreeding [,ɪn'briːdɪŋ] *n* [of animals] croisement *m* ▪ [of people] : **generations of ~** des générations d'alliances consanguines.

inbuilt ['ɪnbɪlt] *adj* **1.** [device] incorporé, intégré **2.** [quality, defect] inhérent.

inc. (*written abbrev of* **inclusive**) : **12-15 April ~** du 12 au 15 avril inclus.

Inc. (*written abbrev of* **incorporated**) *US* ≃ SARL.

Inca ['ɪŋkə] (*pl inv OR pl* **Incas**) *n* Inca *mf*.

incalculable [ɪn'kælkjuləbl] *adj* incalculable.

in camera [,ɪn'kæmərə] *adj* & *adv fml* à huis clos.

incandescent [,ɪnkæn'desnt] *adj* incandescent.

incantation [,ɪnkæn'teɪʃn] *n* incantation *f*.

incapable [ɪn'keɪpəbl] *adj* **1.** [unable] incapable ▪ **to be ~ of doing sthg** être incapable de faire qqch ▪ **she's ~ of such an act** elle est incapable de faire une chose pareille ▪ **he's ~ of speech** il ne peut pas parler **2.** [incompetent] incapable.

incapacitate [,ɪnkə'pæsɪteɪt] *vt* **1.** [cripple] rendre infirme *OR* invalide ▪ **he was temporarily ~d by the accident** à la suite de l'accident, il a été temporairement immobilisé **2.** LAW frapper d'incapacité légale.

incapacity [,ɪnkə'pæsətɪ] (*pl* **incapacities**) *n* [gen - LAW] incapacité *f* ▪ **his ~ for work** son incapacité à travailler ▪ **her ~ to adapt** son incapacité à s'adapter.

incapacity benefit *n UK* prestation *f* d'invalidité.

in-car *adj* AUT : **~ stereo** autoradio *f* (à cassette).

incarcerate [ɪn'kɑːsəreɪt] *vt* incarcérer.

incarceration [ɪn,kɑːsə'reɪʃn] *n* incarcération *f*.

incarnate [ɪn'kɑːneɪt] *lit* ◇ *adj* **1.** incarné ▪ **he's stupidity ~** c'est la bêtise incarnée *OR* personnifiée **2.** [colour] incarnat.
◇ *vt* incarner.

incarnation [,ɪnkɑː'neɪʃn] *n* incarnation *f*.
◆ **Incarnation** *n* : **the Incarnation** l'Incarnation *f*.

incautious [ɪn'kɔːʃəs] *adj* imprudent.

incendiary [ɪn'sendjərɪ] (*pl* **incendiaries**) ◇ *n* **1.** [arsonist] incendiaire *mf* **2.** [bomb] bombe *f* incendiaire **3.** *fig* [agitator] fauteur *m* de troubles.
◇ *adj* **1.** [causing fires] incendiaire ▪ **~ bomb/device** bombe *f* /dispositif *m* incendiaire **2.** [combustible] inflammable **3.** *fig* [speech, statement] incendiaire, séditieux.

incense ◇ *n* ['ɪnsens] encens *m*.
◇ *vt* [ɪn'sens] **1.** [anger] rendre furieux, excéder ▪ **he was ~d by** *OR* **at her indifference** son indifférence l'a rendu furieux **2.** [perfume] encenser.

incentive [ɪn'sentɪv] ◇ *n* **1.** [motivation] motivation *f* ▪ **they have lost their ~** ils ne sont plus très motivés ▪ **he has no ~ to work harder** rien ne le motive à travailler plus dur ▪ **to give sb the ~ to do sthg** motiver qqn à faire qqch **2.** FIN & INDUST incitation *f*, encouragement *m* ▪ **tax ~s** avantages *mpl* fiscaux.
◇ *comp* incitateur, incitatif ▪ **~ bonus** *UK* prime *f* de rendement ▪ **~ scheme** *UK* programme *m* d'encouragement.

incentivize [ɪn'sentɪvaɪz] *vt* motiver.

inception [ɪn'sepʃn] *n* création *f*.

inceptive [ɪn'septɪv] *adj* **1.** [beginning] initial **2.** LING inchoatif.

incessant [ɪn'sesnt] *adj* incessant.

incessantly [ɪn'sesntlɪ] *adv* continuellement, sans cesse.

incest ['ɪnsest] *n* inceste *m*.

incestuous [ɪn'sestjuəs] *adj* incestueux ▪ **publishing is a very ~ business** *fig* le monde de l'édition est très fermé.

inch [ɪntʃ] ◇ *n* pouce *m* ▪ **it's about 6 ~es wide** cela fait à peu près 15 centimètres de large ▪ **the car missed me by ~es** la voiture m'a manqué de peu ▪ **every ~ of the wall was covered with posters** il n'y avait pas un centimètre carré du mur qui ne fût couvert d'affiches, le mur était entièrement couvert

d'affiches ◗ **give him an ~ and he'll take a yard** *OR* **a mile** on lui donne le doigt et il vous prend le bras ▪ **~ by ~** petit à petit, peu à peu ▪ **we'll have to fight every ~ of the way** *fig* nous ne sommes pas au bout de nos peines ▪ **he's every ~ a Frenchman** il est français jusqu'au bout des ongles ▪ **the unions won't budge** *OR* **give an ~** les syndicats ne céderont pas d'un pouce ▪ **to be within an ~ of doing sthg** être à deux doigts de faire qqch.
◇ *vt* : **to ~ one's way in/out** entrer/sortir petit à petit.
◇ *vi* : **to ~ in/out** entrer/sortir petit à petit ▪ **he ~ed along the ledge** il avançait petit à petit le long du rebord.

-inch *in cpds* : **a five~ floppy disk** une disquette cinq pouces.

inchoate [ɪn'kəʊeɪt] *adj fml* [incipient] naissant ▪ [unfinished] inachevé.

inchoative ['ɪnkəʊeɪtɪv] *adj* **1.** LING inchoatif **2.** *fml* [incipient] naissant.

inchworm ['ɪntʃwɜːm] *n* arpenteuse *f*.

incidence ['ɪnsɪdəns] *n* **1.** [rate] taux *m* ▪ **there is a higher/lower ~ of crime** le taux de criminalité est plus élevé/plus faible ▪ **the ~ of the disease in adults** la fréquence de la maladie chez les adultes **2.** GEOM & PHYS incidence *f* ▪ **angle/point of ~** angle *m* /point *m* d'incidence.

incident ['ɪnsɪdənt] ◇ *n* incident *m* ▪ **the match was full of ~** de nombreux incidents ont eu lieu pendant le match ◗ **border** *OR* **frontier ~** incident de frontière.
◇ *adj* **1.** *fml* lié, attaché ▪ **~ to** lié à **2.** PHYS incident.

incidental [,ɪnsɪ'dentl] ◇ *adj* **1.** [minor] secondaire, accessoire ▪ [additional] accessoire ▪ **~ expenses** faux frais *mpl* **2.** [related] : **~ to** en rapport avec, occasionné par.
◇ *n* [chance happening] événement *m* fortuit ▪ [minor detail] détail *m* secondaire.
◆ **incidentals** *npl* [expenses] faux frais *mpl*.

incidentally [,ɪnsɪ'dentəlɪ] *adv* **1.** [by chance] incidemment, accessoirement **2.** [by the way] à propos **3.** [additionally] accessoirement.

incidental music *n* musique *f* d'accompagnement.

incident room *n UK* [in police station] salle *f* des opérations.

incinerate [ɪn'sɪnəreɪt] *vt* incinérer.

incineration [ɪn,sɪnə'reɪʃn] *n* incinération *f*.

incinerator [ɪn'sɪnəreɪtəʳ] *n* incinérateur *m*.

incipient [ɪn'sɪpɪənt] *adj* naissant.

incised [ɪn'saɪzd] *adj* **1.** ART gravé **2.** MED incisé **3.** BOT découpé, incisé.

incision [ɪn'sɪʒn] *n* incision *f*.

incisive [ɪn'saɪsɪv] *adj* [mind] perspicace, pénétrant ▪ [wit, remark] incisif.

incisively [ɪn'saɪsɪvlɪ] *adv* [think] de façon incisive ▪ [ask, remark] de manière perspicace *OR* pénétrante.

incisor [ɪn'saɪzəʳ] *n* incisive *f*.

incite [ɪn'saɪt] *vt* : **to ~ sb to do sthg** inciter qqn à faire qqch ▪ **to ~ sb to violence** inciter qqn à la violence.

incitement [ɪn'saɪtmənt] *n* incitation *f* ▪ **~ to riot/violence** incitation à la révolte/à la violence.

incl. (*written abbrev of* **including**) : **~ VAT** TTC.

inclement [ɪn'klemənt] *adj lit* [weather] inclément.

inclination [,ɪnklɪ'neɪʃn] *n* **1.** [tendency] disposition *f*, prédisposition *f*, tendance *f* ▪ **a decided ~ towards laziness** une nette prédisposition à la paresse **2.** [liking] penchant *m*, inclination *f* ▪ **I do it from necessity, not from ~** je le fais par nécessité, pas par inclination *OR* par goût **3.** [slant, lean] inclinaison *f* ▪ [of body] inclination *f* **4.** [hill] pente *f*, inclinaison *f* **5.** ASTRON & MATHS inclinaison *f*.

incline ◇ *vt* [ɪn'klaɪn] **1.** [dispose] disposer, pousser ▪ **his unhappy childhood ~d him towards cynicism** *OR* **to be cynical** c'est à cause de son enfance malheureuse qu'il a tendance à être cynique **2.** [lean, bend] incliner.
◇ *vi* [ɪn'klaɪn] **1.** [tend] tendre, avoir tendance ▪ **he ~s towards exaggeration** il a tendance à exagérer, il exagère facilement **2.** [lean, bend] s'incliner.
◇ *n* ['ɪnklaɪn] inclinaison *f* ▪ [slope] pente *f*, déclivité *f* ▪ RAIL rampe *f*.

inclined [ɪn'klaɪnd] *adj* **1.** [tending, disposed] avoir tendance à ▪ **I'm ~ to agree** j'aurais tendance à être d'accord ▪ **he's ~ to exaggeration** il a tendance à exagérer, il exagère facilement ▪ **to be well ~ towards sb** être bien disposé envers qqn ▪ **if you are so ~** si ça vous dit, si le cœur vous en dit ▪ **I'm not that way ~** je ne suis pas comme ça **2.** [slanting, leaning] incliné.

inclose [ɪn'kləʊz] = **enclose**.

inclosure [ɪn'kləʊʒəʳ] = **enclosure**.

include [ɪn'kluːd] *vt* comprendre, inclure ▪ **the price ~s VAT** la TVA est comprise (dans le prix) ▪ **everyone was in favour, myself ~d** tout le monde était pour, moi y compris ▪ **don't forget to ~ the cheque** n'oubliez pas de joindre le chèque ▪ **'batteries not ~d'** 'piles non fournies' ▪ **my duties ~ sorting the mail** trier le courrier entre dans mes attributions *OR* fait partie de mon travail ▪ **the children refused to ~ him in their games** les enfants ont refusé de l'inclure dans leurs jeux.

included [ɪn'kluːdɪd] *adj* : **myself ~** y compris moi ▪ **'service not ~'** 'service non compris'.

including [ɪn'kluːdɪŋ] *prep* (y) compris ▪ **14 guests ~ the children** 14 invités y compris les enfants ▪ **14 guests not ~ the children** 14 invités sans compter les enfants ▪ **up to and ~ page 40** jusqu'à la page 40 incluse ▪ **five books, ~ one I hadn't read** cinq livres, dont un que je n'avais pas lu.

inclusion [ɪn'kluːʒn] *n* [gen - GEOL] & MATHS inclusion *f*.

inclusive [ɪn'kluːsɪv] *adj* **1.** inclus, compris ▪ **~ of tax** taxes *fpl* comprises ▪ **from July to September ~** de juillet à septembre inclus ▪ **~ prices** prix *mpl* nets ▪ **all-~ holidays** voyages *mpl* organisés *(où tout est compris)* **2.** [list] exhaustif ▪ [survey] complet, - ète *f*, poussé.

inclusively [ɪn'kluːsɪvlɪ] *adv* inclusivement.

inclusivity [,ɪnkluː'sɪvɪtɪ] *n* inclusion *f*, politique *f* d'inclusion.

incognito [,ɪnkɒg'niːtəʊ] (*pl* **incognitos**) ◇ *adv* incognito ▪ **to remain ~** [witness] garder l'anonymat ; [star, politician] garder l'incognito.
◇ *n* incognito *m*.

incoherence [,ɪnkəʊ'hɪərəns] *n* incohérence *f*.

incoherent [,ɪnkəʊ'hɪərənt] *adj* [person, argument] incohérent ▪ [thought] incohérent, décousu.

incoherently [,ɪnkəʊ'hɪərəntlɪ] *adv* de manière incohérente ▪ **to mutters ~** marmonner des paroles incohérentes.

income ['ɪŋkʌm] *n* revenu *m* ▪ **the ~ from her shares** les revenus de ses actions.

income bracket, income group *n* tranche *f* de revenus ▪ **most people in this area belong to the lower/higher ~** la plupart des habitants de ce quartier sont des économiquement faibles/ont des revenus élevés.

incomer ['ɪn,kʌməʳ] *n* nouveau venu *m*, nouvelle venue *f*.

incomes policy *n UK* politique *f* des revenus.

income support *n prestation complémentaire en faveur des personnes justifiant de faibles revenus.*

income tax *n* impôt *m* sur le revenu (des personnes physiques) ▪ **~ inspector** inspecteur *m* des contributions directes *OR* des impôts ▪ **~ return** déclaration *f* de revenus, feuille *f* d'impôts.

incoming ['ɪn,kʌmɪŋ] *adj* **1.** [in direction] : **~ train/flight** train *m* /vol *m* à l'arrivée ▪ **~ passengers** passagers *mpl* à l'arrivée ▪ **~ mail** courrier *m* (du jour) ▪ **~ calls** appels *mpl* téléphoniques (reçus) ▪ **the ~ tide** la marée montante **2.** [cash, interest] qui rentre **3.** [official, administration, tenant] nouveau *(before vowel or silent 'h'* **nouvel***)*, nouvelle *f*.

◆ **incomings** *npl* [revenue] rentrées *fpl*, recettes *fpl*.

incommensurable [ˌɪnkə'menʃərəbl] *adj* [gen - MATHS] incommensurable.

incommensurate [ˌɪnkə'menʃərət] *adj fml* **1.** [disproportionate] disproportionné, inadéquat ■ **it is ~ with our needs** cela ne correspond pas à nos besoins **2.** = **incommensurable**.

incommode [ˌɪnkə'məʊd] *vt fml* incommoder, indisposer.

incommunicado [ˌɪnkəmju:nɪ'kɑ:dəʊ] *adj* & *adv* sans communication avec le monde extérieur ■ **the prisoners are being kept** *OR* **held ~** les prisonniers sont (gardés) au secret.

incomparable [ɪn'kɒmpərəbl] *adj* incomparable.

incomparably [ɪn'kɒmpərəblɪ] *adv* incomparablement, infiniment.

incompatibility ['ɪnkəmˌpætə'bɪlətɪ] *n* incompatibilité *f* ■ [grounds for divorce] incompatibilité *f* d'humeur.

incompatible [ˌɪnkəm'pætɪbl] *adj* incompatible.

incompetence [ɪn'kɒmpɪtəns], **incompetency** [ɪn'kɒmpɪtənsɪ] *n* incompétence *f*.

incompetent [ɪn'kɒmpɪtənt] ◇ *adj* incompétent.
◇ *n* incompétent *m*, - e *f*, incapable *mf*.

incomplete [ˌɪnkəm'pli:t] *adj* **1.** [unfinished] inachevé **2.** [lacking something] incomplet, - ète *f*.

incompletely [ˌɪnkəm'pli:tlɪ] *adv* incomplètement.

incompleteness [ˌɪnkəm'pli:tnɪs] *n* **1.** caractère *m* incomplet **2.** LOGIC incomplétude *f*.

incomprehensible [ˌɪnkɒmprɪ'hensəbl] *adj* incompréhensible.

incomprehension [ˌɪnkɒmprɪ'henʃn] *n* incompréhension *f*.

inconceivable [ˌɪnkən'si:vəbl] *adj* inconcevable, inimaginable.

inconceivably [ˌɪnkən'si:vəblɪ] *adv* incroyablement.

inconclusive [ˌɪnkən'klu:sɪv] *adj* peu concluant ■ **~ data** données *fpl* peu probantes ■ **the talks have been ~** les pourparlers n'ont pas abouti.

inconclusively [ˌɪnkən'klu:sɪvlɪ] *adv* de manière peu concluante ■ **the meeting ended ~** la réunion n'a abouti à aucune conclusion.

incongruity [ˌɪnkɒŋ'gru:ətɪ] (*pl* **incongruities**) *n* **1.** [strangeness, discordancy] incongruité *f* **2.** [disparity] disparité *f*.

incongruous [ɪn'kɒŋgrʊəs] *adj* [strange, discordant] incongru ■ [disparate] incohérent ■ **he was an ~ figure among the factory workers** on le remarquait tout de suite au milieu des ouvriers de l'usine.

inconsequential [ˌɪnkɒnsɪ'kwenʃl] *adj* sans importance ■ **an ~ detail** un détail insignifiant ■ **an ~ little man** un bonhomme sans importance.

inconsiderable [ˌɪnkən'sɪdərəbl] *adj* insignifiant, négligeable ■ **a not ~ amount of money** une somme d'argent non négligeable.

inconsiderate [ˌɪnkən'sɪdərət] *adj* [person] qui manque de prévenance ■ [action, remark] irréfléchi ■ **he's ~ of other people's feelings** peu lui importe ce que pensent les autres ■ **that was very ~ of you** vous avez agi sans aucun égard pour les autres.

inconsiderately [ˌɪnkən'sɪdərətlɪ] *adv* sans aucune considération.

inconsistency [ˌɪnkən'sɪstənsɪ] (*pl* **inconsistencies**) *n* **1.** [incoherence] manque *m* de cohérence, incohérence *f* **2.** [contradiction] contradiction *f* ■ **there are several inconsistencies in your argument** votre argumentation présente *OR* laisse apparaître plusieurs contradictions.

inconsistent [ˌɪnkən'sɪstənt] *adj* **1.** [person] incohérent *(dans ses comportements)* **2.** [performance] inégal **3.** [reasoning] incohérent **4.** [incompatible] incompatible ■ **~ with** incompatible avec.

inconsolable [ˌɪnkən'səʊləbl] *adj* inconsolable.

inconsolably [ˌɪnkən'səʊləblɪ] *adv* de façon inconsolable.

inconspicuous [ˌɪnkən'spɪkjʊəs] *adj* [difficult to see] à peine visible, qui passe inaperçu ■ [discreet] peu voyant, discret, - ète *f* ■ **she tried to make herself as ~ as possible** elle fit tout son possible pour passer inaperçue.

inconspicuously [ˌɪnkən'spɪkjʊəslɪ] *adv* discrètement.

inconstancy [ɪn'kɒnstənsɪ] *n* **1.** [of phenomenon] variabilité *f*, instabilité *f* **2.** [of person] versatilité *f*, inconstance *f*.

inconstant [ɪn'kɒnstənt] *adj* **1.** [weather] variable **2.** [person] inconstant, volage.

incontestable [ˌɪnkən'testəbl] *adj* incontestable.

incontinence [ɪn'kɒntɪnəns] *n* incontinence *f*.

incontinent [ɪn'kɒntɪnənt] *adj* incontinent.

incontrovertible [ˌɪnkɒntrə'vɜ:təbl] *adj* indiscutable ■ **~ evidence** une preuve irréfutable.

incontrovertibly [ˌɪnkɒntrə'vɜ:təblɪ] *adv* indiscutablement, indéniablement.

inconvenience [ˌɪnkən'vi:njəns] ◇ *n* **1.** [disadvantage] inconvénient *m* **2.** [trouble] : **to cause ~** déranger, gêner ❙ [disadvantages] incommodité *f*, inconvénients *mpl* ■ **the ~ of a small flat** les désagréments d'un petit appartement.
◇ *vt* déranger, incommoder.

inconvenient [ˌɪnkən'vi:njənt] *adj* **1.** [inopportune, awkward] inopportun ■ **if it's not ~** si cela ne vous dérange pas ■ **he has chosen to ignore any ~ facts** il a choisi d'ignorer tout ce qui pouvait poser problème **2.** [impractical - tool, kitchen] peu pratique.

inconveniently [ˌɪnkən'vi:njəntlɪ] *adv* **1.** [happen, arrive] au mauvais moment, inopportunément **2.** [be situated] de façon malcommode, mal.

incorporate [ɪn'kɔ:pəreɪt] ◇ *vt* incorporer ■ **she ~d many folk tunes into her performance** son programme comprenait de nombreux airs folkloriques ■ **the territory was ~d into Poland** le territoire fut incorporé *OR* annexé à la Pologne ■ **to ~ amendments into a text** apporter des modifications à un texte.
◇ *vi* COMM [form a corporation] se constituer en société commerciale ■ [merge] fusionner.

incorporated [ɪn'kɔ:pəreɪtɪd] *adj* constitué en société commerciale ■ **Bradley & Jones Incorporated** ≃ Bradley & Jones SARL.

incorporation [ɪnˌkɔ:pə'reɪʃn] *n* **1.** [gen] incorporation *f*, intégration *f* **2.** COMM constitution *f* en société commerciale.

incorporeal [ˌɪnkɔ:'pɔ:rɪəl] *adj lit* incorporel.

incorrect [ˌɪnkə'rekt] *adj* **1.** [wrong - answer, result] erroné, faux, fausse *f* ; [- sum, statement] inexact, incorrect ■ **~ use of a word** usage *m* impropre d'un mot **2.** [improper] incorrect.

incorrectly [ˌɪnkə'rektlɪ] *adv* **1.** [wrongly] : **I was ~ quoted** j'ai été cité de façon incorrecte ■ **the illness was ~ diagnosed** il y a eu erreur de diagnostic **2.** [improperly] incorrectement.

incorrigible [ɪn'kɒrɪdʒəbl] *adj* incorrigible.

incorruptible [ˌɪnkə'rʌptəbl] *adj* incorruptible.

increase ◇ *vi* [ɪn'kri:s] augmenter, croître ■ **to ~ by 10%** augmenter de 10 % ■ **the attacks have ~d in frequency** la fréquence des attaques a augmenté ■ **to ~ in size** grandir ■ **to ~ in intensity** s'intensifier.
◇ *vt* [ɪn'kri:s] augmenter ■ **to ~ output to 500 units a week** augmenter *OR* faire passer la production à 500 unités par semaine ■ **recent events have ~d speculation** des événements récents ont renforcé les rumeurs.

<> *n* ['ɪnkri:s] augmentation *f* ■ **the ~ in productivity/in the cost of living** l'augmentation de la productivité/du coût de la vie ■ **a 10% pay ~** une augmentation de salaire de 10 % ■ **an ~ in population** un accroissement de la population.
◆ **on the increase** *adj phr* : **crime is on the ~** la criminalité est en hausse ■ **shoplifting is on the ~** les vols à l'étalage sont de plus en plus nombreux.

increased [ɪn'kri:st] *adj* accru ■ **~ investment leads to ~ productivity** l'accroissement des investissements entraînera un accroissement *OR* une augmentation de la productivité.

increasing [ɪn'kri:sɪŋ] *adj* croissant, grandissant ■ **there have been an ~ number of complaints** les réclamations sont de plus en plus nombreuses ■ **they make ~ use of computer technology** ils ont de plus en plus souvent recours à l'informatique.

increasingly [ɪn'kri:sɪŋlɪ] *adv* de plus en plus.

incredible [ɪn'kredəbl] *adj* **1.** [unbelievable] incroyable, invraisemblable **2.** *inf* [fantastic, amazing] fantastique, incroyable.

incredibly [ɪn'kredəblɪ] *adv* **1.** [amazingly] : **~, we were on time** aussi incroyable que cela puisse paraître, nous étions à l'heure **2.** [extremely] incroyablement.

incredulity [,ɪnkrɪ'dju:lətɪ] *n* incrédulité *f*.

incredulous [ɪn'kredjʊləs] *adj* incrédule.

incredulously [ɪn'kredjʊləslɪ] *adv* avec incrédulité.

increment ['ɪnkrɪmənt] <> *n* **1.** [increase] augmentation *f* ■ **a salary with yearly ~s of £500** un salaire assorti d'augmentations annuelles de 500 livres **2.** COMPUT incrément *m* **3.** MATHS accroissement *m*.
<> *vt* COMPUT incrémenter.

incremental [,ɪnkrɪ'mentl] *adj* **1.** [increasing] croissant ■ **~ increases** augmentations *fpl* régulières **2.** COMPUT incrémentiel, incrémental.

incriminate [ɪn'krɪmɪneɪt] *vt* incriminer, mettre en cause ■ **to ~ o.s.** se compromettre.

incriminating [ɪn'krɪmɪneɪtɪŋ] *adj* accusateur, compromettant ■ **~ evidence** pièce *f OR* pièces *fpl* à conviction.

incriminatory [ɪn'krɪmɪnətrɪ] = **incriminating**.

in-crowd *n inf* coterie *f* ■ **to be in with the ~** être branché.

incrust [ɪn'krʌst] = **encrust**.

incubate ['ɪnkjʊbeɪt] <> *vt* **1.** BIOL [eggs - subj: bird] couver ; [- subj: fish] incuber ; [- in incubator] incuber **2.** *fig* [plot, idea] couver.
<> *vi* **1.** BIOL [egg] être en incubation **2.** MED [virus] incuber **3.** *fig* [plan, idea] couver.

incubation [,ɪnkjʊ'beɪʃn] *n* [of egg, virus, disease] incubation *f* ■ **~ period** (période *f* d')incubation.

incubator ['ɪnkjʊbeɪtəʳ] *n* [for premature baby] couveuse *f*, incubateur *m* ■ [for eggs, bacteria] incubateur *m*.

incubus ['ɪnkjʊbəs] (*pl* **incubuses** *OR pl* **incubi** [-baɪ]) *n* **1.** [demon] incube *m* **2.** *lit* [nightmare] cauchemar *m*.

inculcate ['ɪnkʌlkeɪt] *vt* inculquer ■ **to ~ sb with an idea, to ~ an idea in sb** inculquer une idée à qqn.

incumbency [ɪn'kʌmbənsɪ] (*pl* **incumbencies**) *n* [office] office *m*, fonction *f*.

incumbent [ɪn'kʌmbənt] <> *adj fml* **1.** [obligatory] : **it is ~ on** *OR* **upon the manager to check the takings** il incombe *OR* il appartient au directeur de vérifier la recette **2.** [in office] en fonction, en exercice ■ **the ~ mayor** [current] le maire en exercice ; [during election campaign] le maire sortant.
<> *n* [office holder] titulaire *mf*.

incur [ɪn'kɜ:ʳ] (*pret & pp* **incurred**, *cont* **incurring**) *vt* [blame, loss, penalty] s'exposer à, encourir ■ [debt] contracter ■ [losses] subir ■ **the expenses incurred** les dépenses encourues ■ **to ~ sb's wrath** s'attirer les foudres de qqn.

incurable [ɪn'kjʊərəbl] *adj* [illness] incurable, inguérissable ■ *fig* [optimist] inguérissable, infatigable.

incurably [ɪn'kjʊərəblɪ] *adv* : **to be ~ ill** avoir une maladie incurable ■ **to be ~ lazy** *fig* être irrémédiablement paresseux.

incurious [ɪn'kjʊərɪəs] *adj lit* incurieux *lit*, sans curiosité.

incursion [*UK* ɪn'kɜ:ʃn, *US* ɪn'kɜ:ʒn] *n* incursion *f* ■ **an ~ into enemy territory** une incursion en territoire ennemi.

indebted [ɪn'detɪd] *adj* **1.** [for help] redevable ■ **to be ~ to sb for sthg : I am greatly ~ to you for doing me this favour** je vous suis extrêmement reconnaissant de m'avoir rendu ce service **2.** [owing money] endetté.

indebtedness [ɪn'detɪdnɪs] *n* **1.** [for help] dette *f*, obligation *f* ■ **my ~ to her** ma dette envers elle **2.** [financial] endettement *m*.

indecency [ɪn'di:snsɪ] (*pl* **indecencies**) *n* [gen] indécence *f* ■ LAW attentat *m* à la pudeur ■ **gross ~** outrage *m* à la pudeur.

indecent [ɪn'di:snt] *adj* **1.** [obscene] indécent **2.** [unseemly] indécent, inconvenant, déplacé ■ **with ~ haste** avec une précipitation déplacée.

indecent assault *n* attentat *m* à la pudeur.

indecent exposure *n* outrage *m* public à la pudeur.

indecently [ɪn'di:sntlɪ] *adv* indécemment.

indecipherable [,ɪndɪ'saɪfərəbl] *adj* indéchiffrable.

indecision [,ɪndɪ'sɪʒn] *n* indécision *f*.

indecisive [,ɪndɪ'saɪsɪv] *adj* **1.** [hesitating - person] indécis, irrésolu **2.** [inconclusive] peu concluant.

indecisively [,ɪndɪ'saɪsɪvlɪ] *adv* **1.** [hesitatingly] de manière indécise, avec hésitation **2.** [inconclusively] de manière peu convaincante *OR* concluante.

indecisiveness [,ɪndɪ'saɪsɪvnɪs] = **indecision**.

indeclinable [,ɪndɪ'klaɪnəbl] *adj* indéclinable.

indecorous [ɪn'dekərəs] *adj* inconvenant, malséant.

indeed [ɪn'di:d] *adv* **1.** [used to confirm] effectivement, en effet ■ **we are aware of the problem; ~, we are already investigating it** nous sommes conscients du problème; en fait, nous sommes déjà en train de l'étudier **2.** [used to qualify] : **the problem, if ~ there is one, is theirs** c'est leur problème, si problème il y a ■ **it is difficult, ~ virtually impossible, to get in** il est difficile, pour ne pas dire impossible *OR* voire impossible, d'entrer **3.** [used as intensifier] vraiment ■ **thank you very much ~** merci beaucoup ■ **that's praise ~!** ça, c'est un compliment!, voilà ce qui s'appelle un compliment! ‖ [in replies] en effet ■ **I believe you support their policy – I do ~** je crois que vous soutenez leur politique – en effet **4.** [as surprised, ironic response] : **he asked us for a pay rise – ~!** il nous a demandé une augmentation – eh bien! *OR* vraiment?

indefatigable [,ɪndɪ'fætɪgəbl] *adj* infatigable.

indefatigably [,ɪndɪ'fætɪgəblɪ] *adv* infatigablement, sans se fatiguer, inlassablement.

indefensible [,ɪndɪ'fensəbl] *adj* **1.** [conduct] injustifiable, inexcusable ■ [argument] insoutenable, indéfendable **2.** MIL indéfendable.

indefinable [,ɪndɪ'faɪnəbl] *adj* indéfinissable.

indefinite [ɪn'defɪnɪt] *adj* [indeterminate] indéterminé, illimité ■ **for an ~ period** pour une période indéterminée ‖ [vague, imprecise] flou, peu précis.

indefinite article *n* article *m* indéfini.

indefinitely [ɪn'defɪnətlɪ] *adv* **1.** [without limit] indéfiniment ■ **we can't go on ~** on ne peut pas continuer indéfiniment **2.** [imprecisely] vaguement.

indefinite pronoun *n* pronom *m* indéfini.

indelible [ɪn'deləbl] *adj* [ink, stain] indélébile ■ [memory] impérissable ■ **~ marker** *UK* marqueur *m* indélébile.

indelibly [ɪn'deləblɪ] *adv* de manière indélébile ■ **her face remained ~ fixed in his memory** son visage resta à jamais gravé dans sa mémoire.

indelicacy [ɪn'delɪkəsɪ] (*pl* **indelicacies**) *n* **1.** [of behaviour, remark] indélicatesse *f* **2.** [tactless remark, action] manque *m* de tact.

indelicate [ɪn'delɪkət] *adj* [action] déplacé, indélicat ■ [person, remark] indélicat, qui manque de tact.

indemnification [ɪn,demnɪfɪ'keɪʃn] *n* **1.** [act of compensation] indemnisation *f*, dédommagement *m* **2.** [sum reimbursed] indemnité *f*.

indemnify [ɪn'demnɪfaɪ] (*pret & pp* **indemnified**) *vt* **1.** [compensate] indemniser, dédommager ■ **to be indemnified for sthg** être indemnisé *OR* dédommagé de qqch **2.** [insure] assurer, garantir ■ **to be indemnified for** *OR* **against sthg** être assuré contre qqch.

indemnity [ɪn'demnətɪ] (*pl* **indemnities**) *n* **1.** [compensation] indemnité *f*, dédommagement *m* **2.** [insurance] assurance *f* **3.** [exemption - from prosecution] immunité *f*.

indent ◇ *vt* [ɪn'dent] **1.** [line of text] mettre en retrait ■ **~ the first line** commencez la première ligne en retrait *OR* avec un alinéa **2.** [edge] denteler, découper ■ [more deeply] échancrer **3.** [surface] marquer, faire une empreinte dans **4.** *UK* COMM [goods] commander **5.** = **indenture**.
◇ *vi* [ɪn'dent] **1.** [at start of paragraph] faire un alinéa **2.** *UK* COMM passer commande ■ **to ~ on sb for sthg** commander qqch à qqn.
◇ *n* ['ɪndent] **1.** *UK* COMM [order] commande *f* ■ [order form] bordereau *m* de commande **2.** = **indentation** *(sense 1)*.

indentation [,ɪnden'teɪʃn] *n* **1.** [in line of text] renfoncement *m* **2.** [in edge] dentelure *f* ■ [deeper] échancrure *f* ■ [in coastline] découpure *f* **3.** [on surface] empreinte *f* **4.** = **indenture**.

indented [ɪn'dentɪd] *adj* [edge] découpé, dentelé ■ [coastline] découpé.

indenture [ɪn'dentʃər] ◇ *n (often pl)* contrat *m* ■ [of apprentice] contrat *m* d'apprentissage.
◇ *vt* engager par contrat ■ [apprentice] mettre *OR* placer comme apprenti ■ **he was ~d to a carpenter** on le mit comme apprenti *OR* en apprentissage chez un menuisier.

independence [,ɪndɪ'pendəns] *n* [gen - POL] indépendance *f* ■ **the country has recently gained its ~** le pays vient d'accéder à l'indépendance ■ **the (American) War of Independence** la guerre d'Indépendance (américaine).

THE AMERICAN WAR OF INDEPENDENCE

Guerre d'indépendance des 13 colonies de la Nouvelle-Angleterre, en réaction à la dureté de l'administration britannique qui leur imposait de lourdes taxes. Marqué par la Déclaration d'indépendance du 4 juillet 1776, le conflit dura 5 ans et la République fédérée des États-Unis fut reconnue en 1783 au traité de Paris.

Independence Day *n* fête *f* nationale de l'Indépendance *(aux États-Unis)*.

independency [,ɪndɪ'pendənsɪ] (*pl* **independencies**) *n* **1.** [country] État *m* indépendant **2.** = **independence**.

independent [,ɪndɪ'pendənt] ◇ *adj* **1.** indépendant ■ **to become ~** [country] accéder à l'indépendance ■ **she is ~ of her parents** elle ne dépend plus de ses parents ■ **he is incapable of ~ thought** il est incapable de penser par lui-même ▶ **~ income** revenus *mpl* indépendants, rentes *fpl* ■ **a man of ~ means** un rentier **2.** GRAM, PHILOS & MATHS indépendant.
◇ *n* **1.** [gen] indépendant *m*, - e *f* ■ **The Independent** PRESS *quotidien britannique de qualité sans affiliation politique particulière, see also* **broadsheet** **2.** POL indépendant *m*, - e *f*, non-inscrit *m*, - e *f*.

independently [,ɪndɪ'pendəntlɪ] *adv* de manière indépendante, de manière autonome ■ **~ of** indépendamment de.

independent school *n UK* école *f* privée.

in-depth *adj* en profondeur.

indescribable [,ɪndɪ'skraɪbəbl] *adj* indescriptible.

indescribably [,ɪndɪ'skraɪbəblɪ] *adv* incroyablement.

indestructible [,ɪndɪ'strʌktəbl] *adj* indestructible.

indeterminable [,ɪndɪ'tɜːmɪnəbl] *adj* **1.** [fact, amount, distance] indéterminable **2.** [controversy, problem] insoluble.

indeterminate [,ɪndɪ'tɜːmɪnət] *adj* **1.** [undetermined, indefinite] indéterminé ■ **~ sentence** peine *f* (de prison) de durée indéterminée **2.** [vague, imprecise] flou, vague **3.** LING, MATHS & PHILOS indéterminé.

index ['ɪndeks] (*pl* **indexes**) ◇ *n* **1.** [in book, database] index *m* ■ **name ~** index des noms propres **2.** [in library] catalogue *m*, répertoire *m* ■ [on index cards] fichier *m* **3.** [finger] index *m* **4.** (*pl* indices [-dɪsiːz]) ECON & PHYS indice *m* ■ MATHS [subscript] indice *m* ■ [superscript] exposant *m* **5.** (*pl inv*) [pointer on scale] aiguille *f*, indicateur *m* ■ *fig* [sign] indice *m*, indicateur *m* **6.** TYPO [pointing fist] renvoi *m*.
◇ *vt* **1.** [word, book, database] indexer ■ **you'll find it ~ed under "science"** vous trouverez ça indexé à "science" *OR* dans l'index sous (l'entrée) "science" **2.** ECON indexer ■ **~ed to** indexé sur **3.** MECH indexer.

Index *n* RELIG : **Index** Index *m*.

indexation [,ɪndek'seɪʃn] *n* indexation *f*.

index card *n* fiche *f*.

index finger *n* index *m*.

index-linked *adj UK* indexé.

index page *n* index *m*, page *f* d'accueil.

India ['ɪndjə] *pr n* Inde *f* ■ **in ~** en Inde.

India ink *US* = **Indian ink**.

Indian ['ɪndjən] ◇ *n* **1.** [person - in America, Asia] Indien *m*, - enne *f* **2.** LING [in America] langue *f* amérindienne.
◇ *adj* [American or Asian] indien.

Indiana [,ɪndɪ'ænə] *pr n* Indiana *m* ■ **in ~** dans l'Indiana.

Indian elephant *n* éléphant *m* d'Asie.

Indian file *n* : **in ~** en file *f* indienne.

Indian ink *n UK* encre *f* de Chine.

Indian Ocean *pr n* : **the ~** l'océan *m* Indien.

Indian sign *n US* sort *m (jeté sur qqn)*.

Indian summer *n* été *m* de la Saint-Martin, été *m* indien ■ *fig* vieillesse *f* heureuse.

Indian Wars *pr npl US* HIST *guerres entre les Indiens d'Amérique et les colons aux XVIIIe et XIXe siècles*.

India paper *n* papier *m* bible.

India rubber *n UK* [substance] caoutchouc *m* ■ [eraser] gomme *f*.

indicate ['ɪndɪkeɪt] ◇ *vt* **1.** [show, point to] indiquer **2.** [make clear] signaler ■ **as I have already ~d** comme je l'ai déjà signalé *OR* fait remarquer ■ **he ~d his willingness to help** il nous a fait savoir qu'il était prêt à nous aider **3.** *UK* AUT : **to ~ (that one is turning) left/right** mettre son clignotant à gauche/à droite (pour tourner) **4.** [recommend, require] indiquer.
◇ *vi UK* AUT mettre son clignotant.

indication [,ɪndɪ'keɪʃn] *n* **1.** [sign] indication *f* ■ **she gave no ~ that she had seen me** rien ne pouvait laisser supposer qu'elle m'avait vu ■ **he gave us a clear ~ of his intentions** il nous a clairement fait comprendre *OR* clairement indiqué ses intentions ■ **all the ~s are that..., there is every ~ that...** tout porte à croire que... **2.** [act of indicating] indication *f*.

indicative [ɪn'dɪkətɪv] ◇ *adj* **1.** [symptomatic] indicatif ■ **~ of : his handwriting is ~ of his mental state** son écriture est révélatrice de son état mental ■ **it is ~ of a strong personality** cela témoigne d'une forte personnalité **2.** GRAM indicatif ■ **the ~ mood** le mode indicatif, l'indicatif *m*.
◇ *n* GRAM indicatif *m* ■ **in the ~** à l'indicatif.

indicator ['ɪndɪkeɪtəʳ] *n* **1.** [instrument] indicateur *m* ▪ [warning lamp] voyant *m* **2.** AUT clignotant *m* **3.** [at station, in airport] : **arrivals/departures ~** panneau *m* des arrivées/des départs **4.** *fig* indicateur *m* **5.** CHEM indicateur *m* **6.** LING indicateur *m*.

indices [-dɪsi:z] *pl* ▻ **index**.

indict [ɪn'daɪt] *vt* LAW inculper, mettre en examen *spec*.

indictable [ɪn'daɪtəbl] *adj* LAW **1.** [person] passible de poursuites **2.** [crime] passible des tribunaux.

indictment [ɪn'daɪtmənt] *n* **1.** LAW inculpation *f*, mise *f* en examen *spec* ▪ **~ for fraud** inculpation pour fraude **2.** *fig* **a damning ~ of government policy** un témoignage accablant contre la politique gouvernementale.

indie ['ɪndɪ] *adj inf* [band, charts] indépendant *(dont les disques sont produits par des maisons indépendantes)*.

indifference [ɪn'dɪfrəns] *n* **1.** [unconcern] indifférence *f* ▪ **with total ~** avec une indifférence totale ▪ **~ towards** manque *m* d'intérêt **2.** [mediocrity] médiocrité *f* **3.** [unimportance] insignifiance *f* **4.** PHILOS indifférence *f*.

indifferent [ɪn'dɪfrənt] *adj* **1.** [unconcerned, cold] indifférent ▪ **she was ~ to the beauty of the landscape** elle était indifférente à la beauté du paysage ▪ **~ to the danger** insouciant du danger **2.** [unimportant] indifférent ▪ **it's ~ to me whether they go or stay** qu'ils partent ou qu'ils restent, cela m'est égal *OR* indifférent **3.** [mediocre] médiocre, quelconque ▪ **good, bad or ~** bon, mauvais ou ni l'un ni l'autre.

indifferently [ɪn'dɪfrəntlɪ] *adv* **1.** [unconcernedly] indifféremment, avec indifférence **2.** [not well] médiocrement.

indigenous [ɪn'dɪdʒɪnəs] *adj* **1.** [animal, plant, custom] indigène ▪ [population] autochtone ▪ **rabbits are not ~ to Australia** à l'origine, il n'y avait pas de lapins en Australie **2.** [innate] inné, natif *lit*.

indigestible [,ɪndɪ'dʒestəbl] *adj* indigeste.

indigestion [,ɪndɪ'dʒestʃn] *n (U)* indigestion *f* ▪ **to have ~** avoir une indigestion.

indignant [ɪn'dɪgnənt] *adj* indigné, outré ▪ **he was ~ at her attitude** il était indigné par son attitude.

indignantly [ɪn'dɪgnəntlɪ] *adv* avec indignation.

indignation [,ɪndɪg'neɪʃn] *n* indignation *f*.

indignity [ɪn'dɪgnətɪ] (*pl* **indignities**) *n* indignité *f* ▪ **he suffered the ~ of having to ask for a loan** il a dû s'abaisser à solliciter un prêt.

indigo ['ɪndɪgəʊ] (*pl* **indigos** *OR pl* **indigoes**) ◇ *n* **1.** [dye, colour] indigo *m* **2.** [plant] indigotier *m*.
◇ *adj* indigo *(inv)*.

indigo blue = **indigo** *(sense 1)*.

indirect [,ɪndɪ'rekt] *adj* indirect ▪ **an ~ reference** une allusion voilée ▪ **~ free kick** FTBL coup *m* franc indirect.

indirect costs *npl* frais *mpl* généraux.

indirect lighting *n* éclairage *m* indirect.

indirectly [,ɪndɪ'rektlɪ] *adv* indirectement ▪ **I heard about it ~** je l'ai appris indirectement *OR* par personnes interposées.

indirect object *n* objet *m* indirect.

indirect question *n* question *f* indirecte.

indirect speech *n* discours *m* indirect.

indirect tax *n* impôts *mpl* indirects.

indirect taxation *n* fiscalité *f* indirecte.

indiscipline [ɪn'dɪsɪplɪn] *n* indiscipline *f*.

indiscreet [,ɪndɪ'skri:t] *adj* indiscret, - ète *f*.

indiscreetly [,ɪndɪ'skri:tlɪ] *adv* indiscrètement.

indiscretion [,ɪndɪ'skreʃn] *n* indiscrétion *f*.

indiscriminate [,ɪndɪ'skrɪmɪnət] *adj* : **it was ~ slaughter** ce fut un massacre aveugle ▪ **to distribute ~ punishment/praise** distribuer des punitions/des éloges à tort et à travers ▪ **children are ~ in their television viewing** les enfants regardent la télévision sans discernement ▪ **~ admiration** admiration inconditionnelle.

indiscriminately [,ɪndɪ'skrɪmɪnətlɪ] *adv* : **he reads ~** il lit tout ce qui lui tombe sous la main ▪ **I use the two terms ~** j'utilise indifféremment les deux termes.

indispensable [,ɪndɪ'spensəbl] *adj* indispensable ▪ **~ to** indispensable à *OR* pour ▪ **to make o.s. ~ to sb** se rendre indispensable à qqn.

indisposed [,ɪndɪ'spəʊzd] *adj fml* **1.** *euph* [sick] indisposé, souffrant **2.** [unwilling] peu enclin, peu disposé ▪ **to be ~ to do sthg** être peu enclin *OR* peu disposé à faire qqch.

indisposition [,ɪndɪspə'zɪʃn] *n fml euph* [illness] indisposition *f*.

indisputable [,ɪndɪ'spju:təbl] *adj* incontestable, indiscutable.

indissoluble [,ɪndɪ'sɒljʊbl] *adj* indissoluble.

indissolubly [,ɪndɪ'sɒljʊblɪ] *adv* indissolublement.

indistinct [,ɪndɪ'stɪŋkt] *adj* indistinct.

indistinctly [,ɪndɪ'stɪŋktlɪ] *adv* indistinctement.

indistinguishable [,ɪndɪ'stɪŋgwɪʃəbl] *adj* **1.** [alike] impossible à distinguer ▪ **his handwriting is ~ from his brother's** son écriture est impossible à distinguer de celle de son frère **2.** [imperceptible] imperceptible.

individual [,ɪndɪ'vɪdʒʊəl] ◇ *adj* **1.** [for one person] individuel ▪ **she has ~ tuition** elle prend des cours particuliers **2.** [single, separate] particulier ▪ **it's impossible to investigate each ~ complaint** il est impossible d'étudier séparément chaque réclamation **3.** [distinctive] personnel, particulier ▪ **she has a very ~ way of working** elle a une façon très particulière *OR* personnelle de travailler.
◇ *n* [gen - BIOL] & LOGIC individu *m*.

individualism [,ɪndɪ'vɪdʒʊəlɪzm] *n* [gen - PHILOS & POL] individualisme *m*.

individualist [,ɪndɪ'vɪdʒʊəlɪst] *n* individualiste *mf*.

individualistic ['ɪndɪ,vɪdʒʊə'lɪstɪk] *adj* individualiste.

individuality ['ɪndɪ,vɪdʒʊ'ælətɪ] (*pl* **individualities**) *n* individualité *f*.

individualize, ise [,ɪndɪ'vɪdʒʊəlaɪz] *vt* individualiser.

individually [,ɪndɪ'vɪdʒʊəlɪ] *adv* **1.** [separately] individuellement ▪ **~ wrapped fruit** fruits emballés individuellement *OR* séparément **2.** [distinctively] de façon distinctive.

individuate [,ɪndɪ'vɪdʒʊeɪt] *vt* différencier.

indivisible [,ɪndɪ'vɪzəbl] *adj* indivisible.

Indochina [,ɪndəʊ'tʃaɪnə] *pr n* Indochine *f* ▪ **in ~** en Indochine.

Indochinese [,ɪndəʊtʃaɪ'ni:z] ◇ *n* Indochinois *m*, - e *f*.
◇ *adj* indochinois.

indoctrinate [ɪn'dɒktrɪneɪt] *vt* endoctriner ▪ **they were ~d with revolutionary ideas** on leur a inculqué des idées révolutionnaires.

indoctrination [ɪn,dɒktrɪ'neɪʃn] *n* endoctrinement *m*.

Indo-European ['ɪndəʊ,jʊərə'pi:ən] ◇ *n* indo-européen *m*.
◇ *adj* indo-européen.

indolence ['ɪndələns] *n* **1.** [laziness] paresse *f*, indolence *f* **2.** MED indolence *f*.

indolent ['ɪndələnt] *adj* **1.** [lazy] paresseux, indolent **2.** MED indolent.

indomitable [ɪn'dɒmɪtəbl] *adj* indomptable, irréductible.

Indonesia [,ɪndə'ni:zjə] *pr n* Indonésie *f* ▪ **in ~** en Indonésie.

Indonesian [,ɪndə'ni:zjən] ◇ *n* **1.** [person] Indonésien *m*, - enne *f* **2.** LING indonésien *m*.
◇ *adj* indonésien.

indoor [ˈɪndɔːʳ] *adj* [toilet] à l'intérieur ▪ [clothing] d'intérieur ▪ [swimming pool, tennis court] couvert ▪ SPORT pratiqué en salle ▪ **~ games** SPORT jeux *mpl* pratiqués en salle ; [board-games, charades etc] jeux *mpl* d'intérieur ▪ **~ plants** plantes *fpl* d'intérieur *OR* d'appartement.

indoors [ˌɪnˈdɔːz] *adv* à l'intérieur ▪ **I don't like being ~ all day** je n'aime pas rester enfermée toute la journée.

indorse [ɪnˈdɔːs] = **endorse**.

indrawn [ˌɪnˈdrɔːn] *adj* [air] : **~ breath** aspiration *f*, inspiration *f*.

indubitable [ɪnˈdjuːbɪtəbl] *adj* indubitable.

indubitably [ɪnˈdjuːbɪtəblɪ] *adv* assurément, indubitablement.

induce [ɪnˈdjuːs] *vt* **1.** [cause] entraîner, provoquer **2.** [persuade] persuader, décider ▪ **nothing will ~ me to change my mind** rien ne me décidera à *OR* ne me fera changer d'avis **3.** MED [labour] déclencher (artificiellement) **4.** PHILOS [infer] induire **5.** ELEC induire.

-induced [ɪnˈdjuːst] *in cpds* : **work~ injury** accident *m* du travail ▪ **drug~ sleep** sommeil *m* provoqué par des médicaments.

inducement [ɪnˈdjuːsmənt] *n* **1.** [encouragement] persuasion *f* **2.** [reward] incitation *f*, récompense *f* ▪ [bribe] pot-de-vin *m* ▪ **he was offered considerable financial ~s to leave his company** on lui a offert des sommes considérables pour l'inciter à quitter son entreprise.

induct [ɪnˈdʌkt] *vt* **1.** [into office, post] installer **2.** [into mystery, unknown field] initier **3.** *US* MIL appeler (sous les drapeaux) **4.** ELEC = **induce** *(sense 5)*.

inductance [ɪnˈdʌktəns] *n* ELEC **1.** [property] inductance *f* **2.** [component] inducteur *m*.

induction [ɪnˈdʌkʃn] *n* **1.** [into office, post] installation *f* ▪ [into mystery, new field] initiation *f* **2.** [causing] provocation *f*, déclenchement *m* **3.** MED [of labour] déclenchement *m* (artificiel) **4.** PHILOS induction *f* **5.** *US* MIL conscription *f*, appel *m* sous les drapeaux **6.** BIOL, ELEC & TECH induction *f*.

induction coil *n* bobine *f* d'inductance.

induction course *n* stage *m* préparatoire *OR* de formation.

inductive [ɪnˈdʌktɪv] *adj* inductif.

inductor [ɪnˈdʌktəʳ] *n* inducteur *m*.

indulge [ɪnˈdʌldʒ] ◇ *vi* : **to ~ in** se livrer à ▪ **I occasionally ~ in a cigar** je me permets un cigare de temps en temps ▪ **no thank you, I don't ~** [drink] non merci, je ne bois pas ; [smoke] non merci, je ne fume pas.
◇ *vt* **1.** [person] gâter ▪ **she ~s her children** elle gâte ses enfants, elle passe tout à ses enfants ▪ **to ~ o.s.** se faire plaisir **2.** [desire, vice] assouvir ▪ **he ~s her every whim** il se prête à *OR* il lui passe tous ses caprices **3.** COMM [debtor] accorder un délai de paiement à.

indulgence [ɪnˈdʌldʒəns] *n* **1.** [tolerance, kindness] indulgence *f* **2.** [gratification] assouvissement *m* **3.** [privilege] privilège *m* ▪ [treat] gâterie *f* ▪ **smoking is my only ~** mon seul vice, c'est le tabac **4.** RELIG indulgence *f*.

indulgent [ɪnˈdʌldʒənt] *adj* [liberal, kind] indulgent, complaisant ▪ **you shouldn't be so ~ with your children** vous ne devriez pas vous montrer aussi indulgent envers vos enfants.

indulgently [ɪnˈdʌldʒəntlɪ] *adv* avec indulgence.

industrial [ɪnˈdʌstrɪəl] *adj* [gen] industriel ▪ [unrest] social ▶ **~ accident** accident *m* du travail ▪ **~ diamond** diamant *m* industriel *OR* de nature ▪ **~ dispute** conflit *m* social ▪ **~ espionage** espionnage *m* industriel ▪ **the Industrial Revolution** la révolution industrielle ▪ **~ school** *US* école *f* technique ▪ **~ workers** travailleurs *mpl* de l'industrie.

THE INDUSTRIAL REVOLUTION

Processus d'industrialisation qui, au XVIIIe siècle, apporta de profonds changements dans la société britannique en bouleversant ses structures et son fonctionnement traditionnel. Si la richesse nationale augmenta rapidement, apportant à la Grande-Bretagne un rayonnement économique mondial, elle fut synonyme de misère pour la classe ouvrière jusqu'au XXe siècle.

industrial action *n (U) UK* grève *f*, grèves *fpl* ▪ **they threatened (to take) ~** ils ont menacé de faire grève.

industrial arts *npl US* SCH enseignement *m* technologique.

industrial estate *n UK* zone *f* industrielle.

industrialist [ɪnˈdʌstrɪəlɪst] *n* industriel *m*.

industrialization [ɪnˌdʌstrɪəlaɪˈzeɪʃn] *n* industrialisation *f*.

industrialized [ɪnˈdʌstrɪəlaɪzd] *adj* industrialisé.

industrial park *US* = **industrial estate**.

industrial relations *npl* relations *fpl* entre le patronat et les travailleurs ▪ **~ have deteriorated** le climat social s'est dégradé.

industrial tribunal *n* ≃ conseil *m* de prud'hommes.

industrious [ɪnˈdʌstrɪəs] *adj* travailleur.

industry [ˈɪndʌstrɪ] (*pl* **industries**) *n* **1.** [business] industrie *f* ▪ **both sides of ~** syndicats *mpl* et patronat *m*, les partenaires *mpl* sociaux ▪ **the oil/film ~** l'industrie pétrolière/cinématographique **2.** application *f*, diligence *f*.

inebriate *fml* ◇ *vt* [ɪˈniːbrɪeɪt] enivrer, griser.
◇ *adj* [ɪˈniːbrɪət] ivre.
◇ *n* [ɪˈniːbrɪət] ivrogne *mf*, alcoolique *mf*.

inebriated [ɪˈniːbrɪeɪtɪd] *adj fml* ivre ▪ **~ by his success** *fig* grisé par son succès.

inebriation [ɪˌniːbrɪˈeɪʃn] *n fml* enivrement *m* ▪ [habitual] ivrognerie *f*, alcoolisme *m*.

inedible [ɪnˈedɪbl] *adj* **1.** [unsafe to eat] non comestible **2.** [unpleasant to eat] immangeable.

ineffable [ɪnˈefəbl] *adj lit* ineffable, indicible.

ineffective [ˌɪnɪˈfektɪv] *adj* **1.** [person] inefficace, incapable, incompétent **2.** [action] inefficace, sans effet.

ineffectively [ˌɪnɪˈfektɪvlɪ] *adv* sans résultat.

ineffectual [ˌɪnɪˈfektʃʊəl] *adj* incompétent.

inefficiency [ˌɪnɪˈfɪʃnsɪ] (*pl* **inefficiencies**) *n* inefficacité *f*, manque *m* d'efficacité.

inefficient [ˌɪnɪˈfɪʃnt] *adj* inefficace ▪ **an ~ use of resources** une mauvaise utilisation des ressources ▪ **these old machines are too ~** le rendement de ces vieilles machines est vraiment insuffisant.

inefficiently [ˌɪnɪˈfɪʃntlɪ] *adv* inefficacement.

inelegant [ɪnˈelɪgənt] *adj* inélégant.

inelegantly [ɪnˈelɪgəntlɪ] *adv* de façon peu élégante.

ineligibility [ɪnˌelɪdʒəˈbɪlətɪ] *n* **1.** [gen] : **his ~ for unemployment benefit** le fait qu'il n'ait pas droit aux allocations de chômage ▪ **the ~ of most of the applications** l'irrecevabilité *f* de la plupart des demandes **2.** [for election] inéligibilité *f*.

ineligible [ɪnˈelɪdʒəbl] *adj* **1.** [unqualified] non qualifié ▪ **to be ~ for military service** être inapte au service militaire ▪ **they are ~ to vote** ils n'ont pas le droit de voter **2.** [for election] inéligible.

ineluctable [ˌɪnɪˈlʌktəbl] *adj fml* inéluctable.

inept [ɪˈnept] *adj* inepte.

ineptitude [ɪˈneptɪtjuːd] *n* ineptie *f*.

ineptly [ɪˈneptlɪ] *adv* absurdement, stupidement.

inequality [ˌɪnɪˈkwɒlətɪ] (*pl* **inequalities**) *n* inégalité *f*.

inequitable [ɪn'ekwɪtəbl] *adj* inéquitable.

ineradicable [,ɪnɪ'rædɪkəbl] *adj* indéracinable.

inert [ɪ'nɜːt] *adj* inerte.

inert gas *n* gaz *m* inerte.

inertia [ɪ'nɜːʃə] *n* inertie *f*.

inertia-reel seat belt *n* ceinture *f* de sécurité à enrouleur.

inertia selling *n (U) UK* vente *f* forcée.

inescapable [,ɪnɪ'skeɪpəbl] *adj* [outcome] inévitable, inéluctable ■ [fact] indéniable.

inescapably [,ɪnɪ'skeɪpəblɪ] *adv* inévitablement, indéniablement.

inessential [,ɪnɪ'senʃl] *adj* non essentiel.

inestimable [ɪn'estɪməbl] *adj* inestimable, incalculable.

inevitability [ɪn,evɪtə'bɪlətɪ] *n* inévitabilité *f*.

inevitable [ɪn'evɪtəbl] <> *adj* [outcome, consequence] inévitable, inéluctable ■ [end] inévitable, fatal ■ **it's ~ that someone will feel left out** il est inévitable *OR* on ne pourra empêcher que quelqu'un se sente exclu ■ **the ~ cigarette in his mouth** l'éternelle *OR* l'inévitable cigarette au coin des lèvres.
<> *n* inévitable *m* ■ **we had to resign ourselves to the ~** il fallut nous résoudre à accepter l'inévitable.

inevitably [ɪn'evɪtəblɪ] *adv* inévitablement, fatalement.

inexact [,ɪnɪg'zækt] *adj* [imprecise] imprécis ■ [wrong] inexact, erroné.

inexactitude [,ɪnɪg'zæktɪtjuːd] *n* **1.** [imprecision] imprécision *f* ■ [incorrectness] inexactitude *f* **2.** [mistake] inexactitude *f*.

inexcusable [,ɪnɪk'skjuːzəbl] *adj* inexcusable, impardonnable.

inexcusably [,ɪnɪk'skjuːzəblɪ] *adv*: **~ rude** d'une grossièreté impardonnable ■ **he behaved quite ~ at the party** la façon dont il s'est comporté à la soirée est inexcusable.

inexhaustible [,ɪnɪg'zɔːstəbl] *adj* **1.** [source, energy, patience] inépuisable, illimité **2.** [person] infatigable.

inexorable [ɪn'eksərəbl] *adj* inexorable.

inexorably [ɪn'eksərəblɪ] *adv* inexorablement.

inexpensive [,ɪnɪk'spensɪv] *adj* bon marché *(inv)*, peu cher.

inexpensively [,ɪnɪk'spensɪvlɪ] *adv* [sell] (à) bon marché, à bas prix ■ [live] à peu de frais.

inexperience [,ɪnɪk'spɪərɪəns] *n* inexpérience *f*, manque *m* d'expérience.

inexperienced [,ɪnɪk'spɪərɪənst] *adj* inexpérimenté.

inexpert [ɪn'ekspɜːt] *adj* inexpérimenté, inexpert *lit*.

inexplicable [,ɪnɪk'splɪkəbl] *adj* inexplicable.

inexplicably [,ɪnɪk'splɪkəblɪ] *adv* inexplicablement.

inexpressible [,ɪnɪk'spresəbl] *adj* inexprimable, indicible.

inextinguishable [,ɪnɪk'stɪŋgwɪʃəbl] *adj* [fire] impossible à éteindre ■ [thirst] inextinguible ■ [passion] irrépressible, incontrôlable.

in extremis [ɪnɪk'striːmɪs] *adv* in extremis, de justesse.

inextricable [,ɪnɪk'strɪkəbl] *adj* inextricable.

inextricably [,ɪnɪk'strɪkəblɪ] *adv* inextricablement.

infallibility [ɪn,fælə'bɪlətɪ] *n* infaillibilité *f*.

infallible [ɪn'fæləbl] *adj* infaillible.

infallibly [ɪn'fæləblɪ] *adv* infailliblement, immanquablement.

infamous ['ɪnfəməs] *adj* **1.** [notorious] tristement célèbre, notoire **2.** [shocking - conduct] déshonorant, infamant.

infamy ['ɪnfəmɪ] *(pl* **infamies***)* *n* **1.** [notoriety] triste notoriété *f* **2.** [notorious act, event] infamie *f*.

infancy ['ɪnfənsɪ] *(pl* **infancies***)* *n* **1.** [early childhood] petite enfance *f* ■ **a child in its ~** un enfant en bas âge **2.** *fig* débuts *mpl*, enfance *f* ■ **when electronics was still in its ~** quand l'électronique n'en était qu'à ses balbutiements **3.** LAW minorité *f* (légale).

infant ['ɪnfənt] <> *n* **1.** [young child] petit enfant *m*, petite enfant *f*, enfant *mf* en bas âge ■ [baby] bébé *m* ■ [new-born] nouveau-né *m* **2.** *UK* SCH *élève dans les premières années d'école primaire* **3.** LAW mineur *m*, - e *f*.
<> *comp* **1.** [food] pour bébés ■ [disease] infantile **2.** *UK* [teacher, teaching] des premières années d'école primaire.
<> *adj* [organization] naissant.

infanticide [ɪn'fæntɪsaɪd] *n* **1.** [act] infanticide *m* **2.** [person] infanticide *mf*.

infantile ['ɪnfəntaɪl] *adj* **1.** *pej* [childish] infantile, puéril **2.** [of, for infants] infantile.

infantry ['ɪnfəntrɪ] <> *n* infanterie *f*.
<> *adj* de l'infanterie.

infantryman ['ɪnfəntrɪmən] *(pl* **infantrymen** [-mən]*)* *n* soldat *m* d'infanterie, fantassin *m*.

infant school *n UK* école *f* maternelle *(5-7 ans)*.

infatuate [ɪn'fætjʊeɪt] *vt*: **he was ~d with her** il s'était entiché d'elle.

infatuation [ɪn,fætjʊ'eɪʃn] *n* engouement *m* ■ **his ~ for** *OR* **with her** son engouement pour elle.

infect [ɪn'fekt] *vt* **1.** MED [wound, organ, person, animal] infecter ■ **I hope that cut won't get ~ed** j'espère que cette coupure ne s'infectera pas ■ **to ~ sb with sthg** transmettre qqch à qqn **2.** [food, water] contaminer **3.** *fig* [subj: vice] corrompre, contaminer ■ [subj: emotion] se communiquer à.

infected [ɪn'fektɪd] *adj* [wound] infecté ■ [area] contaminé.

infection [ɪn'fekʃn] *n* **1.** MED infection *f* ■ **a throat ~** une infection de la gorge, une angine **2.** *fig* contagion *f*, contamination *f*.

infectious [ɪn'fekʃəs] *adj* **1.** MED [disease] infectieux ■ [person] contagieux **2.** *fig* contagieux, communicatif.

infectious hepatitis *n (U)* hépatite *f* infectieuse, hépatite *f* virale A.

infectious mononucleosis *n (U)* mononucléose *f* infectieuse.

infelicitous [,ɪnfɪ'lɪsɪtəs] *adj lit* malheureux, malchanceux.

infer [ɪn'fɜːr] *(pret & pp* **inferred**, *cont* **inferring***)* *vt* **1.** [deduce] conclure, inférer, déduire ■ **what are we to ~ from their absence?** que devons-nous conclure de leur absence? **2.** [imply] suggérer, laisser supposer ■ **what are you inferring by that?** qu'insinuez-vous par là?

inference ['ɪnfrəns] *n* déduction *f* ■ LOGIC inférence *f* ■ **what ~s can we draw from it?** quelles conclusions pouvons-nous en tirer?, que pouvons-nous en déduire?

inferior [ɪn'fɪərɪər] <> *adj* **1.** [quality, worth, social status] inférieur ■ **he always felt ~ to his brother** il a toujours éprouvé un sentiment d'infériorité par rapport à son frère ■ **to make sb feel ~** donner un sentiment d'infériorité à qqn **2.** [in rank] subalterne **3.** ANAT & SCI [in space, position] inférieur **4.** TYPO : **~ character** (caractère *m* en) indice *m* **5.** BOT : **~ ovary** ovaire *m* infère *OR* adhérent.
<> *n* [in social status] inférieur *m*, - e *f* ■ [in rank, hierarchy] subalterne *mf*, subordonné *m*, - e *f* ■ **he never speaks to his ~s** il n'adresse jamais la parole à ses subordonnés.

inferiority [ɪn,fɪərɪ'ɒrətɪ] *(pl* **inferiorities***)* *n* infériorité *f*.

inferiority complex *n* complexe *m* d'infériorité.

infernal [ɪn'fɜːnl] *adj* **1.** *inf* [awful] infernal ▪ **stop that ~ racket** *OR* **din!** arrêtez ce raffut *OR* boucan infernal! **2.** [of hell] infernal ▪ [diabolical] infernal, diabolique.

inferno [ɪn'fɜːnəʊ] (*pl* **infernos**) *n* **1.** [fire] brasier *m* ▪ **the hotel was a blazing ~** l'hôtel n'était qu'un gigantesque brasier **2.** [hell] enfer *m*.

infertile [ɪn'fɜːtaɪl] *adj* [person, animal] stérile ▪ [land, soil] stérile, infertile *lit*.

infertility [ˌɪnfə'tɪlətɪ] *n* stérilité *f*, infertilité *f lit*.

infest [ɪn'fest] *vt* infester ▪ **~ed with** infesté de ▪ **shark-~ed waters** eaux infestées de requins.

infestation [ˌɪnfe'steɪʃn] *n* infestation *f*.

infibulation [ɪnˌfɪbjʊ'leɪʃn] *n* infibulation *f*.

infidel ['ɪnfɪdəl] ◇ *n* infidèle *mf*.
◇ *adj* infidèle, incroyant.

infidelity [ˌɪnfɪ'delətɪ] (*pl* **infidelities**) *n* **1.** [betrayal] infidélité *f* **2.** [lack of faith] incroyance *f*, irréligion *f*.

infighting ['ɪnˌfaɪtɪŋ] *n (U)* **1.** *UK* [within group] conflits *mpl* internes, luttes *fpl* intestines **2.** [in boxing] corps à corps *m*.

infill ['ɪnfɪl] ◇ *vt* remplir, combler.
◇ *n* matériau *m* de remplissage.

infiltrate ['ɪnfɪltreɪt] ◇ *vt* **1.** [organization] infiltrer, noyauter ▪ **they ~d spies into the organization** ils ont envoyé des espions pour infiltrer l'organisation **2.** [subj: liquid] s'infiltrer dans.
◇ *vi* s'infiltrer.

infiltration [ˌɪnfɪl'treɪʃn] *n* **1.** [of group] infiltration *f*, noyautage *m* **2.** [by liquid] infiltration *f*.

infiltrator ['ɪnfɪltreɪtəʳ] *n* agent *m* infiltré.

infinite ['ɪnfɪnət] ◇ *adj* **1.** [not finite] infini ▪ **~ set** MATHS ensemble *m* infini **2.** *fig* [very great] infini, incalculable ▪ **he showed ~ patience** il a fait preuve d'une patience infinie ▪ **the government, in its ~ wisdom, has decided to close the factory** *iron* le gouvernement, dans son infinie sagesse, a décidé de fermer l'usine.
◇ *n* infini *m*.

infinitely ['ɪnfɪnətlɪ] *adv* infiniment.

infinitesimal [ˌɪnfɪnɪ'tesɪml] *adj* **1.** MATHS infinitésimal **2.** [tiny] infinitésimal, infime.

infinitival [ɪnˌfɪnɪ'taɪvl] *adj* infinitif ▪ **~ clause** proposition *f* infinitive.

infinitive [ɪn'fɪnɪtɪv] ◇ *n* infinitif *m*.
◇ *adj* infinitif.

infinity [ɪn'fɪnətɪ] (*pl* **infinities**) *n* **1.** infinité *f*, infini *m* ▪ **it stretches to ~** cela s'étend jusqu'à l'infini **2.** MATHS & PHOT infini *m*.

infirm [ɪn'fɜːm] ◇ *adj* **1.** [in health, body] invalide, infirme **2.** *lit* [in moral resolution] indécis, irrésolu **3.** LAW invalide.
◇ *npl* : **the ~** les infirmes *mpl*.

infirmary [ɪn'fɜːmərɪ] (*pl* **infirmaries**) *n* [hospital] hôpital *m*, dispensaire *m* ▪ [sickroom] infirmerie *f*.

infirmity [ɪn'fɜːmətɪ] (*pl* **infirmities**) *n* **1.** [physical] infirmité *f* **2.** [moral] défaut *m*, faiblesse *f*.

infix ◇ *vt* [ɪn'fɪks] **1.** [instil] instiller, implanter **2.** LING insérer (comme infixe).
◇ *n* ['ɪnfɪks] LING infixe *m*.

inflame [ɪn'fleɪm] ◇ *vt* **1.** [rouse - person, crowd] exciter, enflammer ▪ [anger, hatred, passion] attiser, exacerber ▪ **she was ~d with anger/passion** elle brûlait de colère/de passion **2.** MED [wound, infection] enflammer ▪ [organ, tissue] irriter, infecter.
◇ *vi* **1.** MED [wound, infection] s'enflammer ▪ [organ, tissue] s'irriter, s'infecter **2.** [catch fire] s'enflammer, s'embraser.

inflamed [ɪn'fleɪmd] *adj* **1.** MED [eyes, throat, tendon] enflammé, irrité **2.** *fig* [passions, hatred] enflammé, ardent.

inflammable [ɪn'flæməbl] ◇ *adj* inflammable ▪ **an ~ situation** *fig* une situation explosive.
◇ *n* matière *f* inflammable.

inflammation [ˌɪnflə'meɪʃn] *n* inflammation *f*.

inflammatory [ɪn'flæmətrɪ] *adj* **1.** [speech, propaganda] incendiaire **2.** MED inflammatoire.

inflatable [ɪn'fleɪtəbl] ◇ *adj* [toy] gonflable ▪ [mattress, boat] pneumatique.
◇ *n* structure *f* gonflable.

inflate [ɪn'fleɪt] ◇ *vt* **1.** [tyre, balloon, boat] gonfler ▪ [lungs] emplir d'air ▪ [chest] gonfler, bomber **2.** [opinion, importance] gonfler, exagérer **3.** ECON [prices] faire monter, augmenter ▪ [economy] provoquer l'inflation de ▪ **to ~ the currency** provoquer une inflation monétaire.
◇ *vi* **1.** [tyre] se gonfler ▪ [lungs] s'emplir d'air ▪ [chest] se gonfler, se bomber **2.** ECON [prices, money] subir une inflation.

inflated [ɪn'fleɪtɪd] *adj* **1.** [tyre] gonflé **2.** [opinion, importance] exagéré ▪ [style] emphatique, pompier ▪ **he has an ~ sense of his own importance** il se fait une idée exagérée de sa propre importance **3.** [price] exagéré.

inflation [ɪn'fleɪʃn] *n* **1.** ECON inflation *f* **2.** [of tyre, balloon, boat] gonflement *m* ▪ [of idea, importance] grossissement *m*, exagération *f*.

inflationary [ɪn'fleɪʃnrɪ] *adj* inflationniste.

inflationist [ɪn'fleɪʃənɪst] *adj* inflationniste.

inflation-proof *adj* protégé contre les effets de l'inflation.

inflect [ɪn'flekt] ◇ *vt* **1.** LING [verb] conjuguer ▪ [noun, pronoun, adjective] décliner ▪ **~ed form** forme *f* fléchie **2.** [tone, voice] moduler **3.** [curve] infléchir.
◇ *vi* LING : **adjectives do not ~ in English** les adjectifs ne prennent pas de désinence en anglais.

inflection [ɪn'flekʃn] *n* **1.** [of tone, voice] inflexion *f*, modulation *f* **2.** LING désinence *f*, flexion *f* **3.** [curve] flexion *f*, inflexion *f*, courbure *f* **4.** MATHS inflexion *f* ▪ **point of ~** point *m* d'inflexion.

inflexibility [ɪnˌfleksə'bɪlətɪ] *n* inflexibilité *f*, rigidité *f*.

inflexible [ɪn'fleksəbl] *adj* inflexible, rigide.

inflexion *etc* [ɪn'flekʃn] *UK* = **inflection**.

inflict [ɪn'flɪkt] *vt* infliger ▪ **to ~ pain/suffering on sb** faire mal à/faire souffrir qqn ▪ **to ~ a defeat on sb** infliger une défaite à qqn ▪ **I don't want to ~ myself** *OR* **my company on you** je ne veux pas vous infliger ma compagnie.

in-flight *adj* en vol, à bord ▪ **~ meal** plateau-repas *m* ▪ **~ video** vidéo *f* projetée en vol ▪ **~ refuelling** ravitaillement *m* en vol.

inflow ['ɪnfləʊ] *n* [of water, gas] arrivée *f*, afflux *m* ▪ **the ~ of capital** l'afflux de capitaux ▪ **cash ~** rentrées *fpl* d'argent.

influence ['ɪnflʊəns] ◇ *n* influence *f* ▪ **to have ~** avoir de l'influence ▪ **to bring one's ~ to bear on sthg** exercer son influence sur qqch ▪ **he is a man of ~** c'est un homme influent ▪ **I have no ~ over them** je n'ai aucune influence sur eux ▪ **he is a bad ~ on them** il a une mauvaise influence sur eux ▪ **she is a disruptive ~** c'est un élément perturbateur ▪ **his music has a strong reggae ~** sa musique est fortement influencée par le reggae ▪ **she was under the ~ of drink/drugs** elle était sous l'emprise de l'alcool/de la drogue ▪ **driving under the ~ of alcohol** conduite en état d'ivresse.
◇ *vt* influencer, influer sur ▪ **~d by cubism** influencé par le cubisme ▪ **to ~ sb to the good** exercer une bonne influence sur qqn ▪ **he is easily ~d** il se laisse facilement influencer, il est très influençable.

influential [ˌɪnflʊ'enʃl] *adj* influent, puissant ▪ [newspaper, TV programme] influent, qui a de l'influence.

influenza [ˌɪnflʊ'enzə] *n (U) fml* grippe *f* ■ **to have ~** avoir la grippe.

influx ['ɪnflʌks] *n* **1.** [inflow] afflux *m* **2.** [of river] embouchure *f*.

info ['ɪnfəʊ] *n (U) inf* tuyaux *mpl*.

infomercial [ˌɪnfəʊ'mɜːʃl] *n US publicité télévisée sous forme de débat sur l'annonceur et son produit.*

inform [ɪn'fɔːm] <> *vt* informer ■ **will you ~ him of your decision?** allez-vous l'informer de votre décision? ■ **I'll keep you ~ed** je vous tiendrai au courant.
<> *vi* : **to ~ on** *OR* **against sb** dénoncer qqn.

informal [ɪn'fɔːml] *adj* **1.** [discussion, meeting] informel ■ [dinner] décontracté **2.** [clothes] : **his dress was ~** il était habillé simplement **3.** [unofficial - arrangement, agreement] officieux ; [- visit, talks] non officiel **4.** [colloquial] familier.

informal economy *n* travail *m* au noir.

informality [ˌɪnfɔː'mælətɪ] (*pl* **informalities**) *n* **1.** [of gathering, meal] simplicité *f* ■ [of discussion, interview] absence *f* de formalité ■ [of manners] naturel *m* **2.** [of expression, language] familiarité *f*, liberté *f*.

informally [ɪn'fɔːməlɪ] *adv* **1.** [casually - entertain, discuss] sans cérémonie ; [- behave] simplement, avec naturel ; [- dress] simplement **2.** [unofficially] officieusement **3.** [colloquially] familièrement, avec familiarité.

informant [ɪn'fɔːmənt] *n* [gen - SOCIOL & LING] informateur *m*, - trice *f*.

informatics [ˌɪnfə'mætɪks] *n (sg)* sciences *fpl* de l'information.

information [ˌɪnfə'meɪʃn] *n* **1.** *(U)* [facts] renseignements *mpl*, informations *fpl* ■ **a piece** *OR* **bit of ~** un renseignement, une information ■ **do you have any ~ on** *OR* **about the new model?** avez-vous des renseignements concernant *OR* sur le nouveau modèle? **2.** [communication] information *f* **3.** *(U)* [knowledge] connaissances *fpl* ■ **for your ~, please find enclosed...** ADMIN à titre d'information, vous trouverez ci-joint... ■ **for your ~, it happened in 1938** je vous signale que cela s'est passé en 1938 **4.** COMPUT & SCI information *f* **5.** *(U)* [service, department] (service *m* des) renseignements *mpl* ■ **ask at the ~ desk** adressez-vous aux renseignements ■ **to call ~** *US* appeler les renseignements **6.** *UK* LAW acte *m* d'accusation ■ **to lay an ~ against sb** porter une accusation contre qqn.

information bureau *UK*, **information office** *n* bureau *m OR* service *m* des renseignements.

information highway *n* = **information superhighway**.

information processing *n* **1.** [action] traitement *m* de l'information **2.** [domain] informatique *f* ■ **~ error** erreur *f* dans le traitement de l'information.

information retrieval *n* recherche *f* documentaire ■ COMPUT recherche *f* d'information.

information science *n* science *f* de l'information.

information scientist *n* informaticien *m*, - enne *f*.

information superhighway *n* autoroute *f* de l'information.

information technology *n* technologie *f* de l'information, informatique *f*.

informative [ɪn'fɔːmətɪv] *adj* [lecture, book, TV programme] instructif ■ [person] : **he wasn't very ~ about his future plans** il ne nous a pas dit grand-chose de ses projets.

informed [ɪn'fɔːmd] *adj* **1.** [having information] informé, renseigné ■ **according to ~ sources** selon des sources bien informées **2.** [based on information] : **an ~ choice** un choix fait en toute connaissance de cause ■ **he made an ~ guess** il a essayé de deviner en s'aidant de ce qu'il sait **3.** [learned, cultured] cultivé.

informer [ɪn'fɔːməʳ] *n* **1.** [denouncer] informateur *m* ■ **police ~** indicateur (de police) **2.** [information source] informateur *m*, - trice *f*.

infotainment ['ɪnfəʊteɪnmənt] *n* info-spectacle *m*, infodivertissement *m*.

infra dig [ˌɪnfrə'dɪg] *adj UK datedinf* dégradant.

infrared [ˌɪnfrə'red] <> *adj* infrarouge ■ **~ photography** photographie *f* (à l')infrarouge.
<> *n* infrarouge *m*.

infrastructure ['ɪnfrəˌstrʌktʃəʳ] *n* infrastructure *f*.

infrequent [ɪn'friːkwənt] *adj* [event] peu fréquent, rare ■ [visitor] épisodique.

infrequently [ɪn'friːkwəntlɪ] *adv* rarement, peu souvent.

infringe [ɪn'frɪndʒ] <> *vt* [agreement, rights] violer, enfreindre ■ [law] enfreindre, contrevenir à ■ [patent] contrefaire ■ **to ~ copyright** enfreindre les lois de copyright.
<> *vi* : **to ~ on** *OR* **upon** empiéter sur.

infringement [ɪn'frɪndʒmənt] *n* [violation] infraction *f*, atteinte *f* ■ [encroachment] empiètement *m* ■ **an ~ on freedom of speech** une atteinte à la liberté d'expression ■ **that's an ~ of my rights** c'est une atteinte à mes droits.

infuriate [ɪn'fjʊərɪeɪt] *vt* [enrage] rendre furieux ■ [exasperate] exaspérer.

infuriated [ɪn'fjʊərɪeɪtɪd] *adj* furieux.

infuriating [ɪn'fjʊərɪeɪtɪŋ] *adj* agaçant, exaspérant.

infuriatingly [ɪn'fjʊərɪeɪtɪŋlɪ] *adv* : **~ stubborn** d'un entêtement exaspérant.

infuse [ɪn'fjuːz] <> *vt* **1.** [inspire] inspirer, insuffler, infuser *lit* ■ **to ~ sb with sthg, to ~ sthg into sb** inspirer *OR* insuffler qqch à qqn **2.** CULIN (faire) infuser.
<> *vi* CULIN infuser.

infuser [ɪn'fjuːzəʳ] *n* : **tea ~** boule *f* à thé.

infusion [ɪn'fjuːʒn] *n* infusion *f*.

ingenious [ɪn'dʒiːnjəs] *adj* [person, idea, device] ingénieux, astucieux.

ingeniously [ɪn'dʒiːnjəslɪ] *adv* ingénieusement.

ingenuity [ˌɪndʒɪ'njuːətɪ] (*pl* **ingenuities**) *n* ingéniosité *f*.

ingenuous [ɪn'dʒenjʊəs] *adj* [naive] ingénu ■ [frank] candide.

ingenuously [ɪn'dʒenjʊəslɪ] *adv* [naively] ingénument ■ [frankly] franchement.

ingest [ɪn'dʒest] *vt* [food, liquid] ingérer.

ingestion [ɪn'dʒestʃn] *n* ingestion *f*.

inglenook ['ɪŋglnʊk] *n* coin *m* du feu ■ **~ fireplace** vaste cheminée *f* à l'ancienne.

inglorious [ɪn'glɔːrɪəs] *adj* [shameful] déshonorant.

ingoing ['ɪnˌgəʊɪŋ] *adj* [tenant, president] nouveau *(before vowel or silent 'h' nouvel)*, nouvelle *f*.

ingot ['ɪŋgət] *n* lingot *m* ■ **gold/cast-iron ~** lingot d'or/de fonte.

ingrained [ˌɪn'greɪnd] *adj* [attitude, fear, prejudice] enraciné, inébranlable ■ [habit] invétéré, tenace ■ [belief] inébranlable ■ **~ dirt** crasse *f*.

ingratiate [ɪn'greɪʃɪeɪt] *vt* : **to ~ o.s. with sb** s'insinuer dans les bonnes grâces de qqn.

ingratiating [ɪn'greɪʃɪeɪtɪŋ] *adj* [manners, person] insinuant ■ [smile] mielleux.

ingratitude [ɪn'grætɪtjuːd] *n* ingratitude *f*.

ingredient [ɪn'griːdjənt] *n* **1.** CULIN ingrédient *m* **2.** [element] élément *m*, ingrédient *m lit*.

in-group *n* groupe *m* d'initiés.

ingrowing toenail ['ɪnˌgrəʊɪŋ-] *n UK* ongle *m* incarné.

ingrown ['ɪn,grəʊn] *adj* **1.** [toenail] incarné **2.** [ingrained - habit] enraciné, tenace.

inhabit [ɪn'hæbɪt] *vt* habiter ■ **the island is no longer ~ed** l'île n'est plus habitée *OR* est maintenant inhabitée.

inhabitable [ɪn'hæbɪtəbl] *adj* habitable.

inhabitant [ɪn'hæbɪtənt] *n* habitant *m*, - e *f*.

inhalation [,ɪnhə'leɪʃn] *n* **1.** [of air] inspiration *f* **2.** [of gas, glue] inhalation *f*.

inhalator ['ɪnhəleɪtər] *n* inhalateur *m*.

inhale [ɪn'heɪl] ◇ *vt* [fumes, gas] inhaler ■ [fresh air, scent] respirer ■ [smoke] avaler.
◇ *vi* [smoker] avaler la fumée ■ [breathe in] aspirer.

inhaler [ɪn'heɪlər] = **inhalator**.

inherent [ɪn'hɪərənt, ɪn'herənt] *adj* inhérent ■ **~ in** *OR* **to** inhérent à.

inherently [ɪn'hɪərəntlɪ, ɪn'herəntlɪ] *adv* intrinsèquement, par nature.

inherit [ɪn'herɪt] ◇ *vt* **1.** [property, right] hériter (de) ■ [title, peerage] accéder à ■ **she ~ed a million dollars** elle a hérité d'un million de dollars **2.** [situation, tradition, attitude] hériter ■ **the problems ~ed from the previous government** les problèmes hérités du gouvernement précédent ■ [characteristic, feature] hériter (de) ■ **she ~ed her father's intelligence** elle a hérité (de) l'intelligence de son père.
◇ *vi* hériter ■ **she stands to ~ when her aunt dies** elle doit hériter à la mort de sa tante.

inheritance [ɪn'herɪtəns] *n* **1.** [legacy] héritage *m* ■ **to come into an ~** faire *OR* toucher un héritage **2.** [succession] succession *f* ■ **to claim sthg by right of ~** revendiquer qqch en faisant valoir son droit à la succession **3.** SCI hérédité *f* **4.** [heritage] héritage *m*, patrimoine *m*.

inheritance tax *n* droits *mpl* de succession.

inheritor [ɪn'herɪtər] *n* héritier *m*, - ère *f*.

inhibit [ɪn'hɪbɪt] *vt* **1.** [hinder - person, freedom] gêner, entraver ■ **were you ~ed by him being there?** est-ce que sa présence vous a gêné? ■ **a law which ~s free speech** une loi qui constitue une entrave à la liberté d'expression **2.** [check - growth, development] freiner, entraver ■ **to ~ progress** entraver la marche du progrès **3.** [suppress - desires, emotions] inhiber, refouler ■ PSYCHOL inhiber **4.** [forbid] interdire **5.** CHEM inhiber.

inhibited [ɪn'hɪbɪtɪd] *adj* inhibé.

inhibiting [ɪn'hɪbɪtɪŋ] *adj* inhibant.

inhibition [,ɪnhɪ'bɪʃn] *n* [gen] inhibition *f*.

inhibitor, inhibiter [ɪn'hɪbɪtər] *n* inhibiteur *m*.

inhospitable [,ɪnhɒ'spɪtəbl] *adj* **1.** [person] peu accueillant ■ **I don't wish to appear ~, but...** je ne voudrais pas vous mettre à la porte, mais... **2.** [weather] rude, rigoureux.

in-house ◇ *adj* interne *(à une entreprise)* ■ [training] maison *(inv)* ■ **a very small ~ staff** un personnel permanent très peu nombreux.
◇ *adv* sur place.

inhuman [ɪn'hju:mən] *adj* [behaviour] inhumain, barbare ■ [person, place, process] inhumain.

inhumane [,ɪnhju:'meɪn] *adj* cruel.

inhumanity [,ɪnhju:'mænətɪ] (*pl* **inhumanities**) *n* **1.** [quality] inhumanité *f*, barbarie *f*, cruauté *f* ■ **man's ~ to man** la cruauté de l'homme pour l'homme **2.** [act] atrocité *f*, brutalité *f*.

inhumation [,ɪnhju:'meɪʃn] *n* *fml* inhumation *f*.

inhume [ɪn'hju:m] *vt* *fml* inhumer.

inimical [ɪ'nɪmɪkl] *adj* **1.** [unfavourable] hostile ■ **~ to** peu favorable à **2.** [unfriendly] inamical.

inimitable [ɪ'nɪmɪtəbl] *adj* inimitable.

iniquitous [ɪ'nɪkwɪtəs] *adj* inique.

iniquity [ɪ'nɪkwətɪ] *n* iniquité *f*.

initial [ɪ'nɪʃl] (*UK pret & pp* **initialled**, *cont* **initialling**) (*US pret & pp* **initialed**, *cont* **initialing**) ◇ *adj* initial ■ **my ~ reaction** ma première réaction ■ **the project is still in its ~ stages** le projet en est encore à ses débuts ▶ **~ letter** initiale *f*.
◇ *n* **1.** [letter] initiale *f* ■ **it's got his ~s on it** il y a ses initiales dessus **2.** TYPO [of chapter] lettrine *f*.
◇ *vt* [memo, page] parapher, parafer, signer de ses initiales.

initialize, ise [ɪ'nɪʃəlaɪz] *vt* COMPUT initialiser.

initially [ɪ'nɪʃəlɪ] *adv* initialement, à l'origine.

initiate ◇ *vt* [ɪ'nɪʃɪeɪt] **1.** [talks, debate] amorcer, engager ■ [policy] lancer ■ [quarrel, reaction] provoquer, déclencher ■ **the pilot has ~d landing procedures** le pilote a entamé *OR* amorcé les procédures d'atterrissage ■ **I find it hard to ~ conversation with him** je trouve difficile d'engager la conversation avec lui **2.** [person] initier ■ **to ~ sb into sthg** initier qqn à qqch.
◇ *n* [ɪ'nɪʃɪət] initié *m*, - e *f*.

initiation [ɪ,nɪʃɪ'eɪʃn] ◇ *n* **1.** [start] commencement *m*, début *m* ■ **he fought for the ~ of new policies** il s'est battu pour la mise en œuvre de politiques différentes **2.** [of person] initiation *f* ■ **her ~ into politics** son initiation à la politique.
◇ *comp* : **~ ceremony** cérémonie *f* d'initiation.

initiative [ɪ'nɪʃətɪv] ◇ *n* **1.** [drive] initiative *f* ■ **to act on one's own ~** agir de sa propre initiative ■ **you'll have to use your ~** vous devrez prendre des initiatives ▶ **citizen's ~** *US* POL initiative *f* populaire **2.** [first step] initiative *f* ■ **to take the ~** prendre l'initiative **3.** [lead] initiative *f* ■ **to have the ~** avoir l'initiative.
◇ *adj* **1.** [preliminary] préliminaire **2.** [ritual] initiatique.

initiator [ɪ'nɪʃɪeɪtər] *n* initiateur *m*, - trice *f*, instigateur *m*, - trice *f*.

inject [ɪn'dʒekt] *vt* **1.** MED faire une piqûre de, injecter ■ **to ~ sb with penicillin** faire une piqûre de pénicilline à qqn ■ **have you been ~ed against tetanus?** êtes-vous vacciné contre le tétanos? ■ INDUST : **the resin is ~ed into the mould** la résine est injectée dans le moule **2.** *fig* injecter ■ **they've ~ed billions of dollars into the economy** ils ont injecté des milliards de dollars dans l'économie ■ **he tried to ~ some humour into the situation** *fig* il a tenté d'introduire un peu d'humour dans la situation.

injection [ɪn'dʒekʃn] *n* MED & *fig* injection *f* ■ **to give sb an ~** MED faire une injection *OR* une piqûre à qqn ▶ **~ moulding** moulage *m* par injection.

injector [ɪn'dʒektər] *n* injecteur *m*.

injudicious [,ɪndʒu:'dɪʃəs] *adj* peu judicieux, imprudent.

injunction [ɪn'dʒʌŋkʃn] *n* **1.** LAW ordonnance *f* ■ **to take out an ~ against sb** mettre qqn en demeure **2.** [warning] injonction *f*, recommandation *f* formelle.

injure ['ɪndʒər] *vt* **1.** [physically] blesser ■ **he ~d his knee skiing** il s'est blessé au genou en faisant du ski ■ **ten people were ~d in the accident** l'accident a fait dix blessés **2.** [damage - relationship, interests] nuire à **3.** [offend] blesser, offenser **4.** [wrong] faire du tort à.

injured ['ɪndʒəd] ◇ *adj* **1.** [physically] blessé ■ **her head is badly ~** elle est grièvement blessée à la tête **2.** [offended - person] offensé ■ **it's just his ~ pride** il est blessé dans son amour-propre, c'est tout.
◇ *npl* : **the ~** les blessés *mpl*.

injurious [ɪn'dʒʊərɪəs] *adj* *fml* **1.** [detrimental] nuisible, préjudiciable ■ **~ to** préjudiciable à **2.** [insulting] offensant, injurieux.

injury ['ɪndʒərɪ] (*pl* **injuries**) *n* **1.** [physical] blessure *f* ■ **the explosion caused serious injuries** l'explosion a fait des blessés graves ■ **the team has had very few injuries this season** SPORT il n'y a eu que très peu de blessés dans l'équipe cette saison ■ **be careful, you'll do yourself an ~!** *UK* fais attention, tu vas te blesser! **2.** *fml* & *lit* [wrong] tort *m*, préjudice *m* **3.** [offence] offense *f* **4.** LAW préjudice *m*.

injury time *n (U)* SPORT arrêts *mpl* de jeu.

injustice [ɪn'dʒʌstɪs] *n* injustice *f* ▪ **to do sb an ~** être injuste envers qqn.

ink [ɪŋk] ◇ *n* **1.** encre *f* ▪ **in ~** à l'encre ➊ **~ drawing** dessin *m* à l'encre **2.** [of squid, octopus etc] encre *f*, noir *m*.
◇ *vt* encrer.
➡ **ink in** *vt sep* [drawing] repasser à l'encre.

inkblot ['ɪŋkblɒt] *n* tache *f* d'encre, pâté *m* ▪ **~ test** test *m* de Rorschach *OR* des taches d'encre.

inkjet printer ['ɪŋkdʒet-] *n* TECH imprimante *f* à jet d'encre.

inkling ['ɪŋklɪŋ] *n* vague *OR* petite idée *f* ▪ **I had some ~ of the** *OR* **as to the real reason** j'avais bien une petite idée de la véritable raison.

inkpad ['ɪŋkpæd] *n* tampon *m* (encreur).

ink pen *n* stylo *m* à encre.

inkpot ['ɪŋkpɒt] *n* encrier *m*.

inkstand ['ɪŋkstænd] *n* encrier *m*.

inkwell ['ɪŋkwel] *n* encrier *m* (encastré).

inky ['ɪŋkɪ] (*comp* **inkier**, *superl* **inkiest**) *adj* **1.** [inkstained] taché d'encre **2.** [dark] noir comme l'encre.

inlaid [ˌɪn'leɪd] ◇ *pt* & *pp* ▷ **inlay**.
◇ *adj* incrusté ▪ [wood] marqueté, incrusté ▪ **an ~ table** une table en marqueterie.

inland ◇ *adj* ['ɪnlənd] **1.** [not coastal - town, sea] intérieur ▪ **~ waterways** voies *fpl* navigables ▪ **~ navigation** navigation *f* fluviale **2.** *UK* [not foreign] intérieur ▪ **~ mail** courrier *m* intérieur.
◇ *adv* [ɪn'lænd] [travelling] vers l'intérieur ▪ [located] à l'intérieur.

Inland Revenue *n UK* **the ~** ≃ le fisc.

in-laws *npl inf* [gen] belle-famille *f* ▪ [parents-in-law] beaux-parents *mpl*.

inlay (*pret & pp* **inlaid**) ◇ *n* [ˌɪn'leɪ] **1.** [gen] incrustation *f* ▪ [in woodwork] marqueterie *f* ▪ [in metalwork] damasquinage *m* ▪ **with ivory ~** incrusté d'ivoire **2.** MED incrustation *f*.
◇ *vt* ['ɪnleɪ] incruster ▪ **inlaid with** incrusté de.

inlet ['ɪnlet] ◇ *n* **1.** [in coastline] anse *f*, crique *f* ▪ [between offshore islands] bras *m* de mer **2.** TECH [intake] arrivée *f*, admission *f* ▪ [opening] (orifice *m* d')entrée *f* ▪ [for air] prise *f* (d'air).
◇ *comp* d'arrivée ▪ **~ pipe** tuyau *m* d'arrivée ▪ **~ valve** soupape *f* d'admission.

in-line skates *npl* patins *mpl* en ligne, rollers *mpl*.

in-line skating *n* SPORT roller *m*.

in loco parentis [ɪnˌləukəupə'rentɪs] *adv* : **to act ~** agir en lieu et place des parents.

inmate ['ɪnmeɪt] *n* [of prison] détenu *m*, - e *f* ▪ [of mental institution] interné *m*, - e *f* ▪ [of hospital] malade *mf* ▪ [of house] occupant *m*, - e *f*, résident *m*, - e *f*.

in memoriam [ˌɪnmɪ'mɔːrɪəm] *prep* à la mémoire de ▪ [on gravestone] in memoriam.

inmost ['ɪnməʊst] = **innermost**.

inn [ɪn] *n* **1.** [pub, small hotel] auberge *f* **2.** *UK* LAW : **the Inns of Court** *associations auxquelles appartiennent les avocats et les juges et dont le siège se trouve dans le quartier historique du même nom à Londres.*

innards ['ɪnədz] *npl inf* entrailles *fpl*.

innate [ɪ'neɪt] *adj* [inborn] inné, naturel.

innately [ɪ'neɪtlɪ] *adv* naturellement.

inner ['ɪnəʳ] ◇ *adj* **1.** [interior - courtyard, pocket, walls, lane] intérieur ; [- structure, workings] interne ▪ **Inner London** *partie centrale de l'agglomération londonienne* **2.** [inward - feeling, conviction] intime ; [- life, voice, struggle, warmth] intérieur ▪ **the ~ meaning** le sens profond ▪ **the ~ man** [spiritual self] l'être *m* intérieur ; *hum* [stomach] l'estomac *m* **3.** [privileged] : **her ~ circle of advisers/friends** le cercle de ses conseillers/amis les plus proches.
◇ *n* [in archery, darts] *zone rouge entourant le centre de la cible.*

inner city (*pl* **inner cities**) *n quartier défavorisé dans le centre d'une grande ville.*

inner ear *n* oreille *f* interne.

innermost ['ɪnəməʊst] *adj* **1.** [feeling, belief] intime ▪ **my ~ thoughts** mes pensées les plus secrètes ▪ **in her ~ being** au plus profond d'elle-même **2.** [central - place, room] le plus au centre ▪ **in the ~ depths of the cave** au plus profond de la grotte.

inner tube *n* [of tyre] chambre *f* à air.

innings ['ɪnɪŋz] (*pl inv*) ◇ *n* [in cricket] tour *m* de batte ▪ **he's had a good ~** *UK fig* il a bien profité de la vie.
◇ *npl* [reclaimed land] polders *mpl*.

innkeeper ['ɪnˌkiːpəʳ] *n* aubergiste *mf*.

innocence ['ɪnəsəns] *n* innocence *f*.

innocent ['ɪnəsənt] ◇ *adj* **1.** [not guilty] innocent ▪ **to be ~ of a crime** être innocent d'un crime ▪ **to prove sb ~** innocenter qqn, reconnaître qqn innocent **2.** [naïve] innocent, naïf **3.** *fml* [devoid] : **~ of** dépourvu de, sans.
◇ *n* innocent *m*, - e *f* ▪ **don't play** *OR* **come the ~!** ne fais pas l'innocent! ➊ **'The Innocents Abroad'** *Twain* 'le Voyage des innocents'.

innocently ['ɪnəsəntlɪ] *adv* innocemment.

innocuous [ɪ'nɒkjʊəs] *adj* inoffensif.

innovate ['ɪnəveɪt] *vi* & *vt* innover.

innovation [ˌɪnə'veɪʃn] *n* innovation *f* ▪ **~s in management techniques** des innovations en matière de gestion.

innovative ['ɪnəvətɪv] *adj* innovateur, novateur.

innovator ['ɪnəveɪtəʳ] *n* innovateur *m*, - trice *f*, novateur *m*, - trice *f*.

innuendo [ˌɪnjuː'endəʊ] (*pl* **innuendos** *OR pl* **innuendoes**) *n* [insinuation] insinuation *f*, sous-entendu *m*.

innumerable [ɪ'njuːmərəbl] *adj* innombrable ▪ **~ times** un nombre incalculable de fois.

innumerate [ɪ'njuːmərət] *adj* qui ne sait pas compter ▪ **he's completely ~** il est incapable d'additionner deux et deux.

inoculate [ɪ'nɒkjʊleɪt] *vt* MED [person, animal] vacciner ▪ **to ~ sb against sthg** vacciner qqn contre qqch ▪ **they ~d guinea pigs with the virus** ils ont inoculé le virus à des cobayes.

inoculation [ɪˌnɒkjʊ'leɪʃn] *n* inoculation *f*.

inoffensive [ˌɪnə'fensɪv] *adj* inoffensif.

inoperable [ɪn'ɒprəbl] *adj* **1.** MED inopérable **2.** [unworkable] impraticable.

inoperative [ɪn'ɒprətɪv] *adj* inopérant.

inopportune [ɪn'ɒpətjuːn] *adj* [remark] déplacé, mal à propos ▪ [time] mal choisi, inopportun ▪ [behaviour] inconvenant, déplacé.

inordinate [ɪn'ɔːdɪnət] *adj* [immense - size] démesuré ; [- pleasure, relief] incroyable ; [- amount of money] exorbitant ▪ **they spent an ~ amount of time on it** ils y ont consacré énormément de temps.

inordinately [ɪn'ɔːdɪnətlɪ] *adv* démesurément, excessivement.

inorganic [ˌɪnɔː'gænɪk] *adj* inorganique.

in-patient *n* hospitalisé *m*, - e *f*, malade *mf*.

input ['ɪnpʊt] (*pret & pp* **input**, *cont* **inputting**) ◇ *n (U)* **1.** [during meeting, discussion] contribution *f* ▪ **we'd like some ~ from marketing before committing ourselves** nous aimerions consulter le service marketing avant de nous engager plus

avant **2.** COMPUT [data] données *fpl* (en entrée) ▪ [entering] entrée *f* (de données) **3.** ELEC énergie *f*, puissance *f* **4.** ECON input *m*, intrant *m*.
◇ *comp* [device, file, program] d'entrée.
◇ *vt* [gen] (faire) entrer, introduire ▪ COMPUT saisir.

input/output *n* COMPUT entrée-sortie *f* ▪ **~ device** périphérique d'entrée-sortie.

inquest ['ɪnkwest] *n* LAW enquête *f* ▪ [into death] *enquête menée pour établir les causes des morts violentes, non naturelles ou mystérieuses.*

inquire [ɪn'kwaɪəʳ] ◇ *vt* [ask] demander ▪ **may I ~ what brings you here?** puis-je vous demander l'objet de votre visite?
◇ *vi* [seek information] se renseigner, demander ▪ **'~ within'** 'se renseigner à l'intérieur' ▪ **to ~ about sthg** demander des renseignements OR se renseigner sur qqch.
◆ **inquire after** *vt insep UK* demander des nouvelles de.
◆ **inquire into** *vt insep* se renseigner sur ▪ [investigate] faire des recherches sur ▪ ADMIN & LAW enquêter sur ▪ **they should ~ into how the money was spent** ils devraient enquêter sur la façon dont l'argent a été dépensé.

inquirer [ɪn'kwaɪərəʳ] *n* investigateur *m*, - trice *f*.

inquiring [ɪn'kwaɪərɪŋ] *adj* [voice, look] interrogateur ▪ [mind] curieux.

inquiringly [ɪn'kwaɪərɪŋlɪ] *adv* d'un air interrogateur.

inquiry [*UK* ɪn'kwaɪərɪ, *US* ɪnkwərɪ] (*pl* **inquiries**) *n* **1.** [request for information] demande *f* (de renseignements) **2.** [investigation] enquête *f* ▪ **to hold** OR **to conduct an ~ into sthg** faire une enquête sur qqch ▪ **the police are making inquiries** la police enquête, une enquête (policière) est en cours ▪ **he is helping police with their inquiries** la police est en train de l'interroger ▪ **upon further ~** après vérification ➔ **commission of ~** commission *f* d'enquête **3.** [questioning] : **a look/tone of ~** un regard/ton interrogateur.

inquisition [,ɪnkwɪ'zɪʃn] *n* **1.** [gen] *pej* inquisition *f* **2.** HIST : **the Inquisition** l'Inquisition *f* **3.** LAW enquête *f*.

inquisitive [ɪn'kwɪzətɪv] *adj* [curious] curieux ▪ *pej* [nosy] indiscret, - ète *f*.

inquisitively [ɪn'kwɪzətɪvlɪ] *adv* [curiously] avec curiosité ▪ *pej* [nosily] de manière indiscrète.

inquisitiveness [ɪn'kwɪzətɪvnɪs] *n* [curiosity] curiosité *f* ▪ *pej* [nosiness] indiscrétion *f*.

inquisitor [ɪn'kwɪzɪtəʳ] *n* **1.** [investigator] enquêteur *m*, - euse *f* ▪ [interrogator] interrogateur *m*, - trice *f* **2.** HIST inquisiteur *m*.

inquisitorial [ɪn,kwɪzɪ'tɔːrɪəl] *adj* inquisitorial.

inroad ['ɪnrəʊd] *n* [raid] incursion *f* ▪ [advance] avance *f*.
◆ **inroads** *npl* **1.** MIL : **to make ~s into enemy territory** avancer en territoire ennemi **2.** *fig* **to make ~s in** OR **into** OR **on** [supplies, funds] entamer ; [spare time, sb's rights] empiéter sur ▪ **they have made significant ~s into our market share** ils ont considérablement mordu sur notre part du marché ▪ **they've made great ~s on the work** ils ont bien avancé le travail.

inrush ['ɪnrʌʃ] *n* afflux *m*.

insalubrious [,ɪnsə'luːbrɪəs] *adj fml* [district, climate] insalubre, malsain.

insane [ɪn'seɪn] ◇ *adj* **1.** [mentally disordered] fou *(before vowel or silent 'h'* **fol***)*, folle *f* ▪ **to go ~** perdre la raison **2.** *fig* [person] fou *(before vowel or silent 'h'* **fol***)*, folle *f* ▪ **it's driving me ~!** ça me rend fou! ▪ [scheme, price] démentiel.
◇ *npl* : **the ~** les malades *mpl* mentaux.

insanely [ɪn'seɪnlɪ] *adv* **1.** [crazily - laugh, behave, talk] comme un fou **2.** [as intensifier - funny, rich] follement ▪ **he was ~ jealous** il était fou de jalousie.

insanitary [ɪn'sænɪtrɪ] *adj* insalubre, malsain.

insanity [ɪn'sænətɪ] *n* folie *f*, démence *f*.

insatiable [ɪn'seɪʃəbl] *adj* insatiable.

inscribe [ɪn'skraɪb] *vt* **1.** [on list] inscrire ▪ [on plaque, tomb etc] graver, inscrire ▪ **his cigar case was ~d with his name** son étui à cigares était gravé à son nom ▪ **it's ~d on my memory** *fig* c'est inscrit OR gravé dans ma mémoire **2.** [dedicate] dédicacer ▪ **an ~d copy of the book** un exemplaire dédicacé du livre **3.** GEOM inscrire **4.** FIN : **~d securities** titres *mpl* nominatifs.

inscription [ɪn'skrɪpʃn] *n* [on plaque, tomb] inscription *f* ▪ [in book] dédicace *f*.

inscrutable [ɪn'skruːtəbl] *adj* [person] énigmatique, impénétrable ▪ [remark] énigmatique.

insect ['ɪnsekt] *n* insecte *m* ▪ **~ bite** piqûre *f* d'insecte ▪ **~ repellent** produit *m* insectifuge.

insecticide [ɪn'sektɪsaɪd] *n* insecticide *m*.

insectivore [ɪn'sektɪvɔːʳ] *n* insectivore *m*.

insectivorous [,ɪnsek'tɪvərəs] *adj* insectivore.

insecure [,ɪnsɪ'kjʊəʳ] *adj* **1.** [person - temporarily] inquiet, - ète *f* ; [- generally] pas sûr de soi, qui manque d'assurance ▪ **he's so ~** il est vraiment mal dans sa peau **2.** [chair, nail, scaffolding etc] peu solide **3.** [place] peu sûr **4.** [future, market] incertain ▪ [peace, job, relationship] précaire.

insecurely [,ɪnsɪ'kjʊəlɪ] *adv* : **~ balanced** en équilibre instable ▪ **~ closed/bolted/attached** mal fermé/verrouillé/attaché.

insecurity [,ɪnsɪ'kjʊərətɪ] (*pl* **insecurities**) *n* **1.** [lack of confidence] manque *m* d'assurance ▪ [uncertainty] incertitude *f* ▪ **job ~** précarité *f* de l'emploi **2.** [lack of safety] insécurité *f*.

inseminate [ɪn'semɪneɪt] *vt* inséminer.

insemination [ɪn,semɪ'neɪʃn] *n* insémination *f*.

insensible [ɪn'sensəbl] *adj fml* **1.** [unconscious] inconscient, sans connaissance ▪ [numb] insensible ▪ **her body was ~ to any pain** son corps était insensible à toute douleur **2.** [cold, indifferent] : **~ to the suffering of others** insensible OR indifférent à la souffrance d'autrui **3.** [unaware] inconscient *fig* ▪ **~ of the risks** inconscient des risques **4.** [imperceptible] insensible, imperceptible.

insensitive [ɪn'sensətɪv] *adj* **1.** [cold-hearted] insensible, dur ▪ **they are ~ brutes** ce sont des brutes épaisses ▪ **the government's reaction was highly ~** le gouvernement a fait preuve d'une indifférence extrême **2.** [unaware] insensible **3.** [physically] insensible ▪ **~ to pain** insensible à la douleur.

insensitively [ɪn'sensətɪvlɪ] *adj* avec un grand manque de tact.

insensitivity [ɪn,sensə'tɪvətɪ], **insensitiveness** [ɪn'sensətɪvnɪs] *n* insensibilité *f*.

inseparable [ɪn'seprəbl] *adj* inséparable.

inseparably [ɪn'seprəblɪ] *adv* inséparablement.

insert ◇ *vt* [ɪn'sɜːt] introduire, insérer ▪ **she ~ed a small ad in the local paper** elle a mis une petite annonce dans le journal local ▪ **before ~ing your contact lenses** avant de mettre vos verres de contact.
◇ *n* ['ɪnsɜːt] **1.** [gen] insertion *f* ▪ [extra text] encart *m* **2.** SEW pièce *f* rapportée ▪ [decorative] incrustation *f*.

insertion [ɪn'sɜːʃn] *n* **1.** [act] insertion *f* **2.** [thing inserted] = **insert 3.** ANAT & BOT insertion *f*.

in-service *adj* : **~ training** formation *f* permanente OR continue.

inset ['ɪnset] (*pret & pp* **inset**, *cont* **insetting**) ◇ *vt* **1.** [detail, map, diagram] insérer en encadré ▪ **town plans are ~ in the main map** des plans de ville figurent en encadrés sur la carte principale **2.** SEW [extra material] rapporter **3.** TYPO rentrer **4.** [jewel] incruster ▪ **~ with** incrusté de.
◇ *n* **1.** [in map, text] encadré *m* ▪ [on video, TV screen] incrustation *f* **2.** [in newspaper, magazine - extra pages] encart *m* **3.** SEW panneau *m* rapporté.

inshore ◇ *adj* ['ɪnʃɔːʳ] **1.** [near shore] côtier **2.** [towards shore] : **~ wind** vent *m* de mer ▪ **~ current** courant *m* qui porte vers la côte.

◇ *adv* [ɪn'ʃɔːr] [near shore] près de la côte ▪ [towards shore] vers la côte.

inside [ɪn'saɪd] ◇ *adv* **1.** [within enclosed space] dedans, à l'intérieur ▪ **it's hollow ~** c'est creux à l'intérieur, l'intérieur est creux
2. [indoors] à l'intérieur ▪ **bring the chairs ~** rentre les chaises ▪ **she opened the door and went ~** elle ouvrit la porte et entra ▪ *UK* [in bus] : **plenty of room ~!** il y a plein de place à l'intérieur!
3. *inf* [in prison] en taule ▪ **he's been ~** il a fait de la taule.
◇ *prep* **1.** [within] à l'intérieur de, dans ▪ **~ the house** à l'intérieur de la maison ▮ *fig* **what goes on ~ his head?** qu'est-ce qui se passe dans sa tête? ▪ **it's just ~ the limit** c'est juste (dans) la limite ▪ **someone ~ the company must have told them** quelqu'un de l'entreprise a dû le leur dire
2. [in less than] en moins de ▪ **I'll have it finished ~ 6 days** je l'aurai terminé en moins de 6 jours.
◇ *n* **1.** [inner part] intérieur *m* ▪ **she has a scar on the ~ of her wrist** elle a une cicatrice à l'intérieur du poignet
2. [of pavement, road] : **walk on the ~** marchez loin du bord ▪ **to overtake on the ~** AUT [driving on left] doubler à gauche ; [driving on right] doubler à droite ▪ **coming up on the ~ is Golden Boy** Golden Boy remonte à la corde
3. *fig* **on the ~ : only someone on the ~ would know that** seul quelqu'un de la maison saurait ça.
◇ *adj* **1.** [door, wall] intérieur ▪ **~ leg measurement** hauteur *f* de l'entrejambe ▪ **the ~ pages** [of newspaper] les pages intérieures ▪ **the ~ lane** [in athletics] la corde ; [driving on left] la voie de gauche ; [driving on right] la voie de droite ▪ **to be on the ~ track** [in horse-racing] tenir la corde ; *fig* être bien placé
2. *fig* **he has ~ information** il a quelqu'un dans la place ▪ **find out the ~ story** essaie de découvrir les dessous de l'histoire ▪ **it looks like an ~ job** on dirait que c'est quelqu'un de la maison qui a fait le coup
3. FTBL : **~ left/right** inter *m* gauche/droite
4. AUT : **the ~ wheel/door** la roue/portière côté trottoir.
◆ **insides** *npl inf* [stomach] estomac *m* ▪ [intestines] intestins *mpl*, tripes *fpl*.
◆ **inside of** *prep phr inf* **1.** [in less than] en moins de
2. *US* [within] à l'intérieur de, dans.
◆ **inside out** *adv phr* **1.** [with inner part outwards] : **your socks are on ~ out** tu as mis tes chaussettes à l'envers ▪ **he turned his pockets ~ out** il a retourné ses poches ▪ **they turned the room ~ out** *fig* ils ont mis la pièce sens dessus dessous
2. [thoroughly] : **she knows her job ~ out** elle connaît parfaitement son travail.

insider [ˌɪn'saɪdər] *n* initié *m*, - e *f* ▪ **according to an ~** selon une source bien informée ▪ **I got a hot tip from an ~** quelqu'un dans la place m'a donné un bon tuyau.

insider dealing, insider trading *n (U)* ST. EX délit *m* d'initiés.

insidious [ɪn'sɪdɪəs] *adj* insidieux.

insidiously [ɪn'sɪdɪəslɪ] *adv* insidieusement.

insight ['ɪnsaɪt] *n* **1.** [perspicacity] perspicacité *f* ▪ **she has great ~** elle est très fine ▪ **his book shows remarkable ~ into the problem** son livre témoigne d'une compréhension très fine du problème **2.** [idea, glimpse] aperçu *m*, idée *f* ▪ **I managed to get** *OR* **gain an ~ into her real character** j'ai pu me faire une idée de sa véritable personnalité ▪ **his book offers us new ~s into human behaviour** son livre nous propose un nouveau regard sur le comportement humain.

insightful ['ɪnsaɪtfʊl] *adj* pénétrant, perspicace.

insignia [ɪn'sɪgnɪə] (*pl inv OR pl* **insignias**) *n* insigne *m*, insignes *mpl*.

insignificance [ˌɪnsɪg'nɪfɪkəns] *n* insignifiance *f*.

insignificant [ˌɪnsɪg'nɪfɪkənt] *adj* **1.** [unimportant] insignifiant, sans importance **2.** [negligible] insignifiant, négligeable.

insincere [ˌɪnsɪn'sɪər] *adj* peu sincère ▪ **his grief turned out to be ~** il s'avéra que son chagrin n'était que feint.

insincerely [ˌɪnsɪn'sɪəlɪ] *adv* sans sincérité, de manière hypocrite.

insincerity [ˌɪnsɪn'serətɪ] *n* manque *m* de sincérité.

insinuate [ɪn'sɪnjʊeɪt] *vt* **1.** [imply] insinuer, laisser entendre ▪ **he ~d that you were lying** il a insinué que vous mentiez **2.** [introduce] insinuer ▪ **he ~d himself into their favour** il s'est insinué dans leurs bonnes grâces.

insinuation [ɪnˌsɪnjʊ'eɪʃn] *n* **1.** [hint] insinuation *f*, allusion *f* **2.** [act, practice] insinuation *f*.

insipid [ɪn'sɪpɪd] *adj* insipide, fade.

insist [ɪn'sɪst] ◇ *vi* **1.** [demand] insister ▪ **to ~ on sthg/doing sthg : he ~ed on a new contract** il a exigé un nouveau contrat ▪ **she ~s on doing it her way** elle tient à le faire à sa façon ▪ **he ~ed on my taking the money** il a tenu à ce que je prenne l'argent **2.** [maintain] : **to ~ on** maintenir ▪ **she ~s on her innocence** elle maintient qu'elle est innocente **3.** [stress] : **to ~ on** insister sur.
◇ *vt* **1.** [demand] insister ▪ **I ~ that you tell no-one** j'insiste pour que vous ne le disiez à personne ▪ **you should ~ that you be paid** vous devriez exiger qu'on vous paye **2.** [maintain] maintenir, soutenir ▪ **she ~s that she locked the door** elle maintient qu'elle a fermé la porte à clef.

insistence [ɪn'sɪstəns] *n* : **their ~ on secrecy has hindered negotiations** en exigeant le secret, ils ont entravé les négociations ▪ **his ~ on his rights** la revendication répétée de ses droits ▪ **at** *OR* **on my ~** sur mon insistance.

insistent [ɪn'sɪstənt] *adj* [person] insistant ▪ [demand] pressant ▪ [denial, refusal] obstiné ▪ **she was most ~** elle a beaucoup insisté.

insistently [ɪn'sɪstəntlɪ] *adv* [stare, knock] avec insistance ▪ [ask, urge] avec insistance, instamment.

in situ [ˌɪn'sɪtjuː] *adv phr* sur place MED & BOT in situ.

insofar as [ˌɪnsəʊ'fɑːr-] *conj phr* dans la mesure où ▪ **~ it's possible** dans la limite *OR* mesure du possible.

insole ['ɪnsəʊl] *n* semelle *f* intérieure.

insolence ['ɪnsələns] *n* insolence *f*.

insolent ['ɪnsələnt] *adj* insolent ▪ **he's ~ to his teachers** il est insolent *OR* il fait preuve d'insolence envers ses professeurs.

insolently ['ɪnsələntlɪ] *adv* insolemment, avec insolence.

insolubility [ɪnˌsɒljʊ'bɪlətɪ] *n* insolubilité *f*.

insoluble [ɪn'sɒljʊbl] *adj* [problem, substance] insoluble.

insolvency [ɪn'sɒlvənsɪ] *n* insolvabilité *f*.

insolvent [ɪn'sɒlvənt] *adj* insolvable.

insomnia [ɪn'sɒmnɪə] *n (U)* insomnie *f*.

insomniac [ɪn'sɒmnɪæk] ◇ *adj* insomniaque.
◇ *n* insomniaque *mf*.

insomuch as [ˌɪnsəʊ'mʌtʃ-] = **inasmuch as**.

insouciant [ɪn'suːsjənt] *adj lit* insoucieux.

inspect [ɪn'spekt] ◇ *vt* **1.** [scrutinize] examiner, inspecter ▪ **she ~ed her body for bruises** elle examina son corps à la recherche de bleus **2.** [check officially - school, product, prison] inspecter ; [- ticket] contrôler ; [- accounts] contrôler **3.** MIL [troops] passer en revue.
◇ *vi* faire une inspection.

inspection [ɪn'spekʃn] *n* **1.** [of object] examen *m* (minutieux) ▪ [of place] inspection *f* ▪ **on closer ~** en regardant de plus près **2.** [official check] inspection *f* ▪ [of ticket, passport] contrôle *m* ▪ [of school, prison] (visite *f* d')inspection *f* **3.** MIL [of troops] revue *f*, inspection *f*.

inspection chamber *n* bouche *f* d'égout.

inspector [ɪn'spektər] *n* **1.** [gen] inspecteur *m*, - trice *f* ▪ [on public transport] contrôleur *m*, - euse *f* ▪ **~ of taxes** *UK* ≃ inspecteur *m*, - trice *f* des impôts ▪ **tax ~** *UK* [sent to firms] polyvalent *m* **2.** *UK* SCH inspecteur *m*, - trice *f* **3.** [in police force] : **(police) ~** ≃ inspecteur *m* (de police).

inspectorate [ɪn'spektərət] *n* [body of inspectors] inspection *f* ▪ [duties, term of office] inspection *f*, inspectorat *m*.

inspector general (*pl* **inspectors general**) *n* **1.** [gen] inspecteur *m* général **2.** MIL ≃ général *m* inspecteur.

inspiration [ˌɪnspəˈreɪʃn] *n* **1.** [source of ideas] inspiration *f* ■ **to draw one's ~ from** s'inspirer de ■ **to be an ~ to sb** être une source d'inspiration pour qqn ■ **the ~ for her screenplay** l'idée de son scénario **2.** [bright idea] inspiration *f* ■ **hey, I've had an ~!** hé! j'ai une idée géniale!

inspirational [ˌɪnspəˈreɪʃənl] *adj* **1.** [inspiring] inspirant **2.** [inspired] inspiré.

inspire [ɪnˈspaɪəʳ] *vt* [person, work of art] inspirer ■ **Moore's sculptures ~d her early work** les sculptures de Moore lui ont inspiré ses œuvres de jeunesse ■ **to ~ sb to do sthg** inciter OR pousser qqn à faire qqch ■ **he ~d her to become a doctor** il suscita en elle une vocation de médecin.

inspired [ɪnˈspaɪəd] *adj* [artist, poem] inspiré ■ [moment] d'inspiration ■ [performance] extraordinaire ■ [choice, decision] bien inspiré, heureux ■ **to make an ~ guess** deviner OR tomber juste.

inspiring [ɪnˈspaɪərɪŋ] *adj* [speech, book] stimulant ■ [music] exaltant.

inst. (*written abbrev of* **instant**) COMM courant ■ **of the 9th ~** du 9 courant OR de ce mois.

instability [ˌɪnstəˈbɪlətɪ] (*pl* **instabilities**) *n* instabilité *f*.

instal *US* = **install**.

install [ɪnˈstɔːl] *vt* **1.** [machinery, equipment, software] installer **2.** [settle - person] installer ■ **she ~ed herself in an armchair** elle s'installa dans un fauteuil **3.** [appoint - manager, president] nommer.

installation [ˌɪnstəˈleɪʃn] *n* [gen - MIL] installation *f*.

installment plan *n US système de paiement à tempérament* ■ **to buy sthg on an ~** acheter qqch à crédit.

instalment *UK*, **installment** *US* [ɪnˈstɔːlmənt] *n* **1.** [payment] acompte *m*, versement *m* partiel ■ **monthly ~s** mensualités *fpl* ■ **to pay in** OR **by ~s** payer par versements échelonnés ■ **to pay off a loan in** OR **by ~s** rembourser un prêt en plusieurs versements OR tranches **2.** [of serial, story] épisode *m* ■ [of book] fascicule *m* ■ [of TV documentary] volet *m*, partie *f* ■ **published in ~s** publié par fascicules **3.** = **installation**.

instance [ˈɪnstəns] ◇ *n* **1.** [example] exemple *m* ■ **as an ~ of** comme exemple de ■ [case] occasion *f*, circonstance *f* ■ **he agrees with me in most ~s** la plupart du temps OR dans la plupart des cas il est d'accord avec moi ■ **our policy, in that ~, was to raise interest rates** notre politique en la circonstance OR l'occurrence a consisté à augmenter les taux d'intérêt **2.** [stage] : **in the first/second ~** en premier/second lieu **3.** *fml* [request] demande *f*, instances *fpl* ■ **at the ~ of** à la demande de.

◇ *vt* donner OR citer en exemple.

◆ **for instance** *adv phr* par exemple.

instant [ˈɪnstənt] ◇ *adj* **1.** [immediate] immédiat ■ **for ~ weight loss** pour perdre du poids rapidement ■ **give yourself an ~ new look** changez de look en un clin d'œil ➤ **~ replay** TV ralenti *m* **2.** CULIN [coffee] instantané, soluble ■ [soup, sauce] instantané, en sachet ■ [milk] en poudre ■ [mashed potato] en flocons ■ [dessert] à préparation rapide.

◇ *n* instant *m*, moment *m* ■ **do it this ~** fais-le tout de suite OR immédiatement OR à l'instant ■ **she read it in an ~** elle l'a lu en un rien de temps ■ **I'll be with you in an ~** je serai à vous dans un instant ■ **call me the ~ you arrive** appelle-moi dès que OR aussitôt que tu seras arrivé ■ **I didn't believe it for one ~** je ne l'ai pas cru un seul instant.

instantaneous [ˌɪnstənˈteɪnjəs] *adj* instantané.

instantaneously [ˌɪnstənˈteɪnjəslɪ] *adv* instantanément.

instantly [ˈɪnstəntlɪ] *adv* [immediately] immédiatement, instantanément ■ **he was killed ~** il a été tué sur le coup.

instead [ɪnˈsted] *adv*: **he didn't go to the office, he went home ~** au lieu d'aller au bureau, il est rentré chez lui ■ **I don't like sweet things, I'll have cheese ~** je n'aime pas les sucreries, je prendrai plutôt du fromage ■ **since I'll be away, why not send Mary ~?** puisque je ne serai pas là, pourquoi ne pas envoyer Mary à ma place?

◆ **instead of** *prep phr* au lieu de, à la place de ■ **~ of reading a book** au lieu de lire un livre ■ **her son came ~ of her** son fils est venu à sa place ■ **I had an apple ~ of lunch** j'ai pris une pomme en guise de déjeuner.

instep [ˈɪnstep] *n* **1.** ANAT cou-de-pied *m* **2.** [of shoe] cambrure *f*.

instigate [ˈɪnstɪgeɪt] *vt* **1.** [initiate - gen] être à l'origine de ; [- project] promouvoir ; [- strike, revolt] provoquer ; [- plot] ourdir **2.** [urge] inciter, pousser ■ **to ~ sb to do sthg** pousser OR inciter qqn à faire qqch.

instigation [ˌɪnstɪˈgeɪʃn] *n* [urging] instigation *f*, incitation *f* ■ **at her ~** à son instigation.

instigator [ˈɪnstɪgeɪtəʳ] *n* instigateur *m*, - trice *f*.

instil *UK*, **instill** *US* [ɪnˈstɪl] *vt* [principles, ideals] inculquer ■ [loyalty, courage, fear] insuffler ■ [idea] faire comprendre.

instinct [ˈɪnstɪŋkt] *n* instinct *m* ■ **by ~** d'instinct ■ **she has an ~ for business** elle a le sens des affaires ■ **her first ~ was to run away** sa première réaction a été de s'enfuir.

instinctive [ɪnˈstɪŋktɪv] *adj* instinctif.

instinctively [ɪnˈstɪŋktɪvlɪ] *adv* instinctivement.

institute [ˈɪnstɪtjuːt] ◇ *vt* **1.** [establish - system, guidelines] instituer, établir ; [- change] introduire, apporter ; [- committee] créer, constituer ; [- award, organization] fonder, créer **2.** [take up - proceedings] engager, entamer ; [- inquiry] ouvrir **3.** [induct] installer ■ RELIG instituer.

◇ *n* institut *m*.

institution [ˌɪnstɪˈtjuːʃn] *n* **1.** [of rules] institution *f*, établissement *m* ■ [of committee] création *f*, constitution *f* ■ [of change] introduction *f* ■ LAW [of action] début *m* ■ [of official] installation *f* **2.** [organization] organisme *m*, établissement *m* ■ [governmental] institution *f* ■ [educational, penal, religious] établissement *m* ■ [private school] institution *f* ■ [hospital] hôpital *m*, établissement *m* hospitalier ■ *euph* [mental hospital] établissement *m* psychiatrique **3.** [custom, political or social structure] institution *f* **4.** *hum* [person] institution *f* ■ **she's a national ~** elle est devenue une véritable institution nationale.

institutional [ˌɪnstɪˈtjuːʃənl] *adj* **1.** [hospital, prison, school etc] institutionnel ■ **~ care** soins *mpl* hospitaliers ■ **he'd be better off in ~ care** il serait mieux dans un établissement OR centre spécialisé ■ **after years of ~ life** après des années d'internement **2.** [belief, values] séculaire **3.** COMM institutionnel.

institutionalize, ise [ˌɪnstɪˈtjuːʃənˌlaɪz] *vt* **1.** [establish] institutionnaliser ■ **to become ~d** s'institutionnaliser **2.** [place in a hospital, home] placer dans un établissement *(médical ou médico-social)* ■ **to be ~d** être interné ■ **to become ~d** ne plus être capable de se prendre en charge *(après des années passées dans des établissements spécialisés)*.

institutional racism, institutionalized racism *n* racisme *m* institutionnel.

instruct [ɪnˈstrʌkt] *vt* **1.** [command, direct] charger ■ **we have been ~ed to accompany you** nous sommes chargés de OR nous avons mission de vous accompagner **2.** [teach] former ■ **to ~ sb in sthg** enseigner OR apprendre qqch à qqn **3.** [inform] informer ■ **I have been ~ed that the meeting has been cancelled** on m'a informé OR avisé que la réunion a été annulée **4.** LAW [jury, solicitor] donner des instructions à.

instruction [ɪnˈstrʌkʃn] *n* **1.** [order] instruction *f* ■ **they were given ~s not to let him out of their sight** ils avaient reçu l'ordre de ne pas le perdre de vue ➤ **~s (for use)** mode *m* d'emploi **2.** *(U)* [teaching] leçons *fpl* ■ MIL instruction *f*.

instruction manual *n* COMM & TECH manuel *m* (d'utilisation et d'entretien).

instructive [ɪnˈstrʌktɪv] *adj* instructif.

instructor [ɪn'strʌktəʳ] *n* **1.** [gen] professeur *m* ■ MIL instructeur *m* ■ **sailing ~** moniteur *m*, - trice *f* de voile **2.** *US* UNIV ≃ assistant *m*, - e *f*.

instructress [ɪn'strʌktrɪs] *n* instructrice *f*, monitrice *f*.

instrument ['ɪnstrʊmənt] ◇ *n* **1.** MED, MUS & TECH instrument *m* ■ **to fly by** *OR* **on ~ s** naviguer à l'aide d'instruments ➤ **~ error** erreur due aux instruments **2.** *fig* [means] instrument *m*, outil *m* **3.** FIN effet *m*, titre *m* ■ LAW instrument *m*, acte *m* juridique.
◇ *comp* AERON [flying, landing] aux instruments (de bord).
◇ *vt* **1.** MUS orchestrer **2.** TECH munir *OR* équiper d'instruments.

instrumental [,ɪnstrʊ'mentl] ◇ *adj* **1.** [significant] : **her work was ~ in bringing about the reforms** elle a largement contribué à faire passer les réformes ■ **an ~ role** un rôle déterminant **2.** MUS instrumental **3.** TECH d'instruments ■ **~ check** [of devices] vérification des instruments ; [by devices] vérification par instruments **4.** LING : **~ case** (cas *m*) instrumental *m*.
◇ *n* **1.** MUS morceau *m* instrumental **2.** LING instrumental *m*.

instrumentalist [,ɪnstrʊ'mentəlɪst] *n* MUS instrumentiste *mf*.

instrumentation [,ɪnstrʊmen'teɪʃn] *n* **1.** [musical arrangement] orchestration *f*, instrumentation *f* ■ [musical instruments] instruments *mpl* **2.** TECH instrumentation *f*.

instrument panel, instrument board *n* AERON & AUT tableau *m* de bord ■ TECH tableau *m* de contrôle.

insubordinate [,ɪnsə'bɔːdɪnət] *adj* insubordonné.

insubordination ['ɪnsə,bɔːdɪ'neɪʃn] *n* insubordination *f*.

insubstantial [,ɪnsəb'stænʃl] *adj* **1.** [structure] peu solide ■ [book] facile, peu substantiel ■ [garment, snack, mist] léger ■ [claim] sans fondement ■ [reasoning] faible, sans substance **2.** [imaginary] imaginaire, chimérique.

insufferable [ɪn'sʌfərəbl] *adj* insupportable, intolérable.

insufferably [ɪn'sʌfərəblɪ] *adv* insupportablement, intolérablement ■ **he's ~ arrogant** il est d'une arrogance insupportable.

insufficiency [,ɪnsə'fɪʃnsɪ] (*pl* **insufficiencies**) *n* insuffisance *f*.

insufficient [,ɪnsə'fɪʃnt] *adj* insuffisant ■ **there is ~ evidence** les preuves sont insuffisantes.

insufficiently [,ɪnsə'fɪʃntlɪ] *adv* insuffisamment.

insular ['ɪnsjʊləʳ] *adj* **1.** [island - tradition, authorities] insulaire ■ [isolated] isolé **2.** *fig* & *pej* [mentality] limité, borné.

insularity [,ɪnsjʊ'lærətɪ] *n* insularité *f* ■ [isolation] isolement *m*.

insulate ['ɪnsjʊleɪt] *vt* **1.** [against cold, heat, radiation] isoler ■ [hot water pipes, tank] calorifuger ■ [soundproof] insonoriser ■ **~d sleeping bag** sac de couchage isolant **2.** ELEC isoler **3.** *fig* [protect] protéger ■ **they are no longer ~d from the effects of inflation** ils ne sont plus à l'abri des effets de l'inflation.

insulating tape ['ɪnsjʊleɪtɪŋ-] *n* chatterton *m*.

insulation [,ɪnsjʊ'leɪʃn] *n* **1.** [against cold] isolation *f* (calorifuge), calorifugeage *m* ■ [sound-proofing] insonorisation *f*, isolation *f* ■ **loft ~** isolation thermique du toit **2.** ELEC isolation *f* **3.** [feathers, foam etc] isolant *m* **4.** *fig* [protection] protection *f*.

insulator ['ɪnsjʊleɪtəʳ] *n* [material] isolant *m* ■ [device] isolateur *m*.

insulin ['ɪnsjʊlɪn] *n* insuline ■ **~ reaction** *OR* **shock** choc *m* insulinique.

insult ◇ *vt* [ɪn'sʌlt] [abuse] insulter, injurier ■ [offend] faire (un) affront à, offenser.
◇ *n* ['ɪnsʌlt] insulte *f*, injure *f*, affront *m* ■ **his remarks were an ~ to their intelligence** ses commentaires étaient une insulte à leur intelligence ■ **their ads are an ~ to women** leurs pubs sont insultantes *OR* une insulte pour les femmes ➤ **to add ~ to injury** pour couronner le tout.

insulting [ɪn'sʌltɪŋ] *adj* [language] insultant, injurieux ■ [attitude] insultant, offensant ■ [behaviour] grossier.

insultingly [ɪn'sʌltɪŋlɪ] *adv* [speak] d'un ton insultant *OR* injurieux ■ [act] d'une manière insultante.

insuperable [ɪn'suːprəbl] *adj* insurmontable.

insupportable [,ɪnsə'pɔːtəbl] *adj* **1.** [unbearable] insupportable, intolérable **2.** [indefensible] insoutenable.

insurable [ɪn'ʃɔːrəbl] *adj* assurable.

insurance [ɪn'ʃɔːrəns] ◇ *n* **1.** *(U)* [against fire, theft, accident] assurance *f* ■ [cover] garantie *f* (d'assurance), couverture *f* ■ [premium] prime *f* (d'assurance) ■ **to take out ~ (against sthg)** prendre *OR* contracter une assurance, s'assurer (contre qqch) ■ **she got £2,000 in ~** elle a reçu 2 000 livres de l'assurance ■ **how much do you pay in ~?** combien payez-vous (de prime) d'assurance? **2.** *fig* [means of protection] garantie *f*, moyen *m* de protection ■ **take Sam with you, just as an ~** emmenez Sam avec vous, on ne sait jamais *OR* au cas où.
◇ *comp* [premium, scheme] d'assurance ■ [company] d'assurances.

insurance broker *n* courtier *m* d'assurance *OR* d'assurances.

insurance claim *n* demande *f* d'indemnité.

insurance policy *n* police *f* d'assurance, contrat *m* d'assurance.

insure [ɪn'ʃɔːʳ] *vt* **1.** [car, building, person] assurer ■ **he ~d himself** *OR* **his life** il a pris *OR* contracté une assurance-vie ■ **~d against** assuré contre **2.** *fig* [protect] : **what strategy can ~ (us) against failure?** quelle stratégie peut nous prévenir contre l'échec *OR* nous garantir que nous n'échouerons pas? ■ **to ~ one's future** assurer son avenir.

insured [ɪn'ʃɔːd] (*pl inv*) ◇ *adj* assuré ■ **~ risk** risque *m* couvert.
◇ *n* assuré *m*, - e *f*.

insurer [ɪn'ʃɔːrəʳ] *n* assureur *m*.

insurgency [ɪn'sɜːdʒənsɪ], **insurgence** [ɪn'sɜːdʒəns] *n* insurrection *f*.

insurgent [ɪn'sɜːdʒənt] ◇ *n* insurgé *m*, - e *f*.
◇ *adj* insurgé.

insurmountable [,ɪnsə'maʊntəbl] *adj* insurmontable.

insurrection [,ɪnsə'rekʃn] *n* insurrection *f*.

intact [ɪn'tækt] *adj* intact.

intake ['ɪnteɪk] *n* **1.** SCH & UNIV admission *f*, inscription *f* ■ MIL recrutement *m* ■ **the ~ of refugees** l'accueil des réfugiés ■ **they've increased their ~ of medical students** ils ont décidé d'admettre davantage d'étudiants en médecine ➤ **~ class** *UK* cours *m* préparatoire **2.** TECH [of water] prise *f*, arrivée *f* ■ [of gas, steam] admission *f* ➤ **air ~** admission d'air ■ **~ valve** soupape *f* d'admission **3.** [of food] consommation *f* ■ **a daily ~ of 2,000 calories** une ration quotidienne de 2 000 calories ■ **there was a sharp ~ of breath** tout le monde/il/elle etc retint son souffle ➤ **oxygen ~** absorption *f* d'oxygène.

intangible [ɪn'tændʒəbl] ◇ *adj* [quality, reality] intangible, impalpable ■ [idea, difficulty] indéfinissable, difficile à cerner ■ **~ assets** COMM immobilisations *fpl* incorporelles ■ **~ property** LAW biens *mpl* incorporels.
◇ *n* impondérable *m*.

integer ['ɪntɪdʒəʳ] *n* MATHS (nombre *m*) entier *m* ■ [whole unit] entier.

integral ['ɪntɪgrəl] ◇ *adj* **1.** [essential - part, element] intégrant, constitutif ■ **it's an ~ part of your job** cela fait partie intégrante de votre travail **2.** [entire] intégral, complet, - ète *f* **3.** MATHS intégral.
◇ *n* MATHS intégrale *f*.

integral calculus *n* calcul *m* intégral.

integrate ['ɪntɪgreɪt] ◇ *vt* **1.** [combine] : **the two systems have been ~d** on a combiné les deux systèmes **2.** [include in a larger unit] intégrer ■ **to ~ sb in a group** intégrer qqn dans un

groupe **3.** [end segregation of] : **the law was intended to ~ racial minorities** cette loi visait à l'intégration des minorités raciales ■ **to ~ a school** mettre fin à la ségrégation raciale dans une école **4.** MATHS intégrer.
◇ *vi* **1.** [fit in] s'intégrer ■ **to ~ into** s'intégrer dans **2.** [desegregate] ne plus pratiquer la ségrégation raciale.

integrated ['ɪntɪgreɪtɪd] *adj* [gen] intégré ● **~ studies** SCH études *fpl* interdisciplinaires ■ **~ neighborhood** *US* quartier *m* multiracial ■ **~ school** *US* *école où se pratique l'intégration (raciale).*

integration [,ɪntɪ'greɪʃn] *n* intégration *f* ■ **racial ~** déségrégation *f* ■ **school ~** *US* déségrégation des établissements scolaires ■ **vertical/horizontal ~** ECON intégration verticale/horizontale.

integrity [ɪn'tegrətɪ] *n* **1.** [uprightness] intégrité *f*, probité *f* **2.** [wholeness] totalité *f* ■ **cultural ~** identité *f* culturelle.

intellect ['ɪntəlekt] *n* **1.** [intelligence] intelligence *f* **2.** [mind, person] esprit *m*.

intellectual [,ɪntə'lektjʊəl] ◇ *adj* [mental] intellectuel ■ [attitude, image] d'intellectuel.
◇ *n* intellectuel *m*, - elle *f*.

intellectualize, ise [,ɪntə'lektjʊəlaɪz] ◇ *vt* intellectualiser.
◇ *vi* tenir des discours intellectuels.

intellectually [,ɪntə'lektjʊəlɪ] *adv* intellectuellement.

intelligence [ɪn'telɪdʒəns] *n (U)* **1.** [mental ability] intelligence *f* ■ **to have the ~ to do sthg** avoir l'intelligence de faire qqch ■ **use your ~!** réfléchis un peu! **2.** [information] renseignements *mpl*, information *f*, informations *fpl* ■ **~ is** *OR* **are working on it** les services de renseignements y travaillent ● **army ~** service *m* de renseignements de l'armée **3.** [intelligent being] intelligence *f*.

intelligence officer *n* officier *m* de renseignements.

intelligence quotient *n* quotient *m* intellectuel.

intelligence service *n* POL service *m* de renseignements.

intelligence test *n* test *m* d'aptitude intellectuelle.

intelligent [ɪn'telɪdʒənt] *adj* intelligent.

intelligently [ɪn'telɪdʒəntlɪ] *adv* intelligemment.

intelligentsia [ɪn,telɪ'dʒentsɪə] *n* intelligentsia *f*.

intelligible [ɪn'telɪdʒəbl] *adj* intelligible.

intelligibly [ɪn'telɪdʒəblɪ] *adj* intelligiblement.

intemperate [ɪn'tempərət] *adj fml* **1.** [overindulgent] intempérant **2.** [uncontrolled - behaviour, remark] excessif, outrancier ■ **her ~ refusal** la violence de son refus **3.** [harsh - climate] rigoureux, rude.

intend [ɪn'tend] *vt* **1.** [plan, have in mind] : **to ~ to do sthg, to ~ doing** *OR* *US* **on doing sthg** avoir l'intention de *OR* projeter de faire qqch ■ **how do you ~ to do it?** comment avez-vous l'intention de vous y prendre? ■ **we arrived later than (we had) ~ed** nous sommes arrivés plus tard que prévu ■ **his statement was ~ed to mislead** la déclaration visait à induire en erreur ■ **we ~ to increase our sales** nous entendons développer nos ventes ■ **the board ~s her to become managing director** le conseil d'administration souhaite qu'elle soit nommée P-DG ■ **to ~ marriage** *lit* avoir l'intention de se marier ■ **I'm sorry, no criticism/insult was ~ed** je suis désolé, je ne voulais pas vous critiquer/offenser ■ **no pun ~ed!** sans jeu de mots! **2.** [destine] destiner ■ **a book ~ed for the general public** un livre destiné *OR* qui s'adresse au grand public ■ **the reform is ~ed to limit the dumping of toxic waste** cette réforme vise à limiter le déversement de déchets toxiques.

intended [ɪn'tendɪd] ◇ *adj* **1.** [planned - event, trip] prévu ; [- result, reaction] voulu ; [- market, public] visé **2.** [deliberate] intentionnel, délibéré.
◇ *n arch & hum* **his ~** sa future, sa promise *arch* ■ **her ~** son futur, son promis *arch*.

intense [ɪn'tens] *adj* **1.** [gen] intense ■ [battle, debate] acharné ■ [hatred] violent, profond ■ [pleasure] vif ■ **to my ~ satisfaction/annoyance** à ma très grande satisfaction/mon grand déplaisir **2.** [person] : **he's so ~** [serious] il prend tout très au sérieux ; [emotional] il prend tout très à cœur.

intensely [ɪn'tenslɪ] *adv* **1.** [with intensity - work, stare] intensément, avec intensité ; [- love] profondément, passionnément **2.** [extremely - hot, painful, curious] extrêmement ; [- moving, affected, bored] profondément.

intensification [ɪn,tensɪfɪ'keɪʃn] *n* intensification *f*.

intensifier [ɪn'tensɪfaɪər] *n* **1.** LING intensif *m* **2.** PHOT renforçateur *m*.

intensify [ɪn'tensɪfaɪ] (*pret & pp* **intensified**) ◇ *vt* [feeling, impression, colour] renforcer ■ [sound] intensifier ■ **the police have intensified their search for the child** la police redouble d'efforts pour retrouver l'enfant.
◇ *vi* s'intensifier, devenir plus intense.

intensity [ɪn'tensətɪ] (*pl* **intensities**) *n* intensité *f* ■ **the emotional ~ of his paintings** la force des sentiments exprimés dans ses tableaux ■ **the ~ of the debate** la véhémence du débat.

intensive [ɪn'tensɪv] ◇ *adj* intensif ● **~ farming** culture *f* intensive ■ **~ security prison** *US* prison *f* où la surveillance est renforcée.
◇ *n* LING intensif *m*.

-intensive *in cpds* qui utilise beaucoup de... ■ **labour~** qui nécessitent une main-d'œuvre importante ■ **energy ~** [appliance, industry] grand consommateur d'énergie.

intensive care *n (U)* MED soins *mpl* intensifs ■ **in ~** en réanimation.

intensive care unit *n* unité *f* de soins intensifs.

intensively [ɪn'tensɪvlɪ] *adv* intensivement.

intent [ɪn'tent] ◇ *n* intention *f*, but *m* ■ **with good/evil ~** dans une bonne/mauvaise intention ■ **with criminal ~** LAW dans un but délictueux ● **declaration of ~** déclaration *f* d'intention.
◇ *adj* **1.** [concentrated] attentif, absorbé ■ **he was silent, ~ on the meal** il était silencieux, tout à son repas **2.** [determined] résolu, déterminé ■ **to be ~ on doing sthg** être déterminé *OR* résolu à faire qqch.
◆ **to all intents and purposes** *adv phr* en fait.

intention [ɪn'tenʃn] *n* intention *f* ■ **despite my ~ to say** *OR* **of saying nothing** malgré mon intention de ne rien dire ■ **he went to Australia with the ~ of making his fortune** il est parti en Australie dans l'intention de *OR* dans le but de faire fortune ■ **it was with this ~ that I wrote to him** c'est dans cette intention *OR* à cette fin que je lui ai écrit.

intentional [ɪn'tenʃənl] *adj* intentionnel, voulu.

intentionally [ɪn'tenʃənəlɪ] *adv* intentionnellement.

intently [ɪn'tentlɪ] *adv* [alertly - listen, watch] attentivement ■ [thoroughly - question, examine] minutieusement.

inter [ɪn'tɜːr] (*pret & pp* **interred**, *cont* **interring**) *vt fml* enterrer, inhumer.

interact [,ɪntər'ækt] *vi* **1.** [person] : **they ~ very well together** le courant passe bien (entre eux), ils s'entendent très bien **2.** [forces] interagir ■ [substances] avoir une action réciproque **3.** COMPUT dialoguer.

interaction [,ɪntər'ækʃn] *n* interaction *f*.

interactive [,ɪntər'æktɪv] *adj* interactif ■ **~ mode** COMPUT mode conversationnel *OR* interactif.

interactivity [,ɪntəræk'tɪvɪtɪ] *n* interactivité *f*.

Interahamwe [,ɪntərə'hæmweɪ] *n* Interahamwe *m* ■ **the ~** l'Interhamwe.

inter alia [,ɪntər'eɪlɪə] *adv phr fml* notamment.

interbreed [,ɪntə'briːd] (*pret & pp* **interbred** [-bred]) ◇ *vt* [crossbreed - animals] croiser ; [- races] métisser.

◇ *vi* **1.** [crossbreed - animals] se croiser ; [- races] se métisser **2.** [within family, community] contracter des mariages consanguins.

intercalate [ɪn'tɜ:kəleɪt] *vt* intercaler.

intercede [,ɪntə'si:d] *vi* intercéder ■ **she ~d with the boss on my behalf** elle a intercédé en ma faveur auprès du patron.

intercept ◇ *vt* [,ɪntə'sept] intercepter ■ **to ~ a blow** parer un coup.
◇ *n* ['ɪntəsept] interception *f*.

intercepter [,ɪntə'septəʳ] = **interceptor**.

interception [,ɪntə'sepʃn] *n* interception *f*.

interceptor [,ɪntə'septəʳ] *n* [plane] intercepteur *m*.

intercession [,ɪntə'seʃn] *n* intercession *f*.

interchange ◇ *vt* [,ɪntə'tʃeɪndʒ] **1.** [exchange - opinions, information] échanger **2.** [switch round] intervertir, permuter ■ **these tyres can be ~d** ces pneus sont interchangeables.
◇ *n* ['ɪntətʃeɪndʒ] **1.** [exchange] échange *m* **2.** [road junction] échangeur *m*.

interchangeable [,ɪntə'tʃeɪndʒəbl] *adj* interchangeable.

intercity [,ɪntə'sɪtɪ] (*pl* **intercities**) *adj* [travel] d'une ville à l'autre, interurbain ■ **~ train** *UK* (train *m*) rapide *m*.

intercollegiate [,ɪntəkə'li:dʒɪət] *adj* entre collèges ■ *US* [between universities] interuniversitaire.

intercom ['ɪntəkɒm] *n* Interphone® *m*.

intercommunicate [,ɪntəkə'mju:nɪkeɪt] *vi* communiquer.

interconnect [,ɪntəkə'nekt] ◇ *vt* [gen] connecter ■ **~ed corridors** couloirs *mpl* communicants ■ **~ed ideas** *fig* idées étroitement reliées.
◇ *vi* [rooms, buildings] communiquer ■ [circuits] être connecté.

interconnecting [,ɪntəkə'nektɪŋ] *adj* [wall, room] mitoyen.

intercontinental ['ɪntə,kɒntɪ'nentl] *adj* intercontinental.

intercontinental ballistic missile *n* missile *m* balistique intercontinental.

intercourse ['ɪntəkɔ:s] *n* **1.** [sexual intercourse] rapports *mpl* (sexuels) ■ **to have ~ (with sb)** avoir des rapports sexuels (avec qqn) **2.** *fml* [communication] relations *fpl*, rapports *mpl* ■ **social ~** communication *f*.

interdenominational ['ɪntədɪ,nɒmɪ'neɪʃənl] *adj* interconfessionnel.

interdepartmental ['ɪntə,di:pɑ:t'mentl] *adj* [in company, hospital] entre services ■ [in university, ministry] interdépartemental.

interdependence [,ɪntədɪ'pendəns] *n* interdépendance *f*.

interdependent [,ɪntədɪ'pendənt] *adj* interdépendant.

interdict ◇ *vt* [,ɪntə'dɪkt] **1.** LAW interdire **2.** RELIG jeter l'interdit sur.
◇ *n* ['ɪntədɪkt] **1.** LAW interdiction *f* **2.** RELIG interdit *m*.

interdiction [,ɪntə'dɪkʃn] *n* LAW & RELIG interdiction *f*.

interdisciplinary [,ɪntə'dɪsɪ,plɪnərɪ] *adj* interdisciplinaire.

interest ['ɪntrəst] ◇ *n* **1.** [curiosity, attention] intérêt *m* ■ **she takes a great/an active ~ in politics** elle s'intéresse beaucoup/activement à la politique ■ **he has** *OR* **takes no ~ whatsoever in music** il ne s'intéresse absolument pas à la musique ■ **to show (an) ~ in sthg** manifester de l'intérêt pour qqch ■ **he lost all ~ in his work** il a perdu tout intérêt pour son travail ■ **to hold sb's ~** retenir l'attention de qqn ■ **the book created** *OR* **aroused a great deal of ~** le livre a suscité un intérêt considérable
2. [appeal] intérêt *m* ■ **of no ~** sans intérêt ■ **politics has** *OR* **holds no ~ for me** la politique ne présente aucun intérêt pour moi ■ **to be of ~ to sb** intéresser qqn
3. [pursuit, hobby] centre d'intérêt *m* ■ **we share the same ~s** nous avons les mêmes centres d'intérêt ■ **his only ~s are television and comic books** la télévision et les bandes dessinées sont les seules choses qui l'intéressent
4. [advantage, benefit] intérêt *m* ■ **it's in your own ~** *OR* **~s** c'est dans votre propre intérêt ■ **it's in all our ~s to cut costs** nous avons tout intérêt à *OR* il est dans notre intérêt de réduire les coûts ■ **I have your ~s at heart** tes intérêts me tiennent à cœur ■ **of public ~** d'intérêt public ■ **in the ~s of hygiene** par mesure d'hygiène
5. [group with common aim] intérêt *m* ■ **big business ~s** de gros intérêts commerciaux ■ **~ group** groupe *m* d'intérêt
6. [share, stake] intérêts *mpl* ■ **he has an ~ in a sawmill** il a des intérêts dans une scierie
7. FIN intérêts *mpl* ■ **to pay ~ on a loan** payer des intérêts sur un prêt ■ **the investment will bear 6% ~** le placement rapportera 6 % ■ **he'll get it back with ~!** *fig* il va le payer cher!
◇ *vt* intéresser ■ **can I ~ you in our new model?** puis-je attirer votre attention sur notre nouveau modèle?

interest-bearing *adj* productif d'intérêts.

interested ['ɪntrestɪd] *adj* **1.** [showing interest] intéressé ■ **to be ~ in sthg** s'intéresser à qqch ■ **would you be ~ in meeting him?** ça t'intéresserait de le rencontrer? ■ **I'm ~ to see how they do it** je suis curieux de voir comment c'est fait ■ **she seems ~ in the offer** elle semble intéressée par la proposition ■ **a group of ~ passers-by** un groupe de passants curieux **2.** [involved, concerned] intéressé ■ **~ party** partie *f* intéressée.

interest-free *adj* FIN sans intérêt.

interesting ['ɪntrəstɪŋ] *adj* intéressant.

interestingly ['ɪntrəstɪŋlɪ] *adv* de façon intéressante ■ **~ enough, they were out** chose intéressante, ils étaient sortis.

interest rate *n* taux *m* d'intérêt.

interface ◇ *n* ['ɪntəfeɪs] [gen - COMPUT] interface *f*.
◇ *vt* [,ɪntə'feɪs] **1.** [connect] connecter **2.** SEW entoiler.
◇ *vi* [,ɪntə'feɪs] COMPUT & TECH faire interface ■ **to ~ with** faire interface avec, s'interfacer à.

interfacing [,ɪntə'feɪsɪŋ] *n* SEW entoilage *m*.

interfere [,ɪntə'fɪəʳ] *vi* **1.** [intrude] s'immiscer, s'ingérer ■ **to ~ in sb's life** s'immiscer *OR* s'ingérer dans la vie de qqn ■ **I warned him not to ~** je l'ai prévenu de ne pas s'en mêler *OR* de rester à l'écart ■ **I hate the way he always ~s** je déteste sa façon de se mêler de tout **2.** [clash, conflict] : **to ~ with** entraver ■ **to ~ with the course of justice** entraver le cours de la justice ■ **it ~s with my work** cela me gêne dans mon travail ■ **he lets his pride ~ with his judgment** il laisse son orgueil troubler son jugement **3.** [meddle] : **to ~ with** toucher (à) ■ **don't ~ with those wires!** laisse ces fils tranquilles! ■ **to ~ with a child** *euph* se livrer à des attouchements sur un enfant **4.** PHYS interférer **5.** RADIO : **local radio sometimes ~s with police transmissions** la radio locale brouille *OR* perturbe parfois les transmissions de la police.

interference [,ɪntə'fɪərəns] *n* **1.** [gen] ingérence *f*, intervention *f* ■ **she won't tolerate ~ in** *OR* **with her plans** elle ne supportera pas qu'on s'immisce dans ses projets **2.** PHYS interférence *f* **3.** *(U)* RADIO parasites *mpl*, interférence *f* **4.** LING interférence *f*.

interfering [,ɪntə'fɪərɪŋ] *adj* [person] importun.

intergalactic [,ɪntəgə'læktɪk] *adj* intergalactique.

inter-governmental *adj* intergouvernemental.

interim ['ɪntərɪm] ◇ *n* intérim *m*.
◇ *adj* [government, measure, report] provisoire ■ [post, function] intérimaire ■ **~ payment** versement *m* provisionnel.
◆ **in the interim** *adv phr* entre-temps.

interior [ɪn'tɪərɪəʳ] ◇ *adj* intérieur ■ **~ monologue** monologue *m* intérieur ■ **~ angle** MATHS angle *m* interne.
◇ *n* **1.** [gen] intérieur *m* ■ **the French Minister of the Interior** le ministre français de l'Intérieur ■ **Secretary/Department of the Interior** *ministre/ministère chargé de l'administration des domaines et des parcs nationaux aux États-Unis* **2.** ART (tableau *m* d')intérieur *m*.

interior decoration *n* décoration *f* (d'intérieurs).

interior decorator *n* décorateur *m*, - trice *f* (d'intérieurs).

interior design *n* architecture *f* d'intérieurs.

interior designer *n* architecte *mf* d'intérieurs.

interiorize, -ise [ɪn'tɪərɪəraɪz] *vt* intérioriser.

interject [ˌɪntə'dʒekt] *vt* [question, comment] placer ▪ **"not like that," he ~ed** "pas comme ça", coupa-t-il.

interjection [ˌɪntə'dʒekʃn] *n* **1.** LING interjection *f* **2.** [interruption] interruption *f*.

interlace [ˌɪntə'leɪs] <> *vt* **1.** [entwine] entrelacer **2.** [intersperse] entremêler.
<> *vi* s'entrelacer, s'entrecroiser.

interlanguage ['ɪntəˌlæŋgwɪdʒ] *n* LING interlangue *f*.

interleaf ['ɪntəli:f] (*pl* **interleaves** [-li:vz]) *n* feuillet *m* intercalé.

interleave [ˌɪntə'li:v] *vt* [book] interfolier ▪ [sheet] intercaler.

interlock <> *vt* [ˌɪntə'lɒk] **1.** TECH enclencher **2.** [entwine] entrelacer.
<> *vi* [ˌɪntə'lɒk] **1.** TECH [mechanism] s'enclencher ▪ [cogwheels] s'engrener ▪ **~ing chairs** *chaises qui s'accrochent les unes aux autres* **2.** [groups, issues] s'imbriquer.
<> *n* ['ɪntəlɒk] **1.** TECH enclenchement *m* **2.** TEX interlock *m*.

interlocutor [ˌɪntə'lɒkjʊtəʳ] *n* interlocuteur *m*, - trice *f*.

interloper ['ɪntələʊpəʳ] *n* intrus *m*, - e *f*.

interlude ['ɪntəlu:d] *n* **1.** [period of time] intervalle *m* ▪ **a pleasant ~ in her troubled life** un moment de répit dans sa vie mouvementée **2.** THEAT intermède *m* ▪ MUS & TV interlude *m*.

intermarriage [ˌɪntə'mærɪdʒ] *n* **1.** [within family, clan] endogamie *f* **2.** [between different groups] mariage *m* mixte.

intermarry [ˌɪntə'mærɪ] (*pret & pp* **intermarried**) *vi* **1.** [within family, clan] pratiquer l'endogamie **2.** [between different groups] : **members of different religions intermarried freely** les mariages mixtes se pratiquaient librement.

intermediary [ˌɪntə'mi:djərɪ] (*pl* **intermediaries**) <> *adj* intermédiaire.
<> *n* intermédiaire *mf*.

intermediate [ˌɪntə'mi:djət] <> *adj* **1.** [gen] intermédiaire **2.** SCH [class] moyen ▪ **~ students** étudiants *mpl* de niveau moyen OR intermédiaire ▪ **an ~ English course** un cours d'anglais de niveau moyen OR intermédiaire.
<> *n* **1.** US [car] voiture *f* de taille moyenne **2.** CHEM produit *m* intermédiaire.

interment [ɪn'tɜ:mənt] *n* enterrement *m*, inhumation *f*.

interminable [ɪn'tɜ:mɪnəbl] *adj* interminable.

interminably [ɪn'tɜ:mɪnəblɪ] *adv* interminablement ▪ **the play seemed ~ long** la pièce semblait interminable ▪ **the discussions dragged on ~** les discussions s'éternisaient.

intermingle [ˌɪntə'mɪŋgl] *vi* se mêler.

intermission [ˌɪntə'mɪʃn] *n* **1.** [break] pause *f*, trêve *f* ▪ [in illness, fever] intermission *f* ▪ **without ~** sans relâche **2.** CIN & THEAT entracte *m*.

intermittent [ˌɪntə'mɪtənt] *adj* intermittent ▪ **~ rain** pluies *fpl* intermittentes, averses *fpl*.

intermittently [ˌɪntə'mɪtəntlɪ] *adv* par intervalles, par intermittence ▪ **the journal has been published only ~** la revue n'a connu qu'une parution irrégulière.

intern <> *vt* [ɪn'tɜ:n] POL interner.
<> *vi* [ɪn'tɜ:n] US MED faire son internat ▪ SCH faire son stage pédagogique ▪ [with firm] faire un stage en entreprise.
<> *n* ['ɪntɜ:n] **1.** MED interne *mf* ▪ US SCH (professeur *m*) stagiaire *mf* ▪ US [in firm] stagiaire *mf* **2.** [internee] interné *m*, - e *f* (politique).

internal [ɪn'tɜ:nl] <> *adj* **1.** [gen] interne, intérieur ▪ **~ bleeding** hémorragie *f* interne ▪ **~ examination** MED examen *m* interne ▪ **~ injuries** lésions *fpl* internes ▪ **~ rhyme** rime *f* intérieure **2.** [inside country] intérieur **3.** [inside organization, institution] interne ▪ **~ memo** note *f* à circulation interne ▪ **~ disputes are crippling the party** des luttes intestines paralysent le parti ▪ **~ examiner** SCH examinateur *m*, - trice *f* d'un établissement scolaire.
<> *n* MED examen *m* gynécologique.

internal-combustion engine *n* moteur *m* à explosion OR à combustion interne.

internalize, ise [ɪn'tɜ:nəlaɪz] *vt* **1.** [values, behaviour] intérioriser **2.** INDUST & FIN internaliser.

internally [ɪn'tɜ:nəlɪ] *adv* intérieurement ▪ **'not to be taken ~'** PHARM 'à usage externe, ne pas avaler'.

Internal Revenue Service *pr n* US fisc *m*.

international [ˌɪntə'næʃənl] <> *adj* international ▶ **~ law** droit *m* international ▪ **~ relations** relations *fpl* internationales ▪ **~ waters** eaux *fpl* internationales.
<> *n* **1.** SPORT [match] match *m* international ▪ [player] international *m*, - e *f* **2.** POL : **the International** l'Internationale *f*.

International Bank for Reconstruction and Development *pr n* Banque *f* internationale pour la reconstruction et le développement.

International Court of Justice *pr n* Cour *f* internationale de justice.

International Date Line *pr n* ligne *f* de changement de date.

Internationale [ˌɪntənæʃə'nɑ:l] *n* : **the ~** l'Internationale *f*.

internationalist [ˌɪntə'næʃnəlɪst] <> *adj* internationaliste.
<> *n* internationaliste *mf*.

internationalize, ise [ˌɪntə'næʃnəlaɪz] *vt* internationaliser.

International Labour Organization *pr n* Bureau *m* international du travail.

internationally [ˌɪntə'næʃnəlɪ] *adv* internationalement ▪ **~ famous** de renommée internationale ▪ **~ (speaking), the situation is improving** sur le OR au plan international, la situation s'améliore.

International Monetary Fund *pr n* Fonds *m* monétaire international.

internecine [UK ˌɪntə'ni:saɪn, US ˌɪntər'ni:sn] *adj fml* **1.** [within a group] intestin ▪ **~ struggles** luttes *fpl* intestines **2.** [mutually destructive] : **~ warfare** guerre *f* qui ravage les deux camps.

internee [ˌɪntɜ:'ni:] *n* interné *m*, - e *f* (politique).

Internet ['ɪntənet] <> *pr n* Internet *m*.
<> *comp* : **~ café** cybercafé *m* ▪ **~ company** cyberentreprise *f*.

Internet access *n (U)* accès *m* à l'Internet.

Internet banking *n* opérations *fpl* bancaires par l'Internet.

Internet-based *adj* [service, trade] sur Internet ▪ **~ firm** cyberentreprise *f*.

Internet connection *n* connexion *f* Internet.

Internet radio *n* radio *f* par Internet.

Internet service provider *n* fournisseur *m* d'accès, portail *m* électronique.

Internet start-up, Internet start-up company *n* start-up *f*, jeune pousse *f* d'entreprise *offic.*

Internet television, Internet TV *n (U)* télévision *f* Internet.

internist [ɪn'tɜ:nɪst] *n* US MED interniste *mf*, spécialiste *mf* de médecine interne.

internment [ɪn'tɜːnmənt] *n* **1.** [gen] internement *m* (politique) ▪ **~ camp** camp *m* d'internement **2.** [in Ireland] *système de détention des personnes suspectées de terrorisme en Irlande du Nord.*

INTERNMENT

En Irlande du Nord, ce terme désigne l'emprisonnement de terroristes présumés auquel avaient recours les autorités britanniques au début des années 70 pour contrôler les activités de l'IRA (***Irish Republican Army***). Cette pratique fut abandonnée en 1975.

internship ['ɪntɜːnʃɪp] *n* *US* MED internat *m* ▪ [with firm] stage *m* en entreprise.

interpenetrate [,ɪntə'penɪtreɪt] *vt* [permeate] imprégner, pénétrer.

interpersonal [,ɪntə'pɜːsənl] *adj* interpersonnel ▪ **~ skills** qualités *fpl* relationnelles.

interplay ['ɪntəpleɪ] *n* [between forces, events, people] interaction *f*.

Interpol ['ɪntəpɒl] *pr n* Interpol.

interpolate [ɪn'tɜːpəleɪt] *vt* **1.** *fml* [passage of text] interpoler ▪ **he ~d several extra passages into the new edition** dans la nouvelle édition, il a interpolé plusieurs passages supplémentaires **2.** *fml* [interrupt] interrompre **3.** MATHS interpoler.

interpolation [ɪn,tɜːpə'leɪʃn] *n* **1.** *fml* [gen] interpolation *f* **2.** MATHS interpolation *f*.

interpose [,ɪntə'pəʊz] ◇ *vt* **1.** [between objects] interposer, intercaler **2.** [interject] lancer ▪ **he ~d a few apt comments** il lança *OR* plaça quelques remarques pertinentes.
◇ *vi* intervenir, s'interposer ▪ **"that simply isn't true!" he ~d** "c'est tout simplement faux!" lança-t-il.

interpret [ɪn'tɜːprɪt] ◇ *vt* interpréter.
◇ *vi* servir d'interprète, interpréter.

interpretation [ɪn,tɜːprɪ'teɪʃn] *n* interprétation *f* ▪ **she puts quite a different ~ on the facts** l'interprétation qu'elle donne des faits est assez différente ▪ **to be open to ~** donner lieu à interprétation.

interpretative [ɪn'tɜːprɪtətɪv] *adj* interprétatif.

interpreter [ɪn'tɜːprɪtəʳ] *n* **1.** [person] interprète *mf* **2.** COMPUT interpréteur *m*.

interpreting [ɪn'tɜːprɪtɪŋ] *n* [occupation] interprétariat *m*.

interracial [,ɪntə'reɪʃl] *adj* [relations] interracial.

interregnum [,ɪntə'regnəm] (*pl* **interregnums** *OR pl* **interregna** [-'regnə]) *n* interrègne *m* ▪ **the Interregnum** *UK* HIST l'Interrègne *m (intervalle (1649-1660) pendant lequel l'Angleterre, sous l'autorité de Cromwell, fut une république)*.

interrelate [,ɪntərɪ'leɪt] ◇ *vt* mettre en corrélation ▪ **~d questions** questions interdépendantes *OR* intimement liées.
◇ *vi* être interdépendant, interagir.

interrelation [,ɪntərɪ'leɪʃn], **interrelationship** [,ɪntərɪ'leɪʃnʃɪp] *n* corrélation *f*.

interrogate [ɪn'terəgeɪt] *vt* [gen - COMPUT] interroger.

interrogation [ɪn,terə'geɪʃn] *n* [gen - LING & COMPUT] interrogation *f* ▪ [by police] interrogatoire *m* ▪ **she's been under ~** elle a subi un interrogatoire.

interrogation mark *n* point *m* d'interrogation.

interrogative [,ɪntə'rɒgətɪv] ◇ *adj* **1.** [inquiring] interrogateur **2.** LING interrogatif.
◇ *n* [word] interrogatif *m* ▪ [grammatical form] interrogative *f* ▪ **in the ~** à la forme interrogative.

interrogator [ɪn'terəgeɪtəʳ] *n* interrogateur *m*, - trice *f*.

interrogatory [,ɪntə'rɒgətrɪ] *adj* interrogateur.

interrupt [,ɪntə'rʌpt] ◇ *vt* **1.** [person, lecture, conversation] interrompre **2.** [process, activity] interrompre ▪ **we ~ this programme for a news flash** nous interrompons notre émission pour un flash d'information **3.** [uniformity] rompre.
◇ *vi* interrompre ▪ **he tried to explain but you kept ~ing** il a essayé de s'expliquer mais vous n'avez cessé de l'interrompre *OR* de lui couper la parole.
◇ *n* COMPUT interruption *f*.

interruption [,ɪntə'rʌpʃn] *n* interruption *f* ▪ **without ~** sans interruption, sans arrêt.

intersect [,ɪntə'sekt] ◇ *vi* se couper, se croiser ▪ **~ing lines** MATHS lignes intersectées.
◇ *vt* couper, croiser.

intersection [,ɪntə'sekʃn] *n* **1.** [road junction] carrefour *m*, croisement *m* **2.** MATHS intersection *f*.

intersperse [,ɪntə'spɜːs] *vt* parsemer, semer ▪ **our conversation was ~d with long silences** notre conversation était ponctuée de longs silences.

interstate ['ɪntəsteɪt] ◇ *adj* [commerce, highway] entre États.
◇ *n* *US* autoroute *f*.

interstellar [,ɪntə'steləʳ] *adj* interstellaire.

interstice [ɪn'tɜːstɪs] *n* interstice *m*.

intertwine [,ɪntə'twaɪn] ◇ *vt* entrelacer ▪ **their lives are inextricably ~d** leurs vies sont inextricablement liées.
◇ *vi* s'entrelacer.

interval ['ɪntəvl] *n* **1.** [period of time] intervalle *m* ▪ **at ~s** par intervalles, de temps en temps ▪ **at regular ~s** à intervalles réguliers ▪ **at short ~s** à intervalles rapprochés ▪ **at weekly ~s** toutes les semaines, chaque semaine **2.** [interlude] pause *f* ▪ *UK* THEAT entracte *m* ▪ SPORT mi-temps *f* **3.** [distance] intervalle *m*, distance *f* **4.** METEOR **: sunny ~s** éclaircies *fpl* **5.** MATHS & MUS intervalle *m*.

interval ownership *n* *US* multipropriété *f*.

intervene [,ɪntə'viːn] *vi* **1.** [person, government] intervenir ▪ **they were unwilling to ~ in the conflict** ils ne souhaitaient pas intervenir dans le conflit ▪ **I warned him not to ~** [in fight] je lui avais bien dit de ne pas intervenir *OR* s'interposer ; [in argument] je lui avais bien dit de ne pas s'en mêler **2.** [event] survenir ▪ **he was about to go to college when war ~d** il allait entrer à l'université lorsque la guerre a éclaté **3.** [time] s'écouler **4.** [interrupt] intervenir.

intervening [,ɪntə'viːnɪŋ] *adj* [period of time] intermédiaire ▪ **during the ~ period** dans l'intervalle, entre-temps.

intervention [,ɪntə'venʃn] *n* intervention *f*.

interventionism [,ɪntə'venʃənɪzm] *n* interventionnisme *m*.

interventionist [,ɪntə'venʃənɪst] ◇ *adj* interventionniste.
◇ *n* interventionniste *mf*.

interview ['ɪntəvjuː] ◇ *n* **1.** [for job, university place etc] entrevue *f*, entretien *m* ▪ **~s will be held at our London offices** les entretiens se dérouleront dans nos bureaux de Londres ▪ **to invite** *OR* **to call sb for ~** convoquer qqn pour une entrevue **2.** PRESS, RADIO & TV interview *f* ▪ **she gave him an exclusive ~** elle lui a accordé une interview en exclusivité.
◇ *vt* **1.** [for university place, job etc] avoir une entrevue *OR* un entretien avec ▪ **shortlisted applicants will be ~ed in March** les candidats sélectionnés seront convoqués pour un entretien en mars ▪ **we have ~ed ten people for the post** nous avons déjà vu dix personnes pour ce poste ▮ [for opinion poll] interroger, sonder **2.** PRESS, RADIO & TV interviewer **3.** [subj: police] interroger, questionner ▪ **he is being ~ed in connection with a series of thefts** on l'interroge pour une série de vols.
◇ *vi* [interviewer] faire passer un entretien ▪ [candidate] **: he ~s well/badly** il s'en sort/ne s'en sort pas bien aux entretiens.

interviewee [,ɪntəvjuː'iː] *n* interviewé *m*, - e *f*.

interviewer ['ɪntəvjuːəʳ] *n* **1.** [for media] interviewer *m*, intervieweur *m*, - euse *f* ▪ [for opinion poll] enquêteur *m*, - euse *f*, - trice *f* **2.** [for job] **: the ~ asked me what my present salary was** la personne qui m'a fait passer l'entretien *OR* l'entrevue m'a demandé quel était mon salaire actuel.

interwar [ˌɪntəˈwɔːʳ] *adj* : **the ~ period** *OR* **years** l'entre-deux-guerres *m*.

interweave [ˌɪntəˈwiːv] (*pret* **interwove** [-ˈwəʊv] *OR* **interweaved**, *pp* **interwoven** [-ˈwəʊvn] *OR* **interweaved**) ◇ *vt* entrelacer ▪ **interwoven with** entrelacé de ▪ **our lives have become closely interwoven** *fig* nos deux vies sont devenues intimement liées.
◇ *vi* s'entrelacer, s'entremêler.

intestate [ɪnˈtesteɪt] ◇ *adj* intestat *(inv)* ▪ **to die ~** décéder intestat.
◇ *n* intestat *mf*.

intestinal [ɪnˈtestɪnl] *adj* intestinal.

intestine [ɪnˈtestɪn] *n (usu pl)* intestin *m* ◐ **large ~** gros intestin ▪ **small ~** intestin grêle.

intimacy [ˈɪntɪməsɪ] (*pl* **intimacies**) *n* **1.** [closeness, warmth] intimité *f* **2.** [privacy] intimité *f* **3.** *(U) euph & fml* [sexual relations] relations *fpl* sexuelles, rapports *mpl*.
◆ **intimacies** *npl* [familiarities] familiarités *fpl* ▪ **they never really exchanged intimacies** ils ont toujours gardé une certaine réserve l'un envers l'autre.

intimate ◇ *adj* [ˈɪntɪmət] **1.** [friend, relationship] intime ▪ **we were never very ~** nous n'avons jamais été (des amis) intimes ▪ **we're on ~ terms with them** nous sommes très amis, ils font partie de nos amis intimes **2.** [small and cosy] intime ▪ **an ~ (little) dinner party** un dîner en tête-à-tête, un petit dîner à deux **3.** *euph & fml* [sexually] : **they were ~ on more than one occasion** ils ont eu des rapports (intimes) à plusieurs reprises **4.** [personal, private] intime **5.** [thorough] profond, approfondi ▪ **she has an ~ knowledge of the field** elle connaît le sujet à fond **6.** [close, direct] étroit.
◇ *n* [ˈɪntɪmət] intime *mf*.
◇ *vt* [ˈɪntɪmeɪt] [hint, imply] laisser entendre, insinuer ▪ **he ~d that he had had an affair with her** il a laissé entendre qu'il avait eu une liaison avec elle.

intimately [ˈɪntɪmətlɪ] *adv* **1.** [talk, behave - in a friendly way] intimement **2.** [know - thoroughly] à fond ; [- closely, directly] étroitement ▪ **I am ~ acquainted with the details of the matter** je connais l'affaire dans ses moindres détails.

intimation [ˌɪntɪˈmeɪʃn] *n fml* [suggestion] suggestion *f* ▪ [sign] indice *m*, indication *f* ▪ [premonition] pressentiment *m* ▪ **we had no ~ that disaster was imminent** rien ne laissait pressentir l'imminence d'une catastrophe.

intimidate [ɪnˈtɪmɪdeɪt] *vt* intimider ▪ **don't let him ~ you** ne le laisse pas t'intimider, ne te laisse pas intimider par lui.

intimidating [ɪnˈtɪmɪdeɪtɪŋ] *adj* intimidant.

intimidation [ɪnˌtɪmɪˈdeɪʃn] *n (U)* intimidation *f*, menaces *fpl*.

into [ˈɪntʊ] *prep* **1.** [indicating direction, movement etc] dans ▪ **come ~ my office** venez dans mon bureau ▪ **planes take off ~ the wind** les avions décollent face au vent **2.** [indicating collision] dans ▪ **the truck ran** *OR* **crashed ~ the wall** le camion est rentré dans *OR* s'est écrasé contre le mur **3.** [indicating transformation] en ▪ **mix the ingredients ~ a paste** mélangez les ingrédients jusqu'à ce qu'ils forment une pâte **4.** [indicating result] : **to frighten sb ~ confessing** faire avouer qqn en lui faisant peur ▪ **they were shocked ~ silence** le choc leur a fait perdre la parole **5.** [indicating division] en ▪ **cut it ~ three** coupe-le en trois ▪ **6 ~ 10 won't go** on ne peut pas diviser 10 par 6 **6.** [indicating elapsed time] : **we worked well ~ the night** nous avons travaillé (jusque) tard dans la nuit ▪ **he must be well ~ his forties** il doit avoir la quarantaine bien passée *OR* sonnée ▪ **a week ~ her holiday and she's bored already** il y a à peine une semaine qu'elle est en vacances et elle s'ennuie déjà **7.** *inf* [fond of] : **to be ~ sthg** être passionné par qqch ▪ **is he ~ drugs?** est-ce qu'il se drogue? **8.** [curious about] : **the baby's ~ everything** le bébé est curieux de tout.

intolerable [ɪnˈtɒlrəbl] *adj* intolérable, insupportable.

intolerably [ɪnˈtɒlrəblɪ] *adv* intolérablement, insupportablement.

intolerance [ɪnˈtɒlərəns] *n* [gen - MED] intolérance *f*.

intolerant [ɪnˈtɒlərənt] *adj* intolérant ▪ **she is very ~ of fools** elle ne supporte absolument pas les imbéciles.

intolerantly [ɪnˈtɒlərəntlɪ] *adv* avec intolérance.

intonation [ˌɪntəˈneɪʃn] *n* intonation *f* ▪ **~ pattern** LING intonation.

intone [ɪnˈtəʊn] *vt* entonner.

intoxicate [ɪnˈtɒksɪkeɪt] *vt* **1.** *liter & fig* enivrer, griser **2.** MED [poison] intoxiquer.

intoxicated [ɪnˈtɒksɪkeɪtɪd] *adj* **1.** [drunk] ivre, en état d'ébriété *fml* **2.** *fig* ivre ▪ **she was ~ by success** son succès l'avait grisée *OR* lui avait fait tourner la tête.

intoxicating [ɪnˈtɒksɪkeɪtɪŋ] *adj liter* enivrant ▪ *fig* grisant, enivrant, excitant ▪ **~ liquor** boisson *f* alcoolisée.

intoxication [ɪnˌtɒksɪˈkeɪʃn] *n* **1.** *liter & fig* ivresse *f* **2.** MED [poisoning] intoxication *f*.

intractable [ɪnˈtræktəbl] *adj* **1.** [person] intraitable, intransigeant **2.** [problem] insoluble ▪ [situation] inextricable, sans issue.

intramural [ˌɪntrəˈmjʊərəl] *adj* SCH & UNIV [courses, sports] interne (à l'établissement).

intranet [ˈɪntrənet] *n* intranet *m*.

intransigence [ɪnˈtrænzɪdʒəns] *n* intransigeance *f*.

intransigent [ɪnˈtrænzɪdʒənt] ◇ *adj* intransigeant.
◇ *n* intransigeant *m*, - e *f*.

intransitive [ɪnˈtrænzətɪv] ◇ *adj* intransitif.
◇ *n* intransitif *m*.

intrastate [ˌɪntrəˈsteɪt] *adj* à l'intérieur d'un même État.

intrauterine device *n* stérilet *m*.

intravenous [ˌɪntrəˈviːnəs] *adj* intraveineux ▪ **~ drugs user** usager *m* de drogue par voie intraveineuse ▪ **~ injection** (injection *f*) intraveineuse *f*.

intravenously [ˌɪntrəˈviːnəslɪ] *adv* par voie intraveineuse ▪ **he's being fed ~** on l'alimente par perfusion.

in-tray *n* corbeille *f* de courrier à traiter *OR* "arrivée".

intrepid [ɪnˈtrepɪd] *adj* intrépide.

intricacy [ˈɪntrɪkəsɪ] (*pl* **intricacies**) *n* **1.** [complicated detail] complexité *f* ▪ **I couldn't follow all the intricacies of her argument** je n'ai pas suivi toutes les subtilités de son raisonnement **2.** [complexity] complexité *f*.

intricate [ˈɪntrɪkət] *adj* complexe, compliqué ▪ **~ patterns** des motifs complexes *OR* très élaborés.

intricately [ˈɪntrɪkətlɪ] *adv* de façon complexe *OR* compliquée.

intrigue [ɪnˈtriːg] ◇ *n* **1.** [plotting] intrigue *f* ▪ **the boardroom was rife with ~** la salle du conseil d'administration sentait l'intrigue **2.** [plot, treason] complot *m* **3.** [love affair] intrigue *f*.
◇ *vt* intriguer ▪ **I'd be ~d to know where they met** je serais curieux de savoir où ils se sont rencontrés.
◇ *vi* intriguer, comploter.

intriguing [ɪnˈtriːgɪŋ] *adj* bizarre, curieux ▪ **it's an ~ idea!** c'est une idée bizarre!

intriguingly [ɪnˈtriːgɪŋlɪ] *adv* bizarrement, curieusement.

intrinsic [ɪnˈtrɪnsɪk] *adj* intrinsèque ▪ **the picture has little ~ value** ce tableau a peu de valeur en soi ▪ **such ideas are ~ to my argument** de telles idées sont essentielles *OR* inhérentes à mon raisonnement.

intrinsically [ɪnˈtrɪnsɪklɪ] *adv* intrinsèquement.

intro [ˈɪntrəʊ] (*pl* **intros**) *n inf* introduction *f*, intro *f*.

introduce [ˌɪntrəˈdjuːs] *vt* **1.** [present - one person to another] présenter ▪ **she ~d me to her sister** elle m'a présenté à sa sœur ▪ **may I ~ you?** permettez-moi de *OR* laissez-moi vous présenter ▪ **let me ~ myself, I'm John** je me présente? John

■ **has everyone been ~d?** les présentations ont été faites? ■ **I don't think we've been ~d, have we?** nous n'avons pas été présentés? je crois? **2.** [radio or TV programme] présenter **3.** [bring in] introduire ■ **her arrival ~d a note of sadness into the festivities** son entrée mit une note de tristesse dans la fête **4.** [laws, legislation] déposer, présenter ■ [reform] introduire **5.** [initiate] initier ■ **to ~ sb to sthg** initier qqn à qqch, faire découvrir qqch à qqn **6.** [start] ouvrir, donner le départ **7.** *fml* [insert, put in] introduire.

introduction [ˌɪntrəˈdʌkʃn] *n* **1.** [of one person to another] présentation *f* ■ **would you do** *inf* OR **make the ~s?** peux-tu faire les présentations? ■ **our next guest needs no ~** inutile de vous présenter l'invité suivant **2.** [first part - of book, speech, piece of music] introduction *f* **3.** [basic textbook, course] introduction *f*, initiation *f* ■ **an ~ to his more difficult work** une introduction aux parties difficiles de son œuvre **4.** [bringing in] introduction *f* ■ **the ~ of computer technology into schools** l'introduction de l'informatique à l'école **5.** [of bill, law] introduction *f*, présentation *f* **6.** [insertion] introduction *f*.

introductory [ˌɪntrəˈdʌktrɪ] *adj* [remarks] préliminaire ■ [chapter, course] d'introduction ■ **~ offer** COMM offre *f* de lancement.

introspection [ˌɪntrəˈspekʃn] *n* introspection *f*.

introspective [ˌɪntrəˈspektɪv] *adj* introspectif.

introversion [ˌɪntrəˈvɜːʃn] *n* introversion *f*.

introvert [ˈɪntrəvɜːt] <> *n* PSYCHOL introverti *m*, - e *f*.
<> *vt* introvertir.

introverted [ˈɪntrəvɜːtɪd] *adj* PSYCHOL introverti.

intrude [ɪnˈtruːd] *vi* **1.** [disturb] déranger, s'imposer ■ **I hope I'm not intruding** j'espère que je ne vous dérange pas **2.** [interfere with] : **I don't let my work ~ on my private life** je ne laisse pas mon travail empiéter sur ma vie privée ■ **I felt I was intruding on their grief** j'ai eu l'impression de les déranger dans leur chagrin.

intruder [ɪnˈtruːdər] *n* [criminal] cambrioleur *m* ■ [outsider] intrus *m*, - e *f*, importun *m*, - e *f*.

intrusion [ɪnˈtruːʒn] *n* **1.** [gen] intrusion *f*, ingérence *f* ■ **it's an ~ into our privacy** c'est une intrusion dans notre vie privée **2.** GEOL intrusion *f*.

intrusive [ɪnˈtruːsɪv] *adj* **1.** [person] importun **2.** GEOL intrusif **3.** LING : **~ consonant** consonne *f* d'appui.

intuit [ɪnˈtjuːɪt] *vt fml* savoir OR connaître intuitivement ■ **I could only ~ what had happened between them** je n'ai pu que deviner ce qui s'était passé entre eux.

intuition [ˌɪntjuːˈɪʃn] *n* intuition *f* ■ **I had an ~ something was wrong** j'avais le sentiment que quelque chose n'allait pas.

intuitive [ɪnˈtjuːɪtɪv] *adj* intuitif.

intuitively [ɪnˈtjuːɪtɪvlɪ] *adv* intuitivement.

Inuit [ˈɪnuɪt] (*pl inv* OR *pl* **Inuits**) <> *n* Inuit *mf*.
<> *adj* inuit.

inundate [ˈɪnʌndeɪt] *vt liter & fig* inonder ■ **we've been ~d with phone calls/letters** nous avons été submergés de coups de fil/courrier ■ **I'm ~d with work just now** pour l'instant je suis débordé (de travail) OR je croule sous le travail.

inundation [ˌɪnʌnˈdeɪʃn] *n* inondation *f*.

inure [ɪˈnjʊər] <> *vt* aguerrir ■ **to become ~d to** s'habituer à.
<> *vi* [law] entrer en vigueur.

invade [ɪnˈveɪd] *vt* **1.** MIL envahir **2.** *fig* envahir ■ **to ~ sb's privacy** s'immiscer dans la vie privée de qqn.

invader [ɪnˈveɪdər] *n* envahisseur *m*, - euse *f*.

invading [ɪnˈveɪdɪŋ] *adj* **1.** [army] d'invasion ■ **the ~ barbarians** l'envahisseur barbare **2.** [plants, insects] envahissant.

invalid¹ <> *n* [ˈɪnvəlɪd] [disabled person] infirme *mf*, invalide *mf* ■ [ill person] malade *mf*.
<> *adj* [ˈɪnvəlɪd] [disabled] infirme, invalide ■ [ill] malade ■ **~ chair** fauteuil *m* roulant.
<> *vt* [ˈɪnvəliːd] **1.** [disable] rendre infirme **2.** UK MIL : **he was ~ed home** il a été rapatrié pour raisons médicales.
◆ **invalid out** *vt sep* MIL : **to ~ sb out of the army** réformer qqn pour raisons médicales.

invalid² [ɪnˈvælɪd] *adj* **1.** [passport, ticket] non valide, non valable **2.** [law, marriage, election] nul **3.** [argument] non valable.

invalidate [ɪnˈvælɪdeɪt] *vt* **1.** [contract, agreement etc] invalider, annuler **2.** [argument] infirmer.

invalid car, invalid carriage *n* UK voiture *f* d'infirme.

invalidity [ˌɪnvəˈlɪdətɪ] *n* **1.** MED invalidité *f* **2.** [of contract, agreement etc] manque *m* de validité, nullité *f* **3.** [of argument] manque *m* de fondement.

invalidity benefit *n* UK prestation *f* d'invalidité *(aujourd'hui remplacée par l'"incapacity benefit")*.

invaluable [ɪnˈvæljʊəbl] *adj* inestimable, très précieux ■ **your help has been ~ (to me)** votre aide m'a été très précieuse.

invariable [ɪnˈveərɪəbl] <> *adj* invariable.
<> *n* MATHS constante *f*.

invariably [ɪnˈveərɪəblɪ] *adv* invariablement ■ **she was almost ~ dressed in black** elle était presque toujours habillée en noir.

invariant [ɪnˈveərɪənt] <> *adj* invariant.
<> *n* invariant *m*.

invasion [ɪnˈveɪʒn] *n* **1.** MIL invasion *f*, envahissement *m* ■ **the Roman ~ of England** l'invasion de l'Angleterre par les Romains **2.** *fig* invasion *f*, intrusion *f* ■ **he considered it an ~ of privacy** il l'a ressenti comme une intrusion dans sa vie privée.

invasive [ɪnˈveɪsɪv] *adj* MED [surgery] invasif ■ *fig* envahissant.

invective [ɪnˈvektɪv] *n (U)* invective *f*, invectives *fpl* ■ **a stream of ~** un torrent d'invectives.

inveigh [ɪnˈveɪ] *vi fml* **to ~ against sb/sthg** invectiver qqn/qqch, pester contre qqn/qqch.

inveigle [ɪnˈveɪgl] *vt* manipuler ■ **he had been ~d into letting them in** on l'avait adroitement manipulé pour qu'il les laisse entrer.

invent [ɪnˈvent] *vt* **1.** [new machine, process] inventer **2.** [lie, excuse] inventer.

invention [ɪnˈvenʃn] *n* **1.** [discovery, creation] invention *f* **2.** [untruth] invention *f*, fabrication *f* ■ **it was pure ~** ce n'était que pure invention, c'était complètement faux.

inventive [ɪnˈventɪv] *adj* [person, mind] inventif ■ [plan, solution] ingénieux.

inventiveness [ɪnˈventɪvnɪs] *n* esprit *m* d'invention, inventivité *f*.

inventor [ɪnˈventər] *n* inventeur *m*, - trice *f*.

inventory [ˈɪnvəntrɪ] (*pl* **inventories**, *pret & pp* **inventoried**) <> *n* **1.** [list] inventaire *m* ■ **to draw up** OR **to make an ~** dresser un inventaire ■ **to take the ~** faire l'inventaire **2.** *(U)* US [stock] stock *m*, stocks *mpl* ■ **~ control** OR **management** gestion *f* des stocks.
<> *vt* inventorier.

inverse [ɪnˈvɜːs] <> *adj* inverse ■ **to be in ~ proportion to** être inversement proportionnel à ■ **in ~ video** COMPUT en vidéo inverse.
<> *n* inverse *m*, contraire *m* ■ MATHS inverse *m*.

inversely [ɪnˈvɜːslɪ] *adv* inversement.

inversion [ɪnˈvɜːʃn] *n* **1.** [gen] inversion *f* ■ [of roles, relations] renversement *m* **2.** MUS [of chord] renversement *m* ■ [in counterpoint] inversion *f* **3.** ANAT, ELEC & MATHS inversion *f*.

invert <> *vt* [ɪnˈvɜːt] **1.** [turn upside down or inside out] inverser, retourner ■ [switch around] intervertir ■ [roles] intervertir, renverser **2.** MUS [chord] renverser ■ [interval] inverser **3.** CHEM [sugar] invertir.
<> *n* [ˈɪnvɜːt] PSYCHOL inverti *m*, - e *f*.

invertebrate [ɪn'vɜ:tɪbreɪt] ◇ *adj* invertébré.
◇ *n* invertébré *m*.

inverted commas [ɪn'vɜ:tɪd-] *npl UK* guillemets *mpl* ■ **in ~** entre guillemets.

inverted snob *n UK personne d'origine modeste qui affiche du mépris pour les valeurs bourgeoises.*

inverter, invertor [ɪn'vɜ:tər] *n* **1.** ELEC onduleur *m* (de courant) **2.** COMPUT inverseur *m*.

invest [ɪn'vest] ◇ *vi* investir ■ **to ~ in shares/in the oil industry/on the stock market** investir en actions/dans l'industrie pétrolière/en Bourse ■ **you ought to ~ in a new coat** *inf* tu devrais t'offrir *OR* te payer un nouveau manteau.
◇ *vt* **1.** [money] investir, placer ■ **they ~ed five million dollars in new machinery** ils ont investi cinq millions de dollars dans de nouveaux équipements **2.** [time, effort] investir ■ **we've ~ed a lot of time and energy in this project** nous avons investi beaucoup de temps et d'énergie dans ce projet **3.** *fml* [confer on] investir ■ **~ed with the highest authority** investi de la plus haute autorité **4.** MIL [besiege, surround] investir.

investigate [ɪn'vestɪgeɪt] ◇ *vt* [allegation, crime, accident] enquêter sur ■ [problem, situation] examiner, étudier.
◇ *vi* enquêter, mener une enquête.

investigation [ɪn,vestɪ'geɪʃn] *n* [into crime, accident] enquête *f* ■ [of problem, situation] examen *m*, étude *f* ■ **his activities are under ~** une enquête a été ouverte sur ses activités ■ **your case is currently under ~** nous étudions actuellement votre cas.

investigative [ɪn'vestɪgətɪv] *adj* PRESS, RADIO & TV d'investigation ■ **~ journalism** journalisme *m* d'investigation *OR* d'enquête.

investigator [ɪn'vestɪgeɪtər] *n* enquêteur *m*, - euse *f*, - trice *f*.

investigatory [ɪn'vestɪgeɪtərɪ] *adj* d'investigation.

investiture [ɪn'vestɪtʃər] *n* investiture *f*.

investment [ɪn'vestmənt] *n* **1.** [of money, capital] investissement *m*, placement *m* ■ **the company has ~s all over the world** la société a des capitaux investis dans le monde entier **2.** [of time, effort] investissement *m* **3.** = **investiture**.

investment analyst *n* analyste *mf* en placements.

investment bank *n* ≃ banque *f* d'affaires.

investment trust *n* société *f* de placement.

investor [ɪn'vestər] *n* investisseur *m* ■ [shareholder] actionnaire *mf*.

inveterate [ɪn'vetərət] *adj* **1.** [habit, dislike] invétéré ■ [hatred] tenace **2.** [drinker, gambler] invétéré ■ [bachelor, liar, smoker] impénitent.

invidious [ɪn'vɪdɪəs] *adj* [unfair] injuste ■ [unpleasant] ingrat, pénible.

invigilate [ɪn'vɪdʒɪleɪt] *vi* & *vt UK* SCH & UNIV surveiller *(pendant un examen)*.

invigilator [ɪn'vɪdʒɪleɪtər] *n UK* SCH & UNIV surveillant *m*, - e *f* *(d'un examen)*.

invigorate [ɪn'vɪgəreɪt] *vt* revigorer, vivifier ■ **she felt ~d by the cold wind** le vent frais la revigorait.

invigorating [ɪn'vɪgəreɪtɪŋ] *adj* [air, climate] tonique, tonifiant, vivifiant ■ [walk] revigorant ■ [bath] tonifiant ■ [discussion] enrichissant.

invincibility [ɪn,vɪnsɪ'bɪlətɪ] *n* invincibilité *f*.

invincible [ɪn'vɪnsɪbl] *adj* [army, troops] invincible ■ [belief] inébranlable.

inviolable [ɪn'vaɪələbl] *adj* inviolable.

inviolate [ɪn'vaɪələt] *adj lit* inviolé.

invisibility [ɪn,vɪzɪ'bɪlətɪ] *n* invisibilité *f*.

invisible [ɪn'vɪzɪbl] *adj* **1.** invisible ■ **~ to the naked eye** invisible à l'œil nu ➲ **~ mending** stoppage *m* **2.** COMM [unrecorded] : **~ assets** biens *mpl* incorporels ■ **~ balance** balance *f* des invisibles ■ **~ earnings** revenus *mpl* invisibles ■ **~ imports** importations *fpl* invisibles.

invisible ink *n* encre *f* invisible *OR* sympathique.

invitation [,ɪnvɪ'teɪʃn] *n* invitation *f* ■ **have you sent out the wedding ~s?** as-tu envoyé les invitations au mariage? ■ **she's here at my ~** c'est moi qui l'ai invitée ■ **at the ~ of** à l'invitation de ■ **by ~ only** sur invitation seulement ■ **a standing ~** une invitation permanente ■ **prison conditions are an (open) ~ to violence** *fig* les conditions de détention sont une véritable incitation à la violence.

invite ◇ *vt* [ɪn'vaɪt] **1.** [ask to come] inviter ■ **to ~ sb for lunch** inviter qqn à déjeuner ■ **I ~d him up for a coffee** je l'ai invité à monter prendre un café **2.** [ask to do sthg] demander, solliciter ■ **I've been ~d for interview** j'ai été convoqué à un entretien **3.** [solicit] : **he ~d comment on his book** il a demandé aux gens leur avis sur son livre ■ **we ~ applications from all qualified candidates** nous invitons tous les candidats ayant le profil requis à postuler ■ **we ~ suggestions from readers** toute suggestion de la part de nos lecteurs est la bienvenue **4.** [trouble, defeat, disaster] aller au devant de ■ [doubt, sympathy] appeler, attirer.
◇ *n* ['ɪnvaɪt] *inf* invitation *f*.
➡ **invite out** *vt sep* inviter (à sortir).

inviting [ɪn'vaɪtɪŋ] *adj* [gesture] d'invitation ■ [eyes, smile] engageant ■ [display] attirant, attrayant ■ [idea] tentant, séduisant ■ [place, fire] accueillant.

in vitro [,ɪn'vi:trəʊ] ◇ *adj* in vitro ■ **~ fertilization** fécondation *f* in vitro.
◇ *adv* in vitro.

invoice ['ɪnvɔɪs] ◇ *n* COMM facture *f* ■ **to make out an ~** établir une facture.
◇ *vt* [goods] facturer ■ **to ~ sb for sthg** facturer qqch à qqn.

invoice clerk *n* facturier *m*, - ère *f*.

invoke [ɪn'vəʊk] *vt* **1.** [cite] invoquer **2.** [call upon] en appeler à, faire appel à **3.** [conjure up] invoquer ■ **to ~ evil spirits** invoquer les mauvais esprits.

involuntarily [ɪn'vɒləntrəlɪ] *adv* involontairement.

involuntary [ɪn'vɒləntrɪ] *adj* involontaire.

involve [ɪn'vɒlv] *vt* **1.** [entail] impliquer, comporter ■ **it ~s a lot of work** cela implique *OR* nécessite *OR* veut dire beaucoup de travail ■ **what does the job ~?** en quoi consiste le travail? ■ **a job which ~s meeting people** un travail où l'on est amené à rencontrer beaucoup de gens ■ **it won't ~ you in much expense** cela ne t'entraînera pas dans de grosses dépenses **2.** [concern, affect] concerner, toucher ■ **there are too many accidents involving children** il y a trop d'accidents dont les enfants sont les victimes **3.** [bring in, implicate] impliquer ■ **it was a huge operation involving thousands of helpers** c'était une opération gigantesque qui a nécessité l'aide de milliers de gens ■ **several vehicles were ~d in the accident** plusieurs véhicules étaient impliqués dans cet accident ■ **we try to ~ the parents in the running of the school** nous essayons de faire participer les parents à la vie de l'école ■ **I'm not going to ~ myself in their private affairs** je ne vais pas me mêler de leur vie privée *OR* de leurs affaires **4.** [absorb, engage] absorber.

involved [ɪn'vɒlvd] *adj* **1.** [complicated] compliqué, complexe **2.** [implicated] impliqué ■ **I don't want to get ~** je ne veux pas être impliqué, je ne veux rien avoir à faire avec cela ■ **they became ~ in a long war** ils se sont trouvés entraînés dans une longue guerre ■ **the amount of work ~ is enormous** la quantité de travail à fournir est énorme ■ **he had no idea of the problems ~** il n'avait aucune idée des problèmes en jeu *OR* en cause ■ **over 100 companies are ~ in the scheme** plus de 100 sociétés sont associées à *OR* parties prenantes dans ce projet ■ **I think he's ~ in advertising** je crois qu'il est dans la publicité ■ **to be ~ in politics** prendre part à la vie politique **3.** [absorbed] absorbé ■ **she's too ~ in her work to notice** elle est trop absorbée par son travail pour remarquer quoi que ce soit **4.** [emotionally] : **to be ~ with sb** avoir une liaison avec qqn ■ **he doesn't want to get ~** il ne veut pas s'engager.

involvement [ɪn'vɒlvmənt] *n* **1.** [participation] participation *f* ■ **they were against American ~ in the war** ils étaient opposés à toute participation américaine au conflit **2.** [commitment] investissement *m*, engagement *m* **3.** [relationship] liaison *f* ■ **he's frightened of emotional ~** il a peur de s'engager sentimentalement, il redoute tout engagement affectif **4.** [complexity] complexité *f*, complication *f*.

invulnerable [ɪn'vʌlnərəbl] *adj* invulnérable ■ **~ to attack** invulnérable à toute attaque, inattaquable.

inward ['ɪnwəd] ◇ *adj* **1.** [thoughts, satisfaction] intime, secret, - ète *f* **2.** [movement] vers l'intérieur.
◇ *adv US* = **inwards**.

inward-looking *adj* [person] introverti, replié sur soi ■ [group] replié sur soi, fermé ■ [philosophy] introspectif ■ *pej* nombriliste ■ **he's become very ~ lately** il s'est beaucoup refermé *OR* replié sur lui-même ces derniers temps.

inwardly ['ɪnwədlɪ] *adv* [pleased, disgusted] secrètement ■ **he smiled ~** il sourit intérieurement ■ **~ I was still convinced that I was right** en mon for intérieur, j'étais toujours convaincu d'avoir raison.

inwards ['ɪnwədz] *adv* **1.** [turn, face] vers l'intérieur **2.** [into one's own heart, soul etc] : **my thoughts turned ~** je me suis replié sur moi-même ■ **he said we should look ~ to find our true selves** il a dit que c'est en nous-mêmes qu'il fallait chercher notre véritable identité.

in-your-face *adj* **1.** [uncompromising - documentary, film] cru **2.** [aggressive - attitude, personality] agressif.

I/O (*written abbrev of* **input/output**) E/S.

IOC (*abbrev of* **International Olympic Committee**) *pr n* CIO *m*.

iodine [*UK* 'aɪədiːn, *US* 'aɪədaɪn] *n* iode *m* ■ PHARM teinture *f* d'iode.

IOM *written abbr of* **Isle of Man**.

ion ['aɪən] *n* ion *m*.

Ionian [aɪ'əʊnjən] ◇ *n* **1.** [person] Ionien *m*, - enne *f* **2.** LING ionien *m*.
◇ *adj* ionien.

Ionic [aɪ'ɒnɪk] *adj* ARCHIT ionique.

ionosphere [aɪ'ɒnə,sfɪəʳ] *n* ionosphère *f*.

iota [aɪ'əʊtə] *n* **1.** [Greek letter] iota *m* **2.** [tiny bit] brin *m*, grain *m*, iota *m* ■ **there's not one ~ of truth in the letter** il n'y a pas un brin *OR* grain de vrai dans cette lettre.

IOU (*abbrev of* **I owe you**) *n reconnaissance de dette*.

IOW *written abbr of* **Isle of Wight**.

Iowa ['aɪəʊə] *pr n* Iowa *m* ■ **in ~** dans l'Iowa.

IPA (*abbrev of* **International Phonetic Alphabet**) *n* API *m*.

iPod® ['aɪpɒd] *n* iPod® *m*.

IQ (*abbrev of* **intelligence quotient**) *n* QI *m*.

IRA ◇ *pr n* (*abbrev of* **Irish Republican Army**) IRA *f*.
◇ *n US* (*abbrev of* **individual retirement account**) *compte d'épargne retraite (à avantages fiscaux)*.

IRA

L'IRA est une organisation luttant pour la réunification de l'Irlande. En 1969, elle s'est scindée en deux et a donné naissance à la *Provisional IRA* et à l'*Official IRA*. En 1994, le processus de paix progressant, l'IRA s'est engagée à ne plus recourir à la violence. Le cessez-le-feu a été rompu plusieurs fois depuis, mais l'IRA, dans sa majorité, a suivi le Sinn Féin dans cette marche vers la paix (marquée en particulier par la signature de l'accord de paix d'Ulster, en avril 1998, le *Good Friday Agreement*). Depuis, deux factions sont apparues: la *Real IRA* et la *Continuity IRA*, prêtes à reprendre la lutte armée pour la réunification de l'Irlande.

Iran [ɪ'rɑːn] *pr n* Iran *m* ■ **in ~** en Iran.

Irangate [ɪ'rɑːngeɪt] *pr n* : **the ~ scandal** *scandale politique sous le mandat Reagan: le Président aurait autorisé la vente d'armes à l'Iran contre la mise en liberté d'otages américains, et versé une partie des revenus de ces opérations aux contras du Nicaragua*.

Iranian [ɪ'reɪnjən] ◇ *n* **1.** [person] Iranien *m*, - enne *f* **2.** LING iranien *m*.
◇ *adj* iranien.

Iraq [ɪ'rɑːk] *pr n* Iraq *m*, Irak *m* ■ **in ~** en Iraq.

Iraqi [ɪ'rɑːkɪ] ◇ *n* Irakien *m*, - enne *f*, Iraquien *m*, - enne *f*.
◇ *adj* irakien.

irascible [ɪ'ræsəbl] *adj* irascible, coléreux.

irate [aɪ'reɪt] *adj* furieux ■ **she got most ~ about it** cela l'a rendue furieuse ■ **an ~ letter** une lettre courroucée.

ire ['aɪəʳ] *n lit* courroux *m*.

Ireland ['aɪələnd] *pr n* Irlande *f* ■ **in ~** en Irlande ■ **the Republic of ~** la république d'Irlande.

iridescence [,ɪrɪ'desəns] *n* irisation *f*.

iridescent [,ɪrɪ'desənt] *adj* irisé, iridescent *lit*.

iris ['aɪərɪs] (*pl* **irises**) *n* **1.** (*pl also* *irides* [ɪrɪdiːz]) ANAT iris *m* **2.** BOT iris *m*.

Irish ['aɪrɪʃ] ◇ *npl* : **the ~** les Irlandais.
◇ *n* LING irlandais *m*.
◇ *adj* irlandais ■ **the ~ Free State** l'État *m* libre d'Irlande ■ **~ joke** *plaisanterie véhiculant une image négative des Irlandais*.

THE IRISH FREE STATE

En 1921, après deux ans de guerre civile, la partition de l'Irlande donna naissance à l'Irlande du Nord et à l'État libre d'Irlande, membre du Commonwealth.

Irish coffee *n* irish-coffee *m*.

Irishman ['aɪrɪʃmən] (*pl* **Irishmen** [-mən]) *n* Irlandais *m*.

Irish Sea *pr n* : **the ~** la mer d'Irlande.

Irish wolfhound *n* lévrier *m* irlandais.

Irishwoman ['aɪrɪʃ,wʊmən] (*pl* **Irishwomen** [-,wɪmɪn]) *n* Irlandaise *f*.

irk [ɜːk] *vt* irriter, agacer.

irksome ['ɜːksəm] *adj* irritant, agaçant.

iron ['aɪən] ◇ *adj* **1.** [made of, containing iron] de fer, en fer ■ **spinach has a high ~ content** les épinards contiennent beaucoup de fer ■ **~ deficiency** MED carence *f* en fer **2.** *fig* [strong] de fer, d'acier ➜ **the Iron Lady** *UK* POL la Dame de Fer ■ **the ~ hand** *OR* **fist in a velvet glove** une main de fer dans un gant de velours.
◇ *vt* [laundry] repasser.
◇ *vi* [laundry] se repasser.
◇ *n* **1.** [mineral] fer *m* ■ **made of ~** de *OR* en fer ■ **she has a will of ~** elle a une volonté de fer ➜ **(as) hard as ~** dur comme *OR* aussi dur que le fer **2.** [for laundry] fer *m* (à repasser) ■ [action] : **your shirt needs an ~** ta chemise a besoin d'un coup de fer *OR* d'être repassée **3.** [tool, appliance] fer *m* ■ **to have many ~s in the fire** avoir plusieurs fers au feu, jouer sur plusieurs tableaux **4.** [golf club] fer *m*.
◆ **irons** *npl* [chains] fers *mpl*.
◆ **iron out** *vt sep* **1.** [crease] repasser **2.** *fig* [problem, difficulty] aplanir ■ [differences] faire disparaître ■ **they've ~ed out their differences** ils ont fait disparaître les différences qui existaient entre eux.

Iron Age *n* : **the ~** l'âge *m* du fer.

Iron Curtain ◇ *n* : **the ~** le rideau *m* de fer.
◇ *adj* : **the ~ countries** les pays *mpl* de l'Est.

iron foundry *n* fonderie *f (de fonte)*.

iron-grey *adj* gris acier.

ironic(al) [aɪ'rɒnɪk(l)] *adj* ironique.

ironically [aɪ'rɒnɪklɪ] *adv* **1.** [smile, laugh] ironiquement **2.** [paradoxically] : **~ enough, he was the only one to remember** paradoxalement, il était le seul à s'en souvenir.

ironing ['aɪənɪŋ] *n* repassage *m* ■ **to do the ~** faire le repassage, repasser.

ironing board *n* planche *f* OR table *f* à repasser.

iron lung *n* MED poumon *m* d'acier.

ironmonger ['aɪən,mʌŋgəʳ] *n* UK quincaillier *m*.

ironmongery ['aɪən,mʌŋgərɪ] *n* UK quincaillerie *f*.

iron ore *n* minerai *m* de fer.

iron tablet *n* MED comprimé *m* de fer.

ironwork ['aɪənwɜ:k] *n* ferronnerie *f*.

ironworks ['aɪənwɜ:ks] (*pl inv*) *n* usine *f* sidérurgique.

irony ['aɪrənɪ] (*pl* **ironies**) *n* [gen - LIT] ironie *f* ■ **the ~ is that it might be true** ce qui est ironique OR ce qu'il y a d'ironique, c'est que cela pourrait être vrai.

irradiate [ɪ'reɪdɪeɪt] *vt* **1.** MED & PHYS [expose to radiation] irradier ■ [food] irradier **2.** [light up] illuminer, éclairer.

irradiation [ɪ,reɪdɪ'eɪʃn] *n* **1.** MED & PHYS [exposure to radiation] irradiation *f* ■ [X-ray therapy] radiothérapie *f* ■ [of food] irradiation *f* **2.** OPT irradiation *f*.

irrational [ɪ'ræʃənl] *adj* **1.** [person, behaviour, feeling] irrationnel ■ [fear] irraisonné ■ [creature, being] incapable de raisonner **2.** MATHS irrationnel.

irrationality [ɪ,ræʃə'nælətɪ] *n* irrationalité *f*.

irrationally [ɪ'ræʃnəlɪ] *adv* irrationnellement.

irreconcilable [ɪ'rekənsaɪləbl] *adj* **1.** [aims, views, beliefs] inconciliable, incompatible **2.** [conflict, disagreement] insoluble ■ **to be ~ enemies** être ennemis jurés.

irrecoverable [,ɪrɪ'kʌvərəbl] *adj* **1.** [thing lost] irrécupérable ■ [debt] irrécouvrable **2.** [loss, damage, wrong] irréparable.

irredeemable [,ɪrɪ'di:məbl] *adj* **1.** [share, bond] non remboursable ■ [paper money] non convertible **2.** [person] incorrigible, impénitent **3.** [loss, damage, wrong] irréparable.

irredeemably [,ɪrɪ'di:məblɪ] *adv* irrémédiablement ■ **to be ~ wicked** être foncièrement méchant.

irreducible [,ɪrɪ'dju:səbl] *adj* irréductible.

irrefutable [,ɪrɪ'fju:təbl] *adj* [argument, proof] irréfutable ■ [fact] certain, indéniable.

irregular [ɪ'regjʊləʳ] ◇ *adj* **1.** [object, shape etc] irrégulier ■ [surface] inégal **2.** [intermittent, spasmodic] irrégulier ■ **~ breathing** respiration irrégulière OR saccadée **3.** *fml* [unorthodox] irrégulier **4.** LING irrégulier.
◇ *n* **1.** MIL irrégulier *m* **2.** US COMM article *m* de second choix.

irregularity [ɪ,regjʊ'lærətɪ] (*pl* **irregularities**) *n* [of surface, work, breathing] irrégularité *f*.
◆ **irregularities** *npl* [errors, intringements] irrégularités *fpl*.

irregularly [ɪ'regjʊləlɪ] *adv* **1.** [spasmodically] irrégulièrement **2.** [unevenly] inégalement.

irrelevance [ɪ'reləvəns] *n* **1.** [of fact, comment] manque *m* de rapport, non-pertinence *f* **2.** [pointless fact or matter] inutilité *f* ■ **don't waste your time on ~s** ne perdez pas votre temps avec des choses sans importance ■ **the committee has become an ~** le comité n'a plus de raison d'être.

irrelevancy [ɪ'reləvənsɪ] (*pl* **irrelevancies**) = **irrelevance**.

irrelevant [ɪ'reləvənt] *adj* sans rapport, hors de propos ■ **your question is totally ~ to the subject in hand** votre question n'a aucun rapport OR n'a rien à voir avec le sujet qui nous intéresse ■ **~ information** information non pertinente ■ **age is ~** l'âge est sans importance OR n'est pas un critère.

irreligious [,ɪrɪ'lɪdʒəs] *adj* irréligieux.

irremediable [,ɪrɪ'mi:djəbl] *adj* irrémédiable.

irreparable [ɪ'repərəbl] *adj* irréparable ■ **he's done ~ harm to his career** il a compromis sa carrière de façon irréparable.

irreplaceable [,ɪrɪ'pleɪsəbl] *adj* irremplaçable.

irrepressible [,ɪrɪ'presəbl] *adj* **1.** [need, desire] irrépressible ■ [good humour] à toute épreuve **2.** [person] jovial.

irreproachable [,ɪrɪ'prəʊtʃəbl] *adj* irréprochable.

irresistible [,ɪrɪ'zɪstəbl] *adj* irrésistible.

irresistibly [,ɪrɪ'zɪstəblɪ] *adv* irrésistiblement.

irresolute [ɪ'rezəlu:t] *adj* irrésolu, indécis.

irrespective [,ɪrɪ'spektɪv] ◆ **irrespective of** *prep phr* sans tenir compte de ■ **~ of race or religion** sans discrimination de race ou de religion.

irresponsibility ['ɪrɪ,spɒnsə'bɪlətɪ] *n* irresponsabilité *f*.

irresponsible [,ɪrɪ'spɒnsəbl] *adj* [person] irresponsable ■ [act] irréfléchi ■ **you're so ~!** tu n'as aucun sens des responsabilités!

irretrievable [,ɪrɪ'tri:vəbl] *adj* [object] introuvable ■ [loss, harm, damage] irréparable.

irretrievably [,ɪrɪ'tri:vəblɪ] *adv* irréparablement, irrémédiablement ■ **~ lost** perdu pour toujours OR à tout jamais.

irreverence [ɪ'revərəns] *n* irrévérence *f*.

irreverent [ɪ'revərənt] *adj* irrévérencieux ■ **an ~ sense of humour** un sens de l'humour insolent OR impertinent.

irreversible [,ɪrɪ'vɜ:səbl] *adj* irréversible.

irrevocable [ɪ'revəkəbl] *adj* irrévocable.

irrevocably [ɪ'revəkəblɪ] *adv* irrévocablement.

irrigate ['ɪrɪgeɪt] *vt* [gen - MED] irriguer.

irrigation [,ɪrɪ'geɪʃn] *n* [gen - MED] irrigation *f* ■ **~ channel** fossé *m* OR rigole *f* d'irrigation.

irritability [,ɪrɪtə'bɪlətɪ] *n* irritabilité *f*.

irritable ['ɪrɪtəbl] *adj* [gen - MED] irritable.

irritable bowel syndrome *n* syndrome *m* du côlon irritable.

irritably ['ɪrɪtəblɪ] *adv* avec irritation.

irritant ['ɪrɪtənt] ◇ *adj* irritant.
◇ *n* irritant *m*.

irritate ['ɪrɪteɪt] *vt* **1.** [annoy] irriter, contrarier, énerver **2.** MED irriter.

irritated ['ɪrɪteɪtɪd] *adj* **1.** [annoyed] irrité, agacé ■ **don't get ~!** ne t'énerve pas! **2.** MED [eyes, skin] irrité.

irritating ['ɪrɪteɪtɪŋ] *adj* **1.** [annoying] irritant, contrariant, énervant **2.** MED irritant, irritatif.

irritatingly ['ɪrɪteɪtɪŋlɪ] *adv* de façon agaçante OR irritante.

irritation [ɪrɪ'teɪʃn] *n* **1.** [annoyance] irritation *f*, agacement *m* **2.** MED irritation *f*.

IRS (*abbrev of* **Internal Revenue Service**) *pr n* : **the ~** *le fisc américain*.

is [ɪz] ▷ **be**.

Isaiah [aɪ'zaɪə] *pr n* Isaïe.

ISBN (*abbrev of* **International Standard Book Number**) *n* ISBN *m*.

ISDN (*abbrev of* **integrated services data network**) *n* RNIS *m*.

Isis ['aɪsɪs] *pr n* Isis.

Islam ['ɪzlɑ:m] *n* Islam *m*.

Islamic [ɪz'læmɪk] *adj* islamique ■ **~ law** la loi islamique.

Islamic fundamentalist *n* fondamentaliste *mf* islamiste, intégriste *mf* islamiste.

Islamist ['ɪzləmɪst] *adj* & *n* islamiste *mf*.

Islamophobia [ɪzˌlæmə'fəʊbɪə] *n* islamophobie *f*.

Islamophobic [ɪzˌlæmə'fəʊbɪk] *adj* islamophobe.

island ['aɪlənd] ◇ *n* GEOG île *f* ■ **they are an ~ race** c'est une race insulaire ■ **an ~ of peace** *fig* une oasis de tranquillité.
◇ *vt* [isolate] isoler.

islander ['aɪləndəʳ] *n* insulaire *mf*.

isle [aɪl] *n* île *f*.

Isle of Dogs *pr n quartier de l'est de Londres faisant partie des Docklands.*

Isle of Man *pr n* : **the ~** l'île *f* de Man ■ **in** *OR* **on the ~** à l'île de Man.

Isle of Wight [-waɪt] *pr n* : **the ~** l'île *f* de Wight ■ **in** *OR* **on the ~** à l'île de Wight.

islet ['aɪlɪt] *n* îlot *m*.

isn't ['ɪznt] = **is not**.

isobar ['aɪsəbɑːʳ] *n* isobare *f*.

isolate ['aɪsəleɪt] *vt* [gen - MED] isoler.

isolated ['aɪsəleɪtɪd] *adj* **1.** [alone, remote] isolé **2.** [single] unique, isolé ■ **an ~ incident** un incident isolé.

isolation [aɪsə'leɪʃn] *n* isolement *m* ■ **in ~** en soi, isolément.

isolation hospital *n* hôpital *m* d'isolement.

isolationism [ˌaɪsə'leɪʃənɪzm] *n* isolationnisme *m*.

isolationist [ˌaɪsə'leɪʃənɪst] *adj* isolationniste.

isolation ward *n* service *m* des contagieux.

isometric [ˌaɪsəʊ'metrɪk] *adj* isométrique ■ **~ exercises** exercices *mpl* isométriques.

isosceles [aɪ'sɒsɪliːz] *adj* isocèle ■ **an ~ triangle** un triangle isocèle.

isotope ['aɪsətəʊp] *n* isotope *m*.

ISP *n* = **Internet service provider**.

I-spy *n jeu d'enfant où l'un des joueurs donne la première lettre d'un objet qu'il voit et les autres doivent deviner de quoi il s'agit.*

Israel ['ɪzreɪəl] *pr n* Israël ■ **in ~** en Israël.

Israeli [ɪz'reɪlɪ] (*pl inv OR pl* **Israelis**) ◇ *n* Israélien *m*, - enne *f*.
◇ *adj* israélien.

Israelite ['ɪzrəlaɪt] *n* Israélite *mf*.

issue ['ɪʃuː] ◇ *n* **1.** [matter, topic] question *f*, problème *m* ■ **where do you stand on the abortion ~?** quel est votre point de vue sur (la question de) l'avortement? ■ **that's not the ~** il ne s'agit pas de ça ■ **it's become an international ~** le problème a pris une dimension internationale ■ **the important ~s of the day** les grands problèmes du moment ■ **at ~** en question ■ **her competence is not at ~** sa compétence n'est pas en cause ■ **to cloud** *OR* **confuse the ~** brouiller les cartes ■ **to avoid** *OR* **duck** *OR* **evade the ~** esquiver la question ■ **to force the ~** forcer la décision
2. [cause of disagreement] différend *m* ■ **the subject has now become a real ~ between us** ce sujet est maintenant source de désaccord entre nous ■ **to be at ~ with sb over sthg** être en désaccord avec qqn au sujet de qqch ■ **to make an ~ of sthg** monter qqch en épingle ■ **to take ~ with sb/sthg** être en désaccord avec qqn/qqch
3. [edition - of newspaper, magazine etc] numéro *m* ■ **the latest ~ of the magazine** le dernier numéro du magazine
4. [distribution - of supplies] distribution *f* ; [- of tickets, official document] délivrance *f* ; [- of shares, money, stamps] émission *f* ■ **date of ~** date *f* de délivrance ▶ **standard ~** modèle *m* standard ■ **army ~** modèle *m* de l'armée
5. *fml* [result, outcome] issue *f*, résultat *m*
6. *arch* & LAW [progeny] descendance *f*, progéniture *f lit* ■ **he died without ~** il est mort sans héritiers.
◇ *vt* **1.** [book, newspaper] publier, sortir ■ [record] sortir ■ **the magazine is ~d on Wednesdays** le magazine sort *OR* paraît le mercredi ‖ [official document, passport] délivrer ■ LAW [warrant, writ] lancer ■ [statement, proclamation] publier ■ [shares, money, stamps] émettre
2. [distribute - supplies, tickets etc] distribuer ■ **we were all ~d with rations** on nous a distribué à tous des rations.
◇ *vi fml* **1.** [come or go out] sortir ■ **delicious smells ~d from the kitchen** des odeurs délicieuses provenaient de la cuisine
2. *fml* [result, originate] : **to ~ from** provenir de.

issuing ['ɪʃuɪŋ] *adj* FIN [company] émetteur ■ **~ bank** *UK* banque *f* d'émission *OR* émettrice.

ISTC (*abbrev of* **Iron and Steels Confederation**) *pr n syndicat britannique des ouvriers de la sidérurgie.*

isthmus ['ɪsməs] (*pl* **isthmuses** *OR pl* **isthmi** [-maɪ]) *n* isthme *m*.

it [ɪt] ◇ *pron* **1.** [referring to specific thing, animal etc - as subject] il, elle *f* ; [- as direct object] le, la *f*, l' *(before vowel or silent 'h')* ; [- as indirect object] lui ■ **is it a boy or a girl?** c'est un garçon ou une fille? ■ **I'd lend you my typewriter but it's broken** je te prêterais bien ma machine à écrire mais elle est cassée ■ **give it a tap with a hammer** donnez un coup de marteau dessus
2. [after preposition] : **he told me all about it** il m'a tout raconté ■ **there was nothing inside it** il n'y avait rien dedans *OR* à l'intérieur ■ **I left the bag under it** j'ai laissé le sac dessous
3. [impersonal uses] : **it's me!** c'est moi! ■ **it's raining/snowing** il pleut/neige ■ **it's 500 miles from here to Vancouver** Vancouver est à 800 kilomètres d'ici ■ **I like it here** je me plais beaucoup ici ■ **I couldn't bear it if she left** je ne supporterais pas qu'elle parte ■ **it might look rude if I don't go** si je n'y vais pas cela pourrait être considéré comme une impolitesse ■ **it's the Johnny Carson Show!** voici le Johnny Carson Show! ■ **it's a goal!** but! ■ **it's his constant complaining I can't stand** ce que je ne supporte pas c'est sa façon de se plaindre constamment.
◇ *n inf* **1.** [in games] : **you're it!** c'est toi le chat!, c'est toi qui y es!
2. [most important person] : **he thinks he's it** il s'y croit.

IT *n* = **information technology**.

Italian [ɪ'tæljən] ◇ *n* **1.** [person] Italien *m*, - enne *f* **2.** LING italien *m*.
◇ *adj* italien ■ **the ~ embassy** l'ambassade *f* d'Italie.

Italianate [ɪ'tæljəneɪt] *adj* italianisant.

italic [ɪ'tælɪk] ◇ *adj* italique.
◇ *n* italique *m* ■ **in ~s** en italique.

italicize, ise [ɪ'tælɪsaɪz] *vt* mettre en italique ■ **the ~d words** les mots en italique.

Italy ['ɪtəlɪ] *pr n* Italie *f* ■ **in ~** en Italie.

itch [ɪtʃ] ◇ *n* **1.** *liter* démangeaison *f* ■ **I've got an ~** ça me démange *OR* me gratte **2.** *inf fig* [desire] envie *f*.
◇ *vi* **1.** [physically] avoir des démangeaisons ■ [insect bite, part of body] : **does it ~?** est-ce que cela te démange? ■ **my back ~es** mon dos me démange *OR* me gratte ■ **that sweater ~es** ce pull me gratte **2.** *inf fig* [desire] : **to be ~ing to do sthg** : **I was ~ing to tell her** ça me démangeait de lui dire ■ **we're ~ing to go** nous ne tenons plus en place.

itching ['ɪtʃɪŋ] *n* démangeaison *f*.

itching powder *n* poil *m* à gratter.

itchy ['ɪtʃɪ] (*comp* **itchier**, *superl* **itchiest**) *adj* qui gratte, qui démange ■ **I've got an ~ leg** ma jambe me démange ▶ **to have ~ feet** *inf* avoir la bougeotte.

it'd ['ɪtəd] **1.** = **it would 2.** = **it had**.

item ['aɪtəm] *n* **1.** [object] article *m* ■ **an ~ of clothing** un vêtement **2.** [point, issue] point *m*, question *f* ■ **I've several ~s of business to attend to** j'ai plusieurs affaires à régler **3.** [in newspaper] article *m* ■ [on T.V. or radio] point *m OR* sujet *m* d'actualité ■ **and here are today's main news ~s** et voici les principaux points de l'actualité **4.** COMPUT article *m* **5.** LING item *m* **6.** [in book-keeping] écriture *f*.

itemize, ise ['aɪtəmaɪz] *vt* détailler ■ **an ~d list/bill** une liste/une facture détaillée.

itinerant [ɪ'tɪnərənt] ◇ *adj* itinérant ■ [actors] ambulant, itinérant ■ **~ teacher** *US* professeur *m* remplaçant.
◇ *n* nomade *mf*.

itinerary [aɪ'tɪnərərɪ] (*pl* **itineraries**) *n* itinéraire *m*.

it'll [ɪtl] = **it will**.

ITN (*abbrev of* **Independent Television News**) *pr n service d'actualités télévisées pour les chaînes relevant de l'IBA*.

its [ɪts] *det* son *m*, sa *f*, ses *mf pl* ▪ **the committee has ~ first meeting on Friday** le comité se réunit pour la première fois vendredi ▪ **the dog wagged ~ tail** le chien a remué la queue ▪ **the jug's lost ~ handle** le pichet n'a plus de poignée.

it's [ɪts] **1.** = **it is 2.** = **it has**.

itself [ɪt'self] *pron* **1.** [reflexive use] se, s' *(before vowel or silent 'h')* ▪ **the cat was licking ~ clean** le chat faisait sa toilette **2.** [emphatic use] lui-même *m*, elle-même *f* ▪ **she's kindness ~** c'est la gentillesse même **3.** [after preposition] : **it switches off by ~** ça s'éteint tout seul ▪ **it's not dangerous in ~** ce n'est pas dangereux en soi ▪ **working with her was in ~ fascinating** le seul fait de travailler avec elle était fascinant.

itsy-bitsy [,ɪtsɪ'bɪtsɪ], **itty-bitty** [,ɪtɪ'bɪtɪ] *adj inf* tout petit, minuscule.

ITV (*abbrev of* **Independent Television**) *pr n sigle désignant les programmes diffusés par les chaînes relevant de l'IBA*.

IUCD (*abbrev of* **intrauterine contraceptive device**) *n* stérilet *m*.

IUD (*abbrev of* **intrauterine device**) *n* stérilet *m*.

I've [aɪv] = **I have**.

IVF (*abbrev of* **in vitro fertilization**) *n* FIV *f*.

Ivorian [aɪ'vɔːrɪən] ◇ *n* Ivoirien *m*, - enne *f*.
◇ *adj* ivoirien.

ivory ['aɪvərɪ] (*pl* **ivories**) ◇ *adj* **1.** [made of ivory] d'ivoire, en ivoire **2.** [ivory-coloured] (couleur) ivoire *(inv)*.
◇ *n* **1.** [substance] ivoire *m* **2.** [object] ivoire *m*.
◆ **ivories** *npl inf* [piano keys] touches *fpl* ▪ **to tickle the ivories** *hum* toucher du piano.

Ivory Coast *pr n* : **the ~** la Côte-d'Ivoire ▪ **in the ~** en Côte-d'Ivoire.

ivory tower *n* tour *f* d'ivoire.

ivy ['aɪvɪ] (*pl* **ivies**) *n* lierre *m*.

Ivy League *n groupe des huit universités les plus prestigieuses du nord-est des États-Unis*.
◆ **Ivy-League** *adj* : **he had an Ivy-League education** il a fait ses études dans une grande université ▪ **her boyfriend's very Ivy-League** *inf* son petit ami est très BCBG.

J

j (*pl* **j's** *OR pl* **js**), **J** (*pl* **J's** *OR pl* **Js**) [dʒeɪ] *n* j *m*, J *m*, *see also* **f**.

J/A *written abbr of* **joint account**.

jab [dʒæb] (*pret & pp* **jabbed**, *cont* **jabbing**) ◇ *vt* [pierce] piquer ▪ **he jabbed my arm with a needle, he jabbed a needle into my arm** il m'a piqué le bras avec une aiguille, il m'a enfoncé une aiguille dans le bras ❙ [poke] : **you almost jabbed me in the eye with that knife!** tu as failli m'éborgner avec ce couteau! ▪ **he jabbed her in the ribs** il lui a enfoncé les doigts dans les côtes ❙ [brandish] pointer, brandir *(d'une façon menaçante)* ▪ **she kept jabbing her finger at the defendant** elle ne cessait de pointer le doigt vers l'accusé *OR* de désigner l'accusé du doigt.
◇ *vi* **1.** [stick] s'enfoncer ▪ **something jabbed into my ribs** j'ai reçu un coup sec dans les côtes **2.** [gesture] : **he jabbed at me with his umbrella** il essaya de me donner un coup de parapluie ▪ **she jabbed wildly at the buttons** elle appuyait frénétiquement sur les boutons **3.** [in boxing] : **he's jabbing with (his) right and left** il lui envoie un direct du droit et du gauche.
◇ *n* **1.** [poke] coup *m (donné avec un objet pointu)* ▪ [in boxing] (coup *m*) droit *m OR* direct *m* **2.** *inf* MED piqûre *f* ▪ **I've got to get a tetanus ~** je dois me faire vacciner contre le tétanos.

jabber ['dʒæbəʳ] *inf* ◇ *vi* [idly] jacasser, caqueter *pej* ▪ [inarticulately] bredouiller, bafouiller ▪ [in foreign tongue] baragouiner.
◇ *vt* : **to ~ (out)** bredouiller, bafouiller.

jabbering ['dʒæbərɪŋ] *n inf* [idle chatter] bavardage *m*, papotage *m* ▪ [in foreign tongue] baragouin *m*.

jack [dʒæk] ◇ *vt* MECH soulever avec un vérin ▪ AUT mettre sur cric.
◇ *n* **1.** [tool - MECH] & MIN vérin *m* ▪ AUT cric *m* **2.** [playing card] valet *m* **3.** [in bowls] cochonnet *m* **4.** ELEC [male] = **jack plug** ▪ [female] = **jack socket** **5.** *phr* **every man ~ (of them)** *UK inf* tous autant qu'ils sont.
◆ **Jack** *pr n* : **I'm all right Jack** *UK inf* moi ça va ▪ **hey, Jack!** *US* [to call stranger] hé, vous là-bas!
◆ **jack in** *vt sep UK inf* plaquer ▪ **oh, ~ it in, will you!** oh, fermela, tu veux!
◆ **jack up** *vt sep* **1.** [car] lever avec un cric **2.** *inf* [price, wage] augmenter, monter.

jackal ['dʒækəl] *n liter & fig* chacal *m*.

jackass ['dʒækæs] *n* **1.** [donkey] âne *m*, baudet *m* **2.** *inf* [imbecile] imbécile *mf*.

jackboot ['dʒækbu:t] *n* botte *f* (de militaire) ▪ **~ tactics** des tactiques dictatoriales.

jackdaw ['dʒækdɔ:] *n* choucas *m*.

jacket ['dʒækɪt] *n* **1.** [for men] veste *f* ▪ [for women] veste *f*, jaquette *f* ▪ **leather ~** blouson *m* de cuir **2.** [of book] jaquette *f* ▪ *US* [of record] pochette *f* **3.** CULIN : **~ potato, potato (cooked) in its ~** pomme de terre *f* en robe des champs *OR* en robe de chambre **4.** TECH [of boiler] chemise *f*.

Jack Frost *n inf personnage imaginaire symbolisant l'hiver*.

jackfruit ['dʒækfru:t] *n* jaque *m*.

jackhammer ['dʒæk,hæməʳ] *n* marteau piqueur *m*.

jack-in-the-box *n* diable *m* (à ressort).

jackknife ['dʒæknaɪf] (*pl* **jackknives** [-naɪvz]) ◇ *n* couteau *m* de poche.
◇ *vi* : **the truck ~d** le camion s'est mis en travers de la route.

jack-of-all-trades *n pej* homme *m* à tout faire ▪ **~ and master of none** *prov* propre à tout et bon à rien.

jack-o'-lantern *n* feu *m* follet.

jack plug *n* jack *m* (mâle), fiche *f* jack.

jackpot ['dʒækpɒt] *n* gros lot *m* ▪ [in cards] pot *m* ▪ **you hit the ~!** tu as décroché le gros lot!

Jack Robinson *n UK inf* **before you could say ~** avant d'avoir pu dire "ouf".

Jack Russell [-'rʌsl] *n* Jack Russell (terrier) *m*.

jack socket *n* jack *m* (femelle), prise *f* jack.

Jack-the-Lad *n inf* jeune frimeur *m*.

Jacobean [,dʒækə'bɪən] *adj* jacobéen *m*, - enne *f*, de l'époque de Jacques Iᵉʳ (d'Angleterre).

Jacobin ['dʒækəbɪn] ◇ *n* Jacobin *m*, - e *f*.
◇ *adj* jacobin.

Jacobite ['dʒækəbaɪt] ◇ *adj* jacobite.
◇ *n* Jacobite *mf*.

THE JACOBITES

Membres du parti légitimiste anglais qui soutint, après la révolution de 1688, d'abord la cause de Jacques II contre Guillaume d'Orange, puis celle des derniers Stuarts contre la maison des Hanovre.

Jacuzzi® [dʒə'ku:zɪ] (*pl* **Jacuzzis**) *n* Jacuzzi® *m*, bain *m* à remous.

jade [dʒeɪd] ◇ *n* **1.** [stone] jade *m* **2.** [colour] vert jade *m inv*.
◇ *adj* **1.** [made of jade] de *OR* en jade **2.** [colour] vert jade *(inv)*.

jaded ['dʒeɪdɪd] *adj* [person] désabusé, blasé, éreinté ▪ [appetite] écœuré, saturé.

jag [dʒæg] (*pret & pp* **jagged**, *cont* **jagging**) ◇ *vt* déchiqueter ▪ [fabric] taillader.
◇ *n* **1.** pointe *f*, aspérité *f* ▪ [of saw] dent *f* **2.** *US inf* [party] orgie *f*.

jagged ['dʒægɪd] *adj* [edge, coastline] déchiqueté ▪ [tear] irrégulier ▪ [rock] râpeux, rugueux.

jaguar ['dʒægjʊəʳ] *n* jaguar *m*.

jail [dʒeɪl] <> *n* prison *f* ▪ **to be in ~** être en prison ▪ **to be sent to ~** être incarcéré *OR* emprisonné ▪ **sentenced to 15 years in ~** condamné à 15 ans de prison.
<> *vt* emprisonner, mettre en prison, incarcérer ▪ **to be ~ed for life** être condamné à perpétuité *OR* à vie.

jailbait ['dʒeɪlbeɪt] *n (U) US inf* mineur *m*, - e *f* ▪ **she's ~** c'est un coup à se retrouver en taule *(pour détournement de mineur)*.

jailbird ['dʒeɪlbɜːd] *n inf* récidiviste *mf*.

jailbreak ['dʒeɪlbreɪk] *n* évasion *f*.

jailer ['dʒeɪləʳ] *n* geôlier *m*, - ère *f*.

jailhouse ['dʒeɪlhaʊs] (*pl* [-haʊzɪz]) *n US* prison *f*.

Jain [dʒaɪn] <> *n* jaïn *m*, - e *f*.
<> *adj* jaïn.

Jakarta [dʒə'kɑːtə] *pr n* Djakarta, Jakarta.

jalapeño [dʒælə'piːnəʊ] *n US* petit piment *m* vert.

jalopy [dʒə'lɒpɪ] (*pl* **jalopies**) *n inf* tacot *m*, guimbarde *f*.

jam [dʒæm] (*pret & pp* **jammed**, *cont* **jamming**) <> *n* **1.** [preserve] confiture *f* ▪ **strawberry ~** confiture de fraises ▪ **it's a case of ~ tomorrow** *UK inf* ce sont des promesses en l'air **2.** [congestion] encombrement *m* **3.** *inf* [predicament] pétrin *m* ▪ **I'm in a bit of a ~** je suis plutôt dans le pétrin.
<> *comp* [tart, pudding, sandwich] à la confiture.
<> *vt* **1.** [crowd, cram] entasser, tasser ▪ **we were jammed in like sardines** on était entassés *OR* serrés comme des sardines ▪ **I was jammed (up) against the wall** j'étais coincé contre le mur ▮ [push roughly, ram] fourrer ▪ **she jammed her hat on** elle enfonça *OR* vissa son chapeau sur sa tête **2.** [make stick] coincer, bloquer ▪ **she jammed the window shut with a wedge** elle coinça *OR* bloqua la fenêtre avec une cale **3.** [congest] encombrer, bloquer, boucher ▪ **the streets were jammed with cars** les rues étaient embouteillées **4.** RADIO brouiller.
<> *vi* **1.** [crowd] se tasser, s'entasser **2.** [become stuck - gen] se coincer, se bloquer ; [- gun] s'enrayer ; [- brakes] se bloquer **3.** *inf* [play in a jam session] faire un bœuf.
◆ **jam on** *vt sep inf* **to ~ on the brakes** piler.

Jamaica [dʒə'meɪkə] *pr n* Jamaïque *f* ▪ **in ~** à la Jamaïque.

Jamaican [dʒə'meɪkn] <> *n* Jamaïcain *m*, - e *f*, Jamaïquain *m*, - e *f*.
<> *adj* jamaïcain, jamaïquain.

jamb [dʒæm] *n* montant *m*.

jambalaya [ˌdʒæmbə'laɪə] *n plat cajun à base de fruits de mer et de poulet.*

jamboree [ˌdʒæmbə'riː] *n* **1.** [gathering] grande fête *f* **2.** [scout rally] jamboree *m*.

James [dʒeɪmz] *pr n* Jacques ▪ **Saint ~** saint Jacques.

jam-full *adj inf* bourré, archiplein.

jamjar ['dʒæmdʒɑːʳ] *n* pot *m* à confiture.

jamming ['dʒæmɪŋ] *n* **1.** coincement *m* ▪ [of brakes] blocage *m* **2.** RADIO brouillage *m*.

jammy ['dʒæmɪ] (*comp* **jammier**, *superl* **jammiest**) *adj UK inf* **1.** [sticky with jam] poisseux ▪ **~ fingers** des doigts poisseux de confiture **2.** [lucky] chanceux ▪ **you ~ beggar!** espèce de veinard!

jam-packed = **jam-full**.

jampot ['dʒæmpɒt] = **jamjar**.

jam session *n inf* bœuf *m*, jam-session *f*.

Jan. (*written abbrev of* **January**) janv.

Jane Doe [dʒeɪn-] *n US* LAW *expression désignant une femme dont on ignore l'identité ou dont on veut préserver l'anonymat.*

jangle ['dʒæŋgl] <> *vi* retentir (avec un bruit métallique *OR* avec fracas) ▪ [more quietly] cliqueter.
<> *vt* faire retentir ▪ [more quietly] faire cliqueter ▪ **my nerves are all ~d** *fig* j'ai les nerfs en boule *OR* en pelote.
<> *n* [of bells] tintamarre *m* ▪ [of money] bruit *m*, cliquetis *m*.

jangling ['dʒæŋglɪŋ] <> *adj* [bells] retentissant ▪ [keys] qui tintent ▪ **a ~ noise** un bruit métallique.
<> *n* vacarme *m*, tintamarre *m* ▪ [quieter] bruit *m* ▪ **a ~ of keys** un bruit de clés.

janitor ['dʒænɪtəʳ] *n* [caretaker] *US & Scotland* gardien *m*, concierge *m* ▪ [doorkeeper] *dated* portier *m*.

Jansenism ['dʒænsənɪzm] *n* jansénisme *m*.

January ['dʒænjʊərɪ] *n* janvier *m*, *see also* **February**.

Jap [dʒæp] *n inf offens* Jap *m*.

japan [dʒə'pæn] <> *n* ART laque *f*.
<> *vt* laquer.

Japan [dʒə'pæn] *pr n* Japon *m* ▪ **in ~** au Japon.

Japanese [ˌdʒæpə'niːz] (*pl inv*) <> *n* **1.** [person] Japonais *m*, - e *f* **2.** LING japonais *m*.
<> *adj* japonais ▪ **the ~ embassy** l'ambassade *f* du Japon.

jape [dʒeɪp] *n inf dated* farce *f*, blague *f*.

japonica [dʒə'pɒnɪkə] *n* cognassier *m* du Japon.

jar [dʒɑːʳ] (*pret & pp* **jarred**, *cont* **jarring**) <> *n* **1.** [container - glass] bocal *m* ; [- for jam] pot *m* ; [- earthenware] pot *m*, jarre *f* **2.** *UK inf* [drink] pot *m* **3.** [jolt] secousse *f*, choc *m*.
<> *vi* **1.** [make harsh noise] grincer, crisser ▪ **there's something about her voice which really ~s** sa voix a quelque chose qui vous écorche les oreilles **2.** [clash - note] détonner ; [- colour] jurer ▪ **his constant complaining ~s on my nerves** ses lamentations continuelles me hérissent.
<> *vt* [shake - structure] secouer, ébranler.

jargon ['dʒɑːgən] *n* jargon *m*.

jarring ['dʒɑːrɪŋ] *adj* [sound] discordant ▪ [colour] criard.

Jarrow Marches ['dʒærəʊ'mɑːtʃɪz] *pr npl* : **the ~** *"marches de la faim", du nord-est de l'Angleterre à Londres, organisées par les chômeurs pour protester contre leur condition, au milieu des années trente.*

jasmine ['dʒæzmɪn] *n* jasmin *m*.

jaundice ['dʒɔːndɪs] *n* **1.** *(U)* MED jaunisse *f* **2.** *fig* [bitterness] amertume *f*.

jaundiced ['dʒɔːndɪst] *adj* [bitter] aigri, cynique ▪ [disapproving] désapprobateur ▪ **she has a very ~ view of English society** elle a une vision très négative de la société anglaise.

jaunt [dʒɔːnt] <> *n* balade *f*.
<> *vi* : **she's always ~ing off to Paris** elle est toujours en balade entre ici et Paris.

jauntily ['dʒɔːntɪlɪ] *adv* [cheerfully] joyeusement, jovialement ▪ [in a sprightly way] lestement.

jaunty ['dʒɔːntɪ] (*comp* **jauntier**, *superl* **jauntiest**) *adj* [cheerful] joyeux, enjoué, jovial ▪ [sprightly] leste, allègre.

Java ['dʒɑːvə] *pr n* Java ▪ **in ~** à Java.

Javanese [ˌdʒɑːvə'niːz] (*pl inv*) <> *n* **1.** [person] Javanais *m*, - e *f* **2.** LING javanais *m*.
<> *adj* javanais.

javelin ['dʒævlɪn] *n* [weapon] javelot *m*, javeline *f* ▪ SPORT javelot *m* ▪ **~ thrower** lanceur *m*, - euse *f* de javelot.

jaw [dʒɔː] <> *n* **1.** ANAT mâchoire *f* ▪ **his ~ dropped in astonishment** il en est resté bouche bée ▪ **snatched from the ~s of death** *fig* arraché aux griffes de la mort ▪ **upper/lower ~** mâchoire supérieure/inférieure ◐ **'Jaws'** *Spielberg* 'les Dents de la mer' **2.** [of tool] mâchoire *f* **3.** *inf* [chat] : **to have a good old ~** tailler une petite bavette, papoter **4.** *inf* [moralizing speech] sermon *m*.
<> *vi inf* [chat] papoter, tailler une bavette.
<> *vt inf* [remonstrate with] sermonner.

jawbone ['dʒɔːbəʊn] *n* maxillaire *m*.

jawline ['dʒɔːlaɪn] *n* menton *m* ■ **a strong ~** un menton saillant.

jay [dʒeɪ] *n* ORNITH geai *m*.

jaywalker ['dʒeɪwɔːkəʳ] *n* US *piéton qui traverse en dehors des passages pour piétons.*

jaywalking ['dʒeɪwɔːkɪŋ] *n* US *délit mineur qui consiste à traverser une rue en dehors des clous ou au feu vert.*

jazz [dʒæz] ◇ *n* **1.** MUS jazz *m* ■ **the Jazz Age** *l'âge d'or du jazz américain* **2.** *inf* [rigmarole] baratin *m*, blabla *m* ➤ **and all that ~** et tout le bataclan.
◇ *comp* [club, record, singer] de jazz ■ **~ band** jazz-band *m*.
➡ **jazz up** *vt sep* **1.** MUS : **to ~ up a song** mettre une chanson sur un rythme (de) jazz **2.** *inf* [enliven] égayer ■ **they've ~ed up the hotel** ils ont refait la déco de l'hôtel.

jazzman ['dʒæzmæn] (*pl* **jazzmen** [-men]) *n* musicien *m* de jazz.

jazzy ['dʒæzɪ] (*comp* **jazzier**, *superl* **jazziest**) *adj* **1.** [music] (de) jazz *(inv)*, sur un rythme de jazz **2.** *inf* [gaudy] tapageur, voyant ■ [smart] chic *(inv)*.

JCB® *n* tractopelle *f*.

JCR (*abbrev of* **junior common room**) *n* UK UNIV ≃ foyer *m* des étudiants.

JD *pr n* = **Justice Department**.

jealous ['dʒeləs] *adj* **1.** [envious] jaloux ■ **he gets terribly ~** il a des crises de jalousie terribles ■ **to be ~ of sb** être jaloux de qqn **2.** [possessive] jaloux, possessif ■ **to be ~ of one's reputation** être jaloux de OR veiller à sa réputation.

jealously ['dʒeləslɪ] *adv* jalousement.

jealousy ['dʒeləsɪ] (*pl* **jealousies**) *n* jalousie *f*.

jeans [dʒiːnz] *npl* jean *m*, blue-jean *m* ■ **a pair of ~** un jean.

Jeep® [dʒiːp] *n* Jeep® *f*.

jeepers ['dʒiːpəz] *interj* US *inf* : **~ (creepers)!** oh la la!

jeer [dʒɪəʳ] ◇ *vi* [scoff] railler, se moquer ■ [boo, hiss] pousser des cris hostiles OR de dérision ■ **everybody ~ed at me** ils se sont tous moqués de moi.
◇ *vt* huer, conspuer.
◇ *n* [scoffing] raillerie *f* ■ [boo, hiss] huée *f*.

jeering ['dʒɪərɪŋ] ◇ *adj* railleur, moqueur.
◇ *n (U)* [scoffing] railleries *fpl* ■ [boos, hisses] huées *fpl*.

Jehovah [dʒɪ'həʊvə] *pr n* Jéhovah ■ **~'s Witness** témoin de Jéhovah.

jejune [dʒɪ'dʒuːn] *adj lit* **1.** [puerile] naïf, puéril **2.** [dull] ennuyeux, morne ■ [unrewarding] ingrat.

Jekyll and Hyde [ˌdʒekɪlənd'haɪd] *n* : **he's a real ~ character** c'est un véritable docteur Jekyll.

jell [dʒel] ◇ *vi* = **gel**.
◇ *n inf* US *inf* = **jelly**.

jellied ['dʒelɪd] *adj* CULIN en gelée.

Jell-o® ['dʒeləʊ] *n* US = **jelly** *(sense 2)*.

jelly ['dʒelɪ] (*pl* **jellies**) ◇ *n* **1.** [gen] gelée *f* ■ **my legs feel like ~** j'ai les jambes en coton OR comme du coton ■ **my legs just turned to ~** j'en ai eu les jambes coupées, je n'avais plus de jambes **2.** UK CULIN [dessert] ≃ gelée *f* **3.** US CULIN [jam] confiture *f*.
◇ *vt* gélifier.

jelly baby (*pl* **jelly babies**) *n* UK bonbon *m* gélifié *(en forme de bébé)*.

jelly bean *n* dragée *f* à la gelée de sucre.

jellyfish ['dʒelɪfɪʃ] (*pl inv* OR *pl* **jellyfishes**) *n* méduse *f*.

jemmy ['dʒemɪ] (*pl* **jemmies**, *pret & pp* **jemmied**) UK *inf* ◇ *n* pince-monseigneur *f*.
◇ *vt* : **to ~ a door (open)** forcer une porte avec une pince-monseigneur.

jenny ['dʒenɪ] (*pl* **jennies**) *n* [female of bird or animal] : **~ wren** roitelet *m* femelle ■ **~ (ass)** ânesse *f*.

jeopardize, ise ['dʒepədaɪz] *vt* compromettre, mettre en péril.

jeopardy ['dʒepədɪ] *n* danger *m*, péril *m* ■ **our future is in ~** notre avenir est en péril OR menacé OR compromis.

Jerba ['dʒɜːbə] = **Djerba**.

Jeremiah [ˌdʒerɪ'maɪə] ◇ *pr n* BIBLE Jérémie.
◇ *n fig* prophète *m* de malheur.

jerk [dʒɜːk] ◇ *vt* **1.** [pull] tirer d'un coup sec, tirer brusquement **2.** [shake] secouer.
◇ *vi* **1.** [jolt] cahoter, tressauter ■ **to ~ to a halt** s'arrêter en cahotant **2.** [person - jump] sursauter ■ [person, muscle - twitch] se contracter.
◇ *n* **1.** [bump] secousse *f*, saccade *f* ■ **the train came to a halt with a ~** le train s'arrêta brutalement **2.** [wrench] coup *m* sec **3.** [brusque movement] mouvement *m* brusque ■ **with a ~ of his head he indicated that I should leave** d'un brusque signe de la tête, il me fit comprendre qu'il me fallait partir ■ **to wake up with a ~** se réveiller en sursaut **4.** △ [person] con△ *m* **5.** = **jerky** *(n)*.
➡ **jerk off**▲ *vi insep* se branler▲.

jerkily ['dʒɜːkɪlɪ] *adv* par à-coups.

jerkin ['dʒɜːkɪn] *n* blouson *m* ■ HIST pourpoint *m*.

jerky ['dʒɜːkɪ] (*comp* **jerkier**, *superl* **jerkiest**) ◇ *n* viande *f* séchée ■ **beef ~** bœuf *m* séché.
◇ *adj* [bumpy] saccadé ■ **a ~ ride** un trajet cahotant.

jeroboam [ˌdʒerə'bəʊəm] *n* jéroboam *m*.

jerry ['dʒerɪ] (*pl* **jerries**) *n* UK *inf* pot *m* de chambre.

Jerry△ ['dʒerɪ] (*pl* **Jerries**) *n dated & offens* [German] Fritz *m*, Boche *m*.

jerry-built *adj pej* [house, building] construit en carton-pâte.

jerry can *n* jerricane *m*.

jersey ['dʒɜːzɪ] *n* **1.** [pullover] pull-over *m*, tricot *m* ■ SPORT maillot *m* **2.** [fabric] jersey *m*.

Jersey ['dʒɜːzɪ] ◇ *pr n* Jersey ■ **in ~** à Jersey.
◇ *n* = **Jersey cow**.

Jersey cow *n* vache *f* jersiaise.

Jerusalem [dʒə'ruːsələm] *pr n* Jérusalem.

Jerusalem artichoke *n* topinambour *m*.

jest [dʒest] ◇ *n* plaisanterie *f* ■ **to say sthg in ~** dire qqch pour rire OR pour plaisanter ➤ **there's many a true word spoken in ~** *prov* il n'y a pas de meilleures vérités que celles dites en riant.
◇ *vi* plaisanter.

jester ['dʒestəʳ] *n* bouffon *m*, fou *m* (du roi).

Jesuit ['dʒezjʊɪt] ◇ *n* jésuite *m*.
◇ *adj* jésuite.

jesuitical [ˌdʒezjʊ'ɪtɪkl] *adj* jésuitique.

Jesus ['dʒiːzəs] ◇ *pr n* Jésus ■ **~ Christ** Jésus-Christ.
◇ *interj* : **~ (Christ)!**, **~ wept!**△ nom de Dieu!△.

jet [dʒet] (*pret & pp* **jetted**, *cont* **jetting**) ◇ *n* **1.** [aircraft] avion *m* à réaction, jet *m* **2.** [stream - of liquid] jet *m*, giclée *f* ; [- of gas, steam] jet *m* **3.** [nozzle, outlet] gicleur *m* ■ [on gas cooker] brûleur *m* **4.** [gem] jais *m*.
◇ *comp* **1.** [fighter, bomber] à réaction ■ [transport, travel] en avion (à réaction) ■ **~ fuel** kérosène *m* **2.** [made of jet - earrings, necklace] en jais.
◇ *vi* **1.** *inf* [travel by jet] voyager en avion (à réaction) ■ **they jetted (over) to Paris for the weekend** ils ont pris l'avion pour passer le week-end à Paris **2.** [issue forth - liquid] gicler, jaillir.
◇ *vt* **1.** [transport by jet] transporter par avion (à réaction) **2.** [direct - liquid] faire gicler.

jet-black *adj* jais *(inv)*, noir de jais.

jet engine *n* moteur *m* à réaction.

jetfoil ['dʒetfɔɪl] *n* hydroglisseur *m*.

jetlag ['dʒetlæg] *n* fatigue *f* due au décalage horaire ▪ **I'm still suffering from ~** je suis encore sous le coup du décalage horaire.

jet-lagged [-lægd] *adj* fatigué par le décalage horaire ▪ **I'm still a bit ~** je ne suis pas complètement remis du décalage horaire.

jet plane *n* avion *m* à réaction.

jet-propelled *adj* à réaction.

jetsam ['dʒetsəm] *n (U)* jet *m* à la mer.

jet set *n inf* jet-set *m*.

jet-setter *n inf* membre *m* du jet-set.

jetski ['dʒetski] *n* scooter *m* de mer, jetski *m*.

jet stream *n* jet-stream *m*, courant-jet *m*.

jettison ['dʒetɪsən] *vt* **1.** NAUT jeter à la mer, jeter par-dessus bord ▪ AERON [bombs, cargo] larguer **2.** *fig* [unwanted possession] se débarrasser de ▪ [theory, hope] abandonner.

jetty ['dʒetɪ] (*pl* **jetties**) *n* [landing stage] embarcadère *m*, débarcadère *m* ▪ [breakwater] jetée *f*, môle *m*.

Jew [dʒu:] *n* Juif *m*, - ive *f*.

jewel ['dʒu:əl] *n* **1.** [precious stone] bijou *m*, joyau *m*, pierre *f* précieuse ▪ [in clockmaking] rubis *m* ▪ **a three-~ wristwatch** une montre trois rubis **2.** *fig* [person, thing] bijou *m*, perle *f*.

jewel case, jewel box *n* boîte *f* de CD.

jeweled *US* = **jewelled**.

jeweler *US* = **jeweller**.

jewelled *UK*, **jeweled** *US* ['dʒu:əld] *adj* orné de bijoux ▪ [watch] à rubis.

jeweller *UK*, **jeweler** *US* ['dʒu:ələr] *n* bijoutier *m*, - ère *f*, joaillier *m*, - ère *f* ▪ **~'s (shop)** bijouterie *f*.

jewellery *UK*, **jewelry** *US* ['dʒu:əlrɪ] *n (U)* bijoux *mpl* ▪ **a piece of ~** un bijou.

Jewess ['dʒu:ɪs] *n arch & pej* Juive *f*.

Jewish ['dʒu:ɪʃ] *adj* juif.

Jewry ['dʒʊərɪ] *n arch & pej* [Jews collectively] la communauté juive.

jew's-harp *n* guimbarde *f*.

Jezebel ['dʒezə,bl] ◇ *pr n* BIBLE Jézabel.
◇ *n lit & hum* dévergondée *f*.

JFK (*abbrev of* **John Fitzgerald Kennedy International Airport**) *pr n aéroport de New York*.

jib [dʒɪb] (*pret & pp* **jibbed**, *cont* **jibbing**) ◇ *n* **1.** NAUT foc *m* ▪ **I don't like the cut of his ~** [look] je n'aime pas son allure ; [manner, behaviour] je n'aime pas ses façons de faire **2.** [of crane] flèche *f*, bras *m*.
◇ *vi UK* [horse] regimber ▪ [person] : **to ~ (at sthg)** regimber *OR* rechigner (à qqch).

jibe [dʒaɪb] ◇ *vi* **1.** *US inf* [agree] s'accorder, coller **2.** = **gibe**.
◇ *n* = **gibe**.

Jibouti [dʒɪ'bu:tɪ] = **Djibouti**.

jiffy ['dʒɪfɪ] (*pl* **jiffies**), **jiff** [dʒɪf] *n inf* **to do sthg in a ~** faire qqch en un rien de temps *OR* en moins de deux ▪ **I'll be back in a ~** je serai de retour dans une minute.

Jiffy bag® *n* enveloppe *f* matelassée.

jig [dʒɪg] (*pret & pp* **jigged**, *cont* **jigging**) ◇ *n* **1.** [dance] gigue *f* **2.** TECH gabarit *m* **3.** FISHING leurre *m*.
◇ *vi* **1.** [dance] danser allègrement **2.** *UK* **to ~ (around** *OR* **about)** sautiller, se trémousser.
◇ *vt* [shake] secouer (légèrement).

jigger ['dʒɪgər] *n* **1.** [spirits measure] mesure *f (42 ml)* **2.** [golf club] fer *m* quatre **3.** [in billiards] chevalet *m*, appui-queue *m inv* **4.** NAUT tapecul *m* **5.** *US inf* [thing] machin *m*, truc *m* **6.** *UK* [flea] chique *f*, puce-chique *f*.

jiggery-pokery [,dʒɪgərɪ'pəʊkərɪ] *n (U) UK inf* micmacs *mpl* ▪ **there's some ~ going on** il se passe des choses pas très catholiques.

jiggle ['dʒɪgl] ◇ *vt* secouer (légèrement) ▪ **you have to ~ the key a bit to get it in** il faut tourner et retourner un peu la clef pour la faire entrer dans la serrure.
◇ *vi* : **to ~ (about** *OR* **around)** se trémousser.
◇ *n* secousse *f* ▪ **give it a ~** secoue-le un peu.

jigsaw ['dʒɪgsɔ:] *n* **1.** [game] : **the pieces of the ~ were beginning to fall into place** *fig* peu à peu tout devenait clair ➲ **~ (puzzle)** puzzle *m* **2.** [tool] scie *f* sauteuse.

jihad [dʒɪ'hɑ:d] *n* djihad *m*.

jilt [dʒɪlt] *vt* quitter.

jimjams ['dʒɪmdʒæmz] *npl UK* **1.** △ [excitement] agitation *f* ▪ [nervousness] frousse *f* ▪ **to have the ~** [excited] être excité comme une puce ; [nervous] avoir la frousse *OR* les foies△ **2.** *inf* [pyjamas] *baby* pyjama *m*.

jimmy ['dʒɪmɪ] (*pl* **jimmies**, *pret & pp* **jimmied**) *US* = **jemmy**.

jingle ['dʒɪŋgl] ◇ *n* **1.** [sound] tintement *m* **2.** RADIO & TV jingle *m*.
◇ *vi* tinter.
◇ *vt* faire tinter.

jingo ['dʒɪŋgəʊ] *n inf dated* **by ~!** crénom de nom!

jingoism ['dʒɪŋgəʊɪzm] *n pej* chauvinisme *m*.

jingoistic [,dʒɪŋgəʊ'ɪstɪk] *adj pej* chauvin, cocardier.

jink [dʒɪŋk] ◇ *n* [movement] esquive *f*.
◇ *vi* zigzaguer, se faufiler ▪ **he ~ed through the defence** SPORT il s'est faufilé à travers la défense adverse.

jinx [dʒɪŋks] *inf* ◇ *n* malchance *f*, sort *m* ▪ **there's a ~ on this car** cette voiture porte malheur *OR* la guigne ▪ **to put a ~ on sb** jeter un sort à qqn.
◇ *vt* porter malheur à, jeter un sort à ▪ **to be ~ed** être poursuivi par le mauvais sort.

jitterbug ['dʒɪtəbʌg] ◇ *n* **1.** [dance] jitterbug *m* **2.** *inf* [nervous person] nerveux *m*, - euse *f*.
◇ *vi* [dance] danser le jitterbug.

jitters ['dʒɪtəz] *npl inf* frousse *f* ▪ **to give sb the ~** flanquer la frousse à qqn.

jittery ['dʒɪtərɪ] *adj inf* [person] nerveux ▪ [situation] tendu, délicat ▪ **he's always ~ before exams** il a toujours le trac avant un examen.

jiu-jitsu [dʒu:'dʒɪtsu:] = **ju-jitsu**.

jive [dʒaɪv] ◇ *n* **1.** [dance] swing *m* **2.** [slang] : **~ (talk)** argot *m (employé par les Noirs américains, surtout les musiciens de jazz)* **3.** △ *US* [lies, nonsense] baratin *m*, blabla *m*.
◇ *vt*△ *US* [deceive, mislead] baratiner, charrier.
◇ *vi* [dance] danser le swing.
◇ *adj*△ *US* [phoney, insincere] bidon *(inv)*.

Jnr (*written abbrev of* **Junior**) : **Michael Roberts ~** Michael Roberts fils.

Joan of Arc [,dʒəʊnəv'ɑ:k] *pr n* Jeanne d'Arc.

job [dʒɒb] (*pret & pp* **jobbed**, *cont* **jobbing**) ◇ *n* **1.** [occupation, employment] emploi *m*, travail *m* ▪ **to find a ~** trouver du travail *OR* un emploi ▪ **to look for a ~** chercher un emploi *OR* du travail ▪ **to be out of a ~** être sans emploi *OR* au chômage ▪ **a Saturday/summer ~** un boulot *OR* un job pour le samedi/l'été ▪ **she's got a very good ~** elle a une très bonne situation *OR* place ▪ **he took a ~ as a rep** il a pris un emploi de représentant ▪ **hundreds of ~s have been lost** des centaines d'emplois ont été supprimés, des centaines de personnes ont été licenciées ▪ **he was sleeping on the ~** il dormait pendant le travail *OR* à son poste ▪ **it's more than my ~'s worth** je risquerais ma place (si je faisais ça) ➲ **~s for the boys** *UK* copinage *m* **2.** [piece of work, task] travail *m*, tâche *f* ▪ **to do a good ~** faire du bon travail *OR* du bon boulot ▪ **try to do a better ~ next time** essayez de faire mieux la prochaine fois ▪ **she made a good ~ of fixing the car** elle s'en est bien sortie pour réparer la voiture ▪ **we need to concentrate on the ~ in hand** il faut se con-

centrer sur ce que nous sommes en train de faire ■ **it's not perfect but it does the ~** *fig* ce n'est pas parfait mais ça fera l'affaire ⊙ **on the ~** [working] pendant le travail ■ **to be on the ~**△ *UK* [having sex] être en pleine action
3. [role, responsibility] travail *m* ■ **it's not my ~** ce n'est pas mon travail ■ **she had the ~ of breaking the bad news** c'est elle qui était chargée d'annoncer les mauvaises nouvelles
4. [difficult time] : **to have a ~ doing sthg** avoir du mal à faire qqch ■ **you've got quite a ~ ahead of you** tu as du travail en perspective *OR* de quoi faire
5. [state of affairs] : **it's a good ~ they were home** heureusement qu'ils étaient à la maison ■ **thanks for the map, it's just the ~** merci pour la carte, c'est exactement ce qu'il me fallait ■ **to give sb/sthg up as a bad ~** laisser tomber qqn/qqch qui n'en vaut pas la peine ■ **we decided to make the best of a bad ~** nous avons décidé de faire avec ce que nous avions
6. *inf* [crime] coup *m* ■ **to pull a ~** faire un casse
7. *inf* [item, specimen] : **he drives a flashy Italian ~** il conduit un petit bolide italien
8. COMPUT tâche *f*.
◇ *vi* **1.** [do piecework] travailler à la pièce ■ [work irregularly] faire des petits travaux *OR* boulots
2. *UK* COMM : **he ~s in used cars** il revend des voitures d'occasion.
◇ *vt UK* ST. EX négocier.

Job [dʒəʊb] *pr n* BIBLE Job ■ **she has the patience of ~** elle a une patience à toute épreuve ⊙ **he's a real ~'s comforter** pour remonter le moral, tu peux lui faire confiance *iron* ■ **as poor as ~** pauvre comme Job.

jobber [ˈdʒɒbəʳ] *n UK* **1.** ST. EX courtier *m*, - ère *f* (en Bourse) **2.** [pieceworker] ouvrier *m*, - ère *f* à la pièce ■ [casual worker] journalier *m*, - ère *f* **3.** COMM [wholesaler] grossiste *mf*.

jobbing [ˈdʒɒbɪŋ] *adj UK* : **~ gardener** jardinier *m* à la journée ■ **~ workman** ouvrier *m* à la tâche.

Jobcentre [ˈdʒɒbˌsentəʳ] *n UK agence locale pour l'emploi*, ≃ ANPE *f*.

job creation *n* création *f* d'emplois.

job description *n* description *f* de poste.

jobholder [ˈdʒɒbˌhəʊldəʳ] *n* salarié *m*, - e *f*.

jobhunter [ˈdʒɒbˌhʌntə] = **jobseeker**.

job hunting *n* recherche *f* d'un emploi ■ **to go/to be ~** aller/être à la recherche d'un emploi.

jobless [ˈdʒɒblɪs] ◇ *adj* au chômage, sans emploi.
◇ *npl* : **the ~** les chômeurs *mpl*, les demandeurs *mpl* d'emploi.

job lot *n UK* COMM lot *m* ■ **they sold off the surplus as a ~** ils ont vendu tout l'excédent en un seul lot.

job satisfaction *n* satisfaction *f* professionnelle.

job security *n* sécurité *f* de l'emploi.

jobseeker [ˈdʒɒbsiːkəʳ] *n UK* demandeur *m* d'emploi ■ **~'s allowance** indemnité de chômage.

jobsharing [ˈdʒɒbʃeərɪŋ] *n* partage *m* du travail.

jobsworth [ˈdʒɒbzwəθ] *n UK inf* petit chef *m (qui invoque le règlement pour éviter toute initiative)*.

job title *n* titre *m* (de fonction).

Jocasta [dʒəˈkæstə] *pr n* Jocaste.

jock [dʒɒk] *n inf* **1.** *US* [sporty type] sportif *m* **2.** [jockey] jockey *m* **3.** [disc jockey] disc-jockey *m*.

Jock [dʒɒk] *n inf* [Scottish soldier] soldat *m* écossais.

jockey [ˈdʒɒkɪ] ◇ *n* **1.** SPORT jockey *m* **2.** *US inf* [driver] conducteur *m*, - trice *f* ■ [operator] opérateur *m*, - trice *f* ■ **truck ~** routier *m*.
◇ *vt* **1.** [horse] monter **2.** [trick] manipuler, manœuvrer ■ **they ~ed him into lending them money** ils l'ont adroitement *OR* habilement amené à leur prêter de l'argent.
◇ *vi* : **to ~ for position** *liter* & *fig* essayer de se placer avantageusement.

Jockey shorts® *npl* slip *m* kangourou.

jockstrap [ˈdʒɒkstræp] *n* suspensoir *m*.

jocose [dʒəˈkəʊs] *lit* = **jocular** *(sense 1)*.

jocular [ˈdʒɒkjʊləʳ] *adj* **1.** [jovial] gai, jovial, enjoué **2.** [facetious] facétieux, badin.

jocularly [ˈdʒɒkjʊləlɪ] *adv* jovialement.

jocund [ˈdʒɒkənd] *adj lit* gai, jovial.

jodhpurs [ˈdʒɒdpəz] *npl* jodhpurs *mpl*.

Joe [dʒəʊ] *n US inf* **1.** [man] type *m*, gars *m* **2.** [GI] soldat *m*, GI *m*.

Joe Bloggs [-blɒgz] *UK*, **Joe Blow** *US* & *Australia n inf* Monsieur Tout le Monde.

Joe Public *n inf* Monsieur Tout le Monde.

Joe Six-pack *n US inf* l'Américain *m* moyen.

joey [ˈdʒəʊɪ] *n Australia inf* **1.** [kangaroo] jeune kangourou *m* **2.** [child] mômе *mf*, marmot *m*.

jog [dʒɒg] (*pret* & *pp* **jogged**, *cont* **jogging**) ◇ *n* **1.** [slow run] jogging *m* ■ EQUIT petit trot *m* ■ **to go for a ~** aller faire un jogging **2.** [push] légère poussée *f* ■ [nudge] coup *m* de coude.
◇ *vi* **1.** [run] courir à petites foulées ■ [for fitness] faire du jogging ■ **she ~s to work every morning** tous les matins, elle va travailler en joggant **2.** [bump] se balancer.
◇ *vt* [nudge] donner un léger coup à ■ **to ~ sb's memory** *fig* rafraîchir la mémoire de qqn.
◆ **jog along** *vi insep* **1.** EQUIT trottiner, aller au petit trot **2.** *fig* suivre son cours ■ **my work is jogging along pretty steadily** mon travail avance assez bien.

jogger [ˈdʒɒgəʳ] *n* jogger *mf*, joggeur *m*, - euse *f*.

jogging [ˈdʒɒgɪŋ] *n* jogging *m* ■ **to go ~** faire du jogging ⊙ **~ suit** jogging *m*.

joggle [ˈdʒɒgl] ◇ *vt* **1.** [shake] secouer (légèrement) **2.** CONSTR fixer, assembler *(au moyen d'une cheville ou d'un goujon)*.
◇ *vi* cahoter, ballotter.
◇ *n* **1.** [shake, jolt] secousse *f* **2.** CONSTR cheville *f*, goujon *m*.

jog trot *n* petit trot *m*.
◆ **jog-trot** *vi* trottiner, aller au petit trot.

john [dʒɒn] *n US* **1.** *inf* [lavatory] waters *mpl*, W-C *mpl* **2.** △ [prostitute's client] micheton△ *m*.

John [dʒɒn] *pr n* : **Saint ~** saint Jean ■ **(Saint) ~ the Baptist** (saint) Jean-Baptiste.

John Birch Society [-bɜːtʃ-] *pr n organisation conservatrice américaine, particulièrement hostile au communisme, influente dans les années 50-60*.

John Doe [-dəʊ] *pr n US* l'Américain *m* moyen ■ LAW *expression désignant un homme dont on ignore l'identité ou dont on veut préserver l'anonymat*.

johnny [ˈdʒɒnɪ] (*pl* **johnnies**) *n UK* **1.** *inf dated* [man] type *m*, gars *m* **2.** △ *UK* [condom] : **(rubber) ~** capote *f* anglaise.

Johnny-come-lately *n inf* [newcomer] nouveau venu *m* ■ *pej* [upstart] parvenu *m*.

John o'Groats [-əˈgrəʊts] *pr n village d'Écosse qui marque le point le plus septentrional de la Grande-Bretagne continentale*.

John Thomas *n inf* [penis] zizi *m*.

join [dʒɔɪn] ◇ *vt* **1.** [political party, club etc] adhérer à ■ **so you've been burgled too? ~ the club!** alors, toi aussi tu as été cambriolé? bienvenue au club! ‖ [armed forces] s'engager dans
2. [join company with, meet] rejoindre ■ **she ~ed the procession** elle se joignit au cortège ■ **I ~ed the queue at the ticket office** j'ai fait la queue au guichet ■ **they ~ed us for lunch** ils nous ont retrouvés pour déjeuner ■ **will you ~ me for** *OR* **in a drink?** vous prendrez bien un verre avec moi? ‖ [in activity or common purpose] se joindre à

3. [attach, fasten] joindre, raccorder ■ **the workmen ~ed the pipes (together)** les ouvriers ont raccordé les tuyaux
4. [unite] relier, unir ■ **to be ~ed in marriage** *OR* **matrimony** être uni par les liens du mariage ■ **to ~ hands** [in prayer] joindre les mains ; [link hands] se donner la main ■ **we must ~ forces (against the enemy)** nous devons unir nos forces (contre l'ennemi) ■ **she ~ed forces with her brother** elle s'est alliée à son frère ■ **to ~ battle (with)** entrer en lutte (avec), engager le combat (avec)
5. [intersect with] rejoindre ■ **we camped where the stream ~s the river** nous avons campé là où le ruisseau rejoint la rivière.
◇ *vi* **1.** [become a member] devenir membre
2. [meet, come together] se rejoindre
3. [form an alliance] s'unir, se joindre ■ **we all ~ with you in your sorrow** [sympathize] nous nous associons tous à votre douleur.
◇ *n* [in broken china, wallpaper] (ligne *f* de) raccord *m* ■ SEW couture *f*.
◆ **join in** ◇ *vi insep* : **she started singing and the others ~ed in** elle a commencé à chanter et les autres se sont mis à chanter avec elle.
◇ *vt insep* participer à ■ **he ~ed in the protest** il s'associa aux protestations ■ **all ~ in the chorus!** reprenez tous le refrain en chœur!
◆ **join on** ◇ *vi insep* s'attacher.
◇ *vt sep* attacher, ajouter.
◆ **join up** ◇ *vi insep* **1.** MIL s'engager
2. [meet] : **to ~ up with sb** rejoindre qqn.
◇ *vt sep* = **join** *(vt sense 3)*.

joined-up [dʒɔɪnd-] *adj* : **can you do ~ writing yet?** tu sais lier les lettres?

joiner ['dʒɔɪnəʳ] *n* **1.** [carpenter] menuisier *m*, -ère *f* **2.** *inf* [person who joins clubs] : **he's not really a ~** il n'est pas très sociable.

joinery ['dʒɔɪnərɪ] *n* menuiserie *f*.

joint [dʒɔɪnt] ◇ *n* **1.** [gen - CONSTR] assemblage *m* ■ MECH joint *m* **2.** ANAT articulation *f*, jointure *f* ■ **to put one's shoulder out of ~** se démettre *OR* se déboîter l'épaule ■ **the change in schedule has put everything out of ~** *fig* le changement de programme a tout chamboulé **3.** *UK* CULIN rôti *m* **4.** *inf* [night club] boîte *f* ■ [bar] troquet *m*, boui-boui *m* ■ [gambling house] tripot *m pej* **5.** *US inf* [house] baraque *f* **6.** △ *drug sl* joint△ *m*.
◇ *adj* **1.** [united, combined] conjugué, commun ■ **to take ~ action** mener une action commune **2.** [shared, collective] joint, commun ■ **~ account** BANK compte *m* joint ■ **~ custody** LAW garde *f* conjointe ■ **~ ownership** copropriété *f* ■ **~ property** biens *mpl* communs ■ **~ responsibility** *OR* **liability** responsabilité *f* conjointe ■ **the project is their ~ responsibility** le projet relève de leur responsabilité à tous les deux ■ **~ tenancy** location *f* commune **3.** [associate] : **~ author** coauteur *m* ■ **~ heir** cohéritier *m* ■ **~ owner** copropriétaire *mf*.
◇ *vt* **1.** MECH assembler, emboîter **2.** *UK* CULIN découper.

Joint Chiefs of Staff *pr npl* : **the ~** *organe consultatif du ministère américain de la Défense, composé des chefs d'état-major des trois armes.*

jointed ['dʒɔɪntɪd] *adj* articulé.

join-the-dots *n (U) UK jeu qui consiste à relier des points numérotés pour découvrir un dessin.*

jointly ['dʒɔɪntlɪ] *adv* conjointement ■ **the house is ~ owned** la maison est en copropriété ■ **~ liable** LAW coresponsable, conjointement responsable.

joint-stock company *n UK* société *f* par actions.

joint venture *n* joint-venture *m*.

joist [dʒɔɪst] *n* solive *f*.

joke [dʒəʊk] ◇ *n* **1.** [verbal] plaisanterie *f* ■ **to tell a ~** raconter une plaisanterie ■ **to make a ~ of** *OR* **about sthg** plaisanter sur *OR* à propos de qqch ■ **we did it for a ~** nous l'avons fait pour rire *OR* pour rigoler ■ **I don't get** *OR* **see the ~** je ne comprends pas l'astuce ■ **he can't take a ~** il n'a pas le sens de l'humour ■ **it's gone beyond a ~** la plaisanterie a assez duré ■ **it's a private ~** c'est une plaisanterie entre nous/eux ■ **it was no ~ climbing that cliff!** escalader cette falaise, ce n'était pas de la tarte *OR* de la rigolade! **2.** [prank] plaisanterie *f*, farce *f* ■ **to play a ~ on sb** jouer un tour à qqn, faire une farce à qqn ■ **the ~ is on you** la plaisanterie s'est retournée contre toi **3.** [laughing stock] risée *f*.
◇ *vi* plaisanter ■ **I was only joking** je ne faisais que plaisanter ■ **you must be joking, you have (got) to be joking!** vous plaisantez!, vous n'êtes pas sérieux! ■ **Tom's passed his driving test – you're joking!** Tom a eu son permis de conduire – sans blague! *OR* tu veux rire? ■ **to ~ about sthg** se moquer de qqch.

joker ['dʒəʊkəʳ] *n* **1.** [funny person] farceur *m*, - euse *f* ■ *pej* [frivolous person] plaisantin *m* **2.** [in cards] joker *m* **3.** △ [man] type *m*, mec△ *m* **4.** [clause] clause *f* contradictoire.

jokey ['dʒəʊkɪ] (*comp* **jokier**, *superl* **jokiest**) *adj inf* comique.

joking ['dʒəʊkɪŋ] ◇ *adj* badin.
◇ *n (U)* plaisanterie *f*, plaisanteries *fpl* ■ **~ apart** *OR* **aside** plaisanterie mise à part, blague à part.

jokingly ['dʒəʊkɪŋlɪ] *adv* en plaisantant, pour plaisanter.

joky ['dʒəʊkɪ] *inf* = **jokey**.

jollity ['dʒɒlətɪ] (*pl* **jollities**) *n* entrain *m*, gaieté *f*.

jolly ['dʒɒlɪ] (*comp* **jollier**, *superl* **jolliest**, *pret & pp* **jollied**)
◇ *adj* **1.** [person] gai, joyeux, jovial **2.** *UK* [enjoyable] agréable, plaisant ■ **we had a very ~ time** nous nous sommes bien amusés ▶ **~ hockey sticks** *expression parodique utilisée pour désigner une femme bourgeoise, éduquée dans une public school, caractérisée par un enthousiasme débordant et une certaine naïveté.*
◇ *adv UK* rudement, drôlement ■ **you'll ~ well do what you're told!** tu feras ce qu'on te dit de faire, un point c'est tout! ■ **it ~ well serves them right!** c'est vraiment bien fait pour eux!
◇ *vt UK* [coax] enjôler, entortiller ■ **he'll come if you ~ him along a bit** il viendra si tu le pousses un peu.
◆ **jolly up** *vt sep UK* égayer ■ **we jollied up the room with some posters** nous avons égayé la pièce avec des affiches.

jolly boat *n* chaloupe *f*, canot *m*.

Jolly Roger [-'rɒdʒəʳ] *n* pavillon *m* noir, drapeau *m* de pirate.

jolt [dʒəʊlt] ◇ *vt* **1.** [physically] secouer **2.** [mentally] secouer, choquer ■ **to ~ sb into action** pousser qqn à agir.
◇ *vi* cahoter ■ **the jeep ~ed along the track** la jeep avançait en cahotant sur la piste.
◇ *n* **1.** [jar] secousse *f*, coup *m* **2.** [start] sursaut *m*, choc *m* ■ **to wake up with a ~** se réveiller en sursaut.

Jonah ['dʒəʊnə] *pr n* Jonas.

Joneses ['dʒəʊnzɪz] *npl* : **to keep up with the ~** *inf* vouloir faire aussi bien que le voisin, ne pas vouloir être en reste.

Jordan ['dʒɔːdn] *pr n* Jordanie *f* ■ **in ~** en Jordanie ■ **the (River) ~** le Jourdain.

Jordanian [dʒɔː'deɪnjən] ◇ *n* Jordanien *m*, - enne *f*.
◇ *adj* jordanien.

Josephine ['dʒəʊzəfiːn] *pr n* : **the Empress ~** l'impératrice *f* Joséphine.

josh [dʒɒʃ] *inf* ◇ *vi* blaguer ■ **I'm only ~ing** je plaisante.
◇ *vt* charrier.

Joshua ['dʒɒʃʊə] *pr n* Josué.

joss stick [dʒɒs-] *n* bâtonnet *m* d'encens.

jostle ['dʒɒsl] ◇ *vi* se bousculer ■ **they were jostling for seats** ils se bousculaient pour avoir des places.
◇ *vt* bousculer, heurter.
◇ *n* bousculade *f*.

jot [dʒɒt] (*pret & pp* **jotted**, *cont* **jotting**) *n* : **it won't change his mind one ~** ça ne le fera absolument pas changer d'avis ■ **there isn't a ~ of truth in what he says** il n'y a pas un brin de vérité dans ce qu'il raconte.
◆ **jot down** *vt sep* noter, prendre note de.

jotter ['dʒɒtəʳ] *n UK* [exercise book] cahier *m*, carnet *m* ■ [pad] bloc-notes *m*.

jottings ['dʒɒtɪŋz] *npl* notes *fpl*.

joule [dʒuːl] *n* joule *m*.

journal [ˈdʒɜːnl] *n* **1.** [publication] revue *f* **2.** [diary] journal *m* intime **3.** NAUT [logbook] journal *m* de bord **4.** LAW procès-verbal *m* **5.** MECH tourillon *m* ■ **~ bearing** palier *m* (de tourillon).

journalese [ˌdʒɜːnəˈliːz] *n pej* jargon *m* journalistique.

journalism [ˈdʒɜːnəlɪzm] *n* journalisme *m*.

journalist [ˈdʒɜːnəlɪst] *n* journaliste *mf*.

journalistic [dʒɜːnəˈlɪstɪk] *adj* journalistique.

journey [ˈdʒɜːnɪ] ◇ *n* **1.** [gen] voyage *m* ■ **to set out on a ~** partir en voyage ■ **she went on a ~ to Europe** elle a fait un voyage en Europe ■ **the ~ back** *OR* **home** le (voyage du) retour ■ **to break one's ~** [in plane, bus] faire escale ; [in car] faire une halte, s'arrêter **2.** [shorter distance] trajet *m* ■ **the ~ to work takes me ten minutes** je mets dix minutes pour aller à mon travail.
◇ *vi fml* voyager.

journeyman [ˈdʒɜːnɪmən] (*pl* **journeymen** [-mən]) *n* [qualified apprentice] compagnon *m*.

joust [dʒaʊst] ◇ *n* joute *f*.
◇ *vi* jouter.

Jove [dʒəʊv] *pr n* Jupiter ■ **by ~!** *UK inf dated* par Jupiter!

jovial [ˈdʒəʊvjəl] *adj* jovial, enjoué.

jowls [dʒaʊlz] *npl* bajoues *fpl*.

joy [dʒɔɪ] *n* **1.** [pleasure] joie *f*, plaisir *m* ■ **to shout with** *OR* **for ~** crier de joie ■ **her grandchildren are a great ~ to her** ses petits-enfants sont la joie de sa vie ■ **the ~s of gardening** les plaisirs *OR* les charmes du jardinage **2.** *inf* [luck, satisfaction] **: they had no ~ at the casino** ils n'ont pas eu de chance au casino ■ **any ~ at the job centre?** tu as trouvé quelque chose à l'agence pour l'emploi? ■ **you'll get no ~ out of her** tu n'as pas grand-chose à attendre d'elle.

Joycean [ˈdʒɔɪsɪən] *adj* de (James) Joyce.

joyful [ˈdʒɔɪfʊl] *adj* joyeux, enjoué.

joyfully [ˈdʒɔɪfʊlɪ] *adv* joyeusement.

joyless [ˈdʒɔɪlɪs] *adj* [unhappy] triste, sans joie ■ [dull] morne, maussade.

joyous [ˈdʒɔɪəs] *adj lit* joyeux.

joyride [ˈdʒɔɪraɪd] (*pret* **joyrode** [-rəʊd], *pp* **joyridden** [-rɪdn]) ◇ *n* **: they went for a ~** ils ont volé une voiture pour aller faire un tour.
◇ *vi* **: to go joyriding** faire une virée dans une voiture volée.

joyrider [ˈdʒɔɪraɪdəʳ] *n personne qui vole une voiture pour faire un tour.*

joyrode [-rəʊd] *pt* ▷ **joyride**.

joystick [ˈdʒɔɪstɪk] *n* **1.** AERON manche *m* à balai **2.** COMPUT manette *f* (de jeux), manche *m* à balai.

JP (*abbrev of* **Justice of the Peace**) *n UK* ≃ juge d'instance.

JUSTICE OF THE PEACE

Les *JPs* sont nommés par le *Lord Chancellor*. Bien que théoriquement chacun ait le droit de poser sa candidature, ce sont en général des notables locaux (médecins, professeurs à la retraite) jouissant d'une bonne réputation.

Jr. (*written abbrev of* **Junior**) junior, fils.

JSA [ˌdʒeɪesˈeɪ] (*abbrev of* **Job Seekers Allowance**) *n UK* allocation *f* chômage.

jubilant [ˈdʒuːbɪlənt] *adj* débordant de joie, radieux ■ **the Prime Minister was ~ at the election results** le Premier ministre fut transporté de joie à la vue des résultats du scrutin ■ **he gave a ~ shout** il poussa un cri de joie.

jubilation [ˌdʒuːbɪˈleɪʃn] *n (U)* [rejoicing] joie *f*, jubilation *f* ■ [celebration] réjouissances *fpl*.

jubilee [ˈdʒuːbɪliː] *n* jubilé *m*.

Judaea [dʒuːˈdɪə] *pr n* Judée *f* ■ **in ~** en Judée.

Judaeo-Christian [dʒuːˈdiːəʊ-] *adj* judéo-chrétien.

Judah [ˈdʒuːdə] *pr n* Juda.

Judaic [dʒuːˈdeɪɪk] *adj* judaïque.

Judaism [ˈdʒuːdeɪˌɪzm] *n* judaïsme *m*.

judas [ˈdʒuːdəs] *n* [peephole] judas.

Judas [ˈdʒuːdəs] ◇ *pr n* BIBLE Judas ■ **~ Iscariot** Judas Iscariote.
◇ *n* [traitor] judas *m*.

judder [ˈdʒʌdəʳ] ◇ *vi UK* [gen] vibrer ■ [brakes, clutch] brouter ■ **the bus ~ed to a halt** le bus s'est arrêté en cahotant.
◇ *n* trépidation *f* ■ [of vehicle, machine] broutement *m*.

Judea [dʒuːˈdɪə] = **Judaea**.

Judeo-Christian [dʒuːˈdiːəʊ-] = **Judaeo-Christian**.

judge [dʒʌdʒ] ◇ *n* **1.** LAW juge *mf* ■ **presiding ~** président *m* du tribunal **2.** [in a competition] membre *m* du jury ■ SPORT juge *mf* ■ **the ~s were divided** le jury était partagé **3.** *fig* juge *m* ■ **I'll let you be the ~ of that** je vous laisse juge ■ **he's a bad ~ of character** il manque de psychologie.
◇ *vt* **1.** [pass judgment on, adjudicate] juger ■ **don't ~ him too harshly** ne le juge pas trop sévèrement **2.** [consider] juger, considérer ■ [estimate] évaluer, estimer ■ **can you ~ the distance?** peux-tu évaluer la distance?
◇ *vi* juger ■ **as far as I can ~** pour autant que je puisse en juger ■ **judging from** *OR* **by what he said** si j'en juge par ce qu'il a dit.
◆ **Judges** *n* **: (the)book of Judges** BIBLE (le livre des) Juges.

judge advocate (*pl* **judge advocates**) *n* MIL assesseur *m* *(d'un tribunal militaire)*.

judgement *etc* [ˈdʒʌdʒmənt] = **judgment**.

judgment [ˈdʒʌdʒmənt] *n* **1.** LAW & RELIG jugement *m* ■ **to pass ~ on sb/sthg** porter un jugement sur qqn/qqch ■ **to sit in ~ on** juger **2.** [opinion] jugement *m*, opinion *f*, avis *m* ■ **to reserve ~ on sthg** réserver son jugement *OR* opinion sur qqch ■ **against my better ~ we decided to go** malgré mon avis, nous avons décidé d'y aller **3.** [discernment] jugement *m*, discernement *m*.

judgmental [dʒʌdʒˈmentl] *adj* [person - by nature] enclin à juger *OR* à critiquer ■ **I'm not being ~** ce n'est pas une critique que je vous fais.

Judgment Day *n* (jour *m* du) Jugement *m* dernier.

judicature [ˈdʒuːdɪkətʃəʳ] *n* LAW **1.** [judge's authority] justice *f* **2.** [court's jurisdiction] juridiction *f* ■ **court of ~** cour *f* de justice **3.** [judges collectively] magistrature *f*.

judicial [dʒuːˈdɪʃl] *adj* **1.** LAW judiciaire ■ **to take** *OR* **to bring ~ proceedings against sb** attaquer qqn en justice ➤ **~ inquiry** enquête *f* judiciaire ■ **~ review** *US* [of ruling] examen *m* d'une décision de justice *(par une juridiction supérieure)* ; [of law] examen de la constitutionnalité d'une loi ■ **~ separation** séparation *f* de corps **2.** [impartial] impartial, critique.

judicially [dʒuːˈdɪʃəlɪ] *adv* judiciairement.

judiciary [dʒuːˈdɪʃərɪ] ◇ *adj* judiciaire.
◇ *n* **1.** [judicial authority] pouvoir *m* judiciaire **2.** [judges collectively] magistrature *f*.

judicious [dʒuːˈdɪʃəs] *adj* judicieux.

judiciously [dʒuːˈdɪʃəslɪ] *adv* judicieusement.

judo [ˈdʒuːdəʊ] *n* judo *m*.

jug [dʒʌg] (*pret & pp* **jugged**, *cont* **jugging**) ◇ *n* **1.** *UK* [small - for milk] pot *m* ; [- for water] carafe *f* ; [- for wine] pichet *m*, carafe *f* ■ [large - earthenware] cruche *f* ; [- metal, plastic] broc *m* ■ **a ~ of wine** une carafe de vin **2.** △ *UK* [jail] tôle△ *f*, taule△ *f*, cabane△ *f* **3.** *US* [narrow-necked] bonbonne *f*.
◇ *vt* CULIN cuire à l'étouffée *OR* à l'étuvée.

jugful [ˈdʒʌgfʊl] *n* (contenu *m* d'un) pot *m*, (contenu *m* d'une) carafe *f*.

jugged hare [dʒʌgd-] *n* lièvre *m* à l'étouffée.

juggernaut ['dʒʌgənɔ:t] *n* **1.** *UK* [large lorry] gros poids lourd *m* **2.** [force] force *f* fatale.

juggle ['dʒʌgl] <> *vi* [as entertainment] jongler ▪ **to ~ with** [figures, dates] jongler avec.
<> *vt liter & fig* jongler avec ▪ **he ~d all the different possibilities** *fig* il envisagea toutes les possibilités.
<> *n* jonglerie *f*.

juggler ['dʒʌglər] *n* **1.** [entertainer] jongleur *m*, - euse *f* **2.** [deceitful person] tricheur *m*, - euse *f*.

juggling ['dʒʌglɪŋ], **jugglery** ['dʒʌglərɪ] *n liter & fig* jonglerie *f*.

Jugoslavia *etc* [,ju:gəʊ'slɑ:vjə] = **Yugoslavia**.

jugular ['dʒʌgjʊlər] <> *adj* jugulaire ▪ **~ vein** jugulaire *f*.
<> *n* jugulaire *f* ▪ **to go for the ~** *inf* attaquer qqn sur ses points faibles.

juice [dʒu:s] <> *n* **1.** CULIN jus *m* ▪ **grapefruit ~** jus de pamplemousse **2.** BIOL suc *m* **3.** *inf* [electricity] jus *m* ▪ [petrol] essence *f* **4.** *US inf* [spirits] tord-boyaux *m* ▪ [wine] pinard *m*.
<> *vt* [fruit] presser.

juicer ['dʒu:sər] *n* presse-fruits *m inv*.

juicy ['dʒu:sɪ] (*comp* **juicier**, *superl* **juiciest**) *adj* **1.** [fruit] juteux **2.** *inf* [profitable] juteux **3.** *inf* [racy] savoureux ▪ **a ~ story** une histoire osée OR piquante ▪ **let's hear all the ~ details** racontenous les détails croustillants.

ju-jitsu [dʒu:'dʒɪtsu:] *n* jiu-jitsu *m inv*.

jukebox ['dʒu:kbɒks] *n* juke-box *m*.

Jul. (*written abbrev of* **July**) juill.

Julian calendar *n* calendrier *m* julien.

Julius Caesar [,dʒu:ljəs'si:zər] *pr n* Jules César.

July [dʒu:'laɪ] *n* juillet *m*, *see also* **February**.

jumble ['dʒʌmbl] <> *n* **1.** [confusion, disorder] fouillis *m*, désordre *m* ▪ **my things are all in a ~** mes affaires sont tout en désordre **2.** *UK* [articles for jumble sale] bric-à-brac *m*.
<> *vt* **1.** [objects, belongings] mélanger ▪ **her clothes were all ~d (up OR together) in a suitcase** ses vêtements étaient fourrés pêle-mêle dans une valise **2.** [thoughts, ideas] embrouiller ▪ **his essay was just a collection of ~d ideas** sa dissertation n'était qu'un fourre-tout d'idées confuses.

jumble sale *n UK vente de charité où sont vendus des articles d'occasion et des produits faits maison.*

jumbo ['dʒʌmbəʊ] (*pl* **jumbos**) *inf* <> *n* **1.** [elephant] éléphant *m*, pachyderme *m* **2.** = **jumbo jet**.
<> *adj* énorme, géant.

jumbo jet *n* (avion *m*) gros-porteur *m*, jumbo *m*, jumbo-jet *m*.

jumbo-size(d) *adj* énorme, géant ▪ **a ~ packet of washing powder** un paquet de lessive familial.

jump [dʒʌmp] <> *vi* **1.** [leap] sauter, bondir ▪ **they ~ed across the crevasse** ils ont traversé la crevasse d'un bond ▪ **to ~ back** faire un bond en arrière ▪ **she ~ed into/out of her car** elle a sauté dans/hors de sa voiture ▪ **he ~ed (down) off the train** il a sauté du train ▪ **he ~ed off the bridge** il s'est jeté du haut du pont ▪ **he ~ed up, he ~ed to his feet** il se leva d'un bond ▪ **why did he ~ out of the window?** pourquoi a-t-il sauté par la fenêtre? ▮ *fig* **this record ~s** ce disque saute ▪ **he ~ed from one topic to another** il passait rapidement d'un sujet à un autre ▪ **to ~ for joy** sauter de joie ▪ **to ~ to conclusions** tirer des conclusions hâtives ➋ **~ to it!** *inf* grouille! ▪ **to ~ down sb's throat** *inf* houspiller OR enguirlander qqn **2.** [start] sursauter, tressauter ▪ **when the phone rang his heart ~ed** il tressaillit en entendant la sonnerie du téléphone **3.** [rise sharply] grimper OR monter en flèche ▪ **prices ~ed dramatically in 1974** les prix ont grimpé de façon spectaculaire en 1974 **4.** *US inf* [be lively] être très animé ▪ **the joint was ~ing** ça chauffait dans la boîte.
<> *vt* **1.** [leap over] sauter ▪ **to ~ a fence** sauter OR franchir un obstacle **2.** [horse] faire sauter **3.** [omit, skip] sauter **4.** *inf* [attack] sauter sur, agresser **5.** *inf* [leave, abscond from] : **to ~ ship** *liter & fig* quitter le navire ▪ **to ~ bail** ne pas comparaître au tribunal *(après avoir été libéré sous caution)* **6.** [not wait one's turn at] : **to ~ the queue** ne pas attendre son tour, resquiller ▪ **she ~ed the lights** elle a grillé OR brûlé le feu (rouge) **7.** *inf* [not pay for, take illegally] : **to ~ a train** *esp US* voyager sans billet.
<> *n* **1.** [leap, bound] saut *m*, bond *m* ▪ **we need to keep one ~ ahead of the competition** *fig* nous devons garder une longueur d'avance sur nos concurrents **2.** [sharp rise] bond *m*, hausse *f* **3.** EQUIT [fence, obstacle] obstacle *m* **4.** COMPUT saut *m* **5.** GAMES prise *f* (de pion).

◆ **jump about** *UK*, **jump around** *vi insep* sautiller.

◆ **jump at** *vt insep* sauter sur, saisir ▪ **he ~ed at the chance to go abroad** il sauta sur l'occasion de partir à l'étranger.

◆ **jump in** *vi insep* **1.** *liter* [into vehicle] monter ▪ [into water, hole] sauter **2.** *inf fig* [intervene] intervenir.

◆ **jump on** *vt insep* **1.** *liter* [bicyle, horse] sauter sur ▪ [bus, train] sauter dans ▪ [person] sauter sur **2.** *fig* [mistake] repérer ▪ **the boss ~s on every little mistake** aucune faute n'échappe au patron.

jumped-up ['dʒʌmpt-] *adj UK inf* parvenu ▪ **she's just a ~ shop assistant** ce n'est qu'une petite vendeuse qui se donne de grands airs OR qui se prend au sérieux.

jumper ['dʒʌmpər] *n* **1.** *UK* [sweater] pull-over *m* **2.** *US* [dress] robe-chasuble *f* **3.** [person] sauteur *m*, - euse *f*.

jumper cables *US* = **jump leads**.

jumping ['dʒʌmpɪŋ] *n* EQUIT jumping *m*.

jumping-off point, jumping-off place *n* point *m* de départ, tremplin *m*.

jump jet *n UK* avion *m* à décollage vertical.

jump leads *npl UK* câbles *mpl* de démarrage.

jump-off *n* EQUIT barrage *m*.

jump rope *n US* corde *f* à sauter.

jump seat *n UK* strapontin *m*.

jump-start *vt* : **to ~ a car** [by pushing or rolling] faire démarrer une voiture en la poussant OR en la mettant dans une pente ; [with jump leads] faire démarrer une voiture avec des câbles *(branchés sur la batterie d'une autre voiture)*.

jumpsuit ['dʒʌmpsu:t] *n* combinaison-pantalon *f*.

jumpy ['dʒʌmpɪ] (*comp* **jumpier**, *superl* **jumpiest**) *adj* **1.** *inf* [edgy] nerveux **2.** ST. EX instab le, fluctuant.

Jun. 1. *written abbr of* **June 2.** (*written abbrev of* **Junior**) junior, fils.

junction ['dʒʌŋkʃn] *n* **1.** [of roads] carrefour *m*, croisement *m* ▪ [of railway lines, traffic lanes] embranchement *m* ▪ [of rivers, canals] confluent *m* **2.** ELEC [of wires] jonction *f*, raccordement *m*.

junction box *n UK* boîte *f* de dérivation.

juncture ['dʒʌŋktʃər] *n* **1.** *fml* [moment] conjoncture *f* ▪ **at this ~** dans la conjoncture actuelle, dans les circonstances actuelles **2.** LING joncture *f*, jointure *f*, frontière *f* **3.** TECH jointure *f*.

June [dʒu:n] *n* juin *m*, *see also* **February**.

June beetle, June bug *n* hanneton *m*.

jungle ['dʒʌŋgl] <> *n* **1.** [tropical forest] jungle *f* ▪ **'The Jungle Book'** *Kipling* 'le Livre de la jungle' **2.** *fig* jungle *f* ▪ **it's a ~ out there** c'est la jungle là-bas **3.** MUS jungle *f*.
<> *comp* [animal] de la jungle.

jungle fever *n (U)* paludisme *m*.

jungle gym *n ensemble de jeux pour les enfants (balançoires, toboggans, etc.)*

junior ['dʒu:njər] <> *n* **1.** [younger person] cadet *m*, - ette *f* ▪ **he is five years her ~** il est de cinq ans son cadet, il a cinq ans de moins qu'elle **2.** [subordinate] subordonné *m*, - e *f*, subalterne *mf* **3.** *UK* [pupil] écolier *m*, - ère *f (entre 7 et 11 ans)* **4.** *US* SCH élève *mf* de troisième année ▪ *US* UNIV étudiant *m*, - e *f* de première année **5.** *US inf* [term of address] fiston *m*.
<> *comp UK* [teaching, teacher] dans le primaire.

◇ *adj* **1.** [younger] cadet, plus jeune **2.** [lower in rank] subordonné, subalterne ■ **he's ~ to her in the department** il est son subalterne dans le service ● **~ doctor** interne *mf* ■ **~ executive** cadre *m* débutant, jeune cadre ■ **the ~ faculty** *US* UNIV les enseignants non titulaires ■ **~ minister** sous-secrétaire *m* d'État ■ **~ partner** associé *m* adjoint **3.** [juvenile] jeune.
◆ **Junior** = **Jnr**.

Junior College *n* [in US] *établissement d'enseignement supérieur où l'on obtient un diplôme en deux ans.*

junior common room *n UK* UNIV salle *f* des étudiants.

junior high school *n US* ≃ collège *m* d'enseignement secondaire.

Junior League *pr n association américaine de jeunes femmes de droite.*

junior school *n UK* école *f* élémentaire *(pour les enfants de 7 à 11 ans)* ■ **a ~ teacher** instituteur *m*, institutrice *f*.

juniper ['dʒu:nɪpəʳ] *n* genévrier *m* ■ **~ berry** baie *f* de genièvre.

junk [dʒʌŋk] ◇ *n* **1.** *inf (U) inf* [anything poor-quality or worthless] pacotille *f*, camelote *f* ■ **this watch is a real piece of ~** cette montre, c'est vraiment de la camelote *OR* c'est de la vraie camelote ■ **all his so-called antiques were just a pile of ~** ses prétendues antiquités n'étaient en fait qu'un ramassis de vieilleries ■ **his latest film is a load of ~** *fig* son dernier film est absolument nul *OR* un vrai navet **2.** *(U)* [second-hand, inexpensive goods] bric-à-brac *m* **3.** *inf (U) inf* [stuff] trucs *mpl*, machins *mpl* ■ **what's all that ~ in the hall?** qu'est-ce que c'est que ce bric-à-brac *OR* ce bazar dans l'entrée? **4.** [boat] jonque *f*.
◇ *vt inf* jeter (à la poubelle), balancer.

junk bond *n* junk bond *m*.

junket ['dʒʌŋkɪt] ◇ *n* **1.** *inf pej* [official journey] voyage *m* aux frais de la princesse **2.** *inf* [festive occasion] banquet *m*, festin *m* **3.** CULIN : ≃ fromage *m* frais (sucré et parfumé).
◇ *vi inf* voyager aux frais de la princesse.

junk food *n inf* nourriture *f* de mauvaise qualité ■ **their kids eat nothing but ~** leurs gosses ne mangent que des cochonneries.

junkie ['dʒʌŋkɪ] *n inf* **1.** [drug addict] drogué *m*, - e *f*, junkie *mf* **2.** *fig* dingue *mf*, accro *mf* ■ **a television/football ~** un dingue de télé/de football.

junk jewellery *n (U)* bijoux *mpl* fantaisie.

junk mail *n* publicité *f* (reçue par courrier).

junk shop *n* magasin *m* de brocante ■ **at the ~** chez le brocanteur.

junky ['dʒʌŋkɪ] = **junkie**.

junkyard ['dʒʌŋkjɑ:d] *n* **1.** [for scrap metal] entrepôt *m* de ferraille ■ **at the ~** chez le ferrailleur **2.** [for discarded objects] dépotoir *m*.

Juno ['dʒu:nəʊ] *pr n* Junon.

junoesque [,dʒu:nəʊ'esk] *adj* [woman] imposant.

Junr = **Jnr**.

junta [*UK* 'dʒʌntə, *US* 'hʊntə] *n* junte *f*.

Jupiter ['dʒu:pɪtəʳ] *pr n* **1.** ASTRON Jupiter *f* **2.** MYTH Jupiter.

Jurassic [dʒʊ'ræsɪk] ◇ *adj* jurassique.
◇ *n* jurassique *m*.

juridical [dʒʊə'rɪdɪkl] *adj* juridique.

jurisdiction [,dʒʊərɪs'dɪkʃn] *n* LAW & ADMIN juridiction *f* ■ **the federal government has no ~ over such cases** de tels cas ne relèvent pas de la compétence *OR* des attributions du gouvernement fédéral ■ **to come** *OR* **to fall within the ~ of** relever de la juridiction de ■ **this territory is within the ~ of the United States** ce territoire est soumis à l'autorité judiciaire des États-Unis.

jurisprudence [,dʒʊərɪs'pru:dəns] *n* jurisprudence *f*.

jurist ['dʒʊərɪst] *n* juriste *mf*.

juror ['dʒʊərəʳ] *n* juré *m*.

jury ['dʒʊərɪ] (*pl* **juries**) ◇ *n* **1.** LAW jury *m* ■ **to serve on a ~** faire partie d'un jury ■ **Ladies and Gentlemen of the ~** Mesdames et Messieurs les jurés ● **the ~ is still out on that one** ça reste à voir **2.** [in contest] jury *m*.
◇ *adj* NAUT de fortune, improvisé.

jury box *n* sièges *mpl* des jurés.

juryman ['dʒʊərɪmən] (*pl* **jurymen** [-mən]) *n* juré *m*.

jury-rigging *n* LAW truquage *m* d'un jury.

jury service *n* participation *f* à un jury.

jurywoman ['dʒʊərɪ,wʊmən] (*pl* **jurywomen** [-,wɪmɪn]) *n* jurée *f*.

just[1] [dʒʌst] *adv* **1.** [indicating immediate past] juste ■ **~ last week** pas plus tard que la semaine dernière ■ **they had (only) ~ arrived** ils venaient (tout) juste d'arriver ■ **she's ~ this moment** *OR* **minute left the office** elle vient de sortir du bureau à l'instant ■ **he's ~ been to Mexico** il revient *OR* rentre du Mexique
2. [indicating present or immediate future] juste ■ **I was ~ going to phone you** j'allais juste *OR* justement te téléphoner, j'étais sur le point de te téléphoner ■ **I'm ~ off** *inf* je m'en vais ■ **~ coming!** *inf* j'arrive tout de suite! ■ **I'm ~ making tea, do you want some?** je suis en train de faire du thé, tu en veux?
3. [only, merely] juste, seulement ■ **~ a little** juste un peu ■ **~ a minute** *OR* **a moment** *OR* **a second, please** une (petite) minute *OR* un (petit) instant, s'il vous plaît ■ **it was ~ a dream** ce n'était qu'un rêve ■ **he's ~ a clerk** ce n'est qu'un simple employé ■ **we're ~ friends** nous sommes amis, c'est tout ■ **he was ~ trying to help** il voulait juste *OR* simplement rendre service ■ **if he could ~ work a little harder!** si seulement il pouvait travailler un peu plus! ■ **don't argue, ~ do it!** ne discute pas, fais-le, c'est tout! ■ **you can't ask ~ anybody to present the prizes** tu ne peux pas demander au premier venu de présenter les prix ■ **this is not ~ any horse race, this is the Derby!** ça n'est pas n'importe quelle course de chevaux, c'est le Derby!
4. [exactly, precisely] exactement, juste ■ **~ at that moment** juste à ce moment-là ■ **that's ~ what I needed** c'est exactement *OR* juste ce qu'il me fallait ; *iron* il ne me manquait plus que ça ■ **~ what are you getting at?** où veux-tu en venir exactement? ■ **he's ~ like his father** c'est son père tout craché ■ **oh, I can ~ picture it!** oh, je vois tout à fait! ■ **you speak French ~ as well as I do** ton français est tout aussi bon que le mien ■ **I'd ~ as soon go tomorrow** j'aimerais autant y aller demain ■ **(it's) ~ my luck!** *iron* c'est bien ma chance! ■ **don't come in ~ yet** n'entre pas tout de suite
5. [barely] (tout) juste, à peine ■ **I could ~ make out what they were saying** je parvenais tout juste à entendre ce qu'ils disaient ■ **I ~ missed a lorry** j'ai failli heurter un camion ▮ [a little] : **it's ~ after/before two o'clock** il est un peu plus/moins de deux heures ■ **~ afterwards** juste après
6. [possibly] : **I may** *OR* **might ~ be able to do it** il n'est pas impossible que je puisse le faire
7. [emphatic use] : **~ think what might have happened!** imagine un peu ce qui aurait pu arriver! ■ **it ~ isn't good enough** c'est loin d'être satisfaisant, c'est tout ■ **he looks terrible in that suit – doesn't he ~!** ce costume ne lui va pas du tout – je ne te le fais pas dire! ■ **don't you ~ love that hat?** adorable, ce chapeau, non? ▮ [with adjective] : **the meal was ~ delicious** le repas était tout simplement *OR* vraiment délicieux ■ **everything is ~ fine** tout est parfait.
◆ **just about** *adv phr* **1.** [very nearly] presque, quasiment ■ **I've ~ about had enough of your sarcasm!** j'en ai franchement assez de tes sarcasmes!
2. [barely] (tout) juste ■ **can you reach the shelf? – ~ about!** est-ce que tu peux atteindre l'étagère? – (tout) juste! ■ **his handwriting is ~ about legible** son écriture est tout juste *OR* à peine lisible
3. [approximately] : **their plane should be taking off ~ about now** leur avion devrait être sur le point de décoller.
◆ **just as** *conj phr* **1.** [at the same time as] juste au moment où
2. [exactly as] : **~ as I thought/predicted** comme je le pensais/prévoyais.
◆ **just in case** ◇ *conj phr* juste au cas où ■ **~ in case we don't see each other** juste au cas où nous ne nous verrions pas.

◇ *adv phr* au cas où ■ **take a coat, ~ in case** prends un manteau, on ne sait jamais *OR* au cas où.
◆ **just like that** *adv phr inf* comme ça ■ **he told me to clear off, ~ like that!** il m'a dit de me tirer, carrément!
◆ **just now** *adv phr* **1.** [at this moment] : **I'm busy ~ now** je suis occupé pour le moment
2. [a short time ago] : **I heard a noise ~ now** je viens juste d'entendre un bruit ■ **when did this happen? – ~ now** quand cela s'est-il passé? – à l'instant.
◆ **just on** *adv phr UK* exactement.
◆ **just so** ◇ *adv phr fml* [expressing agreement] c'est exact.
◇ *adj phr UK* [properly arranged] parfait ■ **she likes everything (to be) ~ so** elle aime que tout soit parfait.
◆ **just then** *adv phr* à ce moment-là.
◆ **just the same** *adv phr* [nonetheless] quand même.

just[2] [dʒʌst] ◇ *adj* **1.** [fair, impartial] juste, équitable ■ [reasonable, moral] juste, légitime ■ **a ~ cause** une juste cause ■ **he has ~ cause for complaint** il a de bonnes raisons pour se plaindre **2.** [deserved] juste, mérité ▶ **he got his ~ deserts** il n'a eu que ce qu'il méritait, ce n'est que justice **3.** [accurate] juste, exact **4.** RELIG [righteous] juste.
◇ *npl* : **the ~** les justes *mpl* ■ **to sleep the sleep of the ~** dormir du sommeil du juste.

justice ['dʒʌstɪs] *n* **1.** LAW justice *f* ■ **a court of ~** une cour de justice ■ **to dispense ~** rendre la justice ■ **to bring sb to ~** traduire qqn en justice ▶ **the Justice Department, the Department of Justice** *US* ≃ le ministère de la Justice **2.** [fairness] justice *f*, équité *f* ■ **there's no ~ in their claim** leur demande est dénuée de fondement ■ **to do sb/sthg ~** [represent fairly] rendre justice à qqn/qqch ■ **to do him ~, he wasn't informed of the decision** il faut lui rendre cette justice que *OR* il faut reconnaître que l'on ne l'avait pas mis au courant de la décision **3.** [punishment, vengeance] justice *f* **4.** [judge] juge *m* ■ **Justice of the Peace** = **JP**.

justifiable ['dʒʌstɪˌfaɪəbl] *adj* justifiable ■ LAW légitime.

justifiable homicide *n* **1.** [killing in self-defence] légitime défense *f* **2.** [state execution] application *f* de la peine de mort.

justifiably ['dʒʌstɪˌfaɪəblɪ] *adv* légitimement, à juste titre ■ **she was ~ angry** elle était fâchée, et à juste titre.

justification [ˌdʒʌstɪfɪ'keɪʃn] *n* **1.** [gen] justification *f* ■ **what ~ do you have for such a statement?** comment justifiez-vous une telle affirmation? ■ **he spoke out in ~ of his actions** il a parlé pour justifier ses actes **2.** COMPUT & TYPO justification *f* ■ **left/right ~** justification à gauche/à droite.

justified ['dʒʌstɪfaɪd] *adj* **1.** [right, fair - action] justifié, légitime ; [- person] : **to be ~ in doing sthg** avoir raison de faire qqch **2.** COMPUT & TYPO [aligned] justifié.

justify ['dʒʌstɪfaɪ] (*pret & pp* **justified**) *vt* **1.** [gen] justifier ■ **she tried to ~ her behaviour to her parents** elle a essayé de justifier son comportement aux yeux de ses parents **2.** COMPUT & TYPO justifier **3.** LAW : **to ~ a lawsuit** justifier une action en justice.

justly ['dʒʌstlɪ] *adv* **1.** [fairly] justement, avec justice **2.** [accurately, deservedly] à juste titre.

justness ['dʒʌstnɪs] *n* [of claim, demand] bien-fondé *m*, légitimité *f* ■ [of idea, reasoning] justesse *f*.

jut [dʒʌt] (*pret & pp* **jutted**, *cont* **jutting**) *vi* : **to ~ out** dépasser, faire saillie ■ **a rocky peninsula ~s (out) into the sea** une péninsule rocheuse avance dans la mer.

jute [dʒu:t] *n* [textile] jute *m*.

Jute [dʒu:t] *n* Jute *mf*.

Jutland ['dʒʌtlənd] *pr n* Jütland *m*, Jylland *m*.

juvenile ['dʒu:vənaɪl] ◇ *adj* **1.** [young, for young people] jeune, juvénile *fml* ■ **~ lead** jeune premier *m* ■ **~ literature** livres *mpl* pour enfants *OR* pour la jeunesse **2.** [immature] puéril, enfantin.
◇ *n* **1.** *fml* mineur *m*, - e *f* **2.** THEAT jeune acteur *m*, - trice *f*.

juvenile court *n* tribunal *m* pour enfants *(10-16 ans)*.

juvenile delinquency *n* délinquance *f* juvénile.

juvenile delinquent *n* jeune délinquant *m*, - e *f*, mineur *m* délinquant, mineure *f* délinquante.

juxtapose [ˌdʒʌkstə'pəuz] *vt* juxtaposer.

juxtaposition [ˌdʒʌkstəpə'zɪʃn] *n* juxtaposition *f*.

k (*pl* **k's** *OR pl* **ks**), **K** (*pl* **K's** *OR pl* **Ks**) [keɪ] *n* [letter] k *m*, K *m*, *see also* **f**.

K ◇ **1.** (*written abbrev of* **kilobyte**) K, Ko **2.** *written abbr of* **Knight**.
◇ *n* (*abbrev of* **thousand**) K.

K-12 [ˌkeɪ'twelv] *n* *US* SCH *terme désignant l'ensemble de l'enseignement public du jardin d'enfant au terme du secondaire.*

Kabul ['kɑ:bʊl] *pr n* Kaboul, Kabul.

Kafkaesque [ˌkæfkə'esk] *adj* kafkaïen.

kaftan ['kæftæn] *n* caftan *m*, cafetan *m*.

Kaiser ['kaɪzəʳ] *n* Kaiser *m*.

Kalahari Desert [ˌkælə'hɑ:rɪ-] *pr n* : **the ~** le (désert du) Kalahari.

kale [keɪl] *n* chou *m* frisé.

kaleidoscope [kə'laɪdəskəʊp] *n* *liter* & *fig* kaléidoscope *m*.

kamikaze [ˌkæmɪ'kɑ:zɪ] ◇ *n* kamikaze *mf*.
◇ *adj* **1.** *liter* **~ pilot** kamikaze *m* ▪ **~ plane** kamikaze *m*, avion-suicide *m* **2.** *fig* suicidaire.

Kampala [kæm'pɑ:lə] *pr n* Kampala.

Kampuchea [ˌkæmpu:'tʃɪə] *pr n* Kampuchéa *m* ▪ **in ~** au Kampuchéa.

Kampuchean [ˌkæmpu:'tʃɪən] ◇ *n* Cambodgien *m*, - enne *f*.
◇ *adj* cambodgien.

kangaroo [ˌkæŋgə'ru:] *n* kangourou *m*.

kangaroo court *n* tribunal *m* illégal ▪ [held by strikers, prisoners etc] ≃ tribunal *m* populaire.

Kansas ['kænzəs] *pr n* Kansas *m* ▪ **in ~** dans le Kansas.

kaolin ['keɪəlɪn] *n* kaolin *m*.

kapok ['keɪpɒk] ◇ *n* kapok *m*.
◇ *comp* de kapok.

kaput [kə'pʊt] *adj* *inf* fichu, foutu.

karaoke [ˌkærə'əʊkɪ] *n* karaoké *m*.

karat *US* = **carat**.

karate [kə'rɑ:tɪ] *n* karaté *m* ▪ **~ chop** coup *m* de karaté *(donné avec le tranchant de la main).*

karma ['kɑ:mə] *n* karma *m*, karman *m*.

kart [kɑ:t] ◇ *n* kart *m*.
◇ *vi* : **to go ~ing** faire du karting.

Kashmir [kæʃ'mɪəʳ] *n* GEOG Cachemire *m*, Kashmir *m*.

Katmandu [ˌkætmæn'du:] *pr n* Katmandou, Katmandu.

katydid ['keɪtɪdɪd] *n* sauterelle *f* (d'Amérique du Nord).

kayak ['kaɪæk] *n* kayak *m*.

Kazakh [kæ'zæk] ◇ *n* Kasakh *m*, - e *f*.
◇ *adj* kasakh.

Kazakhstan [ˌkæzæk'stɑ:n] *pr n* Kazakhstan *m* ▪ **in ~** au Kazakhstan.

kazoo [kə'zu:] *n* mirliton *m*.

KB (*abbrev of* **Kilobyte**) *n* COMPUT ko *m*, Ko *m*.

KC (*abbrev of* **King's Counsel**) *n* *UK* *avocat de la Couronne.*

kebab [kɪ'bæb] *n* chiche-kebab *m* ▪ **~ house** *restaurant grec ou turc.*

kedgeree ['kedʒəri:] *n* *UK* *plat à base de riz, de poisson et d'œufs.*

keel [ki:l] ◇ *n* **1.** NAUT quille *f* ▪ **on an even ~** *liter* à tirant d'eau égal ; *fig* en équilibre **2.** *lit* [ship] navire *m*.
◇ *vi* chavirer.
◇ *vt* faire chavirer, cabaner.

◆ **keel over** ◇ *vi insep* **1.** NAUT chavirer **2.** [fall] s'effondrer ▪ [faint] s'évanouir.
◇ *vt sep* NAUT faire chavirer, cabaner.

keelhaul ['ki:lhɔ:l] *vt* NAUT faire passer sous la quille.

keen [ki:n] ◇ *adj* **1.** *UK* [eager, enthusiastic] passionné, enthousiaste ▪ **she's a ~ gardener** c'est une passionnée de jardinage ▪ **he was ~ to talk to her** il tenait à *OR* voulait absolument lui parler ▪ **I'm not so ~ on the idea** l'idée ne m'enchante *OR* ne m'emballe pas vraiment ▪ **Susan is really ~ on Tom** Susan a vraiment le béguin pour Tom ▶ **to be as ~ as mustard** *inf* [enthusiastic] être très enthousiaste ; [clever] avoir l'esprit vif **2.** [senses, mind, wit] fin, vif ▪ **to have a ~ sense of smell** avoir un odorat subtil ▪ **to have a ~ eye** avoir le coup d'œil **3.** [fierce - competition, rivalry] acharné **4.** *UK* [cold - wind] glacial **5.** *UK* [sharp - blade, knife] affilé **6.** [intense] intense, profond **7.** *UK* [very competitive] : **~ prices** des prix *mpl* imbattables.
◇ *vi* & *vt* *Ireland* [mourn] pleurer.
◇ *n* *Ireland* [dirge] mélopée *f* funèbre.

keenly ['ki:nlɪ] *adv* *UK* **1.** [deeply, intensely] vivement, profondément ▪ [fiercely] âprement ▪ **a ~ contested game** un match âprement disputé **2.** [eagerly] ardemment, avec enthousiasme ▪ [attentively] attentivement.

keenness ['ki:nnɪs] *n* **1.** *UK* [enthusiasm] enthousiasme *m*, empressement *m*, ardeur *f* **2.** [sharpness - of blade, senses] acuité *f*, finesse *f* ▪ **~ of mind** perspicacité *f*, finesse *f* **3.** [intensity, fierceness] intensité *f*, âpreté *f*.

keep [ki:p] (*pret & pp* **kept** [kept]) ◇ *vt*

A.

1. [retain - receipt, change] garder ▪ **please ~ your seats** veuillez rester assis ▪ **to ~ sthg to o.s.** garder qqch pour soi ➊ **they ~ themselves very much to themselves** ce sont des gens plutôt discrets ▪ **if that's your idea of a holiday, you can ~ it!** *inf* si c'est ça ton idée des vacances, tu peux te la garder!
2. [save] garder ▪ **we've kept some cake for you** on t'a gardé du gâteau
3. [store, put] mettre, garder ▪ **she ~s her money in the bank** elle met son argent à la banque ▪ **how long can you ~ fish in the freezer?** combien de temps peut-on garder *OR* conserver du poisson au congélateur? ▪ **where do you ~ the playing cards?** où est-ce que vous rangez les cartes à jouer?

B.

1. *(with adj complement)* [maintain in the specified state or place] : **to ~ sb quiet** faire tenir qqn tranquille ▪ **to ~ sthg warm** garder qqch au chaud ▪ **the doors are kept locked** les portes sont toujours fermées à clef ▪ **to ~ sthg up to date** tenir qqch à jour ▪ *(with adv complement)* **a well-/badly-kept office** un bureau bien/mal tenu ▪ **the weather kept us indoors** le temps nous a empêchés de sortir ▪ **he kept his hands in his pockets** il a gardé les mains dans les poches ▪ **~ your eyes on the red dot** ne quittez pas le point rouge des yeux ▪ **~ the noise to a minimum** essayez de ne pas faire trop de bruit ▪ *(with present participle)* **to ~ sb waiting** faire attendre qqn ▪ **~ the engine running** n'arrêtez pas le moteur ▪ **to ~ sthg going** [organization, business] faire marcher qqch ; [music, conversation] ne pas laisser qqch s'arrêter ▪ **alcohol is the only thing that ~s me going** l'alcool est la seule chose qui me permette de tenir
2. [delay] retenir ▪ **what kept you?** qu'est-ce qui t'a retenu? ▪ [distract] : **I don't want to ~ you from your work** je ne veux pas vous empêcher de travailler
3. [not allow to leave] garder ▪ **to ~ sb in hospital/prison** garder qqn à l'hôpital/en prison

C.

1. [support] : **he hardly earns enough to ~ himself** il gagne à peine de quoi vivre ▪ **she has a husband and six children to ~** elle a un mari et six enfants à nourrir ▪ **it ~s me in cigarette money** ça paie mes cigarettes
2. [have as dependant or employee] *dated* avoir
3. [run - shop, business] tenir
4. COMM [have in stock] vendre
5. [farm animals] élever
6. [diary, list etc] tenir ▪ **my secretary ~s my accounts** ma secrétaire tient *OR* s'occupe de ma comptabilité

D.

1. [fulfil - a promise, one's word] tenir
2. [observe - silence] observer ; [- the Sabbath] respecter ; [- law] respecter, observer
3. [uphold, maintain] maintenir ▪ **to ~ order/the peace** maintenir l'ordre/la paix
4. [guard] garder ▪ **to ~ goal** être gardien de but

E.

1. [prevent] : **to ~ sb from doing sthg** empêcher qqn de faire qqch
2. [withhold] : **to ~ sthg from sb** cacher qqch à qqn ▪ **to ~ information from sb** dissimuler des informations à qqn.

◇ *vi* **1.** *(with present participle)* [continue] continuer ▪ **letters ~ pouring in** les lettres continuent d'affluer ▪ **don't ~ apologizing** arrête de t'excuser ▪ **she had several failures but kept trying** elle a essuyé plusieurs échecs mais elle a persévéré ▪ **to ~ going** [not give up] continuer ▪ **~ going till you get to the crossroads** allez jusqu'au croisement ▪ **with so few customers, it's a wonder the shop ~s going** avec si peu de clients, c'est un miracle que le magasin ne ferme pas **2.** [stay, remain] rester, se tenir ▪ **~ calm!** restez calmes!, du calme! ▪ **she kept warm by jumping up and down** elle se tenait chaud en sautillant sur place ▪ **~ to the path** ne vous écartez pas du chemin ▪ **to ~ in touch with sb** rester en contact avec qqn ▪ **to ~ to o.s.** se tenir à l'écart **3.** [last, stay fresh] se conserver, se garder ▪ **it will ~ for a week in the refrigerator** vous pouvez le garder *OR* conserver au réfrigérateur pendant une semaine ▪ **the news will ~ (until tomorrow)** *fig* la nouvelle peut attendre (jusqu'à demain) **4.** [in health] aller ▪ **I'm ~ing well** je vais bien, ça va (bien).

◇ *n* **1.** [board and lodging] : **he gives his mother £50 a week for his ~** il donne 50 livres par semaine à sa mère pour sa pension ▪ **to earn one's ~** *payer ou travailler pour être nourri et logé* **2.** [in castle] donjon *m* **3.** *phr* **for ~s** *inf* pour de bon.

◆ **keep at** ◇ *vt insep* **1.** [pester] harceler **2.** *phr* **to ~ at it** persévérer.
◇ *vt sep* : **to ~ sb at it : the sergeant kept us hard at it all morning** le sergent nous a fait travailler toute la matinée.

◆ **keep away** ◇ *vt sep* tenir éloigné, empêcher d'approcher ▪ **spectators were kept away by the fear of violence** la peur de la violence tenait les spectateurs à distance.
◇ *vi insep* ne pas s'approcher ▪ **~ away from those people** évitez ces gens-là.

◆ **keep back** ◇ *vt sep* **1.** [keep at a distance - crowd, spectators] tenir éloigné, empêcher de s'approcher **2.** [not reveal - names, facts] cacher ▪ **I'm sure he's ~ing something back (from us)** je suis sûr qu'il (nous) cache quelque chose **3.** [retain] retenir **4.** [detain] retenir ▪ **to be kept back after school** être en retenue **5.** [restrain] retenir.
◇ *vi insep* rester en arrière, ne pas s'approcher.

◆ **keep behind** *vt sep* [after meeting, class] retenir.

◆ **keep down** ◇ *vt sep* **1.** [not raise] ne pas lever ▪ **~ your head down!** ne lève pas la tête!, garde la tête baissée! ▪ **~ your voices down!** parlez doucement! **2.** [prevent from increasing] limiter ▪ **our aim is to ~ prices down** notre but est d'empêcher les prix d'augmenter **3.** [repress] réprimer ▪ [control - vermin, weeds] empêcher de proliférer ▪ **you can't ~ a good man down** rien n'arrêtera un homme de mérite **4.** [food] garder ▪ **she can't ~ solid foods down** son estomac ne garde aucun aliment solide **5.** SCH faire redoubler.
◇ *vi insep* ne pas se lever.

◆ **keep from** *vt insep* s'empêcher de, se retenir de ▪ **I couldn't ~ (myself) from laughing** je n'ai pas pu m'empêcher de rire.

◆ **keep in** *vt sep* [not allow out] empêcher de sortir ▪ SCH donner une consigne à, garder en retenue.

◆ **keep in with** *vt insep* : **to ~ in with sb** rester en bons termes avec qqn.

◆ **keep off** ◇ *vt sep* **1.** [dogs, birds, trespassers] éloigner ▪ [rain, sun] protéger de ▪ **this cream will ~ the mosquitoes off** cette crème vous/le/te *etc* protégera contre les moustiques ▪ **~ your hands off!** pas touche!, bas les pattes! **2.** [coat, hat] ne pas remettre.
◇ *vt insep* **1.** [avoid] éviter ▪ **~ off drink and tobacco** évitez l'alcool et le tabac ▪ **we tried to ~ off the topic** on a essayé d'éviter le sujet **2.** [keep at a distance from] ne pas s'approcher de ▪ **'~ off the grass'** 'pelouse interdite'.
◇ *vi insep* **1.** [keep at a distance] ne pas s'approcher **2.** [weather] : **the rain/snow kept off** il n'a pas plu/neigé.

◆ **keep on** ◇ *vt sep* **1.** [coat, hat] garder **2.** [employee] garder.
◇ *vi insep* **1.** [continue] continuer ▪ **they kept on talking** ils ont continué à parler ▪ **I ~ on making the same mistakes** je fais toujours les mêmes erreurs **2.** *inf* [talk continually] parler sans cesse ▪ **he ~s on about his kids** il n'arrête pas de parler de ses gosses ▪ **don't ~ on about it!** ça suffit, j'ai compris!

◆ **keep on at** *vt insep* [pester] harceler.

◆ **keep out** ◇ *vt sep* empêcher d'entrer ▪ **a guard dog to ~ intruders out** un chien de garde pour décourager les intrus ▪ **a scarf to ~ the cold out** une écharpe pour vous protéger du froid.
◇ *vi insep* ne pas entrer ▪ **'~ out'** 'défense d'entrer', 'entrée interdite' ▪ **to ~ out of an argument** ne pas intervenir dans une discussion.

◆ **keep to** *vt insep* **1.** [observe, respect] respecter ▪ **you must ~ to the deadlines** vous devez respecter les délais **2.** [not deviate from] ne pas s'écarter de ▪ **~ to the point** *OR* **the subject!** ne vous écartez pas du sujet! **3.** [stay in] garder ▪ **to ~ to one's room/bed** garder la chambre/le lit.

◆ **keep together** ◇ *vt sep* ne pas séparer.
◇ *vi insep* rester ensemble.

◆ **keep up** ◇ *vt sep* **1.** [prevent from falling - shelf, roof] maintenir ▪ **I need a belt to ~ my trousers up** j'ai besoin d'une ceinture pour empêcher mon pantalon de tomber ▪ *fig* **it will ~ prices up** ça empêchera les prix de baisser ▪ **it's to ~ the troops' morale up** c'est pour maintenir le moral des troupes **2.** [maintain - attack, bombardment] poursuivre ; [- correspondence, contacts, conversation] entretenir ▪ **you have to ~ up the**

payments on ne peut pas interrompre les versements ▪ **she kept up a constant flow of questions** elle ne cessait de poser des questions ➊ **~ up the good work!** c'est du bon travail, continuez! ▪ **you're doing well, ~ it up!** c'est bien, continuez! **3.** [prevent from going to bed] empêcher de dormir **4.** [not allow to deteriorate - house, garden] entretenir ▪ **she goes to evening classes to ~ up her French** elle suit des cours du soir pour entretenir son français.

◇ *vi insep* **1.** [continue] continuer ▪ **if this noise ~s up much longer, I'll scream** si ce bruit continue, je crois que je vais hurler **2.** [not fall] se maintenir **3.** [not fall behind] suivre ▪ **he's finding it hard to ~ up in his new class** il a du mal à suivre dans sa nouvelle classe.

◆ **keep up with** *vt insep* **1.** [stay abreast of] : **to ~ up with the news** se tenir au courant de l'actualité **2.** [keep in touch with] rester en contact avec.

keeper ['ki:pər] *n* **1.** [gen] gardien *m*, - enne *f* ▪ [in museum] conservateur *m*, - trice *f* ▪ **am I my brother's ~?** BIBLE suis-je le gardien de mon frère? **2.** [goalkeeper] goal *m*, gardien *m* de but **3.** TECH [safety catch] cran *m* de sûreté.

keep-fit *n* culture *f* physique, gymnastique *f* (d'entretien) ▪ **she goes to ~ (classes) every week** toutes les semaines elle va à son cours de gymnastique.

keeping ['ki:pɪŋ] *n* **1.** [care, charge] garde *f* ▪ **he left the manuscript in his wife's ~** il a confié le manuscrit à son épouse ▪ **in safe ~** en sécurité, sous bonne garde **2.** [observing - of rule, custom etc] observation *f*.

◆ **in keeping** *adj phr* conforme à ▪ **their dress was not at all in ~ with the seriousness of the occasion** leur tenue ne convenait pas du tout à la gravité de la circonstance.

◆ **in keeping with** *prep phr* conformément à.

◆ **out of keeping** *adj phr* : **to be out of ~ with** être en désaccord avec.

keepsake ['ki:pseɪk] *n* souvenir *m* *(objet)*.

keg [keg] *n* **1.** [barrel] tonnelet *m*, baril *m* ▪ [of fish] baril ▪ [of beer] tonnelet ▪ [of herring] caque *f* **2.** [beer] bière *f* (à la) pression.

kelly-green ['kelɪ-] *adj US* vert pomme.

kelp [kelp] *n* varech *m*.

kelvin ['kelvɪn] *n* kelvin *m*.

ken [ken] (*pret & pp* **kenned**, *cont* **kenning**) ◇ *n dated & hum* : **it is beyond my ~** cela dépasse mon entendement.

◇ *vi & vt Scotland* connaître, savoir.

Kennedy ['kenɪdɪ] *pr n* Kennedy ▪ **Cape ~** cap *m* Kennedy ▪ **the ~ assassination** l'assassinat *m* de Kennedy.

THE KENNEDY ASSASSINATION

Assassinat, le 22 novembre 1963, du jeune président américain J.F. Kennedy, à Dallas, au Texas. Le meurtrier présumé, Lee Harvey Oswald, fut arrêté puis assassiné à son tour deux jours plus tard. Bien qu'officiellement close, cette affaire n'est pas sans susciter des polémiques, selon lesquelles la CIA pourrait avoir été impliquée.

kennel ['kenl] (*UK pret & pp* **kennelled**) (*US pret & pp* **kenneled**) ◇ *n* **1.** *UK* [doghouse] niche *f* **2.** *US* [for boarding or breeding] chenil *m*.

◇ *vt* mettre dans un chenil.

◆ **kennels** *n UK* [for boarding or breeding] chenil *m*.

Kentucky [ken'tʌkɪ] *pr n* Kentucky *m* ▪ **in ~** dans le Kentucky.

Kenya ['kenjə] *pr n* Kenya *m* ▪ **in ~** au Kenya.

Kenyan ['kenjən] ◇ *n* Kenyan *m*, - e *f*.

◇ *adj* kenyan.

kept [kept] ◇ *pt & pp* ▷ **keep**.

◇ *adj hum & pej* **a ~ man** un homme entretenu ▪ **a ~ woman** une femme entretenue.

keratin ['kerətɪn] *n* kératine *f*.

kerb *UK*, **curb** *US* [kɜ:b] *n* bord *m* du trottoir ▪ **he stepped off the ~** il est descendu du trottoir.

kerb crawler *n individu longeant le trottoir en voiture à la recherche d'une prostituée.*

kerb crawling *n fait de longer le trottoir en voiture à la recherche d'une prostituée.*

kerb market *n* ST. EX marché *m* officieux *(où les valeurs sont échangées en dehors des heures d'ouverture de la Bourse)*.

kerbstone *UK*, **curbstone** *US* ['kɜ:bstəʊn] *n* bordure *f* de trottoir.

kerb weight *n* poids *m* à vide.

kerchief ['kɜ:tʃɪf] *n dated* foulard *m*, fichu *m*.

kerfuffle [kə'fʌfl] *n UK inf* [disorder] désordre *m*, chahut *m* ▪ [fight] bagarre *f*.

kernel ['kɜ:nl] *n* **1.** [of nut, fruit stone] amande *f* ▪ [of cereal] graine *f* **2.** *fig* [heart, core] cœur *m*, noyau *m*.

kerosene, kerosine ['kerəsi:n] ◇ *n US* [for aircraft] kérosène *m* ▪ [for lamps, stoves] pétrole *m*.

◇ *comp* [lamp, stove] à pétrole.

kestrel ['kestrəl] *n* crécerelle *f*.

ketch [ketʃ] *n* ketch *m*.

ketchup ['ketʃəp] *n* ketchup *m*.

kettle ['ketl] *n* **1.** [for water] bouilloire *f* ▪ **to put the ~ on** mettre de l'eau à chauffer ▪ **the ~'s boiling** l'eau bout **2.** [for fish] poissonnière *f* ▪ **that's another** *OR* **a different ~ of fish** *inf* c'est une autre paire de manches ▪ **this is a fine** *OR* **pretty ~ of fish!** *UK inf* quelle salade!, quel sac de nœuds!

kettledrum ['ketldrʌm] *n* timbale *f*.

Kevlar® ['kevlɑ:r] *n (U)* kevlar *m*.

Kew Gardens [kju:-] *pr n parc et jardin botanique dans l'ouest de Londres.*

key [ki:] ◇ *n* **1.** [for lock] clé *f*, clef *f* ▪ [for clock, mechanism etc] clé *f*, remontoir *m* ▪ **the ~ to the drawer** la clé du tiroir ▪ **where are the car ~s?** où sont les clés de la voiture? ➊ **to get the ~ of the door** atteindre sa majorité **2.** *fig* [means] clé *f*, clef *f* ▪ **the ~ to happiness** la clé du bonheur **3.** [on typewriter, computer, piano, organ] touche *f* ▪ [on wind instrument] clé *f*, clef *f* **4.** MUS ton *m* ▪ **in the ~ of B minor** en si mineur ▪ **to play in/off ~** jouer dans le ton/dans le mauvais ton ▪ **to sing in/off ~** chanter juste/faux **5.** [on map, diagram] légende *f* **6.** [answers] corrigé *m*, réponses *fpl* **7.** TECH clé *f* *OR* clef *f* (de serrage) **8.** [island] îlot *m* ▪ [reef] (petit) récif *m (qui s'étend au sud de la Floride)*.

◇ *adj* clé, clef ▪ **~ industries** industries clés, industries-clés ▪ **a ~ factor** un élément décisif ▪ **one of the ~ issues in the election** un des enjeux fondamentaux de ces élections.

◇ *vt* **1.** [data, text] saisir, entrer **2.** [adjust, adapt] adapter.

◆ **key in** *vt sep* COMPUT [word, number] entrer ▪ [data, text] saisir.

key bar *n* [in shop] stand *m* de clef-minute.

keyboard ['ki:bɔ:d] ◇ *n* [of instrument, typewriter, computer] clavier *m* ▪ **who's on ~s?** qui est aux claviers ? ➊ **~ instrument** instrument *m* à clavier ▪ **~ operator** claviste *mf*.

◇ *vt* saisir.

keyboarder ['ki:bɔ:dər] *n* TYPO claviste *mf*.

keyboard shortcut *n* raccourci *m* clavier.

key card *n* badge *m*.

keyed up [ki:d-] *adj* surexcité ▪ **the fans were all ~ for the match** les supporters attendaient le match dans un état de surexcitation.

keyhole ['ki:həʊl] *n* trou *m* de serrure ▪ **he looked through the ~** il regarda par le trou de la serrure.

keyhole surgery *n* cœliochirurgie *f*.

keying ['ki:ɪŋ] *n* saisie *f*.

key money *n* pas *m* de porte.

Keynesian ['keɪnzɪən] *adj* keynésien.

keynote ['kiːnəʊt] ◇ *n* **1.** [main point] point *m* capital **2.** MUS tonique *f*.
◇ *adj* [address] introductif ■ [speaker] principal ■ **~ speech** discours *m* introductif *OR* liminaire.
◇ *vt* insister sur, mettre en relief.

keypad ['kiːpæd] *n* pavé *m* numérique.

keypunch ['kiːpʌntʃ] *n* perforatrice *f* à clavier.

key ring *n* porte-clés *m inv*.

key signature *n* MUS armature *f*, armure *f*.

keystone ['kiːstəʊn] *n* CONSTR & *fig* clé *f OR* clef *f* de voûte ■ **the Keystone State** la Pennsylvanie.

keystroke ['kiːstrəʊk] *n* frappe *f (d'une touche)* ■ **codes are entered with a single ~** une seule touche suffit pour entrer les codes.

key word *n* mot-clef *m*.

kg (*written abbrev of* **kilogram**) kg.

KGB *pr n* KGB *m*.

khaki ['kɑːkɪ] ◇ *adj* kaki *(inv)*.
◇ *n* [colour] kaki *m* ■ [material] treillis *m*.

khaki election *n UK élection dont la date est fixée dans la foulée d'une victoire militaire, assurant ainsi le succès du gouvernement au pouvoir.*

Khmer [kmeəʳ] ◇ *n* **1.** [person] Khmer *m*, - ère *f* ■ **~ Rouge** Khmer rouge **2.** LING khmer *m*.
◇ *adj* khmer.

KHz (*abbrev of* **kilohertz**) *n* KHz *m*.

kibbutz [kɪ'bʊts] (*pl* **kibbutzes** *OR pl* **kibbutzim** [kɪbʊt'sɪm]) *n* kibboutz *m*.

kibosh ['kaɪbɒʃ] *n inf* **to put the ~ on sthg** ficher qqch en l'air△.

kick [kɪk] ◇ *n* **1.** coup *m* de pied ■ **to aim a ~ at sb/sthg** lancer *OR* donner un coup de pied en direction de qqn/qqch ▶ **it was a real ~ in the teeth for him** *inf* ça lui a fait un sacré coup ■ **she needs a ~ up the backside** *inf OR* **in the pants** *inf* elle a besoin d'un coup de pied aux fesses
2. *inf* [thrill] plaisir *m* ■ **to get a ~ from** *OR* **out of doing sthg** prendre son pied à faire qqch ■ **to do sthg for ~s** faire qqch pour rigoler *OR* pour s'amuser
3. *inf* [strength - of drink] : **his cocktail had quite a ~** son cocktail était costaud
4. *inf* [vitality, force] entrain *m*, allant *m*
5. *inf* [fad] engouement *m* ■ **she's on a yoga ~ at the moment** elle est emballée *OR* elle ne jure que par le yoga en ce moment
6. [recoil - of gun] recul *m*.
◇ *vt* **1.** donner un coup de pied à *OR* dans ■ **she ~ed the ball over the wall** elle a envoyé la balle par-dessus le mur (d'un coup de pied) ■ **I ~ed the door open** j'ai ouvert la porte d'un coup de pied ■ **he had been ~ed to death** il avait été tué à coups de pieds ■ **the dancers ~ed their legs in the air** les danseurs lançaient les jambes en l'air ■ **to ~ a penalty** [in rugby] marquer *OR* réussir une pénalité ; [in football] tirer un penalty ▶ **to ~ the bucket** *inf* passer l'arme à gauche, casser sa pipe ■ **you shouldn't ~ a man when he's down** il ne faut jamais frapper un homme à terre ■ **I could have ~ed myself!** je me serais donné des gifles! ■ **to ~ one's heels** *inf* faire le pied de grue, poireauter
2. *phr* **I used to smoke but I've managed to ~ the habit** *inf* je fumais, mais j'ai réussi à m'arrêter.
◇ *vi* **1.** donner *OR* lancer un coup de pied ■ **they dragged him away ~ing and screaming** il se débattait comme un beau diable quand ils l'ont emmené ■ [in rugby] : **to ~ for touch** chercher une touche ▶ **to ~ over the traces** *UK* ruer dans les brancards
2. [in dance] lancer les jambes en l'air
3. [gun] reculer.

◆ **kick about** ◇ *vi insep UK inf* traîner.
◇ *vt sep* = **kick around**.

◆ **kick about with** = **kick around with**.

◆ **kick against** *vt insep inf* regimber contre ▶ **to ~ against the pricks** se rebeller en pure perte.

◆ **kick around** ◇ *vt sep* **1.** *liter* **to ~ a ball around** jouer au ballon ■ **they were ~ing a tin can around** ils jouaient au foot avec une boîte de conserves
2. *inf fig* [idea] débattre ■ **we ~ed a few ideas around** on a discuté à bâtons rompus
3. *inf fig* [mistreat] malmener, maltraiter ■ **I'm not going to let her ~ me around** *OR* **to be ~ed around by her any more** je ne vais plus me laisser faire par elle.
◇ *vi insep inf* traîner ■ **I know my old overalls are ~ing around here somewhere** je suis sûr que mon vieux bleu de travail traîne quelque part par là.

◆ **kick around with** *vt insep inf* traîner avec.

◆ **kick at** *vt insep inf* regimber contre.

◆ **kick back** *vt sep* **1.** [ball] renvoyer du pied
2. *US inf* [money] verser.

◆ **kick down** *vt sep* [person] abattre *OR* faire tomber à coups de pied ■ [door] défoncer à coups de pied.

◆ **kick in** ◇ *vt sep* défoncer à coups de pied ■ **I'll ~ his teeth in!** *inf* je vais lui casser la figure!
◇ *vi insep inf* entrer en action.

◆ **kick off** ◇ *vt sep* **1.** [shoes] enlever d'un coup de pied
2. *inf fig* [start] démarrer
3. SPORT donner le coup d'envoi à.
◇ *vi insep* **1.** SPORT donner le coup d'envoi ■ **they ~ed off an hour late** le match a commencé avec une heure de retard
2. *inf fig* [start] démarrer, commencer.

◆ **kick out** ◇ *vt sep inf* [person] *liter* chasser à coups de pied ■ *fig* foutre dehors.
◇ *vi insep* [person] lancer des coups de pieds ■ [horse, donkey] ruer.

◆ **kick over** *vt sep* renverser du pied *OR* d'un coup de pied.

◆ **kick up** *vt sep* **1.** [dust, sand] faire voler (du pied)
2. *inf fig* **to ~ up a fuss** *OR* **a row (about sthg)** faire toute une histoire *OR* tout un plat(au sujet de qqch) ■ **to ~ up a din** *OR* **a racket** faire un boucan d'enfer.

kick-ass *adj inf* super.

kickback ['kɪkbæk] *n* **1.** *inf* [bribe] dessous-de-table *m inv*, pot-de-vin *m* **2.** TECH recul *m* **3.** [backlash] contrecoup *m*.

kickoff ['kɪkɒf] *n* **1.** SPORT coup *m* d'envoi ■ **the ~ is at 3pm** le coup d'envoi sera donné à 15h **2.** *UK inf fig* **for a ~** pour commencer.

kick-start ◇ *n* = **kick-starter**.
◇ *vt* démarrer (au kick) ■ **measures to ~ the economy** *fig* des mesures pour faire repartir l'économie.

kick-starter *n* kick *m*.

kick turn *n* [in skiing] conversion *f*.

kid [kɪd] (*pret & pp* **kidded**, *cont* **kidding**) ◇ *n* **1.** *inf* [child, young person] gosse *mf*, môme *mf*, gamin *m*, - e *f* ■ **listen to me, ~!** écoute-moi bien, petit! ■ **that's ~s' stuff** c'est pour les bébés **2.** [young goat] chevreau *m*, chevrette *f* **3.** [hide] chevreau *m*.
◇ *adj* **1.** *inf* [young] : **~ brother** petit frère *m*, frérot *m* ■ **~ sister** petite sœur *f*, sœurette *f* **2.** [coat, jacket] en chevreau.
◇ *vi inf* [joke] blaguer ■ **I won it in a raffle – no kidding!** *OR* **you're kidding!** je l'ai gagné dans une tombola – sans blague! *OR* tu rigoles! ■ **don't get upset, I was just kidding** ne te fâche pas, je plaisantais *OR* c'était une blague.
◇ *vt inf* **1.** [tease] taquiner, se moquer de ■ **they kidded him about his accent** ils se moquaient de lui à cause de son accent **2.** [deceive, mislead] charrier, faire marcher ■ **don't ~ yourself!** il ne faut pas te leurrer *OR* te faire d'illusions! ■ **who do you think you're kidding?** tu te fous de moi? ■ **you're not kidding!** je ne te le fais pas dire! ■ **I ~ you not** sans blague, sans rigoler.

◆ **kid around** *vi insep inf* raconter des blagues, rigoler.

kiddie ['kɪdɪ] *inf* = **kiddy**.

kidding ['kɪdɪŋ] *n (U) inf* plaisanterie *f*, plaisanteries *fpl*, blague *f*, blagues *fpl*.

kiddy ['kɪdɪ] (*pl* **kiddies**) *n inf* gosse *mf*, gamin *m*, - e *f*.

kid gloves *npl* gants *mpl* de chevreau ■ **to handle** *OR* **to treat sb with ~** prendre des gants avec qqn.

kidnap ['kɪdnæp] (*UK pret & pp* **kidnapped**, *cont* **kidnapping**) (*US pret & pp* **kidnaped**, *cont* **kidnaping**) ◇ *vt* enlever, kidnapper ■ **'Kidnapped' Stevenson** 'Enlevé'.
◇ *n* enlèvement *m*, rapt *m*, kidnapping *m*.

kidnaping ['kɪdnæpɪŋ] *US* = **kidnapping**.

kidnapper *UK*, **kidnaper** *US* ['kɪdnæpəʳ] *n* ravisseur *m*, - euse *f*, kidnappeur *m*, - euse *f*.

kidnapping *UK*, **kidnaping** *US* ['kɪdnæpɪŋ] *n* enlèvement *m*, rapt *m*, kidnapping *m*.

kidney ['kɪdnɪ] ◇ *n* **1.** ANAT rein *m* **2.** CULIN rognon *m* **3.** *UK lit* [temperament] nature *f*, caractère *f*.
◇ *comp* ANAT [ailment, trouble] des reins, rénal ■ **~ specialist** néphrologue *mf*.

kidney bean *n* haricot *m* rouge *OR* de Soissons.

kidney machine *n* rein *m* artificiel ■ **he's on a ~** il est sous rein artificiel *OR* en dialyse *OR* en hémodialyse.

kidology [kɪ'dɒlədʒɪ] *n UK inf* esbroufe *f*, bluff *m*.

Kilimanjaro [ˌkɪlɪmən'dʒɑːrəʊ] *pr n* : **(Mount) ~** le Kilimandjaro.

kill [kɪl] ◇ *vt* **1.** [person, animal] tuer ■ **to ~ o.s.** se tuer, se donner la mort *fml* ▮ *fig* tuer ■ **I'll finish it even if it ~s me** j'en viendrai à bout même si je dois me tuer à la tâche ■ **if you tell them, I'll ~ you!** si tu leur dis, je te tue! ■ **they were ~ing themselves laughing** *OR* **with laughter** ils étaient morts de rire ▶ **to ~ two birds with one stone** *prov* faire d'une pierre deux coups ■ **to ~ time** tuer le temps **2.** *inf fig* [cause pain to] faire très mal à ■ **these shoes are ~ing me** ces chaussures me font souffrir le martyre ■ **my back's ~ing me** j'ai très *OR* horriblement mal au dos **3.** [put an end to] tuer, mettre fin à ■ **the accident ~ed all his hopes of becoming a dancer** avec son accident, ses espoirs de devenir danseur se sont évanouis *OR* envolés **4.** [alleviate, deaden] atténuer, soulager **5.** *inf* POL [defeat] rejeter, faire échouer **6.** *inf* [cancel, remove] supprimer, enlever ■ [computer file] effacer **7.** *inf* [switch off] arrêter, couper ■ **to ~ the lights** éteindre les lumières.
◇ *vi* tuer ■ **to shoot to ~** tirer dans l'intention de tuer ■ **thou shalt not ~** BIBLE tu ne tueras point ▶ **it's a case of ~ or cure** c'est un remède de cheval.
◇ *n* **1.** mise *f* à mort ▶ **to be in at the ~** assister au coup de grâce ■ **to move in for the ~** donner *OR* porter le coup de grâce **2.** [prey - killed by animal] proie *f* ; [- killed by hunter] chasse *f*.
◆ **kill off** *vt sep* tuer, exterminer ■ **high prices could ~ off the tourist trade** *fig* des prix élevés pourraient porter un coup fatal au tourisme.

killer ['kɪləʳ] ◇ *n* **1.** *liter* tueur *m*, - euse *f* ■ **a convicted ~** une personne reconnue coupable d'homicide ■ **tuberculosis was once a major ~** jadis, la tuberculose faisait de nombreuses victimes *OR* des ravages **2.** *phr* **a real ~** *inf* : **the exam was a real ~** l'examen était d'une difficulté incroyable ■ **this joke is a real ~** cette histoire est à mourir de rire.
◇ *comp* [disease] meurtrier ■ **a ~ shark** un requin tueur.

killer instinct *n fig* : **he's got the ~** c'est un battant ■ **he lacks the ~** il manque d'agressivité *OR* de combativité, il a trop de scrupules.

killer whale *n* épaulard *m*, orque *m*.

killing ['kɪlɪŋ] ◇ *n* **1.** [of person] assassinat *m*, meurtre *m* ■ **the ~ of endangered species is forbidden** il est interdit de tuer un animal appartenant à une espèce en voie de disparition **2.** *inf* [profit] : **to make a ~** se remplir les poches, s'en mettre plein les poches.
◇ *adj UK inf* **1.** [tiring] crevant, tuant **2.** *dated* [hilarious] tordant, bidonnant.

killjoy ['kɪldʒɔɪ] *n* trouble-fête *mf inv* ■ **don't be such a ~!** ne sois pas rabat-joie!

kiln [kɪln] *n* four *m (à céramique, à briques etc).*

kilo ['kiːləʊ] (*pl* **kilos**) (*abbrev of* **kilogram**) *n* kilo *m*.

kilobyte ['kɪləbaɪt] *n* kilobyte *m*, kilo-octet *m*.

kilocalorie ['kɪləˌkælərɪ] *n* kilocalorie *f*, grande calorie *f*.

kilocycle ['kɪləˌsaɪkəl] *n* kilocycle *m*, kilohertz *m*.

kilogram(me) *UK*, **kilogram** *US* ['kɪləˌgræm] *n* kilogramme *m*.

kilohertz ['kɪləˌhɜːts] *n* kilohertz *m*.

kilojoule ['kɪləˌdʒuːl] *n* kilojoule *m*.

kilolitre *UK*, **kiloliter** *US* ['kɪləˌliːtəʳ] *n* kilolitre *m*.

kilometre *UK*, **kilometer** *US* ['kɪləˌmiːtəʳ, kɪ'lɒmɪtəʳ] *n* kilomètre *m*.

kilovolt ['kɪləˌvəʊlt] *n* kilovolt *m*.

kilowatt ['kɪləˌwɒt] *n* kilowatt *m*.

kilowatt-hour *n* kilowatt-heure *m*.

kilt [kɪlt] *n* kilt *m*.

kilted ['kɪltɪd] *adj* [person] en kilt.

kilter ['kɪltəʳ] ◆ **out of kilter** *adj phr* en dérangement, en panne.

kimono [kɪ'məʊnəʊ] (*pl* **kimonos**) *n* kimono *m*.

kin [kɪn] *npl* parents *mpl*, famille *f*.

kind[1] [kaɪnd] *n* **1.** [sort, type] sorte *f*, type *m*, genre *m* ■ **hundreds of different ~s of books** des centaines de livres de toutes sortes ■ **have you got any other ~?** en avez-vous d'autres? ■ **all ~s of people** toutes sortes de gens ■ **what ~ of people go there? – oh, all ~s** quel type de gens y va? – oh, des gens très différents ■ **it's a different ~ of problem** c'est un tout autre problème, c'est un problème d'un autre ordre ■ **I think he's some ~ of specialist** *OR* **a specialist of some ~** je crois que c'est un genre de spécialiste ■ **what ~ of computer have you got?** qu'est-ce que vous avez comme (marque d')ordinateur? ■ **what ~ of person do you think I am?** pour qui me prenez-vous? ■ **it's all right, if you like that ~ of thing** c'est bien si vous aimez ce genre de choses ■ **they're not our ~ of people** [not the sort we mix with] nous ne sommes pas du même monde ■ **Las Vegas is my ~ of town** Las Vegas est le genre de ville que j'aime ■ **she's not the marrying ~** elle n'est pas du genre à se marier ▶ **I said nothing of the ~!** je n'ai rien dit de pareil *OR* de tel! ■ **you were drunk last night – I was nothing of the ~ !** tu étais ivre hier soir – absolument pas *OR* mais pas du tout!
2. [class of person, thing] : **it's one of the finest of its ~** [animal] c'est l'un des plus beaux spécimens de son espèce ; [object] c'est l'un des plus beaux dans son genre
3. *phr* **a ~ of** une sorte de, une espèce de ■ **I had a ~ of (a) feeling you'd come** j'avais comme l'impression que tu viendrais ■ **~ of** *inf* plutôt ■ **it's ~ of big and round** c'est plutôt *OR* dans le genre grand et rond ■ **I'm ~ of sad about it** ça me rend un peu triste ■ **did you hit him? – well, ~ of** tu l'as frappé? – oui, si on veut ■ **of a ~ : they're two of a ~** ils sont de la même espèce ■ **one of a ~** unique (en son genre) ■ **it's work of a ~, but only as a stopgap** c'est un emploi, d'accord, mais pas pour très longtemps.
◆ **in kind** *adv phr* **1.** [with goods, services] en nature ■ **to pay sb in ~** payer qqn en nature
2. [in similar fashion] de même ■ **he insulted me, and I replied in ~** il m'a insulté, et je lui ai rendu la monnaie de sa pièce.

kind[2] [kaɪnd] *adj* **1.** [good-natured, considerate] gentil, aimable ■ **to be ~ to sb** être gentil avec qqn ■ **it's very ~ of you to take an interest** c'est très gentil à vous de vous y intéresser ■ **she was ~ enough to say nothing** elle a eu la gentillesse de ne rien dire ■ **would you be so ~ as to post this for me?** auriez-vous l'amabilité de mettre ceci à la poste pour moi? ▮ [favourable] favorable **2.** [delicate, not harmful] doux, douce *f* ■ **a detergent that is ~ to your hands** une lessive qui n'abîme pas les mains.

kinda△ ['kaɪndə] *US* = **kind of**.

kindergarten ['kɪndəˌgɑːtn] *n* jardin *m* d'enfants, (école *f*) maternelle *f*.

kind-hearted *adj* bon, généreux.

kindle ['kɪndl] ◇ *vt* **1.** [wood] allumer, faire brûler **2.** *fig* [interest] susciter ■ [passion] embraser, enflammer ■ [hatred, jealousy] attiser, susciter.
◇ *vi* **1.** [wood] s'enflammer, brûler **2.** *fig* [passion, desire] s'embraser, s'enflammer ■ [interest] s'éveiller.

kindling ['kɪndlɪŋ] *n* petit bois *m*, bois *m* d'allumage.

kindly ['kaɪndlɪ] (*comp* **kindlier**, *superl* **kindliest**) ◇ *adv* **1.** [affably, warmly] chaleureusement, affablement ■ **he has always treated me ~** il a toujours été gentil avec moi **2.** [obligingly] gentiment, obligeamment ■ **she ~ offered to help us** elle a gentiment offert de nous aider **3.** [favourably] : **to look ~ on sthg** voir qqch d'un bon œil ■ **they don't take ~ to people arriving late** ils n'apprécient pas beaucoup *OR* tellement qu'on arrive en retard ■ **I have always thought ~ of him** j'ai toujours eu une bonne opinion de lui **4.** [in polite requests] : **would *OR* will you ~ pass the salt?** auriez-vous la gentillesse *OR* l'amabilité de me passer le sel? ■ **~ refrain from smoking** prière de ne pas fumer ■ [in anger or annoyance] : **will you ~ sit down!** asseyez-vous, je vous prie!
◇ *adj* [person, attitude] gentil ■ [smile] bienveillant.

kindness ['kaɪndnɪs] *n* **1.** [thoughtfulness] bonté *f*, gentillesse *f* ■ **she did it out of the ~ of her heart** elle l'a fait par bonté d'âme **2.** *UK* [considerate act] service *m* ■ **to do sb a ~** rendre service à qqn ■ **please do me the ~ of replying** *fml* pourriez-vous être assez gentil pour *OR* pourriez-vous avoir l'amabilité de me donner une réponse?

kindred ['kɪndrɪd] ◇ *n* *arch* & *lit* [relationship] parenté *f* ■ [family] famille *f*, parents *mpl*.
◇ *adj* [related] apparenté ■ [similar] similaire, analogue ■ **~ spirits** âmes *fpl* sœurs.

kinetic [kɪ'netɪk] *adj* cinétique.

kinetic art *n* art *m* cinétique.

kinetic energy *n* énergie *f* cinétique.

kinfolk ['kɪnfəʊk] *US* = **kinsfolk**.

king [kɪŋ] *n* **1.** roi *m* ■ **King Henry the Eighth** le roi Henri VIII ■ **the King of Spain/Belgium** le roi d'Espagne/des Belges ■ **the Three Kings** les trois Mages, les Rois mages ■ **the ~ of (the) beasts** *fig* le roi des animaux ■ **the fast-food ~** *fig* le roi *OR* magnat de la restauration rapide ▶ **to live like a ~** vivre en grand seigneur ■ **to pay a ~'s ransom (for sthg)** payer une fortune *OR* un prix fou (pour qqch) ■ **'King Lear'** ***Shakespeare*** 'le Roi Lear' **2.** [in cards & chess] roi *m* ■ [in draughts] dame *f*.
◆ **Kings** *n* : **(the book of) Kings** BIBLE (le livre des) Rois.

King Charles spaniel *n* king-charles *m inv*.

king cobra *n* cobra *m* royal, hamadryade *f*.

kingcup ['kɪŋkʌp] *n* *UK* populage *m*, souci *m* d'eau.

kingdom ['kɪŋdəm] *n* **1.** [realm] royaume *m* ■ **the ~ of God/Heaven** BIBLE le royaume de Dieu/des cieux ▶ **till ~ come** jusqu'à la fin des temps ■ **they were blown to ~ come** ils ont été expédiés dans l'autre monde *OR* dans l'au-delà **2.** [division] règne *m* ■ **the animal/vegetable/mineral ~** le règne animal/végétal/minéral.

kingfisher ['kɪŋ,fɪʃəʳ] *n* martin-pêcheur *m*.

kingly ['kɪŋlɪ] (*comp* **kinglier**, *superl* **kingliest**) *adj* royal, majestueux.

kingmaker ['kɪŋ,meɪkəʳ] *n* HIST faiseur *m* de rois ■ *fig* & POL *personne qui fait ou défait les candidats politiques.*

king penguin *n* manchot *m* royal.

kingpin ['kɪŋpɪn] *n* **1.** TECH pivot *m* **2.** *fig* pivot *m*, cheville *f* ouvrière.

king prawn *n* (grosse) crevette *f*.

King's English *n* *UK* : **the ~** le bon anglais.

King's evidence *n* *UK* : **to turn ~** témoigner contre ses complices.

kingship ['kɪŋʃɪp] *n* royauté *f*.

king-size(d) *adj* [bed, mattress] (très) grand ■ [cigarette] long, longue *f* ■ [packet, container] géant ■ **I've got a ~ hangover** *inf fig* j'ai une méga gueule de bois.

kink [kɪŋk] ◇ *n* **1.** [in rope, wire] nœud *m* ■ [in hair] boucle *f*, frisette *f* **2.** *inf fig* [sexual deviation] perversion *f*, aberration *f* ■ [quirk] bizarrerie *f*, excentricité *f* **3.** *US inf* [flaw] problème *m*.
◇ *vt* [rope, cable] entortiller, emmêler.
◇ *vi* [rope, cable] s'entortiller, s'emmêler.

kinky ['kɪŋkɪ] (*comp* **kinkier**, *superl* **kinkiest**) *adj* **1.** *inf* [behaviour] farfelu ■ [sexually] vicieux, pervers ■ **he likes ~ sex** il a des goûts sexuels un peu spéciaux **2.** [rope, cable] entortillé, emmêlé ■ [hair] crépu, frisé.

kinsfolk ['kɪnzfəʊk] *npl* parents *mpl*, famille *f*.

kinship ['kɪnʃɪp] *n* [relationship] parenté *f* ■ *fig* [closeness] intimité *f*.

kinsman ['kɪnzmən] (*pl* **kinsmen** [-mən]) *n* parent *m*.

kinswoman ['kɪnz,wʊmən] (*pl* **kinswomen** [-,wɪmɪn]) *n* parente *f*.

kiosk ['ki:ɒsk] *n* [for newspapers, magazines] kiosque *m* ■ *US* [for advertisements] ≃ colonne *f* Morris.

kip [kɪp] (*pret & pp* **kipped**, *cont* **kipping**) *UK inf* ◇ *n* [sleep] roupillon *m* ■ **to have a *OR* to get some ~** faire *OR* piquer un roupillon.
◇ *vi* roupiller.
◆ **kip down** *vi insep inf* se pieuter.

kipper ['kɪpəʳ] ◇ *n* hareng *m* fumé, kipper *m*.
◇ *vt* [fish] fumer.

kipper tie *n* large cravate *f*.

KIPS [kɪps] (*abbrev of* **kilo instructions per second**) *n* COMPUT *millier d'instructions par seconde.*

Kirgizia [kɜ:'gɪzɪə] *pr n* Kirghizie *f* ■ **in ~** en Khirgizie.

Kirgizstan [,kɪrgɪz'stɑ:n] *n* Kirghizistan *m*.

Kiribati ['kɪrɪbætɪ] *n* Kiribati *m*.

Kiritimati [kɪ'rɪsɪmætɪ] *n* GEOG Kiritimati *m*.

kirk [kɜ:k] *n* *Scotland* église *f*.

kirsch [kɪəʃ] *n* Kirsch *m*.

kiss [kɪs] ◇ *n* baiser *m* ■ **they gave her a ~** ils l'ont embrassée ■ **give us a ~!** *inf* fais-moi un (gros) bisou! ■ **she gave him a goodnight ~** elle lui a souhaité une bonne nuit en l'embrassant, elle l'a embrassé pour lui souhaiter (une) bonne nuit ▶ **to give sb the ~ of life** faire du bouche-à-bouche à qqn ■ **it could be the ~ of life for the building trade** cela pourrait permettre à l'industrie du bâtiment de retrouver un *OR* son second souffle ■ **~ of death** coup fatal ■ **the new supermarket was the ~ of death for local shopkeepers** l'ouverture du supermarché a entraîné la ruine des petits commerçants.
◇ *vt* **1.** [with lips] embrasser ■ **he ~ed her on the lips/forehead** il l'embrassa sur la bouche/sur le front ■ **he ~ed her hand** il lui a baisé la main, il lui a fait le baisemain *lit* ■ **I ~ed her goodnight** je l'ai embrassée *OR* je lui ai fait une bise pour lui souhaiter (une) bonne nuit ▶ **you can ~ your money goodbye!** *inf* tu peux faire ton deuil de *OR* tu peux faire une croix sur ton fric! **2.** *lit* [touch lightly] caresser.
◇ *vi* s'embrasser ■ **to ~ and make up** s'embrasser et faire la paix.
◆ **kiss away** *vt sep* : **she ~ed away my tears** ses baisers ont séché mes larmes.

kissagram ['kɪsəgræm] *n* baiser *m* par porteur spécial (*service utilisé à l'occasion d'un anniversaire etc*).

kiss-and-tell *adj* PRESS : **another ~ story by an ex-girlfriend** encore des révélations intimes faites *OR* des secrets d'alcôve dévoilés par une ancienne petite amie.

kiss curl *n* *UK* accroche-cœur *m*.

kisser ['kɪsəʳ] *n* **1.** [person] : **is he a good ~?** est-ce qu'il embrasse bien? **2.** *inf* [face, mouth] tronche *f*.

kit [kɪt] (*pret & pp* **kitted**, *cont* **kitting**) *n* **1.** [set] trousse *f* ■ **tool/sewing ~** trousse à outils/à couture **2.** [equipment] affaires *fpl*, matériel *m* ■ **have you got your squash ~?** as-tu tes affaires de squash? ■ **get your ~ off!**[△] *hum* à poil! ▶ **the whole ~ and caboodle** *inf* tout le bazar *OR* bataclan **3.** [soldier's gear] fourniment *m* ■ **in full battle ~** en tenue de combat ■ **~ inspection** revue *f* de détail **4.** [parts to be assembled] kit *m* ■ **it's sold in ~ form** c'est vendu en kit ■ **model aircraft ~** maquette *f* d'avion.

◆ **kit out, kit up** *vt sep UK inf* équiper ▪ **we kitted ourselves out for a long trip** nous nous sommes équipés pour un long voyage ▪ **he was kitted out for golf** il était en tenue de golf.

kit bag *n UK* musette *f*, sac *m* de toile.

kitchen ['kɪtʃɪn] <> *n* cuisine *f*.
<> *comp* [salt, scissors, table, utensil] de cuisine.

kitchen cabinet *n* **1.** [furniture] buffet *m* (de cuisine) **2.** *UK* POL cabinet *m* restreint *(conseillers proches du chef du gouvernement)*.

kitchenette [ˌkɪtʃɪ'net] *n* kitchenette *f*, cuisinette *f offic*.

kitchen foil *n* aluminium *m* ménager, papier *m* d'aluminium *OR* d'alu.

kitchen sink *n* évier *m* ▪ **everything but the ~** *fig & hum* tout sauf les murs ▪ **~ drama** *théâtre et cinéma réalistes des années 50-60 dépeignant l'ennui et la misère des gens ordinaires*.

kitchen unit *n* élément *m* (de cuisine).

kitchenware ['kɪtʃɪnweəʳ] *n* vaisselle *f* et ustensiles *mpl* de cuisine.

kite [kaɪt] *n* **1.** [toy] cerf-volant *m* ▪ **to fly a ~** *liter* faire voler un cerf-volant ; *fig* lancer un ballon d'essai **2.** ORNITH milan *m*.

Kite mark *n label représentant un petit cerf-volant apposé sur les produits conformes aux normes officielles britanniques*.

kitesurfing ['kaɪtsɜːfɪŋ] *n* kitesurf *m*.

kith [kɪθ] *npl* : **~ and kin** amis *mpl* et parents *mpl* ▪ **he's one of our own ~ and kin** il est l'un des nôtres.

kitsch [kɪtʃ] <> *adj* kitsch.
<> *n* kitsch *m*.

kitschy ['kɪtʃɪ] (*comp* **kitschier**, *superl* **kitschiest**) = **kitsch** *(adj)*.

kitten ['kɪtn] *n* chaton *m* ▪ **our cat has had ~s** notre chatte a eu des petits ▶ **he was having ~s** *UK inf* il était dans tous ses états *OR* aux cent coups.

kitty ['kɪtɪ] (*pl* **kitties**) *n* **1.** *inf* [kitten] chaton *m* ▪ **here, ~~** viens, mon minou *OR* minet **2.** [funds held in common] cagnotte *f*, caisse *f* (commune) ▪ [in gambling] cagnotte *f*.

kiwi ['kiːwiː] *n* **1.** ORNITH kiwi *m*, aptéryx *m* **2.** [fruit] kiwi *m*.
◆ **Kiwi** *n inf* [New Zealander] Néo-Zélandais *m*, - e *f* ▪ **the Kiwis** [rugby team] les Kiwis.

kiwi fruit *n* kiwi *m*.

KKK *pr n* = **Ku Klux Klan**.

Kleenex® ['kliːneks] *n* Kleenex® *m inv*, mouchoir *m* en papier.

kleptomania [ˌkleptə'meɪnɪə] *n* kleptomanie *f*, cleptomanie *f*.

kleptomaniac [ˌkleptə'meɪnɪæk] <> *adj* kleptomane, cleptomane.
<> *n* kleptomane *mf*, cleptomane *mf*.

klieg light [kliːg-] *n US* lampe *f* à arc.

Klondike ['klɒndaɪk] *pr n* : **the ~ (River)** le Klondike ▪ **the ~ gold rush** *la ruée vers l'or, aux États-Unis*.

klutz [klʌts] *n inf* balourd *m*, - e *f*, godiche *f*.

km (*written abbrev of* **kilometre**) km.

km/h (*written abbrev of* **kilometres per hour**) km/h.

knack [næk] *n* tour *m* de main, truc *m* ▪ **it's easy, once you get the ~(of it)** c'est facile, une fois qu'on a compris le truc ▪ **she's got a ~ of finding the right word** elle sait toujours trouver le mot juste ▪ **he's got a ~ of turning up at meal-times** *hum* il a le chic pour arriver aux heures des repas.

knacker ['nækəʳ] *UK* <> *vt*△ crever ▪ **that run completely ~ed me** cette course m'a mis sur les genoux.
<> *n* **1.** [slaughterer] équarrisseur *m* ▪ **~'s yard** équarrissoir *m*, abattoir *m* **2.** [in real estate] démolisseur *m*.

knackered△ ['nækəd] *adj* [tired] crevé ▪ [engine] mort.

knapsack ['næpsæk] *n* havresac *m*, sac *m* à dos.

knave [neɪv] *n* **1.** *arch* [rogue] canaille *f* **2.** CARDS & *fml* valet *m*.

knead [niːd] *vt* [dough, clay] pétrir, malaxer ▪ [massage - body] pétrir, malaxer.

knee [niː] <> *n* **1.** ANAT genou *m* ▪ **the snow was up to our ~s, we were up to our ~s in snow** on avait de la neige jusqu'aux genoux ▪ **to go down on one's ~s, to fall to one's ~s** se mettre à genoux ▶ **to be on one's ~s** *liter & fig* être à genoux ▪ **to bring sb to his/her ~s** faire capituler qqn ▪ **the war nearly brought the country to its ~s** la guerre a failli entraîner la ruine du pays **2.** [of trousers] genou *m* ▪ **worn at the ~ (s)** usé aux genoux **3.** [lap] genoux *mpl* ▪ **come and sit on my ~** viens t'asseoir sur mes genoux ▪ **to put sb over one's ~** donner la fessée à *OR* corriger qqn ▶ **I learnt it at my mother's ~** c'est ma mère qui me l'a appris lorsque je n'étais qu'un enfant ▪ **to go down on bended ~** se mettre à genoux.
<> *vt* donner un coup de genou à.

kneecap ['niːkæp] (*pret & pp* **kneecapped**, *cont* **kneecapping**)
<> *n* ANAT rotule *f*.
<> *vt* : **he was kneecapped** on lui a brisé les rotules.

knee-deep *adj* : **the snow was ~** on avait de la neige jusqu'aux genoux ▪ **we were ~ in water** l'eau nous arrivait *OR* nous étions dans l'eau jusqu'aux genoux ▪ **he was ~ in trouble** *fig* il était dans les ennuis jusqu'au cou.

knee-high *adj* [grass] à hauteur de genou ▪ **~ socks** chaussettes *fpl* montantes ▪ **the grass was ~** l'herbe nous arrivait (jusqu')aux genoux ▶ **~ to a grasshopper** *inf hum* haut comme trois pommes.

knee jerk *n* réflexe *m* rotulien.
◆ **knee-jerk** *adj* automatique ▪ **~ reaction** *fig & pej* réflexe *m*, automatisme *m*.

knee joint *n* articulation *f* du genou.

kneel [niːl] (*pret & pp* **knelt** [nelt] *OR* **kneeled**) *vi* s'agenouiller, se mettre à genoux ▪ **to ~ in prayer** s'agenouiller pour prier.
◆ **kneel down** *vi insep* se mettre à genoux, s'agenouiller.

knee-length *adj* : **a ~ skirt** une jupe qui descend jusqu'au genou.

knee level *n* : **at ~** à hauteur du genou.

kneeling ['niːlɪŋ] *adj* agenouillé, à genoux.

knee pad *n* genouillère *f*.

knees-up *n UK inf* [dance] danse *f* (agitée) ▪ [party] fête *f*.

knell [nel] *n lit* glas *m*.

knelt [nelt] *pt & pp* ▷ **kneel**.

knew [njuː] *pt* ▷ **know**.

knickerbocker glory ['nɪkəbɒkəʳ-] *n coupe de glace avec fruits et crème Chantilly*.

knickerbockers ['nɪkəbɒkəz] *npl* knickers *mpl* ▪ [for golf] culotte *f* de golf.

knickers ['nɪkəz] <> *npl UK* [underwear] : **don't get your ~ in a twist!** *inf* [don't panic] ne t'affole pas! ; [don't get angry] du calme!, calme-toi!
<> *interj inf UK inf dated* **~!** mon œil!

knick-knack ['nɪknæk] *n* [trinket] bibelot *m* ▪ [brooch] colifichet *m*.

knife [naɪf] (*pl* **knives** [naɪvz]) <> *n* **1.** [for eating] couteau *m* ▪ **a ~ and fork** une fourchette et un couteau ▪ **her words cut me like a ~** ses paroles m'ont piqué au vif *OR* profondément blessé ▶ **fish ~** couteau *m* à poisson ▪ **like a ~ through butter** comme dans du beurre ▪ **to be *OR* to go under the ~** *inf* passer sur le billard **2.** [as a weapon] couteau *m* ▶ **the knives are out** ils sont à couteaux tirés *OR* en guerre ouverte ▪ **you really stuck the ~ in!** *inf* tu ne l'as pas loupé! ▪ **to turn *OR* to twist the ~ (in the wound)** retourner le couteau dans la plaie.

◇ *comp* : **a ~ wound/attack** une blessure/une attaque à coups de couteau.
◇ *vt* donner un coup de couteau à ▪ **to ~ sb to death** tuer qqn à coups de couteau ▪ **he was ~d in the back** *liter* il a reçu un coup de couteau *OR* on lui a planté un couteau dans le dos ; *fig* on lui a tiré dans le dos *OR* dans les pattes.

knife-edge *n* **1.** [blade] fil *m* d'un couteau ▪ **we were on a ~** *fig* on était sur des charbons ardents ▪ **his decision was (balanced) on a ~** sa décision ne tenait qu'à un fil **2.** [of scales] couteau *m*.

knife-grinder *n* rémouleur *m*.

knife-point *n* : **at ~** sous la menace du couteau.

knife-rest *n* porte-couteau *m*.

knifing ['naɪfɪŋ] *n* agression *f* à coups de couteau.

knight [naɪt] ◇ *n* **1.** HIST chevalier *m* ▪ **a ~ in shining armour** [romantic hero] un prince charmant ; [saviour] un sauveur, un redresseur de torts **2.** *UK* [honorary title] chevalier *m* **3.** [chess piece] cavalier *m*.
◇ *vt* faire chevalier.

knighthood ['naɪthʊd] *n* **1.** *UK* [title] titre *m* de chevalier ▪ **to receive a ~** être fait chevalier, être anobli **2.** HIST chevalerie *f*.

knit [nɪt] (*pret & pp* **knit** *OR* **knitted**, *cont* **knitting**) ◇ *vt* **1.** tricoter ▪ **he knitted himself a scarf** il s'est tricoté une écharpe **2.** [in instructions] : **~ 2 purl 2** (tricoter) 2 mailles à l'endroit, 2 mailles à l'envers **3.** [unite] unir **4.** *phr* **to ~ one's brows** froncer les sourcils.
◇ *vi* tricoter.

◆ **knit together** ◇ *vi insep* [heal - bones] se souder.
◇ *vt sep* [unite] unir ▪ MED [bones] souder.

◆ **knit up** ◇ *vi insep* [yarn] : **this wool ~s up easily** cette laine se tricote facilement.
◇ *vt sep* [garment] tricoter.

knitted ['nɪtɪd] *adj* tricoté, en tricot.

knitter ['nɪtəʳ] *n* tricoteur *m*, - euse *f* ▪ **she's a good/a quick ~** elle tricote bien/vite.

knitting ['nɪtɪŋ] ◇ *n* **1.** [garment] tricot *m* **2.** [activity] tricot *m* ▪ [on industrial scale] tricotage *m* ▪ **to do some ~** faire du tricot ➊ **machine ~** tricots faits à la machine.
◇ *comp* [wool] à tricoter ▪ [pattern] de tricot ▪ [factory] de tricotage.

knitting machine *n* machine *f* à tricoter.

knitting needle, knitting pin *n* aiguille *f* à tricoter.

knitwear ['nɪtweəʳ] *n* [garments] tricots *mpl*, pulls *mpl* ▪ [in department store] rayon *m* pulls.

knives [naɪvz] *pl* ▷ **knife**.

knob [nɒb] *n* **1.** [handle - of door, drawer] poignée *f*, bouton *m* ▪ **the same to you with ~s on!** *inf UK* toi-même! **2.** [control - on appliance] bouton *m* **3.** [ball-shaped end - of walking stick] pommeau *m* ; [- on furniture] bouton *m* **4.** [of butter] noix *f* **5.** [hillock] monticule *m* **6.** ▲ *UK* [penis] queue▲ *f*, bite▲ *f*.

knobbly *UK* ['nɒblɪ], **knobby** *US* ['nɒbɪ] (*UKcomp* **knobblier**, *superl* **knobbliest**) (*UScomp* **knobbier**, *superl* **knobbiest**) *adj* noueux ▪ **~ knees** genoux couverts de bosses.

knock [nɒk] ◇ *vt* **1.** [hit] : **to ~ a nail in** enfoncer un clou ▪ **she ~ed a nail into/she ~ed a hole in the wall** elle a planté un clou/elle a fait un trou dans le mur ▪ **the force of the explosion ~ed us to the floor** la force de l'explosion nous a projetés à terre ▪ **to ~ sb unconscious** *OR* **cold** *inf* assommer qqn ▮ [bump] heurter, cogner ▪ **I ~ed my head on** *OR* **against the low ceiling** je me suis cogné la tête contre le *OR* au plafond
2. *fig* **to ~ holes in a plan/an argument** démolir un projet/un argument ▪ **maybe it will ~ some sense into him** cela lui mettra peut-être du plomb dans la cervelle, cela le ramènera peut-être à la raison ▪ **he ~ed all our hopes on the head** *UK* il a réduit nos espoirs à néant ▪ **he can ~ spots off me at chess/tennis** *UK* il me bat à plate couture aux échecs/au tennis
3. *inf* [criticize - author, film] éreinter ; [- driving, cooking] critiquer ▪ **~ing your colleagues isn't going to help** ce n'est pas en débinant vos collègues *OR* en cassant du sucre sur le dos de vos collègues que vous changerez quoi que ce soit
4. △ *UK* [have sex with] se faire△, se taper△.
◇ *vi* **1.** [hit] frapper ▪ **to ~ on** *OR* **at the door** frapper (à la porte) ▪ **they ~ on the wall when we're too noisy** ils tapent *OR* cognent contre le mur quand on fait trop de bruit
2. [bump] : **to ~ against** *OR* **into** heurter, cogner ▪ **she ~ed into the desk** elle s'est heurtée *OR* cognée contre le bureau
3. [make symptomatic sound] cogner ▪ **my heart was ~ing** je sentais mon cœur cogner dans ma poitrine, j'avais le cœur qui cognait ▪ **the car engine is ~ing** le moteur cogne ▪ **his knees were ~ing** *hum* ses genoux jouaient des castagnettes.
◇ *n* **1.** [blow] coup *m* ▪ **give it a ~ with a hammer** donne un coup de marteau dessus ▪ **there was a ~ at the door/window** on a frappé à la porte/fenêtre ▪ **no one answered my ~** personne n'a répondu quand j'ai frappé ▪ **~! ~!** toc! toc! ▮ [bump] coup *m* ▪ **I got a nasty ~ on the elbow** [in fight, accident] j'ai reçu un sacré coup au coude ; [by one's own clumsiness] je me suis bien cogné le coude ▪ **the car's had a few ~s, but nothing serious** la voiture est un peu cabossée mais rien de grave
2. [setback] coup *m* ▪ **his reputation has taken a hard ~** sa réputation en a pris un sérieux coup ▪ **I've taken a few ~s in my time** *inf* j'ai encaissé des coups moi aussi
3. *inf* [criticism] critique *f* ▪ **she's taken a few ~s from the press** la presse n'a pas toujours été très tendre avec elle
4. AUT [in engine] cognement *m*.

◆ **knock about** *UK*, **knock around** ◇ *vi insep inf* [loiter] traîner ▪ **I ~ed about in Australia for a while** j'ai bourlingué *OR* roulé ma bosse en Australie pendant quelque temps.
◇ *vt insep inf* traîner dans ▪ **these clothes are OK for ~ing about the house in** ces vêtements, ça va pour traîner à la maison.
◇ *vt sep* **1.** [beat] battre ▪ [ill-treat] malmener ▪ **the old car's been ~ed about a bit** la vieille voiture a pris quelques coups ici et là
2. [jolt, shake] ballotter
3. *inf* [discuss] débattre ▪ **we ~ed the idea about for a while** nous en avons vaguement discuté pendant un certain temps.

◆ **knock about with** *UK*, **knock around with** *vt insep inf* fréquenter.

◆ **knock back** *vt sep inf* **1.** [drink] descendre ▪ **she could ~ back five cognacs in an hour** elle pouvait s'envoyer cinq cognacs en une heure
2. [cost] coûter.

◆ **knock down** *vt sep* **1.** [person] renverser ▪ [in fight] envoyer par terre, étendre ▪ **she was ~ed down by a bus** elle a été renversée par un bus
2. [hurdle, vase, pile of books] faire tomber, renverser
3. [demolish - building] démolir ; [- wall] démolir, abattre ; [- argument] démolir
4. [price] baisser ▪ [salesman] faire baisser ▪ **I managed to ~ him down to $500** j'ai réussi à le faire baisser jusqu'à 500 dollars
5. *UK* [at auction] adjuger.

◆ **knock off** ◇ *vt sep* **1.** [from shelf, wall etc] faire tomber ▪ **he was ~ed off his bicycle** le choc l'a fait tomber de sa bicyclette ➊ **to ~ sb's block off** *inf* casser la figure à qqn
2. [reduce by] faire une réduction de ▪ **the salesman ~ed 10% off (for us)** le vendeur nous a fait un rabais *OR* une remise de 10 %
3. *inf* [write rapidly] torcher ▪ **she can ~ off an article in half an hour** elle peut pondre un article en une demi-heure
4. △ [kill] descendre, buter△
5. △ *UK* [steal] piquer, faucher ▪ [rob] braquer△
6. *inf phr* **~ it off!** [stop] arrête ton char△ !
7. ▲ *UK* [have sex with] baiser▲.
◇ *vi insep inf* [stop work] cesser le travail ▪ **we ~ off at 5** on finit à 17h.

◆ **knock on** ◇ *vi insep* **1.** RUGBY faire un en-avant
2. *UK inf* [age] : **my dad's ~ing on a bit now** mon père commence à prendre de la bouteille.
◇ *vt sep* RUGBY : **to ~ the ball on** faire un en-avant.
◇ *vt insep UK inf* **he's ~ing on 60** il va sur la soixantaine.

◆ **knock out** *vt sep* **1.** [nail] faire sortir ▪ [wall] abattre ▪ **one of his teeth was ~ed out** il a perdu une dent
2. [make unconscious] assommer ▪ [in boxing] mettre K-O ▪ *inf* [subj: drug, pill] assommer, mettre K-O
3. *inf* [astound] épater

4. [eliminate] éliminer
5. [put out of action] mettre hors service ▪ **it can ~ out a tank at 2,000 metres** cela peut mettre un tank hors de combat à 2 000 mètres
6. *inf* [exhaust] crever
7. [pipe] : **he ~ed out his pipe** il a débourré sa pipe.
◆ **knock over** *vt sep* renverser, faire tomber.
◆ **knock together** <> *vt sep* [hit together] cogner l'un contre l'autre.
<> *vi insep* s'entrechoquer.
◆ **knock up** <> *vt sep* **1.** *UK inf* [make quickly] faire à la hâte ▪ **he ~ed up a delicious meal in no time** en un rien de temps, il a réussi à nous préparer quelque chose de délicieux
2. *UK* [waken] réveiller (en frappant à la porte)
3. *UK inf* [exhaust] crever ▪ [make ill] rendre malade ▪ **he's ~ed up with the flu** il a chopé la grippe
4. △ [make pregnant] mettre en cloque△
5. [in cricket] marquer.
<> *vi insep UK* [in ball games] faire des balles.

knockabout ['nɒkəbaut] *adj* turbulent, violent ▪ **a ~ comedy** *OR* **farce** une grosse farce ▪ **a ~ comedian** un clown.

knockdown ['nɒk,daun] <> *adj* **1.** [forceful] : **a ~ blow** un coup à assommer un bœuf ▪ **a ~ argument** un argument massue **2.** *UK* [reduced] : **for sale at ~ prices** en vente à des prix imbattables *OR* défiant toute concurrence ▪ **I got it for a ~ price** je l'ai eu pour trois fois rien **3.** [easy to dismantle] démontable.
<> *n* [in boxing] knock-down *m*.

knocker ['nɒkəʳ] *n* **1.** [on door] heurtoir *m*, marteau *m* (de porte) **2.** *inf* [critic] débineur *m*, - euse *f*.
◆ **knockers**△ *npl* [breasts] nichons△ *mpl*.

knock-for-knock *adj* [in insurance] : **~ agreement** *accord à l'amiable selon lequel, lors d'un accident, chaque compagnie d'assurance paie les dégâts de son propre assuré.*

knocking ['nɒkɪŋ] *n* **1.** [noise] bruit *m* de coups, cognement *m* ▪ AUT cognement *m*, cliquetis *m* **2.** *UK inf* [injury, defeat] : **to take a ~** [in fight] se faire rouer de coups ; [in match] se faire battre à plate couture *OR* plates coutures ▪ **their prestige took a ~** leur prestige en a pris un coup.

knocking copy *n (U)* contre-publicité *f*.

knocking-off time *n UK inf* **it's ~** c'est l'heure de se tirer.

knocking shop△ *n UK* bordel△ *m*.

knock-kneed [-'ni:d] *adj* cagneux.

knock-knees *npl* : **to have ~** avoir les genoux cagneux.

knock-on <> *n* RUGBY en-avant *m inv*.
<> *adj* : **~ effect** répercussion *f* ▪ **to have a ~ effect** déclencher une réaction en chaîne.

knockout ['nɒkaut] <> *n* **1.** [in boxing] knock-out *m*, K-O *m* ▪ **to win by a ~** gagner par K-O **2.** *inf* [sensation] : **to be a ~** être sensationnel *OR* génial **3.** SPORT tournoi *m* (par élimination directe).
<> *adj* **1.** : **~ blow** coup *m* qui met K-O ▪ **~ drops** *inf* soporifique *m*, somnifère *m* **2.** SPORT : **~ competition** tournoi *m* par élimination.

knock-up *n UK* SPORT [in ball games] échauffement *m* ▪ **to have a ~** faire des balles.

knoll [nəul] *n* monticule *m*, tertre *m*.

knot [nɒt] (*pret & pp* **knotted**, *cont* **knotting**) <> *n* **1.** [fastening] nœud *m* ▪ *fig* [bond] lien *m* ▪ **to tie sthg in a ~, to tie a ~ in sthg** nouer qqch, faire un nœud à qqch ▪ **to tie/to untie a ~** faire/défaire un nœud ➤ **to tie the (marriage) ~** se marier ▪ **tie a ~ in it!** *UK inf* ferme-la!
2. [tangle] nœud *m* ▪ **the wool is full of ~s** la laine est toute emmêlée ▪ **my stomach was in ~s** *fig* j'avais l'estomac noué ▪ **to get tied up in ~s** *inf*, **to tie o.s. (up) in ~s** *inf* s'emmêler les pinceaux
3. [in wood] nœud *m*
4. ANAT & MED nœud *m*, nodule *m*
5. [cluster of people] petit groupe *m*
6. NAUT nœud *m* ▪ **we are doing 15 ~s** nous filons 15 nœuds ➤ **at a rate of ~s** à toute allure, à un train d'enfer.
<> *vt* [string] nouer, faire un nœud dans ▪ [tie] nouer ▪ **he knotted the rope around his waist** il s'est attaché *OR* noué la corde autour de la taille.
<> *vi* [stomach] se nouer ▪ [muscles] se contracter, se raidir.

knothole ['nɒthəul] *n* trou *m (laissé par un nœud dans du bois).*

knotted ['nɒtɪd] *adj* noué ▪ **get ~!**△ va te faire voir!

knotty ['nɒtɪ] (*comp* **knottier**, *superl* **knottiest**) *adj* [wood, hands] noueux ▪ [wool, hair] plein de nœuds ▪ [problem] épineux.

know [nəu] (*pret* **knew** [nju:], *pp* **known** [nəun]) <> *vt* **1.** [person] connaître ▪ **to ~ sb by sight/by reputation** connaître qqn de vue/de réputation ▪ **I don't ~ him to speak to** je ne le connais pas assez pour lui parler ▪ **~ing him, he'll still be in bed** tel que je le connais, il sera encore au lit ▪ **you'll like her once you get to ~ her better** elle vous plaira une fois que vous la connaîtrez mieux
2. [place] connaître
3. [fact, information] : **do you ~ her phone number?** vous connaissez son numéro de téléphone? ▪ **civilization as we ~ it** la civilisation telle que nous la connaissons ▪ **I ~ for a fact that he's lying** je sais pertinemment qu'il ment ▪ **I don't ~ that it's the best solution** je ne suis pas certain *OR* sûr que ce soit la meilleure solution ▪ **I ~ what I'm talking about** je sais de quoi je parle ▪ **I'll let you ~ how it turns out** je te dirai comment ça s'est passé ▪ **any problems, let me ~** au moindre problème, n'hésitez pas ▪ **she ~s a lot about politics** elle s'y connaît en politique ▪ **she ~s her own mind** elle sait ce qu'elle veut ➤ **it's not an easy job – don't I ~ it!** *inf* ce n'est pas un travail facile – à qui le dis-tu! ▪ **you ~ what I mean** tu vois ce que je veux dire ▪ **well, what do you ~!** *inf* ça alors!, ça par exemple! ▪ **there's no ~ing how he'll react** on ne peut pas savoir comment il réagira ▪ **God** *OR* **Heaven ~s why!** *inf* Dieu sait pourquoi!
4. [language, skill] : **he ~s French** il comprend le français ▪ **I ~ a few words of Welsh** je connais quelques mots de gallois ▪ **she really ~s her job/subject** elle connaît son boulot/sujet ▪ **to ~ how to do sthg** savoir faire qqch ▪ **they knew how to make cars in those days!** en ce temps-là, les voitures, c'était du solide!
5. [recognize] reconnaître ▪ **she ~s a bargain when she sees one** elle sait reconnaître une bonne affaire
6. [distinguish] distinguer, discerner ▪ **she doesn't ~ right from wrong** elle ne sait pas discerner le bien du mal *OR* faire la différence entre le bien et le mal
7. [experience] connaître ▪ **I've never known him to be wrong** je ne l'ai jamais vu se tromper
8. [nickname, call] : **Ian White, known as "Chalky"** Ian White, connu sous le nom de "Chalky" ▪ **they're known as June bugs in America** on les appelle des "June bugs" en Amérique
9. [regard] considérer ▪ **she's known as one of our finest singers** elle est considérée comme l'une de nos meilleures chanteuses.
<> *vi* savoir ▪ **not that I ~ (of)** pas que je sache ▪ **you never ~** on ne sait jamais ▪ **he might** *OR* **should have known better** ce n'était pas très sage de sa part ▪ **to ~ about sthg** être au courant de qqch ▪ **he ~s about cars** il s'y connaît en voitures ▪ **I don't ~ about you, but I'm exhausted** toi, je ne sais pas, mais moi, je suis épuisé ▪ **do you ~ of a good bookshop?** vous connaissez une bonne librairie?
<> *n phr* : **to be in the ~** *inf* être au courant.
◆ **as far as I know** *adv phr* (pour) autant que je sache ▪ **not as far as I ~** pas que je sache.
◆ **you know** *adv phr* **1.** [for emphasis] : **I was right, you ~** j'avais raison, tu sais
2. [indicating hesitancy] : **he was just, you ~, a bit boring** il était juste un peu ennuyeux, si tu vois ce que je veux dire
3. [to add information] : **it was that blonde woman, you ~, the one with the dog** c'était la femme blonde, tu sais, celle qui avait un chien
4. [to introduce a statement] : **you ~, sometimes I wonder why I do this** tu sais, parfois je me demande pourquoi je fais ça.

know-all *UK*, **know-it-all** *US n inf pej* je-sais-tout *mf*, monsieur *m OR* madame *f OR* mademoiselle *f* je-sais-tout.

know-how *n* savoir-faire *m*, know-how *m*.

knowing ['nəʊɪŋ] *adj* [look, laugh] entendu, complice ▪ **she gave him a ~ look** elle l'a regardé d'un air entendu.

knowingly ['nəʊɪŋlɪ] *adv* **1.** [act] sciemment, consciemment **2.** [smile, laugh] d'un air entendu.

know-it-all *US inf* = **know-all**.

knowledgable ['nɒlɪdʒəbl] = **knowledgeable**.

knowledge ['nɒlɪdʒ] *n* **1.** [learning] connaissance *f*, savoir *m* ▪ [total learning] connaissances *fpl* ▪ **she has a good ~ of English** elle a une bonne connaissance de l'anglais ▪ **he has a basic ~ of computing** il a un minimum de connaissances en informatique ▪ **to have a thorough ~ of sthg** connaître qqch à fond **2.** [awareness] connaissance *f* ▪ **it has come to my ~ that...** j'ai appris que... ▪ **to (the best of) my ~** (pour) autant que je sache, à ma connaissance ▪ **not to my ~** pas que je sache ▪ **without my ~** à mon insu, sans que je le sache ▪ **it's (a matter of) common ~** c'est de notoriété publique, personne ne l'ignore.

knowledgeable ['nɒlɪdʒəbl] *adj* **1.** [well researched] bien documenté **2.** [expert] bien informé ▪ **he's very ~ about computing** il connaît bien l'informatique, il s'y connaît en informatique.

knowledgeably ['nɒlɪdʒəblɪ] *adv* en connaisseur ▪ **he speaks very ~ about art** il parle d'art en connaisseur.

known [nəʊn] <> *pp* ▻ **know**.
<> *adj* [notorious] connu, notoire ▪ [recognized] reconnu ▪ **it's a ~ fact** c'est un fait établi ▪ **to make o.s. ~** se faire connaître ▪ **to let it be ~** faire savoir.

knuckle ['nʌkl] *n* **1.** [of human] articulation *f* OR jointure *f* (du doigt) ▪ [of animal] première phalange *f* ▪ **I grazed my ~s on the wall** je me suis écorché les doigts contre le mur ⊙ **near the ~** [joke, remark] osé **2.** [joint of meat] jarret *m*.
◆ **knuckles** *npl US* = **knuckle-duster**.
◆ **knuckle down** *vi insep UK* s'y mettre ▪ **we'd better ~ down to some work** il vaudrait mieux se mettre OR s'atteler au travail.
◆ **knuckle under** *vi insep* céder, se soumettre.

knuckle-duster *n* coup-de-poing *m* américain.

knucklehead ['nʌklhed] *n inf* andouille *f*.

knurl [nɜ:l] <> *n* **1.** [in wood] nœud *m* **2.** [on screw] moletage *m*.
<> *vt* TECH moleter.

KO (*pl* **KO's**, *pret & pp* **KO'd**, *cont* **KO'ing**) (*abbrev of* **knockout**)
<> *vt* mettre K-O ▪ [in boxing] battre par K-O.
<> *n* K-O *m*.

koala [kəʊ'ɑ:lə] *n* : **~ (bear)** koala *m*.

kohlrabi [kəʊl'rɑ:bɪ] *n* chou-rave *m*.

kookie, kooky ['ku:kɪ] (*comp* **kookier**, *superl* **kookiest**) *adj US inf* fêlé, malade.

Koran [kɒ'rɑ:n] *n* : **the ~** le Coran.

Korea [kə'rɪə] *pr n* Corée *f* ▪ **in ~** en Corée ▪ **the Democratic People's Republic of ~** la République démocratique populaire de Corée.

Korean [kə'rɪən] <> *n* **1.** [person] Coréen *m*, - enne *f* **2.** LING coréen *m*.
<> *adj* coréen ▪ **the ~ War** la guerre de Corée.

THE KOREAN WAR

Conflit qui opposa, de 1950 à 1953, la Corée du Nord (régime communiste) aux forces des Nations unies (soutenant la Corée du Sud), dirigées par le général MacArthur, et largement composées de soldats américains. Un traité mit fin à cette guerre en établissant la frontière entre les deux pays sur la ligne de front.

kosher ['kəʊʃə^r] <> *adj* **1.** RELIG kasher, cacher *(inv)* **2.** *inf* [honest] honnête, régulier ▪ **it's not ~** c'est louche, c'est pas catholique.
<> *n* nourriture *f* kasher.

Kosova ['kɑsəvɑ:] *n* Kosovo *m*.

Kosovan ['kɑsəvən], **Kosovar** ['kɑsəvər] <> *n* Kosovar *m*, - e *f*.
<> *adj* kosovar.

Kosovar Albanian <> *n* Albanais *m*, - e *f* du Kosovo.
<> *adj* albanais du Kosovo.

Kosovo ['kɑsəvəʊ] *n* Kosovo *m*.

kowtow [,kaʊ'taʊ] *vi* : **to ~ to sb** faire des courbettes à qqn.

kph (*written abbrev of* **kilometres per hour**) km/h.

Kraut△ [kraʊt] *offens* <> *n* Boche *mf*.
<> *adj* boche.

Kremlin ['kremlɪn] *pr n* Kremlin *m*.

krona ['krəʊnə] *n* couronne *f* suédoise.

krone ['krəʊnə] *n* [in Norway] couronne *f* norvégienne ▪ [in Denmark] couronne *f* danoise.

Krugerrand ['kru:gərænd] *n* Krugerrand *m*.

Krushchev ['krʊstʃɒf] *pr n* : **Nikita ~** Nikita Khrouchtchev.

krypton ['krɪptɒn] *n* krypton *m*.

KS *written abbr of* **Kansas**.

kudos ['kju:dɒs] *n* gloire *f*, prestige *m*.

kudzu vine ['kʊdzu:-] *n plante fourragère très envahissante qui pousse dans le sud des États-Unis.*

kumquat ['kʌmkwɒt] *n* kumquat *m*.

kung fu [,kʌŋ'fu:] *n* kung-fu *m*.

Kurd [kɜ:d] *n* Kurde *mf*.

Kurdish ['kɜ:dɪʃ] <> *n* LING kurde *m*.
<> *adj* kurde.

Kurdistan [,kɜ:dɪ'stɑ:n] *pr n* Kurdistan *m* ▪ **in ~** au Kurdistan.

Kuwait [kʊ'weɪt] *pr n* **1.** [country] Koweït *m* ▪ **in ~** au Koweït **2.** [town] Koweït City.

Kuwaiti [kʊ'weɪtɪ] <> *n* Koweïtien *m*, - enne *f*.
<> *adj* koweïtien.

kW (*written abbrev of* **kilowatt**) kW.

Kwanzaa ['kwænzɑ:] *n* Kwanzaa *f*.

kwashiorkor [,kwɒʃɪ'ɔ:kɔ:r] *n* kwashiorkor *m*.

KY *written abbr of* **Kentucky**.

Kyrgyzstan [,kɜ:gɪ'stɑ:n] *pr n* : **the Republic of ~** la république du Kirghizistan.

L

l (*pl* **l's** *OR pl* **ls**)**, L** (*pl* **L's** *OR pl* **Ls**) [el] *n* [letter] l *m*, L *m*, *see also* **F**.

l (*written abbrev of* **litre**) l.

L 1. *written abbr of* **lake 2.** *written abbr of* **large 3.** (*written abbrev of* **left**) g **4.** (*written abbrev of* **learner**) *lettre apposée sur une voiture et signalant un apprenti conducteur (en Grande-Bretagne)*.

L-DRIVER

En Grande-Bretagne, la lettre « L » apposée sur l'arrière d'un véhicule indique que le conducteur n'a pas encore son permis de conduire mais qu'il est en conduite accompagnée.

la [lɑː] *n* MUS la *m*.

LA ◇ *pr n* = **Los Angeles**.
◇ *written abbr of* **Louisiana**.

lab [læb] *inf* ◇ *n* (*abbrev of* **laboratory**) labo *m*.
◇ *comp* [book] de laboratoire ■ **~ assistant** laborantin *m* (*f* e), assistant *m* (*f* e) de laboratoire.

Lab [læb] *written abbr of* **Labour/Labour Party**.

label ['leɪbl] (*UK pret & pp* **labelled**, *cont* **labelling**) (*US pret & pp* **labeled**, *cont* **labeling**) ◇ *n* *liter* & *fig* étiquette *f* ■ **they brought out the record on the Mega ~** ils ont sorti le disque chez Mega ▶ **designer ~** marque *f*, griffe *f*.
◇ *vt* **1.** [suitcase, jar] étiqueter ■ **you must ~ your clothes clearly** tous vos vêtements doivent être clairement marqués à votre nom ■ **the bottle was labelled "shake before use"** la bouteille portait l'étiquette "agiter avant de s'en servir" **2.** *fig* [person] étiqueter, cataloguer ■ **he's been labelled (as) a troublemaker** on l'a étiqueté *OR* catalogué comme fauteur de troubles.

labelling *UK*, **labeling** *US* ['leɪblɪŋ] *n* étiquetage *m*.

labia ['leɪbɪə] *npl* ANAT lèvres *fpl* ■ **~ minora/majora** petites/grandes lèvres.

labial ['leɪbjəl] LING ◇ *adj* labial.
◇ *n* labiale *f*.

labiodental [,leɪbɪəʊ'dentl] LING ◇ *adj* labiodental.
◇ *n* labiodentale *f*.

labor *etc US* = **labour**.

laboratory [*UK* lə'bɒrətrɪ, *US* 'læbrə,tɔːrɪ] (*pl* **laboratories**) ◇ *n* laboratoire *m*.
◇ *comp* [assistant, equipment] de laboratoire.

Labor Code *n* code *m* du travail *(aux États-Unis)*.

Labor Day *n* fête *f* du travail *(aux États-Unis, célébrée le premier lundi de Septembre)*.

laborious [lə'bɔːrɪəs] *adj* laborieux.

laboriously [lə'bɔːrɪəslɪ] *adv* laborieusement.

labor union *n US* syndicat *m*.

labour *UK*, **labor** *US* ['leɪbər] ◇ *n* **1.** [work] travail *m* ■ [hard effort] labeur *m* ■ **a ~ of love** un travail fait pour le plaisir **2.** INDUST [manpower] main-d'œuvre *f* ■ [workers] ouvriers *mpl*, travailleurs *mpl* **3.** POL : **Labour** le parti travailliste britannique ■ **to vote Labour** voter travailliste **4.** MED travail *m* ■ **to be in ~** être en travail ■ **to go into ~** commencer le travail ▶ **~ pains** douleurs *fpl* de l'accouchement ■ **~ ward** salle *f* d'accouchement.
◇ *comp* **1.** [dispute, movement] social ■ [market] du travail ■ [shortage] de main-d'œuvre ■ **~ costs** coûts *mpl* de la main d'œuvre **2.** POL [government, victory] travailliste.
◇ *vi* **1.** [work] travailler dur **2.** [struggle - person] : **he ~ed up the stairs** il monta péniblement l'escalier ■ **to ~ under a misapprehension** *OR* **a delusion** *fig* se méprendre, être dans l'erreur ■ [move with difficulty - vehicle] peiner.
◇ *vt* [stress] insister sur ■ **there's no need to ~ the point** ce n'est pas la peine de t'étendre *OR* d'insister là-dessus.

labour camp *n* camp *m* de travail.

laboured *UK*, **labored** *US* ['leɪbəd] *adj* **1.** [breathing] pénible, difficile **2.** [clumsy] lourd, laborieux.

labourer *UK*, **laborer** *US* ['leɪbərər] *n* [gen] ouvrier *m*, - ère *f* ■ [on building site] manœuvre *m*.

labour exchange *n UK dated* agence *f* pour l'emploi.

labour force *n* [in country] population *f* active ■ [in firm] main-d'œuvre *f*.

labour-intensive *adj* : **a ~ industry** une industrie à forte main-d'œuvre ■ **craftwork is very ~** le travail artisanal nécessite une main-d'œuvre considérable.

Labour Party *n* parti *m* travailliste.

labour relations *npl* relations *fpl* sociales.

laboursaving *UK*, **laborsaving** *US* ['leɪbə,seɪvɪŋ] *adj* : **~ device** [in home] appareil *m* ménager ; [at work] appareil permettant un gain de temps.

Labrador ['læbrədɔːr] *pr n* GEOG Labrador *m* ■ **in ~** au Labrador.
◆ **labrador** *n* [dog] labrador *m*.

laburnum [lə'bɜːnəm] *n* : **~ (tree)** cytise *m*, faux ébénier *m*.

labyrinth ['læbərɪnθ] *n* labyrinthe *m*, dédale *m*.

labyrinthine [,læbə'rɪnθaɪn] *adj* labyrinthique.

lace [leɪs] ◇ *n* **1.** TEX dentelle *f* **2.** [in shoe, corset] lacet *m*.
◇ *comp* [handkerchief, tablecloth etc] en dentelle.
◇ *vt* **1.** [tie] lacer ■ [put laces in] mettre des lacets à **2.** [add alcohol to] : **he ~d my orange juice with gin** il a mis du gin dans mon jus d'orange.

◆ **lace up** *vt sep UK* [shoes] lacer.

lacemaking ['leɪs,meɪkɪŋ] *n* industrie *f* dentellière.

lacerate ['læsəreɪt] ◇ *vt* lacérer ■ **his hands were ~d by the broken glass** il avait les mains lacérées par le verre brisé.
◇ *adj* BOT : **~ leaves** feuilles *fpl* dentées *OR* dentelées.

laceration [,læsə'reɪʃn] *n* **1.** [action] lacération *f* **2.** MED [gash] : **he had deep ~s on his back** il avait le dos profondément lacéré *OR* entaillé.

lace-up *adj* [shoe, boot] à lacets.
◆ **lace-ups** *npl UK* chaussures *fpl* à lacets.

lachrymal ['lækrɪml] *adj* lacrymal.

lachrymose ['lækrɪməʊs] *adj lit* larmoyant.

lacing ['leɪsɪŋ] *n* [on shoe, garment] laçage *m*.

lack [læk] ◇ *n* manque *m* ■ **through** *OR* **for ~ of** par manque de, faute de ■ **there's no ~ of volunteers** ce ne sont pas les volontaires qui manquent.
◇ *vt* manquer de ■ **they certainly don't ~ confidence** ils ne manquent certes pas de confiance en eux ■ **we ~ the necessary resources** nous n'avons pas les ressources nécessaires.
◆ **lack for** *vt insep* manquer de.

lackadaisical [,lækə'deɪzɪkl] *adj* [person - apathetic] apathique ; [- lazy] indolent ■ [work] tranquille.

lackey ['lækɪ] *n* laquais *m* ■ *pej* larbin *m*.

lacking ['lækɪŋ] *adj* **1.** [wanting] qui manque de ■ **~ in confidence** qui manque de confiance en soi ■ **originality is sadly ~ in his new novel** son nouveau roman manque malheureusement d'originalité **2.** *inf euph* [stupid] demeuré, simple d'esprit.

lacklustre *UK*, **lackluster** *US* ['læk,lʌstər] *adj* terne.

laconic [lə'kɒnɪk] *adj* laconique.

lacquer ['lækər] ◇ *n* **1.** [varnish, hairspray] laque *f* **2.** [varnished object] laque *m*.
◇ *vt* [wood] laquer ■ [hair] mettre de la laque sur.

lacquered ['lækəd] *adj* laqué.

lacquerware ['lækəweər] *n (U)* laques *mpl*.

lacrosse [lə'krɒs] ◇ *n* lacrosse *f*, crosse *f* ■ **~ stick** crosse.
◇ *comp* [player] de crosse.

lactate ◇ *n* ['lækteɪt] CHEM lactate *m*.
◇ *vi* [læk'teɪt] sécréter du lait.

lactation [,læk'teɪʃn] *n* lactation *f*.

lactic acid ['læktɪk-] *n* CHEM acide *m* lactique.

lactose ['læktəʊs] *n* lactose *m*.

lacuna [lə'kju:nə] (*pl* **lacunas** *OR pl* **lacunae** [-ni:]) *n* lacune *f*.

lacy ['leɪsɪ] (*comp* **lacier**, *superl* **laciest**) *adj* [lace-like] semblable à de la dentelle ■ [made of lace] en dentelle.

lad [læd] *n* **1.** [young boy] garçon *m* ■ [son] fils *m* ■ **when I was a ~** quand j'étais jeune **2.** *UK inf* [friend] copain *m* ■ [colleague] collègue *m*, gars *m* **3.** *UK inf* [rake] noceur *m* ■ **he was a bit of a ~ when he was young** il a eu une jeunesse assez tumultueuse.

ladder ['lædər] ◇ *n* **1.** *liter & fig* échelle *f* ■ **to be at the top of the ~** *liter & fig* être arrivé au sommet *OR* en haut de l'échelle **2.** *UK* [in stocking] maille *f* filée ■ **you've got a ~ in your stocking** ton bas a filé, tu as filé ton bas.
◇ *vi & vt UK* filer.

ladderproof ['lædəpru:f] *adj UK* indémaillable.

laden ['leɪdn] *adj* chargé ■ **~ with** chargé de ■ **apple-~ trees** arbres couverts de pommes ■ **a heavily ~ ship** un navire à forte charge.

la-di-da [,lɑ:dɪ'dɑ:] *adj inf pej* [manner] snob, prétentieux ■ [voice] maniéré.

ladies ['leɪdɪz] *n UK* toilettes *fpl* pour dames.

ladies' man *n* don Juan *m*, homme *m* à femmes.

ladies room *US* = **ladies**.

ladle ['leɪdl] ◇ *n* louche *f*.
◇ *vt* servir (à la louche).
◆ **ladle out** *vt sep UK* **1.** [soup] servir (à la louche) **2.** *inf fig* [money, advice] distribuer à droite et à gauche.

lady ['leɪdɪ] (*pl* **ladies**) ◇ *n* **1.** [woman] dame *f* ■ **Ladies and Gentlemen** Mesdames et Messieurs ■ **the ~ of the house** la maîtresse de maison ■ **young ~** [girl] jeune fille ; [young woman] jeune femme ■ **ask the young ~ over there** [in shop] demandez à la demoiselle que vous voyez là-bas ■ **well, young ~, what have you got to say for yourself?** eh bien, ma fille, qu'avez-vous à répondre? ■ **his young ~** *dated* sa petite amie ‖ [by birth or upbringing] dame *f* ■ **she's no ~** elle n'a aucune classe ‖ [term of address] : **my Lady** Madame ‖ [as title] : **Lady Patricia** Lady Patricia ➊ **'Lady Chatterley's Lover'** ***Lawrence*** 'L'Amant de Lady Chatterley' ■ **'Lady Windermere's Fan'** ***Wilde*** 'L'Éventail de Lady Windermere' ■ **'The Lady Vanishes'** ***Hitchcock*** 'Une femme disparaît' **2.** *US inf* [term of address] madame *f* **3.** RELIG : **Our Lady** Notre-Dame *f*.
◇ *comp* femme ■ **a ~ doctor** une femme médecin.

ladybird ['leɪdɪbɜ:d] *n UK* coccinelle *f*.

ladybug ['leɪdɪbʌg] *n US* coccinelle *f*.

Lady Day *n* (fête *f* de) l'Annonciation *f*.

ladyfriend ['leɪdɪfrend] *n dated* petite amie *f*.

Lady Godiva [-gə'daɪvə] *pr n au XIe siècle, dame de haut rang qui aurait parcouru la ville de Coventry en Angleterre nue et à cheval pour forcer son mari à réduire les impôts locaux.*

lady-in-waiting *n* dame *f* d'honneur.

ladykiller ['leɪdɪ,kɪlər] *n inf* bourreau *m* des cœurs.

ladylike ['leɪdɪlaɪk] *adj* [person] distingué, bien élevé ■ [manners] raffiné, élégant ■ **it's not very ~ to smoke in the street!** une fille comme il faut ne fume pas dans la rue!

ladylove ['leɪdɪlʌv] *n lit* **his ~** sa bien-aimée.

Lady Mayoress *n UK* femme *f* du maire.

ladyship ['leɪdɪʃɪp] *n* : **Your** *OR* **Her Ladyship** *liter* Madame (la baronne/la vicomtesse/la comtesse) ; *fig & hum* la maîtresse de ces lieux.

lady's maid *n* femme *f* de chambre.

lady's man *n* don Juan *m*.

lag [læg] (*pret & pp* **lagged**, *cont* **lagging**) ◇ *n* **1.** [gap] décalage *m* **2.** △ *UK* [convict] : **an old ~** un cheval de retour.
◇ *vi* rester en arrière, traîner.
◇ *vt* [pipe] calorifuger.
◆ **lag behind** ◇ *vi insep* [dawdle] traîner, lambiner ■ [be at the back] rester derrière ■ [be outdistanced] se laisser distancer ■ **our country is lagging behind in medical research** notre pays a du retard en matière de recherche médicale.
◇ *vt insep* [competitor] traîner derrière, avoir du retard sur.

lager ['lɑ:gər] *n UK* bière *f* blonde ■ **~ lout** *jeune qui, sous l'influence de l'alcool, cherche la bagarre ou commet des actes de vandalisme.*

lagging ['lægɪŋ] *n* isolant *m*, calorifuge *m*.

lagoon [lə'gu:n] *n* [gen] lagune *f* ■ [in coral reef] lagon *m*.

lah [lɑ:] = **la**.

lah-di-dah [,lɑ:dɪ'dɑ:] = **la-di-da**.

laid [leɪd] *pt & pp* ▷ **lay**.

laid-back *adj inf* décontracté, cool.

lain [leɪn] *pp* ▷ **lie**.

lair [leər] *n* [for animals] tanière *f* ■ *fig* repaire *m*, tanière *f*.

laird [leəd] *n* laird *m*, propriétaire *m* foncier *(en Écosse)*.

lairy ['leərɪ] *adj* **1.** *inf* [object] tape à l'oeil *inv* **2.** [noisy] bruyant.

laisser-faire, laissez-faire [,leseɪ'feə] ◇ *n* non-interventionnisme *m*.
◇ *comp* : **~ economy** économie *f* basée sur le non-interventionnisme ■ **~ policy** politique *f* du laisser-faire.

laity ['leɪətɪ] *n (U)* **1.** RELIG laïcs *mpl* **2.** [non-specialists] profanes *mpl*.

lake [leɪk] *n* **1.** GEOG lac *m* ▪ **a wine ~** *fig* des excédents *mpl* de vin ➋ **go jump in the ~!** *inf* va te faire cuire un œuf! **2.** [pigment] laque *f*.

◆ **Lakes** *pr npl* : **the Lakes** *UK* la région des lacs.

LAKES

Lake Baikal le lac Baïkal ;
Lake Balaton le lac Balaton ;
Lake Como le lac de Côme ;
Lake Constance le lac de Constance ;
Lake Erie le lac Érié ;
Lake Garda le lac de Garde ;
Lake Geneva le lac Léman ou de Genève ;
Lake Huron le lac Huron ;
Lake Ladoga le lac Ladoga ;
Lake Maggiore le lac Majeur ;
Lake Malawi le lac Malawi ;
Lake Michigan le lac Michigan ;
Lake Nasser le lac Nasser ;
Lake Ontario le lac Ontario ;
Lake Superior le lac Supérieur ;
Lake Tanganyika le lac Tanganyika ;
Lake Tiberias le lac de Tibériade ;
Lake Titicaca le lac Titicaca ;
Lake Victoria le lac Victoria ;
Lake Winnipeg le lac Winnipeg.

Lake District *pr n* : **the ~** le Lake District, la région des lacs *(dans le nord-ouest de l'Angleterre)*.

lake dwelling *n* habitation *f* lacustre.

Lakeland ['leɪklənd] *adj* [of or in Lake District] de la région des lacs.

lakeshore ['leɪkʃɔː] ◇ *n* rive *f* d'un lac.
◇ *adj* au bord du lac.

lakeside ['leɪksaɪd] ◇ *n* rive *f* OR bord *m* d'un lac.
◇ *comp* [hotel] (situé) au bord d'un lac.

lam [læm] (*pret & pp* **lammed**, *cont* **lamming**) ◇ *vt inf* [beat] rosser.
◇ *n*△ *US* [escape] cavale△ *f*.

◆ **lam into** *vt insep UK inf* **1.** [physically] rentrer dans **2.** [verbally] enguirlander, sonner les cloches à.

lama ['lɑːmə] *n* RELIG lama *m*.

lamb [læm] ◇ *n* **1.** ZOOL agneau *m* ▪ **like ~s to the slaughter** comme des veaux à l'abattoir **2.** [meat] agneau *m* **3.** *fig* [innocent person] agneau *m* ▪ [lovable person] : **be a ~ and fetch my glasses** sois un ange OR sois gentil, va me chercher mes lunettes **4.** RELIG : **the Lamb of God** l'Agneau de Dieu.
◇ *comp* [chop, cutlet] d'agneau.
◇ *vi* agneler, mettre bas.

lambast [læm'bæst], **lambaste** [læm'beɪst] *vt* [scold] réprimander ▪ [thrash] battre, rosser.

Lambeth Palace ['læmbəθ-] *pr n résidence londonienne de l'archevêque de Cantorbéry.*

lambing ['læmɪŋ] *n* agnelage *m*.

lambskin ['læmskɪn] ◇ *n* (peau *f* d')agneau *m*.
◇ *comp* [coat, gloves] en agneau.

lamb's lettuce *n* mâche *f*.

lambswool ['læmzwʊl] *comp* [scarf, sweater etc] en laine d'agneau, en lambswool.

lame [leɪm] ◇ *adj* **1.** [person, horse] boiteux ▪ **to be ~** boiter ▪ **to go ~** se mettre à boiter ▪ **his left leg is ~, he's ~ in his left leg** il boite de la jambe gauche **2.** [weak - excuse] piètre, bancal ; [- argument, reasoning] boiteux ; [- plot] boiteux, bancal **3.** *US inf* [conventional] vieux jeu *(inv)*.
◇ *vt* estropier.
◇ *npl* : **the ~** les boiteux *mpl*.

lamé ['lɑːmeɪ] *n* lamé *m*.

lame duck *n fig* **1.** [gen - INDUST] canard *m* boiteux **2.** *US* POL *candidat sortant non réélu qui attend l'arrivée de son successeur.*

◆ **lame-duck** *comp* : **a lame-duck president** *un président sortant non réélu.*

lamely ['leɪmlɪ] *adv* de façon peu convaincante, maladroitement.

lament [lə'ment] ◇ *vt* [feel sorrow for] regretter, pleurer ▪ [complain about] se lamenter sur, se plaindre de ▪ **"I'll never finish in time!", she ~ed** "je n'aurai jamais fini à temps!", gémit-elle.
◇ *vi* se lamenter.
◇ *n* **1.** [lamentation, complaint] lamentation *f* **2.** [poem] élégie *f* ▪ [song] complainte *f*.

lamentable ['læməntəbl] *adj* [regrettable] regrettable ▪ [poor] lamentable ▪ **the ~ state of the economy** l'état lamentable OR déplorable de l'économie.

lamentation [,læmen'teɪʃn] *n* lamentation *f* ▪ **the Lamentations (of Jeremiah)** les Lamentations (de Jérémie).

laminate ['læmɪneɪt] ◇ *vt* TECH [bond in layers] laminer ▪ [veneer] plaquer.
◇ *n* stratifié *m*.

laminated ['læmɪneɪtɪd] *adj* [wood] stratifié ▪ [glass] feuilleté.

lamp [læmp] *n* **1.** [gen] lampe *f* ▪ [street-lamp] réverbère *m* ▪ [on car, train] lumière *f*, feu *m* **2.** MED lampe *f* ▪ **infrared ~** lampe à infrarouges.

lamplight ['læmplaɪt] *n* : **her hair shone in the ~** la lumière de la lampe faisait briller ses cheveux ▪ **to read by ~** lire à la lumière d'une OR de la lampe.

lampoon [læm'puːn] ◇ *n* [satire] satire *f* ▪ [written] pamphlet *m*.
◇ *vt* ridiculiser, tourner en dérision.

lampoonist [læm'puːnɪst] *n* [satirist] satiriste *mf* ▪ [in writings] pamphlétaire *mf*.

lamppost ['læmppəʊst] *n* réverbère *m*.

lamprey ['læmprɪ] *n* lamproie *f*.

lampshade ['læmpʃeɪd] *n* abat-jour *m inv*.

lampstand ['læmpstænd] *n* pied *m* de lampe.

LAN *n* = **local area network**.

Lancaster ['læŋkəstəʳ] *pr n* **1.** GEOG Lancaster *m* **2.** HIST Lancastre *f*.

Lancastrian [læŋ'kæstrɪən] *n* **1.** GEOG habitant *m*, - e *f* de Lancaster **2.** HIST lancastrien *m*, - enne *f*.

lance [lɑːns] ◇ *n* **1.** [weapon] lance *f* **2.** MED lancette *f*, bistouri *m*.
◇ *vt* MED percer, inciser.

lance corporal *n* caporal *m*, -e *f (dans l'armée britannique).*

lancer ['lɑːnsəʳ] *n* HIST & MIL lancier *m*.

lancet ['lɑːnsɪt] *n* MED lancette *f*, bistouri *m*.

Lancs *written abbr of* **Lancashire**.

land [lænd] ◇ *vi* **1.** AERON & ASTRONAUT atterrir ▪ **to ~ on the moon** atterrir sur la Lune, alunir ▪ **to ~ in the sea** amerrir ▪ **to ~ on an aircraft carrier** apponter (sur un porte-avions)
2. NAUT [boat] arriver à quai ▪ [passengers] débarquer
3. [ball, high jumper] tomber, retomber ▪ [falling object, bomb, parachutist] tomber ▪ [bird] se poser ▪ **an apple ~ed on her head** elle a reçu une pomme sur la tête
4. *inf* [finish up] finir, atterrir ▪ **the car ~ed (up) in the ditch** la voiture a terminé sa course dans le fossé ▪ **you'll ~ up in jail!** tu finiras en prison!
◇ *vt* **1.** [plane] poser ▪ [cargo, passengers] débarquer ▪ **they have succeeded in ~ing men on the moon** ils ont réussi à envoyer des hommes sur la Lune
2. [fish - onto bank] hisser sur la rive ; [- onto boat] hisser dans le bateau

3. *inf* [job, contract] décrocher
4. *inf* [put, place] ficher ■ **this could ~ us in real trouble** ça pourrait nous attirer de gros ennuis *OR* nous mettre dans le pétrin
5. [blow] flanquer ■ **I ~ed him a blow** *OR* **~ ed him one on the nose** je lui ai flanqué *OR* collé mon poing dans la figure
6. *inf* [encumber] : **to get ~ed with sthg : I got ~ed with the job of organizing the party** c'est moi qui me suis retrouvé avec la fête à organiser, c'est moi qui me suis tapé l'organisation de la fête.
◇ *n* **1.** [for farming, building etc] terre *f* ■ **he works on the ~** il travaille la terre ■ **this is good farming ~** c'est de la bonne terre ■ **building ~** terrain constructible ■ **a piece of ~** [for farming] un lopin de terre ; [for building] un terrain (à bâtir) ■ **to live off the ~** vivre des ressources naturelles de la terre ▶ **to see how the ~ lies, to find out the lie** *OR* **lay of the ~** tâter le terrain
2. [property] terre *f*, terres *fpl* ■ **get off my ~!** sortez de mes terres!
3. [area, region] région *f*
4. [not sea] terre *f* ■ **we travelled by ~ to Cairo** nous sommes allés au Caire par la route ■ **over ~ and sea** sur terre et sur mer
5. [nation, country] pays *m*
6. *fig* [realm] royaume *m*, pays *m* ■ **he is no longer in the ~ of the living** il n'est plus de ce monde.
◇ *comp* [prices - in town] du terrain ; [- in country] de la terre ■ [reform] agraire ■ [tax, ownership] foncier ■ *UK* HIST [army] de terre ■ [worker] agricole.
◆ **lands** *npl* = **land** *(n senses 2 & 3)*.
◆ **land up** *vi insep* = **land** *(vi sense 4)*.

land agent *n* **1.** [administrator] régisseur *m*, intendant *m*, - e *f* **2.** *UK* [estate agent] agent *m* immobilier.

land-based *adj* **1.** ECON basé sur la propriété terrienne **2.** MIL : **~ forces** forces *fpl* terrestres, armée *f* de terre ■ **~ missile** missile *m* terrestre.

land breeze *n* brise *f* de terre.

landed ['lændɪd] *adj UK* foncier ■ **the ~ gentry** la noblesse terrienne.

landfall ['lændfɔːl] *n* NAUT : **to make ~** apercevoir la terre, arriver en vue d'une côte.

landfill ['lændfɪl] *n* ensevelissement *m* de déchets.

landing ['lændɪŋ] *n* **1.** [of plane, spacecraft] atterrissage *m* ■ [on moon] alunissage *m* ■ [of passengers, foods] débarquement *m* ■ SPORT [of skier, high jumper] réception *f* ■ **he made a bad ~** il s'est mal reçu ▶ **the Normandy ~s** HIST le Débarquement (en Normandie) **2.** [in staircase] palier *m* ■ [floor] étage *m* **3.** [jetty] débarcadère *m*, embarcadère *m*.

landing beacon *n* AERON balise *f* d'atterrissage.

landing card *n* carte *f* de débarquement.

landing craft *n* navire *m* de débarquement.

landing field = **landing strip**.

landing gear *n* AERON train *m* d'atterrissage.

landing lights *npl* [on plane] phares *mpl* d'atterrissage ■ [at airport] balises *fpl* (d'atterrissage).

landing stage *n* débarcadère *m*.

landing strip *n* piste *f* d'atterrissage.

landlady ['lænd,leɪdɪ] (*pl* **landladies**) *n* [owner] propriétaire *f* ■ [in lodgings] logeuse *f* ■ [in pub, guesthouse] patronne *f*.

landlocked ['lændlɒkt] *adj* [country] enclavé, sans accès à la mer ■ [sea] intérieur.

landlord ['lændlɔːd] *n* [owner] propriétaire *m* ■ [in lodgings] logeur *m* ■ [in pub, guesthouse] patron *m*.

landlubber ['lænd,lʌbəʳ] *n* **inf hum** marin *m* d'eau douce.

landmark ['lændmɑːk] ◇ *n* **1.** *liter* point *m* de repère ■ **major Paris ~s** les principaux monuments de Paris **2.** *fig* étape *f* décisive, jalon *m* ■ **the trial was a ~ in legal history** *fig* le procès a fait date dans les annales juridiques.
◇ *comp* [decision] qui fait date.

landmass ['lændmæs] *n* zone *f* terrestre ■ **the American ~** le continent américain.

landmine ['lændmaɪn] *n* mine *f* (terrestre).

landowner ['lænd,əʊnəʳ] *n* propriétaire *m* foncier, propriétaire *f* foncière.

land reform *n* réforme *f* agraire.

land registry *n* cadastre *m*.

Land Rover® *n* Land-Rover® *f*.

landscape ['lændskeɪp] ◇ *n* **1.** [gen] paysage *m* ■ **the political ~** *fig* le paysage politique **2.** PRINT : **to print in ~** imprimer à l'italienne.
◇ *adj* **1.** ART : **~ painter** (peintre *m*) paysagiste *m* ■ **~ painting** le paysage **2.** HORT : **~ architect** architecte *mf* paysagiste ■ **~ gardener** jardinier *m* paysagiste, jardinière *f* paysagiste ■ **~ gardening** paysagisme *m* **3.** PRINT à l'italienne.
◇ *vt* [garden] dessiner ■ [waste land] aménager.

landscaping ['lænd,skeɪpɪŋ] *n* aménagement *m* paysager.

Land's End *pr n pointe en Cornouailles qui marque l'extrémité sud-ouest de la Grande-Bretagne*.

landslide ['lændslaɪd] ◇ *n* glissement *m* de terrain.
◇ *comp* [election victory] écrasant.

landslip ['lændslɪp] *n* éboulement *m*.

land tax *n* impôt *m* foncier.

landward ['lændwəd] ◇ *adj* du côté de la terre ■ **~ breeze** vent *m* marin *OR* qui souffle de la mer.
◇ *adv* = **landwards**.

landwards ['lændwədz] *adv* NAUT en direction de la terre ■ [on land] vers l'intérieur (des terres).

lane [leɪn] *n* **1.** [road - in country] chemin *m* ; [- in street names] rue *f*, allée *f* **2.** [for traffic] voie *f* ■ [line of vehicles] file *f* ■ [for shipping, aircraft] couloir *m* ■ [in athletics, swimming] couloir *m* ■ **get into the right-hand ~** mettez-vous dans la file *OR* sur la voie de droite ■ **'keep in ~'** ne changez pas de file.

lane closure *n* fermeture *f* de voies ■ **the traffic was held up by ~s** la circulation a été ralentie par des rétrécissements (dûs à des travaux).

lang SCH & UNIV *written abbr of* **language**.

language ['læŋgwɪdʒ] ◇ *n* **1.** [means of communication] langage *m* ■ **I prefer ~ to literature** je préfère l'étude des langues à celle de la littérature **2.** [specific tongue] langue *f* ■ SCH & UNIV [area of study] langue *f* ■ **the French ~** la langue française ■ **to study ~s** faire des études de langue ■ **to speak the same ~** parler le même langage **3.** [code] langage *m* ■ **a computer ~** un langage machine **4.** [terminology] langue *f*, langage *m* ■ **medical/legal ~** langage médical/juridique ▌[manner of expression] expression *f*, langue *f* ■ **I find his ~ very pompous** je trouve qu'il s'exprime avec emphase *OR* de façon très pompeuse ▌[rude words] gros mots *mpl*, grossièretés *fpl* ■ **mind your ~!** surveille ton langage!
◇ *comp* [acquisition] du langage ■ [course] de langues ■ [barrier] linguistique ■ [student] en langues.

language laboratory, language lab *n* laboratoire *m* de langues.

languid ['læŋgwɪd] *adj* langoureux, alangui.

languidly ['læŋgwɪdlɪ] *adv* langoureusement.

languish ['læŋgwɪʃ] *vi* **1.** [suffer] languir ■ **to ~ in prison** croupir en prison **2.** [become weak] dépérir ■ **to ~ in the heat** [plant] dépérir à la chaleur ; [person] souffrir de la chaleur ■ **the project was ~ing for lack of funds** le projet traînait, faute d'argent **3.** *lit* [pine] languir.

languishing ['læŋgwɪʃɪŋ] = **languid**.

languor ['læŋgəʳ] *n* langueur *f*.

languorous ['læŋgərəs] *adj* langoureux.

lank [læŋk] *adj* [hair] terne, mou *(before vowel or silent 'h' mol)*, molle *f* ■ [plant] étiolé, grêle.

lanky ['læŋkɪ] (*comp* **lankier**, *superl* **lankiest**) *adj* dégingandé.

lanolin(e) ['lænəlɪn] *n* lanoline *f*.

lantern ['læntən] *n* lanterne *f*.

lantern fish *n* poisson-lanterne *m*.

lantern-jawed [-dʒɔ:d] *adj* aux joues creuses.

lanyard ['lænjəd] *n* corde *f*, cordon *m* ■ NAUT ride *f*.

Lao [laʊ] = **Laotian**.

Laos ['laʊs] *pr n* Laos *m* ■ **in ~** au Laos.

Laotian ['laʊʃn] <> *n* [person] Laotien *m*, - enne *f*.
<> *adj* laotien.

lap [læp] (*pret & pp* **lapped**, *cont* **lapping**) <> *n* **1.** [knees] genoux *mpl* ■ **come and sit on my ~** viens t'asseoir sur mes genoux ▶ **don't think it's just going to fall into your ~ !** *inf* ne t'imagine pas que ça va te tomber tout cuit dans le bec! ■ **it's in the ~ of the gods** c'est entre les mains des dieux ■ **the ~ of luxury** le grand luxe **2.** SPORT tour *m* de piste ■ **we ran 2 ~s** nous avons fait 2 tours de piste **3.** [of journey] étape *f* ■ **to be on the last ~ : we're on the last ~** *liter* c'est le dernier tour ; *fig* on arrive au bout de nos peines.
<> *vt* **1.** SPORT [competitor, car] dépasser, prendre un tour d'avance sur ■ [time] chronométrer ■ **Kelly was lapped at over 200 mph** Kelly a été chronométré sur un tour à plus de 300 km/h **2.** [milk] laper **3.** [subj: waves] clapoter contre.
<> *vi* **1.** SPORT tourner, faire un tour de circuit ■ **Kelly was lapping at over 200 mph** Kelly tournait à plus de 300 km/h de moyenne **2.** [waves] clapoter ■ **the waves lapped against the boat** les vagues clapotaient contre le bateau.
◆ **lap over** <> *vt insep* [tiles] chevaucher sur.
<> *vi insep* se chevaucher.
◆ **lap up** *vt sep* **1.** [milk] laper **2.** *inf fig* [praise] boire ■ [information] avaler, gober ■ **to ~ it up : they were all paying her compliments and she was just lapping it up** tous lui faisaient des compliments et elle s'en délectait.

LAPD [,eleɪpi:'di:] (*abbrev of* **Los Angeles Police Department**) *n* LAPD *m*, police *f* de Los Angeles.

lap dance <> *vi* danser *(pour les clients d'un bar)*.
<> *n* danse *f (pour les clients d'un bar)*.

lap dancer *n* danseuse *f* de bar.

lapdog ['læpdɒg] *n* **1.** *liter* petit chien *m* d'appartement **2.** *pej* toutou *m*, caniche *m*.

lapel [lə'pel] *n* revers *m*.

lap-held *adj* [typewriter, computer] portatif *(que l'on peut poser sur ses genoux)*.

lapis lazuli [,læpɪs'læzjʊlaɪ] *n* lapis *m*, lapis-lazuli *m inv*.

Lapland ['læplænd] *pr n* Laponie *f* ■ **in ~** en Laponie.

Laplander ['læplændəʳ] *n* Lapon *m*, - one *f*.

lap of honour *n* SPORT tour *m* d'honneur.

Lapp [læp] <> *n* **1.** [person] Lapon *m*, - one *f* **2.** LING lapon *m*.
<> *adj* lapon *m*.

lapping ['læpɪŋ] *n* [of waves] clapotis *m*.

lap robe *n* US plaid *m*.

lapse [læps] <> *n* **1.** [failure] : **~ of memory** trou *m* de mémoire ■ **~ in** OR **of concentration** moment *m* d'inattention **2.** [in behaviour] écart *m* (de conduite) ■ **she has occasional ~s** elle fait des bêtises de temps en temps ■ **a ~ from virtue** un manquement à la vertu **3.** [interval] laps *m* de temps, intervalle *m* ■ **after a ~ of six months** au bout de six mois **4.** [of contract] expiration *f* ■ [of custom] disparition *f* ■ [of legal right] déchéance *f*.
<> *vi* **1.** [decline] baisser, chuter ■ **to ~ from grace** RELIG pécher **2.** [drift] tomber ■ **to ~ into bad habits** prendre de mauvaises habitudes ■ **to ~ into silence** garder le silence, s'enfermer dans le silence ■ **she kept lapsing into Russian** elle se remettait sans cesse à parler russe **3.** [pass - time] passer **4.** [law, custom] tomber en désuétude ■ [licence, passport] se périmer ■ [subscription] prendre fin, expirer ■ **he let his insurance ~** il a laissé périmer son assurance **5.** RELIG [lose faith] abandonner OR perdre la foi.

lapsed [læpst] *adj* [law] caduc ■ [passport] périmé ■ **a ~ Catholic** un catholique qui ne pratique plus.

laptop ['læptɒp] *n* : **~ (computer)** portable *m*.

lapwing ['læpwɪŋ] *n* vanneau *m*.

larceny ['lɑ:sənɪ] (*pl* **larcenies**) *n* LAW vol *m* simple.

larch [lɑ:tʃ] *n* mélèze *m*.

lard [lɑ:d] <> *n* saindoux *m*.
<> *vt* larder ■ **an essay ~ed with quotations** *fig* une rédaction truffée de citations.

larder ['lɑ:dəʳ] *n* [room] cellier *m* ■ [cupboard] garde-manger *m inv* ■ **to raid the ~** *inf* faire une razzia dans le garde-manger.

large [lɑ:dʒ] <> *adj* **1.** [in size] grand ■ [family] grand, nombreux ■ [person] gros, grosse *f*, grand ■ [organization] gros, grosse *f*, grand ■ **a ~ coat** un grand manteau ■ **on a ~ scale** à grande échelle ■ **to a ~ extent** dans une large mesure ■ **she's a ~ woman** c'est une femme plutôt grosse OR forte ▮ [in number, amount] grand, important ■ **she wrote him a ~ cheque** elle lui a fait un chèque pour une somme importante OR une grosse somme ■ **a ~ helping of potatoes/apple pie** une grosse portion de pommes de terre/part de tarte aux pommes ■ **a ~ number of** beaucoup de ▶ **he was standing there as ~ as life** il était là, en chair et en os ■ **larger than life** exagéré, outrancier **2.** [extensive - changes] considérable, important **3.** [liberal - views, ideas] libéral, large ■ [generous - heart] grand, généreux.
<> *adv* : **to loom ~** menacer, sembler imminent ■ **to be writ ~** être évident.
◆ **at large** <> *adj phr* [at liberty] en liberté ■ [prisoner] en fuite ■ **the rapist is at ~ somewhere in the city** le violeur se promène en (toute) liberté quelque part dans cette ville.
<> *adv phr* [as a whole] dans son ensemble ■ **the country at ~** le pays dans son ensemble.
◆ **by and large** *adv phr* de manière générale.

largely ['lɑ:dʒlɪ] *adv* [mainly] en grande partie, pour la plupart ■ [in general] en général, en gros.

large-scale *adj* à grande échelle.

large-size(d) *adj* [clothes] grande taille ■ [product] grand modèle ■ [envelope] grand format.

largesse [lɑ:'dʒes] *n (U)* largesse *f*, largesses *fpl*.

largo ['lɑ:gəʊ] <> *n* largo *m*.
<> *adj & adv* largo.

lariat ['lærɪət] US <> *n* lasso *m*.
<> *vt* prendre au lasso.

lark [lɑ:k] *n* **1.** ZOOL alouette *f* ■ **to rise** OR **to be up with the ~** se lever avec les poules OR au chant du coq **2.** *inf* [joke] rigolade *f* ■ [prank] blague *f*, farce *f* ■ **for a ~** pour blaguer, pour rigoler **3.** *inf* [rigmarole, business] histoire *f* ■ **I don't like the sound of this fancy dress ~** je n'aime pas beaucoup cette histoire de déguisement, cette idée de déguisement ne me dit rien qui vaille.
◆ **lark about, lark around** *vi insep* UK *inf* faire le fou.

larkspur ['lɑ:kspɜ:ʳ] *n* pied-d'alouette *m*, delphinium *m*.

larva ['lɑ:və] (*pl* **larvae** [-vi:]) *n* larve *f*.

larval ['lɑ:vl] *adj* larvaire.

laryngal [lə'rɪŋgl], **laryngeal** [,lærɪn'dʒi:əl] *adj* MED laryngé, laryngien ■ LING laryngal, glottal.

laryngitis [,lærɪn'dʒaɪtɪs] *n (U)* laryngite *f* ■ **to have ~** avoir une laryngite.

larynx ['lærɪŋks] *n* larynx *m*.

lasagne, lasagna [lə'zænjə] *n (U)* lasagnes *fpl*.

lascivious [lə'sɪvɪəs] *adj* lascif, lubrique.

lasciviously [lə'sɪvɪəslɪ] *adv* lascivement.

laser ['leɪzəʳ] *n* laser *m* ■ **~ surgery** chirurgie *f* (au) laser.

laser beam *n* rayon *m* OR faisceau *m* laser.

laser card *n* carte *f* à puce.

laser disc *n* disque *m* laser.

laser printer *n* imprimante *f* (à) laser.

laser show *n* spectacle *m* laser.

lash [læʃ] ◇ *n* **1.** [whip] lanière *f* ▪ [blow from whip] coup *m* de fouet **2.** *fig* [of scorn, criticism] : **he'd often felt the ~ of her tongue** il avait souvent été la cible de ses propos virulents **3.** [of rain, sea] : **the ~ of the rain on the windows** le bruit de la pluie qui fouette les vitres ▪ **the ~ of the waves against the shore** le déferlement des vagues sur la grève **4.** [eyelash] cil *m*.
◇ *vt* **1.** [with whip] fouetter **2.** [subj: rain, waves] battre, fouetter ▪ **the waves ~ed the shore** les vagues venaient se fracasser sur la grève **3.** [move] : **the tiger ~ed its tail** le tigre fouettait l'air de sa queue **4.** [tie] attacher ▪ **they ~ed the cargo to the deck** ils arrimèrent la cargaison sur le pont.
◇ *vi* : **its tail ~ed wildly** il fouettait l'air furieusement de sa queue ▪ **the hail ~ed against the window** la grêle cinglait la vitre.
◆ **lash down** ◇ *vt sep* [cargo] arrimer, fixer.
◇ *vi insep* [rain, hail] s'abattre, tomber avec violence.
◆ **lash out** *vi insep* **1.** [struggle - with fists] donner des coups de poing ; [- with feet] donner des coups de pied ▪ **she ~ed out in all directions** elle se débattit de toutes ses forces **2.** *fig* [verbally] : **he ~ed out at his critics** il a fustigé ses détracteurs **3.** *UK inf* [spend] : **to ~ out (on sthg)** dépenser un fric monstre (pour qqch).

lashing ['læʃɪŋ] *n* **1.** [with whip] flagellation *f*, fouet *m* **2.** *fig* [scolding] réprimandes *fpl*, correction *f* **3.** [rope] corde *f* ▪ NAUT amarre *f*.
◆ **lashings** *npl UK* [in amount] des montagnes ▪ **with ~s of chocolate sauce** couvert de sauce au chocolat.

lass [læs] *n Scotland* [girl] fille *f*.

Lassa fever ['læsə-] *n* fièvre *f* de Lhassa.

lassie ['læsɪ] *n Scotland & Ireland* fillette *f*, gamine *f*.

lassitude ['læsɪtju:d] *n* lassitude *f*.

lasso, lassoo [læ'su:] ◇ *n* lasso *m*.
◇ *vt* prendre au lasso.

last[1] [lɑ:st] ◇ *adj* **1.** [with dates, times of day] dernier ▪ **~ Monday** lundi dernier ▪ **~ week/year** la semaine/l'année dernière ▪ **~ July** en juillet dernier, l'année dernière au mois de juillet ▪ **~ night** [at night] cette nuit ; [in the evening] hier soir **2.** [final] dernier ▪ **that was the ~ time I saw him** c'était la dernière fois que je le voyais ▪ **at the ~ minute** OR **moment** à la dernière minute ▪ **I'm down to my ~ cigarette** il ne me reste plus qu'une seule cigarette ▪ **I'll sack every ~ one of them!** je vais les virer tous! ▪ **she used up every ~ ounce of energy** elle a utilisé tout ce qui lui restait d'énergie ▪ **to the ~ detail** dans les moindres détails ➲ **she was on her ~ legs** elle était au bout du rouleau ▪ **your car is on its ~ legs** votre voiture ne va pas tarder à vous lâcher ▪ **I'll get my money back if it's the ~ thing I do** je récupérerai mon argent coûte que coûte ▪ **I always clean my teeth ~ thing at night** je me brosse toujours les dents juste avant de me coucher
3. [most recent] : **you said that ~ time** c'est ce que tu as dis la dernière fois ▪ **I've been here for the ~ five years** je suis ici depuis cinq ans, cela fait cinq ans que je suis ici ▪ **I didn't like her ~ film** je n'ai pas aimé son dernier film
4. [least likely] : **he's the ~ person I expected to see** c'est bien la dernière personne que je m'attendais à voir ▪ **that's the ~ thing I wanted** je n'avais vraiment pas besoin de ça.
◇ *adv* **1.** [finally] : **she arrived ~** elle est arrivée la dernière OR en dernier ▪ **..., and ~ but not least......** et en dernier, mais non par ordre d'importance,...
2. [most recently] : **when did you ~ see him?** quand l'avez-vous vu pour la dernière fois? ▪ **they ~ came to see us in 1989** leur dernière visite remonte à 1989 ▪ **it's ~ in, first out** dernier entré, premier sorti
3. = **lastly**.
◇ *n & pron* **1.** [final one] dernier *m*, - ère *f* ▪ **she was the ~ to arrive** elle est arrivée la dernière ▪ **the next to ~, the ~ but one** l'avant-dernier
2. [previous one] : **each more handsome than the ~** tous plus beaux les uns que les autres ▪ **the day before ~** avant-hier ▪ **the night before ~** [at night] la nuit d'avant-hier ; [in the evening] avant-hier soir ▪ **the winter before ~** l'hiver d'il y a deux ans ▪ **the Prime Minister before ~** l'avant-dernier Premier ministre
3. [end] : **that was the ~ I saw of her** c'était la dernière fois que je la voyais ▪ **I hope that's the ~ we see of them** j'espère qu'on ne les reverra plus ▪ **I'll never see the ~ of this!** je n'en verrai jamais la fin!, je n'en viendrai jamais à bout! ▪ **you haven't heard the ~ of this!** vous aurez de mes nouvelles! ➲ **till ~** : **leave the pans till ~** gardez les casseroles pour la fin, lavez les casseroles en dernier
4. [remainder] reste *m* ▪ **we drank the ~ of the wine** on a bu ce qui restait de vin.
◆ **at last** *adv phr* enfin ▪ **free at ~** enfin libre ▪ **at long ~** enfin.
◆ **at the last** *adv phr fml* **she was there at the ~** elle est restée jusqu'au bout.
◆ **to the last** *adv phr* jusqu'au bout ▪ **she insisted to the ~ that she was not guilty** elle a dit jusqu'au bout qu'elle n'était pas coupable.

last[2] [lɑ:st] ◇ *vi* **1.** [continue to exist or function] durer ▪ **it ~ed (for) ten days** cela a duré dix jours ▪ **how long can we ~ without water?** combien de temps tiendrons-nous sans eau? ▪ **he won't ~ long** [in job] il ne tiendra pas longtemps ; [will soon die] il n'en a plus pour longtemps ▪ **built/made to ~** construit/fait pour durer **2.** [be enough] : **we've got enough food to ~ another week** nous avons assez à manger pour une semaine encore **3.** [keep fresh - food] se conserver ▪ **these flowers don't ~ (long)** ces fleurs ne tiennent OR ne durent pas (longtemps).
◇ *vt* : **have we got enough to ~ us until tomorrow?** en avons-nous assez pour tenir OR aller jusqu'à demain? ▪ **that fountain pen will ~ you a lifetime** vous pourrez garder ce stylo plume toute votre vie.
◇ *n* [for shoes] forme *f*.
◆ **last out** ◇ *vi insep* **1.** [survive] tenir **2.** [be enough] suffire ▪ **will our supplies ~ out till the end of the month?** les provisions suffiront-elles jusqu'à la fin du mois?
◇ *vt sep* : **he didn't ~ the night out** il n'a pas passé la nuit, il est mort pendant la nuit ▪ **will the play ~ out the month?** est-ce que la pièce tiendra le mois?

last-ditch *adj* [ultimate] ultime ▪ [desperate] désespéré ▪ **a ~ attempt** OR **effort** un ultime effort.

lasting ['lɑ:stɪŋ] *adj* durable ▪ **to their ~ regret/shame** à leur plus grand regret/plus grande honte.

Last Judgment *n* : **the ~** le Jugement dernier.

lastly ['lɑ:stlɪ] *adv* enfin, en dernier lieu.

last-minute *adj* de dernière minute.

last name *n* nom *m* de famille.

last post *n UK* MIL [at night] extinction *f* des feux ▪ [at funeral] sonnerie *f* aux morts.

last rites *npl* derniers sacrements *mpl*.

Last Supper *n* : **the ~** la (sainte) Cène.

last word *n* **1.** [final decision] dernier mot *m* ▪ **the Treasury has the ~ on defence spending** le ministère des Finances a le dernier mot en matière de dépenses militaires **2.** [latest style] dernier cri *m*.

latch [lætʃ] ◇ *n* loquet *m* ▪ **leave the door on the ~** ne fermez pas la porte à clé ▪ **the door was on the ~** la porte n'était pas fermée à clé.
◇ *vt* fermer au loquet.
◇ *vi* se fermer.
◆ **latch on** *vi insep inf* piger.
◆ **latch onto** *vt insep inf* **1.** [attach o.s. to] s'accrocher à **2.** *UK* [understand] piger **3.** *US* [obtain] se procurer, obtenir.

latchkey child *n enfant dont les parents travaillent et ne sont pas là quand il rentre de l'école.*

late [leɪt] ◇ *adj* **1.** [behind schedule] en retard ▪ **to be ~** être en retard ▪ **to be 10 minutes ~** avoir 10 minutes de retard ▪ **to make sb ~** retarder qqn, mettre qqn en retard ▪ **we apologize for the ~ arrival of flight 906** nous vous prions d'excuser le retard du vol 906
2. [in time] tardif ▪ **to keep ~ hours** veiller, se coucher tard ▪ **in the ~ afternoon** tard dans l'après-midi, en fin d'après-midi ▪ **she's in her ~ fifties** elle approche la soixantaine ▪ **in the ~ seventies** à la fin des années soixante-dix ▪ **in ~ 1970** fin 1970 ▪ **at this ~ stage** à ce stade avancé ▪ **to have a ~ lunch** déjeuner tard ▪ **he was a ~ developer** [physically] il a eu une croissance tardive ; [intellectually] son développement intellectuel fut

un peu tardif ‖ [news, edition] dernier ■ **there have been some ~ developments in the talks** il y a du nouveau dans les discussions ▶ **~ booking** réservation *f* de dernière minute
3. [former] ancien, précédent ■ [deceased] : **the ~ lamented president** le regretté président ■ **the ~ Mr Fox** le défunt M. Fox, feu M. Fox *fml* ■ **her ~ husband** son défunt mari, feu son mari *fml*
4. [recent] récent, dernier.
◇ *adv* **1.** [in time] tard ■ **to arrive/to go to bed ~** arriver/se coucher tard ■ **to arrive 10 minutes ~** arriver avec 10 minutes de retard ■ **it's getting ~** il se fait tard ■ **~ in the afternoon** tard dans l'après-midi ■ **she came to poetry ~ in life** elle est venue à la poésie sur le tard ▶ **~ in the day** *liter* vers la fin de la journée ■ **it's rather ~ in the day to be thinking about that** *fig* c'est un peu tard pour penser à ça
2. [recently] récemment ■ **even as ~ as last year he was still painting** pas plus tard que l'année dernière, il peignait encore
3. *fml* [formerly] autrefois, anciennement.
◆ **of late** *adv phr* récemment ■ **I haven't seen him of ~** je ne l'ai pas vu récemment *OR* ces derniers temps.

latecomer ['leɪt,kʌmər] *n* retardataire *mf* ■ **'~s will not be admitted'** ≃ 'le placement n'est plus assuré après le début de la représentation' ■ **he was a ~ to football** il est venu au football sur le tard.

lately ['leɪtlɪ] *adv* récemment, ces derniers temps, dernièrement.

latency ['leɪtənsɪ] *n* latence *f*.

lateness ['leɪtnɪs] *n* **1.** [of bus, train, person] retard *m* ■ **I find persistent ~ infuriating** les gens qui sont toujours en retard m'exaspèrent **2.** [late time] heure *f* tardive ■ **given the ~ of the hour** étant donné *OR* vu l'heure tardive.

late-night *adj* [play, show, film] ≃ de minuit ■ **~ opening** COMM nocturne *f* ■ **~ shopping** courses *fpl* en nocturne.

latent ['leɪtənt] *adj* latent.

latent period *n* MED incubation *f*.

later ['leɪtər] *(compar of late)* ◇ *adj* ultérieur ■ **we can always catch a ~ train** on peut toujours prendre un autre train, plus tard ■ **a collection of her ~ poems** un recueil de ses derniers poèmes ■ **at a ~ date** à une date ultérieure ■ **at a ~ stage** à un stade plus avancé ■ **in ~ life** plus tard dans la vie.
◇ *adv* plus tard ■ **~ that day** plus tard dans la journée ■ **~ on** plus tard ■ **see you ~!** à plus tard! ■ **no ~ than tomorrow** demain dernier délai, demain au plus tard.

lateral ['lætərəl] ◇ *adj* latéral.
◇ *n* LING (consonne *f*) latérale *f*.

lateral thinking *n* approche *f* originale.

latest ['leɪtɪst] ◇ *adj (superl of late)* dernier ■ **the ~ date/time** la date/l'heure limite ■ **the ~ news** les dernières nouvelles ■ **let's hope her ~ novel won't be her last** espérons que le roman qu'elle vient de publier ne sera pas le dernier.
◇ *n* **1.** [most recent - news] : **have you heard the ~?** vous connaissez la dernière? ■ **what's the ~ on the trial?** qu'y a-t-il de nouveau sur le procès? ■ **tune in at 7 p.m. for the ~ on the elections** soyez à l'écoute à 19 h pour les dernières informations sur les élections ■ **have you met his/her ~?** [boyfriend, girlfriend] avez-vous fait la connaissance de sa dernière conquête?
2. [in time] : **at the ~** au plus tard ■ **when is the ~ you can come?** jusqu'à quelle heure pouvez-vous venir?

latex ['leɪteks] *n* latex *m*.

lath [lɑ:θ] *n* [wooden] latte *f* ■ [in venetian blind] lame *f*.

lathe [leɪð] ◇ *n* tour *m (à bois ou à métal)* ■ **~ operator** tourneur *m*.
◇ *vt* tourner.

lather ['lɑ:ðər] ◇ *n* **1.** [from soap] mousse *f* **2.** [foam - on horse, seawater] écume *f* ■ **to get into a ~ about** *OR* **over sthg** *UK* s'énerver *OR* se mettre dans tous ses états à propos de qqch.
◇ *vt* [clean] savonner.
◇ *vi* **1.** [soap] mousser **2.** [horse] écumer.

Latin ['lætɪn] ◇ *n* **1.** [person] Latin *m*, - e *f* ■ **the ~s** [in Europe] les Latins ; [in US] les Latino-américains *mpl* **2.** LING latin *m*.
◇ *adj* latin ■ [alphabet] latin ■ **the ~ Quarter** le Quartier latin.

Latin America *pr n* Amérique *f* latine ■ **in ~** en Amérique latine.

Latin American ◇ *n* Latino-américain *m*, - e *f*.
◇ *adj* latino-américain.

Latinate ['lætɪneɪt] *adj* [vocabulary] d'origine latine ■ [style] empreint de latinismes.

Latino [læ'ti:nəʊ] *(pl* **Latinos)** *n US* Latino *mf*.

latitude ['lætɪtju:d] *n* **1.** ASTRON & GEOG latitude *f* ■ **at a ~ of 50° south** à 50° de latitude sud ■ **few animals live in these ~s** rares sont les animaux qui vivent sous ces latitudes **2.** [freedom] latitude *f* ■ **they don't allow** *OR* **give the children much ~ for creativity** ils n'encouragent guère les enfants à être créatifs.

latrines [lə'tri:nz] *npl* latrines *fpl*.

latter ['lætər] ◇ *adj* **1.** [in relation to former] dernier, second **2.** [later] dernier, second ■ **in the ~ years of her life** au cours des dernières années de sa vie.
◇ *n* : **the former... the ~** le premier... le second, celui-là... celui-ci ■ **of tigers and cheetahs, the ~ are by far the faster runners** des tigres et des guépards, ces derniers sont de loin les plus rapides.

latter-day *adj* d'aujourd'hui ■ **a ~ St Francis** un saint François moderne ■ **Church of the ~ Saints** Église *f* de Jésus-Christ des saints des derniers jours.

latterly ['lætəlɪ] *adv* [recently] récemment, dernièrement ■ [towards the end] vers la fin.

lattice ['lætɪs] *n* [fence, frame] treillage *m* ■ [design] treillis *m*.

lattice window *n* fenêtre *f* à croisillons.

latticework ['lætɪswɜ:k] *n (U)* treillis *m*.

Latvia ['lætvɪə] *pr n* Lettonie *f* ■ **in ~** en Lettonie.

Latvian ['lætvɪən] ◇ *n* **1.** [person] Letton *m*, - onne *f* **2.** LING letton *m*.
◇ *adj* letton.

laud [lɔ:d] *vt fml & lit* louer, chanter les louanges de, glorifier.

laudable ['lɔ:dəbl] *adj* louable, digne de louanges.

laudably ['lɔ:dəblɪ] *adv* de manière louable ■ **you behaved ~** votre comportement a été admirable.

laudanum ['lɔ:dənəm] *n* laudanum *m*.

laudatory ['lɔ:dətrɪ] *adj fml* laudatif, élogieux.

laugh [lɑ:f] ◇ *vi* **1.** [in amusement] rire ■ **she was ~ing about his gaffe all day** sa gaffe l'a fait rire toute la journée ■ **you have to ~** mieux vaut en rire ■ **to burst out ~ing** éclater de rire ■ **we ~ed until we cried** on a ri aux larmes, on a pleuré de rire ■ **we ~ed about it afterwards** après coup, cela nous a fait bien rire, on en a ri après coup ■ **it's easy for you to ~!** vous pouvez rire! ■ **to ~ aloud** *OR* **out loud** rire aux éclats ■ **he was ~ing to himself** il riait dans sa barbe ■ **they didn't know whether to ~ or cry** ils ne savaient pas s'ils devaient en rire ou en pleurer ▶ **to ~ up one's sleeve** *UK* rire sous cape ■ **I'll make him ~ on the other side of his face** *UK* je lui ferai passer l'envie de rire, moi ■ **he who ~s last ~s longest** *UK OR* **best** *US prov* rira bien qui rira le dernier *prov*
2. [in contempt, ridicule] rire ■ **they ~ed in my face** ils m'ont ri au nez ■ **he ~ed about his mistakes** il a ri de ses erreurs
3. *fig* [be confident] : **once we get the contract, we're ~ing** une fois qu'on aura empoché le contrat, on sera tranquilles ■ **she's ~ing all the way to the bank** elle s'en met plein les poches.
◇ *vt* **1.** [in amusement] : **to ~ o.s. silly** se tordre de rire, être plié en deux de rire
2. [in ridicule] : **he was ~ed off the stage/out of the room** il a quitté la scène/la pièce sous les rires moqueurs ■ **they ~ed him to scorn** ils se sont moqués de lui ▶ **to ~ sthg out of court** tourner qqch en dérision
3. [express] : **she ~ed her scorn** elle eut un petit rire méprisant.
◇ *n* **1.** [of amusement] rire *m* ■ [burst of laughter] éclat *m* de rire ■ **to give a ~** rire ■ **we had a good ~ about it** ça nous a bien fait rire ■ **she left the room with a ~** elle sortit en riant *OR* dans un éclat de rire ‖ [of contempt] rire *m* ■ **we all had a good ~ at his expense** nous nous sommes bien moqués de lui ▶ **to have the last ~** avoir le dernier mot

2. *UK inf* [fun] rigolade *f* ■ **to have (a bit of) a ~** rigoler *OR* se marrer un peu ■ **he's always good for a ~** avec lui, on se marre bien ■ **he's a ~ a minute** il est très marrant
3. *inf* [joke] : **we did it for a ~** *OR* **just for ~s** on l'a fait pour rigoler ■ **what a ~!** qu'est-ce qu'on s'est marré! ■ **home-made cakes? – that's a ~!** *iron* gâteaux faits maison? – c'est une blague *OR* ils plaisantent!
◆ **laugh at** *vt insep* **1.** [in amusement] : **we all ~ed at the joke/the film** la blague/le film nous a tous fait rire
2. [mock] se moquer de, rire de ■ **to ~ at someone else's misfortunes** se moquer des malheurs des autres
3. [disregard] rire de, rester indifférent à.
◆ **laugh off** *vt sep* [difficulty] rire de, se moquer de ■ [difficult situation] désamorcer ■ **how can they just ~ it off like that?** comment osent-ils prendre ça à la légère? ■ **he tried to ~ off the defeat** il s'efforça de ne pas prendre sa défaite trop au sérieux.

laughable ['lɑ:fəbl] *adj* ridicule, dérisoire.

laughing ['lɑ:fɪŋ] *adj* [eyes] riant, rieur ■ **this is no ~ matter** il n'y a pas de quoi rire.

laughing gas *n* gaz *m* hilarant.

laughing hyena *n* hyène *f* tachetée.

laughingly ['lɑ:fɪŋlɪ] *adv* **1.** [cheerfully] en riant **2.** [inappropriately] : **this noise is ~ called folk music** c'est ce bruit qu'on appelle le plus sérieusement du monde de la musique folk.

laughing stock *n* : **they were the ~ of the whole neighbourhood** ils étaient la risée de tout le quartier ■ **they made ~s of themselves** ils se sont couverts de ridicule.

laughter ['lɑ:ftəʳ] *n (U)* rire *m*, rires *mpl* ■ **a burst of ~** un éclat de rire ■ **she continued to speak amid loud ~** elle a continué à parler au milieu des éclats de rire.

launch [lɔ:ntʃ] ◇ *n* **1.** [boat] vedette *f* ■ [long boat] chaloupe *f* ■ **(pleasure) ~** bateau *m* de plaisance **2.** [of ship, spacecraft, new product] lancement *m* ■ **a book ~** le lancement d'un livre.
◇ *vt* **1.** [boat - from ship] mettre à la mer ; [- from harbour] faire sortir ; [- for first time] lancer **2.** COMM lancer ■ FIN [shares] émettre ■ **our firm has ~ed a new perfume on** *OR* **onto the market** notre société a lancé un nouveau parfum **3.** [start] : **that was the audition that ~ed me on my career** cette audition a donné le coup d'envoi de ma carrière ■ **to ~ a military offensive** déclencher *OR* lancer une attaque.
◆ **launch into** *vt insep* [start] se lancer dans ■ **she ~ed into her work with vigour** elle s'est lancée dans son travail avec énergie.
◆ **launch out** *vi insep* se lancer ■ **she's just ~ed out on her own** elle vient de se mettre à son compte.

launch complex *n* ASTRONAUT base *f* *OR* station *f* de lancement.

launcher ['lɔ:ntʃəʳ] *n* ASTRONAUT & MIL lanceur *m*.

launching ['lɔ:ntʃɪŋ] *n* **1.** [of ship, spacecraft] lancement *m* ■ [of lifeboat - from ship] mise *f* à la mer ; [- from shore] sortie *f* **2.** [of new product] lancement *m*.

launching ceremony *n* cérémonie *f* de lancement.

launching pad = **launch pad**.

launching vehicle = **launch vehicle**.

launch pad *n* rampe *f* de lancement.

launch vehicle *n* fusée *f* de lancement.

launder ['lɔ:ndəʳ] *vt* **1.** [clothes] laver ■ [at laundry] blanchir **2.** *fig* [money] blanchir.

Launderette® [,lɔ:ndə'ret] = **laundrette**.

laundress ['lɔ:ndrɪs] *n* blanchisseuse *f*.

laundrette [lɔ:n'dret] *n UK* laverie *f* automatique.

Laundromat® ['lɔ:ndrəmæt] *n US* laverie *f* automatique.

laundry ['lɔ:ndrɪ] (*pl* **laundries**) *n* **1.** [shop] blanchisserie *f* ■ [in house] buanderie *f* **2.** [washing] linge *m* ■ **to do the ~** faire la lessive.

laundry basket *n* panier *m* à linge.

laundryman ['lɔ:ndrɪmən] (*pl* **laundrymen** [-mən]) *n* **1.** [van-driver] livreur *m* de blanchisserie **2.** [worker in laundry] blanchisseur *m*.

laureate ['lɔ:rɪət] *n* **1.** [prize winner] lauréat *m* ■ **a Nobel ~** un prix Nobel **2.** [poet] poète *m* lauréat.

laurel ['lɒrəl] ◇ *n* [tree] laurier *m*.
◇ *comp* [crown, wreath] de lauriers.
◆ **laurels** *npl* [honours] lauriers *mpl* ■ **to look to one's ~s** ne pas s'endormir sur ses lauriers ■ **to rest on one's ~s** se reposer sur ses lauriers.

Lautro ['lautrəu] (*abbrev of* **Life Assurance and Unit Trust Regulatory Organization**) *pr n organisme britannique contrôlant les activités de compagnies d'assurance-vie et de SICAV.*

lav [læv] *n UK inf* cabinets *mpl*, W-C *mpl*.

lava ['lɑ:və] *n* lave *f*.

lavatorial [,lævə'tɔ:rɪəl] *adj* [style, humour] scatologique.

lavatory ['lævətrɪ] (*pl* **lavatories**) ◇ *n UK* toilettes *fpl*, cabinets *mpl* ■ [bowl] cuvette *f* ■ **to go to the ~** aller aux toilettes.
◇ *adj* des W-C ■ [humour] scatologique.

lavender ['lævəndəʳ] ◇ *n* lavande *f*.
◇ *adj* [colour] lavande.

lavender blue ◇ *n* bleu lavande *m inv*.
◇ *adj* bleu lavande *(inv)*.

lavish ['lævɪʃ] ◇ *adj* **1.** [abundant] copieux, abondant ■ [luxurious] somptueux, luxueux **2.** [generous] généreux, magnanime ■ **he was ~ in his praise** il ne tarissait pas d'éloges.
◇ *vt* prodiguer ■ **they ~ all their attention on their son** ils sont aux petits soins pour leur fils ■ **he ~ed praise on the book** il ne tarissait pas d'éloges sur le livre.

lavishly ['lævɪʃlɪ] *adv* **1.** [generously, extravagantly] généreusement, sans compter ■ **he praised us ~** il n'a pas tari d'éloges à notre égard **2.** [luxuriously] luxueusement, somptueusement.

law [lɔ:] ◇ *n* **1.** [legal provision] loi *f* ■ **a ~ against gambling** une loi qui interdit les jeux d'argent ■ **there's no ~ against it!** il n'y a pas de mal à cela! ▶ **Law Lords** *UK membres de la chambre des Lords siégeant en tant que cour d'appel de dernière instance* ■ **the Law Society** *UK conseil de l'ordre des avocats chargé de faire respecter la déontologie* ■ **to be a ~ unto o.s.** ne connaître ni foi ni loi
2. [legislation] loi *f* ■ **it's against the ~ to sell alcohol** la vente d'alcool est illégale ■ **by ~** selon la loi ■ **in** *OR* **under British ~** selon la loi britannique ■ **to break/to uphold the ~** enfreindre/respecter la loi ■ **the bill became ~** le projet de loi a été voté *OR* adopté ■ **the ~ of the land** la loi, les lois ■ **the ~ of the jungle** la loi de la jungle ■ **to lay down the ~** *fig* imposer sa loi, faire la loi ■ **her word is ~** *fig* ses décisions sont sans appel
3. [legal system] droit *m*
4. [justice] justice *f*, système *m* juridique ■ **to go to ~** *UK* aller en justice ■ **to take a case to ~** *UK* porter une affaire en justice *OR* devant les tribunaux ■ **to take the ~ into one's own hands** (se) faire justice soi-même ■ [police] : **the ~** *inf* les flics *mpl* ■ **I'll have the ~ on you!** je vais appeler les flics!
5. [rule - of club, sport] règle *f*
6. SCI [principle] loi *f* ■ **the ~ of supply and demand** ECON la loi de l'offre et de la demande.
◇ *comp* [faculty, school] de droit ■ **he's a ~ student** il est étudiant en droit.

law-abiding *adj* respectueux de la loi ■ **a ~ citizen** un honnête citoyen.

law and order *n* l'ordre public *m* ■ **law-and-order issues** questions *fpl* d'ordre public.

law-breaker *n* personne *f* qui transgresse la loi.

law centre *n* bureau *m* d'aide judiciaire.

law court *n* tribunal *m*, cour *f* de justice.

law-enforcement *adj US* chargé de faire respecter la loi ■ **~ officer** *représentant d'un service chargé de faire respecter la loi.*

lawful ['lɔːfʊl] *adj* [legal] légal ■ [legitimate] légitime ■ [valid] valide ■ **by all ~ means** par tous les moyens légaux ■ **my ~ wedded wife** mon épouse légitime.

lawfully ['lɔːfʊlɪ] *adv* légalement, de manière légale.

lawgiver ['lɔː,gɪvəʳ] *n* législateur *m*, - trice *f*.

lawless ['lɔːlɪs] *adj* [person] sans foi ni loi ■ [activity] illégal ■ [country] livré à l'anarchie ■ **a ~ frontier territory** un territoire sauvage situé aux confins du monde civilisé.

lawlessness ['lɔːlɪsnɪs] *n* non-respect *m* de la loi ■ [anarchy] anarchie *f* ■ [illegality] illégalité *f*.

lawmaker ['lɔː,meɪkəʳ] *n* législateur *m*, - trice *f*.

lawman ['lɔːmæn] (*pl* **lawmen** [-men]) *n* **US** [policeman] policier *m* ■ [sheriff] shérif *m*.

lawn [lɔːn] *n* **1.** [grass] pelouse *f*, gazon *m* **2.** TEX linon *m*.

lawn chair *n* **US** chaise *f* de jardin.

lawnmower ['lɔːn,məʊəʳ] *n* tondeuse *f* à gazon.

lawn party *n* **US** garden party *f*.

lawn tennis ◇ *n* tennis *m* sur gazon.
◇ *comp* [club] de tennis.

Lawrence ['lɒrəns] *pr n* : **~ of Arabia** Lawrence d'Arabie.

Lawrentian [lə'renʃɪən] *adj* lawrencien.

lawsuit ['lɔːsuːt] *n* action *f* en justice ■ **to bring a ~ against sb** intenter une action (en justice) contre qqn.

lawyer ['lɔːjəʳ] *n* **1.** [barrister] avocat *m*, homme *m* de loi **2.** [solicitor - for wills, conveyancing etc] notaire *m* **3.** [legal expert] juriste *mf* ■ [adviser] conseil *m* juridique.

lax [læks] *adj* **1.** [person] négligent ■ [behaviour, discipline] relâché ■ [justice] laxiste ■ **to be ~ about sthg** négliger qqch **2.** [not tense - string] lâche, relâché ■ LING [phoneme] lâche, relâché ■ MED [bowels] relâché **3.** [imprecise - definition] imprécis, vague.

laxative ['læksətɪv] ◇ *adj* laxatif.
◇ *n* laxatif *m*.

laxity ['læksətɪ], **laxness** ['læksnɪs] *n* [slackness] relâchement *m* ■ [negligence] négligence *f*.

lay [leɪ] (*pret & pp* **laid** [leɪd]) ◇ *pt* ⊳ **lie**.
◇ *vt* **1.** [in specified position] poser, mettre ■ **he laid the baby on the bed** il a couché l'enfant sur le lit ■ **she laid her head on my shoulder** elle a posé sa tête sur mon épaule ■ **to ~ sb to rest** *euph* enterrer qqn ❙ [spread out] étendre ■ **she laid the blanket on the ground** elle a étendu la couverture par terre ➊ **to ~ it on the line** *inf* ne pas y aller par quatre chemins **2.** [tiles, bricks, pipes, cable, carpet] poser ■ [foundations] poser ■ [wreath] déposer ■ [mine] poser, mouiller ■ **the plan ~s the basis** OR **the foundation for economic development** *fig* le projet jette les bases du développement économique **3.** [set - table] mettre ■ **~ the table for six** mettez la table pour six (personnes), mettez six couverts **4.** [prepare, arrange - fire] préparer ■ **to ~ a trail** tracer un chemin ■ **they laid a trap for him** ils lui ont tendu un piège **5.** [egg] pondre ■ **'new-laid eggs'** 'œufs frais' **6.** [impose - burden, duty] imposer ■ **to ~ emphasis** OR **stress on sthg** mettre l'accent sur qqch **7.** LAW [lodge] porter ■ **to ~ an accusation against sb** porter une accusation contre qqn ■ **charges have been laid against five men** cinq hommes ont été inculpés **8.** [present, put forward] : **she laid the scheme before him** elle lui soumit le projet **9.** [allay - fears] dissiper ■ [exorcize - ghost] exorciser ■ [refute - rumour] démentir **10.** [bet] parier ■ **I'll ~ you ten to one that she won't come** je te parie à dix contre un qu'elle ne viendra pas **11.** ▲ [have sex with] baiser△ ■ **to get laid** baiser△ **12.** *lit* [strike] : **to ~ a whip across sb's back** fouetter qqn **13.** [with adjective complements] : **to ~ o.s. open to criticism** s'exposer à la critique.
◇ *vi* **1.** [bird, fish etc] pondre **2.** *inf* = **lie** *(vi sense 2)*.
◇ *adj* **1.** [non-clerical] laïque **2.** [not professional] profane, non-spécialiste ■ **~ people** les profanes *mpl*.
◇ *n* **1.** ▲ [person] : **he's/she's a good ~** c'est un bon coup▲ **2.** [poem, song] lai *m*.

◆ **lay about** *vt insep lit* attaquer, taper sur ■ **she laid about him with her umbrella** elle l'a attaqué à coups de parapluie, elle lui a tapé dessus avec son parapluie.

◆ **lay aside** *vt sep* **1.** [put down] mettre de côté ■ **you should ~ aside any personal opinions you might have** *fig* vous devez faire abstraction de toute opinion personnelle **2.** [save] mettre de côté ■ **we have some money laid aside** nous avons de l'argent de côté.

◆ **lay down** *vt sep* **1.** [put down] poser ■ **to ~ down one's arms** déposer OR rendre les armes **2.** [renounce, relinquish] renoncer à ■ **to ~ down one's life** se sacrifier **3.** [formulate, set out - plan, rule] formuler, établir ; [- condition] imposer ■ **as laid down in the contract, the buyer keeps exclusive rights** il est stipulé OR il est bien précisé dans le contrat que l'acheteur garde l'exclusivité **4.** [store - wine] mettre en cave.

◆ **lay in** *vt sep* [stores] faire provision de.

◆ **lay into** *vt insep* [attack - physically] tomber (à bras raccourcis) sur ; [- verbally] prendre à partie, passer un savon à.

◆ **lay off** ◇ *vt sep* **1.** [employees] licencier **2.** [in gambling - bet] couvrir.
◇ *vt insep* laisser tomber ■ **~ off it, will you!** laisse tomber, tu veux! ■ **I told her to ~ off my husband** je lui ai dit de laisser mon mari tranquille.
◇ *vi insep inf* laisser tomber.

◆ **lay on** *vt sep* **1.** [provide] fournir ■ **the meal was laid on by our hosts** le repas nous fut offert par nos hôtes ■ **they had transport laid on for us** ils s'étaient occupés de nous procurer un moyen de transport **2.** UK [install] installer, mettre ■ **the caravan has electricity laid on** la caravane a l'électricité **3.** [spread - paint, plaster] étaler ■ **to ~ it on thick** *inf fig* en rajouter **4.** △ US **to ~ sthg on sb** [give] filer qqch à qqn ; [tell] raconter qqch à qqn **5.** *phr* **if you're not careful, I'll ~ one on you!**△ [hit] fais gaffe ou je t'en mets une!

◆ **lay out** *vt sep* **1.** [arrange, spread out] étaler ■ **he laid his wares out on the ground** il a étalé OR déballé sa marchandise sur le sol **2.** [present, put forward] exposer, présenter ■ **her ideas are clearly laid out in her book** ses idées sont clairement exposées dans son livre **3.** [design] concevoir ■ **the house is badly laid out** la maison est mal conçue **4.** [corpse] faire la toilette de **5.** *inf* [spend] mettre ■ **we've already laid out a fortune on the project** nous avons déjà mis une fortune dans ce projet **6.** *inf* [knock out] assommer, mettre K-O **7.** TYPO faire la maquette de, monter.

◆ **lay over** *vi insep* US [stop off] faire une halte, faire escale.

◆ **lay up** *vt sep* UK **1.** [store, save] mettre de côté ■ **you're just ~ing up trouble for yourself** *fig* tu te prépares des ennuis **2.** *inf* [confine to bed] aliter ■ **she's laid up with mumps** elle est au lit avec les oreillons **3.** [ship] désarmer ■ [car] mettre au garage.

layabout ['leɪəbaʊt] *n* UK *inf* paresseux *m*, - euse *f*, fainéant *m*, - e *f*.

lay-by (*pl* **lay-bys**) *n* **1.** UK AUT aire *f* de stationnement **2.** RAIL voie *f* de garage.

lay days *npl* starie *f*, jours *mpl* de planche.

layer ['leɪəʳ] ◇ *n* **1.** [of skin, paint, wood] couche *f* ■ [of fabric, clothes] épaisseur *f* ■ **the poem has many ~s of meaning** *fig* le poème peut être lu de différentes façons **2.** GEOL strate *f*, couche *f* **3.** HORT marcotte *f* **4.** [hen] pondeuse *f*.
◇ *vt* [hair] couper en dégradé ■ HORT marcotter.

layer cake *n* génoise *f*.

layered ['leɪəd] *adj* SEW : **a ~ skirt** une jupe à volants.

layette [leɪ'et] *n* layette *f*.

laying ['leɪɪŋ] ◇ *n* **1.** [of egg] ponte *f* **2.** [of cables, carpets] pose *f* ■ [of mine] pose *f*, mouillage *m* ■ [of wreath] dépôt *m* ➊ **~ on of hands** RELIG imposition *f* des mains.
◇ *adj* : **~ hen** poule *f* pondeuse.

layman ['leɪmən] (*pl* **laymen** [-mən]) *n* **1.** [non-specialist] profane *mf*, non-initié *m*, - e *f* ■ **a ~'s guide to the stock market** un manuel d'initiation au système boursier **2.** [non-clerical] laïc *m*, laïque *f*.

lay-off *n* **1.** [sacking] licenciement *m* **2.** [inactivity] chômage *m* technique.

layout ['leɪaʊt] *n* **1.** [gen] disposition *f* ■ [of building, park] disposition *f*, agencement *m* ■ [of essay] plan *m* ■ **you've got quite a ~ here!** *inf* c'est pas mal chez vous! **2.** TYPO maquette *f* ■ **~ artist** maquettiste *mf* **3.** [diagram] schéma *m*.

layover ['leɪəʊvəʳ] *n* *US* escale *f*, halte *f*.

lay preacher *n* prédicateur *m* laïque.

lay reader *n* prédicateur *m* laïque.

Lazarus ['læzərəs] *pr n* Lazare.

laze [leɪz] ◇ *vi* [relax] se reposer ▪ [idle] paresser ▪ **to ~ in bed** traîner au lit.
◇ *n* farniente *m* ▪ **to have a ~ in bed** traîner au lit.
◆ **laze about** *UK*, **laze around** *vi insep* paresser, fainéanter.

lazily ['leɪzɪlɪ] *adv* paresseusement, avec paresse.

laziness ['leɪzɪnɪs] *n* paresse *f*, fainéantise *f*.

lazy ['leɪzɪ] (*comp* **lazier**, *superl* **laziest**) *adj* **1.** [idle] paresseux, fainéant ▪ [relaxed] indolent, nonchalant ▪ **we spent a ~ afternoon on the beach** on a passé l'après-midi à paresser sur la plage **2.** [movement] paresseux, lent.

lazybones ['leɪzɪbəʊnz] *n inf* fainéant *m*, - e *f* ▪ **come on, ~!** allez, secoue-toi *OR* remue-toi un peu!

lazy eye *n* amblyopie *f* ▪ **to have a ~** être amblyope.

lb (*written abbrev of* **pound**) ▪ **3 ~** *OR* **~s** 3 livres.

lbw (*abbrev of* **leg before wicket**) *n au cricket, faute d'un joueur qui met une jambe devant le guichet.*

lc (*written abbrev of* **lower case**) bdc.

L/C *written abbr of* **letter of credit**.

LCD (*abbrev of* **liquid crystal display**) *n* LCD *m*.

L-driver (*abbrev of* **learner-driver**) *n* *UK* *personne qui apprend à conduire.*

lea [liː] *n lit* pré *m*.

LEA *n* = **local education authority**.

leach [liːtʃ] *vt* **1.** TECH lessiver, extraire par lessivage **2.** CHEM & PHARM lixivier.

lead[1] [liːd] (*pret & pp* **led** [led]) ◇ *vt* **1.** [take, guide] mener, emmener, conduire ▪ **to ~ sb somewhere** mener *OR* conduire qqn quelque part ▪ **she led him down the stairs** elle lui fit descendre l'escalier ▪ **to ~ an army into battle** mener une armée au combat ▪ **the captain led the team onto the field** le capitaine a conduit son équipe sur le terrain ▪ **he led her to the altar** *lit* il la prit pour épouse ▪ **to ~ the way** montrer le chemin ▪ **police motorcyclists led the way** des motards de la police ouvraient la route ● **to ~ sb up the garden path** mener qqn en bateau
2. [be leader of] être à la tête de, diriger ▪ SPORT [be in front of] mener ▪ **to ~ the prayers/singing** diriger la prière/les chants ▪ **Stardust is ~ing Black Beauty by 10 lengths** Stardust a pris 10 longueurs d'avance sur Black Beauty
3. [induce] amener ▪ **to ~ sb to do sthg** amener qqn à faire qqch ▪ **despair led him to commit suicide** le désespoir l'a poussé au suicide ▪ **he led me to believe (that) he was innocent** il m'a amené à croire qu'il était innocent ▪ **everything ~s us to believe (that) she is still alive** tout porte à croire *OR* nous avons toutes les raisons de croire qu'elle est encore en vie ▪ **he is easily led** il se laisse facilement influencer ❙ *fig* **subsequent events led the country into war** des événements ultérieurs ont entraîné le pays dans la guerre ▪ **this ~s me to my second point** ceci m'amène à ma seconde remarque
4. [life] mener
5. [in cards] demander, jouer
6. LAW [witness] influencer.
◇ *vi* **1.** [go] mener ▪ **where does this door ~ to?** sur quoi ouvre cette porte? ▪ **the stairs lead to the cellar** l'escalier mène *OR* conduit à la cave ▪ **take the street that ~s away from the station** prenez la rue qui part de la gare ▪ **that road ~s nowhere** cette route ne mène nulle part ▪ **this is ~ing nowhere!** *fig* cela ne rime à rien!
2. SPORT mener, être en tête ▪ **to ~ by 2 metres** avoir 2 mètres d'avance ▪ **to ~ by 3 points to 1** mener par 3 points à 1 ❙ [in cards] : **hearts led** cœur (a été) demandé ▪ **Peter to ~** c'est à Peter de jouer
3. [go in front] aller devant ▪ **if you ~, I'll follow** allez-y, je vous suis
4. *UK* PRESS : **to ~ with sthg** mettre qqch à la une ▪ **the "Times" led with news of the plane hijack** le détournement d'avion faisait la une *OR* était en première page du "Times"
5. [in boxing] : **he ~s with his right** il attaque toujours du droit *OR* de la droite
6. [in dancing] conduire.
◇ *n* **1.** SPORT tête *f* ▪ **to be in the ~** être en tête, mener ▪ **to go into** *OR* **to take the ~** [in race] prendre la tête ; [in match] mener ▪ **to have a 10-point/10-length ~** avoir 10 points/10 longueurs d'avance
2. [initiative] initiative *f* ▪ **take your ~ from me** prenez exemple sur moi ▪ **to follow sb's ~** suivre l'exemple de qqn ▪ **it's up to the government to give a ~ on housing policy** c'est au gouvernement (qu'il revient) de donner l'exemple en matière de politique du logement
3. [indication, clue] indice *m*, piste *f* ▪ **the police have several ~s** la police tient plusieurs pistes
4. *UK* PRESS gros titre *m* ▪ **the news made the ~ in all the papers** la nouvelle était à la une de tous les journaux
5. CIN & THEAT [role] rôle *m* principal ▪ [actor] premier rôle *m* masculin ▪ [actress] premier rôle *m* féminin
6. [in cards] : **whose ~ is it?** c'est à qui de jouer?
7. [for dog] laisse *f* ▪ **'dogs must be kept on a ~'** 'les chiens doivent être tenus en laisse'
8. ELEC fil *m*.
◇ *adj* [actor, singer] principal, premier ▪ PRESS [article] de tête.
◆ **lead away** *vt sep* emmener ▪ **he led her away from the scene of the accident** il l'éloigna du lieu de l'accident.
◆ **lead back** ◇ *vt sep* ramener, reconduire.
◇ *vi insep* : **this path ~s back to the beach** ce chemin ramène à la plage.
◆ **lead off** ◇ *vi insep* [in conversation] commencer, débuter ▪ [at dance] ouvrir le bal.
◇ *vt insep* **1.** [begin] commencer, entamer
2. [go from] partir de ▪ **several avenues ~ off the square** plusieurs avenues partent de la place.
◇ *vt sep* conduire ▪ **they were led off to jail** ils ont été conduits *OR* emmenés en prison.
◆ **lead on** ◇ *vi insep* aller *OR* marcher devant ▪ **~ on!** allez-y!
◇ *vt sep* **1.** [trick] : **to ~ sb on** faire marcher qqn
2. [bring on] faire entrer
3. [in progression] amener ▪ **this ~s me on to my second point** ceci m'amène à mon deuxième point.
◆ **lead to** *vt insep* [result in, have as consequence] mener *OR* aboutir à ▪ **the decision led to panic on Wall Street** la décision a semé la panique à Wall Street ▪ **one thing led to another** une chose en amenait une autre ▪ **a course ~ing to a degree** un cursus qui débouche sur un diplôme ▪ **several factors led to his decision to leave** plusieurs facteurs le poussèrent *OR* l'amenèrent à décider de partir ▪ **this could ~ to some confusion** ça pourrait provoquer une certaine confusion.
◆ **lead up to** *vt insep* **1.** [path, road] conduire à, mener à ▪ **a narrow path led up to the house** un étroit sentier menait jusqu'à la maison
2. [in reasoning] : **what are you ~ing up to?** où voulez-vous en venir?
3. [precede, cause] : **the events ~ing up to the war** les événements qui devaient déclencher la guerre ▪ **in the months ~ing up to her death** pendant les mois qui précédèrent sa mort.

lead[2] [led] ◇ *n* **1.** [metal] plomb *m* ▪ **it's made of ~** c'est en plomb ▪ **~ oxide** oxyde *m* de plomb **2.** *inf* [bullets] plomb *m* ▪ **they pumped him full of ~** ils l'ont flingué **3.** [in pencil] mine *f* **4.** [piece of lead - for sounding] plomb *m* (de sonde) ; [- on car wheel, fishing line] plomb *m* ▪ TYPO interligne *m*.
◇ *vt* **1.** [seal] plomber **2.** TYPO interligner.
◇ *adj* [made of lead] de *OR* en plomb ▪ [containing lead] plombifère ▪ **~ pipe/shot** tuyau *m* /grenaille *f* de plomb.

leaded ['ledɪd] *adj* **1.** [door, box, billiard cue] plombé ▪ **~ window** fenêtre *f* avec verre cathédrale **2.** [petrol] au plomb **3.** TYPO interligné.

leaden ['ledn] *adj* **1.** [made of lead] de *OR* en plomb **2.** [dull - sky] de plomb, plombé ▪ [heavy - sleep] de plomb ; [- heart] lourd ▪ [oppressive - atmosphere] lourd, pesant ; [- silence] de mort ● **he walked with ~ steps** il marchait d'un pas lourd.

leader ['li:dəʳ] *n* **1.** [head] chef *m* ▪ POL chef *m*, leader *m*, dirigeant *m*, - e *f* ▪ [of association] dirigeant *m*, - e *f* ▪ [of strike, protest] meneur *m*, - euse *f* ▪ **the ~s of the march were arrested** les organisateurs de la manifestation ont été arrêtés ◐ **the Leader of the House** [in the Commons] *parlementaire de la majorité chargé de certaines fonctions dans la mise en place du programme gouvernemental* ; [in the Lords] *porte-parole du gouvernement* ▪ **the Leader of the Opposition** le chef de l'opposition **2.** SPORT [horse] cheval *m* de tête ▪ [athlete] coureur *m* de tête ▪ [in championship] leader *m* ▪ **she was up with the ~s** elle était parmi les premiers *OR* dans le peloton de tête ▌[main body or driving force] : **the institute is a world ~ in cancer research** l'institut occupe une des premières places mondiales en matière de recherche contre le cancer **3.** MUS : **~ of the orchestra** *UK* premier violon *m* ; *US* chef *m* d'orchestre **4.** [in newspapers - editorial] éditorial *m* **5.** COMM produit *m* d'appel **6.** [for film, tape] amorce *f* **7.** [in climbing] premier *m* de cordée.

leaderless ['li:dəlɪs] *adj* sans chef, dépourvu de chef.

leadership ['li:dəʃɪp] *n* **1.** [direction] direction *f* ▪ **during** *OR* **under her ~** sous sa direction ▪ **he has great ~ qualities** c'est un excellent meneur d'hommes **2.** [leaders] direction *f*, dirigeants *mpl*.

leader writer *n UK* éditorialiste *mf*.

lead-free [led-] *adj* [paint, petrol] sans plomb ▪ [toy] (garanti) sans plomb.

lead glass [led-] *n* verre *m* de *OR* au plomb.

lead guitar *n* première guitare *f*.

lead-in [li:d-] *n UK* **1.** [introductory remarks] introduction *f*, remarques *fpl* préliminaires **2.** [wire] descente *f* d'antenne.

leading[1] ['li:dɪŋ] *adj* **1.** [prominent] premier, de premier plan ▪ [major] majeur, principal, dominant ▪ **~ figure** figure *f* de premier plan ▪ **they played a ~ part in the discussions** ils ont joué un rôle prépondérant dans le débat ▪ **to play the ~ role in a film** être la vedette d'un film ▪ **~ shares** ST. EX valeurs *fpl* vedettes ▪ **~ technology** technologie *f* de pointe **2.** SPORT [in race] de tête ▪ [in championship] premier ▪ **to be in the ~ position** être en tête ▪ **the ~ runners/riders** les coureurs/cavaliers de tête **3.** MATHS [coefficient] premier.

leading[2] ['ledɪŋ] *n* TYPO [process] interlignage *m* ▪ [space] interligne *m*.

leading article ['li:dɪŋ-] *n UK* éditorial *m* ▪ *US* article *m* leader *OR* de tête.

leading edge ['li:dɪŋ-] *n* **1.** AERON bord *m* d'attaque **2.** *fig* **they are on** *OR* **at the ~ of technology** ils sont à la pointe de la technologie.

◆ **leading-edge** *comp* de pointe.

leading lady ['li:dɪŋ-] *n* CIN & THEAT premier rôle *m* (féminin) ▪ **Vivian Leigh was the ~** Vivian Leigh tenait le premier rôle féminin.

leading light ['li:dɪŋ-] *n* personnage *m* (de marque).

leading man ['li:dɪŋ-] *n* CIN & THEAT premier rôle *m* (masculin).

leading question ['li:dɪŋ-] *n* question *f* orientée.

leading reins ['li:dɪŋ-] *npl UK* harnais *m (pour enfant)*.

lead pencil [led-] *n* crayon *m* noir *OR* à papier *OR* à mine de plomb.

lead poisoning [led-] *n* MED intoxication *f* par le plomb, saturnisme *m*.

lead time [li:d-] *n* INDUST délai *m* de préparation ▪ COMM délai *m* de livraison.

leaf [li:f] (*pl* **leaves** [li:vz]) *n* **1.** [on plant, tree] feuille *f* ▪ **to come into ~** se couvrir de feuilles ▪ **the trees are in ~** les arbres sont en feuilles **2.** [page] feuillet *m*, page *f* ▪ **to take a ~ out of sb's book** prendre exemple *OR* modèle sur qqn **3.** [on table - drop-leaf] abattant *m* ; [- inserted board] allonge *f*, rallonge *f* **4.** [of metal] feuille *f*.

◆ **leaf through** *vt insep* [book, magazine] feuilleter, parcourir.

leaflet ['li:flɪt] ◇ *n* **1.** [brochure] prospectus *m*, dépliant *m* ▪ [political] tract *m* ▪ **~ drop** largage *m* de prospectus *OR* de tracts *(par avion)* **2.** [instruction sheet] notice *f* (explicative), mode *m* d'emploi **3.** BOT foliole *f*.

◇ *vt* distribuer des prospectus *OR* des tracts à ▪ **has the area been ~ed?** est-ce qu'on a distribué des tracts dans le quartier?

leaf spring *n* ressort *m* à lames.

leafy ['li:fɪ] (*comp* **leafier**, *superl* **leafiest**) *adj* [tree] feuillu ▪ [woodland] boisé, vert ▪ **a ~ avenue** une avenue bordée d'arbres.

league [li:g] *n* **1.** [alliance] ligue *f* ▪ **to be in ~ (with sb)** être de mèche (avec qqn) ▪ **they're all in ~ against me** ils se sont tous ligués contre moi ◐ **the League of Nations** HIST la Société des Nations **2.** SPORT [competition] championnat *m* ▪ **United are ~ leaders at the moment** United est en tête du championnat en ce moment ▪ **~ match** match *m* de championnat *OR* comptant pour le championnat ▌[division] division *f* **3.** *fig* [class] classe *f* ▪ **he's not in the same ~ as his father** il n'a pas la classe de son père ▪ **to be in the top ~** être parmi les meilleurs **4.** *arch* [distance] lieue *f*.

league champion *n* champion *m* ▪ **to become ~s** remporter le championnat.

league championship *n* championnat *m*.

league table *n* (classement *m* du) championnat *m*.

leak [li:k] ◇ *n* **1.** [in pipe, tank, roof] fuite *f* ▪ [in boat] voie *f* d'eau **2.** [disclosure - of information, secret] fuite *f* **3.** *phr* **to go for** *OR* **to take a ~**△ [urinate] pisser un coup△.

◇ *vi* [pen, pipe] fuir ▪ [boat, shoe] prendre l'eau ▪ **the roof ~s** il y a une fuite dans le toit ▌[gas, liquid] fuir, s'échapper ▪ **the rain ~s through the ceiling** la pluie s'infiltre par le plafond.

◇ *vt* **1.** [liquid] répandre, faire couler ▪ **the can ~ed oil onto my trousers** de l'huile du bidon s'est répandue sur mon pantalon **2.** [information] divulguer ▪ **the budget details were ~ed** il y a eu des fuites sur le budget ▪ **the documents had been ~ed to a local councillor** quelqu'un avait communiqué *OR* avait fait parvenir les documents à un conseiller municipal.

◆ **leak in** *vi insep* s'infiltrer.

◆ **leak out** *vi insep* **1.** [liquid, gas] fuir, s'échapper **2.** [news, secret] filtrer, transpirer ▪ **the truth finally ~ed out** la vérité a fini par se savoir.

leakage ['li:kɪdʒ] *n (U)* fuite *f*.

leakproof ['li:kpru:f] *adj* étanche.

leaky ['li:kɪ] (*comp* **leakier**, *superl* **leakiest**) *adj* [boat, shoes] qui prend l'eau ▪ [pen, roof, bucket] qui fuit.

lean [li:n] (*UK pret & pp* **leaned** *OR* **leant** [lent]) (*US pret & pp* **leaned**) ◇ *vi* [be on incline] pencher, s'incliner ▪ **she/a ladder was ~ing (up) against the wall** elle/une échelle était appuyée contre le mur ▪ **~ on my arm** appuyez-vous *OR* prenez appui sur mon bras ▪ **she was ~ing with her elbows on the window sill** elle était accoudée à la fenêtre.

◇ *vt* **1.** [prop - ladder, bicycle] appuyer ▪ **he leant the ladder/bike (up) against the tree** il appuya l'échelle/le vélo contre un arbre **2.** [rest - head, elbows] appuyer ▪ **she leant her head on his shoulder** elle posa sa tête sur son épaule **3.** [incline] pencher ▪ **to ~ one's head to one side** pencher *OR* incliner la tête.

◇ *adj* **1.** [animal, meat] maigre ▪ [person - thin] maigre ; [- slim] mince **2.** [poor - harvest] maigre, pauvre ; [- period of time] difficile **3.** [deficient - ore, mixture] pauvre.

◇ *n* **1.** [slope] inclinaison *f* **2.** [meat] maigre *m*.

◆ **lean back** ◇ *vi insep* **1.** [person] se pencher en arrière ▪ **he ~ed back against the wall** il s'est adossé au mur ▪ **don't ~ back on your chair!** ne te balance pas sur ta chaise! ▪ **he ~ed back in his armchair** il s'est renversé dans son fauteuil **2.** [chair] basculer ▪ **this chair ~s back if you pull that lever** on peut incliner *OR* faire basculer le siège en poussant ce levier.

◇ *vt sep* pencher en arrière ▪ **to ~ one's head back** pencher *OR* renverser la tête en arrière.

◆ **lean forward** ◇ *vi insep* se pencher en avant.

◇ *vt sep* pencher en avant.

◆ **lean on, lean upon** *vt insep* **1.** [depend] s'appuyer sur ■ **to ~ on sb's advice** compter sur les conseils de qqn ■ **she ~s heavily on her family for financial support** financièrement, elle dépend beaucoup de sa famille **2.** *UK inf* [pressurize] faire pression sur.

◆ **lean out** ◇ *vi insep* se pencher au dehors ■ **don't ~ out of the window!** ne te penche pas par la fenêtre!

◇ *vt sep* pencher au dehors ■ **he ~ed his head out of the window** il a passé la tête par la fenêtre.

◆ **lean over** *vi insep* [person] se pencher en avant ■ [tree, wall] pencher, être penché ■ **he ~ed over to speak to me** il s'est penché vers moi pour me parler ▶ **to ~ over backwards** *liter* se pencher en arrière ; *fig* remuer ciel et terre, se mettre en quatre.

◆ **lean towards** *vt insep* [tend] pencher pour ■ **I rather ~ towards the view that we should sell** je pencherais plutôt pour la vente, j'ai tendance à penser que nous devrions vendre ■ **politically she ~s towards the right** politiquement, elle se situe plutôt à droite.

lean-burn *adj* [engine] fonctionnant avec un mélange pauvre.

leaning ['li:nɪŋ] ◇ *n (usu pl)* tendance *f*, penchant *m* ■ **she has communist/literary ~s** elle a des penchants communistes/ aimerait être écrivain.

◇ *adj* [tree, wall] penché ■ **the Leaning Tower of Pisa** la tour de Pise.

leant [lent] *UK pt & pp* ▷ **lean**.

lean-to *n UK* **a ~ (shed)** un appentis.

leap [li:p] (*UK pret & pp* **leaped** *OR* **leapt** [lept]) (*US pret & pp* **leaped**) ◇ *vi* **1.** [person, animal] bondir, sauter ■ [flame] jaillir ■ **to ~ to one's feet** se lever d'un bond ■ **to ~ for joy** [person] sauter de joie ; [heart] faire un bond ■ **to ~ into the air** sauter en l'air ■ **the cat leapt off the chair onto the table** le chat sauta de la chaise sur la table **2.** *fig* faire un bond ■ **the price of petrol leapt by 10%** le prix du pétrole a fait un bond de 10 % ■ **the answer almost leapt off the page at me** la réponse m'a pour ainsi dire sauté aux yeux ■ **she leapt to the wrong conclusion** elle a conclu trop hâtivement.

◇ *vt* **1.** [fence, stream] sauter (par-dessus), franchir d'un bond **2.** [horse] faire sauter.

◇ *n* **1.** [jump] saut *m*, bond *m* ■ **to take a ~ forward** *liter & fig* faire un bond en avant, sauter en avant ■ **it's a great ~ forward in medical research** c'est un grand bond en avant pour la recherche médicale ▶ **in ~s and bounds** à pas de géant ■ **a ~ in the dark** un saut dans l'inconnu **2.** [in prices] bond *m*.

◆ **leap about** *UK*, **leap around** ◇ *vt insep* gambader dans.

◇ *vi insep* gambader.

◆ **leap at** *vt insep* **1.** [in attack] sauter sur **2.** *fig* **she leapt at the chance** elle a sauté sur l'occasion.

◆ **leap out** *vi insep* bondir ■ **to ~ out at sb** bondir sur qqn ■ **they leapt out from behind the bushes** ils ont surgi de derrière les buissons ■ *fig* **he almost leapt out of his skin** il a failli tomber à la renverse.

◆ **leap up** *vi insep* [into the air] sauter (en l'air) ■ [to one's feet] se lever d'un bond ■ **to ~ up in surprise** sauter au plafond, sursauter ■ **the dog leapt up at him** le chien lui a sauté dessus.

leapfrog ['li:pfrɒg] (*pret & pp* **leapfrogged**, *cont* **leapfrogging**) ◇ *n* saute-mouton *m* ■ **to play ~** jouer à saute-mouton.

◇ *vi UK* : **to ~ over sb** sauter par-dessus qqn ■ **to ~ into the computer age** *fig* se trouver propulsé à l'ère de l'informatique.

◇ *vt UK fig* dépasser.

leapt [lept] *UK pt & pp* ▷ **leap**.

leap year *n* année *f* bissextile.

learn [lɜ:n] (*UK pret & pp* **learned** *OR* **learnt** [lɜ:nt]) (*US pret & pp* **learned**) ◇ *vt* **1.** [by instruction] apprendre ■ **to ~ (how) to do sthg** apprendre à faire qqch ■ **to ~ sthg by heart** apprendre qqch par cœur ■ **he's learnt his lesson now** *fig* cela lui a servi de leçon **2.** [discover, hear] apprendre ■ **I subsequently learnt that he wouldn't be coming** j'ai appris par la suite qu'il ne viendrait pas **3.** *hum* [teach] apprendre ■ **that'll ~ you!** ça t'apprendra!

◇ *vi* **1.** [by instruction, experience] apprendre ■ **to ~ about sthg** apprendre qqch ■ **to ~ from one's mistakes** tirer la leçon de ses erreurs ■ **they learnt the hard way** ils ont été à dure école **2.** [be informed] : **to ~ of sthg** apprendre qqch ■ **we only learnt of her death today** ce n'est qu'aujourd'hui que nous avons appris sa mort.

◆ **learn up** *vt sep UK inf* bûcher, potasser.

learned *adj* **1.** ['lɜ:nɪd] [erudite - person] savant, érudit ; [- subject, book, society] savant **2.** ['lɜ:nɪd] LAW [lawyer] : **my ~ friend** mon éminent confrère **3.** [lɜ:nd] PSYCHOL [behaviour] acquis.

learner ['lɜ:nəʳ] *n* apprenant *m*, - e *f* ■ **to be a quick ~** apprendre vite ▶ **~ (driver)** *UK* apprenti *m* conducteur, apprentie *f* conductrice.

learning ['lɜ:nɪŋ] *n* **1.** [erudition] érudition *f*, savoir *m* ■ **a man of great ~** [in sciences] un grand savant ; [in arts] un homme d'une grande érudition *OR* culture **2.** [acquisition of knowledge] étude *f* ■ **language ~** l'étude *OR* l'apprentissage *m* des langues ■ **~ difficulties,** *US* SCH difficultés *fpl* scolaires ■ **~ disability** *US politiquement correct pour handicap mental* ■ **adults with ~ difficulties** *adultes ayant des difficultés d'apprentissage*.

learning curve *n* courbe *f* d'assimilation.

learning disabilities *n* difficultés *fpl* d'apprentissage.

learning-disabled *adj US* : **to be ~** [child] avoir des difficultés scolaires ; [adult] avoir des difficultés d'apprentissage.

learnt [lɜ:nt] *UK* ◇ *pt & pp* ▷ **learn**.

◇ *adj* PSYCHOL acquis.

lease [li:s] ◇ *n* **1.** LAW bail *m* ■ **to take (out) a ~ on a house, to take a house on ~** prendre une maison à bail **2.** *phr* **the trip has given her a new ~ of** *UK OR* **on** *US* **life** le voyage l'a remise en forme *OR* lui a redonné du tonus ■ **to take on a new ~ of life** retrouver une nouvelle jeunesse.

◇ *vt* [house] louer à bail ■ [car, sailboard] louer.

leaseback ['li:sbæk] *n* cession-bail *f*.

leasehold ['li:shəʊld] ◇ *n* [lease] bail *m* ■ [property] location *f* à bail.

◇ *adj* loué à bail.

leaseholder ['li:s,həʊldəʳ] *n* [tenant] locataire *mf*.

leash [li:ʃ] *n* [for dog] laisse *f*.

leasing ['li:sɪŋ] *n* crédit-bail *m*, leasing *m*.

least [li:st] ◇ *det & pron (superl of little)* **1.** [in quantity, size] : **he's the one who drank the ~ (wine)** c'est lui qui a bu le moins (de vin) ■ **he's got the ~** c'est lui qui en a le moins **2.** [slightest] : **the ~ thing upsets her** un rien la contrarie ■ **I'm not the ~ bit interested** cela ne m'intéresse pas le moins du monde ■ **it was the ~ we could do** c'était la moindre des choses ▶ **that's the ~ of our worries** c'est le moindre *OR* c'est le cadet de nos soucis ■ **~ said, soonest mended** *prov* moins on en dit, mieux on se porte.

◇ *adv* (le) moins ■ **the ~ interesting film I've ever seen** le film le moins intéressant que j'aie jamais vu ■ **it's what we ~ expected** c'est ce à quoi nous nous attendions le moins.

◆ **at least** *adv phr* **1.** [not less than] au moins ■ **at ~ $500** au moins 500 dollars **2.** [as a minimum] au moins ■ **at the very ~ he might have phoned us** la moindre des choses aurait été de nous téléphoner **3.** [indicating an advantage] au moins, du moins ■ **at ~ we've got an umbrella** au moins *OR* du moins on a un parapluie **4.** [used to qualify] du moins ■ **I didn't like him, at ~ not at first** il ne m'a pas plu, en tout cas *OR* du moins pas au début.

◆ **in the least** *adv phr (with negative)* **not in the ~** pas du tout, pas le moins du monde ■ **she didn't seem to mind in the ~** ça ne semblait pas la déranger le moins du monde.

◆ **least of all** *adv phr* surtout pas ■ **nobody could understand it, Jim ~ of all** *OR* **~ of all Jim** personne ne comprenait, surtout pas Jim *OR* Jim encore moins que les autres.

◆ **not least** *adv phr* : **many politicians, not ~ the Foreign Secretary, are in favour** de nombreux hommes politiques y sont favorables, notamment le ministre des Affaires étrangères.

leastways ['li:stweɪz] *adv inf* du moins.

leastwise ['li:stwaɪz] *US inf* = **leastways**.

leather ['leðəʳ] <> *n* **1.** [material] cuir *m* ▪ **real ~** cuir véritable ▪ **made of ~** de *OR* en cuir **2.** [for polishing] : **(wash** *OR* **window) ~** peau *f* de chamois **3.** *inf* [sexual fetish] : **he's into ~** c'est un fétichiste du cuir.
<> *comp* **1.** [jacket, shoes, sofa, bag] de *OR* en cuir ▪ **~ goods** [ordinary] articles *mpl* en cuir ; [finer] maroquinerie *f* **2.** [bar, club] cuir *(inv)*.
<> *vt inf* [punish] tanner le cuir à.

leatherbound ['leðəbaʊnd] *adj* relié (en) cuir.

leatherette [,leðə'ret] <> *n* similicuir *m*.
<> *adj* en similicuir.

leathering ['leðərɪŋ] *n UK inf* raclée *f*.

leathery ['leðərɪ] *adj* [meat] coriace ▪ [skin] parcheminé, tanné.

leave[1] [li:v] *(pret & pp* **left** [left]) <> *vi* **1.** [depart] partir ▪ **when did you ~?** quand est-ce que vous êtes partis? ▪ **we're leaving for Mexico tomorrow** nous partons pour le Mexique demain ▪ **he's just left for lunch** il vient de partir déjeuner ▪ **if you'd rather I left...** si vous voulez que je vous laisse...
2. [quit] partir ▪ **fewer schoolchildren are now leaving at 16** les élèves sont aujourd'hui moins nombreux à quitter l'école à 16 ans
3. [end relationship] : **Charles, I'm leaving!** Charles, je te quitte!
<> *vt* **1.** [depart from - place] quitter ▪ **she left London yesterday** elle est partie de *OR* elle a quitté Londres hier ▪ **he left the room** il est sorti de *OR* il a quitté la pièce ▪ **to ~ the table** se lever de table
2. [quit - job, institution] quitter ▪ **I left home at 18** je suis parti de chez moi *OR* de chez mes parents à 18 ans ▪ **to ~ school** quitter l'école
3. [in specified place or state] laisser ▪ **he left her asleep on the sofa** elle était endormie sur le canapé lorsqu'il la quitta ▪ **I left him to his reading** je l'ai laissé à sa lecture ▪ **I left him to himself** je l'ai laissé seul ▪ **just ~ me alone!** laissez-moi tranquille!
4. [abandon - person] quitter ▪ **she left him for another man** elle l'a quitté pour un autre ▪ **the prisoners were left to die** les prisonniers furent abandonnés à la mort ▪ *fml* [take leave of - person] laisser ▪ **it's getting late, I must ~ you now** il se fait tard, je dois vous laisser ▪ **you may ~ us now** vous pouvez disposer maintenant
5. [deposit, set down] laisser ▪ **it's no trouble to ~ you at the station** ça ne me dérange pas de vous laisser *OR* déposer à la gare
6. [for sb's use, information etc] laisser ▪ **I've left your dinner in the oven for you** je t'ai laissé de quoi dîner dans le four ▪ **he's out, do you want to ~ a message?** il n'est pas là, voulez-vous laisser un message? ▪ **she left word for you to call her back** elle a demandé que vous la rappeliez
7. [forget] laisser, oublier ▪ **I must have left my gloves at the café** j'ai dû oublier mes gants au café
8. [allow or cause to remain] laisser ▪ **if you don't like your dinner, then ~ it** si tu n'aimes pas ton dîner, laisse-le ▪ **~ yourself an hour to get to the airport** prévoyez une heure pour aller à l'aéroport ▪ **don't ~ things to the last minute** n'attendez pas la dernière minute (pour faire ce que vous avez à faire) ▪ **he left his work unfinished** il n'a pas terminé son travail ▪ **their behaviour ~s a lot to be desired** leur conduite laisse beaucoup à désirer ▪ **the decision ~s me in a bit of a quandary** cette décision me place devant un dilemme ▪ **I want to be left on/off the list** je veux que mon nom reste/je ne veux pas que mon nom figure sur la liste ▪ **I was left with the bill** c'est moi qui ai dû payer l'addition ▪ *(passive use)* **to be left** rester ▪ **we finished what was left of the cake** on a fini ce qui restait du gâteau ▪ **there's nothing left** il ne reste (plus) rien ▪ **I've got £10/10 minutes left** il me reste 10 livres/10 minutes ▮ [mark, trace] laisser ▪ **the wine left a stain** le vin a fait une tache
9. [allow] : **can I ~ you to deal with it, then?** vous vous en chargez, alors? ▪ **she ~s me to get on with things** elle me laisse faire ▪ **right then, I'll ~ you to it** bon, eh bien, je te laisse
10. [entrust] laisser ▪ **can I ~ my suitcase with you for a few minutes?** puis-je vous confier ma valise quelques instants? ▪ **you should ~ such tasks to a specialist** vous devriez laisser *OR* confier ce genre de travail à un spécialiste ▪ **~ it to me!** je m'en occupe!, je m'en charge! ▪ **~ it with me** laissez-moi faire, je m'en charge
11. *UK* MATHS : **9 from 16 ~s 7** 16 moins 9 égale 7
12. [bequeath] léguer ▪ **she left all her money to charity** elle légua toute sa fortune à des œuvres de charité
13. [be survived by] : **he ~s a wife and two children** il laisse une femme et deux enfants.
<> *n* **1.** [from work] congé *m* ▪ MIL permission *f* ▪ **to be/to go on ~** [gen] être/partir en congé ; MIL être/partir en permission ➊ **~ of absence** congé (exceptionnel) ; [without pay] congé sans solde
2. *fml* [permission] permission *f*, autorisation *f* ▪ **by** *OR* **with your ~** avec votre permission
3. [farewell] congé *m* ▪ **to take one's ~ (of sb)** prendre congé (de qqn) ▪ **to take ~ of one's senses** *fig* perdre la tête *OR* la raison.

◆ **leave about** *UK*, **leave around** *vt sep* laisser traîner.

◆ **leave aside** *vt sep* laisser de côté ▪ **leaving aside the question of cost for the moment** si on laisse de côté pour le moment la question du coût.

◆ **leave behind** *vt sep* **1.** [not take] laisser ▪ **it's hard to ~ all your friends and relations behind** c'est dur de laisser tous ses amis et sa famille derrière soi ▮ [forget] laisser, oublier
2. [leave as trace] laisser ▪ **the cyclone left behind a trail of destruction** le cyclone a tout détruit sur son passage
3. [outstrip] distancer, devancer ▪ **she soon left the other runners behind** elle a vite distancé tous les autres coureurs ▪ **if you don't work harder you'll soon get left behind** si tu ne travailles pas plus, tu vas vite te retrouver loin derrière les autres.

◆ **leave in** *vt sep* [word, paragraph] garder, laisser.

◆ **leave off** <> *vi insep* [stop] s'arrêter ▪ **we'll carry on from where we left off** nous allons reprendre là où nous nous étions arrêtés ▪ **~ off, will you!** *UK inf* arrête, tu veux!
<> *vt insep inf UK inf* [stop] : **to ~ off doing sthg** arrêter de faire qqch.
<> *vt sep* **1.** [not put on] ne pas remettre ▪ **who left the top of the toothpaste off?** qui a laissé le tube de dentifrice débouché?
2. [not switch or turn on - tap, gas] laisser fermé ; [- light] laisser éteint ▪ [not plug in - appliance] laisser débranché ▪ **we left the heating off while we were away** nous avons arrêté *OR* coupé le chauffage pendant notre absence.

◆ **leave on** *vt sep* **1.** [not take off - garment] garder ; [- top, cover] laisser ▪ **don't ~ the price tag on** enlève l'étiquette
2. [not switch or turn off - tap, gas] laisser ouvert ; [- light] laisser allumé ▪ [not unplug - appliance] laisser branché ▪ **I hope I didn't ~ the gas on** j'espère que j'ai éteint le gaz.

◆ **leave out** *vt sep* **1.** [omit] omettre ▪ **~ out any reference to her husband in your article** dans votre article, évitez toute allusion à son mari
2. [exclude] exclure ▪ **I felt completely left out at the party** j'ai eu le sentiment d'être totalement tenu à l'écart *OR* exclu de leur petite fête
3. [not put away - by accident] ne pas ranger ; [- on purpose] laisser sorti, ne pas ranger ▪ **he left a meal out for the children** il a laissé un repas tout prêt pour les enfants ▪ [leave outdoors] laisser dehors
4. *phr* **~ it out!**△ *UK* lâche-moi!

◆ **leave over** *vt sep* [allow or cause to remain] laisser ▪ **to be left over** rester ▪ **there are still one or two left over** il en reste encore un ou deux.

leave[2] [li:v] *(pret & pp* **leaved**, *cont* **leaving**) *vi* BOT [produce leaves] feuiller.

leaven ['levn] <> *n* [yeast] levain *m*.
<> *vt* **1.** CULIN faire lever **2.** *fig* [occasion] égayer.

leavening ['levnɪŋ] *n liter & fig* levain *m*.

leaves [li:vz] *pl* ▻ **leaf**.

leave-taking *n (U)* adieux *mpl*.

leaving ['li:vɪŋ] *n* départ *m*.

Lebanese [,lebə'ni:z] *(pl inv)* <> *n* Libanais *m*, - e *f*.
<> *adj* libanais.

Lebanon ['lebənən] *pr n* Liban *m* ▪ **in (the) ~** au Liban.

lech [letʃ] *inf* ◇ *vi* : **he's always ~ing after my secretary** il n'arrête pas de reluquer ma secrétaire.
◇ *n* obsédé *m* (sexuel).

lecher ['letʃəʳ] *n* obsédé *m* (sexuel).

lecherous ['letʃərəs] *adj* lubrique.

lecherously ['letʃərəslɪ] *adv* lubriquement, avec lubricité ■ **to look at sb ~** regarder qqn d'un œil lubrique.

lechery ['letʃərɪ] *n* lubricité *f*.

lectern ['lektən] *n* lutrin *m*.

lector ['lektəʳ] *n* RELIG & UNIV lecteur *m*, - trice *f*.

lecture ['lektʃəʳ] ◇ *n* **1.** [talk] conférence *f*, exposé *m* ■ UNIV [as part of course] cours *m* (magistral) ■ **she gave a very good ~ on Yeats** elle a fait un très bon cours sur Yeats ■ **have you been to his linguistics ~s?** avez-vous suivi ses cours de linguistique? **2.** *fig* [sermon] sermon *m*, discours *m* ■ **to give sb a ~** sermonner qqn, faire des remontrances à qqn.
◇ *comp* [notes] de cours ■ **~ hall** *OR* **theatre** salle *f* de cours, amphithéâtre *m*.
◇ *vi* [talk] faire *OR* donner une conférence ■ [teach] faire (un) cours ■ **she ~s in linguistics** elle enseigne la *OR* donne des cours de linguistique ■ **she ~s on Dante** elle donne des cours sur Dante.
◇ *vt* [reprimand] réprimander, sermonner ■ **he's always lecturing his children about their manners** il est toujours à sermonner *OR* réprimander ses enfants sur leurs manières.

lecturer ['lektʃərəʳ] *n* [speaker] conférencier *m*, - ère *f* ■ UNIV [teacher] assistant *m*, - e *f* ■ **she's a ~ in English at the University of Dublin** elle est professeur d'anglais à l'université de Dublin ▶ **assistant ~** ≃ maître-assistant *m* ■ **senior ~** ≃ maître *m* de conférences.

lecture room *n* salle *f* de cours *OR* de conférences.

lectureship ['lektʃəʃɪp] *n* UNIV poste *m* d'assistant ■ **he got a ~ at the University of Oxford** il a été nommé assistant à l'université d'Oxford ▶ **senior ~** ≃ poste de maître de conférences.

led [led] *pt* & *pp* ▷ **lead** *(to guide)*.

LED (*abbrev of* **light-emitting diode**) *n* LED *f* ■ **~ display** affichage *m* (par) LED.

ledge [ledʒ] *n* **1.** [shelf] rebord *m* **2.** GEOG [on mountain] saillie *f* ■ [on rock or cliff face] corniche *f* ■ [on seabed] haut-fond *m* **3.** GEOL [vein] filon *m*.

ledger ['ledʒəʳ] *n* **1.** COMM & FIN grand livre *m* **2.** TECH longrine *f*.

ledger line *n* MUS ligne *f* supplémentaire.

lee [li:] ◇ *n* **1.** NAUT bord *m* sous le vent **2.** [shelter] abri *m*.
◇ *adj* sous le vent.

leech [li:tʃ] ◇ *n* *liter* & *fig* sangsue *f* ■ **to cling to sb like a ~** s'accrocher *OR* coller à qqn comme une sangsue.
◇ *vt* MED saigner (avec des sangsues).

leek [li:k] *n* poireau *m*.

LEEK

Le poireau est l'emblème du pays de Galles.

leer [lɪəʳ] ◇ *n* [malevolent] regard *m* méchant ■ [lecherous] regard *m* concupiscent *OR* lubrique.
◇ *vi* : **to ~ at sb** lorgner qqn.

leery ['lɪərɪ] (*comp* **leerier**, *superl* **leeriest**) *adj* *inf* méfiant ■ **to be ~ of sthg** se méfier de qqch.

lees [li:z] *npl* [sediment] lie *f* ■ **to drink** *OR* **to drain sthg to the ~** *fig* boire qqch jusqu'à la lie.

leeward ['li:wəd] ◇ *adj* sous le vent.
◇ *n* bord *m* sous le vent ■ **to ~** NAUT sous le vent.

leeway ['li:weɪ] *n (U)* **1.** [margin] marge *f* (de manœuvre) ■ **it doesn't give us much ~** cela ne nous laisse pas une grande marge de manœuvre ■ **a quarter of an hour should be enough ~** une marge de sécurité d'un quart d'heure devrait suffire **2.** [lost time] retard *m* **3.** AERON & NAUT [drift] dérive *f*.

left[1] [left] *pt* & *pp* ▷ **leave**.

left[2] [left] ◇ *adj* [foot, eye] gauche ■ **on the ~ side** sur la gauche, du côté gauche ■ **~ hand down a bit!** AUT braquez un peu à gauche! ■ **to make a ~ turn** tourner à gauche ■ **take the ~ fork** prenez à gauche à l'embranchement ▶ **~ back/half** SPORT arrière *m* /demi *m* gauche.
◇ *adv* **1.** [gen] à gauche ■ **turn ~ at the junction** tournez *OR* prenez à gauche au croisement **2.** POL à gauche.
◇ *n* **1.** [gen] gauche *f* ■ **on the ~** sur la gauche, à gauche ■ **to drive on the ~** rouler à gauche ■ **it's to** *OR* **on the ~ of the picture** [in the picture] c'est sur la gauche du tableau ; [next to the picture] c'est à gauche du tableau ■ **move a bit to the ~** déplacez-vous un peu vers la gauche ■ **he doesn't know his ~ from his right** il ne reconnaît pas sa droite de sa gauche **2.** POL gauche *f* ■ **she is further to the ~ than her husband** elle est (politiquement) plus à gauche que son mari **3.** [in boxing] gauche *m*.

left-footed [-'fʊtɪd] *adj* gaucher (du pied).

left-hand *adj* gauche ■ **on the ~ side** à gauche, sur la gauche ■ **on my ~ side, the Grand Palace** à *OR* sur ma gauche, le Grand Palais ■ **a ~ bend** un virage à gauche ■ **~ drive** conduite *f* à gauche.

left-handed [-'hændɪd] ◇ *adj* **1.** [person] gaucher **2.** [scissors, instrument, golf club] pour gauchers **3.** *US* **a ~ compliment** un faux compliment.
◇ *adv* de la main gauche.

left-hander [-'hændəʳ] *n* [person] gaucher *m*, - ère *f* ■ [blow] coup *m* (donné de la main gauche).

leftie ['leftɪ] *inf* = **lefty**.

leftism ['leftɪzm] *n* [gen] idées *fpl* de gauche ■ [extreme left] gauchisme *m*.

leftist ['leftɪst] ◇ *n* [gen] homme *m* de gauche, femme *f* de gauche ■ [extreme left-winger] gauchiste *mf*.
◇ *adj* [gen] de gauche ■ [extremely left-wing] gauchiste.

left luggage *n (U) UK* [cases] bagages *mpl* en consigne ■ [office] consigne *f* ■ **the ~ lockers** la consigne automatique.

left-luggage office *n UK* consigne *f*.

left-of-centre *adj* POL de centre-gauche.

leftover ['leftəʊvəʳ] ◇ *adj* [food, material] qui reste ■ [stock] en surplus ■ **she used the ~ wool to knit a scarf** elle a tricoté une écharpe avec la laine qui restait.
◇ *n* [throwback, vestige] vestige *m* ■ **the gun is a ~ from the war** le fusil est un souvenir de la guerre.

leftovers ['leftəʊvəz] *npl* [food] restes *mpl*.

leftward ['leftwəd] ◇ *adj* de gauche.
◇ *adv US* = **leftwards**.

leftwards ['leftwədz] *adv* à gauche.

left wing *n* **1.** POL gauche *f* ■ **the ~ of the party** l'aile *f* gauche du parti **2.** SPORT [position] aile *f* gauche ■ [player] ailier *m* gauche.
◆ **left-wing** *adj* POL de gauche ■ **she's very left-wing** elle est très à gauche.

left-winger *n* **1.** POL homme *m* de gauche, femme *f* de gauche **2.** SPORT ailier *m* gauche.

lefty ['leftɪ] (*pl* **lefties**) *n* *inf* **1.** *pej* homme *m* de gauche, femme *f* de gauche **2.** *US* [left-handed person] gaucher *m*, - ère *f*.

leg [leg] (*pret* & *pp* **legged**, *cont* **legging**) ◇ *n* **1.** ANAT [of human, horse] jambe *f* ■ [of smaller animals and birds] patte *f* ■ **his ~s went from under him** ses jambes se sont dérobées sous lui ▶ **he hasn't got a ~ to stand on** sa position est indéfendable ■ **to get one's ~ over**[△] se faire quelqu'un[△] ■ **to pull sb's ~** faire marcher qqn **2.** CULIN [of lamb] gigot *m* ■ [of pork, beef] rôti *m* ■ [of chicken] cuisse *f* ■ **frog's ~s** cuisses de grenouille **3.** [of chair, table] pied *m* **4.** [of trousers, pyjamas] jambe *f* **5.** [stage - of journey] étape *f* ; [- of competition] manche *f* ■ **they won the first/second ~** SPORT ils ont gagné le match aller/retour.
◇ *vt* : **to ~ it** *inf* [run] courir ; [walk] aller à pied ; [flee] se sauver, se tirer.

legacy ['legəsɪ] (*pl* **legacies**) *n* **1.** LAW legs *m* ■ **to leave sb a ~** faire un legs *OR* laisser un héritage à qqn ■ **the money is a ~ from my aunt** j'ai hérité cet argent de ma tante, ma tante m'a légué cet argent **2.** *fig* héritage *m*.

legal ['li:gl] *adj* **1.** [lawful] légal ■ [legitimate] légal, légitime ■ **they're below the ~ age** ils n'ont pas atteint l'âge légal ■ **to be above the ~ limit** [for drinking] dépasser le taux légal (d'alcoolémie) ■ **to make sthg ~** légaliser qqch **2.** [judicial - mind, matter, question] juridique ; [- power, investigation, error] judiciaire ■ **to take ~ action** engager des poursuites judiciaires, intenter un procès ■ **to take ~ advice** consulter un juriste *OR* un avocat ■ **he's a member of the ~ profession** c'est un homme de loi ■ **~ system** système *m* juridique.

legal adviser *n* conseil *m* juridique.

legal aid *n* assistance *f* judiciaire.

legal department *n* [in bank, company] (service *m* du) contentieux *m*.

legal eagle *n inf hum* avocat *m*, - e *f*.

legal holiday *n US* jour *m* férié, fête *f* légale.

legalistic [ˌli:gə'lɪstɪk] *adj* légaliste, formaliste.

legality [li:'gælətɪ] *n* légalité *f*.

legalization [ˌli:gəlaɪ'zeɪʃn] *n* légalisation *f*.

legalize, ise ['li:gəlaɪz] *vt* légaliser, rendre légal.

legally ['li:gəlɪ] *adv* légalement ■ **to be ~ binding** avoir force de loi, être juridiquement contraignant ■ **to be held ~ responsible for sthg** être tenu légalement *OR* juridiquement responsable de qqch.

legal pad *n US* bloc-notes *m*.

legal separation *n* LAW séparation *f* de corps.

legal tender *n* monnaie *f* légale ■ **these coins are no longer ~** ces pièces n'ont plus cours *OR* ont été démonétisées.

legate ['legɪt] *n* RELIG légat *m* ■ [gen] messager *m*, - ère *f*.

legation [lɪ'geɪʃn] *n* légation *f*.

legend ['ledʒənd] *n* **1.** [myth] légende *f* ■ **she became a ~ in her own lifetime** elle est entrée dans la légende de son vivant **2.** [inscription] légende *f*.

legendary ['ledʒəndrɪ] *adj* légendaire.

leggings ['legɪŋz] *npl* caleçon *m (porté comme pantalon)*.

leggy ['legɪ] (*comp* **leggier**, *superl* **leggiest**) *adj* [person] tout en jambes ■ [colt, young animal] haut sur pattes.

Leghorn [ˌleg'hɔ:n] *pr n* Livourne.

legibility [ˌledʒɪ'bɪlətɪ] *n* lisibilité *f*.

legible ['ledʒəbl] *adj* lisible.

legibly ['ledʒəblɪ] *adv* lisiblement.

legion ['li:dʒən] <> *n* MIL & *fig* légion *f*.
<> *adj fml* légion *(inv)*.

legionary ['li:dʒənərɪ] (*pl* **legionaries**) <> *n* légionnaire *m*.
<> *adj* de la légion.

legionnaire [ˌli:dʒə'neəʳ] *n* légionnaire *m*.

legionnaire's disease *n* maladie *f* du légionnaire.

leg iron *n* MED appareil *m* orthopédique.

legislate ['ledʒɪsleɪt] *vi* légiférer ■ **you can't ~ for everything** *fig* on ne peut pas tout prévoir.

legislation [ˌledʒɪs'leɪʃn] *n* législation *f* ■ **a piece of ~** une loi ■ **to bring in ~ in favour of/against sthg** légiférer en faveur de/contre qqch.

legislative ['ledʒɪslətɪv] *adj* législatif ■ **~ assembly** assemblée *f* législative.

legislator ['ledʒɪsleɪtəʳ] *n* législateur *m*, - trice *f*.

legislature ['ledʒɪsleɪtʃəʳ] *n* (corps *m*) législatif *m*.

legit [lə'dʒɪt] *adj inf* réglo.

legitimacy [lɪ'dʒɪtɪməsɪ] *n* légitimité *f*.

legitimate <> *adj* [lɪ'dʒɪtɪmət] **1.** [legal, lawful] légitime **2.** [valid] légitime, valable ■ **it would be perfectly ~ to ask them to pay** on serait tout à fait en droit d'exiger qu'ils paient **3.** [theatre] sérieux.
<> *vt* [lɪ'dʒɪtɪmeɪt] légitimer.

legitimately [lɪ'dʒɪtɪmətlɪ] *adv* **1.** [legally, lawfully] légitimement **2.** [justifiably] légitimement, avec raison.

legitimize, ise [lɪ'dʒɪtəmaɪz] *vt* légitimer.

legless ['leglɪs] *adj* **1.** [without legs] cul-de-jatte **2.** *UK inf* [drunk] bourré, soûl.

leg-pull *n inf* canular *m*, farce *f*.

leg-pulling *n (U) inf* blagues *fpl*, mise *f* en boîte.

legroom ['legrʊm] *n* place *f* pour les jambes.

leg-up *n* : **to give sb a ~** *liter* faire la courte échelle à qqn ; *fig* donner un coup de main *OR* de pouce à qqn.

legwarmers ['leg,wɔ:məz] *npl* jambières *fpl*.

legwork ['legwɜ:k] *n inf* **who's going to do the ~?** qui va se taper la marche?

Leicester Square ['lestəʳ-] *pr n place populaire de Londres connue pour ses grands cinémas.*

Leics *written abbr of* **Leicestershire**.

leisure [*UK* 'leʒəʳ, *US* 'li:ʒər] <> *n (U)* **1.** [spare time] loisir *m*, loisirs *mpl*, temps *m* libre ■ **to be at ~ to do sthg** avoir (tout) le loisir de faire qqch ■ **I'll read it at (my) ~** je le lirai à tête reposée **2.** [relaxation] loisir *m* ■ **to lead a life of ~** mener une vie oisive ■ **he's a man of ~** il mène une vie de rentier.
<> *comp* [activity, clothes] de loisir *OR* loisirs ■ **~ industry** industrie *f* des loisirs.

leisure centre *n* centre *m* de loisirs.

leisured [*UK* 'leʒəd, *US* 'li:ʒərd] *adj* oisif, qui mène une vie oisive.

leisurely [*UK* 'leʒəlɪ, *US* 'li:ʒərlɪ] <> *adj* [gesture] mesuré, nonchalant ■ [lifestyle] paisible, indolent ■ **we went for a ~ stroll through the park** nous sommes allés faire une petite balade dans le parc ■ **at a ~ pace** sans se presser ■ **he spoke in a ~ way** il parlait en prenant son temps.
<> *adv* [calmly] paisiblement, tranquillement ■ [unhurriedly] sans se presser.

leisurewear ['leʒəweəʳ] *n* vêtements *mpl* de sport.

leitmotiv, leitmotif ['laɪtməʊ,ti:f] *n* [gen - MUS] leitmotiv *m*.

lemming ['lemɪŋ] *n* lemming *m*.

lemon ['lemən] <> *n* **1.** [fruit] citron *m* ■ [tree] citronnier *m* ■ **~ juice** jus *m* de citron ; [lemon squash] citronnade *f* ; [freshly squeezed] citron pressé ■ **~ squash** citronnade *f*, sirop *m* de citron ■ **~ tea** thé *m* au citron **2.** [colour] jaune citron *m inv* **3.** *UK inf* [awkward person] idiot *m*, - e *f*.
<> *adj* [colour] (jaune) citron *(inv)* ■ [flavour] citron *(inv)*.

lemonade [ˌlemə'neɪd] *n* [in UK] limonade *f* ■ [in US] citron *m* pressé.

lemon balm *n* BOT mélisse *f*, citronnelle *f*.

lemon cheese, lemon curd *n* lemon curd *m*, crème *f* au citron.

lemongrass ['lemənɡrɑ:s] *n (U)* citronnelle *f*.

lemon sole *n* limande-sole *f*.

lemon squeezer *n* presse-citron *m*.

lemur ['li:məʳ] *n* lémur *m*, maki *m*.

lend [lend] (*pret & pp* **lent** [lent]) *vt* **1.** [money, book] prêter ■ **to ~ sthg to sb, to ~ sb sthg** prêter qqch à qqn **2.** [contribute] apporter, conférer ■ **her presence lent glamour to the occasion** sa présence a conféré un certain éclat à l'événement **3.** [give - support] apporter ; [- name] prêter ■ **to ~ sb a hand** donner un coup de main à qqn ■ **you can't expect me to ~ my name to such an enterprise** ne comptez pas sur moi pour prêter mon nom à *OR* cautionner cette affaire ■ **to ~ an ear** *fig* prêter l'oreille

4. [adapt - to circumstances, interpretation] : **the novel doesn't ~ itself to being filmed** le roman ne se prête pas à une adaptation cinématographique.

lender ['lendəʳ] *n* prêteur *m*, - euse *f*.

lending ['lendɪŋ] *n* prêt *m*.

lending library *n* bibliothèque *f* de prêt.

lending rate *n* taux *m* (d'un prêt).

length [leŋθ] *n* **1.** [measurement, distance] longueur *f* ▪ **what ~ is the room?** quelle est la longueur de la pièce? ▪ **the room is 20 metres in ~** la pièce fait 20 mètres de long *OR* de longueur ▪ **a river 200 kilometres in ~** un fleuve long de 200 kilomètres ▪ **we walked the ~ of the garden** nous sommes allés jusqu'au bout du jardin ▪ **flower beds ran the ~ of the street** il y avait des massifs de fleurs tout le long de la rue ▪ **throughout the ~ and breadth of the continent** partout sur le continent **2.** [effort] : **to go to considerable** *OR* **great ~s to do sthg** se donner beaucoup de mal pour faire qqch ▪ **he would go to any ~s to meet her** il ferait n'importe quoi pour la rencontrer **3.** [duration] durée *f*, longueur *f* ▪ **the ~ of time required to do sthg** le temps qu'il faut pour faire qqch ▪ **bonuses are given for ~ of service** les primes sont accordées selon l'ancienneté **4.** [of text] longueur *f* ▪ **articles must be less than 5,000 words in ~** les articles doivent faire moins de 5 000 mots **5.** SPORT [in racing, rowing] longueur *f* ▪ **to win by a ~** gagner d'une longueur ▮ [in swimming] longueur *f* (de bassin) ▪ **I swam ten ~s** j'ai fait dix longueurs **6.** [piece - of string, tubing] morceau *m*, bout *m* ; [- of wallpaper] lé *m* ; [- of fabric] pièce *f* **7.** LING [of syllable, vowel] longueur *f*.

◆ **at length** *adv phr* [finally] finalement, enfin ▪ [in detail, for a long time] longuement ▪ **she went on** *OR* **spoke at some ~ about her experience** elle a parlé assez longuement de son expérience.

-length *in cpds* à hauteur de ▪ **knee~ socks** chaussettes *fpl* (montantes), mi-bas *mpl*.

lengthen ['leŋθən] ◇ *vi* [shadow] s'allonger ▪ [day] rallonger ▪ [holiday, visit] se prolonger.
◇ *vt* [garment] allonger, rallonger ▪ [holiday, visit] prolonger ▪ LING [vowel] allonger.

lengthily ['leŋθɪlɪ] *adv* longuement.

lengthways ['leŋθweɪz], **lengthwise** ['leŋθwaɪz] ◇ *adv* dans le sens de la longueur, longitudinalement.
◇ *adj* en longueur, longitudinal.

lengthy ['leŋθɪ] (*comp* **lengthier**, *superl* **lengthiest**) *adj* (très) long ▪ **after a ~ wait** après avoir attendu très longtemps, après une attente interminable.

leniency ['li:njənsɪ] *n* clémence *f*, indulgence *f*.

lenient ['li:njənt] *adj* [jury, sentence] clément ▪ [attitude, parent] indulgent ▪ **you shouldn't be so ~ with them** vous devriez être plus strict avec eux.

leniently ['li:njəntlɪ] *adv* avec clémence *OR* indulgence ▪ **the magistrate had treated him ~** le magistrat s'était montré indulgent *OR* avait fait preuve d'indulgence à son égard.

Lenin ['lenɪn] *pr n* Lénine.

Leninist ['lenɪnɪst] ◇ *adj* léniniste.
◇ *n* léniniste *mf*.

lens [lenz] *n* **1.** OPT [in microscope, telescope] lentille *f* ▪ [in spectacles] verre *m* ▪ [in camera] objectif *m* ▪ [contact lens] lentille *f* *OR* verre *m* (de contact) **2.** ANAT [in eye] cristallin *m*.

lens cap *n* bouchon *m* d'objectif.

lens hood *n* pare-soleil *m inv*.

lent [lent] *pt & pp* ▻ **lend**.

Lent [lent] *n* RELIG le carême ▪ **I've given up sugar for ~** j'ai renoncé au sucre pour le carême.

lentil ['lentɪl] *n* BOT & CULIN lentille *f* ▪ **~ soup** soupe *f* aux lentilles.

Leo ['li:əʊ] ◇ *pr n* ASTROL & ASTRON Lion *m*.
◇ *n* : **he's a ~** il est (du signe du) Lion.

leonine ['li:ənaɪn] *adj lit* léonin *lit*, de lion.

leopard ['lepəd] *n* léopard *m* ▪ **a ~ cannot change its spots** *prov* chassez le naturel, il revient au galop *prov*.

leopardess ['lepədɪs] *n* léopard *m* femelle.

leopard skin ◇ *n* peau *f* de léopard.
◇ *adj* [coat, rug] en (peau de) léopard.

leotard ['li:ətɑ:d] *n* body *m (pour le sport)*.

leper ['lepəʳ] *n* lépreux *m*, -euse *f* ▪ *fig* pestiféré *m*, - e *f* ▪ **~ colony** léproserie *f*.

lepidopterist [,lepɪ'dɒptərɪst] *n* lépidoptériste *mf*.

leprechaun ['leprəkɔ:n] *n* lutin *m*.

leprosy ['leprəsɪ] *n* lèpre *f*.

lesbian ['lezbɪən] ◇ *adj* lesbien.
◇ *n* lesbienne *f*.

lesbianism ['lezbɪənɪzm] *n* lesbianisme *m*.

lese majesty [,li:z'mædʒɪstɪ] *n* (crime *m* de) lèse-majesté *f inv*.

lesion ['li:ʒn] *n* lésion *f*.

Lesotho [lə'su:tu:] *pr n* Lesotho *m* ▪ **in ~** au Lesotho.

less [les] ◇ *det (compar of little)* moins de ▪ **~ money/time/bread** moins d'argent/de temps/de pain ▪ **of ~ importance/value** de moindre importance/valeur ▪ **I seem to have ~ and ~ energy** on dirait que j'ai de moins en moins d'énergie.
◇ *pron (compar of little)* moins ▪ **there was ~ than I expected** il y en avait moins que je m'y attendais ▪ **we found we had ~ and ~ to say to each other** nous nous sommes rendu compte que nous avions de moins en moins de choses à nous dire ⊙ **~ of : the evening was ~ of a success than she had hoped** la soirée était moins réussie qu'elle ne l'avait espéré ▪ **let's hope we see ~ of them in future** espérons que nous les verrons moins souvent à l'avenir ▪ **~ of your noise!** faites moins de bruit! ▪ **~ than : it took me ~ than five minutes** ça m'a pris moins de cinq minutes ▪ **you won't get another one like it for ~ than $1,000** vous n'en retrouverez pas un comme ça à moins de 1 000 dollars ▪ **nothing ~ than a four-star hotel is good enough for them** il leur faut au moins un quatre étoiles ▪ **in ~ than no time** en un rien de temps, en moins de deux ▪ **it would have been ~ than fair to have kept it from her** ça aurait été vraiment injuste de le lui cacher.
◇ *adv* moins ▪ **the blue dress costs ~** la robe bleue coûte moins cher ▪ **~ and ~ interesting** de moins en moins intéressant ⊙ **I don't think any (the) ~ of her** *OR* **I think no ~ of her because of what happened** ce qui s'est passé ne l'a pas fait baisser dans mon estime ▪ **we don't like her any the ~ for all her faults** nous ne l'aimons pas moins à cause de ses défauts.
◇ *prep* : **that's £300 ~ ten per cent for store card holders** ça fait 300 livres moins dix pour cent avec la carte du magasin.

◆ **much less** *conj phr* encore moins ▪ **he wouldn't even phone her, much ~ visit her** il ne voulait même pas l'appeler, encore moins aller la voir.

◆ **no less** *adv phr* rien de moins ▪ **he won the Booker prize, no ~!** il a obtenu le Booker prize, rien de moins que ça! ▪ **she married a duke, no ~!** elle a épousé un duc, ni plus ni moins! ▪ **she had invited no ~ a person than the President himself** elle avait invité rien moins que le président lui-même.

◆ **no less than** *adv phr* pas moins de ▪ **taxes rose by no ~ than 15%** les impôts ont augmenté de 15 %, ni plus ni moins.

◆ **still less** = much less.

lessee [le'si:] *n* preneur *m*, - euse *f* (à bail).

lessen ['lesn] ◇ *vt* [cost, importance] diminuer, réduire ▪ [impact, effect] atténuer, amoindrir ▪ [shock] amortir.
◇ *vi* s'atténuer, s'amoindrir.

lessening ['lesənɪŋ] *n (U)* [of cost, importance] diminution *f* ▪ [of value, rate] réduction *f*, diminution *f*, baisse *f* ▪ [of powers] réduction *f*, baisse *f* ▪ [of impact, effect] amoindrissement *m* ▪ [of shock] amortissement *m*.

lesser ['lesəʳ] *adj* **1.** [gen] moindre ▪ **to a ~ extent** dans une moindre mesure ▪ **~ mortals like me** *hum* les simples mortels comme moi **2.** BOT, GEOG & ZOOL petit.

lesser-known *adj* moins connu.

lesson ['lesn] *n* **1.** [gen] leçon *f* ■ SCH leçon *f*, cours *m* ■ **an English ~** une leçon *OR* un cours d'anglais ■ **a dancing/driving ~** une leçon de danse/de conduite ■ **to give a ~** donner un cours *OR* une leçon ■ **private ~s** cours *mpl* particuliers **2.** [example] leçon *f* ■ **her downfall was a ~ to us all** sa chute nous a servi de leçon à tous ■ **to teach sb a ~** donner une (bonne) leçon à qqn **3.** RELIG leçon *f*, lecture *f*.

lessor [le'sɔːr] *n* bailleur *m*, - eresse *f*.

lest [lest] *conj lit* de peur que, de crainte que ■ **they whispered ~ the children should hear** ils parlèrent à voix basse de peur *OR* de crainte que les enfants ne les entendent.

let[1] [let] (*pret & pp* **let**, *cont* **letting**) ◇ *vt* **1.** [rent] louer ■ **'to ~'** 'à louer' **2.** *arch & lit &* MED : **to ~ (sb's) blood** faire une saignée (à qqn).
◇ *n* **1.** [rental] location *f* ■ **she took a six-month ~ on a house** elle a loué une maison pour six mois **2.** SPORT [in tennis, squash] : **~ (ball)** let *m* ■ **the ball was a ~** la balle était let **3.** *fml* [hindrance] : **without ~ or hindrance** librement, sans entrave.
◆ **let out** *vt sep* [rent] louer.

let[2] [let] (*pret & pp* **let**, *cont* **letting**) *vt* **1.** [permit] laisser, permettre ■ **she ~ them watch the programme** elle les a laissés regarder l'émission ■ **I couldn't come because my parents wouldn't ~ me** je ne suis pas venu parce que mes parents ne me l'ont pas permis ‖ [allow] laisser ■ **I ~ the cakes burn** j'ai laissé brûler les gâteaux ■ **~ me buy you all a drink** laissez-moi vous offrir un verre ■ **don't ~ me stop you going** je ne veux pas t'empêcher d'y aller ■ **to ~ sb past** laisser passer qqn ■ **they don't ~ anyone near the reactor** ils ne laissent personne approcher du réacteur ■ **to ~ sb have sthg** donner qqch à qqn ■ **don't be selfish, ~ him have a cake!** ne sois pas égoïste, donne-lui un gâteau! ■ **she ~ him know what she thought of him** elle lui a fait savoir ce qu'elle pensait de lui ■ **please ~ me know if there's any change** veuillez me prévenir s'il y a du changement ■ **please God don't ~ anything happen to her!** faites qu'il ne lui arrive rien! ➲ **to ~ sb have it** *inf* [physically] casser la figure à qqn ; [verbally] dire ses quatre vérités à qqn
2. [followed by 'go'] : **to ~ sb go** [allow to leave] laisser partir qqn ; [release] relâcher qqn ; *euph* [dismiss, fire] licencier qqn ■ **to ~ sb/sthg go** [allow to escape] laisser échapper qqn/qqch ■ **to ~ sb/sthg go, to ~ go of sb/sthg** [stop holding] lâcher qqn/qqch ■ **~ me go!, ~ go of me!** lâchez-moi! ■ **to ~ o.s. go** [neglect o.s., relax] se laisser aller ■ **he's really ~ the garden go** il a vraiment négligé le jardin ■ **that remark was uncalled-for but ~ it go** cette réflexion était déplacée mais restons-en là ■ **give me £5 and we'll ~ it go at that** donne-moi 5 livres et on n'en parle plus
3. [in making suggestions] : **~'s go!** allons-y! ■ **don't ~'s go out** *OR* **~'s not go out tonight** ne sortons pas ce soir ■ **shall we have a picnic? – yes, ~'s!** si on faisait un pique-nique? – d'accord!
4. [to focus attention] : **~ me start by saying how pleased I am to be here** laissez-moi d'abord vous dire combien je suis ravi d'être ici ■ **~ me try and explain** attendez que je vous explique
5. [in hesitation] : **~ me think** attends, voyons voir ■ **~ me see, ~'s see** voyons
6. [to express criticism or defiance] : **if she doesn't want my help, ~ her do it herself!** si elle ne veut pas de mon aide, qu'elle le fasse toute seule! ■ **~ them talk!** laisse-les dire!
7. [in threats] : **don't ~ me catch you at it again!** que je ne t'y reprenne plus!
8. [in commands] : **~ the festivities begin!** que la fête commence! ■ **~ them be!** laisse-les tranquilles!, fiche-leur la paix!
9. [in making assumptions] : **~ us suppose that...** supposons que... ■ **~ x equal 17** MATHS soit x égal à 17.
◆ **let alone** *conj phr* : **I wouldn't go out with him, ~ alone marry him** je ne sortirais même pas avec lui, alors pour ce qui est de l'épouser...
◆ **let down** *vt sep* **1.** [disappoint] décevoir ■ **I felt really ~ down** j'étais vraiment déçu ■ **our old car has never ~ us down** notre vieille voiture ne nous a jamais laissés tomber ■ **she ~ us down badly** elle nous a proprement laissés tomber
2. [lower, let fall - object] baisser, (faire) descendre ; [- hair] dénouer ■ **to ~ sb down gently** *fig* traiter qqn avec ménagement
3. SEW rallonger ■ **to ~ (the hem of) a dress down** rallonger une robe
4. [deflate] dégonfler.
◆ **let in** *vt sep* **1.** [person, animal] laisser entrer ■ **to ~ sb in** ouvrir (la porte) à qqn, faire entrer qqn ■ **here's the key to ~ yourself in** voici la clé pour entrer
2. [air, water] laisser passer ■ **the roof ~s the rain in** le toit laisse entrer *OR* passer la pluie ■ **my shoes ~ in water** mes chaussures prennent l'eau
3. AUT : **to ~ in the clutch** embrayer.
◆ **let in for** *vt sep* : **he didn't realize what he was letting himself in for** il ne savait pas à quoi il s'engageait.
◆ **let in on** *vt sep* : **to ~ sb in on sthg** mettre qqn au courant de qqch ■ **have you ~ him in on the secret?** lui avez-vous confié le secret?
◆ **let into** *vt sep* **1.** [allow to enter] laisser entrer
2. [allow to know] : **I'll ~ you into a secret** je vais te confier un secret
3. [insert] encastrer ■ **the pipes are ~ into the wall** les tuyaux sont encastrés dans le mur.
◆ **let off** ◇ *vt sep* **1.** [excuse] dispenser ■ **to ~ sb off doing sthg** dispenser qqn de faire qqch
2. [allow to leave] laisser partir ■ [allow to disembark] laisser descendre ■ **we were ~ off an hour early** on nous a laissés partir une heure plus tôt
3. [criminal, pupil, child] ne pas punir ■ **the judge ~ him off lightly** le juge a fait preuve d'indulgence à son égard ■ **she was ~ off with a fine** elle s'en est tirée avec une amende
4. [bomb, explosive] faire exploser ■ [firework] faire partir ■ [gun] laisser partir
5. [release - steam, liquid] laisser échapper
6. [rent] louer.
◇ *vi insep inf inf* [break wind] péter.
◆ **let on** ◇ *vi insep inf* **she never ~ on** elle ne l'a jamais dit ■ **somebody ~ on about the wedding to the press** quelqu'un a parlé du mariage à *OR* a révélé le mariage à la presse.
◇ *vt sep* [allow to embark] laisser monter.
◆ **let out** *vt sep* **1.** [allow to leave] laisser sortir ■ **the teacher ~ us out early** le professeur nous a laissés sortir plus tôt ■ **my secretary will ~ you out** ma secrétaire va vous reconduire ■ **don't get up, I'll ~ myself out** ne vous levez pas, je connais le chemin
2. [water, air] laisser échapper ■ **someone's ~ the air out of the tyres** quelqu'un a dégonflé les pneus
3. [shout, oath, whistle] laisser échapper
4. [secret] révéler
5. SEW [dress, trousers] élargir
6. AUT : **to ~ out the clutch** débrayer.
◆ **let up** *vi insep* **1.** [stop] arrêter ■ [diminish] diminuer ■ **the rain didn't ~ up all day** il n'a pas cessé *OR* arrêté de pleuvoir de toute la journée
2. [relax] : **he never ~s up** il ne s'accorde aucun répit ■ **don't ~ up now, you're in the lead** ce n'est pas le moment de faiblir, tu es en tête.
◆ **let up on** *vt insep inf* **to ~ up on sb** lâcher la bride à qqn.

letdown ['letdaʊn] *n inf* déception *f* ■ **the party was a bit of a ~** la fête a été plutôt décevante.

lethal ['liːθl] *adj* fatal, mortel ■ MED létal ■ **a ~ weapon** une arme meurtrière ■ **in the hands of a child, a plastic bag can be ~** dans les mains d'un enfant, un sac en plastique peut être dangereux ■ **this substance is ~ to rats** c'est une substance mortelle pour les rats ➲ **~ dose** dose *f* mortelle *OR* létale ■ **~ gene** gène *m* létal.

lethally ['liːθəlɪ] *adv* mortellement.

lethargic [lə'θɑːdʒɪk] *adj* [person, sleep] léthargique ■ [atmosphere] soporifique.

lethargy ['leθədʒɪ] *n* léthargie *f*.

let-out *n UK* [excuse] prétexte *m* ■ [way out] échappatoire *f*.

Letraset® ['letrəset] *n* Letraset®.

let's [lets] = **let us**.

Lett [let] *n* Letton *m*, - on(n)e *f*.

letter ['letər] ◇ *n* **1.** [of alphabet] lettre *f* ■ **the ~ B** la lettre B ■ **a six-~ word** un mot de six lettres ■ **he's got a lot of ~s after his name** il est bardé de diplômes **2.** *fig* [exact meaning] lettre *f* ■ **the ~ of the law** la lettre de la loi ■ **she obeyed the instructions to the ~** elle a suivi les instructions à la lettre *OR* au pied de

la lettre **3.** [communication] lettre *f* ■ [mail] courrier *m* ■ **by ~** par lettre *OR* courrier ■ **he's a good ~ writer** il écrit régulièrement ■ **a ~ of introduction** une lettre de recommandation ■ **~s to the editor** [in newspapers, magazines] courrier des lecteurs ■ **the ~s of D. H. Lawrence** la correspondance de D. H. Lawrence ▶ **~ of credit** COMM lettre de crédit ■ **~s of credence** ADMIN lettres de créance.
◇ *vt* [write] inscrire des lettres sur ■ [engrave] graver (des lettres sur) ■ [manuscript] enluminer ■ **the title was ~ed in gilt** le titre était inscrit en lettres dorées ■ **the rooms are ~ed from A to K** les salles portent des lettres de A à K.
◆ **letters** *npl fml* [learning] belles-lettres *fpl* ■ **a man of ~s** [scholar] un lettré ; [writer] un homme de lettres ■ **English ~s** *UK* littérature *f* anglaise.

letter bomb *n* lettre *f* piégée.

letterbox ['letəbɒks] *n UK* boîte *f* à *OR* aux lettres.

letter card *n* carte-lettre *f*.

letterhead ['letəhed] *n* en-tête *m inv (de lettre)*.

lettering ['letərɪŋ] *n (U)* [inscription] inscription *f* ■ [characters] caractères *mpl*.

letter opener *n* coupe-papier *m inv*.

letter-perfect *adj US* [person] qui connait son texte parfaitement ■ [text] parfait.

letter quality *n* COMPUT qualité *f* courrier ■ **near ~** qualité quasi-courrier *(pour une imprimante)*.
◆ **letter-quality** *adj* qualité courrier *inv*.

letter rack *n* porte-lettres *m inv*.

letters patent *npl* patente *f*.

letting ['letɪŋ] *n* [of house, property] location *f*.

lettuce ['letɪs] *n* [gen - CULIN] salade *f* ■ BOT laitue *f*.

letup ['letʌp] *n* [stop] arrêt *m*, pause *f* ■ [abatement] répit *m* ■ **it's been raining for days without a ~** ça fait des jours qu'il n'arrête pas de pleuvoir *OR* qu'il pleut sans arrêt.

leukaemia *UK*, **leukemia** *US* [lu:'ki:mɪə] *n (U)* leucémie *f* ■ **he has ~** il a une leucémie, il est atteint de leucémie.

levee ['levɪ] *n* **1.** *US* [embankment] levée *f* ■ [surrounding field] digue *f* **2.** *US* [landing place] quai *m* **3.** HIST [in royal chamber] lever *m* (du roi) ■ *UK* [at court] réception *f* à la cour.

level ['levl] (*UK pret & pp* **levelled**, *cont* **levelling**) (*US pret & pp* **leveled**, *cont* **leveling**) ◇ *n* **1.** [height - in a horizontal plane] niveau *m* ; [- in a vertical plane] hauteur *f* ■ **at ground ~** au niveau du sol ■ **water seeks its own ~** c'est le principe des vases communicants ■ **the sink is on a ~ with the work surface** l'évier est au niveau du *OR* de niveau avec le plan de travail ■ **on the same ~** au même niveau
2. [amount] niveau *m* ■ [percentage] taux *m* ■ **noise ~s are far too high** le niveau sonore est bien trop élevé ■ **a low ~ of sugar in the bloodstream** un faible taux de sucre dans le sang ■ **inflation has reached new ~s** l'inflation a atteint de nouveaux sommets ■ **check the oil ~** [in car] vérifiez le niveau d'huile
3. [rank] niveau *m*, échelon *m* ■ **at cabinet/national ~** à l'échelon ministériel/national ■ **at a regional ~** au niveau régional
4. [standard] niveau *m* ■ **her ~ of English is poor** elle n'a pas un très bon niveau en anglais ■ **students at beginners'~** étudiants *mpl* au niveau débutant ■ **she's on a different ~ from the others** elle n'est pas au même niveau que les autres ■ **to come down to sb's ~** se mettre au niveau de qqn ■ **don't descend** *OR* **sink to their ~** ne t'abaisse pas à leur niveau
5. [point of view] : **on a personal ~, I really like him** sur le plan personnel, je l'aime beaucoup ■ **on a practical ~** du point de vue pratique
6. [storey] niveau *m*, étage *m* ■ **the library is on ~ three** la bibliothèque est au niveau trois *OR* au troisième étage
7. [flat land] plat *m* ■ **100 km/h on the ~** 100 km/h sur le plat
8. [for woodwork, building etc] : **(spirit) ~** niveau *m* (à bulle)
9. *inf phr* **on the ~** [honest] honnête, réglo.
◇ *adj* **1.** [flat] plat ■ **a ~ spoonful** une cuillerée rase ■ **to make sthg ~** aplanir qqch
2. [at the same height] au même niveau, à la même hauteur ■ [at the same standard] au même niveau ■ **the terrace is ~ with the pool** la terrasse est au même niveau que *OR* de plain-pied avec la piscine ■ **his head is just ~ with my shoulder** sa tête m'arrive exactement à l'épaule
3. [in horizontal position] : **hold the tray ~** tenez le plateau à l'horizontale *OR* bien à plat ■ **to fly ~** AERON voler en palier
4. [equal] à égalité ■ **the leading cars are almost ~** les voitures de tête sont presque à la même hauteur ■ **to draw ~** se trouver à égalité ■ **the other runners drew ~ with me** les autres coureurs m'ont rattrapé
5. [calm, steady] calme, mesuré ■ **to keep a ~ head** garder la tête froide
6. *inf* [honest] honnête, réglo
7. *inf phr* **to do one's ~ best** faire de son mieux ■ **~ pegging** *UK* à égalité.
◇ *vt* **1.** [flatten] aplanir, niveler
2. [aim] : **to ~ a gun at sb** braquer une arme sur qqn ■ **a lot of criticism has been levelled at me** on m'a beaucoup critiqué.
◇ *vi* : **to ~ with sb** *inf* être franc avec qqn, jouer franc jeu avec qqn.
◆ **level down** *vt sep* [surface] aplanir, niveler ■ [standard] niveler par le bas.
◆ **level off** ◇ *vi insep* **1.** [production, rise, development] s'équilibrer, se stabiliser ■ **the curve on the graph ~s off at this point** la courbe du graphique se stabilise à partir d'ici
2. AERON amorcer un palier.
◇ *vt sep* [flatten] aplatir, niveler.
◆ **level out** ◇ *vi insep* **1.** [road, surface] s'aplanir
2. [stabilize] se stabiliser.
◇ *vt sep* niveler.
◆ **level up** *vt sep* niveler (par le haut).

level crossing *n UK* passage *m* à niveau.

leveler *US* = **leveller**.

level-headed [-'hedɪd] *adj* équilibré, pondéré, réfléchi ■ **he's a ~ boy** c'est un garçon qui a la tête sur les épaules.

leveling *US* = **levelling**.

leveller *UK*, **leveler** *US* ['levələr] *n* POL égalitariste *mf*, niveleur *m*, -euse *f* ■ **death is a great ~** nous sommes tous égaux devant la mort.
◆ **the Levellers** *npl* HIST les niveleurs *mpl*.

levelling *UK*, **leveling** *US* ['levəlɪŋ] ◇ *n* nivellement *m*, aplanissement *m* ■ **a ~ up/down of salaries is desirable** un nivellement des salaires par le haut/par le bas est souhaitable ■ **a ~ off of prices** une stabilisation des prix.
◇ *adj* de nivellement.

lever [*UK* 'li:vər, *US* 'levər] ◇ *n liter & fig* levier *m* ■ [smaller] manette *f*.
◇ *vt* manœuvrer à l'aide d'un levier ■ **they ~ed the engine into position** ils installèrent le moteur à l'aide d'un levier.
◆ **lever out** *vt sep* extraire *OR* extirper (à l'aide d'un levier) ■ *fig* **he ~ed himself out of bed** il s'extirpa du lit ■ **they ~ed the president out of office** ils ont délogé le président de son poste.
◆ **lever up** *vt sep* soulever (au moyen d'un levier) ■ **she ~ed herself up onto the rock** *fig* elle se hissa sur le rocher.

leverage [*UK* 'li:vərɪdʒ, *US* 'levərɪdʒ] *n* **1.** MECH force *f* (de levier) ■ **I can't get enough ~** je n'ai pas assez de prise **2.** [influence] : **the committee's findings give us considerable (political) ~** les conclusions de la commission constituent pour nous des moyens de pression considérables (sur le plan politique) **3.** *US* ECON effet *m* de levier.

leveret ['levərɪt] *n* levraut *m*.

leviathan [lɪ'vaɪəθn] *n* [ship] navire *m* géant ■ [institution, organization] institution *f OR* organisation *f* géante.
◆ **Leviathan** *pr n* Léviathan.

levitate ['levɪteɪt] ◇ *vi* léviter.
◇ *vt* faire léviter, soulever par lévitation.

levitation [,levɪ'teɪʃn] *n* lévitation *f*.

Levite ['li:vaɪt] *n* lévite *m*.

Leviticus [lɪ'vɪtɪkəs] *pr n* le Lévitique.

levity ['levətɪ] (*pl* **levities**) *n* légèreté *f*, manque *m* de sérieux.

levy ['levɪ] ◇ *n* (*pl* **levies**) **1.** [levying] prélèvement *m* ▪ **a capital ~ of 10%** un prélèvement de 10 % sur le capital **2.** [tax, duty] impôt *m*, taxe *f* ▪ **to impose a ~ on sugar imports** taxer les importations de sucre **3.** MIL levée *f*.
◇ *vt* (*pret & pp* **levied**) **1.** [impose - tax] prélever ; [- fine] imposer, infliger ▪ **to ~ a duty on imports** prélever une taxe sur les importations **2.** [collect - taxes, fine] lever, percevoir **3.** MIL [troops] lever **4.** [wage] : **to ~ war on small states** faire la guerre à de petits États.

lewd [lju:d] *adj* [behaviour] lubrique ▪ [speech] obscène.

lexeme ['leksi:m] *n* lexème *m*.

lexical ['leksɪkl] *adj* lexical.

lexicalize, ise ['leksɪkəlaɪz] *vt* lexicaliser.

lexicographer [ˌleksɪ'kɒgrəfəʳ] *n* lexicographe *mf*.

lexicography [ˌleksɪ'kɒgrəfɪ] *n* lexicographie *f*.

lexicologist [ˌleksɪ'kɒlədʒɪst] *n* lexicologue *mf*.

lexicology [ˌleksɪ'kɒlədʒɪ] *n* lexicologie *f*.

lexicon ['leksɪkən] *n* lexique *m*.

lexis ['leksɪs] *n* lexique *m*.

ley line *n ensemble de repères indiquant le tracé probable d'un chemin préhistorique.*

Lhasa ['lɑ:sə] *pr n* Lhassa.

LI *written abbr of* **Long Island**.

liability [ˌlaɪə'bɪlətɪ] (*pl* **liabilities**) *n* **1.** *(U)* LAW [responsibility] responsabilité *f* (légale) ▪ **he refused to admit ~ for the damage** il refusa d'endosser la responsabilité des dégâts **2.** *(U)* [eligibility] assujettissement *m* ▪ **~ for tax** assujettissement à l'impôt ▪ **~ for military service** obligations *fpl* militaires **3.** [hindrance] gêne *f*, handicap *m* ▪ **the house he had inherited was a real ~** la maison dont il avait hérité lui coûtait une petite fortune *OR* lui revenait cher ▪ **that man is a (total) ~** ce type est un vrai poids mort *OR* un véritable boulet.
◆ **liabilities** *npl* FIN [debts] passif *m*, engagements *mpl* financiers ▪ **to meet one's liabilities** faire face à ses engagements ▪ **liabilities on an estate** passif d'une succession.

liability suit *n US* LAW procès *m* en responsabilité civile.

liable ['laɪəbl] *adj* **1.** LAW [responsible] responsable ▪ **to be held ~ for sthg** être tenu (pour) responsable de qqch ▪ **to be ~ for sb's debts** répondre des dettes de qqn ▪ **you'll be ~ for damages** on sera en droit de vous demander *OR* réclamer des dommages et intérêts **2.** [likely] : **~ to** : **the programme is ~ to change** le programme est susceptible d'être modifié, il se peut que le programme subisse des modifications ▪ **he's ~ to arrive at any moment** il peut arriver d'une minute à l'autre ▪ **if you don't remind him, he's ~ to forget** si on ne lui rappelle pas, il risque d'oublier ▪ **~ to headaches** sujet aux maux de tête **3.** ADMIN : **to be ~ for tax** [person] être assujetti à *OR* redevable de l'impôt ; [goods] être assujetti à une taxe ▪ **offenders are ~ to a fine** les contrevenants sont passibles d'une amende ▪ **he is ~ to be prosecuted** il s'expose à des poursuites judiciaires ▮ MIL : **to be ~ for military service** être astreint au service militaire.

liaise [lɪ'eɪz] *vi* : **to ~ with sb** assurer la liaison avec qqn.

liaison [lɪ'eɪzɒn] *n* liaison *f*.

liana [lɪ'ɑ:nə] *n* liane *f*.

liar ['laɪəʳ] *n* menteur *m*, - euse *f*.

lib [lɪb] *n* = **liberation**.

Lib [lɪb] = **Liberal**.

libation [laɪ'beɪʃn] *n lit* [offering] libation *f* ▪ *hum* [drink] libations *fpl*.

Lib Dem [-dem] *n* = **Liberal Democrat**.

libel ['laɪbl] (*UK pret & pp* **libelled**, *cont* **libelling**) (*US pret & pp* **libeled**, *cont* **libeling**) ◇ *n* LAW [act of publishing] diffamation *f* ▪ [publication] écrit *m* diffamatoire ▪ *fig* [calumny] calomnie *f*, mensonge *m* ▪ **the ~ laws** la législation en matière de diffamation ▪ **~ suit** procès *m* en diffamation.
◇ *vt* LAW diffamer ▪ *fig* calomnier.

libellous *UK*, **libelous** *US* ['laɪbələs] *adj* diffamatoire.

liberal ['lɪbərəl] ◇ *adj* **1.** [tolerant - person] libéral, large d'esprit ; [- ideas, mind] libéral, large ; [- education] libéral ▪ **~ studies** ≃ programme *m* de culture générale **2.** [generous] libéral, généreux ▪ [copious - helping, portion] abondant, copieux ▪ **the cook was a bit too ~ with the salt** le cuisinier a eu la main un peu lourde avec le sel.
◇ *n* [moderate] : **she's a ~** elle est de centre-gauche.
◆ **Liberal** ◇ *adj* POL [19th century] libéral ▪ [today] de centre-gauche ▪ **the Liberal Party** le parti Libéral ▪ **the Liberal Democrats** *parti centriste britannique.*
◇ *n* [party member] libéral *m*, -e *f*.

liberal arts *npl* : **the ~** les sciences humaines.

liberalism ['lɪbərəlɪzm] *n* libéralisme *m*.

liberalize, ise ['lɪbərəlaɪz] *vt* libéraliser.

liberally ['lɪbərəlɪ] *adv* libéralement ▪ **a ~ spiced dish** un plat généreusement épicé.

liberal-minded [-maɪndɪd] *adj* large d'esprit.

liberate ['lɪbəreɪt] *vt* [gen] libérer ▪ CHEM libérer, dégager.

liberated ['lɪbəreɪtɪd] *adj* libéré.

liberating ['lɪbəreɪtɪŋ] *adj* libérateur.

liberation [ˌlɪbə'reɪʃn] *n* libération *f*.

liberation movement *n* mouvement *m* de libération.

liberation theology *n* théologie *f* de la libération.

liberator ['lɪbəreɪtəʳ] *n* libérateur *m*, - trice *f*.

Liberia [laɪ'bɪərɪə] *pr n* Liberia *m* ▪ **in ~** au Liberia.

Liberian [laɪ'bɪərɪən] ◇ *n* Libérien *m*, - enne *f*.
◇ *adj* libérien.

libertarian [ˌlɪbə'teərɪən] ◇ *adj* libertaire.
◇ *n* libertaire *mf*.

libertarianism [ˌlɪbə'teərɪənɪzm] *n* [doctrine] doctrine *f* libertaire ▪ [political ideas] convictions *fpl* libertaires.

libertine ['lɪbəti:n] ◇ *adj* libertin.
◇ *n* libertin *m*, - e *f*.

liberty ['lɪbətɪ] (*pl* **liberties**) *n* [in behaviour] liberté *f* ▪ **to take liberties with sb** prendre *OR* se permettre des libertés avec qqn ▪ **to take liberties with the truth** prendre des libertés avec la vérité ▪ **I took the ~ of inviting them** j'ai pris la liberté *OR* je me suis permis de les inviter ▮ [cheek] : **what a ~!** quel toupet!
◆ **at liberty** *adj phr* : **the criminals are still at ~** les criminels sont toujours en liberté *OR* courent toujours ▪ **I'm not at ~ to say** il ne m'est pas possible *OR* permis de le dire.

liberty cap *n* bonnet *m* phrygien *OR* d'affranchi.

libido [lɪ'bi:dəʊ] (*pl* **libidos**) *n* libido *f*.

Libra ['li:brə] ◇ *pr n* ASTROL & ASTRON Balance *f*.
◇ *n* : **he's a ~** il est (du signe de la) Balance.

librarian [laɪ'breərɪən] *n* bibliothécaire *mf*.

librarianship [laɪ'breərɪənʃɪp] *n* [science] bibliothéconomie *f*.

library ['laɪbrərɪ] (*pl* **libraries**) ◇ *n* **1.** [gen] bibliothèque *f* ▪ **the Library of Congress** la bibliothèque du Congrès *(équivalent américain de la Bibliothèque Nationale)* **2.** [published series] bibliothèque *f*, collection *f* **3.** COMPUT bibliothèque *f*.
◇ *comp* [book, card] de bibliothèque.

library edition *n* édition *f* de luxe.

librettist [lɪ'bretɪst] *n* librettiste *mf*.

libretto [lɪ'bretəʊ] (*pl* **librettos** *OR pl* **libretti** [-tɪ]) *n* MUS livret *m*, libretto *m*.

Libya ['lɪbɪə] *pr n* Libye *f* ▪ **in ~** en Libye.

Libyan ['lɪbɪən] ◇ *n* Libyen *m*, - enne *f*.
◇ *adj* libyen ▪ **the ~ Desert** le désert de Libye.

lice [laɪs] *pl* ▷ **louse**.

licence *UK*, **license** *US* ['laɪsəns] *n* **1.** [permit] permis *m* ▪ [for marriage] certificat *m* de publication des bans ▪ [for trade, bar] licence *f* ▪ [for TV, radio] redevance *f* ▪ [for pilot] brevet *m* ▪ [for driver] permis *m* (de conduire) ▪ **do you have a TV ~?** avez-vous payé la redevance (télé) ? ▪ **a ~ to sell alcoholic drinks**

une licence de débit de boissons **2.** ADMIN & COMM [permission] licence *f*, autorisation *f* ■ **to marry by special ~** ≃ se marier sans publication de bans ■ **a ~ to print money** *fig* **: that job's a ~ to print money!** ce travail est une sinécure! **3.** [liberty] licence *f*, liberté *f* ■ **artistic ~** licence artistique **4.** [immoral behaviour] licence *f*, débordements *mpl*.

licence number *n* [on vehicle] numéro *m* d'immatriculation ■ [on driving licence] numéro *m* de permis de conduire.

license ['laɪsəns] ◇ *n US* = **licence**.
◇ *vt* **1.** ADMIN & COMM [premises, trader] accorder une licence OR une autorisation à ■ **~d to practise medicine** habilité à exercer la médecine ■ **to ~ a car** immatriculer une voiture **2.** [allow] **: to ~ sb to do sthg** autoriser qqn à faire qqch, permettre à qqn de faire qqch.

licensed ['laɪsənst] *adj* **1.** COMM fabriqué sous licence ■ [for alcohol] **: these premises are ~ to sell alcoholic drinks** cet établissement est autorisé à vendre des boissons alcoolisées ▶ **~ premises** [bar, pub] débit *m* de boissons ; [restaurant, cafeteria] établissement *m* autorisé à vendre des boissons alcoolisées **2.** [pilot] breveté ■ [driver] qui a son permis (de conduire).

licensed practical nurse *n US* infirmier *m*, - ère *f*.

licensee [,laɪsən'siː] *n* [gen] titulaire *mf* d'une licence OR d'un permis ■ [pub-owner, landlord] débitant *m*, - e *f* (de boissons).

license plate *n US* plaque *f* minéralogique OR d'immatriculation.

licensing ['laɪsənsɪŋ] *n* [of car] immatriculation *f* ■ [of activity] autorisation *f* ■ **~ authority** *organisme chargé de la délivrance des licences.*

licensing hours *npl* [in UK] *heures d'ouverture des pubs.*

LICENSING HOURS

Les heures d'ouverture des pubs ont longtemps été conformes à une réglementation très stricte (liée à la législation sur la vente des boissons alcoolisées), mais celle-ci a été assouplie en 1988. Les pubs peuvent désormais rester ouverts de 11h à 23h (le dimanche de 12h à 22h30). Les personnes de moins de 18 ans n'y sont généralement pas admises, mais certains établissements ont des salles conçues pour l'accueil des familles. On parle aujourd'hui d'éventuels nouveaux assouplissements des heures d'ouverture.

licensing laws *npl* [in UK] *lois réglementant la vente d'alcools.*

licentiate [laɪ'senʃɪət] *n* diplômé *m*, - e *f*.

licentious [laɪ'senʃəs] *adj* licencieux.

lichee [,laɪ'tʃiː] *n* = **lychee**.

lichen ['laɪkən] *n* lichen *m*.

lich-gate ['lɪtʃ-] = **lych-gate**.

licit ['lɪsɪt] *adj* licite.

lick [lɪk] ◇ *vt* **1.** [ice-cream] lécher ■ [stamp] humecter ■ **the dog ~ed her hand** le chien lui a léché la main ■ **he ~ed the jam off the bread** il lécha la confiture de la tartine ■ **to ~ one's chops** *inf* se lécher les babines ■ **the flames ~ed the walls of the house** *fig* les flammes léchaient les murs de la maison ▶ **to ~ sb's boots** lécher les bottes à qqn ■ **to ~ one's lips** *liter* se lécher les lèvres ; *fig* [with satisfaction, lust] se frotter les mains ; [with eager anticipation] se lécher les babines ■ **to ~ one's wounds** panser ses blessures **2.** *inf* [defeat] battre à plate couture ■ [in fight] donner une raclée à ■ **this crossword has got me ~ed** ces mots croisés sont trop forts pour moi ■ **we've finally got the problem ~ed** nous sommes enfin venus à bout du problème.
◇ *n* **1.** [with tongue] coup *m* de langue ■ **to give sthg a ~** lécher qqch ■ **a ~ of paint** un (petit) coup de peinture ▶ **a ~ and a promise** un brin de toilette **2.** *UK inf* [speed] **: at a tremendous ~** à fond la caisse OR de train **3.** AGRIC pierre *f* à lécher.

lickety-split [,lɪkətɪ'splɪt] *adv US inf* à toute pompe, à toutes pompes, à fond la caisse.

licking ['lɪkɪŋ] *n inf* [thrashing] raclée *f*, dégelée *f* ■ [defeat] déculottée *f*.

lickspittle ['lɪk,spɪtl] *n inf* lèche-bottes *mf inv*.

licorice *US* = **liquorice**.

lid [lɪd] *n* **1.** [gen] couvercle *m* **2.** *inf phr* **the scandal put the ~ on the Chicago operation** le scandale mit fin à l'opération de Chicago ■ **that puts the (tin) ~ on it!** *UK* ça, c'est le bouquet! ■ **to take** OR **to lift the ~ off sthg** percer OR mettre qqch à jour **3.** ANAT [eyelid] paupière *f* **4.** *inf* [hat] galure *m*, galurin *m* ■ [helmet] casque *m*.

lidded ['lɪdɪd] *adj* **: heavy-~ eyes** des yeux aux paupières lourdes.

lidless ['lɪdlɪs] *adj* [container] sans couvercle ■ [eyes] sans paupières.

lido ['liːdəʊ] (*pl* **lidos**) *n* [pool] piscine *f* découverte ■ [resort] station *f* balnéaire.

lie [laɪ] (*cont* **lying**, *pret* **lay** [leɪ], *pp* **lain** [leɪn]) ◇ *vi* **1.** (*pret & pp* **lied**) [tell untruth] mentir ■ **he ~d about his age** il a menti sur son âge
2. [person, animal - recline] se coucher, s'allonger, s'étendre ■ **she lay on the beach all day** elle est restée allongée sur la plage toute la journée ■ **she was lying on the couch** elle était couchée OR allongée sur le divan ■ **~ on your back** couchez-vous sur le dos ■ **~ still!** ne bouge pas! ■ **I like lying in bed on Sunday mornings** j'aime rester au lit OR faire la grasse matinée le dimanche matin ■ **she lay awake for hours** elle resta plusieurs heures sans pouvoir s'endormir ▶ **'As I Lay Dying'** ***Faulkner*** 'Tandis que j'agonise'
3. [corpse] reposer ■ **he will ~ in state at Westminster Abbey** son corps sera exposé solennellement à l'abbaye de Westminster ■ **'here ~s John Smith'** 'ci-gît John Smith'
4. [team, competitor - rank] être classé, se classer ■ **she was lying fourth** [in race] elle était en quatrième position
5. [thing - be, be placed] **: a folder lay open on the desk before her** un dossier était ouvert devant elle sur le bureau ■ **snow lay (thick) on the ground** il y avait une (épaisse) couche de neige ■ **the castle now ~s in ruins** le château est aujourd'hui en ruines ■ **all her hopes and dreams lay in ruins** *fig* tous ses espoirs et ses rêves étaient anéantis OR réduits à néant
6. [thing - remain, stay] rester ■ **our machines are lying idle** nos machines sont arrêtées OR ne tournent pas
7. [place - be situated] se trouver, être ■ [land - stretch, extend] s'étendre ■ **a vast desert lay before us** un immense désert s'étendait devant nous
8. [future event] **: they didn't know what lay ahead of them** ils ne savaient pas ce qui les attendait ■ **who knows what may ~ in store for us** qui sait ce qui nous attend OR ce que l'avenir nous réserve
9. [answer, explanation, duty etc] **: the problem ~s in getting them motivated** le problème, c'est de réussir à les motiver ■ **where do our real interests ~?** qu'est-ce qui compte vraiment pour nous? ■ **responsibility for the strike ~s with the management** la responsabilité de la grève incombe à la direction
10. LAW [appeal, claim] être recevable.
◇ *n* **1.** [untruth] mensonge *m* ■ **to tell ~s** dire des mensonges, mentir ■ **a pack** OR **tissue of ~s** un tissu de mensonges ■ **to give the ~ to sthg** *lit* démentir qqch ■ **it was in June, no, I tell a ~, in July** c'était en juin, non, c'est faux, en juillet
2. [of land] configuration *f*, disposition *f*
3. SPORT [of golf ball] position *f*.

➜ **lie about** *UK*, **lie around** *vi insep* **1.** [person] traîner
2. [thing] traîner ■ **don't leave your things lying about** ne laisse pas traîner tes affaires.

➜ **lie back** *vi insep* **: he lay back in his armchair** il s'est renversé dans son fauteuil ■ **just ~ back and take it easy!** *fig* repose-toi un peu!

➜ **lie behind** *vt insep* se cacher derrière ■ **deep insecurity lay behind his apparently successful life** sa vie, en apparence réussie, cachait une profonde insécurité.

➜ **lie down** *vi insep* se coucher, s'allonger, s'étendre ▶ **to take sthg lying down** accepter qqch sans réagir OR sans broncher ■ **I won't take this lying down!** je ne vais pas me laisser faire comme ça!

➜ **lie in** *vi insep* **1.** [sleep in] faire la grasse matinée
2. *arch* & MED être en couches.

◆ **lie off** *vi insep* NAUT rester au large.
◆ **lie to** *vi insep* NAUT se tenir *OR* (se) mettre à la cape.
◆ **lie up** *vi insep* [person] rester au lit, garder le lit ■ [machine] ne pas tourner, être arrêté ■ [car] rester au garage.

Liechtenstein ['lɪktənstaɪn] *pr n* Liechtenstein *m* ■ **in ~** au Liechtenstein.

lie detector *n* détecteur *m* de mensonges.

lie-down *n UK inf* **to have a ~** se coucher, s'allonger.

liege [li:dʒ] *arch* ◇ *adj* **1.** : **~ lord** seigneur *m*, suzerain *m* **2.** [vassal, homage] lige ■ **~ man** homme *m* lige.
◇ *n* seigneur *m*, suzerain *m*.

lie-in *n UK inf* **to have a ~** faire la grasse matinée.

lieu [lju:, lu:] ◆ **in lieu** *adv phr* : **take Monday off in ~** prends ton lundi pour compenser.
◆ **in lieu of** *prep phr* au lieu de, à la place de.

Lieut. (*written abbrev of* **lieutenant**) lieut.

lieutenant [*UK* lef'tenənt, *US* lu:'tenənt] *n* **1.** MIL [in army] lieutenant *m*, -e *f* ■ [in navy] lieutenant *m*, -e *f* de vaisseau **2.** [in US police] inspecteur *m* (de police) **3.** *fig* lieutenant *m*, second *m* **4.** *UK* HIST lieutenant *m*.

lieutenant colonel *n* lieutenant-colonel *m*, lieutenante-colonelle *f*.

lieutenant commander *n* capitaine *mf* de corvette.

lieutenant general *n* [in army] général *m*, -e *f* de corps d'armée ■ [in US airforce] général *m*, -e *f* de corps aérien.

lieutenant governor *n* **1.** [in Canada] lieutenant *m* gouverneur **2.** [in US] gouverneur *m* adjoint.

life [laɪf] (*pl* **lives** [laɪvz]) ◇ *n* **1.** [existence] vie *f* ■ **it's a matter of ~ and death** c'est une question de vie ou de mort ■ **I've worked hard all my ~** j'ai travaillé dur toute ma vie ■ **~ is hard** la vie est dure ■ **there have been several attempts on her ~** elle a été victime de plusieurs attentats ■ **he's in hospital fighting for his ~** il lutte contre la mort à l'hôpital ■ **how's ~?** *inf* comment ça va? ■ **I began ~ as a labourer** j'ai débuté dans la vie comme ouvrier ■ **just relax and enjoy ~!** profite donc un peu de la vie! ■ **I want to live my own ~** je veux vivre ma vie ■ **is ~ worth living?** la vie vaut-elle la peine d'être vécue? ■ **to live ~ to the full** *UK OR* **fullest** *US* croquer la vie à belles dents ■ **hundreds lost their lives** des centaines de personnes ont trouvé la mort ■ **he emigrated in order to make a new ~ for himself** il a émigré pour commencer une nouvelle vie *OR* pour repartir à zéro ■ **we don't want to spend the rest of our lives here** on ne veut pas finir nos jours ici ■ **to save sb's ~** sauver la vie à qqn ■ **to risk one's ~ (to do sthg)** risquer sa vie (à faire qqch) ■ **to take sb's ~** tuer qqn ■ **she took her own ~** elle s'est donné la mort ■ **I've never eaten snails in my ~** je n'ai jamais mangé d'escargots de ma vie ■ **she's the only woman in his ~** c'est la seule femme dans sa vie ■ **I ran the race of my ~!** j'ai fait la course de ma vie! ■ **it gave me the fright of my ~** je n'ai jamais eu aussi peur de ma vie ➊ **my/her** *etc* **~'s work** l'œuvre *f* de to ute ma/sa *etc* vie ■ **to run for one's ~** *OR* **for dear ~** s'enfuir à toutes jambes ■ **for the ~ of me I can't remember where we met** rien à faire, je n'arrive pas à me rappeler où nous nous sommes rencontrés ■ **he can't sing to save his ~** *inf* il chante comme un pied ■ **not on your ~!** jamais de la vie! ■ **to risk ~ and limb** risquer sa peau ■ **to have nine lives** avoir l'âme chevillée au corps ■ **you take your ~ in your hands when cycling in London** on risque sa vie quand on fait du vélo à Londres ■ **that's ~!** c'est la vie! ■ **this is the ~!** (ça, c'est) la belle vie! ■ **I had the time of my ~** je ne me suis jamais autant amusé
2. [mode of existence] vie *f* ■ **they lead a strange ~** ils mènent une drôle de vie ■ **she's not used to city ~** elle n'a pas l'habitude de vivre en ville ■ **married ~** la vie conjugale
3. [living things collectively] vie *f* ■ **is there ~ on Mars?** y a-t-il de la vie sur Mars?
4. *(U)* [physical feeling] sensation *f*
5. [liveliness] vie *f* ■ **there's a lot more ~ in Sydney than in Wellington** Sydney est nettement plus animé que Wellington ■ **to come to ~** s'animer ■ **his arrival put new ~ into the firm** son arrivée a donné un coup de fouet à l'entreprise ■ **there's ~ in the old boy** *OR* **dog yet!** il est envore vert, le bonhomme!, ➊ **she was the ~ and soul of the party** c'est elle qui a mis de l'ambiance dans la soirée
6. [living person] vie *f* ■ **200 lives were lost in the disaster** 200 personnes ont perdu la vie dans la catastrophe, la catastrophe a fait 200 morts
7. [durability] (durée de) vie *f* ■ **double the ~ of your batteries** multipliez par deux la durée de vos piles ■ **during the ~ of the previous government** sous le gouvernement précédent
8. [biography] vie *f* ■ **she's writing a ~ of James Joyce** elle écrit une biographie de James Joyce
9. ART nature *f* ■ **to draw from ~** dessiner d'après nature ‖ LIT réalité *f* ■ **his novels are very true to ~** ses romans sont très réalistes
10. GAMES vie *f*
11. *inf* [imprisonment] prison *f* à vie ■ **the kidnappers got ~** les ravisseurs ont été condamnés à perpétuité *OR* à la prison à vie ■ **he's doing ~** il purge une peine à perpétuité.
◇ *comp* [post, member, president] à vie.
◆ **for life** *adv phr* : **he was crippled for ~** il a été estropié à vie ■ **sent to prison for ~** condamné à perpétuité ■ **a job for ~** un emploi à vie.

life-and-death *adj* : **this is a ~ decision** c'est une décision vitale ■ **a ~ struggle** un combat à mort, une lutte désespérée.

life assurance *UK* = **life insurance**.

life belt *n* bouée *f* de sauvetage.

lifeblood ['laɪfblʌd] *n* élément *m* vital.

lifeboat ['laɪfbəʊt] *n* [shore-based] canot *m* de sauvetage ■ [on ship] chaloupe *f* de sauvetage.

lifeboatman ['laɪfbəʊtmən] (*pl* **lifeboatmen** [-mən]) *n* sauveteur *m* (en mer).

life buoy *n* bouée *f* de sauvetage.

life class *n* cours *m* de dessin d'après nature.

life cycle *n* cycle *m* de vie.

life drawing *n* dessin *m* d'après nature.

life expectancy *n* [of human, animal] espérance *f* de vie ■ [of machine] durée *f* de vie probable.

life-form *n* forme *f* de vie.

life-giving *adj* qui insuffle la vie, vivifiant.

lifeguard ['laɪfgɑ:d] *n* maître *m* nageur.

life history *n* vie *f* ■ **the organism takes on many different forms during its ~** l'organisme prend de nombreuses formes au cours de sa vie *OR* de son existence ■ **she told me her whole ~** elle m'a raconté l'histoire de sa vie.

life imprisonment *n* prison *f* à vie.

life insurance *n* assurance-vie *f* ■ **to take out ~** contracter une assurance-vie.

life jacket *n* gilet *m* de sauvetage.

lifeless ['laɪflɪs] *adj* **1.** [dead body] sans vie **2.** [where no life exists] sans vie **3.** [dull - eyes] éteint ; [- hair] terne ; [- town] mort ; [- style] sans énergie.

lifelike ['laɪflaɪk] *adj* **1.** [portrait] ressemblant **2.** [seeming alive] : **the new robots are extremely ~** ces nouveaux robots ont l'air *OR* paraissent vraiment vivants.

lifeline ['laɪflaɪn] *n* **1.** NAUT [thrown to boat] remorque *f* ■ [stretched across deck] sauvegarde *f*, filière *f* de mauvais temps *OR* de sécurité ■ **they threw the drowning man a ~** ils ont lancé un filin à l'homme qui se noyait **2.** [for diver] corde *f* de sécurité **3.** *fig* lien *m* vital ■ **it's his ~ to the outside world** c'est son lien avec le monde extérieur ■ **to cut off sb's ~** couper les vivres à qqn.

lifelong ['laɪflɒŋ] *adj* de toute une vie ■ **it's been my ~ ambition to meet her** toute ma vie, j'ai espéré la rencontrer.

life-or-death = **life-and-death**.

life peer *n UK membre de la Chambre des lords dont le titre n'est pas héréditaire.*

life preserver *n US* [life belt] bouée *f* de sauvetage ■ [life jacket] gilet *m* de sauvetage.

lifer ['laɪfər] *n inf* condamné *m*, - e *f* à perpète.

life raft *n* radeau *m* de sauvetage.

lifesaver ['laɪf,seɪvəʳ] *n* **1.** [lifeguard] maître nageur *m* **2.** *inf fig* **thank you, you're a ~!** merci, tu m'as sauvé la vie! ▪ **that money was a ~** cet argent m'a sauvé la vie.

life science *n* : **the ~s** les sciences de la vie.

life sentence *n* condamnation *f* à vie *OR* à perpétuité.

life-size(d) *adj* grandeur nature *(inv)*.

life span *n* durée *f* de vie.

life story *n* biographie *f*.

lifestyle ['laɪfstaɪl] *n* style *m OR* mode *m* de vie.

life-support system *n* MED respirateur *m* artificiel ▪ AERON & ASTRON équipement *m* de vie.

life-threatening *adj* [illness] qui peut être mortel.

lifetime ['laɪftaɪm] *n* vie *f* ▪ **it won't happen during our ~** nous ne serons pas là pour voir ça ▪ **win the holiday of a ~!** gagnez les vacances de votre vie! ▪ **a once-in-a-~ experience** une expérience unique *OR* qui ne se renouvellera pas.

life vest = **life jacket**.

lift [lɪft] <> *vt* **1.** [object] soulever, lever ▪ **I ~ed the books out of the crate** j'ai sorti les livres de la caisse ▪ **she ~ed the suitcase down from the top of the wardrobe** elle a descendu la valise de dessus l'armoire ▪ **I feel as if a burden has been ~ed from my shoulders** j'ai l'impression qu'on m'a enlevé un poids des épaules ▮ [part of body] lever ▪ **she ~ed her eyes from her magazine** elle leva les yeux de sa revue ▮ *fml* [voice] élever **2.** [spirits, heart] remonter ▪ **his music never fails to ~ my spirits** sa musique me remonte toujours le moral **3.** [end - blockade, embargo etc] lever ; [- control, restriction] supprimer **4.** *inf* [steal] piquer, faucher ▪ [plagiarize] plagier, piquer **5.** AGRIC [bulbs, potatoes, turnips] arracher **6.** *US* [debt] rembourser **7.** [face] : **she's had her face ~ed** elle s'est fait faire un lifting.

<> *vi* **1.** [rise] se lever, se soulever **2.** [fog, mist] se lever, se dissiper.

<> *n* **1.** [act of lifting] : **to give sthg a ~** soulever qqch **2.** [in morale, energy] : **to give sb a ~** remonter le moral à qqn ▪ **glucose tablets are good if you need a quick ~** les comprimés de glucose sont bons si vous avez besoin d'un coup de fouet **3.** *UK* [elevator] ascenseur *m* ▪ **goods ~** monte-charge *m inv* **4.** [free ride] : **can I give you a ~ home?** est-ce que je peux te raccompagner chez toi (en voiture)? ▪ **I got a ~ in a lorry** j'ai été pris (en auto-stop) par un camion.

◆ **lift off** <> *vi insep* [plane, rocket] décoller.

<> *vt sep* [hat, lid] enlever, ôter.

◆ **lift up** *vt sep* soulever, lever ▪ [part of body] lever ▪ **to ~ up one's head** lever la tête ▮ *fml* [voice] élever ▪ *fml* [heart] élever.

lifting ['lɪftɪŋ] *n* **1.** [of weight] levage *m* ▪ **~ gear** appareil *m* de levage ▪ **~ jack** cric *m* (de levage) **2.** [of blockade, embargo etc] levée *f* ▪ [of control, restriction] suppression *f* **3.** AGRIC arrachage *m*, récolte *f*.

lift-off *n* décollage *m* ▪ **we have ~!** décollage!

lift shaft *n UK* cage *f* d'ascenseur.

ligament ['lɪgəmənt] *n* ligament *m*.

ligature ['lɪgətʃəʳ] <> *n* **1.** [gen - MED] & TYPO ligature *f* **2.** MUS liaison *f*.

<> *vt* ligaturer.

light [laɪt] <> *n* **1.** [luminosity, brightness] lumière *f* ▪ **it looks brown in this ~** on dirait que c'est marron avec cette lumière ▪ **by the ~ of our flashlamps** à la lumière de nos lampes de poche ▪ **the ~ was beginning to fail** le jour commençait à baisser ▪ **she took the picture against the ~** elle a pris la photo à contre-jour ▪ **at first ~** au point *OR* au lever du jour ▪ **you're (standing) in my ~** tu me fais de l'ombre ▮ *fig* **to bring to ~** mettre en lumière ▪ **to be brought** *OR* **to come to ~** être découvert *OR* révélé ▪ **to throw** *OR* **to cast ~ on sthg : the trial will throw** *OR* **cast ~ on their real motives** le procès permettra d'en savoir plus sur *OR* de percer à jour leurs véritables mobiles ▪ **can you throw any ~ on this problem?** peux-tu apporter tes lumières sur ce problème?, peux-tu éclaircir cette question? ➊ **the ~ at the end of the tunnel** le bout du tunnel ▪ **to see the ~** [understand] comprendre ; [be converted] trouver le chemin de la vérité ▪ **to see the ~ of day** voir le jour

2. [light source] lumière *f* ▪ [lamp] lampe *f* ▪ **turn the ~ on/off** allume/éteins (la lumière) ▪ **during the storm the ~s went out** il y a eu une panne d'électricité *OR* de lumière pendant l'orage ➊ **to go out like a ~** [fall asleep] s'endormir tout de suite ; [faint] tomber dans les pommes

3. *fig* [in sb's eyes] lueur *f*

4. AUT [gen] feu *m* ▪ [headlamp] phare *m* ➊ **parking/reversing ~s** feux de stationnement/de recul

5. [traffic light] : **the ~s** le feu (de signalisation) ▪ **turn left at the ~s** tournez à gauche au feu rouge ▪ **she jumped the ~s** elle a brûlé le feu rouge ▪ **the ~s were (on) amber** le feu était à l'orange ▪ **the ~s aren't working** les feux ne marchent pas

6. [aspect, viewpoint] jour *m* ▪ **in a good/bad/new ~** sous un jour favorable/défavorable/nouveau

7. [flame] feu *m* ▪ **could you give me a ~?** pouvez-vous me donner du feu? ▪ **to set ~ to sthg** mettre le feu à qqch

8. [window] fenêtre *f*, jour *m*.

<> *adj* **1.** [bright, well-lit] clair ▪ **it isn't ~ enough to read** il n'y a pas assez de lumière pour lire ▪ **it's getting ~ already** il commence déjà à faire jour ▪ **it stays ~ until 10** il fait jour jusqu'à 10 h du soir

2. [pale] clair ▪ **she has ~ hair** elle a les cheveux clairs ▪ **~ yellow/brown** jaune/marron clair *(inv)*

3. LING [in phonetics] atone

4. [in weight] léger ▪ **~ clothes** vêtements *mpl* légers ➊ **a ~ aircraft** un avion de tourisme ▪ **~ cream** *US* crème *f* liquide ▪ **~ weapons** armes *fpl* légères ▪ **to be ~ on one's feet** être leste

5. [comedy, music etc] léger, facile ▪ **take some ~ reading** prends quelque chose de facile à lire ▪ **~ entertainment** variétés *fpl*

6. [not intense, strong etc] léger ▪ **the traffic was ~** la circulation était fluide ▪ **I had a ~ lunch** j'ai mangé légèrement à midi, j'ai déjeuné léger ▪ **a ~ rain was falling** il tombait une pluie fine ▪ **I'm a ~ sleeper** j'ai le sommeil léger ➊ **~ industry** industrie *f* légère ▪ **to make ~ of sthg** prendre qqch à la légère.

<> *adv* : **to travel ~** voyager avec peu de bagages.

<> *vt* (*pret & pp* **lit** [lɪt] *pret & pp* **lighted**) **1.** [illuminate] éclairer ▪ **I'll ~ the way for you** je vais t'éclairer le chemin

2. [lamp, candle, cigarette] allumer ▪ [match] craquer ▪ **to ~ a fire** allumer un feu, faire du feu.

<> *vi* (*pret & pp* **lit** [lɪt] *pret & pp* **lighted**) **1.** [lamp] s'allumer ▪ [match] s'enflammer ▪ [fire, coal] prendre

2. *lit* [alight] se poser.

◆ **lights** *npl* [lungs] mou *m*.

◆ **in (the) light of** *prep phr* : **in the ~ of these new facts** à la lumière de ces faits nouveaux.

◆ **light into** *vt insep inf* : **to ~ into sb** [attack] rentrer dans le lard à quelqu'un, agresser qqn.

◆ **light on, light upon** *vt insep* tomber (par hasard) sur, trouver par hasard.

◆ **light out** *vi insep US inf* se tirer.

◆ **light up** <> *vt sep* éclairer ▪ **the house was all lit up** la maison était tout *OR* toute éclairée.

<> *vi insep* **1.** [lamp] s'allumer

2. [face, eyes] s'éclairer, s'illuminer

3. *inf* [have a cigarette] allumer une cigarette.

light ale *n UK bière brune légère.*

light bulb *n* ampoule *f* (électrique).

light-coloured *adj* clair, de couleur claire.

lighted ['laɪtɪd] *adj* [room] éclairé ▪ [candle] allumé.

lighten ['laɪtn] <> *vt* **1.** [make brighter] éclairer, illuminer **2.** [make paler] éclaircir **3.** [make less heavy] alléger ▪ **having an assistant will ~ my workload** avec un assistant ma charge de travail sera moins lourde.

<> *vi* **1.** [become light] s'éclairer, s'éclaircir ▪ **her mood ~ed** sa mauvaise humeur se dissipa **2.** [load, burden] s'alléger.

◆ **lighten up** *vi insep inf* se remettre ▪ **oh come on, ~ up!** allez, remets-toi *OR* ne fais pas cette tête!

lighter ['laɪtəʳ] <> *n* **1.** [for cigarettes] briquet *m* ▪ [for gas] allume-gaz *m inv* **2.** [barge] allège *f*, chaland *m* **3.** **firelighter**.

<> *comp* [flint, fuel] à briquet.

light-fingered [-'fɪŋgəd] *adj* chapardeur.

light fitting *n* applique *f* (électrique).

light-footed [-'fʊtɪd] *adj* au pied léger, à la démarche légère.

light-headed *adj* [dizzy] étourdi ▪ [tipsy] ivre, enivré ▪ **to feel ~** avoir des vertiges *OR* la tête qui tourne ▪ **the wine had made me ~** le vin m'était monté à la tête.

light-headedness [-'hedɪdnɪs] *n* [dizziness] vertige *m* ▪ [tipsiness] ivresse *f*.

light-hearted *adj* [person, atmosphere] enjoué, gai ▪ [poem, irony] léger ▪ **a ~ remark** une remarque bon enfant ▪ **this programme takes a ~ look at politics** cette émission pose un regard amusé sur la politique.

light heavyweight <> *n* (poids *m*) mi-lourd *m*.
<> *adj* mi-lourd.

lighthouse ['laɪthaʊs] (*pl* [-haʊzɪz]) *n* phare *m* ▪ **~ keeper** gardien *m* de phare.

lighting ['laɪtɪŋ] *n* **1.** [gen] éclairage *m* ▪ **artificial/neon ~** éclairage *m* artificiel/au néon **2.** *(U)* THEAT éclairages *mpl* ▪ **~ effects** effets *mpl* d'éclairage *OR* de lumière ▪ **~ engineer** éclairagiste *mf*.

lighting-up time *n UK heure où les automobilistes doivent obligatoirement allumer leurs phares.*

lightly ['laɪtlɪ] *adv* **1.** [not heavily] légèrement ▪ **she stepped ~ onto the dance floor** elle entra sur la piste de danse d'un pas léger **2.** [casually] légèrement, à la légère ▪ **to take sthg ~** prendre qqch à la légère **3.** *phr* **to get off ~** s'en tirer à bon compte.

light meter *n* posemètre *m*.

lightness ['laɪtnɪs] *n* **1.** [brightness, light] clarté *f* **2.** [of object, tone, step etc] légèreté *f*.

lightning ['laɪtnɪŋ] <> *n (U)* éclairs *mpl*, foudre *f* ▪ **a flash of ~** un éclair ▪ **to be struck by ~** être frappé par la foudre *OR* foudroyé ◐ **to go like (greased) ~** partir sur les chapeaux de roue.
<> *adj* [raid, visit] éclair *(inv)* ▪ **with** *OR* **at ~ speed** à la vitesse de l'éclair, en un éclair.

lightning arrester *n* parafoudre *m* (de surtension).

lightning conductor, lightning rod *n* paratonnerre *m*.

lightning strike *n* grève *f* surprise *(inv)*.

light opera *n* opéra *m* comique, opérette *f*.

light pen *n* crayon *m* optique, photostyle *m*.

lightship ['laɪtʃɪp] *n* bateau-feu *m*, bateau-phare *m*.

light show *n* spectacle *m* de lumière.

lights-out *n* extinction *f* des feux.

light switch *n* interrupteur *m*.

lightweight ['laɪtweɪt] <> *n* **1.** [in boxing] poids *m* léger **2.** [insignificant person] personne *f* sans envergure ▪ **he's a literary ~** c'est un écrivain sans envergure.
<> *adj* **1.** [clothes, equipment] léger **2.** [in boxing] poids léger *(inv)*.

light-year *n* année-lumière *f* ▪ **it seems ~s away** ça paraît si loin.

ligneous ['lɪgnɪəs] *adj* ligneux.

likable ['laɪkəbl] = **likeable**.

like[1] [laɪk] *vt* **1.** [find pleasant] aimer (bien) ▪ **I ~ her, but I don't love her** je l'aime bien, mais je ne suis pas amoureux d'elle ▪ **I don't ~ him** je ne l'aime pas beaucoup, il ne me plaît pas ▪ **what do you ~ about him?** qu'est-ce qui te plaît chez lui?
2. [enjoy - activity] : **to ~ doing** *OR* **to do sthg** aimer faire qqch ▪ **I don't ~ being talked at** je n'aime pas qu'on me fasse des discours ▪ **how would HE ~ being kept waiting in the rain?** ça lui plairait, à lui, qu'on le fasse attendre sous la pluie?
3. [approve of] aimer ▪ **I ~ people to be frank with me** j'aime qu'on soit franc avec moi ▪ **I don't ~ you swearing, I don't ~ it when you swear** je n'aime pas que tu dises des gros mots ▪ **whether you ~ it or not!** que ça te plaise ou non! ▪ **well, I ~ that!** *iron* ça, c'est le bouquet! ▪ **I ~ the way you say "don't worry"** *hum* "ne t'inquiète pas", c'est facile à dire
4. [want, wish] aimer, vouloir ▪ **do what you ~** fais ce que tu veux *OR* ce qui te plaît ▪ **I didn't ~ to say anything, but...** je ne voulais rien dire mais... ▪ **I'd ~ your opinion on this wine** j'aimerais savoir ce que tu penses de ce vin ▮ [in polite offers, requests] : **would you ~ to go out tonight?** ça te dirait de *OR* tu as envie de sortir ce soir? ▪ **would you ~ tea or coffee?** voulez-vous du thé ou du café? ▪ **would you ~ me to do it for you?** veux-tu que je le fasse à ta place? ▪ **I'd ~ to speak to Mr Smith, please** je voudrais parler à M. Smith, s'il vous plaît
5. [asking opinion] : **how do you ~ my jacket?** comment trouves-tu ma veste? ▪ **how would you ~ a trip to Paris?** ça te dirait d'aller à Paris?
6. [asking preference] : **how do you ~ your coffee, black or white?** vous prenez votre café noir ou avec du lait?
7. [in generalizations] : **I ~ to be in bed by 10 p.m.** j'aime être couché pour 10 h ▪ **one doesn't ~ to interrupt** c'est toujours délicat d'interrompre quelqu'un.

like[2] [laɪk] <> *prep* **1.** [similar to] comme ▪ **there's a car ~ ours** voilà une voiture comme la nôtre ▪ **there's no place ~ home** rien ne vaut son chez-soi ▪ **she's nothing ~ her sister** elle ne ressemble pas du tout à sa sœur ▪ **it's shaped ~ an egg** ça a la forme d'un œuf ▪ **it seemed ~ hours** c'était comme si des heures entières s'étaient écoulées ▪ **it looks ~ rain** on dirait qu'il va pleuvoir
2. [asking for opinion or description] : **what's your new boss ~?** comment est ton nouveau patron? ▪ **what's the weather ~?** quel temps fait-il? ▪ **what does it taste ~?** quel goût ça a?
3. [such as] comme ▪ **I'm useless at things ~ sewing** je ne suis bon à rien quand il s'agit de couture et de choses comme ça
4. [indicating typical behaviour] : **kids are ~ that, what do you expect?** les gosses sont comme ça, qu'est-ce que tu veux! ▪ **it's not ~ him to be rude** ça ne lui ressemble pas *OR* ce n'est pas son genre d'être impoli ▪ **it's just ~ him not to show up!** c'est bien son style *OR* c'est bien de lui de ne pas venir!
5. [in the same manner as] comme ▪ **do it ~ this/that** voici/voilà comment il faut faire ▪ **~ so** comme ça ▪ **sorry to interrupt you ~ this, but...** désolé de vous interrompre ainsi, mais... ▪ **don't talk to me ~ that!** ne me parle pas sur ce ton!
6. [in approximations] : **it cost something ~ £200** ça a coûté dans les 200 livres ▪ **it was more ~ midnight when we got home** il était plus près de minuit quand nous sommes arrivés à la maison ◐ **that's more ~ it!** voilà qui est mieux! ▪ **he ran ~ anything** *OR* **~ hell** *OR* **~ blazes** *inf* il a couru comme un dératé *OR* comme s'il avait le feu aux fesses.
<> *adj* : **we were treated in ~ manner** on nous a traités de la même façon.
<> *conj inf* **1.** [as] comme ▪ **~ I was saying** *inf* comme je disais ▪ **they don't make them ~ they used to!** ils/elles ne sont plus ce qu'ils/elles étaient! ▪ **tell it ~ it is** dis les choses comme elles sont
2. [as if] comme si ▪ **he acted ~ he was in charge** il se comportait comme si c'était lui le chef ▪ **she felt ~ she wanted to cry** elle avait l'impression qu'elle allait pleurer.
<> *adv*△ *UK* **I was hungry, ~, so I went into this café** j'avais faim, tu vois, alors je suis entré dans un café.
<> *n* : **you can only compare ~ with ~** on ne peut comparer que ce qui est comparable ▪ **she goes in for macramé, yoga and the ~** elle fait du macramé, du yoga et d'autres choses comme ça ▪ **I've never seen the ~ of it!** je n'ai jamais rien vu de pareil! ▪ **he was a president the ~** *OR* **~s of which we will probably never see again** *lit* c'était un président comme on n'en verra probablement plus jamais.
◆ **likes** *npl* **1.** [preferences] goûts *mpl* ▪ **try to discover their ~s and dislikes** essayez de découvrir ce qu'ils aiment et ce qu'ils n'aiment pas
2. *phr* **the ~s of us/them** *etc inf* les gens comme nous/eux *etc*.
◆ **(as) like as not** = **like enough**.
◆ **if you like** *adv phr* **1.** [expressing willingness] si tu veux **2.** [as it were] si tu veux.
◆ **like enough** *adv phr inf* probablement ▪ **he's still at the office, ~ enough** il y a des chances qu'il soit encore au bureau.
◆ **like it or not** *adv phr* : **~ it or not, we're heading for a confrontation** qu'on le veuille ou non, nous ne pouvons éviter une confrontation.

-like *in cpds* : **dream~** onirique, de rêve ▪ **ghost~** fantomatique.

likeable ['laɪkəbl] *adj* sympathique, agréable.

likelihood ['laɪklɪhʊd] *n* probabilité *f* ■ **there is little ~ of us still being here** *OR* **that we'll still be here in August** il y a peu de chances (pour) que nous soyons encore là en août ■ **there is every ~ of an agreement** tout porte à croire qu'un accord sera conclu.
◆ **in all likelihood** *adv phr* vraisemblablement, selon toute vraisemblance.

likely ['laɪklɪ] (*comp* **likelier**, *superl* **likeliest**) ◇ *adj* **1.** [probable] probable ■ **it's more than ~ that it will snow** il y a de grandes chances pour qu'il neige ■ **it's not** *OR* **hardly ~ to happen** il est peu probable *OR* il y a peu de chances que cela se produise ■ **rain is ~ in the east** il risque de pleuvoir dans l'est ■ **a ~ story!** *iron* mon œil!, elle est bien bonne! **2.** [promising] prometteur ■ **we found a ~** *OR* **~ -looking spot for a picnic** on a trouvé un endroit qui a l'air idéal pour pique-niquer.
◇ *adv* probablement, sans doute ■ **they'll very ~** *OR* **most ~ forget** ils vont très probablement oublier ■ **as ~ as not she's already home** elle est sûrement déjà rentrée ● **would you do it again? – not ~!** *inf* tu recommencerais? – ça risque pas *OR* y a pas de risque!

like-minded [-'maɪndɪd] *adj* : **~ people** des gens ayant la même vision des choses.

liken ['laɪkn] *vt* comparer ■ **his style has been ~ed to that of Peter Wolfe** on a comparé son style à celui de Peter Wolfe.

likeness ['laɪknɪs] *n* **1.** [resemblance] ressemblance *f* ■ **a family ~** un air de famille ■ **she bears a strong ~ to her mother** elle ressemble beaucoup à sa mère **2.** [portrait] portrait *m* ■ **to paint sb's ~** faire le portrait de qqn ■ **it's a very good ~ of him** c'est tout à fait lui ■ **it isn't a very good ~ of him** ça ne lui ressemble pas beaucoup.

likewise ['laɪkwaɪz] *adv* **1.** [similarly] de même ■ **he worked hard and expected his daughters to do ~** il travaillait beaucoup et attendait de ses filles qu'elles fassent de même ■ **pleased to meet you – ~** ravi de vous rencontrer – moi de même **2.** [by the same token] de même, de plus, en outre.

liking ['laɪkɪŋ] *n* **1.** [affection] sympathie *f*, affection *f* ■ **to take a ~ to sb** se prendre d'amitié pour qqn ■ **I took an instant ~ to Rome** j'ai tout de suite aimé Rome **2.** [taste] goût *m*, penchant *m* ■ **is everything to your ~?** est-ce que tout est à votre convenance? ■ **it's too small for my ~** c'est trop petit à mon goût.

lilac ['laɪlək] ◇ *n* [colour, flower] lilas *m*.
◇ *adj* [colour] lilas *(inv)*.

Lilliputian [,lɪlɪ'pju:ʃn] ◇ *n* lilliputien *m*, - enne *f*.
◇ *adj* lilliputien.

Lilo® ['laɪləʊ] (*pl* **Lilos**) *n* matelas *m* pneumatique.

lilt [lɪlt] *n* **1.** [in voice] modulation *f* ■ **her voice has a ~ to it** sa voix a des inflexions mélodieuses **2.** [in music] rythme *m*, cadence *f* **3.** [in movement] balancement *m* harmonieux.

lilting ['lɪltɪŋ] *adj* **1.** [voice, accent] mélodieux **2.** [music, tune] chantant, mélodieux **3.** [movement] souple, harmonieux.

lily ['lɪlɪ] (*pl* **lilies**) *n* lis *m*, lys *m* ■ **~ of the valley** muguet *m*.

lily-livered [-'lɪvəd] *adj* froussard.

lily pad *n* feuille *f* de nénuphar.

lily-white *adj* d'une blancheur de lis, d'un blanc immaculé.

limb [lɪm] *n* **1.** ANAT membre *m* ■ **let's rest our weary ~s!** *hum* si on soufflait un peu! ■ **I'll tear him ~ from ~!** je le taillerai en pièces! **2.** [of tree] (grosse) branche *f* ■ **to be out on a ~** *inf* [alone] se trouver tout seul ; [without support] être très exposé.

limbo ['lɪmbəʊ] *n* **1.** *(U)* RELIG limbes *mpl* **2.** COMPUT : **~ file** fichier *m* temporaire **3.** (*pl* limbos) DANCE limbo *m* **4.** *fig* **to be in (a state of) ~** être dans l'incertitude.

lime [laɪm] ◇ *n* **1.** AGRIC & CHEM chaux *f* ■ **burnt ~** chaux vive **2.** [fruit] citron *m* vert, lime *f*, limette *f* ■ **~ cordial/juice** sirop *m* /jus *m* de citron vert ■ **lager and ~** bière *f* blonde au sirop de citron vert **3.** [citrus tree] limettier *m* **4.** [linden] : **~ (tree)** tilleul *m*.
◇ *vt* **1.** AGRIC [soil] chauler **2.** [with birdlime - branch, bird] engluer.

limeade [laɪ'meɪd] *n* boisson *f* au citron vert.

lime green *n* vert *m* citron.
◆ **lime-green** *adj* vert citron *(inv)*.

limelight ['laɪmlaɪt] *n (U)* THEAT feux *mpl* de la rampe ■ **to be in the ~** être sous les feux de la rampe, occuper le devant de la scène.

limerick ['lɪmərɪk] *n* limerick *m (poème absurde ou indécent en cinq vers, dont les rimes doivent suivre un ordre précis)*.

limestone ['laɪmstəʊn] *n* calcaire *m*, roche *f* calcaire.

limey ['laɪmɪ] *US inf pej* ◇ *n* **1.** [English person] ≃ Angliche *inf mf* **2.** [English sailor] matelot *m* anglais.
◇ *adj* ≃ angliche *inf*.

limit ['lɪmɪt] ◇ *n* **1.** [boundary, greatest extent, maximum] limite *f* ■ **I know my ~s** je connais mes limites, je sais ce dont je suis capable ■ **there is no ~ to his powers** ses pouvoirs sont illimités ■ **our resources are stretched to the ~** nous sommes au bout de nos ressources ■ **within the ~s of the present regulations** dans le cadre délimité par le présent règlement ■ **I agree with you, within ~s** je suis d'accord avec toi, jusqu'à un certain point ● **off ~s** interdit d'accès ■ **the bar's off ~s to servicemen** le bar est interdit aux militaires ■ **that's the (absolute) ~!** c'est le comble! ■ **she really is the ~!** elle dépasse vraiment les bornes! **2.** [restriction] limitation *f* ■ **to put** *OR* **to set a ~ on sthg** limiter qqch ● **weight ~** limitation de poids ■ **to be over the ~** *UK* [driver] dépasser le taux d'alcoolémie autorisé.
◇ *vt* limiter ■ **they are ~ing their research to one kind of virus** ils limitent leurs recherches à un seul type de virus ■ **she ~s herself to one visit a week** elle se contente d'une visite par semaine.

limitation [,lɪmɪ'teɪʃn] *n* **1.** [restriction, control] limitation *f*, restriction *f* ■ **we will accept no ~ on our freedom** nous n'accepterons aucune entrave à notre liberté ● **arms ~ talks** négociations *fpl* sur la limitation des armements **2.** [shortcoming] limite *f* ■ **to know one's ~s** connaître ses limites **3.** LAW prescription *f*.

limited ['lɪmɪtɪd] *adj* [restricted] limité, restreint ■ **the play met with only ~ success** la pièce n'a connu qu'un succès relatif ■ **to a ~ extent** jusqu'à un certain point.

limited company *n* société *f* à responsabilité limitée, SARL *f*.

limited edition *n* édition *f* à tirage limité.

limited liability *n* responsabilité *f* limitée.

limited liability company = **limited company**.

limiting ['lɪmɪtɪŋ] *adj* contraignant.

limitless ['lɪmɪtlɪs] *adj* illimité ■ **~ resources** des ressources illimitées *OR* inépuisables.

limo ['lɪməʊ] (*pl* **limos**) *inf* = **limousine**.

limousine ['lɪməzi:n] *n* limousine *f*.

limp [lɪmp] ◇ *vi* boiter ■ [slightly] clopiner ■ **she was ~ing badly** elle boitait beaucoup.
◇ *n* : **to walk with a ~** boiter ■ **the accident left him with a ~** depuis son accident il boite.
◇ *adj* **1.** [cloth, lettuce, handshake] mou *(before vowel or silent 'h' mol)*, molle *f* ■ [skin] flasque ■ **his body went completely ~** il s'affaissa **2.** [book - cover, binding] souple.

limpet ['lɪmpɪt] *n* ZOOL patelle *f*, bernique *f*, chapeau *m* chinois ■ **to hold on to sthg** *OR* **to cling to sthg like a ~** se cramponner à qqch de toutes ses forces.

limpet mine *n* mine-ventouse *f*.

limpid ['lɪmpɪd] *adj* limpide.

limply ['lɪmplɪ] *adv* mollement.

limp-wristed [-'rɪstɪd] *adj pej* efféminé.

linchpin ['lɪntʃpɪn] *n* **1.** TECH esse *f* (d'essieu) **2.** *fig* [person] pivot *m* ■ **it's the ~ of government policy** c'est l'axe central de la politique du gouvernement.

Lincs *written abbr of* **Lincolnshire**.

linctus ['lɪŋktəs] *n* sirop *m* (pour la toux).

line [laɪn] ◇ *n* **1.** [mark, stroke] ligne *f*, trait *m* ■ [wrinkle] ride *f* ■ MATHS, SPORT & TV ligne ■ **to draw a ~** tracer *OR* tirer une ligne ■ **straight ~** MATHS droite *f* ; [gen] ligne *f* droite
2. [path] ligne *f* ■ **light travels in a straight ~** la lumière se propage en ligne droite ■ **the two grooves must be exactly in ~** les deux rainures doivent être parfaitement alignées ▶ **I don't follow your ~ of thinking** je ne suis pas ton raisonnement ■ **to be in the ~ of fire** être dans la ligne de tir ■ **~ of sight** *OR* **of vision** ligne de visée ■ **let's try a different ~ of attack** essayons une approche différente ■ **it's all in the ~ of duty** cela fait partie de mes fonctions ■ **to take the ~ of least resistance** *UK* choisir la solution de facilité ■ **there's been a terrible mistake somewhere along the ~** il s'est produit une erreur grave quelque part ■ **I'll support them all along** *OR* **right down the ~** je les soutiendrai jusqu'au bout *OR* sur toute la ligne ■ **the population is split along religious ~s** la population est divisée selon des critères religieux ■ **he reorganized the company along more rational ~s** il a réorganisé l'entreprise sur une base plus rationnelle ■ **another idea along the same ~s** une autre idée dans le même genre ■ **we seem to be thinking along the same ~s** il semble que nous voyions les choses de la même façon ■ **to be on the right ~s** être sur la bonne voie
3. [row - side by side] ligne *f*, rang *m*, rangée *f* ; [- one behind another] rang *m*, file *f* ■ **stand in ~, children** mettez-vous en rang, les enfants ■ **to step into ~** se mettre en rang ■ *US* [queue] file *f* (d'attente), queue *f* ■ *fig* **he's in ~ for promotion** il est sur les rangs pour une promotion ■ **he's next in ~ for promotion** la prochaine promotion sera pour lui ■ **he's first in ~ for the throne** c'est l'héritier du trône
4. *fig* [conformity] : **it's in/out of ~ with company policy** c'est conforme/ce n'est pas conforme à la politique de la société ■ **it's more or less in ~ with what we'd expected** cela correspond plus ou moins à nos prévisions ■ **to bring wages into ~ with inflation** actualiser les salaires en fonction de l'inflation ■ **the rebels have been brought into ~** les rebelles ont été mis au pas ■ **to fall into ~ with government policy** accepter la politique gouvernementale ■ **to step out of ~** s'écarter du droit chemin
5. [of writing, text] ligne *f* ■ **she gave me 100 ~s** SCH elle m'a donné 100 lignes (à faire) ■ [of poem, song] vers *m* ■ THEAT réplique *f* ■ **he forgot his ~s** il a oublié son texte ■ **he gave me the usual ~ about his wife not understanding him** il m'a fait son numéro habituel comme quoi sa femme ne le comprend pas ■ **to shoot a ~** *inf* [boast] frimer ; [smooth talk] baratiner
6. *inf* [letter] mot *m* ■ **to drop sb a ~** envoyer un mot à qqn
7. [rope] corde *f* ■ NAUT bout *m* ■ FISHING ligne *f* ■ **to hang the washing on the ~** mettre le linge à sécher, étendre le linge
8. [pipe] tuyau *m* ■ [pipeline] pipeline *m*
9. *UK* RAIL [track] voie *f* ■ [single rail] rail *m*
10. [travel route] ligne *f* ■ **there's a new coach ~ to London** il y a un nouveau service d'autocars pour Londres ■ **to keep the ~s of communication open** maintenir ouvertes les lignes de communication ■ [transport company] compagnie *f* ■ **shipping ~** compagnie de navigation
11. ELEC ligne *f* ■ **the power station comes on ~ in June** la centrale entre en service en juin
12. TELEC ligne *f* ■ **the ~ went dead** la communication a été coupée ■ **I was on the ~ to Paris** je téléphonais à Paris ■ **then a voice came on the other end of the ~** alors une voix a répondu à l'autre bout du fil ▶ **hold the ~** ne quittez pas ■ **on ~** COMPUT en ligne
13. [outline] ligne *f* ■ **can you explain the main** *OR* **broad ~s of the project to me?** pouvez-vous m'expliquer les grandes lignes du projet?
14. [policy] ligne *f* ■ **they took a hard** *OR* **tough ~ on terrorism** ils ont adopté une politique de fermeté envers le terrorisme ▶ **to follow** *OR* **to toe the party ~** suivre la ligne du parti
15. MIL ligne *f* ■ **they struggled vainly to hold the ~** ils ont vainement tenté de maintenir leur position ▶ **battle ~s** lignes de bataille ■ **the Old Line State** le Maryland
16. [boundary] frontière *f*, limite *f* ■ **the distant ~ of the horizon** la ligne lointaine de l'horizon ▶ **the (dividing) ~ between frankness and rudeness** la limite entre la franchise et l'impolitesse ■ **the poverty ~** le seuil de pauvreté ■ **they crossed the state ~ into Nevada** ils ont franchi la frontière du Nevada ■ **to cross the Line** [equator] traverser l'équateur
17. [field of activity] branche *f* ■ [job] métier *m* ■ **she's in the same~ (of work) as you** elle travaille dans la même branche que toi ■ **what ~ (of business) are you in?, what's your~ (of business)?** qu'est-ce que vous faites dans la vie? ■ **if you need anything doing in the plumbing ~** si vous avez besoin de faire faire des travaux de plomberie ■ [field of interest] domaine *m* ■ **that's more in Katy's ~** c'est plus du domaine de Katy ■ **opera isn't really my ~** l'opéra n'est pas vraiment mon genre
18. [range - of products] ligne *f* ■ **they produce** *OR* **do an interesting ~ in chairs** ils produisent une gamme intéressante de chaises ▶ **product ~** gamme *f OR* ligne de produits
19. [production line] chaîne *f* ■ **the new model will be coming off the ~ in May** le nouveau modèle sortira de l'usine en mai
20. [lineage, ancestry] lignée *f* ■ **the title is transmitted by the male ~** le titre se transmet par les hommes ■ **he comes from a long ~ of doctors** il est issu d'une longue lignée de médecins
21. *inf* [information] : **I'll try and get a ~ on what actually happened** j'essaierai d'avoir des tuyaux sur ce qui s'est réellement passé ■ **the police have got a ~ on him** la police sait des choses sur lui.
◇ *vt* **1.** [road, river] border ■ **the avenue is ~d with trees** l'avenue est bordée d'arbres ■ **crowds ~d the streets** la foule était *OR* s'était massée sur les trottoirs
2. [paper] régler, ligner
3. [clothes, curtains] doubler ■ [container, drawer, cupboard] tapisser, garnir ■ [brakes] garnir ■ **~d with silk** doublé de soie ■ **the tissue that ~s the digestive tract** la paroi interne de l'appareil digestif ■ **the tubes are ~d with plastic** l'intérieur des tubes est revêtu d'une couche de plastique ■ **walls ~d with books** des murs tapissés de livres ▶ **to ~ one's pockets** *inf* s'en mettre plein les poches.
➡ **line up** ◇ *vt sep* **1.** [put in line - objects] aligner, mettre en ligne ; [- people] faire aligner
2. [bring into alignment] aligner
3. *inf* [prepare, arrange] préparer, prévoir ■ **I've got a treat ~d up for the kids** j'ai préparé une surprise pour les gosses ■ **he's ~d up an all-star cast for his new film** la distribution de son nouveau film ne comprend que des stars.
◇ *vi insep* [stand in line] s'aligner, se mettre en ligne ■ *US* [queue up] faire la queue.

lineage ['lɪnɪɪdʒ] *n* [ancestry] ascendance *f*, famille *f* ■ [descendants] lignée *f*, descendance *f* ■ **of noble ~** de famille *OR* d'ascendance noble.

lineal ['lɪnɪəl] *adj* en ligne directe.

linear ['lɪnɪəʳ] *adj* linéaire.

lined [laɪnd] *adj* **1.** [paper] réglé **2.** [face, skin] ridé **3.** [jacket] doublé ■ [box] tapissé.

line dancing *n* line *m* dancing.

line drawing *n* dessin *m* au trait.

line feed *n* saut *m* de ligne.

line judge *n* SPORT juge *m* de ligne.

lineman ['laɪnmən] (*pl* **linemen** [-mən]) *n US* ELEC & TELEC monteur *m OR* ouvrier *m* de ligne.

linen ['lɪnɪn] ◇ *n* **1.** [fabric] (toile *f* de) lin *m* **2.** [sheets, tablecloths, towels etc] linge *m* (de maison) ■ [underclothes] linge *m* (de corps) ■ **dirty ~** linge sale ■ **to wash one's dirty ~ in public** *UK fig* laver son linge sale en public ■ **table ~** linge de table.
◇ *comp* de fil, de lin ■ **~ sheets** draps *mpl* de fil ■ **~ thread** fil *m* de lin.

linen basket *n* corbeille *f* à linge.

linen closet, linen cupboard *n* armoire *f OR* placard *m* à linge.

line-out *n* SPORT touche *f*, remise *f* en jeu.

line printer *n* imprimante *f* ligne à ligne.

liner ['laɪnəʳ] *n* **1.** [ship] paquebot *m* (de grande ligne) **2.** [eye-liner] eye-liner *m* **3.** [for clothing] doublure *f* **4.** TECH chemise *f*.

linesman ['laɪnzmən] (*pl* **linesmen** [-mən]) *n* **1.** SPORT [in rugby, football] juge *m OR* arbitre *m* de touche ■ [in tennis] juge *m* de ligne **2.** *UK* ELEC & TELEC monteur *m OR* ouvrier *m* de ligne.

lineup ['laɪnʌp] *n* 1. [identity parade] séance *f* d'identification ■ [line of suspects] rangée *f* de suspects 2. [composition] : the England ~ for tonight's match la composition de l'équipe anglaise pour le match de ce soir ■ we have an all-star ~ for tonight's programme nous avons un plateau de vedettes pour l'émission de ce soir.

linger ['lɪŋgəʳ] *vi* 1. [persist] persister, subsister ■ a doubt ~ed (on) in my mind il subsistait un doute dans mon esprit 2. [tarry] s'attarder, traîner ■ we ~ed over lunch nous nous sommes attardés à table 3. [stay alive] : she might ~ on for years yet il se pourrait qu'elle tienne encore des années.

lingerie ['lænʒərɪ] *n* lingerie *f*.

lingering ['lɪŋgrɪŋ] *adj* [long] long, longue *f* ■ he gave her a long ~ look il lui lança un long regard langoureux ‖ [persistent] persistant ■ a ~ feeling of dissatisfaction un irréductible sentiment d'insatisfaction ‖ [slow] lent ■ a ~ death une mort lente.

lingo ['lɪŋgəʊ] (*pl* lingoes) *n inf* I don't speak the ~ je ne parle pas la langue du pays.

lingua franca [,lɪŋgwə'fræŋkə] (*pl* lingua francas OR *pl* linguae francae [,lɪŋgwi:'fræŋki:]) *n* lingua franca *f*, langue *f* véhiculaire.

linguist ['lɪŋgwɪst] *n* 1. [in foreign languages - student] étudiant *m*, - e *f* en langues étrangères ; [- specialist] spécialiste *mf* en langues étrangères ■ to be a good ~ être doué pour les langues 2. [in linguistics] linguiste *mf*.

linguistic [lɪŋ'gwɪstɪk] *adj* linguistique.

linguistics [lɪŋ'gwɪstɪks] *n (U)* linguistique *f*.

liniment ['lɪnɪmənt] *n* pommade *f*.

lining ['laɪnɪŋ] *n* 1. [of clothes, curtains] doublure *f* 2. [of container, bearing] revêtement *m* ■ [of brake, clutch] garniture *f* 3. ANAT paroi *f* interne ■ the stomach ~ la paroi de l'estomac.

link [lɪŋk] ◇ *n* 1. [of chain] chaînon *m*, maillon *m* 2. [bond, relationship] lien *m* ■ she's severed all ~s with her family elle a coupé les ponts avec sa famille ■ Britain's trade ~s with Spain les relations commerciales entre la Grande-Bretagne et l'Espagne ■ the ~ between inflation and unemployment le lien OR rapport entre l'inflation et le chômage 3. [physical connection] liaison *f* ■ a road/rail/radio ~ une liaison routière/ferroviaire/radio 4. COMPUT lien *m*.
◇ *vt* 1. [relate] lier ■ how would you ~ these two theories? quel rapport voyez-vous entre ces deux théories? 2. [connect physically] relier ■ they ~ed arms ils se prirent le bras.
◇ *vt sep* relier.
◇ *vi* COMPUT avoir un lien vers ■ to link to sth mettre un lien avec qch.
◆ **link up** *vi insep* 1. [meet - persons] se rejoindre ; [- troops] effectuer une jonction ; [- spacecraft] s'arrimer 2. [form a partnership] s'associer 3. [be connected] se relier ■ it can ~ up to a computer on peut le relier OR connecter à un ordinateur.

linkage ['lɪŋkɪdʒ] *n* lien *m*, rapport *m*.

linkman ['lɪŋkmən] (*pl* linkmen [-mən]) *n* RADIO & TV journaliste *m (qui annonce les reportages des envoyés spéciaux)*.

link road *n* route *f* de jonction.

links [lɪŋks] *npl* (terrain *m* OR parcours *m* de) golf *m*, links *mpl*.

linkup ['lɪŋkʌp] *n* 1. [physical connection] liaison *f* ■ a telephone/satellite ~ une liaison téléphonique/par satellite 2. [of spacecraft, troops] jonction *f*.

linkwoman ['lɪŋk,wʊmən] (*pl* linkwomen [-,wɪmɪn]) *n* journaliste *f (qui annonce les reportages des envoyés spéciaux)*.

linnet ['lɪnɪt] *n* linotte *f*.

lino ['laɪnəʊ] *n UK* lino *m*.

linoleum [lɪ'nəʊljəm] *n* linoléum *m*.

linseed ['lɪnsi:d] *n* graine *f* de lin.

linseed oil *n* huile *f* de lin.

lint [lɪnt] *n (U)* 1. [fabric] tissu *m* gratté ■ ~ bandage charpie *f* 2. [fluff] peluches *fpl*.

lintel ['lɪntl] *n* linteau *m*.

lion ['laɪən] *n* 1. ZOOL lion *m* ▶ the ~'s den l'antre *m* du lion ■ to fight like a ~ se battre comme un lion ■ the ~'s share la part du lion 2. *fig* [courageous person] lion *m*, lionne *f* ■ [celebrity] célébrité *f*.

lion cub *n* lionceau *m*.

lioness ['laɪənes] *n* lionne *f*.

lionhearted ['laɪən,hɑ:tɪd] *adj* courageux comme un lion.

lionize, ise ['laɪənaɪz] *vt* [treat like a celebrity] porter aux nues.

lion-tamer *n* dompteur *m*, - euse *f* (de lions).

lip [lɪp] *n* 1. [human] lèvre *f* ■ [animal] lèvre *f*, babine *f* ■ my ~s are sealed je ne dirai rien ■ her name is on everyone's ~s son nom est sur toutes les lèvres ■ they only pay ~ service to the ideal of equality ils ne souscrivent qu'en paroles à l'idéal d'égalité 2. [of jug] bec *m* ■ [of cup, bowl] rebord *m* ■ [of wound] lèvre *f*, bord *m* ■ [of crater] bord *m* 3. *inf* [impertinence] culot *m* ■ enough of your ~! ne sois pas insolent!

lip gloss *n* brillant *m* à lèvres.

liposuction ['lɪpəʊ,sʌkʃn] *n* liposuccion *f*.

-lipped [lɪpt] *in cpds* : thin~ aux lèvres minces.

lip pencil *n* crayon *m* à lèvres.

lippy ['lɪpɪ] (*comp* lippier, *superl* lippiest) *adj inf* insolent, culotté.

lip-read ['lɪpri:d] (*pret & pp* lip-read ['lɪpred]) ◇ *vi* lire sur les lèvres.
◇ *vt* lire sur les lèvres de.

lip-reading *n* lecture *f* sur les lèvres.

lip salve *n* pommade *f* OR baume *m* pour les lèvres.

lipstick ['lɪpstɪk] *n* 1. [substance] rouge *m* à lèvres 2. [stick] (tube *m* de) rouge *m* à lèvres.

lip-synch [-sɪŋk] ◇ *vi* chanter en play-back.
◇ *vt* : to ~ a song chanter une chanson en play-back.

liquefy ['lɪkwɪfaɪ] (*pret & pp* liquefied) ◇ *vt* liquéfier.
◇ *vi* se liquéfier.

liqueur [lɪ'kjʊəʳ] *n* liqueur *f*.

liqueur chocolate *n* chocolat *m* à la liqueur.

liqueur glass *n* verre *m* à liqueur.

liquid ['lɪkwɪd] ◇ *adj* 1. [fluid] liquide ■ ~ air/nitrogen/fuel/oxygen air *m* /azote *m* /combustible *m* /oxygène *m* liquide ■ to have a ~ lunch *hum* boire de l'alcool en guise de déjeuner 2. FIN liquide ■ ~ assets liquidités *fpl* 3. [clear - eyes, sound] limpide 4. LING [consonant] liquide.
◇ *n* 1. [fluid] liquide *m* 2. LING [consonant] liquide *f*.

liquidate ['lɪkwɪdeɪt] ◇ *vt* 1. *euph* [kill, eliminate] liquider, éliminer 2. FIN & LAW [debt, company, estate] liquider ■ [capital] mobiliser.
◇ *vi* FIN & LAW entrer en liquidation, déposer son bilan.

liquidation [,lɪkwɪ'deɪʃn] *n* 1. *euph* [killing, elimination] liquidation *f* 2. FIN & LAW [of debt, company, estate] liquidation *f* ■ [of capital] mobilisation *f* ■ to go into ~ entrer en liquidation, déposer son bilan.

liquidator ['lɪkwɪdeɪtəʳ] *n* liquidateur *m*, - trice *f*.

liquid crystal display *n* affichage *m* à cristaux liquides.

liquidity [lɪ'kwɪdətɪ] *n* liquidité *f*.

liquidize, ise ['lɪkwɪdaɪz] *vt* 1. CULIN passer au mixeur 2. PHYS liquéfier.

liquidizer ['lɪkwɪdaɪzəʳ] *n UK* mixer *m*, mixeur *m*.

liquid paraffin *n* huile *f* de paraffine.

liquified petroleum gas ['lɪkwɪfaɪd-] *n* gaz *m* de pétrole liquéfié.

liquor ['lɪkəʳ] *n* 1. *US* [alcohol] alcool *m*, boissons *fpl* alcoolisées ■ to be the worse for ~ être ivre 2. CULIN jus *m*, bouillon *m* 3. PHARM solution *f* aqueuse.

liquorice *UK*, **licorice** *US* [ˈlɪkərɪs] *n* [plant, root] réglisse *f* ■ [sweet] réglisse *f* ■ **~ allsorts** *bonbons au réglisse de différentes couleurs.*

liquor store *n US* magasin *m* de vins et spiritueux.

lira [ˈlɪərə] (*pl* **lire** [-rɪ] *OR pl* **liras**) *n* lire *f*.

Lisbon [ˈlɪzbən] *pr n* Lisbonne.

lisp [lɪsp] ◇ *vi* parler avec un cheveu sur la langue, zézayer.
◇ *vt* dire en zézayant.
◇ *n* : **to speak with** *OR* **to have a ~** avoir un cheveu sur la langue, zézayer.

lissom(e) [ˈlɪsəm] *adj lit* souple, agile.

list [lɪst] ◇ *n* **1.** [record] liste *f* ■ **to make** *OR* **to write a ~** faire *OR* dresser une liste **2.** [lean] inclinaison *f* ■ NAUT gîte *f*, bande *f*.
◇ *vt* **1.** [make list of] dresser la liste de ■ [enumerate] énumérer ■ [enter in a list] inscrire (sur une liste) ■ **my name isn't ~ed** mon nom ne figure pas sur la liste **2.** [classify] classer ■ **they are ~ed by family name** ils sont classés par nom de famille **3.** COMPUT lister **4.** ST. EX [shares] coter.
◇ *vi* [lean] pencher, être incliné ■ NAUT [ship] gîter, donner de la bande.

listed building [ˈlɪstɪd-] *n UK* monument *m* classé.

listed company [ˈlɪstɪd-] *n UK* société *f* cotée en Bourse.

listen [ˈlɪsn] ◇ *vi* **1.** [to sound] écouter ■ **~ carefully** écoutez bien ■ **to ~ to sb/sthg** écouter qqn/qqch **2.** [take notice - of advice] écouter ■ **if only I'd ~ed to my mother!** si seulement j'avais écouté ma mère *OR* suivi les conseils de ma mère! ■ **I told him but he wouldn't ~** je le lui ai dit, mais il ne voulait rien entendre.
◇ *n inf* **have a ~ to their latest record** écoute un peu leur dernier disque.
◆ **listen (out) for** *vt insep* guetter, être à l'affût de ■ **she ~s (out) for his steps on the stairs every evening** elle guette le bruit de ses pas dans l'escalier tous les soirs.
◆ **listen in** *vi insep* **1.** [to radio] écouter, être à l'écoute **2.** [eavesdrop] écouter ■ **it's rude to ~ in on other people's conversations** c'est impoli d'écouter les conversations.

listener [ˈlɪsnər] *n* **1.** personne *f* qui écoute ■ **he's a good/bad ~** il sait/il ne sait pas écouter (les autres) **2.** RADIO auditeur *m*, - trice *f*.

listening post [ˈlɪsnɪŋ-] *n* poste *m* d'écoute.

listing [ˈlɪstɪŋ] *n* **1.** [gen - list] liste *f* ; [- entry] entrée *f* ■ **I found no ~ for the company in the directory** je n'ai pas trouvé la société dans l'annuaire **2.** COMPUT listing *m*, listage *m*.
◆ **listings** *npl* : **cinéma/TV ~s** programme *m* des films/émissions de la semaine.

listless [ˈlɪstlɪs] *adj* [torpid, unenergetic] apathique, endormi, avachi ■ [weak] mou *(before vowel or silent 'h' mol)*, molle *f*, inerte ■ [bored] indolent, alangui ■ [indifferent] indifférent, insensible.

listlessly [ˈlɪstlɪslɪ] *adv* [without energy] sans énergie *OR* vigueur, avec apathie ■ [weakly] mollement ■ [without interest] d'un air absent.

list price *n* prix *m* du catalogue ■ **I can get 20% off (the) ~** je peux avoir un rabais de 20 % sur le prix de vente.

lists [lɪsts] *npl* lice *f* ■ **to enter the ~** *liter* & *fig* entrer en lice.

lit [lɪt] ◇ *pt* & *pp* ⊳ **light**.
◇ *adj* éclairé.
◇ *n inf* (*abbrev of* **literature**) ■ **she teaches English ~** elle enseigne la littérature anglaise.

litany [ˈlɪtənɪ] (*pl* **litanies**) *n liter* & *fig* litanie *f*.

liter *US* = **litre**.

literacy [ˈlɪtərəsɪ] *n* [of individual] capacité *f* de lire et d'écrire ■ [of population] alphabétisation *f* ▶ **adult ~** l'alphabétisation des adultes ■ **computer ~** connaissances *fpl* en informatique.

literal [ˈlɪtərəl] *adj* [meaning] propre, littéral ■ [translation] littéral.

literally [ˈlɪtərəlɪ] *adv* **1.** [not figuratively] littéralement, au sens propre ■ [word for word] littéralement ■ **to take sthg ~** prendre qqch au pied de la lettre *OR* à la lettre ■ **to translate ~** faire une traduction littérale **2.** [in exaggeration] littéralement ■ **we've had ~ millions of letters** nous avons reçu littéralement des millions de lettres.

literal-minded *adj* sans imagination, terre à terre.

literary [ˈlɪtərərɪ] *adj* **1.** [style, work etc] littéraire ■ **a ~ man** un homme de lettres ■ **~ criticism** critique *f* littéraire **2.** [formal, written - language] littéraire.

literary agent *n* agent *m* littéraire.

literate [ˈlɪtərət] *adj* **1.** [able to read and write] capable de lire et d'écrire **2.** [educated] instruit, cultivé.

-literate *in cpds* : **to be computer~** avoir des connaissances en informatique.

literati [ˌlɪtəˈrɑːtiː] *npl fml* gens *mpl* de lettres, lettrés *mpl*.

literature [ˈlɪtrətʃər] *n (U)* **1.** [creative writing] littérature *f* **2.** [printed material] documentation *f* ■ **sales ~** documentation *f*, brochures *fpl* de vente.

lithe [laɪð] *adj* [movement, person] agile ■ [body] souple.

lithium [ˈlɪθɪəm] *n* lithium *m*.

lithograph [ˈlɪθəgrɑːf] ◇ *n* lithographie *f (estampe)*.
◇ *vt* lithographier.

lithography [lɪˈθɒgrəfɪ] *n* lithographie *f (procédé)*.

Lithuania [ˌlɪθjʊˈeɪnjə] *pr n* Lituanie *f* ■ **in ~** en Lituanie.

Lithuanian [ˌlɪθjʊˈeɪnjən] ◇ *n* **1.** [person] Lituanien *m*, - enne *f* **2.** LING lituanien *m*.
◇ *adj* lituanien.

litigant [ˈlɪtɪgənt] LAW ◇ *n* plaideur *m*, - euse *f*, partie *f*.
◇ *adj* en litige.

litigate [ˈlɪtɪgeɪt] LAW ◇ *vt* contester (en justice).
◇ *vi* plaider, intenter une action en justice.

litigation [ˌlɪtɪˈgeɪʃn] *n* LAW litige *m* ■ **the case went to ~** le cas est passé en justice ■ **they are in ~** ils sont en procès ■ **the issue is still in ~** l'affaire est toujours devant *OR* entre les mains de la justice.

litigious [lɪˈtɪdʒəs] *adj fml* & *pej* [fond of lawsuits] procédurier.

litmus [ˈlɪtməs] *n* tournesol *m*.

litmus paper *n* papier *m* de tournesol.

litmus test *n* CHEM réaction *f* au tournesol ■ *fig* épreuve *f* de vérité.

litotes [ˈlaɪtəʊtiːz] (*pl inv*) *n* litote *f*.

litre *UK*, **liter** *US* [ˈliːtər] *n* litre *m*.

litter [ˈlɪtər] ◇ *n* **1.** *(U)* [rubbish] détritus *mpl*, ordures *fpl* ■ [dropped in street] papiers *mpl* (gras) ■ **'no ~'** 'respectez la propreté des lieux' **2.** [clutter] fouillis *m* **3.** ZOOL portée *f* **4.** [material - to bed animals] litière *f* ; [- to protect plants] paille *f*, paillis *m* ■ **~ tray** caisse *f* (pour litière).
◇ *vt* **1.** [make untidy - public place] laisser des détritus dans ; [- house, room] mettre du désordre dans ; [- desk] encombrer ■ **don't ~ the table (up) with your tools** n'encombre pas la table avec tes outils **2.** *(usu passive)* [cover, strew] joncher, couvrir ■ *fig* parsemer ■ **his life is ~ed with failed love affairs** sa vie est jalonnée d'échecs amoureux.
◇ *vi* **1.** ZOOL mettre bas **2.** *US* [with rubbish] : **'no littering'** 'respectez la propreté des lieux'.

litter bin *n UK* poubelle *f*.

litter lout *UK*, **litterbug** [ˈlɪtəbʌg] *US n inf personne qui jette des papiers ou des détritus par terre.*

little[1] [ˈlɪtl] *adj* **1.** [in size, quantity] petit ■ **would you like a ~ drop of gin?** tu veux un peu de gin? ■ **would you like a ~ something to eat?** voudriez-vous manger un petit quelque chose? ▶ **the ~ hand** [of clock] la petite aiguille
2. [young - child, animal] petit ■ **when I was ~** quand j'étais petit ■ **my ~ sister** ma petite sœur ■ **my ~ sister** ma petite sœur ▶ ***'Little Women'*** *Alcott* 'Les Quatre filles du docteur March'

3. [short - time, distance] : **we spent a ~ time in France** nous avons passé quelque temps en France ▪ **a ~ while ago** [moments ago] il y a quelques instants ; [days, months ago] il y a quelque temps ▪ **she only stayed (for) a ~ while** elle n'est pas restée très longtemps ▪ **the shop is a ~ way along the street** le magasin se trouve un peu plus loin dans la rue
4. [unimportant] petit ▪ **they had a ~ argument** ils se sont un peu disputés
5. [expressing affection, pleasure, irritation] petit ▪ **what a nice ~ garden!** quel joli petit jardin! ▪ **a ~ old lady** une petite vieille ▪ **poor ~ thing!** pauvre petit!

little² ['lɪtl] (*comp* **less** [les], *superl* **least** [li:st]) ◇ *det* [opposite of 'much'] peu de ▪ **very ~ time/money** très peu de temps/d'argent ▪ **I watch very ~ television** je regarde très peu la télévision ▪ **I'm afraid there's ~ hope left** je crains qu'il n'y ait plus beaucoup d'espoir ▪ **with no ~ difficulty** *fml* non sans peine.
◇ *pron* **1.** [small amount] pas grand-chose ▪ **there's ~ one can say** il n'y a pas grand-chose à dire ▪ **I see very ~ of him now** je ne le vois plus que très rarement ▪ **very ~ is known about his childhood** on ne sait pas grand-chose *OR* on ne sait que très peu de choses sur son enfance ▪ **I gave her as ~ as possible** je lui ai donné le minimum ▪ **you may be paid as ~ as £3 an hour** tu ne seras peut-être payé que 3 livres de l'heure ▪ **so ~** si peu ▪ **to make ~ of** [fail to understand] ne pas comprendre grand-chose à ; [not emphasize] minimiser ; [scorn] faire peu de cas de **2.** [certain amount] : **a ~ of everything** un peu de tout ▪ **the ~ I saw looked excellent** le peu que j'en ai vu paraissait excellent.
◇ *adv* **1.** [to a limited extent] : **it's ~ short of madness** ça frise la folie ▪ **he's ~ more than a waiter** il n'est rien de plus qu'un simple serveur **2.** [rarely] peu ▪ **we go there as ~ as possible** nous y allons le moins possible ▪ **we talk very ~ now** nous ne nous parlons presque plus **3.** *fml* [never] : **I ~ thought** *OR* **~ did I think we would be friends one day** jamais je n'aurais cru que nous serions amis un jour.
◆ **a little** ◇ *det phr* un peu de ▪ **I speak a ~ French** je parle quelques mots de français ➲ **a ~ learning is a dangerous thing** *prov* il est moins dangereux de ne rien savoir que d'en savoir trop peu.
◇ *pron phr* un peu.
◇ *adv phr* **1.** [slightly] un peu ▪ **I'm a ~ tired** je suis un peu fatigué ▪ **not even a ~ interested** pas le moins du monde intéressé **2.** [for a short time or distance] un peu ▪ **I walked on a ~** j'ai marché encore un peu.
◆ **a little bit** *adv phr inf* = a little.
◆ **little by little** *adv phr* peu à peu, petit à petit.

little- *in cpds* : **a ~understood phenomenon** un phénomène (encore) mal compris ▪ **a ~explored area** une zone presque inexplorée *OR* (encore) peu explorée.

Little Bighorn ['lɪtl'bɪg,hɔ:n] *pr n* : **the battle of the ~** la bataille de Little Bighorn.

THE BATTLE OF THE LITTLE BIGHORN

Ultime bataille du général Custer, qui eut lieu en 1876 dans l'État du Montana. Ayant sous-estimé les Sioux de Sitting Bull et de Crazy Horse, le général conduisit ses soldats au massacre. Cet épisode est également connu sous le nom de *Custer's last stand*.

little black dress *n* petite robe *f* noire.

little Englander *n Anglais borné.*

little finger *n* auriculaire *m*, petit doigt *m* ▪ **to twist sb round one's ~** faire ce qu'on veut de qqn.

little green men *npl* petits hommes verts *mpl*, extraterrestres *mf pl*.

little-known *adj* peu connu.

little league *US* ◇ *n championnat de base-ball pour les moins de 12 ans.*
◇ *adj inf* de second rang.

little toe *n* petit orteil *m*.

liturgy ['lɪtədʒɪ] (*pl* **liturgies**) *n* liturgie *f*.

livable ['lɪvəbl] *adj inf* **1.** [inhabitable] habitable ▪ **we're trying to make the house ~ (in)** nous essayons de rendre la maison habitable **2.** [bearable] supportable.

live¹ [lɪv] ◇ *vi* **1.** [be or stay alive] vivre ▪ **as long as I ~** tant que je vivrai, de mon vivant ▪ **was she still living when her grandson was born?** est-ce qu'elle était encore en vie quand son petit-fils est né? ▪ **she didn't ~ long after her son died** elle n'a pas survécu longtemps à son fils ▪ **you'll ~!** *iron* tu n'en mourras pas! ▪ **I won't ~ to see them grow up** je ne vivrai pas assez vieux pour les voir grandir ▪ **to ~ on borrowed time** être en sursis *fig* ▪ **to ~ to a ripe old age** vivre vieux *OR* jusqu'à un âge avancé ▮ *fig* **the dialogue is what makes the characters ~** ce sont les dialogues qui donnent de la vie aux personnages
2. [have a specified way of life] vivre ▪ **to ~ dangerously** vivre dangereusement ▪ **they ~d happily ever after** ils vécurent heureux jusqu'à la fin de leurs jours ▪ **she ~s for her children/for skiing** elle ne vit que pour ses enfants/que pour le ski ▪ **to ~ in poverty/luxury** vivre dans la pauvreté/le luxe ▪ **we ~ in uncertain times** nous vivons une époque incertaine ➲ **~ and let ~!** *prov* laisse faire! ▪ **well, you ~ and learn!** on en apprend tous les jours!
3. [reside] habiter ▪ **they have nowhere to ~** ils sont à la rue ▪ **the giant tortoise ~s mainly in the Galapagos** la tortue géante vit surtout aux Galapagos ▪ **they ~ in Rome** ils habitent (à) Rome, ils vivent à Rome ▪ **to ~ in a flat/a castle** habiter (dans) un appartement/un château ▪ **I ~ in** *OR* **on Bank Street** j'habite Bank Street ▪ **he practically ~s in** *OR* **at the library** il passe sa vie à la bibliothèque ▪ **do you ~ with your parents?** habitez-vous chez vos parents? ▪ **to ~ in sin (with sb)** *dated* & *hum* vivre dans le péché (avec qqn)
4. [support o.s.] vivre ▪ **they don't earn enough to ~** ils ne gagnent pas de quoi vivre ▪ **he ~s by teaching** il gagne sa vie en enseignant ▪ **how does she ~ on that salary?** comment s'en sort-elle avec ce salaire?
5. [obtain food] se nourrir ▪ **we've been living out of cans** *OR* **tins lately** on se nourrit de conserves depuis quelque temps ▪ **he was reduced to living out of rubbish bins** il en était réduit à fouiller les poubelles pour se nourrir
6. [exist fully, intensely] vivre ▪ **she really knows how to ~** elle sait vraiment profiter de la vie ▪ **let's ~ for the moment** *OR* **for today!** vivons l'instant présent! ▪ **if you haven't been to New York, you haven't ~d!** si tu n'es jamais allé à New York, tu n'as rien vu!
◇ *vt* vivre ▪ **to ~ a life of poverty** vivre dans la pauvreté ▪ **to ~ a solitary life** mener une vie solitaire ▪ **to ~ a lie** être dans une situation fausse ▪ **she ~d the life of a film star for six years** elle a vécu comme une star de cinéma pendant six ans ➲ **to ~ it up** *inf* faire la fête ▪ **my father ~s and breathes golf** mon père ne vit que pour le golf.
◆ **live down** *vt sep* [recover from - error, disgrace] : **they'll never let him ~ that down** ils ne lui passeront *OR* pardonneront jamais cela ▪ **you'll never ~ this down!** [ridicule] tu n'as pas fini d'en entendre parler!
◆ **live in** *vi insep* **1.** [domestic] être logé et nourri ▪ [worker, nurse] être logé *OR* habiter sur place
2. [pupil] être interne.
◆ **live off** *vt insep* **1.** [sponge off] vivre aux crochets de ▪ **he ~s off his parents** il vit aux crochets de ses parents
2. [savings] vivre de ▪ [nuts, berries] se nourrir de ▪ **to ~ off the land** vivre de la terre.
◆ **live on** ◇ *vi insep* [person] continuer à vivre ▪ [custom, ideal] persister ▪ **his memory ~s on** son souvenir est encore vivant.
◇ *vt insep* **1.** [food] vivre de, se nourrir de
2. [salary] vivre de ▪ **his pension is all they have to ~ on** ils n'ont que sa retraite pour vivre ▪ **to ~ on $800 a month** vivre avec 800 dollars par mois.
◆ **live out** ◇ *vt sep* **1.** [spend] passer ▪ **she ~d out the rest of her life in Spain** elle a passé le reste de sa vie en Espagne
2. [fulfil] vivre ▪ **to ~ out one's fantasies** réaliser ses rêves.
◇ *vi insep* : **the maid ~s out** la bonne ne loge pas sur place ▪ **he studies here but ~s out** il est étudiant ici mais il n'habite pas sur le campus.
◆ **live through** *vt insep* connaître ▪ **they've ~d through war and famine** ils ont connu la guerre et la famine.
◆ **live together** *vi insep* [as a couple] vivre ensemble, cohabiter.

◆ **live up to** *vt insep* [name, reputation] se montrer à la hauteur de ▪ [expectation] être *OR* se montrer à la hauteur de, répondre à ▪ **we have a reputation to ~ up to!** nous avons une réputation à défendre!

◆ **live with** *vt insep* **1.** [cohabit with] vivre avec
2. [put up with] : **she's not easy to ~ with** elle n'est pas facile à vivre ▪ **I don't like the situation, but I have to ~ with it** cette situation ne me plaît pas, mais je n'ai pas le choix ▪ **I couldn't ~ with myself if I didn't tell him the truth** je ne supporterais pas de ne pas lui dire la vérité.

live[2] [laɪv] ◇ *adj* **1.** [alive - animal, person] vivant ▪ **a real ~ cowboy** *inf* un cowboy, un vrai de vrai ▶ **~ births** naissances *fpl* viables ▪ **~ yoghurt** yaourt *m* actif
2. MUS, RADIO & TV [programme, interview, concert] en direct ▪ **Sinatra ~ at the Palladium** Sinatra en concert au Palladium ▪ **recorded before a ~ audience** enregistré en public ▶ **~ music** musique *f* live ▪ **~ recording** enregistrement *m* live *OR* public
3. ELEC [connected] sous tension ▪ **~ circuit** circuit *m* alimenté *OR* sous tension
4. [unexploded] non explosé ▪ **~ ammunition** balles *fpl* réelles
5. [still burning - coals, embers] ardent
6. [not extinct - volcano] actif
7. [controversial] controversé ▪ **a ~ issue** un sujet controversé.
◇ *adv* en direct ▪ **the match can be seen/is going out ~ at 3.30 p.m.** on peut suivre le match/le match est diffusé en direct à 15 h 30.

liveable ['lɪvəbl] = **livable**.

lived-in ['lɪvdɪn] *adj* [comfortable] confortable ▪ [occupied] habité ▪ **the room had a nice ~ feel** on sentait que la pièce était habitée.

live-in ['lɪv-] *adj* [maid] logé et nourri ▪ [nurse, governess] à demeure ▪ **his ~ girlfriend** sa compagne, la femme avec qui il vit ▪ **she has a ~ lover** son ami habite chez elle.

livelihood ['laɪvlɪhʊd] *n (U)* moyens *mpl* d'existence, gagne-pain *m inv* ▪ **writing isn't a hobby, it's my ~** écrire n'est pas un passe-temps, c'est mon gagne-pain *OR* mon métier.

liveliness ['laɪvlɪnɪs] *n* [of person] vivacité *f* ▪ [of conversation, party] animation *f* ▪ [of debate, style] vigueur *f* ▪ [of music, dance] gaieté *f*, allégresse *f* ▪ [of colours] éclat *m*, gaieté *f*.

lively ['laɪvlɪ] (*comp* **livelier**, *superl* **liveliest**) *adj* **1.** [full of life - person] vif, plein d'entrain ; [- kitten, puppy] plein de vie, espiègle ; [- horse] fringant ; [- music] gai, entraînant **2.** [keen - mind, curiosity, imagination] vif ▪ **to take a ~ interest in sthg** s'intéresser vivement à qqch **3.** [exciting - place, event, discussion] animé ▪ **the town gets a bit livelier in summer** la ville s'anime un peu en été ▪ **a ~ performance** une interprétation très enlevée **4.** [eventful - day, time] mouvementé, agité ▪ **look ~!** *UK inf* grouille-toi! **5.** [brisk - pace] vif **6.** [vivid - colour] vif, éclatant.

liver ['lɪvər] *n* **1.** ANAT foie *m* **2.** CULIN foie *m* ▪ **~ pâté** pâté *m* de foie **3.** [colour] rouge brun *m inv*, brun roux *m inv* **4.** [person] : **fast** *OR* **high ~** fêtard *m*, - e *f*, noceur *m*, - euse *f*.

liveried ['lɪvərɪd] *adj* en livrée.

liverish ['lɪvərɪʃ] *adj* **1.** *inf* [ill] : **to be** *OR* **to feel ~** avoir mal au foie **2.** [peevish] irritable, bilieux.

Liverpudlian [,lɪvə'pʌdlɪən] ◇ *n habitant de Liverpool.*
◇ *adj* de Liverpool.

liver salts *npl* lithiné *m*.

liver sausage *n* pâté *m* de foie.

liver spot *n* tache *f* de vieillesse.

liverwort ['lɪvəwɜːt] *n* BOT hépatique *f*.

liverwurst ['lɪvəwɜːst] *US* = **liver sausage**.

livery ['lɪvərɪ] (*pl* **liveries**) *n* **1.** [uniform] livrée *f* **2.** [of company] couleurs *fpl* ▪ **the cars have been painted in the new company ~** les voitures ont été peintes aux nouvelles couleurs de la maison.

livery stable *n* [for boarding] écurie *f* prenant des chevaux en pension ▪ [for hiring] écurie *f* de chevaux de louage.

lives [laɪvz] *pl* ▷ **life**.

livestock ['laɪvstɒk] *n (U)* bétail *m*, cheptel *m*.

live wire ['laɪv-] *n* **1.** ELEC fil *m* sous tension **2.** *inf fig* **she's a real ~** elle déborde d'énergie.

livid ['lɪvɪd] *adj* **1.** [blue-grey] livide ▪ **a ~ sky** un ciel de plomb **2.** *inf* [angry] furax.

living ['lɪvɪŋ] ◇ *n* **1.** [livelihood] vie *f* ▪ **I have to work for a ~** je suis obligé de travailler pour vivre ▪ **what do you do for a ~?** qu'est-ce que vous faites dans la vie? ▪ **you can't make a decent ~ in this business** on gagne mal sa vie *OR* on a du mal à gagner sa vie dans ce métier **2.** [life, lifestyle] vie *f* **3.** *UK* RELIG bénéfice *m*.
◇ *adj* **1.** [alive] vivant ▪ **he has no ~ relatives** il n'a plus de famille ▶ **it was the worst storm in ~ memory** de mémoire d'homme on n'avait jamais vu une tempête aussi violente ▪ **I didn't see a ~ soul** je n'ai pas vu âme qui vive ▪ **she's ~ proof that the treatment works** elle est la preuve vivante que le traitement est efficace ▪ **they made her life a ~ hell** ils lui ont rendu la vie infernale ▪ **the~ dead** les morts vivants *mpl* ▪ **~ death** vie *f* de souffrances **2.** GEOL : **the ~ rock** la roche non exploitée.
◇ *npl* : **the ~** les vivants *mpl*.
◇ *comp* **1.** [conditions] de vie ▪ **~ expenses** frais *mpl* de subsistance ▪ **~ standards** niveau *m* de vie **2.** [place] : **the ~ area is separated from the bedrooms** la partie séjour est séparée des chambres ▪ **~ quarters** [for servants] logements *mpl* ▪ [on ship] partie *f* habitée ▪ **these are the crew's ~ quarters** ce sont les quartiers de l'équipage.

living room *n* (salle *f* de) séjour *m*.

living wage *n* : **a ~** le minimum vital ▪ **£400 a month isn't a ~** on ne peut pas vivre avec 400 livres par mois.

Livy ['lɪvɪ] *pr n* Tite-Live.

lizard ['lɪzəd] ◇ *n* lézard *m*.
◇ *comp* [belt, shoes] en lézard.

llama ['lɑːmə] *n* ZOOL lama *m*.

LLB (*abbrev of* **Bachelor of Laws**) *n (titulaire d'une) licence de droit.*

LLD (*abbrev of* **Doctor of Laws**) *n docteur en droit.*

lo [ləʊ] *interj phr* **and ~ and behold there he was!** et voilà, il était là!

load [ləʊd] ◇ *vt* **1.** [person, animal, vehicle] charger ▪ **to ~ sthg with sthg** charger qqch sur qqch ▪ **~ the bags into the car** chargez *OR* mettez les sacs dans la voiture ▪ **the ship is ~ing grain** on est en train de charger le navire de céréales
2. [camera, gun, machine] charger ▪ **to ~ a film/tape** mettre une pellicule/une cassette ▪ **~ the cassette into the recorder** introduisez la cassette dans le magnétophone ▪ **to ~ a program (into memory)** COMPUT charger un programme (en mémoire)
3. [insurance premium] majorer, augmenter
4. *phr* **to ~ the dice** piper les dés ▪ **to ~ the dice against sb** *fig* défavoriser qqn ▪ **the dice are ~ed against us** nous n'aurons pas la partie facile.
◇ *vi* **1.** [receive freight] charger ▪ **the ship is ~ing** le navire est en cours de chargement
2. [camera, gun] se recharger ▪ [computer program] se charger.
◇ *n* **1.** [cargo] charge *f*, chargement *m* ▪ [carrying capacity] charge *f* ▪ **we moved all the stuff in ten ~s** nous avons tout transporté en dix voyages
2. *fig* [burden] fardeau *m*, charge *f* ▪ **the reforms should lighten the ~ of classroom teachers** les réformes devraient faciliter la tâche des enseignants ▪ **hire somebody to share the ~** embauchez quelqu'un pour vous faciliter la tâche ▶ **that's a ~ off my mind!** me voilà soulagé d'un poids!
3. [batch of laundry] machine *f*
4. ELEC, CONSTR & TECH charge *f*
5. *phr* **get a ~ of this** *inf* [look] vise un peu ça ; [listen] écoute-moi ça ▪ **to shoot one's ~**▲ [ejaculate] décharger.
◇ *comp* COMPUT [program] de chargement ▪ [module] chargeable ▪ **~ mode** mode *m* chargement.

◆ **a load of** *det phr* : **what a ~ of rubbish!** *UK inf* c'est vraiment n'importe quoi!

◆ **loads** *adv inf* beaucoup.

◆ **loads of** *det phr inf* des tas *OR* des masses de ▪ **it'll be ~s of fun** ça va être super marrant ▪ **she's got ~s of money** elle est bourrée de fric, elle a un fric monstre.

◆ **load down** *vt sep* charger (lourdement) ▪ **he was ~ed down with packages** il avait des paquets plein les bras ▪ **I'm ~ed down with work** je suis surchargé de travail.
◆ **load up** ◇ *vt sep* charger ▪ **~ the wheelbarrow up with bricks** remplissez la brouette de briques.
◇ *vi insep* charger.

load-bearing *adj* [wall] porteur.

loaded ['ləʊdɪd] *adj* **1.** [laden] chargé ▪ **is the lorry fully ~?** le camion est-il vraiment plein? **2.** *fig* **to be ~ with** être chargé de *OR* plein de **3.** [gun, camera] chargé **4.** [dice] pipé **5.** [statement, comment] insidieux ▪ **~ question** question *f* piège **6.** *inf* [rich] plein aux as **7.** △ [drunk] plein, bourré ▪ [high on drugs] défoncé△, cassé△.

loader ['ləʊdəʳ] *n* **1.** [person] chargeur *m*, - euse *f* **2.** ELEC, MIL & PHOT [device] chargeur *m* **3.** CONSTR [machine] chargeuse *f*, loader *m* **4.** COMPUT (programme *m*) chargeur *m*.

loading ['ləʊdɪŋ] *n* [of vehicle, machine, gun, computer program] chargement *m*.

loading bay *n* aire *f* de chargement.

loads [ləʊdz] *adv inf* vachement ▪ **it'll cost ~** ça va coûter un max *OR* vachement cher.

loaf [ləʊf] (*pl* **loaves** [ləʊvz]) ◇ *n* **1.** [of bread] pain *m* ▪ [large round loaf] miche *f* ▪ **two loaves (of bread) please** deux pains, s'il vous plaît **2.** *phr* **use your ~!** *UK inf* fais travailler tes méninges!
◇ *vi inf* fainéanter, traîner.

loafer ['ləʊfəʳ] *n* **1.** *inf* [person] fainéant *m*, - e *f* **2.** [shoe] mocassin *m*.

loam [ləʊm] *n* **1.** AGRIC & HORT terreau *m* **2.** CONSTR pisé *m*.

loan [ləʊn] ◇ *n* **1.** [money lent] prêt *m* ▪ [money borrowed] emprunt *m* ▪ **he asked me for a ~** il m'a demandé de lui prêter de l'argent ▪ **student ~s** des prêts aux étudiants **2.** [act of lending] : **may I have the ~ of your typewriter?** *UK* peux-tu me prêter ta machine à écrire? ▪ **I have three books on ~ from the library** j'ai emprunté trois livres à la bibliothèque ▪ **the book you want is out on ~** le livre que vous voulez est sorti ▪ **the picture is on ~ to an American museum** le tableau a été prêté à un musée américain ▪ **she's on ~ from head office** le siège l'a envoyée chez nous pour un temps **3.** = **loanword**.
◇ *vt* prêter ▪ **to ~ sb sthg, to ~ sthg to sb** prêter qqch à qqn.

loan account *n* compte *m* de prêt.

loan capital *n* capital *m* d'emprunt.

loan shark *n pej* usurier *m*, - ère *f*.

loan translation *n* LING calque *m*.

loanword ['ləʊnwɜːd] *n* LING (mot *m* d')emprunt *m*.

loath [ləʊθ] *adj* : **to be ~ to do sthg** ne pas être disposé à faire qqch ▪ **I'm very ~ to admit it** j'ai beaucoup de mal à l'admettre ▪ **I am somewhat ~ to contradict you, but...** je n'aime pas vous contredire, mais... ▪ **nothing ~** avec plaisir, très volontiers.

loathe [ləʊð] *vt* détester ▪ **I ~ having to get up in the mornings** j'ai horreur d'être obligé de me lever le matin.

loathing ['ləʊðɪŋ] *n* aversion *f*, répugnance *f* ▪ **I have an absolute ~ for people like them** j'ai horreur des gens comme eux ▪ **it fills me with ~** ça me révolte.

loathsome ['ləʊðsəm] *adj* [behaviour] abominable ▪ [person] détestable.

loaves [ləʊvz] *pl* ⊳ **loaf**.

lob [lɒb] (*pret & pp* **lobbed**, *cont* **lobbing**) ◇ *n* SPORT lob *m*.
◇ *vt* **1.** [throw] lancer ▪ **he lobbed the stone into the air** il envoya la pierre en l'air **2.** SPORT [ball] envoyer haut ▪ [opponent] lober.
◇ *vi* SPORT [player] faire un lob.

lobby ['lɒbɪ] (*pl* **lobbies**, *pret & pp* **lobbied**) ◇ *n* **1.** [in hotel] hall *m* ▪ THEAT foyer *m* ▪ [in large house, apartment block] entrée *f* **2.** POL [pressure group] groupe *m* de pression, lobby *m* ▪ [action] pression *f* ▪ **yesterday's ~ of parliament** la pression exercée hier sur le parlement **3.** *UK* POL [hall] salle *f* des pas perdus.
◇ *vi* : **ecologists are ~ing for the closure of the plant** les écologistes font pression pour obtenir la fermeture de la centrale.
◇ *vt* [person, parliament] exercer une pression sur ▪ **a group of teachers came to ~ the minister** un groupe d'enseignants est venu faire pression sur le ministre.

lobby correspondent *n UK* POL journaliste *mf* parlementaire.

lobbying ['lɒbɪɪŋ] *n (U)* POL pressions *fpl* ▪ **there has been intense ~ against the bill** il y a eu de fortes pressions pour que le projet de loi soit retiré.

lobbyist ['lɒbɪɪst] *n* lobbyiste *mf*, membre *m* d'un groupe de pression.

lobe [ləʊb] *n* ANAT, BOT & RADIO lobe *m*.

lobectomy [ləʊ'bektəmɪ] (*pl* **lobectomies**) *n* lobectomie *f*.

lobelia [lə'biːljə] *n* BOT lobélie *f*.

lobotomy [lə'bɒtəmɪ] (*pl* **lobotomies**) *n* lobotomie *f*, leucotomie *f*.

lobster ['lɒbstəʳ] (*pl inv OR pl* **lobsters**) *n* homard *m*.

lobsterpot ['lɒbstəpɒt] *n* casier *m* à homards *OR* à langoustes.

local ['ləʊkl] ◇ *adj* **1.** [of the immediate area - tradition, phone call] local ; [- hospital, shop] de quartier ; [- inhabitants] du quartier, du coin ▪ **~ traders** les commerces *mpl* de proximité **2.** ADMIN & POL [services, council] local, communal, municipal **3.** MED [infection, pain] localisé.
◇ *n* **1.** [person] habitant *m*, - e *f* (du lieu) ▪ **the ~s** les gens *m* du pays *OR* du coin ▪ **ask one of the ~s** demande à quelqu'un du coin **2.** *UK inf* [pub] troquet *m* du coin **3.** *US* [train] omnibus *m* ▪ [bus] bus *m* local **4.** *US* [union branch] section *f* syndicale **5.** *inf* MED anesthésie *f* locale **6.** *US* PRESS [item] nouvelle *f* locale.

local area network *n* COMPUT réseau *m* local.

local authority *n* administration *f* locale ▪ [in town] municipalité *f*.

local colour *n* couleur *f* locale.

locale [ləʊ'kɑːl] *n* [place] endroit *m*, lieu *m* ▪ [scene, setting] cadre *m*.

local education authority *n* direction *f* régionale de l'enseignement *(en Angleterre et au pays de Galles)*.

local government *n* administration *f* municipale ▪ **~ elections** élections *fpl* municipales ▪ **~ official** fonctionnaire *mf* de l'administration municipale.

locality [lə'kælətɪ] (*pl* **localities**) *n* **1.** [neighbourhood] voisinage *m*, environs *mpl* ▪ [general area] région *f* **2.** [location - of building, place] lieu *m*, site *m* ; [- of species] localité *f*.

localization [ˌləʊkəlaɪ'zeɪʃn] *n* COMPUT localisation *f*.

localize, ise ['ləʊkəlaɪz] *vt* **1.** [pinpoint, locate] localiser, situer **2.** [confine] localiser, limiter ▪ **they have tried to ~ the effect of the strike** ils ont essayé de limiter l'effet de la grève **3.** [concentrate - power, money] concentrer.

localized ['ləʊkəlaɪzd] *adj* localisé.

locally ['ləʊkəlɪ] *adv* localement ▪ **she is well known ~** [in region] elle est très connue dans la région ; [in neighbourhood] elle est très connue dans le quartier ▪ **he lives ~** il vit par ici ▪ **we shop ~** nous faisons nos courses dans le quartier ▪ **many issues have to be decided ~, not nationally** de nombreux problèmes doivent être résolus au niveau local, et non au niveau national ▪ **'~ grown potatoes/carrots'** 'pommes de terre/carottes du pays' ▪ **~ manufactured goods** articles *mpl* de fabrication locale.

local time *n* heure *f* locale.

locate [*UK* ləʊ'keɪt, *US* 'ləʊkeɪt] ◇ *vt* **1.** [find] repérer, trouver, localiser ▪ **the police are trying to ~ possible witnesses** la police recherche des témoins éventuels ▪ **we are trying to ~ his sister** nous essayons de savoir où se trouve sa sœur

2. *(usu passive)* [situate] situer ■ **the house is conveniently ~d for shops and public transport** la maison est située à proximité des magasins et des transports en commun.
◇ *vi* **1.** COMM [company, factory] s'établir, s'implanter **2.** *US* [settle] s'installer, s'établir.

location [ləʊ'keɪʃn] *n* **1.** [place, site] emplacement *m*, site *m* ■ **the firm has moved to a new ~** la société a déménagé ‖ [whereabouts] : **what is your present ~?** où te trouves-tu en ce moment? **2.** CIN extérieurs *mpl* ■ **shot on ~** tourné en extérieur **3.** [finding, discovery] repérage *m*, localisation *f* **4.** COMPUT position *f* ■ **memory ~** position (en) mémoire.

locative ['lɒkətɪv] LING ◇ *adj* locatif.
◇ *n* locatif *m*.

loc. cit. (*written abbrev of* **loco citato**) loc. cit.

loch [lɒk, lɒx] *n Scotland* loch *m*, lac *m*.

loci ['ləʊsaɪ, 'ləʊkaɪ] *pl* ▷ **locus**.

lock [lɒk] ◇ *vt* **1.** [door, drawer, car etc] fermer à clef
2. [valuables, person] enfermer ■ **they were ~ed into the agreement *fig*** ils étaient tenus par l'accord
3. [hold tightly] serrer ■ **they were ~ed in a passionate embrace** ils étaient unis *OR* enlacés dans une étreinte passionnée ■ **to ~ arms** [police cordon] former un barrage ■ **the unions were ~ed in a dispute with the management** les syndicats étaient aux prises avec la direction ■ **to be ~ed in combat** être engagé dans un combat ; *fig* être aux prises ➊ **to ~ horns** [stags] s'entremêler les bois ; *fig* être aux prises
4. [device, wheels, brakes] bloquer
5. COMPUT [file] verrouiller.
◇ *vi* **1.** [door, drawer, car etc] (se) fermer à clef
2. [engage] se joindre ■ **push the lever back until it ~s into place** pousse le levier jusqu'à ce qu'il s'enclenche
3. [wheels, brakes, nut] se bloquer.
◇ *n* **1.** [on door, drawer etc] serrure *f* ■ **under ~ and key** [object] sous clef ■ **the whole gang is now safely under ~ and key** toute la bande est désormais sous les verrous
2. [on canal] écluse *f*
3. [grip - gen] prise *f* ■ [in wrestling] clef *f*, prise *f*
4. *UK* AUT (rayon *m* de) braquage *m* ■ **on full ~** braqué à fond
5. TECH [device - gen] verrou *m* ; [- on gun] percuteur *m* ; [- on keyboard] : **shift *OR* caps ~** touche *f* de verrouillage majuscule
6. COMPUT verrouillage *m*
7. RUGBY : **~ (forward)** deuxième ligne *m*
8. [curl] boucle *f* ■ [stray strand] mèche *f*
9. *phr* **~, stock and barrel** en entier ■ **she bought the company ~, stock and barrel** elle a acheté la société en bloc ■ **the family has moved ~, stock and barrel to Canada** la famille est partie avec armes et bagages s'installer au Canada.
◆ **locks** *npl lit* chevelure *f*.
◆ **lock away** *vt sep* [valuables] mettre sous clef ■ [criminal] incarcérer, mettre sous les verrous ■ **we keep the alcohol ~ed away** nous gardons l'alcool sous clef.
◆ **lock in** *vt sep* enfermer ■ **he ~ed himself in** il s'est enfermé (à l'intérieur).
◆ **lock onto** *vt insep* [subj: radar] capter ■ [subj: homing device] se caler sur ■ [subj: missile] se fixer *OR* se verrouiller sur.
◆ **lock out** *vt sep* **1.** [accidentally] enfermer dehors ■ [deliberately] laisser dehors ■ **I've ~ed myself out** j'ai fermé la porte en laissant les clés à l'intérieur, je me suis enfermé dehors **2.** INDUST [workers] lock-outer.
◆ **lock up** ◇ *vt sep* **1.** [house, shop] fermer à clef
2. [valuables, criminal] = **lock away**
3. [capital] immobiliser.
◇ *vi insep* fermer à clef ■ **the last to leave ~s up** le dernier à partir ferme la porte à clef.

lockable ['lɒkəbl] *adj* qu'on peut fermer à clef.

locker ['lɒkər] *n* **1.** [for clothes, valuables etc] casier *m*, petit placard *m* ■ **where are the left-luggage ~s?** où se trouve la consigne automatique? **2.** *US* [freezer] congélateur *m*.

locker room *n US* vestiaire *m (avec casiers)*.
◆ **locker-room** *adj* [humour, joke] corsé, salé.

locket ['lɒkɪt] *n* pendentif *m*.

lock gate *n* porte *f* d'écluse.

locking ['lɒkɪŋ] *adj* [door, briefcase] à serrure, qui ferme à clef ■ **~ mechanism** mécanisme *m* de verrouillage.

lockjaw ['lɒkdʒɔ:] *n* tétanos *m*.

lock keeper *n* éclusier *m*, - ère *f*.

lockout ['lɒkaʊt] *n* [of workers] lock-out *m inv*.

locksmith ['lɒksmɪθ] *n* serrurier *m*.

lockup ['lɒkʌp] *n* **1.** *US* [jail] prison *f* ■ [cell] cellule *f* **2.** *UK* [garage] garage *m* **3.** [act of locking up] fermeture *f*.

lock-up garage *n UK* garage *m*.

loco ['ləʊkəʊ] (*pl* **locos**) ◇ *adj*[△] *US* dingue.
◇ *n inf* RAIL loco *f*.

locomotion [ˌləʊkə'məʊʃn] *n* locomotion *f*.

locomotive [ˌləʊkə'məʊtɪv] ◇ *n* locomotive *f*.
◇ *adj* automobile ■ ANAT locomoteur.

locomotor [ˌləʊkə'məʊtər] *adj* locomoteur.

locum ['ləʊkəm] *n UK* remplaçant *m*, - e *f (de prêtre, de médecin)*.

locus ['ləʊkəs] (*pl* **loci** ['ləʊsaɪ, 'ləʊkaɪ]) *n* **1.** *fml* [place] lieu *m* ■ LAW lieux *mpl* **2.** MATHS lieu *m* (géométrique) **3.** BIOL [of gene] locus *m*.

locust ['ləʊkəst] ◇ *n* **1.** [insect] locuste *f*, criquet *m* migrateur **2.** = **locust tree**.
◇ *comp* : **~ bean** caroube *f*.

locust tree *n* **1.** [false acacia] robinier *m* **2.** [carob tree] caroubier *m*.

locution [lə'kju:ʃn] *n fml* **1.** [phrase] locution *f* **2.** [style] style *m*, phraséologie *f* ■ [manner of speech] élocution *f*.

lode [ləʊd] *n* [vein - of metallic ore] veine *f* ; [- of gold, copper, silver] filon *m*.

lodestar ['ləʊdstɑ:r] *n* (étoile *f*) Polaire *f* ■ *fig* guide *m*, point *m* de repère.

lodestone ['ləʊdstəʊn] *n* MINER pierre *f* à aimant, magnétite *f* ■ *fig* aimant *m*.

lodge [lɒdʒ] ◇ *vt* **1.** [house] héberger, loger **2.** [stick, embed] loger ■ **a fish bone had ~d itself in his throat** une arête s'était logée dans sa gorge ■ **his words were ~d in my memory** ses paroles étaient gravées dans ma mémoire **3.** [make, file - claim] déposer ■ **to ~ a complaint** porter plainte ■ **she ~d a formal complaint with the authorities** elle a déposé une plainte officielle auprès de l'administration ■ **to ~ an accusation against sb** LAW porter plainte contre qqn **4.** [deposit for safekeeping] déposer, mettre en sûreté **5.** [invest - power, authority etc] investir.
◇ *vi* **1.** [stay] loger, être logé ■ **he is lodging at Mrs Smith's *OR* with Mrs Smith** il loge chez Mme Smith ; [with board] il est en pension chez Mme Smith **2.** [stick, become embedded] se loger.
◇ *n* **1.** [cabin - for hunters] pavillon *m* ; [- for skiers] chalet *m* **2.** *UK* [on country estate] maison *f* du gardien ■ [of porter] loge *f* **3.** *US* [in park, resort] bâtiment *m* central **4.** [Masonic] loge *f* **5.** [hotel] hôtel *m*, relais *m* **6.** [beavers'] hutte *f*.

lodger ['lɒdʒər] *n* locataire *mf* ■ [with board] pensionnaire *mf*.

lodging ['lɒdʒɪŋ] *n* hébergement *m*.
◆ **lodgings** *npl UK* chambre *f* meublée *OR* chambres *fpl* meublées *(chez un particulier)*.

lodging house *n* meublé *m*.

loft [lɒft] ◇ *n* **1.** [attic] grenier *m* ■ **~ conversion** combles *mpl* aménagés **2.** [elevated space - in church] tribune *f*, galerie *f* **3.** *US* [warehouse space] loft *m*.
◇ *vt* SPORT [hit] lancer très haut.

loftily ['lɒftɪlɪ] *adv* avec mépris, dédaigneusement.

lofty ['lɒftɪ] (*comp* **loftier**, *superl* **loftiest**) *adj* **1.** [high - summit, building etc] haut, élevé **2.** [supercilious - manner] hautain, dédaigneux, méprisant **3.** [exalted - in spirit] noble, élevé ; [- in rank, position] éminent **4.** [elevated - style, prose] élevé, noble.

log [lɒg] (*pret & pp* **logged**, *cont* **logging**) ◇ *n* **1.** [of wood] rondin *m* ■ [for firewood] bûche *f* **2.** [record] journal *m*, registre *m* ■ NAUT journal *m* *OR* livre *m* de bord ■ AERON carnet *m* de vol ■ [lorry driver's] carnet *m* de route ■ **keep a ~ of all the phone calls** notez tous les appels téléphoniques **3.** (*abbrev of* **logarithm**) log *m* **4.** [cake] : **Yuletide** *OR* **Christmas ~** bûche *f* de Noël.
◇ *comp* : **~ fire** feu *m* de bois.
◇ *vt* **1.** [information - on paper] consigner, inscrire ; [- in computer memory] entrer **2.** [speed, distance, time] : **he has logged 2,000 hours flying time** il a 2 000 heures de vol à son actif, il totalise 2 000 heures de vol **3.** [tree] tronçonner ■ [forest] mettre en coupe.
◇ *vi* [company] exploiter une forêt ■ [person] travailler comme bûcheron.
◆ **log in** ◇ *vi insep* COMPUT entrer dans le système, ouvrir une session.
◇ *vt sep* [user name, password] entrer, introduire.
◆ **log off** = log out.
◆ **log on** = log in.
◆ **log out** *vi insep* COMPUT sortir du système, fermer une session.
◆ **log up** *vt sep UK* [do, achieve] avoir à son actif ■ **they managed to ~ up 80 miles a day** ils ont réussi à faire 130 km par jour.

loganberry ['ləʊgənbərɪ] (*pl* **loganberries**) *n* [plant] framboisier *m* (hybride) ■ [fruit] mûre-framboise *f*.

logarithm ['lɒgərɪðm] *n* logarithme *m*.

logarithmic [,lɒgə'rɪðmɪk] *adj* logarithmique ■ **~ function** fonction *f* logarithme.

logbook ['lɒgbʊk] *n* **1.** [record] journal *m* ■ NAUT journal *m* *OR* livre *m* de bord ■ AERON carnet *m* de vol **2.** *UK* AUT ≃ carte *f* grise.

log cabin *n* cabane *f* en rondins.

LOG CABIN

Certains hommes politiques américains prétendent être nés dans une *log cabin* comme Abraham Lincoln, exprimant ainsi leur souci de proximité vis-à-vis des Américains d'origine modeste.

logger ['lɒgər] *n* **1.** *US* [lumberjack] bûcheron *m* **2.** *UK* [tractor] tracteur *m* forestier.

loggerheads ['lɒgəhedz] *npl* : **to be at ~ (with sb) : he's at ~ with the management over the issue** il est en complet désaccord avec la direction sur cette question.

logging ['lɒgɪŋ] *n* exploitation *f* forestière.

logic ['lɒdʒɪk] *n* [gen - COMPUT] logique *f* ■ [reasoning] raisonnement *m* ■ **if you follow my ~** si tu suis mon raisonnement.

logical ['lɒdʒɪkl] *adj* logique ■ **it's a ~ impossibility** c'est logiquement impossible ■ **he is incapable of ~ argument** il est incapable d'avoir un raisonnement logique.

logically ['lɒdʒɪklɪ] *adv* logiquement ■ **if you think about it ~** si on y réfléchit bien ■ **~, he should win** logiquement *OR* normalement, il devrait gagner.

logician [lə'dʒɪʃn] *n* logicien *m*, - enne *f*.

logistical [lə'dʒɪstɪkl] *adj* logistique.

logistically [lə'dʒɪstɪklɪ] *adv* sur le plan logistique.

logistics [lə'dʒɪstɪks] *npl* logistique *f*.

logjam ['lɒgdʒæm] *n* **1.** [in river] bouchon *m* de bois flottés **2.** *fig* [deadlock] impasse *f*.

logo ['ləʊgəʊ] (*pl* **logos**) *n* logo *m*.

log tables *npl* tables *fpl* de logarithmes.

logy ['ləʊgɪ] (*comp* **logier**, *superl* **logiest**) *adj US inf* patraque.

loin [lɔɪn] *n* CULIN [of pork] longe *f*, échine *f*, filet *m* ■ [of beef] aloyau *m* ■ [of veal] longe *f* ■ [of lamb] carré *m*.
◆ **loins** *npl* ANAT reins *mpl* ■ *euph* [genitals] parties *fpl*.

loincloth ['lɔɪnklɒθ] *n* pagne *m*.

loiter ['lɔɪtər] *vi* **1.** [hang about] traîner ■ [lurk] rôder ■ **'no ~ing'** zone sous surveillance *(où il est interdit de s'attarder)* ■ **~ing with intent** LAW délit *m* d'intention **2.** [dawdle] traîner ■ [lag behind] traîner (en route).

loll [lɒl] *vi* [lounge] se prélasser ■ **he was ~ing against the wall** il était nonchalamment appuyé contre le mur.
◆ **loll about** *UK*, **loll around** *vi insep* [in grass, armchair etc] se prélasser.
◆ **loll out** *vi insep* [tongue] pendre (mollement).

lollipop ['lɒlɪpɒp] *n* **1.** [sweet] sucette *f* **2.** *UK* [ice lolly] esquimau *m*, sucette *f* glacée.

lollipop lady, lollipop man *n inf en Grande-Bretagne, personne chargée d'aider les enfants à traverser une rue en arrêtant la circulation à l'aide d'un panneau en forme de sucette.*

lollop ['lɒləp] *vi* [person] marcher lourdement ■ [animal] galoper.

lolly ['lɒlɪ] (*pl* **lollies**) *n* **1.** *UK inf* = **lollipop** **2.** △ *UK* [money] fric *m*, pognon△ *m*.

lollypop ['lɒlɪpɒp] = **lollipop**.

Lombard ['lɒmbəd] ◇ *n* Lombard *m*, - e *f*.
◇ *adj* Lombard.

Lombard Street *pr n* [in London] *rue de Londres, cœur de l'activité financière* ■ [in San Francisco] *rue de San Francisco que l'on prétend la plus sinueuse du monde.*

Lombardy ['lɒmbədɪ] *pr n* Lombardie *f*.

London ['lʌndən] ◇ *pr n* Londres.
◇ *comp* [museums, shops, traffic] londonien ■ [life] à Londres ■ **~ (Regional) Transport** *régie des transports publics londoniens.*

London Bridge *pr n pont construit sur la Tamise en 1968 pour remplacer l'ancien pont, qui fut vendu et remonté dans l'Arizona.*

Londoner ['lʌndənər] *n* Londonien *m*, - enne *f*, habitant *m*, - e *f* de Londres.

lone [ləʊn] *adj* [unaccompanied - rider, stag] solitaire ■ [isolated - house] isolé ■ [single, unique] unique, seul ➊ **~ parent** parent *m* unique.

loneliness ['ləʊnlɪnɪs] *n* [of person] solitude *f*, isolement *m* ■ [of place] isolement *m*.

lonely ['ləʊnlɪ] (*comp* **lonelier**, *superl* **loneliest**) *adj* **1.** [sad - person] seul ; [- life] solitaire ■ **to be** *OR* **to feel ~** se sentir seul ■ **the house seems ~ without you** la maison paraît vide sans toi ■ **he went home to his ~ room** il regagna la solitude de sa chambre **2.** [unfrequented - spot] isolé ; [- street] peu fréquenté, vide.

lonely hearts *adj* : **~ club** club *m* de rencontres ■ **~ column** rubrique *f* rencontres *(des petites annonces).*

loner ['ləʊnər] *n inf* [person] solitaire *mf*.

lonesome ['ləʊnsəm] ◇ *adj US* = **lonely**.
◇ *n inf* : **on one's ~** tout seul.

lone star *n* : **the Lone Star State** le Texas.

lone wolf = **loner**.

long [lɒŋ] (*comp* **longer** ['lɒŋgər], *superl* **longest** ['lɒŋgɪst])
◇ *adj* **1.** [in space - road, garment, letter] long, longue *f* ■ **how ~ is the pool?** quelle est la longueur de la piscine?, la piscine fait combien de long? ■ **the pool's 33 metres ~** la piscine fait 33 mètres de long ■ **the article is 80 pages ~** l'article fait 80 pages ■ **is it a ~ way (away)?** est-ce loin (d'ici)? ■ **it's a ~ way to the beach** la plage est loin ■ **she can throw a ~ way** elle lance loin ■ **to take the ~ way round** prendre le chemin le plus long ■ **to get** *OR* **grow ~er** [shadows] s'allonger ; [hair, beard] pousser ➊ **~ trousers** *OR* *US* **pants** pantalon *m* long ■ **~ dress** [for evening wear] robe *f* longue ■ **why the ~ face?** pourquoi est-ce que tu fais cette tête de six pieds de long?
2. [in time - pause, speech, separation] long, longue *f* ■ **how ~ will the flight be/was the meeting?** combien de temps durera le vol/a duré la réunion? ■ **her five-year-~ battle with the authorities** sa lutte de cinq années contre les autorités ■ **to have a ~ memory** avoir une bonne mémoire *OR* une mémoire d'élé-

phant ■ **to get ~er** [days, intervals] devenir plus long ■ **they took a ~ look at the view** ils restèrent longtemps à regarder la vue qui s'offrait à eux ■ **it was a ~ two months** ces deux mois ont été longs ■ **I've had a ~ day** j'ai eu une journée bien remplie ■ **I've known her (for) a ~ time** *OR* **while** je la connais depuis longtemps, cela fait longtemps que je la connais ➔ **at ~ last!** enfin!
3. GRAM [vowel, syllable] long, longue *f*
4. *phr* **his speeches are ~ on rhetoric but short on substance** ce n'est pas la rhétorique qui manque dans ses discours, c'est la substance.
◇ *n* **1.** *phr* **the ~ and the short of it is that I got fired** *inf* enfin bref, j'ai été viré
2. GRAM [vowel, syllable] longue *f*.
◇ *adv* **1.** [a long time] longtemps ■ **they live ~er than humans** ils vivent plus longtemps que les êtres humains ■ **I haven't been here ~** je viens d'arriver, j'arrive juste ■ **how ~ will he be/was he in jail?** (pendant) combien de temps restera-t-il/est-il resté en prison? ■ **how ~ has he been in jail?** ça fait combien de temps qu'il est en prison?, depuis combien de temps est-il en prison? ■ **how ~ is it since we last visited them?** quand sommes-nous allés les voir pour la dernière fois? ■ **as ~ ago as 1937** déjà en 1937 ■ **~ before you were born** bien avant que tu sois né ■ **the decision had been taken ~ before** la décision avait été prise depuis longtemps ■ **colleagues ~ since promoted** des collègues promus depuis longtemps ■ **we talked ~ into the night** nous avons parlé jusque tard dans la nuit ■ [with 'be', 'take'] : **will you be ~?** tu en as pour longtemps? ■ **please wait, she won't be ~** attendez, s'il vous plaît, elle ne va pas tarder ■ **don't be** *OR* **take too ~** fais vite ■ **he took** *OR* **it took him so ~ to make up his mind...** il a mis si longtemps à se décider..., il lui a fallu tellement de temps pour se décider... ■ **how ~ does it take to get there?** combien de temps faut-il pour y aller? ■ **this won't take ~** ça va être vite fait ■ [in wishes, toasts etc] : **~ may our partnership continue!** à notre collaboration! ■ **~ live the Queen!** vive la reine!
2. [for a long time] depuis longtemps ■ **it has ~ been known that...** on sait depuis longtemps que... ■ **the ~est-running TV series** le plus long feuilleton télévisé
3. [throughout] : **all day/week ~** toute la journée/la semaine
4. *phr* **so ~!** *inf* salut!, à bientôt!
◇ *vi* : **to ~ for sb/sthg** : **I ~ for him** il me manque énormément ■ **she was ~ing for a letter from you** elle attendait impatiemment que vous lui écriviez ■ **we were ~ing for a cup of tea** nous avions très envie d'une tasse de thé ■ **to ~** *OR* **to be ~ing to do sthg** être impatient *OR* avoir hâte de faire qqch ■ **I was ~ing to tell her the truth** je mourais d'envie de lui dire la vérité.
◆ **as long as** *conj phr* **1.** [during the time that] aussi longtemps que, tant que ■ **as ~ as he's in power, there will be no hope** tant qu'il sera au pouvoir, il n'y aura aucun espoir
2. [providing] à condition que, pourvu que ■ **you can have it as ~ as you give me it back** vous pouvez le prendre à condition que *OR* pourvu que vous me le rendiez ■ **I'll do it as ~ as I get paid for it** je le ferai à condition d'être payé
3. *US inf* [seeing that] puisque.
◆ **before long** *adv phr* [soon] dans peu de temps, sous peu ■ [soon afterwards] peu (de temps) après.
◆ **for long** *adv phr* longtemps ■ **he's still in charge here, but not for ~** c'est encore lui qui s'en occupe, mais plus pour longtemps.
◆ **no longer** *adv phr* ne... plus ■ **not any ~er** plus maintenant ■ **I can't wait any ~er** je ne peux pas attendre plus longtemps, je ne peux plus attendre.
◆ **so long as** = **as long as**.

long. (*written abbrev of* **longitude**) long.

long-awaited [-ə'weɪtɪd] *adj* très attendu.

longboat ['lɒŋbəʊt] *n* chaloupe *f*.

longbow ['lɒŋbəʊ] *n* arc *m*.

long-distance ◇ *adj* **1.** [phone call] interurbain **2.** [runner, race] de fond ■ [pilot, lorry driver] au long cours ■ [journey] vers un pays lointain **3.** [device] (à) longue portée ■ [aircraft] long-courrier.
◇ *adv* : **to call** *OR* **phone ~** appeler *OR* téléphoner par l'interurbain.

long division *n* MATHS division *f* posée ■ **to do ~/a ~** faire des divisions/une division *(à la main)*.

long-drawn-out *adj* interminable, qui n'en finit pas.

long drink *n* long drink *m* ■ [non-alcoholic] *grand verre de jus de fruit, de limonade etc.*

long-eared *adj* aux grandes oreilles.

longed-for ['lɒŋd-] *adj* très attendu.

long-established *adj* [tradition] qui existe depuis longtemps.

longevity [lɒn'dʒevətɪ] *n* longévité *f*.

long-forgotten *adj* oublié depuis longtemps ■ **a ~ tradition** une tradition tombée en désuétude.

longhand ['lɒŋhænd] *n* écriture *f* courante ■ **he writes everything out in ~** [not on a typewriter] il écrit tout à la main ; [not in shorthand] il écrit tout en entier, il ne prend jamais de notes en sténo.

long-haul *adj* [aircraft] long-courrier.

longhorn ['lɒŋhɔːn] *n* AGRIC longhorn *m*.

longing ['lɒŋɪŋ] ◇ *n* envie *f*, désir *m* ■ **I had a ~ to see the sea** j'avais très envie de voir la mer ■ **the sight of her filled him with ~** en la voyant le désir s'empara de lui.
◇ *adj* d'envie, de désir ■ **a ~ look** un regard plein d'envie.

longingly ['lɒŋɪŋlɪ] *adv* [with desire] avec désir *OR* envie ■ [with regret] avec regret.

Long Island *pr n* Long Island ■ **on ~** à Long Island.

longitude ['lɒŋɪtjuːd] *n* longitude *f* ■ **at a ~ of 60° east** par 60° de longitude est.

longitudinal [,lɒndʒɪ'tjuːdɪnl] *adj* longitudinal ■ **~ section** coupe *f* longitudinale.

long johns *npl inf* caleçon *m* long, caleçons *mpl* longs.

long jump *n UK* SPORT saut *m* en longueur.

long jumper *n UK* sauteur *m (qui fait du saut en longueur)*.

long-lasting *adj* durable, qui dure longtemps.

long-legged *adj* [person] aux jambes longues ■ [animal] aux pattes longues.

long-life *adj* [milk] longue conservation *(inv)* ■ [lightbulb, battery] longue durée *(inv)*.

longlist ['lɑŋlɪst] *n* première liste *f*.

long-lived [-lɪvd] *adj* [family, species] d'une grande longévité ■ [friendship] durable ■ [prejudice] tenace, qui a la vie dure.

long-lost *adj* [friend, cousin] perdu de vue depuis longtemps ■ [object] perdu depuis longtemps.

long-playing record *n* 33 tours *m inv*, microsillon *m*.

long-range *adj* **1.** [weapon] à longue portée ■ [vehicle, aircraft] à long rayon d'action **2.** [forecast, plan] à long terme.

long-running *adj* qui tient l'affiche.

longship ['lɒŋʃɪp] *n* drakkar *m*.

longshoreman ['lɒŋʃɔːmən] (*pl* **longshoremen** [-mən]) *n US* docker *m*.

long shot *n* **1.** [in race - runner, horse] *concurrent qui ne figure pas parmi les favoris* **2.** [bet] pari *m* risqué **3.** CIN plan *m* éloigné **4.** *fig* entreprise *f* hasardeuse ■ **it's a bit of a ~** il y a peu de chances pour que cela réussisse ■ **I haven't finished by a ~** je n'ai pas fini, loin de là.

longsighted [,lɒŋ'saɪtɪd] *adj* **1.** MED hypermétrope, presbyte **2.** *fig* [well-judged] prévoyant.

longsightedness [,lɒŋ'saɪtɪdnɪs] *n* **1.** MED hypermétropie *f*, presbytie *f* **2.** *fig* [good judgement] prévoyance *f*, discernement *m*.

long-sleeved *adj* à manches longues.

long-standing *adj* de longue date.

long-suffering *adj* (extrêmement) patient, d'une patience à toute épreuve ■ [resigned] résigné.

long term ◆ **long-term** *adj* à long terme ▪ [situation] prolongé ▪ [unemployment] longue durée ▪ **long-term car park** *UK* parking *m* longue durée ▪ **long-term memory** mémoire *f* à long terme.
◆ **in the long term** *adv phr* à long terme.

long-time *adj* [friend, acquaintance] de longue date ▪ [interest, affiliation] ancien, qui dure depuis longtemps.

long ton *n* TECH tonne *f* anglaise.

long vacation *n* UNIV grandes vacances *fpl*, vacances *fpl* d'été.

long view *n* prévisions *fpl* à long terme.

long wave *n* RADIO grandes ondes *fpl* ▪ **on (the) ~** sur les grandes ondes.
◆ **long-wave** *adj* : **long-wave broadcasts** émissions *fpl* sur grandes ondes.

longways ['lɒŋweɪz] *adv* longitudinalement, dans le sens de la longueur.

longwearing [,lɒŋ'weərɪŋ] *adj US* solide, résistant.

long weekend *n* week-end *m* prolongé.

long-winded *adj* [person] prolixe, bavard ▪ [article, essay, lecture] interminable ▪ [style] verbeux, diffus.

longwise ['lɒŋwaɪz] = **longways**.

Lonsdale Belt ['lɒnzdeɪl-] *n la plus haute distinction pour les boxeurs professionnels en Grande-Bretagne.*

loo [lu:] *n UK inf* cabinets *mpl*, petit coin *m* ▪ **~ roll** rouleau *m* de papier hygiénique.

loofa(h) ['lu:fə] *n* luffa *m*, loofa *m*.

look [lʊk] ◇ *vi* **1.** [gen] regarder ▪ **~, there's Brian!** regarde, voilà Brian! ▪ **what's happening outside? let me ~** qu'est-ce qui se passe dehors? laissez-moi voir ▪ **they crept up on me while I wasn't ~ing** ils se sont approchés de moi pendant que j'avais le dos tourné ▪ **I'm just ~ing** [in shop] je jette un coup d'œil ▪ **~ and see if there's anyone there** regarde voir s'il y a quelqu'un ▪ **she ~ed along the row/down the list** elle a parcouru la rangée/la liste du regard ▪ **he was ~ing out of the window/over the wall/up the chimney** il regardait par la fenêtre/par-dessus le mur/dans la cheminée ▶ **to ~ over sb's shoulder** *liter* regarder par-dessus l'épaule de qqn ; *fig* surveiller ce que fait qqn ▪ **~ before you leap** *prov* il faut réfléchir deux fois avant d'agir
2. [search] chercher ▪ **you can't have ~ed hard enough** tu n'as pas dû beaucoup chercher
3. [in imperative - listen, pay attention] écouter ▪ **~, I can't pay you back just yet** écoute, je ne peux pas te rembourser tout de suite ▪ **~ here!** dites donc!
4. [seem, appear] avoir l'air ▪ **you ~** *OR* **are ~ ing better today** tu as l'air (d'aller) mieux aujourd'hui ▪ **how do I ~?** comment tu me trouves? ▪ **it makes him ~ ten years older/younger** ça le vieillit/rajeunit de dix ans ▪ **he's 70, but he doesn't ~ it** il a 70 ans mais il n'en a pas l'air *OR* mais il ne les fait pas ▪ **I can't hang the picture there, it just doesn't ~ right** je ne peux pas mettre le tableau là, ça ne va pas ▪ **it ~s all right to me** moi, je trouve ça bien ▪ **how does the situation ~ to you?** que pensez-vous de la situation? ▪ **that's not how it ~s to the man in the street** ce n'est pas comme ça que l'homme de la rue voit les choses ▪ **things will ~ very different when you leave school** les choses te sembleront très différentes quand tu quitteras l'école ▪ **it'll ~ bad if I don't contribute** ça fera mauvaise impression si je ne contribue pas ▪ **things are ~ing black for the economy** les perspectives économiques sont assez sombres ▪ **I must have ~ed a fool** j'ai dû passer pour un imbécile ▪ **to make sb ~ a fool** *OR* **an idiot** tourner qqn en ridicule ▪ **to ~ like sb/sthg** [resemble] ressembler à qqn/qqch ▪ **what does she ~ like?** [describe her] comment est-elle? ; [she looks a mess] non mais, à quoi elle ressemble! ▶ **it ~s like rain** on dirait qu'il va pleuvoir ▪ **it ~s (to me) like he was lying** j'ai l'impression qu'il mentait ▪ **is this our room? – it ~s like it** c'est notre chambre? – ça m'en a tout l'air ▪ **the meeting ~ed like going on all day** la réunion avait l'air d'être partie pour durer toute la journée ▪ **you ~ as if you've seen a ghost** on dirait que tu as vu un revenant ▪ **it doesn't ~ as if they're coming** on dirait qu'ils ne vont pas venir ▪ **to ~ good : you're ~ing good** tu as l'air en forme ▪ **he ~s good in jeans** les jeans lui vont bien ▪ **it'll ~ good on your CV** ça fera bien sur ton curriculum ▪ **things are ~ing pretty good here** les choses ont l'air de se présenter plutôt bien ici
5. [face - house, window] : **to ~ (out) onto a park** donner sur un parc ▪ **to ~ north/west** être exposé au nord/à l'ouest
6. [intend] : **to be ~ing to do sthg** chercher à faire qqch.
◇ *vt* **1.** *phr* **to ~ one's last on sthg** jeter un dernier regard à qqch ▪ **to ~ sb up and down** regarder qqn de haut en bas, toiser qqn du regard
2. [in imperative] : **~ who's coming!** regarde qui arrive! ▪ **~ who's talking!** tu peux parler, toi! ▪ **~ what you're doing/where you're going!** regarde un peu ce que tu fais/où tu vas!
◇ *n* **1.** [gen] coup *m* d'œil ▪ **to have** *OR* **to take a ~ (at sthg)** jeter un coup d'œil (sur) *OR* à qqch, regarder (qqch) ▪ **would you like a ~ through my binoculars?** voulez-vous regarder avec mes jumelles? ▪ **one ~ at him is enough to know he's a crook** on voit au premier coup d'œil que c'est un escroc ▪ **it's worth a quick ~** ça vaut le coup d'œil ▪ **we need to take a long hard ~ at our image abroad** il est temps que nous examinions de près notre image de marque à l'étranger ▪ **and now a ~ ahead to next week's programmes** et maintenant, un aperçu des programmes de la semaine prochaine ▪ **do you mind if I take a ~ around?** ça vous gêne si je jette un coup d'œil?
2. [search] : **to have a ~ for sthg** chercher qqch ▪ **have another ~** cherche encore
3. [glance] regard *m* ▪ **she gave me a dirty ~** elle m'a jeté un regard mauvais ▪ **you should have seen the ~s we got from passers-by!** si tu avais vu la façon dont les passants nous regardaient! ▶ **he didn't say anything, but if ~s could kill!** il n'a pas dit un mot, mais il y a des regards qui tuent!
4. [appearance, air] air *m* ▪ [expression] : **he had a strange ~ in his eyes** il avait un drôle de regard ▪ **the old house has a neglected ~** la vieille maison a l'air négligé ▪ **by the ~** *OR* **~s of her, I'd say she failed the exam** à la voir *OR* rien qu'en la voyant, je dirais qu'elle a raté son examen ▪ **there's trouble brewing by the ~ of it** *OR* **things** on dirait que quelque chose se trame ▪ **I quite like the ~ of the next candidate** j'aime assez le profil du prochain candidat ▪ **I don't like the ~ of it** ça ne me dit rien de bon *OR* rien qui vaille ▪ **I didn't like the ~ of her at all** son allure ne m'a pas du tout plu
5. [fashion] mode *f*, look *m*.
◆ **looks** *npl* [beauty] : **she's got everything, ~s, intelligence, youth...** elle a tout pour elle, elle est belle, intelligente, jeune... ▪ **he's lost his ~s** il n'est plus aussi beau qu'avant.
◆ **look after** *vt insep* **1.** [take care of] s'occuper de ▪ **she has a sick mother to ~ after** elle a une mère malade à charge ▪ **you should ~ after your clothes more carefully** tu devrais prendre plus grand soin de tes vêtements ▌ *fig* **~ after yourself!** fais bien attention à toi! ▪ **don't worry, he can ~ after himself** ne t'inquiète pas, il est capable de se débrouiller tout seul
2. [be responsible for] s'occuper de ▪ **they ~ after our interests in Europe** ils s'occupent de nos affaires en Europe
3. [keep temporarily - child] garder ; [- object] surveiller ▪ **Grandma can ~ after the children while we're away** Grand-mère peut garder les enfants pendant notre absence ▪ **can you ~ after my luggage for a few minutes?** pouvez-vous surveiller mes bagages quelques instants?
◆ **look ahead** *vi insep* regarder vers l'avenir ▪ **~ing ahead three or four years** dans trois ou quatre ans ▪ **let's ~ ahead to the next century/to next month's meeting** pensons au siècle prochain/à la réunion du mois prochain.
◆ **look around** = **look round**.
◆ **look at** *vt insep* **1.** *liter* regarder ▪ **she ~ed at herself in the mirror** elle se regarda dans la glace ▪ **they ~ed at each other** ils ont échangé un regard ▪ **it's not much to ~ at** ça ne paie pas de mine ▪ **you wouldn't think, to ~ at him, that he's a multi-millionaire** à le voir on ne croirait pas avoir affaire à un multi-millionnaire
2. [consider] considérer ▪ **that's not the way I ~ at it** ce n'est pas comme ça que je vois les choses ▪ **if you don't have money, he won't even ~ at you** si vous n'avez pas l'argent, il ne vous regardera même pas ▪ **my brother can't ~ at an egg** *inf* mon frère ne supporte pas *OR* déteste les œufs
3. [check] vérifier, regarder ▪ **to have one's teeth ~ed at** se faire examiner les dents.
◆ **look away** *vi insep* détourner les yeux.

◆ **look back** *vi insep* **1.** [in space] regarder derrière soi ▪ **she walked away without ~ing back** elle est partie sans se retourner
2. [in time] regarder en arrière ▪ **the author ~s back on the war years** l'auteur revient sur les années de guerre ▪ **it seems funny now we ~ back on it** ça semble drôle quand on y pense aujourd'hui ▪ **we can ~ back on some happy times** nous avons connu de bons moments ▪ **after she got her first job she never ~ed back** *fig* à partir du moment où elle a trouvé son premier emploi, tout lui a réussi.

◆ **look down** *vi insep* regarder en bas ▪ [in embarrassment] baisser les yeux ▪ **we ~ed down on** *OR* **at the valley** nous regardions la vallée en dessous.

◆ **look down on** *vt insep* [despise] mépriser.

◆ **look for** *vt insep* **1.** [seek] chercher ▪ **are you ~ing for a fight?** tu cherches la bagarre?
2. [expect] attendre ▪ **it's not the result we were ~ing for** ce n'est pas le résultat que nous attendions.

◆ **look forward to** *vt insep* attendre avec impatience ▪ **to ~ forward to doing sthg** être impatient de faire qqch ▪ **I ~ forward to hearing from you soon** [in letter] dans l'attente de votre réponse ▪ **I'm not ~ing forward to the operation** la perspective de cette opération ne m'enchante guère.

◆ **look in** *vi insep* **1.** [inside] regarder à l'intérieur
2. [pay a visit] passer ▪ **to ~ in on sb** rendre visite à *OR* passer voir qqn
3. [watch TV] regarder la télévision.

◆ **look into** *vt insep* examiner, étudier ▪ **it's a problem that needs ~ing into** c'est un problème qu'il faut examiner *OR* sur lequel il faut se pencher.

◆ **look on** ◇ *vi insep* regarder ▪ **the passers-by just ~ed on** les passants se sont contentés de regarder.
◇ *vt insep* considérer ▪ **I ~ on him as my brother** je le considère comme mon frère ▪ **to ~ on sb/sthg with favour/disfavour** voir qqn/qqch d'un œil favorable/défavorable.

◆ **look out** ◇ *vi insep* **1.** [person] regarder dehors
2. [room, window] : **the bedroom ~s out on** *OR* **over the garden** la chambre donne sur le jardin
3. [be careful] faire attention ▪ **~ out, it's hot!** attention, c'est chaud!
◇ *vt sep UK* : **I'll ~/I've ~ed that book out for you** je te chercherai/je t'ai trouvé ce livre.

◆ **look out for** *vt insep* **1.** [be on watch for] guetter ▪ **she's always ~ing out for bargains** elle est toujours à la recherche *OR* à l'affût d'une bonne affaire ▪ **you have to ~ out for snakes** il faut faire attention *OR* se méfier, il y a des serpents
2. *inf phr* **to ~ out for o.s.** penser à soi ▪ **you've got to ~ out for number one!** chacun pour soi!

◆ **look over** *vt insep* [glance over] jeter un coup d'œil sur ▪ [examine] examiner, étudier.

◆ **look round** ◇ *vi insep* **1.** [look at surroundings] regarder (autour de soi) ▪ **I'm just ~ing round** je ne fais que jeter un coup d'œil, je jette simplement un coup d'œil ▪ **I'd rather ~ round on my own than take the guided tour** je préférerais faire le tour moi-même plutôt que de suivre la visite guidée ▪ **I ~ed round for an exit** j'ai cherché une sortie
2. [look back] regarder derrière soi, se retourner.
◇ *vt insep* [museum, cathedral, factory] visiter ▪ [shop, room] jeter un coup d'œil dans.

◆ **look through** *vt insep* **1.** [window, screen] regarder à travers
2. [book, report] jeter un coup d'œil sur *OR* à, regarder
3. *fig* [person] : **he ~ed straight through me** il m'a regardé comme si je n'étais pas là.

◆ **look to** *vt insep* **1.** [turn to] se tourner vers ▪ **it's best to ~ to an expert** il est préférable de consulter un expert *OR* de demander l'avis d'un expert ▪ **don't ~ to her for help** ne compte pas sur elle pour t'aider
2. *fml* [attend to] veiller à ▪ **~ to it that discipline is properly maintained** veillez à ce que la discipline soit bien maintenue.

◆ **look up** ◇ *vi insep* **1.** [raise one's eyes] lever les yeux
2. [improve] s'améliorer ▪ **things are ~ing up for the economy** les perspectives économiques semblent meilleures.
◇ *vt sep* **1.** [in reference work, directory etc] chercher
2. [visit] passer voir, rendre visite à ▪ **~ us up when you're in New York** passe nous voir quand tu seras à New York.

◆ **look upon** = **look on** *(vt insep)*.

◆ **look up to** *vt insep* respecter, avoir du respect pour.

lookalike ['lʊkə,laɪk] *n* [double] sosie *m* ▪ **a John Major ~** un sosie de John Major.

looker ['lʊkər] *n inf* canon *m* ▪ **she's/he's quite a ~** elle/il n'est pas mal (du tout).

look-in *n UK inf* [chance] : **she talked so much that I didn't get a ~** elle ne m'a pas laissé le temps de placer un mot *OR* d'en placer une ▪ **the other people applying for the job don't have a ~** les autres candidats n'ont aucune chance.

-looking ['lʊkɪŋ] *in cpds* : **kind~** qui a l'air gentil ▪ **filthy~** (d'aspect) très sale *OR* répugnant.

looking glass *n dated* miroir *m*, glace *f* ▪ **a looking-glass world** *fig* un monde à l'envers.

lookout ['lʊkaʊt] *n* **1.** [watcher - gen] guetteur *m* ▪ MIL guetteur *m*, sentinelle *f* ▪ NAUT vigie *f* **2.** [watch] guet *m* ▪ **to keep (a) ~** faire le guet ▪ **to keep a ~** *OR* **to be on the ~ for sthg** guetter qqch, être à l'affût de qqch ▪ **I'm on the ~ for a better job** je suis à la recherche d'un meilleur emploi ▪ **~ post/tower** poste *m* /tour *f* de guet **3.** [observation post - MIL] poste *m* de guet ▪ NAUT poste *m* de vigie **4.** *UK inf* [prospect] : **it's a poor ~ when even doctors are on the dole** il y a de quoi s'inquiéter quand même les médecins sont au chômage ➊ **that's your/his ~!** c'est ton/son problème!

look-over *n inf* coup *m* d'œil ▪ **I've given the report a ~** j'ai jeté un coup d'œil sur le rapport.

look-up *n* COMPUT recherche *f*, consultation *f* ▪ **~ table** table *f* de recherche.

loom [lu:m] ◇ *vi* **1.** [appear] surgir ▪ **a figure ~ed in the doorway** une silhouette est apparue dans l'encadrement de la porte **2.** [approach] être imminent ▪ **a sinister-looking character was ~ing up towards them** un personnage à l'air sinistre s'avançait vers eux de façon menaçante **3.** : **to ~ large** [threaten] menacer ▪ **the idea of eviction ~ed large in their minds** l'idée d'être expulsés ne les quittait pas.
◇ *n* TEX métier *m* à tisser ▪ **hand/power ~** métier manuel/mécanique.

◆ **loom up** *vi insep* apparaître indistinctement, surgir.

loon [lu:n] *n* **1.** *inf* [lunatic] dingue *mf* ▪ [simpleton] idiot *m*, - e *f* **2.** *US* ORNITH plongeon *m*.

looney ['lu:nɪ] *inf* = **loony**.

loony ['lu:nɪ] *inf* ◇ *adj* (*comp* **loonier**, *superl* **looniest**) dingue, loufoque ▪ **the ~ left** *UK* POL les extrémistes du parti travailliste.
◇ *n* (*pl* **loonies**) dingue *mf*, malade *mf*.

loony bin *n inf hum* asile *m*.

loop [lu:p] ◇ *n* **1.** [in string, rope] boucle *f* ▪ [in river] méandre *m* ▪ [in drainpipe] siphon *m* ▪ **the film/the tape runs in a ~** le film/la bande défile en continu ▪ **the Loop** *quartier des affaires de Chicago (délimité par une ligne de métro faisant une boucle)* **2.** COMPUT boucle *f* **3.** ELEC [closed circuit] circuit *m* fermé **4.** [contraceptive device] stérilet *m*.
◇ *vt* **1.** [in string, rope etc] faire une boucle à ▪ **~ the rope around your waist/through the ring** passez la corde autour de votre taille/dans l'anneau ▪ **streamers were ~ed across the room** la pièce était tendue de guirlandes **2.** AERON : **to ~ the ~** faire un looping.
◇ *vi* [road] zigzaguer ▪ [river] faire des méandres *OR* des boucles.

loop aerial *n* RADIO cadre *m*.

loopey ['lu:pɪ] = **loopy**.

loophole ['lu:phəʊl] *n* **1.** [gap, defect] lacune *f*, faille *f* ▪ **a ~ in the law** un vide législatif **2.** ARCHIT meurtrière *f*.

loopy ['lu:pɪ] (*comp* **loopier**, *superl* **loopiest**) *adj inf* [crazy] dingue, cinglé.

loose [lu:s] ◇ *adj* **1.** [not tightly fixed - nail] mal enfoncé ; [- screw, bolt] desserré ; [- button] qui pend, mal cousu ; [- knot] qui se défait ; [- floor tile] décollé ; [- shelf] mal fixé ; [- handle, brick] branlant ; [- flooboard] disjoint ; [- slate] mal fixé ; [- tooth] qui bouge ▪ **he prised a brick ~** il a réussi à faire bouger une brique ▪ **remove all the ~ plaster** enlève tout le plâtre qui se détache ▪ **the steering seems ~** il y a du jeu dans la direction

■ **to work ~** [nail] sortir ; [screw, bolt] se desserrer ; [knot] se défaire ; [tooth, slate] bouger ; [button] se détacher ■ **the wind blew some slates ~** le vent a déplacé quelques ardoises ■ **to have a ~ cough** *UK* avoir une toux grasse ■ **~ connection** ELEC mauvais contact *m*
2. [free, unattached] libre ■ **she picked up all the ~ newspapers** elle a ramassé tous les journaux qui traînaient ■ **a ~ sheet of paper** une feuille volante ■ **the cutlery was ~ in the drawer** les couverts étaient en vrac dans le tiroir ■ **her hair hung ~ about her shoulders** ses cheveux flottaient librement sur ses épaules ■ **several pages have come ~** plusieurs pages se sont détachées ■ **I got one hand ~** j'ai réussi à dégager une de mes mains ■ **he decided to cut ~ from his family** il a décidé de couper les ponts avec sa famille ■ **all the cows were ~ in the village** toutes les vaches se promenaient *OR* étaient en liberté dans les rues du village ■ **a lion got ~ from the zoo** un lion s'est échappé du zoo ■ **he set** *OR* **let** *OR* **turned a mouse ~ in the kitchen** il a lâché une souris dans la cuisine ■ **he let ~ a torrent of abuse** *fig* il a lâché un torrent d'injures ‖ COMM [not packaged] en vrac ■ **~ coal** charbon *m* en vrac ■ **I always buy vegetables ~** je n'achète jamais de légumes préemballés
3. [slack - grip, hold] mou *(before vowel or silent 'h'* **mol**), molle *f* ; [- skin, flesh] flasque ; [- bowstring, rope] lâche ■ **she tied the ribbon in a ~ bow** elle noua le ruban sans le serrer ■ **his arms hung ~ at his sides** il avait les bras ballants ■ *fig* [discipline] relâché ■ **to have a ~ tongue** ne pas savoir tenir sa langue ■ **~ talk** des propos lestes
4. [not tight-fitting - dress, jacket] ample, flottant
5. [weak - connection, link] vague ■ **they have ~ ties with other political groups** ils sont vaguement liés à d'autres groupes politiques ■ [informal - organization] peu structuré ; [- agreement] officieux ■ **a ~ political grouping** un regroupement politique peu organisé
6. [imprecise, broad - thinking, application] peu rigoureux ; [- translation, terminology] approximatif ■ **we can make a ~ distinction between the two phenomena** nous pouvons faire une vague distinction entre les deux phénomènes
7. *pej* [woman] facile ■ [morals] léger ■ **~ living** débauche *f*, vie *f* dissolue
8. [not dense or compact - earth] meuble ; [- knit, weave] lâche
9. [relaxed - muscles] détendu, relâché, au repos ■ **to have ~ bowels** avoir la diarrhée
10. FIN disponible ■ **~ money** argent *m* disponible, liquidités *fpl*.
◇ *n* [in rugby] **: in the ~** dans la mêlée ouverte.
◇ *vt lit* **1.** [unleash - dogs] lâcher ; [- panic, chaos] semer ■ **she ~d her tongue** *OR* **fury upon me** elle s'est déchaînée contre moi ■ [let fly - bullet] tirer ; [- arrow] décocher ■ **he ~d a volley of threats/abuse at her** *fig* il s'est répandu en menaces/invectives contre elle
2. [undo - knot] défaire ; [- hair] détacher ■ [unfasten - boat, raft] démarrer, détacher.
◆ **on the loose** *adj phr* **: to be on the ~** [gen] être en liberté ; [on the run] être en fuite ■ **there was a gunman on the ~ in the neighbourhood** il y avait un homme armé qui rôdait dans le quartier.
◆ **loose off** ◇ *vt sep* [bullet] tirer ■ [arrow] décocher ■ [gun] décharger ■ [curses] lâcher.
◇ *vi insep* [with gun] tirer ■ *US fig* [with insults, criticism etc] **: to ~ off at sb** se déchaîner contre qqn, s'en prendre violemment à qqn.

loosebox ['lu:sbɒks] *n UK* EQUIT box *m*.

loose change *n* petite monnaie *f*.

loose cover *n UK* [for armchair, sofa] housse *f*.

loose end *n* **: I have a few ~s to tie up** j'ai encore quelques petits détails à régler ▶ **to be at a ~** *UK OR* **at ~s** *US* être dans un moment creux.

loose-fitting *adj* [garment] ample, large, flottant.

loose-leaf(ed) *adj* à feuilles mobiles *OR* volantes ■ **~ binder** classeur *m* (à feuilles mobiles) ■ **~ paper** feuillets *mpl* mobiles.

loose-limbed *adj* souple, agile.

loosely ['lu:slɪ] *adv* **1.** [not firmly - pack, fit, hold, wrap] sans serrer ■ [not closely - knit, weave] lâchement ■ **the dress was ~ gathered at the waist** la robe était peu ajustée à la taille **2.** [apply, interpret] mollement ■ **~ translated** [freely] traduit librement ; [inaccurately] mal traduit ■ **~ speaking, I'd say...** en gros, je dirais... **3.** [vaguely - connect, relate] vaguement ■ **the book is only ~ based on my research** le livre n'a qu'un rapport lointain avec mes recherches.

loosen ['lu:sn] ◇ *vt* **1.** [make less tight - knot, screw, lid] desserrer ; [- rope, cable] détendre ; [- grip, reins] relâcher ■ **I ~ed my belt a notch** j'ai desserré ma ceinture d'un cran ■ **the punch had ~ed several of his teeth** le coup lui a déchaussé plusieurs dents ■ **~ the cake from the sides of the tin** détachez le gâteau des bords du moule ■ **it ~s the bowels** c'est un laxatif ■ **~ the soil with a hoe** ameublissez le sol avec une binette ■ **the wine soon ~ed his tongue** le vin eut vite fait de lui délier la langue ■ [weaken] affaiblir ■ **they have ~ed their ties with Moscow** leurs liens avec Moscou se sont relâchés **2.** [liberalize - rules, restrictions] assouplir.
◇ *vi* [become less tight - knot, screw] se desserrer ; [- grip] se relâcher, se desserrer.
◆ **loosen up** ◇ *vi insep* **1.** [get less severe] se montrer moins sévère ■ **to ~ up on discipline** relâcher la discipline **2.** [relax socially] se détendre **3.** [limber up - athlete, musician] s'échauffer.
◇ *vt sep* [muscles] échauffer.

looseness ['lu:snɪs] *n* **1.** [of screw, nail, lever] jeu *m* ■ [of rope] relâchement *m*, mou *m* **2.** [of clothing] ampleur *f* **3.** [of thinking, interpretation] manque *m* de rigueur ■ [of translation, terminology] manque *m* de précision.

loose-tongued *adj* bavard.

loose-weave *adj* [fabric] lâche, à mailles lâches.

loot [lu:t] ◇ *vt* [town, goods, tomb] piller.
◇ *vi* piller, se livrer au pillage.
◇ *n* **1.** [stolen goods] butin *m* **2.** △ [money] pognon△ *m*, fric *m*.

looter ['lu:tər] *n* [in war, riot] pillard *m*, - e *f* ■ [of tombs, churches] pilleur *m*, - euse *f*.

looting ['lu:tɪŋ] *n* pillage *m*.

lop [lɒp] (*pret & pp* **lopped**, *cont* **lopping**) *vt* **1.** [tree] élaguer, tailler ■ [branch] couper ■ **farmers have to ~ and top all trees and hedges** les agriculteurs doivent tailler tous les arbres et toutes les haies **2.** *fig* [budget] élaguer, faire des coupes sombres dans ■ [sum of money, item of expenditure] retrancher, supprimer.
◆ **lop off** *vt sep* **1.** [branch] couper, tailler **2.** *fig* [price, time] réduire ■ **the new motorway will ~ 30 minutes off the journey** la nouvelle autoroute va raccourcir le trajet de 30 minutes.

lope [ləʊp] ◇ *vi* [runner] courir à grandes foulées ■ [animal] courir en bondissant.
◇ *n* [of runner] pas *m* de course *(rapide et souple)* ■ [of animal] course *f (avec des bonds)*.

lop-eared *adj UK* aux oreilles tombantes.

lopsided *adj* **1.** [crooked - nose, grin] de travers ■ [out of line - wall, roof, building] de travers ■ [asymmetric] asymétrique ■ [of uneven proportions] disproportionné ■ **her handwriting is all ~** son écriture part dans tous les sens **2.** [unevenly weighted] mal équilibré ■ [unequal - debate, contest] inégal, déséquilibré ■ **the article presents a rather ~ picture of events** l'article présente les événements de façon plutôt partiale.

loquacious [lə'kweɪʃəs] *adj fml* loquace, volubile.

lord [lɔ:d] *n* [master] seigneur *m* ■ [nobleman] noble *m* ■ **the ~s of industry** les barons de l'industrie ■ **to live like a ~** mener grand train, vivre en grand seigneur.
◆ **Lord** ◇ *n UK* [title] lord *m* ■ **Lord (Peter) Snow** lord (Peter) Snow ‖ [term of address] **: my Lord** [to noble] Monsieur le Marquis, Monsieur le Baron ; [to judge] Monsieur le juge ; [to bishop] Monseigneur, Excellence ▶ **'The Lord of the Flies'** *Golding* 'Sa Majesté des Mouches' ■ **'The Lord of the Rings'** *Tolkien* 'le Seigneur des anneaux'.
◇ *pr n* RELIG **: the Lord** le Seigneur ■ **Our Lord Jesus Christ** Notre Seigneur Jésus-Christ ■ **in the year of our Lord 1897** en l'an de grâce 1897 ■ **the Lord's Supper** l'eucharistie *f* ‖ [in interjections and expressions] **: Good Lord!** *inf* Seigneur! ■ **oh Lord!** *inf* mon Dieu! ■ **Lord (only) knows!** Dieu seul le sait!
◇ *vt* **: to ~ it over sb** *UK* prendre des airs supérieurs avec qqn.

Lord Advocate *n* ≃ procureur *m* de la République, ≃ procureur *m* général *(en Écosse)*.

Lord Chancellor *n* lord *m* Chancelier ■ ≃ ministre *m* de la Justice *(en Grande-Bretagne)*.

Lord Chief Justice (*pl* **Lords Chief Justice**) *n* ≃ président *m* de la Haute Cour *(en Grande-Bretagne)*.

Lord High Chancellor = **Lord Chancellor**.

Lord Lieutenant (*pl* **Lords Lieutenant** OR *pl* **Lord Lieutenants**) *n* lord-lieutenant *m (en Grande-Bretagne)*.

lordly ['lɔ:dlɪ] *adj* **1.** [arrogant] arrogant, hautain ■ **with ~ indifference** avec une indifférence souveraine **2.** [noble - gesture] noble, auguste ■ [splendid - feast, occasion, life style] somptueux.

Lord Mayor *n* lord-maire *m*, maire *m*.

Lord Privy Seal (*pl* **Lords Privy Seal**) *n* : **the ~** *titre du doyen du gouvernement britannique*.

Lord's [lɔ:dz] *pr n célèbre terrain de cricket londonien.*

Lordship ['lɔ:dʃɪp] *n* **1.** [form of address] : **Your/His ~** [to noble] Monsieur le Marquis, Monsieur le Baron ; [to judge] Monsieur le juge ; [to bishop] Excellence/Son Excellence ■ **if His ~ would care to sit down** *hum* si votre Altesse daigne s'asseoir **2.** [lands, rights] seigneurie *f* ■ [power] autorité *f*.

Lord's Prayer *n* : **the ~** le Notre Père.

Lords Spiritual *pr npl membres ecclésiastiques de la Chambre des lords.*

Lords Temporal *pr npl membres laïques de la Chambre des lords.*

lore [lɔ:r] *n* **1.** [folk legend] tradition *f*, traditions *fpl*, coutume *f*, coutumes *fpl* **2.** [traditional knowledge] science *f*, savoir *m* ■ **she knows all the countryside ~** elle connaît tous les us et coutumes du pays.

lorgnette [lɔ:'njet] *n* **1.** [spectacles] lorgnon *m*, face-à-main *m* **2.** [opera glasses] jumelles *fpl* de théâtre, lorgnette *f*.

Lorraine [lɒ'reɪn] *pr n* Lorraine *f* ■ **in ~** en Lorraine.

lorry ['lɒrɪ] (*pl* **lorries**) *n UK* camion *m*, poids lourd *m* ■ **~ park** aire *f* de stationnement pour poids lourds ■ **it fell off the back of a ~** *inf* c'est de la marchandise volée.

lorry driver *n UK* chauffeur *m* de camion, routier *m*, -ère *f*.

lorry-load *n UK* chargement *m*.

Los Angeles [lɒs'ændʒɪli:z] *pr n* Los Angeles.

lose [lu:z] (*pret & pp* **lost** [lɒst]) ◇ *vt* **1.** [gen - limb, job, money, patience etc] perdre ■ **to ~ one's way** se perdre, s'égarer ■ **what have you got to ~?** qu'est-ce que tu as à perdre? ■ **you've got nothing to ~** tu n'as rien à perdre ■ **we haven't got a moment to ~** il n'y a pas une seconde à perdre ■ **they are losing their markets to the Koreans** ils sont en train de perdre leurs marchés au profit des Coréens ■ **he lost no time in telling her she was wrong** il ne s'est pas gêné pour lui dire qu'elle avait tort ■ **don't talk so fast, you've lost me** ne parle pas si vite, je n'arrive pas à te suivre ■ **the hint/the suggestion was not lost on him** l'allusion/la suggestion ne lui a pas échappé ■ **your compliment was lost on her** elle ne s'est pas rendu compte que tu lui faisais un compliment ■ **at what age did he ~ his mother?** à quel âge a-t-il perdu sa mère? ■ **30 lives were lost in the fire** 30 personnes ont péri dans l'incendie, l'incendie a fait 30 morts ■ **to ~ one's voice** avoir une extinction de voix ■ **to ~ one's appetite** perdre l'appétit ■ **the plane is losing altitude** OR **height** l'avion perd de l'altitude ■ **to ~ one's balance** perdre l'équilibre ■ **to ~ consciousness** perdre connaissance ■ **to ~ face** perdre la face ■ **to ~ ground** perdre du terrain ■ **to ~ one's head** perdre la tête

2. [not win] perdre ■ **he lost four games to Karpov** il a perdu quatre parties contre Karpov

3. [shed, get rid of] perdre ■ **to ~ weight** perdre du poids ■ [elude, shake off] semer

4. [cause to lose] coûter, faire perdre ■ **it lost him his job** ça lui a fait perdre son emploi

5. [subj: clock, watch] : **my watch ~s five minutes a day** ma montre prend cinq minutes de retard par jour.

◇ *vi* **1.** perdre ■ **they lost by one goal** ils ont perdu d'un but ■ **either way, I can't ~** je suis gagnant à tous les coups ■ **the dollar is losing in value (against the deutschmark)** le dollar baisse (par rapport au Deutsche Mark) ■ **his work ~s a lot in translation** son œuvre se prête très mal à la traduction ■ **if you sell the house now you'll ~ on it** si tu vends la maison maintenant tu vas perdre de l'argent ■ **I lost on the deal** j'ai été perdant dans l'affaire

2. [clock, watch] retarder.

◆ **lose out** *vi insep* perdre, être perdant ■ **to ~ out on a deal** être perdant dans une affaire ■ **will the Americans ~ out to the Japanese in computers?** les Américains vont-ils perdre le marché de l'informatique au profit des Japonais?

loser ['lu:zər] *n* **1.** [gen - SPORT] perdant *m*, - e *f* ■ **he's not a very good ~** il est mauvais perdant OR joueur ■ **they're the ~s by it** *UK fig* ce sont eux les perdants dans cette affaire **2.** *inf* [failure - person] raté *m*, - e *f*.

losing ['lu:zɪŋ] *adj* **1.** [gen - SPORT] perdant ■ **to fight a ~ battle** engager une bataille perdue d'avance **2.** [unprofitable] : **the business was a ~ concern** cette entreprise n'était pas viable ■ **it's a ~ proposition** ce n'est pas rentable.

loss [lɒs] *n* **1.** [gen] perte *f* ■ **it's your gain and their ~** c'est vous qui y gagnez et eux qui y perdent ■ **it's your ~!** tant pis pour vous! ■ **it can cause temporary ~ of vision** cela peut provoquer OR entraîner une perte momentanée de la vue ■ **the ~ of a close relative** la perte OR la mort d'un parent proche ■ **the party suffered heavy ~es in the last elections** le parti a subi de lourdes pertes OR a perdu de nombreux sièges lors des dernières élections ■ **the company announced ~es of** OR **a ~ of a million pounds** la société a annoncé un déficit d'un million de livres ■ **we made a ~ of 10% on the deal** nous avons perdu 10 % dans l'affaire ■ **to sell at a ~** vendre à perte ■ **the closure will cause the ~ of hundreds of jobs** la fermeture provoquera la disparition de centaines d'empl ois ■ **there was terrible ~ of life in the last war** la dernière guerre a coûté beaucoup de vies humaines ■ **they inflicted heavy ~es on the enemy** ils infligèrent de lourdes pertes à l'ennemi **2.** [feeling of pain, unhappiness] malheur *m*, chagrin *m* ■ **a tremendous feeling of ~ overcame him** il réalisa avec angoisse ce qu'il avait perdu **3.** [in insurance] sinistre *m* **4.** *phr* **to be at a ~** ne pas savoir quoi faire, être déconcerté OR dérouté ■ **he's never at a ~** il ne se laisse jamais déconcerter ■ **I was at a ~ for words** je ne savais pas quoi dire, les mots me manquaient ■ **I'm at a ~ as to how to tell him the truth** je ne sais pas comment m'y prendre pour lui dire la vérité.

loss adjuster *n* [for insurance] expert *m* ■ NAUT dispatcheur *m*.

loss leader *n* COMM *article vendu à perte dans le but d'attirer la clientèle.*

lossmaker ['lɒsmeɪkər] *n* gouffre *m* financier.

lost [lɒst] ◇ *pt & pp* ▷ **lose**.

◇ *adj* **1.** [keys, money etc] perdu ■ **all is not yet ~** tout n'est pas perdu ■ **they have discovered a ~ masterpiece** ils ont découvert un chef-d'œuvre disparu ■ **the ~ city of Atlantis** Atlantide, la ville engloutie **2.** [person - in direction] perdu, égaré ■ **can you help me, I'm ~** pouvez-vous m'aider, je me suis perdu OR égaré ■ **to get ~** se perdre ■ **~ in action** MIL mort au combat ■ **a ~ sheep** *liter & fig* une brebis égarée ■ **a ~ soul** une âme en peine ➜ **get ~!** *inf* va te faire voir! **3.** *fig* [engrossed] perdu, plongé, absorbé ■ **~ in a daydream** perdu dans une rêverie **4.** [wasted - time] perdu ; [- opportunity] perdu, manqué ; [- youth] gâché ■ **the allusion was ~ on me** je n'ai pas compris OR saisi l'allusion ■ **your advice would be ~ on them** leur donner un conseil serait peine perdue **5.** [confused, bewildered] perdu ■ [disconcerted] désorienté ■ **I'm ~ for words** je ne sais pas quoi dire **6.** [oblivious] insensible ■ **he was ~ to the world** il avait l'esprit ailleurs.

lost-and-found *n* : **~ (office)** *US* bureau *m* des objets trouvés ■ **I put an advert in the ~ column** j'ai mis une annonce dans la rubrique des objets trouvés.

lost cause *n* cause *f* perdue.

lost property *n* objets *mpl* trouvés.

lost property office *n UK* bureau *m* des objets trouvés.

lot [lɒt] *n* **1.** *inf* [group of people] : **this ~ are leaving today and another ~ are arriving tomorrow** ce groupe part aujourd'hui et un autre (groupe) arrive demain ▪ **I don't want you getting mixed up with that ~** je ne veux pas que tu traînes avec cette bande ▪ **come here, you ~!** venez ici, vous autres! ➡ **he's a bad ~** c'est un sale type
2. [group of things] : **most of the last ~ of fans we had in were defective** presque tous les ventilateurs du dernier lot étaient défectueux ▪ **take all this ~ and dump it in my office** prends tout ça et mets-le dans mon bureau ▪ **I've just been given another ~ of letters to sign** on vient de me donner un autre paquet de lettres à signer
3. [item in auction, in lottery] lot *m*
4. [destiny, fortune] sort *m*, destin *m* ▪ **to be content with one's ~** être content de son sort ▪ **it was his ~ in life to be the underdog** il était destiné à rester un sous-fifre ➡ **it fell to my ~ to be the first to try** le sort a voulu que je sois le premier à essayer ▪ **to throw in one's ~ with sb** se mettre du côté de qqn
5. [random choice] : **the winners are chosen by ~** les gagnants sont choisis par tirage au sort ▪ **to draw** *OR* **cast ~ s** tirer au sort
6. *US* [plot of land] terrain *m* ▪ **a vacant ~** un terrain vague ▪ **a used car ~** un parking de voitures d'occasion
7. *US* CIN studio *m* (de cinéma).
◆ **lots** *inf* ◇ *pron* beaucoup ▪ **do you need any paper/envelopes? I've got ~s** est-ce que tu as besoin de papier/d'enveloppes? j'en ai plein ▪ **there are ~s to choose from** il y a du choix.
◇ *adv* beaucoup.
◆ **a lot** ◇ *pron phr* beaucoup ▪ **there's a ~ still to be done** il y a encore beaucoup à faire ▪ **there's not a ~ you can do about it** tu n'y peux pas grand-chose ▪ **what a ~ of people!** quelle foule!, que de monde! ▪ **there's an awful ~ of work still to be done** il reste encore beaucoup de travail à faire ▪ **she takes a ~ of care over her appearance** elle fait très attention à son apparence ▪ **we see a ~ of them** nous les voyons beaucoup *OR* souvent ▪ **a (fat) ~ of help you were!** *iron*, **you were a (fat) ~ of help!** *iron* ça, pour être utile, tu as été utile! *iron*.
◇ *adv phr* beaucoup ▪ **a ~ better/more** beaucoup mieux/plus ▪ **thanks a ~!** merci beaucoup! ▪ **a (fat) ~ she cares!** *iron* elle s'en fiche pas mal!
◆ **lots of** *det phr inf* beaucoup de ▪ **we had ~s of fun** on s'est bien marrés ▪ **I've been there ~s of times** j'y suis allé plein de fois ▪ **~s of love** [at end of letter] ≃ je t'embrasse, grosses bises *inf*.
◆ **the lot** *pron phr* le tout ▪ **there isn't much, take the ~** il n'y en a pas beaucoup, prenez tout ▪ **there aren't many, take the ~** il n'y en a pas beaucoup, prenez-les tous ▪ **she ate the (whole) ~** elle a tout mangé ▪ **the (whole) ~ of them came** ils sont tous venus ▪ **that's the ~** tout est là ▪ **that's the** *OR* **your ~ for tonight** *inf* c'est tout pour ce soir.

Lot [lɒt] *pr n* BIBLE Lot, Loth.

loth [ləʊθ] = **loath**.

Lothario [lə'θɑːrɪəʊ] (*pl* **Lotharios**) *n* don Juan *m*, libertin *m*.

Lothian Region ['ləʊðjən-] *pr n* la région du Lothian *(Écosse)*.

lotion ['ləʊʃn] *n* lotion *f*.

lottery ['lɒtərɪ] *n* **1.** loterie *f* ▪ **~ ticket** billet *m* de loterie **2.** *fig* [matter of luck] loterie *f*.

lotto ['lɒtəʊ] *n* loto *m (jeu de société)*.

lotus ['ləʊtəs] *n* lotus *m*.

lotus-eater *n* MYTH lotophage *m* ▪ *fig* doux rêveur *m*.

lotus position *n* position *f* du lotus.

loud [laʊd] ◇ *adj* **1.** [noise, shout] grand, puissant ▪ [voice, music] fort ▪ [explosion] fort, violent ▪ **the television is too ~** la télévision est trop forte, le son de la télévision est trop fort ▪ **the door slammed with a ~ bang** la porte a claqué très fort ▪ **a ~ argument was going on in the next room** on se disputait bruyamment dans la pièce voisine ▮ [vigorous - protest, applause] vif ▪ **they were ~ in their support/condemnation of the project** ils ont vigoureusement soutenu/condamné le projet ▪ *pej* [loudmouthed, brash] bruyant, tapageur ▪ **he's a bit ~, isn't he?** ce n'est pas le genre discret! **2.** [garish - colour] criard, voyant ; [- pattern] voyant.
◇ *adv* fort ▪ **can you speak a little ~er?** pouvez-vous parler un peu plus fort? ▪ **the music was turned up ~** on avait mis la musique à fond ▪ **to read out ~** lire à haute voix ▪ **I was thinking out ~** je pensais tout haut ▪ **receiving you ~ and clear** je vous reçois cinq sur cinq.

loudhailer [,laʊd'heɪlər] *n* *UK* porte-voix *m inv*, mégaphone *m*.

loudly ['laʊdlɪ] *adv* **1.** [noisily - speak] d'une voix forte ; [- laugh] bruyamment ▪ **our neighbour banged ~ on the wall** notre voisin a donné de grands coups contre le mur ▪ **the supporters cheered ~** les supporters ont applaudi bruyamment ▪ [vigorously] avec force *OR* vigueur ▪ **we protested ~** nous avons protesté vigoureusement **2.** [garishly] de façon tapageuse *OR* voyante.

loudmouth ['laʊdmaʊθ] (*pl* [-maʊðz]) *n inf* **1.** [noisy person] braillard *m*, - e *f*, gueulard *m*, - e *f* **2.** [boaster] crâneur *m*, - euse *f*, frimeur *m*, - euse *f* **3.** [gossip] commère *f*.

loudmouthed ['laʊdmaʊðd] *adj inf* **1.** [noisy] fort en gueule **2.** [boastful] crâneur ▪ [gossipy] bavard, frimeur.

loudness ['laʊdnɪs] *n* **1.** [of sound] intensité *f*, force *f* ▪ [of voice] intensité *f* ▪ [of cheers] vigueur *f* ▪ **the ~ of the music makes conversation impossible** la musique est tellement forte qu'on ne s'entend pas **2.** [on hi-fi system] : **~ control** bouton *m* de compensation physiologique.

loud pedal *n* MUS pédale *f* forte.

loudspeaker [,laʊd'spiːkər] *n* haut-parleur *m* ▪ [on stereo] enceinte *f*, baffle *m*.

lough [lɒk] *n Ireland* [lake] lac *m*.

Louisiana [luː,iːzɪ'ænə] *pr n* Louisiane *f* ▪ **in ~** en Louisiane.

Louisiana Purchase *pr n* : **the ~** l'achat *m* de la Louisiane.

THE LOUISIANA PURCHASE

Rachat par les États-Unis du territoire de la Louisiane à la France, en 1803. Craignant l'expansion de l'empire napoléonien, Thomas Jefferson négocia cet immense territoire pour 15 000 000 $ en argent liquide. La superficie du pays s'en trouva doublée.

lounge [laʊndʒ] ◇ *n* **1.** [room - in private house, on ship, in hotel] salon *m* ; [- at airport] salle *f* d'attente ▪ [bar] (salle *f* de) bar *m* ▪ *UK* [- in pub] = **lounge bar 2.** [rest] : **to have a ~ in the sun** paresser *OR* se prélasser au soleil.
◇ *vi* **1.** [recline] s'allonger, se prélasser ▪ [sprawl] être allongé ▪ **he ~d against the counter** il était appuyé nonchalamment contre le comptoir **2.** [laze] paresser ▪ [hang about] traîner ▪ [stroll] flâner.
◆ **lounge about** *UK*, **lounge around** = **lounge** *(vi sense 2)*.

lounge bar *n UK salon dans un pub (plus confortable et plus cher que le "public bar")*.

lounge lizard *n inf* salonnard *m*, - e *f*.

lounger ['laʊndʒər] *n* **1.** [sunbed] lit *m* de plage **2.** [person] paresseux *m*, - euse *f*.

lounge suit *n UK* costume *m* de ville ▪ [on invitation] tenue *f* de ville.

lour ['laʊər] = **lower** *((sky, weather))*.

louse [laʊs] ◇ *n* **1.** (*pl* lice [laɪs]) [insect] pou *m* **2.** (*pl* louses) △ [person] salaud△ *m*, chienne△ *f*.
◇ *vt* [remove lice from] épouiller.
◆ **louse up**△ *vt sep* [spoil] foutre en l'air△.

lousy ['laʊzɪ] (*comp* **lousier**, *superl* **lousiest**) *adj* **1.** *inf* [appalling - film, singer] nul ; [- weather] pourri ▪ **we had a ~ holiday!** bonjour les vacances! ▪ **I feel ~ this morning** je suis mal fichu ce matin ▪ **I'm ~ at tennis, I'm a ~ tennis player** je suis nul au tennis, je joue au tennis comme un pied ▪ **you're a ~ liar** [lie badly] tu ne sais pas mentir ; [as intensifier] tu n'es qu'un sale menteur ▪ [annoying] fichu, sacré **2.** *inf* [mean] vache ▪ **that was a ~ trick!** tu parles d'une vacherie! ▪ **I feel ~ about what hap-**

pened ça m'embête, ce qui est arrivé **3.** ***dated inf*** [full] **: the town was ~ with police** la ville grouillait de flics **4.** [lice-infested] pouilleux.

lout [laʊt] *n* [bumpkin] rustre *m* ▪ [hooligan] voyou *m*.

loutish ['laʊtɪʃ] *adj* [behaviour] grossier ▪ [manners] de rustre, mal dégrossi.

louvre ***UK*****, louver** ***US*** ['lu:vəʳ] *n* [slat] lamelle *f* ▪ [window] jalousie *f*, volet *m* à claire-voie, persienne *f*.

louvred ***UK*****, louvered** ***US*** ['lu:vəd] *adj* à claire-voie.

lovable ['lʌvəbl] *adj* charmant, sympathique, attachant.

lovat ['lʌvət] *n couleur bleu-vert ou jaune-vert qu'on trouve en particulier dans les lainages et dans les tweeds.*

love [lʌv] ◇ *vt* **1.** [sweetheart] aimer ▪ [friends, relatives] aimer beaucoup *OR* bien ▪ **I like you but I don't ~ you** je t'aime bien mais je ne suis pas amoureux de toi ➋ **I'll have to ~ you and leave you** ***inf*** ce n'est pas tout mais il faut que j'y aille
2. [enjoy] aimer, adorer ▪ **don't you just ~ that little dress?** cette petite robe est vraiment adorable, tu ne trouves pas? ▪ **I love lying** *OR* **to lie in bed on Sunday mornings** j'adore faire la grasse matinée le dimanche ▪ **I'd ~ to come** j'aimerais beaucoup venir ▪ **I'd ~ you to come** j'aimerais beaucoup que *OR* cela me ferait très plaisir que tu viennes ▪ **would you like to come too? – I'd ~ to** voudriez-vous venir aussi? – avec grand plaisir
3. [prize - one's country, freedom etc] aimer.
◇ *n* **1.** [for person] amour *m* ▪ **we didn't marry for ~** nous n'avons pas fait un mariage d'amour ▪ **he did it out of ~ for her** il l'a fait par amour pour elle ▪ **it was ~ at first sight** ce fut le coup de foudre ▪ **to be in ~ (with sb)** être amoureux (de qqn) ▪ **they were deeply in ~** ils s'aimaient profondément ▪ **to fall in ~ (with sb)** tomber amoureux (de qqn) ▪ **to make ~** faire l'amour ▪ **to make ~ to sb** [have sex with] faire l'amour à qqn ; ***arch*** [court] faire la cour à qqn ▪ **for the ~ of God** *OR* ***UK*** **Mike!** ***inf*** pour l'amour du ciel! ▪ **Harry sends** *OR* **gives you his ~** Harry t'embrasse ▪ **give my ~ to Harry** embrasse Harry de ma part *OR* pour moi ▪ **(lots of) ~ from Jane, all my ~, Jane** [in letter] affectueusement, Jane ➋ **I wouldn't do it for ~ nor money** ***inf*** je ne le ferais pas pour tout l'or du monde, je ne le ferais pour rien au monde ▪ **there's no ~ lost between them** ils se détestent cordialement ▪ **'All For Love'** ***Dryden*** 'Tout pour l'amour' ▪ **'Love's Labour's Lost'** ***Shakespeare*** 'Peines d'amour perdues'
2. [for jazz, one's country etc] amour *m* ▪ **his ~ of good food** sa passion pour la bonne chère ▪ **she fell in ~ with the house immediately** elle a eu le coup de foudre pour la maison ▪ **I don't do this job for the ~ of it** je ne fais pas ce travail pour le *OR* par plaisir
3. [beloved person] amour *m* ▪ **she's the ~ of his life** c'est la femme de sa vie ▪ **isn't he a ~!** ***UK inf*** ce qu'il est mignon *OR* chou! ▮ [favourite activity] passion *f*
4. [term of address] **: thank you, (my) ~** ***inf*** merci, mon chou ▮ [to stranger] **: wait a minute, ~!** ***UK inf*** [to child] attends une minute, mon petit! ; [to adult] attendez une minute
5. SPORT zéro *m*.

loveable ['lʌvəbl] = **lovable**.

love affair *n* liaison *f* (amoureuse) ▪ ***fig*** passion *f* ▪ **his ~ with Paris** sa passion pour Paris.

lovebird ['lʌvbɜ:d] *n* **1.** ORNITH perruche *f* ▪ **~s** inséparables *mpl* **2.** ***hum*** [lover] amoureux *m*, - euse *f*.

lovebite ['lʌvbaɪt] *n* ***UK*** suçon *m*.

love child *n* enfant *mf* de l'amour.

love-hate *adj* **: a ~ relationship** une relation d'amour-haine.

loveless ['lʌvlɪs] *adj* [marriage] sans amour ▪ [person - unloved] mal aimé ; [- unloving] sans cœur, incapable d'aimer.

love letter *n* lettre *f* d'amour, billet *m* doux.

love life *n* vie *f* sentimentale ▪ **how's your ~?** ***inf*** comment vont tes amours?

loveliness ['lʌvlɪnɪs] *n* charme *m*, beauté *f*.

lovelorn ['lʌvlɔ:n] *adj* malheureux en amour.

lovely ['lʌvlɪ] (*comp* **lovelier**, *superl* **loveliest**) ◇ *adj* **1.** [in appearance - person] beau *(before vowel or silent 'h'* **bel***)*, belle *f*, joli ; [- child] joli, mignon ; [- home, scenery] joli **2.** [view, evening, weather] beau *(before vowel or silent 'h'* **bel***)*, belle *f* ▪ [holiday] (très) agréable ▪ [dress] joli ▪ [meal] excellent ▪ **it's a ~ idea** c'est une très bonne idée ▪ **it's ~ to see you** je suis enchanté *OR* ravi de vous voir ▪ **it's ~ and warm by the fire** ***UK*** il fait bon près de la cheminée ▪ **it sounds ~** cela a l'air très bien ▪ **would you like to come to dinner next week? – that'd be ~** tu veux venir dîner la semaine prochaine? – ça serait vraiment bien *OR* avec plaisir **3.** [in character] charmant, très aimable.
◇ *n* ***inf*** mignonne *f*.

lovemaking ['lʌv,meɪkɪŋ] *n* **1.** [sexual intercourse] ébats *mpl* (amoureux) **2.** ***arch*** [courtship] cour *f*.

love match *n* mariage *m* d'amour.

love nest *n* nid *m* d'amour.

love potion *n* philtre *m*.

lover ['lʌvəʳ] *n* **1.** [sexual partner] amant *m*, - e *f* **2.** ***dated*** [suitor] amoureux *m*, soupirant *m* ▪ **the young ~s** les jeunes amoureux *mpl* **3.** [enthusiast] amateur *m*, - trice *f* ▪ **he's a real music ~** c'est un mélomane ▪ **I'm not a dog ~ myself** moi-même je n'aime pas beaucoup les chiens.

lover-boy *n* ***inf hum*** [womanizer] don Juan *m*, tombeur *m*, séducteur *m*.

love scene *n* scène *f* d'amour.

lovesick ['lʌvsɪk] *adj* **: to be ~** se languir d'amour.

love song *n* chanson *f* d'amour.

love story *n* histoire *f* d'amour.

love token *n* gage *m* d'amour.

love triangle *n* triangle *m* amoureux.

lovey-dovey ['lʌvɪ, dʌvɪ] *adj* ***inf pej*** doucereux.

loving ['lʌvɪŋ] *adj* [affectionate] affectueux ▪ [tender] tendre ▪ **~ kindness** bonté *f*.

-loving *in cpds* **: wine~** qui aime le vin, amateur de vin ▪ **music~** amateur de musique, mélomane ▪ **money ~** qui aime l'argent, cupide.

loving cup *n* coupe *f* de l'amitié.

lovingly ['lʌvɪŋlɪ] *adv* [affectionately] affectueusement ▪ [tenderly] tendrement ▪ [passionately] avec amour, amoureusement ▪ [with great care] soigneusement, avec soin.

low [ləʊ] ◇ *adj* **1.** [in height] bas ▪ **this room has a ~ ceiling** cette pièce est basse de plafond ▪ **~ hills** collines peu élevées ▪ **a ~ neckline** un décolleté ▪ **'~ bridge'** AUT 'hauteur limitée'
2. [in scale - temperature] bas ; [- level] faible ▪ **the temperature is in the ~ twenties** il fait un peu plus de vingt degrés ▪ **old people are given very ~ priority** les personnes âgées ne sont absolument pas considérées comme prioritaires ▪ **I've reached a ~ point in my career** j'ai atteint un creux dans ma carrière ▪ **their relationship is at a ~ ebb** leurs relations sont au plus bas ▪ **a ~ blood count** une numération globulaire basse ▪ **~ gear** ***US*** première (vitesse) *f* ▪ **'engage ~ gear'** AUT 'utilisez le frein moteur' ▪ [in degree, intensity - probability, visibility] faible ; [- fire] bas ; [- lighting] faible, tamisé ▪ **cook on a ~ heat** faire cuire à feu doux ▪ **a ~ pressure area** METEOR une zone de basse pression ▪ [in value, amount - figure, price] bas, faible ; [- profit] faible, maigre ▪ **attendance was ~** il y avait peu de monde ▪ **we're only playing for ~ stakes** nous ne jouons que de petites mises, nous ne jouons pas de grosses sommes ▪ **we're rather ~ on whisky** on n'a plus beaucoup de whisky ▪ **~ in calories** pauvre en calories ▪ **the soil is very ~ in nitrogen** la terre est très pauvre en azote ▪ **to play a ~ trump** CARDS jouer un petit atout
3. [poor - intelligence, standard] faible ; [- opinion] faible, piètre ; [- in health] mauvais, médiocre ; [- in quality] mauvais ▪ **he's very ~ at the moment** il est bien bas *OR* bien affaibli en ce moment ▪ **I'm in rather ~ spirits, I feel rather ~** je n'ai pas le moral, je suis assez déprimé
4. [in rank] bas, inférieur ▪ **to be of ~ birth** être de basse extraction *OR* d'origine modeste ▪ **~ ranking officials** petits fonctionnaires *mpl*, fonctionnaires *mpl* subalternes

5. [vulgar - behaviour] grossier ; [- tastes] vulgaire ▪ **to keep ~ company** fréquenter des gens peu recommandables ▪ **that was a ~ trick** c'était un sale tour ◗ **~ comedy** THEAT farce *f*
6. [primitive] : **~ forms of life** des formes de vie inférieures OR peu évoluées
7. [soft - voice, music] bas, faible ; [- light] faible ▪ **keep your voice ~** ne parlez pas trop fort ▪ **turn the radio down ~** mettez la radio moins fort ▪ **turn the lights down ~** baissez les lumières ▪ **we heard a ~ moan** nous avons entendu une plainte étouffée
8. [deep - note, voice] bas.
◇ *adv* **1.** [in height] bas ▪ **~er down** plus bas ▪ **a helicopter flew ~ over the town** un hélicoptère a survolé la ville à basse altitude ▪ **she was sitting very ~ in her chair** elle était avachie sur sa chaise ▪ **he bowed ~** il s'inclina profondément ▪ **to lie ~** [hide] se cacher ; [keep low profile] adopter un profil bas ▪ **to be laid ~** [ill] être immobilisé
2. [in intensity] bas ▪ **stocks are running ~** les réserves baissent ▪ **the batteries are running ~** les piles sont usées
3. [in price] : **to buy ~** acheter à bas prix ; ST. EX acheter quand les cours sont bas
4. [morally] : **I wouldn't stoop** OR **sink so ~ as to tell lies** je ne m'abaisserais pas à mentir.
◇ *n* **1.** [in height] bas *m* ▪ [in intensity] minimum *m* ▪ **the heating is on ~** le chauffage est au minimum
2. [low point] niveau *m* bas, point *m* bas ▪ **the dollar has reached a record ~** le dollar a atteint son niveau le plus bas ▪ **relations between them are at an all-time ~** leurs relations n'ont jamais été si mauvaises
3. METEOR dépression *f*
4. *US* AUT : **in ~** en première OR seconde
5. *lit* [of cattle] meuglement *m*, beuglement *m*.
◇ *vi* meugler, beugler.

low-alcohol *adj* à faible teneur en alcool.

lowboy ['ləʊbɔɪ] *n* commode *f* (basse).

lowbrow ['ləʊbraʊ] ◇ *n pej* personne *f* sans prétentions intellectuelles OR terre à terre.
◇ *adj* [person] peu intellectuel, terre à terre ▪ [book, film] sans prétentions intellectuelles.

low-budget *adj* économique.

low-calorie, low-cal *adj* (à) basses calories.

Low Church *adj* à tendance évangélique *(dans l'Église anglicane).*

low-cost *adj* (à) bon marché.

Low Countries *pr npl* : **the ~** les Pays-Bas *mpl*.

low-cut *adj* décolleté.

lowdown ['ləʊdaʊn] *n (U) inf* renseignements *mpl* ▪ **can you give me the ~ on what happened?** tu peux me mettre au courant de ce qui s'est passé?
◆ **low-down** *adj* **1.** [shameful] honteux, bas ▪ [mean] mesquin ▪ **that was a dirty low-down trick** c'était un sale tour **2.** *US* [depressed] cafardeux.

lower[1] ['ləʊəʳ] ◇ *adj (compar of low)* inférieur, plus bas ▪ **the ~ deck** [of ship] le pont inférieur ▪ **the ~ classes** les classes inférieures ▪ **the ~ middle class** la petite bourgeoisie ▪ **~ vertebrates** vertébrés inférieurs ▪ **'The Lower Depths'** ***Gorky, Renoir*** 'les Bas-Fonds'.
◇ *adv (compar of low)* : **the ~ paid** la tranche inférieure du salariat.
◇ *vt* **1.** [blind] baisser ▪ [eyes] baisser ▪ [sails] abaisser, amener ▪ [lifeboat] mettre à la mer ▪ **~ your aim a bit** visez un peu plus bas ▪ **supplies were ~ed down to us on a rope** on nous a descendu des provisions au bout d'une corde ▪ **she ~ed herself into the water** elle se laissa glisser dans l'eau ◗ **~ed control button** *US dans un ascenseur, bouton accessible aux personnes en fauteuil roulant* ▪ **to ~ one's guard** [in boxing] baisser sa garde ; *fig* prêter le flanc **2.** [reduce - price, pressure, standard] baisser, diminuer ▪ **~ your voice** parlez moins fort, baissez la voix **3.** [morally] : **she wouldn't ~ herself to talk to them** elle ne s'abaisserait pas au point de leur adresser la parole.
◇ *vi* [diminish - pressure] diminuer ; [- price] baisser.

lower[2] ['laʊəʳ] *vi* **1.** [sky, weather] se couvrir ▪ **a ~ing sky** un ciel menaçant OR couvert **2.** [person] regarder d'un air menaçant.

lower-case ['ləʊəʳ-] ◇ *adj* TYPO en bas de casse.
◇ *n* bas *m* de casse.

lower-class ['ləʊəʳ-] *adj* populaire.

lowering[1] ['ləʊərɪŋ] ◇ *n* **1.** [of flag] abaissement *m* ▪ [of boat] mise *f* à la mer **2.** [reduction - of temperature, standards, prices] baisse *f*.
◇ *adj* humiliant.

lowering[2] ['laʊərɪŋ] *adj* [sky] sombre, couvert ▪ [clouds] menaçant.

lowermost ['ləʊəməʊst] *adj fml* le plus bas.

lowest ['ləʊɪst] *adj (superl of low)* le plus bas ▪ **the ~ of the low** le dernier des derniers ▪ **the newspaper panders to the views of the ~ in society** *fig* ce journal flatte les instincts les plus bas de la société ◗ **the ~ common multiple** le plus petit commun multiple ▪ **the ~ common denominator** le plus petit dénominateur commun.

low-fat *adj* [yoghurt, crisps] allégé ▪ [milk] demi-écrémé.

low-flying *adj* volant à basse altitude.

low-frequency *adj* (à) basse fréquence.

Low German *n* bas allemand *m*.

low-grade *adj* [in quality] de qualité inférieure ▪ [in rank] (de rang) inférieur, subalterne.

low-heeled *adj* à talons plats.

lowing ['ləʊɪŋ] *n (U) lit* meuglement *m*, beuglement *m*, mugissement *m*.

low-key *adj* [style] discret, - ète *f* ▪ [person] réservé ▪ **the meeting was a very ~ affair** la réunion s'est tenue dans la plus grande discrétion.

lowland ['ləʊlənd] *n* plaine *f*, basse terre *f* ▪ **the Lowlands** les Basses Terres.

low-level *adj* [talks] à bas niveau ▪ [operation] de faible envergure ▪ **~ flying** AERON vol *m* à basse altitude ▪ **~ language** COMPUT langage *m* non évolué OR de bas niveau ▪ **~ radiation** NUCL PHYS irradiation *f* de faible intensité.

low life *n* pègre *f*.

low-loader *n* RAIL wagon *m* à plate-forme surbaissée ▪ AUT camion *m* à plate-forme surbaissée.

lowly ['ləʊlɪ] (*comp* **lowlier**, *superl* **lowliest**) *adj* [modest] modeste ▪ [meek] humble ▪ [simple] sans prétention OR prétentions.

low-lying *adj* [land - gen] bas ; [- below sea level] au-dessous du niveau de la mer ▪ [cloud] bas.

Low Mass *n* RELIG messe *f* basse.

low-minded *adj* vulgaire, grossier.

low-necked *adj* décolleté.

low-paid ◇ *adj* mal payé.
◇ *npl* : **the ~** les petits salaires *mpl*.

low-pressure *adj* **1.** [gas] sous faible pression, de basse pression ▪ [tyre] à basse pression **2.** [job] peu stressant.

low-price(d) *adj* bon marché, peu cher.

low profile *n* : **to keep a ~** garder un profil bas.
◆ **low-profile** *adj* **1.** = **low-key 2.** AUT : **low-profile tyre** pneu *m* à profil bas.

low-rent *adj* [housing] à loyer modéré.

low-rise *adj* [buildings] de faible hauteur, bas.

low season *n* : **the ~** la basse saison ▪ **~ holidays** vacances *fpl* hors saison.

low-sulphur petrol *n* essence *f* à basse teneur en soufre.

low-tar *adj* : **~ cigarettes** cigarettes *fpl* à faible teneur en goudron.

low-tech *adj* rudimentaire.

low tide *n* marée *f* basse ■ **at ~** à marée basse.

low water *n (U)* basses eaux *fpl*.

loyal ['lɔɪəl] *adj* loyal, fidèle ■ **to be ~ to sb** être loyal envers qqn, faire preuve de loyauté envers qqn ➜ **the ~ toast** *toast porté à la reine d'Angleterre à la fin d'un dîner.*

loyalism ['lɔɪəlɪzm] *n* loyalisme *m*.

loyalist ['lɔɪəlɪst] ◇ *n* loyaliste *mf*.
◇ *adj* loyaliste.
◆ **Loyalist** *n* loyaliste *mf*.

LOYALIST

Dans le contexte britannique, le mot *Loyalist* désigne un protestant d'Irlande du Nord souhaitant que son pays reste rattaché au Royaume-Uni.

loyally ['lɔɪəlɪ] *adv* loyalement, fidèlement.

loyalty ['lɔɪəltɪ] (*pl* **loyalties**) *n* **1.** [faithfulness] loyauté *f*, fidélité *f* ■ **she's always shown great ~** elle a toujours fait preuve d'une grande loyauté ■ **the party demands ~ to the principles of democracy** le parti exige le respect des principes de la démocratie ■ **her ~ to the cause is not in doubt** son dévouement à la cause n'est pas mis en doute **2.** [tie] : **tribal loyalties** liens *mpl* tribaux ■ **my loyalties are divided** je suis déchiré (entre les deux), entre les deux mon cœur balance ***hum***.

loyalty card *n* carte *f* de fidélité.

lozenge ['lɒzɪndʒ] *n* **1.** [sweet] pastille *f* ■ **throat ~** pastille pour la gorge **2.** [rhombus] losange *m*.

LP (*abbrev of* **long-player**) *n* : **an ~** un 33 tours.

LPG [,elpiː'dʒiː] (*abbrev of* **liquified petroleum gas**) *n* GPL *m*.

L-plate *n* ***UK*** *plaque apposée sur la voiture d'un conducteur qui n'a pas encore son permis (L signifie "learner", apprenti).*

LPN (*abbrev of* **licensed practical nurse**) *n aide infirmière diplômée.*

LSD[1] (*abbrev of* **lysergic acid diethylamide**) *n* LSD *m*.

LSD[2], **lsd** (*abbrev of* **librae, solidi, denarii**) *n symboles représentant les pounds, les shillings et les pence de l'ancienne monnaie britannique avant l'adoption du système décimal en 1971.*

LSE (*abbrev of* **London School of Economics**) *pr n établissement universitaire dépendant de l'Université de Londres, spécialisé dans l'économie.*

LSO (*abbrev of* **London Symphony Orchestra**) *pr n orchestre symphonique de Londres.*

Lt. (*written abbrev of* **lieutenant**) Lieut.

LT (*written abbrev of* **low tension**) BT.

Ltd, ltd (*written abbrev of* **limited**) ≃ SARL.

lubricant ['luːbrɪkənt] ◇ *adj* lubrifiant.
◇ *n* lubrifiant *m*.

lubricate ['luːbrɪkeɪt] *vt* [gen] lubrifier ■ [mechanism] lubrifier, graisser, huiler.

lubricated ['luːbrɪkeɪtɪd] *adj* ***inf hum*** [drunk] beurré.

lubrication [,luːbrɪ'keɪʃn] *n* [gen] lubrification *f* ■ [of mechanism] lubrification *f*, graissage *m*, huilage *m*.

lubricious [luː'brɪʃəs] *adj* ***lit*** lubrique.

lucid ['luːsɪd] *adj* **1.** [clear-headed] lucide ■ **he has his ~ moments** il a des moments de lucidité **2.** [clear] clair, limpide ■ **she gave a ~ account of events** elle donna un compte rendu net et précis des événements.

lucidity [luː'sɪdətɪ] *n* **1.** [of mind] lucidité *f* **2.** [of style, account] clarté *f*, limpidité *f*.

lucidly ['luːsɪdlɪ] *adv* lucidement, avec lucidité.

Lucifer ['luːsɪfər] *pr n* Lucifer.

luck [lʌk] *n* **1.** [fortune] chance *f* ■ **to have good ~** avoir de la chance ■ **good ~!** bonne chance! ■ **good ~ in your new job!** bonne chance pour ton nouveau travail! ▌ [good fortune] : **that's a bit of ~!** c'est de la chance! ■ **~ was with us** *OR* **on our side** la chance était avec nous ■ **you're in ~, your ~'s in** vous avez de la chance ■ **we're out of ~** on n'a pas de chance ■ **better ~ next time** vous aurez plus de chance la prochaine fois ■ **any ~ ?** alors, ça a marché? ■ **some people have all the ~!** il y en a qui ont vraiment de la chance! ■ **it would be just my ~ to bump into my boss** ***iron*** ce serait bien ma veine de tomber sur mon patron ▌ [bad fortune] : **we had a bit of bad ~ with the car** on a eu un pépin avec la voiture ■ **you've brought me nothing but bad ~** tu ne m'as causé que des malheurs ■ **it's bad ~ to spill salt** renverser du sel porte malheur ■ **bad** *OR* **hard** *OR* **tough ~ !** pas de chance! ■ **we thought the exam was cancelled – no such ~** nous croyions que l'examen était annulé – ç'aurait été trop beau ■ **to be down on one's ~** avoir la poisse *OR* la guigne ■ **to push one's ~** jouer avec le feu ■ **with (any) ~** avec un peu de chance ■ **worse ~** tant pis **2.** [chance, opportunity] hasard *m* ■ **it's the ~ of the draw** c'est une question de chance ■ **to try one's ~** tenter sa chance ■ **as ~ would have it** [by chance] par hasard ; [by good luck] par bonheur ■ **as ~ would have it I'd forgotten my keys** et comme par hasard, j'avais oublié mes clés.
◆ **luck out** *vi insep* ***US inf*** **1.** [succeed] avoir de la veine **2.** [fail] avoir la poisse.

luckily ['lʌkɪlɪ] *adv* heureusement, par chance ■ **~ for him, he escaped** heureusement pour lui, il s'est échappé.

luckless ['lʌklɪs] *adj* [person] malchanceux ■ [escapade, attempt] malheureux.

lucky ['lʌkɪ] (*comp* **luckier**, *superl* **luckiest**) *adj* **1.** [fortunate - person] chanceux ; [- encounter, winner] heureux ■ **to be ~** avoir de la chance ■ **to get ~** ***inf*** avoir un coup de bol ■ **what a ~ escape!** on l'a échappé belle! ■ **it was ~ for them that we were there** heureusement pour eux que nous étions là ➜ **a ~ break** ***inf*** un coup de pot *OR* de bol ■ **it's my ~ day** c'est mon jour de chance ■ **you ~ devil** *OR* **thing!** ***inf*** sacré veinard! ■ **I'd like a pay rise – you'll be ~** *OR* **you should be so ~!** j'aimerais une augmentation – tu peux toujours courir! ■ **~ you!** vous en avez de la chance! ■ **'Lucky Jim'** ***Amis*** 'Jim-la-Chance' **2.** [token, number] porte-bonheur *(inv)* **3.** [guess] heureux.

lucky dip *n* ***UK*** *jeu d'enfant consistant à chercher des cadeaux enfouis dans une caisse remplie de sciure.*

lucrative ['luːkrətɪv] *adj* [job] bien rémunéré, lucratif ■ [activity, deal] lucratif, rentable.

lucre ['luːkər] *n* ***hum*** & ***pej*** **(filthy) ~** lucre *m*.

Lucretia Borgia [luː'kriːʃə'bɔːdʒə] *pr n* Lucrèce Borgia.

Lucretius [luː'kriːʃəs] *pr n* Lucrèce.

Luddite ['lʌdaɪt] ◇ *n* luddite *m*.
◇ *adj* luddite ■ **the ~ Riots** les émeutes *fpl* luddites.

THE LUDDITE RIOTS

Émeutes ouvrières qui eurent lieu en Grande-Bretagne pendant la crise de 1811-1813. Au nord du pays, des chômeurs détruisirent les machines-outils sous prétexte qu'elles étaient responsables de leur sort. Ces émeutes furent durement réprimées par le gouvernement. Aujourd'hui, le mot *Luddite* peut désigner quelqu'un qui dédaigne les nouvelles technologies et l'informatique.

ludicrous ['luːdɪkrəs] *adj* ridicule, absurde.

ludicrously ['luːdɪkrəslɪ] *adv* ridiculement.

ludo ['luːdəʊ] *n* ≃ (jeu *m* des) petits chevaux *mpl*.

Ludwig ['lʊdvɪg] *pr n* : **~ of Bavaria** Louis de Bavière.

lug [lʌg] (*pret & pp* **lugged**, *cont* **lugging**) ◇ *vt* ***inf*** [carry, pull] trimbaler ■ **I had to ~ my bags all the way from the station** j'ai dû trimbaler mes bagages de la gare jusqu'ici.
◇ *n* **1.** [for fixing] ergot *m*, (petite) patte *f* ■ [handle] anse *f*, poignée *f* **2.** △ ***UK*** = **lughole**.
◆ **lug about** ***UK***, **lug around** *vt sep* ***inf*** trimbaler.

luggage ['lʌgɪdʒ] *n (U)* bagages *mpl* ■ **~ trolley** chariot *m* à bagages.

luggage handler *n* ***UK*** bagagiste *mf*.

luggage rack *n* ***UK*** RAIL [shelf] porte-bagages *m inv* ■ [net] filet *m* (à bagages) ■ AUT galerie *f* (de toit).

luggage van *n* UK RAIL fourgon *m* (à bagages).

lughole△ ['lʌghəʊl] *n* UK [ear] esgourde *f*.

lugubrious [lu:'gu:brɪəs] *adj* lugubre.

Luke [lu:k] *pr n* Luc ▪ **Saint ~** saint Luc.

lukewarm ['lu:kwɔ:m] *adj* [water, soup] tiède ▪ **a ~ reception** *fig* [of person] un accueil peu chaleureux ; [of book, film] un accueil mitigé.

lull [lʌl] ◇ *n* [in weather] accalmie *f* ▪ [in fighting] accalmie *f*, pause *f* ▪ [in conversation] pause *f* ▪ **the ~ before the storm** le calme avant la tempête.
◇ *vt* [calm - anxiety, person] calmer, apaiser ▪ **she ~ed the child to sleep** elle berça l'enfant jusqu'à ce qu'il s'endorme ▪ **they were ~ed into a false sense of security** ils ont fait l'erreur de se laisser rassurer par des propos lénifiants.

lullaby ['lʌləbaɪ] (*pl* **lullabies**) *n* berceuse *f*.

lumbago [lʌm'beɪgəʊ] *n (U)* lumbago *m*, lombalgie *f*.

lumbar puncture *n* ponction *f* lombaire, rachicentèse *f*.

lumber ['lʌmbəʳ] ◇ *n* **1.** US [cut wood] bois *m* (d'œuvre) ▪ [ready for use] bois *m* de construction OR de charpente **2.** UK [junk] bric-à-brac *m inv*.
◇ *vt* US [logs] débiter ▪ [tree] abattre, couper.
◇ *vi* **1.** [large person, animal] marcher pesamment ▪ **I could hear him ~ing down the stairs** je l'entendais descendre l'escalier d'un pas pesant ▮ [heavy vehicle] : **the tanks ~ed into the centre of the town** la lourde colonne de chars avançait vers le centre de la ville **2.** US [fell trees] abattre des arbres *(pour le bois)*.
◆ **lumber with** *vt sep (usu passive) inf* [encumber] : **to ~ sb with sthg** refiler qqch à qqn ▪ **I'll get ~ed with it** ça va me retomber dessus.

lumbering ['lʌmbərɪŋ] ◇ *n* US exploitation *f* forestière.
◇ *adj* [heavy - step] pesant, lourd ; [- person] lourd, maladroit.

lumberjack ['lʌmbədʒæk] *n* bûcheron *m*, - onne *f* ▪ **~ shirt** chemise *f* de bûcheron *(chemise épaisse à grands carreaux)*.

lumber-jacket *n* grosse veste *f* de bûcheron.

lumberman ['lʌmbəmən] (*pl* **lumbermen** [-mən]) US = **lumberjack**.

lumbermill ['lʌmbə,mɪl] *n* US scierie *f*.

lumber room *n* UK débarras *m*.

lumberyard ['lʌmbəjɑ:d] *n* US dépôt *m* de bois.

luminary ['lu:mɪnərɪ] (*pl* **luminaries**) *n* **1.** [celebrity] lumière *f*, sommité *f* **2.** *lit* [heavenly body] astre *m*.

luminosity [,lu:mɪ'nɒsətɪ] *n* luminosité *f*.

luminous ['lu:mɪnəs] *adj* [paint, colour, sky] lumineux ▪ *fig* [explanation, argument] lumineux, limpide.

lump [lʌmp] ◇ *n* **1.** [of sugar] morceau *m* ▪ **one ~ or two?** un ou deux sucres? **2.** [of solid matter - small] morceau *m* ; [- large] masse *f* ▪ [in food] grumeau *m* ▪ [of marble] bloc *m* ▶ **to have a ~ in one's throat** avoir une boule dans la gorge, avoir la gorge serrée **3.** [bump on surface] bosse *f* ▪ **I've got a ~ on my forehead** j'ai une bosse au front ▪ **there are lots of ~s in this mattress** ce matelas est plein de bosses **4.** MED [swelling] grosseur *f*, protubérance *f* ▪ **she has a ~ in her breast** elle a une grosseur au sein **5.** [of money] : **you don't have to pay it all in one ~** vous n'êtes pas obligé de tout payer en une seule fois **6.** *inf pej* [clumsy person] empoté *m*, - e *f* **7.** UK CONSTR : **~ labour** main-d'œuvre *f* non déclarée.
◇ *vt inf* [put up with] : **if you don't like it you can ~ it!** si ça ne te plaît pas, tant pis pour toi!
◆ **lump together** *vt sep* **1.** [gather together] réunir, rassembler ▪ **couldn't you ~ all these paragraphs together under one heading?** ne pourrais-tu pas réunir OR regrouper tous ces paragraphes sous un même titre? **2.** [consider the same] mettre dans la même catégorie.

lumpectomy [,lʌm'pektəmɪ] *n* ablation *f* d'une tumeur au sein.

lumpfish ['lʌmpfɪʃ] (*pl inv* OR *pl* **lumpfishes**) *n* lump *m*, lompe *m*.

lumpish ['lʌmpɪʃ] *adj* [clumsy] maladroit ▪ [dull-witted] idiot, abruti.

lump sugar *n* sucre *m* en morceaux.

lump sum *n* somme *f* forfaitaire ▪ **they pay me a ~** je touche une somme forfaitaire ▪ **to be paid in a ~** être payé en une seule fois.

lumpy ['lʌmpɪ] (*comp* **lumpier**, *superl* **lumpiest**) *adj* [sauce] plein de grumeaux ▪ [mattress] plein de bosses, défoncé.

lunacy ['lu:nəsɪ] (*pl* **lunacies**) *n* **1.** [madness] démence *f*, folie *f* **2.** [folly] folie *f* ▪ **it would be ~ to accept such a proposal** ce serait de la folie d'accepter pareille proposition.

lunar ['lu:nəʳ] *adj* [rock, month, cycle] lunaire ▪ [eclipse] de la Lune ▪ **~ landing** alunissage *m* ▪ **~ module** module *m* lunaire.

lunatic ['lu:nətɪk] ◇ *n* **1.** [madman] aliéné *m*, - e *f*, dément *m*, - e *f* **2.** *inf* [fool] cinglé *m*, - e *f*.
◇ *adj* **1.** [insane] fou *(before vowel or silent 'h'* **fol***)*, folle *f*, dément **2.** *inf* [crazy - person] cinglé, dingue ; [- idea] insensé.

lunatic asylum *n* asile *m* d'aliénés.

lunatic fringe *n pej* extrémistes *mpl* fanatiques.

lunch [lʌntʃ] ◇ *n* déjeuner *m* ▪ **to have ~** déjeuner ▪ **she's gone out for ~** elle est partie déjeuner ▪ **I have a ~ date** je déjeune avec quelqu'un, je suis pris pour le déjeuner ; [for business] j'ai un déjeuner d'affaires ▪ **what did you have for ~?** qu'est-ce que tu as mangé à midi? ▶ **he's out to ~** *liter* il est parti déjeuner ; *inf fig* il débloque.
◇ *vi* déjeuner.

lunchbox ['lʌntʃbɒks] *n* **1.** [for sandwiches *etc*] *boîte dans laquelle on transporte son déjeuner* **2.** *inf* bijoux *mpl* de famille.

luncheon ['lʌntʃən] *n fml* déjeuner *m*.

luncheonette [,lʌntʃə'net] *n* US snack *m*, snack-bar *m*.

luncheon meat *n bloc de viande de porc en conserve*.

luncheon voucher *n* UK Ticket-Restaurant® *m*.

lunch hour *n* heure *f* du déjeuner.

lunchpail ['lʌntʃpeɪl] US = **lunchbox**.

lunchtime ['lʌntʃtaɪm] *n* heure *f* du déjeuner ▪ **I saw him at ~** je l'ai vu à midi OR à l'heure du déjeuner.

lung [lʌŋ] ◇ *n* poumon *m* ▪ **he filled his ~s with air** il inspira profondément.
◇ *comp* [artery, congestion, disease] pulmonaire ▪ [transplant] du poumon ▪ **~ cancer** cancer *m* du poumon ▪ **~ specialist** pneumologue *mf*.

lunge [lʌndʒ] ◇ *n* **1.** [sudden movement] : **to make a ~ for sthg** se précipiter vers qqch **2.** FENCING fente *f* (avant) **3.** EQUIT longe *f*.
◇ *vi* [move suddenly] faire un mouvement brusque en avant ▪ **she ~d at him with a knife** elle se précipita sur lui avec un couteau.
◇ *vt* [horse] mener à la longe.

lungful ['lʌŋfʊl] *n* : **take a ~ of air** inspirez à fond.

lupin ['lu:pɪn] *n* lupin *m*.

lupine ['lu:paɪn] ◇ *n* US = **lupin**.
◇ *adj* de loup.

lurch [lɜ:tʃ] ◇ *vi* [person] tituber, chanceler ▪ [car - swerve] faire une embardée ; [- jerk forwards] avancer par à-coups ▪ [ship] tanguer ▪ **the car ~ed out of control** la voiture livrée à elle-même fit une embardée ▪ **his opinions ~ from one extreme to another** *fig* dans ses opinions, il passe d'un extrême à l'autre.
◇ *n* : **the car gave a sudden ~ and left the road** la voiture fit une embardée et quitta la route ▶ **to leave sb in the ~** laisser qqn en plan.

lure [ljʊəʳ] ◇ *n* **1.** [attraction] attrait *m* ▪ [charm] charme *m* ▪ [temptation] tentation *f* **2.** FISHING & HUNT leurre *m*.
◇ *vt* [person] attirer (sous un faux prétexte) ▪ **he ~d them into a trap** il les a attirés dans un piège.
◆ **lure away** *vt sep* : **she invited me over in order to ~ me away from the office** elle m'a invité chez elle pour m'éloigner du bureau.

Lurex® ['lʊəreks] *n* [thread] Lurex® *m* ▪ [cloth] tissu *m* en Lurex®.

lurgy ['lɜ:gɪ] *n UK inf hum* **I've got the dreaded ~** j'ai attrapé quelque chose.

lurid ['ljʊərɪd] *adj* **1.** [sensational - account, story] macabre, atroce, horrible ■ [salacious] salace, malsain ■ **the book gives a ~ description of life at the castle** le livre donne une description haute en couleur de la vie au château **2.** [glaring - sky, sunset] sanglant, rougeoyant ; [- wallpaper, shirt] criard, voyant ■ **a ~ green dress** une robe d'un vert criard.

lurk [lɜ:k] *vi* [person, animal] se tapir ■ [danger] se cacher, menacer ■ [doubt, worry] persister ■ **the burglar was ~ing behind the trees** le cambrioleur était tapi derrière les arbres.

lurking ['lɜ:kɪŋ] *adj* [suspicion] vague ■ [danger] menaçant.

luscious ['lʌʃəs] *adj* **1.** [fruit] succulent ■ [colour] riche **2.** [woman] séduisant ■ [lips] pulpeux.

lush [lʌʃ] <> *adj* **1.** [vegetation] riche, luxuriant ■ [fruit] succulent ■ *fig* [description] riche **2.** [luxurious] luxueux.
<> *n*[△] poivrot *m*, - e *f*.

lust [lʌst] *n* **1.** [sexual desire] désir *m* sexuel, concupiscence *f* ■ [as sin] luxure *f* **2.** [greed] soif *f*, convoitise *f* ■ **~ for power** soif de pouvoir.
◆ **lust after** *vt insep* [person] désirer, avoir envie de, convoiter ■ [money, property] convoiter.
◆ **lust for** *vt insep* [money] convoiter ■ [revenge, power] avoir soif de.

luster *US* = **lustre**.

lustful ['lʌstfʊl] *adj* **1.** [lecherous] concupiscent, lascif **2.** [greedy] avide.

lustily ['lʌstɪlɪ] *adv* [sing, shout] à pleine gorge, à pleins poumons.

lustre *UK*, **luster** *US* ['lʌstəʳ] *n* **1.** [sheen] lustre *m*, brillant *m* **2.** *fig* [glory] éclat *m*.

lustrous ['lʌstrəs] *adj* **1.** [shiny - pearls, stones] lustré, chatoyant ■ [eyes] brillant ■ [cloth] lustré ■ **~ black hair** cheveux d'un noir de jais **2.** *lit* [illustrious - career] illustre ■ [name] glorieux.

lusty ['lʌstɪ] (*comp* **lustier**, *superl* **lustiest**) *adj* [strong - person, baby] vigoureux, robuste ; [- voice, manner] vigoureux.

lute [lu:t] *n* MUS luth *m*.

Lutetia [lu:'ti:ʃə] *pr n* Lutèce.

Lutheran ['lu:θərən] <> *n* Luthérien *m*, - enne *f*.
<> *adj* luthérien.

Lutheranism ['lu:θərənɪzm] *n* luthéranisme *m*.

luv [lʌv] *n* & *vt UK inf* = **love**.

luvvie ['lʌvɪ] *n inf hum* acteur *m* prétentieux, actrice *f* prétentieuse.

Luxembourg ['lʌksəmbɜ:g] *pr n* **1.** [country] Luxembourg *m* ■ **in ~** au Luxembourg **2.** [town] Luxembourg.

Luxemburger ['lʌksəmbɜ:gəʳ] *n* Luxembourgeois *m*, - e *f*.

luxuriance [lʌg'ʒʊərɪəns] *n* **1.** [luxury] luxe *m*, somptuosité *f* **2.** [of vegetation] luxuriance *f*, richesse *f* ■ [of plants] exubérance *f*, abondance *f* ■ [of hair] abondance *f*.

luxuriant [lʌg'ʒʊərɪənt] *adj* **1.** [luxurious - surroundings] luxueux, somptueux **2.** [vegetation] luxuriant ■ [crops, undergrowth] abondant, riche ■ [countryside] couvert de végétation, luxuriant ■ *fig* [style] luxuriant, riche **3.** [flowing - hair, beard] abondant.

luxuriate [lʌg'ʒʊərɪeɪt] *vi* **1.** [take pleasure] : **to ~ in sthg** se délecter de qqch ■ **to ~ in the sun/in a hot bath** se prélasser au soleil/dans un bain chaud **2.** *lit* [proliferate, flourish] proliférer.

luxurious [lʌg'ʒʊərɪəs] *adj* **1.** [opulent - house, decor, clothes] luxueux, somptueux ; [- car] luxueux **2.** [voluptuous] voluptueux.

luxuriously [lʌg'ʒʊərɪəslɪ] *adv* **1.** [with, in luxury] luxueusement ■ **to live ~** vivre dans le luxe *OR* dans l'opulence **2.** [voluptuously] voluptueusement.

luxury ['lʌkʃərɪ] (*pl* **luxuries**) <> *n* **1.** [comfort] luxe *m* ■ **to live in ~, to lead a life of ~** vivre dans le luxe **2.** [treat] luxe *m* ■ **one of life's little luxuries** un des petits plaisirs de la vie.
<> *comp* [car, restaurant, kitchen] de luxe ■ [apartment] de luxe, de standing.

luxury goods *npl* articles *mpl* de luxe.

LW (*written abbrev of* **long wave**) GO.

LWT (*abbrev of* **London Weekend Television**) *pr n chaîne de télévision relevant de l'IBA*.

lyceum [laɪ'sɪəm] *n* [in names of public buildings] théâtre *m*.

lychee [,laɪ'tʃi:] *n* litchi *m*, lychee *m*.

lych-gate ['lɪtʃ-] *n* porche *m* de cimetière.

Lycra® ['laɪkrə] *n* Lycra® *m*.

lying ['laɪɪŋ] <> *cont* ▻ **lie**.
<> *adj* **1.** [reclining] couché, étendu, allongé **2.** [dishonest - person] menteur ; [- story] mensonger, faux, fausse *f*.
<> *n* **1.** [corpse] : **~ in state** exposition *f* du corps **2.** *(U)* [dishonesty] mensonges *mpl*.

lying-in *n* MED couches *fpl*.

lymph [lɪmf] *n* lymphe *f*.

lymphatic [lɪm'fætɪk] *adj* lymphatique ■ **~ drainage** drainage *m* lymphatique.

lymph gland, lymph node *n* ganglion *m* lymphatique.

lynch [lɪntʃ] *vt* lyncher.

lynching ['lɪntʃɪŋ] *n* lynchage *m*.

lynchpin ['lɪntʃpɪn] = **linchpin**.

lynx [lɪŋks] (*pl inv OR pl* **lynxes**) *n* lynx *m inv*.

Lyon [li:ɔ̃], **Lyons** ['laɪənz] *pr n* Lyon.

lyre ['laɪəʳ] *n* lyre *f*.

lyrebird ['laɪəbɜ:d] *n* oiseau-lyre *m*.

lyric ['lɪrɪk] <> *adj* lyrique.
<> *n* [poem] poème *m* lyrique.
◆ **lyrics** *npl* [of song] paroles *fpl*.

lyrical ['lɪrɪkl] *adj* **1.** *liter* lyrique **2.** *fig* passionné ■ **he was positively ~ about his visit to China** son séjour en Chine l'a véritablement enthousiasmé.

lyrically ['lɪrɪklɪ] *adv* [poetically] avec lyrisme ■ [enthusiastically] avec enthousiasme.

lyricism ['lɪrɪsɪzm] *n* lyrisme *m*.

lyricist ['lɪrɪsɪst] *n* [of poems] poète *m* lyrique ■ [of song, opera] parolier *m*, - ère *f*.

Lysander [laɪ'sændəʳ] *pr n* Lysandre.

lysergic [laɪ'sɜ:dʒɪk] *adj* lysergique.

m (*pl* **m's** *OR pl* **ms**), **M** (*pl* **M's** *OR pl* **Ms**) [em] *n* [letter] m *m*, M *m*, *see also* **F**.

m 1. (*written abbrev of* **metre**) m **2.** (*written abbrev of* **million**) M **3.** *written abbr of* **mile**.

M ◇ *UK* (*abbrev of* **motorway**) ▪ **the M5** l'autoroute M5.
◇ (*written abbrev of* **medium**) M.

ma [mɑː] *n* maman *f*.

MA ◇ *n* **1.** (*abbrev of* **Master of Arts**) [in England, Wales and US] (*titulaire d'une*) *maîtrise de lettres* ▪ [in Scotland] *premier examen universitaire, équivalent de la licence* **2.** = **military academy**.
◇ *written abbr of* **Massachusetts**.

ma'am [mæm] *n* madame *f*.

mac [mæk] *inf* **1.** *UK* (*abbrev of* **macintosh**) imper *m* **2.** *US* & *Scotland* **come here ~!** amène-toi, mec!

macabre [mə'kɑːbrə] *adj* macabre.

macadam [mə'kædəm] ◇ *n* macadam *m*.
◇ *comp* [road] macadamisé, en macadam.

macaroni [ˌmækə'rəʊnɪ] *n (U)* macaronis *mpl* ▪ **~ cheese** gratin *m* de macaronis.

macaroon [ˌmækə'ruːn] *n* CULIN macaron *m*.

Macao [mə'kaʊ] *n* Macao *f*.

macaw [mə'kɔː] *n* ara *m*.

macchiato [mæk'jɑːtəʊ] *n* crème *m*.

mace [meɪs] *n* **1.** [spice] macis *m* **2.** [club] massue *f*, masse *f* d'armes ▪ [ceremonial] masse *f* ▪ **~ bearer** massier *m*.

Mace® [meɪs] ◇ *n* [spray] gaz *m* lacrymogène.
◇ *vt inf US inf* bombarder au gaz lacrymogène.

Macedonia [ˌmæsɪ'dəʊnjə] *pr n* Macédoine *f* ▪ **in ~** en Macédoine.

Macedonian [ˌmæsɪ'dəʊnjən] ◇ *n* **1.** [person] Macédonien *m*, - enne *f* **2.** LING macédonien *m*.
◇ *adj* macédonien.

Mach [mæk] *n* Mach ▪ **to fly at ~ 3** voler à Mach 3.

machete [mə'ʃetɪ] *n* machette *f*.

Machiavelli [ˌmækɪə'velɪ] *pr n* Machiavel.

Machiavellian [ˌmækɪə'velɪən] *adj* machiavélique.

machinations [ˌmækɪ'neɪʃnz] *npl* machinations *fpl*.

machine [mə'ʃiːn] ◇ *n* **1.** [mechanical device] machine *f* ▪ **to do sthg by ~** *OR* **on a ~** faire qqch à la machine ▮ *fig* & *pej* [person] machine *f*, automate *m* **2.** [organization] machine *f*, appareil *m* ▪ **the party ~** l'appareil du parti **3.** [car, motorbike] machine *f* ▪ [plane] appareil *m*.
◇ *comp* : **the ~ age** l'ère *f* de la machine.
◇ *vt* SEW coudre à la machine ▪ INDUST [manufacture] fabriquer à la machine ▪ [work on machine] usiner.

machine code *n* code *m* machine.

machine-finished *adj* [paper] apprêté, calandré ▪ [clothes] fini à la machine.

machine gun *n* mitrailleuse *f*.
◆ **machine-gun** *vt* mitrailler.

machine-gunner *n* mitrailleur *m*.

machine intelligence *n* intelligence *f* artificielle.

machine language *n* langage *m* machine.

machine-made *adj* fait *OR* fabriqué à la machine.

machine operator *n* opérateur *m*, - trice *f* (sur machine).

machine pistol *n* mitraillette *f*, pistolet *m* mitrailleur.

machine-readable *adj* COMPUT exploitable par machine.

machinery [mə'ʃiːnərɪ] (*pl* **machineries**) *n* **1.** *(U)* [machines] machines *fpl*, machinerie *f* ▪ [mechanism] mécanisme *m* **2.** *fig* rouages *mpl* ▪ **the ~ of state/of government** les rouages de l'État/du gouvernement.

machine shop *n* atelier *m* d'usinage.

machine-stitch ◇ *n* point *m* (de piqûre) à la machine.
◇ *vt* piquer (à la machine).

machine tool *n* machine-outil *f*.

machine translation *n* traduction *f* automatique.

machine washable *adj* lavable à la *OR* en machine.

machinist [mə'ʃiːnɪst] *n* INDUST opérateur *m*, - trice *f* (sur machine) ▪ SEW mécanicien *m*, - enne *f*.

machismo [mə'tʃɪzməʊ, mə'kɪzməʊ] *n* machisme *m*.

Mach number *n* nombre *m* de Mach.

macho ['mætʃəʊ] ◇ *adj* macho.
◇ *n* macho *m*.

mack [mæk] = **mac** *(sense 1)*.

mackerel ['mækrəl] (*pl inv OR pl* **mackerels**) *n* maquereau *m*.

mackerel sky *n* ciel *m* pommelé.

mackintosh ['mækɪntɒʃ] *n UK* imperméable *m*.

macramé ['mækrəmeɪ] *n* macramé *m*.

macro ['mækrəʊ] (*pl* **macros**) *n* COMPUT macro-instruction *f*, macro *f*.

macrobiotic [,mækrəʊbaɪ'ɒtɪk] *adj* macrobiotique.
◆ **macrobiotics** *n (U)* macrobiotique *f*.

macroclimate ['mækrəʊ,klaɪmət] *n* macroclimat *m*.

macrocosm ['mækrəʊkɒzm] *n* macrocosme *m*.

macrocosmic [,mækrəʊ'kɒzmɪk] *adj* macrocosmique.

macroeconomics ['mækrəʊ,i:kə'nɒmɪks] *n (U)* macroéconomie *f*.

macron ['mækrɒn] *n* TYPO macron *m*.

macroscopic [,mækrəʊ'skɒpɪk] *adj* macroscopique.

macrostructure ['mækrəʊ,strʌktʃə'] *n* macrostructure *f*.

mad [mæd] <> *adj* **1.** *esp UK* [crazy] fou *(before vowel or silent 'h'* **fol***)*, folle *f* ▪ **to go ~** devenir fou ▪ **to be ~ with joy/grief** être fou de joie/douleur ▪ **it's a case of patriotism gone ~** c'est du patriotisme poussé à l'extrême *OR* qui frise la folie ▪ **to drive sb ~** rendre qqn fou ▶ **to be as ~ as a hatter** *OR* **a March hare** être fou à lier ▪ **MAD (magazine)** PRESS *magazine satirique américain très populaire*
2. [absurd - ambition, plan] fou *(before vowel or silent 'h'* **fol***)*, folle *f*, insensé
3. [angry] en colère, furieux ▪ **he went ~ when he saw them** il s'est mis dans une colère noire en les voyant ▪ **to be ~ at** *OR* **with sb** être en colère *OR* fâché contre qqn ▪ **she makes me ~** elle m'énerve ▪ **don't get ~** ne vous fâchez pas
4. [frantic] : **there was a ~ rush for the door** tous les gens se sont rués vers la porte comme des fous ▪ **I'm in a ~ rush** *inf* je suis très pressé, je suis à la bourre ▪ **don't go ~ and try to do it all yourself** *fig* tu ne vas pas te tuer à essayer de tout faire toi-même? ▶ **like ~** *inf* : **to run like ~** courir comme un fou *OR* un dératé ▪ **they were arguing like ~** ils discutaient comme des perdus
5. *inf esp UK inf* [enthusiastic, keen] fou *(before vowel or silent 'h'* **fol***)*, folle *f* ▪ **to be ~ about** *OR* **on sthg** être fou de qqch ▪ **she's ~ about cats** elle adore les chats ▪ **he's ~ about her** il est fou d'elle
6. [dog] enragé ▪ [bull] furieux.
<> *n US* accès *m* de colère.
<> *adv UK* **to be ~ keen on** *OR* **about sthg** *inf* être dingue *OR* être un mordu de qqch.

MAD [mæd] (*abbrev of* **mutual assured destruction**) *n équilibre de la terreur*.

Madagascan [,mædə'gæskn] <> *n* Malgache *mf*.
<> *adj* malgache.

Madagascar [,mædə'gæskə'] *pr n* Madagascar ▪ **in ~** à Madagascar.

madam ['mædəm] *n* **1.** *fml* madame *f* ▪ **Dear Madam** (Chère) Madame ▪ **~ Chairman** Madame la Présidente **2.** *pej* **she's a little ~** c'est une petite effrontée **3.** [in brothel] tenancière *f*.

madcap ['mædkæp] <> *adj* fou *(before vowel or silent 'h'* **fol***)*, folle *f*, insensé ▪ **a ~ scheme** un projet insensé.
<> *n* fou *m*, folle *f*, hurluberlu *m*, - e *f*.

mad cow disease *n* maladie *f* de la vache folle.

madden ['mædn] *vt* [drive insane] rendre fou ▪ [exasperate] exaspérer, rendre fou.

maddening ['mædnɪŋ] *adj* exaspérant ▪ **a ~ noise** un bruit à vous rendre fou.

maddeningly ['mædnɪŋlɪ] *adv* de façon exaspérante ▪ **~ slow** d'une lenteur exaspérante.

madder ['mædə'] *n* BOT & TEX garance *f*.

made [meɪd] *pt* & *pp* ⊳ **make**.

-made *in cpds* : **factory~** industriel ▪ **British~** fabriqué au Royaume-Uni.

Madeira [mə'dɪərə] <> *pr n* [island] Madère ▪ **in ~** à Madère.
<> *n* [wine] madère *m*.

Madeira cake *n* ≃ quatre-quarts *m inv*.

made-to-measure *adj* (fait) sur mesure.

made-to-order *adj* (fait) sur commande.

made-up *adj* **1.** [wearing make-up] maquillé **2.** [invented - story] fabriqué ; [- evidence] faux, fausse *f*.

madhouse ['mædhaʊs] (*pl* [-haʊzɪz]) *n inf* asile *m* d'aliénés, maison *f* de fous ▪ *fig* maison de fous ▪ **the place was a complete ~ when we arrived** lorsque nous sommes arrivés, on se serait crus dans une maison de fous.

Madison Avenue ['mædɪsn-] *pr n rue de New York dont le nom évoque le milieu de la publicité.*

madly ['mædlɪ] *adv* **1.** [passionately] follement ▪ **~ in love** éperdument *OR* follement amoureux ▪ **~ jealous** fou de jalousie **2.** [frantically] comme un fou, frénétiquement ▪ [wildly] comme un fou, follement ▪ [desperately] désespérément.

madman ['mædmən] (*pl* **madmen** [-mən]) *n* fou *m*, aliéné *m*.

madness ['mædnɪs] *n* **1.** [insanity] folie *f*, démence *f* **2.** [folly] folie *f* ▪ **it's ~ even to think of going away now** il faut être fou pour songer à partir maintenant.

Madonna [mə'dɒnə] *pr n* RELIG Madone *f* ▪ [image] madone *f* ▪ **'~ and Child'** 'Vierge à l'enfant'.

madrigal ['mædrɪgl] *n* MUS madrigal *m*.

madwoman ['mæd,wʊmən] (*pl* **madwomen** [-,wɪmɪn]) *n* folle *f*, aliénée *f*.

Maecenas [mi:'si:næs] *pr n* Mécène.

maelstrom ['meɪlstrɒm] *n* maelström *m*.

maestro ['maɪstrəʊ] (*pl* **maestros**) *n* maestro *m*.

MAFF (*abbrev of* **Ministry of Agriculture, Fisheries and Food**) *pr n ministère anglais de l'agriculture, de la pêche et de l'alimentation.*

mafia ['mæfɪə] *n liter* & *fig* mafia *f*, maffia *f*.

mafioso [,mæfɪ'əʊsəʊ] (*pl* **mafiosi** [-si:]) *n* mafioso *m*, maffioso *m*.

mag [mæg] *n inf* = **magazine**.

magazine [,mægə'zi:n] *n* **1.** [publication] magazine *m*, revue *f* ▪ TV magazine *m* **2.** [in gun] magasin *m* ▪ [cartridges] chargeur *m* **3.** MIL [store] magasin *m* ▪ [for weapons] dépôt *m* d'armes ▪ [munitions] munitions *fpl* **4.** PHOT magasin *m* ▪ [for slides] panier *m*, magasin *m*.

magazine rack *n* porte-revues *m*.

Magellan [mə'gelən] *pr n* Magellan ▪ **the Strait of ~** le détroit de Magellan.

magenta [mə'dʒentə] <> *n* magenta *m*.
<> *adj* magenta *(inv)*.

Maggiore [,mædʒɪ'ɔ:rɪ] *pr n* : **Lake ~** le lac Majeur.

maggot ['mægət] *n* asticot *m*.

Maghreb ['mɑ:grəb] *pr n* : **the ~** le Maghreb ▪ **in the ~** au Maghreb.

Magi ['meɪdʒaɪ] *pr npl* : **the ~** les Rois *mpl* mages.

magic ['mædʒɪk] <> *n* **1.** [enchantment] magie *f* ▪ **like** *OR* **as if by ~** *fig* comme par enchantement *OR* magie ▪ **the medicine worked like ~** le remède a fait merveille ▮ [conjuring] magie *f*, prestidigitation *f* **2.** [special quality] magie *f* ▪ **discover the ~ of Greece** découvrez les merveilles de la Grèce.
<> *adj* **1.** [supernatural] magique ▪ **a ~ spell** un sortilège ▪ **just say the ~ words** il suffit de dire la formule magique ▶ **~ number/square** nombre *m* /carré *m* magique ▪ **'The Magic Flute'** ***Mozart*** 'la Flûte enchantée' **2.** [special - formula, moment] magique **3.** *inf* [marvellous] génial.
◆ **magic away** *vt sep* faire disparaître comme par enchantement.

magical ['mædʒɪkl] *adj* magique.

magically ['mædʒɪklɪ] *adv* magiquement ▪ **don't think it will just happen ~** ne t'imagine pas que cela va se produire comme par enchantement.

magic carpet *n* tapis *m* volant.

magic eye *n* œil *m* cathodique *OR* magique.

magician [mə'dʒɪʃn] *n* magicien *m*, - enne *f*.
magic lantern *n* lanterne *f* magique.
magic mushroom *n inf* champignon *m* hallucinogène.
magic wand *n* baguette *f* magique.
magisterial [,mædʒɪ'stɪərɪəl] *adj* LAW de magistrat ■ *fig* magistral.
magistral [mə'dʒɪstrəl] *adj* magistral.
magistrate ['mædʒɪstreɪt] *n* magistrat *m*.
magistrates' court *n* tribunal *m* de première instance.
magma ['mægmə] *n* magma *m*.
Magna Carta, Magna Charta ['mægnə'kɑ:tə] *pr n UK* HIST la Grande Charte.

MAGNA CARTA

Souvent prise pour le symbole de la lutte contre l'oppression, cette charte, imposée en 1215 au roi Jean sans Terre par les barons anglais, énonce les droits et privilèges des nobles, de l'Église et des « hommes libres » (*freemen*) face à l'arbitraire royal.

magna cum laude [,mægnəkʊm'laʊdeɪ] *adv* UNIV avec mention très bien.
magnanimity [,mægnə'nɪmətɪ] *n* magnanimité *f*.
magnanimous [mæg'nænɪməs] *adj* magnanime.
magnanimously [mæg'nænɪməslɪ] *adv* avec magnanimité, magnanimement.
magnate ['mægneɪt] *n* magnat *m* ■ **a press ~** un magnat de la presse.
magnesia [mæg'ni:ʃə] *n* magnésie *f*.
magnesium [mæg'ni:zɪəm] *n* magnésium *m* ■ **~ oxide** magnésie *f*, oxyde *m* de magnésium.
magnet ['mægnɪt] *n* aimant *m*.
magnetic [mæg'netɪk] *adj* magnétique ■ **a ~ personality** *fig* une personnalité fascinante *OR* charismatique.
magnetic disk *n* disque *m* magnétique.
magnetic field *n* champ *m* magnétique.
magnetic needle *n* aiguille *f* aimantée.
magnetic north *n* nord *m* magnétique.
magnetic storm *n* orage *m* magnétique.
magnetic tape *n* bande *f* magnétique.
magnetism ['mægnɪtɪzm] *n* magnétisme *m*.
magnetize, ise ['mægnɪtaɪz] *vt* aimanter, magnétiser ■ *fig* [charm] magnétiser.
magnification [,mægnɪfɪ'keɪʃn] *n* **1.** OPT grossissement *m* ■ ACOUST amplification *f* **2.** RELIG glorification *f*.
magnificence [mæg'nɪfɪsəns] *n* magnificence *f*, splendeur *f*.
magnificent [mæg'nɪfɪsənt] *adj* magnifique, splendide ➊ **'The Magnificent Seven'** ***Sturges*** 'les Sept Mercenaires'.
magnify ['mægnɪfaɪ] (*pret & pp* **magnified**) *vt* **1.** OPT grossir ■ ACOUST amplifier **2.** [exaggerate] exagérer, grossir ■ **the incident was magnified out of all proportion** on a terriblement exagéré l'importance de cet incident **3.** *lit* [exalt] exalter, magnifier ■ RELIG glorifier.
magnifying glass ['mægnɪfaɪɪŋ-] *n* loupe *f*.
magnitude ['mægnɪtju:d] *n* [scale] ampleur *f*, étendue *f* ■ ASTRON & GEOL magnitude *f* ■ [of problem - importance] importance *f* ; [- size] ampleur *f*.
magnolia [mæg'nəʊljə] <> *n* magnolia *m* ■ **the Magnolia State** le Mississippi.
<> *adj* couleur magnolia *(inv)*, blanc rosé *(inv)*.
magnum ['mægnəm] *n* [wine bottle, gun] magnum *m*.
magnum opus *n* œuvre *f* maîtresse, chef-d'œuvre *m*.
magpie ['mægpaɪ] *n* **1.** ORNITH pie *f* **2.** *inf fig* [chatterbox] pie *f*, moulin *m* à paroles ■ *UK* [hoarder] chiffonnier *m*, - ère *f fig*.
Magyar ['mægjɑ:] <> *n* [person] Magyar *m*, - e *f*.
<> *adj* magyar.
maharaja(h) [,mɑ:hə'rɑ:dʒə] *n* maharaja *m*, maharadjah *m*.
maharani [,mɑ:hə'rɑ:ni:] *n* maharani *f*.
maharishi [,mɑ:hə'ri:ʃɪ] *n* maharishi *m*.
mahatma [mə'hɑ:tmə] *n* mahatma *m*.
mahogany [mə'hɒgənɪ] (*pl* **mahoganies**) <> *n* acajou *m* ■ **~ tree** acajou *m*.
<> *adj* **1.** : **~ (coloured)** acajou *(inv)* **2.** [furniture] en acajou.
Mahomet [mə'hɒmɪt] = **Mohammed**.
Mahometan [mə'hɒmɪtn] *dated* <> *adj* mahométan.
<> *n* Mahométan *m*, - e *f*.
maid [meɪd] *n* **1.** [servant] bonne *f*, domestique *f* ■ [in hotel] femme *f* de chambre ■ **~ of honour** demoiselle *f* d'honneur **2.** *lit* jeune fille *f*, demoiselle *f* ■ **the Maid of Orleans** la pucelle d'Orléans **3.** *pej* **old ~** vieille fille *f*.
maiden ['meɪdn] *n* [young girl] jeune fille *f* ■ [virgin] vierge *f*.
maiden aunt *n* tante *f* célibataire.
maidenhair ['meɪdnheə^r] *n* : **~ (fern)** capillaire *m*, cheveu-de-Vénus *m*.
maidenhead ['meɪdnhed] *n lit* [hymen] hymen *m* ■ [virginity] virginité *f*.
maidenhood ['meɪdnhʊd] *n* virginité *f*.
maiden name *n* nom *m* de jeune fille.
maiden over *n au cricket, série de balles où aucun point n'a été marqué.*
maiden speech *n UK premier discours prononcé par un parlementaire nouvellement élu.*
maiden voyage *n* voyage *m* inaugural.
maid-in-waiting (*pl* **maids-in-waiting**) *n* dame *f* d'honneur.
maidservant ['meɪd,sɜ:vənt] *n* servante *f*.
mail [meɪl] <> *n* **1.** [postal service] poste *f* ■ **the parcel got lost in the ~** le colis a été égaré par la poste ■ **your cheque is in the ~** votre chèque a été posté **2.** [letters] courrier *m* ■ **the ~ is only collected twice a week** il n'y a que deux levées par semaine **3.** *(U)* [armour] mailles *fpl*.
<> *vt US* [parcel, goods, cheque] envoyer *OR* expédier par la poste ■ [letter] poster.
◆ **Mail** *pr n* : **the Mail** PRESS *nom abrégé du «Daily Mail»* ■ **the Mail on Sunday** PRESS *hebdomadaire de centre droit paraissant le dimanche.*
mailbag ['meɪlbæg] *n* sac *m* postal.
mail bomb *n US* [letter] lettre *f* piégée ■ [parcel] colis *m* piégé.
mailbox ['meɪlbɒks] *n* **1.** *esp US* [postbox] boîte *f* à lettres **2.** *US* [letterbox] boîte *f* aux lettres **3.** COMPUT boîte *m* aux lettres électronique.
mail clerk *n US* employé *m*, - e *f* responsable du courrier.
mailcoach ['meɪlkəʊtʃ] *n* RAIL voiture-poste *f* ■ [horse-drawn] malle-poste *f*.
mail drop *n* boîte *f* à *OR* aux lettres.
mailing ['meɪlɪŋ] *n* **1.** [posting] expédition *f*, envoi *m* par la poste **2.** COMM & COMPUT mailing *m*, publipostage *m*.
mailing list *n* [diffusion] fichier *m* d'adresses ■ COMPUT liste *f* de diffusion.
mailman ['meɪlmən] (*pl* **mailmen** [-mən]) *n US* facteur *m*.
mail merge *n* COMPUT publipostage *m*, mailing *m*.

mail order *n* vente *f* par correspondance ▪ **to buy sthg by ~** acheter qqch par correspondance *OR* sur catalogue.
◆ **mail-order** *adj* : **mail-order catalogue** catalogue *m* de vente par correspondance ▪ **mail-order firm** maison *f* de vente par correspondance ▪ **mail-order goods** marchandises *fpl* vendues *OR* achetées par correspondance.

mailroom ['meɪlru:m] *n* service *m* du courrier.

mailshot ['meɪlʃɒt] *n* mailing *m*, publipostage *m*.

mail train *n* train *m* postal.

mail truck *n US* camionnette *f OR* fourgonnette *f* des postes.

mail van *n UK* AUT camionnette *f OR* fourgonnette *f* des postes ▪ RAIL voiture-poste *f*.

maim [meɪm] *vt* [disable] mutiler, estropier ▪ [injure] blesser ▪ **people were badly ~ed in the attack** des gens ont été grièvement blessés au cours de l'attaque ▮ [psychologically] marquer, perturber.

main [meɪn] ◇ *adj* **1.** [principal] principal ▪ [largest] principal, plus important ▪ [essential - idea, theme, reason] principal, essentiel ▪ **the ~ points** les points principaux ▪ **the ~ thing we have to consider is his age** la première chose à prendre en compte, c'est son âge ▪ **you're safe, that's the ~ thing** tu es sain et sauf, c'est le principal ▶ **he always has an eye to the ~ chance** *inf* il ne perd jamais de vue ses propres intérêts ▪ **~ course** plat *m* de résistance ; [on menu] plat *m* ▪ **~ office** [gen] bureau *m* principal ; [headquarters] siège *m* **2.** *lit* [sheer] : **to do sthg by ~ force** employer la force pour faire qqch.
◇ *n* **1.** [for gas, water - public] canalisation *f* principale ▪ [for electricity] conducteur *m* principal **2.** NAUT grand mât *m*.
◆ **in the main** *adv phr* en gros, dans l'ensemble.

main beam *n* **1.** AUT feux *mpl* de route **2.** CONSTR poutre *f* maîtresse.

main bearing *n* palier *m (dans un moteur)*.

mainbrace ['meɪnbreɪs] *n* grand bras *m* de vergue.

main clause *n* GRAM proposition *f* principale.

main deck *n* NAUT pont *m* principal.

Maine [meɪn] *pr n* le Maine ▪ **in ~** dans le Maine.

mainframe ['meɪnfreɪm] *n* : **~ (computer)** gros ordinateur *m*, processeur *m* central.

mainland ['meɪnlənd] ◇ *n* continent *m* ▪ **the Danish ~** le Danemark continental.
◇ *adj* continental ▪ **in ~ Britain** en Grande-Bretagne proprement dite *(par opposition aux îles qui l'entourent)*.

mainlander ['meɪnləndəʳ] *n* habitant *m*, - e *f* du continent, continental *m*, - e *f*.

mainline△ ['meɪnlaɪn] *drug sl* ◇ *vi* se piquer, se shooter.
◇ *vt* : **to ~ heroin** se shooter à l'héroïne.

main line *n* RAIL grande ligne *f* ▪ *US* [road] grande route *f*.
◆ **main-line** *adj* [train, station] de grande ligne.

mainly ['meɪnlɪ] *adv* [chiefly] principalement, surtout ▪ [in the majority] pour la plupart, dans l'ensemble.

main road *n* grande route *f*, route à grande circulation, ≃ nationale *f*.

mains [meɪnz] ◇ *n (with sg OR pl vb)* **1.** [main supply] réseau *m* ▪ **where's the ~?** où est la conduite principale? ▪ **did you turn the electricity/gas off at the ~?** as-tu fermé l'arrivée de gaz/d'électricité? **2.** ELEC secteur *m* ▪ **my shaver works on battery or ~** mon rasoir marche sur piles ou sur (le) secteur.
◇ *comp* : **the village doesn't have ~ electricity** le village n'est pas raccordé au réseau électrique ▪ **~ gas** gaz *m* de ville ▪ **~ supply** réseau *m* de distribution de gaz/d'eau/d'électricité ▪ **~ water** eau *f* courante.

mainsail ['meɪnseɪl, 'meɪnsəl] *n* NAUT grand-voile *f*.

main sewer *n* égout *m* collecteur.

mainsheet ['meɪnshi:t] *n* écoute *f* de (la) grand-voile.

mains-operated *adj* fonctionnant sur secteur.

mainspring ['meɪnsprɪŋ] *n* **1.** TECH ressort *m* moteur **2.** *fig* cause *f* ▪ **his courage was the ~ of his success** son courage était à l'origine de son succès.

mainstay ['meɪnsteɪ] *n* **1.** NAUT étai *m* (de grand mât) **2.** *fig* soutien *m*, point *m* d'appui ▪ **maize is the ~ of their diet** le maïs constitue la base de leur alimentation.

mainstream ['meɪnstri:m] ◇ *adj* : **~ French politics** le courant dominant de la politique française ▪ **~ America** la majorité des américains ▪ **their music is hardly what you'd call ~!** leur musique se démarque de ce qu'on entend habituellement!
◇ *n* courant *m* ▪ **the ~ of modern European literature** la tendance qui prédomine dans la littérature européenne moderne ▪ **to live outside the ~ of society** vivre en marge de la société.

main street *n* **1.** *liter* rue *f* principale **2.** *US fig* **Main Street** *les petits commerçants*.

maintain [meɪn'teɪn] ◇ *vt* **1.** [retain - institution, tradition] conserver, préserver ▪ [preserve - peace, standard] maintenir ▪ **to ~ law and order** maintenir l'ordre ▪ **to ~ a position** MIL & *fig* tenir une position ▪ [look after - roads, machinery] entretenir **2.** [uphold, keep - correspondence, friendship] entretenir ; [- silence, advantage, composure] garder ; [- reputation] défendre **3.** [financially - dependents] entretenir ▪ **they have two children at university to ~** ils ont deux enfants à charge à l'université **4.** [assert - opinion] soutenir, défendre ; [- innocence] affirmer ▪ **I still ~ she's innocent** je soutiens *OR* je maintiens toujours qu'elle est innocente.
◇ *vi US* **I'm ~ing!** [I'm fine] ça va!

maintainable [meɪn'teɪnəbl] *adj* [attitude, opinion, position] soutenable, défendable.

maintenance ['meɪntənəns] ◇ *n* **1.** [of roads, building] entretien *m* ▪ [of machinery, computer] maintenance *f* **2.** [financial support] entretien *m* **3.** LAW [alimony] pension *f* alimentaire **4.** [of order] maintien *m* ▪ [of regulations] application *f* ▪ [of situation] maintien *m*.
◇ *comp* [costs, crew] d'entretien ▪ **~ man** ouvrier *m* chargé de l'entretien *OR* de la maintenance.

maintenance allowance *n* [to student] bourse *f* d'études ▪ [to businessman] indemnité *f* pour frais de déplacement.

maintenance-free *adj* sans entretien, sans maintenance.

maintenance grant = **maintenance allowance**.

maintenance order *n* obligation *f* alimentaire.

Mainz [maɪnts] *pr n* Mayence.

maisonette [,meɪzə'net] *n UK* [small house] maisonnette *f* ▪ [flat] duplex *m*.

maître d' [,metrə'di:] *n* maître *m* d'hôtel.

maître d'hôtel [,metrədəʊ'tel] *n* maître *m* d'hôtel.

maize [meɪz] *n* maïs *m*.

Maj. *(written abbrev of* **Major***)* ≃ Cdt.

majestic [mə'dʒestɪk] *adj* majestueux.

majesty ['mædʒəstɪ] *(pl* **majesties***)* *n* majesté *f* ▪ **His Majesty the King** Sa Majesté le Roi ▪ **Her Majesty the Queen** Sa Majesté la Reine.

major ['meɪdʒəʳ] ◇ *adj* **1.** [main] : **the ~ part of our research** l'essentiel de nos recherches ▪ **the ~ portion of my time is devoted to politics** la majeure partie *OR* la plus grande partie de mon temps est consacrée à la politique ▶ **~ road** route *f* principale *OR* à grande circulation ▪ ≃ nationale *f*
2. [significant - decision, change, factor, event] majeur ▪ **don't worry, it's not a ~ problem** ne t'inquiète pas, ce n'est pas très grave ▪ **of ~ importance** d'une grande importance, d'une importance capitale ▪ **a ~ role** [in play, film] un grand rôle ; [in negotiations, reform] un rôle capital *OR* essentiel
3. [serious - obstacle, difficulty] majeur ▪ **she underwent ~ surgery** elle a subi une grosse opération

4. MUS majeur ▪ **a sonata in E ~** une sonate en mi majeur ➲ **in a ~ key** en (mode) majeur
5. *UK* SCH [elder] : **Smith ~** Smith aîné
6. CARDS majeur ▪ **~ suit** majeure *f.*
◇ *n* **1.** MIL [in air force] commandant *m*, -e *f* ▪ [in infantry] chef *m* de bataillon ▪ [in cavalry] chef *m* d'escadron
2. *fml* [person over 18] personne *f* majeure
3. *US* UNIV [subject] matière *f* principale ▪ **Tina is a physics ~** Tina fait des études de physique
4. MUS (mode *m*) majeur *m*
5. *US* [big company] : **the oil ~s** les grandes compagnies pétrolières ▪ **the Majors** [film companies] *les cinq compagnies de production les plus importantes à Hollywood.*
◇ *vi US* UNIV [specialize] se spécialiser ▪ [be a student] : **she ~ed in sociology** elle a fait des études de sociologie.

Majorca [mə'dʒɔ:kə, mə'jɔ:kə] *pr n* Majorque ▪ **in ~** à Majorque.

Majorcan [mə'dʒɔ:kn, mə'jɔ:kn] ◇ *n* Majorquin *m*, - e *f.*
◇ *adj* majorquin.

majordomo [,meɪdʒə'dəʊməʊ] (*pl* **majordomos**) *n* majordome *m.*

majorette [,meɪdʒə'ret] *n* majorette *f.*

major general *n* général *m* de division.

majority [mə'dʒɒrətɪ] (*pl* **majorities**) ◇ *n* **1.** [of a group] majorité *f*, plupart *f* ▪ **the ~ of people** la plupart des gens ▪ **the ~ was** *OR* **were in favour** la majorité *OR* la plupart d'entre eux était pour ▪ **the vast ~ of the tourists were Japanese** les touristes, dans leur très grande majorité, étaient des Japonais ▮ [in voting, opinions] majorité *f* ▪ **to be in a ~** être majoritaire ▪ **the proposition had an overwhelming ~** la proposition a recueilli une écrasante majorité ▪ **she was elected by a ~ of 6** elle a été élue avec une majorité de 6 voix *OR* par 6 voix de majorité **2.** LAW [voting age] majorité *f.*
◇ *comp* majoritaire ▪ **a ~ government/verdict** un gouvernement/verdict majoritaire.

major league *US* ◇ *n* [gen] première division *f* ▪ **~ team** grande équipe *(sportive)* ▮ [in base-ball] *une des deux principales divisions de base-ball professionnel aux États-Unis.*
◇ *adj* [significant] de premier rang ▪ [as intensifier] : **he's a major-league jerk** c'est un imbécile de première.

make [meɪk] (*pret & pp* **made** [meɪd]) ◇ *vt*

A.

1. [construct, create, manufacture] faire, fabriquer ▪ **to ~ one's own clothes** faire ses vêtements soi-même ▪ **to ~ a meal** préparer un repas ▪ **'made in Japan'** 'fabriqué au Japon' ▪ **a vase made of** *OR* **from clay** un vase en *OR* de terre cuite ▪ **what's it made of?** en quoi est-ce que c'est fait? ▪ **what do you ~ aluminium from?** à partir de quoi est-ce qu'on fabrique l'aluminium? ➲ **they're made for each other** ils sont faits l'un pour l'autre ▪ **we're not made of money!** on n'a pas d'argent à jeter par les fenêtres! ▪ **I'll show them what I'm made of!** je leur montrerai de quel bois je me chauffe *OR* qui je suis!
2. [cause to appear or happen - hole, tear, mess, mistake, noise] faire ▪ **it made a dent in the bumper** ça a cabossé le pare-chocs ▪ **he's always making trouble** il faut toujours qu'il fasse des histoires
3. [establish - law, rule] établir, faire ▪ **I don't ~ the rules** ce n'est pas moi qui fais les règlements
4. [form - circle, line] former
5. CIN & TV [direct] faire ▪ [act in] faire
6. *(delexical use)* [indicating action performed] : **to ~ an offer** faire une offre ▪ **to ~ a request** faire une demande ▪ **to ~ a note of sthg** prendre note de qqch ▪ **to ~ a phone call** passer un coup de fil ▪ **the police are making inquiries** la police procède à une enquête
7. [tidy] : **to ~ one's bed** faire son lit

B.

1. *(with adj or pp complement)* [cause to be] rendre ▪ **to ~ sb happy/mad** rendre qqn heureux/fou ▪ **this will ~ things easier** cela facilitera les choses ▪ **it ~s her tired** ça la fatigue ▪ **what ~s the sky blue?** qu'est-ce qui fait que le ciel est bleu? ▪ **I'd like to ~ it clear that it wasn't my fault** je voudrais qu'on comprenne bien que je n'y suis pour rien ▪ **it was hard to ~ myself heard/understood** j'ai eu du mal à me faire entendre/comprendre
2. *(with noun complement or with 'into')* [change into] faire ▪ **the film made her (into) a star** le film a fait d'elle une vedette ▪ **he was made president for life** il a été nommé président à vie ▪ **they made Bonn the capital** ils ont choisi Bonn pour capitale ▪ **he ~s a joke of everything** il tourne tout en plaisanterie ▪ **the building has been made into offices** l'immeuble a été réaménagé *OR* converti en bureaux ▪ **I can't come in the morning, shall we ~ it 2 pm?** je ne peux pas venir le matin, est-ce que 14 h vous conviendrait?
3. *(with verb complement)* [cause] faire ▪ **what ~s you think they're wrong?** qu'est-ce qui te fait penser qu'ils ont tort? ▪ **you ~ it look easy** à vous voir, on croirait que c'est facile ▪ **the hat/photo ~s you look ridiculous** tu as l'air ridicule avec ce chapeau/sur cette photo
4. [force, oblige] : **to ~ sb do sthg** faire faire qqch à qqn ; [stronger] forcer *OR* obliger *OR* contraindre qqn à faire qqch ▪ **they made me wait, I was made to wait** ils m'ont fait attendre ▪ **she made herself keep running** elle s'est forcée à continuer à courir

C.

1. [attain, achieve - goal] atteindre ▪ **their first record made the top ten** leur premier disque est rentré au top ten ▪ **you won't ~ the team if you don't train** tu n'entreras jamais dans l'équipe si tu ne t'entraînes pas ▪ **the story made the front page** l'histoire a fait la une des journaux
2. [arrive at, get to - place] atteindre ▪ **we should ~ Houston/port by evening** nous devrions arriver à Houston/atteindre le port d'ici ce soir ▪ **did you ~ your train?** as-tu réussi à avoir ton train?
3. [be available for] : **I won't be able to ~ lunch** je ne pourrai pas déjeuner avec toi/elle/vous *etc* ▪ **can you ~ Friday afternoon?** vendredi après-midi, ça vous convient?
4. [earn, win] faire, gagner ▪ **how much do you ~ a month?** combien gagnes-tu par mois? ▪ **what do they ~ out of the deal?** qu'est-ce qu'ils gagnent dans l'affaire?, qu'est-ce que l'affaire leur rapporte?

D.

1. [amount to, add up to] faire ▪ **17 and 19 ~** *OR* **~s 36** 17 plus 19 font *OR* égalent 36 ▪ **how old does that ~ him?** quel âge ça lui fait?
2. [reckon to be] : **I ~ the answer 257** d'après moi, ça fait 257 ▪ **what time do you ~ it?** quelle heure as-tu?
3. *(with noun complement)* [fulfil specified role, function etc] faire ▪ **he'll ~ somebody a good husband** ce sera un excellent mari ▪ **they ~ a handsome couple** ils forment un beau couple ▪ **her reminiscences ~ interesting reading** ses souvenirs sont intéressants à lire
4. [score] marquer

E.

1. [make successful] faire le succès de ▪ **if this deal comes off we're made!** si ça marche, on touche le gros lot! ➲ **you've got it made!** tu n'as plus de souci à te faire! ▪ **what happens today will ~ or break us** notre avenir dépend entièrement de ce qui va se passer aujourd'hui
2. △ [seduce] draguer ▪ [have sex with] se faire△
3. *US* [in directions] : **~ a right/left** tournez à droite/à gauche
4. *phr* **to ~ it** [arrive] arriver ; [be successful] réussir ; [be able to attend] être là ▪ **I'll never ~ it for 10 o'clock** je ne pourrai jamais y être pour 10 h ▪ **I hope she ~s it through the winter** j'espère qu'elle passera l'hiver ▪ **I can't ~ it for supper tomorrow** je ne peux pas dîner avec eux/toi *etc* demain ➲ **to ~ it with sb**△ se faire qqn△.
◇ *vi* [act] : **to ~ (as if) to** faire mine de ▪ **she made (as if) to stand up** elle fit mine de se lever ▪ **~ like you're asleep!** *inf* fais semblant de dormir! ➲ **to ~ believe** imaginer ▪ **to ~ do (with)** [manage] se débrouiller (avec) ; [be satisfied] se contenter (de) ▪ **it's broken but we'll just have to ~ do** c'est cassé mais il faudra faire avec *OR* nous débrouiller avec.
◇ *n* **1.** [brand] marque *f* **2.** *phr* **to be on the ~** *inf* [for power, profit] avoir les dents longues ; [looking for sexual partner] draguer.

◆ **make away with** = make off with.

◆ **make for** *vt insep* **1.** [head towards] se diriger vers ▪ [hastily] se précipiter vers ▪ **he made for his gun** il fit un geste pour saisir son pistolet **2.** [contribute to] mener à ▪ **the treaty should**

~ **for a more lasting peace** le traité devrait mener *OR* aboutir à une paix plus durable ▪ **this typeface ~s for easier reading** cette police permet une lecture plus facile ▪ **a good diet ~s for healthier babies** un bon régime alimentaire donne des bébés en meilleure santé.

◆ **make of** <> *vt sep* **1.** [understand] comprendre à ▪ **can you ~ anything of these instructions?** est-ce que tu comprends quelque chose à ce mode d'emploi? **2.** [give importance to] : **I think you're making too much of a very minor problem** je pense que tu exagères l'importance de ce petit problème ▪ **do you want to ~ something of it, then?** *inf* [threat] tu cherches des histoires ou quoi?

<> *vt insep* [think of] penser de ▪ **what do you ~ of the Smiths?** qu'est-ce que tu penses des Smith?

◆ **make off** *vi insep* partir.

◆ **make off with** *vt insep* partir avec.

◆ **make out** <> *vt sep* **1.** [see] distinguer ▪ [hear] entendre, comprendre ▪ [read] déchiffrer **2.** [understand] comprendre ▪ **I can't ~ her out at all** je ne la comprends pas du tout **3.** [claim] prétendre ▪ **she made out that she was busy** elle a fait semblant d'être occupée ▪ **don't ~ yourself out to be something you're not** ne prétends pas être ce que tu n'es pas **4.** [fill out - form, cheque] remplir ▪ **who shall I ~ the cheque out to?** je fais le chèque à quel ordre? **5.** [draw up - list] dresser, faire ; [- will, contract] faire, rédiger, établir ; [- receipt] faire.

<> *vi insep* **1.** *inf* [manage] se débrouiller ▪ **how did you ~ out at work today?** comment ça s'est passé au boulot aujourd'hui? **2.** △ [neck, pet] se peloter ▪ **to ~ out with sb** [have sex] s'envoyer qqn△.

◆ **make over** *vt sep* **1.** [transfer] transférer, céder **2.** *US* [convert - room, house] réaménager ▪ **the garage had been made over into a workshop** le garage a été transformé en atelier **3.** *US* [change the appearance of] transformer.

◆ **make up** <> *vi insep* **1.** [put on make-up] se maquiller **2.** [become reconciled] se réconcilier.

<> *vt sep* **1.** [put make-up on] maquiller ▪ **to ~ o.s. up** se maquiller ▪ **he was heavily made up** il était très maquillé *OR* fardé **2.** [prepare] faire, préparer ▪ **the chemist made up the prescription** le pharmacien a préparé l'ordonnance ▪ **the fire needs making up** il faut remettre du charbon/du bois sur le feu **3.** [invent] inventer **4.** *phr* **to ~ (it) up with sb** se réconcilier avec qqn.

<> *vt insep* **1.** [constitute] composer, constituer ▪ **the different ethnic groups that ~ up our organization** les différents groupes ethniques qui constituent notre organisation ▪ **the cabinet is made up of 11 ministers** le cabinet est composé de 11 ministres ▪ **it is made up of a mixture of different types of tobacco** c'est un mélange de plusieurs tabacs différents **2.** [compensate for - losses] compenser ▪ **to ~ up lost ground** regagner le terrain perdu ▪ **he's making up time** il rattrape son retard **3.** [complete] : **this cheque will help you ~ up the required sum** ce chèque vous aidera à atteindre le montant requis ▪ **we need two more players to ~ up the team** nous avons besoin de deux joueurs de plus pour que l'équipe soit au complet ▪ **I'll ~ up the difference** je mettrai la différence.

◆ **make up for** *vt insep* compenser ▪ **how can I ~ up for all the trouble I've caused you?** que puis-je faire pour me faire pardonner tous les ennuis que je vous ai causés? ▪ **she's making up for lost time now!** *liter & fig* elle est en train de rattraper le temps perdu!

◆ **make up to** <> *vt insep* : **to ~ up to sb** [try to win favour] essayer de se faire bien voir par qqn ; [make advances] faire du plat à qqn.

<> *vt sep phr* **I promise I'll ~ it up to you someday** tu peux être sûr que je te revaudrai ça (un jour).

◆ **make with** *vt insep inf* ~ **with the drinks!** à boire! ▪ ~ **with the music!** musique!

make-believe <> *n* : **it's only ~** ce n'est qu'illusion ▪ **a world of ~** un monde d'illusions.

<> *adj* imaginaire ▪ **they turned the bed into a ~ raft** ils imaginèrent que le lit était un radeau.

makeover ['meɪkəʊvəʳ] *n liter & fig* [transformation] transformation *f* ▪ **cosmetic ~** démonstration *f* de maquillage.

maker ['meɪkəʳ] *n* **1.** [craftsman] fabricant *m*, - e *f* **2.** RELIG : **Maker** Créateur *m* ▪ **to go to meet one's Maker** *euph & hum* passer de vie à trépas.

-maker *in cpds* **1.** [manufacturer] fabricant *m* ▪ **dress~** couturière *f* **2.** [machine] : **electric coffee~** cafetière *f* électrique ▪ **ice cream~** sorbetière *f*.

makeshift ['meɪkʃɪft] <> *adj* de fortune ▪ **a ~ shelter** un abri de fortune ▪ **the accommodation was very ~** le logement était plutôt improvisé.

<> *n* expédient *m*.

make-up *n* **1.** [cosmetics] maquillage *m*, fard *m* ▪ **she had a lot of ~ on** elle était très maquillée ▪ **eye ~** fard pour les yeux ▶ **~ artist** maquilleur *m*, - euse *f* ▪ **~ bag** trousse *f* de maquillage ▪ **~ remover** démaquillant *m* **2.** [constitution] constitution *f* **3.** [nature, character] nature *f*, caractère *m* **4.** TYPO mise *f* en pages **5.** *US* [test, exam] : **~ (test)** examen *m* de rattrapage.

makeweight ['meɪkweɪt] *n* [on scales] complément *m* de poids ▪ **I'm only here as a ~** *fig* je ne suis là que pour faire nombre.

making ['meɪkɪŋ] *n* **1.** [manufacture, creation] fabrication *f* ▪ **the situation is entirely of his own ~** il est entièrement responsable de la situation dans laquelle il se trouve ▪ **the incident was to be the ~ of his career as a politician** l'incident devait être à l'origine de sa carrière d'homme politique **2.** [preparation - of cake] confection *f*, préparation *f* ; [- of film] tournage *m*.

◆ **in the making** *adj phr* [idea] en gestation ▪ [plan] à l'étude ▪ [building] en construction ▪ **it's history in the ~** c'est une page d'histoire qui s'écrit sous nos yeux.

◆ **makings** *npl* [essential elements] ingrédients *mpl* ▪ **his war stories have the ~s of a good film** il y a de quoi faire un bon film avec ses récits de guerre ▮ [potential] : **that child has the ~s of a genius** cet enfant présente toutes les caractéristiques du génie.

malachite ['mæləkaɪt] *n* malachite *f*.

maladapted [,mælə'dæptɪd] *adj* inadapté.

maladjusted [,mælə'dʒʌstɪd] *adj* **1.** PSYCHOL [child] inadapté **2.** [engine, TV picture] mal réglé ▪ [mechanism] mal ajusté.

maladjustment [,mælə'dʒʌstmənt] *n* **1.** [psychological or social] inadaptation *f* ▪ [emotional] déséquilibre *m* **2.** [of engine, TV] mauvais réglage *m* ▪ [of mechanism] mauvais réglage *m*, mauvais ajustement *m*.

maladroit [,mælə'drɔɪt] *adj* maladroit, gauche, malhabile.

malady ['mælədɪ] (*pl* **maladies**) *n lit* maladie *f*, affection *f*, mal *m*.

Malagasy [,mælə'gæsɪ] <> *n* [person] Malgache *mf*.

<> *adj* malgache.

malaise [mæ'leɪz] *n* malaise *m*.

malapropism ['mæləprɒpɪzm] *n* lapsus *m*.

malaria [mə'leərɪə] *n* malaria *f*, paludisme *m*.

malarkey [mə'lɑ:kɪ] *n (U)* bêtises *fpl*, sottises *fpl*.

Malawi [mə'lɑ:wɪ] *pr n* Malawi *m* ▪ **in ~** au Malawi.

Malawian [mə'lɑ:wɪən] <> *n* Malawite *mf*.

<> *adj* malawite.

Malay [mə'leɪ] <> *n* [person] Malais *m*, - e *f*.

<> *adj* malais.

Malaya [mə'leɪə] *pr n* Malaisie *f*, Malaysia *f* Occidentale ▪ **in ~** en Malaisie.

Malayan [mə'leɪən] <> *n* Malais *m*, - e *f*.

<> *adj* malais.

Malay Peninsula *pr n* : **the ~** (la presqu'île de) Malacca, la presqu'île Malaise.

Malaysia [mə'leɪzɪə] *pr n* Malaysia *f* ▪ **in ~** en Malaysia.

Malaysian [mə'leɪzɪən] <> *n* Malais *m*, - e *f*.

<> *adj* malais.

malcontent ['mælkən,tent] *n fml* mécontent *m*, - e *f*.

Maldives ['mɔ:ldaɪvz] *pr npl* : **the ~** les (îles *fpl*) Maldives *fpl* ■ **in the ~** aux Maldives.

Maldivian [mɔ:l'dɪvɪən] ◇ *n habitant ou natif des Maldives.*
◇ *adj* des Maldives.

male [meɪl] ◇ *adj* **1.** ZOOL & BOT mâle ■ **~ attitudes** l'attitude des hommes ■ **when I phoned her, a ~ voice answered** quand je l'ai appelée, c'est une voix d'homme qui a répondu ■ **the ~ sex** le sexe masculin ▶ **~ voice choir** chœur *m* d'hommes **2.** [virile] mâle, viril **3.** TECH [plug] mâle.
◇ *n* ZOOL & BOT mâle *m* ■ [gen - man] homme *m*.

male chauvinism *n* phallocratie *f*.

male chauvinist *n* phallocrate *m* ■ **~ pig!** sale phallocrate!

malefactor ['mælɪfæktə^r] *n fml* malfaiteur *m*.

maleficent [mə'lefɪsnt] *adj lit* maléfique.

malevolence [mə'levələns] *n* malveillance *f*.

malevolent [mə'levələnt] *adj* malveillant.

malevolently [mə'levələntlɪ] *adv* avec malveillance.

malfeasance [mæl'fi:zns] *n* LAW méfait *m*, malversation *f*.

malformation [,mælfɔ:'meɪʃn] *n* malformation *f*.

malformed [mæl'fɔ:md] *adj* difforme.

malfunction [mæl'fʌŋkʃn] ◇ *n* [fault] fonctionnement *m* défectueux ■ [breakdown] panne *f*, défaillance *f*.
◇ *vi* [go wrong] mal fonctionner ■ [break down] tomber en panne.

malfunction routine *n* COMPUT programme *m* de diagnostic.

Mali ['mɑ:lɪ] *pr n* Mali *m* ■ **in ~** au Mali.

Malian ['mɑ:lɪən] ◇ *n* Malien *m*, - enne *f*.
◇ *adj* malien.

malice ['mælɪs] *n* méchanceté *f*, malveillance *f* ■ **I don't bear any ~ towards them, I don't bear them any ~** je ne leur en veux pas, je ne leur veux aucun mal ■ **out of** *OR* **through ~** par méchanceté, par malveillance ▶ **with ~ aforethought** LAW avec préméditation.

malicious [mə'lɪʃəs] *adj* **1.** [gen] méchant, malveillant ■ **~ gossip** médisances *fpl* **2.** LAW criminel ■ **~ damage** *UK*, **~ mischief** *US* ≃ dommage *m* causé avec intention de nuire.

maliciously [mə'lɪʃəslɪ] *adv* **1.** [gen] méchamment, avec malveillance **2.** LAW avec préméditation, avec intention de nuire.

malign [mə'laɪn] ◇ *vt* [slander] calomnier ■ [criticize] critiquer, dire du mal de ■ **the much-~ed government** le gouvernement, dont on dit beaucoup de mal *OR* que l'on a souvent critiqué.
◇ *adj* **1.** [evil] pernicieux, nocif **2.** MED malin, - igne *f*.

malignancy [mə'lɪgnənsɪ] (*pl* **malignancies**) *n* **1.** [ill will] malignité *f*, malveillance *f*, méchanceté *f* **2.** MED malignité *f*.

malignant [mə'lɪgnənt] *adj* **1.** [person, behaviour, intentions] malveillant, malfaisant, méchant **2.** MED malin, - igne *f* ■ **~ tumour** tumeur *f* maligne.

malignity [mə'lɪgnətɪ] = **malignancy**.

malinger [mə'lɪŋgə^r] *vi* simuler la maladie, faire semblant d'être malade.

malingerer [mə'lɪŋgərə^r] *n* faux malade *m*, personne *f* qui fait semblant d'être malade.

mall [mɔ:l] *n* **1.** [avenue] mail *m*, avenue *f* **2.** = **shopping mall**.
◆ **Mall** *pr n* : **the Mall** [in London] *large avenue reliant Buckingham Palace à Trafalgar Square* ; [in Washington] *jardin public sur lequel donnent les principaux musées de la ville.*

mallard ['mælɑ:d] *n* : **~ (duck)** colvert *m*.

malleable ['mælɪəbl] *adj* [substance] malléable ■ [person] influençable, malléable.

mallet ['mælɪt] *n* maillet *m*.

mallow ['mæləʊ] *n* BOT mauve *f*.

malnourished [,mæl'nʌrɪʃt] *adj* sous-alimenté.

malnutrition [,mælnju:'trɪʃn] *n* malnutrition *f*.

malodorous [mæl'əʊdərəs] *adj hum* malodorant, nauséabond.

malpractice [,mæl'præktɪs] *n (U)* [professional] faute *f* professionnelle ■ [financial] malversation *f*, malversations *fpl* ■ [political] fraude *f*.

malpractice suit *n US* LAW *procès pour faute ou négligence professionnelle.*

malt [mɔ:lt] ◇ *n* **1.** [substance] malt *m* **2.** = **malt whisky 3.** *US* [milk shake] milk-shake *m* au malt.
◇ *comp* [extract, sugar, vinegar] de malt.
◇ *vt* malter.

Malta ['mɔ:ltə] *pr n* Malte ■ **in ~** à Malte.

malted ['mɔ:ltɪd] *n* : **~ (milk)** lait *m* malté.

Maltese [,mɔ:l'ti:z] ◇ *n* **1.** [person] Maltais *m*, - e *f* **2.** LING maltais *m*.
◇ *adj* maltais ■ **the ~ Cross** la croix de Malte.

maltreat [,mæl'tri:t] *vt* maltraiter.

maltreatment [,mæl'tri:tmənt] *n (U)* mauvais traitement *m* *OR* traitements *mpl*, sévices *mpl*.

malt whisky *n* whisky *m* au malt.

malty ['mɔ:ltɪ] (*comp* **maltier**, *superl* **maltiest**) *adj* [in smell] qui sent le malt ■ [in taste] qui a un goût de malt.

mam [mæm] *n inf dial* maman *f*.

mama [1] [mə'mɑ:] *n UK dated* maman *f*.

mama [2] ['mɒmə] *n US* maman *f*.

mama's boy *n US inf* fils *m* à sa maman.

mamba ['mæmbə] *n* mamba *m*.

mambo ['mæmbəʊ] (*pl* **mambos**) *n* mambo *m*.

mamma ['mæmə] *n esp US* **1.** *inf* [mother] maman *f* **2.** △ [woman] môme△ *f*, nana *f*.

mammal ['mæml] *n* mammifère *m*.

mammary ['mæmərɪ] *adj* mammaire ■ **~ gland** glande *f* mammaire.

mammography [mæ'mɒgrəfɪ] *n* MED mammographie *f*.

Mammon ['mæmən] *pr n* Mammon *m*.

mammoth ['mæməθ] ◇ *n* mammouth *m*.
◇ *adj* immense, colossal, gigantesque ■ **a ~ task** un travail de Titan.

mammy ['mæmɪ] (*pl* **mammies**) *n inf* **1.** [mother] maman **2.** *pej & dated* [black nanny] *bonne d'enfants noire*.

man [mæn] ◇ *n* (*pl* **men** [men]) **1.** [adult male] homme *m* ■ **a young ~** un jeune homme ■ **an old ~** un vieillard ■ **he seems a nice ~** il a l'air gentil ■ **a blind ~** un aveugle ■ **he's lived here, ~ and boy, for forty years** c'est ici qu'il a grandi et vécu pendant quarante ans ▶ **he's a ~'s ~** il aime bien être avec ses copains ■ **he's a ~ of the world** c'est un homme d'expérience ■ **the ~ in the moon** le visage de la lune
2. [type] homme *m* ■ **he's not a betting/drinking ~** ce n'est pas un homme qui parie/boit ■ **he's not a ~ to make a mistake** il n'est pas homme à se tromper
3. [appropriate person] homme *m* ■ **I'm your ~** je suis votre homme ■ **he's not the ~ for that kind of work** il n'est pas fait pour ce genre de travail
4. [professional] : **a medical ~** un médecin ■ **a ~ of learning** un savant ■ **a ~ of letters** un homme de lettres
5. [with manly qualities] homme *m* ■ **he took the news like a ~** il a pris la nouvelle avec courage ■ **he's not ~ enough to own up** il n'aura pas le courage d'avouer ■ **a holiday will make a new**

~ of me des vacances me feront le plus grand bien ▪ **this will separate** *OR* **sort the men from the boys** c'est là qu'on verra les vrais hommes
6. [person, individual] homme *m*, individu *m* ▪ **what more can a ~ do?** qu'est-ce qu'on peut faire de plus? ▪ **any ~ would have reacted in the same way** n'importe qui aurait réagi de la même façon ▪ **all men are born equal** tous les hommes naissent égaux ➊ **to be one's own ~** être indépendant *OR* son propre maître ▪ **to the last ~** [without exception] sans exception ; [until defeat] jusqu'au dernier ▪ **it's every ~ for himself** c'est chacun pour soi ▪ **the ~ in the street** l'homme de la rue ▪ **one ~'s meat is another ~'s poison** *prov* le malheur des uns fait le bonheur des autres *prov*
7. [as husband, father] homme *m* ▪ **~ and wife** mari et femme ▪ **to live as ~ and wife** vivre maritalement *OR* en concubinage ▪ **he's a real family ~** c'est un vrai père de famille ▌ *hum* le pater familias ▪ **my old ~** *inf* [husband] mon homme ; [father] mon vieux
8. [boyfriend, lover] homme *m* ▪ **have you met her young ~?** [boyfriend] avez-vous rencontré son petit ami? ; [fiancé] avez-vous rencontré son fiancé?
9. [inhabitant, native] : **I'm a Dublin ~** je suis de Dublin ▪ **he's a local ~** c'est un homme du pays
10. [student] : **he's a Harvard ~** [at present] il fait ses études à Harvard ; [in the past] il a fait ses études à Harvard
11. [servant] valet *m*, domestique *m*
12. [employee - in industry, on farm] ouvrier *m* ; [- in business, shop] employé *m* ▪ **a TV repair ~** un réparateur télé ▪ **we'll send a ~ round to look at it** nous vous envoyons quelqu'un pour voir ▪ **our ~ in Paris** [representative] notre représentant à Paris ; [journalist] notre correspondant à Paris ; [diplomat] notre envoyé diplomatique à Paris
13. [in armed forces - soldier] soldat *m*, homme *m* (de troupe) ; [- sailor] matelot *m*, homme *m* (d'équipage) ▪ **officers and men** [in army] officiers et hommes de troupe ; [in navy] officiers et matelots
14. [player] joueur *m*, équipier *m* ▪ **a 3-~ team** une équipe de 3 joueurs ▪ **twelfth ~** [in cricket] remplaçant *m*
15. [mankind] homme *m* ▪ **primitive/modern ~** l'homme primitif/moderne ▪ **one of the most deadly poisons known to ~** un des plus dangereux poisons connus de l'homme ➊ **~ proposes, God disposes** *prov* l'homme propose, Dieu dispose *prov* ▪ **~ cannot live by bread alone** *prov* l'homme ne vit pas que de pain
16. [as term of address] : **hey, ~, how are you doing?**△ salut, mon pote, comment tu vas?△ ▪ **my good ~** *dated* mon cher monsieur ▪ **good ~!** c'est bien!
17. [in chess] pièce *f* ▪ [in draughts] pion *m*.
◇ *vt* (*pret & pp* **manned**, *cont* **manning**) **1.** MIL [ship] armer, équiper ▪ [pumps] armer ▪ [cannon] servir ▪ **the tanker was manned by Greek seamen** le pétrolier avait un équipage grec ▪ **~ the lifeboats!** mettez les canots à la mer! ▪ **manned spaceflight** vol *m* spatial habité ▪ **the fort was manned by 20 soldiers** le fort était tenu par une garnison de 20 soldats ▪ **can you ~ the fort while I'm at lunch?** *hum* pouvez-vous prendre la relève *OR* me remplacer pendant que je vais déjeuner?
2. [staff - machine] faire tourner, s'occuper de ; [- switchboard] assurer le service *OR* la permanence de ▪ **who's manning the telephone?** qui assure la permanence téléphonique? ▪ **the office is manned by a skeleton staff** le bureau tourne à effectif réduit.
◇ *interj US inf* **~, was it big!** bon sang, qu'est-ce que c'était grand!
◆ **as one man** *adv phr* comme un seul homme.
◆ **to a man** *adv phr* sans exception ▪ **they agreed to a ~** ils ont accepté à l'unanimité.

man-about-town (*pl* **men-about-town**) *n UK* homme *m* du monde, mondain *m*.

manacle ['mænəkl] *vt* [shackle] enchaîner ▪ [handcuff] mettre *OR* passer les menottes à.
◆ **manacles** *npl* [shackles] fers *mpl*, chaînes *fpl* ▪ [handcuffs] menottes *fpl*.

manage ['mænɪdʒ] ◇ *vt* **1.** [business, hotel, shop] gérer, diriger ▪ [property, estate] gérer ▪ [team] être le manager de, diriger ▪ [finances, resources] s'occuper de ▪ **I'm very bad at managing money** je suis incapable de gérer un budget ▌ [crisis, illness] gérer
2. [accomplish] réussir ▪ **you'll ~ it** ça ira ▪ **she ~d a smile** elle trouva la force de sourire ▪ **to ~ to do sthg** réussir *OR* parvenir *OR* arriver à faire qqch ▪ **he ~d to keep a straight face** il est parvenu à garder son sérieux ▪ **he always ~s to arrive at meal times** il se débrouille toujours pour arriver *OR* il trouve toujours le moyen d'arriver à l'heure des repas
3. [handle - person, animal] savoir s'y prendre avec ▪ **she's a difficult child to ~** c'est une enfant difficile, c'est une enfant dont on ne fait pas ce qu'on veut ▪ [manipulate - machine, tool] manier, se servir de
4. [be available for] : **can you ~ 9 o'clock/next Saturday?** pouvez-vous venir à 9 h/samedi prochain? ▪ **can you ~ lunch tomorrow?** pouvez-vous déjeuner avec moi demain?
5. [cope with] : **I can't ~ all this extra work** je ne peux pas faire face à ce surcroît de travail ▪ **can you ~ that rucksack?** pouvez-vous porter ce sac à dos? ▪ **he can't ~ the stairs any more** il n'arrive plus à monter l'escalier ▌ [eat or drink] : **I think I could ~ another slice** j'en reprendrais volontiers une tranche ▪ **I couldn't ~ another thing** je ne peux plus rien avaler ▌ [financially] : **can you ~ £10?** pouvez-vous aller jusqu'à 10 livres?
◇ *vi* [cope] se débrouiller, y arriver ▪ **can you ~?** ça ira? ▪ **give me a fork, I can't ~ with chopsticks** donne-moi une fourchette, je ne m'en sors pas avec des baguettes ▪ **we had to ~ without heating** nous avons dû nous passer de chauffage ▌ [financially] se débrouiller, s'en sortir.

manageable ['mænɪdʒəbl] *adj* [size, amount] raisonnable ▪ [tool, car, boat] maniable ▪ [hair] facile à coiffer.

management ['mænɪdʒmənt] *n* **1.** [control - of firm, finances, property] gestion *f*, direction *f* ▪ **under Gordon's ~ sales have increased significantly** depuis que c'est Gordon qui s'en occupe, les ventes ont considérablement augmenté ▪ **who looks after the ~ of the farm?** qui s'occupe de l'exploitation de la ferme? ▪ [handling] : **she was praised for her ~ of the situation** on a applaudi la façon dont elle s'est comportée dans cette situation ▌ [of crisis, illness etc] gestion *f* ▪ **man ~** *UK* gestion des ressources humaines **2.** [of shop, hotel etc] direction *f* ▪ **'the ~ cannot accept responsibility for any loss or damage'** 'la direction décline toute responsabilité en cas de perte ou de dommage' ▪ **'under new ~'** 'changement de direction *OR* de propriétaire' ▌ INDUST patronat *m*.

management buyout *n UK* rachat *m* d'une entreprise par les salariés.

management consultancy *n* [activity] conseil *m* en gestion (d'entreprise) ▪ [firm] cabinet *m* (de) conseil.

management consultant *n* conseiller *m*, - ère *f* en *OR* de gestion (d'entreprise).

management studies *n (U)* études *fpl* de gestion.

manager ['mænɪdʒəʳ] *n* **1.** [of firm, bank] directeur *m*, - trice *f* ▪ [of shop] directeur *m*, - trice *f*, gérant *m* ▪ [of restaurant] gérant *m*, - e *f* ▪ [of pop star, football team] manager *m* ▪ FIN directeur *m*, - trice *f* ▪ **fund ~** directeur financier ▪ **he's been made ~** il est passé cadre **2.** [organizer] : **she's a good home ~** elle sait tenir une maison.

manageress [ˌmænɪdʒə'res] *n* [of shop] directrice *f*, gérante *f* ▪ [of restaurant] gérante *f* ▪ [of bank] directrice *f*.

managerial [ˌmænɪ'dʒɪərɪəl] *adj* gestionnaire ▪ **~ staff** cadres *mpl*, encadrement *m* ▪ **~ skills** qualités *fpl* de gestionnaire.

managing director ['mænɪdʒɪŋ-] *n* directeur *m* général, directrice *f* générale, P-DG *mf*.

managing editor *n* rédacteur *m*, - trice *f* en chef.

manatee [ˌmænə'tiː] *n* lamantin *m*.

Manchurian [mæn'tʃʊərɪən] ◇ *n* [person] Mandchou *m*, - e *f*.
◇ *adj* mandchou.

Mancunian [mæŋ'kju:njən] ◇ *n* [inhabitant] habitant *m*, - e *f* de Manchester ▪ [native] natif *m*, - ive *f* de Manchester.
◇ *adj* de Manchester.

mandarin ['mændərɪn] *n* **1.** HIST & *fig* mandarin *m* **2.** BOT [tree] mandarinier *m* **3.** [fruit] : ~ **(orange)** mandarine *f*.
◆ **Mandarin** *n* LING : **Mandarin (Chinese)** mandarin *m*.

mandate ◇ *n* ['mændeɪt] **1.** POL mandat *m* ▪ **the government has no ~ to introduce the new tax** le gouvernement n'a pas été mandaté pour mettre en place ce nouvel impôt **2.** [country] (territoire *m* sous) mandat *m* **3.** [task] tâche *f*, mission *f*.
◇ *vt* [,mæn'deɪt] **1.** [give authority] mandater ▪ **to ~ sb to do sthg** donner mandat à qqn de faire qqch **2.** [country] mettre sous mandat, administrer par mandat.

mandatory ['mændətrɪ] (*pl* **mandatories**) ◇ *adj* **1.** [obligatory] obligatoire **2.** [of a mandate] découlant d'un mandat ▪ **~ powers** pouvoirs *mpl* donnés par mandat.
◇ *n* mandataire *mf*.

man-day *n UK* jour-homme *m* ▪ **30 ~s** 30 journées *fpl* de travail.

mandible ['mændɪbl] *n* mandibule *f*.

mandolin ['mændəlɪn] *n* mandoline *f*.

mandrake ['mændreɪk] *n* mandragore *f*.

mandrill ['mændrɪl] *n* : ~ **(ape)** mandrill *m*.

mane [meɪn] *n* [of horse, lion] crinière *f* ▪ **a ~ of golden hair** une crinière blonde.

man-eater *n* [animal] anthropophage *m* ▪ [cannibal] cannibale *m*, anthropophage *m* ▪ *hum* [woman] dévoreuse *f* d'hommes, mante *f* religieuse.

man-eating *adj* [animal] mangeur d'hommes, anthropophage ▪ [people] cannibale, anthropophage.

maneuver *etc US* = **manoeuvre**.

man-for-man *adj UK* SPORT : ~ **marking** marquage *m* individuel.

man Friday *n* [servant] fidèle serviteur *m*.
◆ **Man Friday** *pr n* Vendredi.

manful ['mænfʊl] *adj* [courageous] vaillant, ardent.

manfully ['mænfʊlɪ] *adv* [courageously] vaillamment, courageusement.

manganese ['mæŋgəni:z] *n* manganèse *m*.

mange [meɪndʒ] *n* gale *f*.

mangel-wurzel ['mæŋgl,wɜ:zl] *n* betterave *f* fourragère.

manger ['meɪndʒər] *n* [trough] mangeoire *f* ▪ RELIG crèche *f*.

mangetout [,mɑ̃ʒ'tu:] *n* mange-tout *m*.

mangey ['meɪndʒɪ] = **mangy**.

mangle ['mæŋgl] ◇ *vt* **1.** [body] mutiler, déchiqueter ▪ [vehicle] rendre méconnaissable ▪ [quotation, text] estropier, mutiler ▪ **the ~d wreckage of the two cars** les carcasses déchiquetées des deux voitures **2.** [laundry, linen] essorer.
◇ *n* essoreuse *f* (à rouleaux).

mango ['mæŋgəʊ] (*pl* **mangos** *OR pl* **mangoes**) *n* **1.** [fruit] mangue *f* **2.** [tree] manguier *m*.

mangold(-wurzel) ['mæŋgəld(,wɜ:zl)] = **mangel-wurzel**.

mangrove ['mæŋgrəʊv] *n* manglier *m*, palétuvier *m* ▪ **~ swamp** mangrove *f*.

mangy ['meɪndʒɪ] (*comp* **mangier**, *superl* **mangiest**) *adj* **1.** [having mange - animal] galeux **2.** [shabby - coat, carpet] miteux, pelé.

manhandle ['mæn,hændl] *vt* **1.** [treat roughly] maltraiter, malmener **2.** [move] porter *OR* transporter (à bras d'homme).

Manhattan [mæn'hætn] ◇ *pr n* GEOG Manhattan.
◇ *n* [cocktail] manhattan *m*.

manhole ['mænhəʊl] *n* regard *m* ▪ [into sewer] bouche *f* d'égout ▪ **~ cover** plaque *f* d'égout.

manhood ['mænhʊd] *n* **1.** [age] âge *m* d'homme **2.** [virility] virilité *f* **3.** [men collectively] hommes *mpl*, population *f* masculine.

man-hour *n UK* heure-homme *f* ▪ **300 ~s** 300 heures *fpl* de travail.

manhunt ['mænhʌnt] *n* chasse *f* à l'homme.

mania ['meɪnjə] *n* **1.** PSYCHOL manie *f* ▪ [obsession] obsession *f* **2.** [zeal] manie *f pej*, passion *f* ▪ **he has a ~ for collecting old photographs** il a la manie de collectionner les vieilles photos.

maniac ['meɪnɪæk] ◇ *n* **1.** [dangerous person] fou *m*, folle *f* ▪ [sexual] obsédé *m*, - e *f* ▪ **to drive like a ~** conduire comme un fou **2.** [fan] fou *m*, folle *f* ▪ **he's a football ~** c'est un fan *OR* un mordu de football **3.** PSYCHOL maniaque *mf*.
◇ *adj* **1.** [gen] fou *(before vowel or silent 'h'* **fol***)*, folle *f* **2.** PSYCHOL maniaque.

maniacal [mə'naɪəkl] *adj* **1.** [crazy] fou *(before vowel or silent 'h'* **fol***)*, folle *f* ▪ **~ laughter** rire *m* hystérique **2.** PSYCHOL maniaque.

manic ['mænɪk] ◇ *adj* **1.** [crazy] fou *(before vowel or silent 'h'* **fol***)*, folle *f* **2.** PSYCHOL maniaque.
◇ *n* maniaque *mf*.

manic depression *n* psychose *f* maniaco-dépressive.

manic-depressive ◇ *adj* maniaco-dépressif.
◇ *n* maniaco-dépressif *m*, - ive *f*.

manicure ['mænɪ,kjʊər] ◇ *n* soins *mpl* des mains ▪ **to give sb a ~** faire les mains de qqn, manucurer qqn.
◇ *comp* [case, scissors] de manucure, à ongles.
◇ *vt* faire les mains à, manucurer ▪ **she was manicuring her nails** elle était en train de se faire les ongles ▪ **a ~d lawn** une pelouse impeccable.

manicurist ['mænɪ,kjʊərɪst] *n* manucure *mf*.

manifest ['mænɪfest] ◇ *adj fml* manifeste, évident.
◇ *vt* manifester ▪ **how did this mania ~ itself?** comment cette obsession s'est-elle manifestée?
◇ *vi* [ghost, spirit] se manifester.
◇ *n* [of ship, plane] manifeste *m*.

manifestation [,mænɪfes'teɪʃn] *n* manifestation *f*.

manifestly ['mænɪfestlɪ] *adv* manifestement, à l'évidence.

manifesto [,mænɪ'festəʊ] (*pl* **manifestos** *OR pl* **manifestoes**) *n* manifeste *m*.

manifold ['mænɪfəʊld] ◇ *adj fml* [numerous] multiple, nombreux ▪ [varied] varié, divers.
◇ *n* AUT : **inlet ~** tubulure *f* d'admission.

manikin ['mænɪkɪn] = **mannikin**.

manil(l)a [mə'nɪlə] ◇ *n* [hemp] chanvre *m* de Manille ▪ [paper] papier *m* kraft.
◇ *comp* : **~ envelope** enveloppe *f* en papier kraft.

manil(l)a paper *n* papier *m* kraft.

manioc ['mænɪɒk] *n* manioc *m*.

manipulate [mə'nɪpjʊleɪt] *vt* **1.** [equipment] manœuvrer, manipuler ▪ [tool] manier ▪ [vehicle] manœuvrer **2.** *pej* [person] manipuler, manœuvrer ▪ [facts, figures] manipuler ▪ **he skilfully ~d situations (to his own end)** il avait l'art de tirer profit de toutes les situations **3.** MED : **to ~ bones** pratiquer des manipulations.

manipulation [mə,nɪpjʊ'leɪʃn] *n* [of equipment] manœuvre *f*, manipulation *f* ▪ *pej* [of people, facts, situation] manipulation *f* ▪ MED manipulation *f*.

manipulative [mə'nɪpjʊlətɪv] *adj pej* **he can be very ~** il n'hésite pas à manipuler les gens.

manipulator [mə'nɪpjʊleɪtər] *n* manipulateur *m*, - trice *f*.

Manitoba [,mænɪ'təʊbə] *pr n* Manitoba *m*.

man jack *n UK inf* **every ~ of them** chacun d'eux sans exception.

mankind [mæn'kaɪnd] *n* **1.** [species] humanité *f*, espèce *f* humaine **2.** [men in general] hommes *mpl*.

manky△ ['mæŋkɪ] (*comp* **mankier**, *superl* **mankiest**) *adj UK* [worthless] nul ▪ [dirty] miteux, pourri.

manlike ['mænlaɪk] *adj* **1.** [virile] viril, masculin **2.** [woman] masculin.

manliness ['mænlɪnɪs] *n* virilité *f*.

manly ['mænlɪ] (*comp* **manlier**, *superl* **manliest**) *adj* viril, mâle.

man-made *adj* [fibre] synthétique ▪ [construction, lake] artificiel ▪ [landscape] modelé *OR* façonné par l'homme.

manna ['mænə] *n* manne *f* ▪ **~ from heaven** *fig* manne céleste.

manned [mænd] *adj* [ship, machine] ayant un équipage ▪ **~ spacecraft** vaisseau *m* spatial habité.

mannequin ['mænɪkɪn] *n* mannequin *m*.

manner ['mænər] *n* **1.** [way] manière *f*, façon *f* ▪ **in the same ~** de la même manière *OR* façon ▪ **it's just a ~ of speaking** c'est juste une façon de parler ▪ **she dealt with them in a very gentle ~** elle a été d'une grande douceur avec eux **2.** [attitude] attitude *f*, manière *f* ▪ [behaviour] comportement *m*, manière *f* de se conduire ▪ **to have a pleasant ~** avoir des manières agréables ▪ **I don't like his ~** je n'aime pas ses façons ▪ **he has a good telephone ~** il fait bonne impression au téléphone ▶ **in a ~ of speaking** pour ainsi dire, dans un certain sens ▪ **by all ~ of means** [of course] bien entendu ▪ **not by any ~ of means** en aucune manière, aucunement ▪ **to the ~ born** vraiment fait pour ça **3.** [style] manière *f* ▪ **in the ~ of Rembrandt** dans le style *OR* à la manière de Rembrandt **4.** [kind] sorte *f*, genre *m* ▪ **all ~ of rare books** toutes sortes de livres rares.

◆ **manners** *npl* **1.** [social etiquette] manières *fpl* ▪ **to have good table ~s** savoir se tenir à table ▪ **it's bad ~s to talk with your mouth full** c'est mal élevé *OR* ce n'est pas poli de parler la bouche pleine ▪ **she has no ~s** elle n'a aucune éducation, elle est mal élevée ▪ **where are your ~s?** [say thank you] qu'est-ce qu'on dit quand on est bien élevé? ; [behave properly] est-ce que c'est une façon de se tenir? ▶ **~s maketh the man** *prov* un homme n'est rien sans les manières **2.** *lit* [social customs] mœurs *fpl*, usages *mpl*.

mannered ['mænəd] *adj* maniéré, affecté, précieux.

mannerism ['mænərɪzm] *n* tic *m*, manie *f*.

◆ **Mannerism** *n* ART maniérisme *m*.

mannerly ['mænəlɪ] *adj* bien élevé, courtois, poli.

mannikin ['mænɪkɪn] *n* **1.** [dwarf] nain *m* **2.** = **mannequin**.

mannish ['mænɪʃ] *adj* [woman] masculin.

manoeuvrability *UK*, **maneuverability** *US* [məˌnuːvrə'bɪlətɪ] *n* manœuvrabilité *f*, maniabilité *f*.

manoeuvrable *UK*, **maneuvrable** *US* [mə'nuːvrəbl] *adj* manœuvrable, maniable.

manoeuvre *UK*, **maneuver** *US* [mə'nuːvər] ◇ *n* manœuvre *f* ▪ **to be on ~s** MIL être en manœuvres ▪ **it was only a ~ to get him to resign** ce n'était qu'une manœuvre pour l'amener à démissionner ▪ **room for ~** marge *f* de manœuvre.

◇ *vt* **1.** [physically] manœuvrer ▪ **they ~d the animal into the pen** ils ont fait entrer l'animal dans l'enclos **2.** [by influence, strategy] manœuvrer ▪ **she ~d her way to the top** elle a réussi à se hisser jusqu'au sommet.

◇ *vi* manœuvrer ▪ **to ~ for position** manœuvrer pour se placer avantageusement.

man-of-war [ˌmænə'wɔːr] (*pl* **men-of-war** [ˌmen-]) *n* bâtiment *m* de guerre.

manor ['mænər] *n* **1.** [house] : **~ (house)** manoir *m*, château *m* **2.** HIST seigneurie *f*, domaine *m* seigneurial ▪ **lord of the ~** châtelain *m* ▪ **lady of the ~** châtelaine *f*.

manorial [mə'nɔːrɪəl] *adj* seigneurial.

man-o'-war [ˌmænə'wɔːr] = **man-of-war**.

manpower ['mænˌpaʊər] *n (U)* [personnel] main-d'œuvre *f* ▪ MIL effectifs *mpl* ▪ **we don't have the necessary ~** nous ne disposons pas des effectifs nécessaires.

Manpower Services Commission *n agence britannique pour l'emploi, aujourd'hui remplacée par la Training Agency.*

manse [mæns] *n* presbytère *m*.

manservant ['mænsɜːvənt] *n* [gen] domestique *m* ▪ [valet] valet *m* (de chambre).

mansion ['mænʃn] *n* [in town] hôtel *m* particulier ▪ [in country] château *m*, manoir *m* ▪ **~ block** résidence *f* de standing.

man-size(d) *adj* [job, task] ardu, difficile ▪ [meal] copieux ▪ **~ tissues** grands mouchoirs *mpl* (en papier).

manslaughter ['mænˌslɔːtər] *n* homicide *m* involontaire.

mantel ['mæntl] *n* [shelf] (tablette *f* de) cheminée *f* ▪ [frame] manteau *m*.

mantelpiece ['mæntlpiːs] *n* **1.** [surround] (manteau *m* de) cheminée *f* **2.** [shelf] (tablette *f* de) cheminée *f*.

mantelshelf ['mæntlʃelf] (*pl* **mantelshelves** [-ʃelvz]) = **mantelpiece** *(sense 2)*.

mantilla [mæn'tɪlə] *n* mantille *f*.

mantis ['mæntɪs] *n* mante *f*, *see also* **praying**.

mantle ['mæntl] *n* **1.** [cloak] cape *f* ▪ *fig* manteau *m* ▪ **to take on** *OR* **to assume the ~ of** *fig* assumer le rôle de **2.** ZOOL & GEOL manteau *m* **3.** [of gas-lamp] manchon *m* **4.** = **mantel**.

man-to-man ◇ *adj* **1.** [discussion] entre hommes, d'homme à homme **2.** SPORT = **man-for-man**.

◇ *adv* entre hommes, d'homme à homme.

mantra ['mæntrə] *n* mantra *m inv*.

mantrap ['mæntræp] *n* piège *m* à hommes.

manual ['mænjʊəl] ◇ *adj* manuel ▪ **~ worker** travailleur *m* manuel ▪ **~ labour** travail *m* manuel.

◇ *n* **1.** [handbook] manuel *m* **2.** [of organ] clavier *m*.

manually ['mænjʊəlɪ] *adv* manuellement, à la main.

manufacture [ˌmænjʊ'fæktʃər] ◇ *n* **1.** [making] fabrication *f* ▪ [of clothes] confection *f* **2.** TECH [product] produit *m* manufacturé.

◇ *vt* **1.** [produce] fabriquer, produire ▪ [clothes] confectionner ▪ **~d goods** produits *mpl* manufacturés **2.** [invent - news, story] inventer ; [- evidence] fabriquer.

manufacturer [ˌmænjʊ'fæktʃərər] *n* fabricant *m*, - e *f*.

manufacturing [ˌmænjʊ'fæktʃərɪŋ] ◇ *adj* [city, area] industriel ▪ **~ industry** les industries *fpl* manufacturières *OR* de transformation.

◇ *n* fabrication *f*.

manure [mə'njʊər] ◇ *n* [farmyard] fumier *m* ▪ [fertilizer] engrais *m* ▪ **liquid ~** purin *m*, lisier *m*.

◇ *vt* [with dung] fumer ▪ [with fertilizer] répandre de l'engrais sur.

manuscript ['mænjʊskrɪpt] ◇ *n* manuscrit *m* ▪ **I read the book in ~** j'ai lu le manuscrit du livre ▮ [for music] : **~ (paper)** papier *m* à musique.

◇ *adj* manuscrit, (écrit) à la main.

Manx [mæŋks] ◇ *npl* : **the ~** les Manxois *mpl*.

◇ *n* LING manx *m*.

◇ *adj* manxois.

Manx cat *n* chat *m* (sans queue) de l'île de Man.

Manxman ['mæŋksmən] (*pl* **Manxmen** [-mən]) *n* Manxois *m*.

Manxwoman ['mæŋksˌwʊmən] (*pl* **Manxwomen** [-ˌwɪmɪn]) *n* Manxoise *f*.

many ['menɪ] (*comp* **more** [mɔː], *superl* **most** [məʊst]) ◇ *det & pron* beaucoup de, de nombreux ▪ **~ people** beaucoup de *OR* bien des gens ▪ **she had cards from all her ~ admirers** elle a reçu des cartes de ses nombreux admirateurs ▪ **~ of them** beaucoup d'entre eux ▪ **~'s the time** bien des fois ▪ **they admitted as ~ (people) as they could** ils ont laissé entrer autant de gens que possible ▪ **as ~ again** encore autant ▪ **twice/three times as ~** deux/trois fois plus ▪ **we visited six cities in as ~ days** nous avons visité six villes en autant de jours ▪ **as ~ as 8,000 students enrolled** jusqu'à *OR* près de 8 000 étudiants se sont inscrits ▪ **how ~?** combien? ▪ **how ~ students came?** combien d'étudiants sont venus? ▪ **so ~ people** tant de gens ▪ **we can only fit in so ~** nous n'avons de place que pour un certain nombre de personnes ▪ **too ~ people** trop de gens ▪ **don't give me too ~** ne m'en donne pas trop ▪ **a good ~** un bon nombre ▪ **we met a good ~ times** on s'est vus bien des fois ▪ **a great ~** un grand nombre.
◇ *predet* : **~ a time** bien des fois ▪ **~ a child would be glad of it** bien des enfants s'en contenteraient.
◇ *npl* [masses] : **the ~** la majorité ▪ **the ~ who loved her** tous ceux qui l'aimaient.

Maoism ['maʊɪzm] *n* maoïsme *m*.

Maoist ['maʊɪst] ◇ *adj* maoïste.
◇ *n* maoïste *mf*.

Maori ['maʊrɪ] (*pl inv OR pl* **Maoris**) ◇ *n* **1.** [person] Maori *m*, - e *f* **2.** LING maori *m*.
◇ *adj* maori.

Mao Tse-Tung, Mao Zedong ['maʊtse'tʊŋ] *pr n* Mao Tsé-toung, Mao Zedong.

map [mæp] (*pret & pp* **mapped**, *cont* **mapping**) ◇ *n* **1.** [of country] carte *f* ▪ [of town, network] plan *m* ▪ **to read a ~** lire une carte ▪ **the city was wiped off the ~** *fig* la ville a été rayée de la carte ➊ **to put sthg on the ~** faire connaître qqch ▪ **the election results put them firmly on the political ~** le résultat des élections leur assure une place sur l'échiquier politique **2.** MATHS fonction *f*, application *f*.
◇ *vt* **1.** [country, region] faire *OR* dresser la carte de ▪ [town] faire *OR* dresser le plan de **2.** MATHS : **to ~ sthg onto sthg** représenter qqch sur qqch.
◆ **map out** *vt sep* [itinerary] tracer ▪ [essay] faire le plan de ▪ [plan] établir les grandes lignes de ▪ [career, future] organiser, prévoir ▪ **they have Laura's future all mapped out for her** ils ont déjà planifié l'avenir de Laura.

MAP (*abbrev of* **Modified American Plan**) *n dans un hôtel américain, séjour en demi-pension.*

maple ['meɪpl] *n* érable *m*.

maple leaf *n* feuille *f* d'érable.

maple syrup *n* sirop *m* d'érable.

mapmaker ['mæp,meɪkəʳ] *n* cartographe *mf*.

mapmaking ['mæp,meɪkɪŋ] *n* cartographie *f*.

map reading *n* lecture *f* de carte.

mar [mɑːʳ] (*pret & pp* **marred**, *cont* **marring**) *vt* gâter, gâcher ▪ **today will make or ~ their future** c'est aujourd'hui que se décide *OR* se joue leur avenir.

Mar. *written abbr of* **March**.

maraca [mə'rækə] *n* maraca *f*.

maraschino [,mærə'skiːnəʊ] (*pl* **maraschinos**) *n* marasquin *m* ▪ **~ cherry** cerise *f* au marasquin.

marathon ['mærəθn] ◇ *n* SPORT marathon *m* ▪ **dance ~** *fig* marathon de danse.
◇ *comp* : **~ runner** coureur *m*, - euse *f* de marathon, marathonien *m*, - enne *f*.
◇ *adj* marathon *(inv)* ▪ **a ~ exam** un examen-marathon.

marauder [mə'rɔːdəʳ] *n* [person] maraudeur *m*, - euse *f* ▪ [animal, bird] maraudeur *m*, prédateur *m*.

marauding [mə'rɔːdɪŋ] *adj* maraudeur, en maraude.

marble ['mɑːbl] ◇ *n* **1.** [stone, sculpture] marbre *m* **2.** [for game] bille *f* ▪ **to play ~s** jouer aux billes ➊ **to lose one's ~s** *inf* perdre la boule.
◇ *comp* [fireplace, staircase, statue] de *OR* en marbre ▪ [industry] marbrier ▪ **~ quarry** marbrière *f*, carrière *f* de marbre.
◇ *vt* marbrer.

Marble Arch *pr n grande arche monumentale dans le centre de Londres.*

marble cake *n* gâteau *m* marbré.

marbled ['mɑːbld] *adj* marbré.

marbling ['mɑːblɪŋ] *n* [gen] marbrure *f* ▪ [in meat] marbré *m*.

march [mɑːtʃ] ◇ *n* **1.** MIL marche *f* ▪ **troops on the ~** des troupes en marche ▪ **the ~ of time/events** *fig* la marche du temps/des événements ➊ **quick ~!** en avant, marche! **2.** [demonstration] manifestation *f*, marche *f* ▪ **to go on a ~** manifester, descendre dans la rue ▪ **peace ~** marche pour la paix **3.** [music] marche *f* **4.** *(usu pl)* [frontier] frontière *f* ▪ **the Welsh Marches** les marches *fpl* galloises.
◇ *vi* **1.** MIL marcher (au pas) ▪ **to ~ against the enemy** marcher contre l'ennemi ▪ **to ~ off to war/into battle** partir à la guerre/au combat ▪ **to ~ on a city** marcher sur une ville ▮ [at a ceremony, on parade] défiler ▪ *fig* [time, seasons] avancer, s'écouler ▪ **time ~es on** le temps s'écoule inexorablement **2.** [walk briskly] avancer d'un pas ferme *OR* résolu ▪ **they ~ed off in a huff** ils partirent furieux ▪ **he ~ed upstairs** il monta l'escalier d'un air décidé **3.** [in demonstration] manifester ▪ **the students ~ed alongside the workers** les étudiants manifestèrent aux côtés des ouvriers.
◇ *vt* **1.** MIL faire marcher au pas ▪ **the troops were ~ed out of the citadel** on fit sortir les troupes de la citadelle **2.** [lead forcibly] : **the prisoner was ~ed away/back to his cell** on conduisit/ramena le prisonnier dans sa cellule ▪ **the children were ~ed off to bed** les enfants ont été expédiés au lit (au pas de gymnastique).

March [mɑːtʃ] *n* (mois *m* de) mars *m* ▪ **~ hare** lièvre *m* en rut.

marcher ['mɑːtʃəʳ] *n* [in demonstration] manifestant *m*, - e *f*.

marching ['mɑːtʃɪŋ] ◇ *n* [gen - MIL] marche *f*.
◇ *adj* cadencé ▪ **the sound of ~ feet** le bruit de pas cadencés.

marching orders *npl* **1.** MIL ordre *m* de route **2.** *UK inf fig* **to give sb his/her ~** flanquer qqn à la porte.

marchioness ['mɑːʃənes] *n* [aristocrat] marquise *f*.

march-past *n* défilé *m* (militaire).

Mardi Gras [,mɑːdɪ'grɑː] *n* mardi *m* gras, carnaval *m*.

mare [meəʳ] *n* jument *f*.

mare's nest *n* [illusion] illusion *f* ▪ [disappointment] déception *f*.

margarine [,mɑːdʒə'riːn, ,mɑːgə'riːn] *n* margarine *f*.

margarita [,mɑːgə'riːtə] *n* margarita *f*.

marge [mɑːdʒ] *UK inf* = **margarine**.

margin ['mɑːdʒɪn] *n* **1.** [on page] marge *f* ▪ **written in the ~** écrit dans la *OR* en marge **2.** [leeway] marge *f* ▪ **~ of error** marge *f* d'erreur ▮ [distance, gap] marge *f* ▪ **they won by a narrow/wide ~** ils ont gagné de justesse/avec une marge confortable **3.** [periphery - of field, lake] bord *m* ; [- of wood] lisière *f*, orée *f* ; [- of society] marge *f*.

marginal ['mɑːdʒɪnl] ◇ *adj* **1.** [slight - improvement] léger ; [- effect] minime, insignifiant ; [- importance] mineur, secondaire ; [- case] limite ; [- problem] d'ordre secondaire ➊ **~ land** AGRIC terre *f* de faible rendement **2.** COMM [business, profit] marginal **3.** [in margin - notes] marginal, en marge.
◇ *n* POL = **marginal seat**.

marginalize, ise ['mɑːdʒɪnəlaɪz] *vt* marginaliser.

marginally ['mɑːdʒɪnəlɪ] *adv* à peine, légèrement ▪ **his health has improved only ~** son état ne s'est guère amélioré.

marginal seat *n* POL *en Grande-Bretagne, circonscription dont le député ne dispose que d'une majorité très faible.*

margin release *n* déclenche-marge *m inv*.

Maria [mə'raɪə] **Black Maria**.

Marie-Antoinette ['mærɪ,æntwə'net] *pr n* Marie-Antoinette.

marigold ['mærɪgəʊld] *n* [African] rose *f* d'Inde ■ [French] œillet *m* d'Inde ■ **(pot) ~** souci *m* (des jardins).

marihuana, marijuana [,mærɪ'wɑːnə] *n* marihuana *f*, marijuana *f*.

marina [mə'riːnə] *n* marina *f*.

marinade [,mærɪ'neɪd] ◇ *n* CULIN marinade *f*.
◇ *vt* mariner.

marinate ['mærɪneɪt] *vt* & *vi* CULIN mariner.

marine [mə'riːn] ◇ *adj* **1.** [underwater] marin ■ **~ biology** biologie *f* marine **2.** [naval] maritime ■ **~ engineering** mécanique *f* navale ■ **~ insurance** assurance *f* maritime.
◇ *n* **1.** [ships collectively] marine *f* **2.** [soldier] fusilier *m* marin ■ [British or American] marine *m* ■ **go tell it to the ~s!** *inf* mon œil!, à d'autres!

Marine Corps *pr n US* MIL Marines *mpl*.

mariner ['mærɪnəʳ] *n fml* & *lit* marin *m*.

marionette [,mærɪə'net] *n* marionnette *f*.

marital ['mærɪtl] *adj* [vows, relations, duty] conjugal ■ [problem] conjugal, matrimonial ■ **~ status** situation *f* de famille.

marital aid *n* gadget *m* érotique.

maritime ['mærɪtaɪm] *adj* maritime.

Maritime Provinces, Maritimes *pr npl* : **the ~** les Provinces *fpl* Maritimes.

marjoram ['mɑːdʒərəm] *n* marjolaine *f*, origan *m*.

mark [mɑːk] ◇ *n* **1.** [symbol, sign] marque *f*, signe *m* ■ **to make a ~ on sthg** faire une marque sur qqch, marquer qqch ‖ [on scale, in number, level] marque *f*, niveau *m* ■ **sales topped the 5 million ~** les ventes ont dépassé la barre des 5 millions ■ **to reach the half-way ~** arriver à mi-course ■ **don't go beyond the 50-metre ~** ne dépassez pas les 50 mètres ■ **gas ~ 6** *UK* CULIN thermostat 6 ‖ [model] : **~ 3** COMM modèle *m* OR série *f* 3 ‖ [feature] marque *f* ■ [token] marque *f*, signe *m* ■ **a ~ of affection** une marque d'affection ■ **as a ~ of my esteem/friendship** en témoignage de mon estime/de mon amitié ■ **as a ~ of respect** en signe de respect
2. [trace] trace *f*, marque *f* ■ **the years she spent in prison have left their ~** ses années en prison l'ont marquée ‖ [stain, blemish] tache *f*, marque *f* ■ [wound] trace *f* de coups ■ **there wasn't a ~ on the body** le corps ne portait aucune trace de coups
3. SCH [grade] note *f* ■ **the ~ is out of 100** la note est sur 100 ■ **to get full ~s** obtenir la meilleure note (possible) ‖ [point] point *m* ■ *fig* **it will be a black ~ against his name** ça va jouer contre lui, ça ne va pas jouer en sa faveur ■ **she deserves full ~s for imagination** il faut saluer son imagination ■ **no ~s for guessing the answer!** il ne faut pas être sorcier pour deviner la réponse!
4. [impact] empreinte *f*, impression *f* ■ **to make one's ~** s'imposer, se faire un nom ■ **they left their ~ on 20th-century history** ils ont profondément marqué l'histoire du XXᵉ siècle ‖ [distinction] marque *f* ■ **to be of little ~** *UK* avoir peu d'importance
5. *UK* [standard] : **to be up to the ~** [be capable] être à la hauteur ; [meet expectations] être satisfaisant ‖ [in health] : **I still don't feel quite up to the ~** je ne suis pas encore en pleine forme
6. *UK* [target] but *m*, cible *f* ■ **to hit/to miss the ~** atteindre/manquer la cible
7. SPORT : **on your ~s, (get) set, go!** à vos marques, prêts, partez! ■ *UK fig* **she is quick/slow off the ~** [clever] elle est/n'est pas très maligne, ellea/n'a pas l'esprit très vif ; [in reactions] elle est/n'est pas très rapide ■ **he's sometimes a bit too quick off the ~ in his criticism** il lui arrive d'avoir la critique un peu trop facile
8. RUGBY arrêt *m* de volée
9. [currency] mark *m*.
◇ *vt* **1.** [label] marquer ■ **the towels were ~ed with his name** les serviettes étaient à son nom, son nom était marqué sur les serviettes ■ **~ the text with your initials** inscrivez vos initiales sur ce texte ■ **shall I ~ her absent?** est-ce que je la marque absente? ■ **the table was ~ed "sold"** la table portait l'étiquette "vendue"
2. [stain] tacher, marquer ■ [face, hands] marquer ■ **the scandal ~ed him for life** [mentally] le scandale l'a marqué pour la vie ‖ ZOOL tacheter
3. [indicate] indiquer, marquer ■ **X ~s the spot** l'endroit est marqué d'un X
4. [celebrate - anniversary, event] célébrer, marquer ■ **let's have some champagne to ~ the occasion** ouvrons une bouteille de champagne pour fêter l'événement
5. [distinguish] marquer ■ **he has all the qualities that ~ a good golfer** il possède toutes les qualités d'un bon golfeur
6. SCH [essay, homework] corriger ■ [student] noter ■ **the exam was ~ed out of 100** l'examen a été noté sur 100 ■ **to ~ sthg wrong/right** marquer qqch comme étant faux/juste
7. [pay attention to] : **(you) ~ my words!** souvenez-vous de ce que je vous dis! ■ **~ how he does it** *UK* observez bien la façon dont il s'y prend ■ **~ you, I didn't believe him** *UK* remarquez, je ne l'ai pas cru
8. SPORT [opponent] marquer
9. *phr* **to ~ time** MIL marquer le pas ; *fig* attendre son heure OR le moment propice ■ **the government are just ~ing time until the elections** le gouvernement fait traîner les choses en attendant les élections.
◇ *vi* [garment] être salissant, se tacher facilement.

◆ **mark down** *vt sep* **1.** [write] noter, prendre note de, inscrire
2. [reduce - price] baisser ; [- article] baisser le prix de ■ **~ed down shirts** chemises démarquées OR soldées ■ **prices were ~ed down in early trading** ST. EX les valeurs étaient en baisse OR ont reculé en début de séance ■ SCH [essay, student] baisser la note de ■ **he was ~ed down for bad grammar** il a perdu des points à cause de la grammaire
3. [single out] désigner ■ **I ~ed him down as a troublemaker** j'avais remarqué qu'il n'était bon qu'à créer des ennuis.

◆ **mark off** *vt sep* **1.** [divide, isolate - area, period of time] délimiter ■ **one corner of the field had been ~ed off by a fence** un coin du champ avait été isolé par une barrière
2. [measure - distance] mesurer
3. *UK* [distinguish] distinguer ■ **his intelligence ~ed him off from his school friends** il se distinguait de ses camarades d'école par son intelligence
4. [on list] cocher.

◆ **mark out** *vt sep* **1.** [with chalk, paint - court, pitch] tracer les lignes de ■ [with stakes] jalonner ■ [with lights, flags] baliser ■ **his path in life is clearly ~ed out** *fig* son avenir est tout tracé
2. [designate] désigner ■ **Brian was ~ed out for promotion** Brian était désigné pour obtenir une promotion ■ **they were ~ed out for special treatment** ils ont bénéficié d'un régime particulier
3. *UK* [distinguish] distinguer ■ **her ambition ~s her out from her colleagues** son ambition la distingue de ses collègues.

◆ **mark up** *vt sep* **1.** [on notice] marquer ■ **the menu is ~ed up on the blackboard** le menu est sur le tableau
2. [increase - price] augmenter, majorer ; [- goods] augmenter le prix de, majorer ■ **prices at last began to be ~ed up** ST. EX les cours sont enfin à la hausse
3. [annotate] annoter.

Mark [mɑːk] *pr n* Marc ■ **~ Antony** Marc Antoine ■ **Saint ~** saint Marc.

markdown ['mɑːkdaʊn] *n* démarque *f*.

marked [mɑːkt] *adj* **1.** [noticeable] accentué, marqué, sensible ■ [accent] prononcé **2.** [bearing a mark] marqué ■ **he's a ~ man** c'est l'homme à abattre **3.** LING marqué.

markedly ['mɑːkɪdlɪ] *adv* d'une façon marquée, sensiblement, ostensiblement.

marker ['mɑːkəʳ] ◇ *n* **1.** [pen] feutre *m*, marqueur *m* **2.** [indicator, landmark] jalon *m*, balise *f* **3.** [scorekeeper] marqueur *m*, - euse *f* **4.** SCH correcteur *m*, - trice *f* ■ **to be a hard ~** noter sévèrement **5.** [page marker] marque-page *m*, signet *m* **6.** SPORT marqueur *m* ■ **to lose one's ~** se démarquer (d'un adversaire) **7.** LING marque *f*.
◇ *comp* [pen, buoy] : **~ pen** marqueur *m* ■ **~ buoy** bouée *f* de balisage.

market ['mɑːkɪt] ◇ *n* **1.** [gen] marché *m* ■ **to go to (the) ~** aller au marché, aller faire son marché ■ **~ square** place *f* du marché ■ **~ day** jour *m* de marché **2.** ECON marché *m* ■ **the job ~** le marché de l'emploi ■ **the property ~** le marché immobilier ■ **to put sthg on the ~** mettre qqch en vente OR sur le marché ■ **new products are always coming onto the ~** de nou-

veaux produits apparaissent constamment sur le marché ■ **to be on the open ~** être sur le marché libre ■ **she's in the ~ for Persian rugs** elle cherche à acheter des tapis persans, elle est acheteuse de tapis persans ‖ [demand] demande *f*, marché *m* ■ [outlet] débouché *m*, marché *m* ■ **he's unable to find a ~ for his products** il ne trouve pas de débouchés pour ses produits ‖ [clientele] marché *m*, clientèle *f* ■ **this ad should appeal to the teenage ~** cette pub devrait séduire les jeunes **3.** ST. EX marché *m* ■ [index] indice *m* ■ [prices] cours *mpl* ■ **the ~ has risen 10 points** l'indice est en hausse de 10 points ■ **to play the ~** jouer en bourse, spéculer.
◇ *vt* [sell] vendre, commercialiser ■ [launch] lancer *OR* mettre sur le marché.
◇ *vi US* [go shopping] faire le marché ■ **to go ~ing** aller faire ses courses.

marketable ['mɑːkɪtəbl] *adj* vendable, commercialisable ■ ST. EX négociable.

market analysis *n* analyse *f* de marché.

market economy *n* économie *f* de marché *OR* libérale.

marketeer [ˌmɑːkə'tɪər] *n* **1.** : **black ~** trafiquant *m*, - e *f* (au marché noir) **2.** *UK* POL : **pro-~** partisan *m*, - e *f* du Marché commun ■ **anti-~** adversaire *mf* du Marché commun.

market forces *npl* les forces *fpl* du marché.

market garden *n UK* jardin *m* maraîcher.

market gardening *n UK* culture *f* maraîchère.

marketing ['mɑːkɪtɪŋ] *n* [selling] commercialisation *f*, distribution *f* ■ [promotion, research] marketing *m*.

market leader *n* [product] premier produit *m* sur le marché ■ [firm] leader *m* du marché.

market maker *n* FIN teneur *m* de marché.

marketplace ['mɑːkɪtpleɪs] *n* **1.** [in town] place *f* du marché **2.** COMM marché *m*.

market price *n* COMM prix *m* courant ■ ST. EX cours *m* de (la) Bourse.

market research *n* étude *f OR* études *fpl* de marché ■ **he works in ~** il travaille dans le marketing.

market researcher *n personne qui fait des études de marché.*

market share *n* part *f* de marché.

market town *n* bourg *m*.

market value *n* COMM valeur *f* marchande ■ ST. EX valeur *f* boursière *OR* en bourse.

marking ['mɑːkɪŋ] *n* **1.** ZOOL tache *f*, marque *f* **2.** SCH correction *f* **3.** SPORT marquage *m*.

marksman ['mɑːksmən] (*pl* **marksmen** [-mən]) *n* tireur *m* d'élite.

marksmanship ['mɑːksmənʃɪp] *n* habileté *f* au tir.

markswoman ['mɑːksˌwʊmən] (*pl* **markswomen** [-ˌwɪmɪn]) *n* tireuse *f* d'élite.

markup ['mɑːkʌp] *n* majoration *f*, augmentation *f* (de prix).

marmalade ['mɑːməleɪd] ◇ *n* [gen] confiture *f* d'agrumes ■ [orange] marmelade *f* d'orange ■ **~ orange** orange *f* amère, bigarade *f*.
◇ *adj* [cat] roux, rousse *f*.

Marmite® ['mɑːmaɪt] *n pâte à tartiner végétale à base d'extrait de levure.*

marmoset ['mɑːməzet] *n* ouistiti *m*.

marmot ['mɑːmət] *n* marmotte *f*.

maroon [mə'ruːn] ◇ *vt* [abandon] abandonner *(sur une île ou une côte déserte)* ■ **to be ~ed** [shipwrecked] faire naufrage.
◇ *adj* [colour] bordeaux *(inv)*.
◇ *n* **1.** [colour] bordeaux *m* **2.** [rocket] fusée *f* de détresse.

marque [mɑːk] *n* [brand] marque *f*.

marquee [mɑː'kiː] *n* **1.** *UK* [tent] grande tente *f* ■ [for circus] chapiteau *m* **2.** *US* [canopy at hotel, theatre] marquise *f*.

Marquesas Islands [mɑː'keɪsæs-] *pr npl* : **the ~** les îles *fpl* Marquises ■ **in the ~** aux îles Marquises.

marquess ['mɑːkwɪs] *n* marquis *m*.

marquetry ['mɑːkɪtrɪ] ◇ *n* marqueterie *f*.
◇ *adj* [table] en marqueterie.

marquis ['mɑːkwɪs] = **marquess**.

marriage ['mærɪdʒ] ◇ *n* **1.** mariage *m* ■ [ceremony] mariage *m*, noces *fpl* ■ **to give sb in ~** donner qqn en mariage ■ **to take sb in ~** prendre qqn pour époux/épouse, épouser qqn ■ **he's my uncle by ~** c'est mon oncle par alliance ▶ **'The Marriage of Figaro'** ***Beaumarchais*** 'le Mariage de Figaro' ; ***Mozart*** 'les Noces de Figaro' **2.** *fig* [union] mariage *m*, alliance *f*.
◇ *comp* conjugal, matrimonial ■ **~ ceremony** cérémonie *f* de mariage ■ **~ vows** vœux *mpl* de mariage.

marriageable ['mærɪdʒəbl] *adj* mariable ■ **to be of ~ age** être en âge de se marier.

marriage bureau *n* agence *f* matrimoniale.

marriage certificate *n* extrait *m* d'acte de mariage.

marriage guidance *n* conseil *m* conjugal ■ **~ counsellor** conseiller *m* conjugal, conseillère *f* conjugale.

marriage licence *n* ≃ certificat *m* de non-opposition au mariage.

marriage of convenience *n* mariage *m* de raison.

married ['mærɪd] *adj* [man, woman] marié, mariée ■ [life] conjugal ■ **'just ~'** 'jeunes mariés' ■ **he's ~ to his work** *fig* il passe son temps à travailler ▶ **~ couple** couple *m* marié ■ **~ name** nom *m* d'épouse.

marrow ['mærəʊ] *n* **1.** BIOL & *fig* moelle *f* ■ **frozen** *OR* **chilled to the ~** gelé jusqu'à la moelle des os **2.** [vegetable] courge *f*.

marrowbone ['mærəʊbəʊn] *n* os *f* à moelle.

marry ['mærɪ] (*pret & pp* **married**) ◇ *vt* **1.** [subj: fiancé] épouser, se marier avec ■ **to get married** se marier ■ **to be married (to sb)** être marié (avec qqn) ■ **will you ~ me?** veux-tu m'épouser? **2.** [subj: priest] marier **3.** *fig* [styles] marier, allier.
◇ *vi* se marier ■ **he's not the ~ing type** ce n'est pas le genre à se marier ■ **she married beneath herself/above herself** elle s'est mésalliée/a fait un beau mariage ■ **to ~ for money** faire un mariage d'argent.
◆ **marry off** *vt sep* marier ■ **she married off her daughter to an aristocrat** elle a marié sa fille à un aristocrate.
◆ **marry up** ◇ *vt sep* [join together] marier.
◇ *vi insep* s'associer.

Mars [mɑːz] *pr n* ASTRON & MYTH Mars.

Marseille, Marseilles [mɑː'seɪ] *pr n* Marseille.

marsh [mɑːʃ] *n* marais *m*, marécage *m*.

marshal ['mɑːʃl] (*UK pret & pp* **marshalled**, *cont* **marshalling**) (*US pret & pp* **marshaled**, *cont* **marshaling**) ◇ *n* **1.** MIL maréchal *m* **2.** [at public event] membre *m* du service d'ordre ■ [in law court] huissier *m* ■ [at race-track] commissaire *m* **3.** *US* [police chief] commissaire *m* de police ■ [fire chief] capitaine *m* des pompiers ■ [district police officer] commissaire *m*.
◇ *vt* **1.** MIL [troops] masser, rassembler ■ [people, group] canaliser, diriger **2.** [organize - arguments, thoughts] rassembler ■ **he's trying to ~ support for his project** il essaie d'obtenir du soutien pour son projet.

Marshall Plan ['mɑːʃl-] *pr n* : **the ~** le Plan Marshall.

MARSHALL PLAN

Le plan Marshall, du nom de son auteur le général et secrétaire d'État George C. Marshall, est le programme américain d'aide à la reconstruction économique de l'Europe après la seconde guerre mondiale.

marsh gas *n* gaz *m* des marais, méthane *m*.

marshland ['mɑːʃlænd] *n* marais *m*, terrain *m* marécageux.

marshmallow [*UK* mɑːʃ'mæləʊ, *US* 'mɑrʃˌmeləʊ] *n* BOT guimauve *f* ■ CULIN [sweet] guimauve *f*.

marsh marigold *n* souci *m* d'eau, populage *m*.

marshy ['mɑːʃɪ] (*comp* **marshier**, *superl* **marshiest**) *adj* marécageux.

marsupial [mɑː'suːpjəl] ◇ *adj* marsupial.
◇ *n* marsupial *m*.

mart [mɑːt] *n* **1.** [market] marché *m* ■ **second-hand car ~** magasin *m* de voitures d'occasion **2.** [auction room] salle *f* des ventes.

marten ['mɑːtɪn] *n* marte *f*, martre *f*.

Martha ['mɑːθə] *pr n* Marthe.

martial ['mɑːʃl] *adj* [military] martial ■ [warlike] martial, guerrier ■ **~ music** musique *f* militaire.

martial art *n* art *m* martial.

martial law *n* loi *f* martiale.

Martian ['mɑːʃn] ◇ *n* Martien *m*, - enne *f*.
◇ *adj* martien.

martin ['mɑːtɪn] *n* martinet *m*.

martinet [,mɑːtɪ'net] *n* tyran *m*.

Martini® [mɑː'tiːnɪ] *n* Martini® *m*.

Martinique [,mɑːtɪ'niːk] *pr n* Martinique *f* ■ **in ~** à la *OR* en Martinique.

martyr ['mɑːtə^r] ◇ *n* martyr *m*, - e *f* ■ **to die a ~** mourir en martyr ‖ *fig* **she's always making a ~ of herself** elle joue toujours les martyres ■ **he's a ~ to rheumatism** ses rhumatismes lui font souffrir le martyre.
◇ *vt* martyriser.

martyrdom ['mɑːtədəm] *n* RELIG martyre *m* ■ *fig* martyre *m*, calvaire *m*.

martyred ['mɑːtəd] *adj* de martyr ■ **to put on a ~ look** prendre des airs de martyr.

marvel ['mɑːvl] (*UK pret & pp* **marvelled**, *cont* **marvelling**) (*US pret & pp* **marveled**, *cont* **marveling**) ◇ *n* **1.** [miracle] merveille *f*, miracle *m*, prodige *m* ■ **to do** *OR* **to work ~s** faire des merveilles **2.** [marvellous person] : **you're a ~!** tu es une vraie petite merveille!
◇ *vi* : **to ~ at sthg** s'émerveiller de qqch.
◇ *vt* : **he marvelled that she had kept so calm** il n'en revenait pas qu'elle ait pu rester si calme.

marvellous *UK*, **marvelous** *US* ['mɑːvələs] *adj* [amazing] merveilleux, extraordinaire ■ [miraculous] miraculeux.

marvellously *UK*, **marvelously** *US* ['mɑːvələslɪ] *adv* merveilleusement, à merveille.

Marxism ['mɑːksɪzm] *n* marxisme *m*.

Marxist ['mɑːksɪst] ◇ *adj* marxiste.
◇ *n* marxiste *mf*.

Mary ['meərɪ] *pr n* Marie ■ **~ Magdalene** Marie Madeleine ■ **the Virgin ~** la Vierge Marie.

Maryland ['meərɪlənd] *pr n* Maryland *m* ■ **in ~** dans le Maryland.

marzipan ['mɑːzɪpæn] ◇ *n* pâte *f* d'amandes.
◇ *comp* [cake, sweet etc] à la pâte d'amandes.

mascara [mæs'kɑːrə] *n* mascara *m*.

mascaraed [mæs'kɑːrəd] *adj* : **she had heavily ~ eyelashes** elle portait beaucoup de mascara.

mascot ['mæskət] *n* mascotte *f*.

masculine ['mæskjʊlɪn] ◇ *adj* [gen] masculin ■ [virile] viril ■ **a very ~ fragrance** un parfum très viril.
◇ *n* GRAM masculin *m*.

masculinity [,mæskjʊ'lɪnətɪ] *n* masculinité *f*.

mash [mæʃ] ◇ *n* **1.** *UK inf* CULIN purée *f* (de pommes de terre) **2.** [for horses] mash *m* **3.** [in brewing] moût *m* **4.** *inf* [pulp] pulpe *f*, bouillie *f*.
◇ *vt* **1.** [crush] écraser, broyer **2.** CULIN faire une purée de ■ **~ed potato** *OR* **potatoes** purée *f* (de pommes de terre) **3.** [in brewing] brasser.

MASH [mæʃ] (*abbrev of* **mobile army surgical hospital**) *n hôpital militaire de campagne.*

masher ['mæʃə^r] *n* broyeur *m* ■ [for potatoes] presse-purée *m inv*.

mask [mɑːsk] ◇ *n* **1.** *liter* & *fig* masque *m* ■ PHOT cache *m* **2.** COMPUT masque *m*.
◇ *vt* **1.** [face] masquer **2.** [truth, feelings] masquer, cacher, dissimuler **3.** [house] masquer, cacher ■ [view] boucher, masquer ■ [flavour, smell] masquer, recouvrir **4.** [in painting, photography] masquer, cacher.
◆ **mask out** *vt sep* PHOT masquer, cacher.

masked [mɑːskt] *adj* [face, man] masqué.

masked ball *n* bal *m* masqué.

masking tape ['mɑːskɪŋ-] *n* papier *m* à maroufler.

masochism ['mæsəkɪzm] *n* masochisme *m*.

masochist ['mæsəkɪst] ◇ *adj* masochiste.
◇ *n* masochiste *mf*.

masochistic [,mæsə'kɪstɪk] *adj* masochiste.

mason ['meɪsn] *n* [stoneworker] maçon *m*.
◆ **Mason** *n* [Freemason] Maçon *m*, franc-maçon *m*.

Masonic [mə'sɒnɪk] *adj* maçonnique, franc-maçonnique.

masonry ['meɪsnrɪ] *n* [stonework, skill] maçonnerie *f* ■ **a large piece of ~** un gros bloc de pierre.
◆ **Masonry** *n* [Freemasonry] Maçonnerie *f*, franc-maçonnerie *f*.

masque [mɑːsk] *n* THEAT masque *m*.

masquerade [,mæskə'reɪd] ◇ *n liter* & *fig* mascarade *f*.
◇ *vi* : **to ~ as** [pretend to be] se faire passer pour ; [disguise o.s. as] se déguiser en.

mass [mæs] ◇ *n* **1.** PHYS masse *f* **2.** [large quantity or amount] masse *f*, quantité *f* ■ **the streets were a solid ~ of people/traffic** les rues regorgeaient de monde/de voitures ‖ [bulk] masse *f* **3.** [majority] majorité *f*, plupart *f* ■ **in the ~** dans l'ensemble **4.** GEOG : **land ~** masse *f* continentale.
◇ *adj* [for all - communication, education] de masse ■ [large-scale - starvation, unemployment] à *OR* sur une grande échelle ■ [involving many - resignation] massif, en masse ■ [collective - funeral] collectif ■ **this product will appeal to a ~ audience** ce produit plaira à un large public ■ **~ consumption/culture** consommation *f* /culture *f* de masse ■ **~ demonstration** grande manifestation *f* ■ **~ execution** exécution *f* en masse ■ **~ grave** charnier *m* ■ **~ meeting** grand rassemblement *m* ■ **~ hypnosis/hysteria** hypnose *f* /hystérie *f* collective ■ **~ suicide** suicide *m* collectif ■ **~ murder** tuerie *f* ■ **~ murderer** tueur *m* fou.
◇ *vi* [people] se masser ■ [clouds] s'amonceler.
◇ *vt* [troops] masser.

Mass [mæs] *n* RELIG **1.** [music] messe *f* **2.** [ceremony] messe *f* ■ **to go to ~** aller à la messe ■ **to say ~** dire la messe.

Mass. *written abbr of* **Massachusetts**.

Massachusetts [,mæsə'tʃuːsɪts] *pr n* Massachusetts *m* ■ **in ~** dans le Massachusetts.

massacre ['mæsəkə^r] ◇ *vt* **1.** [kill] massacrer **2.** *inf* SPORT écraser.
◇ *n* massacre *m*.

massage [*UK* 'mæsɑːʒ, *US* mə'sɑːʒ] ◇ *n* massage *m*.
◇ *vt liter* masser ■ *fig* [statistics, facts] manipuler.

massage parlour *n* salon *m* de massage.

massed [mæst] *adj* **1.** [crowds, soldiers] massé, regroupé ■ **~ bands** *UK* ensemble *m* de fanfares **2.** [collective] de masse ■ **the ~ weight of public opinion** le poids de l'opinion publique.

masses ['mæsɪz] *npl* **1.** : **the ~** les masses *fpl* ■ **culture for the ~** la culture à la portée de tous **2.** *inf* [large amount] : **~ of** des masses de, plein de.

masseur [*UK* mæ'sɜːʳ, *US* mæ'suər] *n* masseur *m*.

masseuse [*UK* mæ'sɜːz, *US* mæ'suːz] *n* masseuse *f*.

massive ['mæsɪv] *adj* [in size] massif, énorme ■ [dose, increase] massif ■ [majority] écrasant ■ [change, explosion] énorme ■ [sound] retentissant.

massively ['mæsɪvlɪ] *adv* massivement ■ **he's ~ built** il est solidement bâti.

mass-market *adj* grand public *inv*.

mass media *n & npl* mass media *mpl*.

mass noun *n* nom *m* non comptable.

mass number *n* nombre *m* de masse.

mass-produce *vt* fabriquer en série.

mass production *n* fabrication *f* OR production *f* en série.

mast [mɑːst] *n* **1.** [on ship, for flag] mât *m* ■ [for radio or TV aerial] pylône *m* **2.** [animal food] faine *f (destinée à l'alimentation animale)*.

mastectomy [mæs'tektəmɪ] (*pl* **mastectomies**) *n* mastectomie *f*, mammectomie *f*.

master ['mɑːstəʳ] <> *n* **1.** [of household, dog, servant, situation] maître *m* ■ **to be ~ in one's own house** être maître chez soi ■ **to be one's own ~** être son propre maître ■ **to be (the) ~ of one's fate** être maître de son destin ➲ **~ of ceremonies** [at reception] maître des cérémonies ; [on TV show] présentateur *m* ■ **~ of hounds** OR **foxhounds** maître d'équipage ■ **Master of the Rolls** ≃ président *m* de la cour d'appel *(en Grande-Bretagne)* **2.** [expert] maître *m* ■ **chess ~** maître **3.** SCH [in primary school] instituteur *m*, maître *m* d'école ■ [in secondary school] professeur *m* ■ [private tutor] maître *m* **4.** UNIV : **Master of Arts/Science** [diploma] ≃ maîtrise *f* ès lettres/ès sciences ; [person] ≃ titulaire *mf* d'une maîtrise de lettres/de sciences ■ **she's doing a ~'s (degree) in philosophy** elle prépare une maîtrise de philosophie **5.** *dated & fml* [boy's title] monsieur *m* **6.** ART maître *m* **7.** NAUT [of ship] capitaine *m* ■ [of fishing boat] patron *m* **8.** UNIV [head of college] principal *m* **9.** [original copy] original *m* ■ [standard] étalon *m*.
<> *vt* **1.** [person, animal] maîtriser, dompter ■ [problem, difficulty] surmonter, venir à bout de ■ [emotions] maîtriser, surmonter ■ [situation] maîtriser, se rendre maître de ■ **to ~ o.s.** se maîtriser, se dominer **2.** [subject, technique] maîtriser.
<> *adj* **1.** [overall] directeur, maître ■ **~ plan** stratégie *f* globale **2.** [in trade] maître ■ **~ chef/craftsman** maître chef *m* /artisan *m* ■ **a ~ thief/spy** un voleur/un espion de génie **3.** [controlling] principal ■ **~ switch** interrupteur *m* général **4.** [original] original ■ **~ copy** original *m*.

master (disk) *n* COMPUT disque *m* d'exploitation.

master bedroom *n* chambre *f* principale.

master builder *n* maître *m* bâtisseur.

master class *n* cours *m* de maître ■ MUS master class *m*.

master file *n* COMPUT fichier *m* principal OR maître.

masterful ['mɑːstəfʊl] *adj* **1.** [dominating] autoritaire **2.** = **masterly**.

master key *n* passe-partout *m inv*.

masterly ['mɑːstəlɪ] *adj* magistral ■ **in a ~ fashion** magistralement, avec maestria.

master mariner *n* capitaine *m*.

mastermind ['mɑːstəmaɪnd] <> *n* [genius] cerveau *m*, génie *m* ■ [of crime, operation] cerveau *m*.
<> *vt* diriger, organiser ■ **she ~ed the whole operation** c'est elle qui a dirigé toute l'opération, c'est elle le cerveau de toute l'opération.
◆ **Mastermind** *pr n jeu télévisé britannique portant sur des questions de culture générale.*

masterpiece ['mɑːstəpiːs] *n liter & fig* chef-d'œuvre *m*.

master race *n* race *f* supérieure.

masterstroke ['mɑːstəstrəʊk] *n* coup *m* de maître.

masterwork ['mɑːstəwɜːk] *n* chef-d'œuvre *m*.

mastery ['mɑːstərɪ] (*pl* **masteries**) *n* **1.** [domination, control] maîtrise *f*, domination *f* ■ **~ of** OR **over a situation** maîtrise d'une situation ■ **~ of an opponent** supériorité *f* sur un adversaire **2.** [of art, subject, language] maîtrise *f*, connaissance *f* **3.** [masterly skill] maestria *f*, brio *m*.

masthead ['mɑːsthed] *n* **1.** NAUT tête *f* de mât **2.** PRESS titre *m*.

mastic ['mæstɪk] *n* [resin] mastic *m* de Chio ■ [filler, seal] mastic *m*.

masticate ['mæstɪkeɪt] *vi & vt* mastiquer, mâcher.

mastiff ['mæstɪf] *n* mastiff *m*.

mastoiditis [,mæstɔɪ'daɪtɪs] *n (U)* mastoïdite *f*.

masturbate ['mæstəbeɪt] <> *vi* se masturber.
<> *vt* masturber.

masturbation [,mæstə'beɪʃn] *n* masturbation *f*.

mat [mæt] (*pret & pp* **matted**, *cont* **matting**) <> *adj* = **matt**.
<> *n* **1.** [floor covering] (petit) tapis *m*, carpette *f* ■ [doormat] paillasson *m* ■ [in gym] tapis *m* ■ **to be on the ~** *inf* être sur la sellette ■ **to have sb on the ~** *inf* faire passer un mauvais quart d'heure à qqn **2.** [for sleeping on] natte *f* **3.** [on table] set *m* de table ■ [for hot dishes] dessous-de-plat *m inv*.
<> *vi* **1.** [hair] s'emmêler **2.** [material] (se) feutrer.

matador ['mætədɔːʳ] *n* matador *m*.

match [mætʃ] <> *n* **1.** SPORT match *m*, rencontre *f* ■ **a rugby/boxing ~** un match de rugby/de boxe ■ **game, set and ~** TENNIS jeu, set et match ■ **to play a ~** jouer un match
2. [equal] égal *m*, - e *f* ■ **he's found** OR **met his ~ (in Pauline)** il a trouvé à qui parler (avec Pauline) ■ **he's a ~ for her any day** il est de taille à lui faire face ■ **Dave is no ~ for Rob** Dave ne fait pas le poids contre Rob
3. [couple] couple *m* ■ [marriage] mariage *m* ■ **they are** OR **make a good ~** ils vont bien ensemble ■ **to make a ~** arranger un mariage ■ **to find a (good) ~ for sb** trouver un (beau) parti à qqn
4. [combination] : **these colours are a good ~** ces couleurs se marient bien OR vont bien ensemble ■ **the new paint's not quite a perfect ~** la nouvelle peinture n'est pas exactement de la même couleur que la précédente
5. [for lighting] allumette *f* ■ **to light** OR **to strike a ~** frotter OR craquer une allumette ■ **to put** OR **to set a ~ to sthg** mettre le feu à qqch ■ **a box/book of ~es** une boîte/une pochette d'allumettes
6. [fuse] mèche *f*.
<> *vt* **1.** [be equal to] être l'égal de, égaler ■ **his arrogance is ~ed only by that of his father** son arrogance n'a d'égale que celle de son père
2. [go with - subj: clothes, colour] s'assortir à, aller (bien) avec, se marier (harmonieusement) avec ■ **the gloves ~ the scarf** les gants sont assortis à l'écharpe
3. [coordinate] : **I'm trying to ~ this paint** je cherche une peinture identique à celle-ci ■ **can you ~ the names with the photographs?** pouvez-vous attribuer à chaque photo le nom qui lui correspond? ■ **he and his wife are well ~ed** lui et sa femme vont bien ensemble
4. [oppose] : **to ~ sb against sb** opposer qqn à qqn ■ **he ~ed his skill against the champion's** il mesura son habileté à celle du champion ■ **the two teams are well ~ed** les deux équipes sont de force égale
5. [find equal to] égaler ■ **this restaurant can't be ~ed for quality** ce restaurant n'a pas son pareil pour ce qui est de la qualité.
<> *vi* aller (bien) ensemble, être bien assorti ■ **a red scarf with a bonnet to ~** un foulard rouge avec un bonnet assorti ■ **I can't find two socks that ~** je ne parviens pas à trouver deux chaussettes identiques ■ **none of the glasses ~ed** les verres étaient tous dépareillés.
◆ **match up** <> *vt sep* = **match** *(vt sense 3)*.
<> *vi insep* [dates, figures] correspondre ■ [clothes, colours] aller (bien) ensemble, être bien assorti.

◆ **match up to** *vt insep* valoir ■ **his jokes don't ~ (up to) Mark's** ses plaisanteries ne valent pas celles de Mark ■ **the hotel didn't ~ (up to) our expectations** l'hôtel nous a déçus *OR* ne répondait pas à notre attente.

matchbook ['mætʃbʊk] *n* pochette *f* d'allumettes.

matchbox ['mætʃbɒks] *n* boîte *f* d'allumettes.

match-fit *adj UK* **they only have ten ~ players** ils n'ont que dix joueurs en état de jouer.

matching ['mætʃɪŋ] *adj* assorti.

matchless ['mætʃlɪs] *adj lit* sans égal, sans pareil.

matchmaker ['mætʃ,meɪkəʳ] *n* **1.** [gen] entremetteur *m*, - euse *f* ■ [for marriage] marieur *m*, - euse *f* **2.** [manufacturer] fabricant *m* d'allumettes.

match play *n* GOLF match-play *m*.
◆ **match-play** *adj* : **match-play tournament** match-play *m*.

match point *n* TENNIS balle *f* de match.

matchstick ['mætʃstɪk] *n UK* allumette *f* ■ **~ men** personnages *mpl* stylisés *(dessinés de simples traits)*.

match-winner *n* atout *m* pour gagner, joker *m*.

matchwood ['mætʃwʊd] *n* bois *m* d'allumettes ■ **smashed** *OR* **reduced to ~** *UK* réduit en miettes.

mate [1] [meɪt] ◇ *n* **1.** *inf UK & Australia inf* [friend] pote *m*, copain *m* ■ [term of address] : **listen, ~!** écoute, mon vieux! **2.** [colleague] camarade *mf* (de travail) **3.** [workman's helper] aide *mf* ■ **plumber's ~** aide-plombier *m* **4.** NAUT [in navy] second maître *m* ■ [on merchant vessel] : **(first) ~** second *m* ■ **second ~** lieutenant *m* **5.** ZOOL mâle *m*, femelle *f* ■ *hum* [husband] époux *m* ■ [wife] épouse *f* ■ [lover] partenaire *mf* ■ **some animals pine when separated from their ~** certains animaux dépérissent quand on les sépare de leur compagnon **6.** [in chess] mat *m*.
◇ *vt* **1.** ZOOL accoupler ■ **to ~ a cow with a bull** accoupler une vache à un taureau **2.** [in chess] mettre échec et mat, mater.
◇ *vi* s'accoupler.

mate [2]**, maté** ['mæteɪ] *n* **1.** [tree] (variété *f* de) houx *m* **2.** [drink] maté *m*.

mater ['meɪtəʳ] *n UK dated & hum* mère *f*, maman *f*.

material [mə'tɪərɪəl] ◇ *n* **1.** [wood, plastic, stone etc] matière *f*, substance *f* ■ [as constituent] matériau *m* ■ **building ~s** matériaux de construction **2.** [cloth] tissu *m*, étoffe *f* **3.** *(U)* [ideas, data] matériaux *mpl*, documentation *f* ■ **background ~** documentation de base **4.** [finished work] : **a comic who writes his own ~** un comique qui écrit ses propres textes *OR* sketches ■ **a singer who writes his own ~** un auteur-compositeur interprète **5.** [necessary equipment] matériel *m* ■ **writing ~** matériel pour écrire ■ **teaching ~s** SCH supports *mpl* pédagogiques ■ **reference ~s** documents *mpl* de référence **6.** [suitable person or persons] : **is he officer/university ~?** a-t-il l'étoffe d'un officier/universitaire? ■ **they're not first division ~** ils ne sont pas de taille à jouer en première division.
◇ *adj* **1.** [concrete] matériel ■ **~ comforts** confort *m* matériel ■ **of ~ benefit** d'un apport capital **2.** *fml* [relevant] pertinent ■ **the facts ~ to the investigation** les faits qui présentent un intérêt pour l'enquête ➤ **~ evidence** LAW preuve *f* matérielle *OR* tangible.

materialism [mə'tɪərɪəlɪzm] *n* matérialisme *m*.

materialist [mə'tɪərɪəlɪst] ◇ *adj* matérialiste.
◇ *n* matérialiste *mf*.

materialistic [mə,tɪərɪə'lɪstɪk] *adj* matérialiste.

materialize, ise [mə'tɪərɪəlaɪz] ◇ *vi* **1.** [become fact] se matérialiser, se réaliser ■ [take shape] prendre forme ■ **the promised pay rise never ~d** l'augmentation promise ne s'est jamais concrétisée **2.** *inf* [arrive] : **he eventually ~d around ten** il a fini par se pointer vers dix heures **3.** [ghost, apparition] se matérialiser.
◇ *vt* matérialiser.

materially [mə'tɪərɪəlɪ] *adv* matériellement.

maternal [mə'tɜ:nl] *adj* **1.** [motherly] maternel **2.** [related through mother] maternel.

maternity [mə'tɜ:nətɪ] ◇ *n* maternité *f*.
◇ *comp* [dress] de grossesse ■ [ward] de maternité ■ **~ home** *OR* **hospital** maternité *f*.

maternity allowance *n allocation de maternité versée par l'État à une femme n'ayant pas droit à la "maternity pay"*.

maternity benefit *n* ≃ allocations *fpl* de maternité.

maternity leave *n* congé *m* (de) maternité.

maternity pay *n allocation de maternité versée par l'employeur*.

matey ['meɪtɪ] *inf* ◇ *n UK* pote *m* ■ [term of address] : **listen, ~** écoute, mon vieux.
◇ *adj* [pally] copain ■ **he's very ~ with me** il est très copain avec moi.

math [mæθ] *US* = **maths**.

mathematical [,mæθə'mætɪkl] *adj* mathématique.

mathematically [,mæθə'mætɪklɪ] *adv* mathématiquement.

mathematician [,mæθəmə'tɪʃn] *n* mathématicien *m*, - enne *f*.

mathematics [,mæθə'mætɪks] ◇ *n (U)* [science, subject] mathématiques *fpl*.
◇ *npl* [calculations involved] : **can you explain the ~ of it to me?** pouvez-vous m'expliquer comment on parvient à ce résultat?

maths [mæθs] (*abbrev of* **mathematics**) *n (U) UK* maths *fpl*.

maths coprocessor [-,kəʊ'prəʊsesəʳ] *n* COMPUT coprocesseur *m* mathématique.

matinee, matinée ['mætɪneɪ] *n* CIN & THEAT matinée *f*.

matinee coat *n UK* veste *f* de bébé.

matinee idol *n dated & hum* idole *f* (romantique).

matinee jacket *UK* = **matinee coat**.

mating ['meɪtɪŋ] ◇ *n* accouplement *m*.
◇ *comp* : **~ call** appel *m* du mâle *OR* de la femelle ■ **~ instinct** instinct *m* sexuel ■ **~ season** saison *f* des amours.

matins ['mætɪnz] = **mattins**.

matriarch ['meɪtrɪɑ:k] *n* [ruler, head of family] chef *m* de famille *(dans un système matriarcal)* ■ [old woman] matrone *f*.

matriarchal [,meɪtrɪ'ɑ:kl] *adj* matriarcal.

matriarchy ['meɪtrɪɑ:kɪ] (*pl* **matriarchies**) *n* matriarcat *m*.

matrices ['meɪtrɪsi:z] *pl* ▷ **matrix**.

matricide ['mætrɪsaɪd] *n* **1.** [act] matricide *m* **2.** [person] matricide *mf*.

matriculate [mə'trɪkjʊleɪt] *vi* **1.** [register] s'inscrire, se faire immatriculer ■ [at university] s'inscrire **2.** *UK* SCH ≃ obtenir son baccalauréat.

matriculation [mə,trɪkjʊ'leɪʃn] *n* **1.** [registration] inscription *f*, immatriculation *f* ■ [at university] inscription *f* ■ **~ fees** droits *mpl* d'inscription **2.** *UK* SCH *ancien examen équivalent au baccalauréat*.

matrimonial [,mætrɪ'məʊnjəl] *adj* matrimonial, conjugal.

matrimony ['mætrɪmənɪ, *US* 'mætrɪməʊnɪ] (*pl* **matrimonies**) *n fml* mariage *m*.

matrix ['meɪtrɪks] (*pl* **matrixes** *OR pl* **matrices** ['meɪtrɪsi:z]) *n* matrice *f*.

matron ['meɪtrən] *n* **1.** *UK* [in hospital] infirmière *f* en chef ■ [in school] infirmière *f* **2.** *lit* [married woman] matrone *f*, mère *f* de famille **3.** [in retirement home] surveillante *f* **4.** *US* [in prison] gardienne *f*, surveillante *f*.

matronly ['meɪtrənlɪ] *adj* : **she looks very ~** elle a tout de la matrone.

matron of honour (*pl* **matrons of honour**) *n* dame *f* d'honneur.

matt [mæt] *adj* mat ■ ~ **paint** peinture *f* mate.

matte [mæt] <> *adj* = **matt**.
<> *n* METALL matte *f*, maton *m*.

matted ['mætɪd] *adj* [material] feutré ■ [hair] emmêlé ■ [vegetation, roots] enchevêtré.

matter ['mætər] <> *n* **1.** [affair] affaire *f* ■ [subject] sujet *m* ■ **I reported the ~ to the police** j'ai rapporté les faits à la police ■ **business ~s** affaires *fpl* ■ **money ~s** questions *fpl* d'argent ■ **this is no laughing ~** il n'y a pas de quoi rire ■ **it is no easy ~** c'est une question difficile *OR* un sujet délicat ■ **I will give the ~ my immediate attention** j'accorderai toute mon attention à ce problème ■ **you're not going out, and that's the end of** *OR* **there's an end to the ~!** tu ne sortiras pas, un point c'est tout! **2.** [question] question *f* ■ **there's the small ~ of the £100 you owe me** il y a ce petit problème des 100 livres que tu me dois ■ **a ~ of life and death** une question de vie ou de mort ■ **that's quite another ~, that's a different ~ altogether** ça c'est une (tout) autre affaire ■ **that's a ~ of opinion** ça c'est une question d'opinion ■ **as a ~ of course** tout naturellement ■ **as a ~ of principle** par principe ■ **as a ~ of urgency** d'urgence ■ **she'll do it in a ~ of minutes** cela ne lui prendra que quelques minutes ■ **it's only** *OR* **just a ~ of time** ce n'est qu'une question de temps ■ **it's only** *OR* **just a ~ of filling in a few forms** il ne s'agit que de remplir quelques formulaires
3. [physical substance] matière *f*
4. [written material] : **printed ~** texte *m* imprimé ; [sent by post] imprimés *mpl*
5. MED [pus] pus *m*
6. *phr* **what's the ~?** qu'est-ce qu'il y a?, qu'est-ce qui ne va pas? ■ **what's the ~ with Jim?** qu'est-ce qu'il a, Jim? ■ **what's the ~ with your eyes?** qu'est-ce que vous avez aux yeux? ■ **what's the ~ with the way I dress?** qu'est-ce que vous reprochez à ma façon de m'habiller? ■ **what's the ~ with telling him the truth?** quel mal y a-t-il à lui dire la vérité? ■ **there's something the ~ with my leg** j'ai quelque chose à la jambe ■ **is there something** *OR* **is anything the ~?** il y a quelque chose qui ne va pas?, il y a un problème? ■ **nothing's the** *OR* **there's nothing the ~** il n'y a rien, tout va bien ■ **nothing's the ~ with me** je vais parfaitement bien ■ **there's nothing the ~ with the engine** le moteur est en parfait état de marche ■ **no ~!** peu importe! ■ **no ~ what I do** quoi que je fasse ■ **no ~ what the boss thinks** peu importe ce qu'en pense le patron ■ **don't go back, no ~ how much he begs you** même s'il te le demande à genoux, n'y retourne pas ■ **no ~ what** quoi qu'il arrive ■ **no ~ how hard I try** quels que soient les efforts que je fais ■ **I must speak to her, no ~ how ill she is** je dois lui parler, quel que soit son état de santé ■ **no ~ where I am** où que je sois.
<> *vi* importer, avoir de l'importance ■ **what does it ~?** quelle importance est-ce que ça a?, qu'importe? ■ **it ~s a lot** cela a beaucoup d'importance, c'est très important ■ **it doesn't ~** cela n'a pas d'importance, ça ne fait rien ■ **it doesn't ~ to me what you do with your money** ce que tu fais de ton argent m'est égal ■ **money is all that ~s to him** il n'y a que l'argent qui l'intéresse ■ **she ~s a lot to him** il tient beaucoup à elle, elle compte beaucoup pour lui ■ **she knows all the people who ~** elle connaît tous les gens qui comptent.
◆ **matters** *npl* : **as ~s stand** les choses étant ce qu'elles sont ■ **getting angry won't help ~s at all** se mettre en colère n'arrangera pas les choses.
◆ **as a matter of fact** *adv phr* en fait, à vrai dire, en réalité.
◆ **for that matter** *adv phr* d'ailleurs.

Matterhorn ['mætəhɔ:n] *pr n* : **the ~** le mont Cervin.

matter-of-fact *adj* [down-to-earth] terre à terre *(inv)* ■ [prosaic] prosaïque ■ [unemotional] neutre ■ **Frank has a very ~ approach** Frank a une vision très pratique des choses ■ **he has a very ~ way of speaking** il dit les choses comme elles sont ■ **she took the news in a very ~ way** elle a pris les nouvelles avec beaucoup de sang-froid.

Matthew ['mæθju:] *pr n* Matthieu.

matting ['mætɪŋ] *n (U)* [used as mat] natte *f*, tapis *m*.

mattins ['mætɪnz] *n (U)* RELIG matines *fpl*.

mattock ['mætək] *n* pioche *f*.

mattress ['mætrɪs] *n* matelas *m*.

maturation [,mætjʊ'reɪʃn] *n* BOT & BIOL maturation *f* ■ *fig* mûrissement *m*.

mature [mə'tjʊər] <> *adj* **1.** [person - physically] mûr ; [- mentally] mûr, mature ■ **a man of ~ years** un homme d'âge mûr **2.** [cheese] fait ■ [wine, spirits] arrivé à maturité **3.** FIN échu.
<> *vi* **1.** [person, attitude] mûrir ■ **he has ~d into a very sensible young man** c'est maintenant un jeune homme plein de bon sens **2.** [wine] arriver à maturité ■ [cheese] se faire **3.** FIN arriver à échéance, échoir.
<> *vt* [cheese] faire mûrir, affiner ■ [wine, spirits] faire vieillir.

mature student *n* UNIV *adulte qui fait des études.*

maturity [mə'tjʊərətɪ] *n* **1.** [gen] maturité *f* ■ **to reach ~** [person] devenir majeur **2.** FIN : **~ (date)** échéance *f*.

matzo [mætsəʊ] *(pl* **matzos**) *n* pain *m* azyme.

maudlin ['mɔ:dlɪn] *adj* larmoyant, sentimental.

maul [mɔ:l] <> *vt* **1.** [attack - subj: animal] mutiler ; [- subj: person, crowd] malmener **2.** *inf* [handle clumsily] tripoter **3.** [criticize] démolir, mettre en pièces.
<> *vi* RUGBY faire un maul.
<> *n* RUGBY maul *m*.

Maundy money ['mɔ:ndɪ-] *n (U) pièces de monnaie spéciales offertes par le souverain britannique à certaines personnes âgées le jour du jeudi saint.*

Maundy Thursday ['mɔ:ndɪ-] *n* RELIG jeudi *m* saint.

Mauritania [,mɒrɪ'teɪnjə] *pr n* Mauritanie *f* ■ **in ~** en Mauritanie.

Mauritanian [,mɒrɪ'teɪnjən] <> *n* Mauritanien *m*, - enne *f*.
<> *adj* mauritanien.

Mauritian [mə'rɪʃn] <> *n* Mauricien *m*, - enne *f*.
<> *adj* mauricien.

Mauritius [mə'rɪʃəs] *pr n* l'île *f* Maurice ■ **in ~** à l'île Maurice.

mausoleum [,mɔ:sə'lɪəm] *n* mausolée *m*.

mauve [məʊv] <> *adj* mauve.
<> *n* mauve *m*.

maverick ['mævərɪk] <> *n* **1.** [person] franc-tireur *m*, indépendant *m*, - e *f* **2.** [calf] veau *m* non marqué.
<> *adj* non-conformiste, indépendant.

maw [mɔ:] *n* ZOOL [of cow] caillette *f* ■ [of bird] jabot *m* ■ *fig* gouffre *m*.

mawkish ['mɔ:kɪʃ] *adj* [sentimental] mièvre ■ [nauseating] écœurant.

max. *(written abbrev of* **maximum**) max.

maxi ['mæksɪ] <> *adj* [skirt, dress etc] maxi.
<> *n* maxi *m*.

maxilla [mæk'sɪlə] *(pl* **maxillae** [-li:]) *n* ANAT maxillaire *m*.

maxim ['mæksɪm] *n* maxime *f*.

maxima ['mæksɪmə] *pl* ▷ **maximum**.

maximal ['mæksɪml] *adj* maximal.

maximize, ise ['mæksɪmaɪz] *vt* maximiser, maximaliser.

maximum ['mæksɪməm] *(pl* **maximums** *OR pl* **maxima** ['mæksɪmə]) <> *n* maximum *m* ■ **to the ~** au maximum.
<> *adj* maximum, maximal ■ **~ load** charge *f* maximale *OR* limite ● **~ security prison** prison *f* de haute sécurité.
<> *adv* au maximum.

may[1] [meɪ] *modal vb* **1.** [expressing possibility] : **this ~ take some time** ça prendra peut-être *OR* il se peut que ça prenne du temps ■ **symptoms ~ disappear after a few days** les symptômes peuvent disparaître après quelques jours ■ **you ~ well be right** il est fort possible *OR* il se peut bien que vous ayez raison ■ **what he says ~ be true** ce qu'il dit est peut-être vrai ■ **she ~ not have arrived yet** il se peut *OR* il se pourrait qu'elle ne soit pas encore arrivée ■ **he ~ have been right** il avait peut-être raison

2. [expressing permission] : **you ~ sit down** vous pouvez vous asseoir ▪ **only close relatives ~ attend** seuls les parents proches sont invités à assister à la cérémonie ▪ **I will go home now, if I ~** je vais rentrer chez moi, si vous me le permettez ▪ **if I ~ say so** si je peux *OR* puis me permettre cette remarque ▪ **you ~ well ask!** bonne question!
3. [in polite questions, suggestions] : **~ I interrupt?** puis-je vous interrompre?, vous permettez que je vous interrompe? ▪ **~ I?** vous permettez? ▪ **~ I make a suggestion?** puis-je me permettre de faire une suggestion? ▪ **~ I buy you ladies a drink?** puis-je vous offrir un verre, mesdames? ▪ **~ I come too? – yes, you ~** puis-je venir aussi? – oui ▪ **~ I say how pleased we are that you could come** permettez-moi de vous dire à quel point nous sommes ravis que vous ayez pu venir
4. [contradicting a point of view] : **you ~ think I'm imagining things, but I think I'm being followed** tu vas croire que je divague mais je crois que je suis suivi ▪ **such facts ~ seem insignificant, but they could prove vital** de telles choses peuvent paraître insignifiantes mais elles pourraient se révéler vitales ▪ **he ~ not be very bright, but he's got a heart of gold** il n'est peut-être pas très brillant mais il a un cœur d'or ◆ **that's as ~ be** c'est possible
5. [giving additional information] : **this, it ~ be said, is yet another example of government interference** c'est là, on peut le dire, un autre exemple de l'interventionnisme de l'État
6. *fml* [expressing purpose] : **they work hard so that their children ~ have a better life** ils travaillent dur pour que leurs enfants aient une vie meilleure
7. [expressing wishes, hopes] : **~ she rest in peace** qu'elle repose en paix ▪ **~ the best man win!** que le meilleur gagne!
8. *phr* **~ as well : can I go home now? – you ~ as well** est-ce que je peux rentrer chez moi maintenant? – tu ferais aussi bien ▪ **we ~ as well have another drink** tant qu'à faire, autant prendre un autre verre.

may² [meɪ] *n* [hawthorn] aubépine *f*, épine *f* de mai.

May [meɪ] *n* mai *m*, *see also* **February**.

Maya ['maɪə] (*pl* **- s**) *n* **1.** (*pl inv OR pl* s) [person] Indien *m*, - enne *f* maya ▪ **the ~ (s)** les Mayas *mpl* **2.** LING maya *m*.

Mayan ['maɪən] ◇ *n* **1.** [person] Indien *m*, - enne *f* maya **2.** LING maya *m*.
◇ *adj* maya.

May ball *n bal qui se tient au mois de juin à l'université de Cambridge.*

maybe ['meɪbi:] *adv* peut-être ▪ **~ she'll come tomorrow** elle viendra peut-être demain ▪ **~ so** peut-être bien que oui ▪ **~ not** peut-être bien que non.

May bug *n* hanneton *m*.

Mayday ['meɪdeɪ] *n* [SOS] SOS *m* ▪ **to send out a ~ signal** envoyer un signal de détresse *OR* un SOS.

May Day *n* le Premier Mai.

mayflower ['meɪflaʊər] *n* [gen] fleur *f* printanière ▪ *UK* [marsh marigold] souci *m* d'eau ▪ *UK* [hawthorn] aubépine *f*.
◆ **Mayflower** *pr n* : **the Mayflower** *US* HIST le Mayflower ▪ **the Mayflower Compact** le covenant du Mayflower.

THE MAYFLOWER COMPACT

Accord signé à bord du *Mayflower* par les Pères pèlerins en novembre 1620, avant leur débarquement à Plymouth. Cette convention officialisait la création d'un gouvernement indépendant ; elle est considérée comme la première Constitution de l'Amérique du Nord.

mayfly ['meɪflaɪ] (*pl* **mayflies**) *n* éphémère *m*.

mayhem ['meɪhem] *n* **1.** [disorder] désordre *m* ▪ **to create** *OR* **to cause ~** semer la panique **2.** LAW mutilation *f* du corps humain.

mayn't [meɪnt] *UK* = **may not**.

mayonnaise [ˌmeɪə'neɪz] *n* mayonnaise *f*.

mayor [meər] *n* maire *m*, mairesse *f*.

mayoress ['meərɪs] *n* femme *f* du maire.

maypole ['meɪpəʊl] *n* ≃ arbre *m* de mai *(mât autour duquel on danse le Premier mai).*

May queen *n* reine *f* du Premier mai.

may've ['meɪəv] *inf* = **may have**.

May week *n semaine du mois de juin pendant laquelle se tiennent les "May balls".*

maze [meɪz] *n liter & fig* labyrinthe *m*, dédale *m*.

mazurka [mə'zɜ:kə] *n* mazurka *f*.

MB (*written abbrev of* **megabyte**) Mo.

MBA (*abbrev of* **Master of Business Administration**) *n (titulaire d'une) maîtrise de gestion.*

MBBS (*abbrev of* **Bachelor of Medicine and Surgery**) *n (titulaire d'une) licence de médecine et de chirurgie.*

MBE (*abbrev of* **Member of the Order of the British Empire**) *n (membre de) l'ordre de l'Empire britannique (titre honorifique).*

MBO (*abbrev of* **management buyout**) *n UK* RES *m*.

MC *n* **1.** = **master of ceremonies 2.** *US* = **Member of Congress**.

MCAT (*abbrev of* **Medical College Admissions Test**) *n test d'admission aux études de médecine.*

MCC (*abbrev of* **Marylebone Cricket Club**) *pr n célèbre club de cricket de Londres.*

McCarthyism [mə'kɑ:θɪɪzm] *n* POL maccartisme *m*, maccarthysme *m*.

MCCARTHYISM

Ce mouvement anticommuniste américain vit le jour dans les années 1950, et donna lieu à une chasse aux sorcières dans les milieux artistique, professionnel et politique. Il tire son nom du sénateur McCarthy. Celui-ci fut désavoué en 1954 par le Sénat.

McCoy [mə'kɔɪ] *n inf phr* **it's the real ~** c'est du vrai de vrai, c'est de l'authentique.

MCP (*abbrev of* **male chauvinist pig**) *n inf* phallo *m*.

MD ◇ *n* **1.** = **Doctor of Medicine 2.** = **managing director**.
◇ *written abbr of* **Maryland**.

MDT *n* = **Mountain Daylight Time**.

me¹ [mi:] ◇ *pron* **1.** [direct or indirect object - unstressed] me, m' *(before vowel or silent 'h')* ; [- stressed] moi ▪ **do you love me?** tu m'aimes? ▪ **give me a light** donne-moi du feu ▪ **what, me, tell a lie?** moi, mentir? **2.** [after preposition] moi ▪ **they're talking about me** ils parlent de moi **3.** [used instead of 'I'] moi ▪ **it's me** c'est moi ▪ **is it just me or is it cold in here?** c'est moi, ou bien il fait froid ici? ▪ **she's bigger than me** elle est plus grande que moi ▪ **this hairstyle isn't really me** *fig* cette coiffure, ce n'est pas vraiment mon style **4.** [in interjections] : **poor me!** pauvre de moi! ▪ **silly me!** que je suis bête!
◇ *n* moi *m* ▪ **now I'm going to show you the real me** maintenant je vais te montrer qui je suis ▪ **the me generation** *la génération des années 80, considérées comme celles de l'individualisme.*
◇ *det inf* = **my**.

me² [mi:] MUS = **mi**.

ME ◇ *n (U)* (*abbrev of* **myalgic encephalomyelitis**) myélo-encéphalite *f*.
◇ *written abbr of* **Maine**.

mead [mi:d] *n* [drink] hydromel *m*.

meadow ['medəʊ] *n* pré *m*, prairie *f*.

meadowland ['medəʊlænd] *n* prairie *f*, pâturages *mpl*.

meagre *UK*, **meager** *US* ['mi:gər] *adj* maigre.

meal [mi:l] *n* **1.** repas *m* ▪ **he had an enormous ~** il a mangé comme un ogre ▪ **have a nice ~!, enjoy your ~!** bon appétit! ▪ **they've invited us round for a ~** ils nous ont invités à manger ◆ **evening ~** dîner *m* ▪ **we have our evening ~ early** nous dînons tôt ▪ **to make a ~ of sthg** *inf* faire tout un plat de qqch **2.** [flour] farine *f* **3.** *(U)* *Scotland* [oatmeal] flocons *mpl* d'avoine.

meals on wheels *n service de repas à domicile à l'intention des invalides et des personnes âgées.*

meal ticket *n* **1.** *US* ticket *m* restaurant **2.** *inf* [source of income] gagne-pain *m inv*.

mealtime ['mi:ltaɪm] *n* [lunch] heure *f* du déjeuner ■ [dinner] heure *f* du dîner ■ **at ~s** aux heures des repas.

mealy ['mi:lɪ] (*comp* **mealier**, *superl* **mealiest**) *adj* **1.** [floury] farineux **2.** [pale] pâle.

mealy-mouthed [-'maʊðd] *adj* doucereux, patelin.

mean [mi:n] (*pret & pp* **meant** [ment]) ◇ *adj* **1.** [miserly] avare, radin, pingre ■ **they're very ~ about pay rises** ils accordent les augmentations de salaire au compte-gouttes
2. [nasty, unkind] méchant, vache ■ **don't be ~ to your sister!** ne sois pas méchant avec ta sœur! ■ **to play a ~ trick on sb** jouer un sale tour à qqn ■ **I feel ~ about not inviting her** j'ai un peu honte de ne pas l'avoir invitée ■ **he gets ~ after a few drinks** *US inf* il devient mauvais *OR* méchant après quelques verres ■ **~ weather** *US inf* sale temps
3. [inferior] : **the meanest intelligence** l'esprit le plus borné ■ **he's no ~ architect/guitarist** c'est un architecte/guitariste de talent ■ **it was no ~ feat** ce n'était pas un mince exploit
4. [average] moyen ■ **~ deviation** écart *m* moyen
5. △ [excellent] terrible, super ■ **she plays a ~ guitar** comme guitariste, elle est super ■ **he makes a ~ chocolate cake** pas mal, son gâteau au chocolat
6. [shabby] miteux, misérable ■ **~ slums** taudis misérables
7. *lit* [of lower rank or class] : **of ~ birth** de basse extraction.
◇ *n* **1.** [middle point] milieu *m*, moyen terme *m* ■ **the golden** *OR* **happy ~** le juste milieu
2. MATHS moyenne *f*.
◇ *vt* **1.** [signify - subj: word, gesture] vouloir dire, signifier ; [- subj: person] vouloir dire ■ **what do you ~?** qu'est-ce que tu veux dire? ■ **what do you ~ by "wrong"?** qu'entendez-vous par "faux"? ■ **what do you ~ you don't like the cinema?** comment ça, vous n'aimez pas le cinéma? ■ **do you ~** *OR* **you ~ it's over already?** tu veux dire que c'est déjà fini? ■ **how do you ~?** qu'entendez-vous par là? ■ **does the name Heathcliff ~ anything to you?** est-ce que le nom de Heathcliff vous dit quelque chose? ■ **that was when the word "friendship" still meant something** c'était à l'époque où le mot "amitié" avait encore un sens ■ **that doesn't ~ a thing!** ça ne veut (strictement) rien dire! ■ [requesting or giving clarification] : **do you ~ it?** tu es sérieux? ■ **she always says what she ~s** elle dit toujours ce qu'elle pense ▶ **I ~** [that's to say] je veux dire ■ **why diet? I ~, you're not exactly fat** pourquoi te mettre au régime? on ne peut pas dire que tu sois grosse ■ **I ~ to say...** ce que je veux dire c'est...
2. [imply, entail - subj: event, change] signifier ■ **going to see a film ~s driving into town** pour voir un film, nous sommes obligés de prendre la voiture et d'aller en ville ■ **she's never known what it ~s to be loved** elle n'a jamais su ce que c'est que d'être aimée
3. [matter, be of value] compter ■ **this watch ~s a lot to me** je suis très attaché à cette montre ■ **your friendship ~s a lot to her** votre amitié compte beaucoup pour elle ■ **you ~ everything to me** tu es tout pour moi ■ **he ~s nothing to me** il n'est rien pour moi ■ **I can't tell you what this ~s to me** je ne peux pas te dire ce que ça représente pour moi ■ **$20 ~s a lot to me** 20 dollars, c'est une grosse somme *OR* c'est beaucoup d'argent pour moi
4. [refer to] : **do you ~ us?** tu veux dire nous? ■ **it was you she meant when she said that** c'était à vous qu'elle pensait *OR* qu'elle faisait allusion quand elle a dit ça
5. [intend] avoir l'intention de, vouloir, compter ■ **we ~ to win** nous avons (bien) l'intention de gagner, nous comptons (bien) gagner ■ **I only meant to help** je voulais seulement me rendre utile ■ **I ~ to see him now – and I ~ now!** j'ai l'intention de le voir tout de suite, et quand je dis tout de suite, c'est tout de suite! ■ **I didn't ~ it!** [action] je ne l'ai pas fait exprès! ; [words] je n'étais pas sérieux! ■ **without ~ing to** involontairement ■ **I meant it as a joke** c'était une plaisanterie ■ **that remark was meant for you** cette remarque s'adressait à vous ■ **the present was meant for your brother** le cadeau était destiné à ton frère ■ **they're meant for each other** ils sont faits l'un pour l'autre ■ **it's meant to be a horse** c'est censé représenter un cheval ■ **perhaps I was meant to be a doctor** peut-être que j'étais fait pour être médecin ■ **it was meant to be** c'était écrit ■ **he ~s well** il a de bonnes intentions
6. [consider, believe] : **it's meant to be good for arthritis** il paraît que c'est bon pour l'arthrite ■ **this painting is meant to be by Rembrandt** ce tableau est censé être un Rembrandt
7. [suppose] : **that box isn't meant to be in here** cette boîte n'est pas censée être ici.

meander [mɪ'ændər] ◇ *vi* **1.** [river] serpenter, faire des méandres **2.** [person] errer (sans but), se promener au hasard.
◇ *n* méandre *m*.

meaning ['mi:nɪŋ] ◇ *n* sens *m*, signification *f* ■ **I don't know the ~ of this word** je ne connais pas le sens de ce mot, je ne sais pas ce que veut dire ce mot ■ **he doesn't know the ~ of hard work** il ne sait pas ce que c'est que de travailler dur ■ **they're just good friends, if you get my ~** ils sont seulement bons amis, si vous voyez ce que je veux dire ■ **what's the ~ of this?** [in anger] qu'est-ce que ça veut dire? ■ **the ~ of life** le sens de la vie ■ **our success gives ~ to what we're doing** notre réussite donne un sens à ce que nous faisons.
◇ *adj* [look, smile] significatif, éloquent.

meaningful ['mi:nɪŋfʊl] *adj* **1.** [expressive - gesture] significatif, éloquent ■ **she gave him a ~ look** elle lui adressa un regard qui en disait long **2.** [comprehensible - explanation] compréhensible ■ [significant] significatif **3.** [profound - experience, relationship] profond.

meaningfully ['mi:nɪŋfʊlɪ] *adv* de façon significative.

meaningless ['mi:nɪŋlɪs] *adj* **1.** [devoid of sense] dénué de sens, sans signification ■ **the lyrics of this song are completely ~** les paroles de cette chanson n'ont absolument aucun sens **2.** [futile] futile, vain ■ **a ~ task** une tâche inutile ■ **~ violence** de la violence gratuite.

meanness ['mi:nnɪs] *n* **1.** [stinginess] avarice *f* **2.** *US* [nastiness, spitefulness] méchanceté *f*, mesquinerie *f* **3.** *lit* [poverty] pauvreté *f*.

means [mi:nz] (*pl inv*) ◇ *n* **1.** [way, method] moyen *m* ■ **a ~ of doing sthg** un moyen de faire qqch ■ **is there no ~ of doing it any faster?** n'y a-t-il pas moyen de le faire plus vite? ■ **he has no ~ of support** il est sans ressources ■ **it's just a ~ to an end** ce n'est qu'un moyen d'arriver au but ■ **the end justifies the ~** *prov* la fin justifie les moyens ■ **by ~ of a screwdriver** à l'aide d'un tournevis ■ **they communicate by ~ of signs** ils communiquent par signes ■ **by some ~ or other** *OR* **another** d'une façon ou d'une autre ▶ **~ of transport** moyen de transport ■ **~ of production** moyens de production **2.** *phr* **may I leave? – by all ~!** puis-je partir? – je vous en prie *OR* mais bien sûr! ■ **by no (manner of) ~** pas du tout ■ **it's by no ~ easy** c'est loin d'être facile ■ **she's not his friend by any (manner of) ~** elle est loin d'être son amie.
◇ *npl* [money, resources] moyens *mpl*, ressources *fpl* ■ **to live within one's ~** vivre selon ses moyens ■ **to live beyond one's ~** vivre au-dessus de ses moyens ■ **her family obviously has ~** il est évident qu'elle vient d'une famille aisée.

mean-spirited *adj* mesquin.

means test *n* enquête *f* sur les revenus *(d'une personne désirant bénéficier d'une allocation d'État)* ■ **the grant is subject to a ~** cette allocation est assujettie à des conditions de ressources.
◆ **means-test** *vt* : **is unemployment benefit means-tested?** les allocations de chômage sont-elles attribuées en fonction des ressources *OR* des revenus du bénéficiaire? ■ **all applicants are means-tested** tous les candidats font l'objet d'une enquête sur leurs revenus.

meant [ment] *pt & pp* ⊳ **mean**.

meantime ['mi:n,taɪm] *adv* pendant ce temps.
◆ **in the meantime** *adv phr* entre-temps.
◆ **for the meantime** *adv phr* pour l'instant.

meanwhile ['mi:n,waɪl] *adv* entre-temps, pendant ce temps ■ **I, ~, was stuck in the lift** pendant ce temps, moi, j'étais coincé dans l'ascenseur.

measles ['mi:zlz] *n* rougeole *f.*

measly ['mi:zlɪ] (*comp* **measlier**, *superl* **measliest**) *adj inf* minable, misérable ■ **all that for a ~ £5!** tout ça pour cinq malheureuses livres!

measurable ['meʒərəbl] *adj* **1.** [rate, change, amount] mesurable **2.** [noticeable, significant] sensible, perceptible.

measurably ['meʒərəblɪ] *adv* [noticeably, significantly] sensiblement, notablement.

measure ['meʒər] <> *n* **1.** [measurement] mesure *f* ■ **weights and ~s** les poids *mpl* et mesures ■ **linear/square/cubic ~** mesure de longueur/de superficie/de volume ■ **to give good** *OR* **full ~** [in length, quantity] faire bonne mesure ; [in weight] faire bon poids ■ **to give short ~** [in quantity] tricher sur la quantité ; [in weight] tricher sur le poids ■ **for good ~** *fig* pendant qu'il/elle y est ■ **then he painted the door, just for good ~** et puis, pendant qu'il y était, il a peint la porte ■ **to take** *OR* **to get the ~ of sb** *fig* jauger qqn, se faire une opinion de qqn ■ **this award is a ~ of their success** ce prix ne fait que refléter leur succès ■ **her joy was beyond ~** sa joie était incommensurable ● **'Measure for Measure'** ***Shakespeare*** 'Mesure pour mesure' **2.** [degree] mesure *f* ■ **in some ~** dans une certaine mesure, jusqu'à un certain point ■ **in large ~** dans une large mesure, en grande partie **3.** [device - ruler] mètre *m*, règle *f* ; [- container] mesure *f* ■ **a pint ~** une mesure d'une pinte **4.** [portion] portion *f*, dose *f* **5.** [step, legislation] mesure *f* ■ **as a precautionary ~** par mesure de précaution ■ **we have taken ~s to correct the fault** nous avons pris des mesures pour rectifier l'erreur **6.** MUS & LIT mesure *f.*
<> *vt* **1.** [take measurement of] mesurer ■ **he ~d me for a suit** il a pris mes mesures pour me faire un costume ● **to ~ one's length** s'étaler de tout son long **2.** [judge] jauger, mesurer, évaluer ■ **to ~ oneself** *OR* **one's strength against sb** se mesurer à qqn.
<> *vi* mesurer ■ **the room ~s 18 feet by 12** la pièce mesure 18 pieds sur 12.
◆ **measure off** *vt sep* mesurer.
◆ **measure out** *vt sep* mesurer ■ **he ~d out a double gin** il versa un double gin.
◆ **measure up** <> *vt sep* mesurer ■ **to ~ sb up** *fig* jauger qqn, prendre la mesure de qqn.
<> *vi insep* être *OR* se montrer à la hauteur ■ **to ~ up to sb's expectations** répondre aux espérances de qqn ■ **the hotel didn't ~ up (to our expectations)** l'hôtel nous a déçus.

measured ['meʒəd] *adj* **1.** [distance, length etc] mesuré **2.** [careful, deliberate] mesuré.

measurement ['meʒəmənt] *n* **1.** [dimension] mesure *f* ■ **to take (down) the ~s of a piece of furniture** prendre les dimensions d'un meuble ■ **waist/hip ~** tour *m* de taille/de hanches ■ **what are her ~s?** quelles sont ses mensurations? **2.** [act] mesurage *m.*

measuring ['meʒərɪŋ] *n* mesurage *m.*

measuring jug *n* verre *m* gradué, doseur *m.*

measuring tape *n* mètre *m* à ruban.

meat [mi:t] *n* **1.** viande *f* ■ **cooked** *OR* **cold ~s** viande froide **2.** *lit* [food] nourriture *f* ■ **one man's ~ is another man's poison** *prov* ce qui est bon pour les uns ne l'est pas forcément pour les autres **3.** [substance, core] substance *f* ■ **there's not much ~ in his report** il n'y a pas grand-chose dans son rapport.

meatball ['mi:tbɔ:l] *n* CULIN boulette *f* (de viande).

meat-eater *n* carnivore *mf* ■ **we aren't big ~s** nous ne mangeons pas beaucoup de viande, nous ne sommes pas de gros mangeurs de viande.

meat-eating *adj* carnivore.

meat hook *n* crochet *m* de boucherie.

meat loaf (*pl* **meat loaves**) *n* pain *m* de viande.

meatus [mɪ'eɪtəs] *n* ANAT conduit *m*, méat *m.*

meaty ['mi:tɪ] (*comp* **meatier**, *superl* **meatiest**) *adj* **1.** [taste] de viande ■ **a good, ~ meal** [full of meat] un bon repas riche en viande **2.** [rich in ideas] substantiel, étoffé.

Mecca ['mekə] *pr n* la Mecque.
◆ **mecca** *n fig* **it's a ~ for book lovers** c'est la Mecque des bibliophiles ■ **the ~ of country music** le haut lieu de la country.

mechanic [mɪ'kænɪk] *n* mécanicien *m.*

mechanical [mɪ'kænɪkl] *adj* **1.** [device, process] mécanique ■ **~ shovel** pelle *f* mécanique, pelleteuse *f* **2.** [machine-like] machinal, mécanique ■ **a ~ gesture** un geste machinal.

mechanical drawing *n* dessin *m* aux instruments.

mechanical engineer *n* ingénieur *m* mécanicien.

mechanical engineering *n* [study] mécanique *f* ■ [industry] construction *f* mécanique.

mechanically [mɪ'kænɪklɪ] *adv* mécaniquement ■ *fig* machinalement, mécaniquement ■ **~ recovered meat** viande *f* séparée mécaniquement.

mechanics [mɪ'kænɪks] <> *n (U)* [study] mécanique *f.*
<> *npl* [functioning] mécanisme *m* ■ **the ~ of government** les mécanismes gouvernementaux, les rouages du gouvernement ■ **I haven't got to grips yet with the ~ of the system** je n'ai pas encore compris comment fonctionne le système.

mechanism ['mekənɪzm] *n* mécanisme *m.*

mechanistic [,mekə'nɪstɪk] *adj* mécaniste.

mechanization [,mekənaɪ'zeɪʃn] *n* mécanisation *f.*

mechanize, ise ['mekənaɪz] *vt* **1.** [equip with machinery] mécaniser ■ **a highly ~d industry** une industrie fortement mécanisée **2.** MIL [motorize] motoriser.

MEd [,em'ed] (*abbrev of* **Master of Education**) *n (titulaire d'une) maîtrise en sciences de l'éducation.*

medal ['medl] *n* médaille *f* ■ **gold ~** médaille d'or.

medalist *US* = **medallist.**

medallion [mɪ'dæljən] *n* médaillon *m* ■ **~ man** *hum type du séducteur macho.*

medallist *UK*, **medalist** *US* ['medəlɪst] *n* [winner of medal] médaillé *m*, - e *f* ■ **the bronze ~** le détenteur de la médaille de bronze.

meddle ['medl] *vi* **1.** [interfere] : **to ~ in sthg** se mêler de qqch ■ **he can't resist the temptation to ~** il ne peut pas s'empêcher de se mêler de tout *OR* de ce qui ne le regarde pas **2.** [tamper] : **to ~ with sthg** toucher à qqch, tripoter qqch.

meddler ['medlər] *n* **1.** [busybody] : **she's such a ~** il faut toujours qu'elle fourre son nez partout **2.** [tamperer] touche-à-tout *mf inv.*

meddlesome ['medlsəm] *adj* indiscret, - ète *f*, qui se mêle de tout.

Medea [mɪ'dɪə] *pr n* Médée.

media ['mi:djə] <> *npl* **1.** *(often sg)* **the ~** les médias *mpl* ■ **the power of the ~** la puissance des médias ■ **the news ~** la presse ■ **he knows how to handle the ~** il sait s'y prendre avec les journalistes **2.** ▷ **medium.**
<> *comp* des médias ■ [interest, coverage] médiatique ■ **~ person** homme *m* de communication, femme *f* de communication.

mediaeval *etc* [,medɪ'i:vl] = **medieval.**

media event *n* événement *m* médiatique.

medial ['mi:djəl] <> *adj* **1.** [average] moyen **2.** [middle] médian **3.** LING médial, médian.
<> *n* LING médiale *f.*

median ['mi:djən] <> *adj* médian.
<> *n* **1.** MATHS médiane *f* **2.** *US* AUT = **median strip.**

median strip *n US* terre-plein *m* central.

media studies *npl études de communication.*

mediate ['mi:dɪeɪt] <> *vi* [act as a peacemaker] servir de médiateur ■ **to ~ in a dispute** servir de médiateur dans un conflit ■ **to ~ between** servir d'intermédiaire entre.

◇ *vt* **1.** [agreement, peace] obtenir par médiation ■ [dispute] servir de médiateur dans, se faire le médiateur de ■ **to ~ a dispute** servir de médiateur dans un conflit **2.** [moderate] modérer.

mediation [,mi:dɪ'eɪʃn] *n* médiation *f*.

mediator ['mi:dɪeɪtəʳ] *n* médiateur *m*, - trice *f*.

medic ['medɪk] *n inf* **1.** [doctor] toubib *m* **2.** *UK* [medical student] étudiant *m* en médecine.

Medicaid ['medɪkeɪd] *pr n US* assistance *f* médicale.

medical ['medɪkl] ◇ *adj* médical ■ **~ board** commission *f* médicale ; MIL conseil *m* de révision ■ **~ insurance** assurance *f* maladie ■ **~ officer** INDUST médecin *mf* du travail ; MIL médecin *mf* militaire ■ **Medical Officer of Health** directeur *m*, - trice *f* de la santé publique ■ **~ practitioner** (médecin *mf*) généraliste *mf* ■ **the ~ profession** le corps médical ■ **~ school** faculté *f* de médecine ■ **~ student** étudiant *m*, - e *f* en médecine.
◇ *n* visite *f* médicale ■ **to have a ~** passer une visite médicale ■ **to pass/fail a ~** être déclaré apte/inapte à un travail après un bilan de santé.

medical certificate *n* certificat *m* médical.

medical examination *n* visite *f* médicale.

medically ['medɪklɪ] *adv* médicalement ■ **~ approved** approuvé par les autorités médicales.

Medical Research Council *pr n organisme public de financement des centres de recherche médicale et des hôpitaux en Grande-Bretagne.*

medicament [mɪ'dɪkəmənt] *n* médicament *m*.

Medicare ['medɪkeəʳ] *pr n aux États-Unis, programme fédéral d'assistance médicale pour personnes âgées qui a largement contribué à réhabiliter socialement le 3ᵉ âge.*

medicated ['medɪkeɪtɪd] *adj* traitant.

medication [,medɪ'keɪʃn] *n* médication *f* ■ **to be on ~** être sous médicaments.

medicinal [me'dɪsɪnl] *adj* médicinal.

medicine ['medsɪn] *n* **1.** [art] médecine *f* ■ **to practise ~** exercer la médecine ■ **he studies ~** il est étudiant en médecine **2.** [substance] médicament *m*, remède *m* ■ **don't forget to take your ~** n'oublie pas de prendre tes médicaments ❯ **to take one's ~** *UK* avaler la pilule ■ **to give sb a dose** *OR* **taste of his/her own ~** rendre à qqn la monnaie de sa pièce.

medicine ball *n* medicine-ball *m*, médecine-ball *m*.

medicine cabinet, medicine chest *n* (armoire *f* à) pharmacie *f*.

medicine man *n* sorcier *m*, medicine-man *m*.

medieval [,medɪ'i:vl] *adj* médiéval.

medievalist [,medɪ'i:vəlɪst] *n* médiéviste *mf*.

mediocre [,mi:dɪ'əʊkəʳ] *adj* médiocre.

mediocrity [,mi:dɪ'ɒkrətɪ] (*pl* **mediocrities**) *n* **1.** [gen] médiocrité *f* **2.** [mediocre person] médiocre *mf*, incapable *mf*.

meditate ['medɪteɪt] *vi* **1.** [practise meditation] méditer **2.** [reflect, ponder] réfléchir, songer ■ **to ~ on** *OR* **upon sthg** réfléchir *OR* songer à qqch.

meditation [,medɪ'teɪʃn] *n* méditation *f*, réflexion *f*.

meditative ['medɪtətɪv] *adj* méditatif.

Mediterranean [,medɪtə'reɪnjən] ◇ *pr n* : **the ~ (Sea)** la (mer) Méditerranée.
◇ *adj* méditerranéen.

medium ['mi:djəm] ◇ *n* **1.** (*pl* media ['mi:djə]) [means of communication] moyen *m* (de communication) ■ **the decision was made public through the ~ of the press** la décision fut rendue publique par voie de presse *OR* par l'intermédiaire des journaux ■ **television is a powerful ~ in education** la télévision est un très bon instrument éducatif ■ **his favourite ~ is watercolour** son moyen d'expression favori est l'aquarelle **2.** (*pl* media ['mi:djə] *OR pl* mediums) PHYS [means of transmission] véhicule *m*, milieu *m* ■ **sound travels through the ~ of air** les sons sont propagés *OR* véhiculés par l'air **3.** (*pl* media ['mi:djə] *OR pl* mediums) BIOL [environment] milieu *m* **4.** (*pl* mediums) [spiritualist] médium *m* **5.** (*pl* mediums) [middle course] milieu *m* ■ **the happy ~** le juste milieu **6.** (*pl* mediums) [size] taille *f* moyenne.
◇ *adj* **1.** [gen] moyen ■ **in the ~ term** à moyen terme ■ **~ brown** châtain **2.** CULIN [meat] à point.

medium-dry *adj* [wine] demi-sec.

medium-range *adj* : **~ missile** missile *m* à moyenne portée.

medium-rare *adj* CULIN [meat] entre saignant et à point.

medium-sized *adj* moyen, de taille moyenne.

medium-term *adj* à moyen terme.

medium wave *n (U)* RADIO ondes *fpl* moyennes ■ **on ~** sur (les) ondes moyennes.
◆ **medium-wave** *adj* [broadcast] sur ondes moyennes ■ [station, transmitter] émettant sur ondes moyennes.

medley ['medlɪ] *n* **1.** [mixture] mélange *m* **2.** MUS pot-pourri *m* **3.** [in swimming] quatre nages *m inv*.

medulla [mɪ'dʌlə] *n* ANAT [part of organ, structure] moelle *f* ■ [part of brain] bulbe *m* rachidien.

Medusa [mɪ'dju:zə] *pr n* Méduse.

meek [mi:k] *adj* doux, douce *f*, docile ■ **~ and mild** doux comme un agneau.

meekly ['mi:klɪ] *adv* doucement, docilement.

meerschaum ['mɪəʃəm] *n* **1.** [pipe] pipe *f* en écume **2.** [mineral] écume *f* de mer, magnésite *f*.

meet [mi:t] (*pret & pp* **met** [met]) ◇ *vt* **1.** [by chance] rencontrer ■ **to ~ sb on the stairs** croiser qqn dans l'escalier ■ **fancy ~ing you here!** je ne m'attendais pas à vous trouver ici! ▮ [by arrangement] rejoindre, retrouver ■ **I'll ~ you on the platform in 20 minutes** je te retrouve sur le quai dans 20 minutes ■ **I'm ~ing Gregory this afternoon** j'ai rendez-vous avec Gregory cet après-midi ■ **the train ~s the ferry at Dover** le train assure la correspondance avec le ferry à Douvres
2. [wait for, collect] attendre, aller *OR* venir chercher ■ **nobody was at the station to ~ me** personne ne m'attendait à la gare ■ **I'll be there to ~ the bus** je serai là à l'arrivée du car ■ **he'll ~ us at the station** il viendra nous chercher à la gare ■ **I'll send a car to ~ you** j'enverrai une voiture vous chercher *OR* vous prendre
3. [greet] : **she came to ~ us** elle est venue à notre rencontre
4. [make acquaintance of] rencontrer, faire la connaissance de ■ **I met him last year** je l'ai rencontré *OR* j'ai fait sa connaissance l'année dernière ■ **I'd like you to ~ Mr Jones** j'aimerais vous présenter M. Jones ■ **~ Mrs Dickens** je vous présente Mme Dickens ■ **(I'm very) glad** *OR* **pleased to ~ you** enchanté (de faire votre connaissance)
5. [satisfy] satisfaire, répondre à ■ **supply isn't ~ing demand** l'offre est inférieure à la demande ■ **to ~ sb halfway** *fig* trouver un compromis avec qqn ■ **they decided to ~ each other halfway** ils décidèrent de couper la poire en deux ▮ [settle] régler ■ **I couldn't ~ the payments** je n'ai pas pu régler *OR* payer les échéances
6. [face] rencontrer, affronter ■ **to ~ the enemy** affronter l'ennemi ■ **how are we going to ~ the challenge?** comment allons-nous relever le défi? ■ **to ~ one's death** trouver la mort
7. [come in contact with] rencontrer ■ **it's the first case of this sort I've met** c'est la première fois que je vois un cas semblable ■ **his hand met hers** leurs mains se rencontrèrent ■ **my eyes met his** nos regards se croisèrent *OR* se rencontrèrent
8. [treat] accueillir ■ **his suggestion was met with howls of laughter** sa proposition a été accueillie par des éclats de rire ■ **we shall ~ violence with violence** à la violence, nous répondrons par la violence.
◇ *vi* **1.** [by chance] se rencontrer ■ **we met on the stairs** nous nous sommes croisés dans l'escalier ▮ [by arrangement] se retrouver, se rejoindre, se donner rendez-vous ■ **shall we ~ at the station?** on se retrouve *OR* on se donne rendez-vous à la gare? ■ **they weren't to ~ again for a long time** ils ne devaient

pas se revoir avant longtemps ▪ **until we ~ again!** à la prochaine! ▪ **I think they ~ every day** je crois qu'ils se voient tous les jours
2. [become acquainted] se rencontrer, faire connaissance ▪ **we first met in 1989** nous nous sommes rencontrés pour la première fois en 1989 ▪ **have you two met?** est-ce que vous vous connaissez déjà?, vous vous êtes déjà rencontrés?
3. [assemble] se réunir ▪ **the committee ~s once a month** le comité se réunit une fois par mois
4. [join - lines, wires] se rencontrer, se joindre ▪ **the cross stands where four roads ~** la croix se trouve à la jonction de quatre routes ▪ **their eyes met** leurs regards se rencontrèrent *OR* se croisèrent
5. [teams, opponents] se rencontrer, s'affronter ▪ [armies] s'affronter, se heurter.
◇ *n* **1.** *UK* [in hunting] rendez-vous *m* (de chasse)
2. *US* SPORT rencontre *f*.
◇ *adj arch & fml* [suitable] séant, convenable ▪ [right] juste.
➡ **meet up** *vi insep* [by chance] se rencontrer ▪ [by arrangement] se retrouver, se donner rendez-vous ▪ **to ~ up with sb** retrouver qqn.
➡ **meet with** *vt insep* **1.** [encounter] rencontrer ▪ **they met with considerable difficulties** ils ont rencontré d'énormes difficultés ▪ **the agreement met with general approval** l'accord a reçu l'approbation générale ▪ **to ~ with a refusal** se heurter à *OR* essuyer un refus ▪ **the play met with great success** la pièce a eu beaucoup de succès ▪ **I'm afraid your dog has met with an accident** j'ai bien peur que votre chien n'ait eu un (petit) accident
2. *US* = **meet** *(vt senses 1 & 2)*.
Voir module d'usage

meeting ['mi:tɪŋ] *n* **1.** [assembly] réunion *f* ▪ POL assemblée *f*, meeting *m* ▪ *UK* SPORT rencontre *f*, meeting *m* ▪ **to hold a ~** tenir une réunion ▪ **to call a ~ of the committee/the workforce** convoquer les membres du comité/le personnel ▪ **the (general) ~ of shareholders** l'assemblée (générale) des actionnaires ➔ **athletics ~** rencontre *f OR* meeting *m* d'athlétisme ▪ **committee ~** réunion du comité **2.** [encounter] rencontre *f* **3.** [arranged] rendez-vous *m* ▪ **I have a ~ with the boss this morning** j'ai rendez-vous avec le patron ce matin ▪ **the Governor had a ~ with Church dignitaries** le Gouverneur s'est entretenu avec *OR* a rencontré les dignitaires de l'Église **4.** [junction - of roads] jonction *f*, rencontre *f* ; [- of rivers] confluent *m* **5.** RELIG [Quakers'] culte *m* ▪ **to go to ~** aller au culte.

meetinghouse ['mi:tɪŋhaʊs], [-haʊzɪz] *n* RELIG temple *m*.

meeting place *n* [for gatherings] lieu *m* de réunion ▪ [for rendez-vous] (lieu *m* de) rendez-vous *m*.

mega- ['megə-] *in cpds inf* super, méga-.

megabit ['megəbɪt] *n* COMPUT méga-bit *m*.

megabuck ['megəbʌk] *n US inf* million *m* de dollars.

megabyte ['megəbaɪt] *n* mégaoctet *m*.

megadeath ['megədeθ] *n* million *m* de morts.

megahertz ['megəhɜ:ts] *(pl inv) n* mégahertz *m*.

megalith ['megəlɪθ] *n* mégalithe *m*.

megalithic [,megə'lɪθɪk] *adj* mégalithique.

megalomania [,megələ'meɪnjə] *n* mégalomanie *f*.

megalomaniac [,megələ'meɪnɪæk] ◇ *adj* mégalomane.
◇ *n* mégalomane *mf*.

megalopolis [,megə'lɒpəlɪs] *n* mégapole *f*, mégalopole *f*.

megaphone ['megəfəʊn] *n* porte-voix *m inv*, mégaphone *m*.

megastar ['megəstɑ:ʳ] *n inf* superstar *f*.

megaton ['megətʌn] *n* mégatonne *f*.

megawatt ['megəwɒt] *n* mégawatt *m*.

meiosis [maɪ'əʊsɪs] *(pl* **meioses** [-si:z]*)* *n* **1.** BIOL méiose *f* **2.** [in rhetoric] litote *f*.

melamine ['meləmi:n] *n* mélamine *f*.

melancholia [,melən'kəʊljə] *n* PSYCHOL mélancolie *f*.

melancholic [,melən'kɒlɪk] ◇ *adj* mélancolique.
◇ *n* mélancolique *mf*.

melancholy ['melənkəlɪ] ◇ *n lit* mélancolie *f*.
◇ *adj* [person, mood] mélancolique ▪ [news, sight, thought] sombre, triste.

Melanesia [,melə'ni:zjə] *pr n* Mélanésie *f* ▪ **in ~** en Mélanésie.

Melanesian [,melə'ni:zjən] ◇ *n* **1.** [person] Mélanésien *m*, - enne *f* **2.** LING mélanésien *m*.
◇ *adj* mélanésien.

melanin ['melənɪn] *n* mélanine *f*.

melanoma [,melə'nəʊmə] *n* mélanome *m*.

Melba toast *n tartine de pain grillé très fine.*

Melchior ['melkɪ,ɔ:ʳ] *pr n* Melchior.

meld [meld] ◇ *n* CARDS pose *f*.
◇ *vt US* [merge] fusionner, amalgamer.

melee, mêlée ['meleɪ] *n* mêlée *f*.

mellifluous [me'lɪfluəs], **mellifluent** [me'lɪfluənt] *adj lit* mélodieux, doux, douce *f*.

mellow ['meləʊ] ◇ *adj* **1.** [fruit] mûr ▪ [wine] velouté **2.** [bricks] patiné ▪ [light] doux, douce *f*, tamisé ▪ [colour] doux, douce *f* ▪ [voice, music] doux, douce *f*, mélodieux **3.** [person, mood] serein, tranquille ▪ **to become** *OR* **to grow ~** s'adoucir **4.** *inf* [relaxed] cool, relax, relaxe **5.** *inf* [tipsy] éméché, gai.
◇ *vt* [subj: age, experience] adoucir ▪ [subj: food, alcohol] détendre, décontracter.
◇ *vi* **1.** [fruit] mûrir ▪ [wine] devenir moelleux, se velouter **2.** [light, colour] s'adoucir ▪ [stone, brick, building] se patiner ▪ [sound, music] s'adoucir, devenir plus mélodieux **3.** [person] : **he's mellowed (with age)** il s'est adouci avec l'âge ▪ [with food, alcohol] se décontracter.
➡ **mellow out** *vi insep inf* [relax] se calmer, se détendre.

mellowing ['meləʊɪŋ] ◇ *n* **1.** [of fruit, wine] maturation *f* **2.** [of person, mood, light] adoucissement *m* ▪ [of stone] patine *f*.
◇ *adj* adoucissant.

ARRANGING TO MEET SOMEBODY

On pourrait se voir *OU* **se retrouver quelque part la semaine prochaine.** How about meeting up somewhere next week?

Tu es libre demain à déjeuner ? Are you free for lunch tomorrow?

Mardi 10 h 30, ça te va ? Is Tuesday at 10.30 OK for you?

Nous avons rendez-vous avec l'agent immobilier devant l'immeuble. We're meeting the estate agent in front of the building.

Disons demain, 20 h 30, devant le cinéma. Let's say tomorrow, 8.30, in front of the cinema.

Retrouvons-nous devant l'entrée principale du musée. Let's meet outside the main entrance of the museum.

On se retrouve *OU* **On se donne rendez-vous à l'entrée du parc, d'accord ?** Let's meet at the entrance to the park, OK?

Je passe te prendre chez toi à 8 heures. I'll pick you up at your place at 8 o'clock.

mellowness ['meləʊnɪs] *n* **1.** [of fruit] douceur *f* ■ [of wine] moelleux *m*, velouté *m* **2.** [of light, colour] douceur *f* ■ [of voice, music] douceur *f*, mélodie *f* **3.** [of person, mood] douceur *f*, sérénité *f*.

melodic [mɪ'lɒdɪk] *adj* mélodique.

melodious [mɪ'ləʊdjəs] *adj* mélodieux.

melodrama ['melədrɑːmə] *n* mélodrame *m*.

melodramatic [,melədrə'mætɪk] *adj* mélodramatique.

melodramatically [,melədrə'mætɪklɪ] *adv* de façon mélodramatique.

melody ['melədɪ] (*pl* **melodies**) *n* mélodie *f*.

melon ['melən] *n* melon *m*.

melt [melt] <> *vi* **1.** [become liquid] fondre ■ **that chocolate ~s in your mouth** ce chocolat fond dans la bouche ■ **his heart ~ed** ça l'a attendri **2.** [disappear] : **to ~ (away)** disparaître, s'évaporer ■ **her anger ~ed away** sa colère s'est évanouie ■ **the crowd ~ed (away)** la foule s'est dispersée **3.** [blend] se fondre ■ **he tried to ~ into the crowd** il a essayé de se fondre *OR* de disparaître dans la foule.
<> *vt* [gen] (faire) fondre ■ [metal] fondre ■ **to ~ sb's heart** attendrir (le cœur de) qqn.
◆ **melt down** *vt sep* & *vi insep* fondre.

meltdown ['meltdaʊn] *n* NUCL PHYS fusion *f* (du cœur).

melting ['meltɪŋ] <> *adj* **1.** *liter* fondant ■ **~ ice/snow** de la glace/neige qui fond **2.** *fig* attendrissant.
<> *n* [of ice, snow] fonte *f* ■ [of metal] fusion *f*, fonte *f*.

melting point *n* point *m* de fusion.

melting pot *n* creuset *m* ■ **a ~ of several cultures** *fig* un mélange de plusieurs cultures ■ **the American ~** *fig* le melting-pot américain.

member ['membəʳ] <> *n* **1.** [of club, union, political party etc] membre *m*, adhérent *m*, - e *f* ■ **to become a ~ of a club/society** devenir membre d'un club/d'une association ■ **he became a ~ of the party in 1985** il a adhéré au parti en 1985 **2.** [of group, family, class] membre *m* ■ **you're practically a ~ of the family now** tu fais presque partie de la famille maintenant ■ **it's a ~ of the cat family** il fait partie de *OR* il appartient à la famille des félins ■ **a ~ of the opposite sex** un représentant du sexe opposé ■ **a ~ of the audience** un spectateur **3.** ANAT, ARCHIT & MATHS membre *m* ■ **(male) ~** ANAT membre (viril).
<> *comp* : **~ country/state** pays *m* /état *m* membre.
◆ **Member** *n* [of legislative body] : **Member of Parliament** membre *m* de la Chambre des communes, ≃ député *m*, -e *f* ■ **the Member (of Parliament) for Leicester** le député de Leicester ■ **Member of Congress** membre *m* du Congrès ■ **Member of the House of Representatives** membre *m* de la Chambre des représentants.

membership ['membəʃɪp] *n* **1.** [condition] adhésion *f* ■ **to apply for ~** faire une demande d'adhésion ■ **they have applied for ~ to the EC** ils ont demandé à entrer dans *OR* à faire partie de la CEE ■ **to take up party ~** prendre sa carte du *OR* adhérer au parti ■ **it's hard to get ~ of the golf club** il est difficile de devenir membre du club de golf ◐ **~ card** carte *f* d'adhérent *OR* de membre ■ **~ fee** cotisation *f* **2.** [body of members] : **our club has a large ~** notre club compte de nombreux adhérents *OR* membres ■ **we have a ~ of about 20** nous avons environ 20 adhérents.

membrane ['membreɪn] *n* membrane *f*.

memento [mɪ'mentəʊ] (*pl* **mementos** *OR pl* **mementoes**) *n* souvenir *m*.

memo ['meməʊ] (*pl* **memos**) *n* note *f*.

memoir ['memwɑːʳ] *n* **1.** [biography] biographie *f* **2.** [essay, monograph] mémoire *m*.
◆ **memoirs** *npl* [autobiography] mémoires *mpl*.

memo pad *n* bloc-notes *m*.

memorabilia [,memərə'bɪlɪə] *npl* souvenirs *mpl*.

memorable ['memərəbl] *adj* mémorable, inoubliable.

memorably ['memərəblɪ] *adv* : **a ~ hot summer** un été torride dont on se souvient encore.

memorandum [,memə'rændəm] (*pl* **memoranda** [-də]) *n* **1.** COMM note *f* **2.** LAW sommaire *m* **3.** [diplomatic communication] mémorandum *m*.

memorial [mɪ'mɔːrɪəl] <> *n* **1.** [monument] monument *m* (commémoratif), mémorial *m* **2.** [diplomatic memorandum] mémorandum *m* ■ [petition] pétition *f* ■ [official request] requête *f*, mémoire *m*.
<> *adj* **1.** [commemorative] commémoratif ■ **the Marcel Proust ~ prize** le prix Marcel Proust ■ **~ service** commémoration *f* **2.** [of memory] mémoriel.

Memorial Day *n* US *dernier lundi du mois de mai (férié aux États-Unis en l'honneur des soldats américains morts pour la patrie).*

memorize, ise ['meməraɪz] *vt* mémoriser.

memory ['memərɪ] (*pl* **memories**) *n* **1.** [capacity to remember] mémoire *f* ■ **to have a good/bad ~** avoir (une) bonne/mauvaise mémoire ■ **to have a short ~** avoir la mémoire courte ■ **I've got a very good/bad ~ for names** j'ai/je n'ai pas une très bonne mémoire des noms ■ **to quote a figure from ~** citer un chiffre de mémoire *OR* de tête ■ **to lose one's ~** perdre la mémoire ■ **if (my) ~ serves me well** *OR* **right, to the best of my ~** si j'ai bonne mémoire, autant que je m'en souvienne ■ **within living ~** de mémoire d'homme **2.** [recollection] souvenir *m* ■ **childhood memories** des souvenirs d'enfance ■ **to have good/bad memories of sthg** garder un bon/mauvais souvenir de qqch ■ **to the ~ of** à la mémoire de ■ **to keep the ~ of sthg/sb alive** *OR* **green** garder vivant *OR* entretenir le souvenir de qqch/qqn ■ **I cherish his ~** je chéris sa mémoire *OR* son souvenir ◐ **to take a trip down ~ lane** faire un voyage en arrière **3.** COMPUT mémoire *f* ■ **data is stored in the ~** les données sont (entrées) en mémoire ◐ **~ dump** vidage *m* de mémoire.
◆ **in memory of** *prep phr* en souvenir de.

memory bank *n* bloc *m* de mémoire.

memory card *n* COMPUT carte *f* d'extension mémoire.

memory span *n* empan *m* mnémonique *spec*, capacité *f* de mémorisation (de courte durée).

men [men] *pl* ▻ **man**.

menace ['menəs] <> *n* **1.** [source of danger] danger *m* ■ **some drivers are a public ~** certains conducteurs constituent un véritable danger public *OR* sont de véritables dangers publics **2.** [threat] menace *f* **3.** *inf* [annoying person or thing] plaie *f*.
<> *vt* menacer.

menacing ['menəsɪŋ] *adj* menaçant.

menacingly ['menəsɪŋlɪ] *adv* [speak, act] de manière menaçante ■ [look] d'un air menaçant.

menagerie [mɪ'nædʒərɪ] *n* ménagerie *f*.

Mencap ['menkæp] *pr n association britannique pour les enfants et les adultes handicapés mentaux.*

mend [mend] <> *vt* **1.** [repair - machine, television, broken vase] réparer ; [- clothes] raccommoder ; [- hem] recoudre ■ [darn - socks] repriser, ravauder ■ **to get** *OR* **to have sthg ~ed** faire réparer qqch **2.** [rectify] rectifier, réparer ■ **to ~ matters** arranger les choses ■ **to ~ one's ways** s'amender.
<> *vi* [improve - patient] se remettre, être en voie de guérison ; [- weather] s'améliorer.
<> *n* **1.** [darn] reprise *f* ■ [patch] pièce *f* **2.** *phr* **to be on the ~** *inf* s'améliorer ; [patient] se remettre, être en voie de guérison.

mendacious [men'deɪʃəs] *adj fml* [statement, remark] mensonger, fallacieux ■ [person] menteur.

mendacity [men'dæsətɪ] (*pl* **mendacities**) *n fml (U)* mensonge *m*, mensonges *mpl*.

mendicant ['mendɪkənt] <> *n* mendiant *m*, - e *f*.
<> *adj* mendiant ■ **~ order** RELIG ordre *m* mendiant.

mendicity [men'dɪsətɪ] *n* mendicité *f*.

mending ['mendɪŋ] *n* raccommodage *m*.

Menelaus [ˌmenɪ'leɪəs] *pr n* Ménélas.

menfolk ['menfəʊk] *npl* hommes *mpl*.

menhir ['menˌhɪəʳ] *n* menhir *m*.

menial ['mi:njəl] <> *adj* : ~ **tasks** tâches *fpl* ingrates *OR* sans intérêt.
<> *n* [subordinate] subalterne *mf* ■ [servant] domestique *mf*, laquais *m pej*.

meningitis [ˌmenɪn'dʒaɪtɪs] *n* méningite *f*.

meniscus [mə'nɪskəs] (*pl* **meniscuses** *OR pl* **menisci** [-'nɪsaɪ]) *n* ménisque *m*.

menopausal [ˌmenə'pɔ:zl] *adj* ménopausique.

menopause ['menəpɔ:z] *n* ménopause *f* ■ **the male** ~ l'andropause *f*.

Mensa ['mensə] *pr n association de personnes ayant un QI particulièrement élevé.*

menservants ['mensɜ:vənts] *pl* ▻ **manservant**.

men's room *n US* toilettes *fpl (pour hommes)*.

menstrual ['menstrʊəl] *adj* menstruel ■ ~ **cycle** cycle *m* menstruel.

menstruate ['menstrʊeɪt] *vi* avoir ses règles.

menstruation [ˌmenstrʊ'eɪʃn] *n* menstruation *f*, règles *fpl*.

mensurable ['menʃərəbl] *adj* mesurable.

mensuration [ˌmenʃə'reɪʃn] *n* mesurage *m*, mensuration *f*.

menswear ['menzweəʳ] *n (U)* vêtements *mpl* pour hommes.

mental ['mentl] *adj* **1.** [intellectual] mental ■ **he has a ~ age of seven** il a un âge mental de sept ans **2.** [in the mind] mental ■ **to make a ~ note of sthg** prendre note de qqch ■ **she made a ~ note to speak to him about the matter** elle se promit de lui en parler **3.** [psychiatric] mental ■ **it can cause great ~ strain** cela peut provoquer une grande tension nerveuse ■ **he had a ~ breakdown** il a fait une dépression nerveuse ⊙ ~ **illness** maladie *f* mentale ■ ~ **nurse** infirmier *m*, - ère *f* psychiatrique **4.** △ [crazy] malade, timbré.

mental arithmetic *n* calcul *m* mental.

mental cruelty *n* cruauté *f* mentale.

mental health *n* santé *f* mentale.

mental home, mental hospital *n* hôpital *m* psychiatrique.

mentality [men'tæləti] (*pl* **mentalities**) *n* mentalité *f*.

mentally ['mentəlɪ] *adv* mentalement ■ **the ~ disabled** *OR* **handicapped** les handicapés mentaux ■ ~ **ill** malade *(mentalement)* ■ ~ **defective** (mentalement) déficient ■ ~ **disturbed** déséquilibré (mental) ■ ~ **retarded** (mentalement) arriéré.

menthol ['menθɒl] *n* menthol *m* ■ ~ **cigarette** cigarette *f* au menthol *OR* mentholée.

mentholated ['menθəleɪtɪd] *adj* au menthol, mentholé.

mention ['menʃn] <> *vt* [talk about] mentionner, faire mention de, parler de ■ **the newspapers didn't ~ it** les journaux n'en ont pas fait mention *OR* n'en ont pas parlé ■ **I'll ~ it to him sometime** je lui en toucherai un mot à l'occasion ■ **thank you very much – don't ~ it!** merci beaucoup – il n'y a pas de quoi! *OR* je vous en prie! ■ **it's not worth ~ing** ça ne vaut pas la peine d'en parler ▌[remark, point out] signaler ■ **I should ~ that it was dark at the time** il faut signaler *OR* je tiens à faire remarquer qu'il faisait nuit ■ **she did ~ a couple of good restaurants to me** elle m'a bien donné l'adresse de *OR* elle m'a bien signalé quelques bons restaurants ▌[name, cite] mentionner, citer, nommer ■ **someone, without ~ing any names, has broken my hairdryer** je ne citerai personne, mais quelqu'un a cassé mon séchoir à cheveux ■ **just ~ my name to her** dites-lui que c'est de ma part ■ **to ~ sb in one's will** coucher qqn sur son testament.
<> *n* mention *f* ■ **it got a ~ in the local paper** le journal local en a parlé *OR* y a fait allusion ■ **special ~ should be made of all the people behind the scenes** n'oublions pas tous ceux qui ont travaillé dans l'ombre *OR* en coulisse ⊙ **honourable ~** mention *f*.
◆ **not to mention** *prep phr* sans parler de.

mentor ['mentɔ:ʳ] *n* mentor *m*.

menu ['menju:] *n* **1.** [in restaurant] menu *m*, carte *f* ■ **on the ~** au menu **2.** COMPUT menu *m*.

menu bar *n* COMPUT barre *f* de menu.

menu-driven *adj* COMPUT piloté par menus.

meow [mi:'aʊ] = **miaow**.

MEP (*abbrev of* **Member of the European Parliament**) *n* député *m* à l'Assemblée européenne, membre *m* du Parlement européen.

mephistophelean, mephistophelian [ˌmefɪstə'fi:ljən] *adj* méphistophélique.

Mephistopheles [ˌmefɪ'stɒfɪli:z] *pr n* Méphistophélès.

mercantile ['mɜ:kəntaɪl] *adj* **1.** COMM : ~ **company** société *f* commerciale ■ ~ **law** droit *m* commercial ■ ~ **nation** nation *f* commerçante **2.** ECON [concerning mercantilism] mercantiliste.

mercantilism ['mɜ:kəntɪlɪzm] *n* mercantilisme *m*.

mercenary ['mɜ:sɪnrɪ] (*pl* **mercenaries**) <> *n* mercenaire *m*.
<> *adj* **1.** *pej* intéressé **2.** MIL mercenaire.

merchandise ['mɜ:tʃəndaɪz] <> *n (U)* marchandises *fpl*.
<> *vt* commercialiser.

merchandising ['mɜ:tʃəndaɪzɪŋ] *n* merchandising *m*, marchandisage *m*.

merchant ['mɜ:tʃənt] <> *n* **1.** [trader] négociant *m*, - e *f* ■ [shopkeeper] marchand *m*, - e *f* ■ **wool ~** lainier *m*, négociant en laines ■ **wine ~** marchand de vin ■ **'The Merchant of Venice'** ***Shakespeare*** 'le Marchand de Venise' **2.** *fig* ~ **of death** marchand de mort ■ **a doom ~** un prophète de malheur.
<> *adj* marchand.

merchant bank *n* banque *f* d'affaires.

merchant banker *n* banquier *m* d'affaires.

merchantman ['mɜ:tʃəntmən] (*pl* **merchantmen** [-mən]) = **merchant ship**.

merchant marine *n US* marine *f* marchande.

merchant navy *n UK* marine *f* marchande.

merchant seaman *n* marin *m* de la marine marchande.

merchant ship *n* navire *m* de commerce.

merciful ['mɜ:sɪfʊl] *adj* clément, miséricordieux ■ **to be ~ to** *OR* **towards sb** faire preuve de clémence *OR* de miséricorde envers qqn ■ **her death was a ~ release** sa mort a été une délivrance.

mercifully ['mɜ:sɪfʊlɪ] *adv* **1.** [luckily] heureusement, par bonheur **2.** [with clemency] avec clémence.

merciless ['mɜ:sɪlɪs] *adj* impitoyable, implacable.

mercilessly ['mɜ:sɪlɪslɪ] *adv* sans merci, impitoyablement, implacablement.

mercurial [mɜ:'kjʊərɪəl] *adj* **1.** [changeable] versatile, d'humeur inégale, changeant **2.** [lively] vif, plein de vie, gai **3.** CHEM mercuriel.

mercury ['mɜ:kjʊrɪ] *n* **1.** CHEM mercure *m* **2.** BOT mercuriale *f*.
◆ **Mercury** *pr n* ASTRON & MYTH Mercure.

mercy ['mɜ:sɪ] (*pl* **mercies**) <> *n* **1.** [clemency] clémence *f*, pitié *f*, indulgence *f* ■ **she had** *OR* **showed no ~** elle n'a eu aucune pitié, elle a été sans pitié ■ **to have ~ on sb** avoir pitié de qqn ■ **(have) ~!** (ayez) pitié! ▌RELIG miséricorde *f* **2.** [blessing] chance *f*, bonheur *m* ■ **it's a ~ that he doesn't know** heureusement qu'il ne sait pas, c'est une chance qu'il ne sache pas ■ **we must be thankful for small mercies** il faut savoir

apprécier les moindres bienfaits **3.** [power] merci *f* ▪ **to be at sb's/sthg's ~** être à la merci de qqn/qqch ▪ **to leave sb to the tender mercies of sb** *iron* abandonner qqn aux bons soins de qqn.
◇ *comp* humanitaire, de secours ▪ **on a ~ mission** en mission humanitaire ▪ **~ dash** course *f* contre la mort.

mercy killing *n* euthanasie *f*.

mere [mɪəʳ] ◇ *adj* seul, simple, pur ▪ **I'm a ~ beginner** je ne suis qu'un débutant ▪ **it's a ~ formality** ce n'est qu'une simple formalité ▪ **the ~ thought of it disgusts her** rien que d'y penser ça lui répugne ▪ **the ~ sight of fish makes me queasy** la seule vue du poisson me donne la nausée ▪ **his eyes light up at the merest mention of money** son regard s'allume dès qu'on commence à parler d'argent.
◇ *n* (petit) lac *m*, étang *m*.

merely ['mɪəlɪ] *adv* seulement, (tout) simplement ▪ **I'm ~ a beginner** je ne suis qu'un débutant ▪ **I was ~ wondering if this is the best solution** je me demandais seulement *OR* simplement si c'était la meilleure solution ▪ **she ~ glanced at it** elle n'a fait qu'y jeter *OR* elle s'est contentée d'y jeter un coup d'œil.

meretricious [ˌmerɪ'trɪʃəs] *adj fml* [glamour, excitement] factice ▪ [impression] faux, fausse *f* ▪ [ornamentation, design] clinquant, tape-à-l'œil ▪ [style] ampoulé, pompier.

merge [mɜːdʒ] ◇ *vi* **1.** [join - rivers] se rejoindre, confluer ; [- roads] se rejoindre ; [- colours, voices] se confondre ; [- cultures] se mélanger ▪ POL s'unir **2.** [vanish] se perdre ▪ **the thief ~d into the crowd** le voleur s'est fondu dans la foule **3.** COMM fusionner.
◇ *vt* joindre, fusionner ▪ COMM & COMPUT fusionner ▪ POL unifier.

merger ['mɜːdʒəʳ] *n* COMM fusion *f*.

meridian [mə'rɪdɪən] ◇ *n* **1.** ASTRON, GEOG & MED méridien *m* ▪ **the Greenwich ~** le méridien de Greenwich **2.** MATHS méridienne *f* **3.** *fig* [zenith] zénith *m*, sommet *m*, apogée *m*.
◇ *adj* méridien.

meringue [mə'ræŋ] *n* meringue *f*.

merino [mə'riːnəʊ] (*pl* **merinos**) ◇ *n* [sheep, wool] mérinos *m*.
◇ *adj* en mérinos.

merit ['merɪt] ◇ *n* mérite *m* ▪ **its great ~ is its simplicity** ça a le grand mérite d'être simple ▪ **promotion is on ~ alone** l'avancement se fait uniquement au mérite ▪ **I don't see much ~ in the idea** cette idée ne me paraît pas particulièrement intéressante ▪ **a work of great ~** une œuvre remarquable ▪ **the relative ~s of theatre and cinema** les avantages respectifs du théâtre et du cinéma ▪ **the project has the further ~ of being cheap** le projet a de plus l'avantage d'être bon marché.
◇ *vt* mériter ▪ **the case ~s closer examination** le cas mérite d'être examiné de plus près.

meritocracy [ˌmerɪ'tɒkrəsɪ] (*pl* **meritocracies**) *n* méritocratie *f*.

meritorious [ˌmerɪ'tɔːrɪəs] *adj* [person] méritant ▪ [act] méritoire, louable.

merit system *n US* ADMIN système *m* d'avancement fondé sur le mérite.

merlin ['mɜːlɪn] *n* émerillon *m*.

Merlin ['mɜːlɪn] *pr n* Merlin.

mermaid ['mɜːmeɪd] *n* MYTH sirène *f*.

merman ['mɜːmæn] (*pl* **mermen** [-men]) *n* MYTH triton *m*.

Merovingian [ˌmerə'vɪndʒɪən] ◇ *n* Mérovingien *m*, - enne *f*.
◇ *adj* mérovingien.

merrily ['merɪlɪ] *adv* [happily] joyeusement, gaiement.

merriment ['merɪmənt] *n* [joy] joie *f*, gaieté *f* ▪ [laughter] rire *m*, rires *mpl*, hilarité *f*.

merry ['merɪ] (*comp* **merrier**, *superl* **merriest**) *adj* **1.** [happy] joyeux, gai ▪ **Merry Christmas!** Joyeux Noël! ▪ **the more the merrier** *prov* plus on est de fous, plus on rit *prov* **2.** *inf* [tipsy] éméché, pompette **3.** [good] : **the ~ month of May** le joli mois de mai ▪ **the ~ men** LIT *compagnons de Robin des Bois* ▪ **the Minister and his ~ men** *hum* le ministre et son état-major ◗ **Merry England** la bonne vieille Angleterre ▪ **'The Merry Wives of Windsor'** ***Shakespeare*** 'les Joyeuses Commères de Windsor'.

merry-go-round *n* manège *m* ▪ *fig* [whirl] tourbillon *m*.

merrymaking ['merɪˌmeɪkɪŋ] *n (U)* réjouissances *fpl*, festivités *fpl*.

mescal ['meskæl] *n* **1.** BOT peyotl *m* **2.** [alcohol] mescal *m*, mezcal *m*.

mescaline ['meskəliːn], **mescalin** ['meskəlɪn] *n* mescaline *f*.

mesh [meʃ] ◇ *n* **1.** [of net] mailles *fpl* ▪ [of sieve] grille *f* ▪ **fine-~ stockings** des bas à mailles fines ▪ **a ~ shopping bag** un filet à provisions **2.** [fabric] tissu *m* à mailles ▪ **nylon ~** tulle *m* de nylon **3.** *fig* [trap] rets *mpl*, piège *m* ▪ **caught in a ~ of lies** enfermé dans *OR* prisonnier de ses propres mensonges ▮ [network] réseau *m* **4.** MECH [of gears] engrenage *m* ▪ **in ~** en prise.
◇ *vi* **1.** [be in harmony] s'harmoniser, s'accorder **2.** [tally, coincide] cadrer, concorder ▪ **to ~ with** cadrer *OR* concorder avec **3.** MECH [gears] s'engrener.

mesmerism ['mezmərɪzm] *n* **1.** [hypnotism] hypnotisme *m* **2.** [Mesmer's doctrine] mesmérisme *m*.

mesmerize, ise ['mezməraɪz] *vt* **1.** [hypnotise] hypnotiser **2.** [entrance] ensorceler, envoûter.

mesocarp ['mesəʊkɑːp] *n* mésocarpe *m*.

Mesolithic [ˌmesə'lɪθɪk] ◇ *adj* mésolithique.
◇ *n* mésolithique *m*.

meson ['miːzɒn] *n* méson *m*.

mesosphere ['mesəʊsfɪə] *n* mésosphère *f*.

Mesopotamia [ˌmesəpə'teɪmjə] *pr n* Mésopotamie *f* ▪ **in ~** en Mésopotamie.

Mesopotamian [ˌmesəpə'teɪmjən] *adj* mésopotamien.

Mesozoic [ˌmesə'zəʊɪk] *adj* mésozoïque.

mess [mes] ◇ *n* **1.** [untidiness] désordre *m*, fouillis *m* ▪ **Tom's room is (in) a real ~!** il y a une de ces pagailles *OR* un de ces fouillis dans la chambre de Tom! ▪ **my papers are in a ~** mes papiers sont en désordre ▪ **clear up this ~!** mets un peu d'ordre là-dedans!, range un peu tout ce fouillis! ▪ **my hair's a ~!** je suis coiffé comme l'as de pique! ▪ **I feel a ~** je suis dans un état lamentable ▪ **you're a ~, go and clean up** tu n'es pas présentable, va t'arranger ▮ [dirtiness] saleté *f*, saletés *fpl* ▪ **the cooker is (in) a horrible ~** la cuisinière est vraiment sale *OR* dégoûtante ▪ **the dog has made a ~ on the carpet** le chien a fait des saletés sur le tapis **2.** [muddle] gâchis *m* ▪ **to make a ~ of a job** gâcher un travail ▪ **to make a ~ of one's life** gâcher sa vie ▪ **this country is in a ~!** la situation dans ce pays n'est pas vraiment réjouissante! **3.** *inf* [predicament] pétrin *m* ▪ **he's got himself into a bit of a ~** il s'est fourré dans de beaux draps *OR* dans le pétrin ▪ **thanks for getting me out of that ~** merci de m'avoir tiré de ce pétrin **4.** MIL [canteen] mess *m* **5.** MIL [food] ordinaire *m*, gamelle *f*.
◇ *vt* [dirty] salir, souiller.
◇ *vi* **1.** *inf* [meddle] : **to ~ with sb** embêter qqn ▪ **don't ~ with me!** ne me cherche pas! ▪ **it's true, no ~ing!** c'est vrai, je ne blague pas! **2.** MIL manger *OR* prendre ses repas au mess.
➡ **mess about, mess around** *inf* ◇ *vi insep UK* **1.** [waste time] perdre son temps ▪ [dawdle, hang around] traîner ▪ [potter] bricoler ▪ **he likes ~ing about in the garden** il aime s'occuper dans le jardin ▮ [play the fool] faire l'imbécile **2.** [meddle, fiddle] tripoter, tripatouiller ▪ **don't ~ about with my computer** ne tripote pas mon ordinateur ▮ *fig* **to ~ about with sb** [annoy] embêter qqn ; [have an affair] coucher avec qqn ▪ **if I catch her ~ing about with my husband I'll kill her!** si je l'attrape à faire du gringue à mon mari, je la tue!

◇ *vt sep* [person] embêter ■ **I'm fed up with being ~ed about by men** j'en ai marre des hommes qui se moquent de moi.
◆ **mess up** *vt sep* **1.** [make disorderly - room, papers] mettre en désordre ■ **stop it, you'll ~ my hair up!** arrête, tu vas me décoiffer! **2.** *inf* [spoil] ficher en l'air **3.** [dirty] salir, souiller.

message ['mesɪdʒ] *n* **1.** [communication] message *m*, commission *f* ■ [written] message *m*, mot *m* ■ **to take/to leave a ~** prendre/laisser un message ■ **can you give her a ~?** pouvez-vous lui transmettre un message? **2.** [theme - of book, advert] message *m* ■ [teaching - of prophet] message *m*, enseignement *m* ■ **to get one's ~ across** se faire comprendre ■ **(do you) get the ~?** *inf* tu piges? **3.** *Scotland* commission *f*, course *f* **4.** LING message *m*.

message switching [-'swɪtʃɪŋ] *n* COMPUT commutation *f* de messages.

messenger ['mesɪndʒər] *n* [gen] messager *m*, - ère *f* ■ [errand boy - in office] coursier *m* ■ [in hotel] chasseur *m*, coursier *m* ■ [in post office] télégraphiste *mf* ■ **by special ~** par porteur spécial ➲ **~ boy** coursier *m*, garçon *m* de courses ■ **~ service** messagerie *f*.

messiah [mɪ'saɪə] *n* messie *m*.
◆ **Messiah** *n* Messie *m*.

messianic [,mesɪ'ænɪk] *adj* messianique.

messily ['mesɪlɪ] *adv* **1.** [untidily] mal, de façon peu soignée ■ [in a disorganized way] n'importe comment ■ **the affair ended ~** *fig* l'affaire s'est mal terminée **2.** [dirtily] comme un cochon.

mess jacket *n* MIL veston *m* de tenue de soirée ■ [civilian] veste *f* courte.

messmate ['mesmeɪt] *n* commensal *m*, - e *f*.

mess-room *n* NAUT carré *m*.

Messrs, Messrs. ['mesəz] MM, Messieurs.

mess tin *n* gamelle *f*.

mess-up *n inf* confusion *f* ■ **there was a ~ over the dates** on s'est embrouillé dans les dates.

messy ['mesɪ] (*comp* **messier**, *superl* **messiest**) *adj* **1.** [dirty - hands, clothes] sale, malpropre ; [- job] salissant ■ **don't get all ~** ne te salis pas ■ **he did some painting and got all ~** il a fait de la peinture et il s'en est mis partout **2.** [untidy - place] en désordre, désordonné, mal tenu ; [- person] peu soigné, négligé, débraillé ; [- hair] ébouriffé, en désordre, en bataille **3.** [badly done] bâclé ■ **a ~ piece of homework** un devoir bâclé **4.** *fig* compliqué, embrouillé, délicat ■ **a ~ divorce** un divorce difficile OR compliqué.

met [met] *pt & pp* ⊳ **meet**.

Met [met] *pr n inf* **1.** *US* = **Metropolitan Opera 2.** *US* = **Metropolitan Museum 3.** *UK* = **Metropolitan Police**.

metabolic [,metə'bɒlɪk] *adj* métabolique.

metabolism [mɪ'tæbəlɪzm] *n* métabolisme *m*.

metabolize, ise [mɪ'tæbəlaɪz] *vt* métaboliser.

metacarpus [,metə'kɑ:pəs] (*pl* **metacarpi** [-paɪ]) *n* métacarpe *m*.

metal ['metl] (*UK pret & pp* **metalled**, *cont* **metalling**) (*US pret & pp* **metaled**, *cont* **metaling**) ◇ *n* **1.** [gen - CHEM] métal *m* ■ **made of ~** en métal **2.** TYPO plomb *m* **3.** [for road - building] cailloutis *m*, empierrement *m* **4.** [glass] pâte *f* de verre.
◇ *adj* en métal, métallique.
◇ *vt* **1.** [cover with metal] couvrir de métal **2.** [road] empierrer.
◆ **metals** *npl UK* RAIL voie *f* ferrée, rails *mpl*.

metalanguage ['metə,læŋgwɪdʒ] *n* métalangue *f*, métalangage *m*.

metal detector *n* détecteur *m* de métaux.

metaled *US* = **metalled**.

metalled *UK*, **metaled** *US* ['metld] *adj* [road] revêtu *(de macadam, de pierres etc)*.

metallic [mɪ'tælɪk] *adj* **1.** CHEM métallique **2.** [colour] : **~ blue/grey** bleu/gris métallisé **3.** [voice] métallique ■ [sound] métallique, grinçant.

metallurgist [me'tælədʒɪst] *n* métallurgiste *m*, ingénieur *m* en métallurgie.

metallurgy [me'tælədʒɪ] *n* métallurgie *f*.

metalware ['metəlweər] *n* ustensiles *mpl* (domestiques) en métal.

metalwork ['metəlwɜ:k] *n* **1.** [objects] ferronnerie *f* **2.** [activity] travail *m* des métaux **3.** [metal framework] tôle *f*, métal *m* ■ [of crashed car, plane] carcasse *f*.

metalworker ['metəl,wɜ:kər] *n* **1.** [in factory] métallurgiste *m*, métallo *m* **2.** [craftsman] ferronnier *m*.

metamorphose [,metə'mɔ:fəʊz] ◇ *vi* se métamorphoser ■ **to ~ into sthg** se métamorphoser en qqch.
◇ *vt* métamorphoser.

metamorphosis [,metə'mɔ:fəsɪs, ,metəmɔ:'fəʊsɪs] (*pl* **metamorphoses** [-si:z]) *n* métamorphose *f*.

metaphor ['metəfər] *n* métaphore *f* ■ **it's a ~ for loneliness** c'est une métaphore de la solitude.

metaphorical [,metə'fɒrɪkl] *adj* métaphorique.

metaphorically [,metə'fɒrɪklɪ] *adv* métaphoriquement ■ **~ speaking** métaphoriquement.

metaphysical [,metə'fɪzɪkl] *adj* LIT & PHILOS métaphysique ■ *fig* [abstract] métaphysique, abstrait.

metaphysically [,metə'fɪzɪklɪ] *adv* métaphysiquement.

metaphysician [,metəfɪ'zɪʃn] *n* métaphysicien *m*, - enne *f*.

metaphysics [,metə'fɪzɪks] *n (U)* métaphysique *f*.

metastasis [me'tæstəsɪs] (*pl* **metastases** [-si:z]) *n* métastase *f*.

metatarsus [,metə'tɑ:səs] (*pl* **metatarsi** [-saɪ]) *n* métatarse *m*.

mete [mi:t] ◆ **mete out** *vt sep* [punishment] infliger ■ [judgment, justice] rendre.

meteor ['mi:tɪər] *n* météore *m* ■ **~ shower** pluie *f* d'étoiles filantes, averse *f* météorique.

meteoric [mi:tɪ'ɒrɪk] *adj* **1.** ASTRON météorique **2.** *fig* fulgurant, très rapide.

meteorite ['mi:tjəraɪt] *n* météorite *f*.

meteoroid ['mi:tjərɔɪd] *n* météoroïde *m*.

meteorological [,mi:tjərə'lɒdʒɪkl] *adj* météorologique.

meteorologist [,mi:tjə'rɒlədʒɪst] *n* météorologue *mf*, météorologiste *mf*.

meteorology [,mi:tjə'rɒlədʒɪ] *n* météorologie *f*.

meter ['mi:tər] ◇ *n* **1.** [for water, gas, electricity] compteur *m* ■ **to read the ~** relever le compteur ■ **to feed the ~** mettre des pièces dans le compteur ➲ **(parking) ~** parcmètre *m*, parcomètre *m* ■ **(taxi) ~** taximètre *m*, compteur *m* **2.** *US* = **metre**.
◇ *vt* **1.** [electricity, water, gas] mesurer à l'aide d'un compteur **2.** [mail] affranchir *(avec une machine)*.

metered ['mi:təd] *adj* décomptéà la minute.

meter maid *n inf* contractuelle *f*, aubergine *f*.

methadone ['meθədəʊn] *n* méthadone *f*.

methane ['mi:θeɪn] *n* méthane *m*.

methanol ['meθənɒl] *n* méthanol *m*.

methinks [mɪ'θɪŋks] (*pret* **methought** [-'θɔ:t]) *vb arch & hum* ce me semble.

method ['meθəd] *n* **1.** [means] méthode *f*, moyen *m* ■ [manner] manière *f* ■ [instruction] méthode *f*, mode *m* d'emploi ■ **~ of doing sthg** manière de faire qqch, méthode (employée) pour faire qqch **2.** [procedure] méthode *f*, procédé *m* ■ **their**

~s of investigation have come under fire la façon dont ils mènent leurs enquêtes a été critiquée, on a critiqué leur façon d'enquêter ▮ [theory] théorie *f*, méthode *f* ▪ **the Montessori ~** la méthode Montessori **3.** [organization] méthode *f*, organisation *f* ▪ **there's ~ in her madness** elle n'est pas aussi folle qu'elle en a l'air.
◆ **Method** *n* **: Method acting** la méthode Stanislavski.

methodical [mɪ'θɒdɪkl] *adj* méthodique.

methodically [mɪ'θɒdɪklɪ] *adv* méthodiquement, de façon méthodique, avec méthode.

Methodism ['meθədɪzm] *n* méthodisme *m*.

Methodist ['meθədɪst] <> *adj* méthodiste.
<> *n* méthodiste *mf*.

methodological [,meθədə'lɒdʒɪkl] *adj* méthodologique.

methodology [,meθə'dɒlədʒɪ] (*pl* **methodologies**) *n* méthodologie *f*.

meths [meθs] (*abbrev of* **methylated spirits**) *n* **UK** *inf* alcool *m* à brûler ▪ **~ drinker** *alcoolique qui boit de l'alcool à brûler*.

Methuselah [,mɪ'θju:zələ] <> *pr n* BIBLE Mathusalem ▪ **as old as ~** vieux comme Mathusalem.
<> *n* [bottle] mathusalem *m*.

methyl ['meθɪl] *n* méthyle *m*.

methyl acetate *n* acétate *m* de méthyle.

methyl alcohol *n* méthanol *m*, alcool *m* méthylique.

methylated spirits ['meθɪleɪtɪd] *n* alcool *m* à brûler.

meticulous [mɪ'tɪkjʊləs] *adj* méticuleux.

meticulously [mɪ'tɪkjʊləslɪ] *adv* méticuleusement ▪ **~ honest** d'une honnêteté scrupuleuse.

meticulousness [mɪ'tɪkjʊləsnɪs] *n* minutie *f*, méticulosité *f* *lit* ▪ **with great ~** avec un soin tout particulier.

Met Office [met-] (*abbrev of* **Meteorological Office**) *pr n les services météorologiques britanniques*.

metonym ['metənɪm] *n* métonymie *f*.

metonymy [mɪ'tɒnɪmɪ] *n* métonymie *f*.

metre *UK*, **meter** *US* ['mi:tər] *n* **1.** [measurement] mètre *m* **2.** LIT mètre *m* ▪ **in iambic ~** en vers *mpl* iambiques **3.** MUS mesure *f*.

metric ['metrɪk] *adj* MATHS métrique ▪ **to go ~** adopter le système métrique ▪ **~ hundredweight** 50 kilogrammes *mpl* ▪ **~ ton** tonne *f*.

metrical ['metrɪkl] *adj* LIT métrique.

metrically ['metrɪklɪ] *adv* **1.** LIT en vers **2.** MATHS selon le système métrique.

metrication [,metrɪ'keɪʃn] *n* conversion *f* au système métrique, métrisation *f*.

metro ['metrəʊ] (*pl* **metros**) *n* métro *m*.

metrology [me'trɒlədʒɪ] *n* métrologie *f*.

metronome ['metrənəʊm] *n* métronome *m*.

metropolis [mɪ'trɒpəlɪs] (*pl* **metropolises** [-i:z]) *n* métropole *f*, grande ville *f*, grand centre *m* urbain.

metropolitan [,metrə'pɒlɪtn] <> *adj* **1.** GEOG métropolitain **2.** RELIG métropolitain ▪ **~ bishop** métropolitain *m*.
<> *n* RELIG métropolitain *m* ▪ [in orthodox church] métropolite *m*.

metropolitan district *n* [in UK] circonscription *f* administrative.

Metropolitan Museum of Art *pr n un des principaux musées américains, à New York*.

Metropolitan Police *n* **UK** police *f* londonienne.

metrosexual [,metrə'sekʃʊəl] <> *n* métrosexuel *m*.
<> *adj* métrosexuel,.

Mets [mets] *pr npl* **: the (New York) ~** *l'une des équipes de baseball de New York*.

mettle ['metl] *n* courage *m* ▪ **to show** *OR* **to prove one's ~** montrer ce dont on est capable ▪ **this new challenge has really put him on his ~** ce nouveau défi l'a vraiment forcé à donner le meilleur de lui-même.

mettlesome ['metəlsəm] *adj lit* courageux.

mew [mju:] <> *vi* [cat] miauler ▪ [gull] crier.
<> *n* **1.** [of cat] miaulement *m* ▪ [of gull] cri *m* **2.** [gull] mouette *f*.

mews [mju:z] *n* **UK** **1.** [flat] *appartement chic aménagé dans une écurie rénovée* **2.** [street] ruelle *f*.

Mexican ['meksɪkn] <> *n* Mexicain *m*, - aine *f*.
<> *adj* mexicain ▪ **the ~ War** la guerre du Mexique.

THE MEXICAN WAR

Conflit qui opposa les États-Unis au Mexique de 1846 à 1848. Vaincu, celui-ci renonça à ses prétentions sur le Texas et céda un vaste territoire comprenant plusieurs États américains actuels (dont le Nouveau-Mexique et la Californie).

Mexican wave *n* ola *f*.

Mexico ['meksɪkəʊ] *pr n* Mexique *m* ▪ **in ~** au Mexique ▪ **the Gulf of ~** le golfe du Mexique.

Mexico City *pr n* Mexico.

mezzanine ['metsəni:n] *n* **1.** mezzanine *f* **2.** **US** [in theatre] corbeille *f*.

mezzo-soprano (*pl* **mezzo-sopranos**) *n* **1.** [singer] mezzo-soprano *f* **2.** [voice] mezzo-soprano *m*.

mezzotint ['medzəʊtɪnt] *n* mezzotinto *m inv*.

MFA (*abbrev of* **Master of Fine Arts**) *n (titulaire d'une) maîtrise en beaux-arts*.

mfr *written abbr of* **manufacturer**.

mg (*written abbrev of* **milligram**) mg.

Mgr **1.** (*written abbrev of* **Monseigneur, Monsignor**) Mgr **2.** *written abbr of* **manager**.

MHR *n* = **Member of the House of Representatives**.

MHz (*written abbrev of* **megahertz**) MHz.

mi [mi:] *n* MUS mi *m inv*.

MI *written abbr of* **Michigan**.

MI5 (*abbrev of* **Military Intelligence 5**) *pr n service de contre-espionnage britannique*.

MI6 (*abbrev of* **Military Intelligence 6**) *pr n service de renseignements britannique*.

MIA (*abbrev of* **missing in action**) *adj expression indiquant qu'une personne a disparu lors d'un combat*.

miaow [mi:'aʊ] **UK** <> *vi* miauler.
<> *n* miaulement *m*.
<> *interj* miaou.

miasma [mɪ'æzmə] *n lit* **1.** [vapour] miasme *m* ▪ [of smoke] bouffée *f* **2.** [evil influence] emprise *f*, empire *m*.

mica ['maɪkə] *n* mica *m*.

Micah ['maɪkə] *pr n* Michée.

Micawber [mɪ'kɔ:bər] *pr n* **: Mr ~** *personnage du roman de Charles Dickens 'David Copperfield', qui fait preuve d'un optimisme à toute épreuve malgré des difficultés financières*.

mice [maɪs] *pl* ⊳ **mouse**.

Mich. *written abbr of* **Michigan**.

Michael ['maɪkl] *pr n* **: Saint ~** saint Michel ▪ **are you taking the ~?** **UK** *inf hum* tu me fais marcher ou quoi?

Michaelmas ['mɪkəlməs] *n* RELIG Saint-Michel *f*.

Michaelmas daisy *n* aster *m* (d'automne).

Michelangelo [,maɪkəl'ændʒɪləʊ] *pr n* Michel-Ange.

Michigan ['mɪʃɪgən] *pr n* Michigan *m* ■ **in ~** dans le Michigan ■ **Lake ~** le Lac Michigan.

Mick△ [mɪk] *n terme injurieux désignant un Irlandais.*

mickey ['mɪkɪ] *n* **UK to take the ~ out of sb** *inf* se payer la tête de qqn.

Mickey Mouse ◇ *pr n* Mickey.
◇ *adj inf* [trivial] de pacotille.

MICR (*abbrev of* **magnetic ink character recognition**) *n reconnaissance magnétique de caractères.*

micro ['maɪkrəʊ] (*pl* **micros**) ◇ *adj* très petit, microscopique.
◇ *n* [microcomputer] micro-ordinateur *m*, micro *m*.

microbe ['maɪkrəʊb] *n* microbe *m*.

microbiologist [,maɪkrəʊbaɪ'ɒlədʒɪst] *n* microbiologiste *mf*.

microbiology [,maɪkrəʊbaɪ'ɒlədʒɪ] *n* microbiologie *f*.

microbrewery ['maɪkrəʊbruərɪ] *n* microbrasserie *f*.

microchip ['maɪkrəʊtʃɪp] *n* microprocesseur *m*.

microcircuit ['maɪkrəʊ,sɜːkɪt] *n* microcircuit *m*.

microcomputer [,maɪkrəʊkəm'pjuːtəʳ] *n* micro-ordinateur *m*.

microcomputing [,maɪkrəʊkəm'pjuːtɪŋ] *n* micro-informatique *f*.

microcosm ['maɪkrəʊ,kɒzm] *n* microcosme *m*.

microdot ['maɪkrəʊdɒt] *n* micropoint *m*, micro-image *f*.

microeconomics ['maɪkrəʊ,iːkə'nɒmɪks] *n (U)* microéconomie *f*.

microelectronics ['maɪkrəʊɪ,lek'trɒnɪks] *n* microélectronique *f*.

microfibre *UK*, **microfiber** *US* ['maɪkrə,faɪbəʳ] *n* microfibre *f*.

microfiche ['maɪkrəʊfiːʃ] *n* microfiche *f*.

microfilm ['maɪkrəʊfɪlm] ◇ *n* microfilm *m*.
◇ *vt* microfilmer, mettre sur microfilm.

micrograph ['maɪkrəgrɑːf] ◇ *n* micrographie *f*.
◇ *vt* micrographier.

microlight ['maɪkrəlaɪt] *n* AERON ultra-léger motorisé *m*, ULM *m*.

micromesh ['maɪkrəʊmeʃ] *adj* [tights] surfin.

micrometer [maɪ'krɒmiːtəʳ] *n* [device] micromètre *m (appareil)* ■ **~ screw** vis *f* micrométrique ■ **~ screw gauge** palmer *m*.

micrometre *UK*, **micrometer** *US* ['maɪkrəʊ,miːtəʳ] *n* micromètre *m (mesure)*.

micrometry [maɪ'krɒmətrɪ] *n* micrométrie *f*.

micron ['maɪkrɒn] (*pl* **microns** *OR pl* **micra** [-krə]) *n* micron *m*.

Micronesia [,maɪkrə'niːzjə] *pr n* Micronésie *f*.

Micronesian [,maɪkrə'niːzjən] ◇ *n* [person] Micronésien *m*, - enne *f*.
◇ *adj* micronésien.

microorganism [,maɪkrəʊ'ɔːgənɪzm] *n* micro-organisme *m*.

microphone ['maɪkrəfəʊn] *n* microphone *m* ■ **to talk into a ~** parler dans un micro.

microphotography [,maɪkrəʊfə'tɒgrəfɪ] *n* microphotographie *f*.

microprocessor ['maɪkrəʊ,prəʊsesəʳ] *n* microprocesseur *m*.

microprogram ['maɪkrəʊ,prəʊgræm] *n* microprogramme *m*.

micro scooter *n* trottinette *f* pliante.

microscope ['maɪkrəskəʊp] *n* microscope *m* ■ **to look at sthg under the ~** *liter* observer *OR* examiner qqch au microscope ; *fig* examiner qqch de très près.

microscopic [,maɪkrə'skɒpɪk] *adj* **1.** [tiny] microscopique **2.** [using a microscope] au microscope, microscopique.

microscopically [,maɪkrə'skɒpɪklɪ] *adv* [examine] au microscope ■ **~ small** invisible à l'œil nu.

microsecond ['maɪkrəʊ,sekənd] *n* microseconde *f*.

microsurgery [,maɪkrəʊ'sɜːdʒərɪ] *n* microchirurgie *f*.

microwave ['maɪkrəweɪv] ◇ *n* **1.** PHYS micro-onde *f* **2.** = **microwave oven.**
◇ *vt* faire cuire au micro-ondes.

microwaveable ['maɪkrəʊ,weɪvəbl] *adj* micro-ondable.

microwave oven *n* four *m* à micro-ondes.

microwriter ['maɪkrəʊ,raɪtəʳ] *n* COMPUT micro-ordinateur *m* de traitement de texte.

micturate ['mɪktjʊəreɪt] *vi fml* uriner.

mid [mɪd] ◇ *adj* **1.** [middle] : **in ~ October** à la mi-octobre, au milieu du mois d'octobre ■ **he's in his ~ fifties** il a environ 55 ans ■ **she stopped in ~ sentence** elle s'est arrêtée au milieu de sa phrase, sa phrase est restée en suspens **2.** [half] : **~ green** vert ni clair ni foncé **3.** [central] central, du milieu ■ **~ Wales** le centre *OR* la région centrale du pays de Galles.
◇ *prep* = **amid.**

'mid [mɪd] = **amid.**

midair [mɪd'eəʳ] ◇ *adj* en plein ciel.
◇ *n* : **in ~** en plein ciel.

Midas ['maɪdəs] *pr n* Midas ■ **to have the ~ touch** avoir le sens des affaires.

mid-Atlantic ◇ *adj* [accent] américanisé.
◇ *n* : **in (the) ~** au milieu de l'Atlantique.

midbrain ['mɪdbreɪn] *n* ANAT mésencéphale *m*.

midcourse ['mɪdkɔːs] ◇ *n* : **in ~** à mi-course.
◇ *adj* ASTRON : **~ corrections** corrections *fpl* de trajectoire.

midday ['mɪddeɪ] *n* midi *m* ■ **at ~** à midi ■ **~ meal** repas *m* de midi.

midden ['mɪdn] *n* **1.** *dial* [dung heap] (tas *m* de) fumier *m* **2.** ARCHEOL ordures *fpl* ménagères, rejets *mpl* domestiques.

middle ['mɪdl] ◇ *n* **1.** [in space] milieu *m*, centre *m* ■ **in the ~ (of)** au milieu (de), au centre (de) ■ **two seats in the ~ of the row** deux places en milieu de rangée ■ **in the ~ of London** en plein Londres ■ **right in the ~ of the target** au beau milieu *OR* en plein centre de la cible ▶ **we broke down in the ~ of nowhere** on est tombés en panne dans un endroit perdu **2.** [in time] milieu *m* ■ **in the ~ of the week** au milieu de la semaine ■ **in the ~ of October** à la mi-octobre, au milieu (du mois) d'octobre ■ **in the ~ of the night** en pleine nuit, en plein milieu de la nuit ■ **in the ~ of winter** en plein hiver ▮ [in activity] : **to be in the ~ of (doing) sthg** être en train de faire qqch **3.** [stomach] ventre *m* ■ [waist] taille *f* ■ **he's got rather fat around the ~** il a pris du ventre.
◇ *adj* **1.** [in the centre] du milieu ■ **to take the ~ course** *OR* **way** *fig* trouver le juste milieu ■ **the ~ path** *liter* le chemin du milieu ; *fig* la voie de la modération ■ **~ C** do *m* du milieu du clavier **2.** [average] moyen ■ [intermediate] moyen, intermédiaire ■ **this car is in the ~ price range** cette voiture se situe dans un ordre de prix moyen.
◇ *vt* **1.** NAUT [sail] plier en deux **2.** FTBL centrer.
◆ **Middle** *adj* LING : **Middle Irish/French** moyen gaélique/français.

middle age *n* la cinquantaine ■ **to reach ~** avoir un certain âge ■ **she's well into ~** elle a plus de 50 ans.
◆ **middle-age** *comp* : **he's got middle-age spread** il prend de l'embonpoint.

middle-aged *adj* d'une cinquantaine d'années ■ **a ~ businessman** un homme d'affaires d'un certain âge.

Middle Ages *npl* Moyen Âge *m* ■ **in the ~** au Moyen Âge.

Middle America *pr n* **1.** GEOG Amérique *f* centrale **2.** SOCIOL l'Amérique *f* moyenne ▪ *pej* l'Amérique *f* bien pensante.

Middle American <> *n* **1.** GEOG Américain *m*, - e *f* du Middle-West **2.** *fig* Américain *m* moyen, Américaine *f* moyenne.
<> *adj* **1.** GEOG du Middle-West **2.** *fig* de l'américain moyen.

middlebrow ['mɪdlbraʊ] <> *n* *pej* [reader] lecteur *m* moyen, lectrice *f* moyenne ▪ [audience] spectateur *m* moyen, spectatrice *f* moyenne.
<> *adj* [reader, audience] moyen ▪ **their music's very ~** leur musique s'adresse à un public moyen ▪ **~ programmes** programmes s'adressant à un public moyen.

middle class *n* : **the ~, the ~es** les classes *fpl* moyennes ; *pej* la bourgeoisie *f*.
◆ **middle-class** *adj* des classes moyennes ▪ *pej* bourgeois.

middle distance *n* : **in the ~** à mi-distance ; [in picture] au second plan.
◆ **middle-distance** *adj* SPORT : **middle-distance runner/race** coureur *m*, - euse *f* / course *f* de demi-fond.

middle ear *n* ANAT oreille *f* moyenne.

Middle East *pr n* : **the ~** le Moyen-Orient ▪ **in the ~** au Moyen-Orient.

Middle Eastern *adj* moyen-oriental.

Middle England *n* l'Angleterre *f* moyenne.

Middle Englander [-'ɪŋgləndəʳ] *n* Anglais *m* moyen, Anglaise *f* moyenne.

Middle English *n* LING moyen anglais *m*.

middle finger *n* majeur *m*.

middle ground *n* **1.** [in picture] second plan *m* **2.** *fig* terrain *m* neutre.

Middle High German *n* le moyen haut-allemand.

middleman ['mɪdlmæn] (*pl* **middlemen** [-men]) *n* intermédiaire *mf*.

middle management *n* *(U)* cadres *mpl* moyens.

middlemost ['mɪdlməʊst] *adj* le plus proche du centre.

middle name *n* deuxième prénom *m* ▪ **honesty is her ~** c'est l'honnêteté même.

middle-of-the-road *adj* [opinions, policies] modéré ▪ *pej* timide, circonspect ▪ **~ music** variétés *fpl* OR musique *f* passe-partout *pej*.

middle school *n* *UK* *école pour enfants de 8 à 13 ans* ▪ *US école pour enfants de 10 à 13 ans*, ≃ collège.

middleweight ['mɪdlweɪt] <> *n* poids *m* moyen.
<> *adj* [championship] de poids moyen.

Middle West = **Midwest**.

middling ['mɪdlɪŋ] *adj* *inf* [average] moyen ▪ [mediocre] médiocre ▪ [in health] : **how are you? – fair to ~** ça va? – on fait aller.

Middx *written abbr of* **Middlesex**.

Mideast [,mɪd'i:st] *US* = **Middle East**.

midfield [,mɪd'fi:ld] *n* SPORT milieu *m* du terrain ▪ **~ player** (joueur *m* du) milieu *m* de terrain.

midge [mɪdʒ] *n* moucheron *m*.

midget ['mɪdʒɪt] <> *n* [dwarf] nain *m*, naine *f*.
<> *adj* nain, minuscule.

midi ['mɪdɪ] *n* [coat] manteau *m* à mi-mollet ▪ [skirt] jupe *f* à mi-mollet.

midi system *n* mini-chaîne *f*.

midland ['mɪdlənd] *adj* au centre du pays.

Midlands ['mɪdləndz] *pr npl* : **the ~** les Midlands *(comtés du centre de l'Angleterre)*.

midlife ['mɪdlaɪf] *n* la cinquantaine.

midlife crisis *n* : **he's having** OR **going through a ~** il a du mal à passer le cap de la cinquantaine.

midmorning [,mɪd'mɔ:nɪŋ] *n* milieu *m* de la matinée.

midnight ['mɪdnaɪt] <> *n* minuit *m* ▪ **at ~** à minuit ▶ **'Midnight's Children'** *Rushdie* 'les Enfants de minuit'.
<> *adj* [mass, swim] de minuit ▪ **~ feast** *petit repas pris en cachette la nuit* ▪ **to burn the ~ oil** travailler tard dans la nuit ▪ **the land of the ~ sun** les pays du soleil de minuit *(au nord du cercle polaire arctique)* ▪ **'Midnight Cowboy'** *Schlesinger* 'Macadam cowboy'.

THE MIDNIGHT RIDE

Nom donné à l'acte héroïque de Paul Revere qui, en 1775, pendant la guerre d'Indépendance, réussit à prévenir les patriotes américains du débarquement des troupes anglaises.

midpoint ['mɪdpɔɪnt] *n* [in space, time] milieu *m*.

mid-range *adj* COMM [computer, car] de milieu de gamme.

midrib ['mɪdrɪb] *n* nervure *f* centrale.

midriff ['mɪdrɪf] *n* **1.** [stomach] ventre *m* **2.** ANAT diaphragme *m*.

midrise ['mɪdraɪz] *adj* *US* **~ apartment block** immeuble *m* de hauteur moyenne *(10 étages au maximum)*.

midshipman ['mɪdʃɪpmən] (*pl* **midshipmen** [-mən]) *n* NAUT aspirant *m*, enseigne *m* de vaisseau (deuxième classe).

midst [mɪdst] *n* **1.** [in space] milieu *m*, cœur *m* ▪ **in the ~ of** au milieu OR au cœur de ▪ **there's a spy in our ~** il y a un espion parmi nous **2.** [in time] : **in the ~ of the crisis** en pleine crise.

midstream [mɪd'stri:m] *n* : **in ~** *liter* au milieu du courant ▪ **he stopped talking in ~** *fig* il s'arrêta au beau milieu d'une phrase ▪ **to change horses in ~** se raviser en cours de route.

midsummer ['mɪd,sʌməʳ] *n* : **in ~** au milieu de l'été, en été ▶ **~ madness** folie *f* estivale ▪ **'A Midsummer Night's Dream'** *Shakespeare* 'le Songe d'une nuit d'été'.

Midsummer Day, Midsummer's Day *n* le solstice d'été.

midterm [mɪd'tɜ:m] *n* **1.** SCH & UNIV milieu *m* du trimestre **2.** MED [of pregnancy] milieu *m* **3.** POL : **~ elections** *aux États-Unis, élections législatives qui ont lieu au milieu du mandat présidentiel*.

midtown ['mɪdtaʊn] *n* *US partie d'une ville située à mi-chemin entre le centre et les quartiers périphériques* ▪ **a ~ apartment** un appartement pas très loin du centre.

midway <> *adv* [,mɪd'weɪ] à mi-chemin ▪ **she was ~ through writing the first chapter** elle avait déjà écrit la moitié du premier chapitre ▪ **~ between** à mi-chemin entre.
<> *adj* ['mɪdweɪ] : **~ point** [in time, space] milieu *m* ▪ **we've reached a ~ point in the negotiations** nous avons parcouru la moitié du chemin dans les négociations.

midweek <> *adv* [mɪd'wi:k] [travel, arrive, meet] au milieu de la semaine ▪ RAIL ≃ en période bleue.
<> *adj* ['mɪd'wi:k] [travel, prices, performance] au milieu de la semaine ▪ RAIL ≃ (en) période bleue.

Midwest [,mɪd'west] *pr n* : **the ~** le Midwest ▪ **in the ~** dans le Midwest.

Midwestern [,mɪd'westən] *adj* du Midwest.

midwife ['mɪdwaɪf] (*pl* **midwives** [-waɪvz]) *n* sage-femme *f*.

midwifery ['mɪd,wɪfərɪ] *n* obstétrique *f*.

midwinter [,mɪd'wɪntəʳ] *n* [solstice] solstice *m* d'hiver ▪ **in ~** au milieu de l'hiver.

midyear [,mɪd'jɪəʳ] <> *n* milieu *m* de l'année.
<> *adj* du milieu de l'année.
◆ **midyears** *npl* *US* UNIV ≃ partiels *mpl* du deuxième trimestre.

miffed [mɪft] *adj inf* [person] piqué, fâché ▪ [expression] froissé, fâché.

might[1] [maɪt] *modal vb* **1.** [expressing possibility] : **you ~ well be right** il se pourrait bien que vous ayez raison ▪ **I ~ be home late tonight** je rentrerai peut-être tard ce soir ▪ **why not come with us? – I ~** pourquoi ne viens-tu pas avec nous? – peut-être ▪ **don't eat it, it ~ be poisonous** n'en mange pas, tu pourrais t'empoisonner ▪ **she ~ well have decided to turn back** il se pourrait *OR* il se peut bien qu'elle ait décidé de rentrer ▪ **she ~ have decided not to go** il se peut qu'elle ait décidé de ne pas y aller
2. [past form of 'may'] : **I never considered that she ~ want to come** je n'avais jamais pensé qu'elle pouvait avoir envie de venir ▪ **we feared you ~ be dead** nous avons eu peur que vous ne soyez mort
3. [in polite questions or suggestions] : **~ I interrupt?** puis-je me permettre de vous interrompre? ▪ **~ I** *OR* **if I ~ make a suggestion?** puis-je me permettre de suggérer quelque chose? ▪ **you ~ try using a different approach altogether** vous pourriez adopter une approche entièrement différente
4. [commenting on a statement made] : **that, I ~ add, was not my idea** cela n'était pas mon idée, soit dit en passant ▪ **this, as one ~ expect, did not go down well with the government** le gouvernement, est-il nécessaire de le préciser, n'a guère apprécié
5. [ought to] : **you ~ at least tidy up your room!** tu pourrais au moins ranger ta chambre! ▪ **I ~ have known he'd be the last (to arrive)** j'aurais dû savoir qu'il serait le dernier (à arriver) ▪ **you ~ have warned me!** tu aurais pu me prévenir!
6. [used to contradict or challenge] : **they ~ say they support women, but they do nothing practical to help them** ils disent peut-être qu'ils soutiennent les femmes mais ils ne font rien pour les aider sur le plan concret
7. *fml* & *hum* [in questions] : **and who ~ you be?** et qui êtes-vous donc?
8. *phr* **we ~ as well go home (as stay here)** nous ferions aussi bien de rentrer chez nous (plutôt que de rester ici) ▪ **he's regretting it now, as well he ~!** il le regrette maintenant, et pour cause!

might[2] [maɪt] *n* **1.** [power - of nation] pouvoir *m*, puissance *f* ; [- of army] puissance *f* **2.** [physical strength] force *f* ▪ **with all one's ~** de toutes ses forces ▪ **he started yelling with all his ~** il se mit à crier à tue-tête ➲ **with ~ and main** de toutes ses forces ▪ **~ is right** *prov* force fait loi *prov*.

might-have-been *n* **1.** [opportunity] occasion *f* manquée ▪ [hope] espoir *m* déçu **2.** *inf* [person] raté *m*, - e *f*.

mightily ['maɪtɪlɪ] *adv* **1.** [with vigour] avec vigueur, vigoureusement **2.** [extremely] extrêmement.

mightn't ['maɪtənt] = **might not**.

might've ['maɪtəv] = **might have**.

mighty ['maɪtɪ] (*comp* **mightier**, *superl* **mightiest**) <> *adj* **1.** [powerful] puissant **2.** [impressive] imposant ▪ [enormous] énorme.
<> *adv US inf* rudement.

migraine ['mi:greɪn, 'maɪgreɪn] *n* migraine *f* ▪ **to suffer from ~** avoir des migraines ▪ **I've got a ~** j'ai la migraine.

migrant ['maɪgrənt] <> *n* **1.** [bird, animal] migrateur *m* **2.** [worker - in agriculture] (travailleur *m*) saisonnier *m* ; [- foreign] travailleur *m* immigré.
<> *adj* **1.** [bird, animal] migrateur **2.** [person] : **~ worker** [seasonal] (travailleur *m*) saisonnier *m* ; [foreign] travailleur *m* immigré.

migrate [*UK* maɪ'greɪt, *US* 'maɪgreɪt] *vi* **1.** [bird, animal] migrer **2.** [person, family] migrer, se déplacer, émigrer.

migration [maɪ'greɪʃn] *n* migration *f*.

migratory ['maɪgrətrɪ] *adj* **1.** [bird, fish] migrateur **2.** [habit, movement] migratoire.

mike [maɪk] (*abbrev of* **microphone**) *n inf* micro *m*.

mil [mɪl] *n* **1.** [unit of length] millième *m* de pouce **2.** [thousand] mille *m inv*.

milady [mɪ'leɪdɪ] (*pl* **miladies**) *n arch* madame *f*.

Milanese [,mɪlə'ni:z] <> *n* Milanais *m*, - e *f*.
<> *adj* milanais.

milch cow ['mɪltʃ-] *n* vache *f* laitière ▪ *fig* vache *f* à lait.

mild [maɪld] <> *adj* **1.** [person, manner, voice] doux, douce *f* **2.** [in taste - cheese] doux, douce *f* ; [- curry] pas très fort *OR* épicé ▪ [soap, shampoo] doux, douce *f* ▪ [in strength - sedative, cigarette] léger **3.** [clement - winter] doux, douce *f* ▪ **the weather's ~ for the time of year** il fait (un temps) doux pour la saison **4.** [punishment] léger ▪ [criticism] clément.
<> *n UK bière moins riche en houblon et plus foncée que la "bitter"*.

mildew ['mɪldju:] <> *n* **1.** [on cereals, flowers] rouille *f* ▪ [on vines, potatoes, tomatoes] mildiou *m* **2.** [on paper, leather, food] moisissure *f*.
<> *vi* **1.** [cereals, flowers] se rouiller ▪ [vines, potatoes, tomatoes] être atteint par le mildiou **2.** [paper, leather, food] moisir.

mildewed ['mɪldju:d] *adj* [cereals, flowers] rouillé ▪ [vines, potatoes, tomatoes] mildiousé ▪ [paper, leather, food] moisi.

mildly ['maɪldlɪ] *adv* **1.** [in manner, voice] doucement, avec douceur **2.** [slightly] modérément, légèrement ▪ **that's putting it ~!** c'est le moins qu'on puisse dire!

mild-mannered *adj* doux, douce *f*.

mildness ['maɪldnɪs] *n* **1.** [of manner] douceur *f* **2.** [in taste] : **she appreciated the ~ of the curry** elle apprécia le fait que le curry n'était pas trop épicé **3.** [of weather] douceur *f* **4.** [of rebuke] indulgence *f*, clémence *f*.

mile [maɪl] *n* **1.** [measurement] mille *m* *(1 609,33 m)* ▪ [in athletics] mile *m* ▪ **she lives 30 ~s from Birmingham** elle habite à une cinquantaine de kilomètres de Birmingham ▪ **a 100-~ journey** un voyage de 160 kilomètres **2.** [long distance] : **you can see it a ~ off** ça se voit de loin ▪ **they live ~s apart** ils habitent à des kilomètres l'un de l'autre ▪ **the best doctor for ~s around** le meilleur médecin à des kilomètres à la ronde ▪ **we're ~s from the nearest town** on est à des kilomètres de la ville la plus proche ▪ **it's ~s from anywhere** c'est un endroit complètement isolé ▪ **you can see for ~s and ~s** on voit à des kilomètres à la ronde ▪ **we walked (for) ~s and ~s** on a fait des kilomètres (à pied) **3.** *fig* **they're ~s ahead of their competitors** ils ont une avance considérable sur leurs concurrents ▪ **the two judges are ~s apart on capital punishment** les deux juges ont des points de vue *OR* des avis radicalement opposés sur la peine de mort ➲ **he was ~s away** il était dans la lune ▪ **you could see what was going to happen a ~ off** on voyait d'ici ce qui allait arriver ▪ **your calculations are ~s out** vous vous êtes complètement trompé dans vos calculs ▪ **not a million ~s from here** tout près d'ici, parmi nous ▪ **it's not a million ~s from what we tried to do** cela ressemble assez à ce que nous avons essayé de faire **4.** *inf (adverbial use) inf* [much] : **she's ~s better than me at languages** elle est bien plus forte que moi en langues ▪ **I'm feeling ~s better already** je me sens déjà cent fois mieux.

mileage ['maɪlɪdʒ] *n* **1.** AUT [distance] ≃ kilométrage *m* ▪ **the car's got a very high ~** la voiture a beaucoup roulé *OR* a un kilométrage élevé ▪ **the papers got tremendous ~ out of the scandal** *fig* les journaux ont exploité le scandale au maximum **2.** [consumption] consommation *f* (d'essence).

mileage allowance *n* indemnité *f* kilométrique.

mileometer [maɪ'lɒmɪtə^r] *n* ≃ compteur *m* (kilométrique).

milepost ['maɪlpəʊst] *n* ≃ borne *f* (kilométrique).

miler ['maɪlə^r] *n* coureur *m*, - euse *f* du mile.

milestone ['maɪlstəʊn] *n* **1.** *liter* ≃ borne *f* (kilométrique) **2.** *fig* [important event] jalon *m*, étape *f* importante.

milieu [*UK* 'mi:ljɜ:, *US* mi:l'ju:] *n* environnement *m* (social).

militancy ['mɪlɪtənsɪ] *n* militantisme *m*.

militant ['mɪlɪtənt] <> *adj* militant.
<> *n* **1.** [gen] militant *m*, - e *f* **2.** *UK* = **Militant (Tendency)**.

◆ **Militant (Tendency)** *pr n* POL *tendance d'extrême gauche à l'intérieur du parti travailliste britannique.*

militarism ['mɪlɪtərɪzm] *n* militarisme *m.*

militarist ['mɪlɪtərɪst] *n* militariste *mf.*

militaristic [,mɪlɪtə'rɪstɪk] *adj* militariste.

militarize, ise ['mɪlɪtəraɪz] *vt* militariser.

militarized zone ['mɪlɪtəraɪzd-] *n* zone *f* militarisée.

military ['mɪlɪtrɪ] <> *adj* militaire ▪ **he's a ~ man** c'est un militaire (de carrière) ▶ **~ academy** école *f* militaire ▪ **~ band** fanfare *f* militaire ▪ **~ service** service *m* militaire.
<> *n* : **the ~** l'armée *f.*

Military Cross *n distinction militaire britannique.*

military police *n* police *f* militaire.

military policeman *n membre de la police militaire.*

militate ['mɪlɪteɪt] ◆ **militate against** *vt insep* [facts, actions] militer contre.

militia [mɪ'lɪʃə] *n* **1.** [body of citizens] milice *f* **2.** *US* [reserve army] réserve *f.*

militiaman [mɪ'lɪʃəmən] (*pl* **militiamen** [-mən]) *n* milicien *m.*

milk [mɪlk] <> *n* lait *m* ▪ **mother's ~** lait maternel ▪ **cow's ~** lait de vache ▪ **Milk of Magnesia®** lait de magnésie ▪ **a land flowing with ~ and honey** un pays de cocagne ▪ **the ~ of human kindness** *fig* le lait de la tendresse humaine.
<> *comp* [bottle, churn, jug etc - empty] à lait ; [- full] de lait ▪ **~ can** *US* bidon *m* de lait.
<> *vt* **1.** [cow, goat] traire **2.** [snake] extraire le venin de **3.** *fig* **to ~ a country of its resources** dépouiller un pays de ses ressources ▪ **he really ~s his clients** il plume ses clients ▪ **she ~ed the subject dry** elle a épuisé le sujet.
<> *vi* : **the cow ~s well** la vache donne beaucoup de lait.

milk bar *n* milk-bar *m.*

milk chocolate *n* chocolat *m* au lait.

milker ['mɪlkəʳ] *n* **1.** [cow] : **a good ~** une bonne laitière **2.** [dairy hand] trayeur *m*, - euse *f* **3.** [machine] trayeuse *f.*

milk float *n UK* camionnette *f* du laitier.

milk gland *n* glande *f* lactéale *OR* galactophore.

milking ['mɪlkɪŋ] *n* traite *f* ▪ **to do the ~** traire les vaches ▪ **~ time** l'heure *f* de la traite.

milking machine *n* machine *f* à traire, trayeuse *f.*

milking stool *n* tabouret *m* à traire.

milk loaf *n* pain *m* brioché.

milkmaid ['mɪlkmeɪd] *n* vachère *f*, trayeuse *f.*

milkman ['mɪlkmən] (*pl* **milkmen** [-mən]) *n* [who delivers milk] laitier *m* ▪ *UK* [who milks] vacher *m*, trayeur *m.*

milk powder *n* lait *m* en poudre.

milk pudding *n UK* entremets *m* au lait.

milk round *n UK* **1.** [for milk delivery] tournée *f* du laitier **2.** UNIV *tournée des universités par les employeurs pour recruter des étudiants en fin d'études.*

milk run *n inf* **1.** AERON vol *m* sans histoire, partie *f* de rigolade **2.** [regular journey] trajet *m* habituel, tournée *f* habituelle.

milk shake *n* milk-shake *m.*

milksop ['mɪlksɒp] *n* chiffe *f* molle.

milk tooth *n* dent *f* de lait.

milk train *n* premier train *m.*

milk truck *US* = **milk float**.

milk-white *adj* d'un blanc laiteux.

milky ['mɪlkɪ] (*comp* **milkier**, *superl* **milkiest**) *adj* **1.** [taste] laiteux, de lait ▪ [dessert] lacté, à base de lait ▪ [tea, coffee] avec du lait **2.** [colour] laiteux ▪ [skin] d'un blanc laiteux **3.** [cloudy - liquid] laiteux, lactescent.

Milky Way *pr n* : **the ~** la Voie lactée.

mill [mɪl] <> *n* **1.** [for flour] moulin *m* ▪ [on industrial scale] meunerie *f*, minoterie *f* ▪ **she's been through the ~** elle a souffert ▪ **she put him through the ~** elle lui en a fait voir ▪ **'The Mill on the Floss'** ***Eliot*** 'le Moulin sur la Floss' **2.** [factory] usine *f* ▪ **steel ~** aciérie *f* **3.** [domestic - for coffee, pepper] moulin *m* **4.** TECH [for coins] machine *f* à créneler ▪ [for metal] fraiseuse *f.*
<> *vt* **1.** [grain] moudre ▪ [ore] broyer **2.** [mark - coin] créneler ; [- screw] moleter ; [- surface] strier, rainer.
◆ **mill about** *UK*, **mill around** *vi insep* [crowd, people] grouiller.

millenarian [,mɪlɪ'neərɪən] <> *adj* millénariste.
<> *n* millénariste *mf.*

millennial [mɪ'lenɪəl] *adj* du millenium.

millennium [mɪ'lenɪəm] (*pl* **millenniums** *OR pl* **millennia** [-nɪə]) *n* **1.** [thousand years] millénaire *m* **2.** RELIG & *fig* **the ~** le millénium **3.** [the year 2000] l'an *m* 2000.

millennium bug *n* bogue *m* de l'an 2000.

millepede ['mɪlɪpi:d] = **millipede**.

miller ['mɪləʳ] *n* meunier *m*, - ère *f.*

millet ['mɪlɪt] *n* millet *m.*

millibar ['mɪlɪbɑ:ʳ] *n* millibar *m.*

milligram(me) ['mɪlɪgræm] *n* milligramme *m.*

millilitre *UK*, **milliliter** *US* ['mɪlɪ,li:təʳ] *n* millilitre *m.*

millimetre *UK*, **millimeter** *US* ['mɪlɪ,mi:təʳ] *n* millimètre *m.*

milliner ['mɪlɪnəʳ] *n* modiste *mf.*

millinery ['mɪlɪnrɪ] *n* [manufacture] fabrication *f* de chapeaux de femmes ▪ [sale] vente *f* de chapeaux de femmes.

milling ['mɪlɪŋ] *n* crénelage *m.*

milling machine *n* fraiseuse *f.*

million ['mɪljən] *n* **1.** *liter* million *m* ▪ **two ~ dollars** deux millions de dollars ▪ **~s of pounds** des millions de livres ▪ **the chance of that happening is one in a ~** il y a une chance sur un million que ça arrive ▪ **his secretary is one in a ~** sa secrétaire est une perle rare ▪ **that man is worth several ~** cet homme est plusieurs fois milliardaire **2.** [enormous number] : **there were simply ~s of people at the concert!** il y avait un monde fou au concert! ▪ **I've told you a ~ times not to do that** je t'ai dit cent fois de ne pas faire ça.
◆ **millions** *npl* [masses] masses *fpl.*

millionaire [,mɪljə'neəʳ] *n* ≃ milliardaire *mf* ▪ **he's a dollar ~** il possède des millions de dollars.

millionairess [,mɪljə'neərɪs] *n* ≃ milliardaire *f.*

millionth ['mɪljənθ] <> *det* millionième.
<> *n* **1.** [ordinal] millionième *mf* **2.** [fraction] millionième *m.*

millipede ['mɪlɪpi:d] *n* mille-pattes *m inv.*

millisecond ['mɪlɪ,sekənd] *n* milliseconde *f*, millième *m* de seconde.

millpond ['mɪlpɒnd] *n* retenue *f* de moulin ▪ **the sea was like a ~** *fig* la mer était d'huile.

millrace ['mɪlreɪs] *n* bief *m.*

Mills and Boon® ['mɪlzn,bu:n] *pr n maison d'édition publiant des romans sentimentaux.*

millstone ['mɪlstəʊn] *n* **1.** *liter* meule *f* **2.** *fig* fardeau *m* ▪ **another ~ round the taxpayer's neck** une charge supplémentaire pour le contribuable.

millstream ['mɪlstri:m] *n* courant *m* du bief.

millwheel ['mɪlwi:l] *n* roue *f* (d'un moulin).

millwright ['mɪlraɪt] *n* constructeur *m* de moulins.

milometer [maɪ'lɒmɪtəʳ] = **mileometer**.

milt [mɪlt] *n* [of fish - fluid] laitance *f* ; [- organ] testicule *m.*

mime [maɪm] <> *n* [actor, play] mime *m* ▪ **to explain something in ~** expliquer quelque chose par gestes.

◇ *vi* **1.** THEAT faire du mime **2.** [pop singer] chanter en playback.
◇ *vt* mimer ▪ [derisively] singer.

mimesis [mɪ'mi:sɪs] *n* BIOL mimétisme *m*.

mimic ['mɪmɪk] (*pret & pp* **mimicked**, *cont* **mimicking**) ◇ *vt* **1.** [gestures] mimer ▪ [satirically] parodier, singer **2.** BIOL imiter (par mimétisme).
◇ *n* imitateur *m*, - trice *f*.
◇ *adj* **1.** [mock - battle, warfare] simulé ▪ **~ colouring** mimétisme *m* des couleurs **2.** THEAT mimique.

mimicry ['mɪmɪkrɪ] *n* **1.** [imitation] imitation *f* **2.** BIOL mimétisme *m*.

mimosa [mɪ'məʊzə] *n* mimosa *m*.

min. 1. (*written abbrev of* **minute**) mn, min **2.** (*written abbrev of* **minimum**) min.

Min. *written abbr of* **ministry**.

minaret [mɪnə'ret] *n* minaret *m*.

minatory ['mɪnətrɪ] *adj fml* comminatoire.

mince [mɪns] ◇ *vt* **1.** CULIN hacher **2.** *phr* **he doesn't ~ his words** il ne mâche pas ses mots.
◇ *vi* **1.** [speak] parler avec affectation **2.** [move] marcher en se trémoussant.
◇ *n* **1.** *UK* [meat] viande *f* hachée, haché *m* **2.** *US* = **mincemeat** *(sense 2)*.

mincemeat ['mɪnsmi:t] *n* **1.** [meat] viande *f* hachée **2.** [sweet filling] *mélange de fruits secs et d'épices qui sert de garniture à des tartelettes* **3.** *phr* **to make ~ of sb** *inf* réduire qqn en bouillie OR en chair à pâté.

mince pie *n tartelette fourrée avec un mélange de fruits secs et d'épices que l'on sert à Noël en Grande-Bretagne.*

mincer ['mɪnsəʳ] *n* hachoir *m*, hache-viande *m inv*.

mincing ['mɪnsɪŋ] *adj* affecté, maniéré.

mind [maɪnd] ◇ *n* **1.** [reason] esprit *m* ▪ **the power of ~ over matter** le pouvoir de l'esprit sur la matière ▪ **to be strong in ~ and body** être physiquement et mentalement solide ▪ **to be of sound ~** être sain d'esprit ▪ **his ~ became unhinged** il a perdu la raison, il est devenu fou ▶ **to be/to go out of one's ~** être/devenir fou ▪ **he was out of his ~ with worry** il était fou d'inquiétude ▪ **he isn't in his right ~** il n'a pas tous ses esprits ▪ **no-one in their right ~ would do such a thing** aucune personne sensée n'agirait ainsi
2. [thoughts] : **there's something on her ~** il y a quelque chose qui la tracasse ▪ **I have a lot on my ~** j'ai beaucoup de soucis ▪ **what's going on in her ~?** qu'est-ce qui se passe dans son esprit OR sa tête? ▪ **at the back of one's ~** au fond de soi-même ▪ **to put sthg to the back of one's ~** chasser qqch de son esprit ▪ **I just can't get him out of my ~** je n'arrive absolument pas à l'oublier ▪ **to have sb/sthg in ~** penser à qqn/qqch de précis ▪ **what kind of holiday did you have in ~?** qu'est-ce que tu voulais OR voudrais faire pour les vacances? ▪ **you must put the idea out of your ~** tu dois te sortir cette idée de la tête ▪ **to set one's ~ on doing sthg** se mettre en tête de faire qqch ▪ **to have one's ~ set on sthg** vouloir qqch à tout prix ▪ **a drink will take your ~ off the accident** bois un verre, ça te fera oublier l'accident ▶ **to see things in one's ~'s eye** bien se représenter qqch
3. [attention] : **I can't seem to apply my ~ to the problem** je n'arrive pas à me concentrer sur le problème ▪ **keep your ~ on the job** ne vous laissez pas distraire ▪ **she does crosswords to keep her ~ occupied** elle fait des mots croisés pour s'occuper l'esprit ▪ **don't pay him any ~** *US* ne fais pas attention à lui
4. [memory] : **my ~ has gone blank** j'ai un trou de mémoire ▪ **it brings to ~ the time we were in Spain** cela me rappelle l'époque où nous étions en Espagne ▪ **Churchill's words come to ~** on pense aux paroles de Churchill ▪ **it went clean** OR **right out of my ~** cela m'est complètement sorti de l'esprit OR de la tête ▪ **it puts me in ~ of Japan** cela me fait penser au Japon, cela me rappelle le Japon ▪ **it must have slipped my ~** j'ai dû oublier ▶ **time out of ~ I've warned him not to go there** *UK* cela fait une éternité que je lui dis de ne pas y aller
5. [intellect] esprit *m* ▪ **she has an outstanding ~** elle est d'une très grande intelligence ▪ [intelligent person, thinker] esprit *m*, cerveau *m* ▶ **great ~s think alike** *hum* les grands esprits se rencontrent
6. [way of thinking] : **the Western ~** les modes de pensée occidentaux ▪ **he has a suspicious ~** il est soupçonneux de nature
7. [opinion] : **to be of the same** OR **of like** OR **of one ~** être du même avis ▶ **to my ~** à mon avis, selon moi ▪ **I'm in two ~s about where to go for my holidays** je ne sais pas très bien où aller passer mes vacances ▪ **to make up one's ~** se décider, prendre une décision ▪ **my ~ is made up** ma décision est prise ▪ **to make up one's ~ about sthg** décider qqch ▪ **to make up one's ~ to do sthg** se décider à faire qqch
8. [desire] : **I've half a ~ to give up** j'ai à moitié envie de renoncer ▪ **I've a good ~ to tell him what I think** j'ai bien envie de lui dire ce que je pense ▪ [intention] : **nothing was further from my ~** je n'en avais nullement l'intention ▪ **I've had it in ~ for some time now** j'y songe depuis un moment.
◇ *vt* **1.** [look after - children] garder ; [- bags, possessions] garder, surveiller ; [- shop, business] garder, tenir ; [- plants, garden] s'occuper de, prendre soin de
2. [pay attention to] faire attention à ▪ **~ your own business!** occupe-toi de ce qui te regarde!, mêle-toi de tes oignons! ▪ **~ your language!** surveille ton langage! ▪ **to ~ one's manners** se surveiller ▪ **'~ the step'** 'attention à la marche' ▪ **~ the cat!** attention au chat!
3. *(with verb phrase)* [be sure of] faire attention à ▪ **~ you don't break it** fais bien attention de ne pas le casser ▪ **~ what you say** [pay attention] réfléchissez à OR faites attention à ce que vous dites ; [don't be rude] mesurez vos paroles ▪ **~ what you're doing!** regarde ce que tu fais! ▪ [remember] : **~ you post my letter** n'oubliez surtout pas de poster ma lettre
4. [bother about] faire attention à, s'inquiéter de OR pour ▪ **I really don't ~ what he says/thinks** je me fiche de ce qu'il peut dire/penser
5. [object to] : **I don't ~ him** il ne me dérange pas ▪ **do you ~ me smoking?** cela ne vous ennuie OR dérange pas que je fume? ▪ **did you ~ me inviting her?** tu aurais peut-être préféré que je ne l'invite pas?, ça t'ennuie que je l'aie invitée? ▪ **would you ~ turning out the light, please?** [politely] pourriez-vous éteindre la lumière, s'il vous plaît? ; [aggressively] est-ce que cela vous dérangerait beaucoup d'éteindre la lumière? ▪ **I wouldn't ~ a cup of tea** je prendrais bien OR volontiers une tasse de thé
6. *phr* **~ (you), I'm not surprised** remarque OR tu sais, cela ne m'étonne pas ▪ **~ you, he's a bit young** ceci dit, il est un peu jeune ▪ **never ~ that now** [leave it] ne vous occupez pas de cela tout de suite ; [forget it] ce n'est plus la peine de s'en occuper ▪ **never ~ the consequences** ne vous préoccupez pas des conséquences, peu importent les conséquences ▪ **never ~ what people say/think** peu importe ce que disent/pensent les gens ▪ **never ~ his feelings, I've got a business to run!** je n'ai que faire de ses états d'âme, j'ai une affaire à diriger!
◇ *vi* **1.** [object - esp in requests] : **do you ~ if I open the window?** cela vous dérange si j'ouvre la fenêtre? ▪ **would you ~ if I opened the window?** est-ce que cela vous ennuierait si j'ouvrais la fenêtre? ▪ **I don't ~ in the least** cela ne me dérange pas le moins du monde ▪ **if you don't ~** si vous voulez bien, si vous n'y voyez pas d'inconvénient ▪ **I don't ~ if I do** [in reply to offer] volontiers, je ne dis pas non, ce n'est pas de refus
2. [care, worry] : **I don't ~ if people laugh at me – but you should ~!** je ne me soucie guère que les gens se moquent de moi – mais vous devriez! ▪ **if you don't ~, I haven't finished** si cela ne vous fait rien, je n'ai pas terminé ▪ **do you ~!** *iron* [politely] vous permettez? ; [indignantly] non mais! ▪ **never ~** [it doesn't matter] cela ne fait rien, tant pis ; [don't worry] ne vous en faites pas ▪ **never you ~!** [don't worry] ne vous en faites pas! ; [mind your own business] ce n'est pas votre affaire! ▪ **never ~ about the money now** ne t'en fais pas pour l'argent, on verra plus tard
3. *UK* [be careful] faire attention ▪ **~!** attention!
➡ **mind out** *vi insep UK* faire attention ▪ **~ out!** attention!

mind-altering *adj* [drug] psychotrope.

mind-bending [-bendɪŋ] *adj inf* **1.** [complicated] compliqué **2.** [drugs] psychotrope.

mind-blowing *adj inf* [amazing] époustouflant.

mind-boggling *adj* extraordinaire, stupéfiant.

minded ['maɪndɪd] *adj fml* disposé ■ **she could easily lend us the money, if she were ~ to do so** elle pourrait facilement nous prêter l'argent, si elle y était disposée *OR* le voulait.

-minded [ˌmaɪndɪd] *in cpds* **1.** *(with adj)* **simple~** simple d'esprit ■ **they're so narrow~** ils sont tellement étroits d'esprit **2.** *(with adv)* **to be politically~** s'intéresser beaucoup à la politique ■ **many young people are scientifically~** beaucoup de jeunes ont l'esprit scientifique **3.** *(with n)* **my parents are very money~** mes parents ont un faible pour l'argent *OR* sont très portés sur l'argent.

minder ['maɪndəʳ] *n* **1.** *UK inf* [bodyguard] gorille *m* **2.** [gen] gardien *m*, - enne *f*, surveillant *m*, - e *f*.

mind-expanding *adj* [drugs] hallucinogène, psychédélique.

mindful ['maɪndful] *adj fml* **~ of her feelings on the subject, he fell silent** attentif à ce qu'elle ressentait à ce sujet, il se tut ■ **he was always ~ of his children's future** il a toujours été soucieux *OR* il s'est toujours préoccupé de l'avenir de ses enfants.

mindless ['maɪndlɪs] *adj* **1.** [stupid - film, book] idiot, stupide ■ [senseless - cruelty, violence] insensé, sans nom **2.** [boring] bête, ennuyeux **3.** [heedless] : **~ of the danger, he dived into the river** insouciant du danger, il plongea dans la rivière.

mind-numbing *adj* abrutissant.

mind reader *n* : **he must be a ~** il lit dans les pensées comme dans un livre ■ **I'm not a ~** je ne suis pas devin.

mindset ['maɪndset] *n* façon *f* de voir les choses.

mine¹ [maɪn] ◇ *pron* le mien *m*, la mienne *f*, les miens *mpl*, les miennes *f* ■ **is this pen ~? – no, it's ~!** il est à moi ce stylo? – non, c'est le mien! ■ **this bag is ~** ce sac m'appartient *OR* est à moi ■ **he's an old friend of ~** c'est un vieil ami à moi ■ **where did that brother of ~ get to?** mais où est-ce que mon frère est encore passé? ■ **~ is an exceptional situation** je me trouve dans une situation exceptionnelle.
◇ *det arch* mon *m*, ma *f*, mes *pl*.

mine² [maɪn] ◇ *n* **1.** [for coal, gold, salt etc] mine *f* ■ **he went down the ~** *OR* **~s at 16** il est descendu à la mine à 16 ans **2.** *fig* [valuable source] mine *f* ■ **she's a ~ of information** c'est une véritable mine de renseignements **3.** [explosive] mine *f* ■ **to clear a road of ~s** déminer une route.
◇ *vt* **1.** GEOL [coal, gold etc] extraire ■ **they ~ coal in the area** il y a des mines de charbon dans la région **2.** MIL [road, sea] miner ■ [destroy] : **their jeep was ~d** leur jeep a sauté sur une mine **3.** [undermine - fortification] saper.
◇ *vi* exploiter une mine ■ **to ~ for uranium** [prospect] chercher de l'uranium, prospecter pour trouver de l'uranium ; [extract] exploiter une mine d'uranium.

mine detector *n* détecteur *m* de mines.

minefield ['maɪnfiːld] *n* **1.** *liter* champ *m* de mines **2.** *fig* **the ~ of high-level diplomacy** les chausse-trappes de la haute diplomatie ■ **a political ~** une situation épineuse du point de vue politique.

minehunter ['maɪnˌhʌntəʳ] *n* NAUT chasseur *m* de mines.

minelayer ['maɪnˌleɪəʳ] *n* mouilleur *m* de mines.

miner ['maɪnəʳ] *n* MIN mineur *m*.

mineral ['mɪnərəl] ◇ *n* **1.** GEOL minéral *m* **2.** *UK* [soft drink] boisson *f* gazeuse (non alcoolique), soda *m*.
◇ *adj* minéral.

mineralogical [ˌmɪnərə'lɒdʒɪkl] *adj* minéralogique.

mineralogist [ˌmɪnə'rælədʒɪst] *n* minéralogiste *mf*.

mineralogy [ˌmɪnə'rælədʒɪ] *n* minéralogie *f*.

mineral ore *n* minerai *m*.

mineral water *n* eau *f* minérale.

miner's lung *n* anthracose *f*.

Minerva [mɪ'nɜːvə] *pr n* Minerve.

mineshaft ['maɪnʃɑːft] *n* puits *m* de mine.

minestrone (soup) [ˌmɪnɪ'strəʊnɪ-] *n* minestrone *m*.

minesweeper ['maɪnˌswiːpəʳ] *n* dragueur *m* de mines.

mineworker ['maɪnˌwɜːkəʳ] *n* ouvrier *m*, - ère *f* de la mine, mineur *m*.

mingle ['mɪŋgl] ◇ *vt* mélanger, mêler ■ **he ~d truth with lies** il mélangeait le vrai et le faux.
◇ *vi* se mêler (aux autres) ■ [at party] : **excuse me, I must ~** excusez-moi, il faut que je salue d'autres invités.

minging[△] ['mɪŋɪŋ] *adj UK* horrible.

mingy ['mɪndʒɪ] (*comp* **mingier**, *superl* **mingiest**) *adj UK inf* [mean - person] radin, pingre ; [- portion, quantity] chiche, misérable, maigre.

mini ['mɪnɪ] ◇ *n inf* **1.** [skirt] minijupe *f* **2.** COMPUT mini-ordinateur *m*, mini *m*.
◇ *adj* mini *(inv)*.
◆ **Mini®** *n* [car] (Austin®) mini *f*.

miniature ['mɪnətʃəʳ] ◇ *adj* [in miniature] en miniature ■ [model] miniature ■ [tiny] minuscule ■ **~ golf** golf *m* miniature ■ **~ poodle** caniche *m* nain.
◇ *n* [gen - ART] miniature *f* ■ **in ~** en miniature.

miniaturist ['mɪnətʃərɪst] *n* miniaturiste *mf*.

miniaturized ['mɪnətʃəraɪzd] *adj* miniaturisé.

minibus ['mɪnɪbʌs] (*pl* **minibuses**) *n* minibus *m*.

minicab ['mɪnɪkæb] *n UK voiture de série convertie en taxi.*

minicomputer [ˌmɪnɪkəm'pjuːtəʳ] *n* mini-ordinateur *m*.

MiniDisc® ['mɪnɪdɪsk] *n* Minidisc® *m*.

MiniDisc® player *n* lecteur de MiniDiscs® *m*.

minidish ['mɪnɪdɪʃ] *n* TV mini antenne *f* parabolique.

minidress ['mɪnɪdres] *n* mini-robe *f*.

minim ['mɪnɪm] *n* **1.** *UK* MUS blanche *f* **2.** [measure] ≃ goutte *f* *(0,5 ml)*.

minima ['mɪnɪmə] *pl* ▷ **minimum**.

minimal ['mɪnɪml] *adj* minimal ■ **there has been only a ~ improvement** il n'y a eu qu'une infime amélioration ● **~ art** art *m* minimal ■ **~ pair** LING paire *f* minimale.

minimalism ['mɪnɪməlɪzm] *n* minimalisme *m*.

minimalist ['mɪnɪməlɪst] *n* minimaliste *mf*.

minimalize, ise ['mɪnɪməlaɪz] *vt* minimaliser.

minimally ['mɪnɪməlɪ] *adv* à peine.

minimarket ['mɪnɪˌmɑːkɪt], **minimart** ['mɪnɪmɑːt] *n* supérette *f*, petit supermarché *m*.

minimize, ise ['mɪnɪˌmaɪz] *vt* **1.** [reduce - size, amount] réduire au minimum, diminuer le plus possible **2.** [diminish - importance, achievement] minimiser.

minim rest *n UK* MUS demi-pause *f*.

minimum ['mɪnɪməm] (*pl* **minimums** *OR pl* **minima** ['mɪnɪmə])
◇ *n* minimum *m* ■ **costs were reduced to the** *OR* **a ~** les coûts furent réduits au minimum ■ **there was only the ~ of damage** il n'y a eu que des dégâts minimes ■ **keep expenses to a ~** limitez au minimum les dépenses, dépensez le moins possible ■ **at the (very) ~ it will cost £2,000** (en mettant les choses) au mieux, cela coûtera 2 000 livres ■ **we will need £50 each ~** *OR* **a ~ of £50 each** il nous faudra 50 livres chacun (au) minimum.
◇ *adj* minimum, minimal.

minimum lending rate *n UK* taux *m* d'escompte *OR* de base.

minimum wage *n* salaire *m* minimum *(légal)*, ≃ SMIC *m*.

mining ['maɪnɪŋ] ◇ *n* **1.** MIN exploitation *f* minière, extraction *f* **2.** MIL [on land] pose *f* de mines ■ [at sea] mouillage *m* de mines.
◇ *adj* [town, company] minier ■ [family] de mineurs.

mining engineer *n* ingénieur *m* des mines.

mining engineering *n* ingénierie *f* des mines.

minion ['mɪnjən] *n pej* laquais *m.*

minipill ['mɪnɪpɪl] *n* minipilule *f.*

miniscule ['mɪnɪskju:l] *adj* minuscule.

mini-series *n* TV mini-feuilleton *m.*

miniskirt ['mɪnɪskɜ:t] *n* minijupe *f.*

minister ['mɪnɪstə^r] ◇ *n* **1.** POL ministre *m* ▪ **the Minister of Education/Defence** le ministre de l'Éducation/de la Défense ▪ **~ of state** secrétaire *mf* d'État **2.** [diplomat] ministre *m* **3.** RELIG pasteur *m*, ministre *m* ▪ **~ of God** ministre du culte.
◇ *vi* **1.** [provide care] : **to ~ to sb** secourir qqn, donner des soins à qqn ▪ **to ~ to sb's needs** pourvoir aux besoins de qqn **2.** RELIG : **he ~ ed to St. Luke's for 20 years** il a été le pasteur de l'église St-Luc pendant 20 ans.

ministerial [,mɪnɪ'stɪərɪəl] *adj* **1.** POL [project, crisis] ministériel ▪ [post] de ministre ▪ **~ benches** banc *m* des ministres ▪ **to hold ~ office** être ministre **2.** RELIG pastoral, sacerdotal.

ministering angel ['mɪnɪstrɪŋ-] *n fig* ange *m* de bonté.

ministration [,mɪnɪ'streɪʃn] *n* RELIG ministère *m.*
◆ **ministrations** *npl fml* soins *mpl.*

ministry ['mɪnɪstrɪ] (*pl* **ministries**) *n* **1.** POL [department] ministère *m* ▪ [government] gouvernement *m* ▪ **the Ministry of Defence** le ministère de la Défense **2.** RELIG [collective body] sacerdoce *m*, saint ministère *m* ▪ **to join the ~** [Roman Catholic] se faire ordonner prêtre ; [Protestant] devenir pasteur ▮ [period of office] ministère *m.*

mink [mɪŋk] ◇ *n* [animal, fur] vison *m* ▪ [coat] manteau *m* en *OR* de vison, vison *m.*
◇ *comp* [coat, stole] en *OR* de vison.

Minnesota [,mɪnɪ'səʊtə] *pr n* Minnesota *m* ▪ **in ~** dans le Minnesota.

minnow ['mɪnəʊ] (*pl inv OR pl* **minnows**) *n* **1.** [specific fish] vairon *m* ▪ [any small fish] fretin *m (U)* **2.** *UK fig* [insignificant person] (menu) fretin *m.*

minor ['maɪnə^r] ◇ *adj* **1.** [secondary - road, role, position] secondaire ; [- writer] mineur ; [- importance, interest] secondaire, mineur ; [- share] petit, mineur ▪ **~ orders** ordres *mpl* mineurs **2.** [unimportant - problem, worry] mineur, peu important **3.** [small - alteration, disagreement] mineur, petit ; [- detail, expense] mineur, petit, menu **4.** [not serious - accident] mineur, petit ; [- illness, injury] bénin, - igne *f* ▪ **~ offence** LAW délit *m* mineur ▪ **to have a ~ operation** MED subir une petite intervention chirurgicale *OR* une intervention chirurgicale bénigne **5.** MUS mineur ▪ **in A ~** en la mineur ➊ **in a ~ key** en mode mineur ▪ **~ third** tierce *f* mineure **6.** *US* UNIV [subject] facultatif.
◇ *n* **1.** [in age] mineur *m*, - e *f* **2.** *US* UNIV matière *f* secondaire.
◇ *vi US* UNIV : **she ~ed in French** elle a pris le français comme matière secondaire.

Minorca [mɪ'nɔ:kə] *pr n* Minorque ▪ **in ~** à Minorque.

Minorcan [mɪ'nɔ:kn] ◇ *n* Minorquin *m*, - e *f.*
◇ *adj* minorquin.

minority [maɪ'nɒrətɪ] (*pl* **minorities**) ◇ *n* **1.** [small group] minorité *f* ▪ **to be in a** *OR* **the ~** être dans la minorité ▪ **I'm afraid you're in a ~ of one** *hum* j'ai bien peur que vous ne soyez le seul de cet avis ▪ **the vocal ~** la minorité qui se fait entendre **2.** LAW [age] minorité *f.*
◇ *comp* [government, movement, tastes] minoritaire ▪ **~ group** minorité *f* ▪ **~ report** contre-rapport *m (soumis par une minorité)* ▪ **a ~ TV programme** *une émission de télévision destinée à un public restreint* ▪ **~ verdict** LAW verdict *m* de la minorité.

minor league ◇ *n US* SPORT ≃ division *f* d'honneur.
◇ *adj fig* secondaire, de peu d'importance ▪ **they're ~ compared with some American corporations** ils sont loin d'avoir l'envergure de certaines grandes sociétés américaines.

Minotaur ['maɪnətɔ:^r] *n* : **the ~** le Minotaure.

minster ['mɪnstə^r] *n* [abbey church] (église *f*) abbatiale *f* ▪ [cathedral] cathédrale *f.*

minstrel ['mɪnstrəl] *n* ménestrel *m*, troubadour *m.*

minstrel gallery *n* tribune *f* des musiciens.

mint [mɪnt] ◇ *n* **1.** BOT menthe *f* **2.** [sweet] bonbon *m* à la menthe **3.** [for coins] : **the Mint** l'Hôtel *m* de la Monnaie, la Monnaie **4.** *inf* [fortune] fortune *f* ▪ **to make a ~** faire fortune ▪ **it's worth a ~** cela vaut une fortune.
◇ *comp* [chocolate, sauce, tea] à la menthe.
◇ *adj* [stamps, coins] (tout) neuf ▪ **in ~ condition** *fig* en parfait état, à l'état neuf.
◇ *vt* **1.** [coins] fabriquer, frapper, battre **2.** [invent - word] inventer, créer ; [- expression] forger.

minuet [,mɪnjʊ'et] *n* menuet *m.*

minus ['maɪnəs] (*pl* **minuses** *OR pl* **minusses**) ◇ *prep* **1.** MATHS moins **2.** [in temperature] : **it's ~ 5° outside** il fait moins 5° dehors **3.** *inf* [without] : **he came home ~ his shopping** il est rentré sans ses achats ▪ **that chair is ~ a leg** cette chaise a un pied en moins.
◇ *n* **1.** [sign] moins *m* **2.** [drawback] inconvénient *m.*
◇ *adj* **1.** [number] moins **2.** *fig* négatif ▪ **the one ~ factor in the job is the low salary** le seul aspect négatif de ce poste est le salaire, qui est bas.

minuscule ['mɪnəskju:l] ◇ *adj* **1.** [tiny] minuscule **2.** [lower-case] en (lettres) minuscules.
◇ *n* minuscule *f.*

minus sign *n* signe *m* moins.

minute[1] ['mɪnɪt] ◇ *n* **1.** [period of 60 seconds] minute *f* ▪ [in telling the time] : **two ~s past/to ten** dix heures deux/moins deux **2.** [moment] instant *m*, minute *f* ▪ **it only took him a ~** il en a eu pour une minute ▪ **wait a ~, please** attendez un instant, s'il vous plaît ▪ **just a ~!** un instant! ; [aggressively] une minute! ▪ **come here this ~!** viens ici tout de suite! ▪ **I think of you every ~ of the day** je pense à vous à chaque instant de la journée ▪ **I'll talk to him the ~ he arrives** je lui parlerai dès qu'il arrivera ▪ **any ~ now** d'un instant à l'autre ▪ **at the ~** en ce moment ▪ **right up till the last ~** jusqu'à la toute dernière minute ▪ **the flight took two hours to the ~** le vol a duré deux heures à la minute près *OR* exactement ▪ **she arrived at six o'clock to the ~** *UK* elle est arrivée à six heures précises *OR* à six heures pile **3.** GEOM [of degree] minute *f.*
◇ *vt* **1.** [take down - fact, remark] inscrire au procès-verbal **2.** [time] minuter, chronométrer.
◆ **minutes** *npl* **1.** [of meeting] procès-verbal *m*, compte rendu *m* **2.** [report] note *f.*

minute[2] [maɪ'nju:t] *adj* **1.** [tiny] minuscule, infime ▪ [very slight - difference, improvement] infime, minime **2.** [precise] minutieux, détaillé ▪ **with ~ care** avec un soin minutieux ▪ **in ~ detail** par le menu ▪ **in the minutest detail** dans les moindres détails.

minute hand ['mɪnɪt-] *n* aiguille *f* des minutes.

minutely [maɪ'nju:tlɪ] *adv* **1.** [carefully] minutieusement, avec un soin minutieux ▪ [in detail] en détail, par le menu **2.** [fold] tout petit ▪ [move] imperceptiblement, très légèrement.

Minuteman ['mɪnɪtmæn] (*pl* **Minutemen** [-men]) *n* **1.** [soldier] homme-minute *m (soldat volontaire de la guerre d'Indépendance américaine)* **2.** [missile] Minuteman *m (missile balistique).*

MINUTEMEN

Les « hommes-minute » étaient des soldats qui devaient se tenir prêts à rejoindre les troupes à tout moment pendant la guerre d'Indépendance. Pendant la guerre froide, le nom de *Minuteman* fut donné à un type de missile américain.

minute steak ['mɪnɪt-] *n* entrecôte *f* minute.

minutiae [maɪ'nju:ʃɪaɪ] *npl* menus détails *mpl*, petits détails *mpl* ▪ *pej* [trivialities] vétilles *fpl*, riens *mpl.*

miracle ['mɪrəkl] ◇ *n* **1.** RELIG & *fig* miracle *m* ▪ **to work ~s** faire *OR* accomplir des miracles ▪ **by a ~, disaster was averted** la catastrophe a été évitée par miracle ▮ [achievement] :

economic ~ miracle *m* économique ▪ **a ~ of modern science** un prodige *OR* miracle de la science moderne **2.** = **miracle play**.
◇ *comp* [drug] miracle ▪ [cure] miraculeux ▪ **~ worker** faiseur *m*, - euse *f* de miracles.

miracle play *n* miracle *m (drame)*.

miraculous [mɪ'rækjʊləs] *adj* miraculeux ▪ **they had a ~ escape** c'est un miracle qu'ils s'en soient tirés (vivants).

miraculously [mɪ'rækjʊləslɪ] *adv* **1.** [by a miracle] miraculeusement, par miracle **2.** [extremely] merveilleusement, prodigieusement.

mirage [mɪ'rɑːʒ] *n* mirage *m*.

Miranda [mə'rændə] *pr n* **US** : **~ decision** *décision rendue par la Cour suprême en 1966 obligeant la police à informer toute personne arrêtée de ses droits.*

MIRAS ['maɪ,ræs] (*abbrev of* **mortgage interest relief at source**) *n* **UK** *système d'exonération fiscale sur les intérêts des emprunts immobiliers.*

mire [maɪəʳ] *lit* ◇ *n* boue *f* ▪ [deep] bourbier *m* ▪ **to drag sb's name through the ~** traîner le nom de qqn dans la boue.
◇ *vt (usu passive)* **1.** *lit* [in debt, difficulty] empêtrer **2.** [in mud] embourber.

mirror ['mɪrəʳ] ◇ *n* **1.** [looking glass] miroir *m*, glace *f* ▪ AUT rétroviseur *m* ▪ **to hold up a ~ to sthg** *fig* refléter qqch ▪ **the tabloid press is not necessarily a ~ of national opinion** la presse à sensation ne reflète pas nécessairement l'opinion du pays ▶ **the ~ stage** PSYCHOL le stade du miroir **2.** COMPUT site *m* miroir **3.** PRESS : **the Mirror** *nom abrégé du "Daily Mirror".*
◇ *vt* **1.** [reflect] réfléchir, refléter ▪ **the stars were ~ed in the smooth surface of the lake** les étoiles se réfléchissaient *OR* se reflétaient sur la surface lisse du lac **2.** [imitate] imiter ▪ **her career exactly ~ed her brother's** sa carrière fut calquée exactement sur celle de son frère **3.** COMPUT donner un site miroir à.

mirror image *n* image *f* en miroir, image *f* spéculaire ▪ *fig* copie *f* conforme.

mirror site *n* COMPUT site *m* miroir.

mirth [mɜːθ] *n (U)* rires *mpl*, hilarité *f*.

mirthful ['mɜːθfʊl] *adj lit* rieur, joyeux.

mirthless ['mɜːθlɪs] *adj lit* triste, sombre, morne ▪ [laugh] faux, forcé.

MIS (*abbrev of* **management information system**) *n* système *m* de gestion de l'information, MIS *m*.

misadventure [,mɪsəd'ventʃəʳ] *n* [accident] mésaventure *f* ▪ [misfortune] malheur *m*.

misaligned [,mɪsə'laɪnd] *adj* mal aligné.

misalliance [,mɪsə'laɪəns] *n* mésalliance *f*.

misanthropic [,mɪsən'θrɒpɪk] *adj* [person] misanthrope ▪ [thoughts] misanthropique.

misanthropist [mɪ'sænθrəpɪst] *n* misanthrope *mf*.

misanthropy [mɪ'sænθrəpɪ] *n* misanthropie *f*.

misapplication ['mɪs,æplɪ'keɪʃn] *n* mauvaise utilisation *f*, mauvaise application *f* ▪ [of law] mauvaise application *f* ▪ [of money] détournement *m*.

misapply [,mɪsə'plaɪ] (*pret & pp* **misapplied**) *vt* [learning] mal utiliser, mal exploiter ▪ [law] mal appliquer, appliquer à tort ▪ [money] détourner.

misapprehend ['mɪs,æprɪ'hend] *vt fml* se méprendre sur.

misapprehension ['mɪs,æprɪ'henʃn] *n fml* malentendu *m* ▪ **I'm afraid you are under a** *OR* **some ~** je crains que vous ne vous mépreniez.

misappropriate [,mɪsə'prəʊprɪeɪt] *vt fml* [money, funds] détourner ▪ [property] voler.

misappropriation ['mɪsə,prəʊprɪ'eɪʃn] *n fml* détournement *m*.

misbegotten [,mɪsbɪ'gɒtn] *adj fml* **1.** [plan] mal conçu, bâtard ▪ [child] bâtard, illégitime **2.** [illegally obtained] d'origine douteuse.

misbehave [,mɪsbɪ'heɪv] *vi* : **to ~ (o.s.)** se conduire mal ▪ **stop misbehaving!** sois sage! ▪ **he's misbehaving again!** il fait encore des siennes!

misbehaviour *UK*, **misbehavior** *US* [,mɪsbɪ'heɪvjəʳ] *n* mauvaise conduite *f*.

misc *written abbr of* **miscellaneous**.

miscalculate [,mɪs'kælkjʊleɪt] ◇ *vt* [amount, distance] mal calculer ▪ *fig* mal évaluer.
◇ *vi* MATHS se tromper dans ses calculs ▪ *fig* [judge wrongly] se tromper.

miscalculation [,mɪskælkjʊ'leɪʃn] *n* MATHS erreur *f* de calcul ▪ *fig* mauvais calcul *m*.

miscarriage [,mɪs'kærɪdʒ] *n* **1.** MED fausse couche *f* ▪ **to have a ~** faire une fausse couche **2.** [failure] échec *m* ▪ **~ of justice** erreur *f* judiciaire **3.** *UK* [loss - of mail, cargo] perte *f*.

miscarry [,mɪs'kærɪ] (*pret & pp* **miscarried**) *vi* **1.** MED faire une fausse couche **2.** [fail - plan, hopes] échouer, avorter, mal tourner **3.** *UK* [mail, cargo] s'égarer, se perdre.

miscast [,mɪs'kɑːst] (*pret & pp* **miscast**) *vt* CIN & THEAT [play] se tromper dans la distribution de ▪ [actor] mal choisir le rôle de ▪ **Jim was hopelessly ~ as Romeo** Jim n'était vraiment pas fait pour jouer le rôle de Roméo.

miscellaneous [,mɪsə'leɪnɪəs] *adj* [assorted] divers, varié ▪ [jumbled] hétérogène, hétéroclite, disparate ▪ **~ expenses** frais *mpl* divers.

miscellany [*UK* mɪ'selənɪ, *US* 'mɪsəleɪnɪ] (*pl* **miscellanies**) *n* **1.** [mixture, assortment] amalgame *m*, mélange *m* **2.** [anthology] recueil *m*, anthologie *f*.

mischance [,mɪs'tʃɑːns] *n fml* malheur *m*, malchance *f*.

mischief ['mɪstʃɪf] *n* **1.** *(U)* [naughtiness] espièglerie *f*, malice *f* ▪ **to get up to ~** faire des bêtises *OR* sottises ▪ **to keep sb out of ~** occuper qqn ▪ **to do sthg out of sheer ~** faire qqch par pure espièglerie *OR* par pure malice ▪ **a smile full of ~** un sourire espiègle **2.** *(U)* [trouble] : **to make ~** semer la zizanie **3.** *(U) fml* [damage] dommages *mpl*, dégâts *mpl* **4.** *UK* [injury] : **to do o.s. a ~** *inf* se blesser, se faire mal **5.** *inf hum* [child] polisson *m*, - onne *f*, (petite) canaille *f*.

mischief-maker *n* faiseur *m* d'histoires *OR* d'embarras.

mischievous ['mɪstʃɪvəs] *adj* **1.** [child, trick] espiègle, malicieux ▪ [look] taquin, narquois ▪ [thought] malicieux **2.** [harmful] méchant, malveillant ▪ **~ gossip** médisances *fpl*.

mischievously ['mɪstʃɪvəslɪ] *adv* [naughtily, teasingly] malicieusement ▪ [nastily] méchamment, avec malveillance.

misconceived [,mɪskən'siːvd] *adj* [plan] mal conçu ▪ [idea] faux, - sse *f*, erroné.

misconception [,mɪskən'sepʃn] *n* [poor understanding] mauvaise compréhension *f* ▪ [complete misunderstanding] idée fausse *f*, méprise *f* ▪ **a popular ~** une fausse idée couramment répandue.

misconduct ◇ *n* [,mɪs'kɒndʌkt] **1.** [bad behaviour] mauvaise conduite *f* ▪ [immoral behaviour] inconduite *f* ▪ [adultery] adultère *m* ▪ **(professional) ~** faute *f* professionnelle **2.** [bad management] mauvaise gestion *f*.
◇ *vt* [,mɪskən'dʌkt] [mismanage - business] mal gérer ; [- affair] mal conduire.

misconstruction [,mɪskən'strʌkʃn] *n* **1.** [gen] fausse interprétation *f* ▪ **the law is open to ~** la loi peut prêter à des interprétations erronées **2.** GRAM mauvaise construction *f*.

misconstrue [,mɪskən'struː] *vt* mal interpréter.

miscount ◇ *vt* [,mɪs'kaʊnt] mal compter, faire une erreur en comptant.
◇ *vi* [,mɪs'kaʊnt] se tromper dans le compte.

◇ *n* ['mɪskaʊnt] mécompte *m* ■ **there was a ~** POL une erreur s'est produite dans le décompte des voix.

miscreant ['mɪskrɪənt] *n lit* [villain] scélérat *m*, - e *f*, vaurien *m*, - enne *f*.

misdate [ˌmɪs'deɪt] *vt* mal dater.

misdeal [ˌmɪs'di:l] (*pret & pp* **misdealt** [-'delt]) ◇ *vt* : **to ~ the cards** faire (une) maldonne.
◇ *vi* faire (une) maldonne.
◇ *n* maldonne *f*.

misdeed [ˌmɪs'di:d] *n fml* méfait *m* ■ LAW délit *m*.

misdemeanour *UK*, **misdemeanor** *US* [ˌmɪsdɪ'mi:nəʳ] *n* méfait *m* ■ LAW délit *m*, infraction *f*.

misdirect [ˌmɪsdɪ'rekt] *vt* **1.** [to destination - traveller] mal orienter, mal renseigner ; [- letter] mal adresser **2.** [misuse - efforts, talents] mal employer, mal orienter ■ **~ed energy** énergie mal utilisée **3.** LAW [jury] mal renseigner.

misdirection [ˌmɪsdɪ'rekʃn] *n* **1.** [of traveller] mauvaise orientation *f* **2.** [of efforts, talents] mauvais emploi *m*, mauvais usage *m*.

misdoing [ˌmɪs'du:ɪŋ] *n* méfait *m*.

miser ['maɪzəʳ] *n* **1.** [person] avare *mf* ■ **he's a real ~** c'est un vrai grippe-sou ➲ **'The Miser'** ***Molière*** 'l'Avare' **2.** [tool] tarière *f* à gravier.

miserable ['mɪzrəbl] *adj* **1.** [unhappy] malheureux, triste ■ **to look ~** avoir l'air déprimé *OR* malheureux ■ **I feel really ~ today** je n'ai vraiment pas le moral aujourd'hui ■ **don't be so ~!** allez! ne fais pas cette tête ■ **they make her life ~** ils lui rendent *OR* mènent la vie dure **2.** [unpleasant - evening, sight] pénible ; [- weather, summer] épouvantable, pourri ; [- conditions, holiday] déplorable, lamentable ■ **I've got a ~ cold** j'ai un sale rhume ■ **to have a ~ time** passer un mauvais moment **3.** [poor - hotel] miteux ; [- tenement] misérable ; [- meal] maigre ■ **all their efforts were a ~ failure** tous leurs efforts ont échoué lamentablement **4.** [mean - reward] minable, misérable ; [- salary] de misère ; [- donation, amount] dérisoire ■ **they only gave us five ~ dollars** ils ne nous ont donné que cinq malheureux *OR* misérables dollars **5.** *pej* méchant ■ **you ~ brat!** sale gosse!

miserably ['mɪzrəblɪ] *adv* **1.** [extremely - unhappy, cold] extrêmement ■ [very badly - play] de façon lamentable *OR* déplorable ; [- fail] lamentablement ; [- pay] très mal **2.** [unhappily] malheureusement, d'un air malheureux **3.** [in poverty] misérablement, dans la misère.

miserliness ['maɪzəlɪnɪs] *n* avarice *f*.

miserly ['maɪzəlɪ] *adj* avare.

misery ['mɪzərɪ] (*pl* **miseries**) *n* **1.** [unhappiness] malheur *m*, tristesse *f* ■ **to make sb's life a ~** rendre la vie insupportable à qqn **2.** [suffering] : **she begged to be put out of her ~** elle suppliait qu'on mît fin à ses souffrances ■ **go on, put me out of my ~ and tell me the worst** continue, mets fin à mon supplice, dis-moi tout ■ **to put a sick animal out of its ~** *euph* achever un animal malade **3.** [misfortune] malheur *m*, misère *f* **4.** [poverty] misère *f* **5.** *UK inf* [gloomy person] rabat-joie *m inv*, grincheux *m*, - euse *f*.

misfire ◇ *vi* [ˌmɪs'faɪəʳ] **1.** [gun] faire long feu ■ *fig* [plan, joke] rater, échouer **2.** [engine] avoir des problèmes d'allumage *OR* des ratés.
◇ *n* ['mɪsfaɪəʳ] MIL & AUT raté *m*.

misfit ['mɪsfɪt] *n* inadapté *m*, - e *f*, marginal *m*, - e *f* ■ **a social ~** un inadapté social.

misfortune [mɪs'fɔ:tʃu:n] *n* **1.** [bad luck] malchance *f*, infortune *f* ■ **I had the ~ to meet him in Paris** j'ai eu la malchance de le rencontrer à Paris **2.** [unfortunate event] malheur *m* ■ **to be plagued by ~s** jouer de malchance.

misgiving [mɪs'gɪvɪŋ] *n* doute *m*, appréhension *f* ■ **to have ~s about** avoir des doutes quant à, douter de ■ **the whole idea fills me with ~** l'idée même me remplit d'appréhension.

misgovern [ˌmɪs'gʌvən] *vi & vt* mal gouverner.

misgovernment [ˌmɪs'gʌvənmənt] *n* [of country] mauvais gouvernement *m* ■ [of affairs] mauvaise gestion *f*.

misguidance [ˌmɪs'gaɪdəns] *n* mauvaise influence *f*.

misguided [ˌmɪs'gaɪdɪd] *adj* [attempt] malencontreux ■ [decision] peu judicieux ■ [attack] malavisé, maladroit ■ [idealist] égaré ■ [nationalism] dévoyé ■ **it was very ~ of him to try to intervene** il a commis une grosse bévue en essayant d'intervenir.

mishandle [ˌmɪs'hændl] *vt* **1.** [equipment] mal utiliser, mal se servir de ■ [resources, information] mal exploiter ■ [affair] mal gérer ■ **the case was ~d from the outset** l'affaire a été mal menée depuis le début **2.** [treat insensitively - customer] malmener, traiter avec rudesse.

mishap ['mɪshæp] *n* [misadventure] mésaventure *f*, accident *m* ■ **he arrived without ~** il est arrivé sans encombre.

mishear [ˌmɪs'hɪəʳ] (*pret & pp* **misheard** [-'hɜ:d]) *vt* mal entendre, mal comprendre.

mishit ◇ (*pret & pp* **mishit**) *vt* [ˌmɪs'hɪt] SPORT [ball] mal frapper.
◇ *vi* [ˌmɪs'hɪt] mal frapper la balle.
◇ *n* ['mɪshɪt] mauvais coup *m*, coup *m* manqué.

mishmash ['mɪʃmæʃ] *n inf* méli-mélo *m*, mic-mac *m*.

misinform [ˌmɪsɪn'fɔ:m] *vt* [unintentionally] mal renseigner ■ [intentionally] donner de faux renseignements à, tromper.

misinformation [ˌmɪsɪnfə'meɪʃn] *n* *(U)* fausse information *f*.

misinterpret [ˌmɪsɪn'tɜ:prɪt] *vt* mal comprendre, mal interpréter ■ **now don't ~ what I'm saying** surtout, ne vous méprenez pas sur le sens de mes propos ■ **she ~ed his silence as contempt** elle a pris à tort son silence pour du mépris.

misinterpretation ['mɪsɪnˌtɜ:prɪ'teɪʃn] *n* erreur *f* d'interprétation ■ **the rules are open to ~** l'interprétation du règlement prête à confusion.

misjudge [ˌmɪs'dʒʌdʒ] *vt* [distance, reaction] mal juger, mal évaluer ■ [person] mal juger ■ **I have ~d her** je me suis trompé sur son compte, je l'ai mal jugée.

misjudg(e)ment [ˌmɪs'dʒʌdʒmənt] *n* erreur *f* de jugement.

miskick ◇ *vt* [ˌmɪs'kɪk] SPORT : **he ~ed the ball** il a raté son coup de pied.
◇ *vi* [ˌmɪs'kɪk] rater le ballon.
◇ *n* ['mɪskɪk] coup *m* de pied raté.

mislay [ˌmɪs'leɪ] (*pret & pp* **mislaid** [-'leɪd]) *vt* égarer.

mislead [ˌmɪs'li:d] (*pret & pp* **misled** [-'led]) *vt* tromper, induire en erreur ■ **we were misled into believing he was dead** on nous a fait croire qu'il était mort.

misleading [ˌmɪs'li:dɪŋ] *adj* [false] trompeur, fallacieux ■ [confusing] équivoque ■ **~ advertising** publicité *f* mensongère ■ **the map is very ~** cette carte n'est pas claire du tout.

misled [-'led] *pt & pp* ⊳ **mislead**.

mismanage [ˌmɪs'mænɪdʒ] *vt* mal gérer.

mismanagement [ˌmɪs'mænɪdʒmənt] *n* mauvaise gestion *f*.

mismatch ◇ *vt* [ˌmɪs'mætʃ] **1.** [colours, clothes] mal assortir **2.** [in marriage] : **they were totally ~ed** [socially] ils étaient vraiment mal assortis ; [by temperament] ils n'étaient absolument pas faits pour s'entendre.
◇ *n* ['mɪsmætʃ] **1.** [clash] : **the colours are a ~** ces couleurs ne vont vraiment pas ensemble *OR* sont vraiment mal assorties **2.** [in marriage] mésalliance *f* **3.** SPORT match *m* inégal **4.** COMPUT incohérence *f*.

misname [ˌmɪs'neɪm] *vt* mal nommer.

misnomer [ˌmɪs'nəʊməʳ] *n* nom *m* inapproprié ■ **to call it a democratic country is a complete ~** ce pays ne mérite vraiment pas le nom de démocratie.

misogynist [mɪ'sɒdʒɪnɪst] *n* misogyne *mf*.

misogyny [mɪ'sɒdʒɪnɪ] *n* misogynie *f*.

misplace [ˌmɪs'pleɪs] *vt* **1.** [put in wrong place] mal placer **2.** [mislay] égarer **3.** [trust, confidence] mal placer.

misplaced [ˌmɪs'pleɪst] *adj* [trust, confidence] mal placé.

misprint ◇ *n* ['mɪsprɪnt] faute *f* d'impression, coquille *f*.
◇ *vt* [ˌmɪs'prɪnt] : **my name was ~ed in the newspaper** il y a eu une coquille dans mon nom sur le journal.

mispronounce [ˌmɪsprə'naʊns] *vt* [word] mal prononcer, prononcer incorrectement ▪ [name] estropier, écorcher.

mispronunciation ['mɪsprəˌnʌnsɪ'eɪʃn] *n* faute *f* de prononciation.

misquotation [ˌmɪskwəʊ'teɪʃn] *n* citation *f* inexacte.

misquote ◇ *vt* [ˌmɪs'kwəʊt] [author, text] citer inexactement ▪ [speaker] déformer les propos de ▪ **on your programme you ~d me as saying "..."** dans votre émission vous m'avez attribué à tort la phrase suivante: "...".
◇ *n* ['mɪskwəʊt] *inf* = **misquotation**.

misread ◇ *vt* [ˌmɪs'ri:d] (*pret & pp* **misread** [-red]) [word, text] mal lire ▪ *fig* [actions, motives] mal interpréter, mal comprendre.
◇ *n* ['mɪsri:d] COMPUT erreur *f* de lecture.

misrepresent ['mɪsˌreprɪ'zent] *vt* [facts, events] déformer ▪ [person] donner une image fausse de.

misrepresentation ['mɪsˌreprɪzen'teɪʃn] *n* [of truth] déformation *f* ▪ **what they say is a complete ~ of the facts** ils déforment complètement la réalité.

misrule [ˌmɪs'ru:l] ◇ *vt* mal gouverner.
◇ *n* **1.** [misgovernment] mauvais gouvernement *m* **2.** [anarchy] désordre *m*, anarchie *f*.

miss [mɪs] ◇ *vt* **1.** [bus, film, target] manquer, rater ▪ [opportunity, turn] manquer, laisser passer ▪ **you didn't ~ much** vous n'avez pas manqué grand-chose ▪ **it's too good an opportunity to ~** c'est une occasion trop belle pour qu'on la manque ▶ **to ~ the boat** rater une occasion, manquer le coche ▪ **to ~ one's cue** THEAT manquer sa réplique ; *fig* rater l'occasion
2. [fail to do, find, see etc] manquer ▪ **to ~ school** manquer l'école ▪ **I'm sorry, I ~ed you in the crowd** désolé, je ne vous ai pas vu *OR* remarqué *OR* aperçu dans la foule ▪ **I ~ed seeing them in Australia** [for lack of time] je n'ai pas eu le temps de les voir en Australie ; [for lack of opportunity] je n'ai pas eu l'occasion *OR* la possibilité de les voir en Australie ▪ **I ~ed the beginning of your question** je n'ai pas entendu le début de votre question ▪ **they've ~ed my name off the list** ils ont oublié mon nom sur la liste ▪ **you've ~ed *OR* you're ~ing the point!** vous n'avez rien compris! ▪ **she ~ed her footing *OR* step** *UK* elle a glissé *OR* trébuché ▶ **they never *OR* don't ~ a trick** *UK* rien ne leur échappe
3. [escape, manage to avoid] : **I narrowly *OR* just ~ed being killed** j'ai bien failli me faire tuer
4. [regret the absence of] : **I ~ her** elle me manque ▪ **you'll be ~ed when you retire** on vous regrettera *OR* vous nous manquerez quand vous serez à la retraite
5. [be short of, lack] manquer de ▪ **I'm ~ing two books from my collection** il me manque deux livres dans ma collection, deux livres de ma collection ont disparu
6. [notice disappearance of] : **when did you first ~ your passport?** quand est-ce que vous vous êtes aperçu pour la première fois de la perte de *OR* que vous aviez perdu votre passeport? ▪ **he's got so many records he won't ~ one** il a tellement de disques qu'il ne s'apercevra pas qu'il lui en manque un.
◇ *vi* **1.** [fail to hit target] manquer *OR* rater son coup ▪ **~ed!** raté!
2. [engine] avoir des ratés
3. *phr* **to be ~ing** manquer ▪ **there's one ~ing, one is ~ing** il en manque un.
◇ *n* **1.** [gen - SPORT] coup *m* raté *OR* manqué ▪ **a ~ is as good as a mile** *UK prov* rater de peu ou de beaucoup, c'est toujours rater
2. *inf* [girl] jeune fille *f* ▪ **impudent little ~!** petite effrontée!
3. TEX [size] junior
4. *phr* **to give sthg a ~** *UK* [do without] se passer de qqch ; [avoid] éviter qqch ▪ **I gave work a ~ yesterday** je ne suis pas allé travailler hier ▪ **I gave lessons a ~ last week** je n'ai pas assisté aux cours la semaine dernière.
◆ **Miss** *n* [term of address] mademoiselle *f* ▪ **Dear Miss Brett** Chère Mademoiselle Brett, Chère Mlle Brett ▪ **the Miss Bretts** les demoiselles Brett ▪ **Miss West Indies** Miss Antilles ▪ **please Miss!** *UK* SCH Madame!
◆ **miss out** ◇ *vt sep* [omit] omettre, sauter ▪ [forget] oublier ▪ [in distribution] oublier, sauter.
◇ *vi insep* : **he ~ed out because he couldn't afford to go to college** il a été désavantagé parce qu'il n'avait pas les moyens de poursuivre ses études.
◆ **miss out on** *vt insep* [advantage, opportunity] manquer, rater ▪ **you're ~ing out on all the fun** tu rates une occasion de bien t'amuser ▪ **we ~ed out on the deal** l'affaire nous est passée sous le nez *OR* nous a échappé.

missal ['mɪsl] *n* missel *m*.

misshapen [ˌmɪs'ʃeɪpn] *adj* difforme, tordu, déformé.

missile [*UK* 'mɪsaɪl, *US* 'mɪsəl] *n* **1.** MIL missile *m* **2.** [object thrown] projectile *m*.

missile carrier *n* porte-missiles *m inv*.

missile launcher *n* lance-missiles *m inv*.

missing ['mɪsɪŋ] *adj* **1.** [lacking] manquant ▪ **the table had one leg ~** il manquait un pied à la table **2.** [lost - person] disparu ; [- object] manquant, égaré, perdu ▪ **to go ~** disparaître ; [in war] être porté disparu ▪ **the ~ diamonds were found in her suitcase** les diamants qui avaient disparu ont été retrouvés dans sa valise ▪ **the ~ climbers are safe** les alpinistes dont on était sans nouvelles sont sains et saufs ▶ **~ person** personne *f* disparue ; MIL & POL disparu *m*.

missing link *n* chaînon *m* manquant.

mission ['mɪʃn] *n* **1.** [delegation] mission *f* ▪ **~ of inquiry** mission d'enquête ▪ **he was sent on a rescue ~** il fut envoyé en mission de sauvetage ▪ **a Chinese trade ~** une mission commerciale chinoise **2.** [job, vocation] mission *f* ▪ **she saw it as her ~ in life to provide for the homeless** elle s'est donné pour mission d'aider les sans-abri **3.** [organization, charity] mission *f* **4.** RELIG [campaign, building] mission *f* **5.** MIL, COMM & ASTRONAUT mission *f* ▪ **~ accomplished** mission accomplie.

missionary ['mɪʃənrɪ] (*pl* **missionaries**) ◇ *n* missionnaire *mf*.
◇ *adj* [work] missionnaire ▪ [zeal] de missionnaire ▪ **~ society** société *f* de missionnaires.

missionary position *n* position *f* du missionnaire.

mission control *n* centre *m* de contrôle.

mission controller *n* chef *m* du centre de contrôle.

missis ['mɪsɪz] = **missus**.

Mississippi [ˌmɪsɪ'sɪpɪ] *pr n* **1.** [river] : **the ~ (River)** le Mississippi **2.** [state] Mississippi *m* ▪ **in ~** dans le Mississippi.

missive ['mɪsɪv] *n fml* missive *f*.

Missouri [mɪ'zʊərɪ] *pr n* **1.** [river] : **the ~ (river)** le Missouri **2.** [state] Missouri *m* ▪ **in ~** dans le Missouri ▪ **the ~ Compromise** le compromis du Missouri.

misspell [ˌmɪs'spel] (*pret & pp* **misspelt** [ˌmɪs'spelt] *OR* **misspelled**) *vt* [in writing] mal écrire, mal orthographier ▪ [in speaking] mal épeler.

misspelling [ˌmɪs'spelɪŋ] *n* faute *f* d'orthographe.

misspelt [ˌmɪs'spelt] *pt & pp* ▷ **misspell**.

misspend [ˌmɪs'spend] (*pret & pp* **misspent** [-'spent]) *vt* [money, talents] gaspiller, gâcher ▪ **my misspent youth** mes folles années de jeunesse.

misstate [ˌmɪs'steɪt] *vt* [case, argument] rapporter *OR* exposer incorrectement ▪ [truth] déformer.

misstatement [ˌmɪs'steɪtmənt] *n* [report] rapport *m* inexact ▪ [mistake] inexactitude *f*.

missus ['mɪsɪz] *n* **UK inf 1.** [wife] bourgeoise *f* ■ **I'll have to ask the ~** je dois demander à la patronne **2.** [woman] **: eh, ~!** dites, m'dame *OR* ma p'tite dame!

mist [mɪst] ◇ *n* **1.** [fog] brume *f* ■ **the morning ~ will clear by noon** les brumes matinales se dissiperont avant midi ■ **the ~s of time** *fig* la nuit des temps **2.** [vapour - on window, glasses] buée *f* ; [- from spray] brouillard *m*, nuage *m*.
◇ *vt* **: to ~ (over *OR* up)** embuer ■ **tears ~ed his eyes** ses yeux étaient brouillés par les larmes.
◇ *vi* **: to ~ (over *OR* up)** [window, glasses, eyes] s'embuer.

mistake [mɪ'steɪk] (*pret* **mistook** [-'stʊk], *pp* **mistaken** [-'steɪkn]) ◇ *n* **1.** [error] erreur *f* ■ [in grammar, spelling] faute *f* ■ **to make a ~** faire une erreur *OR* une faute ■ **I made the ~ of losing my temper** j'ai commis l'erreur de *OR* j'ai eu le tort de me fâcher ■ **anybody can make a ~** tout le monde peut se tromper ■ **you're making a big ~** vous faites une grave erreur ■ **make no ~ (about it)** ne vous y trompez pas ■ **there must be some ~** il doit y avoir erreur *OR* un malentendu ■ **she knew it was a ~ ever to have married him** elle savait bien qu'elle n'aurait pas dû commettre l'erreur de l'épouser ■ **sorry, my ~** [my fault] excusez-moi, c'est (de) ma faute ; [I got it wrong] excusez-moi, c'est moi qui me trompe **2.** [inadvertence] **: by *OR* UK in ~** par mégarde *OR* erreur ■ **I took her scarf in ~ for mine** en croyant prendre mon écharpe, j'ai pris la sienne ■ **I went into the wrong room by ~** je suis entré par erreur dans la mauvaise pièce **3.** *phr* **he's a big man and no ~ !** *UK* pour être costaud, il est costaud!
◇ *vt* **1.** [misunderstand - meaning, intention] mal comprendre, se tromper sur ■ **there's no mistaking what she said** on ne peut pas se méprendre sur le sens de ses propos **2.** [fail to distinguish] se tromper sur ■ **you can't ~ our house, it has green shutters** vous ne pouvez pas vous tromper *OR* il n'y a pas de confusion possible, notre maison a des volets verts ■ **there's no mistaking the influence of Brahms on his music** l'influence de Brahms sur sa musique est indéniable **3.** [date, route] se tromper de ■ [person] **: I'm often mistaken for my sister** on me prend souvent pour ma sœur ■ **I mistook his shyness for arrogance** j'ai pris sa timidité pour de l'arrogance.

mistaken [-'steɪkn] ◇ *pp* ▷ **mistake**.
◇ *adj* [wrong - idea, conclusion] erroné, faux, fausse *f* ■ **to be ~** se tromper, être dans l'erreur ■ **if I'm not ~** si je ne me trompe, si je ne m'abuse ➤ **it was a case of ~ identity** il y avait erreur sur la personne ■ **unless I'm very much ~, that's Nick's daughter** si je ne m'abuse, c'est la fille de Nick.

mistakenly [mɪ'steɪknlɪ] *adv* [in error] par erreur ■ [wrongly] à tort.

mister ['mɪstəʳ] *n* *inf* monsieur *m* ■ **~ knowall** *UK*, **~ know-it-all** *US* monsieur je-sais-tout.

mistime [,mɪs'taɪm] *vt* mal calculer (le moment de).

mistle thrush ['mɪsl-] *n* draine *f*.

mistletoe ['mɪsltəʊ] *n* gui *m*.

mistook [-'stʊk] *pt* ▷ **mistake**.

mistranslate [,mɪstræns'leɪt] ◇ *vt* mal traduire.
◇ *vi* faire des contresens.

mistranslation [,mɪstræns'leɪʃn] *n* **1.** [mistake] contresens *m*, faute *f* *OR* erreur *f* de traduction **2.** [faulty text] traduction *f* inexacte, mauvaise traduction *f*.

mistreat [,mɪs'triːt] *vt* maltraiter.

mistreatment [,mɪs'triːtmənt] *n* mauvais traitement *m*.

mistress ['mɪstrɪs] *n* **1.** [woman in control] maîtresse *f* ■ **she was ~ of the situation** elle était maîtresse de la situation, elle maîtrisait la situation ■ **the ~ of the house** la maîtresse de maison **2.** [lover] maîtresse *f* **3.** *UK* SCH [in primary school] maîtresse *f* ■ [in secondary school] professeur *m (femme)* **4.** *UK* [of servants] maîtresse *f* **5.** *arch* [title] **: Mistress Bacon** Madame *OR* Mme Bacon **6.** [of pet] maîtresse *f*.

mistrial ['mɪstraɪəl] *n* erreur *f* judiciaire ■ *US* [with hung jury] *procès annulé par manque d'unanimité parmi les jurés.*

mistrust [,mɪs'trʌst] ◇ *n* méfiance *f*, défiance *f*.
◇ *vt* [be suspicious, wary of] se méfier de ■ [doubt] douter de, ne pas avoir confiance en.

mistrustful [,mɪs'trʌstfʊl] *adj* méfiant ■ **to be ~ of sb** se méfier de qqn.

misty ['mɪstɪ] (*comp* **mistier**, *superl* **mistiest**) *adj* **1.** [weather, morning] brumeux **2.** [window, eyes] embué ■ [horizon, mountain] embrumé **3.** [vague - idea, memory] flou, nébuleux **4.** [like mist] vaporeux ■ **a ~ veil of cloud** un léger voile de nuages ■ **~ blue** bleu pâle.

mistype [,mɪs'taɪp] ◇ *vt* faire une faute de frappe dans.
◇ *n* faute *f* de frappe.

misunderstand [,mɪsʌndə'stænd] (*pret & pp* **misunderstood** [-'stʊd]) *vt* **1.** [misinterpret] mal comprendre, comprendre de travers ■ **I misunderstood the message** j'ai mal compris le message ■ **don't ~ me** comprenez-moi bien **2.** *(usu passive)* [misjudge, underrate] méconnaître ■ **he feels misunderstood** il se sent incompris.

misunderstanding [,mɪsʌndə'stændɪŋ] *n* **1.** [misapprehension] méprise *f*, quiproquo *m*, malentendu *m* ■ **there seems to have been some ~** il semble qu'il y ait eu méprise *OR* une erreur ■ **his statement is open to ~** sa déclaration prête à confusion ■ **to clear up a ~** dissiper un malentendu **2.** *euph* [quarrel] mésentente *f*, brouille *f* ■ **we've had a ~ with the neighbours** nous nous sommes brouillés avec les voisins.

misunderstood [-'stʊd] *pt & pp* ▷ **misunderstand**.

misuse ◇ *vt* [,mɪs'juːz] **1.** [privilege, position etc] abuser de ■ [word, phrase] employer abusivement ■ [equipment, gun] mal employer, mal utiliser ■ [money, time] mal employer **2.** [funds] détourner **3.** [ill-treat] maltraiter, malmener.
◇ *n* [,mɪs'juːs] **1.** [of privilege, one's position] abus *m* ■ [of word, phrase] emploi *m* abusif ■ [of equipment, gun] mauvais usage *m*, mauvaise utilisation *f* ■ [of money, time] mauvais emploi *m* **2.** [of funds] détournement *m*.

MIT (*abbrev of* **Massachusetts Institute of Technology**) *pr n* *l'Institut de Technologie du Massachusetts.*

mite [maɪt] *n* **1.** [insect] mite *f* **2.** *inf* [little bit] grain *m*, brin *m*, tantinet *m* **3.** *inf* [child] mioche *mf* ■ **poor little ~!** pauvre petit! **4.** [coin] denier *m* ■ [donation] obole *f*.

miter *US* = **mitre**.

mitigate ['mɪtɪgeɪt] *vt* [anger, grief, pain] adoucir, apaiser, alléger ■ [conditions, consequences, harm] atténuer.

mitigating ['mɪtɪgeɪtɪŋ] *adj* **: ~ circumstances** LAW circonstances *fpl* atténuantes.

mitigation [,mɪtɪ'geɪʃn] *n* *fml* [of anger, grief, pain] adoucissement *m*, allègement *m* ■ [of conditions, consequences, harm] atténuation *f* ■ **in ~, it is obvious that she was provoked** il est évident qu'elle a été provoquée, ce qui constitue une circonstance atténuante.

mitre *UK*, **miter** *US* ['maɪtəʳ] ◇ *n* **1.** RELIG mitre *f* **2.** [in carpentry] onglet *m*.
◇ *vt* [in carpentry - cut] tailler en onglet ■ [join] assembler en onglet.

mitre block, mitre box *n* boîte *f* à onglet.

mitre joint *n* (assemblage *m* à *OR* en) onglet *m*.

mitt [mɪt] *n* **1.** = **mitten 2.** [glove] gant *m* ■ [boxing glove] gant *m* (de boxe) ■ **oven/baseball ~** gant isolant/de baseball **3.** *inf* [hand] paluche *f*.

mitten ['mɪtn] *n* [with fingers joined] moufle *f* ■ [with cut-off fingers] mitaine *f* ■ [boxing glove] gant *m* (de boxe), mitaine *f*.

mix [mɪks] ◇ *vt* **1.** [combine, blend] mélanger ■ **~ the sugar into the batter** incorporez le sucre à la pâte ■ **the screws and nails were all ~ed together** les vis et les clous étaient tous mélangés ■ **never ~ your drinks** ne faites jamais de mélanges de boissons ■ **to ~ metaphors** faire des amalgames de métaphores ➤ **to ~ it** *UK inf* [fight] chercher la bagarre, être bagarreur **2.** [prepare - cocktail, medicine] préparer ; [- cement, plaster] malaxer **3.** [stir - salad] tourner **4.** CIN, ELECTRON & MUS mixer.

◇ *vi* **1.** [combine, blend] se mélanger **2.** [go together] aller ensemble, faire bon ménage **3.** [socialize] : **she ~es well** elle est très sociable ■ **he ~es with a strange crowd** il fréquente de drôles de gens ■ **my friends and his just don't ~** mes amis et les siens ne sympathisent pas.
◇ *n* **1.** [combination, blend] mélange *m* **2.** *UK* [act of mixing] : **give the paint a (good) ~** mélangez (bien) la peinture **3.** CULIN [in package] préparation *f* ■ [batter] pâte *f* ■ **a packet of soup ~** un sachet de soupe instantanée **4.** CIN, ELECTRON & MUS mixage *m*.
◆ **mix in** ◇ *vt sep* mélanger.
◇ *vi insep* : **she makes no effort to ~ in** elle ne fait aucun effort pour se montrer sociable.
◆ **mix up** *vt sep* **1.** [mistake] confondre ■ **I always ~ her up with her sister** je la confonds toujours avec sa sœur ■ [baffle, confuse] embrouiller ■ **I'm ~ed up about how I feel about him** mes sentiments pour lui sont très confus ■ [scramble] : **you've got the story completely ~ed up** tu t'es complètement embrouillé dans cette histoire **2.** *(usu passive)* [involve] impliquer ■ **he was ~ed up in a burglary** il a été impliqué *OR* mêlé à une affaire de cambriolage ■ **she got ~ed up with some awful people** elle s'est mise à fréquenter des gens épouvantables ■ **I got ~ed up in their quarrel** je me suis trouvé mêlé à leur querelle **3.** [disorder] mélanger **4.** [combine, blend] mélanger.

mix-and-match *adj* [clothes] que l'on peut coordonner à volonté.

mixed [mɪkst] *adj* **1.** [assorted] mélangé ■ **there was a very ~ crowd at the party** il y avait toutes sortes de gens à la fête ■ **we had rather ~ weather** nous avons eu un temps assez variable ➲ **~ economy** économie *f* mixte ■ **~ farming** polyculture *f* ■ **~ grill** assortiment *m* de grillades, mixed grill *m* ■ **~ metaphor** mélange *m* de métaphores ■ **~ vegetables** jardinière *f* de légumes **2.** [not wholly positive] mitigé ■ **to meet with a ~ reception** recevoir un accueil mitigé ■ **I have ~ feelings about it** je ne sais pas très bien ce que j'en pense, je suis partagé à ce sujet ➲ **it's a bit of a ~ bag** *inf* il y a un peu de tout ■ **it's a ~ blessing** il y a du pour et du contre **3.** [sexually, racially] mixte ■ **it's not a proper topic for ~ company** ce n'est pas un sujet à aborder devant les dames ■ **man of ~ race** métis *m* ■ **woman of ~ race** métisse *f* ➲ **~ school/doubles** école *f* /double *m* mixte ■ **~ marriage** mariage *m* mixte **4.** MATHS : **~ number** nombre *m* mixte (fractionnaire).

mixed-ability *adj* [class, teaching] sans niveaux.

mixed-media *adj* multimédia.

mixed-up *adj* [confused] désorienté, déboussolé.

mixer ['mɪksəʳ] *n* **1.** [device - gen] mélangeur *m* ■ CULIN [mechanical] batteur *m* ■ [electric] mixeur *m*, mixer *m* ■ CIN, ELECTRON & MUS mixeur *m*, mélangeur *m* de signaux **2.** [sociable person] : **to be a good/poor ~** être sociable/peu sociable **3.** *inf* [troublemaker] provocateur *m*, - trice *f* **4.** [soft drink] boisson *f* gazeuse *(servant à la préparation des cocktails)*.

mixer tap *n* (robinet *m*) mélangeur *m*.

mixing ['mɪksɪŋ] *n* **1.** [gen] mélange *m* **2.** CIN, ELECTRON & MUS mixage *m* ■ **~ desk** table *f* de mixage.

mixing bowl *n* [big] saladier *m* ■ [smaller] bol *m*.

mixture ['mɪkstʃəʳ] *n* **1.** [gen] mélange *m* **2.** MED mixture *f*.

mix-up *n* confusion *f* ■ **there was a ~ over the bookings** il y a eu confusion dans les réservations.

mizen, mizzen ['mɪzn] *n* artimon *m*.

mizzenmast ['mɪznmɑːst] *n* mât *m* d'artimon.

mk, MK *written abbr of* **mark**.

mkt *written abbr of* **market**.

ml *(written abbrev of* **millilitre**) ml.

MLitt [em'lɪt] *(abbrev of* **Master of Literature, Master of Letters**) *n (titulaire d'une) maîtrise de lettres*.

MLR *n* = **minimum lending rate**.

mm *(written abbrev of* **millimetre**) mm.

MMC *pr n* = **Monopolies and Mergers Commission**.

MMR [,emem'ɑːʳ] *(abbrev of* **measles, mumps & rubella**) *n* MED ROR *m*.

MN ◇ *n* = **Merchant Navy**.
◇ *written abbr of* **Minnesota**.

mnemonic [nɪ'mɒnɪk] ◇ *adj* **1.** [aiding memory] mnémonique, mnémotechnique **2.** [relating to memory] mnémonique.
◇ *n* formule *f* mnémotechnique, aide *f* à la mémoire ■ COMPUT mnémonique *m*.

mo, mo' [məʊ] *n inf* moment *m*, instant *m* ■ **(I) won't be a ~** j'en ai pour une minute.

m.o. *written abbr of* **money order**.

MO ◇ *n* **1.** = **medical officer 2.** = **modus operandi**.
◇ *written abbr of* **Missouri**.

moan [məʊn] ◇ *vi* **1.** [in pain, sadness] gémir **2.** [grumble] ronchonner, grogner ■ **what are you ~ing about now?** de quoi te plains-tu encore?
◇ *vt* maugréer.
◇ *n* [of pain, sadness] gémissement *m* ■ [of complaint] plainte *f* ■ **she gave a ~** elle poussa un gémissement.

moaner ['məʊnəʳ] *n inf* grognon *m*, - onne *f*, râleur *m*, - euse *f*.

moaning ['məʊnɪŋ] ◇ *n (U)* **1.** [in pain, sadness] gémissement *m*, gémissements *mpl* **2.** [complaining] plaintes *fpl*, jérémiades *fpl* ■ **stop your ~!** arrête de ronchonner!
◇ *adj* **1.** [groaning] gémissant ■ **a ~ sound** un gémissement **2.** [complaining] grognon, râleur ■ **she's a real ~ Minnie** *UK inf* quelle râleuse, celle-là!

moat [məʊt] *n* douves *fpl*, fossé *m*, fossés *mpl*.

mob [mɒb] *(pret & pp* **mobbed**) ◇ *n* **1.** [crowd] foule *f*, cohue *f* ■ **~ hysteria** hystérie *f* collective **2.** *pej* [common people] : **the ~** la populace **3.** [of criminals] gang *m* ■ **the Mob** la Mafia **4.** *inf* [bunch, clique] bande *f*, clique *f pej* ■ **he was surrounded by the usual ~ of hangers-on** il était entouré par sa bande habituelle de parasites.
◇ *vt* [person] attaquer, agresser ■ [place] assiéger.

mob cap *n* charlotte *f (bonnet)*.

mobile ['məʊbaɪl] ◇ *adj* **1.** mobile ■ **she's no longer ~** elle ne peut plus se déplacer seule ➲ **~ library** bibliobus *m* **2.** [features, face] mobile, expressif **3.** [socially] : **the middle classes tend to be particularly ~** les classes moyennes se déplacent plus facilement que les autres **4.** *inf* [having transport] : **are you ~?** tu es motorisé?
◇ *n* **1.** ART mobile *m* **2.** *inf* = **mobile phone**.

mobile home *n* caravane *f*.

mobile phone *n* téléphone *m* portable.

mobile shop *n* marchand *m* ambulant.

mobility [mə'bɪlətɪ] *n* mobilité *f* ■ **~ allowance** indemnité *f* de déplacement *(versée aux personnes handicapées)*.

mobilization [,məʊbɪlaɪ'zeɪʃn] *n* mobilisation *f*.

mobilize, ise ['məʊbɪlaɪz] *vi* & *vt* mobiliser.

mob rule *n* loi *f* de la rue.

mobster ['mɒbstəʳ] *n inf* gangster *m*.

moccasin ['mɒkəsɪn] *n* [shoe] mocassin *m*.

mocha ['mɒkə] *n* moka *m*.

mock [mɒk] ◇ *vt* **1.** [deride] se moquer de, tourner en dérision ■ **don't ~ the afflicted!** ne te moque pas des malheureux! **2.** [imitate] singer, parodier **3.** *lit* [thwart] déjouer.
◇ *vi* se moquer.
◇ *adj* **1.** [imitation] faux, fausse *f*, factice ■ **~ turtle soup** consommé *m* à la tête de veau **2.** [feigned] feint **3.** [as practice] : **~ examination** examen *m* blanc.
◇ *n* **1.** *phr* **to make a ~ of sb/sthg** *lit* tourner qqn/qqch en dérision **2.** *UK inf* [examination] examen *m* blanc.
◆ **mock up** *vt sep UK* faire une maquette de.

mocker ['mɒkəʳ] *n* moqueur *m*, - euse *f*.

mockers ['mɒkəz] *npl UK inf* **to put the ~ on sthg** ficher qqch en l'air, bousiller qqch.

mockery ['mɒkərɪ] (*pl* **mockeries**) *n* **1.** [derision] moquerie *f*, raillerie *f* ▪ **to hold sthg up to ~** tourner qqch en ridicule *OR* en dérision **2.** [travesty] parodie *f* ▪ **a ~ of justice** une parodie de justice ▪ **to make a ~ of sthg** rendre qqch ridicule, enlever toute crédibilité à qqch.

mock-heroic *adj* burlesque.

mocking ['mɒkɪŋ] ◇ *n* moquerie *f*, raillerie *f*.
◇ *adj* moqueur, railleur.

mockingbird ['mɒkɪŋbɜ:d] *n* ORNITH moqueur *m*.

mock turtleneck *n US* pull *m* à col cheminée.

mock-up *n* maquette *f*.

mod [mɒd] ◇ *adj inf dated* [fashionable] à la mode.
◇ *n* **1.** *en Angleterre, membre d'un groupe de jeunes des années 60 qui s'opposaient aux rockers* **2.** [festival] *festival de littérature et de musique gaélique en Écosse.*

MoD, MOD *pr n UK* = **Ministry of Defence**.

modal ['məʊdl] *adj* GRAM, PHILOS & MATHS modal ▪ **~ auxiliary** *OR* **verb** auxiliaire *m* modal.

modality [mə'dælətɪ] (*pl* **modalities**) *n* modalité *f*.

mod cons [-kɒnz] (*abbrev of* **modern conveniences**) *npl inf*: **all ~** tout confort, tt. conf.

mode [məʊd] *n* **1.** [manner] mode *m*, manière *f* ▪ **~s of transport** moyens de transport **2.** GRAM, PHILOS & MATHS mode *m* **3.** COMPUT mode *m* ▪ **access/control ~** mode d'accès/de contrôle **4.** [prevailing fashion] mode *f*.

model ['mɒdl] (*UK pret & pp* **modelled**, *cont* **modelling**) (*US pret & pp* **modeled**, *cont* **modeling**) ◇ *n* **1.** [copy, representation] modèle *m*, maquette *f* ▪ [theoretical pattern] modèle *m* **2.** [perfect example] modèle *m* **3.** ART & PHOT [sitter] modèle *m* **4.** [in fashion show] mannequin *m* ▪ **male ~** mannequin (homme) **5.** COMM modèle *m* ▪ **demonstration ~** modèle de démonstration **6.** *US* [showhouse] résidence *f* témoin.
◇ *vt* **1.** [shape] modeler ▪ **to ~ o.s. on sb** prendre modèle sur qqn **2.** [in fashion show] : **she ~s clothes** elle est mannequin ▪ **she ~s hats** elle présente des chapeaux dans des défilés de mode.
◇ *vi* [for artist, photographer] poser ▪ [in fashion show] être mannequin.
◇ *adj* **1.** [miniature] (en) miniature ▪ **~ aeroplane** maquette *f* d'avion ▪ **~ car** [toy] petite voiture *f* ; [for collectors] modèle *m* réduit **2.** [exemplary] modèle ▪ **he's a ~ pupil/husband** c'est un élève/mari modèle.

modelling *UK*, **modeling** *US* ['mɒdəlɪŋ] *n* **1.** [building models] modelage *m* ▪ [as a hobby] construction *f* de maquettes **2.** [in fashion shows] : **~ is extremely well-paid** le travail de mannequin est très bien payé, les mannequins sont très bien payés ▪ **to make a career in ~** faire une carrière de mannequin **3.** MATHS modélisation *f*.

Model T (Ford) *n* AUT *première voiture fabriquée à la chaîne (1909-1927).*

modem ['məʊdem] *n* modem *m*.

moderate ◇ *adj* ['mɒdərət] **1.** [restrained, modest] modéré ▪ **a ~ wage increase** une augmentation raisonnable des salaires ▪ **~ language** langage mesuré **2.** [average] moyen ▪ **pupils of ~ ability** élèves moyens **3.** METEOR tempéré.
◇ *n* ['mɒdərət] POL modéré *m*, - e *f*.
◇ *vt* ['mɒdəreɪt] **1.** [make less extreme] modérer **2.** [preside over - meeting, group, debate] présider **3.** NUCL PHYS [slow down - neutrons] modérer, ralentir.
◇ *vi* **1.** [lessen] se modérer **2.** [preside] présider, être président.

moderately ['mɒdərətlɪ] *adv* [with moderation] modérément, avec modération ▪ **~ priced** d'un prix raisonnable ▪ [slightly] moyennement.

moderation [,mɒdə'reɪʃn] *n* modération *f* ▪ **a slight ~ of temperature** un léger changement de température ▪ **to drink in** *OR* **with ~** boire avec modération.

moderator ['mɒdəreɪtəʳ] *n* **1.** [president] président *m*, - e *f* ▪ [mediator] médiateur *m*, - trice *f* ▪ RELIG modérateur *m* **2.** NUCL PHYS modérateur *m*, ralentisseur *m*.

modern ['mɒdən] ◇ *adj* moderne ▪ **~ English/French/Greek** anglais *m* /français *m* /grec *m* moderne ▪ **~ face** TYPO didot *m* ▪ **~ jazz** jazz *m* moderne ▪ **~ languages** langues *fpl* vivantes.
◇ *n* **1.** [person] moderne *mf* **2.** TYPO didot *m*.

modern-day *adj* d'aujourd'hui ▪ **a ~ Joan of Arc** la Jeanne d'Arc des temps modernes.

modernism ['mɒdənɪzm] *n* **1.** modernisme *m* **2.** [expression, word] néologisme *m*.

modernist ['mɒdənɪst] ◇ *adj* moderniste.
◇ *n* moderniste *mf*.

modernistic [,mɒdə'nɪstɪk] *adj* moderniste.

modernity [mɒ'dɜ:nətɪ] *n* modernité *f*.

modernization [,mɒdənaɪ'zeɪʃn] *n* modernisation *f*.

modernize, ise ['mɒdənaɪz] ◇ *vt* moderniser.
◇ *vi* se moderniser.

modest ['mɒdɪst] *adj* **1.** [unassuming] modeste ▪ **she's very ~ about her success** son succès ne lui est pas monté à la tête **2.** [small, moderate, simple] modeste ▪ [meagre] modique ▪ **we are very ~ in our needs** nous avons besoin de très peu **3.** [decorous] pudique.

modestly ['mɒdɪstlɪ] *adv* **1.** [unassumingly] modestement, avec modestie **2.** [simply] modestement, simplement **3.** [with decorum] avec pudeur, pudiquement.

modesty ['mɒdɪstɪ] *n* **1.** [lack of conceit] modestie *f* ▪ **in all ~** en toute modestie ▪ **false ~** fausse modestie **2.** [moderation] modestie *f* ▪ [meagreness] modicité *f* **3.** [decorum] pudeur *f* ▪ **she lowered her gaze out of ~** la pudeur lui a fait baisser les yeux.

modicum ['mɒdɪkəm] *n* minimum *m* ▪ **she showed a ~ of common sense** elle a fait preuve d'un minimum de bon sens.

modifiable ['mɒdɪfaɪəbl] *adj* modifiable.

modification [,mɒdɪfɪ'keɪʃn] *n* modification *f* ▪ **he made several ~s in** *OR* **to the text** il apporta plusieurs modifications au texte ▪ **the rules need some ~** il faut modifier les règles.

modifier ['mɒdɪfaɪəʳ] *n* GRAM modificateur *m*.

modify ['mɒdɪfaɪ] (*pret & pp* **modified**) *vt* **1.** [alter] modifier **2.** [moderate] modérer **3.** GRAM modifier.

modish ['məʊdɪʃ] *adj* à la mode.

modular ['mɒdjʊləʳ] *adj* modulaire ▪ **~ degree** ≃ licence *f* à UV ▪ **~ furniture** mobilier *m* modulaire *OR* à éléments.

modulate ['mɒdjʊleɪt] *vt* **1.** ELECTRON & MUS moduler ▪ [voice] moduler **2.** [moderate, tone down] adapter, ajuster.

modulated ['mɒdjʊleɪtɪd] *adj* modulé.

modulation [,mɒdjʊ'leɪʃn] *n* modulation *f*.

modulator ['mɒdjʊleɪtəʳ] *n* ELECTRON modulateur *m*.

module ['mɒdju:l] *n* **1.** [gen] module *m* **2.** UNIV ≃ unité *f* de valeur ▪ ≃ UV *f*.

modus operandi ['məʊdəs,ɒpə'rændi:] *n fml & lit* méthode *f* (de travail), procédé *m*.

modus vivendi ['məʊdəsvɪ'vendi:] *n fml & lit* modus vivendi *m*.

moggie, moggy ['mɒgɪ] (*pl* **moggies**) *n UK inf* minou *m*.

mogul ['məʊgl] *n* **1.** [magnate] magnat *m* **2.** [on ski slope] bosse *f*.
◆ **Mogul** ◇ *n* Moghol *m*.
◇ *adj* moghol.

mohair ['məʊheəʳ] ◇ *n* mohair *m*.
◇ *adj* en *OR* de mohair.

Mohammed [mə'hæmɪd] *pr n* Mahommed, Mahomet.

Mohawk ['məʊhɔ:k] (*pl inv* OR *pl* **Mohawks**) *n* Mohawk *m*.

Mohican [məʊ'hi:kən, 'məʊɪkən] (*pl inv* OR *pl* **Mohicans**) ◇ *n* [person] Mohican *m*, - e *f*.
◇ *adj* mohican.
◆ **mohican** *n* [hairstyle] coupe *f* à l'iroquoise.

moist [mɔɪst] *adj* [skin, air, heat] moite ▪ [climate, soil, surface] humide ▪ [cake] moelleux.

moisten ['mɔɪsn] ◇ *vt* humecter, mouiller ▪ **she ~ed her lips** elle s'humecta les lèvres.
◇ *vi* [eyes] se mouiller ▪ [palms] devenir moite.

moistness ['mɔɪstnɪs] *n* moiteur *f*, humidité *f*.

moisture ['mɔɪstʃər] *n* humidité *f* ▪ [on mirror, window etc] buée *f* ▪ **~ content** teneur *f* en humidité OR en eau.

moistureproof ['mɔɪstʃəpru:f] *adj* [clothing, shoes] imperméable ▪ [watch, container] étanche ▪ [finish, sealant] hydrofuge.

moisturize, ise ['mɔɪstʃəraɪz] *vt* [skin] hydrater ▪ [air] humidifier.

moisturizer ['mɔɪstʃəraɪzər] *n* crème *f* hydratante.

molar ['məʊlər] ◇ *adj* [quantity, solution] molaire.
◇ *n* [tooth] molaire *f*.

molasses [mə'læsɪz] *n (U)* mélasse *f*.

mold *etc* US = **mould**.

Moldavia [mɒl'deɪvjə] *pr n* Moldavie *f* ▪ **in ~** en Moldavie.

Moldavian [mɒl'deɪvjən] ◇ *n* Moldave *mf*.
◇ *adj* moldave.

Moldova [mɒl'dəʊvə] *pr n* : **the Republic of ~** la république de Moldova.

Moldovan [mɑl'dəʊvən] ◇ *adj* moldave.
◇ *n* Moldave *mf*.

mole [məʊl] *n* **1.** [on skin] grain *m* de beauté **2.** ZOOL taupe *f* **3.** *fig* [spy] taupe *f* **4.** [breakwater] môle *m*, digue *f* **5.** [unit of substance] mole *f*.

molecular [mə'lekjʊlər] *adj* moléculaire.

molecule ['mɒlɪkju:l] *n* molécule *f*.

molehill ['məʊlhɪl] *n* taupinière *f*.

moleskin ['məʊlskɪn] *n* **1.** [fur] (peau *f* de) taupe *f* **2.** [cotton] coton *m* sergé.

molest [mə'lest] *vt* [bother] importuner, tracasser ▪ [more violently] molester, malmener ▪ [sexually] agresser (sexuellement).

molestation [,məʊle'steɪʃn] *n (U)* brutalité *f*, violences *fpl* ▪ [sexual] attentat *m* à la pudeur.

molester [mə'lestər] *n* agresseur *m* ▪ **child ~** pédophile *mf*.

moll[△] [mɒl] *n* poule *f*, nana *f*.

Moll Flanders [-'flɑndəz] *pr n héroïne haute en couleurs d'un roman de Daniel Defoe.*

mollify ['mɒlɪfaɪ] (*pret & pp* **mollified**) *vt* apaiser, amadouer.

mollusc UK, **mollusk** US ['mɒləsk] *n* mollusque *m*.

mollycoddle ['mɒlɪ,kɒdl] *vt* UK *inf pej* dorloter, materner.

Molotov cocktail ['mɒlətɒf-] *n* cocktail *m* Molotov.

molt US = **moult**.

molten ['məʊltn] *adj* [metal, lava] en fusion.

mom [mɑ:m] *n* US *inf* maman *f*.

MOMA ['məʊmɑ:] (*abbrev of* **Museum of Modern Art**) *pr n musée d'art moderne à New York.*

moment ['məʊmənt] *n* **1.** [period of time] moment *m*, instant *m* ▪ **at the ~** en ce moment ▪ **at that ~** à ce moment-là ▪ **at this (very) ~** en ce moment même ▪ **at this ~ in time** à l'heure qu'il est ▪ **from that ~ on** désormais ▪ **for the ~** pour le moment ▪ **let me think (for) a ~** laissez-moi réfléchir un moment OR une seconde ▪ **for a long ~ he remained silent** pendant un long moment il est resté sans parler ▪ **I'll do it in a ~** je le ferai dans un instant ▪ **I didn't believe them for a** OR **one ~** je ne les ai pas crus un seul instant ▪ **one ~, please** un instant, s'il vous plaît ; [on telephone] ne quittez pas ▪ **just a ~, you haven't paid yet** un instant, vous n'avez pas encore payé ▪ **she's just this ~ gone out** elle vient de sortir ▪ **don't wait until the last ~** n'attendez pas la dernière minute ▪ **without a ~'s hesitation** sans la moindre hésitation ▪ **he fell in love with her the ~ he saw her** il est tombé amoureux d'elle à l'instant même où il l'a vue ▪ **it was her darkest ~** ce fut l'époque la plus sombre de sa vie ▪ **the ~ of truth** l'heure de vérité ▪ **in the heat of the ~** dans le feu de l'action ▪ **the film has its ~s** le film est parfois intéressant OR a de bons passages **2.** *fml* [import, consequence] importance *f*, signification *f*, portée *f* **3.** PHYS moment *m*.

momentarily [UK 'məʊməntərɪlɪ, US ,məʊmen'terɪlɪ] *adv* **1.** [briefly, temporarily] momentanément **2.** US [immediately] immédiatement, tout de suite ▪ **I'll be with you ~** je suis à vous dans une seconde.

momentary ['məʊməntrɪ] *adj* **1.** [brief, temporary] momentané **2.** *lit* [continual] constant, continuel.

momentous [mə'mentəs] *adj* capital, d'une importance capitale ▪ **on this ~ occasion** en cette occasion mémorable.

momentum [mə'mentəm] *n* **1.** [impetus] vitesse *f*, élan *m* ▪ **to gain ~** *liter & fig* atteindre sa vitesse de croisière ▪ **to lose ~** [vehicle] perdre de la vitesse ; [campaign] s'essouffler **2.** MECH & PHYS moment *m*.

momma ['mɒmə] *n* US *inf* maman *f*.

mommy ['mɒmɪ] US *inf* = **mummy** *(sense 2)*.

Mon. (*written abbrev of* **Monday**) lun.

Monacan ['mɒnəkən] = **Monegasque**.

Monaco ['mɒnəkəʊ] *pr n* Monaco.

Mona Lisa ['məʊnə'li:zə] *pr n* : **'The ~'** *Leonardo da Vinci* 'la Joconde'.

monarch ['mɒnək] *n* [gen - ENTOM] monarque *m*.

monarchical [mə'nɑ:kɪkl] *adj* monarchique.

monarchist ['mɒnəkɪst] ◇ *adj* monarchiste.
◇ *n* monarchiste *mf*.

monarchy ['mɒnəkɪ] (*pl* **monarchies**) *n* monarchie *f*.

monastery ['mɒnəstrɪ] (*pl* **monasteries**) *n* monastère *m*.

monastic [mə'næstɪk] *adj* monastique.

monasticism [mə'næstɪsɪzm] *n* monachisme *m*.

Monday ['mʌndeɪ] *n* lundi *m*.

Monegasque [,mɒnɪ'gæsk] ◇ *n* Monégasque *mf*.
◇ *adj* monégasque.

monetarism ['mʌnɪtərɪzm] *n* monétarisme *m*.

monetarist ['mʌnɪtərɪst] ◇ *adj* monétariste.
◇ *n* monétariste *mf*.

monetary ['mʌnɪtrɪ] *adj* monétaire.

money ['mʌnɪ] (*pl* **moneys** OR *pl* **monies**) ◇ *n* **1.** [gen] argent *m* ▪ **have you got any ~ on you?** est-ce que tu as de l'argent OR du liquide sur toi? ▪ **your ~ or your life!** la bourse ou la vie! ▪ **to get one's ~'s worth** en avoir pour son argent ▪ **to put ~ into sthg** investir dans qqch ▪ **it's ~ well spent** c'est une bonne affaire ▪ **the best dictionary that ~ can buy** le meilleur dictionnaire qui existe OR qui soit ▪ **to make ~** [person] gagner de l'argent ; [business, investment] rapporter ▪ **~ is no object** peu importe le prix, l'argent n'entre pas en ligne de compte ▪ **I'm no good with ~** je n'ai pas la notion de l'argent ▪ **there's no ~ in translating** la traduction ne rapporte pas OR ne paie pas ▪ **toys cost ~, you know** les jouets, ce n'est pas gratuit, tu sais ▪ **we paid good ~ for it** cela nous a coûté cher ▪ **I'm not made of ~, you know** tu as l'air de croire que je roule sur l'or ▪ **to put ~ on a horse** miser sur un cheval ▶ **to be in the ~** *inf* être plein aux as ▪ **put your ~ where your mouth is** il est temps de joindre le geste à la parole ▪ **to have ~ to burn** avoir de l'argent à jeter par les fenêtres ▪ **it's ~ for old rope** UK *inf* c'est de l'argent vite gagné OR du fric vite fait ▪ **for my**

~, he's the best candidate à mon avis, c'est le meilleur candidat ■ **~ talks** l'argent peut tout ■ **~ is the root of all evil** *prov* l'argent est la source de tous les maux **2.** FIN [currency] monnaie *f* ■ **to coin** *OR* **to mint ~** battre *OR* frapper de la monnaie ■ **counterfeit ~** fausse monnaie.
◇ *comp* [problems, matters] d'argent, financier.
◆ **moneys, monies** *npl* LAW [sums] sommes *fpl* (d'argent) ■ **public ~** deniers *mpl* publics.

money-back guarantee *n* garantie *f* de remboursement.

moneybags ['mʌnɪbægz] (*pl inv*) *n inf* richard *m*, - e *f*, rupin *m*, - e *f*.

money belt *n* ceinture *f* portefeuille.

moneybox ['mʌnɪbɒks] *n* tirelire *f*.

money changer *n* **1.** [person] cambiste *mf* **2.** *US* [machine] changeur *m* de monnaie.

moneyed ['mʌnɪd] *adj* riche, nanti.

money-grubbing [-ˌgrʌbɪŋ] *inf* ◇ *n* radinerie *f*.
◇ *adj* radin.

moneylender ['mʌnɪˌlendəʳ] *n* FIN prêteur *m*, - euse *f* ■ [usurer] usurier *m*, - ère *f* ■ [pawnbroker] prêteur *m*, - euse *f* sur gages.

moneymaker ['mʌnɪˌmeɪkəʳ] *n* affaire *f* qui rapporte, mine *f* d'or *fig*.

moneymaking ['mʌnɪˌmeɪkɪŋ] *adj* lucratif ■ **it's another of her ~ schemes** c'est encore une de ses idées pour faire fortune.

money market *n* marché *m* monétaire.

money order *n* mandat *m*.

money spider *n* araignée *f* porte-bonheur.

money-spinner *UK inf* = **moneymaker**.

money supply *n* masse *f* monétaire.

mongol ['mɒŋgəl] *dated & offens & MED* ◇ *n* mongolien *m*, - enne *f*.
◇ *adj* mongolien.

Mongol ['mɒŋgəl] ◇ *n* **1.** [person] Mongol *m*, - e *f* **2.** LING mongol *m*.
◇ *adj* mongol.

Mongolia [mɒŋ'gəʊlɪə] *pr n* Mongolie *f* ■ **in ~** en Mongolie ■ **Inner/Outer ~** Mongolie-Intérieure/Extérieure.

Mongolian [mɒŋ'gəʊlɪən] = **Mongol**.

mongolism ['mɒŋgəlɪzm] *n dated & offens & MED* mongolisme *m*, trisomie *f*.

mongoloid ['mɒŋgəlɔɪd] *dated & offens & MED* ◇ *adj* mongoloïde.
◇ *n* mongoloïde *mf*.

Mongoloid ['mɒŋgəlɔɪd] ◇ *adj* mongol, mongolique.
◇ *n* mongol *m*, - e *f*, mongolique *mf*.

mongoose ['mɒŋgu:s] *n* mangouste *f*.

mongrel ['mʌŋgrəl] ◇ *adj* [dog] bâtard ■ [other animal] hybride.
◇ *n* [dog] bâtard *m* ■ [other animal] hybride *m*.

monicker△ ['mɒnɪkəʳ] = **moniker**.

monied ['mʌnɪd] = **moneyed**.

moniker△ ['mɒnɪkəʳ] *n* [name] nom *m* ■ [nickname] surnom *m*.

monitor ['mɒnɪtəʳ] ◇ *n* **1.** MED & TECH [checking device] moniteur *m* **2.** COMPUT & TV [screen] moniteur *m* **3.** SCH ≃ chef *m* de classe **4.** RADIO employé *m*, - e *f* d'un service d'écoute.
◇ *vt* **1.** [check] suivre, surveiller ■ **their progress is carefully ~ed** leurs progrès sont suivis de près **2.** [listen in to - broadcasts] écouter ■ **~ing station** station *f* d'écoute.

monitory ['mɒnɪtərɪ] *adj fml* [warning] d'avertissement ■ [reproving] d'admonition.

monk [mʌŋk] *n* moine *m*, religieux *m*.

monkey ['mʌŋkɪ] *n* **1.** [animal] singe *m* ■ **female ~** guenon *f* ❯ **to make a ~ out of sb** *inf* se payer la tête de qqn ■ **to have a ~ on one's back** *US inf* être accro **2.** *inf* [scamp] polisson *m*, - onne *f*, galopin *m*.
◆ **monkey about** *UK*, **monkey around** *vi insep inf* **1.** [play the fool] faire l'imbécile **2.** [tamper] : **to ~ about** *OR* **around with sthg** tripoter qqch.

monkey business *n (U) inf* [suspect activity] combines *fpl* ■ [mischief] bêtises *fpl* ■ **they're up to some ~** ils sont en train de combiner quelque chose.

monkey jacket *n* veste *f* courte.

monkey nut *n UK* cacahouète *f*, cacahuète *f*.

monkey-puzzle *n* : **~ (tree)** araucaria *m*, désespoir *m* des singes.

monkey suit *n inf* tenue *f* de soirée, habit *m*.

monkey wrench *n* clef *f* anglaise *OR* à molette.

monkfish ['mʌŋkfɪʃ] (*pl inv OR pl* **monkfishes**) *n* [angler fish] baudroie *f*, lotte *f* ■ [angel shark] ange *m* de mer.

monkhood ['mʌŋkhʊd] *n* **1.** [institution] monachisme *m* ■ [way of life] vie *f* monastique **2.** [monks collectively] : **the ~** les moines *mpl*.

monkish ['mʌŋkɪʃ] *adj* monacal, de moine.

mono ['mɒnəʊ] (*pl* **monos**) ◇ *adj* (*abbrev of* **monophonic**) mono *(inv)*, monophonique.
◇ *n* **1.** AUDIO monophonie *f* ■ **in ~** en monophonie **2.** *US inf* MED mononucléose *f* (infectieuse).

monochrome ['mɒnəkrəʊm] ◇ *adj* [photograph] en noir et blanc ■ [television set] en noir et blanc *(inv)* ■ [computer screen] monochrome ■ [painting] en camaïeu ■ **he leads a very ~ existence** *fig* il mène une existence très terne.
◇ *n* **1.** [technique] monochromie *f* ■ PHOT & TV noir et blanc *m* ■ ART camaïeu *m* **2.** [photograph] photographie *f* en noir et blanc ■ [painting] camaïeu *m* ■ [in modern art] monochrome *m*.

monocle ['mɒnəkl] *n* monocle *m*.

monocled ['mɒnəkld] *adj* qui porte un monocle.

monocoque ['mɒnəkɒk] *n* AERON construction *f* monocoque ■ AUT monocoque *f*.

monogamist [mɒ'nɒgəmɪst] *n* monogame *mf*.

monogamous [mɒ'nɒgəməs] *adj* monogame.

monogamy [mɒ'nɒgəmɪ] *n* monogamie *f*.

monogram ['mɒnəgræm] (*pret & pp* **monogrammed**, *cont* **monogramming**) ◇ *n* monogramme *m*.
◇ *vt* marquer d'un monogramme ■ **monogrammed handkerchiefs** mouchoirs avec un monogramme brodé.

monograph ['mɒnəgrɑ:f] *n* monographie *f*.

monokini ['mɒnəki:nɪ] *n* monokini *m*.

monolingual [ˌmɒnə'lɪŋgwəl] *adj* monolingue.

monolith ['mɒnəlɪθ] *n* monolithe *m*.

monolithic [ˌmɒnə'lɪθɪk] *adj* monolithique.

monologue *UK*, **monolog** *US* ['mɒnəlɒg] ◇ *n* monologue *m*.
◇ *vi* monologuer.

monomania [ˌmɒnə'meɪnjə] *n* monomanie *f*.

monomaniac [ˌmɒnə'meɪnɪæk] ◇ *adj* monomaniaque, monomane.
◇ *n* monomaniaque *mf*, monomane *mf*.

mononucleosis ['mɒnəʊˌnju:klɪ'əʊsɪs] *n (U)* mononucléose *f* (infectieuse).

monoplane ['mɒnəpleɪn] *n* monoplan *m*.

monopolist [mə'nɒpəlɪst] *n* monopoliste *mf*, monopoleur *m*, - euse *f*.

monopolistic [məˌnɒpə'lɪstɪk] *adj* monopoliste, monopolistique.

monopolization [mə,nɒpəlaɪ'zeɪʃn] *n* monopolisation *f*.

monopolize, ise [mə'nɒpəlaɪz] *vt* monopoliser.

monopoly [mə'nɒpəlɪ] (*pl* **monopolies**) *n* monopole *m* ■ **to have a ~ of** *OR* **in** *OR* **on sthg** avoir le monopole de qqch ▶ **state ~** monopole d'État ■ **the Monopolies and Mergers Commission** *commission veillant au respect de la législation antitrust en Grande-Bretagne*.
◆ **Monopoly®** *n* [game] Monopoly® *m* ■ **~ money** *fig* billets *mpl* de Monopoly.

monorail ['mɒnəreɪl] *n* monorail *m*.

monosemic [,mɒnəʊ'si:mɪk] *adj* monosémique.

monoski ['mɒnəʊskɪ] *n* monoski *m*.

monosodium glutamate [,mɒnə'səʊdjəm'glu:təmeɪt] *n* CULIN glutamate *m* (de sodium).

monosyllabic [,mɒnəsɪ'læbɪk] *adj* **1.** LING monosyllabe, monosyllabique **2.** [person] qui s'exprime par monosyllabes.

monosyllable ['mɒnə,sɪləbl] *n* monosyllabe *m* ■ **to speak in ~s** parler par monosyllabes.

monotheism ['mɒnəθi:,ɪzm] *n* monothéisme *m*.

monotheist ['mɒnəθi:,ɪst] ◇ *adj* monothéiste.
◇ *n* monothéiste *mf*.

monotone ['mɒnətəʊn] ◇ *n* ton *m* monocorde ■ **to speak in a ~** parler d'un ton monocorde.
◇ *adj* monocorde.

monotonous [mə'nɒtənəs] *adj* monotone.

monotonously [mə'nɒtənəslɪ] *adv* de façon monotone.

monotony [mə'nɒtənɪ] (*pl* **monotonies**) *n* monotonie *f* ■ **her visits broke the ~ of his life** les visites qu'elle lui rendait rompaient la monotonie de son existence ■ **the ~ of the landscape** l'uniformité *OR* la monotonie du paysage.

monotype ['mɒnətaɪp] *n* ART & BIOL monotype *m*.

monoxide [mɒ'nɒksaɪd] *n* monoxyde *m*.

Monroe Doctrine [mən'rəʊ-] *n*: **the ~** la doctrine de Monroe.

MONROE DOCTRINE

La doctrine de Monroe, énoncée en 1823, inaugura une période isolationniste aux États-Unis, pendant laquelle le continent américain se ferma à l'Europe colonialiste et se détourna délibérément des affaires européennes.

monsignor [mɒn'si:njəʳ] (*pl* **monsignors** *OR pl* **monsignori** [-si:'njɔ:rɪ]) *n* monseigneur *m*.

monsoon [mɒn'su:n] *n* mousson *f* ■ **the ~ season** la mousson.

monster ['mɒnstəʳ] ◇ *n* monstre *m*.
◇ *adj* colossal, monstre.

monstrosity [mɒn'strɒsətɪ] (*pl* **monstrosities**) *n* **1.** [monstrous nature] monstruosité *f* **2.** [ugly person, thing] horreur *f*.

monstrous ['mɒnstrəs] *adj* **1.** [appalling] monstrueux, atroce **2.** [enormous] colossal, énorme **3.** [abnormal] monstrueux.

monstrously ['mɒnstrəslɪ] *adv* affreusement.

montage ['mɒntɑ:ʒ] *n* ART, CIN & PHOT montage *m*.

Montana [mɒn'tænə] *pr n* Montana *m* ■ **in ~** dans le Montana.

Mont Blanc [,mɔ̃'blɑ̃] *pr n* mont Blanc *m*.

Monte Carlo [,mɒntɪ'kɑ:ləʊ] *pr n* Monte-Carlo.

Montenegro [,mɒntɪ'ni:grəʊ] *pr n* Monténégro *m*.

month [mʌnθ] *n* mois *m* ■ **how much does she earn a ~?** combien gagne-t-elle par mois? ■ **every ~** tous les mois ■ **in a ~'s time** dans un mois ■ **by the ~** au mois ▶ **she hasn't heard from him in a ~ of Sundays** *inf* ça fait des siècles *OR* un bail qu'elle n'a pas de nouvelles de lui ■ **never in a ~ of Sundays** à la saint-glinglin.

monthly ['mʌnθlɪ] (*pl* **monthlies**) ◇ *adj* mensuel ■ **~ instalment** *OR* **payment** mensualité *f* ■ **~ period** MED règles *fpl* ■ **~ statement** relevé *m* mensuel.
◇ *n* [periodical] mensuel *m*.
◇ *adv* [meet, occur] tous les mois ■ [pay] mensuellement.

Montreal [,mɒntrɪ'ɔ:l] *pr n* Montréal.

Montserrat ['mɑntsəræt] *pr n* Montserrat *f*.

monument ['mɒnjʊmənt] *n* **1.** [memorial] monument *m* **2.** [historic building] monument *m* historique.

monumental [,mɒnjʊ'mentl] *adj* monumental ■ **he's a ~ bore** il est prodigieusement ennuyeux.

monumentally [,mɒnjʊ'mentəlɪ] *adv* **1.** [build] de façon monumentale **2.** [extremely] extrêmement.

moo [mu:] ◇ *n* **1.** [sound] meuglement *m*, beuglement *m*, mugissement *m* **2.** *UK inf* [stupid woman] bécasse *f*.
◇ *vi* meugler, beugler, mugir.
◇ *onom* meuh.

mooch [mu:tʃ] *inf* ◇ *vi UK* [wander aimlessly] traîner ■ **he ~ed down the street** il descendit la rue en flânant.
◇ *vt US* **1.** [cadge] taper ■ **to ~ $10 off** *OR* **from sb** taper qqn de 10 dollars **2.** [steal] chiper, piquer.
◆ **mooch about, mooch around** *vi insep UK inf* [loaf] traîner.

mood [mu:d] *n* **1.** [humour] humeur *f*, disposition *f* ■ **to be in a good/bad ~** être de bonne/mauvaise humeur ■ **she can be quite funny when the ~ takes her** elle peut être plutôt drôle quand l'envie lui en prend ■ **are you in the ~ for a hamburger?** un hamburger, ça te dit? ■ **I'm not in the ~** *OR* **I'm in no ~ to hear his life story** je ne suis pas d'humeur à l'écouter raconter (l'histoire de) sa vie **2.** [bad temper, sulk] mauvaise humeur *f*, bouderie *f* ■ **to be in a ~** être de mauvaise humeur **3.** [atmosphere] ambiance *f*, atmosphère *f* ■ **the ~ is one of cautious optimism** l'ambiance est à l'optimisme prudent ▶ **~ music** musique *f* d'ambiance **4.** GRAM mode *m* ■ **imperative ~** impératif *m*.

moodily ['mu:dɪlɪ] *adv* [behave] maussadement, d'un air morose ■ [talk, reply] d'un ton maussade.

moodiness ['mu:dɪnɪs] *n* **1.** [sullenness] humeur *f* maussade, maussaderie *f* **2.** [volatility] humeur *f* changeante ■ **it's his ~ I can't stand** ce sont ses sautes d'humeur que je ne supporte pas.

mood swing *n* saute *f* d'humeur.

moody ['mu:dɪ] (*comp* **moodier**, *superl* **moodiest**) *adj* **1.** [sullen] de mauvaise humeur, maussade, grincheux **2.** [temperamental] versatile, d'humeur changeante.

moon [mu:n] ◇ *n* **1.** lune *f* ■ **there's a ~ tonight** on voit la lune ce soir ■ **by the light of the ~** au clair de (la) lune ▶ **to be over the ~** *inf* être aux anges ■ **he promised her the ~ (and the stars)** il lui promit la lune *OR* monts et merveilles ■ **once in a blue ~** tous les trente-six du mois **2.** *US inf* [bare backside] lune *f*.
◇ *comp* [base, flight, rocket] lunaire.
◇ *vi inf* [show one's buttocks] montrer son derrière *OR* ses fesses.
◆ **moon about** *UK*, **moon around** *vi insep inf* [idly] paresser, traîner, flemmarder ■ [dreamily] rêvasser ■ [gloomily] se morfondre.
◆ **moon over** *vt insep inf* soupirer après.

moonbeam ['mu:nbi:m] *n* rayon *m* de lune.

moonboots ['mu:nbu:ts] *npl* après-skis *mpl*.

moon buggy (*pl* **moon buggies**) *n* Jeep® *f* lunaire.

moon-faced *adj* joufflu, aux joues rebondies.

Moonie ['mu:nɪ] *n inf* adepte *m* de la secte Moon, mooniste *mf*.

moon landing *n* atterrissage *m* sur la lune, alunissage *m*.

moonless ['mu:nlɪs] *adj* sans lune.

moonlight ['mu:nlaɪt] <> *n* clair *m* de lune ■ **they took a walk by ~** ils se sont promenés au clair de (la) lune ⊙ **'The Moonlight Sonata'** ***Beethoven*** 'la Sonate au clair de lune'.
<> *adj* [walk] au clair de (la) lune.
<> *vi inf* [have second job] avoir un deuxième emploi ■ [illegally] travailler au noir.

moonlighter ['mu:nlaɪtə^r] *n* travailleur *m* non déclaré, travailleuse *f* non déclarée.

moonlight flit *n UK inf* **to do a ~** déménager à la cloche de bois.

moonlighting ['mu:nlaɪtɪŋ] *n* [illegal work] travail *m* au noir.

moonlit ['mu:nlɪt] *adj* éclairé par la lune ■ **a ~ night** une nuit de lune ■ **we walked through the ~ fields** nous avons marché à travers champs, au clair de lune.

moonscape ['mu:nskeɪp] *n* paysage *m* lunaire.

moonshine ['mu:nʃaɪn] *n (U)* **1.** = **moonlight** *(n)* **2.** *inf* [foolishness] sornettes *fpl*, sottises *fpl*, bêtises *fpl* **3.** *US* [illegally made spirits] alcool *m* de contrebande.

moonshining ['mu:nʃaɪnɪŋ] *n US fabrication clandestine d'alcool en milieu rural.*

moon shot *n* lancement *m* d'un vaisseau lunaire.

moonstone ['mu:nstəʊn] *n* pierre *f* de lune, adulaire *f*.

moonstruck ['mu:nstrʌk] *adj* [dreamy] dans la lune ■ [mad] fou *(before vowel or silent 'h' fol)*, folle *f*, détraqué.

moon walk *n* marche *f* sur la lune.

moony ['mu:nɪ] (*comp* **moonier**, *superl* **mooniest**) *adj inf* **1.** [dreamy] rêveur, dans la lune **2.** *UK* [crazy] dingue, timbré.

moor [mʊə] <> *vt* [boat] amarrer ■ [buoy] mouiller.
<> *vi* mouiller.
<> *n* lande *f*.

Moor [mɔ:^r] *n* Maure *m*, Mauresque *f*.

moorage ['mɔ:rɪdʒ] *n* **1.** [place] mouillage *m* **2.** [fee] droit *m* d'ancrage.

moorhen ['mɔ:hen] *n* **1.** [waterfowl] poule *f* d'eau **2.** [female grouse] grouse *f* d'Écosse.

mooring ['mɔ:rɪŋ] *n* **1.** [act] amarrage *m*, mouillage *m* **2.** [place] mouillage *m*.
◆ **moorings** *npl* [cables, ropes etc] amarres *fpl* ■ **the boat was (riding) at her ~s** le bateau tirait sur ses amarres.

Moorish ['mɔ:rɪʃ] *adj* maure.

moorland ['mɔ:lənd] *n* lande *f*.

moose [mu:s] (*pl inv*) *n* orignal *m*.

moot [mu:t] <> *vt* [question, topic] soulever ■ **a change in the rules has been ~ed** il a été question de modifier le règlement.
<> *n* **1.** HIST assemblée *f* **2.** UNIV [in law faculties] tribunal *m* fictif.

moot point *n* : **that's a ~** c'est discutable *OR* ce n'est pas sûr.

mop [mɒp] (*pret & pp* **mopped**, *cont* **mopping**) <> *n* **1.** [for floor - string, cloth] lave-pont *m*, balai *m* (à franges) ; [- sponge] balai-éponge *m* ■ NAUT vadrouille *f* ■ [for dishes] lavette *f* (à vaisselle) **2.** [of hair] tignasse *f* ■ **a ~ of blond hair** une tignasse blonde.
<> *vt* [floor] laver ■ [table, face, spilt liquid] essuyer, éponger ■ **he mopped the sweat from his brow** il s'épongea le front.
◆ **mop up** *vt sep* **1.** [floor, table, spilt liquid] essuyer, éponger ■ **have some bread to ~ up the sauce** prenez un morceau de pain pour saucer votre assiette **2.** *inf* [win, make off with] rafler **3.** MIL [resistance] liquider.

mope [məʊp] *vi* broyer du noir ■ **there's no use moping about** *OR* **over it** ça ne sert à rien de passer ton temps à ressasser ce qui s'est passé.

moped ['məʊped] *n UK* Mobylette® *f*, cyclomoteur *m*, vélomoteur *m*.

moppet ['mɒpɪt] *n inf* chou *m*.

mopping-up operation ['mɒpɪŋ-] *n* opération *f* de nettoyage.

moquette [mɒ'ket] *n* moquette *f (étoffe)*.

moraine [mɒ'reɪn] *n* moraine *f*.

moral ['mɒrəl] <> *adj* moral ■ **he complains about the decline in ~ standards** il se plaint du déclin des valeurs morales *OR* du relâchement des mœurs ■ **to give sb ~ support** soutenir qqn moralement ⊙ **~ philosophy** morale *f*, éthique *f* ■ **~ victory** victoire *f* morale.
<> *n* [lesson] morale *f*.
◆ **morals** *npl* [standards] sens *m* moral, moralité *f*.

morale [mə'rɑ:l] *n* moral *m* ■ **~ is high/low among the troops** les troupes ont bon/mauvais moral, les troupes ont/n'ont pas le moral ■ **she tried to raise their ~** elle a essayé de leur remonter le moral *OR* de leur redonner (du) courage.

morale-booster *n* : **it was a ~** ça nous/leur *etc* a remonté le moral.

moralist ['mɒrəlɪst] *n* moraliste *mf*.

moralistic [,mɒrə'lɪstɪk] *adj* moraliste.

morality [mə'rælətɪ] (*pl* **moralities**) *n* **1.** moralité *f* **2.** : **~ (play)** THEAT moralité *f*.

moralize, ise ['mɒrəlaɪz] <> *vi* moraliser ■ **to ~ about sthg** moraliser sur qqch.
<> *vt* moraliser.

moralizing ['mɒrəlaɪzɪŋ] <> *adj* moralisateur, moralisant.
<> *n (U)* leçons *fpl* de morale, prêches *mpl pej*.

morally ['mɒrəlɪ] *adv* moralement ■ **~ wrong** contraire à la morale.

moral majority *n* : **the ~** les néo-conservateurs *mpl (surtout aux États-Unis)*.

morass [mə'ræs] *n* **1.** [disordered situation] bourbier *m* ■ [of paperwork, information] fouillis *m*, fatras *m* **2.** [marsh] marais *m*, bourbier *m*.

moratorium [,mɒrə'tɔ:rɪəm] (*pl* **moratoriums** *OR pl* **moratoria** [-rɪə]) *n* **1.** [suspension of activity] moratoire *m* ■ **they are calling for a ~ on arms sales** ils appellent à un moratoire sur les ventes d'armes **2.** ECON & LAW moratoire *m* ■ [of debt] moratoire, suspension *f*.

Moravia [mə'reɪvjə] *pr n* Moravie *f* ■ **in ~** en Moravie.

Moravian [mə'reɪvjən] <> *n* Morave *mf*.
<> *adj* morave.

moray ['mɒreɪ] *n* : **~ (eel)** murène *f*.

morbid ['mɔ:bɪd] *adj* **1.** [gen] morbide ■ [curiosity] malsain ■ **he has a ~ outlook on life** il voit les choses en noir **2.** MED [state, growth] morbide ■ **~ anatomy** anatomie *f* pathologique.

morbidity [mɔ:'bɪdətɪ] *n* **1.** [gen] morbidité *f* **2.** : **~ (rate)** MED morbidité *f* (relative).

morbidly ['mɔ:bɪdlɪ] *adv* maladivement.

mordant ['mɔ:dənt] *adj* mordant, caustique.

more [mɔ:^r] <> *det* **1.** *(compar of* **many, much***)* [greater in number, amount] plus de, davantage de ■ **there were ~ boys than girls** il y avait plus de garçons que de filles
2. [further, additional] : **you should eat ~ fish** tu devrais manger davantage de *OR* plus de poisson ■ **I need ~ time** j'ai besoin de plus de temps ■ **three ~ people arrived** trois autres personnes sont arrivées ■ **do you have any ~ stamps?** est-ce qu'il vous reste des timbres? ■ **just wait a few ~ minutes** patiente encore quelques instants ■ **there are no ~** *OR* **there aren't any**

~ green lampshades il n'y a plus d'abat-jour verts ■ **there'll be no ~ skiing this winter** le ski est fini pour cet hiver ■ **there have been several ~ incidents in the same area** plusieurs autres incidents se sont produits dans le même quartier ■ **would you like some ~ soup?** voulez-vous un peu plus de soupe?

◇ *pron* **1.** *(compar of* **many, much***)* [greater amount] plus, davantage ■ [greater number] plus ■ **he earns ~ than I do** *OR* **than me** il gagne plus que moi ■ **I wish I could do ~ for her** j'aimerais pouvoir l'aider plus *OR* davantage ■ **some opted for A, but many ~ chose B** certains ont choisi A, mais ceux qui ont choisi B étaient bien plus nombreux ■ **there are ~ of them than there are of us** ils sont plus nombreux que nous ■ **~ of: he's even ~ of a coward than I thought** il est encore plus lâche que je ne pensais ■ **it's ~ of a problem now than it used to be** ça pose plus de problèmes maintenant qu'avant ■ **she's ~ of a singer than a dancer** c'est une chanteuse plus qu'une danseuse

2. [additional amount] plus, encore ■ **there's ~ if you want it** il y en a encore si tu veux ■ **he asked for ~** il en redemanda ■ **I couldn't eat any ~, thanks** je ne pourrais plus rien avaler, merci ■ **she just can't take any ~** elle n'en peut vraiment plus ■ **please can I have some ~?** [food] puis-je en reprendre, s'il vous plaît? ■ **there are some ~ here that you haven't washed** il en reste ici que tu n'as pas lavés ■ **something/nothing ~** quelque chose/rien de plus ■ **I have something/nothing ~ to say** j'ai encore quelque chose/je n'ai plus rien à dire ■ **what ~ do you want?** que voulez-vous de plus? ■ **what ~ could you ask for!** *hum* que demande le peuple! ■ **but ~ of that later...** mais nous reparlerons de ça plus tard... ■ **that's ~ like it!** voilà, c'est mieux! ➲ **no ~ no less** ni plus ni moins ■ **~ of the same** la même chose ■ **there's plenty ~ where that came from** si vous en revoulez, il n'y a qu'à demander ■ **need I say ~?** si tu vois ce que je veux dire

3. *hum* [additional people] : **any ~ for the ferry?** qui d'autre prend le ferry?

◇ *adv* **1.** [forming comparatives] plus ■ **~ intelligent** plus intelligent

2. [to a greater extent, degree] plus, davantage ■ **you should read ~** tu devrais lire plus *OR* davantage ■ **I like wine ~ than beer** je préfère le vin à la bière, j'aime mieux le vin que la bière ■ **I'll give you £20, not a penny ~** je te donnerai 20 livres, pas un sou de plus ■ [rather] plutôt ■ **she was ~ disappointed than angry** elle était plus déçue que fâchée ■ **do it ~ like this** fais-le plutôt comme ceci

3. [again] : **once/twice ~** encore une/deux fois.

◆ **more and more** ◇ *det phr* de plus en plus.

◇ *adv phr* de plus en plus.

◆ **more or less** *adv phr* **1.** [roughly] plus ou moins **2.** [almost] presque.

◆ **more than** ◇ *prep phr* [with numbers, measurements etc] plus de ■ **for little ~ than £500** pour à peine plus de 500 livres ■ **I won't be ~ than two hours** je n'en ai pas pour plus de deux heures, j'en ai pour deux heures au maximum.

◇ *adv phr* plus que ■ **I'd be ~ than happy to do it** je serais ravi de le faire ■ **this ~ than makes up for his previous mistakes** voilà qui rachète largement ses anciennes erreurs.

◆ **more than a little** *adv phr* vraiment.

◆ **no more** *adv phr* **1.** [neither] non plus **2.** [as little] pas plus ■ **she's no ~ a spy than I am!** elle n'est pas plus espionne que moi! **3.** *lit* [no longer] : **the Empire is no ~** l'Empire n'est plus.

◆ **not... any more** *adv phr* : **we don't go there any ~** nous n'y allons plus ■ **he still works here, doesn't he? – not any ~ (he doesn't)** il travaille encore ici, n'est-ce pas? – non, plus maintenant.

◆ **the more** *adv phr fml* d'autant plus ■ **the ~ so because...** d'autant plus que...

◆ **the more... the more** *conj phr* plus... plus ■ **the ~ they have, the ~ they want** plus ils en ont, plus ils en veulent.

◆ **what is more, what's more** *adv phr* qui plus est.

moreish ['mɔːrɪʃ] *adj UK inf* appétissant.

morello [mə'reləʊ] *(pl* **morellos***) n* : **~ (cherry)** griotte *f*.

moreover [mɔː'rəʊvər] *adv* de plus.

mores ['mɔːreɪz] *npl fml* mœurs *fpl*.

morganatic [,mɔːgə'nætɪk] *adj* morganatique.

morgue [mɔːg] *n* **1.** [mortuary] morgue *f* **2.** *inf* PRESS archives *fpl*.

MORI ['mɒrɪ] *(abbrev of* **Market & Opinion Research Institute***) pr n institut de sondage britannique*.

moribund ['mɒrɪbʌnd] *adj* moribond.

morish ['mɔːrɪʃ] *inf* = **moreish**.

Mormon ['mɔːmən] ◇ *n* mormon *m*, - e *f*.

◇ *adj* mormon.

Mormonism ['mɔːmənɪzm] *n* mormonisme *m*.

morn [mɔːn] *n* **1.** *lit* [morning] matin *m* **2.** *Scotland* **the ~** [tomorrow] demain.

morning ['mɔːnɪŋ] ◇ *n* **1.** matin *m*, matinée *f* ■ **at three/ten o'clock in the ~** à trois/dix heures du matin ■ **I worked all ~** j'ai travaillé toute la matinée ■ **when I awoke it was ~** quand je me suis réveillé il faisait jour ■ **every Saturday/Sunday ~** tous les samedis/dimanches matin ■ **from ~ till night** du matin jusqu'au soir ■ **it's open in the ~** *OR* **~s** c'est ouvert le matin ■ **see you in the ~!** à demain matin! ■ **in the early/late ~** en début/fin de matinée ■ **I'll be back on Monday ~** je serai de retour lundi matin ■ **the cleaning lady comes on Monday ~s** la femme de ménage vient le lundi matin ■ **could I have the ~ off?** puis-je avoir la matinée de libre? ■ **(good) ~!** [hello] bonjour! ; [goodbye] au revoir! ■ **this ~** ce matin ■ **that ~** ce matin-là ■ **the previous ~, the ~ before** la veille au matin ■ **the next ~, the ~ after** le lendemain matin ➲ **the ~ after the night before** *inf* un lendemain de cuite **2.** *lit* [beginning] matin *m*, aube *f*.

◇ *comp* [dew, sun, bath] matinal, du matin ■ [newspaper, broadcast] du matin ■ **we have ~ coffee around 11** nous faisons une pause-café vers 11 h du matin.

morning-after pill *n* pilule *f* du lendemain.

morning coat *n* queue-de-pie *f*.

morning dress *n* **1.** *(U) UK* [suit] *habit porté lors des occasions importantes et comportant queue-de-pie, pantalon gris et haut-de-forme gris* **2.** *US* [dress] robe *f* d'intérieur.

morning glory *n* ipomée *f*, volubilis *m*.

Morning Prayer *n* office *m* du matin *(Église anglicane)*.

morning room *n* petit salon *m*.

mornings ['mɔːnɪŋz] *adv (esp) US* le matin.

morning sickness *n* nausées *fpl* matinales *OR* du matin.

morning star *n* étoile *f* du matin.

Moroccan [mə'rɒkən] ◇ *n* Marocain *m*, - e *f*.

◇ *adj* marocain.

Morocco [mə'rɒkəʊ] *pr n* Maroc *m* ■ **in ~** au Maroc.

◆ **morocco** *n* : **morocco (leather)** maroquin *m*.

moron ['mɔːrɒn] *n* **1.** △ [stupid person] imbécile *mf*, crétin *m*, - e *f* **2.** *dated* [mentally retarded person] débile *m* léger, débile *f* légère.

moronic [mə'rɒnɪk] *adj* imbécile, stupide.

morose [mə'rəʊs] *adj* morose.

morpheme ['mɔːfiːm] *n* morphème *m*.

morphemics [mɔː'fiːmɪks] *n (U)* morphématique *f*.

Morpheus ['mɔːfjuːs] *pr n* Morphée.

morphine ['mɔːfiːn], **morphia** ['mɔːfjə] *n* morphine *f* ■ **~ addict** morphinomane *mf*.

morphological [,mɔːfə'lɒdʒɪkl] *adj* BIOL & LING morphologique.

morphology [,mɔː'fɒlədʒɪ] *n* BIOL & LING morphologie *f*.

morris ['mɒrɪs] *n* : **~ dance** *danse folklorique anglaise* ■ **~ dancer, ~ man** *danseur folklorique anglais* ■ **~ dancing** *danses folkloriques anglaises*.

morrow ['mɒrəʊ] *n* **1.** *lit* [next day] lendemain *m* ■ **on the ~** le lendemain **2.** *arch* & *lit* [morning] matin *m*.

Morse [mɔːs] *n* : ~ **(code)** morse *m* ■ ~ **signals** signaux *mpl* en morse.

morsel ['mɔːsl] *n* [gen] morceau *m* ■ [mouthful] bouchée *f*.

mortal ['mɔːtl] ◇ *adj* **1.** [not immortal] mortel ■ **~remains** ***euph*** dépouille *f* mortelle **2.** [fatal - blow, disease, injury] mortel, fatal ■ [deadly - enemy, danger] mortel ■ **they were locked in ~ combat** ils étaient engagés dans un combat mortel **3.** ***inf dated*** [blessed, damned] sacré, satané **4.** [very great] : **he lived in ~ fear of being found out** il vivait dans une peur mortelle d'être découvert.
◇ *n* mortel *m*, - elle *f*.

mortality [mɔː'tælətɪ] (*pl* **mortalities**) *n* [loss of life] mortalité *f* ■ **no mortalities have been reported** on ne fait état d'aucun mort, aucun décès n'a été enregistré.

mortally ['mɔːtəlɪ] *adv* mortellement ■ ~ **offended** mortellement offensé ■ ~ **wounded** blessé à mort ■ **to be ~ afraid** être mort de peur ***fig***.

mortal sin *n* péché *m* mortel.

mortar ['mɔːtəʳ] ◇ *n* CONSTR, MIL & PHARM mortier *m*.
◇ *vt* CONSTR cimenter.

mortarboard ['mɔːtəbɔːd] *n* **1.** SCH & UNIV ≃ mortier *m* *(couvre-chef de professeur, d'universitaire)* **2.** CONSTR taloche *f*.

mortgage ['mɔːgɪdʒ] ◇ *n* **1.** [to buy house] prêt *m* (immobilier) ■ **a 25-year ~ at 13%** un emprunt sur 25 ans à 13 % ▶ **we can't meet our ~ repayments** nous ne pouvons pas payer les mensualités de notre emprunt ■ **second ~** hypothèque *f* **2.** [surety] hypothèque *f*.
◇ *vt* ***liter*** & ***fig*** hypothéquer, prendre une hypothèque sur ■ **to be ~d to the hilt** [person] crouler sous les remboursements.

mortgage broker *n* courtier *m* en prêts hypothécaires.

mortgagee [ˌmɔːgɪ'dʒiː] *n* créancier *m*, - ère *f* hypothécaire, prêteur *m*, - euse *f* (sur une hypothèque).

mortgage rate *n* taux *m* de crédit immobilier.

mortgagor [ˌmɔːgɪ'dʒɔːʳ] *n* débiteur *m*, - trice *f* hypothécaire, emprunteur *m*, - euse *f* *(sur une hypothèque)*.

mortice ['mɔːtɪs] = **mortise**.

mortician [mɔː'tɪʃn] *n* ***US*** entrepreneur *m* de pompes funèbres.

mortification [ˌmɔːtɪfɪ'keɪʃn] *n* [gen - MED & RELIG] mortification *f*.

mortified ['mɔːtɪfaɪd] *adj* mortifié, gêné.

mortify ['mɔːtɪfaɪ] (*pret* & *pp* **mortified**) ◇ *vt* mortifier.
◇ *vi* MED [become gangrenous] se gangrener ■ [undergo tissue death] se nécroser, se mortifier.

mortise ['mɔːtɪs] ◇ *n* mortaise *f*.
◇ *vt* mortaiser.

mortise lock *n* serrure *f* encastrée.

mortuary ['mɔːtʃʊərɪ] (*pl* **mortuaries**) ◇ *n* morgue *f*.
◇ *adj* mortuaire.

mosaic [məʊ'zeɪɪk] ◇ *n* mosaïque *f*.
◇ *adj* en mosaïque ■ ~ **floor** carrelage *m* en mosaïque.

Mosaic [məʊ'zeɪɪk] *adj* BIBLE mosaïque, de Moïse.

Moscow ['mɒskəʊ] *pr n* Moscou.

Moselle [məʊ'zel] *n* **1.** [region] Moselle *f* ■ **in ~** en Moselle **2.** [wine] (vin *m* de) Moselle *m*.

Moses ['məʊzɪz] *pr n* Moïse.

Moses basket *n* couffin *m*.

mosey ['məʊzɪ] *vi* ***US inf*** [amble] marcher d'un pas tranquille.

mosh [mɒʃ] *vi* ***US inf*** *danser de façon agressive.*

Moslem ['mɒzləm] ◇ *n* musulman *m*, - e *f*.
◇ *adj* musulman.

mosque [mɒsk] *n* mosquée *f*.

mosquito [mə'skiːtəʊ] (*pl* **mosquitos** *OR* *pl* **mosquitoes**) *n* moustique *m*.

mosquito net *n* moustiquaire *f*.

moss [mɒs] *n* BOT mousse *f*.

moss rose *n* rose *f* moussue *OR* mousseuse.

moss stitch *n* point *m* de riz.

mossy ['mɒsɪ] (*comp* **mossier**, *superl* **mossiest**) *adj* moussu, couvert de mousse.

most [məʊst] ◇ *det (superl of many, much)* **1.** [greatest in number, degree etc] : **the candidate who gets (the) ~ votes** le candidat qui obtient le plus de voix *OR* le plus grand nombre de voix ■ **which of your inventions gave you ~ satisfaction?** laquelle de vos inventions vous a procuré la plus grande satisfaction?
2. [the majority of] la plupart de, la majorité de ■ **I like ~ kinds of fruit** j'aime presque tous les fruits ■ **I don't like ~ modern art** en général, je n'aime pas l'art moderne.
◇ *pron (superl of many, much)* **1.** [the greatest amount] : **which of the three applicants has (the) ~ to offer?** lequel des trois candidats a le plus à offrir? ■ **that is the ~ one can say in his defence** c'est tout ce qu'on peut dire en sa faveur ▶ **to make the ~ of** [advantage, chance, good weather] profiter de ; [bad situation, ill-luck] tirer le meilleur parti de ; [resources, skills] employer *OR* utiliser au mieux ■ **he knows how to make the ~ of himself** il sait se mettre en valeur
2. [the greater part] la plus grande *OR* la majeure partie ■ [the greater number] la plupart *OR* majorité ■ **~ of the snow has melted** presque toute la neige a fondu ■ **~ of us/them** la plupart d'entre nous/eux.
◇ *adv* **1.** [forming superlatives] : **it's the ~ beautiful house I've ever seen** c'est la plus belle maison que j'aie jamais vue ■ **she was the one who explained things ~ clearly** c'est elle qui expliquait les choses le plus clairement
2. [to the greatest extent, degree] : **(the) ~** le plus ■ **what worries you ~?, what ~ worries you?** qu'est-ce qui vous inquiète le plus?
3. [as intensifier] bien, fort ■ **a ~ interesting theory** une théorie fort intéressante ■ **we had the ~ awful weather** nous avons eu un temps détestable ■ **~ certainly you may!** mais bien entendu!
4. ***US inf*** [almost] presque.
◆ **at (the) most** *adv phr* au plus, au maximum ■ **at the very ~** tout au plus, au grand maximum.

most-favoured nation *n* nation *f* la plus favorisée ■ **this country has ~ status** ce pays bénéficie de la clause de la nation la plus favorisée.

mostly ['məʊstlɪ] *adv* **1.** [mainly] principalement, surtout ■ **it's ~ sugar** c'est surtout du sucre ■ **the soldiers were ~ young men** il s'agissait pour la plupart *OR* surtout *OR* principalement de jeunes soldats **2.** [usually] le plus souvent, la plupart du temps.

MOT (*pret* & *pp* **MOT'd** [ˌeməʊ'tiːd], *cont* **MOT'ing** [ˌeməʊ'tiːɪŋ]) (*abbrev of* **Ministry of Transport**) ***UK*** ◇ *n* **1.** ***dated*** [ministry] ministère *m* des Transports **2.** AUT : ~ **(certificate)** *contrôle technique annuel obligatoire pour les véhicules de plus de trois ans* ■ **that old car of yours will never pass its ~** ta vieille voiture n'obtiendra jamais son certificat de contrôle technique.
◇ *vt* : **to have one's car ~'d** soumettre sa voiture au contrôle technique.

mote [məʊt] *n* ***lit*** atome *m*, grain *m*, particule *f*.

motel [məʊ'tel] *n* motel *m*.

motet [məʊ'tet] *n* motet *m*.

moth [mɒθ] *n* **1.** ENTOM papillon *m* (nocturne) **2.** [in clothes] mite *f*.

mothball ['mɒθbɔːl] ◇ *n* boule *f* de naphtaline.
◇ *vt* [project] mettre en suspens.

moth-eaten *adj* **1.** ***liter*** [clothing] mité **2.** ***inf fig*** [shabby] miteux.

mother ['mʌðəʳ] <> *n* **1.** [parent] mère *f* ■ **she's a ~ of three** elle est mère de trois enfants ■ **~, this is John** maman, je te présente John ▶ **Mother Earth** la Terre ■ **~'s milk** lait *m* maternel ■ **every ~'s son** tous sans exception **2.** RELIG [woman in authority] mère *f* ■ **~ superior** Mère *f* supérieure ▮ [Virgin Mary] : **Mother of God** Mère *f* de Dieu **3.** [original cause, source] mère *f* ■ **necessity is the ~ of invention** *prov* nécessité est mère d'industrie *OR* d'invention **4.** △ *US* [character] type *m* **5.** △ *US* = **motherfucker**.
<> *adj* **1.** [motherly] maternel **2.** [as parent] : **the ~ bird feeds her young** l'oiseau (femelle) nourrit ses petits ▶ **~ hen** mère *f* poule ■ **~ lode** MIN veine *f* principale ■ **~ ship** MIL ravitailleur *m*.
<> *vt* **1.** [give birth to] donner naissance à **2.** [take care of] servir de mère à ■ [coddle] dorloter, materner.

motherboard ['mʌðəbɔ:d] *n* COMPUT carte *f* mère.

Mothercare® *pr n chaîne de magasins spécialisés dans les articles pour nouveau-nés, jeunes enfants et femmes enceintes.*

mother company *n* maison *f* mère.

mother country *n* (mère) patrie *f*.

mother figure *n* figure *f* maternelle.

motherfucker▲ ['mʌðə,fʌkəʳ] *n US* [person] enculé *m*, - e *f* ▲ ■ [thing] saloperie△ *f*.

motherhood ['mʌðəhʊd] *n* maternité *f*.

Mothering Sunday ['mʌðərɪŋ-] *n UK* la fête des Mères.

mother-in-law (*pl* **mothers-in-law**) *n* belle-mère *f*.

motherland ['mʌðəlænd] *n* (mère) patrie *f*, pays *m* natal.

motherless ['mʌðəlɪs] *adj* sans mère.

motherly ['mʌðəlɪ] *adj* maternel.

Mother Nature *n* la Nature.

mother-of-pearl *n* nacre *f* ■ **~ buttons** boutons *mpl* en *OR* de nacre.

mother's boy *UK*, **mamma's boy** *US n* fils *m* à sa maman, poule *f* mouillée.

Mother's Day *n* la fête des Mères.

mother-to-be (*pl* **mothers-to-be**) *n* future mère *f*.

mother tongue *n* langue *f* maternelle.

mother wit *n* bon sens *m*.

mothproof ['mɒθpru:f] <> *adj* traité à l'antimite.
<> *vt* traiter à l'antimite.

motif [məʊ'ti:f] *n* ART, LIT & MUS motif *m*.

motion ['məʊʃn] <> *n* **1.** [movement] mouvement *m* **2.** [gesture] geste *m*, mouvement *m* ■ **he made a ~ as if to step back** il esquissa un geste de recul ■ **with a swaying ~ of the hips** en ondulant des hanches ▶ **to go through the ~s (of doing sthg)** faire qqch machinalement **3.** [proposal] motion *f*, résolution *f* ■ **to propose** *OR* **to bring a ~** présenter une motion, soumettre une proposition ■ **to table a ~ of no confidence** déposer une motion de censure **4.** LAW [application] requête *f* **5.** MED [faeces] selles *fpl* ■ **to have** *OR* **to pass a ~** aller à la selle **6.** MUS mouvement *m*.
<> *vi* : **to ~ to sb (to do sthg)** faire signe à qqn (de faire qqch).
<> *vt* : **to ~ sb in/away/out** faire signe à qqn d'entrer/de s'éloigner/de sortir.
◆ **in motion** <> *adj* [moving] en mouvement ■ [working] en marche ■ **do not alight while the train is in ~** il est interdit de descendre du train avant l'arrêt complet.
<> *adv phr* : **he set the machine in ~** il mit la machine en marche ■ **to set the wheels in ~** démarrer.

motionless ['məʊʃənlɪs] *adj* immobile.

motion picture *n US* CIN film *m*.

motion sickness *n US* mal *m* des transports.

motivate ['məʊtɪveɪt] *vt* motiver ■ **what ~d you to change your mind?** qu'est-ce qui vous a poussé à changer d'avis?

motivated ['məʊtɪveɪtɪd] *adj* motivé.

motivating ['məʊtɪviitɪŋ] *adj* motivant.

motivation [,məʊtɪ'veɪʃn] *n* motivation *f* ■ **the pupils lack ~** les élèves sont peu motivés.

motivational [,məʊtɪ'veɪʃənl] *adj* motivationnel ■ **~ research** études *fpl* de motivation.

motive ['məʊtɪv] <> *n* **1.** [reason] motif *m*, raison *f* ■ **the ~s for her behaviour** ce qui explique sa conduite, les raisons de sa conduite ■ **my ~ for asking is simple** la raison pour laquelle je pose cette question est simple ▮ LAW mobile *m* **2.** = **motif**.
<> *adj* moteur.

motiveless ['məʊtɪvlɪs] *adj* immotivé, injustifié ■ **an apparently ~ murder** un meurtre sans mobile apparent.

motley ['mɒtlɪ] <> *adj* **1.** [diverse, assorted] hétéroclite, composite, disparate ■ **a ~ crew** une foule bigarrée **2.** [multicoloured] multicolore, bariolé.
<> *n* **1.** [mixture] mélange *m* hétéroclite **2.** *arch* [jester's dress] livrée *f* de bouffon.

motocross ['məʊtəkrɒs] *n* motocross *m*.

motor ['məʊtəʳ] <> *n* **1.** [engine] moteur *m* **2.** *UK inf* [car] auto *f*, automobile *f*, voiture *f* (automobile).
<> *adj* **1.** [equipped with motor] à moteur ■ **~ coach** autocar *m* ■ **~ launch** vedette *f* ■ **~ vehicle** véhicule *m* automobile ■ **~ mouth** *inf hum* moulin *m* à paroles **2.** *UK* [concerning cars] automobile ■ **the ~ industry** l'industrie *f* automobile ■ **~ insurance** assurance *f* automobile ■ **she had a ~ accident** elle a eu un accident de voiture ▶ **the ~ show** le salon de l'automobile **3.** ANAT [nerve, muscle] moteur.
<> *vi UK* **1.** *dated* aller en voiture **2.** *fig* **now we're ~ing!** cette fois on y vient!

Motorail ['məʊtəreɪl] *n* train *m* autocouchette *OR* autoscouchettes.

motorbike ['məʊtəbaɪk] *n* moto *f*.

motorboat ['məʊtəbəʊt] *n* canot *m* automobile *OR* à moteur.

motorcade ['məʊtəkeɪd] *n* cortège *m* (de voitures).

motor car *n fml* automobile *f*, voiture *f*.

motor court *n US* motel *m*.

motorcycle ['məʊtə,saɪkl] <> *n* motocyclette *f*, moto *f* ■ **~ racing** motocyclisme *m* ■ **~ cop** *US inf* motard *m (de la police)*.
<> *vi* aller en moto.

motorcyclist ['məʊtə,saɪklɪst] *n* motocycliste *mf*.

motor home *n US* camping-car *m*.

motoring ['məʊtərɪŋ] *n* l'automobile *f (U)*.

motor inn *n US* motel *m*.

motorist ['məʊtərɪst] *n* automobiliste *mf*.

motorize, ise ['məʊtəraɪz] *vt* motoriser ■ **a ~d wheelchair** un fauteuil roulant à moteur.

motor lodge *n US* motel *m*.

motor mechanic *n* mécanicien *m*.

motor neurone disease *n* maladie *f* de Charcot.

motor racing *n* courses *fpl* automobiles.

motor scooter *n* scooter *m*.

motorsport ['məʊtəspɔ:t] *n* sport *m* mécanique.

motorway ['məʊtəweɪ] *n UK* autoroute *f*.

mottled ['mɒtld] *adj* tacheté, moucheté ■ [skin] marbré.

motto ['mɒtəʊ] (*pl* **mottos** *OR pl* **mottoes**) *n* **1.** [maxim] devise *f* **2.** [in Christmas cracker - joke] blague *f* ; [- riddle] devinette *f*.

mould *UK*, **mold** *US* [məʊld] <> *vt* **1.** [fashion - statue, vase] façonner, modeler ■ **to ~ sthg in** *OR* **from** *OR* **out of clay** sculpter qqch dans de l'argile ■ **to ~ sb's character** *fig* façonner *OR* former le caractère de qqn **2.** ART & METALL [make in a mould] mouler ■ **~ed plastic chairs** chaises *fpl* en plastique moulé **3.** [cling to - body, figure] mouler.
<> *vi* [become mouldy] moisir.

◇ *n* **1.** ART & METALL [hollow form] moule *m* ▪ [prototype] modèle *m*, gabarit *m* ▪ **cake** ~ moule à gâteau ▮ [moulded article] pièce *f* moulée ▪ **rice** ~ gâteau *m* de riz **2.** *fig* [pattern] moule *m* ▪ **cast in a heroic** ~ fait de l'étoffe des héros ▪ **to break the** ~ sortir des sentiers battus ▪ **when they made him they broke the** ~ il n'y en a pas deux comme lui **3.** [mildew] moisissure *f* **4.** [soil] humus *m*, terreau *m*.

moulder *UK*, **molder** *US* ['məʊldəʳ] *vi* **1.** [decay - corpse, compost] se décomposer ; [- house, beams] se délabrer ; [- bread] moisir **2.** [languish - person, article] moisir ; [- economy, institution] dépérir.

moulding *UK*, **molding** *US* ['məʊldɪŋ] *n* **1.** ARCHIT [decorative] moulure *f* ▪ [at join of wall and floor] baguette *f*, plinthe *f* **2.** [moulded article] objet *m* moulé, pièce *f* moulée **3.** [act of shaping] moulage *m*.

mouldy *UK* (*comp* **mouldier**, *superl* **mouldiest**), **moldy** *US* (*comp* **moldier**, *superl* **moldiest**) ['məʊldɪ] *adj* **1.** moisi ▪ **it smells** ~ ça sent le moisi **2.** *inf* [measly] minable ▪ [nasty] vache, rosse.

moult *UK*, **molt** *US* [məʊlt] ◇ *vi* ZOOL muer ▪ [cat, dog] perdre ses poils.
◇ *vt* [hair, feathers] perdre.
◇ *n* mue *f*.

mound [maʊnd] *n* **1.** [of earth, stones] butte *f*, monticule *m*, tertre *m* ▪ **burial** ~ tertre funéraire, tumulus *m* **2.** [heap] tas *m* ▪ **a huge** ~ **of junk mail** une gigantesque pile de prospectus.

mount [maʊnt] ◇ *vt* **1.** [climb - slope, steps] monter ▪ [climb onto - horse, bicycle] monter sur, enfourcher ; [- stage, throne etc] monter sur **2.** [organize, put on - exhibition, campaign etc] monter, organiser **3.** [fix, support] monter ▪ **to** ~ **photographs/stamps** coller des photos/timbres (dans un album) ▪ **they ~ed machine guns on the roofs** ils installèrent des mitrailleuses sur les toits ▪ **an old sword ~ed in a glass case** une épée de collection exposée dans une vitrine **4.** [mate with] monter, saillir, couvrir.
◇ *vi* **1.** [onto horse] monter (à cheval), se mettre en selle **2.** [rise, increase] monter, augmenter, croître ▪ **her anger ~ed** sa colère montait.
◇ *n* **1.** [mountain] mont *m*, montagne *f* **2.** GEOG **: the Mount of Olives** le mont des Oliviers ▪ **Mount Rushmore** le mont Rushmore ▪ **Mount Rushmore State** le Dakota du Sud **3.** [horse] monture *f* **4.** [support - of photo] carton *m*, support *m* ; [- of gem, lens, tool] monture *f* ; [- of machine] support *m* ; [- for stamp in collection] charnière *f* ; [- for object under microscope] lame *f*.
◆ **mount up** *vi insep* **1.** [increase] monter, augmenter, s'accroître **2.** [accumulate] s'accumuler, s'amonceler.

MOUNTAINS BEGINNING WITH 'MOUNT'

Mount Ararat le mont Ararat ;
Mount Athos le mont Athos ;
Mount Etna le mont Etna, l'Etna ;
Mount Everest le mont Everest, l'Everest ;
Mount Fuji le (mont) Fuji-Yama ;
Mount Kilimanjaro le Kilimandjaro ;
Mount Olympus le mont Olympe, l'Olympe ;
Mount Palomar le mont Palomar ;
Mount Parnassus le mont Parnasse ;
Mount Rushmore le mont Rushmore (dans lequel sont sculptés les visages des présidents Washington, Jefferson, Lincoln et Th. Roosevelt) ;
Mount Sinai le (mont) Sinaï ;
Mount Vesuvius le (mont) Vésuve ;
Mount Whitney le mont Whitney.

mountain ['maʊntɪn] ◇ *n* **1.** montagne *f* ▪ **we spent a week in the ~s** on a passé une semaine à la montagne ▪ **the Green Mountain State** le Vermont ▪ **the Mountain State** la Virginie de l'Ouest ◗ **to make a** ~ **out of a molehill** se faire une montagne d'un rien ▪ **to move ~s** déplacer des montagnes, faire l'impossible ▪ **if the** ~ **won't go to Mohammed, Mohammed will have to go to the** ~ si la montagne ne vient pas à Mahomet, Mahomet ira à la montagne **2.** [heap, accumulation] montagne *f*, tas *m* ▪ **I've got ~s of work to get through** j'ai un travail fou *OR* monstre à terminer ◗ **the butter** ~ ECON la montagne de beurre.
◇ *comp* [people] montagnard ▪ [resort, stream, guide] de montagne ▪ [air] de la montagne ▪ [life] en montagne ▪ [flora, fauna] de montagne, des montagnes ▪ **a** ~ **rescue team** une équipe de secours en montagne.

mountain ash *n* **1.** [rowan] sorbier *m* **2.** [eucalyptus] eucalyptus *m*.

mountain bike *n* vélo *m* tout terrain, vélocross *m*.

mountain cat *n* [lynx] lynx *m* ▪ [puma] puma *m*, cougouar *m*.

Mountain Daylight Time *n* heure *f* d'été des montagnes Rocheuses.

mountaineer [,maʊntɪ'nɪəʳ] *n* alpiniste *mf*.

mountaineering [,maʊntɪ'nɪərɪŋ] *n* alpinisme *m*.

mountain goat *n* chamois *m*.

mountain lion *n* puma *m*, cougouar *m*.

mountainous ['maʊntɪnəs] *adj* **1.** [region] montagneux **2.** *fig* [huge] énorme, colossal.

mountain pass *n* col *m*, défilé *m*.

mountain range *n* chaîne *f* de montagnes.

mountain sheep (*pl inv*) *n* bighorn *m*.

mountain sickness *n* mal *m* des montagnes.

mountainside ['maʊntɪnsaɪd] *n* flanc *m* *OR* versant *m* d'une montagne ▪ **a village perched on the** ~ un village juché à flanc de montagne.

Mountain (Standard) Time *n* heure *f* d'hiver des montagnes Rocheuses.

mountain top *n* sommet *m*, cime *f*.

mountebank ['maʊntɪbæŋk] *n* charlatan *m*.

mounted ['maʊntɪd] *adj* [troops] monté, à cheval ▪ **the** ~ **police** la police montée ▪ ~ **policeman** [gen] policier *m* à cheval.

Mountie, Mounty ['maʊntɪ] (*pl* **Mounties**) *n inf* membre *m* de la police montée *(au Canada)* ▪ **the ~s** la police montée *(au Canada)*.

mounting ['maʊntɪŋ] ◇ *n* = **mount** *(sense 4)*.
◇ *adj* [pressure, anxiety] croissant.

mourn [mɔːn] ◇ *vi* [feel grief] pleurer ▪ [be in mourning] être en deuil, porter le deuil ▪ **we** ~ **with you** nous partageons votre douleur ▪ **he ~s for** *OR* **over his lost youth** il se lamente sur *OR* il pleure sa jeunesse perdue.
◇ *vt* [person] pleurer, porter le deuil de ▪ [death, loss] pleurer ▪ **the whole town ~s the tragedy** cette tragédie a plongé la ville entière dans le malheur.

mourner ['mɔːnəʳ] *n* [friend, relative] proche *mf* du défunt ▪ **the ~s followed the hearse** le cortège funèbre suivait le corbillard ▪ **the streets were lined with ~s** la foule en deuil s'était massée sur les trottoirs.

mournful ['mɔːnfʊl] *adj* [person, eyes, mood] triste, mélancolique ▪ [tone, voice] lugubre ▪ [place] lugubre, sinistre.

mourning ['mɔːnɪŋ] ◇ *n (U)* **1.** [period] deuil *m* ▪ [clothes] (vêtements *mpl* de) deuil *m* ▪ **to be in** ~ être en deuil, porter le deuil ▪ **to be in** ~ **for sb** porter le deuil de qqn ▪ **to go into/come out of** ~ prendre/quitter le deuil ▪ **a day of** ~ **was declared** une journée de deuil a été décrétée ◗ **'Mourning Becomes Electra'** ***O'Neill*** 'le Deuil sied à Électre' **2.** [cries] lamentations *fpl*.
◇ *comp* [dress, suit] de deuil.

mouse [maʊs] (*pl* **mice** [maɪs]) ◇ *n* **1.** souris *f* ▪ **'Of Mice and Men'** ***Steinbeck*** 'Des souris et des hommes' **2.** [shy person] timide *mf*, timoré *m*, - e *f* **3.** COMPUT souris *f*.
◇ *vi* [cat] chasser les souris.

mousehole ['maʊshəʊl] *n* trou *m* de souris.

mouse mat, mouse pad *n* COMPUT tapis *m* de souris.

mouse potato *n inf* *personne passant le plus clair de son temps devant son ordinateur.*

mouser ['maʊsəʳ] *n* [cat] chasseur *m*, - euse *f* de souris.

mousetrap ['maʊstræp] *n* souricière *f*.

mousey ['maʊsɪ] = **mousy**.

moussaka [mu:'sɑ:kə] *n* moussaka *f*.

mousse [mu:s] *n* mousse *f* ▪ **chocolate ~** mousse au chocolat.

moustache [mə'stɑ:ʃ] *UK*, **mustache** ['mʌstæʃ] *US* *n* moustache *f*, moustaches *fpl* ▪ **he's growing a ~** il se fait pousser la moustache.

mousy ['maʊsɪ] (*comp* **mousier**, *superl* **mousiest**) *adj* **1.** *pej* [shy] timide, effacé **2.** *pej* [in colour - hair] châtain clair.

mouth (*pl* **mouths** [maʊðz]) ◇ *n* [maʊθ] **1.** [of person] bouche *f* ▪ [of animal] gueule *f* ▪ **don't talk with your ~ full!** ne parle pas la bouche pleine! ▪ **breathe through your ~** respirez par la bouche ▪ **I have five ~s to feed** j'ai cinq bouches à nourrir ▪ **he didn't open his ~ once during the meeting** il n'a pas ouvert la bouche *OR* il n'a pas dit un mot pendant toute la réunion ▪ **keep your ~ shut** n'en parlez à personne, gardez-le pour vous ▪ **he's incapable of keeping his ~ shut** il ne sait pas tenir sa langue ➔ **he's got a big ~** *inf* il ne peut pas s'empêcher de l'ouvrir ▪ **to be down in the ~** *inf* avoir le cafard ▪ **me and my big ~!** j'ai encore perdu une occasion de me taire! ▪ **out of the ~s of babes** *prov* de la bouche des enfants *OR* des innocents **2.** [of river] embouchure *f*, bouche *f*, bouches *fpl* **3.** [opening - gen] ouverture *f*, orifice *m*, bouche *f* ; [- of bottle] goulot *m* ; [- of cave] entrée *f*.
◇ *vt* [maʊð] **1.** [silently - insults, obscenities] dire à voix basse, marmonner ▪ **don't talk/sing, just ~ the words** ne parle/chante pas, fais seulement semblant **2.** [pompously] déclamer ▪ [mechanically] débiter ▪ [insincerely - excuses] dire qqch du bout des lèvres ; [- regrets] formuler sans conviction ▪ **to ~ platitudes** débiter des lieux communs.

◆ **mouth off** *vi insep inf* **1.** [brag] la ramener **2.** [be insolent] se montrer insolent.

-mouthed [maʊðd] *in cpds* : **open~** bouche bée ▪ **wide~** [bottle] à large goulot.

mouthful ['maʊθfʊl] *n* **1.** [of food] bouchée *f* ▪ [of liquid] gorgée *f* ▪ **I couldn't eat another ~!** je ne pourrais rien avaler de plus! **2.** *inf* [word] mot *m* difficile à prononcer ▪ **his name's a bit of a ~** il a un nom *m* à coucher dehors **3.** *US* [important remark] : **you said a ~!** ça, tu peux le dire!, là, tu as parlé d'or!

mouth organ *n* harmonica *m*.

mouthpiece ['maʊθpi:s] *n* **1.** [of musical instrument] bec *m*, embouchure *f* ▪ [of pipe] tuyau *m* ▪ [of telephone] microphone *m* **2.** [spokesperson] porte-parole *m inv* ▪ [newspaper, magazine] organe *m*, porte-parole *m inv*.

mouth-to-mouth *adj* : **to give sb ~ resuscitation** faire du bouche-à-bouche à qqn.

mouth ulcer *n* aphte *m*.

mouthwash ['maʊθwɒʃ] *n* [for cleansing] bain *m* de bouche ▪ [for gargling] gargarisme *m*.

mouth-watering *adj* appétissant, alléchant.

movable ['mu:vəbl] ◇ *adj* mobile ▪ **~ property** LAW biens *mpl* meubles ▪ **~ feast** RELIG fête *f* mobile ▪ **'A Movable Feast'** *Hemingway* 'Paris est une fête'.
◇ *n* : **~s** LAW effets *mpl* mobiliers, biens *mpl* meubles.

move [mu:v] ◇ *vt* **1.** [put elsewhere - object] déplacer ; [- part of body] bouger, remuer ▪ **~ the lever to the left** poussez le levier vers la gauche ▪ **we ~d all the chairs indoors/outdoors** nous avons rentré/sorti toutes les chaises ▪ **we've ~d the couch into the spare room** nous avons mis le canapé dans la chambre d'amis ▪ **~ all those papers off the table!** enlève tous ces papiers de la table!, débarrasse la table de tous ces papiers! ▪ **don't ~ anything on my desk** ne touche à rien sur mon bureau ▪ **~ your head to the left** inclinez la tête vers la gauche ▪ GAMES jouer ▪ **she ~d a pawn** elle a joué un pion ➔ **~ it!** *inf* grouille-toi!
2. [send elsewhere - prisoner, troops etc] transférer ▪ **~ all these people out of the courtyard** faites sortir tous ces gens de la cour ▪ **she's been ~d to the New York office/to accounts** elle a été mutée au bureau de New York/affectée à la comptabilité ▪ **he asked to be ~d to a room with a sea-view** il a demandé qu'on lui donne une chambre avec vue sur la mer ▪ **troops are being ~d into the area** des troupes sont envoyées dans la région
3. [change time or date of] déplacer ▪ **the meeting has been ~d to Friday** [postponed] la réunion a été remise à vendredi ; [brought forward] la réunion a été avancée à vendredi
4. [to new premises, location] : **the company that ~d us** la firme qui s'est chargée de *OR* qui a effectué notre déménagement ▪ **to ~ house** *OR* **flat** *UK* déménager
5. [affect, touch] émouvoir ▪ **I was deeply ~d** j'ai été profondément ému *OR* touché
6. [motivate, prompt] pousser, inciter ▪ **to ~ sb to do sthg** pousser *OR* inciter qqn à faire qqch ▪ **what ~d you to change your mind?** qu'est-ce qui vous a fait changer d'avis?
7. *(usu passive & negative)* [cause to yield] : **we shall not be ~d!** nous ne céderons pas!
8. [propose] proposer ▪ **I ~ that we vote on it** je propose que nous procédions au vote
9. COMM [sell] écouler, vendre
10. MED : **to ~ one's bowels** aller à la selle.
◇ *vi* **1.** [shift, change position] bouger ▪ **I was so scared I couldn't ~** j'étais pétrifié (de terreur) ▪ **the handle won't ~** la poignée ne bouge pas ▪ **she wouldn't ~ out of my way** elle ne voulait pas s'écarter de mon chemin ∥ [be in motion - vehicle] : **the line of cars was moving slowly down the road** la file de voitures avançait lentement le long de la route ▪ **I jumped off while the train was still moving** j'ai sauté avant l'arrêt du train ▪ **the truck started moving backwards** le camion a commencé à reculer ▪ [travel in specified direction] : **the guests ~d into/out of the dining room** les invités passèrent dans/sortirent de la salle à manger ▪ **the depression is moving westwards** la dépression se déplace vers l'ouest ▪ **the demonstrators were moving towards the embassy** les manifestants se dirigeaient vers l'ambassade ▪ **the hands of the clock ~d inexorably towards midnight** les aiguilles de l'horloge s'approchaient inexorablement de minuit ▪ **small clouds ~d across the sky** de petits nuages traversaient le ciel ▪ **the earth ~s round the sun** la Terre tourne autour du Soleil ▪ **public opinion is moving to the left/right** *fig* l'opinion publique évolue vers la gauche/droite ➔ **to ~ in high circles** fréquenter la haute société
2. [leave] partir ▪ **it's getting late, I ought to be** *OR* **get moving** il se fait tard, il faut que j'y aille *OR* que je parte
3. GAMES [player] jouer ▪ [piece] se déplacer
4. [to new premises, location] déménager ▪ **when are you moving to your new apartment?** quand est-ce que vous emménagez dans votre nouvel appartement? ▪ **she's moving to San Francisco** elle va habiter (à) San Francisco ▪ **the company has ~d to more modern premises** la société s'est installée dans des locaux plus modernes
5. [change job, profession etc] : **he's ~d to a job in publishing** il travaille maintenant dans l'édition
6. [develop, progress] avancer, progresser ▪ **to get things moving** faire avancer les choses
7. *inf* [travel fast] filer, foncer ▪ **that car can really ~!** cette voiture a quelque chose dans le ventre!
8. [take action] agir ▪ **the town council ~d to have the school closed down** la municipalité a pris des mesures pour faire fermer l'école ▪ **I'll get moving on it first thing tomorrow** je m'en occuperai demain à la première heure
9. COMM [sell] se vendre, s'écouler
10. MED : **have your bowels ~d today?** êtes-vous allé à la selle aujourd'hui?
◇ *n* **1.** [movement] mouvement *m* ▪ **with one ~ she was by his side** en un éclair, elle fut à ses côtés ▪ **one ~ out of you and you're dead!** un seul geste et tu es mort! ▪ **he made a ~ to take out his wallet** il s'apprêta à sortir son portefeuille ▪ **she made a ~ to leave** elle se leva pour partir ▪ **it's late, I ought to be making a ~** il se fait tard, il faut que j'y aille ➔ **get a ~ on!** *inf* grouille-toi!, active!
2. [change of home, premises] déménagement *m* ▪ **we're considering a ~ to bigger premises** nous envisageons d'emménager dans des locaux plus spacieux
3. [change of job] changement *m* d'emploi ▪ **after ten years in the same firm she felt it was time for a ~** après dix ans dans la même société elle avait le sentiment qu'il était temps de changer d'air *OR* d'horizon
4. [step, measure] pas *m*, démarche *f* ▪ **she made the first ~** elle a fait le premier pas ▪ **she wondered when he would make his ~** elle se demandait quand il allait se décider ▪ **the new management's first ~ was to increase all salaries** la première mesure de la nouvelle direction a été de relever tous les sa-

laires ▪ **what do you think their next ~ will be?** selon vous, que vont-ils faire maintenant? ▪ **they made an unsuccessful ~ to stop the war** ils firent une tentative infructueuse pour arrêter la guerre
5. GAMES [turn to move] tour *m* ▪ **it's my ~** c'est à moi (de jouer) ▮ [act of moving] coup *m* ▪ [way piece moves] marche *f* ➊ **to be on the ~** être en déplacement ▪ **I've been on the ~ all day** je n'ai pas arrêté de la journée ▪ **we're a firm on the ~** nous sommes une entreprise dynamique.

move about *UK* ◇ *vi insep* se déplacer, bouger ▪ **I can hear somebody moving about upstairs** j'entends des bruits de pas là-haut.
◇ *vt sep* déplacer.

move along ◇ *vi insep* avancer ▪ **~ along there, please!** circulez, s'il vous plaît!
◇ *vt sep* [bystanders, busker] faire circuler.

move around = **move about**.

move away ◇ *vi insep* **1.** [go in opposite direction] s'éloigner, partir ▪ **the train ~d slowly away** le train partit lentement
2. [change address] déménager.
◇ *vt sep* éloigner.

move back ◇ *vi insep* **1.** [back away] reculer
2. [return to original position] retourner ▪ **they've ~d back to the States** ils sont retournés habiter *OR* ils sont rentrés aux États-Unis.
◇ *vt sep* **1.** [push back - person, crowd] repousser ; [- chair] reculer
2. [return to original position] remettre.

move down ◇ *vi insep* **1.** [from higher level, floor etc] descendre
2. [make room] se pousser.
◇ *vt insep* : **~ down the bus, please** avancez jusqu'au fond de l'autobus, s'il vous plaît.
◇ *vt sep* [from higher level, floor etc] descendre ▪ **he was ~d down a class** SCH on l'a fait passer dans la classe inférieure.

move forward ◇ *vi insep* avancer.
◇ *vt sep* avancer.

move in ◇ *vi insep* **1.** [into new home, premises] emménager ▪ **his mother-in-law has ~d in with them** sa belle-mère s'est installée *OR* est venue habiter chez eux
2. [close in, approach] avancer, s'approcher ▪ **the police began to ~ in on the demonstrators** la police a commencé à avancer *OR* à se diriger vers les manifestants ▪ **the camera then ~s in on the bed** la caméra s'approche ensuite du lit
3. [take control] : **another gang is trying to ~ in** un autre gang essaie de mettre la main sur l'affaire ▪ **the unions ~d in and stopped the strike** les syndicats prirent les choses en main et mirent un terme à la grève.
◇ *vt sep* [furniture] installer ▪ **the landlord ~d another family in** le propriétaire a loué à une autre famille.

move off *vi insep* s'éloigner, partir ▪ **the train finally ~d off** le train partit *OR* s'ébranla enfin.

move on ◇ *vi insep* **1.** [proceed on one's way] poursuivre son chemin ▪ **we spent a week in Athens, then we ~d on to Crete** on a passé une semaine à Athènes avant de partir pour la Crête ▪ **a policeman told me to ~ on** un policier m'a dit de circuler
2. [progress - to new job, new subject etc] : **she's ~d on to better things** elle a trouvé une meilleure situation ▪ **can we ~ on to the second point?** pouvons-nous passer au deuxième point?
◇ *vt sep* [bystanders, busker] faire circuler.

move out ◇ *vi insep* **1.** [of home, premises] déménager ▪ **his girlfriend has ~d out** son amie l'a quitté
2. MIL [troops] se retirer.
◇ *vt sep* MIL [troops] retirer.

move over *vi insep* **1.** [make room] se pousser
2. [stand down - politician] se désister ▪ **it's time he ~d over to make way for a younger man** il serait temps qu'il laisse la place à un homme plus jeune
3. [change over] : **we're moving over to mass production** nous passons à la fabrication en série.

move up ◇ *vi insep* **1.** [make room] se pousser
2. [in hierarchy] monter ▪ [in company] avoir de l'avancement ▪ **to ~ up a class** SCH passer dans la classe supérieure ➊ **you've ~d up in the world!** tu en as fait du chemin!
3. MIL [troops] avancer ▪ **our battalion's moving up to the front** notre bataillon monte au front.
◇ *vt sep* **1.** [in order to make room] pousser, écarter
2. [in hierarchy] faire monter ▪ **he's been ~d up a class** SCH on l'a fait passer dans la classe supérieure
3. MIL [troops] faire avancer ▪ **another division has been ~d up** une autre division a été envoyée sur place.

moveable ['mu:vəbl] = **movable**.

movement ['mu:vmənt] *n* **1.** [change of position] mouvement *m* ▪ **population/troop ~s** mouvements de populations/de troupes ▪ **the ~ of goods** le transport des marchandises ▪ **there was a general ~ towards the bar** tout le monde se dirigea vers le bar ▪ **she heard ~ in the next room** elle a entendu des bruits dans la pièce voisine ▪ **his ~s are being watched** ses déplacements sont surveillés ▪ **I'm not sure what my ~s are going to be over the next few weeks** je ne sais pas exactement ce que je vais faire *OR* quel sera mon emploi du temps dans les quelques semaines à venir ▪ **freedom of ~** la liberté de circulation ▮ [gesture] mouvement *m*, geste *m* **2.** [change, tendency] mouvement *m*, tendance *f* ▪ **his speeches over the last year show a ~ towards the right** les discours qu'il a prononcés depuis un an font apparaître un glissement vers la droite **3.** [group] mouvement *m* ▪ **liberation ~** mouvement de libération **4.** TECH [mechanism - of clock etc] mouvement *m* **5.** MUS [of symphony, sonata etc] mouvement *m* **6.** MED [faeces] selles *fpl* ▪ **to have a (bowel) ~** aller à la selle.

mover ['mu:vər] *n* **1.** [physical] : **she's a lovely ~** *inf* elle bouge bien ➊ **he's a fast ~** *inf* c'est un tombeur ▪ **the ~s and the shakers** [key people] les hommes *mpl* et les femmes *fpl* d'action **2.** [of a proposal, motion] motionnaire *mf* **3.** *US* [removal company] déménageur *m*.

movie ['mu:vɪ] *esp US* ◇ *n* film *m*.
◇ *comp* [actor] de cinéma ▪ **the ~ industry** l'industrie *f* cinématographique *OR* du cinéma.

movies *npl (esp) US* **to go to the ~s** aller au cinéma ▪ **she's in the ~s** elle travaille dans le cinéma.

movie camera *n US* caméra *f*.

moviegoer ['mu:vɪ,gəʊər] *n US* cinéphile *mf*.

movie house, movie theatre *n US* (salle *f* de) cinéma *m*.

movie star *n* vedette *f OR* star *f* de cinéma.

moving ['mu:vɪŋ] *adj* **1.** [in motion] en mouvement ▪ [vehicle] en marche ▪ [target] mouvant ▪ **slow-/fast-~** qui se déplace lentement/rapidement **2.** [not fixed] mobile ▪ **~ parts** pièces *fpl* mobiles **3.** [touching] émouvant, touchant **4.** [motivating] : **she's the ~ force** *OR* **spirit behind the project** c'est elle l'instigatrice *OR* le moteur du projet **5.** [for moving house] de déménagement ▪ **~ van** *US* camion *m* de déménageurs.

moving pavement *n UK* trottoir *m* roulant.

moving picture *n US dated* film *m*.

moving staircase *n* escalier *m* roulant, escalator *m*.

mow [məʊ] (*pret* **mowed**, *pp* **mowed** *OR* **mown** [məʊn]) *vt* [lawn] tondre ▪ [hay] faucher.

mow down *vt sep* faucher, abattre.

mower ['məʊər] *n* [person] faucheur *m*, - euse *f* ▪ [machine - for lawn] tondeuse *f* ; [- for hay] faucheuse *f*.

mowing ['məʊɪŋ] *n* AGRIC fauchage *m* ▪ **~ machine** faucheuse *f*.

mown [məʊn] *pp* ▷ **mow**.

Mozambican [,məʊzæm'bi:kn] ◇ *n* Mozambicain *m*, - e *f*.
◇ *adj* mozambicain.

Mozambique [,məʊzæm'bi:k] *pr n* Mozambique *m* ▪ **in ~** au Mozambique.

Mozart ['məʊtsɑ:t] *pr n* Mozart.

MP *n* **1.** (*abbrev of* **Military Police**) PM *f* **2.** *UK* & *Canada* (*abbrev of* **Member of Parliament**) ≃ député *m* ▪ **the ~ for Finchley** le député de Finchley **3.** *Canada* = **Mounted Police**.

MP3 [,empi:'θri:] (*abbrev of* **MPEG-1 Audio Layer-3**) *n* COMPUT MP3 *m*.

MPEG ['empeg] (*abbrev of* **Moving Pictures Expert Group**) *n* COMPUT MPEG *m*.

mpg (*abbrev of* **miles per gallon**) *n* consommation *f* d'essence ▪ **my old car did 20 ~** mon ancienne voiture faisait *OR* consommait 3,5 litres au cent.

mph (*abbrev of* **miles per hour**) *n* miles *mpl* à l'heure.

MPhil [ˌem'fɪl] (*abbrev of* **Master of Philosophy**) *n (titulaire d'une) maîtrise de lettres.*

Mr ['mɪstəʳ] (*written abbrev of* **Mister**) M., Monsieur ▪ **~ Brown** M. Brown ▪ **~ President** Monsieur le Président.

MRC (*abbrev of* **Medical Research Council**) *pr n institut de recherche médicale situé à Londres.*

Mr Nice Guy *n inf* : **no more ~!** j'en ai assez d'être la bonne pâte!

MRP *n* = **manufacturer's recommended price**.

Mr Right *n inf* l'homme idéal, le prince charmant ▪ **she's waiting for ~** elle attend le prince charmant *OR* l'homme de ses rêves.

Mrs ['mɪsɪz] Mme, Madame ▪ **~ Brown** Mme Brown.

MRSA (*abbrev of* **methicillin-resistant Staphylococcus aureus**) *n* MED SAMR *m*.

Mrs Mop *n UK inf* [cleaner] femme *f* de ménage.

ms. (*pl* **mss.**) (*written abbrev of* **manuscript**) ms.

Ms [mɪz] *titre que les femmes peuvent utiliser au lieu de madame ou mademoiselle pour éviter la distinction entre les femmes mariées et les célibataires.*

MS ◇ *n* **1.** (*abbrev of* **multiple sclerosis**) SEP *f* **2.** *US* (*abbrev of* **Master of Science**) *(titulaire d'une) maîtrise de sciences.*
◇ **1.** *written abbr of* **Mississippi 2.** (*written abbrev of* **manuscript**) ms.

MSA (*abbrev of* **Master of Science in Agriculture**) *n (titulaire d'une) maîtrise en sciences agricoles.*

MSB (*abbrev of* **most significant bit/byte**) *n bit de poids fort.*

MSc (*abbrev of* **Master of Science**) *n (titulaire d'une) maîtrise de sciences.*

MSC *pr n* = **Manpower Services Commission**.

MSF (*abbrev of* **Manufacturing, Science, Finance**) *pr n confédération syndicale britannique.*

msg [emes'dʒiː] (*written abbrev of* **message**) *n* message *m*.

MSG *n* = **monosodium glutamate**.

Mss *written abbr of* **manuscripts**.

MSS *pl* ▷ **MS, ms**.

MST *n* = **Mountain Standard Time**.

MSW (*abbrev of* **Master of Social Work**) *n (titulaire d'une) maîtrise en travail social.*

Mt (*written abbrev of* **mount**) Mt.

much [mʌtʃ] ◇ *det* beaucoup de ▪ **the tablets didn't do ~ good** les comprimés n'ont pas servi à grand-chose *OR* n'ont pas fait beaucoup d'effet ▪ **~ good may it do you!** *iron* grand bien vous fasse!
◇ *pron* beaucoup ▪ **is there any left? – not ~** est-ce qu'il en reste? – pas beaucoup ▪ **there's still ~ to be decided** il reste encore beaucoup de choses à décider ▪ **there's not ~ anyone can do about it** personne n'y peut grand-chose ▪ **~ of the time** [long period] la majeure partie du temps ; [very often] la plupart du temps ▪ **I agreed with ~ of what she said** j'étais d'accord avec presque tout ce qu'elle a dit ▮ [used to intensify] : **I'm not ~ of a hiker** je ne suis pas un très bon marcheur ▪ **it hasn't been ~ of a holiday** ce n'était pas vraiment des vacances ▶ **what he said didn't amount to ~** il n'avait pas grand-chose d'important à dire ▪ **to make ~ of sb/sthg** : **the defence made ~ of the witness's criminal record** la défense a beaucoup insisté sur le casier judiciaire du témoin ▪ **I couldn't make ~ of the figures** je n'ai pas compris grand-chose aux chiffres ▪ **I don't think ~ of him/of his technique** je n'ai pas une très haute opinion de lui/de sa technique ▪ **there's ~ to be said for the old-fashioned method** la vieille méthode a beaucoup d'avantages ▪ **there's ~ to be said for his suggestions** il y a des choses fort intéressantes dans ce qu'il propose ▪ **it's not up to ~** ça ne vaut pas grand-chose ▪ **he's not up to ~** ce n'est pas une lumière ▪ **there's not ~ to choose between them** ils se valent ▪ **there's not ~ in it** il n'y a pas une grande différence ▪ **he doesn't want** *OR* **ask** *OR* **expect ~, does he?** *inf iron* il n'est pas difficile, lui, au moins! *iron.*
◇ *adv* beaucoup ▪ **~ happier/more slowly** beaucoup plus heureux/plus lentement ▪ **it is ~ to be regretted that...** *fml* il est fort regrettable que... ▪ **~ to my surprise** à mon grand étonnement ▪ **I'm not ~ good at making speeches** je ne suis pas très doué pour faire des discours ▪ **it's ~ the best/the fastest** c'est le meilleur/le plus rapide de beaucoup ▶ **~ the same** presque pareil ▪ **she's still ~ the same as yesterday** son état n'a pas changé depuis hier ▪ **I feel ~ the same as you** je pense plutôt comme vous.

◆ **as much** ◇ *pron phr* [that, the same] : **I thought/suspected as ~** c'est bien ce que je pensais/soupçonnais ▪ **I said as ~ to him yesterday** c'est ce que je lui ai dit hier ▪ **would you do as ~ for me?** en ferais-tu autant pour moi?
◇ *adv phr* [with multiples, fractions] : **twice/three times as ~** deux/trois fois plus ▪ **half as ~** la moitié (de ça).

◆ **as much... as** ◇ *det phr* [the same amount as] : **as much... as** autant de... que.
◇ *conj phr* autant que ▪ **he's as ~ to blame as her** elle n'est pas plus responsable que lui, il est responsable autant qu'elle.

◆ **as much as** ◇ *pron phr* **1.** [the same as] : **it costs as ~ as the Japanese model** ça coûte le même prix que le modèle japonais ▪ **that's as ~ as to say that I'm a liar** ça revient à me traiter de menteur **2.** [all] : **it was as ~ as I could do to keep a straight face** j'ai failli éclater de rire.
◇ *conj phr* autant que ▪ **I hate it as ~ as you do** ça me déplaît autant qu'à vous ▪ **I don't dislike them as ~ as all that** ils ne me déplaisent pas autant que ça.

◆ **however much** ◇ *det phr* : **however ~ money you give him, it won't be enough** vous pouvez lui donner autant d'argent que vous voulez, ça ne suffira pas.
◇ *pron phr* : **however ~ they offer, take it** quelle que soit la somme qu'ils proposent, acceptez-la.
◇ *adv phr* : **however ~ you dislike the idea...** quelle que soit votre aversion pour cette idée... ▪ **however ~ I try, it doesn't work** j'ai beau essayer, ça ne marche pas.

◆ **how much** ◇ *det phr* combien de.
◇ *pron phr* combien ▪ **how ~ do you want?** [gen] combien en voulez-vous? ; [money] combien voulez-vous?

◆ **much as** *conj phr* : **~ as I admire him, I have to admit that...** malgré toute mon admiration pour lui, je dois admettre que... ▪ **~ as I would like to, I can't come** à mon grand regret, il m'est véritablement impossible de venir.

◆ **so much** ◇ *det phr* tant de, tellement de ▪ **it's just so ~ nonsense** c'est tellement bête.
◇ *pron phr* **1.** [such a lot] tant ▪ **I've learnt so ~ on this course** j'ai vraiment appris beaucoup (de choses) en suivant ces cours ▪ **there's still so ~ to do** il y a encore tant à faire **2.** [this amount] : **there's only so ~ one can do** il y a une limite à ce qu'on peut faire ▪ **how ~ water will I put in? – about so ~** combien d'eau est-ce que je dois mettre? – à peu près ça.
◇ *adv phr* tellement ▪ **I wouldn't mind so ~, only he promised to do it** ça ne me gêne pas tellement, mais il avait promis de le faire ▪ **thank you ever so ~** merci infiniment *OR* mille fois.

◆ **so much as** *adv phr* même ▪ **if you so ~ as breathe a word of this...** si seulement tu répètes un mot de tout ça... ▪ **without so ~ as asking permission** sans même demander la permission.

◆ **so much for** *prep phr* : **so ~ for the agenda; now let us consider...** voilà pour ce qui est de l'ordre du jour; maintenant, je voudrais que nous nous penchions sur la question de... ▪ **so ~ for that idea!** on peut oublier cette idée!

◆ **that much** ◇ *det phr* : **there was that ~ food, we thought we'd never finish it** il y avait tellement à manger qu'on pensait ne jamais arriver à finir.
◇ *pron phr* : **was there ~ damage? – not that ~** y a-t-il eu beaucoup de dégâts? – pas tant que ça ▪ **did it cost that ~?** ça a coûté autant que ça? ▪ **how ~ do you want? – about that ~** combien en veux-tu? – à peu près ça.
◇ *adv phr (with compar)* **1.** [a lot] beaucoup plus ▪ **it'll be that ~ easier to organize** ce sera d'autant plus facile à organiser ▪ **not that ~ better** pas beaucoup mieux **2.** [this amount] : **she's that ~ taller than me** elle est plus grande que moi de ça.

◆ **this much** ◇ *det phr* : **there was this ~ coffee left** il restait ça de café.
◇ *pron phr* **1.** [this amount] : **I had to cut this ~ off the hem of my skirt** j'ai dû raccourcir ma jupe de ça **2.** [one thing] une chose ■ **I'll say this ~ for her, she's got guts** il faut reconnaître une chose, c'est qu'elle a du cran.
◆ **too much** ◇ *det phr* trop de.
◇ *pron phr* trop ■ **don't expect too ~** [be too demanding] ne soyez pas trop exigeant, n'en demandez pas trop ; [be too hopeful] ne vous faites pas trop d'illusions.
◇ *adv phr* [work, speak] trop.

muchness ['mʌtʃnɪs] *n UK inf phr* **they're all pretty much of a ~** [objects] c'est du pareil au même ; [people] ils se valent.

muck [mʌk] *(U) inf* ◇ *n* **1.** [mud] boue *f*, gadoue *f* ■ [dirt] saletés *fpl* ■ [manure] fumier *m* ■ [dung - of horse] crottin *m* ; [- of dog] crotte *f* ■ **they think they're Lord and Lady Muck** *UK hum* ils ne se prennent pas pour n'importe qui, ils se croient sortis de la cuisse de Jupiter ■ **where there's ~, there's brass** *UK prov* c'est peut-être sale, mais ça rapporte! *(fait référence aux travaux salissants mais rentables)* **2.** *fig* [inferior literature, films etc] saletés *fpl* ■ [bad food] cochonneries *fpl* **3.** *phr* **to make a ~ of sthg** *UK* [bungle] foutre qqch par terre, bousiller qqch.
◇ *vt* AGRIC fumer.
◆ **muck about, muck around** *UK inf* ◇ *vi insep* **1.** [waste time] traîner, perdre son temps **2.** [be stupid] faire l'imbécile **3.** [interfere] : **to ~ about with sthg** [equipment] toucher à qqch, tripoter qqch ; [belongings] déranger qqch, mettre la pagaille dans qqch.
◇ *vt sep* [person - waste time of] faire perdre son temps à ; [- be inconsiderate to] malmener ■ [belongings, papers] déranger, toucher à.
◆ **muck in** *vi insep UK inf* [share task] mettre la main à la pâte, donner un coup de main ■ [share costs] participer aux frais.
◆ **muck out** *vt sep UK* [horse, stable] nettoyer, curer.
◆ **muck up** *vt sep inf* **1.** [dirty] cochonner **2.** [ruin] bousiller, foutre en l'air.

mucker△ ['mʌkə^r] *n UK* [pal] copain *m*, copine *f*, pote *m*.

muckheap ['mʌkhi:p] *n UK inf* tas *m* de fumier.

muckraking ['mʌkreɪkɪŋ] *n pej* **it's the kind of paper that specializes in ~** c'est le type de journal spécialisé dans les scandales.

muckspreader ['mʌkspredə^r] *n* AGRIC épandeur *m* (d'engrais).

muck-up *n UK inf* pagaille *f*, bordel *m* ■ **to make a ~ of sthg** foutre qqch en l'air, bousiller qqch.

mucky ['mʌkɪ] *(comp* **muckier**, *superl* **muckiest**) *adj inf* **1.** [dirty, muddy - hands] sale, crasseux ; [- shoes] sale, crotté ; [- water, road] sale, boueux **2.** [obscene - book, film] obscène.

mucous ['mju:kəs] *adj* muqueux ■ **~ membrane** muqueuse *f*.

mucus ['mju:kəs] *n* mucus *m*, mucosité *f* ■ [from nose] morve *f*.

mud [mʌd] *(pret & pp* **mudded**, *cont* **mudding**) *n* [gen] boue *f* ■ [in river, lake] vase *f* ■ **my car got stuck in the ~** ma voiture s'est embourbée ➲ **here's ~ in your eye!** *US* à la tienne! ■ **to drag sb** *OR* **sb's name through the ~** traîner qqn dans la boue ■ **my name is ~ in certain circles** *inf* je suis en disgrâce *OR* persona non grata dans certains milieux ■ **to throw** *OR* **to sling ~ at sb** couvrir qqn de boue.

mudbath ['mʌdbɑ:θ] *n* bain *m* de boue.

muddle ['mʌdl] ◇ *n* [confusion] confusion *f* ■ [mess] désordre *m*, fouillis *m* ■ **all her belongings were in a ~** toutes ses affaires étaient en désordre *OR* sens dessus dessous ■ **my finances are in an awful ~** ma situation financière n'est pas claire du tout *OR* est complètement embrouillée ■ **Peter was in a real ~ over the holiday plans** Peter ne savait plus où il en était dans ses projets de vacances ■ **let's try to sort out this ~** essayons de démêler cet écheveau *fig* ■ **there must have been a ~ over the train times** quelqu'un a dû se tromper dans les horaires de train.
◇ *vt* **1.** [mix up - dates] confondre, mélanger ; [- facts] embrouiller, mélanger ■ **the dates got ~d** il y a eu une confusion dans les dates **2.** [confuse - person] embrouiller (l'esprit *OR* les idées de) ■ **now you've got me ~d** maintenant, je ne sais plus où j'en suis.
◆ **muddle along** *vi insep* se débrouiller.
◆ **muddle through** *vi insep* se tirer d'affaire.
◆ **muddle up** *vt sep* = **muddle** *(vt)*.

muddleheaded [,mʌdl'hedɪd] *adj* [person] désordonné, brouillon, écervelé ■ [idea, speech, essay] confus.

muddler ['mʌdlə^r] *n* personne *f* désordonnée.

muddle-up *n* **1.** [misunderstanding] quiproquo *m*, malentendu *m* **2.** [situation] embrouillement *m*, imbroglio *m*.

muddy ['mʌdɪ] *(comp* **muddier**, *superl* **muddiest**) ◇ *adj* **1.** [hand, car] plein *OR* couvert de boue ■ [shoes] plein de boue, crotté ■ [road, stream] boueux **2.** *fig* [complexion] terreux ■ [colour] terne, sale ■ [flavour, drink] boueux ■ [liquid] boueux, trouble **3.** [indistinct - thinking, ideas] confus, embrouillé, peu clair ■ [out of focus - image] brouillé, trouble, flou.
◇ *vt* **1.** [hands, shoes] salir, couvrir de boue ■ [road, stream] rendre boueux **2.** [situation] compliquer, embrouiller.

mudflap ['mʌdflæp] *n* [on car] bavette *f* ■ [on truck] pare-boue *m inv*.

mudflat ['mʌdflæt] *n* laisse *f OR* banc *m* de boue.

mudguard ['mʌdgɑ:d] *n* garde-boue *m inv*.

mud hut *n* case *f* en pisé *OR* en terre.

mudlark ['mʌdlɑ:k] *n lit* gamin *m*, - e *f* des rues.

mudpack ['mʌdpæk] *n* masque *m* à l'argile.

mud pie *n* pâté *m* (de sable).

mudslinging ['mʌd,slɪŋɪŋ] *n* calomnie *f*.

muesli ['mju:zlɪ] *n* muesli *m* ■ **the ~ belt** *UK pej* *quartiers où vit une certaine bourgeoisie de gauche, soucieuse de diététique etc.*

muezzin [mu:'ezɪn] *n* muezzin *m*.

muff [mʌf] ◇ *n* **1.** [for hands] manchon *m* ■ [for ears] oreillette *f* **2.** ORNITH aigrette *f* **3.** [bungled attempt] coup *m* manqué.
◇ *vt* [bungle] rater, manquer.

muffin ['mʌfɪn] *n* muffin *m*.

muffle ['mʌfl] *vt* [quieten - sound] étouffer, assourdir ; [- engine] étouffer le bruit de.

muffled ['mʌfld] *adj* [sound, voice] sourd, étouffé ■ [oars] assourdi ■ [drums] voilé ■ **there was a lot of ~ laughter** on entendait de nombreux rires étouffés.

muffler ['mʌflə^r] *n* **1.** *dated* [scarf] écharpe *f* de laine, cache-nez *m inv* **2.** *US* AUT silencieux *m*.

mufti ['mʌftɪ] *n dated* tenue *f* civile ■ **wearing ~, in ~** en civil.

mug [mʌg] *(pret & pp* **mugged**, *cont* **mugging**) ◇ *n* **1.** [cup, beer glass] chope *f* **2.** △ [face] gueule△ *f* **3.** *UK inf* [dupe] poire *f* ■ [fool] nigaud *m*, - e *f* ■ **it's a ~'s game** [foolish] c'est de la connerie△ ; [trap] c'est de l'arnaque **4.** *US inf* [thug] gangster *m*, voyou *m* **5.** = **mug shot**.
◇ *vt* agresser.

mugful ['mʌgfʊl] *n* [of tea, coffee] tasse *f* (pleine) ■ [of beer] chope *f* (pleine).

mugger ['mʌgə^r] *n* agresseur *m*.

mugging ['mʌgɪŋ] *n* agression *f*.

muggins ['mʌgɪnz] *(pl inv OR pl* **mugginses**) *n UK inf* idiot *m*, - e *f*, poire *f* ■ **I suppose ~ will have to go** je suppose que c'est bibi *OR* ma pomme qui devra y aller.

muggy ['mʌgɪ] *(comp* **muggier**, *superl* **muggiest**) *adj* METEOR lourd et humide.

mugshot ['mʌgʃɒt] *n inf* photo *f* d'identité judiciaire ■ *pej & hum* photo *f* d'identité.

Muhammad [mə'hæmɪd] *pr n* Mohammed, Mahomet.

Muhammedan, Muhammadan [mə'hæmɪdn] ◇ *n* Mahométan *m*, - e *f*.
◇ *adj* mahométan.

mujaheddin [,mu:dʒəhe'di:n] *n* moudjahid *m*.

mulatto [mju:'lætəʊ] (*pl* **mulattos** *OR pl* **mulattoes**) ◇ *adj* mulâtre.
◇ *n* mulâtre *m*, mulâtresse *f*.

mulberry ['mʌlbərɪ] ◇ *n* **1.** [fruit] mûre *f* ■ [tree] mûrier *m* **2.** [colour] violet *m* foncé.
◇ *adj* violet foncé *(inv)*.

mulch [mʌltʃ] HORT ◇ *n* paillis *m*.
◇ *vt* pailler.

mule [mju:l] *n* **1.** [animal - male] mulet *m* ; [- female] mule *f* ■ **(as) stubborn as a ~** têtu comme un mulet *OR* une mule **2.** TECH mule-jenny *f* **3.** [slipper] mule *f*.

muleteer [ˌmju:lɪ'tɪəʳ] *n* muletier *m*, - ère *f*.

mulish ['mju:lɪʃ] *adj* têtu, entêté.

mull [mʌl] *vt* [wine, beer] chauffer et épicer.
◆ **mull over** *vt sep* réfléchir (longuement) à.

mullah ['mʌlə] *n* mollah *m*.

mulled ['mʌld] *adj* : **~ wine** vin *m* chaud.

mullet ['mʌlɪt] (*pl inv OR pl* **mullets**) *n* [grey] muge *m*, mulet *m* gris ■ [red] rouget *m*, mulet *m* rouge.

mulligatawny [ˌmʌlɪgə'tɔ:nɪ] *n UK* mulligatawny *m*, soupe *f* au curry.

mullion ['mʌlɪən] *n* meneau *m* ■ **~ window** fenêtre *f* à meneaux.

multiaccess [ˌmʌltɪ'ækses] *adj* COMPUT multiaccès *(inv)*.

multichannel [ˌmʌltɪ'tʃænl] *adj* multicanal.

multicoloured *UK*, **multicolored** *US* ['mʌltɪˌkʌləd] *adj* multicolore.

multicultural [ˌmʌltɪ'kʌltʃərəl] *adj* multiculturel.

multidisciplinary ['mʌltɪˌdɪsɪ'plɪnərɪ] *adj UK* pluridisciplinaire, multidisciplinaire.

multiethnic [ˌmʌltɪ'eθnɪk] *adj* pluriethnique.

multifaceted [ˌmʌltɪ'fæsɪtɪd] *adj* présentant de multiples facettes.

multifaith ['mʌltɪfeɪθ] *adj* multiconfessionnel ■ **~ organization** organisation *f* multiconfessionnelle.

multifarious [ˌmʌltɪ'feərɪəs] *adj* [varied] (très) divers *OR* varié ■ [numerous] (très) nombreux.

multigym ['mʌltɪdʒɪm] *n* [equipment] appareil *m* de musculation ■ [room] salle *f* de musculation.

multilateral [ˌmʌltɪ'lætərəl] *adj* multilatéral.

multilingual [ˌmʌltɪ'lɪŋgwəl] *adj* multilingue.

multimedia [ˌmʌltɪ'mi:djə] ◇ *n* multimédia *m*.
◇ *comp* multimédia.

multi-million *adj* : **a ~ pound/dollar project** un projet de plusieurs millions de livres/dollars.

multimillionaire ['mʌltɪˌmɪljə'neəʳ] *n* multimillionnaire *mf*.

multinational [ˌmʌltɪ'næʃənl] ◇ *adj* multinational.
◇ *n* multinationale *f*.

multipartite [ˌmʌltɪ'pɑ:taɪt] *adj* **1.** [talks] multipartite, multilatéral **2.** [in many parts] composé de plusieurs parties ■ [with many people] impliquant plusieurs personnes ■ [with many signatories] comportant de nombreux signataires.

multiparty ['mʌltɪˌpɑ:tɪ] *adj* : **the ~ system** le pluripartisme.

multiple ['mʌltɪpl] ◇ *n* MATHS multiple *m* ■ **in ~s of 100** en *OR* par multiples de 100.
◇ *adj* **1.** [gén] multiple ■ **she suffered ~ injuries** elle a été blessée en plusieurs endroits ■ **~ ownership** copropriété *f* **2.** ELEC en parallèle.

multiple-access = **multiaccess**.

multiple-choice *adj* à choix multiples.

multiple sclerosis *n* sclérose *f* en plaques.

multiple shop, multiple store *n* grand magasin *m* à succursales, chaîne *f* de magasins.

multiplex ['mʌltɪpleks] ◇ *n* **1.** TELEC multiplex *m* **2.** CIN complexe *m* multisalles.
◇ *comp* **1.** TELEC multiplex **2.** CIN : **~ cinema** complexe *m* multisalles.
◇ *vt* TELEC multiplexer.

multiplexer, multiplexor ['mʌltɪˌpleksəʳ] *n* TELEC multiplexeur *m*.

multiplicand [ˌmʌltɪplɪ'kænd] *n* multiplicande *m*.

multiplication [ˌmʌltɪplɪ'keɪʃn] *n* [gen - MATHS] multiplication *f*.

multiplication sign *n* signe *m* de multiplication.

multiplication table *n* table *f* de multiplication.

multiplicity [ˌmʌltɪ'plɪsətɪ] *n* multiplicité *f*.

multiplier ['mʌltɪplaɪəʳ] *n* **1.** ECON, ELECTRON & MATHS multiplicateur *m* **2.** COMPUT multiplieur *m*.

multiply ['mʌltɪplaɪ] (*pret & pp* **multiplied**) ◇ *vt* multiplier ■ **it will ~ costs by eight** ça va multiplier les coûts par huit.
◇ *vi* **1.** MATHS faire des multiplications **2.** [reproduce, increase] se multiplier.

multiprocessing ['mʌltɪprəʊsesɪŋ] *n* COMPUT multitraitement *m*.

multiprocessor [ˌmʌltɪ'prəʊsesəʳ] *n* COMPUT multiprocesseur *m*.

multiprogramming [ˌmʌltɪ'prəʊgræmɪŋ] *n* COMPUT multiprogrammation *f*.

multipurpose [ˌmʌltɪ'pɜ:pəs] *adj* à usages multiples, polyvalent.

multiracial [ˌmʌltɪ'reɪʃl] *adj* multiracial.

multistage ['mʌltɪsteɪdʒ] *adj* **1.** [procedure] à plusieurs étapes **2.** [rocket] à plusieurs étages.

multistorey [ˌmʌltɪ'stɔ:rɪ] *UK*, **multistoried** [ˌmʌltɪ'stɔ:rɪd] *US adj* : **~ car park** parking *m* à plusieurs niveaux.

multitasking [ˌmʌltɪ'tɑ:skɪŋ] ◇ *n* multitâche *f*.
◇ *comp* multitâche.

multitrack [ˌmʌltɪ'træk] *adj* multipiste.

multitude ['mʌltɪtju:d] *n* **1.** [large number - of people, animals] multitude *f* ; [- of details, reasons] multitude *f*, foule *f* ■ **it covers a ~ of sins** cela peut être interprété de diverses façons **2.** [ordinary people] : **the ~** la multitude, la foule.

multitudinous [ˌmʌltɪ'tju:dɪnəs] *adj* [countless] innombrable.

multiuser [ˌmʌltɪ'ju:zəʳ] *adj* multiutilisateurs *(inv)*.

multivitamin [*UK* 'mʌltɪvɪtəmɪn, *US* 'mʌltɪvaɪtəmɪn] *n* multivitamine *f*.

multiwindow [ˌmʌltɪ'wɪndəʊ] *adj* COMPUT multifenêtre.

mum [mʌm] ◇ *adj* : **to keep ~** garder le silence ▶ **~'s the word!** *inf* motus et bouche cousue!
◇ *n UK inf* [mother] maman *f*.

mumble ['mʌmbl] ◇ *vi* marmonner ■ **what are you mumbling about?** qu'est-ce que tu as à marmonner comme ça? ■ **he ~d on for half an hour** il a radoté pendant une demi-heure.
◇ *vt* marmonner ■ **to ~ an apology** marmonner des excuses.
◇ *n* paroles *fpl* indistinctes, marmonnement *m*, marmonnements *mpl* ■ **he replied in a ~** il marmonna une réponse.

mumbo jumbo [ˌmʌmbəʊ'dʒʌmbəʊ] *n pej* langage *m* incompréhensible, charabia *m*.

mummer ['mʌməʳ] *n* mime *mf*.

mummify ['mʌmɪfaɪ] (*pret & pp* **mummified**) ◇ *vt* momifier.
◇ *vi* se momifier.

mummy ['mʌmɪ] (*pl* **mummies**) *n* **1.** [body] momie *f* **2.** *UK inf* [mother] maman *f*.

mummy's boy ['mʌmɪz-] *n UK pej* : **he's a ~** c'est le petit chéri à sa maman.

mumps [mʌmps] *n (U)* oreillons *mpl*.

munch [mʌntʃ] ◇ *vt* [crunchy food] croquer ■ [food in general] mâcher.
◇ *vi* : **to ~ on an apple** croquer une pomme ■ **she was ~ing away at some toast** elle mâchonnait un toast.

munchies [ˈmʌntʃɪz] *npl* *inf* **to have the ~** avoir un petit creux.

mundane [mʌnˈdeɪn] *adj* [gen] banal, ordinaire.

mung bean [mʌŋ-] *n* mungo *m*, ambérique *f*.

municipal [mjuːˈnɪsɪpl] *adj* municipal, de la ville.

municipality [mjuːˌnɪsɪˈpælətɪ] (*pl* **municipalities**) *n* municipalité *f*.

munificence [mjuːˈnɪfɪsəns] *n* munificence *f*.

munificent [mjuːˈnɪfɪsənt] *adj* munificent.

munitions [mjuːˈnɪʃnz] *npl* munitions *fpl* ■ **~ dump** dépôt *m* de munitions ■ **~ factory** fabrique *f* de munitions.

mural [ˈmjuːərəl] ◇ *n* [painting] mural *m*, peinture *f* murale.
◇ *adj* mural.

murder [ˈmɜːdəʳ] ◇ *n* **1.** *liter* meurtre *m*, assassinat *m* ■ **he's up on a ~ charge** il est accusé de meurtre ■ **~ trial** procès *m* pour meurtre ■ **the ~ weapon** l'arme *f* du crime ■ **~ one** *US* LAW assassinat *m* ▶ **to get away with ~** faire n'importe quoi impunément ■ **'Murder on the Orient Express'** ***Christie, Lumet*** 'le Crime de l'Orient-Express' **2.** *inf fig* calvaire *m*, enfer *m* ■ **the traffic is ~ on Fridays** il y a une circulation épouvantable le vendredi ■ **it's ~ trying to get her to agree** ce n'est pas une mince affaire que d'obtenir son consentement.
◇ *vt* **1.** [kill] tuer, assassiner ■ [slaughter] tuer, massacrer ■ **I could ~ a beer!** je me taperais bien une bière! **2.** *fig* [language, play] massacrer.
◇ *interj* : **~!** à l'assassin!

murderer [ˈmɜːdərəʳ] *n* meurtrier *m*, - ère *f*, assassin *m*.

murderess [ˈmɜːdərɪs] *n* meurtrière *f*.

murderous [ˈmɜːdərəs] *adj* **1.** [deadly - regime, attack, intention] meurtrier **2.** [hateful - look, expression] meurtrier, assassin, de haine **3.** [dangerous - road, bend] meurtrier, redoutable **4.** *inf* [hellish] infernal, épouvantable.

murk [mɜːk] *n (U)* obscurité *f*, ténèbres *fpl*.

murky [ˈmɜːkɪ] (*comp* **murkier**, *superl* **murkiest**) *adj* **1.** [dark - sky, night] noir, sombre ■ [muddy - water] boueux, trouble ■ [dirty - windows, weather] sale **2.** *fig* [shameful] : **a ~ episode** une histoire sombre *OR* trouble ■ **he's someone from my ~ past** *hum* c'est quelqu'un qui appartient à mon passé trouble.

murmur [ˈmɜːməʳ] ◇ *vi* murmurer ■ **to ~ at** *OR* **against sthg** murmurer contre qqch.
◇ *vt* murmurer.
◇ *n* **1.** [sound] murmure *m* ■ [of conversation] bruit *m*, bourdonnement *m* ■ **there wasn't a ~** on aurait pu entendre une mouche voler ■ **without a ~** sans broncher **2.** MED [of heart] souffle *m*.

murmuring [ˈmɜːmərɪŋ] ◇ *n* murmure *m*.
◇ *adj* murmurant.
◆ **murmurings** *npl* murmures *mpl*.

Murphy bed [ˈmɜːfɪ-] *n* *US* lit *m* escamotable.

Murphy's law [ˈmɜːfɪz-] *n* loi *f* de l'emmerdement maximum.

Murrayfield [ˈmʌrɪfiːld] *pr n terrain de rugby à Édimbourg*.

Mururoa (Atoll) [ˈmʊrʊˌrəʊəˈætɒl] *pr n* Mururoa ■ **on ~** à Mururoa.

MusB [ˈmʌzbiː], **MusBac** [ˈmʌzbæk] (*abbrev of* **Bachelor of Music**) *n* (titulaire d'une) licence de musique.

muscatel [ˌmʌskəˈtel] *n* muscat *m*.

muscle [ˈmʌsl] ◇ *n* **1.** ANAT & ZOOL muscle *m* ■ [strength] muscle *m*, force *f* ▶ **she didn't move a ~** elle est restée parfaitement immobile **2.** [influence, power] puissance *f*, poids *m*.
◇ *vt* muscler.
◆ **muscle in** *vi insep inf* intervenir ■ **to ~ in on sthg** intervenir autoritairement dans qqch ■ **to ~ one's way in** entrer par la force.

muscle-bound *adj* **1.** [muscular] extrêmement musclé **2.** [rigid] inflexible, rigide.

muscleman [ˈmʌslmæn] (*pl* **musclemen** [-men]) *n* [strongman] hercule *m* ■ [bodyguard] garde *m* du corps, homme *m* de main.

muscle relaxant *n* myorelaxant *m*, décontracturant *m*.

muscly [ˈmʌslɪ] *adj* musclé, plein de muscles.

Muscovite [ˈmʌskəvaɪt] ◇ *n* Moscovite *mf*.
◇ *adj* moscovite.

muscular [ˈmʌskjʊləʳ] *adj* **1.** [body] musclé **2.** [pain, tissue] musculaire.

muscular dystrophy *n (U)* myopathie *f*.

musculature [ˈmʌskjʊlətʃəʳ] *n* musculature *f*.

MusD [ˈmʌzdiː], **MusDoc** [ˈmʌzdɒk] (*abbrev of* **Doctor of Music**) *n* (titulaire d'un) doctorat en musique.

muse [mjuːz] ◇ *n* muse *f* ■ **the Muses** les Muses.
◇ *vi* rêvasser, songer ■ **to ~ on** *OR* **upon** *OR* **over sthg** songer à qqch.
◇ *vt* : **"I wonder what happened to him", she ~d** "je me demande bien ce qu'il est devenu", dit-elle d'un air songeur.

museum [mjuːˈziːəm] *n* musée *m*.

museum piece *n liter* & *fig* pièce *f* de musée.

mush[1] [mʌʃ] *n* **1.** [food] bouillie *f* ■ *US* [porridge] bouillie *f* de maïs **2.** *inf fig* [sentimentality] mièvrerie *f*.

mush[2] △ [mʊʃ] *n* *UK* **1.** [face] poire *f*, trombine *f* **2.** [term of address] : **oi, ~!**△ eh, machin!

mushroom [ˈmʌʃrʊm] ◇ *n* BOT & NUCL PHYS champignon *m*.
◇ *comp* **1.** [soup, omelette] aux champignons **2.** [in colour] beige **3.** *fig* **~ growth** poussée *f* *OR* croissance *f* rapide ■ **~ town** ville *f* champignon.
◇ *vi* **1.** [gather mushrooms] : **to go ~ing** aller aux champignons **2.** [spring up] pousser comme des champignons ■ **video shops ~ed in almost every town** les magasins de vidéo se sont multipliés dans presque toutes les villes **3.** [grow quickly] s'étendre, prendre de l'ampleur ■ **the conflict ~ed into full-scale war** le conflit a vite dégénéré en véritable guerre.

mushroom cloud *n* champignon *m* atomique.

mushrooming [ˈmʌʃruːmɪŋ] *n* **1.** [mushroom picking] cueillette *f* des champignons **2.** [sudden growth] croissance *f* exponentielle.

mushy [ˈmʌʃɪ] (*comp* **mushier**, *superl* **mushiest**) *adj* **1.** [vegetables] ramolli ■ [fruit] trop mûr, blet ■ [ground] détrempé ■ **~ peas** purée *f* de petits pois **2.** *inf fig* [sentimental] à l'eau de rose, mièvre.

music [ˈmjuːzɪk] ◇ *n* musique *f* ■ **to set to ~** mettre en musique ‖ [score] partition *f*, musique *f* ■ **to read ~** lire une partition ▶ **the news was ~ to my ears** la nouvelle m'a fait très plaisir *OR* m'a ravi.
◇ *comp* [teacher, lesson, festival] de musique.

musical [ˈmjuːzɪkl] ◇ *adj* **1.** [evening, taste, composition] musical ■ [instrument] de musique **2.** [person] musicien ■ **they are a ~ people** [liking music] c'est un peuple mélomane ; [including musicians] c'est un peuple de musiciens ■ **I'm not very ~** je n'ai pas tellement l'oreille musicale **3.** [pleasant - voice, chimes] musical.
◇ *n* = **musical comedy**.

musical box *UK* = **music box**.

musical chairs *n* **1.** [game] jeu *m* des chaises musicales **2.** *fig* va-et-vient *m inv*, remue-ménage *m inv* ■ POL remaniements *mpl*.

musical comedy *n* comédie *f* musicale, musical *m*.

musical instrument *n* instrument *m* de musique.

musically [ˈmjuːzɪklɪ] *adv* [in a musical way] musicalement ■ [from a musical viewpoint] musicalement, d'un point de vue musical.

music box *n* boîte *f* à musique.

music case *n* porte-musique *m inv*.

music centre *n* chaîne *f* (midi).

music hall ◇ *n* **1.** [theatre] théâtre *m* de variétés **2.** [entertainment] music-hall *m*.
◇ *comp* [song, artist] de music-hall.

musician [mjuːˈzɪʃn] *n* musicien *m*, - enne *f*.

musicianship [mjuːˈzɪʃnʃɪp] *n* sens *m* musical.

music-lover *n* mélomane *mf*.

musicology [ˌmjuːzɪˈkɒlədʒɪ] *n* musicologie *f*.

music paper *n* papier *m* à musique.

music stand *n* pupitre *m* (à musique).

music video *n* clip *m* (vidéo).

musing [ˈmjuːzɪŋ] ◇ *n (U)* songes *mpl*, rêverie *f*.
◇ *adj* songeur, rêveur.

musingly [ˈmjuːzɪŋlɪ] *adv* pensivement ■ **"I don't know", she answered ~** "je ne sais pas", répondit-elle songeuse *OR* d'un air songeur.

musk [mʌsk] *n* musc *m*.

musk deer *n* porte-musc *m*.

musket [ˈmʌskɪt] *n* mousquet *m*.

musketeer [ˌmʌskɪˈtɪəʳ] *n* mousquetaire *m*.

muskrat [ˈmʌskræt] (*pl inv OR pl* **muskrats**) *n* **1.** ZOOL rat *m* musqué, ondatra *m* **2.** [fur] rat *m* d'Amérique, loutre *f* d'Hudson.

musk rose *n* rosier *m* musqué.

musky [ˈmʌskɪ] (*comp* **muskier**, *superl* **muskiest**) *adj* musqué.

Muslim [ˈmʊzlɪm] ◇ *adj* musulman.
◇ *n* musulman *m*, - e *f*.

muslin [ˈmʌzlɪn] ◇ *n* TEX mousseline *f*.
◇ *comp* de *OR* en mousseline.

musquash [ˈmʌskwɒʃ] = **muskrat**.

muss [mʌs] *vt inf* [rumple] friper, froisser ■ [dirty] salir.

mussel [ˈmʌsl] ◇ *n* moule *f*.
◇ *comp* : **~ farm** moulière *f* ■ **~ bed** parc *m* à moules.

must[1] [*weak form* [məs] *OR* [məst], *strong form* [mʌst]]
◇ *modal vb* **1.** [expressing necessity, obligation] devoir ■ **you ~ lock the door** vous devez fermer *OR* il faut que vous fermiez la porte à clé ■ **I ~ go now** il faut que je parte (maintenant) ■ **I ~ admit the idea intrigues me** je dois avouer que l'idée m'intrigue ■ **if I/you** *etc* **~** s'il le faut ■ **if you ~ know, he's asked me out to dinner** si tu veux tout savoir, il m'a invitée à dîner ■ **~ you be so rude?** es-tu obligé d'être aussi grossier? ■ **they told us we ~ leave** ils nous ont dit qu'il fallait que nous partions, ils nous ont dit que nous devions partir ■ **you mustn't smoke** il est interdit de fumer ■ **I mustn't say any more** je n'ai pas le droit d'en dire plus ■ **they told us we mustn't come before 10 o'clock** ils nous ont dit de ne pas arriver avant 10 h **2.** [suggesting, inviting] : **you ~ meet my wife** il faut que vous rencontriez *OR* fassiez la connaissance de ma femme **3.** [expressing likelihood] devoir ■ **you ~ be Alison** vous devez être Alison ■ **you ~ be joking!** tu plaisantes! **4.** *(with 'have' + pp)* [making assumptions] : **she ~ have forgotten** elle a dû oublier, elle a sans doute oublié ■ **has she forgotten? – she ~ have** elle a oublié? – sans doute *OR* certainement ■ **you ~ have known!** vous le saviez sûrement! ■ [stating requirements] : **before applying candidates ~ have successfully completed all their exams** les candidats doivent avoir obtenu tous leurs examens avant de se présenter.
◇ *n inf* **sunglasses are a ~** les lunettes de soleil sont absolument indispensables ■ **this film/his new album is a ~** il faut absolument avoir vu ce film/acheter son dernier album.

must[2] [mʌst] *n* **1.** [mould] moisissure *f* **2.** [for wine] moût *m*.

mustache *US* [ˈmʌstæʃ] = **moustache**.

mustachio [məˈstɑːʃɪəʊ] (*pl* **mustachios**) *n* (longue) moustache *f*.

mustachioed [məˈstɑːʃɪəʊd] *adj* moustachu.

mustang [ˈmʌstæŋ] *n* mustang *m*.

mustard [ˈmʌstəd] ◇ *n* moutarde *f* ■ **~ seed** graine *f* de moutarde ■ **~ and cress** *mélange de cresson alénois et de pousses de moutarde blanche utilisé en salade* ■ **French ~** ≃ moutarde *f* de Dijon ■ **~ pot** moutardier *m*, pot *m* à moutarde.
◇ *adj* [colour] moutarde *(inv)*.

mustard gas *n* gaz *m* moutarde, ypérite *f*.

muster [ˈmʌstəʳ] ◇ *vt* **1.** [gather - troops] rassembler, réunir ; [- courage, energy] rassembler ; [- finance, cash] réunir ■ **they were unable to ~ enough support** ils n'ont pas pu trouver suffisamment de gens pour soutenir leur initiative ■ **to ~ one's courage to do sthg** prendre son courage à deux mains pour faire qqch **2.** [take roll-call] faire l'appel de.
◇ *vi* se rassembler.
◇ *n* **1.** MIL revue *f*, inspection *f* ■ **to pass ~** *UK fig* [in dress, appearance] être présentable ; [in content] être acceptable **2.** [assembly] rassemblement *m*.
◆ **muster up** *vt insep* [courage] rassembler ■ **to ~ up support** chercher à obtenir un soutien *OR* un appui.

mustn't [mʌsnt] = **must not**.

must've [ˈmʌstəv] = **must have**.

musty [ˈmʌstɪ] (*comp* **mustier**, *superl* **mustiest**) *adj* **1.** [smell] de moisi ■ [room] qui sent le renfermé **2.** *fig* [old-fashioned] suranné, vieux jeu *(inv)*.

mutable [ˈmjuːtəbl] *adj* [gen] mutable ■ ASTROL mutable, commun.

mutant [ˈmjuːtənt] ◇ *adj* mutant.
◇ *n* mutant *m*, - e *f*.

mutate [mjuːˈteɪt] *vi* & *vt* muter.

mutation [mjuːˈteɪʃn] *n* mutation *f*.

mute [mjuːt] ◇ *adj* **1.** MED muet **2.** LING [vowel, letter] muet **3.** [silent - person] muet, silencieux ■ [unspoken - feeling] muet.
◇ *vt* [sound] amortir, atténuer ■ [feelings, colour] atténuer.
◇ *n* **1.** MED muet *m*, - ette *f* **2.** MUS sourdine *f*.

muted [ˈmjuːtɪd] *adj* **1.** [sound] assourdi, amorti, atténué ■ [voice] feutré, sourd ■ [colour] doux, douce *f*, pâle ■ [criticism, protest] voilé ■ [applause] faible **2.** MUS en sourdine.

mutely [ˈmjuːtlɪ] *adv* [stare, gaze] en silence.

mute swan *n* cygne *m* muet *OR* tuberculé *OR* domestique.

mutilate [ˈmjuːtɪleɪt] *vt* **1.** [maim - body] mutiler ; [- face] défigurer **2.** [damage - property, thing] mutiler, dégrader, détériorer **3.** [adulterate - text] mutiler.

mutilation [ˌmjuːtɪˈleɪʃn] *n* **1.** [of body] mutilation *f* **2.** [of property] détérioration *f*, dégradation *f* **3.** [of text] mutilation *f*, altération *f*.

mutineer [ˌmjuːtɪˈnɪəʳ] *n* mutin *m*, mutiné *m*, - e *f*.

mutinous [ˈmjuːtɪnəs] *adj* **1.** [rebellious - crew, soldiers] mutiné, rebelle ■ **the inmates of the prison were ~** les détenus étaient au bord de la rébellion **2.** [unruly - child] indiscipliné, rebelle.

mutiny [ˈmjuːtɪnɪ] (*pl* **mutinies**) ◇ *n* [on ship] mutinerie *f* ■ [in prison, barracks] rébellion *f*, mutinerie *f* ■ [in city] soulèvement *m*, révolte *f* ■ **'Mutiny on the Bounty'** ***Nordhoff, Hall*** 'les Révoltés du Bounty'.
◇ *vi* se mutiner, se rebeller.

mutt [mʌt] *n inf* **1.** [dog] clébard *m* **2.** [fool] crétin *m*, - e *f*.

mutter ['mʌtəʳ] <> *vt* [mumble] marmonner, grommeler.
<> *vi* **1.** [mumble] marmonner, parler dans sa barbe OR entre ses dents ■ **what are you ~ing about?** qu'est-ce que tu as à marmonner? ■ **to ~ to o.s.** marmonner tout seul **2.** [grumble] grommeler, grogner.
<> *n* murmure *m*, murmures *mpl*, marmonnement *m* ■ **to speak in a ~** marmonner dans sa barbe.

muttering ['mʌtərɪŋ] *n* marmottement *m*.

mutton ['mʌtn] <> *n* CULIN mouton *m* ■ **she's ~ dressed as lamb** elle joue les jeunesses.
<> *comp* [chop, stew] de mouton.

muttonchops [,mʌtən'tʃɒps], **muttonchop whiskers** *npl* favoris *mpl (bien fournis)*.

mutual ['mju:tʃʊəl] *adj* [reciprocal - admiration, help] mutuel, réciproque ■ [shared - friend, interest] commun ■ **by ~ consent** à l'amiable, par consentement mutuel ■ **the feeling is ~** c'est réciproque.

mutual fund *n US* [unit trust] fonds *m* commun de placement.

mutually ['mju:tʃʊəlɪ] *adv* mutuellement, réciproquement ■ **~ exclusive** OR **contradictory** qui s'excluent l'un l'autre, contradictoires.

Muzak® ['mju:zæk] *n* musique *f* de fond, fond *m* sonore.

muzzle ['mʌzl] <> *n* **1.** [for dog, horse] muselière *f* **2.** *fig* [censorship] bâillon *m*, censure *f* **3.** [of gun] canon *m* **4.** [mouth of animal] gueule *f*.
<> *vt* **1.** [dog, horse] museler, mettre une muselière à **2.** *fig* [speaker] museler, empêcher de s'exprimer librement ■ [press] bâillonner, museler.

muzzle-loader *n arme à feu dont le chargement s'opère par la bouche.*

muzzle velocity *n* vitesse *f* initiale.

muzzy ['mʌzɪ] (*comp* **muzzier**, *superl* **muzziest**) *adj UK* **1.** [person] aux idées embrouillées ■ [mind, head] confus ■ [ideas] embrouillé, flou **2.** [picture] flou, indistinct.

MW (*written abbrev of* **medium wave**) PO.

my [maɪ] <> *det* **1.** [belonging to me] mon *m*, ma *f*, mes *pl* ■ **my dog/car/ear** mon chien/ma voiture/mon oreille ■ **I never use my own car** je n'utilise jamais ma voiture (personnelle) ■ **I have a car of my own** j'ai une voiture (à moi) ■ **this is MY chair** cette chaise est à moi ■ **I've broken my arm** je me suis cassé le bras ■ **she looked into my eyes** elle m'a regardé dans les yeux **2.** [in terms of affection] : **my dear** OR **darling** [to man] mon chéri ; [to woman] ma chérie **3.** [in titles] : **my Lord** [to judge] Monsieur le juge ; [to nobleman] Monsieur le Comte/le Duc ; [to bishop] Monseigneur **4.** [in exclamations] : **oh, my God!** oh! mon Dieu!
<> *interj* eh bien ■ **my, but you've grown!** eh bien dis donc, tu as poussé!

myalgic encephalomyelitis [maɪ'ældʒɪk en,sefələʊ,maɪ'laɪtɪs] = **ME**.

Myanmar [,maɪæn'mɑ:ʳ] *pr n* Myanmar *m* ■ **in ~** au Myanmar.

myelitis [,maɪə'laɪtɪs] *n* myélite *f*.

myeloma [,maɪə'ləʊmə] *n* myélome *m*.

myna(h) ['maɪnə] *n* : **~ (bird)** mainate *m*.

myocardial [,maɪəʊ'kɑ:dɪəl] *adj* : **~ infarction** infarctus *m* du myocarde.

myopic [maɪ'ɒpɪk] *adj* myope.

myriad ['mɪrɪəd] <> *adj lit* innombrable.
<> *n* myriade *f*.

myrrh [mɜ:ʳ] *n* myrrhe *f*.

myrtle ['mɜ:tl] *n* myrte *m*.

myself [maɪ'self] *pron* **1.** [reflexive use] : **may I help ~?** puis-je me servir? ■ **I knitted ~ a cardigan** je me suis tricoté un gilet ■ **it doesn't taste bad, though I say so** OR **it ~** *hum* sans fausse modestie, ça n'est pas mauvais ■ **I can see ~ reflected in the water** je vois mon reflet dans l'eau ■ **I can't see ~ going on holiday this year** je ne crois pas que je pourrai partir en vacances cette année **2.** [replacing 'me'] : **the group included ~ and Jim** Jim et moi faisions partie du groupe ■ **it is meant for people like ~** c'est fait pour les gens comme moi ➲ **I'm not (feeling) ~ today** je ne me sens pas très bien OR je ne suis pas dans mon assiette aujourd'hui **3.** [emphatic use] : **I'm not a great fan of opera ~** personnellement, je ne suis pas un passionné d'opéra ■ **I'm a stranger here ~** je ne suis pas d'ici non plus ■ **I ~** OR **~, I don't believe him** pour ma part, je ne le crois pas ■ **I was left all by ~** on m'a laissé tout seul **4.** [unaided, alone] moi-même ■ **I can do it ~** je peux le faire moi-même OR tout seul.

mysterious [mɪ'stɪərɪəs] *adj* mystérieux.

mysteriously [mɪ'stɪərɪəslɪ] *adv* mystérieusement.

mystery ['mɪstərɪ] (*pl* **mysteries**) <> *n* **1.** [strange or unexplained event] mystère *m* ■ **it's a ~ to me why she came** la raison de sa venue est un mystère pour moi, je n'ai aucune idée de la raison pour laquelle elle est venue ■ **his past is a ~** son passé est bien mystérieux ■ **there's no ~ about that** ça n'a rien de mystérieux, cela n'est un mystère pour personne **2.** [strangeness] mystère *m* ■ **she has a certain ~ about her** il se dégage de sa personne une impression de mystère **3.** THEAT & RELIG mystère *m*.
<> *comp* [man, voice] mystérieux.

mystery play *n* THEAT mystère *m*.

mystery story *n* histoire *f* à suspense, intrigue *f* policière.

mystery tour *n excursion dont la destination est inconnue des participants.*

mystic ['mɪstɪk] <> *adj* mystique.
<> *n* mystique *mf*.

mystical ['mɪstɪkl] *adj* **1.** PHILOS & RELIG mystique **2.** [occult] occulte.

mysticism ['mɪstɪsɪzm] *n* mysticisme *m*.

mystification [,mɪstɪfɪ'keɪʃn] *n* mystification *f*.

mystified ['mɪstɪfaɪd] *adj* perplexe.

mystify ['mɪstɪfaɪ] (*pret & pp* **mystified**) *vt* [puzzle] déconcerter, laisser OR rendre perplexe ■ [deceive] mystifier.

mystifying ['mɪstɪfaɪɪŋ] *adj* inexplicable, déconcertant.

mystique [mɪ'sti:k] *n* mystique *f*, côté *m* mystique.

myth [mɪθ] *n* mythe *m*.

mythical ['mɪθɪkl] *adj* mythique.

mythological [,mɪθə'lɒdʒɪkl] *adj* mythologique.

mythology [mɪ'θɒlədʒɪ] (*pl* **mythologies**) *n* mythologie *f*.

mythomania [,mɪθə'meɪnjə] *n* mythomanie *f*.

myxomatosis [,mɪksəmə'təʊsɪs] *n* myxomatose *f*.

N

n *n* MATHS n *m* ■ **there are ~ possible solutions** *inf* il y a 36 solutions possibles.

n (*pl* **n's** *OR pl* **ns**), **N** (*pl* **N's** *OR pl* **Ns**) [en] *n* [letter] n *m*, N *m*, *see also* **f**.

N (*written abbrev of* **North**) N.

n/a, N/A (*written abbrev of* **not applicable**) s.o.

Naafi ['næfɪ] (*abbrev of* **Navy, Army, and Air Force Institutes**) *pr n organisme approvisionnant les forces armées britanniques en biens de consommation.*

nab [næb] (*pret & pp* **nabbed**, *cont* **nabbing**) *vt inf* **1.** [catch in wrongdoing] pincer, choper **2.** [catch - to speak to] coincer, agrafer **3.** [steal, take] chiper, faucher ■ [occupy - seat] prendre, accaparer ; [- parking place] piquer.

nabob ['neɪbɒb] *n* nabab *m*.

nachos ['nɑːtʃəʊz] *npl chips de maïs servies avec du fromage fondu.*

nacre ['neɪkəʳ] *n* nacre *f*.

nadir ['neɪˌdɪəʳ] *n* **1.** ASTRON nadir *m* **2.** *fig* [lowest point] point *m* le plus bas *OR* profond ■ **to reach a ~** être au plus bas, toucher le fond, atteindre le niveau le plus bas.

naff [næf] *adj UK inf* [very bad] nul, bidon.
◆ **naff off** *vi insep UK inf* **~ off!** [go away] tire-toi! ; [as refusal] arrête ton char!

NAFTA ['næftə] (*abbrev of* **North American Free Trade Agreement**) *n* ALENA *m*.

nag [næg] ◇ *vt* (*pret & pp* **nagged**, *cont* **nagging**) **1.** [pester] houspiller, harceler ■ **she's always nagging him** elle est toujours après lui ■ **he nagged me into buying him a hi-fi** il m'a harcelé jusqu'à ce que je lui achète une chaîne stéréo **2.** [subj: pain, sorrow] ronger, travailler ■ [subj: doubt] tourmenter, ronger.
◇ *vi* (*pret & pp* **nagged**, *cont* **nagging**) trouver à redire, maugréer ■ **to ~ at sb** harceler qqn ■ **his children nagged at him to buy a video** ses enfants lui ont cassé les pieds pour qu'il achète un magnétoscope.
◇ *n* **1.** *inf* [person] rouspéteur *m*, - euse *f*, râleur *m*, - euse *f* ■ **his wife's a real ~** sa femme est toujours sur son dos *OR* ne lui laisse pas une seconde de répit **2.** [horse] rosse *f*.

nagging ['nægɪŋ] ◇ *adj* **1.** [wife, husband] grincheux, acariâtre **2.** [doubt, feeling] tenace, harcelant ■ [pain] tenace.
◇ *n (U)* plaintes *fpl* continuelles.

naiad ['naɪæd] *n* naïade *f*.

nail [neɪl] ◇ *n* **1.** [pin] clou *m* ■ **it's another ~ in his coffin** [ruin] pour lui, c'est un pas de plus vers la ruine ; [death] pour lui, c'est un pas de plus vers la tombe **2.** ANAT ongle *m* ■ **to do one's ~s** se faire les ongles.
◇ *vt* **1.** [attach] clouer ■ **~ the planks together** clouez les planches l'une à l'autre ■ **~ed to the door** cloué sur la porte ■ **the windows are ~ed shut** les fenêtres ont été clouées *OR* sont condamnées ◗ **to ~ one's colours to the mast** exprimer clairement son opinion **2.** *inf* [catch, trap - person] pincer, coincer **3.** *inf* [expose - rumour] démentir ; [- lie] dénoncer, révéler.
◆ **nail down** *vt sep* **1.** [fasten] clouer, fixer avec des clous **2.** [make definite - details, date] fixer (définitivement) ; [- agreement] parvenir à, arriver à ; [- person] amener à se décider ■ **try to ~ her down to a definite date** essayez de faire en sorte qu'elle vous fixe une date précise ■ **he's difficult to ~ down** il est difficile d'obtenir une réponse précise de sa part.
◆ **nail up** *vt sep* **1.** [shut - door, window] condamner *(en fixant avec des clous)* ; [- box] clouer ; [- items in box] : **the pictures were ~ed up in a crate** les tableaux étaient placés dans une caisse fermée par des clous **2.** [fix to wall, door - picture, photo etc] fixer (avec un clou) ; [- notice] clouer, afficher.

nail-biting ◇ *n* [habit] manie *f* de se ronger les ongles ■ *fig* nervosité *f*, inquiétude *f*.
◇ *adj* [situation] angoissant, stressant ■ [finish] haletant.

nail bomb *n* bombe *f* à fragmentation *(bourrée de clous)*.

nailbrush ['neɪlbrʌʃ] *n* brosse *f* à ongles.

nail clippers *npl* coupe-ongles *m inv*, pince *f* à ongles.

nail file *n* lime *f* à ongles.

nail polish *n* vernis *m* à ongles.

nail scissors *npl* ciseaux *mpl* à ongles.

nail varnish *n UK* vernis *m* à ongles ■ **~ remover** dissolvant *m* (pour vernis à ongles).

naive, naïve [naɪ'iːv] *adj* naïf.

naively, naïvely [naɪ'iːvlɪ] *adv* naïvement, avec naïveté.

naivety [naɪ'iːvtɪ] *n* naïveté *f*.

naked ['neɪkɪd] *adj* **1.** [unclothed - body, leg] nu ■ **the ~ ape** *fig* l'homme *m*, l'espèce *f* humaine ■ [bare - tree] nu, dénudé, sans feuilles ; [- landscape] nu, dénudé ; [- wall, room] nu ■ [unprotected - flame, light, sword] nu ; [- wire] nu, dénudé ■ **a ~ lightbulb lit the room** une simple ampoule électrique éclairait la pièce **2.** [undisguised - reality, truth] tout nu, tout cru ; [- facts] brut ; [- fear] pur et simple ; [- aggression] délibéré **3.** [eye] nu ■ **visible with** *OR* **to the ~ eye** visible à l'œil nu **4.** BOT & ZOOL nu.

nakedness ['neɪkɪdnɪs] *n* nudité *f*.

NALGO ['nælgəʊ] (*abbrev of* **National and Local Government Officers' Association**) *pr n ancien syndicat de la fonction publique en Grande-Bretagne.*

Nam [næm] *pr n US inf* Vietnam *m*.

namby-pamby [ˌnæmbɪ'pæmbɪ] ◇ *adj inf* [person] gnangnan *(inv)*, cucul *(inv)* ■ [style] à l'eau de rose, fadasse.
◇ *n* lavette *f*, gnangnan *mf*.

name [neɪm] <> *n* **1.** nom *m* ▪ **what's your ~?** quel est votre nom?, comment vous appelez-vous? ▪ **my ~'s Richard** je m'appelle Richard ▪ **the house is in his wife's ~** la maison est au nom de sa femme ▪ **she knows all the children by ~** elle connaît le nom de tous les enfants ▪ **he is known** *OR* **he goes by the ~ of Penn** il est connu sous le nom de Penn, il se fait appeler Penn ▪ **someone by** *OR* **of the ~ of Penn** quelqu'un du nom de *OR* qui s'appelle Penn ▪ **a guy ~ of Jones** *US inf* un type du nom de Jones ▪ **I know it by** *OR* **under a different ~** je le connais sous un autre nom ▪ **he writes novels under the ~ of A.B. Alderman** il écrit des romans sous le pseudonyme de A.B. Alderman ▪ **have you put your ~ down for evening classes?** est-ce que vous vous êtes inscrit aux cours du soir? ▪ **she was his wife in all but ~** ils n'étaient pas mariés, mais c'était tout comme ▪ **he had his ~ taken** FTBL il a eu un carton jaune ▪ **he is president in ~ only** il n'a de président que le nom, c'est un président sans pouvoir ▪ **what's in a ~?** on n'a pas toujours le nom que l'on mérite ◐ **to call sb ~s** injurier *OR* insulter qqn ▪ **money is the ~ of the game** c'est une affaire d'argent ▪ **ah well, that's the ~ of the game** c'est comme ça!, c'est la vie! **2.** [sake] nom *m* ▪ **in the ~ of freedom** au nom de la liberté ▪ **in God's ~!, in the ~ of God!** pour l'amour de Dieu! ▮ [authority] nom ▪ **in the ~ of the law** au nom de la loi
3. [reputation - professional or business] nom *m*, réputation *f* ▪ **to make** *OR* **to win a ~ for o.s.** se faire un nom *OR* une réputation ▪ **we have the company's (good) ~ to think of** il faut penser au renom de la société ▪ **to have a bad ~** avoir (une) mauvaise réputation
4. [famous person] nom *m*, personnage *m* ▪ **he's a big ~ in the art world** c'est une figure de proue du monde des arts ▪ **all the great political ~s were there** tous les ténors de la scène politique étaient présents.
<> *comp* COMM [product] de marque.
<> *vt* **1.** [give name to - person, animal] nommer, appeler, donner un nom à ; [- ship, discovery] baptiser ▪ **they ~d the baby Felix** ils ont appelé *OR* prénommé le bébé Felix ▪ **she wanted to ~ her son after the President** elle voulait donner à son fils le prénom du Président, elle voulait que son fils porte le prénom du Président ▪ **the building is ~d for Abraham Lincoln** *US* on a donné au bâtiment le nom d'Abraham Lincoln ▪ **the fellow ~d Chip** le dénommé Chip
2. [give name of] désigner, nommer ▪ **the journalist refused to ~ his source** le journaliste a refusé de révéler *OR* de donner le nom de son informateur ▪ **whatever you need, just ~ it** vos moindres désirs seront exaucés ▪ **you ~ it, we've got it** demandez-nous n'importe quoi, nous l'avons! ▪ **~ the books of the Old Testament** citez les livres de l'Ancien Testament ▪ **to ~ names** donner des noms ▮ [cite] citer, mentionner ▪ **he is ~d as one of the consultants** son nom est cité *OR* mentionné en tant que consultant
3. [appoint] nommer, désigner ▪ **she has been ~d as president** elle a été nommée présidente ▪ **June 22nd has been ~d as the date for the elections** la date du 22 juin a été retenue *OR* choisie pour les élections ▪ **~ your price** votre prix sera le mien, dites votre prix ◐ **they've finally ~d the day** ils ont enfin fixé la date de leur mariage
4. *UK* POL : **to ~ an MP** ≃ suspendre un député.
◆ **Name** *n titre réservé aux membres investissant leur fortune personnelle dans la compagnie d'assurances Lloyd's et s'engageant à avoir une responsabilité illimitée en cas de sinistre.*

name-calling *n (U)* insultes *fpl*, injures *fpl*.

name day *n* fête *f*.

name-dropping *n allusion fréquente à des personnes connues dans le but d'impressionner.*

nameless ['neɪmlɪs] *adj* **1.** [anonymous, unmentioned] sans nom, anonyme ▪ [unknown - grave, writer] anonyme, inconnu ▪ **a person who shall be ~** une personne que je ne nommerai pas ▪ **to remain ~** garder l'anonymat **2.** [indefinable - fear, regret] indéfinissable, indicible **3.** [atrocious - crime] innommable, sans nom, inouï.

namely ['neɪmlɪ] *adv* c'est-à-dire, à savoir.

nameplate ['neɪmpleɪt] *n* plaque *f*.

namesake ['neɪmseɪk] *n* homonyme *m* ▪ **she's my ~** nous portons toutes les deux le même nom.

nametape ['neɪmteɪp] *n* marque *f (sur des vêtements)*, griffe *f*.

Namibia [nə'mɪbɪə] *pr n* Namibie *f* ▪ **in ~** en Namibie.

Namibian [nə'mɪbɪən] <> *n* Namibien *m*, - enne *f*.
<> *adj* namibien.

naming ['neɪmɪŋ] *n* **1.** [gen] attribution *f* d'un nom ▪ [of ship] baptême *m* **2.** [citing] mention *f*, citation *f* **3.** [appointment] nomination *f*.

nan *UK* [næn], **nana** ['nænə] *n inf* [grandmother] mémé *f*.

nan bread [nɑ:n-] *n pain plat indien.*

nancy△ ['nænsɪ] *n* : **~ (boy)** pédale *f*△, tapette *f*△.

nanna ['nænə] *UK* = **nan**.

nanny ['nænɪ] (*pl* **nannies**) *n* **1.** [nurse] nurse *f*, bonne *f* d'enfants ▪ **the ~ state** l'État *m* paternaliste **2.** *UK inf* [grandma] mémé *f*, mamie *f*.

nanny goat *n* chèvre *f*.

nanometre, nanometer ['nænəʊ,mi:tər] *US n* nanomètre *m*.

nanosecond ['nænəʊ,sekənd] *n* nanoseconde *f*.

nanotechnology ['nænəʊ,teknɒlədʒɪ] *n* nanotechnologie *f*.

nap [næp] <> *n* **1.** [sleep] somme *m* ▪ **to take** *OR* **to have a ~** faire un (petit) somme ▪ **to take an afternoon ~** faire la sieste **2.** TEX poil *m* **3.** [card game] *jeu de cartes ressemblant au whist.*
<> *vi* (*pret & pp* **napped**, *cont* **napping**) [sleep - gen] faire un (petit) somme ; [- in afternoon] faire la sieste.
<> *vt* (*pret & pp* **napped**, *cont* **napping**) **1.** TEX [cloth] lainer, gratter ▪ [velvet] brosser **2.** [in horse-racing] désigner comme favori, donner gagnant.

napalm ['neɪpɑ:m] <> *n* napalm *m* ▪ **~ bomb** bombe *f* au napalm.
<> *vt* bombarder au napalm.

nape [neɪp] *n* : **the ~ of the neck** la nuque.

naphtha ['næfθə] *n* naphta *m*.

napkin ['næpkɪn] *n* **1.** [on table] serviette *f* (de table) **2.** *UK* [for baby] couche *f*.

napkin ring *n* rond *m* de serviette.

napoleon [nə'pəʊljən] *n* **1.** [coin] napoléon *m* **2.** *US* CULIN mille-feuille *m*.

Napoleon [nə'pəʊljən] *pr n* Napoléon ▪ **~ Bonaparte** Napoléon Bonaparte.

Napoleonic [nə,pəʊlɪ'ɒnɪk] *adj* napoléonien.

nappy ['næpɪ] (*pl* **nappies**) *n UK* couche *f* (pour bébé).

nappy liner *n UK* change *m* (jetable).

nappy rash *n UK* érythème *m* fessier ▪ **babies often get ~** les bébés ont souvent les fesses rouges et irritées.

narcissi [nɑ:'sɪsaɪ] *pl* ▷ **narcissus**.

narcissism ['nɑ:sɪsɪzm] *n* narcissisme *m*.

narcissistic [,nɑ:sɪ'sɪstɪk] *adj* narcissique.

narcissus [nɑ:'sɪsəs] (*pl inv OR pl* **narcissuses** *OR* **narcissi** [nɑ:'sɪsaɪ]) *n* narcisse *m*.

Narcissus [nɑ:'sɪsəs] *pr n* Narcisse.

narcosis [nɑ:'kəʊsɪs] *n* narcose *f*.

narcotic [nɑ:'kɒtɪk] <> *adj* narcotique.
<> *n* **1.** PHARM narcotique *m* **2.** *US* [illegal drug] stupéfiant *m*.

nard *n* nard *m*, spicanard *m*.

nark [nɑ:k] *vt inf* [annoy] mettre en boule *OR* en rogne.

narked [nɑ:kt] *adj UK inf* furibard, furax.

narky ['nɑ:kɪ] (*comp* **narkier**, *superl* **narkiest**) *adj UK inf* rouspéteur, grognon.

narrate [*UK* nə'reɪt, *US* 'næreɪt] *vt* **1.** [relate - story] raconter, narrer *lit* ; [- event] faire le récit de, relater **2.** [read commentary for] : **the film was ~d by an American actor** le commentaire du film a été dit *OR* lu par un acteur américain.

narration [*UK* nə'reɪʃn, *US* næ'reɪʃn] *n* **1.** [narrative] narration *f* **2.** [commentary] commentaire *m*.

narrative ['nærətɪv] ◇ *adj* narratif.
◇ *n* **1.** LIT narration *f* **2.** [story] histoire *f*, récit *m*.

narrator [*UK* nə'reɪtəʳ, *US* 'næreɪtəʳ] *n* narrateur *m*, - trice *f*.

narrow ['nærəʊ] ◇ *adj* **1.** [not wide - street, passage, valley] étroit ■ [tight - skirt, shoe] étroit, serré ■ [long - nose] mince ; [- face] allongé ■ **to grow** *OR* **to become ~** se rétrécir ■ **to have ~ shoulders** être petit de carrure, ne pas être large d'épaules **2.** [scant, small - advantage, budget, majority] petit, faible ■ [close - result] serré ■ **it was another ~ victory/defeat for the French side** l'équipe française l'a encore emporté de justesse/a encore perdu de peu ■ **we had a ~ escape** on l'a échappé belle **3.** [restricted - scope, field, research] restreint, limité ■ [strict - sense, interpretation] restreint, strict ■ **in the ~est sense of the word** au sens strict du mot **4.** [bigoted, illiberal - mind, attitude] borné, étroit ; [- person] borné **5.** *fml* [detailed - search] minutieux, détaillé **6.** LING [vowel] tendu ■ [in phonetics] : **~ transcription** transcription *f* étroite.
◇ *vt* **1.** [make narrow - road] rétrécir ■ **to ~ one's eyes** plisser les yeux **2.** [reduce - difference, gap] réduire, restreindre ■ [limit - search] limiter, restreindre ■ **the police have ~ed their search to a few streets in central Glasgow** la police concentre ses recherches sur quelques rues du centre de Glasgow.
◇ *vi* **1.** [become narrow - road, space] se rétrécir, se resserrer ■ **the old man's eyes ~ed** le vieil homme plissa les yeux **2.** [be reduced - difference, choice] se réduire, se limiter ■ [number, majority] s'amenuiser, se réduire.
◇ *n (usu pl)* [gen] passage *m* étroit ■ [pass] col *m* ■ [strait] détroit *m*.
◆ **narrow down** ◇ *vt sep* [limit - choice, search] limiter, restreindre ■ [reduce - majority, difference] réduire.
◇ *vi insep* [search] se limiter, se restreindre ■ **the choice ~ed down to just two people** il ne restait que deux personnes en lice.

narrow-band *adj* à bande étroite.

narrow boat *n* péniche *f* (étroite).

narrowcast ◇ *vt* diffuser localement.
◇ *vi* diffuser localement des émissions de télévision.

narrow gauge *n* voie *f* étroite.
◆ **narrow-gauge** *adj* [track, line] à voie étroite.

narrowly ['nærəʊlɪ] *adv* **1.** [barely] de justesse, de peu ■ **he ~ avoided capture** il s'en est fallu de peu qu'il (ne) soit capturé **2.** [closely] de près, étroitement **3.** *fml* [strictly] de manière stricte, rigoureusement.

narrow-minded *adj* [person] étroit d'esprit, borné ■ [attitude, opinions] borné.

narrow-mindedness [-'maɪndɪdnɪs] *n* étroitesse *f* d'esprit.

narrowness ['nærəʊnɪs] *n* étroitesse *f*.

narwal, narwhal ['nɑːwəl] *n* narval *m*.

NASA (*abbrev of* **National Aeronautics and Space Administration**) ['næsə] *pr n* NASA *f*.

nasal ['neɪzl] ◇ *adj* **1.** ANAT & LING nasal **2.** [voice, sound] nasillard.
◇ *n* LING nasale *f*.

nasalize, ise ['neɪzəlaɪz] *vt* nasaliser.

nascent ['neɪsənt] *adj* **1.** [in early stages] naissant ■ **a ~ rebellion** un début de rébellion **2.** CHEM naissant.

nastily ['nɑːstɪlɪ] *adv* [unpleasantly - answer, remark] méchamment, avec méchanceté ■ **she cut herself ~ on the knife** elle s'est fait une vilaine blessure avec le couteau.

nastiness ['nɑːstɪnɪs] *n* **1.** [of character] méchanceté *f* **2.** [of injury] gravité *f* **3.** [obscenity] obscénité *f*, indécence *f* **4.** [unpleasantness - of smell, taste] caractère *m* très désagréable.

nasturtium [nəs'tɜːʃəm] *n* capucine *f*.

nasty ['nɑːstɪ] (*comp* **nastier**, *superl* **nastiest**, *pl* **nasties**) ◇ *adj* **1.** [mean, spiteful - person] mauvais, méchant ; [- remark, rumour] désagréable, désobligeant ■ **to be ~ to sb** être méchant avec qqn ■ **he's got a ~ temper** il a un sale caractère **2.** [unpleasant - smell, taste] mauvais, désagréable ; [- impression, surprise] désagréable, déplaisant ; [- weather, job] sale ■ **things started to turn ~** la situation a pris une vilaine tournure ■ [in child language - dragon, giant, wolf] vilain, méchant **3.** [ugly, in bad taste] vilain, laid ● **everything they sell is cheap and ~** ils ne vendent que de la pacotille **4.** [serious - sprain, burn, disease] grave **5.** [dangerous - bend, junction] dangereux **6.** [difficult - problem, question] difficile, épineux **7.** [book, film, scene - violent] violent, dur ; [- obscene] obscène, indécent.
◇ *n inf* [obscene film] film *m* pornographique ■ [violent film] film *m* violent.

NAS/UWT (*abbrev of* **National Association of Schoolmasters/Union of Women Teachers**) *pr n syndicat d'enseignants et de chefs d'établissement en Grande-Bretagne.*

natal ['neɪtl] *adj* natal.

nation ['neɪʃn] *n* **1.** [country] pays *m*, nation *f* ■ **the British ~** la nation britannique ■ **a ~ of shopkeepers** un pays de petits commerçants **2.** [people] nation *f*.

national ['næʃənl] ◇ *adj* national ■ **the ~ newspapers** la presse nationale ■ **the killings caused a ~ outcry** les assassinats ont scandalisé le pays ■ **it's not in the ~ interest** ce n'est pas dans l'intérêt du pays ● **the National Council for Civil Liberties** *en Grande-Bretagne, ligue de défense des droits du citoyen luttant contre toute forme de discrimination* ■ **National Heritage Minister** ≃ ministre *m* de la Culture.
◇ *n* **1.** [person] ressortissant *m*, - e *f* ■ **all EC ~s** tous les ressortissants des pays de la CEE **2.** [newspaper] journal *m* national.

national anthem *n* hymne *m* national.

National Convention *n US* POL *grande réunion du parti démocrate ou républicain pour choisir le "ticket" (candidats à la présidence et à la vice-présidence).*

National Curriculum *n* : **the ~** *programme introduit en 1988 définissant au niveau national (Angleterre et pays de Galles) le contenu de l'enseignement primaire et secondaire.*

national debt *n* : **the ~** la dette publique.

national dress *n* costume *m* national.

National Enquirer *pr n hebdomadaire américain à sensation.*

National Front *pr n* Front *m* national.

national government *n* gouvernement *m* de coalition.

national grid *n* **1.** *UK* ELEC réseau *m* national d'électricité **2.** GEOG réseau *m*.

National Guard *pr n* [in the US] Garde *f* nationale *(armée nationale américaine composée de volontaires).*

National Guardsman *n* membre *m* de la Garde nationale.

National Health Service, National Health *pr n système créé en 1946 en Grande-Bretagne et financé par l'État, assurant la gratuité des soins et des services médicaux,* ≃ Sécurité *f* sociale.

national hunt *n* : **~ (racing)** courses *fpl* d'obstacles.

national income *n* revenu *m* national.

national insurance *n UK système britannique de sécurité sociale (maladie, retraite) et d'assurance chômage* ■ **~ contributions** cotisations *fpl* à la sécurité sociale ■ **~ number** numéro *m* de sécurité sociale.

nationalism ['næʃnəlɪzm] *n* nationalisme *m*.

nationalist ['næʃnəlɪst] <> *adj* nationaliste.
<> *n* nationaliste *mf*.

nationalistic [,næʃnə'lɪstɪk] *adj* nationaliste.

nationality [,næʃə'nælətɪ] (*pl* **nationalities**) *n* nationalité *f*.

nationalization [,næʃnəlaɪ'zeɪʃn] *n* nationalisation *f*.

nationalize, ise ['næʃnəlaɪz] *vt* nationaliser.

nationalized ['næʃnəlaɪzd] *adj* nationalisé.

National League *pr n l'une des deux ligues professionnelles de base-ball aux États-Unis.*

National Lottery *n* Loto *m* britannique.

nationally ['næʃnəlɪ] *adv* nationalement.

national park *n* parc *m* national.

National Power *pr n entreprise privée de production d'électricité en Angleterre et au pays de Galles.*

National Rifle Association *pr n association américaine militant pour le droit au port d'armes.*

national service *n* UK service *m* militaire.

national socialism *n* national-socialisme *m*.

national socialist <> *adj* national-socialiste.
<> *n* national-socialiste *mf*.

National Trust *pr n* : **the ~** *organisme non gouvernemental britannique assurant la conservation de certains paysages et monuments historiques.*

nationhood ['neɪʃənhʊd] *n* statut *m* de nation.

nation-state *n* État-nation *m*.

nationwide ['neɪʃənwaɪd] <> *adj* national, à travers tout le pays.
<> *adv* à l'échelle nationale, dans tout le pays.

native ['neɪtɪv] <> *n* **1.** [of country] natif *m*, - ive *f*, autochtone *mf* ▪ [of town] natif *m*, - ive *f* ▪ **I'm a ~ of Portland** je suis originaire de Portland, je suis né à Portland ▪ **she's a ~ of Belgium** elle est belge de naissance, elle est née en Belgique ▪ **she speaks English like a ~** elle parle anglais comme si c'était sa langue maternelle *OR* comme les Anglais **2.** *pej* [primitive] indigène *m* **3.** BOT [plant] plante *f* indigène ▪ ZOOL [animal] animal *m* indigène ▪ [species] espèce *f* indigène.
<> *adj* **1.** [by birth] natif ▪ **~ Indians** Indiens *mpl* de naissance *OR* de souche ▪ **Portland honours its ~ sons** Portland rend hommage à ses enfants ▮ [of birth - country] natal ; [- language] maternel ▪ **he always writes in his ~ Russian** il écrit toujours en russe, sa langue maternelle **2.** [indigenous - resources] du pays ; [- tribe, customs] indigène **3.** [innate - ability, attraction] inné, naturel **4.** BOT & ZOOL indigène, originaire ▪ **~ to India** originaire de l'Inde **5.** MINER [ore, silver] natif.

Native American *n* Indien *m*, - enne *f* d'Amérique, Amérindien *m*, - enne *f*.

Native Australian *n* aborigène *mf*.

native speaker *n* LING locuteur *m* natif, locutrice *f* native ▪ **a ~ of French/German, a French/German ~** un francophone/germanophone, une personne de langue maternelle française/allemande.

nativity [nə'tɪvətɪ] (*pl* **nativities**) *n* **1.** RELIG : **the Nativity** la Nativité **2.** [birth] horoscope *m*.

Nativity play *n pièce jouée par des enfants et représentant l'histoire de la Nativité.*

NATO ['neɪtəʊ] (*abbrev of* **North Atlantic Treaty Organization**) *pr n* OTAN *f*.

natter ['nætəʳ] *inf* <> *vi* UK papoter.
<> *n* papotage *m* ▪ **to have a ~** tailler une bavette, faire la causette *OR* un brin de causette.

natty ['nætɪ] (*comp* **nattier**, *superl* **nattiest**) *adj inf* **1.** [smart, neat - person] bien sapé ; [- dress] chic, qui a de l'allure **2.** [clever - device] astucieux.

natural ['nætʃrəl] <> *adj* **1.** [created by nature - scenery, resources] naturel ▪ [wild - prairie, woodland] à l'état naturel, sauvage ▪ **the Natural State** l'Arkansas *m* **2.** [not artificial - wood, finish] naturel ▪ **she's a ~ redhead** c'est une vraie rousse **3.** [normal - explanation, reaction, wish] naturel, normal ▪ **it's only ~ for her to be worried** *OR* **that she should be worried** il est tout à fait normal *OR* il est tout naturel qu'elle se fasse du souci ▪ **death from ~ causes** mort *f* naturelle **4.** [unaffected - person, manner] naturel, simple **5.** [innate - talent] inné, naturel ▪ **she's a ~ organizer** c'est une organisatrice née, elle a un sens inné de l'organisation **6.** [free of additives] naturel ▪ **~ yoghurt** yaourt *m* nature **7.** [child] naturel **8.** [real - parents] naturel **9.** MUS naturel ▪ [after accidental] bécarre *(inv)* **10.** MATHS naturel **11.** INDUST : **~ wastage** départs *mpl* naturels ▪ **~ person** LAW personne *f* physique *OR* naturelle.
<> *adv inf* : **try to act ~!** soyez naturel!
<> *n* **1.** *inf* [gifted person] : **she's a ~** elle a ça dans le sang ▪ **he's a ~ for the part of Banquo** il serait parfait dans le rôle de Banquo **2.** MUS bécarre *m*.

natural childbirth *n* accouchement *m* naturel.

natural disaster *n* catastrophe *f* naturelle.

natural gas *n* gaz *m* naturel.

natural history *n* histoire *f* naturelle.

naturalism ['nætʃrəlɪzm] *n* naturalisme *m*.

naturalist ['nætʃrəlɪst] *n* naturaliste *mf*.

naturalistic [,nætʃrə'lɪstɪk] *adj* naturaliste.

naturalize, ise ['nætʃrəlaɪz] <> *vt* [person, expression, custom] naturaliser ▪ [plant, animal] acclimater.
<> *vi* BIOL s'acclimater.

natural justice *n* droits *mpl* naturels.

natural language *n* langage *m* naturel, langue *f* naturelle.

natural law *n* loi *f* naturelle.

naturally ['nætʃrəlɪ] *adv* **1.** [of course] naturellement, bien sûr, bien entendu ▪ **you have got the money? – ~!** tu as l'argent? – cela va de soi! ▪ **I was ~ surprised** évidemment, cela m'a surpris **2.** [by nature - lazy] de nature, par tempérament ; [- difficult] naturellement, par sa nature ▪ **skiing comes ~ to her** on dirait qu'elle a fait du ski toute sa vie **3.** [unaffectedly] naturellement, de manière naturelle **4.** [in natural state - occur] naturellement, à l'état naturel.

naturalness ['nætʃrəlnɪs] *n* **1.** [unaffectedness] naturel *m*, simplicité *f* **2.** [natural appearance] naturel *m*.

natural number *n* nombre *m* naturel.

natural science *n* **1.** *(U)* sciences *fpl* naturelles **2.** *(countable)* **botany is a ~** la botanique fait partie des sciences naturelles.

natural selection *n* sélection *f* naturelle.

nature ['neɪtʃəʳ] *n* **1.** nature *f* ▪ **Nature can be cruel** la nature peut être cruelle ▪ **to go back** *OR* **to return to ~** retourner à la nature ▪ **the ~-nurture debate** le débat sur l'inné et l'acquis *OR* sur la nature et la culture ▪ **to let ~ take its course** laisser faire la nature **2.** [character] nature *f*, caractère *m* ▪ **he has such a kind ~** il a une si bonne nature *OR* un si bon caractère ▪ **it's not in her ~ to struggle** ce n'est pas dans sa nature de lutter ▪ **lazy by ~** paresseux de nature ▪ **to appeal to sb's better ~** faire appel aux bons sentiments de qqn ▪ **human beings are by ~ gregarious** l'homme est, par nature, un être grégaire ▪ **war is by its very ~ destructive** la guerre est destructrice par nature ▪ **in the ~ of things** dans la nature des choses **3.** [type] nature *f*, type *m*, genre *m* ▪ **books of a serious ~** des livres sérieux ▪ **do you sell chocolates or anything of that ~?** est-ce que vous vendez des chocolats ou ce genre de choses?
◆ **in the nature of** *prep phr* en guise de, à titre de.

nature cure *n* naturopathie *f*, naturothérapie *f*.

-natured ['neɪtʃəd] *in cpds* d'une nature..., d'un caractère... ▪ **she's good/ill~** elle a bon/mauvais caractère.

nature lover *n* amoureux *m*, - euse *f* de la nature.

nature-loving *adj* qui adore la nature.

nature reserve *n* réserve *f* naturelle.

nature study *n* SCH sciences *fpl* naturelles, histoire *f* naturelle.

nature trail *n* sentier *m* (de découverte de la) nature.

naturism ['neɪtʃərɪzm] *n* naturisme *m*.

naturist ['neɪtʃərɪst] ◇ *adj* naturiste.
◇ *n* naturiste *mf*.

naugahide® ['nɔːgəhaɪd] *n* US ≃ Skaï®.

naught [nɔːt] ◇ *n* **1.** = **nought** *(sense 1)* **2.** *arch* & *lit* [nothing] : **their plans came to ~** leurs projets ont échoué OR n'ont pas abouti ■ **they set my ideas at ~** ils ne font aucun cas OR ils ne tiennent aucun compte de mes idées.
◇ *adv arch* & *lit* nullement.

naughtily ['nɔːtɪlɪ] *adv* **1.** [mischievously] avec malice, malicieusement ■ **you have behaved very ~** tu as été très vilain **2.** [suggestively] avec grivoiserie.

naughtiness ['nɔːtɪnɪs] *n* **1.** [disobedience] désobéissance *f* ■ [mischievousness] malice *f* **2.** [indecency] grivoiserie *f*, gaillardise *f*.

naughty ['nɔːtɪ] (*comp* **naughtier**, *superl* **naughtiest**) *adj* **1.** [badly behaved - child] méchant, désobéissant, vilain ■ **that was very ~ of you** ce que tu as fait était très vilain ■ **you ~ boy!** petit vilain! ■ [mischievous] coquin, malicieux **2.** [indecent - joke, story, postcard] paillard, osé ; [- word] vilain, gros, grosse *f* **3.** [sexy] sexy *(inv)* ■ **~ underwear** dessous *mpl* sexy.

Nauru ['naʊruː] *n* Nauru *m*.

nausea ['nɔːsjə] *n* nausée *f*.

nauseate ['nɔːsɪeɪt] *vt liter* & *fig* donner la nausée à, écœurer.

nauseating ['nɔːsɪeɪtɪŋ] *adj* [food, sight, idea] écœurant, qui donne la nausée ■ [smell] écœurant, nauséabond ■ [person, behaviour] écœurant, dégoûtant, répugnant ■ **the stench was ~** la puanteur vous levait OR soulevait le cœur.

nauseatingly ['nɔːsɪeɪtɪŋlɪ] *adv* à vous donner la nausée, à vous écœurer.

nauseous [UK 'nɔːsjəs, US 'nɔːʃəs] *adj* **1.** [revolting - smell] nauséabond, qui donne la nausée, écœurant **2.** [unwell - person] écœuré ■ **it made me feel ~** cela m'a levé OR soulevé le cœur **3.** *US inf* [disgusting] dégueulasse.

nautical ['nɔːtɪkl] *adj* nautique.

nautical mile *n* mille *m* marin.

Navajo ['nævəhəʊ] (*pl inv* OR *pl* **Navajos** OR *pl* **Navajoes**) ◇ *n* [person] Navajo *mf* ■ **the ~** les Navajos.
◇ *adj* navajo.

naval ['neɪvl] *adj* [gen] naval ■ [power] maritime ■ **~ base** base *f* navale ■ **~ officer** officier *m* de marine.

naval architect *n* architecte *m* naval, architecte *f* navale ■ [for warships] ingénieur *m* du génie maritime OR en construction navale.

naval architecture *n* construction *f* navale.

nave [neɪv] *n* **1.** [of church] nef *f* **2.** [hub] moyeu *m*.

navel ['neɪvl] *n* nombril *m*.

navel-gazing [-ˌgeɪzɪŋ] *n* nombrilisme *m*.

navigable ['nævɪgəbl] *adj* [water] navigable ■ [craft] dirigeable.

navigate ['nævɪgeɪt] ◇ *vt* **1.** [chart course of - ship] calculer le parcours de ; [- car, aircraft] être le navigateur de ■ **she ~d us successfully through Bombay** elle nous a fait traverser Bombay sans problèmes ■ **he ~d the plane to the nearest airport** il dirigea l'avion sur l'aéroport le plus proche **2.** [sail] : **to ~ the Atlantic** traverser l'Atlantique (en bateau) ■ **they ~d the seven seas** ils naviguaient sur OR parcouraient toutes les mers du globe **3.** *fig* **the stairs are difficult to ~ in the dark** cet escalier est difficile à monter/descendre dans l'obscurité ■ **she ~d her way across the crowded room** elle se fraya un chemin à travers la salle bondée.
◇ *vi* **1.** [plot course] naviguer ■ **to ~ by the stars** naviguer aux étoiles ■ [in car] : **can you ~ for me?** peux-tu m'indiquer la route OR me piloter? **2.** COMPUT naviguer, surfer.

navigation [ˌnævɪ'geɪʃn] *n* **1.** [act, skill of navigating] navigation *f* **2.** *US* [shipping] navigation *f*, trafic *m* (maritime) **3.** COMPUT navigation *f*, surf *m* sur l'Internet.

navigational [ˌnævɪ'geɪʃnl] *adj* de (la) navigation.

navigation lights *npl* AERON feux *mpl* de position ■ NAUT fanaux *mpl*, feux *mpl* de bord OR de route.

navigator ['nævɪgeɪtəʳ] *n* navigateur *m*, - trice *f*.

navvy ['nævɪ] (*pl* **navvies**) *n UK inf* terrassier *m*.

navy ['neɪvɪ] (*pl* **navies**) ◇ *n* **1.** [service] marine *f* (nationale) **2.** [warships collectively] marine *f* de guerre ■ [fleet] flotte *f* **3.** = **navy blue**.
◇ *adj* **1.** de la marine **2.** = **navy-blue**.

navy blue *n* bleu *m* marine.
◆ **navy-blue** *adj* bleu marine *(inv)*.

navy yard *n* arsenal *m* maritime.

nay [neɪ] ◇ *adv arch* & *hum* voire, que dis-je.
◇ *n* vote *m* défavorable ■ **the ~s have it** les non l'emportent.

Nazareth ['næzərəθ] *pr n* Nazareth.

Nazi ['nɑːtsɪ] ◇ *adj* nazi.
◇ *n* nazi *m*, - e *f*.

Nazism ['nɑːtsɪzm], **Naziism** ['nɑːtsɪˌɪzm] *n* nazisme *m*.

NB 1. (*written abbrev of* **nota bene**) NB **2.** *written abbr of* **New Brunswick**.

NBC ◇ *pr n* (*abbrev of* **National Broadcasting Company**) *chaîne de télévision américaine*.
◇ *adj* (*abbrev of* **nuclear, biological and chemical**) NBC.

NC 1. *written abbr of* **no charge 2.** *written abbr of* **North Carolina 3.** (*abbrev of* **network computer**) NC *m*.

NCC (*abbrev of* **Nature Conservancy Council**) *pr n organisme britannique de protection de la nature*.

NCCL *pr n* = **National Council for Civil Liberties**.

NCO (*abbrev of* **non-commissioned officer**) *n* sous-officier *m*.

NCU (*abbrev of* **National Communications Union**) *pr n syndicat des salariés qui travaillent dans les télécommunications*.

ND *written abbr of* **North Dakota**.

NE 1. *written abbr of* **Nebraska 2.** *written abbr of* **New England 3.** (*written abbrev of* **north-east**) N. E.

Neanderthal, neanderthal [nɪ'ændətɑːl] ◇ *adj* **1.** ANTHR néandertalien, de Neandertal **2.** [uncivilized] fruste, inculte, primitif **3.** *inf* POL réac.
◇ *n* néandertalien *m*.

Neanderthal man *n* l'homme *m* de Neandertal.

neap [niːp] ◇ *adj* faible.
◇ *n* = **neap tide**.

Neapolitan [ˌnɪə'pɒlɪtn] ◇ *n* Napolitain *m*, - e *f*.
◇ *adj* napolitain ■ **~ ice cream** tranche *f* napolitaine.

neap tide *n* (marée *f* de) morte-eau *f*.

near [nɪəʳ] (*comp* **nearer**, *superl* **nearest**) ◇ *prep* **1.** [in space] près de ■ **don't go ~ the fire** ne t'approche pas du feu ■ **is there a chemist's ~ here?** est-ce qu'il y a un pharmacien près d'ici OR dans le coin? ■ **~ the end of the book** vers la fin du livre ■ **I haven't been ~ a horse since the accident** je n'ai pas approché un cheval depuis l'accident ■ **you can't trust him ~ a gun** il est dangereux avec une arme à feu ■ **she wouldn't let anyone ~ her** [physically] elle ne voulait pas qu'on l'approche ; [emotionally] elle ne voulait être proche de personne

2. [in time] près de, proche de ■ **it's getting ~ Christmas** c'est bientôt Noël ■ **ask me ~er the time** repose-moi la question quand l'heure viendra ■ **~ the end of the film** vers la fin du film

3. [similar to] près de ■ **that would be ~er the truth** ce serait plus près de la vérité

4. [in amount or number] : **profits were ~ the 30% mark** les bénéfices approchaient la barre des 30 % ■ **it took us ~er three hours to finish** en fait, nous avons mis presque trois heures à finir ■ **it will cost ~er £5,000** ça coûtera plutôt dans les 5 000 livres

5. [on the point of] près de, au bord de ■ **it's ~ freezing** il ne fait pas loin de zéro, la température avoisine zéro degré.

◇ *adv* **1.** [in space] près, à côté, à proximité ■ **to draw ~** s'approcher ■ **the heat was too great for us to get ~** la chaleur était trop intense pour que l'on puisse s'approcher ▶ **so ~ and yet so far!** c'est dommage, si près du but!

2. [in time] proche, près ■ **as the time grew** *OR* **drew ~** à mesure que le moment approchait

3. [with adjective] quasi ■ **a ~ impossible task** une tâche quasi *OR* quasiment *OR* pratiquement impossible

4. *phr* **as ~ as makes no difference** à peu de chose près, à quelque chose près ■ **£50 or as ~ as dammit** *inf* 50 livres à peu de chose près ■ **it's ~ enough** ça va comme ça ■ **it's ~ enough 50 lbs** ça pèse dans les 50 livres ■ **it's nowhere ~ good enough** c'est loin d'être suffisant ■ **there weren't anywhere ~ enough people** il y avait bien trop peu de gens.

◇ *adj* **1.** [in space] proche ■ **the ~ edge** le bord le plus proche ■ **I knew you were ~** je savais que vous étiez dans les environs *OR* parages ■ **the ~ front wheel** [driving on left] la roue avant gauche ; [driving on right] la roue avant droite

2. [in time] proche ■ **when the time is ~** quand le moment approchera ■ **in the ~ future** dans un proche avenir

3. [virtual] : **it was a ~ disaster** on a frôlé la catastrophe ■ **he found himself in ~ darkness** il s'est retrouvé dans une obscurité quasi totale ▶ **it was a ~ thing** on l'a échappé belle, il était moins une ■ **I caught the train, but it was a ~ thing** j'ai eu mon train de justesse ■ **I missed the train, but it was a ~ thing** j'ai manqué mon train de peu ■ **he's the ~est thing we have to a national hero** il est ce que nous avons de mieux en matière de héros national

4. [in amount, number] : **to the ~est £10** à 10 livres près

5. [closely related] proche ■ **your ~est and dearest** *hum* vos proches.

◇ *vt* [approach - place, date, event] approcher de ; [- state] être au bord de ■ **he was ~ing 70 when he got married** il allait sur ses 70 ans quand il s'est marié ■ **the book is ~ing completion** le livre est sur le point d'être terminé.

◇ *vi* [subj: date, place] approcher.

◆ **near to** *prep phr* **1.** [in space] près de ■ [emotionally] proche de

2. [in time] près de, proche de ■ **it's getting ~ to Christmas** Noël approche

3. [in similarity] près de

4. [on the point of] près de, au bord de ■ **to be ~ to death** être sur le point de mourir ■ **to be ~ to tears** être au bord des larmes ■ **I came ~ to leaving several times** j'ai failli partir plusieurs fois.

near- *in cpds* : **~perfect** pratiquement *OR* quasi parfait ■ **~complete** pratiquement *OR* quasi complet.

nearby ◇ *adv* [ˌnɪəˈbaɪ] [near here] près d'ici ■ [near there] près de là ■ **is there a station ~?** est-ce qu'il y a une gare près d'ici *OR* à proximité?

◇ *adj* [ˈnɪəbaɪ] : **we stopped at a ~ post office** nous nous sommes arrêtés dans un bureau de poste situé non loin de là.

Near East *pr n* : **the ~** le Proche-Orient.

nearly [ˈnɪəlɪ] *adv* **1.** [almost] presque, à peu près ■ **we're ~ there** on y est presque ■ **he's ~ 80** il a presque 80 ans ■ **I ~ fell** j'ai failli tomber ■ **I very ~ didn't come** j'ai bien failli ne pas venir ■ **he was ~ crying** *OR* **in tears** il était au bord des larmes **2.** [with negative] : **I didn't buy ~ enough food for everyone** je suis loin d'avoir acheté assez de provisions pour tout le monde ■ **it's not ~ as difficult as I thought** c'est bien moins difficile que je ne l'imaginais.

near miss *n* **1.** [gen - SPORT] coup *m* qui a raté de peu ■ **it was a ~** FTBL il s'en est fallu de peu qu'on marque, on a failli marquer un but ; [answer] la réponse était presque bonne ; [accident] on a frôlé l'accident ■ **that was a ~!** [escape] on l'a échappé belle! **2.** [between planes, vehicles etc] quasi-collision *f*.

nearness [ˈnɪənɪs] *n* proximité *f*.

nearside [ˈnɪəsaɪd] *UK* ◇ *adj* AUT [when driving on right] (du côté) droit, du côté trottoir ■ [when driving on left] (du côté) gauche, du côté trottoir.

◇ *n* [when driving on right] côté *m* droit ■ [when driving on left] côté *m* gauche ■ **get out on the ~** descendez côté trottoir.

nearsighted [ˌnɪəˈsaɪtɪd] *adj US* myope.

neat [niːt] *adj* **1.** [tidy - in dress] net, soigné ; [- desk, room] net, bien rangé ; [- garden] bien tenu *OR* entretenu, soigné ■ [careful - work, handwriting] soigné **2.** [smart, pretty] joli ■ **a ~ little house** une gentille petite maison **3.** [effective - organization] net, efficace ; [- system, plan] bien conçu ; [- solution] élégant **4.** *US inf* [great] chouette **5.** [undiluted - spirits] sec, sèche *f*, sans eau **6.** [tax-free] : **we made a ~ £100** on a fait 100 livres net.

neaten [ˈniːtn] *vt* [room, house] remettre en ordre, ranger ■ [garden] ranger ■ [clothing] arranger, ajuster ■ [hair] arranger, mettre en ordre ■ **you ought to ~ (up) the place before they arrive** tu devrais mettre un peu d'ordre dans la maison avant qu'ils arrivent.

'neath, neath [niːθ] *lit* = **beneath**.

neat-looking *adj US inf* mignon ■ **he's a ~ guy** il est mignon.

neatly [ˈniːtlɪ] *adv* **1.** [tidily] avec soin *OR* ordre ■ [carefully - write, work] avec soin, soigneusement ■ **put the papers ~ on the desk** posez les papiers soigneusement sur le bureau **2.** [skilfully] habilement, adroitement ■ **you got out of the situation very ~** vous vous en êtes magnifiquement tiré.

neatness [ˈniːtnɪs] *n* **1.** [tidiness - of dress] soin *m*, netteté *f* ; [- of room] ordre *m* ■ [carefulness - of work] soin *m* ■ **the ~ of her writing** l'élégance *f* de son écriture **2.** [skilfulness - of phrase, solution] élégance *f* ; [- of scheme] habileté *f*.

Nebraska [nɪˈbræskə] *pr n* Nebraska *m* ■ **in ~** dans le Nebraska.

Nebuchadnezar [ˌnebjʊkədˈnezəʳ] ◇ *n* [bottle] nabuchodonosor *m*.

◇ *pr n* Nabuchodonosor.

nebula [ˈnebjʊlə] (*pl* **nebulas** *OR pl* **nebulae** [-liː]) *n* **1.** ASTRON nébuleuse *f* **2.** MED [of cornea] nébulosité *f* ■ [of urine] aspect *m* trouble.

nebular [ˈnebjʊləʳ] *adj* **1.** ASTRON nébulaire **2.** MED [cornea] nébuleux ■ [urine] trouble.

nebulous [ˈnebjʊləs] *adj* **1.** [vague] vague, flou, nébuleux **2.** ASTRON nébulaire **3.** MED [of cornea] nébuleux **4.** *lit* [misty] brumeux.

NEC (*abbrev of* **National Exhibition Centre**) *pr n centre de conférences et d'expositions près de Birmingham en Angleterre.*

necessarily [ˌnesəˈserɪlɪ] *adv* nécessairement, forcément ■ **we don't ~ have to go** rien ne nous oblige à partir, nous ne sommes pas forcés de partir ■ **not ~** pas forcément.

necessary [ˈnesəsrɪ] (*pl* **necessaries**) ◇ *adj* **1.** [essential] nécessaire, essentiel ■ [indispensable] indispensable ■ [compulsory] obligatoire ■ **water is ~ to** *OR* **for life** l'eau est indispensable à la vie ■ **it is ~ for him to come** il est nécessaire qu'il vienne, il faut qu'il vienne ■ **circumstances made it ~ to delay our departure** les circonstances nous ont obligés à retarder notre départ ■ **I'll do everything ~ to make her agree** je ferai tout pour qu'elle accepte ■ **he did no more than was ~** il n'a fait que le strict nécessaire ■ **if ~** [if forced] s'il le faut ; [if need arises] le cas échéant, si besoin est ■ **a ~ condition** [gen] une condition nécessaire *OR* sine qua non ; PHILOS une condition nécessaire ■ **he took the ~ measures** il a pris les mesures nécessaires *OR* qui s'imposaient **2.** [inevitable] nécessaire, iné-

luctable ▪ **a ~ evil** un mal nécessaire ▪ **you can draw the ~ conclusion yourself** vous pouvez vous-même tirer les conclusions qui s'imposent.
◇ *n* **1.** *UK inf* **to do the ~** faire le nécessaire **2.** *UK inf* [cash] : **have you got the ~?** tu as de quoi payer?

necessitate [nɪ'sesɪteɪt] *vt* nécessiter, rendre nécessaire.

necessitous [nɪ'sesɪtəs] *adj fml* nécessiteux, démuni, pauvre.

necessity [nɪ'sesətɪ] (*pl* **necessities**) *n* **1.** [need] nécessité *f*, besoin *m* ▪ **there is no ~ for drastic measures** il n'y a pas lieu de prendre des mesures draconiennes ▪ **there's no real ~ for us to go** nous n'avons pas vraiment besoin d'y aller, il n'est pas indispensable que nous y allions ▪ **the ~ for** *OR* **of keeping careful records** la nécessité de prendre des notes détaillées ▪ **in case of absolute ~** en cas de force majeure ▪ **out of** *OR* **by** *OR* **through ~** par nécessité, par la force des choses ➜ **~ has no law** *prov* nécessité fait loi *prov* ▪ **~ is the mother of invention** *prov* nécessité est mère d'industrie **2.** *fml* [poverty] besoin *m*, nécessité *f* **3.** [essential] chose *f* nécessaire *OR* essentielle ▪ **the basic** *OR* **bare necessities of life** les choses qui sont absolument essentielles *OR* indispensables à la vie **4.** PHILOS nécessité *f*.
◆ **of necessity** *adv phr* nécessairement.

neck [nek] ◇ *n* **1.** ANAT cou *m* ▪ **he threw his arms round her ~** il s'est jeté à son *OR* il lui a sauté au cou ▪ **the cat had a collar round its ~** le chat avait un collier au cou ▪ **to get a stiff ~** attraper le torticolis ▪ *fig* **he's always breathing down my ~** il est tout le temps sur mon dos ▪ **they were up to their ~s in debt** ils étaient endettés jusqu'au cou ▪ **I'm up to my ~ in trouble** j'ai des ennuis par-dessus la tête ▪ **to risk one's ~** risquer sa peau ➜ **she'll get it in the ~** *UK inf* ça va chauffer pour son matricule ▪ **he was thrown out ~ and crop** *OR* **on his ~** *UK* il a été mis à la porte avec pertes et fracas ▪ **it's ~ or nothing** *UK inf* ça passe ou ça casse ▪ **to stick one's ~ out** prendre des risques
2. CULIN [of lamb] collet *m* ▪ [of beef] collier *m*
3. SPORT : **to win by a ~** gagner d'une encolure ➜ **to be ~ and ~** être à égalité ▪ **the two candidates are ~ and ~** les deux candidats sont au coude à coude
4. [narrow part or extremity - of bottle, flask] goulot *m*, col *m* ; [- of pipe] tuyau *m* ; [- of womb, femur] col *m* ; [- of violin] manche *m* ; [- of bolt, tooth] collet *m*
5. GEOG [peninsula] péninsule *f*, presqu'île *f* ▪ [strait] détroit *m* ▪ **a ~ of land** une langue de terre ➜ **in our ~ of the woods** par chez nous
6. [of dress, pullover] col *m*, encolure *f* ▪ **a dress with a low ~** une robe décolletée ▪ **what ~ size** *OR* **what size ~ do you take?** combien faites-vous de tour de cou?
7. *UK inf* [cheek] toupet *m*, culot *m*.
◇ *vi inf* se bécoter, se peloter.

neckband ['nekbænd] *n* bande *f* d'encolure.

-necked [nekt] *in cpds* à col... ▪ **swan~** en col de cygne ▪ **a V/round~ pullover** un pull en V/ras du cou.

neckerchief ['nekətʃɪf] *n* foulard *m*.

necking ['nekɪŋ] *n inf* pelotage *m*.

necklace ['neklɪs] *n* collier *m*.

neckline ['neklaɪn] *n* col *m*, encolure *f* ▪ **her dress had a low/plunging ~** elle avait une robe décolletée/très décolletée.

necktie ['nektaɪ] *n US* cravate *f* ▪ **~ party** *inf* lynchage *m*.

necrology [ne'krɒlədʒɪ] *n* nécrologie *f*.

necromancy ['nekrəmænsɪ] *n* nécromancie *f*.

necrophilia [ˌnekrə'fɪlɪə] *n* nécrophilie *f*.

necropolis [ne'krɒpəlɪs] *n* nécropole *f*.

nectar ['nektəʳ] *n* BOT & *fig* nectar *m*.

nectarine ['nektərɪn] *n* nectarine *f*.

neddy ['nedɪ] (*pl* **neddies**) *n inf UK* [donkey] baudet *m*.

née, nee [neɪ] *adj fml* **Sarah James, ~ White** Sarah James née White.

need [ni:d] ◇ *vt* **1.** [as basic requirement] avoir besoin de ▪ **have you got everything you ~?** est-ce que tu as tout ce qu'il te faut? ▪ **he likes to feel ~ed** il aime se sentir indispensable ▪ **a lot of money is ~ed if we are to save the company** il va falloir beaucoup d'argent pour empêcher l'entreprise de couler ▪ **you only ~ to ask** vous n'avez qu'à demander ▪ **you don't ~ me to tell you that** vous devez le savoir mieux que moi ▪ **the carpet ~s cleaning** la moquette a besoin d'être nettoyée
2. [would benefit from] : **I ~ a drink/a shower** j'ai besoin de boire quelque chose/de prendre une douche ▪ **it's just what I ~** c'est exactement ce qu'il me faut ▪ **that's all we ~!** *iron* il ne nous manquait plus que ça! ▪ **who ~s money anyway?** de toute façon, l'argent n'a aucune importance ▪ **liquid nitrogen ~s careful handling** *OR* **to be handled with care** l'azote liquide demande à être manié avec précaution ▪ **there are still a few points that ~ to be made** il reste encore quelques questions à soulever
3. [expressing obligation] : **to ~ to do sthg** avoir besoin de *OR* être obligé de faire qqch ▪ **I ~ to be home by ten** il faut que je sois rentré *OR* je dois être rentré pour 10 h ▪ **you ~ to try harder** tu vas devoir faire *OR* il va falloir que tu fasses un effort supplémentaire ▪ **I'll help you – you don't ~ to** je vais t'aider – tu n'es pas obligé.
◇ *modal vb* : **you needn't come if you don't want to** vous n'avez pas besoin de *OR* vous n'êtes pas obligé de venir si vous n'en avez pas envie ▪ **I needn't tell you how important it is** je n'ai pas besoin de vous dire *OR* vous savez à quel point c'est important ▪ **I needn't have bothered** je me suis donné bien du mal pour rien, ce n'était pas la peine que je me donne autant de mal ▪ **the accident ~ never have happened** cet accident aurait pu être évité ▪ **no-one else ~ ever know** ça reste entre nous ▪ **~ I say more?** ai-je besoin d'en dire davantage *OR* plus? ▪ **~ that be the case?** est-ce nécessairement *OR* forcément le cas?
◇ *n* **1.** [necessity] besoin *m* ▪ **I have no ~ of your sympathy** je n'ai que faire de votre sympathie ▪ **phone me if you feel the ~ for a chat** appelle-moi si tu as besoin de parler ▪ **there's no ~ to adopt that tone** inutile d'employer ce ton ▪ **there's no ~ to panic** *OR* **for any panic** inutile de paniquer ▪ **I'll help with the dishes – no ~, I've done them already** je vais vous aider à faire la vaisselle – inutile, c'est terminé ▪ **to be in ~ of sthg** avoir besoin de qqch ▪ **should the ~ arise** si cela s'avérait nécessaire, si le besoin s'en faisait sentir ▪ **your ~ is greater than mine** *hum* vous en avez plus besoin que moi
2. [requirement] besoin *m* ▪ **he saw to her every ~** il subvenait à ses moindres besoins ▪ **the grant is ~s-based** le montant de la bourse est établi selon les besoins du demandeur
3. [poverty] besoin *m*, nécessité *f* ▪ [adversity] adversité *f*, besoin *m* ▪ **to be in ~** être dans le besoin.
◆ **if need(s) be** *adv phr* si besoin est, le cas échéant.

needful ['ni:dfʊl] ◇ *adj fml* nécessaire, requis.
◇ *n UK inf* **1.** *phr* **to do the ~** faire le nécessaire **2.** [money] : **to find the ~** trouver le fric.

needle ['ni:dl] ◇ *n* **1.** MED & SEW aiguille *f* ▪ [for record player] pointe *f* de lecture, saphir *m* ▪ [of pine-tree] aiguille *f* ▪ [spine - of hedgehog] piquant *m* ▪ **it's like looking for a ~ in a haystack** c'est comme si l'on cherchait une aiguille dans une botte de foin **2.** [as indicator - in compass, on dial] aiguille *f* **3.** GEOL [rocky outcrop] aiguille *f*, pic *m* **4.** [monument] aiguille *f*, flèche *f* **5.** *UK inf* **a bit of ~ has crept into the match** les joueurs commencent à s'énerver *OR* disputent le match avec plus d'âpreté ➜ **to get the ~** prendre la mouche ▪ **to give sb the ~** [tease] chambrer qqn ; [annoy] taper sur les nerfs de qqn.
◇ *vt* **1.** *inf* [annoy] asticoter ▪ [tease] chambrer **2.** *US* [drink] corser **3.** SEW coudre.

needlecord ['ni:dlkɔ:d] *n* velours *m* côtelé.

needlecraft ['ni:dlkrɑ:ft] *n* travaux *mpl* d'aiguille.

needle exchange scheme *n* programme *m* d'échange de seringues.

needlepoint ['ni:dlpɔɪnt] ◇ *n* [embroidery] broderie *f*, tapisserie *f* ▪ [lace] dentelle *f* à l'aiguille.
◇ *comp* : **~ lace** dentelle *f* brodée.

needle-sharp *adj* [point] acéré ▪ [eyes] de lynx ▪ [mind] fin, perspicace.

needless 660 neighbour

needless ['ni:dlɪs] *adj* [unnecessary - expense, effort, fuss] superflu, inutile ; [- remark] inopportun, déplacé ▪ **~ to say I won't go** il va sans dire que je n'irai pas.

needlessly ['ni:dlɪslɪ] *adv* inutilement.

needlewoman ['ni:dl,wʊmən] (*pl* **needlewomen** [-,wɪmɪn]) *n* couturière *f*.

needlework ['ni:dlwɜ:k] *n (U)* travaux *mpl* d'aiguille, couture *f*.

needling ['ni:dlɪŋ] *n (U)* taquineries *fpl*.

needn't [ni:dnt] = **need not**.

needs [ni:dz] *adv* ***arch*** & ***hum*** **if ~ must, I shall go** s'il le faut absolument *OR* si c'est indispensable, j'irai ▶ **~ must when the devil drives** ***prov*** nécessité fait loi ***prov***.

needs test *n* ***UK*** examen *m* des conditions de vie *(pour bénéficier d'une aide de l'État)*.

needy ['ni:dɪ] (*comp* **needier**, *superl* **neediest**) ◇ *adj* [financially] nécessiteux, dans le besoin ▪ [emotionally] en manque d'affection.
◇ *npl* : **the ~** les nécessiteux *mpl*.

ne'er [neəʳ] ***lit*** = **never** *(adv)*.

ne'er-do-well *n* bon *m* à rien, bonne *f* à rien.

nefarious [nɪ'feərɪəs] *adj* infâme, vil.

Nefertiti [,nefə'ti:tɪ] *pr n* Néfertiti.

negate [nɪ'geɪt] *vt* **1.** [nullify - law] abroger ; [- order] annuler ; [- efforts] réduire à néant ; [- argument, theory] invalider, rendre non valide **2.** [deny] réfuter, nier.

negation [nɪ'geɪʃn] *n* négation *f*.

negative ['negətɪv] ◇ *adj* négatif ▪ **she's always so ~ about my plans** elle trouve toujours quelque chose à redire à mes projets ▶ **~ earth** ELEC négatif *m*, terre *f* reliée au moins.
◇ *n* **1.** GRAM négation *f* ▪ **in the ~** à la forme négative **2.** [answer] réponse *f* négative, non *m* ▪ **to reply in the ~** répondre négativement *OR* par la négative **3.** PHOT négatif *m* **4.** ELEC & PHYS (pôle *m*) négatif *m*.
◇ *vt* **1.** [cancel - instruction] annuler ▪ [nullify - effect] neutraliser, réduire à néant **2.** [reject - proposition, evidence] rejeter, repousser **3.** [deny] nier, réfuter.

negative equity *n (U) situation où l'acquéreur d'un bien immobilier reste redevable de l'emprunt contracté alors que son logement enregistre une moins-value.*

negative feedback *n* ***fig*** **we got a lot of ~ from the questionnaire** ce questionnaire a révélé de nombreuses réactions négatives.

negatively ['negətɪvlɪ] *adv* négativement.

negative sign *n* signe *m* moins *OR* négatif.

negativism ['negətɪvɪzm] *n* négativisme *m*.

neglect [nɪ'glekt] ◇ *n* **1.** [lack of attention, care - of building, garden] abandon *m*, manque *m* de soins *OR* d'entretien ; [- of child, invalid] manque *m* de soins *OR* d'attention ; [- of people's demands, needs] manque *m* d'égards ▪ **through ~** par négligence *f* ▪ **the roof fell in through ~** le toit s'est effondré faute d'entretien ▪ **to suffer from ~** [person] souffrir d'un manque de soins ; [building, garden] être laissé à l'abandon ▪ **his ~ of his appearance** le peu d'intérêt qu'il accorde à son apparence ▪ [bad condition - of building, garden] délabrement *m* ▪ **to be in a state of ~** être à l'abandon ▪ **the buildings fell into ~** les bâtiments sont tombés en ruine **2.** [disregard - of duty, promise, rules] manquement *m* ▪ **he was reprimanded for ~ of duty** il a été réprimandé pour avoir manqué à ses devoirs.
◇ *vt* **1.** [fail to attend to, to care for - building, garden] négliger, laisser à l'abandon ; [- work] négliger ; [- child, invalid, friend] délaisser, négliger ▪ **he ~s himself** *OR* **his appearance** il se néglige *OR* se laisse aller ▪ **you shouldn't ~ your health** vous devriez vous soucier un peu plus de votre santé ▪ **the house has been ~ed for years** la maison est à l'abandon depuis des années ▪ **he ~ed his wife all evening** il n'a pas prêté la moindre attention à sa femme de toute la soirée ▪ **governments have ~ed the needs of the disabled for long enough** il est temps que les gouvernements cessent d'ignorer les besoins des invalides **2.** [disregard - duty, promise] manquer à ; [- advice] ignorer ▪ [omit, overlook] omettre, oublier ▪ **to ~ to do sthg** oublier *OR* omettre de faire qqch.

neglected [nɪ'glektɪd] *adj* **1.** [uncared for - garden] (laissé) à l'abandon, mal entretenu ; [- building] (laissé) à l'abandon, délabré ; [- appearance] négligé, peu soigné **2.** [emotionally - child, wife] délaissé, abandonné ▪ **to feel ~** se sentir abandonné, avoir l'impression d'être délaissé.

neglectful [nɪ'glektfʊl] *adj* [person, attitude] négligent ▪ **to be ~ of one's duty** négliger ses devoirs ▪ **he's very ~ of his appearance** il ne prend aucun soin de sa tenue.

neglectfully [nɪ'glektfʊlɪ] *adv* [behave] négligemment, avec négligence.

negligee, negligée, negligé ['neglɪʒeɪ] *n* négligé *m*, déshabillé *m*.

negligence ['neglɪdʒəns] *n* [inattention] négligence *f* ▪ **due to** *OR* **through ~** par négligence ▪ [of duties, rules] négligence *f*, manquement *m*.

negligent ['neglɪdʒənt] *adj* **1.** [neglectful] négligent ▪ **to be ~ of one's duties** manquer à *OR* négliger ses devoirs **2.** [nonchalant - attitude, manner] nonchalant, négligent.

negligently ['neglɪdʒəntlɪ] *adv* **1.** [carelessly] négligemment ▪ **he acted ~** il a fait preuve de légèreté ▪ **they behaved ~ towards their children** ils ont négligé leurs enfants **2.** [nonchalantly] négligemment, nonchalamment ▪ **she leaned ~ against the car** elle s'appuya avec nonchalance contre la voiture.

negligible ['neglɪdʒəbl] *adj* négligeable, insignifiant.

negotiable [nɪ'gəʊʃjəbl] *adj* **1.** FIN [bonds] négociable ▪ [price, salary] négociable, à débattre **2.** [road] praticable ▪ [river - navigable] navigable ; [- crossable] franchissable.

negotiate [nɪ'gəʊʃɪeɪt] ◇ *vt* **1.** [gen - FIN] négocier **2.** [manoeuvre round - bend] négocier ; [- rapids, obstacle] franchir ▪ ***fig*** [- difficulty] franchir, surmonter.
◇ *vi* négocier ▪ **the unions will have to ~ with the management for higher pay** il faudra que les syndicats négocient une augmentation de salaire auprès de la direction.

negotiating table [nɪ'gəʊʃɪeɪtɪŋ-] *n* table *f* des négociations.

negotiation [nɪ,gəʊʃɪ'eɪʃn] *n* **1.** [discussion] négociation *f*, pourparlers *mpl* ▪ **to enter into ~** *OR* **~s with sb** entamer des négociations avec qqn ▪ **the project is under ~** le projet est en négociation ▪ **your salary is a matter of ~** nous devons débattre du montant de votre salaire **2.** [of bend, obstacle] franchissement *m*.

negotiator [nɪ'gəʊʃɪeɪtəʳ] *n* négociateur *m*, - trice *f*.

Negress ['ni:grɪs] *n* négresse *f (attention: le terme "Negress", comme son équivalent français, est considéré comme raciste).*

Negro ['ni:grəʊ] (*pl* **Negroes**) ◇ *n* nègre *m (attention: le terme "Negro" est considéré comme raciste, sauf dans le domaine de l'anthropologie).*
◇ *adj* nègre.

negroid ['ni:grɔɪd] ◇ *adj* négroïde.
◇ *n* négroïde *mf*.

Negro spiritual *n* (negro) spiritual *m*.

Nehemiah [,ni:ɪ'maɪə] *pr n* Néhémie.

neigh [neɪ] ◇ *vi* hennir.
◇ *n* hennissement *m*.

neighbor *etc* ***US*** = **neighbour**.

neighbour ***UK***, **neighbor** ***US*** ['neɪbəʳ] ◇ *n* **1.** voisin *m*, - e *f* **2.** [fellow man] prochain *m*, - e *f*.
◇ *comp* : **~ states** pays *mpl* voisins.
➡ **neighbour on** *vt insep* [adjoin] avoisiner, être contigu à.

neighbourhood *UK*, **neighborhood** *US* ['neɪbəhʊd] ◇ *n* **1.** [district] voisinage *m*, quartier *m* ■ **in the ~ of the station** près de la gare ■ **there's some nice scenery in the ~** il y a de jolis paysages dans les environs **2.** *fig* **it'll cost you in the ~ of $1,000** cela vous coûtera dans les *OR* environ 1 000 dollars.
◇ *comp* [police, shop, school] du quartier.

Neighbourhood Watch *n système par lequel les habitants d'un quartier s'entraident pour en assurer la surveillance et la sécurité.*

neighbouring *UK*, **neighboring** *US* ['neɪbərɪŋ] *adj* avoisinant, voisin.

neighbourliness *UK*, **neighborliness** *US* ['neɪbəlɪnɪs] *n* (bons) rapports *mpl* de voisinage, sociabilité *f*, amabilité *f*.

neighbourly *UK*, **neighborly** *US* ['neɪbəlɪ] *adj* [person] amical ■ [relations, visit] de bon voisinage ■ **to be ~** être bon voisin, entretenir de bonnes relations avec ses voisins.

neither [*UK* 'naɪðər *(esp) US* 'ni:ðər] ◇ *pron* : **~ of us** aucun de nous (deux) ■ **which do you prefer? – ~!** lequel des deux préfères-tu? – ni l'un ni l'autre!
◇ *conj* : **~... nor...** ni... ni... ■ **I like ~ tea nor coffee** je n'aime ni le thé ni le café ▸ **that's ~ here nor there** [unimportant] c'est sans importance ; [irrelevant] là n'est pas la question ■ **I ~ know nor care** c'est vraiment le cadet de mes soucis.
◇ *adv* non plus ■ **~ did/do/were we** (et) nous non plus ■ **me ~!** *inf* moi non plus!
◇ *det* aucun (des deux), ni l'un ni l'autre ■ **~ one of them has accepted** ni l'un ni l'autre n'a accepté.

nelly ['nelɪ] *n UK phr* **not on your ~!** *inf* tu peux courir!

nelson ['nelsn] *n* [in wrestling] double clé *f*.

nem con [ˌnem'kɒn] *adv* unanimement, à l'unanimité.

nemesis ['neməsɪs] *n lit* **1.** [retribution] : **it's ~** c'est un juste retour des choses **2.** [agency of retribution] : **she saw the British press as her ~** elle vit dans la presse britannique l'instrument de sa vengeance.

neoclassical [ˌni:əʊ'klæsɪkl] *adj* néoclassique.

neoclassicism [ˌni:əʊ'klæsɪsɪzm] *n* néoclassicisme *m*.

neocolonial [ˌni:əʊkə'ləʊnɪəl] *adj* néocolonial.

neocolonialism [ˌni:əʊkə'ləʊnɪəlɪzm] *n* néocolonialisme *m*.

neofascism [ˌni:əʊ'fæʃɪzm] *n* néofascisme *m*.

neofascist [ˌni:əʊ'fæʃɪst] ◇ *adj* néofasciste.
◇ *n* néofasciste *mf*.

neolithic, Neolithic [ˌni:ə'lɪθɪk] ◇ *adj* néolithique.
◇ *n* néolithique *m*.

neologism [ni:'ɒlədʒɪzm] *n* néologisme *m*.

neon ['ni:ɒn] ◇ *n* néon *m*.
◇ *comp* [lamp] au néon ■ **~ sign** enseigne *f* lumineuse (au néon) ■ **~ lights** néons *mpl*.

neonatal [ˌni:əʊ'neɪtl] *adj* néonatal.

neo-Nazi [ˌni:əʊ'nɑ:tsɪ] ◇ *n* néonazi *m*, - e *f*.
◇ *adj* néonazi.

neorealism [ˌni:əʊ'ri:əlɪzm] *n* néoréalisme *m*.

Nepal [nɪ'pɔ:l] *pr n* Népal *m* ■ **in ~** au Népal.

Nepalese [ˌnepə'li:z] *(pl inv)* ◇ *n* Népalais *m*, - e *f*.
◇ *adj* népalais.

Nepali [nɪ'pɔ:lɪ] *(pl inv OR pl* **Nepalis**) ◇ *n* [person] Népalais *m*, - e *f*.
◇ *adj* népalais.

nephew ['nefju:] *n* neveu *m*.

nepotism ['nepətɪzm] *n* népotisme *m*.

Neptune ['neptju:n] *pr n* ASTRON & MYTH Neptune.

nerd [nɜ:d] *n inf* [stupid] crétin *m* ■ **computer ~** accro *m* d'informatique ■ [studious] binoclard *m*.

nerdy ['nɜ:dɪ] *adj inf pej* [unfashionable] ringard ■ [foolish] débile.

Nero ['nɪərəʊ] *pr n* Néron.

nerve [nɜ:v] ◇ *n* **1.** ANAT nerf *m* ■ **to touch a raw ~** *fig* toucher une corde sensible **2.** [courage] courage *m* ■ [boldness] audace *f* ■ [self-control] assurance *f*, sang-froid *m* ■ **it takes ~ to say no to him** il faut du courage *OR* il faut avoir les nerfs solides pour lui dire non ■ **his ~ failed him, he lost his ~** [backed down] le courage lui a manqué ; [panicked] il a perdu son sang-froid **3.** [cheek, audacity] culot *m* ■ **he had the ~ to refuse** il a eu le culot de refuser ■ **you've got a ~ coming here!** *inf* tu es gonflé de venir ici! ■ **what a ~!** *inf* quel culot *OR* toupet! **4.** [vein - in leaf, marble] veine *f*, nervure *f*.
◇ *vt fml* **to ~ sb to do sthg** encourager *OR* inciter qqn à faire qqch.
◆ **nerves** *npl* **1.** [agitated state] nerfs *mpl* ■ [anxiety] nervosité *f* ■ [before concert, exam, interview] trac *m* ■ **to be in a state of ~s** être sur les nerfs ■ **I'm a bundle of ~s** je suis un paquet de nerfs ■ **I need a drink to steady my ~s** il faut que je boive un verre pour me calmer **2.** [self-control] nerfs *mpl* ■ **to have strong ~s/~s of steel** avoir les nerfs solides/des nerfs d'acier ▸ **he gets on my ~s** *inf* il me tape sur les nerfs *OR* sur le système.

nerve cell *n* cellule *f* nerveuse.

nerve centre *n* **1.** ANAT centre *m* nerveux **2.** *fig* [headquarters] quartier *m* général, poste *m* de commandement.

nerve ending *n* terminaison *f* nerveuse.

nerve gas *n* gaz *m* neurotoxique.

nerveless ['nɜ:vlɪs] *adj* **1.** [numb] engourdi, inerte **2.** [weak] sans force, mou *(before vowel or silent 'h'* **mol**), molle *f* **3.** [calm] impassible, imperturbable ■ [fearless] intrépide.

nerve-racking, nerve-wracking [-ˌrækɪŋ] *adj inf* angoissant, stressant ■ **after a ~ wait he was shown in** après une attente qui mit ses nerfs à rude épreuve, on le fit entrer.

nervous ['nɜ:vəs] *adj* **1.** [anxious, worried] anxieux, appréhensif ■ [shy] timide, intimidé ■ [uneasy] mal à l'aise ■ [agitated] agité, tendu ■ [tense] tendu ■ **don't be ~** détendez-vous, n'ayez pas peur ■ **you're making me ~** vous m'intimidez, vous me faites perdre mes moyens ■ **he is ~ of Alsatians** les bergers allemands lui font peur ■ **I'm ~ about speaking in public** j'ai peur *OR* j'appréhende de parler en public ■ **I'm always ~ before exams** j'ai toujours le trac avant un examen ■ **he's a ~ wreck** *inf* il est à bout de nerfs, il est à cran **2.** ANAT [strain, illness] nerveux ■ **the ~ system** le système nerveux.

nervous breakdown *n* dépression *f* nerveuse ■ **to have a ~** avoir *OR* faire une dépression nerveuse.

nervously ['nɜ:vəslɪ] *adv* [anxiously] anxieusement, avec inquiétude ■ [tensely] nerveusement.

nervy ['nɜ:vɪ] (*comp* **nervier**, *superl* **nerviest**) *adj inf* **1.** *UK* [tense] énervé, excité **2.** *US* [cheeky] culotté.

Ness [nes] *pr n* : **Loch ~** le Loch Ness ■ **the Loch ~ monster** le monstre du Loch Ness.

nest [nest] ◇ *n* **1.** [for birds, wasps, snakes etc] nid *m* ■ [occupants - esp birds] nichée *f* ■ *fig* [den - of brigands] nid *m*, repaire *m* ■ [for machine guns] nid *m* **2.** [set] : **~ of tables/boxes** (série *f*) *OR* ensemble *m* de tables *fpl* /boîtes *fpl* gigognes.
◇ *vi* **1.** [bird] (se) nicher, faire son nid **2.** [person] : **to go ~ing** [find nests] aller chercher des nids ; [steal young] aller dénicher des oisillons ; [steal eggs] aller dénicher des œufs **3.** [fit together] s'emboîter.
◇ *vt* **1.** [animal, bird] servir de nid à **2.** [tables, boxes] emboîter.

nest box *n* [in henhouse] pondoir *m* ■ [in birdhouse] nichoir *m*.

nest egg *n* économies *fpl*, bas *m* de laine, pécule *m*.

nesting ['nestɪŋ] ◇ *n* nidification *f*.
◇ *comp* [bird] nicheur ■ [time, instinct] de (la) nidification.

nesting box = **nest box**.

nestle ['nesl] ◇ *vi* **1.** [against person] se blottir ■ **she ~d (up) against me** elle s'est blottie contre moi ■ [in comfortable place]

se pelotonner ■ **to ~ down in bed** se pelotonner dans son lit **2.** [land, house] être niché *OR* blotti ■ **their house ~s among the pines** leur maison est tapie *OR* blottie au milieu des sapins.
◇ *vt* blottir.

nestling ['neslɪŋ] *n* oisillon *m*.

net [net] ◇ *n* **1.** [gen, for fishing, butterflies etc] filet *m* ■ *fig* [trap] filet *m*, piège *m* ■ **to slip through the ~** glisser *OR* passer à travers les mailles du filet **2.** SPORT filet *m* ■ **to come to the ~** [tennis] monter au filet **3.** [for hair] filet *m* à cheveux, résille *f* **4.** TEX tulle *m*, filet *m* **5.** [network] réseau *m* **6.** [income, profit, weight] net *m*.
◇ *vt* (*pret & pp* **netted**, *cont* **netting**) **1.** [catch - fish, butterfly] prendre *OR* attraper (au filet) ; [- terrorist, criminal] arrêter **2.** [acquire - prize] ramasser, gagner ; [- fortune] amasser **3.** SPORT : **to ~ the ball** [in tennis] envoyer la balle dans le filet ■ **to ~ a goal** FTBL marquer un but **4.** [fruit tree] recouvrir de filets *OR* d'un filet **5.** [income, salary] toucher *OR* gagner net ■ [profit] rapporter net ■ **we netted over $10,000** nous avons réalisé un bénéfice net de plus de 10 000 dollars.
◇ *adj* **1.** [income, price, weight] net ■ **we made a ~ loss/profit of £500** nous avons enregistré une perte sèche/réalisé un bénéfice net de 500 livres **2.** [result] final.

Net ◇ *n* : **the ~** le Net, l'Internet *m*.
◇ *comp* : **net.citizen** cybercitoyen *m*, - enne *f* ■ **net.user** internaute *mf*.

netball ['netbɔ:l] *n* net-ball *m (sport féminin proche du basket-ball)*.

net curtain *n* rideau *m* (de tulle *OR* en filet), voilage *m*.

net domestic product *n* produit *m* intérieur net.

nethead ['nethed] *n inf* fada *mf OR* accro *mf* d'Internet.

nether ['neðəʳ] *adj arch & lit* bas, inférieur ■ [lip] inférieur ■ **the ~ regions** *OR* **world** *fig* l'enfer *m* ■ **the ball hit him in the ~ regions** *hum* le ballon l'a atteint dans les parties basses.

Netherlander ['neðəlændəʳ] *n* Néerlandais *m*, - e *f*.

Netherlands ['neðələndz] *pr npl* : **the ~** les Pays-Bas *mpl* ■ **in the ~** aux Pays-Bas.

nethermost ['neðəməʊst] *adj lit* le plus bas *OR* profond.

netiquette ['netiket] *n* COMPUT nétiquette *f*.

Net surfer *n* internaute *mf*.

nett [net] = **net** *(n sense 6, vt sense 5, adj sense 1)*.

nettie ['netɪ] *n inf* fada *mf OR* accro *mf* d'Internet.

netting ['netɪŋ] *n (U)* **1.** [for strawberries, trees] filet *m*, filets *mpl* ■ [fencing] treillis *m* (métallique), grillage *m* **2.** TEX [for curtains] tulle *m*, filet *m* **3.** [of fish, butterfly] prise *f* au filet.

nettle ['netl] ◇ *n* ortie *f* ■ **to grasp the ~** *UK* prendre le taureau par les cornes.
◇ *vt UK* agacer, énerver.

nettled ['netld] *adj* agacé.

nettle rash *n* urticaire *f*.

network ['netwɜ:k] ◇ *n* **1.** [gen - ELEC] & RAIL réseau *m* ■ [of shops, hotels] réseau *m*, chaîne *f* ■ [of streets] lacis *m* ■ **road ~** réseau routier **2.** TV [national] réseau *m* ■ [channel] chaîne *f* **3.** COMPUT réseau *m*.
◇ *vt* TV diffuser sur l'ensemble du réseau *OR* sur tout le territoire ■ COMPUT mettre en réseau.
◇ *vi* [make contacts] tenter d'établir un réseau de contacts professionnels.

network computer *n* ordinateur *m* réseau.

networking ['netwɜ:kɪŋ] *n* **1.** COMPUT mise *f* en réseau **2.** [gen - COMM] établissement *m* d'un réseau de liens *OR* de contacts.

network TV *n* réseau *m* (de télévision) national.

neural ['njʊərəl] *adj* neural.

neuralgia [njʊə'rældʒə] *n (U)* névralgie *f*.

neuritis [,njʊə'raɪtɪs] *n (U)* névrite *f*.

neurological [,njʊərə'lɒdʒɪkl] *adj* neurologique.

neurologist [,njʊə'rɒlədʒɪst] *n* neurologue *mf*.

neurology [,njʊə'rɒlədʒɪ] *n* neurologie *f*.

neuron ['njʊərɒn], **neurone** ['njʊərəʊn] *n* neurone *m*.

neurophysiology ['njʊərəʊ,fɪzɪ'ɒlədʒɪ] *n* neurophysiologie *f*.

neuroscience ['njʊərəʊsaɪəns] *n* neuroscience *f*.

neurosis [,njʊə'rəʊsɪs] (*pl* **neuroses** [-si:z]) *n* névrose *f*.

neurosurgeon ['njʊərəʊ,sɜ:dʒən] *n* neurochirurgien *m*, - enne *f*.

neurosurgery [,njʊərəʊ'sɜ:dʒərɪ] *n* neurochirurgie *f*.

neurotic [,njʊə'rɒtɪk] ◇ *n* névrosé *m*, - e *f*.
◇ *adj* [person] névrosé ■ [disease] névrotique ■ **he's really ~ about his weight** *fig* il est littéralement obsédé par son poids.

neuroticism [,njʊə'rɒtɪsɪzm] *n* neurasthénie *f fig*.

neuter ['nju:təʳ] ◇ *adj* neutre.
◇ *n* **1.** GRAM neutre *m* **2.** [animal - asexual] animal *m* asexué ; [- castrated] animal *m* châtré ■ [insect, plant] neutre *m*.
◇ *vt* châtrer.

neutral ['nju:trəl] ◇ *adj* neutre ■ [policy] de neutralité.
◇ *n* **1.** AUT point *m* mort ■ **in ~** au point mort **2.** POL [person] habitant *m*, - e *f* d'un pays neutre ■ [state] pays *m* neutre.

neutrality [nju:'trælətɪ] *n* neutralité *f*.

neutralization [,nju:trəlaɪ'zeɪʃn] *n* neutralisation *f*.

neutralize, ise ['nju:trəlaɪz] *vt* neutraliser.

neutron ['nju:trɒn] *n* neutron *m*.

neutron bomb *n* bombe *f* à neutrons.

Nevada [nɪ'vɑ:də] *pr n* Nevada *m* ■ **in ~** dans le Nevada.

never ['nevəʳ] ◇ *adv* **1.** [not ever] jamais ■ **I ~ saw her again** je ne l'ai plus jamais *OR* jamais plus revue ■ **you ~ know** on ne sait jamais ■ **~ before** [until that moment] jamais auparavant *OR* avant *OR* jusque-là ; [until now] jamais jusqu'ici *OR* jusqu'à présent ■ **I'll ~ ever speak to him again** plus jamais de ma vie je ne lui adresserai la parole ■ **~ again!** plus jamais ça! **2.** [used instead of 'did not'] : **she ~ turned up** elle n'est pas venue ■ **I ~ knew you cared** je ne savais pas que tu m'aimais ■ [as intensifier] : **I ~ even asked if you wanted something to drink** je ne vous ai même pas offert (quelque chose) à boire ■ **~ fear** ne craignez rien, n'ayez crainte ➜ **that will ~ do!** [it is unacceptable] c'est inadmissible! ; [it is insufficient] ça ne va pas! **3.** [in surprise, disbelief] : **you ~ did!** vous n'avez pas fait ça! ■ **you've ~ lost your purse again!** ne me dis pas que tu as encore perdu ton porte-monnaie! ➜ **well I ~ (did)!** ça alors!, par exemple!
◇ *interj* : **~!** (ce n'est) pas possible!

never-ending *adj* interminable, qui n'en finit pas.

nevermore [,nevə'mɔ:ʳ] *adv lit* jamais plus, plus jamais.

never-never *inf* ◇ *n UK* **to buy sthg on the ~** acheter qqch à crédit *OR* à tempérament.
◇ *adj* imaginaire, chimérique ■ **~ land** pays *m* de cocagne.

nevertheless [,nevəðə'les] *adv* néanmoins ■ **a small, but ~ significant increase** une augmentation faible mais néanmoins significative ■ **she'd not skied before but she insisted on coming with us ~** elle n'avait jamais fait de ski mais elle a quand même tenu à nous accompagner ■ [at start of clause or sentence] cependant.

new [nju:] (*comp* **newer**, *superl* **newest**) ◇ *adj* **1.** [gen] nouveau *(before vowel or silent 'h'* **nouvel***)*, nouvelle *f* ■ [different] nouveau, nouvelle *f*, autre ■ [unused] neuf, nouveau *(before vowel or silent 'h'* **nouvel***)*, nouvelle *f* ■ **a ~ tablecloth** [brand new] une nouvelle nappe, une nappe neuve ; [fresh] une nouvelle nappe, une nappe propre ■ **she needs a ~ sheet of paper** il lui faut une autre feuille de papier ■ **there are ~ people in the flat next door** il y a de nouveaux occupants dans l'appartement d'à côté ■ **'under ~ management'** 'changement de propriétaire' ➜ **as** *OR* **like ~** comme neuf ; [in advert] 'état neuf' ■ **as good as ~ (again)** [clothing, carpet] (à nouveau) comme neuf ; [watch, electrical appliance] (à nouveau) en parfait état de marche ■ **to feel like a ~ woman/man** se sentir re-

vivre ▪ **to make a ~ woman/man of sb** transformer qqn complètement ▪ **there's nothing ~ under the sun** *prov* (il n'y a) rien de nouveau sous le soleil
2. [latest, recent - issue, recording, baby] nouveau *(before vowel or silent 'h'* **nouvel***)*, nouvelle *f* ▪ **the ~est fashions** la dernière mode ▪ **is there anything ~ on the catastrophe?** est-ce qu'il y a du nouveau sur la catastrophe? ▪ [modern] nouveau *(before vowel or silent 'h'* **nouvel***)*, nouvelle *f*, moderne ▪ **~ maths** *UK* *OR* **math** *US* les maths modernes ▪ **her husband is a New Man** son mari est le type même de l'homme moderne ➲ **what's ~?** quoi de neuf? ▪ **(so) what's ~!, what else is ~!** [dismissive] quelle surprise!
3. [unfamiliar - experience, environment] nouveau *(before vowel or silent 'h*nouvel*)*, nouvelle *f* ▪ **to be ~ to sb : everything's still very ~ to me here** tout est encore tout nouveau pour moi ici ➲ **that's a ~ one on me!** *inf* [joke] celle-là, on ne me l'avait jamais faite! ; [news] première nouvelle! ; [experience] on en apprend tous les jours!
4. [recently arrived] nouveau *(before vowel or silent 'h'* **nouvel***)*, nouvelle *f* ▪ [novice] novice ▪ **you're ~ here, aren't you?** vous êtes nouveau ici, n'est-ce pas? ▪ **she's ~ to the job** elle débute dans le métier ▪ **we're ~ to this area** nous venons d'arriver dans la région
5. CULIN [wine] nouveau *(before vowel or silent 'h'* **nouvel***)*, nouvelle *f* ▪ [potatoes, carrots] nouveau *(before vowel or silent 'h'* **nouvel***)*, nouvelle *f*.
◇ *n* nouveau *m*.

new- *in cpds* : **~won freedom** une liberté toute neuve ▪ **~built** nouvellement construit.

New Age ◇ *n* New Age *m*.
◇ *adj* New Age *(inv)* ▪ **~ traveller** voyageur *m* New Age.

New Ager [-'eɪdʒər] *n* adepte *mf* du New Age.

new blood *n inf* sang *m* neuf.

newborn ['nju:bɔ:n] ◇ *adj* nouveau-né ▪ **a ~ baby girl** une (petite fille) nouveau-née.
◇ *npl* : **the ~** les nouveaux-nés *mpl*.

new boy *n* SCH nouveau *m*, nouvel élève *m* ▪ [in office, team etc] nouveau *m*.

new broom *n* réformateur *m*, - trice *f* ▪ **a ~ sweeps clean** *prov* tout nouveau tout beau *prov*.

New Brunswick *pr n* Nouveau-Brunswick *m* ▪ **in ~** dans le Nouveau-Brunswick.

New Caledonia *pr n* Nouvelle-Calédonie *f* ▪ **in ~** en Nouvelle-Calédonie.

New Caledonian ◇ *n* Néo-Calédonien *m*, - enne *f*.
◇ *adj* néo-calédonien.

newcomer ['nju:ˌkʌmər] *n* **1.** [new arrival] nouveau venu *m*, nouvelle venue *f* ▪ **she's a ~ to the town** elle vient d'arriver dans la ville **2.** [beginner] novice *mf* ▪ **a good book for ~s to computing** un bon livre pour les débutants en informatique ▪ **I'm a ~ to all this** tout cela est nouveau pour moi.

New Deal *pr n* : **the ~** le New Deal *(programme de réformes sociales mises en place aux États-Unis par le président Roosevelt au lendemain de la grande dépression des années 30)*.

New Delhi *pr n* New Delhi.

new-edge *adj* : **~ technology** technologie *f* de pointe.

New England *pr n* Nouvelle-Angleterre *f* ▪ **in ~** en Nouvelle-Angleterre.

New Englander *n* habitant *m*, - e *f* de la Nouvelle-Angleterre.

newfangled [ˌnju:'fæŋgld] *adj pej* [idea, device] nouveau *(before vowel or silent 'h'* **nouvel***)*, nouvelle *f*, dernier cri *(inv)*.

new-found *adj* nouveau *(before vowel or silent 'h'* **nouvel***)*, nouvelle *f*, récent.

Newfoundland ['nju:fəndlənd] *pr n* **1.** GEOG Terre-Neuve ▪ **in ~** à Terre-Neuve **2.** [dog] terre-neuve *m inv*.

Newfoundlander ['nju:fəndləndər] *pr n* Terre-Neuvien *m*, - enne *f*.

new girl *n* SCH nouvelle (élève) *f* ▪ [in office, team] nouvelle *f*.

New Guinea *pr n* Nouvelle-Guinée *f* ▪ **in ~** en Nouvelle-Guinée.

New Hampshire [-'hæmpʃər] *pr n* New Hampshire *m* ▪ **in ~** dans le New Hampshire.

New Jersey *pr n* New Jersey *m* ▪ **in ~** dans le New Jersey.

New Labour *pr n* [in UK] New Labour *m*.

new-laid *adj UK* **a ~ egg** un œuf extra-frais.

newly ['nju:lɪ] *adv* nouvellement, récemment ▪ **the gate has been ~ painted** la barrière vient d'être peinte ▪ **~ elected** nouvellement élu ▪ **their ~ won independence** leur indépendance récemment conquise.

newlyweds ['nju:lɪwedz] *npl* jeunes mariés *mpl*.

New Mexico *pr n* Nouveau-Mexique *m* ▪ **in ~** au Nouveau-Mexique.

new moon *n* nouvelle lune *f*.

new-mown *adj UK* [grass] fraîchement coupé ▪ [lawn] fraîchement tondu ▪ [hay] fraîchement fauché.

newness ['nju:nɪs] *n* **1.** [of building] nouveauté *f* ▪ [of shoes, carpet] état *m* neuf **2.** [of ideas, experience, fashion] nouveauté *f*, originalité *f*.

New Orleans [-'ɔ:lɪənz] *pr n* La Nouvelle-Orléans.

New Quebec *pr n* Nouveau-Québec *m* ▪ **in ~** au Nouveau-Québec.

new rich *npl* nouveaux riches *mpl*.

news [nju:z] ◇ *n (U)* **1.** [information] nouvelles *fpl*, informations *fpl* ▪ **a piece of ~** une nouvelle, une information ▪ **is there any more ~ about** *OR* **on the explosion?** est-ce qu'on a plus d'informations sur l'explosion? ▪ **that's good/bad ~** c'est une bonne/mauvaise nouvelle ▪ **to have ~ of sb** avoir des nouvelles de qqn ▪ **have you had any ~ of her?** avez-vous eu de ses nouvelles? ➲ **have I got ~ for you!** j'ai du nouveau (à vous annoncer)! ▪ **it's ~ to me!** première nouvelle!, je l'ignorais! ▪ **famine isn't ~ any more** la famine ne fait plus la une (des journaux) ▪ **to be in the ~, to make ~** défrayer la chronique, faire parler de soi ▪ **to break the ~ (of sthg) to sb** annoncer la nouvelle (de qqch) à qqn ▪ **he's bad ~** *inf* on a toujours des ennuis avec lui ▪ **no ~ is good ~** *prov* pas de nouvelles, bonnes nouvelles *prov* **2.** RADIO & TV actualités *fpl*, informations *fpl* ▪ [bulletin] chronique *f*, journal *m*, page *f* ▪ **the 9 o'clock ~** TV le journal (télévisé) *OR* les informations de 21 h ; RADIO le journal (parlé) *OR* les informations de 21 h ▪ **the sports/financial ~** la page sportive/financière.
◇ *comp* : **~ desk** (salle *f* de) rédaction *f* ▪ **~ editor** rédacteur *m*, - trice *f* ▪ **~ item** information *f* ▪ **~ value** intérêt *m* médiatique.

news agency *n* agence *f* de presse.

newsagent *UK* ['nju:zˌeɪdʒənt], **news dealer** *US n* marchand *m*, - e *f* de journaux.

news analyst *n US* RADIO & TV commentateur *m*.

newsboy ['nju:zbɔɪ] *n* [in street] crieur *m* de journaux ▪ [delivery boy] livreur *m* de journaux.

news bulletin *n* bulletin *m* d'informations.

newscast ['nju:zkɑ:st] *n* bulletin *m* d'informations ▪ TV journal *m* télévisé, informations *fpl*.

newscaster ['nju:zkɑ:stər] *n* présentateur *m*, - trice *f* du journal.

news conference *n* conférence *f* de presse.

newsflash ['nju:zflæʃ] *n* flash *m* d'informations.

newsgroup ['nju:zgru:p] *n* COMPUT forum *m* de discussion.

news headlines *npl* titres *mpl* de l'actualité.

newshound ['nju:zhaʊnd] *n inf* reporter *m*, journaliste *mf*.

newsletter ['nju:zˌletər] *n* lettre *f*, bulletin *m*.

newsocracy [ˌnju:z'ɒkrəsɪ] *n aux États-Unis, ensemble de la presse et du réseau télévisé à audience nationale*.

New South Wales *pr n* Nouvelle-Galles du Sud *f* ▪ **in ~** en Nouvelle-Galles du Sud.

newspaper ['nju:z,peɪpəʳ] ◇ *n* **1.** [publication] journal *m* ▪ **in the ~** dans le journal ▪ **an evening ~** un journal du soir ▪ **a daily ~** un quotidien **2.** [paper] : **wrapped in ~** enveloppé dans du papier journal.
◇ *comp* [article, report] de journal ▪ **~ reporter** reporter *m* (de la presse écrite).

newspaper clipping, newspaper cutting *n* coupure *f* de presse.

newspaperman ['nju:z,peɪpəmæn] (*pl* **newspapermen** [-men]) *n* journaliste *m* (de la presse écrite).

newspaper rack *n* porte-journaux *m*.

newspeak ['nju:spi:k] *n* jargon *m* bureaucratique, ≃ langue *f* de bois.

newsprint ['nju:zprɪnt] *n* papier *m* journal.

newsreader ['nju:z,ri:dəʳ] = **newscaster**.

newsreel ['nju:zri:l] *n* film *m* d'actualités.

news report *n* bulletin *m* d'informations.

newsroom ['nju:zru:m] *n* **1.** PRESS salle *f* de rédaction **2.** RADIO & TV studio *m*.

news service *n* US *agence de presse qui publie ses informations par le biais d'un syndicat de distribution.*

newssheet ['nju:zʃi:t] = **newsletter**.

newsstand ['nju:zstænd] *n* kiosque *m* (à journaux).

newsvendor ['nju:z,vendəʳ] *n* [gen] marchand *m*, - e *f* de journaux ▪ [in street] crieur *m*, - euse *f* de journaux.

newsworthiness ['nju:z,wɜ:ðɪnɪs] *n* intérêt *m* médiatique.

newsworthy ['nju:z,wɜ:ðɪ] *adj* : **it's not ~** cela n'a aucun intérêt médiatique.

newt [nju:t] *n* ZOOL triton *m*.

new technology *n* nouvelle technologie *f*, technologie *f* de pointe.

New Testament *pr n* Nouveau Testament *m*.

Newtonian [nju:'təʊnjən] *adj* newtonien.

new wave *n* [in cinema] nouvelle vague *f* ▪ [in pop music] new wave *f*.
◆ **new-wave** *adj* [cinema] nouvelle vague *(inv)* ▪ [pop music] new-wave *(inv)*.

New World *pr n* : **the ~** le Nouveau Monde ▶ **'The New World Symphony'** ***Dvorák*** 'Symphonie du Nouveau Monde'.

New Year *n* Nouvel An *m* ▪ **happy ~!** bonne année! ▪ **to see the ~ in** réveillonner *(le 31 décembre)* ▪ **~'s resolutions** résolutions *fpl* du nouvel an.

New Year's *n* US **1.** [day] le premier de l'an **2.** [eve] le soir du réveillon OR du 31 décembre.

New Year's Day *n* jour *m* de l'an.

New Year's Eve *n* Saint-Sylvestre *f*.

New Year's Honours List *pr n* : **the ~** *titres et distinctions honorifiques décernés par la reine d'Angleterre à l'occasion de la nouvelle année et dont la liste est établie officieusement par le Premier ministre.*

New York *pr n* **1.** [city] : **~ (City)** New York ▪ **the ~ subway** le métro new-yorkais ▪ **the ~ Times** *quotidien américain de qualité* **2.** [state] : **~ (State)** l'État *m* de New York ▪ **in (the State of) ~, in ~ (State)** dans l'État de New York.

New Yorker [-'jɔ:kəʳ] *n* New-Yorkais *m*, - e *f* ▪ **the ~** US PRESS *hebdomadaire culturel et littéraire new- yorkais.*

New Zealand [-'zi:lənd] *pr n* Nouvelle-Zélande *f* ▪ **in ~** en Nouvelle-Zélande ▪ **~ butter** beurre néo-zélandais.

New Zealander [-'zi:ləndəʳ] *n* Néo-Zélandais *m*, - e *f*.

next [nekst] ◇ *adj* **1.** [in time - coming] prochain ; [- already past] suivant ▪ **keep quiet about it for the ~ few days** n'en parlez pas pendant les quelques jours qui viennent ▪ **I had to stay in bed for the ~ ten days** j'ai dû garder le lit pendant les dix jours qui ont suivi ▪ **(the) ~ day** le lendemain ▪ **(the) ~ morning/evening** le lendemain matin/soir ▪ **~ Sunday, Sunday ~** dimanche prochain ▪ **the ~ Sunday** le dimanche suivant ▪ **(the) ~ minute/moment : ~ minute she was dashing off out again** *inf* une minute après, elle repartait ▪ **the situation's changing from one moment to the ~** la situation change sans arrêt ▪ **~ time : (the) ~ time I see him** la prochaine fois que je le vois OR verrai ▪ **(the) ~ time I saw him** quand je l'ai revu
2. [in series - in future] prochain ; [- in past] suivant ▪ **translate the ~ sentence** traduisez la phrase suivante ▪ **their ~ child was a girl** ensuite, ils eurent une fille ▪ **they want their ~ child to be a girl** ils veulent que leur prochain enfant soit une fille, la prochaine fois ils veulent une fille ▪ **the ~ 10 pages** les 10 pages suivantes ▪ **the ~ before last** l'avant-dernier ▪ **ask the ~ person you meet** demandez à la première personne que vous rencontrez ▪ **the ~ world** l'au-delà *m* ▪ **this life and the ~** ce monde et l'autre ▪ [in space - house, street] prochain, suivant ▪ **take the ~ street on the left** prenez la prochaine à gauche ▪ **after the kitchen, it's the ~ room on your right** après la cuisine, c'est la première pièce à votre droite ▪ [in queue, line] : **I'm ~** c'est (à) mon tour, c'est à moi ▪ **who's ~?** à qui le tour? ▪ **I'm ~ after you** je suis (juste) après vous ▪ **Helen is ~ in line for promotion** Helen est la suivante sur la liste des promotions ▶ **I can take a joke as well as the ~ person, but...** j'aime plaisanter comme tout le monde, mais... ▪ **(the) ~ thing** ensuite ▪ **and (the) ~ thing I knew, I woke up in hospital** et l'instant d'après je me suis réveillé à l'hôpital.
◇ *adv* **1.** [afterwards] ensuite, après ▪ **what did you do with it ~?** et ensuite, qu'en avez-vous fait? ▪ **~ on the agenda is the question of finance** la question suivante à l'ordre du jour est celle des finances ▪ **what will they think of ~?** *hum* qu'est-ce qu'ils vont bien pouvoir inventer maintenant? ▪ **what OR whatever ~?** [indignantly or in mock indignation] et puis quoi encore?
2. [next time - in future] la prochaine fois ; [- in past] la fois suivante OR d'après ▪ **when we ~ met** quand nous nous sommes revus
3. [with superlative adj] : **the ~ youngest/oldest child** l'enfant le plus jeune/le plus âgé ensuite ▪ **the ~ largest size** la taille juste au-dessus ▪ **watching the match on TV was the ~ best thing to actually being there** l'idéal aurait été de pouvoir assister au match, mais ce n'était déjà pas mal de le voir à la télé.
◇ *n* [next train, person, child] prochain *m*, - e *f* ▪ **~ please!** au suivant, s'il vous plaît! ▪ **~ of kin** plus proche parent *m*.
◇ *prep* US = **next to**.
◆ **next to** *prep* **1.** [near] à côté de ▪ **come and sit ~ to me** venez vous asseoir à côté de OR près de moi ▪ **I love the feel of silk ~ to my skin** j'adore le contact de la soie sur ma peau ▪ [in series] : **~ to last** avant-dernier ▪ **the ~ to bottom shelf** la deuxième étagère en partant du bas
2. [in comparisons] après
3. [almost] presque ▪ **~ to impossible** presque OR quasiment impossible ▪ **I bought it for ~ to nothing** je l'ai acheté pour trois fois rien OR presque rien.

next door ◇ *adv* : **they live ~ to us** ils habitent à côté de chez nous, ce sont nos voisins ▪ **the girl/boy ~** la fille/le garçon d'à côté ▪ **she was just the girl ~** *fig* c'était une fille tout à fait ordinaire.
◇ *n* la maison d'à côté ▪ **~'s children** les enfants qui habitent à côté OR des voisins ▪ **it's the man from ~** c'est le voisin.
◆ **next-door** *adj* : **next-door neighbour** [in private house] voisin *m*, - e *f* (de la maison d'à côté) ; [in apartment building] voisin *m*, - e *f* de palier.

nexus ['neksəs] (*pl inv* OR *pl* **nexuses**) *n* lien *m*, liaison *f*.

NF ◇ *pr n* = **National Front**.
◇ *written abbr of* **Newfoundland**.

NGO (*abbrev of* **non-governmental organization**) *n* ONG *f*.

NH *written abbr of* **New Hampshire**.

NHS *pr n* UK = **National Health Service**.

NI ◇ *n* UK = **national insurance**.
◇ *written abbr of* **Northern Ireland**.

Niagara [naɪ'ægərə] *pr n* : **~ Falls** les chutes *fpl* du Niagara.

nib [nɪb] *n* [of fountain pen] plume *f* ▪ [of ballpoint, tool] pointe *f*.

-nibbed [nɪbd] *in cpds* : **gold~** avec une plume en or ▪ **fine~** [fountain pen] à plume fine ; [ballpoint] à pointe fine.

nibble ['nɪbl] ◇ *vt* **1.** [subj: person, caterpillar] grignoter ■ [subj: rodent] grignoter, ronger ■ [subj: goat, sheep] brouter ■ **the fish ~d the bait** le poisson a mordu à l'hameçon **2.** [playfully - ear] mordiller.
◇ *vi* **1.** [eat] : **to ~ at** *OR* **on sthg** grignoter qqch **2.** [bite] : **to ~ at sthg** mordiller qqch ▶ **to ~ at the bait** *liter & fig* mordre à l'hameçon **3.** *fig* [show interest] : **to ~ at an offer** être tenté par une offre.
◇ *n* **1.** FISHING touche *f* **2.** [snack] : **to have a ~** grignoter quelque chose ■ **~s** amuse-gueules *mpl*.

nibs [nɪbz] *n* **UK inf hum his ~** sa Majesté, son Altesse *hum*.

Nicaragua [,nɪkə'rægjʊə] *pr n* Nicaragua *m* ■ **in ~** au Nicaragua.

Nicaraguan [,nɪkə'rægjʊən] ◇ *n* Nicaraguayen *m*, - enne *f*.
◇ *adj* nicaraguayen.

nice [naɪs] ◇ *adj* **1.** [expressing approval - good] bien, chouette ; [- attractive] beau *(before vowel or silent 'h'* **bel**), belle *f* ; [- pretty] joli ; [- car, picture] beau *(before vowel or silent 'h'* **bel**), belle *f* ; [- food] bon ; [- idea] bon ; [- weather] beau *(before vowel or silent 'h'* **bel**), belle *f* ■ **very ~** [visually] très joli ; [food] très bon ■ **to taste ~** avoir bon goût ■ **to smell ~** sentir bon ■ **she was wearing a very ~ hat** elle portait un très joli chapeau ■ **she always looks ~** elle est toujours bien habillée *OR* mise ■ **we had a ~ meal** on a bien mangé ■ **~ work!** beau travail! ■ **~ work if you can get it** *hum* c'est un travail agréable, encore faut-il le décrocher ■ [pleasant - gen] agréable, bien ; [- person] bien, sympathique ■ **she's very ~** elle est très sympa ■ **have a ~ time** amusez-vous bien ■ **it's ~ to be back again** cela fait plaisir d'être de retour ■ **(it was) ~ meeting you** (j'ai été) ravi de faire votre connaissance ▶ **~ one!** bravo!, chapeau! **2.** [kind] gentil, aimable ■ **to be ~ to sb** être gentil avec qqn ■ **that's ~ of her** c'est gentil *OR* aimable de sa part ■ **it's ~ of you to say so** vous êtes bien aimable de le dire ■ **he was ~ enough to carry my case** il a eu la gentillesse *OR* l'obligeance de porter ma valise
3. [respectable] bien (élevé), convenable ■ **~ people don't blow their noses at table** les gens bien élevés ne se mouchent pas à table
4. [ironic use] : **he made a ~ mess of the job** il a fait un travail de cochon ■ **you're a ~ one to talk!** toi, tu peux parler! ■ **we're in a ~ mess** nous sommes dans de beaux draps *OR* un beau pétrin ■ **that's a ~ way to talk!** en voilà une façon de parler! ▶ **~ one!** *UK* bravo!
5. [subtle - distinction, point] subtil, délicat.
◇ *adv* [as intensifier] : **~ long holidays** des vacances longues et agréables ■ **a ~ cold drink** une boisson bien fraîche ■ **to have a ~ long nap** faire une bonne sieste ▮ [with 'and'] : **take it ~ and easy** allez-y doucement ■ **it's ~ and warm in here** il fait bon ici.

nice-looking *adj* joli, beau *(before vowel or silent 'h'* **bel**), belle *f*.

nicely ['naɪslɪ] *adv* **1.** [well] bien ■ **it's coming along ~** ça progresse bien ■ **~ put!** bien dit! ■ **this bag will do ~** ce sac fera très bien l'affaire ■ **he's doing ~** [at school] il travaille bien ; [after illness] il se remet bien ; [financially] il s'en sort bien, il n'est pas à plaindre ▮ [pleasantly] gentiment, agréablement ■ **she smiled at me ~** elle me sourit gentiment **2.** [politely - behave, eat] bien, comme il faut ■ **ask ~** demandez gentiment **3.** [exactly] exactement, avec précision ■ [subtly] avec précision.

Nicene [naɪ'si:n] *adj* : **the ~ Creed** le symbole de Nicée.

nicety ['naɪsətɪ] (*pl* **niceties**) *n* **1.** [precision] justesse *f*, précision *f* ■ **to a ~** exactement, à la perfection **2.** *(usu pl)* [subtlety] subtilité *f*, finesse *f* ■ **the niceties of chess** les subtilités des échecs ■ **we haven't time for all these social niceties** nous n'avons guère le temps de nous livrer à ces mondanités.

niche [ni:ʃ] *n* **1.** [recess - in church, cliff] niche *f* ■ **to find one's ~** *fig* trouver sa voie **2.** COMM créneau *m* ■ **~ marketing** marketing *m* de créneau.

Nicholas ['nɪkələs] *pr n* : **Saint ~** saint Nicolas ■ **Saint ~' Day** la Saint-Nicolas.

nick [nɪk] ◇ *n* **1.** [notch] encoche *f* ■ [chip - in crockery] ébréchure *f* ■ [cut - on skin] (petite) coupure *f* **2.** △ *UK* [police station] poste *m* (de police) ■ [prison] taule *f* **3.** *UK inf* [condition] état *m* ■ **in good ~** en bon état **4.** *phr* **in the ~ of time** à point nommé.
◇ *vt* **1.** [cut - deliberately] faire une entaille *OR* une encoche sur ■ [accidentally - crockery] ébrécher ; [- metal, paint] faire des entailles dans ; [- skin, face] entailler, couper (légèrement) ■ **he ~ed his chin shaving** il s'est légèrement coupé le menton en se rasant **2.** △ *UK* [arrest] épingler **3.** *UK inf* [steal] faucher, chiper.

nickel ['nɪkl] ◇ *n* **1.** [metal] nickel *m* **2.** *US* [coin] pièce *f* de 5 cents.
◇ *vt* (*UK pret & pp* **nickelled**, *cont* **nickelling**) (*US pret & pp* **nickeled**, *cont* **nickeling**) nickeler.

nickel-and-dime store *n US magasin à prix unique*.

nickel-plated *adj* nickelé.

nickel-plating *n* nickelage *m*.

nickel silver *n* argentan *m*, maillechort *m*.

nick-nack ['nɪknæk] = **knick-knack**.

nickname ['nɪkneɪm] ◇ *n* [gen] surnom *m*, sobriquet *m* ■ [short form] diminutif *m*.
◇ *vt* surnommer.

nicotine ['nɪkəti:n] *n* nicotine *f* ■ **~ addiction** tabagisme *m*.

nicotine patch *n* patch *m OR* timbre *m* antitabac.

niece [ni:s] *n* nièce *f*.

Nietzschean ['ni:tʃɪən] *adj* nietzschéen.

niff△ [nɪf] ◇ *n UK* mauvaise odeur *f*, puanteur *f*.
◇ *vi* schlinguer△.

niffy△ ['nɪfɪ] (*comp* **niffier**, *superl* **niffiest**) *adj UK* puant.

nifty ['nɪftɪ] (*comp* **niftier**, *superl* **niftiest**) *adj inf* **1.** [stylish] chouette, classe *(inv)* **2.** [clever - solution] génial ■ **a ~ piece of work** du bon travail **3.** [quick] rapide ■ [agile] agile.

Niger *pr n* **1.** [ni:'ʒeəʳ] [country] Niger *m* ■ **in ~** au Niger **2.** ['naɪdʒəʳ] [river] : **the (River) ~** le Niger.

Nigeria [naɪ'dʒɪərɪə] *pr n* Nigeria *m* ■ **in ~** au Nigeria.

Nigerian [naɪ'dʒɪərɪən] ◇ *n* Nigérian *m*, - e *f*.
◇ *adj* nigérian.

Nigerien [ni:'ʒeərɪən] ◇ *n* Nigérien *m*, - enne *f*.
◇ *adj* nigérien.

niggard ['nɪgəd] *n* avare *m*.

niggardly ['nɪgədlɪ] *adj* [person] avare, pingre, ladre ■ [quantity] parcimonieux, chiche.

nigger▲ ['nɪgəʳ] *n terme raciste désignant un Noir*, ≃ nègre *m*, négresse *f* ■ **there's a ~ in the woodpile** *UK* [problem] il y a un hic ; [person] il y a un empêcheur de tourner en rond ; [secret] il y a anguille sous roche.

niggle ['nɪgl] ◇ *vi* **1.** [fuss over details] ergoter ■ **to ~ over** *OR* **about sthg** ergoter sur qqch **2.** [nag] trouver à redire.
◇ *vt* **1.** [worry - subj: conscience] harceler, travailler **2.** [nag] harceler.
◇ *n* **1.** [small criticism] objection *f* mineure **2.** [small worry, doubt] léger doute *m*.
◆ **niggle at** *vt insep* : **it's been niggling at me all day** ça me travaille depuis ce matin.

niggling ['nɪglɪŋ] ◇ *adj* **1.** [petty - person] tatillon ; [- details] insignifiant **2.** [fastidious - job] fastidieux **3.** [nagging - pain, doubt] tenace.
◇ *n* chicanerie *f*, pinaillerie *f*.

niggly ['nɪglɪ] (*comp* **nigglier**, *superl* **niggliest**) *adj inf* pinailleur.

nigh [naɪ] *lit* ◇ *adv* : **well ~ 80 years** près de 80 ans ■ **well ~ impossible** presque impossible.
◇ *adj* proche ■ **the hour is ~** c'est bientôt *OR* presque l'heure.
◇ *prep* près de, proche de.
◆ **nigh on** *adv phr* presque.

night [naɪt] ◇ *n* **1.** [late] nuit *f* ■ [evening] soir *m*, soirée *f* ■ **at ~** [evening] le soir ; [late] la nuit ■ **ten o'clock at ~** dix heures du soir ■ **all ~ (long)** toute la nuit ■ **by ~** de nuit ■ **during** *OR* **in the ~** pendant la nuit ■ **(on) Tuesday ~** [evening] mardi soir ; [during night] dans la nuit de mardi à mercredi ■ **last ~** [evening] hier soir ; [during night] cette nuit ■ **the ~ before** [evening] la veille au soir ; [late] la nuit précédente ■ **far** *OR* **late into the ~** jusqu'à une heure avancée de la nuit ■ **it's weeks since we had a ~ out** ça fait des semaines que nous ne sommes pas sortis le soir ■ **Tuesday's our poker ~** le mardi, c'est notre soirée poker, le mardi soir, nous faisons un poker ■ **to have a late ~** se coucher tard ■ **this has been going on ~ after ~** cela s'est prolongé des nuits durant ■ **I had a bad ~** j'ai passé une mauvaise nuit, j'ai mal dormi ■ **let's make a ~ of it!** [have fun] faisons la fête toute la nuit! ➊ **the ~ of the long knives** la nuit des longs couteaux ■ **the ~ is young** *liter* la nuit n'est pas très avancée ; *hum* on a toute la nuit devant nous ■ **'The Night Watch'** ***Rembrandt*** 'la Ronde de nuit' **2.** [darkness] obscurité *f* ■ *fig* ténèbres *fpl* ■ **~ falls early** il fait nuit tôt, la nuit tombe tôt **3.** THEAT soirée *f* ■ **gala ~** soirée de gala.

◇ *comp* [duty, flight, sky] de nuit.

◆ **nights** *adv* de nuit ■ **to work ~s** travailler de nuit ■ **to lie awake ~s** *US* ne pas dormir la nuit.

night bird *n* ORNITH oiseau *m* nocturne *OR* de nuit ■ *fig* noctambule *mf*, oiseau *m* de nuit.

night blindness *n (U)* héméralopie *f*.

nightcap ['naɪtkæp] *n* **1.** [drink - gen] boisson *f (que l'on prend avant d'aller se coucher)* ; [- alcoholic] dernier verre *m (avant d'aller se coucher)* **2.** [headgear] bonnet *m* de nuit.

nightclothes ['naɪtkləʊðz] *npl* [pyjamas] pyjama *m* ■ [nightdress] chemise *f* de nuit.

nightclub ['naɪtklʌb] *n* night-club *m*, boîte *f* de nuit.

nightclubbing ['naɪtklʌbɪŋ] *n* : **to go ~** sortir en boîte.

nightdress ['naɪtdres] *n* chemise *f* de nuit.

night editor *n* rédacteur *m*, - trice *f* de nuit *(dans un journal)*.

nightfall ['naɪtfɔːl] *n* tombée *f* de la nuit *OR* du jour.

night fighter *n* chasseur *m* de nuit.

nightgown ['naɪtgaʊn] = **nightdress**.

nightie ['naɪtɪ] *n inf* chemise *f* de nuit.

nightingale ['naɪtɪŋgeɪl] *n* rossignol *m*.

nightjar ['naɪtdʒɑːʳ] *n* engoulevent *m* (d'Europe).

nightlife ['naɪtlaɪf] *n* vie *f* nocturne ■ **what's the ~ like round here?** qu'est-ce qu'on peut faire le soir, ici?

nightlight ['naɪtlaɪt] *n* veilleuse *f*.

nightlong ['naɪtlɒŋ] ◇ *adj* qui dure toute la nuit ■ **a ~ vigil** une nuit de veille.

◇ *adv* pendant toute la nuit, la nuit durant.

nightly ['naɪtlɪ] ◇ *adj* [happening every night] de tous les soirs, de chaque nuit.

◇ *adv* tous les soirs, chaque soir.

nightmare ['naɪtmeəʳ] ◇ *n liter & fig* cauchemar *m* ■ **I had a ~** j'ai fait un cauchemar.

◇ *comp* [vision, experience] cauchemardesque, de cauchemar.

nightmarish ['naɪtmeərɪʃ] *adj* cauchemardesque, de cauchemar.

night-night *interj inf* **~!** bonne nuit!

night nurse *n* infirmier *m*, - ère *f* de nuit.

night owl *n inf* couche-tard *mf inv*.

night porter *n* portier *m* de nuit.

night safe *n* coffre *m* de nuit.

night school *n* cours *mpl* du soir ■ **to go to ~** suivre des cours du soir ■ **in** *US* *OR* **at** *UK* **~** aux cours du soir.

nightshade ['naɪtʃeɪd] *n* morelle *f*.

night shift *n* [work force] équipe *f* de nuit ■ [period of duty] poste *m* de nuit ■ **to be on the ~** être de nuit.

nightshirt ['naɪtʃɜːt] *n* chemise *f* de nuit.

night soil *n* fumier *m (d'excréments humains)*.

nightspot ['naɪtspɒt] *n inf* boîte *f* (de nuit).

nightstick ['naɪtstɪk] *n US* matraque *f (de policier)*.

night storage heater *n* radiateur *m* à accumulation.

night-time *n* nuit *f* ■ **at ~** la nuit.

night vision *n* vision *f* nocturne.

night watchman *n* veilleur *m* de nuit.

nightwear ['naɪtweəʳ] *n (U)* = **nightclothes**.

nighty ['naɪtɪ] (*pl* **nighties**) *inf* = **nightie**.

nighty-night *inf* = **night-night**.

nihilism ['naɪɪlɪzm] *n* nihilisme *m*.

nihilist ['naɪɪlɪst] ◇ *adj* nihiliste.

◇ *n* nihiliste *mf*.

nihilistic [ˌnaɪɪ'lɪstɪk] *adj* nihiliste.

Nike ['naɪkiː] *pr n* MYTH Nikê.

nil [nɪl] ◇ *n* [gen - SPORT] zéro *m* ■ [on written form] néant *m*.

◇ *adj* nul, zéro *(inv)*.

Nile [naɪl] *pr n* : **the (River) ~** *UK*, **the ~ River** *US* le Nil.

nimbi ['nɪmbaɪ] *pl* ▻ **nimbus**.

nimble ['nɪmbl] *adj* **1.** [agile - body, movements] agile ; [- fingers] adroit, habile ■ **she's very ~ for (someone of) her age** elle est très alerte pour (quelqu'un de) son âge ■ [skilful] habile **2.** [quick - thought, mind] vif, prompt.

nimble-witted *adj* vif (d'esprit), à l'esprit vif *OR* rapide.

nimbly ['nɪmblɪ] *adv* agilement, lestement, prestement.

nimbus ['nɪmbəs] (*pl* **nimbi** ['nɪmbaɪ] *OR pl* **nimbuses**) *n* **1.** METEOR nimbus *m* **2.** [halo] nimbe *m*, auréole *f*.

nincompoop ['nɪŋkəmpuːp] *n inf* cruche *f*.

nine [naɪn] ◇ *det* neuf *(inv)* ■ **a ~-hole golf course** un (parcours de) neuf trous ■ **~ times out of ten** neuf fois sur dix ➊ **a ~ days' wonder** *UK* un feu de paille, *see also* **five**.

◇ *n* **1.** neuf *m inv* ■ **he was dressed up to the ~s** il s'était mis sur son trente et un, *see also* **five** **2.** *US* SPORT équipe *f* (de base-ball).

◇ *pron* neuf.

ninefold ['naɪnfəʊld] ◇ *adj* neuf fois supérieur.

◇ *adv* neuf fois ■ **to increase ~** (se) multiplier par neuf.

ninepin ['naɪnpɪn] *n* [skittle] quille *f* ■ **to go down like ~s** *UK* tomber comme des mouches.

◆ **ninepins** *n* [game] quilles *fpl*.

nineteen [ˌnaɪn'tiːn] ◇ *det* dix-neuf.

◇ *n* dix-neuf *m* ■ **they were talking ~ to the dozen** *UK* ils étaient intarissables, il n'y avait pas moyen de les faire taire, *see also* **five**.

◇ *pron* dix-neuf.

nineteenth [ˌnaɪn'tiːnθ] ◇ *det* dix-neuvième ■ **the ~ hole** *hum* [in golf] le bar (du club), *see also* **fifth**.

◇ *n* **1.** [ordinal] dix-neuvième *mf*, *see also* **fifth** **2.** [fraction] dix-neuvième *m*.

ninetieth ['naɪntɪəθ] ◇ *det* quatre-vingt-dixième, *see also* **fifth**.

◇ *n* **1.** [ordinal] quatre-vingt-dixième *mf*, *see also* **fifth** **2.** [fraction] quatre-vingt-dixième *m*.

nine-to-five ◇ *adv* de neuf heures du matin à cinq heures du soir ■ **to work ~** avoir des horaires de bureau.

◇ *adj* **1.** [job] routinier **2.** [mentality, attitude] de gratte-papier.

ninety ['naɪntɪ] (*pl* **nineties**) ◇ *det* quatre-vingt-dix.

◇ *n* quatre-vingt-dix *m* ■ **~-one** quatre-vingt-onze ■ **~-two** quatre-vingt-douze ■ **~-nine** quatre-vingt-dix-neuf ■ **he's in his nineties** il est nonagénaire, il a quatre-vingt-dix ans passés ■ **in the nineties** dans les années quatre-vingt-dix, *see also* **fifty**.

◇ *pron* quatre-vingt-dix.

ninny ['nɪnɪ] (*pl* **ninnies**) *n inf* empoté *m*, - e *f*, nigaud *m*, - e *f*, bêta *m*, - asse *f*.

ninth [naɪnθ] <> *adj* neuvième, *see also* **fifth**.
<> *n* **1.** [ordinal] neuvième *mf*, *see also* **fifth 2.** [fraction] neuvième *m*.
<> *adv* [in contest] en neuvième position, à la neuvième place.

nip [nɪp] <> *n* **1.** [pinch] pincement *m* ■ [bite] morsure *f* **2.** [cold] froid *m* piquant ■ **there's a ~ in the air** ça pince **3.** [in taste] goût *m* piquant **4.** [of alcohol] goutte *f* **5.** *phr* **~ and tuck** *hum* [plastic surgery] chirurgie *f* esthéthique ■ **to be ~ and tuck** être au coude à coude.
<> *vt* (*pret & pp* **nipped**, *cont* **nipping**) **1.** [pinch] pincer ■ [bite] mordre (légèrement), mordiller ■ **she nipped her finger in the door** elle s'est pincé le doigt dans la porte ■ **the puppy nipped my leg** le chiot m'a mordillé la jambe **2.** HORT [plant, shoot] pincer ■ **to ~ sthg in the bud** *fig* tuer OR écraser OR étouffer qqch dans l'œuf **3.** [numb, freeze] geler, piquer ■ **the vines were nipped by the frost** les vignes ont été grillées par le gel **4.** *US inf* [steal] piquer, faucher.
<> *vi* (*pret & pp* **nipped**, *cont* **nipping**) **1.** [try to bite] : **the dog nipped at my ankles** le chien m'a mordillé les chevilles **2.** *UK inf* [go] faire un saut ■ **to ~ (across OR along OR over) to the butcher's** faire un saut chez le boucher ■ **we just nipped out for a drink** on est sorti prendre un pot en vitesse.
◆ **nip off** <> *vt sep* [cut off] couper ■ HORT pincer.
<> *vi insep UK inf* filer.

Nip▲ [nɪp] *n terme injurieux désignant un Japonais*, ≃ Jap *mf*.

nipper ['nɪpəʳ] *n* **1.** [of crab, lobster] pince *f* **2.** *UK inf* [child] gosse *mf*, môme *mf*.
◆ **nippers** *npl* [tool] pince *f* ■ **a pair of ~s** une pince.

nipple ['nɪpl] *n* **1.** [on breast] mamelon *m* ■ [on animal] tétine *f*, mamelle *f* **2.** [teat - on feeding bottle] tétine *f* **3.** *US* [baby's dummy] tétine *f* **4.** TECH [of pump] embout *m* ■ [for greasing] graisseur *m* ■ [connector] raccord *m*.

nippy ['nɪpɪ] (*comp* **nippier**, *superl* **nippiest**) *adj* **1.** *inf* [weather] frisquet ■ [cold] piquant **2.** *UK inf* [quick] vif, rapide.

nirvana [,nɪə'vɑːnə] *n* nirvana *m*.

nisi ['naɪsaɪ] **decree nisi**.

Nissen hut ['nɪsn-] *n UK* MIL abri *m (en tôle ondulée)*.

nit [nɪt] *n* **1.** ENTOM lente *f* ■ [in hair] pou *m* **2.** *UK inf* [idiot] andouille *f*.

nitpick ['nɪtpɪk] *vi inf* couper les cheveux en quatre, chercher la petite bête, pinailler.

nitpicking ['nɪtpɪkɪŋ] *inf* <> *n* chicanerie *f*, pinaillage *m*.
<> *adj* chicanier.

nitrate ['naɪtreɪt] *n* nitrate *m*, azotate *m*.

nitric acid ['naɪtrɪk-] *n* acide *m* nitrique.

nitrogen ['naɪtrədʒən] *n* azote *m*.

nitroglycerine [,naɪtrəʊ'glɪsəriːn] *n* nitroglycérine *f*.

nitty-gritty [,nɪtɪ'grɪtɪ] *n inf* essentiel *m* ■ **let's get down to the ~** venons-en au cœur du problème.

nitwit ['nɪtwɪt] *n inf* andouille *f*.

nix [nɪks] *US inf* <> *interj* **1.** [no] non **2.** [watch out] attention.
<> *n* rien *m*.
<> *vt* [refuse] rejeter, refuser ■ [veto] opposer un veto à.

NJ *written abbr of* **New Jersey**.

NLQ (*abbrev of* **near letter quality**) *n qualité quasi-courrier*.

NM *written abbr of* **New Mexico**.

no [nəʊ] (*pl* **noes** OR *pl* **nos**) <> *adv* **1.** [expressing refusal, disagreement] non ■ **do you like spinach? - no, I don't** aimez-vous les épinards? - non ■ **oh no you don't!** [forbidding, stopping] oh que non! ➊ **they won't take no for an answer** ils n'accepteront aucun refus
2. [with comparative adj or adv] : **I can go no further** je ne peux pas aller plus loin ■ **we'll go no further than three million** on n'ira pas au-delà de OR nous ne dépasserons pas les trois millions ■ **you're no better than he is** vous ne valez pas mieux que lui ■ **call me, if you're (feeling) no better in the morning** appelez-moi si vous ne vous sentez pas mieux demain matin **3.** *lit* [not] : **whether you wish it or no** que vous le vouliez ou non.
<> *det* **1.** [not any, not one] : **I have no family** je n'ai pas de famille ■ **she has no intention of leaving** elle n'a aucune intention de partir ■ **no sensible person would dispute this** quelqu'un de raisonnable ne discuterait pas ■ **no other washing powder gets clothes so clean** aucune autre lessive ne laisse votre linge aussi propre ■ **no one company can handle all the orders** une seule entreprise ne pourra jamais s'occuper de toutes les commandes ■ **no two experts ever come up with the same answer** il n'y a pas deux experts qui soient d'accord ■ **there's no telling** nul ne peut le dire
2. [not a] : **I'm no expert, I'm afraid** malheureusement, je ne suis pas un expert ■ **it will be no easy task persuading them** ce ne sera pas une tâche facile que de les persuader
3. [introducing a prohibition] : **'no smoking'** 'défense de fumer' ■ **'no swimming'** 'baignade interdite'.
<> *n* non *m inv*.
<> *interj* non.

No., no. (*written abbrev of* **number**) No, no.

no-account *US inf* <> *n* bon *m* à rien, bonne *f* à rien.
<> *adj* bon à rien.

Noah ['nəʊə] *pr n* Noé ■ **~'s Ark** l'arche de Noé.

nob [nɒb] *n inf* **1.** *UK* [wealthy person] richard *m*, - e *f* **2.** [head] caboche *f*.

no-ball *n* SPORT balle *f* nulle.

nobble ['nɒbl] *vt UK inf* **1.** [jury, witness - bribe] graisser la patte à ; [- threaten] manipuler (avec des menaces) **2.** [racehorse] mettre hors d'état de courir ■ [with drugs] droguer **3.** [grab, catch - person] accrocher(au passage), agrafer **4.** [steal] faucher, barboter.

Nobel [nəʊ'bel] *comp* : **~ prize** prix *m* Nobel ■ **~ prizewinner** lauréat *m*, - e *f* du prix Nobel.

nobility [nə'bɪlətɪ] (*pl* **nobilities**) *n* **1.** [aristocracy] noblesse *f*, aristocratie *f* **2.** [loftiness] noblesse *f*, majesté *f*, grandeur *f*.

noble ['nəʊbl] <> *adj* **1.** [aristocratic] noble ■ **of ~ birth** de haute naissance, de naissance noble **2.** [fine, distinguished - aspiration, purpose] noble, élevé ; [- bearing, manner] noble, gracieux, majestueux ; [- person] noble, supérieur ; [- animal] noble ; [- wine] grand **3.** [generous - gesture] généreux, magnanime **4.** [brave - deed, feat] noble, héroïque ■ **the ~ art OR science** la boxe **5.** [impressive - monument] noble, majestueux **6.** CHEM [gas, metal] noble.
<> *n* noble *mf*, aristocrate *mf*.

nobleman ['nəʊblmən] (*pl* **noblemen** [-mən]) *n* noble *m*, aristocrate *m*.

noble-minded *adj* magnanime, généreux.

noblewoman ['nəʊbl,wʊmən] (*pl* **noblewomen** [-,wɪmɪn]) *n* noble *f*, aristocrate *f*.

nobly ['nəʊblɪ] *adv* **1.** [by birth] noblement ■ **~ born** de haute naissance **2.** [majestically, superbly] majestueusement, superbement **3.** [generously] généreusement, magnanimement **4.** [bravely] noblement, courageusement.

nobody ['nəʊbədɪ] (*pl* **nobodies**) <> *pron* personne ■ **~ came** personne n'est venu ■ **~ else** personne d'autre ■ **who was at the party? - ~ you know** qui était à la fête? - personne que tu connais ■ **~ famous** personne de célèbre ➊ **she's ~'s fool** elle n'est pas née d'hier OR tombée de la dernière pluie.
<> *n* [insignificant person] moins que rien *mf*.

no-claim(s) bonus *n UK* [in insurance] bonus *m*.

nocturnal [nɒk'tɜːnl] *adj* nocturne.

nocturne ['nɒktɜːn] *n* nocturne *m*.

nod [nɒd] <> *vt* (*pret & pp* **nodded**, *cont* **nodding**) : **to ~ one's head** [as signal] faire un signe de (la) tête ; [in assent] faire oui de la tête, faire un signe de tête affirmatif ; [in greeting] saluer d'un signe de tête ; [with fatigue] dodeliner de la tête ■ **she nodded her head in approval OR nodded her approval** elle manifesta son approbation d'un signe de tête.
<> *vi* (*pret & pp* **nodded**, *cont* **nodding**) **1.** [as signal] faire un signe de (la) tête ■ [in assent, approval] faire un signe de tête

affirmatif, faire oui de la tête ■ [in greeting] saluer d'un signe de tête **2.** [doze] somnoler **3.** *fig* [flowers] danser, se balancer ■ [crops, trees] se balancer, onduler.
◇ *n* **1.** [sign] signe *m* de (la) tête ■ **to give sb a ~** [as signal] faire un signe de tête à qqn ; [in assent] faire un signe de tête affirmatif à qqn ; [in greeting] saluer qqn d'un signe de tête ➤ **a ~ is as good as a wink (to a blind man)** inutile d'en dire plus ■ **to get the ~** *UK OR* **a ~** *US* [gen] obtenir le feu vert ; [in boxing] gagner aux points ■ **on the ~** *UK* [without formality] : **to approve sthg on the ~** approuver qqch d'un commun accord **2.** [sleep] : **the land of Nod** le pays des rêves.
◆ **nod off** *vi insep inf* s'endormir, s'assoupir.

nodal ['nəʊdl] *adj* nodal.

nodding ['nɒdɪŋ] *adj UK* **to have a ~ acquaintance with sb** connaître qqn de vue *OR* vaguement ■ **a ~ acquaintance with marketing techniques** *fig* quelques notions des techniques de marketing.

noddle ['nɒdl] *n inf* caboche *f*.

noddy ['nɒdɪ] *UK inf adj* : **he's got a ~ job** il fait un boulot peinard.

node [nəʊd] *n* ASTRON, BOT, LING & MATHS nœud *m* ■ ANAT nodosité *f*, nodule *m*.

nodule ['nɒdju:l] *n* nodule *m*.

Noel, Noël [nəʊ'el] *n lit* [Christmas] Noël *m*.

no-fly zone *n* zone *f* d'exclusion aérienne.

no-frills *adj* sans fioritures, (tout) simple, sommaire ■ **a ~ hotel** un hôtel sans confort superflu.

noggin ['nɒgɪn] *n* **1.** [measure] quart *m* de pinte **2.** *inf* [drink] pot *m* **3.** *inf* [head] caboche *f*.

no-go area *n* zone *f* interdite.

no-good *inf* ◇ *adj* propre à rien.
◇ *n* bon *m* à rien, bonne *f* à rien.

no-holds-barred *adj* [report, documentary] sans fard.

no-hoper [-'həʊpər] *n inf* raté *m*, - e *f*, minable *mf*.

nohow ['nəʊhaʊ] *adv inf* aucunement.

noise [nɔɪz] ◇ *n* **1.** [sound] bruit *m*, son *m* ■ **the clock is making a funny ~** la pendule fait un drôle de bruit ■ **I thought I heard a ~ downstairs** j'ai cru entendre du bruit en bas ■ **the humming ~ of the engine** le ronronnement du moteur ➤ **~s off** THEAT bruitage *m* **2.** [din] bruit *m*, tapage *m*, tintamarre *m* ■ [very loud] vacarme *m* ■ **to make a ~** faire du bruit ■ **shut your ~!** *UK inf* ferme-la! ➤ **~ abatement** lutte *f* contre le bruit ■ **~ pollution** nuisances *fpl* sonores, pollution *f* sonore **3.** ELEC & TELEC parasites *mpl* ■ [on line] friture *f*, sifflement *m* **4.** *inf phr* **to make a ~ about sthg** faire du tapage *OR* beaucoup de bruit autour de qqch.
◇ *vt* : **to ~ sthg about** *OR* **abroad** ébruiter qqch.
◆ **noises** *npl inf* [indications of intentions] : **she made vague ~s about emigrating** elle a vaguement parlé d'émigrer ■ **he started making placatory ~s** il se mit à marmonner quelques paroles d'apaisement ■ **they made all the right ~s, but...** ils ont fait semblant de marcher à fond *OR* d'être tout à fait d'accord, mais...

noiseless ['nɔɪzlɪs] *adj* silencieux.

noiselessly ['nɔɪzlɪslɪ] *adv* silencieusement, sans faire de bruit.

noisily ['nɔɪzɪlɪ] *adv* bruyamment.

noisome ['nɔɪsəm] *adj lit* [repellent] répugnant, repoussant ■ [smelly] puant, méphitique *lit* ■ [noxious] nocif, nuisible.

noisy ['nɔɪzɪ] (*comp* **noisier**, *superl* **noisiest**) *adj* **1.** [machine, engine, person] bruyant ■ **my typewriter is very ~** ma machine à écrire est très bruyante *OR* fait beaucoup de bruit **2.** [colour] criard.

nomad ['nəʊmæd] *n* nomade *mf*.

nomadic [nəʊ'mædɪk] *adj* nomade.

no-man's-land *n liter & fig* no man's land *m inv*.

nom de plume [ˌnɒmdə'plu:m] *n* pseudonyme *m*, nom *m* de plume.

nomenclature [*UK* nəʊ'menklətʃər, *US* 'nəʊmənkleɪtʃər] *n* nomenclature *f*.

nominal ['nɒmɪnl] ◇ *adj* **1.** [in name only - owner, leader] de nom (seulement), nominal ; [- ownership, leadership] nominal **2.** [negligible] insignifiant ■ [token] symbolique **3.** GRAM nominal.
◇ *n* GRAM élément *m* nominal ■ [noun phrase] groupe *m* nominal ■ [pronoun] nominal *m*.

nominalization [ˌnɒmɪnəlaɪ'zeɪʃn] *n* nominalisation *f*.

nominally ['nɒmɪnəlɪ] *adv* **1.** [in name only] nominalement **2.** [as token] pour la forme **3.** [theoretically] théoriquement.

nominal value *n* valeur *f* nominale.

nominate ['nɒmɪneɪt] *vt* **1.** [propose] proposer (la candidature de) ■ **to ~ sb for a post** proposer la candidature de qqn à un poste ❙ [for award] sélectionner, nominer ■ **the film was ~d for an Oscar** le film a été sélectionné *OR* nominé pour un Oscar **2.** [appoint] nommer, désigner ■ **he was ~d chairman** *OR* **to the chairmanship** il fut nommé président.

nomination [ˌnɒmɪ'neɪʃn] *n* **1.** [proposal] proposition *f* ■ **who will get the Democratic ~ (for president)?** qui obtiendra l'investiture démocrate (à l'élection présidentielle)? ❙ [for award] nomination *f* ■ **the film got three Oscar ~s** le film a obtenu trois nominations aux Oscars **2.** [appointment] nomination *f*.

nominative ['nɒmɪnətɪv] ◇ *n* GRAM nominatif *m* ■ **in the ~** au nominatif.
◇ *adj* GRAM nominatif ■ **the ~ case** le nominatif.

nominator ['nɒmɪneɪtər] *n* présentateur *m*, - trice *f (d'un candidat)*.

nominee [ˌnɒmɪ'ni:] *n* **1.** [proposed] candidat *m*, - e *f* **2.** [appointed] personne *f* désignée *OR* nommée.

non- [nɒn] *in cpds* **1.** [not] non- ■ **all ~French nationals** tous les ressortissants de nationalité autre que française **2.** [against] anti-.

nonacademic [ˌnɒnækə'demɪk] *adj* **1.** [activity - SCH] extrascolaire ■ UNIV extra-universitaire **2.** SCH & UNIV [staff] non enseignant **3.** [course] pratique, technique.

nonacceptance [ˌnɒnək'septəns] *n* non-acceptation *f*.

nonachiever [ˌnɒnə'tʃi:vər] *n* élève *mf* qui ne réussit pas.

nonaddictive [ˌnɒnə'dɪktɪv] *adj* qui ne crée pas de phénomène d'accoutumance.

nonadmission [ˌnɒnəd'mɪʃn] *n* non-admission *f*.

nonaerosol [ˌnɒn'eərəsɒl] *adj* [container] non pressurisé.

nonaffiliated [ˌnɒnə'fɪlɪeɪtɪd] *adj* non affilié, indépendant.

nonagenarian [ˌnəʊnədʒɪ'neərɪən] ◇ *adj* nonagénaire.
◇ *n* nonagénaire *mf*.

nonaggression [ˌnɒnə'greʃn] *n* non-agression *f* ■ **~ pact** pacte *m* de non-agression.

nonalcoholic [ˌnɒnælkə'hɒlɪk] *adj* non alcoolisé, sans alcool.

nonaligned [ˌnɒnə'laɪnd] *adj* non-aligné.

nonalignment [ˌnɒnə'laɪnmənt] *n* non-alignement *m*.

nonappearance [ˌnɒnə'pɪərəns] *n* LAW non-comparution *f*.

nonarrival [ˌnɒnə'raɪvl] *n* non-arrivée *f*.

nonattendance [ˌnɒnə'tendəns] *n* absence *f*.

nonavailability ['nɒnəˌveɪlə'bɪlətɪ] *n* non-disponibilité *f*.

nonbeliever [ˌnɒnbɪ'li:vər] *n* non-croyant *m*, - e *f*, incroyant *m*, - e *f*.

nonbelligerent [ˌnɒnbɪ'lɪdʒərənt] *adj* non-belligérant.

nonbinding [ˌnɒn'baɪndɪŋ] *adj* sans obligation, non contraignant.

nonbiodegradable ['nɒnˌbaɪəʊdɪ'greɪdəbl] *adj* non biodégradable.

nonce [nɒns] *n lit & hum* **for the ~** pour l'instant.

nonce word *n* mot *m* créé pour l'occasion.

nonchalance [*UK* 'nɒnʃələns, *US* ˌnɒnʃə'lɑːns] *n* nonchalance *f*.

nonchalant [*UK* 'nɒnʃələnt, *US* ˌnɒnʃə'lɑːnt] *adj* nonchalant.

nonchalantly [*UK* 'nɒnʃələntlɪ, *US* ˌnɒnʃə'lɑːntlɪ] *adv* nonchalamment, avec nonchalance.

noncom ['nɒnkɒm] *n inf* sous-off *m*.

noncombatant [*UK* ˌnɒn'kɒmbətənt, *US* ˌnɒnkəm'bætənt] <> *n* non-combattant *m*, - e *f*.
<> *adj* non-combattant.

noncombustible [ˌnɒnkəm'bʌstəbl] *adj* incombustible.

noncommissioned officer [ˌnɒnkə'mɪʃnd-] *n* sous-officier *m*.

noncommittal [ˌnɒnkə'mɪtl] *adj* [statement] évasif, qui n'engage à rien ▪ [attitude, person] réservé ▪ [gesture] peu révélateur ▪ **she gave a ~ grunt** elle émit un petit grognement qui ne l'engageait ni dans un sens, ni dans l'autre ▪ **he was very ~ about his plans** il s'est montré très réservé.

noncompetitive [ˌnɒnkəm'petɪtɪv] *adj* qui n'est pas basé sur la compétition.

noncompliance [ˌnɒnkəm'plaɪəns] *n* non-respect *m*, non-observation *f* ▪ **~ with the treaty** le non-respect du traité.

non compos mentis ['nɒnˌkɒmpɒs'mentɪs] *adj* fou *(before vowel or silent 'h' fol)*, folle *f*, dément, irresponsable.

nonconductor [ˌnɒnkən'dʌktər] *n* non-conducteur *m*.

nonconformism [ˌnɒnkən'fɔːmɪzm] *n* [gen] non-conformisme *m*.
◆ **Nonconformism** *n* RELIG non-conformisme *m*.

nonconformist [ˌnɒnkən'fɔːmɪst] <> *n* [gen] non-conformiste *mf*.
<> *adj* [gen] non-conformiste.
◆ **Nonconformist** RELIG <> *n* non-conformiste *mf*.
<> *adj* non-conformiste.

nonconformity [ˌnɒnkən'fɔːmətɪ] *n* [gen] non-conformité *f*.
◆ **Nonconformity** RELIG = **Nonconformism**.

noncontributory [ˌnɒnkən'trɪbjʊtərɪ] *adj UK* **a ~ pension scheme** un régime de retraite sans retenues *OR* cotisations.

noncooperation ['nɒnkəʊˌɒpə'reɪʃn] *n* refus *m* de coopérer.

non-dairy *adj* qui ne contient aucun produit laitier ▪ **~ cream** *US crème liquide d'origine végétale.*

non-dazzle *adj* antiéblouissement *(inv)*.

nondeductible [ˌnɒndɪ'dʌktəbl] *adj* non déductible.

nondelivery [ˌnɒndɪ'lɪvərɪ] *n* : **in the event of ~** dans l'éventualité où les marchandises ne seraient pas livrées.

nondescript [*UK* 'nɒndɪskrɪpt, *US* ˌnɒndɪ'skrɪpt] *adj* quelconque ▪ **a ~ little man** un petit homme que rien ne distingue des autres *OR* tout à fait anodin.

nondrinker [ˌnɒn'drɪŋkər] *n* abstinent *m*, - e *f* ▪ **she's a ~** elle ne boit pas (d'alcool).

nondrip [ˌnɒn'drɪp] *adj* antigoutte *(inv)*.

nondriver [ˌnɒn'draɪvər] *n* : **I'm a ~** [never learnt] je n'ai pas mon permis ; [out of choice] je ne conduis pas.

none [nʌn] <> *pron* **1.** [with countable nouns] aucun *m*, - e *f* ▪ **~ of the photos is** *OR* **are for sale** aucune des photos n'est à vendre ▪ **there are ~ left** il n'en reste plus ▪ **how many cigarettes have you got? – ~ at all** combien de cigarettes as-tu? – aucune *OR* pas une seule ▮ [with uncountable nouns] : **~ of the mail is for you** il n'y a rien pour vous au courrier ▪ **I've done a lot of work but you've done ~** j'ai beaucoup travaillé, mais toi tu n'as rien fait ▪ **she displayed ~ of her usual good humour** elle était loin d'afficher sa bonne humeur habituelle ▪ **more soup anyone? – ~ for me, thanks** encore un peu de soupe? – pas pour moi, merci ▶ **(I'll have) ~ of your cheek!** je ne tolérerai pas vos insolences! ▪ **~ of that!** [stop it] pas de ça! ▪ **she would have ~ of it** elle ne voulait rien savoir **2.** [not one person] aucun *m*, - e *f* ▪ **~ of us understood his explanation** aucun de nous n'a compris son explication ▪ **there was ~ braver than her** *lit* nul n'était plus courageux qu'elle.
<> *adv US inf* [in double negatives] : **that won't change things ~** ça ne changera rien.
◆ **none but** *adv phr fml & lit* **we use ~ but the finest ingredients** nous n'utilisons que les meilleurs ingrédients.
◆ **none other than** *prep phr* personne d'autre que ▪ **he received a letter from ~ other than the Prime Minister himself** il reçut une lettre dont l'auteur n'était autre que le Premier ministre en personne.
◆ **none the** *adv phr (with compar adj)* **I feel ~ the better/worse for it** je ne me sens pas mieux/plus mal pour autant ▪ **she's ~ the worse for her adventure** son aventure ne lui a pas fait de mal.
◆ **none too** *adv phr* : **he's ~ too bright** il est loin d'être brillant ▪ **and ~ too soon!** ce n'est pas trop tôt!

nonentity [nɒn'entətɪ] *(pl* **nonentities***) n* **1.** [insignificant person] personne *f* insignifiante, nullité *f* **2.** [insignificance] inexistence *f*.

nonessential [ˌnɒnɪ'senʃl] <> *adj* accessoire, non essentiel ▪ **~ details** des détails superflus.
<> *n* : **the ~s** l'accessoire *m*, le superflu ▪ **leave behind all ~s** n'emportez que l'essentiel.

nonetheless [ˌnʌnðə'les] = **nevertheless**.

non-event *n* non-événement *m*.

nonexistent [ˌnɒnɪg'zɪstənt] *adj* non-existant, inexistant ▪ **his help has been almost ~** *inf* il ne s'est pas beaucoup foulé pour nous aider.

nonfat ['nɒnfæt] *adj* sans matière grasse *OR* matières grasses.

nonfattening [ˌnɒn'fætnɪŋ] *adj* qui ne fait pas grossir.

nonfiction [ˌnɒn'fɪkʃn] <> *n (U)* ouvrages *mpl* non romanesques.
<> *comp* : **~ section** [of bookshop] rayon *m* des ouvrages généraux.

nonfigurative [ˌnɒn'fɪgjʊrətɪv] *adj* non-figuratif.

nonflammable [ˌnɒn'flæməbl] *adj* ininflammable.

non-governmental organization *n* organisation *f* non gouvernementale.

non-habit-forming [-ˌfɔːmɪŋ] *adj* qui ne crée pas de phénomène d'accoutumance.

noninfectious [ˌnɒnɪn'fekʃəs] *adj* qui n'est pas infectieux.

noninflammable [ˌnɒnɪn'flæməbl] = **nonflammable**.

noninterference [ˌnɒnɪntə'fɪərəns], **nonintervention** [ˌnɒnɪntə'venʃn] *n* non-intervention *f*, non-ingérence *f*.

noninterventionist [ˌnɒnɪntə'venʃənɪst] *adj* [policy] non interventionniste, de non-intervention.

non-iron *adj* qui ne nécessite aucun repassage.

nonjudg(e)mental [ˌnɒndʒʌdʒ'mentl] *adj* neutre, impartial.

nonmalignant [ˌnɒnmə'lɪgnənt] *adj* bénin.

nonmember ['nɒnˌmembər] *n* non-membre *m* ▪ [of a club] personne *f* étrangère (au club) ▪ **open to ~s** ouvert au public.

nonmetallic [ˌnɒnmɪ'tælɪk] *adj* non-métallique.

non-native *adj* non-indigène ▪ **~ speaker** locuteur *m* étranger *OR* non natif, locutrice *f* étrangère *OR* non native.

non-negotiable *adj* non négociable.

no-no *n inf* interdit *m* ▪ **dating someone from work is a ~** sortir avec un collègue de travail, c'est l'erreur à ne pas faire.

nonobservance [ˌnɒnəb'zɜːvəns] *n* [of rules] non observation *f* ▪ [of treaty] non-respect *m* ▪ RELIG inobservance *f*.

no-nonsense *adj* [efficient] pratique ■ **she's got a very ~ approach** elle va droit au but.

nonoperational [ˌnɒnɒpəˈreɪʃənl] *adj* non-opérationnel.

nonparticipant [ˌnɒnpɑːˈtɪsɪpənt] *n* non participant *m*, - e *f*.

nonparticipation [ˌnɒnpɑːtɪsəˈpeɪʃn] *n* non-participation *f*.

nonpartisan [ˈnɒnˌpɑːtɪˈzæn] *adj* impartial, sans parti pris.

nonparty [ˌnɒnˈpɑːtɪ] *adj* indépendant.

nonpayment [ˌnɒnˈpeɪmənt] *n* non-paiement *m*, défaut *m* de paiement.

nonperson [ˌnɒnˈpɜːsən] *n* **1.** [stateless person] *personne mise au ban de la société* **2.** [insignificant person] personne *f* insignifiante, nullité *f*.

nonplussed [ˌnɒnˈplʌst] *adj* dérouté, perplexe.

nonpractising [ˌnɒnˈpræktɪsɪŋ] *adj* non pratiquant.

nonproductive [ˌnɒnprəˈdʌktɪv] *adj* ECON improductif.

nonprofit [ˌnɒnˈprɒfɪt] *US* = **non-profitmaking.**

non-profitmaking *adj UK* à but non lucratif.

nonproliferation [ˈnɒnprəˌlɪfəˈreɪʃn] *n* non-prolifération *f*.

nonrefundable [ˌnɒnrɪˈfʌndəbl] *adj* non remboursable.

nonrenewable [ˌnɒnrɪˈnjuːəbl] *adj* [resources] non renouvelable.

nonresident [ˌnɒnˈrezɪdənt] ◇ *n* **1.** [of country] non-résident *m*, - e *f* **2.** [of hotel] : **the dining room is open/closed to ~ s** le restaurant est ouvert au public/réservé aux clients.
◇ *adj* non résident.

nonresistance [ˌnɒnrɪˈzɪstəns] *n* [nonviolence] non-violence *f*.

nonresistant [ˌnɒnrɪˈzɪstənt] *adj* non résistant.

nonreturnable [ˌnɒnrɪˈtɜːnəbl] *adj* [bottle, container] non consigné ■ **sales goods are ~** les articles en solde ne sont pas repris.

nonsectarian [ˌnɒnsekˈteərɪən] *adj* tolérant, ouvert.

nonsense [ˈnɒnsəns] ◇ *n (U)* **1.** [rubbish, absurdity] absurdités *fpl*, non-sens *m inv*, sottises *fpl* ■ **you're talking ~!** tu dis des bêtises!, tu racontes n'importe quoi! ■ **his accusations are utter ~** ses accusations n'ont aucun sens ■ **it's ~ to say that things will never improve** il est absurde de dire que les choses n'iront jamais mieux ■ **I've had enough of his ~** j'en ai assez de l'entendre raconter n'importe quoi ■ **to make a ~ of sthg** saboter qqch **2.** [foolishness] sottises *fpl*, bêtises *fpl*, enfantillages *mpl* ■ **stop this** *OR* **no more of this ~!** arrêtez de vous conduire comme des imbéciles! ■ **she took no ~ from her subordinates** elle ne tolérait aucun manquement de la part de ses subordonnés, elle menait ses subordonnés à la baguette ■ **the maths teacher doesn't stand for any ~** le prof de maths ne se laisse pas marcher sur les pieds ■ **there's no ~ about him** c'est un homme très carré.
◇ *interj* taratata.
◇ *adj* dénué de sens ■ **a ~ word** un mot qui ne veut rien dire, un non-sens.

nonsense verse *n* vers *mpl* amphigouriques.

nonsensical [nɒnˈsensɪkl] *adj* [talk, idea, action] absurde, qui n'a pas de sens, inepte.

non sequitur [ˌnɒnˈsekwɪtəʳ] *n* illogisme *m*.

nonsexist [ˌnɒnˈseksɪst] ◇ *adj* non sexiste.
◇ *n* non-sexiste *mf*.

nonshrink [ˌnɒnˈʃrɪŋk] *adj* irrétrécissable.

nonskid [ˌnɒnˈskɪd] *adj* antidérapant.

nonslip [ˌnɒnˈslɪp] *adj* antidérapant.

nonsmoker [ˌnɒnˈsməʊkəʳ] *n* **1.** [person] non-fumeur *m*, - euse *f* **2.** RAIL compartiment *m* non-fumeurs.

nonsmoking [ˌnɒnˈsməʊkɪŋ] *adj* [area] (pour les) non-fumeurs.

nonspecific urethritis [ˌnɒnspɪˌsɪfɪk-] *n (U)* urétrite *f* non spécifique *OR* non gonococcique.

nonstandard [ˌnɒnˈstændəd] *adj* **1.** LING [use of word] critiqué ■ **in ~ English** [colloquial] en anglais familier *OR* populaire ; [dialectal] en anglais dialectal **2.** [product, size, shape etc] non-standard.

nonstarter [ˌnɒnˈstɑːtəʳ] *n* **1.** [horse] non-partant *m* **2.** *inf fig* **this project is a ~** ce projet est condamné d'avance.

nonstick [ˌnɒnˈstɪk] *adj* [coating] antiadhérent, antiadhésif ■ [pan] qui n'attache pas.

nonstop [ˌnɒnˈstɒp] ◇ *adj* [journey] sans arrêt ■ [flight] direct, sans escale, non-stop ■ [train] direct ■ [radio programme] non-stop, sans interruption.
◇ *adv* sans arrêt ■ **to fly ~ from Rome to Montreal** faire Rome-Montréal sans escale.

nontaxable [ˌnɒnˈtæksəbl] *adj* non imposable.

nontoxic [ˌnɒnˈtɒksɪk] *adj* non-toxique.

nontransferable [ˌnɒntrænsˈfɜːrəbl] *adj* nominatif.

nonunion [ˌnɒnˈjuːnjən] *adj* [worker, labour] non syndiqué ■ [firm] qui n'emploie pas de personnel syndiqué.

nonviolence [ˌnɒnˈvaɪələns] *n* non-violence *f*.

nonviolent [ˌnɒnˈvaɪələnt] *adj* non-violent.

nonvoter [ˌnɒnˈvəʊtəʳ] *n* **1.** [person not eligible to vote] personne *f* qui n'a pas le droit de vote **2.** [person not exercising the right to vote] abstentionniste *mf*.

nonvoting [ˌnɒnˈvəʊtɪŋ] *adj* **1.** [person - not eligible to vote] qui n'a pas le droit de vote ; [- not exercising the right to vote] abstentionniste **2.** FIN [shares] sans droit de vote.

nonwhite [ˌnɒnˈwaɪt] ◇ *n* personne *f* de couleur.
◇ *adj* de couleur ■ **a ~ neighbourhood** un quartier où vivent des gens de couleur (et très peu de blancs).

noodle [ˈnuːdl] *n* **1.** CULIN : **chicken ~ soup** soupe *f* de poulet aux vermicelles **2.** *inf* [fool] andouille *f*, nouille *f* **3.** *US inf* [head] tronche *f*.
◆ **noodles** *npl* nouilles *fpl*.

nook [nʊk] *n* **1.** [corner] coin *m*, recoin *m* ■ **in every ~ and cranny** dans le moindre recoin **2.** *lit* [secluded spot] retraite *f*.

nookie, nooky [ˈnʊkɪ] *n inf hum* **a bit of ~** une partie de jambes en l'air.

noon [nuːn] ◇ *n* **1.** [midday] midi *m* ■ **come at ~** venez à midi **2.** *lit* [peak] zénith *m*.
◇ *comp* [break, heat, sun] de midi ■ **~ hour** *US* heure *f* du déjeuner.

noonday [ˈnuːndeɪ] ◇ *n* midi *m*.
◇ *comp* [heat, sun] de midi.

no one, no-one = **nobody.**

noose [nuːs] ◇ *n* [gen] nœud *m* coulant ■ [snare] collet *m* ■ [lasso] lasso *m* ■ **to put one's head in the ~, to put a ~ around one's neck** creuser sa (propre) tombe.
◇ *vt* **1.** [rope] faire un nœud coulant à **2.** [snare] prendre au collet ■ [lasso] attraper *OR* prendre au lasso.

nope [nəʊp] *adv inf* non.

no-place *US* = **nowhere.**

nor [nɔːʳ] ◇ *conj* [following 'neither', 'not'] ni ■ **neither he ~ his wife has ever spoken to me** ni lui ni sa femme ne m'ont jamais adressé la parole ■ **she neither drinks ~ smokes** elle ne boit ni ne fume.
◇ *adv* : **I don't believe him, ~ do I trust him** je ne le crois pas, et je n'ai pas confiance en lui non plus ■ **it's not the first time, ~ will it be the last** ce n'est ni la première ni la dernière fois ■ **I don't like fish – ~ do I** je n'aime pas le poisson – moi non plus ■ **she won't do it and ~ will he** elle ne le fera pas et lui non plus.

Nordic [ˈnɔːdɪk] ◇ *n* Nordique *mf*.
◇ *adj* nordique.

norm [nɔ:m] *n* norme *f* ▪ **unemployment has become the ~ in certain areas** dans certaines régions, le chômage est devenu la règle.

normal ['nɔ:ml] <> *adj* **1.** [common, typical, standard] normal ▪ **it's ~ for it to rain in April** il est normal OR naturel qu'il pleuve en avril ▮ [habitual] habituel, normal ▪ **at the ~ time** à l'heure habituelle **2.** MATHS [in statistics, geometry] normal **3.** CHEM normal.
<> *n* **1.** [gen] normale *f*, état *m* normal ▪ **temperatures above ~** des températures au-dessus de la normale ▪ **the situation has returned to ~** la situation est redevenue normale **2.** GEOM normale *f*.

normality [nɔ:'mælətɪ], **normalcy** ['nɔ:məlsɪ] US *n* normalité *f* ▪ **everything returned to ~** tout est revenu à la normale.

normalization [,nɔ:məlaɪ'zeɪʃn] *n* normalisation *f*.

normalize, ise ['nɔ:məlaɪz] *vt* normaliser.

normally ['nɔ:məlɪ] *adv* **1.** [in a normal manner] normalement **2.** [ordinarily] en temps normal, d'ordinaire.

Norman ['nɔ:mən] <> *n* **1.** [person] Normand *m*, - e *f* **2.** LING normand *m*.
<> *adj* GEOG & HIST normand ▪ **the ~ Conquest** la conquête normande *(de l'Angleterre)* ▮ ARCHIT roman, anglo-normand.

THE NORMAN CONQUEST

Conquête de l'Angleterre par Guillaume le Conquérant, inaugurée par sa victoire sur le roi Harold à la bataille de Hastings, en 1066. Désormais gouverné et régi par les Normands, le pays subit de grands changements dans les domaines politique et social, se voyant notamment imposer le français comme langue officielle.

Normandy ['nɔ:məndɪ] *pr n* Normandie *f* ▪ **in ~** en Normandie.

normative ['nɔ:mətɪv] *adj* normatif.

Norse [nɔ:s] <> *npl* HIST : **the ~** [Norwegians] les Norvégiens *mpl* ; [Vikings] les Vikings *mpl*.
<> *n* LING norrois *m*, nordique *m* ▪ **Old ~** vieux norrois.
<> *adj* [Scandinavian] scandinave, nordique ▪ [Norwegian] norvégien ▪ **~ legends** légendes *fpl* scandinaves.

Norseman ['nɔ:smən] (*pl* **Norsemen** [-mən]) *n* Viking *m*.

north [nɔ:θ] <> *n* GEOG nord *m* ▪ **the region to the ~ of Sydney** la région au nord de Sydney ▪ **I was born in the North** je suis né dans le Nord ▪ **in the ~ of India** dans le nord de l'Inde ▪ **the wind is in the ~** le vent est au nord ▪ **the Old North State** la Caroline du Nord ➲ **the ~-south divide** *ligne fictive de démarcation, en termes de richesse, entre le nord de l'Angleterre et le sud* ▪ **the far ~** le Grand Nord ▪ **'North by Northwest'** ***Hitchcock*** 'la Mort aux trousses'.
<> *adj* **1.** GEOG nord *(inv)*, du nord ▪ **the ~ coast** la côte nord ▪ **in North London** dans le nord de Londres ▪ **the North Atlantic/Pacific** l'Atlantique/le Pacifique Nord **2.** [wind] du nord.
<> *adv* au nord, vers le nord ▪ **the ranch lies ~ of the town** le ranch est situé au nord de la ville ▪ **this room faces ~** cette pièce est exposée au nord ▪ **I drove ~ for two hours** j'ai roulé pendant deux heures en direction du nord ▪ **they live up ~** ils habitent dans le nord.

North Africa *pr n* Afrique *f* du Nord ▪ **in ~** en Afrique du Nord.

North African <> *n* Nord-Africain *m*, - e *f*.
<> *adj* nord-africain, d'Afrique du Nord.

North America *pr n* Amérique *f* du Nord.

North American <> *n* Nord-Américain *m*, - e *f*.
<> *adj* nord-américain, d'Amérique du Nord ▪ **the ~ Indians** les Indiens *mpl* d'Amérique du Nord.

North American Free Trade Agreement *pr n* Accord *m* de libre-échange nord-américain.

Northants *written abbr of* **Northamptonshire**.

northbound ['nɔ:θbaʊnd] *adj* en direction du nord.

North Carolina *pr n* Caroline *f* du Nord ▪ **in ~** en Caroline du Nord.

North Country *pr n* **1.** [in England] Angleterre *f* du Nord ▪ **he's got a ~ accent** il a un accent du nord **2.** [in America] *l'Alaska, le Yukon et les Territoires du Nord-Ouest*.

north-countryman (*pl* **north-countrymen**) *n* Anglais *m* du nord.

Northd *written abbr of* **Northumberland**.

North Dakota *pr n* Dakota *m* du Nord ▪ **in ~** dans le Dakota du Nord.

northeast [,nɔ:θ'i:st] <> *n* GEOG nord-est *m*.
<> *adj* **1.** GEOL nord-est *(inv)*, du nord-est ▪ **in ~ Scotland** dans le nord-est de l'Écosse **2.** [wind] de nord-est.
<> *adv* au nord-est, vers le nord-est.

northeasterly [,nɔ:θ'i:stəlɪ] (*pl* **northeasterlies**) <> *adj* **1.** GEOG nord-est *(inv)*, du nord-est ▪ **in a ~ direction** vers le nord-est **2.** [wind] de nord-est.
<> *adv* au nord-est, vers le nord-est.

northeastern [,nɔ:θ'i:stən] *adj* nord-est *(inv)*, du nord-est.

northeastwards [,nɔ:θ'i:stwədz] *adv* vers le nord-est, en direction du nord-est.

northerly ['nɔ:ðəlɪ] (*pl* **northerlies**) <> *adj* **1.** GEOG nord *(inv)*, du nord ▪ **in these ~ latitudes** sous ces latitudes boréales ▪ **in a ~ direction** vers le nord ▪ **a room with a ~ aspect** une pièce exposée au nord **2.** [wind] du nord.
<> *adv* vers le nord.
<> *n* vent *m* du nord.

northern ['nɔ:ðən] *adj* **1.** GEOG nord *(inv)*, du nord ▪ **she has a ~ accent** elle a un accent du nord ▪ **in ~ Mexico** dans le nord du Mexique ▪ **the ~ migration of swallows in spring** la migration printanière des hirondelles vers le nord **2.** [wind] du nord.

Northerner ['nɔ:ðənəʳ] *n* **1.** [gen] homme *m* /femme *f* du nord ▪ **she is a ~** elle vient du nord ▪ **I find that ~s are more friendly** je trouve que les gens du Nord sont plus accueillants **2.** US HIST nordiste *mf*.

northern hemisphere *n* hémisphère *m* nord OR boréal.

Northern Ireland *pr n* Irlande *f* du Nord ▪ **in ~** en Irlande du Nord.

NORTHERN IRELAND

Partie de l'Irlande à majorité protestante, restée rattachée à la Grande-Bretagne lors de la partition du pays, en 1921. Depuis les émeutes sanglantes de Belfast et de Londonderry, en 1969, le pays a connu trente années de confrontations violentes entre les nationalistes de l'IRA, les extrémistes protestants et les autorités britanniques. En 1985, l'accord anglo-irlandais a donné à la République d'Irlande un droit de regard sur les affaires de l'Irlande du Nord, sans qu'une véritable solution pour la paix ne soit proposée. En 1993, la déclaration faite par le Premier ministre à Downing Street (***Downing Street Declaration***) préparait la voie pour l'arrêt de la violence et, le 31 août 1994, l'IRA promettait de ne plus recourir à la violence. Cette déclaration fut suivie d'un cessez-le-feu loyaliste, rompu par la suite en plusieurs occasions, mais le processus de paix a finalement conduit à la signature de l'accord de paix d'Ulster, en avril 1998 (***Good Friday Agreement***), activement suivi par le Sinn Féin et la majorité des partis unionistes. Bien que le climat demeure très agité, cet accord représente la promesse de paix la plus sérieuse depuis le début du conflit.

northern lights *npl* aurore *f* boréale.

northernmost ['nɔ:ðənməʊst] *adj* le plus au nord.

north-facing *adj* [wall, building] (exposé) au nord.

North Korea *pr n* Corée *f* du Nord.

North Korean <> *n* Nord-Coréen *m*, - enne *f*.
<> *adj* nord-coréen.

north-northeast <> *n* nord-nord-est *m*.
<> *adj* nord-nord-est *(inv)*, du nord-nord-est.
<> *adv* au nord-nord-est, vers le nord-nord-est.

north-northwest <> *n* nord-nord-ouest *m*.

◇ *adj* nord-nord-ouest *(inv)*, du nord-nord-ouest.
◇ *adv* au nord-nord-ouest, vers le nord-nord-ouest.

North Pole *pr n* : **the ~** le pôle Nord.

North Rhine-Westphalia *pr n* Rhénanie-du-Nord-Westphalie *f* ■ **in ~** en Rhénanie-du-Nord-Westphalie.

North Sea ◇ *pr n* : **the ~** la mer du Nord.
◇ *comp* [oil, gas] de la mer du Nord.

North Star *pr n* : **the ~** l'étoile *f* Polaire ■ **the North Star State** le Minnesota.

Northumbrian [nɔː'θʌmbrɪən] *adj* GEOG du Northumberland ■ HIST northumbrien, de la Northumbrie.

North Vietnam *pr n* Nord Viêt-nam *m* ■ **in ~** au Nord Viêt-nam.

North Vietnamese ◇ *n* Nord-Vietnamien *m*, - enne *f*.
◇ *adj* nord-vietnamien.

North Wales *pr n* pays *m* de Galles du nord.

northward ['nɔːθwəd] ◇ *adj* au nord.
◇ *adv* = **northwards**.

northwards ['nɔːθwədz] *adv* vers le nord, en direction du nord.

northwest [,nɔːθ'west] ◇ *n* nord-ouest *m*.
◇ *adj* **1.** GEOG nord-ouest *(inv)*, du nord-ouest ■ **in ~ Canada** dans le nord-ouest du Canada **2.** [wind] de nord-ouest.
◇ *adv* au nord-ouest, vers le nord-ouest.

northwesterly [,nɔːθ'westəlɪ] (*pl* **northwesterlies**) ◇ *adj* **1.** GEOG nord-ouest *(inv)*, du nord-ouest ■ **in a ~ direction** vers le nord-ouest **2.** [wind] du nord-ouest.
◇ *adv* au nord-ouest, vers le nord-ouest.

northwestern [,nɔːθ'westən] *adj* nord-ouest *(inv)*, du nord-ouest.

Northwest Passage *pr n* passage *m* du Nord-Ouest.

Northwest Territories *pr npl* Territoires *mpl* du Nord-Ouest.

northwestwards [,nɔːθ'westwədz] *adv* vers le nord-ouest, en direction du nord-ouest.

North Yemen *pr n* Yémen *m* du Nord ■ **in ~** au Yémen du Nord.

Norway ['nɔːweɪ] *pr n* Norvège *f* ■ **in ~** en Norvège.

Norwegian [nɔː'wiːdʒən] ◇ *n* **1.** [person] Norvégien *m*, - enne *f* **2.** LING norvégien *m*.
◇ *adj* norvégien.

Nos., nos. (*written abbrev of* **numbers**) no.

nose [nəʊz] ◇ *n* **1.** ANAT nez *m* ■ **to hold one's ~** se pincer le nez ■ **the dog has a wet ~** le chien a le nez OR la truffe humide ■ **your ~ is bleeding** tu saignes du nez ■ **your ~ is running** tu as le nez qui coule ■ **to speak through one's ~** parler du nez ■ **I punched him on OR in the ~** je lui ai donné un coup de poing en pleine figure ■ **she's always got her ~ in a book** elle a toujours le nez dans un livre ■ **the favourite won by a ~** [in horse-racing] le favori a gagné d'une demi-tête ■ **it was (right) under my ~ all the time** c'était en plein sous mon nez ■ **they stole it from under the ~ of the police** *fig* ils l'ont volé au nez et à la barbe de la police ● **he can see no further than (the end of) his ~** il ne voit pas plus loin que le bout de son nez ■ **he really gets OR he gets right up my ~!** *inf* il me pompe l'air! ■ **you've got OR hit it right on the ~** *inf* tu as mis en plein dans le mille ■ **to keep one's ~ clean** *inf* se tenir à carreau ■ **keep your (big) ~ out of my business!** *inf* mêle-toi de ce qui te regarde! ■ **to keep OR to have one's ~ to the grindstone** bosser (dur) ■ **to lead sb by the ~** mener qqn par le bout du nez ■ **to look down one's ~ at sb/sthg** traiter qqn/qqch avec condescendance ■ **to pay through the ~ (for sthg)** payer (qqch) la peau des fesses ■ **to put sb's ~ out of joint** *UK inf* contrarier OR dépiter qqn ■ **he's always sticking OR poking his ~ in** *inf* il faut qu'il fourre son nez partout ■ **to turn up one's ~ at sthg** faire la fine bouche devant qqch ■ **he's always walking around with his ~ in the air** il prend toujours un air hautain OR méprisant **2.** [sense of smell] odorat *m*, nez *m* ■ **these dogs have an excellent ~** ces chiens ont un excellent flair OR le nez fin *spec* ■ **she's got a (good) ~ for a bargain** *fig* elle a le nez creux OR du nez pour dénicher les bonnes affaires **3.** [aroma - of wine] arôme *m*, bouquet *m*, nez *m* **4.** [forward part - of aircraft, ship] nez *m* ; [- of car] avant *m* ; [- of bullet, missile, tool] pointe *f* ; [- of gun] canon *m* ■ **the traffic was ~ to tail all the way to London** *UK* les voitures étaient pare-chocs contre pare-chocs jusqu'à Londres.
◇ *vt* **1.** [smell] flairer, renifler **2.** [push with nose] pousser du nez.
◇ *vi* **1.** [advance with care] avancer précautionneusement ■ **the car ~d out into the traffic** la voiture se frayait un chemin au milieu des embouteillages **2.** *inf* [snoop] fouiner.
◆ **nose about** *UK*, **nose around** *vi insep inf* [snoop] fureter, fouiner.
◆ **nose out** *vt sep* **1.** [discover - by smell] flairer ; [- by cunning, intuition] dénicher, débusquer **2.** *inf* [beat narrowly] battre d'une courte tête.

nosebag ['nəʊzbæg] *n UK* musette *f*, mangeoire *f* portative.

noseband ['nəʊzbænd] *n* muserolle *f*.

nosebleed ['nəʊzbliːd] *n* saignement *m* de nez, épistaxis *f spec* ■ **I've got a ~** je saigne du nez.

nose cone *n* [of missile] ogive *f* ■ [of aircraft] nez *m*.

-nosed [nəʊzd] *in cpds* au nez... ■ **red~** au nez rouge.

nosedive ['nəʊzdaɪv] ◇ *n* **1.** [of plane, bird] piqué *m* ■ **I did a ~ onto the concrete** *inf* je suis tombé la tête la première sur le béton **2.** *inf fig* [sharp drop] chute *f*, dégringolade *f* ■ **prices took a ~** les prix ont considérablement chuté ■ **his popularity has taken a ~** sa cote de popularité s'est littéralement effondrée.
◇ *vi* **1.** [plane] piquer, descendre en piqué **2.** *fig* [popularity, prices] être en chute libre, chuter.

nose drops *npl* gouttes *fpl* nasales OR pour le nez.

nosegay ['nəʊzgeɪ] *n lit* (petit) bouquet *m*.

nose job *n inf* intervention *f* de chirurgie esthétique sur le nez ■ **she's had a ~** elle s'est fait refaire le nez.

nose ring *n* anneau *m* de nez.

nose stud *n* clou *m* (de nez).

nosey ['nəʊzɪ] *inf* = **nosy**.

nosh [nɒʃ] *inf dated* ◇ *n* bouffe *f*.
◇ *vi* bouffer.

no-show *n* [for flight, voyage] *passager qui ne se présente pas à l'embarquement* ■ [for show] *spectateur qui a réservé sa place et qui n'assiste pas au spectacle*.

nosh-up *n UK inf* gueuleton *m*.

nosiness ['nəʊzɪnɪs] *n inf* curiosité *f* ■ **his ~ really annoys me** il m'agace sérieusement à fourrer son nez partout.

nostalgia [nɒ'stældʒə] *n* nostalgie *f*.

nostalgic [nɒ'stældʒɪk] *adj* nostalgique ■ **to be OR feel ~ for sthg** regretter qqch.

nostril ['nɒstrɪl] *n* [gen] narine *f* ■ [of horse, cow etc] naseau *m*.

nosy ['nəʊzɪ] (*comp* **nosier**, *superl* **nosiest**) *adj inf* curieux ■ **don't be so ~!** occupe-toi donc de tes affaires OR de tes oignons! ■ **he's very ~** il fourre son nez partout ■ **I didn't mean to be ~** je ne voulais pas être indiscret.

nosy parker *n UK inf pej* curieux *m*, - euse *f*.

not [nɒt] *adv* **1.** [after verb or auxiliary] ne... pas ■ **we are ~ OR aren't sure** nous ne sommes pas sûrs ■ **do ~ OR don't believe her** ne la croyez pas ■ **you've been there already, haven't you OR *fml* have you ~?** vous y êtes déjà allé, non OR n'est-ce pas? ■ [with infinitive] ne pas ■ **I'll try ~ to cry** j'essaierai de ne pas pleurer
2. [as phrase or clause substitute] non, pas ■ **we hope ~** nous espérons que non ■ **will it rain? – I think ~** *fml* est-ce qu'il va pleuvoir? – je crois que non OR je ne crois pas ■ **whether they like it or ~** que ça leur plaise ou non OR ou pas ■ **she really has a nice dress – ~!** *inf* quelle belle robe elle a – façon de parler! OR faut pas être difficile!
3. [with adj, adv, noun etc] pas ■ **it's Thomas, ~ Jake** c'est Thomas, pas Jake ■ **~ all her books are good** ses livres ne sont pas tous bons, tous ses livres ne sont pas bons ■ **~ I** *fml* pas moi

4. [in double negatives] : **~ without some difficulty** non sans quelque difficulté ■ **it's ~ unusual for him to be late** il n'est pas rare qu'il soit en retard ■ **the two events are ~ unconnected** les deux événements ne sont pas tout à fait indépendants l'un de l'autre
5. [less than] moins de ■ **~ five minutes later the phone rang** moins de cinq minutes plus tard, le téléphone a sonné ■ **~ ten metres away** à moins de dix mètres.

notable ['nəʊtəbl] <> *adj* [thing] notable, remarquable ■ [person] notable, éminent ■ **the film was ~ for its lack of violence** le film se distinguait par l'absence de scènes de violence.
<> *n* notable *m*.

notably ['nəʊtəblɪ] *adv* **1.** [particularly] notamment, en particulier **2.** [markedly] manifestement, de toute évidence.

notarize, ise ['nəʊtəraɪz] *vt* certifier, authentifier ■ **~d deed** acte *m* notarié ■ **a ~d copy** ≃ une copie certifiée conforme *(par un notaire)*.

notary ['nəʊtərɪ] (*pl* **notaries**) *n* : **~ (public)** notaire *m* ■ **signed in the presence of a ~** signé par-devant notaire.

notation [nəʊ'teɪʃn] *n* **1.** [sign system] notation *f* ■ **musical ~** notation musicale ■ **mathematical ~** symboles *mpl* mathématiques ■ **in binary ~** en numération binaire, en base 2 **2.** *US* [jotting] notation *f*, note *f*.

notch [nɒtʃ] <> *n* **1.** [cut - in stick] entaille *f*, encoche *f* ■ [hole - in belt] cran *m* ■ **he let out his belt a ~** il a desserré sa ceinture d'un cran **2.** [degree] cran *m* ■ **turn the heating up a ~** monte un peu le chauffage **3.** *US* [gorge] défilé *m*.
<> *vt* **1.** [make cut in - stick] entailler, encocher ; [- gear wheel] cranter, denteler ■ [damage - blade] ébrécher **2.** *fig* = **notch up**.
◆ **notch up** *vt sep* [achieve] accomplir ■ **they've ~ed up six wins in a row** ils ont six victoires consécutives à leur palmarès.

note [nəʊt] <> *n* **1.** [record, reminder] note *f* ■ **to take** *OR* **to make ~s** prendre des notes ■ **she spoke from/without ~s** elle a parlé en s'aidant/sans s'aider de notes ■ **make a ~ of everything you spend** notez toutes vos dépenses ■ **I must make a ~ to myself to ask her about it** *fig* il faut que je pense à le lui demander ■ **he made a mental ~ to look for it later** il se promit de le chercher plus tard ■ **to compare ~s** *fig* échanger ses impressions
2. [short letter] mot *m*
3. [formal communication] note *f* ■ **a doctor's** *OR* **sick ~** un certificat *OR* une attestation du médecin (traitant) ; SCH un certificat (médical)
4. [annotation, commentary] note *f*, annotation *f* ■ **editor's ~** note de la rédaction ▶ **programme ~s** notes sur le programme
5. *UK* [banknote] billet *m* (de banque) ■ **ten-pound ~** billet de dix livres
6. [sound, tone] ton *m*, note *f* ■ **the piercing ~ of the siren** le son strident de la sirène ■ **there was a ~ of contempt in her voice** il y avait du mépris dans sa voix ▮ *fig* [feeling, quality] note *f* ■ **the meeting began on a promising ~** la réunion débuta sur une note optimiste ■ **on a more serious/a happier ~** pour parler de choses plus sérieuses/plus gaies ■ **the flowers add a ~ of colour** les fleurs apportent une touche de couleur ■ **her speech struck a warning ~** son discours était un signal d'alarme ▶ **to strike the right/a false ~** [speech] sonner juste/faux ; [behaviour] être/ne pas être dans le ton
7. MUS note *f* ■ **to hit a high ~** sortir un aigu ■ *UK* [piano key] touche *f*
8. [notice, attention] : **to take ~ of sthg** prendre (bonne) note de qqch
9. COMM : **(promissory) ~, ~ of hand** billet *m* à ordre.
<> *vt* **1.** [observe, notice] remarquer, noter ■ **~ that she didn't actually refuse** notez (bien) qu'elle n'a pas vraiment refusé ■ **please ~ that payment is now due** veuillez effectuer le règlement dans les plus brefs délais
2. [write down] noter, écrire ■ **I ~d (down) her address** j'ai noté son adresse ■ **all sales are ~d in this book** toutes les ventes sont enregistrées *OR* consignées dans ce carnet
3. [mention] (faire) remarquer *OR* observer.
◆ **of note** *adj phr* : **a musician of ~** un musicien éminent *OR* renommé ■ **a musician of some ~** un musicien d'une certaine renommée ■ **everyone of ~ was there** tous les gens importants *OR* qui comptent étaient là ■ **nothing of ~ has happened** il ne s'est rien passé d'important, aucun événement majeur ne s'est produit.
◆ **note down** *vt sep* = **note** *(vt sense 2)*.

notebook ['nəʊtbʊk] *n* carnet *m*, calepin *m* ■ SCH cahier *m*, carnet *m* ■ **~ computer** ordinateur *m* bloc-notes.

noted ['nəʊtɪd] *adj* [person] éminent, célèbre ■ [place, object] réputé, célèbre ■ [fact, idea] reconnu ■ **to be ~ for one's integrity** être connu pour son intégrité ■ **he's not ~ for his flexibility** il ne passe pas pour quelqu'un de particulièrement accommodant ■ **a region ~ for its parks** une région réputée *OR* connue pour ses parcs.

notelet ['nəʊtlɪt] *n UK* carte-lettre *f*.

notepad ['nəʊtpæd] *n* [for notes] bloc-notes *m* ■ [for letters] bloc *m* de papier à lettres.

notepaper ['nəʊtpeɪpər] *n* papier *m* à lettres.

noteworthy ['nəʊt,wɜːðɪ] *adj* notable, remarquable.

nothing ['nʌθɪŋ] <> *pron* ne... rien ■ **she forgets ~** elle n'oublie rien ■ **~ has been decided** rien n'a été décidé ■ **I have ~ else to say** je n'ai rien d'autre à dire ■ **~ serious** rien de grave ■ **they're always fighting over ~** ils passent leur temps à se disputer pour des broutilles *OR* des riens ■ **reduced to ~** réduit à néant ■ **there's ~ for it but to start again** il n'y a plus qu'à recommencer ■ **there's ~ in** *OR* **to these rumours** ces rumeurs sont dénuées de tout fondement ■ **there's ~ to it!** [it's easy] c'est simple (comme bonjour)! ■ **there's ~ like a nice hot bath** rien de tel qu'un bon bain chaud ■ **she says he's ~** *OR* **he means ~ to her** elle dit qu'il n'est rien pour elle ■ **I'll take what's due to me, ~ more, ~ less** je prendrai mon dû, ni plus ni moins ▶ **what a physique! Charles Atlas has got ~ on you!** *inf* quel physique! tu n'as rien à envier à Charles Atlas *OR* Charles Atlas peut aller se rhabiller! ■ **our sacrifices were as ~ compared to his** *lit* nos sacrifices ne furent rien auprès des siens.
<> *n* **1.** [trifle] rien *m*, vétille *f* ■ **$500 may be a mere ~ to you** 500 dollars ne représentent peut-être pas grand-chose pour vous **2.** *inf* [person] nullité *f*, zéro *m* **3.** MATHS zéro *m*.
<> *adj inf* [worthless] nul.
◆ **for nothing** *adv phr* **1.** [gratis] pour rien ■ **I got it for ~ at the flea market** je l'ai eu pour (trois fois) rien aux puces **2.** [for no purpose] pour rien **3.** [for no good reason] pour rien ■ **they don't call him Einstein for ~** ce n'est pas pour rien qu'on le surnomme Einstein.
◆ **nothing but** *adv phr* : **that car's been ~ but trouble** cette voiture ne m'a attiré que des ennuis ■ **~ but a miracle can save us** seul un miracle pourrait nous sauver ■ **she wants ~ but the best** elle ne veut que ce qu'il y a de meilleur ■ **they do ~ but sleep** ils ne font que dormir.
◆ **nothing if not** *adv phr* rien de moins que ■ **she's ~ if not honest** elle n'est rien de moins qu'honnête.
◆ **nothing less than** *adv phr* **1.** [undoubtedly] rien de moins que, tout bonnement ■ **it was ~ less than miraculous/a miracle** c'était tout simplement miraculeux/un miracle **2.** [only] seul.
◆ **nothing like** <> *prep phr* **1.** [completely unlike] : **she's ~ like her mother** elle ne ressemble en rien à sa mère **2.** [nothing as good as] : **there's ~ like a nice cup of tea!** rien de tel qu'une bonne tasse de thé!
<> *adv phr inf* [nowhere near] : **this box is ~ like big enough** cette boîte est beaucoup trop *OR* bien trop petite.
◆ **nothing more than** *adv phr* : **I want ~ more than a word of thanks from time to time** tout ce que je demande, c'est un petit mot de remerciement de temps à autre ■ **he's ~ more than a petty crook** il n'est rien d'autre qu'un vulgaire escroc.

nothingness ['nʌθɪŋnɪs] *n* néant *m* ■ **he stared out into the ~** il avait le regard perdu dans le vide.

notice ['nəʊtɪs] <> *n* **1.** [written announcement] annonce *f* ■ [sign] écriteau *m*, pancarte *f* ■ [poster] affiche *f* ■ [in newspaper - article] entrefilet *m* ; [- advertisement] annonce *f* ■ **a ~ was pinned to the door** il y avait une notice sur la porte
2. [attention] attention *f* ■ **to take ~ of** faire *OR* prêter attention à ■ **take no ~ (of him)!** ne faites pas attention (à lui)! ■ **she considers it beneath her ~** *fml* elle considère que ça ne vaut pas la peine qu'elle s'y arrête ■ **to bring sthg to sb's ~** faire re-

marquer qqch à qqn, attirer l'attention de qqn sur qqch ▪ **her book attracted a great deal of/little ~** son livre a suscité beaucoup/peu d'intérêt ▪ **to escape** *OR* **to avoid ~** passer inaperçu ▪ **my mistake did not escape his ~** mon erreur ne lui a pas échappé ▪ **has it escaped their ~ that something is seriously wrong?** ne se sont-ils pas aperçu qu'il y a quelque chose qui ne va pas du tout?
3. [notification, warning] avis *m*, notification *f* ▪ [advance notification] préavis *m* ▪ **please give us ~ of your intentions** veuillez nous faire part préalablement de vos intentions ▪ **he was given ~** *OR* **~ was served on him** *fml* **to quit** on lui a fait savoir qu'il devait partir ▪ **give me more ~ next time you come up** prévenez-moi plus tôt la prochaine fois que tu viens ▪ **legally, they must give you a month's ~** d'après la loi, ils doivent vous donner un préavis d'un mois *OR* un mois de préavis ▪ **give me a few days' ~** prévenez-moi quelques jours à l'avance ▪ **without previous** *OR* **prior ~** sans prévenir ▪ **he turned up without any ~** il est arrivé à l'improviste ▪ **at a moment's ~** sur-le-champ, immédiatement ▪ **at short ~** très rapidement ▪ **it's impossible to do the work at such short ~** c'est un travail impossible à faire dans un délai aussi court ▪ **until further ~** jusqu'à nouvel ordre *OR* avis
4. [notifying document] avis *m*, notification *f* ▪ [warning document] avertissement *m* ➊ **~ of receipt** COMM accusé *m* de réception
5. [intent to terminate contract - by employer, landlord, tenant] congé *m* ; [- by employee] démission *f* ▪ **fifty people have been given their ~** cinquante personnes ont été licenciées ▪ **to give in** *OR* **to hand in one's ~** remettre sa démission ▪ **we are under ~ to quit** nous avons reçu notre congé
6. [review] critique *f*.
<> *vt* **1.** [spot, observe] remarquer, s'apercevoir de ▪ **he ~d a scratch on the table** il remarqua que la table était rayée ▪ **hello, Sam, I didn't ~ you in the corner** bonjour, Sam, je ne t'avais pas vu dans le coin ▪ **so I've ~d!** c'est ce que j'ai remarqué!
2. [take notice of] faire attention à.

noticeable ['nəʊtɪsəbl] *adj* [mark, defect] visible ▪ [effect, change, improvement] sensible.

noticeably ['nəʊtɪsəblɪ] *adv* sensiblement.

noticeboard ['nəʊtɪsbɔ:d] *n* panneau *m* d'affichage.

notifiable ['nəʊtɪfaɪəbl] *adj* [disease] à déclaration obligatoire.

notification [,nəʊtɪfɪ'keɪʃn] *n* notification *f*, avis *m* ▪ **you will receive ~ by mail** vous serez averti par courrier.

notify ['nəʊtɪfaɪ] (*pret & pp* **notified**) *vt* notifier, avertir ▪ **to ~ sb of sthg** avertir qqn de qqch, notifier qqch à qqn ▪ **have you notified the authorities?** avez-vous averti *OR* prévenu les autorités? ▪ **winners will be notified within ten days** les gagnants seront avisés dans les dix jours.

notion ['nəʊʃn] *n* **1.** [concept] notion *f*, concept *m* ▪ **I lost all ~ of time** j'ai perdu la notion du temps **2.** [opinion] idée *f*, opinion *f* ▪ **where did she get the ~** *OR* **whatever gave her the ~ that we don't like her?** où est-elle allée chercher que nous ne l'aimions pas? **3.** [vague idea] notion *f*, idée *f* **4.** [thought, whim] idée *f* ▪ [urge] envie *f*, désir *m*.
◆ **notions** *npl US* [haberdashery] mercerie *f*.

notional ['nəʊʃənl] *adj* **1.** *UK* [hypothetical] théorique, notionnel ▪ **let's put a ~ price of $2 a kilo on it** pour avoir un ordre d'idées, fixons-en le prix à 2 dollars le kilo **2.** [imaginary] imaginaire **3.** *US* [fanciful] capricieux **4.** LING [word] sémantique, plein ▪ **~ grammar** grammaire *f* notionnelle.

notoriety [,nəʊtə'raɪətɪ] (*pl* **notorieties**) *n* [ill fame] triste notoriété *f* ▪ [fame] notoriété *f* ▪ **these measures brought him ~** ces mesures l'ont rendu tristement célèbre.

notorious [nəʊ'tɔ:rɪəs] *adj pej* [ill-famed - person] tristement célèbre ; [- crime] célèbre ; [- place] mal famé ▪ **a ~ miser/spy** un avare/espion notoire ▪ [well-known] connu ▪ **she's ~ for being late** elle est connue pour ne jamais être à l'heure ▪ **the junction is a ~ accident spot** ce croisement est réputé pour être très dangereux ▪ **the area is ~ for muggings** il est bien connu que c'est un quartier où il y a beaucoup d'agressions.

notoriously [nəʊ'tɔ:rɪəslɪ] *adv* notoirement ▪ **the trains here are ~ unreliable** tout le monde sait qu'on ne peut pas se fier aux horaires des trains ici.

Notting Hill Carnival ['nɒtɪŋ-] *pr n carnaval afro-antillais qui a lieu chaque année à Londres.*

not-too-distant *adj* : **in the ~ future** dans un avenir proche.

Notts *written abbr of* **Nottinghamshire**.

notwithstanding [,nɒtwɪθ'stændɪŋ] *fml* <> *prep* en dépit de.
<> *adv* malgré tout, néanmoins.

nougat ['nu:gɑ:] *n* nougat *m*.

nought [nɔ:t] *n UK* [zero] zéro *m*.

noughts and crosses *n UK (U)* ≃ morpion *m (jeu)*.

noun [naʊn] *n* nom *m*, substantif *m* ▪ **common/proper ~** nom commun/propre ▪ **~ phrase** groupe *m* *OR* syntagme *m* nominal ▪ **~ clause** proposition *f*.

nourish ['nʌrɪʃ] *vt* **1.** [feed] nourrir **2.** [entertain, foster] nourrir, entretenir.

nourishing ['nʌrɪʃɪŋ] *adj* nourrissant, nutritif.

nourishment ['nʌrɪʃmənt] *n (U)* **1.** [food] nourriture *f*, aliments *mpl* ▪ **the patient has taken no ~** le malade ne s'est pas alimenté ▪ **brown rice is full of ~** le riz complet est très nourrissant **2.** [act of nourishing] alimentation *f*.

nous [naʊs] *n* **1.** *UK inf* bon sens *m*, jugeote *f* **2.** PHILOS esprit *m*, intellect *m*.

Nov. (*written abbrev of* **November**) nov.

Nova Scotia [,nəʊvə'skəʊʃə] *pr n* Nouvelle-Écosse *f* ▪ **in ~** en Nouvelle-Écosse.

Nova Scotian [,nəʊvə'skəʊʃn] <> *n* Néo-Écossais *m*, - e *f*.
<> *adj* néo-écossais.

novel ['nɒvl] <> *n* roman *m*.
<> *adj* nouveau *(before vowel or silent 'h' nouvel)*, nouvelle *f*, original ▪ **what a ~ idea!** quelle idée originale!

novelette [,nɒvə'let] *n* **1.** [short novel] nouvelle *f* **2.** *pej* [easy reading] roman *m* de hall de gare ▪ [love story] roman *m* à l'eau de rose.

novelist ['nɒvəlɪst] *n* romancier *m*, - ère *f*.

novella [nə'velə] (*pl* **novellas** *OR pl* **novelle** [-leɪ]) *n* ≃ nouvelle *f (texte plus court qu'un roman et plus long qu'une nouvelle)*.

novelty ['nɒvltɪ] (*pl* **novelties**) *n* **1.** [newness] nouveauté *f*, originalité *f* ▪ **the ~ soon wore off** l'attrait de la nouveauté n'a pas duré ➊ **~ value** attrait *m* de la nouveauté **2.** [thing, idea] innovation *f*, nouveauté *f* ▪ **it was a real ~** c'était une nouveauté, c'était tout nouveau **3.** [trinket] nouveauté *f*, article *m* fantaisie ▪ [gadget] gadget *m*.

November [nə'vembəʳ] *n* novembre *m*, *see also* **February**.

novice ['nɒvɪs] *n* **1.** [beginner] débutant *m*, - e *f*, novice *mf* **2.** RELIG novice *mf*.

novitiate, noviciate [nə'vɪʃɪət] *n* RELIG **1.** [period] noviciat *m* ▪ *fig* noviciat *m*, apprentissage *m* **2.** [place] noviciat *m*.

Novocaine® ['nəʊvəkeɪn] *n* Novocaïne® *f*, procaïne *f*.

now [naʊ] <> *adv* **1.** [at this time] maintenant ▪ **she'll be here any moment** *OR* **any time ~** elle va arriver d'un moment *OR* instant à l'autre ▪ **we are ~ entering enemy territory** nous sommes désormais en territoire ennemi ▪ **it's ~ or never** c'est le moment ou jamais ▪ **~ she tells me!** *hum* c'est maintenant qu'elle me le dit! ▪ **(and) ~ for something completely different** (et) voici à présent quelque chose de tout à fait différent ▪ **as of ~** désormais ▪ **I'd never met them before ~** je ne les avais jamais rencontrés auparavant ▪ **between ~ and next August/next year** d'ici le mois d'août prochain/l'année prochaine ▪ **they must have got the letter by ~** ils ont dû recevoir la lettre à l'heure qu'il est ▪ **that's all for ~** c'est tout pour le moment ▪ **in a few years from ~** d'ici quelques années ▪ **from ~ on** dé-

sormais, dorénavant, à partir de maintenant ■ **we've had no problems till ~ *or* until ~ *or* up to ~** nous n'avons eu aucun problème jusqu'ici
2. [nowadays] maintenant, aujourd'hui, actuellement
3. [marking a specific point in the past] maintenant, alors, à ce moment-là ■ **by ~ we were all exhausted** nous étions alors tous épuisés ■ **up to ~ I'd never agreed with him** jusque-là *OR* jusqu'alors, je n'avais jamais été d'accord avec lui
4. [introducing information] or ■ **~ a Jaguar is a very fast car** or, la Jaguar est une voiture très rapide
5. [to show enthusiasm] : **~ that's what I call a car!** voilà ce que j'appelle une voiture! ❚ [to show surprise] : **well ~!** ça alors! ❚ [to mark a pause] : **~, what was I saying?** voyons, où en étais-je? ■ **~ let me see** voyons voir ❚ [to comfort] : **there ~ *OR* ~, ~, you mustn't cry** allons, allons, il ne faut pas pleurer ❚ [to cajole, warn] : **~ then, it's time to get up!** allons, il est l'heure de se lever! ■ **you be careful ~!** fais bien attention, hein! ❚ [to scold] : **~ that's just silly!** arrête tes bêtises!
◇ *conj* maintenant que, à présent que ■ **~ you come to mention it** maintenant que tu le dis.
◇ *adj inf* **1.** [current] actuel
2. [fashionable] branché.
◆ **now and again, now and then** *adv phr* de temps en temps, de temps à autre.
◆ **now... now** *conj phr* tantôt... tantôt.

nowadays ['naʊədeɪz] *adv* aujourd'hui, de nos jours.

nowhere ['nəʊweəʳ] *adv* **1.** [no place] nulle part ■ **he goes ~ without her** il ne va nulle part sans elle ■ **there's ~ to hide** il n'y a pas d'endroit où se cacher ■ **~ else** nulle part ailleurs ■ **my watch is ~ to be found** impossible de retrouver ma montre ■ **she/the book was ~ to be seen** elle/le livre avait disparu ❚ *fig* **he appeared from ~ *OR* out of ~** il est apparu comme par enchantement ■ **the horse I backed came ~** le cheval sur lequel j'ai parié est arrivé bon dernier *OR* loin derrière ■ **lying will get you ~** mentir ne vous servira à *OR* ne mènera à rien ■ **I got ~ trying to convince him** mes tentatives pour le convaincre sont restées vaines *OR* se sont soldées par un échec ■ **we're getting ~ fast** *inf* on pédale dans la choucroute *OR* la semoule ■ **he's going ~ fast** il n'ira pas loin **2.** *phr* **~ near** : **the hotel was ~ near the beach** l'hôtel était bien loin de la plage ■ **I've ~ near enough time** je suis loin d'avoir assez de temps.

no-win situation *n* situation *f* sans issue.

nowise ['nəʊwaɪz] *US inf* = **noway**.

nowt [naʊt] *UK inf dial* = **nothing** *(pron)*.

noxious ['nɒkʃəs] *adj* [gas, substance] nocif ■ [influence] néfaste.

nozzle ['nɒzl] *n* [gen] bec *m*, embout *m* ■ [for hose, paint gun] jet *m*, buse *f* ■ [in carburettor] gicleur *m* ■ [in turbine] tuyère *f*.

nr *written abbr of* **near**.

NRA *n* = **National Rifle Association**.

NS *written abbr of* **Nova Scotia**.

NSC (*abbrev of* **National Security Council**) *pr n organisme chargé de superviser la politique militaire de défense du gouvernement des États-Unis.*

NSPCC (*abbrev of* **National Society for the Prevention of Cruelty to Children**) *pr n association britannique de protection de l'enfance.*

NSU *n* = **nonspecific urethritis**.

NT ◇ *n* (*abbrev of* **New Testament**) NT.
◇ *pr n* **1.** = **National Trust 2.** (*abbrev of* **(Royal) National Theatre**) *grand théâtre londonien subventionné par l'État.*

nth [enθ] *adj* **1.** MATHS : **to the ~ power** à la puissance n **2.** *inf* [umpteenth] énième ■ **to the ~ degree** au énième degré.

NUAAW (*abbrev of* **National Union of Agricultural and Allied Workers**) *pr n syndicat britannique des employés du secteur agricole.*

nuance [nju:'ɑ:ns] *n* nuance *f*.

nub [nʌb] *n* **1.** [crux] essentiel *m*, cœur *m* ■ **the ~ of the problem** le cœur *OR* le nœud du problème ■ **the ~ of the matter** le vif du sujet **2.** [small piece] petit morceau *m*, (petit) bout *m* ■ [small bump] petite bosse *f*.

Nubia ['nju:bjə] *pr n* Nubie *f*.

nubile [*UK* 'njubaɪl, *US* 'nu:bəl] *adj* nubile.

nuclear ['nju:klɪəʳ] *adj* **1.** PHYS nucléaire ■ **~ power station** centrale *f* nucléaire *OR* atomique **2.** MIL nucléaire ■ **~ bomb** bombe *f* nucléaire ■ **~ war** guerre *f* atomique ■ **France's ~ deterrent** la force de dissuasion nucléaire française ■ **~ testing** essais *mpl* nucléaires ■ **~ disarmament** désarmement *m* nucléaire ■ **~ weapons** armes *fpl* nucléaires **3.** BIOL nucléaire.

nuclear energy *n* énergie *f* nucléaire.

nuclear family *n* SOCIOL famille *f* nucléaire.

nuclear fission *n* fission *f* nucléaire.

nuclear-free zone *n périmètre dans lequel une collectivité locale interdit l'utilisation, le stockage ou le transport des matières radioactives.*

nuclear fusion *n* fusion *f* nucléaire.

nuclear physics *n (U)* physique *f* nucléaire.

nuclear power *n* nucléaire *m*, énergie *f* nucléaire.

nuclear-powered *adj* à propulsion nucléaire ■ **~ submarine** sous-marin *m* nucléaire.

nuclear reactor *n* réacteur *m* nucléaire.

nuclear winter *n* hiver *m* nucléaire.

nuclei ['nju:klɪaɪ] *pl* ▷ **nucleus**.

nucleic acid [nju:'klɪɪk-] *n* acide *m* nucléique.

nucleus ['nju:klɪəs] (*pl* **nucleuses** *OR pl* **nuclei** ['nju:klɪaɪ]) *n* **1.** BIOL & PHYS noyau *m* **2.** *fig* [kernel] noyau *m*, cœur *m* ■ **a ~ for regional development** un centre de développement régional.

NUCPS (*abbrev of* **National Union of Civil and Public Servants**) *pr n syndicat britannique des employés de la fonction publique.*

nude [nju:d] ◇ *adj* [naked] nu ■ **~ photos** nus *mpl* ; [soft pornography] photos *fpl* érotiques ■ **is ~ sunbathing common here?** est-ce qu'il y a beaucoup de nudistes par ici?
◇ *n* **1.** ART nu *m* **2.** [being nude] : **I was in the ~** j'étais (tout) nu ■ **to pose in the ~** poser nu.

nudge [nʌdʒ] ◇ *vt* **1.** [with elbow] pousser du coude ■ **she ~d her friend to wake her up** elle donna un petit coup de coude à son amie pour la réveiller ▶ **he didn't come home last night, ~~, wink wink** *hum UK* il n'est pas rentré hier soir, si tu vois ce que je veux dire **2.** [push] pousser ■ **he cautiously ~d the door open** il poussa tout doucement la porte (pour l'ouvrir) **3.** [encourage] encourager, pousser ■ **to ~ sb's memory** *UK* rafraîchir la mémoire de qqn **4.** [approach] approcher (de).
◇ *n* **1.** [with elbow] coup *m* de coude ■ [with foot, stick etc] petit coup *m* (de pied), de bâton etc ■ **to give sb a ~** pousser qqn du coude **2.** [encouragement] : **he needs a ~ in the right direction** il a besoin qu'on le pousse dans la bonne direction.

nudism ['nju:dɪzm] *n* nudisme *m*, naturisme *m*.

nudist ['nju:dɪst] ◇ *adj* nudiste, naturiste ■ **~ colony/beach** camp *m* /plage *f* de nudistes.
◇ *n* nudiste *mf*, naturiste *mf*.

nudity ['nju:dətɪ] *n* nudité *f*.

nugget ['nʌgɪt] *n* **1.** [piece] pépite *f* ■ **gold ~** pépite d'or **2.** *fig* **~s of wisdom** des trésors de sagesse ■ **an interesting ~ of information** un (petit) renseignement intéressant.

nuisance ['nju:sns] *n* **1.** [annoying thing, situation] : **that noise is a ~** ce bruit est énervant ■ **it's (such) a ~ having to attend all these meetings** c'est (vraiment) pénible de devoir assister à toutes ces réunions ■ **what a ~!** c'est énervant! ▶ **~ call** appel *m* anonyme ■ **they are not politically important but they have a certain ~ value** ils n'ont pas un grand poids politique, mais ils ont le mérite de déranger **2.** [annoying person] empoisonneur *m*, - euse *f* ■ **to make a ~ of o.s.** embêter *OR* empoisonner le monde ■ **stop being a ~** arrête de nous embêter **3.** [hazard] nuisance *f* ■ **that rubbish dump is a public ~** cette décharge est une calamité.

NUJ (*abbrev of* **National Union of Journalists**) *pr n syndicat britannique des journalistes.*

nuke [nju:k] *inf* ◇ *vt* [bomb] lâcher une bombe atomique sur.
◇ *n* **1.** [weapon] arme *f* nucléaire **2.** *US* [power plant] centrale *f* nucléaire.

null [nʌl] *adj* **1.** LAW [invalid] nul ■ [lapsed] caduc ■ **~ and void** nul et non avenu ■ **the contract was rendered ~ (and void)** le contrat a été annulé *OR* invalidé **2.** [insignificant] insignifiant, sans valeur ■ [amounting to nothing] nul **3.** MATHS nul ■ **~ set** ensemble *m* vide.

nullify ['nʌlɪfaɪ] (*pret & pp* **nullified**) *vt* **1.** LAW [claim, contract, election] annuler, invalider **2.** [advantage] neutraliser.

nullity ['nʌlətɪ] (*pl* **nullities**) *n* **1.** LAW nullité *f* ■ **~ suit** demande *f* en nullité de mariage **2.** [person] nullité *f*.

NUM (*abbrev of* **National Union of Mineworkers**) *pr n syndicat britannique des mineurs.*

numb [nʌm] ◇ *adj* engourdi ■ **we were ~ with cold** nous étions transis de froid ■ **my arm has gone ~** mon bras est engourdi ■ **is your jaw still ~?** [anaesthetized] ta mâchoire est-elle encore anesthésiée? ■ **~ with terror** *fig* paralysé par la peur ■ **he was ~ with shock** *fig* il était sous le choc.
◇ *vt* [person, limbs, senses] engourdir ■ [pain] atténuer, apaiser ■ **~ed by grief** *fig* prostré de douleur.

number ['nʌmbəʳ] ◇ *n* **1.** [gen - MATHS] nombre *m* ■ [figure, numeral] chiffre *m* ■ **a six-figure ~** un nombre de six chiffres ■ **in round ~s** en chiffres ronds ■ **to do sthg by ~s** faire qqch en suivant des instructions précises ■ **she taught him his ~s** elle lui a appris à compter ▶ **even/odd/rational/whole ~** nombre pair/impair/rationnel/entier
2. [as identifier] numéro *m* ■ **have you got my work ~?** avez-vous mon numéro (de téléphone) au travail? ■ **the winning ~** le numéro gagnant ■ **we live at ~ 80** nous habitons au (numéro) 80 ■ **he's the President's ~ two** il est le bras droit du président ■ **name, rank and ~!** MIL nom, grade et matricule! ▶ **did you get the car's (registration) ~?** tu as relevé le numéro d'immatriculation de la voiture? ■ **I've got your ~!** *inf* toi, je te vois venir! ■ **his ~'s up** *inf* son compte est bon
3. [quantity] nombre *m* ■ **any ~ can participate** le nombre de participants est illimité ■ **they were eight in ~** ils étaient (au nombre de) huit ■ **in equal ~s** en nombre égal ■ **to be equal in ~** être à nombre égal ■ **we were many/few in ~** nous étions nombreux/en petit nombre ■ **a (certain) ~ of you** un certain nombre d'entre vous ■ **a large ~ of people** un grand nombre de gens, de nombreuses personnes ■ **in a good** *OR* **fair ~ of cases** dans bon nombre de cas ■ **times without ~** à maintes (et maintes) reprises ■ **they defeated us by force of** *OR* **by sheer weight of ~s** ils l'ont emporté sur nous parce qu'ils étaient plus nombreux
4. [group] : **one of their/our ~** un des leurs/des nôtres ■ **she was not of our ~** elle n'était pas des nôtres *OR* avec nous
5. [issue - of magazine, paper] numéro *m*
6. *inf* [job] boulot *m* ■ **a cushy ~** une planque
7. [song, dance, act] numéro *m* ■ **a dance ~** un numéro de danse ■ **they sang some new ~s** ils ont chanté de nouvelles chansons
8. *inf* [thing, person] : **this ~ is a hot seller** ce modèle se vend comme des petits pains ■ **she was wearing a little black ~** elle portait une petite robe noire ■ **he was driving a little Italian ~** il était au volant d'un de ces petits bolides italiens ■ **who's that blonde ~?** qui est cette belle blonde? ▶ **to do** *OR* **to pull a ~ on sb** rouler qqn
9. GRAM nombre *m*.
◇ *vt* **1.** [assign number to] numéroter
2. [include] compter ■ **I'm glad to ~ her among my closest friends** je suis heureux de la compter parmi mes meilleurs amis
3. [total] compter ■ **each team ~s six players** chaque équipe est composée de *OR* compte six joueurs ■ **the crowd ~ed 5,000** il y avait une foule de 5 000 personnes
4. [count] compter ▶ **his days are ~ed** ses jours sont comptés.
◇ *vi* : **she ~s among the great writers of the century** elle compte parmi les grands écrivains de ce siècle ■ **did he ~ among the ringleaders?** faisait-il partie des meneurs?
◆ **any number of** *adj phr* : **there were any ~ of different dishes to choose from** un très grand nombre de plats différents nous furent présentés.
◆ **numbers** *n US* = **numbers game**.
◆ **number off** *vi insep* se numéroter.

number-crunching [-krʌntʃɪŋ] *n inf* COMPUT traitement *m* en masse des chiffres.

numbering ['nʌmbərɪŋ] *n* numérotation *f*, numérotage *m*.

numberless ['nʌmbəlɪs] *adj* **1.** *fml* [countless] innombrable, sans nombre **2.** [without a number] sans numéro, qui ne porte pas de numéro, non numéroté.

number one ◇ *adj* premier ■ **it's our ~ priority** c'est la première de nos priorités ■ **the ~ oil exporter** le premier exportateur de pétrole ■ **my ~ choice** mon tout premier choix ■ **the ~ hit in the charts** le numéro un au hit-parade.
◇ *n* **1.** *inf* [boss] boss *m*, patron *m*, - onne *f* **2.** *inf* [oneself] : **to look out for** *OR* **to take care of ~** penser à soi **3.** [in hit parade] : **her record got to ~** son disque a été classé numéro un au hit-parade **4.** *baby* **to do ~** faire pipi.

numberplate ['nʌmbəpleɪt] *n UK* AUT plaque *f* minéralogique *OR* d'immatriculation ■ **the lorry had a foreign ~** le camion était immatriculé à l'étranger.

Numbers ['nʌmbəz] *n* BIBLE Nombres *mpl* ■ **the book of ~** le livre des Nombres.

numbers game *n US* loterie *f* clandestine.

Number Ten *pr n* : **~ (Downing Street)** *résidence officielle du Premier ministre britannique.*

numbhead ['nʌmhed], **numbskull** ['nʌmskʌl] *inf* = **numskull**.

numbness ['nʌmnɪs] *n* [physical] engourdissement *m* ■ [mental] torpeur *f*, engourdissement *m*.

numeracy ['nju:mərəsɪ] *n (U) UK* notions *fpl* d'arithmétique.

numeral ['nju:mərəl] *n* chiffre *m*, nombre *m*.

numerate ['nju:mərət] *adj UK* [skilled] bon en mathématiques ■ [having basics] sachant compter.

numerator ['nju:məreɪtəʳ] *n* MATHS numérateur *m*.

numerical [nju:'merɪkl] *adj* numérique ■ **in ~ order** par ordre numérique.

numerical control *n* contrôle *m* numérique.

numerically [nju:'merɪklɪ] *adv* numériquement.

numeric keypad *n* COMPUT pavé *m* numérique.

numerous ['nju:mərəs] *adj* nombreux ■ **for ~ reasons** pour de nombreuses raisons.

numinous ['nju:mɪnəs] *adj* [awe-inspiring] terrifiant.

numismatics [,nju:mɪz'mætɪks] *n (U)* numismatique *f*.

numskull ['nʌmskʌl] *n inf* andouille *f*.

nun [nʌn] *n* religieuse *f* ■ **to become a ~** prendre le voile.

nuncio ['nʌnsɪəʊ] (*pl* **nuncios**) *n* nonce *m*.

nunnery ['nʌnərɪ] (*pl* **nunneries**) *n* couvent *m OR* monastère *m* (de femmes).

NUPE ['nju:pɪ] (*abbrev of* **National Union of Public Employees**) *pr n ancien syndicat britannique des employés de la fonction publique.*

nuptial ['nʌpʃl] *adj* nuptial ■ **~ vows** vœux *mpl* du mariage.
◆ **nuptials** *npl lit* noce *f*, noces *fpl*.

nurd [nɜ:d] *inf* = **nerd**.

NURMTW (*abbrev of* **National Union of Rail, Maritime and Transport Workers**) *pr n syndicat britannique des cheminots, gens de mer et routiers.*

nurse [nɜ:s] ◇ *n* **1.** MED [in hospital] infirmier *m*, - ère *f* ■ [at home] infirmier *m*, - ère *f*, garde-malade *mf* ■ **male ~** infirmier *m* **2.** *UK* [nanny] gouvernante *f*, nurse *f* **3.** [wet nurse] nourrice *f*.
◇ *vt* **1.** MED soigner ■ **he ~d her through the worst of it** il l'a soignée pendant qu'elle était au plus mal ■ **she ~d me back to health** elle m'a guérie ▌ *fig* **he was nursing a bad hangover** il essayait de faire passer sa gueule de bois ■ **to ~ one's pride** panser ses blessures (d'amour-propre) ■ **he ~d the company**

through the crisis il a permis à l'entreprise de traverser la crise **2.** [harbour, foster - grudge, hope, desire] entretenir ; [- scheme] mijoter, couver **3.** [breast-feed] allaiter **4.** [hold] bercer (dans ses bras) ▪ **he sat nursing his fourth whisky** il sirotait son quatrième whisky.
◇ *vi* **1.** MED être infirmier/infirmière **2.** [infant] téter.

nurseling ['nɜːslɪŋ] = **nursling**.

nursemaid ['nɜːsmeɪd] *n* gouvernante *f*, nurse *f* ▪ **to play ~ to sb** *fig* tenir qqn par la main.

nursery ['nɜːsərɪ] (*pl* **nurseries**) *n* **1.** [room] nursery *f*, chambre *f* d'enfants **2.** [day-care centre] crèche *f*, garderie *f* **3.** [school] école *f* maternelle ◗ **~ teacher** instituteur *m*, - trice *f* de maternelle **4.** [for plants, trees] pépinière *f*.

nurserymaid ['nɜːsrɪmeɪd] = **nursemaid**.

nursery nurse *n* puéricultrice *f*.

nursery rhyme *n* comptine *f*.

nursery school *n* école *f* maternelle ▪ **~ teacher** instituteur *m*, - trice *f* de maternelle.

nursery slopes *npl* UK pistes *fpl* pour débutants.

nurse's aide *n* US aide-soignante *f*.

nursing ['nɜːsɪŋ] ◇ *n* **1.** [profession] profession *f* d'infirmier **2.** [care] soins *mpl* **3.** [breast-feeding] allaitement *m*.
◇ *adj* **1.** MED d'infirmier ▪ **the ~ staff** le personnel soignant **2.** [suckling] allaitant.

nursing home *n* **1.** [for aged] maison *f* de retraite ▪ [for convalescents] maison *f* de repos ▪ [for mentally ill] maison *f* de santé **2.** UK [private clinic] hôpital *m* privé, clinique *f* privée.

nursing mother *n* mère *f* qui allaite.

nursing officer *n* UK infirmier *m*, - ère *f* en chef.

nursling ['nɜːslɪŋ] *n* nourrisson *m*.

nurture ['nɜːtʃəʳ] ◇ *vt* **1.** [bring up] élever, éduquer ▪ [nourish] nourrir **2.** [foster - hope, desire] entretenir ; [- plan, scheme] mijoter, couver.
◇ *n* **1.** [upbringing] éducation *f* **2.** [food] nourriture *f*.

nut [nʌt] ◇ *n* **1.** BOT & CULIN *terme générique pour les amandes, noisettes, noix etc* ◗ **she's a hard** OR **tough ~ to crack** *inf* on n'en fait pas ce qu'on veut ▪ **it's a hard** OR **tough ~ to crack** c'est difficile à résoudre ▪ **the American market will be a hard** OR **tough ~ to crack** *inf* ça ne sera pas facile de pénétrer le marché américain
2. TECH écrou *m* ◗ **to learn the ~s and bolts of a department/business** apprendre à connaître le fonctionnement d'un service/d'une entreprise
3. *inf* [crazy person] dingue *mf*, timbré *m*, - e *f*, taré *m*, - e *f* ▪ **what a ~!** il est complètement dingue! ▮ [enthusiast] fana ▪ **she's a golf ~** c'est une fana de golf
4. *inf* [head] caboche *f* ◗ **you must be off your ~!** tu es complètement cinglé! ▪ **to do one's ~** piquer sa crise ▪ **she really did her ~** elle a piqué une de ces crises
5. [small lump of coal] noix *f*, tête-de-moineau *f*.
◇ *vt* (*pret* & *pp* **nutted**, *cont* **nutting**) *inf* donner un coup de boule à △.

NUT (*abbrev of* **National Union of Teachers**) *pr n syndicat britannique d'enseignants*.

nut-brown *adj* brun.

nutcase ['nʌtkeɪs] *n inf* dingue *mf*, taré *m*, - e *f*.

nutcracker ['nʌt,krækəʳ] *n* casse-noix *m inv*, casse-noisettes *m inv*.

nutcrackers ['nʌt,krækəz] *npl* = **nutcracker**.

nuthouse ['nʌthaʊs] (*pl* [-haʊzɪz]) *n inf* maison *f* de fous.

nutmeg ['nʌtmeg] *n* BOT [nut] (noix *f* de) muscade *f* ▪ [tree] muscadier *m*.

nut oil *n* [from walnuts] huile *f* de noix ▪ [from hazelnuts] huile *f* de noisettes.

nutrient ['njuːtrɪənt] ◇ *n* substance *f* nutritive.
◇ *adj* nutritif.

nutriment ['njuːtrɪmənt] *n* [food] nourriture *f*.

nutrition [njuː'trɪʃn] *n* nutrition *f* ▪ **cereals have a high ~ content** les céréales sont très nourrissantes OR nutritives.

nutritional [njuː'trɪʃənl] *adj* [disorder, process, value] nutritif ▪ [science, research] nutritionnel.

nutritionist [njuː'trɪʃənɪst] *n* nutritionniste *mf*.

nutritious [njuː'trɪʃəs] *adj* nutritif, nourrissant.

nuts [nʌts] ◇ *adj inf inf* dingue, timbré, fêlé ▪ **that noise is driving me ~** ce bruit me rend dingue ▪ **to go ~** [crazy, angry] piquer une crise ▪ **to be ~ about** OR **on** être fou OR dingue de.
◇ *npl*△ [testicles] couilles△ *fpl*.
◇ *interj*△ **: ~!** des clous!△.

nutshell ['nʌtʃel] *n* coquille *f* de noix *(de noisette etc)* ▪ **in a ~** en un mot ▪ **to put it in a ~** pour résumer l'histoire (en un mot).

nutter ['nʌtəʳ] *n* UK *inf* malade *mf*, timbré *m*, - e *f*, taré *m*, - e *f*.

nutty ['nʌtɪ] (*comp* **nuttier**, *superl* **nuttiest**) *adj* **1.** [tasting of or containing nuts] aux noix *(aux amandes, aux noisettes etc)* ▪ **a ~ flavour** un goût de noix *(de noisette etc)* **2.** *inf* [crazy] dingue, timbré ◗ **as ~ as a fruitcake** complètement dingue.

nuzzle ['nʌzl] ◇ *vt* [push with nose] pousser du nez ▪ [sniff at] renifler ▪ [subj: animal] pousser du museau.
◇ *vi* **1. : to ~ up against, to ~ at** = **nuzzle** *(vt)* **2.** [nestle] se blottir ▪ **they ~d (up) against their mother** ils se blottirent contre leur mère.

NV *written abbr of* **Nevada**.

nvCJD [,enviː,siːdʒeɪ'diː] (*abbrev of* **new variant Creutzfeld-Jacob Disease**) *n* nvMCJ *f*.

NW (*written abbrev of* **north-west**) N-O.

NWT *written abbr of* **Northwest Territories**.

NY *written abbr of* **New York**.

NYC *written abbr of* **New York City**.

nylon ['naɪlɒn] ◇ *n* Nylon® *m*.
◇ *comp* [thread, shirt, stockings] de OR en Nylon.
◆ **nylons** *npl* [stockings] bas *mpl* (de) Nylon.

nymph [nɪmf] *n* MYTH & ZOOL nymphe *f*.

nymphet ['nɪmfət] *n* nymphette *f*.

nympho ['nɪmfəʊ] (*pl* **nymphos**) *n inf* nympho *f*.

nymphomania [,nɪmfə'meɪnɪə] *n* nymphomanie *f*.

nymphomaniac [,nɪmfə'meɪnɪæk] ◇ *adj* nymphomane.
◇ *n* nymphomane *f*.

NYPD [,enwaɪpiː'diː] *n* NYPD *m*, police *f* new-yorkaise.

NYSE *pr n* = **New York Stock Exchange**.

NZ *written abbr of* **New Zealand**.

o (*pl* **o's** *OR pl* **os**), **O** (*pl* **O's** *OR pl* **Os**) [əʊ] *n* [letter] o *m*, O *m* ■ **O positive/negative** MED O positif/négatif, *see also* **f**.

o *interj* **1.** *lit* [as vocative] ô **2.** [as exclamation] = **oh**.

o' [ə] *prep* [of] de.

O *n* [zero] zéro *m* ■ **agent double O seven** agent 007.

oaf [əʊf] *n* [dull, clumsy man] lourdaud *m* ■ [uncouth man] rustre *m*, goujat *m*.

oafish ['əʊfɪʃ] *adj* [dull, clumsy] lourdaud, balourd ■ [uncouth] rustre.

oak [əʊk] ◇ *n* chêne *m*.
◇ *comp* [furniture, door, panelling] de *OR* en chêne ■ **~ forest** forêt *f* de chênes ■ **~ tree** chêne *m*.

oak apple *n* noix *f* de galle.

oakum ['əʊkəm] *n* étoupe *f*, filasse *f*.

OAP (*abbrev of* **old age pensioner**) *n UK* retraité *m*, - e *f* ■ **'students and ~s half price'** ≃ étudiants et carte vermeille demi-tarif.

oar [ɔːr] ◇ *n* **1.** [instrument] rame *f*, aviron *m* ■ **to stick** *OR* **to put one's ~ in** *UK inf* mettre son grain de sel **2.** [person] rameur *m*, - euse *f*.
◇ *vi* & *vt lit* ramer.

oarlock ['ɔːlɒk] *n US* [concave] dame *f* (de nage) ■ [pin] tolet *m*.

oarsman ['ɔːzmən] (*pl* **oarsmen** [-mən]) *n* rameur *m*.

oarsmanship ['ɔːzmənʃɪp] *n (U)* compétences *fpl* de rameur.

oarswoman ['ɔːzˌwʊmən] (*pl* **oarswomen** [-ˌwɪmɪn]) *n* rameuse *f*.

oasis [əʊ'eɪsɪs] (*pl* **oases** [-siːz]) *n liter* & *fig* oasis *f* ■ **an ~ of calm** une oasis *OR* un havre de paix.

oat [əʊt] *n* [plant] avoine *f*.
◆ **oats** *npl* avoine *f* ▶ **is he getting his ~s?** *inf* est-ce qu'il a ce qu'il lui faut au lit?

oatcake ['əʊtkeɪk] *n* gâteau *m* sec (d'avoine).

oatflakes ['əʊtfleɪks] *npl* flocons *mpl* d'avoine.

oath [əʊθ] (*pl* [əʊðz]) *n* **1.** [vow] serment *m* ■ **he took** *OR* **swore an ~ never to return** il fit le serment *OR* il jura de ne jamais revenir ■ **it's true, on my ~!** c'est vrai, je vous le jure! ■ **to be on** *OR* **under ~** LAW être sous serment, être assermenté ■ **to put sb on** *OR* **under ~** LAW faire prêter serment à qqn **2.** [swearword] juron *m* ■ **he let out a string of ~s** il a laissé échapper un torrent d'injures.

oatmeal ['əʊtmiːl] ◇ *n (U)* [flakes] flocons *mpl* d'avoine ■ [flour] farine *f* d'avoine ■ **~ porridge** bouillie *f* d'avoine, porridge *m*.
◇ *adj* [colour] grège.

OAU (*abbrev of* **Organization of African Unity**) *pr n* OUA *f*.

Obadiah [ˌəʊbə'daɪə] *pr n* Abdias.

obduracy ['ɒbdjʊrəsɪ] *n fml* **1.** [hardheartedness] dureté *f* (de cœur), insensibilité *f* **2.** [obstinacy] obstination *f*, entêtement *m* ■ [inflexibility] inflexibilité *f*, intransigeance *f*.

obdurate ['ɒbdjʊrət] *adj fml* **1.** [hardhearted] insensible, dur **2.** [obstinate] obstiné, entêté ■ [unyielding] inflexible.

OBE (*abbrev of* **Officer of the Order of the British Empire**) *n* *distinction honorifique britannique*.

obedience [ə'biːdjəns] *n* **1.** obéissance *f* ■ **to show ~ to sb** obéir à qqn ■ **to owe ~ to sb** *lit* devoir obédience à qqn ■ **in ~ to her wishes** conformément à ses vœux ■ **to command ~** savoir se faire obéir **2.** RELIG obédience *f*.

obedient [ə'biːdjənt] *adj* obéissant, docile ■ **to be ~ to sb** obéir à qqn.

obediently [ə'biːdjəntlɪ] *adv* docilement ■ **they followed him ~** ils le suivirent sans discuter.

obeisance [əʊ'beɪsns] *n lit* **1.** [homage] hommage *m* ■ **to make** *OR* **to pay ~ to sb** rendre hommage à qqn **2.** [bow] révérence *f* ■ [sign] geste *m* de respect.

obelisk ['ɒbəlɪsk] *n* **1.** [column] obélisque *m* **2.** TYPO croix *f* (d'évêque), obel *m*.

obese [əʊ'biːs] *adj* obèse.

obesity [əʊ'biːsətɪ], **obeseness** [əʊ'biːsnɪs] *n* obésité *f*.

obey [ə'beɪ] ◇ *vt* obéir à ■ **he always ~ed his mother/his intuition/the law** il a toujours obéi à sa mère/à son intuition/aux lois ■ **the plane is no longer ~ing the controls** l'avion ne répond plus.
◇ *vi* obéir, obtempérer.

obfuscate ['ɒbfʌskeɪt] *vt fml* [obscure - issue] obscurcir, embrouiller ; [- mind] embrouiller ■ [perplex - person] embrouiller, dérouter.

obit ['ɒbɪt, 'əʊbɪt] *n inf* nécrologie *f*.

obituary [ə'bɪtʃʊərɪ] (*pl* **obituaries**) ◇ *n* nécrologie *f*, notice *f* nécrologique ■ **the ~ column, the obituaries** la rubrique nécrologique.
◇ *adj* nécrologique.

object[1] ['ɒbdʒɪkt] *n* **1.** [thing] objet *m*, chose *f* **2.** [aim] objet *m*, but *m*, fin *f* ■ **with this ~ in mind** dans ce but, à cette fin ■ **that's the (whole) ~ of the exercise** c'est (justement là) le but de l'opération ▶ **money is no ~** peu importe le prix, le prix est sans importance ■ **money is no ~ to them** ils n'ont pas de problèmes d'argent ■ **time is no ~** peu importe le temps que cela prendra **3.** [focus] objet *m* ■ **an ~ of ridicule/interest** un objet de ridicule/d'intérêt **4.** GRAM [of verb] complément *m* d'objet ■ [of preposition] objet *m*.

object² [əb'dʒekt] <> *vi* élever une objection ■ [stronger] protester ■ **to ~ to sthg** protester contre qqch ■ **they ~ to working overtime** ils ne sont pas d'accord pour faire des heures supplémentaires ■ **if you don't ~** si vous n'y voyez pas d'inconvénient ■ **you know how your father ~s to it!** tu sais combien ton père y est opposé! ■ **I ~!** je proteste! ■ **I ~ strongly to your attitude** je trouve votre attitude proprement inadmissible ■ **I wouldn't ~ to a cup of tea** je ne dirais pas non à *OR* je prendrais volontiers une tasse de thé ■ **he ~s to her smoking** il désapprouve qu'elle fume ■ **she ~s to his coming** elle n'est pas d'accord pour qu'il vienne ■ **why do you ~ to all my friends?** pourquoi cette hostilité à l'égard de tous mes amis? ■ **it's not her I ~ to but her husband** ce n'est pas elle qui me déplaît, c'est son mari ■ **to ~ to a witness** LAW récuser un témoin.
<> *vt* objecter.

objection [əb'dʒekʃn] *n* **1.** [argument against] objection *f* ■ **to make** *OR* **to raise an ~** faire *OR* soulever une objection ■ **I have no ~ to his coming** je ne vois pas d'objection à ce qu'il vienne ■ **I have no ~ to his friends** je n'ai rien contre ses amis ■ **if you have no ~** si vous n'y voyez pas d'inconvénient ■ **~!** LAW objection! ■ **~ overruled!** LAW objection rejetée! **2.** [opposition] opposition *f*.

objectionable [əb'dʒekʃnəbl] *adj* [unpleasant] désagréable ■ [blameworthy] répréhensible ■ **to use ~ language** parler vulgairement ■ **I find his views ~** je n'aime pas sa façon de penser ■ **what is so ~ about her behaviour?** qu'est-ce qu'on peut lui reprocher?

objective [əb'dʒektɪv] <> *adj* **1.** [unbiased] objectif, impartial **2.** [real, observable] objectif ➲ **~ symptoms** MED signes *mpl* **3.** GRAM objectif.
<> *n* **1.** [aim] objectif *m*, but *m* ■ **to achieve** *OR* **to reach one's ~** atteindre son but **2.** GRAM accusatif *m*, cas *m* objectif **3.** PHOT objectif *m*.

objectively [əb'dʒektɪvlɪ] *adv* **1.** [unbiasedly] objectivement, impartialement **2.** [really, externally] objectivement.

objectivism [əb'dʒektɪvɪzm] *n* objectivisme *m*.

objectivity [,ɒbdʒek'tɪvətɪ] *n* objectivité *f*.

object lesson *n* **1.** [example] demonstration *f*, illustration *f (d'un principe)* ■ **it was an ~ in persistence** ce fut un parfait exemple de persévérance **2.** SCH leçon *f* de choses.

objector [əb'dʒektəʳ] *n* opposant *m*, - e *f*.

oblate ['ɒbleɪt] <> *adj* GEOM aplati (aux pôles).
<> *n* RELIG oblat *m*, - e *f*.

oblation [ə'bleɪʃn] *n* RELIG [ceremony] oblation *f* ■ [thing offered] oblation *f*, oblats *mpl*.

obligate ['ɒblɪgeɪt] *vt* **1.** *UK fml US* [compel] obliger, contraindre ■ **to be/to feel ~d to do sthg** être/se sentir obligé de faire qqch **2.** *US* FIN [funds, credits] affecter.

obligation [,ɒblɪ'geɪʃn] *n* obligation *f* ■ **to be under an ~ to do sthg** être dans l'obligation de faire qqch ■ **you are under no ~ to reply** vous n'êtes pas tenu de répondre ■ **I am under an ~ to her** j'ai une dette envers elle ■ **to put** *OR* **to place sb under an ~ to do sthg** mettre qqn dans l'obligation de faire qqch ■ **it is my ~ to inform you that...** il est de mon devoir de *OR* je suis tenu de vous informer que... ■ **to meet one's ~s** satisfaire à ses obligations, assumer ses engagements.
Voir module d'usage

obligatory [ə'blɪgətrɪ] *adj* obligatoire.

oblige [ə'blaɪdʒ] <> *vt* **1.** [constrain] obliger ■ **to ~ sb to do sthg** obliger qqn à faire qqch ■ **you're not ~d to come** tu n'es pas obligé de venir **2.** [do a favour to] rendre service à, obliger ■ **I would be ~d if you would refrain from smoking** *fml* vous m'obligeriez beaucoup en ne fumant pas ■ **could you ~ me with a match?** *fml* auriez-vous l'amabilité *OR* l'obligeance de me donner une allumette? ■ **much ~d!** merci beaucoup! ■ **to be ~d to sb for sthg** savoir gré à qqn de qqch ■ **she ~d the guests with a song** elle a consenti à chanter pour les invités.
<> *vi* : **always ready to ~!** toujours prêt à rendre service!

obliging [ə'blaɪdʒɪŋ] *adj* serviable, obligeant ■ **it was very ~ of him** c'était très aimable à lui *OR* de sa part.

obligingly [ə'blaɪdʒɪŋlɪ] *adv* aimablement, obligeamment ■ **the letter you ~ sent me** la lettre que vous avez eu l'obligeance de m'envoyer.

oblique [ə'bli:k] <> *adj* **1.** GEOM [slanted] oblique **2.** [indirect] indirect **3.** BOT oblique **4.** GRAM oblique.
<> *n* **1.** GEOM oblique *f* ■ ANAT oblique *m* **2.** TYPO barre *f* oblique.

obliquely [ə'bli:klɪ] *adv* **1.** obliquement, en biais **2.** [indirectly] indirectement.

obliterate [ə'blɪtəreɪt] *vt* [destroy, erase] effacer ■ [cancel - stamp] oblitérer ■ **the town was ~d** la ville a été effacée de la carte.

obliteration [ə,blɪtə'reɪʃn] *n* [destruction, erasure] effacement *m* ■ [of stamp] oblitération *f*.

oblivion [ə'blɪvɪən] *n* **1.** [being forgotten] oubli *m* ■ **to fall** *OR* **to sink into ~** tomber dans l'oubli ■ **to save sb/sthg from ~** tirer qqn/qqch de l'oubli, sauver qqn/qqch de l'oubli **2.** [unconsciousness] inconscience *f*, oubli *m* ■ **he had drunk himself into ~** il était abruti par l'alcool.

oblivious [ə'blɪvɪəs] *adj* inconscient ■ **she was ~ of** *OR* **to what was happening** elle n'avait pas conscience de *OR* n'était pas consciente de ce qui se passait ■ **he remained ~ to our comments** il est resté sourd à nos remarques.

oblong ['ɒblɒŋ] <> *adj* [rectangular] rectangulaire ■ [elongated] allongé, oblong, - ongue *f*.
<> *n* [rectangle] rectangle *m*.

obloquy ['ɒbləkwɪ] (*pl* **obloquies**) *n (U) fml* **1.** [abuse] insultes *fpl*, injures *fpl* ■ [defamation] diffamation *f* **2.** [disgrace] opprobre *m*.

obnoxious [əb'nɒkʃəs] *adj* [person] odieux, ignoble ■ [behaviour] odieux ■ [smell] ignoble, infect.

oboe ['əʊbəʊ] *n* hautbois *m*.

oboist ['əʊbəʊɪst] *n* hautbois *m (musicien)*, hautboïste *mf*.

OBLIGATION

Est-ce qu'il faut prendre rendez-vous ? Do you have to make an appointment?

Faut-il faire une réservation ? Do you have to make a reservation?

Est-ce que je dois vraiment y aller ? Do I really have to go?

Il faut que tu y sois à 8 heures. You have to be there at 8 o'clock.

Tu dois absolument en parler à ton père. You really must talk to your father about this.

Il lui faudra d'abord repasser chez lui. He'll have to go home first.

La scolarité est obligatoire jusqu'à l'âge de seize ans. Schooling is compulsory up to the age of sixteen.

Vous n'avez pas l'obligation d'acheter. You're under no obligation to buy.

Tu n'es pas obligé de rester. You don't have to stay.

Personne ne t'oblige à y aller. Nobody's forcing you to go.

Vous n'avez pas besoin d'un visa. You don't need a visa.

obscene [əb'si:n] *adj* obscène ■ **an ~ publication** une publication obscène ■ **it's ~ to earn so much money** *fig* c'est indécent de gagner autant d'argent.

obscenely [əb'si:nlɪ] *adv* d'une manière obscène ■ **he's ~ rich** *fig* il est tellement riche que c'en est dégoûtant.

obscenity [əb'senətɪ] (*pl* **obscenities**) *n* **1.** *(U)* [obscene language] obscénité *f*, obscénités *fpl* **2.** [obscene word] obscénité *f*, grossièreté *f* ■ **to shout obscenities** crier des obscénités **3.** *fig* **war is an ~** la guerre est une chose obscène.

obscurantist [ˌɒbskjʊə'ræntɪst] *fml* ◇ *adj* obscurantiste. ◇ *n* obscurantiste *mf*.

obscure [əb'skjʊəʳ] ◇ *adj* **1.** [not clear] obscur ■ **the meaning is rather ~** le sens n'est pas très clair ■ **an ~ feeling of unease** un obscur *OR* vague sentiment de malaise ▮ [little-known] perdu **2.** [dark] obscur, sombre.
◇ *vt* **1.** [hide] cacher ■ [confuse] obscurcir, embrouiller ■ **to ~ the facts/the issue** embrouiller les faits/la question **2.** [darken] obscurcir, assombrir.

obscurely [əb'skjʊəlɪ] *adv* obscurément.

obscurity [əb'skjʊərətɪ] (*pl* **obscurities**) *n* **1.** [insignificance] obscurité *f* ■ **to fall into ~** sombrer dans l'oubli **2.** [difficulty] obscurité *f* **3.** [darkness] obscurité *f*, ténèbres *fpl*.

obsequies ['ɒbsɪkwɪz] *npl fml* obsèques *fpl*.

obsequious [əb'si:kwɪəs] *adj fml* obséquieux.

obsequiousness [əb'si:kwɪəsnɪs] *n fml* obséquiosité *f*.

observable [əb'zɜ:vəbl] *adj* [visible] observable, visible ■ [discernible] perceptible, appréciable ■ **behaviour ~ in humans** un comportement observable *OR* que l'on peut observer chez les humains.

observance [əb'zɜ:vəns] *n* **1.** [recognition - of custom, law etc] observation *f*, observance *f* ; [- of anniversary] célébration *f* **2.** RELIG [rite, ceremony] observance *f*.

observant [əb'zɜ:vnt] *adj* [alert] observateur ■ **how ~ of him!** comme il est observateur!, rien ne lui échappe!

observation [ˌɒbzə'veɪʃn] *n* **1.** [study] observation *f*, surveillance *f* ■ **to be under ~** [patient] être en observation ; [by police] être surveillé par la police *OR* sous surveillance policière **2.** [comment] observation *f*, remarque *f* **3.** [perception] observation *f* ■ **to have great powers of ~** avoir de grandes facultés d'observation **4.** NAUT relèvement *m*.

observational [ˌɒbzə'veɪʃənl] *adj* [faculties, powers] d'observation ■ [technique, research] observationnel.

observation car *n* RAIL voiture *f* panoramique.

observation post *n* MIL poste *m* d'observation.

observation tower *n* tour *f* de guet, mirador *m*.

observatory [əb'zɜ:vətrɪ] (*pl* **observatories**) *n* observatoire *m*.

observe [əb'zɜ:v] *vt* **1.** [see, notice] observer, remarquer **2.** [study, pay attention to] observer ■ **the police are observing his movements** la police surveille ses allées et venues **3.** [comment, remark] (faire) remarquer, (faire) observer **4.** [abide by, keep] observer, respecter ■ **to ~ a minute's silence** observer une minute de silence.

observer [əb'zɜ:vəʳ] *n* **1.** [watcher] observateur *m*, - trice *f* ■ **to the casual ~** pour un non-initié **2.** [at official ceremony, election] observateur *m*, - trice *f* **3.** [commentator] spécialiste *mf*, expert *m* ■ **The Observer** PRESS *journal de qualité politiquement indépendant, paraissant le dimanche et comprenant un supplément magazine, see also* **Sunday**.

obsess [əb'ses] *vt* obséder ■ **he's ~ed with punctuality** c'est un maniaque de la ponctualité ■ **she's ~ed with the idea of becoming an actress** elle n'a qu'une idée, devenir actrice ■ **he became ~ed by the horrific image** cette vision d'horreur se mit à le hanter.

obsession [əb'seʃn] *n* [fixed idea] obsession *f*, idée *f* fixe ■ **it's becoming an ~ with him** ça devient une idée fixe *OR* une obsession chez lui ■ **she has an ~ about punctuality** c'est une maniaque de la ponctualité ▮ [obsessive fear] hantise *f* ■ **his ~ with death** sa hantise de la mort.

obsessional [əb'seʃənl] *adj* obsessionnel.

obsessive [əb'sesɪv] ◇ *adj* **1.** [person] obsédé MED & PSYCHOL obsessionnel ■ [behaviour] obsessionnel **2.** [thought, image] obsédant.
◇ *n* obsessionnel *m*, - elle *f*.

obsessively [əb'sesɪvlɪ] *adv* d'une manière obsessionnelle ■ **he's ~ cautious** il est d'une prudence obsessionnelle ■ **he is ~ attached to the toy** il a un attachement maladif pour ce jouet ■ **she is ~ attached to her mother** elle fait une fixation sur sa mère.

obsolescence [ˌɒbsə'lesns] *n* [of equipment, consumer goods] obsolescence *f* ■ **planned** *OR* **built-in ~** COMM obsolescence planifiée, désuétude *f* calculée.

obsolescent [ˌɒbsə'lesnt] *adj* qui tombe en désuétude ■ [equipment, consumer goods] obsolescent.

obsolete ['ɒbsəli:t] *adj* **1.** [outmoded] démodé, désuet(ète) *f* ■ [antiquated] archaïque ■ [machinery] dépassé **2.** LING obsolète **3.** BIOL atrophié.

obstacle ['ɒbstəkl] *n* obstacle *m* ■ **what are the ~s to free trade?** qu'est-ce qui fait obstacle au libre-échange? ■ **to put ~s in sb's way** mettre des bâtons dans les roues à qqn.

obstacle course, obstacle race *n* course *f* d'obstacles.

obstetric [ɒb'stetrɪk] *adj* obstétrical ■ [nurses] en obstétrique.

obstetrician [ˌɒbstə'trɪʃn] *n* obstétricien *m*, - enne *f*.

obstetrics [ɒb'stetrɪks] *n (U)* obstétrique *f*.

obstinacy ['ɒbstɪnəsɪ] *n* **1.** [stubbornness] obstination *f*, entêtement *m* ■ [tenacity] opiniâtreté *f*, ténacité *f* **2.** [persistence] persistance *f*.

obstinate ['ɒbstənət] *adj* **1.** [stubborn] obstiné, entêté, têtu ■ [tenacious] obstiné, tenace, acharné **2.** [persistent] persistant, tenace.

obstinately ['ɒbstənətlɪ] *adv* [stubbornly] obstinément, avec acharnement.

obstreperous [əb'strepərəs] *adj fml* & *hum* [noisy] bruyant ■ [disorderly] turbulent ■ [recalcitrant] récalcitrant.

obstruct [əb'strʌkt] *vt* **1.** [block - passage, road, traffic] bloquer, obstruer ; [- pipe] boucher ; [- vein, artery] obstruer, boucher ■ **her hat ~ed my view** son chapeau m'empêchait de voir **2.** [impede - progress, measures] faire obstruction *OR* obstacle à, entraver ■ **to ~ progress/justice** entraver la marche du progrès/le cours de la justice ■ **he was arrested for ~ing a policeman in the course of his duty** on l'a arrêté pour avoir entravé un agent dans l'exercice de ses fonctions **3.** SPORT [opponent] faire obstruction à.

obstruction [əb'strʌkʃn] *n* **1.** [impeding - of progress, measures] obstruction *f* **2.** [blockage, obstacle - gen] obstacle *m* ; [- in vein, artery] obstruction *f* ; [- in pipe] bouchon *m* ■ **the accident caused an ~ in the road** l'accident a bloqué la route **3.** SPORT obstruction *f* **4.** LAW obstruction *f* de la voie publique.

obstructive [əb'strʌktɪv] *adj* : **they are being very ~** ils nous mettent constamment des bâtons dans les roues ■ **to use ~ tactics** POL user de tactiques obstructionnistes.

obtain [əb'teɪn] ◇ *vt* obtenir ■ [for oneself] se procurer ■ **to ~ sthg for sb** obtenir qqch pour qqn, procurer qqch à qqn ■ **to ~ sthg from sb** obtenir qqch de qqn ■ **the book may be ~ed from the publisher** on peut se procurer le livre chez l'éditeur.
◇ *vi fml* [prevail] avoir cours, être en vigueur ■ **the situation ~ing in Somalia** la situation (qui règne) en Somalie ■ **this new system will ~ as from next week** ce nouveau système entrera en vigueur dès la semaine prochaine.

obtainable [əb'teɪnəbl] *adj* : **where is this drug ~?** où peut-on se procurer ce médicament? ■ **the catalogue is ~ in our branches** le catalogue est disponible dans nos agences ■ **~ from your local supermarket** en vente dans votre supermarché ■ **this result is easily ~** ce résultat est facile à obtenir.

obtrusive [əb'tru:sɪv] *adj* [intrusive - decor, advertising, hoarding, architecture] trop voyant ; [- smell] tenace, envahissant, pénétrant ; [- person, behaviour] envahissant, importun, indiscret, - ète *f*.

obtrusively [əb'tru:sɪvlɪ] *adv* importunément.

obtuse [əb'tju:s] *adj* **1.** *fml* [slow-witted] obtus ■ **stop being so ~!** ne sois pas si borné! **2.** GEOM [angle] obtus ■ [triangle] obtusangle **3.** [indistinct] vague, sourd.

obverse ['ɒbvɜ:s] ◇ *n* **1.** [of coin] avers *m*, face *f* **2.** [of opinion, argument etc] contraire *m*, opposé *m*.
◇ *adj* : **the ~ side** [of coin] le côté face *OR* l'avers d'une pièce ; *fig* [of opinion, argument etc] le contraire.

obviate ['ɒbvɪeɪt] *vt fml* [difficulty, need] obvier à ■ **this ~s the need for further action** cela rend toute autre démarche inutile.

obvious ['ɒbvɪəs] ◇ *adj* **1.** [evident] évident ■ **it's ~ that he's wrong** il est évident *OR* clair qu'il a tort ■ **her ~ innocence** son innocence manifeste ■ **the ~ thing to do is to leave** la seule chose à faire, c'est de partir **2.** *pej* [predictable] prévisible ■ **his symbolism is too ~** son symbolisme manque de subtilité.
◇ *n* : **to state the ~** enfoncer une porte ouverte ■ **it would be stating the ~ to say that** cela va sans dire.

obviously ['ɒbvɪəslɪ] *adv* **1.** [of course] évidemment, de toute évidence ■ **she's ~ not lying** il est clair *OR* évident qu'elle ne ment pas ■ **~ not!** il semble que non! **2.** [plainly, visibly] manifestement **3.** [beginning a sentence] il va de soi ■ **~, we won't break even until next year** il va de soi que nous ne rentrerons pas dans nos frais avant un an.

ocarina [,ɒkə'ri:nə] *n* ocarina *m*.

OCAS (*abbrev of* **Organization of Central American States**) *pr n* ODEAC *f*.

occasion [ə'keɪʒn] ◇ *n* **1.** [circumstance, time] occasion *f* ■ **he was perfectly charming on that ~** cette fois-là, il fut tout à fait charmant ■ **on the ~ of her wedding** à l'occasion de son mariage ■ **I have been there on quite a few ~s** j'y suis allé à plusieurs occasions *OR* à plusieurs reprises ■ **if the ~ arises, should the ~ arise** si l'occasion se présente, le cas échéant ■ **it wasn't a suitable ~** les circonstances n'étaient pas favorables ▶ **to rise to the ~** se montrer à la hauteur (de la situation) **2.** [special event] événement *m* ■ **to have a sense of ~** savoir marquer le coup **3.** [reason, cause] motif *m*, raison *f*, occasion *f* ■ **there is no ~ for worry** il n'y a pas lieu de s'inquiéter.
◇ *vt* occasionner, provoquer.
◆ **on occasion(s)** *adv phr* de temps en temps, de temps à autre.

occasional [ə'keɪʒənl] *adj* **1.** occasionnel, épisodique ■ **he's an ~ visitor/golfer** il vient/joue au golf de temps en temps ■ **during his ~ visits to her** lorsqu'il allait la voir *OR* lui rendait visite ■ **I like an *OR* the ~ cigar** j'aime (fumer) un cigare à l'occasion *OR* de temps en temps ■ **there will be ~ showers** il y aura quelques averses *OR* pluies intermittentes **2.** [music, play etc] de circonstance.

occasionally [ə'keɪʒnəlɪ] *adv* de temps en temps, quelquefois, occasionnellement.

occasional table *n UK* table *f* d'appoint.

occident ['ɒksɪdənt] *n lit* occident *m*, couchant *m*.
◆ **Occident** *n* : **the Occident** l'Occident *m*.

occidental [,ɒksɪ'dentl] *adj lit* occidental.
◆ **Occidental** ◇ *adj* occidental.
◇ *n* Occidental *m*, - e *f*.

occipital [ɒk'sɪpɪtl] *adj* occipital.

occiput ['ɒksɪpʌt] (*pl* **occiputs** *OR pl* **occipita** [ɒk'sɪpɪtə]) *n* occiput *m*.

occlude [ɒ'klu:d] *vt* occlure.

occluded front [ɒ'klu:dɪd-] *n* METEOR front *m* occlus.

occlusion [ɒ'klu:ʒn] *n* occlusion *f*.

occlusive [ɒ'klu:sɪv] ◇ *adj* occlusif.
◇ *n* LING (consonne *f*) occlusive *f*.

occult [ɒ'kʌlt] ◇ *adj* occulte.
◇ *n* : **the ~** [supernatural] le surnaturel ; [mystical skills] les sciences *fpl* occultes.

occupancy ['ɒkjʊpənsɪ] (*pl* **occupancies**) *n* occupation *f* (*d'un appartement etc*).

occupant ['ɒkjʊpənt] *n* [gen] occupant *m*, - e *f* ■ [tenant] locataire *mf* ■ [of vehicle] passager *m*, - ère *f* ■ [of job] titulaire *mf*.

occupation [,ɒkjʊ'peɪʃn] *n* **1.** [employment] emploi *m*, travail *m* ■ **what's his ~?** qu'est-ce qu'il fait comme travail *OR* dans la vie? ■ **please state your name and ~** veuillez indiquer votre nom et votre profession ■ **I'm not an actor by ~** je ne suis pas acteur de métier ■ **raising a family is a full-time ~** élever des enfants, c'est un travail à plein temps **2.** [activity, hobby] occupation *f* ■ **his favourite ~ is listening to music** ce qu'il aime faire par-dessus tout, c'est écouter de la musique **3.** [of building, offices etc] occupation *f* ■ **the offices are ready for ~** les bureaux sont prêts à être occupés **4.** MIL & POL occupation *f* ■ **army of ~** armée *f* d'occupation ■ **under French ~** sous occupation française ■ **the Occupation** HIST l'Occupation.

occupational [,ɒkju:'peɪʃənl] *adj* professionnel ■ **~ disease** maladie *f* professionnelle ■ **~ hazard** risque *m* professionnel *OR* du métier.

occupational pension *n UK* retraite *f* complémentaire ■ **~ scheme** caisse *f* de retraite complémentaire.

occupational therapist *n* ergothérapeute *mf*.

occupational therapy *n* ergothérapie *f*.

occupied ['ɒkjʊpaɪd] *adj* [country, town] occupé ■ **in ~ France** dans la France occupée.

occupier ['ɒkjʊpaɪə^r] *n* [gen] occupant *m*, - e *f* ■ [tenant] locataire *mf*.

occupy ['ɒkjʊpaɪ] (*pret & pp* **occupied**) *vt* **1.** [house, room etc] occuper ■ **is this seat occupied?** est-ce que cette place est prise? **2.** [keep busy - person, mind] occuper ■ **she occupies herself by doing crosswords** elle s'occupe en faisant des mots croisés ■ **to be occupied in *OR* with (doing) sthg** être occupé à (faire) qqch ■ **try to keep them occupied for a few minutes** essaie de les occuper quelques minutes ■ **I like to keep my mind occupied** j'aime bien m'occuper l'esprit **3.** [fill, take up - time, space] occuper **4.** MIL & POL occuper ■ **~ing army** armée *f* d'occupation **5.** [hold - office, role, rank] occuper.

occur [ə'kɜ:^r] (*pret & pp* **occurred**, *cont* **occurring**) *vi* **1.** [happen] arriver, avoir lieu, se produire ■ **misunderstandings often ~ over the phone** il y a souvent des malentendus au téléphone ■ **many changes have occurred since then** beaucoup de choses ont changé depuis ce temps-là ■ **if a difficulty/the opportunity ~s** si une difficulté/l'occasion se présente ■ **whatever ~s** quoi qu'il arrive **2.** [exist, be found] se trouver, se rencontrer ■ **such phenomena often ~ in nature** on rencontre souvent de tels phénomènes dans la nature **3.** [come to mind] : **to ~ to sb** venir à l'esprit de qqn ■ **it occurred to me later that he was lying** j'ai réalisé plus tard qu'il mentait ■ **didn't it ~ to you to call me?** ça ne t'est pas venu à l'idée de m'appeler? ■ **it would never ~ to me to use violence** il ne me viendrait jamais à l'idée d'avoir recours à la violence.

occurrence [ə'kʌrəns] *n* **1.** [incident] événement *m* ■ **it's an everyday ~** ça arrive *OR* ça se produit tous les jours **2.** [fact or instance of occurring] : **the increasing ~ of racial attacks** le nombre croissant d'agressions racistes ■ **the ~ of the disease in adults is more serious** lorsqu'elle se déclare chez l'adulte, la maladie est plus grave ■ **of rare ~** qui arrive *OR* se produit rarement **3.** LING occurrence *f*.

OCD (*abbrev of* **obsessive compulsive disorder**) *n* PSYCHOL TOC *m*.

ocean ['əʊʃn] *n* **1.** GEOG océan *m* ■ **the ~** *US* la mer ■ **the Ocean State** le Rhode Island **2.** *fig* **~s of** beaucoup de.

ocean bed, ocean floor *n* fond *m* océanique.

oceanfront ['əʊʃnfrʌnt] *US n* bord *m* de mer.

oceangoing ['əʊʃn,gəʊɪŋ] *adj* de haute mer.

Oceania [,əʊʃɪ'ɑ:nɪə] *pr n* Océanie *f* ■ **in ~** en Océanie.

oceanic [,əʊʃɪ'ænɪk] *adj* **1.** [marine] océanique **2.** *fig* [huge] immense.

ocean liner *n* paquebot *m*.

oceanography [ˌəʊʃə'nɒgrəfɪ] *n* océanographie *f*.

och [ɒx] *interj* **Scotland** & **Ireland** oh ▪ **~ aye!** eh oui! *(parfois employé pour parodier les Écossais)*.

ochre, ocher *US* ['əʊkəʳ] <> *n* [ore] ocre *f* ▪ [colour] ocre *m*.
<> *adj* ocre *(inv)*.
<> *vt* ocrer.

o'clock [ə'klɒk] *adv* **1.** [time] : **it's one/two ~** il est une heure/deux heures ▪ **at precisely 9 ~** à 9 h précises ▪ **a flight at 4 ~ in the afternoon** un vol à 16 h ▪ **the 8 ~ bus** le bus de 8 h ▪ **at 12 ~** [midday] à midi ; [midnight] à minuit **2.** [position] : **enemy fighter at 7 ~** chasseur ennemi à 7 h.

OCR *n* **1.** = **optical character reader 2.** (*abbrev of* **optical character recognition**) ROC *f*.

Oct. (*written abbrev of* **October**) oct.

octagon ['ɒktəgən] *n* octogone *m*.

octagonal [ɒk'tægənl] *adj* octogonal.

octal ['ɒktl] <> *adj* octal.
<> *n* octal *m*.

octameter [ɒk'tæmɪtəʳ] *n* LIT vers *m* de huit pieds, octosyllabe *m*.

octane ['ɒkteɪn] *n* octane *m* ▪ **high-~ petrol** *UK OR* **gas** *US* super *m*, supercarburant *m* ▪ **low-~ petrol** *UK OR* **gas** *US* ordinaire *m*, essence *f* ordinaire.

octane number, octane rating *n* indice *m* d'octane.

octave ['ɒktɪv] *n* FENCING, MUS & RELIG octave *f* ▪ LIT huitain *m*.

Octavian [ɒk'teɪvjən] *pr n* Octave.

octavo [ɒk'teɪvəʊ] (*pl* **octavos**) *n* in-octavo *m inv*.

octet [ɒk'tet] *n* **1.** [group] octuor *m* **2.** MUS octuor *m* **3.** LIT huitain *m* **4.** CHEM octet *m*.

October [ɒk'təʊbəʳ] *n* octobre *m*, *see also* **February**.

October Revolution *n* : **the ~** la révolution d'Octobre.

octogenarian [ˌɒktəʊdʒɪ'neərɪən] <> *adj* octogénaire.
<> *n* octogénaire *mf*.

octopus ['ɒktəpəs] (*pl* **octopuses** *OR pl* **octopi** [-paɪ]) *n* **1.** ZOOL pieuvre *f*, poulpe *m* ▪ CULIN poulpe *m* **2.** *fig* pieuvre *f*.

octosyllabic [ˌɒktəʊsɪ'læbɪk] *adj* octosyllabique, octosyllabe.

ocular ['ɒkjʊləʳ] <> *adj* oculaire.
<> *n* oculaire *m*.

oculist ['ɒkjʊlɪst] *n* oculiste *mf*.

OD (*pret & pp* **OD'd**) <> *n inf* (*abbrev of* **overdose**) overdose *f*.
<> *vi inf* être victime d'une overdose ▪ **we rather ~'d on TV last night** *hum* on a un peu forcé sur la télé hier soir.
<> *written abbr of* **overdrawn**.

odalisk, odalisque ['əʊdəlɪsk] *n* odalisque *f*.

odd [ɒd] *adj* **1.** [weird] bizarre, étrange ▪ **he's an ~ character** c'est un drôle d'individu ▪ **the ~ thing is that the room was empty** ce qui est bizarre, c'est que la pièce était vide ▪ **it felt ~ seeing her again** ça m'a fait (tout) drôle de la revoir ▪ **he's a bit ~ in the head** *inf* il lui manque une case
2. [occasional, incidental] : **at ~ moments** de temps en temps ▪ **I smoke the ~ cigarette** il m'arrive de fumer une cigarette de temps en temps ▪ **we took the ~ photo** nous avons pris deux ou trois photos ➤ **~ jobs** petits boulots *mpl*
3. [not matching] dépareillé
4. [not divisible by two] impair ▪ **the ~ pages of a book** les pages impaires d'un livre ➤ **~ number** nombre *m* impair
5. *inf (in combinations) inf* [or so] : **twenty ~** vingt et quelques ▪ **thirty-~ pounds** trente livres et quelques, trente et quelques livres ▪ **he must be forty-~** il doit avoir la quarantaine *OR* dans les quarante ans
6. *phr* **the ~ one** *OR* **man** *OR* **woman out** l'exception *f* ▪ **which of these drawings is the ~ one out?** parmi ces dessins, lequel est l'intrus? ▪ **they all knew each other so well that I felt the ~ one out** ils se connaissaient tous si bien que j'avais l'impression d'être la cinquième roue du carrosse *OR* de la charrette.

oddball ['ɒdbɔːl] *inf* <> *n* excentrique *mf*, original *m*, - e *f*.
<> *adj* excentrique, original.

odd bod *UK inf* = **oddball** *(n)*.

odd-even *adj* COMPUT : **~ check** contrôle *m* de parité.

oddity ['ɒdɪtɪ] (*pl* **oddities**) *n* **1.** [strange person] excentrique *mf*, original *m*, - e *f* ▪ [strange thing] curiosité *f* ▪ **being the only woman there makes her something of an ~** on la remarque du simple fait qu'elle est la seule femme **2.** [strangeness] étrangeté *f*, bizarrerie *f*.

odd-job man *n* homme *m* à tout faire, factotum *m*.

odd-looking *adj* à l'air bizarre.

odd lot *n* COMM lot *m* dépareillé ▪ ST. EX lot *m* fractionné.

oddly ['ɒdlɪ] *adv* bizarrement, curieusement ▪ **~ shaped** d'une forme bizarre ▪ **~ enough, he didn't recognize me** chose curieuse, il ne m'a pas reconnu.

oddment ['ɒdmənt] *n* COMM [of matched set] article *m* dépareillé ▪ [of lot, line] fin *f* de série ▪ [of fabric] coupon *m*.

odds [ɒdz] *npl* **1.** [in betting] cote *f* ▪ **the ~ are ten to one against** la cote est de dix contre un ▪ **the ~ are ten to one on** la cote est de un contre dix ▪ **they're offering long/short ~ against Jackson** Jackson a une bonne/faible cote ▪ **I'll lay** *OR* **give you ~ of twenty to one that she'll leave him** je te parie à vingt contre un qu'elle le quittera ➤ **I ended up paying over the ~** *UK* en fin de compte, je l'ai payé plus cher qu'il ne valait *OR* que sa valeur **2.** [chances] chances *fpl* ▪ **the ~ are she's been lying to us all along** il y a de fortes chances qu'elle nous ait menti depuis le début ▪ **the ~ are on/against her accepting** il y a de fortes chances/il y a peu de chances (pour) qu'elle accepte **3.** [great difficulties] : **against all the ~** contre toute attente ▪ **they won against overwhelming ~** ils ont gagné alors que tout était contre eux **4.** *UK inf* [difference] : **it makes no ~** ça ne change rien **5.** *phr* **~ and sods** *UK inf*, **~ and ends** [miscellaneous objects] objets *mpl* divers, bric-à-brac *m inv* ; [leftovers] restes *mpl*.
◆ **at odds** *adj phr* en conflit ▪ **at ~ with** en conflit avec ▪ **the way she was dressed was completely at ~ with her personality** ce qu'elle portait ne correspondait pas du tout à sa personnalité.

odds-on *adj UK* **it's ~ that he'll win** il y a tout à parier qu'il gagnera ➤ **~ favourite** grand favori *m*.

ode [əʊd] *n* ode *f* ▪ **'Ode to Joy'** ***Beethoven*** 'Hymne à la joie'.

odious ['əʊdjəs] *adj fml* odieux.

odium ['əʊdjəm] *n fml* [condemnation] réprobation *f* ▪ [hatred] haine *f*.

odometer [əʊ'dɒmɪtəʳ] *n US* AUT compteur *m* kilométrique.

odontology [ˌɒdɒn'tɒlədʒɪ] *n* odontologie *f*.

odor *etc US* = **odour**.

odorous ['əʊdərəs] *adj* [fragrant] odorant ▪ [malodorous] malodorant.

odour *UK*, **odor** *US* ['əʊdəʳ] *n* **1.** [smell] odeur *f* ▪ **guaranteed to get rid of unpleasant ~s!** fini les mauvaises odeurs! **2.** [pervasive quality] odeur *f*, parfum *m*, arôme *m* **3.** *UK phr* **to be in good/bad ~ with sb** *fml* être bien/mal vu de qqn.

odourless *UK*, **odorless** *US* ['əʊdəlɪs] *adj* inodore.

Odysseus [ə'diːsɪəs] *pr n* Ulysse.

odyssey ['ɒdɪsɪ] *n* odyssée *f* ▪ **'The Odyssey'** ***Homer*** 'l'Odyssée'.

OECD (*abbrev of* **Organization for Economic Cooperation and Development**) *pr n* OCDE *f*.

oecumenical *etc* [ˌiːkjuː'menɪkl] = **ecumenical**.

oedema *UK*, **edema** *US* [iː'diːmə] (*UK pl* **oedemata** [-mətə]) (*US pl* **edemata** [-mətə]) *n* oedème *m*.

Oedipal ['iːdɪpl] *adj* œdipien.

Oedipus ['iːdɪpəs] *pr n* Œdipe ▪ **'Oedipus Rex'** ***Sophocle*** 'Œdipe roi'.

Oedipus complex *n* complexe *m* d'Œdipe.

oenology [iː'nɒlədʒɪ] *n* œnologie *f*.

o'er ['əʊəʳ] *lit* = **over** *(adv, prep)*.

oesophagus *UK*, **esophagus** *US* [ɪˈsɒfəgəs] (*UK pl* **oesophaguses** *OR pl* **oesophagi** [-gaɪ]) (*US pl* **esophaguses** *OR pl* **esophagi** [-gaɪ]) *n* œsophage *m*.

oestrogen *UK*, **estrogen** *US* [ˈiːstrədʒən] *n* œstrogène *m*.

oestrous *UK*, **estrus** *US* [ˈiːstrəs] *adj* œstral ▪ **~ cycle** cycle *m* œstral.

oestrus *UK*, **estrus** *US* [ˈiːstrəs] *n* œstrus *m*.

of [(*weak form* [əv], *strong form* [ɒv])] *prep* **1.** [after nouns expressing quantity, number, amount] de ▪ **a loaf of bread** un pain ▪ **a piece of cake** un morceau de gâteau ▪ **a pair of trousers** un pantalon ▪ **there are six of us** nous sommes six ▪ **some/many/few of us were present** quelques-uns/beaucoup/peu d'entre nous étaient présents
2. [indicating age] de ▪ **a boy/a girl of three** un garçon/une fille de trois ans ▪ **at the age of nineteen** à dix-neuf ans, à l'âge de dix-neuf ans
3. [indicating composition, content] de ▪ **a map of Spain** une carte d'Espagne
4. [created by] de ▪ **the poems of Byron** les poèmes de Byron
5. [with words expressing attitude or emotion] de ▪ **I'm proud of it** j'en suis fier ▪ **I'm afraid of the dark** j'ai peur du noir
6. [indicating possession, relationship] de ▪ **he's a friend of mine** c'est un ami à moi ▪ **a friend of mine saw me** un de mes amis m'a vu ▪ **the rights of man** les droits de l'homme ▪ **she's head of department** elle est chef de service
7. [indicating subject of action] : **it was kind/mean of him** c'était gentil/méchant de sa part
8. [with names of places] de ▪ **the city of New York** la ville de New York
9. [after nouns derived from verbs] de ▪ **the arrival/departure of Flight 556** l'arrivée/le départ du vol 556
10. [describing a particular feeling or quality] de ▪ **she has the gift of mimicry** elle a un talent d'imitatrice ▮ *fml* **to be of sound mind** être sain d'esprit ▪ **to be of a nervous disposition** avoir une prédisposition à la nervosité
11. [made from] : **a ring of solid gold** une bague en or massif ▪ **a heart of stone** un cœur de pierre
12. [after nouns of size, measurement etc] de ▪ **they reach a height of ten feet** ils atteignent une hauteur de dix pieds
13. [indicating cause, origin, source] de ▪ **to die of cancer** mourir du *OR* d'un cancer ▪ **of which/whom** dont
14. [indicating likeness, similarity] de ▪ **the colour of blood/of grass** la couleur du sang/de l'herbe ▪ **it smells of coffee** ça sent le café ▪ **a giant of a man** un homme très grand
15. [indicating specific point in time or space] de ▪ **the 3rd of May** le 3 mai ▪ **in the middle of August** à la mi-août ▪ **the crash of 1929** le krach de 1929 ▪ **a quarter of nine** *US* neuf heures moins le quart ▪ **in the middle of the road** au milieu de la chaussée
16. [indicating deprivation or absence] : **a lack of food** un manque de nourriture ▪ **to rob sb of sthg** voler qqch à qqn
17. [indicating information received or passed on] : **I've never heard of him** je n'ai jamais entendu parler de lui ▪ **to learn of sthg** apprendre qqch ▪ **her knowledge of French** sa connaissance du français
18. [as intensifier] : **the best/the worst of all** le meilleur/le pire de tout ▪ **today of all days!** il fallait que ça arrive aujourd'hui!
19. *dated* & *dial* **I like to listen to the radio of a morning/an evening** j'aime écouter la radio le matin/le soir.

off [ɒf] ◇ *adv* **1.** [indicating removal] : **to take sthg ~** enlever *OR* ôter qqch ▪ **to come ~** [sticker, handle] se détacher ; [lipstick, paint] partir ▪ **peel ~ the wallpaper** décollez le papier peint ▪ **she cut ~ her hair** elle s'est coupé les cheveux
2. [indicating departure] : **to run ~** partir en courant ▪ **when are you ~ to Dublin?** quand partez-vous pour Dublin? ▪ **they're ~!** SPORT ils sont partis! ▪ **I'm ~!** *inf* j'y vais! ▪ **~ we go!** c'est parti! ▪ **~ to bed with you!** au lit! ▪ **oh no, he's ~ again!** *hum* ça y est, ça le reprend!
3. [indicating movement away from a surface] : **the ball hit the wall and bounced ~** la balle a heurté le mur et a rebondi ▪ **I knocked the glass ~ with my elbow** j'ai fait tomber le verre d'un coup de coude
4. [indicating location] : **it's ~ to the right** c'est sur la droite ▪ **she's ~ playing tennis** elle est partie jouer au tennis
5. [indicating disembarkment, dismounting etc] : **to get ~** descendre ▪ **to jump ~** sauter
6. [indicating absence, inactivity] : **to take a week ~** prendre une semaine de congé ▪ **Monday's my day ~** le lundi est mon jour de congé
7. [indicating distance in time or space] : **Paris/Christmas is still a long way ~** Paris/Noël est encore loin ▪ **it's a few miles ~** c'est à quelques kilomètres d'ici
8. [indicating disconnection] : **to put** *OR* **switch** *OR* **turn the light ~** éteindre la lumière ▪ **to turn the tap ~** fermer le robinet
9. [indicating separation, partition] : **to fence ~ land** clôturer un terrain ▪ **the police have cordoned ~ the area** la police a bouclé le quartier
10. [indicating price reduction] : **'special offer: £5 ~'** 'offre spéciale: 5 livres de réduction' ▪ **the salesman gave me $20/20% ~** le vendeur m'a fait une remise de 20 dollars/20 %
11. [indicating relief from discomfort] : **to sleep/to walk sthg ~** faire passer qqch en dormant/marchant.
◇ *prep* **1.** [indicating movement away from] de ▪ **she knocked the vase ~ the table** elle a fait tomber le vase de la table ▪ **it'll take your mind ~ it** *fig* ça te changera les idées
2. [indicating removal] de ▪ **take the top ~ the bottle** enlève le bouchon de la bouteille
3. [from] : **to buy sthg ~ sb** acheter qqch à qqn ▪ **can I borrow £5 ~ you?** je peux t'emprunter 5 livres?
4. [from the direction of] de ▪ **a cool breeze ~ the sea** une brise fraîche venant du large
5. [indicating location] : **a few miles ~ the coast** à quelques kilomètres de la côte ▪ **we ate in a small restaurant ~ the main road** nous avons mangé dans un petit restaurant à l'écart de la grand-route ▪ **an alley ~ Oxford Street** une ruelle qui part d'Oxford Street ▪ **just ~ Oxford Street there's a pretty little square** à deux pas d'Oxford Street il y a une petite place ravissante
6. [absent from] : **Mr Dale is ~ work today** M. Dale est absent aujourd'hui ▪ **Wayne's ~ school with the flu** Wayne est à la maison avec la grippe
7. [by means of] : **it runs ~ gas/electricity/solar power** ça marche au gaz/à l'électricité/à l'énergie solaire
8. [indicating source of nourishment] de ▪ **to live ~ vegetables** vivre de légumes
9. [reduced from] : **they'll knock** *inf OR* **take something ~ it if you pay cash** ils vous feront une remise si vous payez en liquide
10. *inf* [no longer wanting or needing] : **to be ~ one's food** ne pas avoir faim ▪ **I'm ~ whisky** je n'aime plus le whisky ▪ **I'm ~ him at the moment** j'en ai marre de lui en ce moment ▪ **she's ~ antibiotics now** elle ne prend plus d'antibiotiques maintenant.
◇ *adj* **1.** [not working - electricity, light, radio, TV] éteint ; [- tap] fermé ; [- engine, machine] arrêté, à l'arrêt ; [- handbrake] desserré ▪ **the gas is ~** [at mains] le gaz est fermé ; [under saucepan] le gaz est éteint ; [for safety reasons] le gaz est coupé ▪ **'off'** 'arrêt' ▪ **make sure the switches are in the ~ position** vérifiez que les interrupteurs sont sur (la position) arrêt ▪ **the ~ button** le bouton d'arrêt
2. [bad, tainted] mauvais, avarié ▪ **the milk is ~** le lait a tourné ▪ **it smells/tastes ~** on dirait que ce n'est plus bon
3. [cancelled] annulé ▪ **if that's your attitude, the deal's ~!** si c'est comme ça que vous le prenez, ma proposition ne tient plus!
4. *UK* [not available] : **I'm afraid salmon's ~** je regrette, mais il n'y a plus de saumon
5. [unwell] : **I felt decidedly ~ the next morning** le lendemain matin, je ne me sentais vraiment pas bien ▪ **everyone has their ~ days** on a tous nos mauvais jours
6. *inf* [unacceptable] : **I say, that's a bit ~!** dites donc, vous y allez un peu fort! ▪ **I thought it was a bit ~ the way she just ignored me** je n'ai pas apprécié qu'elle m'ignore comme ça
7. *UK* AUT [when driving on right] (du côté) gauche ▪ [when driving on left] (du côté) droit
8. [having a certain amount of] : **how are we ~ for milk?** combien de lait nous reste-t-il?
◇ *n inf* [start] départ *m* ▪ **they're ready for the ~** ils sont prêts à partir.
◇ *vt*[△] [kill] *US* buter[△].
◆ **off and on** *adv phr* par intervalles ▪ **we lived together ~ and on for three years** on a plus ou moins vécu ensemble pendant trois ans.

offal [ˈɒfl] *n (U)* **1.** *UK* CULIN abats *mpl* **2.** [refuse] ordures *fpl*, déchets *mpl* **3.** [carrion] charogne *f*.

off-balance <> *adj* déséquilibré.
<> *adv* : **to throw** *OR* **to knock sb ~** *liter* faire perdre l'équilibre à qqn ; *fig* couper le souffle à *OR* désarçonner qqn ■ **her question caught me ~** sa question m'a pris au dépourvu.

offbeat ['ɒfbi:t] <> *adj* [unconventional] original, excentrique.
<> *n* MUS temps *m* faible.

off-Broadway *adj US* **an ~ show** *spectacle new-yorkais non conventionnel qui se démarque du style de ceux de Broadway, et qui n'est pas présenté dans un 'Broadway Theatre'* ■ **an ~ director** un metteur en scène de pièces d'avant-garde.

off-centre *UK*, **off-center** *US* <> *adj* **1.** [painting on wall] décentré ■ [rotation] excentrique ■ [gun sights] désaligné ■ **the title is ~** le titre n'est pas centré **2.** *fig* [unconventional] original.
<> *adv* de côté.

off chance ◆ **on the off chance** *adv phr* au cas où ■ **I phoned on the ~ of catching him at home** j'ai appelé en espérant qu'il serait chez lui ■ **she kept it on the ~ (that) it might prove useful** elle l'a gardé pour le cas où cela pourrait servir.

off-colour *adj* **1.** *UK* [ill] mal fichu ■ **she's looking a little ~** elle n'est pas très bien, elle est mal fichue **2.** [indelicate - film, story] de mauvais goût, d'un goût douteux.

offcut ['ɒfkʌt] *n* [of cloth, wood, paper] chute *f* ■ [of meat] reste *m*.

off-day *n* : **he was having an ~** il n'était pas en forme ■ **everyone has their ~s** il y a des jours 'sans'.

off-duty *adj* [policeman, soldier, nurse] qui n'est pas de service ■ **I'm off duty at 6** je finis mon service à 6 h.

offence *UK*, **offense** *US* [ə'fens] *n* **1.** LAW délit *m* ■ **it's his first ~** c'est la première fois qu'il commet un délit ■ **to commit a second** *OR* **subsequent ~** récidiver ■ **arrested for drug ~s** [dealing] arrêté pour trafic de drogue ; [use] arrêté pour consommation de drogue ➊ **motoring** *OR* **driving ~** infraction *f* au Code de la route ■ **sex ~** ≃ attentat *m* à la pudeur **2.** [displeasure, hurt] : **to give** *OR* **to cause ~ to sb** blesser *OR* offenser qqn ■ **to take ~ at sthg** s'offenser *OR* s'offusquer de qqch ■ **he's very quick to take ~** il se vexe pour un rien ■ **I meant no ~** je ne voulais pas vous blesser ■ **no ~ meant – none taken!** je n'avais pas l'intention de te vexer – il n'y a pas de mal! **3.** MIL [attack] attaque *f*, offensive *f* **4.** SPORT [attackers] attaque *f*.

offend [ə'fend] <> *vt* [person] offenser, blesser ■ **she's easily ~ed** elle est susceptible, elle se vexe pour un rien ■ **the film contains scenes which could ~ some viewers** le film contient des scènes pouvant choquer certains spectateurs ‖ [eyes, senses, reason] choquer.
<> *vi* LAW violer la loi, commettre un délit.

◆ **offend against** *vt insep* [law, regulation] enfreindre, violer ■ [custom] aller à l'encontre de ■ [good manners, good taste] être un outrage à.

offended [ə'fendɪd] *adj* offensé, blessé ■ **don't be ~ if I leave early** ne le prends pas mal si je pars de bonne heure.

offender [ə'fendəʳ] *n* **1.** LAW délinquant *m*, - e *f* **2.** [gen - culprit] coupable *mf* ■ **the chemical industry is the worst ~** l'industrie chimique est la première responsable.

offending [ə'fendɪŋ] *adj* blessant ■ **the ~ word was omitted** le mot choquant a été enlevé ■ **the ~ object/article** l'objet/l'article incriminé.

offense *US* = **offence**.

offensive [ə'fensɪv] <> *adj* **1.** [causing indignation, anger] offensant, choquant ■ **to find sthg ~** être choqué par qqch ■ **to be ~ to sb** [person] injurier *OR* insulter qqn ■ **this advertisement is ~ to Muslims/women** cette publicité porte atteinte à la religion musulmane/à la dignité de la femme ■ **~ language** propos *mpl* choquants **2.** [disgusting - smell] repoussant **3.** [aggressive] offensif ■ **they took immediate ~ action** ils sont immédiatement passés à l'offensive ➊ **~ weapon** arme *f* offensive.
<> *n* offensive *f* ■ **to go over to** *OR* **to go on** *OR* **to take the ~** passer à *OR* prendre l'offensive.

offensively [ə'fensɪvlɪ] *adv* **1.** [behave, speak] d'une manière offensante *OR* blessante **2.** MIL & SPORT offensivement.

offer ['ɒfəʳ] <> *vt* **1.** [present] offrir ■ **to ~ sthg to sb, to ~ sb sthg** offrir qqch à qqn ■ **she ~ed me £800 for my car** elle m'a proposé 800 livres pour ma voiture ■ **he ~ed her a chair/his arm** il lui offrit une chaise/son bras ■ **to ~ advantages** présenter des avantages ■ **to have a lot to ~** [town, person] avoir beaucoup à offrir ■ **candidates may ~ one of the following foreign languages** les candidats peuvent présenter une des langues étrangères suivantes **2.** [propose] proposer ■ **to ~ to do sthg** s'offrir pour faire qqch, proposer de faire qqch ■ **I ~ed to help them** je leur ai proposé mon aide ■ **it was kind of you to ~** c'est gentil de me l'avoir proposé ■ **to ~ an opinion** émettre une opinion ■ **to ~ sb advice** donner des conseils à qqn.
<> *n* offre *f* ■ **~s of help are pouring in** les offres d'aide affluent ■ **I'll make you a final ~** je vous ferai une dernière offre ■ **she wants £500, but she's open to ~s** elle veut 500 livres, mais elle est prête à négocier ■ **I made him an ~ he couldn't refuse** je lui ai fait une offre qu'il ne pouvait pas refuser ■ **special ~** offre spéciale ■ **the house is under ~** on a reçu une offre pour la maison.

◆ **on offer** *adv phr* : **these goods are on ~ this week** ces articles sont en promotion cette semaine ■ **there aren't many jobs on ~** les offres d'emploi sont peu nombreuses.

◆ **offer up** *vt sep* [hymn, sacrifice] offrir.
Voir module d'usage

OFFERS

Je peux vous aider ? Can I help you?

Si ça ne vous dérange pas, je veux bien, merci. Please, if it's no trouble.

Non, merci, ce n'est pas la peine/je vais y arriver tout seul. No thanks, it's no bother/I can manage.

Tu veux que j'aille chercher du pain ? Would you like me to go and get some bread?

Ah oui, ça m'arrange. That'd be a great help, thanks.

Non, ne t'en fais pas, j'irai moi-même. No, that's all right, I'll go myself.

Et si je passais te prendre ? Why don't I come and get you?

D'accord, c'est très gentil. Thanks, that's very kind of you.

Non non, ne t'inquiète pas, j'irai par mes propres moyens. No thanks, don't worry about it, I'll make my own way.

Est-ce que j'ouvre une autre bouteille de vin ? Shall I open another bottle of wine?

Excellente idée !/Oui, volontiers. Good idea!/Yes, please!

Non, merci, c'est très bien comme ça. Not for me, thank you, I've had enough.

Je peux vous loger pendant votre séjour à Paris. I can put you up when you come to Paris.

Merci, c'est très gentil de votre part. Thank you, that's very kind of you.

Merci, mais nous avons déjà réservé une chambre d'hôtel. Thank you, but we've already booked a hotel room.

offering ['ɒfərɪŋ] *n* **1.** [action] offre *f* **2.** [thing offered] offre *f*, don *m* ■ **his latest ~ is a novel set in Ireland** *fig* le dernier roman qu'il nous propose se déroule en Irlande **3.** RELIG offrande *f*.

offer price *n* ST. EX cours *m* vendeur *OR* offert.

offertory ['ɒfətrɪ] (*pl* **offertories**) *n* **1.** [prayers, ritual] offertoire *m* **2.** [collection] quête *f*.

off-guard *adj* [moment] : **in an ~ moment** dans un moment d'inattention.
◆ **off guard** *adv phr* : **to catch** *OR* **to take sb off guard** prendre qqn au dépourvu ■ **his offer of help caught her off guard** elle ne s'attendait pas à ce qu'il lui propose son aide.

offhand [,ɒf'hænd] ◇ *adj* **1.** [nonchalant] désinvolte, cavalier **2.** [abrupt] brusque.
◇ *adv* spontanément, au pied levé ■ **~ I'd say it'll take a week** à première vue, je dirais que cela prendra une semaine ■ **I can't give you the figures ~** je ne peux pas vous citer les chiffres de mémoire *OR* de tête.

offhanded [,ɒf'hændɪd] *adj* = **offhand** *(adj)*.

offhandedly [,ɒf'hændɪdlɪ] *adv* [nonchalantly] de façon désinvolte *OR* cavalière, avec désinvolture ■ [with abruptness] brusquement, sans ménagement.

offhandedness [,ɒf'hændɪdnɪs] *n* désinvolture *f*.

office ['ɒfɪs] ◇ *n* **1.** [of firm] bureau *m* ■ **~ space is cheaper in the suburbs** les bureaux sont moins chers en banlieue ▶ **doctor's ~** *US* cabinet *m* médical ■ **lawyer's ~** cabinet *m* d'avocat ■ **~ party** *réception organisée dans un bureau à l'occasion des fêtes de fin d'année* **2.** [government department] bureau *m*, département *m* ▶ **the Office of Fair Trading** *service britannique de la concurrence et des prix* **3.** [distribution point] bureau *m*, guichet *m* **4.** [position, power] fonction *f* ■ **a woman in high ~** une femme haut placée ■ **to be in** *OR* **to hold ~** [political party] être au pouvoir ; [mayor, minister, official] être en fonctions ■ **to be out of ~** avoir quitté ses fonctions ■ **to take ~** [political party] arriver au pouvoir ; [mayor, minister, official] entrer en fonctions ■ **to resign/to leave ~** se démettre de/quitter ses fonctions ■ **to run for** *OR* **to seek ~** se présenter aux élections ■ **elected to the ~ of president** élu à la présidence **5.** RELIG office *m*.
◇ *comp* [furniture, job, staff] de bureau ■ **during ~ hours** pendant les heures de bureau ■ **~ work** travail *m* de bureau ■ **~ worker** employé *m* de bureau.
◆ **offices** *npl* **1.** [help, actions] : **I got the job through the (good) ~s of Mrs Katz** j'ai obtenu ce travail grâce aux bons offices de Mme Katz **2.** *UK* [of large house, estate] office *m*.

office automation *n* bureautique *f*.

office bearer *n UK* [in club, association] membre *m* du bureau.

office block *n UK* immeuble *m* de bureaux.

office boy *n dated* garçon *m* de bureau.

officeholder ['ɒfɪs,həʊldəʳ] *n* **1.** POL titulaire *mf* d'une fonction **2.** *US* = **office bearer**.

office junior *n* stagiaire *mf (en secrétariat)*.

officer ['ɒfɪsəʳ] ◇ *n* **1.** MIL officier *m* **2.** [policeman] agent *m* de police ■ [as form of address - to policeman] Monsieur l'agent ; [- to policewoman] Madame l'agent **3.** [official - in local government] fonctionnaire *mf* ; [- of trade union] représentant *m* permanent ; [- of company] membre *m* de la direction ; [- of association, institution] membre *m* du bureau.
◇ *vt* MIL encadrer.

official [ə'fɪʃl] ◇ *adj* **1.** [formal] officiel ■ **she's here on ~ business** elle est ici en visite officielle ■ **his appointment will be made ~ tomorrow** sa nomination sera (rendue) officielle demain ■ **we decided to make it ~ (and get married)** nous avons décidé de rendre notre liaison officielle (en nous mariant) ■ **to go through the ~ channels** suivre la filière (habituelle) ▶ **~ strike** *grève soutenue par la direction du syndicat* ■ **the Official Secrets Act** *loi britannique sur le secret Défense* **2.** [alleged] officiel ■ **the ~ reason for his visit is to discuss trade** officiellement, il est là pour des discussions ayant trait au commerce.
◇ *n* [representative] officiel *m* ■ [civil servant] fonctionnaire *mf* ■ [subordinate employee] employé *m*, - e *f* ■ SPORT [referee] arbitre *m* ■ **a bank/club/union ~** un représentant de la banque/du club/du syndicat ■ **a government ~** un haut fonctionnaire.

officialdom [ə'fɪʃəldəm] *n pej* bureaucratie *f*.

officialese [ə,fɪʃə'li:z] *n pej* jargon *m* administratif.

officially [ə'fɪʃəlɪ] *adv* **1.** [formally] officiellement ■ **he's now been ~ appointed** sa nomination est désormais officielle **2.** [allegedly] théoriquement, en principe.

Official Receiver *n UK* ADMIN administrateur *m*, - trice *f* judiciaire ■ **the ~ has been called in** on a fait appel à l'administration judiciaire.

officiate [ə'fɪʃɪeɪt] *vi* **1.** [gen] : **she ~d at the ceremony** elle a présidé la cérémonie ■ **the mayor will ~ at the opening of the stadium** le maire inaugurera le stade **2.** RELIG officier.

officious [ə'fɪʃəs] *adj* **1.** [overbearing] impérieux, autoritaire ■ [interfering] importun ■ [zealous] zélé, empressé **2.** [in diplomacy - unofficial] officieux.

officiously [ə'fɪʃəslɪ] *adv* [overbearingly] impérieusement, de manière autoritaire ■ [interferingly] d'une manière importune ■ [zealously] avec zèle, avec empressement.

offie ['ɒfɪ] *n inf* magasin *m* autorisé à vendre des boissons alcoolisées à emporter.

offing ['ɒfɪŋ] *n* **1.** NAUT large *m* **2.** *phr* **to be in the ~** être imminent, être dans l'air.

off-key ◇ *adj* **1.** MUS faux, fausse *f* **2.** *fig* [remark] hors de propos, sans rapport.
◇ *adv* faux.

off-licence *n UK* **1.** [shop] *magasin autorisé à vendre des boissons alcoolisées à emporter* ■ **at the ~** chez le marchand de vins **2.** [licence] licence *f (autorisant la vente de boissons alcoolisées à emporter)*.

off-limits ◇ *adj* interdit.
◇ *adv* en dehors des limites autorisées ■ **to go ~** sortir des limites autorisées.

off-line *adj* **1.** COMPUT [storage, processing] autonome ■ [equipment] hors-circuit **2.** INDUST [production] hors ligne.

offload [ɒf'ləʊd] *vt* **1.** [unload - passengers] débarquer ; [- cargo] décharger **2.** [dump - work, blame] : **she tends to ~ responsibility onto other people** elle a tendance à se décharger de ses responsabilités sur les autres.

off-peak *adj* [consumption, rate, train] aux heures creuses, en dehors des périodes d'affluence *OR* de pointe ■ **~ hours** *OR* **times** heures *fpl* creuses.

off-piste *adj* & *adv* SPORT hors-piste.

offprint ['ɒfprɪnt] ◇ *n* tiré *m* à part.
◇ *vt* : **to ~ an article** faire un tiré à part.

off-putting [-pʊtɪŋ] *adj UK* [smell] repoussant ■ [manner] rébarbatif ■ [person, description] peu engageant ■ **the idea of a five-hour stopover is very ~** l'idée d'une escale de cinq heures n'a rien d'enthousiasmant *OR* de réjouissant.

off-road vehicle *n* véhicule *m* tout terrain.

off sales *npl UK vente à emporter de boissons alcoolisées.*

offscreen CIN & TV ◇ *adj* ['ɒfskri:n] [out of sight] hors champ, off.
◇ *adv* [ɒf'skri:n] **1.** CIN & TV hors champ, off **2.** [in private life] dans le privé ■ **he's less handsome ~** il est moins séduisant dans la réalité.

off-season ◇ *n* morte-saison *f*.
◇ *adj* hors saison *(inv)*.

offset ['ɒfset] (*pret* & *pp* **offset**, *cont* **offsetting**) ◇ *vt* **1.** [make up for] contrebalancer, compenser ■ **we'll have to ~ our research investment against long-term returns** nous devons amortir notre investissement dans la recherche en faisant des bénéfices à long terme **2.** PRINT imprimer en offset.

◇ *n* **1.** [counterbalance] contrepoids *m* ▪ [compensation] compensation *f* **2.** PRINT offset *m* **3.** BOT [shoot] rejeton *m* **4.** CONSTR ressaut *m*.

offshoot [ˈɒfʃuːt] *n* **1.** [of organization, movement] ramification *f* ▪ [spin-off] application *f* secondaire ▪ *fig* [consequence] retombée *f* ▪ [subsidiary] : **the company has ~s in Asia** la société a des succursales en Asie **2.** BOT rejeton *m*.

offshore [ˈɒfʃɔːʳ] *adj* **1.** [in or on sea] marin ▪ [near shore - shipping, fishing, waters] côtier ; [- island] près de la côte ▪ PETR offshore *(inv)*, marin **2.** [towards open sea - current, direction] vers le large ; [- wind] de terre **3.** FIN : **~ fund** placement *m* dans un paradis fiscal.

offside ◇ *adj* [ˌɒfˈsaɪd] *adv* [ˌɒfˈsaɪd] SPORT hors jeu *(inv)* ▪ **to play the ~ trap** jouer le hors-jeu.
◇ *n* [ˈɒfsaɪd] *UK* AUT [when driving on right] côté *m* gauche, côté *m* rue ▪ [when driving on left] côté *m* droit, côté *m* rue.

offspring [ˈɒfsprɪŋ] *(pl inv)* ◇ *n* **1.** *arch* & *hum* [son or daughter] rejeton *m* **2.** *fig* retombée *f*, conséquence *f*.
◇ *npl* [descendants] progéniture *f*.

offstage ◇ *adv* [ˌɒfˈsteɪdʒ] **1.** THEAT dans les coulisses ▪ **she ran ~** elle quitta la scène en courant **2.** [in private life] en privé.
◇ *adj* [ˈɒfˌsteɪdʒ] dans les coulisses.

off-street *adj* : **~ parking** place *f* de parking *(située ailleurs que dans la rue)*.

off-the-cuff ◇ *adj* impromptu, improvisé.
◇ *adv* au pied levé, à l'improviste.

off-the-peg, off-the-rack *US adj* prêt à porter ▪ **~ clothes** prêt-à-porter *m*.
◆ **off the peg, off the rack** *US adv* : **to buy one's clothes off the peg** acheter du prêt-à-porter.

off-the-record *adj* [not to be made public] confidentiel ▪ [not to be put in minutes] à ne pas faire figurer dans le compte rendu.

off-the-wall *adj inf* [crazy] loufoque, dingue ▪ [unexpected] original, excentrique.

off-white ◇ *adj* blanc cassé *(inv)*.
◇ *n* blanc *m* cassé.

Ofgas [ˈɒfgæs] *(abbrev of* **Office of Gas Supply***) pr n organisme britannique chargé de contrôler les activités des compagnies régionales de distribution de gaz.*

Oflot [ˈɒflɒt] *(abbrev of* **Office of the National Lottery***) n organisme britannique chargé de contrôler la loterie nationale.*

Ofsted [ˈɒfsted] *(abbrev of* **Office for Standards in Education***) pr n organisme britannique chargé de contrôler le système d'éducation nationale.*

oft [ɒft] *adv lit* maintes fois, souvent.

oft- *in cpds* : **~quoted** souvent cité.

OFT = **Office of Fair Trading**.

Oftel [ˈɒftel] *(abbrev of* **Office of Telecommunications***) pr n organisme britannique chargé de contrôler les activités des sociétés de télécommunications.*

often [ˈɒfn, ˈɒftn] *adv* souvent ▪ **how ~ do I have to tell you?** combien de fois faudra-t-il que je te le répète? ▪ **how ~ does he write to you?** est-ce qu'il t'écrit souvent? ▪ **she's said that once too ~** elle l'a dit une fois de trop.
◆ **as often as not** *adv phr* la plupart du temps.
◆ **every so often** *adv phr* de temps en temps, de temps à autre.
◆ **more often than not** *adv phr* la plupart du temps.

oftentimes [ˈɒfəntaɪmz] *adv UK arch* souventes fois.

Ofwat [ˈɒfwɒt] *(abbrev of* **Office of Water Supply***) pr n organisme britannique chargé de contrôler les activités des compagnies régionales de distribution des eaux.*

ogive [ˈəʊdʒaɪv] *n* ARCHIT & MATHS ogive *f*.

ogle [ˈəʊgl] *vt* lorgner.

ogre [ˈəʊgəʳ] *n* ogre *m*.

oh [əʊ] *interj* oh, ah ▪ **oh really?** vraiment?, ah bon?

OH *written abbr of* **Ohio**.

Ohio [əʊˈhaɪəʊ] *pr n* Ohio *m* ▪ **in ~** dans l'Ohio.

ohm [əʊm] *n* ohm *m*.

OHMS *(written abbrev of* **On His/Her Majesty's Service***) tampon apposé sur le courrier administratif britannique.*

oho [əˈhəʊ] *interj* oh, ah.

oil [ɔɪl] ◇ *n* **1.** [petroleum] pétrole *m* **2.** [in food, as lubricant] huile *f* ▪ [as fuel] mazout *m*, fuel *m OR* fioul *m* domestique ▪ **sardines in ~** sardines *fpl* à l'huile ▪ **to change the ~** AUT faire la vidange ▶ **~ of lavender/turpentine** essence *f* de lavande/de térébenthine ▪ **to pour ~ on troubled waters** ramener le calme ▪ **suntan ~** huile solaire **3.** ART [paint] (peinture *f* à l')huile *f* ▪ [picture] huile *f* ▪ **she works in ~s** elle travaille avec de la peinture à l'huile.
◇ *comp* **1.** [industry, production, corporation] pétrolier ▪ [drum, deposit, reserves] de pétrole ▪ [magnate, sheikh] du pétrole **2.** [level, pressure] d'huile ▪ [filter] à huile ▪ [heating, burner] à mazout.
◇ *vt* [machine, engine] lubrifier, graisser ▪ [hinge, wood] huiler ▪ [skin] graisser, huiler ▪ **it will help to ~ the wheels** *fig* cela facilitera les choses.
◆ **oils** *npl* ST. EX (valeurs *fpl*) pétrolières *fpl*.

oilcan [ˈɔɪlkæn] *n* [drum] bidon *m* d'huile ▪ [oiler] burette *f* (à huile).

oil change *n* vidange *f*.

oilcloth [ˈɔɪlklɒθ] *n* toile *f* cirée.

oiled [ɔɪld] *adj* **1.** [machine] lubrifié, graissé ▪ [hinge, silk] huilé **2.** *inf* [drunk] : **to be well ~** être complètement bourré.

oiler [ˈɔɪləʳ] *n* **1.** [person] graisseur *m*, - euse *f* **2.** [tanker] pétrolier *m* **3.** [can] burette *f* (à huile) **4.** [well] puits *m* de pétrole.

oilfield [ˈɔɪlfiːld] *n* gisement *m* de pétrole *OR* pétrolier.

oil-fired [-ˌfaɪəd] *adj* à mazout.

oil gauge *n* [for measuring level] jauge *f OR* indicateur *m* de niveau d'huile ▪ [for measuring pressure] indicateur *m* de pression d'huile.

oiliness [ˈɔɪlɪnɪs] *n* [greasiness] nature *f* huileuse ▪ **the ~ of the dish makes it rather indigestible** ce plat contient tellement d'huile qu'il en devient indigeste.

oil lamp *n* [burning oil] lampe *f* à huile ▪ [burning paraffin] lampe *f* à pétrole.

oilman [ˈɔɪlmən] *(pl* **oilmen** [-mən]*) n* pétrolier *m (personne)*.

oil paint *n* peinture *f* à l'huile *(substance)*.

oil painting *n* peinture *f* à l'huile.

oil-producing *adj* producteur de pétrole.

oil refinery *n* raffinerie *f* de pétrole.

oil rig *n* [onshore] derrick *m* ▪ [offshore] plate-forme *f* pétrolière.

oilskin [ˈɔɪlskɪn] ◇ *n* **1.** [cloth] toile *f* cirée **2.** [garment] ciré *m*.
◇ *comp* en toile cirée.

oil slick *n* [on sea] nappe *f* de pétrole ▪ [on beach] marée *f* noire.

oil spill *n* **1.** [event] marée *f* noire **2.** = **oil slick**.

oil stove *n UK* [using fuel oil] poêle *m* à mazout ▪ [using paraffin, kerosene] réchaud *m* à pétrole.

oil tanker *n* [ship] pétrolier *m*, tanker *m* ▪ [lorry] camion-citerne *m (pour le pétrole)*.

oil terminal *n* terminal *m* (pétrolier).

oil well *n* puits *m* de pétrole.

oily ['ɔɪlɪ] (*comp* **oilier**, *superl* **oiliest**) *adj* **1.** [substance] huileux ▪ [rag, fingers] graisseux ▪ [cooking, hair, skin] gras, grasse *f* ▪ **an ~ stain** une tache de graisse **2.** *pej* [smile, person] mielleux, doucereux.

oink [ɔɪŋk] ◇ *n* grognement *m*.
◇ *onom* krouik-krouik.

ointment ['ɔɪntmənt] *n* pommade *f*, onguent *m*.

OJ *n* = **orange juice**.

OK [,əʊ'keɪ] ◇ *interj inf* OK, d'accord, d'ac ▪ **well ~, I'm not a specialist, but...** bon, d'accord, je ne suis pas spécialiste, mais... ▪ **in five minutes, ~?** dans cinq minutes, ça va?
◇ *adj inf* : **you look very pale, are you ~?** tu es très pâle, tu te sens bien? ▪ **that idea sounds ~ to me** ça me semble être une bonne idée ▪ **it's ~ but it could be better** ce n'est pas mal, mais ça pourrait être mieux ▪ **I'll bring my husband if that's ~ with** *OR* **by you** je viendrai avec mon mari, si ça ne vous gêne pas ▪ **thanks for your help – that's ~!** merci de votre aide – de rien! *OR* il n'y a pas de quoi! ▪ **he's ~, he's an ~ guy** c'est un type sympa.
◇ *adv inf* bien ▪ **is the engine working ~?** le moteur, ça va? ▪ **everything is going ~** tout marche bien *OR* va bien ▪ **you're doing ~!** tu t'en tires bien!
◇ *vt* (*pret & pp* **OKed** [,əʊ'keɪd], *cont* **OKing** [,əʊ'keɪɪŋ]) *inf* [approve] approuver ▪ [initial] parafer, parapher.
◇ *n inf* [agreement] accord *m* ▪ [approval] approbation *f* ▪ **I gave him the ~** je lui ai donné le feu vert.
◇ *written abbr of* **Oklahoma**.

okapi [əʊ'kɑːpɪ] (*pl inv OR pl* **okapis**) *n* okapi *m*.

okay [,əʊ'keɪ] = **OK**.

okeydoke(y) [,əʊkɪ'dəʊk(ɪ)] *interj inf* d'ac, OK.

Oklahoma [,əʊklə'həʊmə] *pr n* Oklahoma *m* ▪ **in ~** dans l'Oklahoma.

okra ['əʊkrə] *n* gombo *m*.

ol' [əʊl] *inf* = **old** *(adj)*.

old [əʊld] (*comp* **older**, *superl* **oldest**) ◇ *adj* **1.** [not new or recent] vieux *(before vowel or silent 'h'* **vieil***)*, vieille *f* ▪ **they're ~ friends** ce sont de vieux amis *OR* des amis de longue date ▪ **the ~ country** la mère patrie
2. [not young] vieux *(before vowel or silent 'h'* **vieil***)*, vieille *f* ▪ **an ~ man** un vieil homme ▪ **an ~ woman** une vieille femme ▪ **I don't like that ~ man/woman** je n'aime pas ce vieux/cette vieille ▪ **~ people** personnes *fpl* âgées ▪ **to get** *OR* **grow ~** vieillir ▪ **who will look after me in my ~ age?** qui s'occupera de moi quand je serai vieux? ▪ **I've got a little money put aside for my ~ age** j'ai quelques économies de côté pour mes vieux jours ➊ **~ people's home** maison *f* de retraite
3. [referring to a particular age] : **how ~ is she?** quel âge a-t-elle? ▪ **to be ~ enough to do sthg** être en âge de faire qqch ▪ **she's ~ enough to know better** elle ne devrait plus faire ce genre de chose à son âge ▪ **he's ~ enough to look after himself** il est (bien) assez grand pour se débrouiller tout seul ▪ **he's ~ enough to be my father!** il pourrait être mon père! ▪ **she's two years ~er than him** elle a deux ans de plus que lui ▪ **my boy wants to be a soldier when he's ~er** mon fils veut être soldat quand il sera grand ▪ **the ~er generation** la vieille génération ▪ **my ~er sister** ma sœur aînée ▪ **she's 6 months/25 years ~** elle a 6 mois/25 ans, elle est âgée de 6 mois/25 ans ▪ **they have a 14-year-~ boy** ils ont un garçon de 14 ans
4. [former] ancien ▪ **an ~ admirer of hers** un de ses anciens admirateurs ➊ **in the ~ days** autrefois, jadis ▪ **the good ~ days** le bon vieux temps
5. *inf* [expressing familiarity or affection] vieux *(before vowel or silent 'h'* **vieil***)*, vieille *f*, brave ▪ **hello, ~ thing** *OR* **chap!** *dated* salut, mon vieux *OR* vieille branche!
6. *inf* [as intensifier] : **it's a funny ~ life!** la vie est drôle, quand même! ▪ **silly ~ bat** espèce de vieille folle! ▪ **any ~ bit of wood will do** n'importe quel vieux bout de bois fera l'affaire ▪ **any ~ how** n'importe comment.
◇ *npl* : **the ~** les vieux *mpl*.
◆ **of old** *adv phr* **1.** *lit* [of former times] : **in days of ~** autrefois, jadis
2. [for a long time] : **I know them of ~** je les connais depuis longtemps.

old age pension *n UK* (pension *f* de) retraite *f*.

old age pensioner *n UK* retraité *m*, - e *f*.

Old Bailey *pr n* : **the ~** *la Cour d'assises de Londres*.

Old Bill△ *npl UK* **the ~** les flics *mpl*.

old boy *n UK* **1.** [ex-pupil of school] ancien élève *m* **2.** *inf* [old man] vieux *m* **3.** *inf dated* [form of address] mon vieux.

old boy network *n UK inf contacts privilégiés entre anciens élèves d'un même établissement privé*.

olde [əʊld, 'əʊldɪ] *adj* [in name of inn, shop] d'antan, d'autrefois.

olden ['əʊldn] *adj arch & lit* d'autrefois, d'antan ▪ **in ~ times** *OR* **days** autrefois, jadis.

Old English *n* vieil anglais *m*.

Old English sheepdog *n* bobtail *m*.

olde-worlde [,əʊldɪ'wɜːldɪ] *UK* = **old-world** *(sense 1)*.

old-fashioned [-'fæʃnd] ◇ *adj* **1.** [out-of-date] suranné, désuet, - ète *f*, démodé ▪ [idea] périmé, démodé ▪ **he's a bit ~** il est un peu vieux jeu **2.** [of the past] d'autrefois, ancien ▪ **he needs a good ~ kick in the pants** *inf hum* ce qu'il lui faudrait, c'est un bon coup de pied aux fesses **3.** [quizzical] : **to give sb an ~ look** jeter un regard dubitatif à qqn.
◇ *n US* old-fashioned *m (cocktail au whisky)*.

old flame *n* ancien béguin *m*.

old girl *n UK* **1.** [ex-pupil] ancienne élève *f* **2.** *inf* [old woman] vieille *f* **3.** *inf dated* [form of address] ma chère, chère amie.

Old Glory *pr n US surnom du drapeau américain*.

old guard *n* vieille garde *f*.

old hand *n* vieux routier *m*, vétéran *m* ▪ **he's an ~ at flying these planes** cela fait des années qu'il pilote ces avions.

old hat *adj inf* dépassé, vieux ()before vowel or silent 'h' vieil, vieille *f*.

oldie ['əʊldɪ] *n inf* **1.** [show, song] vieux succès *m* ▪ [pop song] vieux tube *m* **2.** [old person] (petit) vieux *m*, (petite) vieille *f*.

old lady *inf* = **old woman** *(senses 1,2)*.

old maid *n* vieille fille *f*.

old man *n inf* **1.** [husband] homme *m* **2.** [father] vieux *m* **3.** *UK dated* [form of address] mon cher, cher ami.

old master *n* [painter] grand maître *m* (de la peinture) ▪ [painting] tableau *m* de maître.

Old Nick *pr n* Satan *m*, Lucifer *m*.

old school *n* : **of the ~** de la vieille école.

old school tie *n UK* **1.** *liter* cravate *f* aux couleurs de son ancienne école **2.** *fig & pej attitudes et système de valeurs typiques des anciens élèves des écoles privées britanniques*.

old stager *n* vieux routier *m*, vétéran *m*.

Old Testament *n* Ancien Testament *m*.

old-time *adj* d'autrefois, ancien.

old-timer *n US inf* [old person] vieillard *m*, ancien *m*, - enne *f* ▪ [veteran] vétéran *m*, vieux *m* de la vieille.

old wives' tale *n* conte *m* de bonne femme.

old woman *n inf* **1.** [wife] patronne *f*, bourgeoise *f* **2.** [mother] vieille *f* **3.** *fig & pej* **he's such an ~** il est comme une petite vieille.

old-world *adj* **1.** [of the past] d'antan, d'autrefois ▪ [quaint] pittoresque **2.** [of the Old World] de l'Ancien Monde *OR* Continent.

Old World *pr n* : **the ~** l'Ancien Monde.

ole [əʊl] *inf* = **old** *(adj)*.

oleander [,əʊlɪ'ændəʳ] *n* laurier-rose *m*.

O-level *n UK SCH examen qui sanctionnait autrefois la fin des études au niveau de la seconde*, ≃ BEPC *m*.

olfactory [ɒl'fæktərɪ] *adj* olfactif.

oligarchical [ˌɒlɪ'gɑːkɪkl] *adj* oligarchique.

oligarchy ['ɒlɪgɑːkɪ] (*pl* **oligarchies**) *n* oligarchie *f*.

olive ['ɒlɪv] ◇ *n* [fruit] olive *f* ■ [tree] olivier *m* ■ **~ (wood)** (bois *m* d')olivier *m* ■ **~ grove** olivaie *f*, oliveraie *f*.
◇ *adj* [colour] (vert) olive *(inv)* ■ **he has an ~ complexion** il a le teint olive.

olive branch *n* rameau *m* d'olivier ■ **to hold out an ~ to sb** proposer à qqn de faire la paix.

olive drab *US* ◇ *adj* gris-vert (olive) *(inv)*.
◇ *n* [colour] gris-vert *m* (olive) ■ [cloth] toile *f* gris-vert (olive) ■ [uniform] uniforme *m* gris-vert *(surtout celui de l'armée des États-Unis)*.

olive green *n* vert *m* olive.
◆ **olive-green** *adj* vert olive *(inv)*.

olive oil *n* huile *f* d'olive.

Olympia [ə'lɪmpɪə] *pr n* **1.** GEOG Olympie **2.** [in London] *salle d'exposition à Londres*.

Olympiad [ə'lɪmpɪæd] *n* olympiade *f*.

Olympian [ə'lɪmpɪən] ◇ *n* **1.** MYTH Olympien *m*, - enne *f* **2.** *US* SPORT athlète *mf* olympique.
◇ *adj* olympien ■ **it was an ~ task** *fig* cela représentait un travail phénoménal.

Olympic [ə'lɪmpɪk] *adj* olympique ⊙ **the ~ Games** les jeux Olympiques.
◆ **Olympics** *npl* : **the ~s** les jeux Olympiques.

Olympus [əʊ'lɪmpəs] *pr n* : **(Mount) ~** l'Olympe *m*.

O & M (*abbrev of* **organization and method**) *n* O et M *f*.

Oman [əʊ'mɑːn] *pr n* Oman ■ **in ~** à Oman.

Omani [əʊ'mɑːnɪ] ◇ *n* Omanais *m*, - e *f*.
◇ *adj* omanais.

ombudsman ['ɒmbʊdzmən] (*pl* **ombudsmen** [-mən]) *n* ombudsman *m*, médiateur *m* ■ [in Quebec] protecteur *m* du citoyen.

ombudswoman ['ɒmbʊdzˌwʊmən] (*pl* **ombudswomen** [-ˌwɪmɪn]) *n* médiatrice *f* ■ [in Quebec] protectrice *f* du citoyen.

omega ['əʊmɪgə] *n* oméga *m*.

omelette *UK*, **omelet** *US* ['ɒmlɪt] *n* omelette *f* ■ **plain/mushroom ~** omelette nature/aux champignons ⊙ **you can't make an ~ without breaking eggs** *prov* on ne fait pas d'omelette sans casser d'oeufs *prov*.

omen ['əʊmen] *n* augure *m*, présage *m* ■ **a good/bad ~** un bon/mauvais présage ■ **the ~s aren't good** cela ne laisse rien présager de bon.

ominous ['ɒmɪnəs] *adj* [threatening] menaçant, inquiétant ■ [boding ill] de mauvais augure, de sinistre présage ■ **an ~ silence** un silence lourd de menaces ■ **~ black clouds** des nuages menaçants.

ominously ['ɒmɪnəslɪ] *adv* de façon inquiétante *OR* menaçante ■ **the sea was ~ calm** la mer était étrangement calme.

omission [ə'mɪʃn] *n* **1.** [exclusion - accidental] omission *f*, oubli *m* ; [- deliberate] exclusion *f* ■ **their mistakes were sins of ~** ils ont péché par omission **2.** TYPO bourdon *m*.

omit [ə'mɪt] (*pret & pp* **omitted**, *cont* **omitting**) *vt* omettre ■ **a name was omitted from the list** un nom a été omis sur la liste ■ **to ~ to do sthg** omettre de faire qqch.

omnibus ['ɒmnɪbəs] ◇ *n* **1.** *dated* [bus] omnibus *m* **2.** RADIO & TV *rediffusion en continu des épisodes d'un feuilleton*.
◇ *adj* *UK* [edition] complet, - ète *f*.

omnipotence [ɒm'nɪpətəns] *n* omnipotence *f*.

omnipotent [ɒm'nɪpətənt] ◇ *adj* omnipotent, tout-puissant.
◇ *n* : **the Omnipotent** le Tout-Puissant.

omnipresence [ˌɒmnɪ'prezəns] *n* omniprésence *f*.

omnipresent [ˌɒmnɪ'prezənt] *adj* omniprésent.

omniscience [ɒm'nɪsɪəns] *n* omniscience *f*.

omniscient [ɒm'nɪsɪənt] *adj* omniscient.

omnivorous [ɒm'nɪvərəs] *adj* ZOOL omnivore ■ *fig* insatiable, avide.

Omov, OMOV ['əʊmɒv] (*abbrev of* **one member one vote**) *n système de scrutin "un homme, une voix"*.

on [ɒn] ◇ *prep*

A.

1. [specifying position] sur ■ **on the floor** par terre ■ **on the ceiling** au plafond ■ **there are posters on the walls** il y a des affiches aux *OR* sur les murs ■ **a coat was hanging on the hook** un manteau était accroché à la patère ■ **on the left/right** à gauche/droite
2. [indicating writing or painting surface] sur
3. [indicating general location, area] : **he works on a building site** il travaille sur un chantier ■ **they live on a farm** ils habitent une ferme
4. [indicating part of body touched] sur
5. [close to] : **the village is right on the lake/sea** le village est juste au bord du lac/de la mer
6. [indicating movement, direction] : **the mirror fell on the floor** la glace est tombée par terre ■ **they marched on the capital** ils marchèrent sur la capitale

B.

1. [indicating thing carried] sur ■ **I only had £10 on me** je n'avais que 10 livres sur moi ■ **she's got a gun on her** elle est armée
2. [indicating facial expression] : **he had a scornful smile on his face** il affichait un sourire plein de mépris

C.

1. [indicating purpose of money, time, effort spent] sur ■ **she spent £1,000 on her new stereo** elle a dépensé 1 000 livres pour acheter sa nouvelle chaîne hi-fi ■ **what are you working on at the moment?** sur quoi travaillez-vous en ce moment?
2. [indicating activity undertaken] : **to be on strike** être en grève ■ **he's off on a trip to Brazil** il part pour un voyage au Brésil ■ **she was sent on a course** on l'a envoyée suivre des cours ■ **he's on lunch** *US*/**a break** *US* il est en train de déjeuner/faire la pause
3. [indicating special interest, pursuit] : **he's good on modern history** il excelle en histoire moderne ■ **she's very big on equal opportunities** l'égalité des chances, c'est son cheval de bataille
4. [indicating scale of activity] : **on a large/small scale** sur une grande/petite échelle
5. [compared with] par rapport à ■ **it's an improvement on the old system** c'est une amélioration par rapport à l'ancien système

D.

1. [about, on the subject of] sur ■ **we all agree on that point** nous sommes tous d'accord sur ce point
2. [indicating person, thing affected] sur ■ **it has no effect on them** cela n'a aucun effet sur eux ■ **he has survived two attempts on his life** il a échappé à deux tentatives d'assassinat ■ **it's unfair on women** c'est injuste envers les femmes ■ **the joke's on you!** c'est toi qui as l'air ridicule!
3. [indicating cause of injury] : **I cut my finger on a piece of glass** je me suis coupé le doigt sur un morceau de verre
4. [according to] selon ■ **everyone will be judged on their merits** chacun sera jugé selon ses mérites ■ **candidates are selected on their examination results** les candidats sont choisis en fonction des résultats qu'ils ont obtenus à l'examen
5. [indicating reason, motive for action] : **on impulse** sur un coup de tête ■ **the police acted on information from abroad** la police est intervenue après avoir reçu des renseignements de l'étranger ■ **I shall refuse on principle** je refuserai par principe
6. [included in, forming part of] : **your name isn't on the list** votre nom n'est pas sur la liste ■ **on the agenda** à l'ordre du jour
7. [indicating method, system] : **they work on a rota system** ils travaillent par roulement ■ **reorganized on a more rational basis** réorganisé sur une base plus rationnelle
8. [indicating means of transport] : **on foot/horseback** à pied/cheval ■ **on the bus/train** dans le bus/train ■ **she arrived on the midday bus/train** elle est arrivée par le bus/train de midi
9. [indicating instrument played] : **who's on guitar/on drums?** qui est à la guitare/à la batterie?

10. RADIO, TV & THEAT : **I heard it on the radio/on television** je l'ai entendu à la radio/à la télévision ■ **what's on the other channel** *OR* **side?** qu'est-ce qu'il y a sur l'autre chaîne? ■ **on stage** sur scène

11. [indicating where information is stored] : **on file** sur fichier

E.

[indicating date, time etc] : **on the 6th of July** le 6 juillet ■ **on Christmas Day** le jour de Noël ■ **I'll see her on Monday** je la vois lundi ■ **I don't work on Mondays** je ne travaille pas le lundi ■ **on time** à l'heure ■ **it's just on five o'clock** il est cinq heures pile

F.

1. [indicating source of payment] : **have a drink on me** prenez un verre, c'est moi qui offre ■ **the drinks are on me/the house!** c'est ma tournée/la tournée du patron! ■ **you can get it on the National Health** ≃ c'est remboursé par la Sécurité sociale

2. [indicating source or amount of income] : **you can't live on such a low wage** on ne peut pas vivre avec des revenus aussi modestes ■ **they're on the dole** *inf OR* **on unemployment benefit** ils vivent du chômage *OR* des allocations de chômage

3. [indicating source of power] à ■ **it works on electricity** ça marche à l'électricité

4. [indicating source of nourishment] de ■ **we dined on oysters and champagne** nous avons dîné d'huîtres et de champagne

5. [indicating drugs, medicine prescribed] : **is she on the pill?** est-ce qu'elle prend la pilule? ■ **I'm still on antibiotics** je suis toujours sous antibiotiques ■ **the doctor put her on tranquillizers** le médecin lui a prescrit des tranquillisants

6. [at the same time as] à ■ **he'll deal with it on his return** il s'en occupera à son retour ■ **looters will be shot on sight** les pillards seront abattus sans sommation ‖ [with present participle] en ■ **on hearing the news** en apprenant la nouvelle.

◇ *adv* **1.** [in place] : **the lid wasn't on** le couvercle n'était pas mis ■ **put the top back on afterwards** remets le capuchon ensuite **2.** [referring to clothes] : **why have you got your gloves on?** pourquoi as-tu mis tes gants? ■ **he's got nothing on** il est nu **3.** [indicating continued action] : **to read on** continuer à lire ■ **the car drove on** la voiture ne s'est pas arrêtée ■ **they walked on** ils poursuivirent leur chemin ■ **earlier/later/further on** plus tôt/tard/loin **4.** [indicating activity] : **I've got a lot on this week** je suis très occupé cette semaine ■ **have you got anything on tonight?** tu fais quelque chose ce soir? ■ **what's on at the cinema?** qu'est-ce qui passe au cinéma? **5.** [functioning, running] : **put** *OR* **turn** *OR* **switch the television on** allume la télévision ■ **turn the tap on** ouvre le robinet ■ **the car had its headlights on** les phares de la voiture étaient allumés **6.** *inf phr* **to be** *OR* **go on about sthg** parler de qqch sans arrêt ■ **he's on about his new car again** le voilà reparti sur sa nouvelle voiture ■ **what's she on about?** qu'est-ce qu'elle raconte? ■ **to be** *OR* **go on at sb (about sthg)** : **my parents are always on at me about my hair** mes parents n'arrêtent pas de m'embêter avec mes cheveux.

◇ *adj* **1.** [working - electricity, light, radio, TV] allumé ; [- gas, tap] ouvert ; [- engine, machine] en marche ; [- handbrake] serré ■ **the radio was on very loud** la radio hurlait ■ **make sure the switches are in the "on" position** vérifiez que les interrupteurs sont sur (la position) "marche" ■ **the "on" button** le bouton de mise en marche **2.** [happening, under way] : **there's a conference on next week** il y a une conférence la semaine prochaine ■ **the match is still on** [on TV] le match n'est pas terminé ; [going ahead] le match n'a pas été annulé ■ **it's on at the local cinema** ça passe au cinéma du quartier ■ **your favourite TV programme is on tonight** il y a ton émission préférée à la télé ce soir ■ **is our deal still on?** est-ce que notre affaire tient toujours? ■ **the kettle's on for tea** j'ai mis de l'eau à chauffer pour le thé **3.** *inf* [feasible, possible] : **we'll never be ready by tomorrow, it just isn't on** nous ne serons jamais prêts pour demain, c'est tout bonnement impossible **4.** *inf* [in agreement] : **are you still on for dinner tonight?** ça marche toujours pour le dîner de ce soir? ■ **shall we say £10? – you're on!** disons 10 livres? – d'accord *OR* tope là!

◆ **on and off** *adv phr* : **we went out together on and off for a year** on a eu une relation irrégulière pendant un an.

◆ **on and on** *adv phr* sans arrêt ■ **he goes on and on about his minor ailments** il nous rebat les oreilles avec ses petits problèmes de santé ■ **the play dragged on and on** la pièce n'en finissait plus.

ON *written abbr of* **Ontario**.

onanism ['əʊnənɪzm] *n* onanisme *m*.

on-board *adj* COMPUT [built-in] intégré.

ONC (*abbrev of* **Ordinary National Certificate**) *n brevet de technicien en Grande-Bretagne*.

once [wʌns] ◇ *adv* **1.** [on a single occasion] une fois ■ **I've been there ~ before** j'y suis déjà allé une fois ■ **~ or twice** une ou deux fois ■ **I see her ~ every three months** je la vois tous les trois mois ▶ **~ in a while** occasionnellement, une fois de temps en temps ■ **~ more** *OR* **again** encore une fois, une fois de plus ■ **for ~ he isn't late** pour une fois, il n'est pas en retard ■ **~ a liar always a liar** qui a menti mentira ■ **I'll try anything ~** il faut bien tout essayer **2.** [formerly] jadis, autrefois ▶ **~ upon a time there was...** il était une fois...

◇ *predet* : **~ a month/year** une fois par mois/an.

◇ *conj* une fois que, dès que ■ **it'll be easy ~ we've started** une fois qu'on aura commencé, ce sera facile ■ **give me a call ~ you get there** passe-moi un coup de fil quand tu arrives.

◇ *n* : **(just) this ~** (juste) pour cette fois-ci, (juste) pour une fois ■ **she did it just the ~** elle ne l'a fait qu'une seule fois.

◆ **at once** *adv phr* **1.** [at the same time] à la fois, en même temps **2.** [immediately] tout de suite.

◆ **once and for all** *adv phr* une fois pour toutes.

once-over *n inf* **1.** [glance] coup *m* d'œil ■ **I gave the morning paper the ~** j'ai jeté un coup d'oeil sur le journal du matin ■ **I could see her giving me the ~** je la voyais qui me regardait des pieds à la tête **2.** [clean] : **give the stairs/the bookcase a quick ~** passe un coup dans l'escalier/sur la bibliothèque **3.** [beating] raclée *f*.

oncologist [ɒŋ'kɒlədʒɪst] *n* oncologue *mf*, oncologiste *mf*.

oncology [ɒŋ'kɒlədʒɪ] *n* oncologie *f*.

oncoming ['ɒn,kʌmɪŋ] ◇ *adj* **1.** [traffic, vehicle] venant en sens inverse **2.** [year, season] qui arrive, qui approche.

◇ *n* approche *f*.

OND (*abbrev of* **Ordinary National Diploma**) *n brevet de technicien supérieur en Grande-Bretagne*.

one [wʌn] ◇ *det* **1.** *(as numeral)* [in expressions of age, date, measurement etc] un *m*, une *f* ■ **~ and a half kilos** un kilo et demi ■ **~ thousand** mille ■ **at ~ o'clock** à une heure ■ **he'll be ~ (year old) in June** il aura un an en juin ■ **on page ~** [of book] (à la) page un ; [of newspaper] à la une ▶ **~ or two** [a few] un/une ou deux **2.** [referring to a single object or person] un *m*, une *f* ■ **~ American in two** un Américain sur deux ■ **only ~ answer is correct** il n'y a qu'une seule bonne réponse ■ **at any ~ time** au même moment ■ **~ car looks much like another to me** pour moi, toutes les voitures se ressemblent **3.** [only, single] seul, unique ■ **the ~ woman who knows** la seule femme qui soit au courant ■ **no ~ man should have that responsibility** c'est trop de responsabilité pour un seul homme **4.** [same] même ■ **the two wanted men are in fact ~ and the same person** les deux hommes recherchés sont en fait une seule et même personne **5.** [instead of 'a'] : **if there's ~ thing I hate it's rudeness** s'il y a une chose que je n'aime pas, c'est bien la grossièreté ■ **for ~ thing it's too late** d'abord, c'est trop tard **6.** [a certain] : **I was introduced to ~ Ian Bell** on m'a présenté un certain Ian Bell **7.** [indicating indefinite time] : **early ~ morning** un matin de bonne heure **8.** *inf* [as intensifier] : **the room was ~ big mess** il y avait une de ces pagailles dans la pièce! ■ **it's been ~ hell of a day!** quelle journée!

◇ *pron*

A.

1. [person, thing] : **which ~** lequel *m*, laquelle *f* ■ **this ~** celui-ci *m*, celle-ci *f* ■ **the other ~** l'autre *mf* ■ **the right ~** le bon, la bonne *f* ■ **the wrong ~** le mauvais, la mauvaise *f* ■ **which ~s?** lesquels ? *mpl*, lesquelles ? *f* ■ **these ~s** ceux-ci *mpl*, celles-ci *f* ■ **which dog? – the ~ that's barking** quel chien ? – celui qui aboie ■ **he's the ~ who did it** c'est lui qui l'a fait ■ **~ of my colleagues is sick** (l')un/(l')une de mes collègues est malade ■ **she's ~ of us** elle est des nôtres ■ **I've only got ~** je n'en ai qu'un/qu'une ■ **have you seen ~?** en avez-vous vu un/une? ■ **~ or other** l'un d'eux, l'une d'elles *f* ■ **~ after the other** l'un/l'une après l'autre ■ **she's eaten all the ripe ~s** elle a mangé tous ceux qui étaient mûrs/toutes celles qui étaient mûres

■ **the mother and her little ~s** la mère et ses petits ➊ **he's a right ~ he is!** *inf* lui alors! ■ **I'm not much of a ~** *OR* **I'm not a great ~ for cheese** *inf* je ne raffole pas du fromage ■ **she's a great ~ for computers** c'est une mordue d'informatique ■ **she's ~ in a million** *OR* **thousand** c'est une perle rare ■ **I'm not ~ to gossip but...** je ne suis pas du ge nre commère mais... ■ **~ and all** tous (sans exception) ■ **to get ~ over on sb** *inf* avoir l'avantage sur qqn
2. [joke, story, question etc] : **have you heard the ~ about the two postmen?** tu connais celle des deux facteurs? ■ **that's a good ~!** elle est bien bonne celle-là! ■ **that's an easy ~** c'est facile ■ **you'll have to solve this ~ yourself** il faudra que tu règles ça tout seul
3. *inf* [drink] : **do you fancy a quick ~?** on prend un verre en vitesse? ➊ **to have ~ too many** boire un verre de trop
4. *inf* [blow] : **to hit** *OR* **thump** *OR* **belt sb ~** en mettre une à qqn

B.
1. *fml* [as subject] on ■ [as object or after preposition] vous ■ **~ can only do ~'s** *OR* *US* **his best** on fait ce qu'on peut ■ **it certainly makes ~ think** ça fait réfléchir, c'est sûr
2. [with infinitive forms] : **to wash ~'s hands** se laver les mains ■ **to put ~'s hands in ~'s pockets** mettre ses *OR* les mains dans les poches.
◆ **at one** *adv phr fml* **to be at ~ with sb/sthg** être en harmonie avec qqn/qqch.
◆ **for one** *adv phr* : **I for ~ am disappointed** pour ma part, je suis déçu ■ **I know that Eric for ~ is against it** je sais qu'Éric est contre en tout cas.
◆ **in one** *adv phr* **1.** [combined] : **all in ~** à la fois ■ **a useful three-in-~ kitchen knife** un couteau de cuisine très utile avec ses trois fonctions **2.** [at one attempt] du premier coup ■ **he did it in ~** il l'a fait en un seul coup ■ **got it in ~!** *inf* du premier coup!
◆ **in ones and twos** *adv phr* : **they arrived in ~s and twos** ils arrivèrent les uns après les autres ■ **people stood around in ~s and twos** les gens se tenaient là par petits groupes.
◆ **one another** *pron phr* l'un l'autre *m*, l'une l'autre *f*, les uns les autres *mpl*, les unes les autres *f* ■ **they didn't dare talk to ~ another** ils n'ont pas osé se parler ■ **we love ~ another** nous nous aimons ■ **the group meet in ~ another's homes** le groupe se réunit chez l'un ou chez l'autre ■ **they respect ~ another** [two people] ils ont du respect l'un pour l'autre ; [more than two people] ils se respectent les uns les autres.
◆ **one by one** *adv phr* un par un, une par une *f*.

one-act *adj* : **~ play** pièce *f* en un (seul) acte.

one-armed *adj* manchot (d'un bras) ■ **a ~ man** un manchot.

one-armed bandit *n* machine *f* à sous.

one-dimensional *adj* unidimensionnel.

one-eyed *adj* borgne.

one-handed ◇ *adj* [shot, catch] fait d'une (seule) main ■ [tool] utilisable d'une seule main.
◇ *adv* d'une (seule) main.

one-horse *adj* **1.** [carriage] à un cheval **2.** *phr* **a ~ town** *inf* un (vrai) trou, un bled paumé.

one-legged *adj* unijambiste ■ **a ~ man** un unijambiste.

one-liner *n* [quip] bon mot *m* ■ **she has some very good ~s** ses boutades sont très drôles ■ **there are some great ~s in the film** il y a de très bonnes répliques dans ce film.

one-man *adj* [vehicle, canoe] monoplace ■ [task] pour un seul homme ■ [expedition] en solitaire ➊ **~ show** [by artist] exposition *f* individuelle ; [by performer] spectacle *m* solo, one-man-show *m inv*.

one-man band *n* homme-orchestre *m* ■ **the company is very much a ~** *fig* c'est une seule personne qui fait marcher cette entreprise.

oneness ['wʌnnɪs] *n* **1.** [singleness] unité *f* ■ [uniqueness] unicité *f* **2.** [agreement] accord *m* **3.** [wholeness] intégrité *f* **4.** [sameness] identité *f*.

one-night stand *n* **1.** MUS & THEAT représentation *f* unique **2.** *inf* [brief affair] aventure *f* (sans lendemain).

one-off ◇ *adj* unique ■ **he wants a ~ payment** il veut être payé en une seule fois ■ **I'll do it if it's a ~ job** je veux bien le faire mais seulement à titre exceptionnel ■ **this trip is definitely a ~ deal** *US* c'est la première et dernière fois que je fais ce voyage ■ **~ order** COMM commande *f* ponctuelle.
◇ *n* [original] : **it's a ~** [object] c'est unique ; [situation] c'est exceptionnel.

one-on-one *US* = **one-to-one**.

one-parent *adj* : **~ family** famille *f* monoparentale.

one-party *adj* POL à parti unique.

one-piece ◇ *adj* une pièce *(inv)*.
◇ *n* vêtement *m* une pièce.

one-room *adj* à une (seule) pièce ■ **a ~ flat** *OR* **apartment** un studio.

onerous ['əʊnərəs] *adj fml* lourd, pénible.

oneself [wʌn'self] *pron* **1.** [reflexive] se, s' *(before vowel or silent 'h')* ■ [after preposition] soi, soi-même ■ [emphatic] soi-même ■ **to wash ~** se laver ■ **to be pleased with ~** être content de soi *OR* soi-même **2.** [one's normal self] soi-même **3.** *phr* **to be (all) by ~** être tout seul.

one-shot *US inf* = **one-off** *(adj)*.

one-sided *adj* **1.** [unequal] inégal ■ **conversations with him tend to be pretty ~** avec lui, ce n'est pas une conversation, il n'y a que lui qui parle **2.** [biased] partial **3.** [unilateral] unilatéral.

one-stop *adj* [shop, service] *où l'on trouve tout ce dont on a besoin*.

one-time *adj* ancien.

one-to-one *adj* **1.** [discussion, meeting] seul à seul, en tête-à-tête ■ **~ tuition** cours *mpl* particuliers ■ **students receive ~ instruction** le professeur travaille individuellement avec chaque étudiant **2.** [comparison, relationship] terme à terme MATHS biunivoque.

one-touch dialling *UK*, **one-touch dialing** *US* *n* numérotation *f* rapide.

one-track *adj* **1.** RAIL à voie unique **2.** *phr* **he's got a ~ mind** *inf* [thinks only of one thing] c'est une obsession chez lui ; [thinks only of sex] il ne pense qu'à ça.

one-two *n* **1.** [in boxing] *direct suivi d'un crochet de l'autre main* **2.** FTBL une-deux *m inv*.

one-up (*pret & pp* **one-upped**, *cont* **one-upping**) ◇ *adj* : **we're ~ on our competitors** nous avons pris l'avantage sur nos concurrents.
◇ *vt US inf* marquer un point sur.

one-upmanship [-'ʌpmənʃɪp] *n comportement d'une personne qui ne supporte pas de voir d'autres faire mieux qu'elle* ■ **it's pure ~ on her part** elle veut uniquement prouver qu'elle est la meilleure.

one-way *adj* **1.** [street] à sens unique ■ [traffic] en sens unique ■ **he went the wrong way up a ~ street** il a pris un sens interdit **2.** [ticket] simple ■ **a ~ ticket to Rome** un aller simple pour Rome **3.** [mirror] sans tain **4.** [reaction, current] irréversible ■ [decision] unilatéral **5.** [relationship, feeling] à sens unique.

ongoing ['ɒn,gəʊɪŋ] *adj* [continuing] continu ■ [current, in progress] en cours.

onion ['ʌnjən] *n* oignon *m* ■ **~ soup** soupe *f* à l'oignon.

onion dome *n* ARCHIT bulbe *m* (byzantin).

on-line *adj & adv* COMPUT en ligne.

online banking *n* banque *f* en ligne.

online shopping *n* téléachats *mpl*.

onlooker ['ɒn,lʊkər] *n* [during event] spectateur *m*, - trice *f* ■ [after accident] badaud *m*, - e *f*, curieux *m*, - euse *f*.

only ['əʊnlɪ] ◇ *adj* seul, unique ■ **he's/she's an ~ child** il est fils/elle est fille unique ■ **she was the ~ woman there** c'était la seule femme ■ **her ~ answer was to shrug her shoulders** pour toute réponse, elle a haussé les épaules ■ **the ~ thing is, I won't be there** le seul problème, c'est que je ne serai pas là ■ **her one and ~ friend** son seul et unique ami ■ **the one and ~ Billy Shears!** le seul, l'unique Billy Shears!

◇ *adv* **1.** [exclusively] seulement ■ **there are ~ two people I trust** il n'y a que deux personnes en qui j'aie confiance ■ **you'll ~ get him to come if you offer him a lift** tu ne le feras venir que si tu lui proposes de l'amener ■ **'staff ~'** 'réservé au personnel'

2. [just, merely] : **he's ~ a child!** ce n'est qu'un enfant! ■ **it's ~ me!** c'est moi! ■ **you've ~ ruined my best silk shirt (, that's all)!** tu n'as fait qu'abîmer ma plus belle chemise en soie (, c'est tout)! ■ **go on, ask him, he can ~ say no** vas-y, demande-lui, ce qui peut t'arriver de pire c'est qu'il refuse ■ **it's ~ natural she should want to see him** c'est tout naturel qu'elle veuille le voir ■ **I ~ hope we're not too late** j'espère seulement que nous n'arrivons pas trop tard ■ **you ~ have to look at him to see he's guilty** il suffit de le regarder pour voir qu'il est coupable ➲ **you're ~ young once** il faut profiter de sa jeunesse

3. [to emphasize smallness of amount, number etc] ne... que ■ **it ~ cost me £5** ça ne m'a coûté que 5 livres

4. [to emphasize recentness of event] : **it seems like ~ yesterday** c'est comme si c'était hier ■ **I ~ found out this morning** je n'ai appris ça que ce matin

5. [with infinitive] : **I awoke ~ to find he was gone** à mon réveil, il était parti.

◇ *conj inf* **1.** [but, except] mais

2. [were it not for the fact that] mais, seulement.

◆ **not only** *conj phr* : **not ~... but also** non seulement... mais aussi.

◆ **only if, only... if** *conj phr* seulement si ■ **he'll ~ agree if the money's good enough** il n'acceptera que si on lui propose assez d'argent.

◆ **only just** *adv phr* **1.** [not long before] : **I've ~ just woken up** je viens (tout) juste de me réveiller

2. [barely] tout juste ■ **I ~ just finished in time** je n'ai fini qu'au dernier moment ■ **did she win? – yes, but ~ just** a-t-elle gagné? – oui, mais de justesse ■ **I've ~ just got enough** j'en ai tout juste assez.

◆ **only too** *adv phr* : **I was ~ too aware of my own shortcomings** je n'étais que trop conscient de mes propres imperfections ■ **I remember her ~ too well** je ne risque pas de l'oublier.

o.n.o. (*abbrev of* **or near/nearest offer**) *adv UK* **£100 ~** 100 livres à débattre.

on-off *adj* **1.** ELEC : **~ button** bouton *m* de marche-arrêt **2.** [intermittent] : **they have a very ~ relationship** ils ont une relation très peu suivie.

onomastics [ˌɒnə'mæstɪks] *n (U)* onomastique *f*.

onomatopoeia ['ɒnəˌmætə'piːə] *n* onomatopée *f*.

onomatopoeic ['ɒnəˌmætə'piːɪk], **onomatopoetic** ['ɒnəˌmætəpəʊ'etɪk] *adj* onomatopéique.

onrush ['ɒnˌrʌʃ] *n* [of attackers, army] attaque *f*, assaut *m* ■ [of emotion, tears] crise *f* ■ [of anger] accès *m*.

on-screen *adj* & *adv* COMPUT à l'écran ■ **~ help** aide *f* en ligne.

onset ['ɒnˌset] *n* **1.** [assault] attaque *f*, assaut *m* **2.** [beginning] début *m*, commencement *m*.

onshore ['ɒn'ʃɔːʳ] *adj* **1.** [on land] sur terre, terrestre ■ **~ oil production** production *f* pétrolière à terre **2.** [moving towards land] : **~ wind** vent *m* de mer.

onside [ˌɒn'saɪd] *adj* & *adv* SPORT qui n'est pas hors jeu *OR* en position de hors-jeu.

on-site *adj* sur place.

onslaught ['ɒnˌslɔːt] *n* attaque *f*, assaut *m* ■ **the opposition's ~ on government policy** l'attaque violente de l'opposition contre la politique du gouvernement.

onstage ['ɒnsteɪdʒ] *adj* & *adv* sur scène.

Ont. *written abbr of* **Ontario**.

Ontario [ɒn'teərɪəʊ] *pr n* Ontario *m* ■ **in ~** dans l'Ontario ■ **Lake ~** le lac Ontario.

on-the-job *adj* [training] en entreprise ■ [experience] sur le tas.

onto ['ɒntuː] *prep* **1.** [gen] sur ■ **the bedroom looks out ~ a garden** la chambre donne sur un jardin ■ **let's move ~ the next point** passons au point suivant ■ **get ~ the bus** montez dans le bus **2.** [indicating discovery] : **let's just hope the authorities don't get ~ us** espérons qu'on ne sera pas découverts par les autorités ■ **we're ~ something big** nous sommes sur le point de faire une importante découverte ■ **he'd better watch out, I'm ~ him!** qu'il fasse attention, je l'ai dans mon *OR* le collimateur! **3.** [in contact with] : **you should get ~ head office about this** vous devriez contacter le siège à ce sujet.

ontological [ˌɒntə'lɒdʒɪkl] *adj* ontologique.

ontology [ɒn'tɒlədʒɪ] *n* ontologie *f*.

onus ['əʊnəs] *n* [responsibility] responsabilité *f* ■ [burden] charge *f* ■ **the ~ is on you to make good the damage** c'est à vous qu'il incombe de réparer les dégâts.

onward ['ɒnwəd] ◇ *adj* : **the ~ journey** la suite du voyage ■ **there is an ~ flight to Chicago** il y a une correspondance pour Chicago.

◇ *adv US* = **onwards**.

◇ *interj* en avant.

onwards ['ɒnwədz] *adv* [forwards] en avant ■ [further on] plus loin ■ **to go ~** avancer ■ **a trip to Europe, and ~ into Asia** un voyage en Europe, qui se poursuit en Asie.

◆ **from... onwards** *adv phr* à partir de ■ **from her childhood ~** dès *OR* depuis son enfance ■ **from now ~** désormais, dorénavant, à partir de maintenant ■ **from then ~** à partir de ce moment-là.

onyx ['ɒnɪks] ◇ *n* onyx *m*.

◇ *comp* en onyx, d'onyx.

oodles ['uːdlz] *npl inf* des masses *fpl*, des tas *mpl*.

ooh [uː] ◇ *interj* oh!

◇ *vi* : **they were all ~ing and aahing over her baby** ils poussaient tous des cris d'admiration devant son bébé.

oompah ['uːmpɑː] *n* flonflon *m*.

oomph [ʊmf] *n inf* **1.** [energy] punch **2.** [sex appeal] sex-appeal *m*.

oops [ʊps, uːps], **oops-a-daisy** [ˌʊpsə'deɪzɪ] *interj inf* oh la la!

ooze [uːz] ◇ *vi* suinter ■ **blood ~d from the wound** du sang coulait de la blessure ■ **the new father fairly ~d with pride** *fig* le nouveau père débordait de fierté.

◇ *vt* : **the walls ~ moisture** l'humidité suinte des murs ■ **she ~s good health** *fig* elle respire la bonne santé.

◇ *n* boue *f*, vase *f*.

op [ɒp] (*abbrev of* **operation**) *n inf* MED & MIL opération *f*.

op. (*written abbrev of* **opus**) op.

opacity [ə'pæsətɪ] *n* **1.** *liter* opacité *f* **2.** *fig* [of text] inintelligibilité *f*, obscurité *f* ■ [of person] stupidité *f*.

opal ['əʊpl] ◇ *n* opale *f*.

◇ *comp* [brooch, ring] en opale.

opalescence [ˌəʊpə'lesns] *n* opalescence *f*.

opalescent [ˌəʊpə'lesnt] *adj* opalescent *lit*, opalin.

opaque [əʊ'peɪk] *adj* **1.** *liter* opaque **2.** *fig* [text] inintelligible, obscur ■ [person] stupide.

OPEC ['əʊpek] (*abbrev of* **Organization of Petroleum Exporting Countries**) *pr n* OPEP *f* ■ **the ~ countries** les pays membres de l'OPEP.

open ['əʊpn] ◇ *adj* **1.** [not shut - window, cupboard, suitcase, jar, box, sore, valve] ouvert ■ **her eyes were slightly ~/wide ~** ses yeux étaient entrouverts/grands ouverts ■ **he kicked the**

door ~ il a ouvert la porte d'un coup de pied ■ **the panels slide ~** les panneaux s'ouvrent en coulissant ■ **there's a bottle already ~ in the fridge** il y a une bouteille entamée dans le frigo
2. [not fastened - coat, fly, packet] ouvert ■ **his shirt was ~ to the waist** sa chemise était ouverte *OR* déboutonnée jusqu'à la ceinture ■ **the wrapping had been torn ~** l'emballage avait été arraché *OR* déchiré
3. [spread apart, unfolded - arms, book, magazine, umbrella] ouvert ; [- newspaper] ouvert, déplié ; [- legs, knees] écarté ■ **the book lay ~ at page six** le livre était ouvert à la page six ■ **I dropped the coin into his ~ hand** *OR* **palm** j'ai laissé tomber la pièce de monnaie dans le creux de sa main ■ **he ran into my ~ arms** il s'est précipité dans mes bras
4. [for business] ouvert ■ **are you ~ on Saturdays?** ouvrez-vous le samedi? ■ **we're ~ for business as usual** nous sommes ouverts comme à l'habitude
5. [not covered - carriage, wagon, bus] découvert ; [- car] décapoté ; [- grave] ouvert ; [- boat] ouvert, non ponté ; [- courtyard, sewer] à ciel ouvert
6. [not enclosed - hillside, plain] : **the shelter was ~ on three sides** l'abri était ouvert sur trois côtés ■ **the hill was ~ to the elements** la colline était exposée à tous les éléments ■ **our neighbourhood lacks ~ space** notre quartier manque d'espaces verts ■ **the wide ~ spaces of Texas** les grands espaces du Texas ■ **shanty towns sprang up on every scrap of ~ ground** des bidonvilles ont surgi sur la moindre parcelle de terrain vague ■ **they were attacked in ~ country** ils ont été attaqués en rase campagne ■ **ahead lay a vast stretch of ~ water** au loin s'étendait une vaste étendue d'eau ■ **in the ~ air** en plein air ■ **he took to the ~ road** il a pris la route ■ **the ~ sea** la haute mer, le large
7. [unobstructed - road, passage] dégagé ; [- mountain pass] ouvert, praticable ; [- waterway] ouvert à la navigation ; [- view] dégagé ■ **only one lane on the bridge is ~** il n'y a qu'une voie ouverte à la circulation sur le pont
8. [unoccupied, available - job] vacant ; [- period of time] libre ■ **we have two positions ~** nous avons deux postes à pourvoir ■ **I'll keep this Friday ~ for you** je vous réserverai ce vendredi ■ **she likes to keep her weekends ~** elle préfère ne pas faire de projets pour le week-end ■ **it's the only course of action ~ to us** c'est la seule chose que nous puissions faire ■ **he wants to keep his options ~** il ne veut pas s'engager
9. [unrestricted - competition] ouvert (à tous) ; [- meeting, trial] public ; [- society] ouvert, démocratique ■ **club membership is ~ to anyone** aucune condition particulière n'est requise pour devenir membre du club ■ **there are few positions of responsibility ~ to immigrants** les immigrés ont rarement accès aux postes de responsabilité ■ **the field is wide ~ for someone with your talents** pour quelqu'un d'aussi doué que vous, ce domaine offre des possibilités quasi illimitées ■ **to extend an ~ invitation to sb** inviter qqn à venir chez soi quand il le souhaite ➊ **~ classroom** SCH classe *f* primaire à activités libres ■ **they have an ~ marriage** ils forment un couple très libre ■ **~ primary** POL *(élection) primaire américaine ouverte aux non-inscrits d'un parti* ■ **~ seating** AERON & THEAT places *fpl* non réservées ■ **~ ticket** billet *m* open ■ **~ tournament** SPORT (tournoi *m*) open *m*
10. [unprotected, unguarded - flank, fire] ouvert ; [- wiring] non protégé ■ **~ city** MIL & POL ville *f* ouverte ■ **he missed an ~ goal** SPORT il n'y avait pas de défenseurs, et il a raté le but ■ **to lay o.s. ~ to criticism** prêter le flanc à la critique
11. [undecided - question] non résolu, non tranché ■ **the election is still wide ~** l'élection n'est pas encore jouée ■ **I prefer to leave the matter ~** je préfère laisser cette question en suspens ■ **he wanted to leave the date ~** il n'a pas voulu fixer de date
12. [liable] : **his speech is ~ to misunderstanding** son discours peut prêter à confusion ■ **the prices are not ~ to negotiation** les prix ne sont pas négociables ■ **it's ~ to debate whether she knew about it or not** on peut se demander si elle était au courant
13. [receptive] : **to be ~ to suggestions** être ouvert aux suggestions ■ **I don't want to go but I'm ~ to persuasion** je ne veux pas y aller mais je pourrais me laisser persuader ■ **I try to keep an ~ mind about such things** j'essaie de ne pas avoir de préjugés sur ces questions
14. [candid - person, smile, countenance] ouvert, franc, franche *f* ; [- discussion] franc, franche *f*
15. [blatant - contempt, criticism] ouvert ; [- attempt] non dissimulé ; [- scandal] public ; [- rivalry] déclaré ■ **they acted in ~ violation of the treaty** ce qu'ils ont fait constitue une violation flagrante du traité ■ **it's an ~ admission of guilt** cela équivaut à un aveu
16. [loose - weave] lâche ■ **~ mesh** mailles *fpl* lâches ■ **~ pattern** motif *m* aéré
17. LING [vowel, syllable] ouvert
18. ELEC [circuit] ouvert
19. *UK* FIN [cheque] non barré
20. MUS [string] à vide.
◇ *vt* **1.** [window, lock, shop, eyes, border] ouvrir ■ [wound] rouvrir ■ [bottle, can] ouvrir, déboucher ■ [wine] déboucher ■ **she ~ed her eyes very wide** elle ouvrit grand les yeux, elle écarquilla les yeux ▮ *fig* **to ~ one's heart to sb** se confier à qqn
2. [unfasten - coat, envelope, gift, collar] ouvrir
3. [unfold, spread apart - book, umbrella, penknife, arms, hand] ouvrir ; [- newspaper] ouvrir, déplier ; [- legs, knees] écarter
4. [pierce - hole] percer ; [- breach] ouvrir ; [- way, passage] ouvrir, frayer ■ **the agreement ~s the way for peace** l'accord va mener à la paix
5. COMPUT [software] ouvrir ■ [computer] démarrer
6. [start - campaign, discussion, account, trial] ouvrir, commencer ; [- negotiations] ouvrir, engager ; [- conversation] engager, entamer ■ **to ~ fire (on)** *OR* **at sb** ouvrir le feu (sur qqn) ■ **to ~ the betting** [in poker] lancer les enchères
7. [set up - shop, business] ouvrir ■ [inaugurate - hospital, airport, library] ouvrir, inaugurer
8. [clear, unblock - road, lane, passage] dégager ; [- mountain pass] ouvrir.
◇ *vi* **1.** [door, window] (s')ouvrir ■ [suitcase, valve, padlock, eyes] s'ouvrir ■ **the window ~s outwards** la fenêtre (s')ouvre vers l'extérieur ■ **~ wide!** ouvrez grand! ■ **to ~, press down and twist** pour ouvrir, appuyez et tournez ■ **both rooms ~ onto the corridor** les deux chambres donnent *OR* ouvrent sur le couloir ■ **the heavens ~ed and we got drenched** *fig* il s'est mis à tomber des trombes d'eau et on s'est fait tremper
2. [unfold, spread apart - book, umbrella, parachute] s'ouvrir ; [- bud, leaf] s'ouvrir, s'épanouir
3. [gape - chasm] s'ouvrir
4. [for business] ouvrir ■ **what time do you ~ on Sundays?** à quelle heure ouvrez-vous le dimanche?
5. [start - campaign, meeting, discussion, concert, play, story] commencer ■ **the hunting season ~s in September** la chasse ouvre en septembre ■ **she ~ed with a statement of the association's goals** elle commença par une présentation des buts de l'association ■ **the film ~s next week** le film sort la semaine prochaine ■ **when are you ~ing?** THEAT quand aura lieu la première? ■ **when it ~ed on Broadway, the play flopped** lorsqu'elle est sortie à Broadway, la pièce a fait un four ■ **the Dow Jones ~ed at 2461** le Dow Jones a ouvert à 2461.
◇ *n* **1.** [outdoors, open air] : **(out) in the ~** [gen] en plein air, dehors ; [in countryside] au grand air ■ **to sleep in the ~** dormir à la belle étoile
2. [public eye] : **to bring sthg (out) into the ~** exposer *OR* étaler qqch au grand jour ■ **the riot brought the instability of the regime out into the ~** l'émeute a révélé l'instabilité du régime ■ **the conflict finally came out into the ~** le conflit a finalement éclaté au grand jour
3. SPORT : **the British Open** l'open *m* *OR* le tournoi open de Grande-Bretagne.

◆ **open out** ◇ *vi insep* **1.** [unfold - bud, petals] s'ouvrir, s'épanouir ; [- parachute] s'ouvrir ; [- sail] se gonfler ■ **the sofa ~s out into a bed** le canapé est convertible en lit ■ **the doors ~ out onto a terrace** les portes donnent *OR* s'ouvrent sur une terrasse
2. [lie - vista, valley] s'étendre, s'ouvrir ■ **miles of wheatfields ~ed out before us** des champs de blé s'étendaient devant nous à perte de vue
3. [widen - path, stream] s'élargir ■ **the trail finally ~s out onto a plateau** la piste débouche sur un plateau.
◇ *vt sep* [unfold - newspaper, deck chair, fan] ouvrir.

◆ **open up** ◇ *vi insep* **1.** [unlock the door] ouvrir ■ **~ up or I'll call the police!** ouvrez, sinon j'appelle la police! ■ **~ up in there!** ouvrez, là-dedans!
2. [become available - possibility] s'ouvrir ■ **we may have a position ~ing up in May** il se peut que nous ayons un poste disponible en mai

3. [for business - shop, branch etc] (s')ouvrir ■ **a new hotel ~s up every week** un nouvel hôtel ouvre ses portes chaque semaine
4. [start firing - guns] faire feu, tirer ; [- troops, person] ouvrir le feu, se mettre à tirer
5. [become less reserved - person] s'ouvrir ; [- discussion] s'animer ■ **he needs to ~ up about his feelings** il a besoin de dire ce qu'il a sur le cœur *OR* de s'épancher
6. [become interesting] devenir intéressant ■ **things are beginning to ~ up in my field of research** ça commence à bouger dans mon domaine de recherche ■ **the game ~ed up in the last half** le match est devenu plus ouvert après la mi-temps.
◇ *vt sep* **1.** [crate, gift, bag, tomb] ouvrir
2. [for business] ouvrir ■ **he wants to ~ up a travel agency** il veut ouvrir une agence de voyages
3. [for development - isolated region] désenclaver ; [- quarry, oilfield] ouvrir, commencer l'exploitation de ; [- new markets] ouvrir ■ **a discovery which ~s up new fields of research** une découverte qui crée de nouveaux domaines de recherche ■ **the policy ~ed up possibilities for closer cooperation** la politique a créé les conditions d'une coopération plus étroite
4. *inf* [accelerate] : **he ~ed it** *OR* **her up** il a accéléré à fond.

open-air *adj* [market, concert] en plein air ■ [sports] de plein air ■ **~ swimming pool** piscine *f* découverte ■ **~ museum** écomusée *m*.

open-and-shut *adj* [choice] simple, évident ■ **it's an ~ case** la solution est évidente *OR* ne fait pas l'ombre d'un doute.

open bar *n* buvette *f* gratuite, bar *m* gratuit.

opencast ['əʊpnkɑːst] *adj UK* MIN à ciel ouvert.

open day *n UK* journée *f* portes ouvertes.

open-door *adj* [policy] de la porte ouverte.

open-ended [-'endɪd] *adj* [flexible - offer] flexible ; [- plan] modifiable ; [- question] ouvert ■ **an ~ discussion** une discussion libre ■ **~ contract** contrat *m* à durée indéterminée.

opener ['əʊpnəʳ] *n* **1.** [tool] outil *m OR* dispositif *m* servant à ouvrir ■ [for cans] ouvre-boîtes *m inv* **2.** [person - in cards, games] ouvreur *m*, - euse *f* **3.** [first song, act etc] lever *m* de rideau ■ **she chose her latest hit single as an ~ for the show** elle a choisi son dernier tube pour ouvrir le spectacle **4.** *phr* **for ~s** *UK inf* pour commencer ■ **I'm sacking the whole staff, and that's just for ~ s** je licencie toute l'équipe et ce n'est qu'un début.

open-faced *adj US* **~ sandwich** [gen] tartine *f* ; [cocktail food] canapé *m*.

open-handed *adj* généreux.

open-hearted [-'hɑːtɪd] *adj* **1.** [candid] franc, franche *f*, sincère **2.** [kind] bon, qui a bon cœur.

open-hearth *adj* METALL : **~ furnace** four *m* Martin ■ **~ process** procédé *m* Martin.

open-heart surgery *n* chirurgie *f* à cœur ouvert.

open house *n* **1.** *US* = **open day 2.** *US* [party] grande fête *f* **3.** *phr* **to keep ~** *UK* tenir table ouverte.

opening ['əʊpnɪŋ] ◇ *adj* [part, chapter] premier ■ [day, hours] d'ouverture ■ [ceremony] d'ouverture, d'inauguration ■ [remark] préliminaire, préalable ■ **the play's ~ scene** le début de la pièce ■ **~ prices** ST. EX prix *mpl* à l'ouverture ➤ **~ gambit** CHESS gambit *m* ; *fig* premier pas *m*.
◇ *n* **1.** [act of opening] ouverture *f* ■ **at the play's New York ~** lors de la première de la pièce à New York **2.** [gap, hole, entrance] ouverture *f* ■ **an ~ in the clouds** une trouée *OR* une percée dans les nuages **3.** *US* = **clearing** *(sense 1)* **4.** [start, first part] ouverture *f*, début *m* **5.** [opportunity - gen] occasion *f* ; [- for employment] débouché *m* ■ **her remarks about the company gave me the ~ I needed** ses observations au sujet de l'entreprise m'ont fourni le prétexte dont j'avais besoin ■ **there are lots of good ~s in industry** l'industrie offre de nombreux débouchés intéressants ■ **there's an ~ with Smith & Co** il y a un poste vacant chez Smith & Co.

opening night *n* THEAT première *f*.

opening time *n* COMM heure *f* d'ouverture.

open letter *n* lettre *f* ouverte.

openly ['əʊpənlɪ] *adv* visiblement ■ **drugs are on sale ~** la drogue est en vente libre ■ **to weep ~** pleurer sans retenue.

open market *n* marché *m* libre.

open-minded *adj* [receptive] ouvert (d'esprit) ■ [unprejudiced] sans préjugés ■ **my parents are pretty ~ about mixed marriages** mes parents n'ont aucun a priori contre les mariages mixtes.

open-mindedness [-'maɪndɪdnɪs] *n* ouverture *f* d'esprit.

open-mouthed [-'maʊðd] ◇ *adj* [person] stupéfait, interdit ■ **he was sitting there in ~ astonishment** il était assis là, béant d'étonnement.
◇ *adv* : **to watch ~** regarder bouche bée.

open-neck(ed) *adj* à col ouvert.

openness ['əʊpənnɪs] *n* **1.** [candidness] franchise *f* ■ [receptivity] ouverture *f* ■ **I admire her for her ~** ce que j'admire chez elle, c'est qu'elle est très ouverte **2.** [spaciousness] largeur *f*.

open-plan *adj* ARCHIT [design, house] à plan ouvert, sans cloisons ■ **~ kitchen** cuisine *f* américaine ■ **~ office** bureau *m* paysager.

open primary *n US* POL *élection primaire ouverte à tous les électeurs.*

open prison *n* prison *f* ouverte.

open sandwich *n* [gen] tartine *f* ■ [cocktail food] canapé *m*.

open season *n* saison *f* ■ **the ~ for hunting** la saison de la chasse.

open secret *n UK* secret *m* de Polichinelle.

open sesame ◇ *interj* : **~!** sésame, ouvre-toi!
◇ *n UK* [means to success] sésame *m* ■ **good A-level results aren't necessarily an ~ to university** de bons résultats aux A-levels n'ouvrent pas forcément la porte de l'université.

open shop *n* INDUST *UK* [open to non-union members] *entreprise ne pratiquant pas le monopole d'embauche.*

Open University *n UK* ≃ Université *f* ouverte à tous (pratiquant le télé-enseignement).

open verdict *n* LAW verdict *m* de décès sans cause déterminée.

opera ['ɒpərə] ◇ *fml pl* ▷ **opus.**
◇ *n* **1.** [musical play] opéra *m* **2.** [art of opera] opéra *m* ➤ **~ singer** chanteur *m*, - euse *f* d'opéra **3.** [opera house] opéra *m*.

operable ['ɒprəbl] *adj* MED opérable.

opera glasses *npl* jumelles *fpl* de théâtre.

operagoer ['ɒprə,gəʊəʳ] *n* amateur *m* d'opéra.

opera hat *n UK* gibus *m*, (chapeau *m*) claque *m*.

opera house *n* (théâtre *m* de l')opéra *m*.

operand ['ɒpərænd] *n* opérande *m*.

operate ['ɒpəreɪt] ◇ *vt* **1.** [machine, device] faire fonctionner, faire marcher ■ **is it possible to ~ the radio off the mains?** peut-on brancher cette radio sur le secteur? ■ **this clock is battery--d** cette horloge fonctionne avec des piles ■ **a circuit-breaker ~s the safety mechanism** un disjoncteur actionne *OR* déclenche le système de sécurité **2.** [business] gérer, diriger ■ [mine] exploiter ■ [drug ring] contrôler ■ **they ~ several casinos** ils tiennent plusieurs casinos ■ **they ~ a system of rent rebates for poorer families** ils ont un système de loyers modérés pour les familles les plus démunies.
◇ *vi* **1.** [machine, device] marcher, fonctionner ■ [system, process, network] fonctionner ■ **the factory is operating at full capacity** l'usine tourne à plein rendement **2.** MED opérer ■ **to ~ on sb (for sthg)** opérer qqn (de qqch) ■ **he was ~d on for cancer** on l'a opéré *OR* il a été opéré d'un cancer **3.** [be active] opérer ■ **the company ~s out of Chicago** le siège de la société est à Chicago ■ **the company ~s in ten countries** la société est implantée dans dix pays **4.** [produce an effect] opérer, agir

▪ **the drug ~s on the nervous system** le médicament agit sur le système nerveux ▪ **two elements ~ in our favour** deux éléments jouent en notre faveur ▮ [be operative] s'appliquer.

operatic [ˌɒpəˈrætɪk] *adj* d'opéra ▪ **~ repertoire/role** répertoire/rôle lyrique.

operating [ˈɒpəreɪtɪŋ] *adj* [costs, methods etc] d'exploitation ▪ **the factory has reached full ~capacity** l'usine a atteint sa pleine capacité de production ⊙ **~ instructions** mode *m* d'emploi ▪ **~ profit** bénéfice *m* d'exploitation.

operating room *n* *US* salle *f* d'opération.

operating system *n* COMPUT système *m* d'exploitation.

operating table *n* table *f* d'opération.

operating theatre *n* *UK* salle *f* d'opération.

operation [ˌɒpəˈreɪʃn] *n* **1.** [functioning - of machine, device] fonctionnement *m*, marche *f* ; [- of process, system] fonctionnement *m* ; [- of drug, market force] action *f* ▪ **to be in ~** [machine, train service] être en service ; [firm, group, criminal] être en activité ; [law] être en vigueur ▪ **the plant is in ~ round the clock** l'usine fonctionne 24 heures sur 24 ▪ **to put into ~** [machine, train service] mettre en service ; [plan] mettre en application *OR* en œuvre ; [law] faire entrer en vigueur ▪ **to come into ~** [machine, train service] entrer en service ; [law] entrer en vigueur **2.** [running, management - of firm] gestion *f* ; [- of mine] exploitation *f* ; [- of process, system] application *f* ; [- of machine] fonctionnement *m* **3.** [act, activity, deal etc] opération *f* ▪ **a police/rescue ~** une opération de police/de sauvetage ▮ MIL opération *f* **4.** [company] entreprise *f*, société *f* **5.** MED opération *f*, intervention *f* ▪ **she had an ~ for cancer** elle s'est fait opérer d'un cancer ▪ **he had a heart ~** il a subi une opération *OR* il a été opéré du cœur ▪ **to perform an ~** réaliser une intervention **6.** COMPUT & MATHS opération *f*.

operational [ˌɒpəˈreɪʃənl] *adj* **1.** MIL [gen] opérationnel ⊙ **~ costs** frais *mpl* opérationnels ; COMM frais *mpl* d'exploitation **2.** [equipment, engine, system] opérationnel ▪ **as soon as the engine is ~** dès que le moteur sera en état de marche ▪ **~ difficulties** difficultés d'ordre pratique ▪ **we have an ~ malfunction** nous avons un problème de fonctionnement.

operations room *n* base *f* d'opérations.

operative [ˈɒprətɪv] <> *adj* **1.** [law] en vigueur ▪ **to become ~** entrer en vigueur, prendre effet **2.** [operational - system, scheme, skill] opérationnel **3.** MED opératoire **4.** *phr* **the ~ word** le mot qui convient.
<> *n* **1.** opérateur *m*, - trice *f* ▪ **machine ~** conducteur *m*, - trice *f* de machine ▪ **textile ~** ouvrier *m*, - ère *f* du textile **2.** *US* [secret agent] agent *m* secret ▪ [detective] (détective *m*) privé *m*.

operator [ˈɒpəreɪtəʳ] *n* **1.** [technician] opérateur *m*, - trice *f* ▪ **radio ~** radio *mf* **2.** TELEC opérateur *m*, - trice *f* **3.** COMM [director] directeur *m*, - trice *f*, dirigeant *m*, - e *f* ▪ [organizer] organisateur *m*, - trice *f* ▪ **there are too many small ~s in real estate** l'immobilier compte trop de petites entreprises ⊙ **he's a smooth ~** *inf* il sait s'y prendre *OR* se débrouiller, c'est un petit malin **4.** MATHS opérateur *m* **5.** *US* [in bus] machiniste *mf*.

operetta [ˌɒpəˈretə] *n* opérette *f*.

ophthalmic [ɒfˈθælmɪk] *adj* ANAT [nerve] ophtalmique ▪ MED [surgery] ophtalmologique.

ophthalmic optician *n* opticien *m*, - enne *f* (optométriste).

ophthalmologist [ˌɒfθælˈmɒlədʒɪst] *n* oculiste *mf*, ophtalmologiste *mf*, ophtalmologue *mf*.

ophthalmology [ˌɒfθælˈmɒlədʒɪ] *n* ophtalmologie *f*.

ophthalmoscope [ɒfˈθælməskəʊp] *n* ophtalmoscope *m*.

opiate [ˈəʊpɪət] <> *adj* opiacé.
<> *n* opiacé *m*.

opine [əʊˈpaɪn] *vt* *fml* & *lit* (faire) remarquer.

opinion [əˈpɪnjən] *n* **1.** [estimation] opinion *f*, avis *m* ▪ [viewpoint] point *m* de vue ▪ **in my ~** à mon avis ▪ **I am of the ~ that we should wait** je suis d'avis que l'on attende ▪ **what is your ~ on *OR* about the elections?** que pensez-vous des élections? ▪ **my personal ~ is that...** je suis d'avis que..., pour ma part, je pense que... ▪ **to have a good/bad ~ of sthg** avoir une bonne/ mauvaise opinion de qqch ▪ **I have a rather low ~ of him** je n'ai pas beaucoup d'estime pour lui ▪ **he has too high an ~ of himself** il a une trop haute opinion de lui-même **2.** [conviction, belief] opinion *f* ▪ **world/international ~** l'opinion mondiale/ internationale ▪ **a matter of ~** une affaire d'opinion ▮ LAW avis *m* ▪ **it is the ~ of the court that...** la cour est d'avis que... ⊙ **public~ is against them** ils ont l'opinion publique contre eux **3.** [advice] opinion *f*, avis *m* ▪ **a medical/legal ~** un avis médical/juridique.

opinionated [əˈpɪnjəneɪtɪd] *adj* *pej* borné, têtu.

opinion poll *n* sondage *m* d'opinion.

opium [ˈəʊpjəm] *n* opium *m* ▪ **~ addict** opiomane *mf* ▪ **~ addiction** opiomanie *f*.

opium den *n* fumerie *f* d'opium.

opossum [əˈpɒsəm] (*pl inv OR pl* **opossums**) *n* opossum *m*.

opponent [əˈpəʊnənt] <> *n* **1.** [gen - POL] [SPORT] adversaire *mf* ▪ [rival] rival *m*, - e *f* ▪ [competitor] concurrent *m*, - e *f* ▪ [in debate] adversaire *mf* ▪ **political ~** [democratic] adversaire politique ; [of regime] opposant *m*, - e *f* politique ▪ **she has always been an ~ of blood sports** elle a toujours été contre les sports sanguinaires **2.** ANAT antagoniste *m*.
<> *adj* ANAT [muscle] antagoniste.

opportune [ˈɒpətjuːn] *adj* *fml* **1.** [coming at the right time] opportun **2.** [suitable for a particular purpose] propice ▪ **the ~ moment** le moment opportun *OR* propice ▪ **this seems an ~ moment to break for coffee** le moment semble propice pour faire une pause-café.

opportunism [ˌɒpəˈtjuːnɪzm] *n* opportunisme *m*.

opportunist [ˌɒpəˈtjuːnɪst] <> *adj* opportuniste.
<> *n* opportuniste *mf*.

opportunistic [ˌɒpətjuːˈnɪstɪk] *adj* opportuniste.

opportunity [ˌɒpəˈtjuːnətɪ] (*pl* **opportunities**) *n* **1.** [chance] occasion *f* ▪ **to have an ~ to do *OR* of doing sthg** avoir l'occasion de faire qqch ▪ **if ever you get the ~** si jamais vous en avez l'occasion ▪ **to give sb an ~ of doing sthg *OR* the ~ to do sthg** donner à qqn l'occasion de faire qqch ▪ **should the ~ arise** si l'occasion se présente ▪ **I took every ~ of travelling** je n'ai manqué aucune occasion de *OR* j'ai saisi toutes les occasions de voyager ▪ **you missed a golden ~** vous avez manqué *OR* laissé passer une occasion en or ▪ **I'll leave at the first *OR* earliest ~** je partirai à la première occasion *OR* dès que l'occasion se présentera ▪ **at every ~** à la moindre occasion **2.** [prospect] perspective *f* ▪ **job opportunities** perspectives d'emploi.

opportunity cost *n* ECON coût *m* d'opportunité *OR* de renoncement.

opposable [əˈpəʊzəbl] *adj* opposable.

oppose [əˈpəʊz] *vt* **1.** [decision, plan, bill etc] s'opposer à, être hostile à ▪ [verbally] parler contre ▪ **the construction of the power station was ~d by local people** la construction de la centrale s'est heurtée à l'hostilité de la population locale **2.** [in contest, fight] s'opposer à ▪ [combat] combattre **3.** [contrast] opposer.

opposed [əˈpəʊzd] *adj* opposé, hostile ▪ **to be ~ to sthg** être opposé *OR* hostile à qqch ▪ **his views are diametrically ~ to mine** il a des idées radicalement opposées aux miennes.
◆ **as opposed to** *prep phr* par opposition à, plutôt que.

opposing [əˈpəʊzɪŋ] *adj* **1.** [army, team] adverse ▪ [factions] qui s'opposent ▪ [party, minority] d'opposition ▪ **they're on ~ sides** ils sont adversaires, ils ne sont pas du même côté **2.** [contrasting - views] opposé, qui s'oppose.

opposite [ˈɒpəzɪt] <> *adj* **1.** [facing] d'en face, opposé ▪ **the ~ side of the road** l'autre côté de la rue ▪ **'see illustration on ~ page'** 'voir illustration ci-contre' **2.** [opposing - direction, position] inverse, opposé ▪ [rival - team] adverse ▪ **the letter-box is at the ~ end of the street** la boîte à lettres se trouve à l'autre

bout de la rue **3.** [conflicting - attitude, character, opinion] contraire, opposé ▪ **his words had just the ~ effect** ses paroles eurent exactement l'effet contraire **4.** BOT opposé **5.** MATHS opposé.
◇ *adv* en face ▪ **the houses ~** les maisons d'en face ▪ **the lady ~** la dame qui habite en face.
◇ *prep* **1.** en face de ▪ **he lives ~ us** il habite en face de chez nous ▪ **our houses are ~ each other** nos maisons se font face *OR* sont en face l'une de l'autre ▪ **they sat ~ each other** ils étaient assis l'un en face de l'autre **2.** CIN & THEAT : **to play ~ sb** donner la réplique à qqn ▪ **she played ~ Richard Burton in many films** elle fut la partenaire de Richard Burton dans de nombreux films **3.** NAUT en face de, à la hauteur de.
◇ *n* opposé *m*, contraire *m* ▪ **she always does the ~ of what she's told** elle fait toujours le contraire de ce qu'on lui dit de faire ▪ **Mary is the complete ~ of her sister** Mary est tout à fait l'opposé de sa sœur.

opposite number *n* homologue *mf*.

opposite sex *n* sexe *m* opposé.

opposition [ˌɒpəˈzɪʃn] ◇ *n* **1.** [physical] opposition *f*, résistance *f* ▪ **the army met with fierce ~** l'armée se heurta à une vive résistance ▪ **the besieged city put up little ~** la ville assiégée n'opposa guère de résistance ▮ [moral] opposition *f* ▪ **in ~ to** en opposition avec ▪ **the plans met with some ~** les projets suscitèrent une certaine opposition *OR* hostilité **2.** POL : **the ~** l'opposition *f* ▪ **Labour spent the 1980s in ~** les travaillistes furent dans l'opposition pendant toutes les années 80 ▶ **the Opposition benches** les bancs *mpl* de l'opposition **3.** [rivals] adversaires *mpl* ▪ SPORT adversaires *mpl* ▪ COMM concurrents *mpl*, concurrence *f* **4.** [contrast] (mise *f* en) opposition *f*.
◇ *comp* [committee, spokesperson etc] de l'opposition.

oppress [əˈpres] *vt* **1.** [tyrannize] opprimer **2.** *lit* [torment - subj: anxiety, atmosphere] accabler, oppresser.

oppressed [əˈprest] *npl* : **the ~** les opprimés *mpl*.

oppression [əˈpreʃn] *n* **1.** [persecution] oppression *f* **2.** [sadness] angoisse *f*, malaise *m*.

oppressive [əˈpresɪv] *adj* **1.** POL [regime, government] oppressif, tyrannique ▪ [law, tax] oppressif **2.** [hard to bear - debt, situation] accablant **3.** [weather] lourd, étouffant ▪ **the heat was ~** il faisait une chaleur accablante.

oppressively [əˈpresɪvlɪ] *adv* d'une manière oppressante *OR* accablante ▪ **it was ~ hot** il faisait une chaleur étouffante *OR* accablante.

oppressor [əˈpresəʳ] *n* oppresseur *m*.

opprobrious [əˈprəʊbrɪəs] *adj fml* **1.** [scornful] méprisant **2.** [shameful] honteux, scandaleux.

opprobrium [əˈprəʊbrɪəm] *n fml* opprobre *m*.

opt [ɒpt] *vi* : **to ~ for sthg** opter pour qqch, choisir qqch ▪ **she ~ed to study maths** elle a choisi d'étudier les maths.
◆ **opt out** *vi insep* **1.** [gen] se désengager, retirer sa participation ▪ **to ~ out of society** rejeter la société ▪ **I'm ~ing out!** ne comptez plus sur moi!, je me retire de la partie! ▪ **many ~ed out of joining the union** beaucoup ont choisi de ne pas adhérer au syndicat **2.** POL [school, hospital] *choisir l'autonomie vis-à-vis des pouvoirs publics.*

optic [ˈɒptɪk] *adj* optique.

optical [ˈɒptɪkl] *adj* [lens] optique ▪ [instrument] optique.

optical character reader *n* lecteur *m* optique de caractères.

optical character recognition *n* reconnaissance *f* optique de caractères.

optical fibre *n* fibre *f* optique.

optical illusion *n* illusion *f OR* effet *m* d'optique.

optician [ɒpˈtɪʃn] *n* opticien *m*, - enne *f* ▪ **at the ~'s** chez l'opticien.

optics [ˈɒptɪks] *n (U)* optique *f*.

optimal [ˈɒptɪml] *adj* optimal.

optimism [ˈɒptɪmɪzm] *n* optimisme *m*.

optimist [ˈɒptɪmɪst] *n* optimiste *mf*.

optimistic [ˌɒptɪˈmɪstɪk] *adj* [person, outlook] optimiste ▪ [period] d'optimisme.

optimistically [ˌɒptɪˈmɪstɪklɪ] *adv* avec optimisme, d'une manière optimiste.

optimize, ise [ˈɒptɪmaɪz] *vt* optimiser, optimaliser.

optimum [ˈɒptɪməm] (*pl* **optimums** *fml OR pl* **optima** [-mə])
◇ *adj* optimum, optimal.
◇ *n* optimum *m*.

option [ˈɒpʃn] *n* **1.** [alternative] choix *m* ▪ **he has no ~** il n'a pas le choix ▪ **I have no ~ but to refuse** je ne peux faire autrement que de refuser ▪ **they were given the ~ of adopting a child** on leur a proposé d'adopter un enfant ▪ **you leave me no ~** vous ne me laissez pas le choix **2.** [possible choice] option *f*, possibilité *f* ▪ **to keep** *OR* **leave one's ~s open** ne pas prendre de décision, ne pas s'engager ▮ SCH (matière *f* à) option *f* ▪ [accessory] option *f* ▪ **power steering is an ~** la direction assistée est en option **3.** COMM & FIN option *f* ▪ **to take an ~ on sthg** prendre une option sur qqch ▪ **Air France have an ~ to buy 15 planes** Air France a une option d'achat sur 15 appareils **4.** COMPUT option *f* ▪ **~ box** boîte *f* des options ▪ **~s menu** menu *m* des options.

optional [ˈɒpʃənl] *adj* **1.** facultatif ▪ **the tinted lenses are ~** les verres teintés sont en option ▶ **~ extra** option *f* ▪ **the radio is an ~ extra** la radio est en option *OR* en supplément **2.** SCH facultatif, optionnel.

optionally [ˈɒpʃənəlɪ] *adv* facultativement.

optometry [ɒpˈtɒmətrɪ] *n* optométrie *f*.

opulence [ˈɒpjʊləns] *n* opulence *f*.

opulent [ˈɒpjʊlənt] *adj* [lifestyle, figure] opulent ▪ [abundant] abondant, luxuriant ▪ [house, clothes] somptueux.

opus [ˈəʊpəs] (*pl* **opuses** *fml OR pl* **opera** [ˈɒpərə]) *n* opus *m*.

or [ɔːʳ] *conj* **1.** [in positive statements] ou ▪ [in negative statements] ni ▪ **I can go today or tomorrow** je peux y aller aujourd'hui ou demain ▪ **have you got any brothers or sisters?** avez-vous des frères et sœurs? ▪ **he never laughs or smiles** il ne rit ni ne sourit jamais ▪ **or so I thought** du moins c'est ce que je pensais ▪ **...or not, as the case may be**...ou non, peut-être **2.** [otherwise - in negative statements] ou ; [- in positive statements] sinon ▪ **she must have some talent or they wouldn't have chosen her** elle doit avoir un certain talent sinon ils ne l'auraient pas choisie.
◆ **or else** ◇ *conj phr* **1.** [otherwise] sinon **2.** [offering an alternative] ou bien.
◇ *adv phr inf* **give us the money, or else...!** donne-nous l'argent, sinon...!
◆ **or no** *conj phr* ou pas ▪ **I'm taking a holiday, work or no work** travail ou pas, je prends des vacances.
◆ **or other** *adv phr* : **we stayed at San something or other** on s'est arrêté à San quelque chose ▪ **somehow or other we made it home** on a fini par réussir à rentrer, Dieu sait comment ▪ **somebody or other said that...** quelqu'un, je ne sais plus qui, a dit que... ▪ **one or other of us will have to go** il faudra bien que l'un de nous s'en aille ▪ **some actress or other** une actrice (quelconque).
◆ **or so** *adv phr* environ ▪ **ten minutes or so** environ dix minutes ▪ **50 kilos or so** 50 kilos environ, dans les 50 kilos.
◆ **or something** *adv phr inf* ou quelque chose comme ça ▪ **are you deaf or something?** t'es sourd ou quoi?
◆ **or what** *adv phr inf* ou quoi.

OR *written abbr of* **Oregon**.

oracle [ˈɒrəkl] *n* oracle *m*.
◆ **Oracle®** *pr n système de télétexte en Grande-Bretagne.*

oracular [ɒˈrækjʊləʳ] *adj liter* prophétique ▪ *fig* sibyllin.

oral [ˈɔːrəl] ◇ *adj* **1.** [spoken] oral ▪ **~ exam** (examen *m*) oral *m* ▪ **~ literature/tradition** littérature *f* /tradition *f* orale **2.** ANAT [of mouth] buccal, oral ▪ **~ sex** rapports *mpl* buccogénitaux ▮ PHARM [medicine] à prendre par voie orale ▪ **~ contraceptive** contraceptif *m* oral **3.** LING [in phonetics] oral.
◇ *n* (examen *m*) oral *m*.

orally [ˈɔːrəlɪ] *adj* **1.** [verbally] oralement, verbalement, de vive voix **2.** SCH oralement ■ MED par voie orale ■ **'to be taken ~'** 'par voie orale' ■ **'not to be taken ~'** 'ne pas avaler'.

orange [ˈɒrɪndʒ] ◇ *n* **1.** [fruit] orange *f* **2.** [drink] boisson *f* à l'orange ■ **vodka and ~** vodka-orange *f* **3.** [colour] orange *m*.
◇ *adj* **1.** [colour] orange *(inv)*, orangé **2.** [taste] d'orange ■ [liqueur, sauce] à l'orange ■ **~ juice** jus *m* d'orange ■ **~ marmalade** marmelade *f* d'orange, confiture *f* d'orange *OR* d'oranges ■ **~ peel** écorce *f* *OR* peau *f* d'orange ; *fig* [cellulite] peau *f* d'orange ■ **~ tree** oranger *m*.

orangeade [ˌɒrɪndʒˈeɪd] *n* [still] orangeade *f* ■ [fizzy] soda *m* à l'orange.

Orange Lodge *n* association *f* d'orangistes.

Orangeman [ˈɒrɪndʒmən] (*pl* **Orangemen** [-mən]) *n* **1.** *UK* HIST Orangiste *m (partisan de la maison d'Orange)* **2.** [in Ireland] Orangiste *m (protestant)*.

orange-peel skin *n* [cellulite] peau *f* d'orange.

orangery [ˈɒrɪndʒərɪ] (*pl* **orangeries**) *n* orangerie *f*.

Orangewoman [ˈɒrɪndʒˌwʊmən] (*pl* **Orangewomen** [-ˌwɪmɪn]) *n* orangiste *f*.

orangewood [ˈɒrɪndʒwʊd] *n* (bois *m* d') oranger *m*.

orang-(o)utan [ɔːˈrʌŋatan], **orang-(o)utang** [ɔːˈræŋatæŋ] *n* orang-outan *m*, orang-outang *m*.

orate [ɔːˈreɪt] *vi fml* [make speech] prononcer un discours ■ [pompously] pérorer, discourir.

oration [ɔːˈreɪʃn] *n* (long) discours *m*, allocution *f* ■ **funeral ~** oraison *f* funèbre.

orator [ˈɒrətəʳ] *n* orateur *m*, - trice *f*.

oratorical [ˌɒrəˈtɒrɪkl] *adj fml* oratoire.

oratorio [ˌɒrəˈtɔːrɪəʊ] (*pl* **oratorios**) *n* oratorio *m*.

oratory [ˈɒrətrɪ] *n* **1.** [eloquence] art *m* oratoire, éloquence *f* ■ **a superb piece of ~** un superbe morceau de rhétorique **2.** RELIG oratoire *m*.

orb [ɔːb] *n* **1.** [sphere] globe *m* **2.** ASTRON & *lit* orbe *m*.

orbit [ˈɔːbɪt] ◇ *n* **1.** ASTRON orbite *f* ■ **to put a satellite into ~** mettre un satellite sur *OR* en orbite ■ **in ~** en orbite **2.** [influence] orbite *f* ■ **the countries within Washington's ~** les pays qui se situent dans la sphère d'influence de Washington ■ **that's not within the ~ of my responsibility** cela n'est pas de mon ressort, cela ne relève pas de ma responsabilité **3.** ANAT & PHYS [of eye, electron] orbite *f*.
◇ *vt* [subj: planet, comet] graviter *OR* tourner autour de ■ [subj: astronaut] : **the first man to ~ the Earth** le premier homme à être placé *OR* mis en orbite autour de la Terre.
◇ *vi* décrire une orbite.

orbital [ˈɔːbɪtl] *adj* orbital ■ **~ motorway** *UK* (autoroute *f*) périphérique *m*.

Orcadian [ɔːˈkeɪdjən] ◇ *adj* des Orcades.
◇ *n* habitant *m*, - e *f* des Orcades.

orchard [ˈɔːtʃəd] *n* verger *m*.

orchestra [ˈɔːkɪstrə] *n* **1.** [band] orchestre *m* **2.** [in theatre, cinema] fauteuils *mpl* d'orchestre, parterre *m*.

orchestral [ɔːˈkestrəl] *adj* d'orchestre, orchestral ■ **~ music** musique *f* orchestrale.

orchestra pit *n* fosse *f* d'orchestre.

orchestra stalls *npl US* = **orchestra** *(sense 2)*.

orchestrate [ˈɔːkɪstreɪt] *vt* MUS & *fig* orchestrer.

orchestration [ˌɔːkeˈstreɪʃn] *n* MUS & *fig* orchestration *f*.

orchid [ˈɔːkɪd] *n* orchidée *f*.

ordain [ɔːˈdeɪn] *vt* **1.** RELIG ordonner ■ **to be ~ed priest** être ordonné prêtre **2.** [order] ordonner, décréter ■ [declare] décréter, déclarer ■ **it is ~ed in the Bible** c'est la Bible qui le dit | [decide] dicter, décider ■ **fate ~ed that they should meet** le destin a voulu qu'ils se rencontrent.

ordainment [ɔːˈdeɪnmənt] *n* ordination *f*.

ordeal [ɔːˈdiːl] *n* **1.** épreuve *f*, calvaire *m* ■ **to undergo an ~** subir une épreuve ■ **she has been through some terrible ~s** elle a traversé des moments très difficiles ■ **I always find family reunions an ~** j'ai toujours considéré les réunions de famille comme un (véritable) calvaire **2.** HIST ordalie *f*, épreuve *f* judiciaire ■ **~ by fire** épreuve *f* du feu.

order [ˈɔːdəʳ] ◇ *n* **1.** [sequence, arrangement] ordre *m* ■ **in alphabetical/chronological ~** par ordre alphabétique/chronologique ■ **let's do things in ~** faisons les choses en ordre ■ **they have two boys and a girl, in that ~** ils ont deux garçons et une fille, dans cet ordre ■ **in ~ of appearance** THEAT par ordre d'entrée en scène ; CIN & TV par ordre d'apparition à l'écran
2. [organization, tidiness] ordre *m* ■ **to put one's affairs/books in ~** mettre de l'ordre dans ses affaires/livres, ranger ses affaires/livres
3. [command] ordre *m* ■ [instruction] instruction *f* ■ **to give sb ~s to do sthg** ordonner à qqn de faire qqch ■ **Harry loves giving ~s** Harry adore donner des ordres ■ **we have ~s to wait here** on a reçu l'ordre d'attendre ici ■ **I'm just following ~s** je ne fais qu'exécuter les ordres ■ **I don't have to take ~s from you** je n'ai pas d'ordres à recevoir de vous ■ **~s are ~s** les ordres sont les ordres ■ **on my ~, line up in twos** à mon commandement, mettez-vous en rangs par deux ■ **on doctor's ~s** sur ordre du médecin | MIL ordre *m*, consigne *f*
4. COMM [request for goods] commande *f* ■ **to place an ~ for sthg** passer (une) commande de qqch ■ **the books are on ~** les livres ont été commandés | [goods ordered] marchandises *fpl* commandées ■ **your ~ has now arrived** votre commande est arrivée | [in restaurant] : **can I take your ~?** avez-vous choisi? ■ *US* [portion] part *f* ■ **an ~ of French fries** une portion de frites
5. FIN : **(money) ~** mandat *m* ■ **pay to the ~ of A. Jones** payez à l'ordre de A. Jones
6. LAW ordonnance *f*, arrêté *m*
7. [discipline, rule] ordre *m*, discipline *f* ■ **to keep ~** [police] maintenir l'ordre ; SCH maintenir la discipline ■ **children need to be kept in ~** les enfants ont besoin de discipline ■ **to restore ~** rétablir l'ordre | [in meeting] ordre *m* ■ **to call sb to ~** rappeler qqn à l'ordre ■ **to be ruled out of ~** être en infraction avec le règlement ■ **~!** de l'ordre! ■ **he's out of ~** ce qu'il a dit/fait était déplacé
8. [system] ordre *m* établi ■ **in the ~ of things** dans l'ordre des choses ▶ **~ of the day** POL ordre *m* du jour ■ **to be the ~ of the day** [common] être à l'ordre du jour ; [fashionable] être au goût du jour
9. [functioning state] : **in working ~** en état de marche *OR* de fonctionnement
10. [class] classe *f*, ordre *m* ■ [rank] ordre *m* ■ **research work of the highest ~** un travail de recherche de tout premier ordre ■ **a crook of the first ~** *UK* un escroc de grande envergure | [kind] espèce *f*, genre *m*
11. [decoration] ordre *m* ■ **the Order of the Garter/of Merit** l'ordre de la Jarretière/du Mérite
12. RELIG ordre *m*
13. ARCHIT, BOT & ZOOL ordre *m*.
◇ *vt* **1.** [command] ordonner ■ **to ~ sb to do sthg** ordonner à qqn de faire qqch ■ **the doctor ~ed him to rest for three weeks** le médecin lui a prescrit trois semaines de repos ■ **the government ~ed an inquiry into the disaster** le gouvernement a ordonné l'ouverture d'une enquête sur la catastrophe ■ **he was ~ed to pay costs** LAW il a été condamné aux dépens ■ **we were ~ed out of the room** on nous a ordonné de quitter la pièce | MIL : **to ~ sb to do sthg** donner l'ordre à qqn de faire qqch ■ **the troops were ~ed to the Mediterranean** les troupes ont reçu l'ordre de gagner la Méditerranée
2. COMM [meal, goods] commander
3. [organize - society] organiser ; [- ideas, thoughts] mettre de l'ordre dans ; [- affairs] régler, mettre en ordre ■ **a peaceful, well-~ed existence** une existence paisible et bien réglée
4. BOT & ZOOL classer.
◇ *vi* commander, passer une commande ■ **would you like to ~ now?** [in restaurant] voulez-vous commander maintenant?
◆ **by order of** *prep phr* par ordre de ■ **by ~ of the Court** sur décision du tribunal.
◆ **in order** *adj phr* **1.** [valid] en règle

2. [acceptable] approprié, admissible ▪ **it is quite in ~ for you to leave** rien ne s'oppose à ce que vous partiez ▪ **I think lunch is in ~** je pense qu'il est temps de faire une pause pour le déjeuner ▪ **an apology is in ~** des excuses s'imposent.

◆ **in order that** *conj phr* afin que.

◆ **in order to** *conj phr* afin de ▪ **in ~ not to upset you** pour éviter de vous faire de la peine.

◆ **in the order of** *UK*, **of the order of** *UK*, **on the order of** *US prep phr* de l'ordre de.

◆ **out of order** *adj phr* [machine, TV] en panne ▪ [phone] en dérangement ▪ **'out of ~'** 'hors service', 'en panne'.

◆ **to order** *adv phr* sur commande ▪ **he had a suit made to ~** il s'est fait faire un costume sur mesures.

◆ **order about** *UK*, **order around** *vt sep* commander ▪ **he likes ~ing people about** il adore régenter son monde ▪ **I refuse to be ~ed about!** je n'ai pas d'ordres à recevoir!
Voir module d'usage

order book *n* carnet *m* de commandes.

order form *n* bon *m* de commande.

orderliness ['ɔːdəlɪnɪs] *n* **1.** [of room, desk] (bon) ordre *m* **2.** [of person, lifestyle, behaviour] méticulosité *f* **3.** [of crowd] discipline *f*, bonne conduite *f*.

orderly ['ɔːdəlɪ] (*pl* **orderlies**) ◇ *adj* **1.** [tidy - room] ordonné, rangé **2.** [organized - person, mind, lifestyle] ordonné, méthodique ▪ **try to work in an ~ way** essayez de travailler méthodiquement **3.** [well-behaved] ordonné, discipliné ▪ **in case of fire, leave the building in an ~ fashion** en cas d'incendie, quitter les lieux sans précipitation.
◇ *n* **1.** MIL officier *m* d'ordonnance **2.** MED aide-infirmier *m*.

order number *n* numéro *m* de commande.

order paper *n* POL (feuille *f* de l')ordre *m* du jour.

ordinal ['ɔːdɪnl] ◇ *adj* ordinal.
◇ *n* ordinal *m*.

ordinance ['ɔːdɪnəns] *n* ordonnance *f*, décret *m*.

ordinand ['ɔːdɪnænd] *n* ordinand *m*.

ordinarily [*UK* 'ɔːdənrəlɪ, *US* ,ɔːrdn'erəlɪ] *adv* **1.** [in an ordinary way] ordinairement, d'ordinaire ▪ **the questions were more than ~ difficult** les questions étaient plus difficiles que d'ordinaire *OR* qu'à l'accoutumée **2.** [normally] normalement, en temps normal.

ordinary ['ɔːdənrɪ] ◇ *adj* **1.** [usual] ordinaire, habituel ▪ [normal] normal ▪ **the ~ run of things** le cours ordinaire *OR* normal des événements **2.** [average] ordinaire, moyen ▪ **Paul was just an ~ guy before he got involved in films** *inf* Paul était un type comme les autres avant de faire du cinéma ▪ **Miss Brodie was no ~ teacher** Miss Brodie était un professeur peu banal *OR* qui sortait de l'ordinaire **3.** [commonplace] ordinaire, quelconque *pej* ▪ **it's a very ~-looking car** c'est une voiture qui n'a rien de spécial ▪ **she's a very ~-looking girl** c'est une fille quelconque.
◇ *n* **1.** RELIG : **the Ordinary of the mass** l'ordinaire *m* de la messe **2.** ADMIN : **physician in ~ to the king** *UK* médecin *m* (attitré) du roi.

◆ **out of the ordinary** *adj phr* : **as a pianist, she's really out of the ~** c'est vraiment une pianiste exceptionnelle *OR* hors du commun ▪ **nothing out of the ~ ever happens here** il ne se passe jamais rien de bien extraordinaire ici.

ordinary degree *n UK* ≃ licence *f* sans mention *OR* avec la mention passable.

Ordinary level = O-level.

ordinary seaman *n UK* matelot *m* breveté.

ordinary share *n* action *f* ordinaire.

ordinate ['ɔːdənət] *n* ordonnée *f*.

ordination [,ɔːdɪ'neɪʃn] *n* ordination *f*.

ordnance ['ɔːdnəns] *n* **1.** [supplies] (service *m* de l')équipement *m* militaire **2.** [artillery] artillerie *f*.

ordnance corps *n* service *m* du matériel, ≃ train *m*.

ordnance factory *n* usine *f* d'artillerie.

Ordnance Survey *pr n UK* service *m* national de cartographie, ≃ IGN *m* ▪ **~ map** carte *f* d'état-major.

ore [ɔːr] *n* minerai *m* ▪ **copper ~** minerai de cuivre.

oregano [*UK* ,ɒrɪ'gɑːnəʊ, *US* ə'regənəʊ] *n* BOT & CULIN origan *m*.

Oregon ['ɒrɪgən] *pr n* Oregon *m* ▪ **in ~** dans l'Oregon.

Orestes [ɒ'restiːz] *pr n* Oreste.

organ ['ɔːgən] *n* **1.** MUS orgue *m* ▪ [large] (grandes) orgues *fpl* **2.** ANAT organe *m* ▪ *euph* [penis] membre *m* **3.** *fig* [means] organe *m*, instrument *m* ▪ [mouthpiece] organe *m*, porte-parole *m inv*.

organ grinder *n* joueur *m*, - euse *f* d'orgue de Barbarie.

organic [ɔː'gænɪk] *adj* **1.** BIOL & CHEM organique ▪ **~ life** vie *f* organique **2.** [natural - produce] naturel, biologique **3.** [structural] organique ▪ [fundamental] organique, fondamental ▪ **~ change** changement organique.

organically [ɔː'gænɪklɪ] *adv* **1.** BIOL & CHEM organiquement ▪ **~ grown** cultivé sans engrais chimiques, biologique **2.** *fig* organiquement.

organic chemistry *n* chimie *f* organique.

organic farming *n* culture *f* biologique.

organism ['ɔːgənɪzm] *n* BIOL organisme *m*.

organist ['ɔːgənɪst] *n* organiste *mf*.

organization [,ɔːgənaɪ'zeɪʃn] *n* **1.** [organizing] organisation *f* ▶ **~ and method** INDUST organisation *f* scientifique du travail, OST *f* **2.** [association] organisation *f*, association *f* ▪ [official body] organisme *m*, organisation *f* ▪ **a charitable ~** une œuvre de bienfaisance **3.** ADMIN [personnel] cadres *mpl*.

organizational [,ɔːgənaɪ'zeɪʃnl] *adj* [skills, methods] organisationnel, d'organisation ▪ [expenses] d'organisation ▪ [change] dans l'organisation, structurel ▪ **the concert turned out to be an ~ nightmare** l'organisation du concert fut un véritable cauchemar.

organization chart *n* organigramme *m*.

organize, ise ['ɔːgənaɪz] ◇ *vt* **1.** [sort out] organiser ▪ **to get ~d** s'organiser ▪ **I've ~d a visit to a dairy for them** j'ai

GIVING ORDERS

Reculez un peu, s'il vous plaît. Move back a little, please.

Va me chercher mes lunettes, veux-tu ? Go and get my glasses, will you?

Ne rentre pas dans la cuisine, le sol est mouillé. Don't go into the kitchen, the floor's wet.

Tournez à gauche au feu rouge. Turn left at the lights.

Un peu de silence, s'il vous plaît ! Quiet, please!

Pose ça tout de suite, tu m'entends ! Put that down now, do you hear me!

Tu m'appelles dès qu'il arrive, d'accord ? Call me as soon as he arrives, OK?

Sortez (d'ici) ! Get out of here!

organisé la visite d'une laiterie à leur intention ■ **she's good at organizing people** elle est douée pour la gestion du personnel ■ **who's organizing the drinks?** qui est-ce qui s'occupe des boissons? **2.** INDUST syndiquer.
◇ *vi* INDUST se syndiquer.

organized ['ɔːgənaɪzd] *adj* **1.** [trip] organisé ■ **we went on an ~ tour of Scottish castles** nous avons visité les châteaux écossais en voyage organisé **2.** [unionized] syndiqué ■ **~ labour** main-d'œuvre *f* syndiquée **3.** [orderly] organisé ■ [methodical] méthodique.

organized crime *n* le crime organisé.

organized religion *n* religion *f* organisée.

organizer ['ɔːgənaɪzəʳ] *n* **1.** [person] organisateur *m*, - trice *f* **2.** [diary] agenda *m* modulaire, Filofax® *m* **3.** COMPUT organiseur *m*, agenda *m* électronique **4.** BIOL organisateur *m*.

organ loft *n* tribune *f* d'orgue.

organotherapy [ˌɔːgənəʊ'θerəpɪ] *n* opothérapie *f*.

organ stop *n* jeu *m* d'orgue.

organza [ɔː'gænzə] *n* organdi *m*.

orgasm ['ɔːgæzm] *n* orgasme *m*.

orgasmic [ɔː'gæzmɪk] *adj* orgasmique, orgastique.

orgiastic [ˌɔːdʒɪ'æstɪk] *adj* orgiaque.

orgy ['ɔːdʒɪ] (*pl* **orgies**) *n* orgie *f* ■ **a drunken ~** une beuverie ■ **an ~ of killing** *fig* une orgie de meurtres.

orient ['ɔːrɪənt] *vt* orienter ■ **to ~ o.s.** s'orienter ■ **our firm is very much ~ed towards the American market** notre société est très orientée vers le marché américain.

Orient ['ɔːrɪənt] *pr n* : **the ~** l'Orient *m*.

oriental [ˌɔːrɪ'entl] *adj* oriental ■ **~ rug** tapis *m* d'Orient.
◆ **Oriental** *n* Asiatique *mf (attention : le substantif "Oriental" est considéré comme raciste).*

orientalist [ˌɔːrɪ'entəlɪst] *n* orientaliste *mf*.

orientate ['ɔːrɪenteɪt] *vt UK* orienter ■ **to ~ o.s.** s'orienter ■ **the course is very much ~d towards the sciences** le cours est très orienté vers OR axé sur les sciences.

-orientated ['ɔːrɪenteɪtɪd] *UK* = **-oriented**.

orientation [ˌɔːrɪen'teɪʃn] *n* orientation *f*.

oriented ['ɔːrɪentɪd] *adj* orienté.

-oriented *in cpds* orienté vers..., axé sur... ■ **ours is a money~ society** c'est l'argent qui mène notre société ■ **pupil~ teaching** enseignement adapté aux besoins des élèves.

orienteer [ˌɔːrɪen'tɪəʳ] *n* orienteur *m*, - euse *f*.

orienteering [ˌɔːrɪen'tɪərɪŋ] *n* course *f* d'orientation.

orifice ['ɒrɪfɪs] *n* orifice *m*.

origami [ˌɒrɪ'gɑːmɪ] *n* origami *m*.

origin ['ɒrɪdʒɪn] *n* **1.** [source] origine *f* ■ **the ~ of the Nile** la source du Nil ■ **country of ~** pays *m* d'origine ■ **of unknown ~** d'origine inconnue ■ **the present troubles have their ~ in the proposed land reform** le projet de réforme agraire est à l'origine des troubles actuels ■ **the song is Celtic in ~** la chanson est d'origine celte ➲ **'The Origin of Species'** ***Darwin*** 'De l'origine des espèces' **2.** [ancestry] origine *f* ■ **he is of Canadian ~** il est d'origine canadienne ■ **they can trace their ~s back to the time of the Norman conquest** ils ont réussi à remonter dans leur arbre généalogique jusqu'à l'époque de la conquête normande.

original [ɒ'rɪdʒɪnl] ◇ *adj* **1.** [initial] premier, d'origine, initial ■ **the ~ meaning of the word** le sens originel du mot ■ **my ~ intention was to drive there** ma première intention OR mon intention initiale était d'y aller en voiture ■ **most of the ~ 600 copies have been destroyed** la plupart des 600 exemplaires originaux ont été détruits ■ **~ edition** édition originale **2.** [unusual] original ■ **he has some ~ ideas** il a des idées originales ■ **she has an ~ approach to child-rearing** sa conception de l'éducation est originale ▮ [strange] singulier **3.** [new - play, writing] original, inédit.
◇ *n* **1.** [painting, book] original *m* ■ **the film was shown in the ~** le film a été projeté en version originale ■ **I prefer to read Proust in the ~** je préfère lire Proust dans le texte **2.** [model - of hero, character] : **Betty was the ~ of the novel's heroine** Betty inspira le personnage de l'héroïne du roman **3.** [unusual person] original *m*, - e *f*, excentrique *mf*.

originality [əˌrɪdʒə'nælətɪ] (*pl* **originalities**) *n* originalité *f*.

originally [ə'rɪdʒənəlɪ] *adv* **1.** [initially] à l'origine, au début, initialement **2.** [unusually, inventively] d'une façon OR d'une manière originale, originalement.

original sin *n* péché *m* originel.

originate [ə'rɪdʒəneɪt] ◇ *vi* [idea, rumour] : **to ~ in** avoir OR trouver son origine dans ■ **to ~ from** tirer son origine de ■ **this concept ~s from Freudian psychology** ce concept est issu de la psychologie freudienne ■ **the conflict ~d in the towns** le conflit est né dans les villes ■ **I wonder how that saying ~d** je me demande d'où vient ce dicton ▮ [goods] provenir ■ **the cocaine ~s from South America** la cocaïne provient d'Amérique du Sud ▮ [person] : **he ~s from Sydney** il est originaire de Sydney.
◇ *vt* [give rise to] être à l'origine de, donner naissance à ■ [be author of] être l'auteur de.

origination [əˌrɪdʒə'neɪʃn] *n* création *f*.

originator [ə'rɪdʒəneɪtəʳ] *n* [of crime] auteur *m* ■ [of idea] initiateur *m*, - trice *f*, auteur *m*.

Orinoco [ˌɒrɪ'nəʊkəʊ] *pr n* : **the (River) ~** l'Orénoque *m*.

oriole ['ɔːrɪəʊl] *n* loriot *m*.

Orion [ə'raɪən] *pr n* Orion.

Orkney Islands ['ɔːknɪ-], **Orkneys** ['ɔːknɪz] *pr npl* : **the ~** les Orcades *fpl* ■ **in the ~** dans les Orcades.

Orlon® ['ɔːlɒn] ◇ *n* Orlon® *m*.
◇ *comp* en Orlon.

ormolu ['ɔːməluː] ◇ *n* chrysocale *m*, bronze *m* doré.
◇ *comp* [clock] en chrysocale, en bronze doré.

Ormuz [ɔː'muːz] = **Hormuz**.

ornament ◇ *n* ['ɔːnəmənt] **1.** [decorative object] objet *m* décoratif, bibelot *m* ■ [jewellery] colifichet *m* **2.** [embellishment] ornement *m* ■ **rich in ~** richement orné **3.** MUS ornement *m*.
◇ *vt* ['ɔːnəment] orner ■ **his style is highly ~ed** il a un style très fleuri.

ornamental [ˌɔːnə'mentl] *adj* [decorative] ornemental, décoratif ■ [plant] ornemental ■ [garden] d'agrément.

ornamentation [ˌɔːnəmen'teɪʃn] *n* ornementation *f*.

ornate [ɔː'neɪt] *adj* [decoration] (très) orné ■ [style] orné, fleuri ■ [lettering] orné.

ornately [ɔː'neɪtlɪ] *adv* d'une façon très ornée ■ **~ decorated room** pièce richement décorée.

ornery ['ɔːnərɪ] *adj US inf* **1.** [nasty] méchant ■ **an ~ trick** un sale tour **2.** [stubborn] obstiné, entêté.

ornithologist [ˌɔːnɪ'θɒlədʒɪst] *n* ornithologiste *mf*, ornithologue *mf*.

ornithology [ˌɔːnɪ'θɒlədʒɪ] *n* ornithologie *f*.

orphan ['ɔːfn] ◇ *n* **1.** [person] orphelin *m*, - e *f* ■ **to be left an ~** se retrouver OR devenir orphelin **2.** TYPO ligne *f* orpheline.
◇ *adj* orphelin.
◇ *vt* : **to be ~ed** se retrouver OR devenir orphelin.

orphanage ['ɔːfənɪdʒ] *n* orphelinat *m*.

Orpheus ['ɔːfɪəs] *pr n* Orphée ■ **'~ in the Underworld'** ***Offenbach*** 'Orphée aux enfers'.

orthodontics [ˌɔːθə'dɒntɪks] *n (U)* orthodontie *f*.

orthodontist [ˌɔːθə'dɒntɪst] *n* orthodontiste *mf*.

orthodox ['ɔːθədɒks] *adj* orthodoxe.

Orthodox Church *n* : **the ~** l'Église *f* orthodoxe.

orthodoxy ['ɔːθədɒksɪ] (*pl* **orthodoxies**) *n* orthodoxie *f*.

orthographic(al) [ˌɔːθə'græfɪk(l)] *adj* orthographique.

orthography [ɔ:'θɒgrəfɪ] *n* orthographe *f*.

orthopaedic *UK*, **orthopedic** [,ɔ:θə'pi:dɪk] *adj* orthopédique ■ **~ surgeon** (chirurgien *m*, - enne *f*) orthopédiste *mf*.

orthopaedics *UK*, **orthopedics** [,ɔ:θə'pi:dɪks] *n (U)* orthopédie *f*.

orthopaedist *UK*, **orthopedist** [,ɔ:θə'pi:dɪst] *n* orthopédiste *mf*.

oryx ['ɒrɪks] (*pl inv OR pl* **oryxes**) *n* oryx *m*.

O/S *written abbr of* **out of stock**.

Oscar ['ɒskər] *n* CIN Oscar *m*.

oscillate ['ɒsɪleɪt] ◇ *vi* **1.** ELEC & PHYS osciller **2.** [person] osciller.
◇ *vt* faire osciller.

oscillation [,ɒsɪ'leɪʃn] *n* oscillation *f*.

oscillator ['ɒsɪleɪtər] *n* oscillateur *m*.

oscilloscope [ɒ'sɪləskəʊp] *n* oscilloscope *m*.

osculate ['ɒskjʊleɪt] *UK hum* ◇ *vt* donner un baiser à, embrasser.
◇ *vi* s'embrasser.

osier ['əʊzɪər] *n* osier *m*.

osmose ['ɒzməʊs] *vi* subir une osmose.

osmosis [ɒz'məʊsɪs] *n* osmose *f*.

osprey ['ɒsprɪ] *n* [bird] balbuzard *m* ■ [feather] aigrette *f*.

osseous ['ɒsɪəs] *adj* osseux.

ossicle ['ɒsɪkl] *n* osselet *m*.

ossify ['ɒsɪfaɪ] (*pret & pp* **ossified**) ◇ *vt* ossifier.
◇ *vi* s'ossifier.

Ostend [ɒs'tend] *pr n* Ostende.

ostensible [ɒ'stensəbl] *adj* [apparent] apparent ■ [pretended] prétendu ■ [so-called] soi-disant *(inv)* ■ **her ~ reason for not coming was illness** elle a prétendu être malade pour éviter de venir.

ostensibly [ɒ'stensəblɪ] *adv* [apparently] apparemment ■ [supposedly] prétendument, soi-disant ■ **~ they are diplomats** ils se font passer pour des diplomates ‖ [on the pretext] : **he left early, ~ because he was sick** il est parti tôt, prétextant une indisposition.

ostentation [,ɒstən'teɪʃn] *n* ostentation *f*.

ostentatious [,ɒstən'teɪʃəs] *adj* **1.** [showy - display, appearance, decor] ostentatoire, plein d'ostentation ■ [manner, behaviour] prétentieux, ostentatoire **2.** [exaggerated] exagéré, surfait.

ostentatiously [,ɒstən'teɪʃəslɪ] *adv* avec ostentation.

osteoarthritis [,ɒstɪəʊɑ:'θraɪtɪs] *n* ostéo-arthrite *f*.

osteopath ['ɒstɪəpæθ] *n* ostéopathe *mf*.

osteopathy [,ɒstɪ'ɒpəθɪ] *n* ostéopathie *f*.

osteoporosis [,ɒstɪəʊpɔ:'rəʊsɪs] *n* ostéoporose *f*.

ostler ['ɒslər] *n UK arch* valet *m* d'écurie.

ostracism ['ɒstrəsɪzm] *n* ostracisme *m*.

ostracize, ise ['ɒstrəsaɪz] *vt* frapper d'ostracisme, ostraciser ■ **he was ~d by his workmates** ses collègues l'ont mis en quarantaine.

ostrich ['ɒstrɪtʃ] *n* autruche *f*.

Othello [ə'θeləʊ] *pr n* Othello.

other ['ʌðər] ◇ *adj* **1.** [different] autre, différent ■ **it's the same in ~ countries** c'est la même chose dans les autres pays ■ **I had no ~ choice** je n'avais pas le choix *OR* pas d'autre solution ■ **by ~ means** par d'autres moyens ■ **he doesn't respect ~ people's property** il ne respecte pas le bien d'autrui ■ **it always happens to ~ people** cela n'arrive qu'aux autres ■ **can't we discuss it some ~ time?** on ne peut pas en parler plus tard? ■ **in ~ times** autrefois, à une autre époque **2.** [second of two] autre ■ **give me the ~ one** donnez-moi l'autre **3.** [additional] autre ■ **some ~ people came** d'autres personnes sont arrivées **4.** [remaining] autre ■ **the ~ three men** les trois autres hommes **5.** [in expressions of time] autre **6.** [opposite] : **on the ~ side of the room/of the river** de l'autre côté de la pièce/de la rivière.
◇ *pron* **1.** [additional person, thing] autre ■ **some succeed, ~s fail** certains réussissent, d'autres échouent **2.** [opposite, far end] autre **3.** [related person] autre.
◇ *n* [person, thing] autre *mf* ■ **the ~** PHILOS l'autre ■ **politicians, industrialists and ~s** les hommes politiques, les industriels et les autres ■ **can you show me some ~s?** pouvez-vous m'en montrer d'autres?
◆ **other than** ◇ *conj phr* **1.** [apart from, except] autrement que ■ **we had no alternative ~ than to accept their offer** nous n'avions pas d'autre possibilité que celle d'accepter leur offre **2.** [differently from] différemment de ■ **she can't be ~ than she is** elle est comme ça, c'est tout.
◇ *prep phr* sauf, à part ■ **~ than that** à part cela.

otherness ['ʌðənɪs] *n* [difference] altérité *f*, différence *f* ■ [strangeness] étrangeté *f*.

otherwise ['ʌðəwaɪz] ◇ *adv* **1.** [differently] autrement ■ **she is ~ engaged** elle a d'autres engagements ■ **we'll have to invite everyone, we can hardly do ~** nous devrons inviter tout le monde, il nous serait difficile de faire autrement ■ **except where ~ stated** [on form] sauf indication contraire **2.** [in other respects] autrement, à part cela ■ [in other circumstances] sinon, autrement ■ **an ~ excellent performance** une interprétation par ailleurs excellente **3.** [in other words] autrement ■ **Louis XIV, ~ known as the Sun King** Louis XIV, surnommé le Roi-Soleil **4.** [in contrast, opposition] : **through diplomatic channels or ~** par voie diplomatique ou autre.
◇ *conj* [or else] sinon, autrement.
◇ *adj* autre.
◆ **or otherwise** *adv phr* : **it is of no interest, financial or ~** ça ne présente aucun intérêt, que ce soit financier ou autre.

otherworldly [,ʌðə'wɜ:ldlɪ] *adj* **1.** [unrealistic] peu réaliste **2.** [mystical] mystique **3.** [ethereal] éthéré.

otiose ['əʊtɪəʊs] *adj fml* oiseux, inutile.

OTT (*abbrev of* **over-the-top**) *adj UK inf* **that's a bit ~!** c'est pousser le bouchon un peu loin!, c'est un peu fort!

otter ['ɒtər] *n* loutre *f*.

ottoman ['ɒtəmən] *n* **1.** [seat] ottomane *f* **2.** [fabric] ottoman *m*.
◆ **Ottoman** ◇ *n* Ottoman *m*, - e *f*.
◇ *adj* ottoman.

ouch [aʊtʃ] *interj* : **~!** aïe!, ouille!, ouïe!

ought[1] [ɔ:t] *modal vb* **1.** [indicating morally right action] : **you ~ to tell her** vous devriez le lui dire ■ **she thought she ~ to tell you** elle a pensé qu'il valait mieux te le dire ‖ [indicating sensible or advisable action] : **perhaps we ~ to discuss this further** peut-être devrions-nous en discuter plus longuement ■ **I really ~ to be going** il faut vraiment que je m'en aille ■ **do you think I ~?** *fml* pensez-vous que je doive le faire? ■ **that's a nice car - it ~ to be, it cost me a fortune!** c'est une belle voiture - j'espère bien, elle m'a coûté une fortune! **2.** [expressing expectation, likelihood] : **they ~ to be home now** à l'heure qu'il est, ils devraient être rentrés **3.** [followed by 'to have'] : **you ~ to have told me!** vous auriez dû me le dire! ■ **you ~ to have seen her!** si vous l'aviez vue!, il fallait la voir! ■ **they ~ not to have been allowed in** on n'aurait pas dû les laisser entrer.

ought[2] [ɔ:t] = **aught**.

oughta ['ɔ:tə] *US inf* = **ought to**.

oughtn't [ɔ:tnt] = **ought not**.

Ouija® ['wi:dʒə] *n* : **~ (board)** oui-ja *m inv*.

ounce [aʊns] *n* **1.** [weight] once *f* **2.** *fig* **there isn't an ~ of truth in what she says** il n'y a pas une once de vérité dans ce qu'elle raconte ■ **you haven't got an ~ of common sense** tu n'as pas (pour) deux sous de bon sens ■ **it took every ~ of strength she had** cela lui a demandé toutes ses forces **3.** ZOOL once *f*.

our ['aʊər] *det* notre *(sg)*, nos *(pl)* ■ **this is our house** cette maison est à nous ■ **we have a car of ~ own** nous avons une voiture à nous ■ **have you seen ~ Peter?** *inf* avez-vous vu Peter?

Our Father *n* [prayer] Notre Père *m*.

ours ['auəz] *pron* le nôtre *m*, la nôtre *f*, les nôtres *mf pl* ■ **that house is ~** [we live there] cette maison est la nôtre ; [we own it] cette maison est à nous *OR* nous appartient ■ **it's ~ to spend as we like** nous pouvons le dépenser comme nous voulons ■ **it's all ~!** tout cela nous appartient! ■ **~ was a curious relationship** nous avions des rapports assez bizarres ■ **~ is a big family** nous sommes une grande famille ■ **it must be one of ~** ce doit être un des nôtres ■ **she's a friend of ~** c'est une de nos amies ■ **those damned neighbours of ~** *inf* nos fichus voisins.

ourself [auə'self] *pron fml* [regal or editorial plural] nous-même.

ourselves [auə'selvz] *pron* **1.** [reflexive use] nous ■ **we enjoyed ~** nous nous sommes bien amusés ■ **we built ~ a log cabin** nous avons construit une cabane en rondins ■ **we said to ~, why not wait here?** nous nous sommes dit *OR* on s'est dit : pourquoi ne pas attendre ici? **2.** [emphatic use] nous-mêmes ■ **we ~ have much to learn** nous-mêmes avons beaucoup à apprendre ■ **(all) by ~** tout seuls ■ **we had the flat to ~** nous avions l'appartement pour nous tout seuls **3.** [replacing 'us'] nous-mêmes.

oust [aust] *vt* **1.** [opponent, rival] évincer, chasser ■ **the president was ~ed from power** le président a été évincé du pouvoir **2.** [tenant, squatter] déloger, expulser ■ [landowner] déposséder.

ouster ['austər] *n* **1.** LAW dépossession *f*, éviction *f* illicite **2.** *US* [from country] expulsion *f* ■ [from office] renvoi *m*.

out [aut] ◇ *adv*

A.

1. [indicating movement from inside to outside] dehors ■ **to go ~** sortir ■ **she ran/limped/strolled ~** elle est sortie en courant/en boîtant/sans se presser ■ **I met her on my way ~** je l'ai rencontrée en sortant ■ **I had my camera ~ ready** j'avais sorti mon appareil

2. [away from home, office etc] : **Mr Powell's ~, do you want to leave a message?** M. Powell est sorti, voulez-vous laisser un message? ■ **a search party is ~ looking for them** une équipe de secours est partie à leur recherche ■ **to eat ~** aller au restaurant ■ **he stayed ~ all night** il n'est pas rentré de la nuit ■ **the children are playing ~ in the street** les enfants jouent dans la rue

3. [no longer attending hospital, school etc] sorti ■ **what time do you get ~ of school?** à quelle heure sors-tu de l'école?

4. [indicating view from inside] : **I stared ~ of the window** je regardais par la fenêtre ■ **the bedroom looks ~ onto open fields** la chambre donne sur les champs

5. [in the open air] dehors

6. [indicating distance from land, centre, town etc] : **on the trip ~** à l'aller ■ **they live a long way ~** ils habitent loin du centre ■ **she's ~ in Africa** elle est en Afrique

7. [indicating extended position] : **he lay stretched ~ on the bed** il était allongé (de tout son long) sur le lit ■ **hold your arms/your hand ~** tendez les bras/la main

B.

1. [indicating distribution] : **she handed ~ some photocopies** elle a distribué des photocopies

2. [indicating source of light, smell, sound etc] : **it gives ~ a lot of heat** ça dégage beaucoup de chaleur

3. [loudly, audibly] : **read ~ the first paragraph** lisez le premier paragraphe à haute voix

C.

1. [indicating exclusion or rejection] : **'keep ~'** 'défense d'entrer', 'entrée interdite' ■ **throw him ~!** jetez-le dehors!

2. [indicating abandonment of activity] : **get ~ before it's too late** abandonne avant qu'il ne soit trop tard ■ **you can count me ~** ne comptez plus sur moi ■ **I want ~!** *inf* je laisse tomber!

3. [extinguished] : **put** *OR* **turn the lights ~** éteignez les lumières

4. [unconscious] : **to knock sb ~** assommer qqn, mettre qqn K-O

5. [indicating disappearance] : **the stain will wash ~** la tache partira au lavage

D.

1. [revealed, made public] : **the secret is ~** le secret a été éventé ■ **word is ~ that he's going to resign** le bruit court qu'il va démissionner ■ **we must stop the news getting ~** nous devons empêcher la nouvelle de s'ébruiter ■ **~ with it!** *inf* alors, t'accouches?

2. [published, on sale] : **the new model will be** *OR* **come ~ next month** le nouveau modèle sort le mois prochain

3. *inf (with superlative) inf* [in existence] : **it's the best computer ~** c'est le meilleur ordinateur qui existe ■ **she's the biggest liar ~** c'est la pire menteuse qui soit

E.

1. SPORT : **~!** TENNIS faute!, out!

2. [of tide] : **the tide's on its way ~** la mer se retire, la marée descend.

◇ *adj* **1.** [flowering] en fleurs **2.** [shining] : **the sun is ~** il y a du soleil ■ **the moon is ~** la lune s'est levée ■ **the stars are ~** on voit les étoiles **3.** [finished] : **before the year is ~** avant la fin de l'année **4.** [on strike] en grève **5.** GAMES & SPORT : **the ball was ~** la balle était dehors *OR* sortie, la balle était faute ■ **she went ~ in the first round** elle a été éliminée au premier tour **6.** [tide] bas **7.** [wrong] : **your calculations are (way) ~, you're (way) ~ in your calculations** vous vous êtes (complètement) trompé dans vos calculs ■ **I've checked the figures but I'm still £50 ~** j'ai vérifié les chiffres mais il manque toujours 50 livres ■ **it's a few inches ~** [too long] c'est trop long de quelques centimètres ; [too short] c'est trop court de quelques centimètres ■ **it's only a few inches ~** c'est bon à quelques centimètres près **8.** *inf* [impossible] : **that plan's ~ because of the weather** ce projet est à l'eau à cause du temps **9.** *inf* [unfashionable] : **long hair's (right) ~** les cheveux longs c'est (carrément) dépassé **10.** [indicating aim, intent] : **to be ~ to do sthg** avoir l'intention de faire qqch ■ **we're ~ to win** nous sommes partis pour gagner ■ **to be ~ for sthg** vouloir qqch ■ **he's just ~ for himself** il ne s'intéresse qu'à lui-même **11.** *inf* [unconscious] : **to be ~** être K-O **12.** [extinguished] éteint **13.** *inf* [openly gay] qui ne cache pas son homosexualité.

◇ *n* **1.** [way of escape] échappatoire *f* **2.** ▻ **in.**

◇ *interj* **1.** [leave] : **~!** dehors! **2.** TELEC : **(over and) ~!** terminé!

◇ *prep inf inf* hors de ■ **she went ~ that door** elle est sortie par cette porte ■ **look ~ the window** regarde par la fenêtre.

◇ *vi lit* **the truth will ~** la vérité se saura.

◇ *vt* : **to ~ sb** révéler l'homosexualité de qqn.

◆ **out and about** *adv phr* : **where have you been? – oh, ~ and about** où étais-tu? – oh, je suis allé faire un tour ■ **~ and about in Amsterdam** dans les rues d'Amsterdam.

◆ **out of** *prep phr* **1.** [indicating movement from inside to outside] hors de ■ **she came ~ of the office** elle est sortie du bureau ■ **he ran/limped/strolled ~ of the office** il est sorti du bureau en courant/en boitant/sans se presser ■ **to look/to fall ~ of a window** regarder/tomber par une fenêtre **2.** [indicating location] : **we drank ~ of china cups** nous avons bu dans des tasses de porcelaine ■ **she works ~ of York** elle opère à partir de York ■ **he's ~ of town** il n'est pas en ville ■ **it's a long way ~ of town** c'est loin de la ville **3.** [indicating source - of feeling, profit, money etc] : **she did well ~ of the deal** elle a trouvé son compte dans l'affaire ■ **you won't get anything ~ of him** vous ne tirerez rien de lui ■ **she paid for it ~ of company funds/~ of her own pocket** elle l'a payé avec l'argent de la société/payé de sa poche **4.** [indicating raw material] : **it's made ~ of mahogany** c'est en acajou ■ **plastic is made ~ of petroleum** on obtient le plastique à partir du pétrole **5.** [indicating motive] par **6.** [indicating previous tendency, habit] : **I've got ~ of the habit** j'en ai perdu l'habitude ■ **try and stay ~ of trouble** essaie d'éviter les ennuis **7.** [lacking] : **I'm ~ of cigarettes** je n'ai plus de cigarettes ■ **~ of work** au chômage **8.** [in proportions, marks etc] sur ■ **ninety-nine times ~ of a hundred** quatre-vingt-dix-neuf fois sur cent ■ **~ of all the people there, only one spoke German** parmi toutes les personnes présentes, une seule parlait allemand **9.** [indicating similarity to book, film etc] : **it was like something ~ of a Fellini film** on se serait cru dans un film de Fellini **10.** [indicating exclusion or rejection] : **he's ~ of the race** il n'est plus dans la course ■ **you keep ~ of this!** mêlez-vous de ce qui vous regarde! **11.** [indicating avoidance] : **come in ~ of the rain** ne reste pas dehors sous la pluie ■ **stay ~ of the sun** ne restez pas au soleil **12.** [indicating recently completed activity] : **a young girl just ~ of university** une jeune fille tout juste sortie de l'université **13.** *phr* **to be ~ of it** *inf* [unaware of situation] être à côté de la plaque ; [drunk] être bourré ■ **I felt really ~ of it** [excluded] je me sentais complètement exclu.

outa ['aʊtə] *US inf* = **out of.**

outage ['aʊtɪdʒ] *n US* **1.** [breakdown] panne *f* ■ ELEC coupure *f* OR panne *f* de courant **2.** [of service] interruption *f* **3.** COMM [missing goods] marchandises *fpl* perdues *(pendant le stockage ou le transport).*

out-and-out *adj* complet, - ète *f*, total ■ **he's an ~ crook** c'est un véritable escroc.

out-and-outer *n US inf* jusqu'au-boutiste *mf*.

outasight ['aʊtəsaɪt] *adj US inf dated* extra, super, génial.

outback ['aʊtbæk] *n Australia* arrière-pays *m inv*, intérieur *m* du pays.

outbalance [ˌaʊt'bæləns] *vt liter* peser plus lourd que ■ *fig* dépasser.

outbid [aʊt'bɪd] (*pret* **outbid**, *pp* **outbid** OR **outbidden** [-'bɪdn], *cont* **outbidding**) *vt* enchérir sur ■ **we were ~ for the Renoir** quelqu'un a surenchéri sur le Renoir et nous n'avons pu l'acheter.

outboard ['aʊtbɔ:d] ◇ *adj* [position, direction] hors-bord ■ **~ motor** moteur *m* hors-bord.
◇ *n* [motor, boat] hors-bord *m inv*.

outbound ['aʊtbaʊnd] *adj* qui quitte le centre-ville.

outbreak ['aʊtbreɪk] *n* **1.** [of fire, storm, war] début *m* ■ [of violence, disease, epidemic] éruption *f* ■ **there have been ~s of violence throughout the country** il y a eu des explosions de violence dans tout le pays ■ **doctors fear an ~ of meningitis** les médecins redoutent une épidémie de méningite ■ **to have an ~ of spots** avoir une éruption de boutons **2.** METEOR [sudden shower] : **there will be ~s of rain/snow in many places** il y aura des chutes de pluie/de neige un peu partout.

outbuilding ['aʊtˌbɪldɪŋ] *n UK* (bâtiment *m*) annexe *f* ■ [shed] remise *f* ■ **the ~s** [on farm, estate] les dépendances *fpl*.

outburst ['aʊtbɜ:st] *n* accès *m*, explosion *f* ■ **a sudden ~ of violence** [group] une soudaine explosion de violence ; [individual] un accès de brutalité ■ **you must control these ~s** il faut que vous appreniez à garder votre sang-froid.

outcast ['aʊtkɑ:st] ◇ *n* paria *m*.
◇ *adj* proscrit, banni.

outclass [ˌaʊt'klɑ:s] *vt* surclasser, surpasser.

outcome ['aʊtkʌm] *n* [of election, competition] résultat *m* ■ [of sequence of events] conséquence *f* ■ **the ~ of it all was that they never visited us again** résultat, ils ne sont jamais revenus chez nous.

outcrop ◇ *n* ['aʊtkrɒp] GEOL affleurement *m*.
◇ *vi* [ˌaʊt'krɒp] (*pret & pp* **outcropped**, *cont* **outcropping**) affleurer.

outcry ['aʊtkraɪ] (*pl* **outcries**) *n* tollé *m* ■ **the government's decision was greeted by public ~** la décision du gouvernement fut accueillie par un tollé général.

outdated [ˌaʊt'deɪtɪd] *adj* [idea, attitude] démodé, dépassé ■ [clothes] démodé ■ [expression] désuet, - ète *f*.

outdid [ˌaʊt'dɪd] *pt* ▷ **outdo.**

outdistance [ˌaʊt'dɪstəns] *vt* laisser derrière soi ■ **she was easily ~d by the Nigerian** elle fut facilement distancée par la Nigérienne.

outdo [ˌaʊt'du:] (*pret* **outdid** [ˌaʊt'dɪd], *pp* **outdone** [-'dʌn]) *vt* surpasser, faire mieux que, l'emporter sur ■ **Mark, not to be outdone, decided to be ill as well** Mark, pour ne pas être en reste, décida d'être malade lui aussi ■ **she wasn't to be outdone** [in contest] elle refusait de s'avouer vaincue.

outdoor ['aʊtdɔ:ʳ] *adj* **1.** [open-air - games, sports] de plein air ; [- work] d'extérieur ; [- swimming pool] en plein air, découvert **2.** [clothes] d'extérieur ■ **~ shoes** [warm] grosses chaussures ; [waterproof] chaussures imperméables ; [for walking] chaussures de marche **3.** [person] : **to lead an ~ life** vivre au grand air ■ **Kate is a real ~ type** Kate aime la vie au grand air.

outdoors [aʊt'dɔ:z] ◇ *n* : **the great ~** les grands espaces naturels.
◇ *adv* dehors, au dehors ■ **the scene takes place ~** la scène se déroule à l'extérieur ■ **to sleep ~** coucher à la belle étoile.
◇ *adj* [activity] en OR de plein air.

outer ['aʊtəʳ] *adj* **1.** [external] extérieur, externe ■ **~ garments** vêtements *mpl* de dessus **2.** [peripheral] périphérique ■ **~ London** la banlieue londonienne **3.** [furthest - limits] externe ; [- planets] extérieur.

outer ear *n* oreille *f* externe.

outermost ['aʊtəməʊst] *adj* [most distant] le plus (à l')extérieur ■ [most isolated] le plus reculé OR isolé.

outer space *n* espace *m* intersidéral, cosmos *m*.

outfield ['aʊtfi:ld] *n* SPORT **1.** [part of field] champ *m* OR terrain *m* extérieur **2.** [players] joueurs *mpl* de champ.

outfielder ['aʊtfi:ldəʳ] *n US* joueur *m* de champ *(au baseball).*

outfit ['aʊtfɪt] ◇ *n* **1.** [clothes] ensemble *m*, tenue *f* ■ **riding/travelling ~** tenue d'équitation/de voyage ■ **you should have seen the ~ he had on!** tu aurais dû voir comment il était attifé OR fagoté! ■ [child's disguise] panoplie *f* ■ **cowboy's/nurse's ~** panoplie de cowboy/d'infirmière **2.** [equipment, kit - for camping, fishing] matériel *m*, équipement *m* ■ [tools] outils *mpl*, outillage *m* ■ [case] trousse *f* **3.** *inf* [group] équipe *f*, bande *f* **4.** MIL équipe *f*.
◇ *vt* (*pret & pp* **outfitted**, *cont* **outfitting**) [with equipment] équiper.

outfitter ['aʊtfɪtəʳ] *n UK* [shop] : **school ~** OR **~'s** *magasin qui vend des uniformes et autres vêtements scolaires* ■ **(gentlemen's) ~** OR **~'s** magasin de vêtements d'homme.

outflank [ˌaʊt'flæŋk] *vt* MIL déborder ■ *fig* [rival] déjouer les manœuvres de.

outflow ['aʊtfləʊ] *n* **1.** [of fluid] écoulement *m* ■ [place of outflow] décharge *f* **2.** [of capital] sorties *fpl*, fuite *f* ■ [of population] exode *m*, sorties *fpl*, fuite *f*.

outfox [ˌaʊt'fɒks] *vt* se montrer plus rusé que.

outgoing ['aʊtˌgəʊɪŋ] *adj* **1.** [departing - government, minister, tenant] sortant ; [- following resignation] démissionnaire **2.** [train, ship] en partance ■ [letters] à expédier **3.** [tide] descendant **4.** [extrovert] extraverti, plein d'entrain ■ **she's a very ~ person** elle a une personnalité très ouverte.

outgoings ['aʊtˌgəʊɪŋz] *npl* dépenses *fpl*, frais *mpl*.

outgrow [ˌaʊt'grəʊ] (*pret* **outgrew** [-'gru:], *pp* **outgrown** [-'grəʊn]) *vt* **1.** [grow faster than] grandir plus (vite) que ■ **the world is ~ing its resources** la population mondiale croît plus vite que les ressources dont elle dispose **2.** [clothes] devenir trop grand pour ■ **she has outgrown three pairs of shoes this year** elle a pris quatre pointures cette année **3.** [game, habit, hobby] ne plus s'intéresser à *(en grandissant)* ■ [attitude, behaviour, phase] abandonner (en grandissant OR en prenant de l'âge) ■ **Moira has outgrown dolls** Moira est devenue trop grande pour s'intéresser aux poupées ■ **they soon outgrew their first computer** ils ont vite eu fait le tour (des possibilités) de leur premier ordinateur ■ **I think I just outgrew our friendship** je crois qu'avec l'âge, notre amitié a tout simplement perdu son intérêt pour moi.

outgrowth ['aʊtgrəʊθ] *n liter* excroissance *f* ■ *fig* [consequence] conséquence *f*.

outgun [ˌaʊt'gʌn] (*pret & pp* **outgunned**, *cont* **outgunning**) *vt* MIL avoir une puissance de feu supérieure à ■ *fig* vaincre, l'emporter sur.

outhouse ['aʊthaʊs] (*pl* [-haʊzɪz]) *n* **1.** *UK* [outbuilding] remise *f* **2.** *US* [toilet] toilettes *fpl* extérieures.

outing ['aʊtɪŋ] *n* **1.** [trip] sortie *f* ■ [organized] excursion *f* ■ **to go on an ~** faire une excursion ▶ **school ~** sortie scolaire **2.** [of homosexuals] *délation d'homosexuels dans le monde de la politique et du spectacle.*

outlandish [aʊt'lændɪʃ] *adj* [eccentric - appearance, behaviour, idea] bizarre, excentrique ▪ *pej* [language, style] barbare.

outlast [,aʊt'lɑːst] *vt* [subj: person] survivre à ▪ [subj: machine] durer plus longtemps que.

outlaw ['aʊtlɔː] ◇ *n* hors-la-loi *mf inv*.
◇ *vt* [person] mettre hors la loi ▪ [behaviour] proscrire, interdire ▪ [organization] interdire.

outlay ◇ *n* ['aʊtleɪ] [expense] dépense *f* ▪ [investment] investissement *m*, mise *f* de fonds.
◇ *vt* [aʊt'leɪ] (*pret & pp* **outlaid** [-'leɪd]) [spend] dépenser ▪ [invest] investir ▪ **to ~ $10,000 capital** faire une mise de fonds de 10 000 dollars.

outlet ['aʊtlet] ◇ *n* **1.** [for liquid, air, smoke] bouche *f* ▪ [in reservoir, lock] déversoir *m*, dégorgeoir *m* ▪ [tap] vanne *f* d'écoulement ▪ **the pipe/channel provides an ~ for excess water** le tuyau/le canal permet l'écoulement du trop-plein d'eau **2.** [mouth of river] embouchure *f* **3.** [for feelings, energy] exutoire *m* ▪ **children need an ~ for their energies** les enfants ont besoin de se défouler **4.** [for talent] débouché *m* ▪ **the programme provides an ~ for young talent** l'émission permet à de jeunes talents de se faire connaître **5.** COMM [market] débouché *m* ▪ **there are not many sales ~s in Japan** le Japon offre peu de débouchés commerciaux ❚ [sales point] point *m* de vente ▪ **our North American ~s** notre réseau (de distribution) en Amérique du Nord **6.** *US* ELEC prise *f* (de courant).
◇ *comp* [for liquid] d'écoulement ▪ [for gas, smoke] d'échappement.

outline ['aʊtlaɪn] ◇ *n* **1.** [contour, shape] silhouette *f*, contour *m* ▪ [of building, of mountains] silhouette *f* ▪ [of face, figure] profil *m* ▪ ART [sketch] esquisse *f*, ébauche *f* ▪ **to draw sthg in ~** faire un croquis de qqch **2.** [plan - of project, essay] plan *m* d'ensemble, esquisse *f* ; [- of book] canevas *m* ▪ [general idea] idée *f* générale, grandes lignes *fpl* ▪ [overall view] vue *f* d'ensemble ▪ **she gave us an ~ of** *OR* **she explained to us in ~ what she intended to do** elle nous a expliqué dans les grandes lignes ce qu'elle avait l'intention de faire.
◇ *vt* **1.** [plan, theory] expliquer dans les grandes lignes ▪ [facts] résumer, passer en revue ▪ **he ~d the situation briefly** il dressa un bref bilan de la situation ▪ **could you ~ your basic reasons for leaving?** pourriez-vous exposer brièvement les principales raisons de votre départ? **2.** [person, building, mountain] : **the trees were ~d against the blue sky** les arbres se détachaient sur le fond bleu du ciel **3.** ART esquisser (les traits de), tracer ▪ **to ~ sthg in pencil** faire le croquis de qqch ▪ **the figures are ~d in charcoal** les personnages sont esquissés au fusain ▪ **to ~ one's eyes in black** souligner le contour de ses yeux en noir.

outlive [,aʊt'lɪv] *vt* survivre à ▪ **she ~d her husband by only six months** elle n'a survécu à son mari que six mois ▪ **he'll ~ us all at this rate** au train où il va, il nous enterrera tous ▪ **the measures have ~d their usefulness** les mesures n'ont plus de raison d'être.

outlook ['aʊtlʊk] *n* **1.** [prospect] perspective *f* ▪ ECON & POL horizon *m*, perspectives *fpl* (d'avenir) ▪ **the ~ for the New Year is promising** cette nouvelle année s'annonce prometteuse ▪ **it's a bleak ~ for the unemployed** pour les sans-emploi, les perspectives d'avenir ne sont guère réjouissantes ▪ **the ~ for the future is grim** l'avenir est sombre ❚ METEOR prévision *f*, prévisions *fpl* ▪ **the ~ for March is cold and windy** pour mars, on prévoit un temps froid avec beaucoup de vent **2.** [viewpoint] point de vue *m*, conception *f* ▪ **she has pessimistic ~** elle voit les choses en noir *OR* de manière pessimiste **3.** [view - from window] perspective *f*, vue *f*.

outlying ['aʊt,laɪɪŋ] *adj* [remote - area, village] isolé, à l'écart ▪ [far from centre - urban areas] périphérique ▪ **the ~ suburbs** la grande banlieue.

outmanoeuvre *UK*, **outmaneuver** *US* [,aʊtmə'nuːvər] *vt* MIL se montrer meilleur tacticien que ▪ *fig* déjouer les manœuvres de ▪ **we were ~d by the opposition** l'opposition nous a pris de vitesse.

outmoded [,aʊt'məʊdəd] *adj* démodé, désuet, - ète *f*.

outnumber [,aʊt'nʌmbər] *vt* être plus nombreux que ▪ **they were ~ed by the enemy** l'ennemi était supérieur en nombre ▪ **women ~ men by two to one** il y a deux fois plus de femmes que d'hommes.

out-of-bounds *adj* **1.** [barred] interdit ▪ **~ to civilians** interdit aux civils **2.** *US* SPORT hors (du) terrain.

out-of-court *adj* : **~ settlement** arrangement *m* à l'amiable,.

out-of-date *adj* **1.** = **outdated 2.** [expired] périmé.

out-of-doors *UK* ◇ *adv* = **outdoors**.
◇ *adj* = **outdoor**.

out-of-pocket *adj* : **I'm £5 out of pocket** j'en suis pour 5 livres de ma poche ▶ **~ expenses** frais *mpl*.

out-of-the-ordinary *adj* insolite.

out-of-the-way *adj* **1.** [isolated] écarté, isolé ▪ [unknown to most people] peu connu ▪ [not popular] peu fréquenté **2.** [uncommon] insolite.

out-of-work *adj* au chômage.

outpace [,aʊt'peɪs] *vt* [run faster than] courir plus vite que ▪ [overtake] dépasser, devancer.

outpatient ['aʊt,peɪʃnt] *n* malade *mf* en consultation externe ▪ **~s' clinic** *OR* **department** service *m* de consultation externe.

outperform [,aʊtpə'fɔːm] *vt* avoir de meilleures performances que, être plus performant que.

outplacement ['aʊtpleɪsmənt] *n* reconversion *f* externe.

outplay [,aʊt'pleɪ] *vt* jouer mieux que, dominer (au jeu).

outpost ['aʊtpəʊst] *n* avant-poste *m* ▪ **the last ~s of civilization** les derniers bastions de la civilisation.

outpouring ['aʊt,pɔːrɪŋ] *n* épanchement *m* ▪ **~s** effusions *fpl*.

output ['aʊtpʊt] ◇ *n* **1.** [production] production *f* ▪ [productivity] rendement *m* ▪ **his writing ~ is phenomenal** c'est un auteur très prolifique ❚ [power - of machine] rendement *m*, débit *m* ▪ **this machine has an ~ of 6,000 items an hour** cette machine débite 6 000 pièces à l'heure **2.** ELEC puissance *f* ▪ [of amplifier] puissance *f* (de sortie) ▪ COMPUT [device] sortie *f* ▪ [printout] sortie *f* papier, tirage *m*.
◇ *vt* (*pret & pp* **output**, *cont* **outputting**) COMPUT [data] sortir.
◇ *vi* (*pret & pp* **output**, *cont* **outputting**) COMPUT sortir des données.

outrage ['aʊtreɪdʒ] ◇ *n* **1.** [affront] outrage *m*, affront *m* ▪ **it's an ~ against public decency** c'est un outrage aux bonnes mœurs ▪ **it's an ~ against humanity/society** c'est un affront à l'humanité/la société ❚ [scandal] scandale *m* ▪ **it's an ~ that no-one came to their aid** c'est un scandale *OR* il est scandaleux que personne ne soit venu à leur secours **2.** [indignation] indignation *f* **3.** [brutal act] atrocité *f*, acte *m* de brutalité *OR* de violence.
◇ *vt* [person] outrager ▪ [moral sensibility] outrager, faire outrage à.

outraged ['aʊtreɪdʒd] *adj* outré, scandalisé ▪ **to be ~ at** *OR* **by sthg** être outré *OR* scandalisé par qqch.

outrageous [aʊt'reɪdʒəs] *adj* **1.** [scandalous - behaviour, manners] scandaleux ▪ [atrocious - crime, attack etc] monstrueux, atroce **2.** [slightly offensive - humour, style] choquant ; [- joke, remark] outrageant **3.** [extravagant - person, colour] extravagant **4.** [price] exorbitant.

outrageously [aʊt'reɪdʒəslɪ] *adv* **1.** [scandalously] de façon scandaleuse, scandaleusement ▪ [atrociously] atrocement, monstrueusement ▪ **we have been treated ~** on nous a traités d'une façon scandaleuse **2.** [extravagantly] de façon extravagante ▪ **the shop is ~ expensive** les prix pratiqués dans ce magasin sont exorbitants.

outrageousness [aʊt'reɪdʒəsnɪs] *n* [of behaviour] caractère *m* scandaleux *OR* outrageant ■ [of crime, torture] atrocité *f* ■ [of dress] extravagance *f* ■ [of language] outrance *f* ■ [of prices] exagération *f*.

outran [,aʊt'ræn] *pt* ▷ **outrun**.

outrank [aʊt'ræŋk] *vt* avoir un rang plus élevé que ■ MIL avoir un grade supérieur à.

outreach ◇ *vt* [,aʊt'ri:tʃ] **1.** [exceed] dépasser **2.** [in arm length] avoir le bras plus long que ■ [in boxing] avoir l'allonge supérieure à.
◇ *n* ['aʊtri:tʃ] ADMIN *recherche des personnes qui ne demandent pas l'aide sociale dont elles pourraient bénéficier* ■ **~ worker** *employé ou bénévole dans un bureau d'aide sociale.*

outrider ['aʊt,raɪdə^r] *n UK* [motorcyclist] motard *m* (d'escorte) ■ [horseman] cavalier *m*.

outrigger ['aʊt,rɪgə^r] *n* NAUT [gen] balancier *m* ■ [on racing boat] portant *m*, outrigger *m*.

outright ◇ *adj* ['aʊtraɪt] **1.** [absolute, utter - dishonesty, hypocrisy] pur (et simple), absolu ; [- liar] fieffé ; [- ownership] total, absolu ■ [frank - denial, refusal] net, catégorique ■ **he's an ~ fascist!** c'est un vrai fasciste! ■ **it was ~ blackmail** c'était purement et simplement du chantage *OR* du chantage, ni plus ni moins **2.** [clear - win, winner] incontesté **3.** COMM [sale - for cash] au comptant ; [- total] en bloc.
◇ *adv* [aʊt'raɪt] **1.** [frankly - refuse] net, carrément ; [- ask] carrément, franchement **2.** [totally - oppose] absolument ; [- own] totalement **3.** [clearly - win] nettement, haut la main **4.** COMM [sell - for cash] au comptant ; [- totally] en bloc **5.** [instantly] : **they were killed ~** ils ont été tués sur le coup.

outrun [,aʊt'rʌn] (*pret* **outran** [,aʊt'ræn], *pp* **outrun**, *cont* **outrunning**) *vt* **1.** [run faster than] courir plus vite que ■ [pursuer] distancer **2.** [ability, energy, resources] excéder, dépasser.

outsell [,aʊt'sel] (*pret & pp* **outsold** [-'səʊld]) *vt* [subj: article] se vendre mieux que ■ [subj: company] vendre davantage que.

outset ['aʊtset] *n* : **at the ~** au début, au départ ■ **from the ~** dès le début, d'emblée.

outshine [,aʊt'ʃaɪn] (*pret & pp* **outshone** [-'ʃɒn]) *vt* [subj: star] briller plus que ■ *fig* [rival] éclipser, surpasser.

outside ◇ *adv* [aʊt'saɪd] **1.** [outdoors] dehors, à l'extérieur ■ **it's cold ~** il fait froid dehors ■ **to go ~** sortir ■ **seen from ~** vu de l'extérieur ■ **you'll have to park ~** il faudra vous garer dans la rue
2. [on other side of door] dehors
3. [out of prison] dehors.
◇ *prep* [aʊt'saɪd, 'aʊtsaɪd] **1.** [on or to the exterior] à l'extérieur de, hors de ■ **nobody is allowed ~ the house** personne n'a le droit de quitter la maison ■ **put the eggs ~ the window/door** mettez les œufs sur le rebord de la fenêtre/devant la porte ■ **she was wearing her shirt ~ her trousers** elle portait sa chemise par-dessus son pantalon ■ **nobody ~ the office must know** personne ne doit être mis au courant en dehors du bureau ■ **the troublemakers were people from ~ the group** *fig* les fauteurs de troubles ne faisaient pas partie du groupe
2. [away from] : **we live some way ~ the town** nous habitons assez loin de la ville ■ **I don't think anybody ~ France has heard of him** je ne pense pas qu'il soit connu ailleurs qu'en France
3. [in front of] devant
4. [beyond] en dehors de, au-delà de ■ **it's ~ his field** ce n'est pas son domaine ■ **it's ~ my experience** ça ne m'est jamais arrivé ■ **the matter is ~ our responsibility** la question ne relève pas de notre responsabilité ■ **~ office hours** en dehors des heures de bureau.
◇ *adj* ['aʊtsaɪd] **1.** [exterior] extérieur ■ **the ~ world** le monde extérieur ■ **she has few ~ interests** elle s'intéresse à peu de choses à part son travail ■ **an ~ toilet** des toilettes (situées) à l'extérieur ■ **the ~ edge** le bord extérieur ■ **~ lane** [driving on left] file *f OR* voie *f* de droite ; [driving on right] file *f OR* voie *f* de gauche ■ **an ~ line** [on telephone] une ligne extérieure
2. [from elsewhere - help, influence] extérieur ■ **to get an ~ opinion** demander l'avis d'un tiers
3. [poor - possibility] faible ■ **she has only an ~ chance of winning** elle n'a que très peu de chances de gagner
4. [maximum - price] maximum
5. [not belonging to a group] extérieur, indépendant.
◇ *n* [aʊt'saɪd, 'aʊtsaɪd] **1.** [exterior - of building, container] extérieur *m*, dehors *m* ■ **the arms were flown in from ~** les armes ont été introduites dans le pays par avion ■ *fig* **looking at the problem from (the) ~** quand on considère le problème de l'extérieur
2. [out of prison] : **I've almost forgotten what life is like on the ~** j'ai presque oublié ce qu'est la vie dehors *OR* de l'autre côté des barreaux
3. AUT : **to overtake on the ~** [driving on left] doubler à droite ; [driving on right] doubler à gauche
4. [outer edge] extérieur *m*.
◆ **at the outside** *adv phr* **1.** [in number] tout au plus, au maximum
2. [in time] au plus tard.
◆ **outside of** *prep phr esp US* **1.** = **outside**
2. [except for] en dehors de ■ **nobody, ~ of a few close friends, was invited** personne, en dehors de *OR* à part quelques amis intimes, n'était invité
3. [more than] au-delà de ■ **an offer ~ of 10 million** une offre de plus de *OR* supérieure à 10 millions.

outside broadcast *n* reportage *m*.

outside half *n* SPORT demi *m* d'ouverture.

outsider [,aʊt'saɪdə^r] *n* **1.** [person] étranger *m*, - ère *f* ■ **he's always been a bit of an ~** il a toujours été plutôt marginal ■ **I'd be glad to have an ~'s viewpoint** je serais heureux d'avoir un point de vue extérieur **2.** SPORT outsider *m*.

outsize ['aʊtsaɪz] *UK* ◇ *n* [gen] grande taille *f*, grandes tailles *fpl* ■ [for men] très grand patron *m*.
◇ *adj* **1.** [large] énorme, colossal **2.** [in clothes sizes] grande taille *(inv)*.

outsized ['aʊtsaɪzd] *adj* énorme, colossal.

outskirts ['aʊtskɜ:ts] *npl* [of town] banlieue *f*, périphérie *f* ■ [of forest] orée *f*, lisière *f* ■ **we live on the ~ of Copenhagen** nous habitons la banlieue de Copenhague.

outsmart [,aʊt'smɑ:t] *vt* se montrer plus malin que.

outsource ['aʊtsɔ:s] *vt* COMM sous-traiter, externaliser.

outsourcing ['aʊtsɔ:sɪŋ] *n* externalisation *f*, sous-traitance *f*.

outspoken [,aʊt'spəʊkn] *adj* franc, franche *f* ■ **to be ~** parler franchement, avoir son franc-parler ■ **he has always been an ~ critic of the reforms** il a toujours ouvertement critiqué les réformes.

outspokenness [,aʊt'spəʊkənnɪs] *n* franc-parler *m*.

outspread [,aʊt'spred] *adj* écarté ■ **with ~ arms** les bras écartés ■ **with ~ wings** les ailes déployées ■ **an ~ newspaper** un journal déplié.

outstanding [,aʊt'stændɪŋ] *adj* **1.** [remarkable - ability, performance] exceptionnel, remarquable ■ [notable - event, feature] marquant, mémorable ■ **an ~ politician** un politicien hors pair *OR* exceptionnel **2.** [unresolved - problem] non résolu, en suspens ■ **there is still one ~ matter** il reste encore un problème à régler ■ [unfinished - business, work] inachevé, en cours ■ ADMIN en souffrance, en attente ■ **there are about 20 pages ~** il reste environ 20 pages à faire ■ [unpaid - bill] impayé ■ **~ payment** impayé *m* ■ **~ interest/rent** arriérés *mpl* d'intérêt/de loyer **3.** ST. EX émis.

outstandingly [,aʊt'stændɪŋlɪ] *adv* exceptionnellement, remarquablement.

outstation ['aʊtsteɪʃn] *n* **1.** [in colony, isolated region] avant-poste *m* **2.** RADIO station *f* extérieure *OR* satellite.

outstay [,aʊt'steɪ] *vt* **1.** [subj: guests] rester plus longtemps que ■ **to ~ one's welcome** abuser de l'hospitalité de ses hôtes **2.** *UK* SPORT [competitor] tenir plus longtemps que.

outstretched [,aʊt'stretʃt] *adj* [limbs, body] étendu, allongé ■ [wings] déployé ■ **with arms ~, with ~ arms** [gen] les bras écartés ; [in welcome] à bras (grand) ouverts ▪ **the beggar stood outside the church with ~ hands** le mendiant se tenait devant l'église, la main tendue.

outstrip [,aʊt'strɪp] (*pret & pp* **outstripped**, *cont* **outstripping**) *vt UK* dépasser, surpasser.

outtake ['aʊtteɪk] *n* CIN & TV coupure *f*.

out tray *n* corbeille *f* sortie.

outvote [,aʊt'vəʊt] *vt* [bill, reform] rejeter (à la majorité des voix) ▪ [person] mettre en minorité ▪ **I wanted to go to the cinema, but I was ~d** je voulais aller au cinéma, mais les autres ont voté contre.

outward ['aʊtwəd] <> *adj* **1.** [external] extérieur, externe ▪ [apparent] apparent ▪ **to (all) ~ appearances, she's very successful** selon toute apparence, elle réussit très bien ▪ **an ~ show of wealth** un étalage de richesses ▪ **she showed no ~ signs of fear** elle ne montrait aucun signe de peur **2.** [in direction] vers l'extérieur ▪ **the ~ journey** le voyage aller, l'aller *m*.
<> *adv* vers l'extérieur ▪ **~ bound** [ship, train] en partance.

outward bound course *n* école *f* d'endurcissement (en plein air).

outwardly ['aʊtwədlɪ] *adv* en apparence ▪ **~ they seem to get on** ils donnent l'impression de bien s'entendre.

outwards ['aʊtwədz] *adv* vers l'extérieur ▪ **his feet turn ~** il marche les pieds en dehors.

outweigh [aʊt'weɪ] *vt* l'emporter sur ▪ **the advantages easily ~ the disadvantages** les avantages l'emportent largement sur les inconvénients.

outwit [,aʊt'wɪt] (*pret & pp* **outwitted**, *cont* **outwitting**) *vt* se montrer plus malin que ▪ **we've been outwitted** on nous a eus.

outwork ['aʊtwɜ:k] *n UK* [work] travail *m* fait à l'extérieur.
◆ **outworks** *npl* MIL ouvrage *m* défensif avancé.

outworker ['aʊt,wɜ:kər] *n UK* travailleur *m* à domicile.

ouzo ['u:zəʊ] *n* ouzo *m*.

ova ['əʊvə] *pl* ⊳ **ovum**.

oval ['əʊvl] <> *adj* (en) ovale.
<> *n* ovale *m*.
◆ **Oval** *pr n* : **the Oval** *célèbre terrain de cricket dans le centre de Londres.*

Oval Office *pr n* [office] Bureau *m* ovale ▪ [authority] présidence *f* des États-Unis.

ovarian [əʊ'veərɪən] *adj* ovarien.

ovary ['əʊvərɪ] (*pl* **ovaries**) *n* ovaire *m*.

ovate ['əʊveɪt] *adj* oviforme.

ovation [əʊ'veɪʃn] *n* ovation *f* ▪ **to give sb an ~** faire une ovation à qqn.

oven ['ʌvn] *n* four *m* ▪ **to cook sthg in an ~** faire cuire qqch au four ▪ **cook in a hot/medium ~** faire cuire à four chaud/à four moyen ▪ **Athens is like an ~ in summer** *fig* Athènes est une vraie fournaise en été.

ovenable ['ʌvnəbl] *adj* allant au four.

oven glove *n* gant *m* isolant.

ovenproof ['ʌvnpru:f] *adj* allant *OR* qui va au four.

oven-ready *adj* prêt à cuire *OR* à mettre au four.

ovenware ['ʌvnweər] *n* plats *mpl* allant au four.

over ['əʊvər] <> *prep*

A.

1. [above] au-dessus de ▪ **the plane came down ~ France** l'avion s'est écrasé en France
2. [on top of, covering] sur, par-dessus ▪ **put a lace cloth ~ the table** mets une nappe en dentelle sur la table ▪ **she wore a cardigan ~ her dress** elle portait un gilet par-dessus sa robe ▪ **she wore a black dress with a red cardigan ~ it** elle avait une robe noire avec un gilet rouge par-dessus ▪ **I put my hand ~ my mouth** j'ai mis ma main devant ma bouche ▪ **he had his jacket ~ his arm** il avait sa veste sur le bras
3. [across the top or edge of] par-dessus ▪ **he was watching me ~ his newspaper** il m'observait par-dessus son journal
4. [across the entire surface of] : **to cross ~ the road** traverser la rue ▪ **they live ~ the road from me** ils habitent en face de chez moi ▪ **there's a fine view ~ the valley** on a une belle vue sur la vallée ▪ **he ran his eye ~ the article** il a parcouru l'article des yeux ▪ **she ran her hand ~ the smooth marble** elle passa la main sur le marbre lisse ▪ **we travelled for days ~ land and sea** nous avons voyagé pendant des jours par terre et par mer ▪ **a strange look came ~ her face** son visage prit une expression étrange
5. [on the far side of] : **the village ~ the hill** le village de l'autre côté de la colline ▪ **they must be ~ the border by now** ils doivent avoir passé la frontière maintenant

B.

1. [indicating position of control] : **to rule ~ a country** régner sur un pays ▪ **I have no control/influence ~ them** je n'ai aucune autorité/influence sur eux
2. [indicating position of superiority, importance] sur ▪ **a victory ~ the forces of reaction** une victoire sur les forces réactionnaires

C.

1. [with specific figure or amount - more than] plus de ▪ **it took me well/just ~ an hour** j'ai mis bien plus/un peu plus d'une heure ▪ **children ~ (the age of) 7** les enfants (âgés) de plus de 7 ans ▪ **think of a number ~ 100** pensez à un chiffre supérieur à 100
2. [louder than] : **his voice rang out ~ the others** sa voix dominait toutes les autres ▪ **I couldn't hear what she was saying ~ the music** la musique m'empêchait d'entendre ce qu'elle disait
3. MATHS [divided by] : **eight ~ two** huit divisé par deux
4. [during] : **I've got a job ~ the long vacation** je vais travailler pendant les grandes vacances ▪ **what are you doing ~ Easter?** qu'est-ce que tu fais pour Pâques? ▪ **~ the next few decades** au cours des prochaines décennies ▪ **we discussed it ~ a drink/~ a game of golf** nous en avons discuté autour d'un verre/en faisant une partie de golf

D.

1. [concerning] au sujet de ▪ **a disagreement ~ working conditions** un conflit portant sur les conditions de travail ▪ **they're always quarrelling ~ money** ils se disputent sans cesse pour des questions d'argent
2. [by means of, via] : **I heard it ~ the radio** je l'ai entendu à la radio
3. [recovered from] : **are you ~ your bout of flu?** est-ce que tu es guéri *OR* est-ce que tu t'es remis de ta grippe? ▪ **he's ~ the shock now** il s'en est remis maintenant ▪ **we'll soon be ~ the worst** le plus dur sera bientôt passé.

<> *adv*

A.

1. [indicating movement or location, across distance or space] : **an eagle flew ~** un aigle passa au-dessus de nous ▪ **she walked ~ to him and said hello** elle s'approcha de lui pour dire bonjour ▪ **he must have seen us, he's coming ~** il a dû nous voir, il vient vers nous *OR* de notre côté ▪ **pass my cup ~, will you** tu peux me passer ma tasse? ▪ **she glanced ~ at me** elle jeta un coup d'œil dans ma direction ▪ **~ in the States** aux États-Unis ▪ **~ there** là-bas ▪ **come ~ here!** viens (par) ici! ▪ **has Bill been ~?** est-ce que Bill est passé? ▪ **she drove ~ to meet us** elle est venue nous rejoindre en voiture ▪ **let's have *OR* invite them ~ for dinner** si on les invitait à dîner? ▪ **we have guests ~ from Morocco** nous avons des invités qui viennent du Maroc
2. [everywhere] : **she's travelled the whole world ~** elle a voyagé dans le monde entier
3. [indicating movement from a higher to a lower level] : **I fell ~** je suis tombé (par terre) ▪ **she knocked her glass ~** elle a renversé son verre ▪ **they rolled ~ and ~ in the grass** ils se roulaient dans l'herbe
4. [so as to cover] : **the bodies were covered ~ with blankets** les corps étaient recouverts avec des couvertures
5. [into the hands of another person, group etc] : **they handed him ~ to the authorities** ils l'ont remis aux autorités *OR* entre les mains des autorités ‖ RADIO & TV : **and now ~ to David Smith in Paris** nous passons maintenant l'antenne à David Smith à Paris ‖ TELEC : **~ (to you)!** à vous! ▪ **~ and out!** terminé!

B.

1. [left, remaining] : **there were/I had a few pounds (left) ~** il restait/il me restait quelques livres ■ **seven into fifty-two makes seven with three ~** cinquante-deux divisé par sept égale sept, il reste trois
2. [with specific figure or amount - more] plus ■ **men of 30 and ~** les hommes âgés de 30 ans et plus
3. [through] : **read it ~ carefully** lisez-le attentivement ■ **do you want to talk the matter ~?** voulez-vous en discuter?
4. [again, more than once] encore ■ **I had to do the whole thing ~** *US* j'ai dû tout refaire ■ **she won the tournament five times ~** elle a gagné le tournoi à cinq reprises.
◇ *adj* fini.
◆ **over and above** *prep phr* en plus de.
◆ **over and over** *adv phr* : **I've told you ~ and ~ (again)** je te l'ai répété je ne sais combien de fois.

over- *in cpds* **1.** [excessive] : **~activity** suractivité *f* ■ **~cautious** trop prudent, d'une prudence excessive **2.** [more than] : **a club for the ~fifties** un club pour les plus de cinquante ans.

overabundance [ˌəʊvərəˈbʌndəns] *n* surabondance *f*.

overabundant [ˌəʊvərəˈbʌndənt] *adj* surabondant.

overachieve [ˌəʊvərəˈtʃiːv] *vi* réussir brillamment ■ **children who ~** les enfants surdoués.

overachiever [ˌəʊvərəˈtʃiːvər] *n* surdoué *m*, - e *f*.

overact [ˌəʊvərˈækt] *vi* forcer la note, avoir un jeu outré.

overactive [ˌəʊvərˈæktɪv] *adj* : **to have an ~ thyroid** faire de l'hyperthyroïdie.

overage [ˈəʊvərɪdʒ] *n US* [surplus] surplus *m*, excédent *m*.

over-age *adj* [too old] trop âgé.

overall ◇ *adv* [ˌəʊvərˈɔːl] **1.** [in general - consider, examine] en général, globalement **2.** [measure] de bout en bout, d'un bout à l'autre ■ [cost, amount] en tout **3.** [in competition, sport] au classement général.
◇ *adj* [ˈəʊvərɔːl] **1.** [general] global, d'ensemble ■ **my ~ impression** mon impression d'ensemble **2.** [total - cost, amount] total ; [- measurement] total, hors tout.
◇ *n* [ˈəʊvərɔːl] [protective coat] blouse *f* ■ *US* [boiler suit] bleu *m* de travail.
◆ **overalls** *npl UK* [boiler suit] bleu *m* de travail ■ *US* [dungarees] salopette *f*.

overambitious [ˌəʊvəræmˈbɪʃəs] *adj* trop ambitieux.

overanxious [ˌəʊvərˈæŋkʃəs] *adj* **1.** [worried] trop inquiet ■ **don't be ~ about the exam** ne vous inquiétez pas trop au sujet de l'examen **2.** [keen] trop soucieux ■ **he did not seem ~ to meet her** il n'avait pas l'air tellement pressé de faire sa connaissance.

overarm [ˈəʊvərɑːm] ◇ *adv* [serve, bowl] : **to throw a ball ~** lancer une balle par-dessus sa tête ■ **to swim ~** nager à l'indienne.
◇ *adj* : **~ stroke** brasse *f* indienne.

overate [ˌəʊvərˈet] *pt* ▷ **overeat**.

overawe [ˌəʊvərˈɔː] *vt* intimider, impressionner.

overbalance [ˌəʊvəˈbæləns] ◇ *vi* [person] perdre l'équilibre ■ [load, pile] basculer, se renverser ■ [car] capoter ■ [boat] chavirer.
◇ *vt* [person] faire perdre l'équilibre à ■ [pile, vehicle] renverser, faire basculer.

overbearing [ˌəʊvəˈbeərɪŋ] *adj* autoritaire, impérieux.

overbid (*pret & pp* **overbid**, *cont* **overbidding**) ◇ *vt* [ˌəʊvəˈbɪd] enchérir sur.
◇ *vi* [ˌəʊvəˈbɪd] surenchérir.
◇ *n* [ˈəʊvəbɪd] surenchère *f*.

overblown [ˌəʊvəˈbləʊn] *adj* **1.** [flower, beauty] qui commence à se faner **2.** *pej* [prose, style] boursouflé, ampoulé, pompier.

overboard [ˈəʊvəbɔːd] *adv* NAUT par-dessus bord ■ **to jump ~** sauter à la mer ■ **man ~!** un homme à la mer! ▶ **to throw sthg/sb ~** *liter* jeter qqch/qqn par-dessus bord ; *fig* se débarrasser de qqch/qqn ■ **to throw a project ~** abandonner un projet ■ **to go ~** *inf* dépasser la mesure, exagérer ■ **he has really gone ~ with his latest film** il a vraiment dépassé les bornes avec son dernier film ■ **the critics went ~ about her first novel** les critiques se sont enthousiasmés OR emballés pour son premier roman.

overbook [ˌəʊvəˈbʊk] ◇ *vt* [flight, hotel] surréserver.
◇ *vi* [airline, hotel] surréserver.

overbooking [ˌəʊvəˈbʊkɪŋ] *n* surréservation *f*, surbooking *m*.

overburden [ˌəʊvəˈbɜːdn] *vt* surcharger, accabler ■ **~ed with debts** criblé de dettes.

overcame [ˌəʊvəˈkeɪm] *pt* ▷ **overcome**.

overcast ◇ *vt* [ˌəʊvəˈkɑːst] (*pret & pp* **overcast**) SEW surfiler.
◇ *adj* [ˈəʊvəkɑːst] [sky] sombre, couvert ■ [weather] couvert ■ **it's getting ~** le temps se couvre ■ **the sky became ~** le ciel s'assombrit.

overcautious [ˌəʊvəˈkɔːʃəs] *adj* trop prudent, prudent à l'excès.

overcharge [ˌəʊvəˈtʃɑːdʒ] ◇ *vt* **1.** [customer] faire payer trop cher ■ **they ~d me for the coffee** ils m'ont fait payer le café trop cher **2.** ELEC [circuit] surcharger **3.** *UK* [description, picture] surcharger.
◇ *vi* faire payer trop cher ■ **they ~d for the tomatoes** ils ont fait payer les tomates trop cher.

overcloud [ˌəʊvəˈklaʊd] ◇ *vt* : **the sky became ~ed** le ciel se couvrit de nuages.
◇ *vi* se couvrir, devenir nuageux.

overcoat [ˈəʊvəkəʊt] *n* manteau *m*, pardessus *m*.

overcome [ˌəʊvəˈkʌm] (*pret* **overcame** [ˌəʊvəˈkeɪm], *pp* **overcome**) ◇ *vt* **1.** [vanquish - enemy, opposition] vaincre, triompher de ; [- difficulty, shyness] surmonter ; [- fear, repulsion, prejudice] vaincre, surmonter, maîtriser ■ [master - nerves] maîtriser, contrôler **2.** [debilitate, weaken] accabler ■ **the heat overcame me** la chaleur finit par me terrasser ■ **she was ~ by the fumes** les émanations lui ont fait perdre connaissance **3.** (*usu passive*) [overwhelm] : **to be ~ by fear** être paralysé par la peur ■ **to be ~ with joy** être comblé de joie ■ **to be ~ with grief** être accablé par la douleur ■ **I was ~ by the news** la nouvelle m'a bouleversé ■ **in a voice ~ with emotion** d'une voix tremblante d'émotion ■ **how did he take the news? – he was quite ~** comment a-t-il pris la nouvelle? – il est resté muet.
◇ *vi* vaincre.

overcompensate [ˌəʊvəˈkɒmpənseɪt] *vt* surcompenser.

overcomplicated [ˌəʊvəˈkɒmplɪkeɪtɪd] *adj* trop OR excessivement compliqué.

overconfidence [ˌəʊvəˈkɒnfɪdəns] *n* **1.** [arrogance] suffisance *f*, présomption *f* **2.** [trust] confiance *f* aveugle OR excessive.

overconfident [ˌəʊvəˈkɒnfɪdənt] *adj* **1.** [arrogant] suffisant, présomptueux **2.** [trusting] trop confiant ■ **I'm not ~ of his chances of recovery** je ne crois pas trop en ses chances de guérison.

overcook [ˌəʊvəˈkʊk] ◇ *vt* faire trop cuire ■ **the vegetables are ~ed** les légumes sont trop cuits.
◇ *vi* trop cuire.

overcrowded [ˌəʊvəˈkraʊdɪd] *adj* [bus, train, room] bondé, comble ■ [city, country, prison] surpeuplé ■ [streets] plein de monde ■ [class] surchargé ■ **Paris is ~ with tourists in summer** en été, Paris est envahi par les touristes ■ **they live in very ~ conditions** ils vivent très à l'étroit.

overcrowding [ˌəʊvəˈkraʊdɪŋ] *n* surpeuplement *m*, surpopulation *f* ■ [in housing] entassement *m* ■ [in bus, train etc] entassement *m* des voyageurs, affluence *f* ■ [in schools] effectifs *mpl* surchargés ■ [in prisons] surpeuplement *m*.

overdevelop [ˌəʊvədɪˈveləp] *vt* [gen - PHOT] surdévelopper ■ **parts of the coastline have been ~ed** par endroits, le littoral est trop construit.

overdeveloped [,əʊvədɪ'veləpt] *adj* [gen - PHOT] surdéveloppé.

overdevelopment [,əʊvədɪ'veləpmənt] *n* surdéveloppement *m*.

overdo [,əʊvə'du:] (*pret* **overdid** [-'dɪd], *pp* **overdone** [-'dʌn]) *vt* **1.** [exaggerate] exagérer, pousser trop loin ■ **he rather overdoes the penniless student (bit)** il joue un peu trop l'étudiant pauvre ■ **the battle scenes are a bit overdone** les scènes de combat sont un peu exagérées ■ **you've overdone the curry powder** tu as eu la main un peu lourde avec le curry **2.** [eat, drink too much of] : **don't ~ the whisky** n'abuse pas du whisky **3.** *phr* **to ~ it, to ~ things** se surmener ■ **I've been ~ing it again** j'ai de nouveau un peu trop forcé **4.** CULIN trop cuire.

overdone [-'dʌn] <> *pp* ▻ **overdo**.
<> *adj* **1.** [exaggerated] exagéré, excessif **2.** CULIN trop cuit.

overdose <> *n* ['əʊvədəʊs] *liter* dose *f* massive OR excessive ■ **she died from a drugs ~** elle est morte d'une overdose ‖ *fig* dose *f* ■ **I think I've had an ~ of culture today** *hum* je crois que j'ai eu ma dose de culture pour aujourd'hui.
<> *vi* [,əʊvə'dəʊs] prendre une overdose ■ **he ~d on heroin/LSD** il a pris une overdose d'héroïne/de LSD ■ **I've been overdosing on chocolate recently** *hum* j'ai trop forcé sur le chocolat ces derniers temps.
<> *vt* [,əʊvə'dəʊs] [patient] administrer une dose excessive à ■ [drug] prescrire une dose excessive de.

overdraft ['əʊvədrɑ:ft] *n* découvert *m* (bancaire) ■ **to have an ~** avoir un découvert ■ **the bank gave me a £100 ~** la banque m'a accordé un découvert de 100 livres ▶ **~ facilities** autorisation *f* de découvert.

overdraw [,əʊvə'drɔ:] (*pret* **overdrew** [-'dru:], *pp* **overdrawn** [-'drɔ:n]) <> *vt* [account] mettre à découvert.
<> *vi* mettre son compte à découvert.

overdrawn [-'drɔ:n] *adj* à découvert ■ **to be** OR **to go ~** être OR se mettre à découvert ■ **my account is ~** mon compte est à découvert ■ **I'm ~ by £100** j'ai un découvert de 100 livres.

overdress <> *vi* [,əʊvə'dres] *pej* s'habiller avec trop de recherche, porter des toilettes trop recherchées.
<> *n* ['əʊvədres] robe-chasuble *f*.

overdressed [,əʊvə'drest] *adj* habillé avec trop de recherche ■ **I felt ~ in my dinner suit** j'avais la sensation d'être emprunté dans mon smoking.

overdrive ['əʊvədraɪv] *n* AUT (vitesse *f*) surmultipliée *f*, overdrive *m* ■ **to go into ~** *fig* mettre les bouchées doubles.

overdue [,əʊvə'dju:] *adj* **1.** [bus, flight, person] en retard ■ **she is long ~** elle devrait être là depuis longtemps ‖ [payment, rent] en retard, impayé ■ [library book] non retourné ■ **our repayments are two months ~** nous avons un retard de deux mois dans nos remboursements **2.** [apology] tardif ■ **an explanation is ~** le moment semble venu de donner une explication, il est temps de donner une explication ‖ [change, reform] qui tarde, qui se fait attendre ■ **this reform is long ~** cette réforme aurait dû être appliquée il y a longtemps ■ **the car is ~ for a service** la voiture a besoin d'être révisée **3.** [in pregnancy] : **to be ~** être en retard.

overeager [,əʊvər'i:gə^r] *adj* trop empressé ■ **he is ~ to please** il est trop soucieux OR désireux de plaire.

overeat [,əʊvər'i:t] (*pret* **overate** [,əʊvər'et], *pp* **overeaten** [-'i:tn]) *vi* [once] trop manger, faire un repas trop copieux ■ [habitually] se suralimenter.

overeating [,əʊvər'i:tɪŋ] *n* [habitual] suralimentation *f*.

overelaborate [,əʊvərɪ'læbərɪt] *adj* [dress, style] trop recherché ■ [ornamentation] tarabiscoté ■ [explanation, excuse] tiré par les cheveux ■ [description] alambiqué, contourné.

overemotional [,əʊvərɪ'məʊʃənl] *adj* hyperémotif, trop émotif.

overemphasize, ise [,əʊvər'emfəsaɪz] *vt* trop mettre l'accent sur, trop insister sur ■ **I cannot ~ the need for discretion** je n'insisterai jamais assez sur la nécessité de faire preuve de discrétion.

overenthusiastic ['əʊvərɪn,θju:zɪ'æstɪk] *adj* trop enthousiaste.

overestimate [,əʊvər'estɪmeɪt] *vt* surestimer.

overexaggerate [,əʊvərɪg'zædʒəreɪt] *vt* exagérer, attacher trop d'importance à.

overexcite [,əʊvərɪk'saɪt] *vt* surexciter.

overexcited [,əʊvərɪk'saɪtɪd] *adj* surexcité ■ **to become** OR **to get ~** (trop) s'énerver ■ **don't get ~, they haven't arrived yet** ne vous excitez pas, ils ne sont pas encore arrivés ■ **she got ~ and burst into tears** elle s'est mise dans un état d'agitation extrême et a fondu en larmes.

overexcitement [,əʊvərɪk'saɪtmənt] *n* surexcitation *f*.

overexert [,əʊvərɪg'zɜ:t] *vt* surmener ■ **to ~ o.s.** se surmener, s'éreinter.

overexertion [,əʊvərɪg'zɜ:ʃn] *n* surmenage *m*.

overexpose [,əʊvərɪk'spəʊz] *vt* *liter* & *fig* surexposer.

overexposure [,əʊvərɪk'spəʊʒə^r] *n* *liter* & *fig* surexposition *f*.

overfamiliar [,əʊvəfə'mɪljə^r] *adj* **1.** [too intimate, disrespectful] trop familier **2.** [conversant] : **I'm not ~ with the system** je ne connais pas très bien le système.

overfamiliarity ['əʊvəfə,mɪlɪ'ærətɪ] *n* familiarité *f* excessive.

overfeed [,əʊvə'fi:d] (*pret* & *pp* **overfed** [-'fed]) <> *vt* suralimenter.
<> *vi* se suralimenter, trop manger.

overfill [,əʊvə'fɪl] *vt* trop remplir.

overflow <> *vi* [,əʊvə'fləʊ] **1.** [with liquid - container, bath] déborder ■ [river] déborder, sortir de son lit ■ **the glass is full to ~ing** le verre est plein à ras bord ■ **the river frequently ~s onto the surrounding plain** la rivière inonde souvent la plaine environnante ‖ [with people - room, vehicle] déborder, être plein à craquer ■ **the streets were ~ing with people** les rues regorgeaient de monde ■ **the shop was full to ~ing** le magasin était plein à craquer ■ [with objects - box, wastebin] déborder ■ **the contents of the bin ~ed onto the floor** le contenu de la poubelle s'est répandu par terre ■ **her desk was ~ing with papers** son bureau disparaissait sous les papiers **2.** *fig* [with emotion] déborder ■ **his heart was ~ing with joy** son cœur débordait de joie.
<> *vt* [,əʊvə'fləʊ] déborder de ■ **the river ~ed its banks** la rivière est sortie de son lit OR a débordé.
<> *n* ['əʊvəfləʊ] **1.** [drain - from sink, cistern] trop-plein *m* ; [- large-scale] déversoir *m* **2.** [excess - of population, production] excédent *m*, surplus *m* ; [- of energy, emotion] trop-plein *m*, débordement *m* **3.** [flooding] inondation *f* ■ [excess] trop-plein *m* **4.** COMPUT dépassement *m* de capacité, débordement *m*.

overflown [,əʊvə'fləʊn] *pp* ▻ **overfly**.

overflow pipe *n* trop-plein *m*, tuyau *m* d'écoulement.

overfly [,əʊvə'flaɪ] (*pret* **overflew** [,əʊvə'flu:], *pp* **overflown** [,əʊvə'fləʊn]) *vt* survoler.

overfond [,əʊvə'fɒnd] *adj* : **she's not ~ of children** on ne peut pas dire qu'elle ait une passion pour les enfants.

overfull [,əʊvə'fʊl] *adj* trop plein, qui déborde.

overgenerous [,əʊvə'dʒenərəs] *adj* [person, act] (trop) généreux, prodigue ■ [portion] trop copieux, excessif.

overground ['əʊvəgraʊnd] <> *adj* à la surface du sol, en surface ■ **an ~ rail link** une voie ferrée à l'air libre OR aérienne.
<> *adv* à la surface du sol ■ **the line goes ~ when it reaches the suburbs** la ligne fait surface quand elle arrive en banlieue.

overgrown [ˌəʊvə'grəʊn] *adj* [garden, path etc] : **~ with** envahi par ■ **the garden has become very ~** le jardin est devenu une vraie jungle ■ **a wall ~ with ivy** un mur recouvert de lierre ■ **he's just an ~ schoolboy** *fig* c'est un grand enfant.

overhand ['əʊvəhænd] = **overarm**.

overhang ◇ *vt* [ˌəʊvə'hæŋ] (*pret & pp* **overhung** [-'hʌŋ]) **1.** [subj: cliff, ledge, balcony] surplomber, faire saillie au-dessus de ■ [subj: cloud, mist, smoke] planer sur, flotter au-dessus de **2.** *fig* [subj: threat, danger] planer sur, menacer.
◇ *vi* [ˌəʊvə'hæŋ] (*pret & pp* **overhung** [-'hʌŋ]) être en surplomb, faire saillie.
◇ *n* ['əʊvəhæŋ] surplomb *m*.

overhanging [ˌəʊvə'hæŋɪŋ] *adj* **1.** [cliff, ledge, balcony] en surplomb, en saillie ■ **we walked under the ~ branches** nous marchions sous un dais *OR* une voûte de branches **2.** *fig* [threat] imminent.

overhaul ◇ *n* ['əʊvəhɔ:l] [of car, machine] révision *f* ■ [of institution, system] révision *f*, remaniement *m*.
◇ *vt* [ˌəʊvə'hɔ:l] **1.** [car, machine] réviser ■ [system] revoir, remanier **2.** [catch up] rattraper ■ [overtake] dépasser ■ NAUT gagner.

overhead ◇ *adv* [ˌəʊvə'hed] au-dessus ■ **we watched the hawk circling ~** nous regardions le faucon tournoyer dans le ciel *OR* au-dessus de nos têtes.
◇ *adj* ['əʊvəhed] **1.** [cable, railway] aérien ■ [lighting] au plafond ■ SPORT [racket stroke] smashé ■ FTBL [kick] retourné **2.** COMM : **~ costs** frais *mpl* généraux.
◇ *n* ['əʊvəhed] *US* = **overheads**.
◆ **overheads** *npl UK* frais *mpl* généraux.

overhead camshaft *n* arbre *m* à cames en tête.

overhead door *n* porte *f* basculante.

overhead projector *n* rétroprojecteur *m*.

overhear [ˌəʊvə'hɪə^r] (*pret & pp* **overheard** [-'hɜ:d]) *vt* [gen] entendre par hasard ■ [conversation] surprendre ■ **I couldn't help ~ing what you were saying** malgré moi, j'ai entendu votre conversation ■ **she overheard them talking about her** elle les a surpris à parler d'elle.

overheat [ˌəʊvə'hi:t] ◇ *vt* surchauffer.
◇ *vi* chauffer.

overheated [ˌəʊvə'hi:tɪd] *adj* **1.** [too hot - room] surchauffé, trop chauffé ; [- engine] qui chauffe **2.** *fig* [angry] passionné, violent, exalté.

overheating [ˌəʊvə'hi:tɪŋ] *n* échauffement *m* excessif.

overhung [-'hʌŋ] *pt & pp* ▷ **overhang**.

overimpress [ˌəʊvərɪm'pres] *vt* : **she wasn't ~ed by the film** le film ne l'a pas particulièrement impressionnée.

overindulge [ˌəʊvərɪn'dʌldʒ] ◇ *vt* **1.** [appetite, desire] céder à, succomber à **2.** [person] (trop) gâter ■ **she ~s her children** elle cède à tous les caprices de ses enfants ■ **he has a tendency to ~ himself** il a tendance à faire des excès *OR* à se laisser aller.
◇ *vi* [overeat] trop manger ■ [drink] trop boire ■ **you mustn't ~** il ne faut pas abuser des bonnes choses.

overindulgence [ˌəʊvərɪn'dʌldʒəns] *n* **1.** [in food and drink] excès *m*, abus *m* **2.** [towards person] indulgence *f* excessive, complaisance *f*.

overindulgent [ˌəʊvərɪn'dʌldʒənt] *adj* **1.** [in food and drink] : **he's ~** c'est un bon vivant ■ **an ~ weekend** un week-end de bombance **2.** [towards person] trop indulgent, complaisant.

overjoyed [ˌəʊvə'dʒɔɪd] *adj* comblé, transporté, ravi ■ **she was ~ at being home again** elle était ravie d'être rentrée ■ **I was ~ at the news** cette nouvelle m'a ravi *OR* transporté.

overkill ['əʊvəkɪl] *n* **1.** MIL surarmement *m* **2.** *fig* exagération *f*, excès *m* ■ **media ~** médiatisation *f* excessive.

overladen [ˌəʊvə'leɪdn] ◇ *pp* ▷ **overload**.
◇ *adj* surchargé.

overlaid [ˌəʊvə'leɪd] *pt & pp* ▷ **overlay**.

overland ['əʊvəlænd] *adj & adv* par voie de terre ■ **the ~ route to India** le voyage en Inde par la route.

overlap ◇ *vi* [ˌəʊvə'læp] (*pret & pp* **overlapped**, *cont* **overlapping**) [gen] (se) chevaucher, se recouvrir en partie ■ **our visits overlapped** nos visites ont plus ou moins coïncidé ■ **my responsibilities ~ with hers** mes responsabilités empiètent sur les siennes.
◇ *vt* [ˌəʊvə'læp] (*pret & pp* **overlapped**, *cont* **overlapping**) [in space] faire se chevaucher ■ [in time] empiéter sur.
◇ *n* ['əʊvəlæp] **1.** [gen] chevauchement *m* **2.** GEOL nappe *f* de charriage.

overlay ◇ *vt* [ˌəʊvə'leɪ] (*pret & pp* **overlaid** [ˌəʊvə'leɪd]) recouvrir.
◇ *n* ['əʊvəleɪ] **1.** [covering] revêtement *m* **2.** COMPUT recouvrement *m*.

overleaf [ˌəʊvə'li:f] *adv* au dos, au verso ■ **'see ~'** 'voir au verso' ■ **'continued ~'** [in book, magazine] 'suite page suivante'.

overload ◇ *vt* [ˌəʊvə'ləʊd] *pp* **overloaded 1.** (*pp (also)* **overladen** [ˌəʊvə'leɪdn]) [animal, vehicle] surcharger **2.** (*pp* **overloaded**) [electric circuit] surcharger ■ [engine, machine] surmener ■ *fig* [with work] surcharger, écraser.
◇ *n* ['əʊvələʊd] surcharge *f*.

overlong [ˌəʊvə'lɒŋ] ◇ *adj* trop *OR* excessivement long.
◇ *adv* trop longtemps.

overlook [ˌəʊvə'lʊk] *vt* **1.** [have view of] avoir vue sur, donner sur ■ **'villa ~ing the sea'** 'villa avec vue sur la mer' **2.** [fail to notice - detail, small thing] laisser échapper, oublier ■ **it's easy to ~ the small print** on oublie souvent de lire ce qui est en petits caractères ■ [neglect] négliger, ne pas prendre en compte ■ **he seems to have ~ed the fact that I might have difficulties** l'idée que je puisse avoir des difficultés semble lui avoir échappé ■ **his work has been ~ed for centuries** cela fait des siècles que ses travaux sont ignorés ■ [ignore] laisser passer, passer sur ■ **I'll ~ it this time** je veux bien fermer les yeux cette fois-ci **3.** [supervise] surveiller.

overlord ['əʊvəlɔ:d] *n* **1.** HIST suzerain *m* **2.** *fig* grand patron *m*.

overly ['əʊvəlɪ] *adj* trop ■ **she was not ~ friendly** elle ne s'est pas montrée particulièrement aimable.

overmanned [ˌəʊvə'mænd] *adj* [factory, production line] en sureffectif.

overmanning [ˌəʊvə'mænɪŋ] *n (U)* sureffectifs *mpl*.

overmuch [ˌəʊvə'mʌtʃ] *fml* ◇ *adj* trop de.
◇ *adv* outre mesure, trop.

overnice [ˌəʊvə'naɪs] *adj* [distinction] trop subtil ■ [person] trop méticuleux, pointilleux à l'excès.

overnight ◇ *adv* [ˌəʊvə'naɪt] **1.** [during the night] pendant la nuit ■ **to drive/to fly ~** rouler/voler de nuit ■ [until next day] jusqu'au lendemain ■ **they stopped** *OR* **stayed ~ in Birmingham** ils ont passé la nuit à Birmingham ■ **the milk won't keep ~** le lait ne se conservera pas jusqu'à demain **2.** *fig* [suddenly] du jour au lendemain.
◇ *adj* ['əʊvənaɪt] **1.** [stay, guest] d'une nuit ■ [clothes, journey] de nuit ■ **we had an ~ stay in Paris** nous avons passé une nuit à Paris **2.** *fig* [sudden] soudain, subit.
◇ *vi* ['əʊvənaɪt] passer la *OR* une nuit.

overnight bag *n* sac *m* *OR* nécessaire *m* de voyage.

overpaid [ˌəʊvə'peɪd] *pt & pp* ▷ **overpay**.

overpass ['əʊvəpɑ:s] *n* AUT saut-de-mouton *m (route)*.

overpay [ˌəʊvə'peɪ] (*pret & pp* **overpaid** [ˌəʊvə'peɪd]) *vt* [bill, employee] surpayer, trop payer.

overpayment [ˌəʊvə'peɪmənt] *n* trop-perçu *m*.

overplay [ˌəʊvə'pleɪ] ◇ *vt* [importance] exagérer ■ **to ~ one's hand** présumer de ses forces *OR* de ses capacités.
◇ *vi* exagérer son rôle.

overpopulated [ˌəʊvə'pɒpjʊleɪtɪd] *adj* surpeuplé.

overpopulation ['əʊvə,pɒpjʊ'leɪʃn] *n* surpeuplement *m*, surpopulation *f*.

overpower [,əʊvə'paʊəʳ] *vt* **1.** [physically - enemy, opponent] maîtriser, vaincre **2.** [subj: smell] suffoquer ■ [subj: heat, emotion] accabler ■ **they were ~ed by his charm** ils furent ensorcelés *OR* subjugués par son charme.

overpowering [,əʊvə'paʊərɪŋ] *adj* **1.** [heat, sensation] accablant, écrasant ■ [smell] suffocant ■ [perfume] entêtant **2.** [desire, passion] irrésistible ■ [grief] accablant ■ **an ~ sense of guilt** un sentiment irrépressible de culpabilité **3.** [force] irrésistible **4.** [personality, charisma] dominateur, irrésistible.

overprice [,əʊvə'praɪs] *vt* vendre trop cher.

overpriced [,əʊvə'praɪst] *adj* excessivement cher ■ **those books are really ~** le prix de ces livres est vraiment excessif *OR* trop élevé.

overprint ◇ *vt* [,əʊvə'prɪnt] imprimer en surcharge.
◇ *n* ['əʊvəprɪnt] surcharge *f*.

overproduce [,əʊvəprə'dju:s] *vt* surproduire.

overproduction [,əʊvəprə'dʌkʃn] *n* surproduction *f*.

overprotective [,əʊvəprə'tektɪv] *adj* trop protecteur, protecteur à l'excès ■ **she is ~ of** *OR* **towards her son** elle couve trop son fils.

overpublicize, *UK* **ise** [,əʊvə'pʌblɪsaɪz] *vt* faire trop de publicité pour, donner trop de publicité à.

overqualified [,əʊvə'kwɒlɪfaɪd] *adj* surqualifié.

overran [,əʊvə'ræn] *pt* ▷ **overrun**.

overrate [,əʊvə'reɪt] *vt* [person] surestimer ■ [book, film] surfaire.

overrated [,əʊvə'reɪtɪd] *adj* [person] : **he is rather ~ as a novelist** sa réputation de romancier est assez surfaite ▮ [book, film] : **I think champagne is really ~** je pense que le champagne ne mérite pas sa réputation *OR* que la réputation du champagne est surfaite.

overreach [,əʊvə'ri:tʃ] *vt* : **to ~ o.s.** présumer de ses forces, viser trop haut.

overreact [,əʊvərɪ'ækt] *vi* [gen] réagir de façon excessive, dramatiser ■ [panic] s'affoler.

overreaction [,əʊvərɪ'ækʃn] *n* réaction *f* disproportionnée *OR* excessive ■ [panic] affolement *m*.

overridable [,əʊvə'raɪdəbl] *adj* COMPUT annulable.

override [,əʊvə'raɪd] (*pret* **overrode** [-'rəʊd], *pp* **overridden** [-'rɪdn]) *vt* **1.** [instruction, desire, authority] passer outre à, outrepasser ■ [decision] annuler ■ [rights] fouler aux pieds, bafouer **2.** [fact, factor] l'emporter sur **3.** [controls, mechanism] annuler, neutraliser **4.** [horse] harasser.

overriding [,əʊvə'raɪdɪŋ] *adj* **1.** [importance] primordial, capital ■ [belief, consideration, factor] prépondérant, premier, dominant **2.** LAW [clause] dérogatoire.

overripe [,əʊvə'raɪp] *adj* [fruit] trop mûr ■ [cheese] trop fait.

overrode [-'rəʊd] *pt* ▷ **override**.

overrule [,əʊvə'ru:l] *vt* [decision] annuler ■ [claim, objection] rejeter ■ **I was ~d** mon avis a été rejeté.

overrun ◇ *vt* [,əʊvə'rʌn] (*pret* **overran** [,əʊvə'ræn], *pp* **overrun**, *cont* **overrunning**) **1.** [invade] envahir ■ **the garden is ~ with weeds** le jardin est envahi de mauvaises herbes ■ **the building was ~ by rats** l'immeuble était infesté de rats **2.** [exceed - time limit] dépasser ■ [overshoot] dépasser, aller au-delà de ■ **to ~ a signal** RAIL brûler un signal **3.** TYPO [word, sentence - over line] reporter à la ligne suivante ; [- over page] reporter à la page suivante.
◇ *vi* [,əʊvə'rʌn] (*pret* **overran** [,əʊvə'ræn], *pp* **overrun**, *cont* **overrunning**) [programme, speech] dépasser le temps alloué *OR* imparti ■ [meeting] dépasser l'heure prévue ■ **the speech overran by ten minutes** le discours a duré dix minutes de plus que prévu.
◇ *n* ['əʊvərʌn] [in time, space] dépassement *m*.

oversaw [,əʊvə'sɔ:] *pt* ▷ **oversee**.

overscrupulous [,əʊvə'skru:pjʊləs] *adj* [morally] trop scrupuleux ■ [in detail] pointilleux.

overseas ◇ *adv* [,əʊvə'si:z] à l'étranger ■ **to go ~** partir à l'étranger.
◇ *adj* ['əʊvəsi:z] [student, tourist, market] étranger ■ [travel, posting] à l'étranger ■ [mail - from overseas] (en provenance) de l'étranger ; [- to an overseas country] pour l'étranger ■ [trade] extérieur ■ [colony, possession] d'outre-mer ■ **the Ministry of Overseas Development** ≃ le ministère de la Coopération et du Développement ■ **the French ~ territories** les Territoires français d'outre-mer.

oversee [,əʊvə'si:] *vt* (*pret* **oversaw** [,əʊvə'sɔ:], *pp* **overseen** [-'si:n]) [watch] surveiller, contrôler ■ [supervise] superviser.

overseer ['əʊvə,si:əʳ] *n* [foreman] contremaître *m*, chef *m* d'équipe ■ [in mine] porion *m* ■ [in printing works] prote *m* ■ HIST [of slaves] surveillant *m*, - e *f*.

oversell ◇ *vt* [,əʊvə'sel] (*pret & pp* **oversold** [-'səʊld]) **1.** [exaggerate - person, quality] mettre trop en valeur, faire trop valoir **2.** COMM : **the concert was oversold** on a vendu plus de billets pour le concert qu'il n'y avait de places.
◇ *n* ['əʊvəsel] [exaggeration] éloge *m* excessif, panégyrique *m*.

oversensitive [,əʊvə'sensɪtɪv] *adj* trop sensible *OR* susceptible, hypersensible.

oversexed [,əʊvə'sekst] *adj* : **he's ~** il ne pense qu'au sexe.

overshadow [,əʊvə'ʃædəʊ] *vt* **1.** [eclipse - person, event] éclipser **2.** [darken] ombrager ■ **the house is ~ed by a huge flyover** la maison est assombrie par un immense autopont ■ **their lives had been ~ed by the death of their father** *fig* leur vie avait été endeuillée par la mort de leur père.

overshoe ['əʊvəʃu:] *n* galoche *f*.

overshoot ◇ *vt* [,əʊvə'ʃu:t] (*pret & pp* **overshot** [-'ʃɒt]) dépasser, aller au-delà de ➊ **to ~ the mark** aller trop loin.
◇ *vi* [,əʊvə'ʃu:t] (*pret & pp* **overshot** [-'ʃɒt]) [aircraft] dépasser la piste.
◇ *n* ['əʊvəʃu:t] dépassement *m*.

oversight ['əʊvəsaɪt] *n* **1.** [error] omission *f*, oubli *m* ■ **by** *OR* **through an ~** par mégarde, par négligence ■ **due to an ~ your tickets have been sent to your old address** vos billets ont été envoyés par erreur à votre ancienne adresse **2.** [supervision] surveillance *f*, supervision *f*.

oversimplification ['əʊvə,sɪmplɪfɪ'keɪʃn] *n* simplification *f* excessive.

oversimplify [,əʊvə'sɪmplɪfaɪ] *vt* (*pret & pp* **oversimplified**) simplifier à l'excès.

over-sixties *npl* : **the ~** le troisième âge, les plus de soixante ans.

oversize(d) [,əʊvə'saɪz(d)] *adj* **1.** [very big] énorme, démesuré **2.** [too big] trop grand.

oversleep [,əʊvə'sli:p] (*pret & pp* **overslept** [-'slept]) *vi* se réveiller en retard, ne pas se réveiller à temps.

oversold [-'səʊld] *pt & pp* ▷ **oversell**.

overspend ◇ *n* ['əʊvəspend] FIN dépassement *m* budgétaire *OR* du budget.
◇ *vi* [,əʊvə'spend] (*pret & pp* **overspent** [-'spent]) [gen] trop dépenser ■ FIN être en dépassement budgétaire ■ **I've been ~ing recently** j'ai trop dépensé *OR* j'ai dépensé trop d'argent récemment ■ **I've overspent by £5** j'ai dépensé 5 livres de trop.
◇ *vt* [,əʊvə'spend] (*pret & pp* **overspent** [-'spent]) [allowance] dépasser ■ **to have overspent one's budget** FIN être en dépassement budgétaire.

overspill ◇ *vi* [,əʊvə'spɪl] déborder, se répandre.
◇ *n* ['əʊvəspɪl] excédent *m* de population (urbaine).
◇ *comp* : **~ population** excédent *m* de population.

overstaffed [,əʊvə'stɑ:ft] *adj* en sureffectif ■ **the firm is ~** le personnel de la firme est trop nombreux, la firme connaît un problème de sureffectifs.

overstate [ˌəʊvəˈsteɪt] *vt* exagérer.

overstatement [ˌəʊvəˈsteɪtmənt] *n* exagération *f* ▪ **to say that he's a singer would be an ~** il ne mérite pas vraiment le titre de chanteur.

overstay [ˌəʊvəˈsteɪ] *vt* : **to ~ one's welcome** abuser de l'hospitalité de ses hôtes.

oversteer ◇ *n* [ˈəʊvəstɪəʳ] AUT survirage *m*.
◇ *vi* [ˌəʊvəˈstɪəʳ] survirer.

overstep [ˌəʊvəˈstep] *vt* (*pret & pp* **overstepped**, *cont* **overstepping**) dépasser, outrepasser ▶ **to ~ the mark** *OR* **the limit** *fig* dépasser les bornes, aller trop loin.

overstocked [ˌəʊvəˈstɒkt] *adj* **1.** [warehouse] trop approvisionné ▪ [market] encombré, surchargé **2.** [farm] qui a un excès de cheptel ▪ [river] trop poissonneux.

overstrike COMPUT ◇ *n* [ˈəʊvəstraɪk] [character] caractère *m* superposé ▪ [action] frappe *f* superposée.
◇ *vt* [ˌəʊvəˈstraɪk] superposer un caractère à.

oversubscribe [ˌəʊvəsəbˈskraɪb] *vt* : **to be ~d** [concert, play] être en surlocation ▪ **the share issue was ~d** ST. EX la demande d'achats a dépassé le nombre de titres émis ▪ **the school trip is ~d** il y a trop d'élèves inscrits à l'excursion organisée par l'école.

overt [ˈəʊvɜːt, əʊˈvɜːt] *adj* manifeste, évident.

overtake [ˌəʊvəˈteɪk] *vt* (*pret* **overtook** [-ˈtʊk], *pp* **overtaken** [-ˈteɪkn]) **1.** [pass beyond] dépasser, devancer ▪ *UK* AUT dépasser, doubler ▪ **'no overtaking'** 'interdiction de dépasser' **2.** [surprise] surprendre ▪ **overtaken by events** dépassé par les événements ▮ [strike] frapper ▪ **~n by** *OR* **with panic** pris de panique **3.** *lit* [engulf - subj: emotion] s'emparer de.

overtaking lane [ˌəʊvəˈteɪkɪŋ-] *n UK* AUT [when driving on right] voie *f* de gauche ▪ [when driving on left] voie *f* de droite.

overtax [ˌəʊvəˈtæks] *vt* **1.** FIN [person] surimposer ▪ [goods] surtaxer **2.** [strain - patience, hospitality] abuser de ; [- person, heart] surmener.

over-the-counter *adj* **1.** [medicines] vendu sans ordonnance, en vente libre **2.** ST. EX : **~ market** marché *m* hors-cote.

overthrow ◇ *vt* [ˌəʊvəˈθrəʊ] (*pret* **overthrew** [-ˈθruː], *pp* **overthrown** [-ˈθrəʊn]) **1.** [regime, government] renverser ▪ [rival, enemy army] vaincre ▪ [values, standards] bouleverser ▪ [plans] réduire à néant **2.** [ball] envoyer trop loin.
◇ *n* [ˈəʊvəθrəʊ] **1.** [of enemy] défaite *f* ▪ [of regime, government] renversement *m*, chute *f* ▪ [of values, standards] bouleversement *m* **2.** [in cricket - throw] *balle qui dépasse le guichet* ; [- run] *point marqué par une balle hors jeu*.

overtime [ˈəʊvətaɪm] *n (U)* **1.** [work] heures *fpl* supplémentaires ▪ **to do** *OR* **to work ~** faire des heures supplémentaires ▪ **he'll have to work ~ to get those two to agree!** *fig* s'il veut mettre ces deux-là d'accord, il a intérêt à se lever de bonne heure! ▪ **your imagination seems to have been working ~** on dirait que tu as laissé ton imagination s'emballer **2.** [overtime pay] rémunération *f* des heures supplémentaires ▪ **to be paid ~** être payé en heures supplémentaires **3.** *US* SPORT prolongations *fpl* ▪ **the match went into ~** ils ont joué les prolongations.

overtime pay = **overtime** *(sense 2)*.

overtly [əʊˈvɜːtlɪ] *adv* franchement, ouvertement.

overtone [ˈəʊvətəʊn] *n* **1.** [nuance] nuance *f*, accent *m* ▪ **there was an ~ of aggression in what she said** il y avait une pointe d'agressivité dans ses propos ▪ **his speech was full of racist ~s** son discours était truffé de sous-entendus racistes **2.** MUS harmonique *m*.

overtook [-ˈtʊk] *pt* ▷ **overtake**.

overture [ˈəʊvəˌtjʊəʳ] *n* **1.** MUS ouverture *f* **2.** *fig* [proposal] ouverture *f*, avance *f* ▪ **to make ~s to sb** faire des avances à qqn **3.** *fig* [prelude] prélude *m*, début *m*.

overturn [ˌəʊvəˈtɜːn] ◇ *vt* **1.** [lamp, car, furniture] renverser ▪ [ship] faire chavirer **2.** [overthrow - regime, government, plans] renverser ▪ LAW [judgment, sentence] casser ▪ **the bill was ~ed by the Senate** le projet de loi a été rejeté par le Sénat.
◇ *vi* [lamp, furniture] se renverser ▪ [car] se retourner, capoter ▪ [ship] chavirer.

overuse ◇ *vt* [ˌəʊvəˈjuːz] abuser de.
◇ *n* [ˌəʊvəˈjuːs] abus *m*, usage *m* excessif.

overused [ˌəʊvəˈjuːzd] *adj* [word, phrase] galvaudé.

overvalue [ˌəʊvəˈvæljuː] *vt* **1.** [currency] surévaluer ▪ [house, painting] surestimer **2.** [overrate] surestimer, faire trop de cas de.

overview [ˈəʊvəvjuː] *n* vue *f* d'ensemble.

overweening [ˌəʊvəˈwiːnɪŋ] *adj UK* **1.** [pride, ambition etc] sans bornes, démesuré **2.** [person] outrecuidant, présomptueux.

overweight ◇ *adj* [ˌəʊvəˈweɪt] [person] (trop) gros, (trop) grosse *f* ▪ **~ people are more prone to heart disease** les personnes trop grosses *OR* fortes ont plus de risques d'avoir des maladies cardiaques ▪ **I'm a few pounds ~** j'ai quelques kilos de trop ▮ [luggage, parcel] trop lourd.
◇ *n* [ˈəʊvəweɪt] excès *m* de poids.
◇ *vt* [ˌəʊvəˈweɪt] **1.** [overload] surcharger **2.** [overemphasize] accorder trop d'importance à, trop privilégier.

overwhelm [ˌəʊvəˈwelm] *vt* **1.** [devastate] accabler, terrasser ▪ [astound] bouleverser ▪ **~ed with grief** accablé de chagrin ▪ **your generosity ~s me** votre générosité me bouleverse *OR* me va droit au cœur **2.** *liter & fig* [submerge] submerger ▪ **our switchboard has been ~ed by the number of calls** notre standard a été submergé par les appels **3.** [defeat] écraser.

overwhelming [ˌəʊvəˈwelmɪŋ] *adj* **1.** [crushing - victory, defeat] écrasant ▪ **the ~ majority (of people) oppose these measures** la grande majorité des gens est opposée à ces mesures **2.** [extreme, overpowering - grief, heat] accablant ; [- joy] extrême ; [- love] passionnel ; [- desire, urge, passion] irrésistible ▪ **an ~ sense of frustration** un sentiment d'extrême frustration ▪ **their friendliness is somewhat ~** leur amabilité a quelque chose d'excessif.

overwhelmingly [ˌəʊvəˈwelmɪŋlɪ] *adv* **1.** [crushingly] de manière écrasante ▪ **the House of Lords voted ~ against the bill** la Chambre des lords a voté contre le projet à une écrasante majorité **2.** [as intensifier] extrêmement ▪ [predominantly] surtout.

overwind [ˌəʊvəˈwaɪnd] (*pret & pp* **overwound** [-ˈwaʊnd]) *vt* [clock, watch] trop remonter.

overwork ◇ *vt* [ˌəʊvəˈwɜːk] **1.** [person] surmener ▪ **to be ~ed and underpaid** être surchargé de travail et sous-payé **2.** [word] abuser de, utiliser trop souvent.
◇ *vi* [ˌəʊvəˈwɜːk] se surmener.
◇ *n* [ˈəʊvəˌwɜːk] surmenage *m*.

overwrite [ˌəʊvəˈraɪt] (*pret* **overwrote** [-ˈrəʊt], *pp* **overwritten** [-ˈrɪtn]) ◇ *vt* **1.** [write on top of] écrire sur, repasser sur **2.** COMPUT [file] écraser.
◇ *vi* écrire dans un style ampoulé.

overwrought [ˌəʊvəˈrɔːt] *adj* sur les nerfs, à bout.

overzealous [ˌəʊvəˈzeləs] *adj* trop zélé.

Ovid [ˈɒvɪd] *pr n* Ovide.

oviduct [ˈəʊvɪdʌkt] *n* oviducte *m*.

oviparous [əʊˈvɪpərəs] *adj* ovipare.

ovoid [ˈəʊvɔɪd] ◇ *adj* ovoïde, ovoïdal.
◇ *n* figure *f* ovoïde.

ovulate [ˈɒvjʊleɪt] *vi* ovuler.

ovulation [ˌɒvjʊˈleɪʃn] *n* ovulation *f*.

ovule ['ɒvju:l] *n* ovule *m*.

ovum ['əʊvəm] (*pl* **ova** ['əʊvə]) *n* BIOL ovule *m*.

ow [aʊ] *interj* aïe.

owe [əʊ] ◇ *vt* devoir ▪ **to ~ sthg to sb, to ~ sb sthg** devoir qqch à qqn ▪ **how much** *OR* **what do I ~ you?** combien est-ce que *OR* qu'est-ce que je vous dois? ▪ **how much do we still ~ him for** *OR* **on the car?** combien nous reste-t-il à lui payer pour la voiture? ▪ **I think you ~ him an explanation** je pense qu'il a droit à une explication de ta part *OR* que tu lui dois une explication ▪ **we ~ them an apology** nous leur devons des excuses ▪ **you ~ it to yourself to try again** tu te dois d'essayer encore une fois ▪ **to what do we ~ the honour of your visit?** qu'est-ce qui nous vaut l'honneur de votre visite? ▪ **I ~ it all to my parents** je suis redevable de tout cela à mes parents ▪ **he ~s his good looks to his mother** il tient sa beauté de sa mère ▶ **I ~ you one!** à charge de revanche!
◇ *vi* être endetté ▪ **he still ~s for** *OR* **on the house** il n'a pas encore fini de payer la maison.

owing ['əʊɪŋ] *adj (after n)* dû ▪ **the sum ~ on the car** la somme qui reste due sur le prix de la voiture ▪ **to have a lot of money ~** [to owe] devoir beaucoup d'argent ; [to be owed] avoir beaucoup d'argent à récupérer.
◆ **owing to** *prep phr* à cause de, en raison de.

owl [aʊl] *n* hibou *m*, chouette *f* ▪ **he's a wise old ~** c'est la sagesse faite homme, c'est l'image même de la sagesse.

owlet ['aʊlɪt] *n* jeune hibou *m*, jeune chouette *f*.

owlish ['aʊlɪʃ] *adj* : **those glasses give you an ~ look** tu as l'air d'un hibou avec ces lunettes.

own [əʊn] ◇ *adj* propre ▪ **I have my very ~ bedroom** j'ai une chambre pour moi tout seul ▪ **a flat with its ~ entrance** un appartement avec une porte d'entrée indépendante ▪ **these are my ~ skis** ces skis sont à moi *OR* m'appartiennent ▪ **I'll do it (in) my ~ way** je le ferai à ma façon ▪ **it's all my ~ work** c'est moi qui ai tout fait ▪ **it's your ~ fault!** tu n'as à t'en prendre qu'à toi-même! ▪ **you'll have to make up your ~ mind** c'est à toi et à toi seul de décider, personne ne pourra prendre cette décision à ta place.
◇ *pron* : **is that car your ~?** est-ce que cette voiture est à vous? ▪ **I don't need a pen, I've brought my ~** je n'ai pas besoin de stylo, j'ai apporté le mien ▪ **if you want a car, you'll have to buy your ~** si tu veux une voiture, tu n'as qu'à t'en acheter une ▪ **her opinions are identical to my ~** nous partageons exactement les mêmes opinions ▪ **a house/a room/a garden of one's (very) ~** une maison/une pièce/un jardin (bien) à soi ▪ **their son has a car of his ~** leur fils a sa propre voiture ▪ **I shan't be going for reasons of my ~** je n'irai pas pour des raisons personnelles ▪ **the town has a character of its ~** *OR* **all (of) its ~** la ville possède un charme qui lui est propre *OR* un charme bien à elle ▪ **my time is not my ~** je ne suis pas maître de mon temps ▪ **I haven't a single thing I can call my ~** je n'ai rien à moi ▪ **you're on your ~ now!** à toi de jouer maintenant! ▶ **to come into one's ~** [show one's capabilities] montrer de quoi on est capable ; [inherit] toucher son héritage ▪ **to get one's ~ back (on sb)** se venger (de qqn) ▪ **I'll get my ~ back on him for that** je lui revaudrai ça ▪ **to look after one's ~** s'occuper des siens ▪ **to make sthg one's ~** s'approprier qqch.
◇ *vt* **1.** [possess] posséder ▪ **they ~ 51% of the shares** ils détiennent 51 % des actions ▪ **does she ~ the house?** est-elle propriétaire de la maison? ▪ **who ~s this car?** à qui appartient cette voiture? ▶ **they walked in as if they ~ed the place** *inf* ils sont entrés comme (s'ils étaient) chez eux **2.** *lit* [admit] admettre, reconnaître.
◆ **on one's own** *adj phr* (tout) seul ▪ **I'm trying to get him on his ~** j'essaie de le voir seul à seul ▪ **I did it (all) on my ~** je l'ai fait tout seul.
◆ **own to** *vt insep lit* avouer.
◆ **own up** *vi insep* avouer, faire des aveux ▪ **to ~ up to sthg** avouer qqch ▪ **he ~ed up to his mistake** il a reconnu son erreur.

own-brand *adj* : **~ products** *produits vendus sous la marque du distributeur.*

owner ['əʊnəʳ] *n* propriétaire *mf* ▪ **at the ~'s risk** aux risques du propriétaire ▪ **who is the ~ of this jacket?** à qui appartient cette veste? ▪ **they are all car ~s** ils possèdent *OR* ils ont tous une voiture.

ownerless ['əʊnəlɪs] *adj* sans propriétaire.

owner-occupied *adj* occupé par son propriétaire.

owner-occupier *n* occupant *m*, - e *f* propriétaire.

ownership ['əʊnəʃɪp] *n* possession *f* ▪ **we require proof of ~** nous demandons un titre de propriété ▪ **the government encourages home ~** le gouvernement encourage l'accession à la propriété ▪ **'under new ~'** 'changement de propriétaire'.

own goal *n* FTBL but *m* marqué contre son camp ▪ **to score an ~** marquer contre son camp ; *fig* agir contre ses propres intérêts.

own-label *n* = **own-brand**.

ownsome ['əʊnsəm], **owny-o** ['əʊnɪəʊ] *n UK inf* **(all) on one's ~** tout seul.

ox [ɒks] (*pl* **oxen** ['ɒksn]) *n* bœuf *m*.

oxblood ['ɒksblʌd] ◇ *n* [colour] rouge *m* sang.
◇ *adj* rouge sang *(inv)*.

Oxbridge ['ɒksbrɪdʒ] *pr n désignation collective des universités d'Oxford et de Cambridge* ▪ **~ graduates** diplômés des universités d'Oxford ou de Cambridge.

oxcart ['ɒkskɑ:t] *n* char *m* à bœuf *OR* à bœufs.

oxen ['ɒksn] *pl* ▷ **ox**.

Oxfam ['ɒksfæm] (*abbrev of* **Oxford Committee for Famine Relief**) *pr n association caritative britannique.*

Oxford bags *npl* [trousers] pantalon *m* très large.

Oxford English *n l'anglais de l'université d'Oxford, servant parfois de référence pour la 'bonne' prononciation.*

Oxford Street *pr n une des grandes artères commerçantes de Londres.*

oxidation [,ɒksɪ'deɪʃn] *n* oxydation *f*.

oxide ['ɒksaɪd] *n* oxyde *m*.

oxidize, ise ['ɒksɪdaɪz] ◇ *vt* oxyder.
◇ *vi* s'oxyder.

oxidizing agent ['ɒksɪdaɪzɪŋ-] *n* oxydant *m*.

Oxon *written abbr of* **Oxfordshire**.

Oxon. (*written abbrev of* **Oxoniensis**) *de l'université d'Oxford.*

Oxonian [ɒk'səʊnjən] ◇ *n* [student] étudiant *m*, - e *f* de l'université d'Oxford ▪ [townsperson] Oxfordien *m*, - enne *f*.
◇ *adj* oxfordien, d'Oxford.

oxtail ['ɒksteɪl] *n* queue *f* de bœuf ▪ **~ soup** soupe *f* de queue de bœuf.

ox tongue *n* langue *f* de bœuf.

oxyacetylene [,ɒksɪə'setɪli:n] *adj* oxyacétylénique.

oxygen ['ɒksɪdʒən] *n* oxygène *m*.

oxygenation [,ɒksɪdʒə'neɪʃn] *n* oxygénation *f*.

oxygen mask *n* masque *m* à oxygène.

oxygen tent *n* tente *f* à oxygène.

oxymoron [,ɒksɪ'mɔ:rɒn] (*pl* **oxymora** [-rə]) *n* oxymoron *m*.

oyster ['ɔɪstəʳ] *n* huître *f* ▪ **the world is her ~** le monde lui appartient.

oyster bed *n* parc *m* à huîtres.

oystercatcher ['ɔɪstə,kætʃəʳ] *n* huîtrier *m*.

oz. *written abbr of* **ounce**.

ozone ['əʊzəʊn] *n* **1.** [gas] ozone *m* ▪ **~ layer** *OR* **shield** couche *f* d'ozone **2.** *inf* [sea air] bon air *m* marin.

ozone-friendly *adj* qui préserve la couche d'ozone.

P

p (*pl* **p's** *OR pl* **ps**), **P** (*pl* **P's** *OR pl* **Ps**) [pi:] *n* [letter] p *m*, P *m* ▪ **to mind one's p's and q's!** *inf UK* se tenir à carreau, *see also* **f**.

p ◇ (*written abbrev of* **page**) p.
◇ *n* = **penny, pence**.

P45 *n UK formulaire que l'on reçoit en fin de contrat de travail, faisant état des cotisations versées et du montant des impôts acquitté pour l'année écoulée.*

pa [pɑ:] *n inf* papa *m*.

p.a. (*written abbrev of* **per annum**) p.a.

PA ◇ *n* **1.** *UK* (*abbrev of* **personal assistant**) secrétaire *mf* de direction **2.** (*abbrev of* **public address system**) système *m* de sonorisation, sono *f*.
◇ *pr n* = **Press Association**.
◇ *written abbr of* **Pennsylvania**.

PABX (*abbrev of* **private automatic branch exchange**) *n autocommutateur privé.*

PAC (*abbrev of* **political action committee**) *n aux États-Unis, comité qui réunit des fonds pour soutenir une cause politique.*

pace[1] [peɪs] ◇ *n* **1.** [speed] allure *f*, vitesse *f*, train *m* ▪ **she quickened her ~** elle pressa le pas ▪ **we set off at a good** *OR* **brisk** *OR* **smart ~** nous sommes partis à vive allure ▪ **the traffic slowed to (a) walking ~** on roulait au pas ▪ **the slower ~ of country life** le rythme plus paisible de la vie à la campagne ▪ **don't walk so fast, I can't keep ~ with you** ne marche pas si vite, je n'arrive pas à te suivre ▪ **to keep ~ with new developments** se tenir au courant des derniers développements ▪ **output is keeping ~ with demand** la production se maintient au niveau de *OR* répond à la demande ▪ **he couldn't stand** *OR* **take the ~** il n'arrivait pas à suivre le rythme ▪ **do it at your own ~** faites-le à votre propre rythme ▪ **to force the ~** forcer l'allure ▶ **to make** *OR* **to set the ~** SPORT donner l'allure, mener le train ; *fig* donner le ton **2.** [step] pas *m* ▶ **to put sb through his/her ~s** *UK* mettre qqn à l'épreuve ▪ **to go through** *OR* **to show one's ~s** montrer ce dont *OR* de quoi on est capable.
◇ *vi* marcher (à pas mesurés) ▪ **he ~d up and down the corridor** il arpentait le couloir.
◇ *vt* **1.** [corridor, cage, room] arpenter **2.** [regulate] régler l'allure de ▪ **she ~d the first two laps well** elle a trouvé le bon rythme pour les deux premiers tours de piste ▪ **the action is well ~d** le suspense ne faiblit pas.

pace[2] ['peɪsɪ] *prep fml* n'en déplaise à.

pacemaker ['peɪs,meɪkəʳ] *n* **1.** SPORT meneur *m*, - euse *f* de train ▪ *fig* [leader] leader *m* **2.** MED pacemaker *m*, stimulateur *m* cardiaque.

pacer ['peɪsəʳ] *n* SPORT meneur *m*, - euse *f* de train.

pacesetter ['peɪs,setəʳ] = **pacemaker** *(sense 1)*.

pachyderm ['pækɪdɜ:m] *n* pachyderme *m*.

pacific [pə'sɪfɪk] *adj fml* pacifique.

Pacific [pə'sɪfɪk] ◇ *pr n* : **the ~ (Ocean)** le Pacifique, l'océan *m* Pacifique.
◇ *adj* du Pacifique.

Pacific Daylight Time *n* heure *f* d'été du Pacifique.

Pacific Islands *pr npl* îles *fpl* du Pacifique ▪ **in the ~** dans les îles du Pacifique.

Pacific Rim *pr n* : **the ~** *groupe de pays situés au bord du Pacifique, particulièrement les pays industrialisés d'Asie.*

Pacific (Standard) Time *n* heure *f* d'hiver du Pacifique.

pacifier ['pæsɪfaɪəʳ] *n* **1.** [person] pacificateur *m*, - trice *f* **2.** *US* [for baby] tétine *f*, sucette *f*.

pacifism ['pæsɪfɪzm] *n* pacifisme *m*.

pacifist ['pæsɪfɪst] ◇ *adj* pacifiste.
◇ *n* pacifiste *mf*.

pacify ['pæsɪfaɪ] (*pret & pp* **pacified**) *vt* **1.** [soothe] apaiser, calmer **2.** MIL [subdue] pacifier.

pack [pæk] ◇ *vt* **1.** [bags] faire ▪ **to ~ one's case** *OR* **suitcase** faire sa valise ▪ **she ~ed her bags and left** elle a fait ses bagages et elle est partie, elle a plié bagage
2. [container, crate] remplir
3. [put in bags - clothes, belongings] : **I've already ~ed the towels** j'ai déjà mis les serviettes dans la valise ▪ **shall I ~ the camera?** est-ce que j'emporte *OR* je prends l'appareil photo? ▪ **I've ~ed a lunch for you** je t'ai préparé de quoi déjeuner
4. [wrap up - goods for transport] emballer
5. [cram tightly - cupboard, container] bourrer ; [- belongings, people] entasser ▪ **he ~ed his pockets with sweets, he ~ed sweets into his pockets** il a bourré ses poches de bonbons ▪ **we managed to ~ a lot into a week's holiday** *fig* on a réussi à faire énormément de choses en une semaine de vacances ▪ **she ~s the house every night** THEAT elle fait salle comble chaque soir
6. [crowd into - subj: spectators, passengers] s'entasser dans
7. [compress - soil] tasser
8. [fill with supporters] : **to ~ a jury** se composer un jury favorable
9. *inf* [have, carry] : **he ~s a lot of influence in cabinet/ministerial circles** il a beaucoup d'influence au conseil des ministres/ dans les milieux ministériels ▪ **to ~ a gun** *US* être armé
10. [load - horse, donkey] charger.
◇ *vi* **1.** [for journey] faire sa valise *OR* ses bagages
2. [fit - into container] rentrer ▪ **the keyboard will ~ easily into a briefcase** on peut facilement faire tenir le clavier dans un attaché-case

3. [crowd together - spectators, passengers] s'entasser ■ **we all ~ed into her car** nous nous sommes tous entassés dans sa voiture.
◇ *n* **1.** [for carrying - rucksack] sac *m* à dos ; [- bundle] ballot *m* ; [- bale] balle *f* ; [- on animal] charge *f*
2. [packet] paquet *m*
3. *UK* [deck of cards] jeu *m*
4. [group - of children, wolves] bande *f* ; [- of cub scouts] meute *f* ; [- of hunting hounds] meute *f*
5. SPORT [in rugby] pack *m*, paquet *m* (d'avant)
6. MED compresse *f*
7. *phr* **that's a ~ of lies!** *UK* c'est un tissu de mensonges!
◆ **pack away** *vt sep* **1.** [tidy up] ranger
2. = pack off.
◆ **pack in** ◇ *vt sep UK* **1.** [crowd in] entasser ■ **the play is ~ing them in** *inf* la pièce fait salle comble
2. *inf* [task] arrêter ■ [job, boyfriend, girlfriend] plaquer ■ **you should ~ in smoking** tu devrais arrêter de fumer ■ **~ it in!** laisse tomber!, arrête!
◇ *vi insep* **1.** [crowd in] s'entasser (à l'intérieur)
2. *UK inf* [break down - machine, engine] tomber en rade.
◆ **pack off** *vt sep inf* expédier ■ **I ~ed the kids off to bed/school** j'ai envoyé les gosses au lit/à l'école.
◆ **pack up** ◇ *vi insep* **1.** [pack one's suitcase] faire sa valise *OR* ses bagages
2. *UK inf* [break down] tomber en rade
3. *UK inf* [give up] laisser tomber ■ **I'm ~ing up for today** j'arrête pour aujourd'hui.
◇ *vt sep* **1.** [suitcase, bags] faire
2. [clothes, belongings, tools] ranger ■ **help me ~ up the tent** aide-moi à plier la tente.

package ['pækɪdʒ] ◇ *n* **1.** [small parcel] paquet *m*, colis *m* ■ *US* [packet] paquet *m* **2.** [set of proposals] ensemble *m* ■ **we offered them a generous ~** nous leur avons proposé un contrat global très avantageux **3.** COMPUT : **(software) ~** progiciel *m*.
◇ *vt* **1.** [wrap] emballer, conditionner **2.** [in advertising] fabriquer l'image (de marque) de.

package deal *n* transaction *f* globale, accord *m* global ■ **we bought up the lot in a ~** nous avons tout acheté en un seul lot.

package holiday *n* voyage *m* organisé *OR* à prix forfaitaire.

packager ['pækɪdʒəʳ] *n* [in advertising, publishing] packager *m*, packageur *m*.

package tour = **package holiday**.

packaging ['pækɪdʒɪŋ] *n* **1.** [wrapping materials] emballage *m*, conditionnement *m* **2.** [in advertising, publishing] packaging *m*.

pack animal *n* bête *f* de somme.

packed [pækt] *adj* **1.** [crowded - train, room] bondé ; [- theatre] comble ■ **the cinema was ~ (out)** *UK* la salle était comble *OR* pleine à craquer ■ **the meeting was ~** la réunion a fait salle comble **2.** [packaged] emballé, conditionné **3.** [jury] favorable.

-packed *in cpds* [full of] : **a fun~ evening** une soirée pleine de divertissements ■ **an action~ first half** une première moitié pleine d'action.

packed lunch *n* panier-repas *m*, casse-croûte *m inv*.

packer ['pækəʳ] *n* [worker] emballeur *m*, - euse *f*, conditionneur *m*, - euse *f* ■ [machine] emballeuse *f*, conditionneuse *f*.

packet ['pækɪt] *n* **1.** [box] paquet *m* ■ [bag, envelope] sachet *m* ■ **a ~ of soup/seeds** un sachet de soupe/graines **2.** [parcel] paquet *m*, colis *m* **3.** *UK inf* [lot of money] paquet *m* **4.** NAUT : **~ (boat** *OR* **steamer)** paquebot *m*.

packet switching [-,swɪtʃɪŋ] *n* COMPUT commutation *f* par paquets.

packhorse ['pækhɔːs] *n* cheval *m* de bât.

pack ice *n* pack *m*, banquise *f*.

packing ['pækɪŋ] *n (U)* **1.** [of personal belongings] : **have you done your ~?** as-tu fait tes bagages? ■ **the removal men will do the ~** les déménageurs se chargeront de l'emballage **2.** [of parcel] emballage *m* ■ [of commercial goods] emballage *m*, conditionnement *m* ■ **the fish/meat ~ industry** les conserveries de poisson/viande **3.** [wrapping material] emballage *m* **4.** TECH [of piston, joint] garniture *f*.

packing case *n* caisse *f* d'emballage.

pact [pækt] *n* pacte *m* ■ **to make a ~ with the Devil** faire un pacte *OR* pactiser avec le Diable.

pad [pæd] (*pret & pp* **padded**, *cont* **padding**) ◇ *n* **1.** [to cushion shock] coussinet *m* ■ **the skaters wear ~s on their knees and elbows** les patineurs portent des genouillères et des protège-coudes ■ **shin-~** protège-tibia *m* **2.** [for absorbing liquid, polishing etc] tampon *m* **3.** ZOOL [underside of foot] coussinet *m* **4.** [of paper] bloc *m* **5.** AERON & ASTRONAUT aire *f* **6.** *inf* [flat] appart *m* ■ [room] piaule *f* ■ **bachelor ~** garçonnière *f* **7.** BOT [leaf] feuille *f* **8.** [noise] : **the ~ of footsteps behind me** des pas feutrés derrière moi **9.** *inf* [sanitary towel] serviette *f* hygiénique.
◇ *vt* **1.** [clothing] matelasser ■ [shoulder] rembourrer ■ [door, wall] capitonner **2.** = **pad out** *(sense 2)*.
◇ *vi* [walk] avancer à pas feutrés ■ **he padded downstairs in his slippers** il descendit l'escalier en pantoufles ■ **the dog padded along beside the cyclist** le chien trottinait à côté du cycliste.
◆ **pad out** *vt sep* **1.** = pad *(vt sense 1)* **2.** *fig* [essay, article, speech] délayer ■ **he padded out the talk with anecdotes** il a allongé son discours en le truffant d'anecdotes.

padded ['pædɪd] *adj* **1.** [door, bench, steering wheel] capitonné ■ [garment, envelope, oven glove] matelassé ■ [sofa] bien rembourré ■ **~ bra** soutien-gorge *m* à bonnets renforcés ■ **~ cell** cellule *f* capitonnée ■ **~ shoulders** épaules *fpl* rembourrées **2.** [fat] : **he's well ~** il est bien en chair.

padding ['pædɪŋ] *n* **1.** [fabric] ouate *f*, ouatine *f*, garnissage *m* **2.** *fig* [in essay, speech] délayage *m*, remplissage *m*.

paddle ['pædl] ◇ *n* **1.** [for boat, canoe] pagaie *f* **2.** [of waterwheel] palette *f*, aube *f* **3.** *US* [table tennis bat] raquette *f* (de ping-pong) **4.** [of turtle, seal] palette *f* natatoire **5.** [wade] : **to go for** *OR* **to have a ~** aller barboter.
◇ *vi* **1.** [in canoe] pagayer **2.** [wade] barboter.
◇ *vt* **1.** [boat] : **to ~ a canoe** pagayer **2.** *US inf* [spank] donner une fessée à.

paddle boat *n* **1.** = **paddle steamer 2.** [pedalo] Pédalo® *m*.

paddle steamer *n* bateau *m* à roues.

paddling pool *n* pataugeoire *f*.

paddock ['pædək] *n* [gen] enclos *m* ■ [at racetrack] paddock *m*.

paddy ['pædɪ] (*pl* **paddies**) *n* **1.** [field] rizière *f* **2.** [rice] paddy *m*, riz *m* non décortiqué **3.** *UK inf* [fit of temper] : **she was in a real ~** elle était furax.

Paddy ['pædɪ] (*pl* **Paddies**) *n inf offens* Irlandais *m*.

paddy field *n* rizière *f*.

padlock ['pædlɒk] ◇ *n* [for door, gate] cadenas *m* ■ [for bicycle] antivol *m*.
◇ *vt* [door, gate] cadenasser ■ [bicycle] mettre un antivol à.

padre ['pɑːdrɪ] *n* **1.** MIL aumônier *m* **2.** [gen - Catholic] prêtre *m*, curé *m* ; [- Protestant] pasteur *m* ■ [term of address] (mon) Père *m*.

paederast *etc* ['pedəræst] *UK* = **pederast**.

paediatric *etc* [,piːdɪ'ætrɪk] *UK* = **pediatric**.

paedology [piː'dɒlədʒɪ] *UK* = **pedology**.

paedophile *etc* ['piːdəʊ,faɪl] *UK* = **pedophile**.

paella [paɪ'elə] *n* paella *f*.

paeony ['piːənɪ] *UK* = **peony**.

pagan ['peɪgən] ◇ *n* païen *m*, - enne *f*.
◇ *adj* païen.

paganism ['peɪgənɪzm] *n* paganisme *m*.

page [peɪdʒ] ◇ *n* **1.** [of book, newspaper etc] page *f* ▪ **on ~ two** [of book] (à la) page deux ; [of newspaper] (en) page deux ▶ **~ three** *la page 3 du "Sun", où figure chaque jour une pin-up* **2.** [at court] page *m* ▪ [in hotel] chasseur *m*, groom *m* ▪ [at wedding] page *m* ▪ [in legislative body] (jeune) huissier *m*.
◇ *vt* **1.** [paginate] paginer **2.** [call] appeler (par haut-parleur) ▪ **paging Mrs Clark!** on demande Mme Clark! **3.** biper.

pageant ['pædʒənt] *n* [historical parade, show] reconstitution *f* historique ▪ [grand display] spectacle *m* fastueux.

pageantry ['pædʒəntrɪ] *n* apparat *m*, pompe *f*.

page boy *n* **1.** [servant] page *m* ▪ [in hotel] chasseur *m*, groom *m* ▪ [at wedding] page *m* **2.** [hairstyle] : **~ (cut)** coupe *f* à la Jeanne d'Arc.

pager ['peɪdʒəʳ] *n* TELEC récepteur *m* d'appel *OR* de poche.

paginate ['pædʒɪneɪt] *vt* paginer.

pagination [,pædʒɪ'neɪʃn] *n* pagination *f*.

pagoda [pə'gəʊdə] *n* pagode *f*.

paid [peɪd] ◇ *pt* & *pp* ➢ **pay**.
◇ *adj* **1.** payé, rémunéré ▪ **~ holidays** *UK OR* **vacation** *US* congés *mpl* payés ▪ **~ workers** travailleurs *mpl* salariés **2.** *phr* **to put ~ to sthg** gâcher *OR* ruiner qqch.

paid-up *adj* [member] à jour de ses cotisations ▪ *fig* [committed] : **he's a (fully) ~ member of the Communist Party** il a sa carte au Parti Communiste.

pail [peɪl] *n* [bucket] seau *m*.

pain [peɪn] ◇ *vt* [cause distress to] peiner, faire de la peine à ▪ [hurt] faire souffrir.
◇ *n* **1.** [physical] douleur *f* ▪ **he has a ~ in his ear** il a mal à l'oreille ▪ **are you in ~?** avez-vous mal?, est-ce que vous souffrez? ▪ **to cause sb ~** faire mal à qqn **2.** [emotional] peine *f*, douleur *f*, souffrance *f* ▪ **the news will cause her great ~** cette nouvelle va lui faire de la peine **3.** *inf* [annoying person or thing] : **what a ~ he is!** qu'est-ce qu'il est enquiquinant! ▪ **it's a (real)** *OR* **such a ~ trying to cross London during the rush hour** traverser Londres aux heures de pointe, c'est la galère ▶ **he's a ~ in the arse**△ *UK inf OR* **backside** *inf UK OR* **ass**△ *US* il est chiant△, c'est un emmerdeur△ ▪ **she's a ~ in the neck** *inf* elle me casse les pieds **4.** LAW : **on ~ of death** sous peine de mort.
◆ **pains** *npl* [efforts] peine *f*, mal *m* ▪ **he went to great ~s to help us** il s'est donné beaucoup de mal pour nous aider ▪ **is that all we get for our ~s?** c'est comme cela que nous sommes récompensés de nos efforts? ▪ **he was at** *OR* **he took ~s to avoid her** il a tout fait pour l'éviter.

pained [peɪnd] *adj* peiné, affligé.

painful ['peɪnfʊl] *adj* **1.** [sore] douloureux ▪ **these shoes are really ~** ces chaussures me font vraiment mal ▪ **is your back still ~?** avez-vous toujours mal au dos? **2.** [upsetting] pénible **3.** [laborious] pénible, difficile, laborieux **4.** *inf* [very bad] nul.

painfully ['peɪnfʊlɪ] *adv* **1.** [hit, strike, rub] durement ▪ [move, walk] péniblement **2.** [distressingly] douloureusement ▪ [laboriously] laborieusement, avec difficulté **3.** [as intensifier] horriblement ▪ **a ~ boring speech** un discours mortellement ennuyeux ▪ **it was ~ obvious that he didn't understand** il n'était que trop évident qu'il ne comprenait pas ▪ **she's ~ shy** elle est d'une timidité maladive.

painkiller ['peɪn,kɪləʳ] *n* analgésique *m*, calmant *m*.

painkilling ['peɪn,kɪlɪŋ] *adj* analgésique, calmant ▪ **to give sb a ~ injection** injecter un analgésique à qqn.

painless ['peɪnlɪs] *adj* **1.** [injection, operation] sans douleur, indolore ▪ [death] sans souffrance **2.** [unproblematic] facile.

painlessly ['peɪnlɪslɪ] *adv* **1.** [without hurting] sans douleur **2.** [unproblematically] sans peine, sans mal.

painstaking ['peɪnz,teɪkɪŋ] *adj* [research, care] rigoureux, méticuleux ▪ [worker] assidu, soigneux.

painstakingly ['peɪnz,teɪkɪŋlɪ] *adv* soigneusement, méticuleusement.

paint [peɪnt] ◇ *n* **1.** [for a room, furniture, picture] peinture *f* ▪ **a set** *OR* **box of ~s** une boîte de couleurs ▶ **oil/acrylic ~** peinture à l'huile/acrylique **2.** *pej* [make-up] peinture *f*.
◇ *vt* **1.** [room, furniture, picture] peindre ▪ **to ~ one's nails** se vernir les ongles ▪ **to ~ one's face** se maquiller ; *pej* [with make-up] se peinturlurer ▶ **to ~ the town red** *inf* faire la noce *OR* la foire **2.** [apply - varnish] appliquer (au pinceau) **3.** *fig* [describe] dépeindre, décrire ▪ **the author ~s a bleak picture of suburban life** l'auteur dresse un sombre portrait *OR* brosse un sombre tableau de la vie des banlieusards.
◇ *vi* peindre, faire de la peinture ▪ **to ~ in oils** faire de la peinture à l'huile.
◆ **paint out, paint over** *vt sep* recouvrir (d'une couche) de peinture.

paintbox ['peɪntbɒks] *n* boîte *f* de couleurs.

paintbrush ['peɪntbrʌʃ] *n* pinceau *m*.

painted ['peɪntɪd] *adj* **1.** [with paint] peint ▪ **~ blue** peint en bleu **2.** *pej* [with make-up] maquillé, fardé.

painter ['peɪntəʳ] *n* **1.** [artist, decorator] peintre *mf* ▪ **~ and decorator** peintre-décorateur **2.** NAUT amarre *f*.

painting ['peɪntɪŋ] *n* **1.** [activity] peinture *f* **2.** [picture] peinture *f*, tableau *m*.

paint pot *n UK* pot *m* de peinture.

paint stripper *n* décapant *m*.

paintwork ['peɪntwɜ:k] *n (U)* peinture *f* ▪ **the house with the white ~** la maison peinte en blanc.

pair [peəʳ] ◇ *n* **1.** [two related objects or people] paire *f* ▪ **a ~ of shoes/gloves** une paire de chaussures/de gants ▪ **an odd-looking ~** un drôle de tandem ▪ **where's the ~ to this sock?** où est la chaussette qui va avec celle-ci? ▪ **to work in ~s** travailler par deux ▪ **line up in ~s!** mettez-vous en rang (deux) par deux! ▪ **I've only got one ~ of hands!** je n'ai que deux mains! **2.** [single object in two parts] : **a ~ of trousers/shorts/tights** un pantalon/short/collant ▪ **a ~ of scissors** une paire de ciseaux **3.** [husband and wife] couple *m* **4.** [of animals] paire *f* ▪ [of birds] couple *m* **5.** MATHS paire *f* **6.** *UK* POL *deux membres de partis adverses qui se sont entendus pour ne pas participer à un vote ou pour s'abstenir de voter durant une période déterminée* **7.** [in cards, dice] paire *f*.
◇ *vt* [socks] assortir ▪ [animal, birds] apparier, accoupler.
◇ *vi* [animals, birds] s'apparier, s'accoupler.
◆ **pair off** ◇ *vt sep* [arrange in couples - dancers] répartir en couples ; [- team members, children in class] mettre deux par deux ▪ **I got ~ed off with Roger** on m'a mis avec Roger ▪ **our parents are trying to ~ us off** nos parents essaient de nous fiancer.
◇ *vi insep* [dancers] former des couples ▪ [team members, children in class] se mettre deux par deux.
◆ **pair up** ◇ *vt sep* [socks] assortir.
◇ *vi insep* [people] se mettre par deux ▪ **he ~ed up with Bob for the car rally** il a choisi Bob comme équipier pour le rallye.

paisley ['peɪzlɪ] *n* [pattern] (impression *f*) cachemire *m* ▪ [material] tissu *m* cachemire ▪ **a ~ tie** une cravate impression cachemire.

pajama *US* = **pyjama**.

Paki▲ ['pækɪ] *n UK terme raciste désignant un Pakistanais.*

Pakistan [*UK* ,pɑ:kɪ'stɑ:n, *US* 'pækɪstæn] *pr n* Pakistan *m* ▪ **in ~** au Pakistan.

Pakistani [*UK* ,pɑ:kɪ'stɑ:nɪ, *US* ,pækɪ'stænɪ] ◇ *n* Pakistanais *m*, - e *f*.
◇ *adj* pakistanais.

pakora [pə'kɔ:rə] *n beignets de légumes, de poisson, etc ; spécialité indienne.*

pal [pæl] (*pret & pp* **palled**, *cont* **palling**) *n inf* **1.** [friend] copain *m*, copine *f*, pote *m* **2.** [term of address] : **thanks, ~** merci mon pote.
◆ **pal up** *vi insep UK inf* **he/she palled up with George** il est devenu le copain/elle est devenue la copine de George.

PAL [pæl] (*abbrev of* **phase alternation line**) *n* PAL *f*.

palace ['pælɪs] *n* palais *m* ■ **the Palace** *UK* [Buckingham Palace] le palais de Buckingham *(et par extension ses habitants)* ■ **~ spokesman** porte-parole *mf* (du palais) de Buckingham ◐ **the Palace of Westminster** le palais de Westminster *(siège du Parlement britannique)*.

palaeo- *etc UK* = **paleo-**.

palatable ['pælətəbl] *adj* **1.** [food, drink - tasty] savoureux ; [- edible] mangeable **2.** *fig* [idea] acceptable.

palatal ['pælətl] ◇ *adj* **1.** ANAT palatin **2.** LING palatal.
◇ *n* palatale *f*.

palate ['pælət] *n* **1.** ANAT palais *m* **2.** [sense of taste] palais *m* ■ **to have a delicate ~** avoir du palais.

palatial [pə'leɪʃl] *adj* grandiose, magnifique.

palatine ['pælətaɪn] *adj* HIST palatin ■ **the Palatine (Hill)** le mont Palatin.

palaver [pə'lɑːvər] *UK inf* ◇ *n (U)* **1.** [rigmarole, fuss] chichis *mpl*, histoire *f*, histoires *fpl* **2.** [discussion] palabre *m ou f* ■ [tedious] palabres *mpl* OR *fpl*.
◇ *vi* palabrer.

pale [peɪl] ◇ *adj* **1.** [face, complexion] pâle ■ [from fright, shock, sickness] blême, blafard ■ **he turned ~** il a pâli OR blêmi **2.** [colour] pâle, clair ■ [light] pâle, blafard **3.** [feeble] pâle ■ **it was a ~ imitation of the real thing** c'était une pâle copie de l'original.
◇ *vi* [person, face] pâlir, blêmir ■ [sky, colour] pâlir ■ **our problems ~ into insignificance beside hers** nos problèmes sont insignifiants comparés aux siens OR à côté des siens.
◇ *n* **1.** [post] pieu *m* **2.** [fence] palissade *f* ■ **beyond the ~** *UK*: **he's beyond the ~** il n'est pas fréquentable ■ **I find such behaviour beyond the ~** je trouve un tel comportement inadmissible.

pale ale *n* pale-ale *f*, bière *f* blonde légère.

paleface ['peɪlfeɪs] *n pej & hum* Visage *m* pâle.

palefaced ['peɪlfeɪst] *adj* (au teint) pâle.

paleness ['peɪlnɪs] *n* pâleur *f*.

paleo- ['pælɪəʊ] *in cpds* paléo-.

paleography [,pælɪ'ɒgrəfɪ] *n* paléographie *f*.

Paleolithic [,pælɪəʊ'lɪθɪk] ◇ *adj* paléolithique.
◇ *n* paléolithique *m*.

paleontology [,pælɪɒn'tɒlədʒɪ] *n* paléontologie *f*.

Palestine ['pælə,staɪn] *pr n* Palestine *f* ■ **in ~** en Palestine.

Palestine Liberation Organization *pr n* Organisation *f* de libération de la Palestine.

Palestinian [,pælə'stɪnɪən] ◇ *n* Palestinien *m*, - enne *f*.
◇ *adj* palestinien.

palette ['pælət] *n* ART palette *f*.

palette knife *n* ART couteau *m* (à palette) ■ CULIN palette *f*.

palimony ['pælɪmənɪ] *n* pension *f* alimentaire *(accordée à un ex-concubin ou une ex-concubine)*.

palindrome ['pælɪndrəʊm] *n* palindrome *m*.

paling ['peɪlɪŋ] *n* [stake] pieu *m* ■ [fence] palissade *f*.
◆ **palings** *npl* [fence] palissade *f*.

palisade [,pælɪ'seɪd] *n* [fence] palissade *f*.
◆ **palisades** *npl US* [cliffs] ligne *f* de falaises.

pall [pɔːl] ◇ *n* **1.** [cloth] drap *m* mortuaire, poêle *m* **2.** [cloud - of smoke] voile *m* ■ *fig* voile *m*, manteau *m* **3.** *US* [coffin] cercueil *m*.
◇ *vi UK* perdre son charme ■ **it began to ~ on me** j'ai commencé à m'en lasser.

pallbearer ['pɔːl,beərər] *n* : **the ~s** [carrying coffin] les porteurs *mpl* du cercueil ; [accompanying coffin] le cortège funèbre.

pallet ['pælɪt] *n* **1.** [bed] grabat *m* ■ [mattress] paillasse *f* **2.** [for loading, transportation] palette *f* **3.** [potter's instrument] palette *f* **4.** = **palette**.

palliative ['pælɪətɪv] ◇ *adj* palliatif.
◇ *n* palliatif *m*.

palliative care *n (U)* MED soins *mpl* palliatifs.

pallid ['pælɪd] *adj* **1.** [wan] pâle, blême, blafard **2.** [lacking vigour] insipide.

pallor ['pælər] *n* pâleur *f*.

pally ['pælɪ] (*comp* **pallier**, *superl* **palliest**) *adj inf* **to be ~ with sb** être copain/copine avec qqn.

palm [pɑːm] ◇ *n* **1.** [of hand] paume *f* ■ **to have sweaty ~s** avoir les mains moites ■ **to read sb's ~** lire les lignes de la main à qqn ■ **he had them in the ~ of his hand** il les tenait à sa merci OR sous sa coupe ■ **to grease sb's ~** graisser la patte à qqn **2.** [tree] palmier *m* **3.** [branch] palme *f* ■ RELIG rameau *m* ■ **the winner's ~** *UK fig* la palme du vainqueur.
◇ *vt* [coin] cacher dans le creux de la main.
◆ **palm off** *vt sep inf* [unwanted objects] refiler ■ [inferior goods] fourguer ■ **to ~ sb off with sthg, to ~ sthg off on sb** refiler qqch à qqn.

palmist ['pɑːmɪst] *n* chiromancien *m*, - enne *f*.

palmistry ['pɑːmɪstrɪ] *n* chiromancie *f*.

Palm Sunday *n* (le dimanche des) Rameaux *mpl*.

palmtop ['pɑːmtɒp] *n* COMPUT ordinateur *m* de poche.

palm tree *n* palmier *m*.

palmy ['pɑːmɪ] (*comp* **palmier**, *superl* **palmiest**) *adj* **1.** [pleasant] agréable, doux, douce *f* **2.** [beach, coast] bordé de palmiers.

palomino [,pælə'miːnəʊ] (*pl* **palominos**) *n* palomino *m*.

palpable ['pælpəbl] *adj* **1.** [tangible] palpable, tangible **2.** [obvious] évident, manifeste, flagrant ■ **a ~ lie** un mensonge grossier.

palpably ['pælpəblɪ] *adv* **1.** [tangibly] tangiblement **2.** [obviously] manifestement.

palpate ['pælpeɪt] *vt* palper.

palpitate ['pælpɪteɪt] *vi* palpiter.

palpitation [,pælpɪ'teɪʃn] *n* palpitation *f* ■ **to have** OR **to get ~s** MED avoir des palpitations ■ **I get ~s whenever I see her** *hum* mon cœur bat la chamade OR s'emballe chaque fois que je la vois.

palsied ['pɔːlzɪd] *adj* **1.** [paralysed] paralysé **2.** [shaking, trembling] tremblant, tremblotant.

palsy ['pɔːlzɪ] *n* paralysie *f* ■ **shaking ~** maladie *f* de Parkinson.

paltry ['pɔːltrɪ] *adj* **1.** [meagre - wage, sum] misérable, dérisoire ■ **it'll cost you a ~ $100** ça vous coûtera cent malheureux dollars **2.** [worthless - person, attitude] insignifiant, minable ■ **a ~ excuse** une piètre excuse.

pampas ['pæmpəz] *npl* pampa *f*.

pampas grass *n* herbe *f* de la pampa.

pamper ['pæmpər] *vt* choyer, dorloter ■ **~ yourself with a bubble bath** faites-vous plaisir, prenez un bain moussant.

pamphlet ['pæmflɪt] *n* [gen] brochure *f* ■ POL pamphlet *m*.

pamphleteer [,pæmflə'tɪər] *n* [gen - POL] pamphlétaire *mf*.

Pamplona [pæm'pləʊnə] *pr n* Pampelune.

pan [pæn] (*pret & pp* **panned**, *cont* **panning**) ◇ *n* **1.** CULIN casserole *f* ■ **cake ~** *US* moule *m* à gâteau **2.** MIN [for gold] batée *f* **3.** [on scales] plateau *m* **4.** *UK* [toilet bowl] : **(lavatory) ~** cuvette *f* de W-C **5.** CIN & TV panoramique *m* **6.** *inf* [face] bouille *f*.
◇ *vi* **1.** [miner] : **to ~ for gold** chercher de l'or **2.** [camera] faire un panoramique.
◇ *vt* **1.** [camera] : **to ~ the camera** faire un panoramique, panoramiquer *spec* **2.** *inf* [criticize] descendre.
◆ **pan out** *vi insep UK inf* [work out] se dérouler, marcher ■ [succeed] réussir ■ **things should start to ~ out around August** les choses devraient commencer à s'arranger vers le mois d'août.

panacea [,pænə'sɪə] *n* panacée *f*.

panache [pə'næʃ] *n* panache *m*.

Pan-African ◇ *adj* panafricain.
◇ *n* partisan *m*, - e *f* du panafricanisme.

Panama ['pænəmɑ:] ◇ *pr n* Panama *m* ■ **in ~** au Panama ■ **the Isthmus of ~** l'isthme *m* de Panama.
◇ *n* = **Panama hat**.

Panama Canal *pr n* : **the ~** le canal de Panama.

Panama City *pr n* Panama.

Panama hat *n* panama *m*.

Panamanian [,pænə'meɪnjən] ◇ *n* Panaméen *m*, - enne *f*.
◇ *adj* panaméen.

Pan-American *adj* panaméricain ■ **the ~ Highway** la route panaméricaine.

Pan-Arab *adj* panarabe.

panatella [,pænə'telə] *n* panatela *m*, panatella *m*.

pancake ['pæŋkeɪk] ◇ *n* **1.** CULIN [in UK] crêpe *f* ■ [in US] *sorte de petite galette épaisse servie au petit déjeuner* ■ **(as) flat as a ~** plat comme une galette **2.** *inf* [make-up] fond *m* de teint épais ■ **~ make-up** tartine *f* de maquillage **3.** AERON = **pancake landing**.
◇ *vi* AERON atterrir sur le ventre.

Pancake Day *n UK* mardi gras *m*.

pancake landing *n* atterrissage *m* à plat OR brutal.

pancake roll *n* rouleau *m* de printemps.

pancreas ['pæŋkrɪəs] *n* pancréas *m*.

panda ['pændə] *n* panda *m* ■ **~ (car)** *UK* voiture *f* de police.

pandemic [pæn'demɪk] ◇ *adj* **1.** MED pandémique **2.** [universal] universel, général.
◇ *n* MED pandémie *f*.

pandemonium [,pændɪ'məʊnjəm] *n (U)* [chaos] chaos *m* ■ [uproar] tumulte *m*, tohu-bohu *m* ■ **the whole office is in ~** le bureau est sens dessus dessous.

pander ['pændəʳ] *vi* : **to ~ to** [person, weaknesses] flatter (bassement).

pandit ['pændɪt] *n* [wise man] sage *m* ■ [term of address] *titre donné à certains sages en Inde*.

Pandora [pæn'dɔ:rə] *pr n* Pandore ■ **~'s box** la boîte de Pandore.

pane [peɪn] *n* vitre *f*, carreau *m* ■ **a ~ of glass** un carreau ■ **~ glass window** *US* fenêtre *f* panoramique.

panegyric [,pænɪ'dʒɪrɪk] *n fml* panégyrique *m* ■ **he launched into a ~ of** OR **about French cuisine** il s'est lancé dans un éloge dithyrambique de la cuisine française.

panel ['pænl] (*UK pret & pp* **panelled**, *cont* **panelling**) (*US pret & pp* **paneled**, *cont* **paneling**) ◇ *n* **1.** [flat section - of wood, glass etc] panneau *m* ■ **sliding ~** panneau coulissant **2.** [group, committee - gen] comité *m* ; [- to judge exam, contest] jury *m* ; [- in radio or TV quiz] invités *mpl* ; [- in public debate] panel *m* ; [- in public inquiry] commission *f* (d'enquête) **3.** [set of controls] : **(control) ~** tableau *m* de bord ■ **(instrument) ~** AERON & AUT tableau *m* de bord **4.** SEW panneau *m*, lé *m* **5.** LAW [selection list] liste *f* de jurés **6.** ART [backing] panneau *m* ■ [picture] (peinture *f* sur) panneau *m*.
◇ *vt* [wall, hall] lambrisser, revêtir de panneaux ■ **a panelled door** une porte à panneaux ■ **the room is in panelled oak** la pièce est lambrissée de chêne.

panel beater *n* AUT carrossier *m*, tôlier *m*.

panel discussion *n* débat *m*, tribune *f*.

panel game *n UK* RADIO jeu *m* radiophonique ■ TV jeu *m* télévisé.

panelling *UK*, **paneling** *US* ['pænəlɪŋ] *n (U)* panneaux *mpl*, lambris *m*.

panellist *UK*, **panelist** *US* ['pænəlɪst] *n* [jury member] juré *m* ■ [in radio or TV quiz] invité *m*, - e *f* ■ [in public debate] panéliste *mf*.

panel pin *n* pointe *f* à tête d'homme, clou *m* à panneau.

panel truck *n US* camionnette *f*.

pan-fries *npl US* pommes *fpl* (de terre) sautées.

pan-fry *vt* (faire) sauter ■ **pan-fried potatoes** pommes *fpl* (de terre) sautées.

pang [pæŋ] *n* **1.** [of emotion] coup *m* au cœur, pincement *m* de cœur ■ **I felt a ~ of sadness** j'ai eu un serrement de cœur ■ **to feel ~s of conscience** OR **guilt** éprouver des remords **2.** [of pain] élancement *m* ■ **hunger ~s** tiraillements *mpl* d'estomac.

panhandler ['pæn,hændləʳ] *n US inf* mendiant *m*, - e *f*.

panic ['pænɪk] (*pret & pp* **panicked**, *cont* **panicking**) ◇ *n* **1.** [alarm, fear] panique *f*, affolement *m* ■ **it started a ~ on the stock exchange** cela a semé la panique à la Bourse ■ **to throw sb into a ~** affoler qqn **2.** *inf* [rush] hâte *f* ■ **I was in a mad ~ to get to the airport** c'était la panique pour aller à l'aéroport ■ **what's the ~?** ne vous affolez pas! ■ **there's no ~** il n'y a pas le feu **3.** *US inf* [sthg funny] : **it was a ~!** c'était à hurler de rire!
◇ *vi* s'affoler ■ **don't ~!** ne vous affolez pas!
◇ *vt* affoler.

panic button *n* signal *m* d'alarme ■ **to hit the ~** *inf* perdre les pédales.

panic buying *n (U)* achats *mpl* en catastrophe OR de dernière minute.

panicky ['pænɪkɪ] *adj inf* [person, crowd] paniqué ■ [voice, message] affolé ■ [feeling, reaction] de panique.

panicmonger ['pænɪk,mʌŋgəʳ] *n* semeur *m*, - euse *f* de panique.

panic stations *npl inf* **it was ~!** ça a été la panique générale!

panic-stricken *adj* affolé, pris de panique.

pannier ['pænɪəʳ] *n* **1.** [bag - on bicycle, motorbike] sacoche *f* ; [- on donkey] panier *m* de bât **2.** [basket] panier *m*, corbeille *f*.

panoply ['pænəplɪ] *n* panoplie *f*.

panorama [,pænə'rɑ:mə] *n liter & fig* panorama *m*.

panoramic [,pænə'ræmɪk] *adj* panoramique ■ **~ screen** CIN écran *m* panoramique.

panpipes ['pænpaɪps] *npl* flûte *f* de Pan.

pansy ['pænzɪ] (*pl* **pansies**) *n* **1.** BOT pensée *f* **2.** *UK inf pej* [sissy] poule *f* mouillée, femmelette *f* ■ [homosexual] tante *f*.

pant [pænt] ◇ *vi* [puff] haleter, souffler ■ **he ~ed up the stairs** il monta l'escalier en soufflant ■ **to ~ for breath** chercher son souffle.
◇ *vt* [say] dire en haletant OR d'une voix haletante.
◇ *n* [breath] halètement *m*.
◆ **pant for** *vt insep* mourir d'envie de.

pantaloons [,pæntə'lu:nz] *npl* pantalon *m* bouffant.

pantechnicon [pæn'teknɪkən] *n UK* **1.** [van] camion *m* de déménagement **2.** [warehouse] garde-meubles *m*.

pantheist ['pænθi:ɪst] *n* panthéiste *mf*.

pantheon ['pænθɪən] *n* panthéon *m*.

panther ['pænθəʳ] (*pl inv* OR *pl* **panthers**) *n* **1.** [leopard] panthère *f* **2.** *US* [puma] puma *m*.

pantie girdle ['pæntɪ-] = **panty girdle**.

pantie hose = **panty hose**.

panties ['pæntɪz] *npl* (petite) culotte *f*.

pantihose *US* = **panty hose**.

panting ['pæntɪŋ] *adj* [person, dog] haletant.

panto ['pæntəʊ] (*pl* **pantos**) *n UK inf* = **pantomime** *(sense 1)*.

pantograph ['pæntəgrɑ:f] *n* pantographe *m*.

pantomime ['pæntəmaɪm] *n* **1.** *UK* [Christmas show] *spectacle de Noël pour enfants* ■ ~ **dame** *rôle travesti outré et ridicule dans la "pantomime"* **2.** [mime] pantomime *f* **3.** *UK inf fig* comédie *f*, vaudeville *m*.

PANTOMIME

La « pantomime » est un spectacle britannique traditionnel, avec des personnages-types et des interventions du public très codifiées. Le héros (***principal boy***) doit, selon la tradition, être joué par une jeune actrice, alors que le rôle comique, celui de la vieille dame (***pantomime dame***), est tenu par un acteur. Tout au long de la pièce, les spectateurs interviennent au moyen de répliques connues de tous : ***behind you!, Oh, yes he is! - Oh, no he isn't!***. Jouées au moment des fêtes de fin d'année, elles s'inspirent des contes de fées.

pantry ['pæntrɪ] (*pl* **pantries**) *n* [cupboard] garde-manger *m inv* ■ [walk-in cupboard] cellier *m*, office *m*.

pants [pænts] *npl* **1.** *UK* [underpants] : **(pair of)** ~ slip *m*, culotte *f* **2.** *US* [trousers] : **(pair of)** ~ pantalon *m* ■ **a kick in the** ~ un coup de pied aux fesses ■ **he's still in short** ~ il est encore à l'âge des culottes courtes ➲ **to beat the ~ off sb** battre qqn à plates coutures ■ **to catch sb with his ~ down** *inf* surprendre qqn dans une situation embarrassante ■ **he puts his ~ on one leg at a time** *US* il est comme tout le monde ■ **it's his wife who wears the** ~ c'est sa femme qui porte la culotte ■ **he bores the ~ off me** *inf* il me rase ■ **she scares the ~ off me** *UK inf* elle me fiche la trouille.

panty girdle *n* gaine-culotte *f*.

panty hose *UK*, **pantihose** *US* ['pæntɪ,həuz] *npl* collant *m*, collants *mpl*.

panty liner *n* protège-slip *m*.

pap [pæp] *n* **1.** [mush] bouillie *f* **2.** *(U) fig* [drivel] bêtises *fpl*, imbécillités *fpl* ■ **what a load of ~!** n'importe quoi!

papa [pə'pɑ:] *n* papa *m*.

papacy ['peɪpəsɪ] (*pl* **papacies**) *n* [system, institution] papauté *f* ■ [term of office] pontificat *m*.

papadum ['pæpədəm] = **popadum**.

papal ['peɪpl] *adj* papal.

paparazzi [,pæpə'rætsɪ] *npl* paparazzi *mpl*.

papaw [pə'pɔ:] *n* **1.** = **papaya** **2.** [custard apple] anone *f*, pomme-cannelle *f*.

papaya [pə'paɪə] *n* **1.** [fruit] papaye *f* **2.** [tree] papayer *m*.

paper ['peɪpər] <> *n* **1.** *(U)* [material] papier *m* ■ **a piece/sheet of** ~ un bout/une feuille de papier ■ **he wants it on** ~ il veut que ce soit écrit ■ **don't put anything down on ~!** ne mettez rien par écrit! ■ **on ~, they're by far the better side** sur le papier *OR* a priori, c'est de loin la meilleure équipe **2.** [newspaper] journal *m* **3.** *(usu pl)* [document] papier *m*, document *m* ■ **could you fill out this ~?** pourriez-vous remplir ce formulaire? ■ **once you've got the necessary ~s together** une fois que vous aurez réuni les pièces nécessaires ■ **Virginia Woolf's private ~s** les écrits personnels de Virginia Woolf ➲ **(identity) ~s** papiers (d'identité) ■ **ship's ~s** papiers de bord **4.** SCH & UNIV [exam paper] devoir *m*, épreuve *f* ■ [student's answers] copie *f* **5.** [academic treatise - published] article *m* ; [- oral] communication *f* ■ **to give** *OR* **to read a ~ on sthg** faire un exposé sur qqch **6.** [wallpaper] papier peint *m* **7.** POL **green paper**, **white paper**.
<> *adj* **1.** [cup, napkin, towel] en *OR* de papier ■ ~ **currency** billets *mpl* (de banque) **2.** [theoretical] sur le papier, théorique ■ ~ **profits** profits *mpl* fictifs ■ ~ **qualifications** diplômes *mpl* **3.** *pej* [worthless] sans valeur ■ **a ~ victory** une victoire inutile.
<> *vt* [room, walls] tapisser.
◆ **paper over** *vt sep* **1.** *liter* recouvrir de papier peint **2.** *fig* [dispute, facts] dissimuler ■ **they tried to ~ over the cracks** ils ont essayé de masquer les désaccords.

paperback ['peɪpəbæk] <> *n* livre *m* de poche ■ **it's in** ~ c'est en (édition de) poche.
<> *adj* [book, edition] de poche.

paperbacked ['peɪpəbækt] *adj* broché.

paper bag *n* sac *m* en papier.

paperboy ['peɪpəbɔɪ] *n* [delivering papers] livreur *m* de journaux ■ [selling papers] vendeur *m OR* crieur *m* de journaux.

paper chase *n* rallye-papier *m*, ≃ jeu *m* de piste.

paper clip *n* trombone *m*.

paper feed *n* COMPUT & TYPO alimentation *f* en papier.

papergirl ['peɪpəgɜ:l] *n* [delivering papers] livreuse *f* de journaux ■ [selling papers] vendeuse *f* de journaux.

paper handkerchief *n* mouchoir *m* en papier.

paper knife *n* coupe-papier *m inv*.

paperless ['peɪpəlɪs] *adj* [electronic - communication, record-keeping] informatique ■ **the ~ office** le bureau entièrement informatisé.

papermill ['peɪpəmɪl] *n* papeterie *f*, usine *f* à papier.

paper money *n* papier-monnaie *m*.

paper plate *n* assiette *f* en carton.

paper round *n* : **to do a** ~ livrer les journaux à domicile.

paper shop *n* marchand *m* de journaux.

paper shredder *n* broyeur *m*.

paper tape *n* COMPUT bande *f* perforée.

paper-thin *adj* extrêmement mince *OR* fin.

paper tiger *n* tigre *m* de papier.

paper towel *n* serviette *f* en papier.

paper tray *n* bac *m* à papier.

paperweight ['peɪpəweɪt] *n* presse-papiers *m inv*.

paperwork ['peɪpəwɜ:k] *n* travail *m* de bureau ■ *pej* paperasserie *f*.

papery ['peɪpərɪ] *adj* [thin and dry - gen] comme du papier ; [- skin] parcheminé.

papier-mâché [,pæpjeɪ'mæʃeɪ] *n* papier *m* mâché.

papist ['peɪpɪst] <> *adj pej* papiste.
<> *n pej* papiste *mf*.

papoose [pə'pu:s] *n* papoose *m*.

pappy ['pæpɪ] (*comp* **pappier**, *superl* **pappiest**) *adj* gluant.

paprika ['pæprɪkə] *n* paprika *m*.

Papua ['pæpjuə] *pr n* Papouasie *f* ■ **in** ~ en Papouasie.

Papuan ['pæpjuən] <> *n* [person] Papou *m*, - e *f*.
<> *adj* papou.

Papua New Guinea *pr n* Papouasie-Nouvelle-Guinée *f* ■ **in** ~ en Papouasie-Nouvelle-Guinée.

papyrus [pə'paɪərəs] (*pl* **papyruses** *OR pl* **papyri** [-raɪ]) *n* papyrus *m*.

par [pɑ:r] (*pret & pp* **parred**, *cont* **parring**) <> *n* **1.** [equality] égalité *f* ■ **to be on a ~ (with sb/sthg)** être au même niveau (que qqn/qqch) ■ **you can't put him on a ~ with Mozart!** tu ne peux pas le comparer à Mozart! **2.** [normal, average] normale *f*, moyenne *f* ■ **I'm feeling a bit below** *OR* **under ~ these days** je ne me sens pas en forme ces jours-ci ■ **your work is below** *OR* **not up to** ~ votre travail laisse à désirer ➲ **that's about ~ for the course** c'est normal *OR* dans les normes **3.** SPORT [in golf] par *m* ■ **she was two under/over** ~ elle était à deux coups en dessous/au-dessus du par.
<> *vt* [in golf - hole] faire le par à.

para ['pærə] (*abbrev of* **paratrooper**) *n UK inf* para *m*.

parable ['pærəbl] *n* RELIG parabole *f*.

parabola [pə'ræbələ] *n* MATHS parabole *f*.

parabolic [,pærə'bɒlɪk] *adj* parabolique.

paracetamol [,pærə'si:təmɒl] *n* paracétamol *m*.

parachute ['pærəʃu:t] <> *n* parachute *m*.
<> *comp* [harness] de parachute ■ [troops, regiment] de parachutistes ■ ~ **drop** *OR* **landing** parachutage *m* ■ ~ **jump** saut *m* en parachute.

<> *vt* parachuter.
<> *vi* sauter en parachute ▪ **to go parachuting** SPORT faire du parachutisme.

parachutist ['pærəʃu:tɪst] *n* parachutiste *mf*.

parade [pə'reɪd] <> *n* **1.** [procession - gen] défilé *m* ▪ MIL défilé *m*, parade *f* ▪ **fashion ~** défilé de mode ▪ **to be on ~** MIL défiler **2.** [street - of shops] rangée *f* de magasins ; [- public promenade] promenade *f* **3.** [show, ostentation] étalage *m* ▪ **a ~ of force** une démonstration de force **4.** FENCING parade *f* **5.** = **parade ground**.
<> *vi* **1.** [march - gen - MIL] défiler **2.** [strut] se pavaner, parader.
<> *vt* **1.** [troops, prisoners etc] faire défiler **2.** [streets] défiler dans **3.** [show off] faire étalage de.

parade ground *n* terrain *m* de manœuvres.

paradigm ['pærədaɪm] *n* paradigme *m* ▪ **~ shift** changement *m* radical.

paradigmatic [,pærədɪg'mætɪk] *adj* paradigmatique.

paradise ['pærədaɪs] *n* **1.** [heaven] paradis *m* ▪ [Eden] le paradis terrestre ◐ **'Paradise Lost'** ***Milton*** 'Paradis perdu' **2.** *fig* paradis *m* ▪ **it's ~ (here) on earth** c'est le paradis sur terre.

paradox ['pærədɒks] *n* paradoxe *m*.

paradoxical [,pærə'dɒksɪkl] *adj* paradoxal.

paradoxically [,pærə'dɒksɪklɪ] *adv* paradoxalement.

paraffin ['pærəfɪn] <> *n* **1.** UK [fuel - for lamp] pétrole *m* ; [- for stove] mazout *m* ; [- for aircraft] kérosène *m* **2.** CHEM [alkane] paraffine *f*, alcane *m* **3.** = **paraffin wax**.
<> *comp* [lamp] à pétrole ▪ [heater] à mazout.

paraffin wax *n* paraffine *f*.

paragliding ['pærə,glaɪdɪŋ] *n* parapente *m* ▪ **to go ~** faire du parapente.

paragon ['pærəgən] *n* modèle *m* ▪ **~ of virtue** modèle OR parangon *m lit* de vertu.

paragraph ['pærəgrɑ:f] <> *n* **1.** [in writing] paragraphe *m*, alinéa *m* ▪ **begin** OR **start a new ~** (allez) à la ligne ▪ **section A, ~ 3 (of the contract)** article A, alinéa 3 (du contrat) **2.** [short article] entrefilet *m* **3.** TYPO : **~ (mark)** pied de mouche *m*, alinéa *m*.
<> *vt* diviser en paragraphes OR en alinéas.

Paraguay ['pærəgwaɪ] *pr n* Paraguay *m* ▪ **in ~** au Paraguay.

Paraguayan [,pærə'gwaɪən] <> *n* Paraguayen *m*, - enne *f*.
<> *adj* paraguayen.

parakeet ['pærəki:t] *n* perruche *f*.

paralegal ['pærə,li:gəl] *n* US assistant *m*, - e *f (d'un avocat)*.

paralinguistic [,pærəlɪŋ'gwɪstɪk] *adj* paralinguistique.

paralipsis [,pærə'lɪpsɪs] (*pl* **paralipses** [-si:z]) *n* prétérition *f*.

parallax ['pærəlæks] *n* parallaxe *f*.

parallel ['pærəlel] <> *adj* **1.** [gen - MATHS] parallèle ▪ **there is a ditch ~ with** OR **to the fence** il y a un fossé qui longe la clôture ▪ **to run ~ to sthg** longer qqch **2.** [concomitant - change, event] parallèle ▪ **a ~ investigation was mounted in England and Scotland** une enquête a été menée simultanément en Angleterre et en Écosse **3.** COMPUT [interface, operation] parallèle ▪ **~ computer** ordinateur *m* à traitement parallèle ▪ **~ printer** imprimante *f* en parallèle **4.** ELEC : **~ circuit** circuit *m* en parallèle.
<> *n* **1.** [equivalent] équivalent *m* ▪ [similarity] ressemblance *f*, similitude *f* ▪ **the two industries have developed in ~** ces deux industries se sont développées en parallèle ▪ **the disaster is without ~** une telle catastrophe est sans précédent **2.** [comparison] parallèle *m* ▪ **to draw a ~ between** faire OR établir un parallèle entre **3.** MATHS (ligne *f*) parallèle *f* **4.** GEOG parallèle *m* **5.** ELEC parallèle *m* ▪ **in ~** en parallèle.
<> *vt* **1.** [run parallel to] être parallèle à, longer **2.** [match, equal] égaler ▪ **his career has ~ed his father's** sa carrière a suivi une trajectoire semblable à celle de son père.
<> *adv* : **to ski ~, to ~ ski** skier parallèle ▪ **to ~ park** US faire un créneau.

parallel bars *npl* barres *fpl* parallèles.

parallel cable *n* câble *m* parallèle.

parallelism ['pærəlelɪzm] *n* parallélisme *m*.

parallelogram [,pærə'leləgræm] *n* parallélogramme *m*.

parallel port *n* port *m* parallèle.

parallel turn *n* [in skiing] virage *m* parallèle.

paralyse UK, **paralyze** US ['pærəlaɪz] *vt* **1.** MED paralyser **2.** *fig* [city, industry etc] paralyser, immobiliser ▪ [person] paralyser, pétrifier.

paralysed UK, **paralyzed** US ['pærəlaɪzd] *adj* **1.** MED paralysé ▪ **both his legs are ~, he's ~ in both legs** il est paralysé des deux jambes, il a les deux jambes paralysées **2.** *fig* [city, industry etc] paralysé, immobilisé ▪ [person] paralysé, pétrifié ▪ **~ with** OR **by shyness** paralysé par la timidité.

paralysis [pə'rælɪsɪs] *n* **1.** MED paralysie *f* **2.** *fig* [of industry, business] immobilisation *f* ▪ [of government] paralysie *f*.

paralytic [,pærə'lɪtɪk] <> *adj* **1.** MED paralytique **2.** UK *inf* [drunk] ivre mort.
<> *n* paralytique *mf*.

paralyze *etc* US = **paralyse**.

paramedic [,pærə'medɪk] <> *n* aide-soignant *m*, - e *f*, *membre du personnel paramédical* ▪ **'paramedic'** US services *mpl* de secours, ≃ SAMU.
<> *adj* = **paramedical**.

paramedical [,pærə'medɪkl] *adj* paramédical.

parameter [pə'ræmɪtər] *n* [gen - LING] [MATH] paramètre *m* ▪ **according to established ~s of evaluation** selon les critères établis.

paramilitary [,pærə'mɪlɪtrɪ] (*pl* **paramilitaries**) <> *adj* paramilitaire.
<> *n* [group] formation *f* paramilitaire ▪ [person] membre *m* d'une formation paramilitaire.
<> *npl* : **the ~** la milice.

paramount ['pærəmaʊnt] *adj* **1.** [asset, concern] primordial ▪ **the children's interests are ~** l'intérêt des enfants passe avant tout **2.** [ruler] suprême.

paranoia [,pærə'nɔɪə] *n (U)* paranoïa *f*.

paranoiac [,pærə'nɔɪæk], **paranoic** [,pærə'nəʊɪk] <> *adj* paranoïaque.
<> *n* paranoïaque *mf*.

paranoid ['pærənɔɪd] <> *adj* [disorder] paranoïde ▪ [person] paranoïaque.
<> *n* paranoïaque *mf*.

paranormal [,pærə'nɔ:ml] <> *adj* paranormal.
<> *n* : **the ~** le paranormal.

parapet ['pærəpɪt] *n* ARCHIT parapet *m*, garde-fou *m* ▪ MIL parapet *m*.

paraphernalia [,pærəfə'neɪljə] *n (U)* **1.** [equipment] attirail *m* ▪ [belongings] fourbi *m* **2.** *inf* [trappings] tralala *m*.

paraphrase ['pærəfreɪz] <> *n* paraphrase *f*.
<> *vt* paraphraser.

paraplegia [,pærə'pli:dʒə] *n* paraplégie *f*.

paraplegic [,pærə'pli:dʒɪk] <> *adj* paraplégique.
<> *n* paraplégique *mf*.

parapsychology [,pærəsaɪ'kɒlədʒɪ] *n* parapsychologie *f*.

parasailing ['pærə,seɪlɪŋ] *n* parachute *m* ascensionnel *(tracté par bateau)*.

parascending ['pærə,sendɪŋ] *n* parachute *m* ascensionnel *(tracté par véhicule)*.

parasite ['pærəsaɪt] *n* BOT & ZOOL parasite *m* ▪ *fig* parasite *m*.

parasitic [,pærə'sɪtɪk] *adj* **1.** [plant, animal] parasite ▪ *fig* [person] parasite ▪ [existence] de parasite **2.** [illness - caused by parasites] parasitaire.

parasitism ['pærəsaɪ,tɪzm] *n* parasitisme *m*.

parasol ['pærəsɒl] *n* [for woman] ombrelle *f* ▪ [for beach, table] parasol *m*.

parataxis [,pærə'tæksɪs] *n* parataxe *f*, juxtaposition *f*.

paratroop ['pærətru:p] *comp* de parachutistes ▪ [regiment] parachutiste, de parachutistes ▪ [commander] parachutiste.
◆ **paratroops** *npl* MIL parachutistes *mpl*.

paratrooper ['pærətru:pər] *n* MIL parachutiste *m*.

paratyphoid [,pærə'taɪfɔɪd] ◇ *n* paratyphoïde *f*.
◇ *adj* [bacillus] paratyphique ▪ [fever] paratyphoïde.

parboil ['pɑ:bɔɪl] *vt* CULIN blanchir.

parcel ['pɑ:sl] (*UK pret & pp* **parcelled**, *cont* **parcelling**) (*US pret & pp* **parceled**, *cont* **parceling**) ◇ *n* **1.** [package] colis *m*, paquet *m* ▪ **~ delivery** livraison *f* de colis à domicile **2.** [portion of land] parcelle *f* **3.** [group, quantity - gen] groupe *m*, lot *m* ; [- of shares] paquet *m*.
◇ *vt* **1.** [wrap up] emballer, faire un colis de **2.** [divide up] diviser en parcelles.
◆ **parcel out** *vt sep* **1.** [share out] distribuer, partager **2.** [divide up] diviser en parcelles, lotir.

parcel bomb *n* colis *m* piégé.

parcel post *n* : **to send sthg by ~** envoyer qqch par colis postal *OR* en paquet-poste.

parch [pɑ:tʃ] *vt* **1.** [scorch] dessécher, brûler **2.** (*usu passive*) [make thirsty] assoiffer **3.** CULIN griller légèrement.

parched [pɑ:tʃt] *adj* **1.** [very dry - grass] desséché ; [- throat, lips] sec, sèche *f* **2.** *inf* [person] : **I'm ~** je crève de soif.

parchment ['pɑ:tʃmənt] *n* [material, document] parchemin *m* ▪ **skin like ~** peau parcheminée.

pardon ['pɑ:dn] ◇ *vt* **1.** [forgive] pardonner ▪ **to ~ sb for sthg** pardonner qqch à qqn ▪ **please ~ my rudeness** veuillez excuser mon impolitesse ▪ **~ me for asking, but...** excusez-moi de vous poser cette question, mais... ▪ **~ me for breathing!** excuse-moi d'avoir osé ouvrir la bouche! ➤ **he's a bastard, if you'll ~ the expression** *OR* **my French**△ c'est un salaud, si vous voulez bien me passer l'expression **2.** LAW gracier.
◇ *n* **1.** [forgiveness] pardon *m* **2.** LAW grâce *f* **3.** RELIG indulgence *f*.
◇ *interj* : **~ (me)?** [what?] pardon?, comment? ▪ **~ (me)!** [sorry] pardon!, excusez-moi!

pardonable ['pɑ:dnəbl] *adj* pardonnable, excusable.

pare [peər] *vt* **1.** [fruit, vegetable] peler, éplucher ▪ [nails] ronger, couper **2.** [reduce - budget] réduire.
◆ **pare down** *vt sep* [expenses, activity] réduire ▪ [text, speech] raccourcir ▪ **we've got to ~ the report down to 50 pages** il va falloir ramener le rapport à 50 pages.

parent ['peərənt] ◇ *n* **1.** [mother] mère *f* ▪ [father] père *m* ▪ **~s** parents *mpl* ▪ **Anne and Bob have become ~s** Anne et Bob ont eu un enfant **2.** PHYS parent *m*.
◇ *comp* **1.** [cooperation, participation] des parents, parental **2.** [organization] mère **3.** [plant] mère **4.** [animal] parent ▪ **one of the ~ birds/seals** un des parents de l'oiseau/du phoque.

parentage ['peərəntɪdʒ] *n* origine *f* ▪ **a child of unknown ~** un enfant de père et mère inconnus.

parental [pə'rentl] *adj* parental, des parents.

parent company *n* COMM société *f OR* maison *f* mère.

parenthesis [pə'renθɪsɪs] (*pl* **parentheses** [-si:z]) *n* parenthèse *f* ▪ **in ~** entre parenthèses.

parenthetic(al) [,pærən'θetɪk(l)] *adj* entre parenthèses.

parenthetically [,pærən'θetɪklɪ] *adv* entre parenthèses.

parenthood ['peərənthʊd] *n* [fatherhood] paternité *f* ▪ [motherhood] maternité *f* ▪ **the responsibilities of ~** les responsabilités parentales.

parenting ['peərəntɪŋ] *n* fait *m OR* art *m* d'élever un enfant ▪ **the problems of ~** les problèmes qu'on a quand on est parent *OR* quand on a des enfants ▪ **I put it down to bad ~** d'après moi, c'est parce que les parents remplissent mal leur rôle.

parent-teacher association *n association regroupant les parents d'élèves et les enseignants*.

pariah [pə'raɪə] *n* paria *m*.

parietal [pə'raɪɪtl] *adj* ANAT & BOT pariétal.

parings ['peərɪŋz] *npl* [of fruit, vegetables] épluchures *fpl*, pelures *fpl* ▪ [of nails] rognures *fpl*.

Paris ['pærɪs] *pr n* GEOG Paris.

parish ['pærɪʃ] ◇ *n* **1.** RELIG paroisse *f* **2.** POL ≃ commune *f (en Angleterre)*.
◇ *comp* [hall, funds - RELIG] paroissial.

parish church *n* église *f* paroissiale.

parish clerk *n* bedeau *m*.

parish council *n* ≃ conseil *m* municipal *(d'une petite commune en Angleterre)*.

parishioner [pə'rɪʃənər] *n* paroissien *m*, - enne *f*.

parish priest *n* [Catholic] curé *m* ▪ [Protestant] pasteur *m*.

parish-pump *adj UK pej* [parochial - issue] d'intérêt purement local ; [- outlook, mentality, quarrel] de clocher.

parish register *n* registre *m* paroissial.

parish school *n* école *f* communale.

Parisian [pə'rɪzjən] ◇ *n* Parisien *m*, - enne *f*.
◇ *adj* parisien.

parity ['pærətɪ] (*pl* **parities**) *n* **1.** [equality] égalité *f*, parité *f* ▪ **women demanded wage ~ with men** les femmes ont réclamé l'égalité de salaires avec les hommes **2.** ECON & FIN parité *f* ▪ **~ value** valeur *f* au pair **3.** COMPUT, MATHS & PHYS parité *f*.

parity bit *n* COMPUT bit *m* de parité.

park [pɑ:k] ◇ *n* **1.** [public] parc *m* ▪ [smaller] jardin *m* public ▪ [private estate] parc *m*, domaine *m* **2.** AUT [on automatic gearbox] position *f* (de) stationnement.
◇ *vt* **1.** AUT garer ▪ **behind the ~ed coaches** derrière les cars en stationnement **2.** *inf* [dump - person, box] laisser ▪ **he ~ed himself on the sofa** il s'installa sur le canapé.
◇ *vi* AUT se garer, stationner ▪ **I couldn't find anywhere to ~** je n'ai pas trouvé à me garer.

parka ['pɑ:kə] *n* parka *m*.

park-and-ride *n système de contrôle de la circulation qui consiste à garer les voitures à l'extérieur des grandes villes, puis à utiliser les transports en commun*.

parking ['pɑ:kɪŋ] ◇ *n* stationnement *m* ▪ **'no ~'** 'stationnement interdit', 'défense de stationner' ▪ **I'm not very good at ~** je ne suis pas très doué pour me garer.
◇ *comp* [area] de stationnement ▪ **~ space** *OR* **place** place *f* de stationnement ▪ **to look for/to find a ~ place** chercher/trouver à se garer.

parking attendant *n* [in car park] gardien *m*, - enne *f* ▪ [at hotel] voiturier *m*.

parking brake *n US* frein *m* à main.

parking garage *n US* parking *m* couvert.

parking light *n* feu *m* de position.

parking lot *n US* parking *m*, parc *m* de stationnement.

parking meter *n* parcmètre *m*, parcomètre *m*.

parking ticket *n* contravention *f (pour stationnement irrégulier)*, P-V *m*.

Parkinson's disease ['pɑ:kɪnsnz-] *n* maladie *f* de Parkinson.

Parkinson's law *n hum* principe *m* de Parkinson ▪ **it's a case of ~** plus on a de temps, plus on met de temps.

park keeper *n* gardien *m*, - enne *f* de jardin public.

parkland ['pɑːklænd] *n (U)* espace *m* vert, espaces *mpl* verts.

Park Lane *pr n avenue résidentielle très chic à Londres.*

parkway ['pɑːkweɪ] *n* US route *f* paysagère (à plusieurs voies).

parky ['pɑːkɪ] *(comp* **parkier**, *superl* **parkiest**) *adj* UK *inf* [cold] frisquet.

parlance ['pɑːləns] *n fml* langage *m*, parler *m*.

parlay ['pɑːlɪ] *vt* US **1.** [winnings] remettre en jeu **2.** *fig* [talent, project] mener à bien ■ [money] faire fructifier.

parley ['pɑːlɪ] <> *vi* parlementer.
<> *n* pourparlers *mpl*.

parliament ['pɑːləmənt] *n* parlement *m* ■ **she was elected to Parliament in 1988** elle a été élue député en 1988 ■ **the French Parliament** l'Assemblée nationale (française).

parliamentarian [ˌpɑːləmen'teərɪən] <> *adj* parlementaire.
<> *n* parlementaire *mf*.

parliamentary [ˌpɑːlə'mentərɪ] *adj* [system, debate, democracy] parlementaire ■ ~ **elections** élections *fpl* législatives ■ ~ **candidate** candidat *m* aux (élections) législatives.

parliamentary private secretary *n en Grande-Bretagne, député qui assure la liaison entre un ministre et la Chambre des communes.*

parliamentary secretary *n* UK ≃ sous-secrétaire *m* d'État.

parlor *etc* US = **parlour**.

parlour UK, **parlor** US ['pɑːlər] *n* **1.** *dated* [in house] salon *m* **2.** *dated* [in hotel, club] salon *m* ■ [in pub] arrière-salle *f* **3.** [in convent] parloir *m* **4.** US COMM : **beer** ~ bar *m*.

parlour game *n* UK jeu *m* de société.

parlourmaid UK, **parlormaid** US ['pɑːləmeɪd] *n* femme *f* de chambre.

parlous ['pɑːləs] *adj arch & lit* précaire, instable.

Parma ['pɑːmə] *pr n* Parme ■ ~ **ham** jambon *m* de Parme.

Parmesan (cheese) [ˌpɑːmɪ'zæn-] *n* parmesan *m*.

Parnassus [pɑː'næsəs] *pr n* Parnasse *m*.

parochial [pə'rəʊkjəl] *adj* **1.** RELIG paroissial **2.** *pej* borné ■ ~ **attitudes** attitudes de clocher OR bornées.

parochialism [pə'rəʊkjəlɪzm] *n pej* esprit *m* de clocher.

parodist ['pærədɪst] *n* parodiste *mf*.

parody ['pærədɪ] (*pl* **parodies**, *pret & pp* **parodied**) <> *n* parodie *f*.
<> *vt* parodier.

parole [pə'rəʊl] <> *n* **1.** LAW liberté *f* conditionnelle OR sur parole ■ **she was released on** ~ elle a été mise en liberté conditionnelle OR libérée sur parole **2.** US MIL [password] mot *m* de passe **3.** LING parole *f*.
<> *vt* mettre en liberté conditionnelle, libérer sur parole.

parole board *n* ≃ comité *m* de probation et d'assistance aux libérés.

parolee [pə'rəʊlɪ] *n* US prisonnier *m*, - ière *f* en liberté conditionnelle.

paroxysm ['pærəksɪzm] *n* **1.** [outburst - of rage, despair] accès *m* ; [- of tears] crise *f* ■ **his answer sent them into ~s of laughter** sa réponse provoqua l'hilarité générale OR déclencha un fou rire général **2.** MED paroxysme *m*.

parquet ['pɑːkeɪ] <> *n* CONSTR : ~ **(floor** OR **flooring)** parquet *m*.
<> *vt* parqueter.

parquetry ['pɑːkɪtrɪ] *n* parquetage *m*.

parrakeet ['pærəkiːt] = **parakeet**.

parricide ['pærɪsaɪd] *n* **1.** [act] parricide *m* **2.** [killer] parricide *mf*.

parrot ['pærət] *n* perroquet *m*.

parrot fashion *adv* comme un perroquet.

parry ['pærɪ] (*pret & pp* **parried**, *pl* **parries**) <> *vt* **1.** [in boxing, fencing etc] parer **2.** [problem] tourner, éviter ■ [question] éluder ■ [manoeuvre] parer à, contrer.
<> *vi* [in boxing, fencing] parer ■ **he parried with his right** il a paré l'attaque OR le coup d'une droite.
<> *n* parade *f (en boxe, en escrime etc)*.

parse [pɑːz] *vt* faire l'analyse grammaticale de.

Parsee, Parsi [ˌpɑː'siː] <> *n* Parsi *m*, - e *f*.
<> *adj* parsi.

parser ['pɑːzər] *n* COMPUT analyseur *m* syntaxique.

parsimonious [ˌpɑːsɪ'məʊnjəs] *adj fml* parcimonieux.

parsimony ['pɑːsɪmənɪ] *n fml* parcimonie *f*.

parsing ['pɑːzɪŋ] *n* analyse *f* grammaticale.

parsley ['pɑːslɪ] *n* persil *m* ■ **Chinese** ~ coriandre *f* ■ ~ **sauce** sauce *f* au persil OR persillée.

parsnip ['pɑːsnɪp] *n* panais *m (légume courant dans l'alimentation britannique).*

parson ['pɑːsn] *n* [gen] ecclésiastique *m* ■ [Protestant] pasteur *m*.

parsonage ['pɑːsnɪdʒ] *n* presbytère *m*.

parson's nose ['pɑːsnz-] *n* CULIN croupion *m*.

part [pɑːt] <> *n* **1.** [gen - portion, subdivision] partie *f* ■ **(a) ~ of the garden is flooded** une partie du jardin est inondée ■ **(a) ~ of me strongly agrees with them** sur un certain plan, je suis tout à fait d'accord avec eux ■ **that's only ~ of the problem** ce n'est qu'un des aspects du problème ■ **it's very much ~ of the game/of the process** ça fait partie du jeu/du processus ■ **it's very much ~ of the excitement** c'est en partie pour ça que c'est amusant ■ **we've finished the hardest ~** nous avons fait le plus dur ■ **I haven't told you the best ~ yet** je ne t'ai pas encore dit le plus beau OR la meilleure ■ **to be (a) ~ of sthg** [be involved with] faire partie de qqch ■ **to form ~ of sthg** faire partie de qqch ▶ **to be ~ and parcel of sthg** faire partie (intégrante) de qqch
2. [role] rôle *m* ■ **work plays a large ~ in our lives** le travail joue un rôle important dans notre vie ■ **to take ~ (in sthg)** prendre part OR participer (à qqch) ■ **I had no ~ in that affair** je n'ai joué aucun rôle dans cette affaire ■ **he has no ~ in the running of the company** il ne participe pas à OR il n'intervient pas dans la gestion de la société ■ **Joe had no ~ in it** Joe n'y était pour rien ■ **I want no ~ in OR of their schemes** je ne veux pas être mêlé à leurs projets ▶ **to dress the ~** se mettre en tenue de circonstance ■ **to look the ~** avoir la tenue de circonstance ■ **for my/his ~** pour ma/sa part
3. [component - of machine] pièce *f*
4. [area - of country, town etc] : **which ~ of England are you from?** vous êtes d'où en Angleterre?, de quelle région de l'Angleterre venez-vous? ■ **in some ~s of Sydney/Australia** dans certains quartiers de Sydney/certaines régions de l'Australie ■ **it's a dangerous ~ of town** c'est un quartier dangereux ■ **are you new to these ~s?** vous êtes nouveau ici?
5. [instalment - of encyclopedia] fascicule *m* ; [- of serial] épisode *m* ■ **don't miss ~ two!** [of serial] ne manquez pas le deuxième épisode! ; [of programme in two parts] ne manquez pas la deuxième partie!
6. [measure] mesure *f* ■ **one ~ of pastis and four ~s of water** une mesure de pastis et quatre mesures d'eau ■ **a concentration of six ~s per million** CHEM une concentration de six pour un million
7. [side] parti *m*, part *f* ■ **he always takes his mother's ~** il prend toujours le parti de sa mère ▶ **to take sthg in good ~** bien prendre qqch
8. US [in hair] raie *f*
9. GRAM partie *f*
10. MUS partie *f* ■ **the vocal/violin ~** la partie vocale/(pour) violon.
<> *comp* [payment] partiel ■ ~ **owner** copropriétaire *mf*.

◇ *adv* en partie, partiellement ■ **the jacket is ~ cotton, ~ polyester** la veste est un mélange de coton et de polyester *OR* un mélange coton-polyester ■ **he's ~ English, ~ Chinese** il est moitié anglais, moitié chinois.
◇ *vi* **1.** [move apart - lips, curtains] s'ouvrir ; [- branches, legs, crowd] s'écarter ■ [disengage - fighters] se séparer ■ **the clouds ~ed** il y eut une éclaircie
2. [leave one another] se quitter
3. [break - rope] se casser ■ [tear - fabric] se déchirer.
◇ *vt* **1.** [move apart, open - lips, curtains] ouvrir ; [- branches, legs, crowd] écarter ■ **her lips were slightly ~ed** ses lèvres étaient entrouvertes
2. [separate] séparer ■ **the children were ~ed from their parents** les enfants ont été séparés de leurs parents
3. [hair] faire une raie à ■ **her hair's ~ed in the middle** elle a la raie au milieu.
◆ **parts** *npl* [talents] talents *mpl* ■ **a man/woman of many ~s** un homme/une femme de talent.
◆ **for the most part** *adv phr* dans l'ensemble ■ **for the most ~ we get along pretty well** dans l'ensemble, nous nous entendons assez bien.
◆ **in part** *adv phr* en partie ■ **it's true in ~** c'est en partie vrai.
◆ **in parts** *adv phr* par endroits ■ **the book is good in ~s** le livre est bon par endroits, certains passages du livre sont bons.
◆ **on the part of** *prep phr* de la part de.
◆ **part with** *vt insep* se séparer de ■ **he hates ~ing with his money** il a horreur de dépenser son argent.

partake [pɑːˈteɪk] (*pret* **partook** [-ˈtʊk], *pp* **partaken** [-ˈteɪkn]) *vi arch* & *fml* **1.** [eat, drink] : **to ~ of** prendre **2.** [participate] : **to ~ in** [event] participer à ; [joy, grief] partager **3.** [share quality] : **to ~ of** relever de, tenir à.

part exchange *n* COMM reprise *f* ■ **they'll take your old TV set in ~** ils vous font une reprise sur *OR* ils reprennent votre ancien téléviseur.

Parthenon [ˈpɑːθɪnən] *pr n* : **the ~** le Parthénon.

partial [ˈpɑːʃl] *adj* **1.** [incomplete] partiel ■ **the exhibition was only a ~ success** l'exposition n'a connu qu'un succès mitigé **2.** [biased] partial **3.** [fond] : **to be ~ to sthg** avoir un penchant *OR* un faible pour qqch.

partial eclipse *n* éclipse *f* partielle.

partiality [ˌpɑːʃɪˈælətɪ] (*pl* **partialities**) *n* **1.** [bias] partialité *f* **2.** [fondness] faible *m*, penchant *m*.

partially [ˈpɑːʃəlɪ] *adv* **1.** [partly] en partie, partiellement **2.** [in biased way] partialement, avec partialité.

partially sighted ◇ *adj* malvoyant.
◇ *npl* : **the ~** les malvoyants *mpl*.

participant [pɑːˈtɪsɪpənt] *n* participant *m*, - e *f* ■ **the ~s in the debate** les participants au débat.

participate [pɑːˈtɪsɪpeɪt] *vi* participer, prendre part ■ **to ~ in** [race, discussion] prendre part à, participer à.

participation [pɑːˌtɪsɪˈpeɪʃn] *n* participation *f* ■ **they should encourage greater student ~** ils devraient encourager les étudiants à participer plus activement.

participatory [pɑːˌtɪsɪˈpeɪtərɪ] *adj* participatif.

participial [ˌpɑːtɪˈsɪpɪəl] *adj* participial.

participle [ˈpɑːtɪsɪpl] *n* participe *m*.

particle [ˈpɑːtɪkl] *n* **1.** [tiny piece] particule *f*, parcelle *f* ■ [of dust] grain *m* ■ *fig* [jot] brin *m*, grain *m* **2.** LING particule *f* **3.** PHYS particule *f* **4.** RELIG hostie *f*.

particle accelerator *n* accélérateur *m* de particules.

particle beam *n* faisceau *m* de particules.

particle board *n* panneau *m* de particules.

particle physics *n (U)* physique *f* des particules.

parti-coloured [ˈpɑːtɪ-] *adj* bariolé, bigarré.

particular [pəˈtɪkjʊlər] ◇ *adj* **1.** [specific, distinct] particulier ■ **for no ~ reason** sans raison particulière ■ **only that ~ colour will do** il n'y a que cette couleur-là qui fasse l'affaire ■ **the problem is not ~ to this region** le problème n'est pas particulier à *OR* spécifique à *OR* ne se limite pas à cette région **2.** [exceptional, special] particulier, spécial ■ **it's an issue of ~ importance to us** c'est une question qui revêt une importance toute particulière à nos yeux **3.** [fussy] : **to be ~ about hygiene/manners** attacher beaucoup d'importance à l'hygiène/aux bonnes manières ■ **to be ~ about one's food** être difficile pour la nourriture **4.** *fml* [detailed - description, account] détaillé.
◇ *n* **1.** [specific] : **from the general to the ~** du général au particulier **2.** [facts, details] détails *mpl*, points *mpl* ■ **correct in all ~s** correct en tout point ■ **for further ~s phone this number** pour de plus amples renseignements, appelez ce numéro.
◆ **in particular** *adv phr* en particulier ■ **what are you thinking about? – nothing in ~** à quoi penses-tu? – à rien en particulier ■ **what happened? – nothing in ~** que s'est-il passé? – rien de particulier *OR* rien de spécial ■ **no one in ~** personne en particulier ■ **where are you going? – nowhere in ~** où vas-tu? – je vais juste faire un tour.

particularity [pəˌtɪkjʊˈlærətɪ] (*pl* **particularities**) *n* particularité *f*.

particularly [pəˈtɪkjʊləlɪ] *adv* particulièrement ■ **I don't know him ~ well** je ne le connais pas spécialement bien ■ **it was a ~ vicious murder** ce fut un meurtre extrêmement *OR* particulièrement sauvage ■ **I was surprised he wasn't there, ~ as he'd received an official invitation** son absence m'a surpris, d'autant plus qu'il avait reçu une invitation officielle.

parting [ˈpɑːtɪŋ] ◇ *n* **1.** [leave-taking] séparation *f* ■ **they had a tearful ~ at the station** ils se quittèrent en larmes à la gare ▶ **we came to a ~ of the ways** nous sommes arrivées à la croisée des chemins **2.** [opening - in clouds] trouée *f* ■ **the ~ of the Red Sea** le partage des eaux de la mer Rouge **3.** *UK* [in hair] raie *f*.
◇ *adj lit* [words, kiss] d'adieu ■ **he gave me a ~ handshake** il m'a serré la main en partant.

parting shot *n fig* flèche *f* du Parthe ■ **that was his ~** et sur ces mots, il s'en alla.

partisan [ˌpɑːtɪˈzæn] ◇ *adj* partisan ■ **~ politics** politique *f* partisane.
◇ *n* partisan *m*.

partisanship [ˌpɑːtɪˈzænʃɪp] *n* partialité *f*, esprit *m* de parti.

partition [pɑːˈtɪʃn] ◇ *n* **1.** [wall] cloison *f* ■ [screen] paravent *m* **2.** [of country] partition *f* ■ [of property] division *f* ■ [of power] répartition *f*, morcellement *m*.
◇ *vt* **1.** [room] diviser, cloisonner **2.** [country] diviser, démembrer.
◆ **partition off** *vt sep* [part of room] cloisonner ■ **a small office had been ~ed off** on avait aménagé un petit bureau derrière une cloison.

partition wall *n* cloison *f*.

partitive [ˈpɑːtɪtɪv] ◇ *adj* partitif.
◇ *n* partitif *m*.

partly [ˈpɑːtlɪ] *adv* en partie, partiellement.

partner [ˈpɑːtnər] ◇ *n* **1.** [spouse] époux *m*, épouse *f*, conjoint *m*, - e *f* ■ [lover] ami *m*, - e *f* ■ **sexual ~** partenaire *mf* (sexuel) **2.** [in game, dance] partenaire *mf* **3.** [in common undertaking] partenaire *mf* ■ [in firm, medical practice etc] associé *m*, - e *f* ■ **our ~s in NATO** nos partenaires de l'OTAN ■ **to be ~s in crime** être complices dans le crime.
◇ *vt* **1.** [be the partner of] être partenaire de **2.** [dance with] danser avec ■ [play with] faire équipe avec, être le partenaire de.

partnership [ˈpɑːtnəʃɪp] *n* **1.** [gen] association *f* ■ **to work in ~ with sb/sthg** travailler en association avec qqn/qqch ■ **to go into ~ with sb** s'associer avec qqn ■ **they've gone into ~ together** ils se sont associés ■ **they offered him a ~** ils lui ont proposé de devenir leur associé **2.** [firm] ≃ société *f* en nom collectif.

part of speech *n* partie *f* du discours.

partook [-'tʊk] *pt* ▷ **partake**.

part payment *n* acompte *m* ■ **I received £500 in ~ for the car** j'ai reçu un acompte de 500 livres pour la voiture.

partridge ['pɑːtrɪdʒ] (*pl inv* OR *pl* **partridges**) *n* perdrix *f* ■ [immature] perdreau *m*.

part-time *adj* & *adv* à temps partiel ■ **she's got a ~ job** elle travaille à temps partiel.

part-timer *n* travailleur *m*, - euse *f* à temps partiel.

partway ['pɑːtweɪ] *adv* en partie, partiellement ■ **~ through the year, she resigned** elle a démissionné en cours d'année ■ **I'm only ~ through the book** je n'ai pas fini le livre.

part work *n UK* **they published it as a ~** ils l'ont publié sous forme de fascicules.

party ['pɑːtɪ] (*pl* **parties**, *pret & pp* **partied**) ◇ *n* **1.** [social event] fête *f* ■ [more formal] soirée *f*, réception *f* ■ **to give a ~** [formal] donner une réception OR une soirée ; [informal] faire une fête ■ **to have** OR **to throw a ~ for sb** organiser une fête en l'honneur de qqn ■ **I'm having a little cocktail ~ on Friday** je fais un petit cocktail vendredi ■ **New Year's Eve ~** réveillon *m* de fin d'année **2.** POL parti *m* ■ **the Conservative/Democratic Party** le parti conservateur/démocrate **3.** [group of people] groupe *m* ■ **a tour ~** un groupe de touristes ■ **the funeral ~** le cortège funèbre ■ **the wedding ~** les invités *mpl (à un mariage)* ■ **to make dinner reservations for a ~ of six** réserver une table pour six personnes **4.** *fml* & LAW [individual, participant] partie *f* ■ **to be a ~ to** [discussion] prendre part à ; [crime] être complice de ; [conspiracy, enterprise] être mêlé à, tremper dans ■ **the guilty ~** le coupable ■ **the injured ~** la partie lésée ■ **(the) interested parties** les intéressés *mpl* **5.** [person] individu *m*.
◇ *comp* **1.** [atmosphere, clothes] de fête ■ **~ dress** robe *f* habillée ■ **~ invitations** invitations *fpl* ■ **~ snacks** amuse-gueule *mpl* **2.** POL [leader, leadership, funds] du parti ■ [system] des partis.
◇ *vi* faire la fête.

party animal *n inf* fêtard *m* ■ **she's a real ~** elle adore faire la fête.

partygoer ['pɑːtɪgəʊə] *n* fêtard *m*, - e *f*.

partying ['pɑːtɪɪŋ] *n* : **she's a great one for ~** *inf* elle adore faire la fête.

party line *n* **1.** POL ligne *f* du parti ■ **to toe** OR **follow the ~** suivre la ligne du parti **2.** TELEC ligne *f* commune *(à plusieurs abonnés)*.

party piece *n inf* chanson *f* OR poème *m* de circonstance *(à l'occasion d'une fête)*.

party political *adj* [broadcast] réservé à un parti politique ■ [issue] de parti politique.

party politics *npl* politique *f* de parti ■ *pej* politique *f* politicienne.

party pooper *n inf* rabat-joie *m inv*.

party wall *n* mur *m* mitoyen.

par value *n* valeur *f* nominale.

parvenu ['pɑːvənjuː] ◇ *n* parvenu *m*, - e *f*.
◇ *adj* parvenu.

PASCAL [pæ'skæl] *n* PASCAL *m*.

paschal, Paschal ['pæskl] *adj* pascal.

pass [pɑːs] ◇ *vi* **1.** [move in specified direction] passer ■ **the wires ~ under the floorboards** les fils passent sous le plancher ■ **his life ~ed before his eyes** il a vu sa vie défiler devant ses yeux
2. [move past, go by] passer ■ **the road was too narrow for two cars to ~** la route était trop étroite pour que deux voitures se croisent ■ **I happened to be ~ing, so I thought I'd call in** il s'est trouvé que je passais, alors j'ai eu l'idée de venir vous voir
3. [overtake] dépasser, doubler
4. [elapse - months, years] (se) passer, s'écouler ; [- holiday] se passer ■ **the weekend ~ed without surprises** le week-end s'est passé sans surprises ■ **time ~ed rapidly** le temps a passé très rapidement
5. [be transformed] passer, se transformer ■ **the oxygen then ~es to a liquid state** ensuite l'oxygène passe à l'état liquide
6. [take place] se passer, avoir lieu ■ **harsh words ~ed between them** ils ont eu des mots ■ **the party, if it ever comes to ~, should be quite something** la fête, si elle a jamais lieu, sera vraiment un grand moment ■ **and it came to ~ that...** BIBLE et il advint que...
7. [end, disappear - pain, crisis, fever] passer ; [- anger, desire] disparaître, tomber ; [- dream, hope] disparaître
8. [be transferred - power, responsibility] passer ; [- inheritance] passer, être transmis ■ **authority ~es to the Vice-President when the President is abroad** c'est au vice-président que revient la charge du pouvoir lorsque le président se trouve à l'étranger
9. [get through, be approved - proposal] être approuvé ; [- bill, law] être voté ; [- motion] être adopté ■ SCH & UNIV [- student] être reçu OR admis
10. [go unchallenged] passer ■ **the insult ~ed unnoticed** personne ne releva l'insulte ■ **he let the remark/mistake ~** il a laissé passer la remarque/l'erreur sans la relever ■ **I don't like it, but I'll let it ~** je n'aime pas ça, mais je préfère ne rien dire OR me taire
11. [be adequate, acceptable - behaviour] convenir, être acceptable ; [- repair job] passer ■ **in a grey suit you might just ~** avec ton costume gris, ça peut aller
12. [substitute] : **don't try to ~ as an expert** n'essaie pas de te faire passer pour un expert ■ **you could easily ~ for your sister** on pourrait très bien te prendre pour ta sœur ■ **he could ~ for 35** on lui donnerait 35 ans
13. SPORT faire une passe
14. GAMES passer.
◇ *vt* **1.** [move past, go by - building] passer devant ; [- person] croiser ■ **I ~ed her on the stairs** je l'ai croisée dans l'escalier ■ **the ships ~ed each other in the fog** les navires se sont croisés dans le brouillard
2. [go beyond - finishing line, frontier] passer ■ [overtake] dépasser, doubler ■ **we've ~ed the right exit** nous avons dépassé la sortie que nous aurions dû prendre ■ **contributions have ~ed the $100,000 mark** les dons ont franchi la barre des 100 000 dollars ■ **we've ~ed a major turning point** nous avons franchi un cap important
3. [move, run] passer ■ **she ~ed her hand over her hair** elle s'est passé la main dans les cheveux
4. [hand] passer ■ **~ me the sugar, please** passez-moi le sucre, s'il vous plaît ■ [transmit - message] transmettre ■ **can you ~ her the message?** pourriez-vous lui transmettre OR faire passer le message?
5. [spend - life, time, visit] passer
6. [succeed in - exam, driving test] être reçu à, réussir ■ **he didn't ~ his history exam** il a échoué OR il a été recalé à son examen d'histoire
7. [approve - bill, law] voter ; [- motion, resolution] adopter ■ SCH & UNIV [- student] recevoir, admettre ■ **the drug has not been ~ed by the Health Ministry** le médicament n'a pas reçu l'autorisation de mise sur le marché du ministère de la Santé
8. [pronounce - judgment, verdict, sentence] prononcer, rendre ; [- remark, compliment] faire ■ **he declined to ~ comment** il s'est refusé à tout commentaire
9. [counterfeit money, stolen goods] écouler
10. SPORT [ball, puck] passer
11. GAMES : **to ~ one's turn** passer OR sauter son tour
12. PHYSIOL : **to ~ blood** avoir du sang dans les urines ■ **to ~ water** uriner.
◇ *n* **1.** [in mountains] col *m*, défilé *m* ■ **the Brenner Pass** le col du Brenner
2. [authorization - for worker, visitor] laissez-passer *m inv* ■ THEAT invitation *f*, billet *m* de faveur ■ MIL [- for leave of absence] permission *f* ; [- for safe conduct] sauf-conduit *m* ■ **press ~** carte *f* de presse ■ **rail/bus ~** carte *f* d'abonnement (de train)/de bus
3. SCH & UNIV [in exam] moyenne *f*, mention *f* passable ■ **to get a ~** avoir la moyenne ■ **I got three ~es** j'ai été reçu dans trois matières
4. [state of affairs] situation *f* ■ **things have come to a pretty** OR **fine** OR **sorry ~** on est dans une bien mauvaise passe, la situation s'est bien dégradée
5. SPORT [with ball, puck] passe *f* ■ [in fencing] botte *f* ■ [in bull-fighting] passe *f* ■ **to make a ~ at** [in fencing] porter une botte à

6. [by magician] passe *f*
7. COMPUT passe *f*
8. AERON [overflight] survol *m* ■ [attack] attaque *f*
9. *inf phr* **to make a ~ at sb** faire des avances à qqn.
◆ **pass around** *vt sep* [cake, cigarettes] (faire) passer ■ [petition] (faire) circuler ■ [supplies] distribuer.
◆ **pass away** ◇ *vi insep* **1.** *euph* [die] s'éteindre *euph*, décéder
2. [elapse - time] passer, s'écouler.
◇ *vt sep* [while away] passer ■ **we read to ~ the time away** nous avons lu pour tuer *OR* passer le temps.
◆ **pass back** *vt sep* **1.** [give back] rendre
2. RADIO & TV : **I'll now ~ you back to the studio** je vais rendre l'antenne au studio
3. SPORT [to team mate] repasser ■ [backwards] passer en arrière.
◆ **pass by** ◇ *vi insep* **1.** [move past, go by] : **he ~ed by without a word!** il est passé à côté de moi sans dire un mot!
2. [visit] passer.
◇ *vt sep* [disregard] ignorer, négliger ■ **she felt life had ~ed her by** elle avait le sentiment d'avoir raté sa vie.
◆ **pass down** *vt sep* **1.** [reach down] descendre ■ **he ~ed me down my suitcase** il m'a tendu *OR* passé ma valise
2. [transmit - inheritance, disease, tradition] transmettre, passer.
◆ **pass off** ◇ *vi insep* **1.** [take place - conference, attack] se passer, se dérouler
2. [end - fever, fit] passer ■ **the effects of the drug had ~ed off** les effets du médicament s'étaient dissipés.
◇ *vt sep* [represent falsely] faire passer ■ **he ~es himself off as an actor** il se fait passer pour un acteur.
◆ **pass on** ◇ *vi insep* **1.** *euph* [die] trépasser, s'éteindre *euph*
2. [proceed] passer ■ **let's ~ on to the next question** passons à la question suivante.
◇ *vt sep* **1.** [hand on - box, letter] passer
2. [transmit - disease, tradition] transmettre ■ **they ~ the costs on to their customers** ils répercutent les coûts sur leurs clients ■ **we meet at 8, ~ it on** nous avons rendez-vous à 8 h, fais passer (la consigne).
◆ **pass out** ◇ *vi insep* **1.** [faint] s'évanouir, perdre connaissance ■ [from drunkenness] tomber ivre mort ■ [go to sleep] s'endormir
2. MIL [cadet] ≃ finir ses classes.
◇ *vt sep* [hand out] distribuer.
◆ **pass over** ◇ *vt sep* [not take - opportunity] négliger, ignorer ■ [overlook - person] : **he was ~ed over for promotion** on ne lui a pas accordé la promotion qu'il attendait.
◇ *vt insep* **1.** [overlook - fault, mistake] passer sur, ne pas relever
2. [skip - paragraph] sauter.
◆ **pass round** = **pass around**.
◆ **pass through** ◇ *vi insep* passer ■ **are you in Boston for some time or are you just ~ing through?** êtes-vous à Boston pour quelque temps ou êtes-vous juste de passage?
◇ *vt insep* [difficult period] traverser ■ [barrier] franchir ■ **the bullet ~ed through his shoulder** la balle lui a traversé l'épaule ■ **you ~ through a small village** vous traversez un petit village.
◆ **pass up** *vt sep* **1.** [hand up] passer
2. [forego - job, opportunity] manquer, laisser passer ■ **I'll have to ~ up their invitation** je vais devoir décliner leur invitation.

passable ['pɑ:səbl] *adj* **1.** [acceptable] passable, acceptable **2.** [road] praticable ■ [river, canyon] franchissable **3.** [currency] ayant cours.

passably ['pɑ:səblɪ] *adv* passablement, pas trop mal.

passage ['pæsɪdʒ] *n* **1.** [way through] passage *m* ■ **they cleared a ~ through the crowd** ils ouvrirent un passage à travers la foule **2.** [corridor] passage *m*, couloir *m* ■ [alley] ruelle *f* **3.** [in book, music] passage *m* ■ **selected ~s from Churchill's speeches** morceaux choisis des discours de Churchill **4.** ANAT & TECH conduit *m* **5.** [passing - gen] passage *m* ; [- of bill] adoption *f* ■ **their friendship has survived the ~ of time** leur amitié a survécu au temps **6.** [voyage] voyage *m* ■ [crossing] traversée *f* ■ **she worked her ~ to Rio** elle a payé son voyage à Rio en travaillant à bord du navire ▶ **'A Passage to India'** *Forster, Lean* 'la Route des Indes' **7.** *fml* [access] libre passage *m* ■ **to grant sb safe ~ through a country** accorder à qqn le libre passage à travers un pays **8.** *arch* & *fig* **~ of** *OR* **at arms** passe *f* d'armes.

passageway ['pæsɪdʒweɪ] *n* [corridor] passage *m*, couloir *m* ■ [alleyway] ruelle *f*.

passbook ['pɑ:sbʊk] *n* **1.** [bankbook] livret *m* (d'épargne) **2.** *South Africa* laissez-passer *m inv*.

pass degree *n en Grande-Bretagne, licence obtenue avec mention passable (par opposition au "honours degree").*

passé [*UK* 'pæseɪ, *US* pæ'seɪ] *adj pej* dépassé, vieillot, désuet, -ète *f*.

passenger ['pæsɪndʒəʳ] *n* **1.** [in car, bus, aircraft, ship] passager *m*, -ère *f* ■ [in train] voyageur *m*, -euse *f* **2.** *UK pej* [worker, team member] poids *m* mort.

passenger coach *UK*, **passenger car** *US n* RAIL wagon *m OR* voiture *f* de voyageurs.

passenger list *n* liste *f* des passagers.

passenger seat *n* AUT [in front] siège *m* du passager ■ [in back] siège *m* arrière.

passenger train *n* train *m* de voyageurs.

passe-partout [,pæspə'tu:] *n* **1.** [mounting] passe-partout *m inv* **2.** = **passkey**.

passer-by [,pɑ:sə'baɪ] (*pl* **passers-by**) *n* passant *m*, - e *f*.

passim ['pæsɪm] *adv* passim.

passing ['pɑ:sɪŋ] ◇ *adj* **1.** [going by] qui passe ■ **she watched the ~ crowd** elle regardait la foule qui passait ■ **with each ~ day he grew more worried** son inquiétude croissait de jour en jour **2.** [fleeting] éphémère, passager **3.** [cursory, casual] (fait) en passant ■ **he didn't give her absence a ~ thought** c'est tout juste s'il a remarqué son absence, il a à peine remarqué son absence ■ **he made only a ~ reference to her absence** il a fait mention de son absence en passant **4.** AUT : **~ lane** voie *f* de dépassement.
◇ *n* **1.** [of time] passage *m*, fuite *f* ■ [of youth, traditions, old ways] disparition *f* ■ **she regretted the ~ of her beauty** elle regrettait sa beauté envolée ■ **with the ~ of time the pain will ease** la douleur s'atténuera avec le temps **2.** [of train, crowd] passage *m* **3.** *euph* [death] trépas *m*, mort *f*.
◆ **in passing** *adv phr* en passant.

passing-out parade *n* MIL défilé *m* de promotion.

passing place *n* voie *f* de dépassement, aire *f* de croisement.

passing shot *n* [in tennis] passing-shot *m*.

passion ['pæʃn] *n* **1.** [love] passion *f* ■ **to give in to one's ~** s'abandonner à sa passion ■ **crime of ~** crime *m* passionnel ■ **I have a ~ for Chinese food** j'adore la cuisine chinoise **2.** [emotion, feeling] passion *f* ■ **she sings with great ~** elle chante avec beaucoup de passion **3.** *lit* [fit of anger] (accès *m* de) colère *f*.
◆ **Passion** *n* MUS & RELIG : **the Passion** la Passion ■ **'the St Matthew Passion'** *Bach* 'la Passion selon saint Matthieu'.

passionate ['pæʃənət] *adj* passionné ■ **she's ~ about human rights** elle est dévouée à la cause des droits de l'homme.

passionately ['pæʃənətlɪ] *adv* passionnément.

passion fruit *n* fruit *m* de la Passion.

passionless ['pæʃənlɪs] *adj* sans passion.

Passion play *n* mystère *m* de la Passion.

Passion Sunday *n* le dimanche de la Passion.

passive ['pæsɪv] ◇ *adj* **1.** [gen - CHEM] & ELECTRON passif **2.** GRAM passif.
◇ *n* GRAM passif *m* ■ **in the ~** au passif.

passive-aggressive *adj* PSYCHOL passif-agressif.

passively ['pæsɪvlɪ] *adv* **1.** [gen] passivement **2.** GRAM au passif.

passiveness ['pæsɪvnɪs], **passivity** [pæ'sɪvətɪ] *n* passivité *f*.

passive resistance *n* résistance *f* passive.

passive smoker *n non-fumeur dans un environnement fumeur.*

passive smoking *n* tabagisme *m* passif.

passivize, ise ['pæsɪvaɪz] *vt* GRAM passiver.

passkey ['pɑ:ski:] *n* passe-partout *m inv.*

pass mark *n* SCH moyenne *f.*

Passover ['pɑ:s,əʊvər] *n* Pâque *f* (juive), Pesah *m.*

passport ['pɑ:spɔ:t] *n* **1.** passeport *m* ■ **British ~ holders** les détenteurs de passeports britanniques ■ **~ control** contrôle *m* des passeports ■ **~ photo** photo *f* d'identité **2.** *fig* clé *f* ■ **the ~ to happiness** la clé du bonheur.

pass-the-parcel *n* UK *jeu où l'on se passe un colis contenant soit un gage, soit un cadeau.*

password ['pɑ:swɜ:d] *n* mot *m* de passe.

past [pɑ:st] ◇ *n* **1.** [former time] passé *m* ■ **to live in the ~** vivre dans le passé ■ **the great empires of the ~** les grands empires de l'histoire ■ **he's a man with a ~** il a un passé chargé ▶ **politeness seems to have become a thing of the ~** la politesse semble être une chose démodée
2. GRAM passé *m* ■ **in the ~** au passé.
◇ *adj* **1.** [gone by - life] antérieur ; [- quarrels, differences] vieux *(before vowel or silent 'h'* **vieil***)*, vieille *f*, d'autrefois ; [- generation, centuries, mistakes, event] passé ■ **in ~ time** OR **times ~** autrefois, (au temps) jadis ■ [ended, over] : **to be ~** être passé OR terminé
2. [last] dernier ■ **this ~ month has been very busy** le mois qui vient de s'achever a été très chargé ■ **I've not been feeling well for the ~ few days** ça fait quelques jours que je ne me sens pas très bien ■ **he has spent the ~ five years in China** il a passé ces cinq dernières années en Chine
3. [former] ancien
4. GRAM passé.
◇ *prep* **1.** [in time] après ■ **it's ten/quarter/half ~ six** il est six heures dix/et quart/et demie ■ **it's quarter ~ the hour** il est le OR et quart ■ **it's already ~ midnight** il est déjà plus de minuit OR minuit passé ■ **it's long** OR **way ~ my bedtime** je devrais être au lit depuis longtemps ■ **these beans are ~ their best** ces haricots ne sont plus très frais ▶ **to be ~ it** *inf* avoir passé l'âge
2. [further than] plus loin que, au-delà de ■ **it's a few miles ~ the lake** c'est quelques kilomètres après le lac ■ **I didn't manage to get ~ the first page** je n'ai pas réussi à lire plus d'une page
3. [by, in front of] devant
4. [beyond scope of] au-delà de
5. [no longer capable of] : **I'm ~ caring** ça ne me fait plus ni chaud ni froid ▶ **I wouldn't put it ~ him** il en est bien capable.
◇ *adv* **1.** [by] : **to go ~** passer ■ **they ran ~** ils passèrent en courant ■ **the years flew ~** les années passaient à une vitesse prodigieuse
2. [ago] : **one night about three years ~** une nuit il y a environ trois ans ■ **it had long ~ struck midnight** minuit avait sonné depuis longtemps.
◆ **in the past** *adv phr* autrefois, dans le temps.

pasta ['pæstə] *n (U)* pâtes *fpl* (alimentaires).

paste [peɪst] ◇ *n* **1.** [substance - gen] pâte *f* **2.** CULIN [dough] pâte *f* ■ [mashed meat, fish] pâté *m* ■ **tomato ~** concentré *m* de tomate **3.** [glue] colle *f* **4.** [for jewellery] strass *m*, stras *m* ■ **~ necklace/diamonds** collier/diamants en strass OR strass.
◇ *vt* **1.** [stick - stamp] coller ■ [spread glue on] encoller, enduire de colle **2.** [cover - wall] recouvrir.
◆ **paste up** *vt sep* [poster] coller ■ [list] afficher ■ [wallpaper] poser.

pastel ['pæstl] ◇ *n* pastel *m* ■ **~ (drawing)** (dessin *m* au) pastel ■ **a portrait in ~s** un portrait au pastel.
◇ *adj* pastel *(inv)* ■ **~ pink skirts** des jupes rose pastel.

paste-up *n* TYPO maquette *f.*

pasteurize, ise ['pɑ:stʃəraɪz] *vt* pasteuriser.

pasteurized ['pɑ:stʃəraɪzd] *adj* **1.** [milk, beer] pasteurisé **2.** *pej* [version, description] édulcoré, aseptisé.

pastiche [pæ'sti:ʃ] *n* pastiche *m.*

pastille, pastil ['pæstɪl] *n* pastille *f* ■ **cough ~s** pastilles pour OR contre la toux.

pastime ['pɑ:staɪm] *n* passe-temps *m.*

pasting ['peɪstɪŋ] *n inf* [beating, defeat] raclée *f.*

past master *n* expert *m* ■ **he's a ~ at doing as little as possible** *hum* il est passé maître dans l'art d'en faire le moins possible.

pastor ['pɑ:stər] *n* RELIG pasteur *m.*

pastoral ['pɑ:stərəl] *adj* **1.** [gen - ART] & LIT pastoral ▶ **~ land** pâturages *mpl* **2.** RELIG pastoral ■ **~ staff** crosse *f* (d'évêque) **3.** SCH : **~ care** ≃ tutorat *m* ■ **teachers also have a ~ role** les enseignants ont également un rôle de conseillers.

past participle *n* participe *m* passé.

past perfect *n* plus-que-parfait *m.*

pastrami [pə'strɑ:mɪ] *n* pastarmi *m*, pastermi *m.*

pastry ['peɪstrɪ] *(pl* **pastries***)* *n* **1.** [dough] pâte *f* **2.** [cake] pâtisserie *f*, gâteau *m.*

pastry board *n* planche *f* à pâtisserie.

pastry brush *n* pinceau *m* (à pâtisserie).

pastry case *n* croûte *f.*

pastry cook *n* pâtissier *m*, - ère *f.*

pastry shell *n* fond *m* de tarte.

past tense *n* passé *m.*

pasturage ['pɑ:stjʊrɪdʒ] *n* pâturage *m.*

pasture ['pɑ:stʃər] ◇ *n* pâture *f*, pré *m*, pâturage *m* ■ **to put out to ~** [animal] mettre au pâturage ; *hum* [person] mettre à la retraite ; *hum* [car] mettre à la casse ■ **he left for greener ~s** il est parti vers des horizons plus favorables.
◇ *vt* [animal] faire paître.

pastureland ['pɑ:stʃəlænd] *n* herbages *mpl*, pâturages *mpl.*

pasty[1] ['peɪstɪ] *(comp* **pastier**, *superl* **pastiest***)* *adj* [texture] pâteux ■ [sallow] terreux ■ [whitish] blanchâtre.

pasty[2] ['pæstɪ] *(pl* **pasties***)* *n* UK CULIN ≃ petit pâté *m.*

pasty-faced ['peɪstɪ-] *adj* au teint terreux.

pat [pæt] *(pret & pp* **patted**, *cont* **patting***)* ◇ *vt* tapoter ■ **"sit here", she said, patting the place beside her** "assieds-toi ici", dit-elle, désignant la place à côté d'elle ■ **~ your face dry** séchez-vous le visage en le tapotant ■ **he patted the soil/sand down** il a tassé la terre/le sable ▶ **to ~ sb on the back** *liter* tapoter qqn OR donner une petite tape à qqn dans le dos ; *fig* féliciter OR complimenter qqn.
◇ *n* **1.** [tap] (légère) tape *f* ■ **you deserve a ~ on the back** *fig* tu mérites un coup de chapeau **2.** [lump] : **a ~ of butter** une noix de beurre.
◇ *adj* **1.** [glib - remark] tout fait ; [- answer] tout prêt ■ **his story is a little too ~** son histoire colle un peu trop bien **2.** [in poker] : **a ~ hand** une main servie.
◇ *adv* **1.** [exactly] parfaitement, avec facilité ■ **to have sthg off ~** apprendre qqch à la perfection OR par cœur **2.** US [unbending] : **to stand ~** [on decision] rester intraitable.

Patagonia [,pætə'gəʊnjə] *pr n* Patagonie *f* ■ **in ~** en Patagonie.

Patagonian [,pætə'gəʊnjən] ◇ *n* Patagon *m*, - onne *f.*
◇ *adj* patagon.

patch [pætʃ] ◇ *n* **1.** [of fabric] pièce *f* ■ [on inner tube] Rustine® *f* ■ **a jacket with suede ~es on the elbows** une veste avec des pièces en daim aux coudes ▶ **he's not a ~ on you** il ne t'arrive pas à la cheville
2. [over eye] bandeau *m*
3. [sticking plaster] pansement *m* (adhésif)
4. [beauty spot] mouche *f*
5. MIL [on uniform] insigne *m*
6. [plot of land] parcelle *f*, lopin *m* ■ **cabbage/strawberry ~** carré *m* de choux/de fraises ■ **vegetable ~** potager *m*
7. [small expanse - of light, colour] tache *f* ; [- of fog] nappe *f*, poche *f* ■ **snow still lay in ~es on the slopes** les pistes étaient en-

core enneigées par endroits ▪ **we crossed a rough ~ of road** nous sommes passés sur un tronçon de route défoncé ▪ **a bald ~** une (petite) tonsure
8. *UK* [period] période *f*, moment *m* ▪ **to go through a bad** *OR* **sticky** *OR* **rough ~** traverser une période difficile *OR* une mauvaise passe
9. *UK* [district, beat] secteur *m*
10. COMPUT modification *f* (de programme)
11. MED patch *m*, timbre *m*.
◇ *vt* **1.** [mend - clothes] rapiécer ; [- tyre, canoe] réparer ▪ **they ~ed the hole in the roof** ils ont colmaté *OR* bouché le trou dans la toiture
2. COMPUT [program] modifier
3. TELEC raccorder ▪ **I'll ~ you through** je vous passe votre communication.
◆ **patch together** *vt sep* **: they managed to ~ together a government/story** ils sont parvenus à former un gouvernement de fortune/à construire une histoire de toutes pièces.
◆ **patch up** *vt sep* **1.** [repair - clothes] rapiécer ; [- car, boat] réparer ; [- in makeshift way] rafistoler
2. [relationship] **: he's trying to ~ things up with his wife** il essaie de se rabibocher avec sa femme ▪ **they've ~ed up their dispute** ils se sont réconciliés.

patch pocket *n* poche *f* plaquée.

patchwork ['pætʃwɜ:k] *n* **1.** SEW patchwork *m* ▪ *fig* [of colours, fields] mosaïque *f* **2.** [collection] collection *f*.

patchy ['pætʃɪ] (*comp* **patchier**, *superl* **patchiest**) *adj* **1.** [not uniform] inégal, irrégulier ▪ **~ fog** des nappes de brouillard **2.** [incomplete - evidence] incomplet, - ète *f* ; [- knowledge] imparfait.

pate [peɪt] *n arch & hum* tête *f*.

pâté ['pæteɪ] *n* pâté *m*.

patella [pə'telə] (*pl* **patellas** *OR pl* **patellae** [-li:]) *n* **1.** ANAT rotule *f* **2.** archaeology patelle *f*.

patent [*UK* 'peɪtənt, *US* 'pætənt] ◇ *n* **1.** [on invention] brevet *m* ▪ **to take out a ~ on sthg** prendre un brevet sur qqch, faire breveter qqch ▪ **'~ pending'** demande de brevet déposée **2.** = **patent leather 3.** *US* [on land] concession *f*.
◇ *adj* **1.** [product, procedure] breveté **2.** [blatant] patent, manifeste.
◇ *vt* faire breveter.

patented [*UK* 'peɪtəntɪd, 'pætəntɪd] *adj* [product, procedure] breveté.

patentee [*UK* ˌpeɪtən'ti:, *US* ˌpætən'ti:] *n* détenteur *m*, - trice *f* *OR* titulaire *mf* d'un brevet (d'invention).

patent leather *n* cuir *m* verni, vernis *m* ▪ **~ boots** bottes *fpl* vernies *OR* en cuir verni.

patently [*UK* 'peɪtəntlɪ, *US* 'pætəntlɪ] *adv* manifestement, de toute évidence.

patent medicine *n* médicament *m* vendu sans ordonnance ▪ *pej* [cure-all] élixir *m* universel, remède *m* de charlatan *pej*.

Patent Office *n* ≃ Institut *m* national de la propriété industrielle.

paternal [pə'tɜ:nl] *adj* paternel.

paternalism [pə'tɜ:nəlɪzm] *n* paternalisme *m*.

paternalistic [pəˌtɜ:nə'lɪstɪk] *adj* paternaliste.

paternally [pə'tɜ:nəlɪ] *adv* paternellement.

paternity [pə'tɜ:nətɪ] *n* paternité *f*.

paternity leave *n* congé *m* de paternité.

paternity suit *n* action *f* en recherche de paternité.

paternity test *n* test *m* de recherche de paternité.

paternoster [ˌpætə'nɒstər] *n* **1.** [rosary bead] pater *m* **2.** [fishing tackle, lift] pater-noster *m*.
◆ **Paternoster** *n* [prayer] Pater *m*.

path [pɑ:θ] (*pl* **paths** [pɑ:ðz]) *n* **1.** [in garden, park] allée *f* ▪ [in country] chemin *m*, sentier *m* ▪ [along road] trottoir *m* **2.** [way ahead or through] chemin *m*, passage *m* ▪ **to cut a ~ through sthg** se tailler *OR* se frayer un chemin à travers qqch ▪ **the hurricane destroyed everything in its ~** l'ouragan a tout détruit sur son passage ▪ **the ~ to fame** *fig* la route *OR* le chemin qui mène à la gloire **3.** [trajectory - of projectile, planet] trajectoire *f* ▪ **our ~s first crossed in 1965** nos chemins se sont croisés *OR* nous nous sommes rencontrés pour la première fois en 1965 **4.** COMPUT chemin *m* (d'accès).

pathetic [pə'θetɪk] *adj* **1.** [pitiable - lament, waif, smile, story] pitoyable **2.** *pej* [worthless] minable, lamentable.

pathetically [pə'θetɪklɪ] *adv* pitoyablement ▪ **he used to be ~ shy** autrefois, il était d'une timidité qui faisait peine à voir.

pathetic fallacy *n attribution à la nature de sentiments humains.*

pathname ['pɑ:θneɪm] *n* chemin *m* (d'accès).

pathological [ˌpæθə'lɒdʒɪkl] *adj* pathologique ▪ **he's a ~ liar** il ne peut pas s'empêcher de mentir.

pathologist [pə'θɒlədʒɪst] *n* pathologiste *mf*.

pathology [pə'θɒlədʒɪ] (*pl* **pathologies**) *n* pathologie *f*.

pathos ['peɪθɒs] *n* pathétique *m*.

pathway ['pɑ:θweɪ] *n* [in garden] allée *f* ▪ [in country] chemin *m*, sentier *m* ▪ [beside road] trottoir *m*.

patience ['peɪʃns] *n* **1.** patience *f* ▪ **to lose ~ (with sb)** perdre patience (avec qqn) ▪ **he has no ~ with children** les enfants l'exaspèrent ▪ **don't try my ~ any further!** ne mets pas davantage ma patience à l'épreuve!, n'abuse pas davantage de ma patience! ▪ **my ~ is wearing thin** ma patience a des limites, je suis à bout de patience **2.** *UK* [card game] réussite *f*.

patient ['peɪʃnt] ◇ *adj* patient ▪ **be ~!** (un peu de) patience!, soyez patient! ▪ **with a ~ smile** avec un sourire empreint d'une grande patience.
◇ *n* MED malade *mf*, patient *m*, - e *f*.

patiently ['peɪʃntlɪ] *adv* patiemment.

Patient's Charter *pr n* **: the ~** *la charte officielle du National Health Service.*

patina ['pætɪnə] (*pl* **patinas** *OR pl* **patinae** [-ni:]) *n* patine *f*.

patio ['pætɪəʊ] (*pl* **patios**) *n* patio *m* ▪ **~ furniture** meubles *mpl* de jardin.

patio doors *npl* portes *fpl* vitrées *(donnant sur un patio)*.

Patna rice ['pætnə-] *n variété de riz à grains longs.*

patois ['pætwɑ:] (*pl inv* ['pætwɑ:]) *n* patois *m*.

patriarch ['peɪtrɪɑ:k] *n* patriarche *m*.

patriarchal [ˌpeɪtrɪ'ɑ:kl] *adj* patriarcal.

patriarchy ['peɪtrɪɑ:kɪ] (*pl* **patriarchies**) *n* patriarcat *m*.

patrician [pə'trɪʃn] *n* patricien *m*, - enne *f*.

patricide ['pætrɪsaɪd] *n* **1.** [killer] parricide *mf* **2.** [act] parricide *m*.

patrimony [*UK* 'pætrɪmənɪ, *US* 'pætrɪməʊnɪ] (*pl* **patrimonies**) *n* patrimoine *m*.

patriot [*UK* 'pætrɪət, *US* 'peɪtrɪət] *n* patriote *mf*.

Patriot Act *n loi qui donne aux agences gouvernementales américaines des pouvoirs exceptionnels dans la lutte contre le terrorisme.*

patriotic [*UK* ˌpætrɪ'ɒtɪk, *US* ˌpeɪtrɪ'ɒtɪk] *adj* [person] patriote ▪ [song, action etc] patriotique.

patriotically [*UK* ˌpætrɪ'ɒtɪklɪ, *US* ˌpeɪtrɪ'ɒtɪklɪ] *adv* patriotiquement, en patriote.

patriotism [*UK* 'pætrɪətɪzm, *US* 'peɪtrɪətɪzm] *n* patriotisme *m*.

patrol [pə'trəʊl] (*pret & pp* **patrolled**, *cont* **patrolling**) ◇ *n* **1.** [group] patrouille *f* ▪ **highway ~** *US* police *f* des autoroutes **2.** [task] patrouille *f* ▪ **to be on ~** être de patrouille.
◇ *vi* patrouiller.
◇ *vt* [area, streets] patrouiller dans ▪ **the border is patrolled by armed guards** des gardes armés patrouillent le long de la frontière.

patrol boat *n* NAUT patrouilleur *m*.

patrol car *n* voiture *f* de police.

patrol leader *n* chef *m* de patrouille.

patrolman [pə'trəʊlmən] (*pl* **patrolmen** [-mən]) *n* **1.** *US* agent *m* de police *(qui fait sa ronde)* **2.** *UK dépanneur employé par une association d'automobilistes.*

patrol wagon *n US, Australia & New Zealand* fourgon *m* cellulaire.

patrolwoman [pə'trəʊl,wʊmən] (*pl* **patrolwomen** [-,wɪmɪn]) *n US* femme *f* agent de police *(qui fait sa ronde).*

patron ['peɪtrən] *n* **1.** [sponsor - of the arts] mécène *m* ; [- of a festival] parrain *m*, sponsor *m* ▪ **many multinational companies are becoming ~s of the arts** de nombreuses multinationales se lancent dans le mécénat **2.** [customer - of restaurant, hotel, shop] client *m*, - e *f* ; [- of library] usager *m* ; [- of museum] visiteur *m*, - euse *f* ; [- of theatre, cinema] spectateur *m*, - trice *f* ▪ **'~s only'** 'réservé aux clients' **3.** [in ancient Rome] patron *m*.

patronage ['peɪtrənɪdʒ] *n* **1.** [support, sponsorship] patronage *m*, parrainage *m* **2.** COMM clientèle *f* ▪ **I shall take my ~ elsewhere** j'irai me fournir ailleurs **3.** POL pouvoir *m* de nomination ▪ *pej* trafic *m* d'influence ▪ **he got the promotion through the Minister's ~** il a obtenu de l'avancement grâce à l'influence du ministre **4.** [condescension] condescendance *f*.

patronize, ise ['pætrənaɪz] *vt* **1.** [business] donner sa clientèle à ▪ [cinema] fréquenter **2.** [condescend to] traiter avec condescendance ▪ **don't ~ me!** ne prenez pas ce ton condescendant avec moi! **3.** [sponsor] patronner, parrainer.

patronizing ['pætrənaɪzɪŋ] *adj* condescendant.

patronizingly ['pætrənaɪzɪŋlɪ] *adv* [smile] avec condescendance ▪ [say] d'un ton condescendant.

patron saint *n* (saint *m*) patron *m*, (sainte *f*) patronne *f*.

patronymic [,pætrə'nɪmɪk] <> *n* patronyme *m*.
<> *adj* patronymique.

patsy△ ['pætsɪ] (*pl* **patsies**) *n US* [gullible person] pigeon *m*, gogo *m* ▪ [scapegoat] bouc *m* émissaire.

patten ['pætn] *n* socque *m (pour protéger les chaussures contre la boue).*

patter ['pætəʳ] <> *n* **1.** [sound] crépitement *m*, (petit) bruit *m* ➲ **the (pitter) ~ of tiny feet** *hum* un heureux événement **2.** *inf* [of salesman] baratin *m*, boniment *m* ▪ [of entertainer] bavardage *m*, baratin *m* **3.** *inf* [jargon] jargon *m*.
<> *vi* **1.** [raindrops] tambouriner **2.** [person, mouse] trottiner **3.** *inf* [talk] bavarder, baratiner.

pattern ['pætən] <> *n* **1.** [design - decorative] motif *m* ; [- natural] dessin *m* ; [- on animal] marques *fpl* ▪ **a geometric/herringbone ~** un motif géométrique/à chevrons **2.** [physical arrangement] disposition *f*, configuration *f* ▪ **to form a ~** former un motif *OR* un dessin **3.** [abstract arrangement] système *m*, configuration *f* ▪ **research has established that there is a ~ in** *OR* **to the data** la recherche a établi que les données ne sont pas aléatoires ▪ **behaviour ~s in monkeys** types de comportement chez les singes ▪ **there is a definite ~ to the burglaries** on observe une constante bien précise dans les cambriolages ▪ **the ~ of TV viewing in the average household** les habitudes du téléspectateur moyen ▪ **voice ~** empreintes *fpl* vocales **4.** [diagram, shape which guides - TECH] modèle *m*, gabarit *m* ▪ SEW patron *m* ▪ **dress ~** patron de robe **5.** *fig* [example] exemple *m*, modèle *m* ▪ **to set a ~ for** [subj: company, method, work] servir de modèle (à) ; [subj: person] instaurer un modèle (pour).
<> *vt* **1.** [mark - fabric] décorer d'un motif **2.** [copy] modeler ▪ **to ~ o.s. on** *OR* **after sb** prendre modèle *OR* exemple sur qqn.

patterned ['pætənd] *adj* à motifs.

patterning ['pætənɪŋ] *n* **1.** PSYCHOL & SOCIOL acquisition *f* des structures de pensée **2.** ZOOL [markings] marques *fpl*, taches *fpl*.

pattie, patty ['pætɪ] (*pl* **patties**) *n* **1.** *US* **(hamburger) ~** *portion de steak haché* **2.** [pasty] (petit) pâté *m*.

paucity ['pɔːsətɪ] *n fml* pénurie *f*.

Paul [pɔːl] *pr n* : **Saint ~** saint Paul.

paunch [pɔːntʃ] *n* **1.** *pej & hum* [stomach] (gros) ventre *m*, bedaine *f* **2.** ZOOL panse *f*.

paunchy ['pɔːntʃɪ] (*comp* **paunchier**, *superl* **paunchiest**) *adj pej & hum* ventru, pansu, bedonnant ▪ **he's getting ~** il prend du ventre.

pauper ['pɔːpəʳ] *n* pauvre *mf*, pauvresse *f*, indigent *m*, - e *f* ▪ **to end up in a ~'s grave** finir à la fosse commune.

pause [pɔːz] <> *n* **1.** [break] pause *f*, temps *m* d'arrêt ▪ [on tape recorder] 'pause' ▪ **without a ~** sans s'arrêter, sans interruption ▪ **there was a long ~ before she answered** elle garda longtemps le silence avant de répondre ▪ **to give sb ~, to give ~ to sb** *fml* donner à réfléchir à qqn **2.** MUS point *m* d'orgue **3.** LIT césure *f*.
<> *vi* faire *OR* marquer une pause ▪ **he ~d in the middle of his explanation** il s'arrêta *OR* s'interrompit au milieu de son explication ▪ **I signed it without pausing to read the details** je l'ai signé sans prendre le temps d'en lire les détails ▪ **without pausing for breath** sans même reprendre son souffle ▪ **she ~d on the doorstep** elle hésita sur le pas de la porte.

pave [peɪv] *vt* [street, floor - with flagstones, tiles] paver ; [- with concrete, asphalt] revêtir ➲ **to ~ the way for sthg** ouvrir la voie à *OR* préparer le terrain pour qqch.

paved [peɪvd] *adj* : **~ in** *OR* **with** [flagstones, tiles] pavé de ; [concrete, asphalt] revêtu de ▪ **her career was ~ with success** *fig* sa carrière fut jalonnée de succès.

pavement ['peɪvmənt] *n* **1.** *UK* [footpath] trottoir *m* ▪ **~ café** café *m*, terrasse *f* d'un café **2.** *US* [roadway] chaussée *f* **3.** [surfaced area - of cobbles, stones] pavé *m* ; [- of marble, granite] dallage *m* ; [- of concrete] (dalle *f* de) béton *m* ; [- of mosaic] pavement *m*.

pavement artist *n UK* artiste *mf* de trottoir.

pavilion [pə'vɪljən] *n* **1.** [building] pavillon *m* ▪ [at sports ground] vestiaires *mpl* ➲ **(cricket) ~** *bâtiment abritant les vestiaires et le bar sur un terrain de cricket* **2.** [tent] tente *f*.

paving ['peɪvɪŋ] <> *n* [cobbles, flagstones] pavé *m* ▪ [tiles] carrelage *m* ▪ [concrete] dallage *m*, béton *m*.
<> *adj* [measure, legislation] préparatoire.

paving stone *n* pavé *m*.

pavlova [pæv'ləʊvə] *n* vacherin *m*.

Pavlovian [pæv'ləʊvɪən] *adj* pavlovien.

paw [pɔː] <> *n* **1.** [of animal] patte *f* **2.** *inf* [hand] pince *f*, patte *f*.
<> *vt* **1.** [animal] donner un coup de patte à ▪ **the horse ~ed the ground** le cheval piaffait **2.** *inf* [touch, maul] tripoter ▪ [sexually] peloter.
<> *vi* : **the dog ~ed at the door** le chien grattait à la porte.

pawn [pɔːn] <> *n* **1.** [in chess] pion *m* **2.** [at pawnbroker's] : **my watch is in ~** ma montre est en gage ▪ **I got my watch out of ~** *UK* j'ai dégagé ma montre.
<> *vt* mettre *OR* laisser en gage.

pawnbroker ['pɔːn,brəʊkəʳ] *n* prêteur *m* sur gages ▪ **at the ~'s** au mont-de-piété.

pawnshop ['pɔːnʃɒp] *n* boutique *f* de prêteur sur gages, mont-de-piété *m*.

pawn ticket *n* reconnaissance *f* du mont-de-piété.

pawpaw ['pɔːpɔː] *n* papaye *f*.

pay [peɪ] (*pret & pp* **paid** [peɪd]) <> *vt* **1.** [person] payer ▪ **she's paid £2,000 a month** elle est payée *OR* elle touche 2 000 livres par mois **2.** [sum of money] payer ▪ **I paid her £20** je lui ai payé 20 livres ▪ **he paid £20 for the watch** il a payé la montre 20 livres **3.** [bill, debt] payer, régler ▪ [fine, taxes, fare] payer ➲ **to ~ one's way** payer sa part ▪ **is the business ~ing its way?** cette affaire est-elle rentable? **4.** *fig* [benefit] rapporter à ▪ **it'll ~ you to start now** vous avez intérêt à commencer tout de suite ▪ **it'll ~ you to keep quiet!** tu as intérêt à tenir ta langue! **5.** [with various noun objects] : **~ attention!** faites attention! ▪ **to ~ a call on sb, to ~ sb a visit** rendre visite à qqn.

◇ *vi* payer ■ **to ~ by cheque** payer par chèque ■ **to ~ (by) cash** payer en espèces ■ **the job ~s very well** le travail est très bien payé ■ **after two years the business was beginning to ~** après deux ans, l'affaire était devenue rentable ■ **it ~s to be honest** ça rapporte d'être honnête ■ **it's a small price to ~ for peace of mind** c'est faire un bien petit sacrifice pour avoir sa tranquillité d'esprit ◗ **to ~ on the nail** payer rubis sur ongle.
◇ *n* paie *f*, paye *f* ■ **my first month's ~** ma première paie, mon premier salaire ■ **the ~ is good** c'est bien payé ■ **he's in the ~ of the enemy** il est à la solde de l'ennemi.
◇ *comp* **1.** [demand, negotiations] salarial ■ [increase, cut] de salaire **2.** [not free] payant **3.** MIN [deposit] exploitable.
◆ **pay back** *vt sep* **1.** [loan, lender] rembourser ■ **she paid her father back the sum she had borrowed** elle remboursa à son père la somme qu'elle avait empruntée **2.** [retaliate against] rendre la monnaie de sa pièce à ■ **I'll ~ you back for that!** tu me le paieras!
◆ **pay for** *vt insep* **1.** [item, task] payer ■ **to ~ for sthg** payer qqch ■ **I paid good money for that!** ça m'a coûté cher! ■ **you get what you ~ for** la qualité est en rapport avec le prix (que vous payez) ■ **the ticket ~s for itself after two trips** le billet est amorti dès le deuxième voyage **2.** [crime, mistake] payer ■ **you'll ~ for this!** tu me le paieras! ■ **he paid for his mistake with his life** il a payé son erreur de sa vie ■ **to make sb ~ for sthg** faire payer qqch à qqn.
◆ **pay in** *vt sep UK* [cheque] déposer sur un compte.
◆ **pay into** ◇ *vt sep* [money] : **I'd like to ~ this cheque into my account** j'aimerais déposer ce chèque sur mon compte.
◇ *vt insep* : **to ~ into a pension scheme** cotiser à un plan de retraite.
◆ **pay off** ◇ *vt sep* **1.** [debt] payer, régler, s'acquitter de ■ [loan] rembourser **2.** [dismiss, lay off] licencier, congédier **3.** *inf* [bribe] acheter.
◇ *vi insep* payer, rapporter ■ **moving the company out of London really paid off** le transfert de la société hors de Londres a été une affaire rentable.
◆ **pay out** *vt sep* **1.** [money] payer, débourser **2.** [rope] laisser filer.
◆ **pay up** *vi insep* payer.

payable ['peɪəbl] *adj* payable ■ **~ in 24 monthly instalments/in advance** payable en 24 mensualités/d'avance ■ **cheques should be made ~ to Mr Brown** les chèques devraient être libellés *OR* établis à l'ordre de M. Brown.

pay-and-display *adj* : **~ car park** parking *m* à horodateur ■ **~ machine** horodateur *m*.

pay-as-you-earn = **PAYE**.

pay-as-you-go [,pi:di:'ef] *n* système *m* sans forfait.

payback ['peɪbæk] *n* FIN rapport *m (d'un investissement)*.

paybed ['peɪbed] *n UK* lit *m* (d'hôpital) privé.

pay check *US* = **pay packet**.

payday ['peɪdeɪ] *n* jour *m* de paie ■ **tomorrow is ~** nous sommes payés demain.

pay dirt *n US inf* **1.** [earth] gisement *m* **2.** [discovery] trouvaille *f* ■ **to hit ~** trouver un bon filon.

PAYE (*abbrev of* **pay-as-you-earn**) *n* prélèvement *m* à la source *(des impôts)*.

payee [peɪ'i:] *n* bénéficiaire *mf*.

pay envelope *US* = **pay packet**.

payer ['peɪəʳ] *n* **1.** [gen] payeur *m*, - euse *f* **2.** [of cheque] tireur *m*, - euse *f*.

paying ['peɪɪŋ] ◇ *n* paiement *m*.
◇ *adj* **1.** [who pays] payant **2.** [profitable] payant, rentable.

paying guest *n* hôte *m* payant.

paying-in book *n* carnet *m* de versement.

paying-in slip *n UK* bordereau *m* de versement.

payload ['peɪləʊd] *n* **1.** [gen] chargement *m* **2.** TECH [of vehicle, aircraft, rocket] charge *f* utile ■ [of missile, warhead] puissance *f*.

paymaster ['peɪ,mɑ:stəʳ] *n* [gen] payeur *m*, - euse *f*, intendant *m*, - e *f* ■ [in school, institution] économe *mf* ■ [in army] payeur *m* ■ [in administration] trésorier-payeur *m*.

Paymaster General *pr n* : **the ~** le Trésorier-payeur-général britannique.

payment ['peɪmənt] *n* **1.** [sum paid, act of paying] paiement *m*, versement *m* ■ **on ~ of a deposit** moyennant des arrhes ■ **in ~ of your invoice** en règlement de votre facture **2.** [reward, compensation] récompense *f*.

payoff ['peɪɒf] *n* **1.** [act of paying off] paiement *m* **2.** [profit] bénéfice *m*, profit *m* **3.** [consequence] conséquence *f*, résultat *m* ■ [reward] récompense *f* **4.** *inf* [climax] dénouement *m* **5.** *inf* [bribe] pot-de-vin *m*.

payola [peɪ'əʊlə] *n (U) US inf* pots-de-vin *mpl*, dessous-de-table *mpl*.

pay packet *n UK* [envelope] enveloppe *f* contenant le salaire ■ [money] paie *f*, salaire *m*.

pay-per-view *adj* TV à péage.

payphone ['peɪfəʊn] *n* téléphone *m* public ■ **I'm calling from a ~** j'appelle d'une cabine.

pay rise *n* augmentation *f* de salaire.

payroll ['peɪrəʊl] *n* **1.** [personnel] personnel *m* ■ **he's been on our ~ for years** il fait partie du personnel depuis des années ■ **they've added 500 workers to their ~** ils ont embauché 500 travailleurs supplémentaires **2.** [list] registre *m* du personnel.

payslip ['peɪslɪp] *n* fiche *f OR* feuille *f OR* bulletin *m* de paie.

pay station *US* = **payphone**.

pay television *n* chaîne *f* à péage.

pay TV *n* = **pay television**.

PBS (*abbrev of* **Public Broadcasting Service**) *pr n société américaine de production télévisuelle.*

pc (*written abbrev of* **per cent**) p. cent.

pc, PC *n* **1.** (*abbrev of* **personal computer**) PC *m*, micro *m* **2.** = **postcard**.

PC ◇ *n* **1.** = **police constable 2.** = **privy councillor**.
◇ *adj* = **politically correct**.

PCB *n* = **printed circuit board**.

PC card *n* carte *f* PC.

PCP® (*abbrev of* **phencyclidine**) *n* PCP® *f*.

PCV (*abbrev of* **passenger carrying vehicle**) *n UK* véhicule *m* de transport en commun.

PD *n US* = **police department**.

PDA *n* = **personal digital assistant**.

PDF (*abbrev of* **portable document format**) *n* COMPUT PDF *m*.

pdq (*abbrev of* **pretty damn quick**) *adv inf* illico presto.

PDSA (*abbrev of* **People's Dispensary for Sick Animals**) *pr n association de soins aux animaux malades.*

PDT [,pi:di:'ti:] (*abbrev of* **Pacific Daylight Time**) *n* heure *f* du Pacifique.

PE (*abbrev of* **physical education**) *n* EPS *f*.

pea [pi:] *n* BOT pois *m* ■ CULIN (petit) pois *m* ◗ **~ soup** soupe *f* aux pois ■ **they are as alike as two ~s in a pod** ils se ressemblent comme deux gouttes d'eau.

peace [pi:s] ◇ *n* **1.** [not war] paix *f* ■ **the country is at ~ now** la paix est maintenant rétablie dans le pays ■ **I come in ~** je viens en ami ■ **he made (his) ~ with his father** *fig* il a fait la paix *OR* il s'est réconcilié avec son père ■ **the Peace Garden State** le Dakota du Nord ‖ [treaty] (traité *m* de) paix *f* **2.** [tranquillity] paix *f*, tranquillité *f* ■ **to be at ~ with oneself/the world** être en paix avec soi-même/le reste du monde ■ **~ be with you!** que la paix soit avec vous! ■ **we haven't had a moment's ~ all morning** nous n'avons pas eu un moment de tranquillité de toute la matinée ■ **all I want is a bit of ~ and quiet** tout ce que je veux,

c'est un peu de tranquillité ■ **to have ~ of mind** avoir l'esprit tranquille ■ **he'll give you no ~ until you pay him** tant que tu ne l'auras pas payé, il ne te laissera pas tranquille ■ **leave us in ~!** laisse-nous tranquilles!, laisse-nous en paix! ▮ [silence] : **to hold** OR **to keep one's ~** garder le silence, se taire **3.** [law and order] paix *f*, ordre *m* public ■ **to disturb the ~** troubler l'ordre public ■ **to keep the ~** [army, police] maintenir l'ordre.
◇ *comp* [treaty, talks] de paix ■ [rally, movement] pour la paix.

peaceable ['pi:səbl] *adj* **1.** [peace-loving - nation, person] pacifique **2.** [calm - atmosphere] paisible, tranquille ; [- demonstration, methods] pacifique ; [- discussion] calme.

peaceably ['pi:səblɪ] *adv* [live] paisiblement, tranquillement ■ [discuss, listen] calmement, paisiblement ■ [assemble, disperse] pacifiquement, sans incident.

Peace Corps *pr n organisation américaine de coopération avec les pays en voie de développement.*

peaceful ['pi:sfʊl] *adj* **1.** [calm, serene] paisible, tranquille **2.** [non-violent] pacifique.

peacefully ['pi:sfʊlɪ] *adv* [live, rest] paisiblement, tranquillement ■ [protest] pacifiquement ■ **the rally went off ~** le meeting s'est déroulé dans le calme OR sans incident.

peacefulness ['pi:sfʊlnɪs] *n* paix *f*, calme *m*, tranquillité *f*.

peacekeeper ['pi:s,ki:pər] *n* [soldier] soldat *m* de la paix ■ [of United Nations] casque *m* bleu.

peacekeeping ['pi:s,ki:pɪŋ] ◇ *n* maintien *m* de la paix.
◇ *adj* de maintien de la paix ■ **a United Nations ~ force** des forces des Nations unies pour le maintien de la paix.

peace-loving *adj* pacifique.

peacemaker ['pi:s,meɪkər] *n* pacificateur *m*, - trice *f*, conciliateur *m*, - trice *f*.

peacenik ['pi:snɪk] *n inf pej* pacifiste *mf*.

peace offensive *n* offensive *f* de paix.

peace offering *n* offrande *f* de paix.

peace pipe *n* calumet *m* (de la paix).

peacetime ['pi:staɪm] *n* temps *m* de paix ■ **in ~** en temps de paix.

peach [pi:tʃ] ◇ *n* **1.** [fruit] pêche *f* ■ [tree] pêcher *m* ■ **~ blossom** fleurs *fpl* de pêcher ■ **she has a ~es and cream complexion** elle a un teint de pêche ■ **the Peach State** la Géorgie **2.** [colour] couleur *f* pêche **3.** *inf* [expressing approval] : **he played a ~ of a shot** il a joué un coup superbe ■ **thanks, you're a ~!** merci, tu es adorable!
◇ *adj* [colour] pêche *(inv)*.

peach melba *n* pêche *f* melba.

peachy ['pi:tʃɪ] (*comp* **peachier**, *superl* **peachiest**) *adj* **1.** [taste, flavour] de pêche **2.** *inf* [nice] chouette.

peacock ['pi:kɒk] (*pl inv* OR *pl* **peacocks**) ◇ *n* **1.** [bird] paon *m* **2.** [colour] = **peacock blue**.
◇ *adj* = **peacock blue**.

peacock blue *n* bleu *m* paon.
◆ **peacock-blue** *adj* bleu paon *(inv)*.

pea green *n* vert *m* pomme.
◆ **pea-green** *adj* vert pomme *(inv)*.

peahen ['pi:hen] *n* paonne *f*.

peak [pi:k] ◇ *n* **1.** [mountain top] pic *m*, sommet *m* ■ [mountain] pic *m* ■ **snowy ~s** pics enneigés **2.** [pointed part - of roof] faîte *m* ■ **beat the egg whites until they form ~s** battez les blancs d'œufs en neige très ferme **3.** [high point - of fame, career] sommet *m*, apogée *m* ; [- on graph] sommet *m* ■ **emigration was at its ~ in the 1890s** l'émigration a atteint son point culminant OR son sommet dans les années 1890 ■ **the party was at its ~** la fête battait son plein ■ **sales have reached a new ~** les ventes ont atteint un nouveau record **4.** [of cap] visière *f*.
◇ *vi* [production, demand] atteindre un maximum ■ **she ~ed too soon** elle s'est donnée à fond trop tôt.
◇ *adj* maximum ■ **~ viewing hours** TV heures de grande écoute ■ **the team is in ~ condition** l'équipe est à son top niveau ■ **~ hours** OR **period** OR **time** [of electricity use] période *f* de pointe ; [of traffic] heures *fpl* de pointe OR d'affluence ; [in restaurant] coup *m* de feu ■ **~ rate** tarif *m* normal.

peaked [pi:kt] *adj* [roof] pointu ■ [cap] à visière.

peaky ['pi:kɪ] (*comp* **peakier**, *superl* **peakiest**) *adj* **UK** *inf* [unwell] (un peu) malade ■ [tired] fatigué.

peal [pi:l] ◇ *n* **1.** [sound] : **the ~ of bells** la sonnerie de cloches, le carillon ■ **a ~ of thunder** un coup de tonnerre ■ **~s of laughter came from the living room** des éclats de rire se faisaient entendre du salon **2.** [set of bells] carillon *m*.
◇ *vi* : **to ~ (out)** [bells] carillonner ; [thunder] gronder.
◇ *vt* [bells] sonner à toute volée.

peanut ['pi:nʌt] *n* [nut] cacahouète *f*, cacahuète *f* ■ [plant] arachide *f* ▶ **~s** *inf* [small sum] clopinettes *fpl* ■ **to work for ~s** travailler pour des clopinettes ■ **it's worth ~s** ça ne vaut pas un clou.

peanut butter *n* beurre *m* de cacahuètes.

pear [peər] *n* [fruit] poire *f* ■ [tree, wood] poirier *m*.

pearl [pɜ:l] ◇ *n* **1.** [gem] perle *f* ■ **to cast ~s before swine** donner des perles aux cochons OR aux pourceaux **2.** [mother-of-pearl] nacre *f* **3.** *fig* perle *f* ■ **~s of wisdom** trésors *mpl* de sagesse.
◇ *adj* **1.** [made of pearls] de perles ■ **a ~ necklace** un collier de perles **2.** [made of mother-of-pearl] de OR en nacre ■ **~ buttons** boutons en nacre.
◇ *vi* **1.** [form drops] perler **2.** [search for pearls] pêcher des perles.

pearl barley *n* orge *m* perlé.

pearl diver *n* pêcheur *m*, - euse *f* de perles.

pearl grey *n* gris *m* perle.
◆ **pearl-grey** *adj* gris perle *(inv)*.

Pearl Harbor [pɜ:l-] *pr n* Pearl Harbor.

PEARL HARBOR

Base navale américaine située à Hawaii. Attaquée le 7 décembre 1941 par l'aviation japonaise, elle connut de très lourdes pertes humaines et matérielles. Le lendemain, les États-Unis firent leur entrée dans le second conflit mondial en déclarant la guerre au Japon.

pearly ['pɜ:lɪ] (*comp* **pearlier**, *superl* **pearliest**) *adj* **1.** [pearl-like] nacré ■ **~ white teeth** dents de perle OR éclatantes **2.** [decorated with pearls] perlé ■ [made of mother-of-pearl] en OR de nacre.

Pearly Gates *pr n inf* **the ~** les portes *fpl* du paradis.

pear-shaped *adj* en forme de poire, piriforme *lit*.

peasant ['peznt] ◇ *n* **1.** paysan *m*, - anne *f* ■ **the Peasants' Revolt** *UK* HIST la guerre des Gueux **2.** *inf pej* [uncouth person] péquenaud *m*, - e *f*, plouc *m*.
◇ *adj* paysan ■ **~ farmer** paysan.

THE PEASANTS' REVOLT

Première grande révolte populaire dans l'histoire anglaise, provoquée en 1381 par la mise en vigueur de la capitation. Son meneur, Wat Tyler, fut assassiné lors de pourparlers avec le roi Richard II et la révolte s'éteignit sans avoir apporté de changements.

peasantry ['pezntrɪ] *n* paysannerie *f*, paysans *mpl*.

pease pudding *n purée de pois au jambon.*

peashooter ['pi:,ʃu:tər] *n* sarbacane *f*.

pea souper [-'su:pər] *n* [fog] purée *f* de pois.

peat [pi:t] *n* tourbe *f*.

peat bog *n* tourbière *f*.

peat moss *n* sphaigne *f*.

peaty ['pi:tɪ] (*comp* **peatier**, *superl* **peatiest**) *adj* tourbeux.

pebble ['pebl] <> *n* **1.** [stone] caillou *m* ▪ [waterworn] galet *m* ▪ **a ~ beach** une plage de galets **2.** OPT [lens] lentille *f* en cristal de roche ▪ **~ glasses** *inf* lunettes *fpl* à verres très épais.
<> *vt* **1.** [road, path] caillouter ▪ **a ~d drive** une allée de gravillons **2.** [leather] greneler.

pebbledash ['pebldæʃ] *UK* <> *n* crépi *m (incrusté de cailloux).*
<> *vt* crépir.

pecan [*UK* 'pi:kən, *US* pɪ'kæn] <> *n* [nut] (noix *f* de) pecan *m*, (noix *f* de) pacane *f* ▪ [tree] pacanier *m*.
<> *adj* [pie, ice cream] à la noix de pecan.

peccadillo [,pekə'dɪləʊ] (*pl* **peccadillos** *OR pl* **peccadilloes**) *n* peccadille *f*.

peck [pek] <> *vt* **1.** [pick up] picorer, picoter ▪ [strike with beak] donner un coup de bec à **2.** [kiss] faire une bise à.
<> *n* **1.** [with beak] coup *m* de bec **2.** [kiss] bise *f*, (petit) baiser *m* ▪ **she gave me a ~ on the forehead** elle m'a fait une bise sur le front **3.** [measure] ≃ boisseau *m*.
◆ **peck at** *vt insep* **1.** = **peck** *(vt, sense 1)* **2.** : **to ~ at one's food** manger du bout des dents.

pecker ['pekəʳ] *n* **1.** *UK* [spirits] : **keep your ~ up** *inf* il faut garder le moral **2.** △ *US* [penis] quéquette *f*.

pecking order ['pekɪŋ-] *n* [among birds] ordre *m* hiérarchique ▪ [among people] hiérarchie *f*.

peckish ['pekɪʃ] *adj (esp) UK inf* **to be** *OR* **to feel ~** avoir un petit creux.

pecs [peks] *npl inf* [pectorals] pectoraux *mpl*.

pectin ['pektɪn] *n* pectine *f*.

pectoral ['pektərəl] <> *adj* MIL & RELIG pectoral.
<> *n* ANAT, MIL & RELIG pectoral *m*.

pectoral fin *n* nageoire *f* pectorale.

pectoral muscle *n* muscle *m* pectoral.

peculate ['pekjʊleɪt] *vi fml* détourner les fonds *OR* deniers publics.

peculiar [pɪ'kju:ljəʳ] *adj* **1.** [strange] étrange, bizarre **2.** [specific, exclusive] particulier ▪ **it has a ~ taste** ça a un goût spécial ▪ **to be ~ to** être spécifique à ▪ [particular] spécial, particulier.

peculiarity [pɪ,kju:lɪ'ærətɪ] (*pl* **peculiarities**) *n* **1.** [oddness] étrangeté *f*, bizarrerie *f* ▪ **we all have our little peculiarities** nous avons tous nos petites manies **2.** [specific characteristic] particularité *f* ▪ **each region has its own peculiarities** chaque région a son particularisme *OR* ses particularités.

peculiarly [pɪ'kju:ljəlɪ] *adv* **1.** [oddly] étrangement, bizarrement **2.** [especially] particulièrement, singulièrement.

pecuniary [pɪ'kju:njərɪ] *adj* pécuniaire.

pedagogic(al) [,pedə'gɒdʒɪk(l)] *adj* pédagogique.

pedagogue ['pedəgɒg] *n* pédagogue.

pedagogy ['pedəgɒdʒɪ] *n* pédagogie *f*.

pedal ['pedl] (*UK pret & pp* **pedalled**, *cont* **pedalling**) (*US pret & pp* **pedaled**, *cont* **pedaling**) <> *n* **1.** [on bicycle, piano etc] pédale *f* ▪ **clutch/brake ~** pédale d'embrayage/de frein ▪ **loud/soft ~** [of piano] pédale droite *OR* forte/gauche *OR* douce **2.** MUS = **pedal point**.
<> *vi* pédaler ▪ **we pedalled along the back roads** nous roulions (à bicyclette) sur les routes de l'arrière-pays ▪ **it's hard pedalling uphill** c'est dur de grimper une côte à bicyclette *OR* à vélo.
<> *vt* faire avancer en pédalant.

pedal bin *n UK* poubelle *f* à pédale.

pedal boat *n* pédalo *m*.

pedal car *n* voiture *f* à pédales.

pedalo ['pedələʊ] (*pl* **pedalos** *OR pl* **pedaloes**) *n* pédalo *m*.

pedal point *n* MUS pédale *f*.

pedal pushers *npl* (pantalon *m*) corsaire *m*.

pedant ['pedənt] *n* pédant *m*, - e *f*.

pedantic [pɪ'dæntɪk] *adj* pédant.

pedantically [pɪ'dæntɪklɪ] *adv* de manière pédante, avec pédantisme.

pedantry ['pedəntrɪ] (*pl* **pedantries**) *n* **1.** [behaviour] pédantisme *m*, pédanterie *f* **2.** [remark] pédanterie *f*.

peddle ['pedl] <> *vt* **1.** *dated* [wares] colporter ▪ **he didn't want to ~ encyclopedias all his life** il ne voulait pas passer sa vie à faire du porte à porte pour vendre des encyclopédies **2.** [drugs] revendre, faire le trafic de ▪ **drug peddling** trafic *m* de drogue **3.** *pej* [promote - idea, opinion] propager ; [- gossip, scandal] colporter.
<> *vi* faire du colportage.

peddler ['pedləʳ] *n* **1.** [seller] colporteur *m*, - euse *f* **2.** [drug pusher] trafiquant *m*, - e *f* (de drogue), revendeur *m*, - euse *f* **3.** *pej* [promoter - of ideas, opinions] propagateur *m*, - trice *f* ▪ **~s of dreams** marchands *mpl* de rêves.

pederast ['pedəræst] *n* pédéraste *m*.

pederasty ['pedəræstɪ] *n* pédérastie *f*.

pedestal ['pedɪstl] <> *n liter & fig* piédestal *m* ▪ **to place** *OR* **to put sb on a ~** mettre qqn sur un piédestal ▪ **that knocked him off his ~** cela l'a fait tomber de son piédestal.
<> *comp* : **~ basin** lavabo *m* à pied ▪ **~ desk** bureau *m* ministre ▪ **~ table** guéridon *m*.

pedestrian [pɪ'destrɪən] <> *n* piéton *m* ▪ **'~s only'** 'réservé aux piétons'.
<> *comp* [street, area] piéton, piétonnier ▪ **~ overpass** passerelle *f*.
<> *adj* **1.** [prosaic] prosaïque ▪ [commonplace] banal **2.** [done on foot - exercise, outing] pédestre, à pied.

pedestrian crossing *n UK* passage *m* clouté *OR* (pour) piétons.

pedestrianization [pə,destrɪənaɪ'zeɪʃn] *n* transformation *f* en zone piétonne *OR* piétonnière.

pedestrianize, ise [pə'destrɪənaɪz] *vt* transformer en zone piétonne *OR* piétonnière.

pedestrian precinct *UK*, **pedestrian zone** *US n* zone *f* piétonnière.

pediatric [,pi:dɪ'ætrɪk] *adj* pédiatrique.

pediatrician [,pi:dɪə'trɪʃn] *n* pédiatre.

pediatrics [,pi:dɪ'ætrɪks] *n* pédiatrie.

pedicure ['pedɪ,kjʊəʳ] *n* [treatment] pédicurie *f*.

pedigree ['pedɪgri:] <> *n* **1.** [descent - of animal] pedigree *m* ; [- of person] ascendance *f*, lignée *f* ▪ *fig* [background - of person] origine *f* **2.** [document for animal] pedigree *m* **3.** [genealogical table] arbre *m* généalogique.
<> *adj* [horse, cat, dog] de race.

pediment ['pedɪmənt] *n* **1.** ARCHIT fronton *m* **2.** GEOL pédiment *m*.

pedlar ['pedləʳ] = **peddler**.

pedology [pɪ'dɒlədʒɪ] *n* **1.** MED pédologie *f* **2.** GEOL pédologie *f*.

pedophile ['pi:dəʊ,faɪl] *n* pédophile *m*.

pedophilia [,pi:dəʊ'fɪlɪə] *n* pédophilie *f*.

peduncle [pɪ'dʌŋkl] *n* pédoncule *m*.

pee [pi:] *inf* <> *n* pipi *m* ▪ **to have** *OR* **to take a ~** faire pipi.
<> *vi* faire pipi.

peek [pi:k] <> *vi* [glance] jeter un coup d'œil ▪ [look furtively] regarder furtivement ▪ **to ~ at sthg** jeter un coup d'œil à *OR* sur qqch ▪ **someone was ~ing through the keyhole** quelqu'un regardait par le trou de la serrure ▪ **turn around and no ~ing!** retourne-toi et n'essaie pas de voir ce que je fais!
<> *n* coup *m* d'œil ▪ **to have** *OR* **to take a ~ at sthg** jeter un coup d'œil à *OR* sur qqch.

peel [pi:l] ◇ *n* **1.** [of banana] peau *f* ▪ [of orange, lemon] écorce *f* ▪ [of apple, onion, potato] pelure *f* **2.** *(U)* [peeling] épluchures *fpl* ▪ **add a twist of lemon ~** ajouter un zeste de citron.
◇ *vt* [fruit, vegetable] peler, éplucher ▪ [boiled egg] écaler, éplucher ▪ [shrimp] décortiquer ▪ [twig] écorcer ▪ [skin, bark] enlever.
◇ *vi* **1.** [fruit, vegetable] se peler **2.** [plaster on wall, ceiling etc] s'écailler, se craqueler ▪ [paint, varnish] s'écailler ▪ [wallpaper] se décoller **3.** [skin on back, face etc] peler ▪ **I'm ~ing all over** je pèle de partout.
◆ **peel away** ◇ *vi insep* = **peel** *(vi sense 2)*.
◇ *vt sep* [label, wallpaper] détacher, décoller ▪ [bandage] enlever, ôter.
◆ **peel back** *vt sep* [label, wallpaper] détacher, décoller.
◆ **peel off** ◇ *vi insep* **1.** = **peel** *(vi sense 2)* **2.** [turn away] se détacher.
◇ *vt sep* **1.** = **peel away 2.** [item of clothing] enlever ▪ **to ~ off one's clothes** se déshabiller.

peeler ['pi:lər] *n* **1.** [device] éplucheur *m* ▪ [electric] éplucheuse *f* **2.** *UK inf dated* flic *m*.

peelings ['pi:lɪŋz] *npl* épluchures *fpl*, pelures *fpl*.

peep [pi:p] ◇ *vi* **1.** [glance] jeter un coup d'œil ▪ **to ~ at/over/under sthg** jeter un coup d'œil (furtif) à/par-dessus/sous qqch ▪ **the children were ~ing through the keyhole** les enfants épiaient à travers le trou de la serrure **2.** [emerge] se montrer ▪ **the moon ~ed out through the clouds** la lune a percé *OR* est apparue à travers les nuages ▪ **snowdrops were beginning to ~ through** des perce-neiges commençaient à pointer ▪ **her nose ~ed out over her scarf** le bout de son nez pointait *OR* apparaissait par-dessus son écharpe **3.** [bird] pépier.
◇ *n* **1.** [glance] coup *m* d'œil ▪ **to have a ~ at sthg** jeter un coup d'œil à qqch **2.** [of bird] pépiement *m* ▪ *fig* **any news from him? – not a ~!** *inf* tu as eu de ses nouvelles? – pas un mot *OR* que dalle! ▪ **one more ~ out of you and you've had it!** *inf* encore un mot et ton compte est bon!

peepbo ['pi:p,bəʊ] *inf* ◇ *interj* : **~!** coucou!
◇ *n* : **to play ~** jouer à faire coucou.

peephole ['pi:phəʊl] *n* trou *m* ▪ [in house door, cell] judas *m*.

peeping Tom [,pi:pɪŋ'tɒm] *n* voyeur *m*.

peepshow ['pi:pʃəʊ] *n* [device] stéréoscope *m (pour images érotiques)* ▪ [form of entertainment] peep-show *m*.

peep-toe(d) shoes *npl* escarpins *mpl* à bout découpé.

peer [pɪər] ◇ *n* **1.** [nobleman] pair *m*, noble *mf* ▪ **he was made a ~** il a été élevé à la pairie ▪ **~ of the realm** pair du royaume **2.** [equal] pair *m* ▪ **as a negotiator she has no ~** c'est une négociatrice hors pair.
◇ *vi* [look - intently] regarder attentivement ; [- with difficulty] s'efforcer de voir ▪ **she ~ed out into the darkness** elle scruta l'obscurité ▪ **he ~ed at the suspects' faces** il dévisagea les suspects ▪ **she ~ed at the small print** elle lut attentivement ce qui était écrit en petits caractères.

peerage ['pɪərɪdʒ] *n* **1.** [title] pairie *f* ▪ **he was given a ~** il a été élevé à la pairie **2.** [body of peers] pairs *mpl*, noblesse *f* **3.** [book] nobiliaire *m*.

peeress ['pɪərɪs] *n* pairesse *f*.

peer group *n* SOCIOL pairs *mpl*.

peerless ['pɪəlɪs] *adj* sans pareil.

peer pressure *n* influence *f* des pairs *OR* du groupe.

peeve [pi:v] *vt inf* mettre en rogne.

peeved [pi:vd] *adj inf* énervé.

peevish ['pi:vɪʃ] *adj* [person] irritable, grincheux ▪ [report, expression] irrité.

peevishly ['pi:vɪʃlɪ] *adv* [say, refuse] d'un ton irrité ▪ [behave] de façon désagréable ▪ **to complain ~** ronchonner.

peewit ['pi:wɪt] *n* vanneau *m*.

peg [peg] *(pret & pp* **pegged**, *cont* **pegging)** ◇ *n* **1.** [for hat, coat] patère *f* ▪ **a ~ to hang an argument on** *fig* un prétexte de dispute, une excuse pour se disputer **2.** *UK* [clothespeg] pince *f* à linge **3.** [dowel - wooden] cheville *f* ; [- metal] fiche *f* **4.** [for tent] piquet *m* **5.** [in mountaineering] piton *m* **6.** [in croquet] piquet *m* **7.** MUS [on string instrument] cheville *f* **8.** *fig* [degree, notch] degré *m*, cran *m* ▶ **to bring** *OR* **to take sb down a ~ or two** rabattre le caquet à qqn.
◇ *vt* **1.** [fasten - gen] attacher ; [- with dowels] cheviller ▪ [insert - stake] enfoncer, planter ▪ [in mountaineering] pitonner ▪ **he was pegging the washing on the line** il étendait le linge **2.** [set - price, increase] fixer ▪ **export earnings are pegged to the exchange rate** le revenu des exportations varie en fonction du taux de change **3.** *inf* [throw] lancer **4.** *US inf* [classify] classer.
▷ **off-the-peg.**
◆ **peg away** *vi insep UK inf* travailler sans relâche.
◆ **peg down** *vt sep* [fasten down] fixer *OR* attacher (avec des piquets).
◆ **peg out** ◇ *vt sep* **1.** [hang out - washing] étendre **2.** [mark out with pegs] piqueter.
◇ *vi insep inf* [die] crever, claquer.

Pegasus ['pegəsəs] *pr n* Pégase.

pegboard ['pegbɔ:d] *n* plaquette *f* perforée *(utilisée dans certains jeux)*.

peg leg *n inf* jambe *f* artificielle.

pejorative [pɪ'dʒɒrətɪv] ◇ *adj* péjoratif.
◇ *n* péjoratif *m*.

peke [pi:k] *n inf* pékinois *m (chien)*.

Pekinese [,pi:kə'ni:z], **Pekingese** [,pi:kɪŋ'i:z] ◇ *n* **1.** [person] Pékinois *m*, - e *f* **2.** LING pékinois *m* **3.** [dog] pékinois *m*.
◇ *adj* pékinois.

Peking [,pi:'kɪŋ] *pr n* Pékin.

pekoe ['pi:kəʊ] *n* pekoe *m*.

pelican ['pelɪkən] *n* pélican *m* ▪ **the Pelican State** la Louisiane.

pelican crossing *n UK passage piétons à commande manuelle*.

pellet ['pelɪt] *n* **1.** [small ball] boulette *f* ▪ **wax/paper ~s** boulettes de cire/de papier **2.** [for gun] (grain *m* de) plomb *m* **3.** [pill] pilule *f* **4.** ORNITH pelote *f* de régurgitation.

pell-mell [,pel'mel] *adv UK* [pile, throw] pêle-mêle ▪ **the crowd ran ~ into the square** la foule s'est ruée sur la place dans une cohue indescriptible.

pellucid [pe'lu:sɪd] *adj* [membrane, zone] pellucide ▪ [water] limpide ▪ *fig* [prose] clair, limpide.

pelmet ['pelmɪt] *n* [for curtains] cantonnière *f* ▪ [wood, board] lambrequin *m*.

pelota [pə'lɒtə] *n* pelote *f* basque.

pelt [pelt] ◇ *vt* [person, target] bombarder ▪ **they were ~ing each other with snowballs** ils se lançaient des boules de neige.
◇ *vi inf* **1.** [rain] : **it was ~ing** *OR* **~ing down with rain** il pleuvait à verse, il tombait des cordes ▪ **the hail ~ed down** la grêle tombait dru ▪ **I changed the tyre in the ~ing rain** j'ai changé le pneu sous la pluie battante **2.** [run] courir à fond de train *OR* à toute allure.
◇ *n* **1.** [skin] peau *f* ▪ [fur] fourrure *f* **2.** *UK phr* **at full ~** à fond de train.

pelvic ['pelvɪk] *adj* pelvien ▪ **~ bone** ilion *m*.

pelvic girdle *n* ceinture *f* pelvienne.

pelvic inflammatory disease *n* métrite *f*.

pelvis ['pelvɪs] *(pl* **pelvises** *OR pl* **pelves** [-vi:z]) *n* bassin *m*, pelvis *m*.

pen [pen] *(pret & pp* **penned**, *cont* **penning)** ◇ *n* **1.** [for writing] stylo *m* ▪ **another novel from the ~ of Hilary Ratcliff** un nouveau roman de la plume de Hilary Ratcliff ▪ **to put ~ to paper** écrire, prendre sa plume ▶ **a slip of the ~** un lapsus ▪ **the ~ is mightier than the sword** *prov* un coup de langue est pire qu'un coup de lance *prov* **2.** [of squid] plume *f* **3.** [female swan] cygne *m* femelle **4.** [for animals] enclos *m*, parc *m* ▪ **sheep ~** parc à moutons **5.** NAUT : **(submarine) ~** bassin *m* protégé **6.** *US inf* (*abbrev of* **penitentiary**) taule *f*, tôle *f*.

◇ *vt* **1.** [write] écrire ■ **a letter penned in a childish hand** une lettre d'une écriture enfantine **2.** [enclose] : **to ~ in** *OR* **up** [livestock] parquer, enfermer dans un enclos ; [dog] enfermer ; [person] enfermer, cloîtrer, claquemurer.

penal ['pi:nl] *adj* **1.** [law] pénal ■ [establishment] pénitentiaire **2.** [severe - taxation, fine] écrasant.

penal code *n* code *m* pénal.

penal colony *n* colonie *f* pénitentiaire, bagne *m*.

penalization [,pi:nəlaɪ'zeɪʃn] *n* pénalisation *f*, sanction *f*.

penalize, ise ['pi:nəlaɪz] *vt* **1.** [punish] pénaliser, sanctionner **2.** [disadvantage] pénaliser, défavoriser, désavantager.

penal servitude *n* travaux *mpl* forcés, bagne *m*.

penal settlement = **penal colony**.

penalty ['penltɪ] (*pl* **penalties**) *n* **1.** LAW peine *f* ■ **on ~ of** sous peine de ■ **under ~ of death** sous peine de mort ■ **the ~ for that offence is six months' imprisonment** la peine encourue pour ce délit est de six mois d'emprisonnement ■ **'~ for improper use: £25'** 'tout abus est passible d'une amende de 25 livres' **2.** ADMIN & COMM [for breaking contract] pénalité *f*, sanction *f* **3.** *fig* [unpleasant consequence] : **to pay the ~ (for sthg)** subir les conséquences (de qqch) ■ **that's the ~ for being famous** c'est la rançon de la gloire **4.** SPORT [gen] pénalisation *f* ■ [kick - in football] penalty *m* ; [- in rugby] pénalité *f* ■ **to score (from) a ~** [in football] marquer sur (un) penalty ■ **a two-minute (time) ~** [in ice hockey] une pénalité de deux minutes.

penalty area *n* FTBL surface *f* de réparation.

penalty box *n* **1.** [in football] = **penalty area 2.** [in ice hockey] banc *m* de pénalité.

penalty clause *n* LAW clause *f* pénale.

penalty goal *n* [in rugby] but *m* sur pénalité.

penalty kick *n* [in football] penalty *m* ■ [in rugby] (coup *m* de pied de) pénalité *f*.

penalty points *npl* [in quiz, game] gage *m* ■ [for drivers] points *mpl* de pénalité *(dans le système du permis à points)*.

penalty spot *n* [in football] point *m* de penalty.

penalty try *n* [in rugby] essai *m* de pénalité.

penance ['penəns] *n* pénitence *f* ■ **to do ~ for one's sins** faire pénitence.

pen-and-ink *comp* [drawing] à la plume.

pence [pens] *n (pl of penny)* pence *mpl*.

penchant [*UK* pɑ̃ʃɑ̃, *US* 'pentʃənt] *n* penchant *m*, goût *m* ■ **to have a ~ for sthg** avoir un faible pour qqch.

pencil ['pensl] (*UK pret & pp* **pencilled**, *cont* **pencilling**) (*US pret & pp* **penciled**, *cont* **penciling**) ◇ *n* **1.** [for writing, makeup] crayon *m* ■ **the corrections are in ~** les corrections sont (faites) au crayon ➲ **~ box** plumier *m* ■ **~ case** trousse *f* ■ **~ sharpener** taille-crayon *m* **2.** *fig* [narrow beam] : **a ~ of light** un pinceau de lumière.
◇ *comp* au crayon.
◇ *vt* écrire au crayon ■ [hastily] crayonner ■ **to ~ one's eyebrows** se dessiner les sourcils (au crayon).
◆ **pencil in** *vt sep* [date, name, address] noter *OR* inscrire au crayon ■ *fig* fixer provisoirement ■ **I'll ~ the meeting/you in for June 6th** retenons provisoirement la date du 6 juin pour la réunion/notre rendez-vous.

pendant ['pendənt] ◇ *n* **1.** [necklace] pendentif *m* **2.** [piece of jewellery - on necklace] pendentif *m* ; [- on earring] pendeloque *f* ■ **~ earrings** pendants *mpl* d'oreille **3.** [chandelier] lustre *m*.
◇ *adj* = **pendent**.

pendent ['pendənt] *adj fml* **1.** [hanging] pendant, qui pend **2.** [overhanging] en surplomb, en saillie.

pending ['pendɪŋ] ◇ *adj* **1.** [waiting to be settled - gen] en attente ■ LAW en instance, pendant **2.** [imminent] imminent.
◇ *prep* en attendant.

pending tray *n UK* corbeille *f* des dossiers en attente.

pendulous ['pendjʊləs] *adj lit* **1.** [sagging - breasts] tombant ; [- lips] pendant **2.** [swinging] oscillant.

pendulum ['pendjʊləm] *n* pendule *m* ■ [in clock] balancier *m* ■ **a swing of the ~ sent the president's popularity plummeting** *fig* un revirement de l'opinion a fait chuter la cote de popularité du président.

Penelope [pə'neləpɪ] *pr n* Pénélope.

peneplain, peneplane ['pi:nɪpleɪn] *n* pénéplaine *f*.

penetrate ['penɪtreɪt] ◇ *vt* **1.** [find way into or through - jungle] pénétrer dans ; [- blockade, enemy defences] pénétrer ■ **they ~d unknown territory** ils ont pénétré en territoire inconnu ■ **it's not easy to ~ Parisian society** il n'est pas facile de s'introduire dans la société parisienne **2.** [infiltrate - party, movement] s'infiltrer dans, noyauter **3.** [pierce - subj: missile] percer, transpercer ■ **the bullet ~d his right lung** la balle lui a perforé le poumon droit **4.** [pass through - subj: sound, light etc] traverser, transpercer ■ **the cold wind ~d her clothing** le vent glacial passait à travers ses vêtements **5.** COMM s'introduire sur **6.** [see through - darkness, disguise, mystery] percer ■ **to ~ sb's thoughts** lire dans les pensées de qqn **7.** [sexually] pénétrer.
◇ *vi* **1.** [break through] pénétrer ■ **the troops ~d deep into enemy territory** les troupes ont pénétré très avant en territoire ennemi **2.** [sink in] : **I had to explain it to him several times before it finally ~d** j'ai dû le lui expliquer plusieurs fois avant qu'il (ne) finisse par comprendre.

penetrating ['penɪtreɪtɪŋ] *adj* **1.** [sound - pleasant] pénétrant ; [- unpleasant] perçant **2.** [cold] pénétrant, perçant ■ [rain] pénétrant **3.** [look, mind, question] pénétrant.

penetratingly ['penɪtreɪtɪŋlɪ] *adv* **1.** [loudly] : **to scream ~** pousser un cri perçant **2.** *fig* avec perspicacité ■ **she looked at him ~** elle lui lança un regard pénétrant *OR* aigu.

penetration [,penɪ'treɪʃn] *n* **1.** [gen - COMM] pénétration *f* **2.** MIL percée *f* **3.** PHOT profondeur *f* de champ.

penetrative ['penɪtrətɪv] *adj* [force] de pénétration ■ **~ sex** pénétration *f*.

pen friend *n UK* correspondant *m*, - e *f (épistolaire)*.

penguin ['peŋgwɪn] *n* manchot *m*.

penholder ['pen,həʊldər] *n* porte-plume *m inv*.

penicillin [,penɪ'sɪlɪn] *n* pénicilline *f*.

penile ['pi:naɪl] *adj* pénien.

peninsula [pə'nɪnsjʊlə] *n* [large] péninsule *f* ■ [small] presqu'île *f*.

peninsular [pə'nɪnsjʊlər] *adj* péninsulaire.
◆ **Peninsular** *adj* : **the Peninsular War** la guerre d'Espagne *(1808-1814)*.

penis ['pi:nɪs] (*pl* **penises** *OR pl* **penes** [-ɪz]) *n* pénis *m*.

penis envy *n* envie *f* du pénis.

penitence ['penɪtəns] *n* pénitence *f*.

penitent ['penɪtənt] ◇ *adj* **1.** [gen] contrit **2.** RELIG pénitent.
◇ *n* RELIG pénitent *m*, - e *f*.

penitential [,penɪ'tenʃl] ◇ *adj* pénitentiel.
◇ *n* [book] pénitentiel *m*.

penitentiary [,penɪ'tenʃərɪ] (*pl* **penitentiaries**) ◇ *n* **1.** *US* [prison] prison *f* **2.** RELIG [priest] pénitencier *m*.
◇ *adj* **1.** *US* [life, conditions] pénitentiaire ■ [offence] passible d'une peine de prison ■ **~ guard** gardien *m*, - enne *f* de prison **2.** = **penitential**.
◆ **Penitentiary** *n* RELIG : **the Penitentiary** [cardinal] le grand pénitencier ; [tribunal] la Sacrée Pénitencerie, la Pénitencerie apostolique.

penitently ['penɪtəntlɪ] *adv* [say] d'un ton contrit ■ [submit, kneel] avec contrition.

penknife ['pennaɪf] (*pl* **penknives** [-naɪvz]) *n* canif *m*.

penmanship ['penmənʃɪp] *n* calligraphie *f*.

penna ['penə] (*pl* **pennae** [-ni:]) *n* penne *f*.

pen name *n* nom *m* de plume, pseudonyme *m*.

pennant ['penənt] *n* **1.** [flag - gen] fanion *m* **2.** NAUT [for identification] flamme *f* ▪ [for signalling] pavillon *m* **3.** *US* SPORT *drapeau servant de trophée dans certains championnats.*

penniless ['penɪlɪs] *adj* sans le sou ▪ **they're absolutely ~** ils n'ont pas un sou ▪ **the stock market crash left him ~** le krach boursier l'a mis sur la paille.

Pennines ['penaɪnz] *pr npl* : **the ~** les Pennines *fpl*.

pennon ['penən] *n* **1.** [flag - gen] fanion *m* ; [- on lance] pennon *m* **2.** NAUT [for identification] flamme *f* ▪ [for signalling] pavillon *m*.

Pennsylvania [,pensɪl'veɪnjə] *pr n* Pennsylvanie *f* ▪ **in ~** en Pennsylvanie.

Pennsylvania Avenue *pr n* : **1600 ~** *adresse de la Maison Blanche, utilisée par les médias américains pour faire référence au gouvernement.*

Pennsylvania Dutch *npl* : **the ~** *communauté protestante fondée aux États-Unis par les colons allemands aux XVIIe et XVIIIe siècles (en font partie les Amish et les Mennonites).*

penny ['penɪ] *n* **1.** (*pl* pence) [unit of currency - in Britain, Ireland] penny *m* ▪ **it cost me 44 pence** ça m'a coûté 44 pence **2.** (*pl* pennies) [coin - in Britain, Ireland] penny *m*, pièce *f* d'un penny ; [- in US] cent *m*, pièce *f* d'un cent ▪ **it was expensive, but it was worth every ~** c'était cher, mais j'en ai vraiment eu pour mon argent ▪ **it won't cost you a ~** ça ne vous coûtera pas un centime *OR* un sou ▪ **every ~ counts** un sou est un sou ▶ **they haven't got a ~ to their name** *OR* **two pennies to rub together** ils n'ont pas un sou vaillant ▪ **people like him are two** *OR* **ten a ~** *UK inf* des gens comme lui, ce n'est pas ça qui manque ▪ **a ~ for your thoughts** à quoi penses-tu? ▪ **suddenly the ~ dropped** *UK inf* d'un seul coup ça a fait tilt ▪ **he keeps turning up like a bad ~** *UK inf* c'est un vrai pot de colle ▪ **in for a ~ in for a pound** *prov* quand le vin est tiré, il faut le boire *prov* ▪ **take care of the pennies and the pounds will take care of themselves** *prov* les petits ruisseaux font les grandes rivières *prov*.

penny arcade *n US* galerie *f* de jeux.

Penny Black *n premier timbre-poste britannique.*

penny-farthing *n UK* bicycle *m*, vélocipède *m*.

penny loafers *npl US* mocassins *mpl*.

penny-pincher [-,pɪntʃəʳ] *n inf* pingre *mf*, radin *m*, - e *f*.

penny-pinching [-,pɪntʃɪŋ] *inf* ◇ *n* économies *fpl* de bouts de chandelle ▪ **government ~ will ruin the education system** à force de serrer les cordons de la bourse, le gouvernement finira par étrangler le système éducatif.
◇ *adj* qui fait des économies de bouts de chandelle, pingre, radin.

pennyweight ['penɪweɪt] *n UK* ≃ 1,5 grammes.

penny whistle *n* pipeau *m*.

pennyworth ['penɪwɜ:θ, 'penəθ] (*pl inv OR pl* **pennyworths**) *n* **1.** *liter & dated* **she asked for a ~ of toffees** elle demanda pour un penny de caramels **2.** *UK fig* [small quantity] : **if he had a ~ of sense** s'il avait une once de bon sens.

penology [pi:'nɒlədʒɪ] *n* pénologie *f*.

pen pal *n inf* correspondant *m*, - e *f (épistolaire)*.

pen pusher *n pej* gratte-papier *m inv*.

pen pushing *n pej* travail *m* de bureau ▪ **a ~ job** un travail de gratte-papier.

pension ['penʃn] ◇ *n* **1.** [for retired people] retraite *f* ▪ [for disabled people] pension *f* ▪ **to draw a ~** [retired person] toucher une retraite ; [disabled person] toucher une pension, être pensionné ▪ **to pay sb a ~** verser une pension à qqn ▶ **disability ~** pension d'invalidité ▪ **widow's ~** [before retiring age] allocation *f* de veuvage ; [at retiring age] pension de réversion **2.** (*also* ['pɑ̃sjɔ̃]) [small hotel] pension *f* de famille.
◇ *vt* [for retirement] verser une pension de retraite à ▪ [for disability] pensionner, verser une pension à.

◆ **pension off** *vt sep UK* **1.** [person] mettre à la retraite **2.** *hum* [old car, machine] mettre au rancart.

pensionable ['penʃənəbl] *adj* **1.** [person - gen] qui a droit à une pension ; [- for retirement] qui a atteint l'âge de la retraite **2.** [job] qui donne droit à une retraite.

pension book *n* ≃ titre *m* de pension *(en Grande-Bretagne, carnet permettant de retirer sa pension de retraite).*

pensioned ['penʃənd] *adj* retraité.

pensioner ['penʃənəʳ] *n UK* **(old age) ~** retraité *m*, - e *f* ▪ **war ~** ancien combattant *m (titulaire d'une pension militaire d'invalidité).*

pension fund *n* caisse *f* de retraite.

pension plan, pension scheme *n* régime *m* de retraite.

pensive ['pensɪv] *adj* pensif, méditatif, songeur.

pensively ['pensɪvlɪ] *adv* pensivement.

pentacle ['pentəkl] *n* pentacle *m*.

pentagon ['pentəgən] *n* GEOM pentagone *m*.
◆ **Pentagon** *pr n* POL : **the Pentagon** le Pentagone.

PENTAGON

Le Pentagone, immense bâtiment à cinq façades situé à Washington, abrite le secrétariat à la Défense et l'état-major des forces armées des États-Unis. Il fut attaqué lors des attentats du 11 septembre 2001. Le terme désigne plus généralement les autorités militaires américaines.

pentagonal [pen'tægənl] *adj* pentagonal.

pentagram ['pentəgræm] *n* **1.** GEOM pentagone *m* étoilé **2.** [in occultism] pentagramme *m*.

pentameter [pen'tæmɪtəʳ] ◇ *n* pentamètre *m*.
◇ *adj* pentamètre.

pentangle ['pentæŋgl] = **pentacle**.

Pentateuch ['pentətju:k] *n* : **the ~** le Pentateuque.

pentathlete [pen'tæθli:t] *n* pentathlonien *m*, - enne *f*.

pentathlon [pen'tæθln] *n* pentathlon *m*.

Pentecost ['pentɪkɒst] *n* Pentecôte *f*.

Pentecostal [,pentɪ'kɒstl] = **Pentecostalist**.

Pentecostalist [,pentɪ'kɒstəlɪst] ◇ *adj* pentecôtiste.
◇ *n* pentecôtiste *mf*.

penthouse ['penthaʊs] (*pl* [-haʊzɪz]) *n* **1.** [flat] *appartement de luxe avec terrasse généralement au dernier étage d'un immeuble* ▪ **~ suite** [in hotel] suite *f* avec terrasse **2.** [on roof] : **elevator ~** machinerie *f* d'ascenseur *(installée sur un toit)* **3.** [doorway shelter] auvent *m* ▪ [shed] appentis *m*.

pent-up *adj* [emotion] refoulé, réprimé ▪ [force] contenu, réprimé ▪ **his anger is a product of ~ frustration** sa colère vient de ce qu'il est frustré ▪ **to get rid of ~ energy** se défouler ▪ **the children are full of ~ energy** les enfants débordent d'énergie.

penultimate [pe'nʌltɪmət] ◇ *adj* **1.** [gen] avant-dernier **2.** LING pénultième.
◇ *n* **1.** [gen] avant-dernier *m*, - ère *f* **2.** LING pénultième *f*.

penumbra [pɪ'nʌmbrə] (*pl* **penumbras** *OR pl* **penumbrae** [-bri:]) *n* ASTRON & PHYS pénombre *f*.

penurious [pɪ'njʊərɪəs] *adj fml* **1.** [impoverished] indigent, sans ressources **2.** [miserly] parcimonieux, avare.

penury ['penjʊrɪ] *n fml* **1.** [poverty] indigence *f*, dénuement *m* **2.** [scarcity] pénurie *f*.

peon ['pi:ɒn] *n* **1.** AGRIC [in Latin America] péon *m* **2.** MIL [in India, Sri Lanka] fantassin *m* **3.** *US inf* [worker] prolo *mf*.

peony ['pi:ənɪ] (*pl* **peonies**) *n* pivoine *f*.

people ['pi:pl] ◇ *npl* **1.** [gen] personnes *fpl*, gens *mpl* ▪ **500 ~** 500 personnes ▪ **there were ~ everywhere** il y avait des gens *OR* du monde partout ▪ **there were a lot of ~ there** il y avait beaucoup de monde ▪ **some ~ think it's true** certaines per-

sonnes *OR* certains pensent que c'est vrai ▪ **many/most ~ disagree** beaucoup de gens/la plupart des gens ne sont pas d'accord ➊ **really, some ~!** il y a des gens, je vous jure! ▪ **are you ~ coming or not?** et vous (autres), vous venez ou pas? ▪ **it's Meg of all ~!** ça alors, c'est Meg! ▪ **you of all ~ should know that!** si quelqu'un doit savoir ça, c'est bien toi!
2. [in indefinite uses] on ▪ **~ won't like it** les gens ne vont pas aimer ça ▪ **~ say it's impossible** on dit que c'est impossible
3. [with qualifier] gens *mpl* ▪ **clever/sensitive ~** les gens intelligents/sensibles ▪ **rich/poor/blind ~** les riches/pauvres/aveugles ▪ **young ~** les jeunes ▪ **old ~** les personnes âgées ▪ **city/country ~** les citadins/campagnards ▪ **~ who know her** ceux qui la connaissent ▪ **they are theatre/circus ~** ce sont des gens de théâtre/du cirque ▮ [inhabitants, nationals] : **Danish ~** les Danois ▪ **the ~ of Brazil** les Brésiliens ▪ **the ~ of Glasgow** les habitants de Glasgow ▪ **the ~ of Yorkshire** les gens du Yorkshire ▮ [employed in a specified job] : **I'll call the electricity/gas ~ tomorrow** je téléphonerai à la compagnie d'électricité/de gaz demain
4. POL : **the ~** le peuple ▪ **power to the ~!** le pouvoir au peuple! ▪ **a ~'s government/democracy** un gouvernement/une démocratie populaire
5. *dated* [family] famille *f*, parents *mpl*.
◇ *n* **1.** [nation] peuple *m*, nation *f*
2. [ethnic group] population *f*.
◇ *comp* : **to have ~ skills** avoir le sens du contact ▪ **she's a real ~ person** elle a vraiment le sens du contact.
◇ *vt* **1.** *(usu passive)* [inhabit] peupler ▪ **~d by** peuplée de, habité par
2. *fig* **the monsters that ~ his dreams** les monstres qui hantent ses rêves.

people carrier *n* [car] monospace *m*.

People's Republic of China *pr n* : **the ~** la République populaire de Chine.

People's Republic of Congo *pr n* République *f* populaire du Congo.

pep [pep] (*pret & pp* **pepped**, *cont* **pepping**) *n inf* punch *m*.
➡ **pep up** *vt sep inf* **1.** [person - depressed] remonter le moral à ; [- ill, tired] requinquer, retaper **2.** [business] faire repartir, dynamiser ▪ [party] dynamiser, remettre de l'entrain dans ▪ [conversation] égayer, ranimer, relancer.

PEP [pep] (*abbrev of* **personal equity plan**) *n plan d'investissement en actions bénéficiant de conditions fiscales avantageuses.*

pepper ['pepəʳ] ◇ *n* **1.** [condiment] poivre *m* ▪ **~ steak** *UK* steak *m* au poivre **2.** [vegetable - sweet] poivron *m* ; [- hot] piment *m* ▪ **~ sauce** sauce *f* aux piments.
◇ *vt* **1.** CULIN poivrer **2.** [scatter, sprinkle] émailler, parsemer **3.** [pelt] : **the walls were ~ed with lead shot** les murs étaient criblés d'impacts de balles ▪ **they ~ed the houses with machine-gun fire** ils ont mitraillé les maisons.

pepper-and-salt *adj* **1.** [hair, beard] poivre et sel *(inv)* **2.** TEX marengo *(inv)* ▪ **~ cloth** marengo *m*.

pepperbox ['pepəbɒks] *n US* poivrier *m*.

peppercorn ['pepəkɔ:n] *n* grain *m* de poivre.

peppercorn rent *n UK* loyer *m* modique.

pepper mill *n* moulin *m* à poivre.

peppermint ['pepəmɪnt] ◇ *n* **1.** BOT menthe *f* poivrée **2.** [sweet] bonbon *m* à la menthe.
◇ *adj* à la menthe ▪ **~ OR ~-flavoured toothpaste** dentifrice *m* au menthol.

pepper pot *n* CULIN poivrier *m*, poivrière *f*.

peppery ['pepərɪ] *adj* **1.** CULIN poivré **2.** [quick-tempered] coléreux, irascible **3.** [incisive] mordant, piquant.

pep pill *n inf* stimulant *m*, excitant *m*.

peppy ['pepɪ] (*comp* **peppier**, *superl* **peppiest**) *adj inf* [person] qui a du punch.

pepsin ['pepsɪn] *n* pepsine *f*.

pep talk *n inf* discours *m* d'encouragement ▪ **their boss gave them a ~** leur patron leur a dit quelques mots pour leur remonter le moral.

peptic ulcer ['peptɪk-] *spec n* ulcère *m* gastro-duodénal *OR* de l'estomac.

per [pɜ:ʳ] *prep* [for each] par ▪ **~ person** par personne ▪ **~ day/week/month/year** par jour/semaine/mois/an ▪ **they are paid £6 ~ hour** ils sont payés 6 livres de l'heure ▪ **100 miles ~ hour** ≃ 160 kilomètres à l'heure ▪ **it costs £8 ~ kilo** ça coûte 8 livres le kilo.
➡ **as per** *prep phr* suivant, selon ▪ **as ~ specifications** [on bill] conformément aux spécifications requises ▪ **the work is going ahead as ~ schedule** le travail avance selon le calendrier prévu ▪ **as ~ normal** *OR* **usual** *inf* comme d'habitude.

per annum [pər'ænəm] *adv* par an, annuellement.

per capita [pə'kæpɪtə] *fml* ◇ *adj* par personne ▪ **~ income is higher in the south** le revenu par habitant est plus élevé dans le sud.
◇ *adv* par personne.

perceive [pə'si:v] *vt* **1.** [see] distinguer ▪ [hear, smell etc] percevoir ▪ **he was unable to ~ colours** il était incapable de distinguer les couleurs ▪ **verbs of perceiving** LING les verbes de perception **2.** [notice] s'apercevoir de, remarquer **3.** [conceive, understand] percevoir, comprendre.

per cent [pə'sent] (*pl inv*) ◇ *adv* pour cent ▪ **prices went up (by) 10 ~** les prix ont augmenté de 10 pour cent ▪ **it's 50 ~ cotton** il y a 50 pour cent de coton, c'est du coton à 50 pour cent ▪ **to give 100 ~** se donner à fond *OR* à cent pour cent.
◇ *n* [percentage] pourcentage *m*.

percentage [pə'sentɪdʒ] *n* **1.** [proportion] pourcentage *m* ▪ **a high ~ of the staff** une grande partie du personnel **2.** [share of profits, investment] pourcentage *m* ▪ **to get a ~ on sthg** toucher un pourcentage sur qqch **3.** *UK inf* [advantage] avantage *m*, intérêt *m*.

perceptible [pə'septəbl] *adj* perceptible.

perceptibly [pə'septəblɪ] *adv* [diminish, change] sensiblement ▪ [move] de manière perceptible ▪ **she was ~ thinner** elle avait sensiblement maigri.

perception [pə'sepʃn] *n* **1.** [faculty] perception *f* **2.** [notion, conception] perception *f*, conception *f* ▪ **the general public's ~ of the police** l'image que le grand public a de la police **3.** [insight] perspicacité *f*, intuition *f* ▪ **a man of great ~** un homme très perspicace.

perceptive [pə'septɪv] *adj* **1.** [observant - person] perspicace ; [- remark] judicieux **2.** [sensitive] sensible **3.** [organ] sensoriel.

perceptively [pə'septɪvlɪ] *adv* avec perspicacité.

perceptiveness [pə'septɪvnɪs] *n* perspicacité *f*, pénétration *f*.

perceptual [pə'septjʊəl] *adj* [organ] percepteur.

perch [pɜ:tʃ] ◇ *n* **1.** [for bird - in cage] perchoir *m* ; [- on tree] branche *f* **2.** *inf* [for person - seat] perchoir *m* ▪ **to be knocked from OR off one's ~** être détrôné, se faire détrôner **3.** [linear or square measure] ≃ perche *f* **4.** (*pl inv OR pl* perches) [fish] perche *f*.
◇ *vi* [bird, person] se percher.
◇ *vt* [person, object] percher, jucher.

perchance [pə'tʃɑ:ns] *adv arch & lit* **1.** [perhaps] peut-être **2.** [by accident] par hasard, fortuitement.

percipient [pə'sɪpɪənt] *adj* **1.** *fml* [person] perspicace **2.** ANAT [organ] sensoriel.

percolate ['pɜ:kəleɪt] ◇ *vi* **1.** [liquid] filtrer, s'infiltrer ▪ [coffee] passer **2.** [ideas, news] se répandre ▪ **his ideas ~d through to the rank and file** ses idées ont gagné la base **3.** *US inf* [be excited] être (tout) excité.
◇ *vt* [coffee] préparer *(avec une cafetière à pression)* ▪ **~d coffee** café fait avec une cafetière à pression.

percolator ['pɜ:kəleɪtəʳ] *n* cafetière *f* à pression.

percussion [pə'kʌʃn] *n* **1.** MUS percussion *f* ▪ **Jane Stowell on ~** aux percussions, Jane Stowell ▪ **the ~ section** les percussions *fpl* **2.** [collision, shock] percussion *f*, choc *m* **3.** MED & MIL percussion *f*.

percussion cap *n* amorce *f* fulminante.

percussion instrument *n* MUS instrument *m* à percussion.

percussionist [pə'kʌʃənɪst] *n* MUS percussionniste *mf*.

percussive [pə'kʌsɪv] *adj* [instrument] à percussion ▪ [force] de percussion.

perdition [pə'dɪʃn] *n lit* [spiritual ruin] perdition *f* ▪ [hell] enfer *m*, damnation *f*.

peregrination [,perɪgrɪ'neɪʃn] *n lit* & *hum* pérégrinations *fpl*.

peregrinations *npl* = **peregrination**.

peregrine falcon ['perɪgrɪn-] *n* faucon *m* pèlerin.

peremptorily [pə'remptrəlɪ] *adv* de façon péremptoire, impérieusement.

peremptory [pə'remptərɪ] *adj* **1.** [tone, manner] péremptoire ▪ **there was a ~ knock at the door** on a frappé à la porte de façon péremptoire **2.** *UK* LAW : **~ writ** assignation *f* à comparaître en personne.

perennial [pə'renjəl] <> *adj* **1.** BOT vivace **2.** *fig* [everlasting] éternel ▪ [recurrent, continual] perpétuel, sempiternel.
<> *n* BOT plante *f* vivace.

perennially [pə'renjəlɪ] *adv* [everlastingly] éternellement ▪ [recurrently, continually] perpétuellement, continuellement.

perestroika [,perə'strɔɪkə] *n* perestroïka *f*.

perfect <> *adj* ['pɜ:fɪkt] **1.** [flawless - person, performance etc] parfait ▪ **in ~ health** en excellente *OR* parfaite santé ▪ **her hearing is still ~** elle entend encore parfaitement ▪ **nobody's ~** personne n'est parfait **2.** [complete - agreement, mastery etc] parfait, complet, - ète *f* ▪ **there was ~ silence** il y avait un silence total ▪ **you have a ~ right to be here** vous avez parfaitement *OR* tout à fait le droit d'être ici ▪ [as intensifier] véritable, parfait ▪ **he's a ~ idiot** c'est un parfait imbécile **3.** [fine, lovely - conditions] parfait, idéal ; [- weather] idéal, superbe **4.** [fitting, right - gift, example] parfait, approprié ▪ **Monday is ~ for me** lundi me convient parfaitement ▪ **the colour is ~ on you** cette couleur te va à merveille *OR* à la perfection **5.** [exemplary - gentleman, host] parfait, exemplaire **6.** GRAM [participle] passé ▪ **~ participle** participe *m* passé ▪ **the ~ tense** le parfait.
<> *n* ['pɜ:fɪkt] GRAM parfait *m* ▪ **in the ~** au parfait.
<> *vt* [pə'fekt] **1.** [improve - knowledge, skill] perfectionner, parfaire **2.** [bring to final form - plans, method] mettre au point **3.** TYPO imprimer en retiration.

perfect competition *n* ECON concurrence *f* parfaite.

perfectible [pə'fektəbl] *adj* perfectible.

perfection [pə'fekʃn] *n* **1.** [quality] perfection *f* ▪ **to attain ~** atteindre la perfection ▪ **to do sthg to ~** faire qqch à la perfection **2.** [perfecting - of skill, knowledge] perfectionnement *m* ; [- of plans, method] mise *f* au point.

perfectionism [pə'fekʃənɪzm] *n* perfectionnisme *m*.

perfectionist [pə'fekʃənɪst] <> *adj* perfectionniste.
<> *n* perfectionniste *mf*.

perfective [pə'fektɪv] *adj* GRAM perfectif.

perfectly ['pɜ:fɪktlɪ] *adv* **1.** [speak, understand] parfaitement ▪ **~ formed** d'une forme parfaite **2.** [as intensifier] : **you are ~ right** vous avez parfaitement *OR* tout à fait raison ▪ **it's a ~ good raincoat** cet imperméable est tout à fait mettable.

perfect number *n* MATHS nombre *m* parfait.

perfect pitch *n* MUS : **to have ~** avoir l'oreille absolue.

perfidious [pə'fɪdɪəs] *adj lit* perfide.

perfidy ['pɜ:fɪdɪ] (*pl* **perfidies**) *n lit* perfidie *f*.

perforate ['pɜ:fəreɪt] *vt* **1.** [pierce] perforer, percer **2.** TECH [punch holes in] perforer.

perforated ['pɜ:fəreɪtɪd] *adj* perforé, percé ▪ **to have a ~ eardrum** avoir un tympan perforé *OR* crevé ▪ **tear along the ~ line** détacher suivant les pointillés.

perforation [,pɜ:fə'reɪʃn] *n* perforation *f*.

perforce [pə'fɔ:s] *adv lit* forcément, nécessairement.

perform [pə'fɔ:m] <> *vt* **1.** [carry out - manoeuvre, task] exécuter, accomplir ; [- calculation] effectuer, faire ; [- miracle] accomplir ; [- wedding, ritual] célébrer ▪ **to ~ an operation** MED opérer **2.** [fulfil - function, duty] remplir **3.** [stage - play] jouer, donner ; [- ballet, opera] interpréter, jouer ; [- concert] donner ; [- solo] exécuter ▪ **to ~ a part** THEAT jouer *OR* interpréter un rôle ; DANCE danser un rôle.
<> *vi* **1.** [actor, comedian, musician] jouer ▪ [dancer] danser ▪ [singer] chanter ▪ **she ~ed superbly in the role of Lady Chichester** elle a magnifiquement interprété le rôle de Lady Chichester **2.** [in job, situation] se débrouiller ▪ **to ~ well/badly** [person] bien/ne pas bien s'en tirer ; [company] avoir de bons/mauvais résultats ▪ **how does she ~ under pressure?** comment réagit-elle lorsqu'elle est sous pression? ▪ **the Miami branch is not ~ing well** les résultats de la succursale de Miami ne sont pas très satisfaisants **3.** [function - vehicle, machine] marcher, fonctionner ▪ **the car ~s well/badly in wet conditions** cette voiture a une bonne/mauvaise tenue de route par temps de pluie.

performance [pə'fɔ:məns] *n* **1.** [show] spectacle *m*, représentation *f* ▪ CIN séance *f* ▪ **afternoon ~** matinée *f* **2.** [rendition - by actor, musician, dancer] interprétation *f* ▪ [showing - by sportsman, politician etc] performance *f*, prestation *f* ▪ **he gave an excellent ~ in the role of Othello** son interprétation du rôle d'Othello fut remarquable ▪ **the Prime Minister gave the ~ of his career** le Premier ministre n'a jamais été aussi bon de toute sa carrière ▪ **another poor ~ by the French team** encore une contre-performance de l'équipe française ▪ **the country's poor economic ~** les mauvais résultats économiques du pays ▪ **sterling's ~ on the Stock Exchange** le comportement en bourse de la livre sterling ▪ **sexual ~** prouesses sexuelles **3.** [of machine, computer, car] performance *f* ▪ **~ car** voiture *f* performante **4.** [carrying out - of task, manoeuvre] exécution *f* ; [- of miracle, duties] accomplissement *m* ; [- of ritual] célébration *f* **5.** *inf* [rigmarole] histoire *f*, cirque *m* **6.** LING performance *f*.

performance appraisal *n* [system] système *m* d'évaluation ▪ [individual] évaluation *f*.

performance art *n* spectacle *m* total.

performance-related *adj* en fonction du mérite *OR* résultat ▪ **~ pay** salaire *m* au mérite.

performance test *n* PSYCHOL test *m* de performance.

performative [pə'fɔ:mətɪv] <> *adj* LING & PHILOS performatif.
<> *n* LING [verb] performatif *m* ▪ [utterance] énoncé *m* performatif.

performer [pə'fɔ:mər] *n* [singer, dancer, actor] interprète *mf* ▪ **nightclub ~** artiste *mf* de cabaret.

performing [pə'fɔ:mɪŋ] *adj* [bear, dog etc] savant.

performing arts *npl* arts *mpl* du spectacle.

performing rights *npl* THEAT droits *mpl* de représentation ▪ MUS droits *mpl* d'exécution.

perfume <> *n* ['pɜ:fju:m] **1.** [bottled] parfum *m* ▪ **what ~ does she wear** *OR* **use?** quel parfum met-elle?, quel est son parfum? ▶ **~ spray** atomiseur *m* de parfum **2.** [smell] parfum *m*.
<> *vt* [pə'fju:m] parfumer.

perfumed [*UK* 'pɜ:fju:md, *US* pər'fju:md] *adj* parfumé.

perfumery [pə'fju:mərɪ] (*pl* **perfumeries**) *n* parfumerie *f*.

perfunctory [pə'fʌŋktərɪ] *adj* [gesture] négligent ▪ [greeting, kiss] détaché ▪ [explanation, apology, letter] sommaire ▪ [effort] de pure forme ▪ [interrogation, search] fait pour la forme.

pergola ['pɜ:gələ] *n* pergola *f*.

perhaps [pə'hæps] *adv* peut-être ■ **~ they've forgotten** ils ont peut-être oublié, peut-être ont-ils oublié ■ **~ not** peut-être que non ▮ [used in polite requests, offers] : **~ you'd be kind enough...** peut-être aurais-tu la gentillesse...

pericarp ['perɪkɑ:p] *n* péricarpe *m*.

perigee ['perɪdʒi:] *n* périgée *m*.

peril ['perɪl] *n* péril *m*, danger *m* ■ **to be in ~** être en danger ■ **you do it at your ~** *UK* c'est à vos risques et périls.

perilous ['perələs] *adj* périlleux, dangereux.

perilously ['perələslɪ] *adv* périlleusement, dangereusement ■ **he came ~ close to defeat/drowning** il s'en est fallu d'un cheveu qu'il ne perde/qu'il ne se noie.

perimeter [pə'rɪmɪtəʳ] *n* périmètre *m*.

perimeter fence *n* grillage *m*.

perinatal [,perɪ'neɪtl] *adj* périnatal.

perineal [,perɪ'ni:əl] *adj* périnéal.

perineum [,perɪ'ni:əm] (*pl* **perinea** [-'ni:ə]) *n* périnée *m*.

period ['pɪərɪəd] <> *n* **1.** [length of time] période *f* ■ [historical epoch] période *f*, époque *f* ■ **within a ~ of a few months** en l'espace de quelques mois ■ **we have a two-month ~ in which to do it** nous avons un délai de deux mois pour le faire ■ **at that ~ in her life** à cette époque de sa vie ■ **there will be a question/discussion ~ after the lecture** un moment sera consacré aux questions/au débat après la conférence **2.** GEOL période *f* **3.** SCH [lesson] cours *m* ■ **a free ~** [for pupil] une heure de permanence ; [for teacher] une heure de battement **4.** [in ice hockey] période *f* **5.** ASTRON : **~ of rotation** période *f* de rotation **6.** [menstruation] règles *fpl* ■ **I've got my ~** j'ai mes règles **7.** *US* [full stop] point *m* ■ **I said no, ~** j'ai dit non, point final **8.** [sentence] période *f* **9.** CHEM [in periodic table] période *f* **10.** MUS période *f* **11.** COMM : **accounting ~** exercice *m*.
<> *comp* [furniture, costume] d'époque ■ [novel] historique.
<> *adv inf* **you're not going out alone, ~!** tu ne sortiras pas tout seul, un point c'est tout!

periodic [,pɪərɪ'ɒdɪk] *adj* **1.** [gen] périodique **2.** CHEM & MATHS périodique.

periodical [,pɪərɪ'ɒdɪkl] <> *n* [publication] périodique *m*.
<> *adj* périodique.

periodically [,pɪərɪ'ɒdɪklɪ] *adv* périodiquement, de temps en temps.

periodic table *n* classification *f* périodique (des éléments), tableau *m* de Mendeleïev.

periodontics [,perɪə'dɒntɪks] *n (U) branche de la stomatologie qui s'occupe du périodonte.*

period pains *npl* règles *fpl* douloureuses.

period piece *n* objet *m* d'époque.

peripatetic [,perɪpə'tetɪk] *adj* **1.** [itinerant] itinérant **2.** *UK* SCH : **~ teacher** *professeur qui enseigne dans plusieurs établissements scolaires.*

peripheral [pə'rɪfərəl] <> *adj* périphérique ■ **~ vision** vue *f* périphérique.
<> *n* COMPUT : **~ (device** *OR* **unit)** (unité *f*) périphérique *m*.

periphery [pə'rɪfərɪ] (*pl* **peripheries**) *n* **1.** [of circle, vision, city etc] périphérie *f* ■ **on the ~** à la périphérie **2.** [of group, movement] frange *f* ■ **on the ~ of society** en marge de la société.

periphrasis [pə'rɪfrəsɪs] (*pl* **periphrases** [-si:z]) *n* périphrase *f*, circonlocution *f*.

periphrastic [,perɪ'fræstɪk] *adj* périphrastique.

periscope ['perɪskəʊp] *n* périscope *m* ■ **up ~!** sortez le périscope!

perish ['perɪʃ] <> *vi* **1.** *UK* [rot - rubber, leather etc] s'abîmer, se détériorer ; [- food] se gâter, pourrir **2.** *lit* [die] périr ■ **~ the thought** *hum* : **you're not pregnant, are you? – ~ the thought!** tu n'es pas enceinte au moins? -- tu veux rire *OR* j'espère bien que non!
<> *vt* [rubber, leather] abîmer, détériorer ■ [food] gâter.

perishable ['perɪʃəbl] *adj* périssable.
◆ **perishables** *npl* denrées *fpl* périssables.

perished ['perɪʃt] *adj UK inf* [cold] frigorifié.

perisher ['perɪʃəʳ] *n UK inf* galopin *m*.

perishing ['perɪʃɪŋ] *adj UK inf* **1.** [cold - person, hands] frigorifié ■ **it's ~ (cold)** il fait un froid de canard *OR* de loup **2.** [as expletive] sacré, fichu, foutu.

peristalsis [,perɪ'stælsɪs] (*pl* **peristalses** [-si:z]) *n* péristaltisme *m*.

peristyle ['perɪstaɪl] *n* péristyle *m*.

peritonitis [,perɪtə'naɪtɪs] *n (U)* péritonite *f* ■ **to have ~** avoir une péritonite.

periwinkle ['perɪ,wɪŋkl] *n* **1.** BOT pervenche *f* **2.** ZOOL bigorneau *m*.

perjure ['pɜ:dʒəʳ] *vt* : **to ~ o.s.** faire un faux témoignage.

perjured ['pɜ:dʒəd] *adj* : **~ evidence** faux témoignage *m*.

perjurer ['pɜ:dʒərəʳ] *n* faux témoin *m*.

perjury ['pɜ:dʒərɪ] (*pl* **perjuries**) *n* : **to commit ~** faire un faux témoignage.

perk [pɜ:k] *inf* <> *n* [from job] avantage *m* en nature ■ [advantage - gen] avantage *m*.
<> *vi* & *vt* [coffee] passer.
◆ **perk up** <> *vt sep* [cheer up] remonter, ragaillardir, revigorer ■ **the news really ~ed me up** la nouvelle m'a vraiment remonté le moral ▮ [liven up] revigorer ■ **some wine will ~ you up** un peu de vin te remontera.
<> *vi insep* **1.** [cheer up] se ragaillardir, retrouver le moral ■ **he ~ed up in the afternoon** il a retrouvé son entrain l'après-midi **2.** [become interested] dresser l'oreille *OR* la tête **3.** [ears, head] se dresser.

perky ['pɜ:kɪ] (*comp* **perkier**, *superl* **perkiest**) *adj* gai, vif.

perm [pɜ:m] <> *vt* [hair] permanenter ■ **her hair is ~ed** elle a les cheveux permanentés ■ **I've had my hair ~ed** je me suis fait faire une permanente.
<> *n* **1.** permanente *f* ■ **to have a ~** se faire faire une permanente **2.** (*abbrev of* **permutation**) *combinaison jouée dans les paris sur les matches de football en Grande-Bretagne.*

permafrost ['pɜ:məfrɒst] *n* permagel *m*, permafrost *m*, pergélisol *m*.

permanence ['pɜ:mənəns] *n* permanence *f*, caractère *m* permanent.

permanent ['pɜ:mənənt] <> *adj* permanent ■ **no ~ damage was caused** aucun dégât irréparable n'a été occasionné ■ **~ address** domicile *m* ■ **are you here on a ~ basis?** êtes-vous ici à titre définitif? ■ **~ staff** [gen] personnel *m* permanent ; [in public service] personnel *m* titulaire ■ **a ~ post** [gen] un emploi permanent ; [in public service] un poste de titulaire ▸ **~ ink** encre *f* indélébile ■ **~ tooth** dent *f* permanente ■ **Permanent Secretary** *UK* chef *m* de cabinet ■ **Permanent Undersecretary** *UK* ≃ secrétaire général *m*, - e *f (dans la fonction publique).*
<> *n US* [in hair] permanente *f*.

permanently ['pɜ:mənəntlɪ] *adv* **1.** [constantly] en permanence, constamment **2.** [definitively] définitivement, à titre définitif.

permanent-press *adj* : **~ trousers/skirt** pantalon *m* /jupe *f* à pli permanent.

permanent wave *n* permanente *f*.

permanent way *n UK* voie *f* ferrée.

permanganate [pɜ:'mæŋgəneɪt] *n* permanganate *m*.

permeable ['pɜ:mjəbl] *adj* perméable.

permeate ['pɜ:mɪeɪt] <> *vt* **1.** [subj: gas, smell] se répandre dans **2.** [subj: liquid] s'infiltrer dans ■ **damp had ~d the floorboards** le plancher était imprégné *OR* gorgé d'humidité **3.** *fig* [subj: ideas] se répandre dans, se propager à travers

▪ [subj: feelings] envahir, emplir ▪ **an atmosphere of gloom ~s his novels** ses romans sont empreints d'une mélancolie profonde.

<> *vi* **1.** [gas] se répandre, se diffuser ▪ [smell] se répandre **2.** [liquid] filtrer **3.** *fig* [ideas, feelings] se répandre, se propager.

permissible [pə'mɪsəbl] *adj fml* **1.** [allowed] permis, autorisé **2.** [tolerable - behaviour] admissible, acceptable ▪ **degree of ~ error** marge d'erreur admissible *OR* admise.

permission [pə'mɪʃn] *n* permission *f*, autorisation *f* ▪ **to ask for ~ to do sthg** demander la permission *OR* l'autorisation de faire qqch ▪ **to have ~ to do sthg** avoir la permission *OR* l'autorisation de faire qqch ▪ **to give sb ~ to do sthg** donner à qqn la permission de faire qqch ▪ **who gave them ~?** qui le leur a permis ? ▪ **with your ~** avec votre permission, si vous le permettez ▪ **photos published by kind ~ of Larousse** photos publiées avec l'aimable autorisation de Larousse ▪ **you need written ~ to work at home** il faut une autorisation écrite pour travailler chez soi.

Voir module d'usage

permissive [pə'mɪsɪv] *adj* [tolerant - behaviour, parent etc] permissif ▪ **the ~ society** la société permissive.

permissively [pə'mɪsɪvlɪ] *adv* de manière permissive.

permissiveness [pə'mɪsɪvnɪs] *n* [morally] permissivité *f*.

permit <> *vt* [pə'mɪt] (*pret & pp* **permitted**, *cont* **permitting**) **1.** [allow] permettre, autoriser ▪ **to ~ sb to do sthg** permettre à qqn de faire qqch, autoriser qqn à faire qqch ▪ **~ me to inform you that...** laissez-moi vous apprendre que... ▪ **he won't ~ it** il ne le permettra pas ▪ **you are not permitted to enter the building** vous n'avez pas le droit de pénétrer dans l'immeuble ▪ **smoking is not permitted upstairs** il est interdit de fumer à l'étage ▮ [tolerate] tolérer ▪ **he ~s far too much rudeness from his children** il tolère trop de grossièreté chez ses enfants **2.** [enable] permettre ▪ **the statistics ~ the following conclusions** les statistiques permettent (de tirer) les conclusions suivantes.

<> *vi* [pə'mɪt] (*pret & pp* **permitted**, *cont* **permitting**) permettre ▪ **weather permitting** si le temps le permet ▪ **to ~ of** *fml* permettre ▪ **the text ~s of two readings** le texte se prête à deux interprétations différentes.

<> *n* ['pɜːmɪt] [authorization] autorisation *f* ADMIN permis *m* ▪ [pass] laissez-passer *m inv* ▪ **export/drinks ~** licence *f* d'exportation/pour la vente de boissons alcoolisées.

permutation [,pɜːmjuː'teɪʃn] *n* MATHS permutation *f*.

permute [pə'mjuːt] *vt* permuter.

pernicious [pə'nɪʃəs] *adj* **1.** [harmful] pernicieux **2.** [malicious - gossip, lie] malveillant.

pernicious anaemia *n (U)* anémie *f* pernicieuse.

pernickety [pə'nɪkətɪ] *UK*, **persnickety** [pə'snɪkɪtɪ] *US adj inf* **1.** *pej* [person - fussy] tatillon, chipoteur ; [- hard to please] difficile ▪ **she's very ~ about punctuality** elle ne plaisante pas avec *OR* elle est très à cheval sur la ponctualité **2.** [job - fiddly] délicat, minutieux.

perorate ['perəreɪt] *vi fml* discourir, pérorer.

peroration [,perə'reɪʃn] *n* péroraison *f*.

peroxide [pə'rɒksaɪd] <> *n* **1.** CHEM peroxyde *m* **2.** [for hair] eau *f* oxygénée.

<> *vt* [bleach - hair] décolorer, oxygéner *spec*.

peroxide blonde *n* [woman] blonde *f* décolorée.

perpendicular [,pɜːpən'dɪkjʊlər] <> *adj* **1.** GEOM perpendiculaire ▪ **the line AB is ~ to the line CD** la ligne AB est perpendiculaire à la ligne CD **2.** [vertical - cliff] escarpé, abrupt, à pic ; [- slope] raide, à pic.

<> *n* perpendiculaire *f* ▪ **the tower is out of (the) ~** la tour n'est pas verticale *OR* est hors d'aplomb *spec*.

◆ **Perpendicular** *adj* ARCHIT perpendiculaire.

perpetrate ['pɜːpɪtreɪt] *vt fml* [commit - crime] commettre, perpétrer *lit* ▪ **to ~ a hoax** être l'auteur d'une farce.

perpetration [,pɜːpɪ'treɪʃn] *n fml* perpétration *f*.

perpetrator ['pɜːpɪtreɪtər] *n fml* auteur *m*.

perpetual [pə'petʃʊəl] *adj* **1.** [state, worry] perpétuel ▪ [noise, questions] continuel, incessant ▪ **her ~ coughing kept me awake all night** sa toux incessante m'a gardé éveillé toute la nuit ▪ **it's a ~ worry to us** c'est pour nous un sujet d'inquiétude *OR* un souci permanent ▪ **~ snows** neiges *fpl* éternelles **2.** HORT perpétuel.

perpetual calendar *n* calendrier *m* perpétuel.

perpetually [pə'petʃʊəlɪ] *adv* perpétuellement, sans cesse.

perpetual motion *n* mouvement *m* perpétuel.

perpetuate [pə'petʃʊeɪt] *vt* perpétuer.

perpetuation [pə,petʃʊ'eɪʃn] *n* perpétuation *f* ▪ **this leads to the ~ of this type of situation** c'est ce qui permet à ce type de situation de se perpétuer.

perpetuity [,pɜːpɪ'tjuːətɪ] (*pl* **perpetuities**) *n* **1.** [eternity] perpétuité *f lit* ▪ **in** *OR* **for ~** à perpétuité **2.** [annuity] rente *f* perpétuelle.

perplex [pə'pleks] *vt* **1.** [puzzle] rendre *OR* laisser perplexe **2.** [complicate] compliquer.

perplexed [pə'plekst] *adj* perplexe ▪ **I'm ~ about what to do** je ne sais pas trop quoi faire.

perplexing [pə'pleksɪŋ] *adj* inexplicable, incompréhensible ▪ **he asked us some ~ questions** il a posé des questions qui nous ont laissés perplexes.

perplexity [pə'pleksətɪ] *n* **1.** [confusion] perplexité *f* **2.** [complexity - of problem] complexité *f*.

perquisite ['pɜːkwɪzɪt] *fml* = **perk** *(n)*.

perry ['perɪ] (*pl* **perries**) *n* poiré *m*.

per se [pɜː'seɪ] *adv* [as such] en tant que tel ▪ [in itself] en soi.

persecute ['pɜːsɪkjuːt] *vt* **1.** [oppress] persécuter ▪ **they were ~d for their religious beliefs** ils ont été persécutés à cause de leurs convictions religieuses **2.** [pester] persécuter, harceler ▪ **they ~d her with questions** ils l'ont harcelée de questions.

PERMISSION

Est-ce que je peux me servir de l'ordinateur ? Can I use the computer?

Bien sûr, vas-y. Of course you can, go ahead.

Écoute, franchement, ça m'ennuie, il n'est pas à moi. To be honest, I'd rather you didn't. It isn't mine.

Est-ce que je peux m'asseoir ? May I sit here?

Je vous en prie. Yes, of course.

Désolé, la place est prise. Sorry, it's taken.

J'emprunte ta voiture, d'accord ? Is it OK if I borrow your car?

Pas de problème. No problem.

Ah non, pas question, tu n'as qu'à prendre la tienne ! No way, use your own!

Ça te dérange si je fume ? Do you mind if I smoke?

Absolument pas. Not at all.

J'aimerais mieux que tu évites. I'd rather you didn't.

persecution [,pɜːsɪ'kjuːʃn] *n* persécution *f*.

persecution complex *n* délire *m* de persécution.

persecutor ['pɜːsɪkjuːtəʳ] *n* persécuteur *m*, - trice *f*.

Perseus ['pɜːsjuːs] *pr n* Persée.

perseverance [,pɜːsɪ'vɪərəns] *n* persévérance *f*.

persevere [,pɜːsɪ'vɪəʳ] *vi* persévérer ■ **~ in your efforts** persévérez dans vos efforts ■ **you must ~ with your studies** il faut persévérer dans vos études.

persevering [,pɜːsɪ'vɪərɪŋ] *adj* persévérant, obstiné.

Persia ['pɜːʃə] *pr n* Perse *f* ■ **in ~** en Perse.

Persian ['pɜːʃn] ◇ *n* **1.** [person] Persan *m*, - e *f* ■ ANTIQ Perse *mf* **2.** LING [modern] persan *m* ■ [ancient] perse *m*.
◇ *adj* persan ■ ANTIQ perse.

Persian blinds *npl* persiennes *fpl*.

Persian carpet *n* tapis *m* persan.

Persian cat *n* chat *m* persan.

Persian Gulf *pr n* : **the ~** le golfe Persique.

persimmon [pə'sɪmən] *n* [fruit] kaki *m*, plaquemine *f* ■ [tree] plaqueminier *m*.

persist [pə'sɪst] *vi* **1.** [person] persister ■ **to ~ in doing sthg** persister *OR* s'obstiner à faire qqch ■ **he ~s in the belief that...** il persiste à croire que... **2.** [weather, problem etc] persister.

persistence [pə'sɪstəns], **persistency** [pə'sɪstənsɪ] *n* **1.** [perseverance] persistance *f*, persévérance *f* ■ [insistence] persistance *f*, insistance *f* ■ [obstinacy] obstination *f* ■ **his ~ in asking awkward questions** son obstination à poser des questions embarrassantes **2.** [continuation - of rain, problem etc] persistance *f*.

persistent [pə'sɪstənt] *adj* **1.** [continual - demands, rain etc] continuel, incessant ■ **~ offender** récidiviste *mf* **2.** [lingering - smell, fever etc] persistant, tenace **3.** [persevering] persévérant ■ **you must be more ~ in your efforts** il faut être plus persévérant **4.** BOT persistant.

persistently [pə'sɪstəntlɪ] *adv* **1.** [continually] continuellement, sans cesse **2.** [perseveringly] avec persévérance *OR* persistance, obstinément.

persnickety *US inf* = **pernickety**.

person ['pɜːsn] (*pl* **people** ['piːpl] *fml OR pl* **persons**) *n* **1.** personne *f* ■ **a young ~** [female] une jeune personne ; [male] un jeune homme ■ **by a ~ or ~s unknown** LAW par des personnes inconnues *OR* non identifiées ■ **he's not that sort of ~** ce n'est pas du tout son genre ■ **in the ~ of** en la personne de **2.** *fml* [body] personne *f* ■ **to have sthg on *OR* about one's ~** avoir qqch sur soi **3.** GRAM personne *f* ■ **in the first ~ plural** à la première personne du pluriel **4.** RELIG personne *f*.
◆ **in person** *adv phr* en personne ■ **this letter must be delivered to him in ~** cette lettre doit lui être remise en mains propres.

persona [pə'səʊnə] (*pl* **personas** *OR pl* **personae** [-niː]) *n* LIT & PSYCHOL personnage *m* ■ **to take on a new ~** se créer un personnage.

personable ['pɜːsnəbl] *adj* plaisant, charmant.

personage ['pɜːsənɪdʒ] *n fml* personnage *m (individu)*.

personal ['pɜːsənl] ◇ *adj* **1.** [individual - experience, belief etc] personnel ■ **my ~ opinion is that he drowned** personnellement, je crois qu'il s'est noyé ■ **you get more ~ attention in small shops** on s'occupe mieux de vous dans les petits magasins ■ **will you do me a ~ favour?** pourriez-vous m'accorder une faveur?
2. [in person] personnel ■ **the boss made a ~ visit to the scene** le patron est venu lui-même *OR* en personne sur les lieux ■ **'~ callers welcome'** 'vente en gros et au détail'
3. [private - message, letter] personnel ■ **~ and private** [on letter] strictement confidentiel
4. [for one's own use] personnel ■ **~ belongings *OR* possessions** objets *mpl* personnels, affaires *fpl* ■ **this is for my ~ use** ceci est destiné à mon usage personnel ■ **~ pension plan** retraite *f* personnel ■ **~ estate *OR* property** biens *mpl* mobiliers personnels
5. [intimate - feelings, reasons, life] personnel ■ **I'd like to see her on a ~ matter** je voudrais la voir pour des raisons personnelles ■ **just a few ~ friends** rien que quelques amis intimes
6. [offensive] désobligeant ■ **~ remark** remarque *f* désobligeante ■ **there's no need to be so ~!** ce n'est pas la peine de t'en prendre à moi! ■ **nothing ~!** ne le prenez pas pour vous!, n'y voyez rien de personnel! ■ **the discussion was getting rather ~** la discussion prenait un tour un peu trop personnel
7. [bodily - hygiene] corporel
8. GRAM personnel ■ **~ pronoun** pronom *m* personnel.
◇ *n US* [advert] petite annonce *f (pour rencontres)*.

personal account *n* compte *m* personnel.

personal ad *n inf* petite annonce *f (pour rencontres)*.

personal allowance *n* FIN abattement *m (sur l'impôt sur le revenu)*.

personal assistant *n* secrétaire *m* particulier, secrétaire *f* particulière.

personal call *n* TELEC appel *m* personnel *OR* privé.

personal column *n* petites annonces *fpl (pour rencontres)* ■ **to put an ad in the ~** passer une petite annonce.

personal computer *n* ordinateur *m* individuel *OR* personnel, PC *m*.

personal digital assistant *n* agenda *m* électronique, assistant *m* numérique personnel.

personality [,pɜːsə'nælətɪ] (*pl* **personalities**) *n* **1.** [character] personnalité *f*, caractère *m* ■ [of thing, animal etc] caractère *m* **2.** [famous person] personnalité *f* ■ CIN & TV vedette *f* ■ **sports ~** vedette *f* du monde du sport **3.** PSYCHOL personnalité *f*.
◆ **personalities** *npl dated* [offensive remarks] propos *mpl* désobligeants.

personality cult *n* culte *m* de la personnalité.

personality disorder *n* trouble *m* de la personnalité.

personality test *n* test *m* de personnalité, test *m* projectif *spec*.

personality type *n* configuration *f* psychologique.

personalize, ise ['pɜːsənəlaɪz] *vt* **1.** [make personal - gen] personnaliser ; [- luggage, clothes] marquer (à son nom) **2.** [argument, campaign] donner un tour personnel à **3.** [personify] personnifier.

personalized ['pɜːsənəlaɪzd] *adj* [individually tailored] personnalisé ■ **~ stationery** papier *m* à lettres à en-tête.

personally ['pɜːsnəlɪ] *adv* **1.** [speaking for oneself] personnellement, pour ma/sa *etc* part ■ **~ (speaking), I think it's a silly idea** pour ma part *OR* en ce qui me concerne, je trouve que c'est une idée stupide **2.** [in person, directly] en personne, personnellement ■ **I was not ~ involved in the project** je n'ai pas participé directement au projet ■ **deliver the letter to the director ~** remettez la lettre en mains propres au directeur **3.** [not officially] sur le plan personnel **4.** [individually] personnellement ■ **to take things ~** prendre les choses trop à cœur ■ **don't take it ~, but...** ne vous sentez pas visé, mais...

personal organizer *n* organiseur *m*.

personal stereo *n* baladeur *m offic*, Walkman® *m*.

persona non grata [pə'səʊnənɒn'grɑːtə] (*pl* **personae non gratae** [pə'səʊniːnɒn'grɑːtiː]) *n* : **to be ~** être persona non grata ■ **he's definitely ~ in this house** il n'est absolument pas le bienvenu dans cette maison.

personification [pə,sɒnɪfɪ'keɪʃn] *n* personnification *f* ■ **he is the ~ of evil** c'est le mal personnifié *OR* en personne.

personify [pə'sɒnɪfaɪ] (*pret & pp* **personified**) *vt* personnifier ■ **he is evil personified** c'est le mal personnifié *OR* en personne.

personnel [,pɜːsə'nel] *n* **1.** [staff] personnel *m* ■ **~ officer** responsable *m* du personnel **2.** [department] service *m* du personnel **3.** MIL [troops] troupes *fpl*.

personnel carrier *n* (véhicule *m* de) transport *m* de troupes.

person-to-person <> *adv* : **I'd like to speak to her ~** je voudrais lui parler en particulier *OR* seule à seul.
<> *adj* **1.** [conversation] personnel **2.** TELEC : **~ call** communication *f* avec préavis *(se dit d'un appel téléphonique où la communication n'est établie et facturée que lorsque la personne à qui l'on veut parler répond)*.

perspective [pə'spektɪv] <> *n* **1.** ARCHIT & ART perspective *f* ▪ **to draw sthg in ~** dessiner qqch en perspective ▪ **the houses are out of ~** la perspective des maisons est fausse
2. [opinion, viewpoint] perspective *f*, optique *f* ▪ **it gives you a different ~ on the problem** cela vous permet de voir le problème sous un angle *OR* un jour différent ▪ **from a psychological ~** d'un point de vue psychologique ▪ **the latest developments put a new ~ on the case** les derniers événements éclairent l'affaire d'un jour nouveau
3. [proportion] : **we must try to keep our (sense of) ~** *OR* **to keep things in ~** nous devons nous efforcer de garder notre sens des proportions ▪ **to get things out of ~** perdre le sens des proportions ▪ **it should help us to get** *OR* **to put the role she played into ~** cela devrait nous aider à mesurer le rôle qu'elle a joué ▪ **the figures must be looked at in (their proper) ~** il faut étudier les chiffres dans leur contexte
4. [view, vista] perspective *f*, panorama *m*, vue *f*
5. [prospect] perspective *f*.
<> *adj* [drawing] perspectif.

Perspex® ['pɜ:speks] <> *n UK* Plexiglas® *m*.
<> *comp* [window, windscreen etc] en Plexiglas®.

perspicacious [,pɜ:spɪ'keɪʃəs] *adj fml* [person] perspicace ▪ [remark, judgment] pénétrant, lucide.

perspicacity [,pɜ:spɪ'kæsətɪ] *n fml* perspicacité *f*.

perspicuity [,pɜ:spɪ'kju:ətɪ] *n fml* clarté *f*, lucidité *f*.

perspicuous [pə'spɪkjʊəs] *adj fml* clair, lucide.

perspiration [,pɜ:spə'reɪʃn] *n* transpiration *f*, sueur *f*.

perspire [pə'spaɪəʳ] *vi* transpirer ▪ **his hands were perspiring** il avait les mains moites.

persuade [pə'sweɪd] *vt* persuader, convaincre ▪ **to ~ sb to do sthg** persuader *OR* convaincre qqn de faire qqch ▪ **to ~ sb not to do sthg** persuader qqn de ne pas faire qqch, dissuader qqn de faire qqch ▪ **I let myself be ~d into coming** je me suis laissé convaincre qu'il fallait venir ▪ **she finally ~d the car to start** *fig* elle a réussi à faire démarrer la voiture ▪ **I was ~d of her innocence** *fml* j'étais convaincu *OR* persuadé qu'elle était innocente.

persuasion [pə'sweɪʒn] *n* **1.** [act of convincing] persuasion *f* ▪ **the art of gentle ~** l'art de convaincre en douceur ▪ **I used all my powers of ~ on him** j'ai fait tout mon possible *OR* tout ce qui était en mon pouvoir pour le convaincre ▪ **I wouldn't need much ~ to give it up** il ne faudrait pas insister beaucoup pour que j'abandonne **2.** [belief - RELIG] confession *f*, religion *f* ▪ POL tendance *f* ▪ **people, regardless of their political ~** les gens, quelles que soient leurs convictions politiques **3.** *fml* [conviction] conviction *f*.

persuasive [pə'sweɪsɪv] *adj* [manner, speaker] persuasif, convaincant ▪ [argument] convaincant.

persuasively [pə'sweɪsɪvlɪ] *adv* de façon convaincante *OR* persuasive.

persuasiveness [pə'sweɪsɪvnəs] *n* force *f* de persuasion.

pert [pɜ:t] *adj* [person, reply] effronté ▪ [hat] coquet ▪ [nose] mutin ▪ [bottom] ferme.

pertain [pə'teɪn] *vi* **1.** [apply] s'appliquer **2.** : **to ~ to** [concern] avoir rapport à, se rapporter à ; LAW [subj: land, property] se rattacher à, dépendre de.

pertinacity [,pɜ:tɪ'næsətɪ] *n fml* opiniâtreté *f*.

pertinence ['pɜ:tɪnəns] *n* pertinence *f*.

pertinent ['pɜ:tɪnənt] *adj* pertinent, à propos.

pertly ['pɜ:tlɪ] *adv* [reply] avec effronterie ▪ [dress] coquettement.

perturb [pə'tɜ:b] *vt* **1.** [worry] inquiéter, troubler ▪ **they were very ~ed by his disappearance** sa disparition les a beaucoup inquiétés **2.** ASTRON & ELECTRON perturber.

perturbation [,pɜ:tə'beɪʃn] *n* **1.** *fml* [anxiety] trouble *m*, inquiétude *f* **2.** ASTRON & ELECTRON perturbation *f*.

perturbed [pə'tɜ:bd] *adj* troublé, inquiet, - ète *f* ▪ **I was ~ to hear that...** ça m'a troublé *OR* inquiété d'apprendre que...

perturbing [pə'tɜ:bɪŋ] *adj* inquiétant, troublant.

Peru [pə'ru:] *pr n* Pérou *m* ▪ **in ~** au Pérou.

Perugino [peru:'dʒi:nəʊ] *pr n* : **Il ~** le Pérugin.

perusal [pə'ru:zl] *n* [thorough reading] lecture *f* approfondie, examen *m* ▪ [quick reading] lecture *f* sommaire, survol *m*.

peruse [pə'ru:z] *vt* [read thoroughly] lire attentivement, examiner ▪ [read quickly] parcourir, survoler.

Peruvian [pə'ru:vjən] <> *n* Péruvien *m*, - enne *f*.
<> *adj* péruvien.

perv [pɜ:v] *n UK inf* détraqué *m* (sexuel), détraquée *f* (sexuelle).

pervade [pə'veɪd] *vt* **1.** [subj: gas, smell] se répandre dans **2.** [subj: ideas] se répandre dans, se propager à travers ▪ [subj: feelings] envahir ▪ **the fundamental error that ~s their philosophy** l'erreur fondamentale qui imprègne leur philosophie.

pervasive [pə'veɪsɪv] *adj* [feeling] envahissant ▪ [influence] omniprésent ▪ [effect] général ▪ [smell] envahissant, omniprésent ▪ **the ~ influence of television** l'omniprésence de la télévision ▪ **a ~ atmosphere of pessimism** une atmosphère de pessimisme général.

perverse [pə'vɜ:s] *adj* [stubborn - person] têtu, entêté ; [- desire] tenace ▪ [contrary, wayward] contrariant ▪ **he felt a ~ urge to refuse** il fut pris d'une envie de refuser simplement pour le plaisir ▪ **she takes a ~ delight in doing this** elle y prend un malin plaisir.

perversely [pə'vɜ:slɪ] *adv* [stubbornly] obstinément ▪ [unreasonably, contrarily] par esprit de contradiction.

perverseness [pə'vɜ:snɪs] *n* [stubbornness] entêtement *m*, obstination *f* ▪ [unreasonableness, contrariness] esprit *m* de contradiction.

perversion [*UK* pə'vɜ:ʃn, *US* pə'vɜ:rʒn] *n* **1.** [sexual abnormality] perversion *f* **2.** [distortion - of truth] déformation *f*.

perversity [pə'vɜ:sətɪ] *(pl* **perversities***)* *n* **1.** = **perverseness** **2.** [sexual abnormality] perversité *f*.

pervert <> *vt* [pə'vɜ:t] **1.** [corrupt morally - person] pervertir, corrompre ▪ PSYCHOL pervertir **2.** [distort - truth] déformer ; [- words] dénaturer ▪ **to ~ the course of justice** LAW entraver le cours de la justice.
<> *n* ['pɜ:vɜ:t] pervers *m*, - e *f*.

perverted [pə'vɜ:tɪd] *adj* PSYCHOL pervers.

Pesach ['peɪsɔx] *n* Pessah *f*.

peseta [pə'seɪtə] *n* peseta *f*.

pesky ['peskɪ] *(comp* **peskier**, *superl* **peskiest***)* *adj esp US inf* fichu, e.

peso ['peɪsəʊ] *(pl* **pesos***)* *n* peso *m*.

pessary ['pesərɪ] *(pl* **pessaries***)* *n* MED pessaire *m*.

pessimism ['pesɪmɪzm] *n* pessimisme *m*.

pessimist ['pesɪmɪst] *n* pessimiste *mf*.

pessimistic [,pesɪ'mɪstɪk] *adj* pessimiste ▪ **I feel very ~ about her chances of getting the job** je doute fort qu'elle obtienne ce poste ▪ **don't be so ~ about your future** ne regarde pas l'avenir d'un œil si sombre.

pest [pest] *n* **1.** [insect] insecte *m* nuisible ▪ [animal] animal *m* nuisible ▪ **~ control** lutte *f* contre les animaux nuisibles ; [of insects] désinsectisation *f* **2.** *inf* [nuisance] plaie *f*, peste *f* ■ **Christmas shopping is a real ~** c'est une vraie corvée de faire les achats de Noël.

pester ['pestər] *vt* importuner, harceler ■ **stop ~ing your mother!** laisse ta mère tranquille! ■ **they're always ~ing me for money** ils sont toujours à me réclamer de l'argent ■ **he ~ed me into buying him a computer** il m'a harcelé jusqu'à ce que je lui achète un ordinateur.

pesticide ['pestɪsaɪd] *n* pesticide *m*.

pestilence ['pestɪləns] *n lit* peste *f*, pestilence *f lit*.

pestilential [,pestɪ'lenʃl] *adj* **1.** [annoying] agaçant **2.** MED pestilentiel.

pestle ['pesl] *n* CULIN pilon *m*.

pesto ['pestəʊ], **pesto sauce** *n* pesto *m*.

pet [pet] (*pret & pp* **petted**, *cont* **petting**) ◇ *n* **1.** [animal] animal *m* domestique ■ **we don't keep ~s** nous n'avons pas d'animaux à la maison ■ **he keeps a snake as a ~** il a un serpent apprivoisé ■ **~ food** aliments *mpl* pour animaux de compagnie **2.** [favourite] favori *m*, - ite *f*, chouchou *m*, - oute *f pej* ■ **the teacher's ~** le chouchou du prof **3.** *inf* [term of endearment] : **how are you, ~?** comment ça va, mon chou? ■ **she's a real ~** elle est adorable **4.** *inf* [temper] crise *f* de colère.
◇ *adj* **1.** [hawk, snake etc] apprivoisé ■ **they have a ~ budgerigar/hamster** ils ont une perruche/un hamster chez eux **2.** *inf* [favourite - project, theory] favori ■ **it's my ~ ambition to write a novel** ma grande ambition, c'est d'écrire un roman ■ **his ~ subject** *OR* **topic** son dada ■ **Anne is the teacher's ~ pupil** Anne est la chouchoute du prof ■ **~ hate** *OR* **peeve** *US* bête *f* noire.
◇ *vt* **1.** [pamper] chouchouter **2.** [stroke - animal] câliner, caresser **3.** *inf* [caress sexually] caresser.
◇ *vi inf* [sexually] se caresser.

petal ['petl] *n* pétale *m*.

petard [pə'tɑːd] *n* pétard *m*.

Pete [piːt] *pr n* : **for ~'s sake!** *inf* mais nom d'un chien *OR* bon sang!

peter ['piːtər] *n* **1.** *inf* [safe] coffiot△ *m* **2.** △ *US* [penis] quéquette *f*.
◆ **peter out** *vi insep* **1.** [run out - supplies, money] s'épuiser ■ [come to end - path] se perdre ; [- stream] tarir ; [- line] s'estomper, s'évanouir ; [- conversation] tarir **2.** [die away - voice] s'éteindre ; [- fire] s'éteindre, mourir **3.** [come to nothing - plan] tomber à l'eau.

Peter ['piːtər] *pr n* Pierre ■ **~ the Great** Pierre le Grand ■ **Saint ~** saint Pierre ➊ **'~ and the Wolf'** *Prokofiev* 'Pierre et le loup'.

pethidine ['peθɪdiːn] *n* péthidine *f*.

petit bourgeois ['petɪ-] (*pl* **petits bourgeois** ['petɪ-]) = **petty bourgeois**.

petite [pə'tiːt] ◇ *adj* menue.
◇ *n* [clothing size] petites tailles *fpl (pour adultes)*.

petit four ['petɪ'fɔː] (*pl* **petits fours** ['petɪ'fɔːz]) *n* petit-four.

petition [pɪ'tɪʃn] ◇ *n* **1.** [with signatures] pétition *f* ■ **they got up a ~ against the council's plans** ils ont préparé une pétition pour protester contre les projets de la municipalité **2.** [request] requête *f* ■ **the Petition of Right** *UK* HIST la Pétition de droit **3.** LAW requête *f*, pétition *f* ■ **~ for divorce** demande *f* de divorce ■ **~ in bankruptcy** demande *f* de mise en liquidation judiciaire **4.** RELIG prière *f*.
◇ *vt* **1.** [lobby] adresser une pétition à ■ **we are going to ~ to have the wall demolished** nous allons demander que le mur soit démoli **2.** [beg] : **they ~ed the king to save them** ils ont imploré le roi de les sauver **3.** LAW : **to ~ the court** déposer une requête auprès du tribunal.
◇ *vi* **1.** [with signatures] faire signer une pétition ■ **they ~ed for his release** ils ont fait circuler une pétition demandant sa libération **2.** [take measures] : **why don't you ~ against the plan?** pourquoi n'engagez-vous pas un recours contre le projet? **3.** LAW : **to ~ for divorce** faire une demande de divorce.

petitioner [pɪ'tɪʃənər] *n* **1.** LAW pétitionnaire *mf* ■ [in divorce] demandeur *m*, - eresse *f* de divorce **2.** [on petition] signataire *mf*.

pet name *n* surnom *m*.

Petrarch ['petrɑːk] *pr n* Pétrarque.

petrel ['petrəl] *n* pétrel *m*.

Petri dish ['piːtrɪ-] *n* boîte *f* de Petri.

petrified ['petrɪfaɪd] *adj* **1.** [fossilized] pétrifié ■ **~ forest** forêt *f* pétrifiée **2.** [terrified] paralysé *OR* pétrifié de peur ■ [weaker use] terrifié.

petrify ['petrɪfaɪ] (*pret & pp* **petrified**) *vt* **1.** [fossilize] pétrifier **2.** [terrify] paralyser *OR* pétrifier de peur ■ [weaker use] terrifier ■ **the noise petrified me** le bruit me glaça le sang.

petrochemical [,petrəʊ'kemɪkl] *adj* pétrochimique.

petrodollar ['petrəʊ,dɒlər] *n* pétrodollar *m*.

petrol ['petrəl] *UK* ◇ *n* essence *f* ■ **we ran out of ~** nous sommes tombés en panne d'essence.
◇ *comp* [fumes, rationing, shortage] d'essence.

petrolatum [,petrə'leɪtəm] *n US* vaseline *f*.

petrol bomb *n* cocktail *m* Molotov.
◆ **petrol-bomb** *vt* attaquer au cocktail Molotov, lancer un cocktail Molotov contre *OR* sur.

petrol can *n UK* bidon *m* d'essence.

petrol cap *n UK* bouchon *m* d'essence.

petrol-driven *adj UK* [engine] à essence.

petrol engine *n UK* moteur *m* à essence.

petroleum [pɪ'trəʊljəm] ◇ *n* pétrole *m*.
◇ *comp* [industry] du pétrole ■ [imports] de pétrole.

petroleum jelly *n UK* vaseline *f*.

petrol gauge *n UK* jauge *f* à essence.

petrol pump *n UK* [at service station] pompe *f* à essence ■ **prices at the ~ have risen** le prix de l'essence à la pompe a augmenté.

petrol station *n UK* station-service *f*.

petrol tank *n UK* AUT réservoir *m* (d'essence).

petrol tanker *n UK* **1.** [lorry] camion-citerne *m* **2.** [ship] pétrolier *m*, tanker *m*.

Petrushka [pə'truːʃkə] *pr n* Petrouchka.

pet shop *n* magasin *m* d'animaux domestiques.

petticoat ['petɪkəʊt] ◇ *n* [waist slip] jupon *m* ■ [full-length slip] combinaison *f*.
◇ *comp pej* [government, politics] de femmes.

pettifogger ['petɪfɒgər] *n UK* **1.** [quibbler] chicaneur *m*, - euse *f*, ergoteur *m*, - euse *f* **2.** [lawyer] avocat *m* marron.

pettifogging ['petɪfɒgɪŋ] *adj* **1.** [petty - person] chicanier ; [- details] insignifiant **2.** [dishonest] louche.

pettiness ['petɪnɪs] *n* **1.** [triviality - of details] insignifiance *f* ; [- of rules] caractère *m* pointilleux **2.** [small-mindedness] mesquinerie *f*, étroitesse *f* d'esprit.

petting ['petɪŋ] *n (U) inf* [sexual] caresses *fpl* ■ **there was a lot of heavy ~ going on** ça se pelotait dans tous les coins.

petting zoo *n US partie d'un zoo où les enfants peuvent s'approcher des animaux.*

pettish ['petɪʃ] *adj UK* [person] grincheux, acariâtre ■ [mood] maussade ■ [remark] hargneux, désagréable.

petty ['petɪ] (*comp* **pettier**, *superl* **pettiest**) *adj* **1.** *pej* [trivial - detail] insignifiant, mineur ; [- difficulty] mineur ; [- question] tatillon ; [- regulation] tracassier ; [- ambitions] médiocre **2.** *pej* [mean - behaviour, mind, spite] mesquin **3.** [minor, small-scale] petit ■ **~ acts of vandalism** de petits actes de vandalisme ■ **a ~ offence** une infraction mineure ■ **a ~ thief** un petit délinquant ■ **~ expenses** menues dépenses *fpl*.

petty bourgeois ◇ *adj* petit-bourgeois.
◇ *n* petit-bourgeois *m*, petite-bourgeoise *f*.

petty bourgeoisie *n* petite-bourgeoisie *f*.

petty cash *n* petite monnaie *f* ■ **I took the money out of ~** j'ai pris l'argent dans la caisse des dépenses courantes.

petty larceny *n* larcin *m*.

petty-minded *adj* borné, mesquin.

petty-mindedness *n* mesquinerie *f*.

petty officer *n UK* ≃ second maître *m*.

petulance ['petjʊləns] *n* irritabilité *f*.

petulant ['petjʊlənt] *adj* [bad-tempered - person] irritable, acariâtre ; [- remark] acerbe, désagréable ; [- behaviour] désagréable, agressif ■ [sulky] maussade ■ **in a ~ mood** de mauvaise humeur.

petulantly ['petjʊləntlɪ] *adv* [act, speak - irritably] avec irritation ; [- sulkily] avec mauvaise humeur ■ **"no!", she said ~** "non!", dit-elle avec mauvaise humeur.

petunia [pə'tju:njə] *n* pétunia *m*.

pew [pju:] *n* banc *m* d'église.

pewter ['pju:tər] ◇ *n* **1.** [metal] étain *m* **2.** *(U)* [ware] étains *mpl* **3.** [colour] gris étain *m*.
◇ *comp* [tableware, tankard] en étain.

peyote [peɪ'əʊtɪ] *n* peyotl *m*.

PG *n* CIN (*abbrev of* **parental guidance**) *désigne un film dont certaines scènes peuvent choquer*, ≃ pour adultes et adolescents.

p & h *written abbr of* **postage and handling**.

pH *n* pH *m*.

Phaedra ['fi:drə] *pr n* Phèdre.

Phaëthon ['feɪəθən] *pr n* Phaéton.

phagocyte ['fægəsaɪt] *n* phagocyte *m*.

phalange ['fælændʒ] *n* ANAT phalange *f*.

Phalangist [fæ'lændʒɪst] ◇ *adj* phalangiste.
◇ *n* phalangiste *mf*.

phalanx ['fælæŋks] (*pl* **phalanxes** *OR pl* **phalanges** [-lændʒi:z]) *n* **1.** ANTIQ & MIL phalange *f* **2.** ANAT phalange *f* **3.** POL phalange *f*.

phallic ['fælɪk] *adj* phallique.

phallus ['fæləs] (*pl* **phalluses** *OR pl* **phalli** [-laɪ]) *n* phallus *m*.

phantasm ['fæntæzm] *n* fantasme *m*.

phantasmagoria [,fæntæzmə'gɔ:rɪə] *n* fantasmagorie *f*.

phantasmagoric(al) [,fæntæzmə'gɒrɪk(l)] *adj* fantasmagorique.

phantasmal [fæn'tæzml] *adj* fantomatique.

phantasy ['fæntəsɪ] = **fantasy**.

phantom ['fæntəm] ◇ *n* **1.** [ghost] fantôme *m*, spectre *m* **2.** [threat, source of dread] spectre *m* **3.** *lit* [illusion] illusion *f*.
◇ *adj* **1.** [gen] imaginaire, fantôme **2.** MED : **~ limb** membre *m* fantôme ■ **~ pregnancy** *UK* grossesse *f* nerveuse.

pharaoh ['feərəʊ] *n* pharaon *m*.

Pharisee ['færɪsi:] *n* Pharisien *m*, - enne *f*.

pharmaceutical [,fɑ:mə'sju:tɪkl] ◇ *adj* pharmaceutique.
◇ *n* médicament *m*.

pharmacist ['fɑ:məsɪst] *n* pharmacien *m*, - enne *f*.

pharmacological [,fɑ:məkə'lɒdʒɪkl] *adj* pharmacologique.

pharmacologist [,fɑ:mə'kɒlədʒɪst] *n* pharmacologiste *mf*, pharmacologue *mf*.

pharmacology [,fɑ:mə'kɒlədʒɪ] ◇ *n* pharmacologie *f*.
◇ *comp* [laboratory, studies] de pharmacologie, pharmacologique.

pharmacopoeia *UK*, **pharmacopeia** *US* [,fɑ:məkə'pi:ə] *n* pharmacopée *f*.

pharmacy ['fɑ:məsɪ] (*pl* **pharmacies**) *n* **1.** [science] pharmacie *f* **2.** [dispensary, shop] pharmacie *f*.

pharming ['fɑ:mɪŋ] *n culture ou élevage de plantes ou animaux génétiquement modifiés pour la fabrication de produits pharmaceutiques.*

pharyngal [fə'rɪŋgl], **pharyngeal** [,færɪn'dʒi:əl] *adj* **1.** MED [infection] pharyngé ■ [organ] pharyngien **2.** LING pharyngal.

pharyngitis [,færɪn'dʒaɪtɪs] *n (U)* pharyngite *f*.

pharynx ['færɪnks] (*pl* **pharynxes** *OR pl* **pharynges** [fæ'rɪndʒi:z]) *n* pharynx *m*.

phase [feɪz] ◇ *n* **1.** [period - gen] phase *f*, période *f* ; [- of illness] phase *f*, stade *m* ; [- of career, project] étape *f* ; [- of civilization] période *f* ■ **their daughter's going through a difficult ~** leur fille traverse une période difficile ■ **don't worry, it's just a ~ she's going through** ne vous inquiétez pas, ça lui passera **2.** ASTRON [of moon] phase *f* **3.** CHEM, ELEC & PHYS phase *f* ■ **in the solid ~** en phase *OR* à l'état solide ■ **to be in ~** *liter & fig* être en phase ■ **to be out of ~** *liter & fig* être déphasé ■ **the government is out of ~ with the mood of the country** le gouvernement est en décalage complet avec les sentiments de la population.
◇ *vt* **1.** [synchronize] synchroniser, faire coïncider **2.** *US* [prearrange - delivery, development] planifier, programmer **3.** ELEC & TECH mettre en phase.

◆ **phase in** *vt sep* introduire progressivement *OR* par étapes ■ **the increases will be ~d in over five years** les augmentations seront échelonnées sur cinq ans.

◆ **phase out** *vt sep* [stop using - machinery, weapon] cesser progressivement d'utiliser ■ [stop producing - car, model] abandonner progressivement la production de ■ [do away with - jobs, tax] supprimer progressivement *OR* par étapes ; [- grant] retirer progressivement.

phased [feɪzd] *adj* [withdrawal, development] progressif, par étapes.

phase-out *n* suppression *f* progressive.

phatic ['fætɪk] *adj* phatique.

PhD (*abbrev of* **Doctor of Philosophy**) *n (titulaire d'un) doctorat de 3e cycle* ■ **~ students** étudiants *mpl* inscrits en doctorat ■ **her ~ thesis** sa thèse de doctorat.

pheasant ['feznt] (*pl inv OR pl* **pheasants**) *n* faisan *m* ■ [hen] (poule *f*) faisane *f*.

phenix ['fi:nɪks] *US* = **phoenix**.

phenobarbitone [,fi:nəʊ'bɑ:bɪtəʊn], **phenobarbital** [,fi:nəʊ'bɑ:bɪtl] *n* phénobarbital *m*.

phenol ['fi:nɒl] *n* phénol *m*.

phenomena [fɪ'nɒmɪnə] *pl* ▷ **phenomenon**.

phenomenal [fɪ'nɒmɪnl] *adj* phénoménal ■ **a ~ success** un immense succès.

phenomenally [fɪ'nɒmɪnəlɪ] *adv* phénoménalement.

phenomenological [fɪ,nɒmɪnə'lɒdʒɪkl] *adj* phénoménologique.

phenomenology [fɪ,nɒmɪ'nɒlədʒɪ] *n* phénoménologie *f*.

phenomenon [fɪ'nɒmɪnən] (*pl* **phenomena** [fɪ'nɒmɪnə]) *n* phénomène *m*.

pheromone ['ferəməʊn] *n* phéromone *f*, phérormone *f*.

phew [fju:] *interj* [in relief] ouf ■ [from heat] pff ■ [in disgust] berk, beurk.

phial ['faɪəl] *n* fiole *f*.

Phi Beta Kappa ['faɪ,beɪtə'kæpə] *pr n aux États-Unis, association universitaire à laquelle ne peuvent appartenir que les étudiants émérites.*

Philadelphia [,fɪlə'delfjə] *pr n* Philadelphie ■ **in ~** à Philadelphie.

philander [fɪ'lændəʳ] *vi pej* courir le jupon.

philanderer [fɪ'lændərəʳ] *n pej* coureur *m* (de jupons).

philandering [fɪ'lændərɪŋ] *n* donjuanisme *m*.

philanthropic [ˌfɪlən'θrɒpɪk] *adj* philanthropique.

philanthropist [fɪ'lænθrəpɪst] *n* philanthrope *mf*.

philanthropy [fɪ'lænθrəpɪ] *n* philanthropie *f*.

philatelist [fɪ'lætəlɪst] *n* philatéliste *mf*.

philately [fɪ'lætəlɪ] *n* philatélie *f*.

philharmonic [ˌfɪlɑː'mɒnɪk] ◇ *adj* philharmonique.
◇ *n* orchestre *m* philharmonique.

Philip ['fɪlɪp] *pr n* Philippe ■ ~ **the Fair** Philippe le Bel.

Philippians [fɪ'lɪpɪənz] *pr npl* BIBLE : **the** ~ les Philippiens.

philippine ['fɪlɪpiːn] *adj* philippin.

Philippines ['fɪlɪpiːn z] *pr npl* : **the** ~ les Philippines *fpl* ■ **in the** ~ aux Philippines.

Philistine [*UK* 'fɪlɪstaɪn, *US* 'fɪlɪstiːn] ◇ *n* **1.** HIST Philistin *m* **2.** *fig* philistin *m lit*, béotien *m*, - enne *f*.
◇ *adj* philistin.

Philistinism ['fɪlɪstɪnɪzm] *n* philistinisme *m*.

Phillips® ['fɪlɪps] *comp* : ~ **screw/screw-driver** vis *f* /tournevis *m* cruciforme.

philodendron [ˌfɪlə'dendrən] (*pl* **philodendrons** *OR pl* **philodendra** [-drə]) *n* philodendron *m*.

philological [ˌfɪlə'lɒdʒɪkl] *adj* philologique.

philologist [fɪ'lɒlədʒɪst] *n* philologue *mf*.

philology [fɪ'lɒlədʒɪ] *n* philologie *f*.

philosopher [fɪ'lɒsəfəʳ] *n* philosophe *mf* ■ **the ~'s stone** la pierre philosophale.

philosophic(al) [ˌfɪlə'sɒfɪk(l)] *adj* **1.** PHILOS philosophique **2.** [calm, resigned] philosophe ■ **I feel quite ~ about the situation** j'envisage la situation avec philosophie.

philosophically [ˌfɪlə'sɒfɪklɪ] *adv* **1.** PHILOS philosophiquement **2.** [calmly] philosophiquement, avec philosophie.

philosophize, ise [fɪ'lɒsəfaɪz] *vi* philosopher ■ **to ~ about sthg** philosopher sur qqch.

philosophy [fɪ'lɒsəfɪ] (*pl* **philosophies**) *n* philosophie *f* ■ **she's a ~ student** elle est étudiante en philosophie ■ *fig* **we share the same ~ of life** nous avons la même conception de la vie.

phlebitis [flɪ'baɪtɪs] *n (U)* phlébite *f*.

phlegm [flem] *n* **1.** MED [in respiratory passages] glaire *f* **2.** *fig* [composure] flegme *m* **3.** *arch* [bodily humour] flegme *m*.

phlegmatic [fleg'mætɪk] *adj* flegmatique.

phlegmatically [fleg'mætɪklɪ] *adv* avec flegme, flegmatiquement.

phobia ['fəʊbjə] *n* phobie *f* ■ **he has a ~ of spiders** il a la phobie des araignées.

phobic ['fəʊbɪk] ◇ *adj* phobique.
◇ *n* phobique *mf*.

Phoenicia [fɪ'nɪʃɪə] *pr n* Phénicie *f*.

Phoenician [fɪ'nɪʃɪən] ◇ *n* **1.** [person] Phénicien *m*, - enne *f* **2.** LING phénicien *m*.
◇ *adj* phénicien.

phoenix ['fiːnɪks] *n* phénix *m*.

phonate [fəʊ'neɪt] *vi* produire des sons.

phone [fəʊn] ◇ *n* **1.** [telephone] téléphone *m* ■ **I answered the ~** j'ai répondu au téléphone ■ **just a minute, I'm on the ~** un instant, je suis au téléphone ■ **we're not on the ~ yet** nous n'avons pas encore le téléphone ■ **you're wanted on the ~** on vous demande au téléphone ■ **she told me the news by ~** elle m'a appris la nouvelle au téléphone ■ **I don't wish to discuss it over the ~** je préfère ne pas en parler au téléphone **2.** LING phone *m*.
◇ *comp* [bill] de téléphone ■ [line, message] téléphonique.
◇ *vi UK* téléphoner ■ **to ~ for a plumber/a taxi** appeler un plombier/un taxi *(par téléphone)*.
◇ *vt UK* téléphoner à ■ **can you ~ me the answer?** pouvez-vous me donner la réponse par téléphone?
◆ **phone up** ◇ *vi insep* téléphoner.
◇ *vt sep* téléphoner à.

phone book *n* annuaire *m* (téléphonique).

phone booth *n* cabine *f* téléphonique.

phone box *n UK* cabine *f* téléphonique.

phone call *n* coup *m* de téléphone, appel *m* (téléphonique).

phonecard ['fəʊnkɑːd] *n* Télécarte® *f*.

phone-in *n* RADIO & TV : ~ **(programme)** *émission au cours de laquelle les auditeurs ou les téléspectateurs peuvent intervenir par téléphone.*

phoneme ['fəʊniːm] *n* phonème *m*.

phonemic [fə'niːmɪk] *adj* phonémique, phonématique.

phonemics [fə'niːmɪks] *n (U)* phonémique *f*, phonématique *f*.

phone number *n* numéro *m* de téléphone.

phone-tapping [-ˌtæpɪŋ] *n (U)* écoute *f* téléphonique, écoutes *fpl* téléphoniques.

phonetic [fə'netɪk] *adj* phonétique.

phonetically [fə'netɪklɪ] *adv* phonétiquement.

phonetic alphabet *n* alphabet *m* phonétique.

phonetician [ˌfəʊnɪ'tɪʃn] *n* phonéticien *m*, - enne *f*.

phonetics [fə'netɪks] *n (U)* phonétique *f*.

phoney ['fəʊnɪ] *inf* ◇ *adj* (*comp* **phonier**, *superl* **phoniest**) **1.** [false - banknote, jewel, name] faux, fausse *f* ; [- title, company, accent] bidon ; [- tears] de crocodile ; [- laughter] qui sonne faux ■ **his story sounds ~** son histoire a tout l'air d'être (du) bidon ■ **the ~ war** la drôle de guerre **2.** [spurious - person] bidon.
◇ *n* (*pl* **phonies**) **1.** [impostor] imposteur *m* ■ [charlatan] charlatan *m* **2.** [pretentious person] frimeur *m*, - euse *f*, m'as-tu-vu *mf inv*.

phonic ['fəʊnɪk] *adj* phonique.

phonograph ['fəʊnəgrɑːf] *n* [early gramophone] phonographe *m*.

phonological [ˌfəʊnə'lɒdʒɪkl] *adj* phonologique.

phonologist [fəʊ'nɒlədʒɪst] *n* phonologue *mf*.

phonology [fəʊ'nɒlədʒɪ] (*pl* **phonologies**) *n* phonologie *f*.

phony ['fəʊnɪ] = **phoney**.

phooey ['fuːɪ] *interj inf* [as expletive - expressing irritation] zut, flûte ; [- expressing disbelief] mon œil.

phosphate ['fɒsfeɪt] *n* AGRIC & CHEM phosphate *m*.

phosphide ['fɒsfaɪd] *n* phosphure *m*.

phosphor ['fɒsfəʳ] *n* luminophore *m*, phosphore *m (substance phosphorescente)*.

phosphoresce [ˌfɒsfə'res] *vi* être phosphorescent.

phosphorescence [ˌfɒsfə'resns] *n* phosphorescence *f*.

phosphorescent [ˌfɒsfə'resnt] *adj* phosphorescent.

phosphoric [fɒs'fɒrɪk] *adj* phosphorique ■ ~ **acid** acide *m* orthophosphorique.

phosphorism ['fɒsfərɪzm] *n* phosphorisme *m*.

phosphorous ['fɒsfərəs] *adj* phosphorique.

phosphorus ['fɒsfərəs] *n* phosphore *m*.

photo ['fəʊtəʊ] (*pl* **photos**) (*abbrev of* **photograph**) *n* photo *f*.

photoactive [ˌfəʊtəʊ'æktɪv] *adj* [organism] sensible à la lumière.

photo album *n* album *m* de photos.

photobooth ['fəʊtəʊbu:ð] *n* Photomaton®.

photocall ['fəʊtəʊkɔ:l] *n* séance *f* photo *(avec des photographes de presse)*.

photocell ['fəʊtəʊsel] *n* cellule *f* photoélectrique.

photochemical [,fəʊtəʊ'kemɪkl] *adj* photochimique.

photocompose [,fəʊtəʊkəm'pəʊz] *vt* photocomposer.

photocomposition ['fəʊtəʊ,kɒmpə'zɪʃn] *n* photocomposition *f*.

photocopier ['fəʊtəʊ,kɒpɪəʳ] *n* photocopieur *m*, photocopieuse *f*.

photocopy ['fəʊtəʊ,kɒpɪ] (*pl* **photocopies**, *pret & pp* **photocopied**) ◇ *n* photocopie *f*.
◇ *vt* photocopier.

photocopying ['fəʊtəʊ,kɒpɪɪŋ] *n (U)* reprographie *f*, photocopie *f* ▪ **there's some ~ to do** il y a des photocopies à faire.

photodynamics [,fəʊtəʊdaɪ'næmɪks] *n (U)* photodynamique *f*.

photoelectric [,fəʊtəʊɪ'lektrɪk] *adj* photoélectrique ▪ **~ cell** cellule *f* photoélectrique.

photoengraving [,fəʊtəʊɪn'greɪvɪŋ] *n* photogravure *f*.

photo finish *n* **1.** SPORT arrivée *f* groupée ▪ **the race was a ~** il a fallu départager les vainqueurs de la course avec la photo-finish **2.** *fig* partie *f* serrée.

Photofit® ['fəʊtəʊfɪt] *n* : **~ (picture)** photo-robot *f*, portrait-robot *m*.

photogenic [,fəʊtəʊ'dʒenɪk] *adj* photogénique.

photogram ['fəʊtəgræm] *n* photogramme *m*.

photograph ['fəʊtəgrɑ:f] ◇ *n* photographie *f (image)*, photo *f (image)* ▪ **to take a ~** prendre OR faire une photo ▪ **to take a ~ of sb** prendre qqn en photo, photographier qqn ▪ **to have one's ~ taken** se faire photographier ▪ **I'm in this ~** je suis sur cette photo ▪ **she takes a good ~** [is photogenic] elle est photogénique.
◇ *vt* photographier, prendre en photo.
◇ *vi* : **he ~s well** [is photogenic] il est photogénique ▪ **the trees won't ~ well in this light** il n'y a pas assez de lumière pour faire une bonne photo des arbres.

photograph album *n* album *m* de photos.

photographer [fə'tɒgrəfəʳ] *n* photographe *mf* ▪ **I'm not much of a ~** je ne suis pas très doué pour la photographie.

photographic [,fəʊtə'græfɪk] *adj* photographique ▪ **to have a ~ memory** avoir une bonne mémoire visuelle ▪ **~ shop** magasin *m* de photo ▪ **~ society** club *m* d'amateurs de photo ▪ **~ library** photothèque *f*.

photographically [,fəʊtə'græfɪklɪ] *adv* photographiquement.

photography [fə'tɒgrəfɪ] *n* photographie *f (art)*, photo *f (art)*.

photogravure [,fəʊtəʊgrə'vjʊəʳ] *n* photogravure *f*.

photojournalism [,fəʊtəʊ'dʒɜ:nəlɪzm] *n* photojournalisme *m*.

photokinesis [,fəʊtəʊkɪ'ni:sɪs] *n* photocinèse *f*.

photolithography [,fəʊtəʊlɪ'θɒgrəfɪ] *n* photolithographie *f*.

photomap ['fəʊtəʊmæp] (*pret & pp* **photomapped**, *cont* **photomapping**) ◇ *n* photocarte *f*.
◇ *vt* faire une photocarte de.

photomechanical [,fəʊtəʊmɪ'kænɪkl] *adj* photomécanique.

photometer [fəʊ'tɒmɪtəʳ] *n* photomètre *m*.

photometry [fəʊ'tɒmɪtrɪ] *n* photométrie *f*.

photomontage [,fəʊtəʊmɒn'tɑ:ʒ] *n* photomontage *m*.

photon ['fəʊtɒn] *n* photon *m*.

photonovel ['fəʊtə,nɒvl] *n* roman-photo *m*, photo-roman *m*.

photo-offset *n* offset *m*.

photo opportunity *n* séance *f* photoprotocolaire.

photorealism [,fəʊtəʊ'rɪəlɪzm] *n* photoréalisme *m*.

photoreceptor [,fəʊtəʊrɪ'septəʳ] *n* photorécepteur *m*.

photoreconnaissance [,fəʊtəʊrɪ'kɒnɪsns] *n* reconnaissance *f* photographique.

photosensitive [,fəʊtəʊ'sensɪtɪv] *adj* photosensible.

photosensitize, ise [,fəʊtəʊ'sensɪtaɪz] *vt* rendre photosensible.

photoset ['fəʊtəʊset] (*pret & pp* **photoset**, *cont* **photosetting**) *vt* photocomposer.

photostat ['fəʊtəstæt] (*pret & pp* **photostatted**, *cont* **photostatting**) *vt* photocopier.
◆ **Photostat®** *n* photostat *m*, photocopie *f* ▪ **~ copy** photocopie *f*.

photosynthesis [,fəʊtəʊ'sɪnθəsɪs] *n* photosynthèse *f*.

photosynthesize, ise [,fəʊtəʊ'sɪnθəsaɪz] *vt* fabriquer par photosynthèse.

phototransistor [,fəʊtəʊtræn'zɪstəʳ] *n* phototransistor *m*.

phototype ['fəʊtəʊtaɪp] ◇ *n* **1.** [process] phototypie *f* **2.** [print] phototype *m*.
◇ *vt* faire un phototype de.

phototypesetting [,fəʊtəʊ'taɪpsetɪŋ] *n* photocomposition *f*.

phototypography [,fəʊtəʊtaɪ'pɒgrəfɪ] *n* photocomposition *f*.

photovoltaic [,fəʊtəʊvɒl'teɪɪk] *adj* photovoltaïque.

phrasal ['freɪzl] *adj* : **~ conjunction/ preposition** locution *f* conjonctive/prépositive.

phrasal verb *n* verbe *m* à particule.

phrase [freɪz] ◇ *n* **1.** [expression] expression *f*, locution *f* **2.** LING syntagme *m*, groupe *m* **3.** MUS phrase *f*.
◇ *vt* **1.** [letter] rédiger, tourner ▪ [idea] exprimer, tourner ▪ **how shall I ~ it?** comment dire ça? ▪ **he ~ed it very elegantly** il a trouvé une tournure très élégante *(pour le dire)* **2.** MUS phraser.

phrasebook ['freɪzbʊk] *n* guide *m* de conversation.

phrase marker *n* LING indicateur *m* syntagmatique.

phraseology [,freɪzɪ'ɒlədʒɪ] (*pl* **phraseologies**) *n* phraséologie *f*.

phrase structure *n* LING structure *f* syntagmatique ▪ **~ grammar** grammaire *f* syntagmatique.

phrasing ['freɪzɪŋ] *n* **1.** [expressing] choix *m* des mots **2.** MUS phrasé *m*.

phrenetic [frə'netɪk] = **frenetic**.

phrenology [frɪ'nɒlədʒɪ] *n* phrénologie *f*.

phthisis ['θaɪsɪs] *n (U) dated* phtisie *f*.

phut *inf* [fʌt] *inf* ◇ *n* : **the engine made a ~ and stopped** le moteur eut un hoquet puis s'arrêta.
◇ *adv* : **to go ~** *fig* rendre l'âme, lâcher.

phylactery [fɪ'læktərɪ] (*pl* **phylacteries**) *n* RELIG phylactère *m*.

phylogenesis [,faɪləʊ'dʒenɪsɪs] (*pl* **phylogeneses** [-,si:z]) *n* phylogenèse *f*, phylogénie *f*.

phylum ['faɪləm] (*pl* **phyla** [-lə]) *n* phylum *m*.

Phys Ed ['fɪzed] *(abbrev of* **physical education***)* *n* **US** éducation *f* physique.

physiatrics [,fɪzɪ'ætrɪks] *n (U)* **US** kinésithérapie *f*.

physiatrist [,fɪzɪ'ætrɪst] *n* **US** kinésithérapeute *mf*.

physic ['fɪzɪk] *n* **arch** médicament *m*, remède *m*.

physical ['fɪzɪkl] ◇ *adj* **1.** [bodily - fitness, strength, sport] physique ■ **a ~ examination** un examen médical, une visite médicale ■ **I don't get enough ~ exercise** je ne fais pas assez d'exercice (physique) ■ **~ abuse** sévices *mpl* ■ **~ handicap** infirmité *f* **2.** [natural, material - forces, property, presence] physique ; [- manifestation, universe] physique, matériel ■ **it's a ~ impossibility** c'est physiquement *OR* matériellement impossible **3.** CHEM & PHYS physique **4.** GEOG physique ■ **the ~ features of the desert** la topographie du désert.
◇ *n* visite *f* médicale ■ **to go for a ~** passer une visite médicale.

physical education *n* éducation *f* physique.

physical geography *n* géographie *f* physique.

physical jerks *npl* **UK infml to do ~** faire des mouvements de gym.

physically ['fɪzɪklɪ] *adv* physiquement ■ **to be ~ fit** être en bonne forme physique ■ **she is ~ handicapped** elle a un handicap physique.

physical sciences *npl* sciences *fpl* physiques.

physical therapist *n* kinésithérapeute *mf*.

physical therapy *n* kinésithérapie *f* ■ [after accident or illness] rééducation *f*.

physical training = **physical education**.

physician [fɪ'zɪʃn] *n* médecin *mf*.

physicist ['fɪzɪsɪst] *n* physicien *m*, - enne *f*.

physics ['fɪzɪks] *n (U)* physique *f*.

physio ['fɪzɪəʊ] *n* **inf** **1.** *(abbrev of* **physiotherapy***)* kiné *f* **2.** *(abbrev of* **physiotherapist***)* kiné *mf*.

physiognomy [,fɪzɪ'ɒnəmɪ] *(pl* **physiognomies***)* *n* **1.** [facial features] physionomie *f* **2.** GEOG topographie *f*, configuration *f*.

physiological [,fɪzɪə'lɒdʒɪkl] *adj* physiologique.

physiologist [,fɪzɪ'ɒlədʒɪst] *n* physiologiste *mf*.

physiology [,fɪzɪ'ɒlədʒɪ] *n* physiologie *f*.

physiotherapist [,fɪzɪəʊ'θerəpɪst] *n* kinésithérapeute *mf*.

physiotherapy [,fɪzɪəʊ'θerəpɪ] *n* kinésithérapie *f* ■ [after accident or illness] rééducation *f* ■ **to go for** *OR* **to have ~** faire des séances de kinésithérapie.

physique [fɪ'zi:k] *n* constitution *f* physique, physique *m* ■ **to have a fine ~** avoir un beau corps.

phytogenesis [,faɪtəʊ'dʒenɪsɪs] *n* phytogenèse *f*.

pi [paɪ] ◇ *n* MATHS pi *m*.
◇ *adj* **UK inf** & **pej** **1.** [pious] bigot **pej** **2.** [self-satisfied] suffisant.

pianist ['pɪənɪst] *n* pianiste *mf*.

piano[1] [pɪ'ænəʊ] *(pl* **pianos***)* ◇ *n* piano *m*.
◇ *comp* [duet, lesson, stool, teacher, tuner] de piano ■ [music] pour piano ■ [lid, leg] du piano ■ **~ key** touche *f* ■ **the ~ keys** le clavier (du piano) ■ **~ organ** piano *m* mécanique ■ **~ player** pianiste *mf*.

piano[2] ['pjɑ:nəʊ] *adj* & *adv* [softly] piano *(inv)*.

piano accordion [pɪ'ænəʊ-] *n* accordéon *m* (à touches).

pianoforte [pɪ,ænəʊ'fɔ:tɪ] *n* **fml** pianoforte *m*.

Pianola® [,pɪə'nəʊlə] *n* Pianola® *m*.

piano roll [pɪ'ænəʊ-] *n* bande *f* perforée *(pour piano mécanique)*.

piazza [pɪ'ætsə] *n* **1.** [square] place *f*, piazza *f* **2.** **UK** [gallery] galerie *f*.

pic **inf** [pɪk] *(pl* **pics**, *pl* **pix** [pɪks]*)* *n* **inf** [photograph] photo *f* ■ [picture] illustration *f*.

pica ['paɪkə] *n* **1.** TYPO [unit] pica *m* **2.** [on typewriter] pica *m* **3.** MED pica *m*.

picador ['pɪkədɔ:ʳ] *n* picador *m*.

picaninny [,pɪkə'nɪnɪ] *(pl* **picaninnies***)* **inf** = **piccaninny**.

Picardy ['pɪkədɪ] *pr n* Picardie *f* ■ **in ~** en Picardie.

picaresque [,pɪkə'resk] *adj* picaresque.

picayune [,pɪkə'ju:n] **US inf** ◇ *adj* [unimportant] insignifiant ■ [worthless] sans valeur.
◇ *n* pièce *f* de cinq cents ■ **I don't care a ~** je m'en fiche royalement.

piccalilli [,pɪkə'lɪlɪ] *n* piccalilli *m (sauce piquante à base de pickles et de moutarde)*.

piccaninny [,pɪkə'nɪnɪ] *(pl* **piccaninnies***)* *n* **infml** négrillon *m*, - onne *f* **inf** *(attention: le terme "piccaninny", comme son équivalent français, est considéré comme raciste)*.

piccolo ['pɪkələʊ] *(pl* **piccolos***)* *n* piccolo *m*, picolo *m*.

pick [pɪk] ◇ *vt* **1.** [select] choisir ■ **she's been ~ed for the England team** elle a été sélectionnée dans l'équipe d'Angleterre ■ **to ~ a winner** [in racing] choisir un cheval gagnant ■ **you really (know how to) ~ them!** **iron** tu les choisis bien! ➲ **to ~ one's way: they ~ed their way along the narrow ridge** ils avancèrent prudemment le long de la crête étroite **2.** [gather - fruit, flowers] cueillir ; [- mushrooms] ramasser **3.** [remove] enlever ■ **he was ~ing a spot/a scab** il était en train de gratter un bouton/une croûte ■ [remove bits of food, debris etc from] : **they ~ed the bones clean** ils n'ont rien laissé sur les os ■ **to ~ one's nose** se mettre les doigts dans le nez ■ **to ~ one's teeth** se curer les dents ➲ **to ~ sb/sthg to pieces** démolir qqn/qqch **4.** [provoke] : **to ~ a fight** chercher la bagarre ■ **to ~ a quarrel with sb** chercher noise *OR* querelle à qqn **5.** [lock] crocheter **6.** [pluck - guitar string] pincer ; [- guitar] pincer les cordes de.
◇ *vi* : **to ~ and choose** : **I like to be able to ~ and choose** j'aime bien avoir le choix ■ **he always has to ~ and choose** **pej** il faut toujours qu'il fasse le difficile.
◇ *n* **1.** [choice] choix *m* ■ **take your ~** faites votre choix ■ **you can have your ~ of them** vous pouvez choisir celui qui vous plaît ➲ **the ~ of the bunch** **inf** le dessus du panier, le gratin **2.** [tool] pic *m*, pioche *f*.

◆ **pick at** *vt insep* **1.** [pull at - loose end] tirer sur ; [- flake of paint, scab] gratter **2.** [food] manger du bout des dents ■ **he only ~ed at the fish** il a à peine touché au poisson **3.** [criticize pettily] être sur le dos de.

◆ **pick off** *vt insep* **1.** [shoot one by one] abattre (un par un) **2.** [remove - scab, paint] gratter.

◆ **pick on** *vt insep* **1.** [victimize] harceler, s'en prendre à **2.** [single out] choisir.

◆ **pick over, pick through** *vt insep* [fruit, vegetables *etc*] trier.

◆ **pick out** *vt insep* **1.** [choose] choisir **2.** [spot, identify] repérer, reconnaître **3.** [highlight, accentuate] rehausser ■ **the stitching is ~ed out in bright green** un vert vif fait ressortir les coutures **4.** [play - tune] jouer d'une manière hésitante.

◆ **pick up** ◇ *vt insep* **1.** [lift] ramasser ■ **to ~ up the telephone** décrocher le téléphone ■ **to ~ o.s. up** se relever ➲ **they left me to ~ up the bill** **UK** *OR* **the tab** **US** ils m'ont laissé l'addition ■ **to ~ up the pieces** recoller les morceaux **2.** [give lift to] prendre ■ **I never ~ up hitchhikers** je ne prends jamais d'auto-stoppeurs **3.** [collect, fetch] : **my father ~ed me up at the station** mon père est venu me chercher à la gare ■ **helicopters were sent to ~ up the wounded** on a envoyé des hélicoptères pour ramener les blessés ■ **I have to ~ up a parcel at the post office** je dois passer prendre un colis à la poste **4.** [acquire - skill] apprendre ■ **to ~ up bad habits** prendre de mauvaises habitudes ■ [win - reputation] gagner, acquérir ; [- prize] gagner, remporter **5.** [glean - idea, information] glaner **6.** **inf** [buy cheaply] : **to ~ up a bargain** dénicher une bonne affaire ■ **I ~ed it up at the flea market** je l'ai trouvé au marché aux puces **7.** [catch - illness, infection] attraper **8.** **inf** [earn] se faire **9.** **inf** [arrest] pincer **10.** **inf** [start relationship with] draguer **11.** [detect] détecter ■ **the dogs ~ed up the scent again** les

chiens ont retrouvé la piste **12.** RADIO & TV [receive] capter **13.** [notice] relever ▪ **she didn't ~ up on the criticism** elle n'a pas relevé la critique **14.** [criticize] : **nobody ~ed him up on his sexist comments** personne n'a relevé ses remarques sexistes **15.** [resume] reprendre **16.** [return to] revenir sur, reprendre **17.** [gather - speed, momentum] prendre **18.** *inf* [revive] remonter, requinquer.
◇ *vi insep* **1.** [get better - sick person] se rétablir, se sentir mieux **2.** [improve - business, weather] s'arranger, s'améliorer ; [- trade] reprendre ▪ **the market is ~ing up after a slow start** COMM après avoir démarré doucement le marché commence à prendre **3.** [resume] continuer, reprendre.

pickaninny [ˌpɪkəˈnɪnɪ] (*pl* **pickaninnies**) *inf* = **piccaninny**.

pickaxe *UK*, **pickax** *US* [ˈpɪkæks] *n* pic *m*, pioche *f*.

picked [pɪkt] *adj* [products, items] sélectionné ▪ [people] d'élite, trié sur le volet.

picker [ˈpɪkəʳ] *n* [of fruit, cotton etc] cueilleur *m*, - euse *f*, ramasseur *m*, - euse *f* ▪ **grape-~** vendangeur *m*, - euse *f*.

picket [ˈpɪkɪt] ◇ *n* **1.** INDUST [group] piquet *m* de grève ▪ [individual] gréviste *mf*, piquet *m* de grève **2.** [outside embassy, ministry - group] groupe *m* de manifestants ; [- individual] manifestant *m*, - e *f* **3.** MIL piquet *m* **4.** [stake] piquet *m*.
◇ *vt* **1.** INDUST [workplace, embassy] : **the strikers ~ed the factory** les grévistes ont mis en place un piquet de grève devant l'usine ▪ **demonstrators ~ed the consulate at the week-end** des manifestants ont bloqué le consulat ce week-end **2.** [fence] palissader **3.** [tie up] attacher, mettre au piquet.
◇ *vi* INDUST mettre en place un piquet de grève.

picket fence *n* clôture *f* de piquets, palissade *f*.

picketing [ˈpɪkətɪŋ] *n (U)* **1.** [of workplace] piquets *mpl* de grève ▪ **there is heavy ~ at the factory gates** les piquets de grève sont très nombreux aux portes de l'usine **2.** [of ministry, embassy] : **there was ~ outside the embassy today** aujourd'hui, il y a eu des manifestations devant l'ambassade.

picket line *n* piquet *m* de grève ▪ **to be** *OR* **to stand on a ~** faire partie d'un piquet de grève ▪ **to cross a ~** franchir un piquet de grève.

picking [ˈpɪkɪŋ] *n* **1.** [selection - of object] choix *m* ; [- of team] sélection *f* **2.** [of fruit, vegetables] cueillette *f*, ramassage *m* ▪ **cherry-/strawberry-~** cueillette des cerises/des fraises ▪ **mushroom-/potato-~** ramassage des champignons/des pommes de terre **3.** [of lock] crochetage *m*.
◆ **pickings** *npl* **1.** [remains] restes *mpl* **2.** *inf* [spoils] grapillage *m* ▪ **there are rich** *OR* **easy ~s to be had** on pourrait se faire pas mal *inf* d'argent, ça pourrait rapporter gros.

pickle [ˈpɪkl] ◇ *n* **1.** *US* [gherkin] cornichon *m* **2.** [vinegar] vinaigre *m* ▪ [brine] saumure *f* **3.** *inf* [mess, dilemma] pétrin *m* ▪ **to be in a (pretty) ~** être dans le pétrin *OR* dans de beaux draps *inf* **4.** *(U) UK* [food] pickles *mpl (petits oignons, cornichons, morceaux de choux-fleurs etc, macérés dans du vinaigre)*.
◇ *vt* **1.** CULIN [in vinegar] conserver dans le vinaigre ▪ [in brine] conserver dans la saumure **2.** TECH [metal] nettoyer à l'acide *OR* dans un bain d'acide.

pickled [ˈpɪkld] *adj* **1.** CULIN [in vinegar] au vinaigre ▪ [in brine] conservé dans la saumure ▪ **~ herring** rollmops *m inv* **2.** *inf* [drunk] bourré, rond.

picklock [ˈpɪklɒk] *n* **1.** [instrument] crochet *m*, passe-partout *m inv* **2.** [burglar] crocheteur *m* (de serrures).

pick-me-up *n infml* remontant *m*.

pickpocket [ˈpɪkˌpɒkɪt] *n* pickpocket *m*, voleur *m*, - euse *f* à la tire.

pick-up *n* **1.** AUT [vehicle] : **~ (truck)** pick-up *m inv*, camionnette *f* (découverte) **2.** *inf* [casual relationship] partenaire *mf* de rencontre **3.** [act of collecting] : **the truck made several ~s on the way** le camion s'est arrêté plusieurs fois en route pour charger des marchandises ▪ **~ point** [for cargo] aire *f* de chargement ; [for passengers] point *m* de ramassage, lieu *m* de rendez-vous **4.** [on record player] : **~ (arm)** pick-up *m inv dated*, lecteur *m* **5.** *(U) US* AUT [acceleration] reprises *fpl* **6.** [improvement - of business, economy] reprise *f* ▪ **we're hoping for a ~ in sales** nous espérons une reprise des ventes **7.** *inf* [arrest] arrestation *f* **8.** TECH [detector] détecteur *m*, capteur *m* **9.** RADIO & TV [reception] réception *f*.

picky [ˈpɪkɪ] (*comp* **pickier**, *superl* **pickiest**) *adj inf* difficile ▪ **she's really ~ about her food** elle est très difficile pour la nourriture.

picnic [ˈpɪknɪk] (*pret & pp* **picnicked**, *cont* **picnicking**) ◇ *n* **1.** *liter* pique-nique *m* ▪ **to go on** *OR* **for a ~** faire un pique-nique ▪ **we took a ~ lunch** ce midi nous avons pique-niqué **2.** *infml & fig* [easy task] : **it's no ~ showing tourists around London** ce n'est pas une partie de plaisir que de faire visiter Londres aux touristes ▪ **it was no ~ cleaning all the pans** ça n'a pas été du gâteau de nettoyer toutes les casseroles.
◇ *vi* pique-niquer.

picnic basket, picnic hamper *n* panier *m* à pique-nique.

picnicker [ˈpɪknɪkəʳ] *n* pique-niqueur *m*, - euse *f*.

Pict [pɪkt] *n* Picte *mf*.

Pictish [ˈpɪktɪʃ] ◇ *n* langue *f* picte.
◇ *adj* picte.

pictogram [ˈpɪktəgræm], **pictograph** [ˈpɪktəgrɑːf] *n* **1.** LING [symbol] pictogramme *m*, idéogramme *m* **2.** [chart] graphique *m*.

pictorial [pɪkˈtɔːrɪəl] ◇ *adj* **1.** [in pictures] en images ▪ [magazine, newspaper] illustré **2.** [vivid - style] vivant **3.** ART pictural.
◇ *n* illustré *m*.

picture [ˈpɪktʃəʳ] ◇ *n* **1.** [gen] image *f* ▪ [drawing] dessin *m* ▪ [painting] peinture *f*, tableau *m* ▪ [in book] illustration *f* ▪ **to draw/to paint a ~ (of sthg)** dessiner/peindre (qqch) ▪ **to paint a ~ of sb** peindre le portrait de qqn | ▮ [photograph] photo *f*, photographie *f* ▪ **to take a ~** prendre une photo ▪ **to take a ~ of sb, to take sb's ~** prendre une photo de qqn, prendre qqn en photo ▪ **to have one's ~ taken** se faire prendre en photo ▮ [on television] image *f* ➲ **'The Picture of Dorian Gray'** ***Wilde*** 'le Portrait de Dorian Gray' **2.** [film] film *m* ▪ **to go to the ~s** *inf* aller au ciné **3.** [description] tableau *m*, portrait *m* ▪ **the TV series gives a good ~ of life in a mining town** cette série télévisée donne un bon aperçu de la vie dans une ville minière ▪ **the ~ he painted was a depressing one** il a brossé *OR* fait un tableau déprimant de la situation **4.** [idea, image] image *f* ▪ **they have a distorted ~ of the truth** ils se font une fausse idée de la vérité ▪ **he's the ~ of health** il respire la santé, il est resplendissant de santé ▪ **she was the ~ of despair** elle était l'image vivante du désespoir ▪ **he's the ~ of his elder brother** c'est (tout) le portrait de son frère aîné **5.** [situation] situation *f* ▪ **the economic ~ is bleak** la situation économique est inquiétante **6.** *phr* **to be in the ~** *inf* être au courant ▪ **she hates being left out of the ~** elle déteste qu'on la laisse dans l'ignorance ▪ **to put sb in the ~** *inf* mettre qqn au courant ▪ **I get the ~!** je comprends!, j'y suis! ▪ **doesn't she look a ~!** n'est-elle pas adorable *OR* ravissante! ▪ **you're no ~ yourself!** tu n'es pas une beauté non plus! ▪ **her face was a real ~ when she heard the news!** il fallait voir sa tête quand elle a appris la nouvelle! ▪ **the big ~** [overview] une vue d'ensemble.
◇ *vt* **1.** [imagine] s'imaginer, se représenter ▪ **I can't quite ~ him as a teacher** j'ai du mal à me l'imaginer comme enseignant ▪ **just ~ the scene** imaginez un peu la scène **2.** [describe] dépeindre, représenter **3.** [paint, draw etc] représenter ▪ **the artist ~d her on horseback** l'artiste l'a représentée à cheval ▪ **he was ~d with her on the front page of all the papers** une photo où il était en sa compagnie s'étalait à la une de tous les journaux.

picture book *n* livre *m* d'images.

picture card *n* [in card games] figure *f*.

picture frame *n* cadre *m* (pour tableaux).

picture hat *n* capeline *f*.

picture house *n UK dated* cinéma *m*.

picture library *n* banque *f* d'images.

picture palace = **picture house**.

picture-perfect *adj* parfait.

picture postcard *n* ***dated*** carte *f* postale (illustrée).
◆ **picture-postcard** *adj* [view] qui ressemble à une *OR* qui fait carte postale.

picture rail *n* cimaise *f*.

picture research *n* documentation *f* iconographique.

picturesque [ˌpɪktʃəˈresk] *adj* pittoresque.

picture window *n* fenêtre *f OR* baie *f* panoramique.

picture writing *n* écriture *f* idéographique.

piddle [ˈpɪdl] ***inf*** ◇ *vi* faire pipi ***inf.***
◇ *n* **: to have a ~** faire pipi.

piddling [ˈpɪdlɪŋ] *adj* ***inf*** [details] insignifiant ■ [job, pay] minable.

pidgin [ˈpɪdʒɪn] *n* LING pidgin *m*.

pidgin English *n* **1.** LING pidgin *m*, pidgin english *m* **2.** ***pej*** **to speak ~** parler de façon incorrecte.

pie [paɪ] *n* **1.** CULIN [with fruit] tarte *f* ■ [with meat, fish etc] tourte *f* ■ **chicken ~** tourte au poulet ▶ **it's just ~ in the sky** ***inf*** ce sont des paroles *OR* promesses en l'air ■ **I want my piece of the ~** je veux ma part du gâteau **2.** TYPO pâte *f*.

piebald [ˈpaɪbɔːld] ◇ *adj* pie *(inv)*.
◇ *n* cheval *m* pie.

piece [piːs] *n* **1.** [bit - of chocolate, paper, wood] morceau *m*, bout *m* ; [- of land] parcelle *f*, lopin *m* ■ [with uncountable nouns] **: a ~ of bread** un morceau de pain ■ **a ~ of advice** un conseil ■ **~s of advice/information/ news** des conseils/renseignements/ nouvelles ■ **that was a real ~ of luck** cela a vraiment été un coup de chance ■ **it's a superb ~ of craftsmanship** *OR* **workmanship** c'est du très beau travail ■ **to be in ~s** [in parts] être en pièces détachées ; [broken] être en pièces *OR* en morceaux ■ **to be in one ~** [undamaged] être intact ; [uninjured] être indemne ; [safe] être sain et sauf ■ **to be all of a ~** [in one piece] être tout d'une pièce *OR* d'un seul tenant ; [consistent] être cohérent ; [alike] se ressembler ■ **his actions are of a ~ with his opinions** ses actes sont conformes à ses opinions ■ **to break sthg into ~s** mettre qqch en morceaux *OR* en pièces ■ **to pull sthg to ~s** ***liter*** [doll, garment, book] mettre qqch en morceaux ; [flower] effeuiller qqch ; ***fig*** [argument, suggestion, idea] démolir qqch ■ **to pull sb to ~** ***fig*** descendre qqn en flammes ■ **to come to ~s** [into separate parts] se démonter ; [break] se briser ■ **to fall to ~s** partir en morceaux ■ **to go (all) to ~s** ***inf*** [person] s'effondrer, craquer ***inf*** ; [team] se désintégrer ; [market] s'effondrer ■ **to take sthg to ~s** démonter qqch ▶ **it's a ~ of cake** ***inf*** c'est du gâteau ***inf*** ■ **he's a nasty ~ of work** ***inf UK*** c'est un sale type ***inf*** ■ **I gave him a ~ of my mind** ***inf*** [spoke frankly] je lui ai dit son fait *OR* ce que j'avais sur le cœur ; [spoke harshly] je lui ai passé un savon ■ **to say** *OR* **to speak one's ~** dire ce qu'on a sur le cœur **2.** [item] pièce *f* ■ **a ~ of furniture** un meuble ■ **to sell sthg by the ~** vendre qqch à la pièce *OR* au détail ‖ [amount of work] **: to be paid by the ~** être payé à la pièce *OR* à la tâche **3.** [part - of mechanism, set] pièce *f* ; [- of jigsaw] pièce *f*, morceau *m* ■ **to put sthg together ~ by ~** assembler qqch pièce par pièce *OR* morceau par morceau ■ **an 18-~ dinner service** un service de table de 18 pièces ■ **an 18-~ band** un orchestre de 18 musiciens **4.** GAMES [in chess] pièce *f* ■ [in draughts, checkers] pion *m* **5.** [performance] morceau *m* ■ [musical composition] morceau *m*, pièce *f* ■ [sculpture] pièce *f* (de sculpture) ■ **a piano ~** un morceau pour piano **6.** [newspaper article] article *m* **7.** [coin] pièce *f* ■ **a 50p ~** une pièce de 50 pence **8.** ***inf*** [firearm, cannon] pièce *f* **9.** △ [girl] **: she's a nice** *OR* **tasty ~** c'est un beau brin de fille **10.** ***US*** [time] moment *m* ■ [distance] bout *m* de chemin ■ **he walked with me a ~** il a fait un bout de chemin avec moi.
◆ **piece together** *vt insep* **1.** [from parts - broken object] recoller ; [- jigsaw] assembler ■ **the collage was ~d together from scraps of material** le collage était fait *OR* constitué de petits bouts de tissu **2.** [story, facts] reconstituer.

pièce de résistance [ˌpjesdərezɪsˈtɑ̃ːs] (*pl* **pièces de résistance** [ˌpjesdərezɪsˈtɑ̃ːs]) *n* pièce *f* de résistance.

piecemeal [ˈpiːsmiːl] ◇ *adv* [little by little] peu à peu, petit à petit.
◇ *adj* [fragmentary] fragmentaire, parcellaire ■ **the town was rebuilt ~ after the war** la ville a été reconstruite par étapes après la guerre.

piece rate *n* paiement *m* à la pièce ■ **to be on ~** être payé aux pièces.

piecework [ˈpiːswɜːk] *n* travail *m* à la pièce ■ **to be on ~** travailler à la pièce.

pieceworker [ˈpiːswɜːkəʳ] *n* travailleur *m*, - euse *f* à la pièce.

pie chart *n* graphique *m* circulaire, camembert *m*.

piecrust [ˈpaɪkrʌst] *n* couche *f* de pâte *(pour recouvrir une tourte)*.

pied [paɪd] *adj* [gen] bariolé, bigarré ■ [animal] pie *(inv)*.

pied-à-terre [ˌpjeɪdæˈteəʳ] (*pl* **pieds-à-terre** [ˌpjeɪdæˈteəʳ]) *n* pied-à-terre *m inv*.

Piedmont [ˈpiːdmənt] *pr n* Piémont *m* ■ **in ~** dans le Piémont.

Pied Piper (of Hamelin) [-ˈhæmlɪn] *pr n* **: the ~** le joueur de flûte de Hamelin.

pied wagtail *n* bergeronnette *f* grise de Yarrell.

pie-eyed *adj* ***infml*** bourré ***inf.***

pie plate *n* ***US*** plat *m* allant au four.

pier [pɪəʳ] *n* **1.** ***UK*** [at seaside] jetée *f* **2.** [jetty] jetée *f* ■ [landing stage] embarcadère *m* ■ [breakwater] digue *f* **3.** [pillar] pilier *m*, colonne *f* ■ [of bridge] pile *f*.

pierce [pɪəs] *vt* **1.** [make hole in] percer, transpercer ■ **the knife ~d her lung** le couteau lui a perforé *OR* transpercé le poumon ■ **she had her ears ~d** elle s'est fait percer les oreilles ■ **his words ~d my heart** ses paroles me fendirent le cœur **2.** [subj: sound, scream] percer ■ [subj: light] percer ■ [subj: cold] **: we were ~d (through) with cold** nous étions transis *OR* morts de froid ■ **the biting wind ~d his clothing** le vent glacial transperçait ses vêtements **3.** [penetrate - defence, barrier] percer.

pierced [pɪəst] *adj* percé ■ **~ earring** boucle *f* d'oreilles pour oreilles percées ■ **to have ~ ears** avoir les oreilles percées.

piercing [ˈpɪəsɪŋ] ◇ *adj* [scream, eyes, look] perçant ■ [question] lancinant ■ [wind] glacial.
◇ *n* [on face, body] piercing *m*.

piercingly [ˈpɪəsɪŋlɪ] *adv* **: the wind is ~ cold** il fait un vent glacial ■ **a ~ loud scream** un cri perçant.

pierhead [ˈpɪəhed] *n* musoir *m*.

pietism [ˈpaɪətɪzm] *n* piétisme *m*.

piety [ˈpaɪətɪ] (*pl* **pieties**) *n* piété *f*.

piezoelectric [ˌpiːzəʊɪˈlektrɪk] *adj* piézo-électrique.

piffle [ˈpɪfl] ***UK inf*** ◇ *n (U)* balivernes *fpl*, niaiseries *fpl*.
◇ *interj* **: (absolute) ~!** des sottises tout ça!
◇ *vi* dire des bêtises.

piffling [ˈpɪflɪŋ] *adj* ***UK inf*** [excuse, amount] insignifiant.

pig [pɪg] (*pret & pp* **pigged**, *cont* **pigging**) ◇ *n* **1.** ZOOL cochon *m*, porc *m* ■ **~s might fly!** quand les poules auront des dents! ■ **you made a real ~'s ear of that** ça, vous avez fait du beau! ■ **to buy a ~ in a poke** acheter chat en poche **2.** ***inf*** [greedy person] goinfre *m* ■ [dirty eater] cochon *m*, - onne *f* ■ **to eat like a ~** manger comme un cochon *OR* un porc ■ **to make a ~ of o.s.** se goinfrer, s'empiffrer ***inf*** **3.** [dirty person] cochon *m*, - onne *f* ■ **to live like ~s** vivre dans une écurie *OR* porcherie **4.** ***inf*** [unpleasant person] ordure *f* ■ **fascist ~!** sale fasciste! ‖ [unpleasant task] **: it's a real ~ of a job** ce travail est un véritable cauchemar **5.** ***inf pej*** [policeman] flic *m*, poulet *m*.
◇ *vt* ***inf*** **1.** [stuff] **: to ~ o.s. : we really pigged ourselves at Christmas** on s'en est mis plein la lampe à Noël **2.** ***phr*** **to ~ it** vivre comme des cochons.
◇ *vi* [sow] mettre bas.
◆ **pig out** *vi insep* ***inf*** se goinfrer, s'empiffrer.

pigeon ['pɪdʒɪn] *n* **1.** ORNITH pigeon *m* ■ **~ fancier** colombophile *mf* ■ **~ loft** pigeonnier *m* **2.** *UK inf* [business] : **it's not my ~** ce n'est pas mon problème **3.** *inf fig* [dupe] pigeon *m*.

pigeon-breasted [-,brestɪd], **pigeon-chested** [-,tʃestɪd] *adj* : **to be ~** avoir la poitrine bombée.

pigeonhole ['pɪdʒɪnhəʊl] <> *n* casier *m* (à courrier) ■ **he tends to put people in ~s** *fig* il a tendance à étiqueter les gens *OR* à mettre des étiquettes aux gens.
<> *vt* **1.** [file] classer **2.** [postpone] différer, remettre (à plus tard) **3.** [classify] étiqueter, cataloguer.

pigeon-toed *adj* : **to be ~** avoir les pieds tournés en dedans.

piggery ['pɪgərɪ] (*pl* **piggeries**) *n* porcherie *f*.

piggish ['pɪgɪʃ] *adj pej* **1.** [dirty] sale, cochon ■ [greedy] glouton **2.** *UK inf* [stubborn] têtu.

piggy ['pɪgɪ] (*pl* **piggies**) *inf* <> *n* **baby** [pig] (petit) cochon *m* ■ [toe] doigt *m* de pied ■ [finger] doigt *m*.
<> *adj* **1.** [greedy] glouton, goinfre **2.** [features] : **~ eyes** de petits yeux porcins.

piggyback ['pɪgɪbæk] <> *adv* : **to ride** *OR* **to be carried ~** se faire porter sur le dos de qqn.
<> *n* : **to give sb a ~** porter qqn sur le dos.
<> *adj* [ride] sur le dos.

piggybank ['pɪgɪbæŋk] *n* tirelire *f (en forme de petit cochon)*.

pig-headed [-'hedɪd] *adj* têtu, obstiné.

pig-headedness [-'hedɪdnɪs] *n* entêtement *m*, obstination *f*.

pig iron *n* fonte *f* brute.

piglet ['pɪglɪt] *n* cochonnet *m*, porcelet *m*.

pigment <> *n* ['pɪgmənt] pigment *m*.
<> *vt* [pɪg'ment] pigmenter.

pigmentation [,pɪgmən'teɪʃn] *n* pigmentation *f*.

Pigmy ['pɪgmɪ] = **Pygmy**.

pigpen ['pɪgpen] *n US liter* & *fig* porcherie *f*.

pigskin ['pɪgskɪn] <> *n* **1.** [leather] peau *f* de porc **2.** *US* [football] ballon *m (de football américain)*.
<> *comp* [bag, watchstrap] en (peau de) porc.

pigsty ['pɪgstaɪ] (*pl* **pigsties**) *n liter* & *fig* porcherie *f*.

pigswill ['pɪgswɪl] *n* pâtée *f* (pour les cochons).

pigtail ['pɪgteɪl] *n* natte *f*.

pike [paɪk] (*pl inv pl* **pikes**) *n* **1.** [fish] brochet *m* **2.** [spear] pique *f* **3.** *UK dial* [hill] pic *m* **4.** = **turnpike**.

pikestaff ['paɪkstɑ:f] *n* hampe *f* (d'une pique).

pilaf(f) ['pɪlæf] = **pilau**.

pilaster [pɪ'læstəʳ] *n* pilastre *m*.

Pilates [pɪ'lɑ:ti:z] *n* [gymnastics] Pilates *f*.

pilau [pɪ'laʊ] *n* pilaf *m* ■ **~ rice** riz *m* pilaf.

pilchard ['pɪltʃəd] *n* pilchard *m*.

pile [paɪl] <> *n* **1.** [stack] pile *f* ■ [heap] tas *m* ■ **to put books/magazines in a ~** empiler des livres/magazines **2.** *(usu pl) inf* [large quantity] tas *inf m OR mpl*, masses *fpl* ■ **to have ~s of money** avoir plein d'argent, être plein aux as ■ **I've got ~s of work to do** j'ai un tas de boulot *inf OR* un boulot dingue **3.** *inf* [fortune] : **to make one's ~** faire fortune **4.** [large building] édifice *m* **5.** [battery] pile *f* **6.** NUCL PHYS pile *f* **7.** CONSTR pieu *m* ■ [for bridge] pile *f* ■ **built on ~s** sur pilotis **8.** *(U)* TEX fibres *fpl*, poil *m* ■ **a deep-~ carpet** une moquette épaisse.
<> *vt* [stack] empiler ■ **she ~d her clothes into the suitcase** elle a mis tous ses habits pêle-mêle dans la valise ■ **we ~d the toys into the car** on a entassé les jouets dans la voiture ■ **the table was ~d high with papers** il y avait une grosse pile de papiers sur la table ■ **he ~d more coal on the fire** il a remis du charbon dans le feu ■ **he ~d spaghetti onto his plate** il a rempli son assiette de spaghettis ■ **she wears her hair ~d high on her head** ses cheveux sont ramenés en chignon au sommet de sa tête.
<> *vi* : **they all ~d off/onto the bus** ils sont tous descendus du bus/montés dans le bus en se bousculant.
◆ **pile in** *vi insep inf* [enter] entrer en se bousculant ■ [join fight] : **once the first punch was thrown we all ~d in** après le premier coup de poing, on s'est tous lancés dans la bagarre.
◆ **pile into** *vt insep inf* **1.** [crash] rentrer dans **2.** [attack - physically] rentrer dans, foncer dans ; [- verbally] rentrer dans, tomber sur.
◆ **pile off** *vi insep inf* [from bus, train] descendre en se bousculant.
◆ **pile on** *inf* <> *vi insep* [onto bus, train] s'entasser, monter en s'entassant.
<> *vt insep* **1.** [increase - suspense] faire durer ; [- pressure] augmenter ■ **to ~ on the agony** forcer la dose, dramatiser (à l'excès) **2.** *phr* **to ~ it on** [exaggerate] exagérer, en rajouter.
◆ **pile out** *vi insep inf* [off bus, train] descendre en se bousculant ■ [from cinema, lecture hall] sortir en se bousculant.
◆ **pile up** <> *vi insep* **1.** [crash - car] s'écraser **2.** [accumulate - work, debts] s'accumuler, s'entasser ; [- washing, clouds] s'amonceler.
<> *vt insep* **1.** [stack] empiler **2.** [accumulate - evidence, examples] accumuler.

pile driver *n* **1.** CONSTR sonnette *f* **2.** *inf* & *fig* [blow] coup *m* violent.

piles [paɪlz] *npl* MED hémorroïdes *fpl*.

pileup ['paɪlʌp] *n* carambolage *inf m* ■ **there was a 50-car ~ in the fog** 50 voitures se sont télescopées *OR* carambolées dans le brouillard.

pilfer ['pɪlfəʳ] *vi* & *vt* voler *(des objets sans valeur)*.

pilgrim ['pɪlgrɪm] *n* pèlerin *m*.

pilgrimage ['pɪlgrɪmɪdʒ] *n* pèlerinage *m* ■ **to make** *OR* **to go on a ~** faire un pèlerinage.

Pilgrim Fathers *pr npl* : **the ~** les (Pères) Pèlerins *mpl*.

THE PILGRIM FATHERS

Puritains persécutés en Angleterre, les Pères pèlerins parvinrent en Amérique en 1620 à bord du *Mayflower* et fondèrent la première colonie du Nouveau Monde, à Plymouth, dans ce qui devait devenir l'État du Massachusetts.

pill [pɪl] *n* **1.** MED pilule *f*, comprimé *m* ■ **to sugar** *OR* **to sweeten the ~ (for sb)** dorer la pilule (à qqn) **2.** [contraceptive pill] : **the ~** la pilule ■ **to go on the ~** commencer à prendre la pilule.
◆ **Pill** = **pill** *(2)*.

pillage ['pɪlɪdʒ] <> *vt* mettre à sac, piller.
<> *vi* se livrer au pillage.
<> *n* pillage *m*.

pillar ['pɪləʳ] *n* **1.** [structural support] pilier *m* ■ [ornamental] colonne *f* ■ **to go from ~ to post** tourner en rond ■ **he was sent from ~ to post** on l'a envoyé à droite et à gauche **2.** [of smoke] colonne *f* ■ [of water] trombe *f* ■ [mainstay] pilier *m* ■ **a ~ of society** un pilier de la société ■ **you've been a real ~ of strength** vous avez été un soutien précieux.

pillar box *n UK* boîte *f* à lettres.

pillar-box red *adj UK* rouge vif.

pillared ['pɪləd] *adj* à piliers, à colonnes.

pillbox ['pɪlbɒks] *n* **1.** MED boîte *f* à pilules **2.** MIL blockhaus *m inv*, casemate *f* **3.** [hat] toque *f*.

pillion ['pɪljən] <> *n* **1.** [on motorbike] : **~ (seat)** siège *m* arrière ■ **~ passenger** *OR* **rider** passager *m*, - ère *f (sur une moto)* **2.** [on horse] selle *f* de derrière.
<> *adv* : **to ride ~** [on motorbike] voyager sur le siège arrière ; [on horse] monter en croupe.

pillock[△] ['pɪlək] *n UK* con[△] *m*, couillon[△] *m*.

pillory ['pɪlərɪ] <> *n* (*pl* **pillories**) pilori *m*.
<> *vt* (*pret & pp* **pilloried**) HIST & *fig* mettre *OR* clouer au pilori.

pillow ['pɪləʊ] ◇ *n* **1.** [on bed] oreiller *m* **2.** TEX [for lace] carreau *m* (de dentellière) **3.** *US* [on chair, sofa] coussin *m*.
◇ *vt* [rest] reposer.

pillowcase ['pɪləʊkeɪs] *n* taie *f* d'oreiller.

pillow fight *n* bataille *f* de polochons.

pillowslip ['pɪləʊslɪp] *UK*, **pillow sham** *US* = **pillowcase**.

pillow talk *n (U)* confidences *fpl* sur l'oreiller.

pilot ['paɪlət] ◇ *n* **1.** AERON & NAUT pilote *mf* ▪ *fig* [guide] guide *m* **2.** TECH [on tool] guidage *m* **3.** = **pilot light**.
◇ *comp* [error] de pilotage.
◇ *vt* **1.** AERON & NAUT piloter **2.** [guide] piloter, guider ▪ **he's ~ed the company through several crises** il a sorti l'entreprise de la crise *OR* de ses difficultés à plusieurs reprises ▪ **she ~ed the bill through parliament** POL elle s'est assurée que le projet de loi serait voté **3.** [test] tester, expérimenter.
◇ *adj* [trial - study, programme, scheme] d'essai, pilote, expérimental.

pilot boat *n* bateau-pilote *m*.

pilot burner = **pilot light**.

pilot film *n* épisode *m* pilote.

pilot fish *n* (poisson *m*) pilote *m*.

pilot lamp *n* veilleuse *f* (électrique).

pilot light *n* veilleuse *f*.

pilot officer *n* AERON sous-lieutenant *m*.

pilot study *n* avant-projet *m*.

pilot whale *n* globicéphale *m*.

pimento [pɪ'mentəʊ] (*pl* **pimentos**) *n* piment *m*.

pimp *inf* [pɪmp] *inf* ◇ *n* maquereau *inf m*, souteneur *m*.
◇ *vi* faire le maquereau.

pimpernel ['pɪmpənel] *n* mouron *m*.

pimple ['pɪmpl] *n* MED bouton *m*.

pimply ['pɪmplɪ] (*comp* **pimplier**, *superl* **pimpliest**) *adj* boutonneux.

pin [pɪn] (*pret & pp* **pinned**, *cont* **pinning**) ◇ *n* **1.** [for sewing] épingle *f* ▪ [safety pin] épingle *f* ▪ [drawing pin] punaise *f* ▪ [hairpin] épingle *f* ● **for two ~s I'd let the whole thing drop** il ne faudrait pas beaucoup me pousser pour que je laisse tout tomber ▪ **he doesn't care two ~s about it** il s'en moque complètement ▪ **you could have heard a ~ drop** on aurait entendu voler une mouche **2.** *US* [brooch] broche *f* ▪ [badge] insigne *m* **3.** *(usu pl) inf* [leg] quille *f*, guibole *f*, guibolle *f* **4.** [peg - in piano, violin] cheville *f* ; [- in hinge, pulley] goujon *m* ; [- in hand grenade] goupille *f* **5.** ELEC [on plug] broche *f* ▪ **two-~ plug** prise *f* à deux broches **6.** MED [for broken bone] broche *f* **7.** [in skittles, bowling] quille *f* **8.** [in wrestling - gen] prise *f* ; [- shoulders on floor] tombé *m* **9.** [in chess] clouage *m* **10.** [in golf] drapeau *m*.
◇ *vt* **1.** [attach - with pin or pins] épingler ; [- with drawing pin or pins] punaiser ▪ **she had a brooch pinned to her jacket** elle portait une broche épinglée à sa veste ▪ *fig* **to ~ one's hopes on sb/sthg** mettre ses espoirs dans qqn/qqch ▪ **to ~ one's faith on sb** placer sa foi en qqn ▪ **they pinned the blame on the shop assistant** ils ont rejeté la responsabilité sur la vendeuse, ils ont mis ça sur le dos de la vendeuse ▪ **they can't ~ anything on me** il ne peuvent rien prouver contre moi **2.** [immobilize] immobiliser, coincer ▪ **they pinned his arms behind his back** ils lui ont coincé les bras derrière le dos ▪ **to ~ sb to the ground/against a wall** clouer qqn au sol/contre un mur **3.** [in chess] clouer.
◆ **pin back** *vt insep hum* **~ back your ears!** *inf* ouvrez vos oreilles!, écoutez bien!
◆ **pin down** *vt insep* **1.** [with pin or pins] fixer avec une épingle *OR* des épingles ▪ [with drawing pin or pins] fixer avec une punaise *OR* des punaises **2.** [immobilize, trap] immobiliser, coincer **3.** [define clearly - difference, meaning] mettre le doigt sur, cerner avec précision **4.** [commit] amener à se décider ▪ **try to ~ her down to a definite schedule** essayez d'obtenir d'elle un planning définitif ▪ **he doesn't want to be pinned down** il veut avoir les coudées franches, il tient à garder sa liberté de manœuvre.
◆ **pin together** *vt insep* épingler, attacher avec une épingle *OR* des épingles.
◆ **pin up** *vt insep* **1.** [poster] punaiser ▪ [results, names] afficher **2.** [hem] épingler ▪ [hair] relever (avec des épingles).

PIN [pɪn] (*abbrev of* **personal identification number**) *n* : **~ (number)** code *m* confidentiel.

pinafore ['pɪnəfɔːr] *UK n* **1.** [apron] tablier *m* **2.** = **pinafore dress**.

pinafore dress *n* robe *f* chasuble.

pinball ['pɪnbɔːl] *n* [game] flipper *m* ▪ **to play ~** jouer au flipper ▪ **~ machine** *OR* **table** flipper.

pincer ['pɪnsər] *n* [of crab] pince *f*.
◆ **pincers** *npl* [tool] tenaille *f*, tenailles *fpl* ▪ **a pair of ~s** une tenaille, des tenailles.

pincer movement *n* MIL manœuvre *f OR* mouvement *m* d'encerclement.

pinch [pɪntʃ] ◇ *vt* **1.** [squeeze] pincer ▪ **he ~ed her cheek** il lui a pincé la joue ▪ **I had to ~ myself to make sure I wasn't dreaming** je me suis pincé pour voir si je ne rêvais pas ▪ **these new shoes ~ my feet** ces chaussures neuves me font mal aux pieds **2.** *UK inf* [steal] piquer *inf*, faucher ▪ **to ~ sthg from sb** piquer qqch à qqn **3.** *inf* [arrest] pincer.
◇ *vi* **1.** [shoes] serrer, faire mal (aux pieds) **2.** [economize] : **to ~ and scrape** économiser sur tout, regarder (de près) à la dépense.
◇ *n* **1.** [squeeze] pincement *m* ▪ **if it comes to the ~** s'il le faut vraiment, en cas de nécessité absolue ▪ **we're beginning to feel the ~** nous commençons à devoir nous priver **2.** [of salt, snuff] pincée *f* ▪ **you must take what he says with a ~ of salt** il ne faut pas prendre ce qu'il dit pour argent comptant.
◆ **at a pinch** *UK*, **in a pinch** *US adv phr* à la rigueur.

pinched [pɪntʃt] *adj* **1.** [features] tiré ▪ **~ with cold** transi de froid **2.** [lacking] : **I'm a bit ~ for money** je suis à court d'argent ▪ **they're ~ for space in their flat** ils sont à l'étroit *OR* ils n'ont pas beaucoup de place dans leur appartement.

pinch-hit *vi US* **1.** SPORT remplacer un joueur **2.** [gen] effectuer un remplacement.

pinchpenny ['pɪntʃpenɪ] (*pl* **pinchpennies**) ◇ *adj* de bout de chandelle.
◇ *n* grippe-sou *m*.

pincushion ['pɪn,kʊʃn] *n* pelote *f* à épingles.

pine [paɪn] ◇ *n* BOT [tree, wood] pin *m* ▪ **the Pine Tree State** le Maine.
◇ *comp* [furniture] en pin.
◇ *vi* **1.** [long] : **to ~ for sthg** désirer qqch ardemment, soupirer après qqch ▪ **he was pining for home** il avait le mal du pays **2.** [grieve] languir ▪ **she was pining for her lover** elle se languissait de son amant.
◆ **pine away** *vi insep* dépérir.

pineal ['pɪnɪəl] *adj* pinéal, de l'épiphyse.

pineal gland *n* épiphyse *f*.

pineapple ['paɪn,æpl] ◇ *n* ananas *m*.
◇ *comp* [juice, chunks] d'ananas ▪ [ice cream] à l'ananas.

pine cone *n* pomme *f* de pin .

pine kernel *n* BOT pignon *m*, pigne *f*.

pine marten *n* martre *f*.

pine needle *n* aiguille *f* de pin.

pine nut = **pine kernel**.

pinewood ['paɪnwʊd] *n* **1.** [group of trees] pinède *f* **2.** [material] bois *m* de pin, pin *m*.

ping [pɪŋ] ◇ *n & onom* ding *m*.
◇ *vi* **1.** faire ding ▪ [timer] sonner **2.** *US* [car engine] cliqueter.

pinger ['pɪŋər] *n* minuteur *m* (de cuisine).

ping-pong, ping pong ['pɪŋpɒŋ] *n* ping-pong *m* ▪ **~ ball** balle *f* de ping-pong.

pinhead ['pɪnhed] n **1.** *liter* tête f d'épingle **2.** *inf* [fool] andouille f, crétin m.

pinhole ['pɪnhəʊl] n trou m d'épingle.

pinhole camera n appareil m à sténopé.

pinion ['pɪnjən] <> n **1.** ORNITH [wing] aileron m **2.** *lit* [wing] aile f **3.** MECH pignon m.
<> vt **1.** [hold fast] retenir de force ■ **we were ~ed against the wall by the crowd** la foule nous coinçait contre le mur **2.** ORNITH [bird] rogner les ailes à.

pink [pɪŋk] <> n **1.** [colour] rose m **2.** *fig* **to be in the ~ (of health)** se porter à merveille ■ **you're looking in the ~!** *inf* tu as l'air en pleine forme! **3.** [flower] œillet m.
<> adj **1.** [in colour] rose ■ **the sky turned ~** le ciel vira au rose OR rosit ■ **to go** OR **to turn ~ with anger/embarrassment** rougir de colère/confusion ➊ **to see ~ elephants** *hum* voir des éléphants roses **2.** *inf* & POL [left-wing] de gauche, gauchisant.
<> vt **1.** [wound - subj: marksman] blesser (légèrement) ; [- subj: bullet] érafler **2.** SEW cranter **3.** [punch holes in] perforer.
<> vi UK [car engine] cliqueter.

pinkeye ['pɪŋkaɪ] n MED conjonctivite f aiguë contagieuse ■ VET ophtalmie f périodique.

pink gin n cocktail m de gin et d'angustura.

pinking ['pɪŋkɪŋ] n UK AUT cliquetis m, cliquettement m.

pinking scissors, pinking shears npl SEW ciseaux mpl à cranter.

pink pound n UK : **the ~** *le pouvoir d'achat des homosexuels.*

pink slip n US *inf* lettre f OR avis m de licenciement ■ **to get a ~** se faire renvoyer.

pinky ['pɪŋkɪ] (pl **pinkies**) n *inf* petit doigt m.

pin money n argent m de poche.

pinnace ['pɪnɪs] n chaloupe f.

pinnacle ['pɪnəkl] n **1.** [mountain peak] pic m, cime f ■ [rock formation] piton m, gendarme m **2.** *fig* [of fame, career] apogée m, sommet m ■ [of technology] fin m du fin **3.** ARCHIT pinacle m.

pin number n code m confidentiel.

pinny ['pɪnɪ] (pl **pinnies**) n *inf* tablier m.

Pinocchio [pɪ'nəʊkɪəʊ] pr n Pinocchio.

pinpoint ['pɪnpɔɪnt] <> vt **1.** [locate - smell, leak] localiser ; [- on map] localiser, repérer **2.** [identify - difficulty] mettre le doigt sur.
<> n pointe f d'épingle ■ **a ~ of light** un minuscule point lumineux.
<> adj **1.** [precise] très précis ■ **with ~ accuracy** avec une précision parfaite **2.** [tiny] minuscule.

pinprick ['pɪnprɪk] n **1.** [puncture] piqûre f d'épingle **2.** [irritation] agacement m, tracasserie f.

pins and needles n (U) *inf* fourmillements mpl ■ **I've got ~ in my arm** j'ai des fourmis dans le bras, je ne sens plus mon bras ➊ **to be on ~** US trépigner d'impatience, ronger son frein.

pinstripe ['pɪnstraɪp] <> n TEX rayure f (très fine).
<> adj = **pinstriped**.

pinstriped ['pɪnstraɪpt] adj rayé.

pint [paɪnt] n **1.** [measure] pinte f, ≃ demi-litre m **2.** UK *inf* [beer] bière f.

pintail ['pɪnteɪl] n ORNITH pilet m.

pinto ['pɪntəʊ] (pl **pintos** OR pl **pintoes**) <> n US cheval m pie.
<> adj US [gen] tacheté ■ [horse] pie *(inv)*.

pinto bean n coco m rose.

pint-sized adj *inf pej* tout petit, minuscule.

pin tuck n SEW nervure f.

pinup ['pɪnʌp] <> n pin-up f *inv*.
<> adj [photo] de pin-up ■ **~ girl** pin-up f.

pinwheel ['pɪnwi:l] n **1.** [firework] soleil m *(feu d'artifice)* **2.** [cogwheel] roue f dentée **3.** US [windmill] moulin m à vent *(jouet)*.

pinworm ['pɪnwɜ:m] n oxyure m.

pion ['paɪɒn] n PHYS pion m.

pioneer [,paɪə'nɪər] <> n **1.** [explorer, settler] pionnier m, - ère f **2.** [of technique, activity] pionnier m, - ère f ■ **they were ~s in the development of heart surgery** ils ont ouvert la voie en matière de chirurgie cardiaque **3.** MIL pionnier m, sapeur m **4.** BOT espèce f pionnière.
<> comp [work, research] novateur, original.
<> vt : **to ~ research in nuclear physics** être à l'avant-garde de la recherche en physique nucléaire ■ **the town is ~ing a job-creation scheme** la municipalité expérimente un nouveau programme de création d'emplois ■ **the factory ~ed the use of robots** l'usine a été la première à utiliser des robots.

pioneering [,paɪə'nɪərɪŋ] adj [work, spirit] novateur, original.

pious ['paɪəs] adj **1.** [person, act, text] pieux **2.** [falsely devout] cagot *lit*, hypocrite **3.** [unrealistic] irréel.

piously ['paɪəslɪ] adv pieusement.

pip [pɪp] (pret & pp **pipped**, cont **pipping**) <> n **1.** [in fruit] pépin m **2.** UK [sound] bip m ■ [during telephone call] tonalité f *(indiquant une unité supplémentaire)* ■ TELEC [time signal] : **the ~s** le signal sonore, le signal horaire **3.** [on playing card, domino] point m **4.** [on radar screen] spot m **5.** *inf phr* **to give sb the ~** UK *dated* courir sur le haricot à qqn **6.** VET pépie f.
<> vi **1.** [chirrup] pépier **2.** [hatch out] éclore.
<> vt UK **1.** [defeat] battre, vaincre ■ **to ~ sb at the post** coiffer qqn au poteau **2.** *inf* [hit with bullet] atteindre.

pipe [paɪp] <> n **1.** [for smoking] pipe f ■ **he smokes a ~** il fume la pipe ➊ **put that in your ~ and smoke it!** *inf* mets ça dans ta poche et ton mouchoir par-dessus! **2.** [for gas, liquid etc] tuyau m, conduite f ■ [for stove] tuyau m ■ **the ~s have frozen** les canalisations ont gelé **3.** MUS [gen] pipeau m ■ [boatswain's whistle] sifflet m ■ [on organ] tuyau m ■ **the ~s** [bagpipes] la cornemuse ■ **a ~ band** un orchestre de cornemuses **4.** ANAT & ZOOL tube m **5.** [birdsong] pépiement m, gazouillis m **6.** GEOL : **volcanic ~** cheminée f volcanique.
<> comp [bowl, stem] de pipe ■ [tobacco] à pipe.
<> vt **1.** [convey - liquid] acheminer par tuyau ■ **the irrigation system will ~ water to the fields** le système d'irrigation amènera l'eau jusqu'aux champs ■ **untreated sewage is ~d into the lake** les égouts se déversent directement dans le lac ■ **to ~ coolant through a system** faire circuler un produit refroidissant dans un système **2.** MUS [tune] jouer **3.** NAUT [order] siffler ■ **to ~ sb aboard** rendre à qqn les honneurs du sifflet *(quand il monte à bord)* **4.** [say] dire d'une voix flûtée **5.** SEW passepoiler **6.** CULIN : **to ~ cream onto a cake** décorer un gâteau de crème fouettée *(à l'aide d'une poche à douille)*.
<> vi MUS [on bagpipes] jouer de la cornemuse ■ [on simple pipe] jouer du pipeau.
◆ **pipe down** vi insep *inf* la mettre en sourdine.
◆ **pipe up** vi insep **1.** [person] se faire entendre **2.** [band] se mettre à jouer.

pipe bomb n *bombe artisanale fabriquée à partir d'un morceau de tuyau contenant des explosifs.*

pipeclay ['paɪpkleɪ] n terre f de pipe.

pipe cleaner n cure-pipe m.

piped music [paɪpt-] n musique f d'ambiance.

pipe dream n chimère f.

pipeline ['paɪplaɪn] n **1.** [gen] pipeline m ■ [for oil] oléoduc m ■ [for gas] gazoduc m **2.** *fig* **he's got another film/project in the ~** il travaille actuellement sur un autre film/projet ■ **changes are in the ~ for next year** des changements sont prévus pour l'année prochaine.

pipe organ n grandes orgues fpl.

piper ['paɪpər] n [gen] joueur m, - euse f de pipeau ■ [of bagpipes] joueur m, - euse f de cornemuse, cornemuseur m ■ **he who pays the ~ calls the tune** *prov* celui qui paie les pipeaux commande la musique *prov*.

pipette UK, **pipet** US [pɪ'pet] n pipette f.

piping ['paɪpɪŋ] <> *n* **1.** [system of pipes] tuyauterie *f*, canalisations *fpl* ■ **a piece of copper ~** un tuyau de cuivre **2.** SEW passepoil *m* **3.** MUS [gen] son *m* du pipeau *OR* de la flûte ■ [of bagpipes] son de la cornemuse **4.** CULIN décoration *f* (appliquée à la douille).
<> *adv* [as intensifier] : **~ hot** très chaud, brûlant.
<> *adj* [voice] flûté.

piping bag *n* CULIN poche *f* à douille.

pipit ['pɪpɪt] *n* pipit *m*.

pippin ['pɪpɪn] *n* **1.** [apple] (pomme *f*) reinette *f* **2.** [seed] pépin *m*.

pipsqueak ['pɪpskwi:k] *n inf pej* demi-portion *f*.

piquancy ['pi:kənsɪ] *n* **1.** [interest] piquant *m*, piment *m* ■ **it adds ~ to the situation** cela corse un peu la situation **2.** [taste] goût *m* piquant.

piquant ['pi:kənt] *adj* piquant.

pique [pi:k] <> *n* dépit *m*, ressentiment *m* ■ **he resigned in a fit of ~** il a démissionné par pur dépit, il était tellement dépité qu'il a démissionné.
<> *vt* **1.** [vex] dépiter, irriter, froisser **2.** [arouse] piquer, exciter ■ **my curiosity was ~d** cela a piqué ma curiosité **3.** [pride] : **to ~ o.s. on (doing) sthg** se piquer de (faire) qqch.

piqued [pi:kt] *adj* [resentful] vexé, froissé.

piracy ['paɪrəsɪ] (*pl* **piracies**) *n* **1.** [of vessel] piraterie *f* ■ **air ~** piraterie aérienne **2.** [of software, book, tape etc] piratage *m* ■ [of idea] copie *f*, vol *m*.

Piraeus [paɪ'rɪəs] *pr n* Le Pirée.

piranha [pɪ'rɑ:nə] (*pl inv OR pl* **piranhas**) *n* piranha *m*, piraya *m*.

pirate ['paɪrət] <> *n* **1.** [person] pirate *m* ■ [ship] navire *m* de pirates **2.** [of software, book, tape etc] pirate *m* ■ [of idea] voleur *m*, -euse *f*.
<> *comp* [raid, flag] de pirates ■ [video, tape, copy] pirate ■ **~ software** logiciel *m* pirate.
<> *vt* [software, book, tape etc] pirater ■ [idea] s'approprier, voler ■ **~d edition** édition *f* pirate.

pirate radio *n* radio *f* pirate.

piratical [paɪ'rætɪkl] *adj* de pirate.

pirouette [,pɪrʊ'et] <> *n* pirouette *f*.
<> *vi* pirouetter.

Pisa ['pi:zə] *pr n* Pise.

Pisces ['paɪsi:z] <> *pr n* ASTROL & ASTRON Poissons *mpl*.
<> *n* : **she's (a) ~** elle est Poissons.

piss△ [pɪs] <> *vi* **1.** [urinate] pisser ■ **to ~ in the wind** se fatiguer pour rien **2.** [rain] : **it's ~ing with rain** il pleut comme vache qui pisse△.
<> *vt* pisser△.
<> *n* pisse△ *f* ■ **to have** *OR* **to take a ~** pisser (un coup)△ ➋ **to go on the ~** se soûler la gueule△ ■ **to take the ~ out of sb** *UK* [mock] se foutre de la gueule de qqn△ ; *US* [calm down] calmer qqn ■ **it's a piece of ~** *UK* c'est du gâteau.
◆ **piss about**△ *UK*, **piss around**△ <> *vi insep* déconner△, faire le con△ ■ **don't ~ around with my stuff** arrête de tripoter mes affaires *OR* de foutre le bordel dans mes affaires.
<> *vt sep* emmerder△.
◆ **piss down**△ *vi insep* [rain] : **it's ~ing (it) down** il pleut comme vache qui pisse△.
◆ **piss off**△ <> *vi insep* foutre le camp△ ■ **~ off!** fous *OR* fous-moi le camp!
<> *vt sep* faire chier△ ■ **to be ~ed off** [bored] s'emmerder△ ; [angry] être en rogne.

pissed△ [pɪst] *adj* **1.** *UK* [drunk] beurré, schlass△ ■ **to get ~** se soûler la gueule△ ➋ **to be as ~ as a newt** être soûl comme un cochon *OR* complètement noir **2.** *US* [angry] en rogne ■ **I was pretty ~ about it** ça m'a vraiment foutu en rogne.

pisshead△ ['pɪshed] *n* **1.** *UK* [drunkard] poivrot *m*, - e *f*, soûlard *m*, - e *f* **2.** *US* [mean person] salaud△ *m*, salope△ *f* ■ [bore] emmerdeur *m*, - euse *f*△.

piss-poor△ *adj US* minable, nul.

piss-take *UK*△ *n* [mockery] mise *f* en boîte ■ [of book, film] parodie *f*.

piss-up *UK*△ *n* : **to go on** *OR* **to have a ~** se biturer△, se soûler la gueule△ ➋ **he couldn't organise a ~ in a brewery** il n'est pas foutu d'organiser quoi que ce soit△.

pistachio [pɪ'stɑ:ʃɪəʊ] (*pl* **pistachios**) <> *n* **1.** [nut] pistache *f* ■ [tree] pistachier *m* **2.** [colour] (vert *m*) pistache *m*.
<> *adj* (vert) pistache *(inv)*.

piste [pi:st] *n* piste *f* (de ski).

pistil ['pɪstɪl] *n* pistil *m*.

pistol ['pɪstl] *n* pistolet *m* ■ **he's holding a ~ to her head** *fig* il lui met le couteau sur la gorge.

pistol grip *n* [of tool, camera] crosse *f*.

pistol-whip *vt* frapper (au visage) avec un pistolet.

piston ['pɪstən] *n* MECH piston *m*.

piston ring *n* segment *m* (de piston).

piston rod *n* tige *f* de piston, bielle *f*.

pit [pɪt] (*pret & pp* **pitted**, *cont* **pitting**) <> *n* **1.** [hole in ground] fosse *f*, trou *m* ■ [pothole in road] nid *m* de poule **2.** [shallow mark - in metal] marque *f*, piqûre *f* ; [- on skin] cicatrice *f*, marque *f* **3.** [mine] mine *f*, puits *m* ■ [mineshaft] puits *m* de mine ■ **to go down the ~** descendre dans la mine ■ **to work down the ~** travailler à la mine **4.** [quarry] carrière *f* **5.** *UK* THEAT [for orchestra] fosse *f* (d'orchestre) ■ [seating section] parterre *m* **6.** *US* ST. EX parquet *m* (de la Bourse) **7.** *(usu pl)* AUT [at race track] stand *m* (de ravitaillement) ■ **to make a ~ stop** s'arrêter au stand **8.** [in cockfighting] arène *f* **9.** SPORT [for long jump] fosse *f* **10.** ANAT creux *m* ■ **the ~ of the stomach** le creux de l'estomac **11.** *US* [in fruit] noyau *m* **12.** *lit* [hell] : **the ~** l'enfer *m*.
<> *comp* [closure] de mine ■ [worker] de fond ■ [accident] minier ■ **~ pony** cheval *m* de mine ■ **~ prop** poteau *m OR* étau *m* de mine, étançon *m*.
<> *vt* **1.** [mark] marquer ■ **his face was pitted with acne** son visage était criblé d'acné ■ **a road pitted with potholes** une route criblée de nids-de-poule ■ **pitted with rust** piqué par la rouille **2.** [oppose] opposer, dresser ■ **she was pitted against the champion** on l'a opposée à la championne ■ **to ~ one's wits against sb** se mesurer à *OR* avec qqn **3.** *US* [fruit] dénoyauter.
◆ **pits** *npl inf* [awful thing, place] : **it's the ~s!** c'est l'horreur!

pit-a-pat = **pitter-patter**.

pit bull, pit bull terrier *n* pitbull *m*.

pitch [pɪtʃ] <> *vt* **1.** [throw] lancer, jeter ■ **she found herself ~ed into the political arena** *fig* elle se trouva propulsée dans l'arène politique **2.** MUS [note] donner ■ [tune] donner le ton de ■ [one's voice] poser ■ **I can't ~ my voice any higher** je n'arrive pas à chanter dans un ton *OR* un registre plus aigu ■ **the music was ~ed too high/low for her** le ton était trop haut/bas pour elle **3.** [set level of] : **we must ~ the price at the right level** il faut fixer le prix au bon niveau ■ **our prices are ~ed too high** nos prix sont trop élevés ■ **he ~ed his speech at the level of the man in the street** son discours était à la portée de l'homme de la rue, il avait rendu son discours accessible à l'homme de la rue **4.** [set up - camp] établir **5.** [in cricket] lancer ■ [in golf] pitcher **6.** *inf* [tell] raconter.
<> *vi* **1.** [fall over] tomber ■ **to ~ headlong** tomber la tête la première ■ **the passengers ~ed forwards/backwards** les passagers ont été projetés en avant/en arrière **2.** [bounce - ball] rebondir **3.** AERON & NAUT tanguer **4.** [in baseball] lancer, être lanceur ■ **to be in there ~ing** *US inf fig* y mettre du sien **5.** [slope - roof] être incliné.
<> *n* **1.** [tone] ton *m* **2.** [particular level or degree] niveau *m*, degré *m* ■ [highest point] comble *m* ■ **the suspense was at its highest ~** le suspense était à son comble **3.** *UK* [sports field] terrain *m* **4.** [act of throwing] lancer *m*, lancement *m* ■ **the ball went full ~ through the window** la balle passa à travers la vitre sans rebondir **5.** *UK inf* [street vendor's place] place *f*, emplacement *m* **6.** *inf* [spiel] boniment *m* **7.** [slope - of roof etc] pente *f*, inclinaison *f* **8.** [movement - of boat, aircraft] tangage *m* **9.** TECH [of screw, cogwheel, rotor] pas *m* **10.** [in golf] pitch *m* **11.** [natural

tar] poix *f* ■ [distillation residue] brai *m* **12.** *US inf phr* **to make a ~ for sthg** jeter son dévolu sur qqch ■ **he made a ~ at her** il lui a fait du plat, il a essayé de la draguer.

◆ **pitch in** *vi insep* [start work] s'attaquer au travail ■ [lend a hand] donner un coup de main ■ **everybody is expected to ~in** on attend de chacun qu'il mette la main à la pâte.

◆ **pitch into** *vt insep* [attack] : **they ~ed into me** ils me sont tombés dessus ■ **they ~ed into the meal** ils ont attaqué le repas.

◆ **pitch out** *vt sep* [rubbish] jeter ■ [person] expulser, mettre à la porte.

pitch-and-putt *n* pitch-and-putt *m* *(forme simplifiée du golf)*.

pitch-black *adj* [water] noir comme de l'encre ■ [hair] noir ébène *(inv)* ■ [night] noir ■ **it's ~ in here** il fait noir comme dans un four ici.

pitch-dark *adj* [night] noir ■ **it was ~ inside** à l'intérieur, il faisait noir comme dans un four.

pitched [pɪtʃt] *adj* [roof] en pente.

pitched battle *n* MIL & *fig* bataille *f* rangée.

pitcher ['pɪtʃəʳ] *n* **1.** [jug - earthenware] cruche *f* ; [- metal, plastic] broc *m* ■ *US* [smaller - for milk] pot *m* **2.** [in baseball] lanceur *m*.

pitchfork ['pɪtʃfɔ:k] ◇ *n* fourche *f* (à foin).
◇ *vt* **1.** [hay] fourcher **2.** *fig* [person] propulser.

pitch pine *n* pitchpin *m*.

pitch pipe *n* diapason *m* *(sifflet)*.

piteous ['pɪtɪəs] *adj* pitoyable.

piteously ['pɪtɪəslɪ] *adv* pitoyablement.

pitfall ['pɪtfɔ:l] *n* **1.** [hazard] embûche *f*, piège *m* **2.** HUNT piège *m*, trappe *f*.

pith [pɪθ] *n* **1.** [in citrus fruit] peau *f* blanche *(sous l'écorce des agrumes)* **2.** [crux] substance *f*, moelle *f* ■ [force] vigueur *f*, force *f* **3.** [in stem, bone] moelle *f*.

pithead ['pɪthed] *n* carreau *m* de mine ■ **~ ballot** vote *m* des mineurs.

pith helmet *n* casque *m* colonial.

pithiness ['pɪθɪnɪs] *n* concision *f*.

pithy ['pɪθɪ] (*comp* **pithier**, *superl* **pithiest**) *adj* [comment, writing] concis, lapidaire.

pitiable ['pɪtɪəbl] *adj* **1.** [arousing pity] pitoyable **2.** [arousing contempt] piteux, lamentable.

pitiably ['pɪtɪəblɪ] *adv* **1.** [touchingly] pitoyablement **2.** [contemptibly] lamentablement.

pitiful ['pɪtɪfʊl] *adj* **1.** [arousing pity] pitoyable ■ **it's ~ to see people living on the street** cela fait pitié de voir des gens à la rue **2.** [arousing contempt] piteux, lamentable.

pitifully ['pɪtɪfʊlɪ] *adv* **1.** [touchingly] pitoyablement ■ **she was ~ thin** sa maigreur faisait peine à voir, elle était maigre à faire pitié **2.** [contemptibly] lamentablement ■ **a ~ bad performance** une prestation lamentable.

pitiless ['pɪtɪlɪs] *adj* [person] impitoyable, sans pitié ■ [weather] rude, rigoureux.

pitilessly ['pɪtɪlɪslɪ] *adv* impitoyablement, sans pitié.

pitman ['pɪtmən] (*pl* **pitmen** [-mən]) *n* *dial* mineur *m*.

piton ['pi:tɒn] *n* piton *m* (d'alpiniste).

pitta (bread) ['pɪtə-] *n* pita *m*.

pittance ['pɪtəns] *n* somme *f* misérable *OR* dérisoire ■ **to work for a ~** travailler pour un salaire de misère.

pitted ['pɪtɪd] *adj* [olives, cherries] dénoyauté.

pitter-patter ['pɪtə,pætəʳ] ◇ *n* [of rain, hail] crépitement *m* ■ [of feet] trottinement *m* ■ [of heart] battement *m*.
◇ *adv* : **to go ~** [feet] trottiner ; [heart] palpiter ■ **the rain fell ~ on the leaves** la pluie tambourinait doucement sur les feuilles.

pituitary [pɪ'tjʊɪtrɪ] ◇ *n* : **~ (gland)** glande *f* pituitaire, hypophyse *f*.
◇ *adj* pituitaire.

pity ['pɪtɪ] ◇ *n* (*pl* **pities**) **1.** [compassion] pitié *f*, compassion *f* ■ **I feel great ~ for them** j'ai beaucoup de pitié pour eux, je les plains énormément ■ **the sight moved her to ~** le spectacle l'a apitoyée *OR* attendrie ■ **out of ~** par pitié ■ **to take** *OR* **to have ~ on sb** avoir pitié de qqn **2.** [mercy] pitié *f*, miséricorde *f* ■ **have ~ on the children!** ayez pitié des enfants! ■ **he showed no ~ to the traitors** il s'est montré impitoyable envers les traîtres ■ **for ~'s sake!** [entreaty] pitié! ; [annoyance] par pitié! **3.** [misfortune, shame] dommage *m* ■ **what a ~!** c'est dommage! ■ **it's a ~ (that) she isn't here** quel dommage qu'elle ne soit pas là ■ **it seems a ~ not to finish the bottle** ce serait dommage de ne pas finir la bouteille ■ **we're leaving tomorrow, more's the ~** nous partons demain, malheureusement.
◇ *vt* (*pret & pp* **pitied**) avoir pitié de, s'apitoyer sur ■ **he pities himself** il s'apitoie sur son sort ■ **they are greatly to be pitied** ils sont bien à plaindre.

pitying ['pɪtɪɪŋ] *adj* [look, smile] de pitié, compatissant.

pityingly ['pɪtɪɪŋlɪ] *adv* avec compassion, avec pitié.

Pius ['paɪəs] *pr n* Pie.

pivot ['pɪvət] ◇ *n* MECH & MIL & *fig* pivot *m*.
◇ *vi* **1.** *liter* pivoter **2.** *fig* **his life ~s around his family** toute son existence tourne autour de sa famille.
◇ *vt* faire pivoter.

◆ **pivot on** *vt insep fig* dépendre de.

pivotal ['pɪvətl] *adj* [crucial] crucial, central.

pixel ['pɪksl] *n* pixel *m*.

pixie ['pɪksɪ] *n* fée *f*, lutin *m* ■ **~ hat** bonnet *m* pointu ■ **~ boots** bottines *fpl*.

pixy ['pɪksɪ] (*pl* **pixies**) = **pixie**.

pizza ['pi:tsə] *n* pizza *f*.

pizzazz [pɪ'zæz] *n inf* [dynamism] tonus *m*, punch *m* ■ [panache] panache *m*.

pizzeria [,pi:tsə'rɪə] *n* pizzeria *f*.

pizzicato [,pɪtsɪ'kɑ:təʊ] *n* pizzicato *m*.

pl *written abbr of* **plural**.

Pl. *written abbr of* **place**.

P & L *written abbr of* **profit and loss**.

placard ['plækɑ:d] ◇ *n* [on wall] affiche *f*, placard *m* ■ [handheld] pancarte *f*.
◇ *vt* **1.** [wall, town] placarder **2.** [advertisement] placarder, afficher.

placate [plə'keɪt] *vt* apaiser, calmer.

placating [plə'keɪtɪŋ] *adj* apaisant, lénifiant.

placatory [plə'keɪtərɪ] *adj* apaisant, conciliant.

place [pleɪs] ◇ *n* **1.** [gen - spot, location] endroit *m*, lieu *m* ■ **keep the documents in a safe ~** gardez les documents en lieu sûr ■ **'store in a cool ~'** 'à conserver au frais' ■ **this is neither the time nor the ~ to discuss it** ce n'est ni le moment ni le lieu pour en discuter ■ **I had no particular ~ to go** je n'avais nulle part où aller ■ **her leg is fractured in two ~s** elle a deux fractures à la jambe ▶ **to go ~s** [travel] aller quelque part ■ **that girl will go ~s!** *inf* cette fille ira loin! ■ **~ of birth** lieu de naissance ■ **~ of safety order** *ordonnance autorisant une personne ou un organisme à garder des enfants maltraités en lieu sûr* **2.** *US* [in adverbial phrases] : **no ~** nulle part ■ **some ~** quelque part ■ **I've looked every ~** j'ai cherché partout
3. [locality] : **do you know the ~ well?** est-ce que tu connais bien le coin? ■ **the whole ~ went up in flames** [building] tout l'immeuble s'est embrasé ; [house] toute la maison s'est embrasée ■ **how long have you been working in this ~?** depuis combien de temps travaillez-vous ici? ■ **~ of work** lieu *m* de

travail ■ **we had lunch at a little ~ in the country** nous avons déjeuné dans un petit restaurant de campagne ▶ **to shout** *OR* **to scream the ~ down** *inf* hurler comme un forcené
4. [house] maison *f* ■ [flat] appartement *m* ■ **nice ~ you've got here** c'est joli chez vous ■ **your ~ or mine?** on va chez toi ou chez moi?
5. [proper or assigned position] place *f* ■ **take your ~s!** prenez vos places! ■ **suddenly everything fell** *OR* **clicked into ~** *fig* [I saw the light] tout à coup, ça a fait tilt ; [everything went well] tout d'un coup, tout s'est arrangé ■ **I'll soon put him in his ~** j'aurai vite fait de le remettre à sa place ■ **to know one's ~** savoir se tenir à sa place ■ **it's not really my ~ to say** ce n'est pas à moi de le dire
6. [role, function] place *f* ■ **what would you do (if you were) in my ~?** que feriez-vous (si vous étiez) à ma place? ■ **if she leaves there's nobody to take** *OR* **to fill her ~** si elle part, il n'y a personne pour la remplacer
7. [seat - on train, in theatre etc] place *f* ; [- on committee] siège *m* ■ **save me a ~** garde-moi une place ■ **to change ~s with sb** *liter* échanger sa place contre celle de qqn ; *fig* être à la place de qqn ■ **I wouldn't change ~s with her for anything** pour rien au monde je n'aimerais être à sa place
8. [table setting] couvert *m*
9. [post, vacancy] place *f*, poste *m* ■ **to get a ~ at university** être admis à l'université ■ **there is keen competition for university ~s** il y a une forte compétition pour les places en faculté
10. [ranking - in competition, hierarchy etc] place *f* ■ **Brenda took third ~ in the race/exam** Brenda a terminé troisième de la course/a été reçue troisième à l'examen ■ **the team is in fifth ~** l'équipe est en cinquième position ■ **for me, work takes second ~ to my family** pour moi, la famille passe avant le travail
11. [in book, speech etc] : **I've lost my ~** je ne sais plus où j'en étais
12. MATHS : **to 3 decimal ~s, to 3 ~s of decimals** jusqu'à la troisième décimale
13. *phr* **to take ~** avoir lieu.
◇ *vt* **1.** [put, set] placer, mettre ■ **he ~d an ad in the local paper** il a fait passer *OR* mis une annonce dans le journal local ■ **the proposals have been ~d before the committee** les propositions ont été soumises au comité
2. [find work or a home for] placer ■ **to ~ sb in care** placer qqn
3. *(usu passive)* [situate] placer, situer ■ **you are better ~d to judge than I am** vous êtes mieux placé que moi pour en juger ■ **how are you ~d for money at the moment?** quelle est ta situation financière en ce moment?
4. *(usu passive)* [rank - in competition, race etc] placer, classer ■ **the runners ~d in the first five go through to the final** les coureurs classés dans les cinq premiers participent à la finale ■ **the horse we bet on wasn't even ~d** le cheval sur lequel nous avions parié n'est même pas arrivé placé ■ **I would ~ her amongst the best writers of our time** je la classerais parmi les meilleurs écrivains de notre époque
5. [identify] (se) remettre ■ **I can't ~ him** je n'arrive pas à (me) le remettre
6. [order] placer, passer ■ [bet] placer ■ **~ your bets!** [in casino] faites vos jeux!
7. FIN [invest] placer ■ [sell] écouler.
◇ *vi* *US* [in racing] être placé.
◆ **all over the place** *adv phr* [everywhere] partout ■ [in disorder] en désordre ■ **my hair's all over the ~** je suis complètement décoiffé.
◆ **in place** *adv phr* [steady] en place.
◆ **in place of** *prep phr* à la place de.
◆ **in places** *adv phr* par endroits.
◆ **in the first place** *adv phr* : **what drew your attention to it in the first ~?** qu'est-ce qui a attiré votre attention à l'origine *OR* en premier lieu? ■ **I didn't want to come in the first ~** d'abord, je ne voulais même pas venir ■ **in the first ~, it's too big, and in the second ~...** premièrement, c'est trop grand, et deuxièmement..., primo, c'est trop grand, et secundo...
◆ **out of place** *adj phr* : **he felt out of ~ amongst so many young people** il ne se sentait pas à sa place parmi tous les jeunes ■ **such remarks are out of ~ at a funeral** de telles paroles sont déplacées lors d'un enterrement.

placebo [plə'si:bəʊ] *(pl* **placebos** *OR pl* **placeboes)** *n liter & fig* placebo *m.*

placebo effect *n* MED effet *m* placebo.

place card *n carte marquant la place des convives à table.*

place kick *n* SPORT coup *m* de pied placé.

place mat *n* set *m* (de table).

placement ['pleɪsmənt] *n* **1.** [gen - act of putting, sending] placement *m* ■ [situation, position] situation *f*, localisation *f* **2.** [job-seeking] placement *m* ■ **~ office** *US* UNIV centre *m* d'orientation (professionnelle) **3.** [work experience] stage *m* en entreprise.

placename ['pleɪsneɪm] *n* toponyme *m.*

place-name *n* nom *m* de lieu ■ **the study of ~s** la toponymie.

placenta [plə'sentə] *(pl* **placentas** *OR pl* **placentae** [-ti:]) *n* placenta *m.*

place setting *n* couvert *m.*

placid ['plæsɪd] *adj* [person, attitude] placide ■ [lake, town] tranquille, calme.

placidly ['plæsɪdlɪ] *adv* placidement.

placing ['pleɪsɪŋ] *n* [act of putting] placement *m* ■ [situation, position] situation *f*, localisation *f* ■ [arrangement] disposition *f.*

plagiarism ['pleɪdʒjərɪzm] *n* plagiat *m.*

plagiarist ['pleɪdʒjərɪst] *n* plagiaire *mf.*

plagiarize, ise ['pleɪdʒəraɪz] *vt* plagier.

plague [pleɪg] ◇ *n* **1.** [bubonic] : **the ~** la peste ■ **to avoid sb like the ~** fuir qqn comme la peste ■ **he avoids work like the ~** il est allergique au travail *hum* **2.** [epidemic] épidémie *f* ■ **there's been a veritable ~ of burglaries** *fig* il y a eu toute une série de cambriolages **3.** [scourge] fléau *m* ■ BIBLE plaie *f* ■ **a ~ of rats** une invasion de rats **4.** *inf* [annoying person] enquiquineur *m*, - euse *f.*
◇ *vt* **1.** [afflict] tourmenter ■ **the region is ~d by floods** la région est en proie aux inondations ■ **we are ~d with tourists in the summer** l'été, nous sommes envahis par les touristes ■ **it's an old injury that still ~s him** c'est une vieille blessure dont il souffre encore ■ **the industry has been ~d with strikes this year** l'industrie a beaucoup souffert des grèves cette année **2.** [pester] harceler ■ **to ~ sb with telephone calls** harceler qqn de coups de téléphone.

plaice [pleɪs] *(pl inv OR pl* **plaices)** *n* carrelet *m*, plie *f.*

plaid [plæd] ◇ *n* **1.** [fabric, design] tartan *m*, tissu *m* écossais
2. [worn over shoulder] plaid *m.*
◇ *adj* (en tissu) écossais.

Plaid Cymru [,plaɪd'kʌmrɪ] *pr n parti nationaliste gallois.*

plain [pleɪn] ◇ *n* **1.** plaine *f*
2. [in knitting] maille *f* à l'endroit.
◇ *adj* **1.** [not patterned, unmarked] uni ■ **under ~ cover, in a ~ envelope** sous pli discret ■ **~ paper** [unheaded] papier sans en-tête ; [unruled] papier non réglé
2. [simple, not fancy] simple ■ **she was just ~ Sarah Ferguson then** elle s'appelait tout simplement Sarah Ferguson à l'époque ■ **I like good ~ cooking** j'aime la bonne cuisine bourgeoise *OR* simple ■ [with nothing added - omelette, rice] nature *(inv)*
3. [clear, obvious] clair, évident, manifeste ■ **it soon became ~ that I was lost** j'ai vite réalisé *OR* je me suis vite rendu compte que j'étais égaré ■ **the facts are ~** c'est clair, les choses sont claires ■ **I want to make our position absolutely ~ to you** je veux que vous compreniez bien notre position ■ **she made her intentions ~** elle n'a pas caché ses intentions ■ **he made it ~ to us that he wasn't interested** il nous a bien fait comprendre que cela ne l'intéressait pas ■ **I thought I'd made myself ~** je croyais avoir été assez clair ■ **in ~ language** de manière claire ▶ **it's as ~ as a pikestaff** *OR* **as the nose on your face** *inf* c'est clair comme de l'eau de roche, ça saute aux yeux
4. [blunt, unambiguous] franc, franche *f* ■ **the ~ truth of the matter is I'm bored** la vérité, c'est que je m'ennuie ■ **I want a ~ yes or no answer** je veux une réponse claire et nette ■ **the time has come for ~ words** *OR* **speaking** le moment est venu de parler franchement ■ **I told him in ~ English what I thought** je lui ai dit ce que je pensais sans mâcher mes mots
5. [unattractive] pas très beau, quelconque ■ **she's a bit of a ~ Jane** ce n'est pas une beauté *OR* une Vénus

6. [in knitting] : **~ stitch/row** maille *f* /rang *m* à l'endroit.
◇ *adv* **1.** [clearly] franchement, carrément ■ **you couldn't have put it any ~er** tu n'aurais pas pu être plus clair
2. *US inf* [utterly] complètement, carrément.

plain chocolate *n* chocolat *m* noir *OR* à croquer.

plain clothes *npl* : **to be in** *OR* **to wear ~** être en civil.
◆ **plain-clothes** *adj* en civil.

plainclothesman [pleɪnkləðzmən] (*pl* **plainclothesmen** [pleɪnkləðzmən]) *n* policier *m* en civil.

plain flour *n* farine *f* (sans levure).

plainly ['pleɪnlɪ] *adv* **1.** [manifestly] clairement, manifestement **2.** [distinctly - remember, hear] clairement, distinctement **3.** [simply - dress, lunch] simplement **4.** [bluntly, unambiguously] franchement, carrément, sans ambages.

plainness ['pleɪnnɪs] *n* **1.** [of clothes, cooking] simplicité *f* **2.** [clarity, obviousness] clarté *f* **3.** [unattractiveness] physique *m* quelconque *OR* ingrat.

plain sailing *n* : **it's ~ from now on** maintenant ça va marcher tout seul *OR* comme sur des roulettes.

plainsong ['pleɪnsɒŋ] *n* plain-chant *m*.

plain-spoken [-'spəʊkn] *adj* qui a son franc-parler.

plaintiff ['pleɪntɪf] *n* LAW demandeur *m*, - eresse *f*, plaignant *m*, - e *f*.

plaintive ['pleɪntɪv] *adj* [voice, sound] plaintif.

plait [plæt] ◇ *n* [of hair] natte *f*, tresse *f* ■ [of straw] tresse *f*.
◇ *vt* [hair, rope, grass] natter, tresser ■ [garland] tresser.

plan [plæn] (*pret & pp* **planned**, *cont* **planning**) ◇ *n* **1.** [strategy] plan *m*, projet *m* ■ **to draw up** *OR* **to make a ~** dresser *OR* établir un plan ■ **what's your ~ of action** *OR* **campaign?** qu'est-ce que vous comptez faire? ■ **to put a ~ into operation** mettre un plan en œuvre ■ **to go according to ~** se dérouler comme prévu *OR* selon les prévisions ■ **five-year ~** ECON plan quinquennal ■ **flight/career ~** plan de vol/de carrière ■ **we'll have to try ~ B** il faudra qu'on essaie l'autre solution
2. [intention, idea] projet *m* ■ **we had made ~s to stay at a hotel** nous avions prévu de descendre à l'hôtel ■ **what are your ~s for Monday?** qu'est-ce que tu as prévu pour lundi? ■ **the ~ is to meet up at John's** l'idée, c'est de se retrouver chez John
3. [diagram, map] plan *m*
4. [outline - of book, essay, lesson] plan *m* ■ **rough ~** canevas *m*, esquisse *f*
5. ARCHIT plan *m*.
◇ *vt* **1.** [organize in advance - project] élaborer ; [- concert, conference] organiser, monter ; [- crime, holiday, trip, surprise] préparer ■ ECON planifier ■ **~ your time carefully** organisez votre emploi du temps avec soin ■ **they're planning a new venture** ils ont en projet une nouvelle entreprise ■ **the Pope's visit is planned for March** la visite du pape doit avoir lieu en mars ■ **an industrial estate is planned for this site** il est prévu d'aménager un parc industriel sur ce site ■ **everything went as planned** tout s'est déroulé comme prévu
2. [intend] projeter ■ **we're planning to go to the States** nous projetons d'aller aux États-Unis ■ **~ to finish it in about four hours** comptez environ quatre heures pour le terminer
3. [design - house, garden, town] concevoir, dresser les plans de
4. [make outline of - book, essay] faire le plan de, esquisser ; [- lesson] préparer.
◇ *vi* faire des projets ■ **it is important to ~ ahead** il est important de faire des projets pour l'avenir.
◆ **plan for** *vt insep* prévoir.
◆ **plan on** *vt insep* **1.** [intend] projeter ■ **what are you planning on doing?** qu'est-ce que vous projetez de faire *OR* vous avez l'intention de faire?
2. [expect] compter sur ■ **we hadn't planned on it raining** nous n'avions pas prévu qu'il pleuvrait.

plane [pleɪn] ◇ *n* **1.** [aeroplane] avion *m* ■ **~ crash** accident d'avion **2.** ARCHIT, ART & MATHS plan *m* **3.** [level, degree] plan *m* ■ **she's on a higher intellectual ~** elle est d'un niveau intellectuel plus élevé **4.** [tool] rabot *m* **5.** BOT : **~ (tree)** platane *m*.
◇ *adj* [flat] plan, plat ■ MATHS plan.
◇ *vi* **1.** [glide] planer **2.** *inf* [travel by plane] voyager par *OR* en avion.
◇ *vt* [in carpentry] : **~ (down)** raboter.

planet ['plænɪt] *n* planète *f*.

planetarium [,plænɪ'teərɪəm] (*pl* **planetariums** *OR pl* **planetaria** [-rɪə]) *n* planétarium *m*.

planetary ['plænɪtrɪ] *adj* planétaire.

plank [plæŋk] ◇ *n* **1.** [board] planche *f* ■ **to walk the ~** subir le supplice de la planche **2.** POL article *m* ■ **the main ~ of their policy** la pièce maîtresse de leur politique.
◇ *vt* [floor, room] planchéier.

plankton ['plæŋktən] *n* plancton *m*.

planned [plænd] *adj* [trip] projeté ■ [murder] prémédité ■ [baby] désiré, voulu ■ **news of the ~ sale was leaked** le projet de vente s'est ébruité ■ **a demonstration against the ~ nuclear power station** une manifestation contre le projet de centrale nucléaire ➊ **~ economy** ECON économie *f* planifiée ■ **~ obsolescence** INDUST obsolescence *f* planifiée, désuétude *f* calculée ■ **~ parenthood** planning *m* familial.

planner ['plænə^r] *n* **1.** [gen - ECON] planificateur *m*, - trice *f* ■ **(town) ~** urbaniste *mf* **2.** [in diary, on wall] planning *m*.

planning ['plænɪŋ] *n* **1.** [of concert, conference] organisation *f* ■ [of lesson, menu] préparation *f* ■ [of campaign] organisation *f*, préparation *f* ■ **the new product is still in the ~stage** le nouveau produit n'en est encore qu'au stade de projet **2.** [of economy, production] planification *f* ■ **demographic ~** planification des naissances **3.** [of town, city] urbanisme *m*.

planning permission *n (U)* permis *m* de construire.

plant [plɑ:nt] ◇ *n* **1.** BOT plante *f* **2.** [factory] usine *f* **3.** *(U)* [industrial equipment] équipement *m*, matériel *m* ■ [buildings and equipment] bâtiments et matériel **4.** *inf* [frame-up] coup *m* monté ■ **he claims the heroin was a ~ by the police** il prétend que l'héroïne a été mise là par la police (pour le compromettre) **5.** *inf* [infiltrator] agent *m* infiltré, taupe *f*.
◇ *comp* BOT : **~ food** engrais *m (pour plantes d'appartement)* ■ **~ life** flore *f*.
◇ *vt* **1.** [flowers, crops, seed] planter ■ **fields ~ed with wheat** des champs (plantés) de blé **2.** *inf* [firmly place] planter ■ **she ~ed herself in the doorway** elle se planta *OR* se campa dans l'entrée ■ [offload] : **don't try and ~ the blame on me!** *UK* n'essaie pas de me faire porter le chapeau! ■ **they ~ed their kids on us for the weekend** ils nous ont laissé leurs gosses sur les bras pour le week-end **3.** *inf* [give - kick, blow] envoyer, donner ; [- kiss] planter ■ **he ~ed a punch on his nose** il lui a mis un coup de poing sur le nez **4.** [in someone's mind] mettre, introduire **5.** [hide - bomb] mettre, placer ; [- microphone] cacher ■ [infiltrate - spy] infiltrer ■ **to ~ evidence on sb** cacher un objet compromettant sur qqn pour l'incriminer.
◆ **plant out** *vt sep* [young plants] repiquer.

plantain ['plæntɪn] *n* plantain *m*.

plantation [plæn'teɪʃn] *n* plantation *f* ■ **sugar ~** plantation de canne à sucre.

planter ['plɑ:ntə^r] *n* **1.** [person] planteur *m*, - euse *f* **2.** [machine] planteuse *f* **3.** [flowerpot holder] cache-pot *m inv*.

plant kingdom *n* : **the ~** le règne végétal.

plant pot *n* pot *m* (de fleurs).

plaque [plɑ:k] *n* **1.** [on wall, monument] plaque *f* **2.** DENT : **(dental) ~** plaque *f* dentaire.

plash [plæʃ] *lit* ◇ *n* [of waves, oars] clapotement *m*, clapotis *m* ■ [of stream, fountain] murmure *m*.
◇ *vi* [waves] clapoter ■ [oars] frapper l'eau avec un bruit sourd ■ [stream, fountain] murmurer.

plasma ['plæzmə] *n* MED & PHYS plasma *m*.

plaster ['plɑ:stə^r] ◇ *n* **1.** [for walls, modelling] plâtre *m* ■ **~ of Paris** plâtre de Paris *OR* à mouler **2.** [for broken limbs] plâtre *m* ■ **her arm was in ~** *UK* elle avait le bras dans le plâtre **3.** *UK* [for cut] : **(sticking) ~** pansement *m* (adhésif).
◇ *comp* [model, statue] de *OR* en plâtre.

◇ *vt* **1.** CONSTR & MED plâtrer **2.** [smear - ointment, cream] enduire ▪ **she had ~ed make-up on her face, her face was ~ed with make-up** elle avait une belle couche de maquillage sur la figure ▪ **they were ~ed with mud** ils étaient couverts de boue **3.** [make stick] coller ▪ **he tried to ~ his hair down with oil** il mit de l'huile sur ses cheveux pour essayer de les plaquer sur sa tête **4.** [cover] : **to ~ sthg with** couvrir qqch de ▪ **the town was ~ed with election posters** les murs de la ville étaient tapissés *OR* recouverts d'affiches électorales **5.** *inf* [defeat heavily] écraser ▪ [beat up] tabasser, passer à tabac.
◆ **plaster over, plaster up** *vt sep* [hole, crack] boucher (avec du plâtre).

plasterboard ['plɑːstəbɔːd] *n* plaque *f* de plâtre.

plaster cast *n* **1.** MED plâtre *m* **2.** ART moule *m* (en plâtre).

plastered ['plɑːstəd] *adj inf* [drunk] bourré ▪ **to get ~** se soûler.

plasterer ['plɑːstərəʳ] *n* plâtrier *m*.

plastering ['plɑːstərɪŋ] *n* CONSTR plâtrage *m*.

plasterwork ['plɑːstəwɜːk] *n (U)* CONSTR plâtre *m*, plâtres *mpl*.

plastic ['plæstɪk] ◇ *n* **1.** [material] plastique *m*, matière *f* plastique ▪ **the ~s industry** l'industrie du plastique **2.** *inf (U) inf* [credit cards] cartes *fpl* de crédit.
◇ *adj* **1.** [made of plastic] en *OR* de plastique ▪ **~ cups** gobelets *mpl* en plastique **2.** [malleable] plastique, malléable ▪ [adaptable] influençable **3.** ART plastique **4.** *inf pej* [artificial] synthétique ▪ **the ~ rubbish they call bread** cette espèce de caoutchouc qu'ils appellent du pain.

plastic bullet *n* balle *f* en plastique.

plastic explosive *n* plastic *m* ▪ **the laboratory was blown up with ~s** le laboratoire a été plastiqué.

Plasticine® ['plæstɪsiːn] *n* pâte *f* à modeler.

plasticity [plæs'tɪsətɪ] *n* plasticité *f*.

plasticize, ise ['plæstɪsaɪz] *vt* plastifier.

plastic money *n (U) inf* cartes *fpl* de crédit.

plastic surgeon *n* [cosmetic] chirurgien *m*, - enne *f* esthétique ▪ [therapeutic] plasticien *m*, - enne *f*.

plastic surgery *n* [cosmetic] chirurgie *f* esthétique ▪ [therapeutic] chirurgie *f* plastique *OR* réparatrice ▪ **she had ~ on her nose** elle s'est fait refaire le nez.

plastic wrap *n* film *m* alimentaire.

plate [pleɪt] ◇ *n* **1.** [for eating] assiette *f* ▪ [for serving] plat *m* ● **to hand sthg to sb on a ~** donner *OR* apporter qqch à qqn sur un plateau (d'argent) ▪ **to have a lot on one's ~** avoir du pain sur la planche **2.** [piece of metal, glass etc] plaque *f* ▪ [rolled metal] tôle *f* ● **microscope ~** lamelle *f* **3.** [with inscription] plaque *f* **4.** [on cooker] plaque *f* (de cuisson) **5.** [dishes, cutlery - silver] vaisselle *f* en argent ; [- gold] vaisselle *f* en or **6.** [coated metal] plaqué *m* ▪ [metal coating] placage *m* ▪ **the knives are silver ~** les couteaux sont en plaqué argent **7.** TYPO [for printing] cliché *m* ▪ [for engraving] planche *f* ▪ [illustration] planche *f*, hors-texte *m inv* **8.** PHOT plaque *f* (sensible) **9.** [for church collection] plateau *m* (de quête) **10.** ANAT & ZOOL plaque *f* **11.** [denture] dentier *m*, appareil *m OR* prothèse *f* dentaire ▪ [for straightening teeth] appareil *m* (orthodontique) **12.** [in earth's crust] plaque *f* **13.** [trophy, race] trophée *m* **14.** ELEC & ELECTRON plaque *f*.
◇ *vt* **1.** [coat with metal] plaquer **2.** [cover with metal plates] garnir de plaques ▪ [armour plate] blinder **3.** TYPO clicher.

plate armour *n* armure *f (en plaques de fer)*.

plateau ['plætəʊ] (*pl* **plateaus** *OR pl* **plateaux** [-təʊz]) *n* GEOG & *fig* plateau *m* ▪ **to reach a ~** [activity, process] atteindre un palier.

plateful ['pleɪtfʊl] *n* assiettée *f*, assiette *f*.

plate glass *n* verre *m* (à vitres).
◆ **plate-glass** *adj* en verre ▪ **~ window** vitrine *f*.

platelet ['pleɪtlɪt] *n* ANAT plaquette *f* (sanguine).

platen ['plætn] *n* **1.** [on typewriter] rouleau *m*, cylindre *m* **2.** [in printing press] platine *f* **3.** [on machine tool] table *f*, plateau *m*.

plate rack *n* égouttoir *m*.

plate tectonics *n (U)* tectonique *f* des plaques.

platewarmer ['pleɪt,wɔːməʳ] *n* chauffe-plats *m inv*.

platform ['plætfɔːm] *n* **1.** [stage] estrade *f* ▪ [for speakers] tribune *f* ▪ *fig* tribune *f* ▪ **it serves as a ~ for their racist views** *fig* cela sert de tribune pour propager leurs opinions racistes **2.** [raised structure] plate-forme *f* ▪ **gun ~** plate-forme de tir ▪ **loading ~** quai *m* de chargement **3.** [at station] quai *m* **4.** POL [programme] plate-forme *f* **5.** *UK* [on bus] plate-forme *f* **6.** COMPUT plate-forme *f*.

platform shoes *npl* chaussures *fpl* à semelle compensée.

platform soles *npl* semelles *fpl* compensées.

platform ticket *n* ticket *m* de quai.

plating ['pleɪtɪŋ] *n* [gen] placage *m* ▪ [in gold] dorage *m*, dorure *f* ▪ [in silver] argentage *m*, argenture *f* ▪ [in nickel] nickelage *m*.

platinum ['plætɪnəm] ◇ *n* platine *m*.
◇ *comp* [jewellery, pen] en platine.
◇ *adj* [colour] platine *(inv)*.

platinum blonde *n* blonde *f* platine.
◆ **platinum-blonde** *adj* (blond) platine *(inv)*.

platitude ['plætɪtjuːd] *n* **1.** [trite remark] platitude *f*, lieu *m* commun **2.** [triteness] platitude *f*.

Plato ['pleɪtəʊ] *pr n* Platon.

platonic [plə'tɒnɪk] *adj* [love, relationship] platonique.
◆ **Platonic** *adj* PHILOS platonicien.

Platonism ['pleɪtənɪzm] *n* platonisme *m*.

platoon [plə'tuːn] *n* MIL section *f* ▪ [of bodyguards, firemen etc] armée *f*.

platter ['plætəʳ] *n* **1.** [for serving] plat *m* ▪ **seafood ~** plateau *m* de fruits de mer **2.** *US inf* [record] disque *m*.

platypus ['plætɪpəs] *n* ornithorynque *m*.

plaudits ['plɔːdɪts] *npl fml* **1.** [applause] applaudissements *mpl* **2.** [praise] éloges *mpl*.

plausibility [,plɔːzə'bɪlətɪ] *n* plausibilité *f*.

plausible ['plɔːzəbl] *adj* [excuse, alibi, theory] plausible ▪ [person] crédible.

plausibly ['plɔːzəblɪ] *adv* de façon convaincante.

Plautus ['plɔːtəs] *pr n* Plaute.

play [pleɪ] ◇ *vt* **1.** [games, cards] jouer à ▪ **to ~ tennis/poker/dominoes** jouer au tennis/au poker/aux dominos ▪ **the children were ~ing dolls/soldiers** les enfants jouaient à la poupée/aux soldats ▪ **how about ~ing some golf after work?** si on faisait une partie de golf après le travail? ▪ **do you ~ any sports?** pratiquez-vous un sport? ▪ **squash is ~ed indoors** le squash se pratique en salle ● **to ~ the game** SPORT jouer selon les règles ; *fig* jouer le jeu ▪ **I won't ~ his game** je ne vais pas entrer dans son jeu ▪ **she's ~ing games with you** elle te fait marcher ▪ **to ~ it cool** *inf* ne pas s'énerver, garder son calme ▪ **to ~ sb for a fool** rouler qqn ▪ **the meeting's next week, how shall we ~ it?** *inf* la réunion aura lieu la semaine prochaine, quelle va être notre stratégie? ▪ **to ~ (it) safe** ne pas prendre de risque, jouer la sécurité
2. [opposing player or team] jouer contre, rencontrer ▪ **I ~ed him at chess** j'ai joué aux échecs avec lui
3. [match] jouer, disputer ▪ **to ~ a match against sb** disputer un match avec *OR* contre qqn ▪ **how many tournaments has he ~ed this year?** à combien de tournois a-t-il participé cette année? ▪ **the next game will be ~ed on Sunday** la prochaine partie aura lieu dimanche
4. [player] faire jouer

5. [card, chess piece] jouer ■ **to ~ spades/trumps** jouer pique/atout ▶ **she ~ed her ace** *liter* elle a joué son as ; *fig* elle a abattu sa carte maîtresse ■ **he ~s his cards close to his chest** il cache son jeu
6. [position] jouer
7. [shot, stroke] jouer ■ **she ~ed a chip shot to the green** elle a fait un coup coché jusque sur le green ■ **he ~ed the ball to me** il m'a envoyé la balle
8. [gamble on - stock market, slot machine] jouer à ■ **to ~ the horses** jouer aux courses ■ **to ~ the property market** spéculer sur le marché immobilier ■ **he ~ed the red/the black** il a misé sur le rouge/le noir
9. [joke, trick] : **to ~ a trick/joke on sb** jouer un tour/faire une farce à qqn
10. CIN & THEAT [act - role, part] jouer, interpréter ■ **who ~ed the godfather in Coppola's film?** qui jouait le rôle du parrain dans le film de Coppola? ■ *fig* **to ~ a part** *OR* **role in sthg** prendre part *OR* contribuer à qqch ■ **an affair in which prejudice ~s its part** une affaire dans laquelle les préjugés entrent pour beaucoup *OR* jouent un rôle important
11. CIN & THEAT [perform at - theatre, club] : **they ~ed Broadway last year** ils ont joué à Broadway l'année dernière ■ **"Othello" is ~ing the Strand for another week** "Othello" est à l'affiche du Strand pendant encore une semaine ■ **he's now ~ing the club circuit** il se produit maintenant dans les clubs
12. [act as] : **to ~ the fool** faire l'idiot *OR* l'imbécile ■ **some doctors ~ God** il y a des médecins qui se prennent pour Dieu sur terre ■ **to ~ host to sb** recevoir qqn ■ **to ~ the hero** jouer les héros ■ **don't ~ the wise old professor with me!** ce n'est pas la peine de jouer les grands savants avec moi!
13. [instrument] jouer de ■ [note, melody, waltz] jouer ■ **to ~ the blues** jouer du blues ■ **they're ~ing our song/Strauss** ils jouent notre chanson/du Strauss ■ **to ~ scales on the piano** faire des gammes au piano
14. [put on - record, tape] passer, mettre ; [- radio] mettre, allumer ; [- tapedeck, jukebox] faire marcher ■ **don't ~ the stereo so loud** ne mets pas la chaîne si fort ■ **he's in his room ~ing records** il écoute des disques dans sa chambre
15. [direct - beam, nozzle] diriger ■ **he ~ed his torch over the cave walls** il promena le faisceau de sa lampe sur les murs de la grotte
16. [fish] fatiguer.
◇ *vi* **1.** jouer, s'amuser ■ [frolic - children, animals] folâtrer, s'ébattre ■ **I like to work hard and ~ hard** quand je travaille, je travaille, quand je m'amuse, je m'amuse ■ **he didn't mean to hurt you, he was only ~ing** il ne voulait pas te faire de mal, c'était juste pour jouer ■ **don't ~ on the street!** ne jouez pas dans la rue! ■ **to ~ with dolls/with guns** jouer à la poupée/à la guerre
2. GAMES & SPORT jouer ■ **it's her (turn) to ~** c'est à elle de jouer, c'est (à) son tour ■ **to ~ in a tournament** participer à un tournoi ■ **she ~ed into the left corner** elle a envoyé la balle dans l'angle gauche ■ **try ~ing to his backhand** essayez de jouer son revers ■ **to ~ to win** jouer pour gagner ▶ **to ~ dirty** SPORT ne pas jouer franc jeu ; *fig* ne pas jouer le jeu ■ **to ~ fair** SPORT jouer franc jeu ; *fig* jouer le jeu ■ **to ~ into sb's hands** faire le jeu de qqn ■ **to ~ for time** essayer de gagner du temps
3. [gamble] jouer ■ **to ~ for drinks/for money** jouer les consommations/de l'argent
4. MUS [person, band, instrument] jouer ■ [record] passer ■ **I heard a guitar ~ing** j'entendais le son d'une guitare ■ **is that Strauss ~ing?** est-ce que c'est du Strauss que l'on entend? ❙ [radio, stereo] : **a radio was ~ing upstairs** on entendait une radio en haut ■ **the stereo was ~ing full blast** on avait mis la chaîne à fond
5. CIN & THEAT [act] jouer
6. CIN & THEAT [show, play, film] se jouer ■ **the film is ~ing to full houses** le film fait salle comble ■ **the same show has been ~ing there for five years** cela fait cinq ans que le même spectacle est à l'affiche ■ **what's ~ing at the Rex?** qu'est-ce qui passe au Rex? ❙ [give performances] : **the company will be ~ing in the provinces** la compagnie va faire une tournée en province
7. [feign] faire semblant ■ **to ~ dead** faire le mort ■ **to ~ dumb** *inf OR* **innocent** faire l'innocent, jouer les innocents
8. [breeze, sprinkler, light] : **to ~ (on)** jouer (sur) ■ **a smile ~ed on** *OR* **about** *OR* **over his lips** un sourire jouait sur ses lèvres ■ **lightning ~ed across the sky** le ciel était zébré d'éclairs.

◇ *n* **1.** [fun, recreation] jeu *m* ■ **I like to watch the children at ~** j'aime regarder les enfants jouer ▶ **~ on words** jeu *m* de mots, calembour *m*
2. SPORT [course, conduct of game] jeu *m* ■ **~ was interrupted by a shower** le match a été interrompu par une averse ■ **there was some nice ~ from Brooks** Brooks a réussi de belles actions *OR* a bien joué ■ **to keep the ball in ~** garder la balle en jeu ■ **out of ~** sorti, hors jeu ■ *US* [move, manoeuvre] combinaison *f* ■ **she scored off a passing ~** elle a marqué un but après une combinaison de passes
3. [turn] tour *m*
4. [manoeuvre] stratagème *m* ■ **it was a ~ to get money/their sympathy** c'était un stratagème pour obtenir de l'argent/pour s'attirer leur sympathie ■ **he is making a ~ for the presidency** il se lance dans la course à la présidence ■ **she made a ~ for my boyfriend** elle a fait des avances à mon copain
5. [gambling] jeu *m*
6. [activity, interaction] jeu *m* ■ **to come into ~** entrer en jeu ■ **to bring sthg into ~** mettre qqch en jeu
7. THEAT pièce *f* (de théâtre) ■ **to be in a ~** jouer dans une pièce ■ **it's been ages since I've seen** *OR* **gone to see a ~** ça fait des années que je ne suis pas allé au théâtre ▶ **radio ~** pièce radiophonique ■ **television ~** dramatique *f*
8. TECH [slack, give] jeu *m* ■ **give the rope more ~** donnez plus de mou à la corde ■ **to give** *OR* **to allow full ~ to sthg** *fig* donner libre cours à qqch
9. [of sun, colours] jeu *m*
10. *inf* [attention, interest] intérêt *m* ■ **the summit meeting is getting a lot of media ~** les médias font beaucoup de tapage *OR* battage autour de ce sommet ■ **they made a lot of ~** *OR* **a big ~ about his war record** ils ont fait tout un plat de son passé militaire.

◆ **play about** *vi insep UK* [have fun - children] jouer, s'amuser ■ [frolic] s'ébattre, folâtrer.

◆ **play about with** *vt insep* **1.** [fiddle with, tamper with] : **to ~ about with sthg** jouer avec *OR* tripoter qqch
2. [juggle - statistics, figures] jouer avec ■ [consider - possibilities, alternatives] envisager, considérer ■ **she ~ed about with several endings for her novel** elle a essayé plusieurs versions pour le dénouement de son roman
3. *inf* [trifle with] : **to ~ about with sb** faire marcher qqn.

◆ **play along** ◇ *vi insep* [cooperate] coopérer ■ **to ~ along with sb** *OR* **with sb's plans** entrer dans le jeu de qqn.
◇ *vt sep* [tease, deceive] faire marcher.

◆ **play around** *vi insep* **1.** = **play about**
2. *inf* [have several lovers] coucher à droite et à gauche.

◆ **play around with** = **play about with.**

◆ **play at** *vt insep* **1.** [subj: child] jouer à ■ **just what do you think you're ~ing at?** *fig* à quoi tu joues exactement?
2. [dally in - politics, journalism] faire en dilettante ■ **you're just ~ing at being an artist** tu joues les artistes ■ **you can't ~ at being a revolutionary** tu ne peux pas t'improviser révolutionnaire.

◆ **play back** *vt sep* [cassette, film] repasser.

◆ **play by** *vt sep US inf* **~ it by me again** reprenez votre histoire depuis le début.

◆ **play down** *vt sep* [role, difficulty, victory] minimiser ■ **we've been asked to ~ down the political aspects of the affair** on nous a demandé de ne pas insister sur le côté politique de l'affaire.

◆ **play in** *vt sep* **1.** [in basketball] : **to ~ the ball in** remettre la balle en jeu
2. *UK fig* **to ~ o.s. in** s'habituer, se faire la main.

◆ **play off** *vi insep* [teams, contestants] jouer les barrages.

◆ **play off against** *vt sep* : **he ~ed Bill off against his father** il a monté Bill contre son père.

◆ **play on** ◇ *vt insep* [weakness, naivety, trust] jouer sur ■ **the waiting began to ~ on my nerves** l'attente commençait à me porter sur les nerfs.
◇ *vi insep* continuer à jouer.

◆ **play out** *vt sep* **1.** [enact - scene] jouer ; [- fantasy] satisfaire ■ **the drama was ~ed out between rioters and police** les incidents ont eu lieu entre les émeutiers et les forces de police
2. *inf (usu passive)* [exhaust] crever.

◆ **play through** *vi insep* [in golf] dépasser d'autres joueurs.

play up <> *vt sep* **1.** [exaggerate - role, importance] exagérer ▪ [stress] souligner, insister sur ▪ **his speech ~ed up his working-class background** son discours mettait l'accent sur ses origines populaires
2. *UK inf* [bother] tracasser ▪ **my back is ~ing me up** mon dos me joue encore des tours ▪ **don't let the kids ~ you up** ne laissez pas les enfants vous marcher sur les pieds.
<> *vi insep UK inf* [cause problems] : **my back is ~ing up** mon dos me joue encore des tours ▪ **he ~s up when his mother leaves** il pique une crise chaque fois que sa mère s'en va ▪ **the car is ~ing up at the moment** la voiture fait des siennes en ce moment.
play up to *vt insep* : **to ~ up to sb** [flatter] faire de la lèche à qqn.
play upon = **play on** *(vt insep).*
play with *vt insep* **1.** [toy with - pencil, hair] jouer avec ▪ **he only ~ed with his meat** il a à peine touché à sa viande ▶ **to ~ with fire** jouer avec le feu
2. [manipulate - words] jouer sur ; [- rhyme, language] manier
3. [consider - idea] caresser ▪ **we're ~ing with the idea of buying a house** nous pensons à acheter une maison ▪ **here are a few suggestions to ~with** voici quelques suggestions que je soumets à votre réflexion
4. [treat casually - someone's affections] traiter à la légère ▪ **don't you see he's just ~ing with you?** tu ne vois pas qu'il se moque de toi *OR* qu'il te fait marcher?
5. [have available - money, time] disposer de ▪ **how much time have we got to ~ with?** de combien de temps disposons-nous?
6. *inf euph* **to ~ with o.s.** [masturbate] se toucher.

playable ['pleɪəbl] *adj* jouable.

play-act *vi* **1.** *fig* [pretend] jouer la comédie ▪ **stop ~ing!** arrête ton cinéma *OR* de jouer la comédie! **2.** [act in plays] faire du théâtre.

play-acting *n* **1.** [pretence] (pure) comédie *f fig*, cinéma *m fig* **2.** [acting in play] théâtre *m*.

playback ['pleɪbæk] *n* **1.** [replay] enregistrement *m* **2.** [function] lecture *f* ▪ **put it on ~** mettez-le en position lecture ▶ **~ head** tête *f* de lecture.

playbill ['pleɪbɪl] *n* **1.** [poster] affiche *f* (de théâtre) **2.** [programme] programme *m*.

playboy ['pleɪbɔɪ] *n* play-boy *m* ▪ **'The Playboy of the Western World'** ***Synge*** 'le Baladin du monde occidental'.

Play-Doh® ['pleɪˌdəʊ] *n sorte de pâte à modeler.*

player ['pleɪəʳ] *n* **1.** [of game, sport] joueur *m*, - euse *f* ▪ **bridge ~** bridgeur *m*, - euse *f* **2.** [of musical instrument] joueur *m*, - euse *f* ▪ **she's a piano/guitar ~** elle joue du piano/de la guitare **3.** [participant] participant *m*, - e *f* ▪ **France has been a major ~ in this debate** la France a eu un rôle clé dans ce débat **4.** [actor] acteur *m*, - trice *f*.

playfellow ['pleɪˌfeləʊ] *n UK* camarade *mf* (de jeux).

playful ['pleɪfʊl] *adj* [lively - person] gai, espiègle ; [- animal] espiègle ▪ [good-natured - nudge, answer] taquin ▪ **to be in a ~ mood** être d'humeur enjouée.

playfully ['pleɪfʊlɪ] *adv* [answer, remark] d'un ton taquin ▪ [act] avec espièglerie.

playfulness ['pleɪfʊlnɪs] *n* enjouement *m*, espièglerie *f*.

playgoer ['pleɪˌgəʊəʳ] *n* amateur *m* de théâtre.

playground ['pleɪgraʊnd] *n* [at school] cour *f* de récréation ▪ [in park] aire *f* de jeu ▪ **the islands are a ~ for the rich** *fig* les îles sont des lieux de villégiature pour les riches.

playgroup ['pleɪgru:p] *n réunion régulière d'enfants d'âge préscolaire généralement surveillés par une mère.*

playhouse ['pleɪhaʊs] (*pl* [-haʊzɪz]) *n* **1.** [theatre] théâtre *m* **2.** [children's] maison *f* de poupée.

playing ['pleɪɪŋ] *n* MUS : **the pianist's ~ was excellent** le pianiste jouait merveilleusement bien ▪ **guitar ~ is becoming more popular** de plus en plus de gens jouent de la guitare.

playing card ['pleɪɪŋ-] *n* carte *f* à jouer.

playing field ['pleɪɪŋ] *n UK* terrain *m* de sport ▪ **to have a level ~** *fig* être sur un pied d'égalité.

playlist ['pleɪlɪst] *n* RADIO playlist *f (programme des disques à passer).*

playmate ['pleɪmeɪt] *n* camarade *mf* (de jeux).

play-off *n* SPORT (match *m* de) barrage *m*.

playpen ['pleɪpen] *n* parc *m (pour bébés).*

play-reading *n* lecture *f* d'une pièce (de théâtre).

playroom ['pleɪrʊm] *n* [in house] salle *f* de jeux.

playschool ['pleɪsku:l] = **playgroup**.

plaything ['pleɪθɪŋ] *n liter & fig* jouet *m*.

playtime ['pleɪtaɪm] *n* récréation *f* ▪ **at ~** pendant la récréation.

playwright ['pleɪraɪt] *n* dramaturge *m*, auteur *m* dramatique.

plaza ['plɑ:zə] *n* **1.** [open square] place *f* **2.** *US* [shopping centre] centre *m* commercial ▪ **toll ~** péage *m* (d'autoroute).

plc, PLC (*abbrev of* **public limited company**) *n UK* ≃ SARL *f*.

plea [pli:] *n* **1.** [appeal] appel *m*, supplication *f* ▪ **she made a ~ to the nation not to forget the needy** elle conjura la nation de ne pas oublier les nécessiteux **2.** LAW [argument] argument *m* ▪ [defence] défense *f* ▪ **what is your ~?** plaidez-vous coupable ou non coupable? ▪ **to enter a ~ of guilty/not guilty/insanity** plaider coupable/non coupable/la démence **3.** [excuse, pretext] excuse *f*, prétexte *m* ▪ **his ~ of ill health didn't fool anyone** sa prétendue maladie n'a trompé personne.

plea bargaining *n* LAW *possibilité pour un inculpé de se voir notifier un chef d'inculpation moins grave s'il accepte de plaider coupable.*

plead [pli:d] (*UK pret & pp* **pleaded**) (*US pret & pp* **pleaded** *OR* **pled** [pled]) <> *vi* **1.** [beg] supplier ▪ **to ~ for forgiveness** implorer le pardon ▪ **she ~ed to be given more time** elle supplia qu'on lui accorde plus de temps ▪ **to ~ with sb** supplier *OR* implorer qqn **2.** LAW plaider ▪ **to ~ guilty/not guilty** plaider coupable/non coupable ▪ **how does the accused ~?** l'accusé plaide-t-il coupable ou non coupable?
<> *vt* **1.** [beg] implorer, supplier ▪ **she ~ed that her son be forgiven** elle supplia que l'on pardonne à son fils **2.** [gen - LAW] plaider ▪ **to ~ sb's case** défendre qqn ; *fig* plaider la cause de qqn ▪ **to ~ self-defence** plaider la légitime défense **3.** [put forward as excuse] invoquer, alléguer ▪ [pretend] prétexter ▪ **we could always ~ ignorance** nous pourrions toujours prétendre que nous ne savions pas ▪ **she ~ed a prior engagement** elle a prétendu qu'elle était déjà prise.

pleading ['pli:dɪŋ] <> *adj* implorant, suppliant.
<> *n* **1.** [entreaty] supplication *f*, prière *f* **2.** LAW [presentation of case] plaidoyer *m*, plaidoirie *f*.

pleadingly ['pli:dɪŋlɪ] *adv* [look] d'un air suppliant *OR* implorant ▪ [ask] d'un ton suppliant *OR* implorant.

pleasant ['pleznt] *adj* **1.** [enjoyable, attractive] agréable, plaisant **2.** [friendly - person, attitude, smile] aimable, agréable ▪ **she was very ~ to us as a rule** elle était en général très aimable à notre égard.

pleasantly ['plezntlɪ] *adv* **1.** [attractively] agréablement ▪ **the room was ~ arranged** la pièce était aménagée de façon agréable **2.** [enjoyably] agréablement ▪ **~ surprised** agréablement surpris, surpris en bien **3.** [kindly - speak, smile] aimablement.

pleasantry ['plezntrɪ] (*pl* **pleasantries**) *n* [agreeable remark] propos *m* aimable ▪ **to exchange pleasantries** échanger des civilités.

please [pli:z] <> *adv* **1.** [requesting or accepting] s'il vous/te plaît ▪ **could you pass the salt, ~?** pouvez-vous me passer le sel, s'il vous plaît? ▪ **another cup of tea? – (yes) ~!** une autre tasse de thé? – oui, s'il vous plaît! *OR* volontiers! ▪ **may I sit beside you? – ~ do** puis-je m'asseoir près de vous? – mais

bien sûr ▪ **~, make yourselves at home** faites comme chez vous, je vous en prie ▪ **'~ ring'** 'sonnez SVP, veuillez sonner' ▪ **'quiet ~'** 'silence'
2. [pleading] : **~ don't hurt him** je vous en prie, ne lui faites pas de mal
3. [remonstrating] : **Henry, ~, we've got guests!** Henry, voyons, nous avons des invités!
4. [hoping] : **~ let them arrive safely!** faites qu'ils arrivent sains et saufs!
<> *vt* **1.** [give enjoyment to] plaire à, faire plaisir à ▪ [satisfy] contenter ▪ **you can't ~ everybody** on ne peut pas faire plaisir à tout le monde ▪ **to be easy/hard to ~** être facile/difficile à satisfaire
2. *phr* **to ~ oneself** faire comme on veut ▪ **~ yourself!** comme tu veux! ▪ **everything will be all right, ~God!** tout ira bien, plaise à Dieu!
<> *vi* **1.** [give pleasure] plaire, faire plaisir ▪ **to be eager to ~** chercher à faire plaisir
2. [choose] : **she does as** *OR* **what she ~s** elle fait ce qu'elle veut *OR* ce qui lui plaît ▪ **I'll talk to whoever I ~!** je parlerai avec qui je veux! ➊ **as you ~!** *fml* comme vous voudrez!, comme bon vous semblera! ▪ **she told me I was fat, if you ~!** figure-toi qu'elle m'a dit que j'étais gros!

pleased [pli:zd] *adj* content, heureux ▪ **to be ~ with sthg/sb** être content de qqch/qqn ▪ **you're looking very ~ with yourself!** tu as l'air très content de toi! ▪ **I'm very ~ to be here this evening** je suis très heureux d'être ici ce soir ▪ **Mr & Mrs Adams are ~ to announce...** *fml* M. et Mme Adams sont heureux de *OR* ont le plaisir de vous faire part de... ▪ **she would be only too ~ to help us** elle ne demanderait pas mieux que de nous aider ➊ **~ to meet you!** enchanté (de faire votre connaissance)! ▪ **as ~ as Punch** heureux comme un roi.

pleasing ['pli:zɪŋ] *adj* agréable, plaisant.

pleasingly ['pli:zɪŋlɪ] *adv* agréablement, plaisamment.

pleasurable ['pleʒərəbl] *adj* agréable, plaisant.

pleasure ['pleʒər] <> *n* **1.** [enjoyment, delight] plaisir *m* ▪ **to write/to paint for ~** écrire/peindre pour le plaisir ▪ **to take** *OR* **to find ~ in doing sthg** prendre plaisir *OR* éprouver du plaisir à faire qqch ▪ **another beer? – with ~!** une autre bière? – avec plaisir *OR* volontiers! ▪ **it's one of my few ~s in life** c'est un de mes rares plaisirs dans la vie ▪ **thank you very much – my ~!** *OR* **it's a ~!** merci beaucoup – je vous en prie! ▪ **it's a great ~ (to meet you)** ravi de faire votre connaissance ▪ **would you do me the ~ of having lunch with me?** *fml* me feriez-vous le plaisir de déjeuner avec moi? ▪ **may I have the ~ (of this dance)?** *fml* m'accorderez-vous *OR* voulez-vous m'accorder cette danse? ▪ **Mr and Mrs Evans request the ~ of your company at their son's wedding** *fml* M. et Mme Evans vous prient de leur faire l'honneur d'assister au mariage de leur fils **2.** *fml* [desire] : **they are appointed at the chairman's ~** ils sont nommés selon le bon vouloir du président ▪ **detained at His/Her Majesty's ~** *UK* LAW & *euph* emprisonné aussi longtemps qu'il plaira au roi/à la reine **3.** *euph* [sexual gratification] plaisir *m*.
<> *comp* [yacht] de plaisance ▪ [park] de loisirs ▪ [cruise, tour] d'agrément ➊ **~ boat** bateau *m* de plaisance ▪ **~ trip** excursion *f*.
<> *vt arch* & *lit* plaire à, faire plaisir à.

pleasure principle *n* : **the ~** le principe de plaisir.

pleasure-seeker *n* hédoniste *mf*.

pleat [pli:t] <> *n* pli *m*.
<> *vt* plisser.

pleated ['pli:tɪd] *adj* plissé ▪ **a ~ skirt** une jupe plissée.

pleb [pleb] *n* **1.** *pej* [plebeian] plébéien *m*, - enne *f* ▪ **it's not for the ~s** ce n'est pas pour n'importe qui! **2.** *UK inf pej* [vulgar person] plouc *m* **3.** ANTIQ : **the ~s** la plèbe.

plebeian [plɪ'bi:ən] <> *n* plébéien *m*, - enne *f*.
<> *adj* **1.** *pej* [vulgar] plébéien **2.** ANTIQ plébéien.

plebiscite ['plebɪsaɪt] *n* plébiscite *m*.

plectrum ['plektrəm] (*pl* **plectrums** *OR pl* **plectra** [-trə]) *n* médiator *m*, plectre *m*.

pled [pled] *US pt* & *pp* ▷ **plead**.

pledge [pledʒ] <> *vt* **1.** [promise] promettre ▪ **she ~d never to see him again** [to herself] elle s'est promis de ne plus jamais le revoir ; [to sb else] elle a promis de ne plus jamais le revoir **2.** *fml* [commit] engager ▪ **I am ~d to secrecy** j'ai juré de garder le secret ▪ **to ~ one's word** donner *OR* engager sa parole **3.** [offer as security] donner en garantie ▪ [pawn] mettre en gage, engager **4.** *fml* [toast] porter un toast à, boire à la santé de.
<> *n* **1.** [promise] promesse *f* ▪ **manifesto ~** promesse électorale ▪ **a £10 ~** un gage de 10 livres ▪ **thousands of people phoned in with ~s of money** des milliers de personnes ont téléphoné en promettant de donner de l'argent ▪ **you have my ~** vous avez ma parole ▪ **I am under a ~ of secrecy** j'ai juré de garder le secret ➊ **to sign** *OR* **to take the ~** [stop drinking] cesser de boire ▪ **Pledge of Allegiance** *serment de loyauté prononcé à l'occasion du discours d'investiture du président des États-Unis* **2.** [security, collateral] gage *m*, garantie *f* ▪ **in ~** en gage **3.** [token, symbol] gage *m* **4.** *fml* [toast] toast *m*.

Pleiades ['plaɪədi:z] *npl* : **the ~** les Pléiades *fpl*.

plenary ['pli:nərɪ] <> *adj* **1.** POL : **~ powers** pleins pouvoirs *mpl* **2.** [meeting] plénier ▪ **in ~ session** en séance plénière.
<> *n* [plenary meeting] réunion *f* plénière ▪ [plenary session] séance *f* plénière.

plenipotentiary [,plenɪpə'tenʃərɪ] (*pl* **plenipotentiaries**) <> *adj* plénipotentiaire ▪ **ambassador ~** ministre *m* plénipotentiaire.
<> *n* plénipotentiaire *mf*.

plenitude ['plenɪtju:d] *n lit* plénitude *f*.

plentiful ['plentɪfʊl] *adj* [gen] abondant ▪ [meal] copieux ▪ **we have a ~ supply of food** nous avons de la nourriture en abondance.

plentifully ['plentɪfʊlɪ] *adv* abondamment, copieusement.

plenty ['plentɪ] <> *pron* **1.** [enough] (largement) assez, plus qu'assez ▪ **no thanks, I've got ~** non merci, j'en ai (largement) assez ▪ **£20 should be ~** 20 livres devraient suffire (amplement) ▪ **they have ~ to live on** ils ont largement de quoi vivre ▪ **we've got ~ of time** nous avons largement le temps **2.** [a great deal] beaucoup ▪ **there's still ~ to be done** il y a encore beaucoup à faire ▪ **we see ~ of Ray and Janet** on voit beaucoup Ray et Janet.
<> *n lit* [abundance] abondance *f*.
<> *adv inf* **1.** [a lot] beaucoup ▪ **there's ~ more food in the fridge** il y a encore plein de choses à manger dans le frigo **2.** [easily] : **the room is ~ big enough for two** la pièce est largement assez grande pour deux.
<> *det US dial* [a lot of] plein de ▪ **there's ~ work to be done!** ce n'est pas le boulot qui manque!
◆ **in plenty** *adv phr* en abondance.

pleonasm ['pli:ənæzm] *n* pléonasme *m*.

plethora ['pleθərə] *n* pléthore *f*.

pleurisy ['plʊərəsɪ] *n (U)* pleurésie *f*.

Plexiglas® ['pleksɪglɑ:s] *n* Plexiglas® *m*.

plexus ['pleksəs] *n* **1.** ANAT plexus *m* **2.** *fml* [intricate network] enchevêtrement *m*, dédale *m*.

pliability [,plaɪə'bɪlətɪ] *n* **1.** [of material] flexibilité *f* **2.** [of person] malléabilité *f*, docilité *f*.

pliable ['plaɪəbl] *adj* **1.** [material] flexible, pliable **2.** [person] malléable, accommodant, docile.

pliant ['plaɪənt] = **pliable**.

pliers ['plaɪəz] *npl* pince *f* ▪ **a pair of ~** une pince.

plight [plaɪt] <> *n* [bad situation] situation *f* désespérée ▪ **the ~ of the young homeless** la situation désespérée dans laquelle se trouvent les jeunes sans-abri ▪ **seeing my ~ she stopped to help** voyant mon embarras, elle s'est arrêtée pour m'aider.
<> *vt arch* [pledge] promettre, engager ▪ **to ~ one's troth** se fiancer.

plimsoll ['plɪmsəl] *n UK* tennis *m*.

Plimsoll line, Plimsoll mark *n* ligne *f* de flottaison.

plinth [plɪnθ] *n* [of statue] socle *m* ■ [of column, pedestal] plinthe *f*.

Pliny ['plɪnɪ] *pr n* : **~ the Elder** Pline l'Ancien ■ **~ the Younger** Pline le Jeune.

PLO (*abbrev of* **Palestine Liberation Organization**) *pr n* OLP *f*.

plod [plɒd] (*pret & pp* **plodded**, *cont* **plodding**) <> *vi* **1.** [walk] marcher lourdement **2.** *inf* [carry on] : **he'd been plodding along in the same job for years** ça faisait des années qu'il faisait le même boulot ■ **she kept plodding on until it was finished** elle s'est acharnée jusqu'à ce que ce soit fini.
<> *n* : **we maintained a steady ~** nous avons gardé un pas régulier.

plodder ['plɒdəʳ] *n pej* **he's a bit of a ~** il est plutôt lent à la tâche.

plodding ['plɒdɪŋ] *adj pej* [walk, rhythm, style] lourd, pesant ■ [worker] lent.

plonk [plɒŋk] <> *n* **1.** [heavy sound] bruit *m* sourd **2.** *UK inf* [cheap wine] pinard *m*.
<> *vt inf* [put down] poser bruyamment ■ **she ~ed herself down on the sofa** elle s'est affalée sur le canapé.
<> *vi* : **to ~ away on the piano** jouer du piano (mal et assez fort).

plonker△ ['plɒŋkəʳ] *n* **1.** [penis] quéquette▲ *f* **2.** [fool] andouille *f*.

plop [plɒp] (*pret & pp* **plopped**, *cont* **plopping**) <> *n* plouf *m*, floc *m*.
<> *vi* [splash] faire plouf *OR* floc.
<> *vt* [put] poser, mettre.

plosion ['pləʊʒn] *n* LING occlusion *f*.

plosive ['pləʊsɪv] <> *adj* occlusif.
<> *n* occlusive *f*.

plot [plɒt] (*pret & pp* **plotted**, *cont* **plotting**) <> *n* **1.** [conspiracy] complot *m*, conspiration *f* **2.** [story line - of novel, play] intrigue *f* ■ **the ~ thickens** l'affaire se corse **3.** [piece of land] terrain *m* ■ **the land has been split up into 12 ~s** le terrain a été divisé en 12 lotissements ■ **we have a small vegetable ~** nous avons un petit potager *OR* carré de légumes **4.** *US* [graph] graphique *m* **5.** *US* ARCHIT plan *m*.
<> *vt* **1.** [conspire] comploter ■ **they were accused of plotting to overthrow the government** ils ont été accusés de complot *OR* de conspiration contre le gouvernement ■ **I think they're plotting something** je crois qu'ils préparent quelque chose **2.** [course, position] déterminer ■ **they're trying to ~ the company's development over the next five years** *fig* ils essaient de prévoir le développement de la société dans les cinq années à venir **3.** [graph] tracer, faire le tracé de ■ **to ~ figures on *OR* onto a graph** reporter des coordonnées sur un graphique **4.** [map, plan] lever.
<> *vi* [conspire] comploter, conspirer ■ **to ~ against** conspirer contre.

plotter ['plɒtəʳ] *n* **1.** [conspirator] conspirateur *m*, - trice *f* **2.** [device - gen] traceur *m* ■ COMPUT table *f* traçante, traceur *m* de courbes.

plotting ['plɒtɪŋ] *n (U)* **1.** [conspiring] complots *mpl*, conspirations *fpl* **2.** COMPUT & MATHS traçage *m*.

plough *UK*, **plow** *US* [plaʊ] <> *n* **1.** charrue *f* **2.** ASTRON : **the Plough** la Grande Ourse.
<> *vt* **1.** [land] labourer ■ [furrow] creuser **2.** *fig* [invest] investir ■ **to ~ money into sthg** investir de l'argent dans qqch.
<> *vi* **1.** AGRIC labourer **2.** [crash] emboutir, percuter ■ **the truck ~ed into the wall** le camion percuta le mur.
◆ **plough back** *vt sep* [profits] réinvestir.
◆ **plough in** *vt sep* [earth, crops, stubble] enfouir (en labourant).
◆ **plough through** *vt insep* [documents, papers] éplucher.
◆ **plough under** = **plough in**.
◆ **plough up** *vt sep* **1.** AGRIC [field, footpath] labourer **2.** [rip up] labourer.

ploughing *UK*, **plowing** *US* ['plaʊɪŋ] *n* labourage *m*.

ploughman *UK* (*pl* **ploughmen**), **plowman** *US* ['plaʊmən] (*pl* **plowmen** [-mən]) *n* laboureur *m*.

ploughman's (lunch) *n assiette de fromage, de pain et de pickles (généralement servie dans un pub).*

ploughshare *UK*, **plowshare** *US* ['plaʊʃeəʳ] *n* soc *m* ■ **to turn swords into ~s** faire la paix, se réconcilier.

plover ['plʌvəʳ] *n* pluvier *m*.

plow *etc US* = **plough**.

ploy [plɔɪ] *n* **1.** [stratagem, trick] ruse *f*, stratagème *m* **2.** *inf dated* [pastime] passe-temps *m inv* ■ [job] turbin *m*.

pls (*written abbrev of* **please**) *adv* svp.

pluck [plʌk] <> *vt* **1.** [pick - flower, fruit] cueillir **2.** [pull] tirer, retirer ■ **he ~ed the cigarette from my mouth** il m'a arraché la cigarette de la bouche ■ **the ten survivors were ~ed from the sea by helicopter** les dix survivants ont été récupérés en mer par un hélicoptère **3.** [chicken] plumer ■ [feathers] arracher **4.** [instrument] pincer les cordes de ■ [string] pincer **5.** [eyebrow] épiler.
<> *vi* : **he ~ed at my sleeve** il m'a tiré par la manche ■ **she was ~ing at (the strings of) her guitar** elle pinçait les cordes de sa guitare.
<> *n* **1.** [courage] courage *m* **2.** [tug] petite secousse *f* **3.** CULIN fressure *f*.
◆ **pluck up** *vt sep* **1.** [uproot] arracher, extirper **2.** *fig* **to ~ up (one's)courage** prendre son courage à deux mains ■ **to ~ up the courage to do sthg** trouver le courage de faire qqch.

pluckily ['plʌkɪlɪ] *adv* courageusement.

plucky ['plʌkɪ] (*comp* **pluckier**, *superl* **pluckiest**) *adj* courageux.

plug [plʌg] (*pret & pp* **plugged**, *cont* **plugging**) <> *n* **1.** ELEC [on appliance, cable] fiche *f*, prise *f* (mâle) ■ [socket - in wall] prise *f* (de courant) **2.** [stopper - gen] bouchon *m* ; [- in barrel] bonde *f* ; [- for nose] tampon *m* **3.** [for sink, bath] bonde *f* ■ **to pull the ~ out** retirer la bonde ➊ **to pull the ~ on sb/sthg** *inf* : **this will pull the ~ on our competitors** cela va couper l'herbe sous le pied de nos concurrents ■ **he pulled the ~ on our plan** [stopped it] il a mis le holà à notre projet ■ **this pulls the ~ on the whole operation** ça fiche tout par terre **4.** AUT : **(spark) ~** bougie *f* **5.** [for fixing screws] cheville *f* **6.** *inf* [advertising] coup *m* de pub ■ **her book got another ~ on TV last night** on a encore fait de la pub pour son livre à la télé hier soir **7.** [of tobacco] carotte *f* **8.** GEOL : **(volcanic) ~** culot *m* **9.** *US* **(fire) ~** bouche *f* d'incendie **10.** △ [blow] beigne△ *f*, gnon *m*.
<> *vt* **1.** [block - hole, gap] boucher ; [- leak] colmater **2.** [insert] enficher ■ **~ the cable into the socket** branchez le câble sur la prise **3.** *inf* [advertise] faire de la pub à **4.** △ *US* [shoot] flinguer△.
◆ **plug away** *vi insep* travailler dur ■ **he keeps plugging away at his work** il s'acharne sur son travail.
◆ **plug in** <> *vt sep* brancher.
<> *vi insep US* : **we try to ~ in to people's needs** *fig* nous essayons d'être à l'écoute des besoins de la population.

plugged [plʌgd] *adj* [blocked - nose, ear] bouché.

plughole ['plʌghəʊl] *n* trou *m* d'écoulement ■ **that's all our work gone down the ~!** *UK inf* tout notre travail est fichu!

plug-in <> *adj* [radio] qui se branche sur le secteur ■ [accessory for computer, stereo etc] qui se branche sur l'appareil.
<> *n* COMPUT périphérique *m* prêt à brancher.

plug-ugly *inf adj* très moche, laid comme un pou.

plum [plʌm] <> *n* **1.** [fruit] prune *f* **2.** : **~ (tree)** prunier *m* **3.** [colour] couleur *f* lie-de-vin.
<> *comp* [tart] aux prunes.
<> *adj* **1.** [colour] lie-de-vin *(inv)*, prune *(inv)* **2.** *inf* [desirable] : **it's a ~ job** c'est un boulot en or.

plumage ['plu:mɪdʒ] *n* plumage *m*.

plumb [plʌm] <> *n* **1.** [weight] plomb *m* ■ **~ bob** plomb *m* **2.** [verticality] aplomb *m* ■ **the wall is out of ~** le mur n'est pas d'aplomb *OR* à l'aplomb.
<> *adj* **1.** [vertical] vertical, à l'aplomb **2.** *US inf* [utter, complete] complet, - ète *f*, absolu.

◇ *adv* **1.** [in a vertical position] à l'aplomb, d'aplomb ▪ **~ with** d'aplomb avec **2.** *inf* [exactly, right] exactement, en plein ▪ **~ in the middle of the first act** en plein *OR* au beau milieu du premier acte **3.** *US inf* [utterly, completely] complètement, tout à fait.
◇ *vt* sonder ▪ **to ~ the depths** toucher le fond ▪ **his films ~ the depths of bad taste** ses films sont d'un mauvais goût inimaginable.
◆ **plumb in** *vt sep* effectuer le raccordement de ▪ [washing machine] raccorder.

plumber ['plʌmə^r] *n* **1.** [workman] plombier *m* **2.** *inf* [secret agent] plombier *m*.

plumber's friend, plumber's helper *n US* [tool] ventouse *f (pour déboucher)*.

plumbing ['plʌmɪŋ] *n* **1.** [job] plomberie *f* **2.** [pipes] plomberie *f*, tuyauterie *f*.

plumb line *n* CONSTR fil *m* à plomb ▪ NAUT sonde *f*.

plum duff *UK* = **plum pudding**.

plume [plu:m] ◇ *n* **1.** [feather] plume *f* **2.** [on helmet] plumet *m*, panache *m* ▪ [on hat] plumet *m* ▪ [on woman's hat] plume *f* **3.** [of smoke] volute *f* ▪ [of water] jet *m*.
◇ *vt* [preen] lisser ▪ **the swan ~d itself** *OR* **its feathers** le cygne se lissait les plumes.

plumed [plu:md] *adj* **1.** [hat, helmet] emplumé, empanaché **2.** [bird] : **brightly ~ peacocks** des paons au plumage éclatant.

plummet ['plʌmɪt] ◇ *vi* **1.** [plunge, dive] tomber, plonger, piquer ▪ **the plane ~ed towards the earth** l'avion piqua vers le sol **2.** [drop, go down - price, rate, amount] chuter, dégringoler ▪ **his popularity has ~ed** sa cote de popularité a beaucoup baissé ▪ **the value of the pound ~ed** la livre a chuté.
◇ *n* [weight] plomb *m* ▪ [plumb line] fil *m* à plomb.

plummy ['plʌmɪ] (*comp* **plummier**, *superl* **plummiest**) *adj* **1.** *UK pej* [voice, accent] snob **2.** [colour] prune *(inv)*.

plump [plʌmp] ◇ *adj* [person] rondelet, dodu ▪ [arms, legs] dodu, potelé ▪ [fowl] dodu, bien gras ▪ [fruit] charnu.
◇ *adv* [heavily] lourdement ▪ [directly] exactement, en plein.
◇ *vt* **1.** [pillow, cushion] retaper **2.** [fowl] engraisser.
◆ **plump down** *vt sep* : **she ~ed herself/her bag down next to me** elle s'est affalée/a laissé tomber son sac à côté de moi.
◆ **plump for** *vt insep inf* arrêter son choix sur, opter en faveur de.
◆ **plump out** *vi insep* s'arrondir, engraisser.
◆ **plump up** *vt sep* = **plump** *(vt sense 1)*.

plumpness ['plʌmpnɪs] *n* rondeur *f*, embonpoint *m*.

plum pudding *n* plum-pudding *m*.

plunder ['plʌndə^r] ◇ *vt* piller.
◇ *n* **1.** [booty] butin *m* **2.** [act of pillaging] pillage *m*.

plunderer ['plʌndərə^r] *n* pillard *m*, - e *f*.

plundering ['plʌndərɪŋ] ◇ *n* pillage *m*.
◇ *adj* pillard.

plunge [plʌndʒ] ◇ *vi* **1.** [dive] plonger **2.** [throw o.s.] se jeter, se précipiter ▪ [fall, drop] tomber, chuter ▪ **the helicopter ~d to the ground** l'hélicoptère piqua vers le sol ▪ **to ~ to one's death** faire une chute mortelle ▪ **I slipped and ~d forward** j'ai glissé et je suis tombé la tête la première *OR* la tête en avant **3.** *fig* **sales have ~d by 30%** les ventes ont chuté de 30 % ▪ **he ~d into a long and complicated story** il s'est lancé dans une histoire longue et compliquée ▪ **the neckline ~s deeply at the front** le devant est très décolleté **4.** *inf* [gamble] flamber.
◇ *vt* **1.** [immerse] plonger **2.** *fig* plonger ▪ **he ~d his hands into his pockets** il enfonça les mains dans ses poches ▪ **he was ~d into despair by the news** la nouvelle l'a plongé dans le désespoir ▪ **the office was ~d into darkness** le bureau fut plongé dans l'obscurité.
◇ *n* **1.** [dive] plongeon *m* ▪ **to take the ~** se jeter à l'eau **2.** [fall, drop] chute *f* ▪ **prices have taken a ~** les prix ont chuté *OR* se sont effondrés.

plunger ['plʌndʒə^r] *n* **1.** [for sinks, drains] ventouse *f*, déboucheur *m* **2.** [piston] piston *m* **3.** *UK inf* [gambler] flambeur *m*, - euse *f*.

plunging ['plʌndʒɪŋ] *adj* plongeant.

plunk [plʌŋk] *n inf* [sound] bruit *m* sourd ▪ **I could hear the ~ of a guitar** j'entendais quelqu'un gratter sa guitare.
◆ **plunk down** *inf* ◇ *vt sep* = **plunk** *(vt sense 1)*.
◇ *vi insep* se laisser tomber (lourdement), s'affaler.

pluperfect [,plu:'pɜ:fɪkt] ◇ *adj* : **the ~ tense** le plus-que-parfait.
◇ *n* plus-que-parfait *m* ▪ **in the ~** au plus-que-parfait.

plural ['plʊərəl] ◇ *adj* **1.** GRAM [form, ending] pluriel, du pluriel ▪ [noun] au pluriel **2.** [multiple] multiple ▪ [heterogeneous] hétérogène, pluriel ▪ **a ~ system of education** un système d'éducation diversifié ▪ **a ~ society** une société plurielle.
◇ *n* GRAM pluriel *m* ▪ **in the ~** au pluriel.

pluralism ['plʊərəlɪzm] *n* **1.** [gen - PHILOS] pluralisme *m* **2.** [holding of several offices] cumul *m*.

pluralist ['plʊərəlɪst] *n* [gen - PHILOS] pluraliste *mf*.

pluralistic [,plʊərə'lɪstɪk] *adj* pluraliste.

plurality [plʊə'rælətɪ] (*pl* **pluralities**) *n* **1.** [multiplicity] pluralité *f* **2.** *US* POL majorité *f* relative **3.** = **pluralism** *(sense 2)*.

pluralize, ise ['plʊərəlaɪz] *vi* prendre le pluriel.

plus [plʌs] (*pl* **pluses** *OR pl* **plusses**) ◇ *prep* **1.** MATHS plus ▪ **two ~ two is** *OR* **are** *OR* **makes four** deux plus deux *OR* deux et deux font quatre ▪ **~ six** plus six **2.** [as well as] plus ▪ **there were six of us, ~ the children** nous étions six, sans compter les enfants ▪ **£97 ~ VAT** 97 livres plus la TVA.
◇ *adj* **1.** ELEC & MATHS positif **2.** [good, positive] positif ▪ **on the ~ side, it's near the shops** un des avantages, c'est que c'est près des magasins **3.** *(after n)* [over, more than] : **children of twelve ~** les enfants de douze ans et plus ▪ **B ~** [in school marks] B plus.
◇ *n* **1.** MATHS plus *m* **2.** [bonus, advantage] plus *m*, avantage *m*.
◇ *conj inf* (et) en plus.

plus fours *npl* pantalon *m* de golf.

plush [plʌʃ] ◇ *adj* **1.** *inf* [luxurious] luxueux **2.** [made of plush] en peluche.
◇ *n* peluche *f*.

plus sign *n* signe *m* plus.

Plutarch ['plu:tɑ:k] *pr n* Plutarque.

Pluto ['plu:təʊ] *pr n* Pluton.

plutocracy [plu:'tɒkrəsɪ] (*pl* **plutocracies**) *n* ploutocratie *f*.

plutocrat ['plu:təkræt] *n* ploutocrate *mf*.

plutonium [plu:'təʊnɪəm] *n* plutonium *m* ▪ **~ radiation** radiation *f* de plutonium.

pluvial ['plu:vjəl] *adj* pluvial.

pluviometer [,plu:vɪ'ɒmɪtə^r] *n* pluviomètre *m*.

ply [plaɪ] ◇ *n* (*pl* **plies**) **1.** [thickness - gen] épaisseur *f* ▪ [layer - of plywood] pli *m* ▪ [strand - of rope, wool] brin *m* **2.** *inf* = **plywood**.
◇ *vt* (*pret & pp* **plied**) **1.** [supply insistently] : **to ~ sb with sthg** : **she plied us with food all evening** elle nous a gavés toute la soirée ▪ **he plied us with drinks** il nous versait sans arrêt à boire ▪ **we plied her with questions** nous l'avons assaillie de questions **2.** *lit* [perform, practise] exercer ▪ **to ~ one's trade** exercer son métier **3.** *lit* [use - tool] manier **4.** *lit* [travel - river, ocean] naviguer sur ▪ **the barges that ~ the Thames** les péniches qui descendent et remontent le cours de la Tamise.
◇ *vi* (*pret & pp* **plied**) **1.** [seek work] : **to ~ for hire** [taxi] prendre des clients **2.** [travel - ship, boat] : **to ~ between** faire la navette entre.

-ply *in cpds* : **five~ wood** contreplaqué *m* en cinq épaisseurs ▪ **three~ wool** laine *f* à trois fils.

plywood ['plaɪwʊd] *n* contreplaqué *m*.

p.m. (*abbrev of* **post meridiem**) *adv* : **3 ~** 3 h de l'après-midi, 15 h ▪ **11~** 11 h du soir, 23 h.

PM *n* = **Prime Minister**.

PMS (*abbrev of* **premenstrual syndrome**) = **PMT**.

PMT (*abbrev of* **premenstrual tension**) *n* syndrome *m* prémenstruel.

pneumatic [nju:'mætɪk] *adj* pneumatique ▪ ~ **brakes** freins *mpl* à air comprimé.

pneumatic drill *n* marteau piqueur *m*.

pneumoconiosis [ˌnju:məʊkəʊnɪ'əʊsɪs] *n* pneumoconiose *f*.

pneumonia [nju:'məʊnjə] *n (U)* pneumonie *f* ▪ **you'll catch** *OR* **get ~!** tu vas attraper une pneumonie!

po [pəʊ] (*pl* **pos**) *n* **UK** *inf* pot *m* (de chambre).

PO 1. *written abbr of* **post office 2.** *written abbr of* **written**, = **postal order**.

POA (*abbrev of* **Prison Officers' Association**) *pr n syndicat des agents pénitentiaires en Grande-Bretagne*.

poach [pəʊtʃ] <> *vt* **1.** [hunt illegally] prendre en braconnant ▪ **all the game has been ~ed** les braconniers ont tué tout le gibier **2.** *fig* [steal - idea] voler ; [- employee] débaucher ▪ **to ~ sb's shots** [in tennis] piquer les balles de qqn **3.** CULIN pocher ▪ **~ed egg** œuf *m* poché.
<> *vi* braconner ▪ **to ~ for hare** chasser le lièvre sur une propriété privée ▪ **to ~ for salmon** prendre du saumon en braconnant.

poacher ['pəʊtʃə^r] *n* **1.** [person] braconnier *m* **2.** CULIN pocheuse *f* ▪ **egg ~** pocheuse.

poaching ['pəʊtʃɪŋ] *n* braconnage *m*.

POB, PO Box (*abbrev of* **post office box**) *n* boîte *f* postale, BP *f*.

pocked [pɒkt] = **pockmarked**.

pocket ['pɒkɪt] <> *n* **1.** [on clothing] poche *f* ▪ [on car door] compartiment *m* ▪ **it's in your coat ~** c'est dans la poche de ton manteau ▪ **he tried to pick her ~** il a essayé de lui faire les poches ▶ **to have sb in one's ~s** avoir qqn dans sa poche ▪ **we had the deal in our ~** le marché était dans la poche ▪ **they live in each other's ~s** ils vivent entassés les uns sur les autres ▪ **to line one's ~s** se remplir les poches, s'en mettre plein les poches ▪ **to put one's hand in one's ~** mettre la main au portefeuille ▪ **to be out of ~** en être de sa poche **2.** *fig* [financial resources] portefeuille *m*, porte-monnaie *m* ▪ **we have prices to suit all ~s** nous avons des prix pour toutes les bourses **3.** [small area] poche *f* ▪ **~ of air** trou *m* d'air **4.** [on billiard or pool table] blouse *f*.
<> *comp* [diary, camera, revolver etc] de poche.
<> *vt* **1.** [put in one's pocket] mettre dans sa poche, empocher ▪ *fig* **to ~ one's pride** mettre son amour-propre dans sa poche ▪ **to ~ an insult** encaisser une insulte sans rien dire **2.** [steal] : **somebody must have ~ed the money** quelqu'un a dû mettre l'argent dans sa poche **3.** [in billiards, pool] mettre dans le trou *OR* la blouse *spec* **4.** SPORT [another runner] bloquer **5.** **US** POL : **to ~ a bill** *garder un projet de loi sous le coude pour l'empêcher d'être adopté*.

pocket battleship *n* cuirassé *m* de poche.

pocket billiards *n* billard *m* américain.

pocketbook ['pɒkɪtbʊk] *n* **1.** [notebook] calepin *m*, carnet *m* **2.** **US** [handbag] pochette *f*.

pocket calculator *n* calculatrice *f* de poche.

pocketful ['pɒkɪtfʊl] *n* poche *f* pleine.

pocket-handkerchief *n* mouchoir *m* de poche.

pocketknife ['pɒkɪtnaɪf] (*pl* **pocketknives** [-naɪvz]) *n* canif *m*.

pocket money *n* **UK** argent *m* de poche.

pocket-size(d) *adj* **1.** [book, revolver etc] de poche **2.** [tiny] tout petit, minuscule.

pockmark ['pɒkmɑ:k] *n* [on surface] marque *f*, petit trou *m* ▪ [from smallpox] cicatrice *f* de variole ▪ **his face is covered with ~s** il a le visage grêlé *OR* variolé.

pockmarked ['pɒkmɑ:kt] *adj* [face] grêlé ▪ [surface] criblé de petits trous ▪ **~ with rust** piqué par la rouille.

pod [pɒd] (*pret & pp* **podded**, *cont* **podding**) <> *n* **1.** BOT cosse *f* ▪ **bean ~** cosse de haricot **2.** ENTOM oothèque *f* **3.** AERON nacelle *f* ▪ ASTRONAUT capsule *f*.
<> *vt* **UK** écosser.
<> *vi* BOT produire des cosses.

poodle *n* caniche *m*.

podcast ['pɒdkæst] *n* COMPUT podcast *m*.

podgy ['pɒdʒɪ] (*comp* **podgier**, *superl* **podgiest**) *adj* **UK** dodu, replet, - ète *f*.

podiatrist [pə'daɪətrɪst] *n* **US** pédicure *mf*.

podiatry [pə'daɪətrɪ] *n* **US** pédicurie *f*.

podium ['pəʊdɪəm] (*pl* **podiums** *OR pl* **podia** [-dɪə]) *n* [stand] podium *m*.

poem ['pəʊɪm] *n* poème *m*.

poet ['pəʊɪt] *n* poète *m*.

poetess ['pəʊɪtɪs] *n* poétesse *f*.

poetical [pəʊ'etɪkl] *adj* poétique.

poetically [pəʊ'etɪklɪ] *adv* poétiquement.

poeticize, ise [pəʊ'etɪsaɪz] *vt* poétiser.

poetic justice *n* justice *f* immanente ▪ **it's ~ that they ended up losing** ce n'est que justice qu'ils aient fini par perdre.

poetic licence *n* licence *f* poétique.

poetics [pəʊ'etɪks] *n (U)* poétique *f*.

poet laureate (*pl* **poets laureate** *OR pl* **poet laureates**) *n* poète *m* lauréat.

poetry ['pəʊɪtrɪ] *n* poésie *f*.

po-faced ['pəʊfeɪst] *adj* **UK** *inf* à l'air pincé.

pogo stick ['pəʊgəʊ-] *n* bâton *m* sauteur *(jeu)*.

pogrom ['pɒgrəm] *n* pogrom *m*.

poignancy ['pɔɪnjənsɪ] *n* caractère *m* poignant ▪ **a moment of great ~** un moment d'intense émotion.

poignant ['pɔɪnjənt] *adj* poignant.

poignantly ['pɔɪnjəntlɪ] *adv* de façon poignante.

poinsettia [pɔɪn'setɪə] *n* poinsettia *m*.

point [pɔɪnt] <> *n* **1.** [tip - of sword, nail, pencil etc] pointe *f* ▪ **trim one end of the stick into a ~** taillez un des bouts de la branche en pointe ▪ **draw a star with five ~s** dessinez une étoile à cinq branches ▪ **an eight-~ stag** un cerf huit cors
2. [small dot] point *m*
3. [specific place] point *m*, endroit *m* ▪ **~ of intersection, intersection ~** point d'intersection ▪ **'meeting ~'** 'point rencontre' ▪ **the runners have passed the halfway ~** les coureurs ont dépassé la mi-parcours ▪ **to pass/to reach the ~ of no return** passer/atteindre le point de non-retour ▪ **at that ~ you'll see a church on the left** à ce moment-là, vous verrez une église sur votre gauche ▪ **~s south of here get little rainfall** les régions situées au sud d'ici n'ont pas une grande pluviosité
4. [particular moment] moment *m* ▪ [particular period] période *f* ▪ **the country is at a critical ~ in its development** le pays traverse une période *OR* phase critique de son développement ▪ **we are at a critical ~** nous voici à un point critique ▪ **there comes a ~ when a decision has to be made** il arrive un moment où il faut prendre une décision ▪ **at one ~ in my travels** au cours de mes voyages ▪ **at one ~, I thought the roof was going to cave in** à un moment (donné), j'ai cru que le toit allait s'effondrer ▪ **at that ~, I was still undecided** à ce moment-là, je n'avais pas encore pris de décision ▪ **by that ~, I was too tired to move** j'étais alors tellement fatigué que je ne pouvais plus bouger
5. [stage in development or process] point *m* ▪ **thank God we haven't reached that ~!** Dieu merci, nous n'en sommes pas (encore arrivés) là! ▪ **to be at the ~ of death** être sur le point de

mourir ■ **the conflict has gone beyond the ~where negotiations are possible** le conflit a atteint le stade où toute négociation est impossible ■ **the regime is on the ~ of collapse** le régime est au bord de l'effondrement ■ **I was on the ~ of admitting everything** j'étais sur le point de tout avouer ■ **she had worked to the ~ of exhaustion** elle avait travaillé jusqu'à l'épuisement ■ **he was jealous to the ~ of madness** sa jalousie confinait à la folie

6. [for discussion or debate] point *m* ■ **are there any ~s I haven't covered?** y a-t-il des questions que je n'ai pas abordées? ■ **to make** *OR* **to raise a ~** faire une remarque ■ **to make the ~ that...** faire remarquer que... ■ **all right, you've made your ~!** d'accord, on a compris! ■ **let me illustrate my ~** laissez-moi illustrer mon propos ■ **to prove his ~ he showed us a photo** pour prouver ses affirmations, il nous a montré une photo ■ **I see** *OR* **take your ~** je vois ce que vous voulez dire *OR* où vous voulez en venir ■ **~ taken!** c'est juste! ■ **he may not be home – you've got a ~there!** il n'est peut-être pas chez lui – ça c'est vrai! ■ **the fact that he went to the police is a ~ in his favour/a ~ against him** le fait qu'il soit allé à la police est un bon/mauvais point pour lui ▮ [precise detail] : **he rose on a ~ of order** il a demandé la parole pour soulever un point de procédure ■ **she was disqualified on a technical ~** elle a été disqualifiée pour *OR* sur une faute technique ■ **to make a ~ of doing sthg** tenir à faire qqch ■ **kindly make a ~ of remembering next time** faites-moi le plaisir de ne pas oublier la prochaine fois

7. [essential part, heart - of argument, explanation] essentiel *m* ■ [conclusion - of joke] chute *f* ■ **I get the ~** je comprends, je vois ■ **the ~ is (that) we're overloaded with work** le fait est que nous sommes débordés de travail ■ **we're getting off** *OR* **away from the ~** nous nous éloignons *OR* écartons du sujet ■ **that's the (whole) ~!** [that's the problem] c'est là (tout) le problème! ; [that's the aim] c'est ça, le but! ➋ **to be beside the ~ : the money is/your feelings are beside the ~** l'argent n'a/vos sentiments n'ont rien à voir là-dedans ■ **get** *OR* **come to the ~!** dites ce que vous avez à dire!, ne tournez pas autour du pot! ■ **I'll come straight to the ~** je serai bref ■ **to keep to the ~** ne pas s'écarter du sujet

8. [purpose] but *m* ■ [meaning, use] sens *m*, intérêt *m* ■ **there's no ~ in asking him now** ça ne sert à rien *OR* ce n'est pas la peine de le lui demander maintenant ■ **what's the ~ of all this?** à quoi ça sert tout ça? ■ **oh, what's the ~ anyway!** oh, et puis à quoi bon, après tout!

9. [feature, characteristic] point *m* ■ **the boss has his good ~s** le patron a ses bons côtés ■ **it's my weak/strong ~** c'est mon point faible/fort

10. [unit - in scoring, measuring] point *m* ■ **to win/to lead on ~s** [in boxing] gagner/mener aux points ➋ **merit ~s** SCH bons points *mpl*

11. [on compass] point *m* ■ **our people were scattered to all ~s of the compass** *fig* notre peuple s'est retrouvé éparpillé aux quatre coins du monde

12. GEOM point *m*

13. [in decimals] virgule *f*

14. [punctuation mark] point *m* ■ **three** *OR* **ellipsis ~s** points *mpl* de suspension

15. TYPO point *m*

16. GEOG [promontory] pointe *f*, promontoire *m*

17. AUT vis *f* platinée

18. *UK* ELEC [socket] : **(power) ~** prise *f* (de courant)

19. HERALD point *m*.

◇ *vi* **1.** [person] tendre le doigt ■ **to ~ at** *OR* **to** *OR* **towards sthg** montrer qqch du doigt ■ **she ~ed left** elle fit un signe vers la gauche ■ **he ~ed at** *OR* **to me with his pencil** il pointa son crayon vers moi ■ **it's rude to ~** ce n'est pas poli de montrer du doigt

2. [roadsign, needle on dial] : **the signpost ~s up the hill** le panneau est tourné vers le haut de la colline ■ **a compass needle always ~s north** l'aiguille d'une boussole indique toujours le nord ■ **the weather vane is ~ing north** la girouette est orientée au nord ■ **when the big hand ~s to twelve** quand la grande aiguille est sur le douze

3. [be directed, face - gun, camera] être braqué ; [- vehicle] être dirigé, être tourné ■ **hold the gun with the barrel ~ing downwards** tenez le canon de l'arme pointé vers le bas ■ **insert the disk with the arrow ~ing right** insérez la disquette, la flèche pointée *OR* pointant vers la droite ■ **he walks with his feet ~ing outwards** il marche les pieds en dehors

4. [dog] tomber en arrêt.

◇ *vt* **1.** [direct, aim - vehicle] diriger ; [- flashlight, hose] pointer, braquer ; [- finger] pointer, tendre ■ **to ~ one's finger at sb/sthg** montrer qqn/qqch du doigt ■ **he ~ed the rifle/the camera at me** il braqua le fusil/l'appareil photo sur moi ■ **he ~ed the boat out to sea** il a mis le cap vers le large ■ [send - person] : **if anybody shows up, just ~ them in my direction** si quelqu'un arrive, tu n'as qu'à me l'envoyer ■ **just ~ him to the nearest bar** tu n'as qu'à lui indiquer le chemin du bar le plus proche

2. DANCE : **to ~ one's toes** faire des pointes

3. CONSTR [wall, building] jointoyer

4. *lit* [moral, necessity] souligner, faire ressortir

5. [sharpen - stick, pencil] tailler

6. LING mettre des points-voyelles à

7. *phr* **to ~ the way** [subj: arrow, signpost] indiquer la direction *OR* le chemin ; *fig* [subj: person] montrer le chemin ■ **her research ~s the way to a better understanding of the phenomenon** ses recherches vont permettre une meilleure compréhension du phénomène ■ **they ~ the way (in) which reform must go** ils indiquent la direction dans laquelle les réformes doivent aller.

◆ **points** *npl* **1.** *UK* RAIL aiguilles *fpl*

2. DANCE (chaussons *mpl* à)pointes *fpl* ■ **she's already (dancing) on ~s** elle fait déjà des pointes.

◆ **at this point in time** *adv phr* pour l'instant.

◆ **in point of fact** *adv phr* en fait, à vrai dire.

◆ **to the point** *adj phr* pertinent.

◆ **up to a point** *adv phr* jusqu'à un certain point ■ **did the strategy succeed? – up to a ~** est-ce que la stratégie a réussi? – dans une certaine mesure.

◆ **point out** *vt sep* **1.** [indicate] indiquer, montrer

2. [mention, call attention to] signaler, faire remarquer ■ **I'd like to ~ out that it was my idea in the first place** je vous ferai remarquer que l'idée est de moi.

◆ **point to** *vt insep* **1.** [signify, denote] signifier, indiquer ■ [foreshadow] indiquer, annoncer ■ **the facts ~ to only one conclusion** les faits ne permettent qu'une seule conclusion ■ **all the evidence ~s to him** toutes les preuves indiquent que c'est lui

2. [call attention to] attirer l'attention sur ■ **they proudly ~ to the government's record** ils invoquent avec fierté le bilan du gouvernement.

◆ **point up** *vt sep* [subj: person, report] souligner, mettre l'accent sur ■ [subj: event] faire ressortir ■ **the accident ~s up the need for closer cooperation** l'accident fait ressortir le besoin d'une coopération plus étroite.

point-and-shoot *adj* [camera] automatique.

point-blank ◇ *adj* **1.** [shot] (tiré) à bout portant ■ **he was shot at ~ range** on lui a tiré dessus à bout portant **2.** [refusal, denial] catégorique ■ [question] (posé) de but en blanc, (posé) à brûle-pourpoint.

◇ *adv* **1.** [shoot] à bout portant **2.** [refuse, deny] catégoriquement ■ [ask] de but en blanc, à brûle-pourpoint.

point duty *n UK* **to be on ~** diriger la circulation.

pointed ['pɔɪntɪd] *adj* **1.** [sharp] pointu ■ **~ arch** ARCHIT arche *f* en ogive ■ **~ style** ARCHIT style *m* gothique **2.** [meaningful - look, comment] insistant ; [- reference] peu équivoque **3.** [marked] ostentatoire.

-pointed *in cpds* : **five/six~** [gen] à cinq/six pointes ; [star] à cinq/six branches.

pointedly ['pɔɪntɪdlɪ] *adv* **1.** [meaningfully - look, comment] de façon insistante **2.** [markedly] de façon marquée *OR* prononcée ■ **she ~ ignored me all evening** elle m'a ostensiblement ignoré pendant toute la soirée.

pointer ['pɔɪntər] *n* **1.** [for pointing - stick] baguette *f* ; [- arrow] flèche *f* **2.** [on dial] aiguille *f* **3.** [indication, sign] indice *m*, signe *m* ■ **all the ~s indicate an impending economic recovery** tout indique que la reprise économique est imminente ■ **he gave me a few ~s on how to use the computer** il m'a donné quelques tuyaux sur la façon d'utiliser l'ordinateur **4.** COMPUT pointeur *m* **5.** [dog] pointer *m*.

pointing ['pɔɪntɪŋ] *n (U)* CONSTR [act, job] jointoiement *m* ■ [cement work] joints *mpl*.

pointless ['pɔɪntlɪs] *adj* [gen] inutile, vain ■ [crime, violence, vandalism] gratuit ■ **it's ~ trying to convince him** ça ne sert à rien *OR* il est inutile d'essayer de le convaincre.

pointlessly ['pɔɪntlɪslɪ] *adv* [gen] inutilement, vainement ■ [hurt, murder, vandalize] gratuitement.

pointlessness ['pɔɪntlɪsnɪs] *n* [gen] inutilité *f* ■ [of remark] manque *m* d'à-propos ■ [of crime, violence, vandalism] gratuité *f*.

point of order *n* point *m* de procédure.

point of reference *n* point *m* de référence.

point-of-sale *adj* sur le point *OR* sur le lieu de vente ■ **~ advertising** publicité *f* sur le lieu de vente, PLV *f*.

point of view *n* point *m* de vue ■ **from my ~, it doesn't make much difference** en ce qui me concerne, ça ne change pas grand-chose.

pointsman ['pɔɪntsmən] (*pl* **pointsmen** [-mən]) *n UK* RAIL aiguilleur *m*.

point-to-point *n UK rallye hippique pour cavaliers amateurs.*

poise [pɔɪz] ◇ *n* **1.** [composure, coolness] calme *m*, aisance *f*, assurance *f* **2.** [physical bearing] port *m*, maintien *m* ■ [gracefulness] grâce *f*.
◇ *vt* [balance] mettre en équilibre ■ [hold suspended] tenir suspendu.

poised [pɔɪzd] *adj* **1.** [balanced] en équilibre ■ [suspended] suspendu ■ **she held her glass ~ near her lips** elle tenait son verre près de ses lèvres **2.** [ready, prepared] prêt ■ **~ for action** prêt à agir **3.** [composed, self-assured] calme, assuré.

poison ['pɔɪzn] ◇ *n* **1.** poison *m* ■ [of reptile] venin *m* **2.** *fig* poison *m*, venin *m* ■ **the ~ spreading through our society** le mal qui se propage dans notre société ■ **they hate each other like ~** ils se détestent cordialement ◐ **what's your ~?** *hum* qu'est-ce que tu bois ?, qu'est-ce que je t'offre?
◇ *comp* [mushroom, plant] vénéneux ■ [gas] toxique ■ **~ gland** ZOOL glande *f* à venin.
◇ *vt* **1.** *liter* empoisonner ■ **to ~ sb with sthg** empoisonner qqn à qqch ■ **a ~ed arrow/drink** une flèche/boisson empoisonnée **2.** *fig* envenimer, gâcher ■ **his arrival ~ed the atmosphere** son arrivée rendit l'atmosphère insupportable ■ **they are ~ing his mind** ils sont en train de le corrompre ■ **he ~ed our minds against her** il nous a montés contre elle.

poisoned chalice *n fig* cadeau *m* empoisonné.

poisoner ['pɔɪznəʳ] *n* empoisonneur *m*, - euse *f*.

poison gas *n* gaz *m* toxique.

poisoning ['pɔɪznɪŋ] *n* empoisonnement *m* ■ **mercury ~** empoisonnement au mercure.

poison ivy *n* sumac *m* vénéneux.

poisonous ['pɔɪznəs] *adj* **1.** [mushroom, plant] vénéneux ■ [snake, lizard] venimeux ■ [gas, chemical] toxique **2.** *fig* [person] malveillant, venimeux ■ [remark, allegation] venimeux ■ **he's got a ~ tongue** il a une langue de vipère.

poison-pen letter *n* lettre *f* anonyme.

poke [pəʊk] ◇ *vt* **1.** [push, prod - gen] donner un coup à ; [- with elbow] donner un coup de coude à **2.** [stick, thrust] enfoncer ■ **to ~ a hole in sthg** faire un trou dans qqch ■ **he ~d his stick at me** il fit un mouvement avec son bâton dans ma direction ■ **she opened the door and ~d her head in/out** elle ouvrit la porte et passa sa tête à l'intérieur/à l'extérieur ■ **he's always poking his nose in other people's business** il se mêle toujours de ce qui ne le regarde pas **3.** [fire] tisonner **4.** *inf* [punch] flanquer un coup de poing à **5.** △ [have sex with] tirer un coup avec△.
◇ *n* **1.** [push, prod] poussée *f*, (petit) coup *m* ■ **he gave me a ~ in the back** il m'a donné un (petit) coup dans le dos ■ **give the fire a ~** donne un coup de tisonnier dans le feu **2.** *US inf* [punch] gnon *m*, marron *m*.
► **poke about, poke around** *vi insep* fouiller, fourrager ■ **she ~d around in her bag for her purse** elle a fouillé dans son sac pour trouver son porte-monnaie.
► **poke along** *vi insep US* avancer lentement.
► **poke out** ◇ *vi insep* [stick out] dépasser ■ **the new shoots were just poking out of the ground** les nouvelles pousses commençaient tout juste à sortir de terre.
◇ *vt sep* [remove] déloger ■ **to ~ sb's eye out** crever un œil à qqn.

poker ['pəʊkəʳ] *n* **1.** [card game] poker *m* **2.** [for fire] tisonnier *m*.

poker dice ◇ *n* [game] poker *m* d'as.
◇ *npl* [set of dice] dés *mpl* pour le poker d'as.

poker face *n* visage *m* impassible *OR* impénétrable ■ **she kept a ~** son visage n'a pas trahi la moindre émotion *OR* est resté totalement impassible.

poker-faced *adj* (au visage) impassible.

poky ['pəʊkɪ] (*comp* **pokier**, *superl* **pokiest**) *adj inf* **1.** *UK* [house, room - cramped] exigu, - uë *f* **2.** *US* [slow] lambin.

Poland ['pəʊlənd] *pr n* Pologne *f* ■ **in ~** en Pologne.

polar ['pəʊləʳ] *adj* **1.** CHEM, ELEC, GEOG & MATHS polaire ■ **the ~ lights** l'aurore *f* polaire **2.** *fig* [totally opposite - opinions, attitudes] diamétralement opposé.

polar bear *n* ours *m* polaire *OR* blanc.

polarity [pəʊ'lærətɪ] (*pl* **polarities**) *n* polarité *f*.

polarization [,pəʊləraɪ'zeɪʃn] *n* polarisation *f*.

polarize, ise ['pəʊləraɪz] ◇ *vt* polariser.
◇ *vi* se polariser.

Polaroid® ['pəʊlərɔɪd] ◇ *adj* [camera] Polaroid® ■ [film] pour Polaroid® ■ [glasses] à verre polarisé.
◇ *n* [camera] Polaroid® ■ [photo] photo *f* *OR* cliché *m* Polaroid®.
► **Polaroids**® *npl* [sunglasses] lunettes *fpl* de soleil à verre polarisé.

pole [pəʊl] ◇ *n* **1.** ELEC & GEOG pôle *m* ■ **to travel from ~ to ~** parcourir la terre entière ◐ **they are ~s apart** ils n'ont absolument rien en commun ■ **their positions on disarmament are ~s apart** leurs positions sur le désarmement sont diamétralement opposées **2.** [rod] bâton *m*, perche *f* ■ [for tent] montant *m* ■ [in fence, construction] poteau *m*, pieu *m* ■ [for gardening] tuteur *m* ■ [for climbing plants] rame *f* ■ [for polevaulting, punting] perche *f* ■ [for skier] bâton *m* **3.** [mast - for phonelines] poteau *m* ; [- for flags] mât *m* **4.** [for climbing] mât *m* ■ [in firestation] perche *f* ■ **you're up the ~!** *UK inf* [mistaken] tu te gourres! ; [mad] tu es fou *OR* cinglé! ■ **he's driving me up the ~!** *UK* il me rend dingue! **5.** *US* [on racecourse] corde *f* **6.** [unit of measure] ≃ perche *f*.
◇ *vt* **1.** [punt] faire avancer (avec une perche) **2.** [plants] ramer.

Pole [pəʊl] *n* Polonais *m*, - e *f*.

poleaxe *UK*, **poleax** *US* ['pəʊlæks] ◇ *n* **1.** [weapon] hache *f* d'armes **2.** [for slaughter] merlin *m*.
◇ *vt liter* abattre ■ *fig* terrasser.

poleaxed ['pəʊlækst] *adj inf* **1.** [surprised] baba, épaté **2.** [drunk] bourré, beurré.

polecat ['pəʊlkæt] (*pl inv OR pl* **polecats**) *n* **1.** [European, African] putois *m* **2.** *US* [skunk] moufette *f*, mouffette *f*.

pole dancing *n style de danse de strip-tease qui s'exécute autour d'une barre verticale.*

pole jump = **pole vault**.

polemic [pə'lemɪk] ◇ *adj* polémique.
◇ *n* [argument] polémique *f*.
► **polemics** *n (U)* [skill, practice] art *m* de la polémique.

polemical [pə'lemɪkl] *adj* polémique.

polemicist [pə'lemɪsɪst] *n* polémiste *mf*.

pole position *n* [in motor racing] pole position *f* ■ **to be in ~** être en pole position.

Pole Star *n* (étoile *f*) Polaire *f*.

pole vault *n* saut *m* à la perche.
► **pole-vault** *vi* [as activity] faire du saut à la perche ■ [on specific jump] faire un saut à la perche.

pole-vaulter [-ˌvɔːltəʳ] *n* perchiste *mf*.

police [pəˈliːs] ◇ *npl* police *f* ■ **the ~ are on their way** la police arrive, les gendarmes arrivent ■ **a man is helping ~ with their enquiries** un homme est entendu par les policiers dans le cadre de leur enquête ■ **18 ~ were injured** 18 policiers ont été blessés.
◇ *comp* [vehicle, patrol, spy] de police ■ [protection, work] de la police, policier ■ [harassment] policier ■ **he was taken into ~ custody** il a été emmené en garde à vue ■ **a ~ escort** une escorte policière ■ **there was a heavy ~ presence** d'importantes forces de police se trouvaient sur place ➲ **Police Complaints Board** ≃ Inspection *f* générale des services ■ **the Police Federation** *le syndicat de la police britannique*.
◇ *vt* **1.** [subj: policemen] surveiller, maintenir l'ordre dans ■ **the streets are being ~d 24 hours a day** les rues sont surveillées par la police 24 heures sur 24 ■ **the match was heavily ~d** d'importantes forces de police étaient présentes lors du match ■ [subj: guards, vigilantes] surveiller, maintenir l'ordre dans ■ [subj: army, international organization] surveiller, contrôler ■ **the area is ~d by army patrols** des patrouilles militaires veillent au maintien de l'ordre dans la région **2.** [regulate - prices] contrôler ; [- agreement] veiller à l'application *OR* au respect de **3.** *US* [clean - military camp] nettoyer.

police academy *n US* école *f* de police.

police car *n* voiture *f* de police.

police cell *n* cellule *f* d'un poste de police.

police chief *n* ≃ préfet *m* de police.

police commissioner *n US* commissaire *m* de police.

police constable *n UK* ≃ gardien *m* de la paix, ≃ agent *m* (de police).

police court *n* tribunal *m* de police.

police department *n US* service *m* de police.

police dog *n* chien *m* policier.

police force *n* police *f* ■ **to join the ~** entrer dans la police.

police inspector *n* inspecteur *m*, - trice *f* de police.

policeman [pəˈliːsmən] (*pl* **policemen** [-mən]) *n* agent *m* (de police), policier *m*.

police officer *n* policier *m*, -ère *f*, agent *m* de police.

police record *n* casier *m* judiciaire.

police sergeant *n* ≃ brigadier *m* (de police).

police state *n* État *m* *OR* régime *m* policier.

police station *n* [urban] poste *m* de police, commissariat *m* (de police) ■ [rural] gendarmerie *f*.

police wagon *n US* fourgon *m* cellulaire.

policewoman [pəˈliːsˌwʊmən] (*pl* **policewomen** [-ˌwɪmɪn]) *n* femme *f* policier.

policy [ˈpɒləsɪ] (*pl* **policies**) ◇ *n* **1.** POL politique *f* ■ **the government's economic policies** la politique économique du gouvernement **2.** COMM [of company, organization] politique *f*, orientation *f* ■ **this is in line with company ~** ça va dans le sens de la politique de l'entreprise ■ **our ~ is to hire professionals only** nous avons pour politique de n'engager que des professionnels **3.** [personal principle, rule of action] principe *m*, règle *f* ■ **her ~ has been always to tell the truth** elle a toujours eu pour principe de dire la vérité ■ **it's bad ~ to reveal your objectives early on** c'est une mauvaise tactique de dévoiler vos objectifs à l'avance **4.** [for insurance] police *f*.
◇ *comp* [decision, statement] de principe ■ [debate] de politique générale.

policyholder [ˈpɒləsɪˌhəʊldəʳ] *n* assuré *m*, - e *f*.

polio [ˈpəʊlɪəʊ] *n (U)* polio *f*.

poliomyelitis [ˌpəʊlɪəʊmaɪəˈlaɪtɪs] *n (U)* poliomyélite *f*.

polish [ˈpɒlɪʃ] ◇ *vt* **1.** [furniture] cirer, encaustiquer ■ [brass, car] astiquer ■ [mirror] astiquer ■ [shoes] cirer, brosser ■ [gemstone] polir **2.** *fig* [perfect] polir, perfectionner **3.** [person] parfaire l'éducation de ■ **his manners could do with ~ing** ses manières laissent à désirer.
◇ *n* **1.** [for wood, furniture] encaustique *f*, cire *f* ■ [for shoes] cirage *m* ■ [for brass, car, silverware] *produit d'entretien pour le cuivre, la voiture, l'argenterie etc* ■ [for fingernails] vernis *m* **2.** [act of polishing] : **to give sthg a ~** astiquer qqch ■ **give your shoes a quick ~** donne un petit coup de brosse à tes chaussures **3.** [shine, lustre] brillant *m*, éclat *m* ■ **to put a ~ on sthg** faire briller qqch **4.** *fig* raffinement *m*, élégance *f*.
◆ **polish off** *vt sep inf* **1.** [finish - meal] finir, avaler **2.** [complete - job] expédier ; [- book, essay] en finir avec **3.** [defeat] se débarrasser de, écraser ■ [kill] liquider, descendre.
◆ **polish up** ◇ *vi insep* : **brass ~es up well** le cuivre est facile à faire briller.
◇ *vt sep* **1.** [furniture, shoes] faire briller ■ [diamond] polir **2.** *fig* [perfect - maths, language] perfectionner, travailler ; [- technique] parfaire, améliorer.

Polish [ˈpəʊlɪʃ] ◇ *n* LING polonais *m*.
◇ *npl* [people] : **the ~** les Polonais.
◇ *adj* polonais.

polished [ˈpɒlɪʃt] *adj* **1.** [surface] brillant, poli **2.** CULIN [rice] décortiqué **3.** [person] qui a du savoir-vivre, raffiné ■ [manners] raffiné **4.** [performer] accompli ■ [performance] parfait, impeccable ■ [style] raffiné, élégant.

polisher [ˈpɒlɪʃəʳ] *n* [person] cireur *m*, - euse *f* ■ [machine] polissoir *m* ■ [for floors] cireuse *f*.

Politburo [ˈpɒlɪtˌbjʊərəʊ] (*pl* **Politburos**) *n* Politburo *m*.

polite [pəˈlaɪt] *adj* **1.** [person] poli, courtois ■ [remark, conversation] poli, aimable ■ **to be ~ to sb** être poli envers *OR* avec qqn ■ **it is ~ to ask first** quand on est poli, on demande d'abord ■ **to make ~ conversation** faire la conversation ■ **she was very ~ about my poems** elle s'est montrée très diplomate dans ses commentaires sur mes poèmes **2.** [refined - manners] raffiné, élégant ■ **~ society** la bonne société, le beau monde.

politely [pəˈlaɪtlɪ] *adv* poliment, de manière courtoise.

politeness [pəˈlaɪtnɪs] *n* politesse *f*, courtoisie *f* ■ **out of ~** par politesse.

politic [ˈpɒlətɪk] *adj fml* [shrewd] habile, avisé ■ [wise] judicieux, sage.

political [pəˈlɪtɪkl] *adj* **1.** politique **2.** [interested in politics] : **he's always been very ~** il s'est toujours intéressé à la politique.

political correctness *n* le politiquement correct.

political geography *n* géographie *f* politique.

politically [pəˈlɪtɪklɪ] *adv* politiquement.

politically correct *adj* politiquement correct.

POLITICALLY CORRECT

Le mouvement *PC* cherche à établir un nouveau code éthique, bannissant du vocabulaire tout élément discriminatoire. Les termes ou les allusions susceptibles d'offenser certaines parties de la population (minorités ethniques, femmes, personnes âgées, personnes défavorisées, etc.) doivent être évités. Ainsi, on préférera *Native American* à *American Indian*, *Inuit* à *Eskimo*, *differently abled* à *disabled*, *visually impaired* à *blind*, etc. Ce phénomène a pris naissance aux États-Unis au début des années 1970 ; il est apparu en Grande-Bretagne dans les années 1980.

political science *n (U)* sciences *fpl* politiques.

politician [ˌpɒlɪˈtɪʃn] *n* **1.** [gen] homme *m* politique, femme *f* politique **2.** *US pej* politicien *m*, - enne *f*.

politicization [pəˌlɪtɪsaɪˈzeɪʃn] *n* politisation *f*.

politicize, ise [pəˈlɪtɪsaɪz] ◇ *vt* politiser ■ **the whole issue has become highly ~d** on a beaucoup politisé toute cette question.
◇ *vi* faire de la politique.

politicking [ˈpɒlətɪkɪŋ] *n pej activité politique visant uniquement à obtenir des suffrages*.

politico [pəˈlɪtɪkəʊ] (*pl* **politicos** OR *pl* **politicoes**) *n inf pej* politicard *m*, - e *f*.

politics [ˈpɒlətɪks] <> *n (U)* **1.** [as a profession] : **to go into ~** faire de la politique ▪ **local ~** politique locale ▪ **~ has never attracted her** la politique ne l'a jamais intéressée **2.** [art or science] politique *f* ▪ **she studied ~ at university** elle a étudié les sciences politiques à l'université **3.** [activity] politique *f* ▪ **I tried not to be drawn into office ~** j'ai essayé de ne pas me laisser entraîner dans les intrigues de bureau ➊ **sexual ~** *ensemble des idées et des problèmes touchant aux droits des femmes, des homosexuels etc.*
<> *npl* [opinions] idées *fpl* OR opinions *fpl* politiques ▪ **what exactly are her ~?** quelles sont ses opinions politiques au juste?

polity [ˈpɒlətɪ] (*pl* **polities**) *n fml* [state] État *m* ▪ [administration] organisation *f* politique OR administrative ▪ [political unit] entité *f* politique.

polka [ˈpɒlkə] <> *n* polka *f*.
<> *vi* danser la polka.

polka dot *n* TEX pois *m*.
◆ **polka-dot** *adj* à pois.

poll [pəʊl] <> *n* **1.** POL [elections] élection *f*, élections *fpl*, scrutin *m* ▪ **to go to the ~s** voter, se rendre aux urnes ▪ **the party is likely to be defeated at the ~s** le parti sera probablement battu aux élections ‖ [vote] vote *m* ▪ [votes cast] suffrages *mpl* (exprimés), nombre *m* de voix ▪ **there was an unexpectedly heavy ~** contrairement aux prévisions, il y a eu un fort taux de participation au scrutin ▪ **the ecology candidate got 3% of the ~** le candidat écologiste a obtenu OR recueilli 3 % des suffrages OR des voix **2.** [survey - of opinion, intentions] sondage *m* ▪ **to conduct a ~ on** OR **about sthg** faire un sondage d'opinion sur qqch, effectuer un sondage auprès de la population concernant qqch ▪ **the latest ~ puts the Socialists in the lead** le dernier sondage donne les socialistes en tête **3.** [count, census] recensement *m* **4.** [list - of taxpayers] rôle *m* nominatif ; [- of electors] liste *f* électorale.
<> *vt* **1.** POL [votes] recueillir, obtenir **2.** [person] sonder, recueillir l'opinion de ▪ **most of those ~ed were in favour of the plan** la plupart des personnes interrogées OR sondées étaient favorables au projet **3.** *US* [assembly] inscrire le vote de **4.** COMPUT [terminal] appeler ▪ [data] recueillir **5.** [tree] étêter ▪ [cattle] décorner.
<> *vi* [voter] voter.

pollard [ˈpɒləd] <> *n* **1.** BOT têtard *m (arbre)* **2.** ZOOL animal *m* sans cornes.
<> *vt* **1.** BOT étêter **2.** ZOOL décorner.

pollen [ˈpɒlən] *n* pollen *m* ▪ **~ analysis** analyse *f* pollinique.

pollen count *n* indice *m* pollinique (de l'air).

pollinate [ˈpɒləneɪt] *vt* polliniser.

pollination [ˌpɒlɪˈneɪʃn] *n* pollinisation *f*.

polling [ˈpəʊlɪŋ] *n (U)* **1.** POL [voting] vote *m*, suffrage *m* ▪ [elections] élections *fpl*, scrutin *m* ▪ **the first round of ~** le premier tour de scrutin OR des élections ▪ **~ is up on last year** la participation au vote est plus élevée que l'année dernière **2.** [for opinion poll] sondage *m*.

polling booth *n* isoloir *m*.

polling day *n* jour *m* des élections OR du scrutin.

polling station *n* bureau *m* de vote.

pollster [ˈpəʊlstəʳ] *n inf* enquêteur *m*, - euse *f*, - trice *f*, sondeur *m*, - euse *f*.

poll tax *n* **1.** [in UK] *impôt local aboli en 1993, basé sur le nombre d'occupants adultes d'un logement* **2.** [in US] *impôt, aboli en 1964, donnant droit à être inscrit sur les listes électorales* **3.** HIST capitation *f*.

pollutant [pəˈluːtnt] *n* polluant *m*.

pollute [pəˈluːt] *vt* polluer ▪ **the rivers are ~d with toxic waste** les cours d'eau sont pollués par les déchets toxiques.

polluter [pəˈluːtəʳ] *n* pollueur *m*, - euse *f*.

pollution [pəˈluːʃn] *n* **1.** [of environment] pollution *f* **2.** *(U)* [pollutants] polluants *mpl* ▪ **volunteers are helping to clear the beach of ~** des volontaires participent aux opérations d'assainissement de la plage.

Pollyanna [ˌpɒlɪˈænə] *n individu naïvement optimiste*.

polo [ˈpəʊləʊ] (*pl* **polos**) <> *n* SPORT polo *m*.
<> *comp* [match, stick] de polo.

polonaise [ˌpɒləˈneɪz] *n* MUS & SEW polonaise *f*.

polo neck *n UK* [collar] col *m* roulé ▪ [sweater] (pull *m* à) col *m* roulé.
◆ **polo-neck(ed)** *adj UK* à col roulé.

polo shirt *n* polo *m (chemise)*.

poltergeist [ˈpɒltəgaɪst] *n* esprit *m* frappeur, poltergeist *m*.

poly [ˈpɒlɪ] (*pl* **polys**) *UK inf* = **polytechnic**.

polyandry [ˈpɒlɪændrɪ] *n* polyandrie *f*.

polyanthus [ˌpɒlɪˈænθəs] (*pl* **polyanthuses** OR *pl* **polyanthi** [-θaɪ]) *n* **1.** [primrose] primevère *f* **2.** [narcissus] narcisse *m* à bouquet.

poly bag *n UK inf* sac *m* en plastique.

polyester [ˌpɒlɪˈestəʳ] <> *n* polyester *m*.
<> *adj* (de OR en)polyester.

polyethylene [ˌpɒlɪˈeθɪliːn] = **polythene**.

polygamist [pəˈlɪgəmɪst] *n* polygame *m*.

polygamous [pəˈlɪgəməs] *adj* polygame.

polygamy [pəˈlɪgəmɪ] *n* polygamie *f*.

polyglot [ˈpɒlɪglɒt] <> *adj* [person] polyglotte ▪ [edition] multilingue.
<> *n* [person] polyglotte *mf* ▪ [book] édition *f* multilingue.

polygon [ˈpɒlɪgɒn] *n* polygone *m*.

polygonal [pɒˈlɪgənl] *adj* polygonal.

polygraph [ˈpɒlɪgrɑːf] *n* **1.** [lie detector] détecteur *m* de mensonge **2.** [copying device] photocopieuse *f*.

polyhedron [ˌpɒlɪˈhiːdrən] (*pl* **polyhedrons** OR *pl* **polyhedra** [-drə]) *n* polyèdre *m*.

polymer [ˈpɒlɪməʳ] *n* polymère *m*.

polymorphic [ˌpɒlɪˈmɔːfɪk] *adj* polymorphe.

Polynesia [ˌpɒlɪˈniːzjə] *pr n* Polynésie *f* ▪ **in ~** en Polynésie ▪ **French ~** la Polynésie française.

Polynesian [ˌpɒlɪˈniːzjən] <> *n* **1.** [person] Polynésien *m*, - enne *f* **2.** LING polynésien *m*.
<> *adj* polynésien.

polynomial [ˌpɒlɪˈnəʊmjəl] <> *adj* polynomial.
<> *n* polynôme *m*.

polyp [ˈpɒlɪp] *n* polype *m*.

polyphony [pəˈlɪfənɪ] *n* polyphonie *f*.

polypropylene [ˌpɒlɪˈprəʊpəliːn] *n* polypropylène *m*.

polysemous [pəˈlɪsɪməs] *adj* polysémique.

polysemy [pəˈlɪsɪmɪ] *n* polysémie *f*.

polystyrene [ˌpɒlɪˈstaɪriːn] *n* polystyrène *m* ▪ **~ tiles** carreaux *mpl* de polystyrène.

polysyllabic [ˌpɒlɪsɪˈlæbɪk] *adj* polysyllabe, polysyllabique.

polytechnic [ˌpɒlɪˈteknɪk] *n en Grande-Bretagne, avant 1993, établissement d'enseignement supérieur qui appartenait à un système différent de celui des universités ; depuis 1993, les "polytechnics" ont acquis le statut d'universités.*

polytheism [ˈpɒlɪθiːɪzm] *n* polythéisme *m*.

polythene [ˈpɒlɪθiːn] <> *n* polyéthylène *m*, Polythène® *m*.
<> *comp* en plastique, en polyéthylène *spec*, en Polythène® *spec* ▪ **~ bag** sac *m* (en)plastique.

polyunsaturated [ˌpɒlɪʌnˈsætʃəreɪtɪd] *adj* polyinsaturé.

polyurethane [ˌpɒlɪˈjʊərəθeɪn] *n* polyuréthane *m*, polyuréthanne *m*.

pom [pɒm] *Australia & New Zealand inf* = **pommie**.

pomade [pəˈmeɪd] ◇ *n* pommade *f (pour les cheveux)*.
◇ *vt* pommader.

pomander [pəˈmændəʳ] *n* [bag] sachet *m* aromatique ▪ [orange stuck with cloves] pomme *f* d'amour.

pomegranate [ˈpɒmɪˌgrænɪt] *n* grenade *f (fruit)* ▪ **~ tree** grenadier *m*.

pommel [ˈpɒml] (*UK pret & pp* **pommelled**, *cont* **pommelling**) (*US pret & pp* **pommeled**, *cont* **pommeling**) ◇ *n* pommeau *m*.
◇ *vt* = **pummel**.

pommel horse *n* cheval-d'arçons *m inv*.

pommie, pommy [ˈpɒmɪ] (*pl* **pommies**) ◇ *n Australia & New Zealand inf hum* angliche *mf pej*.
◇ *adj* angliche *pej*.

pomp [pɒmp] *n* pompe *f*, faste *m* ▪ **with great ~ (and circumstance)** en grande pompe.

pompadour [ˈpɒmpəˌdʊəʳ] *n* coiffure *f* style Pompadour.

Pompeii [pɒmˈpeɪiː] *pr n* Pompéi.

Pompeiian [pɒmˈpeɪən] ◇ *n* Pompéien *m*, - enne *f*.
◇ *adj* pompéien.

Pompey [ˈpɒmpɪ] *pr n* Pompée.

pompom [ˈpɒmpɒm] *n* **1.** [flower, bobble] pompon *m* **2.** *inf* MIL canon *m* mitrailleur.

pomposity [pɒmˈpɒsətɪ] (*pl* **pomposities**) *n* **1.** *(U)* [of manner] comportement *m* pompeux, manières *fpl* pompeuses **2.** [of ceremony] apparat *m*, pompe *f* ▪ [of style] caractère *m* pompeux.

pompous [ˈpɒmpəs] *adj* [pretentious] pompeux, prétentieux.

pompously [ˈpɒmpəslɪ] *adv* pompeusement.

ponce [pɒns] *UK inf* ◇ *n* **1.** [pimp] maquereau *m* **2.** *pej* [effeminate man] homme *m* efféminé.
◇ *vi* **1.** [pimp] faire le maquereau **2.** *pej* [behave effeminately] faire des simagrées, minauder.
➡ **ponce about, ponce around** *vi insep inf* [mess around] traîner.

poncey, poncy [ˈpɒnsɪ] *adj UK inf pej* efféminé.

poncho [ˈpɒntʃəʊ] (*pl* **ponchos**) *n* poncho *m*.

pond [pɒnd] *n* [small] mare *f* ▪ [large] étang *m* ▪ [in garden] bassin *m* ▪ **~ life** la faune des étangs.

ponder [ˈpɒndəʳ] ◇ *vi* [think] réfléchir ▪ [meditate] méditer.
◇ *vt* réfléchir à *OR* sur ▪ **I sat down and ~ed what to do** je m'assis et considérai ce que j'allais faire.

ponderable [ˈpɒndərəbl] *adj fml* pondérable.

ponderous [ˈpɒndərəs] *adj* [heavy] pesant, lourd ▪ [slow] lent, laborieux ▪ [dull] lourd ▪ **he has a very ~ way of speaking** il s'exprime avec difficulté *OR* laborieusement.

pone [pəʊn] *n US* **~ (bread)** pain *m* au maïs.

pong [pɒŋ] *inf* ◇ *n UK* puanteur *f*.
◇ *vi* cocoter.

pontiff [ˈpɒntɪf] *n* souverain pontife *m*, pape *m*.

pontifical [pɒnˈtɪfɪkl] *adj* **1.** RELIG pontifical **2.** [pompous] pompeux.

pontificate ◇ *vi* [pɒnˈtɪfɪkeɪt] [gen - RELIG] pontifier ▪ **he's always pontificating about** *OR* **on something or other** *pej* il faut toujours qu'il pontifie.
◇ *n* [pɒnˈtɪfɪkɪt] pontificat *m*.

Pontius Pilate [ˈpɒntjəs-] *pr n* Ponce Pilate.

pontoon [pɒnˈtuːn] *n* **1.** [float] ponton *m* ▪ [on seaplane] flotteur *m* **2.** [card game] vingt-et-un *m*.

pontoon bridge *n* pont *m* flottant.

pony [ˈpəʊnɪ] (*pl* **ponies**) *n* **1.** ZOOL poney *m* **2.** [glass] verre *m* à liqueur **3.** *US inf* SCH [crib] antisèche *f*.

pony express *n service postal américain à cheval mis en place en 1860 et détrôné par l'apparition du télégraphe.*

ponytail [ˈpəʊnɪteɪl] *n* queue *f* de cheval.

pony-trekking [-ˌtrekɪŋ] *n* randonnée *f* à dos de poney ▪ **to go ~** faire une randonnée à dos de poney.

poo [puː] *n & vi inf* = **pooh**.

pooch [puːtʃ] *n US inf* toutou *m*.

poodle [ˈpuːdl] *n* caniche *m*.

poof [pʊf] ◇ *n*△ *UK pej* pédé△ *m*.
◇ *interj* : **and then it was gone, ~, just like that** et puis hop! il a disparu d'un coup.

poofter△ [ˈpʊftəʳ] = **poof** *(n)*.

poofy△ [ˈpʊfɪ] (*comp* **poofier**, *superl* **poofiest**) *adj UK pej* efféminé.

pooh [puː] *UK inf* ◇ *interj* [with disgust] pouah ▪ [with disdain] peuh.
◇ *n baby* caca *m*.
◇ *vi baby* faire caca.

pooh-pooh *vt UK* rire de, ricaner de.

pool [puːl] ◇ *n* **1.** [pond - small] mare *f* ; [- large] étang *m* ; [- ornamental] bassin *m* **2.** [puddle] flaque *f* ▪ **a ~ of light** un rond de lumière **3.** [swimming pool] piscine *f* **4.** [in harbour] bassin *m* ▪ [in canal, river] plan *m* d'eau **5.** [of money] cagnotte *f* ▪ [in card games] cagnotte *f*, poule *f* **6.** [of workmen, babysitters] groupe *m*, groupement *m* ▪ [of experts] équipe *f* ▪ [of typists] pool *m* ▪ [of cars - in firm] parc *m* ▪ [of ideas] réserve *f* ▪ [of talent] pépinière *f*, réserve *f* **7.** [consortium] cartel *m*, pool *m* ▪ [group of producers] groupement *m* de producteurs **8.** *US* FIN [group] groupement *m* ▪ [agreement] entente *f*, accord *m* **9.** [American billiards] billard *m* américain ▪ **to shoot ~** *US* jouer au billard américain.
◇ *vt* [resources, cars] mettre en commun ▪ [efforts, ideas] unir.

poolroom [ˈpuːlˌruːm] *n* salle *f* de billard.

pools [puːlz] *npl UK* **the (football) ~** les concours de pronostics (au football) ▪ **to win the (football) ~** gagner aux pronostics (au football) ▪ **~ coupon** fiche *f* de pari, grille *f* de pronostics *(au football)*.

pool table *n* (table *f* de) billard *m*.

poop [puːp] *n* : **~ (deck)** poupe *f*.
➡ **poop out** *vi insep US* [drop out] déclarer forfait.

pooped [puːpt] *adj US inf* **~ (out)** vanné, HS.

pooper-scooper [ˈpuːpəˌskuːpəʳ] *n* ramasse-crotte *m*.

poor [pʊəʳ] ◇ *adj* **1.** [financially - person, area, country] pauvre ▪ **they're too ~ to own a car** ils n'ont pas les moyens d'avoir une voiture ▪ **the oil crisis made these countries considerably ~er** la crise du pétrole a considérablement appauvri ces pays ▶ **~ as a church mouse** pauvre comme Job **2.** [mediocre in quantity - gen] maigre ; [- output, sale figures] faible, médiocre ▪ **there was an unusually ~ turnout** il est venu beaucoup moins de monde que d'habitude ▪ **his pay is very ~** il est très mal payé ▪ [mediocre in quality - land, soil] maigre, pauvre ; [- effort, excuse] piètre ; [- piece of work] médiocre ; [- results] médiocre, piètre ; [- weather, summer] médiocre ; [- quality, condition] mauvais ▪ **the match took place in ~light** le match a eu lieu alors qu'on n'y voyait pratiquement rien ▪ **the joke was in extremely ~ taste** la plaisanterie était du plus mauvais goût ▪ **she has very ~ taste in clothes** elle s'habille avec un goût douteux ▪ **the team put in a ~ performance** l'équipe n'a pas très bien joué ▪ **our side put up a very ~ show** notre équipe a donné un piètre spectacle ▪ **don't be such a ~ loser!** [in game] ne sois pas si mauvais perdant! ▪ **I have only a ~ understanding of economics** je ne comprends pas grand-chose à l'économie ▪ **~ work** SCH travail insuffisant ▪ **our chances of success are very ~** nos chances de réussite sont bien maigres

3. [weak - memory, sight] mauvais ■ **to be in ~ health** être en mauvaise santé ■ **I have rather ~ hearing** j'entends mal
4. [in ability] peu doué ■ **I'm a ~ cook** je ne suis pas doué pour la cuisine ■ **my spelling/French is ~** je ne suis pas fort en orthographe/en français ■ **she's a ~ traveller** elle supporte mal les voyages
5. [inadequate] faible ■ **their food is ~ in vitamins** leur alimentation est pauvre en vitamines
6. [pitiful] pauvre ■ **you ~ thing!** mon pauvre! ■ **~ me!** pauvre de moi! ■ **~ (old) Bill** le pauvre Bill.
◇ *npl* : **the ~** les pauvres *mpl*.

poor box *n* tronc *m* des pauvres.

poorhouse ['puəhaus] (*pl* [-hauzɪz]) *n dans le passé, hospice pour les indigents.*

poor law *n* *UK loi qui régissait autrefois l'assistance publique.*

THE POOR LAWS

Premières lois sociales anglaises, datant de 1597 et de 1601. Motivées autant par la peur du pauvre que par le désir d'améliorer le sort des plus démunis (construction d'hôpitaux, d'écoles, de logements, etc.), tout en condamnant les « oisifs » de la société, elles ouvrirent la voie au système d'aide sociale en Angleterre et en Europe.

poorly ['puəlɪ] (*comp* **poorlier**, *superl* **poorliest**) ◇ *adj UK* malade, souffrant ■ **his condition is described as ~** MED son état est considéré comme sérieux.
◇ *adv* [badly] mal ■ **I did ~ in the maths test** je n'ai pas bien réussi à l'interrogation de maths ■ **to think ~ of sb** avoir une mauvaise opinion de qqn.

poor relation *n UK fig* parent *m* pauvre.

pop [pɒp] (*pret & pp* **popped**, *cont* **popping**) ◇ *onom* pan ■ **to go ~** [cork] sauter ; [balloon] éclater.
◇ *n* **1.** MUS musique *f* pop **2.** [sound] bruit *m* de bouchon qui saute, bruit *m* sec **3.** [drink] boisson *f* gazeuse *OR* pétillante **4.** *US inf* [father] papa *m*.
◇ *comp* [singer, video] pop *(inv)* ■ **~ concert** concert *m* rock ■ **~ group** groupe *m* pop ■ **~ music** musique *f* pop, pop music *f*.
◇ *vi* **1.** [cork, buttons] sauter ■ [bulb, balloon] éclater ■ **to make a popping noise** faire un bruit de bouchon qui saute ■ **to ~ open** [box, bag] s'ouvrir tout d'un coup ; [buttons] sauter **2.** [ears] se déboucher d'un seul coup ■ [eyes] s'ouvrir tout grand ■ **his eyes almost popped out of his head in surprise** de surprise, les yeux lui sont presque sortis de la tête **3.** *UK inf* [go] faire un saut ■ **to ~ into town** faire un saut en ville.
◇ *written abbr of* **population**.
◇ *vt* **1.** [balloon, bag] crever ■ [button, cork] faire sauter ■ [corn] faire éclater **2.** *inf* [put] mettre, fourrer ■ **just ~ the paper through the letterbox** glissez juste le journal dans la boîte aux lettres ■ **she kept popping tablets into her mouth** elle n'arrêtait pas de se fourrer des comprimés dans la bouche ■ **he popped his head over the wall** sa tête surgit en haut du mur **3.** △ *drug sl* **to ~ pills** prendre des comprimés *(pour se droguer)* **4.** *phr* **he's finally popped the question** *inf* il a finalement demandé sa main ■ **to ~ one's clogs** *UK inf* casser sa pipe.
◆ **pop in** *vi insep UK inf* faire une petite visite ■ **to ~ in to see sb** passer voir qqn.
◆ **pop off** *vi insep inf* **1.** [leave] s'en aller, filer **2.** [die] casser sa pipe.
◆ **pop out** *vi insep inf* sortir un instant ■ **to ~ out to the tobacconist's** faire un saut au bureau de tabac.
◆ **pop over** *vi insep UK inf* passer, faire une petite visite.
◆ **pop up** *vi insep inf* **1.** [go upstairs] faire un saut en haut *OR* à l'étage, monter ■ **~ up to see me sometime** monte donc me voir un de ces jours **2.** [crop up] surgir ■ **his name seems to ~ up everywhere** on ne parle que de lui.

popadum ['pɒpədəm] *n galette indienne.*

pop art *n* pop art *m*.

popcorn ['pɒpkɔːn] *n* pop-corn *m inv*.

pope [pəup] *n* **1.** [in Catholic Church] pape *m* **2.** [in Eastern Orthodox Church] pope *m*.

popemobile ['pəupməbiːl] *n inf* papamobile *f*.

pop-eyed *adj inf* ébahi, aux yeux écarquillés.

popgun ['pɒpgʌn] *n* pistolet *m* (d'enfant) à bouchon.

poplar (tree) ['pɒplər-] *n* peuplier *m*.

poplin ['pɒplɪn] ◇ *n* popeline *f*.
◇ *adj* en popeline.

popover ['pɒp,əuvər] *n* **1.** [garment] débardeur *m* **2.** *US* CULIN chausson *m*.

poppadom, poppadum ['pɒpədəm] = **popadum**.

popper ['pɒpər] *n* **1.** *UK* [press-stud] bouton-pression *m*, pression *f* **2.** △ *drug sl* ampoule *f* de nitrite d'amyle.
◆ **poppers** *npl* [drugs] poppers *mpl*.

poppet ['pɒpɪt] *n* **1.** *UK inf* chéri *m*, - e *f*, mignon *m*, - onne *f* **2.** [valve] soupape *f* (à champignon).

poppy ['pɒpɪ] (*pl* **poppies**) *n* **1.** [flower] coquelicot *m* ■ [opium poppy] pavot *m* ■ [paper flower] coquelicot *m* en papier *(vendu le jour de l'Armistice)* ■ **~ seed** graine *f* de pavot **2.** [colour] rouge *m* coquelicot *(inv)*.

poppycock ['pɒpɪkɒk] *n (U) UK inf dated* sottises *fpl*, balivernes *fpl*.

Poppy Day *pr n journée de commémoration pendant laquelle on porte un coquelicot en papier en souvenir des soldats britanniques morts lors des guerres mondiales.*

pops [pɒps] *n US inf* [term of address - to father] papa *m* ; [- to old man] pépé *m*.

Popsicle® ['pɒpsɪkl] *n US* glace *f* en bâtonnet.

populace ['pɒpjuləs] *n* **1.** [population] population *f* **2.** [masses] masses *fpl*, peuple *m*.

popular ['pɒpjulər] *adj* **1.** [well-liked - person] populaire ■ **she's very ~ with her pupils** elle est très populaire auprès de ses élèves, ses élèves l'aiment beaucoup ■ **I'm not going to be very ~ when they find out it's my fault!** je ne vais pas être bien vu quand ils découvriront que c'est de ma faute!
2. [appreciated by many - product, colour] populaire ; [- restaurant, resort] très couru, très fréquenté ■ **the film was very ~ in Europe** le film a été un très grand succès en Europe ■ **the most ~ book of the year** le livre le plus vendu *OR* le best-seller de l'année ■ **videotapes are a ~ present** les vidéocassettes sont des cadeaux très appréciés ■ **it's very ~ with the customers** les clients l'apprécient beaucoup ■ **a ~ line** un article qui se vend bien
3. [common] courant, répandu ■ **a ~ misconception** une erreur répandue *OR* fréquente ‖ [general] populaire ■ **on *OR* by ~ demand** à la demande générale ■ **it's an idea that enjoys great ~ support** c'est une idée qui a l'approbation générale *OR* de tous ■ **~ unrest** mécontentement *m* populaire ▶ **~ front** POL front *m* populaire
4. [aimed at ordinary people] populaire ■ **~ music** musique *f* populaire ■ **a book of ~ mechanics** un livre de mécanique pour tous *OR* à la portée de tous ■ **the ~ press** la presse à grand tirage et à sensation ■ **quality goods at ~ prices** marchandises de qualité à des prix abordables.
◆ **populars** *npl UK inf* presse *f* à grand tirage et à sensation.

popularity [,pɒpju'lærətɪ] *n* popularité *f* ■ **they enjoy a certain ~ with young people** ils jouissent d'une certaine popularité auprès des jeunes.

popularization [,pɒpjuləraɪ'zeɪʃn] *n* **1.** [of trend, activity] popularisation *f* ■ [of science, philosophy] vulgarisation *f* **2.** [book] œuvre *f* de vulgarisation.

popularize, ise ['pɒpjuləraɪz] *vt* **1.** [make popular] populariser ■ **a sport ~d by television** un sport que la télévision a rendu populaire **2.** [science, philosophy] vulgariser.

popularizer ['pɒpjuləraɪzər] *n* [of fashion, ideas] promoteur *m*, - trice *f*.

popularly ['pɒpjuləlɪ] *adv* généralement ■ [commonly] couramment, communément ■ **antirrhinums are ~ known as snapdragons** les antirrhinums sont plus connus sous le nom de gueules-de-loup.

populate ['pɒpjʊleɪt] *vt* [inhabit] peupler, habiter ■ [colonize] peupler, coloniser ■ **a town ~d by miners and their families** une ville habitée par des mineurs et leurs familles ■ **a densely ~d country** un pays fortement peuplé *OR* à forte densité de population.

population [ˌpɒpjʊ'leɪʃn] ◇ *n* population *f* ■ **the whole ~ is in mourning** tous les habitants portent *OR* toute la population porte le deuil ■ **the prison ~** la population carcérale.
◇ *comp* [control, fall, increase] démographique, de la population ■ **~ explosion** explosion *f* démographique.

populism ['pɒpjʊlɪzm] *n* populisme *m.*

populist ['pɒpjʊlɪst] *n* populiste *mf.*

populous ['pɒpjʊləs] *adj* populeux.

pop-up *adj* [book, card] en relief ■ [toaster] automatique ■ **~ menu** COMPUT menu *m* local.

porcelain ['pɔːsəlɪn] ◇ *n* porcelaine *f.*
◇ *comp* [dish, vase, lamp] en porcelaine.

porch [pɔːtʃ] *n* **1.** [entrance] porche *m* **2.** *US* [veranda] véranda *f.*

porcine ['pɔːsaɪn] *adj* porcin.

porcupine ['pɔːkjʊpaɪn] *n* porc-épic *m.*

pore [pɔːʳ] ◇ *n* [in skin, plant, fungus, rock] pore *m.*
◇ *vi* : **to ~ over** [book] être plongé dans *OR* absorbé par ; [picture, details] étudier de près.

pork [pɔːk] ◇ *n* CULIN porc *m.*
◇ *comp* [chop, sausage] de porc.

pork barrel *n US* POL *projet local entrepris par un parlementaire ou un parti à des fins électorales.*

porker ['pɔːkəʳ] *n* **1.** *liter* porcelet *m (engraissé pour la boucherie)* **2.** *inf hum* petit cochon *m.*

pork pie *n* ≃ pâté *m* en croûte *(à la viande de porc).*

pork scratchings *npl petits morceaux croustillants de couenne de porc mangés comme amuse-gueule.*

porky ['pɔːkɪ] (*comp* **porkier**, *superl* **porkiest**) *adj inf pej* [fat] gros, grosse *f*, gras, grasse *f*, adipeux *pej.*

porn [pɔːn] *inf* ◇ *n* porno *m* ■ **hard/soft ~** porno *m* hard/soft ■ **~ shop** sex-shop *m.*
◇ *adj inf* porno.

porno ['pɔːnəʊ] *adj inf* porno.

pornographer [pɔː'nɒgrəfəʳ] *n* pornographe *mf.*

pornographic [ˌpɔːnə'græfɪk] *adj* pornographique.

pornography [pɔː'nɒgrəfɪ] *n* pornographie *f.*

porosity [pɔː'rɒsɪtɪ] (*pl* **porosities**) *n* porosité *f.*

porous ['pɔːrəs] *adj* poreux.

porpoise ['pɔːpəs] (*pl inv OR pl* **porpoises**) *n* marsouin *m.*

porridge ['pɒrɪdʒ] *n* **1.** CULIN porridge *m* **2.** *UK prison sl* peine *f* de prison ■ **to do ~** faire de la tôle△.

porridge oats *npl* flocons *mpl* d'avoine.

port [pɔːt] ◇ *n* **1.** [harbour] port *m* ■ **to come into ~** entrer dans le port ■ **we put into ~ at Naples** nous avons relâché dans le port de Naples ■ **we left ~ before dawn** nous avons appareillé avant l'aube ● **~ of entry** port de débarquement ■ **any ~ in a storm** nécessité fait loi *prov* **2.** [wine] porto *m* **3.** [window - on ship, plane] hublot *m* **4.** [for loading] sabord *m* (de charge) **5.** MIL [in wall] meurtrière *f* ■ [in tank] fente *f* de visée **6.** COMPUT port *m* **7.** TECH [in engine] orifice *m* **8.** NAUT [left side] bâbord *m* **9.** AERON côté *m* gauche, bâbord *m.*
◇ *comp* [authorities, activity, facilities] portuaire ■ [bow, quarter] de bâbord.
◇ *vt* **1.** COMPUT transférer **2.** MIL : **~ arms!** présentez armes! **3.** NAUT : **~ the helm!** barre à bâbord!

portable ['pɔːtəbl] ◇ *adj* **1.** portatif, portable ■ **~ pension** pension *f* transférable ■ **~ TV (set)** télévision *f* portative **2.** COMPUT [software, program] compatible.
◇ *n* [typewriter] machine *f* portative ■ [TV] télévision *f* portative ■ [computer] ordinateur *m* portatif.

Portacrib® ['pɔːtəˌkrɪb] *n US* moïse *m*, porte-bébé *m.*

portage ['pɔːtɪdʒ] *n* **1.** [transport] transport *m* ■ [cost] (frais *mpl* de) port *m* **2.** NAUT portage *m.*

Portakabin® ['pɔːtəˌkæbɪn] *n* [gen] baraquement *m* préfabriqué.

portal ['pɔːtl] *n lit* portail *m* ■ **she found herself standing at the ~s of a new life** *fig* elle se trouvait à l'aube d'une nouvelle vie.

portcullis [ˌpɔːt'kʌlɪs] *n* herse *f (de château fort).*

portend [pɔː'tend] *vt fml & lit* (laisser) présager, annoncer.

portent ['pɔːtənt] *n fml & lit* **1.** [omen] présage *m*, augure *m* ■ [bad omen] mauvais présage *m* **2.** [significance] portée *f*, signification *f.*

portentous [pɔː'tentəs] *adj lit* **1.** [ominous - sign] de mauvais présage *OR* augure **2.** [momentous - event] capital, extraordinaire **3.** [serious] grave, solennel **4.** [pompous] pompeux.

porter ['pɔːtəʳ] *n* **1.** [of luggage] porteur *m* **2.** *UK* [door attendant - in hotel] portier *m* ; [- in block of flats] concierge *mf*, gardien *m*, - enne *f* ; [- on private estate] gardien *m*, - enne *f* ; [- in university, college] appariteur *m* **3.** *US* RAIL [on train] employé *m*, - e *f* des wagons-lits **4.** [beer] porter *m*, bière *f* brune.

porterage ['pɔːtərɪdʒ] *n* [transport] portage *m*, transport *m* (par porteurs) ■ [cost] coût *m* du transport.

porterhouse (steak) ['pɔːtəhaus-] *n* chateaubriand *m*, châteaubriant *m.*

portfolio [ˌpɔːt'fəʊljəʊ] (*pl* **portfolios**) *n* **1.** [briefcase] porte-documents *m inv* **2.** [dossier - of artist] dossier *m* **3.** POL portefeuille *m* **4.** ST. EX portefeuille *m* (financier) *OR* d'investissements.

porthole ['pɔːthəʊl] *n* hublot *m.*

portico ['pɔːtɪkəʊ] (*pl* **porticos** *OR pl* **porticoes**) *n* ARCHIT portique *m.*

portion ['pɔːʃn] *n* **1.** [part, section] partie *f* **2.** [share] part *f* ■ [measure] mesure *f*, dose *f* ■ **he cut the cake into five ~s** il a coupé le gâteau en cinq (parts) **3.** [helping - of food] portion *f* **4.** *lit* [fate] sort *m*, destin *m.*
◆ **portion out** *vt sep* distribuer, répartir.

portliness ['pɔːtlɪnɪs] *n* corpulence *f*, embonpoint *m.*

portly ['pɔːtlɪ] (*comp* **portlier**, *superl* **portliest**) *adj* corpulent, fort.

portmanteau [ˌpɔːt'mæntəʊ] (*pl* **portmanteaus** *OR pl* **portmanteaux** [-təʊz]) ◇ *n* grande valise *f.*
◇ *adj* qui combine plusieurs éléments *OR* styles.

portmanteau word *n* mot-valise *m.*

port of call *n* NAUT escale *f* ■ **her last ~ was the bank** *fig* elle est passée à la banque en dernier.

Porton Down ['pɔːtən-] *pr n ville du Wiltshire.*

PORTON DOWN

Ville célèbre pour son centre de microbiologie, dont les recherches sur les armes bactériologiques et chimiques ainsi que les expériences sur des animaux vivants ont suscité de nombreuses controverses.

portrait ['pɔːtreɪt] ◇ *n* **1.** [gen - ART] portrait *m* ■ **he had his ~ painted** il a fait faire son portrait ● **'A Portrait of the Artist as a Young Man'** *Joyce* 'Portrait de l'artiste jeune par lui-même' ■ **'The Portrait of a Lady'** *James* 'Un portrait de femme' **2.** PRINT : **to print in ~** imprimer à la française.
◇ *comp* : **~ gallery** galerie *f* de portraits ■ **~ painter** portraitiste *mf* ■ **~ painting** le portrait ■ **~ photograph** portrait *m* photographique, photo-portrait *f* ■ **~ photographer** photographe *m* d'art.
◇ *adj* PRINT à la française.

portraitist ['pɔːtreɪtɪst] *n* portraitiste *mf.*

portraiture ['pɔːtrɪtʃəʳ] *n* art *m* du portrait.

portray [pɔː'treɪ] *vt* **1.** [represent] représenter ■ **he ~ed John as a scoundrel** il a représenté John sous les traits d'un voyou **2.** [act role of] jouer le rôle de **3.** [depict in words] dépeindre ■ **she vividly ~s medieval life** elle fait une vivante description de la vie au Moyen Âge **4.** [artist] peindre, faire le portrait de.

portrayal [pɔː'treɪəl] *n* **1.** [description] portrait *m*, description *f* ■ **he disputes the ~ of the protesters as extremists** il conteste la façon dont les médias présentent les protestataires comme des extrémistes **2.** ART portrait *m* **3.** THEAT interprétation *f*.

Portugal ['pɔːtʃʊgl] *pr n* Portugal *m* ■ **in ~** au Portugal.

Portuguese [,pɔːtʃʊ'giːz] (*pl inv*) ◇ *n* **1.** [person] Portugais *m*, - e *f* **2.** LING portugais *m*.
◇ *adj* portugais.

Portuguese man-of-war *n* physalie *f*.

pose [pəʊz] ◇ *n* **1.** [position - gen - ART] & PHOT pose *f* ■ **to take up** *OR* **to strike a ~** prendre une pose **2.** [pretence] façade *f*.
◇ *vi* **1.** ART & PHOT poser ■ **to ~ for a photograph/for an artist** poser pour une photographie/pour un artiste ■ **to ~ in the nude** poser nu ■ **she ~d as a nymph** elle a posé en nymphe **2.** [masquerade] : **he ~d as a hero** il s'est posé en héros, il s'est fait passer pour un héros.
◇ *vt* [constitute - problem] poser, créer ; [- threat] constituer ■ [set - question] poser ■ [put forward - claim, idea] formuler.

poser ['pəʊzəʳ] *n inf* **1.** [question - thorny] question *f* épineuse ; [- difficult] colle *f* **2.** *pej* [show-off] poseur *m*, - euse *f*.

poseur [pəʊ'zɜːʳ] *n pej* poseur *m*, - euse *f*.

posh [pɒʃ] *UK inf* ◇ *adj* [clothes] chic ■ [person] BCBG ■ [car] chic ■ [house] de riches ■ [restaurant] huppé ■ [area] chic ■ [accent] snob ■ **he moves in some very ~ circles** il fréquente des milieux très huppés *OR* des gens de la haute.
◇ *adv* : **to talk ~** parler avec un accent snob.

posit ['pɒzɪt] *vt fml* [idea] avancer ■ [theory] avancer, postuler.

position [pə'zɪʃn] ◇ *n* **1.** [place] position *f*, place *f*, emplacement *m* ■ **to change** *OR* **to shift ~** changer de place ■ **you've changed the ~ of the lamp** vous avez changé la lampe de place ■ **white is now in a strong ~** [in chess] les blancs sont maintenant très bien placés ■ **they put the machine guns in** *OR* **into ~** ils mirent les mitrailleuses en batterie ■ **take up your ~s!, get into ~!** [actors, dancers] à vos places! ; [soldiers, guards] à vos postes!
2. [pose, angle, setting] position *f* ■ **hold the spray can in an upright ~** tenez le vaporisateur en position verticale ■ **the lever should be in the off ~** le levier devrait être en position arrêt
3. [circumstances] situation *f*, position *f* ■ **to be in a bad/good ~** être en mauvaise/bonne posture ■ **you're in a bad ~** *OR* **in no ~ to judge** vous êtes mal placé pour (en)juger ■ **to be in a ~ to do sthg** être en mesure de faire qqch ■ **put yourself in my ~** mettez-vous à ma place ■ **it's an awkward ~ to be in** c'est une drôle de situation ■ **our financial ~ is improving** notre situation financière s'améliore ■ **the present economic ~** la conjoncture économique actuelle
4. [rank - in table, scale] place *f*, position *f* ■ **they're in tenth ~ in the championship** ils sont à la dixième place *OR* ils occupent la dixième place du championnat ■ [in hierarchy] position *f*, situation *f* ■ **a person in my ~ can't afford a scandal** une personne de mon rang ne peut se permettre un scandale ■ **what exactly is his ~ in the government?** quelles sont exactement ses fonctions au sein du gouvernement? ■ [social standing] position *f*, place *f* ■ **she is concerned about her social ~** elle est préoccupée par sa position sociale
5. [standpoint] position *f*, point *m* de vue ■ **could you make your ~ clear on this point?** pouvez-vous préciser votre position à ce sujet? ■ **to take up a ~ on sthg** adopter une position *OR* prendre position sur qqch
6. [job] poste *m*, situation *f* ■ **there were four candidates for the ~ of manager** il y avait quatre candidats au poste de directeur ■ **it is a ~ of great responsibility** c'est un poste à haute responsabilité
7. ADMIN [in bank, post office] guichet *m* ■ **'~ closed'** 'guichet fermé'
8. SPORT [in team, on field] position *f*
9. MIL position *f* ■ **the men took up ~ on the hill** les hommes prirent position sur la colline ■ **to jockey** *OR* **to jostle** *OR* **to manoeuvre for ~** *liter* chercher à occuper le terrain ; *fig* chercher à obtenir la meilleure place.
◇ *vt* **1.** [put in place - cameras, equipment] mettre en place, placer, disposer ; [- precisely] mettre en position ; [- guests, officials] placer ■ **he ~ed himself on the roof** il a pris position sur le toit
2. (*usu passive*) [situate - house, building] situer, placer ■ SPORT placer ■ **the flat is well ~ed** l'appartement est bien situé
3. [post - guards] placer, poster ■ **they have ~ed their ships in the gulf** ils ont envoyé leurs navires dans le golfe
4. COMM [product] positionner.

positional [pə'zɪʃənl] *adj* [warfare] de position, de positions ■ LING [variant] contextuel ■ **~ notation** MATHS numération *f* positionnelle.

positive ['pɒzətɪv] ◇ *adj* **1.** [sure] sûr, certain ■ **are you ~ about that?** en êtes-vous sûr? ■ **it's absolutely ~** c'est sûr et certain
2. [constructive] positif, constructif ■ **haven't you got any ~ suggestions?** n'avez-vous rien à proposer qui fasse avancer les choses? ■ **she has a very ~ approach to the problem** son approche du problème est très positive *OR* constructive ■ **~ thinking** idées *fpl* constructives
3. [affirmative - reply, response] positif, affirmatif ; [- test, result] positif
4. [definite - fact, progress] réel, certain ■ [clear - change, advantage] réel, effectif ■ [precise - instructions] formel, clair ■ **we have ~ evidence of his involvement** nous avons des preuves irréfutables de son implication ■ **his intervention was a ~ factor in the release of the hostages** son intervention a efficacement contribué à la libération des otages ■ **the team needs some ~ support** l'équipe a besoin d'un soutien réel *OR* effectif ➲ **proof ~** *UK*, **~ proof** preuve *f* formelle
5. [as intensifier - absolute] absolu, véritable, pur ■ **a ~ pleasure** un véritable plaisir ■ **it's a ~ lie** c'est un mensonge, ni plus ni moins
6. [assured] assuré, ferme
7. ELEC, MATHS & PHOT positif
8. *US* POL [progressive] progressiste.
◇ *n* **1.** GRAM positif *m* ■ **in the ~** à la forme positive
2. [answer] réponse *f* positive *OR* affirmative, oui *m* ■ **to reply in the ~** répondre par l'affirmative *OR* affirmativement
3. PHOT épreuve *f* positive
4. ELEC borne *f* positive.

positive discrimination *n (U)* discrimination *f* positive *(mesures favorisant les membres de groupes minoritaires)* ■ **~ in favour of people with disabilities** mesures en faveur des handicapés.

positively ['pɒzətɪvlɪ] *adv* **1.** [absolutely] absolument, positivement ■ [definitely] incontestablement, positivement **2.** [constructively] positivement ■ **it's important to act/think ~** il est important d'agir/de penser de façon positive **3.** [affirmatively] affirmativement ■ [with certainty] avec certitude, positivement ■ **the body has been ~ identified** le cadavre a été formellement identifié **4.** ELEC positivement.

positive vetting [-'vetɪŋ] *n* contrôle *m OR* enquête *f* de sécurité *(sur un candidat à un poste touchant à la sécurité nationale)*.

positivism ['pɒzɪtɪvɪzm] *n* positivisme *m*.

poss [pɒs] *adj inf* possible.

posse ['pɒsɪ] *n* **1.** *US* HIST *petit groupe d'hommes rassemblés par le shérif en cas d'urgence* ■ **to get up a ~** réunir un groupe d'hommes **2.**△ [group of friends] bande *f*.

possess [pə'zes] *vt* **1.** [have possession of - permanently] posséder, avoir ; [- temporarily] être en possession de, détenir, avoir ■ **she ~es a clear understanding of the subject** elle connaît bien son sujet, elle a une bonne connaissance du sujet **2.** [obsess] obséder ■ **he was completely ~ed by the idea of going to India** il était complètement obsédé par l'idée d'aller en

Inde ▪ **what on earth ~ed him to do such a thing?** qu'est-ce qui lui a pris de faire une chose pareille? **3.** *fml* & *lit* **to ~ o.s. of sthg** se munir de qqch.

possessed [pəˈzest] *adj* **1.** [controlled - by an evil spirit] possédé ▪ **she/her soul is ~by the devil** elle/son âme est possédée du démon ▪ **he was shouting like one ~** il criait comme un possédé ▪ *lit* [filled] : **~ by curiosity** dévoré de *OR* en proie à la curiosité ➊ **'The Possessed'** ***Dostoievsky*** 'les Possédés' **2.** *fml* & *lit* **~ of : none of her children was ~ of any great talent** aucun de ses enfants n'était particulièrement doué.

possession [pəˈzeʃn] *n* **1.** [gen] possession *f* ▪ **to be in ~ of sthg** être en possession de qqch ▪ **she was charged with ~ of illegal substances** elle a été inculpée pour détention de stupéfiants ▪ **the file is no longer in my ~** le dossier n'est plus en ma possession, je ne suis plus en possession du dossier ▪ **to be in full ~ of one's senses** être en pleine possession de ses moyens ▪ **to be in** *OR* **to have ~ (of the ball)** SPORT avoir le ballon ▪ **certain documents have come into my ~** certains documents sont tombés en ma possession ▪ **to take ~ of sthg** [acquire] prendre possession de qqch ; [by force] s'emparer de *OR* s'approprier qqch ; [confiscate] confisquer qqch ➊ **~ is nine points** *OR* **parts** *OR* **tenths of the law** *UK* possession vaut titre **2.** LAW [of property] possession *f*, jouissance *f* ▪ **to take ~** prendre possession ➊ **immediate ~** jouissance *f* immédiate **3.** [by evil] possession *f*.

◆ **possessions** *npl* **1.** [belongings] affaires *fpl*, biens *mpl* **2.** [colonies] possessions *fpl* ▪ [land] terres *fpl*.

possessive [pəˈzesɪv] ◇ *adj* **1.** [gen] possessif ▪ **he's ~ about his belongings** il a horreur de prêter ses affaires ▪ **she's ~ about her children** c'est une mère possessive **2.** GRAM possessif ▪ **~ adjective/pronoun** adjectif *m* /pronom *m* possessif.
◇ *n* GRAM [case] (cas *m*) possessif *m* ▪ [word] possessif *m*.

possessively [pəˈzesɪvlɪ] *adv* de manière possessive ▪ **she clung ~ to her father's hand** elle agrippa jalousement la main de son père.

possessiveness [pəˈzesɪvnɪs] *n* caractère *m* possessif, possessivité *f*.

possessor [pəˈzesər] *n* possesseur *m*, propriétaire *mf*.

possibility [ˌpɒsəˈbɪlətɪ] (*pl* **possibilities**) *n* **1.** [chance] possibilité *f*, éventualité *f* ▪ **it's a ~** c'est une possibilité, c'est bien possible ▪ **the ~ of a settlement is fading fast** la perspective d'un règlement est de moins en moins probable ▪ **is there any ~ of you coming up for the weekend?** pourriez-vous venir ce week-end?, y a-t-il des chances que vous veniez ce week-end? ▪ **if there's any ~ of leaving early, I'll let you know** s'il y a moyen de partir de bonne heure, je vous le ferai savoir ▪ **there's no ~ of that happening** il n'y a aucune chance *OR* aucun risque que cela se produise ▪ **there's little ~ of any changes being made to the budget** il est peu probable que le budget soit modifié ▪ **there's a strong ~ we'll know the results tomorrow** il est fort possible que nous connaissions les résultats demain ▪ **they hadn't even considered the ~ that he might leave** ils n'avaient même pas envisagé qu'il puisse partir **2.** [person - for job] candidat *m*, - e *f* possible ; [- as choice] choix *m* possible ▪ **she's still a ~** elle conserve toutes ses chances.

◆ **possibilities** *npl* [potential] possibilités *fpl* ▪ **the job has a lot of possibilities** le poste offre de nombreuses perspectives ▪ **job possibilities** possibilités d'emploi.

possible [ˈpɒsəbl] ◇ *adj* **1.** [which can be done] possible ▪ **if ~** si possible ▪ **I'll be there, if at all ~** j'y serai, dans la mesure du possible ▪ **that's ~** c'est possible, ça se peut ▪ **it isn't ~ for her to come** il ne lui est pas possible *OR* il lui est impossible de venir ▪ *(in comparisons)* **as far as ~** [within one's competence] dans la mesure du possible ; [at maximum distance] aussi loin que possible ▪ **as long as ~** aussi longtemps que possible ▪ **as much** *OR* **as many as ~** autant que possible ▪ **as soon as ~** dès que *OR* le plus tôt possible ▪ *(with superl)* **the best/the smallest ~** le meilleur/le plus petit possible ▪ **I mean that in the nicest ~ way** je dis cela sans méchanceté (aucune)
2. [conceivable, imaginable] possible, imaginable ▪ **there's no ~ way out** il n'y a absolument aucune issue ▪ **it doesn't seem ~ that anyone could be so stupid** il est difficile d'imaginer que l'on puisse être aussi bête ▪ **the doctors did everything ~ to save her** les médecins ont fait tout leur possible *OR* tout ce qu'ils ont pu pour la sauver ▪ **what ~ benefit can we get from it?** quel bénéfice peut-on bien en tirer? ▪ **it's ~ (that) he won't come** il se peut qu'il ne vienne pas ▪ **it's just ~ she's forgotten** il n'est pas impossible qu'elle ait oublié ▪ **there is a ~ risk of flooding on low ground** il y a des risques d'inondations en contrebas ▮ [feasible] possible, faisable ▪ **he comes to see me whenever ~** il vient me voir quand il le peut ▪ **the grant made it ~ for me to continue my research** la bourse m'a permis de poursuivre mes recherches
3. [potential] éventuel ▪ **~ risks** des risques éventuels ▪ **~ consequences** des conséquences éventuelles.
◇ *n* **1.** [activity] possible *m*
2. [choice] choix *m* possible ▪ [candidate] candidature *f* susceptible d'être retenue ▪ **we looked at ten houses, of which two were ~s** nous avons visité dix maisons dont deux nous intéressent *OR* sont à retenir ▪ **she is still a ~ for the prize/job** elle garde toutes ses chances d'avoir le prix/d'obtenir le poste ▮ SPORT [player] joueur *m* susceptible d'être choisi.

possibly [ˈpɒsəblɪ] *adv* **1.** [perhaps] peut-être ▪ **~ (so)/~ not, but he had no other choice** peut-être (bien)/peut-être pas, mais il n'avait pas le choix ▪ **will you be there tomorrow? – ~** vous serez là demain? – c'est possible ▪ **could you ~ lend me £5?** vous serait-il possible de me prêter 5 livres? **2.** *(with modal verbs)* [conceivably] : **what advantage can we ~ get from it?** quel avantage pouvons-nous espérer en tirer? ▪ **she can't ~ get here on time** elle ne pourra jamais arriver à l'heure ▪ **where can they ~ have got to?** où peuvent-ils bien être passés? ▪ **run as fast as you ~ can** cours aussi vite que tu peux ▪ **the doctors did all they ~ could to save her** les médecins ont fait tout ce qu'ils ont pu *OR* tout leur possible pour la sauver ▪ **I'll come whenever I ~ can** je viendrai chaque fois que cela me sera possible ▪ **I couldn't ~ accept your offer** je ne puis accepter votre proposition ▪ **she might ~ still be here** il se pourrait qu'elle soit encore ici.

possum [ˈpɒsəm] *n* [American] opossum *m* ▪ [Australian] phalanger *m* ▪ **to play ~** *inf* faire le mort.

post [pəʊst] ◇ *n* **1.** *UK* [letters] courrier *m* ▪ [postal service] poste *f*, courrier *m* ▪ **has the ~ come?** est-ce que le facteur est passé? ▪ **did it come through the ~** *OR* **by ~?** est-ce que c'est arrivé par la poste? ▪ **I sent it by ~** je l'ai envoyé par la poste ▪ **can you put the cheque in the ~?** pouvez-vous poster le chèque? ▮ [delivery] (distribution *f* du)courrier *m* ▪ **a parcel came in this morning's ~** un paquet est arrivé au courrier de ce matin ▮ [collection] levée *f* (du courrier) ▪ **I don't want to miss the ~** je ne veux pas manquer la levée ▪ **will we still catch the ~?** pourrons-nous poster le courrier à temps *OR* avant la levée? ▮ [post office] poste *f* ▪ [letterbox] boîte *f* à lettres ▪ **can you take the letters to the ~?** [post office] pouvez-vous porter les lettres à la poste? ; [post them] pouvez-vous poster les lettres *OR* mettre les lettres à la boîte? **2.** [station] relais *m* de poste ▪ [rider] courrier *m* **3.** [of sign, street lamp, fence] poteau *m* ▪ [of four-poster bed] colonne *f* ▪ [upright - of door] montant *m* **4.** [in racing] poteau *m* **5.** FTBL poteau *m*, montant *m* ▪ **the near/far ~** le premier/deuxième poteau **6.** [job] poste *m*, emploi *m* ▪ **a university/diplomatic ~** un poste universitaire/de diplomate ▪ **a government ~** un poste au gouvernement **7.** [duty station] poste *m* ▪ **a sentry ~** un poste de sentinelle **8.** *US* [trading post] comptoir *m*.
◇ *vt* **1.** [letter - put in box] poster, mettre à la poste ; [- send by post] envoyer par la poste ▪ **to ~ sthg to sb** envoyer qqch à qqn par la poste, poster qqch à qqn ➊ **to keep sb ~ed** tenir qqn au courant **2.** [station] poster **3.** *UK* [transfer - employee] muter, affecter **4.** [publish - banns, names] publier ; [- on bulletin board] afficher ▪ **he has been ~ed missing** il a été porté disparu ▪ **'~ no bills'** *US* 'défense d'afficher' **5.** BANK & ADMIN inscrire, enregistrer ▪ **to ~ an entry** passer une écriture ▪ **to ~ the ledger** tenir le grand-livre à jour **6.** *US* [issue] : **to ~ bail** déposer une caution **7.** COMPUT poster.

◆ **post on** *vt sep* [letters] faire suivre.

◆ **post up** *vt sep* **1.** [notice] afficher **2.** [ledger] mettre à jour *(les écritures)*.

postage [ˈpəʊstɪdʒ] ◇ *n (U)* [postal charges] tarifs *mpl* postaux *OR* d'affranchissement ▪ [cost of posting] frais *mpl* d'ex-

pédition *OR* d'envoi *OR* de port ■ **what's the ~ on this parcel?** c'est combien pour envoyer ce paquet? ➜ **~ and packing** *UK* *OR* **handling** *US* frais de port et d'emballage ■ **~ paid** franco.
◇ *comp* [rates] postal.

postage due stamp *n* timbre *m* taxe.

postage stamp *n* timbre *m*, timbre-poste *m*.

postal ['pəʊstl] *adj* [charge, code, district] postal ■ [administration, service, strike] des postes ■ [delivery] par la poste ■ **~ vote** *UK* vote *m* par correspondance ■ **~ worker** employé *m*, - e *f* des postes.

postal order *n UK* mandat *m* postal.

postbag ['pəʊstbæg] *n UK* **1.** [sack] sac *m* postal **2.** [correspondence] courrier *m*.

postbox ['pəʊstbɒks] *n UK* boîte *f* à *OR* aux lettres.

postcard ['pəʊstkɑːd] *n* carte *f* postale.

post chaise [-ʃeɪz] *n* chaise *f* de poste.

postcode ['pəʊstkəʊd] *n UK* code *m* postal.

postdate [,pəʊst'deɪt] *vt* **1.** [letter, cheque] postdater **2.** [event] assigner une date postérieure à.

postdoctoral [,pəʊst'dɒktərəl], **postdoctorate** [,pəʊst'dɒktərət] *adj* UNIV postdoctoral.

poster ['pəʊstər] *n* [informative] affiche *f* ■ [decorative] poster *m*.

poste restante [,pəʊst'restɑːnt] *n* poste *f* restante.

posterior [pɒ'stɪərɪər] ◇ *adj* **1.** *fml* [in time] postérieur **2.** TECH [rear] arrière.
◇ *n inf hum* [of a person] postérieur *m*, arrière-train *m*.

posterity [pɒ'sterətɪ] *n* postérité *f* ■ **for ~** pour la postérité ■ **to go down to ~** entrer dans la postérité *OR* l'histoire.

postern ['pɒstən] *n* poterne *f*.

poster paint *n* gouache *f*.

post-feminism *n* postféminisme *m*.

post-feminist *adj* & *n* postféministe *mf*.

post-free ◇ *adj* **1.** *UK* [prepaid] port payé **2.** [free of postal charge] dispensé d'affranchissement.
◇ *adv* **1.** *UK* [prepaid] en port payé **2.** [free of postal charge] en franchise postale.

postgraduate [,pəʊst'grædʒʊət] ◇ *n* étudiant *m*, - e *f* de troisième cycle.
◇ *adj* [diploma, studies] de troisième cycle.

posthaste [,pəʊst'heɪst] *adv lit* à toute vitesse, en toute hâte.

postholder ['pəʊst,həʊldər] *n* titulaire *mf*.

post horn *n* trompe *f* (de la malle-poste).

post house *n* relais *m* de poste.

posthumous ['pɒstjʊməs] *adj* posthume.

posthumously ['pɒstjʊməslɪ] *adj* après la mort ■ **the prize was awarded ~** le prix a été décerné à titre posthume.

postil(l)ion [pə'stɪljən] *n* postillon *m*.

postimpressionism [,pəʊstɪm'preʃnɪzm] *n* postimpressionnisme *m*.

postimpressionist [,pəʊstɪm'preʃnɪst] ◇ *n* postimpressionniste *mf*.
◇ *adj* postimpressionniste.

postindustrial [,pəʊstɪn'dʌstrɪəl] *adj* postindustriel.

posting ['pəʊstɪŋ] *n* **1.** *UK* [of diplomat] nomination *f*, affectation *f* ■ [of soldier] affectation *f* ■ **to get an overseas ~** être nommé en poste à l'étranger **2.** COMM [in ledger] inscription *f*, enregistrement *m* **3.** *UK* [of letter] expédition *f* par la poste.

Post-it® *n* Post-it® *m*.

postman ['pəʊstmən] (*pl* **postmen** [-mən]) *n* facteur *m* ADMIN préposé *m*.

postman's knock *n* *jeu d'enfant dans lequel un des joueurs fait semblant de distribuer des lettres, en échange desquelles il reçoit un baiser.*

postmark ['pəʊstmɑːk] ◇ *n* [on letter] cachet *m* de la poste ■ **date as ~** le cachet de la poste faisant foi.
◇ *vt* oblitérer ■ **the letter is ~ed Phoenix** la lettre vient de *OR* a été postée à Phoenix.

postmaster ['pəʊst,mɑːstər] *n* receveur *m* des Postes.

Postmaster General (*pl* **Postmasters General**) *n* ≃ ministre *m* des Postes et Télécommunications.

postmistress ['pəʊst,mɪstrɪs] *n* receveuse *f* des Postes.

post-modern *adj* postmoderne.

post-modernism *n* postmodernisme *m*.

post-modernist ◇ *n* postmoderniste *mf*.
◇ *adj* postmoderniste.

postmortem [,pəʊst'mɔːtəm] ◇ *n* **1.** MED autopsie *f* ■ **to carry out a ~** pratiquer une autopsie **2.** *fig* autopsie *f* ■ **they held a ~ on the game** ils ont disséqué *OR* analysé le match après coup.
◇ *adj* après le décès ■ **~ examination** autopsie *f*.

postnatal [,pəʊst'neɪtl] *adj* postnatal.

post office *n* **1.** [place] (bureau *m* de) poste *f* ■ [service] (service *m* des) postes *fpl*, poste *f* ■ **the Post Office** la Poste ■ **~ and general stores** *petite épicerie de village faisant office de bureau de poste* **2.** *US* = **postman's knock**.

post office box *n* boîte *f* postale.

post office savings *n UK* ≃ Caisse *f* (nationale) d'épargne.

post-op ◇ *adj* postopératoire.
◇ *n* salle *f* de réveil.

postoperative [,pəʊst'ɒpərətɪv] *adj* postopératoire.

postpaid [,pəʊst'peɪd] *adj* & *adv* franco, franc de port.

postpone [,pəʊst'pəʊn] *vt* [meeting, holiday] remettre (à plus tard), reporter ■ [match, game] reporter ■ [decision] différer ■ **the meeting was ~d for three weeks/until a later date** la réunion a été reportée de trois semaines/remise à une date ultérieure.

postponement [,pəʊst'pəʊnmənt] *n* [of meeting, match] renvoi *m* (à une date ultérieure), report *m* ■ [of holiday] report *m*.

postposition [,pəʊstpə'zɪʃn] *n* GRAM postposition *f*.

postprandial [,pəʊst'prændɪəl] *adj fml* postprandial.

postscript ['pəʊsskrɪpt] *n* post-scriptum *m inv*.

poststructuralism [,pəʊs'strʌktʃərəlɪzm] *n* poststructuralisme *m*.

poststructuralist [,pəʊs'strʌktʃərəlɪst] *n* poststructuraliste *mf*.

post-traumatic stress disorder *n (U)* névrose *f* post-traumatique.

postulant ['pɒstjʊlənt] *n* RELIG postulant *m*, - e *f*.

postulate *fml* ◇ *vt* ['pɒstjʊleɪt] **1.** [hypothesize] poser comme hypothèse ■ **to ~ the existence of an underground lake** soutenir l'hypothèse d'un lac souterrain **2.** [take as granted] postuler, poser comme principe ■ **the charter ~s that all men are equal** la charte part du principe que tous les hommes sont égaux.
◇ *n* ['pɒstjʊlət] postulat *m*.

posture ['pɒstʃər] ◇ *n* **1.** [body position] posture *f*, position *f* ■ **to keep an upright ~** se tenir droit **2.** *fig* [attitude] attitude *f*.
◇ *vi* se donner des airs, poser.

posturing ['pɒstʃərɪŋ] *n* pose *f*, affectation *f*.

postviral syndrome [,pəʊst'vaɪərl-] *n* syndrome *m* postviral.

postwar [ˌpəʊst'wɔːr] *adj* d'après-guerre, après la guerre ▪ **the ~ period** l'après-guerre *m ou f* ▪ **in the immediate ~ period** au cours des années qui ont immédiatement suivi la guerre, tout de suite après la guerre.

posy ['pəʊzɪ] (*pl* **posies**) *n* petit bouquet *m* (de fleurs).

pot [pɒt] (*pret & pp* **potted**, *cont* **potting**) ◇ *vt* **1.** [jam] mettre en pot *OR* pots ▪ [fruit] mettre en conserve **2.** [plant] mettre en pot **3.** *UK* [in snooker] : **to ~ the ball** mettre la bille dans la poche *OR* la blouse **4.** *UK* [shoot] tuer.
◇ *vi* **1.** [do pottery] faire de la poterie **2.** *UK* [shoot] : **to ~ at sthg** tirer sur qqch.
◇ *n* **1.** [container - for paint, plant, jam etc] pot *m* ▪ [teapot] théière *f* ▪ [coffeepot] cafetière *f* ▪ **I'll make another ~ of tea/coffee** je vais refaire du thé/café ▪ **a ~ of tea for two** du thé pour deux personnes **2.** [saucepan] casserole *f* ▪ **~s and pans** batterie *f* de cuisine ▪ **(cooking) ~** marmite *f*, fait-tout *m inv* ▪ **it's a case of the ~ calling the kettle black** *UK prov* c'est la Pitié qui se moque de la Charité *prov* **3.** [pottery object] poterie *f*, pot *m* ▪ **to throw a ~** tourner une poterie **4.** *inf* SPORT [trophy] trophée *m*, coupe *f* **5.** *US* [kitty] cagnotte *f* **6.** *inf* [belly] bedaine *f*, brioche *f* **7.** *UK inf* [shot] : **to take a ~ at sthg** tirer sur qqch **8.** *inf* [marijuana] herbe *f* **9.** ELEC potentiomètre *m* **10.** *phr* **to go to ~** *inf* [country] aller à la dérive ; [morals] dégénérer ; [plans] tomber à l'eau ; [person] se laisser aller ▪ **everything has gone to ~** tout est fichu.
◆ **pots** *npl UK inf* [large amount] tas *mpl*, tonnes *fpl* ▪ **to have ~s of money** avoir plein de fric, être plein aux as.

potash ['pɒtæʃ] *n (U)* potasse *f*.

potassium [pə'tæsɪəm] *n (U)* potassium *m*.

potato [pə'teɪtəʊ] (*pl* **potatoes**) ◇ *n* pomme *f* de terre ➊ **the ~ famine** *Ireland* HIST la disette de la pomme de terre.
◇ *comp* [farming, salad] de pommes de terre.

THE POTATO FAMINE

Famine qui sévit en Irlande en 1845, à la suite d'une épidémie qui détruisit les stocks de pommes de terre, aliment de base de la population. Plongeant le pays dans la misère, cette catastrophe poussa plus d'un million de personnes à émigrer aux États-Unis.

potato beetle *n* doryphore *m*.

potato blight *n* mildiou *m* de la pomme de terre.

potato chip *n* **1.** *UK* [French fry] (pomme *f*) frite *f* **2.** *US* [crisp] (pomme *f*) chips *f*.

potato crisp *n UK* (pomme *f*) chips *f*.

potato masher *n* presse-purée *m inv*.

potato peeler *n* [tool] éplucheur *m*, épluche-légumes *m*, (couteau *m*) économe *m* ▪ [machine] éplucheuse *f*.

potato soup *n* soupe *f* de pommes de terre.

potbellied ['pɒtˌbelɪd] *adj* **1.** [person] bedonnant ▪ **to be ~** avoir du ventre **2.** [piece of furniture] : **~ stove** poêle *m*.

potbelly ['pɒtˌbelɪ] (*pl* **potbellies**) *n* **1.** [stomach] ventre *m*, bedon *m* ▪ **to have a ~** avoir du ventre **2.** *US* [stove] poêle *m*.

potboiler ['pɒtˌbɔɪlər] *n inf* gagne-pain *m* ▪ **he only writes ~s** il n'écrit que pour faire bouillir la marmite.

pot-bound *adj* [plant] qui a besoin d'être rempoté.

pot cheese *n US* = **cottage cheese**.

potency ['pəʊtənsɪ] (*pl* **potencies**) *n* **1.** [strength - of spell, influence, argument] force *f*, puissance *f* ; [- of medicine] efficacité *f* ; [- of drink] (forte) teneur *f* en alcool **2.** [virility] puissance *f*, virilité *f*.

potent ['pəʊtənt] *adj* **1.** [spell, influence] fort, puissant ▪ [argument] convaincant ▪ [medicine, poison, antidote] actif ▪ [drink] fort (en alcool) **2.** [virile] viril.

potentate ['pəʊtənteɪt] *n* POL potentat *m* ▪ *fig* magnat *m*.

potential [pə'tenʃl] ◇ *adj* **1.** [possible] possible, potentiel ▪ **that boy is a ~ genius** ce garçon est un génie en puissance ▪ **we mustn't discourage ~investors** il ne faut pas décourager les investisseurs éventuels *OR* potentiels **2.** LING potentiel **3.** ELEC & PHYS potentiel.
◇ *n* **1.** *(U)* [of person] promesse *f*, possibilités *fpl* (d'avenir) ▪ **your son has ~** votre fils a de l'avenir *OR* un avenir prometteur ▪ **she has the ~ to succeed** elle a la capacité de réussir ▪ **they don't have much intellectual ~** ils n'ont pas de grandes capacités intellectuelles ▪ **she has great ~ as an actress** *OR* **great acting ~** elle a toutes les qualités d'une grande actrice ▪ **to fulfil one's ~** donner toute sa mesure ▪ **he never achieved his full ~** il n'a jamais exploité pleinement ses capacités ▮ [of concept, discovery, situation] possibilités *fpl* ▪ **the idea has ~** l'idée a de l'avenir ▪ **your latest invention has great ~for developing countries** votre dernière invention ouvre de grandes perspectives dans les pays en voie de développement ▪ **the scheme has no ~** le projet n'a aucun avenir ▪ **there is little ~ for development in the firm** l'entreprise offre peu de possibilités de développement ▪ **the country's military ~** le potentiel militaire du pays ▮ [of place] possibilités *fpl* ▪ **the area/garden has real ~** le quartier/le jardin offre de nombreuses possibilités **2.** ELEC & MATHS potentiel *m*.

potentiality [pəˌtenʃɪ'ælətɪ] (*pl* **potentialities**) *n* **1.** [likelihood] potentialité *f* **2.** [potential] possibilités *fpl*, perspective *f* (d'avenir).

potentially [pə'tenʃəlɪ] *adv* potentiellement ▪ **she's ~ a great writer** elle pourrait être un grand écrivain ▪ **~ lethal poisons** des poisons qui peuvent être mortels.

potful ['pɒtfʊl] *n* [volume] (contenu *m* d'un) pot *m*.

pothead△ ['pɒthed] *n drug sl* fumeur *m*, - euse *f* de marijuana.

potherb ['pɒthɜːb] *n* [as seasoning] herbe *f* aromatique ▪ [as vegetable] légume *m* vert.

pothole ['pɒthəʊl] *n* **1.** [in road] fondrière *f*, nid-de-poule *m* **2.** [underground] caverne *f*, grotte *f*.

potholer ['pɒtˌhəʊlər] *n UK* spéléologue *mf*.

potholing ['pɒtˌhəʊlɪŋ] *n (U) UK* spéléologie *f* ▪ **to go ~** faire de la spéléologie.

potion ['pəʊʃn] *n* **1.** MED potion *f* **2.** *fig* potion *f*, breuvage *m*.

potluck [ˌpɒt'lʌk] *n inf* **to take ~** [for meal] manger à la fortune du pot ; [take what one finds] s'en remettre au hasard.

pot plant *n UK* plante *f* d'intérieur.

potpourri [ˌpəʊ'pʊərɪ] *n* pot-pourri *m*.

potroast ['pɒtrəʊst] *vt* rôtir à la cocotte.

pot roast *n* rôti *m* à la cocotte.

pot shot *n* : **to take a ~ at sthg** [fire at] tirer à l'aveuglette sur qqch ; [attempt] faire qqch à l'aveuglette.

pottage ['pɒtɪdʒ] *n* potage *m* épais.

potted ['pɒtɪd] *adj* **1.** HORT en pot ▪ **~ plant** plante *f* verte **2.** CULIN [cooked] (cuit) en terrine ▪ [conserved] (conservé) en terrine *OR* en pot ▪ **~ meat** ≃ terrine *f* ▪ **~ shrimps** crevettes *fpl* en conserve **3.** *inf* [condensed - version] condensé, abrégé ▪ **a ~ history of the Second World War** un abrégé d'histoire de la Seconde Guerre mondiale.

potter ['pɒtər] ◇ *n* potier *m*, - ère *f* ▪ **~'s clay** argile *f* de potier, terre *f* glaise ▪ **~'s wheel** tour *m* de potier ▪ **~'s field** *US* cimetière *m* des pauvres.
◇ *vi UK inf* s'occuper de choses et d'autres, bricoler.
◆ **potter about** *UK inf* ◇ *vi insep* s'occuper, bricoler.
◇ *vt insep* : **to ~ about the house/garden** faire de petits travaux *OR* bricoler dans la maison/le jardin.
◆ **potter along** *vi insep UK inf* aller son petit bonhomme de chemin ▪ **I might ~ along to the library later** j'irai peut-être faire un tour à la bibliothèque tout à l'heure.
◆ **potter around** *UK inf* = **potter about**.

Potteries ['pɒtərɪz] *npl* : **the ~** la région des poteries dans le Staffordshire (en Angleterre).

pottery ['pɒtərɪ] (*pl* **potteries**) *n* **1.** *(U)* [craft] poterie *f* **2.** *(U)* [earthenware] poterie *f*, poteries *fpl* ▪ [ceramics] céramiques *fpl* ▪ **a beautiful piece of ~** une très belle poterie **3.** [workshop] atelier *m* de poterie.

potting ['pɒtɪŋ] *n (U)* **1.** HORT rempotage *m* ▪ **~ compost** terreau *m* **2.** [pottery] poterie *f*.

potting shed *n* remise *f OR* resserre *f* (de jardin).

potty ['pɒtɪ] (*pl* **potties**, *comp* **pottier**, *superl* **pottiest**) <> *n* [for children] pot *m* (de chambre).
<> *adj inf UK inf* fou *(before vowel or silent 'h' fol)*, folle *f*, cinglé, dingue ▪ **to be ~ about sthg** être toqué de qqch ▪ **he's absolutely ~ about her** il est absolument fou d'elle.

potty-train *vt* : **to ~ a child** apprendre à un enfant à aller sur son pot.

potty-trained *adj* propre.

pouch [paʊtʃ] *n* **1.** [bag] (petit) sac *m* ▪ [for tobacco] blague *f* ▪ [for money] sac *m*, bourse *f* ▪ [for ammunition] cartouchière *f*, giberne *f* ▪ [for gunpowder] sacoche *f*, sac *m* ▪ [for mail] sac *m* (postal) **2.** ZOOL [of marsupial, in cheeks] poche *f*, abajoue *f* ▪ [pocket of skin] poche *f* **3.** *US* [for diplomats] valise *f* diplomatique.

pouf(fe) [pu:f] *n UK* **1.** [cushion] pouf *m* **2.**△ *UK* = **poof** *(n)*.

poultice ['pəʊltɪs] <> *n* MED cataplasme *m*.
<> *vt* mettre un cataplasme à.

poultry ['pəʊltrɪ] <> *n (U)* [meat] volaille *f*.
<> *npl* [birds] volaille *f*, volailles *fpl*.

poultry farm *n* élevage *m* de volaille *OR* de volailles.

poultry farmer *n* éleveur *m*, - euse *f* de volaille *OR* de volailles, aviculteur *m*, - trice *f*.

poultry farming *n* élevage *m* de volaille *OR* de volailles, aviculture *f*.

pounce [paʊns] <> *vi* sauter, bondir ▪ **a man ~d (out) from behind the bush** un homme a surgi de derrière le buisson.
<> *n* bond *m* ▪ **with a sudden ~** d'un bond.
◆ **pounce on, pounce upon** *vt insep* **1.** [subj: animal] se jeter sur, bondir sur ▪ [subj: bird] se jeter sur, fondre sur ▪ [subj: police] saisir, arrêter **2.** [in criticism] bondir sur, sauter sur **3.** [seize - opportunity] sauter sur, saisir.

pound [paʊnd] <> *n* **1.** [weight] livre *f* ▪ **to sell goods by the ~** vendre des marchandises à la livre ▪ **two dollars a ~** deux dollars la livre ▶ **to get one's ~ of flesh** obtenir ce que l'on exigeait ▪ **he wants his pound of flesh** il veut son dû à n'importe quel prix
2. [money] livre *f* ▪ **two for a ~** deux pour une livre ▪ **the ~ fell yesterday against the dollar** la livre est tombée hier face au dollar ▶ **~ coin** pièce *f* d'une livre ▪ **the ~ sterling** la livre sterling
3. [for dogs, cars] fourrière *f*.
<> *vt* **1.** [crush, pulverize - grain] broyer, concasser ; [- rocks] concasser, écraser
2. [hammer, hit] cogner sur, marteler ▪ **the waves ~ed the rocks/boat** les vagues battaient les rochers/venaient s'écraser violemment contre le bateau ▪ **he began ~ing the typewriter keys** il commença à taper sur *OR* à marteler le clavier de la machine à écrire
3. [bombard, shell] bombarder, pilonner ▪ **they ~ed the enemy positions with mortar fire** ils ont bombardé les positions ennemies au mortier
4. [walk - corridor] faire les cent pas dans, aller et venir dans ▪ **to ~ the streets** battre le pavé ▪ **to ~ the beat** faire sa ronde.
<> *vi* **1.** [hammer - on table, ceiling] cogner, taper ; [- on piano, typewriter] taper ▪ **we had to ~ on the door before anyone answered** il a fallu frapper à la porte à coups redoublés avant d'obtenir une réponse ▪ **the waves ~ed against the rocks** les vagues venaient s'écraser sur *OR* fouettaient les rochers ▪ **the rain was ~ing on the roof** la pluie tambourinait sur le toit
2. [rhythmically - drums] battre ; [- heart] battre fort ; [- with fear, excitement] battre la chamade ▪ **my head was ~ing from the noise** le bruit me martelait la tête
3. [more heavily] : **he ~ed down the stairs** il descendit l'escalier bruyamment ▪ **the elephants ~ed through the jungle** les éléphants se déplaçaient lourdement à travers la jungle.
◆ **pound away** *vi insep* **1.** [at task] travailler avec acharnement
2. [on typewriter, piano, drums] taper
3. [with artillery] : **to ~ away at the enemy lines** pilonner sans arrêt les lignes ennemies.
◆ **pound down** *vt sep* **1.** [crush] piler, concasser ▪ **~ the mixture down to a pulp** réduisez le mélange en bouillie
2. [flatten - earth] pilonner, tasser.
◆ **pound out** *vt sep UK* **1.** [rhythm] marteler
2. [letter, document] taper (avec fougue) ▪ **she ~s out a book a month** elle sort *OR* écrit un livre par mois.

poundage ['paʊndɪdʒ] *n (U)* **1.** [on weight] droits *mpl* perçus par livre de poids **2.** [on value] droits *mpl* perçus par livre de valeur **3.** [weight] poids *m (en livres)*.

pound cake *n* ≃ quatre-quarts *m inv*.

-pounder ['paʊndəʳ] *in cpds* : **a fifteen~** [fish] un poisson de 15 livres ▪ **a six~** [gun] un canon *OR* une pièce de six.

pounding ['paʊndɪŋ] *n* **1.** [noise] martèlement *m* **2.** *(U)* [beating - of heart] battements *mpl* **3.** *inf* [battering] rossée *f* ▪ **he took a real ~ in the first five rounds** il a pris une bonne volée *OR* il s'est drôlement fait rosser pendant les cinq premières reprises ▪ **the jetty/harbour took a ~ in the storm** la jetée/le port en a pris un coup pendant la tempête ▪ **the dollar took a severe ~ last week** le dollar a été sérieusement malmené la semaine dernière **4.** *inf* [severe defeat] déculottée *f*, piquette *f* ▪ **the team took a real ~ last week** l'équipe a subi une lourde défaite *OR* s'est fait battre à plate couture la semaine dernière.

pour [pɔ:ʳ] <> *vt* **1.** [liquid] verser ▪ **she ~ed milk into their mugs** elle a versé du lait dans leurs tasses ▪ **we ~ed the water/wine down the sink** nous avons vidé l'eau/jeté le vin dans l'évier ▪ **her jeans were so tight she looked as if she'd been ~ed into them** son jeans était tellement serré qu'elle semblait avoir été coulée dedans ▪ **to ~ scorn on sb** *fig* traiter qqn avec mépris ▮ [serve] servir, verser ▪ **to ~ a drink for sb** servir à boire à qqn ▪ **may I ~ you some wine?** je vous sers du vin? ▶ **to ~ cold water on** *OR* **over sb's plans** *inf* décourager *OR* refroidir qqn dans ses projets
2. [invest] investir ▪ **he ~ed all his energy into the project** il a mis toute son énergie dans le projet.
<> *vi* **1.** [light, liquid] se déverser, couler à flots ▪ **water ~ed from the gutters** l'eau débordait des gouttières ▪ **tears ~ed down her face** elle pleurait à chaudes larmes ▪ **blood ~ed from the wound** la blessure saignait abondamment ▪ **the sweat was ~ing off his back** son dos ruisselait de sueur ▪ **light ~ed into the church** l'église était inondée de lumière ▪ **smoke ~ed out of the blazing building** des nuages de fumée s'échappaient de l'immeuble en flammes
2. [rain] pleuvoir à verse ▪ **it's ~ing (down), it's ~ing with rain** il pleut à verse *OR* à torrents ▪ **the rain ~ed down** la pluie tombait à verse
3. [crowd] affluer ▪ **spectators ~ed into/out of the cinema** une foule de spectateurs entrait dans le cinéma/sortait du cinéma ▪ **thousands of cars ~ed out of Paris** des milliers de voitures se pressaient aux portes de Paris
4. [pan, jug] : **to ~ well/badly** verser bien/mal.
◆ **pour away** *vt sep* [empty] vider ▪ [throw out] jeter.
◆ **pour down** *vi insep* = **pour** *(vi sense 2)*.
◆ **pour in** *vi insep* **1.** [rain, light] entrer à flots
2. [cars, refugees, spectators] arriver en masse ▪ [information, reports] affluer, arriver en masse ▪ **offers of help ~ed in from all sides** des offres d'aide ont afflué de toutes parts ▪ **money ~ed in for the disaster victims** des milliers de dons ont été envoyés pour les victimes de la catastrophe.
◆ **pour off** *vt sep* [liquid, excess] vider.
◆ **pour out** <> *vt sep* **1.** [liquid] verser
2. [information, propaganda] répandre, diffuser ▪ [substances] : **the industry ~s out tons of dangerous chemicals** l'industrie déverse des tonnes de produits chimiques dangereux
3. [emotions] donner libre cours à ▪ **she ~ed out all her troubles to me** elle m'a raconté tout ce qu'elle avait sur le cœur ▪ **to ~ out one's heart to sb** parler à qqn à cœur ouvert.

◇ *vi insep* [water] jaillir, couler à flots ▪ [tears] couler abondamment ▪ [light] jaillir.

pouring ['pɔːrɪŋ] *adj* **1.** [rain] battant, diluvien **2.** [cream] liquide.

pout [paʊt] ◇ *vi* faire la moue.
◇ *vt* dire en faisant la moue.
◇ *n* **1.** [facial expression] moue *f* ▪ **with a ~** en faisant la moue **2.** (*pl inv* OR *pl* s) [fish - eelpout] lycode *m*, lotte *f* ; [- whiting] tacaud *m*.

POV *written abbr of* **point of view**.

poverty ['pɒvətɪ] *n* **1.** [financial] pauvreté *f*, misère *f* ▪ **to live in ~** vivre dans le besoin **2.** [shortage - of resources] manque *m* ; [- of ideas, imagination] pauvreté *f*, manque *m* ▪ [weakness - of style, arguments] pauvreté *f*, faiblesse *f* **3.** [of soil] pauvreté *f*, aridité *f*.

poverty line *n* seuil *m* de pauvreté ▪ **to live on/below the ~** vivre à la limite/en dessous du seuil de pauvreté.

poverty-stricken *adj* [person] dans la misère, dans le plus grand dénuement ▪ [areas] misérable, où sévit la misère.

poverty trap *n situation inextricable de ceux qui dépendent de prestations sociales qu'ils perdent pour peu qu'ils trouvent une activité, même peu rémunérée.*

pow [paʊ] *onom* [from collision] vlan, v'lan ▪ [from gun] pan.

POW *n* = **prisoner of war**.

powder ['paʊdəʳ] ◇ *n* [gen - MIL] poudre *f* ▪ **in ~ form** en poudre, sous forme de poudre ▪ **to grind sthg to a ~** réduire qqch en poudre, pulvériser qqch ▶ **to keep one's ~ dry** *UK* se tenir prêt, être aux aguets.
◇ *vt* **1.** [crush, pulverize] pulvériser, réduire en poudre **2.** [make up] poudrer ▪ **to ~ one's face** se poudrer le visage ▪ **to ~ one's nose** *euph* [go to the toilet] aller se repoudrer le nez **3.** [sprinkle] saupoudrer.

powder blue *n* bleu *m* pastel.
◆ **powder-blue** *adj* bleu pastel *(inv)*.

powder compact *n* poudrier *m*.

powdered ['paʊdəd] *adj* **1.** [milk] en poudre ▪ [coffee] instantané ▪ **~ sugar** *US* sucre *m* glace **2.** [hair, face] poudré.

powder horn *n* corne *f*, cartouche *f* à poudre.

powder keg *n* [of gunpowder] baril *m* de poudre ▪ *fig* poudrière *f*.

powder puff *n* houppette *f*.

powder room *n euph* toilettes *fpl* (pour dames).

powdery ['paʊdərɪ] *adj* **1.** [covered in powder] couvert de poudre **2.** [like powder] poudreux ▪ **~ snow** (neige *f*) poudreuse *f* **3.** [crumbling] friable.

power ['paʊəʳ] ◇ *n* **1.** [strength, force - gen] puissance *f*, force *f* ▪ **the ~ of the explosion** la puissance OR la force de l'explosion ▪ **economic and industrial ~** la puissance économique et industrielle ▪ PHYS [of engine, lens, microscope] puissance *f* ▪ **at full ~** à plein régime ▪ **the vehicle moves under its own ~** le véhicule se déplace par ses propres moyens OR de façon autonome ▶ **sea/air ~** puissance *f* maritime/aérienne ▪ **more ~ to your elbow!** *UK inf* bonne chance!, bon courage!
2. [influence] pouvoir *m*, puissance *f* ▪ **I'll do everything in my ~ to help you** je ferai tout mon possible OR tout ce qui est en mon pouvoir pour vous aider ▪ **at the height of his ~s** à l'apogée de son pouvoir | [control] pouvoir *m* ▪ **to have sb in one's ~** avoir qqn en son pouvoir ▪ **to fall into sb's ~** tomber au pouvoir de qqn | POL pouvoir *m* ▪ **to be in ~** être au pouvoir ▪ **to come to/to take ~** arriver au/prendre le pouvoir
3. [authority] autorité *f*, pouvoir *m* ▪ [of assembly] pouvoir *m* ▪ **to have the ~ to decide/judge** avoir le pouvoir de décider/juger, avoir autorité pour décider/juger ▪ **it's beyond** OR **outside my ~** cela dépasse ma compétence OR ne relève pas de mon autorité ▪ **no ~ on earth will persuade me to go** rien au monde ne me persuadera d'y aller | [influential group or person] puissance *f* ▪ **the President is the real ~ in the land** c'est le président qui détient le véritable pouvoir dans le pays ▶ **the ~s of darkness** les forces OR puissances des ténèbres ▪ **the ~ behind the throne** [individual] l'éminence *f* grise, celui *m* /celle *f* qui tire les ficelles ; [group] ceux qui tirent les ficelles, les véritables acteurs ▪ **the ~s that be** les autorités constituées
4. POL [state] puissance *f*
5. [ability, capacity] capacité *f*, pouvoir *m* ▪ **he has great ~s as an orator** OR **great oratorical ~s** il a de grands talents oratoires ▪ **it's within her ~ to do it** c'est en son pouvoir, elle est capable de le faire ▪ **to have great ~s of persuasion/suggestion** avoir un grand pouvoir OR une grande force de persuasion/suggestion ▪ **the body's ~s of resistance** la capacité de résistance du corps ▪ **she has great intellectual ~s** elle a de grandes capacités intellectuelles | [faculty] faculté *f*, pouvoir *m* ▪ **her ~s are failing** ses facultés déclinent ▪ **the ~ of sight** la vue ▪ **the ~ of hearing** l'ouïe *f* ▪ **he lost the ~ of speech** il a perdu l'usage de la parole
6. ELEC [current] courant *m*
7. ELEC & PHYS [energy] énergie *f* ▪ **nuclear/solar ~** énergie nucléaire/solaire
8. LAW [proxy] pouvoir *m*
9. MATHS puissance *f* ▪ **5 to the ~ (of) 6** 5 puissance 6
10. *phr* **a ~ of good** *inf*: **the holiday did me a ~ of good** les vacances m'ont fait énormément de bien.
◇ *comp* [source, consumption] d'énergie ▪ [cable] électrique ▪ [brakes, steering] assisté ▪ **~ breakfast** petit déjeuner *m* d'affaires ▪ **~ dressing** *façon de s'habiller qu'adoptent certaines femmes cadres dans le but de projeter une image d'autorité.*
◇ *vt* [give power to] faire fonctionner OR marcher ▪ [propel] propulser ▪ **the boat is ~ed by gas turbines** le bateau est propulsé par des turbines à gaz ▪ **~ed by solar energy** fonctionnant à l'énergie solaire.
◇ *vi* avancer à toute vitesse, foncer ▪ **he ~ed into his opponent** il fonça sur son adversaire.

power-assisted *adj* assisté.

power base *n* assise *f* politique.

powerboat ['paʊəbəʊt] *n* [outboard] hors-bord *m inv* ▪ [inboard] vedette *f* (rapide) ▪ **~ racing** courses *fpl* offshore.

power broker *n* décideur *m* politique.

power cut *n* coupure *f* de courant.

power dive *n* AERON (descente *f* en) piqué *m*.

power drill *n* perceuse *f* électrique.

-powered ['paʊəd] *in cpds* : **high/low~** de haute/faible puissance ▪ **a high~ executive** un cadre très haut placé ▪ **steam/wind~** mû par la vapeur/le vent.

power failure *n* panne *f* de courant.

powerful ['paʊəfʊl] ◇ *adj* **1.** [strong - gen] puissant ; [- smell] fort ; [- kick] violent ; [- imagination] débordant ▪ **a ~ swimmer** un excellent nageur ▪ **~ drugs** médication *f* puissante OR active ▪ **he has been a ~ influence in her life** il a exercé une influence décisive dans sa vie **2.** [influential - person] fort, influent ; [- country, firm] puissant.
◇ *adv UK inf* vachement.

powerfully ['paʊəfʊlɪ] *adv* puissamment ▪ **he's ~ built** il est d'une stature imposante.

power game *n* lutte *f* d'influence, course *f* au pouvoir.

powerhouse ['paʊəhaʊs] (*pl* [-haʊzɪz]) *n* **1.** ELEC centrale *f* électrique **2.** *fig* [person] personne *f* énergique, locomotive *f* ▪ **she's a ~ of energy** elle déborde d'énergie | [place] pépinière *f* ▪ **the university became a ~ of new ideas** l'université est devenue une vraie pépinière d'idées nouvelles.

powerless ['paʊəlɪs] *adj* impuissant, désarmé ▪ **they were ~ to prevent the scandal** ils n'ont rien pu faire pour éviter le scandale ▪ **our arguments were ~ in the face of such conviction** nos arguments sont restés lettre morte devant une telle conviction.

powerlessness ['paʊəlɪsnɪs] *n* impuissance *f*.

power line *n* ligne *f* à haute tension.

power of attorney *n* LAW procuration *f*.

power pack *n* ELEC bloc *m* d'alimentation.

power plant *n* **1.** [factory] centrale *f* électrique **2.** [generator] groupe *m* électrogène **3.** [engine] groupe *m* moteur.

power point *n* prise *f* de courant.

power politics *n (U)* politique *f* du coup de force.

power sharing [-ˌʃeərɪŋ] *n* POL partage *m* du pouvoir.

power station *n* centrale *f* (électrique).

power steering *n* direction *f* assistée.

power structure *n* [system] hiérarchie *f*, répartition *f* des pouvoirs ■ [people with power] *ensemble des personnes qui détiennent le pouvoir.*

power tool *n* outil *m* électrique.

power worker *n* employé *m*, - e *f* de l'électricité.

powwow ['paʊwaʊ] ◇ *n* [of American Indians] assemblée *f* ■ ***fig*** & ***hum*** [meeting] réunion *f* ■ [discussion] discussion *f*, pourparlers *mpl*.
◇ *vi* ***inf*** discuter.

pox [pɒks] *n* ***inf*** vérole *f* ■ **a ~ on him!** ***arch*** qu'il aille au diable!

poxy△ ['pɒksɪ] (*comp* **poxier**, *superl* **poxiest**) *adj* **1.** MED vérolé **2.** *UK* [lousy] merdique△.

pp (*written abbrev of* **per procurationem**) pp.

p & p *written abbr of* **postage and packing**.

PPE (*abbrev of* **philosophy, politics, and economics**) *n* ***UK*** *philosophie, science politique et science économique (cours à l'université).*

ppm (*abbrev of* **parts per million**) ppm.

PPS ◇ *n* ***UK*** = **parliamentary private secretary**.
◇ (*written abbrev of* **post postscriptum**) PPS.

ppsi (*abbrev of* **pounds per square inch**) *livres au pouce carré (mesure de pression).*

PQ *written abbr of* **Province of Quebec**.

Pr. (*written abbrev of* **prince**) Pce.

PR ◇ *n* **1.** = **proportional representation 2.** = **public relations**.
◇ *written abbr of* **Puerto Rico**.

practicability [ˌpræktɪkə'bɪlətɪ] *n* **1.** [of plan, action] faisabilité *f*, viabilité *f* **2.** [of road] praticabilité *f*.

practicable ['præktɪkəbl] *adj* **1.** [feasible] réalisable, praticable ■ [possible] possible **2.** [road] praticable.

practical ['præktɪkl] ◇ *adj* **1.** [convenient, easy to use] pratique, commode **2.** [sensible, commonsense - person] pragmatique, doué de sens pratique ; [- mind, suggestion] pratique ■ **my sister's the ~ one** s'il y a quelqu'un qui a le sens pratique, c'est bien ma sœur ■ **now, be ~, we can't afford a new car** allons, un peu de bon sens, nous n'avons pas les moyens de nous offrir une nouvelle voiture ■ **is white the most ~ colour?** le blanc, c'est ce qu'il y a de plus pratique comme couleur? **3.** [training, experience, question] pratique, concret, - ète *f* ■ **for all ~ purposes** en fait, en réalité ■ **he has a ~ knowledge of German** il connaît l'allemand usuel ▶ **~ nurse** *US* aide-soignant *m*, - e *f* **4.** [virtual] : **it's a ~ impossibility** c'est pratiquement impossible.
◇ *n* ***UK*** SCH & UNIV [class] travaux *mpl* pratiques, TP *mpl* ■ [exam] épreuve *f* pratique.

practicality [ˌpræktɪ'kælətɪ] (*pl* **practicalities**) *n* [of person] sens *m* pratique ■ [of ideas] nature *f* pratique ■ **I'm not too sure about the ~ of his suggestions** je doute que ses propositions puissent trouver une application pratique.
◆ **practicalities** *npl* [details] détails *mpl* pratiques.

practical joke *n* farce *f* ■ **to play a ~ on sb** faire une farce *OR* jouer un tour à qqn.

practical joker *n* farceur *m*, - euse *f*.

practically ['præktɪklɪ] *adv* **1.** [sensibly] de manière pratique ■ **to be ~ dressed** être habillé de façon pratique **2.** [based on practice] pratiquement ■ **the whole course is very much ~based** le cours est fondé en grande partie sur la pratique **3.** [almost] presque, pratiquement **4.** [in practice] dans la pratique ■ **~ speaking** en fait.

practical-minded *adj* : **to be ~** avoir le sens pratique.

practice ['præktɪs] ◇ *n* **1.** [habit] pratique *f*, habitude *f* ■ [custom] pratique *f*, coutume *f*, usage *m* ■ **he makes a ~ of voting against** *OR* **he makes it a ~ to vote against the government** il se fait une règle de voter contre le gouvernement ■ **it's not company ~ to refund deposits** il n'est pas dans les habitudes de la société de rembourser les arrhes ■ **it's normal ~ among most shopkeepers** c'est une pratique courante chez les commerçants ■ **it's our usual ~** c'est ce que nous faisons habituellement, c'est notre politique habituelle ■ **it's standard ~ to make a written request** la procédure habituelle veut que l'on fasse une demande par écrit
2. [exercise - of profession, witchcraft, archery] pratique *f*
3. [training] entraînement *m* ■ [rehearsal] répétition *f* ■ [study - of instrument] étude *f*, travail *m* ■ **I've had a lot of ~ at** *OR* **in dealing with difficult negotiations** j'ai une grande habitude des négociations difficiles ■ **it's good ~ for your interview** c'est un bon entraînement pour votre entrevue ■ **to be in ~** être bien entraîné ■ **to be out of ~** manquer d'entraînement ■ **I'm getting out of ~** [on piano] je commence à avoir les doigts rouillés ; [at sport] je commence à manquer d'entraînement ; [at skill] je commence à perdre la main ■ **it's time for your piano ~** c'est l'heure de travailler ton piano ▶ **fire ~** exercice *m* d'incendie ■ **~ makes perfect** ***prov*** c'est en forgeant qu'on devient forgeron ***prov***
4. [training session] (séance *f* d')entraînement *m* ■ [rehearsal - of choir] répétition *f*
5. [practical application] pratique *f* ■ **to put sthg in** *OR* **into ~** mettre qqch en pratique ■ **in ~** dans la pratique
6. [professional activity] exercice *m* ■ **to be in ~ as a doctor** exercer en tant que médecin ■ **to go into** *OR* **to set up in ~ as a doctor** s'installer comme médecin, ouvrir un cabinet de médecin ▶ **medical/legal ~** l'exercice de la médecine/de la profession d'avocat
7. [office, surgery] cabinet *m* ■ [clientele] clientèle *f* ■ **he has a country ~** il est médecin de campagne.
◇ *comp* [game, run, session] d'entraînement.
◇ *vt* & *vi* ***US*** = **practise**.

practiced *US* = **practised**.

practicing *US* = **practising**.

practise *UK*, **practice** *US* ['præktɪs] ◇ *vt* **1.** [for improvement - musical instrument] s'exercer à, travailler ; [- song] travailler, répéter ; [- foreign language] travailler, pratiquer ; [- stroke, shot] travailler ■ **can I ~ my French on you?** est-ce que je peux parler français *OR* pratiquer mon français avec vous? ■ **to ~ speaking French** s'entraîner à parler français **2.** [put into practice - principle, virtue] pratiquer, mettre en pratique ■ **you should ~ what you preach** vous devriez donner l'exemple **3.** [profession] exercer, pratiquer **4.** [inflict] infliger ■ **the cruelty they ~d on their victims** les cruautés qu'ils infligeaient à *OR* les sévices qu'ils faisaient subir à leurs victimes **5.** [customs, beliefs] observer, pratiquer **6.** RELIG pratiquer **7.** [magic] pratiquer.
◇ *vi* **1.** [gen - MUS] s'entraîner, s'exercer ■ SPORT s'entraîner ■ **to ~ on the guitar** faire des exercices à la guitare **2.** [professionally] exercer **3.** RELIG être pratiquant.

practised *UK*, **practiced** *US* ['præktɪst] *adj* **1.** [experienced] expérimenté, chevronné ■ [skilled] habile **2.** [expert - aim, movement] expert ; [- ear, eye] exercé **3.** [artificial - smile, charm] factice, étudié.

practising *UK*, **practicing** *US* ['præktɪsɪŋ] *adj* **1.** RELIG pratiquant **2.** [professionally - doctor] exerçant ; [- lawyer, solicitor] en exercice **3.** [homosexual] actif.

practitioner [præk'tɪʃnəʳ] *n* **1.** MED : **(medical) ~** médecin *m* **2.** [gen] praticien *m*, - enne *f*.

praetorian [prɪ'tɔːrɪən] *adj* prétorien.

pragmatic [præg'mætɪk] *adj* pragmatique ■ **~ sanction** pragmatique sanction *f*, pragmatique *f*.

pragmatics [præg'mætɪks] *n (U)* LING pragmatique *f*.

pragmatism ['prægmətɪzm] *n* pragmatisme *m*.

pragmatist ['prægmətɪst] *n* pragmatiste *mf*.

prairie ['preərɪ] *n* plaine *f* (herbeuse).
◆ **Prairie** *pr n* : **the Prairie** *OR* **Prairies** [in US] la Grande Prairie ; [in Canada] les Prairies *fpl*.

prairie dog *n* chien *m* de prairie.

prairie oyster *n boisson à base d'œuf cru (remède contre les excès d'alcool).*

prairie wolf *n* coyote *m*.

praise [preɪz] ◇ *n* **1.** [compliments] éloge *m*, louanges *fpl* ▪ **she was full of ~ for their kindness** elle ne tarissait pas d'éloges sur leur gentillesse ▪ **we have nothing but ~ for the way in which he handled the matter** nous ne pouvons que le féliciter de la façon *OR* nous n'avons que des éloges à lui faire pour la façon dont il s'est occupé de l'affaire ▪ **her film has received high ~ from the critics** son film a été couvert d'éloges par la critique ▪ **it is beyond ~** on ne saurait être trop élogieux **2.** RELIG louange *f*, louanges *fpl*, gloire *f* ▪ **to give ~ to the Lord** rendre gloire à Dieu ▪ **~ (be to) the Lord!** Dieu soit loué! ▪ **hymn** *OR* **song of ~** cantique *m*.
◇ *vt* **1.** louer, faire l'éloge de ▪ **he ~d her for her patience** il la loua de *OR* pour sa patience ▪ **to ~ sb to high heaven** *OR* **to the skies** couvrir qqn d'éloges, porter qqn aux nues **2.** RELIG louer, glorifier, rendre gloire à.
◆ **in praise of** *prep phr* : **the director spoke in ~ of his staff** le directeur fit l'éloge de son personnel.

praiseworthy ['preɪz,wɜːðɪ] *adj* [person] digne d'éloges ▪ [action, intention, sentiment] louable, méritoire.

praline ['prɑːliːn] *n* praline *f*.

pram [præm] *n* **1.** *UK* [for baby] voiture *f* d'enfant, landau *m* **2.** NAUT prame *f*.

PRAM [præm] (*abbrev of* **programmable random access memory**) *n* RAM *f* programmable.

prance [prɑːns] ◇ *vi* **1.** [cavort - horse] caracoler, cabrioler ; [- person] caracoler, gambader **2.** [strut] se pavaner, se dandiner ▪ **he came prancing into the room** il entra dans la pièce en se pavanant.
◇ *n* sautillement *m*.

prang [præŋ] *UK inf* ◇ *vt* [car] esquinter ▪ [plane] bousiller.
◇ *n* : **he had a ~** [in car] il a eu un accident (de voiture) *OR* un accrochage ; [in plane] son avion s'est planté.

prank [præŋk] *n* farce *f*, tour *m* ▪ **to play a ~ on sb** jouer un tour *OR* faire une farce à qqn ▪ **it's only a childish ~** c'est seulement une gaminerie.

prankster ['præŋkstəʳ] *n* farceur *m*, - euse *f*.

prat△ [præt] *n UK* couillon△ *m*.

prate [preɪt] *vi dated & pej* jacasser, bavarder.

prattle ['prætl] *UK inf pej* ◇ *vi* [babble] babiller, jacasser ▪ **she ~s away** *OR* **on about her children for hours** elle radote pendant des heures au sujet de ses enfants ▮ [converse] papoter ▪ **they're forever prattling on about politics** ils sont toujours à discutailler politique.
◇ *n* [babble] babillage *m* ▪ [conversation] papotage *m*, bavardage *m*.

prawn [prɔːn] *n* crevette *f* (rose), bouquet *m*.

prawn cocktail *n* cocktail *m* de crevettes.

prawn cracker *n* beignet *m* de crevette.

praxis ['præksɪs] (*pl* **praxes** [-siːz]) *n* pratique *f*.

pray [preɪ] ◇ *vi* prier ▪ **let us ~ to God for guidance** prions Dieu de nous guider ▪ **to ~ for sb/for sb's soul** prier pour qqn/pour l'âme de qqn ▪ **she ~ed to God to save her child** elle pria Dieu qu'il sauve son enfant ▪ **he ~s for release from pain** il prie pour que ses souffrances prennent fin ▪ **the country is past ~ing for at this stage** il n'y a plus d'espoir pour le pays à ce stade ▪ **to ~ for rain** prier pour qu'il pleuve ▪ **let's just ~ for fine weather** espérons qu'il fasse beau.
◇ *vt* **1.** RELIG : **we ~ the rain will stop** nous prions pour que la pluie cesse ▪ **I just ~ he doesn't come back** je prie Dieu *OR* le ciel (pour) qu'il ne revienne pas **2.** *arch & fml* [request] prier ▪ **I ~ you** je vous (en) prie.
◇ *interj arch & fml* **~ be seated** asseyez-vous, je vous en prie.

prayer [preəʳ] *n* **1.** RELIG prière *f* ▪ **to be at ~** être en prière, prier ▪ **to kneel in ~** prier à genoux, s'agenouiller pour prier ▪ **to say a ~ for sb** dire une prière pour qqn ▪ **to say one's ~s** faire sa prière ▪ **remember me in your ~s** pensez à moi *OR* ne m'oubliez pas dans vos prières ▪ **her ~ was answered** sa prière fut exaucée ⊙ **he doesn't have a ~** *inf* il n'a pas la moindre chance *OR* l'ombre d'une chance **2.** [wish] souhait *m* ▪ **it is my earnest ~ that you will succeed** j'espère de tout cœur que vous réussirez, je souhaite sincèrement que vous réussissiez.
◆ **prayers** *npl* [at church] office *m* (divin), prière *f* ▪ *UK* SCH prière *f* du matin.

prayer beads *n* chapelet *m*.

prayer book *n* bréviaire *m*.

prayer mat *n* tapis *m* de prière.

prayer meeting *n* réunion *f* de prière.

prayer rug = **prayer mat**.

prayer stool *n* prie-Dieu *m inv*.

prayer wheel *n* moulin *m* à prières.

praying mantis ['preɪɪŋ-] *n* mante *f* religieuse.

preach [priːtʃ] ◇ *vi* **1.** RELIG prêcher ▪ **to ~ to sb** prêcher qqn ▪ **to ~ to the converted** prêcher un converti **2.** [lecture] prêcher, sermonner ▪ **stop ~ing at me!** arrête tes sermons *OR* de me faire la leçon!
◇ *vt* **1.** RELIG prêcher ▪ **to ~ a sermon** prêcher, faire un sermon **2.** *fig* [recommend] prêcher, prôner.

preacher ['priːtʃəʳ] *n* [gen] prédicateur *m* ▪ *esp US* [minister] pasteur *m*.

preaching ['priːtʃɪŋ] *n (U)* [sermon] prédication *f* ▪ *pej* [moralizing] sermons *mpl*.

preamble [priː'æmbl] *n* préambule *m* ▪ **Preamble to the Constitution** Préambule *m* de la Constitution des États-Unis.

prearrange [,priːə'reɪndʒ] *vt* fixer *OR* régler à l'avance.

prebend ['prebənd] *n* prébende *f*.

prebendary ['prebəndrɪ] (*pl* **prebendaries**) *n* prébendier *m*.

precancerous [,priː'kænsərəs] *adj* précancéreux.

precarious [prɪ'keərɪəs] *adj* précaire.

precariously [prɪ'keərɪəslɪ] *adv* précairement ▪ **~ balanced** en équilibre précaire.

precariousness [prɪ'keərɪəsnɪs] *n* précarité *f*.

precast [,priː'kɑːst] *adj* [concrete element] préfabriqué.

precaution [prɪ'kɔːʃn] *n* précaution *f* ▪ **as a ~** par précaution ▪ **to take ~s** prendre des précautions ▪ **she took the ~ of informing her solicitor** elle prit la précaution d'avertir son avocat ▪ **fire ~s** mesures *fpl* de prévention contre l'incendie.

precautionary [prɪ'kɔːʃənərɪ] *adj* de précaution ▪ **as a ~ measure** par mesure de précaution ▪ **to take ~ measures** *OR* **steps against sthg** prendre des mesures préventives contre qqch.

precede [prɪ'siːd] *vt* **1.** [in order, time] précéder **2.** [in importance, rank] avoir la préséance sur, prendre le pas sur **3.** [preface] (faire) précéder.

precedence ['presɪdəns], **precedency** ['presɪdənsɪ] *n (U)* **1.** [priority] priorité *f* ▪ **to take** *OR* **to have ~over sthg** avoir la priorité sur qqch ▪ **her health must take ~ over all other considerations** sa santé doit passer avant toute autre considération **2.** [in rank, status] préséance *f* ▪ **to have** *OR* **to take ~over sb** avoir la préséance *OR* prendre le pas sur qqn.

precedent ['presɪdənt] <> *n* **1.** LAW précédent *m*, jurisprudence *f* ■ **to set a ~** faire jurisprudence ■ **to follow a ~** s'appuyer sur un précédent, suivre la jurisprudence **2.** [example case] précédent *m* ■ **to create** *OR* **to set** *OR* **to establish a ~** créer un précédent ■ **without ~** sans précédent **3.** [tradition] tradition *f* ■ **to break with ~** rompre avec la tradition.
<> *adj* précédent.

preceding [prɪ'si:dɪŋ] *adj* précédent ■ **the ~ day** le jour précédent, la veille.

precentor [prɪ'sentəʳ] *n* préchantre *m*.

precept ['pri:sept] *n* précepte *m*.

precinct ['pri:sɪŋkt] *n* **1.** [area - round castle, cathedral] enceinte *f* ; [- for pedestrians, shopping] zone *f*, quartier *m* **2.** [boundary] pourtour *m* ■ **the question falls within the ~s of philosophy** la question est du domaine *OR* relève de la philosophie **3.** *US* ADMIN arrondissement *m*, circonscription *f* administrative ■ **~ station** commissariat *m* de quartier *OR* d'arrondissement **4.** *US* POL circonscription *f* électorale.
◆ **precincts** *npl* environs *mpl*, alentours *mpl*.

precious ['preʃəs] <> *adj* **1.** [jewel, material, object] précieux, de grande valeur **2.** [friend, friendship, moment] précieux ■ **my time is ~** mon temps est précieux **3.** [affected - style, person] précieux **4.** *inf* [expressing irritation] : **I don't want your ~ advice** je ne veux pas de vos fichus conseils.
<> *adv inf* très ■ **there's ~ little chance of that happening** il y a bien peu *OR* très peu de chances (pour) que cela se produise ■ **~ few of them turned up** il y en a très peu qui sont venus.
<> *n* : **my ~** mon trésor.

precious metal *n* métal *m* précieux.

precious stone *n* pierre *f* précieuse.

precipice ['presɪpɪs] *n liter* précipice *m* ■ *fig* catastrophe *f*.

precipitant [prɪ'sɪpɪtənt] <> *adj* précipité, hâtif.
<> *n* précipitant *m*.

precipitate <> *vt* [prɪ'sɪpɪteɪt] **1.** [downfall, ruin, crisis] précipiter, hâter **2.** [person, vehicle, object] précipiter **3.** CHEM précipiter.
<> *vi* [prɪ'sɪpɪteɪt] **1.** CHEM se précipiter **2.** METEOR se condenser.
<> *n* [prɪ'sɪpɪteɪt] précipité *m*.
<> *adj* [prɪ'sɪpɪtət] **1.** [hasty - action] précipité ; [- decision, judgment] hâtif ; [- remark] irréfléchi **2.** [steep] abrupt, à pic.

precipitately [prɪ'sɪpɪtətlɪ] *adv* précipitamment, avec précipitation.

precipitation [prɪ,sɪpɪ'teɪʃn] *n (U)* **1.** [haste] précipitation *f* **2.** CHEM précipitation *f* **3.** METEOR précipitations *fpl*.

precipitous [prɪ'sɪpɪtəs] *adj* **1.** [steep - cliff] à pic, escarpé ; [- road, stairs] raide ; [- fall] à pic **2.** [hasty] précipité.

precipitously [prɪ'sɪpɪtəslɪ] *adv* **1.** [steeply] à pic, abruptement **2.** [hastily] précipitamment.

précis [*UK* 'preɪsi:, *US* 'presi:] (*pl inv* [*UK* 'preɪsi:, *US* 'presi:]) <> *n* précis *m*, résumé *m*.
<> *vt* faire un résumé de.

precise [prɪ'saɪs] *adj* **1.** [exact - amount, detail] précis ; [- location] exact ; [- pronunciation] exact, juste ■ **he was very ~ in his description** il a donné une description très précise *OR* détaillée ■ **at that ~ moment** à ce moment précis **2.** [meticulous - person, manner, mind, movement] précis, méticuleux **3.** *pej* [fussy] pointilleux, maniaque.

precisely [prɪ'saɪslɪ] <> *adv* [exactly - explain] précisément, exactement ■ [measure] précisément, avec précision ■ **that's ~ the reason (why) I'm not going** c'est précisément pourquoi je n'y vais pas ■ **she speaks very ~** elle s'exprime avec beaucoup de précision ■ **at 4 o'clock ~** à 4 h précises.
<> *interj* précisément, exactement ■ **do you think it's too risky? – ~!** pensez-vous que ce soit trop risqué? – tout à fait! *OR* exactement!

precision [prɪ'sɪʒn] <> *n* précision *f*.
<> *comp* [instrument, engineering, tool, bombing] de précision.

preclude [prɪ'klu:d] *vt fml* exclure, prévenir ■ **the crisis ~s her (from)going to Moscow** la crise rend impossible son départ pour Moscou *OR* la met dans l'impossibilité de partir pour Moscou.

precocious [prɪ'kəʊʃəs] *adj* précoce.

precognition [,pri:kɒg'nɪʃn] *n* [gift] prescience *f*, don *m* de seconde vue ■ [knowledge] connaissance *f* préalable.

preconceived [,pri:kən'si:vd] *adj* préconçu ■ **~ idea** idée *f* préconçue.

preconception [,pri:kən'sepʃn] *n* préconception *f*, idée *f* préconçue.

precondition [,pri:kən'dɪʃn] <> *n* condition *f* préalable, condition *f* sine qua non.
<> *vt* conditionner.

precooked [pri:'kʊkt] *adj* précuit.

precool [pri:'ku:l] *vt* préréfrigérer.

precursor [,pri:'kɜ:səʳ] *n* [person] précurseur *m* ■ [invention, machine] ancêtre *m* ■ [event] signe *m* avant-coureur *OR* précurseur.

precursory [,pri:'kɜ:sərɪ] *adj* **1.** [anticipatory] précurseur, annonciateur **2.** [introductory] préliminaire, préalable.

predate [pri:'deɪt] *vt* **1.** [give earlier date to - cheque] antidater ; [- historical event] attribuer une date antérieure à **2.** [precede] être antérieur à.

predator ['predətəʳ] *n* **1.** [animal, bird] prédateur *m* **2.** *fig* [person] rapace *m*.

predatory ['predətrɪ] *adj* **1.** [animal, bird] prédateur **2.** *fig* [gen - person, instinct] rapace ; [- attacker] pillard.

predecease [,pri:dɪ'si:s] *vt* mourir avant.

predecessor ['pri:dɪsesəʳ] *n* [person, model] prédécesseur *m* ■ [event] précédent *m*.

predestination [pri:,destɪ'neɪʃn] *n* prédestination *f*.

predestine [,pri:'destɪn] *vt* prédestiner ■ **it was as if they were ~d to lose** on aurait dit qu'ils étaient prédestinés à perdre.

predetermination ['pri:dɪ,tɜ:mɪ'neɪʃn] *n* prédétermination *f*.

predetermine [,pri:dɪ'tɜ:mɪn] *vt* prédéterminer.

predetermined [,pri:dɪ'tɜ:mɪnd] *adj* déterminé ■ **at a ~ date** à une date déterminée *OR* arrêtée d'avance.

predeterminer [,pri:dɪ'tɜ:mɪnəʳ] *n* prédéterminant *m*.

predicable ['predɪkəbl] <> *adj* prédicable.
<> *n* prédicable *m*.

predicament [prɪ'dɪkəmənt] *n* situation *f* difficile *OR* malencontreuse.

predicate <> *vt* ['predɪkeɪt] *fml* **1.** [state] affirmer **2.** [base] : **to ~ one's arguments/policy on sthg** fonder ses arguments/sa politique sur qqch.
<> *n* ['predɪkət] prédicat *m*.
<> *adj* ['predɪkət] prédicatif.

predicative [prɪ'dɪkətɪv] *adj* prédicatif.

predict [prɪ'dɪkt] *vt* prédire ■ **the weathermen are ~ing rain** les météorologues annoncent de la pluie.

predictability [prɪ,dɪktə'bɪlətɪ] *n* prévisibilité *f*.

predictable [prɪ'dɪktəbl] *adj* prévisible.

predictably [prɪ'dɪktəblɪ] *adv* de manière prévisible ■ **~, she forgot to tell him** comme on pouvait le prévoir *OR* comme on pouvait s'y attendre, elle a oublié de le lui dire.

prediction [prɪ'dɪkʃn] *n* [gen] prévision *f* ■ [supernatural] prédiction *f*.

predictive texting [prɪ'dɪktɪv-] *n* TELEC [on mobile phone] écriture *f* prédictive, T9 *m*.

predictor [prɪ'dɪktəʳ] *n* **1.** [prophet] prophète *m* **2.** [in statistics] variable *f* indépendante.

predigested [ˌpriːdaɪˈdʒestɪd] *adj* prédigéré.

predilection [ˌpriːdɪˈlekʃn] *n* prédilection *f* ▪ **to have a ~ for sthg** avoir une prédilection *OR* un faible pour qqch.

predispose [ˌpriːdɪsˈpəuz] *vt* prédisposer ▪ **to be ~d to do sthg** être prédisposé à faire qqch ▪ **I was not ~d in his favour** je n'étais pas prédisposé en sa faveur.

predisposition [ˈpriːˌdɪspəˈzɪʃn] *n* prédisposition *f* ▪ **to have a ~ to** *OR* **towards sthg** avoir une prédisposition à qqch.

predominance [prɪˈdɒmɪnəns], **predominancy** [prɪˈdɒmɪnənsɪ] *n* prédominance *f*.

predominant [prɪˈdɒmɪnənt] *adj* prédominant.

predominantly [prɪˈdɒmɪnəntlɪ] *adv* principalement ▪ **the population is ~ English-speaking** la population est majoritairement anglophone.

predominate [prɪˈdɒmɪneɪt] *vi* **1.** [be greater in number] prédominer ▪ **males still ~ over females in industry** les hommes continuent à être plus nombreux que les femmes dans l'industrie **2.** [prevail] prédominer, prévaloir, l'emporter.

pre-eminence [ˌpriːˈemɪnəns] *n* prééminence *f*.

pre-eminent [ˌpriːˈemɪnənt] *adj* prééminent.

pre-eminently [ˌpriːˈemɪnəntlɪ] *adv* de façon prépondérante, avant tout.

pre-empt [ˌpriːˈempt] ◇ *vt* **1.** [plan, decision] anticiper, devancer **2.** [land, property] acquérir par (droit de)préemption.
◇ *vi* [in bridge] faire une enchère de barrage.

pre-emption [ˌpriːˈempʃn] *n* préemption *f*.

pre-emptive [ˌpriːˈemptɪv] *adj* [right] de préemption ▪ [strike] préventif.

preen [priːn] *vt* **1.** [plumage] lisser ▪ **the bird was ~ing its feathers** *OR* **was ~ing itself** l'oiseau se lissait les plumes ▪ **to ~ o.s.** *fig* se faire beau, se pomponner **2.** [pride] : **to ~ o.s. on sthg** s'enorgueillir de qqch.

preexist [ˌpriːɪgˈzɪst] *vt* préexister à.

prefab [ˈpriːfæb] *n inf* (bâtiment *m*) préfabriqué *m*.

prefabricate [ˌpriːˈfæbrɪkeɪt] *vt* préfabriquer.

prefabricated [ˌpriːˈfæbrɪkeɪtɪd] *adj* : **~ houses** maisons *fpl* en préfabriqué.

preface [ˈprefɪs] ◇ *n* **1.** [to text] préface *f*, avant-propos *m inv* ▪ [to speech] introduction *f*, préambule *m* **2.** RELIG préface *f*.
◇ *vt* [book] préfacer ▪ [speech] faire précéder ▪ **he usually ~s his speeches with a joke** d'habitude, il commence ses discours par une histoire drôle ▪ **I'd like to ~ my lecture by posing this question** en guise d'introduction à cette conférence, je voudrais vous soumettre la question suivante.

prefaded [priːˈfeɪdɪd] *adj* [fabric] délavé.

prefatory [ˈprefətrɪ] *adj* [remarks] préliminaire, préalable ▪ [note] liminaire ▪ [page] de préface.

prefect [ˈpriːfekt] *n* **1.** SCH *élève chargé de la discipline* **2.** ADMIN [in France, Italy etc] préfet *m*.

prefecture [ˈpriːfekˌtjuəʳ] *n* préfecture *f*.

prefer [prɪˈfɜːʳ] *vt* **1.** préférer, aimer mieux ▪ **I ~ Paris to London** je préfère Paris à Londres, j'aime mieux Paris que Londres ▪ **he ~s to walk rather than take the bus** il préfère marcher plutôt que prendre le bus ▪ **do you mind if I smoke? – I'd ~ (that) you didn't** cela vous dérange si je fume? – j'aimerais mieux que vous ne le fassiez pas ▪ **I'd ~ you not to go** je préférerais que vous n'y alliez pas **2.** LAW : **to ~ charges against sb** [civil action] porter plainte contre qqn ; [police action] ≃ déférer qqn au parquet **3.** [submit - argument, petition] présenter **4.** FIN [creditor] privilégier.

preferable [ˈprefrəbl] *adj* préférable ▪ **it is ~ to book seats** il est préférable de *OR* il vaut mieux retenir des places.

preferably [ˈprefrəblɪ] *adv* de préférence, préférablement.

preference [ˈprefərəns] *n* **1.** [liking] préférence *f* ▪ **to have** *OR* **to show a ~ for sthg** avoir une préférence pour qqch ▪ **his ~ is for Mozart** il préfère Mozart ▪ **in order of ~** par ordre de préférence ▪ **he chose the first candidate in ~ to the second** il a choisi le premier candidat plutôt que le second **2.** [priority] préférence *f*, priorité *f* ▪ **to have** *OR* **to be given ~ over** avoir la priorité sur.
Voir module d'usage

preference share *n UK* action *f* privilégiée.

preferential [ˌprefəˈrenʃl] *adj* préférentiel, privilégié ▪ **to get ~ treatment** bénéficier d'un traitement de faveur.

preferment [prɪˈfɜːmənt] *n* [gen - RELIG] avancement *m*, promotion *f*.

preferred [prɪˈfɜːd] *adj* **1.** [best liked] préféré **2.** COMM : **~ creditor** créancier *m* prioritaire.

preferred stock *n (U) US* action *f* privilégiée.

prefigure [priːˈfɪgəʳ] *vt* **1.** [foreshadow] préfigurer **2.** [foresee] se figurer *OR* s'imaginer (d'avance).

prefix [ˈpriːfɪks] ◇ *n* préfixe *m*.
◇ *vt* préfixer.

preflight [ˈpriːflaɪt] *adj* préalable au décollage ▪ **~ checks** vérifications *fpl* avant décollage.

preggers△ [ˈpregəz] *adj* : **she's ~** elle est en cloque△.

pregnancy [ˈpregnənsɪ] (*pl* **pregnancies**) *n* [of woman] grossesse *f* ▪ [of animal] gestation *f*.

pregnancy test *n* test *m* de grossesse.

pregnant [ˈpregnənt] *adj* **1.** [woman] enceinte ▪ [animal] pleine, grosse ▪ **to get** *OR* **to become ~** tomber enceinte ▪ **to get a woman ~** faire un enfant à une femme ▪ **to be six months ~** être enceinte de six mois ▪ **she was ~ with Brian then** à cette époque, elle attendait Brian **2.** *fig* [silence - with meaning] lourd *OR* chargé de sens ; [- with tension] tendu.

preheat [ˌpriːˈhiːt] *vt* préchauffer.

preheated [ˌpriːˈhiːtɪd] *adj* préchauffé.

prehensile [prɪˈhensaɪl] *adj* préhensile.

prehistoric [ˌpriːhɪˈstɒrɪk] *adj liter* & *fig* préhistorique.

prehistory [ˌpriːˈhɪstərɪ] *n* préhistoire *f*.

pre-industrial *adj* préindustriel.

PREFERENCES

Je préfère de loin le cinéma à la télévision. I (much) prefer the cinema to television.

Je préfère aller au cinéma que regarder la télévision. I prefer going to the cinema to watching television.

Je préférerais que tu y ailles à ma place. I'd rather you went instead of me.

J'aime mieux le vin rouge que le vin blanc. I prefer red wine to white wine.

Plutôt que d'y aller en train, j'aimerais mieux y aller en avion. I'd rather fly than go by train.

Samedi me conviendrait davantage. Saturday would suit me better.

prejudge [ˌpriːˈdʒʌdʒ] *vt* [issue, topic] préjuger (de) ■ [person] porter un jugement prématuré sur.

prejudice [ˈpredʒʊdɪs] <> *n* **1.** [bias] préjugé *m* ■ **to have a ~ in favour of/against** avoir un préjugé en faveur de/contre ■ **he's full of/without ~** il est plein de/sans préjugés ■ **racial ~** préjugés raciaux, racisme *m* ■ **I have a certain ~ in favour of the first solution** j'ai une petite préférence pour la première solution **2.** [detriment] préjudice *m*, tort *m* ■ **to the ~ of sb's rights** au préjudice OR au détriment des droits de qqn.
<> *vt* **1.** [influence] influencer, prévenir ■ **to ~ sb against/in favour of sthg** prévenir qqn contre/en faveur de qqch **2.** [jeopardize] compromettre, porter préjudice à, nuire à.

prejudiced [ˈpredʒʊdɪst] *adj* [person] qui a des préjugés OR des idées préconçues ■ **to be ~ against sthg** avoir des préjugés contre qqch ■ **let's not be ~ about this** essayons de ne pas avoir d'idées préconçues là-dessus ■ **he is racially ~** il est raciste ‖ [opinion] partial, préconçu ■ **her politics are ~** ses idées politiques sont fondées sur des préjugés.

prejudicial [ˌpredʒʊˈdɪʃl] *adj* préjudiciable, nuisible ■ **this decision is ~ to world peace** cette décision risque de compromettre la paix mondiale.

prelate [ˈprelɪt] *n* prélat *m*.

prelim [ˈpriːlɪm] (*abbrev of* **preliminary exam**) *n inf* examen *m* préliminaire.
◆ **prelims** *npl* [in book] préliminaires *mpl*.

preliminary [prɪˈlɪmɪnərɪ] (*pl* **preliminaries**) <> *adj* préliminaire, préalable ■ **the ~ stages of the inquiry** les étapes préliminaires OR les débuts de l'enquête ■ **~ to departure** *fml*, **~ to leaving** *fml* avant le départ, avant de partir ■ **~ hearing** LAW première audience *f* ■ **~investigation** LAW instruction *f* (d'une affaire).
<> *n* **1.** [gen] préliminaire *m* ■ **as a ~** en guise de préliminaire, au préalable **2.** [eliminating contest] épreuve *f* éliminatoire.

prelude [ˈprelјuːd] <> *n* [gen - MUS] prélude *m*.
<> *vt* préluder à.

premarital [ˌpriːˈmærɪtl] *adj* prénuptial, avant le mariage ■ **~ sex** rapports *mpl* sexuels avant le mariage.

premature [ˈpreməˌtjʊəʳ] *adj* **1.** [birth, child] prématuré, avant terme ■ **three months ~** né trois mois avant terme **2.** [death, decision, judgment] prématuré.

prematurely [ˈpreməˌtjʊəlɪ] *adv* prématurément ■ **he was born ~** il est né avant terme ■ **to be ~ bald/grey** être chauve/avoir les cheveux gris avant l'âge.

premed [ˈpriːmed] *inf* <> *adj* = **premedical**.
<> *n* **1.** = **premedication 2.** [student] ≃ étudiant *m*, - e *f* en première année de médecine **3.** [studies] ≃ études *fpl* de première année de médecine.

premedical [ˌpriːˈmedɪkl] *adj* [studies] ≃ de première année de médecine.

premedication [ˌpriːmedɪˈkeɪʃn] *n* prémédication *f*.

premeditate [ˌpriːˈmedɪteɪt] *vt* préméditer.

premeditated [ˌpriːˈmedɪteɪtɪd] *adj* prémédité.

premeditation [priːˌmedɪˈteɪʃn] *n* préméditation *f* ■ **without ~** sans préméditation.

premenstrual [priːˈmenstrʊəl] *adj* prémenstruel.

premenstrual tension UK, **premenstrual syndrome** US *n* syndrome *m* prémenstruel.

premier [ˈpremjəʳ] <> *adj* premier, primordial.
<> *n* Premier ministre *m*.

premiere [ˈpremɪeəʳ] <> *n* CIN & THEAT première *f*.
<> *vt* donner la première de ■ **the opera was ~d in Paris** la première de l'opéra a eu lieu à Paris.

Premier League *pr n championnat anglais de football disputé par les plus grands clubs professionnels.*

premiership [ˈpremjəʃɪp] *n* poste *m* de Premier ministre ■ **during her ~** alors qu'elle était Premier ministre.

premise [ˈpremɪs] <> *n* [hypothesis] prémisse *f* ■ **on the ~ that...** en partant du principe que...
<> *vt fml* **to ~ that** poser comme hypothèse que ■ **to be ~d on** être fondé sur.

premises [ˈpremɪsɪz] *npl* **1.** [place] locaux *mpl*, lieux *mpl* ■ **business ~** locaux commerciaux ■ **on the ~** sur les lieux, sur place **2.** LAW préalable *m*.

premiss [ˈpremɪs] = **premise**.

premium [ˈpriːmjəm] <> *n* **1.** [insurance payment] prime *f* (d'assurance) **2.** [bonus, extra cost] prime *f* ■ **fresh fruit is (selling) at a ~** les fruits frais sont très recherchés OR font prime *spec* ■ **honesty is at a ~ these days** l'honnêteté se fait rare OR se perd de nos jours ■ **to put OR to place a (high) ~ on sthg** attacher beaucoup de valeur à OR faire grand cas de qqch **3.** US [fuel] supercarburant *m*.
<> *comp* : **~ price** prix *m* très réduit ■ **~ quality** qualité *f* extra.

premium bond *n* obligation *f* à prime.

premonition [ˌpreməˈnɪʃn] *n* prémonition *f*, pressentiment *m* ■ **to have a ~ of sthg** pressentir qqch, avoir le pressentiment de qqch ■ **I had a ~ he wouldn't come** j'avais le pressentiment qu'il ne viendrait pas.

prenatal [ˌpriːˈneɪtl] *adj* prénatal.

pre-nup (*abbrev of* **pre-nuptual contract**) *n* contrat de mariage *m inf*.

prenuptial [ˌpriːˈnʌpʃl] *adj* prénuptial ■ **~ agreement** contrat *m* de mariage.

preoccupation [priːˌɒkjʊˈpeɪʃn] *n* préoccupation *f* ■ **I don't understand his ~ with physical fitness** je ne comprends pas qu'il soit si préoccupé par sa forme physique.

preoccupied [priːˈɒkjʊpaɪd] *adj* préoccupé ■ **to be ~ by OR with sthg** être préoccupé par OR de *lit* qqch.

preoccupy [priːˈɒkjʊpaɪ] (*pret & pp* **preoccupied**) *vt* préoccuper.

preop [ˈpriːɒp] (*abbrev of* **preoperative**) *inf* <> *adj* préopératoire.
<> *n* : **she's gone for a ~** elle est allée passer un examen préopératoire.

preordain [ˌpriːɔːˈdeɪn] *vt* : **she felt ~ed to be a missionary** elle se sentait prédestinée à devenir missionnaire ■ **our defeat was ~ed** il était dit que nous perdrions.

prep [prep] *inf* SCH <> *n (U)* UK **1.** [homework] devoirs *mpl* **2.** [study period] étude *f (après les cours)*.
<> *vi* US *faire ses études dans un établissement privé.*

prepack [ˌpriːˈpæk], **prepackage** [ˌpriːˈpækɪdʒ] *vt* préemballer, conditionner ■ **the fruit is all ~ed** les fruits sont entièrement conditionnés.

prepaid [*(pt, pp)*ˌpriːˈpeɪd] <> *pt & pp* ▷ **prepay**.
<> *adj* [ˈpriːpeɪd] payé (d'avance).

preparation [ˌprepəˈreɪʃn] *n* **1.** *(U)* préparation *f* ■ **to be in ~** être en préparation ■ **in ~ for publication** en vue d'une publication ■ **in ~ for Christmas** pour préparer Noël ■ **as a ~ for public life** pour préparer à la vie publique **2.** *(countable)* CHEM & PHARM préparation *f* **3.** *(U)* UK SCH = **prep**.
◆ **preparations** *npl* [arrangements] préparatifs *mpl*, dispositions *fpl* ■ **~s for war** préparatifs de guerre.

preparatory [prɪˈpærətrɪ] *adj* [work] préparatoire ■ [measure] préalable, préliminaire ■ **the report is still at the ~ stage** le rapport en est encore au stade préliminaire OR préparatoire.

preparatory school *n* **1.** [in UK] école *f* primaire privée *(pour enfants de sept à treize ans, préparant généralement à entrer dans une "public school")* **2.** [in US] *école privée qui prépare à l'enseignement supérieur.*

prepare [prɪˈpeəʳ] <> *vt* [plan, food, lesson] préparer ■ **to ~ a meal for sb** préparer un repas à OR pour qqn ■ **to ~ a surprise for sb** préparer une surprise à qqn ■ **to ~ the way/the ground for negotiations** ouvrir la voie à/préparer le terrain pour

des négociations ■ we are preparing to leave tomorrow nous nous préparons à partir demain ■ [person] préparer ■ to ~ o.s. for sthg se préparer à qqch ■ ~ yourself for the worst préparez-vous OR attendez-vous au pire.
<> *vi* : to ~ for sthg faire des préparatifs en vue de OR se préparer à qqch ■ to ~ to do sthg se préparer OR s'apprêter à faire qqch ■ to ~ for a meeting/an exam préparer une réunion/un examen ■ ~ for the worst! préparez-vous au pire!

prepared [prɪ'peəd] *adj* [ready - gen] préparé, prêt ; [- answer, excuse] tout prêt ■ I was ~ to leave j'étais préparé OR prêt à partir ■ he wasn't ~ for what he saw [hadn't expected] il ne s'attendait pas à ce spectacle ; [was shocked] il n'était pas préparé à voir cela ■ you must be ~ for anything il faut s'attendre à tout ■ the Minister issued a ~ statement le ministre fit une déclaration préparée à l'avance ■ [willing] prêt, disposé ■ I am ~ to cooperate je suis prêt OR disposé à coopérer.

preparedness [prɪ'peədnɪs] *n* : ~ for war préparation *f* à la guerre.

prepay [,pri:'peɪ] (*pret & pp* **prepaid** [,pri:'peɪd]) *vt* payer d'avance.

preponderance [prɪ'pɒndərəns] *n* [in importance] prépondérance *f* ■ [in number] supériorité *f* numérique.

preponderant [prɪ'pɒndərənt] *adj* prépondérant.

preponderantly [prɪ'pɒndərəntlɪ] *adv* [in importance] de façon prépondérante ■ [especially] surtout.

preponderate [prɪ'pɒndəreɪt] *vi* être prépondérant, prédominer ■ to ~ over sthg l'emporter sur qqch.

preposition [,prepə'zɪʃn] *n* préposition *f*.

prepositional [,prepə'zɪʃnl] *adj* prépositionnel ■ ~ phrase locution *f* prépositive.

prepositionally [,prepə'zɪʃnlɪ] *adv* prépositivement.

prepossessing [,pri:pə'zesɪŋ] *adj* [person] avenant ■ [smile, behaviour] avenant, engageant.

preposterous [prɪ'pɒstərəs] *adj* absurde, grotesque.

preposterously [prɪ'pɒstərəslɪ] *adv* absurdement, ridiculement.

preppie, preppy ['prepɪ] *US inf* <> *n* (*pl* **preppies**) : he's a ~ il est BCBG.
<> *adj* (*pl comp* **preppier**, *superl* **preppiest**) BCBG.

preprandial [,pri:'prændɪəl] *adj lit & hum* [drink] avant le repas.

preprogrammed [,pri:'prəʊgræmd] *adj* préprogrammé.

prep school *n* = **preparatory school**.

prepubescent [,pri:pju:'besənt] *adj* prépubère.

prepuce ['pri:pju:s] *n* prépuce *m*.

prequel ['pri:kwəl] *n film ou roman racontant une histoire antérieure à une histoire principale, traitée dans un autre film ou roman.*

Pre-Raphaelite [,pri:'ræfəlaɪt] <> *adj* préraphaélite.
<> *n* préraphaélite *mf*.

prerecord [,pri:rɪ'kɔ:d] *vt* préenregistrer.

prerecorded [,pri:rɪ'kɔ:dɪd] *adj* préenregistré ■ ~ TV debate débat télévisé préenregistré OR en différé ■ ~ cassette cassette *f* enregistrée.

prerelease [,pri:rɪ'li:s] <> *n* [of film] avant-première *f* ■ [of record] sortie *f* précommerciale.
<> *vt* [film, record] faire sortir en avant-première.

prerequisite [,pri:'rekwɪzɪt] <> *n* (condition *f*) préalable *m*, condition *f* sine qua non ■ to be a ~ for OR of sthg être une condition préalable à qqch.
<> *adj* : ~ condition condition *f* préalable.

prerogative [prɪ'rɒgətɪv] *n* prérogative *f*, apanage *m* ■ to exercise one's ~ exercer ses prérogatives.

Pres. *written abbr of* **president**.

presage ['presɪdʒ] <> *n* présage *m* ■ to have a ~ of doom pressentir un malheur.
<> *vt* présager, annoncer.

Presbyterian [,prezbɪ'tɪərɪən] <> *adj* presbytérien.
<> *n* presbytérien *m*, - enne *f*.

presbytery ['prezbɪtrɪ] *n* **1.** [house] presbytère *m* **2.** [court] presbyterium *m* **3.** [part of church] presbyterium *m*.

preschool [,pri:'sku:l] <> *adj* [playgroup, age] préscolaire ■ [child] d'âge préscolaire.
<> *n US* école *f* maternelle.

prescient ['presɪənt] *adj* prescient.

prescribe [prɪ'skraɪb] *vt* **1.** MED prescrire ■ to ~ sthg for sb prescrire qqch à qqn ■ what can you ~ for migraine? que prescrivez-vous contre la migraine? ■ 'do not exceed the ~d dose' 'ne pas dépasser la dose prescrite' **2.** [advocate] préconiser, recommander **3.** [set - punishment] infliger ■ *UK* SCH [- books] inscrire au programme ■ ~d form/number *UK* formulaire *m* /nombre *m* prescrit **4.** LAW prescrire.

prescription [prɪ'skrɪpʃn] <> *n* **1.** MED ordonnance *f* ■ the doctor wrote out a ~ for her le médecin lui a rédigé OR fait une ordonnance ■ to make up a ~ for sb exécuter OR préparer une ordonnance pour qqn ■ I'll give you a ~ for some antibiotics je vais vous prescrire des antibiotiques ■ to get sthg on ~ obtenir qqch sur ordonnance ■ available OR obtainable only on ~ délivré seulement sur ordonnance **2.** [recommendation] prescription *f* ■ what's your ~ for a happy life? quelle est votre recette du bonheur?
<> *comp* : a ~ drug un médicament délivré seulement sur ordonnance.

prescription charge *n UK* ≃ ticket *m* modérateur.

prescriptive [prɪ'skrɪptɪv] *adj* **1.** LING [grammar, rule] normatif **2.** [dogmatic] dogmatique, strict **3.** [customary] consacré par l'usage.

prescriptivism [prɪ'skrɪptɪvɪzm] *n* normativisme *m*.

preselect [,pri:sə'lekt] *vt* [tracks, channels] prérégler.

presence ['prezns] *n* **1.** présence *f* ■ in the ~ of sb en présence de qqn ■ your ~ is requested at Saturday's meeting vous êtes prié d'assister à la réunion de samedi ■ to show/to have great ~ of mind faire preuve d'une/avoir une grande présence d'esprit **2.** [number of people present] présence *f* ■ there was a large student/police ~ at the demonstration il y avait un nombre important d'étudiants/un important service d'ordre à la manifestation **3.** [personality, magnetism] présence *f* ■ she has great stage ~ elle a beaucoup de présence sur scène **4.** [entity] présence *f* ■ I could sense a ~ in the room je sentais comme une présence dans la pièce.

present <> *n* ['preznt] **1.** [gift] cadeau *m* ■ to give sb a ~ faire un cadeau à qqn ■ to make sb a ~ of sthg faire cadeau de qqch à qqn ■ it's for a ~ [in shop] c'est pour offrir
2. [in time] présent *m* ■ at ~ actuellement, à présent ■ up to the ~ jusqu'à présent, jusqu'à maintenant ■ as things are OR stand at ~ au point où en sont les choses ■ that's enough for the ~ ça suffit pour le moment OR pour l'instant ■ to live only in OR for the ~ vivre pour l'instant présent OR au présent
3. GRAM présent *m* ■ in the ~ au présent.
<> *vt* [prɪ'zent] **1.** [gift] donner, offrir ■ [prize] remettre, décerner ■ to ~ sthg to sb OR sb with sthg donner OR offrir qqch à qqn ■ the singer was ~ed with a bunch of flowers la chanteuse s'est vu offrir OR remettre un bouquet de fleurs ■ she was ~ed with first prize on lui a décerné le premier prix ■ the project ~s us with a formidable challenge le projet constitue pour nous un formidable défi ■ he ~ed us with a fait accompli il nous a mis devant le fait accompli
2. *fml* [introduce] présenter ■ to ~ sb to sb présenter qqn à qqn ■ to be ~ed at Court être présenté à la Cour
3. [put on - play, film] donner ; [- exhibition] présenter, monter
4. RADIO & TV présenter
5. [offer - entertainment] présenter ■ we proudly ~ Donna Stewart nous avons le plaisir OR nous sommes heureux de vous présenter Donna Stewart ■ ~ing Vanessa Brown in the title role avec Vanessa Brown dans le rôle principal

6. [put forward - apology, view, report] présenter ▪ [plan] soumettre ▪ [orally] exposer ▪ **I wish to ~ my complaint in person** je tiens à déposer plainte moi-même ▪ **to ~ a bill in Parliament** présenter *OR* introduire un projet de loi au parlement
7. [pose, offer - problem, difficulty] présenter, poser ; [- chance, view] offrir ▪ **the house ~ed a sorry sight** la maison offrait un triste spectacle ▪ **if the opportunity ~s itself** si l'occasion se présente ▪ **the case ~s all the appearances of murder** tout semble indiquer qu'il s'agit d'un meurtre
8. [show - passport, ticket] présenter ▪ **~ arms!** MIL présentez armes!
9. [arrive, go] : **to ~ o.s.** se présenter
10. MED : **the foetus ~ed itself normally** la présentation (fœtale) était normale.
<> *vi* [prɪ'zent] présenter.
<> *adj* ['preznt] **1.** [in attendance] présent ▪ **to be ~ at a meeting** être présent à *OR* assister à une réunion ▪ **~ company excepted** à l'exception des personnes présentes
2. [current - job, government, price] actuel ▪ **in the ~ case** dans le cas présent ▪ **at the ~ time** actuellement, à l'époque actuelle ▪ **up to the ~ day** jusqu'à présent, jusqu'à aujourd'hui ▪ **given the ~ circumstances** étant donné les circonstances actuelles, dans l'état actuel des choses ▪ **in the ~ writer's opinion** de l'avis de l'auteur de ces lignes
3. GRAM au présent ▪ **indicative ~, ~indicative** présent *m* de l'indicatif.

presentable [prɪ'zentəbl] *adj* [person, room] présentable ▪ [clothes] présentable, mettable ▪ **make yourself ~** arrange-toi un peu.

presentation [ˌprezn'teɪʃn] *n* **1.** [showing] présentation *f* ▪ **on ~ of this voucher** sur présentation de ce bon ▪ **cheque payable on ~** chèque payable à vue ▮ [putting forward - of ideas, facts] présentation *f*, exposition *f* ; [- of petition] présentation *f*, soumission *f* ▪ **he made a very clear ~ of the case** il a très clairement présenté l'affaire **2.** COMM [of product, policy] présentation *f* **3.** [introduction] présentation *f* ▪ **can you make the ~s?** pouvez-vous faire les présentations? **4.** [performance - of play, film] représentation *f* ▪ **in a new ~ of "Hamlet"** dans une nouvelle mise en scène de "Hamlet" **5.** [of piece of work] présentation *f* **6.** [award - of prize, diploma] remise *f* ▪ **to make sb a ~ of sthg** remettre qqch à qqn **7.** [award ceremony] = **presentation ceremony** **8.** MED [of foetus] présentation *f*.

presentation ceremony *n* cérémonie *f* de remise *(d'un prix)*.

presentation copy *n* [specimen] spécimen *m* (gratuit) ▪ [from writer] exemplaire *m* gratuit.

present-day *adj* actuel, contemporain.

presenter [prɪ'zentəʳ] *n* présentateur *m*, - trice *f*.

presentiment [prɪ'zentɪmənt] *n* pressentiment *m*.

presently ['prezəntlɪ] *adv* **1.** *UK* [soon] bientôt, tout à l'heure ▪ **~, she got up and left** au bout de quelques minutes elle se leva et s'en alla **2.** [now] à présent, actuellement.

present participle *n* participe *m* présent.

present perfect *n* passé *m* composé ▪ **in the ~** au passé composé.

presents ['preznts] *npl* LAW : **by these ~** par la présente (lettre).

present tense *n* présent *m* ▪ **in the ~** au présent.

preservation [ˌprezə'veɪʃn] *n* **1.** [upkeep, maintenance - of tradition] conservation *f* ; [- of leather, building, wood] entretien *m* ; [- of peace, life] maintien *m* ▪ **the mummy was in a good state of ~** la momie était en bon état de conservation *OR* était bien conservée **2.** [of food] conservation *f* **3.** [protection] préservation *f*.

preservation order *n* : **to put a ~ on a building** classer un édifice *(monument historique)*.

preservative [prɪ'zɜːvətɪv] <> *n* agent *m* conservateur *OR* de conservation, conservateur *m* ▪ **'contains no artificial ~s'** 'sans conservateurs'.
<> *adj* conservateur.

preserve [prɪ'zɜːv] <> *vt* **1.** [maintain - tradition, building] conserver ; [- leather] conserver, entretenir ; [- silence] garder, observer ; [- peace, life] maintenir ; [- dignity] garder, conserver ▪ **to be well ~d** [building, specimen] être en bon état de conservation ; [person] être bien conservé ▪ **they tried to ~ some semblance of normality** ils essayaient de faire comme si de rien n'était **2.** [protect] préserver, protéger **3.** CULIN mettre en conserve ▪ **~d fruit** fruits *mpl* en conserve.
<> *n* **1.** HUNT réserve *f* (de chasse) **2.** [privilege] privilège *m*, apanage *m* ▪ **it's still very much a male ~** c'est encore un domaine essentiellement réservé aux hommes **3.** CULIN [fruit] confiture *f* ▪ [vegetable] conserve *f*.
◆ **preserves** *npl* CULIN [jam] confitures *fpl* ▪ [vegetables, fruit] conserves *fpl* ▪ [pickles] pickles *mpl*.

preserver [prɪ'zɜːvəʳ] *n* sauveur *m*.

preset [ˌpriː'set] (*pret & pp* **preset**) <> *vt* prérégler, régler à l'avance.
<> *adj* préréglé, réglé d'avance.

preshrunk [ˌpriː'ʃrʌŋk] *adj* irrétrécissable.

preside [prɪ'zaɪd] *vi* présider ▪ **to ~ at a meeting/at table** présider une réunion/la table.
◆ **preside over** *vt insep* **1.** [meeting] présider ▪ [changes] présider à **2.** [subj: statue, building] dominer.

presidency ['prezɪdənsɪ] (*pl* **presidencies**) *n* présidence *f*.

president ['prezɪdənt] *n* **1.** [of state] président *m*, - e *f* ▪ **President Simpson** le président Simpson **2.** [of organization, club] président *m*, - e *f* **3.** *US* [of company, bank] président-directeur général *m*, P-D G *m*.

president-elect *n titre du président des États-Unis nouvellement élu (en novembre) jusqu'à la cérémonie d'investiture présidentielle (le 20 janvier).*

presidential [ˌprezɪ'denʃl] *adj* [elections, candidate] présidentiel ▪ [aeroplane, suite] présidentiel, du président ▪ **it's a ~ year** c'est l'année des élections présidentielles.

presiding officer [prɪ'zaɪdɪŋ-] *n UK* président *m* (de bureau de vote).

presidium [prɪ'sɪdɪəm] (*pl* **presidiums** *OR pl* **presidia** [-dɪə]) *n* praesidium *m*, présidium *m*.

press [pres] <> *vt* **1.** [push - button, bell, trigger, accelerator] appuyer sur ▪ **he ~ed the lid shut** il a fermé le couvercle (en appuyant dessus) ▪ **to ~ sthg flat** aplatir qqch ▪ **to ~ one's way through a crowd/to the front** se frayer un chemin à travers une foule/jusqu'au premier rang ▪ **he was ~ed (up) against the railings** il s'est trouvé coincé contre le grillage ▪ **I ~ed myself against the wall** je me suis collé contre le mur ▪ **she ~ed a note into my hand** elle m'a glissé un billet dans la main ▪ **he ~ed his nose (up)against the windowpane** il a collé son nez à la vitre ▪ **she ~ed the papers down into the bin** elle a enfoncé les papiers dans la poubelle
2. [squeeze - hand, arm] presser, serrer ; [- grapes, olives] presser ▪ **she ~ed her son to her** elle serra son fils contre elle
3. [urge] presser, pousser ▪ **to ~ sb for an answer** presser qqn de répondre ▮ [harass] harceler, talonner ▪ **his creditors were ~ing him hard** ses créanciers le harcelaient *OR* ne lui laissaient pas le moindre répit
4. [force] forcer, obliger ▪ **I was ~ed into signing the contract** j'ai été obligé de signer le contrat
5. [impose, push forward - claim, advantage] appuyer, pousser ; [- opinions] insister sur ▪ **to ~ (home) an advantage** profiter d'un avantage ▪ **I don't want to ~ the point** je ne veux pas insister ▪ **to ~ charges against sb** LAW engager des poursuites contre qqn
6. [iron - shirt, tablecloth] repasser
7. [manufacture in mould - component] mouler ; [- record] presser
8. [preserve by pressing - flower] presser, faire sécher *(dans un livre ou un pressoir)*
9. [in weightlifting] soulever
10. [enlist by force] recruter *OR* enrôler de force ▪ **to ~ into service** *fig* réquisitionner.
<> *vi* **1.** [push] appuyer ▪ **~ here** appuyez *OR* pressez ici
2. [be a burden] *liter* faire pression ▪ *fig* [troubles] peser

3. [insist, campaign] : **he ~ed hard to get the grant** il a fait des pieds et des mains pour obtenir la bourse
4. [surge] : **the crowd ~ed against the barriers/round the President** la foule se pressait contre les barrières/autour du président ▪ **they ~ed forward to get a better view** ils poussaient pour essayer de mieux voir
5. [iron] se repasser
6. *phr* **time ~es!** le temps presse!
◇ *n* **1.** [newspapers] presse *f* ▪ **the national/local ~** la presse nationale/locale ▪ **they advertised in the ~** ils ont fait passer une annonce dans les journaux ➊ **the Press Association** *la principale agence de presse britannique* ▪ **the Press Complaints Commission** *organisme britannique de contrôle de la presse* ▪ **the Press Council** *organisme indépendant veillant au respect de la déontologie dans la presse britannique*
2. [journalists] presse *f* ▪ **the ~ were there** la presse était là ▪ **she's a member of the ~** elle a une carte de presse
3. [report, opinion] presse *f* ▪ **to get (a) good/bad ~** avoir bonne/mauvaise presse ▪ **to give sb (a) good/bad ~** faire l'éloge/la critique de qqn
4. [printing] presse *f* ▪ **to go to ~** [book] être mis sous presse ; [newspaper] partir à l'impression ▪ **the proofs were passed for ~** on a donné le bon à tirer
5. [machine] : **(printing) ~** presse *f*
6. [publisher] presses *fpl*
7. [for tennis racket, handicrafts, woodwork, trousers] presse *f* ▪ [for cider, wine] pressoir *m*
8. [push] : **the machine dispenses hot coffee at the ~of a button** il suffit d'appuyer sur un bouton pour que la machine distribue du café chaud
9. [squeeze] serrement *m* ▪ **he gave my hand a quick ~** il m'a serré la main rapidement
10. [crowd] foule *f* ▪ [rush] bousculade *f* ▪ **in the ~ for the door we became separated** dans la ruée de la foule vers la porte, nous avons été séparés
11. [ironing] coup *m* de fer ▪ **to give sthg a ~** donner un coup de fer à qqch
12. [cupboard] placard *m*
13. [in weightlifting] développé *m*
14. INDUST [forming machine] presse *f*.
◇ *comp* [campaign, card, reporter, photographer] de presse ▪ [advertising, coverage] dans la presse.
➡ **press ahead** = **press on.**
➡ **press for** *vt insep* [demand] exiger, réclamer.
➡ **press in** *vt sep* enfoncer.
➡ **press on** *vi insep* [on journey] poursuivre *OR* continuer son chemin ▪ [in enterprise, job] poursuivre, persévérer ▪ **we ~ed on regardless** nous avons continué malgré tout.
➡ **press on with** *vt insep* [job, negotiations] continuer, poursuivre.

press agency *n* agence *f* de presse.

press agent *n* attaché *m*, - e *f* de presse.

press baron *n* magnat *m* de la presse.

press box *n* tribune *f* de (la)presse.

press button *n* bouton-poussoir *m*.
➡ **press-button** *adj* TELEC : **~ dialling** numérotation *f* à touches.

press conference *n* conférence *f* de presse.

press corps *n* journalistes *mpl*.

press cutting *n* coupure *f* de presse *OR* de journal.

pressed [prest] *adj* **1.** [flower] pressé, séché **2.** [hurried] pressé ▪ [overworked] débordé.
➡ **pressed for** *adj phr* [short of] à court de ▪ **we're ~ for space** nous manquons de place ▪ **we're rather ~ for time** le temps nous est compté.

press gallery *n* tribune *f* de (la)presse *(par exemple au parlement)*.

press-gang ['pres-] ◇ *n* MIL & HIST racoleurs *mpl*, recruteurs *mpl*.
◇ *vt* **1.** *UK* [force] : **to ~ sb into doing sthg** obliger qqn à faire qqch (contre son gré) **2.** MIL & HIST racoler, recruter de force.

pressing ['presɪŋ] ◇ *adj* **1.** [urgent - appointment, business, debt] urgent ▪ **the matter is ~** c'est une affaire urgente **2.** [insistent - demand, danger, need] pressant ▪ **at her ~ invitation, we agreed to go** devant son insistance, nous avons accepté d'y aller **3.** [imminent - danger] imminent.
◇ *n* **1.** [of fruit, record] pressage *m* **2.** [ironing] repassage *m*.

press kit *n* dossier *m* de presse *(distribué aux journalistes)*.

pressman ['presmæn] (*pl* **pressmen** [-men]) *n* **1.** [journalist] journaliste *m* **2.** [printer] typographe *m*.

press officer *n* responsable *mf* des relations avec la presse.

press-on *adj* adhésif.

press pack *n* dossier *m* de presse.

press release *n* communiqué *m* de presse.

press run *n* tirage *m*.

press secretary *n* POL ≃ porte-parole *m inv* du gouvernement.

press stud *n UK* bouton-pression *m*, pression *f*.

press-up *n UK* SPORT pompe *f* ▪ **to do ~s** faire des pompes.

pressure ['preʃər] ◇ *n* **1.** METEOR & PHYS pression *f* ▪ [of blood] tension *f* ▪ **high/low ~ area** [on weather chart] zone *f* de hautes/basses pressions ➊ **oil ~** pression d'huile **2.** [squeezing] pression *f* **3.** *fig* [force, influence] : **to bring ~ to bear** *fml OR* **to put ~ on sb** faire pression *OR* exercer une pression sur qqn ▪ **she did it under ~** elle l'a fait contrainte et forcée ▪ **she came under ~ from her parents** elle est venue parce que ses parents l'y ont obligée **4.** *fig* [strain, stress - of circumstances, events] pression *f* ; [- of doubts, worries] poids *m* ▪ **the ~s of city life** le stress de la vie en ville ▪ **I can't stand any more of this ~** je ne peux plus supporter cette tension ▪ **to work under ~** travailler sous pression ▪ **we're under ~ to finish on time** on nous presse de respecter les délais ▪ **the ~ of work is too much for me** la charge de travail est trop lourde pour moi ▪ **there's a lot of ~ on her to succeed** on fait beaucoup pression sur elle pour qu'elle réussisse ▪ **the ~'s on!** il va falloir mettre les bouchées doubles! ▪ **she's under a lot of ~ just now** elle est vraiment sous pression en ce moment.
◇ *vt* faire pression sur ▪ **they ~d him into resigning** ils l'ont contraint à démissionner.

pressure cabin *n* cabine *f* pressurisée.

pressure chamber *n* MECH réservoir *m* d'air comprimé.

pressure-cook *vt* faire cuire à la cocotte-minute *OR* à l'autocuiseur.

pressure cooker *n* cocotte-minute *f*, autocuiseur *m*.

pressure gauge *n* jauge *f* de pression, manomètre *m*.

pressure group *n* groupe *m* de pression.

pressure point *n* point *m* de compression *(sur une artère)*.

pressure suit *n* scaphandre *m* pressurisé.

pressurization [ˌpreʃəraɪ'zeɪʃn] *n* pressurisation *f*.

pressurize, ise ['preʃəraɪz] *vt* **1.** [person, government] faire pression sur ▪ **to ~ sb to do sthg** *OR* **into doing sthg** faire pression sur qqn pour qu'il fasse qqch **2.** AERON & ASTRONAUT pressuriser.

pressurized ['preʃəraɪzd] *adj* [container] pressurisé ▪ [liquid, gas] sous pression.

Prestel® ['prestel] *pr n service de vidéotexte de la British Telecom.*

prestige [pre'sti:ʒ] ◇ *n* prestige *m*.
◇ *adj* de prestige.

prestigious [pre'stɪdʒəs] *adj* prestigieux.

presto ['prestəʊ] *adv* presto ▪ **hey ~!** et voilà, le tour est joué!

prestressed concrete [ˌpri:'strest-] *n* béton *m* précontraint.

presumably [prɪ'zju:məblɪ] *adv* vraisemblablement ▪ **~, he isn't coming** apparemment, il ne viendra pas.

presume [prɪ'zjuːm] ◇ *vt* **1.** [suppose] présumer, supposer ▪ **I ~ he isn't coming** je présume *OR* suppose qu'il ne viendra pas ▪ **I ~d them to be aware *OR* that they were aware of the difficulties** je supposais qu'ils étaient au courant des difficultés ▪ **missing, ~d dead** MIL manque à l'appel *OR* porté disparu, présumé mort ▪ **every man is ~d innocent until proven guilty** LAW tout homme est présumé innocent tant qu'il n'a pas été déclaré coupable ▪ **I ~ so** je (le) présume *OR* suppose **2.** [take liberty] oser, se permettre **3.** [presuppose] présupposer ▪ **presuming they agree** à supposer qu'ils soient d'accord.
◇ *vi* : **I don't want to ~** je ne voudrais pas m'imposer ▪ **to ~ on *OR* upon sb** abuser de la gentillesse de qqn.

presumption [prɪ'zʌmpʃn] *n* **1.** [supposition] présomption *f*, supposition *f* ▪ **the ~ is that he was drowned** on pense *OR* suppose qu'il s'est noyé ▪ **it's only a ~** ce n'est qu'une hypothèse ▪ **to act on a false ~** agir sur une *OR* à partir d'une fausse supposition ▪ **we worked on the ~ that she would agree** nous avons agi en supposant qu'elle serait d'accord **2.** *(U)* [arrogance] audace *f*, présomption *f*, prétention *f*.

presumptive [prɪ'zʌmptɪv] *adj* [heir] présomptif ▪ **~ proof** preuve *f* par déduction *OR* par présomption.

presumptuous [prɪ'zʌmptʃʊəs] *adj* présomptueux, arrogant.

presuppose [ˌpriːsə'pəʊz] *vt* présupposer.

presupposition [ˌpriːsʌpə'zɪʃn] *n* présupposition *f*.

pre-tax [ˌpriː'tæks] *adj* brut, avant (le prélèvement des) impôts ▪ **~ profits** bénéfices *mpl* bruts *OR* avant impôts.

pretence *UK*, **pretense** *US* [prɪ'tens] *n* **1.** [false display] simulacre *m* ▪ **to make a ~ of doing sthg** faire semblant *OR* mine de faire qqch ▪ **everyone sees through her ~ of being the devoted wife** elle ne trompe personne en jouant les femmes dévouées ▪ **at least SHE made some ~ of sympathy!** elle au moins, elle a fait comme si ça la touchait! **2.** [pretext] prétexte *m* ▪ **under *OR* on the ~ of doing sthg** sous prétexte de faire qqch ▪ **he criticizes her on the slightest ~** il la critique pour un rien *OR* à la moindre occasion **3.** [claim] prétention *f* ▪ **he has *OR* makes no ~ to musical taste** il ne prétend pas *OR* il n'a pas la prétention de s'y connaître en musique **4.** *(U)* [arrogance] prétention *f*.

pretend [prɪ'tend] ◇ *vt* **1.** [make believe] : **to ~ to do sthg** faire semblant de faire qqch, feindre de faire qqch ▪ **they ~ to be rich** ils font semblant d'être riches ▪ **they ~ed not to see *OR* to have seen us** ils ont fait semblant *OR* mine de ne pas nous voir ▪ **he ~ed not to be interested** il a fait semblant de ne pas être intéressé, il a joué les indifférents ▪ **he ~ed to be *OR* that he was their uncle** il s'est fait passer pour leur oncle ▪ **she ~s that everything is all right** elle fait comme si tout allait bien ▪ **it's no use ~ing things will improve** cela ne sert à rien de faire comme si les choses allaient s'améliorer ▮ [in children's play] : **let's ~ you're a prince** on dirait que tu serais un prince
2. [claim] prétendre ▪ **I don't ~ to be an expert** je ne prétends pas être un expert, je n'ai pas la prétention d'être un expert
3. [feign - indifference, ignorance] feindre, simuler.
◇ *vi* **1.** [feign] faire semblant ▪ **there's no point in ~ing (to me)** inutile de faire semblant (avec moi) ▪ **I'm only ~ing!** c'est juste pour rire! ▮ [in children's play] : **to play at let's ~** jouer à faire semblant *OR* comme si ▪ **let's ~** faisons semblant *OR* comme si
2. [lay claim] prétendre ▪ **to ~ to sthg** prétendre à qqch.
◇ *adj inf* [child language - money, fight] pour faire semblant, pour jouer ▪ **it was only ~!** c'était pour rire *OR* pour faire semblant!

pretended [prɪ'tendɪd] *adj* prétendu, soi-disant *inv*.

pretender [prɪ'tendər] *n* **1.** [to throne, title, right] prétendant *m*, - e *f* ▪ **the Young Pretender** HIST le Jeune Prétendant **2.** [impostor] imposteur *m*.

pretense *US* = **pretence**.

pretension [prɪ'tenʃn] *n* **1.** [claim] prétention *f* ▪ **to have ~s to sthg** avoir des prétentions *OR* prétendre à qqch ▪ **I make no ~s to expert knowledge** je n'ai pas la prétention *OR* je ne me flatte pas d'être expert en la matière ▪ **he has literary ~s** il se prend pour un écrivain **2.** *(U)* [pretentiousness] prétention *f* ▪ **he is devoid of ~** il est sans prétention.

pretentious [prɪ'tenʃəs] *adj* prétentieux.

pretentiously [prɪ'tenʃəslɪ] *adv* prétentieusement.

pretentiousness [prɪ'tenʃəsnɪs] *n (U)* prétention *f*.

preterit ['pretərət] *US* = **preterite**.

preterite ['pretərət] ◇ *adj* [form] du prétérit ▪ **the ~ tense** le prétérit.
◇ *n* prétérit *m* ▪ **in the ~** au prétérit.

preternatural [ˌpriːtə'nætʃrəl] ◇ *adj* surnaturel.
◇ *n* surnaturel *m*.

pretext ['priːtekst] *n* prétexte *m* ▪ **on *OR* under the ~ of doing sthg** sous prétexte de faire qqch.

prettify ['prɪtɪfaɪ] (*pret & pp* **prettified**) *vt pej* [room, garden] enjoliver ▪ **to ~ o.s.** se pomponner.

prettily ['prɪtɪlɪ] *adv* joliment.

prettiness ['prɪtɪnɪs] *n* **1.** [of appearance] beauté *f* **2.** *pej* [of style] mièvrerie *f*.

pretty ['prɪtɪ] (*comp* **prettier**, *superl* **prettiest**) ◇ *adj* **1.** [attractive - clothes, girl, place] joli ▪ **it wasn't a ~ sight** ce n'était pas beau *OR* joli à voir ▶ **I'm not just a ~ face!** *inf* il y en a, là-dedans! ▪ **to be as ~ as a picture** [person] être joli comme un cœur ; [place] être ravissant **2.** *iron* **this is a ~ state of affairs!** c'est du joli *OR* du propre! ▪ **things have come to a ~ pass!** nous voilà bien! **3.** *pej* [dainty - style, expression] précieux ▪ [effeminate - boy] mignon ▪ **it's not enough to make ~ speeches** il ne suffit pas de faire de beaux discours **4.** *phr* **a ~ penny : it cost a ~ penny** ça a coûté une jolie petite somme.
◇ *adv inf* **1.** [quite] assez ▪ **it's ~ good/important** c'est pas mal du tout/assez important ▪ **you did ~ well for a beginner** tu t'en es plutôt bien tiré pour un débutant **2.** [almost] presque, à peu près, pratiquement **3.** *phr* **to be sitting ~** avoir la partie belle.

pretty-pretty *adj inf pej* [person] gentillet, mignonnet ▪ [dress] cucul la praline *(inv)* ▪ [painting] gentillet ▪ [garden] mignon, gentil.

pretzel ['pretsl] *n* bretzel *m*.

prevail [prɪ'veɪl] *vi* **1.** [triumph] l'emporter, prévaloir *lit* ▪ **to ~ against sb** l'emporter *OR* prévaloir contre qqn ▪ **to ~ over sb** l'emporter *OR* prévaloir sur qqn ▪ **luckily, common sense ~ed** heureusement, le bon sens a prévalu *OR* l'a emporté **2.** [exist, be widespread - situation, opinion, belief] régner, avoir cours ▪ **the rumour which is now ~ing** le bruit qui court en ce moment ▪ **the conditions ~ing in the Third World** les conditions que l'on rencontre le plus souvent dans le tiers monde.
◆ **prevail on, prevail upon** *vt insep fml* persuader ▪ **can I ~ on your good nature?** puis-je faire appel à votre bonté?

prevailing [prɪ'veɪlɪŋ] *adj* **1.** [wind] dominant **2.** [belief, opinion] courant, répandu ▪ [fashion] en vogue ▪ **in the ~ conditions** [now] dans les conditions actuelles ; [then] à l'époque ▪ **the ~ political climate** le climat politique actuel ▪ **the ~ exchange rate** le taux de change actuel.

prevalence ['prevələns] *n* [widespread existence] prédominance *f* ▪ [of disease] prévalence *f* ▪ [frequency] fréquence *f* ▪ **the ~ of these theories can only do harm** la popularité de ces théories ne peut qu'être nuisible.

prevalent ['prevələnt] *adj* **1.** [widespread] répandu, courant ▪ [frequent] fréquent ▪ **to become ~** se généraliser **2.** [current - today] actuel, d'aujourd'hui ; [- in past] de *OR* à l'époque.

prevaricate [prɪ'værɪkeɪt] *vi fml* tergiverser, user de faux-fuyants.

prevarication [prɪˌværɪ'keɪʃn] *n fml* tergiversation *f*, faux-fuyant *m*, faux-fuyants *mpl*.

prevent [prɪ'vent] *vt* [accident, catastrophe, scandal] éviter ▪ [illness] prévenir ▪ **to ~ sb (from) doing sthg** empêcher qqn de faire qqch ▪ **I couldn't ~ her** je n'ai pas pu l'en empêcher ▪ **we were unable to ~ the bomb from exploding** nous n'avons rien pu faire pour empêcher la bombe d'exploser.

preventable [prɪ'ventəbl] *adj* évitable.

preventative [prɪ'ventətɪv] *adj* préventif.

preventible [prɪ'ventəbl] = **preventable**.

prevention [prɪ'venʃn] *n* prévention *f* ▪ **the ~ of cruelty to animals** la protection des animaux ▶ **the Prevention of Terrorism Act** *loi sur la prévention du terrorisme permettant notamment la garde à vue de toute personne suspectée* ▪ **~ is better than cure** *prov* mieux vaut prévenir que guérir *prov.*

preventive [prɪ'ventɪv] <> *adj* **1.** [medicine] préventif, prophylactique ▪ [measure] préventif **2.** *UK* LAW : **~ detention** *peine de prison allant de 5 à 14 ans.*
<> *n* **1.** [measure] mesure *f* préventive ▪ **as a ~** à titre préventif **2.** MED médicament *m* préventif *OR* prophylactique.

preverbal [,priː'vɜːbl] *adj* **1.** [infant] qui ne parle pas encore ▪ **~ communication** activité *f* préverbale **2.** GRAM avant le verbe.

preview ['priːvjuː] <> *n* **1.** [preliminary showing - of film, show, exhibition] avant-première *f* ; [- of art exhibition] vernissage *m* ▪ **and here is a ~ of tomorrow's programmes** et voici un aperçu des programmes de demain **2.** *US* CIN [trailer] bande-annonce *f.*
<> *vt* : **to ~ a film** [put on] donner un film en avant-première ; [see] voir un film en avant-première ▪ **to ~ the evening's television viewing** passer en revue les programmes télévisés de la soirée.

previous ['priːvjəs] <> *adj* **1.** [prior] précédent ▪ **on a ~ occasion** auparavant ▪ **I have a ~ engagement** j'ai déjà un rendez-vous, je suis déjà pris ▪ **she has had several ~ accidents** elle a déjà eu plusieurs accidents ▪ **do you have any ~ experience of this kind of work?** avez-vous déjà une expérience de ce genre de travail? ▪ **the two months ~ to your arrival** les deux mois précédant votre arrivée ▌LAW : **he has no ~ convictions** il n'a pas de casier judiciaire, il a un casier judiciaire vierge ▪ **he has had several ~ convictions** il a déjà fait l'objet de plusieurs condamnations **2.** [former] antérieur ▪ **in a ~ life** dans une vie antérieure ▪ **his ~ marriages ended in divorce** ses autres mariages se sont soldés par des divorces **3.** [with days and dates] précédent ▪ **the ~ Monday** le lundi précédent ▪ **the ~ June** au mois de juin précédent ▪ **the ~ day** le jour précédent, la veille **4.** *UK inf* [premature, hasty - decision, judgement] prématuré, hâtif ; [- person] expéditif.
<> *adv* antérieurement ▪ **~ to his death** *fml* avant sa mort, avant qu'il ne meure.

previously ['priːvjəslɪ] *adv* **1.** [in the past] auparavant, précédemment ▪ **six weeks ~** six semaines auparavant *OR* plus tôt **2.** [already] déjà.

prevocalic [,priːvə'kælɪk] *adj* prévocalique.

prewar [,priː'wɔːr] *adj* d'avant-guerre ▪ **the ~ years** l'avant-guerre *m ou f.*

prewash ['priːwɒʃ] <> *n* prélavage *m.*
<> *vt* faire un prélavage de.

prey [preɪ] *n (U) liter & fig* proie *f* ▪ **hens are often (a) ~ to foxes** les poules sont souvent la proie des renards ▪ **the sheep fell (a) ~ to some marauding beast** les moutons ont été attaqués par un animal maraudeur ▪ **to be (a) ~ to doubts/nightmares** être en proie au doute/à des cauchemars.
◆ **prey on, prey upon** *vt insep* **1.** [subj: predator] faire sa proie de ▪ **he ~ed on her fears** *fig* il profita de ce qu'elle avait peur ▪ **the thieves ~ed upon old women** *fig* les voleurs s'en prenaient aux *OR* attaquaient les vieilles dames **2.** [subj: fear, doubts] ronger ▪ **the thought continued to ~ on his mind** l'idée continuait à lui ronger l'esprit.

price [praɪs] <> *n* **1.** [cost] prix *m* ▪ **what is the ~ of petrol?** à quel prix est l'essence? ▪ **petrol has gone down in ~** le prix de l'essence a baissé ▪ **~s are rising/falling** les prix sont en hausse/baisse ▪ **I paid a high ~ for it** je l'ai payé cher ▪ **they pay top ~s for antique china** ils achètent la porcelaine ancienne au prix fort ▪ **if the ~ is right** si le prix est correct ▪ **she got a good ~ for her car** elle a obtenu un bon prix de sa voiture ▪ **I got the chair at a reduced/at half ~** j'ai eu la chaise à prix réduit/à moitié prix ▪ **her jewels fetched huge ~s at auction** ses bijoux ont atteint des sommes folles aux enchères ▪ **that's my ~, take it or leave it** c'est mon dernier prix, à prendre ou à laisser ▪ **name** *OR* **state your ~!** votre prix sera le mien! ▪ **every man has his ~** tout homme s'achète
2. [value] prix *m*, valeur *f* ▪ **to argue over the ~ of sthg** débattre le prix de qqch ▪ **to put a ~ on sthg** [definite] fixer le prix *OR* la valeur de qqch ; [estimate] évaluer le prix *OR* estimer la valeur de qqch ▪ **there's a ~ on his head** sa tête a été mise à prix ▪ **you can't put a ~ on love** l'amour n'a pas de prix ▪ **what ~ all her hopes now?** que valent tous ses espoirs maintenant? ▪ **he puts a high ~ on loyalty** il attache beaucoup d'importance *OR* il accorde beaucoup de valeur à la loyauté ▪ **without ~** sans prix
3. ST. EX cours *m*, cote *f* ▪ **today's ~s** les cours du jour
4. *fig* [penalty] prix *m* ▪ **it's a small ~ to pay for peace of mind** c'est bien peu de chose pour avoir l'esprit tranquille ▪ **it's a high ~ to pay for independence** c'est bien cher payer l'indépendance ▪ **that's the ~ of fame** c'est la rançon de la gloire
5. [chance, odds] cote *f* ▪ **what ~ are they giving on Stardust?** quelle est la cote de Stardust? ▪ **what ~ he'll keep his word?** combien pariez-vous qu'il tiendra parole? ▪ **what ~ peace now?** quelles sont les chances de paix maintenant?
6. [quotation] devis *m.*
<> *comp* [bracket, range] de prix ▪ [freeze, rise, level] des prix.
<> *vt* **1.** [set cost of] fixer *OR* établir *OR* déterminer le prix de ▪ **the book is ~d at £17** le livre coûte 17 livres ▪ **his paintings are rather highly ~d** le prix de ses tableaux est un peu élevé ▪ **a reasonably ~d hotel** un hôtel aux prix raisonnables ▌[estimate value of] : **how would you ~ that house?** à combien estimeriez-vous cette maison?
2. [indicate cost of] marquer le prix de ▪ [with label] étiqueter ▪ **this book isn't ~d** le prix de ce livre n'est pas indiqué
3. [ascertain price of] demander le prix de, s'informer du prix de ▪ **she ~d the stereo in several shops before buying it** elle a comparé le prix de la chaîne dans plusieurs magasins avant de l'acheter.
◆ **at any price** *adv phr* : **she wants a husband at any ~** elle veut un mari à tout prix *OR* coûte que coûte ▪ **he wouldn't do it at any ~!** il ne voulait le faire à aucun prix *OR* pour rien au monde!
◆ **at a price** *adv phr* en y mettant le prix ▪ **she'll help you, at a ~** elle vous aidera, à condition que vous y mettiez le prix ▪ **you got what you wanted, but at a ~!** vous avez eu ce que vous souhaitiez, mais à quel prix! *OR* mais vous l'avez payé cher!
◆ **price down** *vt sep UK* baisser le prix de, démarquer.
◆ **price out** *vt sep* : **to ~ o.s.** *OR* **one's goods out of the market** perdre son marché *OR* sa clientèle à cause de ses prix trop élevés ▪ **cheap charter flights have ~d the major airlines out of the market** les vols charters à prix réduit ont fait perdre des parts de marché aux grandes compagnies aériennes ▪ **he ~d himself out of the job** il n'a pas été embauché parce qu'il a demandé un salaire trop élevé.
◆ **price up** *vt sep UK* [raise cost of] augmenter *OR* majorer le prix de, majorer ▪ [on label] indiquer un prix plus élevé sur.

price control *n* contrôle *m* des prix.

price cut *n* rabais *m*, réduction *f* (de prix).

price-cutting *n (U)* réductions *fpl* de prix.

-priced [praɪst] *in cpds* : **high~** à prix élevé, (plutôt)cher ▪ **low~** à bas prix, peu cher ▪ **over~** trop cher.

price-fixing [-fɪksɪŋ] *n* [control] contrôle *m* des prix ▪ [rigging] entente *f* sur les prix.

price index *n* indice *m* des prix.

priceless ['praɪslɪs] *adj* **1.** [precious - jewels, friendship] d'une valeur inestimable **2.** *inf* [funny - joke] tordant, bidonnant ; [- person] impayable.

price list *n* tarif *m*, liste *f* des prix.

price-rigging *n* entente *f* sur les prix.

price tag *n* **1.** [label] étiquette *f* de prix **2.** [value] prix *m*, valeur *f.*

price war *n* guerre *f* des prix.

pricey ['praɪsɪ] (*comp* **pricier**, *superl* **priciest**) *adj inf* chérot.

prick [prɪk] <> *vt* **1.** [jab, pierce] piquer, percer ▪ **she ~ed her finger/herself with the needle** elle s'est piqué le doigt/elle s'est piquée avec l'aiguille ▪ **to ~ holes in sthg** faire des trous dans qqch **2.** [irritate] piquer, picoter ▪ **the smoke was ~ing my eyes** la fumée me piquait les yeux ▪ **his conscience was ~ing him** *fig* il n'avait pas la conscience tranquille, il avait mauvaise conscience.
<> *vi* **1.** [pin, cactus, thorn] piquer **2.** [be irritated] picoter ▪ **my eyes are ~ing from the smoke** j'ai les yeux qui me piquent OR brûlent à cause de la fumée ▪ **her conscience was ~ing (at her)** *fig* elle n'avait pas la conscience tranquille, elle avait mauvaise conscience.
<> *n* **1.** [from insect, pin, thorn] piqûre *f* ▪ **~s of conscience** *fig* remords *mpl* **2.**▲ [penis] bite▲ *f* **3.**△ [person] con△ *m*, connard△ *m*.

prick up <> *vi insep* [ears] se dresser.
<> *vt sep* dresser ▪ **she ~ed up her ears at the sound of her name** elle a dressé OR tendu l'oreille en entendant son nom.

pricking ['prɪkɪŋ] *n* picotement *m* ▪ **the ~s of conscience** les remords *mpl*.

prickle ['prɪkl] <> *n* **1.** [on rose, cactus] épine *f*, piquant *m* ▪ [on hedgehog, porcupine] piquant *m* **2.** [sensation] picotement *m*.
<> *vt* piquer.
<> *vi* [skin] picoter, fourmiller ▪ **her skin ~d with excitement** un frisson d'excitation lui parcourut la peau.

prickly ['prɪklɪ] (*comp* **pricklier**, *superl* **prickliest**) *adj* **1.** [cactus, plant] épineux ▪ [hedgehog] couvert de piquants ▪ [beard] piquant ▪ [clothes] qui pique ▪ **his fingers felt ~** il avait des fourmillements dans les doigts ▪ **his skin felt ~** sa peau le démangeait ▪ **a ~ sensation** une sensation de picotement **2.** *inf* [irritable - person] ombrageux, irritable ; [- character] ombrageux **3.** [delicate - subject, topic] épineux, délicat.

prickly heat *n (U)* fièvre *f* miliaire.

prickly pear *n* [fruit] figue *f* de Barbarie ▪ [tree] figuier *m* de Barbarie.

pricy ['praɪsɪ] *inf* = **pricey**.

pride [praɪd] <> *n* **1.** [satisfaction] fierté *f* ▪ **they take ~ in their town** ils sont fiers de leur ville ▪ **to take (a) ~ in one's appearance** prendre soin de sa personne ▪ **he takes no ~ in his work** il ne prend pas du tout son travail à cœur ▪ **to take (a) ~ in doing sthg** mettre de la fierté à faire qqch, s'enorgueillir de faire qqch **2.** [self-respect] fierté *f*, amour-propre *m* ▪ **a sense of ~** un sentiment d'amour-propre ▪ **he has no ~** il n'a pas d'amour-propre ▪ **her ~ was hurt** elle était blessée dans son amour-propre **3.** *pej* [arrogance] orgueil *m* ▪ **~ comes OR goes before a fall** *prov* plus on est fier, plus dure est la chute **4.** [most valuable thing] orgueil *m*, fierté *f* ▪ **she is her parents' ~ and joy** elle fait la fierté de ses parents ▪ **this painting is the ~ of the collection** ce tableau est le joyau de la collection ◗ **~ of place** place *f* d'honneur ▪ **to have OR to take ~ of place** occuper la place d'honneur **5.** [of lions] groupe *m*.
<> *vt* [satisfaction] : **to ~ o.s. on OR upon sthg** être fier OR s'enorgueillir de qqch.

prier ['praɪəʳ] *n pej* fouineur *m*, - euse *f*.

priest [pri:st] *n* prêtre *m*.

priestess ['pri:stɪs] *n* prêtresse *f*.

priesthood ['pri:sthʊd] *n* [as vocation] prêtrise *f* ▪ [clergy] clergé *m* ▪ **to enter the ~** être ordonné prêtre.

priestly ['pri:stlɪ] (*comp* **priestlier**, *superl* **priestliest**) *adj* sacerdotal, de prêtre.

prig [prɪg] *n* UK **he's such a ~!** il fait toujours son petit saint!

priggish ['prɪgɪʃ] *adj* UK pharisaïque.

prim [prɪm] (*comp* **primmer**, *superl* **primmest**) *adj pej* **1.** [affectedly proper - person] collet monté *(inv)* ; [- attitude, behaviour] guindé, compassé ; [- voice] affecté ▪ **she's very ~ and proper** elle est très collet monté **2.** [neat - clothes] (très) comme il faut, (très) classique ; [- house, hedge, lawn] impeccable.

prima ballerina [,pri:mə-] *n* danseuse *f* étoile.

primacy ['praɪməsɪ] (*pl* **primacies**) *n* **1.** [preeminence] primauté *f*, prééminence *f* **2.** RELIG primatie *f*.

prima donna [,pri:mə'dɒnə] *n* **1.** [opera singer] prima donna *f* **2.** *pej* diva *f* **3.** [star] star *f*.

primaeval [praɪ'mi:vəl] = **primeval**.

prima facie [,praɪmə'feɪʃi:] <> *adv* à première vue, de prime abord.
<> *adj* LAW : **a ~ case** une affaire simple a priori ▪ **it's a ~ case of mistaken identity** a priori, il s'agit d'une erreur sur la personne ▪ **~ evidence** commencement *m* de preuve ▪ **there is no ~ evidence** a priori, il n'y a aucune preuve.

primal ['praɪml] *adj* **1.** [original] primitif, premier ▪ **~ scream** PSYCHOL cri *m* primal **2.** [main] primordial, principal.

primarily [UK 'praɪmərɪlɪ, US praɪ'merəlɪ] *adv* **1.** [mainly] principalement, avant tout **2.** [originally] primitivement, à l'origine.

primary ['praɪmərɪ] (*pl* **primaries**) <> *adj* **1.** [main] principal, premier ▪ [basic] principal, fondamental ▪ **this question is of ~ importance** cette question revêt une importance capitale ▪ **the ~ cause of the accident** la cause principale de l'accident **2.** SCI primaire ▪ **~ circuit** ELEC circuit *m* primaire ▪ **~ tooth** ANAT dent *f* de lait **3.** SCH primaire **4.** ECON primaire ▪ **the ~ sector** le (secteur) primaire.
<> *n* **1.** POL [in US] : **~ (election)** (élection *f*) primaire *f* **2.** [school] école *f* primaire **3.** [colour] couleur *f* primaire **4.** ORNITH rémige *f* **5.** ELEC (enroulement *m*)primaire *m*.

PRIMARIES

> Les primaires américaines sont des élections, directes ou indirectes selon les États, pour sélectionner les candidats représentant les deux grands partis nationaux (Démocrate et Républicain) à l'élection présidentielle.

primary accent *n* accent *m* principal.

primary care trust *n* UK *administration qui gère les services de santé au niveau local.*

primary colour *n* couleur *f* primaire.

primary school *n* école *f* primaire ▪ **~ teacher** instituteur *m*, - trice *f*.

primary stress = **primary accent**.

primate ['praɪmeɪt] *n* **1.** ZOOL primate *m* **2.** RELIG primat *m* ▪ **the Primate of All England** *titre officiel de l'archevêque de Cantorbéry.*

prime [praɪm] <> *adj* **1.** [foremost] premier, primordial ▪ [principal] premier, principal ▪ [fundamental] fondamental ▪ **our ~ concern is to avoid loss of life** notre préoccupation principale est d'éviter de faire des victimes ▪ **of ~ importance** de la plus haute importance, d'une importance primordiale **2.** [perfect] parfait ▪ [excellent] excellent ▪ **in ~ condition** [person] en parfaite santé ; [athlete] en parfaite condition ; [car] en parfait état ▪ **it's a ~ example of what I mean** c'est un excellent exemple de ce que je veux dire ▪ **~ quality** de première qualité ▪ **~ beef** bœuf *m* de première catégorie **3.** MATHS [number] premier.
<> *n* **1.** [best moment] : **to be in one's ~ OR in the ~ of life** être dans la fleur de l'âge ▪ **I'm past my ~** je ne suis plus dans la fleur de l'âge ▪ **these roses look a bit past their ~** ces roses sont plutôt défraîchies ▪ **these curtains look a bit past their ~** ces rideaux ont vu des jours meilleurs ▪ **when Romantic poetry was in its ~** lorsque la poésie romantique était à son apogée **2.** MATHS nombre *m* premier.
<> *vt* **1.** [gun, machine, pump] amorcer ▪ **to ~ sb with drink** faire boire qqn ▪ **he was well ~d** *inf* il était bien parti **2.** [brief - person] mettre au courant, briefer ▪ **to ~ sb for a meeting** préparer qqn à une réunion ▪ **he is well ~d in local politics** il est bien renseigné sur la politique locale **3.** [with paint, varnish] apprêter.

prime cost *n* prix *m* de revient.

prime minister *n* premier ministre *m*.

prime ministership, prime ministry *n* fonctions *fpl* de Premier ministre ▪ **during her ~** pendant qu'elle était Premier ministre.

prime mover *n* **1.** PHYS force *f* motrice **2.** PHILOS cause *f* première **3.** *fig* [person] instigateur *m*, - trice *f*.

prime number *n* nombre *m* premier.

primer ['praɪmər] *n* **1.** [paint] apprêt *m* **2.** [for explosives] amorce *f* **3.** [book - elementary] manuel *m* (élémentaire) ; [- for reading] abécédaire *m*.

prime time *n* heure *f* de grande écoute, prime time *m*.
◆ **prime-time** *adj* [TV programme, advertising] diffusé à une heure de grande écoute, de prime time.

primeval [praɪ'mi:vl] *adj* **1.** [prehistoric] primitif, des premiers âges *OR* temps **2.** [primordial - fears, emotions] atavique, instinctif.

priming ['praɪmɪŋ] *n (U)* **1.** [of pump] amorçage *m* ▪ [of gun] amorce *f* **2.** [paint] première couche *f*.

primitive ['prɪmɪtɪv] <> *adj* primitif.
<> *n* **1.** [primitive person] primitif *m*, - ive *f* **2.** [artist] primitif *m* **3.** COMPUT & MATHS primitive *f*.

primly ['prɪmlɪ] *adv pej* d'une manière guindée *OR* collet monté ▪ **to be ~ dressed** être habillé très comme il faut ▪ **she sat ~ in the corner** elle se tenait assise très sagement dans le coin.

primness ['prɪmnɪs] *n pej* [of person] air *m* collet monté *OR* compassé ▪ [of behaviour] caractère *m* maniéré *OR* compassé ▪ [of dress] aspect *m* collet monté *OR* très comme il faut ▪ [of voice] caractère *m* affecté.

primogeniture [,praɪməʊ'dʒenɪtʃər] *n* primogéniture *f*.

primordial [praɪ'mɔ:djəl] *adj* primordial ▪ **~ ooze** *OR* **soup** soupe *f* primitive.

primp [prɪmp] <> *vi* se faire beau.
<> *vt* : **to ~ o.s. (up)** se faire beau.

primrose ['prɪmrəʊz] <> *n* **1.** BOT primevère *f* **2.** [colour] jaune *m* pâle.
<> *adj* jaune pâle *(inv)*.

primrose path *n* : **the ~** la voie de la facilité.

primrose yellow *adj* jaune pâle *(inv)*.

primula ['prɪmjʊlə] (*pl* **primulas** *OR pl* **primulae** [-li:]) *n* primevère *f*.

Primus® ['praɪməs] *n UK* **~ (stove)** réchaud *m* (de camping).

prince [prɪns] *n liter & fig* prince *m* ▪ **Prince Rupert** le prince Rupert ▪ **the Prince of Darkness** le prince des ténèbres ▪ **the Prince of Peace** le prince de la paix ▪ **the Prince of Wales** le prince de Galles ▪ **he is a ~ among men** c'est un prince parmi les hommes ▪ **to live like a ~** vivre comme un prince.

Prince Charming *n* le Prince Charmant.

prince consort *n* prince *m* consort.

princedom ['prɪnsdəm] *n* principauté *f*.

Prince Edward Island *pr n* l'île *f* du Prince-Édouard.

princeling ['prɪnslɪŋ] *n* petit prince *m*.

princely ['prɪnslɪ] *adj* princier ▪ **a ~ sum** une somme princière.

prince regent *n* prince *m* régent.

princess [prɪn'ses] *n* princesse *f* ▪ **Princess Anne** la princesse Anne ▪ **the Princess of Wales** la princesse de Galles ▪ **she's like a fairytale ~** c'est une princesse de conte de fées.

princess royal *n* : **the ~** la princesse royale.

Princes Street *pr n principale rue commerçante d'Édimbourg.*

principal ['prɪnsəpl] <> *adj* [gen] principal ▪ MUS [violin, oboe] premier.
<> *n* **1.** [head - of school] directeur *m*, - trice *f* ; [- of university] doyen *m*, - enne *f* **2.** LAW [employer of agent] mandant *m*, commettant *m* **3.** [main character - in play] acteur *m* principal, actrice *f* principale ; [- in orchestra] chef *m* de pupitre ; [- in crime] auteur *m* **4.** FIN [capital - gen] capital *m* ; [- of debt] principal *m* **5.** CONSTR [rafter] poutre *f* maîtresse.

principal boy *n jeune héros d'une pantomime dont le rôle est traditionnellement joué par une femme.*

principal clause *n* (proposition *f*) principale *f*.

principality [,prɪnsɪ'pælətɪ] *n* principauté *f* ▪ **the Principality** [Wales] le pays de Galles.

principally ['prɪnsəplɪ] *adv* principalement.

principal parts *npl* GRAM temps *mpl* primitifs.

principle ['prɪnsəpl] *n* **1.** [for behaviour] principe *m* ▪ **she has high ~s** elle a des principes ▪ **she was a woman of ~** c'était une femme de principes *OR* qui avait des principes ▪ **on ~, as a matter of ~** par principe ▪ **it's a matter of ~** c'est une question de principe ▪ **it's against my ~s to eat meat** j'ai pour principe de ne pas manger de viande ▪ **to stick to one's ~s** rester fidèle à ses principes **2.** [fundamental law] principe *m* ▪ **to go back to first ~s** remonter jusqu'au principe **3.** [theory] principe *m* ▪ **in ~** en principe ▪ **basic ~** principe de base ▪ **to be based on false ~s** reposer sur de faux principes *OR* de fausses prémisses ▪ **we acted on the ~ that everybody knew** nous sommes partis du principe que tout le monde était au courant.

principled ['prɪnsəpld] *adj* : **a ~ man** un homme de principes *OR* qui a des principes ▪ **to take a ~ stand** adopter une position de principe.

print [prɪnt] <> *n* **1.** [of publications] : **to appear in ~** être publié *OR* imprimé ▪ **to see o.s./one's name in ~** voir ses écrits imprimés/son nom imprimé ▪ **her work will soon be in ~** son œuvre sera bientôt publiée ▮ [of book] : **to be in/out of ~** être disponible/épuisé ▪ **the book is no longer in ~** le livre est épuisé ▪ **the newspapers had already gone to ~before the news broke** les journaux étaient déjà sous presse lorsque la nouvelle est tombée
2. *(U)* [characters] caractères *mpl* ▪ **in large ~** en gros caractères ▪ **in bold ~** en caractères gras
3. *(U)* [text] texte *m* (imprimé) ◗ **the small** *OR* **fine ~ on a contract** les lignes en petits caractères en bas d'un contrat
4. PHOT épreuve *f*, tirage *m*
5. ART [engraving] gravure *f*, estampe *f* ▪ [reproduction] poster *m*
6. TEX [fabric] imprimé *m* ▪ [dress] robe *f* imprimée
7. [mark - from tyre, foot] empreinte *f* ▪ [fingerprint] empreinte *f* digitale.
<> *comp* **1.** TYPO : **the ~ unions** les syndicats *mpl* des typographes
2. COMPUT : **~ cartridge** cartouche *f* ▪ **~ menu** menu *m* d'impression.
<> *adj* [dress] en tissu imprimé.
<> *vt* **1.** [book, newspaper, money] imprimer ▪ [publish - story, article] publier ▪ **the novel is being ~ed** le roman est sous presse *OR* en cours d'impression ▪ **1,000 copies of the book have already been ~ed** on a déjà tiré le livre à 1 000 exemplaires ▪ **~ed in France** imprimé en France
2. [write] écrire en caractères d'imprimerie ▪ **~ your name clearly** écrivez votre nom lisiblement
3. PHOT tirer
4. TEX imprimer
5. [mark] imprimer ▪ *fig* [in memory] graver, imprimer.
<> *vi* **1.** imprimer ▪ **tomorrow's newspapers haven't started ~ing yet** les journaux de demain ne sont pas encore sous presse *OR* à l'impression ▪ **the drawing should ~ well** le dessin devrait bien ressortir à l'impression
2. [in handwriting] écrire en caractères d'imprimerie
3. PHOT [negative] : **to ~ well** sortir bien au tirage.
◆ **print off** *vt sep* **1.** TYPO imprimer, tirer
2. PHOT tirer.
◆ **print out** *vt sep* COMPUT imprimer.

printable ['prɪntəbl] *adj* imprimable, publiable ▪ **my opinion on the matter is not ~** mon avis sur la question n'est pas très agréable à entendre.

printed ['prɪntɪd] *adj* **1.** [gen] imprimé ▪ **~ matter** imprimés *mpl* ▪ **the ~ word** l'écrit *m* **2.** [notepaper] à en-tête.

printed circuit *n* circuit *m* imprimé.

printer ['prɪntəʳ] *n* **1.** [person - gen] imprimeur *m* ; [- typographer] typographe *mf* ; [- compositor] compositeur *m*, - trice *f* ▪ **it's at the ~'s** c'est chez l'imprimeur *OR* à l'impression ▶ **~'s error** coquille *f* ▪ **~'s ink** encre *f* d'imprimerie ▪ **~'s mark** marque *f* d'imprimeur **2.** COMPUT imprimante *f* ▪ **~ cable** câble *m* d'imprimante ▪ **~ driver** programme *m* de commande d'impression ▪ **~ port** port *m* d'imprimante **3.** PHOT tireuse *f*.

printhead ['prɪnthed] *n* tête *f* d'impression.

printing ['prɪntɪŋ] *n* **1.** [activity] imprimerie *f* ▪ **he works in ~** il travaille dans l'imprimerie **2.** [copies printed] impression *f*, tirage *m* **3.** PHOT tirage *m* **4.** *(U)* [handwriting] (écriture *f* en) caractères *mpl* d'imprimerie.

printing ink *n* encre *f* d'imprimerie.

printing press *n* presse *f* (d'imprimerie).

printout ['prɪntaʊt] *n* [act of printing out] tirage *m*, sortie *f* sur imprimante ▪ **to do a ~** sortir un document sur imprimante, imprimer (un document) ▮ [printed version] sortie *f* papier, tirage *m* ▪ [results of calculation] listing *m* ▪ **here's the ~ of the results** voici le listing des résultats.

print shop *n* imprimerie *f*.

printwheel ['prɪntwi:l] *n* marguerite *f (d'imprimante)*.

prior ['praɪəʳ] <> *adj* **1.** [earlier] antérieur, précédent ▪ **she had a ~ engagement** elle était déjà prise ▮ [preliminary] préalable ▪ **without ~ notice** sans préavis ▪ **without his ~ agreement** sans son accord préalable **2.** [more important] : **to have a ~ claim to** *OR* **on sthg** avoir un droit de priorité *OR* d'antériorité sur qqch ▪ **her son had a ~ claim on her attention** son fils passait avant tout.
<> *n* RELIG (père *m*) prieur *m*.
◆ **prior to** *prep phr* avant, antérieurement à, préalablement à.

prioress ['praɪərɪs] *n* (mère *f*) prieure *f*.

prioritize, ise [praɪ'ɒrɪtaɪz] *vt* donner *OR* accorder la priorité à.

priority [praɪ'ɒrətɪ] (*pl* **priorities**) *n* priorité *f* ▪ **to give ~ to** donner *OR* accorder la priorité à ▪ **to have** *OR* **to take ~ over** avoir la priorité sur ▪ **to do sthg as a (matter of) ~** faire qqch en priorité ▪ **the matter has top ~** l'affaire a la priorité absolue *OR* est absolument prioritaire ▪ **you should get your priorities right** il faudrait que tu apprennes à distinguer ce qui est important de ce qui ne l'est pas ▪ **the government has got its priorities all wrong** le gouvernement n'accorde pas la priorité aux choses les plus importantes.

priory ['praɪərɪ] (*pl* **priories**) *n* prieuré *m*.

prise [praɪz] *vt UK* **to ~ sthg open** ouvrir qqch à l'aide d'un levier ▪ **she managed to ~ her leg free** elle a réussi à dégager sa jambe ▪ **we ~d the top off with a spoon** on a enlevé le couvercle à l'aide d'une cuillère ▪ **we managed to ~ the information out of her** *fig* on a réussi à lui arracher le renseignement.

prism ['prɪzm] *n* prisme *m*.

prison ['prɪzn] <> *n* prison *f* ▪ **to be in ~** être en prison ▪ **he's been in ~** il a fait de la prison ▪ **to go to ~** aller en prison, être emprisonné ▪ **to send sb to ~, to put sb in ~** envoyer *OR* mettre qqn en prison ▪ **to sentence sb to three years in ~** condamner qqn à trois ans de prison ▪ **marriage had become a ~** *fig* le mariage était devenu une prison.
<> *comp* [director, warder, cell] de prison ▪ [food, conditions] en prison, dans les prisons ▪ [system, regulations, administration] pénitentiaire, carcéral ▪ **~ sentence** peine *f* de prison.

prison camp *n* camp *m* de prisonniers.

prison colony *n* bagne *m*, colonie *f* pénitentiaire.

prisoner ['prɪznəʳ] *n* prisonnier *m*, - ère *f*, détenu *m*, - e *f* ▪ **he's a ~ in Wormwood Scrubs** il est détenu à la prison de Wormwood Scrubs ▪ **to take sb ~** faire qqn prisonnier ▪ **to hold sb ~** retenir qqn prisonnier, détenir qqn ▪ **to be taken ~** être fait prisonnier ▪ **to be held ~** être détenu ▪ **she became a ~ of her own fears** *fig* elle devint prisonnière de ses propres peurs ▶ **political ~** prisonnier *OR* détenu politique ▪ **~ of conscience** prisonnier *m* d'opinion ▪ **~ of war** prisonnier de guerre ▪ **to take no ~s** *fig* ne faire aucune concession.

prison van *n* fourgon *m* cellulaire.

prissy ['prɪsɪ] *adj inf* prude, bégueule.

pristine ['prɪsti:n] *adj* **1.** [immaculate] parfait, immaculé ▪ **in ~ condition** en parfait état **2.** [original] primitif, premier.

privacy [*UK* 'prɪvəsɪ, *US* 'praɪvəsɪ] *n* **1.** [seclusion] solitude *f* ▪ **lack of ~** manque *m* d'intimité ▪ **I have no ~ here** je ne peux jamais être seul ici ▪ **can I have some ~ for a few hours?** pouvez-vous me laisser seul quelques heures? ▮ [private life] vie *f* privée ▪ **I value my ~** je tiens à ma vie privée ▪ **an intrusion on sb's ~** une ingérence dans la vie privée de qqn ▪ **in the ~ of one's own home** dans l'intimité de son foyer ▪ **there's no ~ in this world** tout se sait dans ce bas monde **2.** [secrecy] intimité *f*, secret *m* ▪ **to get married in the strictest ~** se marier dans la plus stricte intimité.

private ['praɪvɪt] <> *adj* **1.** [not for the public] privé ▪ **~ land** terrain *m* privé ▪ **~ fishing** pêche *f* gardée ▪ **~ performance** *OR* **showing** THEAT représentation *f* privée ▪ **~ road** voie *f* privée ▪ **'private'** 'privé', 'interdit au public'
2. [independent, not run or controlled by the state] privé ▪ **they operate a ~ pension scheme** ils ont leur propre caisse de retraite
3. [personal] privé, personnel ▪ **don't interfere in my ~ affairs** *OR* **business** ne vous mêlez pas de mes affaires personnelles ▪ **~ agreement** accord *m* à l'amiable ▪ **I thought we had a ~ agreement about it** je croyais que nous avions réglé ce problème entre nous ▪ **it's my ~ opinion** c'est mon opinion personnelle ▪ **it's a ~ joke** c'est une blague que vous ne pouvez pas comprendre ▪ **my ~ address** mon adresse personnelle, mon domicile ▪ **she lives in her own ~ fantasy world** elle vit dans un monde imaginaire bien à elle
4. [confidential] privé, confidentiel, personnel ▪ **a ~ conversation** une conversation privée *OR* à caractère privé ▪ **we had a ~ meeting** nous nous sommes vus en privé ▪ **keep it ~** gardez-le pour vous ▪ **can I tell him? – no, it's ~** je peux le lui dire? – non c'est personnel ▪ **'private'** [on envelope] 'personnel' ▶ **~ hearing** LAW audience *f* à huis clos
5. [individual - bank account] personnel ; [- bathroom, lessons, tuition] particulier ▪ **~ pupil** élève *mf (à qui l'on donne des cours particuliers)* ▪ **~ teacher** précepteur *m*, - trice *f* ▪ **this is a ~ house** c'est une maison particulière *OR* qui appartient à des particuliers ▪ **in my ~ capacity** à titre personnel ▪ **for your ~ use** pour votre usage personnel ▪ **for your ~ information** à titre confidentiel ▶ **~ car** voiture *f* personnelle
6. [quiet, intimate] intime, privé ▪ **he's a very ~ person** c'est quelqu'un de très réservé ▪ **they want a ~ wedding** ils veulent se marier dans l'intimité ▪ **it was a ~ funeral** les obsèques ont eu lieu dans la plus stricte intimité ▪ **do you have a ~ room where we can talk?** avez-vous une pièce où l'on puisse parler tranquillement? ▶ **~ bar** *salon dans un pub*
7. [ordinary] : **a ~ citizen** un (simple) citoyen, un particulier ▪ **~ soldier** (simple) soldat *m*.
<> *n* MIL (simple) soldat *m*, soldat *m* de deuxième classe ▪ **it belongs to Private Hopkins** ça appartient au soldat Hopkins.
◆ **privates** *npl inf euph* parties *fpl (génitales)*.
◆ **in private** *adv phr* [confidentially] en privé, en confidence ▪ [in private life] en privé, dans la vie privée ▪ [personally] en privé, personnellement.

private company *n* entreprise *f OR* société *f* privée.

private detective *n* détective *m* privé.

private enterprise *n* libre entreprise *f*.

privateer [,praɪvə'tɪəʳ] *n* corsaire *m*.

private eye *n inf* privé *m* ▪ **Private Eye** PRESS *magazine satirique britannique*.

private hotel *n* ≃ pension *f* de famille.

private income *n* rentes *fpl* ▪ **to live on** *OR* **off a ~** vivre de ses rentes.

private investigator = **private detective**.

private life *n* vie *f* privée ■ **in (his) ~** dans sa vie privée, en privé.

privately ['praɪvɪtlɪ] *adv* **1.** [not publicly] : **a ~ owned company** une entreprise privée ■ **she sold her house ~** elle a vendu sa maison de particulier à particulier ■ **they were married ~** leur mariage a eu lieu dans l'intimité ■ **to be ~ educated** [at school] faire ses études dans une école privée ; [with tutor] avoir un précepteur ■ **the jury's deliberations took place ~** les délibérations du jury se sont déroulées à huis clos **2.** [personally] dans mon/son *etc* for intérieur, en moi-même/soi-même *etc* ■ **~, he didn't agree** dans son fort intérieur *OR* intérieurement, il n'était pas d'accord | [secretly] secrètement ■ **~, he was plotting to oust his rival** il complotait secrètement *OR* en secret d'évincer son rival **3.** [confidentially] en privé ■ **she informed me ~ that...** elle m'a informé en toute confidence que... ■ **we met ~** nous avons eu une entrevue privée ■ **can I see you ~?** puis-je vous voir en privé *OR* en tête-à-tête? **4.** [as a private individual] à titre personnel.

private means *npl* rentes *fpl*, fortune *f* personnelle ■ **a man of ~** un rentier.

private member's bill *n UK* proposition *f* de loi.

private parts *inf* = **privates** *(informal)*.

private patient *n patient d'un médecin dont les consultations ne sont pas prises en charge par les services de santé.*

private practice *n* médecine *f* privée *OR* non conventionnée ■ **she's in ~** elle a un cabinet (médical) privé.

private property *n* propriété *f* privée.

private school *n* ≃ école *f* libre.

private secretary *n* **1.** COMM secrétaire *m* particulier, secrétaire *f* particulière **2.** *UK* POL *haut fonctionnaire dont le rôle est d'assister un ministre.*

private sector *n* : **the ~** le secteur privé.
◆ **private-sector** *comp* [business, pay, bosses] privé.

private view *n* ART vernissage *m*.

privation [praɪ'veɪʃn] *n* privation *f*.

privative ['prɪvətɪv] ◇ *adj* privatif.
◇ *n* privatif *m*.

privatization [ˌpraɪvɪtaɪ'zeɪʃn] *n* privatisation *f*.

privatize, ise ['praɪvɪtaɪz] *vt* privatiser.

privet ['prɪvɪt] *n* troène *m* ■ **~ hedge** haie *f* de troènes.

privilege ['prɪvɪlɪdʒ] ◇ *n* **1.** [right, advantage] privilège *m* ■ **to grant sb the ~ of doing sthg** accorder à qqn le privilège de faire qqch ■ *(U)* [unfair advantage] : **a struggle against ~** une lutte contre les privilèges **2.** [honour] honneur *m* ■ **it was a ~ to do business with you** ce fut un honneur de travailler avec vous ■ **I had the ~ of attending his wedding** j'ai eu le bonheur *OR* la chance d'assister à son mariage **3.** POL : **parliamentary ~** immunité *f* parlementaire.
◇ *vt* privilégier ■ **I was ~d to meet him after the war** j'ai eu le privilège *OR* la chance de le rencontrer après la guerre.

privileged ['prɪvɪlɪdʒd] ◇ *adj* **1.** [person] privilégié ■ **only a ~ few were invited** seuls quelques privilégiés ont été invités ■ **the ~ few** la minorité privilégiée **2.** LAW [document, information] laissé à la discrétion du témoin ■ **such information is ~** le témoin n'est pas obligé de divulguer une telle information.
◇ *npl* : **the ~** les privilégiés *mpl*.

privy ['prɪvɪ] (*pl* **privies**) ◇ *adj* **1.** *fml* [informed] : **to be ~ to sthg** *fml* être instruit de qqch, être au courant de qqch **2.** *arch* [secret] secret, - ète *f*, caché.
◇ *n arch & hum* [toilet] lieux *mpl* d'aisances.

Privy Council *n* : **the ~** *le Conseil privé du souverain en Grande-Bretagne.*

PRIVY COUNCIL

Présidé par le souverain, le *Privy Council* compte environ 400 membres. En font partie tous les ministres du gouvernement ainsi que d'autres hautes personnalités de la politique. Théoriquement, il peut assumer les pouvoirs du gouvernement en cas de crise nationale, mais en pratique ses fonctions sont purement honorifiques. Les membres du Privy Council ont droit à l'appellation ***Right Honourable*** (***Rt Hon***) devant leur nom.

Privy Councillor *n membre du Conseil privé.*

Privy Purse *n* cassette *f* royale.

Privy Seal *n* : **the ~** le Petit Sceau.

prize [praɪz] ◇ *n* **1.** [for merit] prix *m* ■ **to award a ~ to sb** décerner un prix à qqn ■ **to win (the) first ~ in a contest** remporter le premier prix d'un concours ■ **she won the ~ for the best pupil** elle s'est vu décerner *OR* elle a reçu le prix d'excellence ■ **no ~s for guessing who won** *fig* vous n'aurez aucun mal à deviner le nom du gagnant **2.** [in game] lot *m* **3.** NAUT prise *f*.
◇ *vt* **1.** [for value] chérir, attacher une grande valeur à ■ [for quality] priser ■ **my most ~d possessions** mes biens les plus précieux ■ **original editions are highly ~d** les éditions originales sont très prisées *OR* recherchées **2.** = **prise**.
◇ *adj* **1.** [prizewinning] primé, médaillé **2.** [excellent] parfait, typique ■ **a ~ specimen of manhood** un superbe mâle | [complete] : **a ~ fool** *inf* un parfait imbécile **3.** [valuable] de valeur ■ [cherished] prisé.

prize day *n UK* SCH (jour *m* de la) distribution *f* des prix.

prize draw *n* tombola *f*, loterie *f*.

prizefight ['praɪzfaɪt] *n* combat *m* professionnel.

prizefighter ['praɪzfaɪtər] *n* boxeur *m* professionnel.

prizefighting ['praɪzfaɪtɪŋ] *n* boxe *f* professionnelle.

prize-giving *n* distribution *f OR* remise *f* des prix.

prize money *n* prix *m* en argent.

prize ring *n* ring *m (pour la boxe professionnelle)*.

prizewinner ['praɪzwɪnər] *n* [of exam, essay contest] lauréat *m*, - e *f* ■ [of game, lottery] gagnant *m*, - e *f*.

prizewinning ['praɪzwɪnɪŋ] *adj* [novel, entry] primé ■ [ticket, number, contestant] gagnant.

pro [prəʊ] (*pl* **pros**) ◇ *n inf* **1.** (*abbrev of* **professional**) [gen - SPORT] pro *mf* ■ **to turn ~** passer pro **2.** *UK* (*abbrev of* **prostitute**) professionnelle *f*.
◇ *prep* [in favour of] pour ■ **he's very ~ capital punishment** c'est un partisan convaincu de la peine capitale.
◆ **pros** *npl* : **the ~s and cons** le pour et le contre ■ **the ~s and the antis** ceux qui sont pour et ceux qui sont contre.

PRO [ˌpiːɑː'əʊ] (*abbrev of* **Public Records Office**) *n les archives nationales du RU.*

pro- *in cpds* [in favour of] pro- ■ **~American** proaméricain ■ **they were ~Stalin** ils étaient pour Staline, c'étaient des partisans de Staline.

proactive [prəʊ'æktɪv] *adj* [firm, industry, person] dynamique ■ PSYCHOL proactif.

pro-am ['prəʊ'æm] *adj* SPORT professionnel et amateur ■ **a ~ golf tournament** un open de golf.

probability [ˌprɒbə'bɪlətɪ] (*pl* **probabilities**) *n* **1.** [likelihood] probabilité *f* ■ **the ~ is that he won't come** il est probable qu'il ne viendra pas, il y a de fortes chances (pour) qu'il ne vienne pas ■ **there is a strong ~ of that happening** il y a de fortes chances que cela se produise ■ **in all ~** selon toute probabilité **2.** MATHS calcul *m* des probabilités.

probable ['prɒbəbl] ◇ *adj* **1.** [likely] probable, vraisemblable ■ **it's highly ~ that we won't arrive before 2 o'clock** il est fort probable *OR* plus que probable que nous n'arriverons pas avant 14 h **2.** [plausible] vraisemblable ■ **it doesn't sound very ~ to me** ça ne me paraît pas très vraisemblable.

◇ *n* : **he's a ~ for the team next Saturday** il y a de fortes chances pour qu'il joue dans l'équipe samedi prochain ■ **the Probables and the Possibles** SPORT la sélection A et la sélection B.

probably ['prɒbəblɪ] *adv* probablement, vraisemblablement, selon toute probabilité ■ **~ not** probablement pas ■ **will you be able to come? – ~** pourrez-vous venir? – probablement ■ **will he write to you? – very ~** il t'écrira? – c'est très probable ■ **she's ~ left already** elle est probablement déjà partie, il est probable qu'elle soit déjà partie.

probate ['prəubeɪt] ◇ *n* [authentification] homologation *f*, authentification *f*, validation *f* ■ **to grant/to take out ~ of a will** homologuer/faire homologuer un testament ■ **to value sthg for ~** évaluer *OR* expertiser qqch pour l'homologation d'un testament.
◇ *vt US* [will] homologuer, faire authentifier.

probate court *n* tribunal *m* des successions et des tutelles.

probation [prə'beɪʃn] *n* **1.** LAW probation *f*, ≃ condamnation *f* avec sursis et mise à l'épreuve ■ **to be on ~** ≃ être en sursis avec mise à l'épreuve ■ **to put sb on ~** ≃ condamner qqn avec mise à l'épreuve **2.** [trial employment] essai *m* ■ **to be on ~** être en période d'essai **3.** RELIG probation *f*.

probationary [prə'beɪʃnrɪ] *adj* **1.** [trial] d'essai ■ **~ period** période *f* d'essai ■ **~ teacher** professeur *m* stagiaire ■ **~ year** *UK* SCH année *f* probatoire **2.** LAW de probation **3.** RELIG de probation, de noviciat.

probationer [prə'beɪʃnər] *n* **1.** [employee] employé *m*, -e *f* à l'essai *OR* en période d'essai ■ *UK* [teacher] (professeur *m*) stagiaire *mf* ■ [trainee nurse] élève *m* infirmier, élève *f* infirmière **2.** LAW probationnaire *mf* **3.** RELIG novice *mf*.

probation officer *n* ≃ agent *m* de probation.

probe [prəub] ◇ *n* **1.** [investigation] enquête *f*, investigation *f* ■ **there has been a newspaper ~ into corruption** la presse a fait une enquête sur la corruption **2.** [question] question *f*, interrogation *f* **3.** ASTRONAUT, ELECTRON & MED sonde *f* ■ ZOOL trompe *f*.
◇ *vt* **1.** [investigate] enquêter sur ■ **police are probing the company's accounts** la police épluche les comptes *OR* examine la comptabilité de la société **2.** [examine, sound out - person, motive, reasons] sonder ■ **to ~ sb about sthg** sonder qqn sur qqch **3.** [explore, poke around in] explorer, fouiller, sonder ■ MED sonder.
◇ *vi* **1.** [investigate] enquêter, faire une enquête ■ **the police are probing for clues** les policiers recherchent des indices ■ **to ~ into sthg** enquêter sur qqch ■ **if you ~ into his past, you'll have some surprises** si vous fouillez dans son passé, vous aurez des surprises **2.** MED faire un sondage.

probing ['prəubɪŋ] ◇ *adj* [look] inquisiteur, perçant ■ [mind] pénétrant, clairvoyant ■ [remark, question] perspicace ■ **after hours of ~ questioning** après des heures d'un interrogatoire très poussé.
◇ *n (U)* **1.** [investigation] enquête *f*, investigations *fpl* ■ [questioning] questions *fpl*, interrogatoire *m* **2.** MED sondage *m*.

probity ['prəubətɪ] *n* probité *f*.

problem ['prɒbləm] ◇ *n* problème *m* ■ **to cause ~s for sb** causer des ennuis *OR* poser des problèmes à qqn ■ **he's got ~s with the police** il a des problèmes *OR* ennuis avec la police ■ **the oldest one is a real ~ to me** l'aîné me pose de réels problèmes ■ **that's going to be a bit of a ~** ça va poser un petit problème ■ **thanks for doing that for me – no ~!** *inf* merci d'avoir fait ça pour moi – pas de problème! ■ **I don't see what the ~ is** je ne vois pas où est le problème ■ **it's a ~ knowing** *OR* **to know what to get her for Christmas** c'est difficile de savoir quoi lui offrir pour Noël ■ **what's your ~?** *inf* c'est quoi ton problème?, qu'est-ce qui ne va pas? ■ **she has a bit of a weight ~** elle a des problèmes de poids.
◇ *comp* [child, family, hair] à problèmes ■ [play] à thèse ■ **it's a real ~ case** c'est un cas qui pose de réels problèmes.

problematic(al) [,prɒblə'mætɪk(l)] *adj* problématique, incertain.

problem page *n UK* courrier *m* du cœur.

problem-solving [-,sɒlvɪŋ] *n* résolution *f* de problèmes.

proboscis [prəu'bɒsɪs] (*pl* **proboscises** [-sɪsi:z] *OR pl* **proboscides**) [-sɪdi:z] *n* ZOOL trompe *f* ■ *hum* [nose] appendice *m*.

procedural [prə'si:dʒərəl] *adj* de procédure, procédural.

procedure [prə'si:dʒər] *n* **1.** procédure *f* ■ **what's the correct ~?** comment doit-on procéder?, quelle est la marche à suivre? ◗ **criminal/civil (law) ~** LAW procédure *f* pénale/civile **2.** COMPUT procédure *f*, sous-programme *m*.

proceed [prə'si:d] *vi* **1.** [continue] continuer, poursuivre ■ **before ~ing any further with our investigations...** avant de poursuivre nos investigations..., avant de pousser plus avant nos investigations... ■ **before I ~** avant d'aller plus loin
2. [happen] se passer, se dérouler
3. [move on] passer ■ **let's ~ to item 32** passons à la question 32 ■ **to ~ to do sthg** [start] se mettre à faire qqch ; [do next] passer à qqch ■ **he ~ed to tear up my report** puis, il a déchiré mon rapport
4. [act] procéder, agir ■ **I'm not sure how to ~** je ne vois pas très bien comment faire ■ **~ with caution** agissez avec prudence
5. [go, travel] avancer, aller ■ [car] avancer, rouler ■ **they are ~ing towards Calais** ils se dirigent vers Calais ■ **I then ~ed to the post office** je me suis ensuite rendu au bureau de poste ■ **I was ~ing along Henley Road in a westerly direction** je longeais Henley Road en me dirigeant vers l'ouest
6. LAW : **to ~ with charges against sb** poursuivre qqn en justice, intenter un procès contre qqn
7. [originate] : **to ~ from** provenir de, découler de.
◆ **proceed against** *vt insep* LAW engager des poursuites contre.

proceedings [prə'si:dɪŋz] *npl* **1.** [happening, event] événement *m* ■ **the ~ passed off peacefully** tout s'est déroulé sans incident ■ **we watched the ~ on television** nous avons regardé la retransmission télévisée de la cérémonie **2.** [meeting] réunion *f*, séance *f* **3.** [records - of meeting] compte rendu *m*, procès-verbal *m* ; [- of learned society] actes *mpl* **4.** LAW [legal action] procès *m*, poursuites *fpl* ■ **to take** *OR* **to institute (legal) ~ against sb** intenter une action (en justice) contre qqn, engager des poursuites contre qqn ■ [legal process] procédure *f* ■ **legal ~ are very slow in this country** la procédure judiciaire est très lente dans ce pays.

proceeds ['prəusi:dz] *npl* recette *f*, somme *f* recueillie ■ **all ~ will go to charity** tout l'argent recueilli sera versé aux œuvres de charité.

process ◇ *n* ['prəuses] **1.** [series of events, operation] processus *m* ■ **the ageing ~** le processus de vieillissement ■ **the peace ~** le processus de paix ■ **the whole ~ only takes a few minutes** tout le processus *OR* toute l'opération ne prend que quelques minutes ■ **teaching him French is a slow ~** il en faut du temps pour lui apprendre le français **2.** [method] procédé *m*, méthode *f* ■ **a new manufacturing ~** un nouveau procédé de fabrication ■ **by a ~ of elimination** par élimination ■ **by a ~ of trial and error** en procédant par tâtonnements ■ **to be in ~** être en cours **3.** LAW [legal action] procès *m*, action *f* en justice ■ [writ, summons] citation *f* (en justice), assignation *f* (en justice) **4.** BIOL [outgrowth] processus *m*.
◇ *vt* ['prəuses] **1.** [transform - raw materials] traiter, transformer ; [- cheese, meat, milk] traiter ; [- nuclear waste] retraiter ■ COMPUT [- data] traiter ■ PHOT développer **2.** ADMIN & COMM [deal with - order, information, cheque] traiter ■ **my insurance claim is still being ~ed** ma déclaration de sinistre est toujours en cours de règlement.
◇ *vi* [prə'ses] [march] défiler ■ RELIG défiler en procession.
◆ **in the process** *adv phr* : **I managed to rescue the cat but I twisted my ankle in the ~** j'ai réussi à sauver le chat, mais je me suis tordu la cheville (en le faisant).
◆ **in the process of** *prep phr* en train de ■ **to be in the ~ of doing sthg** être en train de faire qqch ■ **it's in the ~ of being discussed/of being carried out** c'est en cours de discussion/en voie d'exécution ■ **they're in the ~ of getting a divorce** ils sont en instance de divorce.

processed ['prəʊsest] *adj* [food] traité, industriel *pej* ■ **~ cheese** [for spreading] fromage *m* à tartiner ; [in slices] fromage *m* en tranches.

process engineer *n* ingénieur *m* en procédés.

process engineering *n* ingénierie *f* de procédés.

processing ['prəʊsesɪŋ] *n* [gen - COMPUT] traitement *m* ■ **~ plant** [for sewage, nuclear waste etc] usine *f* de traitement.

procession [prə'seʃn] *n* **1.** [ceremony] procession *f*, cortège *m* ■ RELIG procession *f* **2.** [demonstration] défilé *m*, cortège *m* **3.** [continous line] procession *f*, défilé *m* ■ **the soldiers marched in ~ through the town** les soldats ont défilé à travers la ville.

processional [prə'seʃənl] <> *adj* processionnel.
<> *n* RELIG [hymn] hymne *m* processionnel ■ [book] processional *m*.

processor ['prəʊsesəʳ] *n* **1.** COMPUT processeur *m* **2.** CULIN robot *m* ménager.

process printing *n* impression *f* en couleurs.

pro-choice ['prəʊ'tʃɔɪs] *adj* pour l'avortement et l'euthanasie.

proclaim [prə'kleɪm] *vt* **1.** [declare] proclamer, déclarer ■ **to ~ independence** proclamer l'indépendance ■ **many ~ed that he was mad** *OR* **~ed him to be mad** beaucoup de gens ont déclaré qu'il était fou ■ **he ~ed himself emperor** il s'est proclamé empereur ■ **she ~ed her innocence** elle a clamé son innocence **2.** [reveal] révéler, manifester, trahir ■ **his behaviour ~ed his nervousness** son comportement trahissait sa nervosité.

proclamation [,prɒklə'meɪʃn] *n* proclamation *f*, déclaration *f* ■ **to issue** *OR* **to make a ~** faire une proclamation.

proclivity [prə'klɪvətɪ] (*pl* **proclivities**) *n* *fml* propension *f*, inclination *f*, tendance *f* ■ **to have a ~ to** *OR* **towards sthg** avoir une propension à qqch.

proconsul [,prəʊ'kɒnsəl] *n* proconsul *m*.

procrastinate [prə'kræstɪneɪt] *vi* tergiverser, atermoyer, temporiser ■ **if you hadn't ~d** [wasted time] si vous n'aviez pas fait traîner les choses ; [hesitated] si vous n'aviez pas hésité.

procrastination [prə,kræstɪ'neɪʃn] *n* procrastination *f* *lit*, tendance *f* à tout remettre au lendemain ■ **~ is the thief of time** *prov* il ne faut jamais remettre au lendemain ce que l'on peut faire le jour même *prov*.

procreate ['prəʊkrɪeɪt] *fml* <> *vi* procréer.
<> *vt* engendrer.

procreation [,prəʊkrɪ'eɪʃn] *n* *fml* procréation *f*.

Procrustean [prəʊ'krʌstɪən] *adj* de Procruste.

proctor ['prɒktəʳ] <> *n* **1.** LAW [agent] ≃ fondé *m* de pouvoir **2.** UNIV [in UK] représentant *m*, - e *f* du conseil de discipline ■ [in US - invigilator] surveillant *m*, - e *f* (à un examen) **3.** RELIG procureur *m*.
<> *vi* & *vt* *US* surveiller.

procurator ['prɒkjʊreɪtəʳ] *n* **1.** LAW fondé *m* de pouvoir **2.** *Scotland* = **procurator fiscal** **3.** ANTIQ procurateur *m*.

procurator fiscal *n en Écosse, magistrat qui fait office de procureur et qui remplit les fonctions du "coroner" en Angleterre.*

procure [prə'kjʊəʳ] <> *vt* **1.** *fml* [obtain] procurer, obtenir ■ [buy] (se) procurer, acheter ■ **to ~ sthg (for o.s.)** se procurer qqch ■ **to ~ sthg for sb** procurer qqch à qqn **2.** LAW [prostitutes] procurer, prostituer **3.** *arch* [cause] procurer, causer, provoquer.
<> *vi* LAW faire du proxénétisme.

procurement [prə'kjʊəmənt] *n* **1.** [acquisition] obtention *f*, acquisition *f* **2.** COMM [buying] achat *m*, acquisition *f* ■ MIL acquisition *f* de matériel.

procurer [prə'kjʊərəʳ] *n* LAW proxénète *m*.

procuress [prə'kjʊərɪs] *n* LAW proxénète *f*.

procuring [prə'kjʊərɪŋ] *n* **1.** [acquisition] acquisition *f*, obtention *f* **2.** LAW proxénétisme *m*.

prod [prɒd] (*pret & pp* **prodded**, *cont* **prodding**) <> *n* **1.** [with finger] petit coup *m* avec le doigt ■ [with stick] petit coup *m* de bâton ■ **he gave the sausages a ~ with his fork** il a piqué les saucisses avec sa fourchette **2.** *fig* [urging] : **he needs a ~ to make him work** il faut le pousser pour qu'il travaille **3.** [stick] bâton *m*, pique *f*.
<> *vt* **1.** [with finger] donner un coup avec le doigt à, pousser du doigt ■ [with stick] pousser avec la pointe d'un bâton ■ **he prodded me in the back with his pen** il m'a donné un (petit) coup dans le dos avec son stylo **2.** *fig* [urge] pousser, inciter ■ **to ~ sb into doing sthg** pousser *OR* inciter qqn à faire qqch.

prodigal ['prɒdɪgl] <> *adj* prodigue ■ **the ~ son** BIBLE le fils prodigue.
<> *n* prodigue *mf*.

prodigious [prə'dɪdʒəs] *adj* prodigieux.

prodigy ['prɒdɪdʒɪ] (*pl* **prodigies**) *n* **1.** [person] prodige *m* ■ **child** *OR* **infant ~** enfant *mf* prodige **2.** [marvel] prodige *m*.

produce <> *vt* [prə'dju:s] **1.** [manufacture, make] produire, fabriquer ■ **Denmark ~s dairy products** le Danemark est un pays producteur de produits laitiers ■ **we have ~d three new models this year** nous avons sorti trois nouveaux modèles cette année **2.** [yield - minerals, crops] produire ; [- interest, profit] rapporter ■ **halogen lamps ~ a lot of light** les lampes halogènes donnent beaucoup de lumière ■ **my investments ~ a fairly good return** mes investissements sont d'un assez bon rapport **3.** [bring out - book, record] produire, sortir ■ [publish] publier, éditer ■ **he hasn't ~d a new painting for over a year now** cela fait maintenant plus d'un an qu'il n'a rien peint ■ **the publishers ~d a special edition** les éditeurs ont publié *OR* sorti une édition spéciale **4.** BIOL [give birth to - subj: woman] donner naissance à ; [- subj: animal] produire, donner naissance à ■ [secrete - saliva, sweat etc] secréter **5.** [bring about - situation, problem] causer, provoquer, créer ; [- illness, death] causer, provoquer ; [- anger, pleasure, reaction] susciter, provoquer ; [- effect] provoquer, produire ■ **the team has ~d some good results/some surprises this season** l'équipe a obtenu quelques bons résultats/provoqué quelques surprises cette saison **6.** [present, show - evidence, documents] présenter, produire ■ **he ~d a £5 note from his pocket** il a sorti un billet de 5 livres de sa poche ■ **the defendant was unable to ~ any proof** l'accusé n'a pu fournir *OR* apporter aucune preuve ■ **to ~ a witness** faire comparaître un témoin ■ **they ~d some excellent arguments** ils ont avancé d'excellents arguments ■ **she is continually producing new ideas** elle ne cesse d'avoir des idées nouvelles ■ **he finally managed to ~ the money** il a enfin réussi à trouver l'argent *OR* réunir la somme nécessaire ■ **she can ~ a meal from nothing** il lui suffit d'un rien pour cuisiner un bon repas **7.** [film] produire ■ [play - organize, finance] produire ; [- direct] réaliser, mettre en scène ■ [radio or TV programme - organize, finance] produire ; [- direct] réaliser, mettre en ondes **8.** GEOM [line] prolonger, continuer **9.** CHEM, ELEC & PHYS [reaction, spark] produire ■ [discharge] produire, provoquer ■ [vacuum] faire, créer.
<> *vi* [prə'dju:s] **1.** [yield - factory, mine] produire, rendre **2.** THEAT assurer la mise en scène ■ CIN [financer] assurer la production ■ [director] assurer la réalisation.
<> *n* ['prɒdju:s] *(U)* produits *mpl* (alimentaires) ■ **agricultural/dairy ~** produits agricoles/laitiers ■ **farm ~** produits agricoles *OR* de la ferme ■ **home ~** produits du pays ■ **~ of Spain** produit en Espagne.

producer [prə'dju:səʳ] *n* **1.** AGRIC & INDUST producteur *m*, - trice *f* **2.** [of film] producteur *m*, - trice *f* ■ [of play, of TV or radio programme - organizer, financer] producteur *m*, - trice *f* ; [- director] réalisateur *m*, - trice *f*.

-producing [prə,dju:sɪŋ] *in cpds* producteur de ■ **oil~** producteur de pétrole.

product ['prɒdʌkt] *n* **1.** AGRIC, CHEM & INDUST produit *m* ■ **finished ~** INDUST produit fini ; [piece of work] résultat *m* final ■ **food ~s** produits alimentaires, denrées *fpl* alimentaires ■ **~ of India** produit d'Inde **2.** [result] produit *m*, résultat *m* ■ **this book is the ~ of many years' hard work** ce livre est le fruit de longues années d'un travail acharné ■ **that's the ~ of a lively imagination** c'est le produit d'une imagination débordante **3.** MATHS produit *m*.

production [prəˈdʌkʃn] *n* **1.** [process of producing - of goods] production *f*, fabrication *f* ; [- of crops, electricity, heat] production *f* ■ **the workers have halted ~** les travailleurs ont arrêté la production ■ **the model is now in ~** le modèle est en cours de production ■ **this model went into/out of ~ in 1989** on a commencé la fabrication de ce modèle/ce modèle a été retiré de la production en 1989 **2.** [amount produced] production *f* ■ **wine ~ has increased** la production viticole a augmenté **3.** [of film] production *f* ■ [of play, of radio or TV programme - organization, financing] production *f* ; [- artistic direction] réalisation *f*, mise *f* en scène **4.** [show, work of art - CIN] & THEAT spectacle *m* ■ RADIO & TV production *f* ■ ART & LIT œuvre *f* ■ **there's no need to make such a (big) ~ out of it!** *inf fig* il n'y a pas de quoi en faire un plat *OR* toute une histoire! **5.** [presentation - of document, passport, ticket] présentation *f*.

production line *n* chaîne *f* de fabrication ■ **to work on the ~** travailler à la chaîne.

production manager *n* directeur *m*, - trice *f* de la production.

production platform *n* plate-forme *f* de production.

productive [prəˈdʌktɪv] *adj* **1.** [gen - ECON] productif ■ **the ~ forces** les forces productives *OR* de production **2.** [fertile - land] fertile ; [- imagination] fertile, fécond ■ [prolific - writer, artist] prolifique **3.** [useful] fructueux, utile **4.** [of situation, feeling etc] : **to be ~ of** engendrer, créer **5.** LING productif.

productively [prəˈdʌktɪvlɪ] *adv* **1.** ECON d'une manière productive **2.** [usefully] utilement ■ [fruitfully] fructueusement, profitablement, avec profit.

productivity [ˌprɒdʌkˈtɪvətɪ] ◇ *n* productivité *f*, rendement *m*.
◇ *comp* [deal, fall, level] de productivité ■ **~ bonus** prime *f* de rendement *OR* de productivité.

proem [ˈprəʊem] *n* préface *f*.

prof [prɒf] (*abbrev of* **professor**) *n inf* prof *mf*.

Prof. (*written abbrev of* **professor**) Pr.

profane [prəˈfeɪn] ◇ *adj* **1.** [irreligious] sacrilège, impie *lit dated* **2.** [secular] profane, laïque **3.** [uninitiated] profane **4.** [vulgar - language] vulgaire, grossier.
◇ *vt* profaner.

profanity [prəˈfænətɪ] (*pl* **profanities**) *n* **1.** [profane nature - of text] nature *f* *OR* caractère *m* profane ; [- of action] impiété *f* **2.** [oath] grossièreté *f*, juron *m* ■ **to utter profanities** proférer des grossièretés.

profess [prəˈfes] ◇ *vt* **1.** [declare] professer *lit*, déclarer, proclamer ■ **to ~ hatred for** *OR* **of sb** professer sa haine pour qqn ■ **to ~ ignorance** avouer son ignorance **2.** [claim] prétendre, déclarer ■ **she ~es to speak French** elle prétend parler le français **3.** [profession] exercer ■ **to ~ medicine** exercer la profession de médecin.
◇ *vi* RELIG prononcer ses vœux, faire sa profession.

professed [prəˈfest] *adj* **1.** [avowed] déclaré ■ **that is my ~ aim** c'est mon but avoué **2.** [alleged] supposé, prétendu ■ **she's a ~ expert in the field** elle se dit experte en la matière **3.** RELIG profès.

professedly [prəˈfesɪdlɪ] *adv* **1.** [avowedly] : **she has ~ killed three people** d'après elle *OR* d'après ses dires, elle aurait tué trois personnes **2.** [allegedly] soi-disant, prétendument ■ **he came here ~ to help me** à l'en croire, il est venu pour m'aider.

profession [prəˈfeʃn] *n* **1.** [occupation] profession *f* ■ **she's a lawyer by ~** elle exerce la profession d'avocat, elle est avocate (de profession) ■ **I'm not an artist by ~** je ne suis pas un artiste professionnel ■ **the (liberal) ~s** les professions libérales ■ **learned ~** profession intellectuelle **2.** [body] (membres *mpl* d'une) profession *f*, corps *m* ■ **the teaching ~** le corps enseignant, les enseignants *mpl* **3.** [declaration] profession *f*, déclaration *f* ■ **~ of faith** profession de foi.

professional [prəˈfeʃənl] ◇ *adj* **1.** [relating to a profession] professionnel ■ **the surgeon demonstrated his great ~ skill** le chirurgien a montré ses grandes compétences professionnelles ■ **a lawyer is a ~ man** un avocat exerce une profession libérale ■ **a club for ~ people** un club réservé aux membres des professions libérales ■ **it would be against ~ etiquette to tell you** vous le dire serait contraire aux usages *OR* à la déontologie de la profession ■ **may I give you some ~ advice?** puis-je vous donner l'avis d'un professionnel? ■ **to take** *OR* **to get ~ advice** [gen] consulter un professionnel ; [from doctor/lawyer] consulter un médecin/un avocat **2.** [as career, full-time] professionnel, de profession ■ **he's a ~ painter** il vit de sa peinture ■ **a ~ soldier/diplomat** un militaire/diplomate de carrière ■ **a ~ army** une armée de métier ■ **he's a ~ drunk** *fig* il passe son temps à boire ■ SPORT professionnel ■ **to go** *OR* **to turn ~** passer professionnel **3.** [in quality, attitude] professionnel ■ **a ~ piece of work** un travail de professionnel ■ **she is very ~ in her approach to the problem** elle aborde le problème de façon très professionnelle ■ **he works in a very ~ manner** il travaille en professionnel.
◇ *n* professionnel *m*, - elle *f*.

professional foul *n* FTBL faute *f* délibérée.

professionalism [prəˈfeʃnəlɪzm] *n* professionnalisme *m*.

professionally [prəˈfeʃnəlɪ] *adv* **1.** [as profession] professionnellement ■ **he writes ~** il vit de sa plume ■ **she's a ~ qualified doctor** elle est médecin diplômé ■ **he plays ~** SPORT c'est un joueur professionnel ■ **I've only ever met her ~** mes seuls rapports avec elle ont été d'ordre professionnel *OR* ont été des rapports de travail ■ **we had the house painted ~** on a fait peindre la maison par un professionnel *OR* un homme de métier **2.** [skilfully, conscientiously] professionnellement, de manière professionnelle ■ **this work has been done very ~** c'est le travail d'un professionnel.

professor [prəˈfesəʳ] *n* UNIV [in UK - head of department] titulaire *mf* d'une chaire, professeur *m* ■ [in US - lecturer] enseignant *m*, - e *f* (de faculté) *OR* d'université ■ **~ of sociology** *UK* titulaire de la chaire de sociologie, professeur responsable du département de sociologie ; *US* professeur de sociologie ■ **Professor Colin Appleton** le professeur Colin Appleton ■ **Dear Professor Appleton** Monsieur le Professeur ; [less formally] (Cher) Monsieur.

professorial [ˌprɒfɪˈsɔːrɪəl] *adj* professoral.

professorship [prəˈfesəʃɪp] *n* chaire *f* ■ **she has a ~ in French at Durham** elle occupe la chaire *OR* est titulaire de la chaire de français à l'université de Durham.

proffer [ˈprɒfəʳ] *vt fml* **1.** [offer, present - drink, present] offrir, tendre ; [- resignation] présenter, offrir, remettre ; [- advice] donner ; [- excuses] présenter, offrir ■ **to ~ one's hand to sb** tendre la main à qqn **2.** [put forward - idea, opinion] émettre ; [- remark, suggestion] émettre, faire.

proficiency [prəˈfɪʃənsɪ] *n* compétence *f*, maîtrise *f* ■ **she attained a high degree of ~ in French** elle a acquis une grande maîtrise du français.

proficient [prəˈfɪʃənt] *adj* [worker] compétent, expérimenté ■ [driver] expérimenté, chevronné ■ **she's a very ~ pianist** c'est une excellente pianiste ■ **I used to be quite ~ in French** j'avais un assez bon niveau en français.

proficiently [prəˈfɪʃəntlɪ] *adv* de façon (très) compétente, avec (beaucoup de) maîtrise ■ **she speaks French ~** elle parle couramment le français.

profile [ˈprəʊfaɪl] ◇ *n* **1.** ART & ARCHIT profil *m* ■ **to look at/to draw sb in ~** regarder/dessiner qqn de profil **2.** [description - of person] profil *m*, portrait *m* **3.** [of candidate, employee] profil *m* ■ [level of prominence] : **to keep a high ~** occuper le devant de la scène, faire parler de soi ■ **to keep a low ~** adopter un profil bas, se faire tout petit **4.** [graph] profil *m* **5.** GEOG & GEOL profil *m* ■ **a soil ~** le profil d'un sol.
◇ *vt* **1.** [show in profile] profiler ■ **his shadow was ~d against the wall** son ombre se profilait *OR* se découpait sur le mur **2.** [write profile of - person] établir le profil de, brosser le portrait de.

profit ['prɒfɪt] <> *n* **1.** [financial gain] profit *m*, bénéfice *m* ▪ **to make a ~ out of sthg** faire un bénéfice sur qqch ▪ **we made a £200 ~ on the sale** nous avons réalisé un bénéfice de 200 livres sur cette vente ▪ **to be in ~** être bénéficiaire ▪ **to move into ~** devenir bénéficiaire ▪ **to make** *OR* **to turn out a ~** réaliser un bénéfice ▪ **to show a ~** rapporter (un bénéfice *OR* des bénéfices) ▪ **the fair didn't show much of a ~** la foire n'a pas beaucoup rapporté (de bénéfices) ▪ **to sell sthg at a ~** vendre qqch à profit, faire un profit sur la vente de qqch ▶ **~ and loss account** compte *m* de pertes et profits **2.** *fml* [advantage] profit *m*, avantage *m* ▪ **to turn sthg to one's ~, to gain ~ from sthg** tirer profit *OR* avantage de qqch ▪ **to do sthg for ~** faire qqch dans un but intéressé.
<> *vt fml* & *arch* profiter à, bénéficier à.
<> *vi* profiter, tirer un profit *OR* avantage ▪ **to ~ from** *OR* **by sthg** tirer profit *OR* avantage de qqch, profiter de qqch.

profitability [,prɒfɪtə'bɪlətɪ] *n* FIN rentabilité *f* ▪ [of ideas, action] caractère *m* profitable *OR* fructueux.

profitable ['prɒfɪtəbl] *adj* **1.** [lucrative] rentable, lucratif ▪ **it wouldn't be very ~ for me to sell** pour moi il ne serait pas très rentable de vendre, cela ne me rapporterait pas grand-chose de vendre **2.** [beneficial] profitable, fructueux ▪ **we had a very ~ discussion** nous avons eu une discussion très fructueuse.

profitably ['prɒfɪtəblɪ] *adv* **1.** FIN avec profit, d'une manière rentable ▪ **we sold it very ~** on l'a vendu en faisant un bénéfice confortable **2.** [usefully] utilement, avec profit, profitablement ▪ **use your time ~** ne gaspillez pas votre temps.

profit centre *n* centre *m* de profit.

profiteer [,prɒfɪ'tɪə^r] <> *n* profiteur *m*, - euse *f*.
<> *vi* faire des bénéfices exorbitants.

profiteering [,prɒfɪ'tɪərɪŋ] *n* : **they were accused of ~** on les a accusés de faire des bénéfices excessifs.

profiterole [prɒ'fɪtərəʊl] *n* profiterole *f*.

profitless ['prɒfɪtlɪs] *adj* [gen - FIN] sans profit ▪ **we spent a ~ afternoon** nous avons perdu *OR* gaspillé notre après-midi.

profit-making *adj* **1.** [aiming to make profit] à but lucratif ▪ **non ~ organization** association *f* à but non lucratif **2.** [profitable] rentable.

profit margin *n* marge *f* bénéficiaire.

profit motive *n* recherche *f* du profit, appât *m* du gain *pej*.

profit-related pay *n* salaire *m* indexé sur les résultats.

profit-sharing *n* participation *f OR* intéressement *m* aux bénéfices ▪ **we have a ~ agreement/scheme** nous avons un accord/un système de participation (aux bénéfices).

profit squeeze *n* compression *f* des bénéfices.

profligacy ['prɒflɪgəsɪ] *n fml* **1.** [dissoluteness] débauche *f*, licence *f* **2.** [extravagance] (extrême) prodigalité *f*.

profligate ['prɒflɪgɪt] *fml* <> *adj* **1.** [dissolute] débauché, dévergondé **2.** [extravagant] (très) prodigue, dépensier ▪ [wasteful] (très) gaspilleur.
<> *n* **1.** [dissolute person] débauché *m*, - e *f*, libertin *m*, - e *f* **2.** [spendthrift] dépensier *m*, - ère *f*.

pro-form ['prəʊfɔ:m] *n* proforme *f*.

pro forma [,prəʊ'fɔ:mə] <> *adj* pro forma *(inv)*.
<> *adv* pour la forme.
<> *n* = **pro forma invoice**.

pro forma invoice *n* facture *f* pro forma.

profound [prə'faʊnd] *adj* profond.

profoundly [prə'faʊndlɪ] *adv* profondément ▪ **the ~ deaf** les sourds profonds.

profundity [prə'fʌndətɪ] (*pl* **profundities**) *n* profondeur *f*.

profuse [prə'fju:s] *adj* **1.** [abundant, copious] abondant, profus *lit* **2.** [generous - praise, apologies] prodigue, profus ▪ **to be ~ in one's compliments** se répandre en compliments ▪ **to be ~ in one's apologies** se confondre en excuses.

profusely [prə'fju:slɪ] *adv* **1.** [abundantly, copiously] abondamment, en abondance, à profusion ▪ **to sweat ~** transpirer abondamment **2.** [generously, extravagantly] : **they thanked her ~** ils la remercièrent avec effusion ▪ **she was ~ apologetic** elle s'est confondue en excuses.

profusion [prə'fju:ʒn] *n* profusion *f*, abondance *f* ▪ **in ~** à profusion, en abondance.

progenitor [prəʊ'dʒenɪtə^r] *n fml* **1.** [ancestor] ancêtre *m* **2.** [originator] auteur *m* ▪ [precursor] précurseur *m*.

progeny ['prɒdʒənɪ] *n fml* [offspring] progéniture *f* ▪ [descendants] descendants *mpl*, lignée *f*.

progesterone [prə'dʒestərəʊn] *n* progestérone *f*.

prognosis [prɒg'nəʊsɪs] (*pl* **prognoses** [-si:z]) *n fml* & MED pronostic *m*.

prognostic [prɒg'nɒstɪk] <> *n* **1.** MED [symptom] pronostic *m* **2.** *fml* [sign] présage *m* ▪ [forecast] pronostic *m*.
<> *adj* MED pronostique.

prognosticate [prɒg'nɒstɪkeɪt] *vt fml* [foretell] pronostiquer, présager, prédire ▪ [foreshadow] annoncer, présager.

prognostication [prɒg,nɒstɪ'keɪʃn] *n* pronostic *m*.

program ['prəʊgræm] (*pret* & *pp* **programmed** *OR* **programed**, *cont* **programming** *OR* **programing**) <> *n* **1.** *US* = **programme** **2.** COMPUT programme *m*.
<> *vt* **1.** *US* = **programme** **2.** COMPUT programmer.
<> *vi* COMPUT programmer.

programable *US* = **programmable**.

programer *US* = **programmer**.

programmable *UK*, **programable** *US* [prəʊ'græməbl] *adj* programmable ▪ **~ function key** touche *f* de fonction programmable.

programme *UK*, **program** *US* ['prəʊgræm] <> *n* **1.** MUS, POL & THEAT programme *m* ▪ **the ~ includes three pieces by Debussy** il y a trois morceaux de Debussy au programme ▪ **an election ~** *esp US* un programme électoral ▪ **a research ~** un programme de recherches ▪ **what's (on) the ~ for next week?** quel est l'emploi du temps prévu pour la semaine prochaine? **2.** [booklet] programme *m* ▪ [syllabus] programme *m* ▪ [timetable] emploi *m* du temps **3.** RADIO & TV [broadcast] émission *f* ▪ **there's a good ~ about** *OR* **on opera on TV tonight** il y a une bonne émission sur l'opéra à la télévision ce soir ▪ [TV station] chaîne *f* ▪ [radio station] station *f*.
<> *vt* programmer ▪ **the heating is ~d to switch itself off at night** le chauffage est programmé pour s'arrêter la nuit ▪ **his arrival wasn't ~d** son arrivée n'était pas prévue ▪ **all children are ~d to learn language** chez les enfants, la capacité d'apprentissage du langage est innée.

programmed learning ['prəʊgræmd-] *n* enseignement *m* programmé.

programme music *n* musique *f* à programme.

programme notes *npl* THEAT notes *fpl* sur le programme.

programmer *UK*, **programer** *US* ['prəʊgræmə^r] *n* COMPUT **1.** [person] programmeur *m*, - euse *f* **2.** [device] programmateur *m*.

programming ['prəʊgræmɪŋ] *n* programmation *f* ▪ **~ language** langage *m* de programmation.

progress <> *n* ['prəʊgres] *(U)* **1.** [headway] progrès *mpl* ▪ **they have made fast ~** ils ont avancé *OR* ils ont progressé rapidement ▪ **he is making ~ in English** il fait des progrès en anglais ▪ **the patient has made excellent ~** l'état du malade s'est nettement amélioré **2.** [evolution] progrès *m* ▪ **to hinder ~** entraver *OR* freiner le progrès ▪ **you can't stop ~** on ne peut arrêter le progrès **3.** [forward movement] progression *f* **4.** *arch* [journey] voyage *m*.
<> *vi* [prə'gres] **1.** [make headway - negotiations, research] progresser, avancer ; [- situation] progresser, s'améliorer ; [- patient] aller mieux ; [- student] progresser, faire des progrès ▪ **the**

talks are ~ ing well les pourparlers sont en bonne voie **2.** [move forward] avancer ▪ **to ~ towards a place/an objective** se rapprocher d'un lieu/d'un objectif.

◆ **in progress** *adj phr* : **to be in ~** être en cours ▪ **work in ~** travaux *mpl* en cours ▪ **while the exam is in ~** pendant l'examen.

progression [prəˈgreʃn] *n* **1.** [advance - of disease, army] progression *f* **2.** MATHS & MUS progression *f* **3.** [series, sequence] série *f*, suite *f*.

progressive [prəˈgresɪv] <> *adj* **1.** [forward-looking - idea, teacher, jazz] progressiste ; [- education, method] nouveau *(before vowel or silent 'h'* **nouvel***)*, nouvelle *f*, moderne ▪ **he has a very ~ outlook** sa vision des choses est très moderne **2.** [gradual - change] progressif ▪ **~ income tax** impôt *m* progressif ▪ **to do sthg in ~ steps** *OR* **stages** faire qqch par étapes successives ▪ MED [disease] progressif **3.** GRAM [aspect] progressif.

<> *n* **1.** POL progressiste *mf* **2.** GRAM forme *f* progressive, progressif *m* ▪ **in the ~** à la forme progressive.

progressively [prəˈgresɪvlɪ] *adv* **1.** POL & SCH d'une manière progressiste **2.** [gradually] progressivement, graduellement, petit à petit.

progressiveness [prəˈgresɪvnɪs] *n* **1.** [of ideas, teaching] caractère *m* progressiste **2.** [gradualness] progressivité *f*.

progress report *n* [gen] compte-rendu *m* ▪ [on work] rapport *m* sur l'avancement des travaux ▪ [on patient] bulletin *m* de santé ▪ [on pupil] bulletin *m* scolaire.

prohibit [prəˈhɪbɪt] *vt* **1.** [forbid] interdire, défendre, prohiber ▪ **to ~ sb from doing sthg** interdire *OR* défendre à qqn de faire qqch ▪ **drinking alcohol at work is ~ed** il est interdit de boire de l'alcool sur le lieu de travail ▪ **smoking is strictly ~ed** il est formellement interdit de fumer ▪ **'parking ~ed'** 'stationnement interdit' **2.** [prevent] interdire, empêcher ▪ **his pacifism ~s him from joining the army** son pacifisme lui interdit *OR* l'empêche de s'engager dans l'armée.

prohibition [ˌprəʊɪˈbɪʃn] *n* interdiction *f*, prohibition *f* ▪ **the ~ of alcohol** la prohibition de l'alcool ▪ **there should be a ~ on the sale of such goods** il devrait y avoir une loi qui interdise la vente de ce genre de marchandises.

◆ **Prohibition** *n* US HIST la prohibition ▪ **during Prohibition** pendant la prohibition.

PROHIBITION

Le 18e amendement à la Constitution américaine instituant la Prohibition (interdiction de consommer et de vendre de l'alcool) fut voté en 1919 sous la pression de groupes religieux et conservateurs. La prolifération de bars clandestins (*speakeasies*) et l'apparition d'une guerre des gangs (les *bootleggers*) pour le monopole de la vente d'alcool incitèrent le Congrès à voter l'annulation de cette mesure en 1933, et les États l'abandonnèrent progressivement.

Voir module d'usage

prohibitive [prəˈhɪbətɪv] *adj* prohibitif.

prohibitively [prəˈhɪbətɪvlɪ] *adv* : **~ expensive** d'un coût prohibitif.

project <> *n* [ˈprɒdʒekt] **1.** [plan] projet *m* ▪ **a fund-raising ~ to save** *OR* **for saving the shipyard** une collecte de fonds pour sauver le chantier naval ▪ **they're working on a new building ~** ils travaillent sur un nouveau projet de construction ▮ [enterprise, undertaking] opération *f*, entreprise *f* ▪ **the start of the ~ has been delayed** le début de l'opération a été retardé
2. SCH [class work] travaux *mpl* pratiques ▪ [individual work] dossier *m* ▪ **the class has just finished a nature ~** la classe vient de terminer des travaux pratiques de sciences naturelles ▪ **Tina's ~ was the best in the whole class** le dossier de Tina était le meilleur de toute la classe
3. [study, research] étude *f*
4. US (housing) **~** cité *f* HLM.

<> *vt* [prəˈdʒekt] **1.** [plan] prévoir ▪ **two new airports are ~ed for the next decade** il est prévu de construire deux nouveaux aéroports durant la prochaine décennie
2. [foresee, forecast] prévoir
3. [send forth - gen] projeter, envoyer ; [- film, slide etc] projeter ▪ **to ~ one's voice** projeter sa voix ▪ **the missile was ~ed into space** le missile a été envoyé dans l'espace ▪ **try to ~ yourself forward into the 21st century** essayez d'imaginer que vous êtes au XXIe siècle
4. [present] présenter, projeter ▪ **football hooligans ~ a poor image of our country abroad** les hooligans donnent une mauvaise image de notre pays à l'étranger ▪ **to ~ one's personality** mettre sa personnalité en avant ▪ **he tries to ~ himself as a great humanist** il essaie de se faire passer pour un grand humaniste
5. PSYCHOL [transfer] projeter ▪ **to ~ one's feelings onto sb** projeter ses sentiments sur qqn
6. [cause to jut out] faire dépasser
7. GEOM projeter.

<> *vi* [prəˈdʒekt] **1.** [protrude, jut out] faire saillie, dépasser
2. PSYCHOL se projeter
3. [as personality] : **she doesn't ~ well** elle présente mal
4. [with voice] : **to learn to ~** apprendre à projeter sa voix.

projected [prəˈdʒektɪd] *adj* **1.** [planned - undertaking, visit] prévu ▪ **they are opposed to the ~ building scheme** ils sont contre le projet de construction **2.** [forecast - figures, production] prévu.

projectile [prəˈdʒektaɪl] *n* projectile *m*.

projecting [prəˈdʒektɪŋ] *adj* [roof, balcony etc] saillant, en saillie, qui fait saillie.

projection [prəˈdʒekʃn] *n* **1.** CIN, GEOM & PSYCHOL projection *f* **2.** FIN [estimate] projection *f*, prévision *f* ▪ **here are my ~s for the next ten years** voici mes prévisions pour les dix années à venir **3.** [of missile] lancement *m*, envoi *m* **4.** [protrusion] saillie *f*, avancée *f* ▪ [overhang] surplomb *m*.

projectionist [prəˈdʒekʃənɪst] *n* projectionniste *mf*.

projection room *n* cabine *f* de projection.

projective [prəˈdʒektɪv] *adj* projectif.

projective geometry *n* géométrie *f* projective.

PROHIBITION

Il est interdit de fumer dans les salles de cours. Smoking is not permitted in the classroom.

Tu n'as pas le droit de conduire, tu es trop jeune. You're not allowed to drive, you're too young.

Je te défends d'en parler à qui que ce soit. I forbid you to tell anyone about this.

Je t'interdis de sortir, tu m'entends ? You're not going out, do you hear me?

Et ne t'avise pas de recommencer ! There'll be trouble if you do that again!

Pas question que tu ailles à ce concert ! There's no way you're going to that concert!

Nous ne sommes pas censés sortir du lycée entre midi et deux. We're not supposed to leave the school premises during the lunch break.

Vous n'avez pas à lui parler sur ce ton. You've no right talking to him like that.

project manager *n* [gen] chef *m* de projet ■ CONSTR maître *m* d'œuvre.

projector [prəˈdʒektəʳ] *n* projecteur *m*.

prolapse [ˈprəʊlæps] ◇ *n* MED prolapsus *m*, ptôse *f* ■ **~ (of the uterus)** prolapsus *OR* descente *f* de l'utérus.
◇ *vi* descendre, tomber.

prole [prəʊl] *inf pej* ◇ *adj* prolo.
◇ *n* prolo *mf*.

proletarian [ˌprəʊlɪˈteərɪən] ◇ *n* prolétaire *mf*.
◇ *adj* **1.** ECON, POL & SOCIOL prolétarien **2.** *pej* de prolétaire.

proletariat [ˌprəʊlɪˈteərɪət] *n* prolétariat *m*.

pro-life [ˈprəʊˈlaɪf] *adj* contre l'avortement et l'euthanasie.

proliferate [prəˈlɪfəreɪt] *vi* proliférer.

proliferation [prəˌlɪfəˈreɪʃn] *n* **1.** [rapid increase] prolifération *f* **2.** [large amount or number] grande quantité *f*.

prolific [prəˈlɪfɪk] *adj* prolifique.

prolix [ˈprəʊlɪks] *adj fml* prolixe.

prolog [ˈprəʊlɒg] *US* = **prologue**.

prologue [ˈprəʊlɒg] *n liter & fig* prologue *m*, prélude *m* ■ **her arrival was the ~ to yet another row** son arrivée allait être le prélude d'une *OR* préluder à une nouvelle querelle.

prolong [prəˈlɒŋ] *vt* prolonger.

prolongation [ˌprəʊlɒŋˈgeɪʃn] *n* [in time] prolongation *f* ■ [in space] prolongement *m*, extension *f*.

prolonged [prəˈlɒŋd] *adj* long, longue *f*.

prom [prɒm] *n inf* **1.** = **promenade**, = *(senses 1, 4)* **2.** *UK* = **promenade concert**.
▶ **proms** *npl inf festival de concerts-promenades.*

promenade [ˌprɒməˈnɑːd] ◇ *n* **1.** *UK* [at seaside] front *m* de mer, promenade *f* **2.** *UK* MUS = **promenade concert 3.** [walk] promenade *f* **4.** *US* [dance] bal *m (de lycéens ou d'étudiants)*.
◇ *comp* THEAT [performance] *où les auditeurs doivent se déplacer pour suivre l'action de la pièce.*
◇ *vi fml & hum* se promener.
◇ *vt fml & hum* promener.

promenade concert *n* concert-promenade *m (où certains auditeurs se tiennent debout dans un promenoir)*.

promenade deck *n* pont *m* promenade.

promenader [ˌprɒməˈnɑːdəʳ] *n* MUS auditeur *m*, - trice *f* d'un concert-promenade.

Promethean [prəˈmiːθjən] *adj* prométhéen.

Prometheus [prəˈmiːθɪəs] *pr n* Prométhée.

prominence [ˈprɒmɪnəns] *n* **1.** [importance] importance *f* ■ [fame] célébrité *f* ■ **to rise to ~** se hisser au premier rang ■ **to come into** *OR* **to ~** [become important] prendre de l'importance ; [become famous] devenir célèbre **2.** [protuberance] proéminence *f* **3.** ASTRON protubérance *f* solaire.

prominent [ˈprɒmɪnənt] *adj* **1.** [well-known] célèbre ■ [eminent] éminent ■ **she's a very ~ individual** c'est un personnage très en vue ■ **he has a ~ position in the government** il est très haut placé au gouvernement ▮ [important] important ■ **to play a ~part** *OR* **role in sthg** jouer un rôle important *OR* de tout premier plan dans qqch **2.** [striking, salient - detail, difference] frappant, remarquable ; [- fact, feature] saillant, marquant ■ **put that poster in a ~ position** mettez cette affiche (dans un endroit) bien en vue **3.** [clearly visible - bones, muscles] saillant ; [- land, structure, nose] proéminent ; [- teeth] qui avance, proéminent.

prominently [ˈprɒmɪnəntlɪ] *adv* bien en vue ■ **he figures ~ in French politics** il occupe une position importante *OR* de premier plan dans la vie politique française ■ **the medal was ~ displayed** la médaille était mise en évidence.

promiscuity [ˌprɒmɪˈskjuːətɪ] *n* promiscuité *f* sexuelle.

promiscuous [prɒˈmɪskjʊəs] *adj* **1.** [sexually - person] : **to be ~** avoir des mœurs sexuelles libres ■ **~ behaviour** promiscuité *f* sexuelle ■ **he's very ~** il couche avec n'importe qui **2.** *fig* [disorderly] confus.

promise [ˈprɒmɪs] ◇ *n* **1.** [pledge] promesse *f* ■ **to make** *OR* **to give sb a ~** faire une promesse à qqn, donner sa parole à qqn ■ **she always keeps her ~s** elle tient toujours ses promesses, elle tient toujours (sa) parole ■ **I kept** *OR* **held him to his ~** j'ai fait en sorte qu'il tienne parole ■ **to break one's ~** manquer à sa parole, ne pas tenir ses promesses ■ **a ~ of help** une promesse d'assistance ■ **he did it under (the) ~ of a Parliamentary seat** il l'a fait parce qu'on lui a promis un siège de député ■ **I'm under a ~ of secrecy** j'ai promis de garder le secret *OR* de ne rien dire ▶ **a ~ is a ~** chose promise, chose due *prov* ■ **~s, ~s!** toujours des promesses! **2.** [hope, potential] promesse *f* ■ **an artist of ~** un artiste qui promet ■ **to hold out the ~ of sthg to sb** promettre qqch à qqn, faire espérer *OR* miroiter qqch à qqn.
◇ *vt* **1.** [pledge] promettre ■ **to ~ sthg to sb, to ~ sb sthg** promettre qqch à qqn ■ **to ~ sb to do sthg** promettre à qqn de faire qqch ■ **I can't ~ (you) anything** je ne peux rien vous promettre ■ **he ~d himself a good meal** il se promit mentalement de faire un bon repas ■ **you'll get into trouble, I ~ you!** tu auras des ennuis, je te le promets *OR* tu verras ce que je te dis! ■ **the weather forecast ~d us three days of good weather** la météo nous a promis *OR* annoncé trois jours de beau temps **2.** [indicate] promettre, annoncer ■ **the sky ~s fine weather this afternoon** le ciel laisse présager un temps agréable pour cet après-midi ■ **next week already ~s to be difficult** la semaine prochaine promet déjà d'être difficile *OR* s'annonce déjà difficile **3.** [in marriage] : **she was ~d to the King's son at birth** dès sa naissance, elle fut promise au fils du roi.
◇ *vi* **1.** promettre ■ **he wanted to come but he couldn't ~** il espérait pouvoir venir mais ne pouvait rien promettre ■ **OK, I ~!** d'accord, c'est promis! **2.** *fig* **to ~ well** [enterprise] promettre, s'annoncer bien ; [person] être prometteur *OR* plein de promesses ; [results, harvest, negotiations] s'annoncer bien ■ **his first article ~s well** son premier article promet *OR* est prometteur.

Promised Land [ˈprɒmɪst-] *n* BIBLE & *fig* Terre *f* promise.

promising [ˈprɒmɪsɪŋ] *adj* **1.** [full of potential - person] prometteur, qui promet, plein de promesses **2.** [encouraging] prometteur, qui promet ■ **she got off to a ~ start** elle a fait des débuts prometteurs ■ **the forecast isn't very ~ for tomorrow** les prévisions météo n'annoncent rien de bon pour demain.

promisingly [ˈprɒmɪsɪŋlɪ] *adv* d'une façon prometteuse ■ **France started the match ~** la France a bien débuté la partie.

promissory note [ˈprɒmɪsərɪ-] *n* billet *m* à ordre.

promo [ˈprəʊməʊ] (*pl* **promos**) (*abbrev of* **promotion**) *n inf* clip *m* (promotionnel).

promontory [ˈprɒməntrɪ] (*pl* **promontories**) *n* promontoire *m*.

promote [prəˈməʊt] *vt* **1.** [in profession, army] promouvoir ■ **to be** *OR* **to get ~d** être promu, monter en grade, obtenir de l'avancement ■ **she's been ~d (to) regional manager** elle a été promue (au poste de) directrice régionale **2.** SPORT : **the Rovers were ~d to the second division** les Rovers sont montés en deuxième division **3.** [foster] promouvoir, favoriser, encourager ■ **cleanliness ~s health** la propreté est un facteur de santé ■ **to ~ economic growth** promouvoir *OR* favoriser la croissance économique **4.** COMM [advertise, publicize] promouvoir, faire la promotion de.

promoter [prəˈməʊtəʳ] *n* **1.** COMM promoteur *m*, - trice *f* (des ventes) **2.** [organizer - of match, concert] organisateur *m*, - trice *f* ; [- of scheme] promoteur *m*, - trice *f*, instigateur *m*, - trice *f* **3.** [of peace] promoteur *m*, - trice *f*.

promotion [prəˈməʊʃn] *n* **1.** [advancement] promotion *f*, avancement *m* ■ **there are good prospects of ~ in this company** il y a de réelles possibilités de promotion *OR* d'avancement dans cette société **2.** SPORT promotion *f* ■ **the team won ~ to the first division** l'équipe a gagné sa place en première division **3.** [encouragement, development] promotion *f*, développement *m* **4.** COMM promotion *f* ▪ **sales ~** promotion *f* des ventes ▪ **this week's ~** la promotion de la semaine **5.** [in chess] promotion *f*.

promotional [prəˈməʊʃənl] *adj* [material] promotionnel, publicitaire.

prompt [prɒmpt] ◇ *adj* **1.** [quick] rapide, prompt ▪ **a ~ answer/decision** une réponse/décision rapide ▪ **you should give this matter ~ attention** vous devriez vous occuper de cette question sans (plus) attendre *OR* le plus rapidement possible ▪ **to be ~ in paying one's debts** être prompt à payer ses dettes ▪ **~ payment** COMM paiement *m* dans les délais **2.** [punctual] exact, à l'heure.
◇ *adv inf* [exactly] **: we begin at 9 o'clock ~** nous commençons à 9 h précises.
◇ *vt* **1.** [provoke, persuade] pousser, inciter ▪ **he's shy and needs to be ~ed to speak up** il est timide, il faut l'encourager à s'exprimer ▪ **I felt ~ed to intervene** je me suis senti obligé d'intervenir ▪ **what ~ed you to suggest such a thing?** qu'est-ce qui vous a incité à proposer une chose pareille? ▪ **the scandal ~ed his resignation** le scandale a provoqué sa démission **2.** THEAT souffler.
◇ *n* **1.** THEAT **: to give an actor a ~** souffler une réplique à un acteur **2.** COMPUT message-guide *m (au début de la ligne de commande)*.

prompter [ˈprɒmptəʳ] *n* souffleur *m*, -euse *f* ▪ TV télé-prompteur *m*.

prompting [ˈprɒmptɪŋ] *n* **1.** [persuasion] incitation *f* ▪ **no amount of ~ will induce me to go there** rien ne pourra me décider à y aller ▪ **she needed no ~** elle ne s'est pas fait prier, elle l'a fait d'elle-même ▪ **at his mother's ~, he wrote a letter of thanks** à l'instigation *OR* sur l'insistance de sa mère, il a écrit une lettre de remerciement **2.** THEAT **: some actors need frequent ~** certains acteurs ont souvent recours au souffleur.

promptitude [ˈprɒmptɪtjuːd] *fml* = **promptness**.

promptly [ˈprɒmptlɪ] *adv* **1.** [quickly] promptement, rapidement **2.** [punctually] ponctuellement **3.** [immediately] aussitôt, tout de suite.

promptness [ˈprɒmptnɪs] *n* **1.** [quickness] promptitude *f*, rapidité *f* **2.** [punctuality] ponctualité *f*.

promulgate [ˈprɒmlgeɪt] *vt fml* **1.** [decree, law] promulguer **2.** [belief, idea, opinion] répandre, diffuser.

promulgation [ˌprɒmlˈgeɪʃn] *n fml* **1.** [of decree, law] promulgation *f* **2.** [of belief, idea, opinion] diffusion *f*, dissémination *f*.

prone [prəʊn] *adj* **1.** [inclined] sujet, enclin ▪ **to be ~ to do sthg** être sujet *OR* enclin à faire qqch ▪ **to be ~ to accidents/illness** être sujet aux accidents/à la maladie **2.** [prostrate] à plat ventre ▪ **in a ~ position** couché sur le ventre.

proneness [ˈprəʊnnɪs] *n* tendance *f*, prédisposition *f*.

prong [prɒŋ] *n* [of fork] dent *f* ▪ [of tuning fork] branche *f* ▪ [of antler] pointe *f* ▪ [of attack, argument] pointe *f*.

pronged [prɒŋd] *adj* à dents, à pointes.

-pronged *in cpds* **: two~** [fork] à deux dents ; MIL [attack] sur deux fronts ; [argument] double.

pronominal [prəˈnɒmɪnl] *adj* pronominal.

pronoun [ˈprəʊnaʊn] *n* pronom *m*.

pronounce [prəˈnaʊns] ◇ *vt* **1.** [say] prononcer ▪ **how's it ~d?** comment est-ce que ça se prononce? ▪ **you don't ~ the "p" in "psalm"** on ne prononce pas le "p" de "psalm", le "p" de "psalm" est muet **2.** [declare] déclarer, prononcer ▪ **the doctor ~d him dead** le médecin l'a déclaré mort ▪ **judgment has not yet been ~d** le jugement n'est pas encore prononcé *OR* rendu.
◇ *vi* **1.** [articulate] prononcer **2.** [declare] se prononcer ▪ **to ~ for/against sthg** [gen] se prononcer pour/contre qqch ; LAW prononcer pour/contre qqch ▪ **to ~ on** *OR* **upon sthg** se prononcer sur qqch.

pronounced [prəˈnaʊnst] *adj* prononcé, marqué.

pronouncement [prəˈnaʊnsmənt] *n* déclaration *f*.

pronto [ˈprɒntəʊ] *adv inf* illico.

pronunciation [prəˌnʌnsɪˈeɪʃn] *n* prononciation *f*.

proof [pruːf] ◇ *n* **1.** *(U)* [evidence] preuve *f* ▪ **to show** *OR* **to give ~ of sthg** faire *OR* donner la preuve de qqch ▪ **do you have any ~?** vous en avez la preuve *OR* des preuves? ▪ **can you produce any ~ for your accusations?** avez-vous des preuves pour justifier vos accusations? ▪ **you need ~ of identity** vous devez fournir une pièce d'identité ▪ **we have written ~ of it** nous en avons la preuve écrite *OR* par écrit ▪ **by way of ~** comme *OR* pour preuve ▪ **~ of purchase** reçu *m* ▪ **he cited several other cases in ~ of his argument** il a cité plusieurs autres cas pour défendre sa thèse ▪ **he gave her a locket as ~ of his love** il lui a offert un médaillon comme preuve de son amour pour elle *OR* en gage d'amour ➔ **the ~ of the pudding is in the eating** *prov* il faut juger sur pièces **2.** PHOT & TYPO épreuve *f* **3.** [of alcohol] teneur *f* (en alcool) ▪ **45% ~ brandy** ≃ cognac à 45 degrés.
◇ *adj UK* **to be ~ against** [fire, acid, rust] être à l'épreuve de ; [danger, temptation] être à l'abri de *OR* insensible à.
◇ *vt* **1.** [cloth] imperméabiliser **2.** TYPO [proofread] corriger les épreuves de ▪ [produce proof of] préparer les épreuves de.

-proof [pruːf] *in cpds* à l'épreuve de ▪ **acid~** à l'épreuve des acides ▪ **an idiot~ mechanism** un mécanisme (totalement) indéréglable.

proofread [ˈpruːfriːd] *(pret & pp* **proofread** [-red]*) vt* corriger (les épreuves de).

proofreader [ˈpruːfˌriːdəʳ] *n* correcteur *m*, -trice *f* (d'épreuves *OR* d'imprimerie).

proofreading [ˈpruːfˌriːdɪŋ] *n* correction *f* (d'épreuves).

prop [prɒp] *(pret & pp* **propped**, *cont* **propping**) ◇ *n* **1.** [gen] support *m* ▪ CONSTR [for tunnel, wall] étai *m*, étançon *m* ▪ [in pit] étai *m* **2.** [pole, stick - for plant, flowers] tuteur *m* ; [- for beans, peas] rame *f* ; [- for vines] échalas *m* ; [- for washing line] perche *f* **3.** RUGBY pilier *m* **4.** *fig* soutien *m* ▪ **whisky is his ~** le whisky est son réconfort **5.** *(abbrev of* **property**) THEAT accessoire *m* **6.** *inf* = **propeller**.
◇ *vt* **1.** [lean] appuyer ▪ **she propped her bike (up) against the wall** elle a appuyé son vélo contre le mur ▪ **~ yourself** *OR* **your back against these cushions** calez-vous contre *OR* adossez-vous à ces coussins ▪ **he was propping his head (up) in his hands** il tenait sa tête calée entre ses mains **2.** [support] **: to ~ (up)** [wall, tunnel] étayer, étançonner, consolider ; [plants] mettre un tuteur à ; [peas, beans] ramer ▪ **to ~ sthg open : I propped the door open with a chair** j'ai maintenu la porte ouverte avec une chaise.
➔ **prop up** *vt sep* [regime, family, business] soutenir.

prop. *written abbr of* **proprietor**.

propaganda [ˌprɒpəˈgændə] ◇ *n* propagande *f*.
◇ *comp* [film, machine, material, exercise] de propagande.

propagandist [ˌprɒpəˈgændɪst] ◇ *adj* propagandiste.
◇ *n* propagandiste *mf*.

propagate [ˈprɒpəgeɪt] ◇ *vt* propager.
◇ *vi* se propager.

propagation [ˌprɒpəˈgeɪʃn] *n* propagation *f*.

propagator [ˈprɒpəgeɪtəʳ] *n* **1.** [gen] propagateur *m*, -trice *f* **2.** BOT & HORT germoir *m*.

propane [ˈprəʊpeɪn] *n* propane *m*.

propel [prəˈpel] *(pret & pp* **propelled**, *cont* **propelling**) *vt* **1.** [machine, vehicle etc] propulser, faire avancer **2.** [person] propulser, pousser ▪ **he was propelled into the position of manager** on l'a bombardé directeur.

propellant, propellent [prəˈpelənt] ◇ *n* [for rocket] propergol *m* ▪ [for gun] poudre *f* propulsive ▪ [in aerosol] (agent *m*) propulseur *m*.
◇ *adj* propulsif, propulseur.

propeller [prəˈpeləʳ] *n* hélice *f*.

propelling pencil [prəˈpelɪŋ-] *n UK* portemine *m*.

propensity [prə'pensətɪ] (*pl* **propensities**) *n fml* propension *f*, tendance *f*, penchant *m* ■ **he has a ~ for** OR **towards drink** il a tendance à boire (plus que de raison).

proper ['prɒpər] ◇ *adj* **1.** [correct] bon, juste, correct ■ **John wasn't waiting at the ~ place** John n'attendait pas au bon endroit OR là où il fallait ■ **she didn't come at the ~ time** elle s'est trompée d'heure ■ **you're not doing it in the ~ way** vous ne vous y prenez pas comme il faut ■ **he did the ~ thing by her** *dated & hum* [he married her] il a réparé ■ **to think it ~ to do sthg** juger bon de faire qqch ■ **do as you think ~** faites comme bon vous semble
2. [appropriate] convenable, approprié ■ **that wasn't the ~ thing to say/to do** ce n'était pas ce qu'il fallait dire/faire ■ **you must go through the ~ channels** il faut suivre la filière officielle ■ **he wasn't wearing the ~ clothes** il n'était pas vêtu pour la circonstance ■ **evening dress is the ~ thing to wear for a ball** porter une tenue de soirée est de circonstance pour aller au bal ■ **I don't have the ~ tools for this engine** je n'ai pas les outils appropriés pour OR qui conviennent pour ce moteur ■ **put the scissors back in their ~ place** remettez les ciseaux à leur place
3. [real] vrai, véritable ■ **we must give the President a ~ welcome** nous devons réserver au président un accueil digne de ce nom ■ **he's not a ~ doctor** ce n'est pas un vrai docteur ■ **putting letters in envelopes isn't a ~ job** mettre des lettres dans des enveloppes n'a rien d'un vrai travail
4. *UK inf* [as intensifier] vrai, véritable, complet, - ète *f* ■ **her room was in a ~ mess** il y avait un vrai bazar dans sa chambre ■ **I gave him a ~ telling-off** je lui ai passé un bon savon
5. [respectable] correct, convenable, comme il faut ■ **that's not ~ behaviour** ce n'est pas convenable, cela ne se fait pas
6. [predicative use - specifically] proprement dit ■ **he lives outside the city ~** il habite en dehors de la ville même OR proprement dite
7. [characteristic] : **~ to** propre à, typique de.
◇ *adv*△ **1.** *UK* [correctly] comme il faut
2. *UK dial* [very] très, vraiment, complètement.
◇ *n* RELIG propre *m*.

proper fraction *n* fraction *f* inférieure à l'unité.

properly ['prɒpəlɪ] *adv* **1.** [well, correctly] bien, juste, correctement ■ **the lid isn't on ~** le couvercle n'est pas bien mis ■ **the engine isn't working ~** le moteur ne marche pas bien ■ **for once they pronounced my name ~** pour une fois, ils ont prononcé mon nom correctement OR ils ont bien prononcé mon nom ■ **she quite ~ intervened** c'est avec raison OR à juste titre qu'elle est intervenue **2.** [decently] correctement, convenablement, comme il faut ■ **patrons must be ~ dressed** une tenue vestimentaire correcte est exigée de nos clients ■ **I haven't thanked you ~** je ne vous ai pas remercié comme il faut OR comme il convient **3.** [strictly] proprement ■ **he isn't ~ speaking an expert** il n'est pas à proprement parler un expert **4.** *UK inf* [as intensifier] vraiment, complètement, tout à fait.

proper name, proper noun *n* nom *m* propre.

propertied ['prɒpətɪd] *adj fml* possédant ■ **a ~ gentleman** un homme fortuné.

property ['prɒpətɪ] (*pl* **properties**) ◇ *n* **1.** *(U)* [belongings] propriété *f*, biens *mpl* ■ **hands off! that's my ~!** n'y touchez pas, c'est à moi OR ça m'appartient! ■ **this book is the ~ of Theresa Lloyd** ce livre appartient à Theresa Lloyd ■ **government ~** propriété de l'État ‖ LAW biens *mpl* ■ [objects] objets *mpl* ■ **this is stolen ~** ce sont des objets volés **2.** *(U)* [buildings] propriété *f* ■ [real estate] biens *mpl* immobiliers, immobilier *m* ■ [land] terres *fpl* ■ **they own a lot of ~ in the country** [houses] ils ont de nombreuses propriétés à la campagne ; [land] ils ont de nombreuses terres à la campagne **3.** [plot of land] terrain *m* ■ [house, building] propriété *f* **4.** [quality] propriété *f* ■ **healing properties** vertus *fpl* thérapeutiques OR curatives **5.** THEAT accessoire *m*.
◇ *comp* [speculator] immobilier ■ [owner, tax] foncier ■ **~ developer** promoteur *m* (immobilier).

property man *n* THEAT accessoiriste *m*.

property mistress *n* THEAT accessoiriste *f*.

prop forward *n* RUGBY pilier *m*.

prophecy ['prɒfɪsɪ] (*pl* **prophecies**) *n* prophétie *f*.

prophesy ['prɒfɪsaɪ] (*pret & pp* **prophesied**) ◇ *vt* prophétiser, prédire ■ **to ~ that sthg will happen** prédire que qqch va arriver.
◇ *vi* faire des prophéties.

prophet ['prɒfɪt] *n* prophète *m* ■ **a ~ of doom** un prophète de malheur.
◆ **Prophets** *n* BIBLE : **(the Book of) Prophets** le livre des Prophètes.

prophetess ['prɒfɪtɪs] *n* prophétesse *f*.

prophetic [prə'fetɪk] *adj* prophétique.

prophetically [prə'fetɪklɪ] *adv* prophétiquement.

prophylactic [,prɒfɪ'læktɪk] ◇ *adj* prophylactique.
◇ *n* **1.** [drug] médicament *m* prophylactique **2.** [condom] préservatif *m*.

propinquity [prə'pɪŋkwətɪ] *n fml* **1.** [in space, time] proximité *f* **2.** [in kinship] consanguinité *f*.

propitiation [prə,pɪʃɪ'eɪʃn] *n fml* propitiation *f*.

propitious [prə'pɪʃəs] *adj fml* propice, favorable ■ **~ for sthg** propice à OR favorable à qqch ■ **it wasn't really a ~ moment to ask for a rise** le moment était plutôt mal choisi pour demander une augmentation.

proponent [prə'pəʊnənt] *n* avocat *m*, - e *f fig*, partisan *m*, - e *f*.

proportion [prə'pɔːʃn] ◇ *n* **1.** [gen - MATHS] [- ratio] proportion *f*, rapport *m* ■ **the sentence is out of all ~ to the crime** la peine est disproportionnée par rapport au OR est sans commune mesure avec le délit ■ **the ~ of income to** OR **over expenditure** le rapport entre les revenus et les dépenses **2.** [perspective] proportion *f* ■ **to have a sense of ~** avoir le sens des proportions ■ **you seem to have got** OR **blown the problem out of (all) ~** vous semblez avoir exagéré OR grossi le problème ■ **you must try to see things in ~** vous devez essayer de ramener les choses à leur juste valeur ■ **the artist has got the tree out of ~** l'artiste n'a pas respecté les proportions de l'arbre **3.** [dimension] proportion *f*, dimension *f* ■ **the affair has assumed worrying ~s** l'affaire a pris des proportions alarmantes **4.** [share, part] partie *f*, part *f*, pourcentage *m* ■ **what ~ of your income do you spend on tobacco?** quel pourcentage de vos revenus dépensez-vous en tabac?
◇ *vt* proportionner ■ **to ~ one's expenditure to one's resources** proportionner ses dépenses à ses ressources, calculer ses dépenses en fonction de ses ressources.
◆ **in proportion to, in proportion with** *prep phr* par rapport à ■ **his salary is in ~ to his experience** son salaire correspond à son expérience ■ **inflation may increase in ~ with wage rises** l'inflation risque d'augmenter proportionnellement aux augmentations de salaire.

proportional [prə'pɔːʃənl] *adj* proportionnel, en proportion ■ **~ to** proportionnel à.

proportionally [prə'pɔːʃnəlɪ] *adv* proportionnellement.

proportional representation *n* représentation *f* proportionnelle.

proportionate ◇ *adj* [prə'pɔːʃnət] proportionné.
◇ *vt* [prə'pɔːʃəneɪt] = **proportion**.

proportionately [prə'pɔːʃnətlɪ] *adv* proportionnellement, en proportion.

proposal [prə'pəʊzl] *n* **1.** [offer] proposition *f*, offre *f* ■ **to make a ~** faire OR formuler une proposition ‖ [of marriage] demande *f* en mariage **2.** [suggestion] proposition *f*, suggestion *f* **3.** [plan, scheme] proposition *f*, projet *m*, plan *m* ■ **the ~ for a car park/to build a car park** le projet de parking/de construction d'un parking.

propose [prə'pəʊz] ◇ *vt* **1.** [suggest] proposer, suggérer ■ **to ~ sthg to sb** proposer qqch à qqn ■ **to ~ doing sthg** proposer de faire qqch ■ **I ~ (that) we all go for a drink** je propose OR suggère que nous allions tous prendre un verre **2.** [present - policy, resolution, scheme] proposer, présenter, soumettre ■ **to ~ sb's health, to ~ a toast to sb** porter un toast à (la santé

de) qqn ■ **I ~ Jones as** *OR* **for treasurer** je propose Jones comme trésorier ■ [in marriage] : **to ~ marriage to sb** demander qqn en mariage, faire une demande en mariage à qqn **3.** [intend] se proposer, avoir l'intention, compter ■ **I ~ taking** *OR* **to take a few days off work** je me propose de prendre quelques jours de congé.
◇ *vi* **1.** [offer marriage] faire une demande en mariage ■ **to ~ to sb** demander qqn en mariage **2.** *phr* **man ~s, God disposes** l'homme propose, Dieu dispose.

proposed [prəˈpəʊzd] *adj* projeté ■ **the ~ visit** la visite prévue ■ **the building of the ~ car park has been delayed** le projet de construction d'un parking a été suspendu.

proposer [prəˈpəʊzəʳ] *n* **1.** [of motion] auteur *m* (d'une proposition) **2.** [of candidate] parrain *m fig*, marraine *f fig*.

proposition [ˌprɒpəˈzɪʃn] ◇ *n* **1.** [proposal, statement] proposition *f* **2.** [task] affaire *f* ■ **that's quite a ~** c'est une tout autre affaire ■ **climbing that mountain will be no easy ~** ce ne sera pas une petite *OR* mince affaire que de gravir cette montagne ■ **the boss is a tough ~** *inf* le patron n'est pas quelqu'un de commode *OR* facile, le patron est du genre coriace **3.** [available choice] solution *f* ■ **the deal wasn't a paying ~** l'affaire n'était pas rentable **4.** [offer of sex] proposition *f* **5.** MATHS proposition *f*.
◇ *vt* faire des propositions (malhonnêtes) *OR* des avances à.

propound [prəˈpaʊnd] *vt fml* [argument, theory] avancer, mettre en avant ■ [opinion] avancer, émettre ■ [problem] poser.

proprietary [prəˈpraɪətrɪ] *adj* **1.** COMM de marque déposée ■ **~ brand** marque *f* déposée **2.** [attitude, behaviour, function] de propriétaire ■ **his manner towards her was rather ~** il était plutôt possessif avec elle.

proprietor [prəˈpraɪətəʳ] *n* propriétaire *mf*.

proprietorship [prəˈpraɪətəʃɪp] *n* propriété *f*, possession *f* ■ LAW (droit *m* de) propriété *f*.

proprietress [prəˈpraɪətrɪs] *n* propriétaire *f*.

propriety [prəˈpraɪətɪ] (*pl* **proprieties**) *n fml* **1.** [decorum] bienséance *f*, convenance *f* ■ **his behaviour is lacking in ~** son comportement est tout à fait inconvenant *OR* déplacé ■ **contrary to the proprieties** contraire aux bienséances *OR* convenances **2.** [suitability - of action, measure] opportunité *f* ; [- of word, remark] justesse *f*, propriété *f* **3.** [rectitude] rectitude *f*.

propulsion [prəˈpʌlʃn] *n* propulsion *f*.

pro rata [ˌprəʊˈrɑːtə] *adj* & *adv* au prorata.

prorogation [ˌprəʊrəˈgeɪʃn] *n* prorogation *f*.

prorogue [prəˈrəʊg] *vt* proroger.

prosaic [prəʊˈzeɪɪk] *adj* prosaïque.

prosaically [prəʊˈzeɪɪklɪ] *adv* prosaïquement.

proscenium [prəˈsiːnjəm] (*pl* **prosceniums** *OR pl* **proscenia** [-njə]) *n* proscenium *m*.

proscenium arch *n* THEAT ≃ manteau *m* d'Arlequin.

proscribe [prəʊˈskraɪb] *vt* proscrire.

proscription [prəʊˈskrɪpʃn] *n* proscription *f*.

prose [prəʊz] *n* **1.** LIT prose *f* ■ **to write in ~** écrire en prose, faire de la prose **2.** *UK* SCH thème *m*.

prosecute [ˈprɒsɪkjuːt] ◇ *vt* **1.** LAW poursuivre (en justice), engager des poursuites contre ■ **to ~ sb for sthg** poursuivre qqn (en justice) pour qqch **2.** *fml* [pursue - war, investigation] poursuivre.
◇ *vi* LAW [lawyer - in civil case] représenter la partie civile ; [- in criminal case] représenter le ministère public *OR* le parquet.

prosecuting attorney [ˈprɒsɪkjuːtɪŋ-] *n US* ≃ procureur *mf* (de la République).

prosecution [ˌprɒsɪˈkjuːʃn] *n* **1.** LAW [proceedings] poursuites *fpl* (judiciaires) ■ [indictment] accusation *f* ■ **to be liable to ~** s'exposer à des poursuites (judiciaires) ■ **to bring a ~ against sb** poursuivre qqn en justice ■ **this is her second ~** c'est la deuxième fois qu'elle est poursuivie **2.** LAW [lawyer - in civil case] avocat *m OR* avocats *mpl* représentant les plaignants *OR* la partie plaignante ; [- in criminal case] ministère *m* public, accusation *f* ■ **witness for the ~** témoin *m* à charge **3.** *fml* [pursuit] poursuite *f*.

prosecutor [ˈprɒsɪkjuːtəʳ] *n* [person bringing case] plaignant *m*, - e *f* ■ [lawyer] : **(public) ~** procureur *mf*.

proselyte [ˈprɒsəlaɪt] ◇ *n* prosélyte *mf*.
◇ *vi* & *vt esp US* = **proselytize**.

proselytize, ise [ˈprɒsəlɪtaɪz] ◇ *vi* faire du prosélytisme.
◇ *vt* faire un prosélyte de.

prose poem *n* poème *m* en prose.

prosodic [prəˈsɒdɪk] *adj* prosodique.

prosody [ˈprɒsədɪ] *n* prosodie *f*.

prospect ◇ *n* [ˈprɒspekt] **1.** [possibility] chance *f*, perspective *f* ■ **there's little ~ of their winning the match** ils ont peu de chances de remporter *OR* il y a peu d'espoir (pour) qu'ils remportent le match ■ **we had given up all ~ of hearing from you** nous avions renoncé à tout espoir d'avoir *OR* nous pensions ne jamais plus recevoir de vos nouvelles
2. [impending event, situation] perspective *f* ■ **I don't relish the ~ of working for him** la perspective de travailler pour lui ne m'enchante guère ■ **to have sthg in ~** avoir qqch en vue *OR* en perspective ■ **what are the weather ~s for tomorrow?** quelles sont les prévisions météorologiques pour demain?
3. (*usu pl*) [chance of success] perspectives *fpl* d'avenir ■ **the ~s are not very good** les choses se présentent plutôt mal ■ **the ~(s) for the automobile industry** les perspectives d'avenir de l'industrie automobile ■ **her ~s are bleak** ses perspectives d'avenir sont sombres ■ **she's a woman with good ~s** c'est une femme qui a de l'avenir *OR* une femme d'avenir ■ **this company has good ~s/no ~s** cette entreprise a un bel avenir devant elle/n'a pas d'avenir ■ **good promotion ~s** de réelles possibilités d'avancement
4. [person - customer] client *m* potentiel *OR* éventuel, prospect *m* ; [- marriage partner] parti *m dated* ; [- candidate] espoir *m* ■ **he's a good ~ for the manager's job** c'est un candidat potentiel au poste de directeur
5. [view] perspective *f*, vue *f*.
◇ *vi* [prəˈspekt] prospecter ■ **to ~ for oil** chercher du pétrole ■ **to ~ for new customers** rechercher *OR* démarcher de nouveaux clients.
◇ *vt* [prəˈspekt] [area, land] prospecter.

prospecting [prəˈspektɪŋ] *n* MIN & PETR prospection *f*.

prospective [prəˈspektɪv] *adj* **1.** [future] futur ■ **he's our ~ parliamentary candidate** il est notre futur candidat parlementaire **2.** [possible] potentiel, éventuel **3.** [intended, expected] en perspective ■ **my ~ trip to Ireland** le voyage que je projette de faire en Irlande.

prospector [prəˈspektəʳ] *n* prospecteur *m*, - trice *f*, chercheur *m*, - euse *f* ■ **gold ~s** chercheurs d'or.

prospectus [prəˈspektəs] *n* prospectus *m*.

prosper [ˈprɒspəʳ] *vt* prospérer.

prosperity [prɒˈsperətɪ] *n* prospérité *f*.

prosperous [ˈprɒspərəs] *adj* [business, area, family] prospère ■ [period] prospère, de prospérité ■ **~ winds** *lit* vents *mpl* favorables.

prostaglandin [ˌprɒstəˈglændɪn] *n* prostaglandine *f*.

prostate (gland) [ˈprɒsteɪt-] *n* prostate *f*.

prosthesis [prɒsˈθiːsɪs] (*pl* **prostheses** [-siːz]) *n* **1.** MED prothèse *f* **2.** LING prosthèse *f*.

prosthetic [prɒsˈθetɪk] *adj* **1.** MED prothétique **2.** LING prosthétique.

prostitute [ˈprɒstɪtjuːt] ◇ *n* prostituée *f* ■ **male ~** prostitué *m*.
◇ *vt fig* & *liter* prostituer ■ **to ~ o.s.** se prostituer.

prostitution [ˌprɒstɪˈtjuːʃn] *n* prostitution *f*.

prostrate ◇ *adj* ['prɒstreɪt] **1.** [lying flat] (couché) à plat ventre ■ [in submission] prosterné ■ **to lie ~ before sb** être prosterné devant qqn **2.** [exhausted] épuisé, abattu ■ [overwhelmed] prostré, accablé, atterré.
◇ *vt* [prɒ'streɪt] **1.** [in obedience, respect] : **to ~ o.s. before sb** se prosterner devant qqn **2.** [overwhelm] accabler, abattre ■ **to be ~d by illness** être accablé *OR* abattu par la maladie.

prostration [prɒ'streɪʃn] *n* **1.** [lying down] prosternement *m* ■ RELIG prostration *f* **2.** [exhaustion] prostration *f*, épuisement *m*.

prosy ['prəʊzɪ] (*comp* **prosier**, *superl* **prosiest**) *adj* [dull] ennuyeux, prosaïque ■ [long-winded] verbeux.

protagonist [prə'tægənɪst] *n* protagoniste *mf*.

protean [prəʊ'ti:ən] *adj lit* changeant.

protect [prə'tekt] *vt* protéger ■ **to ~ sb/sthg from** *OR* **against sthg** protéger qqn/qqch de *OR* contre qqch ■ **she ~ed her eyes from the sun** elle se protégea les yeux du soleil.

protected [prə'tektɪd] *adj* protégé ■ **~ species** espèce *f* protégée.

protection [prə'tekʃn] *n* **1.** [safeguard] protection *f* ■ **this drug offers ~ against** *OR* **from the virus** ce médicament vous protège *OR* vous immunise contre le virus ■ **cyclists often wear face masks for ~ against car fumes** les cyclistes portent souvent des masques pour se protéger des gaz d'échappement des voitures ■ **environmental ~** protection *f* de l'environnement **2.** [insurance] protection *f* ■ **~ against fire and theft** protection contre l'incendie et le vol **3.** [run by gangsters] : **~ (money)** argent *m* versé aux racketteurs ■ **all the shopkeepers have to pay ~ (money)** tous les commerçants sont rackettés ■ **~ racket** racket *m*.

protectionism [prə'tekʃənɪzm] *n* protectionnisme *m*.

protectionist [prə'tekʃənɪst] ◇ *adj* protectionniste.
◇ *n* protectionniste *mf*.

protective [prə'tektɪv] *adj* **1.** [person] protecteur ■ [behaviour, attitude] protecteur, de protection ■ **she's too ~ towards her children** elle a trop tendance à couver ses enfants **2.** [material, clothes] de protection ■ [cover] protecteur, de protection **3.** ECON [duty, measure] protecteur.

protective custody *n* détention *f* dans l'intérêt de la personne.

protectively [prə'tektɪvlɪ] *adv* [behave, act] de façon protectrice ■ [speak] d'un ton protecteur, d'une voix protectrice ■ [look] d'un œil protecteur.

protectiveness [prə'tektɪvnɪs] *n* attitude *f* protectrice.

protector [prə'tektəʳ] *n* **1.** [person] protecteur *m*, - trice *f* **2.** [on machine] dispositif *m* de protection, protecteur *m*.
◆ **Protector** *n UK* HIST : **the Protector** le Protecteur.

protectorate [prə'tektərət] *n* protectorat *m* ■ **the Protectorate** *UK* HIST le Protectorat.

THE PROTECTORATE

En Angleterre, période allant de 1649 à 1660, succédant à la guerre civile et durant laquelle Oliver Cromwell, se proclamant *Lord Protector*, exerça son autorité sur le pays. Il transmit ensuite cette charge à son fils Richard.

protégé ['prɒtəʒeɪ] *n* protégé *m*, - e *f*.

protein ['prəʊti:n] *n* protéine *f* ■ **~ deficiency** carence *f* en protéines.

pro tem [,prəʊ'tem] *inf*, **pro tempore** ['prəʊ'tempərɪ] ◇ *adv* temporairement.
◇ *adj* intérimaire, temporaire.

protest ◇ *n* ['prəʊtest] **1.** [gen] protestation *f* ■ **to make a ~ against** *OR* **about sthg** élever une protestation contre qqch, protester contre qqch ■ **to register** *OR* **to lodge a ~ with sb** protester auprès de qqn ■ **in ~ against** *OR* **at sthg** en signe de protestation contre qqch ■ **to stage a ~** [complaint] organiser une protestation ; [demonstration] organiser une manifestation ■ **to do sthg under ~** faire qqch en protestant **2.** COMM & LAW protêt *m*.
◇ *comp* [letter, meeting] de protestation ■ **~ demonstration** *OR* **march** manifestation *f* ■ **~ marcher** manifestant *m*, - e *f* ■ **~ vote** vote *m* de protestation.
◇ *vt* [prə'test] **1.** [innocence, love etc] protester de ■ **"no one told me", she ~ed** "personne ne me l'a dit", protesta-t-elle ■ **she ~ed that it was unfair** elle déclara que ce n'était pas juste **2.** *US* [measures, law etc] protester contre.
◇ *vi* protester ■ **to ~ at** *OR* **against/about sthg** protester contre qqch ■ **I must ~ in the strongest terms at** *OR* **about...** je m'élève avec la dernière énergie *fml OR* énergiquement contre...

Protestant ['prɒtɪstənt] ◇ *adj* protestant ■ **the ~ Church** l'Église *f* protestante ■ **the ~ (work) ethic** l'éthique *f* protestante (du travail).
◇ *n* Protestant *m*, - e *f*.

protestation [,prɒte'steɪʃn] *n* protestation *f*.

protester, protestor [prə'testəʳ] *n* [demonstrator] manifestant *m*, - e *f* ■ [complainer] protestataire *mf*.

protocol ['prəʊtəkɒl] *n* [gen - COMPUT] protocole *m*.

proton ['prəʊtɒn] *n* proton *m*.

proton number *n* numéro *m* atomique.

protoplasm ['prəʊtəplæzm] *n* protoplasme *m*, protoplasma *m*.

prototype ['prəʊtətaɪp] *n* prototype *m*.

protozoan [,prəʊtə'zəʊən] (*pl* **protozoans** *OR pl* **protozoa** [-'zəʊə]) *n* protozoaire *m*.

protract [prə'trækt] *vt* prolonger, faire durer.

protracted [prə'træktɪd] *adj* [stay] prolongé ■ [argument, negotiations] qui dure, (très) long.

protraction [prə'trækʃn] *n* prolongation *f*.

protractor [prə'træktəʳ] *n* **1.** GEOM rapporteur *m* **2.** ANAT protracteur *m*.

protrude [prə'tru:d] ◇ *vi* [rock, ledge] faire saillie ■ [eyes, chin] saillir ■ [teeth] avancer ■ **his belly ~d over his trousers** son ventre débordait de son pantalon.
◇ *vt* avancer, pousser en avant.

protruding [prə'tru:dɪŋ] *adj* [ledge] en saillie ■ [chin, ribs] saillant ■ [eyes] globuleux ■ [teeth] proéminent, protubérant ■ [belly] protubérant.

protrusion [prə'tru:ʒn] *n* [ledge] saillie *f* ■ [bump] bosse *f*.

protuberance [prə'tju:bərəns] *n fml* protubérance *f*.

protuberant [prə'tju:bərənt] *adj fml* protubérant.

proud [praʊd] ◇ *adj* **1.** [pleased] fier ■ **to be ~ of sb/sthg** être fier de qqn/qqch ■ **he was ~ to have won** *OR* **of having won** il était fier d'avoir gagné ■ **I'm ~ (that) you didn't give up** je suis fier que tu n'aies pas abandonné ■ **it's nothing to be ~ of!** il n'y a vraiment pas de quoi être fier! ■ **they are now the ~ parents of a daughter** ils sont désormais les heureux parents d'une petite fille ■ **we are ~ to present this concert** nous sommes heureux de vous présenter ce concert ■ **it was a ~ moment for me** pour moi, ce fut un moment de grande fierté ■ **it was her ~est possession** c'était son bien le plus précieux **2.** [arrogant] fier, orgueilleux ➊ **as ~ as a peacock** fier comme un coq **3.** *lit* [stately - tree, mountain] majestueux, altier ; [- bearing, stallion, eagle] fier, majestueux **4.** *UK* [protruding] qui dépasse ■ **it's a few millimetres ~** ça dépasse de quelques millimètres.
◇ *adv inf* **to do sb ~** [entertain lavishly] recevoir qqn comme un roi/une reine ; [honour] faire honneur à qqn.

proudly ['praʊdlɪ] *adv* **1.** [with pride] fièrement, avec fierté ■ **we ~ present...** nous sommes fiers de présenter... **2.** [arrogantly] orgueilleusement **3.** [majestically] majestueusement.

Proustian ['pru:stjən] *adj* proustien.

provable ['pru:vəbl] *adj* prouvable, démontrable.

prove [pruːv] (*UK pret & pp* **proved** *US, pret* **proved**) (*pp* **proved** *OR* **proven** ['pruːvn]) ◇ *vt* **1.** [verify, show] prouver ▪ **the facts ~ her (to be) guilty** les faits prouvent qu'elle est coupable ▪ **the accused is innocent until ~ d** *OR* **proven guilty** l'accusé est innocent jusqu'à preuve du contraire *OR* tant que sa culpabilité n'est pas prouvée ▪ **to ~ sb right/wrong** donner raison/tort à qqn ▪ **they can't ~ anything against us** ils n'ont aucune preuve contre nous ▪ **I think I've ~d my point** je crois avoir apporté la preuve de ce que j'avançais ▪ **she quickly ~d herself indispensable** elle s'est vite montrée indispensable **2.** LOGIC & MATHS [proposition, theorem] démontrer **3.** [put to the test] mettre à l'épreuve ▪ **the method has not yet been ~d** la méthode n'a pas encore fait ses preuves ▪ **to ~ o.s.** faire ses preuves **4.** LAW [will] homologuer **5.** *arch* [experience] éprouver.
◇ *vi* **1.** [turn out] s'avérer, se révéler ▪ **your suspicions ~d (to be) well-founded** vos soupçons se sont avérés fondés ▪ **the arrangement ~d (to be) unworkable** cet arrangement s'est révélé impraticable ▪ **he may ~ (to be) of help to you** il pourrait bien vous être utile ▪ **it has ~d impossible to find him** il a été impossible de le retrouver **2.** CULIN [dough] lever.

proven ['pruːvn] ◇ *pp* ⊳ **prove**.
◇ *adj* **1.** [tested] éprouvé ▪ **a woman of ~ courage** une femme qui a fait preuve de courage ▪ **a ~ method** une méthode qui a fait ses preuves **2.** LAW : **a verdict of not ~** ≃ un non-lieu.

provenance ['prɒvənəns] *n* provenance *f*.

Provençal [ˌprɒvɒn'sɑːl] ◇ *n* **1.** [person] Provençal *m*, - e *f* **2.** LING provençal *m*.
◇ *adj* provençal.

Provence [prɒ'vɛ̃s] *pr n* Provence *f* ▪ **in ~** en Provence.

provender ['prɒvɪndəʳ] *n* **1.** [fodder] fourrage *m*, provende *f* **2.** [food] nourriture *f*.

proverb ['prɒvɜːb] *n* proverbe *m*.
➜ **Proverbs** *n* BIBLE : **(the Book of) Proverbs** le Livre des Proverbes.

proverbial [prə'vɜːbjəl] *adj* proverbial, légendaire.

proverbially [prə'vɜːbjəlɪ] *adv* proverbialement.

provide [prə'vaɪd] ◇ *vt* **1.** [supply] pourvoir, fournir ▪ **to ~ sthg for sb, to ~ sb with sthg** fournir qqch à qqn ▪ **they ~ a car for her use** ils mettent une voiture à sa disposition ▪ **the plane is ~d with eight emergency exits** l'avion dispose de huit sorties de secours ▪ **write the answers in the spaces ~d** écrivez les réponses dans les blancs prévus à cet effet **2.** [offer, afford] offrir, fournir ▪ **the new plant will ~ 2,000 jobs** la nouvelle usine créera 2 000 emplois ▪ **I want to ~ my children with a good education** je veux pouvoir offrir *OR* donner une bonne éducation à mes enfants ▪ **the book ~s a good introduction to maths** ce livre est une bonne introduction aux maths ▪ **milk ~s a good source of protein** le lait constitue un bon apport en protéines **3.** [stipulate - subj: contract, law] stipuler.
◇ *vi* : **to ~ against sthg** se prémunir contre qqch.
➜ **provide for** *vt insep* **1.** [support] : **to ~ for sb** pourvoir *OR* subvenir aux besoins de qqn ▪ **I have a family to ~ for** j'ai une famille à nourrir ▪ **an insurance policy that will ~ for your children's future** une assurance qui subviendra aux besoins de vos enfants ▪ **his widow was left well ~d for** sa veuve était à l'abri du besoin **2.** [prepare] : **to ~ for sthg** se préparer à qqch **3.** [contract, law] : **to ~ for sthg** stipuler *OR* prévoir qqch.

provided [prə'vaɪdɪd] *conj* : **~ (that)** pourvu que, à condition que ▪ **I'll wait for you ~ (that) it doesn't take too long** je t'attendrai à condition que ce ne soit pas trop long.

providence ['prɒvɪdəns] *n* **1.** [fate] providence *f* **2.** [foresight] prévoyance *f* ▪ [thrift] économie *f*.

provident ['prɒvɪdənt] *adj* [foresighted] prévoyant ▪ [thrifty] économe.

providential [ˌprɒvɪ'denʃl] *adj* providentiel.

providently ['prɒvɪdəntlɪ] *adv* avec prévoyance, prudemment.

provident society *n UK* société *f* de prévoyance.

provider [prə'vaɪdəʳ] *n* [gen] fournisseur *m*, - euse *f* ▪ COMPUT fournisseur *m* (d'accès), provider *m* ▪ **she's the family's sole ~** elle subvient seule aux besoins de la famille.

providing [prə'vaɪdɪŋ] = **provided**.

province ['prɒvɪns] *n* **1.** [region, district] province *f* ▪ **the Maritime/Prairie Provinces** [of Canada] les provinces maritimes/des prairies **2.** [field, sphere - of activity] domaine *m* ; [- of responsability] compétence *f* ▪ **politics was once the sole ~ of men** autrefois, la politique était un domaine exclusivement masculin ▪ **staff supervision is not within my ~** la gestion du personnel n'est pas de mon ressort **3.** RELIG province *f* ecclésiastique.
➜ **provinces** *npl UK* [not the metropolis] : **the ~s** la province ▪ **in the ~s** en province.

provincial [prə'vɪnʃl] ◇ *adj* provincial.
◇ *n* **1.** [from provinces] provincial *m*, - e *f* **2.** RELIG provincial *m*.

provincialism [prə'vɪnʃəlɪzm] *n* provincialisme *m*.

proving ground ['pruːvɪŋ-] *n* terrain *m* d'essai.

provision [prə'vɪʒn] ◇ *vt* approvisionner, ravitailler.
◇ *n* **1.** [act of supplying] approvisionnement *m*, fourniture *f*, ravitaillement *m* ▪ **~ of supplies in wartime is a major problem** le ravitaillement en temps de guerre pose de graves problèmes ▪ **one of their functions is the ~ of meals for the homeless** un de leurs rôles est de distribuer des repas aux sans-abri ▪ **the ~ of new jobs** la création d'emplois **2.** [stock, supply] provision *f*, réserve *f* ▪ **to lay in ~s for the winter** faire des provisions pour l'hiver ▪ **the US sent medical ~s** les États-Unis envoyèrent des stocks de médicaments **3.** [arrangement] disposition *f* ▪ **no ~ had been made for the influx of refugees** aucune disposition n'avait été prise pour faire face à l'afflux de réfugiés ▪ **to make ~s for one's family** pourvoir aux besoins de sa famille ▪ **you should think about making ~s for the future** vous devriez penser à assurer votre avenir ▪ **having a lot of children was a ~ for old age** le fait d'avoir de nombreux enfants constituait pour les parents une sorte d'assurance vieillesse **4.** [condition, clause] disposition *f*, clause *f* ▪ **under the ~s of the UN charter/his will** selon les dispositions de la charte de l'ONU/de son testament ▪ **a 4% increase is included in the budget's ~s** une augmentation de 4 % est prévue dans le budget.
➜ **provisions** *npl* [food] vivres *mpl*, provisions *fpl*.

provisional [prə'vɪʒənl] *adj* provisoire ▪ **~ (driving) licence** *UK* permis *m* de conduire provisoire *(autorisation que l'on doit obtenir avant de prendre des leçons)*.
➜ **Provisional** ◇ *adj* POL : **the Provisional IRA** l'IRA *f* provisoire.
◇ *n* membre *m* de l'IRA provisoire.

provisionally [prə'vɪʒnəlɪ] *adv* provisoirement.

proviso [prə'vaɪzəʊ] (*pl* **provisos** *OR* *pl* **provisoes**) *n* stipulation *f*, condition *f* ▪ **with the ~ that the goods be delivered** à la condition expresse *OR* sous réserve que les marchandises soient livrées ▪ **they accept, with one ~** ils acceptent, à une condition.

provisory [prə'vaɪzərɪ] *adj* **1.** [conditional] conditionnel **2.** = **provisional**.

provitamin [prəʊ'vɪtəmɪn, prəʊ'vaɪtəmɪn] *n* provitamine *f*.

provocation [ˌprɒvə'keɪʃn] *n* provocation *f* ▪ **he loses his temper at** *OR* **given the slightest ~** il se met en colère à la moindre provocation ▪ **the crime was committed under ~** ce crime a été commis en réponse à une provocation.

provocative [prə'vɒkətɪv] *adj* **1.** [challenging] provocateur, provocant ▪ **she doesn't really think that, she was just being ~** elle ne le pense pas vraiment, c'est simplement de la provocation **2.** [seductive] provocant **3.** [obscene] : **a ~ gesture** un geste obscène.

provocatively [prə'vɒkətɪvlɪ] *adv* [write, dress] d'une manière provocante ▪ [say] sur un ton provocateur *OR* provocant.

provoke [prə'vəʊk] *vt* **1.** [goad] provoquer ▪ **to ~ sb into doing sthg** pousser qqn à faire qqch ▪ **they'll shoot if in any way ~d** ils tireront à la moindre provocation ▪ **the dog is dangerous when ~d** le chien devient méchant si on le provoque *OR* l'excite ‖ [infuriate] enrager ▪ [vex] exaspérer **2.** [cause - accident, quarrel, anger] provoquer ▪ **the revelations ~d a public outcry** les révélations ont soulevé un tollé général.

provoking [prə'vəʊkɪŋ] *adj* [situation] contrariant ▪ [person, behaviour] exaspérant.

provokingly [prə'vəʊkɪŋlɪ] *adv* par provocation.

provost *n* ['prɒvəst] **1.** UNIV *UK* ≃ recteur *m* ▪ *US* ≃ doyen *m* **2.** RELIG doyen *m* **3.** *Scotland* maire *m* **4.** [prə'vəʊ] MIL ≃ gendarme *m*.

prow [praʊ] *n* proue *f*.

prowess ['praʊɪs] *n (U)* **1.** [skill] (grande) habileté *f* ▪ **~ in negotiating** habileté *OR* savoir-faire en matière de négociations ▪ **he showed great ~ on the sports field** il s'est révélé d'une adresse remarquable sur le terrain de sport ▪ **sexual ~** prouesses *fpl* sexuelles **2.** [bravery] vaillance *f*.

prowl [praʊl] ◇ *vi* rôder.
◇ *vt* [street, jungle] rôder dans.
◇ *n* : **to be on the ~** rôder ▪ **the gang was on the ~ for likely victims** la bande était à la recherche d'une victime.
◆ **prowl about** *UK*, **prowl around** ◇ *vi insep* rôder.
◇ *vt insep* = **prowl** *(vt)*.

prowl car *n US* voiture *f* de police en patrouille.

prowler ['praʊlər] *n* rôdeur *m*, - euse *f*.

prox *written abbr of* **proximo**.

proximity [prɒk'sɪmətɪ] *n* proximité *f* ▪ **in ~ to, in the ~ of** à proximité de.

proxy ['prɒksɪ] (*pl* **proxies**) *n* [person] mandataire *mf*, fondé *m*, - e *f* de pouvoir ▪ [authorization] procuration *f*, mandat *m* ▪ **to vote by ~** voter par procuration.

proxy vote *n* vote *m* par procuration.

Prozac® ['prəʊzæk] *n* Prozac® *m*.

prude [pru:d] *n* prude *f* ▪ **don't be such a ~!** ne sois pas si prude!

prudence ['pru:dns] *n* prudence *f*, circonspection *f*.

prudent ['pru:dnt] *adj* prudent, circonspect.

prudently ['pru:dntlɪ] *adv* prudemment.

prudish ['pru:dɪʃ] *adj* prude, pudibond.

prudishness ['pru:dɪʃnɪs] *n* pruderie *f*, pudibonderie *f*.

prune [pru:n] ◇ *n* **1.** [fruit] pruneau *m* **2.** *UK inf* [fool] patate *f*, ballot *m*.
◇ *vt* **1.** [hedge, tree] tailler ▪ [branch] élaguer **2.** *fig* [text, budget] élaguer, faire des coupes sombres dans ▪ **to ~ (back *OR* down) expenditure** réduire les dépenses.

pruning ['pru:nɪŋ] *n* [of hedge, tree] taille *f* ▪ [of branches] élagage *m* ▪ *fig* [of budget, staff] élagage *m*.

pruning hook *n* ébranchoir *m*.

pruning knife *n* serpette *f*.

prurience ['prʊərɪəns] *n* lubricité *f*, lascivité *f lit*.

prurient ['prʊərɪənt] *adj* lubrique, lascif.

Prussia ['prʌʃə] *pr n* Prusse *f* ▪ **in ~** en Prusse.

Prussian ['prʌʃn] ◇ *n* Prussien *m*, - enne *f*.
◇ *adj* prussien.

prussic acid ['prʌsɪk-] *n* acide *m* prussique.

pry [praɪ] (*pret & pp* **pried**) ◇ *vt US* = **prise**.
◇ *vi* fouiller, fureter ▪ **I didn't mean to ~** je ne voulais pas être indiscret ▪ **I told him not to ~ into my affairs** je lui ai dit de ne pas venir mettre le nez dans mes affaires.

prying ['praɪɪŋ] *adj* indiscret, - ète *f* ▪ **away from ~ eyes** à l'abri des regards indiscrets.

PS (*abbrev of* **postscript**) *n* PS *m*.

psalm [sɑ:m] *n* psaume *m* ▪ **(the Book of) Psalms** (le livre des) Psaumes.

psalmbook ['sɑ:mbʊk] *n* livre *m* de psaumes, psautier *m*.

PSBR *n* = **public sector borrowing requirement**.

psephology [se'fɒlədʒɪ] *n étude statistique et sociologique des élections*.

pseud [sju:d] *inf* ◇ *n* poseur *m*, - euse *f*, prétentieux *m*, - euse *f*.
◇ *adj* = **pseudo**.

pseudo ['sju:dəʊ] *adj inf* [kindness, interest] prétendu ▪ [person] faux, fausse *f*.

pseudo- *in cpds* pseudo-.

pseudonym ['sju:dənɪm] *n* pseudonyme *m*.

pseudonymous [sju:'dɒnɪməs] *adj* pseudonyme.

PSHE (*abbrev of* **personal, social and health education**) *n UK* SCH éducation *f* civique et sexuelle.

psi (*abbrev of* **pounds per square inch**) *n livres au pouce carré (mesure de pression)*.

psoriasis [sɒ'raɪəsɪs] *n (U)* psoriasis *m*.

psst [pst] *interj* psitt, pst.

PSV (*abbrev of* **public service vehicle**) *n* = **PCV**.

psych [saɪk] *vt inf* **1.** [psychoanalyse] psychanalyser **2.** *US* [excite] : **I'm really ~ed about my vacation** je suis surexcité à l'idée de partir en vacances.
◆ **psych out** *vt sep inf* **1.** [sense - sb's motives] deviner ; [- situation] comprendre, piger **2.** [intimidate] : **he soon ~ed out his opponent and the game was his** très vite il a décontenancé son adversaire et il a gagné.
◆ **psych up** *vt sep inf* [motivate] : **to ~ o.s. up for sthg/to do sthg** se préparer psychologiquement à qqch/à faire qqch ▪ **she ~ed herself up before the race** elle s'est concentrée avant la course.

psyche[1] ['saɪkɪ] *n* [mind] psyché *f*, psychisme *m*.

psyche[2] [saɪk] = **psych**.

psychedelic [,saɪkɪ'delɪk] *adj* psychédélique.

psychiatric [,saɪkɪ'ætrɪk] *adj* psychiatrique ▪ **he needs ~ help** il devrait consulter un psychiatre ➲ **~ nurse** infirmier *m*, - ère *f* psychiatrique.

psychiatrist [saɪ'kaɪətrɪst] *n* psychiatre *mf*.

psychiatry [saɪ'kaɪətrɪ] *n* psychiatrie *f*.

psychic ['saɪkɪk] ◇ *adj* **1.** [supernatural] parapsychique ▪ **to be ~, to have ~ powers** avoir le don de double vue *OR* un sixième sens ▪ **I'm not ~!** *hum* je ne suis pas devin! **2.** [mental] psychique.
◇ *n* médium *m*.

psycho ['saɪkəʊ] (*pl* **psychos**) *inf* ◇ *n* psychopathe *mf*.
◇ *adj* psychopathe.

psychoanalyse *UK*, **yze** *US* [,saɪkəʊ'ænəlaɪz] *vt* psychanalyser.

psychoanalysis [,saɪkəʊə'næləsɪs] *n* psychanalyse *f* ▪ **to undergo ~** suivre une psychanalyse, se faire psychanalyser.

psychoanalyst [,saɪkəʊ'ænəlɪst] *n* psychanalyste *mf*.

psychoanalytic(al) ['saɪkəʊ,ænə'lɪtɪk(l)] *adj* psychanalytique.

psychodrama ['saɪkəʊ,drɑ:mə] *n* psychodrame *m*.

psycholinguistics [,saɪkəʊlɪŋ'gwɪstɪks] *n (U)* psycholinguistique *f*.

psychological [,saɪkə'lɒdʒɪkl] *adj* psychologique.

psychological block *n* blocage *m* psychologique.

psychologically [,saɪkə'lɒdʒɪklɪ] *adv* psychologiquement.

psychological warfare *n* guerre *f* psychologique.

psychologist [saɪ'kɒlədʒɪst] *n* psychologue *mf*.

psychology [saɪ'kɒlədʒɪ] *n* psychologie *f* ➲ **child ~** psychologie infantile *OR* de l'enfant.

psychoneurosis [,saɪkəʊnjʊə'rəʊsɪs] (*pl* **psychoneuroses** [-si:z]) *n* psychonévrose *f*.

psychopath ['saɪkəpæθ] *n* psychopathe *mf*.

psychopathic [,saɪkə'pæθɪk] *adj* [person] psychopathe ■ [disorder, personality] psychopathique.

psychopathology [,saɪkəʊpə'θɒlədʒɪ] *n* psychopathologie *f*.

psychosis [saɪ'kəʊsɪs] (*pl* **psychoses** [-si:z]) *n* psychose *f*.

psychosomatic [,saɪkəʊsə'mætɪk] *adj* psychosomatique.

psychotherapist [,saɪkəʊ'θerəpɪst] *n* psychothérapeute *mf*.

psychotherapy [,saɪkəʊ'θerəpɪ] *n* psychothérapie *f*.

psychotic [sa'kɒtɪk] ◇ *adj* psychotique.
◇ *n* psychotique *mf*.

pt 1. *written abbr of* **pint 2.** *written abbr of* **point**.

PT *n* **1.** (*abbrev of* **physical training**) EPS *f* ■ **~ instructor** professeur *m* d'éducation physique **2.** *US* = **physical therapy**.

PTA (*abbrev of* **parent-teacher association**) *n association de parents d'élèves et de professeurs*.

ptarmigan ['tɑ:mɪgən] (*pl inv* OR *pl* **ptarmigans**) *n* lagopède *m* des Alpes.

pterodactyl [,terə'dæktɪl] *n* ptérodactyle *m*.

PTO *UK* (*written abbrev of* **please turn over**) TSVP.

Ptolemy ['tɒləmɪ] *pr n* Ptolémée.

ptomaine ['təʊmeɪn] *n* ptomaïne *f* ■ **~ poisoning** intoxication *f* alimentaire.

PTV *n* **1.** (*abbrev of* **pay television**) *télévision à péage* **2.** (*abbrev of* **public television**) *programmes télévisés éducatifs*.

pub [pʌb] (*abbrev of* **public house**) *n* pub *m* ■ **we had a ~ lunch** nous avons déjeuné dans un pub ■ **~ grub** *inf nourriture (relativement simple) servie dans un pub*.

PUB

Dans l'ensemble des îles britanniques, le *pub* est un des grands foyers de la vie sociale, surtout le vendredi et le samedi soir. Ces établissements généralement interdits aux personnes de moins de 18 ans non accompagnées étaient soumis à des horaires stricts, mais ceux-ci se sont beaucoup assouplis récemment (voir « licensing hours »). De simple débit de boissons, qu'il était souvent, de plus en plus le *pub* évolue vers une sorte de brasserie servant des repas légers. Certains sont devenus de véritables restaurants.

pub. *written abbr of* **published**.

pub crawl *n UK inf* **to go on a ~** ≃ faire la tournée des bars.

puberty ['pju:bətɪ] *n* puberté *f* ■ **to reach ~** atteindre l'âge de la puberté.

pubes ['pju:bi:z] (*pl inv*) *n* [region] pubis *m*, région *f* pubienne ■ [hair] poils *mpl* pubiens ■ [bones] (os *m* du) pubis *m*.

pubescence [pju:'besns] *n* **1.** [puberty] (âge *m* de la) puberté *f* **2.** [of plant, animal] pubescence *f*.

pubescent [pju:'besnt] *adj* **1.** [at puberty] pubère **2.** [plant, animal] pubescent.

pubic ['pju:bɪk] *adj* pubien ■ **~ hair** poils *mpl* pubiens OR du pubis.

pubis ['pju:bɪs] (*pl* **pubes** ['pju:bi:z]) *n* pubis *m*.

public ['pʌblɪk] ◇ *adj* **1.** [of, by the state - education, debt] public ■ **built at ~ expense** construit avec des fonds publics ▶ **~ bill** *UK* POL ≃ projet *m* de loi d'intérêt général ■ **~ housing** *US* logements *mpl* sociaux, ≃ HLM *f inv* ■ **~ housing project** *US* ≃ cité *f* HLM ■ **~ money** deniers *mpl* OR fonds *mpl* publics ■ **to hold ~ office** avoir des fonctions officielles ■ **~ official** fonctionnaire *mf* ■ **~ ownership** nationalisation *f*, étatisation *f* ■ **most airports are under ~ ownership** la plupart des aéroports appartiennent à l'État ■ **the ~ purse** *UK* le Trésor (public) ■ **~ television** *US* (télévision *f* du) service *m* public
2. [open or accessible to all - place, meeting] public ■ **was it a ~ trial?** le public pouvait-il assister au procès? ■ **let's talk somewhere less ~** allons discuter dans un endroit plus tranquille ■ **these gardens are ~ property!** ces jardins appartiennent à tout le monde! ▶ **~ baths** bains *mpl* publics ■ **~ library** bibliothèque *f* municipale ■ **~ phone** cabine *f* téléphonique
3. [of, by the people] public ■ **in the ~ interest** dans l'intérêt général ■ **a ~ outcry** un tollé général ■ **to restore ~ confidence** regagner la confiance de la population ■ **~ awareness of the problem has increased** le public est plus sensible au problème maintenant ■ **the bill has ~ support** l'opinion publique est favorable au projet de loi ■ **the increase in crime is generating great ~ concern** la montée de la criminalité inquiète sérieusement la population ■ **to be in the ~ eye** occuper le devant de la scène (publique) ▶ **~ access channel** *US* TV *chaîne du réseau câblé à laquelle peuvent avoir accès des particuliers*
4. [publicly known, open] public ■ **to make sthg ~** rendre qqch public ■ **a ~ figure** une personnalité très connue ■ **she's active in ~ life** elle prend une part active aux affaires publiques ■ **it created a ~ scandal** ça a provoqué un scandale retentissant ■ **he made a ~ denial of the rumours** il a démenti publiquement les rumeurs, il a apporté un démenti public aux rumeurs ■ **it's ~ knowledge that...** il est de notoriété publique que... ▶ **~ spirit** sens *m* civique, civisme *m*
5. ST. EX : **to go ~** être coté en Bourse.
◇ *n* public *m* ■ **the ~ is** OR **are tired of political scandals** la population est lasse des scandales politiques ■ **her books reach a wide ~** ses livres touchent un public très large ■ **the film-going ~** les amateurs de OR les gens qui vont au cinéma ■ **the viewing ~** les téléspectateurs.
in public *adv phr* en public.

public-address system *n* (système *m* de) sonorisation *f*.

publican ['pʌblɪkən] *n* **1.** *UK* [pub owner] patron *m*, - onne *f* de pub ■ [manager] tenancier *m*, - ère *f* de pub **2.** BIBLE [tax collector] publicain *m*.

public assistance *n US* aide *f* sociale.

publication [,pʌblɪ'keɪʃn] *n* **1.** [of book, statistics, banns] publication *f* ■ [of edict] promulgation *f* ■ **her article has been accepted for ~** son article va être publié **2.** [work] publication *f*, ouvrage *m* publié.

public bar *n UK* salle *f* de bar *(moins confortable et moins cher que le "lounge bar" ou le "saloon bar")*.

public company *n* ≃ société *f* anonyme *(dont les actions sont négociables en Bourse)*.

public convenience *n UK* toilettes *fpl* publiques.

public corporation *n UK & Canada* entreprise *f* publique.

public domain *n* : **to be in the ~** [publication] être dans le domaine public.

public enemy *n* ennemi *m* public.

public footpath *n UK* sentier *m* public.

public gallery *n* tribune *f* réservée au public.

public health *n* santé *f* publique ■ **~ hazard** risque *m* pour la santé publique ■ **the ~ authorities** *administration régionale des services publics de santé* ■ **~ inspector** *dated* inspecteur *m* sanitaire.

public holiday *n* jour *m* férié, fête *f* légale.

public house *n UK* [pub] pub *m*, bar *m* ■ *US* [inn] auberge *f*.

public inquiry *n* enquête *f* officielle ■ **to hold a ~** faire une enquête officielle.

publicist ['pʌblɪsɪst] *n* **1.** [press agent] (agent *m*) publicitaire *mf* **2.** [journalist] journaliste *mf* **3.** LAW publiciste *mf*.

publicity [pʌb'lɪsɪtɪ] ◇ *n* publicité *f* ■ **she/her film is getting** OR **attracting a lot of ~** on fait beaucoup de publicité autour

d'elle/de son film ■ **the incident will mean bad ~ for us** cet incident va être mauvais pour *OR* va faire du tort à notre image de marque.
◇ *comp* [agent, campaign] publicitaire, de publicité ■ [manager] de publicité ■ **~ stunt** coup *m* de pub.

publicity-seeking [-si:kɪŋ] *adj* [person] qui cherche à se faire de la publicité ■ [operation, manœuvre] publicitaire.

publicize, ise ['pʌblɪsaɪz] *vt* **1.** [make known] : **he doesn't like to ~ the fact that he's been in prison** il n'aime pas qu'on dise qu'il a fait de la prison ■ **his much ~d blunders don't help his image** ses célèbres gaffes ne font rien pour arranger son image de marque ■ **the government's environmental reforms have been well ~d in the press** la presse a beaucoup parlé des réformes du gouvernement en matière d'environnement **2.** [advertise - product, event] faire de la publicité pour.

public lavatory *n UK* toilettes *fpl* publiques.

public lending right *n droits que touche un auteur ou un éditeur pour le prêt de ses livres en bibliothèque.*

public limited company *n* société *f* à responsabilité limitée.

publicly ['pʌblɪklɪ] *adv* publiquement, en public ■ **his ~ declared intentions** les intentions qu'il avait affichées ■ **~ owned** ECON nationalisé ■ **the company is 51% ~ controlled** la compagnie est contrôlée à 51 % par des capitaux publics.

public nuisance *n* **1.** [act] : **the pub's late opening hours were creating a ~** les heures d'ouverture tardives du pub portaient atteinte à la tranquillité générale **2.** [person] fléau *m* public, empoisonneur *m*, - euse *f*.

public opinion *n* opinion *f* publique ■ **~ poll** sondage *m* (d'opinion).

public prosecutor *n* ≃ procureur *mf* général, ≃ ministère *m* public.

Public Records Office [,pʌblɪk'rekɔ:dz,ɒfɪs] *n* : **the ~** les Archives nationales du Royaume Uni.

public relations ◇ *n (U)* relations *fpl* publiques.
◇ *adj* : **~ consultant** conseil *m* en relations publiques ■ **~ exercise** opération *f* de relations publiques ■ **~ officer** responsable *mf* des relations publiques.

public school *n* **1.** [in UK] public school *f*, école *f* privée (prestigieuse) **2.** [in US] école *f* publique.

PUBLIC SCHOOL

En Angleterre et au pays de Galles, le terme *public school* désigne une école privée de type traditionnel ; certaines de ces écoles (comme Eton et Harrow, par exemple) sont très réputées. Les *public schools* ont pour vocation de former l'élite de la nation. Aux États-Unis, le terme désigne une école publique.

public schoolboy *n UK* élève *m* d'une "public school".

public schoolgirl *n UK* élève *f* d'une "public school".

public sector *n* secteur *m* public ■ **~ borrowing requirement** emprunts *mpl* d'État.

public servant *n* fonctionnaire *mf*.

public service *n* **1.** *UK* [civil service] fonction *f* publique **2.** [amenity] service *m* public *OR* d'intérêt général ■ ADMIN : **our organization performs a ~** notre association assure un service d'intérêt général.
◆ **public-service** *adj* : **a public-service message** *OR* **announcement** RADIO & TV un communiqué (d'un ministère) ➲ **Public-Service Commission** *US commission chargée de la réglementation des sociétés privées assurant des services publics* ■ **public-service corporation** *US société privée assurant un service public et réglementée par une commission d'État* ■ **public-service vehicle** *UK* autobus *m*.

public speaker *n* orateur *m*, - trice *f*.

public speaking *n* art *m* oratoire ■ **unaccustomed as I am to ~** *hum* bien que je n'aie pas l'habitude de prendre la parole en public.

public spending *n (U)* dépenses *fpl* publiques *OR* de l'État.

public-spirited *adj* [gesture] d'esprit civique ■ [person] : **to be ~** faire preuve de civisme.

public transport *n (U)* transports *mpl* en commun ■ **he went by ~** [bus] il est allé en bus ■ [train] il est allé en train.

public utility *n US* **1.** [company] *société privée assurant un service public et réglementée par une commission d'État* **2.** [amenity] service *m* public.

public works *npl* travaux *mpl* publics.

publish ['pʌblɪʃ] ◇ *vt* **1.** [book, journal] publier, éditer ■ [author] éditer ■ **her latest novel has just been ~ed** son dernier roman vient de paraître ■ **he's a ~ed author** ses livres sont publiés ■ **it's ~ed by Larousse** c'est édité chez Larousse ■ **the magazine is ~ed quarterly** la revue paraît tous les trois mois **2.** [subj: author] : **he's ~ed poems in several magazines** ses poèmes ont été publiés dans plusieurs revues **3.** [make known - statistics, statement, banns] publier.
◇ *vi* **1.** [newspaper] paraître **2.** [author] être publié ■ **she ~es regularly in women's magazines** ses articles sont régulièrement publiés dans la presse féminine.

publishable ['pʌblɪʃəbl] *adj* publiable.

publisher ['pʌblɪʃəʳ] *n* [person] éditeur *m*, - trice *f* ■ [company] maison *f* d'édition.

publishing ['pʌblɪʃɪŋ] ◇ *n* **1.** [industry] édition *f* ■ **she's** *OR* **she works in ~** elle travaille dans l'édition **2.** [of book, journal] publication *f*.
◇ *comp* : **a ~ giant** un géant de l'édition ■ **a ~ empire** un empire de l'édition ■ **~ company** *OR* **house** maison *f* d'édition.

puce [pju:s] ◇ *n* couleur *f* puce.
◇ *adj* puce *(inv)*.

puck [pʌk] *n* **1.** [in ice hockey] palet *m* **2.** [sprite] lutin *m*, farfadet *m*.

pucker ['pʌkəʳ] ◇ *vi* [face, forehead] se plisser ■ [fabric, collar] goder, godailler.
◇ *vt* [face, forehead] plisser ■ [fabric, collar] faire goder, faire godailler ■ **the seam/hem is ~ed** la couture/l'ourlet fait des plis.
◇ *n* [crease] pli *m*.
◆ **pucker up** ◇ *vi insep* **1.** = **pucker** *(vi)* **2.** *inf* [for kiss] avancer les lèvres.
◇ *vt sep* = **pucker** *(vt)*.

puckish ['pʌkɪʃ] *adj* espiègle.

pudding ['pʊdɪŋ] *n* **1.** [sweet dish] : **jam ~** pudding *m* à la confiture ■ **rice/tapioca ~** riz *m* /tapioca *m* au lait **2.** *UK* [part of meal] dessert *m* **3.** [savoury dish] *tourte cuite à la vapeur* **4.** [sausage] boudin *m* ■ **white ~** boudin *m* blanc **5.** *UK inf* [podgy person] boudin *m*.

pudding basin, pudding bowl *n UK jatte dans laquelle on fait cuire le pudding* ■ **~ haircut** coupe *f* au bol.

pudding stone *n* GEOL poudingue *m*.

puddle ['pʌdl] ◇ *n* flaque *f*.
◇ *vt* [clay] malaxer.

pudendum [pju:'dendəm], **pudenda** [pju:'dendə] *n* parties *fpl* génitales.

pudgy ['pʌdʒɪ] (*comp* **pudgier**, *superl* **pudgiest**) = **podgy**.

Pueblo ['pwebləʊ] (*pl inv OR pl* **Pueblos**) *n* Pueblo *mf*.

puerile ['pjʊəraɪl] *adj* puéril.

puerperal [pju:'ɜ:pərəl] *adj* puerpéral.

Puerto Rican [,pwɜ:təʊ'ri:kən] ◇ *pr n* Portoricain *m*, - e *f*.
◇ *adj* portoricain.

Puerto Rico [,pwɜ:təʊ'ri:kəʊ] *pr n* Porto Rico, Puerto Rico ■ **in ~** à Porto Rico, à Puerto Rico.

puff[1] [pʌf] ◇ *vt* **1.** [smoke - cigar, pipe] tirer des bouffées de **2.** [emit, expel] : **to ~ (out) smoke/steam** envoyer des nuages de fumée/des jets de vapeur **3.** [pant] : **"I can't go on", he ~ed** "je

n'en peux plus", haleta-t-il **4.** [swell - sail, parachute] gonfler **5.** *phr* **I'm ~ed (out)!** *inf* je n'ai plus de souffle!, je suis complètement essoufflé!
<> *vi* **1.** [blow - person] souffler ; [- wind] souffler en bourrasques **2.** [pant] haleter ▪ [breathe heavily] souffler ▪ **he was ~ing and panting** il soufflait comme un phoque ▪ **I ~ed along beside her** je courais, tout essoufflé, à ses côtés **3.** [smoke] : **to ~ on one's cigar** tirer sur son cigare **4.** [issue - smoke, steam] sortir **5.** [train] : **the train ~ed into the station** le train entra en gare dans un nuage de fumée.
<> *n* **1.** [gust, whiff] bouffée *f* ▪ [gasp] souffle *m* ▪ **her breath came in short ~s** elle haletait ▪ **all our plans went up in a ~ of smoke** *fig* tous nos projets sont partis en fumée *OR* se sont évanouis **2.** [on cigarette, pipe] bouffée *f* ▪ **to have** *OR* **to take a ~** tirer une bouffée **3.** [sound - of train] teuf-teuf *m* **4.** *UK inf* [breath] souffle *m* ▪ **to be out of ~** être à bout de souffle *OR* essoufflé **5.** [fluffy mass] : **~s of cloud in the sky** des moutons *OR* des petits nuages dans le ciel **6.** [for make-up] : **(powder) ~** houppe *f* (à poudrer), houpette *f* **7.** [pastry] chou *m* **8.** *US* [eiderdown] édredon *m*.
◆ **puff out** <> *vt sep* **1.** [extinguish] souffler, éteindre (en soufflant) **2.** [inflate, make rounded - cheeks, sail] gonfler ; [- chest] bomber ; [- cushion, hair] faire bouffer ▪ **the pigeon ~ed out its feathers** le pigeon fit gonfler ses plumes **3.** [emit] : **to ~ out smoke/steam** envoyer des nuages de fumée/de vapeur.
<> *vi insep* **1.** [parachute, sail] se gonfler **2.** [be emitted - smoke] s'échapper.
◆ **puff up** <> *vt sep* **1.** = **puff out** *(sense 2)* **2.** *(usu passive)* [swell - lip, ankle etc] enfler ▪ **her eyes were ~ed up** elle avait les yeux bouffis ▪ **to be ~ed up with pride** *fig* être bouffi d'orgueil.
<> *vi insep* [lip, ankle etc] enfler, bouffir.

puff² [pʊf] = **poof**.

puff adder [pʌf-] *n* vipère *f* heurtante.

puffball ['pʌfbɔ:l] *n* vesse-de-loup *f*.

puffed [pʌft] *adj* **1.** [rice, oats] soufflé ▪ **~ wheat cereal** céréale *f* de blé soufflé **2.** *UK inf* [out of breath] essoufflé, à bout de souffle.

puffed sleeves = **puff sleeves**.

puffed-up *adj* **1.** [swollen] boursouflé, enflé **2.** [conceited] suffisant, content de soi.

puffer ['pʌfəʳ] *n* **1.** [fish] poisson *m* armé **2.** *UK inf* [train] train *m*.

puffin ['pʌfɪn] *n* macareux *m*.

puffiness ['pʌfɪnɪs] *n* boursouflure *f*.

puff pastry [pʌf-] *UK*, **puff paste** [pʌf-] *US n* [for pies] pâte *f* feuilletée ▪ [for puffs] pâte *f* à choux.

puff sleeves [pʌf-] *npl* manches *fpl* ballon.

puffy ['pʌfɪ] (*comp* **puffier**, *superl* **puffiest**) *adj* [lip, cheek] enflé ▪ [eye] bouffi ▪ **~ clouds** moutons *mpl*.

pug [pʌg] *n* [dog] carlin *m*.

pugilism ['pju:dʒɪlɪzm] *n lit* pugilat *m lit*, boxe *f*.

pugilist ['pju:dʒɪlɪst] *n lit* pugiliste *m lit*, boxeur *m*.

pugnacious [pʌg'neɪʃəs] *adj fml* pugnace, agressif.

pugnacity [pʌg'næsətɪ] *n fml* pugnacité *f*.

pug nose *n* nez *m* camus.

pug-nosed [-nəʊzd] *adj* [face, person] au nez camus ▪ **to be ~** avoir le nez camus.

puke△ [pju:k] <> *vt* dégueuler△, gerber△ ▪ **you make me ~!** tu me dégoûtes!△.
<> *vi* dégueuler.
<> *n* dégueulis△ *m*.
◆ **puke up** <> *vt sep* dégueuler.
<> *vi insep* dégueuler.

pukka ['pʌkə] *adj UK dated & hum* **1.** [genuine] vrai, authentique, véritable **2.** [done well] bien fait, très correct ▪ [excellent] de premier ordre **3.** [socially acceptable] (très) comme il faut.

pull [pʊl] <> *vt* **1.** [object - yank, tug] tirer ; [- drag] traîner ▪ **she ~ed my hair** elle m'a tiré les cheveux ▪ **to ~ the blinds** baisser les stores ▪ **to ~ the curtains** *OR* **drapes** *US* tirer *OR* fermer les rideaux ▪ **he ~ed his chair closer to the fire** il approcha sa chaise de la cheminée ▪ **she ~ed the hood over her face** elle abaissa le capuchon sur son visage ▪ **she came in and ~ed the door shut behind her** elle entra et ferma la porte derrière elle ▪ **~ the rope taut** tendez la corde ▪ [person] tirer, entraîner ▪ **he ~ed himself onto the riverbank** il se hissa sur la berge ▪ **the sound of the doorbell ~ed him out of his daydream** *fig* le coup de sonnette l'a tiré de *OR* arraché à ses rêveries ▮ [remove forcibly] arracher ▪ **she ~ed her hand from mine** elle retira (brusquement) sa main de la mienne ▶ **~ the other one (it's got bells on)!** *UK inf* mon œil!, à d'autres! ▪ **to ~ sthg to bits** *OR* **pieces** *liter* démonter qqch ; *fig* démolir qqch
2. [operate - lever, handle] tirer ▪ **~ the trigger** appuyez *OR* pressez sur la détente
3. [tow, draw - load, trailer, carriage, boat] tirer, remorquer ▪ **carts ~ed by mules** des charrettes tirées par des mules
4. [take out - tooth] arracher, extraire ; [- weapon] tirer, sortir ▪ **he ~ed a gun on me** il a braqué un revolver sur moi
5. [strain - muscle, tendon] : **she ~ed a muscle** elle s'est déchiré un muscle, elle s'est fait un claquage
6. *inf* [bring off] réussir ▪ **to ~ a trick on sb** jouer un tour à qqn ▪ **what are you trying to ~?** qu'est-ce que vous êtes en train de combiner *OR* manigancer? ▪ **don't try and ~ anything!** n'essayez pas de jouer au plus malin!
7. [hold back] : **to ~ one's punches** *liter & fig* retenir ses coups, ménager son adversaire ▪ **she didn't ~ any punches** elle n'y est pas allée de main morte
8. [gut - fowl] vider
9. *inf* [withdraw] retirer ▪ **people complained and they had to ~ the commercial** ils ont dû retirer la pub suite à des plaintes
10. *inf* [attract - customers, spectators] attirer ▪ **the festival ~ed a big crowd** le festival a attiré beaucoup de monde
11. *UK* [serve - draught beer] tirer
12. △ *UK* [seduce] lever.
<> *vi* **1.** [exert force, tug] tirer ▪ **~ harder!** tirez plus fort! ▪ **the steering ~s to the right** la direction tire à droite
2. [rope, cord] : **the rope ~ed easily** la corde filait librement
3. [go, move - vehicle, driver] : **~ into the space next to the Mercedes** mettez-vous *OR* garez-vous à côté de la Mercedes ▪ **he ~ed into the right-hand lane** il a pris la file de droite ▪ **when the train ~s out of the station** quand le train quitte la gare
4. [strain, labour - vehicle] peiner ; [- horse] tirer sur le mors ▪ **the overloaded truck ~ed up the slope** le camion surchargé montait la côte avec difficulté
5. [snag - sweater] filer
6. [row] ramer
7. △ [have sex] : **did you ~ last night?** tu as tiré la nuit dernière?
<> *n* **1.** [tug, act of pulling] coup *m* ▪ **to give sthg a ~, to give a ~ on sthg** tirer (sur) qqch ▪ **I felt a ~ on the fishing line** ça mordait
2. [physical force - of machine] traction *f* ; [- of sun, moon, magnet] attraction *f* ▪ **the gravitational ~ is stronger on Earth** la gravitation est plus forte sur Terre ▪ **we fought against the ~ of the current** nous luttions contre le courant qui nous entraînait
3. [resistance - of bowstring] résistance *f*
4. [psychological, emotional attraction] attrait *m*
5. *inf* [influence, power] influence *f* ▪ **his father's ~ got him in** son père l'a pistonné
6. [climb] montée *f* ▪ **it'll be a long ~ to the summit** la montée sera longue (et difficile) pour atteindre le sommet
7. [in rowing - stroke] coup *m* de rame *OR* d'aviron ▪ **it will be a hard ~ upstream** il faudra ramer dur pour remonter le courant
8. [at cigar] bouffée *f* ▪ [at drink, bottle] gorgée *f* ▪ [on cigarette, pipe] : **to take a ~ at** *OR* **on** tirer sur
9. [knob, handle] poignée *f* ▪ [cord] cordon *m* ▪ [strap] sangle *f*
10. [snag - in sweater] accroc *m*
11. TYPO épreuve *f*.
◆ **pull about** *vt sep* [handle roughly - person] malmener ; [- clothes] tirer sur.
◆ **pull ahead** *vi insep* prendre de l'avance ▪ **to ~ ahead of sb** prendre de l'avance sur qqn.
◆ **pull along** *vt sep* [load, vehicle] tirer ▪ [person] entraîner.
◆ **pull apart** <> *vt sep* **1.** [take to pieces - machine, furniture] démonter
2. [destroy, break] mettre en morceaux *OR* en pièces ▪ **the wreck was ~ed apart by the waves** les vagues ont disloqué l'épave ▪ **tell him where it's hidden or he'll ~ the place apart** *inf* dites-lui où c'est (caché) sinon il va tout saccager

3. ***fig*** [demolish - essay, theory] démolir
4. [separate - fighters, dogs] séparer ; [- papers] détacher, séparer
5. [make suffer] déchirer.
◇ *vi insep* [furniture] se démonter, être démontable.

◆ **pull around** *vt sep* **1.** [cart, toy, suitcase] tirer derrière soi
2. [make turn] tourner, faire pivoter ▪ **he ~ed the horse around** il fit faire demi-tour à son cheval.

◆ **pull at** *vt insep* **1.** [strain at, tug at] tirer sur ▪ **I ~ed at his sleeve** je l'ai tiré par la manche
2. [suck - pipe, cigar] tirer sur ; [- bottle] **: he ~ed at his bottle of beer** il a bu une gorgée de bière.

◆ **pull away** ◇ *vi insep* **1.** [withdraw - person] s'écarter, se détourner ▪ **he had me by the arm but I managed to ~ away** il me tenait par le bras mais j'ai réussi à me dégager
2. [move off - vehicle, ship] démarrer ; [- train, convoy] s'ébranler ▪ **the boat ~ed away from the bank** le bateau quitta la rive
3. [get ahead - runner, competitor] prendre de l'avance ▪ **she's ~ing away from the pack** elle prend de l'avance sur le peloton, elle se détache du peloton.
◇ *vt sep* [withdraw - covering, hand] retirer ▪ **he ~ed me away from the window** il m'éloigna de la fenêtre ▪ [grab] arracher ▪ **she ~ed the book away from him** elle lui arracha le livre.

◆ **pull back** ◇ *vi insep* **1.** [withdraw - troops, participant] se retirer
2. [step backwards] reculer
3. [jib - horse, person] regimber.
◇ *vt sep* **1.** [draw backwards or towards one] retirer ▪ **she ~ed back the curtains** elle ouvrit les rideaux ▪ **~ the lever back** tirez le levier (vers l'arrière)
2. [withdraw - troops] retirer.

◆ **pull down** ◇ *vt sep* **1.** [lower - lever, handle] tirer (vers le bas) ; [- trousers, veil] baisser ; [- suitcase, book] descendre ; [- blind, window] baisser ▪ **~ the blind/the window down** baissez le store/la vitre ▪ **with his hat ~ed down over his eyes** son chapeau rabattu sur les yeux ▪ **she ~ed her skirt down over her knees** elle ramena sa jupe sur ses genoux
2. [demolish - house, wall] démolir, abattre ▪ **it'll ~ down the government** ***fig*** ça va renverser le gouvernement
3. ***inf*** [weaken - subj: illness] affaiblir, abattre ▪ [depress] déprimer, abattre
4. ***US inf*** [earn] gagner, se faire.
◇ *vi insep* [blind] descendre.

◆ **pull in** ◇ *vi insep* [vehicle, driver - stop] s'arrêter ; [- park] se garer ; [- move to side of road] se rabattre ▪ [train] entrer en gare ▪ **I ~ed in for petrol** je me suis arrêté pour prendre de l'essence.
◇ *vt sep* **1.** [line, fishing net] ramener ▪ **to ~ sb in** [into building, car] tirer qqn à l'intérieur, faire entrer qqn ; [into water] faire tomber qqn à l'eau ▮ [stomach] rentrer
2. [attract - customers, investors, investment] attirer ▪ **her show is really ~ing them in** son spectacle attire les foules
3. ***inf*** [earn - subj: person] gagner, se faire ; [- subj: business] rapporter
4. ***inf*** [arrest] arrêter, embarquer.

◆ **pull off** ◇ *vi insep* **1.** [move off] démarrer ▪ [after halt] redémarrer
2. [leave main road] quitter la route ▪ **he ~ed off onto a side road** il bifurqua sur une petite route ▮ [stop] s'arrêter.
◇ *vt sep* **1.** [clothes, boots, ring] enlever, retirer ▪ [cover, bandage, knob] enlever ▪ [page from calendar, sticky backing] détacher ▪ [wrapping, wallpaper] enlever
2. ***inf*** [accomplish - deal, stratagem, mission, shot] réussir ; [- press conference, negotiations] mener à bien ; [- plan] réaliser ▪ **will she (manage to) ~ it off?** est-ce qu'elle va y arriver?

◆ **pull on** ◇ *vt sep* [clothes, boots, pillow slip] mettre, enfiler.
◇ *vt insep* **1.** [tug at - rope, handle etc] tirer sur
2. [draw on - cigarette, pipe] tirer sur.

◆ **pull out** ◇ *vi insep* **1.** [withdraw - troops, ally, participant] se retirer ▪ **they've ~ed out of the deal** ils se sont retirés de l'affaire
2. [move off - car, ship] démarrer ; [- train, convoy] s'ébranler ▪ **she was ~ing out of the garage** elle sortait du garage ▪ [move towards centre of road] **: he ~ed out to overtake** il a déboîté pour doubler ▪ **a truck suddenly ~ed out in front of me** soudain, un camion m'a coupé la route ▪ **to ~ out into traffic** s'engager dans la circulation ▮ AERON **: to ~ out of a dive** sortir d'un piqué, se rétablir
3. [economy] **: to ~ out of a recession/a crisis** sortir de la récession/d'une crise
4. [slide out] **: the sofa ~s out into a bed** le canapé se transforme en lit ▪ **the shelves ~ out** on peut retirer les étagères ▪ **the table top ~s out** c'est une table à rallonges.
◇ *vt sep* **1.** [remove - tooth, hair, weeds] arracher ; [- splinter, nail] enlever ; [- plug, cork] ôter, enlever ▪ [produce - wallet, weapon] sortir, tirer ▪ **she ~ed a map out of her bag** elle sortit une carte de son sac ▪ **~ the paper gently out of the printer** retirez doucement le papier de l'imprimante ▪ **the tractor ~ed us out of the mud/ditch** le tracteur nous a sortis de la boue/du fossé ▪ **to ~ the country out of recession** sortir le pays de la récession
2. [draw towards one - drawer] tirer ▪ [unfold] déplier ▪ **he ~ed a chair out from under the table** il a écarté une chaise de la table
3. [withdraw - troops, contestant] retirer
4. COMPUT [select, produce - data] sortir.

◆ **pull over** ◇ *vt sep* **1.** [draw into specified position] tirer, traîner ▪ **~ the chair over to the window** amenez la chaise près de la fenêtre ▪ **she ~ed the dish over and helped herself** elle a tiré le plat vers *OR* à elle et s'est servie
2. [make fall - pile, person, table] faire tomber, renverser
3. *(usu passive)* [stop - vehicle, driver] arrêter ▪ **I got ~ed over for speeding** je me suis fait arrêter pour excès de vitesse.
◇ *vi insep* [vehicle, driver - stop] s'arrêter ; [- move to side of road] se ranger, se rabattre.

◆ **pull round** *UK* ◇ *vt sep* **1.** = **pull around**
2. [revive] ranimer.
◇ *vi insep* [regain consciousness] revenir à soi, reprendre connaissance ▪ [recover] se remettre.

◆ **pull through** ◇ *vi insep* [recover] s'en sortir, s'en tirer.
◇ *vt sep* **1.** [draw through - rope, thread] faire passer
2. [help survive or surmount] tirer d'affaire.

◆ **pull to** *vt sep* [shut - door, gate] fermer.

◆ **pull together** ◇ *vi insep* [on rope] tirer ensemble ▪ [on oars] ramer à l'unisson ▪ ***fig*** [combine efforts] concentrer ses efforts, agir de concert.
◇ *vt sep* **1.** [place together, join] joindre
2. [organize - demonstration, rescue team] organiser ▪ [prepare] préparer
3. ***phr*** **to ~ o.s. together** se reprendre, se ressaisir ▪ **~ yourself together!** ressaisissez-vous!, ne vous laissez pas aller!

◆ **pull up** ◇ *vi insep* **1.** [stop] s'arrêter ▪ **to ~ up short** s'arrêter net *OR* brusquement
2. ***inf*** [ease up] se détendre, se relâcher
3. [draw even] rattraper ▪ **to ~ up with sb** rattraper qqn
4. [improve - student, athlete, performance] s'améliorer.
◇ *vt sep* **1.** [draw upwards - trousers, sleeve, blanket, lever] remonter ▪ [hoist] hisser ▪ **they ~ed the boat up onto the beach** ils ont tiré le bateau sur la plage
2. [move closer - chair] approcher ▪ **why don't you ~ up a chair and join us?** prenez donc une chaise et joignez-vous à nous!
3. [uproot - weeds] arracher ; [- bush, stump, tree] arracher, déraciner ▪ [rip up - floorboards] arracher
4. [stop - person, vehicle, horse] arrêter ▪ [check - person] retenir ▪ **he was about to tell them everything but I ~ed him up (short)** il était sur le point de tout leur dire mais je lui ai coupé la parole
5. ***inf*** [improve - score, mark] améliorer ; [- average] remonter
6. ***UK inf*** [rebuke] réprimander, enguirlander.

pulldown ['pʊldaʊn] *adj* [bench, counter] à abattant ▪ **~ menu** COMPUT menu *m* déroulant ▪ **~ seat** strapontin *m*.

pullet ['pʊlɪt] *n* poulette *f*.

pulley ['pʊlɪ] *n* [wheel, device] poulie *f* ▪ TECH [set of parallel wheels] molette *f*.

pull-in *n* ***UK*** AUT [café] café *m* au bord de la route, ≃ restaurant *m* routier.

Pullman ['pʊlmən] *(pl* **Pullmans***)* *n* **1.** [sleeping car] **: ~ (carriage** *OR* **car)** (voiture *f*) pullman *m* **2.** [train] rapide *m* de nuit.

pullout ['pʊlaʊt] ◇ *n* **1.** [magazine supplement] supplément *m* détachable **2.** [fold-out] hors-texte *m inv (qui se déplie)*

3. [withdrawal - gen - MIL] retrait *m* ; [- of candidate] désistement *m* ▪ [evacuation] évacuation *f* ▪ **investment ~** désinvestissement *m* **4.** AERON rétablissement *m*.
◇ *adj* [magazine section] détachable ▪ [map, advertising page] hors texte *(inv)* ▪ [legs, shelf] rétractable ▪ **~ bed** canapé-lit *m*.

pullover ['pʊl,əʊvər] *n* pull-over *m*, pull *m*.

pull tab *n* [on can] anneau *m*, bague *f*.

pullulate ['pʌljʊleɪt] *vi* **1.** [teem, breed] pulluler **2.** BOT [germinate] germer.

pull-up *n* **1.** SPORT traction *f (sur une barre ou sur des anneaux)* ▪ **to do ~s** faire des tractions **2.** *UK* = **pull-in**.

pulmonary ['pʌlmənərɪ] *adj* pulmonaire.

pulp [pʌlp] ◇ *n* **1.** [in fruit] pulpe *f* ▪ [for paper] pâte *f* à papier, pulpe *f* ▪ [in tooth] pulpe *f* **2.** [mush] bouillie *f* ▪ **to beat** *OR* **to smash to a ~** réduire en bouillie *OR* en marmelade **3.** MIN pulpe *f*.
◇ *comp pej* [novel, fiction] de hall de gare ▪ **~ magazine** magazine *m* à sensation.
◇ *vt* **1.** [crush - wood] réduire en pâte ; [- fruit, vegetables] réduire en pulpe ; [- book] mettre au pilon **2.** [remove pulp from] ôter la pulpe de **3.** ANAT [cavity, canal] pulpaire.

pulpit ['pʊlpɪt] *n* RELIG chaire *f* ▪ *fig* [clergy] : **the ~** le clergé, les ecclésiastiques *mpl*.

pulpwood ['pʌlpwʊd] *n* bois *m* à pâte.

pulpy ['pʌlpɪ] (*comp* **pulpier**, *superl* **pulpiest**) *adj* **1.** [fruit, tissue] pulpeux **2.** *inf pej* [novel, magazine] à sensation.

pulsar ['pʌlsɑːr] *n* pulsar *m*.

pulsate [pʌl'seɪt] *vi* **1.** [throb - heart] battre fort, pulser MED ; [- music, room] vibrer ▪ **the pulsating beat of the drums** le rythme lancinant des tambours **2.** PHYS subir des pulsations ▪ ASTRON [variable star] pulser.

pulsation [pʌl'seɪʃn] *n* [of heart, arteries] battement *m*, pulsation *f* ▪ ASTRON & PHYS pulsation *f*.

pulse [pʌls] ◇ *n* **1.** MED pouls *m* ▪ [single throb] pulsation *f* ▪ **he took my ~** il a pris mon pouls ▪ **her ~ (rate) is a hundred** son pouls est à cent (pulsations par minute) ▪ **my ~ quickens when I see her** quand je la vois, j'ai le cœur qui bat plus fort **2.** ELECTRON & PHYS [series] série *f* d'impulsions ▪ [single] impulsion *f* **3.** [vibration] rythme *m* régulier **4.** [bustle, life] animation *f* **5.** BOT [plant] légumineuse *f* ▪ CULIN : **(dried) ~s** légumes *mpl* secs.
◇ *vi* [blood] battre ▪ [music, room] vibrer ▪ **a vein ~d in his temple** une veine palpitait sur sa tempe ▪ **the music ~d inside my head** la musique résonnait dans ma tête.

pulverize, ise ['pʌlvəraɪz] *vt liter* & *fig* pulvériser.

puma ['pjuːmə] (*pl inv OR pl* **pumas**) *n* puma *m*.

pumice ['pʌmɪs] ◇ *n* : **~ (stone)** (pierre *f*) ponce *f*.
◇ *vt* poncer, passer à la pierre ponce.

pummel ['pʌml] (*UK pret & pp* **pummelled**, *cont* **pummelling**) (*US pret & pp* **pummeled**, *cont* **pummeling**) *vt* **1.** [punch] donner des coups de poing à, marteler à coups de poing **2.** [massage] masser, palper **3.** [knead - dough] pétrir.

pump [pʌmp] ◇ *n* **1.** MECH pompe *f* ▪ **hand/water ~** pompe à main/à eau ▪ **~ attendant** pompiste *mf* **2.** [shoe - for dancing] ballerine *f* ; [- for gym] tennis *m* **3.** *US inf* [heart] cœur *m*, palpitant△ *m*.
◇ *vt* **1.** [displace - liquid, gas] pomper ▪ **to ~ sthg out of sthg** pomper *OR* aspirer qqch de qqch ▪ **the water is ~ed into a tank** l'eau est acheminée dans un réservoir au moyen d'une pompe ▪ **the factory ~s its waste directly into the river** l'usine déverse ses déchets directement dans la rivière ▪ **coolant is ~ed through the system** une pompe fait circuler le liquide de refroidissement dans le système ▪ **to ~ gas** *US* travailler comme pompiste **2.** [empty - stomach] vider ▪ **he had to have** *OR* **to get his stomach ~ed** on a dû lui faire un lavage d'estomac **3.** [inflate - tyre, ball etc] gonfler **4.** [move back and forth - pedal, handle] appuyer sur *OR* actionner (plusieurs fois) ▪ **~ the brakes or they'll lock** freinez progressivement ou les freins se bloqueront **5.** *inf* [shoot] : **to ~ sb full of lead** cribler qqn de plomb **6.** *inf* [money] investir ▪ **he ~ed a fortune into the business** il a investi une fortune dans cette affaire **7.** *inf* [interrogate] interroger, tirer les vers du nez à ▪ **they ~ed her for information** ils l'ont cuisinée **8.** *phr* **to ~ iron** *inf* faire de la gonflette.
◇ *vi* **1.** [machine, person] pomper ▪ [heart] battre fort **2.** [liquid] couler à flots, jaillir.
◆ **pump in** *vt sep* **1.** [liquid, gas] refouler ▪ **the village ~s in water from the river** l'eau du village est amenée de la rivière à l'aide d'un système de pompage **2.** *inf* [funds, capital] investir, injecter.
◆ **pump out** ◇ *vt sep* **1.** [liquid, gas] pomper ▪ [stomach] vider **2.** *inf pej* [mass-produce - music, graduates, products] produire ; [- books, essays] produire à la chaîne, pondre en série.
◇ *vi* [liquid, blood] couler à flots.
◆ **pump up** *vt sep* **1.** [liquid, mixture] pomper **2.** [inflate] gonfler **3.** *US inf* [excite] : **to be all ~ed up** être tout excité.

pumpernickel ['pʌmpənɪkl] *n* ≃ pain *m* noir, pumpernickel *m*.

pumping station *n* [building] station *f* de pompage ▪ [machinery] installation *f* de pompage.

pumpkin ['pʌmpkɪn] *n* potiron *m* ▪ [smaller] citrouille *f* ▪ **~ pie** tarte *f* au potiron.

pump room *n* [building] pavillon *m* ▪ [room] buvette *f*.

pun [pʌn] (*pret & pp* **punned**, *cont* **punning**) ◇ *n* calembour *m*, jeu *m* de mots.
◇ *vi* faire des calembours.

punch [pʌntʃ] ◇ *n* **1.** [blow] coup *m* de poing ▪ **he gave him a ~ on the chin/in the stomach** il lui a donné un coup de poing dans le menton/dans l'estomac ▪ **to have** *OR* **to pack a powerful ~** avoir du punch **2.** *fig* [effectiveness - of person] punch *m* ▪ [of speech, cartoon, play] mordant *m* ▪ **find a slogan with a bit more ~** trouvez un slogan un peu plus accrocheur **3.** [for holes - in paper] perforateur *m* ; [- in metal] poinçonneuse *f* ▪ [for tickets - by hand] poinçonneuse *f* ; [- machine] composteur *m* ▪ [steel rod, die] poinçon *m* **4.** [for stamping design] machine *f* à estamper **5.** [for nails, bolts] chasse-clou *m* **6.** [drink] punch *m*.
◇ *vt* **1.** [hit - once] donner un coup de poing à ; [- repeatedly] marteler à coups de poing **2.** [key, button] appuyer sur **3.** [pierce - ticket] poinçonner ; [- in machine] composter ; [- paper, computer card] perforer ; [- sheet metal] poinçonner ▪ **to ~ a hole in sthg** faire un trou dans qqch ▪ **to ~ the time clock** *OR* **one's time card** pointer **4.** [stamp] estamper.
◇ *vi* [strike] frapper ▪ **no ~ing!** pas de coups de poing!
◆ **punch in** ◇ *vt sep* **1.** [enter - code, number] taper, composer ; [- figures, data] introduire **2.** [knock in - door] défoncer (à coups de poing) ; [- nails] enfoncer ▪ **I'll ~ your face** *OR* **head** *OR* **teeth in!** *inf* je vais te casser la figure!
◇ *vi insep US* [on time clock] pointer (en arrivant).
◆ **punch out** ◇ *vt sep* **1.** [enter - code, number] taper, composer **2.** [cut out - form, pattern] découper ▪ **the holes are ~ed out by a machine** les trous sont faits par une machine **3.** [remove - nail, bolt] enlever au chasse-clou **4.** [stamp] estamper, emboutir **5.** *US inf* [beat up] tabasser **6.** *inf* AERON [subj: pilot] s'éjecter.
◇ *vi insep US* [on time clock] pointer (en partant).

Punch [pʌntʃ] *pr n* ≃ Polichinelle ▪ **~-and-Judy show** ≃ (spectacle *m* de) guignol *m* ▪ **as pleased as ~** heureux comme un roi.

PUNCH AND JUDY

Le *Punch and Judy show* est un spectacle de marionnettes très apprécié des enfants en Grande-Bretagne. Les représentations ont le plus souvent lieu dans un jardin public ou sur une plage. On y retrouve les personnages de Punch le Bossu, de sa femme Judy, avec qui il se querelle constamment, et de leur chien Toby.

punch bag ['pʌntʃ,bæg] *n UK* **1.** SPORT sac *m* de sable, punching-bag *m* **2.** *fig* [victim] souffre-douleur *m inv*.

punch ball *n UK* punching-ball *m*.

punch bowl *n* bol *m* à punch.

punch card *US* = **punched card**.

punch-drunk *adj* [boxer] groggy ■ *fig* abruti, sonné.

punched card ['pʌntʃt-] *n UK* COMPUT carte *f* perforée.

Punchinello [ˌpʌntʃɪ'neləʊ] *pr n* Polichinelle.

punching bag ['pʌntʃɪŋ-] *US* = **punch bag**.

punch line *n* fin *f (d'une plaisanterie)*.

punch-up *n inf* bagarre *f*.

punchy ['pʌntʃɪ] (*comp* **punchier**, *superl* **punchiest**) *adj inf* **1.** [stimulating, lively] plein de punch **2.** = **punch-drunk**.

punctilious [pʌŋk'tɪlɪəs] *adj* pointilleux.

punctual ['pʌŋktʃʊəl] *adj* [bus] à l'heure ■ [person] ponctuel.

punctuality [ˌpʌŋktʃʊ'ælətɪ] *n* ponctualité *f*, exactitude *f*.

punctually ['pʌŋktʃʊəlɪ] *adv* [begin, arrive] à l'heure ■ [pay] ponctuellement ■ **the flight left ~ at 9/at noon** le vol est parti à 9 h pile/à midi juste.

punctuate ['pʌŋktʃʊeɪt] *vt* ponctuer.

punctuation [ˌpʌŋktʃʊ'eɪʃn] *n* ponctuation *f*.

punctuation mark *n* signe *m* de ponctuation.

puncture ['pʌŋktʃəʳ] ◇ *n* **1.** [in tyre, ball, balloon] crevaison *f* ■ **one of the front tyres had a ~** un des pneus avant était crevé ■ **I had a ~ on the way to work** j'ai crevé en allant travailler ■ **~ repair kit** trousse *f* de réparation pour crevaisons **2.** [gen - hole] perforation *f* **3.** MED ponction *f*.
◇ *vt* **1.** [gen] perforer ■ **the bullet ~d his lung** la balle lui a perforé le poumon **2.** [tyre, ball, balloon] crever **3.** *fig* [pride, self-esteem] blesser, porter atteinte à.
◇ *vi* crever.

pundit ['pʌndɪt] *n* **1.** [expert] expert *m (qui pontifie)* **2.** [Brahmin] pandit *m*.

pungency ['pʌndʒənsɪ] *n* **1.** [of smell, taste] âcreté *f* ■ [of food] piquant *m* **2.** [of wit, remark] causticité *f*, mordant *m*.

pungent ['pʌndʒənt] *adj* **1.** [smell, taste - sour] âcre ; [- spicy] piquant **2.** [wit, remark] caustique, mordant.

Punic ['pju:nɪk] *adj* punique ■ **the ~ Wars** les guerres *fpl* puniques.

punish ['pʌnɪʃ] *vt* **1.** [person, crime] punir ■ **such offences are ~ed by imprisonment** ce genre de délit est passible d'une peine de prison **2.** *inf* [attack relentlessly - opponent, enemy etc] malmener.

punishable ['pʌnɪʃəbl] *adj* punissable ■ **a ~ offence** un délit ■ **~ by prison/a £50 fine** passible d'emprisonnement/d'une amende de 50 livres.

punishing ['pʌnɪʃɪŋ] ◇ *n* **1.** [punishment] punition *f* **2.** *inf* [relentless attack] : **to take a ~** [opponent, team] se faire malmener ; *hum* [bottle] en prendre un coup.
◇ *adj* [heat, climb, effort] exténuant ■ [defeat] écrasant.

punishment ['pʌnɪʃmənt] *n* **1.** [act of punishing] punition *f*, châtiment *m* **2.** [means of punishment] punition *f*, châtiment *m*, sanction *f* ■ LAW peine *f* ■ **to make the ~ fit the crime** adapter le châtiment au délit **3.** *inf* [heavy use] : **the landing gear can take a lot of ~** même soumis à rude épreuve, le train d'atterrissage tiendra le coup.

punitive ['pju:nətɪv] *adj* **1.** [expedition] punitif **2.** [measures, tax] écrasant ■ **to take ~ action** avoir recours à des sanctions ■ **~ damages** dommages *mpl* et intérêts *mpl* dissuasifs.

Punjab [ˌpʌn'dʒɑ:b] *pr n* : **the ~** le Pendjab ■ **in the ~** au Pendjab.

Punjabi [ˌpʌn'dʒɑ:bɪ] ◇ *n* **1.** [person] Pendjabi *mf* **2.** LING pendjabi *m*.
◇ *adj* pendjabi, du Pendjab.

punk [pʌŋk] ◇ *n* **1.** [music, fashion] punk *m* **2.** [punk rocker] punk *mf* **3.** △ *US* [worthless person] vaurien *m*, - enne *f* ■ [hoodlum] voyou *m*.
◇ *adj* **1.** [music, fashion] punk *(inv)* ■ **~ rock** punk *m* ■ **~ rocker** punk *mf* **2.** *US inf* [worthless] nul.

punnet ['pʌnɪt] *n UK* barquette *f*.

punt[1] [pʌnt] ◇ *n* **1.** [boat] *longue barque à fond plat manœuvrée à la perche* **2.** SPORT [kick] coup *m* de pied de volée.
◇ *vt* **1.** [boat] faire avancer à la perche **2.** SPORT [kick] envoyer d'un coup de pied de volée.
◇ *vi* **1.** [in boat] : **to go ~ing** faire un tour en barque **2.** *UK* [gamble] jouer.

punt[2] [pʊnt] *n* [currency] livre *f* irlandaise.

punter ['pʌntəʳ] *n UK* **1.** [gambler] parieur *m*, - euse *f* **2.** *inf* [customer] client *m*, - e *f* ■ **the ~s** le public **3.** △ [prostitute's client] micheton△ *m*.

puny ['pju:nɪ] (*comp* **punier**, *superl* **puniest**) *adj* **1.** [frail - person, animal, plant] malingre, chétif ; [- arms, legs] maigre, grêle **2.** [feeble - effort] pitoyable.

pup [pʌp] (*pret & pp* **pupped**, *cont* **pupping**) ◇ *n* **1.** [young dog] chiot *m* ■ [young animal] jeune animal *m* ■ **seal ~** jeune *OR* bébé phoque *m* ■ **to be in ~** [bitch] être pleine **2.** *inf* [youth] blanc-bec *m*.
◇ *vi* mettre bas.

pupa ['pju:pə] (*pl* **pupas** *OR pl* **pupae** [-pi:]) *n* nymphe *f*, chrysalide *f*, pupe *f*.

pupil ['pju:pl] ◇ *n* **1.** [gen] élève *mf* ■ [of primary school] écolier *m*, - ère *f* ■ [of lower secondary school] collégien *m*, - enne *f* ■ [of upper secondary school] lycéen *m*, - enne *f* ■ [of painter, musician] élève *mf* **2.** LAW [minor ward] pupille *mf* **3.** ANAT pupille *f*.
◇ *comp* SCH [participation, power] des élèves.

puppet ['pʌpɪt] ◇ *n* **1.** [gen] marionnette *f* ■ [string puppet] fantoche *m*, pantin *m* **2.** *fig* pantin *m*, fantoche *m*.
◇ *comp* **1.** [theatre] de marionnettes ■ **~ show** (spectacle *m* de) marionnettes *fpl* **2.** POL [government, president] fantoche.

puppeteer [ˌpʌpɪ'tɪəʳ] *n* marionnettiste *mf*.

puppetry ['pʌpɪtrɪ] *n* [art - of making] fabrication *f* de marionnettes ; [- of manipulating] art *m* du marionnettiste.

puppy ['pʌpɪ] (*pl* **puppies**) *n* chiot *m*.

puppy fat *n UK (U)* rondeurs *fpl* de l'adolescence.

puppy love *n* amourette *f*, amour *m* d'adolescent.

pup tent *n* canadienne *f*.

purchase ['pɜ:tʃəs] ◇ *vt* acheter ■ **to ~ sthg from sb** acheter qqch à qqn ■ **to ~ sthg for sb, to ~ sb sthg** acheter qqch à *OR* pour qqn.
◇ *n* **1.** [buy, buying] achat *m* ■ **to make a ~** faire un achat ■ **date of ~** date *f* d'achat **2.** [grip] prise *f*.

purchase order *n* bon *m* de commande.

purchase price *n* prix *m* d'achat.

purchaser ['pɜ:tʃəsəʳ] *n* acheteur *m*, - euse *f*.

purchase tax *n* taxe *f* à l'achat.

purchasing power ['pɜ:tʃəsɪŋ-] *n* pouvoir *m* d'achat.

purdah ['pɜ:də] *n* : **to be in ~** *liter* être reclus ; *fig* vivre en reclus.

pure [pjʊəʳ] *adj* **1.** [unadulterated, untainted] pur ■ **a ~ silk tie** une cravate (en) pure soie ■ **~ white** blanc *m* immaculé ▶ **as ~ as the driven snow** blanc comme neige **2.** [science, maths, research] pur **3.** [as intensifier] pur ■ **by ~ chance** par pur hasard ■ **it's the truth, ~ and simple** c'est la vérité pure et simple.

purebred ['pjʊəbred] *adj* de race (pure).

puree, purée ['pjʊəreɪ] (*pret & pp* **pureed** *OR* **puréed**, *cont* **pureeing** *OR* **puréeing**) ◇ *n* purée *f* ■ **tomato ~** [gen] purée de tomates ; [in tube] concentré *m* de tomates.
◇ *vt* réduire en purée ■ **~d carrots** purée *f* de carottes.

purely ['pjʊəlɪ] *adj* purement ■ **ours is a ~ professional relationship** nos rapports sont purement *OR* strictement professionnels.

pureness ['pjʊənɪs] *n* pureté *f*.

purgative ['pɜ:gətɪv] ◇ *n* purgatif *m*.

◇ *adj* purgatif.

purgatory ['pɜːgətrɪ] *n* RELIG purgatoire *m* ■ *fig* enfer *m*.

purge [pɜːdʒ] ◇ *vt* **1.** POL [party, organization] purger, épurer ■ [undesirable elements] éliminer **2.** [free, rid] débarrasser, délivrer ■ **~ your mind of such morbid ideas** chassez ces idées morbides de votre esprit **3.** LAW [clear] disculper, innocenter **4.** MED & *dated* [bowels] purger.
◇ *n* **1.** [gen - POL] purge *f*, épuration *f* **2.** MED purge *f*.

purification [,pjʊərɪfɪ'keɪʃn] *n* **1.** [of water, oil] épuration *f* **2.** RELIG purification *f*.

purifier ['pjʊərɪfaɪəʳ] *n* [device - for water, oil] épurateur *m* ; [- for air, atmosphere] purificateur *m*.

purify ['pjʊərɪfaɪ] (*pret & pp* **purified**) *vt* [water, oil] épurer ■ [air, soul] purifier.

Purim ['pʊərɪm] *n* Pourim *m*.

purist ['pjʊərɪst] ◇ *adj* puriste.
◇ *n* puriste *mf*.

puritan ['pjʊərɪtən] ◇ *n* puritain *m*, - e *f*.
◇ *adj* puritain.
◆ **Puritan** RELIG ◇ *n* puritain *m*, - e *f*.
◇ *adj* puritain.

THE PURITANS

Ces protestants anglais radicaux sont apparus au XVIe siècle. Ils souhaitaient débarrasser l'Église anglicane des éléments de faste du culte catholique. Soutenus par la Chambre des communes mais rejetés par Elizabeth Ière, ils réussirent à s'imposer pendant la période du Protectorat d'Olivier Cromwell (1649 à 1660).

puritanical [,pjʊərɪ'tænɪkl] *adj* puritain.

purity ['pjʊərətɪ] *n* pureté *f*.

purl [pɜːl] ◇ *n* [in knitting] : **~ (stitch)** maille *f* à l'envers.
◇ *vt* tricoter à l'envers ■ **knit one, ~ one** une maille à l'endroit, une maille à l'envers.

purlieus ['pɜːljuːz] *npl lit* alentours *mpl*, environs *mpl*.

purloin [pɜː'lɔɪn] *vt fml & hum* dérober, voler.

purple ['pɜːpl] ◇ *n* **1.** [colour] violet *m* **2.** [dye, cloth] pourpre *f* **3.** [high rank] : **the ~** la pourpre.
◇ *adj* **1.** [in colour] violet, pourpre **2.** [prose] emphatique, ampoulé.

purple heart *n inf* [drug] pilule *f* d'amphétamine.
◆ **Purple Heart** *n US médaille décernée aux blessés de guerre.*

purple patch, purple passage *n* morceau *m* de bravoure.

purplish ['pɜːplɪʃ] *adj* violacé.

purport *fml* ◇ *vt* [pə'pɔːt] [claim] prétendre ■ **he ~s to be an expert** il prétend être un expert, il se fait passer pour un expert ■ [sub: film, book] se vouloir.
◇ *n* ['pɜːpɔːt] signification *f*, teneur *f*.

purportedly [pə'pɔːtɪdlɪ] *adv fml* prétendument.

purpose ['pɜːpəs] ◇ *n* **1.** [objective, reason] but *m*, objet *m* ■ **he buys real estate for tax ~s** il investit dans l'immobilier pour des raisons fiscales ■ **it suits my ~s to stay here** j'ai de bonnes raisons de rester ici ■ **to do sthg with a ~ in mind** *OR* **for a ~** faire qqch dans un but précis ■ **for this ~** dans ce but, à cet effet ■ **her remarks were to the ~/not to the ~** ses remarques étaient pertinentes/hors de propos **2.** [use, function] usage *m* ■ [end, result] fin *f* ■ **what is the ~ of this room/object?** à quoi sert cette pièce/cet objet? ■ **the hangar wasn't built for that ~** le hangar n'était pas destiné à cet usage ■ **for our ~s** pour ce que nous voulons faire ■ **for the ~s of this demonstration** pour les besoins de cette démonstration ■ **the funds are to be used for humanitarian ~s** les fonds seront utilisés à des fins humanitaires ■ **the money will be put** *OR* **used to good ~** l'argent sera bien employé ■ **he will use his knowledge to good ~ there** il pourra y mettre à profit ses connaissances ■ **we are arguing to no ~** nous discutons inutilement ■ **my efforts had been to no ~** mes efforts étaient restés vains **3.** [determination] résolution *f*, détermination *f* ■ **she has great strength of ~** elle a une volonté de fer, c'est quelqu'un de très déterminé ■ **to have a sense of ~** avoir un but dans la vie.
◇ *vt lit* avoir l'intention de.
◆ **on purpose** *adv phr* exprès ■ **I avoided the subject on ~** j'ai fait exprès d'éviter *OR* j'ai délibérément évité la question.

purpose-built *adj UK* construit *OR* conçu pour un usage spécifique ■ **~flat** *appartement dans un immeuble (par opposition à un "conversion")* ■ **~ flats for the disabled** appartements *mpl* spécialement adaptés aux besoins des handicapés.

purposeful ['pɜːpəsfʊl] *adj* [person] résolu ■ [look, walk] résolu, décidé ■ [act] réfléchi.

purposefully ['pɜːpəsfʊlɪ] *adv* [for a reason] dans un but précis, délibérément ■ [determinedly] d'un air résolu.

purposeless ['pɜːpəslɪs] *adj* [life] sans but, vide de sens ■ [act, violence] gratuit.

purposely ['pɜːpəslɪ] *adv* exprès, délibérément.

purr [pɜːʳ] ◇ *vi* [cat, engine] ronronner.
◇ *vt* susurrer.
◇ *n* [of cat] ronronnement *m*, ronron *m* ■ [of engine] ronronnement *m*.

purse [pɜːs] ◇ *n* **1.** *UK* [for coins] porte-monnaie *m inv* **2.** *US* [handbag] sac *m* à main **3.** FIN [wealth, resources] bourse *f* ■ **to hold** *OR* **to control the ~ strings** *fig* tenir les cordons de la bourse **4.** SPORT [prize money] bourse *f*.
◇ *vt* [lips] pincer.

purser ['pɜːsəʳ] *n* NAUT commissaire *m* du bord.

purse snatching *n US* vol *m* à l'arraché.

pursuance [pə'sjuːəns] *n fml* exécution *f*, accomplissement *m*.

pursuant [pə'sjʊənt] ◆ **pursuant to** *prep phr fml* [following] à la suite de, suivant ■ [in accordance with] conformément à.

pursue [pə'sjuː] *vt* **1.** [chase, follow] poursuivre ■ *fig* suivre, poursuivre ■ **she was ~d by ill fortune/ill health** elle était poursuivie par la malchance/la maladie **2.** [strive for] poursuivre, rechercher **3.** [carry out] exécuter, mettre en œuvre ■ **the policies ~d by the previous government** la politique menée par le gouvernement précédent ■ [practise] exercer ■ **I have no time to ~ any hobbies** je n'ai pas de temps à consacrer à des hobbies **4.** [take further] poursuivre ■ **if I may ~ that line of argument** si je peux me permettre de pousser plus loin *OR* de développer ce raisonnement ■ **to ~ a point** insister sur *OR* revenir sur un point.

pursuer [pə'sjuːəʳ] *n* poursuivant *m*, - e *f*.

pursuit [pə'sjuːt] *n* **1.** [chasing] poursuite *f* ■ **they went out in ~ of the vandals** ils se sont lancés à la poursuite des vandales ■ **with a pack of dogs in hot ~** avec une meute de chiens à leurs trousses **2.** [striving after] poursuite *f*, quête *f*, recherche *f* **3.** [pastime] occupation *f* ■ **leisure ~s** loisirs *mpl*, passe-temps *m inv* **4.** SPORT [cycle race] poursuite *f*.

purulent ['pjʊərʊlənt] *adj* purulent.

purvey [pə'veɪ] *vt* **1.** [sell] vendre, fournir ■ **to ~ sthg to sb** fournir qqch à qqn, approvisionner qqn en qqch **2.** [communicate - information, news] communiquer ; [- lies, rumours] colporter.

purveyance [pə'veɪəns] *n* fourniture *f*, approvisionnement *m*.

purveyor [pə'veɪəʳ] *n fml* **1.** [supplier] fournisseur *m*, - euse *f* **2.** [spreader - of gossip, lies] colporteur *m*, - euse *f*.

purview ['pɜːvjuː] *n* **1.** *fml* [scope] champ *m*, domaine *m* ■ **the matter falls within/outside the ~ of the committee** la question relève/ne relève pas de la compétence du comité **2.** LAW [body of statute] texte *m*.

pus [pʌs] *n* pus *m*.

push [pʊʃ] ◇ *vt* **1.** [shove, propel] pousser ■ **she ~ed the door open/shut** elle ouvrit/ferma la porte (en la poussant) ■ **he ~ed the branches apart** il a écarté les branches ■ **she ~ed her way to the bar** elle se fraya un chemin jusqu'au bar
2. [insert] enfoncer, introduire ■ [thrust] enfoncer ■ **she ~ed the cork into the bottle** elle enfonça le bouchon dans la bouteille ■ **~ all that mess under the bed** pousse tout ce bazar sous le lit
3. [press - doorbell, pedal, button] appuyer sur
4. [cause to move in specified direction] : **it will ~ inflation upwards** cela va relancer l'inflation ■ **the crisis is ~ing the country towards chaos** la crise entraîne le pays vers le chaos ■ **he is ~ing the party to the right** il fait glisser le parti vers la droite ■ **buying the car will ~ us even further into debt** en achetant cette voiture, nous allons nous endetter encore plus ■ **economic conditions have ~ed the peasants off the land** les paysans ont été chassés des campagnes par les conditions économiques
5. [pressurize] pousser ■ [force] forcer, obliger, contraindre ■ **to ~ sb to do sthg** pousser qqn à faire qqch ■ **to ~ sb into doing sthg** forcer *OR* obliger qqn à faire qqch ■ **their coach doesn't ~ them hard enough** leur entraîneur ne les pousse pas assez ■ **I like to ~ myself hard** j'aime me donner à fond ■ **he ~ed the car to its limits** il a poussé la voiture à la limite de ses possibilités ■ **you're still weak, so don't ~ yourself** tu es encore faible, vas-y doucement ■ **he won't do it if he's ~ed too hard** il ne le fera pas si l'on insiste trop ■ **I won't be ~ed!** je ne céderai pas! ■ **when I ~ed her, she admitted it** quand j'ai insisté, elle a avoué ■ **he keeps ~ing me for the rent** il me relance sans cesse au sujet du loyer
6. [advocate, argue for - idea, method] prôner, préconiser ■ [promote - product] promouvoir ■ **he's trying to ~ his own point of view** il essaie d'imposer son point de vue personnel ■ **the mayor is ~ing his town as the best site for the conference** le maire présente sa ville comme le meilleur endroit pour tenir la conférence
7. [stretch, exaggerate - argument, case] présenter avec insistance, insister sur ■ **if we ~ the comparison a little further** si on pousse la comparaison un peu plus loin ▶ **I'll try to arrive by 7 p.m., but it's ~ing it a bit** *inf* je tâcherai d'arriver à 19 h, mais ça va être juste ■ **that's ~ing it a bit!** *inf* c'est un peu fort!
8. *inf* [sell - drugs] revendre
9. *inf* [approach] friser ■ **to be ~ing thirty** friser la trentaine.
◇ *vi* **1.** [shove] pousser ■ **no ~ing please!** ne poussez pas, s'il vous plaît! ■ **'push'** [on door] 'poussez' ■ **people were ~ing to get in** les gens se bousculaient pour entrer ■ **he ~ed through the crowd to the bar** il s'est frayé un chemin jusqu'au bar à travers la foule ■ **somebody ~ed past me** quelqu'un est passé en me bousculant
2. [press - on button, bell, knob] appuyer
3. [advance] avancer ■ [progress] évoluer
4. [extend - path, fence] s'étendre ■ **the road ~ed deep into the hills** la route s'enfonçait dans les collines.
◇ *n* **1.** [shove] poussée *f* ■ **to give sb/sthg a ~** pousser qqn/qqch ■ **would you give me a ~?** AUT pourriez-vous me pousser? ▶ **to give sb the ~** *UK inf* [from job] virer qqn ; [in relationship] plaquer qqn ■ **when it comes to the ~** *inf*, **when ~ comes to shove** *inf* au moment critique *OR* crucial ■ **I can lend you the money if it comes to the ~** *inf* au pire, je pourrai vous prêter l'argent ■ **I can do it at a ~** *inf* je peux le faire si c'est vraiment nécessaire
2. [act of pressing] : **the door opens at the ~ of a button** il suffit d'appuyer sur un bouton pour que la porte s'ouvre ■ **he expects these things to happen at the ~ of a button** *fig* il s'attend à ce que ça se fasse sur commande
3. *fig* [trend] : **the ~ towards protectionism is gathering strength** la tendance au protectionnisme se renforce
4. [encouragement] mot *m* d'encouragement ■ **he'll do it, but he needs a ~** il le fera, mais il a besoin qu'on le pousse un peu ■ **he just needs a ~ in the right direction** il a juste besoin qu'on le mette sur la bonne voie
5. MIL [advance] poussée *f*
6. [campaign] campagne *f* ■ **a sales ~** une campagne de promotion des ventes
7. [drive, dynamism] dynamisme *m* ■ **he has a lot of ~** il est très dynamique.

◆ **push about** *vt sep UK* **1.** [physically] malmener
2. [bully] donner des ordres à ■ **I won't be ~ed about!** *fig* je ne vais pas me laisser marcher sur les pieds!

◆ **push ahead** *vi insep* [make progress] : **they decided to ~ ahead with the plans to extend the school** ils ont décidé d'activer les projets d'extension de l'école.

◆ **push along** ◇ *vt sep* [trolley, pram] pousser (devant soi).
◇ *vi insep inf* [leave] filer.

◆ **push around** = **push about**.

◆ **push aside** *vt sep* **1.** [objects] pousser
2. [reject - proposal] écarter, rejeter ■ [neglect - problem] : **you can't just ~ aside the problem like that** vous ne pouvez pas faire comme si le problème n'existait pas ■ **I ~ed my doubts aside** je n'ai pas tenu compte de mes doutes.

◆ **push away** *vt sep* repousser ■ **he ~ed his chair away from the fire** il éloigna sa chaise du feu.

◆ **push back** *vt sep* **1.** [person] repousser (en arrière) ■ [bedclothes] rejeter, repousser ■ **he ~ed me back from the door** il m'a éloigné de la porte
2. [repulse - troops] repousser
3. [postpone] repousser.

◆ **push down** ◇ *vt sep* **1.** [lever, handle] abaisser ■ [pedal] appuyer sur ■ **she ~ed the clothes down in the bag** elle a tassé les vêtements dans le sac
2. [knock over] renverser, faire tomber.
◇ *vi insep* [on pedal, lever] appuyer (sur la) pédale/manette *etc.*

◆ **push for** *vt insep* [argue for] demander ■ [campaign for] faire campagne pour ■ [agitate for] militer pour ■ **I'm going to ~ for a bigger budget** je vais faire tout ce qui est en mon pouvoir pour obtenir un budget plus important.

◆ **push forward** ◇ *vt sep liter* pousser (en avant) ■ **to ~ o.s. forward** *fig* se mettre en avant, se faire valoir.
◇ *vi insep* **1.** [advance - person, car] se frayer un chemin ; [- crowd, herd] se presser en avant
2. = **push ahead**.

◆ **push in** ◇ *vt sep* **1.** [drawer] pousser ■ [electric plug, key] enfoncer, introduire ■ [disk] insérer ■ [knife, stake, spade] enfoncer ■ [button, switch] appuyer sur ■ **~ the button right in** appuyer à fond sur le bouton
2. [person] : **they ~ed me in the water** ils m'ont poussé dans l'eau ■ **he opened the door and ~ed me in** il ouvrit la porte et me poussa à l'intérieur
3. [break down - panel, cardboard] enfoncer.
◇ *vi insep* [in queue] se faufiler ■ **no ~ing in!** faites la queue!

◆ **push off** ◇ *vi insep* **1.** *inf* [go away] filer ■ **~ off!** de l'air!, dégage!
2. [in boat] pousser au large.
◇ *vt sep* **1.** [knock off] faire tomber ■ **I ~ed him off the chair** je l'ai fait tomber de sa chaise
2. [boat] déborder.

◆ **push on** ◇ *vi insep* [on journey - set off again] reprendre la route, se remettre en route ; [- continue] poursuivre *OR* continuer son chemin ■ [keep working] continuer, persévérer ■ **they're ~ing on with the reforms** ils poursuivent leurs efforts pour faire passer les réformes.
◇ *vt sep* [urge on] : **to ~ sb on to do sthg** pousser *OR* inciter qqn à faire qqch.

◆ **push out** ◇ *vt sep* **1.** [person, object] : **they ~ed the car out of the mud** ils ont désembourbé la voiture en la poussant ■ **the bed had been ~ed out from the wall** le lit avait été écarté du mur ▶ **to ~ the boat out** *liter* déborder l'embarcation ; *fig* faire la fête
2. [stick out - hand, leg] tendre
3. [grow - roots, shoots] faire, produire
4. [oust] évincer ■ [dismiss from job] mettre à la porte
5. *inf* [churn out - articles, books] produire à la chaîne, pondre en série.
◇ *vi insep* [appear - roots, leaves] pousser ; [- snowdrops, tulips] pointer.

◆ **push over** *vt sep* **1.** [pass - across table, floor] pousser
2. [knock over] faire tomber, renverser ■ [from ledge, bridge] pousser, faire tomber.

◆ **push through** ◇ *vt sep* **1.** [project, decision] faire accepter ■ [deal] conclure ■ [bill, budget] réussir à faire voter *OR* passer

2. [thrust - needle] passer ▪ **she eventually managed to ~ her way through (the crowd)** elle réussit finalement à se frayer un chemin (à travers la foule).
◇ *vi insep* [car, person] se frayer un chemin ▪ [troops, army] avancer.
◆ **push to** *vt sep* [door, drawer] fermer.
◆ **push up** *vt sep* **1.** [push upwards - handle, lever] remonter, relever ; [- sleeves] remonter, retrousser ➲ **he's ~ing up (the) daisies** *inf* il mange les pissenlits par la racine
2. [increase - taxes, sales, demand] augmenter ; [- prices, costs, statistics] faire monter ▪ **the effect will be to ~ interest rates up** cela aura pour effet de faire grimper les taux d'intérêt.

pushbike ['pʊʃbaɪk] *n UK inf* vélo *m*, bécane *f*.

push button *n* bouton *m*.
◆ **push-button** *adj* [telephone] à touches ▪ [car window] à commande automatique ▪ **push-button controls** commandes *fpl* automatiques.

pushcart ['pʊʃkɑ:t] *n US* charrette *f* à bras.

pushchair ['pʊʃtʃeər] *n UK* poussette *f*.

pushed [pʊʃt] *adj* **1.** *inf* [lacking - money, time] : **to be ~ for sthg** manquer de *OR* être à court de qqch ▪ **we're really ~ for time** nous n'avons que très peu de temps ▪ **I'd like to stay longer, but I'm a bit ~** j'aimerais rester plus longtemps, mais je suis assez pressé **2.** [in difficulty] : **to be hard ~ to do sthg** avoir du mal à faire qqch.

pusher ['pʊʃər] *n inf* [drug dealer] trafiquant *m*, - e *f* (de drogue), dealer *m*.

pushiness ['pʊʃɪnɪs] *n inf* [ambitiousness] arrivisme *m* ▪ [forwardness] insistance *f* ▪ **I can't stand his ~** je ne supporte pas sa façon de s'imposer.

pushing ['pʊʃɪŋ] *n* bousculade *f*.

Pushkin ['pʊʃkɪn] *pr n* Pouchkine.

pushover ['pʊʃˌəʊvər] *n* **1.** *inf* [easy thing] jeu *m* d'enfant ▪ **the match will be a ~** le match, c'est du tout cuit *OR* ça va être du gâteau **2.** *inf* [sucker] pigeon *m* **3.** SPORT [in rugby] : **~ try** essai *m* collectif (par les avants).

pushpin ['pʊʃpɪn] *n US* punaise *f*.

pushrod ['pʊʃrɒd] *n* AUT poussoir *m* de soupape.

push-start ◇ *n* AUT : **to give sb a ~** pousser la voiture de qqn pour la faire démarrer.
◇ *vt* faire démarrer en poussant.

push-up *n* pompe *f (exercice physique)*.

pushy ['pʊʃɪ] (*comp* **pushier**, *superl* **pushiest**) *adj inf pej* [ambitious] arriviste ▪ [attention-seeking] qui cherche à se faire valoir *OR* mousser.

pusillanimous [ˌpju:sɪ'lænɪməs] *adj fml* pusillanime.

puss [pʊs] *n inf* [cat] minou *m*.

pussy ['pʊsɪ] (*pl* **pussies**) *n* **1.** *inf* [cat] minou *m* **2.** ▲ [female sex organs] chatte▲ *f*.

pussycat ['pʊsɪkæt] *n inf* minou *m*.

pussyfoot ['pʊsɪfʊt] *vi inf* atermoyer, tergiverser.

pussy willow *n* saule *m* blanc.

pustule ['pʌstju:l] *n* pustule *f*.

put [pʊt] (*pret & pp* **put**, *cont* **putting**) ◇ *vt*

A.
1. [into specified place or position] mettre ▪ **~ the chairs nearer the table** approche les chaises de la table ▪ **he ~ his arm around my shoulders** il passa son bras autour de mes épaules ▪ **to ~ one's head round the door** passer la tête par la porte ▪ **~ some more water on to boil** remettez de l'eau à chauffer ▪ **she ~ a match to the wood** elle a allumé le bois ‖ [send] : **they want to ~ me in an old folks' home** ils veulent me mettre dans une maison pour les vieux ▪ **to ~ a child to bed** mettre un enfant au lit, coucher un enfant ‖ *fig* **I didn't know where to ~ myself!** je ne savais plus où me mettre! ▪ **we ~ a lot of emphasis on creativity** nous mettons beaucoup l'accent sur la créativité ▪ **don't ~ too much trust in what he says** ne te fie pas trop à ce qu'il dit
2. [push or send forcefully] : **he ~ his fist through the window** il a passé son poing à travers la fenêtre ▪ **he ~ a bullet through his head** il s'est mis une balle dans la tête ▪ **she ~ her pen through the whole paragraph** elle a rayé tout le paragraphe d'un coup de stylo
3. [impose - responsibility, tax] mettre ▪ **it ~s an extra burden on our department** c'est un fardeau de plus pour notre service ▪ **the new tax will ~ 5p on a packet of cigarettes** la nouvelle taxe augmentera de 5 pence le prix d'un paquet de cigarettes
4. [into specified state] mettre ▪ **I hope I've not ~ you to too much trouble** j'espère que je ne vous ai pas trop dérangé ▪ **music always ~s him in a good mood** la musique le met toujours de bonne humeur ▪ **the new rules will be ~ into effect next month** le nouveau règlement entrera en vigueur le mois prochain ▪ **to ~ sb out of a job** mettre qqn au chômage ▪ **the money will be ~ to good use** l'argent sera bien employé ▪ **the dog had to be ~ to sleep** il a fallu piquer le chien
5. [write down] mettre, écrire
6. [bring about] : **to ~ an end** *OR* **a stop to sthg** mettre fin *OR* un terme à qqch

B.
1. [say, express] dire, exprimer ▪ **to ~ one's thoughts into words** exprimer sa pensée, s'exprimer ▪ **let me ~ it this way** laissez-moi l'exprimer ainsi ▪ **it was, how shall I ~ it, rather long** c'était, comment dirais-je, un peu long ▪ **he ~ it better than that** il l'a dit *OR* formulé mieux que ça ▪ **to ~ it briefly** *OR* **simply, they refused** bref *OR* en un mot, ils ont refusé
2. [present, submit - suggestion, question] soumettre ; [- motion] proposer, présenter ▪ **he ~ his case very well** il a très bien présenté son cas ▪ **I ~ it to you that you are the real culprit** je vous accuse d'être le véritable coupable ▪ **I ~ it to the delegates that now is the time to act** je tiens à dire aux délégués que c'est maintenant qu'il faut agir

C.
[classify in hierarchy] placer, mettre ▪ **I ~ my family above my job** je fais passer ma famille avant mon travail

D.
1. [set to work] : **they ~ her on the Jones case** ils l'ont mise sur l'affaire Jones
2. [apply, invest - effort] investir, consacrer ▪ **to ~ a lot of time/energy into sthg** consacrer beaucoup de temps/d'énergie à qqch, investir beaucoup de temps/d'énergie dans qqch ▪ **he ~ everything he had into his first service** SPORT il a tout mis dans son premier service
3. [invest - money] placer, investir
4. [bet] parier, miser

E.
SPORT : **to ~ the shot** *OR* **the weight** lancer le poids.
◇ *vi* NAUT : **to ~ to sea** lever l'ancre, appareiller ▪ **we ~ into port at Bombay** nous avons fait escale à Bombay.
◇ *n* **1.** SPORT lancer *m* (du poids) **2.** ST. EX option *f* de vente.
◆ **put about** ◇ *vt sep* **1.** [spread - gossip, story] faire courir **2.** *UK inf* [sexually] : **to ~ o.s. about** coucher à droite à gauche.
◇ *vi insep* NAUT virer de bord.
◆ **put across** *vt sep* **1.** [communicate] faire comprendre ▪ **to ~ sthg across to sb** faire comprendre qqch à qqn ▪ **she's good at putting herself across** elle sait se mettre en valeur **2.** *UK inf phr* **don't try putting anything across on me!** ne me prends pas pour un imbécile!
◆ **put aside** *vt sep* **1.** [stop - activity, work] mettre de côté, poser **2.** [disregard, ignore] écarter, laisser de côté **3.** [save] mettre de côté ▪ **we have a little money ~ aside** nous avons un peu d'argent de côté.
◆ **put at** *vt sep* [estimate] estimer.
◆ **put away** *vt sep* **1.** [tidy] ranger **2.** [lock up - in prison] mettre sous les verrous ; [- in mental home] enfermer **3.** *inf* [eat] enfourner, s'envoyer ▪ [drink] descendre, écluser **4.** [save] mettre de côté ▪ **I have a few pounds ~ away** j'ai un peu d'argent de côté, j'ai quelques économies.
◆ **put back** ◇ *vt sep* **1.** [replace, return] remettre **2.** [postpone] remettre **3.** [slow down, delay] retarder ▪ **the strike has ~ our schedule back at least a month** la grève nous a fait perdre au moins un mois sur notre planning **4.** [turn back - clock] re-

tarder ■ **we ~ the clocks back next weekend** le week-end prochain, on passe à l'heure d'hiver **5.** *inf* [drink] descendre, écluser.

◇ *vi insep* NAUT : **to ~ back (to port)** rentrer au port.

◆ **put by** *vt sep* [save] mettre de côté.

◆ **put down** ◇ *vt sep* **1.** [on table, floor etc] poser ■ **to ~ the phone down** raccrocher ■ **it's one of those books you just can't ~ down** c'est un de ces livres que tu ne peux pas poser avant de l'avoir fini **2.** [drop off - passenger] déposer, laisser **3.** [write down] écrire, inscrire ■ **she ~ us down as Mr and Mrs Smith** elle nous a inscrits sous le nom de M. et Mme Smith ■ **it's never been ~ down in writing** ça n'a jamais été mis par écrit ■ **I can ~ it down as expenses** je peux le faire passer dans mes notes de frais **4.** [on agenda] inscrire à l'ordre du jour ■ **to ~ down a motion of no confidence** déposer une motion de censure **5.** [enrol] inscrire **6.** [quell] réprimer, étouffer **7.** [belittle] rabaisser, critiquer **8.** *UK euph* [kill] : **to have a cat/dog ~ down** faire piquer un chat/chien **9.** [pay as deposit] verser **10.** [store - wine] mettre en cave **11.** [put to bed - baby] coucher **12.** [land - plane] poser.

◇ *vi insep* [land - plane, pilot] atterrir, se poser.

◆ **put down as** *vt sep* classer parmi.

◆ **put down for** *vt sep* inscrire pour ■ **I'll ~ you down for Thursday at 3 o'clock** je vous mets jeudi à 15 h.

◆ **put down to** *vt sep* mettre sur le compte de.

◆ **put forth** *vt insep* **1.** *lit* [sprout - shoots, leaves] produire **2.** *fml* [state] avancer.

◆ **put forward** *vt sep* **1.** [suggest - proposal, idea, hypothesis] avancer ; [- candidate] proposer ■ **she ~ her name forward for the post of treasurer** elle a posé sa candidature au poste de trésorière **2.** [turn forward - clock, hands of clock] avancer ■ **we ~ the clocks forward next weekend** le week-end prochain, on passe à l'heure d'été **3.** [bring forward] avancer.

◆ **put in** ◇ *vt sep* **1.** [place inside bag, container, cupboard] mettre dans ■ **to ~ the ball in** RUGBY remettre la balle en jeu **2.** [insert, include] insérer, inclure **3.** [interject] placer ■ **her name was Alice, the woman ~ in** elle s'appelait Alice, ajouta la femme **4.** [install] installer **5.** [devote - time] passer ■ **I've ~ in a lot of work on that car** j'ai beaucoup travaillé sur cette voiture **6.** [appoint] nommer **7.** [submit - request, demand] déposer, soumettre ■ **to ~ in an application for a job** déposer sa candidature pour *OR* se présenter pour un emploi.

◇ *vi insep* NAUT faire escale.

◆ **put in for** *vt insep* : **to ~ in for sthg** [post] poser sa candidature pour qqch ; [leave, promotion] faire une demande de qqch, demander qqch.

◆ **put off** *vt sep* **1.** [drop off - passenger] déposer, laisser **2.** [postpone] repousser, remettre ■ **the meeting has been ~ off until tomorrow** la réunion a été renvoyée *OR* remise à demain ■ **I kept putting off telling him the truth** je continuais à repousser le moment de lui dire la vérité ■ **I can't ~ him off again** je ne peux pas encore annuler un rendez-vous avec lui **3.** [dissuade] : **once he's made up his mind nothing in the world can ~ him off** une fois qu'il a pris une décision, rien au monde ne peut le faire changer d'avis **4.** [distract] déranger, empêcher de se concentrer ■ **the noise ~ her off her service** le bruit l'a gênée *OR* dérangée pendant son service **5.** [repel] dégoûter, rebuter ■ **don't be ~ off by his odd sense of humour** ne te laisse pas rebuter par son humour un peu particulier ■ **it ~ me off skiing for good** ça m'a définitivement dégoûté du ski ■ **it ~ me off my dinner** ça m'a coupé l'appétit.

◆ **put on** *vt sep* **1.** [clothes, make-up, ointment] mettre **2.** [present, stage - play, opera] monter ; [- poetry reading, whist drive, slide show] organiser **3.** [lay on, provide] : **they ~ on excellent meals on Sundays** ils servent d'excellents repas le dimanche ■ **they have ~ on 20 extra trains** ils ont ajouté 20 trains **4.** [gain - speed, weight] prendre **5.** [turn on, cause to function - light, radio, gas] allumer ; [- record, tape] mettre ; [- handbrake] mettre, serrer ■ **to ~ on the brakes** freiner **6.** [start cooking] mettre (à cuire) ■ **I've ~ the kettle on for tea** j'ai mis de l'eau à chauffer pour le thé **7.** [bet] parier **8.** [assume] prendre ■ **to ~ on airs** prendre des airs ◐ **don't worry, he's just putting it on** ne t'inquiète pas, il fait semblant **9.** *inf* [tease] faire marcher **10.** [apply - pressure] exercer **11.** [add] ajouter ■ **the tax increase will ~ another 10p on a gallon of petrol** l'augmentation de la taxe va faire monter le prix du gallon d'essence de 10 pence **12.** [impose] imposer **13.** [attribute] : **it's hard to ~ a price on it** c'est difficile d'en évaluer *OR* estimer le prix.

◆ **put onto** *vt sep* [help find] indiquer à ■ **I'll ~ you onto a good solicitor** je vous donnerai le nom d'un *OR* je vous indiquerai un bon avocat ■ **to ~ the police/taxman onto sb** dénoncer qqn à la police/au fisc ■ **what ~ you onto the butler, detective inspector?** qu'est-ce qui vous a amené à soupçonner le maître d'hôtel, commissaire?

◆ **put out** ◇ *vt sep* **1.** [place outside] mettre dehors, sortir ■ **I'll ~ the washing out (to dry)** je vais mettre le linge (dehors) à sécher **2.** [remove] : **to ~ sb's eye out** éborgner qqn **3.** [issue - apology, announcement] publier ; [- story, rumour] faire circuler ■ [broadcast] émettre ■ **to ~ out an SOS** lancer un SOS **4.** [extinguish - fire, light, candle] éteindre ; [- cigarette] éteindre, écraser **5.** [lay out, arrange] sortir **6.** [stick out, stretch out - arm, leg] étendre, allonger ; [- hand] tendre ; [- tongue] tirer **7.** [dislocate] : **to ~ one's shoulder out** se démettre l'épaule ■ **I've ~ my back out** je me suis déplacé une vertèbre **8.** [annoy, upset] : **to be ~ out about sthg** être fâché à cause de qqch ■ **he seems quite ~ out about it** on dirait que ça l'a vraiment contrarié **9.** [inconvenience] déranger ■ **she's always ready to ~ herself out for other people** elle est toujours prête à rendre service **10.** [sprout - shoots, leaves] produire **11.** [make unconscious - with drug, injection] endormir **12.** [subcontract] sous-traiter ■ **we ~ most of our work out** nous confions la plus grande partie de notre travail à des sous-traitants **13.** HORT [plant out] repiquer.

◇ *vi insep* **1.** NAUT prendre le large ■ **to ~ out to sea** faire appareiller **2.** *US inf* [sexually] : **everyone knows she ~s out** tout le monde sait qu'elle est prête à coucher.

◆ **put over** = **put across**.

◆ **put over on** *vt sep inf phr* **to ~ one over on sb** avoir *OR* rouler qqn.

◆ **put round** *vt sep* [spread - gossip, story] faire courir.

◆ **put through** *vt sep* **1.** TELEC [connect] passer la communication à ■ **~ the call through to my office** passez-moi la communication dans mon bureau ■ **I'll ~ you through to Mrs Powell** je vous passe Mme Powell **2.** [carry through, conclude] conclure ■ **we finally ~ through the necessary reforms** nous avons fini par faire passer les réformes nécessaires **3.** [subject to] soumettre à ■ **I'm sorry to ~ you through this** je suis désolé de vous imposer ça ◐ **to ~ sb through it** *inf* en faire voir de toutes les couleurs **4.** [pay for] : **he ~ himself through college** il a payé ses études.

◆ **put together** *vt sep* **1.** *(usu passive)* [combine] mettre ensemble, réunir ■ **he's more trouble than the rest of them ~ together** il nous crée plus de problèmes à lui seul que tous les autres réunis **2.** [assemble - kit, furniture, engine] monter, assembler ■ **to ~ sthg (back) together again** remonter qqch **3.** [compile - dossier] réunir ; [- proposal, report] préparer ; [- story, facts] reconstituer **4.** [organize - show, campaign] organiser, monter.

◆ **put under** *vt sep* [with drug, injection] endormir.

◆ **put up** ◇ *vt sep* **1.** [raise, hoist - hand] lever ; [- flag] hisser ; [- hood] relever ; [- umbrella] ouvrir ■ **~ your hands up!** haut les mains! **2.** [erect, build - tent] dresser, monter ; [- house, factory] construire ; [- monument, statue] ériger ■ **they ~ up a statue to her** ils érigèrent une statue en son honneur **3.** [install, put in place] mettre ■ **they've already ~ up the Christmas decorations** ils ont déjà installé les décorations de Noël ■ **the shopkeeper ~ up the shutters** le commerçant a baissé le rideau de fer **4.** [send up - rocket, satellite] lancer **5.** [display - sign] mettre ; [- poster] afficher **6.** [show - resistance] offrir, opposer ■ **to ~ up a good show** bien se défendre ■ **to ~ up a struggle** se défendre, se débattre **7.** [present - argument, proposal] présenter **8.** [offer for sale] : **to ~ sthg up for sale/auction** mettre qqch en vente/aux enchères **9.** [put forward - candidate] présenter ; [- person, name] proposer (comme candidat) **10.** [provide - capital] : **who's putting the money up for the new business?** qui finance la nouvelle entreprise? ■ **we ~ up our own money** nous sommes auto-financés **11.** [increase] faire monter, augmenter **12.** [give hospitality to] loger ■ **to ~ sb up for the night** coucher qqn **13.** [urge, incite] : **to ~ sb up to (doing) sthg** pousser qqn à (faire) qqch.

◇ *vi insep* **1.** *UK* [stay - in hotel] descendre ; [- with friends] loger **2.** [stand - in election] se présenter, se porter candidat **3.** *US* *phr* **~ up or shut up!** *inf* assez parlé, agissez!
◆ **put upon** *vt insep (usu passive)* abuser de ■ **you shouldn't let yourself be ~ upon like that!** tu ne devrais pas te laisser marcher sur les pieds comme ça!
◆ **put up with** *vt insep* supporter, tolérer.

putative ['pju:tətɪv] *adj fml* présumé, putatif.

put-down *n inf* [snub] rebuffade *f*.

put-in *n* RUGBY introduction *f*.

put-off *n US inf* [evasion] faux-fuyant *m* ■ [excuse] prétexte *m*.

put-on ◇ *adj* affecté, simulé.
◇ *n inf* **1.** [pretence] simulacre *m* **2.** [hoax] canular *m* **3.** *US* [charlatan] charlatan *m*.

putrefaction [,pju:trɪ'fækʃn] *n* putréfaction *f*.

putrefy ['pju:trɪfaɪ] (*pret & pp* **putrefied**) ◇ *vi* se putréfier.
◇ *vt* putréfier.

putrescent [pju:'tresnt] *adj fml* putrescent.

putrid ['pju:trɪd] *adj* **1.** [decaying] putride ■ **a ~ smell** une odeur nauséabonde **2.** *inf* [awful] dégueulasse.

putsch [pʊtʃ] *n* putsch *m*, coup *m* d'État.

putt [pʌt] ◇ *n* putt *m*.
◇ *vi & vt* putter.

puttee ['pʌtɪ] *n* bande *f* molletière.

putter ['pʌtə^r] ◇ *n* SPORT **1.** [club] putter *m* **2.** [person] : **he's a good ~** il putte bien.
◇ *vi* **1.** [vehicle] avancer en faisant teuf-teuf **2.** *US* = **potter**.

putting ['pʌtɪŋ] *n* SPORT putting *m*.

putting green *n* green *m*.

putty ['pʌtɪ] (*pret & pp* **puttied**) ◇ *n* [for cracks, holes] mastic *m* ■ [for walls] enduit *m* ■ **my legs feel like ~** j'ai les jambes en coton ● **Max is ~ in her hands** elle fait de Max (tout) ce qu'elle veut, Max ne sait pas lui résister.
◇ *vt* mastiquer.

putty knife *n* couteau *m* à mastiquer, spatule *f* de vitrier.

put-up *adj UK inf* **~ job** coup *m* monté.

put-upon *adj UK* exploité ■ **his poor ~ wife** sa pauvre femme qui lui sert de bonne à tout faire.

put-you-up *n UK* canapé-lit *m*.

puzzle ['pʌzl] ◇ *n* **1.** [game - gen] jeu *m* de patience ■ [jigsaw] puzzle *m* ■ [brainteaser] casse-tête *m inv* ■ [riddle] devinette *f* **2.** [problem] question *f* (difficile) ■ [enigma, mystery] énigme *f*, mystère *m* **3.** [perplexity] perplexité *f* ■ **he was in a ~ about what to do** il ne savait pas trop quoi faire.
◇ *vt* laisser perplexe ■ **I'm still ~d to know how he got out** j'essaie toujours de comprendre comment il s'y est pris pour sortir.
◇ *vi* [wonder] se poser des questions ■ [ponder] réfléchir.
◆ **puzzle out** *vt sep UK* [meaning, solution, route, way] trouver, découvrir ■ [code, enigma, handwriting] déchiffrer ■ [problem] résoudre ■ [behaviour, intentions] comprendre.
◆ **puzzle over** *vt insep* [answer, explanation] essayer de trouver ■ [absence, letter, theory] essayer de comprendre ■ [enigma, crossword] essayer de résoudre ■ [code, handwriting] essayer de déchiffrer ■ **we're still puzzling over why he did it** nous nous demandons toujours ce qui a bien pu le pousser à faire cela.

puzzle book *n* [gen] livre *m* de jeux ■ [of crosswords] livre *m* de mots croisés.

puzzled ['pʌzld] *adj* perplexe.

puzzlement ['pʌzlmənt] *n* perplexité *f*.

puzzler ['pʌzlə^r] *n* énigme *f*, casse-tête *m inv* ■ **his statement is a real ~** sa déclaration est des plus ambiguës.

puzzling ['pʌzlɪŋ] *adj* [behaviour, remark] curieux, qui laisse perplexe ■ [symbol, machine] incompréhensible ■ **it's ~ that he hasn't sent word** c'est curieux qu'il n'ait pas donné signe de vie ■ **it remains a ~ phenomenon** c'est un phénomène encore inexpliqué.

PVC (*abbrev of* **polyvinyl chloride**) *n* PVC *m*.

pw (*written abbrev of* **per week**) p.sem.

PWA (*abbrev of* **person with AIDS**) *n* sidéen *m*, - enne *f*.

Pygmalion [pɪg'meɪljən] *pr n* Pygmalion.

pygmy ['pɪgmɪ] (*pl* **pygmies**) ◇ *n* **1.** ZOOL [small animal] nain *m*, - e *f* **2.** *fig & pej* [person] nain *m*.
◇ *adj* pygmée.
◆ **Pygmy** ◇ *n* Pygmée *mf*.
◇ *adj* pygmée.

pyjama *UK*, **pajama** *US* [pə'dʒɑ:mə] *comp* [jacket, trousers] de pyjama.
◆ **pyjamas** *UK*, **pajamas** *US npl* pyjama *m* ■ **a pair of ~s** un pyjama ■ **he was in his ~s** il était en pyjama.

pylon ['paɪlən] *n* [gen - archaeology] pylône *m*.

pyramid ['pɪrəmɪd] ◇ *n* pyramide *f*.
◇ *vt* **1.** [build in pyramid form] ériger en forme de pyramide **2.** FIN [companies] structurer en holdings.

pyramid selling *n* vente *f* pyramidale.

pyre ['paɪə^r] *n* : **(funeral) ~** bûcher *m* funéraire.

Pyrenean [,pɪrə'ni:ən] *adj* pyrénéen.

Pyrenees [,pɪrə'ni:z] *pr npl* : **the ~** les Pyrénées *fpl*.

Pyrex® ['paɪreks] ◇ *n* Pyrex® *m*.
◇ *comp* [dish] en Pyrex®.

pyrite [paɪ'raɪt], **pyrites** [paɪ'raɪti:z] *n* pyrite *f*.

pyromaniac [,paɪrə'meɪnɪæk] *n* pyromane *mf*.

pyrotechnics [,paɪrəʊ'teknɪks] ◇ *n (U)* [process] pyrotechnie *f*.
◇ *npl* **1.** [display] feu *m* d'artifice **2.** *fig* [display of skill] performance *f* éblouissante.

Pyrrhic victory ['pɪrɪk-] *n* victoire *f* à la Pyrrhus.

Pythagoras [paɪ'θægərəs] *pr n* Pythagore.

Pythagorean [paɪ,θægə'ri:ən] *adj* [relating to Pythagoras] pythagoricien ■ [relating to Pythagoras' theorem] pythagorique.

python ['paɪθn] *n* python *m*.

q (*pl* **q's** *OR pl* **qs**), **Q** (*pl* **Q's** *OR pl* **Qs**) [kju:] *n* [letter] q *m*, Q *m*, *see also* **f**.

q *written abbr of* **quart**.

Qatar [kəˈtaːʳ] *pr n* Qatar *m*.

QC *n UK* (*abbrev of* **Queen's Counsel**) ≃ bâtonnier *m* de l'ordre.

QE2 (*abbrev of* **Queen Elizabeth II**) *pr n grand paquebot de luxe*.

QED (*abbrev of* **quod erat demonstrandum**) *adv* CQFD.

qt *written abbr of* **quart**.

Q-tip® *n US* Coton-Tige® *m*.

qty (*written abbrev of* **quantity**) qté.

qua [kweɪ] *prep fml* en tant que.

quack [kwæk] ◇ *vi* [duck] cancaner, faire coin-coin.
◇ *n* **1.** [of duck] cancanement *m*, coin-coin *m inv* **2.** [charlatan] charlatan *m* **3.** *UK & Australia inf hum* [doctor] toubib *m*.
◇ *adj* [medicine, method] de charlatan, charlatanesque ■ **~ doctor** charlatan *m*.
◇ *onom* : **~ (~)!** coin-coin!

quad [kwɒd] *n* **1.** = **quadruplet 2.** = **quadrangle 3.** = **quadraphonic 4.** TYPO cadrat *m*.

quadrangle [ˈkwɒdræŋgl] *n* **1.** GEOM quadrilatère *m* ■ **complete ~** quadrangle *m* **2.** [courtyard] cour *f*.

quadrangular [kwɒˈdræŋgjʊləʳ] *adj* quadrangulaire.

quadrant [ˈkwɒdrənt] *n* **1.** GEOM quadrant *m* **2.** ASTRON & NAUT quart-de-cercle *m*, quadrant *m*.

quadraphonic [ˌkwɒdrəˈfɒnɪk] *adj* quadriphonique ■ **in ~ sound** en quadriphonie.

quadratic [kwɒˈdrætɪk] ◇ *adj* MATHS quadratique.
◇ *n* équation *f* quadratique *OR* du second degré.

quadrature [ˈkwɒdrətʃəʳ] *n* quadrature *f*.

quadrilateral [ˌkwɒdrɪˈlætərəl] ◇ *adj* quadrilatère, quadrilatéral.
◇ *n* quadrilatère *m*.

quadrille [kwəˈdrɪl] *n* quadrille *m*.

quadriplegia [ˌkwɒdrɪˈpliːdʒə] *n* tétraplégie *f*, quadriplégie *f*.

quadriplegic [ˌkwɒdrɪˈpliːdʒɪk] ◇ *adj* tétraplégique.
◇ *n* tétraplégique *mf*.

quadroon [kwɒˈdruːn] *n* quarteron *m*, - onne *f*.

quadrophonic [ˌkwɒdrəˈfɒnɪk] = **quadraphonic**.

quadruped [ˈkwɒdrʊped] ◇ *adj* quadrupède.
◇ *n* quadrupède *m*.

quadruple [kwɒˈdruːpl] ◇ *adj* quadruple.
◇ *n* quadruple *m*.
◇ *vi* & *vt* quadrupler.

quadruplet [ˈkwɒdrʊplɪt] *n* quadruplé *m*, - e *f*.

quadruplicate [kwɒˈdruːplɪkət] ◇ *adj* quadruple.
◇ *n* : **in ~** en quatre exemplaires.

quads [kwɒdz] *npl inf* quadruplés *mpl*.

quaff [kwɒf] *vt lit* boire.

quagmire [ˈkwægmaɪəʳ] *n liter & fig* bourbier *m*.

quail [kweɪl] (*pl inv OR pl* **quails**) ◇ *n* [bird] caille *f*.
◇ *vi* [feel afraid] trembler ■ [give way, lose heart] perdre courage ■ **to ~ before sb/sthg** trembler devant qqn/qqch.

quaint [kweɪnt] *adj* **1.** [picturesque] pittoresque ■ [old-fashioned] au charme désuet **2.** [odd] bizarre, étrange ■ **what a ~ idea!** quelle drôle d'idée!

quaintly [ˈkweɪntlɪ] *adv* **1.** [picturesquely] de façon pittoresque ■ [in an old-fashioned way] : **they dress very ~** ils s'habillent à l'ancienne (mode) **2.** [oddly] bizarrement, étrangement.

quaintness [ˈkweɪntnɪs] *n* **1.** [picturesqueness] pittoresque *m* ■ [old-fashioned charm] charme *m* vieillot *OR* désuet **2.** [oddness] bizarrerie *f*, étrangeté *f*.

quake [kweɪk] ◇ *vi* **1.** [person] trembler, frémir ■ **to ~ with fear** trembler de peur **2.** [earth] trembler.
◇ *n inf* tremblement *m* de terre.

Quaker [ˈkweɪkəʳ] ◇ *n* quaker *m*, - eresse *f*.
◇ *adj* des quakers.

qualification [ˌkwɒlɪfɪˈkeɪʃn] *n* **1.** [diploma] diplôme *m* ■ **candidates with formal ~s in translating** des candidats possédant un diplôme de traducteur ■ **list your academic ~s** indiquez vos diplômes scolaires et universitaires **2.** [ability, quality] aptitude *f*, compétence *f* ■ [for job] qualification *f* **3.** [restriction] réserve *f* ■ **they accepted the idea with some/without ~** ils acceptèrent l'idée avec quelques réserves/sans réserve **4.** [act of qualifying] qualification *f*.

qualified [ˈkwɒlɪfaɪd] *adj* **1.** [trained] qualifié, diplômé ■ **our staff are highly ~** notre personnel est hautement qualifié **2.** [able, competent] compétent, qualifié ■ **I don't feel ~ to discuss such matters** ces questions sont hors de ma compétence **3.** [limited, conditional] mitigé, nuancé ■ **~ acceptance** acceptation *f* conditionnelle *OR* sous condition.

qualifier [ˈkwɒlɪfaɪəʳ] *n* **1.** SPORT [person] qualifié *m*, - e *f* ■ [contest] (épreuve *f*) éliminatoire *f* **2.** GRAM qualificatif *m*.

qualify [ˈkwɒlɪfaɪ] (*pret & pp* **qualified**) ◇ *vi* **1.** [pass exams, complete training] obtenir son diplôme ■ **to ~ as an accountant/a**

vet obtenir son diplôme de comptable/vétérinaire **2.** [be eligible] : **to ~ for a pension** avoir droit à la retraite ■ **none of the candidates really qualifies for the post** aucun candidat ne répond véritablement aux conditions requises pour ce poste ■ **it hardly qualifies as a success** *fig* c'est loin d'être une réussite **3.** [in competition] se qualifier.
◇ *vt* **1.** [make able or competent] qualifier, habiliter ■ **her experience qualifies her for the post** son expérience lui permet de prétendre à ce poste ■ **what qualifies him to talk about French politics?** en quoi est-il qualifié pour parler de la politique française? **2.** [modify - statement, criticism] mitiger, atténuer ■ [put conditions on] poser des conditions ■ **they qualified their acceptance of the plan** ils ont accepté le projet sous conditions **3.** [describe] qualifier ■ **I wouldn't ~ the play as a masterpiece** je n'irai pas jusqu'à qualifier cette pièce de chef-d'œuvre **4.** GRAM qualifier.

qualifying ['kwɒlɪfaɪɪŋ] *adj* [gen] : **~ examination** [at end of course] examen *m* de fin d'études ; [to get onto course] examen *m* d'entrée ■ **~ heat** *OR* **round** SPORT (épreuve *f*) éliminatoire *f* ■ **~ mark** *UK* SCH moyenne *f*.

qualitative ['kwɒlɪtətɪv] *adj* qualitatif.

qualitatively ['kwɒlɪtətɪvlɪ] *adv* qualitativement.

quality ['kwɒlətɪ] ◇ *n* (*pl* **qualities**) **1.** [standard, nature] qualité *f* ■ **the ~ of life** la qualité de la vie **2.** [high standard, excellence] qualité *f* ■ **we have a reputation for ~** nous sommes réputés pour la qualité de nos produits **3.** [feature, attribute] qualité *f* ■ **he has a lot of good qualities** il a de nombreuses qualités ■ **I don't doubt her intellectual qualities** je ne doute pas de ses capacités intellectuelles **4.** *arch* [high social status] qualité *f* **5.** [tone] timbre *m* **6.** LING [in phonetics] qualité *f*.
◇ *comp* [goods, work, shop] de qualité ■ **~ paper** *UK* *quotidien ou journal du dimanche de qualité (par opposition à la presse populaire).*

quality control *n* contrôle *m* de qualité.

quality time *n* : **I only spend an hour in the evening with my kids, but it's ~** je ne passe qu'une heure avec mes gosses le soir, mais je profite bien d'eux.

qualm [kwɑ:m] *n* **1.** [scruple] scrupule *m* ■ [misgiving] appréhension *f*, inquiétude *f* ■ **she has no ~s about going out alone** elle ne craint pas de sortir seule **2.** [pang of nausea] haut-le-cœur *m inv*, nausée *f*.

quandary ['kwɒndərɪ] (*pl* **quandaries**) *n* dilemme *m* ■ **I'm in a dreadful ~** je suis confronté à un terrible dilemme ■ **she was in a ~ over** *OR* **about whether or not to tell him** elle ne parvenait pas à décider si elle devait le lui dire.

quango ['kwæŋgəʊ] (*abbrev of* **quasiautonomous non-governmental organization**) *n* *UK* *organisme semi-public.*

QUANGO

Un *quango* est un organisme semi-public financé majoritairement par l'État mais disposant d'une certaine autonomie tel que le British Council.

quanta ['kwɒntə] *pl* ▷ **quantum**.

quantifiable [kwɒntɪ'faɪəbl] *adj* quantifiable.

quantifier ['kwɒntɪfaɪəʳ] *n* **1.** GRAM quantificateur *m*, quantifieur *m* **2.** LOGIC & MATHS quantificateur *m*.

quantify ['kwɒntɪfaɪ] (*pret & pp* **quantified**) *vt* **1.** [estimate] quantifier, évaluer quantitativement **2.** LOGIC quantifier.

quantitative ['kwɒntɪtətɪv], **quantitive** ['kwɒntətɪv] *adj* quantitatif.

quantitative analysis *n* analyse *f* quantitative.

quantity ['kwɒntətɪ] (*pl* **quantities**) *n* [gen - LING] & MATHS quantité *f* ■ **in ~** en (grande) quantité ■ **large quantities of** de grandes quantités de.

quantity surveying *n* métrage *m*.

quantity surveyor *n* métreur *m*.

quantum ['kwɒntəm] (*pl* **quanta** ['kwɒntə]) *n* quantum *m*.

quantum jump, quantum leap *n* progrès *m* énorme, bond *m* en avant.

quantum mechanics *n (U)* (mécanique *f*) quantique *f*.

quantum theory *n* théorie *f* des quanta *OR* quantique.

quarantine ['kwɒrənti:n] ◇ *n* MED quarantaine *f* ■ **our dog is in ~** notre chien est en quarantaine.
◇ *vt* mettre en quarantaine.

quark [kwɑ:k] *n* **1.** PHYS quark *m* **2.** [cheese] fromage *m* blanc.

quarrel ['kwɒrəl] (*UK pret & pp* **quarrelled**, *cont* **quarrelling**) (*US pret & pp* **quarreled**, *cont* **quarreling**) ◇ *n* **1.** [dispute] querelle *f*, dispute *f* ■ **they had a ~ over money** ils se sont disputés pour des histoires d'argent ■ **are you trying to start a ~?** tu cherches la dispute? ■ **to pick a ~ with sb** chercher querelle à qqn **2.** [cause for complaint] : **my only ~ with the plan is its cost** la seule chose que je reproche à ce projet, c'est son coût ■ **I have no ~ with her proposal** je n'ai rien contre sa proposition.
◇ *vi* **1.** [argue] se disputer, se quereller ■ **I don't want to ~ with you over** *OR* **about this** je ne veux pas me disputer avec toi à ce sujet *OR* à propos de cela **2.** [take issue] : **I can't ~ with your figures** je ne peux pas contester vos chiffres ■ **critics might ~ with parts of the introduction** les critiques pourraient trouver à redire à certains passages de l'introduction.

quarrelling *UK*, **quarreling** *US* ['kwɒrəlɪŋ] *n (U)* disputes *fpl*, querelles *fpl*.

quarrelsome ['kwɒrəlsəm] *adj* querelleur.

quarry ['kwɒrɪ] (*pl* **quarries**, *pret & pp* **quarried**) ◇ *n* **1.** [excavation] carrière *f* **2.** [prey] proie *f*.
◇ *vt* **1.** [sand, slate, marble etc] extraire **2.** [land, mountain] exploiter ■ **the hills have been extensively quarried** de nombreuses carrières ont été ouvertes dans les collines.
◇ *vi* exploiter ■ **they are ~ing for marble** ils exploitent une carrière de marbre.

quarrying ['kwɒrɪɪŋ] *n* **1.** [of sand, slate, marble etc] extraction *f* **2.** [of land, mountain] exploitation *f*.

quarryman ['kwɒrɪmən] (*pl* **quarrymen** [-mən]) *n* carrier *m*.

quarry tile *n* carreau *m*.

quart [kwɔ:t] *n* ≃ litre *m* ■ **you can't fit a ~ into a pint pot** *UK prov* à l'impossible nul n'est tenu *prov*.

quarter ['kwɔ:təʳ] ◇ *adj* : **a ~ hour/century/pound** un quart d'heure/de siècle/de livre.
◇ *vt* **1.** [divide into four] diviser en quatre
2. [divide by four] diviser par quatre
3. [lodge] loger ■ MIL cantonner
4. [dismember] écarteler
5. [subj: hunting dog] : **to ~ the ground** quêter.
◇ *n* **1.** [one fourth] quart *m* ■ **a ~ of a century/of an hour** un quart de siècle/d'heure ■ **a ton and a ~, one and a ~ tons** une tonne un quart ■ **he ate a ~/three ~s of the cake** il a mangé le quart/les trois quarts du gâteau ■ **it's a ~/three ~s empty** c'est au quart/aux trois quarts vide
2. [in telling time] quart *m* ■ **(a) ~ to six, (a) ~ of six** *US* six heures moins le quart ■ **(a) ~ past six** *UK*, **(a) ~ after six** *US* six heures et quart
3. [3 months] trimestre *m* ■ **published every ~** publié tous les trimestres *OR* tous les trois mois
4. [US and Canadian money] (pièce *f* de) vingt-cinq cents *mpl*
5. [weight - quarter of hundredweight] ≃ 12 kg ; [- quarter pound] quart *m* de livre, 113 g
6. [direction] direction *f*, côté *m* ■ **offers of help poured in from all ~s** des offres d'aide affluèrent de tous côtés ■ **the decision has been criticized in certain ~s** la décision a été critiquée dans certains milieux ■ **the wind is in the port/starboard ~** NAUT le vent souffle par la hanche de bâbord/tribord
7. [part of town] quartier *m*
8. [phase of moon] quartier *m*
9. SPORT [period of play] quart-temps *m inv*
10. [part of butchered animal] quartier *m*
11. *(usu neg) lit* [mercy] quartier *m* ■ **they gave no ~** ils ne firent pas de quartier.

◆ **quarters** *npl* [accommodation] domicile *m*, résidence *f* ▪ **many families live in very cramped ~s** de nombreuses familles vivent dans des conditions de surpeuplement ▪ **the servants' ~s** les appartements des domestiques.

quarterback ['kwɔːtəbæk] ◇ *n* SPORT quarterback *m*, quart-arrière *m* *Canada*.
◇ *vt* *US* **1.** SPORT [team] jouer quarterback dans **2.** *fig* être le stratège de, diriger la stratégie de.

quarterdeck ['kwɔːtədek] *n* **1.** [part of ship - NAUT] plage *f* arrière **2.** [personnel] : **the ~** les officiers.

quarterfinal [ˌkwɔːtə'faɪnl] *n* quart *m* de finale ▪ **knocked out in the ~s** éliminé en quart de finale.

quarterfinalist ['kwɔːtəfaɪnəlɪst] *n* quart-de-finaliste *mf*.

quarter-hourly *adj* & *adv* tous les quarts d'heure.

quarterlight ['kwɔːtəlaɪt] *n* AUT [in UK] déflecteur *m*.

quarterly ['kwɔːtəlɪ] ◇ *adj* trimestriel.
◇ *n* publication *f* trimestrielle.
◇ *adv* trimestriellement, tous les trois mois.

quartermaster ['kwɔːtəˌmɑːstər] *n* **1.** [in army] commissaire *m* ▪ HIST intendant *m* **2.** [in navy] officier *m* de manœuvre.

quarter note *n* *US* MUS noire *f*.

quarter-pounder *n* CULIN gros hamburger.

quarter sessions *npl* **1.** [in England and Wales] ≃ cour *f* d'assises *(remplacée en 1972 par la Crown Court)* **2.** [in US] *dans certains États, tribunal local à compétence criminelle, pouvant avoir des fonctions administratives.*

quarter tone *n* MUS quart *m* de ton.

quartet [kwɔː'tet] *n* **1.** [players - classical] quatuor *m* ; [- jazz] quartette *m* **2.** [piece of music] quatuor *m* **3.** [group of four people] quatuor *m*.

quartette [kwɔː'tet] *n* = **quartet**.

quarto ['kwɔːtəʊ] (*pl* **quartos**) ◇ *n* in-quarto *m inv*.
◇ *adj* in quarto *(inv)*.

quartz [kwɔːts] ◇ *n* quartz *m*.
◇ *comp* [clock, watch] à quartz.

quartz crystal *n* cristal *m* de quartz.

quasar ['kweɪzɑːr] *n* quasar *m*.

quash [kwɒʃ] *vt* *UK* **1.** [annul - verdict] casser ; [- decision] annuler **2.** [suppress - revolt] étouffer, écraser ; [- emotion] réprimer, refouler ; [- suggestion] rejeter, repousser.

quasi- ['kweɪzaɪ] *in cpds* quasi.

quatercentenary [ˌkwætəsen'tiːnərɪ] (*pl* **quatercentenaries**) *n* quatrième centenaire *m*.

quaternary [kwə'tɜːnərɪ] ◇ *adj* CHEM & MATHS quaternaire.
◇ *n* [set of four] ensemble *m* de quatre (éléments).
◆ **Quaternary** GEOL ◇ *adj* quaternaire.
◇ *n* : **the Quaternary** le quaternaire.

quatrain ['kwɒtreɪn] *n* quatrain *m*.

quaver ['kweɪvər] ◇ *vi* [voice] trembloter, chevroter ▪ [person] parler d'une voix tremblotante *OR* chevrotante.
◇ *n* **1.** [of sound, in voice] chevrotement *m*, tremblement *m* **2.** *UK* MUS croche *f*.

quavering ['kweɪvərɪŋ] ◇ *adj* tremblotant, chevrotant.
◇ *n* tremblement *m*, chevrotement *m*.

quavery ['kweɪvərɪ] = **quavering** *(adj)*.

quay [kiː] *n* quai *m*.

quayside ['kiːsaɪd] *n* quai *m* ▪ **we walked along the ~** nous nous sommes promenés le long du quai ▪ **she was waiting at the ~** elle attendait sur le quai.

queasiness ['kwiːzɪnɪs] *n (U)* **1.** [nausea] nausée *f* **2.** [uneasiness] scrupules *mpl*.

queasy ['kwiːzɪ] (*comp* **queasier**, *superl* **queasiest**) *adj* **1.** [nauseous] nauséeux ▪ **I** *OR* **my stomach felt a little ~** j'avais un peu mal au cœur **2.** [uneasy] mal à l'aise, gêné.

Quebec [kwɪ'bek] *pr n* **1.** [province] Québec *m* ▪ **in ~** au Québec **2.** [city] Québec.

Quebecker, Quebecer [kwɪ'bekər] *n* Québécois *m*, - e *f*.

Quebecois, Québécois [kebe'kwɑː] (*pl inv*) *n* Québécois *m*, - e *f*.

queen [kwiːn] ◇ *n* **1.** [sovereign, king's wife] reine *f* ▪ **the Queen of England/Spain/Belgium** la reine d'Angleterre/d'Espagne/de Belgique ▪ **Queen Elizabeth II** la reine Élisabeth II **2.** [woman considered best] reine *f* **3.** [in cards, chess] dame *f*, reine *f* **4.** [of bees, ants] reine *f* **5.** △ *pej* [homosexual] tante *f*, pédale *f*.
◇ *vt* **1.** *UK phr* **to ~ it** *inf* prendre des airs de (grande) marquise **2.** [in chess] : **to ~ a pawn** aller à dame.

queen bee *n* reine *f* des abeilles ▪ **she's the ~ round here** *inf fig* c'est elle la patronne ici.

queen consort *n* reine *f (épouse du roi)*.

queenly ['kwiːnlɪ] *adj* royal, majestueux.

queen mother *n* reine *f* mère.

queen regent *n* reine *f* régente.

Queens [kwiːnz] *pr n* Queens *(quartier de New York)*.

Queen's Bench (Division) *n en Angleterre et au pays de Galles, l'une des trois divisions de la High Court,* ≃ tribunal *m* de grande instance.

Queen's Counsel *n* ≃ bâtonnier *m* de l'ordre *(en Angleterre)*.

Queen's English *n l'anglais britannique correct* ▪ **she speaks the ~** elle s'exprime dans un anglais très soigné.

Queen's evidence *n* *UK* **to turn ~** témoigner contre ses complices.

Queen's Speech *n* [in UK] : **the ~** *allocution prononcée par la reine (mais préparée par le gouvernement) lors de la rentrée parlementaire et dans laquelle elle définit les grands axes de la politique gouvernementale.*

queer [kwɪər] ◇ *adj* **1.** [strange] étrange, bizarre ▪ **he's a ~ fish!** c'est un drôle d'individu! **2.** [suspicious] suspect, louche **3.** *dated inf* [queasy] mal fichu, patraque **4.** *inf* [crazy] timbré, cinglé ▪ **he's a bit ~ in the head** il lui manque une case **5.** △ [homosexual] *pej* pédé *m* ▪ [as used by homosexuals - culture, activism, politics] gay *(inv)*, gai ▪ **~ poetry** poésie *f* gay **6.** *US inf* [counterfeit] : **~ money** fausse monnaie *f*.
◇ *n*△ homo *m* ▪ *pej* pédé *m*.
◇ *vt inf* gâter, gâcher ▪ **to ~ sb's pitch** *UK* couper l'herbe sous les pieds de qqn.

queer-bashing△ [-ˌbæʃɪŋ] *n* *UK pej* chasse *f* aux pédés△.

queerly ['kwɪəlɪ] *adv* étrangement, bizarrement.

queer street *n* *UK* **to be in ~** *inf dated* être dans une mauvaise passe.

quell [kwel] *vt* **1.** [quash - revolt, opposition] réprimer, étouffer **2.** [overcome - emotion] dompter, maîtriser **3.** [allay - pain] apaiser, soulager ; [- doubts, fears] dissiper.

quench [kwentʃ] *vt* **1.** *liter* **to ~ one's thirst** étancher sa soif, se désaltérer **2.** [fire] éteindre **3.** METALL tremper.

querulous ['kwerʊləs] *adj* [person] pleurnicheur ▪ [voice, tone] plaintif, gémissant.

querulously ['kwerʊləslɪ] *adv* d'un ton plaintif.

query ['kwɪərɪ] ◇ *n* (*pl* queries) **1.** [question] question *f* ▪ [doubt] doute *m* ▪ **she accepted my explanation without a ~** elle a accepté mon explication sans poser de questions **2.** *UK* [question mark] point *m* d'interrogation.
◇ *vt* (*pret* & *pp* **queried**) **1.** [express doubt about] mettre en doute ▪ **the accountant queried the figures** le comptable posa des questions sur les chiffres **2.** [ask] demander **3.** *US* [interrogate] interroger.

query language *n* COMPUT langage *m* d'interrogation.

quest [kwest] <> *n* quête *f* ■ **in ~ of truth** en quête de *OR* à la recherche de la vérité.
<> *vi lit* **to ~ for** *OR* **after sthg** se mettre en quête de qqch.

question ['kwestʃn] <> *n* **1.** [query] question *f* ■ **to ask sb a ~** poser une question à qqn ■ **I wish to put a ~ to the chairman** j'aimerais poser une question au président ■ **they obeyed without ~** ils ont obéi sans poser de questions ▶ **(Prime Minister's) Question Time** *session bi-hebdomadaire du Parlement britannique réservée aux questions des députés au Premier ministre*
2. [matter, issue] question *f* ■ [problem] problème *m* ■ **it raises the ~ of how much teachers should be paid** cela soulève *OR* pose le problème du salaire des enseignants ■ **the place/time in ~** le lieu/l'heure en question ■ **the ~ is, will he do it?** toute la question est de savoir s'il le fera ■ **that is the ~** voilà la question ■ **but that's not the ~** mais là n'est pas la question ■ **it's a ~ of how much you want to spend** tout dépend de la somme que vous voulez mettre ■ **it's only a ~ of money/time** ce n'est qu'une question d'argent/de temps
3. *(U)* [doubt] doute *m* ■ **there's no ~ about it, he was murdered** il a été assassiné, cela ne fait aucun doute ■ **his honesty was never in ~** son honnêteté n'a jamais été mise en doute *OR* remise en question ■ **to bring** *OR* **to call sthg into ~** remettre qqch en question ■ **she is without** *OR* **beyond ~ the best** elle est incontestablement la meilleure ■ **whether they are happier now is open to ~** sont-ils plus heureux maintenant? on peut se le demander
4. [possibility] : **there's no ~ of our making the same mistake again** nous ne sommes pas près de refaire la même erreur ■ **there's no ~ of his coming with us, it's out of the ~ that he should come with us** il est hors de question qu'il vienne avec nous.
<> *vt* **1.** [interrogate] interroger, poser des questions à ■ [subj: police] interroger ■ SCH interroger
2. [doubt - motives, honesty, wisdom] mettre en doute, remettre en question ; [- statement, claim] mettre en doute, contester ■ **I ~ed whether it was wise to continue** je me suis demandé s'il était bien sage de continuer.

questionable ['kwestʃənəbl] *adj* **1.** [doubtful] contestable, douteux ■ **his involvement in the affair is ~** sa participation dans cette affaire reste à démontrer *OR* à prouver ■ **it is ~ whether she knew** rien ne prouve qu'elle était au courant **2.** [suspicious - motives] douteux, louche ; [- behaviour] louche **3.** [strange - taste, style] douteux.

questioner ['kwestʃənəʳ] *n* [gen, in quiz show] animateur *m*, -trice *f* ■ LAW interrogateur *m*, - trice *f*.

questioning ['kwestʃənɪŋ] <> *adj* interrogateur.
<> *n* interrogation *f* ■ **he was taken in for ~** LAW il a été interpellé pour être interrogé.

questioningly ['kwestʃənɪŋlɪ] *adv* de manière interrogative.

question mark *n* point *m* d'interrogation ■ *fig* **a ~ hangs over the future of this country** il est impossible de prédire quel sort attend ce pays *OR* sera réservé à ce pays ■ **there is a ~ over her reasons for leaving** on ignore les raisons qui l'ont poussée à partir.

question master *n* meneur *m* de jeu ■ RADIO & TV animateur *m*, - trice *f (d'un jeu)*.

questionnaire [,kwestʃə'neəʳ] *n* questionnaire *m*.

question tag *n tournure en fin de phrase changeant celle-ci en question.*

queue [kju:] *UK* <> *n* queue *f*, file *f* d'attente ■ **they were standing in a ~** ils faisaient la queue ■ **to form a ~** former une queue ■ **a long ~ of cars** une longue file de voitures ■ **we joined the ~ for foreign exchange** nous avons fait la queue devant le bureau de change.
<> *vi* faire la queue ■ **'~ here for tickets'** file d'attente pour les billets.
◆ **queue up** *vi insep UK* faire la queue.

queue-jump *vi UK* essayer de passer avant son tour, resquiller.

queue-jumper *n UK* resquilleur *m*, - euse *f (qui n'attend pas son tour)*.

quibble ['kwɪbl] <> *vi* chicaner ■ **to ~ over details** chicaner sur des détails.
<> *n* chicane *f* ■ **I have one small ~** il y a juste une petite chose qui me gêne.

quibbler ['kwɪbləʳ] *n* chicaneur *m*, - euse *f*, chicanier *m*, - ère *f*.

quibbling ['kwɪblɪŋ] <> *adj* chicaneur, chicanier.
<> *n* chicanerie *f*.

Quiberon ['ki:brɔ̃] *pr n* : **the ~ peninsula** la presqu'île de Quiberon.

quiche [ki:ʃ] *n* quiche *f*.

quick [kwɪk] <> *adj* **1.** [rapid] rapide ■ [easy - profits] rapide, facile ■ **he's a ~ worker** *liter* il travaille vite ; *fig* il ne perd pas de temps ■ **be ~ (about it)!** faites vite!, dépêchez-vous! ■ **to have a ~ look** jeter un rapide coup d'œil ■ **can I have a ~ word?** est-ce que je peux vous parler un instant? ■ **she did the job in double ~ time** elle a fait le travail en deux temps, trois mouvements *OR* en un rien de temps ■ **we had a ~ lunch** nous avons déjeuné sur le pouce ■ **let's have a ~ one** *inf OR* **a ~ drink** prenons un verre en vitesse ▶ **(as) ~ as lightning** *OR* **as a flash** rapide *OR* vif comme l'éclair **2.** [sharp] alerte, éveillé, vif ■ **he is ~ to learn** il apprend vite ■ **she has a ~ ear** elle a l'oreille fine ■ **she has a ~ eye for detail** aucun détail ne lui échappe ■ **I was ~ to notice the difference** j'ai tout de suite remarqué la différence ▶ **she's ~ on the uptake** elle comprend vite ■ **they were very ~ off the mark** *UK* ils n'ont pas perdu de temps **3.** [hasty - judgment] hâtif, rapide ■ **he has a ~ temper** il s'emporte facilement ■ **he is ~ to take offence** il est prompt à s'offenser, il se vexe pour un rien.
<> *adv* rapidement ■ **come ~!** venez vite!
<> *n* [of fingernail] vif *m* ▶ **her remark cut him to the ~** sa remarque l'a piqué au vif.
<> *npl arch* [living] : **the ~ and the dead** les vivants *mpl* et les morts *mpl*.

quick- *in cpds* : **~dry** *OR* **~drying paint** peinture *f* à séchage rapide ■ **~setting cement** ciment *m* à prise rapide.

quick-change artist *n* spécialiste *mf* des transformations rapides.

quicken ['kwɪkn] <> *vt* **1.** [hasten] accélérer, hâter ■ MUS [tempo] presser ■ **to ~ one's pace** *OR* **step** hâter *OR* presser le pas **2.** [stir - imagination] stimuler ; [- hatred, desire] exciter ; [- appetite, interest] stimuler ; [- resolve] hâter.
<> *vi* **1.** [step, pulse] s'accélérer ■ **my heart** *OR* **pulse ~ ed** mon cœur se mit à battre plus vite **2.** [hopes, fire] se ranimer **3.** [foetus] commencer à bouger.

quickening ['kwɪknɪŋ] *n* accélération *f*.

quickfire ['kwɪkfaɪəʳ] *adj* : **he directed ~ questions at me** il m'a mitraillé de questions ■ **a series of ~ questions** un feu roulant de questions.

quick-freeze (*pret* **quick-froze**, *pp* **quick-frozen**) *vt* surgeler.

quickie ['kwɪkɪ] *n inf* **1.** [gen] truc *m* vite fait ■ [question] question *f* rapide **2.** [sex] coup *m* en vitesse *OR* entre deux portes **3.** [drink] pot *m* rapide.

quicklime ['kwɪklaɪm] *n* chaux *f* vive.

quickly ['kwɪklɪ] *adv* rapidement, vite ■ **come as ~ as possible** venez aussi vite que possible ■ **he ~ telephoned the doctor** il se dépêcha d'appeler le médecin.

quickness ['kwɪknɪs] *n* **1.** [rapidity - of movement, pulse] rapidité *f* ; [- of thought, reaction] rapidité, vivacité *f* **2.** [acuteness - of sight, wit] vivacité *f* ; [- of hearing] finesse *f* **3.** [hastiness] : **his ~ of temper** sa promptitude à s'emporter.

quicksand ['kwɪksænd] *n* sables *mpl* mouvants.

quicksands ['kwɪksændz] *npl* = **quicksand**.

quickset ['kwɪkset] *adj UK* **~ hedge** haie *f* vive.

quicksilver ['kwɪk,sɪlvəʳ] <> *n* vif-argent *m*, mercure *m*.

<> *adj* [mind] très vif, comme du vif-argent.

quickstep ['kwɪkstep] *n* quickstep *m*.

quick-tempered *adj* : **he is ~** il s'emporte facilement.

quick-witted *adj* à l'esprit vif ▪ **she is very ~** [in answers] elle a de la repartie ; [in intelligence] elle a l'esprit vif.

quid [kwɪd] *n* **1.** (*pl inv*) *UK inf* [pound] livre *f* **2.** [tobacco] chique *f* **3.** *phr* **we're ~s in** *UK inf* on est peinards.

quid pro quo [ˌkwɪdprəʊ'kwəʊ] (*pl* **quid pro quos**) *n* contrepartie *f*, récompense *f*.

quiescent [kwaɪ'esnt] *adj lit* [passive] passif ▪ [peaceful] tranquille.

quiet ['kwaɪət] <> *adj* **1.** [silent - person] tranquille, silencieux ▪ **be** *OR* **keep ~!** taisez-vous! ▪ **could you try to keep them ~?** pourriez-vous essayer de les faire taire? ▪ **~ please!** silence, s'il vous plaît! ▪ **you're very ~** vous ne dites pas grand-chose ▪ **keep ~ about what you've seen** ne dites rien de ce que vous avez vu ▪ [subdued, soft] tranquille ▪ **we were having a ~ conversation** nous bavardions tranquillement ▪ **can I have a ~ word with you?** est-ce que je peux vous dire un mot en particulier? ▪ **in a ~ voice** d'une voix douce ▶ **it was as ~ as the grave** il régnait un silence de mort ▪ **she was as ~ as a mouse** elle ne faisait pas le moindre bruit
2. [calm, tranquil] calme, tranquille, paisible ▪ FIN [market, business] calme ▪ **the TV keeps the children ~** pendant qu'ils regardent la télé, les enfants se tiennent tranquilles ▪ **to have a ~ drink** boire un verre tranquillement ▪ **all is ~** tout va bien, rien à signaler ▶ **all ~ on the western front** *hum* à l'ouest rien de nouveau ▪ **anything for a ~ life** tout pour avoir la paix
3. [docile - animal] docile ▪ [easy - baby] calme ▪ [uncommunicative] silencieux, peu communicatif
4. [private - wedding] dans l'intimité ; [- party] avec quelques intimes, avec peu d'invités ▪ [secret] secret, - ète *f*, dissimulé ▪ **keep the news ~** gardez la nouvelle pour vous
5. [subtle, discreet - irony] discret, - ète *f* ; [- optimism] tranquille ; [- anger] sourd ; [- despair, resentment] secret, - ète *f*
6. [muted - colour, style] sobre.
<> *n* silence *m* ▪ **to ask for ~** demander le silence.
<> *vt* [calm] calmer ▪ [silence] faire taire.
◆ **on the quiet** *adv phr UK* [in secrecy] en douce, en cachette ▪ [discreetly] discrètement, en douceur ▪ [in confidence] en confiance.
◆ **quiet down** *vi insep US* se calmer.

quieten ['kwaɪətn] <> *vt UK* [child, audience] calmer, apaiser ▪ [conscience] tranquilliser, apaiser ▪ [doubts] dissiper.
<> *vi* [child] se calmer ▪ [music] devenir plus doux.
◆ **quieten down** <> *vi insep* **1.** [become quiet - person] se calmer ; [- storm, wind] se calmer, s'apaiser **2.** [become reasonable] s'assagir.
<> *vt sep* [calm] calmer, apaiser ▪ [shut up] faire taire.

quietist ['kwaɪətɪst] <> *adj* quiétiste.
<> *n* quiétiste *mf*.

quietly ['kwaɪətlɪ] *adv* [silently] silencieusement, sans bruit ▪ [gently, softly] doucement, calmement ▪ [peacefully] tranquillement, paisiblement ▪ **sit ~** restez assis tranquillement ▪ **they got married ~** ils se sont mariés dans l'intimité.

quietness ['kwaɪətnɪs] *n* [stillness] tranquillité *f*, calme *m* ▪ [silence] silence *m*.

quietude ['kwaɪətju:d] *n lit* quiétude *f*.

quiff [kwɪf] *n* [hairstyle] banane *f*.

quill [kwɪl] *n* **1.** [feather] penne *f* ▪ [shaft of feather] hampe *f* creuse ▪ [of hedgehog, porcupine] piquant *m* **2.** [pen] plume *f* (d'oie).

quill pen *n* plume *f* d'oie.

quilt [kwɪlt] *n* [eiderdown] édredon *m* ▪ [bedspread] dessus-de-lit *m inv* ▪ [duvet] couette *f*.

quilt cover *n* housse *f* de couette.

quilted ['kwɪltɪd] *adj* matelassé.

quilting ['kwɪltɪŋ] *n* **1.** [fabric] tissu *m* matelassé ▪ [on furniture] capitonnage *m* **2.** [of clothing] ouatinage *m* ▪ [of furniture covering] capitonnage *m* **3.** [hobby] *réalisation d'ouvrages (vêtements, dessus de lit) en tissu matelassé*.

quin [kwɪn] (*abbrev of* **quintuplet**) *n UK* quintuplé *m*, - e *f*.

quince [kwɪns] <> *n* [fruit] coing *m* ▪ [tree] cognassier *m*.
<> *comp* [jam, jelly] de coing.

quincentenary [ˌkwɪnsen'ti:nərɪ] *n* cinq-centième anniversaire *m*.

quincentennial [ˌkwɪnsen'tenɪəl] <> *n* cinq-centième anniversaire *m*.
<> *adj* cinq-centième.

quinine [kwɪ'ni:n] *n* quinine *f*.

quinquennium [kwɪŋ'kwenɪəm] (*pl* **quinquenniums** *OR pl* **quinquennia** [-nɪə]) *n* quinquennat *m*.

quint [kwɪnt] (*abbrev of* **quintuplet**) *n US* quintuplé *m*, - e *f*.

quintessence [kwɪn'tesns] *n* quintessence *f*.

quintessential [kwɪntə'senʃl] *adj* typique, type ▪ **she's the ~ Parisian** c'est la Parisienne type.

quintet [kwɪn'tet] *n* quintette *m*.

quintette [kwɪn'tet] *n* = **quintet**.

quintuple [kwɪn'tju:pl] <> *adj* quintuple.
<> *n* quintuple *m*.
<> *vi & vt* quintupler.

quintuplet [kwɪn'tju:plɪt] *n* quintuplé *m*, - e *f*.

quip [kwɪp] <> *n* [remark - witty] bon mot *m*, mot *m* d'esprit ; [- sarcastic] sarcasme *m* ▪ [gibe] quolibet *m* ▪ **to make a ~** faire un bon mot *OR* de l'esprit ▪ **he made a nasty ~ about her humble origins** il a fait une remarque désobligeante sur ses origines modestes.
<> *vt* (*pret & pp* **quipped**, *cont* **quipping**) : **"only if I'm asked", he quipped** "seulement si on me le demande", lança-t-il d'un air malicieux.

quire ['kwaɪəʳ] *n* [in bookbinding] cahier *m* ▪ [of paper] main *f* (de papier).

quirk [kw3:k] *n* **1.** [idiosyncrasy] manie *f*, excentricité *f* **2.** [accident] bizarrerie *f*, caprice *m* ▪ **by a strange ~ of fate we met in Sydney** par un caprice du destin, nous nous sommes rencontrés à Sydney **3.** [flourish] fioriture *f*.

quirky ['kw3:kɪ] *adj* bizarre, original.

quisling ['kwɪzlɪŋ] *n pej* collaborateur *m*, - trice *f*.

quit [kwɪt] <> *vt* (*pret & pp* **quit** *OR* **quitted**, *cont* **quitting**) **1.** [leave] quitter **2.** *US* [give up, stop] quitter, cesser ▪ **he ~ his job** il a quitté son travail ▪ **I've ~ smoking** j'ai arrêté *OR* cessé de fumer ▪ **~ it!** arrête!, ça suffit!
<> *vi* (*pret & pp* **quit** *OR* **quitted**, *cont* **quitting**) **1.** [give up] renoncer, abandonner ▪ [resign] démissionner ▪ **I ~!** *inf* j'abandonne! ▪ **I want to ~** j'ai envie de tout laisser tomber **2.** *US* [leave] partir **3.** COMPUT quitter.
<> *adj* : **to be ~ of sb/sthg** être débarrassé de qqn/qqch.

quite [kwaɪt] <> *adv & predet* **1.** [moderately] assez ▪ **the film is ~ good** le film est assez bon ▪ **I'd ~ like to go** ça me plairait assez d'y aller ▪ **~ a difficult job** un travail assez difficile ▪ **~ a lot of people seem to believe it** un bon nombre de gens semblent le croire ▪ **there was ~ a crowd** il y avait pas mal de monde ▪ **I've been here for ~ some time** je suis ici depuis un bon moment *OR* depuis assez longtemps ▪ **he was in France for ~ some time** il a passé pas mal de temps en France **2.** [completely, absolutely] parfaitement, tout à fait ▪ **the story isn't ~ true** l'histoire n'est pas tout à fait *OR* entièrement vraie ▪ **I ~ understand** je comprends tout à fait *OR* parfaitement ▪ **she's ~ brilliant** elle est vraiment très brillante ▪ **if you've ~ finished** si vous avez terminé ▪ **that's ~ another matter!** ça, c'est autre chose! ▪ **not ~ a month ago** il y a un peu moins d'un mois ▪ **you've had ~ enough** vous en avez eu largement assez ▪ **that's ~ enough!** ça suffit comme ça! ▪ **he's ~ the young gentleman** c'est le parfait jeune homme **3.** [exactly] exactement, tout à fait **4.** [expressing approval, appreciation] :

that was ~ a *OR* **~ some party!** ***inf*** ça a été une sacrée soirée! ➋ **his speech was ~ something** son discours était tout à fait remarquable.
<> *interj* : *UK* **~ (so)!** tout à fait!, parfaitement!

Quito ['ki:təʊ] *pr n* Quito.

quits [kwɪts] *adj inf* quitte ▪ **I'm ~ with her now** maintenant, je suis quitte envers elle ▪ **let's call it ~** [financially] disons que nous sommes quittes ; [in fight, argument] restons-en là.

quittance ['kwɪtəns] *n* FIN & LAW quittance *f*.

quitter ['kwɪtəʳ] *n inf* dégonflé *m*, - e *f*.

quiver ['kwɪvəʳ] <> *vi* **1.** [tremble - person] frémir, trembler ; [- lips, hands, voice] trembler ▪ **to ~ with fear/rage** trembler de peur/rage ▪ **to ~ with emotion** frissonner d'émotion **2.** [flutter - heart] trembler, frémir ; [- leaves] frémir, frissonner ; [- flame] trembler, vaciller.
<> *n* **1.** [tremble] tremblement *m* ▪ [of violin] trémolo *m*, frémissement *m* ▪ **a ~ of fear went down my spine** un frisson de peur me parcourut le dos ▪ **he had a ~ in his voice** sa voix tremblait d'émotion ▪ **her heart gave a ~** son cœur fit un bond dans sa poitrine **2.** [for arrows] carquois *m*.

qui vive [ki:'vi:v] *n UK* **on the ~** sur le qui-vive.

Quixote ['kwɪksət] *pr n* : **Don ~** Don Quichotte.

quixotic [kwɪk'sɒtɪk] *adj* [idealistic] idéaliste, chimérique ▪ [chivalrous] généreux, chevaleresque.

quiz [kwɪz] <> *n* (*pl* **quizzes**) **1.** [game - on TV] jeu *m* télévisé ; [- on radio] jeu *m* radiophonique ; [- in newspaper] questionnaire *m* ▪ **~ shows** *OR* **programmes** les jeux télévisés ▪ **general knowledge ~** test *m* de culture générale **2.** *US* SCH [test] interrogation *f* écrite.
<> *vt* (*pret & pp* **quizzed**, *cont* **quizzing**) **1.** [question] interroger, questionner ▪ **to ~ sb about sthg** interroger qqn au sujet de qqch **2.** *US* SCH [test] interroger.

quizmaster ['kwɪz,mɑ:stəʳ] *n* RADIO & TV animateur *m*, - trice *f (d'un jeu)*.

quizzical ['kwɪzɪkl] *adj* [questioning] interrogateur ▪ [ironic] ironique, narquois.

quizzically ['kwɪzɪklɪ] *adv* [questioningly] d'un air interrogateur ▪ [ironically] d'un air ironique *OR* narquois.

quoin [kɔɪn] *n* [cornerstone] pierre *f* d'angle ▪ [keystone] clef *f* de voûte.

quoit [kɔɪt] *n* [in game] anneau *m* ▪ **to play ~s** jouer aux anneaux.

Quonset hut® ['kwɒnsɪt-] *n US* abri *m* préfabriqué *(en tôle ondulée)*.

quorate ['kwɔ:reɪt] *adj UK* où le quorum est atteint.

Quorn® [kwɔ:n] *n aliment aux protéines végétales servant de substitut à la viande*.

quorum ['kwɔ:rəm] *n* quorum *m* ▪ **we don't have a ~** le quorum n'est pas atteint.

quota ['kwəʊtə] *n* **1.** [limited quantity] quota *m*, contingent *m* **2.** [share] part *f*, quota *m*.

quotable ['kwəʊtəbl] *adj* **1.** [worth quoting] digne d'être cité **2.** [on the record] que l'on peut citer ▪ **what he said is not ~** ce qu'il a dit ne peut être répété **3.** ST. EX cotable.

quotation [kwəʊ'teɪʃn] *n* **1.** [remark, sentence] citation *f* **2.** ST. EX cours *m*, cotation *f* **3.** COMM [estimate] devis *m* ▪ [for insurance] cotation *f*.

quotation marks *npl* guillemets *mpl*.

quote [kwəʊt] <> *vt* **1.** [cite - words, example, statistics] citer ▪ **can I ~ you on that?** me permettez-vous de citer ce que vous venez de dire? ▪ **don't ~ me on that** [don't repeat it] ne le répétez pas ; [don't say who told you] ne dites pas que c'est moi qui vous l'ai dit ▪ **he said, ~, get lost, unquote** il a dit, je cite, allez vous faire voir ▪ **their leader was ~d as denying the allegation** leur leader aurait rejeté l'accusation **2.** ADMIN & COMM : **please ~ this reference (number)** prière de mentionner cette référence **3.** [specify - price] indiquer ▪ ST. EX coter ▪ **gold prices were ~d at £500** l'or a été coté à 500 livres.
<> *vi* **1.** [cite] faire des citations ▪ **to ~ from Yeats** citer Yeats **2.** COMM : **to ~ for a job** faire un devis pour un travail.
<> *n* **1.** [quotation] citation *f* ▪ [statement] déclaration *f* **2.** [estimate] devis *m* **3.** [quotation mark] guillemet *m* ▪ **in ~s** entre guillemets.

quoted company ['kwəʊtɪd-] *n UK* société *f* cotée en Bourse.

quoth [kwəʊθ] *vt arch* **"nay", ~ the King** "non", fit *OR* dit le roi.

quotidian [kwɒ'tɪdɪən] *adj fml* quotidien.

quotient ['kwəʊʃnt] *n* quotient *m*.

Qur'an *etc* [kɒ'rɑ:n] = **Koran**.

qv (*written abbrev of* **quod vide**) *expression renvoyant le lecteur à une autre entrée dans une encyclopédie.*

qwerty, Qwerty ['kwɜ:tɪ] *n* : **~ keyboard** clavier *m* qwerty.

R

r (*pl* **r's** *OR pl* **rs**)**, R** (*pl* **R's** *OR pl* **Rs**) [ɑːʳ] *n* [letter] r *m*, R *m* ■ **the three Rs** la lecture, l'écriture et l'arithmétique *(qui constituent les fondements de l'enseignement primaire)*, *see also* **f**.

R ◇ **1.** (*written abbrev of* **right**) dr. **2.** *written abbrev of* **river 3.** *US* (*written abbrev of* **Republican 4.** *UK* (*written abbrev of* **Rex**) *suit le nom d'un roi* **5.** *UK* (*written abbrev of* **Regina**) *suit le nom d'une reine* **6.** *written abbr of* **radius 7.** *written abbrev of* **road 8.** *written abbrev of* **registered (trademark)**.
◇ *adj US* (*abbrev of* **restricted**) *indique qu'un film est interdit aux moins de 17 ans*.

RA ◇ *n* **1.** = **rear admiral 2.** (*abbrev of* **Royal Academician**) *membre de la Royal Academy*.
◇ *pr n* = **Royal Academy**.

rabbet ['ræbɪt] ◇ *n* [groove] feuillure *f*.
◇ *vt* feuiller.

rabbi ['ræbaɪ] *n* rabbin *m* ■ **chief ~** grand rabbin.

rabbinical [rə'bɪnɪkl] *adj* rabbinique.

rabbit ['ræbɪt] ◇ *n* [animal] lapin *m*, - e *f* ■ **doe ~** lapine *f* ■ **young ~** lapereau *m* ■ **wild ~** lapin de garenne.
◇ *comp* [coat] en (peau de) lapin.
◇ *vi* : **to go ~ing** chasser le lapin.
◆ **rabbit on** *vi insep inf* [talk] jacasser ■ **he's been ~ing on about his money problems** il me rebat les oreilles de ses problèmes d'argent ■ **what's she ~ing on about?** de quoi elle cause?

rabbit burrow, rabbit hole *n* terrier *m* (de lapin).

rabbit hutch *n* clapier *m*, cage *f OR* cabane *f* à lapins ■ *fig* [housing] cage *f* à lapins.

rabbit punch *n* coup *m* du lapin.

rabbit warren *n* **1.** *liter* garenne *f* **2.** *fig* labyrinthe *m*, dédale *m*.

rabble ['ræbl] *n* **1.** [mob] : **the ~** *pej* la populace, la racaille **2.** TECH [in foundry] râble *m*.

rabble-rouser *n* agitateur *m*, - trice *f*, démagogue *mf*.

rabble-rousing ◇ *n* démagogie *f*.
◇ *adj* démagogique.

Rabelaisian [ˌræbə'leɪzɪən] *adj* rabelaisien.

rabid ['ræbɪd, 'reɪbɪd] *adj* **1.** MED [animal] enragé ■ [person] atteint de la rage **2.** *fig* [extremist, revolutionary] enragé ■ [hatred] farouche ■ [anger] féroce.

rabies ['reɪbiːz] *n (U)* MED rage *f*.

RAC (*abbrev of* **Royal Automobile Club**) *pr n* : **the ~** *un des deux grands clubs automobiles de Grande-Bretagne*.

raccoon [rə'kuːn] ◇ *n* raton *m* laveur.
◇ *comp* [coat, stole] en (fourrure de) raton laveur.

race [reɪs] ◇ *n* **1.** [competition] course *f* ■ **an 800 metre ~** une course de *OR* sur 800 mètres ■ **to have** *OR* **to run a ~** courir, participer à une course ■ **a ~ against time** une course contre la montre ■ **it'll be a ~ to finish on time** il faudra se dépêcher pour finir à temps ■ **the ~ for the Presidency** la course à la présidence **2.** [ethnic group] race *f* ■ [in anthropology] ethnie *f* **3.** *lit* [passing - of sun, moon] course *f* ; [- of life] cours *m* **4.** [current] fort courant *m* ■ [in sea channel] raz *m* (de courant).
◇ *comp* [discrimination, hatred, prejudice] racial.
◇ *vi* **1.** [compete] faire la course ■ **the cars/drivers were racing against each other** les voitures/conducteurs faisaient la course **2.** [go fast, rush] aller à toute allure *OR* vitesse ■ **to ~ in/out/past** entrer/sortir/passer à toute allure ■ **to ~ for a bus** courir pour attraper un bus ■ **she ~d downstairs** elle a dévalé l'escalier ■ **my pulse was racing** mon cœur battait à tout rompre ■ **a thousand ideas ~d through her mind** mille idées lui sont passées par la tête **3.** [of engine] s'emballer.
◇ *vt* **1.** [compete against] faire la course avec ■ **(I'll) ~ you there!** à qui y arrivera le premier! **2.** [rush] : **the casualties were ~d to hospital** les blessés ont été transportés d'urgence à l'hôpital **3.** [put into a race] : **to ~ a horse** faire courir un cheval ■ **to ~ pigeons** faire des courses de pigeons **4.** AUT : **to ~ the engine** accélérer ; [excessively] faire s'emballer le moteur.

race card *n* programme *m* (des courses).

racecourse ['reɪskɔːs] *n* **1.** champ *m* de courses, hippodrome *m* **2.** *US* [for cars, motorbikes] circuit *m* ■ [for runner, cycles] piste *f*.

racegoer ['reɪsˌgəʊəʳ] *n* turfiste *mf*.

racehorse ['reɪshɔːs] *n* cheval *m* de course.

race meeting *n* courses *fpl*.

racer ['reɪsəʳ] *n* [runner] coureur *m*, - euse *f* ■ [horse] cheval *m* de course ■ [car] voiture *f* de course ■ [cycle] vélo *m* de course.

race relations *npl* relations *fpl* interraciales ■ **~ body** *OR* **board** organisme *m* luttant contre la discrimination raciale.

race riot *n* émeute *f* raciale.

racetrack ['reɪstræk] *n* [gen] piste *f* ■ [for horses] champ *m* de courses, hippodrome *m*.

racewalking ['reɪswɔːkɪŋ] *n* marche *f* athlétique.

raceway ['reɪsweɪ] *n US* **1.** = **racetrack 2.** [millrace] bief *m*.

Rachel ['reɪtʃl] *pr n* BIBLE Rachel.

Rachmaninoff [ræk'mænɪnɒf] *pr n* Rachmaninov.

Rachmanism ['rækmənɪzm] *n pressions exercées par un propriétaire sur ses locataires pour obtenir leur éviction*.

racial ['reɪʃl] *adj* **1.** [concerning a race] racial, ethnique **2.** [between races] racial.

racialism ['reɪʃəlɪzm] *n* racisme *m.*

racialist ['reɪʃəlɪst] ◇ *adj* raciste.
◇ *n* raciste *mf.*

racially ['reɪʃəlɪ] *adv* du point de vue racial ▪ **a ~ motivated attack** une agression raciste ▪ **~ prejudiced** raciste.

racing ['reɪsɪŋ] ◇ *n* [of horses] courses *fpl* de chevaux.
◇ *comp* [bicycle, yacht] de course.

racing car *n* voiture *f* de course.

racing cyclist *n* coureur *m*, - euse *f* cycliste.

racing driver *n* coureur *m*, - euse *f* automobile, pilote *mf* (de course).

racing pigeon *n* pigeon *m* voyageur *(de compétition).*

racism ['reɪsɪzm] *n* racisme *m.*

racist ['reɪsɪst] ◇ *adj* raciste.
◇ *n* raciste *mf.*

rack [ræk] ◇ *n* **1.** [shelf] étagère *f* ▪ [for cooling, drying] grille *f*, claie *f* ▪ [for fodder, bicycles, test tubes, pipes] râtelier *m* ▪ [for bottles] casier *m* ▪ **(luggage) ~** [in train, bus] filet *m* (à bagages) ; [on cycle] porte-bagages *m inv* ▪ **(stereo) ~** meuble *m* pour chaîne hi-fi ▪ **(tool) ~** porte-outils *m inv* ▮ [in shop] présentoir *m* ▪ **(clothes) ~** triangle *m* (à vêtements) ▪ **to buy a suit off the ~** acheter un costume en prêt-à-porter **2.** HIST chevalet *m* ▪ **to put sb on the ~** *liter* faire subir à qqn le supplice du chevalet ; *fig* mettre qqn au supplice **3.** MECH crémaillère *f* **4.** CULIN : **~ of lamb** carré *m* d'agneau **5.** *phr* **to go to ~ and ruin** [house] tomber en ruine ; [garden] être à l'abandon ; [person] dépérir ; [company] péricliter ; [country, institution] aller à vau-l'eau.
◇ *vt* **1.** [torture] faire subir le supplice du chevalet à ▪ *fig* tenailler, ronger ▪ **~ed by guilt** tenaillé par un sentiment de culpabilité ▪ **to ~ one's brains** se creuser la tête **2.** [wine] soutirer.
◆ **rack up** *vt sep US* [points] marquer.

rack and pinion *n* crémaillère *f* ▪ **~ railway = rack railway**.

racket ['rækɪt] ◇ *n* **1.** SPORT [bat] raquette *f* **2.** [snowshoe] raquette *f* **3.** *inf* [din] boucan *m* **4.** [extortion] racket *m* ▪ [fraud] escroquerie *f* ▪ [traffic] trafic *m* ▪ **this lottery is such a ~** cette loterie, c'est de l'arnaque **5.** *inf* [job] boulot *m* ▪ **is she still in the teaching/publishing ~?** est-ce qu'elle est encore dans l'enseignement/l'édition?
◇ *vi* [be noisy] faire du boucan.
◆ **rackets** *n (U)* [game] racket-ball *m.*

racketeer [ˌrækə'tɪəʳ] ◇ *n* racketteur *m.*
◇ *vi* racketter.

racketeering [ˌrækə'tɪərɪŋ] *n* racket *m.*

racket press *n* presse-raquette *m.*

racking ['rækɪŋ] *adj* [pain] atroce, déchirant.

rack railway *n* chemin *m* de fer à crémaillère.

rack rent *n UK* loyer *m* exorbitant.

raconteur [ˌrækɒn'tɜːʳ] *n* raconteur *m*, - euse *f.*

racoon [rə'kuːn] = **raccoon**.

racquet ['rækɪt] = **racket** *(n sense 1).*

racquetball ['rækɪtbɔːl] *n* racquetball *m.*

racy ['reɪsɪ] (*comp* **racier**, *superl* **raciest**) *adj* **1.** [lively] plein de verve *OR* de brio **2.** [suggestive] osé **3.** [wine] racé.

RADA ['rɑːdə] (*abbrev of* **Royal Academy of Dramatic Art**) *pr n conservatoire britannique d'art dramatique.*

radar ['reɪdɑːʳ] ◇ *n* radar *m* ▪ **to navigate by ~** naviguer au radar.
◇ *comp* [image, screen, station] radar ▪ **~ blip** top *m* d'écho (radar) ▪ **~ operator** radariste *mf.*

radar beacon *n* radiophare *m.*

radar trap *n* contrôle *m* radar.

raddled ['rædld] *adj* ravagé.

radial ['reɪdjəl] ◇ *adj* radial ▪ **~ roads** routes *fpl* en étoile.
◇ *n* **1.** [tyre] pneu *m* radial *OR* à carcasse radiale **2.** [line] rayon *m.*

radial engine *n* moteur *m* en étoile.

radial-ply *adj* AUT à carcasse radiale.

radiance ['reɪdjəns] *n* **1.** [of light, sun] éclat *m*, rayonnement *m* ▪ *fig* [beauty, happiness] éclat *m* **2.** PHYS exitance *f.*

radiant ['reɪdjənt] ◇ *adj* **1.** *lit* [bright] radieux **2.** [happy] radieux, rayonnant ▪ **he was ~ with joy** il rayonnait de joie **3.** PHYS radiant, rayonnant **4.** BOT rayonnant.
◇ *n* **1.** PHYS point *m* radiant **2.** ASTRON radiant *m.*

radiant heat *n* chaleur *f* rayonnante.

radiantly ['reɪdjəntlɪ] *adv* [shine, glow] avec éclat ▪ [smile] d'un air radieux ▪ **~ beautiful** d'une beauté éclatante.

radiate ['reɪdɪeɪt] ◇ *vi* **1.** [emit energy] émettre de l'énergie ▪ [be emitted] rayonner, irradier **2.** [spread] rayonner.
◇ *vt* **1.** [heat] émettre, dégager ▪ [light] émettre **2.** *fig* **the children ~ good health/happiness** les enfants respirent la santé/rayonnent de bonheur ▪ **his manner ~d confidence** il semblait très sûr de lui.

radiation [ˌreɪdɪ'eɪʃn] *n* **1.** [energy radiated] rayonnement *m*, rayonnements *mpl* ▪ NUCL PHYS rayons *mpl* ▪ **atomic ~** radiation *f OR* rayonnement atomique ▪ **low-level ~** radiation de faible intensité ▪ **~ therapy** radiothérapie *f* **2.** [act of radiating] rayonnement *m*, radiation *f.*

radiation sickness *n* mal *m* des rayons.

radiator ['reɪdɪeɪtəʳ] *n* [gen - AUT] radiateur *m* ▪ **~ grille** calandre *f.*

radical ['rædɪkl] ◇ *adj* [gen] radical.
◇ *n* **1.** POL radical *m*, - e *f* **2.** LING, MATHS & CHEM radical *m.*

radicalism ['rædɪkəlɪzm] *n* radicalisme *m.*

radically ['rædɪklɪ] *adv* radicalement.

radices ['reɪdɪsiːz] *pl* ▷ **radix**.

radii ['reɪdɪaɪ] *pl* ▷ **radius**.

radio ['reɪdɪəʊ] (*pl* **radios**) ◇ *n* **1.** [apparatus] radio *f* ▪ **to turn the ~ on/off** allumer/éteindre la radio **2.** [system] radio *f* ▪ **by ~** par radio ▮ [industry, activity] radio ▪ **I heard it on the ~** je l'ai entendu à la radio ▪ **to be on the ~** passer à la radio.
◇ *comp* [broadcast, play, programme] radiophonique ▪ [contact, link, silence] radio *(inv)* ▪ [announcer, technician] à la radio.
◇ *vt* **1.** [person] appeler *OR* contacter par radio **2.** [message] envoyer par radio ▪ [position, movement] signaler par radio.
◇ *vi* envoyer un message radio ▪ **she ~ed for help/instructions** elle demanda de l'aide/des instructions par radio.

RADIO

Les principales stations de radio de la BBC sont : Radio 1 (bulletins d'information, musique pop et rock) ; Radio 2 (variétés) ; Radio 3 (musique classique) ; Radio 4 (actualités, reportages, théâtre, programmes éducatifs) ; Radio 5 Live (sports, programmes éducatifs, musique pop et rock). La BBC comprend également 39 stations locales. Il existe d'autre part plus de 100 stations indépendantes.

radioactive [ˌreɪdɪəʊ'æktɪv] *adj* radioactif ▪ **~ dating** datation *f* au carbone 14 ▪ **~ waste** déchets *mpl* radioactifs *OR* nucléaires.

radioactivity [ˌreɪdɪəʊæk'tɪvətɪ] *n* radioactivité *f.*

radio alarm (clock) *n* radioréveil *m.*

radio astronomy *n* radioastronomie *f.*

radio beacon *n* radiobalise *f.*

radio beam *n* faisceau *m* hertzien.

radiobiology [ˌreɪdɪəʊbaɪ'ɒlədʒɪ] *n* radiobiologie *f.*

radio car *n* voiture *f* radio.

radiocarbon [ˌreɪdɪəʊ'kɑːbən] *n* radiocarbone *m*, carbone 14 *m.*

radio cassette *n* radiocassette *f*.

radiocommunication [ˈreɪdɪəʊkəˌmjuːnɪˈkeɪʃn] *n* radiocommunication *f*.

radio compass *n* radiocompas *m*.

radio control *n* télécommande *f* (par) radio, radiocommande *f*.

radio-controlled *adj* radioguidé.

radio frequency *n* fréquence *f* radioélectrique, radiofréquence *f*.

radiogram [ˈreɪdɪəʊˌgræm] *n* **1.** *dated* [radio and record player] radio *f* avec pick-up **2.** [message] radiogramme *m* **3.** = **radiograph**.

radiograph [ˈreɪdɪəʊgrɑːf] *n* radiographie *f*.

radiographer [ˌreɪdɪˈɒgrəfəʳ] *n* radiologue *mf*, radiologiste *mf*.

radiography [ˌreɪdɪˈɒgrəfɪ] *n* radiographie *f*.

radio ham *n* radioamateur *m*.

radiologist [ˌreɪdɪˈɒlədʒɪst] *n* radiologue *mf*, radiologiste *mf*.

radiology [ˌreɪdɪˈɒlədʒɪ] *n* radiologie *f*.

radio microphone *n* microphone *m* sans fil.

radiopager [ˈreɪdɪəʊˌpeɪdʒəʳ] *n* récepteur *m* d'appel *OR* de poche.

radiopaging [ˈreɪdɪəʊˌpeɪdʒɪŋ] *n* radiomessagerie *f*.

radioscopic [ˌreɪdɪəʊˈskɒpɪk] *adj* : **~ image** radiophotographie *f*.

radio station *n* station *f* de radio.

radio taxi *n* radio-taxi *m*.

radiotelephone [ˌreɪdɪəʊˈtelɪfəʊn] *n* radiotéléphone *m*.

radio telescope *n* radiotélescope *m*.

radiotherapist [ˌreɪdɪəʊˈθerəpɪst] *n* radiothérapeute *mf*.

radiotherapy [ˌreɪdɪəʊˈθerəpɪ] *n* radiothérapie *f*.

radio wave *n* onde *f* hertzienne *OR* radioélectrique.

radish [ˈrædɪʃ] *n* radis *m*.

radium [ˈreɪdɪəm] *n* radium *m* ■ **~ therapy** *OR* **treatment** curiethérapie *f*.

radius [ˈreɪdɪəs] (*pl* **radiuses** *OR pl* **radii** [ˈreɪdɪaɪ]) *n* **1.** [gen - MATHS] rayon *m* ■ **within** *OR* **in a ~ of 20 km** dans un rayon de 20 km **2.** ANAT radius *m*.

radix [ˈreɪdɪks] (*pl* **radices** [ˈreɪdɪsiːz]) *n* **1.** MATHS base *f* **2.** LING radical *m*.

radon (gas) [ˈreɪdɒn-] *n* radon *m*.

RAF (*abbrev of* **Royal Air Force**) *pr n armée de l'air britannique*.

raffia [ˈræfɪə] *n* raphia *m*.

raffish [ˈræfɪʃ] *adj* dissolu.

raffle [ˈræfl] ◇ *n* tombola *f* ■ **~ ticket** billet *m* de tombola.
◇ *vt* : **to ~ (off)** mettre en tombola.

raft [rɑːft] ◇ *n* **1.** [craft - gen] radeau *m* ; [- inflatable] matelas *m* pneumatique ■ SPORT raft *m* **2.** [logs] train *m* de flottage **3.** *inf* [large amount] tas *m*, flopée *f* **4.** CONSTR radier *m*.
◇ *vt* : **they ~ wood down the river** ils envoient le bois en aval dans des trains de flottage.
◇ *vi* voyager en radeau ■ **to go ~ing** SPORT faire du rafting.

rafter [ˈrɑːftəʳ] *n* CONSTR chevron *m*.

rag [ræg] (*pret & pp* **ragged**, *cont* **ragging**) ◇ *n* **1.** [cloth] chiffon *m* ■ **a piece of ~** un bout de chiffon ▶ **to chew the ~** *inf* discuter le bout de gras ■ **to lose one's ~** *inf* se mettre en boule ■ **to be like a red ~ to a bull : when he said that to her it was like a red ~ to a bull** elle a vu rouge après ce qu'il lui a dit **2.** [worn-out garment] loque *f* **3.** [shred, scrap] lambeau *m* ■ **torn to ~s** mis en lambeaux **4.** *inf pej* [newspaper] feuille *f* de chou **5.**[△] *US* [sanitary towel] serviette *f* hygiénique **6.** *UK* UNIV : **~ (week)** *semaine pendant laquelle les étudiants préparent des divertissements, surtout au profit des œuvres charitables* **7.** *UK* [joke] farce *f*, canular *m* **8.** MUS ragtime *m*.
◇ *vt* [tease] taquiner ■ **they ragged her about her accent** ils la taquinaient au sujet de son accent.
◆ **rags** *npl* [worn-out clothes] guenilles *fpl*, haillons *mpl*, loques *fpl* ▶ **to go from ~s to riches** passer de la misère à la richesse ■ **a ~s-to-riches story** un véritable conte de fées.

ragamuffin [ˈrægəˌmʌfɪn] *n* [vagrant] va-nu-pieds *m inv*, gueux *m*, gueuse *f* ■ [urchin] galopin *m*, polisson *m*, - onne *f*.

rag-and-bone man *n UK* chiffonnier *m*.

ragbag [ˈrægbæg] *n UK fig* ramassis *m*, bric-à-brac *m inv*, fouillis *m*.

rag doll *n* poupée *f* de chiffon.

rage [reɪdʒ] ◇ *n* **1.** [anger] rage *f*, fureur *f* ■ **the boss was in a ~** le patron était furieux ■ **to fly into a ~** entrer dans une rage folle ■ **a fit of ~** un accès *OR* une crise de rage **2.** *inf* [fashion] mode *f* ■ **to be all the ~** faire fureur **3.** [of sea, elements] furie *f*.
◇ *vi* **1.** [person] être furieux, s'emporter ■ **he was raging against the Government** il pestait contre le gouvernement **2.** [sea] se déchaîner ■ [storm, war] faire rage ■ **the plague was raging throughout Europe** la peste ravageait l'Europe ■ **the argument still ~s** la question est toujours très controversée.

ragga [ˈrægə] *n* MUS ragga *m*.

raggamuffin [ˈrægəˌmʌfɪn] *n* **1.** MUS raggamuffin *m* **2.** *dated* [urchin] va-nu-pieds *mf inv*.

ragged [ˈrægɪd] *adj* **1.** [tattered - clothes] en lambeaux, en loques, en haillons ; [- person] loqueteux, vêtu de loques *OR* de haillons **2.** [uneven] irrégulier ■ **the ~ coastline** la côte échancrée **3.** [erratic - performance] inégal, décousu **4.** *phr* **to run sb ~** *inf* éreinter *OR* crever qqn.

raging [ˈreɪdʒɪŋ] *adj* **1.** [intense - pain] insupportable, atroce ; [- fever] violent ■ **I had a ~ headache** j'avais affreusement mal à la tête ■ **I've got a ~ thirst** je meurs de soif ■ **~ anticlericalism** un anticléricalisme virulent **2.** [storm] déchaîné, violent ■ [sea] démonté ■ [torrent] furieux **3.** [person] furieux.

raglan [ˈræglən] ◇ *n* raglan *m*.
◇ *adj* raglan *(inv)*.

ragout [ˈrægu:] *n* ragoût *m*.

ragtag [ˈrægtæg] *UK* ◇ *adj* de bric et de broc.
◇ *n* : **the ~ and bobtail** la racaille, la populace.

ragtime [ˈrægtaɪm] *n* ragtime *m*.

rag trade *n inf* confection *f* ■ **he's in the ~** il est *OR* travaille dans les fringues.

rag week = **rag** *(n sense 6)*.

raid [reɪd] ◇ *n* **1.** MIL raid *m*, incursion *f* ■ **bombing ~** raid aérien ■ **they fear a terrorist ~ on the palace** ils craignent une attaque terroriste contre le palais **2.** [by police] descente *f*, rafle *f* ■ **a drugs ~** une descente de police (pour saisir de la drogue) **3.** [robbery] hold-up *m*, braquage *m* ■ **a ~ on a bank** un hold-up dans une banque **4.** ST. EX raid *m*.
◇ *vt* **1.** MIL [subj: army] faire un raid *OR* une incursion dans ■ [subj: airforce] bombarder **2.** [subj: police] faire une descente *OR* une rafle dans **3.** [subj: thieves] : **to ~ a bank** dévaliser une banque ■ **to ~ the fridge** *hum* dévaliser le frigo.

raider [ˈreɪdəʳ] *n* **1.** MIL membre *m* d'un commando ■ **the ~s were repelled** le commando a été repoussé **2.** [thief] voleur *m*, - euse *f* **3.** ST. EX : **(corporate) ~** raider *m*.

raiding party [ˈreɪdɪŋ-] *n* commando *m*.

rail [reɪl] ◇ *n* **1.** [bar - gen] barre *f* ; [- in window, on bridge] garde-fou *m* ; [- on ship] bastingage *m* ; [- on balcony] balustrade *f* ; [- on stairway] rampe *f* ; [- for carpet] tringle *f* ■ **towel ~** porte-serviettes *m inv* **2.** [for train, tram] rail *m* ■ [mode of transport] : **to travel by ~** voyager en train ▶ **to go off the ~s** [train] dérailler ; *fig* [person] perdre la tête *OR* le nord **3.** ORNITH râle *m*.

◇ *comp* [traffic, transport, link, tunnel] ferroviaire ■ [ticket, fare] de train ■ [journey, travel] en train ■ [employee, union] des chemins de fer ■ [strike] des chemins de fer, des cheminots ■ **the ~ strike has affected the whole of France** la grève SNCF a touché la France entière.
◇ *vt* [enclose] clôturer.
◇ *vi* [complain bitterly] : **to ~ against** *OR* **at** pester contre.
◆ **rails** *npl* [fencing] grille *f* ■ [in horseracing] corde *f* ■ **to be on the ~s** *fig* [in difficult situation] être sur la corde raide.
◆ **rail in** *vt sep* clôturer.
◆ **rail off** *vt sep* fermer (au moyen d'une barrière).

railcar ['reɪlkɑːr] *n* autorail *m*.

railcard ['reɪlkɑːd] *n UK carte permettant de bénéficier de tarifs avantageux sur les chemins de fer britanniques.*

railing ['reɪlɪŋ] *n* **1.** [barrier - gen] barrière *f* ; [- on bridge] garde-fou *m* ; [- on balcony] balustrade *f* **2.** [upright bar] barreau *m* **3.** = **railings**.
◆ **railings** *npl* [fence] grille *f* ■ **she squeezed through the ~s** elle se glissa entre les barreaux de la grille.

raillery ['reɪlərɪ] *n* raillerie *f*.

railroad ['reɪlrəʊd] ◇ *n US* = **railway**.
◇ *vt* : **to ~ sb into doing sthg** forcer qqn à faire qqch.

railway ['reɪlweɪ] *UK* ◇ *n* **1.** [system, organization] chemin *m* de fer ■ **he works on the ~s** il est cheminot **2.** [track] voie *f* ferrée.
◇ *comp* [bridge, traffic, travel, tunnel] ferroviaire ■ [company] ferroviaire, de chemin de fer ■ [journey] en train ■ [employee, union] des chemins de fer ■ **~ worker** cheminot *m*.

railway carriage *n UK* wagon *m*, voiture *f*.

railway crossing *n UK* passage *m* à niveau.

railway embankment *n UK* remblai *m*.

railway engine *n UK* locomotive *f*.

railway line *n UK* **1.** [route] ligne *f* de chemin de fer **2.** [track] voie *f* ferrée ■ [rail] rail *m*.

railwayman ['reɪlweɪmən] (*pl* **railwaymen** [-mən]) *n UK* cheminot *m*.

railway station *n UK* [gen] gare *f* (de chemin de fer) ■ [in France] gare *f* SNCF.

railway track *n UK* voie *f* ferrée.

railway yard *n UK* dépôt *m*.

raiment ['reɪmənt] *n (U) lit* atours *mpl*.

rain [reɪn] ◇ *n* **1.** *liter* pluie *f* ■ **it was pouring with ~** il pleuvait à verse ■ **the ~ was heavy** il pleuvait beaucoup ■ **a light ~ was falling** il tombait une pluie fine ■ **come in out of the ~** rentre, ne reste pas sous la pluie ■ **it looks like ~** on dirait qu'il va pleuvoir ■ **Venice in the ~** Venise sous la pluie ■ **the ~s** la saison des pluies ◗ **come ~ or shine** quoi qu'il arrive ■ **don't worry, you'll be as right as ~ in a minute** *inf* ne t'inquiète pas, ça va passer **2.** *fig* [of projectiles, blows] pluie *f*.
◇ *vi* pleuvoir ■ **it's ~ing** il pleut ◗ **it's ~ing cats and dogs** *inf* il pleut des cordes, il tombe des hallebardes ■ **it never ~s but it pours** *UK prov*, **when it ~s, it pours** *US prov* tout arrive en même temps *prov*.
◇ *vt* faire pleuvoir.
◆ **rain down** ◇ *vi insep* [projectiles, blows etc] pleuvoir.
◇ *vt sep* [projectiles, blows etc] faire pleuvoir.
◆ **rain off** *vt sep UK* **the game was ~ed off** [cancelled] la partie a été annulée à cause de la pluie ; [abandoned] la partie a été abandonnée à cause de la pluie.
◆ **rain out** *vt sep US* = **rain off**.

rainbow ['reɪnbəʊ] ◇ *n* arc-en-ciel *m* ◗ **to chase ~s** se bercer d'illusions.
◇ *comp* : **~ coalition** *coalition représentant un large éventail de tendances.*

rainbow trout *n* truite *f* arc-en-ciel.

rain check *n US bon pour un autre match (ou spectacle) donné par suite d'une annulation à cause de la pluie* ■ **I'll take a ~ on that** *inf fig* ça sera pour une autre fois.

rain cloud *n* nuage *m* de pluie.

raincoat ['reɪnkəʊt] *n* imperméable *m*.

rain dance *n* danse *f* de la pluie.

raindrop ['reɪndrɒp] *n* goutte *f* de pluie.

rainfall ['reɪnfɔːl] *n* [amount of rain] pluviosité *f*.

rainforest ['reɪn,fɒrɪst] *n* forêt *f* pluviale.

rain gauge *n* pluviomètre *m*.

rainmaker ['reɪn,meɪkər] *n* faiseur *m* de pluie.

rainproof ['reɪnpruːf] ◇ *adj* imperméable.
◇ *vt* imperméabiliser.

rainstorm ['reɪnstɔːm] *n* pluie *f* torrentielle.

rainwater ['reɪn,wɔːtər] *n* eau *f* de pluie *OR* pluviale.

rainwear ['reɪnweər] *n (U)* vêtements *mpl* de pluie.

rainy ['reɪnɪ] (*comp* **rainier**, *superl* **rainiest**) *adj* pluvieux ■ **the ~ season** la saison des pluies ■ **to save sthg for a ~ day** garder qqch pour les mauvais jours.

raise [reɪz] ◇ *vt* **1.** [lift, move upwards - gen] lever ; [- burden, lid] soulever ■ **to ~ one's head** lever la tête ■ **she didn't ~ her eyes from her book** elle n'a pas levé les yeux de son livre **2.** [increase - offer, price, tax] augmenter ; [- interest rates] relever ; [- temperature, tension] faire monter ■ **the speed limit has been ~d to 150 km/h** la limitation de vitesse est passée à 150 km/h ■ **the age limit has been ~d to 18** la limite d'âge a été repoussée à 18 ans **3.** [boost, improve] remonter, élever ■ **to ~ sb's spirits** remonter le moral à qqn ■ **to ~ sb's hopes** donner des espoirs à qqn **4.** [promote] élever, promouvoir **5.** [collect together - support] réunir ; [- army] lever ■ **we have ~d over a million signatures** nous avons recueilli plus d'un million de signatures **6.** [obtain - money] trouver, obtenir ; [- taxes] lever ■ **to ~ funds** collecter des fonds **7.** [make, produce] : **they ~d a cheer when she came in** ils ont poussé des bravos quand elle est entrée ■ **he managed to ~ a smile when he saw us** il a réussi à sourire en nous voyant **8.** [cause as reaction - laugh, welt, blister] provoquer ■ **his jokes didn't even ~ a smile** ses plaisanteries n'ont même pas fait sourire **9.** *esp US* [rear - children, family] élever **10.** *esp US* [breed - livestock] élever ■ [grow - crops] cultiver **11.** [introduce, bring up - point, subject, question] soulever ; [- doubts] soulever, susciter **12.** [erect] élever, ériger **13.** [resuscitate] ressusciter ■ [evoke - spirit] évoquer ■ **they were making enough noise to ~ the dead** ils faisaient un bruit à réveiller les morts **14.** [end - ban, siege] lever **15.** [contact] contacter **16.** [in bridge] monter sur ■ [in poker] relancer ■ **I'll ~ you 5 pounds** je relance de 5 livres **17.** CULIN [dough, bread] faire lever **18.** MATHS élever **19.** NAUT : **to ~ land** arriver en vue de terre.
◇ *vi* [in bridge] monter, enchérir ■ [in poker] relancer.
◇ *n* **1.** *US* [pay increase] augmentation *f* de salaire **2.** [in bridge] enchère *f* ■ [in poker] relance *f*.
◆ **raise up** *vt sep* : **to ~ o.s. up** se soulever ■ **she ~d herself up onto the chair** elle se hissa sur la chaise.

raised [reɪzd] *adj* **1.** [ground, platform, jetty etc] surélevé ■ [pattern] en relief **2.** CULIN levé, à la levure **3.** LING [vowel] haut **4.** TEX lainé, gratté.

raisin ['reɪzn] *n* raisin *m* sec.

raising agent ['reɪzɪŋ-] *n (countable)* levure *f*.

Raj [rɑːdʒ] *n* : **the ~** l'empire *m* britannique (en Inde).

rajah ['rɑːdʒə] *n* raja *m*, rajah *m*, radjah *m*.

rake [reɪk] ◇ *n* **1.** [in garden, casino] râteau *m* **2.** [libertine] roué *m*, libertin *m* **3.** THEAT pente *f* ■ NAUT [of mast, funnel] quête *f*.
◇ *vt* **1.** [soil, lawn, path] ratisser, râteler ■ **she ~d the leaves into a pile** elle ratissa les feuilles en tas **2.** [search] fouiller (dans) **3.** [scan] balayer ■ **a searchlight ~d the darkness** un projecteur fouilla l'obscurité **4.** [strafe] balayer.
◇ *vi* **1.** [search] : **to ~ among** *OR* **through** fouiller dans **2.** [slope] être en pente, être incliné.
◆ **rake in** *vt sep inf* [money] ramasser ■ **to be raking it in** toucher un joli paquet.
◆ **rake off** *vt sep inf* [share of profits] empocher, ramasser.

◆ **rake out** *vt sep* **1.** [fire] enlever les cendres de ▪ [ashes] enlever **2.** [search out] dénicher.
◆ **rake over** *vt sep* **1.** [soil, lawn, path] ratisser **2.** *fig* remuer.
◆ **rake up** *vt sep* **1.** [collect together - leaves, weeds] ratisser ; [- people] réunir, rassembler **2.** [dredge up] déterrer ▪ **to ~ up sb's past** fouiller dans le passé de qqn.

raked [reɪkt] *adj* [inclined] incliné.

rake-off *n inf* petit profit *m*.

rakish ['reɪkɪʃ] *adj* **1.** [jaunty] désinvolte, insouciant **2.** [boat] à la forme élancée, allongé.

rale [rɑ:l] *n* MED râle *m*.

rally ['rælɪ] <> *n* (*pl* **rallies**) **1.** [gathering - gen] rassemblement *m* ▪ MIL [during battle] ralliement *m* ▪ POL rassemblement *m*, (grand) meeting *m* **2.** [recovery - gen] amélioration *f* ▪ ST. EX reprise *f* **3.** AUT rallye *m* ▪ **~ driver** pilote *m* de rallye **4.** SPORT (long) échange *m*.
<> *vi* (*pret & pp* **rallied**) **1.** [assemble, gather - gen] se rassembler ; [- troops, supporters] se rallier ▪ **they rallied to the party/to the defence of their leader** ils se sont ralliés au parti/pour défendre leur chef **2.** [recover - gen] s'améliorer ; [- sick person] aller mieux, reprendre des forces ; [- currency, share prices] remonter ; [- stock market] se reprendre **3.** AUT faire des rallyes.
<> *vt* (*pret & pp* **rallied**) **1.** [gather] rallier, rassembler ▪ **she's trying to ~ support for her project** elle essaie de rallier des gens pour soutenir son projet **2.** [summon up] reprendre ▪ **to ~ one's spirits** reprendre ses esprits ‖ [boost] ranimer ▪ **the news rallied their morale** la nouvelle leur a remonté le moral **3.** *arch* [tease] taquiner.
◆ **rally round** <> *vi insep* : **all her family rallied round** toute sa famille est venue lui apporter son soutien.
<> *vt insep* : **they rallied round her** ils lui ont apporté leur soutien.

rallying ['rælɪɪŋ] *adj* : **~ cry** cri *m* de ralliement.

ram [ræm] (*pret & pp* **rammed**, *cont* **ramming**) <> *n* **1.** ZOOL bélier *m* **2.** HIST [for breaking doors, walls] bélier *m* **3.** TECH [piston] piston *m* ▪ [flattening tool] hie *f*, dame *f* ▪ [pile driver] mouton *m* ▪ [lifting pump] bélier *m* hydraulique.
<> *vt* **1.** [bang into] percuter ▪ NAUT aborder ▪ [in battle] éperonner ▪ **the police car rammed them twice** la voiture de police les a percutés deux fois **2.** [push] pousser (violemment) ▪ **she rammed the papers into her bag** elle fourra les papiers dans son sac ▪ **in order to ~ home the point** *fig* pour enfoncer le clou.
<> *vi* : **to ~ into sthg** entrer dans OR percuter qqch.

RAM [ræm] *n* (*abbrev of* **random access memory**) RAM *f*.

Ramadan [,ræmə'dæn] *n* ramadan *m*.

ramble ['ræmbl] <> *n* [hike] randonnée *f* (pédestre) ▪ [casual walk] promenade *f* ▪ **to go for a ~** aller faire un tour.
<> *vi* **1.** [hike] faire une randonnée **2.** [wander] se balader **3.** [talk] divaguer, radoter ▪ **he ~d on and on about nothing** il n'arrêtait pas de parler pour ne rien dire **4.** [plant] pousser à tort et à travers **5.** [path, stream] serpenter.

rambler ['ræmblər] *n* **1.** [hiker] randonneur *m*, - euse *f* **2.** [in speech] : **he's a bit of a ~** il est du genre radoteur **3.** BOT plante *f* sarmenteuse.

rambling ['ræmblɪŋ] <> *adj* **1.** [building] plein de coins et de recoins **2.** [conversation, style] décousu ▪ [ideas, book, thoughts] incohérent, sans suite ▪ [person] qui divague, qui radote **3.** [plant] sarmenteux ▪ **~ rose** rosier *m* sarmenteux.
<> *n* [hiking] randonnée *f* ▪ **to go ~** aller en randonnée.

Ramboesque [,ræmbəʊ'esk] *adj* digne de Rambo.

ramekin, ramequin ['ræmɪkɪn] *n* ramequin *m*.

Rameses ['ræmɪsi:z] = **Ramses**.

ramification [,ræmɪfɪ'keɪʃn] *n* **1.** [implication] implication *f* **2.** [branching] ramification *f*.

ramify ['ræmɪfaɪ] (*pret & pp* **ramified**) <> *vt* ramifier.
<> *vi* se ramifier.

ramp [ræmp] *n* pente *f*, rampe *f* ▪ [in road works] dénivellation *f*.

rampage [ræm'peɪdʒ] <> *n* fureur *f* ▪ **to be on the ~** être déchaîné ▪ **to go on the ~** se livrer à des actes de violence ▪ **the headmaster's on the ~!** le directeur est déchaîné!
<> *vi* se déchaîner ▪ **a herd of elephants ~d through the bush** un troupeau d'éléphants avançait dans la brousse en balayant tout sur son passage ▪ **they ~d through the town** ils ont saccagé la ville.

rampant ['ræmpənt] *adj* **1.** [unrestrained] déchaîné, effréné ▪ **corruption is ~** la corruption sévit ▪ **the disease is ~** la maladie fait des ravages **2.** [exuberant - vegetation] exubérant, foisonnant **3.** *(after n)* HERALD rampant.

rampart ['ræmpɑ:t] <> *n liter & fig* rempart *m*.
<> *vt* fortifier (d'un rempart).

ramraid ['ræmreɪd] *n* pillage *m*.

ramraider ['ræm,reɪdər] *n personne qui pille les magasins en fracassant les vitrines avec sa voiture.*

ramrod ['ræmrɒd] <> *n* baguette *f (d'arme à feu)* ▪ **to sit/to stand as stiff as a ~** être assis/se tenir raide comme un piquet.
<> *adv* : **the sentry stood ~ straight** la sentinelle se tenait debout, raide comme un piquet.

Ramses ['ræmsi:z] *pr n* Ramsès.

ramshackle ['ræm,ʃækl] *adj* délabré.

ran [ræn] *pt* ▷ **run**.

ranch [rɑ:ntʃ] <> *n* ranch *m* ▪ **chicken ~** élevage *m* de poulets.
<> *comp* : **~ hand** ouvrier *m* agricole ▪ **~ house** *maison basse faisant partie d'un ranch.*
<> *vi* exploiter un ranch.
<> *vt* : **to ~ cattle** élever du bétail (sur un ranch).

rancher ['rɑ:ntʃər] *n* [owner] propriétaire *mf* de ranch ▪ [manager] exploitant *m*, - e *f* de ranch ▪ [worker] garçon *m* de ranch, cow-boy *m*.

ranching ['rɑ:ntʃɪŋ] *n* exploitation *f* d'un ranch ▪ **cattle/chicken ~** élevage *m* de bétail/de poulets.

rancid ['rænsɪd] *adj* rance ▪ **to go** OR **to turn ~** rancir.

rancour *UK*, **rancor** *US* ['ræŋkər] *n* rancœur *f*, rancune *f*.

rand [rænd] (*pl inv*) *n* [money] rand *m*.

R and B *n* = **rhythm and blues**.

R and D *n* = **research and development**.

random ['rændəm] *adj* aléatoire, fait OR choisi au hasard ▪ **a ~ number** un nombre aléatoire ▪ **a ~ sample** un échantillon pris au hasard ▪ **a ~ shot** une balle perdue ▪ **~ violence** violence *f* aveugle.
◆ **at random** *adv phr* au hasard ▪ **to lash out at ~** distribuer des coups à l'aveuglette.

random access *n* COMPUT accès *m* aléatoire OR direct.
◆ **random-access** *adj* COMPUT à accès aléatoire OR direct ▪ **random-access memory** mémoire *f* vive.

randomly ['rændəmlɪ] *adv* au hasard.

R and R (*abbrev of* **rest and recreation**) *n* permission *f*.

randy ['rændɪ] (*comp* **randier**, *superl* **randiest**) *adj UK inf* excité ▪ **he's a ~ devil** c'est un chaud lapin ▪ **a ~ old man** un vieux satyre.

rang [ræŋ] *pt* ▷ **ring**.

range [reɪndʒ] <> *n* **1.** [of missile, sound, transmitter etc] portée *f* ▪ [of vehicle, aircraft] autonomie *f* ▪ **at long/short ~** à longue/courte portée ▪ **out of ~** hors de portée ▪ **within** OR **in ~** [of guns] à portée de tir ; [of voice] à portée de voix ▪ **it can kill a man at a ~ of 800 metres** ça peut tuer un homme à une distance de 800 mètres ▪ **it gives you some idea of the ~ of their powers** ça vous donne une petite idée de l'étendue de leurs pouvoirs
2. [bracket] gamme *f*, éventail *m*, fourchette *f* ❯ **children in the same age ~** les enfants dans la même tranche d'âge ▪ **price ~** gamme OR fourchette de prix ▪ **it's within my price ~** c'est dans mes prix

3. [set, selection] gamme *f* ■ **we stock a wide ~ of office materials** nous avons en stock une large gamme de matériels de bureaux ■ **it provoked a wide ~ of reactions** ça a provoqué des réactions très diverses ▮ COMM : **the new autumn ~** [of clothes] la nouvelle collection d'automne ■ **this car is the top/bottom of the ~** cette voiture est le modèle haut/bas de gamme
4. *fig* [scope] champ *m*, domaine *m* ■ **that is beyond the ~ of the present inquiry** cela ne relève pas de cette enquête ■ **that lies outside the ~ of my responsibility** ça dépasse les limites de ma responsabilité
5. [of mountains] chaîne *f*
6. [prairie] prairie *f*
7. [practice area] champ *m* de tir
8. MUS [of instrument] étendue *f*, portée *f* ■ [of voice] tessiture *f*
9. [cooker] fourneau *m* (de cuisine)
10. [row, line] rang *m*, rangée *f*
11. BIOL [habitat] habitat *m*.
◇ *vi* **1.** [vary] aller, s'étendre ■ **their ages ~ from 5 to 12** *OR* **between 5 and 12** ils ont de 5 à 12 *OR* entre 5 et 12 ans ■ **the quality ~s from mediocre to excellent** la qualité varie de médiocre à excellent
2. [roam] : **to ~ over** parcourir ■ **thugs ~ through the city streets** des voyous rôdent dans les rues de la ville
3. [extend] : **the survey ~d over the whole country** l'enquête couvrait la totalité du pays ■ **our conversation ~d over a large number of topics** nous avons discuté d'un grand nombre de sujets.
◇ *vt* **1.** [roam] parcourir
2. [arrange] ranger ■ [put in a row or in rows] mettre *OR* disposer en rang *OR* rangs ■ **the desks are ~d in threes** les pupitres sont en rangées de trois
3. [join, ally] ranger, rallier
4. [classify] classer, ranger
5. [aim - cannon, telescope] braquer
6. TYPO aligner, justifier.

rangefinder ['reɪndʒˌfaɪndəʳ] *n* télémètre *m*.

ranger ['reɪndʒəʳ] *n* **1.** [in park, forest] garde *m* forestier **2.** *US* [lawman] ≃ gendarme *m* **3.** *US* MIL ranger *m*.
◆ **Ranger (Guide)** *n* guide *m*.

rangy ['reɪndʒɪ] (*comp* **rangier**, *superl* **rangiest**) *adj* **1.** [tall and thin] grand et élancé **2.** [roomy] spacieux.

rank [ræŋk] ◇ *n* **1.** [grade] rang *m*, grade *m* ■ **promoted to the ~ of colonel** promu (au rang de *OR* au grade de) colonel ■ **the ~ of manager** le titre de directeur ▶ **to pull ~** faire valoir sa supériorité hiérarchique
2. [quality] rang *m*
3. [social class] rang *m*, condition *f* (sociale) ■ **the lower ~s of society** les couches inférieures de la société
4. [row, line] rang *m*, rangée *f* ■ [on chessboard] rangée *f* ▶ **to break ~s** MIL rompre les rangs ; *fig* se désolidariser ■ **to close ~s** MIL & *fig* serrer les rangs
5. *UK* **(taxi) ~** station *f* (de taxis)
6. MATHS [in matrix] rang *m*.
◇ *vt* **1.** [rate] classer ■ **she is ~ed among the best contemporary writers** elle est classée parmi les meilleurs écrivains contemporains ■ **I ~ this as one of our finest performances** je considère que c'est une de nos meilleures représentations ■ **he is ~ed number 3** il est classé numéro 3
2. [arrange] ranger
3. *US* [outrank] avoir un grade supérieur à.
◇ *vi* **1.** [rate] figurer ■ **it ~s high/low on our list of priorities** c'est/ce n'est pas une de nos priorités ■ **he hardly ~s as an expert** on ne peut guère le qualifier d'expert
2. *US* MIL être officier supérieur.
◇ *adj* **1.** [as intensifier] complet, véritable ■ **he is a ~ outsider in this competition** il fait figure d'outsider dans cette compétition
2. [foul-smelling] infect, fétide ■ [rancid] rance ■ **his shirt was ~ with sweat** sa chemise empestait la sueur
3. [coarse - person, language] grossier
4. *lit* [profuse - vegetation] luxuriant ; [- weeds] prolifique.
◆ **ranks** *npl* **1.** [members] rangs *mpl* ■ **to join the ~s of the opposition/unemployed** rejoindre les rangs de l'opposition/des chômeurs
2. MIL [rank and file] : **the ~s, other ~s** les hommes du rang ■ **to come up through** *OR* **to rise from the ~s** sortir du rang ■ **to reduce an officer to the ~s** dégrader un officier.

-rank *in cpds* : **top~** grand, majeur ■ **second~** petit, mineur.

rank and file *n* : **the ~** MIL les hommes du rang ; POL la base.
◆ **rank-and-file** *adj* de la base.

ranker ['ræŋkəʳ] *n* MIL [private] homme *m* du rang ■ [officer] officier *m* sorti du rang.

ranking ['ræŋkɪŋ] ◇ *n* classement *m*.
◇ *adj US* **1.** MIL : **~ officer** officier *m* responsable **2.** [prominent] de premier ordre.

-ranking *in cpds* : **high~** de haut rang *OR* grade ■ **low~** de bas rang *OR* grade.

rankle ['ræŋkl] *vi* : **their decision still ~s with me** leur décision m'est restée en travers de la gorge.

ransack ['rænsæk] *vt* **1.** [plunder] saccager, mettre à sac **2.** [search] mettre sens dessus dessous.

ransom ['rænsəm] ◇ *n* rançon *f* ■ **they held her to ~** ils l'ont kidnappée pour avoir une rançon ■ **they're holding the country to ~** *fig* ils tiennent le pays en otage ▶ **a king's ~** une fortune.
◇ *vt* rançonner.

rant [rænt] *vi* fulminer ■ **to ~ at sb** fulminer contre qqn ■ **to ~ and rave** tempêter, tonitruer.

ranting ['ræntɪŋ] ◇ *n (U)* vociférations *fpl*.
◇ *adj* déclamatoire.

rap [ræp] (*pret & pp* **rapped**, *cont* **rapping**) ◇ *vt* **1.** [strike] frapper sur, cogner sur ■ **to ~ sb's knuckles, to ~ sb over the knuckles** *fig* sermonner qqn **2.** [in newspaper headlines] réprimander.
◇ *vi* **1.** [knock] frapper, cogner **2.** *US inf* [chat] bavarder, discuter le bout de gras **3.** MUS jouer du rap.
◇ *n* **1.** [blow, sound] coup *m* (sec) ■ [rebuke] réprimande *f* ■ **to be given a ~ over** *OR* **on the knuckles** *fig* se faire taper sur les doigts ■ **to take the ~ for sthg** *inf* écoper pour qqch **2.**△ *US* [legal charge] accusation *f* ■ **he's up on a murder/drugs ~** il est accusé de meurtre/dans une affaire de drogue ■ **it's a bum ~** c'est un coup monté **3.** *US inf* [chat] : **~ session** bavardage *m* **4.** MUS rap *m*.
◆ **rap out** *vt sep* **1.** [say sharply] lancer, lâcher **2.** [tap out - message] taper.

rapacious [rə'peɪʃəs] *adj* rapace.

rapaciousness [rə'peɪʃəsnɪs], **rapacity** [rə'pæsətɪ] *n* rapacité *f*.

rape [reɪp] ◇ *n* **1.** [sex crime] viol *m* ■ **to commit ~** perpétrer un viol ■ **~ victim** victime *f* d'un viol ■ **the ~ of the countryside** *fig* la dévastation de la campagne ▶ **~ crisis centre** centre d'accueil pour femmes violées **2.** BOT colza *m* **3.** [remains of grapes] marc *m* (de raisin).
◇ *vt* violer.

rape oil *n* huile *f* de colza.

rapeseed ['reɪpsi:d] *n* graine *f* de colza.

Raphael ['ræfeɪəl] *pr n* Raphaël.

rapid ['ræpɪd] *adj* rapide ■ **in ~ succession** en une succession rapide.
◆ **rapids** *npl* rapide *m*, rapides *mpl* ■ **to shoot the ~s** franchir le rapide *OR* les rapides.

rapid eye movement *n mouvement des globes oculaires pendant le sommeil paradoxal.*

rapid-fire *adj* MIL à tir rapide ■ *fig* [questions, jokes] qui se succèdent à toute allure.

rapidity [rə'pɪdətɪ] *n* rapidité *f*.

rapidly ['ræpɪdlɪ] *adv* rapidement.

rapidness ['ræpɪdnɪs] = **rapidity**.

rapid transit *n US* transport *m* urbain rapide.

rapier ['reɪpjəʳ] ◇ *n* rapière *f*.
◇ *comp* : ~ **thrust** coup *m* de rapière ■ **her** ~ **wit** son esprit acerbe.

rapist ['reɪpɪst] *n* violeur *m*.

rapper ['ræpəʳ] *n* **1.** [on door] heurtoir *m* **2.** MUS musicien *m* rap.

rapport [ræ'pɔːʳ] *n* rapport *m* ■ **I have a good ~ with him** j'ai de bons rapports avec lui.

rapt [ræpt] *adj* **1.** [engrossed] absorbé, captivé ■ **the clown held the children ~** le clown fascinait les enfants **2.** [delighted] ravi ■ **~ with joy** transporté de joie.

rapture ['ræptʃəʳ] *n* ravissement *m*, extase *f* ■ **to go into ~s over** *OR* **about sthg** s'extasier sur qqch ■ **they were in ~s about their presents** leurs cadeaux les ont ravis.

rapturous ['ræptʃərəs] *adj* [feeling] intense, profond ■ [gaze] ravi, extasié ■ [praise, applause] enthousiaste.

rapturously ['ræptʃərəslɪ] *adv* [watch] d'un air ravi, avec ravissement ■ [praise, applaud] avec enthousiasme.

rare [reəʳ] *adj* **1.** [uncommon] rare ■ **it's ~ to see such marital bliss nowadays** un tel bonheur conjugal est rare de nos jours ■ **on the ~ occasions when I've seen him angry** les rares fois où je l'ai vu en colère ■ **a ~ opportunity** une occasion exceptionnelle ➲ **he's a ~ bird** c'est un oiseau rare **2.** [exceptional] rare, exceptionnel **3.** *inf* [extreme] énorme ■ [excellent] fameux, génial **4.** [meat] saignant **5.** [rarefied - air, atmosphere] raréfié.

rarebit ['reəbɪt] = **Welsh rarebit**.

rarefied ['reərɪfaɪd] *adj* **1.** [air, atmosphere] raréfié **2.** [refined] raffiné.

rarefy ['reərɪfaɪ] (*pret & pp* **rarefied**) ◇ *vt* raréfier.
◇ *vi* se raréfier.

rarely ['reəlɪ] *adv* rarement.

rareness ['reənɪs] *n* rareté *f*.

raring ['reərɪŋ] *adj inf* impatient ■ **to be ~ to go** ronger son frein.

rarity ['reərətɪ] (*pl* **rarities**) *n* **1.** [uncommon person, thing] rareté *f* ■ **a foreigner's a ~ in these parts** les étrangers sont rares par ici **2.** [scarcity] rareté *f*.

rascal ['rɑːskl] *n* **1.** [naughty child] polisson *m*, - onne *f* **2.** *lit* [rogue] vaurien *m*, gredin *m*.

rascally ['rɑːskəlɪ] *adj lit* [person] coquin ■ [deed] de coquin.

rash [ræʃ] ◇ *n* **1.** MED rougeur *f*, éruption *f* ■ **to come out in a ~** avoir une éruption ■ **oysters bring me out in a ~** les huîtres me donnent des éruptions **2.** [wave, outbreak] vague *f* ■ **last summer's ~ of air disasters** la série noire de catastrophes aériennes de l'été dernier.
◇ *adj* imprudent ■ **it was ~ of her to walk out** c'était imprudent de sa part de partir comme ça ■ **don't be ~** soyez prudent ■ **~ words** des paroles irréfléchies ■ **I bought it in a ~ moment** je l'ai acheté dans un moment de folie *OR* sur un coup de tête.

rasher ['ræʃəʳ] *n UK* tranche *f (de bacon)*.

rashly ['ræʃlɪ] *adv* imprudemment ■ **I rather ~ offered to drive her home** dans un moment de folie j'ai offert de la reconduire chez elle.

rashness ['ræʃnɪs] *n* imprudence *f*.

rasp [rɑːsp] ◇ *n* **1.** [file] râpe *f* **2.** [sound] bruit *m* de râpe.
◇ *vt* **1.** [scrape, file] râper **2.** [say] dire d'une voix rauque.
◇ *vi* [make rasping noise] grincer, crisser.

raspberry ['rɑːzbərɪ] (*pl* **raspberries**) ◇ *n* **1.** [fruit] framboise *f* **2.** *inf* [noise] : **to blow a ~** faire pfft *(en signe de dérision)* ■ **the announcement was greeted with a chorus of raspberries** la nouvelle fut accueillie par des sifflements.
◇ *comp* [jam] de framboises ■ [tart] aux framboises BOT : **~ bush** *OR* **cane** framboisier *m*.
◇ *adj* [colour] framboise *(inv)*.

rasping ['rɑːspɪŋ] ◇ *adj* [noise] grinçant, crissant ■ [voice] grinçant.
◇ *n* [noise] grincement *m*, crissement *m*.

Rasputin [ræ'spjuːtɪn] *pr n* Raspoutine.

Rasta ['ræstə] ◇ *n* (*abbrev of* **Rastafarian**) rasta *mf*.
◇ *adj* rasta *(inv)*.

Rastafarian [ˌræstə'feərɪən] ◇ *n* rastafari *mf*.
◇ *adj* rastafari *(inv)*.

raster ['ræstəʳ] *n* PHYS & TV trame *f*.

rat [ræt] (*pret & pp* **ratted**, *cont* **ratting**) ◇ *n* **1.** ZOOL rat *m* ■ **female ~, she-~** rate *f* ■ **baby ~** raton *m* ➲ **black ~** rat noir ■ **grey** *OR* **sewer ~** rat d'égout, surmulot *m* ■ **to look like a drowned ~** avoir l'air d'un chien mouillé **2.** *inf* [as insult - gen] ordure *f*.
◇ *vi* **1.** *liter* **to go ratting** faire la chasse aux rats **2.** *inf fig* retourner sa veste.
◆ **rat on** *vt insep inf* **1.** [betray] vendre ■ [inform on] moucharder **2.** [go back on] revenir sur.

ratable ['reɪtəbl] = **rateable**.

ratafia [ˌrætə'fɪə] *n* **1.** [liqueur] ratafia *m* **2.** : **~ (biscuit)** macaron *m*.

rat-arsed[△] ['rætɑːst] *adj UK* bourré[△].

rat-a-tat(-tat) ['rætəˌtæt('tæt)] *n* toc-toc *m*.

ratbag ['rætbæg] *n UK inf* peau *f* de vache.

ratcatcher ['rætˌkætʃəʳ] *n* [gen] chasseur *m*, - euse *f* de rats ■ [official] agent *m* de la dératisation.

ratchet ['rætʃɪt] *n* rochet *m*.

rate [reɪt] ◇ *n* **1.** [ratio, level] taux *m* ■ **the birth/death/divorce/suicide ~** le taux de natalité/de mortalité/de divorce/de suicide ■ **how do you explain the high suicide ~?** comment expliquez-vous le nombre élevé de suicides? ➲ **~ of return** taux de rendement ■ **~ of taxation** taux d'imposition ■ **~ of exchange** taux de change **2.** [cost, charge] tarif *m* ■ **his ~s have gone up** ses prix ont augmenté ■ **postal** *OR* **postage ~** tarifs postaux ■ **standard/reduced ~** tarif normal/réduit **3.** [speed] vitesse *f*, train *m* ■ **at the ~ we're going** *OR* **at this ~ we'll never get there** au rythme où nous allons, nous n'y arriverons jamais **4.** *phr* **any ~** *inf* enfin bref.
◇ *vt* **1.** [reckon, consider] considérer ■ **she's ~d as one of the best players in the world** elle est classée parmi les meilleures joueuses du monde ■ **to ~ sb/sthg highly** avoir une haute opinion de qqn/qqch, faire grand cas de qqn/qqch **2.** [deserve] mériter **3.** *inf* [have high opinion of] : **I don't ~ him as an actor** à mon avis, ce n'est pas un bon acteur ■ **I don't ~ their chances much** je ne pense pas qu'ils aient beaucoup de chance **4.** *UK* [fix rateable value of] fixer la valeur locative imposable de.
◇ *vi* [rank high] se classer ■ **he ~s highly in my estimation** je le tiens en très haute estime.
◆ **rates** *npl UK dated* impôts *mpl* locaux.
◆ **at any rate** *adv phr* de toute façon, de toute manière, en tout cas.

-rate *in cpds* : **first~** de premier ordre ■ **second~** de deuxième ordre.

rateable ['reɪtəbl] *adj* : **~ value** *UK* ≃ valeur *f* locative imposable.

rate-capping [-ˌkæpɪŋ] *n* [in UK] *plafonnement des impôts locaux par le gouvernement.*

ratepayer ['reɪtˌpeɪəʳ] *n* [in UK] contribuable *mf*.

rather ['rɑːðəʳ] ◇ *adv* **1.** [slightly, a bit] assez, un peu ■ **it's ~ too small for me** c'est un peu trop petit pour moi ■ **she cut me a ~ large slice** elle m'a coupé une tranche plutôt grande ■ **it tastes ~ like honey** ça a un peu le goût du miel **2.** *UK* [as intensifier] : **I ~ like this town** je trouve cette ville plutôt agréable **3.** [expressing preference] plutôt ■ **I'd ~ not do it today** je préférerais *OR* j'aimerais mieux ne pas le faire aujourd'hui ■ **shall we go out tonight? – I'd ~ not** si on sortait ce soir ? – je n'ai pas très envie ➲ **~ you than me!** je n'aimerais pas être à votre place! **4.** [more exactly] plutôt, plus exactement.
◇ *predet* plutôt ■ **it was ~ a long film** le film était plutôt long.
◇ *interj UK dated* et comment.

◆ **rather than** ◇ *prep phr* plutôt que ■ **it's a melodrama ~ than a tragedy** c'est un mélodrame plus qu'une tragédie.
◇ *conj phr* plutôt que ■ **~ than walk I took the bus** plutôt que d'y aller à pied, j'ai pris le bus.

ratification [ˌrætɪfɪ'keɪʃn] *n* ratification *f*.

ratify ['rætɪfaɪ] (*pret & pp* **ratified**) *vt* ratifier.

rating ['reɪtɪŋ] *n* **1.** [ranking] classement *m* ■ **popularity ~** cote *f* de popularité ■ FIN [of bank, company] notation *f* **2.** [appraisal] évaluation *f*, estimation *f* **3.** NAUT matelot *m*.
◆ **ratings** *npl* RADIO & TV indice *m* d'écoute ■ **to be high in the ~s** avoir un fort indice d'écoute ■ **the ~s battle** *OR* **war** la course à l'Audimat®.

ratio ['reɪʃɪəʊ] (*pl* **ratios**) *n* **1.** [gen] proportion *f*, rapport *m* ■ **in the ~ of six to one** dans la proportion de six contre un ■ **the teacher-student ~ is 1 to 10** le rapport enseignants-étudiants est de 1 pour 10 **2.** MATHS raison *f*, proportion *f* **3.** ECON ratio *m*.

ratiocination [ˌrætɪɒsɪ'neɪʃn] *n fml* raisonnement *m*.

ration ['ræʃn] ◇ *n liter & fig* ration *f* ■ **I've had my ~ of television for today** j'ai eu ma dose de télévision pour aujourd'hui.
◇ *comp* : **~ book** carnet *m* de tickets de rationnement ■ **~ card** carte *f* de rationnement.
◇ *vt* **1.** [food] rationner **2.** [funds] limiter.
◆ **rations** *npl* [food] vivres *mpl* ■ **to be on double/short ~s** toucher une ration double/réduite ■ **half ~s** demi-rations *fpl*.
◆ **ration out** *vt sep* rationner.

rational ['ræʃənl] ◇ *adj* **1.** [capable of reason] doué de raison, raisonnable **2.** [reasonable, logical - person] raisonnable ; [- behaviour, explanation] rationnel ■ **he is incapable of ~ thought** il est incapable de raisonner logiquement **3.** [of sound mind, sane] lucide **4.** MATHS rationnel.
◇ *n* rationnel *m*.

rationale [ˌræʃə'nɑːl] *n* **1.** [underlying reason] logique *f* ■ **what is the ~ for** *OR* **behind their decision?** quelle logique sous-tend leur décision? **2.** [exposition] exposé *m*.

rationalism ['ræʃənəlɪzm] *n* rationalisme *m*.

rationalist ['ræʃənəlɪst] ◇ *adj* rationaliste.
◇ *n* rationaliste *mf*.

rationalistic [ˌræʃənə'lɪstɪk] *adj* rationaliste.

rationality [ˌræʃə'næləti] *n* **1.** [of belief, system etc] rationalité *f* **2.** [faculty] raison *f*.

rationalization [ˌræʃənəlaɪ'zeɪʃn] *n* rationalisation *f*.

rationalize, ise ['ræʃənəlaɪz] *vt* **1.** [gen - COMM] rationaliser **2.** MATHS rendre rationnel.

rationally ['ræʃənəlɪ] *adv* rationnellement.

rationing ['ræʃənɪŋ] *n* [of food] rationnement *m*.

rat race *n* jungle *f fig* ■ **she dropped out of the ~ to live in the country** elle quitta la jungle des affaires pour vivre à la campagne.

rats [ræts] *interj inf hum* zut.

rattan [rə'tæn] ◇ *n* [plant] rotang *m* ■ [substance] rotin *m*.
◇ *comp* [furniture] en rotin.

rat-tat ['ræt,tæt] = **rat-a-tat(-tat)**.

rattle ['rætl] ◇ *vi* [gen] faire du bruit ■ [car, engine] faire un bruit de ferraille ■ [chain, machine, dice] cliqueter ■ [gunfire, hailstones] crépiter ■ [door, window] vibrer ■ **somebody was rattling at the door** quelqu'un secouait la porte ■ **an old car came rattling down the hill** une vieille voiture descendait la côte dans un bruit de ferraille.
◇ *vt* **1.** [box] agiter *(en faisant du bruit)* ■ [key] faire cliqueter ■ [chain, dice] agiter, secouer ■ [door, window] faire vibrer **2.** [disconcert] ébranler, secouer.
◇ *n* **1.** [noise - of chains] bruit *m* ; [- of car, engine] bruit *m* de ferraille ; [- of keys] cliquetis *m* ; [- of gunfire, hailstones] crépitement *m* ; [- of window, door] vibration *f*, vibrations *fpl* **2.** [for baby] hochet *m* ■ [for sports fan] crécelle *f* **3.** ZOOL [of rattlesnake] grelot *m*.
◆ **rattle around** *vi insep* : **you'll be rattling around in that big old house!** tu seras perdu tout seul dans cette grande maison!
◆ **rattle off** *vt sep* [speech, list] débiter, réciter à toute allure ■ [piece of work] expédier ■ [letter, essay] écrire en vitesse.
◆ **rattle on** *vi insep* jacasser.
◆ **rattle through** *vt insep* [speech, meeting etc] expédier.

rattler ['rætlər] *US inf* = **rattlesnake**.

rattlesnake ['rætlsneɪk] *n* serpent *m* à sonnettes, crotale *m*.

rattling ['rætlɪŋ] ◇ *n* = **rattle** *(sense 1)*.
◇ *adj* **1.** [sound] : **there was a ~ noise** on entendait un cliquetis **2.** [fast] rapide ■ **at a ~ pace** à vive allure.
◇ *adv inf dated* **this book is a ~ good read** ce livre est vraiment formidable.

rat trap *n* **1.** *liter* piège *m* à rats, ratière *f* **2.** *US* [building] taudis *m*.

ratty ['rætɪ] (*comp* **rattier**, *superl* **rattiest**) *adj inf* **1.** [irritable] de mauvais poil **2.** *US* [shabby] miteux.

raucous ['rɔːkəs] *adj* **1.** [noisy] bruyant **2.** [hoarse] rauque.

raucously ['rɔːkəslɪ] *adv* **1.** [noisily] bruyamment **2.** [hoarsely] d'une voix rauque.

raunchiness ['rɔːntʃɪnɪs] *n* sensualité *f*.

raunchy ['rɔːntʃɪ] (*comp* **raunchier**, *superl* **raunchiest**) *adj inf* **1.** [woman] d'une sensualité débordante ■ [song, film etc] torride **2.** *US* [slovenly] négligé.

ravage ['rævɪdʒ] *vt* ravager, dévaster ■ **the city had been ~d by war** la ville avait été ravagée par la guerre.
◆ **ravages** *npl* : **the ~s of time** les ravages du temps.

ravaged ['rævɪdʒd] *adj* ravagé.

rave [reɪv] ◇ *vi* **1.** [be delirious] délirer **2.** [talk irrationally] divaguer **3.** [shout] se déchaîner **4.** *inf* [praise] s'extasier ■ **to ~ about sthg/sb** s'extasier sur qqch/qqn **5.** *UK inf* [at party] faire la bringue *OR* la fête.
◇ *n inf* **1.** [praise] critique *f* élogieuse **2.** [fashion, craze] mode *f* **3.** *UK* [party] rave *f*.
◇ *adj inf* **1.** [enthusiastic] élogieux ■ **the play got ~ reviews** *OR* **notices** les critiques de la pièce furent très élogieuses **2.** [trendy] branché.
◆ **rave up** *vt sep UK dated* **to ~ it up** *inf* faire la bringue *OR* la fête.

ravel ['rævl] (*UK pret & pp* **ravelled**, *cont* **ravelling**) (*US pret & pp* **raveled**, *cont* **raveling**) ◇ *vt* [entangle] emmêler, enchevêtrer.
◇ *vi* **1.** [tangle up] s'emmêler, s'enchevêtrer **2.** [fray] s'effilocher **3.** CONSTR [road surface] se détériorer.

raven ['reɪvn] ◇ *n* (grand) corbeau *m*.
◇ *adj lit* noir comme un corbeau *OR* comme du jais.

raven-haired *adj lit* aux cheveux de jais.

ravenous ['rævənəs] *adj* **1.** [hungry] affamé **2.** [rapacious] *lit* vorace.

ravenously ['rævənəslɪ] *adv* voracement ■ [as intensifier] : **to be ~ hungry** avoir une faim de loup.

raver ['reɪvər] *n UK inf* [partygoer] fêtard *m*, - e *f*.

rave-up *n UK inf dated* fête *f*.

ravine [rə'viːn] *n* ravin *m*.

raving ['reɪvɪŋ] ◇ *adj* **1.** [mad] délirant **2.** [as intensifier] : **she's no ~ beauty** elle n'est pas d'une beauté éblouissante ■ **he's a ~ lunatic** *inf* c'est un fou furieux, il est fou à lier.
◇ *adv inf* **~ mad** fou à lier.
◆ **ravings** *npl* divagations *fpl*.

ravioli [ˌrævɪ'əʊlɪ] *n (U)* ravioli *mpl*, raviolis *mpl*.

ravish ['rævɪʃ] *vt* **1.** [delight] *lit* ravir, transporter de joie **2.** *arch & lit* [rape] violer ■ [abduct] ravir.

ravishing ['rævɪʃɪŋ] *adj* ravissant, éblouissant.

ravishingly ['rævɪʃɪŋlɪ] *adv* de façon ravissante ■ [as intensifier] : **~ beautiful** d'une beauté éblouissante.

raw [rɔː] ◇ *adj* **1.** [uncooked] cru **2.** [untreated - sugar, latex, leather] brut ; [- milk] cru ; [- spirits] pur ; [- cotton, linen] écru ; [- silk] grège, écru ; [- sewage] non traité **3.** [data, statistics] brut **4.** [sore - gen] sensible, irrité ; [- wound, blister] à vif ; [- nerves] à fleur de peau ■ **the remark touched a ~ nerve (in him)** *fig* la remarque l'a touché *OR* piqué au vif **5.** [emotion, power, energy] brut **6.** [inexperienced] inexpérimenté ■ **a ~ recruit** un bleu **7.** [weather] rigoureux, rude ■ **a ~ February night** une froide nuit de février **8.** [forthright] franc, franche *f*, direct **9.** *US* [rude, coarse] grossier, cru **10.** *phr* **to give sb a ~ deal** traiter qqn de manière injuste ■ **he got a ~ deal from his last job** il n'était pas gâté dans son dernier emploi ■ **the unemployed get a ~ deal** les chômeurs n'ont pas la part belle.
◇ *n phr* **in the ~** *inf* à poil ■ **to touch sb on the ~** *UK* toucher *OR* piquer qqn au vif.

rawboned ['rɔːbəʊnd] *adj* décharné.

rawhide ['rɔːhaɪd] *n* **1.** [skin] cuir *m* vert *OR* brut **2.** [whip] fouet *m* (de cuir).

Rawlplug® ['rɔːlplʌg] *n* cheville *f*, fiche *f*.

raw material *n (usu pl)* matière *f* première.

rawness ['rɔːnɪs] *n* **1.** [natural state] nature *f* brute **2.** [soreness] irritation *f* **3.** [inexperience] inexpérience *f*, manque *m* d'expérience **4.** [of weather] rigueur *f*, rudesse *f* **5.** [frankness] franchise *f* **6.** *US* [coarseness - of person, language] grossièreté *f*.

ray [reɪ] *n* **1.** [of light] rayon *m* ■ **a ~ of sunlight** un rayon de soleil **2.** *fig* lueur *f* ■ **a ~ of comfort** une petite consolation ■ **a ~ of hope** une lueur d'espoir **3.** [fish] raie *f* **4.** MUS ré *m*.

ray gun *n* pistolet *m* à rayons.

rayon ['reɪɒn] ◇ *n* rayonne *f*.
◇ *adj* en rayonne.

raze [reɪz] *vt* raser ■ **the village was ~d to the ground** le village fut entièrement rasé.

razor ['reɪzə^r] ◇ *n* rasoir *m* ■ **electric/safety ~** rasoir *m* électrique/de sûreté ■ **the company is on a** *OR* **the ~'s edge** l'entreprise est sur le fil du rasoir.
◇ *vt* raser.

razorback ['reɪzəbæk] *n* **1.** [whale] balénoptère *m*, rorqual *m* **2.** *US* [pig] sanglier *m*.

razorbill ['reɪzəbɪl] *n* petit pingouin *m*, torda *m*.

razor blade *n* lame *f* de rasoir.

razor cut *n* [hairstyle] coupe *f* au rasoir.
◆ **razor-cut** *vt* [hair] couper au rasoir.

razor-sharp *adj* **1.** [blade] tranchant comme un rasoir *OR* comme une lame de rasoir ■ [nails] acéré **2.** [person, mind] vif.

razor-shell *n UK* ZOOL couteau *m*.

razor wire *n (U)* barbelés *mpl* tranchants.

razzle^△ ['ræzl] *n UK* **to be** *OR* **to go on the ~** faire la bringue *OR* la nouba.

razzle-dazzle *inf* = **razzmatazz**.

razzmatazz ['ræzmə'tæz] *n inf* clinquant *m* ■ **the ~ of Hollywood** le côté tape-à-l'œil de Hollywood.

R & B (*abbrev of* **rhythm and blues**) *n* R & B *m*.

RC *n* = **Roman Catholic**.

RCAF (*abbrev of* **Royal Canadian Air Force**) *pr n armée de l'air canadienne.*

RCMP (*abbrev of* **Royal Canadian Mounted Police**) *pr n police montée canadienne.*

RCN (*abbrev of* **Royal Canadian Navy**) *pr n marine de guerre canadienne.*

Rd *written abbr of* **road**.

R & D (*abbrev of* **research and development**) *n* R-D *f*.

RDC *n* = **rural district council**.

re[1] [reɪ] *n* MUS ré *m*.

re[2] [riː] *prep* **1.** ADMIN & COMM : **re your letter of the 6th June** en réponse à *OR* suite à votre lettre du 6 juin ■ [in letter heading] : **Re: job application** Objet : demande d'emploi **2.** LAW : **(in) re** en l'affaire de.

RE *n* = **religious education**.

reach [riːtʃ] ◇ *vt* **1.** [arrive at - destination] arriver à ■ **they ~ed port** ils arrivèrent au *OR* gagnèrent le port ■ **the letter hasn't ~ed him yet** la lettre ne lui est pas encore parvenue ■ **the sound of laughter ~ed their ears** des rires parvenaient à leurs oreilles
2. [extend as far as - stage, point, level] arriver à, atteindre ■ **the water ~ed my knees** l'eau m'arrivait aux genoux ■ **to ~ the age of 80** atteindre l'âge de 80 ans
3. [come to - agreement, decision, conclusion] arriver à, parvenir à ; [- compromise] arriver à, aboutir à
4. [be able to touch] atteindre ■ **can you ~ the top shelf?** est-ce que tu peux atteindre la dernière étagère? ■ **his feet don't ~ the floor** ses pieds ne touchent pas par terre
5. [pass, hand] passer
6. [contact] joindre.
◇ *vi* **1.** [with hand] tendre la main ■ **she ~ed for her glass** elle tendit la main pour prendre son verre ➊ **~ for the sky!** haut les mains! ■ **to ~ for the stars** viser haut
2. [extend] s'étendre ■ [carry - voice] porter
3. [be long enough] : **it won't ~** ce n'est pas assez long
4. NAUT faire une bordée.
◇ *n* **1.** [range] portée *f*, atteinte *f* ■ **within ~** à portée de la main ■ **the house is within easy ~ of the shops** la maison est à proximité des magasins ■ **within everyone's ~** [affordable by all] à la portée de toutes les bourses ■ **out of ~** hors de portée ■ **out of ~ of** hors de (la) portée de ■ **nuclear physics is beyond my ~** la physique nucléaire, ça me dépasse complètement
2. [in boxing] allonge *f*
3. NAUT bordée *f*, bord *m*.
◆ **reaches** *npl* étendue *f* ■ **the upper/the lower ~es of a river** l'amont/l'aval d'une rivière ■ **the upper ~es of society** *fig* les échelons supérieurs de la société.
◆ **reach back** *vi insep* [in time] remonter.
◆ **reach down** ◇ *vt sep* descendre.
◇ *vi insep* **1.** [person] se baisser
2. [coat, hair] descendre ■ **her skirt ~ed down to her ankles** sa jupe lui descendait jusqu'aux chevilles.
◆ **reach out** ◇ *vt sep* [arm, hand] tendre, étendre.
◇ *vi insep* tendre *OR* étendre le bras.
◆ **reach up** *vi insep* **1.** [raise arm] lever le bras
2. [rise] : **to ~ up to** arriver à ■ **the water ~ed up to my waist** l'eau m'arrivait à la taille.

reachable ['riːtʃəbl] *adj* **1.** [town, destination] accessible ■ **is it ~ by boat?** peut-on y aller *OR* accéder par bateau? **2.** [contactable] joignable ■ **he's ~ at the following number** on peut le joindre au numéro suivant.

reach-me-down *n UK inf* vieux vêtement *m (que les aînés passent aux cadets).*

react [rɪ'ækt] *vi* réagir ■ **to ~ to sthg** réagir à qqch ■ **to ~ against sb/sthg** réagir contre qqn/qqch ■ **the acid ~s with the metal** l'acide réagit avec le métal.

reaction [rɪ'ækʃn] *n* **1.** [gen - CHEM], MED & PHYS réaction *f* ■ **her work is a ~ against abstract art** son œuvre est une réaction par rapport à l'art abstrait ■ **public ~ to the policy has been mixed** la réaction du public face à cette mesure a été mitigée **2.** [reflex] réflexe *m* ■ **it slows down your ~s** cela ralentit vos réflexes **3.** POL réaction *f* ■ **the forces of ~** les forces réactionnaires.

reactionary [rɪ'ækʃənrɪ] ◇ *adj* réactionnaire.
◇ *n* réactionnaire *mf*.

reactivate [rɪ'æktɪveɪt] *vt* réactiver.

reactive [rɪ'æktɪv] *adj* [gen - CHEM] & PHYS réactif ■ PSYCHOL réactionnel.

reactor [rɪ'æktə^r] *n* réacteur *m*.

read[1] [riːd] (*pret & pp* **read** [red]) ◇ *vt* **1.** [book, magazine etc] lire ■ **I read it in the paper** je l'ai lu dans le journal ■ **for "Barry" ~ "Harry"** lire "Harry" à la place de "Barry" ■ **can you ~ music/braille/Italian?** savez-vous lire la musique/le braille/ l'italien? ▶ **to ~ sb's lips** *liter* lire sur les lèvres de qqn ■ **~ my lips** *fig* écoutez-moi bien ■ **to take sthg as read** considérer qqch comme allant de soi
2. [interpret] interpréter, lire
3. [understand - person, mood] comprendre ■ **to ~ sb's thoughts** lire dans les pensées de qqn ■ **I can ~ him like a book!** je sais comment il fonctionne! ■ **he ~s the game very well** SPORT il a un bon sens du jeu
4. [via radio] recevoir ■ **~ing you loud and clear** je vous reçois cinq sur cinq
5. *UK* [at university] étudier ■ **he read history** il a étudié l'histoire, il a fait des études d'histoire
6. [gauge, dial, barometer] lire ■ **to ~ the meter** relever le compteur
7. [register - subj: gauge, dial, barometer] indiquer
8. [announce - subj: notice] annoncer
9. [proofs] corriger
10. [data, disk] lire.
◇ *vi* **1.** [person] lire ■ **to ~ to sb** faire la lecture à qqn ■ **to ~ to o.s.** lire ■ **I'd read about it in the papers** je l'avais lu dans les journaux ▶ **to ~ between the lines** lire entre les lignes
2. [text] : **her article ~s well/badly** son article se lit facilement/ne se lit pas facilement ■ **the book ~s like a translation** à la lecture, on sent que ce roman est une traduction ■ **article 22 ~s as follows** voici ce que dit l'article 22
3. [gauge, meter etc] : **the dials ~ differently** les cadrans n'indiquent pas le même chiffre
4. [student] : **what's he ~ing?** qu'est-ce qu'il fait comme études? ■ **to ~ for a degree** préparer un diplôme.
◇ *n* **1.** [act of reading] : **to have a ~** lire ■ **can I have a ~ of your paper?** est-ce que je peux jeter un coup d'œil sur ton journal?
2. [reading matter] : **her books are a good ~** ses livres se lisent bien.
◆ **read back** *vt sep* [dictated letter] relire.
◆ **read into** *vt sep* : **you shouldn't ~ too much into their silence** vous ne devriez pas accorder trop d'importance à leur silence.
◆ **read off** *vt sep* **1.** [rapidly] lire d'un trait ■ [aloud] lire (à haute voix)
2. [figure on dial, scale etc] relever.
◆ **read on** *vi insep* lire la suite.
◆ **read out** *vt sep* **1.** [aloud] lire (à haute voix)
2. [subj: computer] lire
3. *US* [expel] expulser.
◆ **read over** *vt sep* relire.
◆ **read through** *vt sep* lire *(du début à la fin)*.
◆ **read up** *vt sep* étudier.
◆ **read up on** *vt insep* = **read up**.

read[2] [red] ◇ *pt & pp* ⊳ **read**.
◇ *adj* : **he's widely ~** c'est un homme cultivé.

readability [ˌriːdəˈbɪlətɪ] *n* lisibilité *f*.

readable [ˈriːdəbl] *adj* **1.** [handwriting] lisible **2.** [book] qui se laisse lire.

readdress [ˌriːəˈdres] *vt* [mail] faire suivre.

reader [ˈriːdəʳ] *n* **1.** [of book] lecteur *m*, - trice *f* ■ **she's an avid ~** c'est une passionnée de lecture ■ **I'm not a fast ~** je ne lis pas vite **2.** COMPUT lecteur *m* ■ **optical character ~** lecteur *m* optique **3.** [reading book] livre *m* de lecture ■ [anthology] recueil *m* de textes **4.** *UK* UNIV ≃ maître-assistant *m*, - e *f* **5.** *US* UNIV ≃ assistant *m*, - e *f*.

readership [ˈriːdəʃɪp] *n* **1.** [of newspaper, magazine] nombre *m* de lecteurs, lectorat *m* ■ **what is their ~ (figure)?** combien ont-ils de lecteurs? **2.** *UK* UNIV ≃ poste *m* de maître-assistant **3.** *US* UNIV ≃ fonction *f* d'assistant.

readily [ˈredɪlɪ] *adv* **1.** [willingly] volontiers **2.** [with ease] facilement, aisément ■ **our products are ~ available** nos produits sont en vente partout.

readiness [ˈredɪnɪs] *n* **1.** [preparedness] : **to be in ~ for sthg** être préparé à qqch ■ **to be in a state of ~** être fin prêt **2.** [willingness] empressement *m* ■ **their ~ to assist us** leur empressement à nous aider.

reading [ˈriːdɪŋ] ◇ *n* **1.** [activity] lecture *f* ■ **~, writing and arithmetic** la lecture, l'écriture et le calcul **2.** [reading material] lecture *f* ■ **his autobiography makes fascinating/dull ~** son autobiographie est passionnante/ennuyeuse à lire **3.** [recital] lecture *f* **4.** [from instrument, gauge] indication *f* ■ **the ~ on the dial was wrong** les indications qui apparaissaient sur le cadran étaient fausses ■ **to take a ~** lire les indications données par un compteur **5.** POL lecture *f* ■ **to give a bill its first/second ~** examiner un projet de loi en première/deuxième lecture **6.** [interpretation] interprétation *f* ■ **a new ~ of Dante** une nouvelle lecture de Dante **7.** [variant] variante *f*.
◇ *comp* : **take some ~ matter** emmenez de quoi lire ■ **the ~ public** le public des lecteurs.

reading age *n UK* niveau *m* de lecture ■ **she has a ~ of 11** elle a le niveau de lecture d'un enfant de 11 ans.

reading glass *n* [magnifying glass] loupe *f (pour lire)*.
◆ **reading glasses** *npl* [spectacles] lunettes *fpl* pour lire.

reading lamp *n* lampe *f* de bureau.

reading light *n* liseuse *f (dans un train)*.

reading list *n* [syllabus] liste *f* des ouvrages au programme ■ [for further reading] liste *f* des ouvrages recommandés.

reading room *n* salle *f* de lecture.

readjust [ˌriːəˈdʒʌst] ◇ *vt* **1.** [readapt] : **to ~ o.s.** se réadapter **2.** [alter - controls, prices, clothing] rajuster, réajuster.
◇ *vi* se réadapter ■ **to ~ to sthg** se réadapter à qqch.

readjustment [ˌriːəˈdʒʌstmənt] *n* **1.** [readaptation] réadaptation *f* **2.** [alteration] rajustement *m*, réajustement *m*.

read-me file *n* COMPUT fichier *m* ouvrez-moi *OR* lisez-moi.

readmit [ˌriːədˈmɪt] *vt* : **she has been readmitted to hospital** elle a été réadmise à l'hôpital ■ **he was readmitted to the concert** on l'a relaissé passer à l'entrée du concert.

read-only [riːd-] *adj* [disk, file] en lecture seule.

read-only memory [riːd-] *n* mémoire *f* morte.

readout [ˈriːdaʊt] *n* COMPUT [gen] lecture *f* ■ [on screen] affichage *m* ■ [on paper] sortie *f* papier *OR* sur imprimante, listing *m*.

read-through [riːd-] *n* : **to have a ~ of sthg** lire qqch *(du début à la fin)*.

readvertise [ˌriːˈædvətaɪz] ◇ *vt* repasser une annonce de.
◇ *vi* repasser une annonce.

readvertisement [ˌriːədˈvɜːtɪsmənt] *n* deuxième annonce *f*.

read-write head [riːd-] *n* tête *f* de lecture-écriture.

ready [ˈredɪ] ◇ *adj* (*comp* **readier**, *superl* **readiest**) **1.** [prepared] prêt ■ **he's just getting ~** il est en train de se préparer ■ **to be ~ to do sthg** être prêt à faire qqch ■ **to be ~ for anything** être prêt à tout ■ **he's not ~ for such responsibility** il n'est pas prêt pour affronter une telle responsabilité ■ **she's always ~ with an answer, she always has an answer ~** elle a toujours réponse à tout ■ **to get sthg ~** préparer qqch ■ **to get ~ to do sthg** se préparer *OR* s'apprêter à faire qqch ■ **we're ~ when you are** nous n'attendons que toi ■ **dinner's ~!** c'est prêt! ■ **are you ~ to order?** vous avez choisi? ■ **the tomatoes are ~ for eating** les tomates sont bonnes à manger ▶ **~, steady, go!** à vos marques, prêts, partez!
2. [willing] prêt, disposé ■ **~ to do sthg** prêt à faire qqch ■ **don't be so ~ to believe him** ne le crois pas systématiquement ■ **you know me, I'm ~ for anything** tu me connais, je suis toujours partant ■ **I'm ~ for bed!** j'ai envie d'aller me coucher!
3. [quick] prompt ■ **she has a ~ wit** elle a l'esprit d'à-propos ■ **she has a ~ tongue** elle n'a pas la langue dans sa poche ■ **he had a ~ smile** il souriait facilement

4. [likely] : **~ to do sthg** sur le point de faire qqch ■ **I'm ~ to collapse!** je suis à bout de forces!, je suis épuisé!
5. [easily accessible] : **a ~ market for our products** un marché tout trouvé pour nos produits ■ **~ to hand** [within reach] à portée de main ; [available] à disposition ■ **~ cash** *OR* **money** (argent *m*) liquide *m*.
◇ *n* (*pl* **readies**) *UK inf* [money] : **the ~, the readies** le fric, le pognon.
◇ *adv UK* **~ cut ham** jambon *m* prétranché ■ **~ salted peanuts** cacahuètes *fpl* salées.
◇ *vt* (*pret & pp* **readied**) préparer ■ **to ~ o.s. for sthg** se préparer pour qqch.
◆ **at the ready** *adj phr* (tout) prêt.

ready-cooked *adj* précuit.

ready-made ◇ *adj* **1.** [clothes] de prêt-à-porter ■ [food] précuit **2.** [excuse, solution, argument] tout prêt.
◇ *n* [garment] vêtement *m* de prêt-à-porter.

ready meal *n* plat *m* cuisiné.

ready-mix *adj* [cake] fait à partir d'une préparation ■ [concrete] prémalaxé.

ready reckoner [-'rekənə^r^] *n* barème *m*.

ready-to-wear *adj* : **~ clothing** prêt-à-porter *m*.

reaffirm [,ri:ə'fɜ:m] *vt* réaffirmer.

reafforest [,ri:ə'fɒrɪst] *vt* reboiser.

reafforestation ['ri:ə,fɒrɪ'steɪʃn] *n* reboisement *m*, reforestation *f*.

reagent [ri:'eɪdʒənt] *n* réactif *m*.

real [rɪəl] ◇ *adj* **1.** [authentic] vrai, véritable ■ **they're ~ silver** ils sont en argent véritable ■ **a ~ man** un vrai homme ■ **we'll never know her ~ feelings** nous ne saurons jamais quels étaient vraiment ses sentiments ■ **we have no ~ cause for concern** nous n'avons aucune raison de nous inquiéter ➜ **it's the ~ thing** [authentic object] c'est du vrai de vrai ; [true love] c'est le grand amour **2.** [actually existing] réel ■ **the ~ world** le monde réel ■ **in ~ life** dans la réalité **3.** [net, overall] réel ■ **salaries have fallen in ~ terms** les salaires ont baissé en termes réels **4.** [as intensifier] vrai, véritable ■ **it was a ~ surprise** ce fut une vraie surprise ■ **she's a ~ pain** elle est vraiment rasante **5.** COMPUT, MATHS, PHILOS & PHYS réel **6.** *phr* **get ~!**△ arrête de délirer!
◇ *adv inf US inf* vachement.
◇ *n* PHILOS : **the ~** le réel.
◆ **for real** *adv & adj phr inf* pour de vrai *OR* de bon ■ **this time it's for ~** cette fois-ci c'est la bonne ■ **is he for ~?**△ d'où il sort, celui-là?

real ale *n UK* bière *f* artisanale.

real estate *n (U)* **1.** *US* [property] biens *mpl* immobiliers ■ **he works in ~** il travaille dans l'immobilier **2.** *UK* LAW biens *mpl* fonciers.
◆ **real-estate** *comp US* immobilier.

realign [,ri:ə'laɪn] ◇ *vt* aligner (de nouveau) ■ POL regrouper.
◇ *vi* s'aligner (de nouveau) ■ POL se regrouper.

realignment [,ri:ə'laɪnmənt] *n* (nouvel) alignement *m* ■ POL regroupement *m*.

realism ['rɪəlɪzm] *n* réalisme *m*.

realist ['rɪəlɪst] ◇ *adj* réaliste.
◇ *n* réaliste *mf*.

realistic [,rɪə'lɪstɪk] *adj* **1.** [reasonable] réaliste **2.** [lifelike] ressemblant.

realistically [,rɪə'lɪstɪklɪ] *adv* de façon réaliste ■ **they can't ~ expect us to do all this** ils ne peuvent pas s'attendre sérieusement à ce que nous fassions tout cela.

reality [rɪ'ælətɪ] (*pl* **realities**) *n* réalité *f* ■ **you have to face ~** il faut que tu regardes la réalité en face.
◆ **in reality** *adv phr* en réalité.

reality TV *n (U)* télévision *f* réalité.

realizable ['rɪəlaɪzəbl] *adj* [gen - FIN] réalisable.

realization [,rɪəlaɪ'zeɪʃn] *n* **1.** [awareness] : **this sudden ~ left us speechless** cette découverte nous a laissés sans voix ■ **there has been a growing ~ on the part of the government that...** le gouvernement s'est peu à peu rendu compte que... ■ **his ~ that he was gay** la prise de conscience de son homosexualité **2.** [of aim, dream, project] réalisation *f* **3.** FIN [of assets] réalisation *f*.

realize, ise ['rɪəlaɪz] *vt* **1.** [be or become aware of] se rendre compte de ■ **do you ~ what time it is?** tu te rends compte de *OR* tu as vu l'heure qu'il est? ■ **it made me ~ what a fool I had been** cela m'a fait comprendre quel imbécile j'avais été ■ **I ~ you're busy, but...** je sais que tu es occupé, mais... **2.** [achieve] réaliser ■ **my worst fears were ~d** ce que je craignais le plus s'est produit *OR* est arrivé ■ **a job where you could ~ your full potential** un travail qui te permettrait de te réaliser complètement **3.** FIN [yield financially] rapporter ■ [convert into cash] réaliser.

real-life *adj* vrai ■ **the ~ drama of her battle against illness** le drame affreux de sa lutte contre la maladie.

reallocate [,ri:'æləkeɪt] *vt* [funds, resources] réaffecter, réattribuer ■ [task, duties] redistribuer.

really ['rɪəlɪ] ◇ *adv* **1.** [actually] vraiment, réellement ■ **did you ~ say that?** as-tu vraiment dis ça? **2.** [as intensifier] vraiment ■ **these cakes are ~ delicious** ces gâteaux sont vraiment délicieux ■ **it ~ doesn't matter** ce n'est vraiment pas important **3.** [softening negative statements] : **it doesn't ~ matter** ce n'est pas vraiment important **4.** [tentative use] : **he's quite nice, ~** il est plutôt sympa, en fait ■ **do you want to go? – I suppose I do ~** tu veux y aller? – pourquoi pas, après tout **5.** [in surprise, interest] : **(oh) ~?** oh, vraiment?, c'est pas vrai?
◇ *interj* [in irritation] : **(well) ~!** enfin!

realm [relm] *n* **1.** [field, domain] domaine *m* ■ **it is within the ~s of possibility** c'est du domaine du possible **2.** [kingdom] *lit* royaume *m*.

real number *n* nombre *m* réel.

real property *n (U)* biens *mpl* immobiliers *OR* immeubles.

real tennis *n* jeu *m* de paume.

real time *n* COMPUT temps *m* réel.
◆ **real-time** *adj* [system, control, processing] en temps réel.

realtor ['rɪəltə^r^] *n US* agent *m* immobilier.

realty ['rɪəltɪ] *n (U) US* biens *mpl* immobiliers.

ream [ri:m] ◇ *n* [of paper] rame *f* ■ **to write ~s** *inf fig* écrire des tartines.
◇ *vt* **1.** TECH fraiser **2.** *US inf* [person] rouler.

reanimate [,ri:'ænɪmeɪt] *vt* réanimer.

reanimation [,ri:ænɪ'meɪʃn] *n* réanimation *f*.

reap [ri:p] ◇ *vt* **1.** [crop] moissonner, faucher **2.** *fig* récolter, tirer ■ **to ~ the benefit** *OR* **the benefits of sthg** récolter les bénéfices de qqch ■ **she ~ed a rich reward** elle a été bien récompensée.
◇ *vi* moissonner, faire la moisson.

reaper ['ri:pə^r^] *n* **1.** [machine] moissonneuse *f* ■ **~ and binder** moissonneuse-lieuse *f* **2.** [person] moissonneur *m*, - euse *f* ■ **the (Grim) Reaper** *lit* la Faucheuse.

reaping ['ri:pɪŋ] *n* moisson *f* ■ **~ machine** moissonneuse *f*.

reappear [,ri:ə'pɪə^r^] *vi* [person, figure, sun] réapparaître ■ [lost object] refaire surface.

reappearance [,ri:ə'pɪərəns] *n* réapparition *f*.

reapply [,ri:ə'plaɪ] (*pret & pp* **reapplied**) *vi* : **to ~ for a job** poser de nouveau sa candidature pour un poste ■ **previous applicants need not ~** les personnes ayant déjà posé leur candidature n'ont pas besoin de le faire à nouveau.

reappoint [,ri:ə'pɔɪnt] *vt* réengager, rengager.

reappraisal [,ri:ə'preɪzl] *n* réexamen *m*.

reappraise [,ri:ə'preɪz] *vt* réexaminer.

rear [rɪəʳ] <> *n* **1.** [of place] arrière *m* ■ **at the ~ of the bus** à l'arrière du bus ■ **the garden at the ~** *UK OR* **in the ~** *US* **of the house** le jardin qui est derrière la maison ■ **they attacked them from the ~** ils les ont attaqués par derrière **2.** MIL arrière *m*, arrières *mpl* ■ **to bring up the ~** MIL & *fig* fermer la marche **3.** *inf* [buttocks] arrière-train *m*.
<> *adj* [door, wheel] arrière *(inv)*, de derrière ■ [engine] arrière ■ [carriages] de queue ■ **is there a ~ entrance?** est-ce qu'il y a une entrée par derrière? ▶ **~ lamp** *OR* **light** *UK* AUT feu *m* arrière ■ **~ window** lunette *f* arrière ■ **'Rear Window'** ***Hitchcock*** 'Fenêtre sur cour'.
<> *vt* **1.** [children, animals] élever ■ [plants] cultiver **2.** [head, legs] lever, relever ■ **racism has ~ed its ugly head again** *fig* le spectre du racisme a refait son apparition.
<> *vi* **1.** [horse] : **to ~ (up)** se cabrer **2.** [mountain, skyscraper] : **to ~ (up)** se dresser.

rear admiral *n* contre-amiral *m*.

rear-engined *adj* avec moteur à l'arrière.

rearguard ['rɪəgɑ:d] *n* arrière-garde *f*.

rearguard action *n* combat *m* d'arrière-garde ■ **to fight a ~** *liter* & *fig* mener un combat d'arrière-garde.

rearm [ri:'ɑ:m] <> *vt* [nation, ship] réarmer.
<> *vi* réarmer.

rearmament [rɪ'ɑ:məmənt] *n* réarmement *m*.

rear-mounted *adj* monté à l'arrière.

rearrange [,ri:ə'reɪndʒ] *vt* **1.** [arrange differently - furniture, objects] réarranger, changer la disposition de ; [- flat, room] réaménager **2.** [put back in place] réarranger ■ **she ~d her hair** elle se recoiffa **3.** [reschedule] changer la date/l'heure de ■ **the meeting has been ~d for Monday** la réunion a été remise à lundi ■ **we'll have to ~ our schedule** il faudra réaménager notre programme.

rearrangement [,ri:ə'reɪndʒmənt] *n* **1.** [different arrangement] réarrangement *m*, réaménagement *m* **2.** [rescheduling] changement *m* de date/d'heure.

rearview mirror ['rɪəvju:-] *n* rétroviseur *m*.

rearward ['rɪəwəd] <> *adj* [part, end] arrière *(inv)* ■ [motion] en arrière, vers l'arrière.
<> *adv* = **rearwards**.
<> *n* arrière *m*.

rearwards ['rɪəwədz] *adv* en arrière, vers l'arrière.

rear-wheel drive *n* AUT traction *f* arrière.

reason ['ri:zn] <> *n* **1.** [cause, motive] raison *f* ■ **what is the ~ for his absence?** quelle est la raison de son absence? ■ **did he give a ~ for being so late?** a-t-il donné la raison d'un tel retard? ■ **the ~ (why) they refused** la raison de leur refus, la raison pour laquelle ils ont refusé ■ **I (can) see no ~ for disagreeing** *OR* **to disagree** je ne vois pas pourquoi je ne serais pas d'accord ■ **why do you ask? – oh, no particular ~** pourquoi est-ce que tu me demandes ça? – oh, comme ça ■ **she wouldn't tell me the ~ why** elle ne voulait pas me dire pourquoi ■ **you have every ~** *OR* **good ~ to be angry** vous avez de bonnes raisons d'être en colère ■ **we have/there is ~ to believe he is lying** nous avons de bonnes raisons de croire/il y a lieu de croire qu'il ment ■ **I chose him for the simple ~ I liked him** je l'ai choisi pour la simple et bonne raison qu'il me plaisait ■ **but that's the only ~ I came!** mais c'est pour ça que je suis venue! ■ **that's no ~ to get annoyed** ce n'est pas une raison pour s'énerver ■ **all the more ~ for trying again** *OR* **to try again** raison de plus pour réessayer ■ **for ~s best known to herself** pour des raisons qu'elle est seule à connaître ■ **for some ~ (or other)** pour une raison ou pour une autre ■ **give me one good ~ why I should believe you!** donne-moi une bonne raison de te croire! ■ **they were upset, and with (good) ~** ils étaient bouleversés, et à juste titre **2.** [common sense] raison *f* ■ **he won't listen to ~** il refuse d'entendre raison ■ **at last he saw ~** il a fini par entendre raison ■ **your demands are beyond all ~** vos exigences dépassent les limites du raisonnable ▶ **it stands to ~** c'est logique, ça va de soi **3.** [rationality] raison *f*.
<> *vi* raisonner ■ **to ~ with sb** raisonner qqn.
<> *vt* **1.** [maintain] maintenir, soutenir ■ [work out] calculer, déduire ■ [conclude] conclure **2.** [persuade] : **she ~ed me into/out of going** elle m'a persuadé/dissuadé d'y aller.
◆ **by reason of** *prep phr* en raison de.
◆ **for reasons of** *prep phr* : **for ~s of space/national security** pour des raisons de place/sécurité nationale.
◆ **within reason** *adv phr* dans la limite du raisonnable.
◆ **reason out** *vt sep* résoudre *(par la raison)*.

reasonable ['ri:znəbl] *adj* **1.** [sensible - person, behaviour, attitude] raisonnable ; [- explanation, decision] raisonnable, sensé **2.** [moderate - price] raisonnable, correct ; [- restaurant] qui pratique des prix raisonnables **3.** [fair, acceptable - offer, suggestion] raisonnable, acceptable ■ **beyond all ~ doubt** indubitablement.

reasonably ['ri:znəblɪ] *adv* **1.** [behave, argue] raisonnablement ■ **one can ~ expect....** on est en droit d'attendre.... ■ **~ priced at $100** au prix raisonnable *OR* modéré de 100 dollars **2.** [quite, rather] : **~ good** assez bien, pas mal.

reasoned ['ri:znd] *adj* [argument, decision] raisonné.

reasoning ['ri:znɪŋ] *n* raisonnement *m*.

reassemble [,ri:ə'sembl] <> *vt* **1.** [people, arguments] rassembler **2.** [machinery] remonter.
<> *vi* se rassembler ■ **Parliament/school ~s in September** la rentrée parlementaire/des classes a lieu en septembre.

reassert [,ri:ə'sɜ:t] *vt* [authority] réaffirmer ■ **you'll have to ~ yourself** vous devrez imposer à nouveau *OR* réaffirmer votre autorité.

reassess [,ri:ə'ses] *vt* **1.** [position, opinion] réexaminer **2.** FIN [damages] réévaluer ■ [taxation] réviser.

reassessment [,ri:ə'sesmənt] *n* **1.** [of position, opinion] réexamen *m* **2.** FIN [of damages] réévaluation *f* ■ [of taxes] révision *f*.

reassign [,ri:ə'saɪn] *vt* réaffecter.

reassurance [,ri:ə'ʃɔ:rəns] *n* **1.** [comforting] réconfort *m* ■ **she turned to me for ~** elle s'est tournée vers moi *OR* est venue à moi pour que je la rassure **2.** [guarantee] assurance *f*, confirmation *f* ■ **despite his ~** *OR* **~s that the contract is still valid** bien qu'il affirme que le contrat est toujours valable ■ **the government has given ~s that....** le gouvernement a assuré que...

reassure [,ri:ə'ʃɔ:ʳ] *vt* **1.** [gen] rassurer **2.** FIN réassurer.

reassuring [,ri:ə'ʃɔ:rɪŋ] *adj* rassurant.

reassuringly [,ri:ə'ʃɔ:rɪŋlɪ] *adv* d'une manière rassurante ■ [as intensifier] : **~ simple** d'une grande simplicité.

reawake [,ri:ə'weɪk] (*pret* **reawoke** [-'wəʊk] *OR* **reawaked**, *pp* **reawoken** [-'wəʊkn] *OR* **reawaked**) *vi* se réveiller de nouveau.

reawaken [,ri:ə'weɪkn] <> *vt* [person] réveiller ■ [concern, interest] réveiller ■ [feelings] faire renaître, raviver.
<> *vi* [person] se réveiller de nouveau.

reawakening [,ri:ə'weɪknɪŋ] *n* [of sleeper] réveil *m* ■ [of interest, concern] réveil *m*.

rebarbative [rɪ'bɑ:bətɪv] *adj* *fml* rébarbatif.

rebate ['ri:beɪt] *n* **1.** [reduction - on goods] remise *f*, ristourne *f* ; [- on tax] dégrèvement *m* ■ [refund] remboursement *m* **2.** = **rabbet**.

rebel (*pret & pp* **rebelled**, *cont* **rebelling**) <> *n* ['rebl] [in revolution] rebelle *mf*, insurgé *m*, - e *f* ■ *fig* rebelle *mf*.
<> *adj* ['rebl] [soldier] rebelle ■ [camp, territory] des rebelles ■ [attack] de rebelles.
<> *vi* [rɪ'bel] se rebeller ■ **to ~ against sthg/sb** se révolter contre qqch/qqn ‖ *hum* [stomach] : **my stomach rebelled** mon estomac a protesté.

rebellion [rɪ'beljən] *n* rébellion *f*, révolte *f* ■ **in open ~** en rébellion ouverte ■ **to rise (up) in ~ against sthg/sb** se révolter contre qqch/qqn.

rebellious [rɪ'beljəs] *adj* [child, hair] rebelle ▪ [troops] insoumis.

rebelliousness [rɪ'beljəsnɪs] *n* [of child, politician] esprit *m* de rébellion ▪ [of soldier] insoumission *f* ▪ [of inhabitants] disposition *f* à la rébellion.

rebirth [,ri:'bɜ:θ] *n* renaissance *f*.

reboot [ri:'bu:t] *vt* [computer] réinitialiser, réamorcer *offic* ▪ [programme] relancer.

reborn [,ri:'bɔ:n] *adj* réincarné ▪ **to be ~** renaître ▪ **I feel ~** je me sens renaître.

rebound ◇ *vi* [rɪ'baʊnd] **1.** [ball] rebondir **2.** *fig* **to ~ on sb** se retourner contre qqn **3.** [recover - business] reprendre, repartir ; [- prices] remonter.
◇ *n* ['ri:baʊnd] **1.** [of ball] rebond *m* ▪ **to catch a ball on the ~** attraper une balle au rebond **2.** *phr* **to be on the ~** [after relationship] être sous le coup d'une déception sentimentale ; [after setback] être sous le coup d'un échec.

re-brand *vt* : **to ~ something** effectuer le rebranding de qqch.

rebroadcast [,ri:'brɔ:dkɑ:st] ◇ *n* retransmission *f*.
◇ *vt* retransmettre.

rebuff [rɪ'bʌf] ◇ *vt* [snub] rabrouer ▪ [reject] repousser.
◇ *n* rebuffade *f* ▪ **to meet with** *OR* **to suffer a ~** [person] essuyer une rebuffade ; [request] être repoussé.

rebuild [,ri:'bɪld] (*pret & pp* **rebuilt** [-'bɪlt]) *vt* [town, economy] rebâtir, reconstruire ▪ [relationship, life] reconstruire ▪ [confidence] faire renaître.

rebuke [rɪ'bju:k] ◇ *vt* [reprimand] réprimander ▪ **to ~ sb for sthg** reprocher qqch à qqn ▪ **to ~ sb for doing** *OR* **having done sthg** reprocher à qqn d'avoir fait qqch.
◇ *n* reproche *m*, réprimande *f*.

rebus ['ri:bəs] *n* rébus *m*.

rebut [ri:'bʌt] (*pret & pp* **rebutted**, *cont* **rebutting**) *vt* réfuter.

rebuttal [ri:'bʌtl] *n* réfutation *f*.

rec [rek] *n UK* **1. = recreation ground 2. = recreation room**.

rec. *written abbr of* **received**.

recalcitrant [rɪ'kælsɪtrənt] *adj fml* récalcitrant.

recall ◇ *vt* [rɪ'kɔ:l] **1.** [remember] se rappeler, se souvenir de ▪ **I don't ~ seeing** *OR* **having seen her** je ne me rappelle pas l'avoir vue ▪ **as far as I can ~** aussi loin que je m'en souvienne ▪ **as I ~** si mes souvenirs sont bons ▪ **as you may ~** comme vous vous en souvenez peut-être **2.** [evoke - past] rappeler **3.** [send for - actor, ambassador] rappeler ; [- Parliament] rappeler (en session extraordinaire) ; [- library book, hire car] demander le retour de ; [- faulty goods] rappeler **4.** MIL rappeler.
◇ *n* ['ri:kɔ:l] **1.** [memory] rappel *m*, mémoire *f* ▪ **total ~** aptitude à se souvenir des moindres détails ▪ **to be beyond** *OR* **past ~** être oublié à tout jamais **2.** MIL rappel *m*.
◇ *comp* : **~ button** [on phone] rappel *m* automatique ▪ **~ slip** [for library book] fiche *f* de rappel.

recant [rɪ'kænt] ◇ *vt* [religion] abjurer ▪ [opinion] rétracter.
◇ *vi* [from religion] abjurer ▪ [from opinion] se rétracter.

recap ['ri:kæp] (*pret & pp* **recapped**, *cont* **recapping**) ◇ *n* [summary] récapitulation *f*.
◇ *vt* [summarize] récapituler.

recapitulate [,ri:kə'pɪtjʊleɪt] *vt* récapituler.

recapitulation ['ri:kə,pɪtjʊ'leɪʃn] *n* récapitulation *f*.

recapture [,ri:'kæptʃər] ◇ *vt* **1.** [prisoner, town] reprendre ▪ [animal] capturer **2.** [regain - confidence] reprendre ; [- feeling, spirit] retrouver ▪ [evoke - subj: film, book, play] recréer, faire revivre **3.** *US* FIN saisir.
◇ *n* **1.** [of escapee, animal] capture *f* ▪ [of town] reprise *f* **2.** *US* FIN saisie *f*.

recast [,ri:'kɑ:st] (*pret & pp* **recast**) ◇ *vt* **1.** [redraft] réorganiser, restructurer **2.** [play] changer la distribution de ▪ [actor] donner un nouveau rôle à **3.** METALL refondre.
◇ *n* METALL refonte *f*.

recce ['rekɪ] (*pret & pp* **recced** *OR* **recceed**) *inf* MIL ◇ *vt* reconnaître.
◇ *vi* faire une reconnaissance.
◇ *n* reconnaissance *f* ▪ **to go on a ~** MIL aller en reconnaissance ; [gen] faire la reconnaissance des lieux.

recd, rec'd *written abbr of* **received**.

recede [ri:'si:d] ◇ *vi* **1.** [move away - object] s'éloigner ; [- waters] refluer ; [- tide] descendre ▪ **to ~ into the distance** disparaître dans le lointain **2.** [fade - hopes] s'évanouir ; [- fears] s'estomper ; [- danger] s'éloigner **3.** [hairline] : **his hair has started to ~** son front commence à se dégarnir **4.** FIN baisser.
◇ *vt* LAW [right] rétrocéder ▪ [land] recéder.

receding [rɪ'si:dɪŋ] *adj* **1.** [hair] : **to have a ~ hairline** avoir le front qui se dégarnit **2.** FIN en baisse.

receipt [rɪ'si:t] ◇ *n* **1.** [for purchase] reçu *m*, ticket *m* de caisse ▪ [for bill] acquit *m* ▪ [for rent, insurance] quittance *f* ▪ [for meal, taxi fare] reçu *m* ▪ [from customs] récépissé *m* **2.** [reception] réception *f* ▪ **to pay on ~** payer à la réception ▪ **to acknowledge ~ of sthg** COMM accuser réception de qqch ▪ **on ~ of your results** dès que vous aurez reçu vos résultats ▪ **I am in ~ of the goods** COMM j'ai bien reçu les marchandises.
◇ *vt UK* acquitter ▪ **a ~ed bill** une facture acquittée.
◆ **receipts** *npl* [money] recettes *fpl*.

receivable [rɪ'si:vəbl] *adj* recevable ▪ COMM [outstanding] à recevoir ▪ **accounts ~** comptes *mpl* clients, créances *fpl*.

receive [rɪ'si:v] ◇ *vt* **1.** [gift, letter] recevoir ▪ **to ~ sthg from sb** recevoir qqch de qqn ▪ **'~d with thanks'** COMM 'acquitté, pour acquit' ▪ **to ~ damages** LAW obtenir *OR* recevoir des dommages-intérêts ▪ **she ~d ten years** LAW elle a été condamnée à dix ans de réclusion
2. [blow] recevoir ▪ [insult, refusal] essuyer ▪ [criticism] être l'objet de ▪ **to ~ treatment (for sthg)** se faire soigner (pour qqch) ▪ **to ~ injuries** être blessé ▪ **he has ~d dreadful/excellent treatment** il a été traité d'une manière épouvantable/avec beaucoup d'égards
3. [greet, welcome] accueillir, recevoir ▪ **the new film was enthusiastically ~d** le nouveau film a été accueilli avec enthousiasme ▪ **their offer was not well ~d** leur proposition n'a pas reçu un accueil favorable ▪ [into club, organization] admettre ▪ **to be ~d into the Church** être reçu *OR* admis dans le sein de l'Église
4. [signal, broadcast] recevoir, capter ▪ **I'm receiving you loud and clear** je vous reçois cinq sur cinq
5. SPORT : **to ~ service** recevoir le service
6. LAW [stolen goods] receler
7. *fml* [accommodate] recevoir, prendre.
◇ *vi* **1.** *fml* [have guests] recevoir
2. SPORT recevoir, être le receveur
3. RELIG recevoir la communion
4. LAW [thief] receler.

received [rɪ'si:vd] *adj* : **~ idea/opinion** idée *f* reçue *OR* toute faite ▪ **~ wisdom** sagesse *f* populaire.

Received Pronunciation *n UK* prononciation *f* standard (de l'anglais).

Received Standard *n US* prononciation *f* standard (de l'américain).

receiver [rɪ'si:vər] *n* **1.** [gen - SPORT] receveur *m*, - euse *f* ▪ [of consignment] destinataire *mf*, consignataire *mf* ▪ [of stolen goods] receleur *m*, - euse *f* **2.** [on telephone] combiné *m*, récepteur *m* ▪ **to lift/to replace the ~** décrocher/raccrocher (le téléphone) **3.** TV récepteur *m*, poste *m* de télévision ▪ RADIO récepteur *m*, poste *m* de radio **4.** FIN administrateur *m* judiciaire ▪ **they have been placed in the hands of the ~, the ~ has been called in** ils ont été placés sous administration judiciaire **5.** CHEM récipient *m*.

receivership [rɪ'si:vəʃɪp] *n* FIN : **to go into ~** être placé sous administration judiciaire.

receiving [rɪ'si:vɪŋ] ◇ *adj* [office] de réception ▪ [country] d'accueil.
◇ *n* [of stolen property] recel *m*.

receiving end *n* **1.** SPORT : **to be at the ~** recevoir (le service) **2.** *phr* **to be on the ~** *inf* **: if anything goes wrong, you'll be on the ~** si ça tourne mal, c'est toi qui vas payer les pots cassés ▪ **she was on the ~ of their bad mood** c'est sur elle qu'ils ont passé leur mauvaise humeur.

recension [rɪ'senʃn] *n* [revision] révision *f* ▪ [text] texte *m* révisé, texte *m* revu et corrigé.

recent ['ri:snt] *adj* [new] récent, nouveau *(before vowel or silent 'h'* **nouvel***)*, nouvelle *f* ▪ [modern] récent, moderne ▪ **in ~ months** ces derniers mois ▪ **~ developments** les derniers événements.

recently ['ri:sntlɪ] *adv* récemment, dernièrement, ces derniers temps ▪ **I saw her as ~ as yesterday** je l'ai vue pas plus tard qu'hier ▪ **until ~** jusqu'à ces derniers temps ▪ **I hadn't heard of it until very ~** je n'en ai entendu parler que très récemment.

receptacle [rɪ'septəkl] *n* **1.** *fml* [container] récipient *m* **2.** *US* ELEC prise *f* de courant (femelle).

reception [rɪ'sepʃn] *n* **1.** [welcome] réception *f*, accueil *m* ▪ **to get a warm ~** recevoir un accueil chaleureux ▪ **to get a cold ~** être reçu froidement **2.** [formal party] réception *f* ▪ **to hold a ~** donner une réception **3.** [in hotel] réception *f* ▪ [in office] accueil *m* ▪ **at ~** à la réception **4.** RADIO & TV réception *f* **5.** *US* SPORT [of ball] réception *f* **6.** *UK* SCH ≃ cours *m* préparatoire ▪ **~ class** première année *f* de maternelle.

reception committee *n* comité *m* d'accueil *hum & liter.*

reception desk *n* [in hotel] réception *f* ▪ [in office] accueil *m*.

receptionist [rɪ'sepʃənɪst] *n* [in hotel] réceptionniste *mf* ▪ [in office] hôtesse *f* d'accueil ▪ **he's a ~ at Larousse** il travaille à l'accueil chez Larousse.

reception room *n* [in hotel] salle *f* de réception ▪ *UK* [in house] salon *m*.

receptive [rɪ'septɪv] *adj* [open] réceptif ▪ **to be ~ to new ideas** être ouvert aux idées nouvelles.

recess [*UK* rɪ'ses, *US* 'ri:ses] ◇ *n* **1.** [alcove - gen] renfoncement *m* ; [- in bedroom] alcôve *f* ▪ [for statue] niche *f* ▪ [in doorway] embrasure *f* **2.** [of mind, memory] recoin *m*, tréfonds *m* **3.** *US* LAW suspension *f* d'audience ▪ **the court went into ~** l'audience a été suspendue **4.** *US* SCH récréation *f* **5.** [closure - of parliament] vacances *fpl* parlementaires, intersession *f* parlementaire ; [- of courts] vacances *fpl* judiciaires, vacations *fpl* ▪ **Parliament is in ~ for the summer** le Parlement est en vacances pour l'été.
◇ *vi* *US* LAW suspendre l'audience ▪ POL suspendre la séance.
◇ *vt* encastrer.

recessed [*UK* rɪ'sest, *US* 'ri:sest] *adj* encastré ▪ **~ lighting** éclairage encastré.

recession [rɪ'seʃn] *n* **1.** ECON récession *f* ▪ **the economy is in ~** l'économie est en récession **2.** *fml* [retreat] recul *m*, retraite *f* **3.** RELIG sortie *f* en procession du clergé **4.** LAW rétrocession *f*.

recessive [rɪ'sesɪv] *adj* **1.** [gene] récessif **2.** [backward - measure] rétrograde.

recharge ◇ *vt* [ˌri:'tʃɑ:dʒ] [battery, rifle] recharger ▪ **to ~ one's batteries** recharger ses batteries.
◇ *n* ['ri:tʃɑ:dʒ] recharge *f*.

rechargeable [ˌri:'tʃɑ:dʒəbl] *adj* rechargeable.

recidivism [rɪ'sɪdɪvɪzm] *n* LAW récidive *f*.

recidivist [rɪ'sɪdɪvɪst] ◇ *adj* récidiviste.
◇ *n* récidiviste *mf*.

recipe ['resɪpɪ] *n* CULIN recette *f* ▪ *fig* recette *f*, secret *m* ▪ **a ~ for success/long life** le secret de la réussite/la longévité ▪ **it's a ~ for disaster** c'est le meilleur moyen pour aller droit à la catastrophe.

recipient [rɪ'sɪpɪənt] *n* **1.** [of letter] destinataire *mf* ▪ [of cheque] bénéficiaire *mf* ▪ [of award, honour] récipiendaire *m* ▪ **he was the proud ~ of a gold watch** il a eu la chance de se voir remettre une montre en or **2.** MED [of transplant] receveur *m*, - euse *f*.

reciprocal [rɪ'sɪprəkl] ◇ *adj* [mutual] réciproque, mutuel ▪ [bilateral] réciproque, bilatéral ▪ GRAM & MATHS réciproque.
◇ *n* MATHS réciproque *f*.

reciprocate [rɪ'sɪprəkeɪt] ◇ *vt* **1.** [favour, invitation, smile] rendre ▪ [love, sentiment] répondre à, rendre **2.** MECH actionner d'un mouvement alternatif.
◇ *vi* **1.** [in praise, compliments] retourner le compliment ▪ [in fight] rendre coup pour coup ▪ [in dispute] rendre la pareille ▪ [in argument] répondre du tac au tac **2.** MECH avoir un mouvement de va-et-vient.

reciprocating [rɪ'sɪprəkeɪtɪŋ] *adj* MECH alternatif.

reciprocation [rɪˌsɪprə'keɪʃn] *n* **: in ~ for** en retour de ▪ **his ~ of her feelings was clear** il était clair que leurs sentiments étaient réciproques.

reciprocity [ˌresɪ'prɒsətɪ] *n* réciprocité *f*.

recital [rɪ'saɪtl] *n* **1.** MUS & LIT récital *m* ▪ **piano/poetry ~** récital de piano/poésie **2.** [narrative] narration *f*, relation *f* ▪ [of details] énumération *f*.

recitation [ˌresɪ'teɪʃn] *n* récitation *f*.

recite [rɪ'saɪt] ◇ *vt* [play, poem] réciter, déclamer ▪ [details, facts] réciter, énumérer.
◇ *vi* réciter ▪ *US* SCH réciter sa leçon.

reckless ['reklɪs] *adj* **1.** [rash] imprudent ▪ [thoughtless] irréfléchi ▪ [fearless] téméraire ▪ **to make a ~ promise** s'engager à la légère **2.** ADMIN & LAW **: ~ driving** conduite *f* imprudente ▪ **~ driver** conducteur *m* imprudent, conductrice *f* imprudente.

recklessly ['reklɪslɪ] *adv* [rashly] imprudemment ▪ [thoughtlessly] sans réfléchir ▪ [fearlessly] avec témérité ▪ **to spend ~** dépenser sans compter ▪ **he drives very ~** il conduit dangereusement.

recklessness ['reklɪsnɪs] *n* [rashness] imprudence *f* ▪ [thoughtlessness] insouciance *f*, étourderie *f* ▪ [fearlessness] témérité *f*.

reckon ['rekn] ◇ *vt* **1.** [estimate] **: there were ~ed to be about fifteen hundred demonstrators** on a estimé à mille cinq cents le nombre des manifestants **2.** [consider] considérer ▪ **I ~ this restaurant to be the best in town** je considère ce restaurant comme le meilleur de la ville ▪ **I don't ~ her chances much** *inf* je ne crois pas qu'elle ait beaucoup de chances **3.** *inf* [suppose, think] croire, supposer ▪ **I ~ you're right** je crois bien que tu as raison ▪ **how old do you ~ he is?** quel âge lui donnez-vous? ▪ **what do you ~?** qu'en pensez-vous? **4.** [expect] compter, penser **5.** *fml* [calculate] calculer.
◇ *vi* [calculate] calculer, compter.

◆ **reckon in** *vt sep* *UK* compter, inclure.

◆ **reckon on** *vt insep* **1.** [rely on] compter sur ▪ **don't ~ on it** n'y comptez pas **2.** [expect] s'attendre à, espérer ▪ **I was ~ing on more** je m'attendais à plus ▪ **I didn't ~ on that extra cost** je n'avais pas prévu ces frais supplémentaires.

◆ **reckon up** ◇ *vt sep* [bill, total, cost] calculer.
◇ *vi insep* faire ses comptes ▪ **to ~ up with sb** régler ses comptes avec qqn.

◆ **reckon with** *vt insep* **1.** [take into account] tenir compte de, songer à ▪ **they didn't ~ with the army/the opposition** ils ont compté sans l'armée/l'opposition ▮ [as opponent] avoir affaire à ▪ **you'll have to ~ with his brother** il faudra compter avec son frère **2.** [cope with] compter avec.

◆ **reckon without** *vt insep* *UK* **1.** [do without] se passer de, se débrouiller sans **2.** *inf* [ignore, overlook] **: he ~ed without the gold price** il n'a pas pris en compte le cours de l'or.

reckoning ['rekənɪŋ] *n* **1.** *(U)* [calculation] calcul *m*, compte *m* ▪ **on** *OR* **by my ~, you owe us £50** d'après mes calculs, vous nous devez 50 livres ▪ **in the final ~** en fin de compte **2.** [estimation] estimation *f* ▪ [opinion] avis *m* ▪ **to the best of my ~** pour autant que je puisse en juger ▪ **by** *OR* **on any ~ she's a fine pianist** personne ne niera que c'est une excellente pianiste **3.** NAUT estime *f*.

reclaim [rɪ'kleɪm] <> *vt* **1.** [land - gen] mettre en valeur ▪ **they have ~ed 1,000 hectares of land from the forest/marshes** ils ont défriché 1 000 hectares de forêt/asséché 1 000 hectares de marais ▪ **they have ~ed 1,000 hectares of land from the sea/the desert** ils ont gagné 1 000 hectares de terres sur la mer/le désert **2.** [salvage] récupérer ▪ [recycle] recycler **3.** [deposit, baggage] récupérer, réclamer **4.** *lit* [sinner, drunkard] ramener dans le droit chemin.
<> *n* : **to be past** *OR* **beyond ~** être irrécupérable.

reclaimable [rɪ'kleɪməbl] *adj* [land] amendable ▪ [waste - for salvage] récupérable ; [- for recycling] recyclable.

reclamation [,reklə'meɪʃn] *n* **1.** [of land - gen] remise *f* en valeur ; [- from forest] défrichement *m* ; [- from sea, marsh] assèchement *m*, drainage *m* ; [- from desert] reconquête *f* **2.** [salvage] récupération *f* ▪ [recycling] recyclage *m*.

reclassify [,riː'klæsɪfaɪ] (*pret & pp* **reclassified**) *vt* reclasser.

recline [rɪ'klaɪn] <> *vt* **1.** [head] appuyer **2.** [seat] baisser, incliner.
<> *vi* **1.** [be stretched out] être allongé, être étendu ▪ [lie back] s'allonger **2.** [seat] être inclinable, avoir un dossier inclinable.

reclining [rɪ'klaɪnɪŋ] *adj* [seat] inclinable, à dossier inclinable ▪ **~ chair** chaise *f* longue.

recluse [rɪ'kluːs] *n* reclus *m*, - e *f* ▪ **to live like a ~** vivre en reclus *OR* en ermite ▪ **she's a bit of a ~** elle aime la solitude.

recognition [,rekəg'nɪʃn] *n* **1.** [identification] reconnaissance *f* ▪ **the town has changed beyond** *OR* **out of all ~** la ville est méconnaissable ▪ **she's changed him beyond** *OR* **out of all ~** elle l'a changé du tout au tout ➋ **optical/speech/character ~** COMPUT reconnaissance optique/de la parole/de caractères **2.** [acknowledgment, thanks] reconnaissance *f* ▪ **in ~ of** en reconnaissance de **3.** [appreciation] : **to win** *OR* **to achieve ~** être (enfin) reconnu ▪ **to seek ~ (for o.s.)** chercher à être reconnu ▪ **his play received little ~** sa pièce est passée quasi inaperçue ▪ **public ~** la reconnaissance du public **4.** [realization - of problem] reconnaissance *f* **5.** [of state, organization, trade union] reconnaissance *f*.

recognizable ['rekəgnaɪzəbl] *adj* reconnaissable.

recognizably ['rekəgnaɪzəblɪ] *adv* d'une manière *OR* façon reconnaissable ▪ **the car was not ~ Japanese** on n'aurait pas dit une voiture japonaise, cette voiture ne ressemblait pas à une voiture japonaise.

recognize, ise ['rekəgnaɪz] *vt* **1.** [identify - person, place etc] reconnaître ▪ **you'll ~ him by his hat** vous le reconnaîtrez à son chapeau ▪ COMPUT reconnaître **2.** [acknowledge - person] reconnaître les talents de ; [- achievement] reconnaître **3.** [be aware of, admit] reconnaître ▪ **I ~ (that) I made a mistake** je reconnais *OR* j'admets que je me suis trompé ▪ **the scale of the disaster has finally been ~d** on a fini par se rendre compte de l'étendue du désastre **4.** ADMIN & POL [state, diploma] reconnaître **5.** *US* [in debate] donner la parole à.

recognized ['rekəgnaɪzd] *adj* [acknowledged] reconnu, admis ▪ **she's a ~ authority on medieval history** c'est une autorité en histoire médiévale ▮ [identified] reconnu ▪ [official] officiel, attitré.

recoil <> *vi* [rɪ'kɔɪl] **1.** [person] reculer ▪ **she ~ed in horror** horrifiée, elle recula ▪ **to ~ from doing sthg** reculer devant l'idée de faire qqch **2.** [firearm] reculer ▪ [spring] se détendre.
<> *n* ['riːkɔɪl] **1.** [of gun] recul *m* ▪ [of spring] détente *f* **2.** [of person] mouvement *m* de recul ▪ *fig* répugnance *f*.

recollect [,rekə'lekt] *vt* se souvenir de, se rappeler ▪ **I don't ~ having asked her** je ne me rappelle pas le lui avoir demandé ▪ **as far as I (can) ~** autant que je m'en souvienne, autant qu'il m'en souvienne.

recollection [,rekə'lekʃn] *n* [memory] souvenir *m* ▪ **I have no ~ of it** je n'en ai aucun souvenir ▪ **to the best of my ~** (pour) autant que je m'en souvienne.

recombinant [riː'kɒmbɪnənt] *adj* : **~ DNA** ADN *m* recombinant.

recombination [,riːkɒmbɪ'neɪʃn] *n* BIOL & PHYS recombinaison *f*.

recommence [,riːkə'mens] *vi & vt* recommencer.

recommend [,rekə'mend] *vt* **1.** [speak in favour of] recommander ▪ **she ~ed him for the job** elle l'a recommandé pour cet emploi ▪ **I'll ~ you to the Minister** j'appuyerai votre candidature auprès du ministre ▮ [think or speak well of] recommander ▪ **it's a restaurant I can thoroughly ~** c'est un restaurant que je recommande vivement ▪ **the town has little to ~ it** la ville est sans grand intérêt **2.** [advise] recommander, conseiller ▪ **I ~ you (to) see the film** je vous recommande *OR* conseille d'aller voir ce film ▪ **not (to be) ~ed** à déconseiller **3.** *arch & fml* [entrust] recommander.

recommendable [,rekə'mendəbl] *adj* recommandable.

recommendation [,rekəmen'deɪʃn] *n* [personal] recommandation *f* ▪ **on your/his ~** sur votre/sa recommandation ▮ [of committee, advisory body] recommandation *f* ▪ **to make a ~** faire une recommandation.

recommended retail price [,rekə'mendɪd-] *n* prix *m* de vente conseillé.

recompense ['rekəmpens] <> *n* **1.** [reward] récompense *f* ▪ **in ~ for your trouble** en récompense de *OR* pour vous récompenser de votre peine **2.** LAW [compensation] dédommagement *m*, compensation *f*.
<> *vt* récompenser ▪ **to ~ sb for sthg** [gen] récompenser qqn de qqch ; LAW dédommager qqn de *OR* pour qqch.

recompose [,riːkəm'pəʊz] *vt* **1.** [text] réécrire ▪ [print] recomposer **2.** [calm] : **to ~ o.s.** se ressaisir.

reconcilable ['rekənsaɪləbl] *adj* [opinions] conciliable, compatible ▪ [people] compatible.

reconcile ['rekənsaɪl] *vt* **1.** [people] réconcilier ▪ [ideas, opposing principles] concilier ▪ **Peter and Jane are ~d at last** Peter et Jane se sont enfin réconciliés **2.** [resign] : **to ~ o.s.** *OR* **to become ~d to sthg** se résigner à qqch ▪ **she ~d herself to the idea of going** elle s'est faite à l'idée de partir **3.** [win over] : **to ~ sb to sthg** faire accepter qqch à qqn **4.** [settle - dispute] régler, arranger.

reconciliation [,rekənsɪlɪ'eɪʃn] *n* [between people] réconciliation *f* ▪ [between ideas] conciliation *f*, compatibilité *f*.

recondite ['rekəndaɪt] *adj fml* [taste] ésotérique ▪ [text, style] abscons, obscur ▪ [writer] obscur.

recondition [,riːkən'dɪʃn] *vt* remettre en état *OR* à neuf.

reconditioned [,riːkən'dɪʃnd] *adj* remis à neuf ▪ *UK* [tyre] rechapé ▪ **~ engine** AUT (moteur *m*) échange *m* standard.

reconfirm [,riːkən'fɜːm] *vt* [booking] confirmer ▪ [opinion, decision] réaffirmer.

reconnaissance [rɪ'kɒnɪsəns] *n* MIL reconnaissance *f* ▪ **~ flight** vol *m* de reconnaissance.

reconnect [,riːkə'nekt] *vt* rebrancher ▪ TELEC reconnecter.

reconnoitre *UK*, **reconnoiter** *US* [,rekə'nɔɪtər] <> *vt* MIL reconnaître.
<> *vi* effectuer une reconnaissance.

reconquer [,riː'kɒŋkər] *vt* reconquérir.

reconsider [,riːkən'sɪdər] <> *vt* [decision, problem] réexaminer ▪ [topic] se repencher sur ▪ [judgment] réviser, revoir.
<> *vi* reconsidérer la question ▪ **I advise you to ~** je vous conseille de revoir votre position.

reconsideration ['riːkən,sɪdə'reɪʃn] *n* [reexamination] nouvel examen *m*, nouveau regard *m* ▪ [of judgment] révision *f*.

reconstitute [,riː'kɒnstɪtjuːt] *vt* reconstituer.

reconstituted [,riː'kɒnstɪtjuːtɪd] *adj* reconstitué.

reconstruct [,riːkən'strʌkt] *vt* [house, bridge] reconstruire, rebâtir ▪ [crime, event] reconstituer ▪ [government, system] reconstituer.

reconstruction [ˌri:kən'strʌkʃn] *n* [of demolished building] reconstruction *f* ■ [of old building] reconstitution *f* ■ [of façade, shop] réfection *f* ■ [of crime, event] reconstitution *f* ■ [of government] reconstitution *f* ■ **the Reconstruction** *US* HIST la Reconstruction.

THE RECONSTRUCTION

Période allant de 1865 à 1877, succédant à la guerre de Sécession et pendant laquelle les États de l'ex-Confédération (États sudistes) étaient réintégrés dans l'Union s'ils avaient adopté les amendements à la Constitution fédérale qui reconnaissaient les droits des Noirs et interdisaient aux confédérés toute activité politique et administrative.

reconvene [ˌri:kən'vi:n] ◇ *vt* reconvoquer.
◇ *vi* : **the meeting ~s at three** la réunion reprend à trois heures.

record ◇ *vt* [rɪ'kɔ:d] **1.** [take note of - fact, complaint, detail] noter, enregistrer ; [- in archives, on computer] enregistrer ■ **your objection has been ~ed** nous avons pris acte de votre objection ■ **to ~ the minutes** *OR* **the proceedings of a meeting** ADMIN faire le procès-verbal *OR* le compte rendu d'une réunion ■ [attest, give account of] attester, rapporter ■ **a photograph was taken to ~ the event** une photographie a été prise pour rappeler cet événement ■ **the book ~s life in medieval England** le livre dépeint *OR* évoque la vie en Angleterre au Moyen Âge ■ **how many votes were ~ed?** POL combien de voix ont été exprimées? ▮ [explain, tell] raconter, rapporter
2. [indicate - measurement] indiquer ; [- permanently] enregistrer ■ **temperatures of 50° were ~ed** on a relevé des températures de 50°
3. [music, tape, TV programme] enregistrer
4. SPORT [score] marquer ■ **he ~ed a time of 10.7 seconds for the 100 metres** il a couru le 100 m en 10.7 secondes.
◇ *vi* [rɪ'kɔ:d] [on tape, video] enregistrer ■ **leave the video, it's ~ing** laisse le magnétoscope, il est en train d'enregistrer.
◇ *n* ['rekɔ:d] **1.** [account, report] rapport *m* ■ [note] note *f* ■ [narrative] récit *m* ■ **to make a ~ of sthg** noter qqch ■ **to strike sthg from the ~** rayer qqch du procès-verbal ■ **they keep a ~ of all deposits/all comings and goings** ils enregistrent tous les versements/toutes les allées et venues ■ **the book provides a ~ of 19th-century Parisian society** le livre évoque la société parisienne au XIXe siècle ▮ [testimony] témoignage *m* ■ [evidence] preuve *f* ■ **there is no ~ of their visit** il n'existe aucune trace de leur visite ■ **do you have any ~ of the transaction?** avez-vous gardé une trace de la transaction? ■ **there's no ~ of it anywhere** ce n'est mentionné nulle part ▮ [from instrument] trace *f* ■ [graph] courbe *f* ➊ **to put** *OR* **to set the ~ straight** mettre les choses au clair
2. [past history] passé *m* ■ [file] dossier *m* ■ **she has an excellent attendance ~** elle a été très assidue, elle n'a presque jamais été absente ■ **the plane has a good safety ~** l'avion est réputé pour sa sécurité ▮ [criminal or police file] casier *m* (judiciaire) ■ **to have a ~** avoir un casier judiciaire ■ **he has a ~ of previous convictions** il a déjà été condamné ▮ [reputation] réputation *f* ➊ **case ~** MED dossier *m* médical ; LAW dossier *m* judiciaire ■ **service** *OR* **army ~** MIL états *mpl* de service ■ **school ~** dossier *m* scolaire
3. [disc] disque *m* ■ [recording] enregistrement *m* ■ **to make** *OR* **to cut a ~** faire *OR* graver un disque
4. [gen - SPORT] record *m* ■ **to set/to break a ~** établir/battre un record ■ **the 200 m ~** le record du 200 m
5. COMPUT enregistrement *m*.
◇ *comp* ['rekɔ:d] **1.** [company, label, producer, shop] de disques **2.** [summer, temperature] record *(inv)* ■ **in ~ time** en un temps record ■ **to reach ~ levels** atteindre un niveau record ■ **a ~ number of spectators** une affluence record.
◆ **records** *npl* [of government, police, hospital] archives *fpl* ■ [of history] annales *fpl* ■ [of conference, learned society] actes *mpl* ■ [register] registre *m* ■ [of proceedings, debate] procès-verbal *m*, compte rendu *m* ■ **the wettest June since ~s began** le mois de juin le plus humide depuis que l'on tient des statistiques ➊ **public ~s office** archives *fpl* nationales.
◆ **for the record** *adv phr* pour mémoire, pour la petite histoire ■ **just for the ~, you started it!** je te signale au passage que c'est toi qui as commencé!
◆ **off the record** ◇ *adj phr* confidentiel ■ **the negotiations were off the ~** [secret] les négociations étaient secrètes ; [unofficial] les négociations étaient officieuses ; [not reported] les négociations n'ont pas été rapportées (dans la presse) ; [not recorded] les négociations n'ont pas été enregistrées ■ **all this is strictly off the ~** *fig* tout ceci doit rester strictement entre nous.
◇ *adv phr* : **he admitted off the ~ that he had known** il a admis en privé qu'il était au courant.
◆ **on record** *adv phr* enregistré ■ **it's on ~ that you were informed** il est établi que vous étiez au courant ■ **we have it on ~ that...** il est attesté *OR* établi que... ■ **it isn't on ~** il n'y en a aucune trace ■ **I wish to go on ~ as saying that...** je voudrais dire officiellement *OR* publiquement que... ■ **it's the wettest June on ~** c'est le mois de juin le plus humide que l'on ait connu ■ **it's the only example on ~** c'est le seul exemple connu.

record-breaker *n* SPORT nouveau recordman *m*, nouvelle recordwoman *f* ■ **the new product is a ~** *UK fig* le nouveau produit bat tous les records.

record-breaking *adj* **1.** SPORT : **a ~ jump** un saut qui a établi un nouveau record **2.** [year, temperatures] record *(inv)*.

record deck *n* platine *f* (tourne-disque).

recorded [rɪ'kɔ:dɪd] *adj* **1.** [music, message, tape] enregistré ■ [programme] préenregistré ■ [broadcast] transmis en différé **2.** [fact] attesté, noté ■ [history] écrit ■ [votes] exprimé ■ **throughout ~ history** pendant toute la période couverte par les écrits historiques.

recorded delivery *n UK* recommandé *m* ■ **to send (by) ~** envoyer en recommandé avec accusé de réception.

recorder [rɪ'kɔ:dəʳ] *n* **1.** [apparatus] enregistreur *m* **2.** [musical instrument] flûte *f* à bec **3.** [keeper of records] archiviste *mf* ■ **court ~** LAW greffier *m* **4.** *UK* LAW *avocat nommé à la fonction de magistrat (à temps partiel)*.

record holder *n* recordman *m*, recordwoman *f*, détenteur *m*, - trice *f* d'un record.

recording [rɪ'kɔ:dɪŋ] ◇ *n* [of music, data] enregistrement *m* ■ **a mono ~** un enregistrement (en) mono.
◇ *comp* **1.** MUS & TV [equipment, session, studio] d'enregistrement ■ [company] de disques ■ [star] du disque ■ **she's a ~ artist for Phonolog** elle enregistre (des disques) chez Phonolog **2.** [indicating - apparatus] enregistreur **3.** ADMIN & LAW [official, clerk - in census] chargé du recensement ; [- in court of law] qui enregistre les débats.

recording head *n* tête *f* d'enregistrement.

recording studio *n* studio *m* d'enregistrement.

record library *n* discothèque *f (de prêt)*.

record player *n* tourne-disque *m*, platine *f* (disques).

record token *n* chèque-disque *m*.

recount [rɪ'kaʊnt] *vt* [story, experience] raconter.

re-count ◇ *vt* [ˌri:'kaʊnt] [count again] recompter, compter de nouveau.
◇ *n* ['ri:kaʊnt] POL nouveau décompte *m* ■ **to demand a ~** exiger un nouveau décompte ■ **there were four ~s** on a compté le nombre de bulletins de vote à quatre reprises.

recoup [rɪ'ku:p] *vt* **1.** [get back - losses, cost] récupérer ■ **to ~ one's investments** rentrer dans ses fonds ■ **to ~ one's costs** rentrer dans *OR* couvrir ses frais **2.** [pay back] rembourser, dédommager **3.** [from taxes] défalquer, déduire.

recourse [rɪ'kɔ:s] *n* **1.** [gen] recours *m* ■ **to have ~ to sthg** recourir à qqch, avoir recours à qqch **2.** FIN recours *m*.

recover [rɪ'kʌvəʳ] ◇ *vt* **1.** [get back - property] récupérer, retrouver ; [- debt, loan, deposit] récupérer, recouvrer ■ [take back] reprendre ■ **to ~ sthg from sb** reprendre qqch à qqn ▮ [regain - territory, ball] regagner ; [- composure, control, hearing] retrouver ; [- advantage] reprendre ■ **to ~ one's breath/footing** reprendre haleine/pied ■ **to ~ one's senses** se ressaisir ■ **to ~ consciousness** reprendre connaissance ■ **to ~ one's strength** reprendre des forces ■ **to ~ lost ground** *liter & fig* regagner du terrain

2. [salvage - wreck, waste] récupérer ; [- from water] récupérer, repêcher
3. LAW : **to ~ damages** obtenir des dommages-intérêts
4. [extract - from ore] extraire.
<> *vi* **1.** [after accident] se remettre ■ [after illness] se rétablir, guérir ■ **to ~ from sthg** se remettre de qqch ■ **to be fully ~ed** être complètement guéri *OR* rétabli ‖ [after surprise, setback] se remettre ■ **I still haven't ~ed from the shock** je ne me suis pas encore remis du choc
2. [currency, economy] se redresser ■ [market] reprendre, se redresser ■ [prices, shares] se redresser, remonter
3. LAW gagner son procès, obtenir gain de cause.

re-cover [ˌriːˈkʌvəʳ] *vt* recouvrir.

recoverable [rɪˈkʌvrəbl] *adj* [debt] recouvrable ■ [losses, mistake] réparable ■ [by-product] récupérable.

recovery [rɪˈkʌvərɪ] (*pl* **recoveries**) *n* **1.** [of lost property, wreck] récupération *f* ■ [of debt] recouvrement *m*, récupération *f* **2.** [from illness] rétablissement *m*, guérison *f* ■ **to make a speedy ~** se remettre vite **3.** [of economy] relance *f*, redressement *m* ■ [of prices, shares] redressement *m*, remontée *f* ■ [of currency] redressement *m* ■ [of market, business] reprise *f* ■ **to stage** *OR* **to make a ~** SPORT reprendre le dessus ■ **the country made a slow ~ after the war** le pays s'est rétabli lentement après la guerre ■ **to be past** *OR* **beyond ~** [situation] être irrémédiable *OR* sans espoir ; [loss] être irrécupérable *OR* irréparable **4.** [of wreck, waste] récupération *f* ■ [from water] récupération *f*, repêchage *m* **5.** COMPUT [of files] récupération *f* **6.** LAW [of damages] obtention *f*.

recovery position *n* MED position *f* latérale de sécurité.

recovery room *n* MED salle *f* de réanimation.

recovery vehicle *n* *UK* dépanneuse *f*.

re-create [ˌriːkrɪˈeɪt] *vt* [past event] reconstituer ■ [place, scene] recréer.

recreation [ˌrekrɪˈeɪʃn] *n* **1.** [relaxation] récréation *f*, détente *f* **2.** SCH récréation *f*.

re-creation *n* [of event, scene] recréation *f*, reconstitution *f*.

recreational [ˌrekrɪˈeɪʃənl] *adj* de loisir ■ **~ drug** drogue *f* douce.

recreational vehicle *US* = **RV**.

recreation ground *n* terrain *m* de jeux.

recreation room *n* [in school, hospital] salle *f* de récréation ■ [in hotel] salle *f* de jeux ■ *US* [at home] salle *f* de jeux.

recriminate [rɪˈkrɪmɪneɪt] *vt fml* récriminer ■ **to ~ against sb** récriminer contre qqn.

recrimination [rɪˌkrɪmɪˈneɪʃn] *n (usu pl)* **~s** récriminations *fpl*.

recrudescent [ˌriːkruːˈdesnt] *adj fml* recrudescent.

recruit [rɪˈkruːt] <> *n* [gen - MIL] recrue *f*.
<> *vt* [member, army] recruter ■ [worker] recruter, embaucher.

recruiting [rɪˈkruːtɪŋ] *n* recrutement *m*.

recruiting office *n* bureau *m* de recrutement.

recruitment [rɪˈkruːtmənt] *n* recrutement *m* ■ **~ campaign** campagne *f* de recrutement.

rectal [ˈrektəl] *adj* rectal.

rectangle [ˈrekˌtæŋgl] *n* rectangle *m*.

rectangular [rekˈtæŋgjʊləʳ] *adj* rectangulaire.

rectifiable [ˈrektɪfaɪəbl] *adj* [gen - CHEM] & MATHS rectifiable, qui peut être rectifié ■ ELEC qui peut être redressé.

rectification [ˌrektɪfɪˈkeɪʃn] *n* **1.** [correction] rectification *f*, correction *f* **2.** CHEM & MATHS rectification *f* ■ ELEC redressement *m*.

rectify [ˈrektɪfaɪ] (*pret & pp* **rectified**) *vt* **1.** [mistake] rectifier, corriger ■ [oversight] réparer ■ [situation] redresser **2.** CHEM & MATHS rectifier ■ ELEC redresser.

rectilinear [ˌrektɪˈlɪnɪəʳ] *adj* rectiligne.

rectitude [ˈrektɪtjuːd] *n* rectitude *f* ■ **moral ~** droiture *f*.

recto [ˈrektəʊ] (*pl* **rectos**) *n* PRINT recto *m*.

rector [ˈrektəʳ] *n* **1.** RELIG [Anglican, Presbyterian] pasteur *m* ■ [Catholic] recteur *m* **2.** *UK* SCH proviseur *mf*, directeur *m*, - trice *f* **3.** *Scotland* UNIV président *m*, - e *f* d'honneur.

rectory [ˈrektərɪ] (*pl* **rectories**) *n* presbytère *m*.

rectum [ˈrektəm] (*pl* **rectums** *OR pl* **recta** [-tə]) *n* rectum *m*.

recumbent [rɪˈkʌmbənt] *adj lit* couché, étendu, allongé ■ **~ figure** ART figure *f* couchée, gisant *m*.

recuperate [rɪˈkuːpəreɪt] <> *vi* se remettre, récupérer ■ [after illness] se rétablir ■ **to ~ from sthg** se remettre de qqch.
<> *vt* [materials, money] récupérer ■ [loss] compenser ■ [strength] reprendre.

recuperation [rɪˌkuːpəˈreɪʃn] *n* **1.** MED rétablissement *m* **2.** [of materials] récupération *f* **3.** FIN [of market] reprise *f*.

recuperative [rɪˈkuːpərətɪv] *adj* [medicine] régénérateur, reconstituant ■ [rest] réparateur ■ [powers] de récupération.

recur [rɪˈkɜːʳ] (*pret & pp* **recurred**, *cont* **recurring**) *vi* **1.** [occur again] se reproduire ■ [reappear] réapparaître, revenir ■ **it's a notion which ~s every now and then** c'est une idée qui revient *OR* qu'on retrouve de temps en temps **2.** [to memory] revenir à la mémoire **3.** MATHS se reproduire, se répéter.

recurrence [rɪˈkʌrəns] *n* [of mistake, notion, event] répétition *f* ■ [of disease, symptoms] réapparition *f* ■ [of subject, problem] retour *m*.

recurrent [rɪˈkʌrənt] *adj* **1.** [repeated] récurrent ■ **I get ~ headaches/bouts of flu** j'ai souvent des maux de tête/la grippe ■ **~ expenses** [gen] dépenses *fpl* courantes ; COMM frais *mpl* généraux **2.** ANAT & MED récurrent.

recurring [rɪˈkɜːrɪŋ] *adj* **1.** [persistent - problem] qui revient *OR* qui se reproduit souvent ; [- dream, nightmare] qui revient sans cesse **2.** MATHS périodique.

recursive [rɪˈkɜːsɪv] *adj* récursif.

recyclable [ˌriːˈsaɪkləbl] *adj* recyclable.

recycle [ˌriːˈsaɪkl] *vt* [materials] recycler ■ [money] réinvestir.

recycle bin *n* COMPUT poubelle *f*, corbeille *f*.

recycled [ˌriːˈsaɪkld] *adj* [materials] recyclé.

recycling [ˌriːˈsaɪklɪŋ] *n* recyclage *m*.

red [red] (*comp* **redder**, *superl* **reddest**) <> *adj* **1.** [gen] rouge ■ [hair] roux, rousse *f* ■ **to go ~** rougir ■ **~ with anger/shame** rouge de colère/honte ■ **to take a ~ pen to sthg** corriger qqch à l'encre rouge ■ **to be ~ in the face** [after effort] avoir la figure toute rouge ; [with embarrassment] être rouge de confusion ➊ **to go into ~ ink** *US* [person] être à découvert ; [company] être en déficit ■ **to be as ~ as a beetroot** être rouge comme une pivoine *OR* une écrevisse ■ **'(Little) Red Riding Hood'** ***Perrault*** 'le Petit Chaperon rouge' **2.** *inf* POL rouge.
<> *n* **1.** [colour] rouge *m* ■ **dressed in ~** habillé en rouge ➊ **to see ~** voir rouge **2.** [in roulette] rouge *m* ■ [in snooker] (bille *f*) rouge *f* **3.** [wine] rouge *m* **4.** *inf pej* [communist] rouge *mf*, coco *mf pej* ■ **~s under the bed** *expression évoquant la psychose du communisme* **5.** [deficit] : **to be in the ~** être dans le rouge ■ **to be £5,000 in the ~** [company] avoir un déficit de 5 000 livres ; [person] avoir un découvert de 5 000 livres ■ **to get out of the ~** [company] sortir du rouge ; [person] combler son découvert.

red admiral *n* ENTOM vulcain *m*.

red alert *n* alerte *f* rouge ■ **to be on ~** être en état d'alerte maximale.

red ant *n* fourmi *f* rouge.

Red Army *pr n* Armée *f* rouge.

red blood cell *n* globule *m* rouge, hématie *f*.

red-blooded [-ˈblʌdɪd] *adj inf* vigoureux, viril.

redbreast [ˈredbrest] *n* rouge-gorge *m*.

red-brick *adj UK* [building] en brique rouge.

redbrick university ['redbrɪk-] *n en Angleterre, ce terme désigne les universités de création relativement récente par opposition à Oxford et Cambridge.*

redcap ['redkæp] *n* **1.** *UK inf* MIL policier *m* militaire **2.** *US* RAIL porteur *m*.

red card *n* SPORT carton *m* rouge.

red carpet *n* tapis *m* rouge ■ **to roll out the ~ for sb** [for VIP] dérouler le tapis rouge en l'honneur de qqn ; [for guest] mettre les petits plats dans les grands en l'honneur de qqn ■ **to give sb the red-carpet treatment** réserver un accueil fastueux *OR* princier à qqn.

red cent *n US inf* **it's not worth a ~** ça ne vaut pas un clou *OR* un centime.

Red China *pr n inf* Chine *f* communiste *OR* populaire.

redcoat ['redkəʊt] *n UK* **1.** HIST soldat *m* anglais **2.** [in holiday camp] animateur *m*, - trice *f*.

red corpuscle *n* globule *m* rouge, hématie *f*.

Red Crescent *pr n* Croissant-Rouge *m*.

Red Cross (Society) *pr n* Croix-Rouge *f*.

redcurrant ['redkʌrənt] *n* groseille *f* (rouge) ■ **~ bush** groseillier *m* rouge ■ **~ jelly** gelée *f* de groseille.

red deer *n* cerf *m* commun.

redden ['redn] ◇ *vt* rougir, rendre rouge ■ [hair] teindre en roux.
◇ *vi* [person, face] rougir, devenir (tout) rouge ■ [leaves] devenir roux, roussir ■ **to ~ with shame** rougir de honte.

redecorate [ˌriː'dekəreɪt] ◇ *vt* [gen - room, house] refaire ■ [repaint] refaire les peintures de ■ [re-wallpaper] retapisser.
◇ *vi* [repaint] refaire les peintures ■ [re-wallpaper] refaire les papiers peints.

redecoration [riːˌdekə'reɪʃn] *n* [painting] remise *f* à neuf des peintures ■ [wallpapering] remise *f* à neuf des papiers peints.

redeem [rɪ'diːm] *vt* **1.** [from pawn] dégager, retirer **2.** [cash - voucher] encaisser ; [- bond, share] réaliser ■ [exchange - coupon, savings stamps] échanger ; [- banknote] compenser **3.** [pay - debt] rembourser, s'acquitter de ; [- bill] honorer ; [- loan, mortgage] rembourser **4.** [make up for - mistake, failure] racheter, réparer ; [- crime, sin] expier ■ **to ~ o.s.** se racheter **5.** [save - situation, position] sauver ; [- loss] récupérer, réparer ; [- honour] sauver ■ RELIG [sinner] racheter **6.** [fulfil - promise] s'acquitter de, tenir ; [- obligation] satisfaire à, s'acquitter de **7.** [free - slave] affranchir.

redeemable [rɪ'diːməbl] *adj* **1.** [voucher] remboursable ■ [debt] remboursable, amortissable ■ **the stamps are not ~ for cash** les timbres ne peuvent être échangés contre des espèces **2.** [error] réparable ■ [sin, crime] expiable, rachetable ■ [sinner] rachetable.

redeemer [rɪ'diːmə^r] *n* RELIG & *fig* rédempteur *m*.

redeeming [rɪ'diːmɪŋ] *adj* [characteristic, feature] qui rachète *OR* compense les défauts ■ **his one ~ feature** sa seule qualité, la seule chose qui le rachète.

redefine [ˌriːdɪ'faɪn] *vt* [restate - objectives, terms] redéfinir ■ [modify] modifier.

redemption [rɪ'dempʃn] *n* **1.** [from pawn] dégagement *m* **2.** [of debt, loan, mortgage, voucher] remboursement *m* ■ ST. EX [of shares] liquidation *f* ■ **~ yield** rendement *m* à l'échéance **3.** [gen - RELIG] rédemption *f*, rachat *m* ■ **past** *OR* **beyond ~** [person] perdu à tout jamais, qui ne peut être racheté ; [situation, position] irrémédiable, irrécupérable ; [book, furniture] irréparable, irrécupérable.

Red Ensign *n pavillon de la marine marchande britannique.*

redeploy [ˌriːdɪ'plɔɪ] *vt* [troops, forces, resources] redéployer ■ [workers] reconvertir.

redesign [ˌriːdɪ'zaɪn] *vt* [plan of room, garden etc] redessiner ■ [layout of furniture, rooms etc] réagencer ■ [system] repenser ■ [book cover, poster etc] refaire le design de.

redevelop [ˌriːdɪ'veləp] *vt* **1.** [region] réexploiter, revitaliser ■ [urban area] rénover, reconstruire ■ [tourism, industry] relancer **2.** [argument] réexposer **3.** PHOT redévelopper.

redeye ['redaɪ] *n US inf* [night flight] vol *m* de nuit.

red eye *n (U)* PHOT *phénomène provoquant l'apparition de taches rouges dans les yeux des personnes photographiées au flash.*

red-eyed *adj* aux yeux rouges.

red-faced [-'feɪst] *adj liter* rougeaud ■ *fig* rouge de confusion *OR* de honte.

red flag *n* [gen - POL] drapeau *m* rouge.
➡ **Red Flag** *n* : **the Red Flag** *hymne du parti travailliste britannique.*

red fox *n* renard *m* roux.

red giant *n* ASTRON géante *f* rouge.

red grouse *n* grouse *f*, coq *m* de bruyère écossais.

Red Guard *pr n* garde *f* rouge.

red-haired [-ˌheəd] *adj* roux, rousse *f*, aux cheveux roux ■ **a ~ girl** une rousse.

red-handed [-'hændɪd] *adv* : **to be caught ~** être pris en flagrant délit *OR* la main dans le sac.

redhead ['redhed] *n* roux *m*, rousse *f*.

red-headed = **red-haired**.

red heat *n* : **to bring** *OR* **to raise a metal to ~** chauffer *OR* porter un métal au rouge.

red herring *n* **1.** *fig* diversion *f* ■ **it's just a ~** ce n'est qu'un truc pour nous dépister *OR* pour brouiller les pistes **2.** CULIN hareng *m* saur.

red-hot *adj* **1.** [metal] chauffé au rouge **2.** [very hot] brûlant **3.** *inf fig* [keen] passionné, enthousiaste **4.** *inf* [recent - news, information] de dernière minute **5.** *inf* [sure - tip, favourite] certain, sûr **6.** *inf* [expert] calé **7.** *inf* [sensational - scandal, story] croustillant, sensationnel.

red-hot poker *n* BOT tritoma *m*.

redial [ˌriː'daɪəl] ◇ *vt* : **to ~ a number** refaire un numéro.
◇ *n* : **automatic ~** système *m* de rappel du dernier numéro.

redid [ˌriː'dɪd] *pt* ▷ **redo**.

Red Indian *n* Peau-Rouge *mf*.

redirect [ˌriːdɪ'rekt] *vt* **1.** [mail] faire suivre, réexpédier ■ [aeroplane, traffic] dérouter ■ **the plane was ~ed to Oslo** l'avion a été dérouté sur Oslo **2.** *fig* [efforts, attentions] réorienter.

rediscover [ˌriːdɪ'skʌvə^r] *vt* redécouvrir.

rediscovery [ˌriːdɪ'skʌvrɪ] (*pl* **rediscoveries**) *n* redécouverte *f*.

redistribute [ˌriːdɪ'strɪbjuːt] *vt* [money, wealth, objects] redistribuer ■ [tasks] réassigner.

redistribution ['riːˌdɪstrɪ'bjuːʃn] *n* redistribution *f*.

red-letter day *n* jour *m* à marquer d'une pierre blanche.

red light *n* AUT feu *m* rouge ■ **to go through a ~** passer au rouge, brûler le feu rouge.
➡ **red-light** *adj* : **red-light district** quartier *m* chaud.

red meat *n* viande *f* rouge.

redneck ['rednek] *US inf pej* ◇ *n Américain d'origine modeste qui a des idées réactionnaires et des préjugés racistes.*
◇ *comp* [attitude] de plouc, borné.

redness ['rednɪs] *n (U)* rougeur *f* ■ [of hair] rousseur *f* ■ [inflammation] rougeurs *fpl*.

redo [ˌriː'duː] (*pret* **redid** [ˌriː'dɪd], *pp* **redone** [-'dʌn]) ◇ *vt* refaire ■ [hair] recoiffer ■ [repaint] refaire, repeindre.
◇ *vi* COMPUT répéter.

redolent ['redələnt] *adj lit* **1.** [perfumed] : **~ of** *OR* **with lemon** qui sent le citron, qui a une odeur de citron **2.** [evocative, reminiscent] : **the style is ~ of James Joyce** le style rappelle celui de James Joyce.

redone [-'dʌn] *pp* ▷ **redo.**

redouble [ˌriː'dʌbl] ◇ *vt* **1.** [in intensity] redoubler **2.** CARDS surcontrer.
◇ *vi* CARDS surcontrer.
◇ *n* CARDS surcontre *m*.

redoubt [rɪ'daʊt] *n* MIL redoute *f* ▪ *fig* forteresse *f*.

redoubtable [rɪ'daʊtəbl] *adj* [formidable] redoutable, terrifiant ▪ [awe-inspiring] impressionnant.

redound [rɪ'daʊnd] *vi fml* **to ~ on** *OR* **upon sb** [negatively] retomber sur qqn ; [positively] rejaillir sur qqn ▪ **to ~ to sb's advantage** être *OR* rejaillir à l'avantage de qqn.

red pepper *n* [spice] (poivre *m* de) cayenne *m* ▪ [vegetable] poivron *m* rouge.

redraft *vt* [ˌriː'drɑːft] [bill, contract] rédiger de nouveau ▪ [demand] reformuler ▪ [text] remanier.

redraw [ˌriː'drɔː] (*pret* **redrew** [-'druː]) (*pp* **redrawn** [-'drɔːn]) *vt* redessiner.

redress [rɪ'dres] ◇ *vt* [grievance, errors] réparer ▪ [wrong] réparer, redresser ▪ [situation] rattraper ▪ **to ~ the balance** rétablir l'équilibre.
◇ *n* [gen - LAW] réparation *f* ▪ **to seek ~ for sthg** demander réparation de qqch.

redrew [-'druː] *pt* ▷ **redraw.**

Red Sea *pr n* : **the ~** la mer Rouge.

red setter *n* setter *m* irlandais.

redshank ['redʃæŋk] *n* (chevalier *m*) gambette *m*.

redskin△ ['redskɪn] *n dated* Peau-Rouge *mf (attention: le terme «redskin» est considéré comme raciste)*.

Red Square *pr n* la place Rouge.

red squirrel *n* écureuil *m* (commun d'Europe).

red tape *n* [bureaucracy] paperasserie *f* ▪ **there's too much ~** il y a trop de paperasserie *OR* de bureaucratie.

reduce [rɪ'djuːs] ◇ *vt* **1.** [risk, scale, time, workload] réduire, diminuer ▪ [temperature] abaisser ▪ [speed] réduire, ralentir ▪ [in length] réduire, raccourcir ▪ [in size] réduire, rapetisser, diminuer ▪ [in weight] réduire, alléger ▪ [in height] réduire, abaisser ▪ [in thickness] réduire, amenuiser ▪ [in strength] réduire, affaiblir ▪ **the record has been ~d by two seconds** le record a été amélioré de deux secondes ▪ **I'm trying to ~ my sugar consumption by half** j'essaie de réduire ma consommation de sucre de moitié **2.** COMM & FIN [price] baisser ▪ [rate, expenses, cost] réduire ▪ [tax] alléger, réduire ▪ [goods] solder, réduire le prix de ▪ **the shirt was ~d to £15** la chemise était soldée à 15 livres **3.** [render] : **to ~ sthg to ashes/to a pulp** réduire qqch en cendres/en bouillie ▪ **to ~ sb to silence/to tears/to poverty/to submission** réduire qqn au silence/aux larmes/à la pauvreté/à l'obéissance ▪ **we were ~d to helpless laughter** nous riions sans pouvoir nous arrêter ▪ **she was ~d to buying her own pencils** elle en était réduite à acheter ses crayons elle-même **4.** CULIN [sauce] faire réduire **5.** CHEM & MATHS réduire **6.** MED [fracture] réduire ▪ [swelling] résorber, résoudre **7.** [dilute] diluer **8.** LAW : **to ~ sthg to writing** consigner qqch par écrit **9.** MIL dégrader.
◇ *vi* **1.** CULIN réduire **2.** [slim] maigrir.

reduced [rɪ'djuːst] *adj* [price, rate, scale] réduit ▪ [goods] soldé, en solde ▪ **on a ~ scale** en plus petit ▪ **'~ to clear'** 'articles en solde' ⊙ **to be in ~ circumstances** *euph* être dans la gêne.

reducible [rɪ'djuːsəbl] *adj* réductible.

reducing [rɪ'djuːsɪŋ] *adj* CHEM & TECH réducteur ▪ [diet] amaigrissant.

reduction [rɪ'dʌkʃn] *n* **1.** [lessening - gen] réduction *f*, diminution *f* ; [- in temperature] baisse *f*, diminution *f* ; [- in length] réduction *f*, raccourcissement *m* ; [- in weight] réduction *f*, diminution *f* ; [- in strength] réduction *f*, affaiblissement *m* ; [- in speed] réduction *f*, ralentissement *m* ▪ **staff ~s** compression *f* de personnel **2.** COMM & FIN [in cost] baisse *f*, diminution *f* ▪ [in rate] baisse *f* ▪ [in expenses] réduction *f*, diminution *f* ▪ [in tax] dégrèvement *m* ▪ [on goods] rabais *m*, remise *f* ▪ **to make a 5% ~ on an article** faire une remise de 5 % sur un article ▪ **cash ~** [discount] remise *f OR* escompte *m* au comptant ; [refund] remise *f* en espèces **3.** CHEM, MATHS & PHOT réduction *f* **4.** TECH [of gear] démultiplication *f* **5.** MED [of fracture] réduction *f* ▪ [of swelling] résorption *f*.

reductionism [rɪ'dʌkʃənɪzm] *n* réductionnisme *m*.

reductive [rɪ'dʌktɪv] *adj* réducteur.

redundancy [rɪ'dʌndənsɪ] (*pl* **redundancies**) ◇ *n* **1.** *UK* [layoff] licenciement *m* ▪ [unemployment] chômage *m* ▪ **voluntary ~** départ *m* volontaire **2.** [superfluousness] caractère *m* superflu ▪ [tautology] pléonasme *m* **3.** COMPUT, LING & TELEC redondance *f*.
◇ *comp* : **~ notice** *UK* lettre *f* de licenciement ▪ **~ payment** *UK* indemnité *f* de licenciement.

redundant [rɪ'dʌndənt] *adj* **1.** INDUST licencié, au chômage ▪ **to become** *OR* **to be made ~** être licencié *OR* mis au chômage **2.** [superfluous] redondant, superflu ▪ [tautologous] pléonastique **3.** COMPUT, LING & TELEC redondant.

reduplication [rɪˌdjuːplɪ'keɪʃn] *n* redoublement *m* ▪ LING réduplication *f*.

redwing ['redwɪŋ] *n UK* mauvis *m*.

redwood ['redwʊd] *n* séquoia *m*.

re-echo [ˌriː'ekəʊ] ◇ *vt* renvoyer en écho.
◇ *vi* retentir.

reed [riːd] ◇ *n* **1.** BOT roseau *m* **2.** MUS anche *f* **3.** *phr* **he's a broken ~** on ne peut pas compter sur lui.
◇ *comp* [chair, mat] en roseau *OR* roseaux, fait de roseaux.

reed bunting *n* bruant *m* des roseaux.

reeding ['riːdɪŋ] *n* ARCHIT rudenture *f*.

reed instrument *n* instrument *m* à anche.

re-edit [ˌriː'edɪt] *vt* rééditer.

reed pipe *n* pipeau *m*, chalumeau *m*.

reed stop *n* jeu *m* d'anches.

re-educate [riː'edʒʊkeɪt] *vt* rééduquer.

re-education *n* rééducation *f*.

reed warbler *n* fauvette *f* des roseaux, rousserolle *f*.

reedy ['riːdɪ] (*comp* **reedier**, *superl* **reediest**) *adj* **1.** [place] envahi par les roseaux **2.** [sound, voice] flûté, aigu, - uë *f*.

reef [riːf] ◇ *n* **1.** [in sea] récif *m*, écueil *m* ▪ *fig* écueil *m* **2.** MIN filon *m* **3.** NAUT ris *m*.
◇ *vt* [spar] rentrer.

reefer ['riːfəʳ] *n* **1.** [garment] : **~ (jacket)** caban *m* **2.** *UK inf* [lorry] camion *m* frigorifique.

reef knot *n* nœud *m* plat.

reek [riːk] ◇ *vi* **1.** [smell] puer, empester ▪ **it ~s of tobacco in here** ça empeste *OR* pue le tabac ici **2.** *Scotland* [chimney] fumer.
◇ *n* puanteur *f*.

reel [riːl] ◇ *n* **1.** [for thread, film, tape] bobine *f* ▪ [for hose] dévidoir *m*, enrouleur *m* ▪ [for cable] enrouleur *m* ▪ [for rope-making] caret *m* ▪ **(fishing) ~** moulinet *m* (de pêche) **2.** [film, tape] bande *f*, bobine *f* **3.** [dance] quadrille *m (écossais ou irlandais)* ▪ MUS branle *m (écossais ou irlandais)*.
◇ *vi* **1.** [stagger] tituber, chanceler ▪ **the blow sent me ~ing across the room** le coup m'a envoyé valser à travers la pièce ▪ **a drunk came ~ing downstairs** un ivrogne descendait l'escalier en titubant **2.** *fig* [whirl - head, mind] tournoyer ▪ **my head is ~ing** j'ai la tête qui tourne ▪ **he is still ~ing from the shock** il ne s'est pas encore remis du choc.
◇ *vt* bobiner.

◆ **reel in** *vt sep* [cable, hose] enrouler ▪ [fish] remonter, ramener ▪ [line] enrouler, remonter.

◆ **reel off** *vt sep* [poem, speech, story] débiter.

re-elect [ˌriːɪ'lekt] *vt* réélire.

re-election [ˌriːɪ'lekʃn] *n* réélection *f* ■ **to stand** *OR* **to run for ~** se représenter aux élections.

reel-to-reel *adj* [system, tape recorder] à bobines.

re-embark [ˌriːɪm'bɑːk] *vi* & *vt* rembarquer.

re-emerge [ˌriːɪ'mɜːdʒ] *vi* [new facts] ressortir ■ [idea, clue] réapparaître ■ [problem, question] se reposer ■ [from hiding, tunnel] ressortir, ressurgir.

re-emergence [ˌriːɪ'mɜːdʒəns] *n* réapparition *f*.

re-emphasize, ise [ˌriː'emfəsaɪz] *vt* insister une fois de plus sur, souligner une nouvelle fois.

re-employ [ˌriːɪm'plɔɪ] *vt* [materials] réemployer, remployer ■ [workers] réembaucher, rembaucher.

re-enact [ˌriːɪ'nækt] *vt* **1.** [scene, crime] reconstituer **2.** ADMIN & POL [legislation] remettre en vigueur.

re-enactment [ˌriːɪ'næktmənt] *n* **1.** [of scene, crime] reconstitution *f* **2.** ADMIN, LAW & POL [of regulation, legislation] remise *f* en vigueur.

re-engage [ˌriːɪn'geɪdʒ] *vt* **1.** [troops] rengager ■ [employee] réengager, rengager **2.** [mechanism] rengréner ■ **to ~ the clutch** rembrayer.

re-enter [ˌriː'entər] ◇ *vi* **1.** [gen] rentrer, entrer à nouveau ■ ASTRONAUT rentrer dans l'atmosphère **2.** [candidate] : **to ~ for an exam** se réinscrire à un examen.
◇ *vt* **1.** [room, country] rentrer dans, entrer à nouveau dans ■ [atmosphere] rentrer dans **2.** COMPUT [data] saisir à nouveau, réintroduire.

re-entry [ˌriː'entrɪ] (*pl* **re-entries**) *n* **1.** [gen - ASTRONAUT] rentrée *f* **2.** MUS [of theme] reprise *f*.

re-equip [ˌriːɪ'kwɪp] *vt* ré-équiper.

re-establish [ˌriːɪ'stæblɪʃ] *vt* **1.** [order] rétablir ■ [practice] restaurer ■ [law] remettre en vigueur **2.** [person] réhabiliter, réintégrer ■ **the team have ~ed themselves as the best in the country** l'équipe s'est imposée de nouveau comme la meilleure du pays.

re-evaluate [ˌriːɪ'væljʊeɪt] *vt* réévaluer.

re-evaluation [ˌriːɪ'væljʊeɪʃn] *n* réévaluation *f*.

re-examination [ˌriːɪgˌzæmɪ'neɪʃn] *n* [of question] réexamen *m* ■ LAW nouvel interrogatoire *m*.

re-examine [ˌriːɪg'zæmɪn] *vt* [question, case] réexaminer, examiner de nouveau ■ [witness] réinterroger, interroger de nouveau ■ [candidate] faire repasser un examen à.

re-export ◇ *vt* [ˌriːek'spɔːt] réexporter.
◇ *n* [ˌriː'ekspɔːt] **1.** [of goods] réexportation *f* **2.** [product] marchandise *f* de réexportation.

ref, ref. (*written abbrev of* **reference**) réf. ■ **your ~** v/réf.

ref [ref] *n UK inf* = **referee**.

refashion [ˌriː'fæʃn] *vt* [object] refaçonner ■ [image] reconstruire.

refectory [rɪ'fektərɪ] (*pl* **refectories**) *n* réfectoire *m*.

refer [rɪ'fɜːr] (*pret & pp* **referred**, *cont* **referring**) *vt* **1.** [submit, pass on] soumettre, renvoyer ■ **I ~ the matter to you for a decision** je m'en remets à vous pour prendre une décision sur la question ■ **to ~ a case to a higher court** renvoyer *OR* déférer une affaire à une instance supérieure ▮ [send, direct] renvoyer ■ **my doctor referred me to the hospital/to a specialist** mon docteur m'a envoyé à l'hôpital/chez un spécialiste ▮ [in writing, reading] renvoyer ■ **I ~ you to Ludlow's book** je vous renvoie au livre de Ludlow ▮ BANK : **to ~ a cheque to drawer** refuser d'honorer un chèque
2. MED : **the pain may be referred to another part of the body** il peut y avoir irradiation de la douleur dans d'autres parties du corps
3. LAW : **to ~ the accused** déférer l'accusé
4. UNIV [student] refuser, recaler ■ [thesis] renvoyer pour révision.

◆ **refer back** *vt sep* **1.** [put off - meeting, decision] ajourner, remettre (à plus tard)
2. [redirect - case] renvoyer.

◆ **refer to** *vt insep* **1.** [allude to] : **to ~ to sthg** faire allusion *OR* référence à qqch, parler de qqch ■ **he keeps referring to me as Dr Rayburn** il ne cesse de m'appeler Dr Rayburn ■ **the revolutionaries are referred to as Mantras** ces révolutionnaires sont connus sous le nom de Mantras ■ **that comment ~s to you** cette remarque s'adresse à vous ■ **they ~ to themselves as martyrs** ils se qualifient eux-mêmes de martyrs
2. [relate to] correspondre à, faire référence à ■ **the numbers ~ to footnotes** les chiffres renvoient à des notes en bas de page ▮ [apply, be connected to] s'appliquer à, s'adresser à ■ **these measures only ~ to taxpayers** ses mesures ne s'appliquent qu'aux contribuables
3. [consult - notes] consulter ; [- book, page, instructions] se reporter à ; [- person] : **I shall have to ~ to my boss** je dois en référer à *OR* consulter mon patron.

referee [ˌrefə'riː] ◇ *n* **1.** SPORT arbitre *m* ■ TENNIS juge *m* arbitre **2.** *UK* [for job] répondant *m*, - e *f* ■ **I was ~** *OR* **I acted as his ~ for his last job** je lui ai fourni une recommandation pour son dernier emploi ■ **you can give my name as a ~** vous pouvez me citer comme référence ■ **please give the names of three ~s** veuillez nous donner le nom de trois personnes susceptibles de fournir une lettre de recommandation **3.** LAW conciliateur *m*, médiateur *m*.
◇ *vt* SPORT arbitrer.
◇ *vi* SPORT être arbitre.

reference ['refrəns] ◇ *n* **1.** [allusion] allusion *f* ■ **to make a ~ to sthg** faire allusion à qqch ■ **look up the ~ in the dictionary** cherchez la référence dans le dictionnaire **2.** [consultation] consultation *f* ■ **without ~ to me** sans me consulter **3.** [recommendation - for job] recommandation *f*, référence *f* ■ **could you give me a ~ please?** pouvez-vous me fournir des références, s'il vous plaît? ■ **banker's ~** références *fpl* bancaires **4.** [in code, catalogue] référence *f* ■ [on map] coordonnées *fpl* ■ [footnote] renvoi *m* ■ COMM référence *f* **5.** [remit - of commission] compétence *f*, pouvoirs *mpl* **6.** LING référence *f* **7.** LAW [of case] renvoi *m*.
◇ *comp* [material, section] de référence ■ [value, quantity] de référence, étalon.
◇ *vt* **1.** [refer to] faire référence à **2.** [thesis] établir la liste des citations dans ■ [quotation] donner la référence de.

◆ **with reference to, in reference to** *prep phr* en ce qui concerne ■ **with ~ to your letter of 25th June...** COMM suite à votre courrier du 25 juin...

reference book *n* ouvrage *m* de référence.

reference library *n* bibliothèque *f* d'ouvrages de référence.

reference number *n* numéro *m* de référence.

referendum [ˌrefə'rendəm] (*pl* **referendums** *OR pl* **referenda** [-də]) *n* référendum *m* ■ **to hold a ~** organiser un référendum.

referent ['refərənt] *n* référent *m*.

referential [ˌrefə'renʃl] *adj* référentiel.

referral [rɪ'fɜːrəl] *n* **1.** [forwarding] renvoi *m* **2.** [consultation] consultation *f* **3.** UNIV [of thesis] renvoi *m* pour révision **4.** [person] patient *m* (*envoyé par son médecin chez un spécialiste*).

refill ◇ *vt* [ˌriː'fɪl] [glass] remplir (à nouveau) ■ [lighter, canister] recharger.
◇ *n* ['riːfɪl] [for pen, lighter] (nouvelle) cartouche *f* ■ [for propelling pencil] mine *f* de rechange ■ [for notebook] recharge *f* ■ [drink] : **do you need a ~?** *inf* je vous en ressers un?
◇ *comp* ['riːfɪl] de rechange.

refillable [ˌriː'fɪləbl] *adj* rechargeable.

refine [rɪ'faɪn] *vt* **1.** [oil, sugar] raffiner ■ [ore, metal] affiner ■ [by distillation] épurer **2.** [model, manners] améliorer ■ [judgment, taste] affiner ■ [lecture, speech] parfaire, peaufiner.

refined [rɪ'faɪnd] *adj* **1.** [oil, sugar] raffiné ▪ [ore] affiné ▪ [by distillation] épuré **2.** [style, person, taste] raffiné.

refinement [rɪ'faɪnmənt] *n* **1.** [of oil, sugar] raffinage *m* ▪ [of metals, ore] affinage *m* ▪ [by distillation] épuration *f* **2.** [of person] délicatesse *f*, raffinement *m* ▪ [of taste, culture] raffinement *m* ▪ [of morals] pureté *f* ▪ **a man of ~** un homme raffiné **3.** [of style, discourse, language] subtilité *f*, raffinement *m* **4.** [improvement] perfectionnement *m*, amélioration *f*.

refiner [rɪ'faɪnəʳ] *n* [of oil, sugar] raffineur *m*, - euse *f* ▪ [of metal] affineur *m*, - euse *f*.

refinery [rɪ'faɪnərɪ] (*pl* **refineries**) *n* [for oil, sugar] raffinerie *f* ▪ [for metals] affinerie *f*.

refit (*pret & pp* **refitted**, *cont* **refitting**) <> *vt* [ˌriː'fɪt] **1.** [repair] remettre en état **2.** [refurbish] rééquiper, renouveler l'équipement de.
<> *vi* [ˌriː'fɪt] [ship] être remis en état.
<> *n* ['riːfɪt] [of plant, factory] rééquipement *m*, nouvel équipement *m* ▪ [of ship] remise *f* en état, réparation *f*.

reflate [ˌriː'fleɪt] *vt* **1.** [ball, tyre] regonfler **2.** ECON relancer.

reflation [ˌriː'fleɪʃn] *n* ECON relance *f*.

reflationary [ˌriː'fleɪʃənrɪ] *adj* ECON [policy] de relance.

reflect [rɪ'flekt] <> *vt* **1.** [image] refléter ▪ [sound, heat] renvoyer ▪ [light] réfléchir ▪ **the mirror ~ed the light from the lamp** le miroir réfléchissait la lumière de la lampe ▪ **her face was ~ed in the mirror/water** son visage se reflétait dans la glace/dans l'eau ▪ **she saw herself ~ed in the window** elle a vu son image dans la vitre ▪ **the plate ~s heat (back) into the room** la plaque renvoie la chaleur dans la pièce ▪ **the sound was ~ed off the rear wall** le son était renvoyé par le mur du fond **2.** *fig* [credit] faire jaillir, faire retomber ▪ **the behaviour of a few ~s discredit on us all** le comportement de quelques-uns porte atteinte à l'honneur de tous **3.** *fig* [personality, reality] traduire, refléter ▪ **many social problems are ~ed in his writing** de nombreux problèmes de société sont évoqués dans ses écrits **4.** [think] penser, se dire ▪ [say] dire, réfléchir.
<> *vi* [think] réfléchir ▪ **to ~ on a question** réfléchir sur une question ▪ **I'll ~ on it** j'y songerai OR réfléchirai ▪ **after ~ing for a while ...** après mûre réflexion ...
◆ **reflect on, reflect upon** *vt insep* [negatively] porter atteinte à, nuire à ▪ [positively] rejaillir sur ▪ [cast doubt on] mettre en doute, jeter le doute sur ▪ **their behaviour ~s well on them** leur comportement leur fait honneur.

reflection [rɪ'flekʃn] *n* **1.** [of light, sound, heat] réflexion *f* **2.** [image] reflet *m* ▪ **a ~ in the mirror/window** un reflet dans la glace/vitre ▪ **the result was not a fair ~ of the game** *fig* le résultat ne reflétait pas la manière dont le match s'était joué ▪ **an accurate ~ of reality** *fig* un reflet exact de la réalité **3.** [comment] réflexion *f*, remarque *f*, observation *f* ▪ **to make a ~ on sthg** faire une réflexion sur qqch ▪ [criticism] critique *f* ▪ **it's no ~ on their integrity** leur intégrité n'est pas en cause ▪ **my comment was not meant to be a ~ on you** ce que j'ai dit ne vous visait pas personnellement **4.** [deliberation] réflexion *f* ▪ [thought] pensée *f* ▪ **on ~** après OR à la réflexion, en y réfléchissant ▪ **on due ~** après mûre réflexion.

reflective [rɪ'flektɪv] *adj* **1.** OPT [surface] réfléchissant, réflecteur ▪ [power, angle] réflecteur ▪ [light] réfléchi **2.** [mind, person] pensif, réfléchi ▪ [faculty] de réflexion.

reflector [rɪ'flektəʳ] *n* réflecteur *m* ▪ AUT catadioptre *m*.

reflex ['riːfleks] <> *n* **1.** [gen - PHYSIOL] réflexe *m* **2.** PHOT (appareil *m*) reflex *m*.
<> *adj* **1.** PHYSIOL réflexe ▪ **~ action** réflexe *m* **2.** OPT & PHYS réfléchi **3.** PHOT reflex *(inv)* ▪ **~ camera** (appareil *m*) reflex *m* **4.** MATHS rentrant.

reflexion [rɪ'flekʃn] *UK* = **reflection**.

reflexive [rɪ'fleksɪv] <> *adj* **1.** GRAM réfléchi **2.** PHYSIOL réflexe **3.** LOGIC & MATHS réflexif.
<> *n* GRAM réfléchi *m*.

reflexively [rɪ'fleksɪvlɪ] *adv* GRAM [in meaning] au sens réfléchi ▪ [in form] à la forme réfléchie.

reflexive pronoun *n* pronom *m* réfléchi.

reflexive verb *n* verbe *m* réfléchi.

reflexology [ˌriːflek'sɒlədʒɪ] *n* réflexothérapie *f*.

refloat [ˌriː'fləʊt] <> *vt fig* & NAUT renflouer.
<> *vi* être renfloué.

reforest [ˌriː'fɒrɪst] = **reafforest**.

reforestation [riːˌfɒrɪ'steɪʃn] = **reafforestation**.

reform [rɪ'fɔːm] <> *vt* **1.** [modify - law, system, institution] réformer **2.** [person] faire perdre ses mauvaises habitudes à ▪ [drunkard] faire renoncer à la boisson ▪ [habits, behaviour] corriger.
<> *vi* se corriger, s'amender.
<> *n* réforme *f*.

re-form [riː'fɔːm] <> *vt* **1.** MIL [ranks] remettre en rang, reformer ▪ [men] rallier **2.** [return to original form] rendre sa forme primitive OR originale à ▪ [in new form] donner une nouvelle forme à ▪ [form again] reformer.
<> *vi* **1.** MIL [men] se remettre en rangs ▪ [ranks] se reformer **2.** [group, band] se reformer.

Reform Act = **Reform Bill**.

reformat [ˌriː'fɔːmæt] (*cont* **reformatting**) (*pret & pp* **reformatted**) *vt* COMPUT reformater.

reformation [ˌrefə'meɪʃn] *n* **1.** [of law, institution] réforme *f* **2.** [of behaviour] réforme *f* ▪ [of criminal, addict] réinsertion *f*.
◆ **Reformation** <> *n* : **the Reformation** la Réforme.
<> *comp* [music, writer] de la Réforme.

reformative [rɪ'fɔːmətɪv] *adj* [concerning reform] de réforme ▪ [reforming] réformateur.

reformatory [rɪ'fɔːmətrɪ] <> *adj* réformateur.
<> *n UK* ≃ maison *f* de redressement ▪ *US* ≃ centre *m* d'éducation surveillée.

Reform Bill *n UK* HIST *loi de réforme du système parlementaire* ▪ **the great ~s** les grandes réformes.

THE GREAT REFORM BILLS

Nom d'une série de réformes réalisées en 1832, 1867, 1884 et 1885 sur le droit de vote et le système de représentation parlementaire. Elles devaient déboucher, bien des années plus tard, sur l'adoption du suffrage universel en Grande-Bretagne.

reformed [rɪ'fɔːmd] *adj* **1.** [person] qui a perdu ses mauvaises habitudes ▪ [prostitute, drug addict] ancien **2.** [institution, system] réformé **3.** RELIG [Christian] réformé ▪ [Jewish] non orthodoxe.

reformer [rɪ'fɔːməʳ] *n* réformateur *m*, - trice *f*.

reformist [rɪ'fɔːmɪst] <> *adj* réformiste.
<> *n* réformiste *mf*.

reform school *n US* ≃ centre *m* d'éducation surveillée.

refract [rɪ'frækt] <> *vt* réfracter.
<> *vi* se réfracter.

refracting [rɪ'fræktɪŋ] *adj* [material, prism] réfringent ▪ [angle] de réfraction.

refracting telescope *n* réfracteur *m*, lunette *f* astronomique.

refraction [rɪ'frækʃn] *n* [phenomenon] réfraction *f* ▪ [property] réfringence *f*.

refractive [rɪ'fræktɪv] *adj* réfringent.

refractor [rɪ'fræktəʳ] *n* **1.** OPT & PHYS [apparatus] appareil *m* de réfraction ▪ [material, medium] milieu *m* réfringent **2.** ASTRON réfracteur *m*, lunette *f* astronomique.

refractory [rɪ'fræktərɪ] *adj* **1.** *fml* [person] réfractaire, rebelle **2.** MED & TECH réfractaire.

refrain [rɪ'freɪn] <> *vi* [hold back] : **to ~ from (doing) sthg** s'abstenir de (faire) qqch ▪ **she ~ed from making a remark** elle s'est

retenue OR abstenue de faire une remarque ▪ **he couldn't ~ from smiling** il n'a pu s'empêcher de sourire ▪ **'please ~ from smoking'** 'prière de ne pas fumer'.
<> *n* MUS & POET & *fig* refrain *m*.

refreeze [,ri:'fri:z] (*pret* **refroze** [-'frəuz], *pp* **refrozen** [-'frəuzn]) *vt* [ice, ice-cream] remettre au congélateur ▪ [food] recongeler.

refresh [rɪ'freʃ] *vt* **1.** [revive - subj: drink, shower, ice] rafraîchir ; [- subj: exercise, swim] revigorer ; [- subj: sleep] reposer, détendre ▪ **I feel ~ed** [after shower, drink] je me sens rafraîchi ; [after exercise] je me sens revigoré ; [after rest] je me sens reposé ▪ **they woke ~ed** ils se sont réveillés frais et dispos **2.** [memory, experience] rafraîchir ▪ **let me ~ your memory** laissez-moi vous rafraîchir la mémoire ▪ **she wanted to ~ her German** elle voulait se remettre à niveau en allemand.

refresher course *n* stage *m* OR cours *m* de recyclage.

refreshing [rɪ'freʃɪŋ] *adj* **1.** [physically - drink, breeze] rafraîchissant ; [- exercise] tonique, revigorant ; [- sleep] réparateur, reposant ; [- holiday] reposant **2.** [mentally - idea] original, stimulant ; [- sight] réconfortant ; [- performance] plein de vie ▪ **a ~ change** un changement agréable OR appréciable.

refreshingly [rɪ'freʃɪŋlɪ] *adv* : **it's ~ different** c'est un changement agréable.

refreshment [rɪ'freʃmənt] *n* [of body, mind] repos *m*, délassement *m* ▪ **would you like some ~?** [food] voulez-vous manger un morceau? ; [drink] voulez-vous boire quelque chose?
◆ **refreshments** *npl* rafraîchissements *mpl* ▪ **'~s available'** 'buvette'.

refried beans [rɪ'fraɪd-] *npl* US *haricots rouges sautés; préparation mexicaine.*

refrigerate [rɪ'frɪdʒəreɪt] *vt* [in cold store] frigorifier, réfrigérer ▪ [freeze] congeler ▪ [put in fridge] mettre au réfrigérateur.

refrigeration [rɪ,frɪdʒə'reɪʃn] *n* réfrigération *f* ▪ **industrial ~** froid *m* industriel.

refrigerator [rɪ'frɪdʒəreɪtər] <> *n* [in kitchen] réfrigérateur *m* ▪ [storeroom] chambre *f* froide OR frigorifique.
<> *comp* [ship, lorry, unit] frigorifique.

refuel [,ri:'fjuəl] (UK *pret & pp* **refuelled**, *cont* **refuelling**) (US *pret & pp* **refueled**, *cont* **refueling**) <> *vt* ravitailler (en carburant).
<> *vi* se ravitailler en carburant ▪ *fig* [eat, drink] se restaurer.

refuelling UK, **refueling** US [,ri:'fjuəlɪŋ] <> *n* ravitaillement *m* (en carburant).
<> *comp* [boom, tanker] de ravitaillement ▪ **to make a ~ stop** AUT s'arrêter pour prendre de l'essence ; AERON faire une escale technique.

refuge ['refju:dʒ] *n* **1.** [shelter - gen] refuge *m*, abri *m* ; [- in mountains] refuge *m* ; [- for crossing road] refuge *m* ▪ **women's ~** foyer *m* pour femmes battues **2.** [protection - from weather] : **to take ~ from the rain** s'abriter de la pluie ▪ [from attack, reality] : **to seek ~** chercher refuge ▪ **he sought ~ from his persecutors** il chercha un asile pour échapper à ses persécuteurs ▪ **to take ~ in fantasy** se réfugier dans l'imagination ▪ **place of ~** [from rain] abri *m* ; [from pursuit] (lieu *m* d')asile *m*.

refugee [,refjʊ'dʒi:] *n* réfugié *m*, - e *f*.

refugee camp *n* camp *m* de réfugiés.

refund <> *vt* [rɪ'fʌnd] **1.** [expenses, excess, person] rembourser ▪ **to ~ sthg to sb** rembourser qqch à qqn **2.** FIN & LAW [monies] restituer.
<> *n* ['ri:fʌnd] **1.** COMM remboursement *m* ▪ **to get** OR **to obtain a ~** se faire rembourser **2.** FIN & LAW [of monies] restitution *f* **3.** US [of tax] bonification *f* de trop-perçu.

refundable [ri:'fʌndəbl] *adj* remboursable.

refurbish [,ri:'fɜ:bɪʃ] *vt* réaménager.

refurbished [,ri:'fɜ:bɪʃt] *adj* [studio, apartment] refait à neuf.

refurbishment [,ri:'fɜ:bɪʃmənt] *n* remise *f* à neuf.

refurnish [,ri:'fɜ:nɪʃ] *vt* [house] remeubler.

refusal [rɪ'fju:zl] *n* **1.** [of request, suggestion] refus *m*, rejet *m* ▪ **to meet with a ~** essuyer OR se heurter à un refus ▪ **we don't understand your ~ to compromise** nous ne comprenons pas les raisons pour lesquelles vous vous opposez à un compromis **2.** EQUIT refus *m* **3.** [denial - of justice, truth] refus *m*, déni *m*.
Voir module d'usage

refuse[1] [rɪ'fju:z] <> *vt* **1.** [turn down - invitation, gift] refuser [- offer] refuser, décliner ; [- request, proposition] refuser, rejeter ▪ **to ~ to do sthg** refuser de OR se refuser à faire qqch ▪ **to be ~d** essuyer un refus ▪ EQUIT refuser ▪ **to ~ a jump** refuser de sauter **2.** [deny - permission] refuser (d'accorder) ; [- help, visa] refuser ▪ **he was ~d entry** on lui a refusé l'entrée.
<> *vi* [person] refuser ▪ [horse] refuser l'obstacle.

refuse[2] ['refju:s] *n* UK [household] ordures *fpl* (ménagères) ▪ [garden] détritus *mpl* ▪ [industrial] déchets *mpl*.

refuse bin ['refju:s-] *n* UK poubelle *f*.

refuse chute ['refju:s-] *n* UK vide-ordures *m inv*.

refuse collection ['refju:s] *n* UK ramassage *m* d'ordures.

refuse collector ['refju:s-] *n* UK éboueur *m*.

refuse disposal ['refju:s-] *n* UK traitement *m* des ordures.

refuse dump ['refju:s-] *n* UK [public] décharge *f* (publique), dépotoir *m*.

refutable ['refjʊtəbl] *adj* réfutable.

refutation [,refju:'teɪʃn] *n* réfutation *f*.

refute [rɪ'fju:t] *vt* [disprove] réfuter ▪ [deny] nier.

reg (*written abbrev of* **registered**) : **~ trademark** marque *f* déposée.

regain [rɪ'geɪn] *vt* **1.** [territory] reconquérir ▪ **to ~ possession of sthg** rentrer en possession de qqch ▪ **to ~ lost time** rattraper le temps perdu ▪ [health] recouvrer ▪ [strength] retrouver ▪ [sight, composure] retrouver, recouvrer ▪ [glory] retrouver ▪ **to ~ consciousness** reprendre connaissance ▪ **to ~ one's balance** retrouver l'équilibre ▪ **to ~ one's footing** reprendre pied **2.** *fml* [get back to - road, place, shelter] regagner.

regal ['ri:gl] *adj* *liter* royal ▪ *fig* [person, bearing] majestueux ▪ [banquet, decor] somptueux.

regale [rɪ'geɪl] *vt* : **to ~ sb with sthg** régaler qqn de qqch.

REFUSALS

Non, je regrette. No, sorry.
Certainement pas ! Certainly not!
Non, je suis désolé, mais je ne peux pas. No, I'm sorry, but I can't.
Je refuse d'y aller. I refuse to go.
Il n'en est pas question ! It's out of the question!
Je ne peux pas accepter vos conditions. I can't accept your conditions.
Je n'irai pas, un point c'est tout *OU* **point final !** I'm not going and that's final!
Alors là, tu peux toujours courir ! *inf* Forget it!
Je m'y oppose catégoriquement. I'm completely against it.

regalia [rɪ'geɪljə] *npl* **1.** [insignia] insignes *mpl* **2.** [finery, robes] accoutrement *m*, atours *mpl* ▪ **to be in full ~** [judge, general] être en grande tenue ; *fig* & *hum* [woman] être paré de tous ses atours.

regally ['ri:gəlɪ] *adv* royalement, majestueusement.

regard [rɪ'gɑ:d] ◇ *vt* **1.** [consider] considérer, regarder ▪ [treat] traiter ▪ **I ~ him as** *OR* **like a brother** je le considère comme un frère ▪ **I ~ their conclusions as correct** *OR* **to be correct** je tiens leurs conclusions pour correctes ▮ [esteem] estimer, tenir en estime ▪ **highly ~ed** très estimé
2. *fml* [observe] regarder, observer
3. [heed - advice, wishes] tenir compte de.
◇ *n* **1.** [notice, attention] considération *f*, attention *f* ▪ **to pay ~ to sthg** tenir compte de qqch, faire attention à qqch ▪ **having ~ to paragraph 24** ADMIN vu le paragraphe 24
2. [care, respect] souci *m*, considération *f*, respect *m* ▪ **to have ~ for sb** avoir de la considération pour qqn ▪ **they have no ~ for your feelings** ils ne se soucient pas de vos sentiments ▪ **Peter has scant ~ for copyright** Peter se soucie peu des droits d'auteur ▪ **they showed no ~ for our wishes** ils n'ont tenu aucun compte de nos souhaits ▪ **with no ~ for his health** sans se soucier de sa santé ▪ **out of ~ for** par égard pour ▪ **with due ~ for your elders** avec les égards dus à vos aînés ▪ **without due ~ to** sans tenir compte de
3. [connection] : **in this ~** à cet égard
4. [esteem] estime *f*, considération *f* ▪ **I hold them in high ~** je les tiens en grande estime
5. *fml* [eyes, look] regard *m*.
◆ **regards** *npl* [in letters] : **~s, Peter** bien cordialement, Peter ▪ **kind ~s** *US*, **best ~s** bien à vous ▮ [in greetings] : **give them my ~s** transmettez-leur mon bon souvenir ▪ **he sends his ~s** vous avez le bonjour de sa part.
◆ **as regards** *prep phr* en ce qui concerne, pour ce qui est de.
◆ **in regard to, with regard to** *prep phr* en ce qui concerne.

regardful [rɪ'gɑ:dfʊl] *adj fml* **to be ~ of** [needs, wishes, difficulties] être attentif à, faire attention à ; [children, interests, image] s'occuper de, soigner.

regarding [rɪ'gɑ:dɪŋ] *prep* quant à, en ce qui concerne, pour ce qui est de ▪ **what are we going to do ~ Fred?** qu'allons-nous faire en ce qui concerne Fred? ▪ **questions ~ management** des questions relatives à la gestion.

regardless [rɪ'gɑ:dlɪs] *adv* [in any case] quand même, en tout cas ▪ [without worrying] sans s'occuper *OR* se soucier du reste.
◆ **regardless of** *prep phr* : **~ of what you think** [without bothering] sans se soucier de ce que vous pensez ; [whatever your opinion] indépendamment de ce que vous pouvez penser ▪ **~ of the expense** sans regarder à la dépense.

regatta [rɪ'gætə] *n* régate *f*.

regd = reg.

regency ['ri:dʒənsɪ] (*pl* **regencies**) *n* régence *f*.
◆ **Regency** *comp* [style, furniture, period] Regency *(inv)*, de la Régence anglaise *(1811-1830)*.

regenerate ◇ *vt* [rɪ'dʒenəreɪt] régénérer.
◇ *vi* [rɪ'dʒenəreɪt] se régénérer.
◇ *adj* [rɪ'dʒenərət] régénéré.

regeneration [rɪˌdʒenə'reɪʃn] *n* [gen] régénération *f* ▪ [of interest] regain *m* ▪ [of urban area] reconstruction *f*, rénovation *f*.

regenerative [rɪ'dʒenərətɪv] *adj* régénérateur.

regent ['ri:dʒənt] *n* **1.** HIST régent *m*, - e *f* **2.** *US membre du conseil d'administration d'une université*.

Regent Street *pr n rue commerçante dans le West End à Londres*.

reggae ['regeɪ] ◇ *n* reggae *m*.
◇ *comp* [song, group, singer] reggae *(inv)*.

regicide ['redʒɪsaɪd] *n* [person] régicide *mf* ▪ [crime] régicide *m*.

regime, régime [reɪ'ʒi:m] *n* POL & SOCIOL régime *m* ▪ **under the present ~** sous le régime actuel.

regiment ◇ *n* ['redʒɪmənt] MIL & *fig* régiment *m*.
◇ *vt* ['redʒɪment] [organize] enrégimenter ▪ [discipline] soumettre à une discipline trop stricte.

regimental [ˌredʒɪ'mentl] *adj* MIL [mess, dress] régimentaire, du régiment ▪ [band, mascot] du régiment ▪ *fig* [organization] trop discipliné, enrégimenté.

regimental sergeant major *n* ≃ adjudant-chef *m*.

regimentation [ˌredʒɪmen'teɪʃn] *n pej* [of business, system] organisation *f* quasi militaire ▪ [in school] discipline *f* étouffante *OR* trop sévère.

regimented ['redʒɪmentɪd] *adj* strict.

region ['ri:dʒən] *n* **1.** GEOG & ADMIN région *f* ▪ **in the Liverpool ~** dans la région de Liverpool ▪ **the lower ~s** *fig* les Enfers
2. [in body] région *f* ▪ **in the ~ of the heart** dans la région du cœur **3.** [of knowledge, sentiments] domaine *m*.
◆ **in the region of** *prep phr* environ ▪ **in the ~ of £500** aux environs de *OR* dans les 500 livres.

regional ['ri:dʒənl] *adj* régional.

regional development *n* [building, land development] aménagement *m* du territoire ▪ [for jobs] action *f* régionale ▪ **~ corporation** *UK organisme pour l'aménagement du territoire*.

regionalism ['ri:dʒənəlɪzm] *n* régionalisme *m*.

regionalize, ise ['ri:dʒənəlaɪz] *vt* régionaliser.

regionally ['ri:dʒnəlɪ] *adv* à l'échelle régionale.

register ['redʒɪstəʳ] ◇ *vt* **1.** [record - name] (faire) enregistrer, (faire) inscrire ; [- birth, death] déclarer ; [- vehicle] (faire) immatriculer ; [- trademark] déposer ; [- on list] inscrire ; [- request] enregistrer ; [- readings] relever, enregistrer ▪ MIL [recruit] recenser ▪ **to ~ a complaint** déposer une plainte ▪ **to ~ a protest** protester ▪ **to ~ one's vote** exprimer son vote, voter ▪ **I'd like officially to ~ my disagreement** je voudrais exprimer officiellement mon désaccord
2. [indicate] indiquer ▪ **the needle is ~ing 700 kg** l'aiguille indique 700 kg ▮ FIN enregistrer ▪ **the pound has ~ed a fall** la livre a enregistré une baisse ▮ [subj: person, face] exprimer ▪ **her face ~ed disbelief** l'incrédulité se lisait sur son visage
3. [obtain - success] remporter ; [- defeat] essuyer
4. *inf* [understand] saisir, piger ▪ **they don't seem to have ~ed (the fact) that the situation is hopeless** ils ne semblent pas se rendre compte que la situation est désespérée
5. [parcel, letter] envoyer en recommandé
6. [at railway station, airport etc - suitcase] (faire) enregistrer
7. TYPO mettre en registre
8. TECH (faire) aligner, faire coïncider.
◇ *vi* **1.** [enrol] s'inscrire, se faire inscrire ▪ [in hotel] s'inscrire sur *OR* signer le registre (de l'hôtel) ▪ **to ~ at night school/for Chinese lessons** s'inscrire aux cours du soir/à des cours de chinois ▪ **foreign nationals must ~ with the police** les ressortissants étrangers doivent se faire enregistrer au commissariat de police ▪ **to ~ with a GP/on the electoral roll** se faire inscrire auprès d'un médecin traitant/sur les listes électorales
2. [be understood] : **the truth slowly began to ~ (with me)** petit à petit, la vérité m'est apparue ▮ [have effect] : **his name doesn't ~ (with me)** son nom ne me dit rien
3. [instrument] donner une indication ▪ **is the barometer ~ing?** est-ce que le baromètre indique quelque chose?
4. TECH coïncider, être aligné ▪ TYPO être en registre.
◇ *n* **1.** [book] registre *m* ▪ [list] liste *f* ▪ SCH registre *m* de présences, cahier *m* d'appel ▪ [on ship] livre *m* de bord ▪ **to call** *OR* **to take the ~** SCH faire l'appel ➡ **electoral ~** liste *f* électorale ▪ **commercial** *OR* **trade ~** registre *m* du commerce ▪ **~ of shipping** registre *m* maritime ▪ **~ of births, deaths and marriages** registre *m* de l'état civil
2. [gauge] enregistreur *m* ▪ [counter] compteur *m* ▪ [cash till] caisse *f* (enregistreuse)
3. [pitch - of voice] registre *m*, tessiture *f* ; [- of instrument] registre
4. LING registre *m*, niveau *m* de langue
5. TYPO registre *m*
6. ART & COMPUT registre *m*.

registered ['redʒɪstəd] *adj* **1.** [student, elector] inscrit ▪ [charity] *UK* agréé ▪ FIN [bond, securities] nominatif ➊ **~ childminder** nourrice *f* agréée ▪ **~ company** société *f* inscrite au registre du commerce **2.** [letter, parcel] recommandé ▪ **send it ~** *UK* envoyez-le en recommandé.

registered disabled *adj UK* **to be ~** avoir une carte d'invalidité.

Registered General Nurse = RGN.

Registered Mental Nurse *n* infirmier *m* psychiatrique diplômé *OR* infirmière *f* psychiatrique diplômée d'État.

Registered Nurse *n* infirmier *m* diplômé *OR* infirmière *f* diplômée d'État.

registered office *n UK* siège *m* social.

registered post *n UK* envoi *m* recommandé.

registered tonnage *n* NAUT jauge *f*.

Registered Trademark *n* marque *f* déposée.

register office ADMIN = **registry office**.

register ton *n* NAUT tonneau *m* (de jauge).

registrar [,redʒɪ'strɑːʳ] *n* **1.** *UK* ADMIN officier *m* de l'état civil **2.** *UK* & *New Zealand* MED chef *m* de clinique **3.** LAW greffier *m* **4.** *US* UNIV chef *m* du service *OR* du bureau des inscriptions ▪ *UK* UNIV président *m (d'une université)* **5.** COMM & FIN : **companies' ~** responsable *mf* du registre des sociétés.

registration [,redʒɪ'streɪʃn] *n* **1.** [of name] enregistrement *m* ▪ [of student] inscription *f* ▪ [of trademark] dépôt *m* ▪ [of vehicle] immatriculation *f* ▪ [of luggage] enregistrement *m* ▪ [of birth, death] déclaration *f* ▪ **land ~** inscription au cadastre **2.** *UK* SCH appel *m* **3.** [of mail] recommandation *f* **4.** MUS [on organ] registration *f*.

registration document *n UK* AUT ≃ carte *f* grise.

registration fee *n* frais *mpl OR* droits *mpl* d'inscription.

registration number *n* **1.** *UK* AUT numéro *m* d'immatriculation ▪ **the car has the ~ E 123 SYK** la voiture est immatriculée E 123 SYK **2.** [of student] numéro *m* d'inscription ▪ [of baggage] numéro *m* d'enregistrement.

registry ['redʒɪstrɪ] (*pl* **registries**) *n* **1.** [registration] enregistrement *m* ▪ UNIV inscription *f* **2.** [office] bureau *m* d'enregistrement **3.** NAUT immatriculation *f* ▪ **port of ~** port *m* d'attache.

registry office *n UK* bureau *m* de l'état civil ▪ **to be married at a ~** ≃ se marier à la mairie.

regress ◇ *vi* [rɪ'gres] **1.** BIOL & PSYCHOL régresser ▪ **to ~ to childhood** régresser à un stade infantile **2.** SCH [go back] reculer, revenir en arrière.
◇ *n* ['riːgres] = **regression**.

regression [rɪ'greʃn] *n* **1.** BIOL & PSYCHOL régression *f* **2.** [retreat] recul *m*, régression *f*.

regressive [rɪ'gresɪv] *adj* BIOL, FIN & PSYCHOL régressif ▪ [movement] de recul.

regret [rɪ'gret] (*pret & pp* **regretted**, *cont* **regretting**) ◇ *vt* **1.** [be sorry about - action, behaviour] regretter ▪ **I ~ to say** [apologize] j'ai le regret de *OR* je regrette de dire ; [unfortunately] hélas, malheureusement ▪ **we ~ to inform you** nous avons le regret de vous informer ▪ **I ~ ever mentioning it** je regrette d'en avoir jamais parlé ▪ **I ~ not being able to come** je regrette *OR* je suis désolé de ne pouvoir venir ▪ **she ~s that she never met Donovan** elle regrette de n'avoir jamais rencontré Donovan ▪ **the accident/error is greatly to be regretted** [gen] l'accident/l'erreur est absolument déplorable ; [in diplomatic language] l'accident/l'erreur est infiniment regrettable ▪ **the airline ~s any inconvenience caused to passengers** la compagnie s'excuse pour la gêne occasionnée **2.** *lit* [lament] regretter.
◇ *n* [sorrow, sadness] regret *m* ▪ **with ~** avec regret ▪ **we announce with ~ the death of our chairman** nous avons le regret de vous faire part de la mort de notre directeur ▪ **much to our ~** à notre grand regret ▪ **to express one's ~s at** *OR* **about sthg** exprimer ses regrets devant qqch ▪ **I have no ~s** je n'ai pas de regrets, je ne regrette rien ▪ **do you have any ~s about** *OR* **for what you did?** regrettez-vous ce que vous avez fait? ▪ **to send sb one's ~s** [condolences] exprimer ses regrets à qqn [apologies] s'excuser auprès de qqn.
Voir module d'usage

regretful [rɪ'gretfʊl] *adj* [person] plein de regrets ▪ [expression, attitude] de regret.

regretfully [rɪ'gretfʊlɪ] *adv* [sadly] avec regret ▪ [unfortunately] malheureusement.

regrettable [rɪ'gretəbl] *adj* [unfortunate] regrettable, malencontreux ▪ [annoying] fâcheux, ennuyeux ▪ **it is most ~ that you were not informed** il est fort regrettable que vous n'ayez pas été informé.

regrettably [rɪ'gretəblɪ] *adv* [unfortunately] malheureusement, malencontreusement ▪ [irritatingly] fâcheusement.

regroup [,riː'gruːp] ◇ *vt* regrouper.
◇ *vi* se regrouper.

regular ['regjʊləʳ] ◇ *adj* **1.** [rhythmical - footsteps, movement, sound] régulier ▪ [even - breathing, pulse] régulier, égal ▪ **as ~ as clockwork** [punctual] réglé comme une horloge ; [frequent] réglé comme du papier à musique **2.** [frequent - meetings, service, salary] régulier ▪ **at ~ intervals** à intervalles réguliers ▪ **it's a ~ occurrence** cela arrive régulièrement **3.** [usual - brand, dentist, supplier] habituel ; [- customer] régulier ▪ [listener, reader] fidèle ▪ **who is your ~ doctor?** qui est votre médecin traitant? ▪ **to be in ~ employment** avoir un emploi régulier ▮ [normal, ordinary - price, model] courant ; [- size] courant, standard ; [- procedure] habituel ▪ **it's ~ practice to pay by cheque** les paiements par chèque sont pratique courante ▪ [permanent - agent] attitré, permanent ; [- police force] permanent, régulier [- army] de métier ; [- soldier] de carrière ➊ **~ (grade) gas** *US* AUT (essence *f*) ordinaire *m* **4.** [even - features, teeth] régulier ▪ [smooth, level] uni, égal **5.** [ordered - hours] régulier ; [- life] bien réglé **6.** GRAM & MATHS régulier ▪ **~ verb** verbe *m* régulier **7.** *inf* [as intensifier] vrai, véritable ▪ **a ~ mess** une vraie pagaille **8.** *US inf* [pleasant] sympathique, chouette **9.** RELIG [clergy] régulier **10.** *US* POL [loyal to party] fidèle au parti.
◇ *n* **1.** [customer - in bar] habitué *m*, - e *f* ; [- in shop] client *m* - e *f* fidèle **2.** [contributor, player] : **she's a ~ on our column** elle contribue régulièrement à notre rubrique **3.** [soldier]

REGRETS

Malheureusement *OU* **Hélas, nous n'avons pas pu arriver à temps.** Unfortunately, we couldn't get there in time.

Je regrette vraiment que vous n'ayez pas pu venir. I'm really sorry you couldn't make it.

S'il y a une chose que je regrette, c'est de ne pas avoir passé mon permis. If there's one thing I regret it's not having taken my driving test.

Je regrette ce que j'ai dit. I regret what I said.

Si seulement je lui en avais parlé plus tôt ! If only I'd told her sooner!

(Quel) dommage que je ne l'aie pas rencontré avant ! What a pity I didn't meet him sooner!

Dire que je ne le reverrai probablement jamais ! To think I'll probably never see him again!

militaire *m* de carrière **4.** RELIG religieux *m* régulier, régulier *m* **5.** *US* [fuel] ordinaire *m* **6.** *US* POL [loyal party member] membre *m* fidèle (du parti).

regularity [,regjʊ'lærətɪ] (*pl* **regularities**) *n* régularité *f.*

regularize, ise ['regjʊləraɪz] *vt* régulariser.

regularly ['regjʊləlɪ] *adv* régulièrement.

regulate ['regjʊleɪt] *vt* **1.** [control, adjust - machine, expenditure] régler ; [- flow] réguler **2.** [organize - habit, life] régler ; [- with rules] réglementer ■ **he followed a well ~d diet** il suivit un régime équilibré.

regulation [,regjʊ'leɪʃn] ◇ *n* **1.** [ruling] règlement *m* ■ **it's contrary to** *OR* **against (the) ~s** c'est contraire au règlement ■ **it complies with EC ~s** c'est conforme aux dispositions communautaires **2.** [adjustment, control - of machine] réglage *m* ; [- of flow] régulation *f.*
◇ *comp* [size, haircut, issue, dress] réglementaire ■ [pistol, helmet] d'ordonnance.

regulator ['regjʊleɪtə^r] *n* **1.** [person] régulateur *m*, - trice *f* **2.** [apparatus] régulateur *m.*

regulatory ['regjʊlətrɪ] *adj* réglementaire.

regurgitate [rɪ'gɜ:dʒɪteɪt] ◇ *vt* [food] régurgiter ■ *fig* [facts] régurgiter, reproduire.
◇ *vi* [bird] dégorger.

rehab ['ri:hæb] *n* *US* **: to be in ~** faire une cure de désintoxication ■ **~ center** centre *m* de désintoxication.

rehabilitate [,ri:ə'bɪlɪteɪt] *vt* **1.** [convict, drug addict, alcoholic] réhabiliter, réinsérer ■ [restore to health] rééduquer ■ [find employment for] réinsérer **2.** [reinstate - idea, style] réhabiliter **3.** [renovate - area, building] réhabiliter.

rehabilitation ['ri:ə,bɪlɪ'teɪʃn] *n* **1.** [of disgraced person, memory, reputation] réhabilitation *f* ■ [of convict, alcoholic, drug addict] réhabilitation *f*, réinsertion *f* ■ [of disabled person] rééducation *f* ■ [of unemployed] réinsertion **2.** [of idea, style] réhabilitation *f* **3.** [of area, building] réhabilitation *f.*

rehabilitation centre *n* [for work training] centre *m* de réadaptation ■ [for drug addicts] centre de réinsertion.

rehash *inf pej* ◇ *vt* [,ri:'hæʃ] **1.** *UK* [rearrange] remanier **2.** [repeat - argument] ressasser ; [- programme] reprendre ; [- artistic material] remanier.
◇ *n* ['ri:hæʃ] réchauffé *m.*

rehear [,ri:'hɪə^r] (*pret & pp* **reheard** [-'hɜ:d]) *vt* LAW entendre de nouveau, réviser.

rehearing [,ri:'hɪərɪŋ] *n* LAW révision *f* de procès.

rehearsal [rɪ'hɜ:sl] *n liter & fig* répétition *f* ■ **she's in ~** elle est en répétition ■ **the play is currently in ~** ils sont en train de répéter.

rehearse [rɪ'hɜ:s] ◇ *vt* **1.** MUS & THEAT & *fig* [play, music, speech, coup d'état] répéter ■ [actors, singers, orchestra] faire répéter ■ **well ~d** [play, performance] bien répété, répété avec soin ; [actor] qui a bien répété son rôle, qui sait son rôle sur le bout des doigts ; [request, coup d'état, applause] bien *OR* soigneusement préparé **2.** [recite - list, facts, complaints] réciter, énumérer ; [- old arguments] répéter, ressasser.
◇ *vi* MUS & THEAT répéter.

reheat [,ri:'hi:t] *vt* réchauffer.

rehouse [,ri:'haʊz] *vt* reloger.

reification [,reɪɪfɪ'keɪʃn] *n* réification *f.*

reify ['reɪɪfaɪ] (*pret & pp* **reified**) *vt* réifier.

reign [reɪn] ◇ *n* règne *m* ■ **in** *OR* **under the ~ of** sous le règne de ■ **~ of terror** règne de terreur.
◇ *vi* **1.** *liter* régner **2.** *fig* [predominate] régner ■ **silence ~s** le silence règne ■ **to ~ supreme** régner en maître.

reigning ['reɪnɪŋ] *adj* **1.** *liter* [monarch, emperor] régnant **2.** [present - champion] en titre **3.** [predominant - attitude, idea] régnant, dominant.

reimburse [,ri:ɪm'bɜ:s] *vt* rembourser ■ **to ~ sb (for) sthg** rembourser qqch à qqn *OR* qqn de qqch ■ **I was ~d** je me suis fait rembourser.

reimbursement [,ri:ɪm'bɜ:smənt] *n* remboursement *m.*

reimport ◇ *vt* [,ri:ɪm'pɔ:t] réimporter.
◇ *n* [,ri:'ɪmpɔ:t] réimportation *f.*

Reims [ri:mz] *pr n* Reims.

rein [reɪn] *n* **1.** [for horse] rêne *f* **2.** *fig* [control] bride *f* ■ **to give (a) free ~ to sb** laisser à qqn la bride sur le cou ■ **to give free ~ to one's emotions/imagination** donner libre cours à ses émotions/son imagination ■ **to keep a ~ on sthg** tenir qqch en bride, maîtriser qqch ■ **to keep a tight ~ on sb** tenir la bride haute à qqn.
◆ **reins** *npl* [for horse, child] rêne *f* ■ *fig* **the ~s of government** les rênes du gouvernement ■ **to hand over the ~s** passer les rênes.
◆ **rein back** ◇ *vi insep* tirer sur les rênes, serrer la bride.
◇ *vt sep* faire ralentir, freiner.
◆ **rein in** ◇ *vi insep* ralentir.
◇ *vt sep* **1.** [horse] serrer la bride à, ramener au pas **2.** *fig* [person] ramener au pas ■ [emotions] maîtriser, réfréner.

reincarnate ◇ *vt* [ri:'ɪnkɑ:neɪt] réincarner.
◇ *adj* [,ri:ɪn'kɑ:nɪt] réincarné.

reincarnation [,ri:ɪnkɑ:'neɪʃn] *n* réincarnation *f.*

reindeer ['reɪn,dɪə^r] (*pl inv*) *n* renne *m.*

reinfect [,ri:ɪn'fekt] *vt* réinfecter.

reinforce [,ri:ɪn'fɔ:s] *vt* **1.** MIL renforcer **2.** [gen - CONSTR] [- wall, heel] renforcer **3.** *fig* [demand] appuyer ■ [argument] renforcer.

reinforced concrete [,ri:ɪn'fɔ:st-] *n* béton *m* armé.

reinforcement [,ri:ɪn'fɔ:smənt] ◇ *n* **1.** [gen - MIL] renfort *m* **2.** [gen - CONSTR] armature *f* **3.** *fig* [strengthening] renforcement *m.*
◇ *comp* [troops, ships, supplies] de renfort.

re-install *vt* réinstaller.

reinstate [,ri:ɪn'steɪt] *vt* [employee] réintégrer, rétablir (dans ses fonctions) ■ [idea, system] rétablir, restaurer.

reinstatement [,ri:ɪn'steɪtmənt] *n* réintégration *f.*

reinsurance [,ri:ɪn'ʃɔ:rəns] *n* réassurance *f.*

reinsure [,ri:ɪn'ʃɔ:^r] *vt* réassurer.

reintegrate [,ri:'ɪntɪgreɪt] *vt* réintégrer.

reintegration ['ri:,ɪntɪ'greɪʃn] *n* réintégration *f.*

reinterpret [,ri:ɪn'tɜ:prɪt] *vt* réinterpréter.

reintroduce ['ri:,ɪntrə'dju:s] *vt* réintroduire.

reintroduction ['ri:,ɪntrə'dʌkʃn] *n* réintroduction *f.*

reinvest [,ri:ɪn'vest] *vt* réinvestir.

reinvigorate [,ri:ɪn'vɪgəreɪt] *vt* revigorer.

reissue [ri:'ɪʃu:] ◇ *vt* **1.** [book] rééditer ■ [film] rediffuser, ressortir **2.** ADMIN & FIN [banknote, shares, stamps] réémettre.
◇ *n* **1.** [of book] réédition *f* ■ [of film] rediffusion *f* **2.** ADMIN & FIN nouvelle émission *f.*

reiterate [ri:'ɪtə,reɪt] *vt* répéter, réaffirmer.

reiteration [ri:,ɪtə'reɪʃn] *n* réitération *f.*

reject ◇ *vt* [rɪ'dʒekt] **1.** [offer, suggestion, unwanted article] rejeter ■ [advances, demands] rejeter, repousser ■ [application, manuscript] rejeter, refuser ■ [suitor] éconduire, repousser ■ [belief, system, values] rejeter **2.** MED [foreign body, transplant] rejeter **3.** COMPUT rejeter.
◇ *n* ['ri:dʒekt] **1.** COMM [in factory] article *m* *OR* pièce *f* de rebut ■ [in shop] (article *m* de) second choix *m* ■ *fig* [person] personne *f* marginalisée **2.** COMPUT rejet *m.*
◇ *comp* ['ri:dʒekt] [merchandise] de rebut ■ [for sale] (de) second choix ■ [shop] d'articles de second choix.

rejection [rɪ'dʒekʃn] *n* **1.** [of offer, manuscript] refus *m* ■ [of advances, demands] rejet *m* ■ **her application met with ~** sa candidature a été rejetée *OR* n'a pas été retenue ■ **to be afraid of ~** [emotional] avoir peur d'être rejeté **2.** MED rejet *m*.

rejig [,ri:'dʒɪg] (*pret & pp* **rejigged**, *cont* **rejigging**) *vt UK* **1.** [re-equip] rééquiper, réaménager **2.** [reorganize] réarranger, revoir.

rejoice [rɪ'dʒɔɪs] ◇ *vi* se réjouir ■ **to ~ at** *OR* **over sthg** se réjouir de qqch ■ **he ~s in the name of French-Edwardes** *hum* il a le privilège de porter le nom de French-Edwardes.
◇ *vt* réjouir, ravir.

rejoicing [rɪ'dʒɔɪsɪŋ] *n* réjouissance *f*.

rejoin[1] [,ri:'dʒɔɪn] *vt* **1.** [go back to] rejoindre ■ **to ~ ship** NAUT rallier le bord **2.** [join again] rejoindre ■ [club] se réinscrire à ■ **to ~ the majority** POL rallier la majorité.

rejoin[2] [rɪ'dʒɔɪn] *vt & vi* [reply] répliquer.

rejoinder [rɪ'dʒɔɪndə^r] *n* réplique *f*.

rejuvenate [rɪ'dʒu:vəneɪt] *vt* rajeunir.

rejuvenating cream [rɪ'dʒu:vəneɪtɪŋ-] *n* crème *f* de beauté rajeunissante.

rekindle [,ri:'kɪndl] ◇ *vt* [fire] rallumer, attiser ■ *fig* [enthusiasm, desire, hatred] raviver, ranimer.
◇ *vi* [fire] se rallumer ■ *fig* [feelings] se ranimer.

relabel [,ri:'leɪbl] *vt* réétiqueter.

relapse [rɪ'læps] ◇ *n* MED & *fig* rechute *f* ■ **to have a ~** faire une rechute, rechuter.
◇ *vi* **1.** MED rechuter, faire une rechute **2.** [go back] retomber ■ **to ~ into silence** redevenir silencieux ■ **to ~ into depression** replonger dans la dépression.

relate [rɪ'leɪt] ◇ *vt* **1.** [tell - events, story] relater, faire le récit de ; [- details, facts] rapporter ■ **strange to ~...** chose curieuse... **2.** [connect - ideas, events] rapprocher, établir un rapport *OR* un lien entre ■ **we can ~ this episode to a previous scene in the novel** nous pouvons établir un lien entre cet épisode et une scène antérieure du roman ■ **she always ~s everything to herself** elle ramène toujours tout à elle.
◇ *vi* **1.** [connect - idea, event] se rapporter, se rattacher ■ **I don't understand how the two ideas ~** je ne comprends pas la relation entre les deux idées ■ **this ~s to what I was just saying** ceci est lié à *OR* en rapport avec ce que je viens de dire **2.** [have relationship, interact] : **at school, they learn to ~ to other children** à l'école, ils apprennent à vivre avec d'autres enfants ■ **I just can't ~ to my parents** je n'arrive pas à communiquer avec mes parents **3.** *inf* [appreciate] : **I can't ~ to his music** je n'accroche pas à sa musique.
◆ **Relate** *pr n organisme britannique de conseil conjugal.*

related [rɪ'leɪtɪd] *adj* **1.** [in family] parent ■ **she is ~ to the president** elle est parente du président ■ **they are ~ on his father's side** ils sont parents par son père ■ **to be ~ by marriage to sb** être parent de qqn par alliance ■ **they aren't ~** ils n'ont aucun lien de parenté | [animal, species] apparenté ■ [language] de même famille, proche ■ **an animal ~ to the cat** un animal apparenté au *OR* de la famille du chat **2.** [connected] connexe, lié ■ [neighbouring] voisin ■ **psychoanalysis and other ~ areas** la psychanalyse et les domaines qui s'y rattachent ■ **problems ~ to health** problèmes qui se rattachent *OR* qui touchent à la santé ■ **the two events are not ~** les deux événements n'ont aucun rapport | ADMIN & LAW afférent ■ **~ to** afférent à **3.** MUS relatif.

-related *in cpds* lié à ■ **business~ activities** des activités liées *OR* ayant rapport aux affaires ■ **performance~ bonus** prime *f* d'encouragement.

relating [rɪ'leɪtɪŋ] ◆ **relating to** *prep phr* ayant rapport à, relatif à, concernant.

relation [rɪ'leɪʃn] *n* **1.** [member of family] parent *m*, - e *f* ■ **they have ~s in Paris** ils ont de la famille à Paris ■ **he's a ~** il est de ma famille ■ **she is no ~ of mine** il n'y a aucun lien de parenté entre nous **2.** [kinship] parenté *f* ■ **what ~ is he to you?** quelle est sa parenté avec vous? **3.** [connection] rapport *m*, relation *f* ■ **to have** *OR* **to bear a ~ to sthg** avoir (un) rapport à qqch, être en rapport avec qqch ■ **your answer bore no ~ to the question** votre réponse n'avait rien à voir avec la question **4.** [relationship, contact] rapport *m*, relation *f* ■ [between people, countries] rapport *m*, rapports *mpl* ■ **to enter into ~** *OR* **~s with sb** entrer *OR* se mettre en rapport avec qqn ■ **to have (sexual) ~s with sb** *fml* avoir des rapports (sexuels) avec qqn ■ **diplomatic ~s** relations diplomatiques **5.** *fml* [narration - of events, story] récit *m*, relation *f* ; [- of details] rapport *m*.
◆ **in relation to, with relation to** *prep phr* par rapport à, relativement à.

relational [rɪ'leɪʃənl] *adj* relationnel.

relational database *n* COMPUT base *f* de données relationnelle.

relationship [rɪ'leɪʃnʃɪp] *n* **1.** [between people, countries] rapport *m*, rapports *mpl*, relation *f*, relations *fpl* ■ **to have a good/bad ~ with sb** [gen] avoir de bonnes/mauvaises relations avec qqn ■ **I'd like to talk to you about our ~** [as a couple] j'aimerais qu'on parle un peu de nous deux *OR* de notre couple ■ **a ~ is something you have to work at** être en couple, ça demande des efforts ■ **our ~ is purely a business one** nos relations sont simplement des relations d'affaires ■ **they have a good/bad ~** ils s'entendent bien/mal ■ **he has a very close ~ with his mother** il est très lié à sa mère **2.** [kinship] lien *m OR* liens *mpl* de parenté ■ **what is your exact ~ to her?** quels sont vos liens de parenté exacts avec elle? **3.** [connection - between ideas, events, things] rapport *m*, relation *f*, lien *m*.

relative ['relətɪv] ◇ *adj* **1.** [comparative] relatif ■ **to live in ~ comfort** vivre dans un confort relatif | [proportional] relatif ■ **taxation is ~ to income** l'imposition est proportionnelle au revenu | [respective] respectif ■ **the ~ qualities of the two candidates** les qualités respectives des deux candidats ➡ **~ atomic mass** poids *m OR* masse *f* atomique **2.** [not absolute] relatif **3.** MUS relatif **4.** GRAM relatif ■ **~ clause** (proposition *f*) relative *f* ■ **~ pronoun** pronom *m* relatif.
◇ *n* **1.** [person] parent *m*, - e *f* ■ **she has ~s in Canada** elle a de la famille au Canada ■ **he's a ~ of mine** il fait partie de ma famille **2.** GRAM relatif *m*.
◆ **relative to** *prep phr* par rapport à.

relatively ['relətɪvlɪ] *adv* relativement.

relativism ['relətɪvɪzm] *n* relativisme *m*.

relativist ['relətɪvɪst] ◇ *adj* relativiste.
◇ *n* relativiste *mf*.

relativity [,relə'tɪvətɪ] *n* relativité *f* ■ **theory of ~** théorie *f* de la relativité.

relativize, ise ['relətɪvaɪz] *vt* relativiser.

relax [rɪ'læks] ◇ *vi* **1.** [person] se détendre, se délasser ■ [in comfort, on holiday] se relaxer, se détendre ■ [calm down] se calmer, se détendre ■ **~!** [calm down] du calme! ; [don't worry] ne t'inquiète pas **2.** [grip] se relâcher, se desserrer ■ [muscle] se relâcher, se décontracter ■ TECH [spring] se détendre ■ **his face ~ed into a smile** son visage s'est détendu et il a souri.
◇ *vt* **1.** [mind] détendre, délasser ■ [muscles] relâcher, décontracter **2.** [grip] relâcher, desserrer ■ MED [bowels] relâcher **3.** *fig* [discipline, restriction] assouplir, relâcher ■ [concentration, effort] relâcher.

relaxant [rɪ'læksənt] ◇ *n* (médicament *m*) relaxant *m*.
◇ *adj* relaxant.

relaxation [,ri:læk'seɪʃn] *n* **1.** [rest] détente *f*, relaxation *f* ■ **he plays golf for ~** il joue au golf pour se détendre **2.** [loosening - of grip] relâchement *m*, desserrement *m* ■ *fig* [- of authority, law] relâchement *m*, assouplissement *m*.

relaxed [rɪ'lækst] *adj* **1.** [person, atmosphere] détendu, décontracté ■ [smile] détendu ■ **he's very ~ about the whole business** cette affaire n'a pas l'air de beaucoup le perturber | [attitude] décontracté **2.** [muscle] relâché ■ [discipline] assoupli.

relaxing [rɪ'læksɪŋ] *adj* [restful - atmosphere, afternoon, holiday] reposant ■ **you need a nice ~ bath** ce qu'il te faut, c'est un bon bain pour te détendre.

relay ['ri:leɪ] ◇ *n* **1.** [team - of athletes, workers, horses] relais *m* ■ **to work in ~s** *UK* travailler par relais, se relayer **2.** RADIO

& TV [transmitter] réémetteur *m*, relais *m* ▪ [broadcast] émission *f* relayée **3.** ELEC & TECH relais *m* **4.** SPORT : **~ (race)** (course *f* de) relais *m*.
◇ *vt* (*pret & pp* **relayed**) **1.** [pass on - message, news] transmettre **2.** RADIO & TV [broadcast] relayer, retransmettre **3.** (*pret & pp* **relaid** [-leɪd]) [cable, carpet] reposer.

relay station *n* relais *m*.

relearn [ˌriːˈlɜːn] (*UK pret & pp* **relearned** *OR* **relearnt** [-ˈlɜːnt]) (*US pret & pp* **relearned**) *vt* réapprendre, rapprendre.

release [rɪˈliːs] ◇ *n* **1.** [from captivity] libération *f* ▪ [from prison] libération *f*, mise *f* en liberté ADMIN élargissement *m* ▪ [from custody] mise *f* en liberté, relaxe *f* ▪ [from work] congé *m* (spécial) ▪ **~ on bail** mise en liberté provisoire (sous caution) ▪ **~ on parole** libération *f* conditionnelle ‖ *fig* [from obligation, promise] libération *f*, dispense *f* ▪ [from pain, suffering] délivrance *f* ➔ **order of ~** ordre *m* de levée d'écrou
2. COMM [from bond, customs] congé *m*
3. [letting go - of handle, switch] déclenchement *m* ; [- of brake] desserrage *m* ; [- of bomb] largage *m*
4. [distribution - of film] sortie *f* ; [- of book, record] sortie *f*, parution *f* ▪ **the film is on general ~** le film est sorti ▪ [new film, book, record] nouveauté *f* ▪ **her latest ~ is called "Chrissy"** son dernier disque s'appelle "Chrissy" ▪ **it's a new ~** ça vient de sortir
5. MECH [lever] levier *m* ▪ [safety catch] cran *m* de sûreté
6. COMPUT version *f*.
◇ *comp* [button, switch] de déclenchement.
◇ *vt* **1.** [prisoner] libérer, relâcher ADMIN élargir ▪ [from custody] remettre en liberté, relâcher, relaxer ▪ [captive person, animal] libérer ▪ [employee, schoolchild] libérer, laisser partir ▪ **to ~ sb from captivity** libérer qqn ▪ **to be ~d on bail** LAW être libéré sous caution ▪ **the children were ~d into the care of their grandparents** on a confié les enfants à leurs grands-parents ▪ **death finally ~d her from her suffering** la mort a mis un terme à ses souffrances ‖ [from obligation] libérer, dégager ▪ [from promise] dégager, relever ▪ [from vows] relever, dispenser ▪ **to ~ sb from a debt** remettre une dette à qqn
2. [let go - from control, grasp] lâcher ; [- feelings] donner *OR* laisser libre cours à ▪ **he ~d his grip on my hand** il m'a lâché la *OR* il a lâché ma main ▪ [bomb] larguer, lâcher ▪ [gas, heat] libérer, dégager
3. [issue - film] sortir ; [- book, record] sortir, faire paraître
4. [goods, new model] mettre en vente *OR* sur le marché ▪ [stamps, coins] émettre
5. [make public - statement] publier ; [- information, story] dévoiler, annoncer ▪ **the company refuses to ~ details of the contract** la compagnie refuse de divulguer *OR* de faire connaître les détails du contrat
6. [lever, mechanism] déclencher ▪ [brake] desserrer ▪ **to ~ the clutch** AUT débrayer ▪ **~ the catch to open the door** pour ouvrir la porte, soulever le loquet
7. FIN [credits, funds] dégager, débloquer
8. [property, rights] céder.

relegate [ˈrelɪgeɪt] *vt* **1.** [person, thought] reléguer ▪ **to ~ sb/sthg to sthg** reléguer qqn/qqch à qqch **2.** SPORT [team] reléguer, déclasser ▪ **to be ~d** FTBL descendre en *OR* être relégué à la division inférieure **3.** [refer - issue, question] renvoyer.

relegation [ˌrelɪˈgeɪʃn] *n* **1.** [demotion - of person, team, thing] relégation *f* **2.** [referral - of issue, matter] renvoi *m*.

relent [rɪˈlent] *vi* **1.** [person] se laisser fléchir *OR* toucher ▪ **they begged him for mercy but he would not ~** ils lui ont demandé grâce mais il est demeuré implacable *OR* impitoyable ▪ **he finally ~ed and let us go** il a finalement accepté de nous laisser partir **2.** [storm] s'apaiser.

relentless [rɪˈlentlɪs] *adj* **1.** [merciless] implacable, impitoyable **2.** [sustained - activity, effort] acharné, opiniâtre ; [- noise] ininterrompu ; [- rain] incessant.

relentlessly [rɪˈlentlɪslɪ] *adv* **1.** [mercilessly] impitoyablement, implacablement **2.** [persistently] avec acharnement *OR* opiniâtreté ▪ **the rain beat down ~** il n'a pas cessé de pleuvoir à verse.

relevance [ˈreləvəns], **relevancy** [ˈreləvənsɪ] *n* pertinence *f*, intérêt *m* ▪ **what is the ~ of this to the matter under discussion?** quel est le rapport avec ce dont on parle?

relevant [ˈreləvənt] *adj* **1.** [pertinent - information, comment, beliefs, ideas] pertinent ▪ **facts ~ to the case** des faits en rapport avec l'affaire ▪ **such considerations are not ~** de telles considérations sont hors de propos ▪ **confine yourself to the ~ facts** ne vous écartez pas du sujet ▪ **her novels no longer seem ~ to modern life** ses romans ne sont plus d'actualité **2.** [appropriate] approprié ▪ **fill in your name in the ~ space** inscrivez votre nom dans la case correspondante.

reliability [rɪˌlaɪəˈbɪlətɪ] *n* **1.** [of person] sérieux *m* ▪ [of information] sérieux *m*, fiabilité *f* ▪ [of memory, judgment] sûreté *f*, fiabilité *f* **2.** [of clock, engine] fiabilité *f*.

reliable [rɪˈlaɪəbl] *adj* **1.** [trustworthy - friend] sur qui on peut compter, sûr ; [- worker] à qui on peut faire confiance, sérieux ; [- witness] digne de confiance *OR* de foi ; [- information] sérieux, sûr ; [- memory, judgment] fiable, auquel on peut se fier ▪ **he's very ~** on peut toujours compter sur lui *OR* lui faire confiance ▪ **the news came from a ~ source** la nouvelle provenait d'une source sûre **2.** [clock, machine, car] fiable.

reliably [rɪˈlaɪəblɪ] *adv* sérieusement ▪ **we are ~ informed that...** nous avons appris de bonne source *OR* de source sûre que...

reliance [rɪˈlaɪəns] *n* **1.** [trust] confiance *f* ▪ **to place ~ on sb/sthg** faire confiance à qqn/qqch **2.** [dependence] dépendance *f* ▪ **her ~ on alcohol** sa dépendance vis-à-vis de l'alcool.

reliant [rɪˈlaɪənt] *adj* **1.** [dependent] dépendant ▪ **we are heavily ~ on your advice** vos conseils nous sont indispensables ▪ **he is too ~ on tranquillizers** il a trop recours aux tranquillisants **2.** [trusting] confiant ▪ **to be ~ on sb** faire confiance à *OR* avoir confiance en qqn.

relic [ˈrelɪk] *n* **1.** RELIG relique *f* ▪ [vestige] relique *f*, vestige *m* **2.** *fig & pej* [old person] croulant *m*, vieux débris *m*.

relief [rɪˈliːf] ◇ *n* **1.** [from anxiety, pain] soulagement *m* ▪ **to bring ~ to sb** soulager qqn, apporter un soulagement à qqn ▪ **the medicine gave** *OR* **brought her little ~ from the pain** le médicament ne la soulagea guère ▪ **he finds ~ in writing** ça le soulage d'écrire ▪ **to our great ~, much to our ~** à notre grand soulagement ▪ **it was a great ~ to her when the exams ended** la fin des examens fut un grand soulagement pour elle
2. [aid] secours *m*, aide *f* ▪ **famine ~** aide *f* alimentaire
3. *US* [state benefit] aide *f* sociale ▪ **to be on ~** recevoir des aides sociales *OR* des allocations
4. [diversion] divertissement *m*, distraction *f* ▪ **she reads detective novels for light ~** elle lit des romans policiers pour se distraire
5. [of besieged city] libération *f*, délivrance *f*
6. [of guard, team] relève *f* ▪ **~s have arrived** [gen] la relève *OR* l'équipe de relève est arrivée ; [troops] les troupes de relève sont arrivées, la relève est arrivée
7. ART relief *m* ▪ **the inscription stood out in ~** l'inscription était en relief ‖ [contrast] relief *m* ▪ **the mountains stood out in bold ~ against the sky** les montagnes se détachaient *OR* se découpaient nettement sur le ciel ▪ **to bring** *OR* **to throw sthg into ~** *fig* mettre qqch en relief *OR* en valeur
8. GEOG relief *m*
9. LAW [redress] réparation *f* ▪ [exemption] dérogation *f*, exemption *f*.
◇ *comp* **1.** [extra - transport, service] supplémentaire ▪ [replacement - worker, troops, team] de relève ; [- bus, machine] de remplacement
2. [for aid - fund, organization] de secours ▪ **~ work** coopération *f* ▪ **~ worker** *membre d'une organisation humanitaire qui travaille sur le terrain.*

relief map *n* carte *f* en relief.

relief printing *n* impression *f* en relief.

relief road *n* itinéraire *m* bis, route *f* de délestage.

relieve [rɪˈliːv] *vt* **1.** [anxiety, distress, pain] soulager, alléger ▪ [poverty] soulager ▪ **the good news ~d her of her anxiety** la bonne nouvelle a dissipé ses inquiétudes ▪ **to ~ congestion** MED & TRANSP décongestionner **2.** [boredom, gloom] dissiper

▪ [monotony] briser ▪ **the darkness of the room was ~d only by the firelight** la pièce n'était éclairée que par la lueur du feu **3.** [unburden] : **to ~ sb of sthg** soulager *OR* débarrasser qqn de qqch ▪ **to ~ sb of their wallet** *hum* délester qqn de son portefeuille ▪ **to ~ sb of an obligation** décharger *OR* dégager qqn d'une obligation ▪ **to ~ sb of his/her duties** *OR* **position** relever qqn de ses fonctions **4.** [aid - population, refugees, country] secourir, venir en aide à **5.** [replace - worker, team] relayer, prendre la relève de ; [- guard, sentry] relever **6.** [liberate - fort, city] délivrer, libérer ▪ [from siege] lever le siège de **7.** *euph* [urinate] : **to ~ o.s.** se soulager.

relieved [rɪ'li:vd] *adj* soulagé ▪ **we were greatly ~ at the news** nous avons été très soulagés d'apprendre la nouvelle.

religion [rɪ'lɪdʒn] *n* **1.** RELIG religion *f* ▪ **the Jewish ~** la religion *OR* la confession juive ▪ **it's against my ~ to work on Sundays** *liter & hum* ma religion m'interdit de travailler le dimanche **2.** *fig* [obsession] religion *f*, culte *m* ▪ **to make a ~ of sthg** se faire une religion de qqch ▪ **sport is a ~ with him** le sport est son dieu.

religious [rɪ'lɪdʒəs] <> *adj* **1.** [authority, order, ceremony, art] religieux ▪ [war] de religion ▪ **~ education** *OR* **instruction** instruction *f* religieuse **2.** [devout] religieux, croyant **3.** *fig* [scrupulous] religieux.
<> *n* [monk, nun] religieux *m*, - euse *f*.

religiously [rɪ'lɪdʒəslɪ] *adv liter & fig* religieusement.

reline [,ri:'laɪn] *vt* [garment] mettre une nouvelle doublure à, redoubler ▪ [picture] rentoiler ▪ **to ~ the brakes** AUT changer les garnitures de freins.

relinquish [rɪ'lɪŋkwɪʃ] *vt* **1.** [give up - claim, hope, power] abandonner, renoncer à ; [- property, possessions] se dessaisir de ; [- right] renoncer à ▪ **he ~ed his voting rights to the chairman** il a cédé son droit de vote au président **2.** [release - grip, hold] : **to ~ one's hold of** *OR* **on sthg** *liter* lâcher qqch ; *fig* relâcher l'étreinte que l'on a sur qqch.

relish ['relɪʃ] <> *n* **1.** [pleasure, enthusiasm] goût *m*, plaisir *m*, délectation *f* ▪ **to do sthg with ~** faire qqch avec délectation *OR* grand plaisir, adorer faire qqch ▪ **he ate with ~** il mangea avec délices *OR* délectation **2.** [condiment, sauce] condiment *m*, sauce *f* **3.** [flavour] goût *m*, saveur *f* ▪ **life had lost its ~ for her** *fig* la vie avait perdu toute saveur pour elle.
<> *vt* **1.** [enjoy] savourer ▪ **I bet he's ~ing this moment** je parie qu'il savoure cet instant ▌ [look forward to] : **I don't ~ the idea** *OR* **prospect** *OR* **thought of seeing them again** l'idée *OR* la perspective de les revoir ne m'enchante *OR* ne me réjouit guère **2.** [savour - food, drink] savourer, se délecter de.

relive [,ri:'lɪv] *vt* revivre.

reload [,ri:'ləʊd] *vt* recharger.

relocate [,ri:ləʊ'keɪt] <> *vt* installer ailleurs, délocaliser ▪ **the facilities were ~d to Scotland** les services ont été réinstallés *OR* délocalisés en Écosse.
<> *vi* s'installer ailleurs, déménager.

relocation [,ri:ləʊ'keɪʃn] *n* [of premises, industry] délocalisation *f*, déménagement *m* ▪ [of population] relogement *m* ▪ **~ expenses** indemnité *f* de déménagement.

reluctance [rɪ'lʌktəns] *n* **1.** [unwillingness] répugnance *f* ▪ **to do sthg with ~** faire qqch à contrecœur *OR* de mauvais gré ▪ **she expressed some ~ to get involved in the matter** elle a dit qu'elle n'avait pas envie de se laisser entraîner dans cette histoire **2.** PHYS réluctance *f*.

reluctant [rɪ'lʌktənt] *adj* **1.** [unwilling] peu enclin *OR* disposé ▪ **to be ~ to do sthg** être peu enclin à faire qqch, n'avoir pas envie de faire qqch **2.** [against one's will - commitment, promise, approval] accordé à contrecœur ▪ **she gave a ~ smile** elle eut un sourire contraint ▪ **she was a ~ sex symbol** c'est bien malgré elle qu'elle était devenue un sex-symbol.

reluctantly [rɪ'lʌktəntlɪ] *adv* à contrecœur.

rely [rɪ'laɪ] (*pret & pp* **relied**) ◆ **rely on, rely upon** *vt insep* **1.** [depend on] compter sur, faire confiance à ▪ **she can always be relied upon to give good advice** on peut toujours compter sur elle pour donner de bons conseils ▪ **we were ~ing on the weather being good** nous comptions sur du beau temps ▪ **we relied on you bringing the records** on comptait sur vous pour apporter les disques ▪ **he can never be relied upon to keep a secret** on ne peut lui confier aucun secret ▪ **I ~ on my daughter to drive me to the shops** je dépends de ma fille pour me conduire aux magasins ▪ **he relies on his family for everything** il dépend de sa famille pour tout ▪ **I'm ~ing on you to find a solution** je compte sur vous pour trouver une solution **2.** LAW [call on] invoquer.

REM (*abbrev of* **rapid eye movement**) *n & comp* : **~ sleep** sommeil *m* paradoxal.

remain [rɪ'meɪn] *vi* **1.** [be left] rester ▪ **six hens ~** il reste six poules ▪ **very little ~s** *OR* **there ~s very little of the original building** il ne reste pas grand-chose du bâtiment d'origine ▪ **much ~s to be discussed** il y a encore beaucoup de choses à discuter ▪ **that ~s to be seen** cela reste à voir ▪ **it ~s to be seen whether he will agree** (il) reste à savoir s'il sera d'accord ▪ **the fact ~s that we can't afford this house** il n'en reste pas moins que *OR* toujours est-il que nous ne pouvons pas nous offrir cette maison ▪ **all that ~ed to be done was to say goodbye** il ne restait plus qu'à se dire au revoir ▪ **it only ~s for me to thank you** il ne me reste plus qu'à vous remercier **2.** [stay] rester, demeurer ▪ **please ~ seated** *OR* **in your seats** veuillez rester assis ▪ **to ~ silent** garder le silence, rester silencieux ▪ **he ~ed behind after the meeting** il est resté après la réunion ▪ **it ~s a mystery whether...** on ignore toujours si... ▪ **the real reasons were to ~ a secret** les véritables raisons devaient demeurer secrètes ▪ **he has ~ed the same despite all that has happened** il n'a pas changé malgré tout ce qui s'est passé ▪ **let things ~ as they are** laissez les choses telles qu'elles sont ▪ **I ~, Sir, your most faithful servant** *fml & dated* veuillez agréer *OR* je vous prie d'agréer, Monsieur, l'expression de mes sentiments les plus respectueux.

remainder [rɪ'meɪndəʳ] <> *n* **1.** [leftover - supplies, time] reste *m* ; [- money] solde *m* ; [- debt] reliquat *m* ; [- people] : **the ~ went on a picnic** les autres sont allés pique-niquer ▪ **for the ~ of his life** pour le restant de ses jours **2.** MATHS reste *m* **3.** [unsold book] invendu *m* ▪ [unsold product] fin *f* de série **4.** LAW usufruit *m* avec réversibilité.
<> *vt* COMM solder.

remaining [rɪ'meɪnɪŋ] *adj* qui reste, restant ▪ **the only ~ member of her family** la seule personne de sa famille (qui soit) encore en vie ▪ **the ~ guests** le reste des invités ▪ **it's our only ~ hope** c'est le seul espoir qui nous reste, c'est notre dernier espoir.

remains [rɪ'meɪnz] *npl* **1.** [of meal, fortune] restes *mpl* ▪ [of building] restes *mpl*, vestiges *mpl* **2.** *euph & fml* [corpse] restes *mpl*, dépouille *f* mortelle.

remake (*pret & pp* **remade** [-'meɪd]) <> *vt* [,ri:'meɪk] refaire.
<> *n* ['ri:meɪk] [film] remake *m*.

remand [rɪ'mɑ:nd] *UK* <> *vt* LAW [case] renvoyer ▪ [defendant] déférer ▪ **to ~ sb in custody** placer qqn en détention préventive ▪ **to ~ sb on bail** mettre qqn en liberté *OR* libérer qqn sous caution.
<> *n* renvoi *m* ▪ **to be on ~** [in custody] être en détention préventive ; [on bail] être libéré sous caution.

remand centre *n UK centre de détention préventive.*

remand home *n UK* ≃ centre *m* d'éducation surveillée.

remark [rɪ'mɑ:k] <> *n* **1.** [comment] remarque *f*, réflexion *f* ▪ **to make** *OR* **to pass a ~** faire une remarque ▪ **to make** *OR* **to pass ~s about sthg/sb** faire des réflexions sur qqch/qqn ▪ **she made the ~ that no one knew the truth** elle fit remarquer *OR* observer que personne ne savait la vérité ▪ **to let sthg pass without ~** laisser passer qqch sans faire de commentaire **2.** *fml* [attention] attention *f*, intérêt *m* ▪ **his behaviour did not escape ~** son comportement n'est pas passé inaperçu.
<> *vt* **1.** [comment] (faire) remarquer, (faire) observer ▪ **"the days are getting longer," she ~ed** "les jours rallongent", fit-elle remarquer **2.** *fml* [notice] remarquer.
◆ **remark on, remark upon** *vt insep* : **to ~ on** *OR* **upon sthg** [comment] faire un commentaire *OR* une observation sur qqch ; [criticize] faire des remarques sur qqch ▪ **he ~ed on the lateness of the hour** il fit remarquer qu'il était tard.

remarkable [rɪ'mɑ:kəbl] *adj* [quality, aspect] remarquable ■ [event, figure] remarquable, marquant ■ **they are ~ for their modesty** ils sont d'une rare modestie *OR* remarquablement modestes.

remarkably [rɪ'mɑ:kəblɪ] *adv* remarquablement.

remarriage [,ri:'mærɪdʒ] *n* remariage *m*.

remarry [,ri:'mærɪ] (*pret & pp* **remarried**) *vi* se remarier.

rematch SPORT ◇ *vt* [,ri:'mætʃ] [players, contestants] opposer de nouveau.
◇ *n* ['ri:mætʃ] [return] match *m* retour ■ [second] deuxième match *m*.

remediable [rɪ'mi:djəbl] *adj* remédiable.

remedial [rɪ'mi:djəl] *adj* **1.** [action] réparateur ■ [measures] de redressement **2.** *UK* SCH [classes, education] de rattrapage, de soutien ■ [pupil, student] qui n'a pas le niveau ■ **~ teaching** rattrapage *m* scolaire **3.** MED [treatment] correctif, curatif ■ **~ exercises** gymnastique *f* corrective.

remedy ['remədɪ] ◇ *n* (*pl* **remedies**) **1.** *liter & fig* remède *m* ■ **it's a good ~ for insomnia** c'est un bon remède contre l'insomnie ■ **to find a ~ for sthg** trouver un remède à qqch **2.** *UK* LAW recours *m* ■ **to have no ~ at law against sb** n'avoir aucun recours légal contre qqn.
◇ *vt* (*pret & pp* **remedied**) MED remédier à ■ *fig* rattraper, remédier à ■ **the situation cannot be remedied** la situation est sans issue.

remember [rɪ'membəʳ] ◇ *vt* **1.** [recollect - face, person, past event] se souvenir de, se rappeler ■ **don't you ~ me?** [in memory] vous ne vous souvenez pas de moi? ; [recognize] vous ne me reconnaissez pas? ■ **I ~ him as a child** je me souviens de lui enfant ■ **I ~ locking the door** je me rappelle avoir *OR* je me souviens d'avoir fermé la porte à clé ■ **I don't ~ ever going** *OR* **having gone there** je ne me rappelle pas y être jamais allé ■ **do you ~ me knocking on your door?** vous souvenez-vous que j'ai frappé à votre porte? ■ **I can't ~ anything else** c'est tout ce dont je me souviens ■ **I ~ when there was no such thing as a paid holiday** je me souviens de l'époque où les congés payés n'existaient pas ■ **I can't ~ her name** son nom m'échappe, je ne me souviens pas de son nom ■ **I can never ~ names** je n'ai aucune mémoire des noms ■ **we have nothing to ~ him by** nous n'avons aucun souvenir de lui ■ **she will always be ~ed as a great poet** on se souviendra toujours d'elle comme d'un grand poète ■ **as you will ~, the door is always locked** vous savez sans doute que la porte est toujours fermée à clef ■ **nobody could ~ such a thing happening before** personne n'avait jamais vu une chose pareille se produire
2. [not forget] penser à, songer à ■ **~ my advice** n'oubliez pas mes conseils ■ **~ to close the door** n'oubliez pas de *OR* pensez à fermer la porte ■ **we can't be expected to ~ everything** nous ne pouvons quand même pas penser à tout ■ **that's a date worth ~ing** voilà une date qu'il faudrait ne pas oublier ▌ [be mindful of] : **~ where you are!** un peu de tenue, voyons! ■ **~ who you're talking to!** à qui croyez-vous parler? ■ **he ~ed himself just in time** il s'est repris juste à temps
3. [give regards to] : **~ me to your parents** rappelez-moi au bon souvenir de vos parents
4. [give tip or present to] : **please ~ the driver** n'oubliez pas le chauffeur ■ **she always ~s me on my birthday** elle n'oublie jamais le jour de mon anniversaire ■ **he ~ed me in his will** il a pensé à moi dans son testament
5. [commemorate - war] commémorer ; [- victims] se souvenir de.
◇ *vi* se souvenir ■ **I ~ now** maintenant, je m'en souviens ■ **as far as I can ~** autant qu'il m'en souvienne ■ **not that I ~** pas que je m'en souvienne ■ **if I ~ rightly** si je me *OR* si je m'en souviens bien, si j'ai bonne mémoire.

remembrance [rɪ'membrəns] *n* **1.** [recollection] souvenir *m*, mémoire *f* **2.** [memory] souvenir *m* **3.** [keepsake] souvenir *m* **4.** [commemoration] souvenir *m*, commémoration *f* ■ **~ service, service of ~** cérémonie *f* du souvenir, commémoration *f*.
◆ **in remembrance of** *prep phr* : **in ~ of sthg/sb** en souvenir *OR* en mémoire de qqch/qqn.

Remembrance Day, Remembrance Sunday *n UK* (commémoration *f* de l')Armistice *m* (*le dimanche avant ou après le 11 novembre*).

REMEMBRANCE SUNDAY

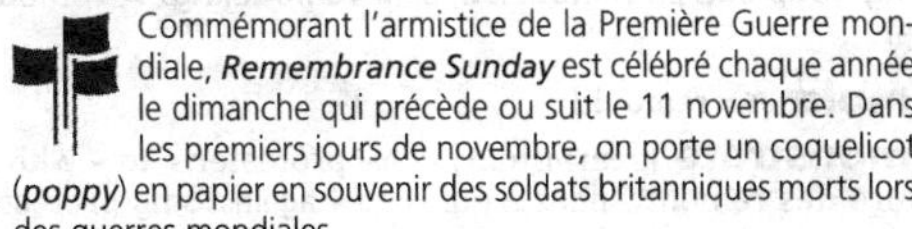

Commémorant l'armistice de la Première Guerre mondiale, *Remembrance Sunday* est célébré chaque année le dimanche qui précède ou suit le 11 novembre. Dans les premiers jours de novembre, on porte un coquelicot (*poppy*) en papier en souvenir des soldats britanniques morts lors des guerres mondiales.

remind [rɪ'maɪnd] *vt* **1.** [tell] rappeler à ■ **to ~ sb to do sthg** rappeler à qqn de faire qqch, faire penser à qqn qu'il faut faire qqch ■ **to ~ sb about sthg** rappeler qqch à qqn ■ **can you ~ me about the bills/to pay the bills?** pouvez-vous me faire penser aux factures/me rappeler qu'il faut payer les factures? ■ **do I need to ~ you of the necessity for discretion?** inutile de vous rappeler que la discrétion s'impose ■ **how many times do they have to be ~ed?** combien de fois faut-il le leur rappeler? ■ **that ~s me!** à propos!, pendant que j'y pense! **2.** [be reminiscent of] : **she ~s me of my sister** elle me rappelle ma sœur.

reminder [rɪ'maɪndəʳ] *n* [spoken] rappel *m* ■ [written] pense-bête *m* ■ ADMIN & COMM rappel *m* ■ **to give sb a ~ to do sthg** rappeler à qqn qu'il doit faire qqch ■ **the picture was a ~ of her life in Paris** cette image lui rappelait sa vie à Paris ■ **we gave him a gentle ~ that it's her birthday tomorrow** nous lui avons discrètement rappelé que demain c'est son anniversaire.

reminisce [,remɪ'nɪs] *vi* raconter ses souvenirs ■ **to ~ about the past** évoquer le passé *OR* parler du passé.

reminiscence [,remɪ'nɪsns] *n* [memory] réminiscence *f*, souvenir *m*.
◆ **reminiscences** *npl* [memoirs] mémoires *mpl*.

reminiscent [,remɪ'nɪsnt] *adj* [suggestive] : **~ of** qui rappelle, qui fait penser à ■ **parts of the book are ~ of Proust** on trouve des réminiscences de Proust dans certaines parties du livre, certaines parties du livre rappellent Proust.

remiss [rɪ'mɪs] *adj fml* négligent ■ **it was rather ~ of you to forget her birthday** c'était un peu négligent *OR* léger de votre part d'oublier son anniversaire.

remission [rɪ'mɪʃn] *n* **1.** *UK* LAW [release - from prison sentence] remise *f* (de peine) ; [- from debt, claim] remise *f* ■ ADMIN [dispensation] dispense *f* **2.** MED & RELIG rémission *f*.

remit (*pret & pp* **remitted**, *cont* **remitting**) ◇ *vt* [rɪ'mɪt] **1.** [release - from penalty, sins] remettre ■ **to ~ sb's debt** remettre la dette de qqn, tenir qqn quitte d'une dette ■ **to ~ sb's sentence** accorder une remise de peine à qqn ■ [dispense, exonerate - fees, tax] remettre ■ **his exam fees were remitted** il a été dispensé des droits d'examen **2.** [send - money] envoyer **3.** LAW [case] renvoyer **4.** *fml* [defer] différer, remettre **5.** *fml* [relax - attention, activity] relâcher.
◇ *vi* [rɪ'mɪt] **1.** [lessen - zeal] diminuer ; [- attention, efforts] se relâcher ; [- storm] s'apaiser, se calmer **2.** MED [fever] tomber, diminuer ■ [disease] régresser.
◇ *n* ['ri:mɪt] attributions *fpl*, pouvoirs *mpl* ■ **that's outside their ~** cela n'entre pas dans (le cadre de) leurs attributions ■ **our ~ is to...** il nous incombe de...

remittal [rɪ'mɪtl] *n* **1.** FIN [of debt] remise *f* **2.** LAW renvoi *m*.

remittance [rɪ'mɪtns] *n* **1.** [payment] versement *m* ■ [settlement] paiement *m*, règlement *m* **2.** [delivery - of papers, documents] remise *f*.

remittee [rɪ,mɪt'i:] *n* ADMIN destinataire *mf* (*d'un envoi de fonds*).

remittent [rɪ'mɪtnt] *adj* MED rémittent.

remitter, remittor [rɪ'mɪtəʳ] *n* FIN remettant *m*, - e *f* ■ [of letter, document] porteur *m*.

remnant ['remnənt] *n* [remains - of meal, material] reste *m* ■ [vestige - of beauty, culture] vestige *m* ■ **the ~s of the army/his fortune** ce qui reste de l'armée/de sa fortune.

◆ **remnants** *npl* COMM [unsold goods] invendus *mpl* ■ [fabric] coupons *mpl* (de tissus) ■ [oddments] fins *fpl* de série.

remodel [,riː'mɒdl] (*UK pret & pp* **remodelled**, *cont* **remodelling**) (*US pret & pp* **remodeled**, *cont* **remodeling**) *vt* remodeler.

remold *US* = **remould**.

remonstrate ['remənstreɪt] *vi fml* protester ■ **to ~ with sb** faire des remontrances à qqn ■ **to ~ against sthg** protester contre qqch.

remorse [rɪ'mɔːs] *n* remords *m* ■ **he was filled with ~ at what he had done** il était pris de remords en songeant à ce qu'il avait fait ■ **she felt no ~** elle n'éprouvait aucun remords ■ **without ~** [with no regret] sans remords ; [pitilessly] sans pitié.

remorseful [rɪ'mɔːsfʊl] *adj* plein de remords.

remorsefully [rɪ'mɔːsfʊlɪ] *adv* avec remords.

remorseless [rɪ'mɔːslɪs] *adj* **1.** [with no regret] sans remords **2.** [relentless] implacable, impitoyable.

remorselessly [rɪ'mɔːslɪslɪ] *adv* **1.** [with no regret] sans remords **2.** [relentlessly] impitoyablement, implacablement.

remortgage [,riː'mɔːgɪdʒ] *vt* [house, property] hypothéquer de nouveau, prendre une nouvelle hypothèque sur.

remote [rɪ'məʊt] *adj* **1.** [distant - place] éloigné, lointain ; [- time, period] lointain, reculé ; [- ancestor] éloigné ■ **in the remotest parts of the continent** au fin fond du continent ■ **a very ~ area** un endroit très isolé **2.** [aloof - person, manner] distant, froid ■ [faraway - look] lointain, vague ; [- voice] lointain **3.** [unconnected - idea, comment] éloigné ■ **your comments are rather ~ from the subject** vos commentaires n'ont pas grand-chose à voir avec le sujet **4.** [slight - chance] petit, faible ; [- ressemblance] vague, lointain ■ **our chances of success are rather ~** nos chances de réussite sont assez minces, nous n'avons que peu de chances de réussir ■ **it's a ~ possibility** c'est très peu probable ■ **I haven't the remotest idea** je n'en ai pas la moindre idée **5.** COMPUT [terminal] commandé à distance.

remote control *n* télécommande *f*, commande *f* à distance.

remote-controlled [-kən'trəʊld] *adj* télécommandé.

remotely [rɪ'məʊtlɪ] *adv* **1.** [slightly] faiblement, vaguement ■ **the two subjects are only very ~ linked** il n'y a qu'un rapport très lointain entre les deux sujets ■ **she's not ~ interested** ça ne l'intéresse pas le moins du monde *OR* absolument pas ■ **I'm not even ~ tired** je ne suis pas fatigué du tout *OR* absolument pas fatigué **2.** [distantly] : **they are ~ related** ils sont parents éloignés **3.** [aloofly] de façon distante *OR* hautaine ■ [dreamily] vaguement, de façon songeuse.

remoteness [rɪ'məʊtnɪs] *n* **1.** [distance - in space] éloignement *m*, isolement *m* ; [- in time] éloignement *m* **2.** [aloofness - of person] distance *f*, froideur *f*.

remould *UK*, **remold** *US* <> *vt* [,riː'məʊld] **1.** ART & TECH remouler, refaçonner **2.** AUT [tyre] rechaper **3.** *fig* [person, character] changer, remodeler.
<> *n* ['riːməʊld] [tyre] pneu *m* rechapé.

remount <> *vt* [,riː'maʊnt] **1.** [horse, bicycle] remonter sur ■ [hill, steps] remonter, gravir à nouveau ■ [ladder] remonter à *OR* sur **2.** [picture] rentoiler ■ [photograph] remplacer le support de ■ [jewel] remonter.
<> *vi* [on horse, bicycle] remonter.

removable [rɪ'muːvəbl] *adj* **1.** [detachable - lining, cover] amovible, détachable **2.** [transportable - furniture, fittings] mobile, transportable.

removal [rɪ'muːvl] <> *n* **1.** [of garment, stain, object] enlèvement *m* ■ [of abuse, evil, threat] suppression *f* ■ MED [of organ, tumour] ablation *f* **2.** [change of residence] déménagement *m* ■ **their ~ from Dublin** leur départ de Dublin ■ **their ~ to Dublin** leur départ pour Dublin ■ [transfer] transfert *m* ■ **the ~ of the prisoner to a safer place** le transfert *OR* le déplacement du prisonnier dans un endroit plus sûr **3.** [dismissal] : **~ from office** révocation *f*, renvoi *m*.
<> *comp UK* [expenses, firm] de déménagement ■ **~ man** déménageur *m* ■ **~ van** camion *m* de déménagement.

remove [rɪ'muːv] <> *vt* **1.** [take off, out - clothes, object] enlever, retirer, ôter ; [- stain] enlever, faire partir ■ MED [- organ, tumour] enlever, retirer ■ **to ~ one's make-up** se démaquiller ■ **to ~ hair from one's legs** s'épiler les jambes ■ [take or send away - object] enlever ; [- person] faire sortir ■ **to ~ a picture from the wall** enlever un tableau du mur, décrocher un tableau ■ **she was ~d to hospital** elle a été transportée à l'hôpital *OR* hospitalisée ■ **the child must be ~d from its mother** il faut retirer l'enfant à sa mère ■ **the soldiers were ~d to the front** on envoya les soldats au front ■ **~ the prisoner!** [in courtroom] qu'on emmène le prisonnier! ■ [dismiss - employee] renvoyer ; [- official] révoquer, destituer ■ **his opponents had him ~d from office** ses opposants l'ont fait révoquer **2.** [suppress - clause, paragraph] supprimer ; [- suspicion, doubt, fear] dissiper ■ **all obstacles have been ~d** tous les obstacles ont été écartés ■ **his name has been ~d from the list** son nom ne figure plus sur la liste ■ *euph* [kill] faire disparaître, tuer.
<> *vi fml* **1.** [firm, premises, family] déménager ■ **our office ~d to Glasgow** notre service s'est installé à Glasgow **2.** [person - go] : **she ~d to her room** elle se retira dans sa chambre.
<> *n* **1.** [distance] distance *f* ■ **this is but one ~ from blackmail** ça frôle le chantage ■ **it's several ~s *OR* a far ~ from what we need** ce n'est vraiment pas ce qu'il nous faut ■ **it's only a slight ~ from his usual themes** ça ne diffère pas beaucoup de ses thèmes habituels **2.** [degree of kinship] degré *m* de parenté.

removed [rɪ'muːvd] *adj* : **to be far ~ from** être très éloigné *OR* loin de ■ **one stage ~ from insanity** au bord de la folie ▶ **first cousin once/twice ~** cousin *m*, cousine *f* au premier/deuxième degré.

remover [rɪ'muːvər] *n* **1.** [of furniture] déménageur *m* **2.** [solvent] : **paint ~** décapant *m (pour peinture)*.

remunerate [rɪ'mjuːnəreɪt] *vt* rémunérer.

remuneration [rɪ,mjuːnə'reɪʃn] *n* rémunération *f* ■ **to receive ~ for sthg** être rémunéré *OR* payé pour qqch.

remunerative [rɪ'mjuːnərətɪv] *adj* rémunérateur.

renaissance [rə'neɪsns] <> *n* renaissance *f* ■ **the Renaissance** ART & HIST la Renaissance.
<> *comp* [art, painter] de la Renaissance ■ [palace, architecture, style] Renaissance *(inv)*.

Renaissance man *n* homme *m* aux talents multiples.

renal ['riːnl] *adj* rénal.

rename [,riː'neɪm] *vt* rebaptiser.

renascent [rɪ'næsnt] *adj* renaissant.

renationalize, ise [riː'næʃnəlaɪz] *vt* renationaliser.

rend [rend] (*pret & pp* **rent** [rent]) *vt lit* **1.** [tear - fabric] déchirer ; [- wood, armour] fendre ■ *fig* [- silence, air] déchirer ■ **the country was rent in two by political strife** le pays était profondément divisé par les conflits politiques ■ **to ~ sb's heart** fendre le cœur à qqn **2.** [wrench] arracher.

render ['rendər] *vt* **1.** [deliver - homage, judgment, verdict] rendre ; [- assistance] prêter ; [- help] fournir ■ [submit - bill, account] présenter, remettre ■ **to ~ an account of sthg** [explain] rendre compte de qqch ; COMM remettre *OR* présenter le compte de qqch ■ **account ~ed** COMM facture *f* de rappel ■ **to ~ sb a service** rendre (un) service à qqn ■ **to ~ thanks to sb** remercier qqn, faire des remerciements à qqn ▶ **~ unto Caesar the things that are Caesar's** BIBLE rendez à César ce qui appartient à César **2.** [cause to become] rendre ■ **a misprint ~ed the text incomprehensible** une coquille rendait le texte incompréhensible **3.** [perform - song, piece of music] interpréter ■ [convey - atmosphere, spirit] rendre, évoquer **4.** [translate] rendre, traduire ■ **~ed into English** rendu *OR* traduit en anglais **5.** CULIN faire fondre **6.** CONSTR crépir, enduire de crépi.

◆ **render up** *vt sep lit* [fortress] rendre ■ [hostage] libérer, rendre ■ [secret] livrer.

rendering ['rendərɪŋ] *n* **1.** [performance - of song, play, piece of music] interprétation *f* **2.** [evocation - of atmosphere, spirit] évocation *f* **3.** [translation] traduction *f* **4.** CONSTR crépi *m*.

rendezvous ['rɒndɪvu:] (*pl inv* ['rɒndɪvu:]) ◇ *n* **1.** [meeting] rendez-vous *m* **2.** [meeting place] lieu *m* de rendez-vous.
◇ *vi* [friends] se retrouver ▪ [group, party] se réunir ▪ **to ~ with sb** rejoindre qqn.

rendition [ren'dɪʃn] *n* **1.** [of poem, piece of music] interprétation *f* **2.** [translation] traduction *f*.

renegade ['renɪgeɪd] ◇ *n* renégat *m*, - e *f*.
◇ *adj* renégat.

renege [rɪ'ni:g] *vi* [in cards] faire une renonce.
◆ **renege on** *vt insep* [responsibilities] manquer à ▪ [agreement] revenir sur.

renegotiate [,ri:nɪ'gəʊʃɪeɪt] *vi* & *vt* renégocier.

renew [rɪ'nju:] *vt* **1.** [extend validity - passport, library book] renouveler ; [- contract, lease] renouveler, reconduire ▪ **to ~ one's subscription to sthg** renouveler son abonnement OR se réabonner à qqch **2.** [repeat - attack, promise, threat] renouveler ▪ [restart - correspondence, negotiations] reprendre ▪ **to ~ one's acquaintance with sb** renouer avec qqn ▪ [increase - strength] reconstituer, reprendre ▪ **to ~ one's efforts to do sthg** redoubler d'efforts pour faire qqch **3.** [replace - supplies] renouveler, remplacer ; [- batteries, mechanism] remplacer, changer.

renewable [rɪ'nju:əbl] *adj* renouvelable ▪ **~ energy** énergie *f* renouvelable.

renewal [rɪ'nju:əl] *n* **1.** [extension - of validity] renouvellement *m* ▪ [restart - of negotiations, hostilities] reprise *f* ; [- of acquaintance] fait *m* de renouer ▪ [increase - of energy, hope] regain *m* ▪ [repetition - of promise, threat] renouvellement *m* **2.** [renovation] rénovation *f* **3.** RELIG renouveau *m*.

renewed [rɪ'nju:d] *adj* [confidence, hope] renouvelé ▪ [vigour, force] accru ▪ **with ~ enthusiasm** avec un regain d'enthousiasme ▪ **~ outbreaks of fighting** une recrudescence des combats.

rennet ['renɪt] *n* **1.** [for cheese, junket] présure *f* **2.** ZOOL caillette *f*.

renounce [rɪ'naʊns] ◇ *vt* [claim, title] abandonner, renoncer à ▪ [faith, principle, habit] renoncer à, renier ▪ [treaty] dénoncer.
◇ *vi* [in cards] renoncer.

renovate ['renəveɪt] *vt* remettre à neuf, rénover.

renovation [,renə'veɪʃn] *n* remise *f* à neuf, rénovation *f*.

renown [rɪ'naʊn] *n* renommée *f*, renom *f*.

renowned [rɪ'naʊnd] *adj* renommé, célèbre, réputé ▪ **to be ~ for sthg** être connu OR célèbre pour qqch.

rent [rent] ◇ *pt* & *pp* ▷ **rend**.
◇ *vt* **1.** [subj: tenant, hirer] louer, prendre en location ▪ **to ~ sthg from sb** louer qqch à qqn **2.** [subj: owner] louer, donner en location ▪ **to ~ sthg (out) to sb** louer qqch à qqn.
◇ *n* **1.** [for flat, house] loyer *m* ▪ [for farm] loyer *m*, fermage *m* ▪ [for car, TV] (prix *m* de) location *f* ▪ **(up)for ~** à louer **2.** ECON loyer *m* **3.** [tear] déchirure *f* **4.** [split - in movement, party] rupture *f*, scission *f*.

rental ['rentl] ◇ *n* **1.** [hire agreement - for car, house, TV, telephone] location *f* **2.** [payment - for property, land] loyer *m* ; [- for TV, car, holiday accommodation] (prix *m* de) location *f* ; [- for telephone] abonnement *m*, redevance *f* **3.** [income] (revenu *m* des) loyers *mpl* **4.** US [apartment] appartement *m* en location ▪ [house] maison *f* en location ▪ [land] terrain *m* en location.
◇ *adj* [agency] de location ▪ **~ agreement** contrat *m* de location ▪ **~ charge** [for telephone] abonnement *m* ; [for TV, car] prix *m* de location ▪ **~ library** US bibliothèque *f* de prêt.

rent book *n* carnet *m* de quittances de loyer.

rent boy *n* jeune prostitué *m (pour hommes)*.

rent collector *n* receveur *m*, - euse *f* des loyers.

rent control *n* contrôle *m* des loyers.

rented ['rentɪd] *adj* loué, de location.

rent-free ◇ *adj* exempt de loyer.
◇ *adv* sans payer de loyer, sans avoir de loyer à payer.

rent rebate *n* réduction *f* de loyer.

renunciation [rɪ,nʌnsɪ'eɪʃn] *n* [of authority, claim, title] renonciation *f*, abandon *m* ▪ [of faith, religion] renonciation *f*, abjuration *f* ▪ [of principle] abandon *m*, répudiation *f* ▪ [of treaty] dénonciation *f*.

reoccupy [,ri:'ɒkjʊpaɪ] (*pret* & *pp* **reoccupied**) *vt* réoccuper.

reoccur [,ri:ə'kɜ:ʳ] (*cont* **reoccurring**, *pret* & *pp* **reoccurred**) = **recur** *(vi senses 1, 2)*.

reoccurrence [,ri:ə'kʌrəns] = **recurrence**.

reopen [,ri:'əʊpn] ◇ *vt* **1.** [door, border, book, bank account] rouvrir **2.** [restart - hostilities] reprendre ; [- debate, negotiations] reprendre, rouvrir.
◇ *vi* **1.** [door, wound] se rouvrir ▪ [shop, theatre] rouvrir ▪ [school - after holiday] reprendre **2.** [negotiations] reprendre.

reopening [,ri:'əʊpnɪŋ] *n* [of shop] réouverture *f* ▪ [of negotiations] reprise *f*.

reorder ◇ *vt* [,ri:'ɔ:dəʳ] **1.** COMM [goods, supplies] commander de nouveau, faire une nouvelle commande de **2.** [rearrange - numbers, statistics, objects] reclasser, réorganiser.
◇ *n* ['ri:ɔ:dəʳ] COMM nouvelle commande *f*.

reorganization ['ri:,ɔ:gənaɪ'zeɪʃn] *n* réorganisation *f*.

reorganize, ise [,ri:'ɔ:gənaɪz] ◇ *vt* réorganiser.
◇ *vi* se réorganiser.

rep [rep] *n* **1.** *inf* COMM (*abbrev of* **representative**) VRP *m* **2.** = **repertory**.

Rep US **1.** *written abbr of* **Representative** **2.** *written abbr of* **Republican**.

repack [,ri:'pæk] *vt* [goods] remballer, emballer de nouveau ▪ [suitcase] refaire.

repackage [,ri:'pækɪdʒ] *vt* **1.** [goods] remballer **2.** US [public image] redorer *fig*.

repaid [ri:'peɪd] *pt* & *pp* ▷ **repay**.

repaint [,ri:'peɪnt] *vt* repeindre.

repair [rɪ'peəʳ] ◇ *vt* **1.** [mend - car, tyre, machine] réparer ; [- road, roof] réparer, refaire ; [- clothes] raccommoder ; [- hull] radouber, caréner ; [- tights] repriser ▪ **to have one's shoes ~ed** faire réparer ses chaussures **2.** [make amends for - error, injustice] réparer, remédier à.
◇ *vi fml* & *hum* aller, se rendre.
◇ *n* **1.** [mending - of car, machine, roof] réparation *f*, remise *f* en état ; [- of clothes] raccommodage *m* ; [- of shoes] réparation *f* ; [- of road] réfection *f*, remise *f* en état ▪ NAUT radoub *m* ▪ **to carry out ~s to** OR **on sthg** effectuer des réparations sur qqch ▪ **to be under ~** être en réparation ▪ **'closed for ~s'** 'fermé pour (cause de) travaux' ▪ **'road ~s'** réfection de la chaussée ▪ **the bridge was damaged beyond ~** le pont avait subi des dégâts irréparables ▪ **the ~s to the car cost him a fortune** les travaux de réparation OR les réparations sur la voiture lui ont coûté une fortune ➲ **~ kit** trousse *f* à outils **2.** [condition] état *m* ▪ **to be in good/bad ~** être en bon/mauvais état ▪ **the road is in a terrible state of ~** la route est très mal entretenue OR en très mauvais état.

repairer [rɪ'peərəʳ] *n* réparateur *m*, - trice *f*.

repairman [rɪ'peəmən] (*pl* **repairmen** [-mən]) *n* réparateur *m*.

repaper [,ri:'peɪpəʳ] *vt* retapisser.

reparable ['repərəbl] *adj* réparable.

reparation [,repə'reɪʃn] *n* **1.** *fml* [amends] réparation *f* ▪ **to make ~s for sthg** réparer qqch *fig* **2.** *(usu pl)* [damages - after war, invasion etc] réparations *fpl*.

repartee [,repɑ:'ti:] *n* **1.** [witty conversation] esprit *m*, repartie *f* ▪ **to be good at ~** avoir la repartie facile, avoir de la repartie **2.** [witty comment] repartie *f*, réplique *f*.

repast [rɪ'pɑ:st] *n fml* repas *m*.

repatriate ◇ *vt* [,ri:'pætrɪeɪt] rapatrier.

◇ *n* [riːˈpætrɪət] rapatrié *m*, - e *f*.

repatriation [ˌriːpætrɪˈeɪʃn] *n* rapatriement *m*.

repay [riːˈpeɪ] (*pret & pp* **repaid** [riːˈpeɪd]) *vt* **1.** [refund - creditor, loan] rembourser ■ **to ~ a debt** *liter* rembourser une dette ; *fig* s'acquitter d'une dette ■ **he repaid her the money she had lent him** il lui a remboursé l'argent qu'elle lui avait prêté **2.** [return - visit] rendre ; [- hospitality, kindness] rendre, payer de retour ■ **how can I ever ~ you (for your kindness)?** comment pourrai-je jamais vous remercier (pour votre gentillesse)? ■ **to ~ good for evil** rendre le bien pour le mal ■ [reward - efforts, help] récompenser ■ **to be repaid for one's efforts/persistence** être récompensé de ses efforts/sa persévérance ■ **her generosity was repaid with indifference** tout ce qu'elle a obtenu en échange de sa générosité, c'est de l'indifférence.

repayable [riːˈpeɪəbl] *adj* remboursable ■ **~ in five years** remboursable sur cinq ans *OR* en cinq annuités.

repayment [riːˈpeɪmənt] *n* **1.** [of money, loan] remboursement *m* **2.** [reward - for kindness, effort] récompense *f*.

repeal [rɪˈpiːl] ◇ *vt* [law] abroger, annuler ■ [prison sentence] annuler ■ [decree] rapporter, révoquer.
◇ *n* [law] abrogation *f* ■ [prison sentence] annulation *f* ■ [decree] révocation *f*.

repeat [rɪˈpiːt] ◇ *vt* **1.** [say again - word, secret, instructions] répéter ; [- demand, promise] répéter, réitérer ■ **you're ~ing yourself** vous vous répétez ■ **it doesn't bear ~ing** [rude] c'est trop grossier pour être répété ; [trivial] ça ne vaut pas la peine d'être répété **2.** [redo, reexecute - action, attack, mistake] répéter, renouveler ■ MUS reprendre ■ **I wouldn't like to ~ the experience** je n'aimerais pas renouveler l'expérience ■ **it's history ~ing itself** c'est l'histoire qui se répète **3.** RADIO & TV [broadcast] rediffuser **4.** COMM [order, offer] renouveler **5.** SCH & UNIV [class, year] redoubler.
◇ *vi* **1.** [say again] répéter ■ **I shall never, ~ never, go there again** je n'y retournerai jamais, mais alors ce qui s'appelle jamais ■ **~ after me** SCH répétez après moi **2.** [recur] se répéter, se reproduire ■ MATHS se reproduire périodiquement **3.** [food] donner des renvois **4.** *US* POL voter plus d'une fois *(à une même élection)* **5.** [watch, clock] être à répétition.
◇ *n* **1.** [gen] répétition *f* **2.** MUS [passage] reprise *f* ■ [sign] signe *m* de reprise **3.** RADIO & TV [broadcast] rediffusion *f*, reprise *f*.
◇ *comp* [order, visit] renouvelé ■ **~ offender** récidiviste *mf* ■ **~ prescription** ordonnance *f (de renouvellement d'un médicament)*.

repeatable [rɪˈpiːtəbl] *adj* susceptible d'être répété ■ **what he said is not ~** je n'ose pas répéter ce qu'il a dit.

repeated [rɪˈpiːtɪd] *adj* répété.

repeatedly [rɪˈpiːtɪdlɪ] *adv* à plusieurs *OR* maintes reprises ■ **you have been told ~ not to play by the canal** on vous a dit cent fois de ne pas jouer près du canal.

repeater [rɪˈpiːtəʳ] *n* **1.** [clock] pendule *f* à répétition ■ [alarm] réveil *m* à répétition **2.** [gun] fusil *m* à répétition **3.** ELEC répéteur *m* **4.** *US* SCH redoublant *m*, - e *f* **5.** *US* POL électeur *m*, - trice *f* qui vote plus d'une fois *(à une même élection)*.

repeating [rɪˈpiːtɪŋ] *adj* **1.** MATHS périodique **2.** [gun] à répétition.

repeat performance *n* THEAT deuxième représentation *f* ■ **we don't want a ~ of last year's chaos** *fig* nous ne voulons pas que le désordre de l'année dernière se reproduise.

repel [rɪˈpel] (*pret & pp* **repelled**, *cont* **repelling**) ◇ *vt* **1.** [drive back - attacker, advance, suggestion] repousser **2.** [disgust - subj: unpleasant sight, smell etc] rebuter, dégoûter **3.** ELEC & PHYS repousser.
◇ *vi* ELEC & PHYS se repousser.

repellent, repellant [rɪˈpelənt] ◇ *adj* repoussant, répugnant ■ **to find sb/sthg ~** éprouver de la répugnance pour qqn/qqch.
◇ *n* **1.** [for insects] insecticide *m* ■ [for mosquitoes] antimoustiques *m inv* **2.** [for waterproofing] imperméabilisant *m*.

repent [rɪˈpent] ◇ *vi* se repentir ■ **to ~ of sthg** se repentir de qqch.
◇ *vt* se repentir de.

repentance [rɪˈpentəns] *n* repentir *m*.

repentant [rɪˈpentənt] *adj* repentant.

repercussion [ˌriːpəˈkʌʃn] *n* **1.** [consequence] répercussion *f*, retentissement *m*, contrecoup *m* ■ **to have ~s on** avoir des répercussions sur **2.** [echo] répercussion *f*.

repertoire [ˈrepətwɑːʳ] *n liter & fig* répertoire *m*.

repertory [ˈrepətrɪ] (*pl* **repertories**) *n* **1.** THEAT : **to be** *OR* **to act in ~** faire partie d'une troupe de répertoire, jouer dans un théâtre de répertoire ■ **~ (theatre)** théâtre *m* de répertoire **2.** = **repertoire**.

repertory company *n* compagnie *f OR* troupe *f* de répertoire.

repetition [ˌrepɪˈtɪʃn] *n* **1.** [of words, orders] répétition *f* **2.** [of action] répétition *f*, renouvellement *m* ■ **I don't want any ~ of this disgraceful behaviour** je ne veux plus vous voir vous conduire de cette façon scandaleuse **3.** MUS reprise *f*.

repetitious [ˌrepɪˈtɪʃəs] *adj* plein de répétitions *OR* de redites.

repetitive [rɪˈpetɪtɪv] *adj* [activity, work, rhythm] répétitif, monotone ■ [song, speech] plein de répétitions ■ [person] qui se répète.

repetitive strain injury, repetitive stress injury ▷ **RSI**.

rephrase [ˌriːˈfreɪz] *vt* reformuler ■ **can you ~ that question?** pouvez-vous formuler cette question autrement?

replace [rɪˈpleɪs] *vt* **1.** [put back] replacer, remettre (à sa place *OR* en place) ■ **to ~ the receiver** [on telephone] reposer le combiné, raccrocher (le téléphone) **2.** [person] remplacer ■ [mechanism, tyres] remplacer ■ **to ~ a worn part by** *OR* **with a new one** remplacer une pièce usée (par une pièce neuve).

replaceable [rɪˈpleɪsəbl] *adj* remplaçable.

replacement [rɪˈpleɪsmənt] ◇ *n* **1.** [putting back] remise *f* en place **2.** [substitution] remplacement *m* **3.** [person] remplaçant *m*, - e *f* **4.** [engine or machine part] pièce *f* de rechange ■ [product] produit *m* de remplacement.
◇ *comp* [part] de rechange.

replant [ˌriːˈplɑːnt] *vt* replanter.

replay ◇ *n* [ˈriːpleɪ] **1.** TV ralenti *m* ■ **the ~ clearly shows the foul** on voit bien la faute au ralenti **2.** SPORT match *m* rejoué.
◇ *vt* [ˌriːˈpleɪ] [match] rejouer ■ [record, piece of film, video] repasser.

replenish [rɪˈplenɪʃ] *vt fml* **1.** [restock - cellar, stock] réapprovisionner **2.** [refill - glass] remplir de nouveau.

replete [rɪˈpliːt] *adj fml* [full] rempli, plein ■ [person - full up] rassasié.

repletion [rɪˈpliːʃn] *n fml* satiété *f*.

replica [ˈreplɪkə] *n* [of painting, model, sculpture] réplique *f*, copie *f* ■ [of document] copie *f* (exacte).

replicate [ˈreplɪkeɪt] ◇ *vt* [reproduce] reproduire ■ **certain cells ~ themselves** BIOL certaines cellules se reproduisent par mitose.
◇ *vi* BIOL se reproduire par mitose.

reply [rɪˈplaɪ] ◇ *n* (*pl* **replies**) **1.** [answer] réponse *f* ■ [retort] réplique *f* ■ **he made no ~** il n'a pas répondu **2.** LAW réplique *f*.
◇ *vt* (*pret & pp* **replied**) [answer] répondre ■ [retort] répliquer, rétorquer ■ **"I don't know," she replied** "je ne sais pas", répondit-elle.
◇ *vi* (*pret & pp* **replied**) répondre ■ **to ~ to sb** répondre à qqn.
◆ **in reply to** *prep phr* en réponse à ■ **to say sthg in ~ to sb/sthg** dire qqch en réponse à qqn/qqch.

reply card *n* coupon-réponse *m*.

reply-paid *adj UK* avec réponse payée.

repoint [,riː'pɔɪnt] *vt* CONSTR rejointoyer.

report [rɪ'pɔːt] ◇ *vt* **1.** [announce] annoncer, déclarer, signaler ▪ **it is ~ed from Delhi that a ten-year contract has been signed** on annonce à Delhi qu'un contrat de dix ans a été signé ▪ **the doctors ~ his condition as comfortable** les médecins déclarent son état satisfaisant
2. [subj: press, media - event, match] faire un reportage sur ; [- winner] annoncer ; [- debate, speech] faire le compte rendu de ▪ **the newspapers ~ heavy casualties** les journaux font état de nombreuses victimes ▪ **our correspondent ~s that troops have left the city** notre correspondant nous signale que des troupes ont quitté la ville ▪ **her resignation is ~ed in several papers** sa démission est annoncée dans plusieurs journaux ▪ **~ing restrictions were not lifted** LAW l'interdiction faite aux journalistes de rapporter les débats n'a pas été levée ▪ [unconfirmed news] : **it is ~ed that a woman drowned** une femme se serait noyée ▪ **he is ~ed to have left** *OR* **as having left the country** il aurait quitté le pays
3. [give account of] faire état de, rendre compte de ▪ **the police have ~ed some progress in the fight against crime** la police a annoncé des progrès dans la lutte contre la criminalité ▪ **to ~ one's findings** [in research] rendre compte des résultats de ses recherches ; [in inquiry, commission] présenter ses conclusions
4. [burglary, disappearance, murder] signaler ▪ [wrongdoer] dénoncer, porter plainte contre ▪ **to ~ sb missing (to the police)** signaler la disparition de qqn (à la police) ▪ **to be ~ed missing/dead** être porté disparu/au nombre des morts ▪ **they were ~ed to the police for vandalism** on les a dénoncés à la police pour vandalisme
5. *fml* [present] : **to ~ o.s. for duty** se présenter au travail.
◇ *vi* **1.** [make a report - committee] faire son rapport, présenter ses conclusions ; [- police] faire un rapport ; [- journalist] faire un reportage ▪ **to ~ on sthg** ADMIN faire un rapport sur qqch ; PRESS faire un reportage sur qqch ▪ **she's ~ing on the train crash** elle fait un reportage sur l'accident de train ▪ **he ~s for the BBC** il est reporter *OR* journaliste à la BBC
2. [in hierarchy] : **to ~ to sb** être sous les ordres de qqn ▪ **I ~ directly to the sales manager** je dépends directement du chef des ventes
3. [present o.s.] se présenter ▪ **to ~ for duty** prendre son service, se présenter au travail ▪ **~ to the sergeant when you arrive** [go and see] présentez-vous au sergent à votre arrivée ; [give account] faites votre rapport au sergent quand vous arriverez ▪ **to ~ to base** MIL [go] se présenter à la base ; [contact] contacter la base ▪ **to ~ to barracks** *OR* **to one's unit** MIL rallier son unité ▪ **to ~ sick** se faire porter malade.
◇ *n* **1.** [account, review] rapport *m* ▪ **to draw up** *OR* **to make a ~ on sthg** faire un rapport sur qqch ▪ **he gave an accurate ~ of the situation** il a fait un rapport précis sur la situation ▮ [summary - of speech, meeting] compte rendu *m* ▪ [official record] procès-verbal *m* ▪ **his ~ on the meeting** son compte rendu de la réunion ▮ COMM & FIN [review] rapport *m* ▪ [balance sheet] bilan *m* ▪ **sales ~** rapport *m OR* bilan *m* commercial
2. [in media] reportage *m* ▪ [investigation] enquête *f* ▪ [bulletin] bulletin *m* ▪ **to do a ~ on sthg** faire un reportage *OR* une enquête sur qqch ▪ **here is a ~ from Keith Owen** RADIO & TV voici le reportage de Keith Owen ▪ **according to newspaper/intelligence ~s** selon les journaux/les services de renseignements ▮ [allegation] allégation *f*, rumeur *f* ▪ [news] nouvelle *f* ▪ **we have had ~s of several burglaries in city stores** on nous a signalé plusieurs cambriolages dans les magasins du centre-ville ▪ **there are ~s of civil disturbances in the North** il y aurait des troubles dans le Nord ▪ **~s are coming in of an earthquake** on parle d'un tremblement de terre
3. *UK* SCH : **(school) ~** bulletin *m* (scolaire) ▪ **end of term ~** bulletin *m* trimestriel
4. LAW [of court proceedings] procès-verbal *m* ▪ **law ~s** recueil *m* de jurisprudence
5. *fml* [repute] renom *m*, réputation *f* ▪ **of good ~** de bonne réputation
6. [sound - of explosion, shot] détonation *f*.
◆ **report back** ◇ *vi insep* **1.** [return - soldier] regagner ses quartiers, rallier son régiment ; [- journalist, salesman] rentrer ▪ **to ~ back to headquarters** MIL rentrer au quartier général ; [salesman, clerk] rentrer au siège ▪ **I have to ~ back to the office** il faut que je repasse au bureau
2. [present report] présenter son rapport ▪ **the commission must first ~ back to the minister** la commission doit d'abord présenter son rapport au ministre ▪ **can you ~ back on what was discussed?** pouvez-vous rapporter ce qui a été dit? ▪ **please ~ back to me before you decide anything** veuillez vous en référer à moi avant de prendre une décision.
◇ *vt sep* [results, decision] rapporter, rendre compte de.
◆ **report out** *vt sep US* POL [bill, legislation] renvoyer après examen.

report card *n* SCH bulletin *m OR* carnet *m* scolaire.

reported [rɪ'pɔːtɪd] *adj* : **there have been ~ sightings of dolphins off the coast** on aurait vu des dauphins près des côtes ▪ **what was their last ~ position?** où ont-ils été signalés pour la dernière fois?

reportedly [rɪ'pɔːtɪdlɪ] *adv* : **300 people have ~ been killed** 300 personnes auraient été tuées.

reported speech *n* GRAM style *m OR* discours *m* indirect ▪ **in ~** en style indirect.

reporter [rɪ'pɔːtə^r] *n* **1.** [for newspaper] journaliste *mf*, reporter *mf* ▪ RADIO & TV reporter *mf* **2.** [scribe - in court] greffier *m*, - ère *f* ; [- in parliament] sténographe *mf*.

report stage *n UK* POL *examen d'un projet de loi avant la troisième lecture* ▪ **the bill has reached ~** ≃ le projet de loi vient de passer en commission.

repose [rɪ'pəʊz] ◇ *vt fml* **1.** [rest] : **to ~ o.s.** se reposer **2.** [place - confidence, trust] mettre, placer.
◇ *vi* **1.** [rest - person] se reposer ; [- the dead] reposer **2.** [be founded - belief, theory] reposer ▪ **to ~ on firm evidence** reposer sur des preuves solides.
◇ *n fml* repos *m* ▪ **in ~** au *OR* en repos.

repository [rɪ'pɒzɪtrɪ] (*pl* **repositories**) *n* **1.** [storehouse - large] entrepôt *m* ; [- smaller] dépôt *m* **2.** [of knowledge, secret] dépositaire *mf*.

repossess [,riːpə'zes] *vt* reprendre possession de ▪ LAW saisir ▪ **they have** *OR* **their house has been ~ed** leur maison a été mise en saisie immobilière.

repossession [,riːpə'zeʃn] *n* reprise *f* de possession ▪ LAW saisie *f*.

repossession order *n* ordre *m* de saisie.

repot [,riː'pɒt] (*pret & pp* **repotted**, *cont* **repotting**) *vt* [plant] rempoter.

reprehend [,reprɪ'hend] *vt* [person] réprimander ▪ [conduct, action] condamner, désavouer.

reprehensible [,reprɪ'hensəbl] *adj* répréhensible.

reprehensibly [,reprɪ'hensəblɪ] *adv* de façon répréhensible.

reprehension [,reprɪ'henʃn] *n fml* [rebuke] réprimande *f* ▪ [criticism] condamnation *f*.

represent [,reprɪ'zent] *vt* **1.** [symbolize - subj: diagram, picture, symbol] représenter ▪ **what does the scene ~?** que représente la scène? **2.** [depict] représenter, dépeindre ▪ [describe] décrire ▪ **he ~ed her as a queen** il l'a peinte sous les traits d'une reine **3.** [constitute - achievement, change] représenter, constituer **4.** POL [voters, members] représenter ▪ **she ~s Tooting** elle est député de *OR* elle représente la circonscription de Tooting ▮ [be delegate for - subj: person] représenter ▪ **I ~ the agency** je viens de la part de l'agence ▪ **the best lawyers are ~ing the victims** les victimes sont représentées par les meilleurs avocats ▪ [opinion] représenter ▪ **the voice of women is not ~ed on the committee** les femmes ne sont pas représentées au comité ▮ [in numbers] représenter ▪ **foreign students are well ~ed in the university** il y a une forte proportion d'étudiants étrangers à l'université **5.** [express, explain - advantages, prospect, theory] présenter **6.** THEAT [subj: actor] jouer, interpréter.

representation [,reprɪzen'teɪʃn] *n* **1.** POL représentation *f* **2.** [description, presentation] représentation *f*.

◆ **representations** *npl* [complaints] plaintes *fpl*, protestations *fpl* ■ [intervention] démarche *f*, intervention *f* ■ **to make ~s to sb** [complain] se plaindre auprès de qqn ; [intervene] faire des démarches auprès de qqn.

representational [ˌreprɪzen'teɪʃənl] *adj* [gen] représentatif ■ ART figuratif.

representative [ˌreprɪ'zentətɪv] <> *adj* **1.** [typical] typique, représentatif ■ **to be ~ of sthg** être représentatif de qqch **2.** POL représentatif.
<> *n* **1.** [gen] représentant *m*, - e *f* ■ **he is our country's ~ abroad** il représente notre pays à l'étranger **2.** COMM : **(sales) ~** représentant *m*, - e *f* (de commerce) **3.** *US* POL ▻ **House of Representatives.**

repress [rɪ'pres] *vt* [rebellion] réprimer ■ PSYCHOL refouler.

repressed [rɪ'prest] *adj* [gen] réprimé ■ PSYCHOL refoulé.

repression [rɪ'preʃn] *n* [gen] répression *f* ■ PSYCHOL refoulement *m*.

repressive [rɪ'presɪv] *adj* [authority, system] répressif ■ [measures] de répression, répressif.

reprieve [rɪ'priːv] <> *vt* **1.** LAW [prisoner - remit] gracier ; [- postpone] accorder un sursis à **2.** *fig* [give respite to - patient] accorder un répit *OR* un sursis à ; [- company] accorder un sursis à.
<> *n* **1.** LAW remise *f* de peine, grâce *f* ■ **the condemned man was given a ~** le condamné a été gracié **2.** *fig* [respite - from danger, illness] sursis *m*, répit *m* ■ [extra time] délai *m*.

reprimand ['reprɪmɑːnd] <> *vt* réprimander ■ **he was ~ed for being late** [worker] il a reçu un blâme pour son retard ; [schoolchild] on lui a donné un avertissement pour son retard.
<> *n* [rebuke] réprimande *f* ■ [professional] blâme *m*.

reprint <> *vt* [ˌriː'prɪnt] réimprimer ■ **the book is being ~ed** le livre est en réimpression.
<> *n* ['riːprɪnt] réimpression *f*.

reprisal [rɪ'praɪzl] *n* représailles *fpl* ■ **to take ~s (against sb)** user de représailles *OR* exercer des représailles (contre qqn) ■ **by way of** *OR* **in ~, as a ~** par représailles.

repro ['riːprəʊ] (*abbrev of* **reproduction**) (*pl* **repros**) *n inf* (épreuve *f*) repro *f*.

reproach [rɪ'prəʊtʃ] <> *n* **1.** [criticism] reproche *m* ■ **in a tone of ~** sur un ton réprobateur *OR* de reproche ■ **above** *OR* **beyond ~** au-dessus de tout reproche, irréprochable **2.** [source of shame] honte *f* ■ **to be a ~ to** être la honte de.
<> *vt* faire des reproches à ■ **to ~ sb with sthg** reprocher qqch à qqn ■ **she ~ed him for** *OR* **with having broken his promise** elle lui reprochait d'avoir manqué à sa parole ■ **I ~ myself for failing to warn them** je m'en veux de ne pas les avoir prévenus ■ **I have nothing to ~ myself for** *OR* **with** je n'ai rien à me reprocher.

reproachful [rɪ'prəʊtʃfʊl] *adj* [voice, look, attitude] réprobateur ■ [tone, words] de reproche, réprobateur.

reproachfully [rɪ'prəʊtʃfʊlɪ] *adv* avec reproche ■ **to look at sb ~** lancer des regards réprobateurs à qqn.

reprobate ['reprəbeɪt] <> *adj* dépravé.
<> *n* dépravé *m*, - e *f*.

reprocess [ˌriː'prəʊses] *vt* retraiter.

reprocessing [ˌriː'prəʊsesɪŋ] *n* retraitement *m* ■ **nuclear ~** retraitement des déchets nucléaires.

reproduce [ˌriːprə'djuːs] <> *vt* reproduire.
<> *vi* se reproduire.

reproduction [ˌriːprə'dʌkʃn] <> *n* **1.** BIOL reproduction *f* **2.** [of painting, document] reproduction *f*, copie *f*.
<> *comp* : **~ furniture** reproduction *f* *OR* copie *f* de meubles d'époque.

reproductive [ˌriːprə'dʌktɪv] *adj* [organs, cells, process] reproducteur, de reproduction.

REPROM [ˌriː'prɒm] *n* COMPUT mémoire *f* morte reprogrammable.

reproof [rɪ'pruːf] *n* réprimande *f*, reproche *m*.

reproval [rɪ'pruːvl] *n* reproche *m*.

reprove [rɪ'pruːv] *vt* [person] réprimander ■ [action, behaviour] réprouver ■ **he was ~d for his conduct** on lui a reproché sa conduite.

reproving [rɪ'pruːvɪŋ] *adj* réprobateur.

reprovingly [rɪ'pruːvɪŋlɪ] *adv* [look] d'un air réprobateur *OR* de reproche ■ [say] d'un ton réprobateur *OR* de reproche.

reptile ['reptaɪl] <> *adj* reptile.
<> *n* reptile *m*.

reptile house *n* vivarium *m*.

reptilian [rep'tɪlɪən] <> *adj* **1.** ZOOL reptilien **2.** *fig* & *pej* reptile.
<> *n* reptile *m*.

Repub *US written abbr of* **Republican.**

republic [rɪ'pʌblɪk] *n* POL & *fig* république *f* ■ **the ~ of letters** la république des lettres ➲ **'The Republic'** ***Plato*** 'la République'.

republican [rɪ'pʌblɪkən] <> *adj* républicain.
<> *n* républicain *m*, - e *f*.

republicanism [rɪ'pʌblɪkənɪzm] *n* républicanisme *m*.

Republican party *pr n* : **the ~** le Parti républicain.

republication ['riːˌpʌblɪ'keɪʃn] *n* [of book] réédition *f*, nouvelle édition *f* ■ [of banns] nouvelle publication *f*.

Republic of Congo *pr n* République *f* du Congo.

repudiate [rɪ'pjuːdɪeɪt] *vt* [reject - opinion, belief] renier, désavouer ; [- evidence] réfuter ; [- authority, accusation, charge] rejeter ; [- spouse] répudier ; [- friend] désavouer ; [- gift, offer] refuser, repousser ■ [go back on - obligation, debt, treaty] refuser d'honorer.

repudiation [rɪˌpjuːdɪ'eɪʃn] *n* **1.** [of belief, opinion] reniement *m*, désaveu *m* ■ [of spouse] répudiation *f* ■ [of friend, accusation] rejet *m* ■ [of gift, offer] refus *m*, rejet *m* **2.** [of obligation, debt] refus *m* d'honorer.

repugnance [rɪ'pʌgnəns] *n* répugnance *f*.

repugnant [rɪ'pʌgnənt] *adj* répugnant ■ **I find the idea ~** cette idée me répugne.

repulse [rɪ'pʌls] <> *vt* [attack, offer] repousser.
<> *n* MIL [defeat] défaite *f*, échec *m* ■ *fig* [refusal] refus *m*, rebuffade *f*.

repulsion [rɪ'pʌlʃn] *n* répulsion *f*.

repulsive [rɪ'pʌlsɪv] *adj* [idea, sight, appearance] répugnant, repoussant ■ PHYS répulsif.

repulsively [rɪ'pʌlsɪvlɪ] *adv* de façon repoussante *OR* répugnante ■ **~ ugly** d'une laideur repoussante.

repurchase [ˌriː'pɜːtʃɪs] <> *n* rachat *m*.
<> *vt* racheter.

reputable ['repjʊtəbl] *adj* [person, family] qui a bonne réputation, honorable, estimable ■ [firm, tradesman] qui a bonne réputation ■ [profession] honorable ■ [source] sûr.

reputation [ˌrepjʊ'teɪʃn] *n* réputation *f* ■ **she has a ~ as a cook** sa réputation de cuisinière n'est plus à faire ■ **they have a ~ for good service** ils sont réputés pour la qualité de leur service ■ **she has a ~ for being difficult** elle a la réputation d'être difficile ■ **he lives up to his ~ as a big spender** il mérite sa réputation de grand dépensier.

repute [rɪ'pjuːt] <> *n* réputation *f*, renom *m* ■ **to be of good ~** avoir (une) bonne réputation ■ **a firm of some ~** une entreprise d'un certain renom ■ **she is held in high ~ by all her colleagues** elle jouit d'une excellente réputation auprès de ses collègues.
<> *vt* [rumoured] : **she is ~d to be wealthy** elle passe pour riche.

reputed [rɪ'pju:tɪd] *adj* réputé ▪ **~ father** LAW père *m* putatif.

reputedly [rɪ'pju:tɪdlɪ] *adv* d'après ce qu'on dit ▪ **he is ~ a millionaire** on le dit milliardaire.

reqd *written abbr of* **required**.

request [rɪ'kwest] <> *n* **1.** [demand] demande *f*, requête *f* ▪ **to make a ~** faire une demande ▪ **to grant** *OR* **to meet sb's ~** accéder à la demande *OR* à la requête de qqn ▪ **at sb's ~** à la demande *OR* requête de qqn ▪ **tickets are available on ~** des billets peuvent être obtenus sur simple demande ▪ **any last ~s?** quelles sont vos dernières volontés? ▪ **by popular ~** à la demande générale **2.** [record - on radio] disque *m* demandé par un auditeur ; [- at dance] *disque ou chanson demandé par un membre du public* ▪ **to play a ~ for sb** passer un disque à l'intention de qqn.
<> *vt* demander ▪ **to ~ sb to do sthg** demander à qqn *OR* prier qqn de faire qqch ▪ **Mr and Mrs Booth ~ the pleasure of your company** M. et Mme Booth vous prient de leur faire l'honneur de votre présence ▪ **I enclose a postal order for £5, as ~ed** selon votre demande, je joins un mandat postal de 5 livres ▪ **to ~ sthg of sb** *fml* demander qqch à qqn.
Voir module d'usage

request programme *n émission de radio où les disques qui passent à l'antenne ont été choisis par les auditeurs.*

request stop *n UK* arrêt *m* facultatif.

requiem ['rekwɪəm] *n* requiem *m*.

requiem mass *n* messe *f* de requiem.

require [rɪ'kwaɪəʳ] *vt* **1.** [need - attention, care etc] exiger, nécessiter, demander ▪ **extreme caution is ~d** une extrême vigilance s'impose ▪ **is that all you ~?** c'est tout ce qu'il vous faut?, c'est tout ce dont vous avez besoin? ▪ **if ~d** si besoin est, s'il le faut ▪ **your presence is urgently ~d** on vous réclame d'urgence **2.** [demand - qualifications, standard, commitment] exiger, requérir, réclamer ▪ **to ~ sthg of sb** exiger qqch de qqn ▪ **to ~ sb to do sthg** exiger que qqn fasse qqch ▪ **candidates are ~d to provide three photographs** les candidats doivent fournir trois photographies ▪ **what do you ~ of me?** que voulez-vous *OR* qu'attendez-vous de moi? ▪ **it is ~d that you begin work at 8 a.m. every morning** on exige de vous que vous commenciez votre travail à 8 h tous les matins ▪ **'formal dress ~d'** [on invitation] 'tenue correcte exigée'.

required [rɪ'kwaɪəd] *adj* [conditions, qualifications, standard] requis, exigé ▪ **in** *OR* **by the ~ time** dans les délais (prescrits) ▪ **~ reading** SCH & UNIV lectures *fpl* à faire.

requirement [rɪ'kwaɪəmənt] *n* **1.** [demand] exigence *f*, besoin *m* ▪ **this doesn't meet our ~s** ceci ne répond pas à nos exigences ▮ [necessity] besoin *m*, nécessité *f* ▪ **energy ~s** besoins énergétiques **2.** [condition, prerequisite] condition *f* requise ▪ **she doesn't fulfil the ~s for the job** elle ne remplit pas les conditions requises pour le poste ▪ **dedication is an essential ~** le dévouement est une condition essentielle ▪ **what are the course ~s?** [for enrolment] quelles conditions faut-il remplir pour s'inscrire à ce cours? ; [as student] quel niveau doit-on avoir pour suivre ce cours?

requisite ['rekwɪzɪt] *adj* requis, nécessaire.

requisition [ˌrekwɪ'zɪʃn] <> *n* **1.** MIL réquisition *f* **2.** COMM demande *f* ▪ **the boss put in a ~ for staplers** le patron a fait une demande d'agrafeuses.
<> *vt* MIL & *fig* réquisitionner.

requite [rɪ'kwaɪt] *vt* **1.** [return - payment, kindness] récompenser, payer de retour ▪ **to ~ sb's love** répondre à l'amour de qqn **2.** [satisfy - desire] satisfaire **3.** [avenge - injury] venger.

reran [ˌri:'ræn] *pt* ▷ **rerun**.

reread [ˌri:'ri:d] (*pret & pp* **reread** [-'red]) *vt* relire.

rerecord [ˌri:rɪ'kɔ:d] *vt* réenregistrer.

rerelease [ˌri:rɪ'li:s] <> *vt* [film, record] ressortir.
<> *n* [film, record] reprise *f*.

reroute [ˌri:'ru:t] *vt* dérouter, changer l'itinéraire de ▪ **the traffic was ~d through the suburbs** la circulation a été déviée vers la banlieue.

rerun <> *n* ['ri:rʌn] [of film] reprise *f* ▪ [of TV serial] rediffusion *f* ▪ **it's a ~ of last year's final** la finale prend la même tournure que celle de l'année dernière.
<> *vt* [ˌri:'rʌn] (*pret* **reran** [ˌri:'ræn], *pp* **rerun**, *cont* **rerunning**) **1.** [film] passer de nouveau ▪ [TV series] rediffuser **2.** [race] courir de nouveau.

resale ['ri:seɪl] *n* revente *f*.

resale shop *n US* magasin *m* d'articles d'occasion.

resat [ˌri:'sæt] *pt & pp* ▷ **resit**.

reschedule [*UK* ˌri:'ʃedju:l, *US* ˌri:'skedʒʊl] *vt* **1.** [appointment, meeting] modifier l'heure ou la date de ▪ [bus, train, flight] modifier l'horaire de ▪ [plan, order] modifier le programme de ▪ **the meeting has been ~d for next week** la réunion a été déplacée à la semaine prochaine **2.** FIN [debt] rééchelonner.

rescind [rɪ'sɪnd] *vt fml* [judgment] casser, annuler ▪ [agreement] annuler ▪ [law] abroger ▪ [contract] résilier.

rescue ['reskju:] <> *vt* [from danger] sauver ▪ [from captivity] délivrer ▪ [in need, difficulty] secourir, venir au secours de ▪ **to ~ sb from drowning** sauver qqn de la noyade ▪ **they were ~d**

REQUESTS

Tu peux me donner un coup de main ? Could you give me a hand?

Si tu veux. If you like.

Est-ce que vous pourriez m'aider à attraper ma valise, s'il vous plaît ? Could you help me get my case down, please?

Oui, bien sûr. Yes, of course.

Tu veux bien m'aider à réviser ma géo ? Help me revise my geography, will you?

Désolé, je n'ai pas le temps. Sorry, I haven't got time.

Tu n'aurais pas le temps de relire cette lettre, par hasard ? You wouldn't have the time to read this letter through for me, would you?

Non, justement, il faut que j'y aille. No, sorry, I'm afraid I have to go.

Je me demandais si tu pourrais *OU* **si tu ne pourrais pas me prêter dix euros ?** I was wondering whether you could lend me ten euros ?

Non, désolé, je suis un peu juste en ce moment. Sorry, I'm a bit short myself at the moment.

Écoute, j'ai vraiment besoin de ta voiture. Listen, I really need to borrow your car.

D'accord, voilà les clefs. OK, here are the keys.

Merci de me rappeler dès que possible. Please phone me back as soon as possible.

Je n'y manquerais pas. Yes, of course.

Ça te dérangerait de m'acheter des timbres en passant ? Would you mind getting me some stamps while you're out?

Non, pas du tout, combien tu en veux? No, not at all. How many do you want?

Tu me passes le sel, s'il te plaît ? Could you pass me the salt, please?

Oui, voilà. Here you are.

from a potentially dangerous situation on les a tirés d'une situation qui aurait pu être dangereuse ■ **the survivors were waiting to be ~d** les survivants attendaient des secours | *fig* **thanks for rescuing me from that boring conversation** merci de m'avoir délivré, cette conversation m'assommait.
◇ *n* [from danger, drowning] sauvetage *m* ■ [from captivity] délivrance *f* ■ [in need, difficulty] secours *m* ■ **to go/to come to sb's ~** aller/venir au secours *OR* à la rescousse de qqn.
◇ *comp* [attempt, mission, operation, party, team] de sauvetage, de secours ■ **~ worker** sauveteur *m*.

rescuer ['reskjuər] *n* sauveteur *m*.

reseal [,ri:'si:l] *vt* [envelope] recacheter ■ [jar] refermer hermétiquement.

research [rɪ'sɜ:tʃ] ◇ *n (U)* recherche *f*, recherches *fpl* ■ **to do ~ into sthg** faire des recherches sur qqch ■ **she's engaged in ~ in genetics/into rare viruses** elle fait des recherches en génétique/sur les virus rares ■ **~ into the problem revealed a worrying trend** les recherches sur le problème ont révélé une tendance inquiétante ■ **an excellent piece of ~** un excellent travail de recherche ■ **~ and development** recherche *f* et développement *m*, recherche-développement *f* ■ **scientific ~** la recherche scientifique.
◇ *comp* [establishment, work] de recherche ■ **~ worker** chercheur *m*, - euse *f*.
◇ *vt* [article, book, problem, subject] faire des recherches sur ■ **your essay is not very well ~ed** votre travail n'est pas très bien documenté.
◇ *vi* faire des recherches *OR* de la recherche.

researcher [rɪ'sɜ:tʃər] *n* chercheur *m*, - euse *f*.

research student *n* étudiant *m*, - e *f* qui fait de la recherche *(après la licence)*.

reseat [,ri:'si:t] *vt* **1.** [person - sit again] faire rasseoir ; [- change place] assigner une nouvelle place à ■ **to ~ o.s.** [sit down] se rasseoir ; [change place] changer de place **2.** [chair] refaire le fond de ■ [trousers] remettre un fond à **3.** MECH [valve] roder.

resell [,ri:'sel] *(pret & pp* **resold** [-'səʊld]) *vt* revendre.

resemblance [rɪ'zembləns] *n* ressemblance *f* ■ **to bear a ~ to sb** ressembler vaguement à qqn ■ **the brothers show a strong family ~** les frères se ressemblent beaucoup.

resemble [rɪ'zembl] *vt* ressembler à ■ **they ~ each other greatly** ils se ressemblent beaucoup.

resent [rɪ'zent] *vt* [person] en vouloir à, éprouver de la rancune à l'égard de ■ [remark, criticism] ne pas apprécier ■ **to ~ sthg strongly** un vif ressentiment à l'égard de qqch ■ **I ~ that!** je proteste! ■ **her presence in the country was strongly ~ed** sa présence dans le pays a été très mal acceptée ■ **I ~ them taking over** *OR* **the fact that they have taken over** je leur en veux de prendre tout en charge.

resentful [rɪ'zentfʊl] *adj* plein de ressentiment ■ **to feel ~ about** *OR* **at sthg** éprouver du ressentiment à l'égard de qqch, mal accepter qqch ■ **to be ~ about** *OR* **of sb's achievements** envier sa réussite à qqn ■ **don't be so ~!** ne soyez pas si rancunier!

resentfully [rɪ'zentfʊlɪ] *adv* avec ressentiment.

resentment [rɪ'zentmənt] *n* ressentiment *m*.

reservation [,rezə'veɪʃn] ◇ *n* **1.** [doubt] réserve *f*, restriction *f* ■ **to have ~s about sthg** faire *OR* émettre des réserves sur qqch ■ **I have ~s about letting them go abroad** j'hésite à les laisser partir à l'étranger ■ **without ~** *OR* **~s** sans réserve ■ **he expressed some ~s about the plan** il a émis quelques doutes à propos *OR* au sujet du projet **2.** [booking] réservation *f* ■ **to make a ~** [on train] réserver une *OR* sa place ; [in hotel] réserver *OR* retenir une chambre ; [in restaurant] réserver une table ■ **the secretary made all the ~s** la secrétaire s'est occupée de toutes les réservations **3.** [enclosed area] réserve *f* **4.** RELIG : **the Reservation (of the sacrament)** la Sainte Réserve.
◇ *comp* [desk] des réservations.

reserve [rɪ'zɜ:v] ◇ *vt* **1.** [keep back] réserver, mettre de côté ■ **to ~ one's strength** garder *OR* ménager ses forces ■ **to ~ the right to do sthg** se réserver le droit de faire qqch ■ **to reserve (one's) judgment about sthg** ne pas se prononcer sur qqch
2. [book] réserver, retenir ■ **these seats are ~d for VIPs** ces places sont réservées aux personnalités.
◇ *n* **1.** [store - of energy, money, provisions] réserve *f* ■ **to draw on one's ~s** puiser dans ses réserves ■ **the body's food ~s** les réserves nutritives du corps ■ **the nation's coal ~s** les réserves de charbon du pays ■ **cash ~s** réserves de caisse
2. [storage] réserve *f* ■ **to have** *OR* **to keep in ~** avoir *OR* garder en réserve ■ **luckily, they have some money in ~** heureusement, ils ont (mis) un peu d'argent de côté
3. *UK* [doubt, qualification] réserve *f* ■ **with all proper ~s** sous toutes réserves
4. [reticence] réserve *f*, retenue *f* ■ **to break through sb's ~** amener qqn à sortir de sa réserve
5. MIL réserve *f* ■ **to call up the ~** *OR* **~s** faire appel à la réserve *OR* aux réservistes
6. [area of land] réserve *f*
7. SPORT remplaçant *m*, - e *f*
8. [at auction] prix *m* minimum.
◇ *comp* **1.** FIN [funds, currency, resources, bank] de réserve
2. SPORT remplaçant ■ **the ~ goalkeeper** le gardien de but remplaçant ■ **the ~ team** l'équipe *f* de réserve.

reserved [rɪ'zɜ:vd] *adj* **1.** [shy - person] timide, réservé **2.** [doubtful] : **he has always been rather ~ about the scheme** il a toujours exprimé des doutes sur ce projet **3.** [room, seat] réservé ■ **all rights ~** tous droits réservés.

reservedly [rɪ'zɜ:vɪdlɪ] *adv* avec réserve, avec retenue.

reserve price *n* prix *m* minimum.

reservist [rɪ'zɜ:vɪst] *n* réserviste *m*.

reservoir ['rezəvwɑ:r] *n* *liter* & *fig* réservoir *m*.

reset ◇ *vt* [,ri:'set] *(pret & pp* **reset**, *cont* **resetting**) **1.** [jewel] remonter **2.** [watch, clock] remettre à l'heure ■ [alarm] réenclencher ■ [counter] remettre à zéro **3.** COMPUT réinitialiser **4.** [limb] remettre en place ■ [fracture] réduire **5.** [lay] : **to ~ the table** [in restaurant] remettre le couvert ; [in home] remettre la table.
◇ *n* ['ri:set] COMPUT réinitialisation *f*.

resettle [,ri:'setl] ◇ *vt* [refugees, population] établir *OR* implanter (dans une nouvelle région) ■ [territory] repeupler.
◇ *vi* se réinstaller.

resettlement [,ri:'setlmənt] *n* [of people] établissement *m* *OR* implantation *f* (dans une nouvelle région) ■ [of territory] repeuplement *m*.

reshape [,ri:'ʃeɪp] *vt* [clay, material] refaçonner ■ [novel, policy] réorganiser, remanier.

reshuffle [,ri:'ʃʌfl] ◇ *vt* **1.** POL [cabinet] remanier **2.** [cards] rebattre, battre de nouveau.
◇ *n* **1.** POL remaniement *m* ■ **a Cabinet ~** un remaniement ministériel **2.** [in cards] : **to have a ~** battre les cartes à nouveau.

reside [rɪ'zaɪd] *vi fml* **1.** [live] résider ■ **they ~ in New York** ils résident *OR* ils sont domiciliés à New York **2.** *fig* [be located] : **authority ~s in** *OR* **with the Prime Minister** c'est le Premier ministre qui est investi de l'autorité ■ **the problem ~s in the fact...** le problème est dû au fait que...

residence ['rezɪdəns] *n* **1.** [home] résidence *f*, demeure *f* ■ **town/country ~** résidence en ville/à la campagne ■ **official summer ~** résidence officielle d'été ■ **'desirable ~ for sale'** [in advert] 'belle demeure *OR* demeure de caractère à vendre' ■ **they took up ~ in Oxford** ils se sont installés *OR* ils ont élu domicile à Oxford ■ **Lord Bellamy's ~** *fml* la résidence de Lord Bellamy ▶ **to be in ~** [monarch] être en résidence ■ **writer/artist in ~** écrivain *m* /artiste *mf* en résidence ■ **place of ~** [on form] domicile *m* **2.** UNIV : **(university) ~** résidence *f* (universitaire) **3.** [period of stay] résidence *f*, séjour *m* ■ **after three years' ~ abroad** après avoir résidé pendant trois ans à l'étranger.

residence permit *n* ≃ permis *m* de séjour.

residency ['rezɪdənsɪ] (*pl* **residencies**) *n* **1.** *fml* [home] résidence *f* officielle **2.** *US* MED *période d'études spécialisées après l'internat.*

resident ['rezɪdənt] <> *n* **1.** [of town] habitant *m*, - e *f* ▪ [of street] riverain *m*, - e *f* ▪ [in hotel, hostel] pensionnaire *mf* ▪ [foreigner] résident *m*, - e *f* ▪ **(local) ~s' association** [in building] association *f* des copropriétaires ; [in neighbourhood] association *f* de riverains ▪ **are you a ~ of an EU country?** ADMIN êtes-vous ressortissant d'un pays membre de l'Union européenne? ▪ **'~s only'** [in street] 'interdit sauf aux riverains' ; [in hotel] 'réservé à la clientèle de l'hôtel' **2.** *US* MED interne *mf* **3.** ZOOL résident *m*.
<> *adj* **1.** [as inhabitant] résidant ▪ **to be ~ in a country** résider dans un pays ▪ **to have permanent ~ status** avoir le statut de résident permanent ▪ **the swallow is ~ to the area** l'hirondelle réside dans la région **2.** [staff] qui habite sur place, à demeure ▪ **our ~ pianist** notre pianiste attitré **3.** COMPUT résident.

residential [,rezɪ'denʃl] *adj* [district, accommodation] résidentiel ▪ [status] de résident ▪ [course, job] sur place ▪ **~ care** *mode d'hébergement supervisé pour handicapés, délinquants etc* ▪ **~ treatment facility** *US fml* hôpital *m* psychiatrique.

residents' association *n association des résidents d'un immeuble.*

residual [rɪ'zɪdjʊəl] <> *adj* [gen] restant ▪ CHEM & GEOL résiduel ▪ PHYS [magnetism] rémanent.
<> *n* MATHS reste *m* ▪ CHEM & GEOL résidu *m*.

residue ['rezɪdju:] *n* [leftovers] reste *m*, restes *mpl* ▪ [of money] reliquat *m* ▪ CHEM & PHYS résidu *m* ▪ MATHS reste *m*, reliquat *m*.

resign [rɪ'zaɪn] <> *vi* **1.** [from post] démissionner, donner sa démission ▪ **she ~ed from her job/from the committee** elle a démissionné de son emploi/du comité **2.** CHESS abandonner.
<> *vt* **1.** [give up - advantage] renoncer à ; [- job] démissionner de ; [- function] se démettre de, démissionner de **2.** [give away] céder ▪ **to ~ sthg to sb** céder qqch à qqn **3.** [reconcile] : **I had ~ed myself to going alone** je m'étais résigné à y aller seul.

resignation [,rezɪg'neɪʃn] *n* **1.** [from job] démission *f* ▪ **to hand in** *OR* **to tender** *fml* **one's ~** donner sa démission **2.** [acceptance - of fact, situation] résignation *f*.

resigned [rɪ'zaɪnd] *adj* résigné ▪ **to become ~ to (doing) sthg** se résigner à (faire) qqch ▪ **she gave me a ~ look/smile** elle m'a regardé/souri avec résignation.

resilience [rɪ'zɪlɪəns] *n* **1.** [of rubber, metal - springiness] élasticité *f* ; [- toughness] résistance *f* **2.** [of character, person] énergie *f*, ressort *m* ▪ [of institution] résistance *f*.

resilient [rɪ'zɪlɪənt] *adj* **1.** [rubber, metal - springy] élastique ; [- tough] résistant **2.** [person - in character] qui a du ressort, qui ne se laisse pas abattre *OR* décourager ; [- in health, condition] très résistant.

resin ['rezɪn] *n* résine *f*.

resinous ['rezɪnəs] *adj* résineux.

resist [rɪ'zɪst] <> *vt* [temptation, attack, change, pressure] résister à ▪ [reform] s'opposer à ▪ **he couldn't ~ having just one more drink** il n'a pas pu résister à l'envie de prendre un dernier verre ▪ **I can't ~ it!** c'est plus fort que moi! ▪ **he was charged with ~ing arrest** *fml* il a été inculpé de résistance aux forces de l'ordre.
<> *vi* résister, offrir de la résistance.

resistance [rɪ'zɪstəns] <> *n* ELEC, MED, PHYS & PSYCHOL résistance *f* ▪ **their ~ to all reform** leur opposition (systématique) à toute réforme ▪ **they offered no ~ to the new measures** ils ne se sont pas opposés aux nouvelles mesures ▪ **they put up fierce ~ to their attackers** ils opposèrent une vive résistance à leurs agresseurs ▪ **her ~ to infection is low** elle offre peu de résistance à l'infection ▶ **air/wind ~** résistance de l'air/du vent.
<> *comp* [movement] de résistance ▪ [group] de résistants ▪ **~ fighter** résistant *m*, - e *f*.

resistant [rɪ'zɪstənt] <> *adj* [gen - ELEC], MED & PHYS résistant ▪ **she is very ~ to change** elle est très hostile au changement.
<> *n* résistant *m*, - e *f*.

-resistant *in cpds* : **heat~** qui résiste à la chaleur ▪ **water~** résistant à l'eau ▪ **flame~** ignifugé.

resistor [rɪ'zɪstər] *n* ELEC résistance *f (objet).*

resit *UK* <> *vt* [,ri:'sɪt] (*pret & pp* **resat** [,ri:'sæt], *cont* **resitting**) [exam] repasser.
<> *n* ['ri:sɪt] examen *m* de rattrapage.

resold [-'səʊld] *pt & pp* ▷ **resell**.

resole [,ri:'səʊl] *vt* ressemeler.

resolute ['rezəlu:t] *adj* [determined - person, expression, jaw] résolu ▪ [steadfast - faith, courage, refusal] inébranlable ▪ **he is ~ in his decision** il est inébranlable dans sa décision.

resolutely ['rezəlu:tlɪ] *adv* [oppose, struggle, believe] résolument ▪ [refuse] fermement ▪ **she marched forward ~** elle avança d'un pas résolu.

resolution [,rezə'lu:ʃn] *n* **1.** [decision] résolution *f*, décision *f* ▪ **she made a ~ to stop smoking** elle a pris la résolution d'arrêter de fumer **2.** [formal motion] résolution *f* ▪ **they passed/adopted/rejected a ~ to limit the budget** ils ont voté/adopté/rejeté une résolution pour limiter le budget **3.** [determination] résolution *f* ▪ **to say/to act with ~** dire/agir avec fermeté **4.** [settling, solving] résolution *f* ▪ **in Act V we see the ~ of the tragedy** au cinquième acte, nous assistons au dénouement de la tragédie **5.** COMPUT, OPT & TV résolution *f* ▪ **high ~ screen** écran *m* à haute résolution **6.** MED & MUS résolution *f*.

resolvable [rɪ'zɒlvəbl] *adj* résoluble, soluble.

resolve [rɪ'zɒlv] <> *vt* **1.** [work out - quarrel, difficulty, dilemma] résoudre ; [- doubt] dissiper ▪ MATHS [- equation] résoudre **2.** [decide] (se) résoudre ▪ **to ~ to do sthg** décider de *OR* se résoudre à faire qqch ▪ **I ~d to resign** j'ai pris la décision de démissionner ▪ **it was ~d that...** il a été résolu *OR* on a décidé que... **3.** [break down, separate] résoudre, réduire ▪ **the problem can be ~d into three simple questions** le problème peut se résoudre en *OR* être ramené à trois questions simples **4.** OPT & PHYS [parts, peaks] distinguer ▪ [image] résoudre **5.** MED résoudre, faire disparaître **6.** MUS résoudre.
<> *vi* **1.** [separate, break down] se résoudre **2.** MUS [chord] être résolu.
<> *n* **1.** [determination] résolution *f* ▪ **it only strengthened our ~** ça n'a fait que renforcer notre détermination **2.** [decision] résolution *f*, décision *f*.

resolved [rɪ'zɒlvd] *adj* résolu, décidé, déterminé ▪ **I was firmly ~ to go** j'étais fermement décidé à partir.

resonance ['rezənəns] *n* résonance *f*.

resonant ['rezənənt] *adj* **1.** [loud, echoing] retentissant, sonore **2.** ACOUST, MUS & PHYS résonant, résonnant.

resonate ['rezəneɪt] *vi* [noise, voice, laughter, place] résonner, retentir ▪ **the valley ~d with their cries** la vallée retentissait de leurs cris.

resonator ['rezəneɪtər] *n* résonateur *m*.

resort [rɪ'zɔ:t] *n* **1.** [recourse] recours *m* ▪ **without ~ to threats** sans avoir recours aux menaces ▪ **as a last ~** en dernier ressort ▪ **call me only as a last** *OR* **in the last ~** ne m'appelez qu'en dernier ressort ▪ **flight was the only ~ left to me** *OR* **my only ~** il ne me restait plus qu'à fuir **2.** [for holidays] station *f* ▪ **ski ~** station de sports d'hiver ▪ **luxury ~ hotel** hôtel *m* de tourisme de luxe **3.** [haunt, hang-out] repaire *m*.
◆ **resort to** *vt insep* [violence, sarcasm etc] avoir recours à, recourir à ▪ **you ~ed to lying to your wife** vous en êtes venu à mentir à votre femme.

resound [rɪ'zaʊnd] *vi* **1.** [noise, words, explosion] retentir, résonner ▪ **the trumpet ~ed through the barracks** le son de la trompette retentissait dans toute la caserne **2.** [hall, cave, hills, room] retentir ▪ **the woods ~ed with birdsong** les bois étaient pleins de chants d'oiseaux **3.** *fml & lit* [spread - rumour] se propager.

resounding [rɪ'zaʊndɪŋ] *adj* **1.** [loud - noise, blow, wail] retentissant ; [- voice] sonore, claironnant ▪ [explosion] violent **2.** [unequivocal] retentissant, éclatant.

resoundingly [rɪ'zaʊndɪŋlɪ] *adv* **1.** [loudly] bruyamment **2.** [unequivocally - win] d'une manière retentissante *OR* décisive ; [- criticize, condemn] sévèrement ▪ **the team was ~ beaten** l'équipe a été battue à plate couture.

resource [rɪ'sɔːs] ◇ *n* **1.** [asset] ressource *f* ▪ **there's a limit to the ~s we can invest** il y a une limite à la somme que nous pouvons investir ▪ **your health is a precious ~** ta santé est un précieux capital ▪ **natural/energy ~s** ressources naturelles/énergétiques **2.** [human capacity] ressource *f* ▪ **the task called for all my ~s of tact** cette tâche a demandé toute ma diplomatie ◆ **left to their own ~s, they're likely to mess everything up** livrés à eux-mêmes, ils risquent de tout gâcher **3.** [ingenuity] ressource *f.*
◇ *comp* SCH & UNIV : **~** *OR* **~s centre/room** centre *m* /salle *f* de documentation ▪ **~ materials** [written] documentation *f* ; [audio-visual] aides *fpl* pédagogiques ▪ **~ person** [in career centre] conseiller *m*, - ère *f* d'orientation ; [in library] bibliothécaire *mf (chargé d'orienter les usagers et d'entreprendre certaines recherches bibliographiques)*.

resourceful [rɪ'sɔːsfʊl] *adj* ingénieux, plein de ressource *OR* ressources.

resourcefully [rɪ'sɔːsfʊlɪ] *adv* ingénieusement.

resourcefulness [rɪ'sɔːsfʊlnɪs] *n* ressource *f*, ingéniosité *f.*

respect [rɪ'spekt] ◇ *vt* **1.** [esteem - person, judgment, right, authority] respecter ▪ **if you don't ~ yourself, no one else will** si vous ne vous respectez pas vous-même, personne ne vous respectera
2. [comply with - rules, customs, wishes] respecter.
◇ *n* **1.** [esteem] respect *m*, estime *f* ▪ **I have (an) enormous ~ for her competence** je respecte infiniment sa compétence ▪ **I don't have much ~ for his methods** je n'ai pas beaucoup de respect pour ses méthodes ▪ **she is held in great ~ by her colleagues** elle est très respectée *OR* elle est tenue en haute estime par ses collègues ▪ **you have to get** *OR* **to gain the children's ~** il faut savoir se faire respecter par les enfants ▪ **you have lost all my ~** je n'ai plus aucun respect pour toi ▪ **he has no ~ for authority/money** il méprise l'autorité/l'argent
2. [care, politeness] respect *m*, égard *m* ▪ **he should show more ~ for local customs** il devrait se montrer plus respectueux des coutumes locales ▪ **to do sthg out of ~ for sthg/sb** faire qqch par respect pour qqch/qqn ▪ **I stood up in ~** je me suis levé respectueusement ▪ **guns should be treated with ~** les armes à feu doivent être maniées avec précaution ▪ **with (all due) ~, Mr Clark...** avec tout le respect que je vous dois, M. Clark...
3. [regard, aspect] égard *m* ▪ **in every ~** à tous les égards ▪ **in some/other ~s** à certains/d'autres égards ▪ **in many ~s** à bien des égards
4. [compliance, observance] respect *m*, observation *f.*
◆ **respects** *npl* [salutations] respects *mpl*, hommages *mpl* ▪ **give my ~s to your father** présentez mes respects à votre père ▪ **to pay one's ~s to sb** présenter ses respects *OR* ses hommages à qqn ▪ **I went to the funeral to pay my last ~s** je suis allé à l'enterrement pour lui rendre un dernier hommage.
◆ **with respect to** *prep phr* quant à, en ce qui concerne.

respectability [rɪˌspektə'bɪlətɪ] *n* respectabilité *f.*

respectable [rɪ'spektəbl] *adj* **1.** [socially proper, worthy] respectable, convenable, comme il faut ▪ **I'm a ~ married woman!** je suis une femme mariée et respectable! ▪ **that's not done in ~ society** ça ne se fait pas dans la bonne société ▪ **to be outwardly ~** avoir l'apparence de la respectabilité ▪ **I'm sure he had a very ~ reason** je suis sûr qu'il avait une raison tout à fait respectable *OR* honorable ▪ **to make o.s. (look) ~** se préparer **2.** [fair - speech, athlete] assez bon ; [- amount, wage etc] respectable, correct ▪ **a ~ first novel** un premier roman qui n'est pas dénué d'intérêt ▪ **I play a ~ game of golf** je joue passablement bien au golf.

respectably [rɪ'spektəblɪ] *adv* [properly] convenablement, comme il faut.

respected [rɪ'spektɪd] *adj* respecté.

respecter [rɪ'spektəʳ] *n* : **she is no ~ of tradition** elle ne fait pas partie de ceux qui respectent la tradition ▪ **disease is no ~ of class** nous sommes tous égaux devant la maladie.

respectful [rɪ'spektfʊl] *adj* respectueux.

respectfully [rɪ'spektfʊlɪ] *adv* respectueusement.

respecting [rɪ'spektɪŋ] *prep* concernant, en ce qui concerne.

respective [rɪ'spektɪv] *adj* respectif.

respectively [rɪ'spektɪvlɪ] *adv* respectivement.

respiration [ˌrespə'reɪʃn] *n* respiration *f.*

respirator ['respəreɪtəʳ] *n* [mask, machine] respirateur *m.*

respiratory [*UK* rɪ'spɪrətrɪ, *US* 'respərətɔːrɪ] *adj* respiratoire ▪ **~ problem** *OR* **problems** troubles *mpl* respiratoires.

respire [rɪ'spaɪəʳ] *vi* & *vt lit* respirer.

respite ['respaɪt] ◇ *n* **1.** [pause, rest] répit *m* ▪ **without ~** sans répit *OR* relâche ▪ **there wasn't a moment's ~ from the noise** il y avait un bruit ininterrompu ▪ **he never has any ~ from the pain** la douleur ne lui laisse aucun répit **2.** [delay] répit *m*, délai *m* ▪ [stay of execution] sursis *m* ▪ **we've been given a week's ~ before we need to pay** on nous a accordé un délai d'une semaine pour payer.
◇ *vt fml* accorder un sursis à.

respite care *n (U) accueil temporaire, dans un établissement médicalisé, de personnes malades, handicapées etc, destiné à prendre le relais des familles.*

resplendent [rɪ'splendənt] *adj* [splendid] magnifique, splendide ▪ [shining] resplendissant ▪ **Joe, ~ in his new suit** Joe, resplendissant *OR* magnifique dans son nouveau costume.

resplendently [rɪ'splendəntlɪ] *adv* [dress, decorate] somptueusement ▪ [shine] avec éclat.

respond [rɪ'spɒnd] ◇ *vi* **1.** [answer - person, guns] répondre ▪ **to ~ to a request** répondre à une demande ▪ **she ~ed with a smile** elle a répondu par un sourire **2.** [react] répondre, réagir ▪ **the steering is slow to ~** la direction ne répond pas bien ▪ **the patient is ~ing** le malade réagit positivement ▪ **her condition isn't ~ing to treatment** le traitement ne semble pas agir sur sa maladie ‖ [person] : **they'll ~ to the crisis by raising taxes** ils répondront à la crise en augmentant les impôts ▪ **are people ~ing to the candidate's message?** l'opinion publique réagit-elle favorablement au message du candidat? ▪ **he doesn't ~ well to criticism** il réagit mal à la critique ▪ **to ~ to flattery** être sensible à la flatterie.
◇ *vt* répondre.
◇ *n* **1.** ARCHIT [for arch] pilier *m* butant ▪ [ending colonnade] colonne *f* engagée **2.** RELIG répons *m.*

respondent [rɪ'spɒndənt] ◇ *n* **1.** LAW défendeur *m*, - eresse *f* **2.** [in opinion poll] sondé *m*, - e *f* ▪ **10% of the ~s** 10 % des personnes interrogées **3.** PSYCHOL [reflex] répondant *m.*
◇ *adj* PSYCHOL répondant.

response [rɪ'spɒns] *n* **1.** [answer] réponse *f* ▪ **have you had any ~ to your request yet?** avez-vous obtenu une réponse à votre demande? ▪ **when asked, she gave** *OR* **made no ~** quand on lui a posé la question, elle n'a pas répondu ▪ **he smiled in ~** il a répondu par un sourire **2.** [reaction] réponse *f*, réaction *f* ▪ **their proposals met with a favourable/lukewarm ~** leurs propositions ont été accueillies favorablement/ont reçu un accueil mitigé **3.** [in bridge] réponse *f* **4.** RELIG répons *m* **5.** MED réaction *f.*
◆ **in response to** *prep phr* en réponse à ▪ **he resigned in ~ to the party's urging/to the pressure** il a démissionné, cédant à l'insistance du parti/à la pression.

response time *n* COMPUT temps *m* de réponse ▪ MED & PSYCHOL temps *m* de réaction.

responsibility [rɪˌspɒnsəˈbɪlətɪ] (*pl* **responsibilities**) *n* **1.** [control, authority] responsabilité *f* ▪ **to have ~ for sthg** avoir la charge *OR* la responsabilité de qqch ▪ **a position of great ~** un poste à haute responsabilité ▪ **how much ~ for the operation did the president really have?** jusqu'à quel point le président était-il responsable de l'opération? ▪ **can he handle all that ~?** est-il capable d'assumer toutes ces responsabilités? ▪ **he authorized it on his own ~** il l'a autorisé de son propre chef, il a pris sur lui de l'autoriser **2.** [accountability] responsabilité *f* ▪ **he has no sense of ~** il n'a aucun sens des responsabilités ▪ **to accept *OR* to assume ~ for one's mistakes** assumer la responsabilité de ses erreurs ▪ **I take full ~ for the defeat** je prends (sur moi) l'entière responsabilité de la défaite **3.** [task, duty] responsabilité *f* ▪ **responsibilities include product development** vous assurerez entre autres le développement des nouveaux produits ▪ **it's his ~!** ça le regarde! ▪ **to have a ~ to sb** avoir une responsabilité envers qqn ▪ **to shirk one's responsibilities** fuir ses responsabilités ▪ **children are a big ~** c'est une lourde responsabilité que d'avoir des enfants.

responsible [rɪˈspɒnsəbl] *adj* **1.** [in charge, in authority] responsable ▪ **who's ~ for research?** qui est chargé de la recherche? ▪ **he was ~ for putting the children to bed** c'était lui qui couchait les enfants ▪ **a ~ position** un poste à responsabilité **2.** [accountable] responsable ▪ **~ for sthg** responsable de qqch ▪ **human error/a malfunction was ~ for the disaster** la catastrophe était due à une erreur humaine/à une défaillance technique ▪ **I hold you personally ~** je vous tiens personnellement responsable ▪ **he is ~ only to the managing director** il n'est responsable que devant le directeur général **3.** [serious, trustworthy] sérieux, responsable ▪ **it wasn't very ~ of him** ce n'était pas très sérieux de sa part ▪ **the chemical industry has become more environmentally ~** l'industrie chimique se préoccupe davantage de l'environnement ▪ **they aren't ~ parents** ce ne sont pas des parents dignes de ce nom.

responsibly [rɪˈspɒnsəblɪ] *adv* de manière responsable ▪ **to behave ~** avoir un comportement responsable.

responsive [rɪˈspɒnsɪv] *adj* **1.** [person - sensitive] sensible ; [- receptive] ouvert ; [- enthusiastic] enthousiaste ; [- affectionate] affectueux ▪ **I asked him for advice, but he wasn't very ~** je lui ai demandé des conseils mais il semblait peu disposé à me répondre ▪ **to be ~ to praise** être sensible aux compliments **2.** [brakes, controls, keyboard] sensible ▪ **the patient isn't proving ~ to treatment** le malade ne réagit pas au traitement **3.** [answering - smile, nod] en réponse.

responsiveness [rɪˈspɒnsɪvnɪs] *n* **1.** [of person - sensitivity] sensibilité *f* ; [- receptiveness] ouverture *f* ; [- enthusiasm] enthousiasme *m* ; [- affection] affection *f*, tendresse *f* **2.** [of brakes, controls, keyboard] sensibilité *f*.

respray ◇ *vt* [ˌriːˈspreɪ] [car] repeindre.
◇ *n* [ˈriːspreɪ] : **I took the car in for a ~** j'ai donné la voiture à repeindre.

rest [rest] ◇ *n* **1.** [remainder] : **take the ~ of the cake** prenez le reste *OR* ce qui reste du gâteau ▪ **take the ~ of the cakes** prenez les autres gâteaux *OR* les gâteaux qui restent ▪ **the ~ of the time they watch television** le reste du temps, ils regardent la télévision ▪ **he's the only amateur, the ~ of them are professionals** c'est le seul amateur, les autres sont des professionnels ▸ **and all the ~ (of it)** *inf*, **and the ~** *inf* et tout le reste *OR* tout le tralala
2. [relaxation] repos *m* ▪ [pause] repos *m*, pause *f* ▪ **(a) ~ will do him good** un peu de repos lui fera du bien ▪ **try to get some ~** essayez de vous reposer (un peu) ▪ **I had *OR* I took a ten-minute ~** je me suis reposé pendant dix minutes, j'ai fait une pause de dix minutes ▪ **you need a week's ~/a good night's ~** vous avez besoin d'une semaine de repos/d'une bonne nuit de sommeil ▪ **after a moment's ~** après s'être reposé quelques instants ▪ **after her afternoon ~** après sa sieste ▪ **she had to take several ~s while climbing the stairs** en montant l'escalier elle a été obligée de s'arrêter à plusieurs reprises ▪ **he needs a ~ from the pressure/the children** il a besoin de se détendre/d'un peu de temps sans les enfants ▪ **he gave her no ~ until she consented** il ne lui a pas laissé une minute de répit jusqu'à ce qu'elle accepte ▪ **you'd better give the skiing a ~** vous feriez mieux de ne pas faire de ski pendant un certain temps ▸ **~ and recuperation** *US* MIL permission *f* ; *hum* vacances *fpl* ▪ **to put *OR* to set sb's mind at ~** tranquilliser *OR* rassurer qqn ▪ **give it a ~!** *inf* arrête, tu veux?
3. [motionlessness] repos *m* ▪ **the machines are at ~** les machines sont au repos ▪ **to come to ~** [vehicle, pendulum, ball] s'immobiliser, s'arrêter ; [bird, falling object] se poser
4. *euph* [death] paix *f* ▪ **he's finally at ~** il a finalement trouvé la paix ▪ **to lay sb to ~** porter qqn en terre ▪ **to lay *OR* to put to ~** [rumour] dissiper ; [allegation, notion] abandonner
5. [support] support *m*, appui *m* ▪ [in snooker] repose-queue *m*
6. MUS silence *m* ▪ **minim *UK OR* half *US* ~** demi-pause *f* ▪ **crotchet *UK OR* quarter *US* ~** soupir *m* ▪ **quaver *UK OR* eighth *US* ~** demi-soupir *m*
7. [in poetry] césure *f*.
◇ *vi* **1.** [relax, stop working] se reposer ▪ **we shall not ~ until the fight is won** nous n'aurons de cesse que la lutte ne soit gagnée
2. [be held up or supported] reposer ▪ **his arm ~ed on the back of the sofa** son bras reposait sur le dossier du canapé ▮ [lean - person] s'appuyer ; [- bicycle, ladder] être appuyé ▪ **she was ~ing on her broom** elle était appuyée sur son balai
3. [depend, be based - argument, hope] reposer ▪ **the theory ~s on a false assumption** la théorie repose sur une hypothèse fausse
4. [be, remain] être ▪ **~ assured we're doing our best** soyez certain que nous faisons de notre mieux ▪ **their fate ~s in your hands** leur sort est entre vos mains ▪ **that's how things ~ between us** voilà où en sont les choses entre nous ▪ **can't you let the matter ~?** ne pouvez-vous pas abandonner cette idée? ▪ **he just won't let it ~** il y revient sans cesse
5. [reside, belong] résider ▪ **power ~s with the committee** c'est le comité qui détient le pouvoir ▪ **the decision doesn't ~ with me** la décision ne dépend pas de moi
6. [alight - eyes, gaze] se poser
7. *euph* [lie dead] reposer ▪ **'~ in peace'** 'repose en paix'
8. LAW : **the defence ~s** la défense conclut sa plaidoirie
9. AGRIC [lie fallow] être en repos *OR* en jachère.
◇ *vt* **1.** [allow to relax] laisser reposer ▪ **sit down and ~ your legs** assieds-toi et repose-toi les jambes
2. [support, lean] appuyer ▪ **she ~ed her bicycle against a lamppost** elle appuya sa bicyclette contre un réverbère ▪ **I ~ed my suitcase on the step** j'ai posé ma valise sur la marche ▪ **he ~ed his arm on the back of the sofa** son bras reposait sur le dossier du canapé
3. *phr* **I ~ my case** LAW j'ai conclu mon plaidoyer ; *fig* je n'ai rien d'autre à ajouter.
◆ **for the rest** *adv phr* pour le reste, quant au reste.
◆ **rest up** *vi insep inf* se reposer (un peu), prendre un peu de repos.

rest area *n* AUT aire *f* de repos.

restart ◇ *vt* [ˌriːˈstɑːt] **1.** [activity] reprendre, recommencer ▪ [engine, mechanism] remettre en marche **2.** COMPUT [system] relancer, redémarrer ▪ [program] relancer.
◇ *vi* [ˌriːˈstɑːt] **1.** [job, project] reprendre, recommencer ▪ [engine, mechanism] redémarrer **2.** COMPUT [system] redémarrer ▪ [program] reprendre.
◇ *n* [ˈriːstɑːt] **1.** [of engine, mechanism] remise *f* en marche **2.** COMPUT [of system] redémarrage *m* ▪ [of program] reprise *f* ▪ **~ point** point *m* de reprise.

restate [ˌriːˈsteɪt] *vt* **1.** [reiterate - argument, case, objection] répéter, réitérer ; [- one's intentions, innocence, faith] réaffirmer **2.** [formulate differently] reformuler.

restatement [ˌriːˈsteɪtmənt] *n* **1.** [repetition - of argument, case, objection] répétition *f* ; [- of intentions, innocence, faith] réaffirmation *f* **2.** [different formulation] reformulation *f*.

restaurant [ˈrestərɒnt] *n* restaurant *m*.

restaurant car *n UK* wagon-restaurant *m*, voiture-restaurant *f*.

restaurateur [ˌrestɒrəˈtɜːr] *n* restaurateur *m*, - trice *f* (*tenant un restaurant*).

rest cure *n* cure *f* de repos.

rested [ˈrestɪd] *adj* reposé.

restful ['restful] *adj* reposant, délassant, paisible.

rest home *n* maison *f* de retraite.

resting place ['restɪŋ-] *n* **1.** *liter* lieu *m* de repos **2.** *fig & lit* [grave] dernière demeure *f*.

restitution [,restɪ'tju:ʃn] *n* restitution *f* ▪ **the company was ordered to make full ~ of the monies** la société a été sommée de restituer l'intégralité de la somme.

restive ['restɪv] *adj* **1.** [nervous, fidgety] nerveux, agité **2.** [unmanageable] rétif, difficile.

restless ['restlɪs] *adj* **1.** [fidgety] nerveux, agité ▪ [impatient] impatient ▪ **I get ~ after a few days in the country** après quelques jours à la campagne, je ne tiens plus en place ▪ **the audience was beginning to grow ~** le public commençait à s'impatienter **2.** [constantly moving] agité ▪ **her ~ mind** son esprit en ébullition **3.** [giving no rest] : **a ~ night** une nuit agitée.

restlessly ['restlɪslɪ] *adv* **1.** [nervously] nerveusement ▪ [impatiently] impatiemment, avec impatience ▪ **to pace ~ up and down** faire les cent pas **2.** [sleeplessly] : **she tossed ~ all night** elle a eu une nuit très agitée.

restlessness ['restlɪsnɪs] *n* [fidgeting, nervousness] nervosité *f*, agitation *f* ▪ [impatience] impatience *f*.

restock [,ri:'stɒk] *vt* **1.** [with food, supplies] réapprovisionner **2.** [with fish] empoissonner ▪ [with game] réapprovisionner en gibier.

restoration [,restə'reɪʃn] *n* **1.** [giving back] restitution *f* **2.** [re-establishment] restauration *f*, rétablissement *m* **3.** [repairing, cleaning - of work of art, building] restauration *f*.

◆ **Restoration** HIST <> *n* : **the Restoration** la Restauration anglaise.

<> *comp* [literature, drama] de (l'époque de) la Restauration (anglaise).

THE RESTORATION

La restauration, en 1660, de la monarchie britannique avec l'avènement de Charles II, mit fin à la période d'austérité débutée sous le Protectorat de Cromwell.

restorative [rɪ'stɒrətɪv] <> *adj* fortifiant, remontant.

<> *n* fortifiant *m*, remontant *m*.

restore [rɪ'stɔ:ʳ] *vt* **1.** [give back] rendre, restituer ▪ **the jewels have been ~d to their rightful owners** les bijoux ont été rendus *OR* restitués à leurs propriétaires légitimes **2.** [re-establish - peace, confidence etc] restaurer, rétablir ; [- monarchy] restaurer ; [- monarch] remettre sur le trône ▪ **~d to his former post** rétabli *OR* réintégré dans ses anciennes fonctions ▪ **if the left-wing government is ~d to power** si le gouvernement de gauche revient au pouvoir ▪ **it ~d my faith in human nature** cela m'a redonné confiance en la nature humaine ▪ **the treatment should soon ~ his health** *OR* **him to health** le traitement devrait très vite le remettre sur pied **3.** [repair, clean - work of art, building] restaurer.

restorer [rɪ'stɔ:rəʳ] *n* ART restaurateur *m*, - trice *f (de tableaux)*.

restrain [rɪ'streɪn] *vt* **1.** [hold back, prevent] retenir, empêcher ▪ **I couldn't ~ myself from making a remark** je n'ai pas pu m'empêcher de faire une remarque **2.** [overpower, bring under control - person] maîtriser **3.** [repress - emotion, anger, laughter] contenir, réprimer **4.** [imprison] emprisonner.

restrained [rɪ'streɪnd] *adj* **1.** [person] retenu, réservé ▪ [emotion] contenu, maîtrisé **2.** [colour, style] sobre, discret, - ète *f*.

restraining order *n* injonction *f*.

restraint [rɪ'streɪnt] *n* **1.** [self-control] retenue *f* ▪ **with remarkable ~** avec une retenue remarquable **2.** [restriction] restriction *f*, contrainte *f* ▪ **certain ~s should be put on the committee's powers** il faudrait restreindre les pouvoirs du comité **3.** [control] contrôle *m* ▪ **a policy of price ~** une politique de contrôle des prix.

restrict [rɪ'strɪkt] *vt* restreindre, limiter ▪ **I ~ myself to ten cigarettes a day** je me limite à dix cigarettes par jour.

restricted [rɪ'strɪktɪd] *adj* **1.** [limited] limité, restreint ➔ **~ area** [out of bounds] zone *f* interdite ; *UK* AUT [with parking restrictions] zone *f* à stationnement réglementé ; [with speed limit] zone *f* à vitesse limitée **2.** ADMIN [secret - document, information] secret, - ète *f*, confidentiel **3.** [narrow - ideas, outlook] étroit, borné.

restriction [rɪ'strɪkʃn] *n* **1.** [limitation] restriction *f*, limitation *f* ▪ **they'll accept no ~ of their liberty** ils n'accepteront pas qu'on restreigne leur liberté ▪ **to put** *OR* **to place** *OR* **to impose ~s on sthg** imposer des restrictions sur qqch ➔ **speed ~** limitation de vitesse **2.** LOGIC & MATHS condition *f*.

restrictive [rɪ'strɪktɪv] *adj* **1.** [clause, list] restrictif, limitatif ▪ [interpretation] strict **2.** LING [clause] déterminatif.

restrictive practice *n* [by union] pratique *f* syndicale restrictive ▪ [by traders] atteinte *f* à la libre concurrence.

restring [,ri:'strɪŋ] (*pret & pp* **restrung** [-'strʌŋ]) *vt* [bow] remplacer la corde de ▪ [musical instrument] remplacer les cordes de ▪ [tennis racket] recorder ▪ [beads] renfiler.

rest room *n US* toilettes *fpl*.

restructure [,ri:'strʌktʃəʳ] *vt* restructurer.

rest stop *n US* AUT aire *f* de stationnement *OR* de repos.

restyle [,ri:'staɪl] *vt* [car] changer le design de ▪ [hair, clothes] changer de style de ▪ [magazine] changer la présentation de.

result [rɪ'zʌlt] <> *n* **1.** [consequence] résultat *m*, conséquence *f* ▪ **the net ~** le résultat final ▪ **these problems are the ~ of a misunderstanding** ces problèmes sont dus à un malentendu ▪ **I overslept, with the ~ that I was late for work** je ne me suis pas réveillé à temps, et du coup, je suis arrivé à mon travail en retard **2.** [success] résultat *m* ▪ **our policy is beginning to get** *OR* **show ~s** notre politique commence à porter ses fruits ▪ **they're looking for sales staff who can get ~s** ils cherchent des vendeurs capables d'obtenir de bons résultats **3.** [of match, exam, election] résultat *m* ▪ **she got good A-level ~s** *UK* ≃ elle a obtenu de bons résultats au baccalauréat ▪ **our team needs a ~ next week** SPORT [win] notre équipe a besoin de gagner la semaine prochaine ▪ **the company's ~s are down on last year** FIN les résultats financiers de l'entreprise sont moins bons que (ceux de) l'année dernière **4.** MATHS [of sum, equation] résultat *m*.

<> *vi* résulter ▪ **the fire ~ed from a short circuit** c'est un court-circuit qui a provoqué l'incendie ▪ **a price rise would inevitably ~** il en résulterait *OR* il s'ensuivrait inévitablement une augmentation des prix ▪ **to ~ in** avoir pour résultat ▪ **the dispute ~ed in her resigning** la dispute a entraîné sa démission ▪ **the attack ~ed in heavy losses on both sides** l'attaque s'est soldée par d'importantes pertes des deux côtés.

◆ **as a result** *adv phr* : **as a ~, I missed my flight** à cause de cela, j'ai manqué mon avion.

◆ **as a result of** *prep phr* à cause de ▪ **I was late as a ~ of the strike** j'ai été en retard en raison de la grève.

resultant [rɪ'zʌltənt] <> *adj* [gen - MATHS] & MUS résultant.

<> *n* MATHS & PHYS résultante *f*.

resume [rɪ'zju:m] <> *vt* **1.** [seat, activity, duties etc] reprendre ▪ [story, journey] poursuivre **2.** *arch* [sum up] résumer.

<> *vi* reprendre, continuer.

résumé ['rezju:meɪ] *n* **1.** [summary] résumé *m* **2.** *US* [curriculum vitae] curriculum vitae *m inv*.

resumption [rɪ'zʌmpʃn] *n* reprise *f*.

resurface [,ri:'sɜ:fɪs] <> *vi liter & fig* refaire surface.

<> *vt* [road] refaire.

resurgence [rɪ'sɜ:dʒəns] *n* réapparition *f*, renaissance *f*.

resurgent [rɪ'sɜ:dʒənt] *adj* renaissant.

resurrect [,rezə'rekt] *vt liter & fig* ressusciter ▪ **~ed from the dead** ressuscité des *OR* d'entre les morts ▪ **the minister succeeded in ~ing his career** le ministre réussit à faire redémarrer sa carrière.

resurrection [ˌrezə'rekʃn] *n* résurrection *f*.

resuscitate [rɪ'sʌsɪteɪt] *vt* ranimer, réanimer.

resuscitation [rɪˌsʌsɪ'teɪʃn] *n* réanimation *f*.

resuscitator [rɪ'sʌsɪteɪtəʳ] *n* [apparatus] respirateur *m* ▪ [person] réanimateur *m*, - trice *f*.

retail ['ri:teɪl] <> *n* (vente *f* au) détail *m*.
<> *adj* de détail ▪ **they run a ~ hifi business** ils ont un magasin de matériel hi-fi ▶ **~ goods** marchandises *fpl* vendues au détail ▪ **~ outlet** point *m* de vente (au détail) ▪ **the ~ price** le prix de *OR* au détail ▪ **~ price index** *UK* indice *m* des prix de détail ▪ **~ shop** magasin *m* de détail ▪ **~ trade** commerce *m* (de détail).
<> *adv* au détail.
<> *vt* **1.** COMM vendre au détail **2.** *fml* [story, event, experience] raconter ▪ [gossip, scandal] répandre, colporter *pej*.
<> *vi* [goods] se vendre (au détail) ▪ **they ~ at £10 each** ils se vendent à 10 livres la pièce.

retailer ['ri:teɪləʳ] *n* détaillant *m*, - e *f*.

retain [rɪ'teɪn] *vt* **1.** [keep] garder ▪ **the village has ~ed its charm** le village a conservé son charme **2.** [hold, keep in place] retenir **3.** [remember] retenir, garder en mémoire **4.** [reserve - place, hotel room] retenir, réserver **5.** [engage - solicitor] engager ▪ **~ing fee** provision *f OR* avance *f* sur honoraires.

retainer [rɪ'teɪnəʳ] *n* **1.** [servant] domestique *mf*, serviteur *m arch* **2.** [retaining fee] provision *f* **3.** [nominal rent] loyer *m* nominal.

retake (*pret* **retook** [-'tʊk], *pp* **retaken** [-'teɪkn]) <> *vt* [ˌri:'teɪk] **1.** [town, fortress] reprendre **2.** [exam] repasser **3.** CIN [shot] reprendre, refaire ▪ [scene] refaire une prise (de vues) de.
<> *n* ['ri:teɪk] **1.** [of exam] nouvelle session *f* **2.** CIN nouvelle prise *f* (de vues).

retaliate [rɪ'tælɪeɪt] *vi* se venger, riposter ▪ **she ~d against her critics** elle a riposté à l'attaque de ses critiques.

retaliation [rɪˌtælɪ'eɪʃn] *n (U)* représailles *fpl*, vengeance *f* ▪ **in ~ (for sthg)** en *OR* par représailles (contre qqch).

retaliatory [rɪ'tælɪətrɪ] *adj* de représailles, de rétorsion ▪ **a ~ attack** une riposte.

retard [rɪ'tɑ:d] <> *vt fml* & SCI retarder.
<> *n US offens* retardé *m*, - e *f*.

retardant [rɪ'tɑ:dnt] <> *n* SCI retardateur *m*.
<> *adj fml* & SCI retardateur.

retarded [rɪ'tɑ:dɪd] <> *adj* **1.** [mentally] arriéré **2.** [delayed] retardé.
<> *npl dated* **the (mentally) ~** les arriérés *mpl* mentaux.

retch [retʃ] <> *vi* avoir un *OR* des haut-le-cœur.
<> *n* haut-le-cœur *m inv*.

retd *written abbr of* **retired**.

retell [ˌri:'tel] (*pret* & *pp* **retold** [-'təʊld]) *vt* raconter de nouveau.

retelling [ˌri:'telɪŋ] *n* nouvelle version *f* ▪ **the story gained in the ~** l'histoire gagnait à être racontée de nouveau.

retention [rɪ'tenʃn] *n* **1.** [keeping] conservation *f* **2.** MED [holding] rétention *f* ▪ **fluid ~** rétention d'eau **3.** [memory] rétention *f*.

retentive [rɪ'tentɪv] *adj* [memory] qui retient bien.

rethink (*pret* & *pp* **rethought** [-'θɔ:t]) <> *vt* [ˌri:'θɪŋk] repenser.
<> *n* ['ri:θɪŋk] : **a ~ of the whole project is necessary** il faut repenser le projet dans son ensemble ▪ **to have a ~ about sthg** réfléchir de nouveau à qqch.

reticence ['retɪsəns] *n* réticence *f*.

reticent ['retɪsənt] *adj* réticent ▪ **he's ~ about explaining his reasons** il hésite *OR* est peu disposé à expliquer ses raisons.

retina ['retɪnə] (*pl* **retinas** *OR pl* **retinae** [-ni:]) *n* rétine *f*.

retinal ['retɪnl] *adj* rétinien.

retinue ['retɪnju:] *n* suite *f*, cortège *m*.

retire [rɪ'taɪəʳ] <> *vi* **1.** [from job] prendre sa retraite ▪ [from business, politics] se retirer ▪ **to ~ from the political scene** se retirer de la scène politique **2.** *fml* & *hum* [go to bed] aller se coucher **3.** [leave] se retirer ▪ **shall we ~ to the lounge?** si nous passions au salon? ▪ **to ~ hurt** SPORT abandonner à la suite d'une blessure **4.** MIL [pull back] se replier.
<> *vt* **1.** [employee] mettre à la retraite **2.** MIL [troops] retirer **3.** FIN [coins, bonds, shares] retirer de la circulation.

retired [rɪ'taɪəd] *adj* **1.** [from job] retraité, à la retraite **2.** [secluded] retiré ▪ **a ~ spot** un endroit retiré *OR* isolé.

retiree [ˌrɪtaɪə'ri:] *n US* retraité *m*, - e *f*.

retirement [rɪ'taɪəmənt] *n* **1.** [from job] retraite *f* ▪ **to take early ~** partir en préretraite **2.** [seclusion] isolement *m*, solitude *f* **3.** MIL [pulling back] repli *m*.

retirement age *n* âge *m* de la retraite.

RETIREMENT AGE

En Grande-Bretagne, l'âge de la retraite est actuellement de 65 ans pour les hommes et 60 ans pour les femmes : il est cependant question de la mettre aussi à 65 ans pour les femmes. Aux États-Unis, il est fixé à 65 ans pour les deux sexes.

retirement pay *n* retraite *f*.

retirement pension *n* (pension *f* de) retraite *f*.

retirement plan *n US* régime *m* de retraite.

retiring [rɪ'taɪərɪŋ] *adj* **1.** [reserved] réservé **2.** [leaving - official, MP] sortant **3.** [employee] qui part à la retraite.

retold [-'təʊld] *pt* & *pp* ⊳ **retell**.

retool [ˌri:'tu:l] <> *vt* **1.** INDUST rééquiper **2.** *US inf* [reorganize] réorganiser.
<> *vi* **1.** INDUST se rééquiper **2.** *inf US* [reorganize] se réorganiser.

retort [rɪ'tɔ:t] <> *vi* & *vt* rétorquer, riposter.
<> *n* **1.** [reply] riposte *f*, réplique *f* **2.** CHEM cornue *f*.

retouch [ˌri:'tʌtʃ] *vt* [gen - PHOT] retoucher.

retrace [rɪ'treɪs] *vt* **1.** [go back over - route] refaire ▪ **to ~ one's steps** rebrousser chemin, revenir sur ses pas **2.** [reconstitute - past events, sb's movements] reconstituer.

retract [rɪ'trækt] <> *vt* **1.** [withdraw - statement, confession] retirer, rétracter *lit* ▪ [go back on - promise, agreement] revenir sur **2.** [draw in - claws, horns] rétracter, rentrer ▪ AERON [- wheels] rentrer, escamoter.
<> *vi* **1.** [recant] se rétracter, se désavouer **2.** [be drawn in - claws, horns] se rétracter ▪ AERON [- wheels] rentrer.

retractable [rɪ'træktəbl] *adj* **1.** [aerial, undercarriage] escamotable **2.** [statement] que l'on peut rétracter *OR* désavouer.

retraction [rɪ'trækʃn] *n* [of false information] démenti *m*.

retrain [ˌri:'treɪn] <> *vt* recycler.
<> *vi* se recycler.

retraining [ˌri:'treɪnɪŋ] *n* recyclage *m*.

retread <> *vt* [ˌri:'tred] (*pret* **retrod** [-'trɒd], *pp* **retrodden** [-'trɒdn] *pp* **retrod** [-'trɒd]) AUT rechaper.
<> *n* ['ri:tred] pneu *m* rechapé.

retreat [rɪ'tri:t] <> *vi* **1.** MIL battre en retraite, se replier ▪ **the management was forced to ~ on this point** *fig* la direction a été obligée de céder sur ce point **2.** [gen] se retirer ▪ **to ~ to the country** se retirer à la campagne.
<> *n* **1.** [gen - MIL] retraite *f*, repli *m* ▪ **to beat/to sound the ~** battre/sonner la retraite ▪ **this is a ~ from the unions' original position** les syndicats ont fait là des concessions par rapport à leur position initiale ▶ **to beat a hasty ~** prendre ses jambes à son cou **2.** [refuge] refuge *m*, asile *m* **3.** RELIG retraite *f* ▪ **to go on a ~** faire une retraite.

retrench [ri:'trentʃ] <> *vt* [costs, expenses] réduire, restreindre.

◇ *vi* faire des économies, se restreindre.

retrenchment [riː'trentʃmənt] *n* [of costs, expenses] réduction *f*, compression *f*.

retrial [ˌriː'traɪəl] *n* nouveau procès *m*.

retribution [ˌretrɪ'bjuːʃn] *n* punition *f*, châtiment *m* ▪ **it is divine ~** c'est le châtiment de Dieu.

retributive [rɪ'trɪbjʊtɪv] *adj* [involving punishment] de punition, de châtiment ▪ [avenging] vengeur ▪ **~ measures will be taken against the culprits** les coupables seront punis.

retrievable [rɪ'triːvəbl] *adj* [object] récupérable ▪ [fortune, health] recouvrable ▪ [error, loss] réparable ▪ [situation] rattrapable.

retrieval [rɪ'triːvl] *n* **1.** [getting back - of object] récupération *f* ; [- of fortune, health] recouvrement *m* **2.** COMPUT récupération *f*, extraction *f* ▪ **data ~** recherche *f* de données **3.** [making good - of mistake] réparation *f* ▪ **the situation is beyond ~** il n'y a plus rien à faire (pour sauver la situation).

retrieve [rɪ'triːv] ◇ *vt* **1.** [get back - lost object] récupérer ; [- health, fortune] recouvrer, retrouver ▪ **I ~d my bag from the lost property office** j'ai récupéré mon sac au bureau des objets trouvés **2.** [save] sauver ▪ **she managed to ~ her coat from the fire** elle réussit à sauver son manteau du feu **3.** COMPUT [data] récupérer, extraire **4.** [make good - mistake] réparer ; [- situation] rattraper, sauver **5.** HUNT rapporter.
◇ *vi* HUNT rapporter le gibier.

retriever [rɪ'triːvər] *n* [gen] retriever *m* ▪ [golden retriever] Golden retriever *m* ▪ [Labrador retriever] Labrador retriever.

retro ['retrəʊ] *adj* rétro *(inv)* ▪ **~ fashions** la mode rétro.

retroactive [ˌretrəʊ'æktɪv] *adj* rétroactif.

retroflexed ['retrəʊflekst] *adj* **1.** LING rétroflexe **2.** ANAT rétrofléchi.

retrograde ['retrəgreɪd] ◇ *adj* rétrograde.
◇ *vi* **1.** [gen] rétrograder **2.** *US* MIL [retreat] battre en retraite.

retrogress ['retrəgres] *vi fml* **1.** [degenerate] régresser **2.** [move backwards] rétrograder.

retrogression [ˌretrə'greʃn] *n* rétrogression *f*, régression *f*.

retrogressive [ˌretrə'gresɪv] *adj* rétrogressif, régressif.

retrorocket ['retrəʊˌrɒkɪt] *n* rétrofusée *f*.

retrospect ['retrəspekt] ◆ **in retrospect** *adv phr* rétrospectivement, avec le recul.

retrospection [ˌretrə'spekʃn] *n* rétrospection *f*.

retrospective [ˌretrə'spektɪv] ◇ *adj* rétrospectif.
◇ *n* ART rétrospective *f*.

retrospectively [ˌretrə'spektɪvlɪ] *adv* rétrospectivement.

retry [ˌriː'traɪ] *(pret & pp* **retried***)* *vt* LAW refaire le procès de, juger à nouveau.

retune [ˌriː'tjuːn] ◇ *vt* **1.** MUS réaccorder **2.** RADIO régler.
◇ *vi* RADIO : **to ~ to medium wave** régler son poste sur ondes moyennes.

return [rɪ'tɜːn] ◇ *vi* **1.** [go back] retourner ▪ [come back] revenir ▪ **as soon as she ~s** dès son retour ▪ **to ~ home** rentrer (à la maison *OR* chez soi)
2. [to subject, activity, former state] revenir ▪ **let's ~ to your question** revenons à votre question ▪ **to ~ to work** reprendre le travail ▪ **she ~ed to her reading** elle reprit sa lecture ▪ **he soon ~ed to his old ways** il est vite retombé dans *OR* il a vite repris ses anciennes habitudes ▪ **the situation should ~ to normal next week** la situation devrait redevenir normale la semaine prochaine
3. [reappear - fever, pain, good weather, fears] réapparaître.
◇ *vt* **1.** [give back] rendre ▪ [take back] rapporter ▪ [send back] renvoyer, retourner ▪ **I have to ~ the library books today** il faut que je rapporte les livres à la bibliothèque aujourd'hui ▪ **'~ to sender'** 'retour à l'expéditeur' ▪ **she ~ed my look** elle me regarda à son tour ▪ **the soldiers ~ed our fire** les soldats répondirent à notre tir
2. [replace, put back] remettre ▪ **she ~ed the file to the drawer** elle remit le dossier dans le tiroir
3. [repay - greeting, kindness, compliment] rendre (en retour) ▪ **how can I ~ your favour?** comment vous remercier? ▪ **they ~ed our visit the following year** ils sont venus nous voir à leur tour l'année suivante ▪ [reciprocate - affection] rendre
4. SPORT [hit or throw back] renvoyer
5. *UK* [elect] élire ▪ **she was ~ed as member for Tottenham** elle a été élue député de Tottenham
6. [reply] répondre
7. LAW [pronounce - verdict] rendre, prononcer
8. FIN [yield - profit, interest] rapporter
9. [in bridge] rejouer.
◇ *adj* [fare] aller (et) retour ▪ [trip, flight] de retour ▪ **the ~ journey** le (voyage du) retour.
◇ *n* **1.** [going or coming back] retour *m* ▪ **on her ~** à son retour ▶ **the point of no ~** le point de non-retour
2. [giving or taking back] retour *m* ▪ [sending back] renvoi *m*, retour *m* ▪ **by ~ (of post)** *UK* par retour du courrier
3. *UK* [round trip] aller et retour *m* ▪ **two ~s to Edinburgh, please** deux allers et retours pour Édimbourg, s'il vous plaît
4. [to subject, activity, earlier state] retour *m* ▪ **a ~ to normal** un retour à la normale ▪ **the strikers' ~ to work** la reprise du travail par les grévistes
5. [reappearance - of fever, pain, good weather] réapparition *f*, retour *m*
6. FIN [yield] rapport *m* ▪ **a 10% ~ on investment** un rendement de 10 % sur la somme investie
7. [for income tax] (formulaire *m* de) déclaration *f* d'impôts
8. SPORT [esp in tennis] retour *m*
9. ARCHIT retour *m*.
◆ **returns** *npl* **1.** [results] résultats *mpl* ▪ [statistics] statistiques *fpl*, chiffres *mpl* ▪ **the election ~s** les résultats des élections
2. [birthday greetings] : **many happy ~s (of the day)!** bon *OR* joyeux anniversaire!
◆ **in return** *adv phr* en retour, en échange.
◆ **in return for** *prep phr* en échange de.

returnable [rɪ'tɜːnəbl] *adj* **1.** [container, bottle] consigné **2.** [document] à retourner ▪ **~ by July 1st** à renvoyer avant le 1er juillet.

returner [rɪ'tɜːnər] *n* [person returning to work] *personne réintégrant la vie professionnelle après une période d'inactivité volontaire.*

returning officer [rɪ'tɜːnɪŋ-] *n* président *m*, - e *f* du bureau de vote.

return key *n* COMPUT touche *f* entrée, touche *f* retour de chariot.

return match *n* match *m* retour.

return ticket *n UK* (billet *m* d')aller (et) retour *m*.

reunification [ˌriːjuːnɪfɪ'keɪʃn] *n* réunification *f*.

reunify [ˌriː'juːnɪfaɪ] *(pret & pp* **reunified***)* *vt* réunifier.

reunion [ˌriː'juːnjən] *n* réunion *f*.

Reunion [ˌriː'juːnjən] *pr n* : **~ (Island)** (l'île *f* de) la Réunion ▪ **in ~** à la Réunion.

reunite [ˌriːjuː'naɪt] ◇ *vt* réunir ▪ **when the hostages were ~d with their families** quand les otages ont retrouvé leur famille.
◇ *vi* se réunir.

reupholster [ˌriːʌp'həʊlstər] *vt* rembourrer (de nouveau).

reusable [riː'juːzəbl] *adj* réutilisable, recyclable.

re-use ◇ *vt* [ˌriː'juːz] réutiliser, remployer, recycler.
◇ *n* [ˌriː'juːs] réutilisation *f*, remploi *m*, recyclage *m*.

rev [rev] *(pret & pp* **revved**, *cont* **revving***)* *inf* ◇ *n* *(abbrev of* **revolution***)* AUT tour *m*.
◇ *vt & vi* = **rev up**.
◆ **rev up** *inf* ◇ *vt sep* [engine] emballer.

◇ *vi insep* [driver] appuyer sur l'accélérateur ■ [engine] s'accélérer.

Rev. *written abbr of* **Reverend**.

revaluation [ˌriːvæljʊ'eɪʃn] *n* [of currency, property etc] réévaluation *f*.

revalue [ˌriː'væljuː] *vt* **1.** [currency] réévaluer **2.** [property] réévaluer, estimer à nouveau la valeur de.

revamp [ˌriː'væmp] *vt inf* rafistoler, retaper.

revanchist [rɪ'væntʃɪst] ◇ *adj* revanchiste.
◇ *n* revanchiste *mf*.

rev counter *n inf* compte-tours *m inv*.

Revd *written abbr of* **reverend**.

reveal [rɪ'viːl] *vt* **1.** [disclose, divulge] révéler ■ **to ~ a secret** révéler *OR* divulguer un secret **2.** [show] révéler, découvrir, laisser voir ■ **he tried hard not to ~ his true feelings** il s'efforça de ne pas révéler ses vrais sentiments ■ **the undertaking ~ed itself to be impossible** l'entreprise s'est révélée impossible.

revealing [rɪ'viːlɪŋ] *adj* **1.** [experience, action] révélateur **2.** [dress] décolleté, qui ne cache rien ■ [neckline] décolleté.

revealingly [rɪ'viːlɪŋlɪ] *adv* **1.** [significantly] : **~, not one of them speaks a foreign language** il est révélateur qu'aucun d'entre eux ne parle une langue étrangère **2.** [exposing the body] : **a ~ short dress** une robe courte qui laisse tout voir.

reveille [*UK* rɪ'vælɪ, *US* 'revəlɪ] *n* MIL réveil *m*.

revel ['revl] (*UK pret & pp* **revelled**, *cont* **revelling**) (*US pret & pp* **reveled**, *cont* **reveling**) *vi* **1.** [bask, wallow] se délecter ■ **to ~ in sthg** se délecter de *OR* à qqch **2.** [make merry] s'amuser.
◆ **revels** *npl* festivités *fpl*.

revelation [ˌrevə'leɪʃn] *n* révélation *f* ■ **her talent was a ~ to me** son talent a été une révélation pour moi ➤ **the Revelation (of Saint John the Divine), Revelations** l'Apocalypse *f* (de saint Jean l'Évangéliste).

revelatory [ˌrevə'leɪtərɪ] *adj* révélateur.

reveller *UK*, **reveler** *US* ['revələʳ] *n* fêtard *m*, - e *f*, noceur *m*, - euse *f*.

revelry ['revəlrɪ] *n* festivités *fpl*.

revelries *npl* = **revelry**.

revenge [rɪ'vendʒ] ◇ *n* **1.** [vengeance] vengeance *f*, revanche *f* ■ **I'll get** *OR* **I'll take my ~ on him for this!** il va me le payer! ■ **she did it out of ~** elle l'a fait pour se venger *OR* par vengeance **2.** SPORT revanche *f*.
◇ *vt* venger ■ **how can I ~ myself on them for this insult?** comment leur faire payer cette insulte?

revenger [rɪ'vendʒəʳ] *n* vengeur *m*, - eresse *f*.

revenue ['revənjuː] ◇ *n* revenu *m* ■ **state ~** *OR* **~s** les recettes publiques *OR* de l'État.
◇ *comp* [department, official] du fisc ■ **~ expenditure** dépenses *fpl* de fonctionnement.

revenue stamp *n* timbre *m* fiscal.

reverberate [rɪ'vɜːbəreɪt] ◇ *vi* **1.** [sound] résonner, retentir ■ **the building ~d with their cries** l'immeuble retentissait de leurs cris **2.** [light] se réverbérer **3.** *fig* [spread] retentir ■ **the scandal ~d through the country** ce scandale a secoué tout le pays.
◇ *vt* **1.** [sound] renvoyer, répercuter **2.** [light] réverbérer.

reverberation [rɪˌvɜːbə'reɪʃn] *n* **1.** [of sound, light] réverbération *f* **2.** *fig* [repercussion] retentissement *m*, répercussion *f* ■ **the crisis had ~s in neighbouring countries** la crise a eu des répercussions dans les pays voisins.

revere [rɪ'vɪəʳ] *vt* révérer, vénérer ■ **she was a much ~d figure** c'était une personnalité très respectée.

reverence ['revərəns] ◇ *n* **1.** [respect] révérence *f*, vénération *f* **2.** [term of address] : **Your Reverence** mon révérend (Père) ■ **His Reverence the Archbishop** Son Excellence l'archevêque.
◇ *vt* révérer, vénérer.

reverend ['revərənd] ◇ *adj* **1.** RELIG : **a ~ gentleman** un révérend père ■ **the Reverend Paul James** le révérend Paul James **2.** [gen - respected] vénérable, révéré.
◇ *n* [Protestant] pasteur *m* ■ [Catholic] curé *m*.

Reverend Mother *n* Révérende Mère *f*.

reverent ['revərənt] *adj* respectueux, révérencieux *lit*.

reverential [ˌrevə'renʃl] *adj* révérenciel.

reverently ['revərəntlɪ] *adv* avec révérence, révérencieusement *lit*.

reverie ['revərɪ] *n lit* [gen - MUS] rêverie *f*.

reversal [rɪ'vɜːsl] *n* **1.** [change - of situation] retournement *m* ; [- of opinion] revirement *m* ; [- of order, roles] interversion *f*, inversion *f* ; [- of policy] changement *m* **2.** [setback] revers *m* ■ **the patient has suffered a ~** le malade a fait une rechute **3.** LAW [annulment] annulation *f* **4.** PHOT inversion *f*.

reverse [rɪ'vɜːs] ◇ *vt* **1.** [change - process, trend] renverser ; [- situation] retourner ; [- order, roles, decline] inverser ■ **this could ~ the effects of all our policies** ceci pourrait annuler les effets de toute notre politique ■ **the unions have ~d their policy** les syndicats ont fait volte-face
2. [turn round - garment] retourner ; [- photo] inverser
3. [annul - decision] annuler ■ LAW casser, annuler
4. [cause to go backwards - car] mettre en marche arrière ; [- machine] renverser la marche de ■ **this lever ~s the belt** ce levier permet d'inverser la marche de la courroie ■ **she ~d the car up the street** elle remonta la rue en marche arrière
5. TELEC : **to ~ the charges** appeler en PCV.
◇ *vi* AUT [car, driver] faire marche arrière ■ **the driver in front ~d into me** la voiture qui était devant moi m'est rentrée dedans en marche arrière.
◇ *n* **1.** AUT marche *f* arrière ■ **in ~** en marche arrière ■ **he put the bus into ~** le conducteur de l'autobus passa en marche arrière ■ **the company's fortunes are going into ~** *fig* l'entreprise connaît actuellement un revers de fortune
2. [contrary] contraire *m*, inverse *m*, opposé *m* ■ **did you enjoy it? – quite the ~** cela vous a-t-il plu? – pas du tout ■ **she is the ~ of shy** elle est tout sauf timide ■ **try to do the same thing in ~** essayez de faire la même chose dans l'ordre inverse
3. [other side - of cloth, leaf] envers *m* ; [- of sheet of paper] verso *m* ; [- of coin, medal] revers *m*
4. [setback] revers *m*, échec *m* ■ [defeat] défaite *f* ■ **his condition has suffered a ~** il a rechuté
5. TYPO noir *m* au blanc ■ **in ~** en réserve.
◇ *adj* **1.** [opposite, contrary] inverse, contraire, opposé ■ **we are now experiencing the ~ trend** actuellement, c'est l'inverse qui se produit ■ **in ~ order** en ordre inverse
2. [back] : **the ~ side** [of cloth, leaf] l'envers ; [of sheet of paper] le verso ; [of coin, medal] le revers
3. [turned around] inversé ■ **a ~ image** une image inversée
4. AUT : **~ gear** marche *f* arrière.

reverse-charge call *n UK* appel *m* en PCV.

reverser [rɪ'vɜːsəʳ] *n* TECH inverseur *m*.

reversible [rɪ'vɜːsəbl] *adj* [coat, process] réversible ■ [decision] révocable.

reversing light [rɪ'vɜːsɪŋ-] *n* feu *m* de recul.

reversion [rɪ'vɜːʃn] *n* **1.** [to former condition, practice] retour *m* **2.** BIOL & LAW réversion *f*.

revert [rɪ'vɜːt] *vi* retourner, revenir ■ **they ~ed to barbarism** ils ont à nouveau sombré dans la barbarie ■ **he soon ~ed to his old ways** il est vite retombé dans *OR* il a vite repris ses anciennes habitudes ■ **to ~ to childhood** retomber en enfance ■ **the property ~s to the spouse** LAW les biens reviennent à l'époux ■ **to ~ to type** retrouver sa vraie nature.

review [rɪ'vjuː] ◇ *n* **1.** [critical article] critique *f* ■ **the play got good/bad ~s** la pièce a eu de bonnes/mauvaises critiques **2.** [magazine] revue *f* ■ [radio or TV programme] magazine *m* **3.** [assessment - of situation, conditions] étude *f*, examen *m*, bilan *m* ■ **she first gave us a brief ~ of the situation** elle nous a d'abord présenté un court bilan de la situation ■ **pollution controls are under ~** on est en train de réexaminer la réglementation en matière de pollution ■ **~ board** commission *f*

d'étude **4.** [reassessment - of salary, prices, case] révision *f* ■ **my salary comes** *OR* **is up for ~ next month** mon salaire doit être révisé le mois prochain **5.** MIL [inspection] revue *f* **6.** *US* SCH & UNIV [revision] révision *f* **7.** = **revue**.
◇ *vt* **1.** [write critical article on] faire la critique de ■ **she ~s books for an Australian paper** elle est critique littéraire pour un journal australien **2.** [assess] examiner, étudier, faire le bilan de ■ [reassess] réviser, revoir ■ LAW [case] réviser ■ **to ~ a decision** reconsidérer une décision **3.** [go back over, look back on] passer en revue **4.** MIL [troops] passer en revue **5.** [revise] réviser ■ **she quickly ~ed her notes before the speech** elle jeta un dernier coup d'œil sur ses notes avant le discours ■ **he's ~ing his French** *US* il révise son français.

review copy *n* exemplaire *m* de service de presse.

reviewer [rɪ'vju:ər] *n* PRESS critique *m*.

revile [rɪ'vaɪl] *vt lit* vilipender, injurier.

revise [rɪ'vaɪz] ◇ *vt* **1.** [alter - policy, belief, offer, price] réviser **2.** [read through - text, manuscript] revoir, corriger **3.** [update] mettre à jour, corriger **4.** *UK* SCH & UNIV réviser.
◇ *vi UK* SCH & UNIV réviser.
◇ *n* TYPO deuxième épreuve *f*.

revised [rɪ'vaɪzd] *adj* **1.** [figures, estimate] révisé **2.** [edition] revu et corrigé.

Revised Version *n* : **the ~** *traduction anglaise de la Bible faite en 1885.*

reviser [rɪ'vaɪzər] *n* [gen] réviseur *m*, - euse *f* ■ TYPO correcteur *m*, - trice *f*.

revision [rɪ'vɪʒn] *n* **1.** [alteration etc] révision *f* ■ **the book has undergone several ~s** ce livre a été révisé *OR* remanié plusieurs fois **2.** *UK* SCH & UNIV révision *f*.

revisionism [rɪ'vɪʒnɪzm] *n* révisionnisme *m*.

revisionist [rɪ'vɪʒnɪst] ◇ *adj* révisionniste.
◇ *n* révisionniste *mf*.

revisit [ˌri:'vɪzɪt] *vt* [place] revisiter ■ [person] retourner voir ■ **Dickens ~ed** *fig* Dickens revisité ▶ **'Brideshead Revisited'** ***Waugh*** 'le Retour au château'.

revitalize, ise [ˌri:'vaɪtəlaɪz] *vt* revitaliser.

revival [rɪ'vaɪvl] *n* **1.** [resurgence] renouveau *m*, renaissance *f* ■ **a ~ of interest in Latin poets** un regain d'intérêt pour les poètes latins ■ **a religious ~** un renouveau de la religion **2.** [bringing back - of custom, language] rétablissement *m* **3.** [of play, TV series] reprise *f* **4.** [from a faint] reprise *f* de connaissance ■ [from illness] récupération *f*.

revivalist [rɪ'vaɪvəlɪst] ◇ *n* **1.** RELIG revivaliste *mf* **2.** [of past] traditionaliste *mf*.
◇ *adj* RELIG revivaliste.

revive [rɪ'vaɪv] ◇ *vi* **1.** [regain consciousness] reprendre connaissance, revenir à soi ■ [regain strength or form] récupérer **2.** [flourish again - business, the economy] reprendre ; [- movement, group] renaître, ressusciter ; [- custom, expression] réapparaître ■ **interest in her work is beginning to ~** on assiste à un renouveau *OR* regain d'intérêt pour son œuvre.
◇ *vt* **1.** [restore to consciousness] ranimer ■ MED réanimer ■ [restore strength to] remonter **2.** [make flourish again - discussion, faith etc] ranimer, raviver ; [- business, the economy] relancer, faire redémarrer ; [- interest, hope etc] raviver, faire renaître ■ **a plan to ~ the city centre** un projet destiné à dynamiser le centre-ville ■ **~d interest in the art of this period** un renouveau *OR* regain d'intérêt pour l'art de cette époque **3.** [bring back - law] remettre en vigueur ; [- fashion] relancer ; [- style, look] remettre en vogue ; [- custom, language, movement] raviver, ressusciter **4.** [play, TV series] reprendre.

revivify [ri:'vɪvɪfaɪ] *vt* revivifier.

revocation [ˌrevə'keɪʃn] *n* [of decision] annulation *f* ■ [of measure, law] abrogation *f*, annulation *f*, révocation *f* ■ [of will] révocation *f*, annulation *f* ■ [of title, diploma, permit] retrait *m*.

revoke [rɪ'vəʊk] *vt* [decision] annuler ■ [measure, law] abroger, annuler, révoquer ■ [will] révoquer, annuler ■ [title, diploma, permit, right] retirer.

revolt [rɪ'vəʊlt] ◇ *vi* [rise up] se révolter, se rebeller, se soulever.
◇ *vt* dégoûter ■ **she is ~ed by the idea** l'idée la dégoûte *OR* la révolte.
◇ *n* **1.** [uprising] révolte *f*, rébellion *f* ■ **the peasants rose up in ~** les paysans se sont révoltés *OR* soulevés ■ **they are in ~ against the system** ils se rebellent contre le système **2.** [disgust] dégoût *m* ■ [indignation] indignation *f*.

revolting [rɪ'vəʊltɪŋ] *adj* **1.** [disgusting - story, scene] dégoûtant ; [- person, act] ignoble ; [- food, mess] écœurant, immonde **2.** *inf* [nasty] affreux.

revoltingly [rɪ'vəʊltɪŋlɪ] *adv* de façon dégoûtante ■ **he's ~ ugly/dirty** il est d'une laideur/d'une saleté repoussante ▌[as intensifier] : **she's so ~ clever!** ça m'écœure qu'on puisse être aussi intelligent!

revolution [ˌrevə'lu:ʃn] *n* **1.** POL & *fig* révolution *f* ■ **a ~ in computer technology** une révolution dans le domaine de l'informatique **2.** [turn] révolution *f*, tour *m* ■ [turning] révolution *f*.

revolutionary [ˌrevə'lu:ʃnərɪ] (*pl* **revolutionaries**) ◇ *adj* révolutionnaire.
◇ *n* révolutionnaire *mf*.

revolutionize, ise [ˌrevə'lu:ʃənaɪz] *vt* **1.** [change radically] révolutionner **2.** POL [country] faire une révolution dans ■ [people] insuffler des idées révolutionnaires à.

revolve [rɪ'vɒlv] ◇ *vi* **1.** [rotate] tourner ■ **the moon ~s around** *OR* **round the earth** la Lune tourne autour de la Terre **2.** [centre, focus] tourner ■ **their conversation ~d around** *OR* **round two main points** leur conversation tournait autour de deux points principaux ■ **his whole life ~s around his work** sa vie tout entière est centrée *OR* axée sur son travail **3.** [recur] revenir ■ **the seasons ~** les saisons se succèdent.
◇ *vt* **1.** [rotate] faire tourner **2.** *fml* [ponder] considérer, ruminer.

revolver [rɪ'vɒlvər] *n* revolver *m*.

revolving [rɪ'vɒlvɪŋ] *adj* [gen] tournant ■ [chair] pivotant ■ TECH rotatif ■ ASTRON en rotation.

revolving door *n* tambour *m (porte).*

revue [rɪ'vju:] *n* THEAT revue *f*.

revulsion [rɪ'vʌlʃn] *n* **1.** [disgust] répulsion *f*, dégoût *m* ■ **she turned away in ~** elle s'est détournée, dégoûtée **2.** [recoiling] (mouvement *m* de) recul *m* **3.** MED révulsion *f*.

reward [rɪ'wɔ:d] ◇ *n* récompense *f* ■ **they're offering a $500 ~** ils offrent 500 dollars de récompense *OR* une récompense de 500 dollars ■ **as a ~ for his efforts** en récompense de ses efforts ■ **I do everything for him, and what do I get in ~ ?** je fais tout pour lui, et tu vois comment il me remercie?
◇ *vt* récompenser ■ **he was handsomely ~ed with a cheque for £1,000** on l'a généreusement récompensé par un chèque de 1 000 livres ■ **our patience has finally been ~ed** notre patience est enfin récompensée ■ **his alibi might ~ investigation** ça vaut peut-être la peine d'enquêter sur son alibi.

rewarding [rɪ'wɔ:dɪŋ] *adj* gratifiant ■ **the conference was most ~** le colloque était très enrichissant ■ **financially ~** rémunérateur, lucratif.

rewind ◇ *vt* [ˌri:'waɪnd] (*pret & pp* **rewound** [ˌri:'waʊnd]) rembobiner.
◇ *vi* [ˌri:'waɪnd] (*pret & pp* **rewound** [ˌri:'waʊnd]) se rembobiner.
◇ *n* ['ri:waɪnd] rembobinage *m* ■ **it has automatic ~** ça se rembobine automatiquement ■ **~ button** bouton *m* de rembobinage.

rewire [ˌri:'waɪər] *vt* [house] refaire l'électricité dans ■ [machine] refaire les circuits électriques de.

reword [ˌri:'wɜ:d] *vt* reformuler.

rework [ˌri:'wɜ:k] *vt* **1.** [speech, text] retravailler ■ **his last novel ~s the same theme** son dernier roman reprend le même thème **2.** INDUST retraiter.

reworking [ˌriːˈwɜːkɪŋ] *n* reprise *f* ▪ **the film is a ~ of the "doppelgänger" theme** le film reprend le thème du double.

rewound [ˌriːˈwaʊnd] *pt* & *pp* ⊳ **rewind.**

rewrite ◇ *vt* [ˌriːˈraɪt] (*pret* **rewrote** [-ˈrəʊt], *pp* **rewritten** [-ˈrɪtn]) récrire, réécrire ▪ [for publication] récrire, rewriter.
◇ *n* [ˈriːraɪt] **1.** *inf* [act] réécriture *f*, rewriting *m* ▪ **can you do a ~ job on this?** pouvez-vous me récrire *OR* rewriter ça? **2.** [text] nouvelle version *f*.

rewritten [-ˈrɪtn] *pp* ⊳ **rewrite.**

rewrote [-ˈrəʊt] *pt* ⊳ **rewrite.**

RGN (*abbrev of* **registered general nurse**) *n UK* infirmier *m* diplômé, infirmière *f* diplômée d'État (*remplacé en 1992 par RN*).

Rh (*written abbrev of* **rhesus**) Rh.

rhapsodic [ræpˈsɒdɪk] *adj* **1.** [ecstatic] extatique ▪ [full of praise] dithyrambique **2.** MUS rhapsodique, rapsodique.

rhapsodize, ise [ˈræpsədaɪz] *vi* s'extasier ▪ **to ~ about sthg** s'extasier sur qqch.

rhapsody [ˈræpsədɪ] (*pl* **rhapsodies**) *n* **1.** [ecstasy] extase *f* ▪ **to go into rhapsodies about sthg** s'extasier sur qqch **2.** MUS & LIT rhapsodie *f*, rapsodie *f*.

rhea [ˈriːə] *n* nandou *m*.

Rheims [riːmz] *pr n* Reims.

rheme [riːm] *n* commentaire *m* ▪ LING rhème *m*.

Rhenish [ˈriːnɪʃ] ◇ *adj* rhénan, du Rhin ▪ **~ wine** vin *m* du Rhin.
◇ *n* vin *m* du Rhin.

rhenium [ˈriːnɪəm] *n* rhénium *m*.

rheostat [ˈriːəstæt] *n* rhéostat *m*.

rhesus baby [ˈriːsəs-] *n bébé souffrant de la maladie hémolytique du nouveau-né.*

rhesus factor *n* facteur *m* Rhésus.

rhesus monkey *n* ZOOL rhésus *m*.

rhesus negative *adj* Rhésus négatif.

rhesus positive *adj* Rhésus positif.

rhetoric [ˈretərɪk] *n* rhétorique *f*.

rhetorical [rɪˈtɒrɪkl] *adj* rhétorique.

rhetorically [rɪˈtɒrɪklɪ] *adv* en rhétoricien ▪ **"who knows?" she asked ~** "qui sait?", demanda-t-elle sans vraiment attendre de réponse ▪ **I was only asking ~** je demandais ça simplement pour la forme.

rhetorical question *n* question *f* posée pour la forme.

rhetorician [ˌretəˈrɪʃn] *n* [speaker] rhétoricien *m*, - enne *f*, rhéteur *m pej* ▪ [teacher of rhetoric] rhéteur *m*.

rheumatic [ruːˈmætɪk] ◇ *adj* [symptom] rhumatismal ▪ [person] rhumatisant ▪ [limbs] atteint de rhumatismes.
◇ *n* rhumatisant *m*, - e *f*.

rheumatic fever *n* rhumatisme *m* articulaire aigu.

rheumatics [ruːˈmætɪks] *npl inf* rhumatismes *mpl*.

rheumatism [ˈruːmətɪzm] *n* rhumatisme *m*.

rheumatoid [ˈruːmətɔɪd] *adj* rhumatoïde.

rheumatoid arthritis *n* polyarthrite *f* rhumatoïde.

rheumatology [ˌruːməˈtɒlədʒɪ] *n* rhumatologie *f*.

rheumy [ˈruːmɪ] (*comp* **rheumier**, *superl* **rheumiest**) *adj* chassieux.

Rh factor = **rhesus factor**.

Rhine [raɪn] *pr n* : **the (River) ~** le Rhin.

Rhineland [ˈraɪnlænd] *pr n* Rhénanie *f*.

Rhineland-Palatinate *pr n* Rhénanie-Palatinat *f*.

rhinestone [ˈraɪnstəʊn] *n* fausse pierre *f* ▪ [smaller] strass *m*.

rhino [ˈraɪnəʊ] (*pl inv OR pl* **rhinos**) *n* rhinocéros *m*.

rhinoceros [raɪˈnɒsərəs] (*pl inv OR pl* **rhinoceroses** *OR pl* **rhinoceri** [-raɪ]) *n* rhinocéros *m*.

Rhode Island [rəʊd-] *pr n* Rhode Island *m* ▪ **in ~** dans le Rhode Island.

Rhodes [rəʊdz] *pr n* Rhodes ▪ **in ~** à Rhodes ▪ **the Colossus of ~** le colosse de Rhodes.

Rhodesia [rəʊˈdiːʃə] *pr n* Rhodésie *f* ▪ **in ~** en Rhodésie.

Rhodes Scholarship *n bourse permettant aux étudiants étrangers d'étudier à l'université d'Oxford.*

rhodium [ˈrəʊdɪəm] *n* rhodium.

rhododendron [ˌrəʊdəˈdendrən] *n* rhododendron *m*.

rhombic [ˈrɒmbɪk] *adj* **1.** GEOM rhombique **2.** MINER [crystal] orthorhombique.

rhomboid [ˈrɒmbɔɪd] ◇ *n* parallélogramme *m* (*dont les côtés adjacents sont inégaux*).
◇ *adj* rhomboïdal, rhombiforme.

rhombus [ˈrɒmbəs] (*pl* **rhombuses** *OR pl* **rhombi** [-baɪ]) *n* losange *m*.

Rhône [rəʊn] *pr n* : **the (River) ~** le Rhône.

rhubarb [ˈruːbɑːb] *n* **1.** BOT rhubarbe *f* **2.** THEAT brouhaha *m*, murmures *mpl*.

rhyme [raɪm] ◇ *n* **1.** [sound] rime *f* ▪ **the use of ~** l'emploi de la rime ▪ **give me a ~ for "mash"** trouve-moi un mot qui rime avec "mash" ⊙ **without ~ or reason** sans rime ni raison ▪ **their demands have neither ~ nor reason** leurs revendications ne riment à rien **2.** (*U*) [poetry] vers *mpl* ▪ **in ~** en vers **3.** [poem] poème *m*.
◇ *vi* **1.** [word, lines] rimer **2.** [write verse] écrire *OR* composer des poèmes.
◇ *vt* faire rimer.

rhymed [raɪmd] *adj* rimé.

rhymer [ˈraɪməʳ] = **rhymester**.

rhyme royal *n* septain *m* (*combinaison ABABBCC*).

rhymester [ˈraɪmstəʳ] *n pej* rimeur *m*, - euse *f*, rimailleur *m*, - euse *f*.

rhyming slang [ˈraɪmɪŋ-] *n sorte d'argot qui consiste à remplacer un mot par un groupe de mots choisis pour la rime.*

RHYMING SLANG

Cet argot londonien, qui consiste à remplacer un mot par une expression avec laquelle il rime, est traditionnellement employé par les *Cockneys*, mais certaines expressions sont passées dans la langue courante, comme *pork pie* (pour dire *lie*), *brown bread* (*dead*), etc. On ne retient parfois que le premier élément de l'expression : *my old china* (qui vient de *china plate* pour dire *mate*) ; *to have a butcher's* (*butcher's hook* ; *look*).

rhythm [ˈrɪðm] *n* rythme *m* ▪ **she's got ~** elle a le sens du rythme.

rhythm and blues *n* rhythm and blues *m inv*.

rhythm guitar *n* guitare *f* rythmique.

rhythmic(al) [ˈrɪðmɪk(l)] *adj* [pattern, exercice] rythmique ▪ [music, noise] rythmé ▪ **the ~ rattling of the train** le bruit régulier du train.

rhythmically [ˈrɪðmɪklɪ] *adv* rythmiquement.

rhythmic gymnastics *nsg* gymnastique *f* rythmique, rhythmique *f*.

rhythm method *n* méthode *f* des températures.

RI *written abbr of* **Rhode Island**.

rib [rɪb] (*pret & pp* **ribbed**, *cont* **ribbing**) ◇ *n* **1.** ANAT côte *f* ▪ **he dug** *OR* **he poked her in the ~s** il lui a donné un petit coup de coude ⊙ **floating ~** côte flottante **2.** CULIN côte *f* **3.** [of vault, leaf, aircraft or insect wing] nervure *f* ▪ [of ship's hull] couple

m, membre *m* ▪ [of umbrella] baleine *f* **4.** [in knitting] côte *f* **5.** [on mountain - spur] éperon *m* ; [- crest] arête *f* **6.** [vein of ore] veine *f*, filon *m*.
◇ *vt inf* [tease] taquiner, mettre en boîte.

RIBA *pr n* = **Royal Institute of British Architects**.

ribald [ˈrɪbəld] *adj lit* [joke, language] grivois, paillard ▪ [laughter] égrillard.

ribbed [rɪbd] *adj* **1.** [leaf, vault] à nervures **2.** [sweater, fabric] à côtes.

ribbing [ˈrɪbɪŋ] *n* **1.** *(U)* TEX côtes *fpl* **2.** *inf* [teasing] taquinerie *f*, mise *f* en boîte.

ribbon [ˈrɪbən] ◇ *vt* **1.** [adorn with ribbon] enrubanner **2.** *fig* [streak] sillonner, zébrer **3.** [cut] couper en rubans ▪ [shred] mettre en lambeaux.
◇ *n* **1.** [for hair, typewriter, parcel etc] ruban *m* **2.** *fig* [of road] ruban *m* ▪ [of land] bande *f* ▪ [of cloud] traînée *f*.

ribbon development *n* UK croissance *f* urbaine linéaire *(le long des grands axes routiers)*.

ribcage [ˈrɪbkeɪdʒ] *n* cage *f* thoracique.

riboflavin [ˌraɪbəʊˈfleɪvɪn] *n* riboflavine *f*.

rice [raɪs] *n* riz *m* ▪ **~ paddy** rizière *f*.

rice bowl *n* **1.** *liter* bol *m* à riz **2.** *fig* [region] région *f* productrice de riz.

ricefield [ˈraɪsfiːld] *n* rizière *f*.

rice paper *n* papier *m* de riz.

rice pudding *n* riz *m* au lait.

ricer [ˈraɪsəʳ] *n* US presse-purée *m inv*.

rice wine *n* alcool *m* de riz, saké *m*.

rich [rɪtʃ] ◇ *adj* **1.** [wealthy, affluent] riche ▪ **they want to get ~ quick** ils veulent s'enrichir très vite **2.** [elegant, luxurious] riche, luxueux, somptueux **3.** [abundant, prolific] riche, abondant ▪ **~ in vitamins/proteins** riche en vitamines/protéines ▪ **~ vegetation** végétation luxuriante ▪ **there are ~ pickings to be had** *liter & fig* ça peut rapporter gros **4.** [fertile] riche, fertile **5.** [full, eventful] riche ▪ **she led a very ~ life** elle a eu une vie bien remplie **6.** [strong, intense - colour] riche, chaud, vif ; [- voice, sound] chaud, riche ; [- smell] fort **7.** CULIN [food] riche ▪ [meal] lourd **8.** [funny] drôle ▪ **I say, that's a bit ~!** *inf* c'est un peu fort (de café)!, ça, c'est le comble!
◇ *npl* : **the ~** les riches *mpl*.
◆ **riches** *npl* richesses *fpl*.

-rich *in cpds* riche en... ▪ **vitamin~ foods** aliments *mpl* riches en vitamines.

Richard [ˈrɪtʃəd] *pr n* : **~ the Lionheart** Richard Cœur de Lion.

richly [ˈrɪtʃlɪ] *adv* **1.** [handsomely, generously] largement, richement **2.** [thoroughly] largement, pleinement ▪ **the punishment she so ~ deserved** le châtiment qu'elle méritait amplement **3.** [abundantly] abondamment, richement **4.** [elegantly, luxuriously] somptueusement, luxueusement **5.** [vividly] : **~ coloured** aux couleurs riches *OR* vives.

richness [ˈrɪtʃnɪs] *n* **1.** [wealth, affluence] richesse *f* **2.** [elegance, luxury] luxe *m*, richesse *f* **3.** [abundance] abondance *f*, richesse *f* **4.** [fertility] richesse *f*, fertilité *f* ▪ **the ~ of the soil/of her imagination** la richesse du sol/de son imagination **5.** [fullness, eventfulness] richesse *f* **6.** [strength, intensity - of colour, sound] richesse *f* ; [- of smell] intensité *f*.

Richter scale [ˈrɪktə-] *n* échelle *f* de Richter.

rick [rɪk] ◇ *n* **1.** AGRIC meule *f (de foin etc)* **2.** [in ankle, wrist] entorse *f* ▪ [in neck] torticolis *m*.
◇ *vt* **1.** AGRIC mettre en meules **2.** UK [sprain] se faire une entorse à ▪ **to ~ one's neck** attraper un torticolis.

rickets [ˈrɪkɪts] *n (U)* rachitisme *m* ▪ **to have ~** souffrir de rachitisme, être rachitique.

rickety [ˈrɪkətɪ] *adj* **1.** [shaky - structure] branlant ; [- chair] bancal ; [- vehicle] (tout) bringuebalant **2.** [feeble - person] frêle, chancelant **3.** MED rachitique.

rickshaw [ˈrɪkʃɔː] *n* [pulled] pousse *m inv*, pousse-pousse *m inv* ▪ [pedalled] cyclo-pousse *m inv*.

ricochet [ˈrɪkəʃeɪ] (*pret & pp* **ricocheted** [-ʃeɪd] *OR* **ricochetted** [-ʃetɪd], *cont* **ricocheting** [-eɪɪŋ] *OR* **ricochetting** [-ʃetɪŋ]) ◇ *n* ricochet *m*.
◇ *vi* ricocher ▪ **to ~ off sthg** ricocher sur qqch.

rid [rɪd] (*pret & pp* **rid** *OR* **ridded**, *cont* **ridding**) ◇ *vt* débarrasser ▪ **we must ~ the country of corruption** il faut débarrasser le pays de la corruption ▪ **you should ~ yourself of such illusions!** arrêtez de vous bercer d'illusions!
◇ *adj* : **to get ~ of** se débarrasser de ▪ **to be ~ of** être débarrassé de.

riddance [ˈrɪdəns] *n* débarras *m* ▪ **good ~ (to bad rubbish)!** *inf* bon débarras!

ridden [ˈrɪdn] ◇ *pp* ▷ **ride**.
◇ *adj* affligé, atteint.

-ridden *in cpds* : **flea~** infesté de puces ▪ **disease~** infesté de maladies ▪ **debt~** criblé de dettes.

riddle [ˈrɪdl] ◇ *n* **1.** [poser] devinette *f* ▪ **to ask sb a ~** poser une devinette à qqn **2.** [mystery] énigme *f* ▪ **to talk** *OR* **to speak in ~s** parler par énigmes **3.** [sieve] crible *m*, tamis *m*.
◇ *vt* **1.** [pierce] cribler ▪ **they ~d the car with bullets** ils criblèrent la voiture de balles **2.** [sift] passer au crible, cribler.

riddled [ˈrɪdld] *adj* plein ▪ **~ with** plein de.

ride [raɪd] (*pret* **rode** [rəʊd], *pp* **ridden** [ˈrɪdn]) ◇ *vt* **1.** [horse] monter à ▪ [camel, donkey, elephant] monter à dos de ▪ **they were riding horses/donkeys/camels** ils étaient à cheval/à dos d'âne/à dos de chameau ▪ **she rode her mare in the park each day** elle montait sa jument chaque jour dans le parc ▪ **she rode her horse back** elle est revenue à cheval ▪ **they rode their horses across the river** ils ont traversé la rivière sur leurs chevaux
2. [bicycle, motorcycle] monter sur ▪ **I don't know how to ~ a bike/a motorbike** je ne sais pas faire du vélo/conduire une moto ▪ **she was riding a motorbike** elle était à *OR* en moto ▪ **she ~s her bicycle everywhere** elle se déplace toujours à bicyclette ▪ **he ~s his bike to work** il va travailler à vélo, il va au travail à vélo
3. [go about - fields, valleys] parcourir ▪ **you can ~ this highway to Tucson** US vous pouvez prendre *OR* suivre cette route jusqu'à Tucson
4. [participate in - race] faire ▪ **she's ridden four races this year** elle a fait quatre courses cette année
5. US [have a go on - roundabout, fairground attraction] faire un tour de ▪ [lift, ski lift] prendre
6. US [travel on - bus, subway, train, ferry] prendre
7. [move with - sea, waves] se laisser porter par ▪ **to ~ the rapids** descendre les rapides ▪ **surfers were riding the waves** des surfeurs glissaient sur les vagues ➊ **to ~ one's luck** compter sur sa chance ▪ **to ~ the storm** NAUT étaler la tempête ; *fig* surmonter la crise
8. [take, recoil with - punch, blow] encaisser
9. US [nag] harceler ▪ **you ~ the kids too hard** tu es trop dur avec les gosses
10. US *inf* [tease] taquiner, mettre en boîte
11. [copulate with - subj: animal] monter ; [- subj: person]△ grimper△
12. US [give a lift to] amener ▪ **hop in and I'll ~ you home** monte, je te ramène chez toi
13. US *phr* **to ~ sb out of town** [drive out] chasser qqn de la ville ; [ridicule] tourner qqn en ridicule *OR* en dérision.
◇ *vi* **1.** [ride a horse] monter (à cheval), faire du cheval ▪ **I was stiff after riding all day** j'avais des courbatures après avoir chevauché toute la journée *OR* après une journée entière à cheval ➊ **Zorro/Nixon ~s again!** *hum* Zorro/Nixon est de retour!
2. [go - on horseback] aller (à cheval) ; [- by bicycle] aller (à bicyclette) ; [- by car] aller (en voiture) ▪ **we rode along the canal and over the bridge** nous avons longé le canal et traversé le pont ▪ **he rode by on a bicycle/on a white horse/on a donkey** il passa à bicyclette/sur un cheval blanc/monté sur un âne ▪ **they ~ to work on the bus/train** ils vont travailler en autobus/train ▪ **she was riding in the back seat** elle était assise à l'arrière ▪ **you can ~ on the handlebars/my shoulders** tu peux

monter sur le guidon/mes épaules ■ **to ~ off** [leave] partir ; [move away] s'éloigner ▶ **to be riding for a fall** courir à l'échec
3. [float, sail] voguer ■ **to ~ with the current** voguer au fil de l'eau ■ **to ~ at anchor** être ancré ▶ **we'll have to ~ with it** *inf* il faudra faire avec ■ **to ~ with the punches** *US inf* encaisser (les coups)
4. [be sustained - person] être porté ■ **she was riding on a wave of popularity** elle était portée par une vague de popularité ■ **he rode to victory on a policy of reform** il a obtenu la victoire grâce à son programme de réformes ■ **the team is riding high** l'équipe a le vent en poupe
5. [depend] dépendre ■ **my reputation is riding on the outcome** ma réputation est en jeu
6. [money in bet] miser ■ **they have a fortune riding on this project** ils ont investi une fortune dans ce projet
7. [continue undisturbed] : **he decided to let the matter ~** il a décidé de laisser courir ■ **let it ~!** laisse tomber!
◇ *n* **1.** [trip - for pleasure] promenade *f*, tour *m* ■ **to go for a car/motorcycle ~** (aller) faire un tour *OR* une promenade en voiture/en moto ■ **we went on long bicycle/horse ~s** nous avons fait de longues promenades à bicyclette/à cheval ■ **a donkey ~** une promenade à dos d'âne ■ **how about a ~ in my new car?** et si on faisait un tour dans ma nouvelle voiture? ■ **give Tom a ~** *OR* **let Tom have a ~ on your tricycle** laisse Tom monter sur ton tricycle ■ **his sister came along for the ~** sa sœur est venue faire un tour avec nous ■ [when talking about distance] parcours *m*, trajet *m* ■ **she has a long car/bus ~ to work** elle doit faire un long trajet en voiture/en bus pour aller travailler ■ **it's a long bus ~ to Mexico** c'est long d'aller en car au Mexique ■ **it's a 30-minute ~ by bus/train/car** il faut 30 minutes en bus/train/voiture
2. [quality of travel] : **this type of suspension gives a smoother ~** ce type de suspension est plus confortable ▶ **the journalists gave her a rough ~** les journalistes ne l'ont pas ménagée ■ **it looks as if we're in for a bumpy ~** *fig* ça promet!
3. *US* [lift - in car] : **can you give me a ~ to the station?** peux-tu me conduire à la gare? ■ **get a ~ to the party with Bill** demande à Bill s'il peut t'emmener à la fête ■ **don't accept ~s from strangers** ne montez pas dans la voiture de quelqu'un que vous ne connaissez pas
4. [in fairground - attraction] manège *m* ; [- turn] tour *m* ■ **it's 50p a ~** c'est 50 pence le tour ■ **to have a ~ on the big wheel** faire un tour sur la grande roue
5. [bridle path] piste *f* cavalière ■ [wider] allée *f* cavalière
6. *inf phr* **to take sb for a ~** [deceive] faire marcher qqn ; [cheat] arnaquer *OR* rouler qqn ; *US* [kill] descendre *OR* liquider qqn ■ **take a ~ !** *US* fous-moi la paix!
◆ **ride about** *UK*, **ride around** *vi insep* : **she ~s about** *OR* **around in a limousine** elle se déplace en limousine.
◆ **ride down** *vt sep* **1.** [knock over] renverser ■ [trample] piétiner
2. [catch up with] rattraper.
◆ **ride in** *vt sep* [horse] préparer *(pour un concours)*.
◆ **ride out** ◇ *vt insep* [difficulty, crisis] surmonter ■ [recession] survivre à ■ **if we can ~ out the next few months** si nous pouvons tenir *OR* nous maintenir à flot encore quelques mois ▶ **to ~ out the storm** NAUT étaler la tempête ; *fig* surmonter la crise, tenir.
◇ *vi insep* sortir *(à cheval, à bicyclette etc)*.
◆ **ride up** *vi insep* [garment] remonter.

rider ['raɪdəʳ] *n* **1.** [of horse, donkey] cavalier *m*, - ère *f* ■ [of bicycle] cycliste *mf* ■ [of motorcycle] motocycliste *mf* **2.** [proviso] condition *f*, stipulation *f* ■ **I'd like to add one small ~ to what my colleague said** j'aimerais apporter une petite précision à ce qu'a dit mon collègue **3.** [annexe - to contract] annexe *f* ■ *UK* LAW [jury recommendation] recommandation *f* **4.** [on scales] curseur *m*.

ridership ['raɪdəʃɪp] *n US* nombre *m* de voyageurs.

ridge [rɪdʒ] ◇ *n* **1.** [of mountains] crête *f*, ligne *f* de faîte ■ [leading to summit] crête *f*, arête *f* **2.** [raised strip or part] arête *f*, crête *f* ■ AGRIC [in ploughed field] crête *f* ■ **the wet sand formed ~s** le sable mouillé était couvert de petites rides ■ **a ~ of high pressure** METEOR une crête de haute pression, une dorsale barométrique *spec* **3.** [of roof] faîte *m*.
◇ *vt* [crease] sillonner, rider.

ridgepole ['rɪdʒpəʊl] *n* [for tent] faîtière *f*.

ridge tent *n* tente *f* à faîtière.

ridicule ['rɪdɪkju:l] ◇ *n* ridicule *m* ■ **to pour ~ on sthg, to hold sthg up to ~** tourner qqch en ridicule ■ **to lay o.s. open to ~** s'exposer au ridicule.
◇ *vt* ridiculiser, tourner en ridicule.

ridiculous [rɪ'dɪkjʊləs] ◇ *adj* ridicule ■ **you look ~ in that hat** tu as l'air ridicule avec ce chapeau ■ **£500? don't be ~!** 500 livres? vous plaisantez! ■ **to make o.s. look ~** se ridiculiser, se couvrir de ridicule.
◇ *n* : **the ~** le ridicule.

ridiculously [rɪ'dɪkjʊləslɪ] *adv* ridiculement ■ **it's ~ expensive** [price] c'est un prix exorbitant ; [article, shop] c'est beaucoup trop cher ■ **it's ~ cheap** [price] c'est un prix dérisoire ; [article, shop] c'est très bon marché.

ridiculousness [rɪ'dɪkjʊləsnɪs] *n* ridicule *m* ■ **the ~ of the situation** le (côté) ridicule de la situation.

riding ['raɪdɪŋ] ◇ *n* **1.** EQUIT : **(horse) ~** équitation *f* ■ **to go ~** faire de l'équitation *OR* du cheval ■ **do you like ~?** aimez-vous l'équitation *OR* monter à cheval? **2.** [in Yorkshire] division *f* administrative **3.** [in Canada, New Zealand] circonscription *f* électorale.
◇ *comp* [boots, jacket] de cheval ■ [techniques] d'équitation.

riding breeches *npl* culotte *f* de cheval.

riding crop *n* cravache *f*.

riding habit *n* tenue *f* d'amazone.

riding school *n* école *f* d'équitation.

rife [raɪf] *adj* **1.** [widespread] répandu ■ **corruption is ~** la corruption est chose commune **2.** [full] : **~ with** abondant en ■ **the garden is ~ with caterpillars** le jardin est envahi par les chenilles ■ **the office is ~ with rumour** les langues vont bon train au bureau.

riffle ['rɪfl] *vt* **1.** [magazine, pages] feuilleter **2.** [cards] battre, mélanger.

riffraff ['rɪfræf] *n* racaille *f*.

rifle ['raɪfl] ◇ *vt* **1.** [search] fouiller (dans) **2.** [rob] dévaliser **3.** [steal] voler **4.** [gun barrel] rayer.
◇ *vi* : **to ~ through sthg** fouiller dans qqch.
◇ *n* [gun] fusil *m*.
◇ *comp* [bullet, butt, shot] de fusil.

rifleman ['raɪflmən] (*pl* **riflemen** [-mən]) *n* fusilier *m*.

rifle range *n* **1.** [for practice] champ *m* de tir **2.** [distance] : **within ~** à portée de tir *OR* de fusil.

rift [rɪft] ◇ *n* **1.** [gap, cleavage] fissure *f*, crevasse *f* ■ GEOL [fault] faille *f* ■ **a ~ in the clouds** une trouée dans les nuages **2.** *fig* [split] cassure *f*, faille *f* ■ POL scission *f* ■ [quarrel] désaccord *m*, querelle *f* ■ **in order to prevent a ~ in our relationship** pour éviter une rupture ■ **there is a deep ~ between them** un abîme les sépare ■ **she hasn't seen her family since that ~** elle n'a pas vu sa famille depuis cette dispute.
◇ *vt* scinder.
◇ *vi* se scinder.

rift valley *n* fossé *m* d'effondrement.

rig [rɪg] (*pret & pp* **rigged**, *cont* **rigging**) ◇ *vt* **1.** [fiddle] truquer ■ **the whole affair was rigged!** c'était un coup monté du début jusqu'à la fin! ■ **to ~ a jury** manipuler un jury **2.** NAUT gréer **3.** [install] monter, bricoler.
◇ *n* **1.** [gen - equipment] matériel *m* **2.** NAUT gréement *m* **3.** PETR [on land] derrick *m* ■ [offshore] plate-forme *f* **4.** *inf* [clothes] tenue *f*, fringues *fpl* **5.** *US* [truck] semi-remorque *m*.
◆ **rig out** *vt sep* **1.** *inf* [clothe] habiller ■ **he was rigged out in a cowboy costume** il était habillé *OR* déguisé en cowboy ■ **look at the way she's rigged out!** *pej* regarde comme elle est fagotée! **2.** [equip] équiper.
◆ **rig up** *vt sep* [install] monter, installer.

rigger ['rɪgəʳ] *n* **1.** NAUT gréeur *m* **2.** PETR *personne qui travaille sur un chantier de forage*.

rigging ['rɪgɪŋ] *n* **1.** NAUT gréement *m* **2.** THEAT machinerie *f* **3.** [fiddling] trucage *m*.

right [raɪt] ◇ *adj* **1.** [indicating location, direction] droit ■ **raise your ~ hand** levez la main droite ■ **take the next ~ (turn)** prenez la prochaine à droite
2. [accurate, correct - prediction] juste, exact ; [- answer, address] bon ■ **he didn't give me the ~ change** il ne m'a pas rendu la monnaie exacte ■ **the clock is ~** l'horloge est juste *OR* à l'heure ■ **have you got the ~ time?** est-ce que vous avez l'heure (exacte)? ■ **the sentence doesn't sound/look quite ~** la phrase sonne/a l'air un peu bizarre ■ **there's something not quite ~ in what he says** il y a quelque chose qui cloche dans ce qu'il dit ■ [person] **: to be ~** avoir raison ■ **you were ~ about him** vous aviez raison à son sujet ■ **I was ~ in thinking he was an actor** j'avais raison de penser que c'était un acteur ■ **you're the eldest, am I ~** *OR* **is that ~?** c'est (bien) toi l'aîné, ou est-ce que je me trompe? ■ **I owe you $5, ~?** je te dois 5 dollars, c'est (bien) ça? ■ **and I'm telling you you still owe me £10, ~!** et moi je te dis que tu me dois encore 10 livres, vu? ■ **that's ~** c'est juste, oui ■ **he got the pronunciation/spelling ~** il l'a bien prononcé/épelé ■ **she got the answer ~** elle a donné la bonne réponse ■ **make sure you get your figures/her name ~** faites attention de ne pas vous tromper dans vos calculs/ sur son nom ■ **get your facts ~!** vérifiez vos renseignements! ■ **let's get this ~** mettons les choses au clair ■ **time proved her ~** le temps lui a donné raison ▶ **to put sb ~ (about sthg/sb)** détromper qqn (au sujet de qqch/qqn) ■ **to put** *OR* **set ~** [object] redresser, remettre d'aplomb ; [clock] remettre à l'heure ; [machine, mechanism] réparer ; [text, record] corriger ; [oversight, injustice] réparer ■ **to put things** *OR* **matters ~** [politically, financially etc] redresser *OR* rétablir la situation ; [in relationships] arranger les choses ■ **he made a mess of it and I had to put things ~** il a raté son coup et j'ai dû réparer les dégâts
3. [appropriate - diploma, tool, sequence, moment] bon ■ [best - choice, decision] meilleur ■ **are we going in the ~ direction?** est-ce que nous allons dans le bon sens? ■ **when the time is ~** au bon moment, au moment voulu ■ **to be in the ~ place at the ~ time** être là où il faut quand il faut ■ **I can't find the ~ word** je ne trouve pas le mot juste ■ **if the price is ~** si le prix est intéressant ■ **the colour is just ~** la couleur est parfaite ■ **the magazine has just the ~ mix of news and commentary** la revue a juste ce qu'il faut d'informations et de commentaires ■ **she's the ~ woman for the job** c'est la femme qu'il faut pour ce travail ■ **the ~ holiday for your budget** les vacances qui conviennent le mieux à votre budget ■ **teaching isn't ~ for you** l'enseignement n'est pas ce qu'il vous faut ■ **place the document ~ side down/up** placez le document face en bas/vers le haut ■ **turn the socks ~ side in/out** mettez les chaussettes à l'envers/à l'endroit ■ **it wasn't the ~ thing to say** ce n'était pas la chose à dire ■ **you've done the ~ thing to tell us about it** vous avez bien fait de nous en parler ■ **he did the ~ thing, but for the wrong reasons** il a fait le bon choix, mais pour de mauvaises raisons ■ **you're not doing it the ~ way!** ce n'est pas comme ça qu'il faut faire *OR* s'y prendre!
4. [fair, just] juste, équitable ■ [morally good] bien *(inv)* ■ [socially correct] correct ■ **it's not ~ to separate the children** ce n'est pas bien de séparer les enfants ■ **I don't think capital punishment is ~** je ne crois pas que la peine de mort soit juste ■ **I thought it ~ to ask you first** j'ai cru bon de vous demander d'abord ■ **I don't feel ~ leaving you alone** ça me gêne de te laisser tout seul ■ **it's only ~ that you should know** il est juste que vous le sachiez ■ **I only want to do what is ~** je ne cherche qu'à bien faire ▶ **to do the ~ thing (by sb)** bien agir (avec qqn)
5. [functioning properly] **: there's something not quite ~ with the motor** le moteur ne marche pas très bien
6. [healthy] bien *(inv)* ■ **my knee doesn't feel ~** j'ai quelque chose au genou ■ **a rest will put** *OR* **set you ~ again** un peu de repos te remettra ■ **to be ~ in the head** *inf* **: he's not quite ~ in the head** ça ne va pas très bien dans sa tête ■ **nobody in their ~ mind would refuse such an offer!** aucune personne sensée ne refuserait une telle offre!
7. [satisfactory] bien *(inv)* ■ **things aren't ~ between them** ça ne va pas très bien entre eux ■ **does the hat look ~ to you?** le chapeau, ça va? ▶ **to come ~** *inf* s'arranger
8. [indicating social status] bien *(inv)*, comme il faut ■ **you'll only meet her if you move in the ~ circles** vous ne la rencontrerez que si vous fréquentez le beau monde ■ **to know the ~ people** connaître des gens bien placés
9. GEOM [angle, line, prism, cone] droit ■ **~ triangle** *US* triangle *m* rectangle
10. *UK inf* [as intensifier] vrai, complet ■ **I felt like a ~ idiot** je me sentais vraiment bête
11. *inf dial* [ready] prêt.
◇ *adv* **1.** [in directions] à droite ■ **turn ~ at the traffic lights** tournez à droite au feu (rouge) ■ **the party is moving further ~** le parti est en train de virer plus à droite
2. [accurately, correctly - hear] bien ; [- guess] juste ; [- answer, spell] bien, correctement ■ **if I remember ~** si je me rappelle bien
3. [properly] bien, comme il faut ■ **the top isn't on ~** le couvercle n'est pas bien mis ■ **if we organize things ~, there'll be enough time** si nous organisons bien les choses, il y aura assez de temps ■ **nothing is going ~ today** tout va de travers aujourd'hui ■ **he can't do anything ~** il ne peut rien faire correctement *OR* comme il faut ■ **do it ~ the next time!** ne vous trompez pas la prochaine fois!
4. [emphasizing precise location] **: the lamp's shining ~ in my eyes** j'ai la lumière de la lampe en plein dans les yeux *OR* en pleine figure ■ **it's ~ opposite the post office** c'est juste en face de la poste ■ **it's ~ in front of/behind you** c'est droit devant vous/juste derrière vous ■ **I'm ~ behind you there** *fig* je suis entièrement d'accord avec vous là-dessus ■ **the hotel was ~ on the beach** l'hôtel donnait directement sur la plage ■ **I left it ~ here** je l'ai laissé juste ici ■ **stay ~ there** ne bougez pas
5. [emphasizing precise time] juste, exactement ■ **I arrived ~ at that moment** je suis arrivé juste à ce moment-là ■ **~ in the middle of the fight** au beau milieu de la bagarre
6. [all the way] **: it's ~ at the back of the drawer/at the front of the book** c'est tout au fond du tiroir/juste au début du livre ■ **~ down to the bottom** jusqu'au fond ■ **~ from the start** dès le début ■ **his shoes were worn ~ through** ses chaussures étaient usées jusqu'à la corde ■ **the car drove ~ through the road-block** la voiture est passée à travers le barrage ■ **that girl is going ~ to the top** *fig* cette fille ira loin ■ **we worked ~ up until the last minute** nous avons travaillé jusqu'à la toute dernière minute
7. [immediately] tout de suite ■ **I'll be ~ over** je viens tout de suite
8. [justly, fairly] bien ■ [properly, fittingly] correctement ■ **you did ~** tu as bien fait ■ **to do ~ by sb** agir correctement envers qqn
9.△ *dial* [very] bien.
◇ *n* **1.** [in directions] droite *f* ■ **look to the** *OR* **your ~** regardez à droite *OR* sur votre droite ■ **keep to the** *OR* **your ~** restez à droite ■ **from ~ to left** de droite à gauche
2. POL droite *f* ■ **the ~ is** *OR* **are divided** la droite est divisée
3. [in boxing] droit *m*, droite *f*
4. [entitlement] droit *m* ■ **the ~ to vote/of asylum** le droit de vote/d'asile ■ **to have a ~ to sthg** avoir droit à qqch ■ **to have a** *OR* **the ~ to do sthg** avoir le droit de faire qqch ■ **you have every ~ to be angry** tu as toutes les raisons d'être en colère ■ **the ~ to life** le droit à la vie ▶ **in one's own ~ : she's rich in her own ~** elle a une grande fortune personnelle ■ **he became a leader in his own ~** il est devenu leader par son seul talent
5. [what is good, moral] bien *m* ■ **to know ~ from wrong** distinguer ce qui est bien de ce qui est mal ■ **to be in the ~** être dans le vrai, avoir raison ■ **he put himself in the ~ by apologizing** il s'est racheté en s'excusant.
◇ *interj* **: come tomorrow – ~ (you are)!** venez demain – d'accord! ■ **~, let's get to work!** bon *OR* bien, au travail! ■ **~ (you are) then, see you later** bon alors, à plus tard.
◇ *vt* **1.** [set upright again - chair, ship] redresser ■ **the raft will ~ itself** le radeau se redressera (tout seul)
2. [redress - situation] redresser, rétablir ; [- damage] réparer ; [- injustice] réparer ■ **to ~ a wrong** redresser un tort ■ **to ~ the balance** rétablir l'équilibre ■ **the problem won't just ~ itself** ce problème ne va pas se résoudre de lui-même *OR* s'arranger tout seul.
◇ *vi* [car, ship] se redresser.
◆ **rights** *npl* **1.** [political, social] droits *mpl* ■ **you'd be within your ~s to demand a refund** vous seriez dans votre (bon) droit si vous réclamiez un remboursement ■ **read him his ~s** *US* [on arresting a suspect] prévenez-le de ses droits
2. COMM droits *mpl* ■ **who has the mineral/film/distribution ~s?** qui détient les droits miniers/d'adaptation cinématographique/de distribution?
3. FIN **: (application) ~** *OR* **~s** droits *mpl* *OR* privilège *m* de souscription

4. *phr* **to put** *OR* **to set to ~s** [room] mettre en ordre ; [firm, country] redresser ; [situation] arranger ▪ **to set the world to ~s** *hum* refaire le monde.
◆ **by right(s)** *adv phr* en principe.
◆ **right away** *adv phr* [at once] tout de suite, aussitôt ▪ [from the start] dès le début ▪ [first go] du premier coup.
◆ **right now** *adv phr* **1.** [at once] tout de suite **2.** [at the moment] pour le moment.
◆ **right off** *US* = **right away**.

right-about turn *n* demi-tour *m*.

right angle *n* angle *m* droit ▪ **a line at ~s to the base** une ligne perpendiculaire à la base ▪ **the path made a ~** le sentier formait un coude.

right-angled *adj* [hook, turn] à angle droit.

right-angled triangle *n UK* triangle *m* rectangle.

righten ['raɪtn] *vt* redresser.

righteous ['raɪtʃəs] *adj* **1.** [just] juste ▪ [virtuous] vertueux **2.** *pej* [self-righteous] suffisant ▪ **~ indignation** colère indignée.

righteously ['raɪtʃəslɪ] *adv* **1.** [virtuously] vertueusement **2.** *pej* [self-righteously] avec suffisance.

righteousness ['raɪtʃəsnɪs] *n* vertu *f*, rectitude *f*.

right-footed [-'futɪd] *adj* qui se sert de son pied droit.

rightful ['raɪtful] *adj* légitime.

rightfully ['raɪtfulɪ] *adv* légitimement.

right-hand *adj* droit ▪ **on the ~ side** à droite ▪ **the ~ side of the road** le côté droit de la route ▪ **it's in the ~ drawer** c'est dans le tiroir de droite ▪ **a ~ bend** un virage à droite.

right-hand drive *n* AUT conduite *f* à droite ▪ **a ~ vehicle** un véhicule avec la conduite à droite.

right-handed [-'hændɪd] *adj* **1.** [person] droitier **2.** [punch] du droit **3.** [scissors, golf club] pour droitiers ▪ [screw] fileté à droite.

right-hander [-'hændər] *n* **1.** [person] droitier *m*, - ère *f* **2.** [blow] coup *m* du droit.

right-hand man *n* bras *m* droit.

Right Honourable *adj UK titre utilisé pour s'adresser à certains hauts fonctionnaires ou à quelqu'un ayant un titre de noblesse.*

rightist ['raɪtɪst] ◇ *n* homme *m*, femme *f* de droite. ◇ *adj* de droite.

rightly ['raɪtlɪ] *adv* **1.** [correctly] correctement, bien ▪ **I don't ~ know** *inf* je ne sais pas bien **2.** [with justification] à juste titre, avec raison ▪ **he was ~ angry, he was angry and ~ so** il était en colère à juste titre.

right-minded *adj* raisonnable, sensé ▪ **every ~ citizen/ Christian** tout citoyen/chrétien honnête.

righto ['raɪtəu] *interj UK inf* OK, d'ac.

right-of-centre *adj* centre droit.

right of way (*pl* **rights of way**) *n* **1.** AUT priorité *f* ▪ **it's your ~** vous avez (la) priorité ▪ **to have (the) ~** avoir (la) priorité **2.** [right to cross land] droit *m* de passage **3.** [path, road] chemin *m* ▪ *US* [for power line, railroad etc] voie *f*.

right-on *adj inf* idéologiquement correct.

Right Reverend *adj UK* **the ~ James Brown** [Protestant] le très révérend James Brown ; [Catholic] monseigneur Brown.

rights issue *n* droit *m* préférentiel de souscription.

right-thinking *adj* raisonnable, sensé.

right-to-life *adj* [movement, candidate] antiavortement.

right-to-lifer *n* adversaire *mf* de l'avortement.

right-to-work movement *n syndicat s'opposant à la pratique du "syndicat unique" aux États-Unis.*

right wing *n* **1.** POL droite *f* ▪ **the ~ of the party** l'aile droite du parti **2.** SPORT [position] aile *f* droite ▪ [player] ailier *m* droit.
◆ **right-wing** *adj* POL de droite ▪ **she's more right-wing than the others** elle est plus à droite que les autres.

right-winger *n* **1.** POL homme *m*, femme *f* de droite ▪ **he's a ~** il est de droite **2.** SPORT ailier *m* droit.

rigid ['rɪdʒɪd] *adj* **1.** [structure, material] rigide ▪ [body, muscle] raide ▪ **he was ~ with fear** il était paralysé par la peur ▪ **it shook me ~!** *inf* ça m'a fait un de ces coups! **2.** [person, ideas, policy] rigide, inflexible ▪ [discipline] strict, sévère.

rigidity [rɪ'dʒɪdətɪ] *n* **1.** [of structure, material] rigidité *f* ▪ [of body, muscle] raideur *f* **2.** [of person, ideas, policy] rigidité *f*, inflexibilité *f* ▪ [of discipline] sévérité *f*.

rigidly ['rɪdʒɪdlɪ] *adv* rigidement, avec raideur ▪ **the rules are ~ applied** le règlement est rigoureusement appliqué.

rigmarole ['rɪgmərəul] *n* **1.** [procedure] cirque *m* ▪ **I don't want to go through all the ~ of applying for a licence** je ne veux pas m'embêter à déposer une demande de permis **2.** [talk] charabia *m*, galimatias *m*.

rigor ['rɪgər] *n* **1.** *US* = **rigour 2.** *(U)* MED [before fever] frissons *mpl* ▪ [in muscle] crampe *f*.

rigor mortis [ˌrɪgə'mɔːtɪs] *n* rigidité *f* cadavérique.

rigorous ['rɪgərəs] *adj* rigoureux.

rigorously ['rɪgərəslɪ] *adv* rigoureusement, avec rigueur.

rigour *UK*, **rigor** *US* ['rɪgər] *n* rigueur *f*.

rigout ['rɪgaut] *n inf* accoutrement *m*.

rile [raɪl] *vt* [person] agacer, énerver.

Riley ['raɪlɪ] *pr n* : **to live the life of ~** *inf* mener une vie de pacha.

rill [rɪl] *n* **1.** *lit* [brook] ruisselet *m* **2.** [on moon] vallée *f* **3.** [from erosion] ravine *f*.

rim [rɪm] (*pret & pp* **rimmed**, *cont* **rimming**) ◇ *n* **1.** [of bowl, cup] bord *m* ▪ [of eye, lake] bord *m*, pourtour *m* ▪ [of well] margelle *f* **2.** [of spectacles] monture *f* **3.** [of wheel] jante *f* **4.** [of dirt] marque *f* ▪ **a ~ of coffee left in the cup** des traces de café à l'intérieur de la tasse ▪ **there was a black ~ around the bath** il y avait une trace de crasse tout autour de la baignoire. ◇ *vt* border.

rimless ['rɪmlɪs] *adj* [spectacles] sans monture.

-rimmed [rɪmd] *in cpds* : **gold/steel~ spectacles** lunettes *fpl* à monture en or/d'acier.

rind [raɪnd] *n* [on bacon] couenne *f* ▪ [on cheese] croûte *f* ▪ [on fruit] écorce *f* ▪ [of bark] couche *f* extérieure.

rindless ['raɪndlɪs] *adj* [bacon] sans couenne.

ring [rɪŋ] (*pret & pp* **ringed**) ◇ *n* **1.** [sound of bell] sonnerie *f* ▪ **there was a ~ at the door** on a sonné (à la porte) ▪ **give two long ~s and one short one** sonnez trois fois, deux coups longs et un coup bref ▪ **the ~ of the church bells** le carillonnement des cloches de l'église
2. [sound] son *m* ▪ [resounding] retentissement *m* ▪ *fig* [note] note *f*, accent *m* ▪ **his words had a ~ of truth** il y avait un accent de vérité dans ses paroles ▪ **the name has a familiar ~** ce nom me dit quelque chose ▪ **that excuse has got a familiar ~!** j'ai déjà entendu ça quelque part!
3. [telephone call] coup *m* de téléphone ▪ **give me a ~ tomorrow** passez-moi un coup de téléphone *OR* appelez-moi demain
4. [set of bells] jeu *m* de cloches
5. [on finger] anneau *m*, bague *f* ▪ [in nose, ear] anneau *m* ◗ **'The Ring of the Nibelung'** ***Wagner*** 'l'Anneau du Nibelung'
6. [round object] anneau *m* ▪ [for serviette] rond *m* ▪ [for swimmer] bouée *f* ▪ [for identifying bird] bague *f* ▪ [of piston] segment *m* ▪ **the ~s** [in gym] les anneaux *mpl*
7. [circle] cercle *m*, rond *m* ▪ [of smoke] rond *m* ▪ [in or around tree trunk] anneau *m* ▪ **she looked round the ~ of faces** elle regarda les visages tout autour d'elle ▪ **the glasses left ~s on the piano** les verres ont laissé des ronds *OR* marques sur le piano ▪ **the ~s of Saturn** les anneaux de Saturne ▪ **there's a ~**

around the moon la lune est cernée d'un halo ▪ **he has ~s round his eyes** il a les yeux cernés ⊳ **to run** OR **to make ~s round sb** *inf* éclipser OR écraser qqn
8. [for boxing, wrestling] ring *m* ▪ [in circus] piste *f*
9. UK [for cooking - electric] plaque *f* ; [- gas] feu *m*, brûleur *m*
10. [group of people] cercle *m*, clique *f pej* ▪ **price-fixing ~** cartel *m* ▪ **spy/drug ~** réseau *m* d'espions/de trafiquants de drogue
11. CHEM [of atoms] chaîne *f* fermée.
<> *vt* **1.** (*pret* **rang** [ræŋ], *pp* **rung** [rʌŋ]) [bell, alarm] sonner ▪ **I rang the doorbell** j'ai sonné à la porte ⊳ **the name/title ~s a bell** ce nom/titre me dit quelque chose ▪ **to ~ the bell** *inf* [succeed] décrocher le pompon ▪ **to ~ the changes** [on church bells] carillonner ; *fig* changer ▪ **to ~ the changes on sthg** apporter des changements à qqch
2. (*pret* **rang** [ræŋ], *pp* **rung** [rʌŋ]) UK [phone] téléphoner à, appeler
3. [surround] entourer, encercler
4. [draw circle round] entourer d'un cercle ▪ **~ the right answer** entourez la bonne réponse
5. [bird] baguer ▪ [bull, pig] anneler
6. [in quoits, hoopla - throw ring round] lancer un anneau sur.
<> *vi* (*pret* **rang** [ræŋ], *pp* **rung** [rʌŋ]) **1.** [chime, peal - bell, telephone, alarm] sonner ▪ [with high pitch] tinter ▪ [long and loud] carillonner ▪ **the doorbell rang** on a sonné (à la porte) ▪ **the line is ~ing for you** ≃ ne quittez pas, je vous le/la passe
2. [resound] résonner, retentir ▪ **their laughter rang through the house** leurs rires résonnaient dans toute la maison ▪ **the theatre rang with applause** la salle retentissait d'applaudissements ▪ **my ears are ~ing** j'ai les oreilles qui bourdonnent ▪ **to ~ true/false/hollow** sonner vrai/faux/creux
3. [summon] sonner ▪ **to ~ for the maid** sonner la bonne ▪ **I rang for a glass of water** j'ai sonné pour qu'on m'apporte un verre d'eau
4. UK [phone] téléphoner.
◆ **ring around** = ring round.
◆ **ring back** *vi insep & vt sep* UK [phone back] rappeler.
◆ **ring down** *vt sep* : **to ~ down the curtain** THEAT baisser le rideau ▪ **to ~ down the curtain on sthg** *fig* mettre un terme à qqch.
◆ **ring in** <> *vi insep* UK téléphoner.
<> *vt sep phr* **to ~ the New Year in** sonner les cloches pour annoncer la nouvelle année.
◆ **ring off** *vi insep* UK raccrocher.
◆ **ring out** <> *vi insep* retentir.
<> *vt sep* : **to ~ out the old year** sonner les cloches pour annoncer la fin de l'année.
<> *vt insep* : **to ~ out the old and ~ in the new** se débarrasser du vieux pour faire place au neuf.
◆ **ring round** *vt insep* UK téléphoner à, appeler.
◆ **ring up** *vt sep* UK **1.** [phone] téléphoner à, appeler
2. [on cash register - sale, sum] enregistrer
3. *phr* **to ~ up the curtain** THEAT lever le rideau ▪ **to ~ up the curtain on sthg** *fig* inaugurer qqch, marquer le début de qqch.

ring-a-ring-a-roses *n chanson que chantent les enfants en faisant la ronde.*

ring binder *n* classeur *m* (à anneaux).

ringer ['rɪŋəʳ] *n* **1.** [of bells] sonneur *m*, carillonneur *m*, - euse *f* **2.** *inf* [double] sosie *m* ▪ **he's a (dead) ~ for you** vous vous ressemblez comme deux gouttes d'eau.

ring-fence *vt* [money] allouer *(à des fins pré-établies par le gouvernement).*

ring finger *n* annulaire *m*.

ringing ['rɪŋɪŋ] <> *adj* sonore, retentissant.
<> *n* **1.** [of doorbell, phone, alarm] sonnerie *f* ▪ [of cowbell] tintement *m* ▪ [of church bells] carillonnement *m* **2.** [of cries, laughter] retentissement *m* ▪ [in ears] bourdonnement *m*.

ringing tone *n* sonnerie *f*, signal *m* d'appel.

ringleader ['rɪŋ,li:dəʳ] *n* meneur *m*, - euse *f*.

ringlet ['rɪŋlɪt] *n* boucle *f* (de cheveux).

ringmaster ['rɪŋ,mɑ:stəʳ] *n* ≃ Monsieur Loyal *m*.

ring-pull *n* UK anneau *m*, bague *f (sur une boîte de boisson)*.

ring road *n* rocade *f*.

ringside ['rɪŋsaɪd] *n (U)* SPORT premiers rangs *mpl* ▪ **to have a ~ seat** *fig* être aux premières loges.

ring tone *n* sonnerie *f*.

ringworm ['rɪŋwɜ:m] *n* teigne *f*.

rink [rɪŋk] *n* [for ice-skating] patinoire *f* ▪ [for roller-skating] piste *f (pour patins à roulettes)*.

rinse [rɪns] <> *vt* rincer ▪ **she ~d her hands/her mouth** elle se rinça les mains/la bouche.
<> *n* **1.** [gen] rinçage *m* ▪ **I gave the shirt a good ~** j'ai bien rincé la chemise **2.** [for hair] rinçage *m*.
◆ **rinse out** *vt sep* rincer.

riot ['raɪət] <> *n* **1.** [civil disturbance] émeute *f* ▪ **race ~s** émeutes raciales **2.** *inf* [funny occasion] : **the party was a ~** on s'est éclatés à la fête ▮ [funny person] : **Jim's a ~** Jim est désopilant OR impayable **3.** [profusion] profusion *f* ▪ **the garden is a ~ of colour** le jardin offre une véritable débauche de couleurs.
<> *vi* participer à OR faire une émeute.
<> *adv* : **to run ~** : **a group of youths ran ~** un groupe de jeunes a provoqué une émeute ▪ **her imagination ran ~** son imagination s'est déchaînée ▪ **the garden is running ~** le jardin est une vraie jungle.

riot act *n* loi *f* antiémeutes ▪ **to read the ~** *inf* faire acte d'autorité ▪ **she read me the ~** elle m'a passé un savon magistral.

rioter ['raɪətəʳ] *n* émeutier *m*, - ère *f*.

rioting ['raɪətɪŋ] *n (U)* émeutes *fpl*.

riotous ['raɪətəs] *adj* **1.** [mob] déchaîné ▪ [behaviour] séditieux **2.** [debauched] débauché ▪ [exuberant, noisy] tapageur, bruyant ▪ **a ~ party was going on upstairs** à l'étage au-dessus, des fêtards s'en donnaient à cœur joie **3.** [funny] désopilant, tordant.

riotously ['raɪətəslɪ] *adv* **1.** [seditiously] de façon séditieuse **2.** [noisily] bruyamment **3.** [as intensifier] : **it's ~ funny** *inf* c'est à mourir OR à hurler de rire.

riot police *npl* police *f* OR forces *fpl* antiémeutes.

riot shield *n* bouclier *m* antiémeutes.

riot squad *n* brigade *f* antiémeutes.

rip [rɪp] (*pret & pp* **ripped**, *cont* **ripping**) <> *vt* **1.** [tear] déchirer (violemment) ▪ **he ripped the envelope open** il déchira l'enveloppe ▪ **to ~ sthg to shreds** OR **pieces** mettre qqch en morceaux OR en lambeaux **2.** [snatch] arracher **3.** US *inf* [rob] voler.
<> *vi* **1.** [tear] se déchirer **2.** *inf* [go fast] aller à fond de train OR à fond la caisse ⊳ **let it ~!** [go ahead] vas-y! ; [accelerate] appuie sur le champignon! ▪ **now they're gone we can really let ~** maintenant qu'ils sont partis, on va pouvoir s'éclater ▪ **to let ~ at sb** enguirlander qqn.
<> *n* déchirure *f*.
◆ **rip off** *vt sep* **1.** [tear off] arracher **2.** *inf* [cheat, overcharge] arnaquer **3.** *inf* [rob] dévaliser ▪ **they ripped off a bank** ils ont braqué une banque ▮ [steal] faucher, piquer ▪ **he ripped off our idea** il nous a piqué notre idée.
◆ **rip out** *vt sep* arracher.
◆ **rip through** *vt insep* [subj: explosion, noise] déchirer ▪ **we ripped through the work in no time** *fig* on a expédié le travail en un rien de temps.
◆ **rip up** *vt sep* [paper, cloth] déchirer *(violemment)*, mettre en pièces ▪ [road surface, street] éventrer.

RIP (*written abbrev of* **rest in peace**) RIP.

ripcord ['rɪpkɔ:d] *n* poignée *f* d'ouverture *(de parachute)*.

ripe [raɪp] *adj* **1.** [fruit, vegetable] mûr ▪ [cheese] fait, à point **2.** [age] : **to live to a ~ old age** vivre jusqu'à un âge avancé ▪ **he married at the ~ old age of 80** il s'est marié au bel âge de 80 ans **3.** [ready] prêt, mûr ▪ **the time is ~ to sell** c'est le moment de vendre **4.** [full - lips] sensuel, charnu ▪ [breasts] plantureux **5.** [pungent - smell] âcre **6.** *inf* [vulgar] égrillard.

ripen ['raɪpn] <> *vi* [gen] mûrir ▪ [cheese] se faire.
<> *vt* [subj: sun] mûrir ▪ [subj: farmer] (faire) mûrir ▪ **sun-~ed oranges** oranges mûries au soleil.

ripeness ['raɪpnɪs] *n* maturité *f*.

rip-off *n inf* **1.** [swindle] escroquerie *f*, arnaque *f* **2.** [theft] vol *m*, fauche *f* ■ **it's a ~ from an Osborne play** ils ont pompé l'idée dans une pièce d'Osborne.

riposte [*UK* rɪ'pɒst, *US* rɪ'pəʊst] ◇ *n* **1.** [retort] riposte *f*, réplique *f* **2.** FENCING riposte *f*.
◇ *vi* riposter.

ripper ['rɪpər] *n* **1.** [criminal] éventreur *m* ■ **Jack the Ripper** Jack l'Éventreur **2.** [machine] scarificateur *m*.

ripple ['rɪpl] ◇ *n* **1.** [on water] ride *f*, ondulation *f* ■ [on wheatfield, hair, sand] ondulation *f* **2.** [sound - of waves] clapotis *m* ; [- of brook] gazouillis *m* ; [- of conversation] murmure *m* ■ **a ~ of laughter ran through the audience** des rires discrets parcoururent l'assistance **3.** [repercussion] répercussion *f*, vague *f* ■ **her resignation hardly caused a ~** sa démission a fait très peu de bruit ■ **~ effect** effet *m* de vague **4.** CULIN : **strawberry/chocolate ~ (ice cream)** glace *f* marbrée à la fraise/au chocolat **5.** ELECTRON oscillation *f*.
◇ *vi* **1.** [undulate - water] se rider ; [- wheatfield, hair] onduler ■ **moonlight ~d on the surface of the lake** le clair de lune scintillait sur la surface du lac ■ **rippling muscles** muscles saillants *OR* puissants **2.** [murmur - water, waves] clapoter **3.** [resound, have repercussions] se répercuter.
◇ *vt* [water, lake] rider.

rip-rap *n* enrochement *m*.

rip-roaring *adj inf* [noisy] bruyant, tapageur ■ [great, fantastic] génial, super ■ **a ~ success** un succès monstre.

RISC (*abbrev of* **reduced instruction set computer**) *n* RISC *m*.

rise [raɪz] (*pret* **rose** [rəʊz], *pp* **risen** ['rɪzn]) ◇ *vi* **1.** [get up - from chair, bed] se lever ; [- from knees, after fall] se relever ■ **he rose (from his chair) to greet me** il s'est levé (de sa chaise) pour me saluer ■ **to ~ to one's feet** se lever, se mettre debout ▶ **~ and shine!** debout!
2. [sun, moon, fog] se lever ■ [smoke, balloon] s'élever, monter ■ [tide, river level] monter ■ [river] prendre sa source ■ [land] s'élever ■ [fish] mordre ■ THEAT [curtain] se lever ■ CULIN [dough] lever ■ [soufflé] monter ■ **to ~ into the air** [bird, balloon] s'élever (dans les airs) ; [plane] monter *OR* s'élever (dans les airs) ■ **to ~ to the surface** [swimmer, whale] remonter à la surface ■ **the colour rose in** *OR* **to her cheeks** le rouge lui est monté aux joues ■ **his eyebrows rose in surprise** il leva les sourcils de surprise ■ **laughter/cheers rose from the crowd** des rires/des hourras montèrent de la foule ■ **to ~ from the dead** RELIG ressusciter d'entre les morts ■ **to ~ into heaven** RELIG monter au ciel ■ **to ~ to the occasion** se montrer à la hauteur de la situation
3. [increase - value] augmenter ; [- number, amount] augmenter, monter ; [- prices, costs] monter, augmenter, être en hausse ; [- temperature, pressure] monter ; [- barometer] monter, remonter ; [- wind] se lever ; [- tension, tone, voice] monter ; [- feeling, anger, panic] monter, grandir ■ **to ~ by 10 dollars/by 10%** augmenter de 10 dollars/de 10 % ■ **his spirits rose when he heard the news** il a été soulagé *OR* heureux d'apprendre la nouvelle
4. [mountains, buildings] se dresser, s'élever ■ **the mountain ~s to 2,500 m** la montagne a une altitude de *OR* culmine à *OR* s'élève à 2 500 m ■ **many new apartment blocks have risen in the past ten years** de nombreux immeubles neufs ont été construits au cours des dix dernières années ▶ **to ~ from the ashes** renaître de ses cendres
5. [socially, professionally] monter, réussir ■ **to ~ in the world** faire son chemin dans le monde ■ **to ~ to fame** devenir célèbre ■ **to ~ in sb's esteem** monter dans l'estime de qqn ■ **to ~ from the ranks** sortir du rang ■ **she rose to the position of personnel manager** elle a réussi à devenir chef du personnel
6. [revolt] se soulever, se révolter ■ **to ~ in revolt (against sb/sthg)** se révolter (contre qqn/qqch) ■ **to ~ in protest against sthg** se soulever contre qqch
7. [adjourn - assembly, meeting] lever la séance ; [- Parliament, court] clore la session ■ **Parliament rose for the summer recess** la session parlementaire est close pour les vacances d'été.
◇ *n* **1.** [high ground] hauteur *f*, éminence *f* ■ [slope] pente *f* ■ [hill] côte *f*
2. [of moon, sun, curtain] lever *m* ■ [to power, influence] montée *f*, ascension *f* ■ INDUST [development] essor *m* ■ **the ~ and fall of the tide** le flux et le reflux de la marée ■ **the ~ and fall of the Roman Empire** la croissance et la chute *OR* la grandeur et la décadence de l'Empire romain ■ **the ~ and fall of the fascist movement** la montée et la chute du mouvement fasciste ■ **the actor's ~ to fame was both rapid and spectacular** cet acteur a connu un succès à la fois rapide et spectaculaire
3. [increase - of price, crime, accidents] hausse *f*, augmentation *f* ; [- in bank rate, interest] relèvement *m*, hausse *f* ; [- of temperature, pressure] hausse *f* ; [- of affluence, wealth] augmentation *f* ■ **to be on the ~** être en hausse ■ **there has been a steep ~ in house prices** les prix de l'immobilier ont beaucoup augmenté ■ **there was a 10% ~ in the number of visitors** le nombre de visiteurs a augmenté de 10 % ■ **there has been a steady ~ in the number of accidents** les accidents sont en augmentation régulière ■ **~ in value** appréciation *f* ■ **to speculate on a ~** ST. EX miser sur la hausse ■ *UK* [in salary] augmentation *f* (de salaire) ■ **to be given a ~** être augmenté
4. [of river] source *f*
5. *phr* **to give ~ to sthg** donner lieu à qqch, entraîner qqch ■ **their disappearance gave ~ to great scandal/suspicion** leur disparition a provoqué un énorme scandale/éveillé de nombreux soupçons ■ **to get** *OR* **to take a ~ out of sb** *UK inf* faire réagir qqn, faire marcher qqn.
➜ **rise above** *vt insep* [obstacle, fear] surmonter ■ [figure] dépasser.
➜ **rise up** *vi insep* **1.** [get up] se lever ■ [go up] monter, s'élever ■ **the smoke/the balloon rose up into the sky** la fumée/le ballon s'élevait dans le ciel
2. [revolt] se soulever, se révolter ■ **to ~ up against an oppressor** se soulever contre un oppresseur
3. RELIG ressusciter
4. [appear] apparaître ■ **a shadowy figure rose up out of the mist** une ombre surgit de la brume.

risen ['rɪzn] ◇ *pp* ▷ **rise**.
◇ *adj* ressuscité.

riser ['raɪzər] *n* **1.** [person] : **to be an early/late ~** être un lève-tôt (*inv*)/lève-tard (*inv*) **2.** [of step] contremarche *f* **3.** [in plumbing] conduite *f* montante.

risible ['rɪzəbl] *adj fml* risible, ridicule.

rising ['raɪzɪŋ] ◇ *n* **1.** [revolt] insurrection *f*, soulèvement *m* **2.** [of sun, moon, of theatre curtain] lever *m* **3.** [of prices] augmentation *f*, hausse *f* **4.** [of river] crue *f* ■ [of ground] élévation *f* **5.** [from dead] résurrection *f* **6.** [of Parliament, an assembly] ajournement *m*, clôture *f* de séance.
◇ *adj* **1.** [sun] levant **2.** [tide] montant ■ [water level] ascendant **3.** [ground, road] qui monte **4.** [temperature, prices] en hausse ■ FIN [market] orienté à la hausse **5.** [up-and-coming] : **he's a ~ celebrity** c'est une étoile montante **6.** [emotion] croissant.

rising damp *n* humidité *f* ascensionnelle *OR* par capillarité.

risk [rɪsk] ◇ *n* **1.** [gen] risque *m* ■ **to take a ~** prendre un risque ■ **to run the ~** courir le risque ■ **is there any ~ of him making another blunder?** est-ce qu'il risque de commettre un nouvel impair? ■ **it's not worth the ~** c'est trop risqué ■ **that's a ~ we'll have to take** c'est un risque à courir ■ **do it at your own ~** faites-le à vos risques et périls ■ **'cars may be parked here at the owner's ~'** les automobilistes peuvent stationner ici à leurs risques (et périls) ■ **at the ~ of one's life** au péril de sa vie ■ **at the ~ of sounding ignorant, how does one open this box?** au risque de passer pour un idiot, j'aimerais savoir comment on ouvre cette boîte? **2.** [in insurance] risque *m* ■ **fire ~** risque d'incendie ■ **he's a bad ~** c'est un client à risques.
◇ *vt* risquer, hasarder *fml* ■ **to ~ defeat** risquer d'être battu ▶ **to ~ one's neck** *OR* **skin, to ~ life and limb** risquer sa peau.
➜ **at risk** *adj phr* : **there's too much at ~** les risques *OR* les enjeux sont trop importants ■ **our children are at ~ from all kinds of violence** nos enfants ont toutes sortes de violences à craindre ■ **all our jobs are at ~** tous nos emplois sont menacés ■ **to be at ~** MED & SOCIOL être vulnérable, être une personne à risque.

risk capital *n (U) UK* capitaux *mpl* à risques.

risk-taking *n (U) fait de prendre des risques* ■ **we knew there would be some ~ involved** nous savions que ce ne serait pas sans risques.

risky ['rɪskɪ] (*comp* **riskier**, *superl* **riskiest**) *adj* [hazardous] risqué, hasardeux ■ **~ business** entreprise hasardeuse.

risotto [rɪ'zɒtəʊ] (*pl* **risottos**) *n* risotto *m*.

risqué ['ri:skeɪ] *adj* [story, joke] risqué, osé, scabreux.

rissole ['rɪsəʊl] *n* CULIN rissole *f*.

rite [raɪt] *n* rite *m* ■ **initiation/fertility ~s** rites d'initiation/de fertilité ■ **~ of passage** cérémonie *f* d'initiation ■ **'The Rite of Spring'** ***Stravinsky*** 'le Sacre du printemps'.

ritual ['rɪtʃʊəl] ◇ *n* rituel *m*.
◇ *adj* rituel.

ritualistic [,rɪtʃʊə'lɪstɪk] *adj* ritualiste.

ritually ['rɪtʃʊəlɪ] *adv* rituellement.

ritzy ['rɪtsɪ] (*comp* **ritzier**, *superl* **ritziest**) *adj inf* classe, très chic, luxueux.

rival ['raɪvl] (*UK pret & pp* **rivalled**, *cont* **rivalling**) (*US pret & pp* **rivaled**, *cont* **rivaling**) ◇ *n* [gen] rival *m*, - e *f* ■ COMM rival *m*, - e *f*, concurrent *m*, - e *f*.
◇ *adj* [gen] rival ■ COMM concurrent, rival.
◇ *vt* [gen] rivaliser avec ■ COMM être en concurrence avec ■ **no-one can ~ her when it comes to business acumen** son sens des affaires n'a pas d'égal ■ **your stubbornness is rivalled only by your narrow-mindedness** votre entêtement n'a d'égal que votre étroitesse d'esprit.

rivalry ['raɪvlrɪ] (*pl* **rivalries**) *n* rivalité *f* ■ **there's a lot of ~ between the two brothers** il y a une forte rivalité entre les deux frères.

riven ['rɪvn] *adj* déchiré, divisé.

river ['rɪvər] ◇ *n* **1.** [as tributary] rivière *f* ■ [flowing to sea] fleuve *m* ▶ **to be up the ~** *US inf* [in prison] être en taule **2.** *fig* [of mud, lava] coulée *f* ■ **a ~ of blood** un fleuve de sang.
◇ *comp* [port, system, traffic] fluvial ■ [fish] d'eau douce.

riverbank ['rɪvəbæŋk] *n* rive *f*, berge *f*.

river basin *n* bassin *m* fluvial.

riverbed ['rɪvəbed] *n* lit *m* de rivière OR de fleuve.

riverside ['rɪvəsaɪd] ◇ *n* bord *m* d'une rivière OR d'un fleuve, rive *f* ■ **we walked along the ~** nous nous sommes promenés le long de la rivière.
◇ *adj* au bord d'une rivière OR d'un fleuve.

rivet ['rɪvɪt] ◇ *n* rivet *m*.
◇ *vt* **1.** TECH riveter, river **2.** *fig* **to be ~ed to the spot** rester cloué OR rivé sur place ■ **the children were ~ed to the television set** les enfants étaient rivés au poste de télévision **3.** [fascinate] fasciner.

riveter ['rɪvɪtər] *n* [person] riveur *m* ■ [machine] riveteuse *f*.

riveting ['rɪvɪtɪŋ] *adj* fascinant, passionnant, captivant.

Riviera [,rɪvɪ'eərə] *pr n* : **the French ~** la Côte d'Azur ■ **on the French ~** sur la Côte d'Azur ■ **the Italian ~** la Riviera italienne ■ **on the Italian ~** sur la Riviera italienne.

rivulet ['rɪvjʊlɪt] *n* (petit) ruisseau *m*, ru *m lit*.

RMT (*abbrev of* **National Union of Rail, Maritime and Transport Workers**) *pr n syndicat britannique des cheminots et des gens de mer*.

RN ◇ *pr n* = **Royal Navy**.
◇ *n UK* **1.** (*abbrev of* **registered nurse**) [nurse] infirmier *m* diplômé (d'État); infirmière *f* diplômée (d'État) **2.** [qualification] diplôme *m* (d'État) d'infirmier.

RNLI (*abbrev of* **Royal National Lifeboat Institution**) *pr n société britannique de sauvetage en mer*.

roach [rəʊtʃ] *n* **1.** (*pl* roach OR *pl* roaches) [fish] gardon *m* **2.** *inf* [cockroach] cafard *m*, cancrelat *m* **3.** △ *drug sl* [of marijuana cigarette] filtre *m*.

road [rəʊd] ◇ *n* **1.** *liter* route *f* ■ [small] chemin *m* ■ **by ~** par la route ■ **is this the (right) ~ for OR to Liverpool?** est-ce la (bonne) route pour Liverpool? ■ **are we on the right ~?** sommes-nous sur la bonne route? ■ **on the ~ to Liverpool, the car broke down** en allant à Liverpool, la voiture est tombée en panne ■ **to take to the ~** [driver] prendre la route OR le volant ; [tramp] partir sur les routes ■ **to be on the ~** [pop star, troupe] être en tournée ■ **we've been on the ~ since 6 o'clock this morning** nous roulons depuis 6 h ce matin ■ **his car shouldn't be on the ~** sa voiture devrait être retirée de la circulation ■ **someone of his age shouldn't be on the ~** une personne de son âge ne devrait pas prendre le volant ■ **my car is off the ~ at the moment** ma voiture est en panne OR chez le garagiste ■ [street] rue *f* ■ **he lives just down the ~** il habite un peu plus loin dans la même rue ■ **he lives across the ~ from us** il habite en face de chez nous ■ [roadway] route *f*, chaussée *f* ■ **to stand in the middle of the ~** se tenir au milieu de la route OR de la chaussée ▶ **let's get this show on the ~!** bon, on y va! ■ **one for the ~** *inf* un petit coup avant de partir ■ **the ~ to hell is paved with good intentions** *prov* l'enfer est pavé de bonnes intentions *prov*
2. *fig* [path] chemin *m*, voie *f* ■ **if we go down that ~** si nous nous engageons sur cette voie ■ **to be on the right ~** être sur la bonne voie ■ **to be on the ~ to success/recovery** être sur le chemin de la réussite/en voie de guérison ■ **down the ~** [in the future] à l'avenir ■ **you're in my ~!** *UK inf* [I can't pass] vous me bouchez le passage! ; [I can't see] vous me bouchez la vue!
3. *US* [railway] chemin de fer *m*, voie *f* ferrée
4. (*usu pl*) NAUT rade *f*
5. [in mine] galerie *f*
6. *UK inf dial* & *phr* **any ~ (up)** de toute façon.
◇ *comp* [traffic, transport, bridge] routier ■ [accident] de la route ■ [conditions, construction, repairs] des routes ■ **~ atlas** atlas *m* routier.

roadbed ['rəʊdbed] *n* CONSTR empierrement *m* ■ RAIL ballast *m*.

roadblock ['rəʊdblɒk] *n* barrage *m* routier.

road hog *n inf* chauffard *m*.

roadholding ['rəʊd,həʊldɪŋ] *n* tenue *f* de route.

roadhouse ['rəʊdhaʊs] (*pl* [-haʊzɪz]) *n* relais *m* routier.

roadie ['rəʊdɪ] *n inf technicien qui accompagne les groupes de rock en tournée*.

roadkill ['rəʊdkɪl] *n* animal *m* tué sur une route.

road manager *n* responsable *m* de tournée *(d'un chanteur ou d'un groupe pop)*.

road map *n* carte *f* routière.

road racing *n* compétition *f* automobile *(sur route)*.

road rage *n* agressivité *f* au volant *(se traduisant parfois par un acte de violence)*.

road roller *n* rouleau *m* compresseur.

road safety *n* sécurité *f* routière.

road sense *n* [for driver] sens *m* de la conduite ■ [for pedestrian] : **children have to be taught ~** on doit apprendre aux enfants à faire attention à la circulation.

roadshow ['rəʊdʃəʊ] *n* [gen] tournée *f* ■ [radio show] *animation en direct proposée par une station de radio en tournée*.

roadside ['rəʊdsaɪd] ◇ *n* bord *m* de la route, bas-côté *m* ■ **we stopped the car by the ~** nous avons arrêté la voiture au bord OR sur le bord de la route.
◇ *adj* au bord de la route ■ **~ inn** auberge située au bord de la route.

road sign *n* panneau *m* de signalisation.

roadster ['rəʊdstər] *n* **1.** [car] roadster *m* **2.** [bicycle] bicyclette *f* (de tourisme).

roadsweeper ['rəʊd,swi:pər] *n* [person] balayeur *m*, - euse *f* ■ [vehicle] balayeuse *f*.

road tax *n UK* taxe *f* sur les automobiles ■ **~ disc** vignette *f* (automobile).

road test *n* essai *m* sur route.
◆ **road-test** *vt* essayer sur route.

roadtrip ['rəʊdtrɪp] *n* **US** [short] promenade *f* en voiture.

road-user *n* usager *m*, - ère *f* de la route.

roadway ['rəʊdweɪ] *n* chaussée *f*.

road works *npl* travaux *mpl* (d'entretien des routes).

roadworthiness ['rəʊd,wɜːðɪnɪs] *n* état *m* général *(d'un véhicule)*.

roadworthy ['rəʊd,wɜːðɪ] *adj* [vehicle] en état de rouler.

roam [rəʊm] ◇ *vt* **1.** [travel - world] parcourir ; [- streets] errer dans ▪ **to ~ the seven seas** aller aux quatre coins du monde **2.** [hang about - streets] traîner dans.
◇ *vi* [wander] errer, voyager sans but ▪ **he allowed his imagination/his thoughts to ~** *fig* il a laissé vagabonder son imagination/ses pensées.
◆ **roam about** *UK*, **roam around** *vi insep* **1.** [travel] vagabonder, bourlinguer **2.** [aimlessly] errer, traîner.

roaming ['rəʊmɪŋ] ◇ *adj* vagabond, errant.
◇ *n* vagabondage *m*.

roan [rəʊn] ◇ *adj* rouan.
◇ *n* rouan *m*.

roar [rɔːr] ◇ *vi* [lion] rugir ▪ [bull] beugler, mugir ▪ [elephant] barrir ▪ [person] hurler, crier ▪ [crowd] hurler ▪ [radio, music] beugler, hurler ▪ [sea, wind] mugir ▪ [storm, thunder] gronder ▪ [fire] ronfler ▪ [cannon] tonner ▪ [car, motorcycle, engine] vrombir ▪ **to ~ with anger** rugir *OR* hurler de colère ▪ **to ~ with laughter** se tordre de rire ▪ **the car ~ed past** [noisily] la voiture est passée en vrombissant ; [fast] la voiture est passée à toute allure.
◇ *vt* [feelings, order] hurler.
◇ *n* [of lion] rugissement *m* ▪ [of bull] mugissement *m*, beuglement *m* ▪ [of elephant] barrissement *m* ▪ [of sea, wind] mugissement *m* ▪ [of thunder, storm] grondement *m* ▪ [of fire] ronflement *m* ▪ [of cannons] grondement *m* ▪ [of crowd] hurlements *mpl* ▪ [of engine] vrombissement *m* ▪ **~s of laughter** gros *OR* grands éclats de rire ▪ **the ~ of the traffic outside my window is awful** le vacarme de la circulation sous ma fenêtre est épouvantable.

roaring ['rɔːrɪŋ] ◇ *adj* **1.** [lion] rugissant ▪ [bull] mugissant, beuglant ▪ [elephant] qui barrit ▪ [person, crowd] hurlant ▪ [sea, wind] mugissant ▪ [thunder, storm] qui gronde ▪ [engine] vrombissant ▪ **a ~ fire** une bonne flambée **2.** *fig* [excellent] : **a ~ success** un succès fou ▪ **to do a ~ trade** *UK* faire des affaires en or ▪ **they did a ~ trade in pancakes** ils ont vendu énormément de crêpes.
◇ *adv inf* **~ drunk** ivre mort, complètement bourré.

Roaring Forties *npl* NAUT quarantièmes *mpl* rugissants.

Roaring Twenties *npl* : **the ~** les Années *fpl* folles.

roast [rəʊst] ◇ *vt* **1.** [meat] rôtir ▪ [peanuts, chestnuts] griller ▪ [coffee] griller, torréfier **2.** [minerals] calciner **3.** *fig* [by sun, fire] griller, rôtir ▪ **I sat ~ing my toes by the fire** j'étais assis devant le feu pour me réchauffer les pieds.
◇ *vi* **1.** [meat] rôtir **2.** *fig* [person] avoir très chaud ▪ **we spent a week ~ing in the sun** nous avons passé une semaine à nous rôtir au soleil.
◇ *adj* rôti ▪ **~ beef** rôti *m* de bœuf, rosbif *m* ▪ **~ chicken** poulet *m* rôti ▪ **~ potatoes** pommes de terre *fpl* rôties au four.
◇ *n* **1.** [joint of meat] rôti *m* **2.** *US* [barbecue] barbecue *m* ▪ **to have a ~** faire un barbecue.

roasting ['rəʊstɪŋ] ◇ *n* **1.** [of meat] rôtissage *m* ▪ [of coffee] torréfaction *f* ▪ **~ spit** tournebroche *m* ▪ **~ tin** plat *m* à rôtir **2.** *UK inf fig* [harsh criticism] : **to give sb a ~** *inf* passer un savon à qqn.
◇ *adj inf* [weather] torride ▪ **it was ~ in her office** il faisait une chaleur à crever dans son bureau ▪ **I'm ~!** je crève de chaud!

rob [rɒb] (*pret & pp* **robbed**, *cont* **robbing**) *vt* **1.** [person] voler ▪ [bank] dévaliser ▪ [house] cambrioler ▪ **to ~ sb of sthg** voler *OR* dérober qqch à qqn ▪ **I've been robbed!** au voleur! ▪ **someone has robbed the till!** on a volé l'argent de la caisse! **2.** *fig* [deprive] priver ▪ **to ~ sb of sthg** priver qqn de qqch ▪ **the team was robbed of its victory** l'équipe s'est vue ravir la victoire ▶ **to ~ Peter to pay Paul** déshabiller Pierre pour habiller Paul.

robber ['rɒbər] *n* [of property] voleur *m*, - euse *f*.

robber baron *n* HIST baron *m* pillard ▪ *fig* [tough businessman] requin *m* de l'industrie.

robbery ['rɒbərɪ] (*pl* **robberies**) *n* **1.** [of property] vol *m* ▪ [of bank] hold-up *m* ▪ [of house] cambriolage *m* ▪ **~ with violence** vol *m* avec coups et blessures, vol *m* qualifié *spec* **2.** *inf* [overcharging] vol *m* ▪ **it's just plain ~!** c'est de l'escroquerie *OR* du vol manifeste!

robe [rəʊb] ◇ *n* **1.** [dressing gown] peignoir *m*, robe *f* de chambre **2.** [long garment - gen] robe *f* ; [- for judge, academic] robe *f*, toge *f*.
◇ *vt* [dress - gen] habiller, vêtir ; [- in robe] vêtir d'une robe ▪ **~d in red** vêtu de rouge.
◇ *vi* [judge] revêtir sa robe.

robin ['rɒbɪn] *n* **1.** [European] : **~ (redbreast)** rouge-gorge *m* **2.** [American] merle *m* américain.

Robin Hood *pr n* Robin des Bois.

robot ['rəʊbɒt] ◇ *n liter & fig* [automaton] robot *m*, automate *m*.
◇ *comp* [pilot, vehicle, system] automatique.

robotic [rəʊ'bɒtɪk] *adj* robotique.

robotics [rəʊ'bɒtɪks] *n (U)* robotique *f*.

robust [rəʊ'bʌst] *adj* [person] robuste, vigoureux, solide ▪ [health] solide ▪ [appetite] robuste, solide ▪ [wine] robuste, corsé ▪ [structure] solide ▪ [economy, style, car] robuste ▪ [response, defence] vigoureux, énergique.

robustly [rəʊ'bʌstlɪ] *adv* solidement, avec robustesse.

rock [rɒk] ◇ *n* **1.** [substance] roche *f*, roc *m* ▪ **the lighthouse is built on ~** le phare est construit sur le roc
2. [boulder] rocher *m* ▪ **the boat struck the ~s** le bateau a été jeté sur les rochers ▶ **to be on the ~s** *inf* [person] être dans la dèche ; [firm] être en faillite ; [enterprise, marriage] mal tourner, tourner à la catastrophe ▪ **to go on the ~s** [firm] faire faillite ; [enterprise, marriage] mal tourner ▪ **on the ~s** [drink] avec des glaçons ▪ **to be caught between a ~ and a hard place** être pris dans un dilemme ▪ **'Brighton Rock'** *Greene* 'le Rocher de Brighton'
3. [music, dance] rock *m*
4. [in place names] rocher *m*, roche *f* ▪ **the Rock** le rocher de Gibraltar
5. *US* [stone] pierre *f*
6. *UK* [sweet] ≃ sucre *m* d'orge
7. RELIG [stronghold] rocher *m*, roc *m*
8.△ [diamond] diam△ *m*
9.△ *(usu pl)* [testicle] couille△ *f*
10. *drug sl* caillou *m (de crack)*.
◇ *comp* [film] rock ▪ [band, record] (de) rock ▪ [radio station] de rock ▪ **a ~ guitarist** un guitariste rock.
◇ *vt* **1.** [swing to and fro - baby] bercer ; [- chair] balancer ; [- lever] basculer ; [- boat] ballotter, tanguer ▪ **to ~ a baby to sleep** bercer un bébé pour l'endormir ▪ **the boat was ~ed by the waves** [gently] le bateau était bercé par les flots ; [violently] le bateau était ballotté par les vagues ▶ **to ~ the boat** jouer les trouble-fête, semer le trouble
2. [shake] secouer, ébranler ▪ **the stock market crash ~ed the financial world to its core** le krach boursier a ébranlé en profondeur le monde de la finance.
◇ *vi* **1.** [sway] se balancer
2. [quake] trembler ▪ **to ~ with laughter** se tordre de rire
3. [jive] danser le rock.

rockabilly ['rɒkə,bɪlɪ] *n* rockabilly *m*.

rock and roll *n* rock *m* (and roll) ▪ **to do the ~** danser le rock.

rock bottom *n fig* **to hit ~** [person] avoir le moral à zéro, toucher le fond ; [firm, funds] atteindre le niveau le plus bas.
◆ **rock-bottom** *adj* [price] le plus bas.

rock bun, rock cake *n* rocher *m (gâteau)*.

rock candy *n US* sucre *m* d'orge.

rock climber *n* varappeur *m*, - euse *f*.

rock climbing *n* escalade *f* (de rochers), varappe *f* ■ **to go ~** faire de l'escalade *OR* de la varappe.

rocker ['rɒkəʳ] *n* **1.** [of cradle, chair] bascule *f* ■ **to be off one's ~** *inf* être cinglé, débloquer **2.** [rocking chair] fauteuil *m* à bascule **3.** *UK* [youth] rocker *m*.

rockery ['rɒkərɪ] (*pl* **rockeries**) *n* (jardin *m* de) rocaille *f*.

rocket ['rɒkɪt] ◇ *n* **1.** AERON & ASTRONAUT fusée *f* ■ **to fire** *OR* **to send up a ~** lancer une fusée ▶ **to go off like a ~** partir comme une fusée ■ **to get a ~ (from sb)** *UK inf* se faire enguirlander(par qqn) ■ **to give sb a ~** *UK inf* enguirlander qqn **2.** MIL [missile] roquette *f* ■ **to fire a ~** lancer une roquette **3.** [signal, flare] fusée *f* **4.** [firework] fusée *f* **5.** BOT & CULIN roquette *f*.
◇ *comp* [propulsion] par fusée ■ [engine] de fusée.
◇ *vt* **1.** [missile, astronaut] lancer (dans l'espace) **2.** [record, singer] faire monter en flèche.
◇ *vi* [price, sales] monter en flèche ■ **to ~ to fame** devenir célèbre du jour au lendemain ■ **the car ~ed down the road/round the track** la voiture a descendu la rue/fait le tour de la piste à une vitesse incroyable.

rocket launcher *n* AERON & ASTRONAUT lance-fusées *m inv* ■ MIL lance-roquettes *m inv*.

rocketry ['rɒkɪtrɪ] *n* **1.** [science] fuséologie *f* **2.** [rockets collectively] arsenal *m* de fusées.

rock face *n* paroi *f* rocheuse.

rockfall ['rɒkfɔːl] *n* chute *f* de pierres *OR* de rochers.

rockfish ['rɒkfɪʃ] (*pl inv OR pl* **rockfishes**) *n* gobie *m*, rascasse *f*.

rock garden *n* jardin *m* de rocaille.

rock-hard *adj* dur comme le roc.

Rockies ['rɒkɪz] *pr npl* : **the ~** les Rocheuses *fpl*.

rocking ['rɒkɪŋ] *n* **1.** [of chair, boat] balancement *m* ■ [of baby] bercement *m* ■ [of head - to rhythm] balancement *m* **2.** MECH oscillation *f*.

rocking chair *n* fauteuil *m* à bascule, rocking-chair *m*.

rocking horse *n* cheval *m* à bascule.

rock music *n* rock *m*.

rock'n'roll [ˌrɒkn'rəʊl] = **rock and roll**.

rock pool *n* petite cuvette *f* d'eau de mer dans les rochers.

rock salt *n* sel *m* gemme.

rock-solid *adj* inébranlable.

rocky ['rɒkɪ] (*comp* **rockier**, *superl* **rockiest**) *adj* **1.** [seabed, mountain] rocheux ■ [path, track] rocailleux **2.** [unstable - situation] précaire, instable ; [- government] peu stable.

Rocky Mountains *pr npl* : **the ~** les montagnes *fpl* Rocheuses.

rococo [rə'kəʊkəʊ] ◇ *adj* rococo.
◇ *n* rococo *m*.

rod [rɒd] *n* **1.** [of iron] barre *f* ■ [of wood] baguette *f* ■ [for curtains, carpet] tringle *f* ■ [for fishing] canne *f* ■ [for punishment] baguette *f* ■ [flexible] verge *f* ■ SCH [pointer] baguette *f* ▶ **~ and line** FISHING canne à pêche ■ **~ fishing** pêche *f* à la ligne ■ **~ of office** (symbole *m* de) pouvoir *m* ■ **to rule with a ~ of iron** gouverner d'une main *OR* poigne de fer ■ **to make a ~ for one's own back** donner des bâtons pour se faire battre **2.** [of uranium] barre *f* **3.** MECH [in engine] tige *f* ■ [mechanism] : **~s** tringlerie *f*, timonerie *f* **4.** [for surveying] mire *f* **5.** ANAT [in eye] bâtonnet *m* **6.** [linear or square measure] ≃ perche *f* **7.**△ *US* [gun] flingue△ *m* **8.**△ [car] voiture *f* gonflée **9.**▲ [penis] bite△ *f*.

rode [rəʊd] *pt* ▷ **ride**.

rodent ['rəʊdənt] ◇ *adj* rongeur.
◇ *n* rongeur *m*.

rodeo ['rəʊdɪəʊ] (*pl* **rodeos**) *n* rodéo *m*.

Rodeo Drive *pr n luxueuse rue commerçante à Hollywood.*

roe [rəʊ] (*pl inv OR pl* **roes**) *n (U)* [eggs] œufs *mpl* de poisson ■ [sperm] laitance *f* ■ **cod ~** œufs de cabillaud.

roebuck ['rəʊbʌk] *n* chevreuil *m* mâle.

roe deer *n* chevreuil *m*.

rogation [rəʊ'geɪʃn] *n (usu pl)* rogations *fpl*.

Rogation Sunday *n* dimanche *m* des rogations.

roger ['rɒdʒəʳ] *interj* TELEC reçu et compris, d'accord ■ **~ and out** message reçu, terminé.

rogue [rəʊg] ◇ *n* **1.** [scoundrel] escroc *m*, filou *m* ■ [mischievous child] polisson *m*, - onne *f*, coquin *m*, - e *f* **2.** [animal] solitaire *m*.
◇ *adj* **1.** [animal] solitaire **2.** *US* [delinquent] dévoyé.

rogues' gallery *n* [in police files] photographies *fpl* de repris de justice ■ **they're a real ~!** ils ont des mines patibulaires!

roguish ['rəʊgɪʃ] *adj* [mischievous] espiègle, malicieux, coquin.

Rohypnol® [rəʊ'hɪpnɒl] *n* Rohypnol® *m*.

roisterous ['rɔɪstərəs] *adj* [behaviour] tapageur ■ [crowd] bruyant.

role, rôle [rəʊl] *n* rôle *m* ■ **to have** *OR* **to play the leading ~** jouer le rôle principal ■ **she had** *OR* **she played an important ~ in this project** elle a joué un rôle important dans ce projet ▶ **~ model** modèle *m* ■ **~ play** SCH & PSYCHOL jeu *m* de rôles ■ **~ playing** *(U)* jeux *mpl* de rôles.

roll [rəʊl] ◇ *vt* **1.** [ball] (faire) rouler ■ [dice] jeter, lancer ■ [cigarette, umbrella] rouler ■ [coil] enrouler ■ **the hedgehog ~ed itself into a tight ball** le hérisson s'est mis en boule ■ **to ~ sthg in** *OR* **between one's fingers** rouler qqch entre ses doigts ■ **the boy ~ed the modelling clay into a long snake** le garçon roula la pâte à modeler pour en faire un long serpent ■ **he ~ed his sleeves above his elbows** il a roulé *OR* retroussé ses manches au-dessus du coude ■ **to ~ dice** jouer aux dés ■ **to ~ one's r's** rouler les r ■ **to ~ one's hips/shoulders** rouler les hanches/épaules ■ **to ~ one's eyes in fright** rouler les yeux de frayeur ■ **she's a company executive, wife and housekeeper all ~ed into one** *fig* elle cumule les rôles de cadre dans sa société, d'épouse et de ménagère ■ **to ~ one's own** *UK* [cigarettes] rouler ses cigarettes
2. [flatten - grass] rouler ; [- pastry, dough] étendre ; [- gold, metal] laminer ; [- road] cylindrer
3. *US inf* [rob] dévaliser.
◇ *vi* **1.** [ball] rouler ■ **to ~ in the mud** [gen] se rouler dans la boue ; [wallow] se vautrer dans la boue ■ **his eyes ~ed in horror** il roulait des yeux horrifiés ■ **the ball ~ed under the car/down the stairs** la balle roula sous la voiture/en bas de l'escalier ■ **the car ~ed down the hill/the slope** la voiture dévalait la colline/la pente ■ **the car ~ed to a halt** la voiture s'est arrêtée lentement ■ [sweat] dégouliner ■ [tears] rouler ■ **tears ~ed down her face** des larmes roulaient sur ses joues ■ **sweat ~ed off his back** la sueur lui dégoulinait dans le dos ▶ **to be ~ing in money** *OR* **~ing in it** *inf* rouler sur l'or, être plein aux as ■ **he had them ~ing in the aisles** il les faisait mourir de rire
2. [ship] avoir du roulis ■ [plane - with turbulence] avoir du roulis ; [- in aerobatics] faire un tonneau *OR* des tonneaux ■ ASTRONAUT tourner sur soi-même
3. [machine, camera] tourner ■ **the credits started to ~** [of film] le générique commença à défiler ▶ **to get** *OR* **to start things ~ing** mettre les choses en marche ■ **to keep the ball** *OR* **the show ~ing** COMM faire tourner la boutique ; THEAT faire en sorte que le spectacle continue ■ **let the good times ~** que la fête continue
4. [drums] rouler ■ [thunder] gronder ■ [voice] retentir ■ [music] retentir, résonner ■ [organ] résonner, sonner.
◇ *n* **1.** [of carpet, paper] rouleau *m* ■ [of banknotes] liasse *f* ■ [of tobacco] carotte *f* ■ [of butter] coquille *f* ■ [of fat, flesh] bourrelet *m* ■ [of film] rouleau *m*, bobine *f* ■ [of tools] trousse *f*
2. : **(bread) ~** petit pain *m*
3. [of ball] roulement *m* ■ [of dice] lancement *m* ■ [of car, ship] roulis *m* ■ [of plane - in turbulence] roulis *m* ; [- in aerobatics]

tonneau *m* ▪ [of hips, shoulders] balancement *m* ▪ [of sea] houle *f* ▪ [somersault] galipette *f* ▪ **to have a ~ in the hay** *inf* [make love] se rouler dans le foin
4. [list - of members] liste *f*, tableau *m* ▪ ADMIN & NAUT rôle *m* ▪ SCH liste *f* des élèves ▪ **to call the ~** faire l'appel ▶ **~ of honour** MIL liste des combattants morts pour la patrie ; SCH tableau *m* d'honneur
5. [of drum] roulement *m* ▪ [of thunder] grondement *m*
6. *phr* **to be on a ~** avoir le vent en poupe ▪ **now we're on a ~, let's carry on** puisque nous sommes lancés, continuons.

◆ **roll about** *vi insep UK* rouler ça et là ▪ **to ~ about on the floor/grass** se rouler par terre/dans l'herbe ▪ **to ~ about with laughter** *fig* se tordre de rire, se tenir les côtes.

◆ **roll along** ◇ *vi insep* **1.** [river] couler ▪ [car] rouler ▪ **the car was ~ing along at 140 km/h** la voiture roulait à 140
2. *fig* [project] avancer
3. *inf* [go] passer, se pointer, s'amener.
◇ *vt sep* [hoop, ball] faire rouler ▪ [car window] baisser ▪ [car, wheelbarrow] pousser.

◆ **roll around** = **roll about**.

◆ **roll away** ◇ *vi insep* [car, clouds] s'éloigner ▪ [terrain] s'étendre ▪ **the ball ~ed away into the street** la balle a roulé jusque dans la rue.
◇ *vt sep* [take away] emmener ▪ [put away] ranger.

◆ **roll back** ◇ *vt sep* **1.** [push back - carpet] rouler, enrouler ; [- blankets] replier ; [- enemy, difficulties] faire reculer ; [- trolley, wheelchair] reculer *fig*
2. [bring back] ramener
3. [prices] casser
4. [time] faire reculer ▪ **it would be nice to ~ back the years** ce serait bien de revenir des années en arrière.
◇ *vi insep* [waves] se retirer ▪ [memories, time] revenir.

◆ **roll by** *vi insep* **1.** [time] s'écouler, passer
2. [car] passer.

◆ **roll down** ◇ *vi insep* rouler en bas, descendre en roulant ▪ [tears, sweat] couler.
◇ *vt sep* [blind] baisser ▪ [sleeves] redescendre ▪ [blanket] replier ▪ [hoop, ball] faire rouler ▪ [car window] baisser.

◆ **roll in** ◇ *vi insep* **1.** [arrive] arriver ▪ [come back] rentrer
2. [car] entrer ▪ [waves] déferler
3. *inf* [money] rentrer ▪ [crowds] affluer.
◇ *vt sep* [bring in] faire entrer ▪ [barrel, car] faire entrer en roulant.

◆ **roll off** ◇ *vi insep* [fall] tomber en roulant ▪ [on floor] rouler par terre.
◇ *vt sep* [print] imprimer.
◇ *vt insep* TYPO : **to ~ off the presses** sortir des presses.

◆ **roll on** ◇ *vi insep* **1.** [ball] continuer à rouler
2. [time] s'écouler
3. *phr UK* **~ on Christmas!** vivement (qu'on soit à) Noël!
◇ *vt sep* **1.** [paint] appliquer au rouleau ▪ [deodorant] appliquer
2. [stockings] enfiler.

◆ **roll out** ◇ *vi insep* sortir ▪ **to ~ out of bed** [person] sortir du lit.
◇ *vt sep* **1.** [ball] rouler (dehors) ▪ [car] rouler OR pousser dehors ▪ [map] dérouler ▪ [pastry] étendre (au rouleau)
2. [produce - goods, speech] débiter.

◆ **roll over** ◇ *vi insep* [person, animal] se retourner ▪ [car] faire un tonneau ▪ **to ~ over and over** [in bed] se retourner plusieurs fois ; [car] faire une série de tonneaux.
◇ *vt sep* retourner.
◇ *vt insep* rouler sur ▪ [subj: car] écraser.

◆ **roll past** ◇ *vt insep* passer devant.
◇ *vi insep* passer.

◆ **roll up** ◇ *vt sep* [map, carpet] rouler ▪ [sleeves] retrousser ▪ [trousers] remonter, retrousser ▪ US [window] remonter ▪ **to ~ sthg up in a blanket** enrouler OR envelopper qqch dans une couverture.
◇ *vi insep* **1.** [carpet] se rouler ▪ **the map keeps ~ing up on its own** impossible de faire tenir cette carte à plat ▪ **to ~ up into a ball** se rouler en boule
2. *inf* [arrive] se pointer, s'amener.
◇ *interj* : **~ up! ~ up!** approchez!

roll bar *n* arceau *m* de sécurité.

roll call *n* appel *m* ▪ **to take (the) ~** faire l'appel.

roll collar *n* col *m* roulé.

rolled [rəʊld] *adj* **1.** [paper] en rouleau ▪ [carpet] roulé **2.** [iron, steel] laminé **3.** [tobacco] en carotte ▪ **~ oats** flocons *mpl* d'avoine.

rolled gold *n* plaqué *m* or.

rolled-up *adj* roulé, enroulé.

roller ['rəʊlər] *n* **1.** [cylinder - for paint, pastry, garden, hair] rouleau *m* ; [- for blind] enrouleur *m* ; [- of typewriter] rouleau *m*, cylindre *m* ▪ TEX calandre *f* ▪ METALL laminoir *m* ▪ **she had her hair in ~s** elle s'était mis des bigoudis **2.** [wheel - for marking, furniture] roulette *f* ; [- in machine] galet *m* **3.** [of sea] rouleau *m*.

roller bearing *n* roulement *m* à rouleaux.

roller blind *n* store *m* à enrouleur.

rollerblade ['rəʊləbleɪd] *vi* SPORT faire du roller ▪ **to go rollerblading** faire du roller.

Rollerblades® *npl* patins *mpl* en ligne.

rollerblading ['rəʊləbleɪdɪŋ] *n (U)* SPORT roller *m*.

roller coaster *n* montagnes *fpl* russes, grand huit *m*.

roller derby *n* course *f* en patins à roulettes.

roller disco *n discothèque où l'on porte des patins à roulettes.*

roller skate *n* patin *m* à roulettes.
◆ **roller-skate** *vi* faire du patin à roulettes.

roller-skating *n* patinage *m* à roulettes.

roller towel *n* essuie-mains *m (monté sur un rouleau)*.

rollicking ['rɒlɪkɪŋ] *inf* ◇ *adj* [joyful] joyeux ▪ [noisy] bruyant ▪ **we had a ~ (good) time** on s'est amusés comme des fous.
◇ *n UK* **to get a ~** se faire enguirlander.

rolling ['rəʊlɪŋ] ◇ *adj* **1.** [object] roulant, qui roule **2.** [countryside, hills] ondulant ▪ **to have a ~ gait** rouler les hanches **3.** [sea] houleux ▪ [boat] qui a du roulis **4.** [fog] enveloppant ▪ [thunder] grondant **5.** [mobile - target] mobile, mouvant **6.** [strikes] tournant.
◇ *n* **1.** [of ball, marble] roulement *m* ▪ [of dice] lancement *m* **2.** [of boat] roulis *m* **3.** [of drum] roulement *m* ▪ [of thunder] grondement *m* **4.** [of shoulders] roulement *m* **5.** METALL laminage *m*.
◇ *adv UK inf* **to be ~ drunk** être complètement soûl.

rolling mill *n* [factory] usine *f* de laminage ▪ [equipment] laminoir *m*.

rolling pin *n* rouleau *m* à pâtisserie.

rolling stock *n* matériel *m* roulant.

rolling stone *n* [person] vadrouilleur *m*, - euse *f* ▪ **to be a ~** rouler sa bosse, avoir une âme de vagabond ▪ **a ~ gathers no moss** *prov* pierre qui roule n'amasse pas mousse *prov*.

rollmop ['rəʊlmɒp] *n* rollmops *m*.

roll neck *n* col *m* roulé.
◆ **roll-neck** = **roll-necked**.

roll-necked *adj* à col roulé.

roll-on ◇ *n* **1.** [deodorant] déodorant *m* à bille **2.** [corset] gaine *f*, corset *m*.
◇ *adj* : **~ deodorant** déodorant *m* à bille.

roll-on/roll-off ◇ *n* [ship] (navire *m*) transbordeur *m*, ferry-boat *m* ▪ [system] roll on-roll off *m inv*, manutention *f* par roulage.
◇ *adj* [ferry] transbordeur, ro-ro *(inv)*.

rollover ['rəʊləʊvər] ◇ *n* FIN rééchelonnement *m* ▪ UK [in national lottery] remise *f* en jeu des prix.
◇ *adj* FIN renouvelable ▪ UK [in national lottery] : **it's a ~ week** cette semaine il y a remise en jeu des prix.

rolltop ['rəʊltɒp] *n* : **~ (desk)** bureau *m* à cylindre.

roll-up ◇ *adj* [map] qui s'enroule.
◇ *n inf UK inf* cigarette *f* roulée.

roly-poly [ˌrəʊlɪ'pəʊlɪ] (*pl* **roly-polies**) <> *adj inf* grassouillet, rondelet.
<> *n* **1.** *inf* [plump person] : **she's a real ~** elle est vraiment grassouillette **2.** CULIN : **~ (pudding)** gâteau *m* roulé à la confiture.

ROM [rɒm] (*abbrev of* **read only memory**) *n* ROM *f*.

roman ['rəʊmən] TYPO <> *n* romain *m*.
<> *adj* romain.

Roman ['rəʊmən] <> *n* Romain *m*, - e *f* ▪ **the Epistle of Paul to the ~s** l'Épître de saint Paul aux Romains.
<> *adj* **1.** [gen - RELIG] romain ▪ **~ Britain** *période de domination romaine en Grande-Bretagne allant du Ier siècle av. J.C. au IVer siècle ap. J.C.* **2.** [nose] aquilin.

Roman alphabet *n* alphabet *m* romain.

Roman calendar *n* calendrier *m* romain.

Roman candle *n* chandelle *f* romaine.

Roman Catholic <> *adj* catholique.
<> *n* catholique *mf*.

romance [rəʊ'mæns] <> *n* **1.** [love affair] liaison *f* (amoureuse) ▪ **to have a ~ with sb** [affair] avoir une liaison avec qqn ; [idyll] vivre un roman d'amour avec qqn ▪ **a holiday ~** un amour de vacances **2.** [love] amour *m* (romantique) **3.** [romantic novel] roman *m* d'amour, roman *m* à l'eau de rose *pej* ▪ [film] film *m* romantique, film *m* à l'eau de rose *pej* ▪ **historical ~** *roman d'amour situé à une époque ancienne* **4.** [attraction, charm] charme *m*, poésie *f* ▪ [excitement] attrait *m* **5.** [fantasy] fantaisie *f* ▪ [invention] invention *f* **6.** LIT roman *m* **7.** MUS romance *f*.
<> *comp* : **~ writer** romancier *m*, - ère *f*, auteur *m* d'histoires romanesques.
<> *vi* laisser vagabonder son imagination, fabuler.
◆ **Romance** <> *n* LING roman *m*.
<> *adj* : **the Romance languages** les langues *fpl* romanes.

Roman Empire *n* : **the ~** l'Empire *m* romain.

Romanesque [ˌrəʊmə'nesk] <> *adj* ARCHIT roman.
<> *n* ARCHIT roman *m*.

Romania [ru:'meɪnjə] *pr n* Roumanie *f* ▪ **in ~** en Roumanie.

Romanian [ru:'meɪnjən] <> *n* **1.** [person] Roumain *m* Roumain, e *f* **2.** LING roumain *m*.
<> *adj* roumain.

Romanic [rəʊ'mænɪk] <> *adj* romain, des Romains.
<> *n* LING roman *m*.

Roman law *n* droit *m* romain.

Roman numeral *n* chiffre *m* romain.

Romans(c)h [rəʊ'mænʃ] <> *n* romanche *m*.
<> *adj* romanche.

romantic [rəʊ'mæntɪk] <> *adj* **1.** romantique ▪ **~ love** l'amour romantique ▪ **they had a ~ attachment** ils ont eu une liaison amoureuse **2.** [unrealistic] romanesque.
<> *n* romantique *mf* ▪ **he's an incurable ~** c'est un éternel romantique.
◆ **Romantic** *adj* ART, LIT & MUS romantique.

romantically [rəʊ'mæntɪklɪ] *adv* de manière romantique, romantiquement *lit* ▪ **we're ~ involved** nous avons une liaison amoureuse.

romanticism [rəʊ'mæntɪsɪzm] *n* romantisme *m*.
◆ **Romanticism** *n* ART, LIT & MUS romantisme *m*.

romanticize, ise [rəʊ'mæntɪsaɪz] *vt* [idea, event] idéaliser ▪ **they have a ~d view of life in Britain** ils ont une vision très romantique de la vie en Grande-Bretagne.

Romany ['rəʊmənɪ] (*pl* **Romanies**) <> *n* **1.** [person] Bohémien *m*, - enne *f*, Rom *mf* **2.** LING rom *m*.
<> *adj* bohémien, rom.

Rome [rəʊm] *pr n* Rome ▪ **when in ~, do as the Romans do** *prov* quand tu seras à Rome, fais comme les Romains *prov* ▪ **~ wasn't built in a day** Rome ne s'est pas faite *OR* Paris ne s'est pas fait en un jour ▪ **all roads lead to ~** tous les chemins mènent à Rome.

Romeo ['rəʊmɪəʊ] <> *pr n* Roméo ▪ **'~ and Juliet'** *Shakespeare, Berlioz* 'Roméo et Juliette'.
<> *n* : **he's a real ~** *fig* c'est un vrai Roméo.

Romish ['rəʊmɪʃ] *adj pej* papiste.

romp [rɒmp] <> *vi* s'ébattre (bruyamment) ▪ **the favourite ~ed home ten lengths ahead** le favori est arrivé avec dix bonnes longueurs d'avance.
<> *n* **1.** [frolic] ébats *mpl*, gambades *fpl* **2.** [film, play] farce *f*, comédie *f* **3.** *UK inf* [easy win] : **it was a ~** c'était du gâteau.
◆ **romp through** *vt insep* : **she ~ed through the test** elle a réussi le test haut la main.

rompers ['rɒmpəz], **romper suit** *(n) npl* barboteuse *f*.

rood [ru:d] <> *n* **1.** [cross] crucifix *m*, croix *f (qui surplombe le jubé)* **2.** *UK* [square measure] ≃ 1000m².
<> *comp* [arch, beam] du jubé.

rood screen *n* jubé *m*.

roof [ru:f] (*pl* **roofs** *OR pl* **rooves** [ru:vz]) <> *n* **1.** [of building] toit *m* ▪ [of cave, tunnel] plafond *m* ▪ [of branches, trees] voûte *f* ▪ [of car] toit *m*, pavillon *m* ▪ **to live under the same ~** vivre sous le même toit ▪ **to be without a ~ over one's head** être à la rue ➊ **to go through** *OR* **to hit the ~** *inf* [person] piquer une crise, sortir de ses gonds ; [prices] flamber ▪ **to raise the ~** [make noise] faire le diable à quatre ; [cause fuss] protester à grands cris **2.** [roof covering] toiture *f* **3.** ANAT : **~ of the mouth** voûte *f* du palais.
<> *vt* couvrir d'un toit.

-roofed [ru:ft] *in cpds* : **flat~ warehouses** des entrepôts à toits plats *OR* en terrasse.

roof garden *n* jardin *m* sur le toit.

roofing ['ru:fɪŋ] *n* toiture *f*, couverture *f*.

roofing felt *n* carton *m* bitumé *OR* goudronné.

roofless ['ru:flɪs] *adj* sans toit, à ciel ouvert.

roof light *n* AUT plafonnier *m* ▪ [window] lucarne *f*.

roof rack *n* AUT galerie *f*.

rooftop ['ru:ftɒp] *n* toit *m* ▪ **to shout** *OR* **to proclaim sthg from the ~s** *fig* crier qqch sur les toits.

rook [rʊk] <> *n* **1.** [bird] freux *m*, corbeau *m* **2.** [in chess] tour *f*.
<> *vt inf* rouler, escroquer.

rookery ['rʊkərɪ] (*pl* **rookeries**) *n* [of rooks] colonie *f* de freux ▪ **a ~ of seals/penguins** une colonie de phoques/manchots.

rookie ['rʊkɪ] *n US inf* [recruit] bleu *m* ▪ [inexperienced person] novice *mf*.

room [ru:m, rʊm] <> *n* **1.** [in building, public place] salle *f* ▪ [in house] pièce *f* ▪ [in hotel] chambre *f* ▪ **'~ to let** *OR* **to rent'** 'chambre à louer' ▪ **his ~s are in Bayswater** il habite à Bayswater ➊ **~ and board** chambre avec pension ▪ **'A Room with a View'** *Forster* 'Avec vue sur l'Arno' ▪ *Ivory* 'Chambre avec vue' **2.** [space, place] place *f* ▪ **is there enough ~ for everybody?** y a-t-il assez de place pour tout le monde? ▪ **it takes up too much ~** ça prend trop de place ▪ **to make ~ for sb** faire une place *OR* de la place pour qqn ; *fig* laisser la place à qqn ▪ **~ to** *OR* **for manoeuvre** *liter* place pour manœuvrer ; *fig* marge de manœuvre ▪ **there's ~ for improvement** [make better] il y a des progrès à faire ; [below standard] ça laisse à désirer ▪ **there's still ~ for discussion/hope** on peut encore discuter/espérer ▪ **there's no ~ for doubt** il n'y a plus aucun doute possible **3.** [people in room] salle *f*.
<> *vi US* loger ▪ **to ~ with sb** [share flat] partager un appartement avec qqn ; [in hotel] partager une chambre avec qqn.

-roomed [ru:md] *in cpds* : **a five~ flat** un appartement de cinq pièces, un cinq-pièces.

roomer ['ru:mər] *n US* pensionnaire *mf*.

roomful ['ru:mfʊl] *n* pleine salle *f OR* pièce *f* ▪ **a ~ of furniture** une pièce pleine de meubles.

rooming house ['ru:mɪŋ-] *n US* immeuble *m (avec chambres à louer)*.

roommate ['ru:mmeɪt] *n* [in boarding school, college] camarade *mf* de chambre ▪ *US* [in flat] *personne avec qui l'on partage un logement.*

room service *n* service *m* dans les chambres *(dans un hôtel).*

room temperature *n* température *f* ambiante ▪ **this plant must be kept at ~** cette plante doit être placée dans une pièce chauffée ▪ **'to be served at ~'** [wine] 'servir chambré'.

roomy ['ru:mɪ] (*comp* **roomier**, *superl* **roomiest**) *adj* [house, office] spacieux ▪ [suitcase, bag] grand ▪ [coat] ample.

roost [ru:st] ◇ *n* perchoir *m*, juchoir *m*.
◇ *vi* [bird] se percher, (se) jucher ▪ **his misdeeds came home to ~** ses méfaits se sont retournés contre lui.

rooster ['ru:stəʳ] *n US* coq *m*.

root [ru:t] ◇ *n* **1.** BOT & *fig* racine *f* ▪ **to pull up a plant by its ~s** déraciner une plante ▪ **to take ~** BOT & *fig* prendre racine ▪ **to put down ~s** BOT & *fig* prendre racine, s'enraciner **2.** ANAT [of tooth, hair etc] racine *f* **3.** [source] source *f* ▪ [cause] cause *f* ▪ [bottom] fond *m* ▪ **the ~ of all evil** la source de tout mal ▪ **to get at** *OR* **to the ~ of the problem** aller au fond du problème ▪ **poor housing is at the ~ of much delinquency** la mauvaise qualité des logements est souvent à l'origine de la délinquance **4.** LING [in etymology] racine *f* ▪ [baseform] radical *m*, base *f* **5.** MATHS racine *f* **6.** MUS fondamentale *f*.
◇ *comp* [cause, problem] fondamental, de base.
◇ *vt* enraciner ▪ **he stood ~ed to the spot** *fig* il est resté cloué sur place.
◇ *vi* **1.** [plant] s'enraciner, prendre racine **2.** [pigs] fouiller *(avec le groin).*
◆ **roots** *npl* [of person - origin] racines *fpl*, origines *fpl* ▪ **their actual ~s are in Virginia** en fait, ils sont originaires de Virginie.
◆ **root about** *UK*, **root around** *vi insep* [animal] fouiller *(avec le museau)* ▪ [person] fouiller ▪ **to ~ about for sthg** fouiller pour trouver qqch.
◆ **root for** *vt insep* [team] encourager, soutenir.
◆ **root out** *vt sep* **1.** [from earth] déterrer ▪ [from hiding place] dénicher **2.** [suppress] supprimer, extirper.
◆ **root up** *vt sep* [plant] déraciner ▪ [subj: pigs] déterrer.

root-and-branch *adj* [reform] complet, - ète *f*.
◆ **root and branch** *adv* : **corruption must be eliminated root and branch** il faut éradiquer la corruption.

root beer *n boisson gazeuse à base d'extraits végétaux.*

root canal *n* canal *m* dentaire ▪ **~ treatment** traitement *m* canalaire.

root crop *n* racine *f* comestible.

rooted ['ru:tɪd] *adj* [prejudice, belief, habits] enraciné ▪ **deeply ~ superstitions** des superstitions bien enracinées *OR* profondément ancrées.

rootless ['ru:tlɪs] *adj* sans racine *OR* racines.

rootstock ['ru:tstɒk] *n* rhizome *m*.

root vegetable *n* racine *f* comestible.

rope [rəʊp] ◇ *n* **1.** [gen] corde *f* ▪ [collectively] cordage *m* ▪ [of steel, wire] filin *m* ▪ [cable] câble *m* ▪ [for bell, curtains] cordon *m* ▪ **a piece** *OR* **length of ~** un bout de corde, une corde ➲ **to come to the end of one's ~** être au bout du rouleau ▪ **to give sb more ~** laisser à qqn une plus grande liberté d'action, lâcher la bride à qqn ▪ **give him enough ~ and he'll hang himself** si on le laisse faire, il creusera sa propre tombe **2.** [in mountaineering] cordée *f* **3.** [of pearls] collier *m* ▪ [of onions] chapelet *m*.
◇ *vt* **1.** [package] attacher avec une corde, corder ▪ **the climbers were ~d together** les alpinistes étaient encordés **2.** *US* [cattle, horses] prendre au lasso.
◆ **ropes** *npl* **1.** BOX cordes *fpl* ▪ **to be on the ~s** [boxer] être dans les cordes ; *fig* être aux abois **2.** [know-how] : **to know the ~s** connaître les ficelles *OR* son affaire ▪ **to show** *OR* **to teach sb the ~s** montrer les ficelles du métier à qqn ▪ **to learn the ~s** se mettre au courant, apprendre à se débrouiller.
◆ **rope in** *vt sep* **1.** [land] entourer de cordes, délimiter par des cordes **2.** [cattle] mettre dans un enclos **3.** *fig* **to ~ sb in to do sthg** enrôler qqn pour faire qqch ▪ **he got himself ~d in as chairman** il a été forcé d'accepter la présidence.
◆ **rope off** *vt sep* [part of hall, of church] délimiter par une corde ▪ [street, building] interdire l'accès de.
◆ **rope up** ◇ *vi insep* s'encorder.
◇ *vt sep* **1.** [parcel] attacher avec une corde, corder **2.** [climbers] encorder.

rope ladder *n* échelle *f* de corde.

rope trick *n tour de prestidigitation réalisé avec une cordelette.*

ropewalker ['rəʊpˌwɔ:kəʳ] *n* funambule *mf*.

rop(e)y ['rəʊpɪ] (*comp* **ropier**, *superl* **ropiest**) *adj UK* **1.** *inf* [mediocre] médiocre, pas fameux ▪ [ill] mal fichu **2.** [substance] visqueux.

ro-ro ['rəʊrəʊ] = **roll-on/roll-off**.

rosary ['rəʊzərɪ] (*pl* **rosaries**) *n* **1.** RELIG [beads] chapelet *m*, rosaire *m* ▪ [prayers] rosaire *m* ▪ **to tell** *OR* **to say the ~** dire son rosaire **2.** [rose garden] roseraie *f*.

rose [rəʊz] ◇ *pt* ⊳ **rise**.
◇ *n* **1.** BOT [flower] rose *f* ▪ [bush] rosier *m* ▪ **life isn't just a bed of ~s, life isn't all ~s** tout n'est pas rose dans la vie ▪ **there's no ~ without a thorn** il n'y a pas de roses sans épines, chaque médaille a son revers ▪ **to come up ~s** [enterprise] marcher comme sur des roulettes ; [person] réussir, avoir le vent en poupe ▪ **that'll put the ~s back into your cheeks** ça va te redonner des couleurs **2.** [rose shape - on hat, dress] rosette *f* ; [- on ceiling] rosace *f* **3.** [colour] rose *m* **4.** [on hosepipe, watering can] pomme *f*.
◇ *adj* rose, de couleur rose.

rosé ['rəʊzeɪ] *n* (vin *m*) rosé *m*.

roseate ['rəʊzɪət] *adj lit* rose.

rosebay ['rəʊzbeɪ] *n* laurier-rose *m*.

rosebed ['rəʊzbed] *n* parterre *m OR* massif *m* de roses.

Rose Bowl [rəʊz-] *pr n* : **the ~** *match de football universitaire organisé le Jour de l'An à Pasadena, en Californie.*

rosebud ['rəʊzbʌd] *n* bouton *m* de rose.

rosebush ['rəʊzbʊʃ] *n* rosier *m*.

rose-coloured *adj* rose, rosé ▪ **to see life through ~ spectacles** voir la vie en rose.

rose garden *n* roseraie *f*.

rose hip *n* gratte-cul *m*, cynorhodon *m spec* ▪ **~ syrup** sirop *m* d'églantine.

rosemary ['rəʊzmərɪ] (*pl* **rosemaries**) *n* romarin *m*.

rose-tinted *adj* teinté en rose.

rose tree *n* rosier *m*.

rosette [rəʊ'zet] *n* **1.** [made of ribbons] rosette *f* ▪ SPORT cocarde *f* **2.** ARCHIT rosace *f* **3.** BOT rosette *f*.

rosewater ['rəʊzˌwɔ:təʳ] *n* eau *f* de rose.

rose window *n* rosace *f*.

rosewood ['rəʊzwʊd] ◇ *n* bois *m* de rose.
◇ *comp* en bois de rose.

Rosh Hashanah *n* Ro(s)ch ha-Shana *m*.

Rosicrucian [ˌrəʊzɪ'kru:ʃn] ◇ *n* rosicrucien *m*, - enne *f*, rose-croix *m inv*.
◇ *adj* rosicrucien.

rosin ['rɒzɪn] ◇ *n* colophane *f*, arcanson *m*.
◇ *vt* traiter à la colophane, enduire de colophane.

roster ['rɒstəʳ] ◇ *n* [list] liste *f* ▪ [for duty] tableau *m* de service ▪ **by ~** à tour de rôle.
◇ *vt* inscrire au tableau de service *OR* au planning.

rösti [rɜ:ʃtɪ] *n (U)* rösti *m*.

rostrum ['rɒstrəm] (*pl* **rostrums** *OR pl* **rostra** [-trə]) *n* **1.** [platform - for speaker] estrade *f*, tribune *f* ; [- for conductor] estrade *f* ■ SPORT podium *m* ■ **to take the ~** monter sur l'estrade *OR* à la tribune **2.** HIST & NAUT rostres *mpl*.

rosy ['rəuzɪ] (*comp* **rosier**, *superl* **rosiest**) *adj* [in colour] rose, rosé ■ **to have ~ cheeks** avoir les joues roses ❙ *fig* [future, situation] brillant, qui se présente bien ■ **to paint a ~ picture of a situation** peindre une situation en rose.

rot [rɒt] (*pret & pp* **rotted**, *cont* **rotting**) ◇ *vi* **1.** [fruit, vegetable] pourrir, se gâter ■ [teeth] se carier **2.** *fig* [person] pourrir ■ **to ~ in prison** pourrir *OR* croupir en prison.
◇ *vt* [vegetable, fibres] (faire) pourrir ■ [tooth] carier, gâter.
◇ *n* **1.** [of fruit, vegetable] pourriture *f* ■ [of tooth] carie *f* **2.** *fig* [in society] pourriture *f* ■ **the ~ has set in** ça commence à se gâter ■ **to stop the ~** redresser la situation **3.** *(U)* [nonsense - spoken] bêtises *fpl*, sottises *fpl* ; [- written] bêtises *fpl* ; [- on TV] émission *f* idiote, émissions *fpl* idiotes ■ **that's utter ~!** c'est vraiment n'importe quoi!
◆ **rot away** *vi insep* tomber en pourriture.

rota ['rəutə] *n* roulement *m* ■ [for duty] tableau *m* de service, planning *m* ■ **on a ~ basis** à tour de rôle, par roulement.
◆ **Rota** *n* RELIG rote *f*.

Rotarian [rəu'teərɪən] ◇ *adj* rotarien.
◇ *n* rotarien *m*.

rotary ['rəutərɪ] (*pl* **rotaries**) ◇ *adj* rotatif.
◇ *n* US rond-point *m*.

Rotary Club *pr n* Rotary Club *m*.

rotary engine *n* moteur *m* rotatif.

rotary tiller *n* US pulvériseur *m*.

rotate ◇ *vt* [rəu'teɪt] **1.** [turn] faire tourner ■ [on pivot] faire pivoter **2.** AGRIC [crops] alterner **3.** [staff] faire un roulement de ■ [jobs] faire à tour de rôle *OR* par roulement.
◇ *vi* [rəu'teɪt] **1.** [turn] tourner ■ [on pivot] pivoter **2.** [staff] changer de poste par roulement.
◇ *adj* ['rəuteɪt] BOT rotacé.

rotating [rəu'teɪtɪŋ] *adj* **1.** *liter* tournant, rotatif **2.** AGRIC : **~ crops** cultures *fpl* alternantes *OR* en rotation.

rotation [rəu'teɪʃn] *n* **1.** [of machinery, planets] rotation *f* ■ **~s per minute** tours *mpl* par minute **2.** [of staff, jobs] roulement *m* ■ **in** *OR* **by ~** par roulement, à tour de rôle **3.** [of crops] rotation *f*.

rotavate ['rəutəveɪt] = **rotovate**.

Rotavator® ['rəutəveɪtər] = **Rotovator**.

rote [rəut] ◇ *n* routine *f* ■ **to learn sthg by ~** apprendre qqch par cœur.
◇ *adj* : **~ learning** apprentissage *m* par cœur.

rotgut△ ['rɒtgʌt] *n (U)* [spirits] tord-boyaux *m inv* ■ [wine] piquette *f*.

rotisserie [rəu'tɪːsərɪ] *n* [spit] rôtissoire *f*.

rotogravure [ˌrəutəgrə'vjuər] *n* rotogravure *f*.

rotor ['rəutər] *n* rotor *m*.

rotor arm *n* [of helicopter] rotor *m* ■ [of engine] rotor *m*, balai *m*.

rotor blade *n* pale *f* de rotor.

rotovate ['rəutəveɪt] *vt* labourer avec un motoculteur.

Rotovator® ['rəutəveɪtər] *n* UK motoculteur *m*.

rotten ['rɒtn] *adj* **1.** [fruit, egg, wood] pourri ■ [tooth] carié, gâté
2. [corrupt] pourri, corrompu ■ **~ through and through** *OR* **to the core** complètement pourri, corrompu jusqu'à la moelle
3. *inf* [person - unfriendly] rosse, peu aimable ■ **to be ~ to sb** être dur avec qqn ■ **what a ~ thing to say!** c'est moche de dire des choses pareilles! ■ **I feel ~ about what happened** je ne suis pas très fier de ce qui est arrivé ■ **what a ~ trick!** quel sale tour!
4. *inf* [ill] mal en point ■ **I feel ~** je ne me sens pas du tout dans mon assiette
5. *inf* [bad] lamentable, nul ■ [weather] pourri ■ [performer] mauvais, nul ■ **he's a ~ goalkeeper** il est nul *OR* il ne vaut rien comme gardien de but ■ **what ~ luck!** quelle poisse! ■ **I've had a ~ time recently** j'ai traversé une sale période récemment ❙ [in indignation] fichu ■ **keep your ~ (old) sweets!** tes bonbons pourris, tu peux te les garder!

rottenly ['rɒtnlɪ] *adv* abominablement ■ **to behave ~ to sb** se conduire d'une manière inqualifiable avec qqn.

rotter ['rɒtər] *n* UK *inf dated* crapule *f*.

rottweiler ['rɒtvaɪlər] *n* rottweiler *m*.

rotting ['rɒtɪŋ] *adj* qui pourrit, pourri.

rotund [rəu'tʌnd] *adj* **1.** [shape] rond, arrondi ■ [person] rondelet **2.** [style, speech] grandiloquent.

rotunda [rəu'tʌndə] *n* rotonde *f*.

rouble ['ruːbl] *n* rouble *m*.

rouge [ruːʒ] ◇ *n* rouge *m* (à joues).
◇ *vt* : **she had ~d cheeks** elle s'était mis du rouge aux joues.

rough [rʌf] ◇ *adj* **1.** [uneven - surface, skin] rugueux, rêche ; [- road] accidenté, rocailleux ; [- coast] accidenté ; [- cloth] rêche ; [- edge] rugueux ■ **~ linen** gros lin *m* ■ **~ ground** [bumpy] terrain *m* rocailleux *OR* raboteux ; [waste] terrain *m* vague
2. [violent, coarse - behaviour] brutal ; [- manners] rude, fruste ; [- neighbourhood] dur, mal fréquenté ■ **they came in for some ~ treatment** ils ont été malmenés ■ **they're ~ kids** ce sont des petites brutes *OR* des petits voyous ■ **he's a ~ customer** c'est un dur ■ **~ play** SPORT jeu *m* brutal ■ **they were ~ with** *OR* **on the new recruits** ils n'ont pas été tendres avec les nouvelles recrues ▶ **to give sb the ~ edge of one's tongue** réprimander qqn, ne pas ménager ses reproches à qqn
3. [unpleasant, harsh] rude, dur ■ **she's had a ~ time of it** elle en a vu des dures *OR* de toutes les couleurs ■ **they gave him a ~ time** *OR* **ride** ils lui ont mené la vie dure ■ **we got a ~ deal** on n'a pas eu de veine ■ **to make things ~ for sb** mener la vie dure à qqn ■ **~ justice** justice *f* sommaire
4. [not finalized] : **~ draft** *OR* **work** brouillon *m* ■ **~ sketch** croquis *m*, ébauche *f* ■ **just give me a ~ sketch** *OR* **outline of your plans** donnez-moi juste un aperçu de vos projets ■ **~ paper** papier *m* brouillon ❙ [approximate] approximatif ■ **at a ~ guess** grosso modo, approximativement ■ **I only need a ~ estimate** je n'ai pas besoin d'une réponse précise ■ **to have a ~ idea of sthg** avoir une idée approximative de qqch ❙ [crude - equipment] grossier, rudimentaire
5. [sea] agité, houleux ■ [climate] rude ■ **we had a ~ crossing** on a eu une traversée agitée ■ **~ weather** gros temps *m* ■ **~ passage** *liter* traversée *f* difficile ■ **the bill had a ~ passage through the House** *fig* le projet de loi a eu des difficultés à passer à la Chambre
6. [sound, voice] rauque ■ [tone] brusque ■ [speech, accent] rude, grossier
7. [taste] âcre ■ **~ wine** vin *m* râpeux
8. [ill] mal en point ■ **I'm feeling a bit ~** je ne suis pas dans mon assiette.
◇ *n* **1.** [ground] terrain *m* rocailleux ■ GOLF rough *m* ■ **to take the ~ with the smooth** prendre les choses comme elles viennent
2. [draft] brouillon *m* ■ **in ~** à l'état de brouillon *OR* d'ébauche
3. *inf* [hoodlum] dur *m*, voyou *m*.
◇ *adv* [play] brutalement ■ [speak] avec rudesse ■ **to live ~** vivre à la dure ■ **to sleep ~** UK coucher à la dure *OR* dans la rue.
◇ *vt phr* **to ~ it** *inf* vivre à la dure.
◆ **rough out** *vt sep* UK [drawing, plan] ébaucher, esquisser.
◆ **rough up** *vt sep* **1.** [hair] ébouriffer ■ [clothes] mettre en désordre
2. *inf* [person] tabasser, passer à tabac.

roughage ['rʌfɪdʒ] *n (U)* fibres *fpl* (alimentaires).

rough-and-ready *adj* **1.** [makeshift - equipment, apparatus] rudimentaire, de fortune ■ [careless - work] grossier, fait à la hâte ; [- methods] grossier, expéditif **2.** [unrefined - person] sans façons, rustre ; [- living conditions] dur.

rough-and-tumble ◇ *adj* [life - hectic] mouvementé ; [- disorderly] désordonné.

<> *n* [fight] bagarre *f* ■ [hurly-burly] tohu-bohu *m inv* ■ **I enjoyed the ~ of circus life** la vie mouvementée du cirque me plaisait.

roughcast ['rʌfkɑ:st] <> *adj* crépi.
<> *n* crépi *m*.
<> *vt* crépir.

rough diamond *n liter* diamant *m* brut ■ **he's a ~** *UK fig* il est bourru mais il a un cœur d'or.

rough-dry (*pret & pp* **rough-dried**) <> *vt* sécher sans repasser *OR* repassage.
<> *adj* séché sans repassage.

roughen ['rʌfn] <> *vt* [surface] rendre rugueux ■ [hands] rendre rugueux *OR* rêche.
<> *vi* devenir rugueux.

rough-hewn *adj* taillé grossièrement ■ **his ~ features** *fig* son visage taillé à coups de serpe.

roughhouse ['rʌfhaʊs] *inf* <> *n* bagarre *f*.
<> *vt* bousculer.
<> *vi* [children] faire du chahut.

roughly ['rʌflɪ] *adv* **1.** [brutally] avec brutalité, brutalement **2.** [sketchily - draw] grossièrement ■ [crudely - make] grossièrement, sans soin **3.** [approximately] approximativement, à peu près ■ **~ 500** à peu près *OR* environ 500 ■ **~ speaking** en gros, approximativement ■ **she told me ~ how to get there** elle m'a expliqué en gros comment y aller.

roughneck ['rʌfnek] *n* **1.** *inf* [thug] voyou *m*, dur *m* **2.** [oil-rig worker] *ouvrier travaillant sur une plate-forme pétrolière*.

roughness ['rʌfnɪs] *n* **1.** [of surface, hands] rugosité *f* ■ [of road, ground] inégalités *fpl* **2.** [of manner] rudesse *f* ■ [of reply, speech] brusquerie *f* ■ [of person] rudesse *f*, brutalité *f* ■ [of living conditions] rudesse *f*, dureté *f* **3.** [of sea] agitation *f*.

roughrider ['rʌf,raɪdər] *n* dresseur *m*, - euse *f* de chevaux.

roughshod ['rʌfʃɒd] <> *adj UK* [horse] ferré à glace.
<> *adv phr* **to ride** *OR* **run ~ over** faire peu de cas de.

rough sleeper *n* [homeless person] SDF *mf*.

rough-spoken *adj* [vulgar] au langage grossier.

roulette [ru:'let] *n* roulette *f*.

Roumania *etc* [ru:'meɪnjə] = **Romania**.

round [raʊnd] <> *adj* **1.** [circular] rond, circulaire ■ [spherical] rond, sphérique ■ **she looked up, her eyes ~ with surprise** elle leva des yeux écarquillés de surprise
2. [in circumference] : **the tree is 5 metres ~** l'arbre fait 5 mètres de circonférence
3. [curved - belly, cheeks] rond ■ **to have ~ shoulders** avoir le dos rond *OR* voûté ▶ **~ arch** arc *m* en plein cintre
4. [figures] rond ■ **500, in ~ numbers** 500 tout rond ■ **a ~ dozen** une douzaine tout rond
5. *lit* [candid] net, franc, franche *f*
6. LING [vowel] arrondi.
<> *prep* **1.** [on all sides of] autour de ■ **to sit ~ the fire/table** s'asseoir autour du feu/de la table ■ **the story centres ~ one particular family** l'histoire est surtout centrée autour d'une famille
2. [measuring the circumference of] : **the pillar is three feet ~ the base** la base du pilier fait trois pieds de circonférence
3. [in the vicinity of, near] autour de ■ **they live somewhere ~ here** ils habitent quelque part par ici
4. [to the other side of] : **the nearest garage is just ~ the corner** le garage le plus proche est juste au coin de la rue ■ **she disappeared ~ the back of the house** elle a disparu derrière la maison ■ **the orchard is ~ the back** le verger est derrière ■ **to go ~ the corner** passer le coin, tourner au coin ■ **there must be a way ~ the problem** *fig* il doit y avoir un moyen de contourner ce problème
5. [so as to cover] : **he put a blanket ~ her legs** il lui enveloppa les jambes d'une couverture
6. [so as to encircle] autour de ■ **he put his arm ~ her shoulders/waist** il a passé son bras autour de ses épaules/de sa taille ■ **the shark swam ~ the boat** le requin faisait des cercles autour du bateau ■ **Drake sailed ~ the world** Drake a fait le tour du monde en bateau
7. [all over, everywhere in] : **all ~ the world** dans le monde entier, partout dans le monde ■ **she looked ~ the room** elle a promené son regard autour de la pièce ■ **to walk ~ the town** faire le tour de la ville (à pied) ■ **we went for a stroll ~ the garden** nous avons fait une balade dans le jardin ■ **there's a rumour going ~ the school** une rumeur circule dans l'école
8. [approximately] environ, aux environs de ■ **~ 6 o'clock** aux environs de *OR* vers les 6 h ■ **~ Christmas** aux environs de Noël.
<> *adv* **1.** [on all sides] autour ■ **there are trees all the way ~** il y a des arbres tout autour ▶ **taking things all ~** à tout prendre, tout compte fait
2. [to other side] : **you'll have to go ~, the door's locked** il faudra faire le tour, la porte est fermée à clé ■ **we drove ~ to the back** nous avons fait le tour (par derrière)
3. [in a circle or cycle] : **turn the wheel right ~** *OR* **all the way ~** faites faire un tour complet à la roue ■ **the shark swam ~ in circles** le requin tournait en rond ■ **all year ~** tout au long de *OR* toute l'année ■ **summer will soon be** *OR* **come ~ again** l'été reviendra vite
4. [in the opposite direction] : **turn ~ and look at me** retournez-vous et regardez-moi ■ **she looked ~ at us** elle se retourna pour nous regarder ■ **we'll have to turn the car ~** on va devoir faire demi-tour
5. [to various parts] : **we spent the summer just travelling ~** on a passé l'été à voyager ■ **can I have a look ~?** je peux jeter un coup d'œil?
6. [from one person to another] : **hand the sweets ~, hand ~ the sweets** faites passer les bonbons ■ **there wasn't enough to go ~** il n'y en avait pas assez pour tout le monde
7. [to a particular place] : **she came ~ to see me** elle est passée me voir ■ **let's invite some friends ~** et si on invitait des amis? ■ **come ~ for supper some time** viens dîner un soir ■ **take these cakes ~ to her house** apportez-lui ces gâteaux
8. [to a different place, position] : **she's always moving the furniture ~** elle passe son temps à changer les meubles de place
9. [by indirect route] : **we had to take the long way ~** on a dû faire le grand tour *OR* un grand détour ■ **she went ~ by the stream** elle fit un détour par le ruisseau.
<> *n* **1.** [circle] rond *m*, cercle *m*
2. [slice - of ham, cheese, bread, toast] tranche *f* ■ [sandwich] sandwich *m*
3. [one in a series - of discussions, negotiations] série *f* ; [- of elections] tour *m* ; [- of increases] série *f*, train *m* ■ **the next ~ of talks will be held in Moscow** les prochains pourparlers auront lieu à Moscou ■ **his life is one long ~ of parties** il passe sa vie à faire la fête
4. [delivery] ronde *f* ■ **a paper/milk ~** une distribution de journaux/de lait ■ **to do** *OR* **make the ~s** circuler ■ **she's doing** *OR* **making the ~s of literary agents** elle fait le tour des agents littéraires ■ **to go on one's ~s** [paperboy, milkman] faire sa tournée ; [doctor] faire ses visites ▶ **to go the ~s** circuler ■ **there's a joke/rumour/virus going the ~s in the office** il y a une blague/une rumeur/un virus qui circule au bureau
5. [routine] : **the daily ~** le train-train quotidien, la routine quotidienne
6. [in golf] partie *f*
7. [in boxing, wrestling] round *m*, reprise *f*
8. [in cards] partie *f*
9. [in showjumping] : **there were six clear ~s** six chevaux avaient fait un sans-faute
10. [stage of competition] tour *m*, manche *f* ■ **she's through to the final ~** elle participera à la finale
11. [of drinks] tournée *f* ■ **it's my ~** c'est ma tournée ■ **let's have another ~** prenons encore un verre
12. [of cheering] salve *f* ■ **a ~ of applause** des applaudissements *mpl* ■ **they got a ~ of applause** ils se sont fait applaudir
13. [of ammunition] cartouche *f*
14. [song] canon *m*
15. THEAT : **theatre in the ~** théâtre *m* en rond.
<> *vt* **1.** [lips, vowel] arrondir
2. [corner] tourner ■ NAUT [cape] doubler, franchir.

◆ **round about** <> *prep phr* environ ■ **~ about midnight** vers minuit.
<> *adv phr* alentour, des alentours.

◆ **round and round** ◇ *adv phr* : **to go ~ and ~** tourner ▪ **we drove ~ and ~ for hours** on a tourné en rond pendant des heures ▪ **my head was spinning ~ and ~** j'avais la tête qui tournait.
◇ *prep phr* : **we drove ~ and ~ the field** on a fait plusieurs tours dans le champ ▪ **the helicopter flew ~ and ~ the lighthouse** l'hélicoptère a tourné plusieurs fois autour du phare.
◆ **round down** *vt sep* arrondir au chiffre inférieur ▪ **their prices were ~ed down to the nearest £10** ils ont arrondi leurs prix aux 10 livres inférieures.
◆ **round off** *vt sep* **1.** [finish, complete] terminer, clore ▪ **he ~ed off his meal with a glass of brandy** il a terminé son repas par un verre de cognac
2. [figures - round down] arrondir au chiffre inférieur ; [- round up] arrondir au chiffre supérieur.
◆ **round on** *vt insep* attaquer, s'en prendre à.
◆ **round up** *vt sep* **1.** [cattle, people] rassembler ▪ [criminals] ramasser
2. [figures] arrondir au chiffre supérieur.

roundabout ['raʊndəbaʊt] ◇ *n* UK **1.** [at fair] manège *m* **2.** AUT rond-point *m*.
◇ *adj* détourné, indirect ▪ **to take a ~ route** prendre un chemin détourné ▪ **he has a ~ way of doing things** il a une façon détournée de faire les choses.

rounded ['raʊndɪd] *adj* **1.** [shape] arrondi ▪ [cheeks] rond, rebondi ▪ [vowel] arrondi **2.** [number] arrondi **3.** [style] harmonieux.

roundel ['raʊndl] *n* **1.** LIT rondeau *m* **2.** AERON cocarde *f* **3.** [window] œil-de-bœuf *m* ▪ [panel, medal] médaillon *m*.

rounders ['raʊndəz] *n (U)* UK *sport proche du base-ball.*

round-eyed *adj* **liter** aux yeux ronds ▪ *fig* [surprised] avec des yeux ronds.

round-faced *adj* au visage rond.

Roundhead ['raʊndhed] *n* HIST : **the ~s** les têtes rondes *(partisans du Parlement pendant la guerre civile anglaise, de 1642 à 1646).*

rounding ['raʊndɪŋ] *n* COMPUT & MATHS arrondi *m*, arrondissage *m*.

roundly ['raʊndlɪ] *adv* *fig* [severely] vivement, sévèrement ▪ UK [plainly] carrément.

round robin *n* **1.** [letter] pétition *f (où les signatures sont disposées en rond)* **2.** US [contest] poule *f*.

round-shouldered [-'ʃəʊldəd] *adj* : **to be ~** avoir le dos rond, être voûté.

roundsman ['raʊndzmən] (*pl* **roundsmen** [-mən]) *n* UK livreur *m*.

round table *n* table *f* ronde.
◆ **round-table** *adj* : **round-table discussions** OR **negotiations** table *f* ronde.
◆ **Round Table** *pr n* : **the Round Table** la Table ronde.

round-the-clock *adj* 24 heures sur 24 ▪ **a ~ vigil** une permanence nuit et jour.
◆ **round the clock** *adv* 24 heures sur 24 ▪ **we worked round the clock** nous avons travaillé 24 heures d'affilée ▪ **he slept round the clock** il a fait le tour du cadran.

round trip *n* (voyage *m*) aller et retour *m*.

round-trip ticket *n* US (billet *m*) aller-retour *m*.

roundup ['raʊndʌp] *n* **1.** [of cattle, people] rassemblement *m* ▪ [of criminals] rafle *f* **2.** [of news] résumé *m* de l'actualité.

roundworm ['raʊndwɜ:m] *n* ascaride *m*.

rouse [raʊz] *vt* **1.** [wake - person] réveiller ▪ **the burglar ~d them (from their sleep)** le cambrioleur les a réveillés OR les a tirés de leur sommeil ▪ **he was ~d from his thoughts by the doorbell** la sonnette l'a arraché à ses pensées ▪ **she did everything to ~ him from his apathy** elle a tout fait pour le faire sortir de son apathie **2.** [provoke - interest, passion] éveiller, exciter ; [- hope] éveiller ; [- suspicion] éveiller, susciter ; [- admiration, anger, indignation] susciter, provoquer ▪ **to ~ sb to action** pousser OR inciter qqn à agir ▪ **to ~ sb to anger, to ~ sb's anger** susciter la colère de qqn, mettre qqn en colère **3.** HUNT [game] lever.

rousing ['raʊzɪŋ] *adj* [speech] vibrant, passionné ▪ [march, music] entraînant ▪ [applause] enthousiaste.

roust [raʊst] *vt* : **to ~ sb (out) from bed** faire sortir qqn du lit.

rout [raʊt] ◇ *n* **1.** MIL déroute *f*, débâcle *f* ▪ **to put an enemy/army to ~** mettre un ennemi/une armée en déroute **2.** LAW attroupement *m* illégal.
◇ *vt* MIL mettre en déroute OR en fuite ▪ *fig* [team, opponent] battre à plate couture, écraser.
◇ *vi* fouiller.
◆ **rout about** *vi insep* fouiller.
◆ **rout out** *vt sep* **1.** [find] dénicher **2.** [remove, force out] déloger, expulser.

route [UK ru:t, US raʊt] ◇ *n* **1.** [way - gen] route *f*, itinéraire *m* ▪ **the climbers took the easy ~ up the south face** les alpinistes ont emprunté l'itinéraire OR la voie la plus facile, par la face sud ▪ **a large crowd lined the ~** il y avait une foule nombreuse sur tout le parcours ▪ **the ~ to success** *fig* le chemin de la réussite ▪ **giving up one's studies is hardly the best ~ to success** *fig* le meilleur moyen de réussir ce n'est pas d'abandonner ses études ▪ **sea/air ~** voie maritime/aérienne **2.** [for buses] trajet *m*, parcours *m* ▪ **we need a map of the bus ~s** il nous faut un plan des lignes d'autobus ▪ **are they on a bus ~?** sont-ils desservis par les autobus? **3.** MED voie *f* ▪ **by oral ~** par voie orale **4.** US [for deliveries] tournée *f* ▪ **he's got a paper ~** il livre des journaux à domicile **5.** US [highway] ≃ route *f* (nationale), ≃ nationale *f*.
◇ *vt* **1.** [procession, motorist] fixer l'itinéraire de, diriger ▪ [train, bus] fixer l'itinéraire de ▪ **the police ~d the marchers via Post Street** la police a fait passer les manifestants par Post Street **2.** [luggage, parcel] expédier, acheminer.
◆ **en route** *adv phr* en route ▪ **we were en ~ for the park when it started to hail** nous nous dirigions vers le parc quand il a commencé à grêler.

route map *n* [for roads] carte *f* routière ▪ [for buses] plan *m* du réseau ▪ [for trains] carte *f* du réseau.

route march *n* marche *f* d'entraînement.

router ['ru:tə, US 'raʊtər] *n* COMPUT routeur *m*.

routine [ru:'ti:n] ◇ *n* **1.** [habit] routine *f*, habitude *f* **2.** *pej* routine *f* ▪ **daily ~** la routine quotidienne, le train-train quotidien **3.** [formality] formalité *f* ▪ **it's just ~** c'est une simple formalité **4.** [dance, play] numéro *m*, séquence *f* ▪ **they taught us some new dance ~s** ils nous ont appris de nouveaux enchaînements de danse **5.** [insincere act] : **don't give me that old ~!** arrête, je la connais celle-là ! **6.** COMPUT sous-programme *m*, routine *f*.
◇ *adj* **1.** [ordinary, regular - flight, visit] de routine ; [- investigation] de routine, d'usage **2.** [everyday] de routine **3.** [monotonous] routinier, monotone.

routinely [ru:'ti:nlɪ] *adv* systématiquement.

roux [ru:] (*pl inv* [ru:]) *n* CULIN roux *m*.

rove [rəʊv] ◇ *vi* **1.** [person] errer, vagabonder **2.** [eyes] errer.
◇ *vt* [country] parcourir, errer dans ▪ [streets] errer dans.

rover ['rəʊvər] *n* vagabond *m*, - e *f*.

roving ['rəʊvɪŋ] ◇ *adj* vagabond, nomade ▪ **~ reporter** reporter *m* ▪ **he has a ~ eye (for the girls)** *fig* il aime bien lorgner les filles.
◇ *n* vagabondage *m*.

row[1] [rəʊ] ◇ *n* **1.** [of chairs, trees] rangée *f* ▪ [of vegetables, seeds] rang *m* ▪ [of people - next to one another] rangée *f* ; [- behind one another] file *f*, queue *f* ▪ [of cars] file *f* ▪ [in knitting] rang *m* ▪ **for the third time in a ~** pour la troisième fois de suite ▪ **she put the boxes in a ~** elle aligna les boîtes ▪ **they sat/stood in a ~** ils étaient assis/debout en rang **2.** [in cinema, hall] rang *m* ▪ **in the third ~** au troisième rang **3.** RUGBY ligne *f* **4.** UK [in street names] rue *f* **5.** COMPUT ligne *f* **6.** [in boat] promenade *f* (en bateau à rames).

◇ *vi* [in boat] ramer ■ **to ~ across a lake** traverser un lac à la rame ■ SPORT faire de l'aviron.
◇ *vt* [boat] faire avancer à la rame *OR* à l'aviron ■ [passengers] transporter en canot ■ **Morgan ~ed the tourists across the lake** Morgan fit traverser le lac aux touristes dans un bateau à rames ■ **to ~ a race** faire une course d'aviron.

row² [raʊ] ◇ *n* **1.** [quarrel] dispute *f*, querelle *f* ■ **to have a ~ with sb** se disputer avec qqn ■ **to get into a ~** se faire gronder ■ **a ~ broke out as a result of the new legislation** la nouvelle loi a fait beaucoup de raffut **2.** [din] tapage *m*, vacarme *m* ■ **to make a ~** faire du tapage *OR* du vacarme ■ **stop that ~!** arrêtez ce boucan!
◇ *vi* se disputer ■ **to ~ with sb** se disputer avec qqn.

rowan ['raʊən, 'rəʊən] *n* [tree] sorbier *m* ■ [fruit] sorbe *f*.

rowboat ['rəʊbəʊt] *n US* bateau *m* à rames.

rowdiness ['raʊdɪnɪs] *n* tapage *m*, chahut *m*.

rowdy ['raʊdɪ] (*comp* **rowdier**, *superl* **rowdiest**, *pl* **rowdies**)
◇ *adj* [person] chahuteur, bagarreur ■ [behaviour] chahuteur.
◇ *n* bagarreur *m*, voyou *m* ■ [at football matches] hooligan *m*.

rower ['rəʊəʳ] *n* rameur *m*, - euse *f*.

row house [rəʊ-] *n US maison attenante aux maisons voisines.*

rowing ['rəʊɪŋ] *n* [gen] canotage *m* ■ SPORT aviron *m* ■ **to go ~** faire du canotage *OR* de l'aviron.

rowing boat *n UK* bateau *m* à rames.

rowing machine *n* rameur *m*.

rowlock ['rɒlək] *n* dame *f* de nage.

royal ['rɔɪəl] ◇ *adj* **1.** *liter* [seal, residence] royal ■ [horse, household, vehicle] royal, du roi, de la reine ■ **by ~ charter** par acte du souverain ▸ **~ assent** *signature royale qui officialise une loi* **2.** *fig & fml* [splendid] royal, princier ■ **they gave us a (right) ~ welcome** ils nous ont accueillis comme des rois **3.** [paper] (format) grand raisin.
◇ *n inf membre de la famille royale* ■ **the Royals** la famille royale.

Royal Academy (of Arts) *pr n* Académie *f* royale britannique.

Royal Air Force *pr n* armée *f* de l'air britannique.

Royal Ascot *pr n événement hippique annuel qui entre dans le calendrier mondain de la haute société anglaise.*

royal blue *n* bleu roi *m*.
◆ **royal-blue** *adj* bleu roi *(inv)*.

Royal Enclosure *n* : **the ~** *tribune de la famille royale à Royal Ascot.*

Royal Engineers *pr npl* génie *m* militaire britannique.

Royal Highness *n* : **His ~, the Prince of Wales** Son Altesse Royale, le prince de Galles.

royal icing *n UK* CULIN *glaçage à base de sucre glace et de blancs d'œufs (utilisé pour les cakes).*

Royal Institution *pr n* Académie *f* des sciences britannique.

royalist ['rɔɪəlɪst] ◇ *adj* royaliste.
◇ *n* royaliste *mf*.

royal jelly *n* gelée *f* royale.

royally ['rɔɪəlɪ] *adv liter & fig* royalement ■ [like a king] en roi ■ [like a queen] en reine.

Royal Mail *pr n* : **the ~** *la Poste britannique.*

Royal Marines *pr npl* Marines *mpl* (britanniques).

Royal Mint *pr n* : **the ~** *administration britannique de la monnaie.*

Royal Navy *pr n* marine *f* nationale britannique.

Royal Show *n* : **the ~** *le salon annuel de l'agriculture en Grande-Bretagne.*

Royal Society *pr n* Académie *f* des sciences britannique.

THE ROYAL SOCIETY

Société à vocation scientifique fondée par Charles II en 1660. Elle contribua à renforcer la crédibilité des hommes de science, qui jouirent également d'une plus grande liberté. En firent notamment partie Isaac Newton et Robert Boyle.

royalty ['rɔɪəltɪ] ◇ *n* **1.** [royal family] famille *f* royale **2.** [rank] royauté *f*.
◇ *comp* : **~ payments** [for writer] (paiement *m* des) droits *mpl* d'auteur ; [for patent] (paiement *m* des) royalties *fpl*.
◆ **royalties** *npl* [for writer, musician] droits *mpl* d'auteur ■ [for patent] royalties *fpl*, redevance *f*.

Royal Ulster Constabulary *pr n* : **the ~** *corps de police d'Irlande du Nord.*

RP (*abbrev of* **received pronunciation**) *n prononciation standard de l'anglais britannique.*

RPI (*abbrev of* **retail price index**) *n UK* indice *m* des prix à la consommation.

rpm (*written abbrev of* **revolutions per minute**) tr/min.

RR *US written abbr of* **railroad**.

RRP *written abbr of* **recommended retail price**.

RSA (*abbrev of* **Royal Society of Arts**) *pr n* société *f* royale des arts.

RSC (*abbrev of* **Royal Shakespeare Company**) *pr n célèbre troupe de théâtre basée à Stratford-on-Avon et à Londres.*

RSFSR (*abbrev of* **Russian Soviet Federal Socialist Republic**) *pr n* RSFSR *f* ■ **in the ~** en RSFSR.

RSI (*abbrev of* **repetitive strain/stress injury**) *n (U) maladie professionnelle, se traduisant par une tendinite du poignet, du coude ou des épaules et due à des gestes répétitifs.*

RSPB (*abbrev of* **Royal Society for the Protection of Birds**) *pr n ligue britannique pour la protection des oiseaux.*

RSPCA (*abbrev of* **Royal Society for the Prevention of Cruelty to Animals**) *pr n société britannique protectrice des animaux,* ≃ SPA *f*.

RSVP (*written abbrev of* **répondez s'il vous plaît**) RSVP.

Rt Hon *written abbr of* **Right Honourable**.

Rt Rev *written abbr of* **Right Reverend**.

RU (*abbrev of* **Rugby Union**) ◇ *n* SPORT rugby *m* (à quinze).
◇ *pr n* [authority] fédération *f* de rugby.

rub [rʌb] (*pret & pp* **rubbed**, *cont* **rubbing**) ◇ *vt* **1.** [gen] frotter ■ **to ~ sthg with a pad/cloth** frotter qqch avec un tampon/chiffon ■ **these shoes ~ my heels** ces chaussures me blessent aux talons ■ **to ~ one's eyes** se frotter les yeux ■ **to ~ one's hands (in delight)** se frotter les mains (de joie) ■ **we rubbed ourselves dry with a towel** nous nous sommes séchés *OR* essuyés avec une serviette ▸ **to ~ shoulders with sb** côtoyer *OR* coudoyer qqn ■ **she really rubbed his nose in it** elle a retourné le couteau dans la plaie **2.** [ointment, lotion] : **~ the ointment into the skin** faire pénétrer la pommade ■ **~ your chest with the ointment** frottez-vous la poitrine avec la pommade **3.** [polish] astiquer, frotter.
◇ *vi* frotter ■ **the cat rubbed against my leg** le chat s'est frotté contre ma jambe ■ **her leg rubbed against mine** sa jambe a effleuré la mienne ■ **my shoe is rubbing** ma chaussure me fait mal.
◇ *n* **1.** [rubbing] frottement *m* ■ [massage] friction *f*, massage *m* ■ **can you give my back a ~?** pouvez-vous me frotter le dos? ■ **give it a ~ !** [after injury] frotte! **2.** [with rag, duster] coup *m* de chiffon ■ [with brush] coup *m* de brosse ■ [with teatowel] coup *m* de torchon ■ **give the table/glasses a ~** passez un coup de chiffon sur la table/les verres **3.** SPORT [unevenness] inégalité *f* (du terrain) **4.** *UK phr* **there's the ~!** voilà le nœud du problème!, c'est là que le bât blesse!
◆ **rub along** *vi insep UK inf* **1.** [manage] se débrouiller **2.** [get on - people] s'entendre ■ **they ~ along (together)** ils s'entendent tant bien que mal.

◆ **rub away** ◇ *vt sep* **1.** [stain, writing] faire disparaître en frottant ▪ **the inscription has been rubbed away** l'inscription a été effacée **2.** [wipe - tears, sweat] essuyer ▪ **she rubbed away the sweat with a towel** elle s'épongea avec une serviette.
◇ *vi insep* disparaître en frottant.
◆ **rub down** *vt sep* **1.** [horse] bouchonner ▪ [dog] frotter *(pour sécher)* ▪ **to ~ o.s. down** se sécher **2.** [clean - wall] frotter, nettoyer en frottant ▪ [with sandpaper] frotter, poncer.
◆ **rub in** *vt sep* [lotion, oil] faire pénétrer (en frottant) ▪ **~ the butter into the mixture** CULIN travailler la pâte (du bout des doigts) pour incorporer le beurre ➊ **to ~ it in** remuer le couteau dans la plaie, insister lourdement ▪ **he is always rubbing it in that he was right all along** il ne manque jamais de rappeler qu'il avait raison depuis le début.
◆ **rub off** ◇ *vt sep* [erase - writing] effacer ; [- mark, dirt] enlever en frottant.
◇ *vi insep* **1.** [mark] s'en aller, partir ▪ **the red dye has rubbed off on my shirt/hands** la teinture rouge a déteint sur ma chemise/m'a déteint sur les mains ▪ **the newspaper ink rubbed off on the cushions** l'encre du journal a noirci les coussins **2.** *fig* [quality] déteindre ▪ **with a bit of luck, her common sense will ~ off on him** avec un peu de chance, son bon sens déteindra sur lui.
◆ **rub on** *vt sep* [spread] étaler (en frottant) ▪ [apply] appliquer (en frottant).
◆ **rub out** ◇ *vt sep* **1.** [erase - stain, writing] effacer **2.**△ *US* [kill] liquider, descendre.
◇ *vi insep* [mark, stain] partir, s'en aller (en frottant).
◆ **rub together** *vt sep* frotter l'un contre l'autre.
◆ **rub up** ◇ *vi insep* **1.** [animal] se frotter ▪ **to ~ up against sb** *fig* côtoyer qqn, coudoyer qqn **2.** *UK inf* [revise] : **to ~ up on sthg** revoir qqch, réviser qqch.
◇ *vt sep* **1.** [polish] frotter, astiquer **2.** *inf* [revise] potasser **3.** *phr* **to ~ sb up the wrong way** prendre qqn à rebrousse-poil.

rubber ['rʌbər] ◇ *adj* [ball, gloves, hose] en *OR* de caoutchouc ▪ [bullet] en caoutchouc ▪ **~ boots** *US* bottes *fpl* en caoutchouc ▪ **~ dinghy** canot *m* pneumatique ▪ **~ ring** bouée *f (de natation)*.
◇ *n* **1.** [material] caoutchouc *m* **2.** *UK* [eraser - for pencil] gomme *f* ▪ **(board) ~** tampon *m (pour essuyer le tableau)* **3.** *US inf* [condom] préservatif *m*, capote *f* **4.** [in bridge, whist] robre *m*, rob *m*.
◆ **rubbers** *npl US* [boots] caoutchoucs *mpl*, bottes *fpl* en caoutchouc.

rubber band *n* élastique *m*.

rubber cheque *n inf fig* chèque *m* sans provision, chèque *m* en bois.

rubberneck ['rʌbənek] *inf* ◇ *n* **1.** [onlooker] badaud *m*, - e *f* **2.** [tourist] touriste *mf*.
◇ *vi* faire le badaud.

rubber plant *n* caoutchouc *m*.

rubber stamp *n* tampon *m OR* timbre *m* en caoutchouc.
◆ **rubber-stamp** *vt* **1.** *liter* tamponner **2.** *fig* [decision] approuver sans discussion.

rubber tree *n* hévéa *m*.

rubbery ['rʌbərɪ] *adj* caoutchouteux.

rubbing ['rʌbɪŋ] *n* **1.** [gen] frottement *m* **2.** ART décalque *m* ▪ **to take a ~ of an inscription** décalquer une inscription *(en frottant)*.

rubbish ['rʌbɪʃ] ◇ *n (U)* **1.** [from household] ordures *fpl* (ménagères) ▪ [from garden] détritus *mpl* ▪ [from factory] déchets *mpl* ▪ [from building site] gravats *mpl* ▪ **~ van** *UK* camion *m* d'éboueurs **2.** *inf* [worthless goods] camelote *f*, pacotille *f* **3.** *inf* [nonsense] bêtises *fpl*, sottises *fpl* ▪ **~!** mon œil!, et puis quoi encore! ▪ **this film is absolute ~!** ce film est complètement nul!
◇ *vt inf* débiner.

rubbish bin *n UK* poubelle *f*.

rubbish chute *n UK* [in building] vide-ordures *m inv* ▪ [at building site] gaine *f* d'évacuation des gravats.

rubbish dump *n UK* décharge *f* (publique), dépotoir *m*.

rubbish heap *n UK* [household] tas *m* d'ordures ▪ [garden] tas *m* de détritus ▪ [public] décharge *f*, dépotoir *m*.

rubbishy ['rʌbɪʃɪ] *adj UK inf* [poor quality - goods] de pacotille ▪ [stupid - idea, book] débile, quelle émission débile!

rubble ['rʌbl] *n (U)* **1.** [ruins] décombres *mpl* ▪ [debris] débris *mpl* ▪ [stones] gravats *mpl* ▪ **the building was reduced to (a heap of) ~** l'immeuble n'était plus qu'un amas de décombres **2.** [for roadmaking, building] blocage *m*, blocaille *f*.

rubdown ['rʌbdaʊn] *n* friction *f* ▪ **to give sb a ~** frictionner qqn ▪ **to give a horse a ~** bouchonner un cheval.

rubella [ru:'belə] *n (U)* MED rubéole *f*.

Rubicon ['ru:bɪkən] *pr n* Rubicon *m* ▪ **to cross** *OR* **to pass the ~** franchir le Rubicon.

rubicund ['ru:bɪkənd] *adj* rubicond.

rubric ['ru:brɪk] *n* rubrique *f*.

ruby ['ru:bɪ] (*pl* **rubies**) ◇ *n* **1.** [jewel] rubis *m* **2.** [colour] couleur *f* (de) rubis, couleur *f* vermeille.
◇ *adj* **1.** [in colour] vermeil, rubis *(inv)* ▪ **~ (red) lips** des lèvres vermeilles ▪ **~ port** porto *m* rouge **2.** [made of rubies] de rubis **3.** [anniversary] : **~ wedding (anniversary)** noces *fpl* de vermeil.

RUC *pr n* = **Royal Ulster Constabulary**.

ruched [ru:ʃt] *adj* à ruchés.

ruck [rʌk] ◇ *n* **1.** SPORT [in rugby] mêlée *f* ouverte ▪ [in race] peloton *m* **2.** [fight] bagarre *f* **3.** [crease] faux pli *m*, godet *m* **4.** [masses] : **the (common) ~** les masses *fpl*, la foule.
◇ *vi* **1.** SPORT former une mêlée ouverte **2.** [crease] se froisser, se chiffonner.
◇ *vt* [crease] froisser, chiffonner.
◆ **ruck up** *vi insep* se froisser.

rucksack ['rʌksæk] *n* sac *m* à dos.

ruckus ['rʌkəs] *n US inf* boucan *m*.

ructions ['rʌkʃnz] *npl inf* grabuge *m*.

rudder ['rʌdər] *n* [of boat, plane] gouvernail *m*.

rudderless ['rʌdəlɪs] *adj* [boat] sans gouvernail ▪ *fig* à la dérive.

ruddy ['rʌdɪ] (*comp* **ruddier**, *superl* **ruddiest**) ◇ *adj* **1.** [red - gen] rougeâtre, rougeoyant ; [- face] rougeaud, rubicond ▪ **to have a ~ complexion** avoir le teint rouge, être rougeaud **2.** *UK inf dated* [as intensifier] fichu, sacré.
◇ *adv UK inf dated* [as intensifier] sacrément, vachement.

rude [ru:d] *adj* **1.** [ill-mannered] impoli, mal élevé ▪ [stronger] grossier ▪ [insolent] insolent ▪ **to be ~ to sb** être impoli envers qqn ▪ **he was very ~ about my new hairstyle** il a fait des commentaires très désagréables sur ma nouvelle coiffure **2.** [indecent, obscene] indécent, obscène, grossier ▪ **a ~ joke** une histoire grivoise *OR* scabreuse ▪ **~ words** gros mots *mpl* **3.** [sudden] rude, violent, brutal ▪ **it was a ~ awakening for us** nous avons été rappelés brutalement à la réalité **4.** *lit* [rudimentary, rough - tool, hut] rudimentaire, grossier **5.** *lit* [primitive - tribesman, lifestyle] primitif, rude **6.** *lit* [vigorous] vigoureux ▪ **to be in ~ health** être en pleine santé.

rudely ['ru:dlɪ] *adv* **1.** [impolitely] impoliment, de façon mal élevée ▪ [stronger] grossièrement ▪ [insolently] insolemment **2.** [indecently, obscenely] indécemment, d'une manière obscène **3.** [suddenly] violemment, brutalement **4.** [in a rudimentary way] grossièrement.

rudeness ['ru:dnɪs] *n* **1.** [impoliteness] impolitesse *f* ▪ [stronger] grossièreté *f* ▪ [insolence] insolence *f* **2.** [indecency, obscenity] indécence *f*, obscénité *f* **3.** [suddenness] violence *f*, brutalité *f* **4.** [rudimentary nature] caractère *m* rudimentaire ▪ [primitive nature] caractère *m* primitif.

rudiment ['ru:dɪmənt] *n* ANAT rudiment *m*.
◆ **rudiments** *npl* [of a language, a skill] rudiments *mpl*, notions *fpl* élémentaires.

rudimentary [,ru:dɪ'mentərɪ] *adj* [gen - ANAT] rudimentaire.

rue [ru:] ◇ *vt lit & hum* regretter ▪ **I ~ the day I met him** je maudis le jour où je l'ai rencontré.

◇ *n* BOT rue *f*.

rueful ['ru:fʊl] *adj* [sad] triste, chagrin *lit*.

ruefully ['ru:fʊlɪ] *adv* [sadly] tristement ■ [regretfully] avec regret.

ruff [rʌf] ◇ *n* **1.** [collar] fraise *f* ■ ZOOL [on bird] collier *m* **2.** ORNITH [sandpiper] combattant *m* **3.** [in cards] action *f* de couper.
◇ *vt* [in cards] couper.

ruffian ['rʌfjən] *n* voyou *m* ■ *hum* [naughty child] petit vaurien *m*.

ruffle ['rʌfl] ◇ *vt* **1.** [hair, fur, feathers] ébouriffer ■ [clothes] friper, froisser, chiffonner ➤ **to ~ sb's feathers** froisser qqn **2.** [lake, sea, grass] agiter **3.** [upset - person] troubler, décontenancer.
◇ *n* **1.** [frill - on dress] ruche *f* **2.** [ripple - on lake, sea] ride *f*.

ruffled ['rʌfld] *adj* **1.** [flustered] décontenancé **2.** [rumpled - sheets] froissé ; [- hair] ébouriffé **3.** [decorated with frill] ruché, plissé.

rug [rʌg] *n* **1.** [for floor] carpette *f*, (petit) tapis *m* ■ **to pull the ~ from under sb's feet** couper l'herbe sous le pied à qqn ■ **to sweep sthg under the ~** *US fig* enterrer qqch **2.** *UK* [blanket] couverture *f* ■ **tartan ~** plaid *m*.

rugby ['rʌgbɪ] ◇ *n* : **~ (football)** rugby *m*.
◇ *comp* [ball, match, team] de rugby ■ **~ player** joueur *m*, - euse *f* de rugby, rugbyman *m* ■ **~ shirt** maillot *m* de rugby.

rugby league *n* rugby *m* OR jeu *m* à treize.

rugby tackle *n* plaquage *m*.
◆ **rugby-tackle** *vt* plaquer.

rugby union *n* rugby *m* à quinze.

rugged ['rʌgɪd] *adj* **1.** [countryside, region] accidenté ■ [road, path - bumpy] cahoteux, défoncé ; [- rocky] rocailleux ■ [coastline] échancré, découpé **2.** [face, features] rude ■ **he had ~ good looks** il était d'une beauté sauvage **3.** [unrefined - person, character, manners] rude, mal dégrossi ; [- lifestyle] rude, fruste ■ [determined - resistance] acharné **4.** [healthy] vigoureux, robuste ■ [tough - clothing, equipment, vehicle] solide, robuste.

ruggedness ['rʌgɪdnɪs] *n (U)* **1.** [of countryside, region] caractère *m* accidenté ■ [of road, path] inégalités *fpl* ■ [of coastline] échancrures *fpl* ■ **the ~ of the terrain** les inégalités du terrain **2.** [of face, features] irrégularité *f* **3.** [of person, manners, lifestyle] rudesse *f*.

rugger ['rʌgəʳ] *n UK inf* rugby *m*.

ruin ['ru:ɪn] ◇ *n* **1.** *(usu pl)* [remains] ruine *f* ■ **the ~s of an old castle** les ruines d'un vieux château ■ **in ~s** en ruine **2.** [destruction] ruine *f* ■ **this spelt the ~ of our hopes** c'était la fin de nos espoirs ■ **to fall into ~** tomber en ruine ■ **you will be my ~** OR **the ~ of me** tu me perdras **3.** [bankruptcy] ruine *f* ■ **the business was on the brink of (financial) ~** l'affaire était au bord de la ruine.
◇ *vt* **1.** [destroy] ruiner, détruire, abîmer ■ [spoil] gâter, gâcher ■ **that's ~ed our chances** ça nous a fait perdre toutes nos chances ■ **you're ~ing your eyesight** tu es en train de t'abîmer la vue OR les yeux **2.** [bankrupt] ruiner.

ruination [ru:ɪ'neɪʃn] *n* ruine *f*, perte *f* ■ **the ~ of the countryside** la destruction de la campagne.

ruined ['ru:ɪnd] *adj* **1.** [house, reputation, health] en ruine, ruiné ■ [clothes] abîmé **2.** [person - financially] ruiné.

ruinous ['ru:ɪnəs] *adj* **1.** [expensive] ruineux **2.** [disastrous] désastreux.

ruinously ['ru:ɪnəslɪ] *adv* de façon ruineuse ■ **~ expensive** ruineux.

rule [ru:l] ◇ *n* **1.** [law, tenet] règle *f* ■ [regulation] règlement *m* ■ **the ~s of chess/grammar** les règles du jeu d'échecs/de la grammaire ■ **to break the ~s** ne pas respecter les règles ■ **to play according to the ~s** OR **by the ~s (of the game)** jouer suivant les règles (du jeu) ■ **the ~s and regulations** le règlement ■ **smoking is against the ~s, it's against the ~s to smoke** le règlement interdit de fumer ■ **to stretch** OR **to bend the ~s (for sb)** faire une entorse au règlement (pour qqn) ➤ **~ of thumb** point *m* de repère
2. [convention, guideline] règle *f* ■ **~s of conduct** règles de conduite ■ **the ~s for a happy marriage** comment réussir son mariage ■ **he makes it a ~ not to trust anyone** il a comme OR pour règle de ne faire confiance à personne
3. [normal state of affairs] règle *f* ■ **tipping is the ~ here** les pourboires sont de règle ici ■ **long hair was the ~ in those days** tout le monde avait les cheveux longs à cette époque
4. [government] gouvernement *m*, autorité *f* ■ [reign] règne *m* ■ **a return to majority/mob ~** un retour à la démocratie/à l'anarchie ■ **the territories under French ~** les territoires sous autorité française ■ **the ~ of law** (l'autorité de) la loi
5. [for measuring] règle *f* ■ **folding ~** mètre *m* pliant ■ **metre ~** mètre *m*.
◇ *vt* **1.** [govern - country] gouverner ■ **if I ~d the world** si j'étais maître du monde
2. [dominate - person] dominer ; [- emotion] maîtriser ■ **their lives are ~d by fear** leur vie est dominée par la peur ■ **don't be ~d by what he says** ce n'est pas à lui de vous dire ce que vous avez à faire ➤ **to ~ the roost** faire la loi
3. [judge, decide] juger, décider
4. [draw - line, margin] tirer à la règle ■ [draw lines on - paper] régler.
◇ *vi* **1.** [govern - monarch, dictator] régner ; [- elected government] gouverner ■ **he ~d over a vast kingdom** il régna sur un vaste royaume ■ **Chelsea ~ OK!** *inf* vive l'équipe de Chelsea! ■ **'Rule Britannia'** *chant patriotique britannique*
2. [prevail] régner
3. LAW [decide] statuer ■ **to ~ on a dispute** statuer sur un litige ■ **to ~ against/in favour of sb** décider OR prononcer contre/en faveur de qqn.
◆ **as a (general) rule** *adv phr* en règle générale.
◆ **rule off** *vt sep* tirer une ligne sous.
◆ **rule out** *vt sep* [possibility, suggestion, suspect] exclure, écarter ■ **she cannot be ~d out of the inquiry** elle n'a pas encore été mise hors de cause ■ **the injury ~s him out of Saturday's game** sa blessure ne lui permettra pas de jouer samedi.

rulebook ['ru:lbʊk] *n* règlement *m* ■ **to do sthg by the ~** faire qqch strictement selon les règles ■ **to go by the ~** suivre scrupuleusement le règlement.

ruled [ru:ld] *adj* [paper, block] réglé.

ruler ['ru:ləʳ] *n* **1.** [sovereign] souverain *m*, - e *f* ■ [president, prime minister etc] homme *m* d'État, dirigeant *m* **2.** [for measuring] règle *f*.

ruling ['ru:lɪŋ] ◇ *adj* **1.** [governing - monarch] régnant ; [- party] au pouvoir ; [- class] dirigeant ■ **football's ~ body** les instances dirigeantes du football **2.** [dominant - passion, factor] dominant.
◇ *n* LAW [finding] décision *f*, jugement *m*.

rum [rʌm] (*comp* **rummer**, *superl* **rummest**) ◇ *n* [drink] rhum *m*.
◇ *comp* [ice cream, toddy] au rhum.
◇ *adj UK inf dated* [odd] bizarre.

Rumania *etc* [ru:'meɪnjə] = **Romania**.

rumba ['rʌmbə] ◇ *n* rumba *f*.
◇ *vi* danser la rumba.

rum baba *n* baba *m* au rhum.

rumble ['rʌmbl] ◇ *n* **1.** [of thunder, traffic, cannons] grondement *m* ■ [of conversation] murmure *m*, bourdonnement *m* ■ [in stomach] borborygme *m*, gargouillis *m*, gargouillement *m* **2.** *US inf* [street fight] bagarre *f*, castagne *f (entre gangs)*.
◇ *vi* [thunder, traffic, cannons] gronder ■ [stomach] gargouiller ■ **trucks were rumbling past all night** toute la nuit, on entendait le grondement des camions.
◇ *vt* **1.** *UK inf* [discover - plan] découvrir ■ [understand - person, trick] piger **2.** [mutter - comment, remark] grommeler, bougonner.
◆ **rumble on** *vi insep* [person] palabrer ■ [conversation, debate] ne pas en finir ■ **the dispute's been rumbling on for weeks now** le conflit dure depuis des semaines.

rumble seat *n US* strapontin *m*.

rumble strip *n* AUT bande *f* rugueuse.

rumbling ['rʌmblɪŋ] *n* [of thunder, traffic, cannons] grondement *m* ■ [of stomach] borborygmes *mpl*, gargouillis *mpl*, gargouillements *mpl*.
◆ **rumblings** *npl* [of discontent] grondement *m*, grondements *mpl* ■ [omens] présages *mpl*.

rumbustious [rʌm'bʌstʃəs] *adj UK inf* [boisterous] exubérant, tapageur, bruyant ■ [unruly] turbulent, indiscipliné.

ruminant ['ru:mɪnənt] ◇ *adj* **1.** ZOOL ruminant **2.** *lit* = **ruminative**.
◇ *n* ZOOL ruminant *m*.

ruminate ['ru:mɪneɪt] ◇ *vi* **1.** ZOOL ruminer **2.** *fml* [person] ruminer ■ **to ~ over** *OR* **about** *OR* **on** réfléchir longuement.
◇ *vt* **1.** ZOOL ruminer **2.** *fml* [person] ruminer.

ruminative ['ru:mɪnətɪv] *adj* [person] pensif, méditatif ■ [look, mood] pensif.

rummage ['rʌmɪdʒ] ◇ *n* **1.** [search] : **to have a ~ through** *OR* **around in sthg** fouiller (dans) qqch **2.** *US* [jumble] bric-à-brac *m*.
◇ *vi* fouiller ■ **he ~d in** *OR* **through his pockets** il fouilla dans ses poches.
◆ **rummage about** *UK*, **rummage around** = **rummage** *(vi)*.

rummage sale *n US* vente *f* de charité.

rummy ['rʌmɪ] (*pl* **rummies**, *comp* **rummier**, *superl* **rummiest**) ◇ *n* [card game] rami *m*.
◇ *adj* = **rum**.

rumour *UK*, **rumor** *US* ['ru:mər] ◇ *n* rumeur *f*, bruit *m* (qui court) ■ **there's a ~ going round** *OR* **~ has it that he's going to resign** le bruit court qu'il va démissionner.
◇ *vt* : **it is ~ed that...** le bruit court que... ■ **she is ~ed to be extremely rich** on la dit extrêmement riche.

rumourmonger *UK*, **rumormonger** *US* ['ru:mə,mʌŋgər] *n* commère *f*.

rump [rʌmp] *n* **1.** [of mammal] croupe *f* ■ CULIN culotte *f* ■ [of bird] croupion *m* ■ *hum* [of person] postérieur *m*, derrière *m* **2.** [remnant] : **the organization was reduced to a ~** il ne restait pas grand-chose de l'organisation.

rumple ['rʌmpl] *vt* [clothes] friper, froisser, chiffonner ■ [banknote, letter] froisser ■ [hair, fur] ébouriffer.

Rump Parliament *pr n* : **the ~** le Parlement croupion *(nom du Parlement anglais pendant la période du Protectorat de Cromwell, de 1649 à 1660)*.

rump steak *n* romsteck *m*, rumsteck *m*.

rumpus ['rʌmpəs] *n inf* raffut *m*, boucan *m* ■ **the announcement caused a ~** la nouvelle fit l'effet d'une bombe ■ **to kick up a ~** faire du chahut *OR* des histoires.

rumpus room *n esp US* salle *f* de jeu *(souvent située au sous-sol et également utilisée pour des fêtes)*.

run [rʌn] (*pret* **ran** [ræn], *pp* **run**, *cont* **running**) ◇ *vi*

A.

1. [gen] courir ■ **they ran out of the house** ils sont sortis de la maison en courant ■ **to ~ upstairs/downstairs** monter/descendre l'escalier en courant ■ **I had to ~ for the train** j'ai dû courir pour attraper le train ■ **~ and fetch me a glass of water** cours me chercher un verre d'eau ■ **I've been running all over the place looking for you** j'ai couru partout à ta recherche ■ **to ~ to meet sb** courir *OR* se précipiter à la rencontre de qqn ‖ *fig* **I didn't expect her to go running to the press with the story** je ne m'attendais pas à ce qu'elle coure raconter l'histoire à la presse ■ **don't come running to me with your problems** ne viens pas m'embêter avec tes problèmes
2. [compete in race] courir ■ **to ~ in a race** [horse, person] participer à une course ‖ [be positioned in race] arriver ■ [in cricket, baseball] marquer ■ **Smith is running second** Smith est en seconde position
3. [flee] se sauver, fuir ■ **if the night watchman sees you, ~ (for it)** *inf* ! si le veilleur de nuit te voit, tire-toi *OR* file! ■ **he turned and ran** il prit ses jambes à son cou ■ **~ for your lives!** sauve qui peut!

B.

1. [road, railway, boundary] passer ■ **the railway line ~s through a valley/over a viaduct** le chemin de fer passe dans une vallée/sur un viaduc ■ **the road ~s alongside the river/parallel to the coast** la route longe la rivière/la côte ■ **a canal running from London to Birmingham** un canal qui va de Londres à Birmingham ■ **a high fence ~s around the building** une grande barrière fait le tour du bâtiment ■ **the lizard has red markings running down its back** le dos du lézard est zébré de rouge ■ **our lives seem to be running in different directions** *fig* il semble que nos vies prennent des chemins différents
2. [hand, fingers] : **his fingers ran over the controls** ses doigts se promenèrent sur les boutons de commande ■ **her eyes ran down the list** elle parcourut la liste des yeux
3. [travel - thoughts, sensation] : **a shiver ran down my spine** un frisson me parcourut le dos
4. [describing song, poem, theory etc] : **their argument** *OR* **reasoning ~s something like this** voici plus ou moins leur raisonnement
5. [occur - inherited trait, illness] : **twins ~ in our family** les jumeaux sont courants dans la famille ■ **heart disease ~s in the family** les maladies cardiaques sont fréquentes dans notre famille
6. [spread - rumour, news] se répandre
7. [move or travel freely - ball, vehicle] rouler ■ **the truck ran off the road** le camion a quitté la route ■ [slip, slide - rope, cable] filer
8. [drive] faire un tour *OR* une promenade ■ **why don't we ~ down to the coast/up to London?** si on faisait un tour jusqu'à la mer/jusqu'à Londres?
9. NAUT [boat] : **to ~ (before the wind)** filer vent arrière

C.

1. [flow - water, tap, nose] couler ■ [paint] goutter ■ **the water's ~ cold** l'eau est froide au robinet ■ **your bath is running** ton bain est en train de couler ■ **your nose is running** tu as le nez qui coule ■ **her mascara had ~** son mascara avait coulé ■ **the hot water ~s along/down this pipe** l'eau chaude passe/descend dans ce tuyau ■ **their faces were running with sweat** *UK* leurs visages ruisselaient de transpiration ■ **tears ran down her face** des larmes coulaient sur son visage
2. [river, stream] couler ■ **the river ran red with blood** les eaux de la rivière étaient rouges de sang ■ **the Jari ~s into the Amazon** le Jari se jette dans l'Amazone
3. [butter, ice cream, wax] fondre ■ [cheese] couler
4. [in wash - colour, fabric] déteindre
5. [tide] monter

D.

1. [operate - engine, machine, business] marcher, fonctionner ■ **to ~ on** *OR* **off electricity/gas/diesel** fonctionner à l'électricité/au gaz/au diesel ■ **the tape recorder was still running** le magnétophone était encore en marche ■ **leave the engine running** laissez tourner le moteur ■ **the new assembly line is up and running** la nouvelle chaîne de montage est en service ■ **do not interrupt the program while it is running** COMPUT ne pas interrompre le programme en cours d'exécution ■ **everything is running smoothly** *fig* tout marche très bien
2. [public transport] circuler ■ **some bus lines ~ all night** certaines lignes d'autobus sont en service toute la nuit

E.

1. [last] durer ■ **I'd like the ad to ~ for a week** je voudrais que l'annonce passe pendant une semaine
2. [be performed - play, film] tenir l'affiche ■ **this soap opera has been running for 20 years** ça fait 20 ans que ce feuilleton est diffusé ■ **America's longest-running TV series** la plus longue série télévisée américaine
3. [be valid, remain in force - contract] être *OR* rester valide ; [- agreement] être *OR* rester en vigueur ■ **the lease has another year to ~** le bail n'expire pas avant un an ■ **your subscription will ~ for two years** votre abonnement sera valable deux ans
4. FIN [be paid, accumulate - interest] courir
5. [range] aller

F.

1. [indicating current state or condition] : **feelings were running high** les passions étaient exacerbées ■ **their ammunition was running low** ils commençaient à manquer de munitions ■ **to ~ late** être en retard, avoir du retard ■ **programmes are running ten minutes late** les émissions ont toutes dix minutes de retard ■ **events are running in our favour** les événements tournent en notre faveur
2. [reach] : **inflation was running at 18%** le taux d'inflation était de 18 %

G.

1. [be candidate, stand] se présenter ■ **to ~ for president** *OR* **the presidency** être candidat aux élections présidentielles *OR* à la présidence
2. [ladder - stocking, tights] filer.

<> *vt*

A.

1. [manage - company, office] diriger, gérer ; [- shop, restaurant, club] tenir, diriger ; [- theatre] diriger ; [- house] tenir ; [- country] gouverner, diriger ■ **a badly ~ organization** une organisation mal gérée ■ **the library is ~ by volunteer workers** la bibliothèque est tenue par des bénévoles ■ **the farm was too big for him to ~ alone** la ferme était trop grande pour qu'il puisse s'en occuper seul ■ **I wish she'd stop trying to ~ my life!** j'aimerais bien qu'elle arrête de me dire comment vivre ma vie!
2. [organize, lay on - service, course, contest] organiser ■ [train, bus] mettre en service ■ **several private companies ~ buses to the airport** plusieurs sociétés privées assurent un service d'autobus pour l'aéroport
3. [operate, work - piece of equipment] faire marcher, faire fonctionner ■ **you can ~ it off solar energy/the mains** vous pouvez le faire fonctionner à l'énergie solaire/sur secteur ■ [vehicle] : **I can't afford to ~ a car any more** *UK* je n'ai plus les moyens d'avoir une voiture
4. [conduct - experiment, test] effectuer
5. COMPUT [program] exécuter

B.

1. [do or cover at a run - race, distance] courir ■ **I can still ~ 2 km in under 7 minutes** j'arrive encore à courir *OR* à couvrir 2 km en moins de 7 minutes ■ **the children were running races** les enfants faisaient la course ■ **the race will be ~ in Paris next year** la course aura lieu à Paris l'année prochaine ■ **to ~ messages** *OR* **errands** faire des commissions *OR* des courses ◐ **he'd ~ a mile if he saw it** il prendrait ses jambes à son cou s'il voyait ça ■ **it looks as if his race is ~** on dirait qu'il a fait son temps
2. [cause to run] : **you're running the poor boy off his feet!** le pauvre, tu es en train de l'épuiser! ■ **to be ~ off one's feet** être débordé ■ **to ~ o.s. to a standstill** courir jusqu'à l'épuisement
3. [enter for race - horse, greyhound] faire courir
4. [chase] chasser ■ **the outlaws were ~ out of town** les hors-la-loi furent chassés de la ville
5. [hunt] chasser

C.

1. [transport - goods] transporter ■ [give lift to - person] accompagner ■ **I'll ~ you to the bus stop** je vais te conduire à l'arrêt de bus
2. [smuggle] faire le trafic de
3. [drive - vehicle] conduire ■ **I ran my car into a lamppost** je suis rentré dans un réverbère (avec ma voiture) ■ **he tried to ~ me off the road!** il a essayé de me faire sortir de la route!

D.

1. [pass, quickly or lightly] passer ■ **she ran her hands over the controls** elle promena ses mains sur les boutons de commande ■ **he ran his hand/a comb through his hair** il passa sa main/un peigne dans ses cheveux ■ **she ran her finger down the list/her eye over the text** elle parcourut la liste du doigt/le texte des yeux
2. [send via specified route] : **we could ~ a cable from the house** nous pourrions amener un câble de la maison ■ **it would be better to ~ the wires under the floorboards** ce serait mieux de faire passer les fils sous le plancher

E.

1. [go through or past - blockade] forcer ; [- rapids] franchir ■ *US* [- red light] brûler
2. [cause to flow] faire couler ■ **to ~ a bath** faire couler un bain
3. [publish] publier ■ **to ~ an ad (in the newspaper)** passer *OR* faire passer une annonce (dans le journal)
4. [enter for election] présenter
5. MED : **to ~ a temperature** *OR* **fever** avoir de la fièvre
6. [expose o.s. to] : **to ~ the danger** *OR* **risk of doing sthg** courir le risque de faire qqch ■ **you ~ the risk of a heavy fine** vous risquez une grosse amende.

<> *n* **1.** [action] course *f* ■ **to go for a ~** aller faire du jogging ■ **to go for a five-mile ~** courir huit kilomètres ■ **I took the dog for a ~ in the park** j'ai emmené le chien courir dans le parc ■ **two policemen arrived at a ~** deux policiers sont arrivés au pas de course ■ **to break into a ~** se mettre à courir ■ **to make a ~ for it** prendre la fuite, se sauver ◐ **we have the ~ of the house while the owners are away** nous disposons de toute la maison pendant l'absence des propriétaires ■ **we give the au pair the ~ of the place** nous laissons à la jeune fille au pair la libre disposition de la maison ■ **to be on the ~ : the murderer is on the ~** le meurtrier est en cavale ■ **she was on the ~ from her creditors/the police** elle essayait d'échapper à ses créanciers/à la police ■ **we've got them on the ~!** MIL & SPORT nous les avons mis en déroute! ■ **you've had a good ~ (for your money), it's time to step down** tu en as bien profité, maintenant il faut laisser la place à un autre ■ **they gave the Russian team a good ~ for their money** ils ont donné du fil à retordre à l'équipe russe **2.** [race] course *f* **3.** [drive] excursion *f*, promenade *f* ■ **she took me for a ~ in her new car** elle m'a emmené faire un tour dans sa nouvelle voiture ■ **I do the school ~ in the morning** c'est moi qui emmène les enfants à l'école tous les matins ‖ [for smuggling] passage *m* ■ **the gang used to make ~s across the border** le gang passait régulièrement la frontière **4.** [route, itinerary] trajet *m*, parcours *m* ■ **the buses on the London to Glasgow ~** les cars qui font le trajet *OR* qui assurent le service Londres-Glasgow **5.** AERON [flight] vol *m*, mission *f* ■ **bombing ~** mission de bombardement **6.** SPORT [in cricket, baseball] point *m* **7.** [track - for skiing, bobsleighing] piste *f* **8.** [series, continuous period] série *f*, succession *f*, suite *f* ■ **they've had a ~ of ten defeats** ils ont connu dix défaites consécutives ■ **you seem to be having a ~ of good/bad luck** on dirait que la chance est/n'est pas de ton côté en ce moment ‖ [series of performances] : **the play had a triumphant ~ on Broadway** la pièce a connu un succès triomphal à Broadway ◐ **in the long/short ~** à long/court terme **9.** [in card games] suite *f* **10.** INDUST [production] lot *m*, série *f* ◐ **print ~** TYPO tirage *m* **11.** [general tendency, trend] tendance *f* ■ **I was lucky and got the ~ of the cards** j'avais de la chance, les cartes m'étaient favorables ■ **the usual ~ of colds and upset stomachs** les rhumes et les maux de ventre habituels ■ **she's well above the average** *OR* **ordinary ~ of students** elle est bien au-dessus de la moyenne des étudiants ■ **in the ordinary ~ of things,...** normalement,... **12.** [great demand] ruée *f* ■ **a ~ on the banks** une panique bancaire ‖ ST. EX : **there was a ~ on the dollar** il y a eu une ruée sur le dollar **13.** [operation - of machine] opération *f* ■ **computer ~** passage *m* machine **14.** [bid - in election] candidature *f* ■ **his ~ for the presidency** sa candidature à la présidence **15.** [ladder - in stocking, tights] échelle *f*, maille *f* filée **16.** [enclosure - for animals] enclos *m* ■ **chicken ~** poulailler *m* **17.** MUS roulade *f*.

◆ **runs** *npl inf* [diarrhoea] courante *f* ■ **to have the ~s** avoir la courante.

◆ **run about** *UK vi insep* courir (çà et là) ■ **I've been running about all day looking for you!** j'ai passé ma journée à te chercher partout!

◆ **run across** <> *vi insep* traverser en courant.
<> *vt insep* [meet - acquaintance] rencontrer par hasard, tomber sur ■ [find - book, reference] trouver par hasard, tomber sur.

◆ **run after** *vt insep liter & fig* courir après.

◆ **run along** *vi insep* [go away] s'en aller, partir ■ **it's getting late, I must be running along** il se fait tard, il faut que j'y aille.

◆ **run around** *vi insep* **1.** = run about **2.** [husband] courir après les femmes ■ [wife] courir après les hommes.

◆ **run away** *vi insep* **1.** [flee] se sauver, s'enfuir ▪ **their son has ~ away from home** leur fils a fait une fugue ▪ **to ~ away from one's responsibilities** *fig* fuir ses responsabilités **2.** [elope] partir.

◆ **run away with** *vt insep* **1.** [secretly or illegally] partir avec ▪ **he ran away with his best friend's wife** il est parti avec la femme de son meilleur ami **2.** [overwhelm] : **she tends to let her imagination ~ away with her** elle a tendance à se laisser emporter par son imagination **3.** [get - idea] : **don't go running away with the idea** *OR* **the notion that it will be easy** n'allez pas vous imaginer que ce sera facile **4.** [win - race, match] emporter haut la main ; [- prize] remporter.

◆ **run back** ◇ *vi insep* **1.** *liter* retourner *OR* revenir en courant **2.** [review] : **to ~ back over sthg** passer qqch en revue.
◇ *vt sep* **1.** [drive back] raccompagner (en voiture) **2.** [rewind - tape, film] rembobiner.

◆ **run by** *vt sep* : **to ~ sthg by sb** [submit] soumettre qqch à qqn ▪ **you'd better ~ that by the committee** vous feriez mieux de demander l'avis du comité ▪ **~ that by me again** répétez-moi ça.

◆ **run down** ◇ *vi insep* **1.** *liter* descendre en courant **2.** [clock, machine] s'arrêter ▪ [battery - through use] s'user ; [- through a fault] se décharger.
◇ *vt sep* **1.** [reduce, diminish] réduire ▪ **the government was accused of running down the steel industry** le gouvernement a été accusé de laisser dépérir la sidérurgie **2.** *inf* [criticize, denigrate] rabaisser ▪ **stop running yourself down all the time** cesse de te rabaisser constamment **3.** AUT [pedestrian, animal] renverser, écraser ▪ **he was ~ down by a bus** il s'est fait renverser par un bus **4.** [track down - animal, criminal] (traquer et) capturer ; [- object] dénicher.

◆ **run in** ◇ *vi insep* **1.** *liter* entrer en courant **2.** *UK* [car, engine] : **'running in'** 'en rodage'.
◇ *vt sep* **1.** *UK* [car, engine] roder **2.** *inf* [arrest] pincer.

◆ **run into** *vt insep* **1.** [encounter - problem, difficulty] rencontrer **2.** [meet - acquaintance] rencontrer (par hasard), tomber sur **3.** [collide with - subj: car, driver] percuter, rentrer dans **4.** [amount to] s'élever à **5.** [merge into] se fondre dans, se confondre avec.

◆ **run off** ◇ *vi insep* **1.** = **run away 2.** [liquid] s'écouler.
◇ *vt sep* **1.** [print] tirer, imprimer ▪ [photocopy] photocopier ▪ **~ me off five copies of this report** faites-moi cinq copies de ce rapport **2.** SPORT [race] disputer ▪ **the heats will be ~ off tomorrow** les éliminatoires se disputeront demain **3.** [lose - excess weight, fat] perdre en courant **4.** [liquid] laisser s'écouler.

◆ **run on** ◇ *vi insep* **1.** [continue] continuer, durer ▪ [drag on] s'éterniser **2.** *inf* [talk nonstop] parler sans cesse **3.** [line of text] suivre sans alinéa ▪ [verse] enjamber.
◇ *vt sep* [lines of writing] ne pas découper en paragraphes ▪ [letters, words] ne pas séparer, lier.

◆ **run out** ◇ *vi insep* **1.** *liter* [person, animal] sortir en courant ▪ [liquid] s'écouler **2.** [be used up - supplies, money etc] s'épuiser, (venir à) manquer ; [- time] filer ▪ **hurry up, time is running out!** dépêchez-vous, il ne reste plus beaucoup de temps! ▪ **their luck finally ran out** la chance a fini par tourner, leur chance n'a pas duré **3.** [expire - contract, passport, agreement] expirer, venir à expiration.
◇ *vt sep* **1.** [cable, rope] laisser filer **2.** [in cricket] : **to ~ a batsman out** mettre un batteur hors jeu.

◆ **run out of** *vt insep* manquer de ▪ **to ~ out of patience** être à bout de patience ▪ **he's ~ out of money** il n'a plus d'argent ▪ **to ~ out of petrol** tomber en panne d'essence.

◆ **run out on** *vt insep* [spouse, colleague] laisser tomber, abandonner.

◆ **run over** ◇ *vt sep* [pedestrian, animal] écraser, renverser.
◇ *vt insep* [review] revoir ▪ [rehearse] répéter ▪ [recap] récapituler ▪ **let's ~ over the arguments one more time before the meeting** reprenons les arguments une dernière fois avant la réunion.
◇ *vi insep* **1.** [overflow] déborder ▪ **my cup runneth over** *lit* je nage dans le bonheur **2.** [run late] dépasser l'heure ▪ RADIO & TV dépasser le temps d'antenne.

◆ **run past** ◇ *vi insep* passer en courant.
◇ *vt sep* = **run by**.

◆ **run through** ◇ *vt insep* **1.** *liter* traverser en courant **2.** [pervade - thought, feeling] : **a strange idea ran through my mind** une idée étrange m'a traversé l'esprit ▪ **a thrill of excitement ran through her** un frisson d'émotion la parcourut ▪ **his words kept running through my head** ses paroles ne cessaient de retentir dans ma tête ▪ **an air of melancholy ~s through the whole film** une atmosphère de mélancolie imprègne tout le film **3.** [review] revoir ▪ [rehearse] répéter ▪ [recap] récapituler ▪ **she ran through the arguments in her mind** elle repassa les arguments dans sa tête **4.** [read quickly] parcourir (des yeux), jeter un coup d'œil sur **5.** [squander - fortune] gaspiller.
◇ *vt sep* : **to ~ sb through (with a sword)** transpercer qqn (d'un coup d'épée).

◆ **run to** *vt insep* **1.** [amount to] se chiffrer à ▪ **her essay ran to 20 pages** sa dissertation faisait 20 pages **2.** [afford, be enough for] : **your salary should ~ to a new computer** ton salaire devrait te permettre d'acheter un nouvel ordinateur **3.** *phr* **to ~ to fat** devenir gros.

◆ **run up** ◇ *vi insep* [climb rapidly] monter en courant ▪ [approach] approcher en courant ▪ **a young man ran up to me** un jeune homme s'approcha de moi en courant.
◇ *vt sep* **1.** [debt, bill] laisser s'accumuler ▪ **I've ~ up a huge overdraft** j'ai un découvert énorme **2.** [flag] hisser **3.** [sew quickly] coudre (rapidement) *OR* à la hâte.

◆ **run up against** *vt insep* [encounter] se heurter à.

runabout ['rʌnəbaʊt] *n inf* [car] petite voiture *f*, voiture *f* de ville ▪ [boat] runabout *m* ▪ [plane] petit avion *m*.

runaround ['rʌnəraʊnd] *n inf* **to give sb the ~** raconter des salades à qqn ; [husband, wife] tromper qqn.

runaway ['rʌnəweɪ] ◇ *n* [gen] fugitif *m*, - ive *f* ▪ [child - from home, school etc] fugueur *m*, - euse *f*.
◇ *adj* **1.** [convict] fugitif ▪ [child] fugueur ▪ [horse] emballé ▪ [train, car] fou *(before vowel or silent 'h'* **fol***)*, folle *f* ▪ **a ~ marriage** un mariage clandestin **2.** [rampant, extreme - inflation] galopant ; [- success] fou *(before vowel or silent 'h'* **fol***)*, folle *f* ▪ **a ~ victory** une victoire remportée haut la main.

rundown ['rʌndaʊn] *n* **1.** [reduction] réduction *f*, déclin *m* **2.** *inf* [report] compte rendu *m* ▪ **to give sb a ~ of** *OR* **on sthg** mettre qqn au courant de qqch.

run-down *adj inf* **1.** [tired] vanné, crevé ▪ **I think you're just a bit ~** je pense que c'est juste un peu de surmenage **2.** [dilapidated] délabré.

rune [ru:n] *n* rune *f*.

rung [rʌŋ] ◇ *pp* ▷ **ring** *(bell)*.
◇ *n* [of ladder] barreau *m*, échelon *m* ▪ [of chair] barreau *m* ▪ *fig* [in hierarchy] échelon *m*.

runic ['ru:nɪk] *adj* runique.

run-in *n inf* [quarrel] engueulade *f*, prise *f* de bec ▪ **I had a bit of a ~ with the police last week** j'ai eu un petit accrochage avec la police la semaine dernière.

runner ['rʌnəʳ] *n* **1.** [in race - person] coureur *m*, - euse *f* ; [- horse] partant *m* ▪ **he's a good/fast ~** il court bien/vite **2.** [messenger] coursier *m*, - ère *f* **3.** *(usu in cpds)* [smuggler] contrebandier *m*, - ère *f*, trafiquant *m*, - e *f* ▪ **drug ~** trafiquant *m* de drogue **4.** [slide - for door, drawer etc] glissière *f* ; [- on sledge] patin *m* ; [- on skate] lame *f* **5.** BOT coulant *m*, stolon *m* **6.** [stair carpet] tapis *m* d'escalier **7.** *phr* **to do a ~** *UK inf* partir sans payer.

runner bean *n UK* haricot *m* d'Espagne.

runner-up (*pl* **runners-up**) *n* second *m*, - e *f* ▪ **her novel was ~ for the Prix Goncourt** son roman était le second favori pour le prix Goncourt ▪ **there will be 50 consolation prizes for the runners-up** il y aura 50 lots de consolation pour les autres gagnants.

running ['rʌnɪŋ] ◇ *n* **1.** SPORT course *f* (à pied) ▪ **~ is forbidden in the corridors** il est interdit de courir dans les couloirs ▶ **to make the ~** SPORT mener le train ; *fig* prendre l'initiative ▪ **to be in the ~ for sthg** être sur les rangs pour obtenir qqch ▪ **to be out of the ~** ne plus être dans la course
2. [management] gestion *f*, direction *f* ▪ [organization] organisation *f*
3. [working, functioning] marche *f*, fonctionnement *m*

4. [operating] conduite *f*, maniement *m*
5. [smuggling] contrebande *f* ▪ **drug ~** trafic *m* de drogue.
◇ *comp* [shoe, shorts, track] de course (à pied).
◇ *adj* **1.** [at a run - person, animal] courant, qui court ▶ **~ jump** *liter* saut *m* avec élan ▪ **(go)take a ~ jump!** *inf* va te faire voir (ailleurs)!
2. *(after n)* [consecutive] de suite ▪ **three times/weeks/years ~** trois fois/semaines/années de suite
3. [continuous] continu, ininterrompu ▪ **~ account** FIN compte *m* courant ▪ **~ battle** lutte *f* continuelle ▪ **~ total** montant *m* à reporter
4. [flowing] : **the sound of ~ water** le bruit de l'eau qui coule ▪ **all the rooms have ~ water** toutes les chambres ont l'eau courante ▪ **a ~ sore** une plaie suppurante
5. [working, operating] : **in ~ order** en état de marche ▶ **to be up and ~** être opérationnel ▪ **~ costs** frais *mpl* d'exploitation ; [of car] frais *mpl* d'entretien ▪ **~ repairs** réparations *fpl* courantes
6. [cursive - handwriting] cursif.

running board *n* marchepied *m*.

running commentary *n* RADIO & TV commentaire *m* en direct ▪ **she gave us a ~ on what the neighbours were doing** *fig* elle nous a expliqué en détail ce que les voisins étaient en train de faire.

running mate *n* *US* POL *personne choisie par un candidat à la présidence des États-Unis pour être son vice-président s'il est élu.*

runny ['rʌnɪ] (*comp* **runnier**, *superl* **runniest**) *adj* **1.** [sauce, honey] liquide ▪ [liquid] (très) fluide ▪ [omelette] baveux ▪ **a ~ egg** un œuf dont le jaune coule **2.** [nose] qui coule ▪ [eye] qui pleure ▪ **I've got a ~ nose** j'ai le nez qui coule.

run-off *n* **1.** SPORT [final] finale *f* ▪ [after tie] belle *f* **2.** [water] trop-plein *m*.

run-of-the-mill *adj* ordinaire, banal.

run-on *n* **1.** [in printed matter] texte *m* composé à la suite *(sans alinéa)* **2.** [in dictionary] sous-entrée *f*.

runt [rʌnt] *n* **1.** [animal] avorton *m* **2.** *inf* [person] avorton *m*.

run-through *n* [review] révision *f* ▪ [rehearsal] répétition *f* ▪ [recap] récapitulation *f*.

run-up *n* **1.** SPORT élan *m* **2.** [period before] période *f* préparatoire ▪ **the ~ to the elections** la période qui précède les élections *OR* pré-électorale **3.** *US* [increase] augmentation *f*, hausse *f*.

runway ['rʌnweɪ] *n* AERON piste *f* (d'atterrissage *OR* d'envol) ▪ **~ lights** feux *mpl* de piste.

rupee [ruː'piː] *n* roupie *f*.

rupture ['rʌptʃər] ◇ *n* **1.** [split] rupture *f* **2.** [hernia] hernie *f*.
◇ *vt* **1.** [split] rompre **2.** MED : **to ~ o.s.** se faire une hernie.

rural ['rʊərəl] *adj* [life, country, scenery] rural.

Ruritania [,rʊərɪ'teɪnjə] *pr n* *nom d'un petit pays imaginaire d'Europe centrale, théâtre par excellence d'intrigues et d'aventures romanesques.*

ruse [ruːz] *n* ruse *f*.

rush [rʌʃ] ◇ *vi* **1.** [hurry, dash - individual] se précipiter ; [- crowd] se ruer, se précipiter ; [- vehicle] foncer ▪ **people ~ed out of the blazing house** les gens se ruèrent hors de la maison en flammes ▪ **there's no need to ~** pas besoin de se presser ▪ **passers-by ~ed to help the injured man** des passants se sont précipités au secours du blessé ▪ **he ~ed in/out/past** il est entré précipitamment/sorti précipitamment/passé à toute allure
2. [act overhastily] : **to ~ into a decision** prendre une décision à la hâte ▪ **now don't ~ into anything** ne va pas foncer tête baissée
3. [surge - air] s'engouffrer ; [- liquid] jaillir ▪ **the cold water ~ed over her bare feet** l'eau froide déferla sur ses pieds nus ▪ **the blood ~ed to her head** le sang lui est monté à la tête.
◇ *vt* **1.** [do quickly] expédier ▪ [do overhastily] faire à la hâte *OR* à la va-vite ▪ **don't ~ your food** ne mange pas trop vite
2. [cause to hurry] bousculer, presser ▪ [pressurize] faire pression sur, forcer la main à ▪ **don't ~ me!** ne me bouscule pas! ▪ **to ~ sb into sthg** *OR* **doing sthg** forcer qqn à faire qqch à la hâte ▪ **don't be ~ed into signing** ne signez pas sous la pression
3. [attack - person] attaquer, agresser ; [- place] attaquer, prendre d'assaut
4. [transport quickly] transporter d'urgence ▪ [send quickly] envoyer *OR* expédier d'urgence
5. *US inf* [court] courtiser.
◇ *n* **1.** [hurry] précipitation *f*, hâte *f* ▪ **to do sthg in a ~** faire qqch à la hâte ▪ **to be in a ~** être (très) pressé ▪ **what's the ~?** pourquoi tant de précipitation? ▪ **there's no (great) ~** rien ne presse ▪ **it'll be a bit of a ~, but we should make it** il faudra se dépêcher mais on devrait y arriver ▪ **your essay was written in too much of a ~** vous avez fait votre dissertation à la va-vite
2. [stampede] ruée *f*, bousculade *f* ▪ **there was a ~ for the door** tout le monde s'est rué vers la porte ▮ [great demand] ruée ▪ **there's been a ~ on** *OR* **for tickets** les gens se sont rués sur les billets ▪ **there's a ~ on that particular model** ce modèle est très demandé
3. [busy period] heure *f* de pointe *OR* d'affluence ▪ **the six o'clock ~** la foule de six heures ▮ [in shops, post office etc] : **I try to avoid the lunchtime ~** j'essaie d'éviter la foule de l'heure du déjeuner ▪ **the holiday ~** [leaving] les grands départs en vacances ; [returning] les embouteillages des retours de vacances
4. [attack] attaque *f*, assaut *m* ▪ **to make a ~ at** *OR* **for sb** se jeter sur qqn
5. [surge - of water] jaillissement *m* ; [- of air] bouffée *f* ; [- of emotion, nausea] accès *m*, montée *f* ▪ **I could hear nothing above the ~ of water** le bruit de l'eau (qui bouillonnait) m'empêchait d'entendre quoi que ce soit ▪ **she had a ~ of blood to the head** le sang lui est monté à la tête
6. BOT jonc *m* ▪ [for seats] paille *f* ▪ **~ mat** natte *f* (de jonc) ▪ **the floor is covered with ~ matting** des nattes (de jonc) recouvrent le sol
7.△ *drug sl* [from drugs] flash△ *m*.
◇ *adj* **1.** [urgent] urgent ▪ **it's a ~ job for Japan** c'est un travail urgent pour le Japon ▪ **~ order** commande *f* urgente
2. [hurried] fait à la hâte *OR* à la va-vite ▪ **I'm afraid it's a bit of a ~ job** je suis désolé, le travail a été fait un peu vite *OR* a été un peu bâclé
3. [busy - period] de pointe, d'affluence.
◆ **rushes** *npl* CIN rushes *mpl*, épreuves *fpl* de tournage.
◆ **rush about** *UK*, **rush around** *vi insep* courir çà et là.
◆ **rush in** *vi insep* **1.** *liter* entrer précipitamment *OR* à toute allure
2. [decide overhastily] : **you always ~ in without thinking first** tu fonces toujours tête baissée sans réfléchir.
◆ **rush out** ◇ *vi insep* sortir précipitamment *OR* à toute allure.
◇ *vt sep* [book, new product] sortir rapidement.
◆ **rush through** *vt sep* [job] expédier ▪ [goods ordered] envoyer d'urgence ▪ [order, application] traiter d'urgence ▪ [bill, legislation] faire voter à la hâte.
◆ **rush up** ◇ *vi insep* accourir.
◇ *vt sep* envoyer d'urgence ▪ **troops were ~ed up as reinforcements** on envoya d'urgence des troupes en renfort.

rushed [rʌʃt] *adj* [person] bousculé ▪ [work] fait à la hâte *OR* à la va-vite, bâclé ▪ **she was too ~ to stay and talk** elle était trop pressée pour rester bavarder ▪ **he doesn't like to be ~** il n'aime pas qu'on le bouscule ▪ **the meal was a bit ~** on a dû se dépêcher pour manger.

rush hour *n* heure *f* de pointe *OR* d'affluence ▪ **I never travel at ~** je ne me déplace jamais aux heures de pointe.
◆ **rush-hour** *comp* [crowds, traffic] des heures de pointe *OR* d'affluence.

rusk [rʌsk] *n* biscotte *f*.

russet ['rʌsɪt] ◇ *n* **1.** [colour] brun roux *m inv* **2.** [apple] reinette *f*.
◇ *adj* [colour] brun roux *(inv)*.

Russia ['rʌʃə] *pr n* Russie *f* ▪ **in ~** en Russie.

Russian ['rʌʃn] ◇ *n* **1.** [person] Russe *mf* **2.** LING russe *m*.
◇ *adj* russe.

Russian Federation *pr n* : **the Russian ~** la Fédération de Russie.

Russian roulette *n* roulette *f* russe.

Russky ['rʌskɪ] (*pl* **Russkies**) *n inf* Ruskof *m*, Ruski *mf*.

rust [rʌst] ◇ *n* **1.** [on metal - BOT] rouille *f* **2.** [colour] couleur *f* rouille.
◇ *adj* rouille *(inv)*.
◇ *vi* rouiller, se rouiller ▪ **it's completely ~ed through** il est complètement mangé par la rouille.
◇ *vt* rouiller.
◆ **rust up** *vi insep* rouiller, se rouiller ▪ **the hinges have ~ed up** les gonds sont bloqués par la rouille.

rusted ['rʌstɪd] *adj esp US* rouillé.

rustic ['rʌstɪk] ◇ *adj* rustique.
◇ *n* paysan *m*, - anne *f*, campagnard *m*, - e *f*.

rustle ['rʌsl] ◇ *vi* **1.** [make sound - gen] produire un froissement *OR* bruissement ; [- leaves] bruire ; [- dress, silk] froufrouter ▪ **something was rustling against the window** quelque chose frottait contre la fenêtre **2.** [steal cattle] voler du bétail.
◇ *vt* **1.** [leaves] faire bruire ▪ [papers] froisser ▪ [dress, silk] faire froufrouter **2.** [cattle] voler.
◇ *n* [sound - gen] froissement *m*, bruissement *m* ; [- of dress, silk] froufrou *m*, froufroutement *m*.
◆ **rustle up** *vt sep inf* [meal] faire en vitesse.

rustler ['rʌslər] *n* [of cattle] voleur *m*, - euse *f* de bétail ▪ **horse ~** voleur de chevaux.

rustling ['rʌslɪŋ] *n* **1.** [sound - gen] froissement *m*, bruissement *m* ; [- of leaves] bruissement *m* ; [- of dress, silk] froufrou *m*, froufroutement *m* **2.** [of cattle] vol *m* de bétail ▪ **horse ~** vol *m* de chevaux.

rustproof ['rʌstpru:f] ◇ *adj* [metal, blade] inoxydable ▪ [paint] antirouille *(inv)*.
◇ *vt* traiter contre la rouille.

rust-resistant = **rustproof** *(adj)*.

rusty ['rʌstɪ] (*comp* **rustier**, *superl* **rustiest**) *adj liter & fig* rouillé ▪ **my German is a bit ~** mon allemand est un peu rouillé ▪ **a ~ brown dress** une robe brun rouille.

rut [rʌt] (*pret & pp* **rutted**, *cont* **rutting**) ◇ *n* **1.** [in ground] ornière *f* **2.** *fig* routine *f* ▪ **to be (stuck) in a ~** s'encroûter ▪ **to get out of the ~** sortir de l'ornière **3.** ZOOL rut *m* ▪ **in ~** en rut.
◇ *vt* [ground] sillonner ▪ **the track had been deeply rutted by tractors** des tracteurs avaient creusé de profondes ornières dans le chemin.
◇ *vi* ZOOL être en rut.

rutabaga [,ru:tə'beɪgə] *n US* rutabaga *m*, chou-navet *m*.

ruthless ['ru:θlɪs] *adj* [person, behaviour - unpitying] impitoyable, cruel ; [- determined] résolu, acharné ▪ [criticism] impitoyable, implacable.

ruthlessly ['ru:θlɪslɪ] *adv* [pitilessly] impitoyablement, sans pitié ▪ [relentlessly] implacablement.

ruthlessness ['ru:θlɪsnɪs] *n* [of person, behaviour - pitilessness] caractère *m* impitoyable, dureté *f* ; [- determination] acharnement *m* ▪ [of criticism] dureté *f*.

rutted ['rʌtɪd] *adj* sillonné ▪ **a badly ~ road** une route complètement défoncée.

RV *n* **1.** = **revised version 2.** *US* (*abbrev of* **recreational vehicle**) camping-car *m*.

Rwanda [rʊ'ændə] ◇ *pr n* GEOG Ruanda *m*, Rwanda *m* ▪ **in ~** au Ruanda.
◇ *n* LING ruanda *m*.

Rwandan [rʊ'ændən] ◇ *n* Ruandais *m*, - e *f*.
◇ *adj* ruandais.

rye [raɪ] *n* **1.** [cereal] seigle *m* ▪ **'The Catcher in the Rye'** ***Salinger*** 'l'Attrape-cœur' **2.** [drink] = **rye whiskey**.

rye bread *n* pain *m* de seigle.

rye whiskey *n* whisky *m* (de seigle).

S

s (*pl* **s's** *OR pl* **ss**), **S** (*pl* **S's** *OR pl* **Ss**) [es] *n* [letter] s *m*, S *m*, *see also* **f**.

S (*written abbrev of* **south**) S.

Saar [sɑ:ʳ] *pr n* : **the ~** la Sarre.

Saarbrücken [ˌsɑ:ˈbrʊkən] *pr n* Sarrebruck.

Saarland [ˈsɑ:lænd] *pr n* Sarre *f* ■ **in ~** dans la Sarre.

Sabbath [ˈsæbəθ] *n* RELIG [Christian] dimanche *m*, jour *m* du Seigneur ■ [Jewish] sabbat *m* ■ **to observe/to break the ~** [Christian] observer/violer le repos du dimanche ; [Jew] observer/violer le sabbat.

sabbatical [səˈbætɪkl] ◇ *adj* [gen - RELIG] sabbatique.
◇ *n* congé *m* sabbatique.

saber *US* = **sabre**.

sable [ˈseɪbl] ◇ *n* [animal, fur] zibeline *f*.
◇ *comp* [coat] de *OR* en zibeline ■ [paintbrush] en poil de martre.
◇ *adj* [colour] noir ■ HERALD sable *(inv)*.

sabot [ˈsæbəʊ] *n* **1.** [shoe] sabot *m* **2.** MIL sabot *m*.

sabotage [ˈsæbətɑ:ʒ] ◇ *n* sabotage *m*.
◇ *vt* saboter.

saboteur [ˌsæbəˈtɜ:ʳ] *n* saboteur *m*, - euse *f*.

sabra [ˈsæbrə] *n* *US inf* sabra *mf*.

sabre *UK*, **saber** *US* [ˈseɪbəʳ] *n* sabre *m*.

sabre-rattling ◇ *n (U) liter* bruits *mpl* de sabre ■ *fig* intimidation *f*, bruit *m* de bottes.
◇ *adj* belliqueux.

sabre-toothed tiger *n* machairodonte *m*.

sac [sæk] *n* ANAT & BOT sac *m*.

saccharide [ˈsækəraɪd] *n* saccharide *m*, glucide *m*.

saccharin [ˈsækərɪn] *n* saccharine *f*.

saccharine [ˈsækərɪn] ◇ *adj* **1.** CHEM saccharin **2.** *fig* & *pej* [exaggeratedly sweet - smile] mielleux ; [- politeness] onctueux ; [- sentimentality] écœurant, sirupeux.
◇ *n* = **saccharin**.

sachet [ˈsæʃeɪ] *n* sachet *m*.

sack [sæk] ◇ *n* **1.** [bag] (grand) sac *m* **2.** *UK inf* [dismissal] licenciement *m* ■ **to give sb the ~** virer qqn ■ **to get the ~** se faire virer **3.** [pillage] sac *m*, pillage *m* **4.** *inf* [bed] pieu *m*, plumard *m* ■ **to hit the ~** se pieuter **5.** *arch* [wine] vin *m* blanc sec.
◇ *vt* **1.** *inf* [dismiss] mettre à la porte, virer **2.** [pillage] mettre à sac, piller.
◆ **sack out** *vi insep US inf* s'endormir.

sackbut [ˈsækbʌt] *n* saqueboute *f*.

sackcloth [ˈsækklɒθ] *n* toile *f* à sac *OR* d'emballage ■ **to wear ~ and ashes** RELIG faire pénitence avec le sac et la cendre ■ **to be in ~ and ashes** *fig* être contrit.

sackful [ˈsækfʊl] *n* sac *m* ■ **we've been getting letters by the ~** nous avons reçu des sacs entiers de lettres.

sacking [ˈsækɪŋ] *n* **1.** TEX toile *f* à sac *OR* d'emballage **2.** *inf* [dismissal] licenciement *m* **3.** [pillaging] sac *m*, pillage *m*.

sacrament [ˈsækrəmənt] *n* sacrement *m*.
◆ **Sacrament** *n* : **the Blessed** *OR* **holy Sacrament** le saint sacrement.

sacramental [ˌsækrəˈmentl] ◇ *adj* [rite] sacramentel ■ [theology] sacramentaire.
◇ *n* sacramental *m*.

sacred [ˈseɪkrɪd] *adj* **1.** [holy] sacré, saint ■ **~ to their gods** consacré à leurs dieux ■ **~ to his memory** voué *OR* dédié à sa mémoire ■ **~ music** musique *f* sacrée *OR* religieuse **2.** [solemn, important - task, duty] sacré, solennel ; [- promise, right] inviolable, sacré ■ [revered, respected] sacré ■ **nothing was ~ in his eyes** il n'y avait rien de sacré pour lui ■ **is nothing ~ any more?** on ne respecte donc plus rien aujourd'hui?

sacred cow *n fig* vache *f* sacrée.

Sacred Heart *n* RELIG Sacré-Cœur *m*.

sacrifice [ˈsækrɪfaɪs] ◇ *n* RELIG & *fig* sacrifice *m* ■ **to offer sthg (up) as a ~ to the gods** offrir qqch en sacrifice aux dieux ■ **I've made a lot of ~s for you** j'ai fait beaucoup de sacrifices pour vous.
◇ *vt* RELIG & *fig* sacrifier ■ **she ~d herself for her children** elle s'est sacrifiée pour ses enfants.

sacrificial [ˌsækrɪˈfɪʃl] *adj* [rite, dagger] sacrificiel ■ [victim] du sacrifice.

sacrilege [ˈsækrɪlɪdʒ] *n liter* & *fig* sacrilège *m*.

sacrilegious [ˌsækrɪˈlɪdʒəs] *adj liter* & *fig* sacrilège.

sacristan [ˈsækrɪstn] *n* sacristain *m*.

sacristy [ˈsækrɪstɪ] (*pl* **sacristies**) *n* sacristie *f*.

sacrosanct [ˈsækrəʊsæŋkt] *adj liter* & *fig* sacro-saint.

sacrum [ˈseɪkrəm] (*pl* **sacra** [-krə]) *n* sacrum *m*.

sad [sæd] (*comp* **sadder**, *superl* **saddest**) *adj* **1.** [unhappy, melancholy] triste ■ [stronger] affligé ■ **I shall be ~ to see you leave** je serai désolé de vous voir partir ■ **the flowers look** *OR* **are a bit ~** les fleurs ont triste mine **2.** [depressing - news, day, story] triste ; [- sight, occasion] triste, attristant ; [- painting, music etc] lugubre, triste ; [- loss] cruel, douloureux ■ **but ~ to say it didn't last long** mais, malheureusement, cela n'a pas duré ■ **the ~ fact is that he's incompetent** c'est malheureux à dire, mais c'est un incapable **3.** [regrettable] triste, regrettable ■ **it's a ~ state of affairs when this sort of thing can go unpunished**

il est vraiment regrettable que de tels actes restent impunis ■ **it's a ~ reflection on modern society** ça n'est pas flatteur pour la société moderne.

SAD *n* = **seasonal affective disorder**.

sadden ['sædn] *vt* rendre triste, attrister ■ [stronger] affliger.

saddle ['sædl] ◇ *n* **1.** [on horse, bicycle] selle *f* ■ **to be in the ~** *liter* & *fig* être en selle **2.** CULIN [of lamb, mutton] selle *f* ■ [of hare] râble *m* **3.** GEOG col *m*.
◇ *vt* **1.** [horse] seller **2.** *inf* [lumber] : **to ~ sb with sthg** refiler qqch à qqn ■ **she was ~d with the children** elle s'est retrouvée avec les enfants sur les bras ■ **I don't want to ~ myself with any more work** je ne veux pas me taper du travail supplémentaire.
◆ **saddle up** *vi insep* seller sa monture.

saddlebacked ['sædlbækt] *adj* [horse] ensellé.

saddlebag ['sædlbæg] *n* [for bicycle, motorcycle] sacoche *f* ■ [for horse] sacoche *f* de selle.

saddle horse *n* cheval *m* de selle.

saddler ['sædlər] *n* sellier *m*.

saddlery ['sædlərɪ] (*pl* **saddleries**) *n* [trade, shop, goods] sellerie *f*.

saddle sore *n* [on rider] *meurtrissures provoquées par de longues heures en selle* ■ [on horse] écorchure *f* OR excoriation *f* sous la selle.
◆ **saddle-sore** *adj* : **he was saddle-sore** il avait les fesses meurtries par de longues heures à cheval.

Sadducee ['sædjʊsi:] *n* Saducéen *m*, - enne *f*, Sadducéen *m*, - enne *f*.

sadism ['seɪdɪzm] *n* sadisme *m*.

sadist ['seɪdɪst] *n* sadique *mf*.

sadistic [sə'dɪstɪk] *adj* sadique.

sadly ['sædlɪ] *adv* **1.** [unhappily] tristement **2.** [unfortunately] malheureusement **3.** [regrettably] déplorablement ■ **you are ~ mistaken** vous vous trompez du tout au tout ■ **the house had been ~ neglected** la maison était dans un état déplorable.

sadness ['sædnɪs] *n* tristesse *f*.

sadomasochism [,seɪdəʊ'mæsəkɪzm] *n* sadomasochisme *m*.

sadomasochist [,seɪdəʊ'mæsəkɪst] *n* sadomasochiste *mf*.

sadomasochistic ['seɪdəʊ,mæsə'kɪstɪk] *adj* sadomasochiste.

Saducee ['sædjʊsi:] = **Sadducee**.

s.a.e., sae *n* UK = **stamped addressed envelope**.

safari [sə'fɑ:rɪ] *n* safari *m* ■ **they've gone on** OR **they're on ~** ils font un safari.

safari jacket *n* saharienne *f*.

safari park *n* safari park *m*.

safari suit *n* saharienne *f*.

safe [seɪf] ◇ *adj* **1.** [harmless, not dangerous - car, machine, area] sûr ; [- structure, building, fastening] solide ; [- beach] pas dangereux ■ **they claim nuclear power is perfectly ~** ils prétendent que l'énergie nucléaire n'est pas du tout dangereuse ■ **this medicine is/isn't ~ for young children** ce médicament convient/ne convient pas aux enfants en bas âge ■ **is it ~ to come out now?** est-ce qu'on peut sortir (sans danger OR sans crainte) maintenant? ■ **is it ~ to swim here?** est-ce qu'on peut OR est-ce dangereux de nager ici? ■ **the bomb has been made ~** la bombe a été désamorcée ■ **the police kept the crowd at a ~ distance** les policiers ont empêché la foule d'approcher de trop près ▶ **~ sex** le sexe sans risque ■ **~r sex** le sexe à moindre risque
2. [not risky, certain - course of action] sans risque OR risques, sans danger ; [- investment] sûr ; [- guess] certain ; [- estimate] raisonnable ■ **I played it ~ and arrived an hour early** pour ne pas prendre de risques, je suis arrivé une heure en avance ■ **you're always ~ ordering a steak** on ne prend jamais de risques en commandant un steak ■ **it's a ~ bet that he'll be late** on peut être sûr qu'il arrivera en retard ■ **the safest option** l'option la moins risquée ■ **I think it's ~ to say that everybody enjoyed themselves** je pense que l'on peut dire avec certitude que ça a plu à tout le monde ■ **it is a ~ assumption that...** on peut présumer sans risque que... ■ **take an umbrella (just) to be on the ~ side** prends un parapluie, c'est plus sûr OR au cas où ▶ **~ seat** UK POL *siège de député qui traditionnellement va toujours au même parti* ■ **it's as ~ as houses** cela ne présente pas le moindre risque ■ **better ~ than sorry** *prov* deux précautions valent mieux qu'une *prov*
3. [secure - place] sûr ■ **keep it in a ~ place** gardez-le en lieu sûr ■ **in ~ hands** en mains sûres ■ **in ~ custody** [child] sous bonne garde ; [securities, assets etc] en dépôt ▶ **~ haven** zone *f* protégée ■ **~ house** [for spies, wanted man] lieu *m* sûr
4. [reliable] : **is he ~ with the money/the children?** est-ce qu'on peut lui confier l'argent/les enfants (sans crainte)? ■ **she's a very ~ driver** c'est une conductrice très sûre, elle ne prend pas de risques au volant
5. [protected, out of danger] en sécurité, hors de danger ■ **the money's ~ in the bank** l'argent est en sécurité à la banque ■ **keep ~!** US prends bien soin de toi! ■ **the secret will be ~ with her** elle ne risque pas d'ébruiter le secret ■ **~ from attack/from suspicion** à l'abri d'une attaque/des soupçons ■ **no woman is ~ with him** c'est un coureur invétéré ■ **you don't look very ~ standing on that chair** tu as l'air d'être en équilibre instable debout sur cette chaise ■ **(have a) ~ journey!** bon voyage!
6. [unharmed, undamaged] sain et sauf ■ **we shall pay upon ~ delivery of the goods** nous payerons après réception des marchandises ■ **he arrived ~ (and sound)** il est arrivé sain et sauf.
◇ *n* **1.** [for money, valuables etc] coffre-fort *m*
2. [for food] garde-manger *m inv*.

safebreaker ['seɪf,breɪkər] *n* perceur *m*, - euse *f* de coffres-forts.

safe-conduct [-'kɒndʌkt] *n* sauf-conduit *m*.

safecracker ['seɪf,krækər] US = **safebreaker**.

safe-deposit box *n* coffre *m (dans une banque)*.

safeguard ['seɪfgɑ:d] ◇ *vt* sauvegarder ■ **to ~ sb/sthg against sthg** protéger qqn/qqch contre qqch.
◇ *n* sauvegarde *f* ■ **as a ~ against theft** comme précaution contre le vol.

safekeeping [,seɪf'ki:pɪŋ] *n* (bonne) garde *f* ■ **she was given the documents for ~** on lui a confié les documents.

safelight ['seɪflaɪt] *n* PHOT lampe *f* inactinique.

safely ['seɪflɪ] *adv* **1.** [without danger] sûrement ■ **drive ~!** soyez prudent sur la route! ■ **an area where women can ~ go out at night** un quartier où les femmes peuvent sortir la nuit en toute tranquillité ■ **you can ~ invest with them** vous pouvez investir chez eux en toute tranquillité **2.** [confidently, certainly] avec confiance OR certitude **3.** [securely] en sécurité, à l'abri ■ **all the doors and windows are ~ locked** toutes les portes et les fenêtres sont bien fermées **4.** [without incident] sans incident ■ **I'm just phoning to say I've arrived ~** je téléphone juste pour dire que je suis bien arrivé.

safety ['seɪftɪ] ◇ *n* [absence of danger] sécurité *f* ■ **the injured were helped to ~** on a aidé les blessés à se mettre à l'abri ■ **there are fears for the ~ of the hostages** on craint pour la vie des otages ■ **we are concerned about the ~ of imported toys** nous craignons que les jouets importés présentent certains dangers ■ **he ran for ~** il a couru se mettre à l'abri ■ **he reached ~** il arriva en lieu sûr ■ **in a place of ~** en lieu sûr ■ **there's ~ in numbers** plus on est nombreux, plus on est en sécurité ■ **~ first!** ne prenez pas de risques!
◇ *comp* [device, feature, measures etc] de sécurité ■ **~ regulations** consignes *fpl* de sécurité.

safety belt *n* ceinture *f* de sécurité.

safety catch *n* **1.** [on gun] cran *m* de sécurité **2.** [on window, door] cran *m* de sûreté.

safety chain *n* [on door] chaîne *f* de sûreté ■ [on bracelet] chaînette *f* de sûreté.

safety curtain *n* THEAT rideau *m* de fer.

safety-first *adj* [campaign, measures] de sécurité ■ [investment, shares] de toute sécurité.

safety glass *n* verre *m* de sécurité.

safety helmet *n* casque *m* (de protection).

safety island *n US* refuge *m (sur une route)*.

safety lamp *n* lampe *f* de mineur.

safety match *n* allumette *f* de sûreté.

safety net *n liter & fig* filet *m*.

safety officer *n* responsable *mf* de la sécurité.

safety pin *n* **1.** [fastener] épingle *f* de nourrice *OR* de sûreté **2.** [of grenade, bomb] goupille *f* de sûreté.

safety razor *n* rasoir *m* de sûreté.

safety valve *n liter & fig* soupape *f* de sûreté.

saffron ['sæfrən] ◇ *n* **1.** BOT & CULIN safran *m* **2.** [colour] jaune *m* safran.
◇ *adj* (jaune) safran *(inv)*.

sag [sæg] (*pret & pp* **sagged**, *cont* **sagging**) ◇ *vi* **1.** [rope] être détendu ■ [roof, beam, shelf, bridge] s'affaisser ■ [branch] ployer ■ [jowls, cheeks, hemline] pendre ■ [breasts] tomber ■ **the bed ~s in the middle** le lit s'affaisse au milieu **2.** [prices, stocks, demand] fléchir, baisser ■ [conversation] traîner ■ **the novel ~s a bit in the middle** le roman perd un peu de son intérêt au milieu ■ **their spirits sagged** ils perdirent courage.
◇ *n* [in prices, stocks, demand] fléchissement *m*, baisse *f*.

saga ['sɑ:gə] *n* **1.** [legend, novel, film] saga *f* **2.** [complicated story] : **I heard the whole ~ of her trip to France** elle m'a raconté son voyage en France en long et en large ■ **it's a ~ of bad management and wrong decisions** c'est une longue histoire de mauvaise gestion et de mauvaises décisions.

sagacious [sə'geɪʃəs] *adj lit* [person] sagace, perspicace, avisé ■ [remark] judicieux.

sage [seɪdʒ] ◇ *n* **1.** *lit* [wise person] sage *m* **2.** BOT & CULIN sauge *f*.
◇ *adj lit* [wise] sage, judicieux.

sagging ['sægɪŋ], **saggy** ['sægɪ] *adj* **1.** [rope] détendu ■ [bed, roof, bridge] affaissé ■ [shelf, beam] qui ploie ■ [hemline] qui pend ■ [jowls, cheeks] pendant ■ [breasts] tombant **2.** [prices, demand] en baisse ■ [spirits] abattu, découragé.

Sagittarius [,sædʒɪ'teərɪəs] ◇ *pr n* ASTROL & ASTRON Sagittaire *m*.
◇ *n* : **he's a ~** il est (du signe du) Sagittaire.

sago ['seɪgəʊ] *n* sagou *m* ■ **~ pudding** sagou au lait.

Sahara [sə'hɑ:rə] *pr n* : **the ~ (Desert)** le (désert du) Sahara.

Saharan [sə'hɑ:rən] *adj* saharien.

said [sed] ◇ *pt & pp* ▷ **say**.
◇ *adj* : **the ~ Howard Riley** le dit *OR* dénommé Howard Riley ■ **the ~ articles** les dits articles.

sail [seɪl] ◇ *n* **1.** [on boat] voile *f* ■ **in full ~** toutes voiles dehors ■ **the boat was under ~** le bateau était sous voiles ■ **to set ~** [boat] prendre la mer, appareiller ; [person] partir (en bateau)
2. [journey] voyage *m* en bateau ■ [pleasure trip] promenade *f* en bateau ■ **to go for a ~** faire un tour en bateau ■ **it's a few hours' ~ from here** c'est à quelques heures d'ici en bateau
3. [of windmill] aile *f*.
◇ *vi* **1.** [move over water - boat, ship] naviguer ■ **the trawler was ~ing north** le chalutier se dirigeait *OR* cinglait vers le nord ■ **the boat ~ed up/down the river** le bateau remonta/descendit le fleuve ▶ **to ~ close to the wind** naviguer au (plus) près ; *fig* jouer un jeu dangereux
2. [set off - boat, passenger] partir, prendre la mer, appareiller
3. [travel by boat] voyager (en bateau) ■ **are you flying or ~ing?** est-ce que vous y allez en avion ou en bateau?
4. [as sport or hobby] : **to ~, to go ~ing** faire de la voile
5. *fig* **swans ~ed by on the lake** des cygnes glissaient sur le lac ■ **birds ~ed across the sky** des oiseaux passaient dans le ciel ■ **a sports car ~ed past me** une voiture de sport m'a doublé à toute vitesse ■ **the balloons ~ed into the air** les ballons se sont envolés ■ **the ball ~ed over the wall** la balle est passée pardessus le mur ■ **she ~ed across the room to greet me** elle traversa la pièce d'un pas majestueux pour venir à ma rencontre.
◇ *vt* **1.** [boat - subj: captain] commander ; [- subj: helmsman, yachtsman] barrer ■ **she ~ed the boat into port** elle a manœuvré *OR* piloté le bateau jusque dans le port
2. [cross - sea, lake] traverser ■ **to ~ the seas** parcourir les mers.
◆ **sail into** *vt insep inf* [attack] tomber à bras raccourcis sur.
◆ **sail through** *vt insep & vi insep* [succeed] réussir haut la main.

sailboard ['seɪlbɔ:d] *n* planche *f* à voile.

sailboarder ['seɪl,bɔ:dər] *n* véliplanchiste *mf*.

sailboarding ['seɪl,bɔ:dɪŋ] *n* planche *f* à voile *(activité)*.

sailboat ['seɪlbəʊt] *n US* voilier *m*, bateau *m* à voile.

sailcloth ['seɪlklɒθ] *n* toile *f* à voile *OR* à voiles.

sailing ['seɪlɪŋ] *n* **1.** [activity] navigation *f* ■ [hobby] voile *f*, navigation *f* de plaisance ■ [sport] voile *f* **2.** [departure] départ *m*.

sailing boat *n* voilier *m*, bateau *m* (à voiles).

sailing dinghy *n* canot *m* à voile.

sailing ship *n* (grand) voilier *m*, navire *m* à voile *OR* à voiles.

sailmaker ['seɪl,meɪkər] *n* voilier *m (personne)*.

sailor ['seɪlər] *n* **1.** [gen] marin *m*, navigateur *m*, - trice *f* ■ **I'm a good/bad ~** j'ai/je n'ai pas le pied marin **2.** [as rank] matelot *m*.

sailor suit *n* costume *m* marin.

sailplane ['seɪlpleɪn] *n* planeur *m*.

saint [seɪnt] *n* saint *m*, - e *f* ■ **Saint David** saint David ■ **Saint David's day** la Saint-David.

Saint Bernard [*UK* -'bɜ:nəd, *US* -bər'nɑ:rd] *n* [dog] saint-bernard *m inv*.

sainted ['seɪntɪd] *adj* [person] sanctifié ■ [place] sacré, consacré.

Saint Elmo's fire [-'elməʊ-] *n* feu *m* Saint-Elme.

Saint Gotthard Pass [-'gɒtəd-] *pr n* : **the ~** le col du Saint-Gothard.

Saint Helena [-ɪ'li:nə] *pr n* Sainte-Hélène ■ **on ~** à Sainte-Hélène.

sainthood ['seɪnthʊd] *n* sainteté *f*.

Saint John's wort [-wɜ:t] *n* millepertuis *m*.

Saint Lawrence [-'lɒrəns] *pr n* : **the ~ (River)** le Saint-Laurent.

Saint Lawrence Seaway *pr n* GEOG voie *f* maritime du Saint-Laurent.

saintliness ['seɪntlɪnɪs] *n* sainteté *f*.

Saint Lucia [-'lu:ʃə] *pr n* Sainte-Lucie.

saintly ['seɪntlɪ] (*comp* **saintlier**, *superl* **saintliest**) *adj* [life, behaviour, humility, virtue] de saint ■ **she was a ~ woman** c'était une vraie sainte.

Saint Petersburg [-'pi:təzbɜ:g] *pr n* Saint-Pétersbourg.

saint's day *n* fête *f (d'un saint)*.

Saint Vitus' dance [-'vaɪtəs] *n* MED danse *f* de Saint-Guy, chorée *f*.

saith [seθ] *vt (pres sg) arch* & BIBLE ▷ **say**.

sake[1] [seɪk] *n* : **for sb's ~** [for their good] pour (le bien de) qqn ; [out of respect for] par égard pour qqn ; [out of love for] pour l'amour de qqn ■ **do it for my ~/for your own ~** fais-le pour moi/pour toi ■ **please come, for both our ~s** viens s'il te plaît, fais-le pour nous deux ■ **they decided not to divorce for the ~ of the children** ils ont décidé de ne pas divorcer à cause des enfants ■ **I walk to work for its own ~, not to save money** je vais travailler à pied pour le plaisir, pas par esprit d'économie ■ **they're just talking for the ~ of talking** *OR* **of it** ils parlent pour ne rien dire ■ **art for art's ~** l'art pour l'art ■ **for the ~ of higher profits** pour réaliser de plus gros bénéfices ■ **all that for the ~ of a few dollars** tout ça pour quelques malheureux dollars ■ **for old times' ~** en souvenir du passé ■ **for the ~ of argument, let's assume it costs £100** (pour les besoins de la discussion,) admettons que ça coûte 100 livres ■ **for goodness** *OR* **God's** *OR* **Christ's** *OR* **pity's** *OR* **heaven's ~!** pour l'amour du ciel *OR* de Dieu!

sake[2] ['sɑ:kɪ] *n* [drink] saké *m*.

salable ['seɪləbl] *adj* vendable.

salacious [sə'leɪʃəs] *adj fml* [joke, book, look] salace, grivois, obscène.

salad ['sæləd] *n* salade *f* ■ **tomato/fruit/mixed ~** salade de tomates/de fruits/mixte.

salad bar *n* [restaurant] *restaurant où l'on mange des salades* ■ [area] salad bar *m*.

salad bowl *n* saladier *m*.

salad cream *n UK sorte de mayonnaise (vendue en bouteille).*

salad days *npl fig & lit* années *fpl* de jeunesse.

salad dressing *n* [gen] sauce *f (pour salade)* ■ [French dressing] vinaigrette *f*.

salad oil *n* huile *f* pour assaisonnement.

salad servers *npl* couverts *mpl* à salade.

salamander ['sælə,mændər] *n* salamandre *f*.

salami [sə'lɑ:mɪ] *n* salami *m*, saucisson *m* sec.

salaried ['sælərɪd] *adj* salarié ■ **a ~ job** [gen] un emploi salarié ; [as opposed to wage-earning] *emploi dont le salaire est mensuel et non hebdomadaire.*

salary ['sælərɪ] (*pl* **salaries**) ◇ *n* salaire *m*.
◇ *comp* [bracket, level, scale] des salaires ■ **~ earner** salarié *m*, - e *f*.

sale [seɪl] ◇ *n* **1.** [gen] vente *f* ■ **to make a ~** conclure une vente ■ **the branch with the highest ~s** la succursale dont le chiffre d'affaires est le plus élevé ■ **'for ~'** 'à vendre' ■ **I'm afraid that article is not for ~** je regrette, cet article n'est pas à vendre ■ **to put sthg up for ~** mettre qqch en vente ■ **on ~** en vente ➲ **~ of work** vente *f* de charité **2.** [event] soldes *mpl* ■ **I got it in a ~** je l'ai acheté en solde ➲ **closing-down ~** liquidation *f* ■ **~ price** prix *m* soldé **3.** [auction] vente *f* (aux enchères).
◇ *comp* [goods] soldé.
◆ **sales** *comp* [department, executive] des ventes, commercial ■ [drive, force, team] de vente ■ [promotion, forecasts, figures] des ventes ■ **~s assistant** vendeur *m*, - euse *f* ■ **~s conference** conférence *f* du personnel des ventes.

saleable ['seɪləbl] = **salable**.

saleroom ['seɪlrum] *n UK* salle *f* des ventes.

salesclerk ['seɪlzklɜ:rk] *n US* vendeur *m*, - euse *f*.

salesgirl ['seɪlzgɜ:l] *n* vendeuse *f*.

salesman ['seɪlzmən] (*pl* **salesmen** [-mən]) *n* [in shop] vendeur *m* ■ [rep] représentant *m* (de commerce) ■ **an insurance ~** un représentant en assurances.

sales manager *n* directeur *m* commercial, directrice *f* commerciale.

salesmanship ['seɪlzmənʃɪp] *n* art *m* de la vente, technique *f* de vente.

salesperson ['seɪlz,pɜ:sn] (*pl* **salespeople** [-,pi:pl]) *n* [in shop] vendeur *m*, - euse *f* ■ [rep] représentant *m*, - e *f* (de commerce).

sales pitch = **sales talk**.

sales rep, sales representative *n* représentant *m*, - e *f* (de commerce).

salesroom ['seɪlzrum] *US* = **saleroom**.

sales slip *n US* ticket *m* de caisse.

sales talk *n* boniment *m*.

sales tax *n US* taxe *f* à la vente.

saleswoman ['seɪlz,wumən] (*pl* **saleswomen** [-,wɪmɪn]) *n* [in shop] vendeuse *f* ■ [rep] représentante *f* (de commerce).

salient ['seɪljənt] ◇ *adj* saillant.
◇ *n* ARCHIT & MIL saillant *m*.

salina [sə'laɪnə] *n* [marsh] marais *m* salant ■ [spring] source *f* saline ■ [lake] lac *m* salé.

saline ['seɪlaɪn] *adj* salin ■ **~ drip** MED perfusion *f* saline.

saliva [sə'laɪvə] *n* salive *f*.

salivary gland ['sælɪvərɪ-] *n* glande *f* salivaire.

salivate ['sælɪveɪt] *vi* saliver.

sallow ['sæləu] ◇ *adj* [gen] jaunâtre ■ [face, complexion] jaunâtre, cireux.
◇ *n* BOT saule *m*.

sally ['sælɪ] *n* (*pl* **sallies**) **1.** [gen - MIL] sortie *f* **2.** *fml* [quip] saillie *f lit*.
◆ **sally forth, sally out** *vi insep* (*pret & pp* **sallied**) *lit* sortir ■ **we all sallied forth** *OR* **out into the snow** nous sommes tous partis gaillardement sous la neige.

Sally Army *n UK inf* = **Salvation Army**.

salmon ['sæmən] (*pl inv OR pl* **salmons**) *n* saumon *m* ■ **young ~** tacon *m*.

salmonella [,sælmə'nelə] (*pl* **salmonellae** [-li:]) *n* salmonella *f inv*, salmonelle *f* ■ **~ poisoning** salmonellose *f*.

salmon pink *n* (rose *m*) saumon *m*.
◆ **salmon-pink** *adj* (rose) saumon *(inv)*.

salmon trout *n* truite *f* saumonée.

Salome [sə'ləumɪ] *pr n* Salomé.

salon ['sælɒn] *n* salon *m*.

saloon [sə'lu:n] *n* **1.** *UK* = **saloon car 2.** [public room] salle *f*, salon *m* ■ [on ship] salon *m* **3.** *US* [bar] bar *m* ■ [in Wild West] saloon *m* **4.** *UK* = **saloon bar**.

saloon bar *n UK* salon *m (dans un pub)*.

saloon car *n UK* conduite *f* intérieure, berline *f*.

salopettes [,sælə'pets] *npl* combinaison *f* de ski.

salsa ['sælsə] *n* **1.** MUS salsa *f* **2.** *sauce pimentée servie en accompagnement de plats mexicains.*

salt [sɔ:lt, sɒlt] ◇ *n* **1.** CHEM & CULIN sel *m* ■ **there's too much ~ in the soup** la soupe est trop salée ■ **the ~ of the earth** le sel de la terre ➲ **to rub ~ into the wound** remuer le couteau dans la plaie **2.** *inf* [sailor] : **old ~** (vieux) loup *m* de mer.
◇ *vt* **1.** [food] saler **2.** [roads] saler, répandre du sel sur.
◇ *adj* salé ■ **~ pork** porc *m* salé, petit salé *m*.
◆ **salts** *npl* PHARM sels *mpl* ■ **like a dose of ~s** rapidement.
◆ **salt away** *vt sep inf fig* [money] mettre de côté.
◆ **salt down** *vt sep* saler, conserver dans du sel.

SALT [sɔ:lt, sɒlt] (*abbrev of* **Strategic Arms Limitation Talks/Treaty**) *n* SALT *m* ■ **~ talks** négociations *fpl* SALT.

salt box *n* **1.** = **salt cellar 2.** *US* ARCHIT *maison à toit mansardé ayant deux étages à l'avant et un étage à l'arrière.*

salt cellar *n* salière *f*.

salted ['sɔ:ltɪd] *adj* salé.

salt flat *n* salant *m*.

salt-free *adj* sans sel.

salt lake *n* lac *m* salé.

saltlick ['sɔ:ltlɪk] *n* **1.** [block] pierre *f* à lécher **2.** [place] salant *m*.

salt marsh *n* marais *m* salant.

salt mine *n* mine *f* de sel.

saltpan ['sɔ:ltpæn] *n* marais *m* salant.

saltpetre *UK*, **saltpeter** *US* [,sɔ:lt'pi:tə^r] *n* salpêtre *m*.

salt shaker *n US* salière *f*.

salt tax *n* HIST gabelle *f*.

salt water *n* eau *f* salée.
◆ **saltwater** *adj* [fish, plant] de mer.

saltworks ['sɔ:ltwɜ:ks] (*pl inv*) *n* saline *f*, salines *fpl*.

salty ['sɔ:ltɪ] (*comp* **saltier**, *superl* **saltiest**) *adj* [food, taste] salé ▪ [deposit] saumâtre.

salubrious [sə'lu:brɪəs] *adj* **1.** [respectable] respectable, bien ▪ **it's not the most ~ of bars** c'est un bar plutôt mal famé **2.** [healthy] salubre, sain.

salutary ['sæljʊtrɪ] *adj* salutaire.

salutation [,sælju'teɪʃn] *n* **1.** [greeting] salut *m*, salutation *f* **2.** [on letter] formule *f* de début de lettre.

salute [sə'lu:t] ◇ *n* **1.** MIL [with hand] salut *m* ▪ **to give (sb) a ~** faire un salut (à qqn) ▪ **to stand at ~** garder le salut ▪ **to take the ~** passer les troupes en revue ‖ [with guns] salve *f* ▪ **a twenty-one gun ~** une salve de vingt et un coups de canon **2.** [greeting] salut *m*, salutation *f* **3.** [tribute] hommage *m*.
◇ *vt* **1.** MIL [with hand] saluer ▪ [with guns] tirer une salve en l'honneur de **2.** [greet] saluer **3.** [acknowledge, praise] saluer, acclamer.
◇ *vi* MIL faire un salut.

Salvador ['sælvədɔ:^r] *pr n* Salvador *(port)*.

salvage ['sælvɪdʒ] ◇ *vt* **1.** [vessel, cargo, belongings] sauver ▪ [old newspapers, scrap metal] récupérer **2.** *fig* [mistake, meal] rattraper ▪ [situation] rattraper, sauver ▪ **to ~ one's reputation** sauver sa réputation.
◇ *n* **1.** [recovery - of vessel, cargo, belongings, furniture] sauvetage *m* ; [- of old newspapers, scrap metal] récupération *f* **2.** *(U)* [things recovered - from shipwreck, disaster] objets *mpl* sauvés ; [- for re-use, recycling] objets *mpl* récupérés **3.** [payment] indemnité *f* OR prime *f* de sauvetage.
◇ *comp* [company, operation, vessel] de sauvetage.

salvation [sæl'veɪʃn] *n* **1.** RELIG salut *m* **2.** *fig* salut *m* ▪ **writing has always been my ~** écrire m'a toujours sauvé.

Salvation Army *pr n* : **the ~** l'Armée *f* du salut.

salvationist [sæl'veɪʃənɪst] *n* **1.** [member of evangelical sect] salutiste *mf* **2.** [member of Salvation Army] salutiste *mf*.

salve [sælv] ◇ *n* **1.** [ointment] baume *m*, pommade *f* **2.** *fig* [relief] baume *m lit*, apaisement *m*.
◇ *vt* **1.** [relieve] calmer, soulager ▪ **I did it to ~ my conscience** je l'ai fait par acquit de conscience **2.** [salvage] sauver.

salver ['sælvə^r] *n* plateau *m* (de service).

salvo ['sælvəʊ] (*pl* **salvos** OR *pl* **salvoes**) *n* **1.** MIL salve *f* **2.** *fig* [of applause] salve *f* ▪ [of laughter] éclat *m* ▪ [of insults] torrent *m*.

Samaritan [sə'mærɪtn] ◇ *n* RELIG Samaritain *m*, - e *f*.
◇ *adj* samaritain.
◆ **Samaritans** *pr npl* : **the ~s** *association proposant un soutien moral par téléphone aux personnes déprimées,* ≃ SOS Amitié.

samba ['sæmbə] ◇ *n* samba *f*.
◇ *vi* danser la samba.

same [seɪm] ◇ *adj* même ▪ **the two suitcases are exactly the ~ colour/shape** les deux valises sont exactement de la même couleur/ont exactement la même forme ▪ **they are one and the ~ thing** c'est une seule et même chose ▪ **they are one and the ~ person** ils ne font qu'un ▪ **it all boils down to the ~ thing** cela revient au même ▪ **see you ~ time, ~ place** je te retrouve à la même heure, au même endroit ➊ **~ difference!** *inf* c'est du pareil au même!
◇ *pron* **1.** : **the ~** [unchanged] le même *m*, la même *f*, les mêmes *mf pl* ▪ **it's the ~ as before** c'est comme avant ▪ **life's just not the ~ now they're gone** les choses ont changé depuis qu'ils sont partis ▪ **it's not spelt the ~** ça ne s'écrit pas de la même façon ‖ [identical] identique ▪ **the two vases are exactly the ~** les deux vases sont identiques **2.** [used in comparisons] : **the ~** la même chose ▪ **it's always the ~** c'est toujours la même chose OR toujours pareil ➊ **aren't you Freddie Fortescue? – the very ~** vous n'êtes pas Freddie Fortescue? – lui-même ▪ **(the) ~ again, please** la même chose (, s'il vous plaît) ▪ **if it's all the ~ to you, I'll go now** si cela ne vous fait rien, je vais partir maintenant ▪ **it's all** OR **just the ~ to me what you do** tu peux faire ce que tu veux, ça m'est bien égal ▪ **the ~ is true of, the ~ holds for** il en va de même pour ▪ **I was really cross – ~ here!** *inf* j'étais vraiment fâché – et moi donc! ▪ **Happy Christmas – (and the) ~ to you!** Joyeux Noël – à vous aussi OR de même! ▪ **stupid idiot – and the ~ to you!** *inf* espèce d'imbécile! – imbécile toi-même! **3.** LAW : **the ~** [aforementioned] le susdit *m*, la susdite *f* **4.** COMM : **and for delivery of ~** et pour livraison de ces (mêmes) articles.
◆ **all the same, just the same** *adv phr* quand même ▪ **all the ~, I still like her** je l'aime bien quand même.

same-day *adj* COMM [processing, delivery] dans la journée.

sameness ['seɪmnɪs] *n* **1.** [similarity] similitude *f*, ressemblance *f* **2.** [tedium] monotonie *f*, uniformité *f*.

samey ['seɪmɪ] *adj UK inf pej* monotone, ennuyeux.

Samoa [sə'məʊə] *pr n* Samoa *m* ▪ **in ~** à Samoa.

Samoan [sə'məʊən] ◇ *n* **1.** [person] Samoan *m*, - e *f* **2.** LING samoan *m*.
◇ *adj* samoan.

samosa [sə'məʊsə] (*pl inv* OR *pl* **samosas**) *n petit pâté indien à la viande ou aux légumes.*

samovar ['sæmə,vɑ:^r] *n* samovar *m*.

sampan ['sæmpæn] *n* sampan *m*, sampang *m*.

sample ['sɑ:mpl] ◇ *n* **1.** [gen - COMM] & SOCIOL échantillon *m* ▪ **a free ~** un échantillon gratuit **2.** GEOL, MED & SCI échantillon *m*, prélèvement *m* ▪ [of blood] prélèvement *m* ▪ [of urine] échantillon *m* ▪ **to take a ~** prélever un échantillon, faire un prélèvement ▪ **to take a blood ~** faire une prise de sang.
◇ *comp* : **a ~ bottle/pack** *etc* un échantillon ▪ **a ~ section of the population** un échantillon représentatif de la population ▪ **do the ~ exercise first** faites d'abord l'exercice donné à titre d'exemple.
◇ *vt* **1.** [food, drink] goûter (à), déguster ▪ [experience] goûter à **2.** MUS échantillonner, sampler **3.** [opinion, market] sonder.

sampler ['sɑ:mplə^r] *n* **1.** SEW modèle *m* de broderie **2.** [collection of samples] échantillonnage *m*, sélection *f* **3.** MUS échantillonneur *m*, sampler *m*.

sampling ['sɑ:mplɪŋ] *n* [gen - COMPUT] échantillonnage *m* ▪ MUS échantillonnage *m*, sampling *m*.

samurai ['sæmʊraɪ] (*pl inv*) *n* samouraï *m*, samourai *m inv*.

San Andreas Fault [sænæn'dreɪəs-] *pr n* : **the ~** la faille de San Andreas *(faille géologique à l'origine de nombreux tremblements de terre en Californie)*.

sanatorium [,sænə'tɔ:rɪəm] (*pl* **sanatoriums** OR *pl* **sanatoria** [-rɪə]) *n* [nursing home] sanatorium *m* ▪ [sick bay] infirmerie *f*.

sanctification [,sæŋktɪfɪ'keɪʃn] *n* sanctification *f*.

sanctify ['sæŋktɪfaɪ] (*pret & pp* **sanctified**) *vt* sanctifier.

sanctimonious [,sæŋktɪ'məʊnjəs] *adj* moralisateur ▪ **I hate his ~ manner** je ne supporte pas ses airs de petit saint.

sanction ['sæŋkʃn] ◇ *n* **1.** [approval] sanction *f*, accord *m*, consentement *m* ▪ **it hasn't yet been given official ~** ceci n'a pas encore été officiellement approuvé OR sanctionné, ceci n'a pas encore eu l'approbation OR sanction officielle ▪ **it has the ~ of long usage** c'est consacré par l'usage **2.** [punitive measure] sanction *f* ▪ **the firm was accused of ~s busting** la société a été accusée d'avoir contourné les sanctions ▪ **to impose (economic) ~s on a country** prendre des sanctions (économiques) à l'encontre d'un pays.
◇ *vt* sanctionner, entériner ▪ [behaviour] approuver.

sanctity ['sæŋktətɪ] *n* [of person, life] sainteté *f* ▪ [of marriage, property, place - holiness] caractère *m* sacré ; [- inviolability] inviolabilité *f*.

sanctuary ['sæŋktʃʊərɪ] (*pl* **sanctuaries**) *n* **1.** [holy place] sanctuaire *m* **2.** [refuge] refuge *m*, asile *m* ▶ **wildlife ~** réserve *f* animale.

sanctum ['sæŋktəm] (*pl* **sanctums** *OR pl* **sancta** ['sæŋktə]) *n* **1.** [holy place] sanctuaire *m* **2.** *hum* [private place] refuge *m*, retraite *f*, tanière *f*.

sand [sænd] ◇ *n* **1.** [substance] sable *m* ▪ **shifting ~** sables mouvants ▪ **the ~s of time** le temps qui passe ▪ **to build on ~** *fig* bâtir sur le sable **2.** △ *US* [courage] cran *m*.
◇ *comp* [dune] de sable.
◇ *vt* **1.** [polish, smooth] poncer **2.** [spread sand on] sabler.
❖ **sand down** *vt sep* [wood, metal] poncer au papier de verre, décaper.

sandal ['sændl] *n* **1.** [footwear] sandale *f* **2.** = **sandalwood**.

sandalwood ['sændlwʊd] *n* bois *m* de santal.

sandbag ['sændbæg] (*pret & pp* **sandbagged**) ◇ *n* sac *m* de sable *OR* de terre.
◇ *vt* **1.** [shore up] renforcer avec des sacs de sable ▪ [protect] protéger avec des sacs de sable **2.** *inf* [hit] assommer **3.** *US inf* [coerce] : **to ~ sb into doing sthg** forcer qqn à faire qqch.

sandbank ['sændbæŋk] *n* banc *m* de sable.

sandbar ['sændbɑːʳ] *n* barre *f* (*dans la mer, dans un estuaire*).

sandblast ['sændblɑːst] ◇ *vt* décaper à la sableuse, sabler.
◇ *n* jet *m* de sable.

sandblaster ['sænd,blɑːstəʳ] *n* sableuse *f*.

sandblasting ['sænd,blɑːstɪŋ] *n* décapage *m* à la sableuse, sablage *m*.

sandbox ['sændbɒks] *n* **1.** RAIL sablière *f* **2.** [for children] bac *m* à sable.

sandcastle ['sænd,kɑːsl] *n* château *m* de sable.

sander ['sændəʳ] *n* [tool] ponceuse *f*.

sand flea *n* [sandhopper] puce *f* de mer, talitre *m* ▪ [chigoe] chique *f*.

sand fly *n* phlébotome *m*, mouche *f* des sables.

sandhopper ['sænd,hɒpəʳ] *n* puce *f* de mer.

sanding ['sændɪŋ] *n* **1.** [of wood, plaster] ponçage *m* **2.** [of roads] sablage *m*.

Sandinista [,sændɪ'niːstə] ◇ *adj* sandiniste.
◇ *n* sandiniste *mf*.

sand lot *n US* terrain *m* vague.

S and M *n inf* sadomasochisme *m*.

sandman ['sændmæn] *n* marchand *m* de sable *fig*.

sand martin *n* hirondelle *f* de rivage.

sandpaper ['sænd,peɪpəʳ] ◇ *n* papier *m* de verre.
◇ *vt* poncer (au papier de verre).

sandpie ['sændpaɪ] *n* pâté *m* de sable.

sandpiper ['sænd,paɪpəʳ] *n* bécasseau *m*, chevalier *m*.

sandpit ['sændpɪt] *n UK* **1.** [for children] bac *m* à sable **2.** [quarry] sablonnière *f*.

sandshoe ['sændʃuː] *n UK* (chaussure *f* de) tennis *m*.

sandstone ['sændstəʊn] *n* grès *m*.

sandstorm ['sændstɔːm] *n* tempête *f* de sable.

sand trap *n US* bunker *m* (de sable).

sandwich ['sænwɪdʒ] ◇ *n* [bread] sandwich *m* ▪ **a ham ~** un sandwich au jambon.
◇ *vt* **1.** *inf* [place] intercaler ▪ **I'll try to ~ you (in) between appointments** j'essaierai de vous caser entre deux rendez-vous **2.** *inf* [trap] prendre en sandwich, coincer **3.** [join - gen] joindre ; [- with glue] coller.

sandwich bar *n UK* ≃ snack *m* (*où on vend des sandwiches*).

sandwich board *n* panneau *m* publicitaire (*porté par un homme-sandwich*).

sandwich cake *n UK* gâteau *m* fourré.

sandwich course *n UK formation en alternance*.

sandwich loaf *n* ≃ pain *m* de mie.

sandwich man *n* homme-sandwich *m*.

sandy ['sændɪ] (*comp* **sandier**, *superl* **sandiest**) *adj* **1.** [beach, desert] de sable ▪ [soil, road] sablonneux ▪ [water, alluvium] sableux ▪ [floor, clothes] couvert de sable **2.** [in colour] (couleur) sable (*inv*) ▪ **he has ~ OR ~-coloured hair** il a les cheveux blond roux.

sand yacht *n* char *m* à voile.

sane [seɪn] *adj* **1.** [person] sain d'esprit ▪ **to be of ~ mind** être sain d'esprit ▪ **how do you manage to stay ~ in this environment?** comment fais-tu pour ne pas devenir fou dans une ambiance pareille? **2.** [action] sensé ▪ [attitude, approach, policy] raisonnable, sensé.

sanely ['seɪnlɪ] *adv* raisonnablement.

sang [sæŋ] *pt* ▷ **sing**.

sangfroid [,sɒŋ'frwɑː] *n* sang-froid *m*.

sangria [sæŋ'grɪə] *n* sangria *f*.

sanguine ['sæŋgwɪn] ◇ *adj* **1.** [optimistic - person, temperament] optimiste, confiant ; [- attitude, prospect] **: he was ~ about the company's prospects** il voyait l'avenir de l'entreprise avec optimisme **2.** *lit* [ruddy - complexion] sanguin, rubicond.
◇ *n* ART sanguine *f*.

sanitary ['sænɪtrɪ] *adj* **1.** [hygienic] hygiénique **2.** [arrangements, conditions, measures, equipment] sanitaire.

sanitary engineer *n* technicien *m* du service sanitaire.

sanitary inspector *n* inspecteur *m* de la santé publique.

sanitary towel *UK*, **sanitary napkin** *US n* serviette *f* hygiénique.

sanitation [,sænɪ'teɪʃn] *n* [public health] hygiène *f* publique ▪ [sewers] système *m* sanitaire ▪ [plumbing] sanitaires *mpl*.

sanitation worker *n US* éboueur *m*.

sanitize, ise ['sænɪtaɪz] *vt* **1.** [disinfect] désinfecter **2.** *fig* [expurgate] expurger ▪ **this is the ~d image he would like to project** c'est l'image proprette *OR* aseptisée qu'il voudrait présenter.

sanitorium [,sænɪ'tɔːrɪəm], **sanitarium** [,sænɪ'teərɪəm] *US* = **sanatorium**.

sanity ['sænətɪ] *n* **1.** [mental health] santé *f* mentale ▪ **to lose one's ~** perdre la raison **2.** [reasonableness] bon sens *m*, rationalité *f*.

sank [sæŋk] *pt* ▷ **sink**.

San Marino [,sænmə'riːnəʊ] *pr n* Saint-Marin.

sans [sænz] *prep arch* sans.

Sanskrit ['sænskrɪt] ◇ *adj* sanskrit.
◇ *n* sanskrit *m*.

sansserif [,sæn'serɪf] *n* (*U*) TYPO caractères *mpl* bâton *OR* sans empattement.

Santa ['sæntə] *inf*, **Santa Claus** ['sæntə,klɔːz] *pr n* le père Noël.

sap [sæp] (*pret & pp* **sapped**, *cont* **sapping**) ◇ *n* **1.** BOT sève *f* **2.** *US inf* [fool] bêta *m*, - asse *f*, andouille *f* ▪ [gullible person] nigaud *m*, - e *f* **3.** *US inf* [cosh] matraque *f*, gourdin *m* **4.** MIL sape *f*.
◇ *vt* **1.** *fig* [strength, courage] saper, miner **2.** *US inf* [cosh] assommer (d'un coup de gourdin) **3.** MIL saper.

sapient ['seɪpjənt] *adj fml* sage.

sapling ['sæplɪŋ] *n* **1.** BOT jeune arbre *m* **2.** *lit* [youth] jouvenceau *m*.

sapper ['sæpəʳ] *n UK* MIL soldat *m* du génie, sapeur *m*.

Sapphic ['sæfɪk] <> *adj* **1.** [relating to Sappho] saphique **2.** LIT : **~ metre** vers *m* saphique.
<> *n* LIT saphique *m*.

sapphire ['sæfaɪəʳ] <> *n* [gem, colour] saphir *m*.
<> *comp* [ring, pendant] de saphir.
<> *adj* [in colour] saphir *(inv)*.

Sappho ['sæfəʊ] *pr n* Sapho, Sappho.

sappy ['sæpɪ] (*comp* **sappier**, *superl* **sappiest**) *adj* **1.** [tree, leaves] plein de sève ▪ [wood] vert **2.** *US inf* [stupid] cloche **3.** *US inf* [corny] nunuche.

sapwood ['sæpwʊd] *n* aubier *m*.

sarcasm ['sɑːkæzm] *n (U)* sarcasme *m*.

sarcastic [sɑː'kæstɪk] *adj* sarcastique.

sarcastically [sɑː'kæstɪklɪ] *adv* d'un ton sarcastique.

sarcoma [sɑː'kəʊmə] (*pl* **sarcomas** *OR pl* **sarcomata** [-mətə]) *n* sarcome *m*.

sarcophagus [sɑː'kɒfəgəs] (*pl* **sarcophaguses** *OR pl* **sarcophagi** [-gaɪ]) *n* sarcophage *m*.

sardine [sɑː'diːn] *n* sardine *f* ▪ **we were packed in like ~s** nous étions serrés comme des sardines.

Sardinia [sɑː'dɪnjə] *pr n* Sardaigne *f* ▪ **in ~** en Sardaigne.

Sardinian [sɑː'dɪnjən] <> *n* **1.** [person] Sarde *mf* **2.** LING sarde *m*.
<> *adj* sarde.

sardonic [sɑː'dɒnɪk] *adj* sardonique.

sardonically [sɑː'dɒnɪklɪ] *adv* sardoniquement.

Sargasso Sea *pr n* : **the ~** la mer des Sargasses.

sarge [sɑːdʒ] (*abbrev of* **sergeant**) *n inf* sergent *m*.

sari ['sɑːrɪ] *n* sari *m*.

Sark [sɑːk] *pr n* Sercq.

sarky ['sɑːkɪ] (*comp* **sarkier**, *superl* **sarkiest**) *adj UK inf* sarcastique.

sarong [sə'rɒŋ] *n* sarong *m*.

SARS (*abbrev of* **severe acute respiratory syndrome**) ['særz] *n* MED SRAS *m*.

sartorial [sɑː'tɔːrɪəl] *adj* vestimentaire ▪ **his ~ elegance** son élégance vestimentaire, l'élégance de sa mise.

Sartrean, Sartrian ['sɑːtrɪən] *adj* sartrien.

SAS (*abbrev of* **Special Air Service**) *pr n commando d'intervention spéciale de l'armée britannique*.

SASE *n US* = **self-addressed stamped envelope**.

sash [sæʃ] *n* **1.** [belt] ceinture *f* (en étoffe) ▪ [sign of office] écharpe *f* **2.** [frame of window, door] châssis *m*, cadre *m*.

sashay ['sæʃeɪ] *vi US inf* [saunter] flâner ▪ [strut] parader, se pavaner ▪ **he ~ed in and said hello** [casually] il entra d'un pas nonchalant et dit bonjour ; [ostentatiously] il entra en se pavanant et dit bonjour.

sash cord *n* corde *f (d'une fenêtre à guillotine)*.

sash window *n* fenêtre *f* à guillotine.

Saskatchewan [sæs'kætʃɪwən] *pr n* Saskatchewan *m* ▪ **in ~** dans le Saskatchwan.

sasquatch ['sæskwætʃ] *n animal légendaire (sorte de yeti) du Canada et du nord des États-Unis*.

sass [sæs] *US inf* <> *n* culot *m*, toupet *m*.
<> *vt* répondre (avec impertinence) à.

Sassenach ['sæsənæk] *n Scotland inf pej terme péjoratif par lequel les Écossais désignent les Anglais*.

sassy ['sæsɪ] (*comp* **sassier**, *superl* **sassiest**) *adj US inf* culotté, gonflé.

sat [sæt] *pt & pp* ▷ **sit**.

Sat. (*written abbrev of* **Saturday**) sam.

SAT [sæt] (*abbrev of* **Scholastic Aptitude Test**) *n examen d'entrée à l'université aux États-Unis*.

Satan ['seɪtn] *pr n* Satan.

satanic [sə'tænɪk] *adj* satanique ▪ **'The Satanic Verses'** ***Rushdie*** 'les Versets sataniques'.

satanism ['seɪtənɪzm] *n* satanisme *m*.

satanist ['seɪtənɪst] <> *adj* sataniste.
<> *n* sataniste *mf*.

satchel ['sætʃəl] *n* cartable *m*.

sate [seɪt] *vt* [satisfy - person] rassasier ; [- hunger] assouvir ; [- thirst] étancher.

sated ['seɪtɪd] *adj* [person] rassasié ▪ [hunger] assouvi ▪ [thirst] étanché.

sateen [sæ'tiːn] *n* satinette *f*.

satellite ['sætəlaɪt] <> *n* **1.** ASTRON & TELEC satellite *m* ▪ **broadcast live by ~** transmis en direct par satellite **2.** [country] pays *m* satellite **3.** [in airport] satellite *m*.
<> *comp* **1.** [broadcast, broadcasting, network, relay] par satellite ▪ **~ dish** antenne *f* de télévision par satellite ▪ **~ television** télévision *f* par satellite **2.** [country] satellite ▪ **~ state** état *m* satellite.

satiate ['seɪʃɪeɪt] *vt lit* **1.** [satisfy - hunger, desire] assouvir ; [- thirst] étancher **2.** [gorge] rassasier ▪ **~d with pleasure** repu de plaisir.

satiation [,seɪʃɪ'eɪʃn] *n* satiété *f* ▪ **to the point of ~** à satiété, jusqu'à satiété.

satiety [sə'taɪətɪ] = **satiation**.

satin ['sætɪn] <> *n* satin *m*.
<> *comp* **1.** [dress, shirt] en *OR* de satin **2.** [finish] satiné.

satin stitch *n* passé *m* plat.

satinwood ['sætɪnwʊd] *n* citronnier *m* de Ceylan.

satire ['sætaɪəʳ] *n* satire *f* ▪ **it's a ~ on the English** c'est une satire contre les Anglais ▪ **her novels are full of ~** ses romans sont pleins d'observations satiriques.

satirical [sə'tɪrɪkl] *adj* satirique.

satirically [sə'tɪrɪklɪ] *adv* satiriquement.

satirist ['sætərɪst] *n* satiriste *mf*.

satirize, ise ['sætəraɪz] *vt* faire la satire de.

satisfaction [,sætɪs'fækʃn] *n* **1.** [fulfilment - of curiosity, hunger, demand, conditions] satisfaction *f* ; [- of contract] exécution *f*, réalisation *f* ; [- of debt] acquittement *m*, remboursement *m* **2.** [pleasure] satisfaction *f*, contentement *m* ▪ **is everything to your ~?** est-ce que tout est à votre convenance? ▪ **the plan was agreed to everyone's ~** le projet fut accepté à la satisfaction générale ▪ **to the ~ of the court** d'une manière qui a convaincu le tribunal ▪ **I don't get much job ~** je ne tire pas beaucoup de satisfaction de mon travail **3.** [pleasing thing] satisfaction *f* **4.** [redress - of a wrong] réparation *f* ; [- of damage] dédommagement *m* ; [- of an insult] réparation *f*.

satisfactorily [,sætɪs'fæktərəlɪ] *adv* de façon satisfaisante.

satisfactory [,sætɪs'fæktərɪ] *adj* satisfaisant ▪ **their progress is only ~** leurs progrès sont satisfaisants, sans plus ▪ **I hope she has a ~ excuse** j'espère qu'elle a une excuse valable ▪ **the patient's condition is ~** l'état du malade n'est pas inquiétant.

satisfied ['sætɪsfaɪd] *adj* **1.** [happy] satisfait, content ▪ **a ~ customer** un client satisfait ▪ **a ~ sigh** un soupir de satisfaction ▪ **the teacher isn't ~ with their work** le professeur n'est pas satisfait de leur travail ▪ **are you ~ now you've made her cry?** tu es content de l'avoir fait pleurer? ▪ **they'll have to be ~ with what they've got** ils devront se contenter de ce qu'ils ont **2.** [convinced] convaincu, persuadé ▪ **I'm not entirely ~ with the truth of his story** je ne suis pas tout à fait convaincu que son histoire soit vraie.

satisfy ['sætɪsfaɪ] (*pret & pp* **satisfied**) <> *vt* **1.** [please] satisfaire, contenter ▪ **Richard Fox has satisfied the examiners in the following subjects** SCH Richard Fox a été reçu dans les

matières suivantes **2.** [fulfil - curiosity, desire, hunger] satisfaire ; [- thirst] étancher ; [- demand, need, requirements] satisfaire à, répondre à ; [- conditions, terms of contract] remplir ; [- debt] s'acquitter de **3.** [prove to - gen] persuader, convaincre ; [- authorities] prouver à ■ **I satisfied myself that all the windows were closed** je me suis assuré que toutes les fenêtres étaient fermées.
◇ *vi* donner satisfaction.

satisfying ['sætɪsfaɪɪŋ] *adj* [job, outcome, evening] satisfaisant ■ [meal] substantiel.

satsuma [ˌsæt'suːmə] *n UK* mandarine *f*.

saturate ['sætʃəreɪt] *vt* **1.** *fig* [swamp] saturer ■ **to ~ sb with sthg** saturer qqn de qqch **2.** [drench] tremper **3.** CHEM saturer.

saturated ['sætʃəreɪtɪd] *adj* **1.** CHEM saturé ■ **~ fats** graisses *fpl* saturées **2.** [very wet] trempé.

saturation [ˌsætʃə'reɪʃn] *n* saturation *f*.

saturation bombing *n* bombardement *m* intensif.

saturation point *n* point *m* de saturation ■ **we've reached ~** nous sommes arrivés à saturation ■ **the market is at** *OR* **has reached ~** le marché est saturé.

Saturday ['sætədeɪ] *n* samedi *m* ■ **'~ Night Fever'** *Badham* 'la Fièvre du samedi soir', *see also* **Friday**.

Saturn ['sætən] *pr n* ASTRON & MYTH Saturne.

saturnalia [ˌsætə'neɪljə] *n* saturnales *fpl*.

satyr ['sætəʳ] *n* satyre *m*.

sauce [sɔːs] *n* **1.** CULIN [with savoury dishes] sauce *f* ■ [with desserts] coulis *m* ■ **raspberry ~** coulis de framboises ■ **chocolate ~** sauce au chocolat ■ **what's ~ for the goose is ~ for the gander** *prov* ce qui est bon pour l'un est bon pour l'autre **2.** *inf* [insolence] culot *m*, toupet *m*.

sauce boat *n* saucière *f*.

saucepan ['sɔːspən] *n* casserole *f*.

saucer ['sɔːsəʳ] *n* soucoupe *f*.

saucily ['sɔːsɪlɪ] *adv inf* **1.** [cheekily] avec effronterie **2.** [provocatively] de manière provocante.

sauciness ['sɔːsɪnɪs] *n inf* **1.** [cheekiness] effronterie *f* **2.** [provocativeness] provocation *f*, aspect *m* provocant.

saucy ['sɔːsɪ] (*comp* **saucier**, *superl* **sauciest**) *adj inf* **1.** [cheeky] effronté **2.** [provocative - action] provocant ; [- postcard, joke] grivois.

Saudi (Arabian) ['saʊdɪ-] ◇ *n* Saoudien *m*, - enne *f*.
◇ *adj* saoudien.

Saudi Arabia *pr n* Arabie Saoudite *f* ■ **in ~** en Arabie Saoudite.

sauerkraut ['saʊəkraʊt] *n* choucroute *f*.

Saul [sɔːl] *pr n* Saül.

sauna ['sɔːnə] *n* sauna *m*.

saunter ['sɔːntəʳ] ◇ *vi* se promener d'un pas nonchalant, flâner ■ **I think I'll ~ down to the library** je pense que je vais aller faire un petit tour jusqu'à la bibliothèque.
◇ *n* petite promenade *f*.

saurian ['sɔːrɪən] ◇ *adj* saurien.
◇ *n* saurien *m*.

sausage ['sɒsɪdʒ] *n* saucisse *f* ■ [of pre-cooked meats] saucisson *m* ◗ **pork ~s** saucisses *fpl* de porc ■ **not a ~!** *UK inf* que dalle!, des clous!

sausage dog *n UK hum* teckel *m*.

sausage meat *n* chair *f* à saucisse.

sausage roll *n sorte de friand à la saucisse*.

sauté [*UK* 'səʊteɪ, *US* səʊ'teɪ] (*pret & pp* **sautéed**, *cont* **sautéing**)
◇ *vt* faire sauter.
◇ *adj* : **~ potatoes** pommes de terre sautées.
◇ *n* sauté *m*.

savage ['sævɪdʒ] ◇ *adj* **1.** [ferocious - person] féroce, brutal ; [- dog] méchant ; [- fighting, tiger] féroce ■ [reply, attack] violent, féroce ■ **he came in for some ~ criticism from the press** il a été violemment critiqué dans la presse ■ **the new policy deals a ~ blow to the country's farmers** la nouvelle politique porte un coup très dur *OR* fatal aux agriculteurs **2.** [primitive - tribe] primitif ; [- customs] barbare, primitif.
◇ *n* sauvage *mf*.
◇ *vt* **1.** [subj: animal] attaquer ■ **she was ~d by a tiger** elle a été attaquée par un tigre **2.** [subj: critics, press] attaquer violemment.

savagely ['sævɪdʒlɪ] *adv* sauvagement, brutalement.

savageness ['sævɪdʒnɪs] = **savagery** *(sense 1)*.

savagery ['sævɪdʒrɪ] *n* **1.** [brutality] sauvagerie *f*, férocité *f*, brutalité *f* **2.** [primitive state] : **the tribe still lives in ~** la tribu vit toujours à l'état sauvage.

savanna(h) [sə'vænə] *n* savane *f*.

save [seɪv] ◇ *vt* **1.** [rescue] sauver ■ **she ~d my life** elle m'a sauvé la vie ■ **to ~ sb from a fire/from drowning** sauver qqn d'un incendie/de la noyade ■ **the doctors managed to ~ her eyesight** les médecins ont pu lui sauver la vue ■ **he ~d me from making a terrible mistake** il m'a empêché de faire une erreur monstrueuse ■ **to ~ a species from extinction** sauver une espèce en voie de disparition ■ **~d by the bell!** sauvé par le gong! ◗ **to ~ one's neck** *OR* **skin** *OR* **hide** *OR* **bacon** *inf* sauver sa peau ■ **to ~ face** sauver la face ■ **to ~ the day** sauver la mise **2.** [put by - money] économiser, épargner, mettre de côté ■ **how much money have you got ~d?** à combien se montent vos économies?, combien d'argent avez-vous mis de côté? ■ [collect] collectionner ■ **do you still ~ stamps?** est-ce que tu collectionnes toujours les timbres? **3.** [economize on - fuel, electricity] économiser, faire des économies de ; [- money] économiser ; [- effort] économiser ; [- time, space] gagner ; [- strength] ménager, économiser ■ **their advice ~d me a fortune** leurs conseils m'ont fait économiser une fortune ■ **a computer would ~ you a lot of time** un ordinateur vous ferait gagner beaucoup de temps **4.** [spare - trouble, effort] éviter, épargner ; [- expense] éviter ■ **thanks, you've ~d me a trip/having to go myself** merci, vous m'avez évité un trajet/d'y aller moi-même **5.** [protect - eyes, shoes] ménager **6.** [reserve] garder, mettre de côté ■ **I'll ~ you a place** je te garderai une place ■ **I always ~ the best part till last** je garde toujours le meilleur pour la fin **7.** FTBL [shot, penalty] arrêter ■ **to ~ a goal** arrêter *OR* bloquer un tir **8.** RELIG [sinner, mankind] sauver, délivrer ■ [soul] sauver **9.** COMPUT sauvegarder.
◇ *vi* **1.** [spend less] faire des économies, économiser ■ **to ~ on fuel** économiser sur le carburant **2.** [put money aside] faire des économies, épargner.
◇ *n* **1.** FTBL arrêt *m* **2.** COMPUT sauvegarde *f*.
◇ *prep fml* sauf, hormis.
◆ **save for** *prep phr* à part ■ **~ for the fact we lost, it was a great match** à part le fait qu'on a perdu, c'était un très bon match.
◆ **save up** ◇ *vt sep* = **save** *(vt sense 2)*.
◇ *vi insep* = **save** *(vi sense 2)*.

save as you earn *n UK* plan *m* d'épargne *(avec prélèvements automatiques sur le salaire)*.

saveloy ['sævəlɔɪ] *n* cervelas *m*.

saver ['seɪvəʳ] *n* **1.** [person] épargnant *m*, - e *f* **2.** [product] bonne affaire *f* ■ **super ~ (ticket)** billet *m* à tarif réduit.

-saver *in cpds* : **it's a real money~** ça permet d'économiser de l'argent *OR* de faire des économies.

Save the Children Fund *pr n organisme international d'assistance à l'enfance*.

Savile Row [ˌsævɪl'rəʊ] *pr n rue de Londres célèbre pour ses tailleurs de luxe*.

saving ['seɪvɪŋ] ◇ *n* **1.** [thrift] épargne *f* **2.** [money saved] économie *f* ■ **to make a ~** faire une économie.
◇ *prep fml* sauf, hormis.

-saving *in cpds* : **energy~** [device] d'économie, d'énergie ■ **time~** qui fait gagner du temps.

saving grace *n bon côté qui rachète des défauts* ▪ **her sense of humour is her ~** on lui pardonne tout parce qu'elle a de l'humour.

savings account *n* compte *m* sur livret.

savings and loan association *n* *US* caisse *f* d'épargne logement.

savings bank *n* caisse *f* d'épargne.

savings bond *n* *US* bon *m* d'épargne.

savings book *n* *UK* livret *m* (de caisse) d'épargne.

savings certificate *n* *UK* bon *m* d'épargne.

savings stamp *n* *UK* timbre-épargne *m*.

saviour *UK*, **savior** *US* ['seɪvjəʳ] *n* sauveur *m* ▪ **the Saviour** le Sauveur.

savoir-faire [ˌsævwɑː'feəʳ] *n* [know-how] savoir-faire *m* ▪ [social skills] savoir-vivre *m*.

savor *etc* *US* = **savour**.

savory ['seɪvərɪ] *n* BOT sarriette *f*.

savour *UK*, **savor** *US* ['seɪvəʳ] ◇ *n* **1.** [taste] goût *m*, saveur *f* **2.** [interest, charm] saveur *f*.
◇ *vt* [taste] goûter (à), déguster ▪ [enjoy - food, experience, one's freedom] savourer.
◇ *vi* : **to ~ of sthg** sentir qqch.

savoury *UK*, **savory** *US* ['seɪvərɪ] ◇ *adj* **1.** [salty] salé ▪ [spicy] épicé ▪ **~ biscuits** biscuits salés **2.** [appetizing] savoureux **3.** *fml* [wholesome] : **it's not a very ~ subject** c'est un sujet peu ragoûtant ▪ **he's not a very ~ individual** c'est un individu peu recommandable.
◇ *n petit plat salé servi soit comme hors d'œuvre, soit en fin de repas après le dessert*.

Savoy [sə'vɔɪ] ◇ *pr n* Savoie *f* ▪ **in ~** en Savoie.
◇ *adj* savoyard.

savoy cabbage *n* chou *m* frisé de Milan.

savvy ['sævɪ] *inf* ◇ *n* [know-how] savoir-faire *m* ▪ [shrewdness] jugeote *f*, perspicacité *f*.
◇ *adj* *US* [well-informed] bien informé, calé ▪ [shrewd] perspicace, astucieux.

saw [sɔː] (*UK pret* **sawed**, *pp* **sawed** *OR* **sawn** [sɔːn]) (*US pret & pp* **sawed**) ◇ *pt* ▷ **see**.
◇ *n* **1.** [tool] scie *f* ▪ **to cut sthg up with a ~** couper *OR* débiter qqch à la scie ▪ **metal ~** scie à métaux **2.** [saying] dicton *m*.
◇ *vt* : **to ~ a tree into logs** débiter un arbre en rondins ▪ **he ~ed the table in half** il a scié la table en deux ▪ **his arms ~ed the air** *fig* il battait l'air de ses bras.
◇ *vi* scier ▪ **he was ~ing away at the cello** *fig* il raclait le violoncelle.
➡ **saw down** *vt sep* [tree] abattre.
➡ **saw off** *vt sep* scier, enlever à la scie.
➡ **saw up** *vt sep* scier en morceaux, débiter à la scie.

sawdust ['sɔːdʌst] *n* sciure *f* (de bois).

sawed-off ['sɔːd-] *US* = **sawn-off**.

sawhorse ['sɔːhɔːs] *n* chevalet *m* *(pour scier du bois)*, chèvre *f*.

sawmill ['sɔːmɪl] *n* scierie *f*.

sawn [sɔːn] *pp* ▷ **saw**.

sawn-off *adj* [truncated] scié, coupé (à la scie) ▪ **~ shotgun** carabine *f* à canon scié.

sawtoothed ['sɔːtuːθt] *adj* en dents de scie.

sawyer ['sɔːjəʳ] *n* scieur *m*.

sax [sæks] (*abbrev of* **saxophone**) *n* saxo *m*.

saxifrage ['sæksɪfrɪdʒ] *n* saxifrage *f*.

Saxon ['sæksn] ◇ *n* **1.** [person] Saxon *m*, - onne *f* **2.** LING saxon *m*.
◇ *adj* saxon.

Saxony ['sæksənɪ] *pr n* Saxe *f* ▪ **in ~** en Saxe ▪ **Lower ~** Basse-Saxe *f*.

saxophone ['sæksəfəʊn] *n* saxophone *m*.

saxophonist [*UK* sæk'sɒfənɪst, *US* 'sæksəfəʊnɪst] *n* saxophoniste *mf*.

say [seɪ] (*pret & pp* **said** [sed]) (*3rd pers pres sing says* [sez]) ◇ *vt*

A.

1. [put into words] dire ▪ **to ~ sthg (to sb)** dire qqch (à qqn) ▪ **I think you can ~ goodbye to your money** *fig* je crois que vous pouvez dire adieu à votre argent ▪ **I wouldn't ~ no!** je ne dis pas non!, ce n'est pas de refus! ▪ **I wouldn't ~ no to a cold drink** je prendrais volontiers une boisson fraîche ▪ **I said to myself "let's wait a bit"** je me suis dit "attendons un peu" ▪ **to ~ a prayer (for)** dire une prière (pour) ▪ **to ~ one's prayers** faire sa prière ▪ **I can't ~ Russian names properly** je n'arrive pas à bien prononcer les noms russes ▪ [expressing fact, idea, comment] : **what did he ~ about his plans?** qu'a-t-il dit de ses projets? ▪ **don't ~ too much about our visit** ne parlez pas trop de notre visite ▪ **what did you ~ in reply?** qu'avez-vous répondu? ▪ **I can't think of anything to ~** je ne trouve rien à dire ▪ **I have nothing to ~** [gen] je n'ai rien à dire ; [no comment] je n'ai aucune déclaration à faire ▪ **I have nothing more to ~ on the matter** je n'ai rien à ajouter là-dessus ▪ **nothing was said about going to Moscow** on n'a pas parlé d'aller *OR* il n'a pas été question d'aller à Moscou ▪ **let's ~ no more about it** n'en parlons plus ▪ **can you ~ that again?** pouvez-vous répéter ce que vous venez de dire? ▪ **~ what you mean** dites ce que vous avez à dire ▪ **he didn't have a good word to ~ about the plan** il n'a dit que du mal du projet ▪ **he didn't have much to ~ for himself** [spoke little] il n'avait pas grand-chose à dire ; [no excuses] il n'avait pas de véritable excuse à donner ▪ **he certainly has a lot to ~ for himself** il n'a pas la langue dans la poche ▪ **as you might ~** pour ainsi dire ▪ **so ~ing, he walked out** sur ces mots, il est parti ▪ **to ~ nothing of the overheads** sans parler des frais ▪ **just ~ the word, you only have to ~ (the word)** *UK* vous n'avez qu'un mot à dire ➤ **having said that** ceci (étant) dit ▪ **to ~ one's piece** dire ce qu'on a à dire ▪ **it goes without ~ing that we shall travel together** il va sans dire *OR* il va de soi que nous voyagerons ensemble ▪ **you can ~ that again!** c'est le cas de le dire!, je ne vous le fais pas dire! ▪ **you said it!** *inf* tu l'as dit! ▪ **~ no more** n'en dis pas plus ▪ **enough said** [I understand] je vois ▪ **well said!** bien dit! ▪ **~ when** dis-moi stop
2. [with direct or indirect speech] dire ▪ **she said (we were) to come** elle a dit qu'on devait venir ▪ **they said it was going to rain** ils ont annoncé de la pluie
3. [claim, allege] dire ▪ **you know what they ~, no smoke without fire** tu sais ce qu'on dit, il n'y a pas de fumée sans feu ▪ **these fans are said to be very efficient** ces ventilateurs sont très efficaces, d'après ce qu'on dit ▪ **he is said to have emigrated** on dit qu'il a émigré ▪ **don't ~ you've forgotten!** ne (me) dites pas que vous avez oublié! ▪ **who can ~?** qui sait? ▪ **who can ~ when he'll come?** qui peut dire quand il viendra?
4. [expressing personal opinion] dire ▪ **so he ~s** c'est ce qu'il dit ▪ **I must ~ she's been very helpful** je dois dire qu'elle nous a beaucoup aidés ▪ **well this is a fine time to arrive, I must ~!** *iron* en voilà une heure pour arriver! ▪ **I'll ~ this for him, he certainly tries hard** je dois reconnaître qu'il fait tout son possible ▪ **you might as well ~ we're all mad!** autant dire qu'on est tous fous! ▪ **I should ~ so** bien sûr que oui, je pense bien ▪ **as they ~** comme ils disent *OR* on dit ▪ **if you ~ so** si *OR* puisque tu le dis ▪ **and so ~ all of us** et nous sommes tous d'accord *OR* de cet avis ➤ **there's no ~ing what will happen** impossible de prédire ce qui va arriver ▪ **to ~ the least** c'est le moins qu'on puisse dire ▪ **I was surprised, not to ~ astounded** j'étais surpris, pour ne pas dire stupéfait ▪ **there's something to be said for the idea** l'idée a du bon ▪ **there's not much to be said for the idea** l'idée ne vaut pas grand-chose ▪ **there's a lot to be said for doing sport** il y a beaucoup d'avantages à faire du sport ▪ **that's not ~ing much** ça ne veut pas dire grand-chose ▪ **it doesn't ~ much for his powers of observation** cela en dit long sur son sens de l'observation ▪ **that isn't ~ing much for him** ce n'est pas à son honneur ▪ **it ~s a lot for his courage/about his real motives** cela en dit long sur son courage/ses intentions réelles

B.

1. [think] dire, penser ▪ **I ~ you should leave** je pense que vous devriez partir ▪ **what do you ~ we drive over** *OR* **to driving over**

to see them? que diriez-vous de prendre la voiture et d'aller les voir? ■ **what do you ~?** [do you agree?] qu'en dites-vous? ■ **what did they ~ to your offer?** qu'ont-ils dit de votre proposition? ■ **when would you ~ would be the best time for us to leave?** quel serait le meilleur moment pour partir, à votre avis? ■ **to look at them, you wouldn't ~ they were a day over forty** à les voir, on ne leur donnerait pas plus de quarante ans
2. [suppose, assume] : **(let's) ~ your plan doesn't work, what then?** admettons que votre plan ne marche pas, qu'est-ce qui se passe? ■ **~ he doesn't arrive, who will take his place?** si jamais il n'arrive pas, qui prendra sa place? ■ **look at, ~, Jane Austen or George Eliot...** prends Jane Austen ou George Eliot, par exemple... ■ **shall we ~ Sunday?** disons dimanche, d'accord?
3. [indicate, register] indiquer, marquer ■ **the clock ~s 10.40** la pendule indique 10 h 40 ■ **it ~s "shake well"** c'est marqué "bien agiter" ■ **the instructions ~ (to) open it out of doors** dans le mode d'emploi, on dit qu'il faut l'ouvrir dehors
4. [express - subj: intonation, eyes] exprimer, marquer ■ **his expression said everything** son expression était très éloquente *OR* en disait long
5. [mean] : **it's short, that's to ~, about 20 pages** c'est court, ça fait 20 pages ■ **that's not to ~ I don't like it** cela ne veut pas dire que je ne l'aime pas.
◇ *vi* [tell] dire ■ **he won't ~** il ne veut pas le dire ■ **I'd rather not ~** je préfère ne rien dire ■ **I can't ~ exactly** je ne sais pas au juste ■ **it's not for me to ~** [speak] ce n'est pas à moi de le dire ; [decide] ce n'est pas à moi de décider ■ **I can't ~ fairer than that** je ne peux pas mieux dire ▶ **so to ~** pour ainsi dire ■ **I ~!** [expressing surprise] eh bien! ; [to attract attention] dites! ■ **you don't ~!** *inf* sans blague!, ça alors!
◇ *n* : **to have a ~ in sthg** avoir son mot à dire dans qqch ■ **I had no ~ in choosing the wallpaper** on ne m'a pas demandé mon avis pour le choix du papier peint ■ **to have one's ~** dire ce qu'on a à dire ■ **now you've had your ~, let me have mine** maintenant que vous avez dit ce que vous aviez à dire, laissez-moi parler.
◇ *interj US* dites donc!
◆ **when all's said and done** *adv phr* tout compte fait, au bout du compte.

saying ['seɪɪŋ] *n* dicton *m*, proverbe *m* ■ **as the ~ goes** [proverb] comme dit le proverbe ; [as we way] comme on dit.

say-so *n UK* **1.** [authorization] : **I'm not going without her ~** je n'irai pas sans qu'elle m'y autorise *OR* sans son accord ■ **he refused to do it without the boss's ~** il a refusé de le faire sans avoir l'aval du patron **2.** [assertion] : **I won't believe it just on his ~** ce n'est pas parce qu'il l'a dit que j'y crois.

SC *written abbr of* **South Carolina**.

S/C *written abbr of* **self contained**.

scab [skæb] (*pret & pp* **scabbed**, *cont* **scabbing**) ◇ *n* **1.** MED [from cut, blister] croûte *f* **2.** BOT & ZOOL gale *f* **3.** *inf pej* [strikebreaker] jaune *mf* **4.** *inf* [cad] crapule *f*, sale type *m*.
◇ *vi* **1.** MED former une croûte **2.** *UK inf pej* briser une grève, refuser de faire grève.

scabbard ['skæbəd] *n* [for sword] fourreau *m* ■ [for dagger, knife] gaine *f*, étui *m*.

scabby ['skæbɪ] (*comp* **scabbier**, *superl* **scabbiest**) *adj* **1.** MED [skin] croûteux, recouvert d'une croûte **2.** *inf pej* [mean - person] mesquin ; [- attitude] moche.

scabies ['skeɪbi:z] *n (U)* gale *f*.

scabrous ['skeɪbrəs] *adj lit* **1.** [joke, story] scabreux, osé ■ [subject] scabreux, risqué **2.** [skin] rugueux, rêche.

scaffold ['skæfəʊld] *n* **1.** CONSTR échafaudage *m* **2.** [for execution] échafaud *m* ■ **to go to the ~** monter à l'échafaud.

scaffolding ['skæfəldɪŋ] *n* [framework] échafaudage *m*.

scalawag ['skæləwæg] *n US* = **scallywag**.

scald [skɔ:ld] ◇ *vt* **1.** [hands, skin] ébouillanter ■ **the hot tea ~ed my tongue** le thé bouillant m'a brûlé la langue **2.** CULIN [tomatoes] ébouillanter ■ [milk] porter presque à ébullition **3.** [sterilize] stériliser.
◇ *vi* brûler.
◇ *n* brûlure *f (causée par un liquide, de la vapeur)* ■ **I got a nasty ~** je me suis bien ébouillanté.

scalding ['skɔ:ldɪŋ] ◇ *adj* **1.** [water] bouillant ■ [metal, tea, soup, tears] brûlant **2.** [sun] brûlant ■ [heat] suffocant, torride ■ [weather] très chaud, torride **3.** [criticism] cinglant, acerbe.
◇ *adv* : **~ hot** [coffee] brûlant ; [weather] torride.

scale [skeɪl] ◇ *n* **1.** [of model, drawing] échelle *f* ■ **the sketch was drawn to ~** l'esquisse était à l'échelle ■ **the ~ of the map is 1 to 50,000** la carte est au 50 millième ■ **the drawing is out of ~** *OR* **is not to ~** le croquis n'est pas à l'échelle
2. [for measurement, evaluation] échelle *f* ■ [of salaries, taxes] échelle *f*, barème *m* ■ [of values] échelle *m* ■ **the social ~** l'échelle sociale ■ **at the top of the ~** en haut de l'échelle ■ [graduation] échelle *f* (graduée), graduation *f*
3. [extent] échelle *f*, étendue *f* ■ [size] importance *f* ■ **the ~ of the devastation** l'étendue des dégâts ■ **the sheer ~ of the problem** l'ampleur même du problème ■ **to do sthg on a large ~** faire qqch sur une grande échelle ■ **on an industrial ~** à l'échelle industrielle ▶ **economies of ~** économies d'échelle
4. MUS gamme *f* ■ **to practise** *OR* **to do one's ~s** faire ses gammes
5. [of fish, reptile] écaille *f* ■ [of epidermis] squame *f* ■ **the ~s fell from her eyes** *fig* les écailles lui sont tombées des yeux
6. [in kettle, pipes] tartre *m*, (dépôt *m*) calcaire *m* ■ [on teeth] tartre *m*
7. [of paint, plaster, rust] écaille *f*, écaillure *f*
8. [scale pan] plateau *m* (de balance)
9. *US* [for weighing] pèse-personne *m*, balance *f*.
◇ *vt* **1.** [climb over - wall, fence] escalader
2. [drawing] dessiner à l'échelle
3. [test] graduer, pondérer
4. [fish, paint] écailler ■ [teeth, pipes] détartrer.
◇ *vi* [paint, rust] s'écailler ■ [skin] peler.
◆ **scales** *npl* [for food] balance *f* ■ [for letters] pèse-lettre *m* ■ [for babies] pèse-bébé *m* ■ [public] bascule *f* ■ **(a pair of) kitchen ~s** une balance de cuisine ■ **(a pair of) bathroom ~s** un pèse-personne.
◆ **scale down** *vt sep* **1.** [drawing] réduire l'échelle de **2.** [figures, demands] réduire, baisser, diminuer.
◆ **scale off** ◇ *vi insep* [paint, rust] s'écailler.
◇ *vt sep* écailler.
◆ **scale up** *vt sep* **1.** [drawing] augmenter l'échelle de **2.** [figures, demands] réviser à la hausse, augmenter.

scaled [skeɪld] *adj* [pipe, kettle, tooth] entartré.

scale drawing *n* dessin *m* à l'échelle.

scale model *n* [of car, plane] modèle *m* réduit ■ [of buildings, town centre] maquette *f*.

scalene ['skeɪli:n] *adj* scalène.

scallion ['skæljən] *n US* CULIN [spring onion] oignon *m* blanc ■ [leek] poireau *m* ■ [shallot] échalote *f*.

scallop ['skɒləp] ◇ *vt* **1.** CULIN [fish, vegetable] gratiner **2.** SEW [edge, hem] festonner.
◇ *n* CULIN & ZOOL coquille Saint-Jacques *f*.
◆ **scallops** *npl* SEW festons *mpl*.

scalloped ['skɒləpt] *adj* **1.** CULIN : **~ potatoes** *fines tranches de pommes de terre sautées ou cuites au four* **2.** SEW [edge, hem] festonné.

scallywag ['skælɪwæg] *n inf* [rascal] voyou *m*, coquin *m*.

scalp [skælp] ◇ *n* **1.** [top of head] cuir *m* chevelu **2.** [Indian trophy] scalp *m* **3.** *fig* [trophy] trophée *m* ■ HUNT trophée *m* de chasse.
◇ *vt* **1.** [person, animal] scalper **2.** *inf* [tickets] vendre en réalisant un bénéfice substantiel ■ **to ~ shares** *OR* **securities** *US* boursicoter **3.** *inf* [cheat] arnaquer.

scalpel ['skælpəl] *n* scalpel *m*.

scalper ['skælpər] *n US* revendeur *m*, - euse *f* de tickets à la sauvette *(pour un concert, un match etc)*.

scaly ['skeɪlɪ] (*comp* **scalier**, *superl* **scaliest**) *adj* [creature] écailleux ■ [paint] écaillé ■ [skin] squameux ■ [pipe] entartré.

scam△ [skæm] *n* escroquerie *f*, arnaque *f*.

scamp [skæmp] *inf n* [child] garnement *m*, coquin *m*, - e *f* ▪ [rogue] voyou *m*.

scamper ['skæmpər] <> *vi* **1.** [small animal] trottiner ▪ [children] gambader, galoper ▪ **the kids ~ed into the house/up the stairs** les gosses sont entrés dans la maison/ont monté l'escalier en courant **2.** *inf* [work quickly] : **I positively ~ed through the book** j'ai lu le livre à toute vitesse.
<> *n* trottinement *m*.
◆ **scamper about** *vi insep* [animal] courir OR trottiner çà et là ▪ [children] gambader.
◆ **scamper away, scamper off** *vi insep* détaler, se sauver.

scampi ['skæmpɪ] *n (U)* scampi *mpl*.

scan [skæn] (*pret & pp* **scanned**, *cont* **scanning**) <> *vt* **1.** [look carefully at] scruter, fouiller du regard ▪ [read carefully] lire attentivement **2.** [consult quickly - report, notes] lire en diagonale, parcourir rapidement ; [- magazine] feuilleter ; [- screen, image] balayer ; [- tape, memory] lire **3.** PHYS [spectrum] balayer, parcourir ▪ [subj: radar, searchlight] balayer **4.** MED examiner au scanner, faire une scanographie de **5.** ELECTRON & TV balayer **6.** LIT scander **7.** COMPUT scanner.
<> *vi* LIT se scander.
<> *n* **1.** MED scanographie *f*, examen *m* au scanner **2.** LIT scansion *f* **3.** ELECTRON & TV balayage *m*.
◆ **scan in** *vt sep* COMPUT insérer par scanneur.

scandal ['skændl] *n* **1.** [disgrace] scandale *m* ▪ **to cause a ~** provoquer un scandale ▪ **it's a ~ that people like them should be let free** c'est scandaleux de laisser des gens pareils en liberté ▪ **it's a national ~** c'est une honte nationale OR un scandale public **2.** *(U)* [gossip] ragots *mpl* ▪ [evil] médisance *f*, médisances *fpl*, calomnie *f* ▪ **this newspaper specializes in ~** c'est un journal à scandale ▪ **the latest society ~** les derniers potins mondains.

scandalize, ise ['skændəlaɪz] *vt* scandaliser, choquer ▪ **he was ~d by what she said** il a été scandalisé par ses propos ▪ **she's easily ~d** elle se scandalise OR s'indigne vite.

scandalmonger ['skændl,mʌŋgər] *n* mauvaise langue *f*, colporteur *m*, - euse *f* de ragots.

scandalous ['skændələs] *adj* **1.** [conduct] scandaleux, choquant ▪ [news, price] scandaleux ▪ **it's absolutely ~!** c'est un véritable scandale! **2.** [gossip] calomnieux.

scandalously ['skændələslɪ] *adv* **1.** [act] scandaleusement **2.** [speak, write] de manière diffamatoire.

scandal sheet *n* journal *m* à scandale.

Scandinavia [,skændɪ'neɪvjə] *pr n* Scandinavie *f* ▪ **in ~** en Scandinavie.

Scandinavian [,skændɪ'neɪvjən] <> *n* **1.** [person] Scandinave *mf* **2.** LING scandinave *m*.
<> *adj* scandinave.

scanner ['skænər] *n* **1.** MED & ELECTRON scanner *m* **2.** [for radar] antenne *f* **3.** COMPUT : **(optical) ~** scanner *m*.

scansion ['skænʃn] *n* LIT scansion *f*.

scant [skænt] <> *adj* maigre ▪ **to pay ~ attention to sb/sthg** ne prêter que peu d'attention à qqn/qqch ▪ **they showed ~ regard for our feelings** ils ne se sont pas beaucoup souciés OR ils se sont peu souciés de ce que nous pouvions ressentir ▪ **a ~ teaspoonful** une cuillerée à café rase.
<> *vt* **1.** [skimp on] lésiner sur ▪ [restrict] restreindre **2.** [treat superficially] traiter de manière superficielle.

scantily ['skæntɪlɪ] *adv* [furnished] pauvrement, chichement ▪ [dressed] légèrement.

scanty ['skæntɪ] (*comp* **scantier**, *superl* **scantiest**) *adj* **1.** [small in number, quantity - meal, crops] maigre, peu abondant ; [- income, payment] maigre, modeste ; [- information, knowledge] maigre, limité ; [- applause] maigre, peu fourni ; [- audience] clairsemé ; [- praise, aid] limité **2.** [brief - clothing] léger ▪ **she was wearing only a ~ negligee** elle ne portait qu'un négligé qui ne cachait pas grand-chose *hum*.

scapegoat ['skeɪpgəʊt] *n* bouc *m* émissaire.

scapula ['skæpjʊlə] (*pl* **scapulas**, *pl* **scapulae** [-li:]) *n* omoplate *f*.

scar [skɑ:r] (*pret & pp* **scarred**, *cont* **scarring**) <> *n* **1.** [from wound, surgery] cicatrice *f* ▪ [from deep cut on face] balafre *f* **2.** *fig* [on land, painted surface, tree] cicatrice *f*, marque *f* ▪ [emotional] cicatrice *f* ▪ **the ~s of battle** les traces de la bataille ▪ **the mine was like an ugly ~ on the landscape** la mine déparait terriblement le paysage **3.** [rock] rocher *m* escarpé ▪ [in river] écueil *m*.
<> *vt* **1.** [skin, face] laisser une cicatrice sur ▪ **his hands were badly scarred** il avait sur les mains de profondes cicatrices ▪ **smallpox had scarred his face** il avait le visage grêlé par la variole **2.** *fig* [surface] marquer ▪ [emotionally] marquer ▪ **she was permanently scarred by the experience** cette expérience l'avait marquée pour la vie.
<> *vi* [form scar] se cicatriser ▪ [leave scar] laisser une cicatrice.
◆ **scar over** *vi insep* [form scar] former une cicatrice ▪ [close up] se cicatriser.

scarab ['skærəb] *n* scarabée *m*.

scarce ['skeəs] <> *adj* [rare] rare ▪ [infrequent] peu fréquent ▪ [in short supply] peu abondant ▪ **sugar is ~ at the moment** il y a une pénurie de sucre en ce moment ▪ **to become ~** se faire rare ▪ **water is becoming ~** l'eau commence à manquer ▪ **rain is ~ in this region** il ne pleut pas souvent dans cette région ▶ **to make o.s. ~** *inf* [run away] se sauver, décamper ; [get out] débarrasser le plancher ▪ **can you make yourself ~ for half an hour?** peux-tu disparaître pendant une demi-heure?
<> *adv lit* à peine.

scarcely ['skeəslɪ] *adv* **1.** [no sooner] à peine ▪ **we had ~ begun** OR **~ had we begun when the bell rang** nous avions tout juste commencé quand OR à peine avions-nous commencé que la cloche a sonné **2.** [barely] : **he ~ spoke to me** c'est tout juste s'il m'a adressé la parole ▪ **she's ~ more than a child** elle n'est encore qu'une enfant ▪ **~ any** presque pas de ▪ **~ anybody** presque personne ▪ **~ anything** presque rien ▪ **I know ~ any of those people** je ne connais pratiquement personne parmi ces gens OR pratiquement aucune de ces personnes ▪ **he has ~ any hair left** il n'a presque plus de cheveux **3.** [indicating difficulty] à peine, tout juste ▪ **I could ~ tell his mother, now could I!** je ne pouvais quand même pas le dire à sa mère, non? ▪ **I ~ know where to begin** je ne sais pas trop par où commencer ▪ **I can ~ wait to meet her** j'ai hâte de la rencontrer ▪ **I can ~ believe what you're saying** j'ai du mal à croire ce que vous dites.

scarcity ['skeəsətɪ] (*pl* **scarcities**) *n* [rarity] rareté *f* ▪ [lack] manque *m* ▪ [shortage] manque *m*, pénurie *f* ▪ **there is a ~ of new talent today** les nouveaux talents se font rares.

scarcity value *n* valeur *f* de rareté.

scare [skeər] <> *vt* effrayer, faire peur à ▪ **thunder really ~s me** le tonnerre me fait vraiment très peur ▶ **the film ~d me stiff!** *inf* le film m'a flanqué une de ces frousses! ▪ **to ~ the wits** OR **the living daylights** OR **the life out of sb** *inf* flanquer une peur bleue OR une trouille pas possible à qqn ▪ **he ~d the hell** *inf* OR **the shit**▲ **out of me** il m'a foutu les jetons△.
<> *vi* s'effrayer, prendre peur ▪ **I don't ~ easily** je ne suis pas peureux.
<> *n* **1.** [fright] peur *f*, frayeur *f* ▪ **to give sb a ~** effrayer qqn, faire peur à qqn **2.** [alert] alerte *f* ▪ [rumour] bruit *m* alarmiste, rumeur *f* ▪ **a bomb/fire ~** une alerte à la bombe/au feu.
<> *comp* [sensational - headlines] alarmiste.
◆ **scare away, scare off** *vt sep* [bird, customer] faire fuir.
◆ **scare up** *vt sep* US *inf* dénicher.

scarecrow ['skeəkrəʊ] *n* [for birds] épouvantail *m* ▪ *fig* [person - thin] squelette *m* ; [- badly dressed] épouvantail *m*.

scared ['skeəd] *adj* [frightened] effrayé ▪ [nervous] craintif, peureux ▪ **to be ~ (of sthg)** avoir peur (de qqch) ▪ **he was ~ to ask** il avait peur de demander ▪ **he's ~ of being told off/that she might tell him off** il craint de se faire gronder/qu'elle ne le gronde ▪ **to be ~ stiff** *inf* OR **to death** *inf* avoir une peur bleue ▪ **I was ~ out of my wits!** *inf* j'étais mort de peur!

scaredy cat ['skeədɪ-] *n inf* froussard *m*, - e *f*.

scaremonger ['skeə,mʌŋgəʳ] *n* alarmiste *mf*.

scaremongering ['skeə,mʌŋgrɪŋ] *n* alarmisme *m*.

scarey ['skeərɪ] = **scary**.

scarf [skɑ:f] *n* **1.** (*pl* scarfs *OR pl* scarves [skɑ:vz]) [long] écharpe *f* ▪ [headscarf, cravat] foulard *m* **2.** CONSTR [cut] entaille *f*.

scarlatina [,skɑ:lə'ti:nə] *n (U)* MED scarlatine *f*.

scarlet ['skɑ:lət] ◇ *adj* [gen] écarlate ▪ [face - from illness, effort] cramoisi ; [- from shame] écarlate, cramoisi.
◇ *n* écarlate *f*.

scarlet fever *n (U)* scarlatine *f*.

scarlet pimpernel *n* BOT mouron *m* rouge ▪ **'The Scarlet Pimpernel'** ***Orczy*** 'le Mouron rouge'.

scarlet woman *n UK hum* femme *f* de mauvaise vie.

scarp [skɑ:p] *n* escarpement *m*.

scarper ['skɑ:pəʳ] *vi UK inf* déguerpir, se barrer.

scar tissue *n* tissu *m* cicatriciel.

scarves [skɑ:vz] *pl* ▷ **scarf** *(sense 1)*.

scary ['skeərɪ] (*comp* **scarier**, *superl* **scariest**) *adj inf* **1.** [frightening - place, person] effrayant ; [- story] qui donne le frisson **2.** [fearful] peureux.

scathing ['skeɪðɪŋ] *adj* [criticism, remark] caustique, cinglant ▪ **to give sb a ~ look** foudroyer qqn du regard ▪ **he can be very ~** il sait se montrer acerbe *OR* cinglant.

scathingly ['skeɪðɪŋlɪ] *adv* [retort, criticize] de manière cinglante.

scatological [,skætə'lɒdʒɪkl] *adj* scatologique.

scatter ['skætəʳ] ◇ *vt* **1.** [strew] éparpiller, disperser ▪ **papers had been ~ed all over the desk** le bureau était jonché *OR* couvert de papiers **2.** [spread] répandre ▪ [sprinkle] saupoudrer ▪ **she ~ed crumbs for the birds** elle a jeté des miettes de pain aux oiseaux ▪ **to ~ seeds** semer des graines à la volée **3.** [disperse - crowd, mob] disperser ; [- enemy] mettre en fuite ; [- clouds] dissiper, disperser **4.** PHYS [light] disperser.
◇ *vi* **1.** [people, clouds] se disperser ▪ **they told us to ~** ils nous ont dit de partir **2.** [beads, papers] s'éparpiller.
◇ *n* **1.** [of rice, bullets] pluie *f* ▪ **a ~ of farms on the hillside** quelques fermes éparpillées à flanc de coteau **2.** [in statistics] dispersion *f*.
◆ **scatter about** *UK*, **scatter around** *vt sep* éparpiller.

scatter bomb *n* obus *m* à mitraille, shrapnel *m*, shrapnell *m*.

scatterbrain ['skætəbreɪn] *n* tête *f* de linotte, étourdi *m*, - e *f*.

scatterbrained ['skætəbreɪnd] *adj* écervelé, étourdi.

scatter cushion *n* petit coussin *m*.

scattered ['skætəd] *adj* **1.** [strewn] éparpillé ▪ **papers/toys lying ~ all over the floor** des papiers/des jouets éparpillés par terre **2.** [sprinkled] parsemé ▪ **the tablecloth was ~ with crumbs** la nappe était parsemée de miettes **3.** [dispersed - population] dispersé, disséminé ; [- clouds] épars ; [- villages, houses] épars ; [- light] diffus ; [- fortune] dissipé ▪ **she tried to collect her ~ thoughts** elle essaya de mettre de l'ordre dans ses idées ▪ **~ showers** averses *fpl* intermittentes.

scatter-gun *n* fusil *m* de chasse.

scattering ['skætərɪŋ] *n* **1.** [small number] : **a ~ of followers** une poignée d'adeptes ▪ **there was a ~ of farms** il y avait quelques fermes çà et là **2.** [dispersion] dispersion *f*.

scatty ['skætɪ] (*comp* **scattier**, *superl* **scattiest**) *adj inf* [forgetful] étourdi, écervelé ▪ [silly] bêta, - asse *f*.

scavenge ['skævɪndʒ] ◇ *vi* **1.** [bird, animal] : **to ~ (for food)** chercher sa nourriture **2.** [person] : **he was scavenging among the dustbins** il fouillait dans *OR* faisait les poubelles.
◇ *vt* **1.** [material, metals] récupérer ▪ **he managed to ~ a meal** il a finalement trouvé quelque chose à se mettre sous la dent **2.** [streets] nettoyer.

scavenger ['skævɪndʒəʳ] *n* **1.** ZOOL charognard *m* **2.** [salvager] ramasseur *m* d'épaves ▪ [in rubbish] pilleur *m* de poubelles **3.** *UK* [street cleaner] éboueur *m*.

scenario [sɪ'nɑ:rɪəʊ] (*pl* **scenarios**) *n* scénario *m*.

scene [si:n] *n* **1.** [sphere of activity, milieu] scène *f*, situation *f* ▪ **the world political ~** la scène politique internationale ▪ **she's a newcomer on** *OR* **to the sports ~** c'est une nouvelle venue sur la scène sportive *OR* dans le monde du sport ▪ **the drug ~** le monde de la drogue ▪ **she came on the ~ just when we needed her** elle est arrivée juste au moment où nous avions besoin d'elle ▪ **he disappeared from the ~ for a few years** il a disparu de la circulation *OR* de la scène pendant quelques années **2.** CIN & THEAT [in film] scène *f*, séquence *f* ▪ [in play] scène *f* ▪ **to set the ~** planter le décor ▪ **the ~ is set** *OR* **takes place in Bombay** la scène se passe *OR* l'action se déroule à Bombay ▪ **behind the ~s** en coulisses ▪ **the ~ was set for the arms negotiations** ***fig*** tout était prêt pour les négociations sur les armements **3.** [place, spot] lieu *m*, lieux *mpl*, endroit *m* ▪ **the ~ of the disaster** l'endroit où s'est produit la catastrophe ▪ **the ~ of the crime** le lieu du crime ▪ **the police were soon on the ~** la police est rapidement arrivée sur les lieux *OR* sur place ▪ **~ of operations** MIL théâtre *m* des opérations
4. [image] scène *f*, spectacle *m* ▪ [incident] scène *f*, incident *m* ▪ **~s of horror/violence** scènes d'horreur/de violence ▪ **~s from** *OR* **of village life** scènes de la vie villageoise ▪ **just picture the ~** essayez de vous représenter la scène ▮ [view] spectacle *m*, perspective *f*, vue *f* ▪ **a change of ~ will do you good** un changement d'air *OR* de décor vous fera du bien ▮ ART tableau *m*, scène *f* ▪ **city/country ~s** scènes de ville/champêtres
5. [fuss, row] scène *f* ▪ **to make a ~** faire une scène ▪ **to have a ~ with sb** se disputer avec qqn ▪ **he made an awful ~ about it** il en a fait toute une histoire
6. *inf* [favourite activity] : **jazz isn't really my ~** le jazz, ça n'est pas vraiment mon truc.

scene change *n* changement *m* de décors.

scenery ['si:nərɪ] *n* **1.** [natural setting] paysage *m* ▪ **mountain ~** paysage de montagne ▪ **the ~ round here is lovely** les paysages sont très beaux par ici ▪ **she needs a change of ~** ***fig*** elle a besoin de changer de décor *OR* d'air **2.** THEAT décor *m*, décors *mpl*.

sceneshifter ['si:n,ʃɪftəʳ] *n* THEAT machiniste *m*.

scenic ['si:nɪk] *adj* **1.** [surroundings] pittoresque ▪ **let's take the ~ route** prenons la route touristique **2.** ART & THEAT scénique.

scenic railway *n* **1.** [for tourists] petit train *m* (touristique) **2.** [in fairground] montagnes *fpl* russes.

scent [sent] ◇ *n* **1.** [smell] parfum *m*, odeur *f* **2.** HUNT [of animal] fumet *m* ▪ [of person] odeur *f* ▪ [track] trace *f*, piste *f* ▪ **the hounds are on the ~** *OR* **have picked up the ~ of a fox** les chiens sont sur la trace d'un renard *OR* ont dépisté un renard ▪ **they've lost the ~** ils ont perdu la piste ▪ **to put** *OR* **to throw sb off the ~** semer qqn ▪ **we're on the ~ of a major scandal** nous flairons un gros scandale **3.** *UK* [perfume] parfum *m*.
◇ *vt* **1.** [smell - prey] flairer ▪ [detect - danger, treachery] flairer, subodorer **2.** [perfume] parfumer ▪ **~ed notepaper** papier *m* à lettres parfumé.

scentless ['sentlɪs] *adj* [odourless - substance] inodore ; [- flower] sans parfum.

scepter *US* = **sceptre**.

sceptic *UK*, **skeptic** *US* ['skeptɪk] ◇ *adj* sceptique.
◇ *n* sceptique *mf*.

sceptical *UK*, **skeptical** *US* ['skeptɪkl] *adj* sceptique.

scepticism *UK*, **skepticism** *US* ['skeptɪsɪzm] *n* scepticisme *m*.

sceptre *UK*, **scepter** *US* ['septəʳ] *n* sceptre *m*.

schedule [*UK* 'ʃedju:l, *US* 'skedʒʊl] ◇ *n* **1.** [programme] programme *m* ▪ [calendar] programme *m*, calendrier *m* ▪ [timetable] programme *m*, emploi *m* du temps ▪ [plan] prévisions

fpl, plan *m* ■ **I have a busy ~** [for visit] j'ai un programme chargé ; [in general] j'ai un emploi du temps chargé ; [over period] j'ai un calendrier chargé ■ **everything went according to ~** tout s'est déroulé comme prévu ■ **the work was carried out according to ~** le travail a été effectué selon les prévisions ■ **we are on ~** *OR* **up to ~** nous sommes dans les temps ■ **our work is ahead of/behind ~** nous sommes en avance/en retard dans notre travail ■ **the bridge was opened on/ahead of ~** le pont a été ouvert à la date prévue/en avance sur la date prévue ■ **to fall behind ~** prendre du retard sur les prévisions de travail
2. [timetable - for transport] horaire *m* ■ **the train is on/is running behind ~** le train est à l'heure/a du retard
3. [list - of prices] barème *m* ; [- of contents] inventaire *m* ; [- of payments] échéancier *m* ■ [for taxes] rôle *m* ■ **~ of charges** tarifs *mpl*
4. LAW [annexe] annexe *f*, avenant *m*.
◇ *vt* **1.** [plan - event] fixer la date *OR* l'heure de ; [- appointment] fixer ■ **the meeting was ~d for 3 o'clock/Wednesday** la réunion était prévue pour 15 heures/mercredi ■ **the plane was ~d to touch down at 18.45** il était prévu que l'avion arrive *OR* l'arrivée de l'avion était prévue à 18 h 45 ■ **which day is the film ~d for?** quel jour a été retenu pour le film? ■ **it's ~d for Saturday** il est programmé pour samedi ■ **you aren't ~d to sing until later** d'après le programme, vous devez chanter plus tard (dans la soirée)
2. [period, work, series] organiser ■ **to ~ one's time** aménager *OR* organiser son temps ■ **to ~ a morning** établir l'emploi du temps d'une matinée ■ **that lunch hour is already ~d** ce déjeuner est déjà réservé
3. [topic, item] inscrire ■ **it's ~d as a topic for the next meeting** c'est inscrit à l'ordre du jour de la prochaine réunion
4. *UK* ADMIN [monument] classer.

scheduled [*UK* 'ʃedju:ld, *US* 'skedʒʊld] *adj* **1.** [planned] prévu ■ **at the ~ time** à l'heure prévue ■ **we announce a change to our ~ programmes** TV nous annonçons une modification de nos programmes **2.** [regular - flight] régulier ; [- stop, change] habituel **3.** [official - prices] tarifé **4.** *UK* ADMIN : **~ building** bâtiment *m* classé (monument historique) ■ **the ~ territories** la zone sterling.

schema ['ski:mə] (*pl* **schemata** [-mətə]) *n* **1.** [diagram] schéma *m* **2.** PHILOS & PSYCHOL schème *m*.

schematic [skɪ'mætɪk] ◇ *adj* schématique.
◇ *n* schéma *m*.

scheme [ski:m] ◇ *n* **1.** [plan] plan *m*, projet *m* ■ **a ~ to get rich quick** un procédé pour s'enrichir rapidement ■ **he's always dreaming up mad ~s for entertaining the children** il a toujours des idées lumineuses pour distraire les enfants ■ **the ~ of things** l'ordre des choses ■ **where does he fit into the ~ of things?** quel rôle joue-t-il dans cette affaire? ■ **it just doesn't fit into her ~ of things** cela n'entre pas dans sa conception des choses **2.** [plot] intrigue *f*, complot *m* ■ [unscrupulous] procédé *m* malhonnête **3.** *UK* ADMIN plan *m*, système *m* ■ **the firm has a profit-sharing/a pension ~** l'entreprise a un système de participation aux bénéfices/un régime de retraites complémentaires ■ **government unemployment ~s** plans antichômage du gouvernement ▶ **National Savings Scheme** ≃ Caisse *f* nationale d'épargne **4.** [arrangement] disposition *f*, schéma *m*.
◇ *vi* intriguer ■ **to ~ to do sthg** projeter de faire qqch.
◇ *vt* combiner, manigancer.

schemer ['ski:mər] *n* intrigant *m*, - e *f* ■ [in conspiracy] conspirateur *m*, - trice *f*.

scheming ['ski:mɪŋ] ◇ *n* (*U*) intrigues *fpl*, machinations *fpl*.
◇ *adj* intrigant, conspirateur.

schism ['sɪzm, 'skɪzm] *n* schisme *m*.

schizo△ ['skɪtsəʊ] (*pl* **schizos**) ◇ *adj* schizophrène, schizo.
◇ *n* schizophrène *mf*, schizo *mf*.

schizoid ['skɪtsɔɪd] ◇ *adj* schizoïde.
◇ *n* schizoïde *mf*.

schizophrenia [ˌskɪtsə'fri:njə] *n* schizophrénie *f* ■ **to suffer from ~** être atteint de schizophrénie, être schizophrène.

schizophrenic [ˌskɪtsə'frenɪk] ◇ *adj* schizophrène.
◇ *n* schizophrène *mf*.

schlep(p)△ [ʃlep] (*pret & pp* **schlepped**, *cont* **schlepping**) *esp US vt* trimbaler ■ **I've got to ~ all this stuff over to the office** il faut que je trimballe *OR* transbahute tous ces trucs au bureau.

schmal(t)z [ʃmɔ:lts] *n inf* sentimentalité *f*.

schmal(t)zy ['ʃmɔ:ltsɪ] *adj inf* à l'eau de rose.

schmuck△ [ʃmʌk] *n* connard△ *m*.

schnap(p)s [ʃnæps] (*pl inv*) *n* schnaps *m*.

schnorkel ['ʃnɔ:kl] *UK* = **snorkel**.

scholar ['skɒlər] *n* **1.** [academic] érudit *m*, - e *f*, savant *m* ■ [specialist] spécialiste *mf* ■ [intellectual] intellectuel *m*, - elle *f* ■ **an Egyptian ~** un spécialiste de l'Égypte **2.** [holder of grant] boursier *m*, - ère *f* **3.** *dated* [pupil] élève *mf*.

scholarly ['skɒləlɪ] *adj* **1.** [person] érudit, cultivé **2.** [article, work] savant **3.** [approach] rigoureux, scientifique **4.** [circle] universitaire.

scholarship ['skɒləʃɪp] *n* **1.** SCH & UNIV [grant] bourse *f* ■ **to win a ~ to Stanford** obtenir une bourse pour Stanford *(sur concours)* ■ **~ student** *OR* **holder** boursier *m*, - ère *f* **2.** [knowledge] savoir *m*, érudition *f*.

scholastic [skə'læstɪk] ◇ *adj* **1.** [ability, record, supplier] scolaire ■ [profession] d'enseignant ■ [competition] inter-écoles **2.** [philosophy, approach, argument] scolastique.
◇ *n* scolastique *m*.

scholasticism [skə'læstɪsɪzm] *n* scolastique *f*.

school [sku:l] ◇ *n* **1.** [educational establishment] école *f*, établissement *m* scolaire ■ [secondary school - to age 15] collège *m* ; [- 15 to 18] lycée *m* ■ **to go to ~** aller à l'école *OR* au collège *OR* au lycée ■ **to be at** *OR* **in ~** être à l'école *OR* en classe ■ **to go back to ~** [after illness] reprendre l'école ; [after holidays] rentrer ■ **to send one's children to ~** envoyer ses enfants à l'école ■ **I was at ~ with him** j'étais en classe avec lui, c'était un de mes camarades de classe ■ **to go skiing/sailing with the ~** ≃ aller en classe de neige/de mer ■ [classes] école *f*, classe *f*, classes *fpl*, cours *mpl* ■ **there's no ~ today** il n'y a pas (d')école *OR* il n'y a pas classe aujourd'hui ■ **~ starts back next week** c'est la rentrée (scolaire *OR* des classes) la semaine prochaine ▮ [pupils] école *f* ■ **the whole ~ is** *OR* **are invited** toute l'école est invitée ▮ *fig* école *f* ■ **the ~ of life** l'école de la vie ■ **I went to the ~ of hard knocks** j'ai été à rude école ▶ **~s broadcasting** émissions *fpl* scolaires ■ **'The School for Scandal'** *Sheridan* 'l'École de la médisance'
2. [institute] école *f*, académie *f* ■ **~ of dance, dancing ~** académie *OR* école de danse ■ **~ of music** [gen] école de musique ; [superior level] conservatoire *m* ■ **~ of motoring** auto-école *f*, école *f* de conduite
3. UNIV [department] département *m*, institut *m* ■ [faculty] faculté *f* ■ [college] collège *m* ■ *US* [university] université *f* ■ **~ of medicine** faculté de médecine ■ **London School of Economics** *institut d'études économiques de l'université de Londres* ■ **she's at law ~** elle fait des études de droit, elle fait son droit ▮ [at Oxbridge] salle *f* d'examens
4. [of art, literature] école *f* ■ **a doctor of the old ~** *fig* un médecin de la vieille école *OR* de la vieille garde ▶ **~ of thought** *liter* école *f* de pensée ; *fig* théorie *f*
5. [training session] stage *m*
6. HIST : **the Schools** l'École *f*, la scolastique
7. [of fish, porpoise] banc *m*.
◇ *comp* [doctor, report] scolaire ■ **~ day** journée *f* scolaire *OR* d'école ■ **~ dinners** repas *mpl* servis à la cantine (de l'école) ■ **~ fees** frais *mpl* de scolarité ■ **~ governor** *UK* membre *m* du conseil de gestion de l'école.
◇ *vt* **1.** [send to school] envoyer à l'école, scolariser
2. [train - person] entraîner ; [- animal] dresser ■ **to be ~ed in monetary/military matters** être rompu aux questions monétaires/militaires ■ **she is well ~ed in diplomacy** elle a une bonne formation diplomatique.

COMPREHENSIVE SCHOOLS

Les *comprehensive schools* furent établies en Grande-Bretagne au cours des années 60 et 70 par les gouvernements travailliste et conservateur. Ils devaient remplacer le système bipolaire des *grammar schools* (l'équivalent des lycées) et *secondary moderns* (l'équivalent des CES) qui ne profitait qu'à une minorité d'élèves. En accueillant dans un même établissement des élèves de tous les niveaux de compétence, les *comprehensives* ont réalisé d'assez bons résultats sur le plan social et éducatif. Mais leur caractère souvent impersonnel (beacoup d'entre elles comptant plus de 1000 élèves) et leur tendance à refléter les problèmes sociaux du milieu environnant ont suscité de vives critiques de la part des parents et des pédagogues. On évolue aujourd'hui vers un système qui se caractérisera par un plus grand éventail d'écoles diverses, mais où le recrutement sélectif aura fait sa réapparition.

school age *n* âge *m* scolaire.

schoolbag ['sku:lbæg] *n* cartable *m*.

schoolbook ['sku:lbʊk] *n* livre *m* OR manuel *m* scolaire.

schoolboy ['sku:lbɔɪ] *n* écolier *m* ■ **~ slang** argot *m* scolaire.

school bus *n* car *m* de ramassage scolaire.

schoolchild ['sku:ltʃaɪld] (*pl* **schoolchildren** [-tʃɪldrən]) *n* écolier *m*, - ère *f*.

schooldays ['sku:ldeɪz] *npl* années *fpl* d'école.

school district *n aux États-Unis, autorité locale décisionnaire dans le domaine de l'enseignement primaire et secondaire.*

schoolgirl ['sku:lgɜ:l] ◇ *n* écolière *f*.
◇ *comp* : **~ complexion** teint *m* de jeune fille ■ **she had the usual ~ crush on the gym teacher** comme toutes les filles de son âge, elle était tombée amoureuse de son prof de gym.

school holiday *n* jour *m* de congé scolaire ■ **during the ~s** pendant les vacances OR congés scolaires.

school hours *npl* heures *fpl* de classe OR d'école ■ **in ~** pendant les heures de classe ■ **out of ~** en dehors des heures de classe.

schoolhouse ['sku:lhaʊs] (*pl* [-haʊzɪz]) *n* école *f* (du village).

schooling ['sku:lɪŋ] *n* **1.** [education] instruction *f*, éducation *f* ■ [enrolment at school] scolarité *f* **2.** [of horse] dressage *m*.

schoolkid ['sku:lkɪd] *n inf* écolier *m*, - ère *f* ■ **he's only a ~** ce n'est qu'un gosse.

school-leaver [-,li:vəʳ] *n UK jeune qui entre dans la vie active à la fin de sa scolarité.*

school-leaving age [-'li:vɪŋ-] *n* fin *f* de la scolarité obligatoire ■ **the ~ was raised to 16** l'âge légal de fin de scolarité a été porté à 16 ans.

schoolma'am, schoolmarm ['sku:lmɑ:m] *n inf* **1.** *hum* [teacher] maîtresse *f* d'école **2.** *UK pej* [prim woman] bégueule *f*.

schoolmarmish ['sku:lmɑ:mɪʃ] *adj UK inf pej* **she's very ~** elle fait très maîtresse d'école.

schoolmaster ['sku:l,mɑ:stəʳ] *n UK* [at primary school] maître *m*, instituteur *m* ■ [at secondary school] professeur *m*.

schoolmate ['sku:lmeɪt] *n* camarade *mf* d'école.

schoolmistress ['sku:l,mɪstrɪs] *n UK* [primary school] maîtresse *f*, institutrice *f* ■ [secondary school] professeur *m*.

schoolroom ['sku:lrʊm] *n* (salle *f* de) classe *f*.

schoolteacher ['sku:l,ti:tʃəʳ] *n* [at any level] enseignant *m*, - e *f* ■ [at primary school] instituteur *m*, - trice *f* ■ [at secondary school] professeur *mf*.

schoolteaching ['sku:l,ti:tʃɪŋ] *n* enseignement *m*.

school tie *n cravate propre à une école et faisant partie de l'uniforme.*

schooltime ['sku:ltaɪm] *n* [school hours] heures *fpl* d'école ■ [outside holidays] année *f* scolaire.

school uniform *n* uniforme *m* scolaire.

schoolwork ['sku:lwɜ:k] *n (U)* travail *m* scolaire ■ [at home] devoirs *mpl*, travail *m* à la maison.

school year *n* année *f* scolaire ■ **my ~s** ma scolarité, mes années d'école.

schooner ['sku:nəʳ] *n* **1.** NAUT schooner *m* **2.** [for sherry, beer] grand verre *m*.

Schubert ['ʃu:bət] *pr n* Schubert.

schuss [ʃʊs] ◇ *n* schuss *m*.
◇ *vi* descendre tout schuss.

schwa [ʃwɑ:] *n* [in phonetics] schwa *m*.

sciatic [saɪ'ætɪk] *adj* sciatique ■ **~ nerve** nerf *m* sciatique.

sciatica [saɪ'ætɪkə] *n (U)* sciatique *f*.

science ['saɪəns] ◇ *n (U)* [gen] science *f*, sciences *fpl* ■ **modern ~** la science moderne ■ **she studied ~** elle a fait des études de science OR scientifiques ■ [branch] science *f* ■ **farming is becoming more and more of a ~** l'agriculture devient de plus en plus scientifique.
◇ *comp* [exam] de science ■ [teacher] de science, de sciences ■ [student] en sciences ■ [lab, subject] scientifique.

science fiction *n* science-fiction *f*.

science park *n* parc *m* scientifique.

scientific [,saɪən'tɪfɪk] *adj* **1.** [research, expedition] scientifique **2.** [precise, strict] scientifique, rigoureux.

scientifically [,saɪən'tɪfɪklɪ] *adv* scientifiquement, de manière scientifique ■ **~ speaking** d'un OR du point de vue scientifique.

scientist ['saɪəntɪst] *n* [worker] scientifique *m* ■ [academic] scientifique *mf*, savant *m*.

Scientology® [,saɪən'tɒlədʒɪ] *n* RELIG scientologie *f*.

sci-fi [,saɪ'faɪ] *n inf* = **science fiction**.

Scilly Isles ['sɪlɪ-], **Scillies** ['sɪlɪz] *pr npl* : **the ~** les îles *fpl* Sorlingues ■ **in the ~** aux îles Sorlingues.

scimitar ['sɪmɪtəʳ] *n* cimeterre *m*.

scintillate ['sɪntɪleɪt] *vi* [stars] scintiller, briller ■ *fig* [person - in conversation] briller, être brillant ■ **to ~ with wit** briller par son esprit, pétiller d'esprit.

scintillating ['sɪntɪleɪtɪŋ] *adj* [conversation, wit] brillant, pétillant, étincelant ■ [person, personality] brillant.

scissor ['sɪzəʳ] *vt* couper avec des ciseaux.
◆ **scissors** *npl* : **(a pair of) ~s** (une paire de) ciseaux *mpl*.

scissors jump *n* SPORT saut *m* en ciseaux, ciseau *m*.

scissors kick *n* SPORT ciseau *m*.

sclerosis [sklə'rəʊsɪs] *n (U)* [BOT - MED] & *fig* sclérose *f*.

sclerotic [sklə'rɒtɪk] *adj* **1.** MED sclérosé **2.** BOT scléreux, sclérosé.

scoff [skɒf] ◇ *vi* **1.** [mock] se moquer, être méprisant ■ **they ~ed at my efforts/ideas** ils se sont moqués de mes efforts/idées **2.** *inf* [eat] s'empiffrer.
◇ *vt UK inf* [eat] bouffer, s'empiffrer de.

scoffer ['skɒfəʳ] *n* railleur *m*, - euse *f*.

scoffing ['skɒfɪŋ] ◇ *n* moquerie *f*, sarcasme *m*.
◇ *adj* railleur, sarcastique.

scold [skəʊld] ◇ *vt* gronder, réprimander.
◇ *vi* rouspéter.

scolding ['skəʊldɪŋ] *n* gronderie *f*, gronderies *fpl*, réprimande *f*, réprimandes *fpl* ■ **to give sb a ~ for doing sthg** gronder qqn pour avoir fait qqch.

scone [skɒn] *n* scone *m (petit pain rond).*

scoop [sku:p] ◇ *n* **1.** PRESS scoop *m*, exclusivité *f* ■ **to get** OR **to make a ~** faire un scoop **2.** [utensil, ladle - for ice-cream, potatoes] cuillère *f* à boule ; [- for flour, grain] pelle *f* ; [- for water] écope *f* ▪ [on crane, dredger] pelle *f* ▪ [on bulldozer] lame *f* **3.** [amount scooped - of ice-cream, potatoes] boule *f* ; [- of flour, grain] pelletée *f* ; [- of earth, rocks] pelletée *f* **4.** *UK inf* FIN [profit] bénéfice *m* (important).

◇ *vt* **1.** [take, measure, put] prendre (avec une mesure) ▪ **the ice-cream was ~ed into a dish** on a mis la glace dans un plat (à l'aide d'une cuillère) ▪ **she ~ed the papers into her case** elle a ramassé les journaux dans sa mallette ▪ **she ~ed the grain out of the bucket** elle a pris le grain dans le seau à l'aide d'une mesure | [serve] servir (avec une cuillère) **2.** FIN [market] s'emparer de ▪ [competitor] devancer ▪ **to ~ the field** *OR* **the pool** *fig* tout rafler **3.** PRESS [story] publier en exclusivité ▪ [competitor] publier avant, devancer.

◆ **scoop out** *vt sep* **1.** [take - with scoop] prendre (avec une cuillère) ; [- with hands] prendre (avec les mains) **2.** [hollow - wood, earth] creuser ▪ [empty, remove] vider ▪ **~ out the flesh from the grapefruit** évidez le pamplemousse.

◆ **scoop up** *vt sep* **1.** [take, pick up - in scoop] prendre *OR* ramasser à l'aide d'une pelle *OR* d'un récipient ; [- in hands] prendre *OR* ramasser dans les mains ▪ **she ~ed the papers up in her arms** elle a ramassé une brassée de journaux **2.** [gather together] entasser.

scoop neck *n* décolleté *m*.

scoot [sku:t] *inf vi* filer ▪ **the children ~ed across the fields/up the stairs** les enfants ont filé à travers champs/ont monté les escaliers à toute vitesse ▪ **to ~ over** [move over] se pousser ▪ **~!** fichez le camp!, allez, ouste!

scooter ['sku:tər] *n* **1.** [child's] trottinette *f* **2.** [moped] : **(motor) ~** scooter *m* **3.** *US* [ice yacht] yacht *m* à glace.

scope [skəʊp] *n* **1.** [range] étendue *f*, portée *f* ▪ [limits] limites *fpl* ▪ **does the matter fall within the ~ of the law?** est-ce que l'affaire tombe sous le coup de la loi? ▪ **it is beyond the ~ of this study/of my powers** cela dépasse le cadre de cette étude/de mes compétences ▪ **to extend the ~ of one's activities/of an enquiry** élargir le champ de ses activités/le cadre d'une enquête | [size, extent - of change] étendue *f* ; [- of undertaking] étendue *f*, envergure *f* **2.** [opportunity, room] occasion *f*, possibilité *f* ▪ **there's plenty of ~ for development/for improvement** les possibilités de développement/d'amélioration ne manquent pas ▪ **the job gave him full/little ~ to demonstrate his talents** son travail lui fournissait de nombreuses/peu d'occasions de montrer ses talents ▪ **I'd like a job with more ~** j'aimerais un poste qui me donne plus de perspectives d'évolution **3.** *inf* [telescope] télescope *m* ▪ [microscope] microscope *m* ▪ [periscope] périscope *m*.

scorch [skɔ:tʃ] ◇ *vt* **1.** [with iron - clothing, linen] roussir, brûler légèrement ▪ [with heat - skin] brûler ; [- meat] brûler, carboniser ; [- woodwork] brûler, marquer **2.** [grass, vegetation - with sun] roussir, dessécher ; [- with fire] brûler.

◇ *vi* **1.** [linen] roussir **2.** *UK inf* [in car] filer à toute allure ▪ [on bike] pédaler comme un fou *OR* à fond de train.

◇ *n* [on linen] marque *f* de roussi ▪ [on hand, furniture] brûlure *f* ▪ **there's a ~ (mark) on my shirt** ma chemise a été roussie.

scorched-earth policy *n* politique *f* de la terre brûlée.

scorcher ['skɔ:tʃər] *n inf* [hot day] journée *f* torride ▪ **yesterday was a real ~** hier c'était une vrai fournaise.

scorching ['skɔ:tʃɪŋ] ◇ *adj* **1.** [weather, tea, surface] brûlant **2.** [criticism] cinglant.

◇ *adv* : **a ~ hot day** une journée torride.

score [skɔ:r] ◇ *n* **1.** SPORT score *m* ▪ CARDS points *mpl* ▪ **the ~ was five-nil** le score était de cinq à zéro ▪ **there was still no ~ at half-time** à la mi-temps, aucun but n'avait encore été marqué ▪ **to keep the ~** GAMES compter *OR* marquer les points ; SPORT tenir le score ; [on scorecard] tenir la marque | [in exam, test - mark] note *f* ; [- result] résultat *m* ▪ **to get a good ~** obtenir une bonne note ▪ **the final ~** FTBL le score final ; [gen - CARDS] le résultat final ▪ **what's the ~?** FTBL quel est le score? ; [gen - CARDS] on a marqué combien de points? ; [in tennis] où en est le jeu? ; *fig* on en est où? ➊ **to know the ~** *inf* connaître le topo

2. *fig* [advantage - in debate] avantage *m*, points *mpl*

3. [debt] compte *m* ▪ **I prefer to forget old ~s** je préfère oublier les vieilles histoires

4. [subject, cause] sujet *m*, titre *m* ▪ **don't worry on that ~** ne vous inquiétez pas à ce sujet ▪ **on what ~ was I turned down?** à quel titre *OR* sous quel prétexte ai-je été refusé?

5. [twenty] vingtaine *f* ▪ [many] : **~s of people** beaucoup de gens ▪ **I've told you ~s of times** je vous l'ai dit des centaines de fois

6. MUS partition *f* ▪ CIN & THEAT musique *f* ▪ **Cleo wrote the (film) ~** Cleo est l'auteur de la musique (du film) ▪ **to follow the ~** suivre (sur) la partition

7. [mark - on furniture] rayure *f* ▪ [notch, deep cut] entaille *f* ▪ [in leather] entaille *f*, incision *f* ▪ GEOL strie *f*.

◇ *vt* **1.** SPORT [goal, point] marquer ▪ **to ~ a hit** [with bullet, arrow, bomb] atteindre la cible ; [in fencing] toucher ; *fig* réussir ▪ **the bomber ~d a direct hit** le bombardier a visé en plein sur la cible ▪ **to ~ a success** remporter un succès | [in test, exam - marks] obtenir ▪ **she ~d the highest mark** elle a obtenu *OR* eu la note la plus élevée ▪ **he's always trying to ~ points off me** *fig* il essaie toujours d'avoir le dessus avec moi

2. [scratch] érafler ▪ [make shallow cut in - paper] marquer ; [- rock] strier ; [- pastry, meat] inciser, faire des incisions dans

3. MUS [symphony, opera] orchestrer ▪ **the piece is ~d for six trombones/treble voices** le morceau est écrit pour six trombones/pour soprano | CIN & THEAT composer la musique de

4. *US* [grade, mark - test] noter.

◇ *vi* **1.** SPORT [team, player] marquer un point *OR* des points ▪ FTBL marquer un but *OR* des buts ▪ [scorekeeper] marquer les points ▪ **the team didn't ~** l'équipe n'a pas marqué | [in test] : **to ~ high/low** obtenir un bon/mauvais score

2. [succeed] avoir du succès, réussir ▪ **that's where we ~** c'est là que nous l'emportons, c'est là que nous avons l'avantage

3.△ [sexually] avoir une touche ▪ **did you ~?** tu as réussi à tomber une fille?

4.△ *drug sl* [get drugs] se procurer de la drogue.

◆ **score off** ◇ *vt insep* prendre l'avantage sur, marquer des points sur.

◇ *vt sep* rayer, barrer.

◆ **score over** *vt insep* **1.** = score off *(vt insep)*

2. [be more successful than] avoir l'avantage sur.

◆ **score out, score through** *vt sep* biffer, barrer.

scoreboard ['skɔ:bɔ:d] *n* tableau *m* d'affichage *(du score)*.

scorecard ['skɔ:kɑ:d] *n* **1.** [for score - in game] fiche *f* de marque *OR* de score ; [- in golf] carte *f* de parcours **2.** [list of players] liste *f* des joueurs.

score draw *n* FTBL match *m* nul *(où chaque équipe a marqué)*.

scorekeeper ['skɔ:,ki:pər] *n* marqueur *m*, - euse *f*.

scoreline ['skɔ:laɪn] *n* score *m*.

scorer ['skɔ:rər] *n* **1.** FTBL [regularly] buteur *m* ▪ [of goal] marqueur *m* ▪ **Watkins was the ~** c'est Watkins qui a marqué le but **2.** [scorekeeper] marqueur *m*, - euse *f* **3.** [in test, exam] : **the highest ~** le candidat qui obtient le meilleur score.

scoresheet ['skɔ:ʃi:t] *n* feuille *f* de match.

scoring ['skɔ:rɪŋ] *n (U)* **1.** [of goals] marquage *m* d'un but ▪ [number scored] buts *mpl* (marqués) **2.** CARDS & GAMES [scorekeeping] marquage *m* des points, marque *f* ▪ [points scored] points *mpl* marqués ▪ **I'm not sure about the ~** je ne suis pas sûr de la manière dont on marque les points **3.** [scratching] rayures *fpl*, éraflures *fpl* ▪ [notching] entaille *f*, entailles *fpl* ▪ GEOL striage *m* **4.** MUS [orchestration] orchestration *f* ▪ [arrangement] arrangement *m* ▪ [composition] écriture *f*.

scorn [skɔ:n] ◇ *n* **1.** [contempt] mépris *m*, dédain *m* ▪ **I feel nothing but ~ for them** ils ne m'inspirent que du mépris **2.** [object of derision] (objet *m* de) risée *f*.

◇ *vt* **1.** [be contemptuous of] mépriser **2.** [reject - advice, warning] rejeter, refuser d'écouter ; [- idea] rejeter ; [- help] refuser, dédaigner.

scornful ['skɔ:nfʊl] *adj* dédaigneux, méprisant ▪ **she's rather ~ about** *OR* **of my ideas** elle manifeste un certain mépris envers mes idées.

scornfully ['skɔ:nfʊlɪ] *adv* avec mépris, dédaigneusement ▪ **"of course not", he said ~** « bien sûr que non », dit-il d'un ton méprisant.

Scorpio ['skɔ:pɪəʊ] <> *pr n* ASTROL & ASTRON Scorpion *m*.
<> *n* : **he's a ~** il est Scorpion.

scorpion ['skɔ:pjən] *n* ZOOL scorpion *m*.

Scot [skɒt] *n* Écossais *m*, - e *f*.

scotch [skɒtʃ] *vt* **1.** [suppress - revolt, strike] mettre fin à, réprimer, étouffer ; [- rumour] étouffer ▪ **we'll have to ~ that idea** il faudra abandonner cette idée **2.** [hamper - plans] entraver, contrecarrer **3.** [block - wheel] caler.

Scotch [skɒtʃ] <> *n* [whisky] scotch *m*.
<> *npl* [people] : **the ~** les Écossais *mpl*.
<> *adj* écossais.

Scotch broth *n soupe écossaise à base de légumes et d'orge perlée.*

Scotch egg *n œuf dur entouré de chair à saucisse et enrobé de chapelure.*

Scotch mist *n* bruine *f*.

Scotch tape® *n* US Scotch® *m*.
◆ **scotch-tape** *vt* scotcher.

Scotch whisky *n* scotch *m*, whisky *m* écossais.

scot-free *adj* impuni ▪ **they were let off ~** on les a relâchés sans les punir.

Scotland ['skɒtlənd] *pr n* Écosse *f* ▪ **in ~** en Écosse.

Scotland Yard *pr n ancien nom du siège de la police à Londres (aujourd'hui New Scotland Yard)*, ≃ Quai *m* des Orfèvres.

Scots [skɒts] <> *n* [language - Gaelic] écossais *m*, erse *m* ; [- Lallans] anglais *m* d'Écosse.
<> *adj* [accent, law etc] écossais.

Scotsman ['skɒtsmən] (*pl* **Scotsmen** [-mən]) *n* Écossais *m* ▪ **the ~** PRESS *un des grands quotidiens écossais.*

Scotswoman ['skɒtswʊmən] (*pl* **Scotswomen** [-,wɪmɪn]) *n* Écossaise *f*.

scottie ['skɒtɪ] = **Scottish terrier**.

Scottish ['skɒtɪʃ] <> *n* LING écossais *m*.
<> *npl* : **the ~** les Écossais *mpl*.
<> *adj* écossais.

Scottish Gaelic *n* LING gaélique *m* d'Écosse, erse *m*.

Scottish National Party *pr n parti indépendantiste écossais fondé en 1934.*

Scottish Office *pr n ministère des affaires écossaises, basé à Édimbourg.*

Scottish terrier *n* scottish-terrier *m*, scotch-terrier *m*.

scotty ['skɒtɪ] (*pl* **scotties**) = **Scottish terrier**.

scoundrel ['skaʊndrəl] *n* bandit *m*, vaurien *m* ▪ [child] vilain *m*, - e *f*, coquin *m*, - e *f*.

scour ['skaʊəʳ] <> *vt* **1.** [clean - pan] récurer ; [- metal surface] décaper ; [- floor] lessiver, frotter ; [- tank] vidanger, purger **2.** [scratch] rayer **3.** [subj: water, erosion] creuser **4.** [search - area] ratisser, fouiller ▪ **the police spent the weekend ~ing the woods** la police a passé le week-end à battre les bois ▪ **I've ~ed the whole library looking for her** j'ai fouillé toute la bibliothèque pour la trouver.
<> *n* : **give the pans a good ~** récurez bien les casseroles.

scourer ['skaʊərəʳ] *n* tampon *m* à récurer.

scourge [skɜ:dʒ] <> *n* **1.** [bane] fléau *m* ▪ **the ~ of war/of disease** le fléau de la guerre/de la maladie **2.** [person] peste *f* **3.** [whip] fouet *m*.
<> *vt* **1.** [afflict] ravager **2.** [whip] fouetter.

scouring pad ['skaʊərɪŋ-] *n* tampon *m* à récurer.

scouring powder *n* poudre *f* à récurer.

Scouse [skaʊs] UK *inf* <> *n* **1.** [person] *surnom donné aux habitants de Liverpool* **2.** [dialect] *dialecte de la région de Liverpool.*
<> *adj* de Liverpool.

scout [skaʊt] <> *n* **1.** [boy] scout *m*, éclaireur *m* ▪ [girl] scoute *f*, éclaireuse *f* **2.** MIL [searcher] éclaireur *m* ▪ [watchman] sentinelle *f*, guetteur *m* ▪ [ship] vedette *f* ▪ [aircraft] avion *m* de reconnaissance **3.** [for players, models, dancers] dénicheur *m* de vedettes **4.** [exploration] tour *m* ▪ **to have** OR **to take a ~ around** (aller) reconnaître le terrain **5.** UK AUT [patrolman] dépanneur *m*.
<> *comp* [knife, uniform] (de) scout, d'éclaireur ▪ **~ camp** camp *m* scout ▪ **the ~ movement** le mouvement scout, le scoutisme.
<> *vt* [area] explorer ▪ MIL reconnaître.
<> *vi* partir en reconnaissance.
◆ **scout about** UK, **scout around** *vi insep* explorer les lieux ▪ MIL partir en reconnaissance ▪ **to ~ about for an excuse** chercher un prétexte.
◆ **Scout** = scout *(sense 1)*.

scout car *n* scout-car *m*.

scouting ['skaʊtɪŋ] *n* **1.** [movement] : **~, Scouting** scoutisme *m* **2.** MIL reconnaissance *f*.

scoutmaster ['skaʊt,mɑ:stəʳ] *n* chef *m* scout.

scowl [skaʊl] <> *n* [angry] mine *f* renfrognée OR hargneuse, air *m* renfrogné ▪ [threatening] air *m* menaçant ▪ **she had an angry ~ on her face** la colère se lisait sur son visage.
<> *vi* [angrily] se renfrogner, faire la grimace ▪ [threateningly] prendre un air menaçant ▪ **to ~ at sb** jeter un regard mauvais à qqn.

scowling ['skaʊlɪŋ] *adj* [face] renfrogné, hargneux.

SCR (*abbrev of* **senior common room**) *n* UK *salle des étudiants de 3ᵉ cycle.*

scrabble ['skræbl] <> *vi* **1.** [search] : **she was scrabbling in the grass for the keys** elle cherchait les clés à tâtons dans l'herbe ▪ **the man was scrabbling for a handhold on the cliff face** l'homme cherchait désespérément une prise sur la paroi de la falaise **2.** [scrape] gratter.
<> *n* [scramble] : **there was a wild ~ for the food** les gens se ruèrent sur la nourriture.
◆ **scrabble about** UK, **scrabble around** *vi insep* [grope] fouiller, tâtonner ▪ **she was scrabbling about on all fours looking for her contact lens** à quatre pattes, elle cherchait à tâtons son verre de contact.

Scrabble® ['skræbl] *n* Scrabble® *m*.

scrag [skræg] (*pret & pp* **scragged**, *cont* **scragging**) <> *n* **1.** [person] personne *f* très maigre ▪ [horse] haridelle *f* **2.** [neck] cou *m* **3.** = **scrag end**.
<> *vt inf* tordre le cou à.

scrag end *n* UK CULIN collet *m* (*de mouton ou de veau*).

scraggy ['skrægɪ] (*comp* **scraggier**, *superl* **scraggiest**) *adj* **1.** [thin - neck, person] efflanqué, maigre, décharné ; [- horse, cat] efflanqué, étique *lit* **2.** [jagged] déchiqueté.

scram [skræm] (*pret & pp* **scrammed**, *cont* **scramming**) <> *vi* **1.** [get out] déguerpir, ficher le camp **2.** [reactor] être arrêté d'urgence.
<> *vt* [reactor] arrêter d'urgence.
<> *n* [of reactor] arrêt *m* d'urgence.

scramble ['skræmbl] <> *vi* **1.** [verb of movement - hurriedly or with difficulty] : **they ~d for shelter** ils se sont précipités pour se mettre à l'abri ▪ **he ~d to his feet** il s'est levé précipitamment ▪ **to ~ away** s'enfuir à toutes jambes ▪ **to ~ down** dégringoler ▪ **to ~ up** grimper avec difficulté ▪ **to ~ over rocks** escalader des rochers en s'aidant des mains ▪ **the soldiers ~d up the hill** les soldats ont escaladé la colline tant bien que mal **2.** [scrabble, fight] : **to ~ for seats** se bousculer pour trouver une place assise, se ruer sur les places assises ▪ **everyone was scrambling to get to the telephones** tout le monde se ruait vers les téléphones ▪ **young people are having to ~ for jobs** les jeunes doivent se battre OR se démener pour trouver un boulot
3. AERON & MIL décoller sur-le-champ
4. SPORT : **to go scrambling** faire du trial.
<> *vt* **1.** RADIO & TELEC brouiller
2. [jumble] mélanger
3. AERON & MIL ordonner le décollage immédiat de
4. CULIN [eggs] brouiller.

◇ *n* **1.** [rush] bousculade *f*, ruée *f* ▪ **there was a ~ for seats** *liter* on s'est bousculé pour avoir une place assise, on s'est rué sur les places assises ; [for tickets] on s'est arraché les places ▪ **there was a ~ for the door** tout le monde s'est rué vers la porte ▪ **a ~ for profits/for jobs** une course effrénée au profit/à l'emploi
2. SPORT [on motorbikes] course *f* de trial
3. AERON & MIL décollage *m* immédiat
4. [in rock climbing] grimpée *f* à quatre pattes.

scrambled egg ['skræmbld-], **scrambled eggs** *(npl)* *n* œufs *mpl* brouillés.

scrambler ['skræmblər] *n* RADIO & TELEC brouilleur *m*.

scrambling ['skræmblɪŋ] *n* **1.** *UK* SPORT trial *m* **2.** [in rock climbing] grimpée *f* à quatre pattes.

scrap [skræp] (*pret & pp* **scrapped**, *cont* **scrapping**) ◇ *n* **1.** [small piece - of paper, cloth] bout *m* ; [- of bread, cheese] petit bout *m* ; [- of conversation] bribe *f* ▪ **~s of news/of information** des bribes de nouvelles/d'informations ▪ **there isn't a ~ of truth in the story** il n'y a pas une parcelle de vérité *OR* il n'y a absolument rien de vrai dans cette histoire ▪ **it didn't do me a ~ of good** [action] cela ne m'a servi absolument à rien ; [medicine] cela ne m'a fait aucun bien ▪ **what I say won't make a ~ of difference** ce que je dirai ne changera rien du tout **2.** [waste] : **we sold the car for ~** on a vendu la voiture à la ferraille *OR* à la casse ▪ **~ (metal)** ferraille *f* **3.** *inf* [fight] bagarre *f* ▪ **to get into** *OR* **to have a ~ with sb** se bagarrer avec qqn.
◇ *comp* [value] de ferraille ▪ **~ lead** plomb *m* de récupération ▪ **~ iron** *OR* **metal** ferraille *f* ▪ **~ merchant** *UK* ferrailleur *m* ▪ **~ (metal) dealer** ferrailleur *m*.
◇ *vt* **1.** [discard - shoes, furniture] jeter ; [- idea, plans] renoncer à, abandonner ; [- system] abandonner, mettre au rancart ; [- machinery] mettre au rebut *OR* au rancart ▪ **you can ~ the whole idea** vous pouvez laisser tomber *OR* abandonner cette idée **2.** [send for scrap - car, ship] envoyer *OR* mettre à la ferraille *OR* à la casse.
◇ *vi* *inf* [fight] se bagarrer.
◆ **scraps** *npl* [food] restes *mpl* ▪ [fragments] débris *mpl*.

scrapbook ['skræpbʊk] *n* album *m (de coupures de journaux, de photos etc)*.

scrape [skreɪp] ◇ *vt* **1.** [rasp, rub - boots, saucepan, earth] gratter, racler ; [- tools] gratter, décaper ; [- vegetables, windows] gratter ▪ **~ the mud off your shoes** enlève *OR* gratte la boue de tes chaussures ▪ **to ~ sthg clean/smooth** gratter qqch pour qu'il soit propre/lisse ▪ **the boat ~d the bottom** [ran aground] le bateau a touché le fond ; [on beach] le bateau s'est échoué sur le sable ▪ [drag] traîner ▪ **don't ~ the chair across the floor like that** ne traîne pas la chaise par terre comme ça ➊ **to ~ the bottom of the barrel** racler les fonds de tiroir **2.** [touch lightly] effleurer, frôler ▪ [scratch - paint, table, wood] rayer ▪ **the plane just ~d the surface of the water** l'avion frôla *OR* rasa la surface de l'eau **3.** [skin, knee] érafler ▪ **I ~d my knee** je me suis éraflé le genou **4.** [with difficulty] : **to ~ a living** arriver tout juste à survivre, vivoter ▪ **to ~ acquaintance with sb** *UK* se débrouiller pour faire la connaissance de qqn.
◇ *vi* **1.** [rub] frotter ▪ [rasp] gratter ▪ **the door ~d shut** la porte s'est refermée en grinçant **2.** *fig* [avoid with difficulty] : **she just ~d clear of the bus in time** elle a évité le bus de justesse ▪ **the ambulance just ~d past** l'ambulance est passée de justesse **3.** [economize] faire des petites économies **4.** [be humble] faire des courbettes *OR* des ronds de jambes.
◇ *n* **1.** [rub, scratch] : **he had a nasty ~ on his knee** il avait une méchante éraflure au genou, il s'était bien éraflé le genou ▪ **just give the saucepan a quick ~** frotte *OR* gratte un peu la casserole **2.** *inf* [dilemma, trouble] pétrin *m* ▪ **to get into a ~** se mettre dans le pétrin **3.** [scraping] grattement *m*, grincement *m* **4.** = **scraping** *(sense 2)*.
◆ **scrape along** *vi insep* [financially] se débrouiller, vivre tant bien que mal.
◆ **scrape away** ◇ *vt sep* enlever en grattant.
◇ *vi insep* gratter ▪ **to ~ away at a violin** racler du violon.
◆ **scrape by** *vi insep* [financially] se débrouiller ▪ **I have just enough to ~ by (on)** j'ai juste assez d'argent pour me débrouiller.
◆ **scrape in** *vi insep* [in election] être élu de justesse ▪ **I just ~d in as the doors were closing** j'ai réussi à entrer juste au moment où les portes se fermaient.
◆ **scrape into** *vt insep* : **he just ~d into university/parliament** il est entré à l'université/au parlement d'extrême justesse.
◆ **scrape off** ◇ *vt sep* [mud, paint] enlever au grattoir *OR* en grattant ▪ [skin] érafler.
◇ *vi insep* s'enlever au grattoir ▪ **this paint ~s off easily** pour enlever cette peinture, il suffit de la gratter.
◆ **scrape out** *vt sep* **1.** [saucepan] récurer, racler ▪ [residue] enlever en grattant *OR* raclant **2.** [hollow] creuser.
◆ **scrape through** ◇ *vt insep* [exam] réussir de justesse ▪ [doorway, gap] passer (de justesse) ▪ **the government will probably just ~ through the next election** le gouvernement va probablement l'emporter de justesse aux prochaines élections.
◇ *vi insep* [in exam] réussir de justesse ▪ [in election] être élu *OR* l'emporter de justesse ▪ [financially] se débrouiller tout juste ▪ [through gap] passer de justesse.
◆ **scrape together** *vt sep* **1.** [two objects] frotter l'un contre l'autre **2.** [into pile] mettre en tas **3.** [collect - supporters, signatures] réunir *OR* rassembler à grand-peine ; [- money for o.s.] réunir en raclant les fonds de tiroirs ; [- money for event] réunir avec beaucoup de mal.
◆ **scrape up** = **scrape together** *(sense 3)*.

scraper ['skreɪpər] *n* grattoir *m* ▪ [for muddy shoes] décrottoir *m*.

scrapheap ['skræphi:p] *n* **1.** *liter* décharge *f* **2.** *fig* rebut *m* ▪ **to be thrown on** *OR* **consigned to the ~** être mis au rebut.

scrapie ['skreɪpɪ] *n* VET tremblante *f*.

scraping ['skreɪpɪŋ] ◇ *adj* [sound] de grattement.
◇ *n* **1.** [sound] grattement *m* ▪ **the ~ of chalk on the blackboard** le crissement *OR* le grincement de la craie sur le tableau **2.** [thin layer] mince couche *f*.
◆ **scrapings** *npl* [food] déchets *mpl*, restes *mpl* ▪ [from paint, wood] raclures *fpl*.

scrap paper *n* (papier *m*) brouillon *m*.

scrappy ['skræpɪ] (*comp* **scrappier**, *superl* **scrappiest**) *adj* **1.** [disconnected] décousu ▪ **I had rather a ~ education** je n'ai pas bénéficié d'une instruction très suivie **2.** *US inf* [quarrelsome] bagarreur, chamailleur.

scrapyard ['skræpjɑ:d] *n* chantier *m* de ferraille, casse *f*.

scratch [skrætʃ] ◇ *vt* **1.** [itch, rash] gratter ▪ **to ~ one's head** se gratter la tête ▮ [earth, surface] gratter ▪ **you've barely ~ed the surface** *fig* vous avez fait un travail très superficiel, vous avez seulement effleuré la question ▪ **they ~ a living selling secondhand books** *UK fig* ils gagnent péniblement leur vie en vendant des livres d'occasion ➊ **you ~ my back, and I'll ~ yours** si vous me rendez ce service, je vous le revaudrai *OR* je vous renverrai l'ascenseur
2. [subj: cat] griffer ▪ [subj: thorn, nail] égratigner, écorcher ▪ **the cat ~ed my hand** le chat m'a griffé la main ▪ **she ~ed her hand on the brambles** elle s'est écorché *OR* égratigné la main dans les ronces ▮ [mark - woodwork, marble] rayer, érafler ; [- glass, record] rayer ▪ **the car's hardly ~ed** la voiture n'a presque rien *OR* n'a pratiquement aucune éraflure ▪ **someone has ~ed their initials on the tree** quelqu'un a gravé ses initiales sur l'arbre
3. [irritate] gratter ▪ **this wool ~es my skin** cette laine me gratte la peau
4. SPORT [cancel - match] annuler
5. *US* POL rayer de la liste.
◇ *vi* **1.** [person, monkey] se gratter
2. [hen] gratter (le sol) ▪ [pen] gratter
3. [cat] griffer ▪ [brambles, nail] griffer, écorcher.
◇ *n* **1.** [for itch] grattement *m* ▪ **the dog was having a good ~** le chien se grattait un bon coup
2. [from cat] coup *m* de griffe ▪ [from fingernails] coup *m* d'ongle ▪ [from thorns, nail] égratignure *f*, écorchure *f* ▪ **how did you get that ~?** comment est-ce que tu t'es égratigné? ▪ **I've got a ~ on my hand** je me suis égratigné la main ▪ **her hands were covered in ~es** elle avait les mains tout écorchées *OR* couvertes d'égratignures

3. [mark - on furniture] rayure *f*, éraflure *f* ; [- on glass, record] rayure *f*
4. *phr* **to be up to ~** [in quality] avoir la qualité voulue ; [in level] avoir le niveau voulu ■ **her work still isn't up to ~** son travail n'est toujours pas satisfaisant ■ **their performance wasn't up to** *OR* **didn't come up to ~** leur performance n'était pas suffisante *OR* à la hauteur.
◇ *adj* [team, meal] improvisé ■ [player] scratch *(inv)*, sans handicap ■ [shot] au hasard.
◆ **from scratch** *adv phr* à partir de rien *OR* de zéro ■ **I learnt Italian from ~ in six months** j'ai appris l'italien en six mois en ayant commencé à zéro.
◆ **scratch off** *vt sep* enlever en grattant.
◆ **scratch out** *vt sep* [name] raturer ■ **to ~ sb's eyes out** arracher les yeux à qqn ■ **I'll ~ your eyes out!** *fig* je vais t'écorcher vif !
◆ **scratch together** *vt sep UK* [team] réunir (difficilement) ■ [sum of money] réunir *OR* rassembler (en raclant les fonds de tiroir).
◆ **scratch up** *vt sep* **1.** [dig up - bone, plant] déterrer **2.** *UK* [money] réunir (en raclant les fonds de tiroir).

scratch card ['skrætʃkɑ:d] *n* carte *f* à gratter.

scratch mark *n* [on hand] égratignure *f* ■ [on leather, furniture] rayure *f*, éraflure *f*.

scratchpad ['skrætʃpæd] *n US* bloc-notes *m* ■ **~ memory** COMPUT mémoire *f* bloc-notes.

scratch paper *US* = **scrap paper**.

scratchy ['skrætʃɪ] (*comp* **scratchier**, *superl* **scratchiest**) *adj* **1.** [prickly - jumper, blanket] rêche, qui gratte ; [- bush] piquant **2.** [pen] qui gratte **3.** [drawing, writing] griffonné **4.** [record] rayé.

scrawl [skrɔ:l] ◇ *n* griffonnage *m*, gribouillage *m* ■ **I thought I recognized his ~** je pensais bien avoir reconnu ses gribouillis ■ **her signature is just a ~** sa signature est totalement illisible.
◇ *vt* griffonner, gribouiller.
◇ *vi* gribouiller.

scrawny ['skrɔ:nɪ] (*comp* **scrawnier**, *superl* **scrawniest**) *adj* **1.** [person, neck] efflanqué, décharné ■ [cat, chicken] efflanqué, étique *lit* **2.** [vegetation] maigre.

scream [skri:m] ◇ *vi* **1.** [shout] crier, pousser des cris, hurler ■ [baby] crier, hurler ■ [birds, animals] crier ■ **to ~ at sb** crier après qqn ■ **to ~ in anger/with pain** hurler de colère/de douleur ■ **she ~ed for help** elle cria à l'aide *OR* au secours ■ **they were ~ing with laughter** ils se tordaient de rire, ils riaient aux éclats **2.** [tyres] crisser ■ [engine, siren] hurler.
◇ *vt* **1.** [shout] hurler ■ **she just stood there ~ing insults at me** elle est restée plantée là à me couvrir d'insultes **2.** [order, answer] hurler ■ **"come here at once!", she ~ed** "viens ici tout de suite!", hurla-t-elle **3.** [newspaper] étaler ■ **headlines ~ed the news of his defeat** la nouvelle de sa défaite s'étalait en gros titres.
◇ *n* **1.** [cry] cri *m* perçant, hurlement *m* ■ **she gave a loud ~** elle a poussé un hurlement ■ **~s of laughter** des éclats de rire **2.** [of tyres] crissement *m* ■ [of sirens, engines] hurlement *m* **3.** [person] : **he's an absolute ~** il est vraiment désopilant *OR* impayable ■ **you do look a ~ in that hat!** vous êtes à mourir de rire avec ce chapeau! ■ [situation, event] : **the party was a ~** on s'est amusés comme des fous à la soirée.
◆ **scream out** ◇ *vi insep* pousser de grands cris ■ **to ~ out in pain** hurler de douleur ■ **to be ~ing out for sthg** *fig* avoir sacrément besoin de qqch.
◇ *vt sep* hurler.

screaming ['skri:mɪŋ] *adj* [fans] qui crie, qui hurle ■ [tyres] qui crisse ■ [sirens, jets] qui hurle ■ [need] criant ■ **~ headlines** grandes manchettes *fpl*.

screamingly ['skri:mɪŋlɪ] *adv inf* **~ funny** on ne peut plus drôle, à se tordre *OR* à mourir de rire.

scree [skri:] *n (U)* éboulis *m*, pierraille *f*.

screech [skri:tʃ] ◇ *vi* **1.** [owl] ululer, hululer, huer ■ [gull] crier, piailler ■ [parrot] crier ■ [monkey] hurler **2.** [person - in high voice] pousser des cris stridents *OR* perçants ; [- loudly] hurler ■ [singer] crier, chanter d'une voie stridente **3.** [tyres] crisser ■ [brakes, machinery] grincer (bruyamment) ■ [siren, jets] hurler ■ **the car ~ed to a halt** la voiture s'est arrêtée dans un crissement de pneus ■ **the car came ~ing round the corner** la voiture a pris le virage dans un crissement de pneus.
◇ *vt* [order] hurler, crier à tue-tête ■ **"never," she ~ed** "jamais", dit-elle d'une voix stridente.
◇ *n* **1.** [of owl] ululement *m*, hululement *m* ■ [of gull] cri *m*, piaillement *m* ■ [of parrot] cri *m* ■ [of monkey] hurlement *m* ■ **the parrot gave a loud ~** le perroquet a poussé un grand cri **2.** [of person] cri *m* strident *OR* perçant ■ [with pain, rage] hurlement *m* ■ **we heard ~es of laughter coming from next door** on entendait des rires perçants qui venaient d'à côté **3.** [of tyres] crissement *m* ■ [of brakes] grincement *m* ■ [of sirens, jets] hurlement *m* ■ **we stopped with a ~ of brakes/tyres** on s'arrêta dans un grincement de freins/dans un crissement de pneus.

screech owl *n* chat-huant *m*, hulotte *f*.

screed [skri:d] *n* **1.** [essay, story] longue dissertation *f* ■ [letter] longue lettre *f* ■ [speech] laïus *m* **2.** CONSTR [level] règle *f* à araser le béton ■ [depth guide] guide *m* ■ [plaster] plâtre *m* de ragrément *OR* de ragréage.

screen [skri:n] ◇ *n* **1.** CIN, PHOT & TV écran *m* ■ **stars of stage and ~** des vedettes de théâtre et de cinéma ■ **the book was adapted for the ~** le livre a été porté à l'écran **2.** [for protection - in front of fire] pare-étincelles *m inv* ; [- over window] moustiquaire *f* **3.** [for privacy] paravent *m* ■ **a ~ of trees** un rideau d'arbres ■ **the rooms are divided by sliding ~s** les pièces sont séparées par des cloisons coulissantes **4.** *fig* [mask] écran *m*, masque *m* **5.** [sieve] tamis *m*, crible *m* ■ [filter - for employees, candidates] filtre *m*, crible *m* **6.** SPORT écran *m*.
◇ *comp* [actor, star] de cinéma.
◇ *vt* **1.** CIN & TV [film] projeter, passer **2.** [shelter, protect] protéger ■ **he ~ed his eyes from the sun with his hand** il a mis sa main devant ses yeux pour se protéger du soleil ■ [hide] cacher, masquer ■ **to ~ sthg from sight** cacher *OR* masquer qqch aux regards **3.** [filter, check - employees, applications, suspects] passer au crible ■ **we ~ all our security staff** nous faisons une enquête préalable sur tous les candidats aux postes d'agent de sécurité ■ **the hospital ~s thousands of women a year for breast cancer** MED l'hôpital fait passer un test de dépistage du cancer du sein à des milliers de femmes tous les ans **4.** [sieve - coal, dirt] cribler, passer au crible.
◆ **screen off** *vt sep* **1.** [put screens round - patient] abriter derrière un paravent ; [- bed] entourer de paravents ■ **the police had ~ed off the garden** la police avait mis des bâches autour du jardin **2.** [divide, separate - with partition] séparer par une cloison ; [- with curtain] séparer par un rideau ; [- with folding screen] séparer par un paravent **3.** [hide - with folding screen] cacher derrière un paravent ; [- with curtain] cacher derrière un rideau ; [- behind trees, wall] cacher.
◆ **screen out** *vt sep* filtrer, éliminer ■ **this cream ~s out UV rays** cette crème protège des UV, cette crème absorbe *OR* filtre les UV.

screen break *n* COMPUT pause *f*.

screen door *n US* porte *f* avec moustiquaire.

screen dump *n* COMPUT vidage *m* d'écran.

screening ['skri:nɪŋ] *n* **1.** CIN projection *f* (en salle) ■ TV passage *m* (à l'écran), diffusion *f* **2.** [of applications, candidates] tri *m*, sélection *f* ■ [for security] contrôle *m* ■ MED [for cancer, tuberculosis] test *m* *OR* tests *mpl* de dépistage ■ **she went for cancer ~** elle est allée passer un test de dépistage du cancer **3.** [mesh] grillage *m* **4.** [of coal] criblage *m*.

screen memory *n* souvenir écran *m*.

screenplay ['skri:npleɪ] *n* scénario *m*.

screen print *n* sérigraphie *f*.

screen printing *n* sérigraphie *f*.

screen process *n* sérigraphie *f*.

screen saver *n* COMPUT économiseur *m* (d'écran).

screenshot ['skri:nʃɒt] *n* copie *f* d'écran.

screen test *n* CIN bout *m* d'essai.
◆ **screen-test** *vt* faire faire un bout d'essai à.

screenwriter ['skri:n,raɪtəʳ] *n* scénariste *mf*.

screw [skru:] <> *n* **1.** [for wood] vis *f* ▪ [bolt] boulon *m* ▪ [in vice] vis *f* ▪ **to turn the ~** *OR* **~s** *fig* serrer la vis ⊳ **to put the ~s on sb** *inf* faire pression sur qqn ▪ **to have a ~ loose** *inf* avoir la tête fêlée, être fêlé **2.** [turn] tour *m* de vis **3.** [thread] pas *m* de vis **4.** [propeller] hélice *f* **5.** *UK* [of salt, tobacco] cornet *m* **6.**△ *prison sl* [guard] maton *m* **7.**△ *UK* [salary] salaire *m*, paye *f* **8.**▲ [sexual] : **to have a ~** *UK* baiser△, s'envoyer en l'air△.
<> *vt* **1.** [bolt, screw] visser ▪ [handle, parts] fixer avec des vis ▪ [lid on bottle] visser ▪ **to ~ sthg shut** fermer qqch (en vissant) **2.** [crumple] froisser, chiffonner ▪ **I ~ed the letter/my handkerchief into a ball** j'ai fait une boule de la lettre/de mon mouchoir **3.** [wrinkle - face] : **he ~ed his face into a grimace** une grimace lui tordit le visage **4.** *inf* [obtain] arracher ▪ **to ~ a promise/an agreement out of sb** arracher une promesse/un accord à qqn **5.**△ [con] arnaquer△, baiser△ **6.**▲ [sexually] baiser△ **7.**△ [as invective] : **~ the expense!** et merde△, je peux bien m'offrir ça! ▪ **~ you!** va te faire foutre!△.
<> *vi* **1.** [bolt, lid] se visser **2.**△ [sexually] baiser△.
◆ **screw around** *vi insep* **1.**△ *US* [waste time] glander△ ▪ [fool about] déconner△ **2.**▲ [sleep around] baiser avec n'importe qui△, coucher à droite à gauche.
◆ **screw down** <> *vt sep* visser.
<> *vi insep* se visser.
◆ **screw off** <> *vt sep* dévisser.
<> *vi insep* se dévisser.
◆ **screw on** <> *vt sep* visser ▪ **the cupboard was ~ed on to the wall** le placard était vissé au mur.
<> *vi insep* se visser ▪ **it ~s on to the wall** ça se visse dans le mur.
◆ **screw up** *vt sep* **1.** [tighten, fasten] visser **2.** [crumple - handkerchief, paper] chiffonner, faire une boule de **3.** *UK* [eyes] plisser ▪ **to ~ up one's courage** prendre son courage à deux mains **4.** *inf* [mess up - plans, chances] bousiller, foutre en l'air ; [- person] faire perdre ses moyens à, angoisser, mettre dans tous ses états ▪ **the divorce really ~ed her up** le divorce l'a complètement perturbée *OR* déboussolée.

screwball ['skru:bɔ:l] *US inf* <> *n* **1.** [crazy] cinglé *m*, - e *f*, dingue *mf* **2.** [in baseball] *balle qui dévie de sa trajectoire.*
<> *adj* cinglé, dingue.

screwdriver ['skru:,draɪvəʳ] *n* **1.** [tool] tournevis *m* **2.** [drink] vodka-orange *f*.

screwed-up *adj* **1.** [crumpled] froissé, chiffonné **2.** *inf* [confused] paumé ▪ [neurotic] perturbé, angoissé.

screw jack *n* cric *m* à vis.

screw thread *n* pas *m* *OR* filet *m* de vis.

screw top *n* couvercle *m* qui se visse ▪ **the jar has a ~** le couvercle du pot se visse.
◆ **screwtop** *adj* dont le couvercle se visse.

screwy ['skru:ɪ] (*comp* **screwier**, *superl* **screwiest**) *adj inf* [person] timbré, cinglé.

scribble ['skrɪbl] <> *vt* **1.** [note, drawing] gribouiller, griffonner ▪ **she left me a hastily ~d note** elle m'a laissé un mot gribouillé à la hâte ▪ **she ~d a few lines to her sister** elle griffonna quelques lignes à l'intention de sa sœur **2.** [wool] carder.
<> *vi* gribouiller.
<> *n* gribouillis *m*, gribouillage *m*, griffonnage *m*.
◆ **scribble down** *vt sep* [address, number] griffonner, noter (rapidement).
◆ **scribble out** *vt sep* **1.** [cross out] biffer, raturer **2.** [write] griffonner.

scribbler ['skrɪbləʳ] *n UK pej* [author] écrivaillon *m*.

scribbling ['skrɪblɪŋ] *n* gribouillis *m*, gribouillage *m*.

scribbling pad *n* bloc-notes *m*.

scribe [skraɪb] <> *n* scribe *m*.
<> *vt* graver.

scrimmage ['skrɪmɪdʒ] <> *n* **1.** SPORT mêlée *f* **2.** [brawl] mêlée *f*, bagarre *f*.
<> *vi* SPORT faire une mêlée.
<> *vt* SPORT [ball] mettre dans la mêlée.

scrimp [skrɪmp] <> *vi* lésiner ▪ **she ~s on food** elle lésine sur la nourriture ▪ **to ~ and save** économiser sur tout, se serrer la ceinture.
<> *vt* [children, family] se montrer pingre avec ▪ [food] lésiner sur.

scrip [skrɪp] *n* **1.** ST. EX titre *m* provisoire **2.** [of paper] morceau *m*.

scrip issue *n* ST. EX émission *f* d'actions gratuites.

script [skrɪpt] <> *n* **1.** [text] script *m*, texte *m* ▪ CIN script *m* **2.** *(U)* [handwriting] script *m*, écriture *f* script ▪ **the letter is written in beautiful ~** la lettre est superbement calligraphiée ▪ **to write in ~** écrire en script ‖ [lettering, characters] écriture *f*, caractères *mpl*, lettres *fpl* ▪ **Arabic ~** caractères arabes, écriture arabe ▪ **in italic ~** en italique **3.** [copy - LAW] original *m* ▪ UNIV copie *f* (d'examen).
<> *vt* CIN écrire le script de.

scripted ['skrɪptɪd] *adj* [speech, interview etc] (dont le texte a été) écrit d'avance.

script girl *n* scripte *mf*, script girl *f*.

scriptural ['skrɪptʃərəl] *adj* biblique.

Scripture ['skrɪptʃəʳ] *n* **1.** [Christian] Écriture *f* (sainte) ▪ **a reading from the ~s** une lecture biblique *OR* de la Bible **2.** [non-Christian] : **the ~s** les textes *mpl* sacrés.

scriptwriter ['skrɪpt,raɪtəʳ] *n* scénariste *mf*.

scrofula ['skrɒfjʊlə] *n (U)* scrofule *f*.

scrofulous ['skrɒfjʊləs] *adj* scrofuleux.

scroll [skrəʊl] <> *n* **1.** [of parchment] rouleau *m* **2.** [manuscript] manuscrit *m* (ancien) **3.** [on column, violin, woodwork] volute *f*.
<> *vt* COMPUT faire défiler.
<> *vi* COMPUT défiler.
◆ **scroll through** *vt insep* COMPUT faire défiler d'un bout à l'autre.

scroll bar *n* COMPUT barre *f* de défilement.

scrolling ['skrəʊlɪŋ] *n* COMPUT défilement *m*.

scrooge [skru:dʒ] *n* grippe-sou *m*, harpagon *m*.
◆ **Scrooge** *pr n personnage de Dickens incarnant l'avarice.*

scrotum ['skrəʊtəm] (*pl* **scrotums** *OR pl* **scrota** [-tə]) *n* scrotum *m*.

scrounge [skraʊndʒ] *inf* <> *vt* [sugar, pencil] emprunter, piquer ▪ [meal] se faire offrir ▪ [money] se faire prêter ▪ **he tried to ~ $10 off me** il a essayé de me taper de 10 dollars.
<> *vi* : **to ~ on** *OR* **off sb** [habitually] vivre aux crochets de qqn ▪ **he's always scrounging off his friends** il fait toujours le pique-assiette chez ses amis, il tape toujours ses amis ▪ **I'm sorry to be always scrounging** je suis désolé d'être toujours à quémander.
<> *n* : **to be on the ~** [for food] venir quémander de quoi manger ; [for cigarette] venir quémander une cigarette ▪ **he's always on the ~** il vit toujours aux crochets des autres.

scrounger ['skraʊndʒəʳ] *n inf* pique-assiette *mf*, parasite *m*.

scrub [skrʌb] (*pret & pp* **scrubbed**, *cont* **scrubbing**) <> *vt* **1.** [clean, wash] brosser *(avec de l'eau et du savon)* ▪ [floor, carpet] nettoyer à la brosse, frotter avec une brosse ▪ [saucepan, sink] frotter, récurer ▪ [clothes, face, back] frotter ▪ [fingernails] brosser ▪ **to ~ sthg clean** nettoyer qqch à fond, récurer qqch ▪ **~ yourself all over** frotte-toi bien partout ▪ **have you scrubbed your hands clean?** est-ce que tu t'es bien nettoyé les mains? **2.** [cancel - order] annuler ; [- plans, holiday] annuler, laisser tomber ▪ [recording, tape] effacer **3.** TECH [gas] laver.
<> *vi* : **I spent the morning scrubbing** j'ai passé la matinée à frotter les planchers *OR* les sols.
<> *n* **1.** [with brush] coup *m* de brosse ▪ **give the floor a good ~** frotte bien le plancher ▪ **can you give my back a ~?** peux-tu me frotter le dos? **2.** [vegetation] broussailles *fpl* **3.** *US* SPORT [team] équipe *f* de seconde zone ▪ [player] joueur *m*, - euse *f* de second ordre **4.** *inf Australia* [wilderness] cambrousse *inf f*.
◆ **scrub away** <> *vt sep* [mark, mud] faire partir en brossant.
<> *vi insep* partir à la brosse.

◆ **scrub down** *vt sep* [wall, paintwork] lessiver ■ [horse] bouchonner.
◆ **scrub out** ◇ *vt sep* **1.** [dirt, stain] faire partir à la brosse ■ [bucket, tub] nettoyer à la brosse ■ [pan] récurer ■ [ears] nettoyer, bien laver **2.** [erase - graffiti, comment] effacer ; [- name] barrer, biffer.
◇ *vi insep* partir à la brosse.
◆ **scrub up** *vi insep* MED [before operation] se laver les mains.

scrubber ['skrʌbəʳ] *n* **1.** [for saucepans] tampon *m* à récurer **2.**△ *UK pej* [whore] pute△ *f*.

scrubbing brush *UK* ['skrʌbɪŋ-], **scrub brush** *US n* brosse *f* à récurer.

scrubby ['skrʌbɪ] (*comp* **scrubbier**, *superl* **scrubbiest**) *adj* **1.** [land] broussailleux **2.** [tree, vegetation] rabougri.

scrubland ['skrʌblænd] *n* maquis *m*, garrigue *f*.

scrubwoman ['skrʌbˌwʊmən] (*pl* **scrubwomen** [-ˌwɪmɪn]) *n US* femme *f* de ménage.

scruff [skrʌf] *n* **1.** *UK inf* [untidy person] individu *m* débraillé *OR* dépenaillé *OR* peu soigné ■ [ruffian] voyou *m* **2.** *phr* **by the ~ of the neck** par la peau du cou.

scruffily ['skrʌfɪlɪ] *adv* : **~ dressed** dépenaillé, mal habillé.

scruffy ['skrʌfɪ] (*comp* **scruffier**, *superl* **scruffiest**) *adj* [appearance, clothes] dépenaillé, crasseux ■ [hair] ébouriffé ■ [building, area] délabré, miteux ■ **he's a ~ dresser** il s'habille mal.

scrum [skrʌm] (*pret & pp* **scrummed**, *cont* **scrumming**) ◇ *n* **1.** RUGBY mêlée *f* **2.** [brawl] mêlée *f*, bousculade *f*.
◇ *vi* former une mêlée.
◆ **scrum down** *vi insep* former une mêlée ■ **~ down!** [as instruction] mêlée!

scrum-cap *n* casquette *f (de joueur de rugby)*.

scrumhalf [ˌskrʌm'hɑːf] *n* demi *m* de mêlée.

scrummage ['skrʌmɪdʒ] ◇ *n* **1.** RUGBY mêlée *f* **2.** [brawl] mêlée *f*, bousculade *f* ■ **there was a ~ for the best bargains** les gens se sont arrachés les soldes les plus intéressants.
◇ *vi* RUGBY former une mêlée.

scrump [skrʌmp] *UK inf* ◇ *vi* : **to go ~ing (for apples)** aller chaparder(des pommes).
◇ *vt* [apples] chaparder.

scrumptious ['skrʌmpʃəs] *adj inf* délicieux, succulent.

scrumpy ['skrʌmpɪ] *n cidre brut et sec fabriqué dans le sud-ouest de l'Angleterre.*

scrunch [skrʌntʃ] ◇ *vt* [biscuit, apple] croquer ■ [snow, gravel] faire craquer *OR* crisser ■ [paper - noisily] froisser (bruyamment).
◇ *vi* [footsteps - on gravel, snow] craquer, faire un bruit de craquement ■ [gravel, snow - underfoot] craquer, crisser.
◇ *n* [of gravel, snow, paper] craquement *m*, bruit *m* de craquement.
◇ *onom* crac! crac!
◆ **scrunch up** *vt sep* **1.** [crumple - paper] froisser ■ **he ~ed up his face in disgust** il a fait une grimace de dégoût **2.** *US* [hunch] : **she was sitting with her shoulders ~ed up** elle était assise, les épaules rentrées.

scrunchie, scrunchy ['skrʌntʃɪ] *n* chouchou *m*.

scruple ['skruːpl] ◇ *n* scrupule *m* ■ **he has no ~s** il n'a aucun scrupule ■ **he had ~s about accepting payment** il avait des scrupules à accepter qu'on le paie.
◇ *vi (only in negative uses)* **they don't ~ to cheat** ils n'ont aucun scrupule *OR* ils n'hésitent pas à tricher.

scrupulous ['skruːpjʊləs] *adj* **1.** [meticulous] scrupuleux, méticuleux ■ **she's very ~ about her dress** elle prête une attention scrupuleuse à la façon dont elle s'habille ■ **they're rather ~ about punctuality** ils tiennent beaucoup à la ponctualité **2.** [conscientious] scrupuleux.

scrupulously ['skruːpjʊləslɪ] *adv* [meticulously] scrupuleusement, parfaitement ■ [honestly] scrupuleusement, avec scrupule ■ **~ clean** d'une propreté impeccable ■ **~ honest** d'une honnêteté irréprochable ■ **~ punctual** parfaitement à l'heure.

scrutineer [ˌskruːtɪ'nɪəʳ] *n UK* POL scrutateur *m*, - trice *f*.

scrutinize, ise ['skruːtɪnaɪz] *vt* scruter, examiner attentivement.

scrutiny ['skruːtɪnɪ] (*pl* **scrutinies**) *n* **1.** [examination] examen *m* approfondi ■ [watch] surveillance *f* ■ [gaze] regard *m* insistant ■ **to be under ~** [prisoners] être sous surveillance ; [accounts, staff] faire l'objet d'un contrôle ■ **to come under ~** être contrôlé ■ **everything we do is under close ~** tous nos actes sont surveillés de près ■ **her work does not stand up to close ~** son travail ne résiste pas à un examen minutieux **2.** *UK* POL deuxième pointage *m* (des suffrages).

scuba ['skuːbə] *n* scaphandre *m* autonome.

scuba dive *vi* faire de la plongée sous-marine.

scuba diver *n* plongeur *m* sous-marin, plongeuse *f* sous-marine.

scuba diving *n* plongée *f* sous-marine.

scud [skʌd] (*pret & pp* **scudded**, *cont* **scudding**) *vi* glisser, filer ■ **clouds scudded across the sky** des nuages filaient dans le ciel.

scuff [skʌf] ◇ *vt* **1.** [shoe, leather] érafler, râper **2.** [drag] : **to ~ one's feet** marcher en traînant les pieds, traîner les pieds.
◇ *vi* marcher en traînant les pieds.
◇ *n* : **~ (mark)** éraflure *f*.

scuffle ['skʌfl] ◇ *n* **1.** [fight] bagarre *f*, échauffourée *f* **2.** [of feet] piétinement.
◇ *vi* **1.** [fight] se bagarrer, se battre **2.** [with feet] marcher en traînant les pieds.
◇ *vt* : **they stood at the door, scuffling their feet** ils piétinaient devant la porte.

scuffling ['skʌflɪŋ] *n* bruit *m* étouffé.

scull [skʌl] ◇ *n* **1.** [double paddle] godille *f* ■ [single oar] aviron *m* **2.** [boat] yole *f*.
◇ *vt* [with double paddle] godiller ■ [with oars] ramer.
◇ *vi* ramer en couple ■ **to go ~ing** faire de l'aviron.

scullery ['skʌlərɪ] (*pl* **sculleries**) *n UK* arrière-cuisine *f*.

scullery maid *n UK* fille *f* de cuisine.

sculpt [skʌlpt] ◇ *vt* sculpter.
◇ *vi* faire de la sculpture.

sculptor ['skʌlptəʳ] *n* sculpteur *m*.

sculptress ['skʌlptrɪs] *n* (femme *f*) sculpteur *m*.

sculptural ['skʌlptʃərəl] *adj* sculptural.

sculpture ['skʌlptʃəʳ] ◇ *n* **1.** [art] sculpture *f* **2.** [object] sculpture *f*.
◇ *vt* sculpter.
◇ *vi* sculpter ■ **to ~ in bronze** sculpter dans le bronze.

scum [skʌm] ◇ *n* [on liquid, sea] écume *f* ■ [in bath] (traînées *fpl* de) crasse *f* ■ METALL écume *f*, scories *fpl* ■ **to take the ~ off** [liquid] écumer ; [bath] nettoyer.
◇ *npl inf* [people] rebut *m*, lie *f* ■ **the ~ of the earth** le rebut de l'humanité ■ **they treated us like ~** on nous a traités comme des moins que rien *OR* des chiens.

scumbag△ ['skʌmbæg] *n* salaud△ *m*, ordure△ *f*.

scummy ['skʌmɪ] (*comp* **scummier**, *superl* **scummiest**) *adj* **1.** [liquid] écumeux **2.** △ [person] salaud△.

scuncheon ['skʌntʃən] *n* ARCHIT battée *f*.

scupper ['skʌpəʳ] ◇ *vt UK* **1.** [ship] saborder **2.** [plans, attempt] saborder, faire capoter ■ **we're completely ~ed unless we can find the cash** on est finis si on ne trouve pas l'argent.
◇ *n* NAUT dalot *m*.

scurrilous ['skʌrələs] *adj* [lying] calomnieux, mensonger ■ [insulting] outrageant, ignoble ■ [bitter] fielleux ■ [vulgar] grossier, vulgaire.

scurry ['skʌrɪ] ◇ *vi* (*pret & pp* **scurried**) se précipiter, courir ■ **the sound of ~ing feet** le bruit de pas précipités.
◇ *n* (*pl* **scurries**) **1.** [rush] course *f* (précipitée), débandade *f* ■ **there was a ~ for the door** tout le monde s'est rué vers la porte **2.** [sound - of feet] bruit *m* de pas précipités.
◆ **scurry away, scurry off** *vi insep* [animal] détaler ■ [person] décamper, prendre ses jambes à son cou.
◆ **scurry out** *vi insep* [animal] détaler ■ [person] sortir à toute vitesse.

S-curve *n US* double virage *m*, virage *m* en S.

scurvy ['skɜ:vɪ] (*comp* **scurvier**, *superl* **scurviest**) ◇ *n (U)* scorbut *m*.
◇ *adj* [trick] honteux, ignoble.

scuttle ['skʌtl] ◇ *vi insep* [run] courir à pas précipités, se précipiter.
◇ *vt* **1.** NAUT saborder **2.** [hopes] ruiner ■ [plans] saborder, faire échouer.
◇ *n* **1.** [run] course *f* précipitée, débandade *f* **2.** : **(coal) ~** seau *m* à charbon **3.** NAUT écoutille *f*.
◆ **scuttle away, scuttle off** *vi insep* [animal] détaler ■ [person] déguerpir, se sauver.
◆ **scuttle out** *vi insep* sortir précipitamment.

scythe [saɪð] ◇ *n* faux *f*.
◇ *vt* faucher.

SD *written abbr of* **South Dakota**.

SDI (*abbrev of* **Strategic Defense Initiative**) *pr n* IDS *f*.

SDLP *pr n* = **Social Democratic and Labour Party**.

SDP *pr n* = **Social Democratic Party**.

SDRs (*abbrev of* **special drawing rights**) *npl* DTS *mpl*.

SE (*written abbrev of* **south-east**) S-E.

sea [si:] ◇ *n* **1.** GEOG mer *f* ■ **to travel by ~** voyager par mer *OR* par bateau ■ **the goods were sent by ~** les marchandises ont été expédiées par bateau ■ **at ~** [boat, storm] en mer ; [as sailor] de *OR* comme marin ■ **life at ~** la vie en mer *OR* de marin ■ **to swim in the ~** nager *OR* se baigner dans la mer ■ **to put (out) to ~** prendre la mer ■ **to go to ~** [boat] prendre la mer ; [sailor] se faire marin ■ **to run away to ~** partir se faire marin ■ **to look out to ~** regarder vers le large ■ **the little boat was swept** *OR* **washed out to ~** le petit bateau a été emporté vers le large ■ **across** *OR* **over the ~** *OR* **~s** outre-mer ■ **a heavy ~, heavy ~s** une grosse mer ➲ **the Sea of Tranquillity** la mer de la Tranquillité ■ **~ and air search** recherches *fpl* maritimes et aériennes ■ **to be at ~** *UK inf* [be lost] nager ; [be mixed-up] être déboussolé *OR* désorienté ■ **he's been all at ~ since his wife left him** il est complètement déboussolé *OR* il a complètement perdu le nord depuis que sa femme l'a quitté **2.** [seaside] bord *m* de la mer ■ **they live by** *OR* **beside the ~** ils habitent au bord de la mer **3.** [large quantity - of blood, mud] mer *f* ; [- of problems, faces] multitude *f*.
◇ *comp* [fish] de mer ■ **~ bathing** bains *mpl* de mer ■ **~ battle** bataille *f* navale ■ **~ breeze** brise *f* marine ■ **~ traffic** navigation *f OR* trafic *m* maritime ■ **~ view** vue *f* sur la mer.

SEA (*abbrev of* **Single European Act**) *pr n* AUE *m*.

sea air *n* air *m* marin *OR* de la mer.

sea anemone *n* anémone *f* de mer.

sea bass *n* ZOOL & CULIN loup *m* de mer.

seabed ['si:bed] *n* fond *m* de la mer *OR* marin.

seabird ['si:bɜ:d] *n* oiseau *m* de mer.

seaboard ['si:bɔ:d] *n* littoral *m*, côte *f* ■ **on the Atlantic ~** sur la côte atlantique.

seaborne ['si:bɔ:n] *adj* [trade] maritime ■ [goods, troops] transporté par mer *OR* par bateau.

sea bream *n* daurade *f*, dorade *f*.

sea captain *n* capitaine *m* de la marine marchande.

sea change *n* changement *m* radical, profond changement *m*.

seacoast [ˌsi:'kəʊst] *n* côte *f*, littoral *m*.

sea cow *n* vache *f* marine, sirénien *m*.

sea cucumber *n* concombre *m* de mer, holothurie *f*.

sea dog *n* **1.** [fish] roussette *f*, chien *m* de mer ■ [seal] phoque *m* **2.** *lit & hum* [sailor] (vieux) loup *m* de mer **3.** [in fog] arc-en-ciel *m (aperçu dans le brouillard)*.

seafarer ['si:ˌfeərər] *n* marin *m*.

seafaring ['si:ˌfeərɪŋ] ◇ *adj* [nation] maritime, de marins ■ [life] de marin.
◇ *n* vie *f* de marin.

seafloor ['si:flɔ:r] *n* fond *m* de (la) mer *OR* marin.

seafood ['si:fu:d] *n (U)* (poissons *mpl* et) fruits *mpl* de mer.

seafront ['si:frʌnt] *n* bord *m* de mer, front *m* de mer.

seagoing ['si:ˌgəʊɪŋ] *adj* [trade, nation] maritime ■ [life] de marin ■ **a ~ man** un marin, un homme de mer ■ **a ~ ship** un navire de haute mer, un (navire) long-courrier.

sea green *n* vert *m* glauque.

seagull ['si:gʌl] *n* mouette *f* ■ [large] goéland *m*.

seahorse ['si:hɔ:s] *n* hippocampe *m*.

seal [si:l] ◇ *n* **1.** ZOOL phoque *m*
2. [tool] sceau *m*, cachet *m* ■ [on document, letter] sceau *m* ■ [on crate] plombage *m* ■ [on battery, gas cylinder] bande *f* de garantie ■ [on meter] plomb *m* ■ **given under my hand and ~** *UK* ADMIN & LAW signé et scellé par moi ■ **to put one's ~ to a document** apposer son sceau à un document ■ **does the project have her ~ of approval?** est-ce qu'elle a approuvé le projet? ■ **to put** *OR* **to set the ~ on sthg** [confirm] sceller qqch ; [bring to end] mettre fin à qqch
3. *(U)* LAW [on door] scellé *m*, scellés *mpl* ■ **under ~** sous scellés ■ **under (the) ~ of secrecy/of silence** *fig* ≃ sous le sceau du secret/du silence
4. COMM label *m* ■ **~ of quality** label de qualité
5. [joint - for engine, jar, sink] joint *m* d'étanchéité ■ [putty] mastic *m*
6. [stamp] : **Christmas ~** timbre *m* de Noël.
◇ *vt* **1.** [document] apposer son sceau à, sceller ■ **~ed with a kiss** scellé d'un baiser ■ **her fate is ~ed** *fig* son sort est réglé ■ **they finally ~ed the deal** *fig* ils ont enfin conclu l'affaire
2. [close - envelope, package] cacheter, fermer ; [- with sticky tape] coller, fermer ; [- jar] sceller, fermer hermétiquement ; [- can] souder ; [- tube, mineshaft] sceller ■ [window, door - for insulation] isoler ■ **~ed orders** des ordres scellés sous pli ■ **my lips are ~ed** *fig* mes lèvres sont scellées
3. LAW [door] apposer des scellés sur ■ [evidence] mettre sous scellés ■ [at customs - goods] (faire) sceller
4. CULIN [meat] saisir.
◇ *vi* ZOOL : **to go ~ing** aller à la chasse au phoque.
◆ **seal in** *vt sep* enfermer hermétiquement ■ **the flavour is ~ed in by freeze-drying** le produit garde toute sa saveur grâce à la lyophilisation.
◆ **seal off** *vt sep* [passage, road] interdire l'accès de ■ [entrance] condamner ■ **the street had been ~ed off** la rue avait été fermée (à la circulation).
◆ **seal up** *vt sep* [close - envelope] cacheter, fermer ; [- with sticky tape] coller, fermer ; [- jar] sceller, fermer hermétiquement ; [- can] souder ; [- tube, mineshaft] sceller ■ [window, door - for insulation] isoler.

sea lane *n* couloir *m* de navigation.

sealant ['si:lənt] *n* **1.** [paste, putty] produit *m* d'étanchéité ■ [paint] enduit *m* étanche ■ [for radiator] antifuite *m* **2.** [joint] joint *m* d'étanchéité.

sealed [si:ld] *adj* [document] scellé ■ [envelope] cacheté ■ [orders] scellé sous pli ■ [jar] fermé hermétiquement ■ [mineshaft] obturé, bouché ■ [joint] étanche.

sealed-beam *adj* : **~ headlight** phare *m* type sealed-beam.

sea legs *npl* : **to find** *OR* **to get one's ~** s'amariner, s'habituer à la mer.

sealer ['si:lər] *n* **1.** [hunter] chasseur *m* de phoques ■ [ship] navire *m* équipé pour la chasse aux phoques **2.** [paint, varnish] enduit *m*, première couche *f*.

sea level *n* niveau *m* de la mer ■ **above/below ~** au-dessus/au-dessous du niveau de la mer.

sealing ['si:lɪŋ] *n* **1.** [hunting] chasse *f* aux phoques **2.** [of document] cachetage *m* ■ [of crate] plombage *m* ■ [of door] scellage *m* ■ [of shaft, mine] fermeture *f*, obturation *f*.

sealing wax *n* cire *f* à cacheter.

sea lion *n* otarie *f*.

sea-lord *n UK* NAUT lord *m* de l'Amirauté.

sealskin ['si:lskɪn] ◇ *n* peau *f* de phoque.
◇ *adj* en peau de phoque.

seam [si:m] ◇ *n* **1.** [on garment, stocking] couture *f* ■ [in airbed, bag] couture *f*, joint *m* ■ [weld] soudure *f* ■ [between planks] joint *m* ■ **your coat is coming** *OR* **falling apart at the ~s** votre manteau se découd ■ **my suitcase was bulging** *OR* **bursting at the ~s** ma valise était pleine à craquer ■ **their marriage is coming** *OR* **falling apart at the ~s** *fig* leur mariage craque **2.** [of coal, ore] filon *m*, veine *f* ■ [in rocks] couche *f*.
◇ *comp* [in cricket] : **a ~ bowler** *un lanceur qui utilise les coutures de la balle pour la faire dévier.*
◇ *vt* [garment] faire une couture dans, coudre ■ [plastic, metal, wood] faire un joint à.

seaman ['si:mən] (*pl* **seamen** [-mən]) *n* **1.** [sailor] marin *m* **2.** [in US Navy] quartier-maître *m* de 2e classe.

seamanship ['si:mənʃɪp] *n (U)* qualités *fpl* de marin.

seamed [si:md] *adj* [furrowed] ridé, sillonné ■ **the rock was ~ with quartz** la roche était veinée de quartz.

seamen [-mən] *pl* ⊳ **seaman**.

sea mile *n* mille *m* marin.

sea mist *n* brume *f* de mer.

seamless ['si:mlɪs] *adj* sans couture ■ *fig* homogène, cohérent.

seamstress ['semstrɪs] *n* couturière *f*.

seamy ['si:mɪ] (*comp* **seamier**, *superl* **seamiest**) *adj* sordide, louche ■ **the ~ side of life** le côté sordide de la vie.

séance ['seɪɑ:ns] *n* **1.** [for raising spirits] séance *f* de spiritisme **2.** [meeting] séance *f*, réunion *f*.

seaplane ['si:pleɪn] *n* hydravion *m*.

seaport ['si:pɔ:t] *n* port *m* maritime.

sear [sɪəʳ] ◇ *vt* **1.** [burn] brûler ■ [brand] marquer au fer rouge ■ MED cautériser ■ **the scene ~ed itself on my memory** la scène est restée gravée *OR* marquée dans ma mémoire **2.** [wither] dessécher, flétrir.
◇ *n* [burn] (marque *f* de) brûlure *f*.
◆ **sear through** *vt insep* [metal, wall] traverser, percer.

search [sɜ:tʃ] ◇ *vt* **1.** [look in - room] chercher (partout) dans ; [- pockets, drawers] fouiller (dans), chercher dans ■ **we've ~ed the whole house for the keys** nous avons cherché dans toute la maison pour retrouver les clés **2.** [subj: police, customs] fouiller ■ [with warrant] perquisitionner, faire une perquisition dans ■ **the flat was ~ed for drugs** on a fouillé l'appartement pour trouver de la drogue ▶ **~ me!** *inf* je n'en ai pas la moindre idée! **3.** [examine, consult - records] chercher dans ; [- memory] chercher dans, fouiller ; [- conscience] sonder ■ COMPUT [file] consulter ■ **I ~ed her face for some sign of emotion** j'ai cherché sur son visage des signes d'émotion.
◇ *vi* chercher ■ **to ~ for sthg** chercher qqch, rechercher qqch ■ **to ~ after the truth** rechercher la vérité ‖ COMPUT : **to ~ for a file** rechercher un fichier ■ **'searching'** 'recherche'.
◇ *n* **1.** [gen] recherche *f*, recherches *fpl* ■ **in the ~ for** *OR* **in my ~ for ancestors, I had to travel to Canada** au cours des recherches *OR* de mes recherches pour retrouver mes ancêtres, j'ai dû me rendre au Canada ■ **the ~ for the missing climbers has been resumed** les recherches ont repris pour retrouver les alpinistes disparus ■ **helicopters made a ~ for survivors** des hélicoptères ont fait *OR* effectué des recherches pour retrouver des survivants ▶ **~ and rescue operation** opération *f* de recherche et secours **2.** [by police, customs - of house, person, bags] fouille *f* ; [- with warrant] perquisition *f* ■ **the police made a thorough ~ of the premises** la police a fouillé les locaux de fond en comble ■ **customs carried out a ~ of the van** les douaniers ont procédé à la fouille de la camionnette **3.** COMPUT recherche *f*.
◆ **in search of** *prep phr* à la recherche de.
◆ **search out** *vt sep* [look for] rechercher ■ [find] trouver, dénicher.
◆ **search through** *vt insep* [drawer, pockets] fouiller (dans) ■ [case, documents] fouiller ■ [records] consulter, faire des recherches dans ■ [memory] fouiller, chercher dans.

search engine *n* COMPUT moteur *m* de recherche.

searcher ['sɜ:tʃəʳ] *n* chercheur *m*, - euse *f*.

searching ['sɜ:tʃɪŋ] *adj* **1.** [look, eyes] pénétrant ■ **he gave me a ~ look** il m'a lancé un regard pénétrant **2.** [examination] rigoureux, minutieux ■ **he asked me some ~ questions** il m'a posé des questions inquisitrices.

searchingly ['sɜ:tʃɪŋlɪ] *adv* [look] de façon pénétrante ■ [examine] rigoureusement ■ [question] minutieusement.

searchlight ['sɜ:tʃlaɪt] *n* projecteur *m* ■ **in the ~** à la lumière des projecteurs.

search party *n* équipe *f* de secours.

search warrant *n* mandat *m* de perquisition.

searing ['sɪərɪŋ] *adj* **1.** [pain] fulgurant ■ [light] éclatant, fulgurant **2.** [attack, criticism] sévère, impitoyable.

Sears Roebuck® [ˌsɪəz'rəʊbʌk] *pr n grande chaîne de magasins américaine.*

sea salt *n* sel *m* marin *OR* de mer.

seascape ['si:skeɪp] *n* **1.** [view] paysage *m* marin **2.** ART marine *f*.

sea shanty *n* chanson *f* de marins.

seashell ['si:ʃel] *n* coquillage *m*.

seashore ['si:ʃɔ:ʳ] *n* [edge of sea] rivage *m*, bord *m* de (la) mer ■ [beach] plage *f*.

seasick ['si:sɪk] *adj* : **to be ~** avoir le mal de mer.

seasickness ['si:sɪknɪs] *n* mal *m* de mer.

seaside ['si:saɪd] ◇ *n* bord *m* de (la) mer ■ **we spent the afternoon at the ~** nous avons passé l'après-midi au bord de la mer *OR* à la mer ■ **we live by** *OR* **at the ~** nous habitons au bord de la mer.
◇ *comp* [holiday, vacation] au bord de la mer, à la mer ■ [town, hotel] au bord de la mer, de bord de mer.

sea slug *n* nudibranche *m*.

sea snake *n* serpent *m* de mer.

season ['si:zn] ◇ *n* **1.** [summer, winter etc] saison *f*
2. [for trade] saison *f* ■ **the start of the tourist/of the holiday ~** le début de la saison touristique/des vacances ■ **at the height of the Christmas ~** en pleine période de Noël ■ **it's a busy ~ for tour operators** c'est une époque très chargée pour les voyagistes ■ **the low/high ~** la basse/haute saison ■ **in ~** en saison ■ **off ~** hors saison
3. [for fruit, vegetables] saison *f* ■ **strawberries are in/out of ~** les fraises sont/ne sont pas de saison, c'est/ce n'est pas la saison des fraises
4. [for breeding] époque *f*, période *f* ■ **to be in ~** [animal] être en chaleur
5. [for sport, entertainment] saison *f* ■ [for show, actor] saison *f* ■ **he did a ~ at Brighton** il a fait la saison de Brighton ■ **a new ~ of French drama** RADIO & TV un nouveau cycle de pièces de théâtre français ‖ [for hunting] saison *f*, période *f* ■ **the hunting/fishing ~** la saison de la chasse/de la pêche ■ **the start of the ~** HUNT l'ouverture de la chasse ; FISHING l'ouverture de la pêche ‖ [for socializing] saison *f* ■ **the social ~** la saison mondaine
6. [Christmas] : **'Season's Greetings'** 'Joyeux Noël et Bonne Année'
7. *lit* [suitable moment] moment *m* opportun ■ **in due ~** en temps voulu, au moment opportun.
◇ *vt* **1.** [food - with seasoning] assaisonner ; [- with spice] épicer ■ **his speech was ~ed with witty remarks** *fig* son discours était parsemé *OR* agrémenté de remarques spirituelles

2. [timber] (faire) sécher, laisser sécher ▪ [cask] abreuver **3.** *fml* [moderate] modérer, tempérer.

seasonable ['si:znəbl] *adj* **1.** [weather] de saison **2.** [opportune] à propos, opportun.

seasonal ['si:zənl] *adj* saisonnier ▪ **~ worker** saisonnier *m* ▪ **~ affective disorder** troubles *mpl* de l'humeur saisonniers.

seasonally ['si:znəlı] *adv* de façon saisonnière ▪ **~ adjusted statistics** statistiques corrigées des variations saisonnières, statistiques désaisonnalisées.

seasoned ['si:znd] *adj* **1.** [food] assaisonné, épicé ▪ **highly ~** bien épicé *OR* relevé **2.** [wood] desséché, séché **3.** [experienced] expérimenté, chevronné, éprouvé ▪ **a ~ traveller** un voyageur expérimenté.

seasoning ['si:znıŋ] *n* **1.** [for food] assaisonnement *m* ▪ **there isn't enough ~** ce n'est pas assez assaisonné **2.** [of wood] séchage *m* ▪ [of cask] abreuvage *m*.

season ticket *n* (carte *f* d')abonnement *m* ▪ **to take out a ~** prendre un abonnement ▪ **~ holder** abonné *m*, - e *f*.

seat [si:t] <> *n* **1.** [chair, stool] siège *m* ▪ [on bicycle] selle *f* ▪ [in car - single] siège *m* ; [- bench] banquette *f* ▪ [on train, at table] place *f* ▪ **take a ~** asseyez-vous, prenez un siège ▪ **please stay in your ~s** restez assis s'il vous plaît ▪ **keep a ~ for me** gardez-moi une place
2. [accommodation, place - in theatre, cinema, train] place *f* ▪ [space to sit] place *f* assise ▪ **please take your ~s** veuillez prendre *OR* gagner vos places
3. [of trousers] fond *m* ▪ [of chair] siège *m* ▪ [buttocks] derrière *m* ➋ **they grabbed him by the ~ of his pants** ils l'ont attrapé par le fond du pantalon ▪ **by the ~ of one's pants** *inf* de justesse
4. POL siège *m* ▪ **he kept/lost his ~** il a été/il n'a pas été réélu ▪ **she has a ~ in Parliament** elle est député ▪ **he was elected to a ~ on the council** [municipal] il a été élu conseiller municipal ; [commercial] il a été élu au conseil ▪ **the government has a 30-~ majority** le gouvernement a une majorité de 30 sièges
5. [centre - of commerce] centre *m* ▪ ADMIN siège *m* ▪ MED [- of infection] foyer *m* ▪ **the ~ of government/of learning** le siège du gouvernement/du savoir
6. [manor] : **(country) ~** manoir *m*
7. EQUIT : **to have a good ~** se tenir bien en selle, avoir une bonne assiette ▪ **to lose one's ~** être désarçonné.
<> *vt* **1.** [passengers, children] faire asseoir ▪ [guests - at table] placer ▪ **please be ~ed** veuillez vous asseoir ▪ **please remain ~ed** restez *OR* veuillez rester assis
2. [accommodate] avoir des places assises pour ▪ **the plane can ~ 400** l'avion a une capacité de 400 personnes ▪ **how many does the bus ~?** combien y a-t-il de places assises dans le bus? ▪ **how many does the table ~?** combien de personnes peut-on asseoir autour de la table?
3. [chair] mettre un fond à ▪ [with straw] rempailler ▪ [with cane] canner.
<> *vi* [skirt, trousers] se déformer (à l'arrière).

seat belt *n* ceinture *f* de sécurité.

-seater ['si:təʳ] *in cpds* : **two/four~ (car)** voiture *f* à deux/quatre places.

seating ['si:tıŋ] <> *n (U)* **1.** [seats] sièges *mpl* ▪ [benches, pews] bancs *mpl* **2.** [sitting accommodation] places *fpl* (assises) ▪ **there's ~ for 300 in the hall** il y a 300 places dans la salle ▪ **there's ~ for eight round this table** on peut asseoir huit personnes autour de cette table **3.** [plan] affectation *f* des places ▪ **who's in charge of the ~?** qui est chargé de placer les gens? **4.** [material - cloth, canvas] (tissu *m* du) siège *m* ; [- wicker] cannage *m*.
<> *comp* : **~ accommodation** *OR* **capacity** nombre *m* de places assises ▪ **the theatre has a ~ capacity of 500** il y a 500 places dans le théâtre ▪ **the ~ arrangements** le placement *m* *OR* la disposition *f* des gens ▪ **~ plan** [in theatre] plan *m* de la disposition des places ; [at table] plan *m* de table.

SEATO ['si:təʊ] (*abbrev of* **Southeast Asia Treaty Organization**) *pr n* OTASE *f*.

sea trout *n* truite *f* de mer.

sea urchin *n* oursin *m*.

sea wall *n* digue *f*.

seaward ['si:wəd] <> *adj* de (la) mer ▪ **~ breeze** brise *f* de mer ▪ **on the ~ side** du côté de la mer.
<> *adv* = **seawards**.

seawater ['si:,wɔ:təʳ] *n* eau *f* de mer.

seaway ['si:weı] *n* route *f* maritime.

seaweed ['si:wi:d] *n (U)* algues *fpl*.

seaworthy ['si:,wɜ:ðı] *adj* [boat] en état de naviguer.

sebaceous [sı'beıʃəs] *adj* sébacé.

Sebastian [sı'bæstjən] *pr n* : **Saint ~** saint Sébastien.

sec [sek] (*abbrev of* **second**) *n inf* seconde *f*, instant *m* ▪ **in a ~!** une seconde!

Sec. *written abbr of* **second**.

SEC (*abbrev of* **Securities and Exchange Commission**) *pr n* commission *f* américaine des opérations de Bourse, ≃ COB *f*.

secant ['si:kənt] *n* sécante *f*.

secateurs [,sekə'tɜ:z] *npl* *UK* **(pair of) ~** sécateur *m*.

secede [sı'si:d] *vi* faire sécession, se séparer ▪ **they voted to ~ from the federation** ils ont voté en faveur de leur sécession de la fédération.

secession [sı'seʃn] *n* sécession *f*, scission *f*.

seclude [sı'klu:d] *vt* éloigner du monde, isoler.

secluded [sı'klu:dıd] *adj* [village] retiré, à l'écart ▪ [garden] tranquille ▪ **to live a ~ life** mener une vie solitaire, vivre en reclus.

seclusion [sı'klu:ʒn] *n* **1.** [isolation - chosen] solitude *f*, isolement *m* ▪ **he lives a life of total ~** il vit en solitaire *OR* retiré du monde **2.** [isolation - imposed] isolement *m*.

second[1] ['sekənd] <> *n* **1.** [unit of time] seconde *f* ▪ **the ambulance arrived within ~s** l'ambulance est arrivée en quelques secondes
2. [instant] seconde *f*, instant *m* ▪ **I'll be with you in a ~** je serai à vous dans un instant ▪ **I'll only be a ~** j'en ai seulement pour deux secondes ▪ **just a** *OR* **half a ~!** une seconde!
3. MATHS seconde *f*
4. [in order] second *m*, - e *f*, deuxième *mf* ▪ **I was the ~ to arrive** je suis arrivé deuxième *OR* le deuxième ▪ **to come a close ~** [in race] être battu de justesse
5. [in duel] témoin *m*, second *m* ▪ [in boxing] soigneur *m* ▪ **~s out!** soigneurs hors du ring!
6. AUT seconde *f* ▪ **in ~** en seconde
7. *UK* UNIV : **an upper/lower ~** une licence avec mention bien/assez bien
8. MUS seconde *f*.
<> *det* **1.** [in series] deuxième ▪ [of two] second ▪ **he's ~ only to his teacher as a violinist** en tant que violoniste, il n'y a que son professeur qui le surpasse *OR* qui lui soit supérieur ▪ **every ~ person** une personne sur deux ▪ **to be ~ in command** [in hierarchy] être deuxième dans la hiérarchie ; MIL commander en second ▪ **he's ~ in line for promotion** il sera le second à bénéficier d'une promotion ▪ **he's ~ in line for the throne** c'est le deuxième dans l'ordre de succession au trône ▪ **~ floor** *UK* deuxième étage *m* ; *US* premier étage ▪ **in the ~ person singular/plural** GRAM à la deuxième personne du singulier/pluriel ▪ **to take ~ place** [in race] prendre la deuxième place ; [in exam] être deuxième ▪ **his wife took ~ place to his career** sa femme venait après sa carrière ▪ **and in the ~ place...** [in demonstration, argument] et en deuxième lieu... ➋ **it's ~ nature to her** c'est une deuxième nature chez elle ▪ **~ teeth** deuxième dentition *f*, dentition *f* définitive ▪ **~ violin** MUS deuxième violon *m* ▪ **as a goalkeeper, he's ~ to none** comme gardien de but, il n'a pas son pareil
2. [additional, extra] deuxième, second, autre ▪ **he was given a ~ chance (in life)** on lui a accordé une seconde chance (dans la vie) ▪ **you are unlikely to get a ~ chance to join the team** il est peu probable que l'on vous propose à nouveau de faire partie de l'équipe ▪ **to take a ~ helping** se resservir ▪ **would you like a ~ helping/a ~ cup?** en reprendrez-vous (un peu/une

goutte)? ▪ **they have a ~ home in France** ils ont une résidence secondaire en France ▪ **I'd like a ~ opinion** [doctor] je voudrais prendre l'avis d'un confrère ; [patient] je voudrais consulter un autre médecin ▪ **I need a ~ opinion on these results** j'aimerais avoir l'avis d'un tiers sur ces résultats.

<> *adv* **1.** [in order] en seconde place ▪ **to come ~** [in race] arriver en seconde position
2. [with superl adj] : **the ~-oldest** le cadet ▪ **the ~-largest/~-richest** le second par la taille/second par le revenu
3. [secondly] en second lieu, deuxièmement.

<> *vt* [motion] appuyer ▪ [speaker] appuyer la motion de ▪ **I'll ~ that!** je suis d'accord!

◆ **seconds** *npl* **1.** [goods] marchandises *fpl* de second choix ▪ [crockery] vaisselle *f* de second choix
2. *inf* [of food] rab *m*.

second² [sɪ'kɒnd] *vt UK* [employee] affecter (provisoirement), envoyer en détachement ▪ MIL détacher ▪ **she was ~ed to the UN** elle a été détachée à l'ONU.

secondary ['sekəndrɪ] (*pl* **secondaries**) <> *adj* **1.** [gen - MED] secondaire ▪ [minor] secondaire, de peu d'importance ▪ **this issue is of ~ importance** cette question est d'une importance secondaire ▪ **any other considerations are ~ to her well being** son bien-être prime sur toute autre considération ➲ **~ cause** PHILOS cause *f* seconde ▪ **~ cell** ELEC accumulateur *m* ▪ **~ colour** couleur *f* secondaire *OR* binaire ▪ **~ era** GEOL (ère *f*) secondaire *m* ▪ **~ product** sous-produit *m* **2.** SCH secondaire *m* ▪ **~ education** enseignement *m* secondaire *OR* du second degré.

<> *n* **1.** [deputy] subordonné *m*, - e *f*, adjoint *m*, - e *f* **2.** ASTRON satellite *m* **3.** MED [tumour] tumeur *f* secondaire, métastase *f*.

secondary modern (school) *n UK établissement secondaire d'enseignement général et technique, aujourd'hui remplacé par la "comprehensive school".*

secondary picketing *n (U) UK* INDUST piquets *mpl* de grève de solidarité.

secondary school *n établissement secondaire* ▪ **~ teacher** professeur *m* du secondaire.

secondary stress *n* accent *m* secondaire.

second best <> *n* pis-aller *m inv* ▪ **I refuse to make do with ~** je refuse de me contenter d'un pis-aller.

<> *adv* : **to come off ~** être battu, se faire battre.

◆ **second-best** *adj* [clothes, objects] de tous les jours.

second chamber *n* [gen] deuxième chambre *f* ▪ [in UK] Chambre *f* des lords ▪ [in US] Sénat *m*.

second childhood *n* gâtisme *m*, seconde enfance *f* ▪ **he's in his ~** il est retombé en enfance.

second class *n* RAIL seconde *f* (classe *f*).

◆ **second-class** <> *adj* **1.** RAIL de seconde (classe) ▪ **two second-class returns to Glasgow** deux allers (et) retours pour Glasgow en seconde (classe) **2.** [hotel] de seconde catégorie **3.** [mail] à tarif réduit *OR* lent **4.** *UK* UNIV : **a second-class honours degree** ≃ une licence avec mention (assez) bien **5.** [inferior] de qualité inférieure.

<> *adv* **1.** RAIL en seconde (classe) **2.** [for mail] : **to send a parcel second-class** expédier un paquet en tarif réduit.

SECOND-CLASS MAIL

Le tarif postal réduit est utilisé en Grande-Bretagne pour les lettres et les paquets non urgents. Aux États-Unis, il est réservé aux magazines et aux journaux.

second-class citizen *n* citoyen *m*, - enne *f* de seconde zone.

Second Coming *n* RELIG : **the ~** le deuxième avènement du Messie.

second cousin *n* cousin *m*, - e *f* au second degré, cousin *m* issu *OR* cousine *f* issue de germains.

second-degree burn *n* brûlure *f* au deuxième degré.

seconder ['sekəndəʳ] *n* **1.** [in debate - of motion] personne *f* qui appuie une motion **2.** [of candidate] deuxième parrain *m*.

second-generation *adj* [immigrant, computer] de la seconde génération.

second-guess *vt inf* **1.** [after event] comprendre après coup **2.** [before event] essayer de prévoir *OR* d'anticiper.

second hand *n* [of watch, clock] aiguille *f* des secondes, trotteuse *f*.

◆ **second-hand** <> *adj* **1.** [car, clothes, books] d'occasion ▪ **second-hand shop** magasin *m* d'occasions ▪ **second-hand clothes shop** friperie *f* **2.** [information] de seconde main ▪ **to hear** *OR* **to discover sthg at second-hand** apprendre *OR* découvrir qqch de seconde main.

<> *adv* **1.** [buy] d'occasion **2.** [indirectly] : **I heard the news second-hand** j'ai appris la nouvelle indirectement.

second-in-command *n* MIL commandant *m* en second ▪ NAUT second *m*, officier *m* en second ▪ [in hierarchy] second *m*, adjoint *m*.

second lieutenant *n* sous-lieutenant *m*.

secondly ['sekəndlɪ] *adv* deuxièmement, en deuxième lieu.

secondment [sɪ'kɒndmənt] *n UK fml* détachement *m*, affectation *f* provisoire ▪ **to be on ~** [teacher] être en détachement ; [diplomat] être en mission.

second name *n* nom *m* de famille.

second officer *n* NAUT (officier *m* en) second *m*.

second-rate *adj* [goods, equipment] de qualité inférieure ▪ [film, book] médiocre ▪ [politician, player] médiocre, de second ordre.

second sight *n* seconde *OR* double vue *f* ▪ **to have ~** avoir un don de double vue.

second-string *adj US* SPORT remplaçant.

second thought *n* : **to have ~s** avoir des doutes ▪ **he left his family without a ~** il a quitté sa famille sans réfléchir *OR* sans se poser de questions ▪ **on ~s** *UK OR* **on ~** *US* **I'd better go myself** toute réflexion faite, il vaut mieux que j'y aille moi-même.

secrecy ['si:krəsɪ] *n (U)* secret *m* ▪ **the negotiations were carried out in the strictest ~** les négociations ont été menées dans le plus grand secret ‖ [mystery] mystère *m* ▪ **there's no ~ about their financial dealings** ils ne font aucun mystère de leurs affaires financières.

secret ['si:krɪt] <> *n* **1.** [information kept hidden] secret *m* ▪ **it's a ~ between you and me** c'est un secret entre nous ▪ **I have no ~s from her** je ne lui cache rien ▪ **can you keep a ~?** pouvez-vous garder un secret? ▪ **shall we let them into the ~?** est-ce qu'on va les mettre dans le secret *OR* dans la confidence? ▪ **I'll tell you** *OR* **I'll let you into a ~** je vais vous dire *OR* révéler un secret ▪ **I make no ~ of** *OR* **about my humble origins** je ne cache pas mes origines modestes **2.** [explanation] secret *m* ▪ **the ~ is to warm the dish first** le secret consiste à chauffer le plat d'abord **3.** [mystery] secret *m*, mystère *m* ▪ **these locks have** *OR* **hold no ~ for me** ces serrures n'ont pas de secret pour moi.

<> *adj* **1.** [meeting, plan] secret, - ète *f* ▪ **~ funds** caisse *f* noire, fonds *mpl* secrets ▪ **the news was kept ~** la nouvelle a été gardée *OR* tenue secrète, on n'a pas révélé la nouvelle ▪ **to keep sthg ~** tenir qqch secret ‖ [personal] secret, - ète *f* ▪ **it's my ~ belief that he doesn't really love her** je crois secrètement *OR* en mon for intérieur qu'il ne l'aime pas vraiment ➲ **~ ballot** vote *m* à bulletin secret **2.** [hidden - door] caché, dérobé ; [- compartment, safe] caché ▪ **a ~ hiding place** une cachette secrète **3.** [identity] inconnu **4.** [secluded - beach, garden] retiré, secret, - ète *f*.

◆ **in secret** *adv phr* en secret, secrètement.

secret agent *n* agent *m* secret.

secretarial [ˌsekrəˈteərɪəl] *adj* [tasks] de secrétaire, de secrétariat ■ [course, college] de secrétariat ■ **she does ~ work** elle fait un travail de secrétariat *OR* de secrétaire ■ **~ skills** notions *fpl* de secrétariat ■ **the ~ staff** le secrétariat.

secretariat [ˌsekrəˈteərɪət] *n* secrétariat *m*.

secretary *(UK* [ˈsekrətrɪ], *US* [ˈsekrəˌterɪ]*)* (*pl* **secretaries**) *n* **1.** [gen - COMM] secrétaire *mf* **2.** POL [in UK - minister] ministre *m* ; [- non-elected official] secrétaire *m* d'État ■ [in US] secrétaire *m* d'Etat ■ **~ of state** [in UK] ministre ; [in US] secrétaire *m* d'État, ministre des Affaires étrangères **3.** [diplomat] secrétaire *m* d'ambassade.

secretary bird *n* ORNITH serpentaire *m*, secrétaire *m*.

secretary-general *n* secrétaire *m* général, secrétaire *f* générale.

secrete [sɪˈkriːt] *vt* **1.** ANAT & MED sécréter **2.** *fml* [hide] cacher.

secretion [sɪˈkriːʃn] *n* ANAT & MED sécrétion *f*.

secretive [ˈsiːkrətɪv] *adj* [nature] secret, - ète *f* ■ [behaviour] cachottier ■ **she's very ~ about her new job** elle ne dit pas grand-chose de son nouveau travail.

secretively [ˈsiːkrətɪvlɪ] *adv* en cachette, secrètement.

secretiveness [ˈsiːkrətɪvnɪs] *n (U)* [of character] réserve *f* ■ [keeping secrets] cachotteries *fpl*.

secretly [ˈsiːkrɪtlɪ] *adv* [do, act] en secret, secrètement ■ [believe, think] en son for intérieur, secrètement.

secret police *n* police *f* secrète.

secret service *n* services *mpl* secrets.

◆ **Secret Service** *n* [in US] : **the ~** *service de protection du président, du vice-président des États-Unis et de leurs familles.*

sect [sekt] *n* secte *f*.

sectarian [sekˈteərɪən] *adj* sectaire ■ **~ violence** violence *f* d'origine religieuse.

sectarianism [sekˈteərɪənɪzm] *n* sectarisme *m*.

section [ˈsekʃn] ◇ *n* **1.** [sector] section *f*, partie *f* ■ **the business ~ of the community** les commerçants et les hommes d'affaires de notre communauté ■ **the residential ~ of the town** les quartiers résidentiels de la ville | [division - of staff, services] section *f* ; [- in army] groupe *m* de combat ; [- in orchestra] section *f* **2.** [component part - of furniture] élément *m* ; [- of tube] section *f* ; [- of track, road] section *f*, tronçon *m* ■ RAIL section *f* **3.** [subdivision - of law] article *m* ; [- of book, exam, text] section *f*, partie *f* ; [- of library] section *f* ■ [of newspaper - page] page *f* ; [- pages] pages *fpl* ■ **the sports/women's ~** les pages des sports/réservées aux femmes ■ [in department store] rayon *m* **4.** *US* RAIL [train] train *m* supplémentaire ■ [sleeper] compartiment-lits *m* **5.** [cut, cross-section - drawing] coupe *f*, section *f* ■ GEOM section *f* ■ [for microscope] coupe *f*, lamelle *f* ■ [in metal] profilé *m* **6.** MED sectionnement *m* **7.** *US* [land] *division (administrative) d'un mille carré.*

◇ *vt* **1.** [divide into sections] sectionner **2.** *UK* [confine to mental hospital] interner.

◆ **section off** *vt sep* séparer ■ **part of the church was ~ed off** l'accès à une partie de l'église était interdit.

sectional [ˈsekʃənl] *adj* **1.** [furniture] modulaire **2.** [interests] d'un groupe **3.** [drawing] en coupe.

sector [ˈsektəʳ] ◇ *n* **1.** [area, realm] secteur *m*, domaine *m* ■ ECON secteur *m* ■ [part, subdivision] secteur *m*, partie *f* ■ COMPUT [of screen] secteur *m* ■ **whole ~s of society live below the poverty line** des catégories sociales entières vivent en dessous du seuil de pauvreté **2.** MIL secteur *m*, zone *f* **3.** GEOM secteur *m* **4.** [for measuring] compas *m* de proportion.

◇ *vt* diviser en secteurs ■ ADMIN & GEOG sectoriser.

secular [ˈsekjʊləʳ] *adj* **1.** [life, clergy] séculier **2.** [education, school] laïque **3.** [music, art] profane **4.** [ancient] séculaire **5.** ASTRON séculaire.

secularism [ˈsekjʊlərɪzm] *n* laïcisme *m*.

secularize, ise [ˈsekjʊləraɪz] *vt* séculariser ■ [education] laïciser.

secure [sɪˈkjʊəʳ] ◇ *adj* **1.** [protected] sûr, en sécurité, en sûreté ■ **put the papers in a ~ place** mettez les papiers en lieu sûr ■ **I feel ~ from** *OR* **against attack** je me sens à l'abri des attaques **2.** [guaranteed - job] sûr ; [- victory, future] assuré **3.** [calm, confident] tranquille, sécurisé ■ **I was ~ in the belief that all danger was past** j'étais intimement persuadé que tout danger était écarté **4.** [solid - investment, base] sûr ; [- foothold, grasp] sûr, ferme ■ [solidly fastened - bolt, window] bien fermé ; [- scaffolding, aerial] solide, qui tient bien ; [- knot] solide ■ **can you make the door/the rope ~?** pouvez-vous vous assurer que la porte est bien fermée/la corde est bien attachée ?

◇ *vt* **1.** *fml* [obtain] se procurer, obtenir ■ [agreement] obtenir ■ [loan] obtenir, se voir accorder ■ **to ~ a majority** [gen] obtenir une majorité ; POL emporter la majorité ■ **to ~ the release of sb** obtenir la libération de qqn **2.** [fasten, fix - rope] attacher ; [- parcel] ficeler ; [- ladder, aerial] bien fixer ; [- window, lock] bien fermer ■ **~ the ladder against the wall first** assurez-vous d'abord que l'échelle est bien appuyée contre le mur **3.** [guarantee - future] assurer ; [- debt] garantir **4.** [from danger] préserver, protéger.

secured [sɪˈkjʊəd] *adj* FIN [debt, loan] garanti.

securely [sɪˈkjʊəlɪ] *adv* **1.** [firmly] fermement, solidement ■ **the door was ~ fastened** la porte était bien fermée *OR* verrouillée **2.** [safely] en sécurité, en sûreté.

secure unit *n* [in psychiatric hospital] quartier *m* de haute sécurité ■ [for young offenders] centre *m* d'éducation surveillée.

security [sɪˈkjʊərətɪ] (*pl* **securities**) ◇ *n* **1.** [safety] sécurité *f* ■ **the President's national ~ advisers** les conseillers du président en matière de sécurité nationale ■ **they slipped through the ~ net** ils sont passés au travers des mailles du filet des services de sécurité | [police measures, protection etc] sécurité *f* ■ **there was maximum ~ for the President's visit** des mesures de sécurité exceptionnelles ont été prises pour la visite du président ■ **maximum ~ wing** [in prison] quartier *m* de haute surveillance

2. *(U)* [assurance] sécurité *f* ■ **job ~** sécurité de l'emploi ■ **to have ~ of tenure** [in job] être titulaire, avoir la sécurité de l'emploi ; [as tenant] avoir un bail qui ne peut être résilié

3. [guarantee] garantie *f*, caution *f* ■ **what ~ do you have for the loan?** quelle garantie avez-vous pour couvrir ce prêt? ■ **have you anything to put up as ~?** qu'est-ce que vous pouvez fournir comme garantie? | [guarantor] garant *m*, - e *f* ■ **to stand ~ for sb** *UK* se porter garant de qqn ■ **to stand ~ for a loan** avaliser un prêt

4. [department] sécurité *f* ■ **please call ~** appelez la sécurité s'il vous plaît

5. COMPUT sécurité *f*.

◇ *comp* [measures, forces] de sécurité ■ **~ device** sécurité *f*.

◆ **securities** *npl* FIN titres *mpl*, actions *fpl*, valeurs *fpl* ■ **government securities** titres *mpl* d'État ■ **the securities market** le marché des valeurs.

security blanket *n* doudou *m*.

Security Council *n* Conseil *m* de Sécurité.

security guard *n* garde *m* (chargé de la sécurité) ■ [for armoured van] convoyeur *m* de fonds.

security leak *n* fuite *f* de documents *OR* d'informations concernant la sécurité.

security officer *n* [on ship] officier *m* chargé de la sécurité ■ [in firm] employé *m* chargé de la sécurité ■ [inspector] inspecteur *m* de la sécurité.

security police *n* (services *mpl* de la) sûreté *f*.

security risk *n* : **she's considered to be a ~** on considère qu'elle représente un risque pour la sécurité.

secy (*written abbrev of* **secretary**) secr.

sedan [sɪˈdæn] *n* **1.** *US* [car] berline *f* **2.** [chair] : **~ (chair)** chaise *f* à porteurs.

sedate [sɪˈdeɪt] ◇ *adj* [person, manner] calme, posé ■ [behaviour] calme, pondéré.

◇ *vt* donner des sédatifs à ■ **he's heavily ~d** on lui a donné de fortes doses de calmants.

sedately [sɪ'deɪtlɪ] *adv* posément, calmement ▪ **she walked ~ back to her house** elle est revenue chez elle d'un pas lent *OR* tranquille.

sedation [sɪ'deɪʃn] *n* sédation *f* ▪ **under ~** sous calmants.

sedative ['sedətɪv] <> *adj* calmant.
<> *n* calmant *m*.

sedentary ['sedntrɪ] *adj* sédentaire.

sedge [sedʒ] *n* laîche *f*, carex *m*.

sediment ['sedɪmənt] <> *n* **1.** GEOL sédiment *m* **2.** [in liquid] sédiment *m*, dépôt *m* ▪ [in wine] dépôt *m*, lie *f*.
<> *vt* déposer.
<> *vi* se déposer.

sedimentary [,sedɪ'mentərɪ] *adj* sédimentaire ▪ **~ rock** roche *f* sédimentaire.

sedition [sɪ'dɪʃn] *n* sédition *f*.

seditious [sɪ'dɪʃəs] *adj* séditieux.

seduce [sɪ'dju:s] *vt* **1.** [sexually] séduire **2.** [attract] séduire, attirer ▪ [draw] entraîner ▪ **she was ~d away from the company** on l'a persuadée de *OR* incitée à quitter la société.

seducer [sɪ'dju:səʳ] *n* séducteur *m*, -trice *f*.

seduction [sɪ'dʌkʃn] *n* séduction *f*.

seductive [sɪ'dʌktɪv] *adj* [person] séduisant ▪ [personality] séduisant, attrayant ▪ [voice, smile] aguichant, séducteur ▪ [offer] séduisant, alléchant.

seductively [sɪ'dʌktɪvlɪ] *adv* [dress] d'une manière séduisante ▪ [smile] d'une manière enjôleuse.

sedulous ['sedjʊləs] *adj fml* diligent, persévérant.

sedum ['si:dəm] *n* sedum *m*.

see [si:] (*pret* **saw** [sɔ:], *pp* **seen** [si:n])
<> *vt*

A.

1. [perceive with eyes] voir ▪ **can you ~ me?** est-ce que tu me vois? ▪ **she could ~ a light in the distance** elle voyait une lumière au loin ▪ **he saw her talk** *OR* **talking to the policeman** il l'a vue parler *OR* qui parlait au policier ▪ **let me ~ your hands** fais-moi voir *OR* montre-moi tes mains ▪ **can I ~ your newspaper a minute?** puis-je voir votre journal *OR* jeter un coup d'œil sur votre journal un instant? ▪ **I ~ her around a lot** je la croise assez souvent ▪ **there wasn't a car to be seen** il n'y avait pas une seule voiture en vue ▪ **nothing more was ever seen of her** on ne l'a plus jamais revue ▮ [imagine] : **there's nothing there, you're ~ing things!** il n'y a rien, tu as des hallucinations! ➊ **could you ~ your way (clear) to lending me £20?** est-ce que vous pourriez me prêter 20 livres? ▪ **to ~ the back** *OR* **last of sthg** en avoir fini avec qqch ▪ **I'll be glad to ~ the back** *OR* **last of her** je serai content d'être débarrassé d'elle
2. [watch - film, play, programme] voir
3. [refer to - page, chapter] voir ▪ **~ page 317** voir page 317

B.

1. [meet by arrangement, consult] voir ▪ **you should ~ a doctor** tu devrais voir *OR* consulter un médecin ▪ **I'll be ~ing the candidates next week** je verrai les candidats la semaine prochaine
2. [meet by chance] voir, rencontrer
3. [visit - person, place] voir ▪ **to ~ the world** voir le monde
4. [receive a visit from] recevoir, voir ▪ **he's too ill to ~ anyone** il est trop malade pour voir qui que ce soit
5. [spend time with socially] voir ▪ **is he ~ing anyone at the moment?** [going out with] est-ce qu'il a quelqu'un en ce moment?
6. *inf phr* **~ you!, (I'll) be ~ing you!** salut! ▪ **~ you later!** à tout à l'heure! ▪ **~ you around!** à un de ces jours! ▪ **~ you tomorrow!** à demain! ▪ **~ you in London!** on se verra à Londres!

C.

1. [understand] voir, comprendre ▪ **I ~ what you mean** je vois *OR* comprends ce que vous voulez dire ▪ **can I borrow the car? – I don't ~ why not** est-ce que je peux prendre la voiture? – je n'y vois pas d'inconvénients ▪ **will you finish in time? – I don't ~ why not** vous aurez fini à temps? – il n'y a pas de raison ▪ **I could ~ his point** je voyais ce qu'il voulait dire
2. [consider, view] voir ▪ **we ~ things differently** nous ne voyons pas les choses de la même façon ▪ **he doesn't ~ his drinking as a problem** il ne se considère pas comme un alcoolique ▪ **how do you ~ the current situation?** que pensez-vous de la situation actuelle? ▪ **as I ~ it, it's the parents who are to blame** à mon avis, ce sont les parents qui sont responsables
3. [imagine, picture] voir, s'imaginer ▪ **I can't ~ him getting married** je ne le vois pas *OR* je ne me l'imagine pas se mariant

D.

1. [try to find] voir ▪ **I'll ~ if I can fix it** je vais voir si je peux le réparer ▪ **she called by to ~ what had happened** elle est venue pour savoir ce qui s'était passé
2. [become aware of] voir ▪ **what can she possibly ~ in him?** qu'est-ce qu'elle peut bien lui trouver?
3. [discover, learn] voir ▪ **I ~ (that) he's getting married** j'ai appris qu'il allait se marier ▪ **as we shall ~ in a later chapter** comme nous le verrons dans un chapitre ultérieur
4. [make sure] s'assurer, veiller à ▪ **~ that all the lights are out before you leave** assurez-vous que *OR* veillez à ce que toutes les lumières soient éteintes avant de partir ➊ **she'll ~ you right** *inf* elle veillera à ce que tu ne manques de rien, elle prendra bien soin de toi
5. [inspect - file, passport, ticket] voir

E.

1. [experience] voir, connaître ▪ **he thinks he's seen it all** il croit tout savoir ▪ **our car has seen better days** notre voiture a connu des jours meilleurs
2. [witness] voir ▪ **this old house has seen some changes** cette vieille maison a subi quelques transformations ▪ **I never thought I'd ~ the day when he'd admit he was wrong** je n'aurais jamais cru qu'un jour il admettrait avoir tort

F.

1. [accompany] accompagner ▪ **he saw her into a taxi/onto the train** il l'a mise dans un taxi/le train
2. [in poker] voir.

<> *vi* **1.** [perceive with eyes] voir ▪ **I can't ~ without (my) glasses** je ne vois rien sans mes lunettes ▪ **to ~ into the future** voir *OR* lire dans l'avenir ▪ **for all to ~** au vu et au su de tous **2.** [find out] voir **3.** [understand] voir, comprendre ▪ **it makes no difference as far as I can ~** autant que je puisse en juger, ça ne change rien ▪ **I was tired, you ~, and...** j'étais fatigué, voyez-vous, et... ▪ **now ~ here, young man!** écoutez-moi, jeune homme! ▪ **I haven't quite finished – so I ~** je n'ai pas tout à fait terminé – c'est ce que je vois ▪ **I don't want any trouble, ~?** *inf* je ne veux pas d'histoires, OK? **4.** [indicating a pause or delay] : **let me** *OR* **let's ~** voyons voir.
<> *n* RELIG [of bishop] siège *m* épiscopal, évêché *m* ▪ [of archbishop] archevêché *m*.

➡ **see about** *vt insep* s'occuper de ▪ **I'll ~ about making the reservations** je m'occuperai des réservations ▪ **they're sending someone to ~ about the gas** ils envoient quelqu'un pour vérifier le gaz ▪ **they won't let us in – we'll (soon) ~ about that!** *inf* ils ne veulent pas nous laisser entrer – c'est ce qu'on va voir!

➡ **see in** <> *vt sep* **1.** [escort] faire entrer **2.** [celebrate] : **to ~ in the New Year** fêter le Nouvel An.
<> *vi insep* voir à l'intérieur.

➡ **see off** *vt sep* **1.** [say goodbye to] dire au revoir à **2.** [chase away] chasser **3.** [repel - attack] repousser.

➡ **see out** *vt sep* **1.** [accompany to the door] reconduire *OR* raccompagner à la porte ▪ **can you ~ yourself out?** pouvez-vous trouver la sortie tout seul? ▪ **goodbye, I'll ~ myself out** au revoir, ce n'est pas la peine de me raccompagner **2.** [last] : **we've got enough food to ~ the week out** nous avons assez à manger pour tenir jusqu'à la fin de la semaine **3.** [celebrate] : **to ~ out the Old Year** fêter le Nouvel An.

➡ **see over** *vt insep* = see round.

➡ **see round** *vt insep* visiter.

➡ **see through** <> *vt insep* **1.** [window, fabric] voir à travers **2.** [be wise to - person] ne pas être dupe de, voir dans le jeu de ; [- trick, scheme, behaviour] ne pas se laisser tromper par.
<> *vt sep* **1.** [bring to a successful end] mener à bonne fin ▪ **we can count on her to ~ the job through** on peut compter sur elle pour mener l'affaire à bien **2.** [support, sustain] : **I've got enough money to ~ me through the week** j'ai assez d'argent

pour tenir jusqu'à la fin de la semaine ■ **her good humour will always ~ her through any difficulties** sa bonne humeur lui permettra toujours de traverser les moments difficiles.

◆ **see to** *vt insep* **1.** [look after] s'occuper de ■ **~ to it that everything's ready by 5 p.m.** veillez à ce que tout soit prêt pour 17 h ■ **she saw to it that our picnic was ruined** elle a fait en sorte de gâcher notre pique-nique **2.** [repair] réparer.

seed [si:d] ◇ *n* **1.** BOT & HORT *(countable)* graine *f* ■ *(U)* graines *fpl*, semence *f* ■ **grass ~** semence pour gazon ▶ **to go** *OR* **to run to ~** HORT monter en graine ; *fig* [physically] se laisser aller, se décatir ; [mentally] perdre ses facultés **2.** [in fruit, tomatoes] pépin *m* **3.** [source] germe *m* ■ **the ~s of doubt/of suspicion** les germes du doute/de la suspicion **4.** BIBLE & *lit* [offspring] progéniture *f* ■ [sperm] semence *f* **5.** SPORT tête *f* de série ■ **the top ~s** les meilleurs joueurs classés.
◇ *vt* **1.** BOT & HORT [garden, field] ensemencer ■ [plants] planter **2.** [take seeds from - raspberries, grapes] épépiner **3.** SPORT : **~ed player** tête *f* de série ■ **he's ~ed number 5** il est tête de série numéro 5.
◇ *vi* [lettuce] monter en graine ■ [corn] grener.

seedbed ['si:dbed] *n* semis *m*, couche *f* à semis ■ **a ~ of revolution** *fig* les germes d'une révolution.

seedbox ['si:dbɒks] *n* germoir *m*.

seedcake ['si:dkeɪk] *n* gâteau *m* aux graines de carvi.

seedcorn ['si:dkɔ:n] *n* blé *m* de semence.

seediness ['si:dɪnɪs] *n* [appearance] aspect *m* miteux *OR* minable.

seeding machine ['si:dɪŋ-] *n* semoir *m*.

seedless ['si:dlɪs] *adj* sans pépins.

seedling ['si:dlɪŋ] *n* [plant] semis *m*, jeune plant *m* ■ [tree] jeune plant *m*.

seed merchant *n* grainetier *m*, - ère *f*.

seed money *n* capital *m* initial *OR* de départ, mise *f* de fonds initiale.

seedpod ['si:dpɒd] *n* BOT cosse *f*.

seed potato *n* pomme *f* de terre de semence.

seedy ['si:dɪ] (*comp* **seedier**, *superl* **seediest**) *adj* **1.** [person, hotel, clothes] miteux, minable ■ [area] délabré **2.** [fruit] plein de pépins.

seeing ['si:ɪŋ] ◇ *n* [vision] vue *f*, vision *f* ■ **~ is believing** *prov* il faut le voir pour le croire.
◇ *conj* vu que ■ **~ (that** *OR* **as how)** *inf* **no-one came, we left** vu que *OR* étant donné que personne n'est venu, nous sommes partis.

seeing eye (dog) *n* US chien *m* d'aveugle.

seek [si:k] (*pret & pp* **sought** [sɔ:t]) ◇ *vt* **1.** [search for - job, person, solution] chercher, rechercher ■ **he constantly sought her approval** il cherchait constamment à obtenir son approbation ■ **we'd better ~ help** il vaut mieux aller chercher de l'aide ■ **they sought shelter from the rain** ils ont cherché à se mettre à l'abri de la pluie ■ **to ~ one's fortune** chercher fortune ■ **to ~ re-election** chercher à se faire réélire ■ **'gentleman; 50s, ~s mature woman...'** 'homme, la cinquantaine, recherche femme mûre...' **2.** [ask for - advice, help] demander, chercher ■ **I sought professional advice** j'ai demandé conseil à un professionnel, j'ai cherché conseil auprès d'un professionnel **3.** [attempt] : **to ~ to do sthg** chercher à faire qqch, tenter de faire qqch **4.** [move towards] chercher ■ **water ~s its own level** l'eau atteint spontanément son niveau ■ **heat-seeking missile** missile *m* thermoguidé.
◇ *vi* chercher.

◆ **seek after** *vt insep* rechercher.

◆ **seek out** *vt sep* **1.** [go to see] aller voir **2.** [search for] chercher, rechercher ■ [dig out] dénicher.

seeker ['si:kəʳ] *n* chercheur *m*, - euse *f* ■ **a ~ after truth** une personne qui recherche la vérité.

seem [si:m] *vi*

A.

1. [with adjective] sembler, paraître, avoir l'air ■ **he ~s very nice** il a l'air très gentil ■ **things aren't always what they ~ (to be)** les apparences sont parfois trompeuses ■ **just do whatever ~s right** fais ce que tu jugeras bon de faire ■ **the wind makes it ~ colder than it is** on dirait qu'il fait plus froid à cause du vent ■ **how does the situation ~ to you? – it ~s hopeless** que pensez-vous de la situation? – elle me semble désespérée
2. [with infinitive] sembler, avoir l'air ■ **the door ~ed to open by itself** la porte sembla s'ouvrir toute seule ■ **he didn't ~ to know, he ~ed not to know** il n'avait pas l'air de savoir ■ **you ~ to think you can do as you like here** vous avez l'air de croire que vous pouvez faire ce que vous voulez ici ■ **I ~ to sleep better with the window open** je crois que je dors mieux avec la fenêtre ouverte ▌[used to soften a statement, question etc] : **I ~ to remember (that)...** je crois bien me souvenir que... ■ **I'm sorry, I ~ to have forgotten your name** excusez-moi, je crois que j'ai oublié votre nom ■ **now, what ~s to be the problem?** alors, quel est le problème d'après vous? ▌[with 'can't', 'couldn't'] : **I can't ~ to do it** je n'y arrive pas ■ **I can't ~ to remember** je n'arrive pas à me souvenir
3. [with noun, often with 'like'] sembler, paraître ■ **he ~s (like) a nice boy** il a l'air très sympathique *OR* d'un garçon charmant ■ **after what ~ed (like) ages, the doctor arrived** après une attente qui parut interminable, le médecin arriva ■ **it ~s like only yesterday** il me semble que c'était hier

B.

1. [impersonal use] : **it ~ed that** *OR* **as if nothing could make her change her mind** il semblait que rien ne pourrait la faire changer d'avis ■ **it ~ed as though we'd known each other for years** nous avions l'impression de nous connaître depuis des années ■ **it ~s to me that...** j'ai l'impression *OR* il me semble que... ■ **there ~s to be some mistake** on dirait qu'il y a une erreur ■ **there doesn't ~ (to be) much point in going on** je ne crois pas qu'il y ait grand intérêt à continuer ■ **we've been having a spot of bother – so it ~s** *OR* **would ~!** nous avons eu un petit problème – on dirait bien!
2. [indicating that information is hearsay or second-hand] paraître ■ **it ~s** *OR* **it would ~ (that) he already knew** il semble *OR* il semblerait qu'il était déjà au courant ■ **he doesn't ~ to have known about the operation** apparemment, il n'était pas au courant de l'opération ■ **it would ~ so** il paraît que oui ■ **it would ~ not** il paraît que non, apparemment pas.

seeming ['si:mɪŋ] *adj* apparent ■ **I don't trust him, for all his ~ concern over our welfare** je n'ai aucune confiance en lui bien qu'il semble se préoccuper de notre bien-être.

seemingly ['si:mɪŋlɪ] *adv* **1.** [judging by appearances] apparemment, en apparence ■ **she has ~ limitless amounts of money** les sommes d'argent dont elle dispose semblent être illimitées **2.** [from reports] à ce qu'il paraît ■ **~ so/not** il paraît que oui/non.

seemly ['si:mlɪ] (*comp* **seemlier**, *superl* **seemliest**) *adj lit* **1.** [of behaviour] convenable, bienséant ■ **it is not ~ to ask personal questions** cela ne se fait pas de poser des questions personnelles **2.** [of dress] décent.

seen [si:n] *pp* ▷ **see**.

seep [si:p] *vi* filtrer, s'infiltrer ■ **water was ~ing through the cracks in the floor** l'eau s'infiltrait par *OR* filtrait à travers les fissures du sol.

◆ **seep away** *vi insep* s'écouler goutte à goutte.

◆ **seep in** *vi insep* **1.** [liquid] s'infiltrer **2.** *fig* faire son effet.

◆ **seep out** *vi insep* **1.** [blood, liquid] suinter ■ [gas, smoke] se répandre **2.** [information, secret] filtrer.

seepage ['si:pɪdʒ] *n* [gradual - process] suintement *m*, infiltration *f* ; [- leak] fuite *f*.

seer ['sɪəʳ] *n lit* prophète *m*, prophétesse *f*.

seersucker ['sɪə,sʌkəʳ] *n* crépon *m* de coton, seersucker *m*.

seesaw ['si:sɔ:] ◇ *n* balançoire *f* (à bascule).
◇ *comp* [motion] de bascule.
◇ *vi* osciller.

seethe [siːð] *vi* **1.** [liquid, lava] bouillir, bouillonner ■ [sea] bouillonner **2.** [with anger, indignation] bouillir ■ **he was seething with anger** il bouillait de rage **3.** [teem] grouiller ■ **the streets seethed with shoppers** les rues grouillaient de gens qui faisaient leurs courses.

seething ['siːðɪŋ] *adj* **1.** [liquid, sea] bouillonnant **2.** [furious] furieux **3.** [teeming] grouillant ■ **a ~ mass of people** une masse fourmillante de gens.

see-through *adj* transparent.

segment <> *n* ['segmənt] **1.** [piece - gen - ANAT] & GEOM segment *m* ; [- of fruit] quartier *m* ■ **in ~s** par segments **2.** [part - of book, film, programme] partie *f* **3.** LING segment *m*.
<> *vt* [seg'ment] [seg'ment] segmenter, diviser *OR* partager en segments.
<> *vi* [seg'ment] se segmenter.

segmented [seg'mentɪd] *adj* segmentaire.

segregate ['segrɪgeɪt] <> *vt* [separate] séparer ■ [isolate] isoler ■ **he went to a school where the sexes were ~d** l'école qu'il a fréquentée n'était pas mixte ■ **the children were ~d into racial groups** les enfants ont été regroupés en fonction de leur race.
<> *vi* [in genetics] se diviser.

segregated ['segrɪgeɪtɪd] *adj* POL *où la ségrégation raciale est pratiquée.*

segregation [ˌsegrɪ'geɪʃn] *n* **1.** POL ségrégation *f* **2.** [separation - of sexes, patients] séparation *f* **3.** [in genetics] division *f*.

segregationist [ˌsegrɪ'geɪʃnɪst] <> *adj* ségrégationniste.
<> *n* ségrégationniste *mf*.

seine [seɪn] *n* : **~ (net)** senne *f*.

Seine [seɪn] *pr n* : **the (River) ~** la Seine.

seismic ['saɪzmɪk] *adj* sismique, séismique.

seismograph ['saɪzməgrɑːf] *n* sismographe *m*, séismographe *m*.

seismology [saɪz'mɒlədʒɪ] *n* sismologie *f*, séismologie *f*.

seize [siːz] <> *vt* **1.** [grasp] attraper, saisir ■ [in fist] saisir, empoigner ■ **my mother ~d me by the arm/the collar** ma mère m'a attrapé par le bras/le col ■ **she ~d the rail to steady herself** elle s'agrippa à la rampe pour ne pas tomber ■ **to ~ hold of sthg** saisir *OR* attraper qqch **2.** [by force] s'emparer de, saisir ■ **to ~ power** s'emparer du pouvoir ■ **the rebels have ~d control of the radio station** les rebelles se sont emparés de la station de radio ■ **five hostages were ~d during the hold-up** les auteurs du hold-up ont pris cinq otages **3.** [arrest - terrorist, smuggler] se saisir de, appréhender, capturer ■ [capture, confiscate - contraband, arms] se saisir de, saisir ■ LAW [property] saisir **4.** [opportunity] saisir, sauter sur **5.** [understand - meaning] saisir **6.** [overcome] saisir ■ **to be ~d with fright** être saisi d'effroi ■ **she was ~d with a desire to travel** elle fut prise d'une envie irrésistible de voyager ■ **the story never really ~s your imagination** l'histoire ne parvient jamais à vraiment frapper l'imagination ■ **I was ~d with a sudden sneezing fit** j'ai soudain été pris d'éternuements.
<> *vi* [mechanism] se gripper.
◆ **seize on** *vt insep* [opportunity] saisir, sauter sur ■ [excuse] saisir ■ [idea] saisir, adopter.
◆ **seize up** *vi insep* **1.** [machinery] se gripper **2.** [system] se bloquer **3.** [leg] s'ankyloser ■ [back] se bloquer ■ [heart] s'arrêter.
◆ **seize upon** = **seize on**.

seizure ['siːʒəʳ] *n* **1.** *(U)* [of goods, property] saisie *f* ■ [of city, fortress] prise *f* ■ [of ship] capture *f* ■ [arrest] arrestation *f* ■ **the police made a big arms ~** la police a saisi un important stock d'armes **2.** MED crise *f*, attaque *f* ■ **to have a ~** *liter & fig* avoir une attaque ■ **heart ~** crise cardiaque.

seldom ['seldəm] *adv* rarement ■ **I ~ see her** je la vois rarement, je la vois peu ■ **he ~ comes** il ne vient que *OR* il vient rarement ■ **he ~, if ever, visits his mother** il rend rarement, pour ne pas dire jamais, visite à sa mère.

select [sɪ'lekt] <> *vt* **1.** [gen] choisir ■ [team] sélectionner ■ **you have been ~ed from among our many customers** vous avez été choisie parmi nos nombreux clients **2.** COMPUT sélectionner.
<> *adj* **1.** [elite - restaurant, neighbourhood] chic, sélect ; [- club] fermé, sélect ■ **the membership is very ~** les membres appartiennent à la haute société ■ **she invited a few ~ friends** elle a invité quelques amis choisis ■ **only a ~ few were informed** seuls quelques privilégiés furent informés **2.** [in quality - goods] de (premier) choix.

select committee *n* POL commission *f* d'enquête parlementaire.

selected [sɪ'lektɪd] *adj* [friends, poems] choisi ■ [customers] privilégié ■ [fruit, cuts of meat] de (premier) choix.

selection [sɪ'lekʃn] <> *n* **1.** [choice] choix *m*, sélection *f* ■ [of team] sélection *f* ■ **no one thought he stood a chance of ~** personne ne pensait qu'il serait sélectionné **2.** [of stories, music] choix *m*, sélection *f* ■ **~s from Balzac** morceaux *mpl* choisis de Balzac **3.** COMPUT sélection .
<> *comp* [committee, criteria] de sélection.

selective [sɪ'lektɪv] *adj* **1.** [gen] sélectif ■ **you should be more ~ in your choice of friends/in your reading** vous devriez choisir vos amis/vos lectures avec plus de discernement ■ **there was a wave of ~ strikes** il y eut une série de grèves tournantes ➔ **~ entry** SCH sélection *f* ■ **~ service** *US* service *m* militaire obligatoire, conscription *f* ■ **~ welfare** allocations *fpl* sociales sélectives **2.** ELECTRON sélectif.

selectively [sɪ'lektɪvlɪ] *adv* sélectivement, de manière sélective.

selectivity [ˌsɪlek'tɪvətɪ] *n* **1.** [choice] discernement *m* **2.** ELECTRON sélectivité *f*.

selector [sɪ'lektəʳ] *n* **1.** [gen - SPORT] sélectionneur *m* **2.** TELEC & TV sélecteur *m*.

selenium [sɪ'liːnɪəm] *n* sélénium *m*.

self [self] (*pl* **selves** [selvz]) <> *n* **1.** [individual] : **she's back to her old** *OR* **usual ~** elle est redevenue elle-même *OR* comme avant ■ **she's only a shadow of her former ~** elle n'est plus que l'ombre d'elle-même ■ **he was his usual tactless ~** il a fait preuve de son manque de tact habituel ■ **they began to reveal their true selves** ils ont commencé à se montrer sous leur véritable jour **2.** PSYCHOL moi *m* **3.** [self-interest] : **all she thinks of is ~, ~, ~** elle ne pense qu'à sa petite personne **4.** [on cheque] : **pay ~** payez à l'ordre de soi-même.
<> *adj* [matching] assorti.

self- *in cpds* **1.** [of o.s.] de soi-même, auto- ■ **~actualization** épanouissement *m* de la personnalité ■ **~accusation** autoaccusation *f* ■ **~admiration** narcissisme *m* **2.** [by o.s.] auto-, par soi-même ■ **~financing** qui s'autofinance **3.** [automatic] auto-, automatique ■ **~checking** à contrôle automatique ■ **~opening** à ouverture automatique.

self-absorbed [-əb'sɔːbd] *adj* égocentrique.

self-abuse *n pej* onanisme *m*, masturbation *f*.

self-addressed [-ə'drest] *adj* : **send three ~ (stamped) envelopes** envoyez trois enveloppes (timbrées) à votre adresse.

self-adhesive *adj* autocollant, autoadhésif.

self-analysis *n* autoanalyse *f*.

self-appointed [-ə'pɔɪntɪd] *adj* qui s'est nommé *OR* proclamé lui-même ■ **she is our ~ guide** elle a assumé d'elle-même le rôle de guide au sein de notre groupe.

self-assembly *adj* [furniture] en kit.

self-assertive *adj* sûr de soi, impérieux.

self-assurance *n* confiance *f* en soi, aplomb *m*.

self-assured *adj* : **he's very ~** il est très sûr de lui.

self-aware *adj* conscient de soi-même.

self-awareness *n* conscience *f* de soi.

self-catering *adj* *UK* [flat, accommodation] indépendant *(avec cuisine)* ■ [holiday] dans un appartement *OR* un logement indépendant.

self-centred *UK*, **self-centered** *US* [-'sentəd] *adj* égocentrique.

self-certification *n* certificat *m* de maladie *(rédigé par un employé)*.

self-cleaning *adj* autonettoyant.

self-coloured *UK*, **self-colored** *US* *adj* uni.

self-composure *n* calme *m*, sang-froid *m* ■ **to keep/to lose one's ~** garder/perdre son sang-froid.

self-confessed [-kən'fest] *adj* [murderer, rapist] qui reconnaît sa culpabilité ■ **he's a ~ drug addict** il avoue lui-même qu'il se drogue.

self-confidence *n* confiance *f* en soi, assurance *f* ■ **she is full of/she lacks ~** elle a une grande/elle manque de confiance en elle.

self-confident *adj* sûr de soi, plein d'assurance.

self-confidently *adv* avec assurance *OR* aplomb.

self-congratulatory *adj* satisfait de soi.

self-conscious *adj* **1.** [embarrassed] timide, gêné ■ **to make sb feel ~** intimider qqn ■ **he's very ~ about his red hair** il fait un complexe de ses cheveux roux ■ **I feel very ~ in front of all these people** je me sens très mal à l'aise devant tous ces gens **2.** [style] appuyé.

self-consciously *adv* timidement.

self-consciousness *n* timidité *f*, gêne *f*.

self-contained *adj* **1.** [device] autonome **2.** [flat] indépendant **3.** [person] réservé.

self-contradictory *adj* qui se contredit.

self-control *n* sang-froid *m*, maîtrise *f* de soi ■ **to lose one's ~** perdre son sang-froid.

self-controlled *adj* maître de soi.

self-critical *adj* qui fait son autocritique.

self-criticism *n* autocritique *f*.

self-defeating [-dɪ'fi:tɪŋ] *adj* contraire au but recherché.

self-defence *n* **1.** [physical] autodéfense *f* **2.** LAW légitime défense *f* ■ **it was ~** j'étais/il était etc en état de légitime défense ■ **I shot him in ~** j'ai tiré sur lui en état de légitime défense.

self-denial *n* abnégation *f*, sacrifice *m* de soi.

self-deprecating [-'deprɪkeɪtɪŋ] *adj* : **to be ~** se déprécier.

self-destruct ◇ *vi* s'autodétruire.
◇ *adj* [mechanism] autodestructeur.

self-destruction *n* **1.** [of spacecraft, missile] autodestruction *f* **2.** PSYCHOL [of personality] autodestruction *f* **3.** [suicide] suicide *m*.

self-destructive *adj* autodestructeur.

self-determination *n* POL autodétermination *f*.

self-discipline *n* [self-control] maîtrise *f* de soi ■ [good behaviour] autodiscipline *f*.

self-disciplined *adj* [self-controlled] maître de soi ■ [well-behaved] qui fait preuve d'autodiscipline.

self-doubt *n* doute *m* de soi-même.

self-drive *adj* : **~ car** voiture *f* sans chauffeur.

self-educated *adj* autodidacte.

self-effacing [-ɪ'feɪsɪŋ] *adj* modeste, effacé.

self-employed ◇ *adj* indépendant, qui travaille à son compte.
◇ *npl* : **the ~** les travailleurs *mpl* indépendants.

self-esteem *n* respect *m* de soi, amour-propre *m*.

self-evident *adj* évident, qui va de soi, qui saute aux yeux.

self-examination *n* examen *m* de conscience.

self-explanatory *adj* qui se passe d'explications, évident.

self-expression *n* expression *f* libre.

self-financing [-faɪ'nænsɪŋ] *adj* autofinancé.

self-focusing [-'fəʊkəsɪŋ] *adj* autofocus *(inv)*, à mise au point automatique.

self-fulfilling *adj* : **~ prophecy** *prophétie défaitiste qui se réalise*.

self-fulfilment *n* épanouissement *m*.

self-funding *adj* qui s'autofinance.

self-governing *adj* POL autonome.

self-government *n* POL autonomie *f*.

self-help ◇ *n* autonomie *f* ■ [in welfare] entraide *f*.
◇ *comp* : **~ group** groupe *m* d'entraide ■ **~ guide** guide *m* pratique.

self-image *n* image *f* de soi-même.

self-importance *n* suffisance *f*.

self-important *adj* vaniteux, suffisant.

self-imposed [-ɪm'pəʊzd] *adj* que l'on s'impose à soi-même ■ **~ exile** exil *m* volontaire.

self-improvement *n* perfectionnement *m* des connaissances personnelles.

self-induced *adj* que l'on provoque soi-même.

self-indulgence *n* complaisance *f* envers soi-même, habitude *f* de ne rien se refuser.

self-indulgent *adj* [person] qui ne se refuse rien ■ [book, film] complaisant.

self-inflicted [-ɪn'flɪktɪd] *adj* : **his wounds were ~** il s'était auto-infligé ses blessures.

self-interest *n* intérêt *m* personnel ■ **to act out of ~** agir par intérêt personnel.

self-interested *adj* intéressé, qui agit par intérêt personnel.

selfish ['selfɪʃ] *adj* égoïste ■ **you're acting out of purely ~ motives** vous agissez par pur égoïsme.

selfishness ['selfɪʃnɪs] *n* égoïsme *m*.

self-justification *n* autojustification *f*.

self-knowledge *n* connaissance *f* de soi.

selfless ['selflɪs] *adj* altruiste, désintéressé.

selflessly ['selflɪslɪ] *adv* de façon désintéressée, avec désintéressement.

selflessness ['selflɪsnɪs] *n* altruisme *m*, désintéressement *m*.

self-loading *adj* [gun] automatique.

self-locking *adj* à verrouillage automatique.

self-made *adj* qui a réussi tout seul *OR* par ses propres moyens ■ **a ~ man** un self-made man.

self-mockery *n* autodérision *f*.

self-opinionated *adj* sûr de soi.

self-pity *n* apitoiement *m* sur son sort ■ **she's full of ~** elle s'apitoie beaucoup sur son sort.

self-pitying *adj* qui s'apitoie sur son (propre) sort.

self-portrait *n* [in painting] autoportrait *m* ■ [in book] portrait *m* de l'auteur par lui-même.

self-possessed *adj* maître de soi, qui garde son sang-froid.

self-possession *n* sang-froid *m*.

self-preservation *n* instinct *m* de conservation.

self-proclaimed [-prə'kleɪmd] *adj* : **she's a ~ art critic** elle se proclame critique d'art.

self-propelled [-prə'peld] *adj* autopropulsé.

self-raising *UK* [-ˌreɪzɪŋ], **self-rising** *US* [-ˌraɪzɪŋ] *adj* : **~ flour** farine *f* avec levure incorporée.

self-regard *n* égoïsme *m*.

self-regulating [-'regjʊleɪtɪŋ] *adj* autorégulateur.

self-reliant *adj* indépendant.

self-respect *n* respect *m* de soi, amour-propre *m*.

self-respecting [-rɪ'spektɪŋ] *adj* qui se respecte ▪ **no ~ girl would be seen dead going out with him** une fille qui se respecte ne sortirait pour rien au monde avec lui.

self-restraint *n* retenue *f* ▪ **to exercise ~** se retenir.

self-righteous *adj* suffisant.

self-righteousness *n* suffisance *f*, pharisaïsme *m* *fml*.

self-righting [-'raɪtɪŋ] *adj* inchavirable.

self-rising *US* = **self-raising**.

self-rule *n* POL autonomie *f*.

self-sacrifice *n* abnégation *f* ▪ **there's no need for ~** vous n'avez pas besoin de vous sacrifier.

selfsame ['selfseɪm] *adj* même, identique.

self-satisfied *adj* [person] suffisant, content de soi ▪ [look, smile, attitude] suffisant, satisfait.

self-sealing *adj* [envelope] autocollant, autoadhésif ▪ [tank] à obturation automatique.

self-seeking [-'si:kɪŋ] *adj* égoïste.

self-service <> *adj* en self-service, en libre service ▪ **~ restaurant** self-service *m* ▪ **~ shop** libre-service *m*.
<> *n* [restaurant] self-service *m* ▪ [garage, shop] libre-service *m*.

self-serving *adj* intéressé.

self-starter *n* **1.** AUT starter *m* automatique **2.** [person] personne *f* pleine d'initiative.

self-styled [-'staɪld] *adj* prétendu, soi-disant.

self study <> *n* autoformation *f*.
<> *adj* d'autoformation.

self-sufficiency *n* **1.** [of person - independence] indépendance *f* ; [- self-assurance] suffisance *f* **2.** ECON [of nation, resources] autosuffisance *f* ▪ POL : **(economic) ~** autarcie *f*.

self-sufficient *adj* **1.** [person - independent] indépendant ; [- self-assured] plein de confiance en soi, suffisant **2.** ECON [nation] autosuffisant ▪ **~ in copper** autosuffisant en cuivre ▮ POL autarcique.

self-supporting *adj* **1.** [financially] indépendant **2.** [framework] autoporteur, autoportant.

self-tapping [-'tæpɪŋ] *adj* : **~ screw** vis *f* autotaraudeuse.

self-taught *adj* autodidacte.

self-willed [-'wɪld] *adj* têtu, obstiné.

self-winding [-'waɪndɪŋ] *adj* [watch] qui n'a pas besoin d'être remonté, (à remontage) automatique.

sell [sel] (*pret & pp* **sold** [səʊld]) <> *vt* **1.** [goods] vendre ▪ **to ~ sb sthg** *OR* **sthg to sb** vendre qqch à qqn ▪ **he sold me his car for $1,000** il m'a vendu sa voiture (pour) 1 000 dollars ▪ **he ~s computers for a living** il gagne sa vie en vendant des ordinateurs ▪ **the book sold 50,000 copies, 50,000 copies of the book were sold** le livre s'est vendu à 50 000 exemplaires ▪ **to ~ sthg for cash** vendre qqch au comptant ▪ **they ~ the cassettes at £3 each** ils vendent les cassettes 3 livres pièce ▪ **what really ~s newspapers is scandal** ce sont les scandales qui font vraiment vendre les journaux ▪ **he'd ~ his own grandmother for a pint of beer** il vendrait son âme pour une bière ▪ **to ~ one's soul (to the devil)** vendre son âme (au diable) ▪ **we'd ~ our souls for a holiday in the Caribbean** *hum* nous ferions n'importe quoi pour passer des vacances aux Caraïbes ▶ **we were sold a pup** *inf dated OR* **a dud** *inf* [cheated] on nous a roulés ; [sold rubbish] on nous a vendu de la camelote
2. [promote - idea] faire accepter ▪ **as a politician, it is important to be able to ~ yourself** les hommes politiques doivent savoir se mettre en valeur
3. *phr* **to ~ sb short** *inf* [cheat] rouler qqn ; [disparage] débiner qqn ▪ **don't ~ yourself short** il faut vous mettre en valeur ▪ **to ~ sb down the river** trahir qqn
4. [make enthusiastic about] convaincre ▪ **I'm completely sold on the idea** je suis emballé par l'idée.
<> *vi* se vendre ▪ **the cakes ~ for** *OR* **at 70 pence each** les gâteaux se vendent (à) *OR* valent 70 pence pièce ▪ **sorry, I'm not interested in ~ing** désolé, je ne cherche pas à vendre ▶ **to sell like hot cakes** se vendre comme des petits pains.
<> *n* **1.** COMM vente *f*
2. *inf* [disappointment] déception *f* ▪ [hoax] attrape-nigaud *m*.

◆ **sell back** *vt sep* revendre.

◆ **sell off** *vt sep* [at reduced price] solder ▪ [clear] liquider ▪ [get cash] vendre ▪ [privatize] privatiser.

◆ **sell on** *vt sep* revendre *(en faisant du bénéfice)*.

◆ **sell out** <> *vt sep* **1.** *(usu passive)* [concert, match] : **the match was sold out** le match s'est joué à guichets fermés
2. [betray] trahir
3. ST. EX vendre, réaliser.
<> *vi insep* **1.** COMM [sell business] vendre son commerce ▪ [sell stock] liquider (son stock) ▪ [run out] vendre tout le stock ▪ **he sold out to some Japanese investors** il a vendu à des investisseurs japonais
2. [be traitor] trahir ▪ **to ~ out to the enemy** passer à l'ennemi ▪ **critics accuse her of ~ing out as a writer** les critiques l'accusent d'être un écrivain vendu *OR* sans principes.

◆ **sell up** <> *vt sep* **1.** FIN & LAW [goods] opérer la vente forcée de, procéder à la liquidation de
2. COMM [business] vendre, liquider.
<> *vi insep* [shopkeeper] vendre son fonds de commerce *OR* son affaire ▪ [businessman] vendre son affaire.

Sellafield ['seləfi:ld] *pr n usine de retraitement des déchets radioactifs dans le nord de l'Angleterre.*

sell-by date *n* date *f* limite de vente.

seller ['selər] *n* **1.** [person - gen] vendeur *m*, - euse *f* ; [- merchant] vendeur *m*, - euse *f*, marchand *m*, - e *f* ▪ **it's a ~'s market** c'est un marché vendeur *OR* favorable aux vendeurs **2.** [goods] : **it's one of our biggest ~s** c'est un des articles qui se vend le mieux.

selling ['selɪŋ] *n (U)* vente *f*.

selling point *n* avantage *m*, atout *m*, point *m* fort.

selling price *n* prix *m* de vente.

selloff ['selɒf] *n* [gen] vente *f* ▪ [of shares] dégagement *m*.

Sellotape® ['seləteɪp] *n UK* Scotch® *m*, ruban *m* adhésif.
◆ **sellotape** *vt UK* scotcher, coller avec du ruban adhésif.

sell-out *n* **1.** COMM liquidation *f* **2.** [betrayal] trahison *f* ▪ [capitulation] capitulation *f* **3.** [of play, concert etc] : **it was a ~** on a vendu tous les billets ▪ **the match was a ~** le match s'est joué à guichets fermés.

selvage, selvedge ['selvɪdʒ] *n* lisière *f (d'un tissu)*.

selves [selvz] *pl* ▷ **self**.

semantic [sɪ'mæntɪk] *adj* sémantique.

semantically [sɪ'mæntɪklɪ] *adv* du point de vue sémantique.

semantics [sɪ'mæntɪks] *n (U)* sémantique *f*.

semaphore ['seməfɔ:r] <> *n* **1.** *(U)* [signals] signaux *mpl* à bras **2.** RAIL & NAUT sémaphore *m*.
<> *vt* transmettre par signaux à bras.

semblance ['sembləns] *n* semblant *m*, apparence *f* ▪ **we need to show at least some ~ of unity** nous devons au moins montrer un semblant d'unité.

semen ['si:men] *n (U)* sperme *m*, semence *f*.

semester [sɪ'mestər] *n* semestre *m*.

semi ['semɪ] *n* **1.** *UK inf* = **semi-detached house 2.** *inf* = **semi-final 3.** *US* = **semitrailer**.

semi- *in cpds* **1.** [partly] semi-, demi- ▪ **~arid** semi-aride ▪ **in ~darkness** dans la pénombre *OR* la semi-obscurité ▪ **he's in ~retirement** il est en semi-retraite **2.** [twice] : **~annual** semestriel.

semi-automatic ◇ *adj* semi-automatique.
◇ *n* arme *f* semi-automatique.

semibreve ['semɪbriːv] *n UK* MUS ronde *f* ▪ **~ rest** pause *f*.

semicircle ['semɪ,sɜːkl] *n* demi-cercle *m*.

semicircular [,semɪ'sɜːkjʊlər] *adj* demi-circulaire, semi-circulaire.

semicolon [,semɪ'kəʊlən] *n* point-virgule *m*.

semiconductor [,semɪkən'dʌktər] *n* semi-conducteur *m*.

semiconscious [,semɪ'kɒnʃəs] *adj* à demi *OR* moitié conscient.

semiconsonant [,semɪ'kɒnsənənt] *n* semi-consonne *f*.

semidarkness [,semɪ'dɑːknɪs] *n* pénombre *f*.

semidetached [,semɪdɪ'tætʃt] *adj* : **~ house** maison *f* jumelée.

semifinal [,semɪ'faɪnl] *n* demi-finale *f* ▪ **she lost in the ~s** elle a perdu en demi-finale.

semifinalist [,semɪ'faɪnəlɪst] *n* demi-finaliste *mf*.

seminal ['semɪnl] *adj* **1.** ANAT & BOT séminal **2.** [important] majeur, qui fait école.

seminar ['semɪnɑːr] *n* **1.** [conference] séminaire *m*, colloque *m* **2.** UNIV [class] séminaire *m*, travaux *mpl* dirigés.

seminary ['semɪnərɪ] (*pl* **seminaries**) *n* RELIG & SCH [for boys, priests] séminaire *m* ▪ [for girls] pensionnat *m* de jeunes filles.

semiotic [,semɪ'ɒtɪk] *adj* sémiotique.

semiotics [,semɪ'ɒtɪks] *n (U)* sémiotique *f*.

semiprecious ['semɪ,preʃəs] *adj* semi-précieux.

semiquaver ['semɪ,kweɪvər] *n* double croche *f*.

semiretired [,semɪrɪ'taɪəd] *adj* en semi-retraite.

semiskilled [,semɪ'skɪld] *adj* [worker] spécialisé.

semi-skimmed [-'skɪmd] *adj* [milk] demi-écrémé.

Semite ['siːmaɪt] *n* Sémite *mf*.

Semitic [sɪ'mɪtɪk] ◇ *n* LING langue *f* sémitique, sémitique *m*.
◇ *adj* sémite, sémitique.

semitone ['semɪtəʊn] *n* demi-ton *m*.

semitrailer [,semɪ'treɪlər] *n US* semi-remorque *f*.

semitropical [,semɪ'trɒpɪkl] *adj* semi-tropical.

semivowel ['semɪ,vaʊəl] *n* semi-voyelle *f*.

semolina [,semə'liːnə] *n* semoule *f* ▪ **~ pudding** gâteau *m* de semoule.

sempiternal [,sempɪ'tɜːnl] *adj lit* sempiternel, éternel.

sempstress ['sempstrɪs] = **seamstress**.

sen. *written abbr of* **senior**.

Sen. *written abbr of* **Senator**.

SEN (*abbrev of* **State Enrolled Nurse**) *n infirmier ou infirmière diplômé(e) d'État.*

senate ['senɪt] *n* **1.** POL sénat *m* ▪ **the United States Senate** le Sénat américain **2.** UNIV Conseil *m* d'Université.

SENATE

Le Sénat constitue, avec la Chambre des représentants, l'organe législatif américain ; il est composé de 100 membres (deux par État). Le mandat d'un sénateur est de six ans.

senator ['senətər] *n* sénateur *m*.

senatorial [,senə'tɔːrɪəl] *adj* sénatorial.

send [send] (*pret & pp* **sent** [sent]) ◇ *vt* **1.** [letter, parcel, money] envoyer, expédier ▪ **to ~ sb a letter, to ~ a letter to sb** envoyer une lettre à qqn ▪ **he sent (us) word that he would be delayed** il (nous) a fait savoir qu'il aurait du retard ▪ **she ~s her love** *OR* **regards** elle vous envoie ses amitiés ▪ **~ them our love** embrassez-les pour nous ▪ **~ them our best wishes** faites-leur nos amitiés ▪ **I sent my luggage by train** j'ai fait expédier *OR* envoyer mes bagages par le train ▪ **what will the future ~ us?** que nous réserve l'avenir? ▪ **we sent help to the refugees** nous avons envoyé des secours aux réfugiés ▮ [to carry out task] envoyer ▪ **she sent her daughter for the meat** *OR* **to get the meat** elle a envoyé sa fille chercher la viande ▪ **the dogs were sent after him** on lança les chiens à sa poursuite *OR* à ses trousses ▶ **to ~ sb packing** *inf OR* **about his business** envoyer promener qqn, envoyer qqn sur les roses
2. [to a specific place] envoyer ▪ **~ the children indoors** faites rentrer les enfants ▪ **~ him to my office** dites-lui de venir dans mon bureau, envoyez-le moi ▪ **the collision sent showers of sparks/clouds of smoke into the sky** la collision fit jaillir une gerbe d'étincelles/provoqua des nuages de fumée ▪ **the sound sent shivers down my spine** le bruit m'a fait froid dans le dos ▪ **the news sent a murmur of excitement through the hall** la nouvelle provoqua un murmure d'agitation dans la salle ▪ **heavy smoking sent him to an early grave** il est mort prématurément parce qu'il fumait trop ▮ [order] : **I was sent to bed/to my room** on m'a envoyé me coucher/dans ma chambre ▪ **to ~ sb home** [from school] renvoyer qqn chez lui ; [from abroad] rapatrier qqn ; INDUST [lay off] mettre qqn en chômage technique ▪ **to ~ sb to prison** envoyer qqn en prison
3. *(with present participle)* [propel] envoyer, expédier ▪ **a gust of wind sent the papers flying across the table** un coup de vent balaya les papiers qui se trouvaient sur la table ▪ **I sent the cup flying** j'ai envoyé voler la tasse ▪ **the blow sent me flying** le coup m'a envoyé rouler par terre ▪ **a sudden storm sent us all running for shelter** un orage soudain nous força à courir nous mettre à l'abri
4. [into a specific state] rendre ▪ **the noise is ~ing me mad** *OR* **out of my mind** le bruit me rend fou ▪ **the news sent them into a panic** les nouvelles les ont fait paniquer ▪ **to ~ sb to sleep** *liter & fig* endormir qqn
5. *inf dated* [into raptures] emballer.
◇ *vi* **1.** [send word] : **he sent to say he couldn't come** il nous a fait savoir qu'il ne pouvait pas venir
2. [for information, equipment] : **we sent to Paris for a copy** nous avons demandé une copie à Paris.

◆ **send away** ◇ *vt sep* **1.** [letter, parcel] expédier, mettre à la poste
2. [person] renvoyer, faire partir ▪ **the children were sent away to school** les enfants furent mis en pension.
◇ *vi insep* : **to ~ away for sthg** [by post] se faire envoyer qqch ; [by catalogue] commander qqch par correspondance *OR* sur catalogue.

◆ **send back** *vt sep* **1.** [return - books, goods] renvoyer
2. [order - person] : **we sent her back to fetch a coat** *OR* **for a coat** nous l'avons envoyée prendre un manteau.

◆ **send down** ◇ *vt sep* **1.** [person, lift] faire descendre, envoyer en bas
2. [prices, temperature] faire baisser, provoquer la baisse de
3. *UK* UNIV [student] expulser, renvoyer
4. *inf* [to prison] envoyer en prison.
◇ *vi insep* [by message or messenger] : **to ~ down for sthg** (se) faire monter qqch.

◆ **send for** *vt insep* **1.** [doctor, taxi] faire venir, appeler ▪ [mother, luggage] faire venir ▪ [police] appeler ▪ [help] envoyer chercher ▪ [food, drink] commander
2. [by post, from catalogue] se faire envoyer, commander ▪ [catalogue, price list] demander.

◆ **send forth** *vt insep lit* **1.** [army, messenger] envoyer
2. [produce - leaves] produire ; [- light] produire, émettre ; [- smell] répandre ; [- cry] pousser.

◆ **send in** *vt sep* **1.** [visitor] faire entrer ▪ [troops, police] envoyer
2. [submit - report, form] envoyer ; [- suggestions, resignation] envoyer, soumettre ▪ **why don't you ~ your name in for the competition?** pourquoi ne pas vous inscrire au concours? ▪ **please ~ in a written application** veuillez envoyer une demande écrite ; [for job] veuillez poser votre candidature par écrit.

◆ **send off** ◇ *vt sep* **1.** [by post] expédier, mettre à la poste
2. [person] envoyer ■ **they sent us off to bed/to get washed** ils nous ont envoyés nous coucher/nous laver
3. SPORT expulser
4. [to sleep] : **to ~ sb off (to sleep)** *liter & fig* endormir qqn.
◇ *vi insep* : **to ~ off for sthg** [by catalogue] commander qqch par correspondance *OR* sur catalogue ; [by post] se faire envoyer qqch.

◆ **send on** *vt sep* **1.** [mail] faire suivre ■ [luggage] expédier ■ **if you've forgotten anything, we'll ~ it on** si vous avez oublié quelque chose, nous vous le renverrons
2. [person] : **they sent us on ahead** *OR* **in front** ils nous ont envoyés en éclaireurs
3. SPORT [player] faire entrer (sur le terrain).

◆ **send out** ◇ *vt sep* **1.** [by post - invitations] expédier, poster
2. [messengers, search party] envoyer, dépêcher ■ [patrol] envoyer ■ **they sent out a car for us** ils ont envoyé une voiture nous chercher ▮ [transmit - message, signal] envoyer ■ **a call was sent out for Dr Bramley** on a fait appeler le Dr Bramley
3. [outside] envoyer dehors ■ [on errand, mission] envoyer ■ **we sent her out for coffee** nous l'avons envoyée chercher du café
4. [produce, give out - leaves] produire ; [- light, heat] émettre, répandre, diffuser ; [- fumes, smoke] répandre.
◇ *vi insep* : **to ~ out for coffee/sandwiches** [to shop] envoyer quelqu'un chercher du café/des sandwiches.

◆ **send round** *vt sep* **1.** [circulate - petition] faire circuler ■ **to ~ round the hat** faire la quête
2. [dispatch - messenger, repairman] envoyer ; [- message] faire parvenir ■ **they sent a car round** ils ont envoyé une voiture.

◆ **send up** *vt sep* **1.** [messenger, luggage, drinks] faire monter ■ [rocket, flare] lancer ■ [plane] faire décoller ■ [smoke] répandre
2. [raise - price, pressure, temperature] faire monter
3. *inf* [ridicule] mettre en boîte, se moquer de
4. *US inf* [to prison] envoyer en prison, coffrer.

sender ['sendəʳ] *n* expéditeur *m*, - trice *f* ■ **return to ~** retour à l'expéditeur.

send-off *n* : **to give sb a ~** dire au revoir à qqn, souhaiter bon voyage à qqn ■ **he was given a warm ~ by all his colleagues** tous les collègues sont venus lui faire des adieux chaleureux.

send-up *n inf* parodie *f*.

Seneca ['senɪkə] *pr n* Sénèque *m*.

Senegal [,senɪ'gɔ:l] *pr n* Sénégal *m* ■ **in ~** au Sénégal.

Senegalese [,senɪgə'li:z] (*pl inv*) ◇ *n* Sénégalais *m*, - e *f*.
◇ *adj* sénégalais.

senescent [sɪ'nesnt] *adj* sénescent.

senile ['si:naɪl] *adj* sénile ■ **~ decay** dégénérescence *f* sénile ■ **~ dementia** démence *f* sénile.

senility [sɪ'nɪlətɪ] *n* sénilité *f*.

senior ['si:njəʳ] ◇ *adj* **1.** [in age] plus âgé, aîné ■ [in rank] (de grade) supérieur ■ **I am ~ to them** [higher position] je suis leur supérieur ; [longer service] j'ai plus d'ancienneté qu'eux ■ **~ airport officials** la direction de l'aéroport ■ **~ clerk** commis *m* principal, chef *m* de bureau ■ **~ executive** cadre *m* supérieur ■ **~ government official** haut fonctionnaire *m* ■ **George is the ~ partner in our firm** Georges est l'associé principal de notre société **2.** SCH : **~ master** *UK* professeur *m* principal ■ *US* **~ high school** lycée *m* ■ **~ year** terminale *f*, dernière année *f* d'études secondaires.
◇ *n* **1.** [older person] aîné *m*, - e *f* ■ **he is my ~ by six months, he is six months my ~** il a six mois de plus que moi, il est de six mois mon aîné **2.** *US* SCH élève *mf* de terminale ■ UNIV étudiant *m*, - e *f* de licence **3.** *UK* SCH : **the ~s** ≃ les grands *mpl*, les grandes *fpl* **4.** [in hierarchy] supérieur *m*, - e *f*.

◆ **Senior** *adj* [in age] : **John Brown ~** John Brown père.

senior citizen *n* personne *f* âgée *OR* du troisième âge.

Senior Common Room *n UK* UNIV salle *f* des professeurs.

seniority [,si:nɪ'ɒrətɪ] *n* **1.** [in age] priorité *f* d'âge ■ **he became chairman by virtue of ~** il est devenu président parce qu'il était le plus âgé *OR* le doyen **2.** [in rank] supériorité *f* ■ **to have ~ over sb** être le supérieur de qqn ▮ [length of service] ancienneté *f* ■ **according to** *OR* **by ~** en fonction de *OR* à l'ancienneté.

Senior Service *n UK* marine *f*.

senna ['senə] *n* séné *m*.

sensation [sen'seɪʃn] *n* **1.** *(U)* [sensitivity] sensation *f* ■ **the cold made me lose all ~ in my hands** le froid m'a complètement engourdi les mains **2.** [impression] impression *f*, sensation *f* ■ **I had a strange ~ in my leg** j'avais une drôle de sensation dans la jambe ■ **I had the ~ of falling** j'avais la sensation *OR* l'impression de tomber **3.** [excitement, success] sensation *f* ■ **to cause** *OR* **to be a ~** faire sensation.

sensational [sen'seɪʃənl] *adj* **1.** [causing a sensation] sensationnel, qui fait sensation **2.** [press] à sensation **3.** [wonderful] formidable, sensationnel ■ **you look ~** tu es superbe.

sensationalism [sen'seɪʃnəlɪzm] *n* **1.** [in press, novels etc] sensationnalisme *m* **2.** PHILOS sensationnisme *m* **3.** PSYCHOL sensualisme *m*.

sensationalist [sen'seɪʃnəlɪst] ◇ *n* [writer] auteur *m* à sensation ■ [journalist] journaliste *mf* à sensation.
◇ *adj* à sensation.

sensationally [sen'seɪʃnəlɪ] *adv* d'une manière sensationnelle ■ [as intensifier] : **we found this ~ good restaurant** *inf* on a découvert un restaurant vraiment génial.

sense [sens] ◇ *n* **1.** [faculty] sens *m* ■ **~ of hearing** ouïe *f* ■ **~ of sight** vue *f* ■ **~ of smell** odorat *m* ■ **~ of taste** goût *m* ■ **~ of touch** toucher *m*
2. [sensation] sensation *f* ■ [feeling] sentiment *m* ■ **I felt a certain ~ of pleasure** j'ai ressenti un certain plaisir ■ **I felt a ~ of shame** je me suis senti honteux ■ **children need a ~ of security** les enfants ont besoin de se sentir en sécurité ▮ [notion] sens *m*, notion *f* ■ **she seems to have lost all ~ of reality** elle semble avoir perdu le sens des réalités ■ **I lost all ~ of time** j'ai perdu toute notion de l'heure ■ **to have a (good) ~ of direction** avoir le sens de l'orientation ■ **she lost her ~ of direction when her husband died** *fig* elle a perdu le nord après la mort de son mari ■ **he has a good ~ of humour** il a le sens de l'humour ■ **I try to teach them a ~ of right and wrong** j'essaie de leur inculquer la notion du bien et du mal ■ **she acted out of a ~ of duty/of responsibility** elle a agi par sens du devoir/des responsabilités ■ **they have no business ~ at all** ils n'ont aucun sens des affaires ■ **he has an overdeveloped ~ of his own importance** il est trop imbu de lui-même
3. [practicality, reasonableness] bon sens *m* ■ **to show good ~** faire preuve de bon sens ■ **to see ~** entendre raison ■ **oh, come on, talk ~!** voyons, ne dis pas n'importe quoi! ■ **there's no ~ in all of us going** cela ne sert à rien *OR* c'est inutile d'y aller tous ■ **they didn't even have enough ~ to telephone** ils n'ont même pas eu l'idée de téléphoner ➊ **'Sense and Sensibility'** *Austen* 'Bon sens et sensibilité'
4. [meaning - of word, expression] sens *m*, signification *f* ; [- of text] sens *m* ■ **don't take what I say in its literal ~** ne prenez pas ce que je dis au sens propre *OR* au pied de la lettre ■ **in every ~ of the word** dans tous les sens du terme ■ **I think we have, in a very real ~, grasped the problem** je crois que nous avons parfaitement saisi le problème
5. [coherent message] sens *m* ■ **to make ~** [words] avoir un sens ; [be logical] tenir debout, être sensé ■ **can you make (any) ~ of this message?** est-ce que vous arrivez à comprendre ce message? ■ **it makes/doesn't make ~ to wait** c'est une bonne idée/idiot d'attendre ■ **to talk ~** dire des choses sensées
6. [way] : **in a ~** dans un sens ■ **in no ~** en aucune manière ■ **in the ~ that...** en ce sens que..., dans le sens où...
◇ *vt* **1.** [feel - presence] sentir ; [- danger, catastrophe] pressentir ■ **I ~d as much** c'est bien l'impression *OR* le sentiment que j'avais ■ **I ~d her meaning** j'ai compris ce qu'elle voulait dire
2. ELECTRON détecter ■ COMPUT lire.

◆ **senses** *npl* [sanity, reason] raison *f* ■ **to come to one's ~s** [become conscious] reprendre connaissance ; [be reasonable] revenir à la raison ■ **to take leave of one's ~s** perdre la raison *OR* la tête ■ **to bring sb to his/her ~s** ramener qqn à la raison.

senseless ['senslɪs] *adj* **1.** [futile] insensé, absurde ▪ **it's ~ trying to persuade her** inutile d'essayer *OR* on perd son temps à essayer de la persuader **2.** [unconscious] sans connaissance ▪ **to knock sb ~** assommer qqn.

senselessly ['senslɪslɪ] *adv* stupidement, de façon absurde.

sense organ *n* organe *m* sensoriel *OR* des sens.

sensibility [,sensɪ'bɪlətɪ] (*pl* **sensibilities**) *n* [physical or emotional] sensibilité *f*.
◆ **sensibilities** *npl* susceptibilité *f*, susceptibilités *fpl* ▪ **we must avoid offending our viewers' sensibilities** nous devons éviter de heurter la sensibilité de nos spectateurs.

sensible ['sensəbl] *adj* **1.** [reasonable - choice] judicieux, sensé ; [- reaction] sensé, qui fait preuve de bon sens ; [- person] sensé, doué de bon sens ▪ **it's a very ~ idea** c'est une très bonne idée ▪ **the most ~ thing to do is to phone** la meilleure chose à faire, c'est de téléphoner **2.** [practical - clothes, shoes] pratique ▪ **you need ~ walking shoes** il vous faut de bonnes chaussures de marche **3.** *fml* [notable - change] sensible, appréciable **4.** *fml* & *lit* [aware] : **I am ~ of the fact that things have changed between us** j'ai conscience du fait que les choses ont changé entre nous.

sensibly ['sensəblɪ] *adv* **1.** [reasonably] raisonnablement ▪ **they very ~ decided to give up before someone got hurt** ils ont pris la décision raisonnable de renoncer avant que quelqu'un ne soit blessé ▪ **to be ~ dressed** porter des vêtements pratiques **2.** *fml* [perceptibly] sensiblement, perceptiblement.

sensing ['sensɪŋ] *n (U)* ELECTRON exploration *f*, sondage *m*.

sensitive ['sensɪtɪv] *adj* **1.** [eyes, skin] sensible ▪ **my eyes are very ~ to bright light** j'ai les yeux très sensibles à la lumière vive **2.** [emotionally] sensible ▪ **to be ~ to sthg** être sensible à qqch **3.** [aware] sensibilisé ▪ **the seminar made us more ~ to the problem** le séminaire nous a sensibilisés au problème **4.** [touchy - person] susceptible ; [- age] où l'on est susceptible ; [- public opinion] sensible ▪ **she's very ~ about her height** elle n'aime pas beaucoup qu'on lui parle de sa taille ▪ [difficult - issue, topic] délicat, épineux ▪ **you're touching on a ~ area** vous abordez un sujet délicat *OR* épineux ▪ [information] confidentiel **5.** [instrument] sensible ▪ PHOT [film] sensible ▪ [paper] sensibilisé **6.** ST. EX [market] instable.

-sensitive *in cpds* sensible ▪ **heat~** sensible à la chaleur, thermosensible ▪ **price~** sensible aux fluctuations des prix ▪ **voice~** sensible à la voix.

sensitively ['sensɪtɪvlɪ] *adv* avec sensibilité.

sensitivity [,sensɪ'tɪvətɪ] *n* **1.** [physical] sensibilité *f* **2.** [emotional] sensibilité *f* ▪ [touchiness] susceptibilité *f* **3.** [of equipment] sensibilité *f* **4.** ST. EX instabilité *f*.

sensitize, ise ['sensɪtaɪz] *vt* sensibiliser, rendre sensible.

sensor ['sensəʳ] *n* détecteur *m*, capteur *m*.

sensory ['sensərɪ] *adj* [nerve, system] sensoriel ▪ **~ deprivation** isolation *f* sensorielle.

sensual ['sensjʊəl] *adj* sensuel.

sensualism ['sensjʊəlɪzm] *n* [gen] sensualité *f* ▪ PHILOS sensualisme *m*.

sensualist ['sensjʊəlɪst] *n* [gen] personne *f* sensuelle ▪ PHILOS sensualiste *mf*.

sensuality [,sensjʊ'ælətɪ] *n* sensualité *f*.

sensuous ['sensjʊəs] *adj* [music, arts] qui affecte les sens ▪ [lips, person] sensuel.

sensuously ['sensjʊəslɪ] *adv* voluptueusement, sensuellement.

sensuousness ['sensjʊəsnɪs] *n* volupté *f*.

sent [sent] *pt* & *pp* ⊳ **send**.

sentence ['sentəns] ◇ *n* **1.** GRAM phrase *f* ▪ **~ structure** structure *f* de phrase **2.** LAW condamnation *f*, peine *f*, sentence *f* ▪ **to pass ~ on sb** prononcer une condamnation contre qqn ▪ **to pronounce ~** prononcer la sentence ▪ **under ~ of death** condamné à mort ▪ **he got a 5-year ~ for burglary** il a été condamné à 5 ans de prison *OR* à une peine de 5 ans pour cambriolage.
◇ *vt* LAW condamner ▪ **to ~ sb to life imprisonment** condamner qqn à la prison à perpétuité.

sententious [sen'tenʃəs] *adj* sentencieux, pompeux.

sentient ['senʃɪənt] *adj fml* doué de sensation.

sentiment ['sentɪmənt] *n* **1.** [feeling] sentiment *m* ▪ [opinion] sentiment *m*, avis *m*, opinion *f* ▪ **my ~s exactly** c'est exactement ce que je pense, voilà mon sentiment **2.** [sentimentality] sentimentalité *f*.

sentimental [,sentɪ'mentl] *adj* sentimental ▪ **the photos have ~ value** ces photos ont une valeur sentimentale.

sentimentalism [,sentɪ'mentəlɪzm] *n* sentimentalisme *m*.

sentimentalist [,sentɪ'mentəlɪst] *n* sentimental *m*, - e *f*.

sentimentality [,sentɪmen'tælətɪ] (*pl* **sentimentalities**) *n* sentimentalité *f*, sensiblerie *f pej*.

sentimentalize, ise [,sentɪ'mentəlaɪz] ◇ *vt* [to others] présenter de façon sentimentale ▪ [to o.s.] percevoir de façon sentimentale.
◇ *vi* faire du sentiment.

sentimentally [,sentɪ'mentəlɪ] *adv* sentimentalement, de manière sentimentale.

sentinel ['sentɪnl] *n* sentinelle *f*, factionnaire *m*.

sentry ['sentrɪ] (*pl* **sentries**) *n* sentinelle *f*, factionnaire *m*.

sentry box *n* guérite *f*.

sentry duty *n* MIL faction *f* ▪ **to be on ~** être en *OR* de faction.

Seoul [səʊl] *pr n* Séoul.

sepal ['sepəl] *n* sépale *m*.

separable ['seprəbl] *adj* séparable.

separate ◇ *adj* ['seprət] [different, distinct - category, meaning, issue] distinct, à part ; [- incident] différent ▪ **that's quite a ~ matter** ça, c'est une toute autre affaire ▪ **they sleep in ~ rooms** [children] ils ont chacun leur chambre ; [couple] ils font chambre à part ▪ **administration and finance are in ~ departments** l'administration et les finances relèvent de services différents ▪ **the canteen is ~ from the main building** la cantine se trouve à l'extérieur du bâtiment principal ▪ **begin each chapter on a ~ page** commencez chaque chapitre sur une nouvelle page ▪ **it happened on four ~ occasions** cela s'est produit à quatre reprises ▪ **she likes to keep her home life ~ from the office** elle tient à ce que son travail n'empiète pas sur sa vie privée ▪ **the peaches must be kept ~ from the lemons** les pêches et les citrons ne doivent pas être mélangés ▪ **he was kept ~ from the other children** on le tenait à l'écart *OR* on l'isolait des autres enfants ▪ [independent - entrance, living quarters] indépendant, particulier ; [- existence, organization] indépendant ▪ **they lead very ~ lives** ils mènent chacun leur vie ➋ **they went their ~ ways** *liter* [after meeting] ils sont partis chacun de leur côté ; *fig* [in life] chacun a suivi sa route.
◇ *n* ['seprət] **1.** [in stereo] élément *m* séparé **2.** *US* [offprint] tiré *m* à part.
◇ *vt* ['sepəreɪt] **1.** [divide, set apart] séparer ▪ **the Bosphorus ~s Europe from Asia** le Bosphore sépare l'Europe de l'Asie ▪ **the seriously ill were ~d from the other patients** les malades gravement atteints étaient isolés des autres patients ▪ **the records can be ~d into four categories** les disques peuvent être divisés *OR* classés en quatre catégories ▮ [detach - parts, pieces] séparer, détacher ▪ **the last three coaches will be ~d from the rest of the train** les trois derniers wagons seront détachés du reste du train **2.** [keep distinct] séparer, distinguer ▪ **to ~ reality from myth** distinguer le mythe de la réalité, faire la distinction entre le mythe et la réalité **3.** CULIN [milk] écrémer ▪ [egg] séparer.
◇ *vi* ['sepəreɪt] **1.** [go different ways] se quitter, se séparer **2.** [split up - couple] se séparer, rompre ; [- in boxing, duel] rompre ▪ POL [party] se scinder **3.** [come apart, divide - liquid] se

séparer ; [- parts] se séparer, se détacher, se diviser ▪ **the boosters ~ from the shuttle** les propulseurs auxiliaires se détachent de la navette ▪ **the model ~s into four parts** la maquette se divise en quatre parties.
◆ **separates** *npl* [clothes] coordonnés *mpl*.
◆ **separate out** ◇ *vt sep* séparer, trier.
◇ *vi insep* se séparer.
◆ **separate up** *vt sep* séparer, diviser.

separated ['sepəreɪtɪd] *adj* [not living together] séparé.

separately ['seprətlɪ] *adv* **1.** [apart] séparément, à part **2.** [individually] séparément ▪ **they don't sell yogurts ~** ils ne vendent pas les yaourts à l'unité.

separation [ˌsepə'reɪʃn] *n* **1.** [division] séparation *f* ▪ **her ~ from her family caused her great heartache** sa séparation d'avec sa famille l'a beaucoup chagrinée **2.** [of couple] séparation *f*.

separation allowance *n* **1.** MIL allocation *f* mensuelle *(versée par l'armée à la femme d'un soldat)* **2.** [alimony] pension *f* alimentaire.

separatism ['seprətɪzm] *n* séparatisme *m*.

separatist ['seprətɪst] ◇ *adj* séparatiste.
◇ *n* séparatiste *mf*.

sepia ['si:pjə] ◇ *n* [pigment, print] sépia *f*.
◇ *adj* sépia *(inv)*.

sepoy ['si:pɔɪ] *n* cipaye *m*.

Sept. (*written abbrev of* **September**) sept.

September [sep'tembəʳ] *n* septembre *m*, *see also* **February**.

septet [sep'tet] *n* septuor *m*.

septic ['septɪk] *adj* septique ▪ [wound] infecté ▪ **to go** *OR* **to become ~** s'infecter ▪ **I have a ~ finger** j'ai une blessure infectée au doigt ▪ **~ poisoning** septicémie *f*.

septicaemia *UK*, **septicemia** *US* [ˌseptɪ'si:mɪə] *n (U)* septicémie *f*.

septic tank *n* fosse *f* septique.

septuagenarian [ˌseptjuədʒɪ'neərɪən] ◇ *adj* septuagénaire.
◇ *n* septuagénaire *mf*.

Septuagint ['septjuədʒɪnt] *n* : **the~** la version des Septante.

septum ['septəm] *n* ANAT septum *m*.

septuplet [sep'tju:plɪt] *n* **1.** [baby] septuplé *m*, - e *f* **2.** MUS septolet *m*.

sepulcher *US* = **sepulchre**.

sepulchral [sɪ'pʌlkrəl] *adj* [figure, voice] sépulcral ▪ [atmosphere] funèbre, lugubre.

sepulchre *UK*, **sepulcher** *US* ['sepəlkəʳ] *n* sépulcre *m*.

sequel ['si:kwəl] *n* **1.** [result, aftermath] conséquence *f*, suites *fpl*, conséquences *fpl* ▪ [to illness, war] séquelles *fpl* ▪ **as a ~ to this event** à la suite de cet événement **2.** [to novel, film etc] suite *f*.

sequence ['si:kwəns] ◇ *n* **1.** [order] suite *f*, ordre *m* ▪ **in ~** [in order] par ordre, en série ; [one after another] l'un après l'autre ▪ **numbered in ~** numérotés dans l'ordre ▪ **in historical ~** par ordre chronologique ▪ **~ of tenses** GRAM concordance *f* des temps **2.** [series] série *f* ▪ [in cards] séquence *f* ▪ **the ~ of events** le déroulement *OR* l'enchaînement des événements **3.** CIN & MUS séquence *f* ▪ **dance ~** numéro *m* de danse **4.** LING & MATHS séquence *f* **5.** BIOL & CHEM séquençage *m*.
◇ *vt* **1.** [order] classer, ordonner **2.** BIOL & CHEM séquencer, faire le séquençage de.

sequencer ['si:kwənsəʳ] *n* séquenceur *m*.

sequential [sɪ'kwenʃl] *adj* **1.** COMPUT séquentiel **2.** *fml* [following] subséquent.

sequentially [sɪ'kwenʃəlɪ] *adv* [follow, happen] séquentiellement.

sequester [sɪ'kwestəʳ] *vt* **1.** *fml* [set apart] isoler, mettre à part **2.** *fml* [shut away] séquestrer **3.** LAW [goods, property] séquestrer, placer sous séquestre.

sequestered [sɪ'kwestəd] *adj lit* [place] retiré, isolé ▪ **to lead a ~ life** vivre à l'écart, mener une vie de reclus.

sequestrate [sɪ'kwestreɪt] *vt* **1.** LAW séquestrer, placer sous séquestre **2.** *fml* [confiscate] saisir.

sequestration [ˌsi:kwe'streɪʃn] *n* LAW mise *f* sous séquestre ▪ *fml* [confiscation] saisie *f*.

sequin ['si:kwɪn] *n* paillette *f*.

sequined ['si:kwɪnd] *adj* pailleté.

sequoia [sɪ'kwɔɪə] *n* séquoia *m*.

serac ['seræk] *n* sérac *m*.

seraglio [se'rɑ:lɪəʊ] (*pl* **seraglios**) *n* sérail *m*.

seraph ['serəf] (*pl* **seraphs** *OR pl* **seraphim** ['serəfɪm]) *n* séraphin *m*.

Serb [sɜ:b] ◇ *n* Serbe *mf*.
◇ *adj* serbe.

Serbia ['sɜ:bjə] *pr n* Serbie *f* ▪ **in ~** en Serbie.

Serbian ['sɜ:bjən] ◇ *n* **1.** [person] Serbe *mf* **2.** LING serbe *m*.
◇ *adj* serbe.

Serbo-Croat [ˌsɜ:bəʊ'krəʊæt], **Serbo-Croatian** [ˌsɜ:bəʊkrəʊ'eɪʃn] ◇ *n* LING serbo-croate *m*.
◇ *adj* serbo-croate.

serenade [ˌserə'neɪd] ◇ *n* sérénade *f*.
◇ *vt* [sing] chanter une sérénade à ▪ [play] jouer une sérénade à.

serendipity [ˌserən'dɪpətɪ] *n lit don de faire des découvertes (accidentelles)*.

serene [sɪ'ri:n] *adj* [person, existence, sky] serein ▪ [sea, lake] calme ▪ **His/Her Serene Highness** *fml* Son Altesse Sérénissime.

serenely [sɪ'ri:nlɪ] *adv* sereinement, avec sérénité ▪ **she was ~ unaware of what was going on** elle vivait dans la douce inconscience de ce qui se passait autour d'elle.

serenity [sɪ'renətɪ] *n* sérénité *f*.

serf [sɜ:f] *n* serf *m*, serve *f*.

serfdom ['sɜ:fdəm] *n* servage *m*.

serge [sɜ:dʒ] ◇ *n* serge *f*.
◇ *comp* [cloth, trousers] de *OR* en serge.

sergeant ['sɑ:dʒənt] *n* **1.** [in army] sergent *m*, -e *f* ▪ [in air force] *UK* sergent-chef *m*, sergente-chef *f* ▪ *US* caporal-chef *m*, caporale-chef *f* **2.** [in police] brigadier *m*, -ère *f*.

sergeant-at-arms *n* huissier *m*, -ère *f* d'armes.

sergeant major *n* sergent-chef *m*.

serial ['sɪərɪəl] ◇ *n* **1.** RADIO & TV feuilleton *m* ▪ **TV ~** feuilleton télévisé ▮ [in magazine] feuilleton *m* ▪ **published in ~ form** publié sous forme de feuilleton **2.** [periodical] périodique *m*.
◇ *adj* **1.** [in series] en série ▪ [from series] d'une série ▪ [forming series] formant une série ▪ **in ~ order** en ordre sériel **2.** [music] sériel **3.** COMPUT [processing, transmission] série *(inv)* ▪ **~ port** port *m* série.

serial cable *n* câble *f* série.

serialization, isation [ˌsɪərɪəlaɪ'zeɪʃn] *n* [of book] publication *f* en feuilleton ▪ [of play, film] adaptation *f* en feuilleton.

serialize, ise ['sɪərɪəlaɪz] *vt* [book] publier en feuilleton ▪ [play, film] adapter en feuilleton ▪ [in newspaper] publier *OR* faire paraître en feuilleton.

serial killer *n* tueur *m* en série.

serial killing *n* : **~s** meurtres *mpl* en série.

serially ['sɪərɪəlɪ] *adv* **1.** MATHS en série **2.** PRESS [as series] en feuilleton, sous forme de feuilleton ▪ [periodically] périodiquement, sous forme de périodique.

serial number *n* [of car, publication] numéro *m* de série ▪ [of cheque, voucher] numéro *m* ▪ [of soldier] (numéro *m*) matricule *m*.

serial rights *npl* droits *mpl* de reproduction en feuilleton.

series ['sɪəri:z] (*pl inv*) *n* **1.** [set, group - gen - CHEM] & GEOL série *f* ▪ [sequence - gen - MATHS] séquence *f*, suite *f* **2.** LING & MUS série *f*, séquence *f* ▪ **a whole ~ of catastrophes** toute une série de catastrophes **3.** [of cars, clothes] série *f* ▪ **~ IV computer** ordinateur série IV **4.** RADIO & TV série *f* ▪ **TV ~** série télévisée ‖ [in magazine, newspaper] série *f* d'articles **5.** [collection - of stamps, coins, books] collection *f*, série *f* **6.** ELEC série *f* ▪ **wired in ~** branché en série **7.** SPORT série *f* de matches.

series connection *n* ELEC montage *m* en série.

serious ['sɪərɪəs] *adj* **1.** [not frivolous - suggestion, subject, worker, publication, writer, theatre] sérieux ; [- occasion] solennel ▪ **the book is meant for the ~ student of astronomy** le livre est destiné aux personnes qui possèdent déjà de solides connaissances en astronomie ▪ **can I have a ~ conversation with you?** est-ce qu'on peut parler sérieusement? ▪ **she's a ~ actress** [cinema] elle fait des films sérieux ; [theatre] elle joue dans des pièces sérieuses ▪ **the ~ cinemagoer** le cinéphile averti
2. [in speech, behaviour] sérieux ▪ **I'm quite ~** je suis tout à fait sérieux, je ne plaisante absolument pas ▪ **is she ~ about Peter?** est-ce que c'est sérieux avec Peter?
3. [thoughtful - person, expression] sérieux, plein de sérieux ; [- voice, tone] sérieux, grave ▪ **don't look so ~** ne prends pas cet air sérieux ▪ [careful - examination] sérieux, approfondi ; [- consideration] sérieux, sincère ▪ **to give ~ thought** *OR* **consideration to sthg** songer sérieusement à qqch
4. [grave - mistake, problem, illness] sérieux, grave ▪ **the situation is ~** la situation est préoccupante ▪ **~ crime** crime *m* ▪ **it poses a ~ threat to airport security** cela constitue une menace sérieuse pour la sécurité des aéroports ▪ **his condition is described as ~** MED son état est jugé préoccupant ▪ [considerable - damage] important, sérieux ; [- loss] lourd ; [- doubt] sérieux **5.** *inf* [as intensifier] : **we're talking ~ money here** il s'agit de grosses sommes d'argent ▪ **they go in for some really ~ drinking at the weekends** le week-end, qu'est-ce qu'ils descendent!

seriously ['sɪərɪəslɪ] *adv* **1.** [earnestly] sérieusement, avec sérieux ▪ **to take sb/sthg ~** prendre qqn/qqch au sérieux ▪ **he takes himself too ~** il se prend trop au sérieux ▪ **are you ~ suggesting we sell it?** pensez-vous sérieusement que nous devrions vendre? ▪ **think about it ~ before you do anything** réfléchissez-y bien avant de faire quoi que ce soit ▪ **~ though, what are you going to do?** sérieusement, qu'est-ce que vous allez faire? ▪ **you can't ~ expect me to believe that!** vous plaisantez, j'espère? **2.** [severely - damage] sérieusement, gravement ; [- ill] gravement ; [- injured, wounded] grièvement ▪ **she is ~ worried about him** elle se fait énormément de souci à son sujet **3.**△ [very] : **he's ~ rich** il est bourré de fric.

serious-minded *adj* sérieux.

seriousness ['sɪərɪəsnɪs] *n* **1.** [of person, expression] sérieux *m* ▪ [of voice, manner] (air *m*) sérieux *m* ▪ [of intentions, occasion, writing] sérieux *m* ▪ **in all ~** sérieusement, en toute sincérité **2.** [of illness, situation, loss] gravité *f* ▪ [of allegation] sérieux *m* ▪ [of damage] importance *f*, étendue *f* ▪ **it is a matter of some ~** c'est une affaire assez sérieuse.

serjeant ['sɑ:dʒənt] = **sergeant**.

sermon ['sɜ:mən] *n* **1.** RELIG sermon *m* ▪ **to give** *OR* **to preach a ~** faire un sermon ▪ **the Sermon on the Mount** BIBLE le Sermon sur la Montagne **2.** *fig* & *pej* sermon *m*, laïus *m*.

seronegative [ˌsɪərəʊ'negətɪv] *adj* séronégatif.

seropositive [ˌsɪərʊ'pɒzɪtɪv] *adj* séropositif.

serpent ['sɜ:pənt] *n* serpent *m*.

serpentine ['sɜ:pəntaɪn] ◇ *adj lit* [winding] sinueux, qui serpente.
◇ *n* MINER serpentine *f*.

SERPS [sɜ:ps] (*abbrev of* **State Earnings-Related Pension Scheme**) *n régime de retraite minimal en Grande-Bretagne.*

serrated [sɪ'reɪtɪd] *adj* [edge] en dents de scie, dentelé ▪ [knife, scissors, instrument] cranté, en dents de scie.

serration [sɪ'reɪʃn] *n* dentelure *f*.

serried ['serɪd] *adj* serré ▪ **in ~ ranks** en rangs serrés.

serum ['sɪərəm] (*pl* **serums** *OR pl* **sera** [-rə]) *n* sérum *m*.

servant ['sɜ:vənt] *n* **1.** [in household] domestique *mf* ▪ [maid] bonne *f*, servante *f* ▪ **~s' quarters** appartements *mpl* des domestiques **2.** [of God, of people] serviteur *m* ▪ **politicians are the ~s of the community** les hommes politiques sont au service de la communauté.

servant girl *n* servante *f*, bonne *f*.

serve [sɜ:v] ◇ *vt* **1.** [employer, monarch, country, God] servir ▪ **she has ~d the company well over the years** elle a bien servi la société pendant des années ⊳ **you cannot ~ two masters** *prov* nul ne peut servir deux maîtres *prov*
2. [in shop, restaurant - customer] servir ▪ **to ~ sb with sthg** servir qqch à qqn ▪ **are you being ~d?** est-ce qu'on s'occupe de vous?
3. [provide - with electricity, gas, water] alimenter ; [- with transport service] desservir ▪ **the village is ~d with water from the Roxford reservoir** le village est alimenté en eau depuis le réservoir de Roxford
4. [food, drink] servir ▪ **dinner is ~d** le dîner est servi ▪ **coffee is now being ~d in the lounge** le café est servi au salon ▪ **the wine should be ~d at room temperature** le vin doit être servi chambré ▪ **this recipe ~s four** cette recette est prévue pour quatre personnes ▪ **to ~ mass** RELIG servir la messe
5. [be suitable for] servir ▪ **the plank ~d him as a rudimentary desk** la planche lui servait de bureau rudimentaire ▪ **this box will ~ my purpose** cette boîte fera l'affaire ▪ **when the box had ~d its purpose, he threw it away** quand il n'eut plus besoin de la boîte, il la jeta ▪ **it ~s no useful purpose** cela ne sert à rien de spécial
6. [term, apprenticeship] faire ▪ **he has ~d two terms (of office) as president** il a rempli deux mandats présidentiels ▪ **to ~ one's apprenticeship as an electrician** faire son apprentissage d'électricien ▪ **to ~ one's time** MIL faire son service ‖ [prison sentence] faire ▪ **to ~ time** faire de la prison ▪ **he has ~d his time** il a purgé sa peine ▪ **she ~d four years for armed robbery** elle a fait quatre ans (de prison) pour vol à main armée
7. LAW [summons, warrant, writ] notifier, remettre ▪ **to ~ sb with a summons, to ~ a summons on sb** remettre une assignation à qqn ▪ **to ~ sb with a writ, to ~ a writ on sb** assigner qqn en justice
8. SPORT servir
9. AGRIC servir
10. *phr* **it ~s you right** c'est bien fait pour toi ▪ **it ~s them right for being so selfish!** ça leur apprendra à être si égoïstes!
◇ *vi* **1.** [in shop or restaurant, at table] servir ▪ **Violet ~s in the dining-room in the evenings** Violet s'occupe du service dans la salle à manger le soir ▪ **could you ~, please?** pourriez-vous faire le service, s'il vous plaît? ‖ [be in service - maid, servant] servir
2. [as soldier] servir ▪ **her grandfather ~d under General Adams** son grand-père a servi sous les ordres du général Adams ‖ [in profession] : **he ~d as treasurer for several years** il a exercé les fonctions de trésorier pendant plusieurs années ‖ [on committee] : **she ~s on the housing committee** elle est membre de la commission au logement
3. [function, act - as example, warning] servir ▪ **let that ~ as a lesson to you!** que cela vous serve de leçon! ▪ **it only ~s to show that you shouldn't listen to gossip** cela prouve qu'il ne faut pas écouter les commérages ▪ **the tragedy should ~ as a reminder of the threat posed by nuclear power** cette tragédie devrait rappeler à tous la menace que représente l'énergie nucléaire ▪ [be used as] : **this stone will ~ to keep the door open** cette pierre servira à maintenir la porte ouverte ▪ **their bedroom had to ~ as a cloakroom for their guests** leur chambre a dû servir *OR* faire office de vestiaire pour leurs invités
4. SPORT servir, être au service ▪ **Smith to ~** au service, Smith ▪ **he ~d into the net** son service a échoué dans le filet
5. RELIG servir la messe.
◇ *n* SPORT service *m*.

◆ **serve out** ◇ *vt sep* **1.** [food] servir ▪ [provisions] distribuer

2. [period of time] faire ▪ **the president retired before he had ~d his term out** le président a pris sa retraite avant d'arriver à *OR* d'atteindre la fin de son mandat ▪ **to ~ out a prison sentence** purger une peine (de prison).
◇ *vi insep* SPORT sortir son service.
◆ **serve up** *vt sep* [meal, food] servir ▪ *fig* [facts, information] servir, débiter ▪ **she ~s up the same old excuse every time** elle ressort chaque fois la même excuse.

server ['sɜːvəʳ] *n* **1.** [at table] serveur *m*, - euse *f* **2.** SPORT serveur *m*, - euse *f* **3.** RELIG servant *m* **4.** [utensil] couvert *m* de service **5.** COMPUT serveur *m*.

servery ['sɜːvərɪ] (*pl* **serveries**) *n* [hatch] guichet *m*, passe-plat *m* ▪ [counter] comptoir *m*.

service ['sɜːvɪs] ◇ *n* **1.** [to friend, community, country, God] service *m* ▪ **in the ~ of one's country** au service de sa patrie ▪ **to require the ~s of a priest/of a doctor** avoir recours aux services d'un prêtre/d'un médecin ▪ **many people gave their ~s free** beaucoup de gens donnaient des prestations bénévoles ▪ **at your ~** à votre service, à votre disposition ▪ **to be of ~ to sb** rendre service à qqn, être utile à qqn ▪ **she's always ready to be of ~** elle est très serviable, elle est toujours prête à rendre service ▪ **the jug had to do ~ as a teapot** le pichet a dû faire office de *OR* servir de théière ▪ **to do sb a ~** rendre (un) service à qqn ▪ **the car has given us/has seen good ~** la voiture nous a bien servi/a fait long usage
2. [employment - in firm] service *m* ▪ **bonuses depend on length of ~** les primes sont versées en fonction de l'ancienneté ▪ [as domestic servant] service ▪ **to be in ~** être domestique ▪ **he's in lord Bellamy's ~** il est au service de Lord Bellamy
3. [in shop, hotel, restaurant] service *m* ▪ **you get fast ~ in a supermarket** on est servi rapidement dans un supermarché ▪ **'10% ~ included/not included'** 'service 10 % compris/non compris' ▪ **~ with a smile** [slogan] servi avec le sourire
4. MIL service *m* ▪ **he saw active ~ in Korea** il a servi en Corée, il a fait la campagne de Corée ▪ **the ~s** les (différentes branches des) forces armées ▪ **their son is in the ~s** leur fils est dans les forces armées
5. ADMIN [department, scheme] service *m* ▪ **a new 24-hour banking ~** un nouveau service bancaire fonctionnant 24 heures sur 24 ▪ **a bus provides a ~ between the two stations** un autobus assure la navette entre les deux gares
6. RELIG [Catholic] service *m*, office *m* ▪ [Protestant] service *m*, culte *m* ▪ **to attend (a) ~** assister à l'office *OR* au culte
7. [of car, machine - upkeep] entretien *m* ; [- overhaul] révision *f*
8. [working order - esp of machine] service *m* ▪ **to bring a machine into ~** mettre une machine en service ▪ **to come into ~** [system, bridge] entrer en service ▪ **the cash dispenser isn't in ~ at the moment** le distributeur automatique de billets est hors service *OR* n'est pas en service en ce moment
9. [set of tableware] service *m*
10. SPORT service *m* ▪ **Smith broke his opponent's ~** Smith a pris le service de son adversaire *OR* a fait le break
11. LAW [of summons, writ] signification *f*, notification *f*.
◇ *comp* **1.** [entrance, hatch, stairs] de service
2. AUT & MECH [manual, record] d'entretien
3. MIL [family, pay] de militaire ▪ [conditions] dans les forces armées.
◇ *vt* **1.** [overhaul - central heating, car] réviser
2. FIN [debt] assurer le service de
3. AGRIC [subj: bull, stallion] servir.
◆ **services** *npl* **1.** *UK* [on motorway] aire *f* de service
2. COMM & ECON services *mpl* ▪ **more and more people will be working in ~s** de plus en plus de gens travailleront dans le tertiaire.

serviceable ['sɜːvɪsəbl] *adj* **1.** [durable - clothes, material] qui fait de l'usage, qui résiste à l'usure ; [- machine, construction] durable, solide **2.** [useful - clothing, tool] commode, pratique **3.** [usable] utilisable, qui peut servir **4.** [ready for use] prêt à servir.

service area *n* **1.** AUT [on motorway] aire *f* de service **2.** RADIO zone *f* desservie *OR* de réception.

service charge *n* service *m*.

service company *n* entreprise *f* prestataire de services.

service game *n* TENNIS jeu *m* de service.

service industry *n* industrie *f* de services.

service line *n* SPORT ligne *f* de service.

serviceman ['sɜːvɪsmən] (*pl* **servicemen** [-mən]) *n* **1.** MIL militaire *m* **2.** *US* [mechanic] dépanneur *m*.

service provider *n* fournisseur *m* de services.

service road *n* [behind shops, factory] *voie d'accès réservée aux livreurs* ▪ [on motorway] *voie d'accès réservée à l'entretien et aux services d'urgence*.

service station *n* station-service *f*.

servicewoman ['sɜːvɪsˌwʊmən] (*pl* **servicewomen** [-ˌwɪmɪn]) *n* femme *f* soldat.

servicing ['sɜːvɪsɪŋ] *n* **1.** [of heating, car] entretien *m* **2.** [by transport] desserte *f*.

serviette [ˌsɜːvɪ'et] *n UK* serviette *f* (de table) ▪ **~ ring** rond *m* de serviette.

servile ['sɜːvaɪl] *adj* [person, behaviour] servile, obséquieux ▪ [admiration, praise] servile ▪ [condition, task] servile, d'esclave.

serving ['sɜːvɪŋ] ◇ *n* **1.** [of drinks, meal] service *m* **2.** [helping] portion *f*, part *f*.
◇ *adj* ADMIN [member, chairman] actuel, en exercice.

servitude ['sɜːvɪtjuːd] *n* servitude *f*.

servo ['sɜːvəʊ] (*pl* **servos**) ◇ *adj* servo-.
◇ *n* [mechanism] servomécanisme *m* ▪ [motor] servomoteur *m*.

servo-assisted [-ə'sɪstɪd] *adj* TECH assisté ▪ **~ brakes** freinage *m* assisté, servofreins *mpl*.

servomotor ['sɜːvəʊˌməʊtəʳ] *n* servomoteur *m*.

sesame ['sesəmɪ] *n* sésame *m* ▪ **open ~!** sésame, ouvre-toi!

sesame oil *n* huile *f* de sésame.

sesame seed *n* graine *f* de sésame.

session ['seʃn] *n* **1.** ADMIN, LAW & POL séance *f*, session *f* ▪ **this court is now in ~** l'audience est ouverte ▪ **the House is not in ~ during the summer months** la Chambre ne siège pas pendant les mois d'été ▪ **to go into secret ~** siéger à huis clos **2.** [interview, meeting, sitting] séance *f* ▪ [for painter, photographer] séance *f* de pose ▪ **a drinking ~** une beuverie **3.** SCH [classes] cours *mpl* **4.** *US* & *Scotland* UNIV [term] trimestre *m* ▪ [year] année *f* universitaire **5.** RELIG conseil *m* presbytéral.

session musician *n* musicien *m*, - enne *f* de studio.

set [set] (*pret & pp* **set**, *cont* **setting**) ◇ *vt*

A.

1. [put in specified place or position] mettre, poser ▪ **she ~ the steaming bowl before him** elle plaça le bol fumant devant lui ▪ **to ~ sb ashore** débarquer qqn
2. (*usu passive*) [locate, situate - building, story] situer ▪ **the house is ~ in large grounds** la maison est située dans un grand parc ▪ **his eyes are ~ too close together** ses yeux sont trop rapprochés ▪ **the story is ~ in Tokyo** l'histoire se passe *OR* se déroule à Tokyo
3. [adjust - gen] régler ; [- mechanism] mettre ▪ **I've ~ the alarm for six** j'ai mis le réveil à (sonner pour) six heures ▪ **how do I ~ the margins?** comment est-ce que je fais pour placer les marges? ▪ **~ the timer for one hour** mettez le minuteur sur une heure ▪ **~ your watches an hour ahead** avancez vos montres d'une heure ▪ **I ~ my watch to New York time** j'ai réglé ma montre à l'heure de New York ▪ **he's so punctual you can ~ your watch by him!** il est si ponctuel qu'on peut régler sa montre sur lui!
4. [fix into position] mettre, fixer ▪ [jewel, diamond] sertir, monter ▪ **to ~ a bone** réduire une fracture ▪ **the brooch was ~ with pearls** la broche était sertie de perles ▪ **the handles are ~ into the drawers** les poignées sont encastrées dans les tiroirs ▪ **there was a peephole ~ in the door** il y avait un judas dans la porte
5. [lay, prepare in advance - table] mettre ; [- trap] poser, tendre ▪ **~ an extra place at table** rajoutez un couvert

6. [place - in hierarchy] placer ■ **they ~ a high value on creativity** ils accordent une grande valeur à la créativité
7. [establish - date, schedule, price, terms] fixer, déterminer ; [- rule, guideline, objective, target] établir ; [- mood, precedent] créer ■ **you've ~ yourself a tough deadline** *OR* **a tough deadline for yourself** vous vous êtes fixé un délai très court ■ **a deficit ceiling has been ~** un plafonnement du déficit a été imposé *OR* fixé *OR* décidé ■ **how are exchange rates ~?** comment les taux de change sont-ils déterminés? ■ **to ~ a new fashion** *OR* **trend** lancer une nouvelle mode ■ **to ~ a new world record** établir un nouveau record mondial ■ **to ~ the tone for** *OR* **of sthg** donner le ton de qqch

B.
1. [indicating change of state or activity] : **to ~ sthg alight** *OR* **on fire** mettre le feu à qqch ■ **it ~s my nerves on edge** ça me crispe ■ **to ~ sb against sb** monter qqn contre qqn ■ **to ~ the dogs on sb** lâcher les chiens sur qqn ■ **to ~ sb against sb** monter qqn contre qqn ■ **the incident ~ the family against him** l'incident a monté la famille contre lui ■ **it will ~ the country on the road to economic recovery** cela va mettre le pays sur la voie de la reprise économique ■ **his failure ~ him thinking** son échec lui a donné à réfléchir ■ **the scandal will ~ the whole town talking** le scandale va faire jaser toute la ville ■ **to ~ a machine going** mettre une machine en marche
2. [solidify - yoghurt, jelly, concrete] faire prendre ■ **pectin will help to ~ the jam** la pectine aidera à épaissir la confiture
3. [make firm, rigid] : **his face was ~ in a frown** son visage était figé dans une grimace renfrognée ■ **she ~ her jaw and refused to budge** elle serra les dents et refusa de bouger
4. [pose - problem] poser ■ [assign - task] fixer ■ **I ~ them to work tidying the garden** je les ai mis au désherbage du jardin ■ **I've ~ myself the task of writing to them regularly** je me suis fixé la tâche de leur écrire régulièrement
5. *UK* SCH [exam] composer, choisir les questions de ■ [books, texts] mettre au programme ■ **she ~ the class a maths exercise, she ~ a maths exercise for the class** elle a donné un exercice de maths à la classe
6. [hair] : **to ~ sb's hair** faire une mise en plis à qqn
7. HORT [plant] planter
8. TYPO [text, page] composer
9. MUS [poem, words] : **to ~ sthg to music** mettre qqch en musique.
◇ *vi* **1.** [sun, stars] se coucher **2.** [become firm - glue, cement, plaster, jelly, yoghurt] prendre **3.** [bone] se ressouder **4.** *(with infinitive)* [start] se mettre ■ **he ~ to work** il s'est mis au travail **5.** [plant, tree] prendre racine **6.** [hen] couver **7.** [wind] : **the wind looks ~ fair to the east** on dirait un vent d'ouest.
◇ *n* **1.** [of facts, conditions, characteristics] ensemble *m* ■ [of people] groupe *m* ■ [of events, decisions, questions] série *f*, suite *f* ■ [of numbers, names, instructions, stamps, weights] série *f* ■ [of tools, keys, golf clubs, sails] jeu *m* ■ [of books] collection *f* ■ [of furniture] ensemble *m* ■ [of dishes] service *m* ■ [of tyres] train *m* ■ PRINT [of proofs, characters] jeu *m* ■ **they make a ~** ils vont ensemble ■ **they've detected two ~s of fingerprints** ils ont relevé deux séries d'empreintes digitales *OR* les empreintes digitales de deux personnes ■ **given another ~ of circumstances, things might have turned out differently** dans d'autres circonstances, les choses auraient pu se passer différemment ■ **he made me a duplicate ~** [keys] il m'a fait un double des clés ; [contact lenses] il m'en a fait une autre paire ■ **the first ~ of reforms** la première série *OR* le premier train de réformes ■ **a full ~ of the encyclopedia** une encyclopédie complète ■ **they ran a whole ~ of tests on me** ils m'ont fait subir toute une série d'examens ■ **the cups/the chairs are sold in ~s of six** les tasses/les chaises sont vendues par six ■ **I can't break up the ~** je ne peux pas les dépareiller ■ **a ~ of matching luggage** un ensemble de valises assorties ■ **a ~ of table/bed linen** une parure de table/de lit ▶ **badminton/chess ~** jeu de badminton/d'échecs ■ **they're playing with Damian's train ~** ils jouent avec le train de Damian **2.** [social group] cercle *m*, milieu *m* ■ **the riding/yachting ~** le monde de l'équitation/du yachting **3.** MATHS ensemble *m* **4.** [electrical device] appareil *m* ■ RADIO & TV poste *m* ■ **a colour TV ~** un poste de télévision *OR* un téléviseur couleur **5.** SPORT set *m*, manche *f* **6.** [scenery - CIN], THEAT & TV décor *m* ■ [place - CIN] & TV plateau *m* ■ THEAT scène *f* ■ **on (the) ~** CIN & TV sur le plateau ; THEAT sur scène ▶ **~ designer** CIN & TV chef décorateur *m* **7.** [part of performance - by singer, group] : **he'll be playing two ~s tonight** il va jouer à deux reprises ce soir ■ **her second ~ was livelier** la deuxième partie de son spectacle a été plus animée **8.** [for hair] mise *f* en plis **9.** [posture - of shoulders, body] position *f*, attitude *f* ; [- of head] port *m* ■ **I could tell he was angry by the ~ of his jaw** rien qu'à la façon dont il serrait les mâchoires, j'ai compris qu'il était en colère **10.** [direction - of wind, current] direction *f* **11.** PSYCHOL [tendency] tendance *f* **12.** HORT [seedling] semis *m* ■ [cutting] bouture *f* ■ **tomato/tulip ~s** tomates/tulipes à repiquer **13.** [clutch of eggs] couvée *f*.
◇ *adj* **1.** [specified, prescribed - rule, quantity, sum, wage] fixe ■ **meals are at ~ times** les repas sont servis à heures fixes ■ **there are no ~ rules for raising children** il n'y a pas de règles toutes faites pour l'éducation des enfants ■ **the tasks must be done in the ~ order** les tâches doivent être accomplies dans l'ordre prescrit ▶ **~ menu** *OR* **meal** *UK* menu *m* **2.** [fixed, rigid - ideas, views] arrêté ; [- smile, frown] figé ■ **her day followed a ~ routine** sa journée se déroulait selon un rituel immuable ■ **to become ~ in one's ways/one's views** devenir rigide dans ses habitudes/ses opinions ■ **~ expression** *OR* **phrase** GRAM expression *f* figée **3.** [intent, resolute] résolu, déterminé ■ **to be ~ on** *OR* **upon sthg** vouloir qqch à tout prix ■ **I'm (dead) ~ on finishing it tonight** je suis (absolument) déterminé à le finir ce soir ■ **he's dead ~ against it** il s'y oppose formellement **4.** [ready, in position] prêt **5.** [likely] probablement ■ **he seems well ~ to win** il semble être sur la bonne voie *OR* être bien parti pour gagner ■ **house prices are ~ to rise steeply** les prix de l'immobilier vont vraisemblablement monter en flèche **6.** *UK* SCH [book, subject] au programme.

➡ **set about** *vt insep* **1.** [start - task] se mettre à ■ **I didn't know how to ~ about it** je ne savais pas comment m'y prendre ■ **how does one ~ about getting a visa?** comment fait-on pour obtenir un visa? **2.** [attack] attaquer, s'en prendre à.

➡ **set against** *vt sep* **1.** FIN [offset] : **some of these expenses can be ~ against tax** certaines de ces dépenses peuvent être déduites des impôts **2.** [friends, family] monter contre.

➡ **set ahead** *vt sep US* **to ~ the clock ahead** avancer l'horloge ■ **we're setting the clocks ahead tonight** on change d'heure cette nuit.

➡ **set apart** *vt sep* **1.** *(usu passive)* [place separately] mettre à part *OR* de côté ■ **there was one deck chair ~ slightly apart from the others** il y avait une chaise longue un peu à l'écart des autres **2.** [distinguish] distinguer ■ **her talent ~s her apart from the other students** son talent la distingue des autres étudiants.

➡ **set aside** *vt sep* **1.** [put down - knitting, book] poser **2.** [reserve, keep - time, place] réserver ; [- money] mettre de côté ■ [arable land] mettre en friche ■ **the room is ~ aside for meetings** la pièce est réservée aux réunions **3.** [overlook, disregard] mettre de côté, oublier, passer sur **4.** [reject - dogma, proposal, offer] rejeter ■ [annul - contract, will] annuler ■ LAW [verdict, judgment] casser.

➡ **set back** *vt sep* **1.** [towards the rear] : **the building is ~ back slightly from the road** l'immeuble est un peu en retrait par rapport à la route **2.** [delay - plans, progress] retarder ■ **his illness ~ him back a month in his work** sa maladie l'a retardé d'un mois dans son travail **3.** *inf* [cost] coûter.

➡ **set down** *vt sep* **1.** [tray, bag etc] poser **2.** *UK* [passenger] déposer **3.** [note, record] noter, inscrire ■ **try and ~ your thoughts down on paper** essayez de mettre vos pensées par écrit **4.** [establish - rule, condition] établir, fixer ■ **it is clearly ~ down that drivers must be insured** il est clairement signalé *OR* indiqué que tout conducteur doit être assuré.

➡ **set forth** ◇ *vi insep lit* = **set off**.
◇ *vt insep fml* [expound - plan, objections] exposer, présenter ■ **the recommendations are ~ forth in the last chapter** les recommandations sont détaillées *OR* énumérées dans le dernier chapitre.

➡ **set in** ◇ *vi insep* [problems] survenir, surgir ■ [disease] se déclarer ■ [winter] commencer ■ [night] tomber ■ **if infection ~s in** si la plaie s'infecte ■ **the bad weather has ~ in for the winter** le mauvais temps s'est installé pour tout l'hiver ■ **panic ~ in** [began] la panique éclata ; [lasted] la panique s'installa.
◇ *vt sep* SEW [sleeve] rapporter.

➡ **set off** ◇ *vi insep* partir, se mettre en route ■ **after lunch, we ~ off again** après le déjeuner, nous avons repris la route.
◇ *vt sep* **1.** [alarm] déclencher ■ [bomb] faire exploser ■ [fireworks] faire partir **2.** [reaction, process, war] déclencher,

provoquer ■ **to ~ sb off laughing** faire rire qqn ■ **it ~ her off on a long tirade against bureaucracy** cela eut pour effet de la lancer dans une longue tirade contre la bureaucratie **3.** [enhance] mettre en valeur **4.** FIN [offset] : **some of these expenses can be ~ off against tax** certaines de ces dépenses peuvent être déduites des impôts.

set on = set upon.

set out <> *vi insep* **1.** = set off **2.** [undertake course of action] entreprendre ■ **he has trouble finishing what he ~s out to do** il a du mal à terminer ce qu'il entreprend ■ **I can't remember now what I ~ out to do** je ne me souviens plus de ce que je voulais faire à l'origine ■ **they all ~ out with the intention of changing the world** au début, ils veulent tous changer le monde ■ **she didn't deliberately ~ out to annoy you** il n'était pas dans ses intentions de vous froisser.

<> *vt sep* **1.** [arrange - chairs, game pieces] disposer ■ [spread out - merchandise] étaler **2.** [design] concevoir **3.** [present] exposer, présenter.

set to *vi insep* [begin work] commencer, s'y mettre.

set up <> *vt sep* **1.** [install - equipment, computer] installer ■ [put in place - roadblock] installer, disposer ; [- experiment] préparer ■ **everything's ~ up for the show** tout est préparé *OR* prêt pour le spectacle ■ **~ the chairs up in a circle** mettez *OR* disposez les chaises en cercle ■ **he ~ the chessboard up** il a disposé les pièces sur l'échiquier ■ *fig* **to ~ up a meeting** organiser une réunion ■ **the system wasn't ~ up to handle so many users** le système n'était pas conçu pour gérer autant d'usagers ■ **he ~ the situation up so she couldn't refuse** il a arrangé la situation de telle manière qu'elle ne pouvait pas refuser **2.** [erect, build - tent, furniture kit, crane, flagpole] monter ; [- shed, shelter] construire ; [- monument, statue] ériger ■ **to ~ up camp** installer *OR* dresser le camp **3.** [start up, institute - business, scholarship] créer ; [- hospital, school] fonder ; [- committee, task force] constituer ; [- system of government, republic] instaurer ; [- programme, review process, system] mettre en place ; [- inquiry] ouvrir ■ **to ~ up house** *OR* **home** s'installer ■ **they ~ up house together** ils se sont mis en ménage ■ **to ~ up a dialogue** entamer le dialogue ■ **you'll be in charge of setting up training programmes** vous serez responsable de la mise en place des programmes de formation **4.** [financially, in business] installer, établir ■ **he ~ his son up in a dry-cleaning business** il a acheté à son fils une entreprise de nettoyage à sec ■ **she could finally ~ herself up as an accountant** elle pourrait enfin s'installer comme comptable ■ **the money would ~ him up for life** l'argent le mettrait à l'abri du besoin pour le restant de ses jours **5.** [provide] : **we're well ~ up with supplies** nous sommes bien approvisionnés ■ **she can ~ you up with a guide/the necessary papers** elle peut vous procurer un guide/les papiers qu'il vous faut ■ **I can ~ you up with a girlfriend of mine** je peux te présenter à *OR* te faire rencontrer une de mes copines **6.** [restore energy to] remonter, remettre sur pied **7.** *inf* [frame] monter un coup contre ■ **she claims she was ~ up** elle prétend qu'elle est victime d'un coup monté.

<> *vi insep* s'installer, s'établir ■ **he's setting up in the fast-food business** il se lance dans la restauration rapide ■ **to ~ up on one's own** [business] s'installer à son compte ; [home] prendre son propre appartement.

set upon *vt insep* [physically or verbally] attaquer, s'en prendre à.

set-aside *n* mise *f* en jachère.

setback ['setbæk] *n* revers *m*, échec *m* ■ [minor] contretemps *m*.

set designer *n* THEAT, CIN & TV décorateur *m*, - trice *f*.

set piece *n* **1.** [ART - LIT] & MUS morceau *m* de bravoure **2.** [fireworks] pièce *f* (de feu) d'artifice **3.** [of scenery] élément *m* de décor.

set point *n* TENNIS balle *f* de set.

setsquare ['setskweəʳ] *n* équerre *f* (*à dessiner*).

sett [set] *n* **1.** [for paving] pavé *m* **2.** [of badger] terrier *m* (de blaireau).

settee [se'ti:] *n* canapé *m*.

setter ['setəʳ] *n* **1.** [dog] setter *m* **2.** [of jewels] sertisseur *m*.

set theory *n* théorie *f* des ensembles.

setting ['setɪŋ] *n* **1.** [of sun, moon] coucher *m* **2.** [situation, surroundings] cadre *m*, décor *m* ■ THEAT décor *m* ■ **they photographed the foxes in their natural ~** ils ont photographié les renards dans leur milieu naturel ■ **the film has Connemara as its ~** le film a pour cadre le Connemara **3.** [position, level - of machine, instrument] réglage *m* **4.** [for jewels] monture *f* ■ [of jewels] sertissage *m* **5.** [at table] set *m* de table **6.** MUS [of poem, play] mise *f* en musique ■ [for instruments] arrangement *m*, adaptation *f* **7.** [of fracture] réduction *f* ■ [in plaster] plâtrage *m* **8.** [of jam] prise *f* ■ [of cement] prise *f*, durcissement *m* **9.** TYPO composition *f*.

setting lotion *n* lotion *f* pour mise en plis.

setting-up *n* [of company, organization] lancement *m*, création *f* ■ [of enquiry] ouverture *f*.

settle ['setl] <> *vt* **1.** [solve - question, issue] régler ; [- dispute, quarrel, differences] régler, trancher ■ **the case was ~d out of court** l'affaire a été réglée à l'amiable ■ **to ~ old scores** régler des comptes

2. [determine, agree on - date, price] fixer ■ **it was ~d that I would go to boarding school** il fut convenu *OR* décidé que j'irais en pension ■ **you must ~ that among yourselves** il va falloir que vous arrangiez cela entre vous ■ **nothing is ~d yet** rien n'est encore décidé *OR* arrêté ■ **that's one point ~d** voilà déjà un point d'acquis ■ **that's that ~d then!** voilà une affaire réglée! ■ **that's ~d then, I'll meet you at 8 o'clock** alors c'est entendu *OR* convenu, on se retrouve à 8 h ■ **that ~s it, the party's tomorrow!** c'est décidé, la fête aura lieu demain! ■ **that ~s it, he's fired** trop c'est trop, il est renvoyé!

3. [pay - debt, account, bill] régler ■ **to ~ one's affairs** mettre ses affaires en ordre, régler ses affaires ■ **to ~ a claim** [insurance] régler un litige

4. [install] installer ■ **he ~d the children for the night** il a mis les enfants au lit, il est allé coucher les enfants ■ **to get ~d** s'installer (confortablement) ■ [arrange, place - on table, surface] installer, poser (soigneusement)

5. [colonize] coloniser ■ **Peru was ~d by the Spanish** le Pérou a été colonisé par les Espagnols, les Espagnols se sont établis au Pérou

6. [calm - nerves, stomach] calmer, apaiser ■ **the rain ~d the dust** la pluie a fait retomber la poussière

7. LAW [money, allowance, estate] constituer ■ **to ~ an annuity on sb** constituer une rente à qqn ■ **she ~d all her money on her nephew** elle a légué toute sa fortune à son neveu ■ **how are you ~d for money at the moment?** *fig* est-ce que tu as suffisamment d'argent en ce moment?

<> *vi* **1.** [go to live - gen] s'installer, s'établir ; [- colonist] s'établir

2. [become calm - nerves, stomach, storm] s'apaiser, se calmer ; [- situation] s'arranger ■ **wait for things to ~ before you do anything** attends que les choses se calment *OR* s'arrangent avant de faire quoi que ce soit

3. [install o.s. - in new flat, bed] s'installer ■ **to ~ for the night** s'installer pour la nuit ■ [adapt - to circumstances] s'habituer ■ **I just can't ~ to my work somehow** je ne sais pas pourquoi, mais je suis incapable de me concentrer sur mon travail

4. [come to rest - snow] tenir ; [- dust, sediment] se déposer ; [- bird, insect, eyes] se poser ■ **let your dinner ~ before you go out** prends le temps de digérer avant de sortir

5. [spread] : **a look of utter contentment ~d on his face** son visage prit une expression de profonde satisfaction ■ **an eerie calm ~d over the village** un calme inquiétant retomba sur le village ■ **the cold ~d on his chest** le rhume lui est tombé sur la poitrine

6. CONSTR [road, wall, foundations] se tasser ■ **'contents may ~ during transport'** le contenu risque de se tasser pendant le transport

7. [financially] : **to ~ with sb for sthg** régler le prix de qqch à qqn ■ **to ~ out of court** régler une affaire à l'amiable

8. [decide] se décider ■ **they've ~d on a Volkswagen** ils se sont décidés pour une Volkswagen ■ **they've ~d on Rome for their honeymoon** ils ont décidé d'aller passer leur lune de miel à Rome ■ **they ~d on a compromise solution** ils ont finalement choisi le compromis.

<> *n* [seat] banquette *f* à haut dossier.

settle down <> *vi insep* **1.** [in armchair, at desk] s'installer ■ [in new home] s'installer, se fixer ■ [at school, in job]

s'habituer, s'adapter ▪ **to ~ down to watch television** s'installer (confortablement) devant la télévision ▪ **to ~ down to work** se mettre au travail
2. *fig* [become stable - people] se ranger, s'assagir ▪ **it's about time Tom got married and ~d down** il est temps que Tom se marie et s'installe dans la vie ▪ **they never ~ down anywhere for long** ils ne se fixent jamais nulle part bien longtemps
3. [concentrate, apply o.s.] : **to ~ down to do sthg** se mettre à faire qqch ▪ **I can't seem to ~ down to anything these days** je n'arrive pas à me concentrer sur quoi que ce soit ces jours-ci
4. [become calm - excitement] s'apaiser ; [- situation] s'arranger.
◇ *vt sep* [person] installer ▪ **to ~ o.s. down in an armchair** s'installer (confortablement) dans un fauteuil.

◆ **settle for** *vt insep* accepter, se contenter de ▪ **I won't ~ for less than £200** 200 livres, c'est mon dernier prix, je ne descendrai pas au-dessous de 200 livres ▪ **they ~d for a compromise** ils ont choisi une solution de compromis.

◆ **settle in** *vi insep* [at new house] s'installer ▪ [at new school, job] s'habituer, s'adapter ▪ **once we're ~d in, we'll invite you round** une fois que nous serons installés, nous t'inviterons.

◆ **settle into** ◇ *vt insep* [job, routine] s'habituer à, s'adapter à ▪ **life soon ~d into the usual dull routine** la vie reprit bientôt son rythme monotone.
◇ *vt sep* installer dans.

◆ **settle up** ◇ *vi insep* régler (la note) ▪ **I must ~ up with the plumber** il faut que je règle le plombier ▪ **can we ~ up?** est-ce qu'on peut faire les comptes?
◇ *vt sep* régler.

settled ['setld] *adj* **1.** [stable, unchanging - person] rangé, établi ; [- life] stable, régulier ; [- habits] régulier ▪ **he's very ~ in his ways** il est très routinier, il a ses petites habitudes **2.** MÉTÉOR [calm] beau *(before vowel or silent 'h'* **bel***)*, belle *f* ▪ **the weather will remain ~** le temps demeurera au beau fixe **3.** [inhabited] peuplé ▪ [colonized] colonisé **4.** [fixed - population] fixe, établi **5.** [account, bill] réglé.

settlement ['setlmənt] *n* **1.** [resolution - of question, dispute] règlement *m*, solution *f* ▪ [of problem] solution *f* **2.** [payment] règlement *m* ▪ **out-of-court ~** règlement à l'amiable **3.** [agreement] accord *m* ▪ **to reach a ~** parvenir à OR conclure un accord ▪ **wage ~** accord salarial **4.** [decision - on details, date] décision *f* ▪ **~ of the final details will take some time** il faudra un certain temps pour régler les derniers détails **5.** LAW [financial] donation *f* ▪ [dowry] dot *f* ▪ [of annuity] constitution *f* ▪ **to make a ~ on sb** faire une donation à OR en faveur de qqn **6.** [colony] colonie *f* ▪ [village] village *m* ▪ [dwellings] habitations *fpl* **7.** [colonization] colonisation *f*, peuplement *m* ▪ **signs of human ~** des traces d'une présence humaine **8.** [of contents, road] tassement *m* ▪ [of sediment] dépôt *m*.

settler ['setlər] *n* colonisateur *m*, - trice *f*, colon *m*.

settling ['setlɪŋ] *n* **1.** [of question, problem, dispute] règlement *m* **2.** [of account, debt] règlement *m* **3.** [of contents] tassement *m* **4.** [of country] colonisation *f*.

◆ **settlings** *npl* [sediment] dépôt *m*, sédiment *m*.

set-to (*pl* **set-tos**) *n inf* [fight] bagarre *f* ▪ [argument] prise *f* de bec.

set-top box *n* boîtier *m* électronique.

set-up *n* **1.** [arrangement, system] organisation *f*, système *m* ▪ **the project manager explained the ~ to me** le chef de projet m'a expliqué comment les choses fonctionnaient OR étaient organisées ▪ **this is the ~** voici comment ça se passe **2.** *inf* [frame-up] coup *m* monté.

seven ['sevn] ◇ *det* sept.
◇ *n* sept *m inv*.
◇ *pron* sept, *see also* **five**.

seven-eleven *n supérette ouverte tard le soir.*

sevenfold ['sevnfəuld] ◇ *adj* septuple.
◇ *adv* au septuple ▪ **profits have increased ~** les bénéfices ont été multipliés par sept.

seven seas *npl* : **the ~** toutes les mers (du monde) ▪ **to sail the ~** parcourir les mers.

seventeen [,sevn'ti:n] ◇ *det* dix-sept.
◇ *n* dix-sept *m inv*.
◇ *pron* dix-sept, *see also* **five**.

seventeenth [,sevn'ti:nθ] ◇ *det* dix-septième.
◇ *n* [ordinal] dix-septième *mf* ▪ [fraction] dix-septième *m*, *see also* **fifth**.

seventh ['sevnθ] ◇ *det* septième.
◇ *n* [ordinal] septième *mf* ▪ [fraction] septième *m* ▪ MUS septième *f*.
◇ *adv* [in contest] en septième position, à la septième place, *see also* **fifth**.

seventh heaven *n* le septième ciel ▪ **to be in (one's) ~** être au septième ciel.

seventieth ['sevntjəθ] ◇ *det* soixante-dixième.
◇ *n* [ordinal] soixante-dixième *mf* ▪ [fraction] soixante-dixième *m*, *see also* **fifth**.

seventy ['sevntɪ] (*pl* **seventies**) ◇ *det* soixante-dix.
◇ *n* soixante-dix *m inv*.
◇ *pron* soixante-dix, *see also* **fifty**.

seventy-eight *n* [record] 78 tours *m inv*.

seven-year itch *n hum* tentation *f* d'infidélité *(après sept ans de mariage)*.

sever ['sevər] ◇ *vt* **1.** [cut off - rope, limb] couper, trancher ▪ **his hand was ~ed (at the wrist)** il a eu la main coupée (au poignet) ▪ **the roadworks ~ed a watermain** les travaux ont crevé une canalisation d'eau ▪ **communications with outlying villages have been ~ed** les communications avec les villages isolés ont été rompues **2.** [cease - relationship, contact] cesser, rompre ▪ **she ~ed all ties with her family** elle a rompu tous les liens avec sa famille.
◇ *vi* se rompre, casser, céder.

several ['sevrəl] ◇ *det* plusieurs ▪ **on ~ occasions** à plusieurs occasions OR reprises.
◇ *pron* plusieurs ▪ **~ of us** plusieurs d'entre nous ▪ **there are ~ of them** ils sont plusieurs.
◇ *adj* LAW [separate] distinct.

severally ['sevrəlɪ] *adv fml* séparément, individuellement.

severance ['sevrəns] *n* [of relations] rupture *f*, cessation *f* ▪ [of communications, contact] interruption *f*, rupture *f*.

severance pay *n (U)* indemnité *f* OR indemnités *fpl* de licenciement.

severe [sɪ'vɪər] *adj* **1.** [harsh - criticism, punishment, regulations] sévère, dur ; [- conditions] difficile, rigoureux ; [- storm] violent ; [- winter, climate] rude, rigoureux ; [- frost] intense ; [- competition] rude, serré ▪ **~ weather conditions** conditions *fpl* météorologiques très rudes ▪ [strict - tone, person] sévère **2.** [serious - illness, handicap] grave, sérieux ; [- defeat] grave ; [- pain] vif, aigu, - uë *f* ▪ **I've got ~ backache/toothache** j'ai très mal au dos/une rage de dents ▪ **to suffer ~ losses** subir de lourdes pertes ▪ **his death was a ~ blow to them/to their chances** sa mort les a sérieusement ébranlés/a sérieusement compromis leurs chances ▪ **it will be a ~ test of our capabilities** cela mettra nos aptitudes à rude épreuve **3.** [austere - style, dress, haircut] sévère, strict ▪ **the building has a certain ~ beauty** l'édifice a une certaine beauté austère.

severely [sɪ'vɪəlɪ] *adv* **1.** [harshly - punish, treat, criticize] sévèrement, durement ▪ [strictly] strictement, sévèrement ▪ **he spoke ~ to them** il leur parla d'un ton sec **2.** [seriously - ill, injured, disabled] gravement, sérieusement ▪ **to be ~ handicapped** être gravement handicapé **3.** [austerely] d'une manière austère, sévèrement.

severity [sɪ'verətɪ] *n* **1.** [harshness - of judgment, treatment, punishment, criticism] sévérité *f*, dureté *f* ; [- of climate, weather] rigueur *f*, dureté *f* ; [- of frost, cold] intensité *f* **2.** [seriousness - of illness, injury, handicap] gravité *f*, sévérité *f* **3.** [austerity] austérité *f*, sévérité *f*.

sew [səu] (*pret* **sewed**, *pp* **sewn** [səun] OR **sewed**) ◇ *vt* coudre ▪ **to ~ a button on(to) a shirt** coudre OR recoudre un bouton sur une chemise ▪ **she can't even ~ a button on** elle ne sait même pas coudre un bouton.

<> *vi* coudre, faire de la couture.

◆ **sew up** *vt sep* **1.** [tear, slit] coudre, recoudre ▪ [seam] faire ▪ MED [wound] coudre, recoudre, suturer ▪ [hole] raccommoder **2.** *inf fig* [arrange, settle - contract] régler ; [- details] régler, mettre au point ▪ **the deal is all sewn up** l'affaire est dans le sac ▪ [control] contrôler, monopoliser ▪ **multinationals have sewn up the economy** les multinationales contrôlent l'économie ▪ **they've got the election all sewn up** l'élection est gagnée d'avance.

sewage ['su:ɪdʒ] *n (U)* vidanges *fpl*, eaux *fpl* d'égout, eaux-vannes *fpl* ▪ **the ~ system** les égouts *mpl* ▪ **~ disposal** évacuation *f* des eaux usées.

sewage farm, sewage works *n* station *f* d'épuration.

sewage tanker *n* camion-citerne *m*.

sewer ['suəʳ] *n* [drain] égout *m*.

sewerage ['suərɪdʒ] *n (U)* **1.** [disposal] évacuation *f* des eaux usées **2.** [system] égouts *mpl*, réseau *m* d'égouts **3.** [sewage] eaux *fpl* d'égout.

sewing ['səuɪŋ] <> *n* **1.** [activity] couture *f* **2.** [piece of work] couture *f*, ouvrage *m*.
<> *comp* [basket, kit] à couture ▪ [cotton] à coudre ▪ [class] de couture.

sewing machine *n* machine *f* à coudre.

sewn [səun] *pp* ▻ **sew**.

sex [seks] <> *n* **1.** [gender] sexe *m* ▪ **the club is open to both ~es** le club est ouvert aux personnes des deux sexes ▪ **single ~ school** établissement *m* scolaire non mixte **2.** *(U)* [sexual intercourse] relations *fpl* sexuelles, rapports *mpl* (sexuels) ▪ **to have ~ with sb** avoir des rapports (sexuels) OR faire l'amour avec qqn **3.** [sexual activity] sexe *m* ▪ **all he ever thinks about is ~** c'est un obsédé (sexuel).
<> *comp* sexuel ▪ **~ drive** pulsion *f* sexuelle, pulsions *fpl* sexuelles, libido *f* ▪ **~ life** vie *f* sexuelle ▪ **~ scandal** affaire *f* de mœurs ▪ **~ worker** prostitué *m*, - e *f*.
<> *vt* [animal] déterminer le sexe de.

sexagenarian [ˌseksədʒɪ'neərɪən] <> *adj* sexagénaire.
<> *n* sexagénaire *mf*.

sex appeal *n* sex-appeal *m*.

sex change *n* changement *m* de sexe ▪ **to have a ~** changer de sexe.

sexed [sekst] *adj* BIOL & ZOOL sexué ▪ **to be highly ~** [person] avoir une forte libido.

sex education *n* éducation *f* sexuelle.

sex hormone *n* hormone *f* sexuelle.

sexily ['seksɪlɪ] *adv* de façon sexy.

sexism ['seksɪzm] *n* sexisme *m*.

sexist ['seksɪst] <> *adj* sexiste.
<> *n* sexiste *mf*.

sex kitten *n inf* bombe *f* sexuelle.

sexless ['sekslɪs] *adj* **1.** BIOL asexué **2.** [person - asexual] asexué ; [- frigid] frigide ▪ [marriage] blanc, blanche *f*.

sex-mad *adj inf* **he's/she's ~** il/elle ne pense qu'à ça.

sex maniac *n* obsédé *m* sexuel, obsédée *f* sexuelle.

sex object *n* objet *m* sexuel.

sex offender *n* auteur *m* d'un délit sexuel.

sexologist [sek'sɒlədʒɪst] *n* sexologue *mf*.

sexology [sek'sɒlədʒɪ] *n* sexologie *f*.

sex organ *n* organe *m* sexuel.

sexploitation [ˌseksplɔɪ'teɪʃn] *n exploitation commerciale du sexe dans l'industrie cinématographique et la publicité*.

sexpot ['sekspɒt] *n inf hum* homme *m* très sexy, femme *f* très sexy.

sex shop *n* sex-shop *m*.

sex-starved *adj hum* (sexuellement) frustré.

sex symbol *n* sex-symbol *m*.

sextant ['sekstənt] *n* sextant *m*.

sextet [seks'tet] *n* sextuor *m*.

sex therapist *n* sexologue *mf*.

sexton ['sekstən] *n* sacristain *m*, bedeau *m*.

sextuplet ['sekstjuplɪt] *n* sextuplé *m*, - e *f*.

sexual ['sekʃuəl] *adj* sexuel.

sexual abuse *n (U)* sévices *mpl* sexuels.

sexual harassment *n* harcèlement *m* sexuel.

sexual intercourse *n (U)* rapports *mpl* sexuels.

sexuality [ˌsekʃu'ælətɪ] *n* sexualité *f*.

sexually ['sekʃuəlɪ] *adv* sexuellement ▪ **to be ~ assaulted** être victime d'une agression sexuelle ▪ **~ transmitted disease** maladie *f* sexuellement transmissible.

sexy ['seksɪ] (*comp* **sexier**, *superl* **sexiest**) *adj inf liter* [person] sexy *(inv)* ▪ *inf fig* [product] sympa.

Seychelles [seɪ'ʃelz] *pr npl* : **the ~** les Seychelles *fpl* ▪ **in the ~** aux Seychelles.

SF [es'ef] (*abbrev of* **science-fiction**) *n (U)* SF *f*.

SFO (*abbrev of* **Serious Fraud Office**) *n service britannique de la répression des fraudes*.

Sgt (*written abbrev of* **sergeant**) Sgt.

sh [ʃ] *interj* : **sh!** chut!

Shabbat [ʃə'bæt] *n* Sabbat *m*, Shabbat *m*.

shabbily ['ʃæbɪlɪ] *adv* **1.** [dressed, furnished] pauvrement **2.** [behave, treat] mesquinement, petitement ▪ **I think she's been very ~ treated** je trouve qu'on l'a traitée de manière très mesquine.

shabbiness ['ʃæbɪnɪs] *n* **1.** [poor condition - of dress, person] pauvreté *f* ; [- of house, street] délabrement *m* ; [- of carpet] mauvais état *m* **2.** [meanness - of behaviour, treatment, trick] mesquinerie *f*, petitesse *f* **3.** [mediocrity - of excuse, reasoning] médiocrité *f*.

shabby ['ʃæbɪ] (*comp* **shabbier**, *superl* **shabbiest**) *adj* **1.** [clothes] râpé, élimé ▪ [carpet, curtains] usé, élimé ▪ [person] pauvrement vêtu ▪ [hotel, house] miteux, minable ▪ [furniture] pauvre, minable ▪ [street, area] misérable, miteux **2.** [mean - behaviour, treatment] mesquin, vil, bas **3.** [mediocre - excuse] piètre ; [- reasoning] médiocre.

shack [ʃæk] *n* cabane *f*, case *f*, hutte *f*.

◆ **shack up** *vi insep inf* **to ~ up with sb** s'installer avec qqn.

shackle ['ʃækl] *vt liter* enchaîner, mettre aux fers ▪ *fig* entraver.

◆ **shackles** *npl liter* chaînes *fpl*, fers *mpl* ▪ *fig* chaînes *fpl*, entraves *fpl*.

shade [ʃeɪd] <> *n* **1.** [shadow] ombre *f* ▪ **45 degrees in the ~** 45 degrés à l'ombre ▪ **in the ~ of a tree** à l'ombre d'un arbre ▪ **these trees give plenty of ~** ces arbres font beaucoup d'ombre ▮ ART ombre *f*, ombres *fpl* ▪ **the use of light and ~ in the painting** l'utilisation des ombres et des lumières OR du clair-obscur dans le tableau ▶ **to put sb in the ~** éclipser qqn **2.** [variety - of colour] nuance *f*, ton *m* ▪ [nuance - of meaning, opinion] nuance *f* ▪ **all ~s of political opinion were represented** toutes les nuances politiques étaient représentées, tous les courants politiques étaient représentés **3.** [for lamp] abat-jour *m inv* ▪ [for eyes] visière *f* ▪ US [blind - on window] store *m* **4.** *lit* [spirit] ombre *f*.
<> *vt* **1.** [screen - eyes, face] abriter ; [- place] ombrager, donner de l'ombre à ▪ **he ~d his eyes (from the sun) with his hand** il a mis sa main devant ses yeux pour se protéger du soleil **2.** [cover - light, lightbulb] masquer, voiler **3.** ART [painting] ombrer ▪ [by hatching] hachurer ▪ **I've ~d the background green** j'ai coloré l'arrière-plan en vert.
<> *vi* [merge] se dégrader, se fondre ▪ **the blue ~s into purple** le bleu se fond en violet.

◆ **shades** *npl* **1.** *lit* [growing darkness] : **the ~s of evening** les ombres du soir **2.** *inf* [sunglasses] lunettes *fpl* de soleil **3.** [reminder, echo] échos *mpl*.

◆ **a shade** *adv phr* : **she's a ~ better today** elle va un tout petit peu mieux aujourd'hui.

◆ **shade in** *vt sep* [background] hachurer, tramer ■ [with colour] colorer.

shadiness [ˈʃeɪdɪnɪs] *n* **1.** [of place] ombre *f* **2.** [of behaviour, dealings] caractère *m* louche *OR* suspect.

shading [ˈʃeɪdɪŋ] *n (U)* ART [in painting] ombres *fpl* ■ [hatching] hachure *f*, tramage *m*, hachures *fpl* ■ *fig* [difference] nuance *f*.

shadow [ˈʃædəʊ] ◇ *n* **1.** [of figure, building] ombre *f* ■ **the ~ of suspicion fell on them** on a commencé à les soupçonner ■ **she's a ~ of her former self** elle n'est plus que l'ombre d'elle-même ▶ **he's afraid of his own ~** il a peur de son ombre ■ **to live in sb's ~** vivre dans l'ombre de qqn ■ **to cast a ~ on** *OR* **over sthg** *liter* & *fig* projeter *OR* jeter une ombre sur qqch **2.** [under eyes] cerne *m* **3.** [shade] ombre *f*, ombrage *m* ■ **she was standing in (the) ~** elle se tenait dans l'ombre **4.** [slightest bit] ombre *f* ■ **without** *OR* **beyond a** *OR* **the ~ of a doubt** sans l'ombre d'un doute **5.** [detective] : **I want a ~ put on him** je veux qu'on le fasse suivre **6.** [companion] ombre *f* ■ **he follows me everywhere like a ~** il me suit comme mon ombre, il ne me lâche pas d'une semelle **7.** MED [on lung] voile *m*.

◇ *vt* **1.** [follow secretly] filer, prendre en filature ■ **our job was to ~ enemy submarines** nous étions chargés de suivre les sous-marins ennemis **2.** [screen from light] *lit* ombrager.

◇ *adj* *UK* POL : **~ cabinet** cabinet *m* fantôme ■ **the Shadow Education Secretary/Defence Secretary** le porte-parole de l'opposition pour l'éducation/pour la défense nationale.

◆ **shadows** *npl lit* [darkness] ombre *f*, ombres *fpl*, obscurité *f*.

SHADOW CABINET

Le cabinet fantôme est composé des parlementaires du principal parti de l'opposition, qui deviendraient ministres si leur parti arrivait au pouvoir.

shadow-boxing *n* SPORT boxe *f* à vide ■ **let's stop all this ~ and get down to business** *fig* arrêtons de tourner autour du pot et parlons sérieusement.

shadowy [ˈʃædəʊɪ] *adj* **1.** [shady - woods, path] ombragé ■ **he looked into the ~ depths** il scruta les profondeurs insondables **2.** [vague - figure, outline] vague, indistinct ; [- plan] vague, imprécis.

shady [ˈʃeɪdɪ] (*comp* **shadier**, *superl* **shadiest**) *adj* **1.** [place] ombragé **2.** *inf* [person, behaviour] louche, suspect ■ [dealings] louche.

shaft [ʃɑːft] ◇ *n* **1.** [of spear] hampe *f* ■ [of feather] tuyau *m* ■ ARCHIT [of column] fût *m* ■ ANAT [of bone] diaphyse *f* **2.** [of axe, tool, golf club] manche *m* **3.** [of cart, carriage] brancard *m*, limon *m* **4.** MECH [for propeller, in machine] arbre *m* **5.** [in mine] puits *m* ■ [of ventilator, chimney] puits *m*, cheminée *f* ■ [of lift] cage *f* **6.** [of light] rai *m* ■ **a ~ of wit** *fig* un trait d'esprit **7.** *lit* [arrow] flèche *f* **8.**△ *US phr* **he got the ~** [got shouted at] qu'est-ce qu'il s'est pris! ; [got fired] il s'est fait viré.

◇ *vt* **1.**△ [cheat] : **to get ~ed** se faire rouler **2.**▲ [have sex with] baiser△.

shag [ʃæg] (*pret & pp* **shagged**) ◇ *n* **1.** [of hair, wool] toison *f* ■ **~ (pile) carpet** moquette *f* à poils longs **2.** : **~ (tobacco)** tabac *m* (très fort) **3.** ORNITH cormoran *m* huppé **4.**▲ [sex] : **to have a ~** baiser△ **5.** *US* [ballboy] ramasseur *m* de balles.

◇ *vt* **1.**△ [tire] crever ■ **to be shagged (out)** être complètement crevé *OR* HS **2.**▲ [have sex with] baiser△ **3.** *US* [fetch] aller chercher.

◇ *vi*▲ [have sex] baiser△.

shaggy [ˈʃægɪ] (*comp* **shaggier**, *superl* **shaggiest**) *adj* [hair, beard] hirsute, touffu ■ [eyebrows] hérissé, broussailleux ■ [dog, pony] à longs poils (rudes) ■ [carpet, rug] à longs poils.

shaggy-dog story *n* histoire *f* sans queue ni tête.

shah [ʃɑː] *n* chah *m*, shah *m*.

shake [ʃeɪk] (*pret* **shook** [ʃʊk], *pp* **shaken** [ˈʃeɪkn]) ◇ *vt* **1.** [rug, tablecloth, person] secouer ■ [bottle, cocktail, dice] agiter ■ [subj: earthquake, explosion] ébranler, faire trembler ■ **she shook me by the shoulders** elle m'a secoué par les épaules ■ **the wind shook the branches** le vent agitait les branches ■ **they shook the apples from the tree** ils secouèrent l'arbre pour (en) faire tomber les pommes ■ **to ~ sugar onto sthg** saupoudrer qqch de sucre ■ **to ~ vinegar onto sthg** asperger qqch de vinaigre ■ **to ~ salt/pepper onto sthg** saler/poivrer qqch ■ **'~ well before use'** 'bien agiter avant l'emploi' ■ **the dog shook itself (dry)** le chien s'est ébroué (pour se sécher) ■ **they shook themselves free** ils se sont libérés d'une secousse ■ **he needs to be shaken out of his apathy** il a besoin qu'on le secoue (pour le tirer de son apathie) ■ **he shook his head** [in refusal] il a dit *OR* fait non de la tête ; [in resignation, sympathy] il a hoché la tête ▶ **~ a leg!** *inf* secoue-toi!, remue-toi! ■ **to ~ the dust from one's feet** partir le cœur léger

2. [brandish] brandir ■ **he shook his fist at him** il l'a menacé du poing ▶ **he's made more films than you can ~ a stick at** *inf* il a réalisé un nombre incroyable de films

3. [hand] serrer ■ **to ~ hands with sb, to ~ sb's hand** serrer la main à qqn ■ **they shook hands** ils se sont serré la main

4. [upset - faith, confidence, health, reputation] ébranler ■ **they were rather shaken by the news** ils ont été plutôt secoués par la nouvelle

5. [amaze] bouleverser, ébranler ■ **she shook everyone with her revelations** tout le monde a été bouleversé par ses révélations ■ **I bet that shook him!** voilà qui a dû le secouer!

◇ *vi* **1.** [ground, floor, house] trembler, être ébranlé ■ [leaves, branches] trembler, être agité ■ **the child shook free of his captor** l'enfant a échappé à son ravisseur

2. [with emotion - voice] trembler, frémir ; [- body, knees] trembler ■ **to ~ with laughter** se tordre de rire ■ **to ~ with fear** trembler de peur ■ **to ~ with cold** trembler de froid, grelotter ■ **to ~ like a jelly** *OR* **leaf** trembler comme une feuille ■ **to ~ in one's shoes** avoir une peur bleue, être mort de peur ■ **his hands were shaking uncontrollably** il ne pouvait empêcher ses mains de trembler

3. [in agreement] : **let's ~ on it!** tope-là! ■ **they shook on the deal** ils ont scellé leur accord par une poignée de main.

◇ *n* **1.** secousse *f*, ébranlement *m* ■ **to give sb/sthg a ~** secouer qqn/qqch ■ **with a ~ of his head** [in refusal, in resignation, sympathy] avec un hochement de tête ■ **to be all of a ~** *UK inf* être tout tremblant

2. *inf* [moment] instant *m* ■ **in two ~s (of a lamb's tail)** en un clin d'œil

3. *US inf* [earthquake] tremblement *m* de terre

4. *US inf* [milk shake] milk-shake *m*

5. *US inf* [deal] : **he'll give you a fair ~** il ne te roulera pas

6. MUS trille *m*.

◆ **shake down** ◇ *vi insep* **1.** *inf* [go to bed] coucher

2. *inf* [adapt - to new situation, job] s'habituer

3. [contents of packet, bottle] se tasser.

◇ *vt sep* **1.** [from tree] faire tomber en secouant

2. [after fall] : **to ~ o.s. down** s'ébrouer, se secouer

3. *US inf* **to ~ sb down** [rob] racketter qqn ; [search] fouiller qqn

4. *US inf* [test] essayer, tester.

◆ **shake off** *vt sep* **1.** [physically] secouer ■ **to ~ the sand/water off sthg** secouer le sable/l'eau de qqch

2. [get rid of - cold, pursuer, depression] se débarrasser de ; [- habit] se défaire de, se débarrasser de.

◆ **shake out** ◇ *vt sep* **1.** [tablecloth, rug] (bien) secouer ■ [sail, flag] déferler, déployer ■ [bag] vider en secouant

2. [rouse - person] : **I can't seem to ~ him out of his apathy** je n'arrive pas à le tirer de son apathie.

◇ *vi insep* MIL se disperser, se disséminer.

◆ **shake up** *vt sep* **1.** [physically - pillow] secouer, taper ; [- bottle] agiter

2. *fig* [upset - person] secouer, bouleverser

3. [rouse - person] secouer ■ **he needs shaking up a bit** il a besoin qu'on le secoue un peu

4. *inf* [overhaul - organization, company] remanier, réorganiser de fond en comble.

◆ **shakes** *npl* **1.** : **to have the ~s** avoir la tremblote

2. *inf phr* **it's no great ~s** [film, book, restaurant, etc] ça ne casse pas des briques ■ **he's no great ~s** il est insignifiant ■ **he's no great ~s at painting** *OR* **as a painter** il ne casse rien *OR* pas des briques comme peintre.

shakedown ['ʃeɪkdaʊn] ◇ *n* **1.** [bed] lit *m* improvisé *OR* de fortune **2.** *inf* [of ship, plane - test] essai *m* ■ [flight, voyage] voyage *m OR* vol *m* d'essai **3.**△ *US* [search] fouille *f* **4.**△ *US* [extortion] racket *m*.
◇ *adj* [test, flight, voyage] d'essai.

shaken ['ʃeɪkn] ◇ *pp* ▷ **shake**.
◇ *adj* [upset] secoué ■ [stronger] bouleversé, ébranlé.

shaker ['ʃeɪkəʳ] *n* [for cocktails] shaker *m* ■ [for salad] panier *m* à salade ■ [for dice] cornet *m*.

Shakespearean [ʃeɪk'spɪərɪən] *adj* shakespearien.

shake-up *n inf* **1.** [of company, organization] remaniement *m*, restructuration *f* **2.** [emotional] bouleversement *m*.

shakily ['ʃeɪkɪlɪ] *adv* **1.** [unsteadily - walk] d'un pas chancelant *OR* mal assuré ; [- write] d'une main tremblante ; [- speak] d'une voix tremblante *OR* chevrotante **2.** [uncertainly] d'une manière hésitante *OR* peu assurée ■ **she started ~ then went on to win the game** au début, elle n'était pas très sûre d'elle, mais elle a fini par gagner la partie.

shaky ['ʃeɪkɪ] (*comp* **shakier**, *superl* **shakiest**) *adj* **1.** [unsteady - chair, table] branlant, peu solide ; [- ladder] branlant, peu stable ; [- hand] tremblant, tremblotant ; [- writing] tremblé ; [- voice] tremblotant, chevrotant ; [- steps] chancelant ■ **he's a bit ~ on his legs** il ne tient pas bien sur ses jambes ■ **I'm still ~ after my accident** je ne me suis pas encore complètement remis de mon accident ■ **to be based** *OR* **built on ~ foundations** avoir des bases chancelantes **2.** [uncertain, weak - health, faith] précaire, vacillant ; [- authority, regime] incertain, chancelant ; [- future, finances] incertain, précaire ; [- business] incertain ■ **her memory is a bit ~** sa mémoire n'est pas très sûre ■ **things got off to a ~ start** les choses ont plutôt mal commencé ■ **my knowledge of German is a bit ~** mes notions d'allemand sont plutôt vagues ■ **he came up with some very ~ arguments** ses arguments étaient très peu convaincants.

shall (*weak form* [ʃəl], *strong form* [ʃæl]) *modal vb* **1.** [as future auxiliary] : **I ~** *OR* **I'll come tomorrow** je viendrai demain ■ **I ~ not** *OR* **I shan't be able to come** je ne pourrai pas venir ■ **I ~ now attempt a triple somersault** je vais à présent essayer d'exécuter un triple saut périlleux **2.** [in suggestions, questions] : **~ I open the window?** voulez-vous que j'ouvre la fenêtre? ■ **I'll shut that window, ~ I?** je peux fermer cette fenêtre, si vous voulez ■ **we'll all go then, ~ we?** dans ce cas, pourquoi n'y allons-nous pas tous? **3.** *fml* [emphatic use] : **it ~ be done** ce sera fait ■ **thou shalt not kill** BIBLE tu ne tueras point.

shallot [ʃə'lɒt] *n* échalote *f*.

shallow ['ʃæləʊ] *adj* **1.** [water, soil, dish] peu profond ■ **the ~ end** [of swimming pool] le petit bain **2.** [superficial - person, mind, character] superficiel, qui manque de profondeur ; [- conversation] superficiel, futile ; [- argument] superficiel **3.** [breathing] superficiel.
◆ **shallows** *npl* bas-fond *m*, bas-fonds *mpl*, haut-fond *m*, hauts-fonds *mpl*.

shallow-minded *adj* : **to be ~** être superficiel *OR* futile.

shallowness ['ʃæləʊnɪs] *n* **1.** [of water, soil, dish] faible profondeur *f* **2.** [of mind, character, sentiments] manque *m* de profondeur ■ [of person] esprit *m* superficiel, manque *m* de profondeur ■ [of talk, ideas] futilité *f*.

shalt [ʃælt] *vb (2nd pers sg) arch* ▷ **shall**.

sham [ʃæm] (*pret & pp* **shammed**, *cont* **shamming**) ◇ *n* **1.** [pretence - of sentiment, behaviour] comédie *f*, farce *f*, faux-semblant *m* ■ **her illness/grief is a ~** sa maladie/son chagrin n'est qu'une mascarade ■ **their marriage is a complete ~** leur mariage est une véritable farce **2.** [impostor - person] imposteur *m* ; [- organization] imposture *f*.
◇ *adj* **1.** [pretended - sentiment, illness] faux, fausse *f*, feint, simulé ; [- battle] simulé **2.** [mock - jewellery] imitation *(adj)*, faux, fausse *f* ■ **a ~ election** un simulacre d'élections.
◇ *vt* feindre, simuler ■ **to ~ illness** faire semblant d'être malade.
◇ *vi* faire semblant, jouer la comédie.

shaman ['ʃæmən] *n* chaman *m*, -e *f*.

shamble ['ʃæmbl] *vi* : **to ~ in/out/past** entrer/sortir/passer en traînant les pieds ■ **a shambling gait** une démarche traînante.

shambles ['ʃæmblz] *n* **1.** [place] désordre *m* ■ **your room is a total ~!** ta chambre est dans un état! ■ **the house was in a ~** la maison était sens dessus dessous **2.** [situation, event] désastre *m* ■ **his life is (in) a real ~** sa vie est un véritable désastre ■ **to make a ~ of a job** saboter un travail.

shambolic [ʃæm'bɒlɪk] *adj UK* désordonné.

shame [ʃeɪm] ◇ *n* **1.** [feeling] honte *f*, confusion *f* ■ **to my great ~** à ma grande honte ■ **he has no sense of ~** il n'a aucune honte ■ **have you no ~?** vous n'avez pas honte ? **2.** [disgrace, dishonour] honte *f* ■ **to bring ~ on one's family/country** déshonorer sa famille/sa patrie, couvrir sa famille/sa patrie de honte ■ **to put sb to ~** faire honte à qqn ■ **she works so hard, she puts you to ~** elle vous ferait honte, tellement elle travaille ■ **the ~ of it!** quelle honte ! ■ **~ on him!** c'est honteux !, quelle honte ! ■ **for ~!** *lit & hum* c'est une honte ! ■ *UK* [in Parliament] : **her speech brought cries of "~!"** son discours provoqua des huées **3.** [pity] dommage *m* ■ **it's a ~!** c'est dommage ! ■ **what a ~!** quel dommage ! ■ **it's a ~ he can't come** c'est dommage qu'il ne puisse pas venir ■ **it would be a great ~ if she missed it** ce serait vraiment dommage qu'elle ne le voie pas.
◇ *vt* [disgrace - family, country] être la honte de, faire honte à, déshonorer ■ [put to shame] faire honte à, humilier ■ **it ~s me to admit it** j'ai honte de l'avouer ■ **to ~ sb into doing sthg** obliger qqn à faire qqch en lui faisant honte ■ **she was ~d into admitting the truth** elle avait tellement honte qu'elle a dû avouer la vérité.

shamefaced [,ʃeɪm'feɪst] *adj* honteux, penaud ■ **he was a bit ~ about it** il en avait un peu honte.

shamefacedly [,ʃeɪm'feɪstlɪ] *adv* d'un air honteux *OR* penaud.

shameful ['ʃeɪmfʊl] *adj* honteux, indigne.

shamefully ['ʃeɪmfʊlɪ] *adv* honteusement, indignement ■ **she has been treated ~** elle a été traitée de façon honteuse ■ **he was ~ ignorant about the issue** son ignorance sur la question était honteuse.

shameless ['ʃeɪmlɪs] *adj* effronté, sans vergogne ■ **that's a ~ lie!** c'est un mensonge éhonté! ■ **they are quite ~ about it!** ils ne s'en cachent pas!

shamelessly ['ʃeɪmlɪslɪ] *adv* sans honte, sans vergogne, sans pudeur ■ **to lie ~** mentir effrontément ■ **they were walking about quite ~ with nothing on** ils se promenaient tout nus sans la moindre gêne *OR* sans que ça ait l'air de les gêner.

shaming ['ʃeɪmɪŋ] *adj* mortifiant, humiliant.

shammy ['ʃæmɪ] *n* : **~ (leather)** peau *f* de chamois.

shampoo [ʃæm'pu:] ◇ *n* shampooing *m* ■ **~ and set** shampooing *m* (et) mise en plis *f*.
◇ *vt* [person, animal] faire un shampooing à ■ [carpet] shampouiner ■ **to ~ one's hair** se faire un shampooing, se laver les cheveux.

shamrock ['ʃæmrɒk] *n* trèfle *m*.

SHAMROCK
Le trèfle est l'emblème de l'Irlande.

shandy ['ʃændɪ] (*pl* **shandies**) *n UK* panaché *m*.

shanghai [,ʃæŋ'haɪ] *vt* **1.** NAUT embarquer de force *(comme matelot)* **2.** *inf fig* **to ~ sb into doing sthg** forcer qqn à faire qqch.

shank [ʃæŋk] *n* **1.** ANAT jambe *f* ■ [of horse] canon *m* ■ CULIN jarret *m* **2.** [stem - of screw, anchor] manche *m* ; [- of glass] pied *m*.

shanks's pony ['ʃæŋksɪz-] *n inf hum* **to go on ~** aller pedibus *OR* à pattes.

shan't [ʃɑ:nt] = **shall not**.

shanty [ˈʃæntɪ] (*pl* **shanties**) *n* **1.** [shack] baraque *f*, cabane *f* **2.** [song] chanson *f* de marins.

shantytown [ˈʃæntɪtaʊn] *n* bidonville *m*.

shape [ʃeɪp] ◇ *n* **1.** [outer form] forme *f* ■ **the room was triangular in ~** la pièce était de forme triangulaire *OR* avait la forme d'un triangle ■ **a sweet in the ~ of a heart** un bonbon en forme de cœur ■ **all the pebbles are different ~ s** *OR* **a different ~** chaque caillou a une forme différente ■ **they come in all ~s and sizes** il y en a de toutes les formes et de toutes les tailles ■ **she moulded the clay into ~** elle façonna l'argile ■ **he bent/beat the copper into ~** il plia/martela le cuivre ■ **my pullover lost its ~ in the wash** mon pull s'est déformé au lavage
2. [figure, silhouette] forme *f*, silhouette *f*
3. [abstract form or structure] forme *f* ■ **the ~ of our society** la structure de notre société ■ **to take ~** prendre forme *OR* tournure ■ **her plan was beginning to take ~** son projet commençait à se concrétiser *OR* à prendre forme ■ **to give ~ to sthg** donner forme à qqch ■ **she plans to change the whole ~ of the company** elle a l'intention de modifier complètement la structure de l'entreprise
4. [guise] forme *f* ■ **help eventually arrived in the ~ of her parents** ce sont ses parents qui finirent par arriver pour lui prêter secours ■ **he can't take alcohol in any ~ or form** il ne supporte l'alcool sous aucune forme ■ **the ~ of things to come** ce qui nous attend, ce que l'avenir nous réserve
5. [proper condition, fitness, effectiveness etc] forme *f* ■ **to be in good/bad ~** [person] être en bonne/mauvaise forme, être/ne pas être en forme ; [business, economy] marcher bien/mal ■ **I need to get (back) into ~** j'ai besoin de me remettre en forme ■ **the economy is in poor ~ at the moment** l'économie est mal en point *OR* dans une mauvaise passe actuellement ■ **to keep o.s.** *OR* **to stay in ~** garder la *OR* rester en forme ■ **what sort of ~ was he in?** dans quel état était-il?, comment allait-il? ➲ **to knock** *OR* **to lick sthg into ~** *inf* arranger qqch, mettre qqch au point ■ **I'll soon knock** *OR* **lick them into ~ !** *inf* [soldiers] j'aurai vite fait de les dresser, moi! ; [team] j'aurai vite fait de les remettre en forme, moi!
6. [apparition, ghost] apparition *f*, fantôme *m*
7. [mould - gen] moule *m* ; [- for hats] forme *f*.
◇ *vt* **1.** [mould - clay] façonner, modeler ; [- wood, stone] façonner, tailler ■ **he ~d a pot from the wet clay** il a façonné un pot dans l'argile ■ **the paper had been ~d into a cone** le papier avait été plié en forme de cône
2. [influence - events, life, future] influencer, déterminer ■ **to ~ sb's character** former le caractère de qqn
3. [plan - essay] faire le plan de ; [- excuse, explanation, statement] formuler
4. SEW ajuster.
◇ *vi* [develop - plan] prendre forme *OR* tournure ■ **things are shaping well** les choses se présentent bien *OR* prennent une bonne tournure ■ [person] se débrouiller.
◆ **shape up** *vi insep* **1.** [improve] se secouer ■ **you'd better ~ up, young man!** il est temps que tu te secoues, jeune homme!
2. *US* [get fit again] retrouver la forme
3. [progress, develop] prendre (une bonne) tournure ■ **the business is beginning to ~ up** les affaires commencent à bien marcher ■ **the new team is shaping up well** la nouvelle équipe commence à bien fonctionner ■ **how is she shaping up as a translator?** comment se débrouille-t-elle *OR* comment s'en sort-elle en tant que traductrice?

shaped [ʃeɪpt] *adj* **1.** [garment] ajusté ■ [wooden or metal object] travaillé **2.** [in descriptions] : **~ like a triangle** en forme de triangle ■ **a rock ~ like a man's head** un rocher qui a la forme d'une tête d'homme.

-shaped *in cpds* en forme de ■ **pear~** en forme de poire, piriforme *spec.*

shapeless [ˈʃeɪplɪs] *adj* [mass, garment, heap] informe ■ **to become ~** se déformer.

shapelessness [ˈʃeɪplɪsnɪs] *n* absence *f* de forme, aspect *m* informe.

shapeliness [ˈʃeɪplɪnɪs] *n* [of legs] galbe *m* ■ [of figure] beauté *f*, belles proportions *fpl*.

shapely [ˈʃeɪplɪ] (*comp* **shapelier**, *superl* **shapeliest**) *adj* [legs] bien galbé, bien tourné ■ [figure, woman] bien fait ■ **a ~ pair of legs** une belle paire de jambes.

shard [ʃɑːd] *n* **1.** [of glass] éclat *m* ■ [of pottery] tesson *m* **2.** ZOOL élytre *m*.

share [ʃeəʳ] ◇ *vt* **1.** [divide - money, property, food, chores] partager ■ **he ~d the chocolate with his sister** il a partagé le chocolat avec sa sœur ■ **they must ~ the blame for the accident** ils doivent se partager la responsabilité de l'accident **2.** [use jointly - tools, flat, bed] partager ■ **~d line** TELEC ligne *f* partagée, raccordement *m* collectif **3.** [have in common - interest, opinion] partager ; [- characteristic] avoir en commun ; [- worry, sorrow] partager, prendre part à, compatir à ■ **I ~ your hope that war may be avoided** j'espère comme vous qu'on pourra éviter la guerre ■ **we ~ the same name** nous avons le même nom ■ **we ~ a common heritage** nous avons un patrimoine commun.
◇ *vi* partager ■ **to ~ in** [cost, work] participer à, partager ; [profits] avoir part à ; [credit, responsibility] partager ; [joy, sorrow] prendre part à, partager ; [grief] compatir à ➲ **~ and ~ alike** *prov* à chacun sa part.
◇ *n* **1.** [portion - of property, cost, food, credit, blame] part *f* ■ **there's your ~** voici votre part *OR* ce qui vous revient ■ **they've had their ~ of misfortune** ils ont eu leur part de malheurs ■ **he's come in for his full ~ of criticism** il a été beaucoup critiqué ■ **we've had more than our (fair) ~ of rain this summer** nous avons eu plus que notre compte de pluie cet été ■ **they all had a ~ in the profits** ils ont tous eu une part des bénéfices ■ **to pay one's ~** payer sa part *OR* quote-part *OR* son écot ■ **they went ~s in the cost of the present** ils ont tous participé à l'achat du cadeau ■ **I went half ~s with her** on a payé la moitié chacun ■ **to have a ~ in a business** être l'un des associés dans une affaire **2.** [part, role - in activity, work] part *f* ■ **what was her ~ in it all?** quel rôle a-t-elle joué dans tout cela? ■ **to do one's ~ (of the work)** faire sa part du travail ■ **to have a ~ in doing sthg** contribuer à faire qqch ■ **she must have had a ~ in his downfall** elle doit être pour quelque chose dans sa chute **3.** ST. EX action *f* ■ **~ prices have fallen** le prix des actions est tombé **4.** AGRIC soc *m* (de charrue).
◆ **share out** *vt sep* partager, répartir ■ **the profits were ~d out among them** ils se sont partagé les bénéfices.

share capital *n* capital-actions *m*.

share certificate *n* certificat *m OR* titre *m* d'actions.

sharecropper [ˈʃeəˌkrɒpəʳ] *n* métayer *m*, - ère *f*.

sharecropping [ˈʃeəˌkrɒpɪŋ] *n US système de métayage en usage dans le sud des États-Unis après la guerre de Sécession.*

shareholder [ˈʃeəˌhəʊldəʳ] *n* actionnaire *mf*.

shareholding [ˈʃeəˌhəʊldɪŋ] *n* actionnariat *m*.

share index *n* indice *m* boursier.

share option scheme *n* plan *m* de participation par achat d'actions.

share-out *n* partage *m*, répartition *f*.

shareware [ˈʃeəweəʳ] *n (U)* COMPUT logiciel *m* contributif *OR* libre essai, shareware *m*.

sharia law [ˈʃɑːrɪə] *n* charia *f*.

sharing [ˈʃeərɪŋ] ◇ *adj* [person] partageur.
◇ *n* [of money, power] partage *m*.

shark [ʃɑːk] *n* **1.** ZOOL requin *m* **2.** *inf fig* [swindler] escroc *m*, filou *m* ■ [predator - in business] requin *m* **3.** *US inf* [genius] génie *m* ■ **to be a ~ at sthg** être calé en qqch **4.** *US* [at match] revendeur *m* de billets à la sauvette.

sharkskin [ˈʃɑːkskɪn] ◇ *n* peau *f* de requin.
◇ *comp* en peau de requin.

sharp [ʃɑːp] ◇ *adj* **1.** [blade, scissors, razor] affûté, bien aiguisé ■ [edge] tranchant, coupant ■ [point] aigu, - uë *f*, acéré ■ [teeth, thorn] pointu ■ [claw] acéré ■ [needle, pin - for sewing] pointu ; [- for pricking] qui pique ■ [pencil] pointu, bien taillé ■ **these scissors are ~** ces ciseaux coupent bien ■ **give me a ~ knife** donnez-moi un couteau qui coupe ▌[nose] pointu ■ **she has ~ features** elle a des traits anguleux

2. [clear - photo, line, TV picture] net ; [- contrast, distinction] net, marqué
3. [abrupt, sudden - blow, bend, turn] brusque ; [- rise, fall, change] brusque, soudain ▪ **the car made a ~ turn** la voiture a tourné brusquement
4. [piercing - wind, cold] vif, fort
5. [intense - pain, disappointment] vif
6. [sour, bitter - taste, food] âpre, piquant
7. [harsh - words, criticism] mordant, cinglant ; [- reprimand] sévère ; [- voice, tone] âpre, acerbe ; [- temper] vif ▪ **he can be very ~ with customers** il lui arrive d'être très brusque avec les clients ▪ **she has a ~ tongue** elle a la langue bien affilée
8. [keen - eyesight] perçant ; [- hearing, senses] fin ▪ **he has a ~ eye** il a le coup d'œil ▪ **keep a ~ lookout!** restez à l'affût! ▪ [in intellect, wit - person] vif ; [- child] vif, éveillé ; [- judgment] vif ▪ **she was too ~ for them** elle était trop maligne pour eux ⊳ **he's as ~ as a needle** [intelligent] il est malin comme un singe ; [shrewd] il est très perspicace, rien ne lui échappe
9. [quick, brisk - reflex, pace] : **be ~ (about it)!** dépêche-toi!
10. [shrill - sound, cry] aigu, - uë *f*, perçant
11. MUS : **C ~ minor** do dièse mineur ▪ **to be ~** [singer] chanter trop haut ; [violinist] jouer trop haut
12. *pej* [unscrupulous - trading, lawyer] peu scrupuleux, malhonnête ▪ **accused of ~ practice** accusé de procédés indélicats *OR* malhonnêtes
13. *inf* [smart] classe ▪ **he's always been a ~ dresser** il s'est toujours habillé très classe.
<> *adv* **1.** [precisely] : **at 6 o'clock ~** à 6 h pile *OR* précises
2. [in direction] : **turn ~ left** tournez tout de suite à gauche ▪ **the road turns ~ left** la route tourne brusquement à gauche
3. MUS [sing, play] trop haut, faux
4. *inf phr* **look ~ (about it)!** dépêche-toi!, grouille-toi!
<> *n* MUS dièse *m*.
<> *vt US* MUS [sharpen] diéser.

sharpen ['ʃɑ:pn] <> *vt* **1.** [blade, knife, razor] affiler, aiguiser, affûter ▪ [pencil] tailler ▪ [stick] tailler en pointe **2.** [appetite, pain] aviver, aiguiser ▪ [intelligence] affiner ▪ **you'll need to ~ your wits** il va falloir te secouer **3.** [outline, image] mettre au point, rendre plus net ▪ [contrast] accentuer, rendre plus marqué **4.** *UK* MUS diéser.
<> *vi* [tone, voice] devenir plus vif *OR* âpre ▪ [pain] s'aviver, devenir plus vif ▪ [appetite] s'aiguiser ▪ [wind, cold] devenir plus vif.

sharpener ['ʃɑ:pnə^r] *n* [for knife - machine] aiguisoir *m* (à couteaux) ; [- manual] fusil *m* (à aiguiser) ▪ [for pencil] taille-crayon *m inv*.

sharp-eyed *adj* [with good eyes] qui a l'œil vif ▪ [with insight] à qui rien n'échappe.

sharpish ['ʃɑ:pɪʃ] *adv UK inf* [quickly] en vitesse, sans tarder ▪ **look ~!** grouille-toi!

sharply ['ʃɑ:plɪ] *adv* **1.** : **~ pointed** [knife] pointu ; [pencil] à pointe fine, taillé fin ; [nose, chin, shoes] pointu **2.** [contrast, stand out] nettement ▪ [differ] nettement, clairement ▪ **this contrasts ~ with her usual behaviour** voilà qui change beaucoup de son comportement habituel **3.** [abruptly, suddenly - curve, turn] brusquement ; [- rise, fall, change] brusquement, soudainement ▪ **the car took the bend too ~** la voiture a pris le virage trop vite ▪ **the road rises/drops ~** la route monte/descend en pente raide ▪ **inflation has risen ~ since May** l'inflation est montée en flèche depuis mai **4.** [harshly - speak] vivement, sèchement, de façon brusque ; [- criticize] vivement, sévèrement ; [- reply, retort] vertement, vivement ▪ **I had to speak to her ~ about her persistent lateness** j'ai dû lui faire des observations sévères au sujet de ses retards répétés **5.** [alertly - listen] attentivement.

sharpness ['ʃɑ:pnɪs] *n* **1.** [of blade, scissors, razor] tranchant *m* ▪ [of needle, pencil, thorn] pointe *f* aiguë ▪ [of features] aspect *m* anguleux **2.** [of outline, image, contrast] netteté *f* **3.** [of bend, turn] angle *m* brusque ▪ [of rise, fall, change] soudaineté *f* **4.** [of wind, cold, frost] âpreté *f* **5.** [of word, criticism, reprimand] sévérité *f* ▪ [of tone, voice] brusquerie *f*, aigreur *f* ▪ **there was a certain ~ in the way he spoke to me** il m'a parlé sur un ton plutôt sec **6.** [of eyesight, hearing, senses] finesse *f*, acuité *f* ▪ [of appetite, pain] acuité *f* ▪ [of mind, intelligence] finesse *f*, vivacité *f* ▪ [of irony, wit] mordant *m*.

sharpshooter ['ʃɑ:p,ʃu:tə^r] *n* tireur *m* d'élite.

sharp-tempered *adj* coléreux, soupe au lait *(inv)*.

sharp-tongued [-'tʌŋd] *adj* caustique.

sharp-witted [-'wɪtɪd] *adj* à l'esprit vif *OR* fin.

shat▲ [ʃæt] *pt & pp* ⊳ **shit**.

shatter ['ʃætə^r] <> *vt* **1.** [break - glass, window] briser, fracasser ; [- door] fracasser ▪ **a stone ~ed the windscreen** un caillou a fait éclater le pare-brise ▪ **the noise ~ed my eardrums** le bruit m'a assourdi **2.** *fig* [destroy - career, health] briser, ruiner ; [- nerves] démolir, détraquer ; [- confidence, faith, hope] démolir, détruire ▪ **they were ~ed by the news, the news ~ed them** ils ont été complètement bouleversés par la nouvelle, la nouvelle les a complètement bouleversés.
<> *vi* [glass, vase, windscreen] voler en éclats ▪ **her whole world ~ed** son univers tout entier s'est écroulé *OR* a été anéanti.

shattered ['ʃætəd] *adj* **1.** [upset] bouleversé ▪ **~ dreams** des rêves brisés **2.** *UK inf* [exhausted] crevé.

shattering ['ʃætərɪŋ] *adj* **1.** [emotionally - news, experience] bouleversant ▪ [disappointment] fort, cruel **2.** [extreme - defeat] écrasant ▪ **a ~ blow** *liter* un coup violent ; *fig* un grand coup **3.** *UK inf* [tiring] crevant.

-shattering *in cpds* : **an ear~ noise** un bruit à vous déchirer les tympans.

shatterproof ['ʃætəpru:f] *adj* : **~ glass** verre *m* sans éclats *OR* Securit®.

shave [ʃeɪv] <> *vt* **1.** raser ▪ **to ~ one's legs/one's head** se raser les jambes/la tête **2.** [wood] raboter **3.** [graze] raser, frôler **4.** [reduce] réduire ▪ **to ~ a few pence off the price** faire un rabais de quelques centimes ▪ **a few percentage points have been ~d off their lead** ils ont perdu un peu de leur avantage.
<> *vi* se raser.
<> *n* : **to have a ~** se raser ▪ **you need a ~** tu as besoin de te raser ▪ **to give sb a ~** raser qqn.
◆ **shave off** *vt sep* **1.** : **to ~ off one's beard/moustache/hair** se raser la barbe/la moustache/la tête **2.** = **shave** *(vt sense 2)*.

shaven ['ʃeɪvn] *adj* [face, head] rasé.

shaver ['ʃeɪvə^r] *n* [razor] rasoir *m* (électrique).

Shavian ['ʃeɪvjən] <> *adj* [writings] de George Bernard Shaw ▪ [style] à la Shaw ▪ [society] consacré à Shaw.
<> *n* partisan *m OR* disciple *mf* de George Bernard Shaw.

shaving ['ʃeɪvɪŋ] <> *n* [act] rasage *m*.
<> *comp* [cream, foam] à raser ▪ **~ brush** blaireau *m* ▪ **~ soap** savon *m* à barbe ▪ **~ stick** (bâton *m* de) savon *m* à barbe.
◆ **shavings** *npl* [of wood] copeaux *mpl* ▪ [of metal] copeaux *mpl*, rognures *fpl* ▪ [of paper] rognures *fpl*.

shawl [ʃɔ:l] *n* châle *m*.

she [ʃi:] <> *pron* **1.** [referring to woman, girl] elle ▪ **~'s a teacher/an engineer** elle est enseignante/ingénieur ▪ **~'s a very interesting woman** c'est une femme très intéressante ▪ **SHE can't do it** elle? elle ne peut pas le faire ▮ [referring to boat, car, country] : **~'s a fine ship** c'est un bateau magnifique ▪ **~ can do over 120 mph** elle fait plus de 150 km à l'heure **2.** [referring to female animal] : **~'s a lovely dog** c'est une chienne adorable.
<> *n* [referring to animal, baby] : **it's a ~** [animal] c'est une femelle ; [baby] c'est une fille.

she- *in cpds* : **~elephant** éléphant *m* femelle ▪ **~bear** ourse *f* ▪ **~dog** chienne *f* ▪ **~wolf** louve *f*.

s/he *(written abbrev of* **she/he***)* il ou elle.

sheaf [ʃi:f] *(pl* **sheaves** [ʃi:vz]*)* <> *n* **1.** [of papers, letters] liasse *f* **2.** [of barley, corn] gerbe *f* ▪ [of arrows] faisceau *m*.
<> *vt* gerber, engerber.

shear [ʃɪə^r] *(pret* **sheared**, *pp* **sheared** *OR* **shorn** [ʃɔ:n]*)* <> *vt* **1.** [sheep, wool] tondre ▪ **to be shorn of sthg** *fig* être dépouillé de qqch **2.** [metal] couper (net), cisailler.
<> *vi* céder.

◆ **shears** *npl* [for gardening] cisaille *f* ■ [for sewing] grands ciseaux *mpl* ■ [for sheep] tondeuse *f* ■ **a pair of ~s** HORT une paire de cisailles ; SEW une paire de grands ciseaux.

◆ **shear off** ◇ *vt sep* [wool, hair] tondre ■ [branch] couper, élaguer ■ [something projecting] couper, enlever ■ **the tail section of the car had been ~ed off on impact** la partie arrière de la voiture avait été arrachée par le choc.
◇ *vi insep* [part, branch] se détacher.

shearing ['ʃɪərɪŋ] *n* [process] tonte *f*.
◆ **shearings** *npl* : **~s (of wool)** laine *f* tondue.

sheath [ʃi:θ] (*pl* **sheaths** [ʃi:ðz]) *n* **1.** [scabbard, case - for sword] fourreau *m* ; [- for dagger] gaine *f* ; [- for scissors, tool] étui *m* **2.** [covering - for cable] gaine *f* ; [- for water pipe] gaine *f*, manchon *m* ■ BOT, ANAT & ZOOL gaine *f* **3.** *UK* [condom] préservatif *m* **4.** = **sheath dress**.

sheath dress *n* (robe *f*) fourreau *m*.

sheathe [ʃi:ð] *vt* **1.** [sword, dagger] rengainer **2.** [cable] gainer ■ [water pipe] gainer, mettre dans un manchon protecteur ■ **she was ~d from head to foot in black satin** *fig* elle était moulée dans du satin noir de la tête aux pieds.

sheath knife *n* couteau *m* à gaine.

sheave [ʃi:v] *vt* gerber, engerber.

sheaves [ʃi:vz] *pl* ▷ **sheaf**.

Sheba ['ʃi:bə] *pr n* Saba ■ **the Queen of ~** la reine de Saba.

shebang [ʃɪ'bæŋ] *n inf* **the whole ~** tout le tremblement.

she-cat *n liter* chatte *f* ■ *fig* furie *f*.

shed [ʃed] (*pret & pp* **shed**, *cont* **shedding**) ◇ *n* **1.** [in garden] abri *m*, remise *f*, resserre *f* ■ [lean-to] appentis *m* **2.** [barn] grange *f*, hangar *m* ■ [for trains, aircraft, vehicles] hangar *m* **3.** [in factory] atelier *m*.
◇ *vt* **1.** [cast off - leaves, petals] perdre ; [- skin, shell] se dépouiller de ; [- water] ne pas absorber ■ **the snake regularly ~s its skin** le serpent mue ■ **the dog has ~ her hairs all over the carpet** la chienne a laissé des poils partout sur la moquette ■ [take off - garments] enlever **2.** [get rid of - inhibitions, beliefs] se débarrasser de, se défaire de ; [- staff] congédier **3.** [tears, blood] verser, répandre ■ [weight] perdre ■ **they came to power without shedding civilian blood** ils ont pris le pouvoir sans faire couler le sang des civils **4.** [eject, lose] déverser ■ ASTRONAUT larguer **5.** *phr* **to ~ light on** *liter* éclairer ; *fig* éclairer, éclaircir.

she'd [(*weak form* [ʃɪd], *strong form* [ʃi:d])] = **she had**, = **she would**.

she-devil *n* furie *f*.

sheen [ʃi:n] *n* [on satin, wood, hair, silk] lustre *m* ■ [on apple] poli *m* ■ **the cello had a beautiful red ~** le violoncelle avait de magnifiques reflets rouges.

sheep [ʃi:p] (*pl inv*) ◇ *n* mouton *m* ■ [ewe] brebis *f* ■ **they're just a load of ~** *pej* ils se comportent comme des moutons (de Panurge) *OR* un troupeau de moutons ► **to separate** *OR* **to sort out the ~ from the goats** séparer le bon grain de l'ivraie.
◇ *comp* [farm, farming] de moutons.

sheep-dip *n* bain *m* parasiticide (pour moutons).

sheepdog ['ʃi:pdɒg] *n* chien *m* de berger.

sheepfold ['ʃi:pfəʊld] *n* parc *m* à moutons, bergerie *f*.

sheepish ['ʃi:pɪʃ] *adj* penaud.

sheepishly ['ʃi:pɪʃlɪ] *adv* d'un air penaud.

sheep's eyes *npl inf* **to cast** *OR* **to make ~ at sb** *dated* faire les yeux doux à qqn.

sheepshearer ['ʃi:p,ʃɪərər] *n* [person] tondeur *m*, - euse *f* (de moutons) ■ [machine] tondeuse *f* (à moutons).

sheepshearing ['ʃi:p,ʃɪərɪŋ] *n* tonte *f* (des moutons).

sheepskin ['ʃi:pskɪn] ◇ *n* **1.** TEX peau *f* de mouton **2.** *US inf* UNIV [diploma] parchemin *m*.
◇ *comp* [coat, rug] en peau de mouton.

sheer [ʃɪər] ◇ *adj* **1.** [as intensifier] pur ■ **it was ~ coincidence** c'était une pure coïncidence ■ **the ~ scale of the project was intimidating** l'envergure même du projet était impressionnante ■ **the ~ boredom of her job drove her mad** elle s'ennuyait tellement dans son travail que ça la rendait folle ■ **by ~ accident** *OR* **chance** tout à fait par hasard, par pur hasard ■ **out of** *OR* **in ~ boredom** par pur ennui ■ **in ~ desperation** en désespoir de cause ■ **that's ~ nonsense!** c'est complètement absurde! ■ **it's ~ folly!** c'est de la folie pure! **2.** [steep - cliff] à pic, abrupt ■ **it's a ~ 50 metre drop** cela descend à pic sur 50 mètres ■ **a ~ drop to the sea** un à-pic jusqu'à la mer ■ **we came up against a ~ wall of water** nous nous sommes trouvés devant un véritable mur d'eau **3.** TEX [stockings] extra fin.
◇ *adv* à pic, abruptement.
◇ *vi* NAUT [ship] faire une embardée.

◆ **sheer away** *vi insep* **1.** [ship] larguer les amarres, prendre le large **2.** [animal, shy person] filer, détaler ■ **to ~ away from** éviter.

◆ **sheer off** *vi insep* **1.** [ship] faire une embardée **2.** *fig* [person] changer de chemin *OR* de direction.

sheet [ʃi:t] ◇ *n* **1.** [for bed] drap *m* ■ [for furniture] housse *f* ■ [shroud] linceul *m* ■ [tarpaulin] bâche *f* **2.** [of paper] feuille *f* ■ [of glass, metal] feuille *f*, plaque *f* ■ [of cardboard, plastic] feuille *f* ■ [of iron, steel] tôle *f*, plaque *f* ► **order ~** bulletin *m* de commande **3.** [newspaper] feuille *f*, journal *m* **4.** [of water, snow] nappe *f*, étendue *f* ■ [of rain] rideau *m*, torrent *m* ■ [of flames] rideau *m* ■ **a ~ of ice** une plaque de glace ; [on road] une plaque de verglas ■ **the rain came down in ~s** il pleuvait des hallebardes *OR* à torrents **5.** CULIN : **baking ~** plaque *f* de four *OR* à gâteaux **6.** NAUT écoute *f* ■ **to be three ~s to the wind** *inf fig* en tenir une bonne.
◇ *vt* [figure, face] draper, couvrir d'un drap ■ [furniture] couvrir de housses ■ **~ed (over) in snow** *fig* couvert de neige.

◆ **sheet down** *vi insep* [rain, snow] tomber à torrents.

sheet anchor *n* NAUT ancre *f* de veille ■ *fig* ancre *f* de salut.

sheet bend *n* nœud *m* d'écoute.

sheet-fed *adj* [printer] feuille à feuille.

sheet feed *n* COMPUT alimentation *f* feuille à feuille.

sheet feeder *n* COMPUT dispositif *m* d'alimentation en papier.

sheet ice *n* plaque *f* de glace ■ [on road] (plaque *f* de) verglas *m*.

sheeting ['ʃi:tɪŋ] *n* **1.** [cloth] toile *f* pour draps **2.** [plastic, polythene] feuillet *m* ■ [metal] feuille *f*, plaque *f*.

sheet lightning *n* éclair *m* en nappe *OR* en nappes.

sheet metal *n* tôle *f*.

sheet music *n (U)* partitions *fpl*.

sheet steel *n* tôle *f* d'acier.

sheik(h) [ʃeɪk] *n* cheikh *m*.

sheik(h)dom ['ʃeɪkdəm] *n* territoire *m* sous l'autorité d'un cheikh.

sheila ['ʃi:lə] *n Australia & New Zealand inf* nana *f*.

sheldrake ['ʃeldreɪk] *n* tadorne *m*.

shelduck ['ʃeldʌk] *n* tadorne *m*, harle *m*.

shelf [ʃelf] (*pl* **shelves** [ʃelvz]) *n* **1.** [individual] planche *f*, étagère *f* ■ [as part of set, in fridge] étagère *f* ■ [short] tablette *f* ■ [in oven] plaque *f* ■ [in shop] étagère *f*, rayon *m* ■ **to buy sthg off the ~** acheter qqch tout fait ■ **you can't buy alcohol off the ~ in that shop** l'alcool n'est pas en vente libre dans ce magasin ■ **to stay on the shelves** [goods] se vendre difficilement ► **to be left on the ~** [woman] rester vieille fille ; [man] rester vieux garçon **2.** GEOL banc *m*, rebord *m*, saillie *f* ■ [under sea] écueil *m*, plate-forme *f*.

shelf life *n* COMM durée *f* de conservation avant vente ■ **bread has a short ~** le pain ne se conserve pas très longtemps.

shell [ʃel] ◇ *n* **1.** BIOL [gen - of egg, mollusc, nut] coquille *f* ; [- of peas] cosse *f* ; [- of crab, lobster, tortoise] carapace *f* ■ [empty - on seashore] coquillage *m* ■ **to come out of one's ~** *liter & fig* sortir de sa coquille ■ **to go back** *OR* **to retire into one's ~** *liter & fig* rentrer dans sa coquille **2.** [of building] carcasse *f* ■ [of car,

ship, machine] coque *f* ■ **he's just an empty ~** il n'est plus que l'ombre de lui-même **3.** CULIN fond *m* (de tarte) **4.** MIL obus *m* ■ *US* [cartridge] cartouche *f* **5.** [boat] outrigger *m*.
◇ *comp* [ornament, jewellery] de *OR* en coquillages.
◇ *vt* **1.** [peas] écosser, égrener ■ [nut] décortiquer, écaler ■ [oyster] ouvrir ■ [prawn, crab] décortiquer **2.** MIL bombarder (d'obus).
◆ **shell out** *inf* ◇ *vi insep* casquer ■ **to ~ out for sthg** casquer pour qqch, payer qqch.
◇ *vt insep* payer, sortir.

she'll [ʃi:l] = **she will**.

shellac [ʃə'læk] (*pret & pp* **shellacked**) ◇ *n* gomme-laque *f*.
◇ *vt* [varnish] laquer.

shellacking [ʃə'lækɪŋ] *n US inf* raclée *f*.

shelled [ʃeld] *adj* [peas] écossé, égrené ■ [nut, shellfish] décortiqué.

shellfire ['ʃelfaɪəʳ] *n (U)* tirs *mpl* d'obus.

shellfish ['ʃelfɪʃ] (*pl inv*) *n* **1.** ZOOL [crab, lobster, shrimp] crustacé *m* ■ [mollusc] coquillage *m* **2.** *(U)* CULIN fruits *mpl* de mer.

shelling ['ʃelɪŋ] *n* MIL pilonnage *m*.

shellproof ['ʃelpru:f] *adj* MIL blindé, à l'épreuve des obus.

shell shock *n (U)* psychose *f* traumatique *(due à une explosion)*.

shell-shocked [-,ʃɒkt] *adj* commotionné *(après une explosion)* ■ **I'm still feeling pretty ~ by it all** *fig* je suis encore sous le choc après toute cette histoire.

shell suit *n* survêtement *m (en polyamide froissé et doublé)*.

shelter ['ʃeltəʳ] ◇ *n* **1.** [cover, protection] abri *m* ■ **to take** *OR* **to get under ~** se mettre à l'abri *OR* à couvert ■ **they took ~ from the rain under a tree** ils se sont abrités de la pluie sous un arbre ■ **we ran for ~** nous avons couru nous mettre à l'abri ‖ [accommodation] asile *m*, abri *m* ■ **to give ~ to sb** [hide] donner asile à *OR* cacher qqn ; [accommodate] héberger qqn ■ **they gave us food and ~** il nous ont offert le gîte et le couvert **2.** [enclosure - gen] abri *m* ; [- for sentry] guérite *f* ■ **(bus) ~** Abribus® *m*.
◇ *vt* [protect - from rain, sun, bombs] abriter ; [- from blame, suspicion] protéger ■ **to ~ sb from sthg** protéger qqn de qqch ■ **the trees ~ed us from the wind** les arbres nous abritaient du vent ■ **we were ~ed from the rain/from danger** nous étions à l'abri de la pluie/du danger ■ [give asylum to - fugitive, refugee] donner asile à, abriter.
◇ *vi* s'abriter, se mettre à l'abri ■ [from bullets] se mettre à couvert.
◆ **Shelter** *pr n association britannique d'aide aux sans-abri.*

sheltered ['ʃeltəd] *adj* **1.** [place] abrité **2.** [protected - industry] protégé *(de la concurrence)* ; [- work] dans un centre pour handicapés ■ **to lead a ~ life** vivre à l'abri des soucis ■ **she led a very ~ life as a child** elle a eu une enfance très protégée.

sheltered accommodation, sheltered housing *n logement dans une résidence pour personnes âgées ou handicapées.*

shelve [ʃelv] ◇ *vt* **1.** [put aside, suspend] laisser en suspens ■ **the project was ~d for two years** le projet a été abandonné pendant deux ans **2.** [books - in shop] mettre sur les rayons ; [- at home] mettre sur les étagères **3.** [wall, room - in shop] garnir de rayons ; [- at home] garnir d'étagères.
◇ *vi* [ground] être en pente douce ■ **the beach ~s steeply** la plage descend en pente raide.

shelves [ʃelvz] *pl* ▷ **shelf**.

shelving ['ʃelvɪŋ] *n (U)* **1.** [in shop] rayonnage *m*, rayonnages *mpl*, étagères *fpl* ■ [at home] étagères *fpl* **2.** [suspension - of plan, question etc] mise *f* en attente *OR* en suspens **3.** GEOL plateau *m*.

shenanigans [ʃɪ'nænɪgənz] *npl inf* **1.** [mischief] malice *f*, espièglerie *f* **2.** [scheming, tricks] manigances *fpl*, combines *fpl*.

shepherd ['ʃepəd] ◇ *n* **1.** berger *m*, pâtre *m lit* ■ **~'s crook** bâton *m* de berger, houlette *f* **2.** RELIG & *lit* pasteur *m*, berger *m* ■ **the Good Shepherd** le bon pasteur *OR* berger.
◇ *vt* **1.** [tourists, children] guider, conduire ■ **to ~ sb out of a room** escorter qqn jusqu'à la porte ■ **to ~ sb into a room** faire entrer *OR* introduire qqn dans une pièce **2.** [sheep] garder, surveiller.

shepherd boy *n* jeune berger *m OR* pâtre *m lit*.

shepherdess [,ʃepə'des] *n* bergère *f*.

shepherd's pie *n* hachis *m* Parmentier.

sherbet ['ʃɜ:bət] *n* **1.** *UK* [powder] poudre *f* acidulée **2.** *US* [ice] sorbet *m*.

sheriff ['ʃerɪf] *n* **1.** *US* [in Wild West and today] shérif *m* **2.** *UK* [crown officer] shérif *m*, officier *m* de la Couronne **3.** *Scotland* LAW ≃ juge *m* au tribunal de grande instance.

sherry ['ʃerɪ] (*pl* **sherries**) *n* sherry *m*, xérès *m*, vin *m* de Xérès.

Sherwood forest [ʃɜ:wʊd-] *pr n ancienne région de forêts au centre de l'Angleterre où Robin des Bois aurait vécu.*

she's [ʃi:z] **1.** = **she has 2.** = **she is**.

Shetland ['ʃetlənd] ◇ *pr n* GEOG : **the ~s, the ~ Isles, the ~ Islands** les (îles *fpl*) Shetland *fpl* ■ **in the ~s** *OR* **the ~ Isles** *OR* **the ~ Islands** dans les Shetland.
◇ *adj* **1.** GEOG shetlandais **2.** TEX [pullover] en shetland ■ **~ wool** laine *f* d'Écosse *OR* de Shetland.

Shetlander ['ʃetləndəʳ] *n* Shetlandais *m*, - e *f*.

Shetland sheepdog *n* berger *m* des Shetland.

shh [ʃ] *interj* chut.

shibboleth ['ʃɪbə,leθ] *n* **1.** [custom, tradition] vieille coutume *f*, vieille tradition *f* ■ [idea, principle] vieille idée *f*, vieux principe *m* **2.** [catchword] mot *m* d'ordre.

shield [ʃi:ld] ◇ *n* **1.** [carried on arm] écu *m* heraldique bouclier *m* **2.** *fig* bouclier *m*, paravent *m* ■ **to provide a ~ against sthg** protéger contre qqch **3.** TECH [on machine] écran *m* de protection *OR* de sécurité ■ [on nuclear reactor, spacecraft] bouclier *m* ■ **nuclear ~** bouclier atomique ■ **sun ~** pare-soleil *m inv* **4.** [trophy] trophée *m*.
◇ *vt* protéger ■ **to ~ sb from sthg** protéger qqn de *OR* contre qqch ■ **we need a shelter to ~ us from the wind/sun** il nous faut un abri contre le vent/soleil ■ **she ~ed him with her own body** elle lui a fait un rempart de son corps.

shift [ʃɪft] ◇ *vt* **1.** [move, put elsewhere] déplacer, bouger ■ **help me ~ the bed nearer the window** aide-moi à rapprocher le lit de *OR* pousser le lit vers la fenêtre ■ **they're trying to ~ the blame onto me** ils essaient de rejeter la responsabilité sur moi ‖ [part of body] bouger, remuer ■ **she kept ~ing from one foot to the other** elle n'arrêtait pas de se balancer d'un pied sur l'autre ■ **~ yourself!** *inf* [move] pousse-toi!, bouge-toi! ; [hurry] remue-toi!, grouille-toi! ‖ [employee - to new job or place of work] muter ; [- to new department] affecter ■ THEAT [scenery] changer
2. [change] changer de ■ **they won't be ~ed from their opinion** impossible de les faire changer d'avis ■ **we're trying to ~ the balance towards exports** nous essayons de mettre l'accent sur les exportations ■ **the latest developments have ~ed attention away from this area** les événements récents ont détourné l'attention de cette région ■ **to ~ gears** *US* changer de vitesse
3. [remove - stain] enlever, faire partir
4. *inf* COMM [sell] écouler.
◇ *vi* **1.** [move] se déplacer, bouger ■ **could you ~ up a bit, please?** pourrais-tu te pousser un peu, s'il te plaît?
2. [change, switch - gen] changer ; [- wind] tourner ■ **their policy has ~ed over the last week** leur politique a changé *OR* s'est modifiée au cours de la semaine ■ **in the second act the scene ~s to Venice** dans le deuxième acte, l'action se déroule à Venise ■ **to ~ into fourth (gear)** *US* AUT passer en quatrième (vitesse)
3. *inf* [travel fast] filer
4. [manage] : **to ~ for o.s.** se débrouiller tout seul
5. [stain] partir, s'enlever

6. *UK inf* COMM [sell] se vendre.
◇ *n* **1.** [change] changement *m* ■ **a ~ in position/opinion** un changement de position/d'avis ■ **there was a sudden ~ in public opinion/the situation** il y a eu un revirement d'opinion/de situation ■ **there was a light ~ in the wind** le vent a légèrement tourné ■ **a ~ in meaning** LING un glissement de sens ▶ **(gear) ~** *US* AUT changement *m* de vitesse
2. [move] déplacement *m*
3. [turn, relay] relais *m* ■ **to do sthg in ~s** se relayer ■ **I'm exhausted, can you take a ~ at the wheel?** je suis épuisé, peux-tu me relayer au volant?
4. INDUST [period of time] poste *m*, équipe *f* ■ **what ~ are you on this week?** à quel poste avez-vous été affecté cette semaine? ■ **I'm on the night/morning ~** je suis dans l'équipe de nuit/du matin ■ **she works long ~s** elle fait de longues journées ■ **to work ~s, to be on ~s** travailler en équipe, faire les trois-huit ■ [group of workers] équipe *f*, brigade *f* ■ **when does** *OR* **do the morning ~ arrive?** à quelle heure arrive l'équipe du matin?
5. *dated* [expedient] expédient *m* ■ **to make ~ with sthg** se contenter de qqch
6. *UK dated US* [woman's slip] combinaison *f* ■ [dress] (robe *f*) fourreau *m*
7. COMPUT [in arithmetical operation] décalage *m* ■ [in word processing, telegraphy etc] touche *f* de majuscule
8. *US* AUT = **shift stick**.
◆ **shift over, shift up** *vi insep inf* se pousser, se déplacer.

shifter ['ʃɪftəʳ] *US* = **shift stick**.

shiftily ['ʃɪftɪlɪ] *adv* sournoisement.

shifting ['ʃɪftɪŋ] *adj* [ideas, opinions] changeant ■ [alliances] instable ■ [ground, sand] mouvant.

shift key *n* touche *f* de majuscule.

shiftless ['ʃɪftlɪs] *adj* [lazy] paresseux, fainéant ■ [apathetic] apathique, mou *(before vowel or silent 'h' mol)*, molle *f* ■ [helpless] sans ressource, perdu.

shift lock *n* touche *f* de blocage des majuscules.

shift stick *n US* AUT levier *m* de (changement de) vitesse.

shift work *n* travail *m* en équipe ■ **she does ~** elle fait les trois-huit.

shift worker *n personne qui fait les trois-huit.*

shifty ['ʃɪftɪ] (*comp* **shiftier**, *superl* **shiftiest**) *adj inf* [look] sournois, furtif, fuyant ■ **he looks a ~ customer** *inf* il a l'air louche.

shiitake [ʃɪ'tɑːkɪ] *n* [mushroom] shiitaké *m*.

Shiite ['ʃiːaɪt] ◇ *n* : **~ (Muslim)** chiite *mf*.
◇ *adj* chiite.

shilling ['ʃɪlɪŋ] *n* **1.** shilling *m (ancienne pièce britannique valant 12 pence, soit un vingtième de livre)* **2.** [in Kenya, Tanzania etc] shilling *m*.

shilly-shally ['ʃɪlɪˌʃælɪ] (*pret & pp* **shilly-shallied**) *vi inf pej* hésiter ■ **stop ~ing (around)!** décide-toi enfin!

shimmer ['ʃɪməʳ] ◇ *vi* [sequins, jewellery, silk] chatoyer, scintiller ■ [water] miroiter ■ **the pavements ~ed in the heat** l'air tremblait au-dessus des trottoirs brûlants.
◇ *n* [of sequins, jewellery, silk] chatoiement *m*, scintillement *m* ■ [of water] miroitement *m*.

shimmering ['ʃɪmərɪŋ] *adj* [light] scintillant ■ [jewellery, silk] chatoyant ■ [water] miroitant.

shin [ʃɪn] ◇ *n* **1.** ANAT tibia *m* **2.** CULIN [of beef] gîte *m OR* gîte-gîte *m* (de bœuf) ■ [of veal] jarret *m* (de veau).
◇ *vi* (*pret & pp* **shinned**) grimper ■ **to ~ (up) a lamp post** grimper à un réverbère ■ **I shinned down the drainpipe** je suis descendu le long de la gouttière.

shinbone ['ʃɪnbəʊn] *n* tibia *m*.

shindig ['ʃɪndɪg] *n inf* **1.** [party] (grande) fête *f* **2.** [fuss] tapage *m*.

shine [ʃaɪn] ◇ *vi* (*pret & pp* **shone** [ʃɒn]) **1.** [sun, moon, lamp, candle] briller ■ [surface, glass, hair] briller, luire ■ **the sun was shining** le soleil brillait, il y avait du soleil ■ **the sun was shining in my eyes** j'avais le soleil dans les yeux, le soleil m'éblouissait ■ **a small desk lamp shone on the table** une petite lampe de bureau éclairait la table ■ **his eyes shone with excitement** ses yeux brillaient *OR* son regard brillait d'émotion ■ **her face shone with joy** son visage rayonnait de joie **2.** [excel] briller ■ **John ~s at sports** John est très bon en sport.
◇ *vt* **1.** (*pret & pp* **shone** [ʃɒn]) [focus] braquer, diriger ■ **the guard shone his torch on the prisoner** le gardien a braqué sa lampe sur le prisonnier ■ **don't ~ that lamp in my eyes** ne m'éblouis pas avec cette lampe **2.** (*pret & pp* **shined**) [polish] faire briller, faire reluire, astiquer.
◇ *n* **1.** [polished appearance] éclat *m*, brillant *m*, lustre *m* ■ **to put a ~ on sthg, to give sthg a ~** faire reluire *OR* briller qqch ■ **to take the ~ off sthg** faire perdre son éclat à qqch, ternir qqch ▶ **to take a ~ to sb** *inf* [take a liking to] se prendre d'amitié pour qqn ; [get a crush on] s'enticher de qqn **2.** [polish] polissage *m* ■ **your shoes need a ~** tes chaussures ont besoin d'un coup de brosse *OR* chiffon.
◆ **shine down** *vi insep* briller ■ **the hot sun shone down on us** le soleil tapait dur.
◆ **shine out, shine through** *vi insep* [light] jaillir ■ *fig* [courage, skill, generosity] rayonner, briller ■ **she ~s out from the others in the class** elle dépasse tous ses camarades de classe de la tête et des épaules.
◆ **shine up to** *vt insep US inf* faire de la lèche à.

shiner ['ʃaɪnəʳ] *n inf* [black eye] coquart *m*, œil *m* au beurre noir.

shingle ['ʃɪŋgl] ◇ *n* **1.** *(U)* [pebbles] galets *mpl* ■ **~ beach** plage *f* de galets **2.** CONSTR [for roofing] bardeau *m*, aisseau *m* ■ **~ roof** toit *m* en bardeaux **3.** *US* [nameplate] plaque *f*.
◇ *vt* [roof] couvrir de bardeaux *OR* d'aisseaux.

shingles ['ʃɪŋglz] *n (U)* MED zona *m*.

shingly ['ʃɪŋglɪ] *adj* [ground] couvert de galets ■ [beach] de galets.

shinguard ['ʃɪngɑːd] = **shinpad**.

shininess ['ʃaɪnɪnɪs] *n* éclat *m*, brillant *m*.

shining ['ʃaɪnɪŋ] *adj* **1.** [gleaming - glass, metal, shoes] luisant, reluisant ; [- eyes] brillant ; [- face] rayonnant **2.** [outstanding] éclatant, remarquable ■ **a ~ example of bravery** un modèle de courage.

shinpad ['ʃɪnpæd] *n* jambière *f*.

Shinto ['ʃɪntəʊ] ◇ *n* shinto *m*.
◇ *adj* shintoïste.

Shintoist ['ʃɪntəʊɪst] ◇ *adj* shintoïste.
◇ *n* shintoïste *mf*.

shiny ['ʃaɪnɪ] (*comp* **shinier**, *superl* **shiniest**) *adj* **1.** [gleaming - glass, metal, shoes] luisant, reluisant ■ **my nose is ~** j'ai le nez qui brille **2.** [clothing - with wear] lustré.

ship [ʃɪp] (*pret & pp* **shipped**) ◇ *n* **1.** NAUT navire *m*, vaisseau *m*, bateau *m* ■ **on board** *OR* **aboard ~** à bord ■ **the ~'s papers** les papiers *mpl* de bord ▶ **sailing ~** bateau *m* à voiles, voilier *m* ■ **the ~ of the desert** le vaisseau du désert ■ **the ~ of State** le char de l'État ■ **when my ~ comes in** *OR* **home** *inf* [money] quand je serai riche, quand j'aurai fait fortune ; [success] quand j'aurai réussi dans la vie **2.** [airship] dirigeable *m* ■ [spaceship] vaisseau *m* (spatial).
◇ *vt* **1.** [send by ship] expédier (par bateau *OR* par mer) ■ [carry by ship] transporter (par bateau *OR* par mer) **2.** [send by any means] expédier ■ [carry by any means] transporter **3.** [embark - passengers, cargo] embarquer **4.** [take into boat - gangplank, oars] rentrer ; [- water] embarquer.
◇ *vi* [passengers, crew] embarquer, s'embarquer.
◆ **ship off** *vt sep inf* expédier.

ship broker *n* courtier *m* maritime.

shipbuilder ['ʃɪpˌbɪldəʳ] *n* constructeur *m*, - trice *f* de navires.

shipbuilding ['ʃɪpˌbɪldɪŋ] *n* construction *f* navale ■ **the ~ industry** (l'industrie *f* de) la construction navale.

ship canal *n* canal *m* maritime.

shipload ['ʃɪpləʊd] *n* cargaison *f*, fret *m*.

shipmate [ˈʃɪpmeɪt] *n* compagnon *m* de bord.

shipment [ˈʃɪpmənt] *n* **1.** [goods sent] cargaison *f* ▪ **arms ~** cargaison d'armes **2.** [sending of goods] expédition *f*.

shipowner [ˈʃɪp,əʊnəʳ] *n* armateur *m*.

shipper [ˈʃɪpəʳ] *n* [charterer] affréteur *m*, chargeur *m* ▪ [transporter] transporteur *m* ▪ [sender] expéditeur *m*, - trice *f*.

shipping [ˈʃɪpɪŋ] ◇ *n (U)* **1.** [ships] navires *mpl* ▪ [traffic] navigation *f* ▪ **dangerous to ~** dangereux pour la navigation ▪ **~ has been warned to steer clear of the area** on a prévenu les navires qu'il fallait éviter le secteur ▪ **the decline of British merchant ~** le déclin de la marine marchande britannique **2.** [transport - gen] transport *m* ; [- by sea] transport *m* maritime ▪ **cost includes ~** le coût du transport est compris **3.** [loading] chargement *m*, embarquement *m*.
◇ *comp* [company, line] maritime, de navigation ▪ [sport, trade, intelligence] maritime ▪ **~ forecast** météo *f* OR météorologie *f* marine.

shipping agent *n* agent *m* maritime.

shipping clerk *n* expéditionnaire *mf*.

shipping lane *n* voie *f* de navigation.

ship's biscuit *n* biscuit *m* de mer.

ship's chandler *n* shipchandler *m*, marchand *m*, - e *f* d'articles de marine.

shipshape [ˈʃɪpʃeɪp] *adj* en ordre, rangé ➊ **all ~ and Bristol fashion!** *inf hum* tout est impeccable!

shipwreck [ˈʃɪprek] ◇ *n* **1.** [disaster at sea] naufrage *m* **2.** [wrecked ship] épave *f*.
◇ *vt* **1.** *liter* **they were ~ed on a desert island** ils ont échoué sur une île déserte **2.** *fig* [ruin, spoil] ruiner.

shipwrecked [ˈʃɪprekt] *adj* : **to be ~** [boat] faire naufrage ; [crew, passenger] être naufragé.

shipwright [ˈʃɪpraɪt] *n* [company] constructeur *m* de navires ▪ [worker] ouvrier *m*, - ère *f* de chantier naval.

shipyard [ˈʃɪpjɑːd] *n* chantier *m* naval.

shire [ˈʃaɪəʳ] *n UK* **1.** [county] comté *m* **2.** = **shire horse**.
◆ **Shires** *pr npl* : **the Shires** *les comtés (ruraux) du centre de l'Angleterre.*

shire horse *n* shire *m*.

shirk [ʃɜːk] ◇ *vt* [work, job, task] éviter de faire, échapper à ▪ [duty] se dérober à ▪ [problem, difficulty, question] esquiver, éviter ▪ **she doesn't ~ her responsibilities** elle n'essaie pas de se dérober à ses responsabilités.
◇ *vi* tirer au flanc.

shirker [ˈʃɜːkəʳ] *n* tire-au-flanc *mf inv*.

shirt [ʃɜːt] *n* [gen] chemise *f* ▪ [footballer's, cyclist's etc] maillot *m* ▪ **~ collar/cuff** col *m* /manchette *f* de chemise ➊ **keep your ~ on!** *inf* ne vous énervez pas! ▪ **to lose one's ~** *inf* y laisser sa chemise, perdre tout ce qu'on a ▪ **to put one's ~ on sthg** miser toute sa fortune sur qqch.

shirtfront [ˈʃɜːtfrʌnt] *n* plastron *m*.

shirtsleeves [ˈʃɜːtsliːvz] *npl* : **to be in (one's) ~** être en manches OR bras de chemise.

shirttail [ˈʃɜːtteɪl] *n* pan *m* de chemise.

shirtwaister [ˈʃɜːt,weɪstəʳ] *UK*, **shirtwaist** [ˈʃɜːtweɪst] *US* *n* robe *f* chemisier.

shirty [ˈʃɜːtɪ] (*comp* **shirtier**, *superl* **shirtiest**) *adj UK inf* désagréable.

shish kebab [ˈʃɪʃkə,bæb] *n* chiche-kebab *m*.

shit▲ [ʃɪt] (*pret & pp* **shat** [ʃæt], *cont* **shitting**) ◇ *n* **1.** [excrement] merde△ *f* ▪ **to have a ~** (aller) chier▲ ▪ **to have the ~s** avoir la chiasse▲ ➊ **tough ~!** tant pis pour ma/ta/sa *etc* gueule!△ ▪ **to kick** OR **to beat** OR **to knock the ~ out of sb** casser la gueule à qqn△ ▪ **to scare the ~ out of sb** foutre la trouille à qqn△ ▪ **I don't give a ~** je m'en fous△, j'en ai rien à foutre ▪ **to give sb a lot of ~** faire chier qqn▲ ▪ **to be in the ~** être dans la merde△ ▪ **no ~?** *US* sans blague? ▪ **when the ~ hits the fan** quand nous serons dans la merde (jusqu'au cou) **2.** *(U)* [nonsense, rubbish] conneries△ *fpl* ▪ **that's a load of ~!** c'est des conneries, tout ça! ▪ **to be full of ~** raconter des conneries **3.** [disliked person] salaud△ *m*, salope△ *f*, connard▲ *m*, connasse▲ *f* **4.** *drug sl* [hashish] shit△ *m*, hasch *m* **5.** *US* [anything] : **I can't see ~** j'y vois que dalle△.
◇ *vi* chier▲.
◇ *vt* : **to ~ oneself** chier dans son froc▲.
◇ *interj* merde.

shite▲ [ʃaɪt] = **shit** *(n senses 1, 2, 3 & interj)*.

shithead▲ [ˈʃɪthed] *n* [disliked person] salaud△ *m*, salope△ *f*.

shit-hot▲ *adj US* vachement bon△ ▪ **he's ~ as an actor** il est vachement bon comme acteur.

shithouse▲ [ˈʃɪthaʊs] (*pl* [-haʊzɪz]) *n* chiottes△ *fpl*.

shitless▲ [ˈʃɪtlɪs] *adj* : **to be scared ~** avoir une trouille bleue△ ▪ **to be bored ~** se faire chier à mort △.

shitload▲ [ˈʃɪtləʊd] *n* : **~s of sthg** des tonnes de qqch.

shit-scared▲ *adj* : **to be ~** avoir une trouille bleu△.

shitty▲ [ˈʃɪtɪ] (*comp* **shittier**, *superl* **shittiest**) *adj* **1.** [worthless] merdique△ **2.** [mean] dégueulasse△.

shiver [ˈʃɪvəʳ] ◇ *vi* **1.** [with cold, fever, fear] grelotter, trembler ▪ [with excitement] frissonner, trembler **2.** NAUT [sail] faseyer **3.** [splinter] se fracasser, voler en éclats.
◇ *n* **1.** [from cold, fever, fear] frisson *m*, tremblement *m* ▪ [from excitement] frisson *m* ▪ **it gives me the ~s** *inf* ça me donne le frisson OR des frissons **2.** [fragment] éclat *m*.

shivery [ˈʃɪvərɪ] *adj* [cold] frissonnant ▪ [frightened] frissonnant, tremblant ▪ [feverish] fiévreux, grelottant de fièvre.

shoal [ʃəʊl] ◇ *n* **1.** [of fish] banc *m* **2.** *fig* [large numbers] foule *f* **3.** [shallows] haut-fond *m* **4.** [sandbar] barre *f* ▪ [sandbank] banc *m* de sable.
◇ *vi* [fish] se mettre OR se rassembler en bancs.

shock [ʃɒk] ◇ *n* **1.** [surprise] choc *m*, surprise *f* ▪ **she got a ~ when she saw me again** ça lui a fait un choc de me revoir ▪ **what a ~ you gave me!** qu'est-ce que tu m'as fait peur! **2.** [upset] choc *m* ▪ **that comes as no ~ to me** ça ne m'étonne pas ▪ **the news of his death came as a terrible ~ to me** la nouvelle de sa mort a été un grand choc pour moi **3.** ELEC décharge *f* (électrique) ▪ **to get a ~** recevoir OR prendre une décharge (électrique) **4.** [impact - of armies, vehicles] choc *m*, heurt *m* ▪ [vibration - from explosion, earthquake] secousse *f* **5.** MED choc *m* ▪ **to be in a state of ~, to be suffering from ~** être en état de choc ▪ **postoperative ~** choc *m* postopératoire **6.** *US inf* AUT = **shock absorber** **7.** [bushy mass] : **a ~ of hair** une crinière *fig*.
◇ *comp* [measures, argument, headline] choc *(inv)* ▪ [attack] surprise *(inv)* ▪ [result, defeat] inattendu.
◇ *vt* **1.** [stun] stupéfier, bouleverser, secouer ▪ **I was ~ed to hear that she had left** j'ai été stupéfait d'apprendre qu'elle était partie **2.** [offend, scandalize] choquer, scandaliser **3.** [incite, force] : **to ~ sb out of sthg** secouer qqn pour le sortir de qqch ▪ **to ~ sb into action** pousser qqn à agir ▪ **to ~ sb into doing sthg** secouer qqn jusqu'à ce qu'il fasse qqch **4.** ELEC donner une secousse OR un choc électrique à.

shock absorber [-əb,zɔːbəʳ] *n* amortisseur *m*.

shocked [ʃɒkt] *adj* **1.** [stunned] bouleversé, stupéfait ▪ **a ~ meeting was told of the takeover** c'est avec stupéfaction que l'assemblée a appris le rachat de l'entreprise ▪ **they all listened in ~ silence** ils ont tous écouté, muets de stupéfaction **2.** [offended, scandalized] choqué, scandalisé.

shocker [ˈʃɒkəʳ] *n inf* **1.** [book] livre *m* à sensation ▪ [film] film *m* à sensation ▪ [news] nouvelle *f* sensationnelle ▪ [play] pièce *f* à sensation ▪ [story] histoire *f* sensationnelle ▪ **that's a real ~ of a story** cette histoire est vraiment choquante **2.** *hum* [atrocious person] : **you little ~!** petit monstre!

shockheaded [ˈʃɒkhedɪd] *adj* hirsute.

shocking [ˈʃɒkɪŋ] ◇ *adj* **1.** [scandalous] scandaleux, choquant **2.** [horrifying] atroce, épouvantable **3.** *inf* [very bad] affreux, épouvantable ▪ **he's a ~ actor** il est nul comme acteur.

<> *adv inf*: **it was raining something ~!** il fallait voir ce qu'il *OR* comme ça tombait!

shockingly ['ʃɒkɪŋlɪ] *adv* **1.** [as intensifier] affreusement, atrocement ▪ **the weather has been ~ bad lately** la météo est vraiment affreuse depuis quelque temps **2.** [extremely badly] très mal, lamentablement.

shocking pink <> *n* rose *m* bonbon.
<> *adj* rose bonbon *(inv)*.

shockproof ['ʃɒkpru:f] *adj* résistant aux chocs.

shock tactics *npl*: **to use ~** employer la manière forte.

shock therapy, shock treatment *n* MED (traitement *m* par) électrochoc *m*, sismothérapie *f*.

shock troops *npl* troupes *fpl* de choc.

shock wave *n* onde *f* de choc ▪ *fig* répercussion *f*.

shod [ʃɒd] *pt & pp* ▷ **shoe**.

shoddily ['ʃɒdɪlɪ] *adv* **1.** [built, made] mal **2.** [meanly, pettily] de façon mesquine.

shoddy ['ʃɒdɪ] (*comp* **shoddier**, *superl* **shoddiest**) <> *adj* **1.** [of inferior quality] de mauvaise qualité ▪ **~ workmanship** du travail mal fait ▪ **a ~ imitation** une piètre *OR* médiocre imitation **2.** [mean, petty] sale.
<> *n* tissu *m* shoddy *OR* de renaissance.

shoe [ʃu:] (*pret & pp* **shod** [ʃɒd]) <> *n* **1.** [gen] chaussure *f* ▪ **a pair of ~s** une paire de chaussures ▪ **to put on one's ~s** mettre ses chaussures, se chausser ▶ **I wouldn't like to be in his ~s** je n'aimerais pas être à sa place ▪ **put yourself in my ~s** mettez-vous à ma place ▪ **to step into** *OR* **to fill sb's ~s** prendre la place de qqn, succéder à qqn ▪ **if the ~ fits, wear it** qui se sent morveux (qu'il) se mouche *prov* **2.** : **(horse) ~** fer *m* (à cheval) **3.** [in casino - for baccarat etc] sabot *m* **4.** [on electric train] frotteur *m*.
<> *comp* [cream, leather] pour chaussures ▪ **~ cleaner** produit *m* pour chaussures ▪ **~ repairer** cordonnier *m* ▪ **~ size** pointure *f*.
<> *vt* **1.** [horse] ferrer **2.** *(usu passive) lit* [person] chausser.

shoe box *n* boîte *f* à chaussures.

shoebrush ['ʃu:brʌʃ] *n* brosse *f* à chaussures.

shoehorn ['ʃu:hɔ:n] *n* chausse-pied *m*.

shoelace ['ʃu:leɪs] *n* lacet *m* (de chaussures).

shoe leather *n* cuir *m* pour chaussures ▪ **save your ~ and take the bus** prenez l'autobus au lieu d'user vos souliers.

shoemaker ['ʃu:ˌmeɪkəʳ] *n* [craftsman] bottier *m* ▪ [manufacturer] fabricant *m*, - e *f* de chaussures, chausseur *m*.

shoe polish *n* cirage *m*.

shoeshine ['ʃu:ʃaɪn] *n* **1.** cirage *m* ▪ **to get a ~** se faire cirer les chaussures **2.** *inf* = **shoeshine boy**.

shoeshine boy *n* (petit) cireur *m* (de chaussures).

shoe shop *n* magasin *m* de chaussures.

shoestring ['ʃu:strɪŋ] <> *n* **1.** *US* [shoelace] lacet *m* (de chaussure) **2.** *inf phr* **on a ~** avec trois fois rien ▪ **the film was made on a ~** c'est un film à très petit budget ▪ **cookery on a ~** la cuisine économique *OR* bon marché.
<> *comp*: **~ budget** petit budget *m*.

shoetree ['ʃu:tri:] *n* embauchoir *m*.

shone [ʃɒn] *pt & pp* ▷ **shine**.

shoo [ʃu:] (*pret & pp* **shooed**) <> *interj* oust, ouste.
<> *vt* chasser ▪ **to ~ sb/sthg away** chasser qqn/qqch.

shoo-in *n US inf* **he's/she's a ~** il/elle gagnera à coup sûr ▪ **it's a ~** *inf* c'est couru d'avance.

shook [ʃʊk] <> *pt* ▷ **shake**.
<> *n* AGRIC gerbe *f*, botte *f*.

shook-up *adj inf* bouleversé.

shoot [ʃu:t] (*pret & pp* **shot** [ʃɒt]) <> *vi* **1.** [with gun] tirer ▪ **~!** tirez!, feu! ▪ **to ~ at sb/sthg** tirer sur qqn/qqch ▪ **to ~ on sight** tirer à vue ▪ **to ~ to kill** tirer pour tuer ▪ **to ~ into the air** tirer en l'air ▪ **to ~ from the hip** *fig* parler franchement
2. [hunt] chasser ▪ **to go ~ing** aller à la chasse
3. [go fast] : **I shot out after her** j'ai couru après elle ▪ **she shot along the corridor** elle a couru à toutes jambes le long du couloir ▪ **~ along to the baker's and get a loaf, will you?** est-ce que tu peux filer à la boulangerie acheter du pain? ▪ **the rabbit shot into its burrow** le lapin s'est précipité dans son terrier ▪ **the car shot out in front of us** [changed lanes] la voiture a déboîté tout d'un coup devant nous ; [from another street] la voiture a débouché devant nous ▪ **the water shot out of the hose** l'eau a jailli du tuyau d'arrosage ▪ **debris shot into the air** des débris ont été projetés en l'air ▪ **Paul has shot ahead at school recently** Paul a fait d'énormes progrès à l'école ces derniers temps ▪ **a violent pain shot up my leg** j'ai senti une violente douleur dans la jambe
4. CIN tourner ▪ **~!** moteur!, on tourne!
5. SPORT tirer, shooter
6. *inf* [go ahead, speak] : **can I ask you something? – ~!** je peux te poser une question? – vas-y!
7. BOT [sprout] pousser ▪ [bud] bourgeonner
8. *US* **to ~ for** *OR* **at** [aim for] viser.
<> *vt* **1.** [hit] atteindre ▪ [injure] blesser ▪ **he's been badly shot** il a été grièvement blessé par balle *OR* balles ▪ **she was shot in the arm/leg** elle a reçu une balle dans le bras/la jambe ▮ [kill] abattre, descendre, tuer (d'un coup de pistolet *OR* de fusil) ▪ **to ~ o.s.** se tuer, se tirer une balle ▮ [execute by firing squad] fusiller ▶ **you'll get me shot** *inf hum* je vais me faire incendier à cause de toi ▪ **to ~ o.s. in the foot** *inf* ramasser une pelle
2. [fire - gun] tirer un coup de ; [- bullet] tirer ; [- arrow] tirer, lancer, décocher ; [- rocket, dart, missile] lancer ▪ **they were ~ing their rifles in the air** ils tiraient des coups de feu en l'air ▪ **to ~ it out with sb** *inf* s'expliquer avec qqn à coups de revolver *OR* de fusil ▪ **to ~ questions at sb** *fig* bombarder *OR* mitrailler qqn de questions ▪ **she shot a shy smile at him** *fig* elle lui jeta un petit sourire timide
3. [hunt] chasser, tirer ▪ **to ~ grouse** chasser la grouse
4. CIN tourner ▪ PHOT prendre (en photo) ▪ **the photos were all shot on location in Paris** les photos ont toutes été prises à Paris
5. GAMES & SPORT [play] jouer ▪ **to ~ pool** jouer au billard américain ▪ **to ~ dice** jouer aux dés ▮ [score] marquer ▪ **to ~ a goal/basket** marquer un but/panier ▪ **he shot 71 in the first round** GOLF il a fait 71 au premier tour
6. [send] envoyer ▪ **the explosion shot debris high into the air** l'explosion a projeté des débris dans les airs ▪ **she shot out a hand** elle a étendu le bras d'un geste vif
7. [go through - rapids] franchir ; [- traffic lights] : **the car shot the lights** la voiture a brûlé le feu rouge
8. [bolt - close] fermer ; [- open] ouvrir, tirer
9.△ *drug sl* [drugs] se shooter à△
10. *US phr* **to ~ the breeze** *OR* **(the) bull** *inf OR* **the shit**▲ tailler une bavette, discuter le bout de gras ▪ **to ~ one's wad**△ tirer son coup△.
<> *n* **1.** BOT pousse *f*
2. HUNT [party] partie *f* de chasse ▪ [land] (terrain *m* de) chasse *f* ▪ **'private ~'** 'chasse gardée'
3. *US* [chute - for coal, rubbish etc] glissière *f*
4. MIL tir *m*
5. CIN tournage *m*
6. PHOT séance *f* photo, prise *f* de vues
7. *US* [rapid] rapide *m*
8. *phr* **the whole (bang) ~** *inf* tout le tremblement.
<> *interj inf US* zut, mince.

◆ **shoot down** *vt sep* [person, plane, helicopter] abattre ▪ **my proposal was shot down by the chairman** *inf* ma proposition a été démolie par le président ▶ **to ~ sb/sthg down in flames** *liter & fig* descendre qqn/qqch en flammes ▪ **well,~ me down! if it isn't Willy Power!** *US inf* ça alors! mais c'est Willy Power!

◆ **shoot off** <> *vi insep* s'enfuir à toutes jambes.
<> *vt sep* **1.** [weapon] tirer, décharger
2. [limb] emporter, arracher
3.△ *phr* **to ~ one's mouth off** ouvrir sa gueule△ ▪ **don't go ~ing your mouth off about it** ne va pas le gueuler sur les toits△.

◆ **shoot up** ◇ *vi insep* **1.** [move skywards - flame, geyser, lava] jaillir ; [- rocket] monter en flèche
2. [increase - inflation, price] monter en flèche
3. [grow - plant] pousser rapidement *OR* vite ; [- person] grandir
4.△ *drug sl* [with drug] se shooter.
◇ *vt sep* **1.** *US inf* [with weapon - saloon, town] terroriser en tirant des coups de feu
2.△ *drug sl* [drug] se shooter à.

shooting ['ʃu:tɪŋ] ◇ *n* **1.** *(U)* [firing] coups *mpl* de feu, fusillade *f* ▪ **we heard a lot of ~ in the night** nous avons entendu de nombreux coups de feu dans la nuit **2.** [incident] fusillade *f* ▪ **four people died in the ~** quatre personnes ont trouvé la mort au cours de la fusillade ▮ [killing] meurtre *m* ▪ **there have been several ~s in the area** plusieurs personnes ont été tuées *OR* abattues dans le secteur **3.** [ability to shoot] tir *m* **4.** *UK* HUNT chasse *f* **5.** CIN tournage *m*.
◇ *comp* **1.** [with weapon] : **~ incident** fusillade *f* ▪ **~ practice** entraînement *m* au tir **2.** HUNT de chasse ▪ **the~ season** la saison de la chasse.
◇ *adj* [pain] lancinant.

shooting brake *n UK* AUT break *m*.

shooting gallery *n* stand *m* de tir.

shooting range *n* champ *m* de tir.

shooting stick *n* canne-siège *f*.

shoot-out *n inf* fusillade *f*.

shop [ʃɒp] (*pret & pp* **shopped**, *cont* **shopping**) ◇ *n* **1.** *UK* [store] magasin *m* ▪ [smaller] boutique *f* ▪ **she's gone out to the ~s** elle est sortie faire des courses ▪ **to have** *OR* **to keep a ~** être propriétaire d'un magasin, tenir un magasin ➊ **at the fruit ~** chez le marchand de fruits, chez le fruitier, à la fruiterie ▪ **to set up ~** *liter* ouvrir un magasin ; *fig* s'établir, s'installer ▪ **to shut up ~** *liter & fig* fermer boutique ▪ **all over the ~** *inf* [everywhere] partout ; [in disorder] en pagaille ▪ **to talk ~** parler métier *OR* boutique **2.** [shopping trip] : **to do one's weekly ~** faire les courses *OR* les achats de la semaine **3.** *UK* [workshop] atelier *m* ▪ **the repair/paint/assembly ~** l'atelier de réparations/de peinture/de montage.
◇ *vi* [for food, necessities] faire les *OR* ses courses ▪ [for clothes, gifts etc] faire les magasins, faire du shopping ▪ **to go shopping** faire des courses, courir les magasins ▪ **I went shopping for a new dress** je suis allée faire les magasins pour m'acheter une nouvelle robe.
◇ *vt UK inf* [to the police] donner, balancer.
◆ **shop around** *vi insep* comparer les prix ▪ **prices vary a lot, so ~ around** les prix varient énormément, il vaut mieux faire plusieurs magasins avant d'acheter ▪ **I shopped around before opening a bank account** j'ai comparé plusieurs banques *OR* je me suis renseigné auprès de plusieurs banques avant d'ouvrir un compte ▪ **our company is shopping around for new premises** notre société est à la recherche de nouveaux locaux.

shopaholic [,ʃɒpə'hɒlɪk] *n* : **he's a real ~** il adore faire les boutiques.

shop assistant *n UK* vendeur *m*, - euse *f*.

shopfitter ['ʃɒp,fɪtər] *n UK* décorateur *m*, - trice *f* de magasin.

shop floor *n* [place] atelier *m* ▪ [workers] : **the ~** les ouvriers *mpl* ▪ **he was on the ~ for 22 years** il a travaillé 22 ans comme ouvrier.
◆ **shop-floor** *comp* : **~ worker** ouvrier *m*, - ère *f* ▪ **the decision was taken at ~ level** la décision a été prise par la base.

shopfront ['ʃɒpfrʌnt] *n UK* devanture *f* (de magasin).

shopgirl ['ʃɒpgɜ:l] *n UK* vendeuse *f*.

shopkeeper ['ʃɒp,ki:pər] *n UK* commerçant *m*, - e *f* ▪ **small ~** petit commerçant.

shoplift ['ʃɒplɪft] *vt* voler à l'étalage.

shoplifter ['ʃɒp,lɪftər] *n* voleur *m*, - euse *f* à l'étalage.

shoplifting ['ʃɒp,lɪftɪŋ] *n* vol *m* à l'étalage.

shopper ['ʃɒpər] *n* **1.** [person] personne *f* qui fait ses courses ▪ **the streets were crowded with Christmas ~s** les rues étaient bondées de gens qui faisaient leurs courses pour Noël **2.** [shopping bag] cabas *m*.

shopping ['ʃɒpɪŋ] ◇ *n (U)* **1.** [for food, necessities] courses *fpl* ▪ [for clothes, gifts etc] courses *fpl*, shopping *m* ▪ **we're going into town to do some ~** nous allons en ville pour faire des courses *OR* pour faire le tour des magasins ▪ **to do a bit of ~** faire quelques (petites) courses *OR* emplettes **2.** [goods bought] achats *mpl*, courses *fpl*, emplettes *fpl* ▪ **there were bags of ~ everywhere** il y avait des cabas remplis de provisions partout.
◇ *comp* [street, area] commerçant.

shopping bag *n* sac *m OR* filet *m* à provisions, cabas *m*.

shopping basket *n* panier *m* (à provisions).

shopping cart *n US* ▪ = **shopping trolley**.

shopping centre *n* centre *m* commercial.

shopping list *n* liste *f* des courses.

shopping mall *n* centre *m* commercial.

shopping trolley, shopping cart *US n* chariot *m*, Caddie® *m*.

shopsoiled ['ʃɒpsɔɪld] *adj UK liter & fig* défraîchi.

shoptalk ['ʃɒptɔ:k] *n* : **all I ever hear from you is ~** tu ne fais que parler boutique *OR* travail.

shopwalker ['ʃɒp,wɔ:kər] *n UK* chef *m* de rayon.

shop window *n* vitrine *f* (de magasin).

shopworn ['ʃɒpwɔ:n] *US* = **shopsoiled**.

shore [ʃɔ:r] ◇ *n* **1.** [edge, side - of sea] rivage *m*, bord *m* ; [- of lake, river] rive *f*, rivage *m*, bord *m* ▪ [coast] côte *f*, littoral *m* ▪ [dry land] terre *f* ▪ **all the crew members are on ~** tous les membres de l'équipage sont à terre ▪ **to go on ~** débarquer **2.** [prop] étai *m*, étançon *m*.
◇ *vt* étayer, étançonner.
◆ **shores** *npl lit* [country] rives *fpl*.
◆ **shore up** *vt sep* **1.** *liter* étayer, étançonner **2.** *fig* étayer, appuyer, consolider ▪ **the government must act to ~ up the pound** le gouvernement doit prendre des mesures visant à renforcer la livre.

shorebird ['ʃɔ:bɜ:d] *n* oiseau *m* des rivages.

shore leave *n* permission *f* à terre.

shoreline ['ʃɔ:laɪn] *n* littoral *m*.

shore patrol *n US* police *f* militaire (de la Marine).

shorewards ['ʃɔ:wədz] *adv* vers le rivage *OR* la côte.

shorn [ʃɔ:n] ◇ *pp* ▷ **shear**.
◇ *adj* **1.** [head, hair] tondu **2.** *fig* **~ of** dépouillé de.

short [ʃɔ:t] ◇ *adj* **1.** [in length] court ▪ **to have ~ hair** avoir les cheveux courts ▪ **skirts are getting ~er and ~er** les jupes raccourcissent de plus en plus *OR* sont de plus en plus courtes ▪ **the editor made the article ~er by a few hundred words** le rédacteur a raccourci l'article de quelques centaines de mots ▪ **she made a ~ speech** elle a fait un court *OR* petit discours ▪ **he read out a ~ statement** il a lu une courte *OR* brève déclaration ▪ **I'd just like to say a few ~ words** j'aimerais dire quelques mots très brefs ▪ **~ and to the point** bref et précis ➊ **~ and sweet** *inf* court mais bien ▪ **to be in ~ trousers** être en culottes courtes
2. [in distance] court, petit ▪ **a straight line is the ~est distance between two points** la ligne droite est le plus court chemin entre deux points ▪ **to go for a ~ walk** faire une petite promenade ▪ **a few ~ miles away** à quelques kilomètres de là à peine ▪ **at ~ range** à courte portée ▪ **how could he have missed at such ~ range?** comment a-t-il pu rater de si près? ▪ **it's only a ~ distance from here** ce n'est pas très loin (d'ici) ▪ **they continued for a ~ distance** ils ont poursuivi un peu leur chemin
3. [in height] petit, de petite taille
4. [period, interval] court, bref ▪ **a ~ stay** un court séjour ▪ **you should take a ~ holiday** vous devriez prendre quelques jours de vacances ▪ **after a ~ time** après un court intervalle *OR* un petit moment ▪ **to have a ~ memory** avoir la mémoire courte

■ **she was in London for a ~ time** elle a passé quelque temps à Londres ■ **I met him a ~ time** *OR* **while later** je l'ai rencontré peu (de temps) après ■ **it's rather ~ notice to invite them for tonight** c'est un peu juste pour les inviter ce soir ■ **time's getting ~** il ne reste plus beaucoup de temps ■ **a few ~ hours/ years ago** il y a à peine quelques heures/années ■ **the days are getting ~er** les jours raccourcissent ■ **to demand ~er hours/a ~er working week** exiger une réduction des heures de travail/une réduction du temps de travail hebdomadaire ➊ **in the ~ run** à court terme ■ **to be on ~ time** *UK* faire des journées réduites
5. FIN : **~ loan/investment** prêt *m* /investissement *m* à court terme
6. [abbreviated] : **HF is ~ for high frequency** HF est l'abréviation de haute fréquence ■ **Bill is ~ for William** Bill est un diminutif de William
7. [gruff] brusque, sec, sèche *f* ■ **she tends to be a bit ~ with people** elle a tendance à être un peu brusque avec les gens ■ **to have a ~ temper** être irascible
8. [sudden - sound, action] brusque ■ **her breath came in ~ gasps** elle avait le souffle court ■ **he gave a ~ laugh** il eut un rire bref ■ **~, sharp shock** *punition sévère mais de courte durée*
9. [lacking, insufficient] : **to give sb ~ weight** ne pas donner le bon poids à qqn ■ **whisky is in ~ supply** on manque *OR* on est à court de whisky ■ **to be ~ of breath** [in general] avoir le souffle court ; [at the moment] être hors d'haleine ■ **to be ~ of staff** manquer de personnel ■ **to be ~ of sleep** n'avoir pas assez dormi ■ **I'm a bit ~ (of money) at the moment** je suis un peu à court (d'argent) en ce moment ■ **he's a bit ~ on imagination** *fig* il manque un peu d'imagination
10. *UK* [drink] : **a ~ drink** un petit verre
11. LING bref ■ **~ syllable/vowel** syllabe/voyelle brève
12. CULIN [pastry] ≃ brisé
13. ST. EX [sale] à découvert
14. [in betting - odds] faible.
◇ *adv* **1.** [suddenly] : **to stop ~** s'arrêter net ➊ **to pull** *OR* **to bring sb up ~** interrompre qqn ■ **to be taken** *OR* **caught ~** *UK inf* être pris d'un besoin pressant
2. *phr* **to fall ~ of** [objective, target] ne pas atteindre ; [expectations] ne pas répondre à ■ **his winnings fell far ~ of what he had expected** ses gains ont été bien moindres que ce à quoi il s'attendait ■ **to go ~ (of sthg)** manquer (de qqch) ■ **to run ~ (of sthg)** être à court (de qqch).
◇ *vt* ELEC court-circuiter.
◇ *vi* ELEC se mettre en court-circuit.
◇ *n* **1.** *inf* ELEC court-circuit *m*
2. *UK* [drink] *alcool servi dans de petits verres*
3. CIN court-métrage *m*.
◆ **shorts** *npl* [short trousers] short *m* ■ **a pair of khaki ~s** un short kaki ‖ [underpants] caleçon *m*.
◆ **for short** *adv phr* : **they call him Ben for ~** on l'appelle Ben pour faire plus court ■ **trinitrotoluene, or TNT for ~** le trinitrotoluène ou TNT en abrégé.
◆ **in short** *adv phr* (en) bref.
◆ **short of** *prep phr* sauf ■ **he would do anything ~ of stealing** il ferait tout sauf voler ■ **nothing ~ of a miracle can save him now** seul un miracle pourrait le sauver maintenant ■ **~ of resigning, what can I do?** à part démissionner, que puis-je faire?

shortage [ˈʃɔːtɪdʒ] *n* [of labour, resources, materials] manque *m*, pénurie *f* ■ [of food] disette *f*, pénurie *f* ■ [of money] manque *m* ■ **a petrol ~, a ~ of petrol** une pénurie d'essence ■ **the housing/energy ~** la crise du logement/de l'énergie ■ **there's no ~ of good restaurants in this part of town** les bons restaurants ne manquent pas dans ce quartier.

short back and sides *n* coupe *f* courte *OR* dégagée sur la nuque et derrière les oreilles.

shortbread [ˈʃɔːtbred] *n* sablé *m* ■ **~ biscuit** *UK* sablé *m*.

shortcake [ˈʃɔːtkeɪk] *n* **1.** *UK* CULIN [biscuit] = **shortbread** **2.** [cake] tarte *f* sablée.

short-change *vt* **1.** *liter* **to ~ sb** ne pas rendre assez (de monnaie) à qqn **2.** *inf* [swindle] rouler, escroquer.

short circuit *n* court-circuit *m*.
◆ **short-circuit** ◇ *vt* ELEC & *fig* court-circuiter.
◇ *vi* se mettre en court-circuit.

shortcoming [ˈʃɔːtˌkʌmɪŋ] *n* défaut *m*.

shortcrust pastry [ˈʃɔːtkrʌst-] *n* pâte *f* brisée.

short cut *n liter* & *fig* raccourci *m* ■ **to take a ~** prendre un raccourci.

shorten [ˈʃɔːtn] ◇ *vt* **1.** [in length - garment, string] raccourcir ; [- text, article, speech] raccourcir, abréger ■ **the name James is often ~ed to Jim** Jim est un diminutif courant de James **2.** [in time] écourter ■ **the new railway line will ~ the journey time to London** la nouvelle ligne de chemin de fer réduira le temps de trajet jusqu'à Londres.
◇ *vi* **1.** [gen] (se) raccourcir **2.** [in betting - odds] devenir moins favorable.

shortening [ˈʃɔːtnɪŋ] *n* **1.** CULIN matière *f* grasse **2.** [of garment, string] raccourcissement *m* ■ [of text, speech] raccourcissement *m*, abrègement *m* ■ [of time, distance] réduction *f*.

shortfall [ˈʃɔːtfɔːl] *n* insuffisance *f*, manque *m* ■ **there's a ~ of $100** il manque 100 dollars.

short-haired *adj* [person] à cheveux courts ■ [animal] à poil ras.

shorthand [ˈʃɔːthænd] *n* sténographie *f*, sténo *f* ■ **to take notes in ~** prendre des notes en sténo.

shorthanded [ˌʃɔːtˈhændɪd] *adj* à court de personnel.

shorthand typist *n* sténodactylo *mf*.

short-haul *adj* [transport] à courte distance ■ **~ aircraft** court-courrier *m*.

shorthorn [ˈʃɔːthɔːn] *n* shorthorn *m (race de bovins)*.

shortie [ˈʃɔːtɪ] *n inf* = **shorty**.

short list *n UK* liste *f* de candidats présélectionnés.
◆ **short-list** *vt UK* **five candidates have been ~ed** cinq candidats ont été présélectionnés.

short-lived [-ˈlɪvd] *adj* [gen] de courte durée, éphémère, bref ■ [animal, species] éphémère.

shortly [ˈʃɔːtlɪ] *adv* **1.** [soon] bientôt, sous peu, avant peu ■ **~ afterwards** peu (de temps) après **2.** [gruffly] sèchement, brusquement **3.** [briefly] brièvement, en peu de mots.

short-order cook *n* cuisinier *m*, - ère *f* dans un snack-bar.

short-range *adj* **1.** [weapon] de courte portée ■ [vehicle, aircraft] à rayon d'action limité **2.** [prediction, outlook] à court terme.

shortsighted [ˌʃɔːtˈsaɪtɪd] *adj* **1.** *liter* myope **2.** *fig* [person] qui manque de perspicacité *OR* de prévoyance ■ [plan, policy] à courte vue.

shortsightedness [ˌʃɔːtˈsaɪtɪdnɪs] *n* **1.** *liter* myopie *f* **2.** *fig* myopie *f*, manque *m* de perspicacité *OR* de prévoyance.

short-sleeved *adj* à manches courtes.

short-staffed [-ˈstɑːft] *adj* à court de personnel.

short-stay *adj* : **~ car park** parking *m* courte durée ■ **~ patient** patient *m* hospitalisé pour une courte durée.

short story *n* nouvelle *f*.

short-tempered *adj* irascible, irritable.

short tennis *n* tennis *m* pour enfants.

short-term *adj* à court terme ■ **~ loan** prêt *m* à court terme.

short-time *adj UK* **to be on ~ working** être en chômage partiel.

short ton *n* tonne *f* (américaine), short ton *f*.

short wave *n* onde *f* courte ■ **on ~** sur ondes courtes.
◆ **short-wave** *comp* [radio] à ondes courtes ■ [programme, broadcasting] sur ondes courtes.

shorty [ˈʃɔːtɪ] (*pl* **shorties**) *n inf* petit *m*, - e *f*, minus *m*.

Shostakovich [ˌʃɒstəˈkəʊvɪtʃ] *pr n* Chostakovitch.

shot [ʃɒt] ◇ *pt & pp* ▷ **shoot**.
◇ *n* **1.** [instance of firing] coup *m* (de feu) ▪ **to have** *OR* **to fire** *OR* **to take a ~ at sthg** tirer sur qqch ▶ **a ~ across the bows** *liter & fig* un coup de semonce ▪ **it was a ~ in the dark** j'ai/il a *etc* dit ça au hasard ▪ **the dog was off like a ~** *inf* le chien est parti comme une flèche ▪ **I'd accept the offer like a ~** *inf* j'accepterais l'offre sans la moindre hésitation ▪ **the ~ heard around the world** *expression évoquant le début de la guerre d'Indépendance américaine*
2. [sound of gun] coup *m* de feu
3. *(U)* [shotgun pellets] plomb *m*, plombs *mpl*
4. [marksman] tireur *m*, - euse *f*, fusil *m* ▪ **she's a good ~** c'est une excellente tireuse, elle tire bien ▪ **she's a poor ~** elle tire mal
5. SPORT [at goal - in football, hockey etc] tir *m* ▪ [stroke - in tennis, cricket, billiards etc] coup *m* ▪ [throw - in darts] lancer *m* ▪ **good ~!** bien joué! ▶ **to call the ~s** mener le jeu ▪ **to call one's ~** *US inf* annoncer la couleur
6. SPORT : **to put the ~** lancer le poids
7. ASTRONAUT [launch] tir *m*
8. PHOT photo *f* ▪ CIN plan *m*, prise *f* de vue ▪ **the opening ~s of the film** les premières images du film
9. *inf* [try] tentative *f*, essai *m* ▪ **I'd like to have a ~ at it** j'aimerais tenter le coup ▪ **give it your best ~** fais pour le mieux
10. [injection] piqûre *f* ▪ **a ~ in the arm** *fig* un coup de fouet *fig*
11. [drink] (petit) verre *m*.
◇ *adj* **1.** *UK* [rid] : **to get ~ of sthg/sb** *inf* se débarrasser de qqch/qqn
2. [streaked] strié ▪ **~ silk** soie *f* changeante ▪ **the book is ~ through with subtle irony** *fig* le livre est plein d'une ironie subtile
3. *inf esp US inf* [exhausted] épuisé, crevé ▪ [broken, spoilt] fichu, bousillé ▪ **my nerves are ~** je suis à bout de nerfs.

THE SHOT HEARD AROUND THE WORLD

Titre d'un poème de Ralph Waldo Emerson, en hommage au premier coup de feu échangé entre les *Minutemen* américains et les forces anglaises, en avril 1775, à Lexington. L'écrivain y loue la détermination des colons et salue l'avènement d'une nouvelle nation.

shotgun ['ʃɒtgʌn] ◇ *n* fusil *m* de chasse.
◇ *adj* forcé ▪ **a ~ merger** une fusion imposée.
◇ *adv US* **to ride ~** voyager comme passager.

shotgun wedding *n* mariage *m* forcé.

shot put *n* lancer *m* du poids.

shot putter *n* lanceur *m*, - euse *f* de poids.

should [ʃʊd] *modal vb* **1.** [indicating duty, necessity] : **I ~ be working, not talking to you** je devrais être en train de travailler au lieu de parler avec vous ▪ **papers ~ not exceed ten pages** les devoirs ne devront pas dépasser dix pages ‖ [indicating likelihood] : **they ~ have arrived by now** ils devraient être arrivés maintenant ‖ [indicating what is acceptable, desirable etc] : **you shouldn't have done that!** tu n'aurais pas dû faire ça! ▪ **you ~ have seen the state of the house!** si tu avais vu dans quel état était la maison! ▪ **you ~ hear the way he talks!** il faut voir comment il s'exprime! ▪ **~ he tell her? – yes he ~** est-ce qu'il devrait le lui dire? – oui, sans aucun doute ▪ **I'm very sorry – and so you ~ be!** je suis vraiment désolé – il y a de quoi! ▪ **why shouldn't I enjoy myself now and then?** pourquoi est-ce que je n'aurais pas le droit de m'amuser de temps en temps? ‖ [prefacing an important remark] : **I ~ perhaps say, at this point, that...** à ce stade, je devrais peut-être dire que...
2. *(forming conditional tense)* [would] : **I ~ like to meet your parents** j'aimerais rencontrer vos parents ▪ **I ~ have thought the answer was obvious** j'aurais pensé que la réponse était évidente ▪ **~ you be interested, I know a good hotel there** si cela vous intéresse, je connais un bon hôtel là-bas ▪ **how ~ I know?** comment voulez-vous que je le sache? ▪ **I ~ think so/not!** j'espère bien/bien que non!
3. [were to - indicating hypothesis, speculation] : **if I ~ forget** si (jamais) j'oublie ▪ **I'll be upstairs ~ you need me** je serai en haut si (jamais) vous avez besoin de moi
4. [after 'that' and in expressions of feeling, opinion etc] : **it's strange (that) she ~ do that** c'est bizarre qu'elle fasse cela ▪ **I'm anxious that she ~ come** je tiens à ce qu'elle vienne ▪ **lest it ~ rain** *lit* de crainte *OR* de peur qu'il ne pleuve
5. *(after 'who' or 'what')* [expressing surprise] : **and who ~ I meet but Betty!** et sur qui je tombe? Betty!
6. *inf iron* [needn't] : **he ~ worry (about money), he owns half of Manhattan!** tu parles qu'il a des soucis d'argent, la moitié de Manhattan lui appartient!

shoulder ['ʃəʊldəʳ] ◇ *n* **1.** [part of body, of garment] épaule *f* ▪ **he's got broad ~s** il est large d'épaules *OR* de carrure ▪ **you can carry it over your ~** tu peux le porter en bandoulière ▪ **I looked over my ~** j'ai jeté un coup d'œil derrière moi ▶ **to cry on sb's ~** pleurer sur l'épaule de qqn ▪ **we all need a ~ to cry on** nous avons tous besoin d'une épaule pour pleurer ▪ **to put one's ~ to the wheel** s'atteler à la tâche ▪ **to stand ~ to ~** être coude à coude **2.** CULIN épaule *f* **3.** [along road] accotement *m*, bas-côté *m* **4.** [on hill, mountain] replat *m* ▪ [of bottle] renflement *m*.
◇ *vt* **1.** [pick up] charger sur son épaule ▪ **to ~ arms** MIL se mettre au port d'armes ▪ **~ arms!** MIL portez armes! **2.** *fig* [take on - responsibility, blame] assumer ▪ [cost] faire face à **3.** [push] pousser (de l'épaule) ▪ **he ~ed me aside** il m'écarta d'un coup d'épaule ▪ **I ~ed my way through the crowd** je me suis frayé un chemin à travers la foule (en jouant des épaules).

shoulder bag *n* sac *m* à bandoulière.

shoulder blade *n* omoplate *f*.

shoulder-high ◇ *adj* qui arrive (jusqu')à l'épaule.
◇ *adv* : **to carry sb ~** porter qqn en triomphe.

shoulder holster *n* holster *m*.

shoulder pad *n* [in garment] épaulette *f (coussinet de rembourrage)* ▪ SPORT protège-épaule *m*.

shoulder strap *n* [on dress, bra, accordion] bretelle *f* ▪ [on bag] bandoulière *f*.

shouldn't ['ʃʊdnt] = **should not**.

should've ['ʃʊdəv] = **should have**.

shout [ʃaʊt] ◇ *n* **1.** [cry] cri *m*, hurlement *m* ▪ **give me a ~ if you need a hand** appelle-moi si tu as besoin d'un coup de main **2.** *inf UK & Australia* [round of drinks] tournée *f* ▪ **whose ~ is it?** c'est à qui de payer la tournée?
◇ *vi* [cry out] crier, hurler ▪ **to ~ at the top of one's voice** crier à tue-tête ▪ **to ~ (out) for help** appeler au secours ▪ **he ~ed at me for being late** il a crié parce que j'étais en retard ▶ **my new job is nothing to ~ about** *inf* mon nouveau travail n'a rien de bien passionnant.
◇ *vt* [cry out] crier ▪ **the sergeant ~ed (out) an order** le sergent hurla un ordre ▪ **they ~ed themselves hoarse** ils crièrent jusqu'à en perdre la voix.
► **shout down** *vt sep* [speaker] empêcher de parler en criant ▪ [speech] couvrir par des cris ▪ **she was ~ed down** les gens ont hurlé tellement fort qu'elle n'a pas pu parler.

shouting ['ʃaʊtɪŋ] *n (U)* cris *mpl*, vociférations *fpl* ▶ **it's all over bar the ~** l'affaire est dans le sac.

shove [ʃʌv] ◇ *vt* **1.** [push] pousser ▪ [push roughly] pousser sans ménagement ▪ **he ~d me out of the way** il m'a écarté sans ménagement ‖ [insert, stick] enfoncer ▪ **he ~d an elbow into my ribs** il m'enfonça son coude dans les côtes **2.** *inf* [put hurriedly or carelessly] mettre, flanquer, ficher ▪ **~ a few good quotes in and it'll be fine** tu y ajoutes quelques citations bien choisies et ce sera parfait.
◇ *vi* **1.** [push] pousser ▪ [jostle] se bousculer ▪ **people kept pushing and shoving** les gens n'arrêtaient pas de se bousculer **2.** *UK inf* [move up] se pousser ▪ **~ up** *OR* **over** *OR* **along a bit** pousse-toi un peu.
◇ *n* **1.** [push] poussée *f* ▪ **to give sb/sthg a ~** pousser qqn/qqch **2.** *inf phr* **to give sb the ~** sacquer qqn ▪ **to get the ~** se faire sacquer.
► **shove about** *UK*, **shove around** *vt sep* [jostle] bousculer ▪ [mistreat] malmener ▪ **don't let him ~ you about!** ne le laisse pas te marcher sur les pieds!
► **shove off** ◇ *vi insep* **1.** *inf* [go away] se casser, se tirer **2.** [boat] pousser au large.

<> *vt sep* [boat] pousser au large, déborder.

shovel ['ʃʌvl] (*UK pret & pp* **shovelled**, *cont* **shovelling**) (*US pret & pp* **shoveled**, *cont* **shoveling**) <> *n* pelle *f* ■ [on excavating machine] pelle *f*, godet *m* ■ **coal ~** pelle mécanique.

<> *vt* [coal, earth, sand] pelleter ■ [snow] déblayer (à la pelle) ■ **they shovelled the gravel onto the drive** avec une pelle, ils ont répandu les gravillons sur l'allée ■ **to ~ food into one's mouth** *inf* enfourner de la nourriture.

show [ʃəʊ] (*pret* **showed**, *pp* **shown** [ʃəʊn]) <> *vt* **1.** [display, present] montrer, faire voir ■ **to ~ sthg to sb, to ~ sb sthg** montrer qqch à qqn ■ **you have to ~ your pass/your ticket on the way in** il faut présenter son laissez-passer/son billet à l'entrée ■ **I had very little to ~ for my efforts** mes efforts n'avaient donné que peu de résultats ■ **three months' work, and what have we got to ~ for it?** trois mois de travail, et qu'est-ce que cela nous a rapporté? ■ **if he ever ~s himself round here again, I'll kill him!** si jamais il se montre encore par ici, je le tue! ■ **to ~ one's age** faire son âge ▮ [reveal - talent, affection, readiness, reluctance] montrer, faire preuve de ■ **she never ~s any emotion** elle ne laisse jamais paraître *OR* ne montre jamais ses sentiments ■ **to ~ a preference for sthg** manifester une préférence pour qqch ■ **they will be shown no mercy** ils seront traités sans merci ■ **the audience began to ~ signs of restlessness** le public a commencé à s'agiter ■ **the situation is ~ing signs of improvement** la situation semble être en voie d'amélioration

2. [prove] montrer, démontrer, prouver ■ **it just goes to ~ that nothing's impossible** c'est la preuve que rien n'est impossible ■ **the Show Me State** le Missouri

3. [register - subj: instrument, dial, clock] marquer, indiquer

4. [represent, depict] montrer, représenter

5. [point out, demonstrate] montrer, indiquer ■ **~ me how to do it** montrez-moi comment faire ■ **to ~ (sb) the way** montrer le chemin (à qqn) ■ **to ~ the way** *fig* donner l'exemple ▶ **I'll ~ you!** *inf* tu vas voir!

6. [escort, accompany] : **let me ~ you to your room** je vais vous montrer votre chambre ■ **will you ~ this gentleman to the door?** veuillez reconduire Monsieur à la porte ■ **an usherette ~ed us to our seats** une ouvreuse nous a conduits à nos places

7. [profit, loss] faire ■ **prices ~ a 10% increase on last year** les prix sont en hausse *OR* ont augmenté de 10 % par rapport à l'an dernier

8. [put on - film, TV programme] passer ■ **the film has never been shown on television** le film n'est jamais passé à la télévision ■ **'as shown on TV'** 'vu à la télé'

9. [exhibit - work of art, prize, produce] exposer.

<> *vi* **1.** [be visible - gen] se voir ; [- petticoat] dépasser ■ **she doesn't like him, and it ~s** elle ne l'aime pas, et ça se voit ■ **their tiredness is beginning to ~** ils commencent à donner des signes de fatigue

2. [be on - film, TV programme] passer

3. *UK* [in a vote] lever la main

4. *US inf* [turn up] arriver, se pointer.

<> *n* **1.** [demonstration, display] démonstration *f*, manifestation *f* ■ [pretence] semblant *m*, simulacre *m* ■ **she put on a ~ of indifference** elle a fait semblant d'être indifférente ▮ [ostentation] ostentation *f*, parade *f* ■ **he always makes such a ~ of his knowledge** il faut toujours qu'il fasse étalage de ses connaissances ■ **the metal strips are just for ~** les bandes métalliques ont une fonction purement décorative ▶ **a ~ of strength** une démonstration de force ■ **a ~ of hands** un vote à main levée

2. THEAT spectacle *m* ■ TV émission *f* ▶ **the ~ must go on** THEAT & *fig* le spectacle continue

3. [exhibition] exposition *f* ■ [trade fair] foire *f*, salon *m* ■ **I dislike most of the paintings on ~** je n'aime pas la plupart des tableaux exposés ■ **the agricultural/motor ~** le salon de l'agriculture/de l'auto

4. *inf* [business, affair] affaire *f* ■ **she planned and ran the whole ~** c'est elle qui a tout organisé et qui s'est occupée de tout ■ **it's up to you, it's your ~** c'est à toi de décider, c'est toi le chef ▶ **let's get this ~ on the road!** il faut y aller maintenant!

5. [achievement, performance] performance *f*, prestation *f* ■ **the team put up a pretty good ~** l'équipe s'est bien défendue ■ **it's a pretty poor ~ when your own mother forgets your birthday** c'est un peu triste que ta propre mère oublie ton anniversaire ▶ **(jolly) good ~, Henry!** *dated* bravo, Henry!

◆ **show around** *vt sep* faire visiter ■ **my secretary will ~ you around (the factory)** ma secrétaire va vous faire visiter (l'usine).

◆ **show in** *vt sep* faire entrer.

◆ **show off** <> *vi insep* crâner, frimer, se faire remarquer ■ **stop ~ing off!** arrête de te faire remarquer!

<> *vt sep* **1.** [parade] faire étalage de ■ **to ~ off one's skill** faire étalage de son savoir-faire

2. [set off] mettre en valeur.

◆ **show out** *vt sep* reconduire *OR* raccompagner (à la porte).

◆ **show over** *UK* = show around.

◆ **show round** = show around.

◆ **show through** *vi insep* se voir (à travers), transparaître.

◆ **show up** <> *vi insep* **1.** *inf* [turn up, arrive] arriver

2. [be visible] se voir, être visible ■ **the difference is so slight it hardly ~s up at all** la différence est tellement minime qu'elle se remarque à peine.

<> *vt sep UK* **1.** [unmask] démasquer ■ **the investigation ~ed him up for the coward he is** l'enquête a révélé sa lâcheté

2. [draw attention to - deficiency, defect] faire apparaître, faire ressortir

3. [embarrass] faire honte à.

showbiz ['ʃəʊbɪz] *n inf* show-biz *m*, monde *m* du spectacle.

show business *n* show-business *m*, monde *m* du spectacle ■ **a show-business personality** une personnalité du monde du spectacle.

showcase ['ʃəʊkeɪs] <> *n* vitrine *f*.

<> *adj* [role] prestigieux ■ [operation] de prestige.

<> *vt* servir de vitrine à *fig*.

showdown ['ʃəʊdaʊn] *n* **1.** [confrontation] confrontation *f*, épreuve *f* de force **2.** [in poker] étalement *m* du jeu.

shower ['ʃaʊər] <> *n* **1.** [for washing] douche *f* ■ **to have** *OR* **to take a ~** prendre une douche **2.** METEOR averse *f* ■ **scattered ~s** averses intermittentes ■ **a snow ~** une chute de neige **3.** [stream - of confetti, sparks, gravel] pluie *f* ; [- of praise, abuse] avalanche *f* ; [- of blows] pluie *f*, volée *f*, grêle *f* **4.** *US* [party] *fête au cours de laquelle les invités offrent des cadeaux* **5.** *UK inf pej* [group] bande *f* ■ **what a ~!** quelle bande de crétins!

<> *vi* **1.** [have a shower] prendre une douche, se doucher **2.** [rain] pleuvoir par averses ■ **it's started to ~** il a commencé à pleuvoir **3.** *fig* [rain down] pleuvoir.

<> *vt* : **passers-by were ~ed with broken glass** des passants ont été atteints par des éclats de verre ■ **they ~ed him with gifts, they ~ed gifts on him** ils l'ont comblé de cadeaux ■ **to ~ sb with kisses** couvrir qqn de baisers.

shower cap *n* bonnet *m* de douche.

shower gel *n* gel *m* douche.

showerproof ['ʃaʊəpru:f] *adj* imperméable.

showery ['ʃaʊərɪ] *adj* : **it will be rather a ~ day tomorrow** il y aura des averses demain.

showgirl ['ʃəʊgɜ:l] *n* girl *f*.

showground ['ʃəʊgraʊnd] *n* parc *m* d'expositions.

show house *n* maison *f* témoin.

showily ['ʃəʊɪlɪ] *adv* de façon voyante *OR* ostentatoire.

showing ['ʃəʊɪŋ] *n* **1.** [of paintings, sculpture] exposition *f* ■ [of film] projection *f*, séance *f* ■ **a special midnight ~** une séance spéciale à minuit **2.** [performance] performance *f*, prestation *f* ■ **on its present ~ our party should win hands down** à en juger par ses performances actuelles, notre parti devrait gagner haut la main.

showing off *n* : **I've had enough of his ~** j'en ai assez de sa vantardise.

show jumper *n* [rider] cavalier, - ère *f m* (*participant à des concours de saut d'obstacle*) ■ [horse] sauteur *m*.

show jumping *n* jumping *m*, concours *m* de saut d'obstacles.

showman ['ʃəʊmən] (*pl* **showmen** [-mən]) *n* THEAT metteur *m* en scène ■ [in fairground] forain *m* ■ [circus manager] propriétaire *m* de cirque.

showmanship ['ʃəʊmənʃɪp] *n* sens *m* de la mise en scène.

shown [ʃəʊn] *pp* ▷ **show**.

show-off *n inf* frimeur *m*, - euse *f*.

showpiece ['ʃəʊpi:s] *n* : **that carpet is a real ~** ce tapis est une pièce remarquable ■ **the ~ of his collection** le joyau de sa collection ■ **the school had become a ~ of educational excellence** l'école est devenue un modèle quant à la qualité de l'enseignement.

showroom ['ʃəʊrʊm] *n* salle *f* OR salon *m* d'exposition.

showstopper ['ʃəʊ,stɒpəʳ] *n* numéro *m* sensationnel ■ **her song was a real ~** sa chanson a eu OR remporté un succès fou.

show trial *n* procès *m* à grand spectacle.

showy ['ʃəʊɪ] (*comp* **showier**, *superl* **showiest**) *adj* voyant, ostentatoire.

shrank [ʃræŋk] *pt* ▷ **shrink**.

shrapnel ['ʃræpnl] *n* **1.** *(U)* [fragments] éclats *mpl* d'obus ■ **a piece of ~** un éclat d'obus **2.** [shell] shrapnel *m*.

shred [ʃred] ◇ *n* **1.** [of paper, fabric etc] lambeau *m* ■ **in ~s** en lambeaux ■ **to tear sthg to ~s** *liter* déchirer qqch en petits morceaux ; *fig* démolir qqch **2.** [of truth, evidence] parcelle *f*.
◇ *vt* **1.** [tear up - paper, fabric] déchiqueter **2.** CULIN râper.

shredder ['ʃredəʳ] *n* **1.** CULIN [manual] râpe *f* ■ [in food processor] disque-râpeur *m* **2.** [for documents] destructeur *m* de documents.

shrew [ʃru:] *n* **1.** ZOOL musaraigne *f* **2.** *pej* [woman] mégère *f*, harpie *f*.

shrewd [ʃru:d] *adj* [person - astute] perspicace ; [- crafty] astucieux, rusé, habile ■ [judgment] perspicace ■ **to make a ~ guess** deviner juste ■ **a ~ investment** un placement judicieux.

shrewdly ['ʃru:dlɪ] *adv* [act] avec perspicacité OR sagacité ■ [answer, guess] astucieusement.

shrewish ['ʃru:ɪʃ] *adj* [woman, character] acariâtre, hargneux.

shriek [ʃri:k] ◇ *vi* hurler, crier ■ **to ~ with pain** pousser un cri de douleur ■ **to ~ with laughter** hurler de rire.
◇ *vt* hurler, crier.

shrift [ʃrɪft] *n* **1.** *arch* [confession] confession *f* ■ [absolution] absolution *f* **2.** *phr* **to give sb short ~** envoyer promener qqn.

shrike [ʃraɪk] *n* pie-grièche *f*.

shrill [ʃrɪl] ◇ *adj* perçant, aigu, - uë *f*, strident.
◇ *vi* [siren, whistle] retentir.
◇ *vt* crier d'une voix perçante.

shrilly ['ʃrɪlɪ] *adv* [say, sing] d'une voix perçante OR aiguë ■ [whistle] d'une manière stridente.

shrimp [ʃrɪmp] (*US*) ◇ *n* **1.** ZOOL crevette *f* ■ **~ cocktail** cocktail *m* de crevettes **2.** *inf pej* [small person] minus *m*, avorton *m*.
◇ *vi* : **to go ~ing** aller aux crevettes.

shrine [ʃraɪn] *n* **1.** [place of worship] lieu *m* saint **2.** [container for relics] reliquaire *m* **3.** [tomb] tombe *f*, mausolée *m* **4.** *fig* haut lieu *m*.

shrink [ʃrɪŋk] (*pret* **shrank** [ʃræŋk], *pp* **shrunk** [ʃrʌŋk]) ◇ *vi* **1.** [garment, cloth] rétrécir **2.** [grow smaller - gen] rétrécir, rapetisser ; [- economy] se contracter ; [- meat] réduire ; [- person] rapetisser ; [- numbers, profits, savings] diminuer, baisser ; [- business, trade] se réduire ■ **the village seems to have shrunk** le village semble plus petit ■ **the size of computers has shrunk dramatically** les ordinateurs sont devenus nettement plus compacts ■ **my savings have shrunk (away) to nothing** mes économies ont complètement fondu **3.** [move backwards] reculer ■ **they shrank (away** OR **back) in horror** ils reculèrent, horrifiés ■ **to ~ into o.s.** se refermer OR se replier sur soi-même **4.** [shy away] se dérober ■ [hesitate] répugner ■ **he ~s from any responsibility** il se dérobe devant n'importe quelle responsabilité ■ **she shrank from the thought of meeting him again** l'idée de le revoir lui faisait peur.
◇ *vt* (faire) rétrécir ■ **old age had shrunk him** il s'était tassé avec l'âge.
◇ *n inf pej* [psychiatrist, psychoanalyst] psy *mf*.

shrinkage ['ʃrɪŋkɪdʒ] *n (U)* **1.** [gen] rétrécissement *m*, contraction *f* ■ **allow for ~** tenir compte du rétrécissement ■ **they forecast a further ~ in output** ils prévoient une nouvelle diminution de la production **2.** COMM [of goods in transit] pertes *fpl* ■ [of goods stolen] vol *m* (des stocks).

shrinking violet *n* personne *f* sensible et timide.

shrink-wrap (*pret* & *pp* **shrink-wrapped**, *cont* **shrink-wrapping**) *vt* emballer sous film plastique.

shrivel ['ʃrɪvl] (*UK pret* & *pp* **shrivelled**, *cont* **shrivelling**) (*US pret* & *pp* **shriveled**, *cont* **shriveling**) ◇ *vi* [fruit, vegetable] se dessécher, se ratatiner ■ [leaf] se recroqueviller ■ [flower, crops] se flétrir ■ [face, skin] se flétrir ■ [meat, leather] se racornir.
◇ *vt* [fruit, vegetable] dessécher, ratatiner ■ [leaf] dessécher ■ [flower, crops] flétrir ■ [face, skin] flétrir, rider, parcheminer ■ [meat, leather] racornir ■ **a shrivelled old woman** une vieille femme toute ratatinée.
◆ **shrivel up** *vi insep* & *vt sep* = **shrivel**.

shroud [ʃraʊd] ◇ *n* **1.** [burial sheet] linceul *m*, suaire *m* **2.** *fig* [covering] voile *m*, linceul *m* ■ **a ~ of mist/mystery** un voile de brume/mystère **3.** [shield - for spacecraft] coiffe *f* **4.** [rope, cord - for aerial, mast etc] hauban *m* ; [- on parachute] suspente *f*.
◇ *vt* **1.** [body] envelopper dans un linceul OR suaire **2.** [obscure] voiler, envelopper ■ **the town was ~ed in mist/darkness** la ville était noyée dans la brume/plongée dans l'obscurité ■ **its origins are ~ed in mystery** ses origines sont entourées de mystère.

Shrovetide ['ʃrəʊvtaɪd] *n* les jours *mpl* gras *(précédant le Carême)*.

Shrove Tuesday [ʃrəʊv-] *pr n* Mardi gras.

shrub [ʃrʌb] *n* arbrisseau *m*, arbuste *m*.

shrubbery ['ʃrʌbərɪ] (*pl* **shrubberies**) *n* [shrub garden] jardin *m* d'arbustes ■ [scrubland] maquis *m*.

shrug [ʃrʌg] (*pret* & *pp* **shrugged**, *cont* **shrugging**) ◇ *vt* : **to ~ one's shoulders** hausser les épaules.
◇ *vi* hausser les épaules.
◇ *n* haussement *m* d'épaules.
◆ **shrug off** *vt sep* [disregard] dédaigner ■ **to ~ off one's problems** faire abstraction de ses problèmes ■ **it's not a problem you can simply ~ off** on ne peut pas faire simplement comme si le problème n'existait pas.

shrunk [ʃrʌŋk] *pp* ▷ **shrink**.

shrunken ['ʃrʌŋkn] *adj* [garment, fabric] rétréci ■ [person, body] ratatiné, rapetissé ■ [head] réduit.

shuck [ʃʌk] *US* ◇ *n* [pod] cosse *f* ■ [of nut] écale *f* ■ [of chestnut] bogue *f* ■ [of maize] spathe *f* ■ [of oyster] coquille *f*.
◇ *vt* **1.** [beans, peas] écosser ■ [nuts] écaler ■ [chestnuts, maize] éplucher ■ [oysters] écailler **2.** *inf* [discard] se débarrasser de ■ **to ~ (off) one's clothes** se déshabiller.

shucks [ʃʌks] *interj inf* (ah) zut.

shudder ['ʃʌdəʳ] *vi* **1.** [person] frissonner, frémir, trembler ■ **I ~ to think how much it must have cost!** je frémis rien que de penser au prix que ça a dû coûter! ■ **I wonder what they're doing now? – I ~ to think!** je me demande ce qu'ils sont en train de faire – je préfère ne pas savoir! **2.** [vehicle, machine] vibrer ■ [stronger] trépider ■ **the train ~ed to a halt** le train s'arrêta dans une secousse.

shuffle ['ʃʌfl] ◇ *vi* **1.** [walk] traîner les pieds ■ **he ~d shamefacedly into the room** il est entré tout penaud dans la pièce **2.** [fidget] remuer, s'agiter **3.** [in card games] battre les cartes.

◇ *vt* **1.** [walk] : **to ~ one's feet** traîner les pieds **2.** [move round - belongings, papers] remuer **3.** [cards] battre, brasser ▪ [dominoes] mélanger, brasser.
◇ *n* **1.** [walk] pas *m* traînant **2.** [of cards] battage *m* ▪ **it's your ~** c'est à toi de battre (les cartes).
◆ **shuffle off** ◇ *vi insep* partir en traînant les pieds ▪ **to ~ off this mortal coil** *lit & hum* quitter cette vie.
◇ *vt sep* [responsibility] se dérober à.

shun [ʃʌn] (*pret & pp* **shunned**, *cont* **shunning**) *vt* fuir, éviter.

shunt [ʃʌnt] ◇ *vt* **1.** [move] déplacer **2.** *UK* RAIL [move about] manœuvrer ▪ [direct] aiguiller ▪ [marshal] trier ▪ **the carriages had been ~ed into a siding** les wagons avaient été mis sur une voie de garage **3.** ELEC [circuit] monter en dérivation ▪ [current] dériver.
◇ *vi* **1.** RAIL manœuvrer **2.** [travel back and forth] faire la navette.
◇ *n* **1.** RAIL manœuvre *f* (de triage) **2.** ELEC shunt *m*, dérivation *f* **3.** MED shunt *m* **4.** *UK inf* [car crash] collision *f*.

shunting ['ʃʌntɪŋ] ◇ *n* **1.** RAIL manœuvres *fpl* (de triage) **2.** ELEC shuntage *m*, dérivation *f*.
◇ *comp* [engine, track] de manœuvre.

shush [ʃʊʃ] ◇ *interj* chut.
◇ *vt* : **he kept ~ing us** il n'arrêtait pas de nous dire de nous taire.

shut [ʃʌt] (*pret & pp* **shut**, *cont* **shutting**) ◇ *vt* **1.** [close] fermer ▪ **~ your eyes!** fermez les yeux! ➋ **~ your mouth** *inf* OR **your face** *inf* ! *inf* boucle-la!, la ferme! **2.** [trap] : **her skirt got ~ in the door** sa robe est restée coincée dans la porte ▪ **I ~ my finger in the door** je me suis pris le doigt dans la porte.
◇ *vi* **1.** [door, window, container etc] (se) fermer ▪ **the door won't ~** la porte ne ferme pas **2.** [shop, gallery etc] fermer.
◇ *adj* fermé ▪ **keep your mouth** OR **trap ~!** *inf* ferme-la!, boucle-la!
◆ **shut away** *vt sep* [criminal, animal] enfermer ▪ [precious objects] mettre sous clé ▪ **I ~ myself away for two months to finish my novel** je me suis enfermé pendant deux mois pour terminer d'écrire mon roman.
◆ **shut down** ◇ *vt sep* [store, factory, cinema] fermer ▪ [machine, engine] arrêter ▪ [lamp] éteindre.
◇ *vi insep* [store, factory, cinema] fermer.
◆ **shut in** *vt sep* enfermer ▪ **he went to the bathroom and ~ himself in** il est allé à la salle de bains et s'y est enfermé.
◆ **shut off** ◇ *vt sep* **1.** [cut off - supplies, water, electricity] couper ; [- radio, machine] éteindre, arrêter ; [- light] éteindre **2.** [isolate] couper, isoler ▪ **the village was ~ off from the rest of the world** le village a été coupé du reste du monde **3.** [block] boucher.
◇ *vi insep* se couper, s'arrêter ▪ **it ~s off automatically** ça s'arrête automatiquement.
◆ **shut out** *vt sep* **1.** [of building, room] : **she ~ us out** elle nous a enfermés dehors ▪ **we got ~ out** nous ne pouvions plus rentrer **2.** [exclude] exclure ▪ **he drew the curtains to ~ out the light** il tira les rideaux pour empêcher la lumière d'entrer **3.** [block out - thought, feeling] chasser (de son esprit) **4.** SPORT [opponent] empêcher de marquer.
◆ **shut up** ◇ *vi insep* **1.** *inf* [be quiet] se taire ▪ **~ up!** taistoi! **2.** [close] fermer.
◇ *vt sep* **1.** [close - shop, factory] fermer **2.** [lock up] enfermer **3.** *inf* [silence] faire taire.

shutdown ['ʃʌtdaʊn] *n* fermeture *f* définitive.

shut-eye *n inf* **to get a bit of ~** faire un somme, piquer un roupillon.

shut-in ◇ *adj* confiné, enfermé.
◇ *n US* malade *m* qui reste confiné, malade *f* qui reste confinée.

shutoff ['ʃʌtɒf] *n* **1.** [device] : **the automatic ~ didn't work** le dispositif d'arrêt automatique n'a pas fonctionné **2.** [action] arrêt *m*.

shutout ['ʃʌtaʊt] *n* **1.** INDUST lock-out *m* **2.** SPORT *US* victoire écrasante *(remportée sans que l'adversaire marque un seul point)*.

shutter ['ʃʌtər] *n* **1.** [on window] volet *m* ▪ **to put up the ~s** [gen] mettre les volets ; [on shop] fermer boutique **2.** PHOT obturateur *m*.

shuttered ['ʃʌtəd] *adj* [with shutters fitted] à volets ▪ [with shutters closed] aux volets fermés.

shutter release *n* déclencheur *m* d'obturateur.

shutter speed *n* vitesse *f* d'obturation.

shuttle ['ʃʌtl] ◇ *n* **1.** [vehicle, service] navette *f* ▪ **there is a ~ bus service from the station to the stadium** il y a une navette d'autobus entre la gare et le stade **2.** [on weaving loom, sewing machine] navette *f* **3.** = **shuttlecock**.
◇ *vi* faire la navette.
◇ *vt* : **a helicopter ~d the injured to hospital** un hélicoptère a fait la navette pour transporter les blessés à l'hôpital ▪ **passengers are ~d to the airport by bus** les passagers sont transportés en bus à l'aéroport.

shuttlecock ['ʃʌtlkɒk] *n* volant *m (au badminton)*.

shuttle diplomacy *n* navette *f* diplomatique.

shy [ʃaɪ] ◇ *adj* (*comp* **shyer**, *superl* **shyest**) **1.** [person - timid] timide ; [- ill at ease] gêné, mal à l'aise ; [- unsociable] sauvage ▪ **she gave a ~ smile** elle sourit timidement ▪ **he's ~ of adults** il est timide avec les adultes ▪ **she's camera ~** elle n'aime pas être prise en photo ▪ **to make sb ~** intimider qqn ▪ **most people are ~ of speaking in public** la plupart des gens ont peur de parler en public ▪ **don't be ~ of asking for more** n'hésitez pas à en redemander **2.** [animal, bird] peureux **3.** *US* [short, lacking] : **to be ~ of** manquer de, être à court de.
◇ *n* (*pret & pp* **shied**) *UK* **1.** [throw] lancer *m*, jet *m* **2.** [attempt] essai *m*, tentative *f*.
◇ *vi* (*pret & pp* **shied**) [horse] broncher ▪ **his horse shied at the last fence** son cheval a bronché devant le dernier obstacle.
◇ *vt* (*pret & pp* **shied**) lancer, jeter.
◆ **shy away from** *vt insep* éviter de.

Shylock ['ʃaɪlɒk] *n pej* usurier *m*, - ère *f*.

shyly ['ʃaɪlɪ] *adv* timidement.

shyness ['ʃaɪnɪs] *n* timidité *f*.

shyster ['ʃaɪstər] *n esp US inf* [crook] escroc *m*, filou *m* ▪ [corrupt lawyer] avocat *m* marron.

si [si:] *n* MUS si *m inv*.

SI (*abbrev of* **Système International**) *n* SI *m* ▪ **~ unit** unité *f* SI.

Siamese cat *n* chat *m* siamois.

Siamese twins *npl* [male] frères *mpl* siamois ▪ [female] sœurs *fpl* siamoises.

SIB (*abbrev of* **Securities and Investments Board**) *pr n organisme mis en place en 1986 pour superviser le marché financier londonien.*

Siberia [saɪ'bɪərɪə] *pr n* Sibérie *f* ▪ **in ~** en Sibérie.

Siberian [saɪ'bɪərɪən] ◇ *n* Sibérien *m*, - enne *f*.
◇ *adj* sibérien.

sibilance ['sɪbɪləns] *n* sifflement *m*.

sibilant ['sɪbɪlənt] *adj* sifflant.

sibilate ['sɪbɪleɪt] ◇ *vt* prononcer en sifflant.
◇ *vi* siffler.

sibling ['sɪblɪŋ] ◇ *n* [brother] frère *m* ▪ [sister] sœur *f* ▪ **all his ~s** sa fratrie *spec*, tous ses frères et sœurs.
◇ *adj* : **~ rivalry** rivalité *f* entre frères et sœurs.

sibyl ['sɪbl] *n* sibylle *f*.

sic [sɪk] *adv* sic.

siccative ['sɪkətɪv] *n* siccatif *m*.

Sicilian [sɪ'sɪljən] ◇ *n* **1.** [person] Sicilien *m*, - enne *f* **2.** LING sicilien *m*.
◇ *adj* sicilien.

Sicily ['sɪsɪlɪ] *pr n* Sicile *f* ▪ **in ~** en Sicile.

sick [sɪk] ◇ *adj* **1.** [unwell - person, plant, animal] malade ; [- state] maladif ▪ **to fall ~, to get** OR **to take ~** *US* tomber malade

■ **my secretary is off ~** ma secrétaire est en congé de maladie ■ **they care for ~ people** ils soignent les malades ■ **to go** *inf* *OR* **to report ~** MIL se faire porter malade *OR* pâle ■ **are you ~ in the head or something?** *inf* tu n'es pas un peu malade? ■ **to be ~ with fear/worry** être malade de peur/d'inquiétude ■ **you're so good at it you make me look ~!** *US inf* tu le fais si bien que j'ai l'air complètement nul! **2.** [nauseous] : **to be ~** vomir ■ **to feel ~** avoir envie de vomir *OR* mal au cœur ■ **I get ~ at the sight of blood** la vue du sang me rend malade *OR* me soulève le cœur ■ **oysters make me ~** les huîtres me rendent malade ■ **you'll make yourself ~ if you eat too fast** tu vas te rendre malade si tu manges trop vite ■ **I felt ~ to my stomach** j'avais mal au cœur ▶ **to be ~ as a dog** *inf* être malade comme un chien **3.** [fed up, disgusted] écœuré, dégoûté ■ **I'm ~ (and tired) of telling you!** j'en ai assez de te le répéter! ■ **you make me ~!** tu m'écœures *OR* me dégoûtes! ■ **he was ~ of living alone** il en avait assez de vivre seul ▶ **to be ~ to death of sb/sthg** *inf* en avoir vraiment assez *OR* ras le bol de qqn/qqch ■ **I was as ~ as a parrot!** *UK hum* j'en étais malade! ■ **to be ~ at heart** *lit* avoir la mort dans l'âme **4.** *inf* [unwholesome] malsain, pervers ■ [morbid - humour] malsain ; [- joke] macabre ■ **that's the ~est thing I ever heard!** je n'ai jamais entendu quelque chose d'aussi écœurant!

◇ *npl* : **the ~** les malades *mpl*.

◇ *n inf UK inf* [vomit] vomi *m*.

◆ **sick up** *vt sep UK inf* vomir, rendre.

sickbag *n sachet mis à la disposition des passagers malades dans les avions.*

sickbay ['sɪkbeɪ] *n* infirmerie *f*.

sickbed ['sɪkbed] *n* lit *m* de malade.

sick building syndrome *n effets néfastes du séjour dans un environnement muni de l'air conditionné.*

sick call *n* **1.** [visit - by doctor] visite *f* à domicile ; [- by priest] visite *f* aux malades **2.** *US* = **sick parade**.

sicken ['sɪkn] ◇ *vt* **1.** [disgust, distress] écœurer, dégoûter **2.** [make nauseous] donner mal au cœur à, écœurer ■ [make vomit] faire vomir ■ **the smell ~s me** cette odeur me soulève le cœur *OR* me donne des hauts-le-cœur.

◇ *vi* **1.** [fall ill - person, animal] tomber malade ; [- plant] dépérir ■ **he's ~ing for something** *UK* il couve quelque chose **2.** *lit* [become weary] se lasser.

sickening ['sɪknɪŋ] *adj* **1.** [nauseating - smell, mess] nauséabond, écœurant ; [- sight] écœurant **2.** *fig* écœurant, répugnant ■ **he fell with a ~ thud** il est tombé avec un bruit qui laissait présager le pire ■ **she's so talented it's ~!** *hum* elle est si douée que c'en est écœurant!

sickeningly ['sɪknɪŋlɪ] *adv* : **he's ~ pious** il est d'une piété écœurante ■ **she's ~ successful** *hum* elle réussit si bien que c'en est écœurant.

sickle ['sɪkl] *n* faucille *f* ■ **a ~ moon** un mince croissant de lune.

sick leave *n* congé *m* (de) maladie ■ **to be (away) on ~** être en congé (de) maladie.

sick list *n* liste *f* des malades ■ **to be on the ~** se faire porter malade.

sickly ['sɪklɪ] (*comp* **sicklier**, *superl* **sickliest**) *adj* **1.** [person] chétif, maladif ■ [complexion, pallor] maladif ■ [plant] chétif ■ [dawn, light, glare] blafard ■ [smile] pâle **2.** [nauseating] écœurant ■ [sentimentality] mièvre ■ **a ~ sweet smell** une odeur écœurante *OR* douceâtre **3.** *arch* [unwholesome - vapour, climate] insalubre, malsain.

sick-making *adj inf* dégueulasse.

sickness ['sɪknɪs] *n* **1.** [nausea] nausée *f* **2.** [illness] maladie *f*.

sickness benefit *n (U) UK* prestations *fpl* de l'assurance maladie, ≃ indemnités *fpl* journalières.

sick note *n* mot d'absence *(pour cause de maladie)*.

sicko ['sɪkəʊ] *adj US inf* dérangé, malade.

sick parade *n UK* MIL : **to go on ~** se faire porter malade.

sick pay *n* indemnité *f* de maladie *(versée par l'employeur)*.

sickroom ['sɪkrʊm] *n* [sickbay] infirmerie *f* ■ [in home] chambre *f* de malade.

side [saɪd] ◇ *n* **1.** [part of body - human] côté *m* ; [- animal] flanc *m* ■ **lie on your ~** couchez-vous sur le côté ■ **I've got a pain in my right ~** j'ai mal au côté droit ■ **her fists were clenched at her ~s** ses poings étaient serrés le long de son corps ■ **I sat down at** *OR* **by his ~** je me suis assis à ses côtés *OR* à côté de lui ■ **she was called to the president's ~** elle a été appelée auprès du président ■ **to get on sb's good/bad ~** s'attirer la sympathie/l'antipathie de qqn

2. [as opposed to top, bottom, front, back] côté *m* ■ **the bottle was on its ~** la bouteille était couchée ■ **lay the barrel on its ~** mettez le fût sur le côté ■ **her hair is cut short at the ~s** ses cheveux sont coupés court sur les côtés ■ **the car was hit from the ~** la voiture a subi un choc latéral

3. [outer surface - of cube, pyramid] côté *m*, face *f* ■ [flat surface - of biscuit, sheet of paper, cloth] côté *m* ; [- of coin, record, tape] côté *m*, face *f* ■ **write on both ~s of the paper** écrivez recto verso ■ **'this ~ up'** 'haut' ■ **the right/wrong ~ of the cloth** l'endroit *m* /l'envers *m* du tissu ■ [inner surface - of bathtub, cave, stomach] paroi *f* ■ **the ~s of the crate are lined with newspaper** l'intérieur de la caisse est recouvert de papier journal ▶ **to know which ~ one's bread is buttered on** ne pas perdre le nord

4. [edge - of triangle, lawn] côté *m* ; [- of road, pond, river, bed] bord *m* ■ **she held on to the ~ of the pool** elle s'accrochait au rebord de la piscine ■ **a wave washed him over the ~** une vague l'emporta par-dessus bord ■ **she was kneeling by the ~ of the bed** elle était agenouillée à côté du lit

5. [slope - of mountain, hill, valley] flanc *m*, versant *m*

6. [opposing part] côté *m* ■ **on the other ~ of the room/wall** de l'autre côté de la pièce/du mur ■ **on** *OR* **to one ~ of the door** d'un côté de la porte ■ **you're driving on the wrong ~!** vous conduisez du mauvais côté! ■ **she got in on the driver's ~** elle est montée côté conducteur ■ **the dark ~ of the moon** la face cachée de la lune ■ **the lamppost leaned to one ~** le réverbère penchait d'un côté ■ **move the bags to one ~** écartez *OR* poussez les sacs ■ **to jump to one ~** faire un bond de côté ■ **to take sb to one ~** prendre qqn à part ■ **leaving that on one ~ for the moment...** en laissant cela de côté pour l'instant... ■ **Manhattan's Lower East Side** le quartier sud-est de Manhattan ■ **it's way on the other ~ of town** c'est à l'autre bout de la ville ■ **on every ~, on all ~s** de tous côtés, de toutes parts ■ **they were attacked on** *OR* **from all ~s** ils ont été attaqués de tous côtés *OR* de toutes parts ■ **he's on the right/wrong ~ of forty** il n'a pas encore/il a dépassé la quarantaine ■ **stay on the right ~ of the law** restez dans la légalité ■ **he operates on the wrong ~ of the law** il fait des affaires en marge de la loi ■ **there's no other hotel this ~ of Reno** il n'y a pas d'autre hôtel entre ici et Reno ■ **I can't see myself finishing the work this ~ of Easter** je ne me vois pas finir ce travail d'ici Pâques ■ **it's a bit on the pricey/small ~** c'est un peu cher/petit

7. [facet, aspect - of problem] aspect *m*, côté *m* ; [- of person] côté *m* ■ **to examine all ~s of an issue** examiner un problème sous tous ses aspects ■ **she's very good at the practical ~ of things** elle est excellente sur le plan pratique ■ **she has her good ~** elle a ses bons côtés ■ **I've seen his cruel ~** je sais qu'il peut être cruel ■ **she showed an unexpected ~ of herself** elle a révélé une facette inattendue de sa personnalité ■ **I've kept my ~ of the deal** j'ai tenu mes engagements dans cette affaire

8. [group, faction] côté *m*, camp *m* ■ [team] équipe *f* ■ POL [party] parti *m* ■ **the winning ~** le camp des vainqueurs ■ **to pick** *OR* **to choose ~s** former des équipes ■ **whose ~ is he on?** de quel côté est-il? ■ **there is mistrust on both ~s** il y a de la méfiance dans les deux camps ■ **there's still no concrete proposal on** *OR* **from their ~** il n'y a toujours pas de proposition concrète de leur part ■ **to go over to the other ~, to change ~s** changer de camp ■ **luck is on our ~** la chance est avec nous ■ **time is on their ~** le temps joue en leur faveur ■ **he really let the ~ down** il nous/leur *etc* a fait faux bond ■ **don't let the ~ down!** nous comptons sur vous! ■ **she tried to get the committee on her ~** elle a essayé de mettre le comité de son côté ■ **to take ~s** prendre parti ■ **he took Tom's ~ against me** il a pris le parti de Tom contre moi

9. [position, point of view] point *m* de vue ▪ **there are two ~s to every argument** dans toute discussion il y a deux points de vue ▪ **he's told me his ~ of the story** il m'a donné sa version de l'affaire
10. [line of descent] : **she's a Smith on her mother's ~** c'est une Smith par sa mère ▪ **my grandmother on my mother's/father's ~** ma grand-mère maternelle/paternelle ▪ **she gets her love for music from her mother's ~ of the family** elle tient son goût pour la musique du côté maternel de sa famille
11. CULIN : **~ of pork** demi-porc *m* ▪ **~ of beef/lamb** quartier *m* de bœuf/d'agneau
12. *UK* [page of text] page *f*
13. *UK inf* [TV channel] chaîne *f*
14. *UK* [in snooker, billiards etc] effet *m*
15. *UK inf* [cheek] culot *m* ▪ [arrogance] fierté *f*.
<> *vi* : **to ~ with sb** se ranger OR se mettre du côté de qqn, prendre parti pour qqn ▪ **they all ~d against her** ils ont fait cause commune contre elle.
<> *adj* **1.** [situated on one side - panel, window] latéral, de côté ▪ **~ aisle** [in church] bas-côté *m* ; THEAT allée *f* latérale ▪ **~ door** porte *f* latérale ▪ **~ entrance** entrée *f* latérale ▪ **~ pocket** poche *f* extérieure ▪ **~ rail** [on bridge] garde-fou *m* ; NAUT rambarde *f*
2. [directional - view] de côté, de profil ; [- elevation, kick] latéral ▪ **to put ~ spin on a ball** SPORT donner de l'effet à une balle
3. [additional] en plus ▪ **a ~ order of toast** une portion de toast en plus OR en supplément.
◆ **on the side** *adv phr* : **to make a bit of money on the ~** [gen] se faire un peu d'argent en plus OR supplémentaire ; [dishonestly] se remplir les poches ▪ **she's an artist but works as a taxi driver on the ~** elle est artiste mais elle fait le chauffeur de taxi pour arrondir ses fins de mois ▪ **a hamburger with salad on the ~** un hamburger avec une salade ▪ **anything on the ~, sir?** [in restaurant] *US* et avec cela, Monsieur?
◆ **side by side** *adv phr* côte à côte ▪ **the road and the river run ~ by ~** la route longe la rivière ▪ **we'll be working ~ by ~ with the Swiss on this project** nous travaillerons en étroite collaboration avec les Suisses sur ce projet.

sidearm ['saɪdɑːm] *n* arme *f* de poing.

sideboard ['saɪdbɔːd] *n* [for dishes] buffet *m* bas.
◆ **sideboards** *UK* = **sideburns**.

sideburns ['saɪdbɜːnz] *npl* pattes *fpl*.

sidecar ['saɪdkɑːʳ] *n* **1.** [on motorbike] side-car *m* **2.** [drink] side-car *m* *(cocktail composé de cognac, de cointreau et de jus de citron)*.

-sided ['saɪdɪd] *in cpds* : **three/five~** à trois/cinq côtés ▪ **a many~ figure** une figure polygonale ▪ **a glass~ box** une boîte à parois de verre ▪ **elastic~ boots** bottes avec de l'élastique sur les côtés ▪ **a steep~ valley** une vallée encaissée.

side dish *n* plat *m* d'accompagnement ▪ [of vegetables] garniture *f*.

side drum *n* caisse *f* claire.

side effect *n* effet *m* secondaire.

side glance *n liter* regard *m* oblique OR de côté ▪ *fig* [allusion] allusion *f*.

side issue *n* question *f* secondaire.

sidekick ['saɪdkɪk] *n inf* acolyte *m*.

sidelight ['saɪdlaɪt] *n* **1.** *UK* AUT feu *m* de position **2.** NAUT feu *m* de position **3.** [information] : **to give (sb) a ~ on sthg** donner à qqn un aperçu de qqch.

sideline ['saɪdlaɪn] <> *n* **1.** SPORT [gen] ligne *f* de côté ▪ [touchline] (ligne *f* de) touche *f*, ligne *f* de jeu ▪ **to wait on the ~s** SPORT attendre sur la touche ; *fig* attendre dans les coulisses ▪ **I prefer to stand on the ~s** *fig* je préfère ne pas m'en mêler **2.** [job] activité *f* OR occupation *f* secondaire ▪ **as a ~ he takes wedding photos** il fait des photos de mariage pour arrondir ses fins de mois **3.** COMM [product line] ligne *f* de produits secondaires ▪ **they've made recycling a profitable ~** ils ont fait du recyclage une activité secondaire rentable ▪ **it's only a ~ for us** ce n'est pas notre spécialité.
<> *vt* SPORT & *fig* mettre sur la touche.

sidelong ['saɪdlɒŋ] <> *adj* oblique, de côté ▪ **they exchanged ~ glances** ils ont échangé un regard complice.
<> *adv* en oblique, de côté.

side-on <> *adv* de profil ▪ **the car was hit ~** la voiture a subi un choc latéral.
<> *adj* [photo] de profil ▪ [collision] latéral.

side order *n esp US* portion *f* ▪ **I'd like a ~ of fries** je voudrais aussi des frites.

side plate *n* petite assiette *f (que l'on met à gauche de chaque convive)*.

sidereal [saɪ'dɪərɪəl] *adj* sidéral.

side road *n* [minor road - in country] route *f* secondaire ; [- in town] petite rue *f* ▪ [road at right angles] rue *f* transversale.

sidesaddle ['saɪd,sædl] <> *n* selle *f* de femme.
<> *adv* : **to ride ~** monter en amazone.

side salad *n* salade *f (pour accompagner un plat)*.

sideshow ['saɪdʃəʊ] *n* **1.** [in fair - booth] stand *m*, baraque *f* foraine ; [- show] attraction *f* **2.** [minor event] détail *m*.

sideslip ['saɪdslɪp] (*pret & pp* **sideslipped**, *cont* **sideslipping**) <> *n* **1.** AERON glissade *f* sur l'aile **2.** AUT dérapage *m*.
<> *vi* AERON glisser sur l'aile.

sidesman ['saɪdzmən] (*pl* **sidesmen** [-mən]) *n UK* RELIG ≃ bedeau *m*.

sidesplitting ['saɪd,splɪtɪŋ] *adj inf* [story, joke] tordant, bidonnant.

sidestep ['saɪdstep] (*pret & pp* **sidestepped**, *cont* **sidestepping**) <> *n* crochet *m* ▪ SPORT esquive *f*.
<> *vt* **1.** [opponent, tackle - in football, rugby] crocheter ; [- in boxing] esquiver **2.** [issue, question] éluder, éviter ▪ [difficulty] esquiver ▪ **they'll ~ the regulations/the law** ils contourneront le règlement/la loi.
<> *vi* **1.** [dodge] esquiver **2.** [in skiing] : **to ~ up a slope** monter une pente en escalier **3.** [be evasive] rester évasif.

side street *n* [minor street] petite rue *f* ▪ [at right angles] rue *f* transversale.

sidestroke ['saɪdstrəʊk] *n* nage *f* indienne ▪ **to swim ~** nager à l'indienne.

sideswipe ['saɪdswaɪp] <> *n* **1.** [blow - glancing] coup *m* oblique ; [- severe] choc *m* latéral **2.** [remark] allusion *f* désobligeante.
<> *vt US* faucher.

side table *n* petite table *f* ▪ [for dishes] desserte *f* ▪ [beside bed] table *f* de chevet.

sidetrack ['saɪdtræk] <> *vt* [person - in talk] faire dévier de son sujet ; [- in activity] distraire ▪ [enquiry, investigation] détourner ▪ **the speaker kept getting ~ed** le conférencier s'écartait sans cesse de son sujet ▪ **sorry, I got ~ed for a moment** pardon, je m'égare.
<> *n* **1.** [digression] digression *f* ▪ **he went off on a ~** [topic] il s'est écarté de son sujet ; [activity] il s'est laissé distraire **2.** *US* RAIL [in yard] voie *f* de garage ▪ [off main line] voie *f* d'évitement.

sidewalk ['saɪdwɔːk] *n US* trottoir *m* ▪ **to hit the ~s** *inf* chercher du boulot.

sidewalk café *n US* café *m* avec terrasse.

sideways ['saɪdweɪz] <> *adv* [lean] d'un côté ▪ [glance] obliquement, de côté ▪ [walk] en crabe ▪ **to step ~** faire un pas de côté ▪ **I was thrown ~** j'ai été projeté sur le côté ▪ **now turn ~** maintenant mettez-vous de profil ▪ **the pieces can move only ~** les pièces ne peuvent que se déplacer latéralement ▶ **the news really knocked him ~** *inf* [astounded him] la nouvelle l'a vraiment époustouflé ; [upset him] la nouvelle l'a vraiment mis dans tous ses états.
<> *adj* [step] de côté ▪ [look] oblique, de côté ▪ **the job is a ~ move** c'est une mutation et non pas une promotion.

side-wheeler *n US* bateau *m* à aubes.

side-whiskers *npl* favoris *mpl*.

sidewinder ['saɪd,waɪndəʳ] *n* *US* **1.** [blow] grand coup *m* de poing **2.** [snake] crotale *m*, serpent *m* à sonnettes **3.** ARM : **Sidewinder missile** missile *m* Sidewinder *(missile air-air tactique américain)*.

siding ['saɪdɪŋ] *n* **1.** RAIL [in yard] voie *f* de garage ■ [off main track] voie *f* d'évitement **2.** *US* CONSTR pavement *m*.

sidle ['saɪdl] *vi* se faufiler ■ **to ~ up** *OR* **over to sb** se glisser vers *OR* jusqu'à qqn ■ **to ~ in/out** entrer/sortir furtivement.

SIDS *n* = **sudden infant death syndrome**.

siege [si:dʒ] ◇ *n* MIL & *fig* siège *m* ■ **to lay ~ to sthg** assiéger qqch ■ **to be under ~** être assiégé ■ **a state of ~ has been declared** l'état de siège a été déclaré.
◇ *comp* [machine, warfare] de siège ■ **to have a ~ mentality** être toujours sur la défensive.

siege economy *n* économie *f* protectionniste.

sienna [sɪ'enə] ◇ *n* **1.** [earth] terre *f* de Sienne ■ **raw/burnt ~** terre de Sienne naturelle/brûlée **2.** [colour] ocre *m* brun.
◇ *adj* ocre brun *(inv)*.

sierra [sɪ'erə] *n* sierra *f*.

Sierra Leone [sɪ'erəlɪ'əʊn] *pr n* Sierra Leone *f* ■ **in ~** en Sierra Leone.

Sierra Leonean [sɪ'erəlɪ'əʊnjən] ◇ *n habitant de la Sierra Leone*.
◇ *adj* de la Sierra Leone.

siesta [sɪ'estə] *n* sieste *f* ■ **to have** *OR* **to take a ~** faire la sieste.

sieve [sɪv] ◇ *n* [gen] tamis *m* ■ [kitchen utensil] passoire *f* ■ [for gravel, ore] crible *m* ■ **I've got a memory** *OR* **mind like a ~!** ma mémoire est une vraie passoire!
◇ *vt* [flour, sand, powder] tamiser, passer au tamis ■ [purée, soup] passer ■ [gravel, ore] cribler, passer au crible.

sift [sɪft] ◇ *vt* **1.** [ingredients, soil] tamiser, passer au tamis ■ [gravel, seed, ore] cribler, passer au crible ■ **~ a little sugar onto the cakes** saupoudrez un peu de sucre sur les gâteaux **2.** [scrutinize - evidence, proposal] passer au crible *fig* **3.** = **sift out**.
◇ *vi* **1.** [search] fouiller ■ **they ~ed through the garbage/the ruins** ils fouillaient (dans) les ordures/les ruines **2.** [pass, filter] filtrer ■ **I let the sand ~ through my fingers** j'ai laissé le sable couler entre mes doigts.
◆ **sift out** *vt sep* **1.** [remove - lumps, debris] enlever (à l'aide) d'un tamis *OR* d'un crible **2.** [distinguish] dégager, distinguer.

sifting ['sɪftɪŋ] *n* [of flour, powder, soil] tamisage *m* ■ [of seed, gravel, ore] criblage *m*.
◆ **siftings** *npl* [residue] résidu *m* ■ AGRIC criblure *f*.

sigh [saɪ] ◇ *vi* **1.** [gen] soupirer, pousser un soupir ■ **to ~ with relief** pousser un soupir de soulagement **2.** *lit* [lament] se lamenter ■ **to ~ over sthg** se lamenter sur qqch ■ [grieve] soupirer ■ **to ~ for** *OR* **over sb/sthg** soupirer pour qqn/qqch **3.** [wind] murmurer ■ [tree, reed] bruire.
◇ *vt* : **"it's so lovely here," she ~ed** "c'est tellement joli ici", soupira-t-elle.
◇ *n* soupir *m* ■ **to give** *OR* **to heave a ~ of relief** pousser un soupir de soulagement.

sighing ['saɪɪŋ] *n (U)* [of person] soupirs *mpl* ■ [of wind] murmure *m* ■ [of trees] bruissement *m*.

sight [saɪt] ◇ *n* **1.** [faculty, sense] vue *f* ■ **to lose/to recover one's ~** perdre/recouvrer la vue
2. [act, instance of seeing] vue *f* ■ **it was my first ~ of the Pacific** c'était la première fois que je voyais le Pacifique ■ **to catch ~ of sb/sthg** apercevoir *OR* entrevoir qqn/qqch ■ **to lose ~ of sb/sthg** perdre qqn/qqch de vue ■ **at first ~ the place seemed abandoned** à première vue, l'endroit avait l'air abandonné ■ **it was love at first ~** ce fut le coup de foudre ■ **I can't stand** *OR* **bear the ~ of him!** je ne le supporte pas! ■ **to know sb by ~** connaître qqn de vue ■ **to buy sthg ~ unseen** acheter qqch sans l'avoir vu ■ **he can play music at** *OR US* **by ~** il sait déchiffrer une partition ■ **to shoot at** *OR* **on ~** tirer à vue
3. [range of vision] (portée *f* de) vue *f* ■ **the plane was still in ~** l'avion était encore en vue ■ **is the end in ~?** est-ce que tu en vois la fin? ■ **keep that car/your goal in ~** ne perdez pas cette voiture/votre but de vue ■ **the mountains came into ~** les montagnes sont apparues ■ **out of ~** hors de vue ■ **I watched her until she was out of ~** je l'ai regardée jusqu'à ce qu'elle disparaisse de ma vue ■ **keep out of ~!** ne vous montrez pas!, cachez-vous! ■ **she never lets him out of her ~** elle ne le perd jamais de vue ■ **get out of my ~!** disparais de ma vue! ■ **a peace settlement now seems within ~** un accord de paix semble maintenant possible ■ **it was impossible to get within ~ of the accident** il était impossible de s'approcher du lieu de l'accident pour voir ce qui se passait ▶ **out of ~, out of mind** *prov* loin des yeux, loin du cœur *prov*
4. [spectacle] spectacle *m* ■ **the cliffs were an impressive ~** les falaises étaient impressionnantes à voir ■ **beggars are a common ~ on the streets** on voit beaucoup de mendiants dans les rues ■ **it was not a pretty ~** ça n'était pas beau à voir ■ **the waterfalls are a ~ worth seeing** les cascades valent la peine d'être vues ▶ **you're a ~ for sore eyes!** [you're a welcome sight] Dieu merci te voilà! ■ [you look awful] tu fais vraiment peine à voir
5. [tourist attraction] curiosité *f* ■ **one of the ~s of Rome** une des choses à voir à Rome ■ **I'll show you** *OR* **take you round the ~s tomorrow** je vous ferai visiter *OR* voir la ville demain
6. *lit* [opinion, judgment] avis *m*, opinion *f* ■ **in my father's ~ she could do no wrong** aux yeux de mon père, elle était incapable de faire du mal ■ **we are all equal in the ~ of God** nous sommes tous égaux devant Dieu
7. *inf* [mess] pagaille *f* ■ [ridiculously dressed person] tableau *m* *fig* ■ **the kitchen was a ~!** quelle pagaille dans la cuisine! ■ **your hair is a ~!** tu as vu tes cheveux? ■ **I must look a ~!** je ne dois pas être beau à voir!
8. [aiming device] viseur *m* ■ [on mortar] appareil *m* de pointage ■ **to have sthg in one's ~s** *liter* avoir qqch dans sa ligne de tir ; *fig* avoir qqch en vue ■ **to lower one's ~s** viser moins haut ■ **to set one's ~s on sthg** viser qqch ■ **to set one's ~s on doing sthg** avoir pour ambition de faire qqch.
◇ *vt* **1.** [see] voir, apercevoir ■ [spot] repérer
2. [aim - gun] pointer.
◆ **a sight** *adv phr* *UK inf* beaucoup ■ **you'd earn a ~ more money working in industry** votre salaire serait beaucoup plus important si vous travailliez dans l'industrie ■ **it's a (far) ~ worse than before** c'est bien pire qu'avant.

sighted ['saɪtɪd] *adj* voyant ■ **partially ~** mal voyant.

sight gag *n* gag *m* visuel.

sighting ['saɪtɪŋ] *n* : **UFO ~s have increased** un nombre croissant de personnes déclarent avoir vu des ovnis.

sightless ['saɪtlɪs] *adj* [blind] aveugle.

sightline ['saɪtlaɪn] *n* : **to block sb's ~** boucher la vue de qqn, champ *m* de vision.

sight-read [-ri:d] *(pret & pp* **sight-read** [-red]*)* *vi* & *vt* MUS déchiffrer.

sight-reading *n* MUS déchiffrage *m*.

sightseeing ['saɪt,si:ɪŋ] ◇ *n* tourisme *m* ■ **to do some ~** faire du tourisme ; [in town] visiter la ville.
◇ *comp* : **I went on a ~ tour of Rome** j'ai fait une visite guidée de Rome.

sightseer ['saɪt,si:əʳ] *n* touriste *mf*.

sign [saɪn] ◇ *n* **1.** [gen - LING], MATHS & MUS signe *m* ■ **this ~ means "real leather"** ce symbole signifie "cuir véritable"
2. [gesture, motion] signe *m*, geste *m* ■ **to make a ~ to sb** faire signe à qqn ■ **the chief made ~s for me to follow him** le chef m'a fait signe de le suivre ■ **to make the ~ of the cross** faire le signe de croix ■ **the victory ~** le signe de la victoire
3. [arranged signal] signal *m* ■ **a lighted lamp in the window is the ~ that it's safe** une lampe allumée à la fenêtre signifie qu'il n'y a pas de danger ■ **when I give the ~, run** à mon signal, courez
4. [written notice - gen - AUT] panneau *m* ; [- hand-written] écriteau *m* ; [- on shop, bar, cinema etc] enseigne *f* ■ **I didn't see the stop ~** je n'ai pas vu le stop ■ **traffic ~s** panneau *m* de signalisation
5. [evidence, indication] signe *m*, indice *m* ■ MED signe *m* ■ **as a ~ of respect** en témoignage *OR* en signe de respect ■ **it's a ~**

of the times c'est un signe des temps ■ **if he's making jokes it's a good ~** c'est bon signe s'il fait des plaisanteries ■ **at the first ~ of trouble, he goes to pieces** *inf* au premier petit problème, il craque ■ **were there any ~s of a struggle?** y avait-il des traces de lutte? ■ **all the ~s are that the economy is improving** tout laisse à penser que l'économie s'améliore ■ **there's no ~ of her changing her mind** rien n'indique qu'elle va changer d'avis ■ **there's no ~ of the file anywhere** on ne trouve trace du dossier nulle part ■ **he gave no ~ of having heard me** il n'a pas eu l'air de m'avoir entendu ■ **is there any ~ of Amy yet? – not a ~** est-ce qu'on a eu des nouvelles de Amy? – pas la moindre nouvelle
6. ASTROL signe *m* ■ **what ~ are you?** de quel signe êtes-vous?
7. RELIG [manifestation] signe *m* ■ **a ~ from God** un signe de Dieu.
◇ *vt* **1.** [document, book] signer ■ **~ your name here** signez ici ■ **a ~ed Picasso lithograph** une lithographie signée par Picasso ■ **he gave me a ~ed photo of himself** il m'a donné une photo dédicacée ■ **she ~s herself A.M. Hall** elle signe A.M. Hall ■ **the deal will be ~ed and sealed tomorrow** l'affaire sera définitivement conclue demain
2. SPORT [contract] signer ■ [player] engager
3. [provide with signs] signaliser.
◇ *vi* **1.** [write name] signer ■ **he ~ed with an X** il a signé d'une croix ■ **to ~ on the dotted line** *liter* signer à l'endroit indiqué ; *fig* s'engager
2. [signal] : **to ~ to sb to do sthg** faire signe à qqn de faire qqch
3. [use sign language] communiquer par signes.
◆ **sign away** *vt sep* [right, land, inheritance] se désister de ■ [independence] renoncer à ■ [power, control] abandonner ■ **I felt I was ~ing away my freedom** j'avais l'impression qu'en signant je renonçais à ma liberté.
◆ **sign in** ◇ *vi insep* **1.** [at hotel] remplir sa fiche (d'hôtel) ■ [in club] signer le registre
2. [worker] pointer (en arrivant).
◇ *vt sep* **1.** [guest] faire signer en arrivant ■ **guests must be ~ed in** les visiteurs doivent se faire inscrire dès leur arrivée
2. [file, book] rendre, retourner.
◆ **sign for** *vt insep* **1.** [accept] signer ■ **to ~ for a delivery/a registered letter** signer un bon de livraison/le récépissé d'une lettre recommandée ■ **the files have to be ~ed for** il faut signer pour retirer les dossiers
2. [undertake work] signer (un contrat d'engagement).
◆ **sign off** *vi insep* **1.** RADIO & TV terminer l'émission
2. [in letter] : **I'll ~ off now** je vais conclure ici.
◆ **sign on** *UK* ◇ *vi insep* **1.** = **sign up** *(sense 3)*
2. [register as unemployed] s'inscrire au chômage ■ **you have to ~ on every two weeks** il faut pointer (au chômage) toutes les deux semaines.
◇ *vt sep* = **sign up** *(sense 2)*.
◆ **sign out** ◇ *vi insep* [gen] signer le registre (en partant) ■ [worker] pointer (en partant).
◇ *vt sep* **1.** [file, car] retirer (contre décharge) ■ [library book] emprunter ■ **the keys are ~ed out to Mr Hill** c'est M. Hill qui a signé pour retirer les clés
2. [hospital patient] autoriser le départ de ■ **he ~ed himself out** il est parti sous sa propre responsabilité.
◆ **sign over** *vt sep* transférer ■ **the house is being ~ed over to its new owners tomorrow** les nouveaux propriétaires entrent en possession de la maison demain.
◆ **sign up** ◇ *vi insep* **1.** [for job] se faire embaucher
2. MIL [enlist] s'engager ■ **to ~ up for the Marines** s'engager dans les marines
3. [enrol] s'inscrire ■ **she ~ed up for an evening class** elle s'est inscrite à des cours du soir.
◇ *vt sep* **1.** [employee] embaucher ■ MIL [recruit] engager
2. [student, participant] inscrire.

signal ['sɪgnl] (*UK pret & pp* **signalled**, *cont* **signalling**) (*US pret & pp* **signaled**, *cont* **signaling**) ◇ *n* **1.** [indication] signal *m* ■ **to give sb the ~ to do sthg** donner à qqn le signal de faire qqch ■ **he'll give the ~ to attack** il donnera le signal de l'attaque ■ **it was the first ~ (that) the regime was weakening** c'était le premier signe de l'affaiblissement du régime ■ **they are sending the government a clear signal that...** ils indiquent clairement au gouvernement que... ▶ **to send smoke ~s** envoyer des signaux de fumée **2.** RAIL sémaphore *m* **3.** RADIO, TELEC & TV signal *m* ■ **station ~** RADIO indicatif *m* (de l'émetteur).
◇ *comp* **1.** NAUT : **~ book** code *m* international des signaux ■ **~ beacon** *OR* **light** AERON & NAUT balise *f* **2.** RADIO & TELEC [strength, frequency] de signal.
◇ *adj fml* insigne.
◇ *vt* **1.** [send signal to] envoyer un signal à ■ **he signalled the plane forward** il a fait signe au pilote d'avancer ■ **to ~ sb** *US* faire signe à qqn **2.** [indicate - refusal] indiquer, signaler ; [- malfunction] signaler, avertir de ■ **the parachutist signalled his readiness to jump** le parachutiste fit signe qu'il était prêt à sauter **3.** [announce, mark - beginning, end, change] marquer.
◇ *vi* **1.** [gesture] faire des signes ■ **to ~ to sb to do sthg** faire signe à qqn de faire qqch ■ **she was signalling for us to stop** elle nous faisait signe de nous arrêter **2.** [send signal] envoyer un signal **3.** AUT [with indicator] mettre son clignotant ■ [with arm] indiquer de la main un changement de direction.

signal box *n* RAIL poste *m* de signalisation.

signaling *US* = **signalling**.

signalize, ise ['sɪgnəlaɪz] *vt fml* [distinguish, mark] marquer.

signalling *UK*, **signaling** *US* ['sɪgnəlɪŋ] ◇ *n* **1.** AERON, AUT, NAUT & RAIL signalisation *f* **2.** [warning] avertissement *m* **3.** [of electronic message] transmission *f*.
◇ *comp* [error, equipment] de signalisation ■ **~ flag** NAUT pavillon *m* de signalisation ; MIL drapeau *m* de signalisation.

signally ['sɪgnəlɪ] *adv fml* **they have ~ failed to achieve their goal** ils n'ont manifestement pas pu atteindre leur but.

signalman ['sɪgnlmən] (*pl* **signalmen** [-mən]) *n* RAIL aiguilleur *m* ■ MIL & NAUT signaleur *m*.

signal tower *n US* poste *m* d'aiguillage.

signatory ['sɪgnətrɪ] (*pl* **signatories**) ◇ *n* signataire *mf* ■ **Namibia is a ~ to** *OR* **of the treaty** la Namibie a ratifié le traité.
◇ *adj* signataire.

signature ['sɪgnətʃər] ◇ *n* **1.** [name] signature *f* ■ **to put one's ~ to sthg** apposer sa signature sur qqch **2.** [signing] signature *f* ■ **to witness a ~** signer comme témoin ■ **the bill is awaiting ~** *US* POL le projet de loi attend la signature du président **3.** *US* PHARM [instructions] posologie *f* **4.** TYPO [section of book] cahier *m* ■ [mark] signature *f*.
◇ *comp* : **Chanel and her ~ two-piece suit** Chanel et le tailleur (deux-pièces) qui lui est si caractéristique.

signature tune *n UK* RADIO & TV indicatif *m* (musical).

signboard ['saɪnbɔːd] *n* [gen] panneau *m* ■ [for notices] panneau *m* d'affichage ■ [for ads] panneau publicitaire ■ [on shop, bar, cinema etc] enseigne *f*.

signet ['sɪgnɪt] *n* sceau *m*, cachet *m*.

signet ring *n* chevalière *f*.

significance [sɪg'nɪfɪkəns] *n* **1.** [importance, impact] importance *f*, portée *f* ■ **what happened? – nothing of any ~** qu'est-ce qui s'est passé? – rien d'important *OR* de spécial ■ **his decision is of no ~ to our plans** sa décision n'aura aucune incidence sur nos projets **2.** [meaning] signification *f*, sens *m* ■ **sounds take on a new ~ at night** la nuit, les bruits se chargent d'un autre sens *OR* acquièrent une autre signification.

significant [sɪg'nɪfɪkənt] *adj* **1.** [notable - change, amount, damage] important, considérable ; [- discovery, idea, event] de grande portée ■ **no ~ progress has been made** aucun progrès notable n'a été réalisé ▶ **~ other** partenaire *mf (dans une relation affective)* **2.** [meaningful, indicative - look, pause] significatif **3.** [in statistics] significatif.

significantly [sɪg'nɪfɪkəntlɪ] *adv* **1.** [differ, change, increase] considérablement, sensiblement ■ **unemployment figures are not ~ lower** le nombre de chômeurs n'a pas considérablement baissé **2.** [nod, frown, wink] : **she smiled ~** elle a eu un sourire lourd de signification *OR* qui en disait long ■ **~, she arrived early** fait révélateur, elle est arrivée en avance **3.** [in statistics] de manière significative.

signification [,sɪgnɪfɪ'keɪʃn] *n* signification *f*.

signified ['sɪgnɪfaɪd] *n* LING signifié *m*.

signifier ['sɪgnɪfaɪər] *n* LING signifiant *m*.

signify ['sɪgnɪfaɪ] (*pret & pp* **signified**) ◇ *vt* **1.** [indicate, show] signifier, indiquer ■ **she stood up, ~ing that the interview was over** elle se leva, signifiant ainsi que l'entrevue était terminée **2.** [mean] signifier, vouloir dire ■ **for him, socialism signified chaos** pour lui, le socialisme était synonyme de chaos.
◇ *vi inf* être important ■ **it doesn't ~!** c'est sans importance!

signing ['saɪnɪŋ] *n traduction simultanée en langage par signes.*

sign language *n (U)* langage *m* des signes ■ **to speak in ~** parler par signes ■ **using ~, he managed to ask for food** (en s'exprimant) par signes, il s'est débrouillé pour demander à manger.

signpost ['saɪnpəʊst] ◇ *n* **1.** *liter* poteau *m* indicateur **2.** *fig* [guide] repère *m* ■ [omen] présage *m*.
◇ *vt liter & fig* [indicate] indiquer ■ [provide with signs] signaliser, baliser ■ **the village is clearly ~ed** le chemin du village est bien indiqué.

signposting ['saɪn,pəʊstɪŋ] *n* signalisation *f*, balisage *m*.

signwriter ['saɪn,raɪtər] *n* peintre *mf* en lettres.

Sikh [si:k] ◇ *n* Sikh *mf*.
◇ *adj* sikh.

Sikhism ['si:kɪzm] *n* sikhisme *m*.

silage ['saɪlɪdʒ] *n* ensilage *m*.

silence ['saɪləns] ◇ *n* silence *m* ■ **a ~ fell between them** un silence s'installa entre eux ■ **to suffer in ~** souffrir en silence ■ **to pass sthg over in ~** passer qqch sous silence ■ **his ~ on the issue/about his past intrigues me** le silence qu'il garde à ce sujet/sur son passé m'intrigue ■ **to observe a minute's ~** observer une minute de silence ▶ **~ is golden** *prov* le silence est d'or *prov*.
◇ *vt* **1.** [person] réduire au silence, faire taire ■ [sound] étouffer ■ [guns] faire taire **2.** [stifle - opposition] réduire au silence ; [- conscience, rumours, complaints] faire taire.

silencer ['saɪlənsər] *n* **1.** [on gun] silencieux *m* **2.** *UK* AUT pot *m* d'échappement, silencieux *m*.

silent ['saɪlənt] ◇ *adj* **1.** [saying nothing] silencieux ■ **to fall ~** se taire ■ **to keep** *OR* **to be ~** garder le silence, rester silencieux ■ **history remains** *OR* **is ~ on this point** l'histoire ne dit rien sur ce point ▶ **to give sb the ~ treatment** *inf* rester silencieux pour mettre qqn mal à l'aise **2.** [taciturn] silencieux, taciturne ■ **Hal's the strong, ~ type** Hal est du genre fort et taciturne **3.** [unspoken - prayer, emotion, reproach] muet **4.** [soundless - room, forest] silencieux, tranquille ; [- tread] silencieux ; [- film] muet ■ **the machines/the wind fell ~** le bruit des machines/du vent cessa ▶ **as ~ as the grave** muet comme la tombe **5.** LING muet.
◇ *n* CIN film *m* muet ■ **the ~s** le (cinéma) muet.

silently ['saɪləntlɪ] *adv* silencieusement.

silent majority *n* majorité *f* silencieuse.

silent partner *n US* COMM (associé *m*) commanditaire *m*, bailleur *m* de fonds.

silex ['saɪleks] *n* silex *m*.

silhouette [,sɪlu:'et] ◇ *n* silhouette *f*.
◇ *vt (usu passive)* **to be ~d against sthg** se découper contre qqch ■ **she stood at the window, ~d against the light** elle se tenait à la fenêtre, sa silhouette se détachant à contre-jour.

silica ['sɪlɪkə] *n* silice *f* ■ **~ gel/glass** gel *m* /verre *m* de silice.

siliceous, silicious [sɪ'lɪʃəs] *adj* siliceux.

silicon ['sɪlɪkən] *n* silicium *m*.

silicon chip *n* puce *f*.

silicone ['sɪlɪkəʊn] *n* silicone *f* ■ **she's had a ~ implant** elle s'est fait poser des implants en silicone.

Silicon Valley *pr n* Silicon Valley *f (centre de l'industrie électronique américaine, situé en Californie).*

silicosis [,sɪlɪ'kəʊsɪs] *n (U)* silicose *f*.

silk [sɪlk] ◇ *n* **1.** [fabric] soie *f* ■ [thread] fil *m* de soie **2.** [filament - from insect, on maize] soie *f* **3.** *UK* LAW : **to take ~** être nommé avocat de la couronne.
◇ *comp* [scarf, blouse etc] de *OR* en soie ■ **the ~ industry** l'industrie *f* de la soie ■ **~ merchant** *OR* **trader** marchand *m*, - e *f* de soierie, soyeux *m spec* ■ **~ finish paint** peinture *f* satinée.
◆ **silks** *npl* [jockey's jacket] casaque *f*.

silken ['sɪlkn] *adj lit* **1.** [made of silk] de *OR* en soie **2.** [like silk - hair, cheek etc] soyeux ; [- voice, tone] doux, douce *f*.

silk hat *n* haut-de-forme *m*, chapeau *m* haut de forme.

silk screen *n* : **~ (printing** *OR* **process)** sérigraphie *f*.
◆ **silk-screen** *vt* sérigraphier, imprimer en sérigraphie.

silkworm ['sɪlkwɜ:m] *n* ver *m* à soie ■ **~ breeding** sériciculture *f*.

silky ['sɪlkɪ] (*comp* **silkier**, *superl* **silkiest**) *adj* **1.** [like silk - hair, cheek] soyeux **2.** [suave - tone, manner] doux, douce *f* **3.** [made of silk] de *OR* en soie.

sill [sɪl] *n* **1.** [ledge - gen] rebord *m* ; [- of window] rebord *m*, appui *m* ; [- of door] seuil *m* **2.** AUT marchepied *m* **3.** MIN [deposit] filon *m*, gisement *m*.

silliness ['sɪlɪnɪs] *n* bêtise *f*, stupidité *f*.

silly ['sɪlɪ] (*comp* **sillier**, *superl* **silliest**) ◇ *adj* **1.** [foolish - person] bête, stupide ; [- quarrel, book, grin, question] bête, stupide, idiot ■ [infantile] bébête ■ **I'm sorry, it was a ~ thing to say** excusez-moi, c'était bête de dire ça ■ **don't do anything ~** ne fais pas de bêtises ■ **how ~ of me!** que je suis bête! ■ **it's ~ to worry** c'est idiot de s'inquiéter ■ **you ~ idiot!** espèce d'idiot *OR* d'imbécile! ■ **you look ~ in that tie** tu as l'air ridicule avec cette cravate **2.** [comical - mask, costume, voice] comique, drôle.
◇ *adv inf* [senseless] : **the blow knocked me ~** le coup m'a étourdi ■ **I was bored ~** je m'ennuyais à mourir ■ **I was scared ~** j'avais une peur bleue ■ **he drank himself ~** il s'est complètement soûlé.

silly-billy (*pl* **silly-billies**) *n inf* gros bêta *m*, grosse bêtasse *f*.

silly season *n UK* PRESS : **the ~** la période creuse *(pour les journalistes)*.

silo ['saɪləʊ] (*pl* **silos**) *n* AGRIC & MIL silo *m*.

silt [sɪlt] *n* GEOL limon *m* ■ [mud] vase *f*.
◆ **silt up** ◇ *vi insep* [with mud] s'envaser ■ [with sand] s'ensabler.
◇ *vt sep* [subj: mud] envaser ■ [subj: sand] ensabler.

Silurian [saɪ'lʊərɪən] ◇ *adj* silurien.
◇ *n* silurien *m*.

silver ['sɪlvər] ◇ *n* **1.** [metal] argent *m* ■ **the Silver State** le Nevada **2.** *(U)* [coins] pièces *fpl* (d'argent) ■ **~ collection** quête *f* **3.** *(U)* [dishes] argenterie *f* ■ [cutlery - gen] couverts *mpl* ; [- made of silver] argenterie *f*, couverts *mpl* en argent **4.** [colour] (couleur *f*) argent *m* **5.** SPORT [medal] médaille *f* d'argent.
◇ *adj* **1.** [of silver] d'argent, en argent ■ **is your ring ~?** est-ce que votre bague est en argent? **2.** [in colour] argenté, argent *(inv)* **3.** [sound] argentin ■ **she has a ~ tongue** elle sait parler.
◇ *vt liter & fig* argenter.

silver birch *n* bouleau *m* blanc.

silver chloride *n* chlorure *m* d'argent.

silvered ['sɪlvəd] *adj lit* argenté.

silver fir *n* [gen] sapin *m* blanc *OR* pectiné ■ [ornamental] sapin *m* argenté.

silverfish ['sɪlvəfɪʃ] (*pl inv OR pl* **silverfishes**) *n* [insect] poisson *m* d'argent, lépisme *m*.

silver foil *n* papier *m* d'aluminium.

silver fox *n* renard *m* argenté.

silver grey *n* gris *m* argenté.
◆ **silver-grey** *adj* gris argenté *(inv)*.

silver-haired *adj* aux cheveux argentés.

silver jubilee *n* (fête *f* du) vingt-cinquième anniversaire *m* ▪ **the Queen's ~** le vingt-cinquième anniversaire de l'accession au trône de la reine.

silver medal *n* SPORT médaille *f* d'argent.

silver nitrate *n* nitrate *m* d'argent.

silver paper *n* papier *m* d'aluminium.

silver plate *n* **1.** [coating] plaquage *m* d'argent ▪ **the cutlery is ~** les couverts sont en plaqué argent **2.** [tableware] argenterie *f*.
◆ **silver-plate** *vt* argenter.

silver-plated [-'pleɪtɪd] *adj* argenté, plaqué argent ▪ **~ tableware** argenterie *f*.

silver plating *n* argentage *m* ▪ [layer] argenture *f*.

silver screen *n dated* **the ~** le grand écran, le cinéma.

silverside ['sɪlvəsaɪd] *n UK* CULIN ≃ gîte *m* à la noix.

silversmith ['sɪlvəsmɪθ] *n* orfèvre *m*.

silver surfer *n inf* internaute *mf* senior.

silverware ['sɪlvəweəʳ] *n* **1.** [gen] argenterie *f* **2.** *US* [cutlery] couverts *mpl*.

silver wedding *n* : **~ (anniversary)** noces *fpl* d'argent.

silvery ['sɪlvərɪ] *adj* [hair, fabric] argenté ▪ [voice, sound] argentin.

simian ['sɪmɪən] ◇ *adj* simien ▪ [resembling ape] simiesque.
◇ *n* simien *m*.

similar ['sɪmɪləʳ] *adj* **1.** [showing resemblance] similaire, semblable ▪ **they're very ~** ils se ressemblent beaucoup ▪ **other customers have had ~ problems** d'autres clients ont eu des problèmes similaires *OR* analogues *OR* du même ordre ▪ **they are very ~ in content** leurs contenus sont pratiquement identiques ▪ **the print is ~ in quality to that of a typewriter** la qualité de l'impression est proche de celle d'une machine à écrire ▪ **it's an assembly ~ to the US Senate** c'est une assemblée comparable au Sénat américain ▪ **a fruit ~ to the orange** un fruit voisin de l'orange **2.** GEOM [triangles] semblable.

similarity [ˌsɪmɪ'lærətɪ] *n* [resemblance] ressemblance *f*, similarité *f* ▪ **there is a certain ~ to her last novel** ça ressemble un peu à son dernier roman ▪ **there are points of ~ in their strategies** leurs stratégies ont des points communs *OR* présentent des similitudes.
◆ **similarities** *npl* [features in common] ressemblances *fpl*, points *mpl* communs ▪ **the molecules show similarities in structure** les molécules présentent des analogies de structure.

similarly ['sɪmɪləlɪ] *adv* **1.** [in a similar way] d'une façon similaire ▪ **the houses are ~ constructed** les maisons sont construites sur le même modèle **2.** [likewise] de même.

simile ['sɪmɪlɪ] *n* LIT comparaison *f*.

similitude [sɪ'mɪlɪtju:d] *n* similitude *f*.

simmer ['sɪməʳ] ◇ *vi* **1.** [water, milk, sauce] frémir ▪ [soup, stew] mijoter, mitonner ▪ [vegetables] cuire à petit feu **2.** [smoulder - violence, quarrel, discontent] couver, fermenter ▪ [seethe - with anger, excitement] être en ébullition ▪ **tempers are ~ing** les passions s'échauffent ▪ **his anger ~ed just below the surface** il bouillait de colère **3.** [be hot] rôtir ▪ [when humid] mijoter ▪ **the city ~ed in the heat** la ville était accablée par la canicule.
◇ *vt* [milk, sauce] laisser frémir ▪ [soup, stew] mijoter, mitonner ▪ [vegetables] faire cuire à petit feu.
◇ *n* faible ébullition *f*.
◆ **simmer down** *vi insep inf* [person] se calmer ▪ **~ down!** calme-toi!, du calme!

Simon says *n* GAMES Jacques a dit *m*.

simper ['sɪmpəʳ] ◇ *vi* minauder.
◇ *vt* : **"of course, madam," he ~ed** "bien sûr, chère Madame", dit-il en minaudant.
◇ *n* sourire *m* affecté.

simpering ['sɪmpərɪŋ] *n (U)* minauderies *fpl*.

simple ['sɪmpl] *adj* **1.** [easy] simple, facile ▪ [uncomplicated] simple ▪ **getting there was the ~ part** ce n'est pas d'y aller qui était difficile ▪ **it's a ~ meal to prepare** c'est un repas facile à préparer ▪ **it should be a ~ matter to change your ticket** tu ne devrais avoir aucun mal à changer ton billet ▪ **to yearn for the ~ life** aspirer au retour à la nature ▪ **let's hear your story, then, but keep it ~** bon, racontez votre histoire, mais passez-moi les détails
2. [plain - tastes, ceremony, life, style] simple ▪ **she wore a ~ black dress** elle portait une robe noire toute simple ▪ **I want a ~ "yes" or "no"** répondez-moi simplement par "oui" ou par "non" ▪ **let me explain in ~ terms** *OR* **language** laissez-moi vous expliquer ça en termes simples ▪ **I did it for the ~ reason that I had no choice** je l'ai fait pour la simple raison que je n'avais pas le choix
3. [unassuming] simple, sans façons
4. [naive] simple, naïf ▪ [feeble-minded] simple, niais ▪ **he's a bit ~** il est un peu simplet
5. [basic, not compound - substance, fracture, sentence] simple ▪ BIOL [eye] simple ▪ **~ equation** MATHS équation *f* du premier degré.

simple fraction *n* fraction *f* ordinaire.

simple fracture *n* fracture *f* simple.

simple-hearted *adj* [person] candide, ouvert ▪ [wisdom, gesture] simple, naturel.

simple interest *n (U)* intérêts *mpl* simples.

simple-minded *adj* [naive] naïf, simplet ▪ [feeble-minded] simple d'esprit ▪ **it's a very ~ view of society** c'est une vision très simpliste de la société.

Simple Simon *n* naïf *m*, nigaud *m*.

simple tense *n* temps *m* simple.

simpleton ['sɪmpltən] *n dated* nigaud *m*, - e *f*.

simplex ['sɪmpleks] ◇ *adj* COMPUT & TELEC simplex *(inv)*, unidirectionnel.
◇ *n* COMPUT & TELEC simplex *m*, transmission *f* unidirectionnelle ▪ GEOM simplexe *m* ▪ LING [sentence] unité *f* proportionnelle ▪ [word] mot *m* simple.

simplicity [sɪm'plɪsətɪ] (*pl* **simplicities**) *n* simplicité *f* ▪ **the instructions are ~ itself** les instructions sont simples comme bonjour *OR* tout ce qu'il y a de plus simple.

simplification [ˌsɪmplɪfɪ'keɪʃn] *n* simplification *f*.

simplify ['sɪmplɪfaɪ] (*pret & pp* **simplified**) *vt* simplifier.

simplistic [sɪm'plɪstɪk] *adj* simpliste.

simplistically [sɪm'plɪstɪklɪ] *adv* de manière simpliste.

simply ['sɪmplɪ] *adv* **1.** [in a simple way] simplement, avec simplicité ▪ **put quite ~, it's a disaster** c'est tout simplement une catastrophe **2.** [just, only] simplement, seulement ▪ **it's not ~ a matter of money** ce n'est pas une simple question d'argent **3.** [as intensifier] absolument ▪ **I ~ don't understand you** je ne vous comprends vraiment pas ▪ **we ~ must go now** il faut absolument que nous partions maintenant.

simulate ['sɪmjʊleɪt] *vt* **1.** [imitate - blood, battle, sound] simuler, imiter **2.** [feign - pain, pleasure] simuler, feindre **3.** COMPUT & TECH simuler.

simulated ['sɪmjʊleɪtɪd] *adj* simulé.

simulation [ˌsɪmjʊ'leɪʃn] *n* simulation *f* ▪ **~ model** COMPUT modèle *m* de simulation.

simulator ['sɪmjʊleɪtəʳ] *n* simulateur *m*.

simulcast [*UK* 'sɪməlkɑ:st, *US* 'saɪməlkæst] ◇ *vt* diffuser simultanément à la télévision et à la radio.
◇ *adj* radiotélévisé.
◇ *n* émission *f* radiotélévisée.

simultaneous [*UK* ˌsɪməl'teɪnjəs, *US* ˌsaɪməl'teɪnjəs] *adj* simultané ▪ **~ translation** traduction *f* simultanée.

simultaneous equations *npl* système *m* d'équations différentielles.

simultaneously [*UK* ˌsɪməl'teɪnjəslɪ, *US* ˌsaɪməl'teɪnjəslɪ] *adv* simultanément, en même temps.

sin [sɪn] (*pret & pp* **sinned**, *cont* **sinning**) ◇ *n* péché *m* ▪ **to commit a ~** pécher, commettre un péché ▪ **it's a ~ to tell a lie** mentir *OR* le mensonge est un péché ▪ **it would be a ~ to sell it** ce serait un crime de le vendre ▶ **for my ~s, I'm the person in charge of all this** *hum* malheureusement pour moi, c'est moi le responsable de tout ça ▪ **to live in ~** RELIG & *hum* vivre dans le péché.
◇ *vi* pécher ▪ **to ~ against sthg** pécher contre qqch ▪ **to be more sinned against than sinning** être plus victime que coupable.

Sinai ['saɪnaɪ] *pr n* [region] Sinaï *m* ▪ **the ~ (Desert)** le (désert du) Sinaï ▪ **(Mount) ~** le (mont) Sinaï.

Sinbad ['sɪnbæd] *pr n* : **~ the Sailor** Sinbad le marin.

sin bin *n inf* SPORT banc *m* des pénalités, prison *f*.

since [sɪns] ◇ *prep* depuis ▪ **he has been talking about it ~ yesterday/~ before Christmas** il en parle depuis hier/depuis avant Noël ▪ **the fair has been held annually ever ~ 1950** la foire a lieu chaque année depuis 1950 ▪ **how long is it ~ their divorce?** ça fait combien de temps qu'ils ont divorcé? ▪ **that was in 1966, ~ when the law has been altered** c'était en 1966; depuis, la loi a été modifiée ▪ **~ when have you been married?** depuis quand êtes-vous marié?
◇ *conj* **1.** [in time] depuis que ▪ **I've worn glasses ~ I was six** je porte des lunettes depuis que j'ai six ans *OR* depuis l'âge de six ans ▪ **how long has it been ~ you last saw Hal?** ça fait combien de temps que tu n'as pas vu Hal? ▪ **it's been ages ~ we've gone to a play** ça fait une éternité que nous ne sommes pas allés au théâtre ▪ **~ leaving New York, I...** depuis que j'ai quitté New York, je... ▪ **it had been ten years ~ I had seen him** cela faisait dix ans que je ne l'avais pas revu **2.** [expressing cause] puisque, comme.
◇ *adv* depuis ▪ **she used to be his assistant, but she's ~ been promoted** elle était son assistante, mais depuis elle a été promue.
◆ **ever since** ◇ *conj phr* depuis que ▪ **ever ~ she resigned, things have been getting worse** depuis qu'elle a démissionné *OR* depuis sa démission, les choses ont empiré.
◇ *prep phr* depuis ▪ **ever ~ that day he's been afraid of dogs** depuis ce jour-là, il a peur des chiens.
◇ *adv phr* depuis ▪ **he arrived at 9 o'clock and he's been sitting there ever ~** il est arrivé à 9 h et il est assis là depuis.
◆ **long since** *adv phr* : **I've long ~ forgotten why** il y a longtemps que j'ai oublié pourquoi.

sincere [sɪn'sɪəʳ] *adj* sincère ▪ **please accept my ~ apologies** veuillez accepter mes sincères excuses.

sincerely [sɪn'sɪəlɪ] *adv* sincèrement ▪ **~ held views** des opinions auxquelles on croit sincèrement ▪ **I ~ hope we can be friends** j'espère sincèrement que nous serons amis ▪ **Yours ~** [formally] je vous prie d'agréer, Monsieur (*OR* Madame), mes sentiments les meilleurs ; [less formally] bien à vous.

sincerity [sɪn'serətɪ] *n* sincérité *f* ▪ **in all ~, I must admit that...** en toute sincérité, je dois admettre que...

sine [saɪn] *n* MATHS sinus *m*.

sinecure ['saɪnɪˌkjʊəʳ] *n* sinécure *f*.

sine qua non [ˌsaɪnɪkweɪ'nɒn] *n* condition *f* sine qua non.

sinew ['sɪnjuː] *n* [tendon] tendon *m* ▪ [muscle] muscle *m* ▪ *lit* [strength] force *f*, forces *fpl*.
◆ **sinews** *npl lit* [source of strength] nerf *m*, vigueur *f*.

sinewy ['sɪnjuːɪ] *adj* **1.** [muscular - person, body, arm] musclé ; [- neck, hands] nerveux **2.** [with tendons - tissue] tendineux ▪ **~ meat** viande *f* nerveuse *OR* tendineuse **3.** *lit* [forceful - style] vigoureux, nerveux.

sinful ['sɪnfʊl] *adj* [deed, urge, thought] coupable, honteux ▪ [world] plein de péchés, souillé par le péché ▪ **his ~ ways** sa vie de pécheur ▪ **~ man** pécheur *m* ▪ **it's downright ~!** c'est un vrai scandale!

sing [sɪŋ] (*pret* **sang** [sæŋ], *pp* **sung** [sʌŋ]) ◇ *vi* **1.** [person] chanter ▪ **she ~s of a faraway land** elle chante une terre lointaine ▶ **'Singin' in the Rain'** *Kelly, Donen* 'Chantons sous la pluie' **2.** [bird, kettle] chanter ▪ [wind, arrow] siffler ▪ [ears] bourdonner, siffler ▪ **bullets sang past his ears** des balles sifflaient à ses oreilles **3.** *US inf* [act as informer] parler.
◇ *vt* **1.** [song, note, mass] chanter ▪ **to ~ opera/jazz** chanter de l'opéra/du jazz ▪ **who ~s tenor?** qui est ténor? ▪ **to ~ sb to sleep** chanter pour endormir qqn ▶ **now they're ~ing another** *OR* **a different tune** ils ont changé de ton **2.** [laud] célébrer, chanter ▪ **to ~ sb's praises** chanter les louanges de qqn.
◆ **sing along** *vi insep* chanter (tous) ensemble ▪ **to ~ along to** *OR* **with the radio** chanter en même temps que la radio.
◆ **sing out** *vi insep* **1.** [sing loudly] chanter fort **2.** *inf* [shout] crier ▪ **when you're ready, ~ out** quand tu seras prêt, fais-moi signe.
◆ **sing up** *vi insep* chanter plus fort.

sing-along *n* chants *mpl* en chœur.

Singapore [ˌsɪŋə'pɔːʳ] *pr n* Singapour.

Singaporean [ˌsɪŋə'pɔːrɪən] ◇ *n* Singapourien *m*, - enne *f*.
◇ *adj* singapourien.

singe [sɪndʒ] (*cont* **singeing**) ◇ *vt* **1.** [gen] brûler légèrement ▪ [shirt, fabric, paper] roussir **2.** CULIN [carcass, chicken] flamber, passer à la flamme.
◇ *vi* [fabric] roussir.
◇ *n* [burn] brûlure *f* (légère) ▪ **~ (mark)** marque *f* de brûlure.

singer ['sɪŋəʳ] *n* chanteur *m*, - euse *f* ▪ **I'm a terrible ~** je chante affreusement mal.

Singhalese [ˌsɪŋhə'liːz] = **Sinhalese**.

singing ['sɪŋɪŋ] ◇ *n* **1.** [of person, bird] chant *m* ▪ [of kettle, wind] sifflement *m* ▪ [in ears] bourdonnement *m*, sifflement *m* ▪ **the ~ went on until dawn** on a chanté *OR* les chants ont continué jusqu'à l'aube **2.** [art] chant *m* ▪ **to study ~** étudier le chant.
◇ *adj* [lesson, teacher, contest] de chant ▪ **she's got a fine ~ voice** elle a une belle voix ▪ **it's a ~ role** c'est un rôle qui comporte des passages chantés.

singing telegram *n vœux présentés sous forme chantée, généralement à l'occasion d'un anniversaire.*

single ['sɪŋgl] ◇ *adj* **1.** [sole] seul, unique ▪ **the room was lit by a ~ lamp** la pièce était éclairée par une seule lampe ▪ **I can't think of one ~ reason why I should do it** je n'ai aucune raison de le faire ▪ **there wasn't a ~ person in the street** il n'y avait pas un chat dans la rue ▪ **not a ~ one of her friends came** pas un seul de ses amis *OR* aucun de ses amis n'est venu ▪ **I couldn't think of a ~ thing to say** je ne trouvais absolument rien à dire ▶ **~ currency** monnaie *f* unique ▪ **the Single European Act** l'Acte unique européen ▪ **the Single Market** le Marché unique (européen)
2. [individual, considered discretely] individuel, particulier ▪ **he gave her a ~ red rose** il lui a donné une rose rouge ▪ **our ~ most important resource is oil** notre principale ressource est le pétrole ▪ **we sell ~ items at a higher price per unit** le prix unitaire est plus élevé ▪ **in any ~ year, average sales are ten million** sur une seule année, les ventes sont en moyenne de dix millions ▪ **every ~ apple** *OR* **every ~ one of the apples was rotten** toutes les pommes sans exception étaient pourries ▪ **every ~ time I take the plane, there's some problem** chaque fois que je prends l'avion, il y a un problème
3. [not double - flower, thickness] simple ; [- combat] singulier ▪ **the score is still in ~ figures** le score est toujours inférieur à dix
4. [for one person] : **~ room** chambre *f* pour une personne *OR* individuelle ▪ **a ~ sheet** un drap pour un lit d'une personne
5. [unmarried] célibataire ▪ **he's a ~ parent** c'est un père célibataire
6. *UK* [one way] : **a ~ ticket to Oxford** un aller (simple) pour Oxford.
◇ *n* **1.** [hotel room] chambre *f* pour une personne *OR* individuelle
2. [record] 45 tours *m inv*, single *m*
3. *UK* [ticket] billet *m*, aller *m* simple ▪ **we only have ~s left** THEAT il ne nous reste que des places séparées
4. (*usu pl*) [money] *UK* pièce *f* d'une livre ▪ *US* billet *m* d'un dollar
5. [in cricket] point *m*.

◆ **single out** *vt sep* [for attention, honour] sélectionner, distinguer ■ **a few candidates were ~d out for special praise** quelques candidats ont eu droit à des félicitations supplémentaires.

single-action *adj* [firearm] *que l'on doit réarmer avant chaque coup.*

single bed *n* lit à une place.

single-breasted [-'brestɪd] *adj* [jacket, coat] droit.

single-celled [-seld] *adj* BIOL unicellulaire.

single-click ◇ *n* clic *m*.
◇ *vi* cliquer une fois (sur).

single cream *n* *UK* crème *f* (fraîche) liquide.

single-decker [-'dekəʳ] *n* : ~ **(bus)** autobus *m* sans impériale.

single-density *adj* COMPUT : ~ **disk** disquette *f* simple densité.

single-engined [-,endʒɪnd] *adj* [plane] monomoteur.

single entry bookkeeping *n* comptabilité *f* en partie simple.

single file *n* file *f* indienne ■ **to walk in ~** marcher en file indienne *OR* à la queue leu leu.

single-handed [-'hændɪd] ◇ *adv* [on one's own] tout seul, sans aucune aide.
◇ *adj* **1.** [unaided - voyage] en solitaire **2.** [using one hand] à une main.

single-handedly [-'hændɪdlɪ] *adv* **1.** [on one's own] tout seul **2.** [with one hand] d'une seule main.

single-income *adj* [family, couple] à salaire unique.

single-lens reflex *n* reflex *m* (mono-objectif).

single-minded *adj* résolu, acharné ■ **to be ~ about sthg** s'acharner sur qqch ■ **he is ~ in his efforts to block the project** il fait tout ce qu'il peut pour bloquer le projet.

single-mindedly [-'maɪndɪdlɪ] *adv* avec acharnement.

single-mindedness [-'maɪndɪdnɪs] *n* résolution *f*, acharnement *m*.

single parent *n* parent *m* isolé.

single-parent family *n* famille *f* monoparentale.

single quotes *npl* guillemets *mpl*.

singles ['sɪŋglz] (*pl inv*) ◇ *n* SPORT simple *m* ■ **the men's ~ champion** le champion du simple messieurs.
◇ *comp* [bar, club, magazine] pour célibataires.

single-seater *n* AERON (avion *m*) monoplace *m*.

single-sex *adj* SCH non mixte.

single-space *vt* [on typewriter] taper avec un interligne simple ■ [on printer] imprimer avec un interligne simple.

singlet ['sɪŋglɪt] *n* *UK* [undergarment] maillot *m* de corps ■ SPORT maillot *m*.

single track *n* RAIL voie *f* unique.
◆ **single-track** *adj* à voie unique.

singly ['sɪŋglɪ] *adv* **1.** [one at a time] séparément **2.** [alone] seul **3.** [individually - packaged] individuellement ■ **you can't buy them ~** vous ne pouvez pas les acheter à la pièce.

singsong ['sɪŋsɒŋ] ◇ *n* **1.** [melodious voice, tone] : **to speak in a ~** parler d'une voix chantante **2.** *UK* [singing] chants *mpl* (en chœur) ■ **let's have a ~** chantons tous ensemble *OR* en chœur.
◇ *adj* [voice, accent] chantant.

singular ['sɪŋgjʊləʳ] ◇ *adj* **1.** [remarkable] singulier ■ [odd] singulier, bizarre **2.** GRAM singulier.
◇ *n* GRAM singulier *m* ■ **in the third person ~** à la troisième personne du singulier.

singularity [,sɪŋgjʊ'lærətɪ] (*pl* **singularities**) *n* singularité *f*.

singularly ['sɪŋgjʊləlɪ] *adv* singulièrement.

Sinhalese [,sɪnhə'li:z] ◇ *n* **1.** [person] Cinghalais *m*, - e *f* **2.** LING cinghalais *m*.
◇ *adj* cinghalais.

sinister ['sɪnɪstəʳ] *adj* **1.** [ominous, evil] sinistre **2.** HERALD senestre, sénestre.

sink [sɪŋk] (*pret* **sank** [sæŋk], *pp* **sunk** [sʌŋk]) ◇ *n* **1.** [for dishes] évier *m* ■ [for hands] lavabo *m* ■ **double ~** évier à deux bacs ■ **~ board** *US* égouttoir *m*
2. [cesspool] puisard *m*
3. GEOL doline *f*.
◇ *vi* **1.** [below surface - boat] couler, sombrer ; [- person, stone, log] couler ■ **to ~ like a stone** couler à pic ■ **the prow had not yet sunk beneath the surface** la proue n'était pas encore submergée ■ **Atlantis sank beneath the seas** l'Atlantide a été engloutie par les mers ■ **the sun/moon is ~ ing** le soleil/la lune disparaît à l'horizon ■ **to ~ without (a) trace** [whereabouts unknown] disparaître sans laisser de trace ; *fig* [no longer famous] tomber dans l'oubli ▶ **it was a case of ~ or swim** il a bien fallu se débrouiller
2. [in mud, snow etc] s'enfoncer ■ **the wheels sank into the mud** les roues s'enfonçaient dans la boue
3. [subside - level, water, flames] baisser ; [- building, ground] s'affaisser ■ **Venice is ~ing** Venise est en train de s'affaisser
4. [sag, slump - person] s'affaler, s'écrouler ; [- hopes] s'écrouler ■ **I sank back in my seat** je me suis enfoncé dans mon fauteuil ■ **her head sank back on the pillow** sa tête retomba sur l'oreiller ■ **to ~ to the ground** s'effondrer ■ **she sank down on her knees** elle tomba à genoux ■ **my heart** *OR* **spirits sank when I saw I was too late** j'ai perdu courage en voyant que j'arrivais trop tard ■ **his heart ~s every time he gets a letter from her** il a un serrement de cœur chaque fois qu'il reçoit une lettre d'elle
5. [decrease, diminish - wages, rates, temperature] baisser ■ [more dramatically] plonger, chuter ■ **the dollar has sunk to half its former value** le dollar a perdu la moitié de sa valeur ■ **profits have sunk to an all-time low** les bénéfices sont au plus bas ■ [voice] se faire plus bas ■ **her voice had sunk to a whisper** [purposefully] elle s'était mise à chuchoter ; [weakly] sa voix n'était plus qu'un murmure
6. [slip, decline] sombrer, s'enfoncer ■ **to ~ into apathy/depression** sombrer dans l'apathie/dans la dépression ■ **the house sank into decay and ruin** la maison est tombée en ruines ■ **how could you ~ to this?** comment as-tu pu tomber si bas? ■ **to ~ to new depths** tomber plus bas ■ **the patient is ~ing fast** le malade décline rapidement ■ **I sank into a deep sleep** j'ai sombré dans un sommeil profond
7. [penetrate - blade, arrow] s'enfoncer.
◇ *vt* **1.** [boat, submarine] couler, envoyer par le fond ■ **to be sunk in thought** *fig* être plongé dans ses pensées
2. [ruin - plans] faire échouer ■ **this latest scandal looks certain to ~ him** ce dernier scandale va sûrement le couler ■ **if they don't come we're sunk!** *inf* s'ils ne viennent pas, nous sommes fichus!
3. [forget] oublier ■ **they'll have to learn to ~ their differences** il faudra qu'ils apprennent à oublier leurs différends
4. [plunge, drive - knife, spear] enfoncer ■ **they're ~ing the piles for the jetty** ils sont en train de mettre en place les pilotis de la jetée ■ **I sank my teeth into the peach** j'ai mordu dans la pêche ■ **the dog sank its teeth into my leg** le chien m'enfonça *OR* me planta ses crocs dans la jambe
5. [dig, bore - well, mine shaft] creuser, forer
6. [invest - money] mettre, investir ; [- extravagantly] engloutir
7. SPORT [score - basket] marquer ; [- putt] réussir ■ **to ~ a shot** [in snooker] couler une bille ; [in basketball] réussir un tir *OR* un panier
8. [debt] s'acquitter de, payer ■ FIN amortir
9. *UK inf* [drink down] s'envoyer, siffler.
◆ **sink in** *vi insep* **1.** [nail, blade] s'enfoncer
2. [soak - varnish, cream] pénétrer
3. [register - news] être compris *OR* assimilé ; [- allusion] faire son effet ■ **I heard what you said, but it didn't ~ in at the time** je vous ai entendu, mais je n'ai pas vraiment saisi sur le moment ■ **I paused to let my words ~ in** j'ai marqué une pause pour que mes paroles fassent leur effet.

sinker ['sɪŋkəʳ] *n* [weight] plomb *m (pour la pêche)*.

sinkhole ['sɪŋkhəʊl] *n* GEOL entonnoir *m*.

sinking ['sɪŋkɪŋ] <> *n* **1.** [of ship - accidental] naufrage *m* ; [- deliberate] torpillage *m* **2.** [of building, ground] affaissement *m* **3.** [of money] engloutissement *m*.
<> *adj* : ~ **feeling : I experienced that ~ feeling you get when you've forgotten something** j'ai eu cette angoisse que l'on ressent quand on sait que l'on a oublié quelque chose.

sinking fund *n* FIN caisse *f* OR fonds *mpl* d'amortissement.

sink school *n inf pej* école *f* dépotoir.

sink tidy (*pl* **sink tidies**) *n rangement pour ustensiles sur un évier*.

sink unit *n* bloc-évier *m*.

sinner ['sɪnər] *n* pécheur *m*, - eresse *f*.

Sinn Féin [ˌʃɪn'feɪn] *pr n* le Sinn Féin *(faction politique de l'IRA)*.

SINN FÉIN

Mouvement nationaliste et républicain irlandais fondé en 1902, luttant pour l'indépendance et la renaissance de la culture gaélique. Force politique vitale en Irlande à partir de 1916, il devient, après la Seconde Guerre mondiale, la branche politique de l'IRA (*Irish Republican Army*).

Sino- ['saɪnəʊ] *in cpds* sino-.

sinology [saɪ'nɒlədʒɪ] *n* sinologie *f*.

sinuous ['sɪnjʊəs] *adj* [road, neck, movement, reasoning] sinueux.

sinus ['saɪnəs] *n* sinus *m* ■ **for fast ~ relief** pour dégager rapidement les sinus.

sinusitis [ˌsaɪnə'saɪtɪs] *n (U)* sinusite *f*.

Sioux [suː] (*pl inv* [suː]) <> *n* **1.** [person] Sioux *mf inv* **2.** LING sioux *m*.
<> *adj* sioux *(inv)* ■ **the ~ Indians** les Sioux *mpl*.

sip [sɪp] (*pret & pp* **sipped**, *cont* **sipping**) <> *vt* [drink slowly] boire à petites gorgées OR à petits coups ■ [savour] siroter.
<> *vi* : **he was at the bar, sipping at a cognac** il était au comptoir, sirotant un cognac.
<> *n* petite gorgée *f* ■ **can I have a ~?** je peux goûter OR en boire un peu?

siphon ['saɪfn] <> *n* siphon *m*.
<> *vt* **1.** [liquid, petrol] siphonner **2.** [money, resources] transférer ■ [illicitly] détourner ■ **huge sums were ~ed into public housing** des sommes énormes ont été injectées dans les logements sociaux.
◆ **siphon off** *vt sep* **1.** [liquid, petrol] siphonner **2.** [remove - money] absorber, éponger ■ [divert illegally] détourner ■ **the private sector is ~ing off the best graduates** le secteur privé absorbe les meilleurs diplômés.

sir [sɜːr] *n* **1.** [term of address] monsieur *m* ■ **no, ~** [gen - SCH] non, Monsieur ; MIL [to officer] non, mon général/mon colonel *etc* ■ **(Dear) Sir** [in letter] (Cher) Monsieur ▶ **not for me, no ~** *inf* [emphatic] pas pour moi, ça non OR pas question! **2.** [title of knight, baronet] : **Sir Ian Hall** sir Ian Hall ■ **to be made a ~** être anobli **3.** UK *inf* [male teacher] : **Sir's coming!** le maître arrive!

sire ['saɪər] <> *n* **1.** [animal] père *m* **2.** [term of address] : **no, ~** [to king] non, sire ; *arch* [to lord] non, seigneur.
<> *vt* engendrer ■ **Buttons, ~d by Goldfly** Buttons, issu de Goldfly.

siren ['saɪərən] *n* **1.** [device] sirène *f* ■ **ambulance/police ~** sirène d'ambulance/de voiture de police **2.** MYTH sirène *f* ■ *fig* [temptress] sirène *f*, femme *f* fatale.

sirloin ['sɜːlɔɪn] *n* aloyau *m* ■ **a ~ steak** un bifteck dans l'aloyau.

sirocco [sɪ'rɒkəʊ] (*pl* **siroccos**) *n* sirocco *m*, siroco *m*.

sis [sɪs] *n inf* [sister] frangine *f*, sœurette *f*.

sisal ['saɪsl] <> *n* sisal *m*.
<> *adj* en OR de sisal.

sissy ['sɪsɪ] (*pl* **sissies**) <> *n* [coward] peureux *m*, - euse *f* ■ [effeminate person] : **he's a real ~** c'est une vraie mauviette.
<> *adj* [cowardly] peureux ■ [effeminate] : **don't be so ~** t'es une mauviette, ou quoi?

sister ['sɪstər] <> *n* **1.** sœur *f* ■ **my big/little ~** ma grande/petite sœur **2.** [nun] religieuse *f*, (bonne) sœur *f* ■ **Sister Pauline** sœur Pauline **3.** UK [nurse] infirmière *f* en chef **4.** POL [comrade] sœur *f*.
<> *adj (especially with f nouns)* sœur ■ *(especially with m nouns)* frère ■ **~ countries** pays *mpl* frères, nations *fpl* sœurs ■ **~ ship** [belonging to same company] navire *m* de la même ligne ; [identical] navire-jumeau *m*, sister-ship *m*.

sisterhood ['sɪstəhʊd] *n* **1.** [group of women - gen - RELIG] communauté *f* de femmes **2.** [solidarity] solidarité *f* entre femmes.

sister-in-law (*pl* **sisters-in-law**) *n* belle-sœur *f*.

sisterly ['sɪstəlɪ] *adj* [kiss, hug] sororal *lit*, fraternel ■ [advice] de sœur.

Sistine Chapel ['sɪstiːn-] *pr n* : **the ~** la chapelle Sixtine.

Sisyphus ['sɪsɪfəs] *pr n* Sisyphe.

sit [sɪt] (*pret & pp* **sat** [sæt], *cont* **sitting**) <> *vi* **1.** [take a seat] s'asseoir ■ [be seated] être assis ■ **she came and sat next to me** elle est venue s'asseoir à côté de moi ■ **she sat by me all evening** elle était assise à côté de moi toute la soirée ■ **~ in the back of the car** mettez-vous à l'arrière (de la voiture) ■ **~ still!** tiens-toi OR reste tranquille! ■ **~!** [to dog] assis! ■ **they sat over the meal for hours** ils sont restés à table pendant des heures ■ **he ~s in front of the television all day** il passe toute la journée devant la télévision ▶ **~ tight, I'll be back in a moment** *inf* ne bouge pas, je reviens tout de suite ■ **we just have to ~ tight and wait for things to get better** on ne peut qu'attendre patiemment que les choses s'arrangent
2. ART & PHOT [pose] poser
3. [be a member] : **to ~ on a board** faire partie OR être membre d'un conseil d'administration
4. [be in session] être en séance, siéger ■ **the council was still sitting at midnight** à minuit, le conseil siégeait toujours OR était toujours en séance
5. [baby-sit] : **I'll ask Amy to ~ for us** je demanderai à Amy de garder les enfants
6. UK SCH & UNIV [be a candidate] : **to ~ for an exam** se présenter à OR passer un examen
7. [be situated - building] être, se trouver ; [- vase] être posé ■ **your keys are sitting right in front of you** tes clés sont là, devant ton nez ■ **a tank sat in the middle of the road** un char d'assaut était planté au milieu de la route
8. [remain inactive or unused] rester ■ **the plane sat waiting on the runway** l'avion attendait sur la piste ■ **the letter sat unopened** la lettre n'avait pas été ouverte
9. [fit - coat, dress] tomber ■ **the jacket ~s well on you** la veste vous va parfaitement ■ *fig* **age ~s well on him** la maturité lui va bien ■ **the thought sat uneasily on my conscience** cette pensée me pesait sur la conscience
10. [bird - perch] se percher, se poser ; [- brood] couver ■ **they take turns sitting on the eggs** ils couvent les œufs à tour de rôle.
<> *vt* **1.** [place] asseoir, installer ■ **he sat the child in the pram** il a assis l'enfant dans le landau
2. [invite to be seated] faire asseoir ■ **she sat me in the waiting room** elle m'a fait asseoir dans la salle d'attente
3. UK [examination] se présenter à, passer.
◆ **sit about** UK, **sit around** *vi insep* rester à ne rien faire, traîner ■ **I'm not going to ~ around waiting for you** je ne vais pas passer mon temps à t'attendre.
◆ **sit back** *vi insep* **1.** [relax] s'installer confortablement ■ **just ~ back and close your eyes** installe-toi bien et ferme les yeux ■ **~ back and enjoy it** détends-toi et profites-en
2. [refrain from intervening] : **I can't just ~ back and watch!** je ne peux pas rester là à regarder sans rien faire! ■ **we can't just ~ back and ignore the danger** nous ne pouvons tout de même pas faire comme s'il n'y avait pas de danger.
◆ **sit by** *vi insep* rester sans rien faire.
◆ **sit down** <> *vi insep* s'asseoir ■ **please ~ down** asseyez-vous, je vous en prie ■ **I was just sitting down to work when the phone rang** j'étais sur le point de me mettre au travail

quand le téléphone a sonné ▪ **to ~ down to table** se mettre à table, s'attabler ▪ **the two sides have decided to ~ down together at the negotiating table** les deux camps ont décidé de s'asseoir à la table des négociations.
◇ *vt sep* [place - person] asseoir, installer ▪ **~ yourself down and have a drink** asseyez-vous et prenez un verre.
◆ **sit in** *vi insep* **1.** [attend] : **to ~ in on a meeting/a class** assister à une réunion/un cours
2. [replace] : **to ~ in for sb** remplacer qqn
3. [hold a sit-in] faire un sit-in.
◆ **sit on** *vt insep inf* **1.** [suppress, quash - file, report] garder le silence sur ; [- suggestion, proposal] repousser, rejeter
2. [take no action on] ne pas s'occuper de ▪ **his office has been sitting on those recommendations for months now** ça fait des mois que son bureau a ces recommandations sous le coude
3. [silence - person] faire taire ▪ [rebuff] rabrouer.
◆ **sit out** ◇ *vi insep* [sit outside] s'asseoir *OR* se mettre dehors.
◇ *vt sep* **1.** [endure] attendre la fin de ▪ **it was very boring but I sat it out** c'était très ennuyeux, mais je suis restée jusqu'au bout
2. [not take part in] : **I think I'll ~ the next one out** [dance] je crois que je ne vais pas danser la prochaine danse ; [in cards] je crois que je ne jouerai pas la prochaine main.
◆ **sit through** *vt insep* attendre la fin de ▪ **I can't bear to ~ through another of his speeches** je ne supporterai pas un autre de ses discours ▪ **we sat through dinner in silence** nous avons passé tout le dîner sans rien dire.
◆ **sit up** ◇ *vi insep* **1.** [raise o.s. to sitting position] s'asseoir ▪ [sit straight] se redresser ▪ **she was sitting up in bed reading** elle lisait, assise dans son lit ▪ **the baby can ~ up now** le bébé peut se tenir assis maintenant ▪ **~ up straight!** redresse-toi!, tiens-toi droit!
2. [not go to bed] rester debout, ne pas se coucher ▪ **I'll ~ up with her until the fever passes** je vais rester avec elle jusqu'à ce que sa fièvre tombe
3. *inf* [look lively] : **the public began to ~ up and take notice** le public a commencé à montrer un certain intérêt.
◇ *vt sep* [child, patient] asseoir, redresser.

sitar [sɪ'tɑːʳ] *n* sitar *m*.

sitcom ['sɪtkɒm] *n* comédie *f* de situation, sitcom *m*.

sit-down ◇ *n inf* [rest] pause *f*.
◇ *adj* : **~ dinner** dîner pris à table ▪ **~ strike** *UK* grève *f* sur le tas.

site [saɪt] ◇ *n* **1.** [piece of land] terrain *m* **2.** [place, location] emplacement *m*, site *m* ▪ **there's been a church on this ~ for centuries** cela fait des siècles qu'il y a une église à cet endroit *OR* ici ▪ **this forest has been the ~ of several battles** cette forêt a été le théâtre de plusieurs batailles **3.** CONSTR : **(building) ~** chantier *m* ▪ **demolition ~** chantier de démolition **4.** archaeology site *m*.
◇ *comp* CONSTR [office, inspection, visit] de chantier.
◇ *vt* placer, situer.
◆ **on site** *adv phr* sur place.

sit-in *n* **1.** [demonstration] sit-in *m inv* ▪ **to stage** *OR* **to hold a ~** faire un sit-in **2.** [strike] grève *f* sur le tas.

siting ['saɪtɪŋ] *n* : **the ~ of the nuclear plant is highly controversial** le choix de l'emplacement de la centrale nucléaire provoque une vive controverse ▪ **access is important in the ~ of the stadium** l'accessibilité est un facteur important dans le choix du site pour le stade.

sitter ['sɪtəʳ] *n* **1.** [babysitter] baby-sitter *mf* **2.** ART [model] modèle *m* **3.** [hen] couveuse *f* **4.** *UK inf* SPORT [easy chance] coup *m* facile.

sitting ['sɪtɪŋ] ◇ *n* [for meal] service *m* ▪ ART [for portrait] séance *f* de pose ▪ [of assembly, committee] séance *f* ▪ **I read the book at** *OR* **in one ~** j'ai lu le livre d'une traite.
◇ *adj* **1.** [seated] assis **2.** [in office] en exercice ▪ **the ~ member for Leeds** le député actuel de Leeds.

sitting duck *n inf* [target] cible *m* facile ▪ [victim] proie *f* facile, pigeon *m*.

sitting room *n UK* salon *m*, salle *f* de séjour.

sitting target *n UK* cible *f* facile.

sitting tenant *n UK* locataire *mf* en place.

situate ['sɪtjʊeɪt] *vt fml* [in place] situer, implanter ▪ [in context] resituer.

situated ['sɪtjʊeɪtɪd] *adj* **1.** [physically] situé ▪ **the house is conveniently ~ for shops and public transport** la maison est située à proximité des commerces et des transports en commun ▪ **the town is well/badly ~ for tourist development** la situation de la ville est/n'est pas favorable à son développement touristique **2.** [circumstantially] : **how are we ~ as regards the competition?** comment est-ce qu'on est situés par rapport à la concurrence?

situation [,sɪtjʊ'eɪʃn] *n* **1.** [state of affairs] situation *f* ▪ **I've got myself into a ridiculous ~** je me suis mis dans une situation ridicule ▪ **what would you do in my ~?** qu'est-ce que tu ferais à ma place *OR* dans ma situation? ▪ **the firm's financial ~ isn't good** la situation financière de la société n'est pas bonne ▪ **a crisis ~** une situation de crise ▪ **it won't work in a classroom ~** ça ne marchera pas dans une salle de classe **2.** [job] situation *f*, emploi *m* ▪ **~s vacant/wanted** offres *fpl* /demandes *fpl* d'emploi **3.** [location] situation *f*, emplacement *m*.

situation comedy *n* comédie *f* de situation.

sit-up *n* SPORT redressement *m* assis.

six [sɪks] ◇ *n* **1.** [number] six *m* ▪ **to be at ~es and sevens** *UK* être sens dessus dessous ▪ **it's ~ of one and half a dozen of the other** *inf* c'est blanc bonnet et bonnet blanc, c'est kif-kif ▪ **to get ~ of the best** *UK inf dated* & SCH se faire fouetter, *see also* **five** **2.** [ice hockey team] équipe *f* ▪ [cub or brownie patrol] patrouille *f* **3.** [in cricket] six points *mpl*.
◇ *det* six ▪ **to be ~ feet under** *inf* être six pieds sous terre, manger les pissenlits par la racine.
◇ *pron* six, *see also* **five**.

Six Counties *pr npl* : **the ~** (les six comtés *mpl* de) l'Irlande *f* du Nord.

sixfold ['sɪksfəʊld] ◇ *adj* sextuple.
◇ *adv* au sextuple ▪ **profits are up ~ on last year** les bénéfices sont six fois plus importants que *OR* se sont multipliés par six depuis l'année dernière.

six-pack *n* pack *m* de six.

sixpence ['sɪkspəns] *n* [coin] (ancienne) pièce *f* de six pence.

six-shooter *n US inf* pistolet *m* à six coups, six-coups *m inv*.

sixteen [sɪks'tiːn] ◇ *det* seize ▪ **she was sweet ~** c'était une jolie jeune fille de seize ans.
◇ *n* seize *m*.
◇ *pron* seize, *see also* **fifteen**.

sixteenth [sɪks'tiːnθ] ◇ *det* seizième.
◇ *n* **1.** [ordinal] seizième *m* **2.** [fraction] seizième *m*, *see also* **fifteenth**.

sixteenth note *n US* MUS double croche *f*.

sixth [sɪksθ] ◇ *det* sixième.
◇ *n* **1.** [ordinal] sixième *mf* **2.** [fraction] sixième *m* **3.** MUS sixte *f* **4.** *UK* SCH : **to be in the lower/upper ~** ≃ être en première/en terminale.
◇ *adv* **1.** [in contest] en sixième position, à la sixième place **2.** = **sixthly**, *see also* **fifth**.

sixth form *n UK* SCH *classe terminale de l'enseignement secondaire en Grande-Bretagne, préparant aux A-levels*, ≃ classes *fpl* de première et de terminale.
◆ **sixth-form** *adj* [student, teacher, subject] de première *OR* terminale ▪ **sixth-form college** *établissement préparant aux A-levels*.

sixth former *n UK* SCH élève *mf* de première *OR* de terminale.

sixthly ['sɪksθlɪ] *adv* sixièmement.

sixth sense *n* sixième sens *m* ▪ **some ~ told me she wouldn't come** j'avais l'intuition qu'elle ne viendrait pas.

sixtieth ['sɪkstɪəθ] ◇ *det* soixantième.
◇ *n* **1.** [ordinal] soixantième *m* **2.** [fraction] soixantième *m*, *see also* **fifth**.

Sixtus ['sɪkstəs] *pr n* Sixte.

sixty ['sɪkstɪ] (*pl* **sixties**) ◇ *det* soixante.
◇ *n* soixante *m* ■ **she's in her sixties** elle a entre soixante et soixante-dix ans ■ **sixties pop music** la musique pop des années soixante.
◇ *pron* soixante, *see also* **fifty**.

sizable *etc* ['saɪzəbl] = **sizeable**.

size [saɪz] ◇ *n* **1.** [gen] taille *f* ■ [of ball, tumour] taille *f*, grosseur *f* ■ [of region, desert, forest] étendue *f*, superficie *f* ■ [of difficulty, operation, protest movement] importance *f*, ampleur *f* ■ [of debt, bill, sum] montant *m*, importance *f* ■ **the two rooms are the same ~** les deux pièces sont de la même taille *OR* ont les mêmes dimensions ■ **it's about the ~ of a dinner plate** c'est à peu près de la taille d'une assiette ■ **the kitchen is the ~ of a cupboard** la cuisine est grande comme un placard ■ **my garden is half the ~ of hers** mon jardin fait la moitié du sien ■ **average family ~ is four persons** la famille moyenne est composée de quatre personnes ■ **it's a city of some ~** c'est une ville assez importante ■ **the town has no hotels of any ~** la ville n'a pas d'hôtel important ■ **we weren't expecting a crowd of this ~** nous ne nous attendions pas à une foule aussi nombreuse ■ **the tumour is increasing in ~** la tumeur grossit ■ **the army has doubled in ~** les effectifs de l'armée ont doublé ■ **a block of marble one cubic metre in ~** un bloc de marbre d'un mètre cube ■ **the cupboards can be built to ~** les placards peuvent être construits sur mesure ► **that's about the ~ of it!** *inf* en gros, c'est ça! **2.** [of clothes - gen] taille *f* ■ [of shoes, gloves, hat] pointure *f*, taille *f* ■ **what ~ are you?, what ~ do you take?** quelle taille faites-vous? ■ **I take (a) ~ 40** je fais du 40 ■ **I take a ~ 5 shoe** ≃ je chausse du 38 ■ **I need a ~ larger/smaller** il me faut la taille au-dessus/au-dessous ■ **we've nothing in your ~** nous n'avons rien dans votre taille ■ **try this jacket on for ~** essayez cette veste pour voir si c'est votre taille ► **collar ~** encolure *f* **3.** [for paper, textiles, leather] apprêt *m* ■ [for plaster] enduit *m*.
◇ *vt* **1.** [sort] trier selon la taille **2.** [make] fabriquer aux dimensions voulues **3.** [paper, textiles, leather] apprêter ■ [plaster] enduire.
◆ **size up** *vt sep* [stranger, rival] jauger ■ [problem, chances] mesurer ■ **she ~d up the situation immediately** elle a tout de suite compris ce qui se passait.

-size = **-sized**.

sizeable ['saɪzəbl] *adj* [piece, box, car] assez grand ■ [apple, egg, tumour] assez gros, assez grosse *f* ■ [sum, income, quantity, crowd] important ■ [town] assez important ■ [error] de taille ■ **they were elected by a ~ majority** ils ont été élus à une assez large majorité.

sizeably ['saɪzəblɪ] *adv* considérablement.

-sized [-saɪzd] *in cpds* : **medium~** de taille moyenne ■ **small and medium~ businesses** petites et moyennes entreprises *fpl*, PME *fpl* ■ **a fair~ crowd** une foule assez nombreuse.

sizzle ['sɪzl] ◇ *vt* **1.** [sputter] grésiller **2.** *inf* [be hot] : **the city ~d in the heat** la ville étouffait sous la chaleur.
◇ *n* grésillement *m*.

sizzler ['sɪzlər] *n inf* journée *f* torride.

sizzling ['sɪzlɪŋ] ◇ *adj* **1.** [sputtering] grésillant **2.** *inf* [hot] brûlant.
◇ *adv inf* **~ hot** brûlant.

skat [skæt] *n jeu de cartes à 3 personnes, comprenant 32 cartes.*

skate [skeɪt] ◇ *n* **1.** [ice] patin *m* à glace ■ [roller] patin *m* à roulettes ■ **to get** *OR* **to put one's ~s on** *inf* se dépêcher, se grouiller **2.** (*pl* skate *OR pl* skates) [fish] raie *f*.
◇ *vi* **1.** [gen] patiner ■ **to go skating** [ice] faire du patin *OR* du patinage ; [roller] faire du patin à roulettes ■ **couples ~d around the rink** des couples patinaient autour de la piste ► **to ~ on thin ice** être sur un terrain dangereux, avancer en terrain miné **2.** [slide - pen, plate] glisser **3.** [person] glisser.
◆ **skate around, skate over** *vt insep* [problem, issue] esquiver, éviter.

skateboard ['skeɪtbɔːd] ◇ *n* skateboard *m*, planche *f* à roulettes.
◇ *vi* faire du skateboard *OR* de la planche à roulettes.

skateboarder ['skeɪtbɔːdər] *n* personne qui fait du skateboard *OR* de la planche à roulettes.

skateboarding ['skeɪtbɔːdɪŋ] *n* : **to go ~** faire de la planche à roulettes *OR* du skateboard.

skater ['skeɪtər] *n* [on ice] patineur *m*, - euse *f* ■ [on roller skates] patineur *m*, - euse *f* à roulettes.

skating ['skeɪtɪŋ] ◇ *n* [on ice] patin *m* (à glace) ■ [on roller skates] patin *m* (à roulettes).
◇ *adj* de patinage.

skating rink *n* [for ice skating] patinoire *f* ■ [for roller skating] piste *f* pour patin à roulettes.

skedaddle [skɪ'dædl] *vi inf* mettre les voiles, se tirer, déguerpir ■ **I'd better ~** il faut que je me sauve *OR* que je file.

skein [skeɪn] *n* **1.** [of wool, silk] écheveau *m* **2.** [flight - of geese] vol *m*.

skeletal ['skelɪtl] *adj* squelettique.

skeleton ['skelɪtn] ◇ *n* **1.** ANAT squelette *m* ■ **he was little more than a ~** il n'avait plus que la peau sur les os ► **to have a ~ in the cupboard** *UK OR* **closet** *US* avoir quelque chose à cacher **2.** CONSTR & CHEM [structure] squelette *m* **3.** [outline - of book, report] ébauche *f*, esquisse *f* ; [- of project, strategy, speech] schéma *m*, grandes lignes *fpl*.
◇ *comp* [crew, staff, team] (réduit au) minimum, squelettique *pej*.

skeleton key *n* passe-partout *m inv*, passe *m*.

skeptic *etc US* = **sceptic**.

sketch [sketʃ] ◇ *n* **1.** [drawing] croquis *m*, esquisse *f* **2.** [brief description] résumé *m* ■ **a biographical ~ of the author** une biographie succincte de l'auteur ; [on book jacket] une notice bibliographique sur l'auteur ■ [preliminary outline - of book] ébauche *f* ; [- of proposal, speech, campaign] grandes lignes *fpl* ■ **give us a rough ~ of your plan** donnez-nous un aperçu de ce que vous proposez **3.** THEAT sketch *m*.
◇ *vt* **1.** [person, scene] faire un croquis *OR* une esquisse de, croquer, esquisser ■ [line, composition, form] esquisser, croquer ■ [portrait, illustration] faire (rapidement) **2.** [book] ébaucher, esquisser ■ [proposal, speech] ébaucher, préparer dans les grandes lignes.
◆ **sketch in** *vt sep* **1.** [provide - background, main points] indiquer ■ **Harry will ~ a few more details in for you** Harry va vous donner encore quelques précisions **2.** [draw] ajouter, dessiner.
◆ **sketch out** *vt sep* **1.** [book] ébaucher, esquisser ■ [plan, speech] ébaucher, préparer dans les grandes lignes ■ [details, main points] indiquer **2.** [draw] ébaucher.

sketchblock ['sketʃblɒk] *n* bloc *m* à dessins.

sketchbook ['sketʃbʊk] *n* carnet *m* à dessins.

sketchily ['sketʃɪlɪ] *adv* [describe, report] sommairement ■ **his article is very ~ researched** son article repose sur des recherches très superficielles.

sketchpad ['sketʃpæd] *n* carnet *m* à dessins.

sketchy ['sketʃɪ] (*comp* **sketchier**, *superl* **sketchiest**) *adj* [description, account] sommaire ■ [research, work, knowledge] superficiel ■ [idea, notion] vague ■ [plan] peu détaillé.

skew [skjuː] ◇ *vt* [distort - facts, results] fausser ; [- idea, truth] dénaturer ; [- statistics] : **it will ~ the sample** ça va fausser l'échantillonnage.
◇ *vi* obliquer, dévier de sa trajectoire ■ **he ~ed off the road** il a quitté la route.
◇ *adj UK* **1.** [crooked - picture] de travers ; [- pole] penché **2.** [distorted - notion, view] partial ■ **~ distribution** [in statistics] distribution *f* asymétrique **3.** [angled, slanting] oblique, en biais.
◇ *n UK* **to be on the ~** être de travers.

skewbald ['skju:bɔ:ld] ◇ *adj* fauve et blanc, pie-rouge *(inv)*.
◇ *n* cheval *m* fauve et blanc OR pie-rouge.

skewed [skju:d] = **skew** *(adj)*.

skewer ['skjʊəʳ] ◇ *n* CULIN brochette *f* ▪ [larger] broche *f*.
◇ *vt* CULIN [roast, duck] embrocher ▪ [meat, mushrooms, tomatoes] mettre en brochette ▪ *fig* [person] transpercer.

skew-whiff [ˌskju:'wɪf] *adj* & *adv* UK *inf* de traviole, de travers.

skewy ['skju:ɪ] (*comp* **skewier**, *superl* **skewiest**) *adj inf* **1.** [crooked - picture, hat] de traviole, de travers **2.** [weird, odd] farfelu.

ski [ski:] ◇ *n* **1.** SPORT ski *m (equipment)* ▪ **(a pair of) ~s** (une paire de) skis **2.** AERON patin *m*, ski *m*.
◇ *vi* faire du ski, skier ▪ **to go ~ing** [activity] faire du ski ; [on holiday] partir aux sports d'hiver OR faire du ski ▪ **they ~ed down the slope** ils descendirent la pente à ski.
◇ *comp* [clothes, boots, lessons] de ski ▪ **~ instructor** moniteur *m*, - trice *f* de ski ▪ **~ pass** forfait *m* de remonte-pente ▪ **~ pole** OR **stick** bâton *m* de ski ▪ **~ wax** fart *m* (pour skis).
◇ *vt* : **I've never ~ed the red run** je n'ai jamais descendu la piste rouge.

skibob ['ski:bɒb] *n* ski-bob *m*, véloski *m*.

skid [skɪd] (*pret & pp* **skidded**, *cont* **skidding**) ◇ *vi* **1.** [on road - driver, car, tyre] déraper ▪ **the car skidded across the junction** la voiture a traversé le carrefour en dérapant ▪ **to ~ to a halt** s'arrêter en dérapant **2.** [slide - person, object] déraper, glisser.
◇ *n* **1.** AUT dérapage *m* ▪ **to go into a ~** partir en dérapage, déraper ▪ **to get out of** OR **to correct a ~** redresser OR contrôler un dérapage **2.** [wedge] cale *f* **3.** US [log] rondin *m* ▪ [dragging platform] traîneau *m*, ≃ schlitte *f* ➤ **to put the ~s on** OR **under sb** mettre des bâtons dans les roues à qqn ▪ **to hit the ~s** *inf* devenir clochard.

skid-lid *n* UK *inf* casque *m* (de moto).

skid mark *n* trace *f* de pneus *(après un dérapage)*.

skidpan ['skɪdpæn] *n* UK piste *f* d'entraînement au dérapage.

skidproof ['skɪdpru:f] *adj* antidérapant.

skid row *n* US *inf* quartier *m* des clochards ▪ **you'll end up on ~!** tu es sur une mauvaise pente!

skier ['ski:əʳ] *n* skieur *m*, - euse *f*.

skiff [skɪf] *n* skiff *m*, yole *f*.

skiffle ['skɪfl] *n* skiffle *m (type de musique pop des années 50 jouée avec des guitares et des instruments à percussion improvisés)*.

skiing ['ski:ɪŋ] ◇ *n* ski *m (activité)*.
◇ *comp* [lessons, accident, clothes] de ski ▪ **to go on a ~ holiday** partir aux sports d'hiver ▪ **~ instructor** moniteur *m*, - trice *f* de ski.

ski jump ◇ *n* [ramp] tremplin *m* de ski ▪ [event, activity] saut *m* à skis.
◇ *vi* faire du saut à skis.

skilful UK, **skillful** US ['skɪlfʊl] *adj* habile, adroit ▪ **a ~ carpenter** un menuisier habile ▪ **a ~ pianist** un pianiste accompli ▪ **she's very ~ with the scissors** elle sait se servir d'une paire de ciseaux.

skilfully UK, **skillfully** US ['skɪlfʊlɪ] *adv* habilement, avec habileté, adroitement.

ski lift *n* [gen] remontée *f* mécanique ▪ [chair lift] télésiège *m*.

skill [skɪl] *n* **1.** [ability] compétence *f*, aptitude *f* ▪ [dexterity] habileté *f*, adresse *f* ▪ [expertise] savoir-faire *m inv* ▪ **you don't need any special ~** ça ne demande aucune compétence précise ▪ **it involves a lot of ~** ça demande beaucoup d'habileté ▪ **with great ~** [in manoeuvre] avec une grande habileté ; [diplomacy] avec un grand savoir-faire ; [dexterity] avec beaucoup d'adresse ▪ **his work shows ~ and imagination** son travail est plein de talent et d'imagination **2.** [learned technique] aptitude *f*, technique *f* ▪ [knowledge] connaissances *fpl* ▪ **management ~s** techniques de gestion ▪ **language ~s** aptitudes linguistiques ▪ **computer technology requires us to learn new ~s** l'informatique nous oblige à acquérir de nouvelles compétences.

skilled [skɪld] *adj* **1.** INDUST [engineer, labour, worker] qualifié ▪ [task] de spécialiste **2.** [experienced - driver, negotiator] habile, expérimenté ▪ [expert] habile, expert ▪ [manually] adroit ▪ [clever - gesture] habile, adroit ▪ **~ in the art of public speaking** versé dans l'art oratoire, rompu aux techniques oratoires ▪ **to be ~ at doing sthg** être doué pour faire qqch.

skillet ['skɪlɪt] *n* US poêle *f* (à frire).

skillful *etc* US = **skilful**.

skim [skɪm] (*pret & pp* **skimmed**, *cont* **skimming**) ◇ *vt* **1.** [milk] écrémer ▪ [jam] écumer ▪ [floating matter - with skimmer] écumer, enlever avec une écumoire ; [- with spatula] enlever avec une spatule ▪ **to ~ the cream from the milk** écrémer le lait **2.** [glide over - surface] effleurer, frôler ▪ **the seagull skimmed the waves** la mouette volait au ras de l'eau OR rasait les vagues ▪ **the stone skimmed the lake** la pierre a ricoché à la surface du lac ▪ **the book only ~s the surface** *fig* le livre ne fait qu'effleurer OR que survoler la question **3.** [stone] faire ricocher ▪ **the children were skimming stones over the lake** les enfants faisaient des ricochets sur le lac **4.** [read quickly - letter, book] parcourir, lire en diagonale ; [- magazine] parcourir, feuilleter.
◇ *vi* : **to ~ over the ground/across the waves** [bird] raser le sol/ les vagues ▪ **to ~ over** OR **across the lake** [stone] faire des ricochets sur le lac.
◆ **skim off** *vt sep* **1.** [cream, froth] enlever (avec une écumoire) ▪ **the book dealers skimmed off the best bargains** *fig* les marchands de livres ont fait les meilleures affaires **2.** [steal - money] : **he skimmed a little off the top for himself** il s'est un peu servi au passage.
◆ **skim over** *vt insep* [letter, report] parcourir, lire en diagonale ▪ [difficult passage] lire superficiellement, parcourir rapidement.
◆ **skim through** *vt insep* [letter, page] parcourir, lire en diagonale ▪ [magazine] feuilleter.

skimmed milk [skɪmd-] *n* lait *m* écrémé.

skimmer ['skɪməʳ] *n* **1.** ORNITH bec-en-ciseaux *m* **2.** CULIN écumoire *f*.

skimming ['skɪmɪŋ] *n* US *inf* [tax fraud] fraude *f* fiscale.

skimp [skɪmp] ◇ *vi* lésiner ▪ **to ~ on sthg** lésiner sur qqch.
◇ *vt* [resources, food] économiser sur, lésiner sur ▪ [job] faire à la va-vite.

skimpily ['skɪmpɪlɪ] *adv* [scantily] : **~ dressed** légèrement vêtu.

skimpy ['skɪmpɪ] (*comp* **skimpier**, *superl* **skimpiest**) *adj* **1.** [mean - meal, offering] maigre, chiche ; [- praise, thanks] maigre, chiche **2.** [clothes, dress - too small] trop juste ; [- light] léger ▪ **a ~ skirt** une jupe étriquée.

skin [skɪn] (*pret & pp* **skinned**, *cont* **skinning**) ◇ *n* **1.** [of person] peau *f* ▪ **to have dark/fair ~** avoir la peau brune/claire ▪ **to have bad/good ~** avoir une vilaine/jolie peau ▪ **you're nothing but ~ and bone** tu n'as que la peau et les os ▪ **we're all human under the ~** au fond, nous sommes tous humains ➤ **she escaped by the ~ of her teeth** elle l'a échappé belle, elle s'en est tirée de justesse ▪ **she nearly jumped out of her ~** elle a sauté au plafond ▪ **it's no ~ off my nose** *inf* ça ne me coûte rien *fig*, ça ne me gêne pas ▪ **he really gets under my ~** *inf* il me tape sur les nerfs, celui-là ▪ **to save one's ~** sauver sa peau ▪ **to be soaked to the ~** être trempé jusqu'aux os **2.** [from animal] peau *f* **3.** [on fruit, vegetable, sausage] peau *f* ▪ [on onion] pelure *f* ▪ **potatoes cooked in their ~s** des pommes de terre en robe des champs **4.** [on milk, pudding] peau *f* **5.** [of plane] revêtement *m* ▪ [of building] revêtement *m* extérieur ▪ [of drum] peau *f* **6.** [for wine] outre *f* **7.** *inf* [skinhead] skin *m*.
◇ *comp* [cancer, disease, tone] de la peau.
◇ *vt* **1.** [animal] dépouiller, écorcher ▪ [vegetable] éplucher ▪ **if I find him I'll ~ him alive** *fig* si je le trouve, je l'écorche

vif ▶ **there's more than one way to ~ a cat** *prov* il y a bien des moyens d'arriver à ses fins **2.** [graze - limb] écorcher **3.** *UK inf* [rob] plumer.
◆ **skin up** *vi inf* rouler un joint.

skincare ['skɪnkeəʳ] *n (U)* soins *mpl* de la peau.

skin-deep ◇ *adj* superficiel.
◇ *adv* superficiellement.

skin diver *n* plongeur *m*, - euse *f*.

skin diving *n* plongée *f* sous-marine.

skinflint ['skɪnflɪnt] *n* avare *mf*.

skinful ['skɪnfʊl] *n UK inf* **he's had a ~** il est beurré.

skin graft *n* greffe *f* de la peau ▪ **to have a ~** subir une greffe de la peau.

skinhead ['skɪnhed] *n* skinhead *m*.

-skinned [skɪnd] *in cpds* à la peau... ▪ **she's dark~** elle a la peau foncée.

skinny ['skɪnɪ] (*comp* **skinnier**, *superl* **skinniest**) *adj* très mince.

skinny-dipping [-'dɪpɪŋ] *n inf* baignade *f* à poil.

skint [skɪnt] *adj UK inf* fauché, raide.

skin test *n* MED cuti-réaction *f*.

skin-tight *adj* moulant.

skip [skɪp] (*pret & pp* **skipped**, *cont* **skipping**) ◇ *vi* **1.** [with skipping rope] sauter à la corde **2.** [jump] sautiller ▪ **he skipped out of the way** il s'est écarté d'un bond ▪ **the children were skipping around in the garden** les enfants gambadaient dans le jardin ▪ **the book keeps skipping from one subject to another** *fig* le livre passe sans arrêt d'un sujet à l'autre **3.** *inf* [go] faire un saut, aller ▪ **we skipped across to Paris for the weekend** on a fait un saut à Paris pour le week-end.
◇ *vt* **1.** [omit] sauter, passer ▪ **let's ~ the next chapter** sautons le chapitre suivant ▮ [miss - meeting, meal] sauter ▪ SCH [- class] sécher ▪ **my heart skipped a beat** *fig* mon cœur s'est arrêté de battre pendant une seconde ▶ **~ it!** *inf* laisse tomber! **2.** *inf* [leave] fuir, quitter.
◇ *n* **1.** *inf* = **skipper 2.** [jump] (petit) saut *m* **3.** [on lorry, for rubbish] benne *f*.
◆ **skip off** *vi insep inf* **1.** [disappear] décamper **2.** [go] faire un saut ▪ **we skipped off to Greece for a holiday** on est allés passer quelques jours de vacances en Grèce.
◆ **skip over** *vt insep* [omit] sauter, passer.

ski pants *npl* fuseau *m*, pantalon *m* de ski.

ski plane *n* avion *m* à skis.

skipper ['skɪpəʳ] ◇ *n* **1.** NAUT [gen] capitaine *mf* ▪ [of yacht] skipper *m* **2.** SPORT capitaine *mf*, chef *m* d'équipe **3.** *inf* [boss] patron *m*.
◇ *vt* **1.** [ship, plane] commander, être le capitaine de ▪ [yacht] skipper **2.** SPORT [team] être le capitaine de.

skipping ['skɪpɪŋ] *n* saut *m* à la corde.

skipping rope *n UK* corde *f* à sauter.

skirmish ['skɜːmɪʃ] ◇ *n fig* & MIL escarmouche *f*, accrochage *m* ▪ **I had a bit of a ~ with the authorities** j'ai eu un différend avec les autorités.
◇ *vi* MIL s'engager dans une escarmouche ▪ **to ~ with sb over sthg** *fig* avoir un accrochage OR s'accrocher avec qqn au sujet de qqch.

skirt [skɜːt] ◇ *n* **1.** [garment] jupe *f* ▪ [part of coat] pan *m*, basque *f* **2.** MECH jupe *f* **3.** *UK* [cut of meat] ≃ flanchet *m* **4.**△ *(U) UK* [woman] : **a bit of ~** une belle nana.
◇ *vt* **1.** [go around] contourner **2.** [avoid - issue, problem] éluder, esquiver.
◆ **skirt round** *vt insep* = **skirt** *(vt)*.

skirting (board) ['skɜːtɪŋ-] *n UK* plinthe *f*.

ski run *n* piste *f* de ski.

skit [skɪt] *n* parodie *f*, satire *f* ▪ **to do a ~ on sthg** parodier qqch.

ski tow *n* téléski *m*.

skitter ['skɪtəʳ] *vi* **1.** [small animal] trottiner ▪ [bird] voleter **2.** [ricochet] faire des ricochets.

skittish ['skɪtɪʃ] *adj* **1.** [person - playful] espiègle ; [- frivolous] frivole **2.** [horse] ombrageux, difficile.

skittle ['skɪtl] *n* quille *f*.
◆ **skittles** *n* (jeu *m* de) quilles *fpl* ▪ **to play ~s** jouer aux quilles, faire une partie de quilles.

skittle alley *n* piste *f* de jeu de quilles.

skive [skaɪv] *vi UK inf* [avoid work] tirer au flanc ▪ SCH sécher les cours.
◆ **skive off** *UK inf* ◇ *vi insep* se défiler.
◇ *vt insep* [work, class, school] sécher.

skiver ['skaɪvəʳ] *n UK inf* tire-au-flanc *m inv*.

skivvy ['skɪvɪ] (*pl* **skivvies**) *UK inf* ◇ *vi* faire la boniche.
◇ *n pej* bonne *f* à tout faire.
◆ **skivvies** *US inf npl* [for men] sous-vêtements *mpl* (masculins).

skulduggery [skʌl'dʌgərɪ] *n (U)* combines *fpl* OR manœuvres *fpl* douteuses.

skulk [skʌlk] *vi* rôder ▪ **there's somebody ~ing (about) in the garden/bushes** il y a quelqu'un qui rôde dans le jardin/qui se cache dans les buissons ▪ **to ~ away** OR **off** s'éclipser.

skull [skʌl] *n* crâne *m* ▪ **can't you get it into your thick ~ that she doesn't like you!** *inf fig* tu n'as toujours pas compris qu'elle ne t'aime pas!

skull and crossbones *n* [motif] tête *f* de mort ▪ [flag] pavillon *m* à tête de mort.

skullcap ['skʌlkæp] *n* **1.** [headgear] calotte *f* **2.** BOT scutellaire *f*.

skullduggery [skʌl'dʌgərɪ] = **skulduggery**.

skunk [skʌŋk] ◇ *n* **1.** (*pl* skunk OR *pl* skunks) [animal] moufette *f*, mouffette *f*, sconse *m* ▪ [fur] sconse *m* **2.** (*pl* skunks) *inf* [person] canaille *f*, ordure *f*.
◇ *vt inf US inf* [opponent] battre à plate couture, flanquer une déculottée à.

sky [skaɪ] ◇ *n* (*pl* **skies**) [gen] ciel *m* ▪ **the ~ at night** le ciel nocturne ▪ **to sleep under the open ~** dormir à la belle étoile ▶ **the ~'s the limit** *inf* tout est possible.
◇ *vt* (*pret & pp* **skied** OR **skyed**) **1.** FTBL [ball] envoyer au ciel **2.** [in rowing] : **to ~ the oars** lever les avirons trop haut.
◆ **skies** *npl* [climate] cieux *mpl* ▪ [descriptive] ciels *mpl* ▪ **we spend the winter under sunnier skies** nous passons l'hiver sous des cieux plus cléments ▪ **Turner is famous for his skies** Turner est renommé pour ses ciels.

sky blue *n* bleu ciel *m*.
◆ **sky-blue** *adj* bleu ciel *(inv)*.

skycap ['skaɪkæp] *n US* porteur *m (dans un aéroport)*.

skydiver ['skaɪˌdaɪvəʳ] *n* parachutiste *mf*.

skydiving ['skaɪˌdaɪvɪŋ] *n* parachutisme *m*.

sky-high ◇ *adj liter* très haut dans le ciel ▪ *fig* [prices] inabordable, exorbitant.
◇ *adv* **1.** *liter* très haut dans le ciel **2.** *fig* [very high] : **prices soared** OR **went ~** les prix ont grimpé en flèche ▪ **the explosion blew the building ~** l'explosion a complètement soufflé le bâtiment ▪ **our plans were blown ~** nos projets sont complètement tombés à l'eau.

skyjack ['skaɪdʒæk] *vt* [plane] détourner.

skylark ['skaɪlɑːk] ◇ *n* alouette *f* des champs.
◇ *vi inf dated* faire le fou, chahuter.

skylight ['skaɪlaɪt] *n* lucarne *f*.

skyline ['skaɪlaɪn] *n* [horizon] horizon *m* ▪ [urban] : **the New York ~** la silhouette (des immeubles) de New York.

sky marshal *n* garde *m* de sécurité à bord d'un avion.

skyscape ['skaɪskeɪp] *n* ART & PHOT ciel *m*.

skyscraper ['skaɪˌskreɪpəʳ] *n* gratte-ciel *m inv*.

skyward ['skaɪwəd] *adj* & *adv* vers le ciel.

skywards ['skaɪwədz] *adv* vers le ciel.

skywriting ['skaɪ,raɪtɪŋ] *n* publicité *f* aérienne *(tracée dans le ciel par un avion)*.

slab [slæb] (*pret* & *pp* **slabbed**, *cont* **slabbing**) <> *n* **1.** [block - of stone, wood] bloc *m* ▪ [flat] plaque *f*, dalle *f* ▪ [for path] pavé *m* ▪ **a concrete ~** une dalle de béton **2.** [piece - of cake] grosse tranche *f* ; [- of chocolate] tablette *f* ; [- of meat] pavé *m* **3.** [table, bench - of butcher] étal *m* ▪ **on the ~** [in mortuary] sur la table d'autopsie ; [for operation] *inf* sur la table d'opération.
<> *vt* [cut - stone] tailler en blocs ; [- log] débiter.

slack [slæk] <> *adj* **1.** [loose - rope, wire] lâche, insuffisamment tendu ; [- knot] mal serré, desserré ; [- chain] lâche ; [- grip] faible **2.** [careless - work] négligé ; [- worker, student] peu sérieux, peu consciencieux ▪ **he's becoming very ~ about his appearance/his work** il commence à négliger son apparence/son travail ▪ **her work has become rather ~ lately** il y a eu un certain laisser-aller dans son travail dernièrement **3.** [slow, weak - demand] faible ; [- business] calme ▪ **the ~ season for tourists** la période creuse pour le tourisme ▪ **after lunch is my ~ period** après le déjeuner, c'est mon heure creuse ▪ **business is ~ at the moment** les affaires marchent au ralenti en ce moment **4.** [lax - discipline, laws, control] mou *(before vowel or silent 'h'* **mol***)*, molle *f*, relâché ; [- parents] négligent ▪ **they're rather ~ about discipline** ils sont plutôt laxistes **5.** NAUT : **~ water, ~ tide** mer *f* étale.
<> *n* **1.** [in rope] mou *m* ▪ [in cable joint] jeu *m* ▪ NAUT [in cable] battant *m* ▪ **to take up the ~ in a rope** tendre une corde ▪ **cut me some ~!** *US fig* fiche-moi la paix! **2.** *fig* [in economy] secteurs *mpl* affaiblis ▪ **to take up the ~ in the economy** relancer les secteurs faibles de l'économie **3.** [still water] eau *f* morte ▪ [tide] mer *f* étale **4.** [coal] poussier *m*.
<> *vi* se laisser aller.

slacken ['slækn] <> *vt* **1.** [loosen - cable, rope] détendre, relâcher ; [- reins] relâcher ; [- grip, hold] desserrer **2.** [reduce - pressure, speed] réduire, diminuer ; [- pace] ralentir.
<> *vi* **1.** [rope, cable] se relâcher ▪ [grip, hold] se desserrer **2.** [lessen - speed, demand, interest] diminuer ; [- business] ralentir ; [- wind] diminuer de force ; [- standards] baisser.
◆ **slacken off** <> *vt sep* **1.** [rope] relâcher, donner du mou à **2.** [speed, pressure] diminuer ▪ [efforts] relâcher.
<> *vi insep* **1.** [rope] se relâcher **2.** [speed, demand] diminuer.
◆ **slacken up** *vi insep* [speed] diminuer ▪ [person] se relâcher.

slackening ['slæknɪŋ] *n* [in speed] diminution *f*, réduction *f* ▪ [in interest] diminution *f* ▪ [in demand] affaiblissement *m* ▪ [in knot] desserrement *m* ▪ [in rope] relâchement *m* ▪ [in standards] abaissement *m*.

slacker ['slækər] *n inf* fainéant *m*, - e *f*.

slackly ['slæklɪ] *adv* [work] négligemment, sans soin ▪ [hang] mollement.

slacks [slæks] *npl* : **(a pair of) ~** un pantalon.

slag [slæg] (*pret* & *pp* **slagged**, *cont* **slagging**) *n* **1.** *(U)* [waste - from mine] stériles *mpl* ; [- from foundry] scories *fpl*, crasses *fpl* ; [- from volcano] scories *fpl* volcaniques **2.**△ *UK pej* [woman] garce *f*, salope△ *f*.
◆ **slag off** *vt sep UK inf* dénigrer, débiner.

slagheap ['slæghi:p] *n* terril *m*, crassier *m*.

slain [sleɪn] <> *pp* ▻ **slay**.
<> *npl lit* **the ~** les soldats tombés au champ d'honneur.

slake [sleɪk] *vt lit* [thirst] étancher ▪ [desire] assouvir.

slaked lime [sleɪkt-] *n* chaux *f* éteinte.

slalom ['slɑ:ləm] <> *n* [gen - SPORT] slalom *m*.
<> *vi* slalomer, faire du slalom.

slam [slæm] (*pret* & *pp* **slammed**, *cont* **slamming**) <> *vt* **1.** [close - window, door] claquer ; [- drawer] fermer violemment ▪ **to ~ the door shut** claquer la porte ▪ **I tried to explain but she slammed the door in my face** j'ai essayé de lui expliquer mais elle m'a claqué la porte au nez ▪ [bang] : **he slammed the books on the desk** il a posé bruyamment les livres sur le bureau ▪ **he slammed the ball into the net** il a envoyé le ballon dans le filet d'un grand coup de pied **2.** *inf* [defeat] écraser **3.** *inf* [criticize] descendre.
<> *vi* [door, window] claquer ▪ **the door slammed shut** la porte a claqué.
<> *n* **1.** [of door, window] claquement *m* ▪ **give the door a good ~** claque la porte un bon coup **2.** CARDS chelem *m*.
◆ **slam down** *vt sep* [lid] refermer en claquant ▪ [books, keys] poser bruyamment ▪ **she slammed the money down on the table** elle a jeté l'argent sur la table.
◆ **slam on** *vt sep* : **to ~ on the brakes** freiner brutalement.
◆ **slam to** *vt sep* refermer en claquant.

slam dunk *US* SPORT <> *n* smash *m* au panier, slam-dunk *m*.
<> *vt* & *vi* smasher.

slammer△ ['slæmər] *n* [jail] tôle△ *f*.

slander ['slɑ:ndər] <> *vt* [gen] calomnier, dire du mal de ▪ LAW diffamer.
<> *n* [gen] calomnie *f* ▪ LAW diffamation *f*.

slanderer ['slɑ:ndərər] *n* [gen] calomniateur *m*, - trice *f* ▪ LAW diffamateur *m*, - trice *f*.

slanderous ['slɑ:ndrəs] *adj* [gen] calomniateur ▪ LAW diffamatoire ▪ **~ gossip** calomnies *fpl*.

slang [slæŋ] <> *n* [gen - LING] argot *m* ▪ **he uses a lot of ~** il emploie beaucoup de mots d'argot ▪ **prison ~** argot carcéral *OR* de prison.
<> *adj* argotique, d'argot.
<> *vt inf UK inf* traiter de tous les noms.

slanging match ['slæŋɪŋ-] *n UK inf* échange *m* d'insultes.

slangy ['slæŋɪ] (*comp* **slangier**, *superl* **slangiest**) *adj* argotique.

slant [slɑ:nt] <> *n* **1.** [line] ligne *f* oblique ▪ [slope] inclinaison *f* ▪ **the table has a ~** *OR* **is on a ~** la table penche *OR* n'est pas d'aplomb **2.** [point of view] perspective *f*, point *m* de vue ▪ **his articles usually have an anti-government ~** il a tendance à critiquer le gouvernement dans ses articles.
<> *vt* **1.** [news, evidence] présenter avec parti pris *OR* de manière peu objective **2.** [line, perspective] incliner, faire pencher.
<> *vi* [line, handwriting] pencher ▪ [ray of light] passer obliquement.

slant-eyed *adj* aux yeux bridés, qui a les yeux bridés.

slanting ['slɑ:ntɪŋ] *adj* [floor, table] en pente, incliné ▪ [writing] penché ▪ [line] oblique, penché.

slantwise ['slɑ:ntwaɪz] *adv* [hang, fall] en oblique, obliquement ▪ [write] d'une écriture penchée.

slap [slæp] (*pret* & *pp* **slapped**, *cont* **slapping**) <> *vt* **1.** [hit] donner une claque à ▪ **she slapped his face, she slapped him across the face** elle l'a giflé, elle lui a donné une gifle ▪ **to ~ sb on the back** [for hiccups, in greeting] donner à qqn une tape dans le dos ; [in praise] féliciter qqn en lui donnant une tape dans le dos ➊ **to ~ sb's wrist** *OR* **wrists, to ~ sb on the wrist** *OR* **wrists** taper sur les doigts de qqn **2.** [put] : **just ~ some paint over it** passe un coup de pinceau dessus ▪ **~ some Sellotape across it** mets juste un bout de Scotch dessus.
<> *vi* : **the waves slapped against the harbour wall** les vagues battaient contre la digue.
<> *n* **1.** [smack] claque *f* ▪ [on face] gifle *f* ▪ [on back] tape *f* dans le dos **2.** [noise] : **the ~ of the waves against the side of the boat** le clapotis des vagues contre la coque.
<> *adv inf* en plein ▪ **~ in the middle of the meeting** en plein *OR* au beau milieu de la réunion.
◆ **slap down** *vt sep* **1.** [book, money] poser avec violence ▪ **she slapped £1,000 down on the table** elle a jeté 1 000 livres sur la table **2.** *inf* [suggestion] rejeter ▪ [person] rembarrer, envoyer promener *OR* paître.
◆ **slap on** *vt sep* **1.** [paint] appliquer n'importe comment *OR* à la va-vite ▪ [jam, butter] étaler généreusement ▪ **~ some paint on the door** donne un coup de pinceau sur la porte

■ **hang on, I'll just ~ some make-up on** attends, je vais juste me maquiller vite fait **2.** [tax, increase] : **they slapped on a 3% surcharge** ils ont mis une surtaxe de 3 %.

slap and tickle *n UK inf* pelotage *m*.

slap-bang *adv inf* en plein, tout droit ■ **she went ~(-wallop) into a tree** elle est rentrée en plein *OR* tout droit dans un arbre ■ **he walked ~ into his boss** *fig* il s'est trouvé nez à nez avec son patron.

slapdash ['slæpdæʃ] <> *adv* à la va-vite, sans soin, n'importe comment.
<> *adj* [work] fait n'importe comment *OR* à la va-vite ■ [person] négligent.

slaphappy ['slæp,hæpɪ] *adj inf* relax.

slapjack ['slæpdʒæk] *n US* CULIN crêpe *f*.

slapstick ['slæpstɪk] <> *n* grosse farce *f*, bouffonnerie *f*.
<> *adj* [humour] bouffon ■ **~ comedy** comédie *f* bouffonne.

slap-up *adj UK inf* **a ~ meal** un repas de derrière les fagots ■ **he invited me out for a ~ lunch** il m'a invité à déjeuner dans un restaurant chic.

slash [slæʃ] <> *vt* **1.** [cut - gen] taillader ; [- face] balafrer ■ **he ~ed my arm with a knife** il m'a tailladé le bras avec un couteau ■ **the bus seats had been ~ed by vandals** les sièges du bus avaient été lacérés par des vandales **2.** [hit - with whip] frapper, cingler ; [- with stick] battre ■ **she ~ed the bushes with a stick** elle donnait des coups de bâton dans les buissons **3.** *US* [verbally] critiquer violemment **4.** [prices] casser ■ [cost, taxes] réduire considérablement ■ **prices have been ~ed by 40%** les prix ont été réduits de 40 % **5.** SEW : **a green jacket ~ed with blue** une veste verte avec des crevés laissant apercevoir du bleu.
<> *vi* : **to ~ at sb with a knife** donner des coups de couteau en direction de qqn ■ **he ~ed at the bushes with a stick** il donna des coups de bâton dans les buissons.
<> *n* **1.** [with knife] coup *m* de couteau ■ [with sword] coup *m* d'épée ■ [with whip] coup *m* de fouet ■ [with stick] coup *m* de bâton **2.** [cut] entaille *f* ■ [on face] balafre *f* **3.** SEW crevé *m* **4.** TYPO (barre *f*) oblique *f* **5.** *UK phr* **to have a ~**△ pisser un coup△.

slash-and-burn *adj* sur brûlis.

slasher movie *n inf* film *m* d'horreur.

slat [slæt] *n* [in blinds, louvre] lamelle *f* ■ [wooden] latte *f* ■ AERON aileron *m*.

slate [sleɪt] <> *n* **1.** CONSTR & SCH ardoise *f* ■ **put it on the ~** *UK inf fig* mettez-le sur mon compte **2.** *US* POL liste *f* provisoire de candidats.
<> *comp* [mine] d'ardoise ■ [roof] en ardoise *OR* ardoises ■ [industry] ardoisier ■ **~ quarry** carrière *f* d'ardoise, ardoisière *f*.
<> *vt* **1.** [cover - roof] couvrir d'ardoises **2.** *US* POL proposer *(un candidat)* **3.** *US* [destine] : **she was ~d for a gold medal/for victory** elle devait remporter une médaille d'or/la victoire ‖ [expect] prévoir ■ **we're slating a full house** nous comptons faire salle comble **4.** *UK inf* [criticize - film, actor] descendre.

slate-grey *adj* gris ardoise *(inv)*.

slater ['sleɪtəʳ] *n* [roofer] couvreur *m*.

slating ['sleɪtɪŋ] *n* **1.** *(U)* CONSTR [of roof] couverture *f* ■ [material] ardoises *fpl* **2.** *UK inf phr* **to get a ~** [criticism] se faire descendre *(par la critique)* ; [scolding] se faire enguirlander.

slatted ['slætɪd] *adj* à lattes.

slattern ['slætən] *n* souillon *f*.

slaty ['sleɪtɪ] *adj* [in colour] ardoise *(inv)* ■ [in appearance, texture] qui ressemble à l'ardoise.

slaughter ['slɔːtəʳ] <> *vt* **1.** [kill - animal] abattre, tuer ; [- people] massacrer, tuer (sauvagement) **2.** *inf fig* [defeat - team, opponent] massacrer.
<> *n* [of animal] abattage *m* ■ [of people] massacre *m*, tuerie *f*.

slaughterhouse ['slɔːtəhaʊs] (*pl* [-haʊzɪz]) *n* abattoir *m*.

Slav [slɑːv] <> *adj* slave.
<> *n* Slave *mf*.

slave [sleɪv] <> *n liter & fig* esclave *mf* ■ **to be a ~ to fashion/habit** être esclave de la mode/de ses habitudes.
<> *vi* travailler comme un esclave *OR* un forçat, trimer ■ **he ~d over his books all day long** il était plongé dans ses livres à longueur de journée.

slave cylinder *n* cylindre *m* récepteur.

slave driver *n liter* meneur *m* d'esclaves ■ *fig* négrier *m*.

slave labour *n* [work] travail *m* fait par des esclaves ■ *fig* travail *m* de forçat ■ **I'm not working there any more, it's ~** je ne travaillerai plus pour eux, c'est le *OR* un vrai bagne.

slaver[1] ['sleɪvəʳ] *n* **1.** [trader] marchand *m* d'esclaves **2.** [ship] (vaisseau *m*) négrier *m*.

slaver[2] ['slævəʳ] <> *vi* [dribble] baver.
<> *n* [saliva] bave *f*.

slavery ['sleɪvərɪ] *n* esclavage *m* ■ **to be sold into ~** être vendu comme esclave.

slave ship *n* négrier *m (bateau)*.

slave trade *n* commerce *m* des esclaves ■ [of Africans] traite *f* des Noirs.

slave trader *n* marchand *m* d'esclaves, négrier *m*.

Slavic ['slɑːvɪk] = **Slavonic**.

slavish ['sleɪvɪʃ] *adj* [mentality, habits] d'esclave ■ [devotion] servile ■ [imitation] sans aucune originalité, servile.

slavishly ['sleɪvɪʃlɪ] *adv* [work] comme un forçat ■ [copy, worship] servilement.

Slavonic [slə'vɒnɪk] <> *n* LING slave *m* ■ HIST slavon *m*.
<> *adj* slave.

slay [sleɪ] (*pret* **slew** [sluː], *pp* **slain** [sleɪn]) *vt* **1.** [kill] tuer **2.** *UK inf* [impress] impressionner **3.** *UK inf* [amuse] faire crever de rire.

sleaze [sliːz] *n inf* [squalidness] aspect *m* miteux, caractère *m* sordide ■ [pornography] porno *m* ■ POL [corruption] corruption *f*.

sleazy ['sliːzɪ] (*comp* **sleazier**, *superl* **sleaziest**) *adj inf* [squalid] miteux, sordide ■ [disreputable] mal famé.

sled [sled] <> *n UK* = **sledge** *(senses 1, 2)* ■ *US* = **sledge** *(sense 1)*.
<> *vi UK* = **sledge** *(senses 1,2)* ■ *US* = **sledge** *(senses 1)*.
<> *vt US* transporter en luge.

sledge [sledʒ] <> *n* **1.** [for fun or sport] luge *f* **2.** [pulled by animals] traîneau *m*.
<> *vi* **1.** *UK* [for fun or sport] faire de la luge ■ **to go sledging** faire de la luge ■ **children were sledging down the slope** des enfants descendaient la pente sur une *OR* en luge **2.** [pulled by animals] faire du traîneau.
<> *vt US* transporter en traîneau.

sledgehammer ['sledʒ,hæməʳ] *n* masse *f (outil)* ■ **a ~ blow** *fig* un coup très violent.

sleek [sliːk] *adj* **1.** [fur, hair] luisant, lustré, lisse ■ [feathers] brillant, luisant ■ [bird] aux plumes luisantes ■ [cat] au poil soyeux *OR* brillant **2.** [person - in appearance] soigné, tiré à quatre épingles ; [- in manner] onctueux, doucereux **3.** [vehicle, plane] aux lignes pures.

sleekly ['sliːklɪ] *adv* **1.** [glossily] : **its fur shone ~** il avait le poil luisant **2.** [elegantly - dress] élégamment, avec chic.

sleekness ['sliːknɪs] *n* [of fur, hair] brillant *m*, luisant *m*.

sleep [sliːp] (*pret & pp* **slept** [slept]) <> *vi* **1.** [rest] dormir ■ **~ well** *OR* **tight!** bonne nuit! ■ **did you ~ well?** avez-vous bien dormi? ■ **to ~ soundly** dormir profondément *OR* à poings fermés ■ **to ~ rough** coucher sur la dure ■ **she slept through the storm** la tempête ne l'a pas réveillée ‖ [spend night] coucher, passer la nuit ■ **can I ~ at your place?** est-ce que je peux coucher *OR* dormir chez vous? ■ **where did you ~ last night?** où est-ce que tu as passé la nuit? ➲ **to ~ like a log** dormir comme une souche *OR* comme un loir *OR* du sommeil du

juste ▪ **'The Sleeping Beauty'** ***Perrault, Tchaikovsky*** 'la Belle au bois dormant' **2.** [daydream] rêvasser, rêver **3.** *euph* & *lit* [be dead] dormir du dernier sommeil.
◇ *vt* **1.** [accommodate] : **the sofa bed ~s two** deux personnes peuvent coucher dans le canapé-lit ▪ **the house ~s four** on peut loger quatre personnes dans cette maison **2.** *phr* **I didn't ~ a wink all night** je n'ai pas fermé l'œil de la nuit.
◇ *n* **1.** [rest] sommeil *m* ▪ **to talk in one's ~** parler en dormant *OR* dans son sommeil ▪ **to walk in one's ~** être somnambule ▪ **to be in a deep ~** dormir profondément ▪ **to have a good ~** bien dormir ▪ **I only had two hours' ~** je n'ai dormi que deux heures ▪ **you need (to get) a good night's ~** il te faut une bonne nuit de sommeil ▪ **I couldn't get to ~** je n'arrivais pas à m'endormir ▪ **to go to ~** s'endormir ▪ **my legs have gone to ~** *fig* [numb] j'ai les jambes engourdies ; [tingling] j'ai des fourmis dans les jambes ▪ **you're not going to lose ~ over it!** tu ne vas pas en perdre le sommeil! ▪ **to put to ~** [patient] endormir ; *euph* [horse, dog] piquer ▪ **to send sb to ~** *liter* endormir qqn ; *fig* [bore] endormir qqn, assommer qqn **2.** *UK* [nap] : **the children usually have a ~ in the afternoon** en général les enfants font la sieste l'après-midi ▪ **I could do with a ~** je ferais bien un petit somme **3.** [substance in eyes] chassie *f* ▪ **to rub the ~ out of one's eyes** se frotter les yeux *(au réveil)*.
◆ **sleep around** *vi insep inf* coucher à droite et à gauche.
◆ **sleep in** *vi insep* **1.** [lie in - voluntarily] faire la grasse matinée ; [- involuntarily] se lever en retard **2.** [sleep at home] coucher à la maison ▪ [staff] être logé sur place.
◆ **sleep off** *vt sep* [hangover, fatigue] dormir pour faire passer ▪ **he's ~ing off the effects of the journey** il dort pour se remettre de la fatigue du voyage ▪ **he's ~ing it off** *inf* il cuve son vin.
◆ **sleep on** ◇ *vi insep* continuer à dormir ▪ **let her ~ on a bit** laisse-la dormir encore un peu.
◇ *vt insep phr* : **~ on it** la nuit porte conseil *prov.*
◆ **sleep out** *vi insep* [away from home] découcher ▪ [in the open air] coucher à la belle étoile ▪ [in tent] coucher sous la tente.
◆ **sleep over** *vi insep* : **can I ~ over?** est-ce que je peux rester dormir?,
◆ **sleep through** ◇ *vi insep* : **he slept through till five o'clock** il a dormi jusqu'à cinq heures.
◇ *vt insep* : **I slept through the last act** j'ai dormi pendant tout le dernier acte ▪ **she slept through her alarm** elle n'a pas entendu son réveil.
◆ **sleep together** *vi insep* coucher ensemble.
◆ **sleep with** *vt insep euph* coucher avec.

sleeper ['sli:pəʳ] *n* **1.** [sleeping person] dormeur *m*, - euse *f* ▪ **to be a light/heavy ~** avoir le sommeil léger/lourd **2.** [train] train-couchettes *m* ▪ [sleeping car] wagon-lit *m*, voiture-lit *f* ▪ [berth] couchette *f* **3.** *US* [sofa bed] canapé-lit *m* **4.** RAIL *UK* [track support] traverse *f* **5.** [spy] agent *m* dormant **6.** *UK* [earring] clou *m* **7.** *inf* [unexpected success] révélation *f*.

sleepily ['sli:pɪlɪ] *adv* [look] d'un air endormi ▪ [speak] d'un ton endormi.

sleepiness ['sli:pɪnɪs] *n* [of person] envie *f* de dormir ▪ [of town] torpeur *f*.

sleeping ['sli:pɪŋ] *adj* qui dort, endormi.

sleeping bag *n* sac *m* de couchage.

sleeping berth *n* RAIL & NAUT couchette *f*.

sleeping car *n* wagon-lit *m*.

sleeping draught *n UK* soporifique *m*.

sleeping partner *n UK* COMM (associé *m*) commanditaire *m*, bailleur *m* de fonds.

sleeping pill *n* somnifère *m*.

sleeping policeman *n UK* casse-vitesse *m inv*, ralentisseur *m*.

sleeping sickness *n* maladie *f* du sommeil.

sleeping tablet = **sleeping pill**.

sleepless ['sli:plɪs] *adj* [without sleep] sans sommeil ▪ **I had** *OR* **spent a ~ night** j'ai passé une nuit blanche, je n'ai pas fermé l'œil de la nuit.

sleeplessness ['sli:plɪsnɪs] *n (U)* insomnie *f*, insomnies *fpl*.

sleep mode *n* COMPUT mode *m* de veille.

sleepwalk ['sli:pwɔ:k] *vi* : **he was ~ing last night** il a eu une crise de somnambulisme hier soir.

sleepwalker ['sli:p,wɔ:kəʳ] *n* somnambule *mf*.

sleepwalking ['sli:p,wɔ:kɪŋ] *n* somnambulisme *m*.

sleepy ['sli:pɪ] (*comp* **sleepier**, *superl* **sleepiest**) *adj* **1.** [person] qui a envie de dormir, somnolent ▪ **I'm** *OR* **I feel ~** j'ai sommeil, j'ai envie de dormir **2.** [town] plongé dans la torpeur.

sleepyhead ['sli:pɪhed] *n inf* **come on, ~, it's time for bed!** allez, va au lit, tu dors debout!

sleet [sli:t] ◇ *n* neige *f* fondue *(tombant du ciel)*.
◇ *vi* : **it's ~ing** il tombe de la neige fondue.

sleeve [sli:v] *n* **1.** [on garment] manche *f* ▪ **to have** *OR* **to keep something up one's ~** avoir plus d'un tour dans son sac ▪ **I wonder what else she's got up her ~** je me demande ce qu'elle nous réserve encore comme surprise **2.** TECH [tube] manchon *m* ▪ [lining] chemise *f* **3.** *UK* [for record] pochette *f*.

sleeveless ['sli:vlɪs] *adj* sans manches.

sleeve notes *npl UK* *texte figurant au dos des pochettes de disques.*

sleigh [sleɪ] *n* traîneau *m* ▪ **~ ride** promenade *f* en traîneau.

sleight of hand [,slaɪt-] *n* [skill] dextérité *f* ▪ [trick] tour *m* de passe-passe ▪ **by ~** par un tour de passe-passe.

slender ['slendəʳ] *adj* **1.** [slim, narrow - figure] mince, svelte ; [- fingers, neck, stem] fin ▪ **Peter is tall and ~** Peter est grand et élancé ; [- margin] étroit **2.** [limited - resources] faible, maigre, limité ; [- majority] étroit, faible ; [- hope, chance] maigre, faible.

slept [slept] *pt* & *pp* ▻ **sleep**.

sleuth [slu:θ] *inf hum* ◇ *n* (fin) limier *m*, détective *m*.
◇ *vi* enquêter.

sleuthing ['slu:θɪŋ] *n inf hum* travail *m* de détective.

S-level (*abbrev of* **Special level**) *n* SCOL *matière supplémentaire à haut niveau pour l'examen A-level.*

slew [slu:] ◇ *pt* ▻ **slay**.
◇ *vi* **1.** [pivot - person] pivoter, se retourner ▪ **he ~ed round in his chair** il a pivoté sur sa chaise **2.** [vehicle - skid] déraper ; [- swerve] faire une embardée ; [- turn] virer.
◇ *vt* **1.** [turn, twist] faire tourner *OR* pivoter ▪ NAUT [mast] virer, dévirer **2.** [vehicle] faire déraper.
◇ *n inf* **a ~ of, ~s of** un tas de.

slewed [slu:d] *adj UK inf* rond, ivre.

slice [slaɪs] ◇ *n* **1.** [of bread, meat, cheese] tranche *f* ▪ [of pizza] part *f* ▪ [round] rondelle *f*, tranche *f* **2.** *fig* [share, percentage] part *f*, partie *f* **3.** [utensil] pelle *f*, spatule *f* ▪ **cake ~** pelle *f* à gâteau **4.** SPORT slice *m*.
◇ *vt* **1.** [cut into pieces - cake, bread] couper (en tranches) ; [- sausage, banana] couper (en rondelles) ▪ **any way you ~ it** *US inf* il n'y a pas à tortiller **2.** [cut] couper, trancher **3.** SPORT couper, slicer.
◇ *vi* [knife] couper ▪ [bread] se couper ▪ **this bread doesn't ~ very easily** ce pain n'est pas très facile à couper.
◆ **slice off** *vt sep* [branch] couper ▪ **his finger was ~d off** il a eu le doigt coupé.
◆ **slice through** *vt insep* **1.** [cut - rope, cable] couper (net), trancher **2.** [go, move] traverser (rapidement), fendre ▪ **the boat ~d through the water** le bateau fendait l'eau.
◆ **slice up** *vt sep* [loaf, cake] couper (en tranches) ▪ [banana] couper (en rondelles).

sliced bread [slaɪst-] *n* pain *m* (coupé) en tranches ▪ **it's the best thing since ~** *inf* il n'y a pas mieux dans le genre.

slicer ['slaɪsəʳ] *n* [gen] machine *f* à trancher ▪ [for bread] machine *f* à couper le pain ▪ [for meat] machine *f* à couper la viande ▪ [for salami, ham] coupe-jambon *m inv*.

slick [slɪk] ◇ *adj* **1.** *pej* [glib] qui a du bagout ■ [in speech] enjôleur ■ [in manner] doucereux ■ [in content] superficiel ■ **he always has a ~ answer** il a toujours réponse à tout ■ **the explanation was rather too ~** l'explication était trop bonne (pour être vraie) **2.** [smoothly efficient] habile ■ **she made a ~ gear change** elle effectua un changement de vitesse en souplesse ■ **a ~ campaign** une campagne astucieuse **3.** [style, magazine] beau *(before vowel or silent 'h' bel)*, belle *f* **4.** [smart, chic] chic, tiré à quatre épingles **5.** [hair] lisse, lissé, luisant ■ [road surface] glissant, gras ■ [tyre] lisse **6.** *US* [slippery] glissant ■ [greasy] gras, grasse *f* **7.** *US* [cunning] malin, -igne *f*, rusé.
◇ *n* **1.** [oil spill - on sea] nappe *f* de pétrole ; [- on beach] marée *f* noire **2.** [tyre] pneu *m* lisse **3.** *US* [glossy magazine] *magazine en papier glacé contenant surtout des articles et des photos sur la vie privée des stars.*
◆ **slick back, slick down** *vt sep* : **to ~ one's hair back** *OR* **down** se lisser les cheveux.

slicker ['slɪkəʳ] *n US* [raincoat] imperméable *m*, ciré *m*.

slickly ['slɪklɪ] *adv* [answer] habilement ■ [perform] brillamment ■ **his hair shone ~** il avait les cheveux luisants.

slickness ['slɪknɪs] *n* **1.** [of hair] brillant *m*, luisant *m* **2.** *pej* [in speech] bagout *m* ■ [in manner] caractère *m* doucereux ■ [in style] brillance *f* (apparente) **3.** [of deal, sale] rapidité *f*, efficacité *f*.

slide [slaɪd] (*pret & pp* **slid** [slɪd]) ◇ *vi* **1.** [on ice, slippery surface] glisser ■ **he slid on the ice** il a glissé sur la glace ■ **he slid down the bannisters** il a descendu l'escalier en glissant sur la rampe ■ **tears slid down her face** des larmes roulèrent sur son visage **2.** [move quietly] : **the car slid away into the dark** la voiture s'enfonça dans l'obscurité ■ **she slid into/out of the room** elle s'est glissée dans la pièce/hors de la pièce ■ **the door slid open/shut** la porte s'est ouverte/fermée en glissant **3.** [go gradually] glisser ■ **the sheet music slid (down) behind the piano** la partition a glissé derrière le piano ■ **he's sliding into bad habits** il est en train de prendre de mauvaises habitudes ■ **to let things ~** laisser les choses aller à la dérive **4.** [prices, value] baisser.
◇ *vt* faire glisser, glisser ■ **~ the lid into place** faites glisser le couvercle à sa place.
◇ *n* **1.** [in playground] toboggan *m* ■ [on ice, snow] glissoire *f* ■ [for logs] glissoire *f* **2.** [act of sliding] glissade *f* ■ **to go into a ~** faire une glissade **3.** [fall - in prices] baisse *f* ■ **the stock exchange is on a downward ~** la Bourse est en baisse ■ **the ~ in standards** la dégradation des valeurs **4.** PHOT diapositive *f*, diapo *f* ■ [for microscope] porte-objet *m* **5.** *UK* [in hair] barrette *f* **6.** [runner - in machine, trombone] coulisse *f* **7.** MUS coulé *m*.
◆ **slide off** *vi insep* **1.** [lid] s'enlever en glissant ■ **this part ~s off easily** il suffit de faire coulisser cette pièce pour l'enlever **2.** [fall] glisser ■ **the book keeps sliding off** le livre n'arrête pas de glisser **3.** [go away - visitor] s'en aller discrètement, s'éclipser ■ **she slid off to the bar in the interval** elle s'est éclipsée à l'entracte pour aller au bar.

slide projector *n* projecteur *m* de diapositives.

slide rule *n* règle *f* à calcul.

slide show *n* diaporama *m*.

slide valve *n* (soupape *f* à) clapet *m*.

sliding ['slaɪdɪŋ] ◇ *adj* [part] qui glisse ■ [movement] glissant ■ [door] coulissant ■ [panel] mobile.
◇ *n* glissement *m*.

sliding roof *n* AUT toit *m* ouvrant.

sliding scale *n* [for salaries] échelle *f* mobile ■ [for prices] barème *m* des prix ■ [for tax] barème *m* des impôts.

slight [slaɪt] ◇ *adj* **1.** [person - slender] menu, mince ; [- frail] frêle ■ [structure] fragile, frêle ■ **she is of ~ build** elle est fluette **2.** [minor, insignificant - error, increase, movement] faible, léger, petit ; [- difference] petit ; [- cut, graze] léger ■ **there's a ~ drizzle/wind** il y a un peu de crachin/de vent ■ **he has a ~ accent** il a un léger accent ■ **she has a ~ temperature** elle a un peu de température ■ **she has a ~ cold** elle est un peu enrhumée ■ **a ~ piece of work** un ouvrage insignifiant ■ [in superl form] : **it makes not the ~est bit of difference** ça ne change absolument rien ■ **I haven't the ~est idea** je n'en ai pas la moindre idée ■ **he gets angry at the ~est thing** il se fâche pour un rien ■ **not in the ~est** pas le moins du monde, pas du tout.
◇ *vt* [snub] manquer d'égards envers ■ [insult] insulter ■ [offend] froisser, blesser.
◇ *n* [snub, insult] manque *m* d'égards, vexation *f*, affront *m* ■ **it's a ~ on her reputation** c'est une offense à sa réputation.

slighting ['slaɪtɪŋ] *adj* offensant, désobligeant.

slightingly ['slaɪtɪŋlɪ] *adv* : **to speak ~ of sb** faire des remarques désobligeantes sur qqn.

slightly ['slaɪtlɪ] *adv* **1.** [a little] un peu, légèrement ■ **~ better** légèrement mieux, un peu mieux ■ **a ~ higher number** un chiffre un peu plus élevé **2.** [slenderly] : **~ built** fluet, frêle.

slim [slɪm] (*comp* **slimmer**, *superl* **slimmest**, *pret & pp* **slimmed**)
◇ *adj* **1.** [person, waist, figure] mince, svelte ■ [wrist] mince, fin, délicat ■ **a ~-hipped young man** un jeune homme aux hanches étroites **2.** [volume, wallet, diary] mince **3.** [faint, feeble - hope, chance] faible, minime ; [- pretext] mince, piètre, dérisoire ■ **they have only a ~ chance of winning the next election** ils n'ont que de faibles chances de gagner les prochaines élections.
◇ *vi* [get thin] maigrir, mincir ■ [diet] faire *OR* suivre un régime.
◇ *vt* [subj: diet, exercise] faire maigrir.
◆ **slim down** ◇ *vt sep* **1.** [subj: diet] faire maigrir ■ [subj: clothes] amincir **2.** *fig* [industry] dégraisser ■ [workforce] réduire ■ [ambitions, plans] limiter, réduire ■ [design, car] épurer, alléger.
◇ *vi insep* **1.** [person] maigrir, suivre un régime **2.** [industry] être dégraissé.

slime [slaɪm] *n* [sticky substance] substance *f* gluante *OR* poisseuse ■ [from snail] bave *f* ■ [mud] vase *f*.

slimline ['slɪmlaɪn] *adj* **1.** [butter] allégé ■ [milk, cheese] sans matière grasse, minceur *(inv)* ■ [soft drink] light *(inv)* **2.** *fig* **clothes for the new ~ you** des vêtements pour votre nouvelle silhouette allégée ■ **the ~ version of the 1990 model** la version épurée du modèle 90.

slimmer ['slɪməʳ] *n* personne *f* qui suit un régime (amaigrissant).

slimming ['slɪmɪŋ] ◇ *n* amaigrissement *m* ■ **~ can be bad for you** les régimes amaigrissants ne sont pas toujours bons pour la santé.
◇ *adj* [diet] amaigrissant ■ [cream, product] amincissant ■ [exercises] pour maigrir ■ [meal] à faible teneur en calories.

slimness ['slɪmnɪs] *n* [of person, waist, figure] minceur *f*, sveltesse *f* ■ [of wrist, ankle] minceur *f*, finesse *f*, délicatesse *f*.

slimy ['slaɪmɪ] (*comp* **slimier**, *superl* **slimiest**) *adj* **1.** [with mud] vaseux, boueux ■ [with oil, secretion] gluant, visqueux ■ [wall] suintant **2.** *UK* [obsequious - person] mielleux ; [- manners] doucereux, obséquieux.

sling [slɪŋ] (*pret & pp* **slung** [slʌŋ]) ◇ *vt* **1.** [fling] jeter, lancer ■ **the children were ~ing stones at the statue** les enfants lançaient des pierres sur la statue ■ **she slung the case into the back of the car** elle a jeté la valise à l'arrière de la voiture ■ **if he's not careful, he'll get slung off the course** *inf* s'il ne fait pas attention, il se fera virer du cours ▶ **to ~ one's hook** *inf* mettre les bouts, ficher le camp **2.** [lift, hang - load] hisser ■ NAUT élinguer ■ **the hammock was slung between two trees** le hamac était suspendu *OR* accroché entre deux arbres ■ **the soldiers wore rifles slung across** *OR* **over their shoulders** les soldats portaient des fusils en bandoulière ■ **he slung his jacket over his shoulder** il a jeté sa veste par-dessus son épaule.
◇ *n* **1.** [for broken arm] écharpe *f* ■ **she had her arm in a ~** elle avait le bras en écharpe **2.** [for baby] porte-bébé *m* **3.** [for loads NAUT & CONSTR élingue *f* ■ [belt] courroie *f* ■ [rope] corde *f*, cordage *m* ■ [for removal men] corde *f*, courroie *f* ■ [for rifle] bretelle *f* ■ [for mast] cravate *f* **4.** [weapon] fronde *f* ■ [toy] lance-pierres *m inv* **5.** [for climber] baudrier *m* **6.** [cocktail] sling *m (cocktail à base de spiritueux et de jus de citron, allongé d'eau plate ou gazeuse)*.
◆ **sling out** *vt sep UK inf* [person] flanquer *OR* ficher à la porte ■ [rubbish, magazines etc] bazarder, ficher en l'air.

➔ **sling over** *vt sep* ***UK inf*** lancer, envoyer.

slingback ['slɪŋbæk] *n* ***UK*** chaussure *f* à talon découvert.

slingshot ['slɪŋʃɒt] *n* ***US*** lance-pierres *m inv*.

slink [slɪŋk] (*pret & pp* **slunk** [slʌŋk]) *vi* : **to ~ in/out** entrer/sortir furtivement ■ **to ~ away** s'éclipser.

slinky ['slɪŋkɪ] (*comp* **slinkier**, *superl* **slinkiest**) *adj* ***inf*** [manner] aguichant ■ [dress] sexy *(inv)* ■ [walk] ondoyant, chaloupé.

slip [slɪp] (*pret & pp* **slipped**, *cont* **slipping**) ◇ *vi* **1.** [lose balance, slide] glisser ■ **I slipped on the ice** j'ai glissé sur une plaque de verglas ■ **he slipped and fell** il glissa et tomba | [move unexpectedly] glisser ■ **the knife slipped and cut my finger** le couteau a glissé et je me suis coupé le doigt ■ **my hand slipped** ma main a glissé ■ **the cup slipped out of my hands** la tasse m'a glissé des mains ■ **the prize slipped from her grasp** *OR* **from her fingers** ***fig*** le prix lui a échappé ■ **somehow, the kidnappers slipped through our fingers** ***fig*** je ne sais comment les ravisseurs nous ont filé entre les doigts
2. [go gradually] glisser ■ **the patient slipped into a coma** le patient a glissé *OR* s'est enfoncé peu à peu dans le coma ■ **she slipped into the habit of visiting him every day** petit à petit elle a pris l'habitude d'aller le voir tous les jours
3. [go down] baisser ■ **prices have slipped (by) 10%** les prix ont baissé de 10 %
4. [go discreetly or unnoticed] se glisser, se faufiler ■ **she slipped quietly into the room** elle s'est glissée discrètement dans la pièce ■ **the thieves managed to ~ through the road blocks** les voleurs ont réussi à passer à travers les barrages routiers ■ **why don't you ~ through the kitchen/round the back?** pourquoi ne passez-vous pas par la cuisine/par derrière? ■ **some misprints have slipped into the text** des coquilles se sont glissées dans le texte | [go quickly] se faufiler ■ **we slipped through the rush hour traffic** on s'est faufilés dans les embouteillages des heures de pointe | [into clothes] : **I'll ~ into something cooler** je vais enfiler *OR* mettre quelque chose de plus léger
5. [slide - runners, drawer] glisser ■ **the back should just ~ into place** l'arrière devrait glisser à sa place
6. ***inf*** [be less efficient] : **you're slipping!** tu n'es plus ce que tu étais!
7. AUT [clutch] patiner
8. ***phr*** **to let ~** [opportunity] laisser passer *OR* échapper ; [word] lâcher, laisser échapper ■ **she let (it) ~ that she was selling her house** elle a laissé échapper qu'elle vendait sa maison.
◇ *vt* **1.** [give or put discreetly] glisser ■ **to ~ sb a note** glisser un mot à qqn ■ **to ~ a letter into sb's hand/pocket** glisser une lettre dans la main/la poche de qqn ■ **~ the key under the door** glissez la clé sous la porte
2. [escape] : **it slipped my mind** ça m'est sorti de la tête ■ **her name has completely slipped my memory** j'ai complètement oublié son nom
3. [release] : **he slipped the dog's lead** ***UK*** il a lâché la laisse du chien ■ **the dog slipped its lead** ***UK*** le chien s'est dégagé de sa laisse ■ **to ~ anchor/a cable** filer l'ancre/un câble ■ **to ~ a stitch** glisser une maille ■ **to ~ a disc, to have a slipped disc** MED avoir une hernie discale
4. AUT [clutch] faire patiner.
◇ *n* **1.** [piece of paper] : **~ (of paper)** feuille *f OR* bout *m* de papier ■ **withdrawal ~** [in bank] bordereau *m* de retrait ■ **delivery ~** COMM bordereau *m* de livraison
2. [on ice, banana skin] glissade *f*
3. [mistake] erreur *f* ■ [blunder] bévue *f* ■ [careless oversight] étourderie *f* ■ [moral] écart *m*, faute *f* légère ■ **~ of the tongue** *OR* **pen** lapsus *m* ■ **there's many a ~ twixt cup and lip** ***UK prov*** il y a loin de la coupe aux lèvres ***prov***
4. [landslide] éboulis *m*, éboulement *m*
5. [petticoat - full length] combinaison *f*, fond *m* de robe ; [- skirt] jupon *m*
6. BOT bouture *f*
7. *(usu pl)* NAUT cale *f*
8. TECH [glaze] engobe *m*
9. ***phr*** **a ~ of a girl** ***UK*** une petite jeune ■ **a ~ of a boy** ***UK*** un petit jeune ■ **to give sb the ~** semer qqn.
➔ **slips** *npl* **1.** THEAT coulisses *fpl*
2. SPORT [in cricket] *partie du terrain ou joueurs situés à droite du guichet, du point de vue du lanceur, si le batteur est gaucher (et vice versa).*

➔ **slip along** *vi insep* **1.** [go quickly] faire un saut ■ **I'll just ~ along to the chemist's** je fais juste un saut à la pharmacie
2. [discreetly] aller en cachette.
➔ **slip away** *vi insep* [person] s'éclipser, partir discrètement ■ [moment] passer ■ [boat] s'éloigner doucement ■ **I felt my life slipping away** j'avais l'impression que ma vie me glissait entre les doigts.
➔ **slip back** *vi insep* [car] glisser (en arrière) ■ [person] revenir discrètement ■ **he slipped back into a coma** il est retombé dans le coma ■ **he slipped back into his old habits** il est retombé dans ses vieilles habitudes.
➔ **slip by** *vi insep* [time] passer ■ [person] se faufiler.
➔ **slip down** *vi insep* [fall - picture, car, socks, skirt] glisser.
➔ **slip in** ◇ *vi insep* [person] entrer discrètement *OR* sans se faire remarquer ■ [boat] entrer lentement ■ **some misprints have slipped in somehow** des fautes de frappe se sont glissées dans le texte.
◇ *vt sep* [moving part] faire glisser à sa place ■ [quotation, word] glisser, placer ■ **to ~ the clutch in** AUT embrayer.
➔ **slip off** ◇ *vi insep* **1.** [go away] s'éclipser
2. [fall - bottle, hat, book] glisser (et tomber).
◇ *vt sep* [remove - coat, hat] enlever, ôter ; [- shoe, ring, sock] enlever ; [- top, lid] faire glisser pour ouvrir.
➔ **slip on** *vt sep* [dress, ring, coat] mettre, enfiler ■ [lid] mettre *OR* remettre (en faisant glisser).
➔ **slip out** ◇ *vi insep* **1.** [leave - person] sortir discrètement, s'esquiver
2. [escape - animal, child] s'échapper ■ **the word slipped out before he could stop himself** le mot lui a échappé
3. [go out] sortir (un instant).
◇ *vt sep* sortir.
➔ **slip over** ◇ *vi insep* aller ■ **we slipped over to Blackpool to see them** nous sommes allés à Blackpool pour les voir.
◇ *vt sep* ***phr*** **to ~ one over on sb** ***inf*** rouler qqn.
➔ **slip past** *vi insep* [time] passer ■ [person] se faufiler.
➔ **slip round** *vi insep* ***UK*** **1.** [go] passer ■ **can you ~ round after supper?** peux-tu passer (chez moi) après souper?
2. [saddle] se retourner ■ [skirt] tourner.
➔ **slip through** *vi insep* [person] passer sans se faire remarquer ■ [mistake] passer inaperçu.
➔ **slip up** *vi insep* ***inf*** faire une gaffe ■ **you've slipped up badly here** tu t'es bien planté.

slipcase ['slɪpkeɪs] *n* [for single volume] étui *m* ■ [for several volumes, for records] coffret *m*.

slipcover ['slɪpkʌvəʳ] *n* ***US*** **1.** [for furniture] housse *f* **2.** = **slipcase.**

slipknot ['slɪpnɒt] *n* nœud *m* coulant.

slip-on ◇ *adj* [shoe] sans lacets.
◇ *n* chaussure *f* sans lacets.

slippage ['slɪpɪdʒ] *n* **1.** MECH patinage *m* **2.** [in targeting] retard *m (par rapport aux prévisions)* ■ [in standards] baisse *f*.

slipped disc [ˌslɪpt-] *n* hernie *f* discale.

slipper ['slɪpəʳ] ◇ *n* [soft footwear] chausson *m*, pantoufle *f* ■ [mule] mule *f* ■ [for dancing] escarpin *m*.
◇ *vt* ***UK*** [hit] : **to ~ sb** donner une fessée à qqn *(avec une pantoufle)*.

slippery ['slɪpərɪ] *adj* **1.** [surface, soap] glissant ■ **we're on the ~ slope to bankruptcy** ***fig*** nous allons droit à la faillite **2.** ***inf*** [person - evasive] fuyant ■ [unreliable] sur qui on ne peut pas compter.

slippy ['slɪpɪ] (*comp* **slippier**, *superl* **slippiest**) *adj* [slippery] glissant.

slip road *n* ***UK*** bretelle *f* d'accès.

slipshod ['slɪpʃɒd] *adj* [appearance] négligé, débraillé ■ [habits, behaviour] négligent ■ [style] peu soigné, négligé ■ [work] négligé, mal fait.

slip stitch *n* SEW point *m* perdu.

slipstream ['slɪpstriːm] ◇ *n* AUT sillage *m*.
◇ *vt* [driver] rester dans le sillage de.

slip-up *n* ***inf*** bévue *f*, gaffe *f*.

slipway ['slɪpweɪ] *n* NAUT [for repairs] cale *f* de halage ▪ [for launching] cale *f* de lancement.

slit [slɪt] (*pret & pp* **slit**, *cont* **slitting**) ◇ *n* [narrow opening] fente *f* ▪ [cut] incision *f* ▪ **the skirt has a ~ at the back** la jupe a une fente *OR* est fendue dans le dos.
◇ *vt* **1.** [split] fendre ▪ [cut] inciser, couper ▪ **the skirt was ~ up the side** la jupe était fendue sur le côté ▪ **the mattress had been ~ open** le matelas avait été éventré ▪ **to ~ sb's throat** égorger qqn ▪ **she ~ her wrists** elle s'est ouvert les veines **2.** [open - parcel, envelope] ouvrir (avec un couteau *OR* un coupe-papier).
◇ *adj* [skirt] fendu ▪ [eyes] bridé.

slither ['slɪðəʳ] *vi* **1.** [snake] ramper, onduler **2.** [car, person - slide] glisser, patiner ; [- skid] déraper.

slithery ['slɪðərɪ] *adj* [surface] glissant ▪ [snake] ondulant.

sliver ['slɪvəʳ] *n* **1.** [of glass] éclat *m* **2.** [small slice - of cheese, cake] tranche *f* fine.

Sloane [sləʊn] *n inf* ~ **(Ranger)** *personne de la haute bourgeoisie (généralement une jeune femme) portant des vêtements sports mais chics et parlant de façon affectée* ▪ ≃ NAP *mf*.

Sloaney ['sləʊnɪ] *adj inf* ≃ NAP.

slob [slɒb] *n inf* [dirty] souillon *mf* ▪ [uncouth] plouc *m* ▪ [lazy] flemmard *m*, - e *f*.
◆ **slob about** *UK*, **slob around** *inf* ◇ *vi insep* traînasser.
◇ *vt insep* traînasser.

slobber ['slɒbəʳ] ◇ *vi* **1.** [dribble - baby, dog] baver ▪ **to ~ over** baver sur **2.** *fig* **to ~ over** [possession, pet] s'extasier sur *OR* devant ; [person] faire des ronds de jambe à.
◇ *n* [dribble] bave *f*.

slobbery ['slɒbərɪ] *adj* [kiss] baveux.

sloe [sləʊ] *n* [berry] prunelle *f* ▪ [tree] prunellier *m*.

sloe-eyed *adj* aux yeux de biche.

sloe gin *n* gin *m* à la prunelle.

slog [slɒg] (*pret & pp* **slogged**, *cont* **slogging**) *inf* ◇ *n* **1.** [hard task] travail *m* d'Hercule ▪ [chore] corvée *f*, travail *m* pénible ▪ [effort] (gros) effort *m* ▪ **it was a real ~ to finish in time** on a dû bosser comme des malades pour finir à temps ▪ **what a ~!** quelle corvée! ▪ **it's been a long hard ~ for her to get where she is** elle en a bavé pour arriver là où elle est **2.** *UK* [hit] grand coup *m*.
◇ *vi* **1.** [work hard] trimer, bosser ▪ **she spent all weekend slogging away at that report** elle a passé tout le week-end à trimer sur ce rapport ▪ **she slogged on until ten o'clock** elle est restée bosser jusqu'à 10h ▪ **do we really have to ~ through all this paperwork?** est-ce qu'il est indispensable de se farcir toute cette paperasse? **2.** [walk, go] avancer péniblement ▪ **we slogged slowly up the hill** nous avons gravi la côte à pas lents.
◇ *vt* **1.** [move] : **we slogged our way through the snow** nous nous sommes péniblement frayé un chemin dans la neige **2.** *UK* [hit - ball] donner un grand coup dans ; [- person] cogner sur ▪ **to ~ it out** [fight] se tabasser ; [argue] s'enguirlander.

slogan ['sləʊgən] *n* slogan *m*.

slo-mo ['sləʊməʊ] *n inf* ralenti *m* ▪ **in ~** au ralenti.

sloop [slu:p] *n* sloop *m*.

slop [slɒp] (*pret & pp* **slopped**, *cont* **slopping**) ◇ *vi* [spill] renverser ▪ [overflow - liquid] déborder ▪ **the soup slopped onto the cooker** la soupe a débordé sur la cuisinière.
◇ *vt* renverser ▪ **he slopped soup onto the tablecloth** il a renversé *OR* répandu de la soupe sur la nappe.
◇ *n (U)* [liquid waste - for pigs] pâtée *f* ; [- from tea, coffee] fond *m* de tasse ▪ [tasteless food] mixture *f pej*.
◆ **slop about** *UK*, **slop around** ◇ *vi insep* **1.** [liquid] clapoter **2.** [paddle] patauger **3.** *inf* [be lazy] traînasser.
◇ *vt sep* [paint] éclabousser ▪ [tea] renverser.
◇ *vt insep inf* **he ~s about the house doing nothing** il traîne à la maison à ne rien faire.
◆ **slop out** *vi insep* [prisoner] vider les seaux hygiéniques.

slop basin *n UK* vide-tasses *m inv*.

slop bucket *n* [gen] seau *m* (à ordures) ▪ [in prison] seau *m* hygiénique.

slope [sləʊp] ◇ *n* **1.** [incline - of roof] inclinaison *f*, pente *f* ; [- of ground] pente *f* ▪ **rifle at the ~** MIL fusil sur l'épaule **2.** [hill - up] côte *f*, montée *f* ; [- down] pente *f*, descente *f* ▪ [mountainside] versant *m*, flanc *m* ▪ **tea is grown on the higher ~s** on cultive le thé plus haut sur les versants de la montagne **3.** [for skiing] piste *f*.
◇ *vi* [roof] être en pente *OR* incliné ▪ [writing] pencher ▪ **the beach ~d gently to the sea** la plage descendait en pente douce vers la mer ▪ **the table ~s** la table penche *OR* n'est pas droite.
◇ *vt* MIL : **~ arms!** portez arme!
◆ **slope off** *vi insep inf* filer.

sloping ['sləʊpɪŋ] *adj* [table, roof] en pente, incliné ▪ [writing] penché ▪ [shoulders] tombant.

sloppily ['slɒpɪlɪ] *adv* **1.** [work] sans soin ▪ [dress] de façon négligée **2.** *UK inf* [sentimentally] avec sensiblerie.

sloppiness ['slɒpɪnɪs] *n* [of work] manque *m* de soin *OR* de sérieux ▪ [in dress] négligence *f*, manque *m* de soin ▪ [of thought] flou *m*, manque *m* de précision.

sloppy ['slɒpɪ] (*comp* **sloppier**, *superl* **sloppiest**) *adj* **1.** [untidy - appearance] négligé, débraillé ▪ [careless - work] bâclé, négligé ; [- writing] peu soigné ; [- thinking] flou, vague, imprécis **2.** *inf* [loose - garment] large, lâche **3.** *inf* [sentimental - person, letter] sentimental ; [- book, film] à l'eau de rose.

sloppy joe *n inf* **1.** *UK* [sweater] gros pull *m* **2.** *US* [hamburger] hamburger *m*.

slosh [slɒʃ] *inf* ◇ *vt* **1.** [spill] renverser, répandre ▪ [pour - onto floor] répandre ; [- into glass, bucket] verser ▪ [apply - paint, glue] flanquer ▪ **she ~ed whitewash on** *OR* **over the wall** elle a barbouillé le mur de blanc de chaux **2.** *UK* [hit] flanquer un coup de poing à^△^.
◇ *vi* **1.** [liquid] se répandre ▪ **the juice ~ed all over the cloth** le jus s'est renversé partout sur la nappe ▪ **water ~ed over the edge** l'eau a débordé **2.** [move - in liquid, mud] patauger.
◇ *onom* plouf.
◆ **slosh about** *UK*, **slosh around** *vi insep* [liquid] clapoter ▪ [person] patauger.

sloshed [slɒʃt] *adj inf* rond, soûl ▪ **to get ~** prendre une cuite.

slot [slɒt] (*pret & pp* **slotted**, *cont* **slotting**) ◇ *n* **1.** [opening - for coins, papers] fente *f* ▪ [groove] rainure *f* **2.** [in schedule, timetable] tranche *f* *OR* plage *f* horaire, créneau *m* ▪ RADIO & TV créneau *m* ▪ [opening] créneau *m* ▪ **there's a ~ for someone with marketing skills** il y a un créneau pour quelqu'un qui s'y connaît en marketing **3.** AERON fente *f*.
◇ *vt* **1.** [insert] emboîter ▪ **~ this bit in here** [in machine, model] introduisez cette pièce ici ; [in jigsaw] posez *OR* mettez cette pièce ici **2.** [find time for, fit] insérer, faire rentrer ▪ **she managed to ~ me into her timetable** elle a réussi à me réserver un moment *OR* à me caser dans son emploi du temps.
◇ *vi* **1.** [fit - part] rentrer, s'encastrer, s'emboîter ▪ **the blade ~s into the handle** la lame rentre dans le manche **2.** [in timetable, schedule] rentrer, s'insérer ▪ **where do we ~ into the scheme?** où intervenons-nous dans le projet?
◆ **slot in** ◇ *vt sep* [into schedule] faire rentrer ▪ **when can you ~ me in?** quand pouvez-vous me caser *OR* trouver un moment pour moi?
◇ *vi insep* [part] s'emboîter, s'encastrer ▪ [programme] s'insérer.
◆ **slot together** ◇ *vt sep* emboîter, encastrer ▪ **~ these two parts together** emboîtez ces deux pièces l'une dans l'autre.
◇ *vi insep* s'emboîter, s'encastrer ▪ **the two parts ~ together** les deux pièces s'emboîtent l'une dans l'autre.

sloth [sləʊθ] *n* **1.** [laziness] paresse *f* **2.** ZOOL paresseux *m*.

slothful ['sləʊθfʊl] *adj* paresseux.

slot machine *n* [for vending] distributeur *m* (automatique) ▪ [for gambling] machine *f* à sous.

slot meter *n UK* compteur *m* à pièces.

slotted spatula ['slɒtɪd-] *n US* pelle *f* à poisson.

slotted spoon *n* écumoire *f*.

slouch [slaʊtʃ] ◇ *vi* : **she was ~ing against the wall** elle était nonchalamment adossée au mur ▪ **stop ~ing!** redresse-toi! ▪ **to ~ in/out** entrer/sortir en traînant les pieds.
◇ *vt* : **to ~ one's shoulders** rentrer les épaules.
◇ *n* **1.** [in posture] : **to have a ~** avoir le dos voûté **2.** *inf* [person] : **he's no ~** ce n'est pas un empoté.
◆ **slouch about** *UK*, **slouch around** *vi insep* se traîner.

slouch hat *n* chapeau *m* à larges bords.

slough[1] [slaʊ] *n* [mud pool] bourbier *m* ▪ [swamp] marécage *m* ▶ **the Slough of Despond** le tréfonds du désespoir.

slough[2] [slʌf] ◇ *n* **1.** [skin - of snake] dépouille *f*, mue *f* ▪ MED escarre *f* **2.** CARDS carte *f* défaussée.
◇ *vt* : **the snake ~s its skin** le serpent mue.
◆ **slough off** *vt sep* [skin] se dépouiller de ▪ **the snake ~s off its skin** le serpent mue ▮ *fig* [worries] se débarrasser de ▪ [habit] perdre, se débarrasser de.

Slovak ['sləʊvæk] ◇ *n* [person] Slovaque *mf*.
◇ *adj* slovaque.

Slovakia [slə'vækɪə] *pr n* Slovaquie *f* ▪ **in ~** en Slovaquie.

Slovakian [slə'vækɪən] ◇ *n* Slovaque *mf*.
◇ *adj* slovaque.

Slovene ['sləʊviːn] ◇ *n* [person] Slovène *mf*.
◇ *adj* slovène.

Slovenia [slə'viːnjə] *pr n* Slovénie *f* ▪ **in ~** en Slovénie.

Slovenian [slə'viːnjən] ◇ *n* Slovène *mf*.
◇ *adj* slovène.

slovenliness ['slʌvnlɪnɪs] *n* [of dress] négligé *m*, débraillé *m* ▪ [of habits] laisser-aller *m* ▪ [of work] manque *m* de soin.

slovenly ['slʌvnlɪ] *adj* [appearance] négligé, débraillé ▪ [habits] relâché ▪ [work] peu soigné ▪ [style, expression] relâché, négligé.

slow [sləʊ] ◇ *adj* **1.** [not fast - movements, speed, service, traffic] lent ▪ **he's a ~ worker** il travaille lentement ▪ **it's ~ work** c'est un travail qui n'avance pas vite *OR* de longue haleine ▪ **to make ~ progress** [in work, on foot] avancer lentement ▪ **a ~ dance** un slow ▪ **it was ~ going, the going was ~** ça n'avançait pas ▪ **with ~ steps** d'un pas lent ▪ **we had a painfully ~ journey** le voyage a duré un temps fou ▪ **the pace of life is ~** on vit au ralenti ▪ **the fog was ~ to clear** le brouillard a mis longtemps à se dissiper ▪ [in reactions] lent ▪ **he was rather ~ to make up** *OR* **in making up his mind** il a mis assez longtemps à se décider ▪ **she wasn't ~ to offer her help/in accepting the cheque** elle ne se fit pas prier pour proposer son aide/pour accepter le chèque ▪ **I was rather ~ to understand** *OR* **in understanding** il m'a fallu assez longtemps pour comprendre ▪ **you were a bit ~ there** là, tu t'es laissé prendre de vitesse ▪ **she's very ~ to anger** il lui en faut beaucoup pour se mettre en colère ▮ [in progress] lent ▪ **the company was ~ to get off the ground** la société a été lente à démarrer ▮ [intellectually] lent ▪ **he's a ~ learner/reader** il apprend/lit lentement ▶ **the ~ lane** AUT [when driving on left] la file de gauche ; [when driving on right] la file de droite ▪ **~ train** omnibus *m* ▪ **to be ~ off the mark** *UK liter* être lent à démarrer ; *fig* avoir l'esprit lent **2.** [slack - business, market] calme ▪ **business is ~** les affaires ne marchent pas fort ▪ **~ economic growth** une faible croissance économique **3.** [dull - evening, film, party] ennuyeux **4.** [clock] qui retarde ▪ **your watch is (half an hour) ~** ta montre retarde (d'une demi-heure) **5.** CULIN : **~ burner** feu *m* doux ▪ **bake in a ~ oven** faire cuire à four doux.
◇ *adv* lentement ▪ **go a bit ~er** ralentissez un peu ▪ **the clock is going** *OR* **running ~** l'horloge prend du retard ▪ **'slow'** [road marking] 'ralentir' ▪ **~ astern!** NAUT arrière doucement! ▶ **to go ~** faire une grève perlée.
◇ *vt* ralentir ▮ **I ~ed the horse to a trot** j'ai mis le cheval au trot.
◆ **slow down** ◇ *vt sep* **1.** [in speed - bus, machine, progress] ralentir ; [- person] (faire) ralentir ▪ [in achievement, activity] ralentir ▪ **production is ~ed down during the winter** pendant l'hiver, la production tourne au ralenti **2.** [delay] retarder.
◇ *vi insep* [driver, train, speed] ralentir ▪ *fig* [person] ralentir (le rythme) ▪ **~ down!** moins vite! ▪ **growth ~ed down in the second quarter** il y a eu une diminution *OR* un ralentissement de la croissance au cours du deuxième trimestre.
◆ **slow up** = **slow down**.

slow-acting *adj* à action lente.

slow burn *n US* **to do a ~** sentir la colère monter.

slowcoach ['sləʊkəʊtʃ] *n UK inf* [in moving] lambin *m*, - e *f*, traînard *m*, - e *f* ▪ [in thought] balourd *m*, - e *f* ▪ **come on ~** allez, du nerf!

slow cooker *n* mijoteuse *f*.

slowdown ['sləʊdaʊn] *n* **1.** *US* [go-slow] grève *f* perlée **2.** [slackening] ralentissement *m*.

slow handclap *n UK* applaudissements *mpl* rythmés *(pour montrer sa désapprobation)* ▪ **they gave him the ~** ≃ ils l'ont sifflé.

slowly ['sləʊlɪ] *adv* **1.** [not fast] lentement ▪ **could you walk/speak more ~?** pouvez-vous marcher/parler moins vite? ▪ **~ but surely** lentement mais sûrement **2.** [gradually] peu à peu.

slow motion *n* CIN & TV ralenti *m* ▪ **in ~** au ralenti.
◆ **slow-motion** *adj* (tourné) au ralenti ▪ **slow-motion replay** TV ralenti *m*.

slow-moving *adj* [person, car] lent ▪ [film, plot] dont l'action est lente ▪ [market] stagnant ▪ **~ target** cible *f* qui bouge lentement.

slowness ['sləʊnɪs] *n* **1.** [of progress, reaction, service, traffic] lenteur *f* ▪ [of plot, play] lenteur *f*, manque *m* d'action **2.** [of intellect] lenteur *f* (d'esprit) **3.** [of trading, market] stagnation *f* **4.** [of watch] retard *m*.

slowpoke ['sləʊpəʊk] *US inf* = **slowcoach**.

slow-witted [-'wɪtɪd] *adj* (intellectuellement) lent.

slowworm ['sləʊwɜːm] *n* orvet *m*.

SLR (*abbrev of* **single-lens reflex**) *n* reflex *m* (mono-objectif).

sludge [slʌdʒ] *n (U)* **1.** [mud] boue *f*, vase *f* ▪ [snow] neige *f* fondue **2.** [sediment] dépôt *m*, boue *f* **3.** [sewage] vidanges *fpl*.

slue [sluː] *US* = **slew** *(vi, vt)*.

slug [slʌg] (*pret & pp* **slugged**, *cont* **slugging**) ◇ *n* **1.** ZOOL limace *f* **2.** *inf fig* [lazy person] mollusque *m* **3.** PRINT [of metal] lingot *m* **4.** *US* [token] jeton *m* **5.** *inf* [hit] beigne *f* **6.** *inf* [drink] coup *m* ▪ [mouthful] lampée *f* ▪ **to take a ~ of whisky** boire une gorgée de whisky **7.** *inf* [bullet] balle *f*.
◇ *vt inf* **1.** [hit] frapper (fort), cogner **2.** *phr* **to ~ it out** *inf* [fight] se taper dessus ; [argue] s'enguirlander.

sluggish ['slʌgɪʃ] *adj* **1.** [lethargic] mou *(before vowel or silent 'h' mol)*, molle *f*, apathique **2.** [slow - traffic, growth, reaction] lent ; [- digestion] lent, paresseux ; [- market, business] calme, stagnant ▪ **trading is always rather ~ on Mondays** les affaires ne marchent jamais très bien *OR* très fort le lundi **3.** [engine] qui manque de reprise *OR* de nervosité.

sluggishly ['slʌgɪʃlɪ] *adv* [slowly] lentement ▪ [lethargically] mollement ▪ **the market reacted ~** la bourse a réagi faiblement ▪ **the car started ~** la voiture a démarré avec difficulté.

sluice [sluːs] ◇ *n* **1.** [lock] écluse *f* ▪ [gate] porte *f OR* vanne *f* d'écluse ▪ [channel] canal *m* à vannes ▪ *(U)* [lock water] eaux *fpl* retenues par la vanne **2.** [wash] : **to give sthg a ~ (down)** laver qqch à grande eau ▪ **to give sb a ~ (down)** asperger qqn d'eau.
◇ *vt* **1.** [drain] drainer ▪ [irrigate] irriguer **2.** [wash] laver à grande eau ▪ MIN [ore] laver ▪ **to ~ sthg (down)** laver qqch à grande eau.

sluice gate, sluice valve *n* porte *f OR* vanne *f* d'écluse.

slum [slʌm] (*pret & pp* **slummed**, *cont* **slumming**) ◇ *n liter & fig* taudis *m* ▪ [district] quartier *m* pauvre, bas quartiers *mpl* ▪ **~ dwelling** taudis *m*.
◇ *vt UK* **to ~ it** *inf* s'encanailler.
◇ *vi inf hum* **we're slumming tonight** on va s'encanailler ce soir.

slumber ['slʌmbər] ◇ *n lit* sommeil *m* (profond).

◇ *vi* dormir.

slumber party *n* ***US*** soirée *f* entre copines *(au cours de laquelle on regarde des films, on discute et on dort toutes ensemble).*

slum clearance *n* ***UK*** rénovation *f* ***OR*** aménagement *m* des quartiers insalubres.

slummy ['slʌmɪ] (*comp* **slummier**, *superl* **slummiest**) *adj* [area, house, lifestyle] sordide, misérable.

slump [slʌmp] ◇ *n* **1.** [in attendance, figures, popularity] chute *f*, forte baisse *f*, baisse *f* soudaine ■ **there has been a ~ in investment** les investissements sont en forte baisse ■ **a ~ in prices/demand** une forte baisse des prix/de la demande **2.** ECON [depression] crise *f* économique ■ [recession] récession *f* ■ ST. EX effondrement *m* (des cours), krach *m* (boursier) **3.** ***US*** SPORT passage *m* à vide.
◇ *vi* **1.** [flop - with fatigue, illness] s'écrouler, s'effondrer **2.** [shoulders] avoir le dos voûté **3.** [collapse - business, prices, market] s'effondrer ■ [morale, attendance] baisser soudainement.
◇ *vt (usu passive)* **to be ~ed in an armchair** être affalé ***OR*** affaissé dans un fauteuil ■ **he was ~ed over the wheel** [in car] il était affaissé sur le volant.

slung [slʌŋ] *pt* & *pp* ▷ **sling**.

slunk [slʌŋk] *pt* & *pp* ▷ **slink**.

slur [slɜːʳ] (*pret* & *pp* **slurred**, *cont* **slurring**) ◇ *n* **1.** [insult] insulte *f*, affront *m* ■ [blot, stain] tache *f* ■ **it's a ~ on his character** c'est une tache à sa réputation ■ **to cast a ~ on sb** porter atteinte à la réputation de qqn **2.** MUS liaison *f*.
◇ *vt* **1.** [speech] mal articuler **2.** [denigrate] dénigrer **3.** MUS lier.
◇ *vi* [speech, words] devenir indistinct.

slurp [slɜːp] *inf* ◇ *vt* & *vi* boire bruyamment.
◇ *n* : **a loud ~** un lapement bruyant ■ **can I have a quick ~ of your tea?** je peux boire une gorgée de ton thé?

slurred [slɜːd] *adj* mal articulé ■ **his speech was ~** il articulait.

slurry ['slʌrɪ] *n* [cement, clay] barbotine *f* ■ [manure] purin *m*.

slush [slʌʃ] *n* **1.** [snow] neige *f* fondue ■ [mud] gadoue *f* **2.** *inf* [sentimentality] sensiblerie *f*.

slush fund *n* caisse *f* noire *(servant généralement au paiement des pots-de-vin).*

slushy ['slʌʃɪ] (*comp* **slushier**, *superl* **slushiest**) *adj* **1.** [snow] fondu ■ [ground] détrempé ■ [path] couvert de neige fondue **2.** [film, book] à l'eau de rose.

slut [slʌt] *n pej* [slovenly woman] souillon *f* ■ [immoral woman] fille *f* facile.

sluttish ['slʌtɪʃ] *adj pej* [appearance] de souillon, sale ■ [morals] dépravé ■ [behaviour] débauché, dépravé.

sly [slaɪ] (*comp* **slyer** ***OR*** **slier**, *superl* **slyest** ***OR*** **sliest**) ◇ *adj* **1.** [cunning, knowing] rusé ■ **he's a ~ (old) devil** ***OR*** **dog** c'est une fine mouche ■ **he gave me a ~ look/smile** il m'a regardé/souri d'un air rusé **2.** [deceitful - person] sournois ; [- behaviour] déloyal ; [- trick] malhonnête **3.** [mischievous] malin, - igne *f*, espiègle **4.** [secretive] dissimulé ■ **he's a ~ one!** c'est un petit cachottier!
◇ *n phr* **on the ~** *inf* en douce.

slyly ['slaɪlɪ] *adv* **1.** [cunningly] de façon rusée, avec ruse **2.** [deceitfully] sournoisement **3.** [mischievously] avec espièglerie, de façon espiègle **4.** [secretly] discrètement.

slyness ['slaɪnɪs] *n* **1.** [cunning] ruse *f* **2.** [deceitfulness] fausseté *f* **3.** [mischief] espièglerie *f* **4.** [secrecy] dissimulation *f*.

s/m *n* = **sadomasochism**.

S&M *n* = **sadomasochism**.

smack [smæk] ◇ *n* **1.** [slap] grande tape *f*, claque *f* ■ [on face] gifle *f* ■ [on bottom] fessée *f* ■ **to give sb a ~ in the face** gifler qqn ■ **a ~ in the face** ***OR*** **eye** *fig* une gifle, une rebuffade **2.** [sound] bruit *m* sec ■ [of whip] claquement *m* **3.** [taste] léger ***OR*** petit goût *m* ■ CULIN soupçon *m* **4.** [boat] smack *m*, sémaque *m* **5.** [kiss] gros baiser *m* **6.** △ ***drug sl*** [heroin] poudre *f*, blanche *f*.
◇ *vt* donner une grande tape à, donner une claque à ■ [in face] donner une gifle à, gifler ■ [on bottom] donner une fessée à ■ **to ~ sb's bottom** [in punishment] donner la fessée à qqn ; [in play] donner une tape sur les fesses de qqn ■ **to ~ one's lips** se lécher les babines.
◇ *vi* : **to ~ of sthg** *liter* & *fig* sentir qqch ■ **the whole thing ~s of corruption** tout ça, ça sent la corruption.
◇ *adv* **1.** [forcefully] en plein ■ **she kissed him ~ on the lips** elle l'a embrassé en plein sur la bouche **2.** [exactly] en plein ■ **we arrived ~ in the middle of the meeting** nous sommes arrivés au beau milieu de la réunion.

smack-dab *esp* ***US***, **smack-bang** = **smack** *(adv sense 2).*

smacker ['smækəʳ] *n inf* **1.** [kiss] grosse bise *f* **2.** [banknote] ***US*** dollar *m* ■ ***UK*** [pound] livre *f*.

smacking ['smækɪŋ] ◇ *n* fessée *f* ■ **I gave the child a good ~** j'ai donné une bonne fessée à l'enfant.
◇ *adj* ***UK*** *inf* **at a ~ pace** à vive allure, à toute vitesse.

small [smɔːl] ◇ *adj* **1.** [in size - person, town, garden] petit ■ **~ children** les jeunes enfants ■ **in ~ letters** en (lettres) minuscules ■ **to make ~er** [garment] diminuer ; [hole] réduire ■ **to make o.s. ~** se faire tout petit ● **the ~est room** *euph* le petit coin ■ **to feel ~** se trouver ***OR*** se sentir bête ■ **to make sb look** ***OR*** **feel ~** humilier qqn **2.** [in number - crowd] peu nombreux ; [- family] petit ; [- population] faible ■ [in quantity - amount, percentage, resources] petit, faible ; [- supply] petit ; [- salary, sum] petit, modeste ; [- helping] petit, peu copieux ; [- meal] léger ■ **the ~est possible number of guests** le moins d'invités possible ■ **to get** ***OR*** **to grow ~ er** diminuer, décroître ■ **the problems don't get any ~er** les problèmes ne vont pas (en) s'amenuisant ■ **to make ~er** [income] diminuer ; [staff] réduire **3.** [in scale, range] petit ■ [minor] petit, mineur ■ **down to the ~est details** jusqu'aux moindres détails ■ **it's no ~ achievement** c'est une réussite non négligeable ■ **there's the ~ matter of the £150 you still owe me** il reste ce petit problème des 150 livres que tu me dois ■ **he felt responsible in his own ~ way** il se sentait responsable à sa façon ■ COMM : **~ businessmen** les petits entrepreneurs *mpl* ***OR*** patrons *mpl* ■ **~ businesses** [firms] les petites et moyennes entreprises *fpl*, les PME *fpl* ; [shops] les petits commerçants *mpl* **4.** [mean, narrow] petit, mesquin ■ **they've got ~ minds** ce sont des esprits mesquins.
◇ *adv* : **to cut sthg up ~** couper qqch en tout petits morceaux ■ **to roll sthg up ~** [long] rouler qqch bien serré ; [ball] rouler qqch en petite boule.
◇ *n* : **he took her by the ~ of the waist** il l'a prise par la taille ■ **I have a pain in the ~ of my back** j'ai mal aux reins ***OR*** au creux des reins.
◆ **smalls** *npl inf hum* sous-vêtements *mpl*.

small ad *n* petite annonce *f*.

small arms *npl* armes *fpl* portatives.

small beer *n* ***UK*** *inf* **it's ~** c'est de la petite bière ■ **we're very ~ in the advertising world** nous ne représentons pas grand-chose dans le monde de la publicité.

small-bore *adj* de petit calibre.

small change *n* petite monnaie *f*.

small-claims court *n* LAW tribunal *m* d'instance.

small fry *n* menu fretin *m* ■ **he's ~** ***UK*** ***OR*** **a ~** ***US*** il ne compte pas.

smallholder ['smɔːl,həʊldəʳ] *n* ***UK*** petit propriétaire *m*.

smallholding ['smɔːl,həʊldɪŋ] *n* ***UK*** petite propriété *f*.

small hours *npl* petit matin *m* ■ **in the ~** au petit matin.

small letter *n* (lettre *f*) minuscule *f* ■ **in ~s** en (lettres) minuscules.

small-minded *adj* [attitude, person] mesquin.

small-mindedness [-'maɪndɪdnɪs] *n* mesquinerie *f*, petitesse *f*.

small potatoes *npl* ***US*** *inf* = **small beer**.

smallpox ['smɔːlpɒks] *n* variole *f*.

small print *n* : **in ~** en petits caractères, écrit petit ■ **make sure you read the ~ before you sign** lisez bien ce qui est écrit en petits caractères avant de signer.

small scale *n* petite échelle *f* ■ **on a ~** sur une petite échelle.
◆ **small-scale** *adj* [replica, model] à taille réduite, réduit ■ [operation] à petite échelle.

small screen *n* : **the ~** le petit écran.

small talk *n (U)* papotage *m*, menus propos *mpl* ■ **to make ~** échanger des banalités.

small-time *adj* peu important, de petite envergure ■ **a ~ thief/crook** un petit voleur/escroc.

small-town *adj* provincial ■ **~ America** l'Amérique profonde.

smarm [smɑːm] *UK inf pej* ◇ *vt* faire du plat OR lécher les bottes à ■ **you won't ~ your way out of this one!** tu ne t'en tireras pas avec des flatteries, cette fois-ci!
◇ *vi* : **to ~ up to sb** passer de la pommade à OR lécher les bottes à qqn.
◇ *n* obséquiosité *f*.

smarmy ['smɑːmɪ] (*comp* **smarmier**, *superl* **smarmiest**) *adj UK inf pej* [toadying] lèche-bottes *(inv)* ■ [obsequious] obséquieux.

smart [smɑːt] ◇ *adj* **1.** *UK* [elegant - person, clothes] chic, élégant ■ **she's a ~ dresser** elle s'habille avec beaucoup de chic ■ **you look very ~ in your new suit** vous avez beaucoup d'allure avec votre nouveau costume ■ [fashionable - hotel, district] élégant, chic ■ **the ~ set** les gens chics, le beau monde
2. [clever - person] malin, - igne *f*, habile ; [- reply] habile, adroit ; [- shrewd person] habile, astucieux ■ [witty - person, remark] spirituel ■ **he's a ~ lad** il n'est pas bête ■ **he's trying to be ~** il essaie de faire le malin ■ **it was ~ of her to think of it** c'était futé de sa part d'y penser ■ **she was too ~ for them** elle était trop maligne OR futée pour eux
3. [impertinent] impertinent, audacieux ■ **don't get ~ with me!** n'essaie pas de jouer au plus malin avec moi!
4. [quick - pace, rhythm] vif, prompt ■ **that was ~ work!** voilà du travail rapide!, voilà qui a été vite fait! ■ **look ~!** *inf* grouille-toi!
5. [sharp - reprimand] bon, bien envoyé
6. COMPUT intelligent
7. ARM [bomb, weapon] intelligent.
◇ *vi* **1.** [eyes, wound] picoter, brûler ■ **the onion made her eyes ~** les oignons lui piquaient les yeux OR la faisaient pleurer ■ **my face was still ~ing from the blow** le visage me cuisait encore du coup que j'avais reçu
2. [person] être piqué au vif ■ **he's still ~ing from the insult** il n'a toujours pas digéré l'insulte.
◇ *adv* [quickly - walk] vivement, à vive allure ; [- act] vivement, promptement.
◇ *n* **1.** [pain] douleur *f* cuisante ■ *fig* effet *m* cinglant **2.** *US inf* [useful hint] tuyau *m*, combine *f*.

smart aleck *n inf* je-sais-tout *mf inv*.
◆ **smart-aleck** *adj inf* gonflé.

smartarse[△] *UK*, **smartass**[△] *US* ['smɑːtɑːs] = **smart aleck**.

smart card *n* carte *f* à puce.

smart drug *n* nootrope *m*, smart drug *f*.

smarten ['smɑːtn] *vt* **1.** [improve appearance] : **to ~ o.s.** se faire beau **2.** *UK* [speed up] : **to ~ one's pace** accélérer l'allure.
◆ **smarten up** ◇ *vi insep* **1.** [person] se faire beau ■ [restaurant] devenir plus chic, être retapé ■ [town, street] devenir plus pimpant **2.** *UK* [output, speed] s'accélérer.
◇ *vt sep* **1.** [person] pomponner ■ [room, house, town] arranger ■ **a coat of paint would help ~ up the restaurant/the car** une couche de peinture et le restaurant/la voiture aurait déjà meilleure allure ■ **to ~ o.s. up** se faire beau, soigner son apparence **2.** [production] accélérer.

smartly ['smɑːtlɪ] *adv* **1.** [elegantly] avec beaucoup d'allure OR de chic, élégamment **2.** [cleverly] habilement, adroitement **3.** [briskly - move] vivement ; [- act, work] rapidement, promptement **4.** [sharply - reprimand] vertement ; [- reply] du tac au tac, sèchement.

smart money *n inf* **all the ~ is on him to win the presidency** il est donné pour favori aux élections présidentielles.

smarty ['smɑːtɪ] (*pl* **smarties**) *n inf* (Monsieur OR Madame OR Mademoiselle) je-sais-tout *mf inv*.

smarty-pants (*pl inv*) *n inf* **you're a real ~, aren't you?** tu crois vraiment tout savoir!

smash [smæʃ] ◇ *n* **1.** [noise - of breaking] fracas *m* ■ **the vase fell with a ~** le vase s'est fracassé en tombant **2.** [blow] coup *m* OR choc *m* violent **3.** *inf* [collision] collision *f* ■ [accident] accident *m* ■ [pile-up] carambolage *m* **4.** ECON & FIN [collapse - of business, market] débâcle *f* (financière), effondrement *m* (financier) ■ ST. EX krach *m*, effondrement *m* des cours ■ [bankruptcy] faillite *f* **5.** SPORT smash *m* **6.** *inf* [success] succès *m* bœuf ■ **it was a ~** ça a fait un tabac.
◇ *onom* patatras.
◇ *adv* : **to go** OR **to run ~ into a wall** heurter un mur avec violence, rentrer en plein dans un mur.
◇ *vt* **1.** [break - cup, window] fracasser, briser ■ **to ~ sthg to pieces** briser qqch en morceaux ■ **I've ~ed my glasses** j'ai cassé mes lunettes ■ **to ~ sthg open** ouvrir qqch d'un grand coup ■ PHYS [atom] désintégrer **2.** [crash, hit] écraser ■ **he ~ed his fist (down) on the table** il écrasa son poing sur la table ■ **they ~ed their way in** ils sont entrés par effraction *(en enfonçant la porte ou la fenêtre)* ■ **the raft was ~ed against the rocks** le radeau s'est fracassé contre OR sur les rochers **3.** SPORT : **to ~ the ball** faire un smash, smasher **4.** [destroy - conspiracy, organization] briser, démolir ; [- resistance, opposition] briser, écraser ; [- chances, hopes, career] ruiner, briser ; [- opponent, record] pulvériser.
◇ *vi* [break, crash] se briser, se fracasser ■ **to ~ into bits** se briser en mille morceaux ■ **the car ~ed into the lamppost** la voiture s'est écrasée contre le réverbère.
◆ **smash down** *vt sep* [door] fracasser, écraser.
◆ **smash in** *vt sep* [door, window] enfoncer ■ **to ~ sb's face** OR **head in** *inf* démolir le portrait à qqn.
◆ **smash up** *vt sep* [furniture] casser, démolir ■ [room, shop] tout casser OR démolir dans ■ [car] démolir.

smash-and-grab (raid) *n cambriolage commis en brisant une devanture.*

smashed [smæʃt] *adj inf* [on alcohol] rond ■ [on drugs] défoncé.

smasher ['smæʃər] *n UK inf* **1.** [person] : **she's a real ~** [in appearance] c'est un vrai canon ; [in character] elle est vraiment sensass **2.** [object] : **it's a real ~!** c'est sensass!

smash hit *n* [song, record] gros succès *m*.

smashing ['smæʃɪŋ] *adj UK inf* super, terrible ■ **we had a ~ time!** on s'est super bien amusés!

smash-up *n* [accident] accident *m* ■ [pile-up] carambolage *m*, télescopage *m*.

smattering ['smætərɪŋ] *n (U)* [of knowledge] notions *fpl* vagues ■ [of people, things] poignée *f*, petit nombre *m* ■ **she has a ~ of Italian** elle a quelques notions d'italien, elle sait un peu d'italien ■ **there was the usual ~ of artists at the party** comme toujours, il y avait un petit groupe d'artistes à la réception.

SME (*abbrev of* **small and medium-sized enterprise**) *n* PME *f*.

smear [smɪər] ◇ *n* **1.** [mark - on glass, mirror, wall] trace *f*, tache *f* ■ [longer] traînée *f* ■ [of ink] pâté *m*, bavure *f* **2.** [slander] diffamation *f* ■ **a ~ on sb's integrity/reputation** une atteinte à l'honneur/à la réputation de qqn ■ **to use ~ tactics** avoir recours à la calomnie **3.** MED frottis *m*, prélèvement *m*.
◇ *vt* **1.** [spread - butter, oil] étaler ■ [coat] barbouiller ■ **she ~ed the dish with butter** elle a beurré le plat ■ **to ~ paint/chocolate on one's face** se barbouiller le visage de peinture/de chocolat **2.** [smudge] : **the ink on the page was ~ed** l'encre a coulé sur la page ■ **don't ~ the wet paint/varnish** ne faites pas de taches de peinture/de vernis ■ **the mirror was ~ed with fingermarks** il y avait des traces de doigts sur la glace **3.** [slander] : **to ~ sb** salir la réputation de qqn, calomnier qqn **4.** *US inf* [thrash] battre à plates coutures.
◇ *vi* [wet paint, ink] se salir, se maculer.

smear campaign *n* campagne *f* de diffamation *OR* dénigrement.

smear test *n* MED frottis *m*.

smell [smel] (*UK pret & pp* **smelled** *OR* **smelt** [smelt]) (*US pret & pp* **smelled**) <> *vt* **1.** [notice an odour of] sentir ▪ **to ~ gas** sentir le gaz ▪ **I can ~ (something) burning** (je trouve que) ça sent le brûlé ▪ **she smelt** *OR* **she could ~ alcohol on his breath** elle s'aperçut que son haleine sentait l'alcool **2.** *fig* [sense - trouble, danger] flairer, pressentir ▪ **to ~ a rat** flairer quelque chose de louche **3.** [sniff at - food] sentir, renifler ; [- flower] sentir, humer.
<> *vi* **1.** [have odour] sentir ▪ **to ~ good** *OR* **sweet** sentir bon ▪ **to ~ bad** sentir mauvais ▪ **it ~s awful!** ça pue! ▪ **it ~s musty** ça sent le renfermé ▪ **what does it ~ of** *OR* **like?** qu'est-ce que ça sent? ▪ **it ~s of lavender** ça sent la lavande ▪ **it ~s like lavender** on dirait de la lavande ▪ **to ~ of treachery/hypocrisy** *fig* sentir la trahison/l'hypocrisie ⊙ **to ~ fishy** sembler louche **2.** [have bad odour] sentir (mauvais) ▪ **his breath ~s** il a mauvaise haleine **3.** [perceive odour] : **he can't ~** il n'a pas d'odorat.
<> *n* **1.** [sense - of person] odorat *m* ; [- of animal] odorat *m*, flair *m* ▪ **he has no sense of ~** il n'a pas d'odorat ▪ **to have a keen sense of ~** avoir le nez fin **2.** [odour] odeur *f* ▪ [bad odour] mauvaise odeur *f*, relent *m* ▪ [stench] puanteur *f* ▪ **there was a ~ of burning in the kitchen** il y avait une odeur de brûlé dans la cuisine ▪ **there was a lovely ~ of lavender** ça sentait bon la lavande ▪ **does it have a ~?** est-ce que ça sent quelque chose?, est-ce que ça a une odeur? ▪ **natural gas has no ~** le gaz naturel n'a pas d'odeur *OR* est inodore ▪ **what an awful ~!** qu'est-ce que ça sent mauvais! ▪ **the ~ of defeat/fear** *fig* l'odeur de la défaite/de la peur **3.** [sniff] : **have a ~ of this** sentez-moi ça.
◆ **smell out** *vt sep* [subj: dog] dénicher en flairant ▪ *fig* [subj: person] découvrir, dépister ▪ [secret, conspiracy] découvrir.

smelling salts ['smelɪŋ-] *npl* sels *mpl*.

smelly ['smelɪ] (*comp* **smellier**, *superl* **smelliest**) *adj* [person, socks etc] qui sent mauvais, qui pue ▪ **to have ~ feet** sentir des pieds.

smelt [smelt] (*pl inv OR pl* **smelts**) <> *pt & pp* ▷ **smell**.
<> *n* [fish] éperlan *m*.
<> *vt* METALL [ore] fondre ▪ [metal] extraire par fusion.

smidgen, smidgin ['smɪdʒɪn] *n inf* **a ~ of** un tout petit peu de.

smile [smaɪl] <> *n* sourire *m* ▪ **"of course," he said with a ~** "bien sûr", dit-il en souriant ▪ **come on, give us a ~!** allez? fais-nous un sourire! ▪ **to have a ~ on one's face** avoir le sourire ▪ **take that ~ off your face!** arrête de sourire comme ça! ▪ **to knock** *OR* **to wipe the ~ off sb's face** *inf fig* faire passer à qqn l'envie de sourire ▪ **to be all ~s** être tout souriant *OR* tout sourire.
<> *vi* sourire ▪ **to ~ at sb** sourire à qqn ▪ **to ~ to o.s.** sourire pour soi ▪ **she ~d at his awkwardness** sa maladresse l'a fait sourire ▪ **he ~d to think of it** il a souri en y pensant, y penser le faisait sourire ▪ **keep smiling!** gardez le sourire! ▪ **heaven ~d on them** *fig* le ciel leur sourit.
<> *vt* : **to ~ one's approval** exprimer son approbation par un sourire ▪ **she ~d a sad smile** elle eut un sourire triste.

smiley ['smaɪlɪ] *n* smiley *m*, émoticon *m*, souriant *m*.

smiling ['smaɪlɪŋ] *adj* souriant.

smirk [smɜːk] <> *vi* [smugly] sourire d'un air suffisant *OR* avec suffisance ▪ [foolishly] sourire bêtement.
<> *n* [smug] petit sourire *m* satisfait *OR* suffisant ▪ [foolish] sourire *m* bête.

smite [smaɪt] (*pret* **smote** [sməʊt], *pp* **smitten** ['smɪtn]) *vt* **1.** *lit & arch* [strike - object] frapper ; [- enemy] abattre **2.** *(usu passive)* [afflict] : **to be smitten with remorse** être accablé de remords ▪ **they were smitten with blindness/fear** ils ont été frappés de cécité/frayeur **3.** BIBLE [punish] châtier.

smith [smɪθ] *n* [blacksmith - gen] forgeron *m* ▪ EQUIT maréchal-ferrant *m*.

smithereens [ˌsmɪðə'riːnz] *npl* morceaux *mpl* ▪ **to smash sthg to ~** briser qqch en mille morceaux ▪ **the house was blown to ~ in the explosion** la maison a été complètement soufflée par l'explosion.

Smithsonian Institution [smɪθ'səʊnɪən-] *pr n complexe réunissant un grand nombre de musées à Washington.*

smithy ['smɪðɪ] (*pl* **smithies**) *n* forge *f*.

smitten ['smɪtn] <> *pp* ▷ **smite**.
<> *adj* : **he was ~with** *OR* **by her beauty** il a été ébloui par sa beauté ▪ **he's really ~ (with that girl)** il est vraiment très épris (de cette fille).

smock [smɒk] <> *n* [loose garment] blouse *f* ▪ [maternity wear - blouse] tunique *f* de grossesse ; [- dress] robe *f* de grossesse.
<> *vt* faire des smocks à.

smocking ['smɒkɪŋ] *n (U)* smocks *mpl*.

smog [smɒg] *n* smog *m*.

smoggy ['smɒgɪ] (*comp* **smoggier**, *superl* **smoggiest**) *adj* : **it's ~** il y a du smog.

smoke [sməʊk] <> *n* **1.** [from fire, cigarette] fumée *f* ▪ **to go up in ~** [building] brûler ; [plans] partir *OR* s'en aller en fumée ▪ **there's no ~ without fire** *prov* il n'y a pas de fumée sans feu *prov* **2.** [act of smoking] : **to have a ~** fumer **3.** *inf dated* [cigarette] clope *m ou f* **4.**△ *UK drug sl* [hashish] shit△ *m* **5.** *UK inf* [city] : **the Smoke** [any city] la grande métropole ; [London] Londres.
<> *vi* **1.** [fireplace, chimney, lamp] fumer **2.** [person] fumer ⊙ **to ~ like a chimney** *inf* fumer comme un pompier *OR* un sapeur.
<> *vt* **1.** [cigarette, pipe, opium etc] fumer ▪ **to ~ a pipe** fumer la pipe **2.** CULIN & INDUST [fish, meat, glass] fumer.
◆ **smoke out** *vt sep* **1.** [from den, hiding place - fugitive, animal] enfumer ▪ *fig* [discover - traitor] débusquer, dénicher ; [- conspiracy, plot] découvrir **2.** [room] enfumer.

smoke bomb *n* bombe *f* fumigène.

smoked [sməʊkt] *adj* fumé ▪ **~ salmon** saumon *m* fumé ▪ **~ glass** verre *m* fumé.

smoke-dried *adj* fumé.

smoke-filled [-fɪld] *adj* enfumé.

smokeless fuel ['sməʊklɪs-] *n* combustible *m* non polluant.

smokeless zone *n zone dans laquelle seul l'usage de combustibles non polluants est autorisé.*

smoker ['sməʊkəʳ] *n* **1.** [person] fumeur *m*, - euse *f* ▪ **to have a ~'s cough** avoir une toux de fumeur **2.** [on train] compartiment *m* fumeurs.

smokescreen ['sməʊkskriːn] *n* MIL écran *m OR* rideau *m* de fumée ▪ *fig* paravent *m*, couverture *f*.

smoke signal *n* signal *m* de fumée.

smokestack ['sməʊkstæk] *n* cheminée *f*.

smokestack industry *n* industrie *f* lourde.

smoking ['sməʊkɪŋ] *n* : **I've given up ~** j'ai arrêté de fumer ▪ **'no ~'** 'défense de fumer' ▪ **~ can cause cancer** le tabac peut provoquer le cancer.

smoking compartment *n* compartiment *m* fumeurs.

smoking gun *n fig* **the ~** l'arme *f* du crime.

smoking jacket *n* veste *f* d'intérieur.

smoking room *n* fumoir *m (pour fumeurs)*.

smoky ['sməʊkɪ] (*comp* **smokier**, *superl* **smokiest**) *adj* **1.** [atmosphere, room] enfumé **2.** [chimney, lamp, fire] qui fume **3.** [in flavour - food] qui sent le fumé, qui a un goût de fumé **4.** [in colour] gris cendré *(inv)*.

smolder *etc US* = **smoulder**.

smooch [smuːtʃ] *inf* <> *n* : **to have a ~** [kiss] se bécoter ; [pet] se peloter.
<> *vi* **1.** [kiss] se bécoter ▪ [pet] se peloter **2.** *UK* [dance] danser joue contre joue.

smooth [smu:ð] ◇ *adj* **1.** [surface] lisse ▪ [pebble, stone] lisse, poli ▪ [skin] lisse, doux, douce *f* ▪ [chin - close-shaven] rasé de près ; [- beardless] glabre, lisse ▪ [hair, fabric, road] lisse ▪ [sea, water] calme **2.** [ride, flight] confortable ▪ [takeoff, landing] en douceur ▪ **they had a ~ crossing** la traversée a été calme **3.** [steady, regular - flow, breathing, working, supply] régulier ; [- organization] qui marche bien ; [- rhythm, style] coulant ▪ **the ~ running of the service** la bonne marche du service ▪ **the ~ running of the operation** le bon déroulement de l'opération **4.** [trouble-free - life, course of events] paisible, calme ▪ **to get off to a ~ start** démarrer en douceur ▪ **to make the way ~ for sb** aplanir les difficultés pour qqn ▪ **the bill had a ~ passage through Parliament** le projet de loi a été voté sans problèmes au Parlement **5.** CULIN [in texture] onctueux, homogène ▪ [in taste] moelleux **6.** *pej* [slick, suave] doucereux, onctueux, suave ▪ **he's a ~ operator** *inf* il sait y faire ▪ **he's a ~ talker** c'est un beau parleur.
◇ *vt* **1.** [tablecloth, skirt] défroisser ▪ [hair, feathers] lisser ▪ [wood] rendre lisse, planer ▪ **to ~ the way for sb, to ~ sb's path** aplanir les difficultés pour qqn **2.** [rub - oil, cream] masser ▪ **to ~ oil into one's skin** mettre de l'huile sur sa peau *(en massant doucement)* **3.** [polish] lisser, polir.
◆ **smooth back** *vt sep* [hair] lisser en arrière ▪ [sheet] rabattre en lissant.
◆ **smooth down** *vt sep* [hair] lisser ▪ [sheets, dress] lisser, défroisser ▪ [wood] planer, aplanir ▪ *fig* [person] apaiser, calmer.
◆ **smooth out** *vt sep* [skirt, sheet, curtains] lisser, défroisser ▪ [crease, pleat, wrinkle] faire disparaître (en lissant) ▪ *fig* [difficulties, obstacles] aplanir, faire disparaître.
◆ **smooth over** *vt sep* **1.** [gravel, sand] rendre lisse (en ratissant) ▪ [soil] aplanir, égaliser **2.** *fig* [difficulties, obstacles] aplanir ▪ [embarrassing situation] : **to ~ things over** arranger les choses.

smooth-faced *adj liter* au visage lisse ▪ [after shaving] rasé de près ▪ *fig* & *pej* trop suave OR poli, onctueux.

smoothie ['smu:ðɪ] *n inf pej* **he's a real ~** [in manner] il roule les mécaniques ; [in speech] c'est vraiment un beau parleur.

smoothly ['smu:ðlɪ] *adv* **1.** [easily, steadily - operate, drive, move] sans à-coups, en douceur ▪ **to run ~** [engine] tourner bien ; [operation] marcher comme sur des roulettes ▪ **things are not going very ~ between them** ça ne va pas très bien entre eux ▪ **the meeting went off quite ~** la réunion s'est déroulée sans heurt OR accroc **2.** [gently - rise, fall] doucement, en douceur **3.** *pej* [talk] doucereusement ▪ [behave] (trop) suavement.

smoothness ['smu:ðnɪs] *n* **1.** [of surface] égalité *f*, aspect *m* uni OR lisse ▪ [of fabric, of skin, of hair] douceur *f* ▪ [of road] surface *f* lisse ▪ [of sea] calme *m* ▪ [of stone] aspect *m* lisse OR poli ▪ [of tyre] aspect *m* lisse **2.** [of flow, breathing, pace, supply] régularité *f* ▪ [of engine, machine] bon fonctionnement *m* ▪ [of life, course of events] caractère *m* paisible OR serein ▪ *fig* [of temperament] calme *m*, sérénité *f* **3.** CULIN [of texture] onctuosité *f* ▪ [of taste] moelleux *m* **4.** *pej* [suaveness] caractère *m* doucereux OR mielleux, onctuosité *f*.

smooth-running *adj* [machine] qui fonctionne bien OR sans à-coups ▪ [engine] qui tourne bien ▪ [car] confortable *(qui roule sans secousses)* ▪ [business, organization] qui marche bien ▪ [plan, operation] qui se déroule bien.

smooth-shaven *adj* rasé de près.

smooth-spoken *adj* qui sait parler.

smooth-talk *vt* : **don't let him ~ you** ne te laisse pas enjôler par lui ▪ **she was ~ed into accepting the job** ils l'ont convaincu d'accepter le travail à force de belles paroles.

smooth-talking [-,tɔ:kɪŋ] *adj* doucereux, mielleux.

smoothy ['smu:ðɪ] *inf* = **smoothie**.

smote [sməʊt] *pt* ▷ **smite**.

smother ['smʌðəʳ] ◇ *vt* **1.** [suppress - fire, flames] étouffer ; [- sound] étouffer, amortir ; [- emotions, laughter, yawn] réprimer ▪ [suppress - scandal, opposition] étouffer **2.** [suffocate - person] étouffer **3.** [cover] couvrir, recouvrir ▪ **strawberries ~ed in** OR **with cream** des fraises couvertes de crème ▪ **she was ~ed in furs** elle était emmitouflée dans des fourrures **4.** [overwhelm - with kindness, love] combler ▪ **to ~ sb with kisses** couvrir OR dévorer qqn de baisers ▪ **to ~ sb with attention** être aux petits soins pour qqn.
◇ *vi* [person] étouffer.

smoulder UK, **smolder** US ['sməʊldəʳ] *vi* **1.** [fire - before flames] couver ; [- after burning] fumer **2.** [feeling, rebellion] couver ▪ **her eyes ~ed with passion** son regard était plein de désir.

smouldering UK, **smoldering** US ['sməʊldərɪŋ] *adj* [fire, anger, passion] qui couve ▪ [embers, ruins] fumant ▪ [eyes] de braise.

SMS [,esem'es] (*abbrev of* **short message service**) *n* service *m* SMS ▪ **~ (message)** (message *m*) SMS *m*, mini-message *m*, texto *m*.

smudge [smʌdʒ] ◇ *n* **1.** [on face, clothes, surface] (petite) tache *f* ▪ [of make-up] traînée *f* ▪ [on page of print] bavure *f* **2.** US [fire] feu *m* (de jardin).
◇ *vt* [face, hands] salir ▪ [clothes, surface] tacher, salir ▪ [ink] répandre ▪ [writing] étaler ▪ **you've made me ~ my lipstick** à cause de toi je me suis mis du rouge à lèvres partout.
◇ *vi* [ink, make-up] faire des taches ▪ [print] être maculé ▪ [wet paint] s'étaler.

smudgy ['smʌdʒɪ] (*comp* **smudgier**, *superl* **smudgiest**) *adj* [make-up, ink] étalé ▪ [print, page] maculé ▪ [writing] à demi effacé ▪ [face] sali, taché ▪ [outline] estompé, brouillé.

smug [smʌg] (*comp* **smugger**, *superl* **smuggest**) *adj pej* [person] content de soi, suffisant ▪ [attitude, manner, voice] suffisant ▪ **he's so ~!** ce qu'il peut être suffisant OR content de sa petite personne!

smuggle ['smʌgl] ◇ *vt* [contraband] passer en contrebande ▪ [into prison - mail, arms] introduire clandestinement ▪ **to ~ sthg through customs** passer qqch en fraude à la douane ▪ **the terrorists were ~d over the border** les terroristes ont passé la frontière clandestinement ▪ **they are suspected of smuggling arms/heroin** on les soupçonne de trafic d'armes/d'héroïne ▪ *fig* [into classroom, meeting etc] introduire subrepticement.
◇ *vi* faire de la contrebande.
◆ **smuggle in** *vt sep* [on a large scale - drugs, arms] faire entrer OR passer en contrebande ▪ [as tourist - cigarettes, alcohol] introduire en fraude ▪ [move secretly - books, mail etc] introduire clandestinement ▪ **he managed to ~ a knife into the prison** il a réussi à faire entrer OR passer clandestinement un couteau dans la prison.
◆ **smuggle out** *vt sep* [goods] faire sortir en fraude OR en contrebande ▪ **he was ~d out of the country** il a quitté le pays clandestinement OR en secret.

smuggler ['smʌgləʳ] *n* contrebandier *m*, - ère *f* ▪ **drug ~** trafiquant *m*, - e *f* de drogue.

smuggling ['smʌglɪŋ] *n* contrebande *f*.

smugly ['smʌglɪ] *adv* [say] d'un ton suffisant, avec suffisance ▪ [look, smile] d'un air suffisant, avec suffisance.

smut [smʌt] (*pret* & *pp* **smutted**, *cont* **smutting**) *n* **1.** *inf (U) inf* [obscenity] cochonneries *fpl* ▪ [pornography] porno *m* **2.** UK [speck of dirt] poussière *f* ▪ [smudge of soot] tache *f* de suie **3.** AGRIC charbon *m* OR nielle *f* du blé.

smutty ['smʌtɪ] (*comp* **smuttier**, *superl* **smuttiest**) *adj* **1.** *inf* [obscene] cochon ▪ [pornographic] porno **2.** [dirty - hands, face, surface] sali, noirci.

snack [snæk] ◇ *n* **1.** [light meal] casse-croûte *m inv*, en-cas *m inv* ▪ **to have a ~** casser la croûte, manger un morceau ▪ **to have a ~ lunch** déjeuner sur le pouce **2.** *(usu pl)* [appetizer - esp at party] amuse-gueule *m*.
◇ *vi* US grignoter.

snack bar *n* snack *m*, snack-bar *m*.

snaffle ['snæfl] ◇ *vt* **1.** UK *inf* [get] se procurer ▪ [steal] piquer, faucher **2.** EQUIT mettre un bridon à.
◇ *n* EQUIT : **~ (bit)** mors *m* brisé, bridon *m*.

snag [snæg] (*pret & pp* **snagged**, *cont* **snagging**) ◇ *n* **1.** [problem] problème *m*, difficulté *f*, hic *m* ▪ **to come across** *OR* **to run into a ~** tomber sur un hic *OR* sur un os ▪ **there are several ~s in your plan** il y a plusieurs choses qui clochent dans ton projet ▪ **the only ~ is that you have to pay first** le seul problème, c'est qu'il faut payer d'abord **2.** [tear - in garment] accroc *m* ; [- in stocking] fil *m* tiré **3.** [sharp protuberance] aspérité *f* ▪ [tree stump] chicot *m*.
◇ *vt* **1.** [tear - cloth, garment] faire un accroc à, déchirer ▪ **she snagged her stocking on the brambles** elle a accroché son bas *OR* fait un accroc à son bas dans les ronces **2.** *US inf* [obtain] s'emparer de.
◇ *vi* s'accrocher ▪ **the rope snagged on the ledge** la corde s'est trouvée coincée sur le rebord.

snail [sneɪl] *n* escargot *m* ▪ **at a ~'s pace** [move] comme un escargot ; [change, progress] très lentement.

snail mail *n inf* poste *f*.

snake [sneɪk] ◇ *n* **1.** ZOOL serpent *m* **2.** [person] vipère *f* ▶ **a ~ in the grass** un faux frère **3.** ECON serpent *m* (monétaire).
◇ *vi* serpenter, sinuer *lit* ▪ **the smoke ~d upwards** une volute de fumée s'élevait vers le ciel.
◇ *vt* : **the river/road ~s its way down to the sea** le fleuve serpente/la route descend en lacets jusqu'à la mer.

snakebite ['sneɪkbaɪt] *n liter* morsure *f* de serpent.

snake charmer *n* charmeur *m*, - euse *f* de serpent.

snakes and ladders *n (U) jeu d'enfants ressemblant au jeu de l'oie.*

snakeskin ['sneɪkskɪn] ◇ *n* peau *f* de serpent.
◇ *comp* [shoes, handbag] en (peau de) serpent.

snaky ['sneɪkɪ] (*comp* **snakier**, *superl* **snakiest**) *adj* **1.** [sinuous - river, road, movement] sinueux **2.** [person] insidieux, perfide ▪ [cunning, acts] perfide.

snap [snæp] (*pret & pp* **snapped**, *cont* **snapping**) ◇ *vt* **1.** [break - sharply] casser net ; [- with a crack] casser avec un bruit sec ▪ **to ~ sthg in two** *OR* **in half** casser qqch en deux d'un coup sec
2. [make cracking sound] faire claquer ▪ **she snapped her case shut** elle ferma sa valise d'un coup sec ▪ **she only needs to ~ her fingers and he comes running** il lui suffit de claquer des doigts pour qu'il arrive en courant ▪ **to ~ one's fingers at sb** faire claquer ses doigts pour attirer l'attention de qqn ; [mockingly] faire la nique à qqn
3. [say brusquely] dire d'un ton sec *OR* brusque
4. [seize - gen] saisir ; [- subj : dog] happer
5. *inf* PHOT prendre une photo de.
◇ *vi* **1.** [break - branch] se casser net *OR* avec un bruit sec, craquer ; [- elastic band] claquer ; [- rope] se casser, rompre ▪ **to ~ in two** se casser net
2. [make cracking sound - whip, fingers] claquer ▪ **to ~ open** s'ouvrir avec un bruit sec *OR* avec un claquement ▶ **~ to it!** *inf* grouille-toi!, magne-toi!
3. *fig* [person, nerves] craquer
4. [speak brusquely] : **to ~ at sb** parler à qqn d'un ton sec ▪ **there's no need to ~!** tu n'as pas besoin de parler sur ce ton-là!
5. [try to bite] : **to ~ at** chercher à *OR* essayer de mordre ▪ **the fish snapped at the bait** les poissons cherchaient à happer l'appât ▪ **the taxmen were beginning to ~ at his heels** *fig* les impôts commençaient à le talonner.
◇ *n* **1.** [of whip] claquement *m* ▪ [of sthg breaking, opening, closing] bruit *m* sec ▪ **with a ~ of his fingers** en claquant des doigts ▪ **to open/to close sthg with a ~** ouvrir/refermer qqch d'un coup sec ▪ **the branch broke with a ~** la branche a cassé avec un bruit sec
2. [of jaws] : **to make a ~ at sb/sthg** essayer de mordre qqn/qqch ▪ **the dog made a ~ at the bone** le chien a essayé de happer l'os
3. *inf* PHOT photo *f*, instantané *m* ▪ **to take a ~ of sb** prendre qqn en photo ▪ **holiday ~s** photos de vacances
4. *UK* CARDS ≃ bataille *f*
5. METEOR : **a cold ~, a ~ of cold weather** une vague de froid
6. *inf* [effort] effort *m* ▪ [energy] énergie *f*
7. *US inf* [easy task] : **it's a ~!** c'est simple comme bonjour!
8. CULIN biscuit *m*, petit gâteau *m* sec
9. [clasp, fastener] fermoir *m*.
◇ *adj* **1.** [vote] éclair ▪ [reaction] immédiat ▪ [judgment] irréfléchi, hâtif ▪ **she made a ~ decision to go to Paris** elle décida tout à coup d'aller à Paris ▪ **the President made a ~ decision to send troops** le Président décida immédiatement d'envoyer des troupes ▪ **to call a ~ election** procéder à une élection surprise
2. *US inf* [easy] facile.
◇ *adv* : **to go ~** casser net.
◇ *interj UK* **1.** CARDS : **~ !** ≃ bataille!
2. *inf* [in identical situation] : **~!** tiens!, quelle coïncidence!

➡ **snap off** ◇ *vt sep* casser ▶ **to ~ sb's head off** *inf* envoyer promener qqn.
◇ *vi insep* casser net.

➡ **snap on** *vt sep US* : **to ~ a light on** allumer une lampe.

➡ **snap out** ◇ *vi insep* : **to ~ out of** [depression, mood, trance] se sortir de, se tirer de ; [temper] dominer, maîtriser ▪ **~ out of it!** [depression] ne te laisse pas aller comme ça! ; [bad temper] ne t'énerve pas comme ça!
◇ *vt sep* [question] poser d'un ton sec ▪ [order, warning] lancer brutalement.

➡ **snap up** *vt sep* **1.** [subj: dog, fish] happer, attraper
2. *fig* [bargain, offer, opportunity] sauter sur, se jeter sur ▪ **the records were snapped up in no time** les disques sont partis *OR* se sont vendus en un rien de temps
3. *US inf phr* **~ it up!** dépêchons!

snap bean *n US* haricot *m* vert.

snapdragon ['snæp,drægən] *n* muflier *m*, gueule-de-loup *f*.

snap fastener *n* [press stud] bouton-pression *m*, pression *f* ▪ [clasp - on handbag, necklace] fermoir *m* (à pression).

snap-on *adj* [collar, cuffs, hood] détachable, amovible (à pressions).

snappy ['snæpɪ] (*comp* **snappier**, *superl* **snappiest**) *adj inf* **1.** [fashionable] : **she's a ~ dresser** elle sait s'habiller **2.** [lively - pace, rhythm] vif, entraînant ; [- dialogue, debate] plein d'entrain, vivant ; [- style, slogan] qui a du punch ; [- reply] bien envoyé ▪ **look ~!** grouille-toi!, active! ▪ **make it ~!** et que ça saute! **3.** [unfriendly - person] hargneux ; [- answer] brusque ; [- voice] cassant ▪ **you're a bit ~ today!** tu es de mauvais poil aujourd'hui! ▪ **a ~ little dog** un petit roquet.

snapshot ['snæpʃɒt] *n* instantané *m*.

snare [sneəʳ] ◇ *n* **1.** [trap - gen] piège *m* ; [- made of rope, wire] lacet *m*, collet *m*, lacs *m* ▪ *fig* piège *m*, traquenard *m* ▪ **to set a ~** tendre un piège ▪ **to be caught in a ~** [animal] être pris dans un piège ; *fig* [person] être pris au piège **2.** MUS : **~ (drum)** caisse *f* claire.
◇ *vt* [animal - gen] piéger ; [- in wire or rope trap] prendre au lacet *OR* au collet ▪ *fig* [person] prendre au piège, piéger.

snarl [snɑːl] ◇ *vi* **1.** [dog] gronder, grogner ▪ [person] gronder ▪ **the dog ~ed at me as I walked past** le chien a grogné quand je suis passé ▪ **the lions ~ed at their tamer** les lions rugissaient contre leur dompteur **2.** [thread, rope, hair] s'emmêler ▪ [traffic] se bloquer ▪ [plan, programme] cafouiller.
◇ *vt* **1.** [person] lancer d'une voix rageuse, rugir ▪ **"shut up," she ~ed** "tais-toi", lança-t-elle d'un ton hargneux **2.** [thread, rope, hair] enchevêtrer, emmêler ▪ **you hair is all ~ed** tu as les cheveux tout emmêlés.
◇ *n* **1.** [sound] grognement *m*, grondement *m* ▪ **to give a ~** [subj: dog] pousser un grognement ; [subj: tiger] feuler ; [subj: person] gronder ▪ **she answered him with a ~** elle lui a répondu d'un ton hargneux **2.** [tangle - in thread, wool, hair] nœud *m*, nœuds *mpl*.

➡ **snarl up** ◇ *vi insep* = **snarl** *(vi sense 2)*.
◇ *vt sep (usu passive)* **1.** [thread, rope, hair] emmêler, enchevêtrer ▪ **to get ~ed up** s'emmêler, s'enchevêtrer **2.** [traffic] bloquer, coincer ▪ [plans] faire cafouiller ▪ **the postal service is completely ~ed up** le service des postes est complètement bloqué.

snarl-up *n* [of traffic] bouchon *m*, embouteillage *m* ▪ [of plans] cafouillage *m*.

snatch [snætʃ] ◇ *vt* **1.** [seize - bag, money] saisir ; [- opportunity] saisir, sauter sur ▪ **to ~ sthg from sb** *OR* **from sb's hands** arracher qqch des mains de qqn ▪ **a boy on a motorbike ~ed her bag** un garçon en moto lui a arraché son sac ▪ **his mother ~ed him out of the path of the bus** sa mère l'a attrapé par le bras pour l'empêcher d'être renversé par le bus **2.** [manage to get - meal, drink] avaler à la hâte ; [- holiday, rest] réussir à avoir ▪ **to ~ some sleep** réussir à dormir un peu ▪ **to ~ a glance at sb** lancer un coup d'œil furtif à qqn **3.** [steal] voler ▪ [kiss] voler, dérober ▪ [victory] décrocher **4.** [kidnap] kidnapper.
◇ *vi* [to child] : **don't ~!** [from hand] prends-le doucement! ; [from plate] prends ton temps! ▪ **to ~ at sthg** essayer de saisir *OR* d'attraper qqch ▪ **she ~es at the slightest hope/opportunity** *fig* elle s'accroche au moindre espoir/saute sur la moindre occasion.
◇ *n* **1.** [grab] geste *m* vif de la main *(pour attraper qqch)* ▪ **to make a ~ at sthg** essayer de saisir *OR* d'attraper qqch ▪ **to make a ~ at victory** *fig* essayer de s'emparer de la victoire **2.** *UK inf* [robbery] vol *m* à l'arraché ▪ **bag ~** vol (de sac) à l'arraché **3.** *inf* [kidnapping] kidnapping *m* **4.** [fragment - of conversation] fragment *m*, bribes *fpl* ; [- of song, music] fragment *m*, mesure *f* ; [- of poetry] fragment *m*, vers *m* **5.** [short spell] courte période *f* ▪ **to sleep in ~es** dormir par intervalles *OR* de façon intermittente **6.** [in weightlifting] arraché *m*.
◆ **snatch away** *vt sep* [letter, plate etc] arracher, enlever d'un geste vif ▪ [hope] ôter, enlever ▪ **to ~ sthg away from sb** arracher qqch à qqn ▪ **she ~ed her hand away from the hot stove** elle a vite enlevé sa main du fourneau brûlant ▪ **victory was ~ed from them in the last minute** la victoire leur a été soufflée à la dernière minute.
◆ **snatch up** *vt sep* ramasser vite *OR* vivement *OR* d'un seul coup ▪ **she ~ed up her child** elle a saisi *OR* empoigné son enfant.

-snatcher ['snætʃəʳ] *in cpds* arracheur *m*, - euse *f* ▪ **bag~** voleur *m*, - euse *f* (de sac) à l'arraché.

snatch squad *n UK groupe de policiers chargé d'arrêter les meneurs (lors d'une manifestation).*

snazzy ['snæzɪ] (*comp* **snazzier**, *superl* **snazziest**) *adj inf* [garment] chic, qui a de l'allure ▪ [car, house] chouette ▪ **she's a ~ dresser** elle s'habille avec chic, elle est toujours bien sapée.

sneak [sniːk] (*UK pret & pp* **sneaked**) (*US pret & pp* **sneaked** *OR* **snuck** [snʌk]) ◇ *vi* **1.** [verb of movement] se glisser, se faufiler ▪ [furtively] se glisser furtivement ▪ [quietly] se glisser à pas feutrés *OR* sans faire de bruit ▪ [secretly] se glisser sans se faire remarquer ▪ **to ~ up/down the stairs** monter/descendre l'escalier furtivement ▪ **we ~ed in at the back** nous nous sommes glissés dans le fond discrètement *OR* sans nous faire remarquer ▪ **they ~ed into the cinema without paying** ils se sont introduits dans le cinéma sans payer ▪ **we managed to ~ past the guards/window** nous avons réussi à passer devant les gardes/la fenêtre sans nous faire remarquer ▪ **I ~ed round to the back door** je me suis glissé sans bruit jusqu'à la porte de derrière **2.** *UK inf* SCH moucharder, cafter ▪ **to ~ on sb** moucharder qqn.
◇ *vt* **1.** [give - letter, message] glisser en douce *OR* sans se faire remarquer **2.** [take] enlever, prendre ▪ **to ~ a look at sthg** lancer *OR* jeter un coup d'œil furtif à qqch **3.** *inf* [steal] chiper, piquer, faucher.
◇ *n inf* **1.** [devious person] faux jeton *m* **2.** *UK* SCH cafardeur *m*, - euse *f*, mouchard *m*, - e *f*.
◇ *adj* [attack] furtif.
◆ **sneak away, sneak off** *vi insep* se défiler, s'esquiver.
◆ **sneak up** *vi insep* s'approcher à pas feutrés *OR* furtivement ▪ **to ~ up on** *OR* **behind sb** s'approcher de qqn à pas feutrés.

sneaker ['sniːkəʳ] *n US* (chaussure *f* de) tennis *m ou f*, basket *m ou f*.

sneaking ['sniːkɪŋ] *adj* [feeling, respect] inavoué, secret, - ète *f* ▪ **she had a ~ suspicion that he was guilty** elle ne pouvait (pas) s'empêcher de penser qu'il était coupable ▪ **I had a ~ feeling that he was right** quelque chose me disait qu'il avait raison.

sneak preview *n* avant-première *f* privée.

sneak thief *n UK* chapardeur *m*, - euse *f*.

sneaky ['sniːkɪ] (*comp* **sneakier**, *superl* **sneakiest**) *adj* [person] sournois ▪ [action] faite en cachette, faite à la dérobée ▪ **I caught him having a ~ cigarette** je l'ai surpris en train de fumer une cigarette en cachette.

sneer [snɪəʳ] ◇ *vi* ricaner, sourire avec mépris *OR* d'un air méprisant ▪ **don't ~** ne sois pas si méprisant ▪ **to ~ at sb/sthg** se moquer de qqn/qqch ▪ **an achievement not to be ~ed at** un exploit qu'il ne faudrait pas minimiser.
◇ *n* [facial expression] ricanement *m*, rictus *m* ▪ [remark] raillerie *f*, sarcasme *m* ▪ **"who do you think you are?", he said with a ~** "pour qui est-ce que tu te prends?", dit-il en ricanant *OR* ricana-t-il.

sneering ['snɪərɪŋ] ◇ *adj* ricaneur, méprisant.
◇ *n (U)* ricanement *m*, ricanements *mpl*.

sneeze [sniːz] ◇ *n* éternuement *m*.
◇ *vi* éternuer ▪ **an offer not to be ~d at** *inf fig* une proposition qui n'est pas à dédaigner *OR* sur laquelle il ne faut pas cracher.

snick [snɪk] ◇ *n* [notch] petite entaille *f*, encoche *f*.
◇ *vt* [cloth, wood] faire une petite entaille *OR* une encoche dans.

snicker ['snɪkəʳ] ◇ *n* **1.** [snigger] ricanement *m* **2.** [of horse] (petit) hennissement *m*.
◇ *vi* **1.** [snigger] ricaner **2.** [horse] hennir doucement.

snide [snaɪd] *adj* [sarcastic] narquois, railleur ▪ [unfriendly] inamical, insidieux ▪ **I've had enough of your ~ remarks!** j'en ai assez de tes sarcasmes!

sniff [snɪf] ◇ *vi* **1.** [from cold, crying etc] renifler **2.** [scornfully] faire la grimace *OR* la moue.
◇ *vt* **1.** [smell - food, soap] renifler, sentir l'odeur de ; [- rose, perfume] humer, sentir l'odeur de ▪ [subj: dog] renifler, flairer **2.** [inhale - air] humer, respirer ; [- smelling salts] respirer ; [- cocaine] sniffer, priser ; [- snuff] priser ; [- glue] respirer, sniffer **3.** [say scornfully] dire d'un air méprisant *OR* dédaigneux.
◇ *n* [gen] reniflement *m* ▪ **to give a ~** *liter* renifler ; [scornfully] faire la grimace *OR* la moue ▪ **to have** *OR* **to take a ~ of sthg** renifler *OR* flairer qqch ▪ **one ~ of that stuff is enough to knock you out** *inf* une bouffée de ce truc et tu tombes raide.
◆ **sniff at** *vt insep* **1.** *liter* **to ~ at sthg** [subj: person] renifler qqch ; [subj: dog] renifler *OR* flairer qqch **2.** *fig* faire la grimace *OR* la moue devant ▪ **their offer is not to be ~ed at** leur offre n'est pas à dédaigner.
◆ **sniff out** *vt sep* [subj: dog] découvrir en reniflant *OR* en flairant ▪ [criminal] découvrir, dépister ▪ [secret] découvrir.

sniffer dog ['snɪfəʳ-] *n* chien *m* policier *(dressé pour le dépistage de la drogue, des explosifs).*

sniffle ['snɪfl] ◇ *vi* [sniff] renifler ▪ [have runny nose] avoir le nez qui coule.
◇ *n* [sniff] (léger) reniflement *m* ▪ [cold] petit rhume *m* de cerveau ▪ **to have the ~s** *inf* avoir le nez qui coule.

sniffy ['snɪfɪ] (*comp* **sniffier**, *superl* **sniffiest**) *adj inf* méprisant, dédaigneux.

snifter ['snɪftəʳ] *n* **1.** *UK inf* [drink] petit verre *m* (d'alcool) **2.** *US* [glass] verre *m* à dégustation.

snigger ['snɪgəʳ] ◇ *vi* ricaner, rire dans sa barbe ▪ **to ~ at** [suggestion, remark] ricaner en entendant ; [appearance] se moquer de, ricaner à la vue de.
◇ *n* rire *m* en dessous ▪ [sarcastic] ricanement *m* ▪ **to give a ~** ricaner.

sniggering ['snɪgərɪŋ] ◇ *n (U)* rires *mpl* en dessous ▪ [sarcastic] ricanements *mpl*.
◇ *adj* ricaneur.

snip [snɪp] (*pret & pp* **snipped**, *cont* **snipping**) ◇ *n* **1.** [cut] petit coup *m* de ciseaux, petite entaille *f OR* incision *f* **2.** [sound] clic *m* ▪ **he could hear the ~ of scissors** il entendait le clic-clac de ciseaux **3.** [small piece - of cloth, paper] petit bout *m* ; [- of hair] mèche *f* (coupée) **4.** *UK inf* [bargain] (bonne) affaire *f* ▪ [horse] tuyau *m* sûr **5.** *UK inf* [cinch] : **it's a ~!** c'est du gâteau!, c'est simple comme bonjour!
◇ *vt* couper *(en donnant de petits coups de ciseaux).*

<> *vi* : **he was snipping at the hedge** il coupait la haie.
◆ **snip off** *vt sep* couper *OR* enlever (à petits coups de ciseaux).

snipe [snaɪp] (*pl inv*) <> *n* bécassine *f*.
<> *vi* **1.** [shoot] tirer (d'une position cachée) ▪ **to ~ at sb** *liter* tirer sur qqn ; *fig* [criticize] critiquer qqn par en dessous ▪ **sniping criticism** critiques insidieuses **2.** HUNT aller à la chasse aux bécassines.

sniper ['snaɪpər] *n* tireur *m* embusqué *OR* isolé ▪ **killed by a ~'s bullet** abattu par un tireur (embusqué).

snippet ['snɪpɪt] *n* [of material, paper] petit bout *m* ▪ [of conversation, information] bribe *f* ▪ **a ~ of news** une petite nouvelle.

snippy ['snɪpɪ] (*comp* **snippier**, *superl* **snippiest**) *adj US* brusque, vif.

snitch [snɪtʃ] *inf* <> *n* **1.** [person] cafardeur *m*, - euse *f*, mouchard *m*, - e *f* **2.** *UK phr* **it's a ~** [easy] c'est simple comme bonjour ; [bargain] c'est une (bonne) occase.
<> *vi* [tell tales] moucharder ▪ **to ~ on sb** moucharder *OR* cafarder qqn.
<> *vt* [steal] chiper, piquer, faucher.

snivel ['snɪvl] (*UK pret & pp* **snivelled**, *cont* **snivelling**) (*US pret & pp* **sniveled**, *cont* **sniveling**) <> *vi* [whine] pleurnicher ▪ [because of cold] renifler (continuellement) ▪ [with runny nose] avoir le nez qui coule.
<> *vt* : **"it wasn't my fault", he snivelled** "ce n'était pas de ma faute", fit-il en pleurnichant.
<> *n* [sniffing] reniflement *m*, reniflements *mpl* ▪ [tears] pleurnichements *mpl*.

snivelling *UK*, **sniveling** *US* ['snɪvlɪŋ] <> *adj* pleurnicheur, larmoyant.
<> *n (U)* [crying] pleurnichements *mpl* ▪ [because of cold] reniflement *m*, reniflements *mpl* ▪ **stop your ~!** [tears] arrête de pleurnicher comme ça! ; [sniffing] arrête de renifler comme ça!

snob [snɒb] *n* snob *mf* ▪ **she's an awful ~/a bit of a ~** elle est terriblement/un peu snob ▪ **to be an intellectual/a literary ~** être un snob intellectuel/en matière de littérature ▪ **inverted** *UK OR* **reverse ~** *personne d'origine modeste qui affiche un mépris pour les valeurs bourgeoises.*

snobbery ['snɒbərɪ] *n* snobisme *m*.

snobbish ['snɒbɪʃ] *adj* snob.

snobby ['snɒbɪ] (*comp* **snobbier**, *superl* **snobbiest**) *inf* = **snobbish**.

snog [snɒg] (*pret & pp* **snogged**, *cont* **snogging**) *UK inf* <> *vi* se rouler une pelle.
<> *vt* rouler une pelle à.
<> *n* : **to have a ~** se rouler une pelle.

snogging ['snɒgɪŋ] *n UK inf* **there was a lot of ~ going on** ça s'embrassait dans tous les coins.

snook [snu:k] *n* **1.** ZOOL brochet *m* de mer **2.** ▷ **cock**.

snooker ['snu:kər] <> *n* snooker *m (sorte de billard joué avec 22 boules).*
<> *vt* **1.** *UK inf* [thwart] mettre dans l'embarras, mettre dans une situation impossible ▪ [trick] arnaquer, avoir ▪ **we're ~ed!** [stuck] on est coincé! ; [tricked] on s'est fait avoir! **2.** GAMES laisser dans une position difficile.

snoop [snu:p] *inf* <> *vi* fourrer son nez dans les affaires des autres ▪ **someone has been ~ing about in my room** quelqu'un est venu fouiner dans ma chambre ▪ **to ~ on sb** espionner qqn ▪ **he's always ~ing around** il est toujours à se mêler des affaires des autres *OR* de ce qui ne le regarde pas.
<> *n* **1.** [search] : **to have a ~ around** fouiller, fouiner **2.** = **snooper**.

snooper ['snu:pər] *n* fouineur *m*, - euse *f*.

snooty ['snu:tɪ] (*comp* **snootier**, *superl* **snootiest**) *adj inf* [person] snobinard ▪ [restaurant] snob ▪ **she's very ~** c'est une vraie pimbêche.

snooze [snu:z] *inf* <> *n* petit somme *m*, roupillon *m* ▪ **to have a ~** faire un petit somme, piquer un roupillon ▪ [in afternoon] faire la sieste ▪ **~ (position)** [on alarm clock] (position *f*) sommeil *m*.
<> *vi* sommeiller, piquer un roupillon ▪ [in afternoon] faire la sieste.

snooze button *n* bouton *m* de veille.

snore [snɔ:r] <> *vi* ronfler.
<> *n* ronflement *m*.

snorer ['snɔ:rər] *n* ronfleur *m*, - euse *f*.

snoring ['snɔ:rɪŋ] *n (U)* ronflement *m*, ronflements *mpl*.

snorkel ['snɔ:kl] (*UK pret & pp* **snorkelled**, *cont* **snorkelling**) (*US pret & pp* **snorkeled**, *cont* **snorkeling**) <> *n* [of swimmer] tuba *m* ▪ [on submarine] schnorchel *m*.
<> *vi* nager sous l'eau *(avec un tuba)*.

snorkelling *UK*, **snorkeling** *US* ['snɔ:klɪŋ] *n* : **to go ~** faire de la plongée avec un tuba.

snort [snɔ:t] <> *vi* **1.** [horse] s'ébrouer ▪ [pig] grogner ▪ [bull] renâcler **2.** [person - in anger] grogner, ronchonner ▪ **to ~ with laughter** s'étouffer *OR* pouffer de rire ▪ **he ~ed in disbelief** il eut un petit grognement incrédule.
<> *vt* **1.** [angrily] grogner ▪ [laughingly] dire en pouffant de rire **2.** △ *drug sl* [cocaine] sniffer.
<> *n* **1.** [of bull, horse] ébrouement *m* ▪ [of person] grognement *m* ▪ **the horse gave a loud ~** le cheval s'ébroua bruyamment ▪ **he gave a ~ of contempt** il poussa un grognement de mépris ▪ **he gave a ~ of laughter** il pouffa de rire **2.** *inf* [drink] petit verre *m* (d'alcool).

snot [snɒt] *n inf* **1.** [in nose] morve *f* **2.** [person] morveux *m*, - euse *f*.

snotty ['snɒtɪ] (*comp* **snottier**, *superl* **snottiest**, *pl* **snotties**) *inf adj* **1.** [nose] qui coule ▪ [face, child] morveux **2.** [uppity] crâneur, snobinard ▪ **a ~ letter** une lettre agressive.

snotty-nosed *adj inf liter & fig* morveux.

snout [snaʊt] *n* **1.** [of pig] groin *m*, museau *m* ▪ [of other animal] museau *m* **2.** [projection] saillie *f* ▪ [of gun] canon *m* **3.** *inf hum* [nose] pif *m*.

snow [snəʊ] <> *n* **1.** *liter* neige *f* ▪ **heavy ~ is forecast** la météo prévoit d'abondantes chutes de neige ▪ **the roads are covered with ~** les routes sont enneigées ▶ **'Snow White and the Seven Dwarfs'** *Grimm, Disney* 'Blanche-Neige et les sept nains' **2.** *fig* [on screen] neige *f* **3.** △ *drug sl* [cocaine] neige *f drug sl*.
<> *vi* neiger ▪ **it's ~ing** il neige.
<> *vt US inf* [sweet-talk] baratiner.
◆ **snow in** *vt sep* : **to be ~ed in** être bloqué par la neige.
◆ **snow under** *vt sep fig* **to be ~ed under with work** être débordé *OR* complètement submergé de travail ▪ **they're ~ed under with applications/offers** ils ont reçu une avalanche de demandes/d'offres.
◆ **snow up** *vt sep* : **to be ~ed up** [house, village, family] être bloqué par la neige ; [road] être complètement enneigé.

snowball ['snəʊbɔ:l] <> *n* **1.** boule *f* de neige ▪ **they had a ~ fight** ils ont fait une bataille de boules de neige ▶ **he hasn't a ~'s chance in hell** *inf* il n'a pas l'ombre d'une chance **2.** [cocktail] snowball *m (advokaat allongé de limonade)*.
<> *comp* : **~ effect** effet *m* boule de neige.
<> *vt* bombarder de boules de neige, lancer des boules de neige à.
<> *vi fig* faire boule de neige.

snowbike ['snəʊbaɪk] *n* motoneige *f*.

snow-blind *adj* : **to be ~** être atteint de *OR* souffrir de la cécité des neiges.

snow blindness *n* cécité *f* des neiges.

snowboard ['snəʊ,bɔ:d] <> *n* surf *m* des neiges.
<> *vi* faire du surf des neiges.

snowboarder ['snəʊ,bɔ:dər] *n* surfeur *m*, - euse *f* (des neiges).

snowboarding ['snəʊ,bɔːdɪŋ] *n* surf *m* (des neiges).

snow-boot *n* après-ski *m*.

snowbound ['snəʊbaʊnd] *adj* [person, house, village] bloqué par la neige ■ [road] enneigé.

snow-capped [-kæpt] *adj* couronné de neige.

snowcat ['snəʊkæt] *n* autoneige *f*, motoneige *f*.

snow chains *npl* AUT chaînes *fpl*.

snowdrift ['snəʊdrɪft] *n* congère *f*.

snowdrop ['snəʊdrɒp] *n* perce-neige *m* OR *f inv*.

snowfall ['snəʊfɔːl] *n* **1.** [snow shower] chute *f* de neige **2.** [amount] enneigement *m*.

snow fence *n* pare-neige *m inv*.

snowfield ['snəʊfiːld] *n* champ *m* de neige.

snowflake ['snəʊfleɪk] *n* flocon *m* de neige.

snow goose *n* oie *f* des neiges.

snow leopard *n* léopard *m* des neiges, once *f*.

snowline ['snəʊlaɪn] *n* limite *f* des neiges éternelles.

snowman ['snəʊmæn] (*pl* **snowmen** [-men]) *n* bonhomme *m* de neige.

snow pea *n* US mange-tout *m inv*.

snowplough UK, **snowplow** US ['snəʊplaʊ] ◇ *n* **1.** [vehicle] chasse-neige *m inv* **2.** [in skiing] chasse-neige *m inv*.
◇ *vi* [in skiing] faire du chasse-neige.

snowshoe ['snəʊʃuː] *n* raquette *f* (*pour marcher sur la neige*).

snowstorm ['snəʊstɔːm] *n* tempête *f* de neige.

snow tyre *n* pneu *m* neige.

snow-white *adj* blanc comme neige.

snowy ['snəʊɪ] (*comp* **snowier**, *superl* **snowiest**) *adj* **1.** [weather, region etc] neigeux ■ [countryside, roads etc] enneigé, couvert OR recouvert de neige ■ [day] de neige **2.** *fig* [hair, beard] de neige ■ [sheets, tablecloth] blanc comme neige.

snowy owl *n* chouette *f* blanche, harfang *m*.

SNP *pr n* = **Scottish National Party**.

Snr (*written abbrev of* **Senior**) *utilisé après le nom de quelqu'un pour le distinguer d'un autre membre de la famille, plus jeune et portant le même nom.*

snub [snʌb] (*pret & pp* **snubbed**, *cont* **snubbing**) ◇ *n* rebuffade *f*.
◇ *vt* [person] remettre à sa place, rabrouer ■ [offer, suggestion] repousser (dédaigneusement) ■ **to be snubbed** essuyer une rebuffade.
◇ *adj* [nose] retroussé.

snub-nosed *adj* au nez retroussé.

snuck [snʌk] *pt & pp* ➡ **sneak**.

snuff [snʌf] ◇ *n* tabac *m* à priser ■ **to take ~** priser ■ **a pinch of ~** une prise (de tabac).
◇ *vi* [sniff] priser.
◇ *vt* **1.** [candle] moucher **2.** *phr* **to ~ it** *inf hum* casser sa pipe **3.** [sniff] renifler, flairer.
◆ **snuff out** *vt sep* [candle] éteindre, moucher ■ *fig* [hope] ôter, supprimer ■ [rebellion] étouffer ■ [enthusiasm] briser.

snuffbox ['snʌfbɒks] *n* tabatière *f* (*pour tabac à priser*).

snuffer ['snʌfər] *n* : **(candle) ~** éteignoir *m*.

snuffle ['snʌfl] ◇ *vi* **1.** [sniffle] renifler **2.** [in speech] parler du nez, nasiller.
◇ *vt* dire OR prononcer d'une voix nasillarde.
◇ *n* **1.** [sniffle] reniflement *m* ■ **to have the ~s** être un peu enrhumé **2.** [in speech] voix *f* nasillarde.

snuff movie *n inf film pornographique comportant une scène de meurtre filmée en direct.*

snug [snʌg] ◇ *adj* **1.** [warm and cosy - bed, room] douillet, (bien) confortable ; [- sleeping bag, jacket] douillet, bien chaud ■ **it's very ~ in this room** on est bien OR il fait bon dans cette pièce ■ **I wish I was home and ~ in bed** j'aimerais être bien au chaud dans mon lit ▶ **to be (as) ~ as a bug in a rug** *inf* être bien au chaud **2.** [fit] bien ajusté ■ **my skirt is a ~ fit** ma jupe me va comme un gant **3.** [harbour] bien abrité ■ [hideout] sûr.
◇ *n* UK [in pub] petite arrière-salle *f*.

snuggle ['snʌgl] ◇ *vi* se blottir, se pelotonner.
◇ *vt* [child, kitten] serrer contre soi, câliner.
◇ *n* câlin *m* ■ **to have a ~** (se) faire un câlin.
◆ **snuggle down** *vi insep* se blottir, se pelotonner ■ **to ~ down under the blankets** s'enfouir sous les couvertures.
◆ **snuggle up** *vi insep* : **to ~ up to sb** se blottir OR se serrer contre qqn.

snugly ['snʌglɪ] *adv* **1.** [cosily] douillettement, confortablement ■ **soon they were settled ~ by the fire** ils se retrouvèrent bientôt réunis autour d'un bon feu **2.** [in fit] : **the skirt fits ~** la jupe est très ajustée ■ **the two parts fit together ~** les deux pièces s'emboîtent parfaitement.

so[1] [səʊ] ◇ *adv* **1.** *(before adj, adv)* [to such an extent] si, tellement ■ **I'm so glad to see you** ça me fait tellement plaisir OR je suis si content de te voir ■ **she makes me so angry** elle a le don de me mettre en colère ■ **I've never been so surprised in all my life** jamais de ma vie je n'avais eu une surprise pareille OR une telle surprise ■ **his handwriting's so bad (that) it's illegible** il écrit si mal que c'est impossible à lire ■ **would you be so kind as to carry my case?** auriez-vous l'amabilité OR la gentillesse de porter ma valise? ■ *(after verb)* comme ça, ainsi ■ **you mustn't worry so** il ne faut pas te faire du souci comme ça ■ *(with 'that' clause)* **she so detests him** OR **she detests him so that she won't even speak to him** elle le hait au point de refuser OR elle le déteste tellement qu'elle refuse de lui parler ■ **he was upset, so much so that he cried** il était bouleversé, à tel point qu'il en a pleuré ■ *(in negative comparisons)* si, aussi ■ **I'm not so sure** je n'en suis pas si sûr ■ **it's not so bad, there's only a small stain** ça n'est pas si grave que ça, il n'y a qu'une petite tache ■ **the young and the not so young** les jeunes et les moins jeunes ■ **he was not so ill (that) he couldn't go out** il n'était pas malade au point de ne pas pouvoir sortir
2. [indicating a particular size, length etc] : **the table is about so high/wide** la table est haute/large comme ça à peu près
3. [referring to previous statement, question, word etc] : **I believe/think/suppose so** je crois/pense/suppose ■ **I don't believe/think so** je ne crois/pense pas ■ **I don't suppose so** je suppose que non ■ **I hope so** [answering question] j'espère que oui ; [agreeing] j'espère bien, je l'espère ■ **who says so?** qui dit ça? ■ **I told you so!** je vous l'avais bien dit! ■ **if so** si oui ■ **perhaps so** peut-être bien ■ **quite so** tout à fait, exactement ■ **so I believe/see** c'est ce que je crois/vois ■ **so I've been told/he said** c'est ce qu'on m'a dit/qu'il a dit ■ **isn't that Jane over there? – why, so it is!** ce ne serait pas Jane là-bas? – mais si (c'est elle)! ■ **he was told to leave the room and did so immediately** on lui a ordonné de quitter la pièce et il l'a fait immédiatement ■ **she was furious and understandably/and justifiably so** elle était furieuse et ça se comprend/et c'est normal ■ **the same only more so** tout autant sinon plus ■ **he's very sorry – so he should be!** il est désolé – c'est la moindre des choses OR j'espère bien! ■ [used mainly by children] : **I can so!** *inf* si, je peux! ■ **I didn't say that! – you did so!** *inf* je n'ai pas dit ça! – si, tu l'as dit! ▶ **so be it!** *arch & hum* soit!, qu'il en soit ainsi! ■ **so help me God!** *fml* que Dieu me vienne en aide!
4. [likewise] aussi ■ **we arrived early and so did he** nous sommes arrivés tôt et lui aussi
5. [like this, in this way] ainsi ■ **hold the pen (like) so** tenez le stylo ainsi OR comme ceci ■ **any product so labelled is guaranteed lead-free** tous les produits portant cette étiquette sont garantis sans plomb ■ **the laptop computer is so called because...** l'ordinateur lap-top tient son nom de... ■ [in such a way] : **the helmet is so constructed as to absorb most of the impact** le casque est conçu de façon à amortir le choc ▶ **it (just) so happens that...** il se trouve (justement) que... ■ **she likes everything (to be) just so** elle aime que tout soit parfait ■ **it has to be positioned just so or it won't go in** il faut le mettre comme ça sinon ça n'entre pas

6. [introducing the next event in a sequence] : **and so we come to the next question** et maintenant nous en venons à la question suivante ▪ **so then she left** alors elle est partie ❙ [requesting more information] : **so what's the problem?** alors, qu'est-ce qui ne va pas? ❙ [summarizing, inferring] : **so we can't go after all** donc nous ne pouvons plus y aller ❙ [in exclamations] alors ▪ **so you're Anna's brother!** alors (comme ça) vous êtes le frère d'Anna? ▪ **so publish it!** eh bien *OR* alors allez-y, publiez-le! ❙ [introducing a concession] et alors ▪ **so I'm late, who cares?** je suis en retard, et alors, qu'est-ce que ça peut faire? ▪ **so?** et alors?, et après? ▶ **he'll be angry – so what?** il va se fâcher! – qu'est-ce que ça peut (me) faire *OR* et alors? ▪ **so what if she does find out!** qu'est-ce que ça peut faire si elle s'en rend compte?

◇ *conj* **1.** [indicating result] donc, alors

2. [indicating purpose] pour que, afin que ▪ **give me some money so I can buy some sweets** donne-moi de l'argent pour que je puisse acheter des bonbons

3. [in the same way] de même ▪ **as 3 is to 6, so 6 is to 12** le rapport entre 6 et 12 est le même qu'entre 3 et 6 ▪ **as he has lived so will he die** il mourra comme il a vécu.

◇ *adj* ainsi, vrai ▪ **is that so?** c'est vrai? ; *iron* vraiment? ▪ **if that is so** si c'est le cas, s'il en est ainsi.

◆ **or so** *adv phr* environ, à peu près.

◆ **so as** *conj phr inf* pour que, afin que.

◆ **so as to** *conj phr* pour, afin de.

◆ **so that** *conj phr* **1.** [in order that] pour que, afin que ▪ **they tied him up so that he couldn't escape** ils l'ont attaché afin qu'il *OR* pour qu'il ne s'échappe pas ▪ **I took a taxi so that I wouldn't be late** j'ai pris un taxi pour ne pas être en retard

2. [with the result that] si bien que, de façon à ce que ▪ **she didn't eat enough, so that in the end she fell ill** elle ne mangeait pas assez, de telle sorte *OR* si bien qu'elle a fini par tomber malade.

◆ **so to speak, so to say** *adv phr* pour ainsi dire.

so² [səʊ] *n* MUS sol *m*.

SO *n* = **standing order**.

soak [səʊk] ◇ *vt* **1.** [washing, food] faire *OR* laisser tremper ▪ **to ~ o.s. (in the bath)** faire trempette dans la baignoire **2.** [drench - person, dog etc] tremper ▪ **to be ~ed through** *OR* **to the skin** être trempé jusqu'aux os ▪ **I got ~ed waiting in the rain** je me suis fait tremper en attendant sous la pluie ▪ **his shirt was ~ed in blood/in sweat** sa chemise était maculée de sang/trempée de sueur **3.** *fig* [immerse] imprégner **4.** *inf* [exploit - by swindling] rouler, arnaquer ; [- through taxation] faire casquer.

◇ *vi* [washing] tremper ▪ **he put the washing (in) to ~** il a mis le linge à tremper ▪ **to ~ in the bath** faire trempette dans la baignoire.

◇ *n* **1.** [in water] trempage *m* ▪ **these shirts need a good ~** il faut laisser *OR* bien faire tremper ces chemises ▪ **I had a nice long ~ in the bath** je suis resté longtemps plongé dans un bon bain **2.** *inf* [heavy drinker] soûlard *m*, - e *f*, pochard *m*, - e *f*.

◆ **soak in** *vi insep* **1.** [water] pénétrer, s'infiltrer **2.** *inf fig* [comment, news] faire son effet.

◆ **soak out** ◇ *vi insep* [dirt, stains] partir (au trempage).

◇ *vt sep* [dirt, stains] faire disparaître *OR* partir (en faisant tremper).

◆ **soak through** *vi insep* [liquid] filtrer au travers, s'infiltrer.

◆ **soak up** *vt sep* **1.** [absorb] absorber ▪ **we spent a week ~ing up the sun** nous avons passé une semaine à lézarder *OR* à nous faire dorer au soleil ▪ **they come to Europe to ~ up the culture** ils viennent en Europe pour s'imbiber de culture **2.** *inf hum* [drink] : **he can really ~ it up** il peut vraiment boire comme un trou.

soaked [səʊkt] *adj fig* [immersed] imprégné ▪ **the place is ~ in history** l'endroit est imprégné d'histoire.

soaking ['səʊkɪŋ] ◇ *adj* trempé ▪ **I'm ~ (wet)!** je suis trempé jusqu'aux os!

◇ *n* **1.** [gen] trempage *m* ▪ **these clothes need a good ~** il faut laisser tremper ces vêtements ❙ *inf* [in rain] *inf* **to get a ~** se faire tremper *OR* saucer **2.** *inf* [financial loss] perte *f* financière.

so-and-so *n inf* **1.** [referring to stranger] untel *m*, unetelle *f* ▪ **Mr ~** Monsieur Untel ▪ **Mrs ~** Madame Unetelle **2.** [annoying person] : **you little ~!** espèce de petit minable!

soap [səʊp] ◇ *n (U)* **1.** savon *m* ▪ **a bar of ~** un savon, une savonnette ▪ **~ bubble** bulle *f* de savon **2.** *US inf phr* **no ~!** des clous!, des nèfles! **3.** *inf* RADIO & TV = **soap opera**.

◇ *vt* savonner.

◆ **soap down** *vt sep* savonner.

soapbox ['səʊpbɒks] ◇ *n* **1.** *liter* caisse *f* à savon ▪ *fig* [for speaker] tribune *f* improvisée *OR* de fortune ▪ **get off your ~!** ne monte pas sur tes grands chevaux! **2.** [go-kart] chariot *m*, ≃ kart *m (sans moteur)*.

◇ *comp* [orator] de carrefour ▪ [oratory] de démagogue.

soapdish ['səʊpdɪʃ] *n* porte-savon *m*.

soapflakes ['səʊpfleɪks] *npl* paillettes *fpl* de savon, savon *m* en paillettes.

soap opera *n* RADIO & TV soap opera *m*.

soap powder *n* lessive *f* (en poudre), poudre *f* à laver.

soapsuds ['səʊpsʌdz] *npl* [foam] mousse *f* de savon ▪ [soapy water] eau *f* savonneuse.

soapy ['səʊpɪ] (*comp* **soapier**, *superl* **soapiest**) *adj* **1.** [water, hands, surface] savonneux ▪ [taste] de savon **2.** *inf fig* [person, manner, voice] onctueux, mielleux.

soar [sɔːʳ] *vi* **1.** [bird, plane] monter en flèche ▪ [flames] jaillir ▪ **to ~ into the sky** *OR* **the air** [bird, balloon etc] s'élever dans les airs ▪ **the ball ~ed over the fence/our heads** le ballon s'est envolé au-dessus de la clôture/de nos têtes **2.** [spire] se dresser vers le ciel ▪ [mountain] s'élever vers le ciel ▪ **the mountain seemed to ~ into the clouds** la montagne paraissait s'élancer dans les nuages **3.** [temperature, profits, prices] monter *OR* grimper en flèche ▪ [suddenly] faire un bond **4.** [spirits] remonter en flèche ▪ [hopes, imagination] grandir démesurément ▪ [reputation] monter en flèche **5.** [sound, music] s'élever.

soaring ['sɔːrɪŋ] ◇ *adj* **1.** [bird, glider] qui s'élève dans le ciel ▪ [spire, tower] qui s'élance vers le ciel ▪ [mountain] qui s'élève vers le ciel **2.** [prices, inflation] qui monte *OR* qui grimpe en flèche ▪ [imagination] débordant ▪ [hopes, reputation] grandissant.

◇ *n* [of bird] essor *m*, élan *m* ▪ [of plane] envol *m* ▪ [of prices] envolée *f*, explosion *f*.

sob¹ [sɒb] (*pret & pp* **sobbed**, *cont* **sobbing**) ◇ *n* sanglot *m* ▪ **she answered him with a ~** elle lui répondit dans un sanglot ▪ **it wasn't me, he said with a ~** ce n'est pas moi, dit-il en sanglotant.

◇ *vi* sangloter.

◇ *vt* : **to ~ o.s. to sleep** s'endormir à force de sangloter *OR* en sanglotant ▪ **"I can't remember!", he sobbed** "je ne me rappelle pas", dit-il en sanglotant.

◆ **sob out** *vt sep* raconter en sanglotant ▪ **to ~ one's heart out** sangloter de tout son corps, pleurer à gros sanglots.

sob², SOB ['esəubiː] *n US inf* = **son of a bitch**.

sobbing ['sɒbɪŋ] ◇ *n (U)* sanglots *mpl*.

◇ *adj* sanglotant.

sober ['səʊbəʳ] *adj* **1.** [not drunk] : **are you sure he was ~?** tu es sûr qu'il n'avait pas bu? ❙ [sobered up] dessoûlé ▪ **wait until he's ~ again** attends qu'il dessoûle ▶ **to be as ~ as a judge** [serious] être sérieux comme un pape ; [temperate] être sobre comme un chameau **2.** [moderate - person] sérieux, posé, sensé ; [- attitude, account, opinion] modéré, mesuré ; [- manner] sérieux, posé **3.** [serious, solemn - atmosphere, occasion] solennel, plein de solennité ; [- expression] grave, plein de gravité ; [- voice] grave, empreint de gravité ; [- reminder] solennel **4.** [subdued - colour, clothing] discret, - ète *f*, sobre ▪ **of ~ appearance** d'aspect sobre **5.** [plain - fact, reality] (tout) simple ; [- truth] simple, tout nu ; [- tastes] simple, sobre.

◆ **sober up** *vi insep & vt sep* dessoûler.

sobering ['səʊbərɪŋ] *adj* : **it's a ~ thought** cela donne à réfléchir ▪ **what she said had a ~ effect on everyone** ce qu'elle a dit donnait à réfléchir à tous.

soberly ['səʊbəlɪ] *adv* [act, speak] avec sobriété *OR* modération *OR* mesure ■ [dress] sobrement, discrètement ■ **he said ~** [calmly] dit-il d'un ton posé *OR* mesuré ; [solemnly] dit-il d'un ton grave.

sobriety [səʊ'braɪətɪ] *n* **1.** [non-drunkenness] sobriété *f* **2.** [moderation - of person] sobriété *f*, sérieux *m* ; [- of opinion, judgement] mesure *f*, modération *f* ; [- of manner, style, tastes] sobriété *f* **3.** [solemnity - of occasion] solennité *f* ; [- of voice] ton *m* solennel *OR* grave ; [- of mood] sobriété *f* **4.** [of colour, dress] sobriété *f*.

sobriquet ['səʊbrɪkeɪ] *n lit* sobriquet *m*.

sob story *n inf pej* histoire *f* larmoyante, histoire *f* à vous fendre le cœur ■ **he told us some ~ about his deprived childhood** il nous a parlé de son enfance malheureuse *OR* à faire pleurer dans les chaumières.

Soc [sɒk] (*abbrev of* **Society**) *n* ≃ club *m* (*abréviation utilisée dans la langue parlée notamment par les étudiants pour désigner les différents clubs universitaires*).

so-called [-kɔːld] *adj* soi-disant (*inv*), prétendu ■ **~ social workers** des soi-disant assistants sociaux ■ **her ~ boudoir** son boudoir, comme elle l'appelle.

soccer ['sɒkəʳ] ◇ *n* football *m*, foot *m*.
◇ *comp* [pitch, match, team] de football, de foot ■ [supporter] d'une équipe de foot ■ **~ hooligans** hooligans *mpl* (*lors de matches de football*) ■ **~ player** footballeur *m*, - euse *f*.

sociable ['səʊʃəbl] ◇ *adj* **1.** [enjoying company] sociable, qui aime la compagnie (des gens) ■ [friendly] sociable, amical ■ [evening] amical, convivial ■ **try to be more ~** [go out more] essaie de sortir un peu et de rencontrer des gens ; [mix more] essaie d'être un peu plus sociable ■ **I'm not in a ~ mood** je ne suis pas d'humeur sociable, je n'ai pas envie de voir de monde **2.** SOCIOL & ZOOL sociable.
◇ *n US* fête *f*.

social ['səʊʃl] ◇ *adj* **1.** [background, behaviour, conditions, reform, tradition] social ■ [phenomenon] social, de société ■ **to bow to ~ pressures** se plier aux pressions sociales ■ **they are our ~ equals** ils sont de même condition sociale que nous ■ **~ benefits** prestations *fpl* sociales ▶ **they move in high** *OR* **the best ~ circles** ils évoluent dans les hautes sphères de la société ■ **~ conscience** conscience *f* sociale ■ **~ order** ordre *m* social ■ **~ outcast** paria *m* ■ **~ structure** structure *f* sociale **2.** [in society - activities] mondain ■ [leisure] de loisir *OR* loisirs ■ **his life is one mad ~ whirl** il mène une vie mondaine insensée **3.** [evening, function] amical ■ **~ event** rencontre *f* ■ **it was the ~ event of the year** c'était l'événement mondain de l'année **4.** ZOOL social ■ **man is a ~ animal** l'homme est un animal social.
◇ *n* soirée *f* (dansante).

social chapter *n* volet *m* social.

Social Charter *n* Charte *f* sociale.

social climber *n* arriviste *mf*.

social club *n* club *m*.

social contract *n* contrat *m* social.

social democracy *n* **1.** [system] social-démocratie *f* **2.** [country] démocratie *f* socialiste.

social democrat *n* social-démocrate *mf*.

Social Democratic and Labour Party *pr n parti travailliste d'Irlande du Nord.*

Social Democratic Party *pr n* Parti *m* social-démocrate.

social disease *n* [gen] maladie *f* provoquée par des facteurs socio-économiques ■ *euph* [venereal] maladie *f* vénérienne.

social drinker *n* : **he's purely a ~** il ne boit pas seul, il boit seulement en société *OR* en compagnie.

social engineering *n* manipulation *f* des structures sociales.

social fund *n caisse d'aide sociale.*

social insurance *n (U)* prestations *fpl* sociales.

socialism ['səʊʃəlɪzm] *n* socialisme *m*.

socialist ['səʊʃəlɪst] ◇ *adj* socialiste.
◇ *n* socialiste *mf*.

socialite ['səʊʃəlaɪt] *n* mondain *m*, - e *f*, personne *f* qui fréquente la haute société.

socialize, ise ['səʊʃəlaɪz] ◇ *vi* [go out] sortir, fréquenter des gens ■ [make friends] se faire des amis ■ **to ~ with sb** frayer avec qqn ■ **he finds it difficult to ~** il a du mal à lier connaissance, il est très peu sociable.
◇ *vt* POL & PSYCHOL socialiser.

socializing ['səʊʃəlaɪzɪŋ] *n* fait *m* de fréquenter des gens ■ **~ between teachers and pupils is discouraged** les relations entre élèves et professeurs ne sont pas encouragées.

social life *n* vie *f* mondaine ■ **to have a busy ~** [be fashionable] mener une vie très mondaine ; [go out often] sortir beaucoup ■ **there isn't much of a ~ in this town** les gens ne sortent pas beaucoup dans cette ville, il ne se passe rien dans cette ville.

socially ['səʊʃəlɪ] *adv* socialement ■ **~ acceptable behaviour** comportement socialement acceptable ■ **we've never met ~** on ne s'est jamais rencontrés en société.

social science *n* sciences *fpl* humaines.

social scientist *n* spécialiste *mf* des sciences humaines.

social security *n* **1.** [gen] prestations *fpl* sociales ■ **to be on ~** toucher une aide sociale **2.** *UK* [money paid to unemployed] ≃ allocations *fpl* de chômage.

social services *npl* services *mpl* sociaux.

social studies *npl* sciences *fpl* sociales.

social work *n* assistance *f* sociale, travail *m* social.

social worker *n* assistant social *m*, assistante sociale *f*, travailleur social *m*, travailleuse sociale *f*.

society [sə'saɪətɪ] (*pl* **societies**) ◇ *n* **1.** [social community] société *f* ■ **it is a danger to ~** cela constitue un danger pour la société ■ **woman's place in ~** la place de la femme dans la société **2.** [nation, group] société *f* ■ **Western ~** la société occidentale **3.** [fashionable circles] : **(high) ~** la haute société, le (beau *OR* grand) monde **4.** *lit* [company] société *f*, compagnie *f* ■ **in polite ~** dans la bonne société *OR* le (beau) monde **5.** [association, club] société *f*, association *f* ■ [for sports] club *m*, association *f* ■ SCH & UNIV [for debating, study etc] société *f* ■ **charitable ~** œuvre *f* de charité, association *f* caritative ■ **the Society of Friends** la Société des Amis (*les quakers*).
◇ *comp* [gossip, news, wedding] mondain ■ **the ~ column** PRESS la chronique mondaine ■ **a ~ man/woman** un homme/une femme du monde.

sociocultural [,səʊsɪəʊ'kʌltʃərəl] *adj* socioculturel.

socioeconomic ['səʊsɪəʊ,iːkə'nɒmɪk] *adj* socio-économique.

sociolinguistic [,səʊsɪəʊlɪŋ'gwɪstɪk] *adj* sociolinguistique.

sociolinguistics [,səʊsɪəʊlɪŋ'gwɪstɪks] *n (U)* sociolinguistique *f*.

sociological [,səʊsjə'lɒdʒɪkl] *adj* sociologique.

sociologist [,səʊsɪ'ɒlədʒɪst] *n* sociologue *mf*.

sociology [,səʊsɪ'ɒlədʒɪ] *n* sociologie *f*.

sociopolitical [,səʊsɪəʊpə'lɪtɪkl] *adj* sociopolitique.

sock [sɒk] ◇ *n* **1.** [garment] chaussette *f* ■ **it'll knock your ~s off!** *inf* tu vas tomber à la renverse! ■ **to pull one's ~s up** *inf* se secouer (les puces) ■ **put a ~ in it!** *UK inf* la ferme! **2.** [insole] semelle *f* (intérieure) **3.** [of horse] paturon *m* **4.** AERON & METEOR : **(wind) ~** manche *f* à air **5.** *inf* [blow] gnon *m*, beigne *f*.

<> *vt inf* [hit] flanquer une beigne à ➋ **~ it to him!, ~ him one!** fous-lui une beigne!, cogne-le! ▪ **~ it to them!** [in performance] allez, montrez-leur un peu de quoi vous êtes capables! ▪ **~ it to me then!** allez, accouche!△.

socket ['sɒkɪt] *n* **1.** ELEC [for bulb] douille *f* ▪ *UK* [in wall] prise *f* (de courant) **2.** TECH cavité *f* ▪ [in carpentry] mortaise *f* ▪ **it fits into a ~** ça s'emboîte dans un support prévu à cet effet **3.** ANAT [of arm, hipbone] cavité *f* articulaire ▪ [of tooth] alvéole *f* ▪ [of eye] orbite *f* ▪ **her arm was pulled out of its ~** elle a eu l'épaule luxée ▪ **her eyes almost popped** *OR* **jumped out of their ~s** *fig* les yeux lui en sont presque sortis de la tête.

socket joint *n* **1.** [in carpentry] joint *m* à rotule **2.** ANAT énarthrose *f*.

socket set *n* coffret *m* de douilles.

socket wrench *n* clef *f* à douille.

sockeye ['sɒkaɪ] *n* ZOOL saumon *m* rouge.

socking ['sɒkɪŋ] *adv UK inf* [as intensifier] vachement.

Socrates ['sɒkrəti:z] *pr n* Socrate.

Socratic [sɒ'krætɪk] *adj* socratique *(inv)*.

sod [sɒd] (*pret & pp* **sodded**, *cont* **sodding**) <> *n* **1.**△ *UK* [obnoxious person] enfoiré△ *m*, con△ *m* **2.**△ *UK* [fellow] bougre *m*, con△ *m* **3.**△ *UK* [difficult or unpleasant thing] corvée *f* ▪ **it's a ~ of a job** c'est vraiment chiant comme boulot△ ➋ **that's ~'s law** c'est la poisse **4.** [of turf] motte *f* (de gazon) ▪ [earth and grass] terre *f* ▪ [lawn] gazon *m* ▪ **the ~ of old Ireland** la bonne vieille terre d'Irlande.
<> *vt*△ *UK* **~ it!** merde!△ ▪ **~ him!** qu'il aille se faire foutre!△.
◆ **sod off**△ *vi insep UK* foutre le camp△ ▪ **~ off!** va te faire foutre!△.

soda ['səʊdə] *n* **1.** CHEM soude *f* **2.** [fizzy water] eau *f* de Seltz ▪ **a whisky and ~** un whisky soda **3.** *US* [soft drink] soda *m*.

soda biscuit *n UK biscuit sec à la levure chimique.*

soda bread *n* pain *m* à la levure chimique.

soda fountain *n US* **1.** [café] ≃ café *m* ▪ [counter] buvette *f (où sont servis des sodas)* **2.** = **soda siphon**.

sod all△ *n UK* **he does ~ around the house** il n'en fout pas une dans la maison ▪ **I'll tell you what you'll get out of him: ~!** tu sais ce qu'il te donnera : que dalle !

soda siphon *n* siphon *m* (d'eau de Seltz).

soda water *n* eau *f* de Seltz.

sodden ['sɒdn] *adj* [ground] détrempé ▪ [clothes] trempé.

sodding△ ['sɒdɪŋ] *UK* <> *adj* foutu△.
<> *adv* [very] vachement ▪ [as intensifier] : **you can ~ well do it yourself!** tu n'as qu'à le faire toi-même, merde!△.

sodium ['səʊdɪəm] *n* sodium *m*.

sodium bicarbonate *n* bicarbonate *m* de soude.

sodium chloride *n* chlorure *m* de sodium.

Sodom ['sɒdəm] *pr n* : **~ and Gomorrah** Sodome et Gomorrhe.

sodomite ['sɒdəmaɪt] *n* sodomite *m*.

sodomize, ise ['sɒdəmaɪz] *vt* sodomiser.

sodomy ['sɒdəmɪ] *n* sodomie *f*.

sofa ['səʊfə] *n* sofa *m*, canapé *m*.

sofa bed *n* canapé-lit *m*.

soft [sɒft] <> *adj* **1.** [to touch - skin, hands] doux, douce *f* ; [- wool, fur, pillow] doux, douce *f*, moelleux ; [- leather] souple ; [- material, hair] doux, douce *f*, soyeux ▪ **the cream will make your hands/the leather ~** la crème t'adoucira les mains/assouplira le cuir
2. [yielding to pressure - bed, mattress] moelleux ; [- collar, ground, snow] mou *(before vowel or silent 'h'* **mol**), molle *f* ; [- butter] mou *(before vowel or silent 'h* **mol**), molle *f*, ramolli ; [- muscles, body] ramolli, avachi, flasque ▪ [too yielding - bed, mattress] mou *(before vowel or silent 'h'* **mol**), molle *f* ▪ **the butter has gone ~** le beurre s'est ramolli ▪ **mix to a ~ paste** mélanger jusqu'à obtention d'une pâte molle ▪ **these chocolates have ~ centres** ces chocolats sont mous à l'intérieur ▪ **the brakes are ~** *fig* il y a du mou dans les freins ▪ **the going is ~** [in horseracing] le terrain est mou ➋ **~ cheese** fromage *m* à pâte molle
3. [malleable - metal, wood, stone] tendre ; [- pencil] gras, grasse *f*, tendre ▪ **~ contact lenses** lentilles *fpl* souples
4. [gentle - breeze, rain, words] doux, douce *f* ; [- expression, eyes] doux, douce *f*, tendre ; [- curve, shadow] doux, douce *f* ; [- climate, weather] doux, douce *f*, clément ▪ **she suits a ~er hairstyle** ce qui lui va bien, c'est une coiffure plus souple ▪ **it's a ~ day** *UK* il bruine aujourd'hui
5. [quiet, not harsh - voice, music] doux, douce *f* ; [- sound, accent] doux, douce *f*, léger ; [- tap, cough] petit, léger ; [- step] feutré
6. [muted - colour, glow] doux, douce *f* ; [- shade] doux, douce *f*, pastel *(inv)* ; [- light] doux, douce *f*, tamisé
7. [blurred - outline] estompé, flou
8. [kind, gentle - person] doux, douce *f*, tendre ; [- reply] gentil, aimable ; [- glance] doux, douce *f*, gentil ▪ [lenient] indulgent ▪ **to be ~ on sb** se montrer indulgent envers qqn, faire preuve d'indulgence envers qqn ▪ **to be ~ on terrorism** faire preuve de laxisme envers le terrorisme
9. [weak - physically] mou *(before vowel or silent 'h* **mol**), molle *f* ▪ **the boy's too ~** ce garçon n'a pas de caractère ▪ **city life has made you ~** la vie citadine t'a ramolli
10. *inf* [mentally] : **he's going ~ in his old age** il devient gâteux en vieillissant ▪ **you must be ~ in the head!** ça va pas, non? ▪ **don't be ~** [stop crying] arrête de pleurer ; [silly] arrête de dire des bêtises
11. [fond] : **to be ~ on sb** *inf* avoir le béguin pour qqn ▪ **to have a ~ spot for sb** avoir un faible pour qqn
12. [easy - life] doux, douce *f*, tranquille, facile ; [- job] facile ▪ **to have a ~ time of it** *inf* se la couler douce ▪ **it's the ~ option** c'est la solution de facilité
13. [moderate] modéré ▪ **to take a ~ line on sthg** adopter une ligne modérée sur qqch ; [compromise] adopter une politique de compromis sur qqch
14. ECON & FIN [currency] faible ▪ [market] faible, lourd ▪ **~ terms** conditions *fpl* favorables ▪ **~ loan** prêt *m* avantageux *OR* à des conditions avantageuses
15. [water] doux, douce *f*
16. LING [consonant] doux, douce *f*
17. [drug] doux, douce *f*.
<> *adv lit* [softly] doucement.

softball ['sɒftbɔ:l] *n US* [game] *sorte de base-ball joué sur un terrain plus petit et avec une balle moins dure.*

soft-boiled [-bɔɪld] *adj* : **~ egg** œuf *m* (à la) coque.

soft-centred *adj* [chocolate, sweet] mou *(before vowel or silent 'h' mol)*, molle *f*.

soft-core *adj* [pornography] soft *(inv)*.

soft drink *n* boisson *f* non alcoolisée.

soften ['sɒfn] <> *vt* **1.** [butter, ground] ramollir ▪ [skin, water] adoucir ▪ [fabric, wool, leather] assouplir ▪ **centuries of erosion had ~ed the stone** des siècles d'érosion avaient rendu la pierre tendre **2.** [voice, tone] adoucir, radoucir ▪ [colour, light, sound] adoucir, atténuer ▪ **to ~ one's voice** [less strident] parler d'une voix plus douce ; [quieter] parler moins fort **3.** [make less strict] assouplir ▪ **he has ~ed his stance on vegetarianism** son attitude envers le végétarisme est plus modérée qu'avant **4.** [lessen - pain, emotion] soulager, adoucir, atténuer ; [- shock, effect, impact] adoucir, amoindrir ; [- opposition, resistance] réduire, amoindrir ▪ **to ~ the blow** *liter & fig* amortir le choc.
<> *vi* **1.** [butter, ground etc] se ramollir ▪ [skin] s'adoucir ▪ [cloth, wool, leather] s'assouplir **2.** [become gentler - eyes, expression, voice] s'adoucir ; [- breeze, rain] s'atténuer ; [- lighting, colour] s'atténuer, s'adoucir ; [- angle, outline] s'adoucir, s'estomper **3.** [become friendlier, more receptive] : **to ~ towards sb** se montrer plus indulgent envers qqn ▪ **their attitude towards immigration has ~ed noticeably** leur position par rapport à l'immigration est nettement plus tolérante ▪ **his face ~ed** son expression se radoucit ▪ **her heart ~ed at the sound of his voice** elle s'attendrit en entendant sa voix.
◆ **soften up** <> *vt sep* **1.** *inf* [make amenable - gen] attendrir, rendre plus souple ; [- by persuasion] amadouer ; [- aggressively] intimider **2.** MIL affaiblir **3.** [make softer - butter, ground] ramollir ; [- skin] adoucir ; [- leather] assouplir.

<> *vi insep* **1.** [ground] devenir mou, se ramollir ■ [butter] se ramollir ■ [leather] s'assouplir ■ [skin] s'adoucir **2.** [become gentler - person, voice] s'adoucir ■ **to ~ up on sb** faire preuve de plus d'indulgence envers qqn.

softener ['sɒfnəʳ] *n* **1.** [for water] adoucisseur *m* (d'eau) ■ [for fabric] assouplissant *m* (textile) **2.** *inf* [bribe] pot-de-vin *m*.

softening ['sɒfnɪŋ] *n* [of substance, ground] ramollissement *m* ■ [of fabric, material] assouplissement *m*, adoucissement *m* ■ [of attitude, expression, voice] adoucissement *m* ■ [of colours, contrasts] atténuation *f* ■ **there has been no ~ of attitude on the part of the management** la direction n'a pas modéré son attitude ➤ **~ of the brain** MED ramollissement *m* cérébral.

soft focus *n* PHOT flou *m* artistique.

soft fruit *n (U)* ≃ fruits *mpl* rouges.

soft furnishings *npl* *UK* tissus *mpl* d'ameublement.

soft goods *npl* *UK* tissus *mpl*, textiles *mpl*.

softhearted [,sɒft'hɑːtɪd] *adj* (au cœur) tendre.

softie ['sɒftɪ] (*pl* **softies**) *n* *inf* **1.** [weak] mauviette *f*, mollasson *m*, - onne *f* ■ [coward] poule *f* mouillée, dégonflé *m*, - e *f* **2.** [softhearted] sentimental *m*, - e *f*.

soft landing *n* atterrissage *m* en douceur.

softly ['sɒftlɪ] *adv* **1.** [quietly - breathe, say] doucement ; [- move, walk] à pas feutrés, (tout) doucement **2.** [gently - blow, touch] doucement, légèrement **3.** [fondly - smile, look] tendrement, avec tendresse.

softly-softly *UK* <> *adv* tout doucement, avec prudence.
<> *adj* prudent ■ **try a ~ approach** allez-y doucement.

softness ['sɒftnɪs] *n* **1.** [to touch - of skin, hands, hair] douceur *f* ; [- of fabric, wool, fur, pillow] douceur *f*, moelleux *m* ; [- of leather] souplesse *f* **2.** [to pressure - of bed, ground, snow, butter] mollesse *f* ; [- of collar] souplesse *f* ; [- of wood] tendreté *f* **3.** [gentleness - of breeze, weather, voice, music] douceur *f* ; [- of expression, manner] douceur *f*, gentillesse *f* ; [- of eyes, light, colour] douceur *f* ; [- of outline, curve] flou *m*, douceur *f* **4.** [kindness - of person] douceur *f* ; [- of heart] tendresse *f* ■ [indulgence] indulgence *f*.

soft palate *n* voile *m* du palais.

soft pedal (*UK pret & pp* **soft-pedalled**, *cont* **soft-pedalling**) (*US pret & pp* **soft-pedaled**, *cont* **soft-pedaling**) *n* [on piano] pédale *f* douce, sourdine *f*.
◆ **soft-pedal** <> *vi* **1.** MUS mettre la sourdine **2.** *fig* **to ~ on reforms** ralentir le rythme des réformes.
<> *vt fig* glisser sur, atténuer.

soft sell *n* COMM *méthodes de vente non agressives*.

soft shoulder = **soft verge**.

soft soap *n* **1.** MED savon *m* vert **2.** *(U) inf* [flattery] flagornerie *f*, flatterie *f*, flatteries *fpl*.
◆ **soft-soap** *vt* passer de la pommade à.

soft-spoken *adj* à la voix douce.

soft top *n inf* AUT (voiture *f*) décapotable *f*.

soft touch *n UK inf* pigeon *m* ■ **he's a real ~** [easily fooled] il se laisse berner facilement ; [for money] il se laisse avoir *OR* rouler facilement.

soft toy *n* (jouet *m* en) peluche *f*.

soft verge *n* [on road] accotement *m* non stabilisé.

software ['sɒftweəʳ] <> *n* COMPUT logiciel *m*, software *m*.
<> *comp* : **~ company** fabricant *m* de logiciels ■ **~ house** société *f* de services et d'ingénierie informatique ■ **~ piracy** piratage *m* de logiciels.

software package *n* logiciel *m*.

softwood ['sɒftwʊd] *n* bois *m* tendre.

softy ['sɒftɪ] *inf* = **softie**.

soggy ['sɒgɪ] (*comp* **soggier**, *superl* **soggiest**) *adj* [ground] détrempé, imbibé d'eau ■ [clothes] trempé ■ [bread, cake] mou *(before vowel or silent 'h' mol)*, molle *f* ■ [rice] trop cuit, collant.

soh [səʊ] *n* MUS sol *m*.

Soho ['səʊhəʊ] *pr n quartier chaud de Londres connu pour ses restaurants*.

SoHo ['seʊhəʊ] *pr n quartier de Manhattan réunissant un grand nombre de galeries d'art*.

soil [sɔɪl] <> *n* **1.** [earth] terre *f* ■ **to work the ~** travailler la terre **2.** [type of earth] terre *f*, sol *m* ■ **good farming ~** de la bonne terre agricole **3.** *fig* [land] terre *f*, sol *m* ■ **his native ~** sa terre natale ■ **on Irish ~** sur le sol irlandais **4.** *(U)* [excrement] excréments *mpl*, ordures *fpl* ■ [sewage] vidange *f*.
<> *vt* **1.** [dirty - clothes, linen, paper] salir ■ *fig & lit* souiller ■ **she refused to ~ her hands with such work** elle a refusé de se salir les mains avec ce genre de travail **2.** *fig* [reputation] salir, souiller, entacher.
<> *vi* [clothes, material] se salir.

soiled [sɔɪld] *adj* [dressings] usagé ■ [bedlinen] souillé ■ [goods] défraîchi.

soil pipe *n* tuyau *m* de chute unique.

solace ['sɒləs] *lit* <> *n* consolation *f*, réconfort *m*.
<> *vt* [person] consoler, réconforter ■ [pain, suffering] soulager.

solar ['səʊləʳ] *adj* **1.** [of, concerning the sun - heat, radiation] solaire, du soleil ; [- cycle, year] solaire **2.** [using the sun's power - energy, heating] solaire.

solar cell *n* pile *f* solaire, photopile *f*.

solar flare *n* éruption *f* solaire.

solarium [sə'leərɪəm] (*pl* **solariums** *OR pl* **solaria** [-rɪə]) *n* solarium *m*.

solar panel *n* panneau *m* solaire.

solar plexus *n* plexus *m* solaire.

solar power *n* énergie *f* solaire.

solar-powered [-'paʊəd] *adj* à énergie solaire.

solar system *n* système *m* solaire.

sold [səʊld] <> *pt & pp* ⊳ **sell**.
<> *adj* **1.** COMM vendu **2.** *inf fig* **to be ~ on sb/sthg** être emballé par qqn/qqch ■ **he's really ~ on her** il est vraiment entiché *OR* toqué d'elle.
◆ **sold out** *adj phr* **1.** [goods] épuisé ■ **'~ out'** [for play, concert] 'complet' ■ **the concert was completely ~ out** tous les billets pour le concert ont été vendus **2.** [stockist] : **we're ~ out of bread** nous avons vendu tout le pain, il ne reste plus de pain.

solder ['səʊldəʳ] <> *vt* souder.
<> *n* soudure *f*, métal *m* d'apport ■ **soft ~** soudure à l'étain, brasure *f* tendre.

soldering iron ['səʊldərɪŋ-] *n* fer *m* à souder.

soldier ['səʊldʒəʳ] <> *n* **1.** soldat *m*, militaire *m* ■ **to become a ~** se faire soldat, entrer dans l'armée ■ **to play (at) ~s** [children] jouer aux soldats *OR* à la guerre ; *pej* [country, adults] jouer à la guerre *OR* à la guéguerre ➤ **~ of fortune** soldat de fortune ■ **old ~** MIL vétéran *m* ■ **don't come** *inf OR* **play the old ~ with me** ne prenez pas de grands airs avec moi **2.** ENTOM soldat *m* **3.** [strip of bread] mouillette *f*.
<> *vi* être soldat, servir dans l'armée.
◆ **soldier on** *vi insep UK* continuer *OR* persévérer (malgré tout).

soldiering ['səʊldʒərɪŋ] *n* carrière *f OR* vie *f* (de) militaire ■ **after many years' ~** après avoir servi pendant de nombreuses années dans l'armée.

sole [səʊl] <> *adj* **1.** [only] seul, unique ■ **the ~ survivor** le seul survivant **2.** [exclusive] exclusif ■ **to have ~ rights on sthg** avoir l'exclusivité des droits sur qqch ■ **to have ~ responsibility for sthg** être entièrement responsable de qqch ➤ **~ agent** COMM concessionnaire *mf* ■ **~ legatee** LAW légataire *m* universel, légataire *f* universelle ■ **~ trader** *UK* COMM entreprise *f* individuelle *OR* unipersonnelle.
<> *n* **1.** [of foot] plante *f* **2.** [of shoe, sock] semelle *f* **3.** (*pl* sole *OR pl* soles) [fish] sole *f*.
<> *vt* ressemeler.

solecism ['sɒlɪsɪzm] *n* **1.** GRAM solécisme *m* **2.** *fml* [violation of good manners] manque *m* de savoir-vivre.

-soled [səʊld] *in cpds* à semelle de ▪ **rubber~ shoes** chaussures *fpl* à semelles de caoutchouc.

solely ['səʊllɪ] *adv* **1.** [only] seulement, uniquement **2.** [entirely] entièrement.

solemn ['sɒləm] *adj* **1.** [grave, serious] sérieux, grave, solennel ▪ [sombre] sobre **2.** [formal - agreement, promise] solennel **3.** [grand - occasion, music] solennel ▪ **~ mass** grand-messe *f*, messe *f* solennelle.

solemnity [sə'lemnətɪ] (*pl* **solemnities**) *n* **1.** [serious nature] sérieux *m*, gravité *f* **2.** [formality] solennité *f* ▪ **she was received with great ~** elle fut accueillie très solennellement **3.** *(usu pl) lit* [solemn event] solennité *f*.

solemnize, ise ['sɒləmnaɪz] *vt lit* [gen] solenniser *lit* ▪ [mariage] célébrer.

solemnly ['sɒləmlɪ] *adv* **1.** [seriously, gravely] gravement, solennellement ▪ **"it's time I left", he said ~** "il est temps que je parte", dit-il d'un ton grave ▪ **she ~ believes that what she did was right** elle croit fermement que ce qu'elle a fait était juste **2.** [formally] solennellement **3.** [grandly] solennellement, avec solennité.

sol-fa [,sɒl'fɑ:] *n* solfège *m*.

solicit [sə'lɪsɪt] <> *vt* **1.** [business, support, information] solliciter ▪ [opinion] demander **2.** [subj: prostitute] racoler.
<> *vi* [prostitute] racoler.

soliciting [sə'lɪsɪtɪŋ] *n* [by prostitute] racolage *m*.

solicitor [sə'lɪsɪtər] *n* **1.** *UK* LAW ≃ avocat *m*, - e *f*, ≃ conseil *m* juridique **2.** *US* ADMIN conseil *m* juridique d'une municipalité **3.** [person who solicits] solliciteur *m*, - euse *f* ▪ **'caution, unofficial ~s'** *US* attention aux démarcheurs non autorisés.

solicitor general (*pl* **solicitors general** *OR pl* **solicitor generals**) *n* **1.** [in UK] conseil *m* juridique de la Couronne **2.** [in US] représentant *m* du gouvernement *(auprès de la Cour suprême)*.

solicitous [sə'lɪsɪtəs] *adj* [showing consideration, concern] plein de sollicitude ▪ [eager, attentive] empressé ▪ [anxious] soucieux.

solicitude [sə'lɪsɪtju:d] *n* [consideration, concern] sollicitude *f* ▪ [eagerness, attentiveness] empressement *m* ▪ [anxiety] souci *m*, préoccupation *f*.

solid ['sɒlɪd] <> *adj* **1.** [not liquid or gas] solide ▪ **frozen ~** complètement gelé ▪ **she can't eat ~ food** elle ne peut pas absorber d'aliments solides
2. [of one substance] massif ▪ **her necklace is ~ gold** son collier est en or massif ▪ **~ oak furniture** meubles *mpl* en chêne massif ▪ **they dug until they reached ~ rock** ils ont creusé jusqu'à ce qu'ils atteignent la roche compacte ▪ **caves hollowed out of ~ rock** des grottes creusées à même la roche
3. [not hollow] plein ▪ **~ tyres** pneus pleins
4. [unbroken, continuous] continu ▪ **a ~ yellow line** une ligne jaune continue ▪ **I worked for eight ~ hours** *OR* **eight hours ~** j'ai travaillé sans arrêt pendant huit heures, j'ai travaillé huit heures d'affilée ▪ **we had two ~ weeks of rain** nous avons eu deux semaines de pluie ininterrompue ▪ **~ compound** GRAM composé *m* écrit en un seul mot
5. *US* [of one colour] uni
6. [dense, compact] dense, compact ▪ **the concert hall was packed ~** la salle de concert était bondée
7. [powerful - blow] puissant
8. [sturdy, sound - structure, understanding, relationship] solide ; [- evidence, argument] solide, irréfutable ; [- advice] valable, sûr ▪ **a man of ~ build** un homme bien charpenté ▪ **he's a good ~ worker** c'est un bon travailleur ◐ **to be on ~ ground** *liter* être sur la terre ferme ; *fig* être en terrain sûr
9. [respectable, worthy] respectable, honorable
10. POL [firm] massif ▪ [unanimous] unanime ▪ **we have the ~ support of the electorate** nous avons le soutien massif des électeurs ▪ **the strike was 100% ~** la grève était totale ▪ **the committee was ~ against the proposal** le comité a rejeté la proposition à l'unanimité
11. MATHS : **~ figure** solide *m*.
<> *n* GEOM & PHYS solide *m*.
◆ **solids** *npl* **1.** [solid food] aliments *mpl* solides ▪ **I can't eat ~s** je ne peux pas absorber d'aliments solides
2. CHEM particules *fpl* solides ▪ **milk ~s** extrait *m* du lait.

solidarity [,sɒlɪ'dærətɪ] <> *n* solidarité *f* ▪ **they went on strike in ~ with the miners** ils ont fait grève par solidarité avec les mineurs.
<> *comp* [strike] de solidarité.

solid fuel *n* combustible *m* solide.
◆ **solid-fuel** *adj* à combustible solide.

solid geometry *n* MATHS géométrie *f* des solides.

solidification [sə,lɪdɪfɪ'keɪʃn] *n* solidification *f*.

solidify [sə'lɪdɪfaɪ] (*pret & pp* **solidified**) <> *vi* **1.** [liquid, gas] se solidifier **2.** [system, opinion] se consolider.
<> *vt* **1.** [liquid, gas] solidifier **2.** [system, opinion] consolider.

solidity [sə'lɪdətɪ] *n* solidité *f*.

solidly ['sɒlɪdlɪ] *adv* **1.** [sturdily] solidement ▪ [person] : **to be ~ built** avoir une forte carrure **2.** [thoroughly] très, tout à fait ▪ **a ~ established reputation** une réputation solidement établie **3.** [massively] massivement, en masse **4.** [continuously] sans arrêt ▪ **I worked ~ for five hours** j'ai travaillé sans interruption pendant cinq heures.

solid-state *adj* **1.** PHYS des solides **2.** ELECTRON à semi-conducteurs.

soliloquize, ise [sə'lɪləkwaɪz] *vi* soliloquer, monologuer.

soliloquy [sə'lɪləkwɪ] (*pl* **soliloquies**) *n* soliloque *m*, monologue *m*.

solipsism ['sɒlɪpsɪzm] *n* solipsisme *m*.

solitaire [,sɒlɪ'teər] *n* **1.** [pegboard] solitaire *m* **2.** *US* [card game] réussite *f*, patience *f* **3.** [gem] solitaire *m*.

solitary ['sɒlɪtrɪ] (*pl* **solitaries**) <> *adj* **1.** [alone - person, life, activity] solitaire **2.** [single] seul, unique **3.** [remote - place] retiré, isolé **4.** [empty of people] vide, désert.
<> *n* **1.** *inf* = **solitary confinement 2.** [person] solitaire *mf*.

solitary confinement *n* isolement *m (d'un prisonnier)*.

solitude ['sɒlɪtju:d] *n* solitude *f* ▪ **to live in ~** vivre dans la solitude.

solo ['səʊləʊ] (*pl* **solos**) <> *n* **1.** MUS solo *m* ▪ **he played a violin/drum ~** il a joué un solo de violon/de batterie **2.** [flight] vol *m* solo **3.** = **solo whist**.
<> *adj* **1.** MUS solo ▪ **she plays ~ violin** elle est soliste de violon, elle est violon solo **2.** [gen] en solitaire ▪ **a ~ act** un one-man-show, un one-woman-show ▪ **the first ~ attempt on the north face** la première tentative d'escalade de la face nord en solitaire ▪ **her first ~ flight** son premier vol en solo.
<> *adv* **1.** MUS en solo ▪ **to play/to sing ~** jouer/chanter en solo **2.** [gen] seul, en solitaire, en solo ▪ **to fly ~** voler en solo.

soloist ['səʊləʊɪst] *n* soliste *mf*.

Solomon ['sɒləmən] *pr n* Salomon.

Solothurn ['sɒlə,θɜ:n] *pr n* Soleure ▪ **in ~** en Soleure.

solo whist *n* solo *m (variante du whist)*.

solstice ['sɒlstɪs] *n* solstice *m*.

solubility [,sɒlju'bɪlətɪ] *n* solubilité *f*.

soluble ['sɒljʊbl] *adj* **1.** [substance] soluble **2.** [problem] soluble.

solution [sə'lu:ʃn] *n* **1.** [answer - to problem, equation, mystery] solution *f* **2.** [act of solving - of problem, equation, mystery] résolution *f* ▪ **our main aim should be the rapid ~ of the problem** notre principal objectif devrait être de résoudre rapidement le problème **3.** CHEM & PHARM solution *f* ▪ **salt in ~** sel en solution.

solvable ['sɒlvəbl] *adj* soluble.

solve [sɒlv] *vt* [equation] résoudre ■ [problem] résoudre, trouver la solution de ■ [crime, mystery] élucider ■ **I couldn't ~ a single clue in the Times crossword** je n'ai pas réussi à trouver une seule définition dans les mots croisés du Times.

solvency ['sɒlvənsɪ] *n* solvabilité *f.*

solvent ['sɒlvənt] ◇ *adj* **1.** [financially] solvable **2.** [substance, liquid] dissolvant.
◇ *n* solvant *m*, dissolvant *m*.

solvent abuse *n fml* usage *m* de solvants hallucinogènes.

Solzhenitsyn [,sɒlʒə'nɪtsɪn] *pr n* Soljenitsyne.

Som. *written abbr of* **Somerset.**

Somali [sə'mɑ:lɪ] ◇ *n* **1.** [person] Somalien *m*, -enne *f* **2.** LING somali *m*.
◇ *adj* somalien.

Somalia [sə'mɑ:lɪə] *pr n* Somalie *f* ■ **in ~** en Somalie.

Somalian [sə'mɑ:lɪən] = **Somali.**

Somali Democratic Republic *pr n* : **the ~** la République démocratique de Somalie.

Somaliland [sə'mɑ:lɪlænd] *pr n* Somalie *f* ■ **British/Italian ~** Somalie britannique/italienne.

somatic [sə'mætɪk] *adj* somatique.

somber *US* = **sombre.**

sombre *UK*, **somber** *US* ['sɒmbəʳ] *adj* **1.** [dark - colour, place] sombre **2.** [grave, grim - outlook, person, day] sombre, morne ■ **a ~ episode in the history of Europe** un épisode sombre dans l'histoire de l'Europe.

sombrero [sɒm'breərəʊ] (*pl* **sombreros**) *n* sombrero *m*.

some [sʌm] ◇ *det* **1.** *(before uncountable nouns)* [a quantity of] : **don't forget to buy ~ cheese/beer/garlic** n'oublie pas d'acheter du fromage/de la bière/de l'ail ■ **let me give you ~ advice** laissez-moi vous donner un conseil ■ *(before plural nouns)* [a number of] des ■ **we've invited ~ friends round** nous avons invité des amis à la maison ■ **I met ~ old friends last night** j'ai rencontré de vieux amis hier soir
2. *(before uncountable nouns)* [not all] : **~ wine/software is very expensive** certains vins/logiciels coûtent très cher ■ **~ petrol still contains lead** il existe encore de l'essence avec plomb ■ *(before plural nouns)* certains *mpl*, certaines *f* ■ **~ cars shouldn't be allowed on the road** il y a des voitures qu'on ne devrait pas laisser circuler
3. *(before uncountable nouns)* [a fairly large amount of] un certain *m*, une certaine *f* ■ **I haven't been abroad for ~ time** ça fait un certain temps que je ne suis pas allé à l'étranger ■ **it happened (quite) ~ time ago** ça s'est passé il y a (bien) longtemps ■ **it's ~ distance from here** c'est assez loin d'ici ■ **the money should go ~ way towards compensating them** l'argent devrait les dédommager dans une certaine mesure ■ *(before plural nouns)* [a fairly large number of] certains *mpl*, certaines *f*, quelques *mf pl* ■ **it happened ~ years ago** ça s'est passé il y a quelques années
4. *(before uncountable nouns)* [a fairly small amount of] un peu de ■ **you must have ~ idea of how much it will cost** vous devez avoir une petite idée de combien ça va coûter ■ **I hope I've been of ~ help to you** j'espère que je vous ai un peu aidé ■ *(before plural nouns)* [a fairly small number of] : **I'm glad ~ people understand me!** je suis content qu'il y ait quand même des gens qui me comprennent!
5. [not known or specified] : **we must find ~ alternative** il faut que nous trouvions une autre solution ■ **he's gone to ~ town in the north** il est parti dans une ville quelque part dans le nord ■ **she works for ~ publishing company** elle travaille pour je ne sais quelle maison d'édition ■ **I'll get even with them ~ day!** je me vengerai d'eux un de ces jours OR un jour ou l'autre! ■ **come back ~ other time** revenez un autre jour
6. *inf* [expressing scorn] : **did you go to the party? – ~ party!** est-ce que tu es allé à la fête? – tu parles d'une fête! ■ **~ hope we've got of winning!** comme si on avait la moindre chance de gagner! ■ [expressing irritation, impatience] : **~ people!** il y a des gens, je vous assure!
7. *inf* [expressing admiration, approval] : **that was ~ party!** ça c'était une fête! ■ **he's ~ tennis player!** c'est un sacré tennisman!
◇ *pron* **1.** [an unspecified number or amount - as subject] quelques-uns *mpl*, quelques-unes *f*, certains *mpl*, certaines *f* ■ **~ say it wasn't an accident** certains disent OR il y a des gens qui disent que ce n'était pas un accident ■ [as object] en ■ **I've got too much cake, do you want ~?** j'ai trop de gâteau, en voulez-vous un peu? ■ **can I have ~ more?** est-ce que je peux en reprendre? ▶ **he wants the lot and then ~** il veut tout et puis le reste
2. [not all] : **~ of the snow had melted** une partie de la neige avait fondu ■ **I only believe ~ of what I read in the papers** je ne crois pas tout ce que je lis dans les journaux ■ **~ of the most beautiful scenery in the world is in Australia** quelques-uns des plus beaux paysages du monde se trouvent en Australie ■ **~ of us/them** certains d'entre nous/eux ■ **if you need pencils, take ~ of these/mine** si vous avez besoin de crayons à papier, prenez quelques-uns de ceux-ci/des miens.
◇ *adv* **1.** [approximately] quelque, environ ■ **it's ~ fifty kilometres from London** c'est à environ cinquante kilomètres OR c'est à une cinquantaine de kilomètres de Londres
2. *US inf* [a little] un peu ■ [a lot] beaucoup, pas mal.

somebody ['sʌmbədɪ] *pron* **1.** [an unspecified person] quelqu'un ■ **~ else** quelqu'un d'autre ■ **~ big/small** quelqu'un de grand/de petit ■ **there's ~ on the phone for you** on vous demande au téléphone ■ **~'s at the door, there's ~ at the door** on a frappé ■ **~ has left their/his/her umbrella behind** quelqu'un a oublié son parapluie ■ **~ or other** quelqu'un, je ne sais qui **2.** [an important person] : **you really think you're ~, don't you?** tu te crois vraiment quelqu'un, n'est-ce pas?

someday ['sʌmdeɪ] *adv* un jour (ou l'autre), un de ces jours.

somehow ['sʌmhaʊ] *adv* **1.** [in some way or another] d'une manière ou d'une autre, d'une façon ou d'une autre ■ **she'd ~ (or other) managed to lock herself in** elle avait trouvé moyen de s'enfermer **2.** [for some reason] pour une raison ou pour une autre, je ne sais pas trop pourquoi ■ **it ~ doesn't look right** je ne sais pas pourquoi mais il me semble qu'il y a quelque chose qui ne va pas.

someone ['sʌmwʌn] = **somebody.**

someplace ['sʌmpleɪs] *US* = **somewhere** *(sense 1).*

somersault ['sʌməsɔ:lt] ◇ *n* [roll] culbute *f* ■ [by car] tonneau *m* ■ [acrobatic feat - in air] saut *m* périlleux ■ **to do** OR **to turn ~s** faire des culbutes.
◇ *vi* faire la culbute OR un saut périlleux OR des sauts périlleux ■ [car] faire un tonneau OR des tonneaux.

Somerset House ['sʌməset-] *pr n édifice sur le Strand à Londres.*

SOMERSET HOUSE

Cet édifice du XVIIIe siècle abritait autrefois les services de l'état civil, des impôts et d'autres administrations.

something ['sʌmθɪŋ] ◇ *pron* **1.** [an unspecified object, event, action etc] quelque chose ■ **I've got ~ in my eye** j'ai quelque chose dans l'œil ■ **I've thought of ~** j'ai eu une idée ■ **~ else** quelque chose d'autre, autre chose ■ **~ or other** quelque chose ■ **~ big/small** quelque chose de grand/de petit ■ **I've done/said ~ stupid** j'ai fait/dit une bêtise ■ **I've got a feeling there's ~ wrong** j'ai le sentiment que quelque chose ne va pas ■ **take ~ to read on the train** prenez quelque chose à lire OR prenez de quoi lire dans le train ■ **he gave them ~ to eat/drink** il leur a donné à manger/boire ■ **a film with ~ for everybody** un film qui peut plaire à tout le monde ■ **they all want ~ for nothing** ils veulent tous avoir tout pour rien ■ **you can't get ~ for nothing** on n'a rien pour rien ■ **there's ~ about him/in the way he talks that reminds me of Gary** il y a quelque chose chez lui/dans sa façon de parler qui me rappelle Gary ■ **there must be ~ in** OR **to all these rumours** il doit y avoir quelque chose de vrai dans toutes ces rumeurs ■ **she's ~ in the City/in insurance** elle travaille dans la finance/dans les assurances ▶ **would you like a little ~ to drink?** voulez-vous un petit quelque chose à boire? ■ **she slipped the head waiter a little ~** elle a glissé un petit pourboire au maître d'hôtel ■ **he's got a certain ~** il a un petit quelque chose ■ **I'm sure she's got ~ going with him** *inf* je suis sûr qu'il y a quelque chose en-

tre elle et lui ■ **I think you've got ~ there!** je crois que vous avez un début d'idée, là! ■ **at least they've replied to my letter, that's ~** au moins, ils ont répondu à ma lettre, c'est mieux que rien *OR* c'est toujours ça ■ **wow, that's ~ else!** *inf* ça, c'est génial! ■ **well, isn't that ~?** *inf* et bien, ça alors! ■ **it was really ~ to see those kids dancing!** c'était quelque chose de voir ces gosses danser! ■ **the new model is really ~** *inf* le nouveau modèle est sensationnel
2. *inf* [in approximations] : **the battle took place in 1840 ~** la bataille a eu lieu dans les années 1840 ■ **he's forty ~** il a dans les quarante ans ■ **it cost £7 ~** ça a coûté 7 livres et quelques ■ [replacing forgotten word, name etc] : **her friend, Maisie ~ (or other)** son amie, Maisie quelque chose
3. *phr* **~ of : he's ~ of an expert in the field** c'est en quelque sorte un expert dans ce domaine ■ **she became ~ of a legend** elle est devenue une sorte de légende ■ **how they do it remains ~ of a mystery** comment ils s'y prennent, ça c'est un mystère ■ **to be** *OR* **have ~ to do with** avoir un rapport avec ■ **I don't know what it means, I think it's got ~ to do with nuclear physics** je ne sais pas ce que ça veut dire, je crois que ça a (quelque chose) à voir avec la physique nucléaire ■ **I'm sure the weather has ~ to do with it** je suis sûre que le temps y est pour quelque chose *OR* que ça a un rapport avec le temps.
◇ *adv* **1.** [a little] un peu ■ [somewhere] : **~ in the region of $10,000** quelque chose comme 10 000 dollars ■ **an increase of ~ between 10 and 15 per cent** une augmentation de 10 à 15 pour cent
2. *inf* [as intensifier] vraiment, vachement ■ **it hurts ~ awful** ça fait vachement mal.
◆ **or something** *adv phr inf* **would you like a cup of tea or ~?** veux-tu une tasse de thé, ou autre chose? ■ **she must be ill or ~** elle doit être malade ou quelque chose dans ce genre-là ■ **are you deaf or ~?** tu es sourd ou quoi?
◆ **something like** *prep phr* **1.** [rather similar to] : **it looks ~ like a grapefruit** ça ressemble un peu à un pamplemousse ▶ **now that's ~ like it!** c'est déjà mieux!
2. [roughly] environ ■ **it costs ~ like £500** ça coûte quelque chose comme *OR* dans les 500 livres.

sometime ['sʌmtaɪm] ◇ *adv* **1.** [in future] un jour (ou l'autre), un de ces jours ■ **you must come and see us ~** il faut que vous veniez nous voir un de ces jours ■ **I hope we'll meet again ~ soon** j'espère que nous nous reverrons bientôt ■ **you'll have to face up to it ~ or other** un jour ou l'autre il faudra bien voir les choses en face ■ **her baby is due ~ in May** elle attend son bébé pour le mois de mai ■ **~ after/before next April** après le mois/d'ici au mois d'avril ■ **~ next year** dans le courant de l'année prochaine **2.** [in past] : **she phoned ~ last week** elle a téléphoné (dans le courant de) la semaine dernière ■ **it happened ~ before/after the Second World War** ça s'est passé avant/après la Seconde Guerre mondiale ■ **~ around 1920** vers 1920.
◇ *adj* **1.** [former] ancien ■ **Mrs Evans, the club's ~ president** l'ancienne présidente du club, Mme Evans **2.** *US* [occasional] intermittent.

sometimes ['sʌmtaɪmz] *adv* quelquefois, parfois ■ **I ~ think that it's a waste of time** parfois je me dis que c'est une perte de temps ■ **~ (they're) friendly, ~ they're not** tantôt ils sont aimables, tantôt (ils ne le sont) pas.

someway ['sʌmweɪ] *US inf* = **somehow** *(sense 1).*

somewhat ['sʌmwɒt] *adv* quelque peu, un peu ■ **everybody came, ~ to my surprise** tout le monde est venu, ce qui n'a pas été sans me surprendre ▶ **I was in ~ of a hurry to get home** j'étais quelque peu pressé de rentrer chez moi ■ **it was ~ of a failure** c'était plutôt un échec.

somewhere ['sʌmweəʳ] *adv* **1.** [indicating an unspecified place] quelque part ■ **she's ~ around** elle est quelque part par là, elle n'est pas loin ■ **let's go ~ else** allons ailleurs *OR* autre part ■ **but it's got to be ~ or other!** mais il doit bien être quelque part! ■ **I'm looking for ~ to stay** je cherche un endroit où loger ■ **she's found ~ more comfortable to sit** elle a trouvé un siège plus confortable ▶ **now we're getting ~!** nous arrivons enfin à quelque chose! **2.** [approximately] environ ■ **she earns ~ around $2,000 a month** elle gagne quelque chose comme 2 000 dollars par mois ■ **~ between five and six hundred people were there** il y avait entre cinq et six cents personnes ■ **he must be ~ in his forties** il doit avoir entre 40 et 50 ans.

somnambulism [sɒm'næmbjʊlɪzm] *n* somnambulisme *m.*

somnambulist [sɒm'næmbjʊlɪst] *n* somnambule *mf.*

somnolence ['sɒmnələns] *n* somnolence *f.*

somnolent ['sɒmnələnt] *adj* somnolent.

son [sʌn] *n* **1.** fils *m* ■ **she's got two ~s** elle a deux fils *OR* garçons ■ **the ~s of Ireland** *fig* les fils de l'Irlande ▶ **~ and heir** héritier *m* **2.** *inf* [term of address] fiston *m.*
◆ **Son** *n* RELIG Fils *m* ■ **the Son of God** le Fils de Dieu ■ **the Son of Man** le Fils de l'Homme.

sonar ['səʊnɑːʳ] *n* sonar *m.*

sonata [sə'nɑːtə] *n* sonate *f* ■ **piano/violin ~** sonate pour piano/violon.

sonde [sɒnd] *n* ASTRONAUT & METEOR sonde *f.*

song [sɒŋ] *n* **1.** chanson *f* ▶ **a ~ and dance act** un numéro de comédie musicale ■ **the Song of Songs, the Song of Solomon** BIBLE le Cantique des cantiques ■ **it was going for a ~** ça se vendait pour une bouchée de pain *OR* trois fois rien ■ **to make a ~ and dance about sthg** *UK inf* faire toute une histoire pour qqch ■ **she gave me that old ~ and dance about being broke** *inf* elle m'a ressorti son couplet habituel, comme quoi elle était fauchée ■ **to be on ~** *UK inf* être en super forme **2.** [songs collectively, act of singing] chanson *f* ■ **an anthology of British ~** une anthologie de la chanson britannique ■ **they all burst into ~** ils se sont tous mis à chanter **3.** [of birds, insects] chant *m.*

songbird ['sɒŋbɜːd] *n* oiseau *m* chanteur.

songster ['sɒŋstəʳ] *n* **1.** [person] chanteur *m*, - euse *f* **2.** *lit* [bird] oiseau *m* chanteur.

song thrush *n* grive *f* musicienne.

songwriter ['sɒŋ,raɪtəʳ] *n* [of lyrics] parolier *m*, - ère *f* ■ [of music] compositeur *m*, - trice *f* ■ [of lyrics and music] auteur-compositeur *m.*

sonic ['sɒnɪk] *adj* **1.** [involving, producing sound] acoustique **2.** [concerning speed of sound] sonique.

sonic barrier = **sound barrier**.

sonic boom *n* bang *m.*

son-in-law (*pl* **sons-in-law**) *n* gendre *m*, beau-fils *m.*

sonnet ['sɒnɪt] *n* sonnet *m.*

sonny ['sʌnɪ] *n inf* fiston *m.*

son-of-a-bitch△ (*pl* **sons-of-bitches**) *n US* salaud△ *m*, fils *m* de pute△.

son-of-a-gun (*pl* **sons-of-guns**) *n US inf* **you old ~!** sacré bonhomme!

sonority [sə'nɒrətɪ] *n* sonorité *f.*

sonorous ['sɒnərəs] *adj* **1.** [resonant] sonore **2.** [grandiloquent] grandiloquent.

soon [suːn] *adv* **1.** [in a short time] bientôt, sous peu ■ **(I'll) see you** *OR* **speak to you ~!** à bientôt! ■ **write ~!** écris-moi vite! ■ **I'll be back ~** je serai vite de retour ■ **a burglar can ~ open a lock like that** un cambrioleur a vite fait d'ouvrir une serrure comme celle-ci ■ **she phoned ~ after you'd left** elle a téléphoné peu après ton départ **2.** [early] tôt ■ **it's too ~ to make any predictions** il est trop tôt pour se prononcer ■ **how ~ can you finish it?** pour quand pouvez-vous le terminer? ■ **the police have arrived, and not a moment too ~** les policiers sont arrivés, et ce n'est pas trop tôt.
◆ **as soon as** *conj phr* dès que, aussitôt que ■ **as ~ as possible** dès *OR* aussitôt que possible ■ **phone me as ~ as you hear anything** téléphonez-moi dès que vous aurez des nouvelles ■ **he came as ~ as he could** il est venu dès *OR* aussitôt qu'il a pu.
◆ **(just) as soon** *adv phr* : **I'd (just) as ~ go by boat as by plane** j'aimerais autant *OR* mieux y aller en bateau qu'en avion

■ **I'd just as ~ he came tomorrow** j'aimerais autant *OR* mieux qu'il vienne demain ■ **I'd as ~ die as do that!** plutôt mourir que de faire ça!

sooner ['su:nəʳ] <> *adv (compar of soon)* **1.** [earlier] plus tôt ■ **the ~ the better** le plus tôt sera le mieux ■ **the ~ it's over the ~ we can leave** plus tôt ce sera fini, plus tôt nous pourrons partir ■ **no ~ said than done!** aussitôt dit, aussitôt fait! ■ **no ~ had I sat down than the phone rang again** je venais juste de m'asseoir quand le téléphone a de nouveau sonné ■ **it was bound to happen ~ or later** cela devait arriver tôt ou tard **2.** [indicating preference] : **would you ~ I called back tomorrow?** préférez-vous que je rappelle demain? ■ **shall we go out tonight? – I'd ~ not** si on sortait ce soir? – j'aimerais mieux pas ■ **I'd ~ die than go through that again!** plutôt mourir que de revivre ça!
<> *n* **US** [pioneer] pionnier *m*, - ère *f* du Far West *(se dit surtout de ceux qui s'installaient sans posséder de titre légal de propriété)* ■ **the Sooner State** l'Oklahoma *m*.

soot [sʊt] *n* suie *f*.
◆ **soot up** *vt sep* [dirty] couvrir *OR* recouvrir de suie ■ [clog] encrasser.

sooth [su:θ] *n arch* **in ~** en vérité.

soothe [su:ð] *vt* **1.** [calm, placate] calmer, apaiser **2.** [relieve - pain] calmer, soulager ■ **this will ~ your sore throat** ça va soulager votre mal de gorge.

soothing ['su:ðɪŋ] *adj* **1.** [music, words, voice] apaisant ■ [atmosphere, presence] rassurant ■ **the music had a ~ effect on them** la musique les a calmés ■ **the chairman made the usual ~ noises** *inf* le président a fait son laïus habituel pour calmer les esprits **2.** [lotion, ointment] apaisant, calmant.

soothsayer ['su:θ,seɪəʳ] *n* devin *m*, devineresse *f*.

sooty ['sʊtɪ] (*comp* **sootier**, *superl* **sootiest**) *adj* **1.** [dirty] couvert de suie, noir de suie **2.** [dark] noir comme de la suie.

sop [sɒp] *n* [concession] : **they threw in the measure as a ~ to the ecologists** ils ont ajouté cette mesure pour amadouer les écologistes ■ **she said it as a ~ to their pride/feelings** elle l'a dit pour flatter leur amour-propre/pour ménager leur sensibilité.

sophist ['sɒfɪst] *n* [false reasoner] sophiste *mf*.
◆ **Sophist** *n* PHILOS sophiste *m*.

sophisticate [sə'fɪstɪkeɪt] *n* personne *f* raffinée.

sophisticated [sə'fɪstɪkeɪtɪd] *adj* **1.** [person, manner, tastes - refined] raffiné ; [- chic] chic, élégant ; [- well-informed] bien informé ; [- mature] mûr ■ **the electorate has become too ~ to believe that promise** l'électorat est désormais trop bien informé *OR* trop averti pour croire à cette promesse **2.** [argument, novel, film - subtle] subtil ; [- complicated] complexe **3.** [machine, system, technology - advanced] sophistiqué, perfectionné.

sophistication [sə,fɪstɪ'keɪʃn] *n* **1.** [of person, manners, tastes - refinement] raffinement *m* ; [- chic] chic *m*, élégance *f* ; [- maturity] maturité *f* **2.** [of argument, novel, film - subtlety] subtilité *f* ; [- complexity] complexité *f* **3.** [of system, technology] sophistication *f*, perfectionnement *m*.

sophistry ['sɒfɪstrɪ] (*pl* **sophistries**) *n* **1.** [argumentation] sophistique *f* **2.** [argument] sophisme *m*.

Sophocles ['sɒfəkli:z] *pr n* Sophocle.

sophomore ['sɒfəmɔ:ʳ] *n* **US** étudiant *m*, - e *f* de seconde année.

soporific [,sɒpə'rɪfɪk] <> *adj* soporifique.
<> *n* soporifique *m*, somnifère *m*.

sopping ['sɒpɪŋ] *adj* & *adv* *inf* ~ **(wet)** [person] trempé (jusqu'aux os) ; [shirt, cloth] détrempé.

soppy ['sɒpɪ] (*comp* **soppier**, *superl* **soppiest**) *adj* **UK** *inf* **1.** [sentimental - person] sentimental, fleur bleue *(inv)* ; [- story, picture] sentimental, à l'eau de rose **2.** [silly] bébête **3.** [in love] : **to be ~ about sb** avoir le béguin pour qqn.

soprano [sə'prɑ:nəʊ] (*pl* **sopranos** *OR* *pl* **soprani** [-ni:]) <> *n* [singer] soprano *mf* ■ [voice, part, instrument] soprano *m* ■ **to sing ~** avoir une voix de soprano.
<> *adj* [voice, part] de soprano ■ [music] pour soprano ■ **~ saxophone** saxophone *m* soprano.

sorbet ['sɔ:beɪ] *n* **1.** **UK** sorbet *m* **2.** **US** *pulpe de fruit glacée.*

sorbic acid ['sɔ:bɪk-] *n* acide *m* sorbique.

sorcerer ['sɔ:sərəʳ] *n* sorcier *m* ■ **'The Sorcerer's Apprentice'** *Dukas* 'l'Apprenti sorcier'.

sorceress ['sɔ:sərɪs] *n* sorcière *f*.

sorcery ['sɔ:sərɪ] *n* sorcellerie *f*.

sordid ['sɔ:dɪd] *adj* **1.** [dirty, wretched] sordide, misérable **2.** [base, loathsome] sordide, infâme, vil ■ **a ~ affair** une affaire sordide ■ **I'll spare you the ~ details** je vous épargnerai les détails sordides.

sore [sɔ:ʳ] <> *adj* **1.** [aching] douloureux ■ **I'm ~ all over** j'ai mal partout ■ **I've a ~ throat** j'ai mal à la gorge ■ **my arms/legs are ~** j'ai mal aux bras/jambes, mes bras/jambes me font mal ■ **where is it ~?** où as-tu mal? ■ **it's a ~ point with her** *fig* elle est très sensible sur ce point *OR* là-dessus **2.** **US** *inf* [angry] en boule ■ **are you still ~ at me?** est-ce que tu es toujours en boule contre moi? ■ [resentful] vexé, amer **3.** *lit* [great] grand ■ **to be in ~ need of sthg** avoir grand besoin de qqch.
<> *n* plaie *f* ■ **open ~s** des plaies ouvertes.
<> *adv arch* grandement.

sorely ['sɔ:lɪ] *adv* **1.** [as intensifier] grandement ■ **the house is ~ in need of a new coat of paint** la maison a grandement *OR* bien besoin d'être repeinte ■ **she will be ~ missed** elle nous manquera cruellement ■ **I was ~ tempted to accept her offer** j'ai été très tenté d'accepter sa proposition **2.** *lit* [painfully] : **~ wounded** grièvement blessé.

sorghum ['sɔ:gəm] *n* sorgho *m*.

sorority [sə'rɒrətɪ] (*pl* **sororities**) *n* **US** UNIV *association d'étudiantes très sélective.*

sorrel ['sɒrəl] <> *n* **1.** BOT & CULIN oseille *f* **2.** [colour] roux *m*, brun rouge *m* **3.** [horse] alezan *m* clair.
<> *adj* [gen] roux ■ [horse] alezan clair *(inv)*.

sorrow ['sɒrəʊ] <> *n* chagrin *m*, peine *f*, tristesse *f* ■ [stronger] affliction *f*, douleur *f* ■ **I am writing to express my ~ at your sad loss** je vous écris pour vous faire part de la tristesse que j'ai éprouvée en apprenant votre deuil ■ **to our great ~** à notre grand regret ■ **more in ~ than in anger** avec plus de tristesse que de colère ■ **his son's failure was a great ~ to him** l'échec de son fils lui a fait *OR* causé beaucoup de peine.
<> *vi lit* éprouver du chagrin *OR* de la peine.

sorrowful ['sɒrəʊfʊl] *adj* [person] triste ■ [look, smile] affligé.

sorrowfully ['sɒrəʊflɪ] *adv* tristement.

sorrowing ['sɒrəʊɪŋ] *adj* attristé, affligé.

sorry ['sɒrɪ] (*comp* **sorrier**, *superl* **sorriest**) *adj* **1.** [in apologies] désolé ■ **I'm ~ we won't be able to fetch you** je regrette que *OR* je suis désolé que nous ne puissions venir vous chercher ■ **(I'm) ~ to have bothered you** (je suis) désolé de vous avoir dérangé ■ **I'm ~ to say there's little we can do** malheureusement, nous ne pouvons pas faire grand-chose ■ **I'm so** *OR* **very** *OR* **terribly ~** je suis vraiment navré ■ **ouch, that's my foot! – (I'm) ~!** aïe! mon pied! – je suis désolé *OR* excusez-moi! ■ **(I'm) ~ about the mess** excusez le désordre ■ **I'm ~ about the mix-up** excusez-moi pour la confusion ■ **~ about forgetting your birthday** désolé d'avoir oublié ton anniversaire ■ **he said he was ~** il a présenté ses excuses ■ **say (you're) ~ to the lady** demande pardon à la dame ■ **what's the time? – ~?** quelle heure est-il? – pardon? *OR* comment? ■ **they're coming on Tuesday, ~, Thursday** ils viennent mardi, pardon, jeudi
2. [regretful] : **I'm ~ I ever came here!** je regrette d'être venu ici! ■ **you'll be ~ for this** tu le regretteras
3. [expressing sympathy] désolé, navré, peiné ■ **I was ~ to hear about your father's death** j'ai été désolé *OR* peiné *OR* navré d'apprendre la mort de votre père
4. [pity] : **to be** *OR* **to feel ~ for sb** plaindre qqn ■ **there's no need to feel ~ for them** ils ne sont pas à plaindre ■ **she felt ~ for him**

and gave him a pound elle eut pitié de lui et lui donna une livre ■ **to be** *OR* **to feel ~ for o.s.** s'apitoyer sur soi-même *OR* sur son propre sort ■ **he's just feeling a bit ~ for himself** il est juste un peu déprimé
5. [pitiable, wretched] triste, piteux ■ **to cut a ~ figure** faire triste *OR* piètre figure ■ **they were a ~ sight after the match** ils étaient dans un triste état après le match ■ **the garden was in a ~ state** le jardin était en piteux état *OR* dans un triste état ■ **it's a ~ state of affairs** c'est bien triste.

sort [sɔ:t] <> *n* **1.** [kind, type] sorte *f*, espèce *f*, genre *m* ■ [brand] marque *f* ■ **it's a strange ~ of film** c'est un drôle de film ■ **it's a different ~ of problem** c'est un autre type de problème ■ **I've got a ~ of feeling about what the result will be** j'ai comme un pressentiment sur ce que sera le résultat ■ **I think that he's some ~ of specialist** *OR* **that he's a specialist of some ~** je crois que c'est un genre de spécialiste ■ **she's not the ~ (of woman) to let you down** elle n'est pas du genre à vous laisser tomber ■ **I love these** *inf OR* **this ~ of biscuits** j'adore ces biscuits-là ■ **there's too much of this ~ of thing going on** il se passe trop de choses de ce genre ■ **they're not our ~ (of people)** nous ne sommes pas du même monde ■ **I know your ~!** les gens de ton espèce, je les connais! ■ **what ~ of fish are we having?** qu'est-ce qu'on mange comme poisson? ■ **what ~ of dog is that?** qu'est-ce que c'est comme chien *OR* comme race de chien? ■ **what ~ of woman is she?** quel genre de femme est-ce? ■ **what ~ of way is that to speak to your grandmother?** en voilà une façon de parler à ta grand-mère! ■ **good luck, and all that ~ of thing!** bonne chance, et tout et tout! ■ **I've heard all ~s of good things about you** j'ai entendu dire beaucoup de bien de vous ➊ **I said nothing of the ~!** je n'ai rien dit de pareil *OR* de tel! ■ **you were drunk last night – I was nothing of the ~!** tu étais ivre hier soir – absolument pas! *OR* mais pas du tout! ■ **I feel out of ~s** je ne suis pas dans mon assiette ■ **it takes all ~s (to make a world)** *prov* il faut de tout pour faire un monde *prov*
2. *inf* [person] : **she's a good ~** [young woman] c'est une brave fille ; [older woman] c'est une brave femme
3. [gen - COMPUT] [- act of sorting] tri *m* ■ **I've had a ~ through all the winter clothes** *inf* j'ai trié tous les vêtements d'hiver ➊ **~ routine** routine *f* de tri.
<> *vt* **1.** [classify] classer, trier ■ [divide up] répartir ■ [separate] séparer ■ COMPUT trier ■ **to ~ mail** trier le courrier ■ **I've ~ed the index cards into alphabetical order** j'ai classé *OR* trié les fiches par ordre alphabétique ■ **~ the cards into two piles** répartissez les cartes en deux piles ■ **~ the letters into urgent and less urgent** répartissez les lettres entre celles qui sont urgentes et celles qui le sont moins
2. [organize] = **sort out** *(sense 2)*.
◆ **of a sort, of sorts** *adj phr* : **they served us champagne of a ~** *OR* **of ~s** ils nous ont servi une espèce de champagne.
◆ **sort of** *adv phr* : **I'm ~ of glad that I missed them** je suis plutôt content de les avoir ratés ■ **it's ~ of big and round** c'est du genre grand et rond ■ **did you hit him? – well, ~ of** tu l'as frappé? – en quelque sorte, oui.
◆ **sort out** *vt sep* **1.** [classify] = **sort** *(vt sense 1)*
2. [select and set aside] trier
3. [tidy up - papers, clothes, room, cupboard] ranger ■ [put in order - finances, ideas] mettre en ordre ■ **she needs to get her personal life ~ed out** il faut qu'elle règle ses problèmes personnels
4. [settle, resolve - problem, dispute] régler, résoudre ■ **everything's ~ed out now** tout est arrangé maintenant ■ **once the initial confusion had ~ed itself out** une fois que la confusion du début se fut dissipée ■ **things will ~ themselves out in the end** les choses finiront par s'arranger
5. [work out] : **have you ~ed out how to do it?** est-ce que tu as trouvé le moyen de le faire? ■ **I'm trying to ~ out what's been going on** j'essaie de savoir *OR* de comprendre ce qui s'est passé ▮ [arrange] arranger, fixer ■ **we still have to ~ out a date for the next meeting** il nous faut encore arranger *OR* choisir une date pour la prochaine réunion
6. *UK inf* [solve the problems of - person] : **he's very depressed, you should try to ~ him out** il est très déprimé, tu devrais essayer de l'aider à s'en sortir ■ **she needs time to ~ herself out** il lui faut du temps pour régler ses problèmes
7. *UK inf* [punish] régler son compte à.
◆ **sort through** *vt insep* trier.

sorta ['sɔ:tə] *inf* = **sort of**.

sort code *n* BANK code *m* guichet.

sorter ['sɔ:tər] *n* **1.** [person] trieur *m*, - euse *f* ■ **letter ~** employé *m*, - e *f* au tri postal **2.** [machine - gen] trieur *m* ; [- for punched cards] trieuse *f*.

sortie ['sɔ:ti:] *n* MIL sortie *f*.

sorting ['sɔ:tɪŋ] *n* tri *m*.

sorting office *n* centre *m* de tri.

sort-out *n UK inf* [tidying] rangement *m*.

SOS (*abbrev of* **save our souls**) *n* SOS *m* ■ **to send out an ~** lancer un SOS.

so-so *adj inf* pas fameux ■ [in health] comme ci comme ça, couci-couça.

sot [sɒt] *n lit* ivrogne *m*, - esse *f*.

sottish ['sɒtɪʃ] *adj lit* sot, sotte *f*, stupide, abruti.

soufflé ['su:fleɪ] *n* soufflé *m* ■ **cheese/chocolate ~** soufflé au fromage/au chocolat ■ **~ dish** moule *m* à soufflé.

sough [saʊ] *lit* <> *vi* murmurer, susurrer.
<> *n* murmure *m*, susurrement *m (du vent)*.

sought [sɔ:t] *pt* & *pp* ▻ **seek**.

sought-after *adj* recherché.

soul [səʊl] *n* **1.** RELIG âme *f* ■ **God rest his ~!** que Dieu ait son âme! ■ **All Soul's Day** le jour des Morts, la Toussaint ■ **you've got no ~!** tu n'as pas de cœur! ▮ [emotional depth] profondeur *f* **2.** [leading figure] âme *f* **3.** [perfect example] modèle *m* ■ **the ~ of discretion** la discrétion même *OR* personnifiée **4.** [person] personne *f*, âme *f* ■ **poor old ~!** le pauvre!, la pauvre! ■ **there wasn't a ~ in the streets** il n'y avait pas âme qui vive dans les rues ■ **I won't tell a ~** je ne le dirai à personne ▮ *lit* **the ship went down with all ~s** le navire a sombré corps et biens **5.** [music] (musique *f*) soul *f*, soul music *f*.

soul-destroying [-dɪ,strɔɪɪŋ] *adj* [job] abrutissant ■ [situation, place] déprimant.

soul food *n inf* cuisine *f* afroaméricaine.

soulful ['səʊlfʊl] *adj* [song, performance, sigh] émouvant, attendrissant ■ [look, eyes] expressif.

soul mate *n* âme *f* sœur.

soul music *n* musique *f* soul, soul music *f*.

soul-searching *n* introspection *f* ■ **after much ~ she decided to leave** après mûre réflexion *OR* après avoir mûrement réfléchi, elle décida de partir.

soul-stirring *adj* (profondément) émouvant.

sound [saʊnd] <> *n* **1.** [noise - of footsteps, thunder, conversation] bruit *m* ; [- of voice, musical instrument] son *m* ■ **I was woken by the ~ of voices/laughter** j'ai été réveillé par un bruit de voix/par des éclats de rires ■ **don't make a ~!** surtout ne faites pas de bruit! ➊ **'The Sound of Music'** ***Wise*** 'la Mélodie du bonheur'
2. PHYS son *m* ■ **the speed of ~** la vitesse du son
3. LING son *m* ■ **the English vowel ~s** les sons vocaliques de l'anglais
4. RADIO & TV son *m* ■ **to turn the ~ up/down** monter/baisser le son *OR* volume
5. [type of music] style *m* de musique, musique *f* ■ **a brand new ~ has hit the charts** un son complètement nouveau a fait son entrée au hit-parade
6. [impression, idea] : **I don't like the ~ of these new measures** ces nouvelles mesures ne me disent rien qui vaille ■ **it's pretty easy by the ~ of it** ça a l'air assez facile
7. [earshot] : **within the ~ of the church bells** à portée du son des cloches de l'église
8. MED [probe] sonde *f*
9. NAUT [sounding line] (ligne *f* de) sonde *f*
10. GEOG [channel] détroit *m*, bras *m* de mer
11. ZOOL [air bladder] vessie *f* natatoire.
<> *comp* [level, recording] sonore ■ [broadcasting] radiophonique ■ LING [change] phonologique ■ **~ crew** équipe *f* du son.
<> *adj* **1.** [structure, building, wall - sturdy] solide ; [- in good condition] en bon état, sain

2. [healthy - person] en bonne santé ; [- body, mind, limbs] sain ■ **to be of ~ mind** être sain d'esprit ➋ **to be as ~ as a bell** être en parfaite santé
3. [sensible, well-founded - advice, idea, strategy] sensé, judicieux ; [- argument, claim] valable, fondé, solide ■ **to show ~ judgment** faire preuve de jugement
4. [reliable, solid] solide, compétent ■ **we need somebody with a ~ grasp of the subject** il nous faut quelqu'un ayant de solides connaissances en la matière ■ **Crawford seems a ~ enough chap** Crawford semble être quelqu'un en qui on peut avoir confiance ■ **is she politically ~?** ses convictions politiques sont-elles solides?
5. [safe - investment] sûr ; [- company, business] solide
6. [severe - defeat] total ; [- hiding] bon
7. [deep - sleep] profond ■ **I'm a very ~ sleeper** j'ai le sommeil profond.
◇ *adv* : **to be ~ asleep** dormir profondément OR à poings fermés.
◇ *vi* **1.** [make a sound] sonner, résonner, retentir ■ **it ~s hollow if you tap it** ça sonne creux lorsqu'on tape dessus ■ **their voices ~ed very loud in the empty house** leurs voix résonnaient bruyamment dans la maison vide ■ **sirens ~ed in the streets** des sirènes retentissaient dans les rues ■ **if the alarm ~s, run** si vous entendez l'alarme, enfuyez-vous
2. *UK* [be pronounced] se prononcer ■ **in English words are rarely spelt as they ~** en anglais, les mots s'écrivent rarement comme ils se prononcent
3. [seem] sembler, paraître ■ **it doesn't ~ very interesting to me** ça ne m'a pas l'air très intéressant ■ **(that) ~s like a good idea** ça semble être une bonne idée ■ **two weeks in Crete, that ~s nice!** deux semaines en Crète, pas mal du tout! ■ **the name ~ed French** le nom avait l'air d'être OR sonnait français ■ **you ~ as though** OR **as if** OR **like you've got a cold** on dirait que tu es enrhumé ■ **it ~s to me as though they don't want to do it** j'ai l'impression qu'ils ne veulent pas le faire ■ **it doesn't ~ to me as though they want to do it** je n'ai pas l'impression qu'ils veuillent le faire ■ **you ~ just like your brother on the phone** tu as la même voix que ton frère OR on dirait vraiment ton frère au téléphone ■ **it's an instrument which ~s rather like a flute** c'est un instrument dont le son ressemble assez à OR est assez proche de la flûte ■ **that ~s like the postman now** je crois entendre le facteur.
◇ *vt* **1.** [bell, alarm] sonner ■ [wind instrument] sonner de ■ **to ~ the horn** klaxonner ■ **the bugler ~ed the reveille** le clairon sonna le réveil ■ **to ~ a warning** lancer un avertissement
2. [pronounce] prononcer ■ **the "p" isn't ~ed** le "p" ne se prononce pas
3. MED [chest, lungs] ausculter ■ [cavity, passage] sonder
4. NAUT sonder
5. [person] sonder ■ **I'll try to ~ their feelings on the matter** j'essaierai de connaître leur sentiment à cet égard.
◆ **sound off** *vi insep inf* **1.** [declare one's opinions] crier son opinion sur tous les toits ■ [complain] râler ■ **he's always ~ing off about the management** il est toujours à râler contre la direction ■ **to ~ off at sb** [angrily] passer un savon à△ qqn
2. [boast] se vanter.
◆ **sound out** *vt sep fig* [person] sonder.

sound archives *npl* phonothèque *f* ■ **a recording from the BBC ~** un enregistrement qui vient des archives de la BBC.

sound barrier *n* mur *m* du son ■ **to break the ~** franchir le mur du son.

soundbite ['saʊndbaɪt] *n* petite phrase *f (prononcée par un homme politique à la radio ou à la télévision pour frapper les esprits).*

soundboard ['saʊndbɔ:d] *n* **1.** [over pulpit, rostrum] abat-voix *m inv* **2.** MUS table *f* d'harmonie.

sound card *n* COMPUT carte *f* son.

sound effects *npl* bruitage *m*.

sound engineer *n* ingénieur *m* du son.

sounder ['saʊndər] *n* NAUT sondeur *m*.

sound hole *n* [of violin, viola etc] ouïe *f*, esse *f* ■ [of guitar, lute etc] rosace *f*, rose *f*.

sounding ['saʊndɪŋ] *n* **1.** AERON, METEOR & NAUT [measuring] sondage *m* **2.** [of bell, horn] son *m* ■ **wait for the ~ of the alarm** attendez le signal d'alarme OR que le signal d'alarme retentisse.
◆ **soundings** *npl* [investigations] sondages *mpl* ■ **to take ~s** faire des sondages.

-sounding *in cpds* : **a foreign~ name** un nom à consonance étrangère.

sounding board *n* **1.** *fig* [person] : **she uses her assistants as a ~ for any new ideas** elle essaie toutes ses nouvelles idées sur ses assistants **2.** [over pulpit, rostrum] abat-voix *m inv*.

soundless ['saʊndlɪs] *adj* **1.** [silent] silencieux **2.** *lit* [deep] insondable.

soundlessly ['saʊndlɪslɪ] *adv* [silently] silencieusement, sans bruit.

soundly ['saʊndlɪ] *adv* **1.** [deeply - sleep] profondément **2.** [sensibly - advise, argue] judicieusement, avec bon sens **3.** [safely - invest] de façon sûre, sans risque OR risques **4.** [competently - work, run] avec compétence **5.** [thoroughly - defeat] à plate couture OR plates coutures ■ **he deserves to be ~ thrashed** il mérite une bonne correction.

soundproof ['saʊndpru:f] ◇ *adj* insonorisé.
◇ *vt* insonoriser.

soundproofing ['saʊndpru:fɪŋ] *n* insonorisation *f*.

sound shift *n* mutation *f* phonologique.

sound system *n* [hi-fi] chaîne *f* hifi ■ [PA system] sonorisation *f*.

soundtrack ['saʊndtræk] *n* bande *f* sonore.

sound wave *n* onde *f* sonore.

soup [su:p] *n* **1.** CULIN soupe *f* ■ [thin or blended] soupe *f*, potage *m* ■ [smooth and creamy] velouté *m* ■ **onion/fish/leek ~** soupe à l'oignon/de poisson/aux poireaux ■ **cream of mushroom ~** velouté de champignons ➋ **to be in the ~** *inf* être dans le pétrin ■ **from ~ to nuts** *US inf* du début à la fin **2.**△ [nitroglycerine] nitroglycérine *f*, nitro *f*.

souped-up [su:pt-] *adj inf* [engine] gonflé, poussé ■ [car] au moteur gonflé OR poussé ■ [machine, computer program] perfectionné.

soup kitchen *n* soupe *f* populaire.

soup plate *n* assiette *f* creuse OR à soupe.

soup spoon *n* cuillère *f* OR cuiller *f* à soupe.

soupy ['su:pɪ] (*comp* **soupier**, *superl* **soupiest**) *adj* **1.** [thick] épais, - aisse *f*, dense **2.** *US inf* [sentimental] à l'eau de rose.

sour ['saʊər] ◇ *adj* **1.** [flavour, taste] aigre, sur **2.** [rancid - milk] tourné, aigre ; [- breath] fétide ■ **the milk has gone** OR **turned ~** le lait a tourné **3.** [disagreeable - person, character, mood] aigre, revêche, hargneux ; [- look] hargneux ; [- comment, tone] aigre, acerbe **4.** [wrong, awry] : **to go** OR **to turn ~** mal tourner ■ **their marriage went ~** leur mariage a tourné au vinaigre **5.** [too acidic - soil] trop acide.
◇ *vi* **1.** [wine] surir, s'aigrir ■ [milk] tourner, aigrir **2.** [person, character] aigrir ■ [relationship] se dégrader, tourner au vinaigre ■ [situation] mal tourner.
◇ *vt* **1.** [milk, wine] aigrir **2.** [person, character] aigrir ■ [relationship] gâter, empoisonner ■ [situation] gâter ■ **the experience ~ed his view of life** cette expérience l'a aigri.

source [sɔ:s] ◇ *n* **1.** [gen] source *f* ■ **they have traced the ~ of the power cut** ils ont découvert l'origine de la panne de courant ■ **at ~** à la source ■ **~ of infection** MED foyer *m* d'infection **2.** [of information] source *f* **3.** [of river] source *f*.
◇ *comp* : **~ material** OR **materials** [documents] documentation *f*.
◇ *vt* : **the quotations are ~d in footnotes** la source des citations figure dans les notes en bas de page.

source language *n* **1.** LING langue *f* source **2.** COMPUT langage *m* source.

source program *n* COMPUT programme *m* source.

sour cream *n* crème *f* aigre.

sour-faced *adj* à la mine revêche ▪ **what are you looking so ~ about?** pourquoi cet air maussade *OR* cette mine revêche?

sour grapes *n* jalousie *f*, envie *f*.

sourly ['saʊəlɪ] *adj* aigrement, avec aigreur.

sourpuss ['saʊəpʊs] *n inf* grincheux *m*, - euse *f*.

sousaphone ['su:zəfəʊn] *n* sousaphone *m*.

souse [saʊs] <> *vt* **1.** CULIN [in vinegar] (faire) mariner dans du vinaigre ▪ [in brine] (faire) mariner dans de la saumure **2.** [immerse] immerger, plonger ▪ [drench] tremper **3.** *inf* [make drunk] soûler.
<> *n* CULIN [vinegar] marinade *f* de vinaigre ▪ [brine] saumure *f*.

south [saʊθ] <> *n* **1.** GEOG sud *m* ▪ **the region to the ~ of Birmingham** la région qui est au sud de Birmingham ▪ **I was born in the ~** je suis né dans le Sud ▪ **in the South of France** dans le Midi (de la France) ▪ **the wind is in the ~** le vent vient du sud ▮ [in US] : **the South** le Sud, les États du Sud **2.** CARDS sud *m*.
<> *adj* **1.** GEOG sud *(inv)*, du sud, méridional ▪ **the ~ coast** la côte sud ▪ **in ~ India** dans le sud de l'Inde ➔ **the South Atlantic** l'Atlantique *m* **2.** [wind] du sud.
<> *adv* au sud, vers le sud ▪ **the village lies ~ of York** le village est situé au sud de York ▪ **the living room faces ~** la salle de séjour est exposée au sud ▪ **the path heads (due) ~** le chemin va *OR* mène (droit) vers le sud ▪ **they live down ~** ils habitent dans le Sud.

South Africa *pr n* Afrique *f* du Sud ▪ **in ~** en Afrique du Sud ▪ **the Republic of ~** la République d'Afrique du Sud.

South African <> *n* Sud-Africain *m*, - e *f*.
<> *adj* sud-africain, d'Afrique du Sud.

South America *pr n* Amérique *f* du Sud ▪ **in ~** en Amérique du Sud.

South American <> *n* Sud-Américain *m*, - e *f*.
<> *adj* sud-américain, d'Amérique du Sud.

South Bank *pr n* : **the ~** *complexe sur la rive sud de la Tamise réunissant des salles de concert, des théâtres et des musées.*

southbound ['saʊθbaʊnd] *adj* en direction du sud ▪ **the ~ carriageway of the motorway is closed** l'axe sud de l'autoroute est fermé (à la circulation).

South Carolina *pr n* Caroline *f* du Sud ▪ **in ~** en Caroline du Sud.

South Dakota *pr n* Dakota *m* du Sud ▪ **in ~** dans le Dakota du Sud.

southeast [,saʊθ'i:st] <> *n* sud-est *m*.
<> *adj* **1.** GEOG sud-est *(inv)*, du sud-est ▪ **in ~ England** dans le sud-est de l'Angleterre **2.** [wind] de sud-est.
<> *adv* au sud-est, vers le sud-est ▪ **it's 50 miles ~ of Liverpool** c'est à 80 kilomètres au sud-est de Liverpool.

Southeast Asia *pr n* Asie *f* du Sud-Est ▪ **in ~** en Asie du Sud-Est.

southeasterly [,saʊθ'i:stəlɪ] (*pl* **southeasterlies**) <> *adj* **1.** GEOG sud-est *(inv)*, du sud-est **2.** [wind] de sud-est.
<> *adv* au sud-est, vers le sud-est.
<> *n* vent *m* de sud-est.

southeastern [,saʊθ'i:stən] *adj* sud-est *(inv)*, du sud-est.

southeastwards [,saʊθ'i:stwədz] *adv* vers le sud-est, en direction du sud-est.

southerly ['sʌðəlɪ] (*pl* **southerlies**) <> *adj* **1.** GEOG sud *(inv)*, du sud ▪ **in a ~ direction** vers le sud **2.** [wind] du sud.
<> *adv* vers le sud.
<> *n* vent *m* du sud.

southern ['sʌðən] *adj* GEOG sud *(inv)*, du sud, méridional ▪ **he has a ~ accent** il a un accent du sud ▪ **~ Africa** l'Afrique *f* australe ▪ **~ Europe** l'Europe *f* méridionale ▪ **in ~ India** dans le sud de l'Inde ➔ **the ~ hemisphere** l'hémisphère *m* Sud *OR* austral ▪ **the Southern States** *aux États-Unis, les États entre la Pennsylvanie et la Virginie occidentale.*

Southern Cross *n* : **the ~** la Croix du Sud.

southerner ['sʌðənəʳ] *n* [gen] homme *m*, femme *f* du sud ▪ [in continental Europe] méridional *m*, - e *f*.

Southern Ireland *pr n* Irlande *f* du Sud ▪ **in ~** en Irlande du Sud.

southernmost ['sʌðənməʊst] *adj* le plus au sud ▪ **the ~ town in Chile** la ville la plus au sud du Chili.

south-facing *adj* [house, wall] (exposé) au sud *OR* au midi.

South Korea *pr n* Corée *f* du Sud ▪ **in ~** en Corée du Sud.

South Korean <> *n* Sud-Coréen *m*, - enne *f*, Coréen *m*, - enne *f* du Sud.
<> *adj* sud-coréen.

South Pacific *pr n* : **the ~** le Pacifique Sud.

southpaw ['saʊθpɔ:] <> *n US inf* gaucher *m*, - ère *f*.
<> *adj* gaucher.

South Pole *pr n* pôle *m* Sud ▪ **at the ~** au pôle Sud.

South Sea Bubble *pr n* : **the ~** *krach financier de 1720 en Angleterre.*

THE SOUTH SEA BUBBLE

Krach financier qui eut lieu en 1720, après que la *South Sea Company* eut repris à son compte la dette nationale britannique en échange du monopole du commerce sur les mers du Sud ; cette nouvelle provoqua une ruée sur les actions de la compagnie et une forte spéculation, qui entraîna la chute des cours et la ruine de nombreux investisseurs.

South Seas *pr npl* : **the ~** les mers *fpl* du Sud.

south-southeast <> *n* sud-sud-est *m*.
<> *adj* sud-sud-est *(inv)*, du sud-sud-est.
<> *adv* au sud-sud-est, vers le sud-sud-est.

south-southwest <> *n* sud-sud-ouest *m*.
<> *adj* sud-sud-ouest *(inv)*, du sud-sud-ouest.
<> *adv* au sud-sud-ouest, vers le sud-sud-ouest.

South Vietnam *pr n* Sud Viêt-Nam *m* ▪ **in ~** au Sud Viêt-Nam.

South Vietnamese <> *n* Sud-Vietnamien *m*, - enne *f* ▪ **the ~** les Sud-Vietnamiens.
<> *adj* sud-vietnamien.

southward ['saʊθwəd] <> *adj* au sud.
<> *adv* vers le sud, en direction du sud.

southwards ['saʊθwədz] = **southward** ***(adv)***.

southwest [,saʊθ'west] <> *n* sud-ouest *m*.
<> *adj* **1.** GEOG sud-ouest *(inv)*, du sud-ouest **2.** [wind] de sud-ouest.
<> *adv* au sud-ouest, vers le sud-ouest ▪ **it's ~ of London** c'est au sud-ouest de Londres.

southwesterly [,saʊθ'westəlɪ] (*pl* **southwesterlies**) <> *adj* **1.** GEOG sud-ouest *(inv)*, du sud-ouest **2.** [wind] de sud-ouest.
<> *adv* au sud-ouest, vers le sud-ouest.
<> *n* vent *m* de sud-ouest, suroît *m*.

southwestern [,saʊθ'westən] *adj* sud-ouest *(inv)*, du sud-ouest ▪ **the ~ States** les États du sud-ouest.

southwestwards [,saʊθ'westwədz] *adv* vers le sud-ouest, en direction du sud-ouest.

South Yemen *pr n* Yémen *m* du Sud ▪ **in ~** au Yémen du Sud.

souvenir [,su:və'nɪəʳ] *n* souvenir *m (objet)*.

sou'wester [saʊ'westəʳ] *n* **1.** [headgear] suroît *m* **2.** [wind] = **southwesterly**.

sovereign ['sɒvrɪn] <> *n* **1.** [monarch] souverain *m*, - e *f* **2.** [coin] souverain *m*.

◇ *adj* **1.** POL [state, territory] souverain ■ [powers] souverain, suprême ■ [rights] de souveraineté **2.** *lit* [excellent - remedy] souverain ■ [utmost - scorn, indifference] souverain, absolu.

sovereignty ['sɒvrɪntɪ] (*pl* **sovereignties**) *n* souveraineté *f*.

soviet ['səʊvɪət] *n* [council] soviet *m*.

◆ **Soviet** ◇ *n* [inhabitant] Soviétique *mf*.
◇ *adj* soviétique ■ **the Union of Soviet Socialist Republics** l'Union *f* des républiques socialistes soviétiques.

Soviet Union *pr n* : **the ~** l'Union *f* soviétique ■ **in the ~** en Union soviétique.

sow[1] [səʊ] (*pret* **sowed**, *pp* **sowed** OR **sown** [səʊn], *cont* **sowing**) ◇ *vt* **1.** [seed, crop] semer ■ [field] ensemencer **2.** *fig* semer ■ **he ~ed (the seeds of) doubt in their minds** il a semé le doute dans leur esprit ■ **it was at this time that the seeds of the Industrial Revolution were sown** c'est à cette époque que remontent les origines de la révolution industrielle ➲ **~ the wind and reap the whirlwind** *prov* qui sème le vent récolte la tempête *prov*.
◇ *vi* semer ■ **as you ~ so shall you reap** BIBLE comme tu auras semé tu moissonneras.

sow[2] [saʊ] *n* [pig] truie *f*.

sower ['səʊəʳ] *n* [person] semeur *m*, - euse *f* ■ [machine] semoir *m*.

sowing ['səʊɪŋ] *n* **1.** [act] ensemencement *m* **2.** *(U)* [work, period, seed] semailles *fpl*.

sown [səʊn] *pp* ▷ **sow**.

sox [sɒks] *npl* US *inf* chaussettes *fpl*.

soya ['sɔɪə] *n* soja *m* ■ **~ flour/milk** farine *f* /lait *m* de soja.

soya bean UK, **soybean** ['sɔɪbi:n] US *n* graine *f* de soja.

soy sauce *n* sauce *f* de soja.

sozzled ['sɒzld] *adj* UK *inf* soûl, paf.

spa [spɑ:] *n* **1.** [resort] ville *f* d'eau **2.** [spring] source *f* minérale **3.** [whirlpool bath] : **~ (bath)** bain *m* à remous, spa *m* **4.** [health club] centre *m* de fitness.

space [speɪs] ◇ *n* **1.** ASTRON & PHYS espace *m* ■ **the first man in ~** le premier homme dans l'espace ■ **she sat staring into ~** elle était assise, le regard perdu dans le vide **2.** [room] espace *m*, place *f* ■ **there's too much wasted ~ in this kitchen** il y a trop de place perdue OR d'espace inutilisé dans cette cuisine ■ **your books take up an awful lot of ~** tes livres prennent énormément de place ■ **the large windows give an impression of ~** les grandes fenêtres donnent une impression d'espace ■ **he cleared a** OR **some ~ on his desk for the tray** il a fait un peu de place sur son bureau pour le plateau ■ **the author devotes a lot of ~ to philosophical speculations** l'auteur fait une large part aux spéculations philosophiques **3.** [volume, area, distance] espace *m* ■ **there are at least five pubs in the ~ of a few hundred yards** il y a au moins cinq pubs sur quelques centaines de mètres ➲ **advertising ~** espace *m* publicitaire **4.** [gap] espace *m*, place *f* ■ [on page, official form] espace *m*, case *f* ■ **leave a ~ for the teacher's comments** laissez un espace pour les remarques du professeur ■ **please add any further details in the ~ provided** veuillez ajouter tout détail supplémentaire dans la case prévue à cet effet **5.** TYPO [gap between words] espace *m*, blanc *m* ■ [blank type] espace *m* **6.** [period of time, interval] intervalle *m*, espace *m* (de temps), période *f* ■ **in** OR **within the ~ of six months** en (l'espace de) six mois ■ **it'll all be over in a very short ~ of time** tout sera fini dans très peu de temps OR d'ici peu **7.** [seat, place] place *f*.
◇ *comp* [programme, research, travel, flight] spatial.
◇ *vt* = **space out**.
◆ **space out** *vt sep* **1.** [in space] espacer ■ **~ yourselves out a bit more** écartez-vous un peu plus les uns des autres **2.** [in time] échelonner, espacer ■ **~d out over a period of ten years** échelonné sur une période de dix ans.

space age *n* : **the ~** l'ère *f* spatiale.
◆ **space-age** *adj* **1.** SCI de l'ère spatiale **2.** [futuristic] futuriste.

space bar *n* [on typewriter] barre *f* d'espacement.

space blanket *n* couverture *f* de survie.

space cadet *n inf* taré *m*, - e *f*.

spacecraft ['speɪskrɑ:ft] *n* vaisseau *m* spatial.

-spaced [speɪst] *in cpds* **1.** [gen] : **the buildings are closely/widely~** les bâtiments sont proches les uns des autres/largement espacés **2.** TYPO : **single/double~** à interligne simple/double.

spaced-out△ *adj* shooté△.

space heater *n* radiateur *m*.

Space Invaders® *npl jeu vidéo dont le but est de détruire des envahisseurs venant de l'espace.*

spacelab ['speɪslæb] *n* laboratoire *m* spatial.

spaceman ['speɪsmæn] (*pl* **spacemen** [-men]) *n* [gen] spationaute *m* ■ [American] astronaute *m* ■ [Russian] cosmonaute *m*.

space platform = **space station**.

space probe *n* sonde *f* spatiale.

space race *n* course *f* pour la suprématie dans l'espace.

space rocket *n* fusée *f* spatiale OR interplanétaire.

space-saving *adj* qui fait gagner de la place.

spaceship ['speɪsʃɪp] *n* vaisseau *m* spatial habité.

space shot *n* lancement *m* spatial.

space shuttle *n* navette *f* spatiale.

space sickness *n* mal *m* de l'espace.

space station *n* station *f* spatiale OR orbitale.

spacesuit ['speɪssu:t] *n* combinaison *f* spatiale.

space-time continuum *n* continuum *m* espace-temps OR spatio-temporel.

space travel *n* voyages *mpl* dans l'espace, astronautique *f spec*.

space walk ◇ *n* marche *f* dans l'espace.
◇ *vi* marcher dans l'espace.

spacewoman ['speɪs,wʊmən] (*pl* **spacewomen** [-,wɪmɪn]) *n* [gen] spationaute *f*, astronaute *f* ■ [Russian] cosmonaute *f*.

spacey△ ['speɪsɪ] (*comp* **spacier**, *superl* **spaciest**) *adj* **1.** [music] planant **2.** [person] : **to feel ~** être dans les vapes.

spacial ['speɪʃl] = **spatial**.

spacing ['speɪsɪŋ] *n* **1.** [of text on page - horizontal] espacement *m* ; [- vertical] interligne *m* ■ **typed in single/double ~** tapé avec interligne simple/double **2.** [between trees, columns, buildings etc] espacement *m*, écart *m*.

spacious ['speɪʃəs] *adj* [house, room, office] spacieux, grand ■ [park, property] étendu, grand.

spade [speɪd] *n* **1.** [tool] bêche *f* ■ **to call a ~ a ~** appeler un chat un chat ■ **to have sthg in ~s** US *inf* avoir des tonnes de qqch **2.** [in cards] pique *m*.

spadeful ['speɪdfʊl] *n* pelletée *f*.

spadework ['speɪdwɜ:k] *n* travail *m* de préparation OR de déblayage.

spaghetti [spə'getɪ] *n (U)* spaghetti *mpl*, spaghettis *mpl*.

Spaghetti Junction *pr n surnom d'un échangeur sur l'autoroute M6 au nord de Birmingham.*

spaghetti western *n* western-spaghetti *m*.

Spain [speɪn] *pr n* Espagne *f* ■ **in ~** en Espagne.

spam [spæm] ◇ *n inf* COMPUT publicité *f* électronique importune ■ *Québec* pourriel *m*.
◇ *vt* (*pret & pp* **spammed**, *cont* **spamming**) envoyer un spam.

Spam® [spæm] *n pâté de jambon en conserve.*

spammer ['spæməʳ] *n* spammeur *m*.

spamming ['spæmɪŋ] *n (U)* spam *m*, arrosage *m offic*.

span [spæn] (*pret & pp* **spanned**, *cont* **spanning**) ◇ *n* **1.** [duration] durée *f*, laps *m* de temps ■ **a short attention ~** une

capacité d'attention limitée ▌[interval] intervalle *m* ■ **his work covers a ~ of twenty-odd years** son œuvre s'étend sur une vingtaine d'années **2.** [range] gamme *f* ■ **we cover only a limited ~ of subjects** nous ne couvrons qu'un nombre restreint de sujets **3.** [of hands, arms, wings] envergure *f* **4.** [of bridge] travée *f* ■ [of arch, dome, girder] portée *f* **5.** [unit of measurement] empan *m* **6.** [matched pair - of horses, oxen] paire *f*.
◇ *vt* **1.** [encompass, stretch over - in time, extent] couvrir, embrasser ■ **her career spanned more than 50 years** sa carrière s'étend sur plus de 50 ans **2.** [cross - river, ditch etc] enjamber, traverser **3.** [build bridge over] jeter un pont sur.
◇ *pt arch* ▷ **spin**.

spandex ['spændeks] *n textile proche du Lycra.*

spangle ['spæŋgl] ◇ *n* paillette *f*.
◇ *vt* pailleter, décorer de paillettes ■ **stars ~d the night sky** le ciel était semé d'étoiles.

Spaniard ['spænjəd] *n* Espagnol *m*, - e *f*.

spaniel ['spænjəl] *n* épagneul *m*.

Spanish ['spænɪʃ] ◇ *adj* espagnol ■ **~ guitar** guitare *f* classique.
◇ *n* LING espagnol *m*.
◇ *npl* : **the ~** les Espagnols *mpl*.

Spanish America *pr n* Amérique *f* hispanophone.

Spanish-American ◇ *n* **1.** [in the US] Hispanique *mf* **2.** [in Latin America] Hispano-Américain *m*, - e *f*.
◇ *adj* **1.** [in the US] hispanique **2.** [in Latin America] hispano-américain **3.** US HIST : **the ~ War** la guerre hispano-américaine.

THE SPANISH-AMERICAN WAR

Conflit qui opposa, en 1898 aux Caraïbes, les États-Unis à l'Espagne. Se posant en défenseurs des Cubains opprimés par les Espagnols, les Américains remportèrent une victoire facile qui leur permit d'étendre leur influence sur le Pacifique et les Caraïbes tout en conférant à leur pays le statut de puissance mondiale.

Spanish Armada *pr n* : **the ~** l'Invincible Armada *f*.

THE SPANISH ARMADA

Flotte envoyée par Philippe II d'Espagne en 1588 pour envahir l'Angleterre et y rétablir le catholicisme. Bien que supérieure en nombre et très préparée, la flotte espagnole fut vaincue, victime d'une série de contretemps et d'une plus grande maniabilité de la flotte britannique.

Spanish fly *n* **1.** [insect] cantharide *f* **2.** [product] poudre *f* de cantharide.

Spanish Inquisition *n* : **the ~** l'Inquisition *f* espagnole.

Spanish Main *pr n* : **the ~** la mer des Caraïbes.

spank [spæŋk] ◇ *vt* donner une fessée à, fesser.
◇ *vi* [go at a lively pace] : **to be** OR **to go ~ing along** aller bon train OR à bonne allure.
◇ *n* tape *f* sur les fesses.

spanking ['spæŋkɪŋ] ◇ *n* fessée *f* ■ **to give sb a ~** donner une fessée à qqn.
◇ *adj inf* **1.** [excellent] excellent **2.** [brisk] vif ■ **to go at a ~ pace** aller bon train OR à bonne allure.
◇ *adv inf* **~ new** flambant neuf ■ **~ clean** propre comme un sou neuf.

spanner ['spænəʳ] *n* clé *f*, clef *f (outil)* ■ **to throw** OR **to put a ~ in the works** poser des problèmes.

spar [spɑːʳ] (*pret & pp* **sparred**, *cont* **sparring**) ◇ *vi* **1.** SPORT [in boxing - train] s'entraîner (avec un sparring-partner) ; [- test out opponent] faire des feintes *(pour tester son adversaire)* ■ **they sparred with each other for a few rounds** ils boxèrent amicalement durant quelques rounds **2.** [argue] se disputer.
◇ *n* **1.** [pole - gen] poteau *m*, mât *m* ■ NAUT espar *m* **2.** AERON longeron *m* **3.** MINER spath *m*.

spare [speəʳ] ◇ *adj* **1.** [not in use] dont on ne se sert pas, disponible ■ [kept in reserve] de réserve, de rechange ■ [extra, surplus] de trop, en trop ■ **take a ~ pullover** prenez un pull de rechange ■ **have you got a ~ piece of paper?** est-ce que tu as une feuille de papier à me prêter? ■ **we had no ~ cash left to buy souvenirs** nous n'avions plus assez d'argent pour acheter des souvenirs ■ **I've got two ~ tickets for the match** j'ai deux billets en plus pour le match ■ **I'll have some more cake if there's any going ~** *inf* je vais reprendre du gâteau s'il en reste
2. [free] libre, disponible ■ **call in next time you have a ~ moment** passez la prochaine fois que vous aurez un moment de libre
3. [lean] maigre, sec, sèche *f*
4. [austere - style, decor] austère ■ [frugal - meal] frugal
5. UK *inf* [mad] : **to go ~** devenir dingue.
◇ *n* [spare part] pièce *f* de rechange ■ [wheel] roue *f* de secours ■ [tyre] pneu *m* de rechange.
◇ *vt* **1.** [make available, give] accorder, consacrer ■ **come and see us if you can ~ the time** venez nous voir si vous avez le temps ■ **~ a thought for their poor parents!** pensez un peu à leurs pauvres parents! ■ **can you ~ (me) a few pounds?** vous n'auriez pas quelques livres (à me passer)? ▌[do without] se passer de ■ **I'm afraid we can't ~ anyone at the moment** je regrette mais nous ne pouvons nous passer de personne OR nous avons besoin de tout le monde en ce moment ■ **I need £50, if you think you can ~ it** j'aurais besoin de 50 livres si c'est possible
2. [refrain from harming, punishing, destroying] épargner ■ **to ~ sb's life** épargner la vie de qqn ■ **to ~ sb's feelings** ménager les sentiments de qqn ■ **to ~ sb's blushes** épargner qqn
3. [save - trouble, suffering] épargner, éviter ■ **I could have ~d myself the bother** j'aurais pu m'épargner le dérangement ■ **he was ~d the shame of a public trial** la honte d'un procès public lui a été épargnée
4. [economize] ménager ■ **they ~d no expense on the celebrations** ils n'ont reculé devant aucune dépense pour les fêtes ■ **the first prize is a real luxury trip, with no expense ~ d** le premier prix est un voyage de rêve pour lequel on n'a pas regardé à la dépense ■ **we shall ~ no effort to push the plan through** nous ne reculerons devant aucun effort pour faire accepter le projet ▶ **~ the rod and spoil the child** *prov* qui aime bien châtie bien *prov*.
◆ **to spare** *adj phr* : **young people with money to ~** des jeunes qui ont de l'argent à dépenser ■ **do you have a few minutes to ~?** avez-vous quelques minutes de libres OR devant vous? ■ **we got to the airport with over an hour to ~** nous sommes arrivés à l'aéroport avec plus d'une heure d'avance ■ **I caught the train with just a few seconds to ~** à quelques secondes près je ratais le train.

spare part *n* pièce *f* de rechange, pièce *f* détachée.

sparerib [speə'rɪb] *n* travers *m* de porc ■ **barbecue ~s** travers de porc grillés sauce barbecue.

spare room *n* chambre *f* d'amis.

spare time *n* temps *m* libre ■ **what do you do in your ~?** que faites-vous pendant votre temps libre OR pendant vos moments de loisirs?
◆ **spare-time** *adj* : **spare-time activities** loisirs *mpl*.

spare tyre *n* **1.** AUT pneu *m* de secours OR de rechange **2.** *inf* [roll of fat] bourrelet *m (à la taille)*.

spare wheel *n* roue *f* de secours.

sparing ['speərɪŋ] *adj* **1.** [economical - person] économe ■ **she's very ~ with her compliments** elle est très avare de compliments ■ **they were ~ in their efforts to help us** ils ne se sont pas donnés beaucoup de mal pour nous aider **2.** [meagre - quantity] limité, modéré ; [- use] modéré, économe ■ **to make ~ use of sthg** utiliser qqch avec parcimonie OR modération.

sparingly ['speərɪŋlɪ] *adv* [eat] frugalement ■ [drink, use] avec modération ■ [praise] chichement, avec parcimonie ■ **use your strength ~** ménagez vos forces.

spark [spɑːk] ◇ *vt* [trigger - interest, argument] susciter, provoquer ■ **the incident was the catalyst that ~ed the revolution**

c'est l'incident qui a déclenché la révolution ■ **the news ~ed (off) an intense debate** la nouvelle déclencha un débat animé.
◇ *vi* **1.** [produce sparks - gen] jeter des étincelles **2.** AUT [spark plug, ignition system] allumer *(par étincelle)*.
◇ *n* **1.** [from flame, electricity] étincelle *f* ■ *fig* **whenever they meet the ~s fly** chaque fois qu'ils se rencontrent, ça fait des étincelles **2.** [flash, trace - of excitement, wit] étincelle *f*, lueur *f* ; [- of interest, enthusiasm] : **she hasn't a ~ of common sense** elle n'a pas le moindre bon sens.
◆ **spark off** *vt sep* = **spark**.

sparking plug ['spɑːkɪŋ-] *UK* = **spark plug**.

sparkle ['spɑːkl] ◇ *vi* **1.** [jewel, frost, glass, star] étinceler, briller, scintiller ■ [sea, lake] étinceler, miroiter ■ [eyes] étinceler, pétiller **2.** [person] briller ■ [conversation] être brillant **3.** [wine, cider, mineral water] pétiller.
◇ *n* **1.** [of jewel, frost, glass, star] étincellement *m*, scintillement *m* ■ [of sea, lake] étincellement *m*, miroitement *m* ■ [of eyes] éclat *m* ■ **she has a ~ in her eye** elle a des yeux pétillants **2.** [of person, conversation, wit, performance] éclat *m*.

sparkler ['spɑːklər] *n* **1.** [firework] cierge *m* magique **2.**△ *UK* [diamond] diam△ *m*.

sparkling ['spɑːklɪŋ] ◇ *adj* **1.** [jewel, frost, glass, star] étincelant, scintillant ■ [sea, lake] étincelant, miroitant ■ [eyes] étincelant, pétillant **2.** [person, conversation, wit, performance] brillant **3.** [soft drink, mineral water] gazeux, pétillant.
◇ *adv* : **~ clean/white** d'une propreté/blancheur éclatante.

sparkling wine *n* vin *m* mousseux.

spark plug *n* AUT bougie *f*.

sparring match ['spɑːrɪŋ-] *n* **1.** [in boxing] combat *m* d'entraînement **2.** [argument] discussion *f* animée.

sparring partner *n* **1.** [in boxing] sparring-partner *m* **2.** *fig* adversaire *m*.

sparrow ['spærəʊ] *n* moineau *m*.

sparrow hawk *n* : **(Eurasian) ~** épervier *m* ■ **American ~** faucon *m* des moineaux.

sparse [spɑːs] *adj* clairsemé, rare.

sparsely ['spɑːslɪ] *adv* [wooded, populated] peu ■ **the room was ~ furnished** la pièce contenait peu de meubles.

Sparta ['spɑːtə] *pr n* Sparte.

Spartacus ['spɑːtəkəs] *pr n* Spartacus.

spartan ['spɑːtn] *adj fig* spartiate ■ **a ~ room** une chambre austère *OR* sans aucun confort.
◆ **Spartan** HIST ◇ *n* Spartiate *mf*.
◇ *adj* spartiate.

spasm ['spæzm] *n* **1.** [muscular contraction] spasme *m* **2.** [fit] accès *m* ■ **he had a ~ of coughing** il a eu une quinte de toux ■ **she went into ~s of laughter** elle a été prise d'une crise de fou rire.

spasmodic [spæz'mɒdɪk] *adj* **1.** [intermittent] intermittent, irrégulier **2.** MED [pain, contraction] spasmodique.

spasmodically [spæz'mɒdɪklɪ] *adv* de façon intermittente, par à-coups.

spastic ['spæstɪk] ◇ *n* MED [gen] handicapé *m*, - e *f* (moteur) ■ [person affected by spasms] spasmophile *mf*.
◇ *adj* **1.** MED [gen] handicapé (moteur) ■ [affected by spasms] spasmophile ■ **~ paralysis** tétanie *f* **2.** △ *offens* [clumsy] empoté, gourde.

spat [spæt] ◇ *pt & pp* ▷ **spit**.
◇ *n* **1.** [gaiter] guêtre *f* **2.** *inf* [quarrel] prise *f* de bec **3.** [shellfish] naissain *m*.

spate [speɪt] *n* **1.** [of letters, visitors] avalanche *f* ■ [of abuse, insults] torrent *m* ■ **a ~ of murders/burglaries** une série de meurtres/cambriolages **2.** *UK* [flood] crue *f* ■ **the river was in ~** le fleuve était en crue ■ **to interrupt sb in full ~** *fig* interrompre qqn en plein discours.

spatial ['speɪʃl] *adj* spatial.

spatiotemporal [ˌspeɪʃɪəʊ'temprəl] *adj* spatio-temporel.

spatter ['spætər] ◇ *vt* [splash] éclabousser ■ **the car ~ed me with mud, the car ~ ed mud over me** l'auto m'a éclaboussé *OR* aspergé de boue.
◇ *vi* [liquid] gicler ■ [oil] crépiter ■ **rain ~ed on the windowpane** la pluie crépitait sur la vitre.
◇ *n* [on garment] éclaboussure *f*, éclaboussures *fpl* ■ [sound - of rain, oil, applause] crépitement *m*.

spatula ['spætjʊlə] *n* **1.** CULIN spatule *f* **2.** MED abaisse-langue *m inv*, spatule *f*.

spawn [spɔːn] ◇ *n (U)* **1.** ZOOL [of frogs, fish] œufs *mpl*, frai *m* **2.** BOT [of mushrooms] mycélium *m* **3.** *fig & pej* [offspring] progéniture *f*.
◇ *vt* **1.** ZOOL pondre **2.** *fig* [produce] engendrer.
◇ *vi* ZOOL frayer.

spay [speɪ] *vt* stériliser.

SPCA (*abbrev of* **Society for the Prevention of Cruelty to Animals**) *pr n société américaine protectrice des animaux*, ≃ SPA.

SPCC (*abbrev of* **Society for the Prevention of Cruelty to Children**) *pr n société américaine pour la protection de l'enfance*.

speak [spiːk] (*pret* **spoke** [spəʊk], *pp* **spoken** ['spəʊkn]) ◇ *vi* **1.** [talk] parler ■ **to ~ to** *OR esp US* **with sb** parler à *OR* avec qqn ■ **to ~ about** *OR* **of sthg** parler de qqch ■ **to ~ to sb about sthg** parler à qqn de qqch ■ **to ~ in a whisper** chuchoter ■ **~ to me!** dites (-moi) quelque chose! ■ **~ when you're spoken to!** ne parlez que lorsque l'on s'adresse à vous! ■ **don't ~ with your mouth full** ne parle pas la bouche pleine ■ **it seems I spoke too soon** on dirait que j'ai parlé un peu vite ‖ [on telephone] parler ■ **who's ~ing?** [gen] qui est à l'appareil? ; [switchboard] c'est de la part de qui? ■ **Kate Smith ~ing** Kate Smith à l'appareil, c'est Kate Smith ■ **may I ~ to Kate? – ~ing** puis-je parler à Kate? – c'est moi ➋ **~ now or forever hold your peace** parlez maintenant ou gardez le silence pour toujours
2. [in debate, meeting etc - make a speech] faire un discours, parler ; [- intervene] prendre la parole, parler ■ **the chair called upon Mrs Fox to ~** le président a demandé à Mme Fox de prendre la parole ■ **he was invited to ~ to us on** *OR* **about Chile** il a été invité à venir nous parler du Chili ■ **to ~ to** *OR* **on a motion** soutenir une motion ■ **to ~ from the floor** intervenir dans un débat
3. [be on friendly terms] : **she isn't ~ing to me** elle ne me parle plus ■ **I don't know them to ~ to** je ne les connais que de vue ■ **to be on ~ing terms with sb** connaître qqn *(assez pour lui parler)* ■ **we're no longer on ~ing terms** nous ne nous parlons plus
4. [as spokesperson] : **to ~ for sb** [on their behalf] parler au nom de qqn ; [in their favour] parler en faveur de qqn ■ **let her ~ for herself!** laisse-la s'exprimer! ■ **~ for yourself!** *hum* parle pour toi! ■ **the facts ~ for themselves** *fig* les faits parlent d'eux-mêmes ■ **the title ~s for itself** *fig* le titre se passe de commentaire
5. [in giving an opinion] : **generally ~ing** en général ■ **personally ~ing** en ce qui me concerne, quant à moi ■ **~ing of which** justement, à ce propos ■ **financially ~ing** financièrement parlant, du point de vue financier ■ **~ing as a politician** en tant qu'homme politique ■ **you shouldn't ~ ill of the dead** tu ne devrais pas dire du mal des morts ■ **he always ~s well/highly of you** il dit toujours du bien/beaucoup de bien de vous ■ **the gift ~s well of her concern for old people** son don témoigne de l'intérêt qu'elle porte aux personnes âgées
6. *fig* [give an impression] : **his paintings ~ of terrible loneliness** ses peintures expriment une immense solitude
7. *lit* [sound - trumpet] sonner, retentir ; [- organ pipe] parler ; [- gun] retentir.
◇ *vt* **1.** [say, pronounce] dire, prononcer ■ **to ~ one's mind** dire sa pensée *OR* façon de penser ■ **she spoke my name in her sleep** elle a prononcé mon nom dans son sommeil ■ **he didn't ~ a word** il n'a pas dit un mot ■ **to ~ the truth** dire la vérité ■ **his silence ~s volumes** son silence en dit long
2. [language] parler ■ **'English spoken'** 'ici on parle anglais' ■ **we just don't ~ the same language** *fig* nous ne parlons pas le même langage, c'est tout.

◆ **not to speak of** *prep phr* sans parler de ▪ **his plays are hugely popular, not to ~ of his many novels** ses pièces sont extrêmement populaires, sans parler de ses nombreux romans.

◆ **so to speak** *adv phr* pour ainsi dire.

◆ **to speak of** *adv phr* : **there's no wind/mail to ~ of** il n'y a presque pas de vent/de courrier.

◆ **speak for** *vt insep (usu passive)* **these goods are already spoken for** ces articles sont déjà réservés *OR* retenus ▪ **she's already spoken for** elle est déjà prise.

◆ **speak out** *vi insep* parler franchement, ne pas mâcher ses mots ▪ **to ~ out for sthg** parler en faveur de qqch ▪ **to ~ out against sthg** s'élever contre qqch ▪ **she spoke out strongly against the scheme** elle a condamné le projet avec véhémence.

◆ **speak up** *vi insep* **1.** [louder] parler plus fort ▪ [more clearly] parler plus clairement
2. [be frank] parler franchement ▪ **to ~ up for sb** parler en faveur de qqn, défendre les intérêts de qqn ▪ **why didn't you ~ up?** pourquoi n'avez-vous rien dit?

-speak *in cpds pej* **computer~** langage *m OR* jargon *m* de l'informatique.

speakeasy ['spi:k,i:zɪ] (*pl* **speakeasies**) *n* bar *m* clandestin *(pendant la prohibition)*.

speaker ['spi:kəʳ] *n* **1.** [gen] celui *m* /celle *f* qui parle ▪ [in discussion] interlocuteur *m*, - trice *f* ▪ [in public] orateur *m*, - trice *f* ▪ [in lecture] conférencier *m*, - ère *f* ▪ **she's a good ~** elle sait parler *OR* s'exprimer en public **2.** LING locuteur *m*, - trice *f* ▪ **native ~s of English** ceux dont la langue maternelle est l'anglais ▪ **Spanish ~** hispanophone *mf* ▪ **my parents are Welsh ~s** mes parents sont galloisants *OR* parlent (le) gallois **3.** POL speaker *m*, président *m*, - e *f* de l'assemblée ➔ **the Speaker (of the House of Commons)** *le président de la Chambre des communes* ▪ **the Speaker of the House** *le président de la Chambre des représentants américaine* **4.** [loudspeaker] haut-parleur *m* ▪ [in stereo system] enceinte *f*, baffle *m*.

SPEAKER OF THE HOUSE

Le président de la Chambre des représentants est l'une des personnalités politiques les plus influentes de la Maison-Blanche : il vient en deuxième position, après le vice-président, pour remplacer le président des États-Unis en cas de force majeure.

speaker phone *n* téléphone *m* avec haut-parleur.

Speakers' Corner *pr n angle nord-est de Hyde Park où chacun peut venir le week-end haranguer la foule sur des tribunes improvisées.*

speaking ['spi:kɪŋ] <> *adj* **1.** [involving speech] : **do you have a ~ part in the play?** est-ce que vous avez du texte? ▪ **she has a good ~ voice** elle a une belle voix **2.** [which speaks - robot, machine, doll] parlant.
<> *n* art *m* de parler.

-speaking *in cpds* **1.** [person] : **they're both German/Spanish~** ils sont tous deux germanophones/hispanophones ▪ **a child of Polish~ parents** un enfant dont les parents sont de langue *OR* d'origine polonaise **2.** [country] : **French/English~ countries** les pays francophones/anglophones ▪ **the Arab~ world** le monde arabophone.

speaking clock *n UK* horloge *f* parlante.

speaking tube *n* tuyau *m* acoustique.

spear [spɪəʳ] <> *n* **1.** [weapon] lance *f* ▪ [harpoon] harpon *m* **2.** [of asparagus, broccoli etc] pointe *f*.
<> *vt* **1.** [enemy] transpercer d'un coup de lance ▪ [fish] harponner **2.** [food] piquer.

speargun ['spɪəgʌn] *n* fusil *m* (de pêche sous-marine).

spearhead ['spɪəhed] <> *n liter & fig* fer *m* de lance.
<> *vt* [attack] être le fer de lance de ▪ [campaign, movement] mener, être à la tête de.

spearmint ['spɪəmɪnt] <> *n* **1.** [plant] menthe *f* verte ▪ [flavour] menthe *f* **2.** [sweet] bonbon *m* à la menthe.
<> *adj* [flavour] de menthe ▪ [toothpaste, chewing gum] à la menthe.

spec [spek] *n* **1.** *phr* **on ~** *UK inf* au hasard ▪ **he bought the car on ~** il a risqué le coup en achetant la voiture **2.** = **specification**.

special ['speʃl] <> *adj* **1.** [exceptional, particular - offer, friend, occasion, ability] spécial ; [- reason, effort, pleasure] particulier ; [- powers] extraordinaire ▪ **pay ~ attention to the details** faites particulièrement attention aux détails ▪ **this is a very ~ moment for me** c'est un moment particulièrement important pour moi ▪ **as a ~ treat** [present] comme cadeau ; [outing] pour vous faire plaisir ▪ **can you do me a ~ favour?** pouvez-vous me rendre un grand service? ▪ **I'll do it as a ~ favour to you** je le ferai, mais c'est bien pour toi *OR* parce que c'est toi ▪ **it's a ~ case** c'est un cas particulier *OR* à part ▪ **a ~ feature** [in paper] un article spécial ; [on TV] une émission spéciale ▪ **they put on a ~ train for the match** ils ont prévu un train supplémentaire pour le match ➔ **~ agent** agent *m* secret ▪ **~ interest holidays** vacances *fpl* à thème ▪ **the ~ relationship** POL *relations d'amitié entre les USA et la Grande-Bretagne* **2.** [specific - need, problem] spécial, particulier ; [- equipment] spécial ; [- adviser] particulier ▪ **you need ~ permission** il vous faut une autorisation spéciale **3.** [peculiar] particulier **4.** [valued] cher ▪ **you're very ~ to me** je tiens beaucoup à toi.
<> *n* **1.** [train] train *m* supplémentaire ▪ [bus] car *m* supplémentaire **2.** [in restaurant] spécialité *f* ▪ **the chef's/the house ~** la spécialité du chef/de la maison ▪ **today's ~** le plat du jour **3.** TV émission *f* spéciale ▪ PRESS [issue] numéro *m* spécial ▪ [feature] article *m* spécial **4.** *US* COMM offre *f* spéciale ▪ **sugar is on ~ today** le sucre est en promotion aujourd'hui.

Special Air Service *pr n commando d'intervention spéciale de l'armée britannique.*

Special Branch *pr n renseignements généraux britanniques.*

special correspondent *n* PRESS envoyé *m* spécial.

special effects *npl* CIN & TV effets *mpl* spéciaux.

specialism ['speʃəlɪzm] *n* spécialisation *f* ▪ **my ~ is maths** je me spécialise dans les maths.

specialist ['speʃəlɪst] <> *n* **1.** [gen - MED] spécialiste *mf* ▪ **she's a heart ~** elle est cardiologue ▪ **he's a ~ in rare books** c'est un spécialiste en livres rares **2.** *US* MIL officier *m* technicien.
<> *adj* [skills, vocabulary] spécialisé, de spécialiste ▪ [writing, publication] pour spécialistes ▪ **to seek ~ advice** demander conseil à *OR* consulter un spécialiste ▪ **~ teacher** professeur *m* spécialisé ▪ **she's a ~ maths teacher** elle n'enseigne que *OR* enseigne uniquement les maths.

speciality [,speʃɪ'ælətɪ] *UK* (*pl* **specialities**), **specialty** ['speʃltɪ] *US* (*pl* **specialties**) *n* **1.** [service, product] spécialité *f* ▪ **a local ~** une spécialité de la région ▪ **he made a ~ of croissants** il s'est spécialisé dans les croissants ▪ **our ~ is electronic components** nous nous spécialisons *OR* nous sommes spécialisés dans les composants électroniques **2.** [area of study] spécialité *f* ▪ **her ~ is Chinese** elle est spécialisée en chinois.

specialization [,speʃəlaɪ'zeɪʃn] *n* spécialisation *f* ▪ **his ~ is computers** il est spécialisé en informatique.

specialize, ise ['speʃəlaɪz] *vi* [company, restaurant, student] se spécialiser ▪ **to ~ in sthg** se spécialiser en *OR* dans qqch.

specialized ['speʃəlaɪzd] *adj* spécialisé ▪ **highly ~ equipment** un matériel hautement spécialisé ▪ **we need somebody with ~ knowledge** il nous faut un spécialiste.

special licence *n UK* dispense *f* de bans ▪ **to be married by ~** se marier avec dispense de bans.

specially ['speʃəlɪ] *adv* **1.** [above all] spécialement, particulièrement, surtout ▪ **I would ~ like to hear that song** j'aimerais beaucoup écouter cette chanson **2.** [on purpose, specifically] exprès, spécialement ▪ **I made your favourite meal ~** j'ai fait exprès ton repas préféré ▪ **we've driven 500 miles ~ to see you** nous avons fait 800 kilomètres spécialement pour venir te voir **3.** [particularly] spécialement ■ **the chocolate mousse is ~ good here** la mousse au chocolat est particulièrement bonne ici.

special needs *npl* : **children with ~** enfants ayant des difficultés scolaires ■ **~ teacher** enseignant *m*, - e *f* spécialisé s'occupant d'enfants ayant des difficultés scolaires.

special offer *n* promotion *f* ■ **to be on ~** être en promotion.

special powers *n* POL pouvoirs *mpl* d'exception.

special school *n* *UK* [for the physically handicapped] établissement *m* d'enseignement spécialisé *(pour enfants handicapés)* ■ [for the mentally handicapped] établissement *m* d'enseignement spécialisé *(pour enfants inadaptés)*.

specialty ['speʃltɪ] (*pl* **specialties**) *n* **1.** *US* = **speciality 2.** LAW contrat *m* sous seing privé.

species ['spi:ʃi:z] (*pl inv*) *n* **1.** BIOL espèce *f* **2.** *fig* espèce *f*.

specific [spə'sɪfɪk] ◇ *adj* **1.** [explicit] explicite ■ [precise] précis ■ [clear] clair ■ [particular] particulier ■ **give me a ~ example** donnez-moi un exemple précis ■ **she was quite ~ about it** elle s'est montrée très claire *OR* précise à ce sujet **2.** BIOL & BOT : **~ name** nom *m* spécifique *OR* d'espèce.
◇ *n* MED (remède *m*) spécifique *m*.
◆ **specifics** *npl* détails *mpl*.

specifically [spə'sɪfɪklɪ] *adv* **1.** [explicitly] explicitement ■ [precisely] précisément, de façon précise ■ [clearly] clairement, expressément ■ **I ~ asked to speak to Mr Day** j'avais bien spécifié *OR* précisé que je voulais parler à M. Day ■ **I ~ told you to telephone** je t'avais bien dit de téléphoner **2.** [particularly] particulièrement ■ [specially] spécialement ■ [purposely] exprès, expressément ■ **our kitchens are ~ designed for the modern family** nos cuisines sont (tout) spécialement conçues pour la famille moderne.

specification [,spesɪfɪ'keɪʃn] *n* **1.** *(often pl)* [in contract, of machine, building materials etc] spécifications *fpl* ■ **made (according) to ~** construit en fonction de spécifications techniques ■ **the builder didn't follow the architect's ~s** le constructeur n'a pas respecté le cahier des charges rédigé par l'architecte **2.** [stipulation] spécification *f*, précision *f* ■ **there was no ~ as to age** l'âge n'était pas précisé.

specific gravity *n* densité *f*.

specify ['spesɪfaɪ] (*pret & pp* **specified**) *vt* spécifier, préciser ■ **unless otherwise specified** sauf indication contraire ■ **the person previously specified** la personne précitée *OR* déjà nommée ■ **on a specified date** à une date précise.

specimen ['spesɪmən] ◇ *n* **1.** [sample - of work, handwriting] spécimen *m* ; [- of blood] prélèvement *m* ; [- of urine] échantillon *m* **2.** [single example] spécimen *m* ■ **a fine ~ of Gothic architecture** un bel exemple d'architecture gothique **3.** *inf pej* [person] spécimen *m*.
◇ *comp* [page, letter, reply] spécimen ■ **they will ask you for a ~ signature** ils vous demanderont un exemplaire de votre signature ■ **~ copy** spécimen *m (livre, magazine)*.

specious ['spi:ʃəs] *adj* [argument, reasoning] spécieux ■ [appearance] trompeur.

speck [spek] ◇ *n* **1.** [of dust, dirt] grain *m* ■ [in eye] poussière *f* **2.** [stain, mark - gen] petite tache *f* ; [- on skin, fruit] tache *f*, tavelure *f* ; [- of blood] petite tache *f* **3.** [dot - on horizon, from height] point *m* noir **4.** [tiny amount] tout petit peu *m* ■ **there isn't a ~ of truth in the rumour** il n'y a pas la moindre vérité *OR* un atome de vérité dans cette rumeur.
◇ *vt (usu passive)* tacheter.

speckle ['spekl] ◇ *n* moucheture *f*.
◇ *vt* tacheter, moucheter ■ **~d with yellow** tacheté *OR* moucheté de jaune.

speckled ['spekld] *adj* tacheté, moucheté.

specs [speks] (*abbrev of* **spectacles**) *npl inf* lunettes *fpl*, binocles *mpl*.

spectacle ['spektəkl] *n* **1.** [sight] spectacle *m* ■ **he was a sorry** *OR* **sad ~** il était triste à voir ■ **to make a ~ of o.s.** se donner en spectacle **2.** CIN, THEAT & TV superproduction *f*.

spectacled ['spektəkld] *adj* [gen - ZOOL] à lunettes.

spectacles ['spektəklz] *npl* lunettes *fpl* ■ **a pair of ~** une paire de lunettes.

spectacular [spek'tækjʊlər] ◇ *adj* [event, defeat, result, view] spectaculaire ■ **there has been a ~ rise in house prices** le prix des maisons a fait un bond spectaculaire.
◇ *n* CIN, THEAT & TV superproduction *f*.

spectacularly [spek'tækjʊləlɪ] *adv* [big, beautiful] spectaculairement ■ **it went ~ wrong** ça s'est vraiment très mal passé.

spectate [spek'teɪt] *vi* assister à.

spectator [spek'teɪtər] *n* spectateur *m*, - trice *f*.

spectator sport *n* sport *m* grand public.

specter *US* = **spectre**.

spectra ['spektrə] *pl* ▷ **spectrum**.

spectral ['spektrəl] *adj* [gen - PHYS] spectral.

spectre *UK*, **specter** *US* ['spektər] *n* spectre *m*.

spectrogram ['spektrəgræm] *n* spectrogramme *m*.

spectrograph ['spektrəgrɑ:f] *n* spectrographe *m*.

spectrum ['spektrəm] (*pl* **spectrums** *OR pl* **spectra** ['spektrə]) *n* **1.** PHYS spectre *m* **2.** *fig* [range] gamme *f* ■ **right across the ~** sur toute la gamme ■ **the political ~** l'éventail *m* politique.

speculate ['spekjʊleɪt] *vi* **1.** [wonder] s'interroger, se poser des questions ■ [make suppositions] faire des suppositions ■ PHILOS spéculer ■ **the press is speculating about the future of the present government** la presse s'interroge sur l'avenir du gouvernement actuel **2.** COMM & FIN spéculer ■ **to ~ on the stock market** spéculer *OR* jouer en Bourse.

speculation [,spekjʊ'leɪʃn] *n* **1.** *(U)* [supposition, conjecture] conjecture *f*, conjectures *fpl*, supposition *f*, suppositions *fpl* ■ PHILOS spéculation *f* ■ **it's pure ~** ce n'est qu'une hypothèse ■ **there's been a lot of ~ about her motives** tout le monde s'est demandé quels étaient ses motifs **2.** [guess] supposition *f*, conjecture *f* **3.** COMM & FIN spéculation *f* ■ **~ in oil** spéculation sur le pétrole.

speculative ['spekjʊlətɪv] *adj* spéculatif.

speculator ['spekjʊleɪtər] *n* COMM & ST. EX spéculateur *m*, - trice *f*.

speculum ['spekjʊləm] (*pl* **speculums** *OR pl* **specula** [-lə]) *n* MED spéculum *m* ■ OPT miroir *m*, réflecteur *m*.

sped [sped] *pt & pp* ▷ **speed**.

speech [spi:tʃ] *n* **1.** [ability to speak] parole *f* ■ [spoken language] parole *f*, langage *m* parlé ■ **to express o.s. in ~** s'exprimer oralement *OR* par la parole ● **~ is silver but silence is golden** *prov* la parole est d'argent, mais le silence est d'or *prov* **2.** [manner of speaking] façon *f* de parler, langage *m* ■ [elocution] élocution *f*, articulation *f* ■ **his ~ was slurred** il bafouillait **3.** [dialect, language] parler *m*, langage *m* **4.** [talk] discours *m*, allocution *f fml* ■ [shorter, more informal] speech *m* ■ **to make a ~ on** *OR* **about sthg** faire un discours sur qqch ● **the Queen's Speech** POL le discours du Trône **5.** THEAT monologue *m*.

speech act *n* LING acte *m* de parole.

speech day *n* *UK* SCH distribution *f* des prix ■ **on ~** le jour de la distribution des prix.

SPEECH DAY

À la fin de l'année scolaire en Grande-Bretagne, il est de coutume, dans certaines écoles, d'inviter une personnalité qui préside la cérémonie de remise des prix et prononce un discours.

speech defect *n* défaut *m* de prononciation, trouble *m* du langage *spec*.

speechify ['spi:tʃɪfaɪ] (*pret & pp* **speechified**) *vi pej* discourir, faire de beaux discours.

speech-impaired *adj* muet.

speech impediment *n* défaut *m* d'élocution *OR* de prononciation.

speechless ['spi:tʃlɪs] *adj* **1.** [with amazement, disbelief] muet, interloqué ▪ [with rage, joy] muet ▪ **to leave sb ~** laisser qqn sans voix ▪ **I'm ~!** *inf* je ne sais pas quoi dire!, les bras m'en tombent! **2.** [inexpressible - rage, fear] muet.

speechmaking ['spi:tʃ,meɪkɪŋ] *n (U)* discours *mpl* ▪ *pej* beaux discours *mpl.*

speech pattern *n* schéma *m* linguistique.

speech recognition *n* COMPUT reconnaissance *f* de la parole.

speech sound *n* LING phone *m*, son *m* linguistique.

speech synthesizer *n* synthétiseur *m* de parole.

speech therapist *n* orthophoniste *mf.*

speech therapy *n* orthophonie *f.*

speechwriter ['spi:tʃ,raɪtəʳ] *n* personne *f* qui écrit des discours ▪ **she's the mayor's ~** c'est elle qui écrit les discours du maire.

speed [spi:d] <> *n* **1.** [rate, pace - of car, progress, reaction, work] vitesse *f* ▪ **I was driving** *OR* **going at a ~ of 65 mph** je roulais à 100 km/h ▪ **to do a ~ of 100 km/h** faire du 100 km/h ▪ **at (a) great** *OR* **high ~** à toute vitesse, à grande vitesse ▪ **at top** *OR* **full ~** [drive] à toute vitesse *OR* allure ; [work] très vite, en quatrième vitesse ▪ **at the ~ of light/sound** à la vitesse de la lumière/du son ➊ **reading ~** vitesse *f* de lecture ▪ **typing/shorthand ~** nombre *m* de mots-minute en dactylo/en sténo **2.** [rapid rate] vitesse *f*, rapidité *f* ▪ **I hate having to work at ~** *UK* j'ai horreur de devoir travailler vite ▪ **to pick up/to lose ~** prendre/perdre de la vitesse **3.** [gear - of car, bicycle] vitesse *f* **4.** PHOT [of film] rapidité *f*, sensibilité *f* ▪ [of shutter] vitesse *f* ▪ [of lens] luminosité *f* **5.** △ *drug sl* speed△ *m*, amphétamines *fpl.*
<> *vi* **1.** (*pret & pp* **sped** [sped]) [go fast] aller à toute allure ▪ **we sped across the field** nous avons traversé le champ à toute allure ▪ **he sped away** il est parti à toute vitesse, il a pris ses jambes à son cou ▪ **time seems to ~ by** le temps passe comme un éclair ▪ **the jetplane sped through the sky** le jet traversa le ciel comme un éclair **2.** (*pret & pp* **speeded**) AUT [exceed speed limit] faire des excès de vitesse.
<> *vt* (*pret & pp* **sped** [sped] *pret & pp* **speeded**) [person] : **to ~ sb on his way** souhaiter bon voyage à qqn ▪ **God ~ (you)!** *arch* (que) Dieu vous garde!
◆ **speed up** <> *vi insep* [gen] aller plus vite ▪ [driver] rouler plus vite ▪ [worker] travailler plus vite ▪ [machine, film] accélérer.
<> *vt sep* [worker] faire travailler plus vite ▪ [person] faire aller plus vite ▪ [work] activer, accélérer ▪ [pace] presser ▪ [production] accélérer, augmenter ▪ [reaction, film] accélérer.

speedboat ['spi:dbəʊt] *n* vedette *f* (rapide) ▪ [with outboard engine] hors-bord *m inv.*

speed bump *n* ralentisseur *m*, casse-vitesse *m.*

speed camera *n* cinémomètre *m.*

speed-dialling, speed-dialing *n (U)* *US* TELEC numérotation *f* rapide.

speeder ['spi:dəʳ] *n* [fast driver] *personne qui conduit vite* ▪ [convicted driver] *automobiliste condamné pour excès de vitesse.*

speed gun *n* radar *m* à main.

speedily ['spi:dɪlɪ] *adv* [quickly] vite, rapidement ▪ [promptly] promptement, sans tarder ▪ [soon] bientôt.

speeding ['spi:dɪŋ] <> *n* AUT excès *m* de vitesse ▪ **I was stopped for ~** j'ai été arrêté pour excès de vitesse.
<> *comp* : **a ~ ticket** un P-V pour excès de vitesse.

speed limit *n* limitation *f* de vitesse ▪ **the ~ is 60** la vitesse est limitée à 60.

speedo ['spi:dəʊ] (*pl* **speedos**) *UK inf* = **speedometer**.

speedometer [spɪ'dɒmɪtəʳ] *n* compteur *m* de vitesse.

speed-reading *n* lecture *f* rapide.

speed trap *n* contrôle *m* de vitesse ▪ **radar ~** contrôle radar.

speed-up *n* accélération *f.*

speedway ['spi:dweɪ] *n* **1.** [racing] speedway *m* **2.** *US* [track] piste *f* de vitesse pour motos **3.** *US* [expressway] voie *f* express *OR* rapide.

Speedwriting® ['spi:d,raɪtɪŋ] *n* sténo *f* alphabétique.

speedy ['spi:dɪ] (*comp* **speedier**, *superl* **speediest**) *adj* **1.** [rapid] rapide ▪ [prompt] prompt ▪ **her help brought a ~ end to the dispute** son aide a permis de mettre rapidement fin au différend **2.** [car] rapide, nerveux.

speleologist [,spi:lɪ'ɒlədʒɪst] *n* spéléologue *mf.*

speleology [,spi:lɪ'ɒlədʒɪ] *n* spéléologie *f.*

spell [spel] (*pret & pp* **spelled** *OR UK* **spelt** [spelt] *OR* **spelled**) <> *vt* **1.** [write] écrire, orthographier ▪ **they've spelt my name wrong** ils ont mal écrit mon nom ▪ **his name is spelt J-O-N** son nom s'écrit J-O-N ▪ **how do you ~ it?** comment est-ce que ça s'écrit? ▪ [aloud] épeler ▪ **shall I ~ my name for you?** voulez-vous que j'épelle mon nom? **2.** [subj: letters] former, donner ▪ **C-O-U-G-H ~s "cough"** C-O-U-G-H donnent "cough" **3.** *fig* [mean] signifier ▪ **the floods ~ disaster for our region** les inondations signifient le désastre pour notre région **4.** (*UK pret & pp* **spelled**) [worker, colleague] relayer.
<> *vi* : **to learn to ~** apprendre l'orthographe ▪ **he ~s badly** il est mauvais en orthographe.
<> *n* **1.** [period] (courte) période *f* ▪ **a ~ of cold weather** une période de (temps) froid ▪ **scattered showers and sunny ~s** des averses locales et des éclaircies ▪ **she did** *OR* **had a ~ as a reporter** elle a été journaliste pendant un certain temps ▪ **he had a dizzy ~** il a été pris de vertige **2.** [of duty] tour *m* ▪ **do you want me to take** *OR* **to do a ~ at the wheel?** voulez-vous que je vous relaie au volant *OR* que je conduise un peu? **3.** [magic words] formule *f* magique, incantation *f* **4.** [enchantment] charme *m*, sort *m*, sortilège *m* ▪ **to cast** *OR* **to put a ~ on sb** jeter un sort *OR* un charme à qqn, ensorceler *OR* envoûter qqn ▪ **to break the ~** rompre le charme ▪ **to be under sb's ~** *liter & fig* être sous le charme de qqn.
◆ **spell out** *vt sep* **1.** [read out letter by letter] épeler ▪ [decipher] déchiffrer **2.** [make explicit] expliquer bien clairement ▪ **do I have to ~ it out for you?** est-ce qu'il faut que je mette les points sur les i?

spellbinding ['spel,baɪndɪŋ] *adj* ensorcelant, envoûtant.

spellbound ['spelbaʊnd] *adj* [spectator, audience] captivé, envoûté ▪ **the film held me ~ from start to finish** le film m'a tenu en haleine *OR* m'a captivé du début jusqu'à la fin.

spell-check <> *n* vérification *f* orthographique ▪ **to do** *OR* **run a ~ on a document** effectuer la vérification orthographique d'un document.
<> *vt* faire la vérification orthographique de.

spell-checker *n* correcteur *m OR* vérificateur *m* orthographique.

speller ['speləʳ] *n* **1.** [person] : **he is a good/bad ~** il est bon/mauvais en orthographe **2.** [book] livre *m* d'orthographe.

spelling ['spelɪŋ] <> *n* **1.** [word formation] orthographe *f* ▪ **what is the ~ of this word?** quelle est l'orthographe de *OR* comment s'écrit ce mot? **2.** [ability to spell] : **he is good at ~** il est fort en orthographe.
<> *comp* [error, test, book] d'orthographe ▪ [pronunciation] orthographique ▪ **~ mistake** faute *f* d'orthographe.

spelling bee *n* *US* concours *m* d'orthographe.

spelling checker = **spell-checker**.

spelt [spelt] <> *pt & pp* ▻ **spell** *(vi & vt senses 1, 2 & 3).*
<> *n* BOT épeautre *m.*

spelunker [spɪ'lʌŋkəʳ] *n* *US* spéléologue *mf.*

spelunking [spɪ'lʌŋkɪŋ] *n* *US* spéléologie *f.*

spend [spend] *(pret & pp* **spent** [spent]*)* ◇ *vt* **1.** [money, fortune] dépenser ■ **to ~ money on** [food, clothes] dépenser de l'argent en ; [house, car] dépenser de l'argent pour, consacrer de l'argent à ■ **how much do you ~ on the children's clothes?** combien (d'argent) dépensez-vous pour habiller vos enfants? ■ **he ~s all his money (on) gambling** il dépense tout son argent au jeu ■ **he ~s most of his pocket money on (buying) records** la plus grande partie de son argent de poche passe dans l'achat de disques ■ **I consider it money well spent** je considère que c'est un bon investissement ■ **without ~ing a penny** sans dépenser un centime, sans bourse délier ▶ **to ~ a penny** *UK inf euph* aller au petit coin **2.** [time - pass] passer ; [- devote] consacrer ■ **to ~ time on sthg/on doing sthg** passer du temps sur qqch/à faire qqch ■ **I spent three hours on the job** le travail m'a pris *OR* demandé trois heures ■ **what a way to ~ Easter!** quelle façon de passer les vacances de Pâques! ■ **I spent a lot of time and effort on this** j'y ai consacré beaucoup de temps et d'efforts ■ **she spent her life helping the underprivileged** elle a consacré sa vie à aider les défavorisés **3.** [exhaust, use up] épuiser.
◇ *vi* dépenser, faire des dépenses.
◇ *n UK* [allocated money] allocation *f* ■ **we must increase our marketing ~** nous devons augmenter le budget marketing.

spendaholic [ˌspendəˈhɒlɪk] *n* grand dépensier *m*, grande dépensière *f*.

spender [ˈspendəʳ] *n* dépensier *m*, - ère *f* ■ **she's a big ~** elle est très dépensière.

spending [ˈspendɪŋ] *n (U)* dépenses *fpl* ■ **public** *OR* **government ~** dépenses publiques ■ **a cut in defence ~** une réduction du budget de la défense.

spending money *n* argent *m* de poche.

spending power *n* pouvoir *m* d'achat.

spending spree *n* : **we went on a ~** nous avons fait des folies, nous avons dépensé des sommes folles.

spendthrift [ˈspendθrɪft] ◇ *n* dépensier *m*, - ère *f*.
◇ *adj* dépensier.

spent [spent] ◇ *pt & pp* ▷ **spend**.
◇ *adj* **1.** [used up - fuel, bullet, match] utilisé ■ [cartridge] brûlé ■ **the party is a ~ force in politics** le parti n'a plus l'influence qu'il avait en politique ■ **her courage was ~** elle n'avait plus de courage **2.** [tired out] épuisé.

sperm [spɜːm] *(pl inv OR pl* **sperms***)* *n* **1.** [cell] spermatozoïde *m* ■ **~ count** spermogramme *m* **2.** [liquid] sperme *m*.

spermatic [spɜːˈmætɪk] *adj* spermatique ■ **~ cord** cordon *m* spermatique ■ **~ fluid** sperme *m*.

sperm bank *n* banque *f* de sperme.

spermicidal [ˌspɜːmɪˈsaɪdl] *adj* spermicide ■ **~ cream/jelly** crème *f* /gelée *f* spermicide.

spermicide [ˈspɜːmɪsaɪd] *n* spermicide *m*.

sperm whale *n* cachalot *m*.

spew [spjuː] ◇ *vt* **1.**[△] *liter* dégueuler **2.** *fig* vomir.
◇ *vi* **1.**[△] *liter* dégueuler **2.** *fig* [pour out] gicler.
◆ **spew up**[△] *vi insep & vt sep* vomir.

sphere [sfɪəʳ] *n* **1.** [globe] sphère *f* ■ *lit* [sky] cieux *mpl* **2.** *fig* [of interest, activity] sphère *f*, domaine *m* ■ **her ~ of activity** [professional] son domaine d'activité ; [personal] sa sphère d'activité ■ **the question is outside the committee's ~** la question ne relève pas des compétences du comité ■ **the guests came from various social and professional ~ s** les invités venaient de divers horizons sociaux et professionnels ■ **in the public ~** [industry] dans le domaine public ; [politics] dans la vie politique.

spherical [ˈsferɪkl] *adj* sphérique.

spheroid [ˈsfɪərɔɪd] *n* sphéroïde *m*.

sphincter [ˈsfɪŋktəʳ] *n* sphincter *m*.

Sphinx [sfɪŋks] *pr n* : **the ~** le sphinx.

spic[▲] [spɪk] *n US terme injurieux désignant les Américains hispanophones, en particulier les Portoricains.*

spice [spaɪs] ◇ *n* **1.** CULIN épice *f* ■ **it needs more ~** ce n'est pas assez épicé *OR* relevé ▶ **mixed ~** *(U)* épices *fpl* mélangées ■ **~ cake** gâteau *m* aux épices ■ **~ rack** étagère *f OR* présentoir *m* à épices **2.** *fig* piquant *m*, sel *m* ■ **the story lacks ~** l'histoire manque de sel *OR* de piquant.
◇ *vt* **1.** CULIN épicer, parfumer ■ **~d with nutmeg** parfumé à la muscade **2.** *fig* pimenter, corser ■ **the story is ~d with political anecdotes** l'histoire est pimentée d'anecdotes politiques.

spick-and-span [ˈspɪkənˌspæn] *adj* [room] impeccable, reluisant de propreté ■ [appearance] tiré à quatre épingles.

spicy [ˈspaɪsɪ] *(comp* **spicier**, *superl* **spiciest***)* *adj* **1.** [food] épicé **2.** *fig* [book, story] piquant, corsé.

spider [ˈspaɪdəʳ] *n* **1.** ZOOL araignée *f* ■ **~'s web** toile *f* d'araignée **2.** *UK* [for luggage] araignée *f* (à bagages) **3.** *US* CULIN poêle *f* (à trépied).

spider crab *n* araignée *f* (de mer).

spider monkey *n* singe *m* araignée, atèle *m*.

spider plant *n* chlorophytum *m*.

spiderweb [ˈspaɪdəweb] *n US* toile *f* d'araignée.

spidery [ˈspaɪdərɪ] *adj* [in shape] en forme d'araignée ■ [finger] long et mince ■ **~ writing** pattes *fpl* de mouches.

spiel [ʃpiːl] *inf* ◇ *n* **1.** [speech] laïus *m*, baratin *m* **2.** [sales talk] baratin *m*.
◇ *vi* baratiner.

spiffy [ˈspɪfɪ] *(comp* **spiffier**, *superl* **spiffiest***)* *adj US* chic.

spigot [ˈspɪgət] *n* **1.** [in cask] fausset *m* **2.** [part of tap] clé *f* **3.** *US* [tap] robinet *m* (extérieur).

spike [spaɪk] ◇ *vt* **1.** [shoes, railings] garnir de pointes **2.** [impale] transpercer **3.** *inf* [drink] corser ■ **my coffee was ~d with brandy** mon café était arrosé de cognac **4.** PRESS [story] rejeter.
◇ *vi* [in volleyball] smasher.
◇ *n* **1.** [on railings, shoe] pointe *f* ■ [on cactus] épine *f* ■ [on tyre] clou *m* ■ [for paper] pique-notes *m inv* **2.** [peak - on graph] pointe *f* **3.** [nail] gros clou *m* **4.** [antler] dague *f* **5.** [in volleyball] smash *m*.
◆ **spikes** *npl inf* [shoes] chaussures *fpl* à pointes.

spiked [spaɪkt] *adj* [railings] à pointes de fer ■ [shoes] à pointes ■ [tyre] clouté, à clous.

spiky [ˈspaɪkɪ] *(comp* **spikier**, *superl* **spikiest***)* *adj* **1.** [branch, railings] garni *OR* hérissé de pointes ■ [hair] en épis ■ [writing] pointu **2.** *UK inf* [bad-tempered] chatouilleux, ombrageux.

spill [spɪl] *(UK pret & pp* **spilt** [spɪlt] *OR* **spilled** *US OR* **spilled***)* ◇ *vt* **1.** [liquid, salt etc] renverser, répandre ■ **she spilt coffee down** *OR* **over her dress** elle a renversé du café sur sa robe ■ **she spilt the contents of her handbag onto the bed** elle vida (le contenu de) son sac à main sur le lit **2.** *fig* [secret] dévoiler ■ **to ~ the beans** *inf* vendre la mèche **3.** [blood] verser, faire couler **4.** [person] : **he was ~ed from his motorbike** il est tombé de sa moto **5.** NAUT : **to ~ (wind from) a sail** étouffer une voile *OR* la toile.
◇ *vi* **1.** [liquid, salt etc] se renverser, se répandre **2.** [crowd] se déverser ■ **the huge crowd ~ed into the square** l'immense foule se répandit *OR* se déversa sur la place.
◇ *n* **1.** [spillage - of liquid] renversement *m* **2.** [fall - from horse, bike] chute *f*, culbute *f* ■ *dated* [accident] accident *m* ■ **to take a ~** faire la culbute **3.** [channel] déversoir *m* **4.** [for fire] longue allumette *f*.
◆ **spill out** ◇ *vt sep* **1.** [contents, liquid] renverser, répandre **2.** *fig* [secret] dévoiler, révéler.
◇ *vi insep* **1.** [contents, liquid] se renverser, se répandre **2.** *fig* [crowd] se déverser, s'échapper ■ **the commuters ~ed out of the train** un flot de banlieusards s'est échappé du train.
◆ **spill over** *vi insep* **1.** [liquid] déborder, se répandre **2.** *fig* [overflow] se déverser, déborder ■ **her work ~s over into her family life** son travail empiète sur sa vie familiale.

spillage ['spɪlɪdʒ] *n* [act of spilling] renversement *m*, fait *m* de renverser ■ [liquid spilt] liquide *m* renversé ■ **we managed to avoid too much ~** nous avons réussi à ne pas trop en renverser.

spillover ['spɪl,əʊvəʳ] *n* **1.** [act of spilling] renversement *m* ■ [quantity spilt] quantité *f* renversée **2.** [excess] excédent *m* **3.** ECON retombées *fpl* (économiques).

spillway ['spɪlweɪ] *n* déversoir *m*.

spilt [spɪlt] *UK pt & pp* ▷ **spill**.

spin [spɪn] (*pret & pp* **spun** [spʌn], *cont* **spinning**) ◇ *vt* **1.** [cause to rotate - wheel, chair] faire tourner ; [- top] lancer, faire tournoyer ■ SPORT [- ball] donner de l'effet à ■ **to ~ the wheel** [in casino] faire tourner la roue ; [in car] braquer
2. [yarn, glass] filer ■ [thread] fabriquer
3. [subj: spider, silkworm] tisser
4. [invent - tale] inventer, débiter ■ **he ~s a good yarn** il raconte bien les histoires
5. [in spin-dryer] essorer.
◇ *vi* **1.** [rotate] tourner, tournoyer ■ SPORT [ball] tournoyer ■ **the skater/ballerina spun on one foot** le patineur/la ballerine virevolta sur un pied ■ **a strange shape was spinning across the sky** une forme étrange traversait le ciel en tournoyant sur elle-même ■ **the wheels were spinning in the mud** les roues patinaient dans la boue ■ **to ~ out of control** [plane] tomber en vrille ; [car] faire un tête-à-queue
2. *fig* [grow dizzy] tourner ■ **my head is spinning** j'ai la tête qui (me) tourne ■ **these figures make your head ~** ces chiffres vous donnent le tournis *OR* le vertige
3. [spinner] filer ■ [spider] tisser sa toile
4. [in spin-dryer] essorer
5. FISHING : **to ~ for pike** pêcher le brochet à la cuiller.
◇ *n* **1.** [rotation] tournoiement *m* ■ **give the wheel a ~** faites tourner la roue ■ **the plane went into a ~** [accidentally] l'avion a fait une chute en vrille ; [in aerobatics] l'avion a effectué une descente en vrille ■ **the car went into a ~** la voiture a fait un tête-à-queue ■ **my head is in a ~** *fig* j'ai la tête qui tourne
2. *inf* [panic] : **to be in a flat ~** être dans tous ses états
3. SPORT [on ball] effet *m* ■ **to put ~ on a ball** donner de l'effet à une balle
4. [in spin-dryer] essorage *m* ■ **to give sthg a ~** essorer qqch
5. *inf* [ride - in car] tour *m*, balade *f* ■ **to go for a ~** faire une (petite) balade en voiture
6. *inf* [try] : **to give sthg a ~** essayer *OR* tenter qqch.
◆ **spin off** *vt sep* [hive off] : **they spun off their own company** ils ont monté leur propre affaire.
◆ **spin out** *vt sep* [story, idea] faire durer, délayer ■ [supplies, money] faire durer, économiser.
◆ **spin round** *UK*, **spin around** ◇ *vi insep* **1.** [planet, wheel] tourner (sur soi-même) ■ [skater, top] tournoyer, tourner
2. [face opposite direction] se retourner ■ **he suddenly spun round** il pivota sur ses talons *OR* se retourna brusquement.
◇ *vt sep* faire tourner.

spina bifida [,spaɪnə'bɪfɪdə] *n* spina-bifida *m inv*.

spinach ['spɪnɪdʒ] *n (U)* épinards *mpl*.

spinal ['spaɪnl] *adj* [nerve, muscle] spinal ■ [ligament, disc] vertébral ■ **a ~ injury** une blessure à la colonne vertébrale.

spinal column *n* colonne *f* vertébrale.

spinal cord *n* moelle *f* épinière.

spindle ['spɪndl] *n* **1.** [for spinning - by hand] fuseau *m* ; [- by machine] broche *f* **2.** TECH broche *f*, axe *m* ■ [in motor, lathe] arbre *m* ■ [of valve] tige *f*.

spindly ['spɪndlɪ] (*comp* **spindlier**, *superl* **spindliest**) *adj* [legs] grêle, comme des allumettes ■ [body] chétif, maigrichon ■ [tree] grêle ■ [plant] étiolé.

spin doctor *n au sein d'un parti politique, personne chargée de promouvoir l'image de celui-ci.*

spin-drier *n* essoreuse *f*.

spindrift ['spɪndrɪft] *n (U)* embruns *mpl*.

spin-dry *vi & vt* essorer.

spine [spaɪn] *n* **1.** ANAT colonne *f* vertébrale ■ ZOOL épine *f* dorsale **2.** [prickle - of hedgehog] piquant *m* ; [- of plant, rose] épine *f* **3.** [of book] dos *m* **4.** [of hill] crête *f* **5.** *US* [courage] résolution *f*, volonté *f*.

spine-chilling *adj* à vous glacer le sang, terrifiant.

spineless ['spaɪnlɪs] *adj* **1.** [weak] mou (*before vowel or silent 'h'* **mol**), molle *f* ■ [cowardly] lâche **2.** ZOOL invertébré **3.** BOT sans épines.

spinet [spɪ'net] *n* épinette *f*.

spinnaker ['spɪnəkəʳ] *n* spinnaker *m*, spi *m*.

spinner ['spɪnəʳ] *n* **1.** TEX [person] fileur *m*, - euse *f* **2.** [in fishing] cuiller *f* **3.** [spin-dryer] essoreuse *f (à linge)* **4.** *UK* SPORT [bowler in cricket] lanceur *m* ■ [ball] balle *f* qui a de l'effet.

spinney ['spɪnɪ] *n UK* bosquet *m*, boqueteau *m*, petit bois *m*.

spinning ['spɪnɪŋ] ◇ *n* **1.** TEX [by hand] filage *m* ■ [by machine] filature *f* **2.** [in fishing] pêche *f* à la cuiller.
◇ *adj* tournant, qui tourne.

spinning jenny *n* jenny *f*.

spinning top *n* toupie *f*.

spinning wheel *n* rouet *m*.

spin-off *n* **1.** [by-product] retombée *f*, produit *m* dérivé **2.** [work derived from another] : **the book is a ~ from the TV series** le roman est tiré de la série télévisée ■ **the TV series gave rise to a number of ~s** la série télévisée a donné lieu à plusieurs produits dérivés.

spinster ['spɪnstəʳ] *n* ADMIN & LAW célibataire *f* ■ *pej* vieille fille *f*.

spiny ['spaɪnɪ] (*comp* **spinier**, *superl* **spiniest**) *adj* épineux, couvert d'épines.

spiny lobster *n* langouste *f*.

spiral ['spaɪərəl] (*UK pret & pp* **spiralled**, *cont* **spiralling**) (*US pret & pp* **spiraled**, *cont* **spiraling**) ◇ *n* **1.** [gen - ECON] & GEOM spirale *f* ■ **in a ~** en spirale ■ **a ~ of smoke rose into the sky** une volute de fumée s'éleva dans le ciel ■ **inflationary ~** spirale *f* inflationniste **2.** AERON vrille *f*.
◇ *adj* [motif, shell, curve] en (forme de) spirale ■ [descent, spring] en spirale ■ **the plane went into a ~ descent** l'avion commença une descente en vrille ■ **~ binding** reliure *f* spirale.
◇ *vi* **1.** [in flight - plane] vriller ; [- bird] voler en spirale ■ [in shape - smoke, stairs] former une spirale **2.** [prices, inflation] s'envoler, monter en flèche ■ **to ~ downwards** chuter.
◆ **spiral up** *vi insep* [plane, smoke] monter en spirale ■ [prices] monter en flèche.

spiral-bound *adj* [notebook] à spirale.

spiral galaxy *n* galaxie *f* spirale.

spiral staircase *n* escalier *m* en colimaçon.

spire ['spaɪəʳ] *n* **1.** ARCHIT flèche *f* **2.** [of blade of grass] tige *f* ■ [of mountain, tree] cime *f*.

spirit ['spɪrɪt] ◇ *n* **1.** [non-physical part of being, soul] esprit *m* ■ **the poor in ~** les pauvres d'esprit ■ **the ~ is willing but the flesh is weak** l'esprit est prompt mais la chair est faible ■ **he is with us in ~** il est avec nous en esprit *OR* par l'esprit
2. [supernatural being] esprit *m* ■ **to call up the ~s of the dead** évoquer les âmes des morts ▶ **evil ~s** esprits malins ■ **the ~ world** le monde des esprits
3. [person] esprit *m*, âme *f* ■ **he is one of the great ~s of modern philosophy** c'est un des grands esprits de la philosophie moderne
4. [attitude, mood] esprit *m*, attitude *f* ■ **you mustn't do it in a ~ of vengeance** il ne faut pas le faire par esprit de vengeance ■ **she took my remarks in the wrong ~** elle a mal pris mes remarques ▶ **to enter into the ~ of things** [at party] se mettre au diapason ; [in work] participer de bon cœur ■ **that's the ~!** voilà comment il faut réagir!, à la bonne heure!
5. [deep meaning] esprit *m*, génie *m* ■ **the ~ of the law** l'esprit de la loi

6. [energy] énergie *f*, entrain *m* ▪ [courage] courage *m* ▪ [character] caractère *m* ▪ **he replied with ~** il a répondu énergiquement ▪ **a man of ~** un homme de caractère ▪ **his ~ was broken** il avait perdu courage
7. *(usu pl)* UK [alcoholic drink] alcool *m*, spiritueux *m*
8. CHEM essence *f*, sel *m* ▪ **~** *OR* **~s of ammonia** ammoniaque *m* liquide ▪ **~ of turpentine** (essence de) térébenthine *f*.
◇ *vt* [move secretly] : **they ~ed her in/out by a side door** ils l'ont fait entrer/sortir discrètement par une porte dérobée ▪ **he seems to have been ~ed into thin air** il semble avoir disparu comme par enchantement.
◆ **spirits** *npl* [mood, mental state] humeur *f*, état *m* d'esprit ▪ [morale] moral *m* ▪ **to be in good ~s** être de bonne humeur, avoir le moral ▪ **to feel out of ~s** avoir le cafard ▪ **to be in low ~s** être déprimé ▪ **you must keep your ~s up** il faut garder le moral, il ne faut pas vous laisser abattre ▪ **to raise sb's ~s** remonter le moral à qqn.
◆ **spirit away, spirit off** *vt sep* [carry off secretly] faire disparaître (comme par enchantement) ▪ [steal] escamoter, subtiliser.

spirited ['spɪrɪtɪd] *adj* **1.** [lively - person] vif, plein d'entrain ; [- horse] fougueux ; [- manner] vif ; [- reply, argument] vif ; [- music, rhythm, dance] entraînant **2.** [courageous - person, action, decision, defence] courageux ▪ **to put up a ~ resistance** résister courageusement, opposer une résistance courageuse.

spirit gum *n* colle *f* gomme.

spirit lamp *n* lampe *f* à alcool.

spiritless ['spɪrɪtlɪs] *adj* [lifeless] sans vie, sans entrain, apathique ▪ [depressed] démoralisé, déprimé ▪ [cowardly] lâche.

spirit level *n* niveau *m* à bulle.

spirit stove *n* réchaud *m* à alcool.

spiritual ['spɪrɪtʃʊəl] ◇ *adj* **1.** [relating to the spirit] spirituel ▪ **a very ~ man** un homme d'une grande spiritualité ▪ **China is her ~ home** la Chine est sa patrie d'adoption **2.** [religious, sacred] religieux, sacré ▪ **~ adviser** conseiller *m* spirituel.
◇ *n* [song] (negro) spiritual *m*.

spiritualism ['spɪrɪtʃʊəlɪzm] *n* RELIG spiritisme *m* ▪ PHILOS spiritualisme *m*.

spiritualist ['spɪrɪtʃʊəlɪst] ◇ *adj* RELIG spirite ▪ PHILOS spiritualiste.
◇ *n* RELIG spirite *mf* ▪ PHILOS spiritualiste *mf*.

spirituality [,spɪrɪtʃʊ'ælətɪ] *n* spiritualité *f*.

spiritually ['spɪrɪtʃʊəlɪ] *adv* spirituellement, en esprit.

spit [spɪt] (*pret & pp* **spit** *OR* **spat** [spæt], *cont* **spitting**) ◇ *vi* **1.** [in anger, contempt] cracher ▪ **to ~ at sb** cracher sur qqn ▪ **to ~ in sb's face** cracher à la figure de qqn ▪ **she spat at him** elle lui a craché dessus **2.** [while talking] postillonner, envoyer des postillons **3.** [hot fat] sauter, grésiller **4.** *phr* **it's spitting (with rain)** il bruine, il pleut légèrement.
◇ *vt liter & fig* cracher.
◇ *n* **1.** *(U)* [spittle - in mouth] salive *f* ; [- spat out] crachat *m* ; [- ejected while speaking] postillon *m* ▪ [act of spitting] crachement *m* ▪ **~ and polish** MIL astiquage *m* ▪ **~ and sawdust** *expression évoquant un pub miteux* **2.** UK *inf* [likeness] : **he's the ~ of his dad** c'est son père tout craché **3.** [of insects] écume *f* printanière, crachat *m* de coucou **4.** CULIN broche *f* **5.** GEOG pointe *f*, langue *f* de terre.
◆ **spit out** *vt sep* [food, medicine, words, invective] cracher ▪ **come on, ~ it out!** *inf* allez, accouche!

spit curl *n* US accroche-cœur *m*.

spite [spaɪt] ◇ *n* [malice] dépit *m*, malveillance *f* ▪ **to do sthg out of ~** faire qqch par dépit.
◇ *vt* contrarier, vexer.
◆ **in spite of** *prep phr* en dépit de, malgré ▪ **in ~ of myself** malgré moi ▪ **in ~ of the fact that we have every chance of winning** bien que nous ayons toutes les chances de gagner.

spiteful ['spaɪtfʊl] *adj* [person, remark, character] malveillant ▪ **that was a ~ thing to say** c'était méchant de dire ça ▪ **to have a ~ tongue** avoir une langue de vipère.

spitefully ['spaɪtfʊlɪ] *adv* par dépit, par méchanceté, méchamment.

spitfire ['spɪtfaɪəʳ] *n* : **she's a real ~** elle est très soupe au lait.

spit roast *n* rôti *m* à la broche.
◆ **spit-roast** *vt* faire rôtir à la broche.

spitting ['spɪtɪŋ] *n* : **'no ~'** 'défense de cracher' ▸ **he was within ~ distance of me** *inf* il était à deux pas de moi.

spitting image *n inf* **to be the ~ of sb : he's the ~ of his father** c'est son père tout craché.

spittle ['spɪtl] *n* [saliva - of person] salive *f* ; [- of dog] bave *f* ; [- on floor] crachat *m*.

spittoon [spɪ'tu:n] *n* crachoir *m*.

spiv [spɪv] *n* UK *inf* filou *m*.

splash [splæʃ] ◇ *vt* **1.** [with water, mud] éclabousser ▪ **the bus ~ed us with mud** *OR* **~ed mud over us** le bus nous a éclaboussés de boue ▪ **I ~ed my face with cold water** *OR* **cold water onto my face** je me suis aspergé le visage d'eau froide *OR* avec de l'eau froide ▪ **he ~ed his way across the river** il a traversé la rivière en pataugeant **2.** [pour carelessly] répandre ▪ **I ~ed disinfectant round the sink** j'ai aspergé le tour de l'évier de désinfectant **3.** [daub] barbouiller **4.** PRESS étaler ▪ **the story was ~ed across the front page** l'affaire était étalée à la une des journaux.
◇ *vi* **1.** [rain, liquid] faire des éclaboussures ▪ **the tea ~ed onto the floor/over the book** le thé éclaboussa le sol/le livre ▪ **heavy drops of rain ~ed on the ground** de grosses gouttes de pluie s'écrasaient sur le sol **2.** [walk, run etc] patauger, barboter ▪ **he ~ed through the mud/puddles** il a traversé la boue/les flaques d'eau en pataugeant.
◇ *n* **1.** [noise] floc *m*, plouf *m* ▪ **he fell/jumped in with a ~** il est tombé/il a sauté dedans avec un grand plouf **2.** [of mud, paint] éclaboussure *f* ▪ [of colour, light] tache *f* ▪ **to give sthg a ~ of colour** donner une touche de couleur à qqch ▪ **~es of white** des taches blanches **3.** [small quantity - of whisky] goutte *f* ; [- of soda, tonic] : **would you like a ~ of soda in your whisky?** voulez-vous un peu de soda dans votre whisky? **4.** *inf fig* [sensation] sensation *f* ▪ **to make a ~** faire sensation.
◇ *adv* : **to go/to fall ~ into the water** entrer/tomber dans l'eau en faisant plouf.
◆ **splash about** UK, **splash around** ◇ *vi insep* [duck, swimmer] barboter.
◇ *vt sep* [liquid] faire des éclaboussures de ▪ [money] dépenser sans compter.
◆ **splash down** *vi insep* [spaceship] amerrir.
◆ **splash out** *inf* ◇ *vi insep* [spend] faire des folies ▪ **to ~ out on sthg** se payer qqch.
◇ *vt insep* [money] claquer.

splashback ['splæʃbæk] *n* revêtement *m* *(derrière un évier, un lavabo)*.

splashdown ['splæʃdaʊn] *n* [of spaceship] amerrissage *m*.

splashy ['splæʃɪ] *adj* US *inf* tape-à-l'œil.

splat [splæt] ◇ *n* floc *m*.
◇ *adv* : **to go ~** faire floc.

splatter ['splætəʳ] ◇ *vt* éclabousser ▪ **~ed with mud/blood** éclaboussé de boue/sang.
◇ *vi* [rain] crépiter ▪ [mud] éclabousser.
◇ *n* **1.** [mark - of mud, ink] éclaboussure *f* **2.** [sound - of rain] crépitement *m*.

splay [spleɪ] ◇ *vt* [fingers, legs] écarter ▪ [feet] tourner en dehors.
◇ *vi* [fingers, legs] s'écarter ▪ [feet] se tourner en dehors.

spleen [spli:n] *n* **1.** ANAT rate *f* **2.** [bad temper] humeur *f* noire, mauvaise humeur *f* ▪ **to vent one's ~ on sthg/sb** décharger sa bile sur qqch/qqn.

splendid ['splendɪd] ◇ *adj* **1.** [beautiful, imposing - dress, setting, decor] splendide, superbe, magnifique **2.** [very good - idea, meal] excellent, magnifique ; [- work] excellent, superbe.
◇ *interj* excellent!, parfait!

splendidly ['splendɪdlɪ] *adv* **1.** [dress, decorate, furnish] magnifiquement, superbement ▪ [entertain] somptueusement ▪ **he was ~ turned out in military uniform** il était vraiment superbe en uniforme militaire **2.** [perform] superbement ▪ **my work is going ~** mon travail avance à merveille.

splendour *UK*, **splendor** *US* ['splendəʳ] *n* splendeur *f*.

splenetic [splɪ'netɪk] *adj lit* [ill-humoured] atrabilaire.

splice [splaɪs] ◇ *vt* **1.** [join] : **to ~ (together)** [film, tape] coller ; [rope] épisser ; [pieces of wood] enter ▶ **to ~ the mainbrace** *inf* NAUT ≃ distribuer une ration de rhum ; [gen] boire un coup **2.** *UK inf hum* [marry] : **to get ~d** convoler (en justes noces).
◇ *n* [in tape, film] collure *f* ▪ [in rope] épissure *f* ▪ [in wood] enture *f*.

spliff [splɪf] *n drug sl* joint *m*.

splint [splɪnt] ◇ *n* MED éclisse *f*, attelle *f* ▪ **her arm was in a ~** *OR* **in ~s** elle avait le bras dans une attelle.
◇ *vt* éclisser, mettre dans une attelle.

splinter ['splɪntəʳ] ◇ *n* [of glass, wood] éclat *m* ▪ [of bone] esquille *f* ▪ [in foot, finger] écharde *f*.
◇ *vt* [glass, bone] briser en éclats ▪ [wood] fendre en éclats.
◇ *vi* [glass, bone] se briser en éclats ▪ [marble, wood] se fendre en éclats ▪ [political party] se scinder, se fractionner.

splinter group *n* groupe *m* dissident *OR* scissionniste.

split [splɪt] (*pret & pp* **split**, *cont* **splitting**) ◇ *vt* **1.** [cleave - stone] fendre, casser ; [- slate] cliver ; [- wood] fendre ▪ **to ~ sthg in two** *OR* **in half** casser *OR* fendre qqch en deux ▪ **to ~ sthg open** ouvrir qqch *(en le coupant en deux ou en le fendant)* ▪ **he ~ his head open on the concrete** il s'est fendu le crâne sur le béton ▪ **they ~ open the mattress in their search for drugs** ils ont éventré le matelas à la recherche de stupéfiants ▪ **to ~ the atom** PHYS fissionner l'atome ▶ **to ~ one's sides (laughing)** se tordre de rire
2. [tear] déchirer ▪ **the plastic sheet had been ~ right down the middle** la bâche en plastique avait été fendue en plein milieu ▪ **I've ~ my trousers** j'ai déchiré mon pantalon
3. [divide - family] diviser ▪ POL [- party] diviser, créer *OR* provoquer une scission dans ▪ **we were ~ into two groups** on nous a divisés en deux groupes ▪ **the committee is ~ on this issue** le comité est divisé sur cette question ▪ **the vote was ~ down the middle** les deux camps avaient obtenu exactement le même nombre de voix ▪ **we were ~ 30-70** on était 30 % d'un côté et 70 % de l'autre
4. [share - profits] (se) partager, (se) répartir ; [- bill] (se) partager ▪ FIN [- stocks] faire une redistribution de ▪ **they decided to ~ the work between them** ils ont décidé de se partager le travail ▪ **to ~ the profits four ways** diviser les bénéfices en quatre ▪ **to ~ the difference** [share out] partager la différence ; [compromise] couper la poire en deux
5. GRAM : **to ~ an infinitive** *intercaler un adverbe ou une expression adverbiale entre "to" et le verbe*
6.△ [leave] quitter ▪ **I'm going to ~ this scene** je me tire *OR* barre.
◇ *vi* **1.** [break - wood, slate] se fendre, éclater ▪ **the ship ~ in two** le navire s'est brisé (en deux) ▪ **my head is splitting** *fig* j'ai un mal de tête atroce
2. [tear - fabric] se déchirer ; [- seam] craquer ▪ **the bag ~ open** le sac s'est déchiré
3. [divide - gen] se diviser, se fractionner ; [- political party] se scinder ; [- cell] se diviser ; [- road, railway] se diviser, bifurquer ▪ **the hikers ~ into three groups** les randonneurs se sont divisés en trois groupes
4. [separate - couple] se séparer ; [- family, group] s'éparpiller, se disperser ▪ **she has ~ with her old school friends** elle ne voit plus ses anciennes camarades de classe
5.△ [leave] se casser, mettre les bouts.
◇ *n* **1.** [crack - in wood, rock] fissure *f* ▪ **there is a long ~ in the wood** le bois est fendu sur une bonne longueur
2. [tear] déchirure *f*
3. [division] division *f* ▪ [separation] séparation *f* ▪ [quarrel] rupture *f* ▪ POL scission *f*, schisme *m* ▪ RELIG schisme *m* ▪ [gap] fossé *m*, écart *m* ▪ **there was a three-way ~ in the voting** les votes étaient répartis en trois groupes
4. [share] part *f*
5. *US* [bottle] : **soda ~** petite bouteille de soda.
◇ *adj* [lip, skirt] fendu.

◆ **splits** *npl* : **to do the ~s** *UK*, **to do ~s** *US* faire le grand écart.

◆ **split off** ◇ *vi insep* **1.** [branch, splinter] se détacher **2.** [separate - person, group] se séparer ▪ **a radical movement ~ off from the main party** un mouvement radical s'est détaché du gros du parti.
◇ *vt sep* **1.** [break, cut - branch, piece] enlever (en fendant) **2.** [person, group] séparer ▪ **our branch was ~ off from the parent company** notre succursale a été séparée de la maison mère.

◆ **split on** *vt insep UK inf* [inform on] vendre, moucharder.

◆ **split up** ◇ *vi insep* **1.** [wood, marble] se fendre ▪ [ship] se briser
2. [couple] se séparer, rompre ▪ [friends] rompre, se brouiller ▪ [meeting, members] se disperser ▪ POL se diviser, se scinder ▪ **to ~ up with sb** rompre avec qqn ▪ **the search party ~ up into three groups** l'équipe de secours s'est divisée en trois groupes.
◇ *vt sep* **1.** [wood] fendre ▪ [cake] couper en morceaux
2. [divide - profits] partager ; [- work] répartir ▪ **let's ~ the work up between us** répartissons-nous le travail ▪ **the teaching syllabus is ~ up into several chapters** le programme d'enseignement est divisé en plusieurs chapitres
3. [disperse] disperser ▪ **the teacher ~ the boys up** le professeur a séparé les garçons ▪ **the police ~ up the meeting/crowd** la police a mis fin à la réunion/dispersé la foule.

split decision *n* SPORT [in boxing] victoire *f*, décision *f* aux points.

split end *n* fourche *f*.

split infinitive *n* GRAM *infinitif où un adverbe ou une expression adverbiale est intercalé entre "to" et le verbe.*

split-level *adj* [house, flat] à deux niveaux ▪ **~ cooker** cuisinière *f* à éléments de cuisson séparés.

split pea *n* pois *m* cassé.

split personality *n* double personnalité *f*, dédoublement *m* de la personnalité.

split pin *n UK* goupille *f* fendue.

split screen *n* CIN écran *m* divisé.

split second *n* : **in a ~** en une fraction de seconde.

◆ **split-second** *adj* [timing, reaction] au quart de seconde.

split ticket *n US* POL panachage *m*.

splitting ['splɪtɪŋ] ◇ *n* **1.** [of wood, marble] fendage *m* ▪ **the ~ of the atom** PHYS la fission de l'atome **2.** [of fabric, seams] déchirure *f* **3.** [division] division *f* **4.** [sharing] partage *m*.
◇ *adj* : **I have a ~ headache** j'ai un mal de tête atroce.

split-up *n* [gen] rupture *f*, séparation *f* ▪ POL scission *f*.

splodge ['splɒdʒ] *inf* ◇ *n* **1.** [splash - of paint, ink] éclaboussure *f*, tache *f* ; [- of colour] tache *f* **2.** [dollop - of cream, of jam] bonne cuillerée *f*.
◇ *vt* éclabousser, barbouiller.
◇ *vi* s'étaler, faire des pâtés.

splotch [splɒtʃ] *US inf* = **splodge**.

splurge [splɜːdʒ] *inf* ◇ *n* **1.** [spending spree] folie *f*, folles dépenses *fpl* ▪ **I went on** *OR* **I had a ~ and bought a fur coat** j'ai fait une folie, je me suis acheté un manteau de fourrure **2.** [display] fla-fla *m*, tralala *m* ▪ **the book came out in a ~ of publicity** le livre est sorti avec un grand battage publicitaire ▪ **a great ~ of colour** une débauche de couleur.
◇ *vt* [spend] dépenser ▪ [waste] dissiper ▪ **she ~d her savings on a set of encyclopedias** toutes ses économies ont été englouties par l'achat d'une encyclopédie.

◆ **splurge out** *vi insep* faire une folie *OR* des folies ▪ **to ~ out on sthg** se payer qqch.

splutter ['splʌtəʳ] ◇ *vi* **1.** [spit - speaker] postillonner ; [- flames, fat] crépiter, grésiller ; [- pen, ink] cracher **2.** [stutter - speaker] bredouiller ; [- engine] tousser, avoir des ratés ▪ **she was ~ing with rage** elle bredouillait de rage.
◇ *vt* [protest, apology, thanks] bredouiller, balbutier.
◇ *n* **1.** [spitting - in speech] crachotement *m* ; [- of fat, flames] crépitement *m*, grésillement *m* **2.** [stutter - in speech] bredouillement *m*, balbutiement *m* ; [- of engine] toussotement *m*.

spoil [spɔɪl] (*pret & pp* **spoilt** [spɔɪlt] *OR* **spoiled**) ◇ *vt* **1.** [make less attractive or enjoyable] gâter, gâcher ■ **our holiday was spoilt by the wet weather** le temps pluvieux a gâché nos vacances ■ **the ending spoilt the film for me** la fin m'a gâché le film ■ **don't ~ the ending for me** ne me raconte pas la fin, ça va tout gâcher **2.** [damage] abîmer, endommager ■ **if you eat those chocolates, you'll ~ your appetite for dinner** si tu manges ces chocolats, tu n'auras plus faim *OR* plus d'appétit à l'heure du dîner ■ **the dinner was spoilt because they were late** le dîner a été gâché par leur retard ➤ **to ~ the ship for a hap'orth of tar** faire des économies de bouts de chandelle **3.** [pamper] gâter ■ **she's spoilt rotten** *inf* elle est super gâtée, c'est une enfant pourrie ■ **to ~ o.s.** s'offrir une petite folie **4.** POL [ballot paper] rendre nul.
◇ *vi* [fruit, food] se gâter, s'abîmer ■ [in store, hold of ship] s'avarier, devenir avarié.
◇ *n (U)* **1.** = **spoils** *(sense 1)* **2.** [earth, diggings] déblai *m*, déblais *mpl*.
◆ **spoils** *npl* **1.** [loot] butin *m*, dépouilles *fpl* ■ [profit] bénéfices *mpl*, profits *mpl* ■ [prize] prix *m* ■ **the ~s of war** les dépouilles de la guerre **2.** *US* POL assiette *f* au beurre.
◆ **spoil for** *vt insep* : **to be ~ing for a fight/an argument** chercher la bagarre/la dispute.

spoilage ['spɔɪlɪdʒ] *n (U)* [damage] détérioration *f* ■ [spoilt matter] déchets *mpl*.

spoiled [spɔɪld] = **spoilt**.

spoiler ['spɔɪlər] *n* AUT becquet *m* ■ AERON aérofrein *m*.

spoilsport ['spɔɪlspɔːt] *n* trouble-fête *mf inv*, rabat-joie *m inv*, empêcheur *m*, - euse *f* de tourner en rond.

spoilt [spɔɪlt] ◇ *pt & pp* ▷ **spoil**.
◇ *adj* **1.** [child] gâté ■ [behaviour] d'enfant gâté ■ **we were ~ for choice** nous n'avions que l'embarras du choix **2.** [harvest] abîmé ■ [food, dinner] gâché, gâté **3.** POL [ballot paper] nul.

spoke [spəʊk] ◇ *pt* ▷ **speak**.
◇ *n* [in wheel] rayon *m* ■ [in ladder] barreau *m*, échelon *m* ■ [on ship's wheel] manette *f* ■ **to put a ~ in sb's wheel** *UK* mettre des bâtons dans les roues à qqn.

spoken ['spəʊkn] ◇ *pp* ▷ **speak**.
◇ *adj* [dialogue] parlé, oral ■ **the ~ word** la langue parlée, la parole ■ **~ language** oral *m*.

-spoken *in cpds* : **soft~** à la voix douce ■ **well~** qui s'exprime bien.

spokeshave ['spəʊkʃeɪv] *n* vastringue *f*.

spokesman ['spəʊksmən] (*pl* **spokesmen** [-mən]) *n* porte-parole *mf inv* ■ **a government ~, a ~ for the government** un porte-parole du gouvernement.

spokesperson ['spəʊks,pɜːsn] *n* porte-parole *mf inv*.

spokeswoman ['spəʊks,wʊmən] (*pl* **spokeswomen** [-,wɪmɪn]) *n* porte-parole *m inv (femme)*.

sponge [spʌndʒ] ◇ *n* **1.** ZOOL [in sea] éponge *f* **2.** [for cleaning, washing] éponge *f* ■ **I gave the table a ~** j'ai passé un coup d'éponge sur la table ➤ **to throw in the ~** jeter l'éponge **3.** *inf pej* [scrounger] parasite *m* **4.** *UK* [cake] gâteau *m* de Savoie ■ **jam/cream ~** gâteau de Savoie fourré à la confiture/à la crème.
◇ *vt* **1.** [wipe - table, window] donner un coup d'éponge sur ; [- body] éponger **2.** [soak up] éponger ■ **can you ~ the milk off the table?** peux-tu éponger le lait renversé sur la table? **3.** *inf* [cadge - food, money] taper ■ **I ~d £20 off *OR* from him** je l'ai tapé de 20 livres.
◇ *vi inf* [cadge] : **to ~ on *OR* from sb** vivre aux crochets de qqn ■ **she's always sponging** c'est un vrai parasite.
◆ **sponge down** *vt sep* éponger, laver à l'éponge.

sponge bag *n UK* trousse *f OR* sac *m* de toilette.

sponge cake *n* gâteau *m* de Savoie.

sponge-down *n* coup *m* d'éponge.

sponge finger *n* boudoir *m (biscuit)*.

sponge pudding *n dessert chaud fait avec une pâte de gâteau de Savoie.*

sponger ['spʌndʒər] *n inf pej* parasite *m*.

spongy ['spʌndʒɪ] (*comp* **spongier**, *superl* **spongiest**) *adj* spongieux.

sponsor ['spɒnsər] ◇ *n* **1.** COMM & SPORT [of sportsman, team, tournament] sponsor *m* ■ [of film, TV programme] sponsor *m*, commanditaire *m* ■ [of artist, musician] commanditaire *m*, mécène *m* ■ [of student, studies] parrain *m* ■ [for charity] donateur *m*, - trice *f* ■ **to act as ~ for sb** sponsoriser qqn **2.** [of would-be club member] parrain *m*, marraine *f* ■ [guarantor - for loan] répondant *m*, - e *f*, garant *m*, - e *f* ■ [backer - for business] parrain *m*, bailleur *m* de fonds ■ **he was the ~ of the proposal** c'est lui qui a lancé la proposition ■ **her uncle stood (as) ~ to her** [for loan] son oncle a été son répondant ; [for business] son oncle l'a parrainée **3.** *US* [of godchild] parrain *m*, marraine *f*.
◇ *vt* **1.** COMM & SPORT sponsoriser ■ RADIO & TV [programme] sponsoriser, parrainer ■ [concert, exhibition] parrainer, commanditer ■ [studies, student] parrainer **2.** [for charity] : **I ~ed him to swim 10 miles** je me suis engagé à lui donner de l'argent (pour des œuvres charitables) s'il parcourait 10 milles à la nage **3.** [appeal, proposal] présenter ■ [would-be club member] parrainer ■ [loan, borrower] se porter garant de ■ [firm] patronner ■ **to ~ a bill** POL présenter un projet de loi **4.** [godchild] être le parrain/la marraine de.

sponsored walk ['spɒnsəd-] *n marche parrainée.*

SPONSORED WALK

Les *sponsored walks* sont destinées à rassembler des fonds, chaque marcheur établissant une liste des personnes ayant accepté de donner une certaine somme d'argent par kilomètre parcouru. On utilise ce principe pour d'autres activités sportives : *sponsored swim, sponsored parachute jump*, etc.

sponsorship ['spɒnsəʃɪp] *n* **1.** COMM & SPORT sponsoring *m* **2.** [of appeal, proposal] présentation *f* ■ POL [of bill] proposition *f*, présentation *f* ■ [of would-be club member, godchild] parrainage *m* ■ [of loan, borrower] cautionnement *m*.

spontaneity [,spɒntə'neɪətɪ] *n* spontanéité *f*.

spontaneous [spɒn'teɪnjəs] *adj* spontané.

spontaneous combustion *n* combustion *f* spontanée.

spontaneously [spɒn'teɪnjəslɪ] *adv* spontanément.

spoof [spuːf] *inf* ◇ *n* **1.** [mockery] satire *f*, parodie *f* ■ **it's a ~ on horror films** c'est une parodie des films d'horreur **2.** [trick] blague *f*, canular *m*.
◇ *adj* prétendu, fait par plaisanterie.
◇ *vt* [book, style] parodier ■ [person] faire marcher.

spook [spuːk] *inf* ◇ *n* **1.** [ghost] fantôme *m* **2.** *US* [spy] barbouze *mf*.
◇ *vt US* **1.** [frighten] faire peur à, effrayer **2.** [haunt] hanter.

spooky ['spuːkɪ] (*comp* **spookier**, *superl* **spookiest**) *adj inf* **1.** [atmosphere] qui donne la chair de poule, qui fait froid dans le dos **2.** *US* [skittish] peureux **3.** [odd] bizarre.

spool [spuːl] ◇ *n* [of film, tape, thread] bobine *f* ■ [for fishing] tambour *m* ■ [of wire] rouleau *m* ■ SEW & TEX cannette *f*.
◇ *vt* [gen] bobiner.

spoon [spuːn] ◇ *n* **1.** [utensil] cuiller *f*, cuillère *f* **2.** [quantity] cuillerée *f* **3.** FISHING cuiller *f*, cuillère *f* **4.** [in golf] spoon *m*.
◇ *vt* [food - serve] servir ; [- transfer] verser ■ **to ~ the fat from *OR* off the gravy** dégraisser la sauce à l'aide d'une cuiller ■ **he ~ed the ice cream into a bowl** il a servi la glace dans un bol (avec une cuiller).
◆ **spoon out** *vt sep* [serve] servir à l'aide d'une cuiller ■ [transfer] verser à l'aide d'une cuillère.
◆ **spoon up** *vt sep* [eat] manger avec une cuiller ■ [clear up] ramasser avec une cuiller.

spoonbill ['spuːnbɪl] *n* ORNITH spatule *f*.

spoonerism ['spuːnərɪzm] *n* contrepèterie *f*.

spoon-feed *vt* **1.** *liter* [child, sick person] nourrir à la cuiller **2.** *fig* **to ~ sb** mâcher le travail à qqn.

spoonful ['spu:nfʊl] *n* cuillerée *f*.

spoor [spɔ:ʳ] *n* trace *f*, traces *fpl*, empreintes *fpl*.

sporadic [spə'rædɪk] *adj* sporadique.

sporadically [spə'rædɪklɪ] *adv* sporadiquement.

spore [spɔ:ʳ] *n* spore *f*.

sporran ['spɒrən] *n* escarcelle *f (portée avec le kilt)*.

sport [spɔ:t] ◇ *n* **1.** [physical exercise] sport *m* ▪ **she does a lot of ~** elle fait beaucoup de sport, elle est très sportive ▪ **I hated ~** *OR* **~s at school** je détestais le sport *OR* les sports à l'école ▶ **the ~ of kings** [horse racing] un sport de rois **2.** *lit* [hunting] chasse *f* ▪ [fishing] pêche *f* **3.** *lit* [fun] amusement *m*, divertissement *m* ▪ **to say sthg in ~** dire qqch pour rire *OR* en plaisantant ▪ **to make ~ of sb/sthg** se moquer de qqn/qqch, tourner qqn/qqch en ridicule **4.** *inf* [friendly person] chic type *m*, chic fille *f* ▪ **go on, be a ~!** allez, sois sympa! **5.** [good loser] : **to be a (good) ~** être beau joueur **6.** [gambler] joueur *m*, -euse *f* ▪ [high flyer] bon vivant *m* **7.** BIOL variété *f* anormale.
◇ *vt* [wear] porter, arborer.
◇ *vi lit* batifoler, s'ébattre.
◆ **sports** ◇ *npl* [athletics meeting] meeting *m* d'athlétisme.
◇ *comp* [equipment, programme, reporter] sportif ▪ [fan] de sport.

sporting ['spɔ:tɪŋ] *adj* **1.** SPORT [fixtures, interests] sportif **2.** [friendly, generous - behaviour] chic *(inv)* **3.** [fairly good - chance] assez bon ▪ **we're in with a ~ chance** on a une assez bonne chance de gagner.

sportingly ['spɔ:tɪŋlɪ] *adv* (très) sportivement.

sport jacket *US* = **sports jacket**.

sports car *n* voiture *f* de sport.

sportscast ['spɔ:tskɑ:st] *n US* émission *f* sportive.

sportscaster ['spɔ:ts,kɑ:stəʳ] *n US* reporter *m* sportif.

sports coat *US* = **sports jacket**.

sports day *n UK* SCH *réunion sportive annuelle où les parents sont invités.*

sports jacket *n* veste *f* sport.

sportsman ['spɔ:tsmən] (*pl* **sportsmen** [-mən]) *n* **1.** [player of sport] sportif *m* **2.** [person who plays fair] : **he's a real ~** il est très sport *OR* beau joueur.

sportsmanlike ['spɔ:tsmənlaɪk] *adj* sportif.

sportsmanship ['spɔ:tsmənʃɪp] *n* sportivité *f*, sens *m* sportif.

sportsperson ['spɔ:ts,pɜ:sn] (*pl* **sportspeople** [-,pi:pl]) *n* sportif *m*, sportive *f*.

sports scholarship *n US bourse pour les élèves bons en sport.*

sports shoe *n* training *m (chaussure)*.

sportswear ['spɔ:tsweəʳ] *n (U)* vêtements *mpl* de sport.

sportswoman ['spɔ:ts,wʊmən] (*pl* **sportswomen** [-,wɪmɪn]) *n* sportive *f*.

sporty ['spɔ:tɪ] (*comp* **sportier**, *superl* **sportiest**) *adj* [person] sportif ▪ [garment] de sport.

spot [spɒt] (*pret & pp* **spotted**, *cont* **spotting**) ◇ *n* **1.** [dot - on material, clothes] pois *m* ; [- on leopard, giraffe] tache *f*, moucheture *f* ; [- on dice, playing card] point *m* ▪ **a tie with red ~s** une cravate à pois rouges ▪ **I've got ~s before my eyes** j'ai des points lumineux *OR* des taches devant les yeux **2.** [stain, unwanted mark] tache *f* ▪ [on fruit] tache *f*, tavelure *f* ▪ [splash] éclaboussure *f* ▪ **a dirty ~** une tache, une salissure **3.** *UK* [pimple] bouton *m* ▪ [freckle] tache *f* de son *OR* de rousseur ▪ **to come out in ~s** avoir une éruption de boutons ▪ **to suffer from ~s** souffrir d'acné **4.** [blemish - on character] tache *f*, souillure *f* ▪ **there isn't a ~ on his reputation** sa réputation est sans tache **5.** [small amount - of liquid] goutte *f* ; [- of salt] pincée *f* ; [- of irony, humour] pointe *f*, soupçon *m* ▪ **there were a few ~s of rain** il est tombé quelques gouttes (de pluie) ▪ **I've got a ~ of bad news** *inf* j'ai une mauvaise nouvelle ▪ **I'm having a ~ of bother with the neighbours** *inf* j'ai quelques ennuis *OR* problèmes avec les voisins **6.** [place] endroit *m*, coin *m* ▪ [site] site *m* ▪ [on body] endroit *m*, point *m* ▪ **a tender** *OR* **sore ~** un point sensible ▶ **that hits the ~!** ça fait du bien! **7.** [aspect, feature, moment] : **the only bright ~ of the week** le seul bon moment de la semaine **8.** [position, job] poste *m*, position *f* **9.** *inf* [difficult situation] embarras *m* ▪ **to be in a ~** être dans l'embarras ▶ **to put sb on the ~** prendre qqn au dépourvu, coincer qqn **10.** RADIO & TV [for artist, interviewee] numéro *m* ▪ [news item] brève *f* ▪ **he got a ~ on the Margie Warner show** [as singer, comedian] il a fait un numéro dans le show de Margie Warner ; [interview] il s'est fait interviewer *OR* il est passé dans le show de Margie Warner ▶ **advertising ~** message *m OR* spot *m* publicitaire **11.** [spotlight] spot *m*, projecteur *m* **12.** [in billiards] mouche *f*.
◇ *comp* **1.** COMM [price] comptant ▪ [transaction, goods] payé comptant **2.** [random - count, test] fait à l'improviste **3.** TV : **~ advertisement** spot *m* publicitaire ▪ **~ announcement** flash *m*.
◇ *vt* **1.** [notice - friend, object] repérer, apercevoir ; [- talent, mistake] trouver, déceler ▪ **I could ~ him a mile off** je pourrais le repérer à des kilomètres ▪ **well spotted!** bien vu! **2.** [stain] tacher ▪ [mark with spots] tacheter **3.** *US* [opponent] accorder un avantage à **4.** *US* [remove - stain] enlever ▪ **a chemical for spotting clothes** un produit pour détacher les vêtements.
◇ *vi* **1.** [garment, carpet] se tacher, se salir **2.** [rain] : **it's spotting with rain** il tombe quelques gouttes de pluie **3.** MIL servir d'observateur.
◆ **on the spot** *adv phr* [at once] sur-le-champ ▪ [at the scene] sur les lieux, sur place ▪ **he was killed on the ~** il a été tué sur le coup ▪ **the man on the ~** [employee, diplomat] l'homme qui est sur place *OR* sur le terrain ; [journalist] l'envoyé spécial ▪ **to run on the ~** courir sur place.
◆ **on-the-spot** *adj phr* [fine] immédiat ▪ [report] sur place *OR* sur le terrain.

spot check *n* [investigation] contrôle *m* surprise ▪ [for quality] sondage *m* ▪ [by customs] fouille *f* au hasard.
◆ **spot-check** *vt* contrôler au hasard ▪ [for quality] sonder.

spotless ['spɒtlɪs] *adj* [room, appearance] impeccable ▪ [character] sans tache.

spotlessly ['spɒtlɪslɪ] *adv* : **~ clean** reluisant de propreté, d'une propreté impeccable.

spotlight ['spɒtlaɪt] (*pret & pp* **spotlit** [-lɪt]) ◇ *n* **1.** [in theatre] spot *m*, projecteur *m* ▪ **in the ~** *liter & fig* sous le feu *OR* la lumière des projecteurs ▪ **to turn the ~ on sb** *liter* braquer les projecteurs sur qqn ; *fig* mettre qqn en vedette ▪ **the ~ was on her** *liter* les projecteurs étaient braqués sur elle ; *fig* elle était en vedette **2.** [lamp - in home, on car] spot *m*.
◇ *vt* **1.** THEAT diriger les projecteurs sur **2.** *fig* [personality, talent] mettre en vedette ▪ [pinpoint - flaws, changes] mettre en lumière, mettre le doigt sur.

spotlit [-lɪt] *adj* éclairé par des projecteurs.

spot market *n* marché *m* au comptant.

spot-on *inf* ◇ *adj UK* **1.** [correct - remark, guess] en plein dans le mille ; [- measurement] pile, très précis **2.** [perfect] parfait.
◇ *adv* [guess] en plein dans le mille ▪ **he timed it ~** il a calculé son coup à la seconde près.

spotted ['spɒtɪd] ◇ *pt & pp* ▷ **spot**.
◇ *adj* **1.** [leopard, bird] tacheté, moucheté ▪ [apple, pear] tavelé **2.** [tie, dress] à pois **3.** [stained - carpet, wall] taché.

spotted dick *n UK dessert chaud fait avec une pâte à gâteau et des raisins.*

spotter ['spɒtəʳ] ◇ *n* **1.** [observer] observateur *m*, -trice *f* ▪ [lookout] dénicheur *m* **2.** *UK* [enthusiast] : **train/plane ~** passionné *m*, -e *f* de trains/d'avions **3.** *US inf* COMM surveillant *m*, -e *f* du personnel.
◇ *comp* [plane] de recherche *OR* recherches.

spotty ['spɒtɪ] (*comp* **spottier**, *superl* **spottiest**) *adj* **1.** [covered with spots - skin, person] boutonneux ; [- wallpaper] piqué *OR* tacheté d'humidité ; [- mirror] piqueté, piqué ▪ [stained] taché **2.** [patterned - fabric, tie] à pois **3.** [patchy] irrégulier.

spouse [spaʊs] *n fml* époux *m*, épouse *f* ▪ ADMIN & LAW conjoint *m*, -e *f*.

spout [spaʊt] ◇ *n* **1.** [of teapot, kettle, tap, watering can] bec *m* ■ [of carton] bec *m* verseur ■ [of pump, gutter] dégorgeoir *m* ■ [of pipe] embout *m* **2.** [of water - from fountain, geyser] jet *m* ; [- from whale] jet *m*, souffle *m* d'eau ■ [of flame] colonne *f* ■ [of lava] jet *m* **3.** *UK phr* **to be up the ~** *inf* [ruined] être fichu *OR* foutu ; [pregnant] être enceinte ■ **our plans are up the ~** nos projets sont tombés à l'eau.
◇ *vi* **1.** [water, oil] jaillir, sortir en jet ■ [whale] souffler ■ **water ~ed out of the pipe** de l'eau jaillit du tuyau **2.** *inf pej* [talk] dégoiser ■ **he's always ~ing (on) about politics** il est toujours à dégoiser sur la politique.
◇ *vt* **1.** [water, oil] faire jaillir un jet de ■ [fire, smoke] vomir, émettre un jet de **2.** *inf pej* [words, poetry] débiter, sortir.

sprain [spreɪn] ◇ *vt* [joint] fouler, faire une entorse à ■ [muscle] étirer ■ **she has ~ed her ankle** *OR* **has a ~ed ankle** elle s'est fait une entorse à la cheville *OR* s'est foulé la cheville.
◇ *n* entorse *f*, foulure *f*.

sprang [spræŋ] *pt* ⊳ **spring**.

sprat [spræt] *n* sprat *m*.

sprawl [sprɔːl] ◇ *vi* **1.** [be sitting, lying] être affalé *OR* vautré ■ [sit down, lie down] s'affaler, se laisser tomber ■ **she was ~ing in the armchair/on the bed** elle était avachie dans le fauteuil/vautrée sur le lit ■ **the blow sent him ~ing** le coup l'a fait tomber de tout son long **2.** [spread] s'étaler, s'étendre ■ **the new industrial estate is beginning to ~ into the countryside** la nouvelle zone industrielle commence à grignoter *OR* envahir la campagne.
◇ *vt (usu passive)* **she was ~ed in the armchair/on the pavement** elle était vautrée dans le fauteuil/étendue de tout son long sur le trottoir.
◇ *n* **1.** [position] position *f* affalée **2.** [of city] étendue *f* ■ **the problem of urban ~** le problème de l'expansion urbaine.

sprawling [ˈsprɔːlɪŋ] *adj* [body] affalé ■ [suburbs, metropolis] tentaculaire ■ [handwriting] informe.

spray [spreɪ] ◇ *vt* **1.** [treat - crops, garden] faire des pulvérisations sur, traiter ; [- field] pulvériser ; [- hair, house plant] vaporiser ■ [sprinkle - road] asperger ■ **I got ~ed with cold water** je me suis fait arroser *OR* asperger d'eau froide ■ **they ~ed the bar with bullets/with machine-gun fire** *fig* ils arrosèrent le bar de balles/de rafales de mitrailleuses **2.** [apply - water, perfume] vaporiser ; [- paint, insecticide] pulvériser ; [- coat of paint, fixer] mettre, appliquer ; [- graffiti, slogan] écrire, tracer (à la bombe) ■ **she ~ed perfume behind her ears** elle se vaporisa du parfum derrière les oreilles ■ **they ~ed water on the flames** ils vaporisèrent de l'eau sur les flammes.
◇ *vi* **1.** [liquid] jaillir ■ **the water ~ed (out) over** *OR* **onto the road** l'eau a jailli sur la route **2.** [against crop disease] pulvériser, faire des pulvérisations.
◇ *n* **1.** [droplets] gouttelettes *fpl* fines ■ [from sea] embruns *mpl* ■ **the liquid comes out in a fine ~** le liquide est pulvérisé **2.** [container - for aerosol] bombe *f*, aérosol *m* ; [- for perfume] atomiseur *m* ; [- for cleaning fluids, water, lotion] vaporisateur *m* ■ **throat ~** vaporisateur pour la gorge **3.** [act of spraying - of crops] pulvérisation *f* ; [- against infestation] traitement *m* (par pulvérisation) ; [- of aerosol product] coup *m* de bombe ■ **I'll give your hair a light ~** je vais donner un petit coup de laque sur vos cheveux **4.** *fig* [of bullets] grêle *f* ■ **the welding sent up ~s** *OR* **a ~ of bright sparks** la soudure faisait voler des gerbes d'étincelles **5.** [cut branch] branche *f* **6.** [bouquet] (petit) bouquet *m* **7.** [brooch] aigrette *f*.
◇ *comp* [insecticide, deodorant] en aérosol.
◆ **spray on** ◇ *vt sep* appliquer (à la bombe) ■ **~ the paint on evenly** vaporisez la peinture de façon uniforme.
◇ *vi insep* [paint, polish, cleaner] s'appliquer (par pulvérisation) ■ **the product ~s on** le produit est présenté sous forme d'aérosol.

spray can *n* [for aerosol] bombe *f*, aérosol *m* ■ [refillable] vaporisateur *m*.

spray gun *n* [for paint] pistolet *m* (à peinture).

spray-on *adj* en bombe, en aérosol ■ **~ deodorant** déodorant *m* en bombe *OR* en spray.

spray paint *n* peinture *f* en bombe ■ **a can of ~** une bombe de peinture.

◆ **spray-paint** *vt* [with can] peindre à la bombe ■ [with spray gun] peindre au pistolet.

spread [spred] (*pret & pp* **spread**) ◇ *vt* **1.** [apply - jam, icing, plaster, glue] étaler ; [- asphalt] répandre ; [- manure] épandre ■ **he ~ butter on a slice of toast** *OR* **a slice of toast with butter** il a tartiné de beurre une tranche de pain grillé
2. [open out, unfold - wings, sails] étendre, déployer ; [- arms, legs, fingers] écarter ; [- map, napkin, blanket] étaler ; [- rug] étendre ; [- fan] ouvrir ▶ **it's time you ~ your wings** il est temps que vous voliez de vos propres ailes
3. [lay out, arrange - photos, cards, possessions] étaler ■ **her hair was ~ over the pillow** ses cheveux s'étalaient sur l'oreiller
4. [disseminate - disease, fire] propager, répandre ; [- news, idea, faith] propager ; [- rumour] répandre, faire courir ; [- terror, panic] répandre ■ **trade helped to ~ the new technology to Asia** le commerce a facilité la diffusion *OR* la dissémination de cette nouvelle technologie en Asie ■ **the attack is at noon, ~ the word!** l'attaque est pour midi, faites passer *OR* passez le mot! ■ **to ~ the gospel** prêcher *OR* répandre l'Évangile
5. [scatter - over an area] répandre ; [- over a period of time] échelonner, étaler ■ **the floor was ~ with straw** le sol était recouvert de paille ■ **the explosion had ~ debris over a large area** l'explosion avait dispersé des débris sur une grande superficie ■ **their troops are ~ (out) too thinly to be effective** leurs troupes sont trop dispersées pour être efficaces ■ **to ~ o.s. too thinly** disperser ses efforts ■ **the tourist season is now ~ over six months** la saison touristique s'étale maintenant sur six mois ■ **to ~ (out) the losses over five years** répartir les pertes sur cinq ans
6. [divide up - tax burden, work load] répartir
7. MUS [chord] arpéger.
◇ *vi* **1.** [stain] s'élargir ■ [disease, suburb] s'étendre ■ [fire, desert, flood] gagner du terrain, s'étendre ■ [rumour, ideas, faith, terror, crime, suspicion] se répandre ■ **panic ~ through the crowd** la panique a envahi *OR* gagné la foule ■ **the epidemic is ~ing to other regions** l'épidémie gagne de nouvelles régions ■ **the cancer had ~ through her whole body** le cancer s'était généralisé ■ **the flood waters have ~ across** *OR* **over the whole plain** l'inondation a gagné toute la plaine ■ **a ~ing waistline** une taille qui s'épaissit
2. [extend - over a period of time, a range of subjects] s'étendre ■ **their correspondence ~s over 20 years** leur correspondance s'étend sur 20 ans
3. [butter, glue] s'étaler.
◇ *n* **1.** [diffusion, growth - of epidemic, fire] propagation *f*, progression *f* ; [- of technology, idea] diffusion *f*, dissémination *f* ; [- of religion] propagation *f* ■ **they are trying to prevent the ~ of unrest to other cities** ils essaient d'empêcher les troubles d'atteindre *OR* de gagner d'autres villes
2. [range - of ages, interests] gamme *f*, éventail *m* ■ **the commission represented a broad ~ of opinion** la commission représentait un large éventail d'opinions ■ **maximum May temperatures show a ten-point ~** les températures maximales du mois de mai montrent une variation de dix degrés
3. [wingspan] envergure *f*
4. [period] période *f* ■ **growth occurred over a ~ of several years** la croissance s'étala sur une période de plusieurs années
5. [expanse] étendue *f*
6. [cover - for bed] couvre-lit *m* ■ [tablecloth] nappe *f* ■ [dust-cover] housse *f*
7. CULIN [paste] pâte *f* à tartiner ■ [jam] confiture *f* ■ **salmon ~** beurre *m* de saumon ■ **chocolate ~** chocolat *m* à tartiner
8. PRESS & TYPO [two pages] double page *f* ■ [advertisement] double page *f* publicitaire
9. *inf* [meal] festin *m*
10. *US inf* [farm] ferme *f* ■ [ranch] ranch *m* ■ **nice ~ you've got here!** belle propriété que vous avez là!
11. ST. EX spread *m*
12. *US* [bedspread] couvre-lit *m*.
◇ *adj* **1.** [arms, fingers, legs] écarté
2. LING [vowel] non arrondi.
◆ **spread out** ◇ *vi insep* **1.** [town, forest] s'étendre
2. [disperse] se disperser ■ [in formation] se déployer ■ **the search party had ~ out through the woods** l'équipe de secours s'était déployée à travers les bois
3. [open out - sail] se déployer, se gonfler
4. [make o.s. at ease] s'installer confortablement.

◇ *vt sep* **1.** *(usu passive)* [disperse] disperser, éparpiller ■ **the runners are now ~ out (along the course)** les coureurs sont maintenant éparpillés le long du parcours ■ **the population is very ~ out** la population est très dispersée
2. = **spread** *(vt senses 2 & 3)*.

spread eagle *n* **1.** HERALD aigle *f* éployée **2.** [in skating] grand aigle *m*.
◆ **spread-eagle** ◇ *vt* [knock flat] envoyer par terre ■ **he was ~d by the blow** le coup l'a fait tomber à la renverse.
◇ *adj* **1.** = **spread-eagled 2.** *US inf* chauvin.

spread-eagled [-,i:gld] *adj* bras et jambes écartés ■ **the police had him ~ against the wall** les policiers l'ont plaqué contre le mur, bras et jambes écartés.

spreader ['spredəʳ] *n* AGRIC & TECH [for fertilizer, manure, asphalt] épandeur *m*, épandeuse *f*.

spreadsheet ['spredʃi:t] *n* tableur *m*.

spree [spri:] *n* fête *f* ■ **to go** *OR* **to be on a ~** faire la fête ■ **her drinking/gambling ~s** les périodes où elle boit/joue ■ **to go on a shopping ~** faire des folies dans les magasins.

sprig [sprɪg] *n* brin *m*.

sprightly ['spraɪtlɪ] (*comp* **sprightlier**, *superl* **sprightliest**) *adj* [person] alerte, guilleret ■ [step] vif ■ [tune, whistle] gai.

spring [sprɪŋ] (*pret* **sprang** [spræŋ] *OR* **sprung** [sprʌŋ], *pp* **sprung**) ◇ *n* **1.** [season] printemps *m* ■ **in (the) ~** au printemps ■ **the Spring Bank Holiday** *UK le dernier lundi de mai, jour férié en Grande-Bretagne*
2. [device, coil] ressort *m* ■ **the ~s** AUT la suspension
3. [natural source] source *f*
4. [leap] bond *m*, saut *m*
5. [resilience] élasticité *f* ■ **the diving board has plenty of ~** le plongeoir est très élastique ■ **the mattress has no ~ left** le matelas n'a plus de ressort ■ **he set out with a ~ in his step** il est parti d'un pas alerte.
◇ *comp* **1.** [flowers, weather, colours] printanier, de printemps ■ **his new ~ collection** sa nouvelle collection de printemps ■ **~ term** SCH & UNIV ≃ dernier trimestre *m*
2. [mattress] à ressorts ■ **~ binding** reliure *f* à ressort
3. [water] de source.
◇ *vi* **1.** [leap] bondir, sauter ■ **to ~ at** bondir *OR* se jeter sur ■ **the couple sprang apart** le couple se sépara hâtivement ■ **he sprang ashore** il sauta à terre ■ **~ing out of the armchair** bondissant du fauteuil ■ **I sprang to my feet** je me suis levé d'un bond ■ **to ~ to attention** bondir au garde-à-vous
2. [be released] : **to ~ shut/open** se fermer/s'ouvrir brusquement ■ **the branch sprang back** la branche s'est redressée d'un coup
3. *fig* **the police sprang into action** les forces de l'ordre passèrent rapidement à l'action ■ **the engine sprang to** *OR* **into life** le moteur s'est mis soudain en marche *OR* a brusquement démarré ■ **she sprang to my defence** elle a vivement pris ma défense ■ **to ~ to the rescue** se précipiter pour porter secours ■ **tears sprang to his eyes** les larmes lui sont montées *OR* venues aux yeux ■ **just say the first thing which ~s to mind** dites simplement la première chose qui vous vient à l'esprit ■ **you didn't notice anything strange? – nothing that ~s to mind** vous n'avez rien remarqué d'anormal? – rien qui me frappe particulièrement ■ **where did you ~ from?** *inf* d'où est-ce que tu sors?
4. [originate] venir, provenir ■ **the problem ~s from a misunderstanding** le problème provient *OR* vient d'un malentendu
5. [plank - warp] gauchir, se gondoler ; [- crack] se fendre
6. *US inf* [pay] : **to ~ for sthg** casquer pour qqch.
◇ *vt* **1.** [trap] déclencher ■ [mine] faire sauter ■ [bolt] fermer ■ **the mousetrap had been sprung but it was empty** la souricière *OR* tapette avait fonctionné, mais elle était vide
2. [make known - decision, news] annoncer de but en blanc *OR* à brûle-pourpoint ■ **I hate to have to ~ it on you like this** cela m'embête d'avoir à vous l'annoncer de but en blanc comme ça ■ **he doesn't like people ~ing surprises on him** il n'aime pas les surprises *OR* qu'on lui réserve des surprises ■ **to ~ a question on sb** poser une question à qqn de but en blanc
3. [develop] : **to ~ a leak** [boat] commencer à prendre l'eau ; [tank, pipe] commencer à fuir ■ **the radiator has sprung a leak** il y a une fuite dans le radiateur
4. [jump over - hedge, brook] sauter
5. [plank - warp] gauchir, gondoler ; [- crack] fendre
6. HUNT [game] lever
7. *inf* [prisoner] faire sortir ■ **the gang sprung him from prison with a helicopter** le gang l'a fait évader de prison en hélicoptère.
◆ **spring up** *vi insep* **1.** [get up] se lever d'un bond
2. [move upwards] bondir, rebondir ■ **the lid sprang up** le couvercle s'est ouvert brusquement ■ **several hands sprang up** plusieurs mains se sont levées
3. [grow in size, height] pousser ■ **hasn't Lisa sprung up this year!** comme Lisa a grandi cette année!
4. [appear - towns, factories] surgir, pousser comme des champignons ; [- doubt, suspicion, rumour, friendship] naître ; [- difficulty, threat] surgir ; [- breeze] se lever brusquement ■ **new companies are ~ing up every day** de nouvelles entreprises apparaissent chaque jour.

springboard ['sprɪŋbɔ:d] *n* SPORT & *fig* tremplin *m*.

spring chicken *n* **1.** *US* poulet *m (à rôtir)* **2.** [young person] : **he's no ~** il n'est plus tout jeune.

spring-clean ◇ *vi* faire un nettoyage de printemps.
◇ *vt* nettoyer de fond en comble.
◇ *n UK* nettoyage *m* de printemps ■ **to give the house a ~** nettoyer la maison de fond en comble ■ **the accounting department needs a ~** *fig* le service comptabilité a besoin d'un bon coup de balai.

spring-cleaning *n* nettoyage *m* de printemps.

springer spaniel *n* springer *m*.

spring fever *n* agitation *f* printanière.

spring greens *npl* choux *mpl* précoces.

spring-loaded *adj* à ressort.

spring lock *n* serrure *f* à fermeture automatique.

spring onion *n* petit oignon *m* blanc.

spring roll *n* rouleau *m* de printemps.

spring tide *n* grande marée *f* ■ [at equinox] marée *f* d'équinoxe (de printemps).

springtime ['sprɪŋtaɪm] *n* printemps *m*.

springy ['sprɪŋɪ] (*comp* **springier**, *superl* **springiest**) *adj* [mattress, diving board] élastique ■ [step] souple, élastique ■ [floor] souple ■ [moss, carpet] moelleux ■ [hair] dru.

sprinkle ['sprɪŋkl] ◇ *vt* **1.** [salt, sugar, spices, breadcrumbs, talc] saupoudrer ■ [parsley, raisins] parsemer ■ **I ~d sugar on** *OR* **over my cereal, I ~d my cereal with sugar** j'ai saupoudré mes céréales de sucre ■ **~ with grated cheese** recouvrez de fromage râpé ■ **he ~d sawdust on the floor** il a répandu de la sciure par terre ■ [liquid] : **to ~ water on sthg** *OR* **sthg with water** asperger qqch d'eau ■ **he ~d vinegar on** *OR* **over his chips** il mit un peu de vinaigre sur ses frites **2.** *(usu passive)* [strew, dot] parsemer, semer ■ **the sky was ~d with stars** le ciel était parsemé d'étoiles ■ **a speech ~d with metaphors** un discours émaillé de métaphores ■ **a few policemen were ~d among the crowd** quelques policiers étaient disséminés dans la foule.
◇ *vi* [rain] tomber des gouttes.
◇ *n* **1.** [rain] petite pluie *f* **2.** = **sprinkling**.

sprinkler ['sprɪŋkləʳ] *n* **1.** AGRIC & HORT arroseur *m* (automatique) ■ **~ truck** arroseuse *f* **2.** [fire-extinguishing device] sprinkler *m* ■ **~ system** installation *f* d'extinction automatique d'incendie **3.** [for holy water] goupillon *m*, aspersoir *m*.

sprinkling ['sprɪŋklɪŋ] *n* [small quantity] petite quantité *f* ■ [pinch] pincée *f* ■ **it was a male audience with a ~ of women** c'était une assistance masculine avec quelques rares femmes ■ **there was a ~ of grey in her hair** elle avait quelques cheveux gris.

sprint [sprɪnt] ◇ *n* SPORT [dash] sprint *m* ■ [race] course *f* de vitesse, sprint *m* ■ **the 60 metre ~** le 60 mètres ■ **to break into** *OR* **to put on a ~** [gen] piquer un sprint.

◇ *vi* sprinter ▪ **she ~ed to** *OR* **for her car** elle sprinta jusqu'à sa voiture.

sprinter ['sprɪntəʳ] *n* sprinter *m*.

sprite [spraɪt] *n* MYTH [male] lutin *m* ▪ [female] nymphe *f* ▪ **water ~** MYTH naïade *f*.

spritzer ['sprɪtsəʳ] *n mélange de vin blanc et de soda.*

sprocket ['sprɒkɪt] *n* [wheel] pignon *m*.

sprog [sprɒg] *n UK inf* **1.** [child] gosse *mf*, môme *mf* **2.** MIL [novice] bleu *m*, nouvelle recrue *f*.

sprout [spraʊt] ◇ *n* **1.** [on plant, from ground] pousse *f* ▪ [from bean, potato] germe *m* **2.** : **(Brussels) ~s** choux *mpl* de Bruxelles.
◇ *vi* **1.** [germinate - bean, seed, onion] germer **2.** [grow - leaves, hair] pousser ▪ **he had hair ~ing from his ears** des touffes de poils lui sortaient des oreilles **3.** [appear] apparaître, surgir.
◇ *vt* **1.** [grow - leaves] pousser, produire ; [- beard] faire pousser ▪ **some lizards can ~ new tails** la queue de certains lézards repousse **2.** [germinate - seeds, beans, lentils] faire germer.
◆ **sprout up** *vi insep* **1.** [grow - grass, wheat, plant] pousser, pointer ; [- person] pousser **2.** [appear - towns, factories] pousser comme des champignons, surgir.

spruce [spru:s] (*pl inv*) ◇ *n* BOT épicéa *m* ▪ [timber] épinette *f*.
◇ *adj* [person, car, building, town] pimpant ▪ [haircut] net ▪ [garment] impeccable.
◆ **spruce up** *vt sep* [car, building, town] donner un coup de neuf à ▪ [paintwork] refaire ▪ [child] faire beau ▪ **a coat of paint will ~ the room up** une couche de peinture rafraîchira la pièce ▪ **to ~ o.s. up, to get ~d up** se faire beau.

sprucely ['spru:slɪ] *adv* [painted, polished, starched] impeccablement ▪ **~ dressed** tiré à quatre épingles.

sprung [sprʌŋ] ◇ *pt & pp* ▷ **spring**.
◇ *adj* [mattress] à ressorts.

spry [spraɪ] (*comp* **sprier** *OR* **spryer**, *superl* **spriest** *OR* **spryest**) *adj* [person] alerte, leste.

spryly ['spraɪlɪ] *adv* agilement, lestement.

SPUC [spʌk] (*abbrev of* **Society for the Protection of the Unborn Child**) *pr n ligue contre l'avortement.*

spud [spʌd] *n* **1.** *inf* [potato] patate *f* **2.** [gardening tool] sarcloir *m*.

spun [spʌn] ◇ *pt & pp* ▷ **spin**.
◇ *adj* filé ▪ **her hair was like ~ gold** elle avait des cheveux d'or.

spunk [spʌŋk] *n* **1.** *inf* [pluck] cran *m*, nerf *m* **2.** ▲ *UK* [semen] foutre△ *m*.

spunky ['spʌŋkɪ] (*comp* **spunkier**, *superl* **spunkiest**) *adj inf* [person] plein de cran, qui a du cran ▪ [retort, fight] courageux.

spun silk *n* schappe *f*.

spun yarn *n* bitord *m*.

spur [spɜ:ʳ] (*pret & pp* **spurred**, *cont* **spurring**) ◇ *n* **1.** EQUIT éperon *m* ▪ **to win one's ~s** HIST gagner son épée de chevalier ; *fig* faire ses preuves **2.** *fig* [stimulation] aiguillon *m* ▪ **the ~ of competition** l'aiguillon de la concurrence ▪ **easy credit is a ~ to consumption** le crédit facile pousse *OR* incite à la consommation ▪ **on the ~ of the moment** sur le coup, sans réfléchir **3.** GEOG [ridge] éperon *m*, saillie *f* **4.** RAIL [siding] voie *f* latérale *OR* de garage ▪ [branch line] embranchement *m* **5.** [on motorway] bretelle *f* **6.** [breakwater] brise-lames *m inv*, digue *f* **7.** BOT & ZOOL éperon *m* ▪ [on gamecock] ergot *m*.
◇ *vt* **1.** [horse] éperonner **2.** *fig* inciter ▪ **her words spurred me into action** ses paroles m'ont incité à agir.
◆ **spur on** *vt sep* **1.** [horse] éperonner **2.** *fig* éperonner, aiguillonner ▪ **to ~ sb on to do sthg** inciter *OR* pousser qqn à faire qqch.

spurious ['spʊərɪəs] *adj* **1.** [false - gen] faux, fausse *f* ; [- comparison, argument, reason, objection] spécieux ▪ **your claim is a ~ one** votre revendication est sans fondement **2.** [pretended - enthusiasm, sympathy] simulé ; [- flattery, compliment] hypocrite **3.** [of doubtful origin - text] apocryphe, inauthentique.

spurn [spɜ:n] *vt* [gen] dédaigner, mépriser ▪ [suitor] éconduire, rejeter.

spur-of-the-moment *adj* [purchase, phone call] fait sur le coup *OR* sans réfléchir ▪ [excuse, tactics, invitation] improvisé ▪ **I made a ~ decision** je me suis décidé sur le moment.

spurred [spɜ:d] *adj* [boots] à éperons.

spurt [spɜ:t] ◇ *vi* **1.** [water, blood] jaillir, gicler ▪ [flames, steam] jaillir ▪ **beer ~ed (out) from the can** la bière a giclé de la boîte ▪ **the milk ~ed into the pail** le lait gicla dans le seau ▪ **some lemon juice ~ed into my eye** j'ai reçu une giclée de jus de citron dans l'œil **2.** [dash - runner, cyclist] sprinter, piquer un sprint ▪ **he ~ed past us** il nous a dépassés comme une flèche.
◇ *vt* [gush - subj: pierced container] laisser jaillir ▪ [spit - subj: gun, chimney] cracher ▪ **his wound ~ed blood** le sang gicla *OR* jaillit de sa blessure.
◇ *n* **1.** [of steam, water, flame] jaillissement *m* ▪ [of blood, juice] giclée *f* **2.** [dash] accélération *f* ▪ [at work] coup *m* de collier ▪ [revival] regain *m* ▪ [flash - of temper, jealousy, sympathy] sursaut *m* ▪ **to put on a ~** [while running, cycling] piquer un sprint ; [while working] donner un coup de collier ▪ **after a brief ~ of economic growth** après un bref regain de croissance économique ▪ **her inspiration came in ~s** l'inspiration lui venait par à-coups.
◆ **spurt out** *vi insep* = **spurt** *(vi sense 1).*

Sputnik ['spʊtnɪk] *n* Spoutnik *m*.

sputter ['spʌtəʳ] ◇ *vi* **1.** [motor] toussoter, crachoter ▪ [fire, candle] crépiter ▪ **the engine ~ed to a halt** le moteur s'arrêta dans un toussotement **2.** [stutter] bredouiller, bafouiller **3.** [spit - gen] crachoter ; [- when talking] postillonner.
◇ *vt* [apology, curses] bredouiller, bafouiller.
◇ *n* **1.** [of motor] toussotement *m*, hoquet *m* ▪ [of fire, candle] crépitement *m* **2.** [stuttering] bredouillement *m*.
◆ **sputter out** *vi insep* [candle, enthusiasm, anger] s'éteindre.

sputum ['spju:təm] (*pl* **sputa** [-tə]) *n* MED crachat *m*, expectoration *f*.

spy [spaɪ] ◇ *n* (*pl* **spies**) espion *m*, - onne *f*.
◇ *comp* [novel, film, scandal] d'espionnage ▪ [network] d'espions ▪ **~ ring** réseau *m* d'espions ▪ **~ satellite** satellite *m* espion.
◇ *vi* (*pret & pp* **spied**) [engage in espionage] faire de l'espionnage ▪ **accused of ~ing for the enemy** accusé d'espionnage au profit de l'ennemi.
◇ *vt lit* [notice] apercevoir ▪ [make out] discerner.
◆ **spy on** *vt insep* espionner ▪ **you've been ~ing on me!** tu m'as espionné!
◆ **spy out** *vt sep* [sb's methods, designs] chercher à découvrir (subrepticement) ▪ [landing sites] repérer ▪ **to ~ out the land** *liter & fig* reconnaître le terrain.

spyglass ['spaɪglɑ:s] *n* longue-vue *f*.

spyhole ['spaɪhəʊl] *n* judas *m*.

spying ['spaɪɪŋ] *n* [gen - INDUST] espionnage *m*.

spymaster ['spaɪˌmɑ:stəʳ] *n* chef *m* des services secrets.

sq., Sq. *written abbr of* **square**.

squab [skwɒb] (*pl inv OR pl* **squabs**, *comp* **squabber**, *superl* **squabbest**) ◇ *n* **1.** ORNITH pigeonneau *m* **2.** [person] homme *m* rond *OR* rondelet, femme *f* ronde *OR* rondelette **3.** [cushion] coussin *m* bien rembourré ▪ [sofa] sofa *m* ▪ AUT [of car seat] dossier *m*.
◇ *adj* **1.** [tubby] rond, enrobé **2.** ORNITH sans plumes.

squabble ['skwɒbl] ◇ *vi* se disputer, se quereller.
◇ *n* dispute *f*, querelle *f*.

squabbling ['skwɒblɪŋ] *n (U)* chamailleries *fpl*, disputes *fpl*.

squad [skwɒd] *n* **1.** [group - gen] équipe *f*, escouade *f* **2.** MIL escouade *f*, section *f* **3.** [of police detachment] brigade *f*.

squad car *n* voiture *f* de patrouille de police.

squaddie *n UK inf* MIL bidasse *m*, troufion *m*.

squadron ['skwɒdrən] *n* [in air force] escadron *m* ■ [in navy - small] escadrille *f* ; [- large] escadre *f* ■ [in armoured regiment, cavalry] escadron *m*.

squadron leader *n* [in air force] commandant *m*.

squalid ['skwɒlɪd] *adj* sordide.

squall [skwɔːl] ◇ *n* **1.** METEOR [storm] bourrasque *f*, rafale *f*, grain *m* NAUT ■ [rain shower] grain *m* **2.** [argument] dispute *f* **3.** [bawling] braillement *m*.
◇ *vi* **1.** [bawl] brailler **2.** NAUT : **it was ~ing** on a pris un grain.
◇ *vt* : **"no!", he ~ed** "non!", brailla-t-il.

squally ['skwɔːlɪ] (*comp* **squallier**, *superl* **squalliest**) *adj* [wind] qui souffle par *OR* en rafales ■ [rain] qui tombe par rafales ■ **the weather will be ~** il y aura des bourrasques.

squalor ['skwɒlər] *n (U)* [degrading conditions] conditions *fpl* sordides ■ [filth] saleté *f* repoussante ■ **to live in ~** vivre dans des conditions sordides *OR* dans une misère noire ■ **the ~ of** *OR* **in the stairwell** la saleté repoussante de la cage d'escalier.

squander ['skwɒndər] *vt* [resources, time, money] gaspiller ■ [inheritance] dissiper ■ [opportunity] gâcher, passer à côté de ■ **huge sums were ~ed on unworkable schemes** des sommes énormes ont été dépensées en pure perte pour des projets irréalisables.

square [skweər] ◇ *n* **1.** [shape - gen - GEOM] carré *m* ■ **she arranged the pebbles in a ~** elle a disposé les cailloux en carré ▶ **to be on the ~** *inf* être réglo
2. [square object - gen] carré *m* ; [- tile] carreau *m* ■ **a silk ~** un carré de soie ■ **a ~ of chocolate** un carré *OR* morceau de chocolat
3. [square space - in matrix, crossword, board game] case *f* ▶ **back to ~ one!** retour à la case départ! ■ **we're back at** *OR* **to ~ one** *fig* nous voilà revenus à la case départ ■ **I had to start from ~ one again** j'ai dû repartir à zéro
4. [open area - with streets] place *f* ; [- with gardens] square *m* ■ MIL [parade ground] place *f* d'armes ■ **barrack ~** cour *f* de caserne ■ **the town ~** la place, la grand-place
5. MATHS [multiple] carré *m*
6. [instrument] équerre *f*
7. *inf pej* [person] ringard *m*, - e *f*.
◇ *adj* **1.** [in shape - field, box, building, face] carré ■ **a tall man with ~ shoulders** un homme grand aux épaules carrées ▶ **to be a ~ peg in a round hole** être comme un chien dans un jeu de quilles
2. [mile, inch etc] carré ■ **10 ~ kilometres** 10 kilomètres carrés ■ **the room is 15 feet ~** la pièce fait 5 mètres sur 5
3. [at right angles] à angle droit ■ **the shelves aren't ~** les étagères ne sont pas droites ▶ **~ pass** SPORT passe *f* latérale
4. [fair, honest] honnête ■ **to give sb a ~ deal** agir correctement avec qqn ■ **I got a ~ deal on the car rental** je n'ai rien à redire au prix de location de la voiture ■ **the farmers aren't getting a ~ deal** les perdants dans l'affaire, ce sont les agriculteurs
5. [frank, blunt - person] franc, franche *f* ; [- denial] clair, net, catégorique
6. [even, equal] : **we're all ~** [in money] nous sommes quittes ■ **they were (all) ~ at two games each** SPORT ils étaient à égalité deux parties chacun ■ **did you get things ~ with Julia?** est-ce que tu as pu arranger les choses avec Julia?
7. *inf* [old-fashioned] vieux jeu.
◇ *adv* **1.** = **squarely**
2. [at right angles] : **she set the box ~ with** *OR* **to the edge of the paper** elle a aligné la boîte sur les bords de la feuille de papier
3. [directly] : **he hit the ball ~ in the middle of the racket** il frappa la balle avec le milieu de sa raquette ■ **she looked him ~ in the face** elle le regarda bien en face.
◇ *vt* **1.** [make square - pile of paper] mettre droit, aligner ; [- stone] carrer ; [- log] équarrir ; [- shoulders] redresser ■ **it's like trying to ~ the circle** c'est la quadrature du cercle
2. MATHS carrer, élever au carré ■ **three ~d is nine** trois au carré égale neuf
3. [reconcile] concilier ■ **I couldn't ~ the story with the image I had of him** je n'arrivais pas à faire coïncider cette histoire avec l'image que j'avais de lui
4. [settle - account, bill] régler ; [- debt] acquitter ; [- books] balancer, mettre en ordre ■ **to ~ accounts with sb** *fig* régler son compte à qqn
5. SPORT : **his goal ~d the match** son but a mis les équipes à égalité
6. *inf* [arrange] arranger ■ **can you ~ it with the committee?** pourriez-vous arranger cela avec le comité?
7. *inf* [bribe] soudoyer.
◇ *vi* cadrer, coïncider ■ **his story doesn't ~ with the facts** son histoire ne cadre *OR* ne coïncide pas avec les faits.
➡ **square away** *vt sep (usu passive)* *US inf* régler, mettre en ordre.
➡ **square off** ◇ *vi insep* [opponents, boxers] se mettre en garde.
◇ *vt sep* **1.** [piece of paper, terrain] quadriller
2. [stick, log] carrer, équarrir.
➡ **square up** *vi insep* **1.** [settle debt] faire les comptes ■ **to ~ up with sb** régler ses comptes avec qqn *liter*
2. = **square off**.
➡ **square up to** *vt insep* [confront - situation, criticism] faire face *OR* front à ; [- in physical fight] se mettre en position de combat contre ■ **the unions are squaring up to the management** les syndicats cherchent la confrontation avec la direction.

square-bashing *n UK (U) inf* MIL exercice *m*.

square bracket *n* PRINT crochet *m* ■ **in ~s** entre crochets.

square-cut *adj* [gem, rock] coupé à angle droit *OR* d'équerre ■ [log] équarri ■ *fig* [jaw] carré.

squared [skweəd] *adj* [paper] quadrillé.

square dance *n* quadrille *m* américain.

square knot *n US* [reef knot] nœud *m* plat.

squarely ['skweəlɪ] *adv* **1.** [firmly] fermement, carrément ■ [directly] en plein ■ **~ opposed to** fermement opposé à ■ **to look sb ~ in the eye** regarder qqn droit dans les yeux **2.** [honestly] honnêtement ■ **to deal ~ with sb** agir avec qqn de façon honnête.

square meal *n* : **I haven't had a ~ in days** ça fait plusieurs jours que je n'ai pas fait de vrai repas.

Square Mile *pr n* : **the ~** *la City de Londres, dont la superficie fait environ un mile carré.*

square number *n* carré *m*.

square-rigged *adj* NAUT [boat] gréé en carré.

square root *n* racine *f* carrée.

squarial ['skweərɪəl] *n UK antenne carrée permettant de recevoir la télévision par satellite.*

squash [skwɒʃ] ◇ *vt* **1.** [crush] écraser ■ **you're ~ing me!** tu m'écrases! ■ **I was ~ed between two large ladies** j'étais serré *OR* coincé entre deux grosses dames ■ **we were ~ed in like sardines** nous étions serrés comme des sardines **2.** [cram, stuff] fourrer ■ **she ~ed the laundry down in the bag** elle a tassé le linge dans le sac **3.** [silence, repress - person] remettre à sa place ; [- objection] écarter ; [- suggestion] repousser ; [- argument] réfuter ; [- hopes] réduire à néant ; [- rumour] mettre fin à ; [- rebellion] réprimer ■ **she ~ed him with a look** elle l'a foudroyé du regard.
◇ *vi* **1.** [push - people] s'entasser **2.** [fruit, package] s'écraser.
◇ *n* **1.** [crush of people] cohue *f* ■ **with five of us it'll be a bit of a ~** à cinq, nous serons un peu serrés **2.** SPORT squash *m* **3.** *UK* [drink] : **lemon/orange ~** sirop *m* de citron/d'orange **4.** *US* [vegetable] courge *f*.
◇ *comp* [ball, court, champion, racket] de squash ■ **~ rackets** *UK* [game] squash *m*.
➡ **squash in** *vi insep* [people] s'entasser ■ **I ~ed in between two very fat men** je me suis fait une petite place entre deux hommes énormes.
➡ **squash together** ◇ *vi insep* [people] se serrer (les uns contre les autres), s'entasser.
◇ *vt sep* serrer, tasser.

squashy ['skwɒʃɪ] (*comp* **squashier**, *superl* **squashiest**) *adj* [fruit, package] mou *(before vowel or silent 'h' mol)*, molle *f* ■ [cushion, sofa] moelleux ■ [ground] spongieux.

squat [skwɒt] *(pret & pp* **squatted**, *cont* **squatting**, *comp* **squatter**, *superl* **squattest)** ◇ *vi* **1.** [crouch - person] s'accroupir ; [- animal] se tapir ▪ **we ate squatting (down) on our haunches** nous avons mangé accroupis **2.** [live] vivre dans un squat ▪ **they're allowed to ~ in abandoned buildings** on leur permet de squatter dans des immeubles abandonnés.
◇ *vt* [building] squatter, squattériser.
◇ *n* **1.** [building] squat *m* ▪ [action] squat *m*, occupation *f* de logements vides **2.** [crouch] accroupissement *m* **3.**△ *US* [nothing] que dalle.
◇ *adj* [person, figure, building] trapu.

squatter ['skwɒtəʳ] *n* squatter *m* ▪ *Australia* [rancher] squatter *m*, éleveur *m*.

squaw [skwɔː] *n* [American Indian] squaw *f*.

squawk [skwɔːk] ◇ *vi* **1.** [bird] criailler ▪ [person] brailler **2.** *inf* [complain] criailler, râler **3.** *inf* [inform] moucharder, vendre la mèche.
◇ *vt* : **"let go of me!", she ~ed** "lâchez-moi!", brailla-t-elle.
◇ *n* [of bird] criaillement *m*, cri *m* ▪ [of person] cri *m* rauque ▪ **to let out** *OR* **to give a ~** pousser un cri rauque.

squeak [skwiːk] ◇ *vi* **1.** [floorboard, chalk, wheel] grincer ▪ [animal] piauler, piailler ▪ [person] glapir ▪ **she ~ed with delight** elle poussa un cri de joie **2.** *inf* [succeed narrowly] : **the team ~ed into the finals** l'équipe s'est qualifiée de justesse pour la finale.
◇ *vt* : **"who, me?", he ~ed** "qui? moi?", glapit-il.
◇ *n* [of floorboard, hinge, chalk etc] grincement *m* ▪ [of animal] piaillement *m* ▪ [of person] petit cri *m* aigu, glapissement *m* ▪ [of soft toy] couinement *m* ▪ **don't let me hear one more ~ out of you!** et que je ne t'entende plus!
◆ **squeak by, squeak through** *vi insep inf* **1.** [pass through] se faufiler **2.** [succeed narrowly] réussir de justesse ▪ [in exam] être reçu de justesse ▪ [in election] l'emporter de justesse.

squeaky ['skwiːkɪ] *(comp* **squeakier**, *superl* **squeakiest)** *adj* [floorboard, bed, hinge] grinçant ▪ [voice] aigu, - uë *f*.

squeaky clean *adj inf* **1.** [hands, hair] extrêmement propre **2.** [reputation] sans tache.

squeal [skwiːl] ◇ *vi* **1.** [person] pousser un cri perçant ▪ [tyres, brakes] crisser ▪ [pig] couiner ▪ **to ~ with pain** pousser un cri de douleur ▪ **to ~ with laughter** hurler de rire ▪ **the car ~ed around the corner** la voiture prit le virage dans un crissement de pneus ◗ **he was ~ing like a stuck pig** il criait comme un cochon qu'on égorge **2.** △ [inform] moucharder ▪ **to ~ on sb** balancer qqn.
◇ *vt* : **"ouch!", she ~ed** "aïe!", cria-t-elle.
◇ *n* [of person] cri *m* perçant ▪ [of tyres, brakes] crissement *m* ▪ **he gave a ~ of delight** il poussa un cri de joie.

squeamish ['skwiːmɪʃ] *adj* hypersensible ▪ **I'm very ~ about the sight of blood** je ne supporte pas la vue du sang ▪ **this film is not for the ~** ce film n'est pas conseillé aux âmes sensibles.

squeegee ['skwiːdʒiː] *n* [with rubber blade] raclette *f* ▪ [sponge mop] balai-éponge *m* ▪ PHOT [roller] rouleau *m (en caoutchouc)*.

squeeze [skwiːz] ◇ *vt* **1.** [press - tube, sponge, pimple] presser ; [- trigger] presser sur, appuyer sur ; [- package] palper ; [- hand, shoulder] serrer ▪ **I ~d as hard as I could** j'ai serré aussi fort que j'ai pu ▪ **I kept my eyes ~d tight shut** j'ai gardé les yeux bien fermés
2. [extract, press out - liquid] exprimer ; [- paste, glue] faire sortir ▪ **a glass of freshly ~d orange juice** une orange pressée ▪ **to ~ the air out of** *OR* **from sthg** faire sortir l'air de qqch en appuyant dessus
3. *fig* [money, information] soutirer ▪ **you won't ~ another penny out of me!** tu n'auras pas un sou de plus! ▪ **they want to ~ more concessions from the EC** ils veulent forcer la CEE à faire de nouvelles concessions ▪ **she's squeezing a lot of publicity out of the issue** elle exploite le sujet au maximum pour se faire de la publicité
4. [cram, force] faire entrer (avec difficulté) ▪ **I can't ~ another thing into my suitcase** je ne peux plus rien faire entrer dans ma valise ▪ **she ~d the ring onto her finger** elle enfila la bague avec difficulté ▪ **he ~d his huge bulk behind the steering wheel** il parvint à glisser son corps volumineux derrière le volant ▪ **20 men were ~d into one small cell** 20 hommes étaient entassés dans une petite cellule ▪ **the airport is ~d between the sea and the mountains** l'aéroport est coincé entre la mer et les montagnes
5. [constrain - profits, budget] réduire ; [- taxpayer, workers] pressurer ▪ **universities are being ~d by the cuts** les réductions (de budget) mettent les universités en difficulté ▪ **I'm a bit ~d for time/money** *inf* question temps/argent, je suis un peu juste
6. [in bridge] squeezer.
◇ *vi* : **the lorry managed to ~ between the posts** le camion a réussi à passer de justesse entre les poteaux ▪ **they all ~d onto the bus** ils se sont tous entassés dans le bus ▪ **can you ~ into that parking space?** y a-t-il assez de place pour te garer là?
◇ *n* **1.** [amount - of liquid, paste] quelques gouttes *fpl* ▪ **a ~ of toothpaste** un peu de dentifrice
2. [crush of people] cohue *f* ▪ **it was a tight ~** [in vehicle, room] on était très serré ; [through opening] on est passé de justesse
3. [pressure, grip] pression *f* ▪ [handshake] poignée *f* de main ▪ [hug] étreinte *f* ▪ **he gave my hand a reassuring ~** il a serré ma main pour me rassurer ◗ **to put the ~ on sb** *inf* faire pression sur qqn
4. *inf* [difficult situation] situation *f* difficile
5. ECON : **(credit) ~** resserrement *m* du crédit
6. [in bridge] squeeze *m*
7. *US inf* [friend] copain *m*, copine *f*.
◆ **squeeze in** ◇ *vi insep* [get in] se faire une petite place.
◇ *vt sep* [in schedule] réussir à faire entrer ▪ **she's hoping to ~ in a trip to Rome too** elle espère avoir aussi le temps de faire un saut à Rome ▪ **the dentist says he can ~ you in** le dentiste dit qu'il peut vous prendre entre deux rendez-vous.
◆ **squeeze out** *vt sep* **1.** [sponge, wet clothes] essorer **2.** [liquid] exprimer ▪ TECH [plastic] extruder ▪ **I ~d out the last of the glue** j'ai fini le tube de colle
3. [replace - candidate, competitor] l'emporter sur ▪ **the Japanese are squeezing them out of the market** ils sont en train de se faire évincer du marché par les Japonais.
◆ **squeeze up** *vi insep* se serrer, se pousser.

squeezer ['skwiːzəʳ] *n* CULIN presse-agrumes *m inv*.

squelch [skweltʃ] ◇ *vi* **1.** [walk - in wet terrain] patauger ; [- with wet shoes] marcher les pieds trempés **2.** [make noise - mud] clapoter ▪ **I heard something soft ~ beneath my foot** j'ai entendu quelque chose de mou s'écraser sous mon pied.
◇ *vt* [crush] écraser.
◇ *n* [noise] clapotement ▪ **I heard the ~ of tyres in mud** j'ai entendu le bruit des pneus dans la boue.

squib [skwɪb] *n* **1.** [firecracker] pétard *m* **2.** [piece of satire] pamphlet *m*.

squid [skwɪd] *(pl inv OR pl* **squids)** *n* cal(a)mar *m*, encornet *m*.

squidgy ['skwɪdʒɪ] *(comp* **squidgier**, *superl* **squidgiest)** *adj UK inf* mou *(before vowel or silent 'h' mol)*, molle *f*, spongieux.

squiffy ['skwɪfɪ] *(comp* **squiffier**, *superl* **squiffiest)** *adj UK inf dated* éméché, pompette.

squiggle ['skwɪgl] *n* **1.** [scrawl, doodle] gribouillis *m* **2.** [wavy line, mark] ligne *f* ondulée.

squiggly ['skwɪglɪ] *adj inf* pas droit, ondulé.

squinch [skwɪntʃ] *vt US inf* **to ~ one's eyes** plisser les yeux.

squint [skwɪnt] ◇ *n* **1.** MED strabisme *m* ▪ **to have a ~** loucher **2.** *inf* [glimpse] coup *m* d'œil.
◇ *vi* **1.** MED loucher **2.** [half-close one's eyes] plisser les yeux.

squint-eyed *adj* **1.** *inf* [cross-eyed] qui louche, bigleux **2.** [sidelong] de côté.

squire ['skwaɪəʳ] *n* **1.** [landowner] propriétaire *m* terrien ▪ **Squire Greaves** le squire Greaves **2.** [for knight] écuyer *m* **3.** *dated* [escort] cavalier *m* **4.** *UK inf* [term of address] : **evening, ~!** bonsoir, chef !

squirearchy ['skwaɪərɑːkɪ] *(pl* **squirearchies)** *n* propriétaires *mpl* terriens.

squirm [skwɜːm] ◇ *vi* **1.** [wriggle] se tortiller ■ **he ~ed out of my grasp** il a échappé à mon étreinte en se tortillant ■ **she ~ed with impatience** elle était tellement impatiente qu'elle ne tenait plus en place **2.** [be ill-at-ease] être gêné, être très mal à l'aise ■ [be ashamed] avoir honte ■ **to ~ with embarrassment** être mort de honte ■ **his speech was so bad it made me ~** son discours était si mauvais que j'en ai eu honte pour lui.
◇ *n* : **she gave a ~ of embarrassment** elle ne put cacher sa gêne.

squirrel [*UK* 'skwɪrəl, *US* 'skwɜːrəl] (*UK pret & pp* **squirrelled**, *cont* **squirrelling**) (*US pret & pp* **squirreled**, *cont* **squirreling**) *n* **1.** ZOOL écureuil *m* **2.** *fig* [hoarder] : **she's a real ~** c'est une vraie fourmi.
◆ **squirrel away** *vt sep* [hoard, store] engranger *fig* ■ [hide] cacher.

squirt [skwɜːt] ◇ *vt* [liquid] faire gicler ■ [mustard, ketchup, washing-up liquid] faire jaillir ■ **~ some oil on the hinges** mettez quelques gouttes d'huile sur les gonds ■ **they were ~ing each other with water, they were ~ing water at each other** ils s'aspergeaient d'eau mutuellement ■ **he ~ed some soda water into his whisky** il versa une rasade d'eau de Seltz dans son whisky.
◇ *vi* [juice, blood, ink] gicler ■ [water] jaillir.
◇ *n* **1.** [of juice, ink] giclée *f* ■ [of water] jet *m* ■ [of mustard, ketchup, washing-up liquid] dose *f* ■ [of oil, perfume] quelques gouttes *fpl* **2.** *inf pej* [person] minus *m* ■ [short person] avorton *m* ■ [child] mioche *mf*.

squirt gun *n US* pistolet *m* à eau.

squish [skwɪʃ] *inf* ◇ *vt US* [crush] écrabouiller ■ **he ~ed his nose against the glass** il a écrasé son nez contre la vitre.
◇ *vi* **1.** *US* [squash - insect, fruit] s'écrabouiller **2.** [squelch] clapoter.

squishy ['skwɪʃɪ] (*comp* **squishier**, *superl* **squishiest**) *adj inf* [fruit, wax] mou *(before vowel or silent 'h' mol)*, molle *f* ■ [chocolate] ramolli ■ [ground] boueux ■ **a ~ blob of dough** un petit tas de pâte molle.

Sr 1. (*written abbrev of* **senior**) ■ **Ralph Todd ~** Ralph Todd père **2.** *written abbr of* **sister**.

Sri Lanka [ˌsriː'læŋkə] *pr n* Sri Lanka *m* ■ **in ~** au Sri Lanka.

Sri Lankan [ˌsriː'læŋkn] ◇ *n* Sri Lankais *m*, - e *f*.
◇ *adj* sri lankais.

SRN *n* = **State Registered Nurse**.

SS ◇ (*abbrev of* **steamship**) *initiales précédant le nom des navires de la marine marchande* ■ **the ~ "Norfolk"** le "Norfolk".
◇ *pr n* (*abbrev of* **Schutzstaffel**) ■ **the ~** les SS.

ssh [ʃ] *interj* : ~! chut!

SSSI (*abbrev of* **Site of Special Scientific Interest**) *n en Grande-Bretagne, site déclaré d'intérêt scientifique*.

St 1. (*written abbrev of* **saint**) St, Ste **2.** *written abbr of* **street**.

ST *n* = **Standard Time**.

stab [stæb] (*pret & pp* **stabbed**, *cont* **stabbing**) ◇ *vt* **1.** [injure - with knife] donner un coup de couteau à, poignarder ; [- with bayonet] blesser d'un coup de baïonnette ; [- with spear] blesser avec une lance ■ **he stabbed me in the arm** il me donna un coup de couteau dans le bras ■ **they were stabbed to death** ils ont été tués à coups de couteau ■ **he was stabbed to death with a kitchen knife** il a été tué avec un couteau de cuisine ▶ **to ~ sb in the back** *liter & fig* poignarder qqn dans le dos **2.** [thrust, jab] planter ■ **I stabbed myself in the thumb with a pin** je me suis enfoncé une épingle dans le pouce ■ **I stabbed my finger in his eye** je lui ai enfoncé mon doigt dans l'œil ■ **I stabbed a turnip with my fork** j'ai piqué un navet avec ma fourchette.
◇ *vi* : **he stabbed at the map with his finger** il frappa la carte du doigt ■ **he stabbed at the leaves with his walking stick** il piquait les feuilles de la pointe de sa canne.
◇ *n* **1.** [thrust] coup *m* (de couteau *OR* de poignard) ■ **he made a vicious ~ at me with the broken bottle** il fit un mouvement agressif vers moi avec la bouteille cassée ■ **she felt the ~ of the needle in her finger** elle a senti la piqûre de l'aiguille dans son doigt ▶ **~ wound** blessure *f* par arme blanche ■ **a man was rushed to hospital with ~ wounds** un homme blessé à coups de couteau a été transporté d'urgence à l'hôpital ■ **it was a ~ in the back** c'était un véritable coup de poignard dans le dos **2.** *lit* [of neon, colour] éclat *m* **3.** [of pain] élancement *m* ■ **I felt a ~ of envy** je sentis un pincement de jalousie **4.** *inf* [try] : **to have** *OR* **to make** *OR* **to take a ~ at (doing) sthg** s'essayer à (faire) qqch.

stabbing ['stæbɪŋ] ◇ *n* [knife attack] agression *f* (à l'arme blanche) ■ **there were two fatal ~s at the football match** deux personnes ont été tuées à coups de couteau au match de football.
◇ *adj* [pain] lancinant.

stability [stə'bɪlətɪ] *n* stabilité *f* ■ **it will undermine the ~ of their marriage** cela va ébranler leur mariage ■ **his mental ~** son équilibre mental.

stabilization [ˌsteɪbəlaɪ'zeɪʃn] *n* stabilisation *f*.

stabilize, ise ['steɪbəlaɪz] ◇ *vt* stabiliser.
◇ *vi* se stabiliser.

stabilizer ['steɪbəlaɪzəʳ] *n* **1.** AERON, AUT & ELEC [device] stabilisateur *m* ■ NAUT stabilisateur *m* ■ [on bicycle] stabilisateur *m* **2.** CHEM [in food] stabilisateur *m*, stabilisant *m*.

stable ['steɪbl] ◇ *adj* **1.** [steady, permanent - gen] stable ; [- marriage] solide ■ **the patient's condition is ~** l'état du malade est stationnaire **2.** [person, personality] stable, équilibré **3.** CHEM & PHYS stable.
◇ *n* **1.** [building] écurie *f* ■ **riding ~** *OR* **~ s** centre *m* d'équitation **2.** [group - of racehorses, racing drivers etc] écurie *f*.
◇ *vt* [take to stable] mettre à l'écurie ■ **her horse is ~d at Dixon's** son cheval est en pension chez Dixon.

stable boy *n* valet *m* d'écurie.

stable door *n* porte *f* d'écurie, porte *f* à deux vantaux *OR* battants ■ **to shut** *OR* **to close the ~ after the horse has bolted** *fig* envoyer les pompiers après l'incendie.

stablemate ['steɪblmeɪt] *n* **1.** [horse] compagnon *m* d'écurie **2.** *fig* [person - at work] collègue *mf* de travail ; [- from same school] camarade *mf* d'études.

stabling ['steɪblɪŋ] *n (U)* écuries *fpl*.

staccato [stə'kɑːtəʊ] ◇ *adj* **1.** MUS [note] piqué ■ [passage] joué en staccato **2.** [noise, rhythm] saccadé.
◇ *adv* MUS staccato.

stack [stæk] ◇ *n* **1.** [pile] tas *m*, pile *f* **2.** *inf* [large quantity] tas *m* ■ **I've written a ~ of** *OR* **~s of postcards** j'ai écrit un tas de cartes postales **3.** AGRIC [of hay, straw] meule *f* **4.** [chimney] cheminée *f* **5.** AERON avions *mpl* en attente, empilage *m* **6.** COMPUT [file] pile *f* **7.** MIL [of rifles] faisceau *m* **8.** [in library] : **the ~** *OR* **~s** les rayons *mpl*.
◇ *vt* **1.** [pile - chairs, boxes etc] empiler **2.** AGRIC [hay] mettre en meule *OR* meules **3.** [fill - room, shelf] remplir ■ **his desk was ~ed high with files** des piles de dossiers s'entassaient sur son bureau **4.** COMPUT empiler **5.** AERON [planes] mettre en attente (à altitudes échelonnées) **6.** [fix, rig - committee] remplir de ses partisans ; [- cards, odds etc] : **to ~ the cards** *OR* **the deck** truquer les cartes ■ **he's playing with a ~ed deck** *fig* [in his favour] les dés sont pipés en sa faveur ; [against him] les dés sont pipés contre lui ■ **the cards** *OR* **the odds are ~ed against us** *fig* nous sommes dans une mauvaise situation ■ **a woman lawyer starts with the cards ~ed against her** une femme avocat part avec un handicap.
◇ *vi* s'empiler.
◆ **stacks** *adv UK inf* vachement.
◆ **stack up** ◇ *vt sep* [pile up] empiler.
◇ *vi insep* **1.** *US inf* [add up, work out] : **I don't like the way things are ~ing up** je n'aime pas la tournure que prennent les événements **2.** [compare] se comparer ■ **how does he ~ up against** *OR* **with the other candidates?** que vaut-il comparé aux autres candidats?

stacked [stækt] *adj* **1.** : **~ heel** talon *m* compensé **2.**△ [woman] : **she's (well) ~** il y a du monde au balcon.

stacker ['stækəʳ] *n* [worker] manutentionnaire *mf* ■ [pallet truck] transpalette *m*.

stadium ['steɪdjəm] (*pl* **stadiums** *OR pl* **stadia** [-djə]) *n* stade *m*.

staff [stɑːf] (*pl* **staffs**) ◇ *n* **1.** [work force] personnel *m* ▪ [teachers] professeurs *mpl*, personnel *m* enseignant ▪ **the company has a ~ of fifty** l'effectif de la société est de cinquante personnes ▪ **we have ten lawyers on the ~** notre personnel comprend dix avocats ▪ **is he ~ OR a member of ~?** est-ce qu'il fait partie du personnel? ▪ **~/student ratio** taux *m* d'encadrement des étudiants **2.** MIL & POL état-major *m* **3.** *(pl also staves* [stɑːvz]*)* [rod] bâton *m* ▪ [flagpole] mât *m* ▪ [for shepherd] houlette *f* ▪ [for bishop] crosse *f*, bâton *m* pastoral ▪ *UK* [in surveying] jalon *m* TECH ▪ *fig* [support] soutien *m* ▪ **the ~ of life** [bread] l'aliment de base ; *fig* le pain et le sel de la vie **4.** *(pl also staves* [stɑːvz]*)* MUS portée *f*.
◇ *comp* [canteen, outing etc] du personnel ▪ **~ training** formation *f* du personnel.
◇ *vt (usu passive)* pourvoir en personnel ▪ **the branch is ~ed by OR with competent people** le personnel de la succursale est compétent ▪ **the committee is completely ~ed by volunteers** le comité est entièrement composé de bénévoles.

staff college *n* MIL école *f* supérieure de guerre.

staff corporal *n* MIL ≃ sergent-major *m*.

staffer ['stɑːfər] *n* PRESS rédacteur *m*, - trice *f*.

staffing ['stɑːfɪŋ] *n* [recruiting] recrutement *m* ▪ **~ levels** effectifs *mpl*.

staff nurse *n* infirmier *m*, - ère *f*.

staff officer *n* MIL officier *m* d'état-major.

staffroom ['stɑːfrʊm] *n* SCH salle *f* des enseignants *OR* des professeurs.

Staffs *written abbr of* **Staffordshire**.

staff sergeant *n* MIL *UK* ≃ sergent-chef *m* ▪ *US* ≃ sergent *m*.

stag [stæg] (*pl inv OR pl* **stags**) *n* **1.** ZOOL cerf *m* **2.** *UK* ST. EX spéculateur *m*, - trice *f* sur un titre nouveau.

stag beetle *n* cerf-volant *m* ENTOM lucane *m*.

stage [steɪdʒ] ◇ *n* **1.** [period, phase - of development, project etc] stade *m* ; [- of illness] stade *m*, phase *f* ▪ **the bill is at the committee ~** le projet de loi va maintenant être examiné par un comité ▪ **we'll deal with that at a later ~** nous nous en occuperons plus tard ▪ **the conflict is still in its early ~s** le conflit n'en est encore qu'à ses débuts ▪ **by OR in ~s** par paliers ▪ **the changes were instituted in ~s** les changements ont été introduits progressivement ▪ **to do sthg ~ by ~** faire qqch par étapes *OR* progressivement
2. [stopping place, part of journey] étape *f*
3. THEAT [place] scène *f* ▪ **the ~** [profession, activity] le théâtre ▪ **on ~** sur scène ▪ **~ right/left** côté jardin/cour ▪ **to go on ~** monter sur (la) scène ▪ **to go on the ~** [as career] monter sur les planches, faire du théâtre ▪ **to write for the ~** écrire pour la scène ▪ **she was the first to bring the play to the London ~** elle a été la première à monter cette pièce sur la scène londonienne ▪ *fig* **the political ~** la scène politique ▪ **his concerns always take centre ~** ses soucis à lui doivent toujours passer avant tout ▪ **to set the ~ for sthg** préparer le terrain pour qqch
4. ASTRONAUT étage *m*
5. [platform - gen] plate-forme *f* ; [- on microscope] platine *f* ▪ [scaffolding] échafaudage *m*
6. [stagecoach] diligence *f*
7. ELECTRON [circuit part] étage *m*.
◇ *comp* [design] scénique ▪ [version] pour le théâtre ▪ **she has great ~ presence** elle a énormément de présence sur scène.
◇ *vt* **1.** THEAT [put on - play] monter ▪ [set] situer ▪ **it's the first time the play has been ~d** c'est la première fois qu'on monte cette pièce ▪ **Macbeth was very well ~d** la mise en scène de Macbeth était très réussie
2. [organize - ceremony, festival] organiser ▪ [carry out - robbery] organiser ▪ **to ~ a hijacking** détourner un avion ▪ **to ~ a diversion** créer une *OR* faire diversion ▪ **the handshake was ~d for the TV cameras** la poignée de main était une mise en scène destinée aux caméras de télévision
3. [fake - accident] monter, manigancer ▪ **they ~d an argument for your benefit** ils ont fait semblant de se disputer parce que vous étiez là ▪ **the murder was ~d to look like a suicide** le meurtre a été maquillé en suicide.

stagecoach ['steɪdʒkəʊtʃ] *n* diligence *f* ▪ **'Stagecoach'** *Ford* 'la Chevauchée fantastique'.

stage designer *n* décorateur *m* de théâtre.

stage direction *n* indication *f* scénique.

stage door *n* entrée *f* des artistes.

stage effect *n* effet *m* scénique.

stage fright *n* trac *m* ▪ **to have ~** avoir le trac, être pris de trac.

stagehand ['steɪdʒhænd] *n* THEAT machiniste *mf*.

stage-manage *vt* **1.** THEAT [play, production] s'occuper de la régie de **2.** [press conference, appearance] orchestrer, mettre en scène.

stage manager *n* THEAT régisseur *m*, -euse *f*.

stage name *n* nom *m* de scène.

stager ['steɪdʒər] *n* [veteran] : **old ~** vieux *m* de la vieille.

stage set *n* THEAT décor *m*.

stage whisper *n* aparté *m* ▪ **"it's midnight," he announced in a loud ~** "il est minuit", chuchota-t-il, suffisamment fort pour que tout le monde l'entende.

stagflation [stæg'fleɪʃn] *n* stagflation *f*.

stagger ['stægər] ◇ *vi* [totter - person, horse] chanceler, tituber ▪ **to ~ out** sortir en chancelant *OR* titubant ▪ **I ~ed under the weight** je titubais sous le poids ▪ **we ~ed into bed at 3 o'clock in the morning** nous nous sommes écroulés sur nos lits à 3 h du matin.
◇ *vt* **1.** *(usu passive)* [payments] échelonner ▪ [holidays] étaler ▪ **they plan to bring in ~ed working hours** ils ont l'intention de mettre en place un système d'échelonnement des heures de travail ▪ **~ed start** SPORT [on oval track] départ *m* décalé ▪ **~ed wings** AERON ailes *fpl* décalées **2.** *(usu passive)* [astound] : **to be ~ed** être atterré, être stupéfait ▪ **I was ~ed to learn of his decision** j'ai été stupéfait d'apprendre sa décision.
◇ *n* [totter] pas *m* chancelant.
◆ **staggers** *n* [in diver] ivresse *f* des profondeurs ▪ **(blind) ~s** [in sheep] tournis *m*, cœnurose *f* ; [in horses] vertigo *m*.

staggering ['stægərɪŋ] ◇ *adj* [news, amount] stupéfiant, ahurissant ▪ [problems] énorme ▪ **it was a ~ blow** *liter & fig* ce fut un sacré coup ▪ **the price tag is a ~ $500,000** c'est au prix astronomique de 500 000 dollars.
◇ *n* **1.** [of vacations] étalement *m* ▪ [of payments] échelonnement *m* **2.** [unsteady gait] démarche *f* chancelante.

staghound ['stæghaʊnd] *n* chien *m* d'équipage.

staging ['steɪdʒɪŋ] ◇ *n* **1.** THEAT [of play] mise *f* en scène **2.** [scaffolding] échafaudage *m* ▪ [shelving] rayonnage *f* **3.** ASTRONAUT largage *m (d'un étage de fusée)*.
◇ *comp* MIL : **~ area OR point** lieu *m* de rassemblement.

staging post *n* lieu *m OR* point *m* de ravitaillement.

stagnancy ['stægnənsɪ] *n* stagnation *f*.

stagnant ['stægnənt] *adj* **1.** [water, pond - still] stagnant ; [- stale] croupissant ▪ [air - still] confiné ; [- stale] qui sent le renfermé **2.** [trade, career] stagnant ▪ [society] statique, en stagnation.

stagnate [stæg'neɪt] *vi* **1.** [water - be still] stagner ; [- be stale] croupir **2.** [economy, career] stagner ▪ [person] croupir.

stagnation [stæg'neɪʃn] *n* stagnation *f*.

stag night, stag party *n* [gen] soirée *f* entre hommes ▪ [before wedding day] : **we're having OR holding a ~ for Bob** nous enterrons la vie de garçon de Bob.

staid [steɪd] *adj* [person] rangé, collet monté *(inv) pej* ▪ [colours] sobre, discret, - ète *f* ▪ [job] très ordinaire ▪ **the party was all very ~** la soirée fut sans surprises *OR* très banale.

staidly ['steɪdlɪ] *adv* [sit, watch] calmement ▪ [walk, dance] dignement ▪ [dress] sobrement.

stain [steɪn] <> *n* **1.** [mark, spot] tache *f* ▪ **to leave a ~** laisser une tache ▪ **I couldn't get the ~ out** je n'ai pas réussi à enlever *OR* faire disparaître la tache **2.** *fig* [on character] tache *f* ▪ **it was a ~ on his reputation** cela a entaché sa réputation **3.** [colour, dye] teinte *f*, teinture *f* ▪ **a wood ~** une teinture pour bois ▪ **oak/mahogany ~** teinte chêne/acajou.
<> *vt* **1.** [soil, mark] tacher ▪ **the sink was ~ed with rust** l'évier était taché de rouille ▪ **smoking ~s your teeth** le tabac jaunit les dents ▪ **his hands are ~ed with blood** *liter* & *fig* il a du sang sur les mains **2.** [honour, reputation] tacher, entacher, ternir **3.** [colour, dye - wood] teindre ; [- glass, cell specimen] colorer.
<> *vi* **1.** [mark - wine, oil etc] tacher **2.** [become marked - cloth] se tacher.

stained [steɪnd] *adj* **1.** [soiled - collar, sheet] taché ; [- teeth] jauni **2.** [coloured - gen] coloré ; [- wood] teint.

-stained *in cpds* taché ▪ **his sweat~ shirt** sa chemise tachée de transpiration ▪ **nicotine~** jauni par la nicotine.

stained glass *n* vitrail *m*.
◆ **stained-glass** *adj* : **stained-glass window** vitrail *m*.

stainless ['steɪnlɪs] *adj* **1.** [rust-resistant] inoxydable **2.** *fig* sans tache, pur.

stainless steel <> *n* acier *m* inoxydable, Inox® *m*.
<> *comp* en acier inoxydable, en Inox®.

stain remover *n* détachant *m*.

stair [steəʳ] *n* **1.** [step] marche *f* ▪ **the bottom ~** la première marche **2.** *lit* [staircase] escalier *m*.
◆ **stairs** *npl* [stairway] escalier *m*, escaliers *mpl* ▪ **I slipped on the ~s** j'ai glissé dans l'escalier ▪ **at the top of the ~s** en haut de l'escalier ▪ **at the bottom** *OR* **the foot of the ~s** en bas *OR* au pied de l'escalier ➲ **above/below ~s** *UK* chez les patrons/les domestiques.

staircase ['steəkeɪs] *n* escalier *m*.

stair-rod *n* tringle *f* d'escalier.

stairway ['steəweɪ] = **staircase**.

stairwell ['steəwel] *n* cage *f* d'escalier.

stake [steɪk] <> *n* **1.** [post, pole] pieu *m* ▪ [for plant] tuteur *m* ▪ [in surveying] piquet *m*, jalon *m* ▪ [for tent] piquet *m* ▪ [for execution] poteau *m* ▪ **to die** *OR* **to be burned at the ~** mourir sur le bûcher ➲ **to (pull) up ~s** *US* [leave place, job] faire ses valises ; [continue journey] se remettre en route
2. [in gambling] enjeu *m*, mise *f* ▪ **to play for high ~s** jouer gros jeu ▪ **the ~s are too high for me** l'enjeu est trop important pour moi ▪ **to lose one's ~** perdre sa mise
3. [interest, share] intérêt *m*, part *f* ▪ [investment] investissement *m*, investissements *mpl* ▪ [shareholding] participation *f* ▪ **she has a 10% ~ in the company** elle a une participation de 10 % dans la société, elle détient 10 % du capital de la société ▪ **the company has a big ~ in nuclear energy** la société a misé gros sur *OR* a fait de gros investissements dans le nucléaire ▪ **we all have a ~ in the education of the young** l'éducation des jeunes nous concerne tous
4. *US* [savings] (petit) pécule *m*, bas *m* de laine.
<> *vt* **1.** [bet - sum of money, valuables] jouer, miser ▪ *fig* [- reputation] jouer, risquer ▪ **he ~d $10 on Birdy** il a joué *OR* misé *OR* mis 10 dollars sur Birdy ▪ **he had ~d everything** *OR* **his all on getting the job** il avait tout misé sur l'acceptation de sa candidature ▪ **I'd ~ my all** *OR* **my life on it** j'en mettrais ma main au feu
2. *US* [aid financially] financer ▪ **he is staking the newspaper for half a million dollars** il investit un demi-million de dollars dans le journal
3. [fasten - boat, animal] attacher (à) un pieu *OR* un piquet ; [- tent] attacher avec des piquets ; [- plant] tuteurer
4. [put forward] : **to ~ a** *OR* **one's claim to sthg** revendiquer qqch ▪ **each gang has ~d its claim to a piece of the territory** chaque gang a délimité sa part de territoire ▪ **she has ~d her claim to a place in the history of our country** elle mérite une place d'honneur dans l'histoire de notre pays
5. *phr* **to be at ~** être en jeu ▪ **what** *OR* **how much is at ~?** quels sont les enjeux?, qu'est-ce qui est en jeu? ▪ **she has a lot at ~** elle joue gros jeu, elle risque gros.
◆ **stakes** *npl* [horse race] course *f* de chevaux ▪ [money prize] prix *m* ▪ **the promotion ~s** *fig* la course à l'avancement.
◆ **stake off** *vt sep* = **stake out** *(sense 1)*.
◆ **stake out** *vt sep* **1.** [delimit - area, piece of land] délimiter (avec des piquets) ; [- boundary, line] marquer, jalonner ▪ *fig* [- sphere of influence] définir ; [- market] se tailler ; [- job, research field] s'approprier
2. *US* [keep watch on] mettre sous surveillance, surveiller.

stakeout ['steɪkaʊt] *n* *US* [activity] surveillance *f* ▪ [place] locaux *mpl* sous surveillance.

stalactite ['stæləktaɪt] *n* stalactite *f*.

stalagmite ['stæləgmaɪt] *n* stalagmite *f*.

stale [steɪl] <> *adj* **1.** [bread, cake] rassis, sec, sèche *f* ▪ [chocolate, cigarette] vieux *(before vowel or silent 'h'* **vieil***)*, vieille *f* ▪ [cheese - hard] desséché ; [- mouldy] moisi ▪ [fizzy drink] éventé, plat ▪ [air - foul] vicié ; [- confined] confiné ▪ **~ breath** haleine *f* fétide ▪ **to go ~** [bread] (se) rassir ; [chocolate, cigarette] perdre son goût ; [cheese] se dessécher ; [beer] s'éventer **2.** [idea, plot, joke] éculé, rebattu ▪ [discovery, news] éventé, dépassé ▪ [pleasure] émoussé, qui n'a plus de goût ▪ [beauty] fané, défraîchi ▪ **his arguments were ~ and unconvincing** ses arguments étaient éculés et peu convaincants ▪ **her marriage had gone ~** son bonheur conjugal s'était fané, elle s'était lassée de son mariage ▪ **he's getting ~ in that job** il sèche sur pied dans ce poste **3.** LAW [warrant] périmé ▪ [debt] impayable ▪ **~ cheque** FIN chèque *m* prescrit.
<> *vi* *lit* [novelty, place, activity] perdre son charme.

stalemate ['steɪlmeɪt] <> *n* **1.** [in chess] pat *m* ▪ **the game ended in ~** la partie s'est terminée par un pat **2.** [deadlock] impasse *f* ▪ **the argument ended in (a) ~** la discussion s'est terminée dans une impasse ▪ **the announcement broke the ~ in the negotiations** l'annonce a fait sortir les négociations de l'impasse.
<> *vt (usu passive)* [in chess - opponent] faire pat à ▪ **the negotiations were ~d** *fig* les négociations étaient dans l'impasse.

Stalin ['stɑːlɪn] *pr n* Staline.

Stalinist ['stɑːlɪnɪst] <> *adj* stalinien.
<> *n* stalinien *m*, - enne *f*.

stalk [stɔːk] <> *n* **1.** BOT [of flower, plant] tige *f* ▪ [of cabbage, cauliflower] trognon *m* ▪ **(grape) ~s** râpe *f*, rafle *f* **2.** ZOOL pédoncule *m* ▪ **his eyes stood out on ~s** *inf* il avait les yeux qui lui sortaient de la tête **3.** [gen - long object] tige *f*.
<> *vt* **1.** [game, fugitive etc] traquer **2.** [subj: wolf, ghost] rôder dans ▪ **enemy patrols ~ed the hills** des patrouilles ennemies rôdaient dans les collines **3.** *lit* [subj: disease, terror] régner dans, rôder dans.
<> *vi* **1.** [person] : **she ~ed out angrily/in disgust** elle sortit d'un air furieux/dégoûté ▪ **he was ~ing up and down the deck** il arpentait le pont **2.** [prowl - tiger, animal] rôder ▪ [hunt] chasser.

stalker ['stɔːkəʳ] *n* [criminal] *criminel suivant sa victime à la trace*.

stalking horse ['stɔːkɪŋ-] *n* **1.** *liter* cheval *m* d'abri **2.** *fig* stratagème *m*.

stall [stɔːl] <> *n* **1.** [at market] étal *m*, éventaire *m* ▪ [at fair, exhibition] stand *m* ▪ **I bought some peaches at a fruit ~** j'ai acheté des pêches chez un marchand de fruits ▪ **flower ~** *UK* [on street] kiosque *m* de fleuriste **2.** [for animal] stalle *f* ▪ **(starting) ~s** EQUIT stalles de départ **3.** [cubicle] cabine *f* **4.** [in church] stalle *f* **5.** *UK* CIN & THEAT orchestre *m*, fauteuil *m* d'orchestre ▪ **the ~s** l'orchestre **6.** *US* [in parking lot] emplacement *m (de parking)* **7.** [for finger] doigtier *m* **8.** AERON décrochage *m* ▪ AUT calage *m (du moteur)* **9.** [delaying tactic] manœuvre *f* dilatoire ▪ [pretext] prétexte *m*.
<> *vi* **1.** [motor, vehicle, driver] caler ▪ [plane] décrocher ▪ [pilot] faire décrocher son avion **2.** [delay] : **to ~ for time** essayer de gagner du temps ▪ **I think they're ~ing on the loan until we make more concessions** je crois qu'ils vont retarder le prêt jusqu'à ce que nous leur fassions davantage de concessions.

◇ *vt* **1.** [motor, vehicle] caler ▪ [plane] faire décrocher **2.** [delay - sale, decision] retarder ; [- person] faire attendre ▪ **try to ~ him (off)!** essayez de gagner du temps! ▪ **the project/his career is ~ ed** le projet/sa carrière en est au point mort **3.** [animal] mettre à l'étable.

stallholder ['stɔ:l,həʊldər] *n* [in market] marchand *m*, - e *f* de *OR* des quatre-saisons ▪ [in fair] forain *m*, - e *f* ▪ [in exhibition] exposant *m*, - e *f*.

stalling ['stɔ:lɪŋ] ◇ *n (U)* atermoiements *mpl*, manœuvres *fpl* dilatoires.
◇ *adj* : **~ tactic** manœuvre *f* dilatoire.

stallion ['stæljən] *n* étalon *m (cheval)*.

stalwart ['stɔ:lwət] ◇ *adj* [person] robuste ▪ [citizen, fighter] vaillant, brave ▪ [work, worker] exemplaire ▪ **he was a ~ supporter of the England team** c'était un supporter inconditionnel de l'équipe d'Angleterre.
◇ *n* fidèle *mf*.

stamen ['steɪmən] (*pl* **stamens** *OR pl* **stamina** ['stæmɪnə]) *n* BOT étamine *f*.

stamina ['stæmɪnə] *n* [physical] résistance *f*, endurance *f* ▪ [mental] force *f* intérieure, résistance *f* ▪ **to build up one's ~** SPORT développer son endurance ▪ **she has more ~ than he does** elle est plus résistante que lui.

stammer ['stæmər] ◇ *vi* [through fear, excitement] balbutier, bégayer ▪ [through speech defect] bégayer, être bègue.
◇ *vt* bredouiller, bégayer ▪ **I managed to ~ (out) an apology** j'ai réussi à bredouiller des excuses.
◇ *n* [through fear, excitement] balbutiement *m*, bégaiement *m* ▪ [through speech defect] bégaiement *m* ▪ **to have a ~** bégayer, être bègue ▪ **he has a bad ~** il est affligé d'un bégaiement prononcé.

stammerer ['stæmərər] *n* bègue *mf*.

stammering ['stæmərɪŋ] *n* [through fear, excitement] bégaiement *m*, balbutiement *m* ▪ [speech defect] bégaiement *m*.

stamp [stæmp] ◇ *n* **1.** [sticker, token] timbre *m* ▪ **fiscal** *OR* **revenue ~** timbre fiscal ▪ **television (licence) ~** timbre pour la redevance ➊ **(national insurance) ~** *UK* cotisation *f* de sécurité sociale ▪ **(postage) ~** timbre, timbre-poste *m* ▪ **the Stamp Act** *US* HIST le Stamp Act
2. [instrument - rubber stamp] tampon *m*, timbre *m* ; [- for metal] poinçon *m* ; [- for leather] fer *m*
3. [mark, impression - in passport, library book etc] cachet *m*, tampon *m* ; [- on metal] poinçon *m* ; [- on leather] motif *m* ; [- on antique] estampille *f* ▪ [postmark] cachet *m* (d'oblitération de la poste) ▪ **he has an Israeli ~ in his passport** il a un tampon de la douane israélienne sur son passeport ▪ **~ of approval** *fig* approbation *f*, aval *m*
4. [distinctive trait] marque *f*, empreinte *f* ▪ **his story had the ~ of authenticity** son histoire semblait authentique ▪ **poverty has left its ~ on him** la pauvreté a laissé son empreinte sur lui *OR* l'a marqué de son sceau ▪ **their faces bore the ~ of despair** le désespoir se lisait sur leur visage
5. [type, ilk, class] genre *m*, acabit *m pej* ▪ [calibre] trempe *f* ▪ **of the old ~** [servant, worker] comme on n'en fait plus ; [doctor, disciplinarian] de la vieille école
6. [noise - of boots] bruit *m* (de bottes) ; [- of audience] trépignement *m*.
◇ *comp* [album, collection, machine] de timbres, de timbres-poste.
◇ *vt* **1.** [envelope, letter] timbrer, affranchir
2. [mark - document] tamponner ; [- leather, metal] estamper ▪ **incoming mail is ~ed with the date received** le courrier qui arrive est tamponné à la date de réception ▪ **the machine ~s the time on your ticket** la machine marque *OR* poinçonne l'heure sur votre ticket
3. [affect, mark - society, person] marquer ▪ **as editor she ~ed her personality on the magazine** comme rédactrice en chef, elle a marqué la revue du sceau de sa personnalité
4. [characterise, brand] étiqueter ▪ **recent events have ~ed the president as indecisive** le président a été taxé d'indécision au vu des derniers événements
5. [foot] : **she ~ed her foot in anger** furieuse, elle tapa du pied ▪ **the audience were ~ing their feet and booing** la salle trépignait et sifflait ▪ **he ~ed the snow off his boots** il a tapé du pied pour enlever la neige de ses bottes.
◇ *vi* **1.** [in one place - person] taper du pied ; [- audience] trépigner ; [- horse] piaffer ▪ **I ~ed on his fingers** je lui ai marché sur les doigts
2. [walk] : **to ~ in/out** [noisily] entrer/sortir bruyamment ; [angrily] entrer/sortir en colère ▪ **he ~ed up the stairs** il monta l'escalier d'un pas lourd.

◆ **stamp down** *vt sep* [loose earth, snow] tasser avec les pieds ▪ [peg] enfoncer du pied.

◆ **stamp on** *vt insep* [rebellion] écraser ▪ [dissent, protest] étouffer ▪ [proposal] repousser.

◆ **stamp out** *vt sep* **1.** [fire] éteindre avec les pieds *OR* en piétinant
2. [end - disease, crime] éradiquer ; [- strike, movement] supprimer ; [- dissent, protest] étouffer ; [- corruption, ideas] extirper
3. [hole] découper (à l'emporte-pièce) ▪ [medal] frapper ▪ [pattern] estamper.

THE STAMP ACT

Impôt britannique auquel furent soumises les colonies américaines à partir de 1765. Portant sur un certain nombre de publications (actes juridiques, journaux, etc.), il doit son nom au timbre justifiant de son acquittement. Premier impôt direct levé par la Couronne, il souleva une violente opposition chez les colons, qui obtinrent sa suppression un an plus tard.

stamp book *n* **1.** [of postage stamps] carnet *m* de timbres *OR* de timbres-poste **2.** [for trading stamps] carnet *m* pour coller les vignettes-épargne.

stamp collecting *n* philatélie *f*.

stamp collector *n* collectionneur *m*, - euse *f* de timbres *OR* de timbres-poste, philatéliste *mf*.

stamped [stæmpt] *adj* [letter, envelope] timbré ▪ **send a ~ addressed envelope** envoyez une enveloppe timbrée à votre adresse.

stampede [stæm'pi:d] ◇ *n* **1.** [of animals] fuite *f*, débandade *f* **2.** [of people - flight] sauve-qui-peut *m inv*, débandade *f* ; [- rush] ruée *f* ▪ **there was a ~ for seats** il y a eu une ruée vers *OR* sur les sièges.
◇ *vi* [flee] s'enfuir (pris d'affolement) ▪ [rush] se ruer, se précipiter ▪ **the cattle ~d across the river** pris d'affolement, le bétail a traversé la rivière.
◇ *vt* **1.** [animals] faire fuir ▪ [crowd] semer la panique dans **2.** [pressurize] forcer la main à.

stamping ground ['stæmpɪŋ-] *n inf* lieu *m* favori.

stance [stæns] *n* **1.** [physical posture] posture *f* ▪ **she altered her ~ slightly** elle changea légèrement de position ▪ **he took up a boxer's ~** il adopta la position d'un boxeur ▪ **he took up his usual ~ in front of the fire** il s'est planté devant le feu à sa place habituelle ▪ **widen your ~** SPORT écartez les jambes
2. [attitude] position *f* ▪ **to adopt** *OR* **to take a tough ~ on sthg** adopter *OR* prendre une position ferme sur qqch.

stand [stænd] (*pret & pp* **stood** [stud]) ◇ *vi*

A.

1. [rise to one's feet] se lever, se mettre debout
2. [be on one's feet] être *OR* se tenir debout ▪ **I've been ~ing all day** je suis resté debout toute la journée ▪ **I had to ~ all the way** j'ai dû voyager debout pendant tout le trajet ▪ **she was so tired she could hardly ~** elle était si fatiguée qu'elle avait du mal à tenir debout *OR* sur ses jambes ▪ **I don't mind ~ing** ça ne me gêne pas de rester debout ▮ [in a specified location] être (debout), rester (debout) ▪ **don't ~ near the edge** ne restez pas près du bord ▪ **don't just ~ there, do something!** ne restez pas là à ne rien faire! ▪ **~ clear!** écartez-vous! ▪ **where should I ~? – beside Yvonne** où dois-je me mettre? – à côté d'Yvonne ▪ **small groups of men stood talking at street corners** des hommes discutaient par petits groupes au coin des rues ▪ **is there a chair I can ~ on?** y a-t-il une chaise sur laquelle je puisse monter? ▪ **they were ~ing a little way off** ils se tenaient un peu à l'écart ▪ **excuse me, you're ~ing on my**

foot excusez-moi, vous me marchez sur le pied ▪ **to ~ in line** *US* faire la queue ▮ [in a specified posture] se tenir ▪ **to ~ upright** *OR* **erect** se tenir droit ▪ **he was so nervous he couldn't ~ still** il était si nerveux qu'il ne tenait pas en place ▪ **I stood perfectly still, hoping they wouldn't see me** je me suis figé sur place en espérant qu'ils ne me verraient pas ▪ **~ still!** ne bougez pas!, ne bougez plus! ▪ **~ with your feet apart** écartez les pieds ➊ **~ and deliver!** la bourse ou la vie!

3. [be upright - post, target etc] être debout ▪ **not a stone was left ~ing** il ne restait plus une seule pierre debout ▪ **the aqueduct has stood for centuries** l'aqueduc est là depuis des siècles

4. [be supported, be mounted] reposer ▪ **the coffin stood on trestles** le cercueil reposait sur des tréteaux ▪ **the house ~s on solid foundations** la maison repose *OR* est bâtie sur des fondations solides

5. [be located - building, tree, statue] se trouver ; [- clock, vase, lamp] être, être posé ▪ **the piano stood in the centre of the room** le piano était au centre *OR* occupait le centre de la pièce ▪ **a wardrobe stood against one wall** il y avait une armoire contre un mur

B.

1. [indicating current state of affairs, situation] être ▪ **how do things ~?** où en est la situation? ▪ **I'd like to know where I ~ with you** j'aimerais savoir où en sont les choses entre nous ▪ **as things ~** telles que les choses se présentent ▪ **he's dissatisfied with the contract as it ~s** il n'est pas satisfait du contrat tel qu'il a été rédigé ▪ **just print the text as it ~s** faites imprimer le texte tel quel ▪ **he ~s accused of rape** il est accusé de viol ▪ **I ~ corrected** je reconnais m'être trompé *OR* mon erreur ▪ **the party ~s united behind him** le parti est uni derrière lui ▪ **to ~ at** [gauge, barometer] indiquer ; [score] être de ; [unemployment] avoir atteint ▪ **their turnover now ~s at three million pounds** leur chiffre d'affaires atteint désormais les trois millions de livres ▪ **the exchange rate ~s at 5 francs to the dollar** le taux de change est de 5 francs pour un dollar ▪ **it's the only thing ~ing between us and financial disaster** c'est la seule chose qui nous empêche de sombrer dans un désastre financier ➊ **to ~ in sb's way** *liter* être sur le chemin de qqn ; *fig* gêner qqn ▪ **don't ~ in my way!** ne reste pas sur mon chemin! ▪ **nothing ~s in our way now** maintenant, la voie est libre ▪ **if you want to leave school I'm not going to ~ in your way** si tu veux quitter l'école, je ne m'y opposerai pas ▪ **their foreign debt ~s in the way of economic recovery** leur dette extérieure constitue un obstacle à la reprise économique

2. [remain] rester ▪ [be left undisturbed - marinade, dough] reposer ; [- tea] infuser ▪ **the machines stood idle** les machines étaient arrêtées ▪ **time stood still** le temps semblait s'être arrêté ▪ **the car has been ~ing in the garage for a year** ça fait un an que la voiture n'a pas bougé du garage ▪ **let the mixture ~ until the liquid is clear** laissez reposer le mélange jusqu'à ce que le liquide se clarifie

3. [be valid, effective - offer, law] rester valable ; [- decision] rester inchangé ▪ **my invitation still ~s** vous êtes toujours le bienvenu ▪ **the verdict ~s unless there's an appeal** le jugement reste valable à moins que l'on ne fasse appel

C.

1. [measure - person, tree] mesurer ▪ **she ~s 5 feet in her stocking feet** elle mesure moins de 1,50 m pieds nus ▪ **the building ~s ten storeys high** l'immeuble compte dix étages

2. [rank] se classer, compter ▪ **this hotel ~s among the best in the world** cet hôtel figure parmi les meilleurs du monde ▪ **she ~s first/last in her class** *US* elle est la première/la dernière de sa classe

3. [on issue] : **how** *OR* **where does he ~ on the nuclear issue?** quelle est sa position *OR* son point de vue sur la question nucléaire? ▪ **you ought to tell them where you ~** vous devriez leur faire part de votre position

4. [succeed] : **the government will ~ or fall on the outcome of this vote** le maintien ou la chute du gouvernement dépend du résultat de ce vote ➊ **united we ~, divided we fall** l'union fait la force

5. [be likely] : **to ~ to lose** risquer de perdre ▪ **to ~ to win** avoir des chances de gagner ▪ **they ~ to make a huge profit on the deal** ils ont des chances de faire un bénéfice énorme dans cette affaire

6. *UK* [run in election] se présenter, être candidat ▪ **will he ~ for re-election?** va-t-il se représenter aux élections? ▪ **she's ~ing as an independent** elle se présente en tant que candidate indépendante

7. *US* [stop] se garer *(pour un court instant)* ▪ **'no ~ing'** 'arrêt interdit'

8. *US* [pay] payer la tournée ▪ **you're ~ing** c'est ta tournée.

◇ *vt* **1.** [set, place] mettre, poser ▪ **she stood her umbrella in the corner** elle a mis son parapluie dans le coin ▪ **to ~ sthg on (its) end** faire tenir qqch debout ▪ **help me ~ the bedstead against the wall** aide-moi à dresser le sommier contre le mur **2.** [endure, withstand] supporter ▪ **it will ~ high temperatures without cracking** cela peut résister à *OR* supporter des températures élevées sans se fissurer ▪ **she's not strong enough to ~ another operation** elle n'est pas assez forte pour supporter une nouvelle opération ▮ *fig* **he certainly doesn't ~ comparison with Bogart** il n'est absolument pas possible de le comparer avec Bogart ▪ **their figures don't ~ close inspection** leurs chiffres ne résistent pas à un examen sérieux **3.** [put up with, bear - toothache, cold] supporter ; [- behaviour] supporter, tolérer ▪ **I can't ~ it any longer!** je n'en peux plus! ▪ **how can you ~ working with him?** comment est-ce que vous faites pour *OR* comment arrivez-vous à travailler avec lui? ▪ **I've had as much as I can ~ of your griping!** j'en ai assez de tes jérémiades! ▪ **if there's one thing I can't ~, it's hypocrisy** s'il y a quelque chose que je ne supporte pas, c'est bien l'hypocrisie ▪ **I can't ~ (the sight of) him!** je ne peux pas le supporter!, je ne peux pas le voir en peinture! ▪ **she can't ~ Wagner/smokers/flying** elle déteste Wagner/les fumeurs/prendre l'avion **4.** *inf* [do with, need] supporter, avoir besoin de ▪ **oil company profits could certainly ~ a cut** une diminution de leurs bénéfices ne ferait aucun mal aux compagnies pétrolières **5.** [perform duty of] remplir la fonction de ▪ **to ~ witness for sb** [at marriage] être le témoin de qqn **6.** *inf* [treat to] : **I'll ~ you a drink** *UK*, **I'll ~ you to a drink** *US* je t'offre un verre **7.** *phr* **you don't ~ a chance!** vous n'avez pas la moindre chance! ▪ **the plans ~ little chance of being approved** les projets ont peu de chances d'être approuvés.

◇ *n* **1.** [stall, booth - gen] stand *m* ; [- in exhibition] stand *m* ; [- in market] étal *m*, éventaire *m* ; [- for newspapers] kiosque *m* ▪ **a shooting ~** un stand de tir **2.** [frame, support - gen] support *m* ; [- for lamp, sink] pied *m* ; [- on bicycle, motorbike] béquille *f* ; [- for pipes, guns] râtelier *m* ▪ COMM [- for magazines, sunglasses] présentoir *m* ▪ [lectern] lutrin *m* ▪ **bicycle ~** [in street] râtelier à bicyclettes ▪ **revolving ~** COMM tourniquet *m*, présentoir rotatif **3.** [platform - gen] plate-forme *f* ; [- for speaker] tribune *f* ▪ [pulpit] chaire *f* **4.** [in sports ground] tribune *f* **5.** [for taxis] : **(taxi) ~** station *f* de taxis **6.** *US* [in courtroom] barre *f* ▪ **the first witness took the ~** le premier témoin est venu à la barre **7.** *liter* & *fig* [position] position *f* ▪ **to take a ~ on sthg** prendre position à propos de qqch ▪ **he refuses to take a ~** il refuse de prendre position **8.** MIL & *fig* [defensive effort] résistance *f*, opposition *f* ▪ **to make a ~** résister ▪ **Custer's last ~** HIST la dernière bataille de Custer **9.** [of trees] bosquet *m*, futaie *f* ▪ [of crop] récolte *f* sur pied.

◆ **stand about** *UK*, **stand around** *vi insep* rester là, traîner *pej* ▪ **we stood about** *OR* **around waiting for the flight announcement** nous restions là à attendre que le vol soit annoncé ▪ **the prisoners stood about** *OR* **around in small groups** les prisonniers se tenaient par petits groupes ▪ **after Mass, the men ~ about** *OR* **around in the square** après la messe, les hommes s'attardent sur la place ▪ **I'm not just going to ~ about waiting for you to make up your mind!** je n'ai pas l'intention de poireauter là en attendant que tu te décides!

◆ **stand aside** *vi insep* [move aside] s'écarter ▪ **he politely stood aside to let us pass** il s'écarta *OR* s'effaça poliment pour nous laisser passer ▪ **to ~ aside in favour of sb** [gen] laisser la voie libre à qqn ; POL se désister en faveur de qqn.

◆ **stand back** *vi insep* **1.** [move back] reculer, s'écarter ▪ **~ back from the doors!** écartez-vous des portes! ▪ **she stood back to look at herself in the mirror** elle recula pour se regarder dans la glace ▪ **the painting is better if you ~ back from it** le tableau est mieux si vous prenez du recul **2.** [be set back] être en retrait *OR* à l'écart ▪ **the house ~s back from the road** la maison est en retrait de la route **3.** [take mental distance] prendre du recul.

◆ **stand by** ◇ *vi insep* **1.** [not intervene] rester là (sans rien faire) **2.** [be ready - person] être *OR* se tenir prêt ; [- vehicle] être prêt ; [- army, embassy] être en état d'alerte ▪ **the police were**

~ing by to disperse the crowd la police se tenait prête à disperser la foule ■ **we have an oxygen machine ~ing by** nous avons une machine à oxygène prête en cas d'urgence ■ **~ by!** attention! ■ **~ by for takeoff** préparez-vous pour le décollage ■ **~ by to receive** RADIO prenez l'écoute.
◇ *vt insep* **1.** [support - person] soutenir ■ **I'll ~ by you through thick and thin** je te soutiendrai *OR* je resterai à tes côtés quoi qu'il arrive **2.** [adhere to - promise, word] tenir ; [- decision, offer] s'en tenir à.

◆ **stand down** ◇ *vi insep* **1.** *UK* POL [withdraw] se désister ■ [resign] démissionner **2.** [leave witness box] quitter la barre **3.** MIL [troops] être déconsigné *(en fin d'alerte).*
◇ *vt sep* [workers] licencier.

◆ **stand for** *vt insep* **1.** [represent] représenter ■ **what does DNA ~ for?** que veut dire l'abréviation ADN? ■ **the R ~s for Ryan** le R signifie Ryan ■ **we want our name to ~ for quality and efficiency** nous voulons que notre nom soit synonyme de qualité et d'efficacité ■ **she supports the values and ideas the party once stood for** elle soutient les valeurs et les idées qui furent autrefois celles du parti ■ **I detest everything that they ~ for!** je déteste tout ce qu'ils représentent! **2.** [tolerate] tolérer, supporter ■ [allow] permettre ■ **I'm not going to ~ for it!** je ne le tolérerai *OR* permettrai pas!

◆ **stand in** *vi insep* assurer le remplacement ■ **to ~ in for sb** remplacer qqn.

◆ **stand off** ◇ *vi insep* **1.** [move away] s'écarter **2.** NAUT [take up position] croiser ■ [sail away] mettre le cap au large.
◇ *vt sep UK* [workers] mettre en chômage technique.
◇ *vt insep* NAUT [coast, island] croiser au large de ■ **they have an aircraft carrier ~ing off Aden** ils ont un porte-avions qui croise au large d'Aden.

◆ **stand out** *vi insep* **1.** [protrude - vein] saillir ; [- ledge] faire saillie, avancer **2.** [be clearly visible - colour, typeface] ressortir, se détacher ; [- in silhouette] se découper ■ **the pink ~s out against the green background** le rose ressort *OR* se détache sur le fond vert ■ **the masts stood out against the sky** les mâts se découpaient *OR* se dessinaient contre le ciel ■ **the name on the truck stood out clearly** le nom sur le camion était bien visible **3.** [be distinctive] ressortir, se détacher ■ **this one book ~s out from all his others** ce livre-ci surclasse tous les autres livres qu'il a écrits ■ **she ~s out above all the rest** elle surpasse *OR* surclasse tous les autres ■ **I don't like to ~ out in a crowd** je n'aime pas me singulariser ■ **the day ~s out in my memory** cette journée est marquée d'une pierre blanche dans ma mémoire **4.** [resist, hold out] tenir bon, tenir ■ **to ~ out against** [attack, enemy] résister à ; [change, tax increase] s'opposer avec détermination à ■ **they are ~ing out for a pay increase** ils réclament une augmentation de salaire.

◆ **stand over** ◇ *vt insep* [watch over] surveiller ■ **I can't work with someone ~ing over me** je ne peux pas travailler quand quelqu'un regarde par-dessus mon épaule ■ **she stood over him until he'd eaten every last bit** elle ne l'a pas lâché avant qu'il ait mangé la dernière miette.
◇ *vt sep UK* [postpone] remettre (à plus tard).
◇ *vi insep UK* être remis (à plus tard) ■ **we have two items ~ing over from the last meeting** il nous reste deux points à régler depuis la dernière réunion.

◆ **stand to** *vi insep* MIL se mettre en état d'alerte ■ **~ to!** à vos postes!

◆ **stand up** ◇ *vi insep* **1.** [rise to one's feet] se lever, se mettre debout ▶ **to ~ up and be counted** avoir le courage de ses opinions **2.** [be upright] être debout ■ **I can't get the candle to ~ up straight** je n'arrive pas à faire tenir la bougie droite **3.** [last] tenir, résister ■ **how is that repair job ~ing up?** est-ce que cette réparation tient toujours? **4.** [be valid - argument, claim] être valable, tenir debout ■ **his evidence won't ~ up in court** son témoignage ne sera pas valable en justice.
◇ *vt sep* **1.** [set upright - chair, bottle] mettre debout ■ **they stood the prisoner up against a tree** ils ont adossé le prisonnier à un arbre ■ **~ the ladder up against the wall** mettez *OR* appuyez l'échelle contre le mur **2.** *inf* [fail to meet] poser un lapin à, faire faux bond à.

◆ **stand up for** *vt insep* défendre ■ **to ~ up for o.s.** se défendre.

◆ **stand up to** *vt insep* : **to ~ up to sthg** résister à qqch ■ **to ~ up to sb** tenir tête à *OR* faire face à qqn.

stand-alone *adj* COMPUT [system] autonome.

standard ['stændəd] ◇ *n* **1.** [norm] norme *f* ■ [level] niveau *m* ■ [criterion] critère *m* ■ **most of the goods are** *OR* **come up to ~** la plupart des marchandises sont de qualité satisfaisante ■ **your work isn't up to ~** *OR* **is below ~** votre travail laisse à désirer ■ **he sets high ~s for himself** il est très exigeant avec lui-même ■ **to set quality ~s for a product** fixer des normes de qualité pour un produit ■ **high safety ~s** des règles de sécurité très strictes ■ **their salaries are low by European ~s** leurs salaires sont bas par rapport aux salaires européens ■ **she's an Olympic ~ swimmer** c'est une nageuse de niveau olympique ■ **it's a difficult task by any ~** *OR* **by anybody's ~s** c'est indiscutablement une tâche difficile ■ **we apply the same ~s to all candidates** nous jugeons tous les candidats selon les mêmes critères ▶ **~ of living** niveau de vie
2. [moral principle] principe *m* ■ **to have high moral ~s** avoir de grands principes moraux
3. [for measures, currency - model] étalon *m* ■ [in coins - proportion] titre *m*
4. [established item] standard *m* ■ [tune] standard *m* ■ **a jazz ~** un classique du jazz
5. *US* [car] : **I can't drive a ~** je ne sais conduire que les voitures à boîte de vitesse automatique
6. [flag] étendard *m* ■ [of sovereign, noble] bannière *f* ■ **under the ~ of Liberty** *fig* sous l'étendard de la liberté
7. [support - pole] poteau *m* ; [- for flag] mât *m* ; [- for lamp] pied *m* ; [- for power-line] pylône *m*
8. *UK* [lamp] lampadaire *m* (de salon)
9. AGRIC & HORT [fruit tree] haute-tige *f*
10. BOT [petal] étendard *m*.
◇ *adj* **1.** [ordinary, regular - gen] normal ; [- model, size] standard ■ **catalytic converters are now ~ features** les pots catalytiques sont désormais la norme ■ **there's a ~ procedure for reporting accidents** il y a une procédure bien établie pour signaler les accidents ■ **any ~ detergent will do** n'importe quel détergent usuel fera l'affaire ■ **an apartment with all the ~ amenities** un appartement doté de tout le confort moderne ■ **it was just a ~ hotel room** c'était une chambre d'hôtel ordinaire ■ **she has a ~ speech for such occasions** elle a un discours tout prêt pour ces occasions ■ **~ gear shift** *US* AUT changement *m* de vitesse manuel
2. [measure - metre, kilogramme etc] étalon *(inv)*
3. [text, work] classique, de base ■ **the ~ works in English poetry** les ouvrages classiques de la poésie anglaise
4. LING [pronunciation, spelling etc] standard ■ **~ English** l'anglais correct
5. AGRIC & HORT [fruit tree, shrub] à haute tige ■ **~ rose** rose *f* tige.

standard bearer *n* **1.** [of cause] porte-drapeau *m* ■ [of political party] chef *m* de file **2.** [of flag] porte-étendard *m*.

standard deviation *n* [in statistics] écart-type *m*.

standard gauge RAIL *n* voie *f* normale.

◆ **standard-gauge** *adj* [line] à voie normale ■ [carriage, engine] pour voie normale.

standardization [ˌstændədaɪ'zeɪʃn] *n* **1.** [gen] standardisation *f* ■ [of dimensions, terms etc] normalisation *f* **2.** TECH [verification] étalonnage *m*.

standardize, ise ['stændədaɪz] *vt* **1.** [gen] standardiser ■ [dimensions, products, terms] normaliser ■ **~d parts** pièces *fpl* standardisées *OR* standard **2.** TECH [verify] étalonner.

standard lamp *n UK* lampadaire *m* (de salon).

standard time *n* heure *f* légale.

standby ['stændbaɪ] (*pl* **standbys**) ◇ *adj* **1.** [equipment, provisions etc] de réserve ■ [generator] de secours ■ **the ~ team can take over operations within an hour** l'équipe de secours est prête à prendre le contrôle des opérations en moins d'une heure ■ **in ~ position** RADIO en écoute **2.** AERON [ticket, fare] stand-by *(inv)* ■ [passenger] stand-by *(inv)*, en attente ■ **~ list** liste *f* d'attente **3.** FIN : **~ credit** crédit *m* stand-by *OR* de soutien ■ **~ loan** prêt *m* conditionnel.
◇ *n* **1.** [substitute - person] remplaçant *m*, - e *f* ■ THEAT [understudy] doublure *f* ■ **to be on ~** [doctor] être de garde *OR* d'astreinte ; [flight personnel, emergency repairman] être d'astreinte ; [troops, police, firemen] être prêt à intervenir ■ **we have a repair crew on ~** nous avons une équipe de réparateurs prête à intervenir en cas de besoin ■ **make sure you have a ~** [equipment]

vérifiez que vous en avez un *OR* une de secours ; [person] assurez-vous que vous pouvez vous faire remplacer ▪ **I'll keep the old typewriter as a ~** je garderai la vieille machine à écrire en cas de besoin *OR* au cas où **2.** AERON [system] stand-by *m inv* ▪ [passenger] (passager *m*, - ère *f*) stand-by *m inv* ▪ **to be on ~** [passenger] être en stand-by *OR* sur la liste d'attente.
◇ *adv* [travel] en stand-by.

stand-in ◇ *n* [gen] remplaçant *m*, - e *f* ▪ CIN [for lighting check] doublure *f* ▪ [stunt person] cascadeur *m*, - euse *f* ▪ THEAT [understudy] doublure *f* ▪ **she asked him to go as her ~** elle lui a demandé de la remplacer.
◇ *adj* [gen] remplaçant ▪ [office worker] intérimaire ▪ [teacher] suppléant, qui fait des remplacements ▪ **I can't find a ~ speaker for tomorrow's session** je ne trouve personne qui puisse remplacer le conférencier prévu pour demain.

standing ['stændɪŋ] ◇ *adj* **1.** [upright - position, person, object] debout *(inv)* ▪ **~ room** *OR* **places** places *fpl* debout ▪ **it was ~ room only at the meeting** il n'y avait plus de places assises *OR* la salle était pleine à craquer lors de la réunion ▶ **~ lamp** *US* lampadaire *m* (de salon) ▪ **~ ovation** ovation *f* ▪ **to get a ~ ovation** se faire ovationner
2. [stationary] : **~ jump** SPORT saut *m* à pieds joints ▪ **~ start** SPORT départ *m* debout ; AUT départ *m* arrêté ▪ **~ wave** PHYS onde *f* stationnaire
3. [grain, timber] sur pied
4. [stagnant - water] stagnant
5. [permanent - army, offer etc] permanent ; [- claim] de longue date ▪ **it's a ~ joke with us** c'est une vieille plaisanterie entre nous ▶ **~ committee** comité *m* permanent ▪ **to pay by ~ order** *UK* payer par prélèvement (bancaire) automatique ▪ **I get paid by ~ order** je reçois mon salaire par virement bancaire ▪ **~ orders** *UK* POL règlement *m* intérieur *(d'une assemblée délibérative).*
◇ *n* **1.** [reputation] réputation *f* ▪ [status] standing *m* ▪ **an economist of considerable ~** un économiste de grand renom *OR* très réputé ▪ **people of lower/higher social ~** des gens d'une position sociale moins/plus élevée ▪ **they are a family of some ~ in the community** c'est une famille qui jouit d'une certaine position dans la communauté ▪ **Mr Pym is a client in good ~ with our bank** M. Pym est un client très estimé de notre banque
2. [ranking] rang *m*, place *f* ▪ SCH & SPORT [ordered list] classement *m* ▪ **her ~ in the opinion polls is at its lowest yet** sa cote de popularité dans les sondages est au plus bas ▪ **what's their ~ in the league table?** quel est leur classement dans le championnat?
3. [duration] durée *f* ▪ **of long ~** de longue date ▪ **of 15 years' ~** [collaboration, feud] qui dure depuis 15 ans ; [treaty, account] qui existe depuis 15 ans ; [friend, member] depuis 15 ans ▪ **an employee of 10 years' ~** un salarié qui a 10 ans d'ancienneté dans l'entreprise
4. *US* AUT : **'no ~'** 'arrêt interdit'
5. *US* LAW position *f* en droit.

standing stone *n* pierre *f* levée.

standoff ['stændɒf] *n* **1.** POL [inconclusive clash] affrontement *m* indécis ▪ [deadlock] impasse *f* ▪ **their debate ended in a ~** leur débat n'a rien donné **2.** *US* SPORT [tie] match *m* nul.

standoffish [,stænd'ɒfɪʃ] *adj* distant, froid ▪ **there's no need to be ~** ce n'est pas la peine de prendre cet air supérieur.

standout ['stændaʊt] *n US* : **his article was a real ~** son article sortait vraiment du lot.

standpipe ['stændpaɪp] *n* **1.** [in street - for fire brigade] bouche *f* d'incendie ; [- for public] point *m* d'alimentation en eau de secours **2.** [in pumping system] tuyau *m* ascendant, colonne *f* d'alimentation.

standpoint ['stændpɔɪnt] *n* point *m* de vue.

standstill ['stændstɪl] *n* arrêt *m* ▪ **to come to a ~** [vehicle, person] s'immobiliser ; [talks, work etc] piétiner ▪ **to bring to a ~** [vehicle, person] arrêter ; [talks, traffic] paralyser ▪ **to be at a ~** [talks, career] être au point mort ; [traffic] être paralysé ; [economy] piétiner, stagner.

stand-up *adj* [collar] droit ▪ [meal] (pris) debout ▪ **a ~ fight** [physical] une bagarre en règle ; [verbal] une discussion violente ▶ **~ comic** *OR* **comedian** comique *mf (qui se produit seul en scène)* ▪ **~ counter** *OR* **diner** *US* buvette *f*.

Stanford ['stænfəd] *pr n prestigieuse université près de San Francisco.*

stank [stæŋk] *pt* ▷ **stink.**

Stanley knife® ['stænlɪ-] *n* cutter *m*.

stanza ['stænzə] *n* **1.** [in poetry] strophe *f* **2.** *US* SPORT période *f*.

staple ['steɪpl] ◇ *n* **1.** [for paper] agrafe *f* **2.** [for wire] cavalier *m*, crampillon *m* **3.** [foodstuff] aliment *m* *OR* denrée *f* de base ▪ **kitchen** *OR* **household ~s** provisions *fpl* de base **4.** COMM & ECON [item] article *m* de base ▪ [raw material] matière *f* première **5.** [constituent] partie *f* intégrante ▪ **divorce cases are a ~ of his law practice** son cabinet s'occupe essentiellement de divorces **6.** TEX fibre *f* artificielle à filer.
◇ *vt* [paper, upholstery etc] agrafer ▪ **posters were ~d on** *OR* **onto** *OR* **to the walls** des posters étaient agrafés aux murs.
◇ *adj* **1.** [food, products] de base ▪ [export, crop] principal ▪ **a ~ diet of rice and beans** un régime à base de riz et de haricots ▪ **the ~ diet of these TV channels consists of soap operas** *fig* les programmes de ces chaînes de télévision sont essentiellement constitués de feuilletons **2.** TEX : **~ fibre** fibre *f* artificielle à filer.

staple gun *n* agrafeuse *f* (professionnelle).

stapler ['steɪplər] *n* agrafeuse *f* (de bureau).

staple remover *n* ôte-agrafes *m inv*.

star [stɑːr] ◇ *n* **1.** [in sky] étoile *f* ▪ **to sleep (out) under the ~s** dormir *OR* coucher à la belle étoile ▪ **the Lone Star State** le Texas ▪ **the North Star State** le Minnesota ▶ **the morning/evening star** l'étoile du matin/du soir ▪ **falling** *OR* **shooting ~** étoile filante ▪ **to have ~s in one's eyes** être sur un petit nuage ▪ **to see ~s** voir trente-six chandelles ▪ **The Star** PRESS *nom abrégé du Daily Star*
2. [symbol of fate, luck] étoile *f* ▪ ASTROL astre *m*, étoile *f* ▪ **his ~ is rising** son étoile brille chaque jour davantage ▪ **his ~ is on the wane** son étoile pâlit ▪ **to be born under a lucky ~** être né sous une bonne étoile ▪ **I thanked my (lucky) ~s I wasn't chosen** j'ai remercié le ciel de ne pas avoir été choisi ▪ **the influence of the ~s** l'influence des astres ▪ **what do my ~s say today?** *inf* que dit mon horoscope aujourd'hui? ▪ **it's written in the ~s** c'est le destin
3. [figure, emblem] étoile *f* ▪ SCH bon point *m* ▪ **the restaurant has gained another ~** le restaurant s'est vu décerner une étoile supplémentaire ▶ **the Star of David** l'étoile de David ▪ **the Stars and Bars** le drapeau des États Confédérés ▪ **the Stars and Stripes** *le drapeau américain*
4. [asterisk] astérisque *m*
5. [celebrity] vedette *f*, star *f* ▪ **he's a rising ~ in the Labour party** il est en train de devenir un personnage important du parti travailliste
6. [blaze - on animal] étoile *f*.
◇ *comp* **1.** CIN & THEAT : **the ~ attraction of tonight's show** la principale attraction du spectacle de ce soir ▪ **the ~ turn** la vedette ▪ **to give sb ~ billing** mettre qqn en tête d'affiche ▪ **the hotel gives all its clients ~ treatment** cet hôtel offre à sa clientèle un service de première classe
2. [salesman, pupil etc] meilleur ▪ **he's our ~ witness** c'est notre témoin-vedette *OR* notre témoin principal
3. ELEC : **~ connection** couplage *m* en étoile ▪ **~ point** point *m* neutre.
◇ *vt* (*pret & pp* **starred**, *cont* **starring**) **1.** CIN & THEAT avoir comme *OR* pour vedette ▪ **the play starred David Caffrey** la pièce avait pour vedette David Caffrey ▪ **"Casablanca", starring Humphrey Bogart and Ingrid Bergman** "Casablanca", avec Humphrey Bogart et Ingrid Bergman (dans les rôles principaux)
2. [mark with asterisk] marquer d'un astérisque
3. *lit* [adorn with stars] étoiler.
◇ *vi* (*pret & pp* **starred**, *cont* **starring**) CIN & THEAT être la vedette ▪ **who starred with Redford in "The Sting"?** qui jouait avec Redford dans "l'Arnaque"? ▪ **he's starring in a new TV serial** il est la vedette d'un nouveau feuilleton télévisé.

STARS AND STRIPES

Stars and Stripes (« la bannière étoilée ») n'est que l'une des nombreuses appellations populaires du drapeau américain, au même titre que *Old Glory* ou *Stars and Bars*. Les 50 étoiles représentent les 50 États actuels, alors que les rayures rouges et blanches symbolisent les 13 États fondateurs de l'Union. Les Américains sont très fiers de leur drapeau et il n'est pas rare de le voir flotter devant les maisons particulières. Le fait de détruire ou déshonorer l'emblème est considéré comme un crime fédéral.

-star *in cpds* : **a two~ hotel** un hôtel deux étoiles ■ **a four~ general** un général à quatre étoiles ■ **two~ petrol** *UK* (essence *f*) ordinaire *m* ■ **four~ petrol** *UK* super *m*.

starboard ['stɑ:bəd] <> *n* NAUT tribord *m* ■ AERON tribord *m*, droite *f*.
<> *adj* NAUT [rail, lights] de tribord ■ AERON [door, wing] droit, de tribord.
<> *vt* NAUT : **to ~ the helm** *OR* **rudder** mettre la barre à tribord.

starch [stɑ:tʃ] <> *n* **1.** [for laundry] amidon *m*, empois *m* **2.** [in cereals] amidon *m* ■ [in root vegetables] fécule *f* ■ **try and avoid ~** *OR* **~es** essayez d'éviter les féculents **3.** *inf (U) inf* [formality] manières *fpl* guindées **4.** *US phr* **to take the ~ out of sb** [critic, bully] rabattre le caquet à qqn.
<> *vt* empeser, amidonner.

Star Chamber *n UK* HIST tribunal *m* correctionnel ■ *fig & pej* tribunal *m* arbitraire *OR* inquisitorial.
◆ **star-chamber** *adj pej* [decision] arbitraire ■ [trial, procedure] arbitraire, inquisitorial.

starched [stɑ:tʃt] *adj* amidonné.

starchy ['stɑ:tʃɪ] (*comp* **starchier**, *superl* **starchiest**) *adj* **1.** [diet] riche en féculents ■ [taste] farineux ■ **~ foods** féculents *mpl* **2.** *pej* [person] guindé, compassé.

star-crossed *adj lit* maudit par le sort.

stardom ['stɑ:dəm] *n* célébrité *f*, vedettariat *m* ■ **to rise to ~** devenir célèbre, devenir une vedette.

stardust ['stɑ:dʌst] *n (U)* [illusions] chimères *fpl*, illusions *fpl* ■ [sentimentality] sentimentalité *f* ■ **to have ~ in one's eyes** [be deluded] être en proie aux chimères ; [be a romantic] être très fleur bleue.

stare [steəʳ] <> *vi* regarder (fixement) ■ **to ~ at sb/sthg** regarder qqn/qqch fixement ■ **it's rude to ~!** ça ne se fait pas de regarder les gens comme ça! ■ **stop it, people are staring!** arrête, les gens nous regardent! ■ **I ~d into his eyes** je l'ai regardé dans le blanc des yeux ■ **she ~d at me in disbelief** elle m'a regardé avec des yeux incrédules ■ **to ~ in amazement** regarder d'un air ébahi ■ **she sat staring into the distance** elle était assise, le regard perdu (au loin) ■ **I ~d out of the train window** j'ai regardé longuement par la fenêtre du train ■ **doesn't being ~d at in the street bother you?** ça ne vous gêne pas d'attirer les regards des gens dans la rue?
<> *vt* **1.** [intimidate] : **to ~ sb into silence** faire taire qqn en le fixant du regard **2.** *phr* **the answer is staring you in the face!** mais la réponse saute aux yeux! ■ **I'd looked everywhere for my keys and there they were staring me in the face** j'avais cherché mes clefs partout alors qu'elles étaient là sous mon nez.
<> *n* regard *m* (fixe).
◆ **stare out** *UK*, **stare down** *US vt sep* faire baisser les yeux à.

starfish ['stɑ:fɪʃ] (*pl inv OR pl* **starfishes**) *n* étoile *f* de mer.

starfruit ['stɑ:fru:t] *n* carambole *f*.

stargazer ['stɑ:,geɪzəʳ] *n* **1.** [astronomer] astronome *mf* ■ [astrologer] astrologue *mf* **2.** [daydreamer] rêveur *m*, - euse *f*, rêvasseur *m*, - euse *f* **3.** [fish] uranoscope *m*.

stargazing ['stɑ:,geɪzɪŋ] *n* **1.** [astronomy] observation *f* des étoiles ■ [astrology] astrologie *f* **2.** *(U)* [daydreaming] rêveries *fpl*, rêvasseries *fpl*.

staring ['steərɪŋ] <> *adj* [bystanders] curieux ■ **with ~ eyes** [fixedly] aux yeux fixes ; [wide-open] aux yeux écarquillés ; [blank] aux yeux vides.
<> *adv* ▻ **stark**.

stark [stɑ:k] <> *adj* **1.** [bare, grim - landscape] désolé ; [- branches, hills] nu ; [- crag, rock] âpre, abrupt ; [- room, façade] austère ; [- silhouette] net ■ **in the ~ light of day** à la lumière crue du jour **2.** [blunt - description, statement] cru, sans ambages ; [- refusal, denial] catégorique ■ [harsh - words] dur ■ **the ~ realities of war** les dures réalités de la guerre ■ **those are the ~ facts** ce sont les faits tels qu'ils sont **3.** [utter - brutality, terror] absolu ; [- madness] pur ■ **in ~ violation of the ceasefire** en violation flagrante du cessez-le-feu ■ **their foreign policy success is in ~ contrast to the failure of their domestic policies** la réussite de leur politique étrangère contraste nettement avec l'échec de leur politique intérieure.
<> *adv* complètement ■ **~ raving** *OR* **staring mad** *inf* complètement fou *OR* dingue ■ **~ naked** à poil.

starkers ['stɑ:kəz] *adj & adv UK inf* à poil.

starkly ['stɑ:klɪ] *adv* [describe] crûment ■ [tell] carrément, sans ambages ■ [stand out] nettement.

starkness ['stɑ:knɪs] *n* [of landscape, scene] désolation *f* ■ [of room, façade] austérité *f* ■ [of branches] nudité *f* ■ [of light] crudité *f* ■ [of life, reality] dureté *f*.

starless ['stɑ:lɪs] *adj* sans étoile.

starlet ['stɑ:lɪt] *n* starlette *f*.

starlight ['stɑ:laɪt] *n* lumière *f* des étoiles ■ **by ~** à *OR* sous la lumière des étoiles.

starling ['stɑ:lɪŋ] *n* étourneau *m*, sansonnet *m*.

starlit ['stɑ:lɪt] *adj* [night] étoilé ■ [landscape] illuminé par les étoiles ■ [beach, sea] baigné par la lumière des étoiles.

starry ['stɑ:rɪ] (*comp* **starrier**, *superl* **starriest**) *adj* **1.** [adorned with stars] étoilé **2.** [sparkling] étincelant, brillant **3.** *lit & fig* [lofty] élevé.

starry-eyed *adj* [idealistic] idéaliste ■ [naive] naïf, ingénu ■ [dreamy] rêveur, dans la lune.

star shell *n* MIL obus *m* éclairant.

star sign *n* signe *m* (du zodiaque).

Star-Spangled Banner *n* : **the ~** la bannière étoilée.

star-studded *adj* [show, film] à vedettes ■ **a ~ cast** une distribution où figurent de nombreuses vedettes *OR* qui réunit une brochette de stars.

star system *n* **1.** CIN & THEAT star-system *m* **2.** ASTRON système *m* stellaire.

start [stɑ:t] <> *vt* **1.** [begin - gen] commencer ; [- climb, descent] amorcer ■ **to ~ doing** *OR* **to do sthg** commencer à *OR* se mettre à faire qqch ■ **it's ~ing to rain** il commence à pleuvoir ■ **it had just ~ed raining** *OR* **to rain when I left** il venait juste de commencer à pleuvoir quand je suis parti ■ **she ~ed driving** *OR* **to drive again a month after her accident** elle a recommencé à conduire *OR* elle s'est remise à conduire un mois après son accident ■ **he ~ed work at sixteen** il a commencé à travailler à seize ans ■ **he ~ed life as a delivery boy** il débuta dans la vie comme garçon livreur ■ **frogs ~ life as tadpoles** les grenouilles commencent par être des têtards ■ **I like to finish anything I ~** j'aime aller au bout de tout ce que j'entreprends ■ **I think I'm ~ing a cold** je crois que j'ai attrapé un rhume ■ **to get ~ed : I got ~ed on the dishes** je me suis mis à la vaisselle ■ **once he gets ~ed there's no stopping him** une fois lancé, il n'y a pas moyen de l'arrêter ■ **I need a coffee to get me ~ed in the morning** j'ai besoin d'un café pour commencer la journée ■ **shall we get ~ed on the washing-up?** si on attaquait la vaisselle?
2. [initiate, instigate - reaction, revolution, process] déclencher ; [- fashion] lancer ; [- violence] déclencher, provoquer ; [- conversation, discussion] engager, amorcer ; [- rumour] faire naître ■ **which side ~ed the war?** quel camp a déclenché la guerre? ■ **the referee blew his whistle to ~ the match** l'arbitre siffla pour signaler le début du match ■ **to ~ a fire** [in fireplace] allumer le feu ; [campfire] faire du feu ; [by accident, bomb] mettre le feu

■ **the fire was ~ed by arsonists** l'incendie a été allumé par des pyromanes ▶ **are you trying to ~ something?** *inf*, **just what are you trying to ~?** *inf* tu cherches la bagarre, ou quoi?
3. [cause to behave in specified way] faire ■ **it ~ed her (off) crying/laughing** cela l'a fait pleurer/rire ■ **I'll ~ a team working on it right away** je vais mettre une équipe là-dessus tout de suite
4. [set in motion - motor, car] (faire) démarrer, mettre en marche ; [- machine, device] mettre en marche ; [- meal] mettre en route ■ **how do I ~ the tape (going)?** comment est-ce que je dois faire pour mettre le magnétophone en marche? ■ **I couldn't get the car ~ed** je n'ai pas réussi à faire démarrer la voiture ■ **to ~ the printer again, press this key** pour remettre en marche l'imprimante, appuyez sur cette touche
5. [begin using - bottle, pack] entamer
6. [establish, found - business, school, political party] créer, fonder ; [- restaurant, shop] ouvrir ; [- social programme] créer, instaurer ■ **to ~ a family** fonder un foyer
7. [person - in business, work] installer, établir ■ **he ~ed his son in the family business** il a fait entrer son fils dans l'entreprise familiale ■ **his election success ~ed him on his political career** son succès aux élections l'a lancé dans sa carrière d'homme politique ■ **they ~ new pilots on domestic flights** ils font débuter les nouveaux pilotes sur les vols intérieurs ■ **I ~ on $500 a week** je débute à 500 dollars par semaine
8. SPORT : **to ~ the race** donner le signal du départ
9. HUNT [flush out] lever.
◇ *vi* **1.** [in time] commencer ■ **before the New Year/the rainy season ~s** avant le début de l'année prochaine/de la saison des pluies ■ **before the cold weather ~s** avant qu'il ne commence à faire froid ■ **~ing (from) next week** à partir de la semaine prochaine ■ **to ~ again** *OR* **afresh** recommencer ■ **to ~ all over again, to ~ again from scratch** recommencer à zéro ■ **school ~s on September 5th** la rentrée a lieu *OR* les cours reprennent le 5 septembre ‖ [story, speech] : **calm down and ~ at the beginning** calmez-vous et commencez par le commencement ■ **I didn't know where to ~** je ne savais pas par quel bout commencer ■ **she ~ed with a joke/by introducing everyone** elle a commencé par une plaisanterie/par faire les présentations ■ **the book ~s with a quotation** le livre commence par une citation ‖ [in career, job] débuter ■ **she ~ed in personnel/as an assistant** elle a débuté au service du personnel/comme assistante ■ **gymnasts have to ~ young** les gymnastes doivent commencer jeunes ▶ **I'll have the soup to ~ (with)** pour commencer, je prendrai du potage ■ **she was an architect to ~ with, then a journalist** elle a d'abord été architecte, puis journaliste ■ **isn't it time you got a job? – don't YOU ~!** il serait peut-être temps que tu trouves du travail – tu ne vas pas t'y mettre, toi aussi!
2. [in space - desert, fields, slope, street] commencer ; [- river] prendre sa source ■ **there's an arrow where the path ~s** il y a une flèche qui indique le début du sentier
3. [car, motor] démarrer, se mettre en marche ■ **why won't the car ~?** pourquoi la voiture ne veut-elle pas démarrer?
4. [set off - person, convoy] partir, se mettre en route ; [- train] s'ébranler ■ **the tour ~s at** *OR* **from the town hall** la visite part de la mairie ■ **I'll have to ~ for the airport soon** il va bientôt falloir que je parte pour l'aéroport ■ **the train was ~ing across** *OR* **over the bridge** le train commençait à traverser le pont *OR* abordait le pont ■ **she ~ed along the path** elle s'engagea sur le sentier
5. [range - prices] commencer ■ **houses here ~ at $100,000** ici, le prix des maisons démarre à 100 000 dollars ■ **return fares ~ from £299** on trouve des billets aller retour à partir de 299 livres
6. [jump involuntarily - person] sursauter ; [- horse] tressaillir, faire un soubresaut ■ [jump up] bondir ■ **he ~ed in surprise** il a tressailli de surprise ■ **she ~ed from her chair** elle bondit de sa chaise
7. [gush] jaillir, gicler ■ **tears ~ed to his eyes** les larmes lui sont montées aux yeux.
◇ *n* **1.** [beginning - gen] commencement *m*, début *m* ; [- of inquiry] ouverture *f* ■ **the ~ of the school year** la rentrée scolaire ■ **the ~ of the footpath is marked by an arrow** le début du sentier est signalé par une flèche ■ **it was an inauspicious ~ to his presidency** c'était un début peu prometteur pour sa présidence ■ **things are off to a bad/good ~** ça commence mal/bien, on est mal/bien partis ■ **my new boss and I didn't get off to a very good ~** au début, mes rapports avec mon nouveau patron n'ont pas été des meilleurs ■ **to get a good ~ in life** prendre un bon départ dans la vie *OR* l'existence ■ **we want an education that will give our children a good ~** nous voulons une éducation qui donne à nos enfants des bases solides ■ **a second honeymoon will give us a fresh ~** une deuxième lune de miel nous fera repartir d'un bon pied ■ **the programme will give ex-prisoners a fresh** *OR* **new ~ (in life)** le programme va donner aux anciens détenus une seconde chance (dans la vie) ■ **to make a ~ (on sthg)** commencer (qqch) ■ **to make** *OR* **to get an early ~** [gen] commencer de bonne heure ; [on journey] partir de bonne heure ■ **I was lonely at the ~** au début je me sentais seule ■ **at the ~ of the war** au début de la guerre ▶ **from the ~** dès le début *OR* commencement ■ **the trip was a disaster from ~ to finish** le voyage a été un désastre d'un bout à l'autre ■ **I laughed from ~ to finish** j'ai ri du début à la fin
2. SPORT [place] (ligne *f* de) départ *m* ■ [signal] signal *m* de départ ■ **they are lined up for** *OR* **at the ~** ils sont sur la ligne de départ
3. [lead, advance] avance *f* ■ **he gave him 20 metres' ~** *OR* **a 20-metre ~** il lui a accordé une avance de 20 mètres ■ **our research gives us a ~ over our competitors** nos recherches nous donnent de l'avance sur nos concurrents
4. [jump] sursaut *m* ■ **she woke up with a ~** elle s'est réveillée en sursaut ■ **to give a ~** sursauter, tressaillir ■ **to give sb a ~** faire sursauter *OR* tressaillir qqn.

➤ **for a start** *adv phr* d'abord, pour commencer.

➤ **for starts** *US inf* = **for a start**.

➤ **to start with** *adv phr* pour commencer, d'abord ■ **to ~ (off) with, my name isn't Jo** pour commencer *OR* d'abord, je ne m'appelle pas Jo.

➤ **start back** *vi insep* **1.** [turn back] rebrousser chemin
2. [start again] recommencer ■ **the children ~ back at school tomorrow** c'est la rentrée scolaire demain.

➤ **start in on** *vt insep* s'attaquer à ■ **once he ~s in on liberty and democracy, there's no stopping him** une fois qu'il est lancé sur le sujet de la liberté et de la démocratie, il n'y a plus moyen de l'arrêter ■ **to ~ in on sb** *inf* s'en prendre à qqn, tomber à bras raccourcis sur qqn.

➤ **start off** ◇ *vi insep* **1.** [leave] partir, se mettre en route ■ **when do you ~ off on your trip?** quand est-ce que vous partez en voyage?
2. [begin - speech, film] commencer ■ **it ~s off with a description of the town** ça commence par une description de la ville ■ **I ~ed off agreeing with him** au début, j'étais d'accord avec lui
3. [in life, career] débuter ■ **he ~ed off as a cashier** il a débuté comme caissier ■ **she ~ed off as a Catholic** elle était catholique à l'origine.
◇ *vt sep* **1.** [book, campaign, show] commencer
2. [person - on new task] : **here's some wool to ~ you off** voici de la laine pour commencer
3. [set off] déclencher ■ **if you mention it it'll only ~ her off again** n'en parle pas, sinon elle va recommencer ■ **to ~ sb off laughing/crying** faire rire/pleurer qqn.

➤ **start on** *vt insep* **1.** [begin - essay, meal] commencer ; [- task, dishes] se mettre à ; [- new bottle, pack] entamer ■ **after they'd searched the car they ~ed on the luggage** après avoir fouillé la voiture, ils sont passés aux bagages
2. [attack, berate] s'en prendre à.

➤ **start out** *vi insep* **1.** = **start off**
2. [begin career] se lancer, s'installer, s'établir ■ **he ~ed out in business with his wife's money** il s'est lancé dans les affaires avec l'argent de sa femme ■ **when she ~ed out there were only a few women lawyers** quand elle a commencé sa carrière, il y avait très peu de femmes avocats.

➤ **start over** *vi insep* & *vt sep* *US* recommencer (depuis le début).

➤ **start up** ◇ *vt sep* **1.** [establish, found - business, school, political party] créer, fonder ; [- restaurant, shop] ouvrir
2. [set in motion - car, motor] faire démarrer ; [- machine] mettre en marche.
◇ *vi insep* **1.** [guns, music, noise, band] commencer ■ [wind] se lever ■ **the applause ~ed up again** les applaudissements ont repris
2. [car, motor] démarrer, se mettre en marche ■ [machine] se mettre en marche
3. [set up business] se lancer, s'installer, s'établir.

starter ['stɑːtər] *n* **1.** AUT [motor, button] démarreur *m* ▪ [on motorbike] kick *m*, démarreur *m* au pied ▪ **~ switch** bouton *m* de démarrage ▪ **~ handle** *US* AUT manivelle *f* **2.** [runner, horse] partant *m* ▪ [in relay race] premier coureur *m*, première coureuse *f* ▪ **to be a slow ~** [gen - SPORT] être lent à démarrer, avoir du retard à l'allumage **3.** SPORT [official] starter *m*, juge *m* de départ ▪ **~'s pistol** *OR* **gun** pistolet *m* du starter ▪ **to be under ~'s orders** [in horseracing] être sous les ordres du starter **4.** [fermenting agent] ferment *m* **5.** *UK* [hors d'œuvre] hors-d'œuvre *m inv* ▪ **for ~s** [in meal] comme hors-d'œuvre ; *fig* *inf* pour commencer ▪ **that was just for ~s** ce n'était qu'un hors-d'œuvre.

starter home *n* première maison *f (achetée par un individu ou un couple).*

starter motor *n* démarreur *m*.

starter pack *n* kit *m* de base.

starter set *n US* [dishes] service *m* pour six.

starting ['stɑːtɪŋ] <> *n* commencement *m*.
<> *adj* initial ▪ **the ~ line-up** la composition initiale de l'équipe ▪ **~ salary** salaire *m* d'embauche.

starting block *n* starting-block *m*.

starting gate *n* SPORT [for horse] starting-gate *f* ▪ [for skier] porte *f* de départ.

starting grid *n* [in motor racing] grille *f* de départ.

starting handle *n UK* AUT manivelle *f*.

starting line = **starting post**.

starting pistol *n* pistolet *m* du starter.

starting point *n* point *m* de départ.

starting post *n* SPORT ligne *f* de départ.

starting price *n* [gen] prix *m* initial ▪ [in horseracing] cote *f* au départ ▪ [at auction] mise *f* à prix, prix *m* d'appel.

startle ['stɑːtl] <> *vt* [person - surprise] surprendre, étonner ; [- frighten, alarm] faire peur à, alarmer ; [- cause to jump] faire sursauter ▪ [animal, bird, fish] effaroucher ▪ **I didn't mean to ~ you** je ne voulais pas vous faire peur ▪ **the noise ~d him out of his reverie** le bruit l'a brusquement tiré de ses rêveries.
<> *vi* s'effaroucher.

startled ['stɑːtld] *adj* [person] étonné ▪ [expression, shout, glance] de surprise ▪ [animal] effarouché.

startling ['stɑːtlɪŋ] *adj* étonnant, surprenant ▪ [contrast, resemblance] saisissant.

start-up <> *adj* [costs] de démarrage ▪ **~ loan** prêt *m* initial.
<> *n* start-up *f*, jeune pousse *f* d'entreprise *offic*.

status bar *n* COMPUT barre *f* d'état.

starvation [stɑː'veɪʃn] *n* faim *f* ▪ **to die of** *OR* **from ~** mourir de faim.

starvation diet *n liter* ration *f* de famine ▪ *fig* régime *m* draconien ▪ **the prisoners subsisted on a ~ of rice and water** les prisonniers devaient se contenter de riz et d'eau.

starve [stɑːv] <> *vi* [suffer] souffrir de la faim, être affamé ▪ **to ~ (to death)** [die] mourir de faim ▪ **I'm starving!** *inf* je meurs de faim!
<> *vt* **1.** [cause to suffer] affamer ▪ **he ~d himself to feed his child** il s'est privé de nourriture pour donner à manger à son enfant ▪ **I'm ~d!** *inf* je meurs de faim! **2.** [cause to die] laisser mourir de faim **3.** [deprive] priver ▪ **the libraries have been ~d of funds** les bibliothèques manquent cruellement de subventions ▪ **to be ~d of affection** être privé d'affection.
◆ **starve out** *vt sep* [rebels, inmates] affamer, réduire par la faim ▪ [animal] obliger à sortir en l'affamant.

starving ['stɑːvɪŋ] *adj* affamé ▪ **think of all the ~ people in the world** pense à tous ces gens qui meurent de faim dans le monde.

Star Wars <> *pr n* la guerre des étoiles *(nom donné à l'Initiative de Défense Stratégique, programme militaire spatial mis en place dans les années 80 par le président Reagan).*
<> *comp* [policy, advocate, weapon] de la guerre des étoiles ▪ **~ research** la recherche sur la défense stratégique.

stash [stæʃ] *inf* <> *vt* **1.** [hide] planquer, cacher ▪ **he's got a lot of money ~ed (away) somewhere** il a plein de fric planqué quelque part **2.** [put away] ranger.
<> *n* **1.** [reserve] réserve *f* ▪ **a ~ of money** un magot ▪ **the police found a big ~ of guns/of cocaine** la police a découvert une importante cache d'armes/un important stock de cocaïne **2.** [hiding place] planque *f*, cachette *f* **3.** △ *drug sl* cache *f*.
◆ **stash away** *vt sep inf* = **stash** *(vt)*.

stasis ['steɪsɪs] (*pl* **stases** [-siːz]) *n* **1.** MED stase *f* **2.** [equilibrium] équilibre *m*, repos *m* ▪ [stagnation] stagnation *f*.

state [steɪt] <> *n* **1.** [condition] état *m* ▪ **the country is in a ~ of war/shock** le pays est en état de guerre/choc ▪ **a ~ of confusion prevailed** la confusion régnait ▪ **chlorine in its gaseous/liquid ~** le chlore à l'état gazeux/liquide ▪ **to be in a good/bad ~** [road, carpet, car] être en bon/mauvais état ; [person, economy, friendship] aller bien/mal ▪ **he was in a ~ of confusion** il ne savait plus où il en était ▪ **she was in no (fit) ~ to make a decision** elle était hors d'état de *OR* elle n'était pas en état de prendre une décision ▪ **to get into a ~** *inf* se mettre dans tous ses états ▪ **there's no need to get into such a ~ about it** ce n'est pas la peine de te mettre dans un état pareil *OR* de t'affoler comme ça
2. POL [nation, body politic] État *m* ▪ **the member ~s** les États membres ▪ **the head of ~** le chef de l'État ▪ **heads of ~** chefs d'État ➲ **~ lottery** *US* *loterie d'État dont les gros lots sont soumis à l'impôt et sont versés au gagnant sur une période de 10 ou 20 ans* ▪ **the State Opening of Parliament** *ouverture officielle du Parlement britannique en présence de la reine*
3. [in US, Australia, India etc - political division] État *m* ▪ **the States** *inf* les États-Unis, les US ▪ **the State of Ohio** l'État de l'Ohio
4. *US* [department] : **State** le Département d'État
5. [pomp] apparat *m*, pompe *f* ▪ **the carriages are used only on ~ occasions** les carrosses sont réservés aux cérémonies d'apparat.
<> *comp* **1.** [secret] d'État ▪ [subsidy, intervention] de l'État ▪ ECON [sector] public ▪ **~ buildings** bâtiments *mpl* publics ▪ **the ~ airline** la compagnie d'aviation nationale ▪ **a ~ funeral** des funérailles nationales
2. *UK* SCH [education system] public
3. *US* [not federal - legislature, policy, law] de l'État ▪ **the ~ capital** la capitale de l'État ▪ **a ~ university** une université d'État *OR* publique ▪ **a ~ park** un parc régional
4. [official, ceremonious] officiel.
<> *vt* [utter, say] déclarer ▪ [express, formulate - intentions] déclarer ; [- demand] formuler ; [- proposition, problem, conclusions, views] énoncer, formuler ; [- conditions] poser ▪ **the president ~d emphatically that the rumours were untrue** le président a démenti catégoriquement les rumeurs ▪ **I have already ~d my position on that issue** j'ai déjà fait connaître ma position à ce sujet ▪ **the regulations clearly ~ that daily checks must be made** le règlement dit *OR* indique clairement que des vérifications quotidiennes doivent être effectuées ▪ **please ~ salary expectations** veuillez indiquer le salaire souhaité ▪ **~ your name and address** donnez vos nom, prénoms et adresse ▪ **the man refused to ~ his business** l'homme a refusé d'expliquer ce qu'il faisait ▪ **as ~d above** comme indiqué plus haut ▪ **to ~ one's case** présenter ses arguments ▪ **to ~ the case for the defence/the prosecution** LAW présenter le dossier de la défense/de l'accusation.
◆ **in state** *adv phr* en grand apparat, en grande pompe ▪ **to lie in ~** être exposé solennellement ▪ **to live in ~** mener grand train.

state apartments *npl* appartements *mpl* de parade.

state control *n* contrôle *m* étatique ▪ [doctrine] étatisme *m* ▪ **to be put** *OR* **placed under ~** être nationalisé.

state-controlled *adj* [industry] nationalisé ▪ [economy] étatisé ▪ [activities] soumis au contrôle de l'État ▪ **the oil company is 51% ~** l'État détient 51 % des actions de la compagnie pétrolière.

statecraft ['steɪtkrɑːft] *n* [skill - in politics] habileté *f* politique ; [- in diplomacy] (art *m* de la) diplomatie *f*.

stated ['steɪtɪd] *adj* [amount, date] fixé ▪ [limit] prescrit ▪ [aim] déclaré ▪ **it will be finished within the ~ time** cela va être terminé dans les délais prescrits *OR* prévus ▪ **at the ~ price** au prix fixé *OR* convenu.

State Department *n US* ministère *m* des Affaires étrangères.

State Enrolled Nurse *n UK* aide-soignant *m* diplômé, aide-soignante *f* diplômée.

statehood ['steɪthʊd] *n* : **the struggle for ~** la lutte pour l'indépendance ▪ **to achieve ~** devenir un État.

Statehouse ['steɪthaʊs] (*pl* [-haʊzɪz]) *n siège de l'assemblée législative d'un État aux États-Unis.*

stateless ['steɪtlɪs] *adj* apatride ▪ **~ person** apatride *mf*.

state line *n US* frontière *f* entre États.

stateliness ['steɪtlɪnɪs] *n* [of ceremony, building, monument] majesté *f*, grandeur *f* ▪ [of person, bearing] dignité *f*.

stately ['steɪtlɪ] (*comp* **statelier**, *superl* **stateliest**) *adj* [ceremony, building] majestueux, imposant ▪ [person, bearing] noble, plein de dignité.

stately home *n château ou manoir à la campagne, généralement ouvert au public.*

statement ['steɪtmənt] *n* **1.** [declaration - gen] déclaration *f*, affirmation *f* ; [- to the press] communiqué *m* ▪ **a written/policy ~** une déclaration écrite/de principe ▪ **to put out** *OR* **to issue** *OR* **to make a ~ about sthg** émettre un communiqué concernant qqch ▪ **a ~ to the effect that...** une déclaration selon laquelle...
2. [act of stating - of theory, opinions, policy, aims] exposition *f* ; [- of problem] exposé *m*, formulation *f* ; [- of facts, details] exposé *m*, compte-rendu *m*
3. LAW déposition *f* ▪ **to make a ~ to the police** faire une déposition dans un commissariat de police ▪ **a sworn ~** une déposition faite sous serment ➲ **~ of claim** demande *f* introductive d'instance
4. COMM & FIN relevé *m*
5. LING affirmation *f*
6. COMPUT instruction *f*.

Staten Island ['stætn-] *pr n* Staten Island *(quartier de New York).*

state of affairs *n* circonstances *fpl* actuelles ▪ **nothing can be done in the present ~** vu les circonstances actuelles, on ne peut rien faire ▪ **this is an appalling ~** c'est une situation épouvantable ▪ **this is a fine ~ !** *iron* c'est du propre !

state of emergency (*pl* **states of emergency**) *n* état *m* d'urgence ▪ **a ~ has been declared** l'état d'urgence a été déclaré.

state of mind (*pl* **states of mind**) *n* état *m* d'esprit ▪ **in your present ~ of mind** dans l'état d'esprit dans lequel vous êtes ▪ **is he in a better ~ of mind?** est-ce qu'il est dans de meilleures dispositions?

state of the art *n* [of procedures, systems] pointe *f* du progrès.
◆ **state-of-the-art** *adj* [design, device] de pointe ▪ **it's ~** *inf* c'est ce qui se fait de mieux, c'est du dernier cri.

State of the Union address *n* : **the ~** le discours sur l'état de l'Union.

STATE OF THE UNION ADDRESS

Une fois par an, le président des États-Unis prononce un discours devant le Congrès, dans lequel il dresse le bilan de son programme et en définit les orientations. Ce discours est retransmis à la radio et à la télévision.

state-owned [-'əʊnd] *adj* nationalisé.

state prison *n US* prison *f* d'État *(pour les longues peines).*

State Registered Nurse *n UK* infirmier *m* diplômé, infirmière *f* diplômée *(remplacé en 1992 par "Registered Nurse").*

stateroom ['steɪtrʊm] *n* **1.** [in ship] cabine *f* de grand luxe ▪ *US* [in railway coach] compartiment *m* privé **2.** [in public building] salon *m* (de réception).

state school *n UK* école *f* publique.

state's evidence *n US* **to turn ~** *témoigner contre ses complices en échange d'une remise de peine.*

States General *npl* États généraux *mpl*.

stateside ['steɪtsaɪd] *adj* & *adv US inf* aux États-Unis, ≃ au pays *inf*.

statesman ['steɪtsmən] (*pl* **statesmen** [-mən]) *n* homme *m* d'État.

statesmanlike ['steɪtsmənlaɪk] *adj* [protest, reply] diplomatique ▪ [solution] de grande envergure ▪ [caution] pondéré.

statesmanship ['steɪtsmənʃɪp] *n* qualités *fpl* d'homme d'État.

State Supreme Court *n aux États-Unis, la plus haute instance judiciaire de chaque État.*

state's witness *n US* : **to turn ~** *témoigner contre ses complices en échange d'une remise de peine.*

state trooper *n US* ≃ gendarme *m*.

state visit *n* POL visite *f* officielle ▪ **he's on a ~ to Japan** il est en voyage officiel au Japon.

state-wide <> *adj US* [support, protest, celebration] dans tout l'État.
<> *adv* dans tout l'État.

static ['stætɪk] <> *adj* **1.** [stationary, unchanging] stationnaire, stable **2.** ELEC statique ▪ **~ electricity** électricité *f* statique.
<> *n (U)* **1.** RADIO & TELEC parasites *mpl* **2.** ELEC électricité *f* statique **3.** *US inf* [aggravation, criticism] : **to give sb ~ about** *OR* **over sthg** passer un savon à qqn à propos de qqch ▪ **to get a lot of ~ (about)** *OR* **(over)sthg** se faire enguirlander(pour qqch).

station ['steɪʃn] <> *n* **1.** TRANSP gare *f* ▪ [underground] station *f* (de métro) **2.** [establishment, building] station *f*, poste *m* **3.** MIL [gen - position] poste *m* ▪ **to take up one's ~** prendre position ▪ **action** *OR* **battle ~s!** à vos postes! **4.** MIL [base] poste *m*, base *f* ▪ **airforce ~** *UK* base aérienne **5.** RADIO & TV [broadcaster] station *f* ▪ [smaller] poste *m* émetteur ▪ **commercial radio ~** station de radio commerciale, radio *f* commerciale ▮ [on radio or TV set] chaîne *f* ▪ **to change ~s** changer de chaîne **6.** [social rank] rang *m*, condition *f*, situation *f* ▪ **to marry below one's ~** faire une mésalliance ▪ **to marry above one's ~** se marier au-dessus de sa condition sociale **7.** COMPUT station *f* **8.** RELIG : **the Stations of the Cross** le chemin de la Croix.
<> *comp* [buffet, platform etc] de gare.
<> *vt* **1.** [position] placer, poster **2.** MIL [garrison] : **British troops ~ed in Germany** les troupes britanniques stationnées en Allemagne.

stationary ['steɪʃnərɪ] *adj* **1.** [not moving] stationnaire ▪ **he hit a ~ vehicle** il a heurté un véhicule à l'arrêt *OR* en stationnement **2.** [fixed] fixe ▪ **~ engine/shaft** MECH moteur *m* /arbre *m* fixe.

station break *n US* pause *f OR* page *f* de publicité.

stationer ['steɪʃnər] *n UK* papetier *m*, - ère *f* ▪ **~'s (shop)** papeterie *f* ▪ **at the ~'s** à la papeterie.

stationery ['steɪʃnərɪ] *n* [in general] papeterie *f* ▪ [writing paper] papier *m* à lettres ▪ **a letter written on hotel ~** une lettre écrite sur le papier à en-tête d'un hôtel ▪ **school/office ~** fournitures *fpl* scolaires/de bureau.

station house *n US* [police station] poste *m* de police, commissariat *m* ▪ [fire station] caserne *f* de pompiers.

stationmaster ['steɪʃn,mɑːstər] *n* chef *m* de gare.

station wagon *n US* break *m*.

statistic [stə'tɪstɪk] *n* chiffre *m*, statistique *f*.

statistical [stə'tɪstɪkl] *adj* [analysis, technique] statistique ▪ [error] de statistique ▪ **it's a ~ certainty** c'est statistiquement certain.

statistically [stəˈtɪstɪklɪ] *adv* statistiquement.

statistician [ˌstætɪˈstɪʃn] *n* statisticien *m*, - enne *f*.

statistics [stəˈtɪstɪks] <> *n (U)* [science] statistique *f*.
<> *npl* **1.** [figures] statistiques *fpl*, chiffres *mpl* **2.** *inf* [of woman] mensurations *fpl*.

stative [ˈsteɪtɪv] *adj* : **~ verb** verbe *m* d'état.

stats [stæts] *inf* = **statistics**.

statue [ˈstætʃuː] *n* statue *f* ▪ **the Statue of Liberty** la statue de la Liberté.

statuesque [ˌstætjuˈesk] *adj* : **a ~ woman** une femme d'une beauté sculpturale.

statuette [ˌstætjuˈet] *n* statuette *f*.

stature [ˈstætʃəʳ] *n* **1.** [height] stature *f*, taille *f* ▪ **he is rather short in** *OR* **of ~** il est plutôt petit **2.** [greatness] envergure *f*, calibre *m* ▪ **he doesn't have the ~ to be prime minister** il n'a pas l'envergure d'un premier ministre.

status [*UK* ˈsteɪtəs, *US* ˈstætəs] <> *n* **1.** [position - in society, hierarchy etc] rang *m*, position *f*, situation *f* ▪ **she quickly achieved celebrity ~** elle est vite devenue une célébrité **2.** [prestige] prestige *m*, standing *m* **3.** [legal or official standing] statut *m* ▪ **legal ~** statut légal **4.** [general state or situation] état *m*, situation *f*, condition *f* ▪ **to make a ~ report on sthg** faire le point sur qqch.
<> *comp* [car, club] de prestige, prestigieux.

status line *n* COMPUT ligne *f* d'état.

status meeting *n* réunion *f* de bilan.

status quo [ˌsteɪtəsˈkwəʊ] *n* statu quo *m* ▪ **to maintain** *OR* **to preserve the ~** maintenir le statu quo.

status symbol *n* marque *f* de prestige.

statute [ˈstætjuːt] *n* **1.** LAW loi *f* ▪ **~ of limitations** loi *f* de prescription, prescription *f* légale **2.** [of club, company, university] règle *f* ▪ **the ~s** le règlement, les statuts *mpl*.

statute book *n UK* code *m* (des lois), recueil *m* de lois ▪ **the new law is not yet on the ~** la nouvelle loi n'est pas encore entrée en vigueur.

statute law *n* droit *m* écrit.

statutory [ˈstætjʊtrɪ] *adj* **1.** [regulations] statutaire ▪ [rights, duties, penalty] statutaire, juridique ▪ [holiday] légal ▪ [offence] prévu par la loi ▪ [price controls, income policy] obligatoire ▪ **~ rape** *US* détournement *m* de mineur ▪ **~ sick pay** *indemnité de maladie versée par l'employeur* ▪ **~ tenant** locataire *mf* en place **2.** *UK* [token] : **the ~ woman** la femme-alibi *(présente pour que soit respectée la réglementation sur l'égalité des sexes)*.

staunch [stɔːntʃ] <> *adj* [loyal] loyal, dévoué ▪ [unswerving] constant, inébranlable ▪ **he's my ~est ally** c'est mon allié le plus sûr.
<> *vt* [liquid, blood] étancher ▪ [flow] arrêter, endiguer.

staunchly [ˈstɔːntʃlɪ] *adv* [loyally] loyalement, avec dévouement ▪ [unswervingly] avec constance, fermement ▪ **their house is in a ~ Republican area** ils habitent un quartier résolument républicain.

staunchness [ˈstɔːntʃnɪs] *n* [loyalty] loyauté *f*, dévouement *m* ▪ [firmness] constance *f*, fermeté *f*.

stave [steɪv] *(pret & pp* **staved** *OR* **stove** [stəʊv]) *n* **1.** MUS portée *f* **2.** [stanza] stance *f*, strophe *f* **3.** [part of barrel] douve *f*, douelle *f*.
◆ **stave in** *vt sep* enfoncer, défoncer.
◆ **stave off** *vt sep* [defeat] retarder ▪ [worry, danger] écarter ▪ [disaster, threat] conjurer ▪ [misery, hunger, thirst] tromper ▪ [questions] éluder.

staves [steɪvz] *pl* ▷ **staff**, ▷ **stave**.

stay [steɪ] <> *vi* **1.** [remain] rester ▪ **~ here** *OR* **~ put until I come back** restez ici *OR* ne bougez pas jusqu'à ce que je revienne ▪ **would you like to ~ for** *OR* **to dinner?** voulez-vous rester dîner? ▪ **I don't want to ~ in the same job all my life** je ne veux pas faire le même travail toute ma vie ▪ **to ~ awake all night** rester éveillé toute la nuit, ne pas dormir de la nuit ▪ **let's try and ~ calm** essayons de rester calmes ▪ **she managed to ~ ahead of the others** elle a réussi à conserver son avance sur les autres ▪ **personal computers have come to ~** *OR* **are here to ~** l'ordinateur personnel est devenu indispensable
2. [reside temporarily] : **how long are you ~ing in New York?** combien de temps restez-vous à New York? ▪ **we decided to ~ an extra week** nous avons décidé de rester une semaine de plus *OR* de prolonger notre séjour d'une semaine ▪ **I always ~ at the same hotel** je descends toujours au même hôtel ▪ **she's ~ing with friends** elle séjourne chez des amis ▪ **to look for a place to ~** chercher un endroit où loger ▪ **you can ~ here for the night, you can ~ the night here** tu peux coucher ici cette nuit *OR* passer la nuit ici
3. *lit* [stop, pause] s'arrêter.
<> *vt* **1.** [last out] aller jusqu'au bout de, tenir jusqu'à la fin de ▪ **to ~ the course** *liter* finir la course ; *fig* tenir jusqu'au bout
2. [stop] arrêter, enrayer ▪ [delay] retarder ▪ **to ~ sb's hand** retenir qqn ▪ **to ~ one's hand** se retenir
3. [prop up - wall] étayer ▪ [secure with cables - mast] haubaner.
<> *n* **1.** [sojourn] séjour *m* ▪ **enjoy your ~!** bon séjour! ▪ **an overnight ~ in hospital** une nuit d'hospitalisation
2. LAW [suspension] suspension *f* ▪ **~ of execution** ordonnance *f* à surseoir (à un jugement)
3. [support, prop] étai *m*, support *m*, soutien *m*
4. [in corset] baleine *f*
5. [cable, wire - for mast, flagpole etc] étai *m*, hauban *m*.
◆ **stays** *npl dated* corset *m*.
◆ **stay away** *vi insep* ne pas aller, s'abstenir d'aller ▪ **people are ~ing away from the beaches** les plages sont désertées en ce moment ▪ **~ away from my sister!** ne t'approche pas de ma sœur!
◆ **stay behind** *vi insep* rester ▪ **a few pupils ~ed behind to talk to the teacher** quelques élèves sont restés (après le cours) pour parler au professeur.
◆ **stay down** *vi insep* **1.** [gen] rester en bas
2. *UK* SCH redoubler ▪ **she had to ~ down a year** elle a dû redoubler
3. [food] : **I do eat, but nothing will ~ down** je mange, mais je ne peux rien garder.
◆ **stay in** *vi insep* **1.** [stay at home] rester à la maison, ne pas sortir ▪ [stay indoors] rester à l'intérieur, ne pas sortir
2. [be kept in after school] être consigné, être en retenue
3. [not fall out] rester en place, tenir.
◆ **stay on** *vi insep* rester ▪ **more pupils are ~ing on at school after the age of 16** de plus en plus d'élèves poursuivent leur scolarité au-delà de l'âge de 16 ans.
◆ **stay out** *vi insep* **1.** [not come home] ne pas rentrer ▪ **she ~ed out all night** elle n'est pas rentrée de la nuit
2. [remain outside] rester dehors
3. [remain on strike] rester en grève
4. [not get involved] ne pas se mêler ▪ **~ out of this!** ne te mêle pas de ça!
◆ **stay over** *vi insep* **1.** [not leave] s'arrêter un certain temps ▪ **we decided to ~ over until the weekend** nous avons décidé de prolonger notre séjour jusqu'au week-end
2. [stay the night] passer la nuit.
◆ **stay up** *vi insep* **1.** [not go to bed] veiller, ne pas se coucher
2. [not fall - building, mast] rester debout ; [- socks, trousers] tenir ▪ [remain in place - pictures, decorations] rester en place.
◆ **stay with** *vt insep inf* **just ~ with it, you can do it** accroche-toi, tu peux y arriver.

stay-at-home *inf pej* <> *n* pantouflard *m*, - e *f*.
<> *adj* pantouflard, popote *(inv)*.

stayer [ˈsteɪəʳ] *n inf* **he's a real ~** il est drôlement résistant.

staying power [ˈsteɪɪŋ-] *n* résistance *f*, endurance *f*.

staysail [ˈsteɪseɪl] *n* voile *f* d'étai.

St. Bernard [*UK* ˌseɪntˈbɜːnəd, *US* ˌseɪntbərˈnɑːrd] *n* [dog] saint-bernard *m inv*.

STD *n* **1.** *UK* TELEC (*abbrev of* **subscriber trunk dialling**) automatique *m* (interurbain) ▪ **~ code** indicatif *m* de zone **2.** (*abbrev of* **sexually transmitted disease**) MST *f*.

stead [sted] *n* UK **in sb's ~** *fml* à la place de qqn ◐ **to stand sb in good ~** rendre grand service *OR* être très utile à qqn.

steadfast ['stedfɑ:st] *adj* **1.** [unswerving] constant, inébranlable ▪ [loyal] loyal, dévoué ▪ **to be ~ in one's support of sb** apporter un soutien inconditionnel à qqn **2.** [steady - stare, gaze] fixe.

steadfastly ['stedfɑ:stlɪ] *adv* avec constance, fermement.

Steadicam® ['stedɪkæm] *n* Steadicam® *m*.

steadily ['stedɪlɪ] *adv* **1.** [regularly - increase, decline] régulièrement, progressivement ; [- breathe] régulièrement ▪ [nonstop - rain] sans interruption, sans cesse **2.** [firmly - stand] planté *OR* campé sur ses jambes ; [- walk] d'un pas ferme ; [- gaze] fixement, sans détourner les yeux.

steadiness ['stedɪnɪs] *n* **1.** [regularity - of increase, speed, pulse etc] régularité *f* **2.** [stability - of ladder, relationship, market etc] stabilité *f* ▪ [firmness - of voice] fermeté *f* ; [- of hand] sûreté *f* ▪ **the ~ of her gaze** la fixité de son regard.

steady ['stedɪ] <> *adj* (*comp* **steadier**, *superl* **steadiest**) **1.** [regular, constant - growth, increase, decline] régulier, progressif ; [- speed, pace] régulier, constant ; [- pulse] régulier, égal ; [- work] stable ; [- income] régulier ▪ **inflation remains at a ~ 5%** l'inflation s'est stabilisée à 5 % ▪ **he's never been able to hold down a ~ job** il n'a jamais pu garder un emploi stable ▪ **~ boyfriend** petit ami *m* régulier *OR* attitré **2.** [firm, stable - ladder, boat, relationship] stable ; [- structure, desk, chair] solide, stable ▪ **hold the ladder ~ for me** tiens-moi l'échelle ▪ **to have a ~ hand** avoir la main sûre ▪ [calm - voice] ferme ; [- gaze] fixe ; [- nerves] solide **3.** [reliable - person] sérieux.
<> *adv* : **to go ~ with sb** sortir avec qqn ▪ **are Diana and Paul going ~?** c'est sérieux entre Diana et Paul?
<> *interj* : **~ (on)!** [be careful] attention! ; [calm down] du calme!
<> *vt* (*pret & pp* **steadied**) **1.** [stabilize] stabiliser ▪ [hold in place] maintenir, retenir ▪ **he almost fell off, but he managed to ~ himself** il a failli tomber, mais il a réussi à se rattraper ▪ **she rested her elbows on the wall to ~ the camera** elle appuya ses coudes sur le mur pour que l'appareil photo ne bouge pas **2.** [calm] calmer ▪ **drink this, it'll ~ your nerves** bois ça, ça te calmera (les nerfs) ▪ **living with Edith has had a ~ing influence on him** il s'est assagi *OR* calmé depuis qu'il vit avec Edith.
<> *vi* (*pret & pp* **steadied**) [boat, prices, stock market] se stabiliser ▪ [pulse, breathing] devenir régulier ▪ [person - regain balance] retrouver son équilibre ; [- calm down] se calmer.

steak [steɪk] *n* **1.** [beefsteak - for frying, grilling] steak *m*, bifteck *m* ▪ **~ and chips** steak frites *m* **2.** [beef - for stews, casseroles] bœuf *m* à braiser ▪ **~ and kidney pie** *tourte à la viande et aux rognons cuite au four* ▪ **~ and kidney pudding** *tourte à la viande et aux rognons cuite à la vapeur* **3.** [cut - of veal, turkey] escalope *f* ; [- of horse meat] steak *m*, bifteck *m* ; [- of other meat] tranche *f* ; [- of fish] tranche *f*, darne *f*.

steakhouse ['steɪkhaʊs] (*pl* [haʊzɪz]) *n* grill *m*, grill-room *m*.

steak knife *n* couteau *m* à steak *OR* à viande.

steak tartare [-tɑ:'tɑ:ʳ] *n* steak *m* tartare.

steal [sti:l] (*pret* **stole** [stəʊl], *pp* **stolen** ['stəʊln]) <> *vt* **1.** [money, property] voler ▪ **to ~ sthg from sb** voler qqch à qqn ▪ **he stole money from her purse** il a volé de l'argent dans son porte-monnaie ▪ **several paintings have been stolen from the museum** plusieurs tableaux ont été volés au musée **2.** *fig* [time] voler, prendre ▪ [attention, affection] détourner ▪ **to ~ sb's heart** séduire qqn ▪ **to ~ all the credit for sthg** s'attribuer tout le mérite de qqch ▪ **may I ~ a few moments of your precious time?** pouvez-vous m'accorder quelques instants de votre temps si précieux? ▪ **to ~ a glance at sb** jeter un regard furtif à qqn ◐ **to ~ a march on sb** UK prendre qqn de vitesse, couper l'herbe sous le pied de qqn ▪ **to ~ the show from sb** ravir la vedette à qqn ▪ **he really stole the show with that act of his!** son numéro a été le clou du spectacle! ▪ **to ~ sb's thunder** éclipser qqn.
<> *vi* **1.** [commit theft] voler ▪ **he was caught ~ing** il a été pris en train de voler ▪ **thou shalt not ~** BIBLE tu ne voleras point **2.** [move secretively] : **to ~ in/out** entrer/sortir à pas furtifs *OR* feutrés ▪ **to ~ into a room** se glisser *OR* se faufiler dans une pièce ▪ **she stole up on me from behind** elle s'est approchée de moi par derrière sans faire de bruit ▪ *fig* **shadows began to ~ across the courtyard** *lit* des ombres commencèrent à envahir la cour.
<> *n inf* US [bargain] affaire *f*.
◆ **steal away** *vi insep* partir furtivement, s'esquiver.

stealing ['sti:lɪŋ] *n* vol *m*.

stealth [stelθ] *n* **1.** [of animal] ruse *f* **2.** *(U)* [underhandedness] moyens *mpl* détournés ▪ **the documents were obtained by ~** nous nous sommes procuré les documents en cachette *OR* par des moyens détournés.

Stealth bomber, Stealth plane *n* avion *m* furtif.

stealthily ['stelθɪlɪ] *adv* furtivement, subrepticement.

stealthy ['stelθɪ] (*comp* **stealthier**, *superl* **stealthiest**) *adj* furtif.

steam [sti:m] <> *n* **1.** [vapour] vapeur *f* ▪ [condensation] buée *f* ▪ **she wiped the ~ from the mirror** elle essuya la buée sur la glace **2.** MECH & RAIL [as power] vapeur *f* ▪ **to run on** *OR* **to work by ~** marcher à la vapeur ◐ **at full ~** à toute vapeur, à pleine vitesse ▪ **full ~ ahead!** en avant toute! ▪ **to do sthg under one's own ~** faire qqch par ses propres moyens ▪ **to get up** *OR* **to pick up ~** [vehicle] prendre de la vitesse ; [campaign] être lancé ▪ **to let off ~** se défouler ▪ **to run out of ~** s'essouffler, s'épuiser.
<> *comp* [boiler, locomotive etc] à vapeur.
<> *vt* **1.** [unstick with steam] : **~ the stamps off the envelope** passez l'enveloppe à la vapeur pour décoller les timbres ▪ **to ~ open an envelope** décacheter une enveloppe à la vapeur **2.** CULIN (faire) cuire à la vapeur ▪ **~ed vegetables** légumes *mpl* (cuits) à la vapeur.
<> *vi* **1.** [soup, kettle, wet clothes] fumer **2.** [go - train, ship] : **the train ~ed into/out of the station** le train entra en gare/quitta la gare ▪ **my brother ~ed on ahead** *fig* mon frère filait devant ▪ **she ~ed into/out of the room** *fig* elle est entrée dans/sortie de la pièce comme une furie.
◆ **steam up** <> *vi insep* [window, glasses] s'embuer, se couvrir de buée.
<> *vt sep* [window, glasses] embuer.

steam bath *n* bain *m* de vapeur.

steamboat ['sti:mbəʊt] *n* bateau *m* à vapeur, vapeur *m*.

steam-driven *adj* à vapeur.

steamed-up [sti:md-] *adj inf* [angry] énervé, dans tous ses états.

steam engine *n* MECH moteur *m* à vapeur ▪ RAIL locomotive *f* à vapeur.

steamer ['sti:məʳ] *n* **1.** NAUT bateau *m* à vapeur, vapeur *m* **2.** CULIN [pan] marmite *f* à vapeur ▪ [basket inside pan] panier *m* de cuisson à la vapeur.

steaming ['sti:mɪŋ] <> *adj* **1.** [very hot] fumant **2.** *inf* [angry] furibard, furax.
<> *adv* : **~ hot** fumant.

steam iron *n* fer *m* (à repasser) à vapeur.

steamroll ['sti:mrəʊl] *vt* [road] cylindrer.

steamroller ['sti:m,rəʊləʳ] <> *n liter & fig* rouleau *m* compresseur ▪ **to use ~ tactics** *fig* employer la technique du rouleau compresseur.
<> *vt* **1.** [crush - opposition, obstacle] écraser **2.** [force] : **to ~ a bill through Parliament** *faire passer une loi à la Chambre sans tenir compte de l'opposition* ▪ **to ~ sb into doing sthg** forcer qqn à faire qqch **3.** = **steamroll**.

steamroom ['sti:mru:m] *n* hammam *m*.

steamship ['sti:mʃɪp] *n* navire *m* à vapeur, vapeur *m*.

steamy ['sti:mɪ] (*comp* **steamier**, *superl* **steamiest**) *adj* **1.** [room] plein de vapeur ▪ [window, mirror] embué **2.** *inf* [erotic] érotique, d'un érotisme torride.

steed [sti:d] *n lit* coursier *m*.

steel [stiːl] ◇ *n* **1.** [iron alloy] acier *m* ■ **to have nerves of ~** avoir des nerfs d'acier **2.** [steel industry] industrie *f* sidérurgique, sidérurgie *f* **3.** [for sharpening knives] aiguisoir *m* **4.** *lit* [sword] fer *m*.
◇ *comp* [industry, plant] sidérurgique ■ [strike] des sidérurgistes ■ **~ manufacturer** sidérurgiste *mf*.
◇ *adj* [helmet, cutlery etc] en acier.
◇ *vt* **1.** *UK* [harden] : **to ~ o.s. against sthg** se cuirasser contre qqch ■ **I had ~ed myself for the worst** je m'étais préparé au pire **2.** METALL aciérer.

steel band *n* MUS steel band *m*.

steel blue *n* bleu *m* acier.
◆ **steel-blue** *adj* bleu acier *(inv)*.

steel wool *n* paille *f* de fer.

steelworker ['stiːlˌwɜːkəʳ] *n* sidérurgiste *mf*.

steelworks ['stiːlwɜːks] *(pl inv)* *n* aciérie *f*, usine *f* sidérurgique.

steely ['stiːlɪ] *adj* **1.** [in colour] d'acier, gris acier *(inv)* **2.** [strong - determination, will] de fer ; [- look] d'acier.

steelyard ['stiːljɑːd] *n* balance *f* romaine.

steep [stiːp] ◇ *adj* **1.** [hill] raide, abrupt, escarpé ■ [slope] fort, raide ■ [cliff] abrupt ■ [road, path] raide, escarpé ■ [staircase] raide ■ **it's a ~ climb to the village** la montée est raide pour arriver au village ■ **the plane went into a ~ dive** l'avion se mit à piquer du nez **2.** [increase, fall] fort ■ **a ~ drop in share prices** une forte chute du prix des actions **3.** *inf* [fee, price] excessif, élevé **4.** *inf* [unreasonable] : **it's a bit ~ asking us to do all that work by Friday** c'est un peu fort *OR* un peu raide de nous demander de faire tout ce travail pour vendredi.
◇ *vt* [soak] (faire) tremper ■ CULIN (faire) macérer, (faire) mariner ■ **I want to ~ myself in the atmosphere of the place** *fig* je veux m'imprégner de l'atmosphère de l'endroit.
◇ *vi* [gen] tremper ■ CULIN macérer, mariner.

steeped [stiːpt] *adj* : **~ in tradition/mystery** imprégné de tradition/mystère.

steepen ['stiːpn] *vi* **1.** [slope, road, path] devenir plus raide *OR* escarpé **2.** [increase - inflation, rate] croître.

steeple ['stiːpl] *n* clocher *m*, flèche *f*.

steeplechase ['stiːpltʃeɪs] *n* [in horse racing, athletics] steeple *m*, steeple-chase *m*.

steeplejack ['stiːpldʒæk] *n* *UK* *réparateur de clochers et de cheminées*.

steeply ['stiːplɪ] *adv* en pente raide, à pic ■ **costs are rising ~** les coûts montent en flèche.

steer ['stɪəʳ] ◇ *vt* **1.** [car] conduire ■ **she ~ed the car into the garage/out onto the main road** elle a rentré la voiture au garage/conduit la voiture jusqu'à la route principale ‖ NAUT [boat] gouverner, barrer ■ **to ~ a course for** mettre le cap sur ■ **the management has decided to ~ a radically different course** *fig* la direction a décidé de changer radicalement de cap ▶ **~ed course** route *f* au compas *OR* apparente **2.** [person] guider, diriger ■ **try to ~ him away from the bar** essayez de l'éloigner du bar **3.** [conversation, project etc] diriger ■ **I tried to ~ the conversation round to/away from the subject** j'ai essayé d'amener la conversation sur le sujet/de détourner la conversation du sujet ■ **she successfully ~ed the company through the crisis** elle a réussi à sortir la société de la crise ■ **to ~ a bill through Parliament** réussir à faire voter un projet de loi par le Parlement.
◇ *vi* **1.** [driver] conduire ■ **I ~ed carefully into the garage** j'ai manœuvré avec soin pour entrer dans le garage ‖ NAUT [helmsman] gouverner, barrer ■ **~ for that buoy** mettez le cap sur cette bouée ▶ **to ~ clear of sthg/sb** éviter qqch/qqn **2.** [car] : **this car ~s very well/badly** cette voiture a une excellente/très mauvaise direction ‖ NAUT [boat] se diriger.
◇ *n* AGRIC bœuf *m*.

steerage ['stɪərɪdʒ] *n* NAUT **1.** *dated* [accommodation] entrepont *m* **2.** [steering] conduite *f*, pilotage *m*.

steering ['stɪərɪŋ] ◇ *n* **1.** AUT [apparatus, mechanism] direction *f* ■ [manner of driving] conduite *f* **2.** NAUT conduite *f*, pilotage *m*.
◇ *comp* AUT [arm, lever] de direction.

steering committee *n* comité *m* directeur.

steering lock *n* AUT **1.** [turning circle] rayon *m* de braquage **2.** [antitheft device] antivol *m* de direction.

steering wheel *n* **1.** AUT volant *m* **2.** NAUT roue *f* du gouvernail, barre *f*.

stein ['staɪn] *n* chope *f*.

stellar ['steləʳ] *adj* **1.** ASTRON stellaire **2.** *inf* CIN & THEAT : **the play boasts a ~ cast** cette pièce a une distribution éblouissante.

stem [stem] *(pret & pp* **stemmed**, *cont* **stemming***)* ◇ *n* **1.** BOT [of plant, tree] tige *f* ■ [of fruit, leaf] queue *f* **2.** [of glass] pied *m* **3.** [of tobacco pipe] tuyau *m* **4.** LING [of word] radical *m* **5.** TECH [in lock, watch] tige *f* **6.** [vertical stroke - of letter] hampe *f* ; [- of musical note] queue *f* **7.** NAUT [timber, structure] étrave *f* ■ [forward section] proue *f* **8.** BIBLE [family, stock] souche *f*.
◇ *vt* **1.** [check, stop - flow, spread, bleeding] arrêter, endiguer ; [- blood] étancher ; [- river, flood] endiguer, contenir ■ **they are trying to ~ the tide of protest** ils essaient d'endiguer le nombre croissant de protestations **2.** SPORT : **to ~ one's skis** faire un stem *OR* stemm.
◇ *vi* **1.** [derive] : **to ~ from** avoir pour cause, être le résultat de **2.** SPORT faire du stem *OR* stemm.

stem cell *n* MED cellule *f* souche.

stem glass *n* verre *m* à pied.

-stemmed [stemd] *in cpds* **1.** BOT à tige... ■ **a long/short/thin~ plant** une plante à tige longue/courte/mince **2.** [gen] : **a long/short~ glass** un verre à pied haut/bas ■ **a long/short~ pipe** une pipe à tuyau long/court.

stench [stentʃ] *n* puanteur *f*, odeur *f* nauséabonde.

stencil ['stensl] *(UK pret & pp* **stencilled**, *cont* **stencilling**, *US pret & pp* **stenciled**, *cont* **stenciling***)* ◇ *n* **1.** [for typing] stencil *m* **2.** [template] pochoir *m* **3.** [pattern] dessin *m* au pochoir.
◇ *vt* dessiner au pochoir.

Sten gun [sten-] *n* mitraillette *f* légère.

stenographer [stəˈnɒgrəfəʳ] *n* *US* sténographe *mf*.

stenography [stəˈnɒgrəfɪ] *n* sténographie *f*.

step [step] *(pret & pp* **stepped**, *cont* **stepping***)* ◇ *n* **1.** [pace] pas *m* ■ **take two ~s forwards/backwards** faites deux pas en avant/en arrière ■ **I heard her ~ *OR* ~s on the stairs** j'ai entendu (le bruit de) ses pas dans l'escalier ■ **that's certainly put a spring in her ~** ça a dû lui donner un peu de ressort ■ **he was following a few ~s behind me** il me suivait à quelques pas ■ **it's only a (short) ~ to the shops** les magasins sont à deux pas d'ici ▶ **watch *OR* mind your ~!** *liter* faites attention où vous mettez les pieds! ; *fig* faites attention!
2. [move, action] pas *m* ■ [measure] mesure *f*, disposition *f* ■ **it's a great ~ forward for mankind** c'est un grand pas en avant pour l'humanité ■ **to take ~s to do sthg** prendre des mesures pour faire qqch ■ **it's a ~ in the right direction** c'est un pas dans la bonne direction
3. [stage] étape *f* ■ **the different ~s in the manufacturing process** les différentes étapes du processus de fabrication ■ **this promotion is a big ~ up for me** cette promotion est un grand pas en avant pour moi ■ **we are still one ~ ahead of our competitors** nous conservons une petite avance sur nos concurrents ■ **if I may take your argument one ~ further** si je peux pousser votre raisonnement un peu plus loin ■ **we'll support you every ~ of the way** nous vous soutiendrons à fond *OR* sur toute la ligne
4. [stair - gen] marche *f* ; [- into bus, train etc] marchepied *m* ■ **a flight of ~s** un escalier ■ **the church ~s** le perron de l'église ■ **'mind the ~'** 'attention à la marche'
5. DANCE pas *m* ■ **do try and keep ~!** essaie donc de danser en mesure!
6. [in marching] pas *m* ■ **in ~** au pas ■ **to march in ~** marcher au pas ■ **to be out of ~** ne pas être en cadence ■ **to break ~** rompre le pas ■ **to change ~** changer de pas ■ **to fall into ~ with sb**

liter s'aligner sur le pas de qqn ; *fig* se ranger à l'avis de qqn ▪ **he fell into ~ beside me** arrivé à ma hauteur, il régla son pas sur le mien ▪ **to keep ~** marcher au pas ➋ **to be in ~ with the times/with public opinion** être au diapason de son temps/de l'opinion publique ▪ **to be out of ~ with the times/with public opinion** être déphasé par rapport à son époque/à l'opinion publique
7. *US* MUS [interval] seconde *f*.
<> *vi* **1.** [take a single step] faire un pas ▪ [walk, go] marcher, aller ▪ **~ this way, please** par ici, je vous prie ▪ **~ inside!** entrez! ▪ **he carefully stepped round the sleeping dog** il contourna prudemment le chien endormi ▪ **I stepped onto/off the train** je suis monté dans le/descendu du train ▪ **she stepped lightly over the ditch** elle enjamba le fossé lestement
2. [put one's foot down, tread] marcher ▪ **I stepped on a banana skin/in a puddle** j'ai marché sur une peau de banane/dans une flaque d'eau ➋ **~ on it!** *inf* appuie sur le champignon! ▪ **to ~ out of line** s'écarter du droit chemin.
<> *vt* **1.** [measure out] mesurer
2. [space out] échelonner.
◆ **steps** *npl UK* [stepladder] : **(pair of) ~s** escabeau *m*.
◆ **step aside** *vi insep* **1.** [move to one side] s'écarter, s'effacer
2. = **step down** *(sense 2)*.
◆ **step back** *vi insep* **1.** *liter* reculer, faire un pas en arrière
2. *fig* prendre du recul.
◆ **step down** <> *vi insep* **1.** [descend] descendre
2. [quit position, job] se retirer, se désister ▪ **he stepped down in favour of a younger person** il a cédé la place à quelqu'un de plus jeune.
<> *vt sep* ELEC [voltage] abaisser.
◆ **step forward** *vi insep* **1.** *liter* faire un pas en avant
2. *fig* [volunteer] se présenter, être volontaire.
◆ **step in** *vi insep* **1.** [enter] entrer
2. [intervene] intervenir.
◆ **step out** *vi insep* **1.** [go out of doors] sortir
2. [walk faster] presser le pas.
◆ **step up** <> *vi insep* s'approcher ▪ **to ~ up to sb** s'approcher de qqn.
<> *vt sep* **1.** [increase - output, pace] augmenter, accroître ; [- activity, efforts] intensifier
2. ELEC [voltage] augmenter.

step aerobics *n* step *m*.

stepbrother ['step,brʌðər] *n* demi-frère *m*.

step-by-step <> *adv* [gradually] pas à pas, petit à petit.
<> *adj* [point by point] : **a ~ guide to buying your own house** un guide détaillé pour l'achat de votre maison.

stepchild ['step,tʃaɪld] (*pl* **stepchildren** [-,tʃɪldrən]) *n* beau-fils *m*, belle-fille *f (fils ou fille du conjoint)*.

stepdaughter ['step,dɔːtər] *n* belle-fille *f (fille du conjoint)*.

step-down *n* : **~ transformer** abaisseur *m* de tension.

stepfather ['step,fɑːðər] *n* beau-père *m (conjoint de la mère)*.

Stephen ['stiːvn] *pr n* : **Saint ~** saint Etienne.

stepladder ['step,lædər] *n* escabeau *m*.

stepmother ['step,mʌðər] *n* belle-mère *f (conjointe du père)*.

stepparent ['step,peərənt] *n* beau-père *m*, belle-mère *f*.

steppe [step] *n* steppe *f*.

stepped-up [stept↓] *adj* [output] accru, augmenté ▪ [pace] plus rapide ▪ [activity, efforts, war] intensifié.

stepping-stone ['stepɪŋ-] *n* **1.** *liter* pierre *f* de gué **2.** *fig* tremplin *m* ▪ **a ~ to a new career** un tremplin pour (se lancer dans) une nouvelle carrière.

stepsister ['step,sɪstər] *n* demi-sœur *f*.

stepson ['stepsʌn] *n* beau-fils *m (fils du conjoint d'un précédent mariage)*.

stereo ['sterɪəʊ] (*pl* **stereos**) <> *n* **1.** [stereo sound] stéréo *f* ▪ **broadcast in ~** retransmis en stéréo **2.** [hifi system] chaîne *f* (stéréo).
<> *adj* [cassette, record, record player] stéréo *(inv)* ▪ [recording, broadcast] en stéréo.

stereophonic [,sterɪə'fɒnɪk] *adj* stéréophonique.

stereoscopic [,sterɪə'skɒpɪk] *adj* stéréoscopique.

stereoscopy [,sterɪ'ɒskəpɪ] *n* stéréoscopie *f*.

stereo system *n* chaîne *f* stéréo.

stereotype ['sterɪətaɪp] <> *n* **1.** [idea, trait, convention] stéréotype *m* **2.** TYPO cliché *m*.
<> *vt* **1.** [person, role] stéréotyper **2.** TYPO clicher.

stereotyped ['sterɪəʊtaɪpt] *adj* stéréotypé.

stereotypical [,sterɪəʊ'tɪpɪkl] *adj* stéréotypé.

stereotyping ['sterɪəʊ,taɪpɪŋ] *n* : **we want to avoid sexual ~** nous voulons éviter les stéréotypes sexuels.

sterile ['steraɪl] *adj* stérile.

sterility [ste'rɪlətɪ] *n* stérilité *f*.

sterilization [,sterəlaɪ'zeɪʃn] *n* stérilisation *f*.

sterilize, ise ['sterəlaɪz] *vt* stériliser.

sterilized ['sterəlaɪzd] *adj* [milk] stérilisé.

sterilizer ['sterəlaɪzər] *n* stérilisateur *m*.

sterling ['stɜːlɪŋ] <> *n* **1.** [currency] sterling *(m inv)* ▪ **~ area** zone *f* sterling **2.** [standard] titre *m* **3.** [silverware] argenterie *f*.
<> *comp* [reserves, balances] en sterling ▪ [traveller's cheques] en livres sterling.
<> *adj* **1.** [gold, silver] fin **2.** *fml* [first-class] excellent, de premier ordre.

stern [stɜːn] <> *adj* **1.** [strict, harsh - person, measure] sévère, strict ; [- appearance] sévère, austère ; [- discipline, punishment] sévère, rigoureux ; [- look, rebuke] sévère, dur ; [- warning] solennel, grave **2.** [robust] solide, robuste ▪ **his wife is made of ~er stuff** sa femme est d'une autre trempe.
<> *n* **1.** NAUT arrière *m*, poupe *f* **2.** [of horse] croupe *f*.

sterna ['stɜːnə] *pl* ▷ **sternum**.

sternly ['stɜːnlɪ] *adv* sévèrement.

sternum ['stɜːnəm] (*pl* **sternums** *OR pl* **sterna** ['stɜːnə]) *n* sternum *m*.

steroid ['stɪərɔɪd] *n* stéroïde *m* ▪ **the doctor put him on a course of ~s** le médecin lui a prescrit *OR* donné un traitement stéroïdien.

stethoscope ['steθəskəʊp] *n* stéthoscope *m*.

Stetson® ['stetsn] *n* Stetson® *m*, chapeau *m* de cow-boy.

stevedore ['stiːvədɔːr] <> *n US* docker *m*, débardeur *m*.
<> *vi* travailler comme docker *OR* débardeur.

stew [stjuː] <> *n* CULIN ragoût *m* ▪ **lamb/vegetable ~** ragoût d'agneau/de légumes (mijotés) ▪ **to be in a ~** *UK inf* [bothered] être dans tous ses états ; [in a mess] être dans de beaux draps *OR* dans le pétrin.
<> *vt* [meat] préparer en ragoût, cuire (en ragoût) ▪ [fruit] (faire) cuire en compote.
<> *vi* CULIN [meat] cuire en ragoût, mijoter ▪ [fruit] cuire ▪ [tea] infuser trop longtemps ➋ **to let sb ~ (in his/her own juice)** *UK inf* laisser cuire *OR* mijoter qqn dans son jus.

steward ['stjʊəd] *n* **1.** [on aeroplane, ship] steward *m* **2.** [at race, sports event] commissaire *m* ▪ **~'s enquiry** *UK* enquête *f* des commissaires **3.** [at dance, social event] organisateur *m*, - trice *f* ▪ [at meeting, demonstration] membre *m* du service d'ordre **4.** [of property] intendant *m*, - e *f* ▪ [estate, finances] régisseur *m*, - euse *f* ▪ [in college] économe *mf*.

stewardess ['stjʊədɪs] *n* hôtesse *f*.

stewbeef ['stjuːbiːf] *US* = **stewing steak**.

stewed [stju:d] *adj* **1.** CULIN : ~ **meat** ragoût *m* ▪ **we had ~ lamb for supper** au dîner, nous avons mangé un ragoût d'agneau ▪ ~ **fruit** compote *f* de fruits **2.** [tea] trop infusé **3.** *inf* [drunk] bourré, cuité.

stewing steak [stju:ɪŋ-] *n UK* bœuf *m* à braiser.

St. Ex. *written abbr of* **stock exchange**.

stg *written abbr of* **sterling**.

STI (*abbrev of* **sexually transmitted infection**) *n* MED MST *f*.

stick [stɪk] (*pret & pp* **stuck** [stʌk]) ◇ *n* **1.** [piece of wood] bout *m* de bois ▪ [branch] branche *f* ▪ [twig] petite branche *f*, brindille *f* ▪ **gather some ~s, we'll make a fire** ramassez du bois, on fera du feu
2. [wooden rod - as weapon] bâton *m* ▪ [walking stick] canne *f*, bâton *m* ▪ [drumstick] baguette *f* ▪ [for plants] rame *f*, tuteur *m* ▪ [for lollipop] bâton *m* ▪ **she had legs like ~s** elle avait des jambes comme des allumettes ▪ **the threat of redundancy has become a ~ with which industry beats the unions** *fig* pour le patronat, la menace du licenciement est devenue une arme contre les syndicats ▪ **we don't have one ~ of decent furniture** nous n'avons pas un seul meuble convenable ▶ **to get (hold of) the wrong end of the ~** mal comprendre, comprendre de travers ▪ **you've got (hold of) the wrong end of the ~ about this business** vous avez tout compris de travers dans cette histoire ▪ **she got the short** *OR* **dirty end of the ~ as usual** c'est tombé sur elle comme d'habitude ▪ **~s and stones may break my bones but words will never hurt me** *prov* la bave du crapaud n'atteint pas la blanche colombe *prov*
3. [piece - of chalk] bâton *m*, morceau *m* ; [- of cinnamon, incense, liquorice, dynamite] bâton *m* ; [- of charcoal] morceau *m* ; [- of chewing gum] tablette *f* ; [- of glue, deodorant] bâton *m*, stick *m* ; [- of celery] branche *f* ; [- of rhubarb] tige *f*
4. GAMES & SPORT [in lacrosse] crosse *f* ▪ [in hockey] crosse *f*, stick *m* ▪ [ski pole] bâton *m* (de ski) ▪ [baseball bat] batte *f* ▪ [billiard cue] queue *f* de billard ▪ [in pick-up sticks] bâton *m*, bâtonnet *m*, jonchet *m*
5. *inf (U) UK inf* [criticism] critiques *fpl* (désobligeantes) ▪ **to get** *OR* **to come in for a lot of ~ : the police got a lot of ~ from the press** la police s'est fait éreinter *OR* démolir par la presse ▪ **he got a lot of ~ from his friends about his new hairstyle** ses amis l'ont bien charrié avec sa nouvelle coupe
6. *inf* [control lever - AERON] manche *m* à balai ▪ AUT levier *m* de vitesse
7. MIL [cluster - of bombs] chapelet *m* ; [- of parachutists] stick *m*
8. *UK inf dated* [person] type *m* ▪ **she's not a bad old ~, she's a nice old ~** elle est plutôt sympa.
◇ *vt* **1.** [jab, stab - spear, nail, knife] planter, enfoncer ; [- needle] piquer, planter ; [- pole, shovel] planter ; [- elbow, gun] enfoncer ▪ **don't ~ drawing pins in the wall** ne plantez pas de punaises dans le mur ▪ **there were maps with coloured pins stuck in them** il y avait des cartes avec des épingles de couleur ▪ **a ham stuck with cloves** un jambon piqué de clous de girofle ▪ **she stuck the revolver in his back** elle lui a enfoncé le revolver dans le dos ▪ **he pulled out his gun and stuck it in my face** *inf* il a sorti son arme et l'a brandie sous mon nez
2. [insert] insérer, mettre, ficher ▪ [put] mettre ▪ **he stuck a rose in his lapel** il s'est mis une rose à la boutonnière ▪ **here, ~ this under the chair leg** tenez, calez la chaise avec ça ▪ **he stuck his foot in the door** il glissa son pied dans l'entrebâillement de la porte ▪ **he stood there with a cigar stuck in his mouth/with his hands stuck in his pockets** il était planté là, un cigare entre les dents/les mains enfoncées dans les poches ▪ **she stuck her head into the office/out of the window** elle a passé la tête dans le bureau/par la fenêtre ▮ *inf* [put casually] mettre, ficher ▪ **mix it all together and ~ it in the oven** mélangez bien (le tout) et mettez au four ▪ **can you ~ my name on the list?** tu peux ajouter mon nom sur la liste? ▶ **he can ~ the job!**△ *UK* il sait où il peut se le mettre, son boulot!△ ▪ **~ it!**△ tu peux te le mettre où je pense△ *OR* quelque part!△
3. [fasten] fixer ▪ [pin up] punaiser ▪ **it was stuck on the notice-board with tacks** c'était punaisé au tableau d'affichage
4. [with adhesive] coller ▪ **help me ~ this vase together** aide-moi à recoller le vase ▪ **to ~ a stamp on an envelope** coller un timbre sur une enveloppe ▪ **he had posters stuck to the walls with Sellotape** il avait scotché des posters aux murs ▪ **'~ no bills'** 'défense d'afficher'
5. [kill - pig] égorger
6. *UK inf* [bear - person, situation] supporter ▪ **I can't ~ him** je ne peux pas le sentir ▪ **what I can't ~ is her telling me how to run my life** ce que je ne supporte pas c'est qu'elle me dise comment je dois vivre ▪ **I'm amazed she stuck a term, let alone three years** je suis étonné qu'elle ait tenu (le coup) un trimestre, et à plus forte raison trois ans
7. *inf* [with chore, burden] : **to ~ sb with a fine/the blame** coller une amende/faire endosser la responsabilité à qqn ▪ **I always get stuck with the dishes** je me retrouve toujours avec la vaisselle sur les bras, c'est toujours moi qui dois me taper la vaisselle.
◇ *vi* **1.** [arrow, dart, spear] se planter ▪ **you'll find some tacks already ~ing in the notice-board** vous trouverez quelques punaises déjà plantées dans le tableau d'affichage
2. [attach, adhere - wet clothes, bandage, chewing gum] coller ; [- gummed label, stamp] tenir, coller ; [- burr] s'accrocher ▪ **the dough stuck to my fingers** la pâte collait à mes doigts ▪ **the damp has made the stamps ~ together** l'humidité a collé les timbres les uns aux autres ▪ **the dust will ~ to the wet varnish** la poussière va coller sur le vernis frais ▪ **these badges ~ to any surface** ces autocollants adhèrent sur toutes les surfaces ▪ **food won't ~ to these pans** ces casseroles n'attachent pas ▪ **they had straw ~ing in their hair** ils avaient des brins de paille dans les cheveux
3. [become jammed, wedged - mechanism, drawer, key] se coincer, se bloquer ▪ **the lorry stuck fast in the mud** le camion s'est complètement enlisé dans la boue ▪ **I have a fishbone stuck in my throat** j'ai une arête (de poisson) coincée dans la gorge ▶ **it ~s in my throat** *inf OR UK* **gullet** *inf* ça me reste sur l'estomac *OR* en travers de la gorge ▪ **having to ask him for a loan really ~s in my throat** ça me coûte vraiment d'avoir à lui demander un prêt
4. [remain, keep] rester ▪ **she has the kind of face that ~s in your memory** elle a un visage qu'on n'oublie pas *OR* dont on se souvient ▪ **his bodyguards ~ close to him at all times** ses gardes du corps l'accompagnent partout *OR* ne le quittent jamais d'une semelle ▪ **~ to the main road** suivez la route principale
5. *inf* [be upheld] : **to make the charge** *OR* **charges ~** prouver la culpabilité de qqn ▪ **the important thing now is to make the agreement ~** ce qui compte maintenant, c'est de faire respecter l'accord
6. [extend, project] : **the antenna was ~ing straight up** l'antenne se dressait toute droite ▪ **his ticket was ~ing out of his pocket** son billet sortait *OR* dépassait de sa poche ▪ **only her head was ~ing out of the water** seule sa tête sortait *OR* émergeait de l'eau
7. [in card games] : **(I) ~** j'arrête, je ne veux pas d'autre carte.

◆ **sticks** *npl inf* [backwoods] cambrousse *f* ▪ **they live way out in the ~s** ils habitent en pleine cambrousse.

◆ **stick around** *vi insep inf* [stay] rester (dans les parages) ▪ [wait] attendre.

◆ **stick at** *vt insep* **1.** : **to ~ at it** *UK* [persevere] persévérer
2. [stop] : **to ~ at nothing** ne reculer *OR* n'hésiter devant rien.

◆ **stick by** *vt insep* **1.** [person] soutenir ▪ **don't worry, I'll always ~ by you** sois tranquille, je serai toujours là pour te soutenir
2. [one's decision] s'en tenir à ▪ **I ~ by what I said** je maintiens ce que j'ai dit.

◆ **stick down** ◇ *vt sep* **1.** [flap, envelope] coller
2. *inf UK* [note down] noter ▪ [scribble] griffonner
3. *inf* [place] poser.
◇ *vi insep* [flap, envelope] (se) coller.

◆ **stick in** ◇ *vt sep* **1.** [nail, knife, spear] planter, enfoncer ▪ [needle] piquer, enfoncer ▪ [pole, shovel] enfoncer, planter
2. [insert - coin, bank card] insérer ; [- electric plug] brancher ; [- cork, sink plug] enfoncer ; [- word, sentence] ajouter ▪ **I stuck my hand in to test the water temperature** j'y ai plongé la main pour vérifier la température de l'eau ▪ **he stuck his head in through the door** il passa la tête par la porte
3. [glue in] coller.
◇ *vi insep* [dart, arrow, spear] se planter.

◆ **stick on** ◇ *vt sep* **1.** [fasten on - gummed badge, label, stamp] coller ; [- china handle] recoller ; [- broom head] fixer
2. *inf* [jacket, boots] enfiler ▪ **he hurriedly stuck a hat on** il s'est collé en vitesse un chapeau sur la tête.
◇ *vi insep* coller, se coller.

◆ **stick out** ◇ *vt sep* **1.** [extend - hand, leg] tendre, allonger ; [- feelers, head] sortir ▪ **to ~ one's tongue out (at sb)** tirer

la langue (à qqn) ▪ **he stuck his foot out to trip me up** il a allongé la jambe pour me faire un croche-pied ▪ **I opened the window and stuck my head out** j'ai ouvert la fenêtre et j'ai passé la tête au dehors ▪ **to ~ one's chest out** bomber le torse ▪ **to ~ out one's lower lip** faire la moue
2. *phr* **to ~ it out** *inf* tenir le coup jusqu'au bout.
◇ *vi insep* **1.** [protrude - nail, splinter] sortir ; [- teeth] avancer ; [- plant, shoot] pointer ; [- ledge, balcony] être en saillie ▪ **his belly stuck out over his belt** son ventre débordait au-dessus de sa ceinture ▪ **her ears ~ out** elle a les oreilles décollées ▪ **my feet stuck out over the end of the bed** mes pieds dépassaient du lit
2. [be noticeable - colour] ressortir ▪ **the red Mercedes really ~s out** on ne voit que la Mercedes rouge ▪ **I don't like to ~ out in a crowd** je n'aime pas me singulariser *OR* me faire remarquer ▪ **it's her accent that makes her ~ out** c'est à cause de son accent qu'on la remarque.
◆ **stick out for** *vt insep* s'obstiner à vouloir, exiger ▪ **the union is ~ing out for a five per cent rise** le syndicat continue à revendiquer une augmentation de cinq pour cent.
◆ **stick to** *vt insep* : **it won't be easy to ~ to this schedule** ce ne sera pas facile de tenir *OR* respecter ce planning ▪ **I can never ~ to diets** je n'arrive jamais à suivre un régime longtemps ▪ **we must ~ to our plan** nous devons continuer à suivre notre plan ▪ **once I make a decision I ~ to it** une fois que j'ai pris une décision, je m'y tiens *OR* je n'en démords pas ▪ **to ~ to one's word** *OR* **promises** tenir (sa) parole ▪ **to ~ to one's principles** rester fidèle à ses principes ▪ **she's still ~ing to her story** elle maintient ce qu'elle a dit ▪ **~ to the point!** ne vous éloignez pas du sujet! ▪ **~ to the facts!** tenez-vous-en aux faits! ▪ **can we ~ to the business in hand?** peut-être pourrions-nous en finir avec les digressions? ▪ **the author would be better off ~ing to journalism** l'auteur ferait mieux de se cantonner au journalisme.
◆ **stick together** *vi insep inf* [people] rester ensemble ▪ *fig* se serrer les coudes.
◆ **stick up** ◇ *vt sep* **1.** [sign, notice, poster] afficher ▪ [postcard] coller ▪ [with drawing pins] punaiser
2. [raise - pole] dresser ▪ **to ~ one's hand up** lever la main ➊ **~ 'em up!** *inf* haut les mains!
3. *US inf* [rob - person, bank, supermarket] braquer.
◇ *vi insep* [point upwards - tower, antenna] s'élever ; [- plant shoots] pointer ▪ **a branch was ~ing up out of the water** une branche sortait de l'eau.
◆ **stick up for** *vt insep* : **to ~ up for sb** prendre la défense *OR* le parti de qqn ▪ **~ up for yourself!** ne te laisse pas faire! ▪ **he has trouble ~ing up for himself/his rights** il a du mal à défendre ses intérêts/à faire valoir ses droits.
◆ **stick with** *vt insep* **1.** [activity, subject] s'en tenir à, persister dans ▪ **now I've started the job, I'm going to ~ with it** maintenant que j'ai commencé ce travail, je ne le lâche pas
2. [person] : **~ with me, kid, and you'll be all right** *inf* reste avec moi, petit, et tout ira bien.

stick deodorant *n* déodorant *m* en stick.

sticker ['stɪkəʳ] *n* **1.** [adhesive label] autocollant *m* **2.** *inf* [determined person] : **she's a ~** elle est persévérante, elle va au bout de ce qu'elle entreprend.

stickiness ['stɪkɪnɪs] *n* [of hands, substance, surface, jamjar] caractère *m* gluant *OR* poisseux.

sticking plaster ['stɪkɪŋ-] *n UK* pansement *m*, sparadrap *m*.

sticking point *n fig* point *m* de friction.

stick insect *n* phasme *m*.

stick-in-the-mud *n inf* [fogey] vieux croûton *m* ▪ [killjoy] rabat-joie *m inv*.

stickleback ['stɪklbæk] *n* épinoche *f (de rivière)*.

stickler ['stɪkləʳ] *n* : **to be a ~ for** [regulations, discipline, good manners] être à cheval sur ; [tradition, routine] insister sur.

stick-on *adj* autocollant.

stickpin ['stɪkpɪn] *n US* épingle *f* de cravate.

stick shift *n US* AUT levier *m* de vitesse.

stick-up *n US inf* braquage *m*, hold-up *m*.

sticky ['stɪkɪ] (*comp* **stickier**, *superl* **stickiest**) *adj* **1.** [adhesive] adhésif, gommé **2.** [tacky, gluey - hands, fingers] collant, poisseux ; [- substance, surface, jamjar] gluant, poisseux ▪ **to have ~ fingers** *liter* avoir les doigts collants *OR* poisseux ; *fig inf* être porté sur la fauche **3.** [sweaty] moite **4.** [humid - weather] moite, humide **5.** *inf* [awkward - situation] difficile, délicat ▪ **to be (batting) on a ~ wicket** *UK* être dans une situation difficile ▪ **to come to a ~ end** *UK* mal finir.

sticky-fingered *adj inf* **to be ~** être porté sur la fauche.

sticky tape *n* ruban *m* adhésif.

stiff [stɪf] ◇ *adj* **1.** [rigid] raide, rigide ▪ **~ paper/cardboard** papier/carton rigide ▪ **a ~ brush** une brosse à poils durs ▪ **to be ~ with terror** être glacé de terreur ➊ **as ~ as a poker** raide comme un piquet ▪ **to keep a ~ upper lip** garder son flegme
2. [thick, difficult to stir] ferme, consistant ▪ **beat the mixture until it is ~** battez jusqu'à obtention d'une pâte consistante ▪ **beat the eggwhites until ~** battre les blancs en neige jusqu'à ce qu'ils soient (bien) fermes
3. [difficult to move] dur ▪ **the drawers have got a bit ~** les tiroirs sont devenus un peu durs à ouvrir
4. [aching] courbaturé, raide ▪ **I'm still ~ after playing squash the other day** j'ai encore des courbatures d'avoir joué au squash l'autre jour ▪ **to have a ~ back** avoir mal au dos ▪ **to have a ~ neck** avoir un *OR* le torticolis
5. [over-formal - smile, welcome] froid ; [- person, manners, behaviour] froid, guindé ; [- style] guindé
6. [difficult] dur, ardu ▪ **to face ~ competition** avoir affaire à forte concurrence
7. [severe] sévère ▪ **I sent them a ~ letter** je leur ai envoyé une lettre bien sentie
8. [strong - breeze, drink] fort ▪ **she poured herself a ~ whisky** elle s'est versé un whisky bien tassé
9. [high - price, bill] élevé
10. [determined - resistance, opposition] tenace, acharné ; [- resolve] ferme, inébranlable
11. *UK inf* [full] plein (à craquer).
◇ *adv inf* **to be bored ~** mourir d'ennui ▪ **to be worried/scared ~** être mort d'inquiétude/de peur.
◇ *n*△ [corpse] macchabée *m*.

stiffen ['stɪfn] ◇ *vt* **1.** [paper, fabric] raidir, renforcer **2.** [thicken - batter, concrete] donner de la consistance à ; [- sauce] lier **3.** [make painful - arm, leg, muscle] courbaturer ▪ **his joints had become ~ed by arthritis** ses articulations s'étaient raidies à cause de l'arthrite **4.** [strengthen - resistance, resolve] renforcer.
◇ *vi* **1.** [harden - paper, fabric] devenir raide *OR* rigide **2.** [tense, stop moving] se raidir **3.** [thicken - batter, concrete] épaissir, devenir ferme ; [- sauce] se lier **4.** [become hard to move - hinge, handle, door] se coincer **5.** [start to ache] s'ankyloser **6.** [strengthen - resistance, resolve] se renforcer ; [- breeze] forcir.

stiffener ['stɪfnəʳ] *n* **1.** [in collar] baleine *f* **2.** *UK inf* [drink] remontant *m*.

stiffening ['stɪfnɪŋ] *n* renforcement *m*.

stiffly ['stɪflɪ] *adv* **1.** [rigidly] : **~ starched** très empesé *OR* amidonné ▪ **he stood ~ to attention** il se tenait raide au garde-à-vous **2.** [painfully - walk, bend] avec raideur **3.** [coldly - smile, greet] froidement, d'un air distant.

stiff-necked *adj liter* qui a le torticolis ▪ *fig* opiniâtre, entêté.

stiffness ['stɪfnɪs] *n* **1.** [of paper, fabric] raideur *f*, rigidité *f* **2.** [of batter, dough, concrete] consistance *f*, fermeté *f* **3.** [of hinge, handle, door] dureté *f* **4.** [of joints, limbs] raideur *f*, courbatures *fpl* **5.** [of manners, smile, welcome] froideur *f*, distance *f* ▪ [of style] caractère *m* guindé **6.** [difficulty - of exam, competition] difficulté *f*, dureté *f* **7.** [severity - of sentence, warning] sévérité *f*.

stifle ['staɪfl] ◇ *vt* **1.** [suppress - resistance, creativity, progress] réprimer, étouffer ; [- tears, anger, emotion] réprimer ▪ **to ~ a cough** réprimer une envie de tousser ▪ **I tried to ~ my laughter/a yawn** j'ai essayé de ne pas rire/bailler **2.** [suffocate] étouffer, suffoquer.
◇ *vi* étouffer, suffoquer.

stifling ['staɪflɪŋ] *adj* suffocant, étouffant ▪ **open the window, it's ~ in here!** ouvre la fenêtre, on étouffe ici!

stigma ['stɪgmə] *n* **1.** [social disgrace] honte *f* ■ **the ~ attached to having been in prison** l'opprobre qui ne quitte pas ceux qui ont fait de la prison **2.** BOT, MED & ZOOL stigmate *m*.

stigmata [stɪg'mɑːtə] *npl* RELIG stigmates *mpl*.

stigmatism ['stɪgmətɪzm] *n* OPT stigmatisme *m*.

stigmatize, ise ['stɪgmətaɪz] *vt* stigmatiser.

stile [staɪl] *n* **1.** [over fence] échalier *m* **2.** [turnstile] tourniquet *m* **3.** CONSTR [upright] montant *m*.

stiletto [stɪ'letəʊ] (*pl* **stilettos**) *n* **1.** [heel] talon *m* aiguille **2.** [knife] stylet *m*.
➡ **stilettos** *npl* (chaussures *fpl* à) talons *mpl* aiguilles.

stiletto heel *n* talon *m* aiguille.

still[1] [stɪl] *adv* **1.** [as of this moment] encore, toujours ■ **we're ~ waiting for the repairman to come** nous attendons toujours que le réparateur vienne ■ **there's ~ a bit of cake left** il reste encore un morceau de gâteau ■ **the worst was ~ to come** le pire n'était pas encore arrivé **2.** [all the same] quand même ■ **it's a shame we lost – ~, it was a good game** (c'est) dommage que nous ayons perdu – quand même, c'était un bon match ■ **~ and all** *inf* quand même **3.** *(with compar)* [even] encore ■ **~ more/less** encore plus/moins ■ **~ further, further ~** encore plus loin ■ **the sea was getting ~ rougher** la mer était de plus en plus agitée.

still[2] [stɪl] ◇ *adj* **1.** [motionless - person, air, surface] immobile ■ **be ~!** arrête de remuer! ➤ **~ waters run deep** *prov* méfie-toi de l'eau qui dort *prov* **2.** [calm] calme, tranquille ■ [quiet] silencieux **3.** [not fizzy] plat.
◇ *adv* sans bouger ■ **stand ~!** ne bougez pas! ■ **my heart stood ~** mon cœur a cessé de battre ■ **they're so excited they can't sit ~** ils sont tellement excités qu'ils ne peuvent pas rester en place ■ **try to hold the camera ~** essaie de ne pas bouger l'appareil photo.
◇ *vt lit* **1.** [silence] faire taire **2.** [allay - doubts, fears] apaiser, calmer.
◇ *n* **1.** *lit* [silence] silence *m* **2.** CIN photo *f* (de plateau) ■ **~ photographer** photographe *mf* de plateau **3.** [apparatus] alambic *m*.

stillbirth ['stɪlbɜːθ] *n* [birth] mort *f* à la naissance ■ [fœtus] enfant *m* mort-né, enfant *f* mort-née.

stillborn ['stɪlbɔːn] *adj* **1.** MED mort-né **2.** *fig* [idea, plan] avorté.

still life (*pl* **still lifes**) *n* nature *f* morte.

stillness ['stɪlnɪs] *n* **1.** [motionlessness] immobilité *f* **2.** [calm] tranquillité *f*, paix *f*.

stilt [stɪlt] *n* **1.** [for walking] échasse *f* **2.** ARCHIT pilotis *m*.

stilted ['stɪltɪd] *adj* [speech, writing, person] guindé, emprunté ■ [discussion] qui manque de naturel.

Stilton® ['stɪltn] *n* stilton *m*, fromage *m* de Stilton.

stimulant ['stɪmjʊlənt] ◇ *n* stimulant *m* ■ **devaluation acts as a ~ to exports** la dévaluation stimule les exportations.
◇ *adj* stimulant.

stimulate ['stɪmjʊleɪt] *vt* stimuler ■ **the bracing sea air ~d me** l'air de la mer m'a revigoré ■ **to ~ sb to do sthg** inciter OR encourager qqn à faire qqch ■ **sexually ~d** excité (sexuellement).

stimulating ['stɪmjʊleɪtɪŋ] *adj* **1.** [medicine, drug] stimulant **2.** [work, conversation, experience] stimulant, enrichissant.

stimulation [,stɪmjʊ'leɪʃn] *n* **1.** [of person] stimulation *f* **2.** [stimulus] stimulant *m*.

stimulus ['stɪmjʊləs] (*pl* **stimuli** [-laɪ, -liː]) *n* **1.** [incentive] stimulant *m*, incitation *f* **2.** PHYSIOL stimulus *m*.

sting [stɪŋ] (*pret & pp* **stung** [stʌŋ]) ◇ *vt* **1.** [subj: insect, nettle, scorpion] piquer ■ [subj: smoke] piquer, brûler ■ [subj: vinegar, acid, disinfectant] brûler ■ [subj: whip, rain] cingler **2.** [subj: remark, joke, criticism] piquer (au vif), blesser ■ **to ~ sb into action** inciter OR pousser qqn à agir **3.** *inf* [cheat] arnaquer ■ **they stung me for £20** ils m'ont arnaqué de 20 livres.
◇ *vi* **1.** [insect, nettle, scorpion] piquer ■ [vinegar, acid, disinfectant] brûler, piquer ■ [whip, rain] cingler **2.** [eyes, skin] piquer, brûler ■ **my eyes are ~ing** j'ai les yeux qui piquent.
◇ *n* **1.** [organ - of bee, wasp, scorpion] aiguillon *m*, dard *m* ; [- of nettle] poil *m* (urticant) ■ **there's a ~ in the tail** *UK* il y a une mauvaise surprise à la fin ■ **his remarks often have a ~ in the tail** ses remarques sont rarement innocentes ■ **to take the ~ out of sthg** rendre qqch moins douloureux, adoucir qqch **2.** [wound, pain, mark - from insect, nettle, scorpion] piqûre *f* ; [- from vinegar, acid, disinfectant] brûlure *f* ; [- from whip] douleur *f* cinglante **3.** *inf* [trick] arnaque *f* ■ **~ (operation)** coup *m* monté *(où les policiers se font passer pour des complices)*.

stinginess ['stɪndʒɪnɪs] *n* [of person, behaviour] avarice *f*, pingrerie *f* ■ [of amount, helping] insuffisance *f*.

stinging ['stɪŋɪŋ] *adj* **1.** [wound, pain] cuisant ■ [bite, eyes] qui pique ■ [lash, rain] cinglant **2.** [remark, joke, criticism] cinglant, mordant.

stinging nettle *n* ortie *f*.

stingray ['stɪŋreɪ] *n* pastenague *f*.

stingy ['stɪndʒɪ] *adj inf* [person] radin ■ [amount, helping] misérable ■ **they're never ~ about food** ils ne lésinent jamais sur la nourriture.

stink [stɪŋk] (*pret* **stank** [stæŋk], *pp* **stunk** [stʌŋk]) ◇ *vi* **1.** [smell] puer, empester ■ **the room stank of cigarette smoke** la pièce puait OR empestait la fumée de cigarette **2.** *inf* [be bad] : **I think your idea ~s!** je trouve ton idée nulle! ■ **this town ~s!** cette ville est pourrie!
◇ *n* **1.** [stench] puanteur *f*, odeur *f* nauséabonde ■ **what a ~!** *inf* qu'est-ce que ça pue! **2.** *inf* [fuss] esclandre *m* ■ **to kick up** OR **to make** OR **to raise a ~ about sthg** faire un esclandre OR un scandale à propos de qqch.
➡ **stink out** *vt sep inf* **1.** [drive away] chasser par la mauvaise odeur **2.** [fill with a bad smell] empester.

stink-bomb *n* boule *f* puante.

stinker ['stɪŋkər] *n inf* **1.** [person] peau *f* de vache **2.** [unpleasant thing] : **the exam was a real ~!** cet examen était vraiment vache! ■ **today's crossword's a ~** les mots croisés d'aujourd'hui sont vraiment coriaces.

stinking ['stɪŋkɪŋ] ◇ *adj* **1.** [smelly] puant, nauséabond **2.** *inf* [as intensifier] : **I've got a ~ cold** j'ai un rhume carabiné.
◇ *adv inf* vachement ■ **to be ~ rich** être plein de fric OR plein aux as.

stint [stɪnt] ◇ *n* **1.** [period of work] période *f* de travail ■ [share of work] part *f* de travail ■ **she did a ~ in Africa/as a teacher** elle a travaillé pendant un certain temps en Afrique/comme professeur ■ **I'll take** OR **I'll do another ~ at the wheel** je vais reprendre le volant **2.** *fml* [limitation] : **without ~** [spend] sans compter ; [give] généreusement ; [work] inlassablement.
◇ *vt UK* **1.** [skimp on] lésiner sur **2.** [deprive] priver ■ **he's incapable of ~ing himself of anything** il est incapable de se priver de quoi que ce soit.
◇ *vi UK* **to ~ on sthg** lésiner sur qqch.

stipend ['staɪpend] *n* traitement *m*, appointements *mpl*.

stipendiary [staɪ'pendjərɪ] (*pl* **stipendiaries**) ◇ *adj* [work, person] rémunéré.
◇ *n* [clergyman] *prêtre percevant un traitement* ■ [magistrate] *juge d'un tribunal de police correctionnelle*.

stippled ['stɪpld] *adj* tacheté, moucheté ■ **~ with yellow** tacheté OR moucheté de jaune.

stipulate ['stɪpjʊleɪt] ◇ *vt* stipuler.
◇ *vi fml* : **to ~ for sthg** stipuler qqch.

stipulation [,stɪpjʊ'leɪʃn] *n* stipulation *f* ■ **they accepted, but with the ~ that the time limit be extended** ils ont accepté sous réserve que les délais soient prolongés.

stir [stɜːr] (*pret & pp* **stirred**, *cont* **stirring**) ◇ *vt* **1.** [mix] remuer, tourner ■ **~ the flour into the sauce** incorporez la farine à la sauce en remuant **2.** [move] agiter, remuer ■ **a light breeze stirred the leaves** une brise légère agitait les feuilles ➤ **~ yourself** OR **your stumps** *inf*, **it's time to go!** *UK inf* grouille-toi, il est l'heure de partir! **3.** [touch] émouvoir

4. [rouse, excite] éveiller, exciter **to ~ sb's curiosity/sympathy** éveiller la curiosité/sympathie de qqn **to ~ sb to do sthg** inciter *OR* pousser qqn à faire qqch **to ~ sb into action** pousser qqn à agir.
◇ *vi* **1.** [move - person] bouger, remuer ; [- leaves] remuer **I shan't ~ from my bed until midday** je ne bougerai pas de mon lit avant midi **2.** [awaken, be roused - feeling, anger] s'éveiller **3.** *inf* [cause trouble] faire de la provocation *OR* des histoires.
◇ *n* **1.** [act of mixing] : **to give sthg a ~** remuer qqch **2.** [commotion] émoi *m*, agitation *f* **to cause** *OR* **to create** *OR* **to make quite a ~** soulever un vif émoi, faire grand bruit **3.** [movement] mouvement *m* **a ~ of excitement** un frisson d'excitation.
◆ **stir in** *vt sep* CULIN ajouter *OR* incorporer en remuant.
◆ **stir up** *vt sep* **1.** [disturb - dust, mud] soulever **2.** [incite, provoke - trouble] provoquer ; [- emotions] exciter, attiser ; [- dissent] fomenter ; [- memories] réveiller ; [- crowd, followers] ameuter **he likes stirring it** *OR* **things up** il aime provoquer.

stir-crazy *adj inf* fou *(à cause d'une période de détention).*

stir-fry ◇ *vt* CULIN faire sauter à feu vif *(tout en remuant).*
◇ *adj* sauté **~ pork** porc sauté.

stirrer ['stɜːrəʳ] *n* **1.** *inf* [troublemaker] provocateur *m*, - trice *f* **2.** CULIN [implement] fouet *m*.

stirring ['stɜːrɪŋ] ◇ *adj* [music, song] entraînant [story] excitant, passionnant [speech] vibrant.
◇ *n* : **he felt vague ~s of guilt** il éprouva un vague sentiment de culpabilité **the first ~s of what was to become the Romantic movement** les premières manifestations de ce qui allait devenir le mouvement romantique.

stirrup ['stɪrəp] *n* EQUIT étrier *m* **to put one's feet in the ~s** chausser les étriers.
◆ **stirrups** *npl* MED étriers *mpl*.

stirrup leather *n* étrivière *f*.

stirrup pump *n* seau-pompe *m*.

stitch [stɪtʃ] ◇ *n* **1.** SEW point *m* [in knitting] maille *f* **to drop a ~** sauter une maille **to pick up a ~** reprendre une maille ◗ **I didn't have a ~ (of clothing) on** *inf* j'étais nu comme un ver, j'étais dans le plus simple appareil **a ~ in time saves nine** *prov* un point à temps en vaut cent *prov* **2.** MED point *m* de suture **I'm having my ~es taken out tomorrow** on m'ôte les fils demain **3.** [pain] point *m* de côté **to get a ~** attraper un point de côté **4.** *phr* **to be in ~ es** *inf* se tordre *OR* être écroulé de rire **his story had us in ~es** son histoire nous a fait pleurer de rire.
◇ *vt* **1.** [material, shirt, hem] coudre **he ~ed the button back on his shirt** il a recousu son bouton de chemise **2.** MED suturer **3.** [in bookbinding] brocher.
◆ **stitch down** *vt sep* rabattre.
◆ **stitch up** *vt sep* **1.** [material, shirt, hem] coudre **2.** MED suturer **3.** *inf* [deal] conclure, sceller **4.** *inf* [frame - person] : **he reckons the police ~ed him up** il pense que la police a monté un coup contre lui.

stitching ['stɪtʃɪŋ] *n* **1.** [gen] couture *f* **2.** [in bookbinding] brochage *m*.

St John Ambulance *pr n organisme bénévole de secours d'urgence en Grande-Bretagne.*

St John's wort [-wɜːt] *n* millepertuis *m*.

stoat [stəʊt] *n* hermine *f*.

stock [stɒk] ◇ *n* **1.** [supply] réserve *f*, provision *f*, stock *m* COMM & INDUST stock *m* **we got in a ~ of food** nous avons fait tout un stock de nourriture **in ~** en stock, en magasin **out of ~** épuisé **I'm afraid we're out of ~** je regrette, nous n'en avons plus en stock ◗ **to take ~** *liter* faire l'inventaire ; *fig* faire le point **2.** [total amount] parc *m* **the housing ~** le parc de logements **3.** *(usu pl)* ST. EX [gen] valeur *f* mobilière [share] action *f* [bond] obligation *f* **to invest in ~s and shares** investir dans des actions et obligations *OR* en portefeuille **government ~s** obligations *fpl OR* titres *mpl* d'État **4.** FIN [equity] capital *m* **5.** *fig* [value, credit] cote *f* **to put ~ in sthg** faire (grand) cas de qqch **6.** [descent, ancestry] souche *f*, lignée *f* **of peasant/noble ~** de souche paysanne/noble **7.** AGRIC [animals] cheptel *m* **8.** CULIN bouillon *m* **vegetable ~** bouillon de légumes **9.** [handle, butt - of gun, plough] fût *m* ; [- of whip] manche *m* ; [- of fishing rod] gaule *f* **10.** BOT giroflée *f* **11.** [tree trunk] tronc *m* [tree stump] souche *f* **12.** HORT [stem receiving graft] porte-greffe *m*, sujet *m* [plant from which graft is taken] plante *f* mère *(sur laquelle on prélève un greffon)* **13.** [in card games, dominoes] talon *m*, pioche *f* **14.** THEAT répertoire *m* **15.** [neckcloth] lavallière *f*, foulard *m*.
◇ *vt* **1.** COMM [have in stock] avoir (en stock), vendre **2.** [supply] approvisionner [fill] remplir **they have a well ~ed cellar** ils ont une cave bien approvisionnée **3.** [stream, lake] empoissonner [farm] monter en bétail.
◇ *adj* **1.** [common, typical - phrase, expression] tout fait ; [- question, answer, excuse] classique **2.** COMM [kept in stock] en stock [widely available] courant **~ control** contrôle *m* des stocks **3.** AGRIC [for breeding] destiné à la reproduction **4.** THEAT [play] du répertoire.
◆ **stocks** *npl* **1.** [instrument of punishment] pilori *m* **2.** NAUT [frame] cale *f* **on the ~s** en chantier.
◆ **stock up** ◇ *vi insep* s'approvisionner **to ~ up on** *OR* **with sthg** s'approvisionner en qqch.
◇ *vt sep* approvisionner, garnir.

stockade [stɒ'keɪd] ◇ *n* **1.** [enclosure] palissade *f* **2.** *US* MIL [prison] prison *f* (militaire).
◇ *vt* palissader.

stockbreeder ['stɒk,briːdəʳ] *n* éleveur *m*, - euse *f* de bétail.

stockbreeding ['stɒk,briːdɪŋ] *n* élevage *m* de bétail.

stockbroker ['stɒk,brəʊkəʳ] *n* agent *m* de change.

stockbuilding ['stɒk,bɪldɪŋ] *n* achat *m* d'actions.

stock car *n* **1.** AUT stock-car *m* **~ racing** (courses *fpl* de) stock-car *m* **2.** *US* RAIL wagon *m* à bestiaux.

stock certificate *n US* FIN titre *m*.

stock cube *n* bouillon *m* Kub®.

stock exchange *n* Bourse *f* **he lost a fortune on the ~** il a perdu une fortune à la Bourse.
◆ **stock-exchange** *comp* boursier, de la Bourse **~ prices** cours *m* des actions.

stockfish ['stɒkfɪʃ] *n* stockfisch *m*, poisson *m* séché.

stockholder ['stɒk,həʊldəʳ] *n* actionnaire *mf*.

Stockholm ['stɒkhəʊm] *pr n* Stockholm.

stockily ['stɒkɪlɪ] *adv* : **~ built** trapu, râblé.

stocking ['stɒkɪŋ] *n* **1.** [for women] bas *m* **~ mask** bas *m (utilisé par un bandit masqué)* **2.** *dated* [sock] bas *m* de laine.

stockinged ['stɒkɪŋd] *adj* : **in one's ~ feet** sans chaussures, en chaussettes.

stocking filler *n petit cadeau destiné à remplir le bas de laine à Noël.*

stocking stitch *n* point *m* de jersey.

stock-in-trade *n* **1.** COMM marchandises *fpl* en stock *OR* en magasin **2.** *fig* **charm is part of an actor's ~** le charme est l'un des outils du comédien.

stockist ['stɒkɪst] *n* stockiste *mf*.

stockman ['stɒkmən] (*pl* **stockmen** [-mən]) *n* [cowherd] vacher *m*, - ère *f*, bouvier *m*, - ère *f* [breeder] éleveur *m*, - euse *f* (de bétail).

stock market *n* Bourse *f* (des valeurs), marché *m* financier **he lost a fortune on the ~** il a perdu une fortune à la Bourse.
◆ **stock-market** *comp* boursier, de la Bourse **the ~ crash** le krach boursier **~ prices** cours *m* des actions.

stockpile ['stɒkpaɪl] ◇ *n* stock *m*, réserve *f*.
◇ *vt* [goods] stocker, constituer un stock de [weapons] amasser, accumuler.
◇ *vi* faire des stocks.

stockpiling ['stɒkpaɪlɪŋ] *n* : **to accuse sb of ~** [food] accuser qqn de faire des réserves de nourriture ; [weapon] accuser qqn de faire des réserves d'armes.

stockroom ['stɒkrʊm] *n* magasin *m*, réserve *f*.

stock-still *adv* (complètement) immobile.

stocktaking ['stɒk,teɪkɪŋ] *n* **1.** COMM inventaire *m* **2.** *fig* **to do some ~** faire le point.

stocky ['stɒkɪ] (*comp* **stockier**, *superl* **stockiest**) *adj* trapu, râblé.

stockyard ['stɒkjɑːd] *n* parc *m* à bestiaux.

stodge [stɒdʒ] *n (U) UK inf* **1.** [food] aliments *mpl* bourratifs, étouffe-chrétien *m inv* ▪ **the canteen food is pure ~** ce qu'on mange à la cantine est vraiment bourratif **2.** [writing] littérature *f* indigeste.

stodgy ['stɒdʒɪ] (*comp* **stodgier**, *superl* **stodgiest**) *adj inf* **1.** [food, meal] bourratif, lourd **2.** [style] lourd, indigeste **3.** [person, manners, ideas] guindé.

stoic ['stəʊɪk] ◇ *adj* stoïque.
◇ *n* stoïque *mf*.
◆ **Stoic** *n* PHILOS stoïcien *m*, - enne *f*.

stoical ['stəʊɪkl] *adj* stoïque.

stoically ['stəʊɪklɪ] *adv* stoïquement, avec stoïcisme.

stoicism ['stəʊɪsɪzm] *n* stoïcisme *m*.
◆ **Stoicism** *n* PHILOS stoïcisme *m*.

stoke [stəʊk] *vt* **1.** [fire, furnace] alimenter, entretenir ▪ [locomotive, boiler] chauffer **2.** *fig* [emotions, feelings, anger] entretenir, alimenter.
◆ **stoke up** ◇ *vi insep* **1.** [put fuel on - fire] alimenter le feu ; [- furnace] alimenter la chaudière **2.** *UK inf* [fill one's stomach] s'empiffrer.
◇ *vt sep* = **stoke**.

stoked [stəʊkd] *adj US inf* : **to be ~ about sthg** [excited] être tout excité à cause de qqch.

stoker ['stəʊkəʳ] *n* chauffeur *m OR* chargeur *m (d'un four, d'une chaudière etc)*.

stole [stəʊl] ◇ *pt* ▷ **steal**.
◇ *n* **1.** étole *f*, écharpe *f* **2.** RELIG étole *f*.

stolen ['stəʊln] *pp* ▷ **steal**.

stolid ['stɒlɪd] *adj* flegmatique, impassible.

stolidly ['stɒlɪdlɪ] *adv* flegmatiquement, avec flegme, de manière impassible.

stomach ['stʌmək] ◇ *n* **1.** [organ] estomac *m* ▪ **to have an upset ~** avoir l'estomac barbouillé ▪ **I can't work on an empty ~** je ne peux pas travailler l'estomac vide ▪ **to have a pain in one's ~** avoir mal à l'estomac ; [lower] avoir mal au ventre ▪ **the sight was enough to turn your ~** le spectacle avait de quoi vous soulever le cœur ▶ **an army marches on its ~** une armée ne peut pas se battre l'estomac vide **2.** [region of body] ventre *m* ▪ **he has a fat ~** il a du ventre ▪ **lie on your ~** couchez-vous sur le ventre **3.** *(usu neg)* [desire, appetite] envie *f*, goût *m* ▪ **she has no ~ for spicy food** elle supporte mal la cuisine épicée ▪ **I've no ~ for his vulgar jokes this evening** je n'ai aucune envie d'écouter ses plaisanteries vulgaires ce soir.
◇ *comp* [infection] de l'estomac, gastrique ▪ [ulcer, operation] à l'estomac ▪ [pain] à l'estomac, au ventre.
◇ *vt* **1.** [tolerate] supporter, tolérer ▪ **I just can't ~ the thought of him being my boss** je ne supporte simplement pas l'idée qu'il soit mon patron **2.** [digest] digérer ▪ **I can't ~ too much rich food** je ne digère pas bien la cuisine riche.

stomachache ['stʌməkeɪk] *n* mal *m* de ventre ▪ **to have (a) ~** avoir mal au ventre.

stomach pump *n* pompe *f* stomacale.

stomp [stɒmp] *inf* ◇ *vi* marcher d'un pas lourd.
◇ *n* **1.** [tread] pas *m* lourd **2.** [dance] *jazz que l'on danse en frappant du pied pour marquer le rythme*.

stone [stəʊn] (*pl* **stones**) ◇ *n* **1.** [material] pierre *f* ▪ **the houses are built of ~** les maisons sont en pierre ▪ **are you made of ~?** *fig* n'as-tu donc pas de cœur? ▪ **a heart of ~** *fig* un cœur de pierre
2. [piece of rock] pierre *f*, caillou *m* ▪ [on beach] galet *m* ▪ **to fall like a ~** tomber comme une pierre ▶ **to leave no ~ unturned** remuer ciel et terre ▪ **it's within a ~'s throw of the countryside** c'est à deux pas de la campagne
3. [memorial] stèle *f*, pierre *f*
4. [gem] pierre *f*
5. MED calcul *m*
6. [in fruit] noyau *m*
7. (*pl* stone *OR pl* stones) [unit of weight] ≃ 6 kg ▪ **she weighs about 8 ~ *OR* ~s** elle pèse dans les 50 kilos.
◇ *adj* de *OR* en pierre.
◇ *vt* **1.** [fruit, olive] dénoyauter
2. [person, car] jeter des pierres sur, bombarder de pierres ▪ [as punishment] lapider
3. *UK phr* **~ the crows!** *inf*, **~ me!** *inf* mince alors!

Stone Age *n* : **the ~** l'âge *m* de (la) pierre.
◆ **Stone-Age** *comp* [man, dwelling, weapon] de l'âge de (la) pierre.

stone-broke *inf* = **stony-broke**.

stonechat ['stəʊntʃæt] *n* traquet *m* (pâtre).

stone-cold ◇ *adj* complètement froid.
◇ *adv inf* **~ sober** pas du tout soûl.

stonecrop ['stəʊnkrɒp] *n* orpin *m*.

stonecutter ['stəʊn,kʌtəʳ] *n* **1.** [person - of stone] tailleur *m* de pierre ; [- of precious stones] lapidaire *m* **2.** [machine] lapidaire *m*.

stoned△ [stəʊnd] *adj* [drunk] bourré△, schlass△ ▪ [drugged] défoncé△.

stone-dead *adj* raide mort.

stone-deaf *adj* complètement sourd.

stone-ground *adj* moulu à la pierre.

Stonehenge ['stəʊnhendʒ] *pr n monument mégalithique dans le sud de l'Angleterre*.

stonemason ['stəʊn,meɪsn] *n* tailleur *m* de pierre.

stonewall [,stəʊn'wɔːl] *vi* **1.** [filibuster] monopoliser la parole *(pour empêcher les autres de parler)* ▪ [avoid questions] donner des réponses évasives **2.** SPORT jouer très prudemment, bétonner.

stoneware ['stəʊnweəʳ] *n* (poterie *f* en) grès *m*.

stonewashed ['stəʊnwɒʃt] *adj* [jeans, denim] délavé *(avant l'achat)*.

stonework ['stəʊnwɜːk] *n* maçonnerie *f*, ouvrage *m* en pierre.

stonily ['stəʊnɪlɪ] *adv* froidement.

stony ['stəʊnɪ] (*comp* **stonier**, *superl* **stoniest**) *adj* **1.** [covered with stones - ground, soil, road, land] pierreux, caillouteux, rocailleux ; [- beach] de galets ▪ **his requests fell on ~ ground** *fig* ses démarches n'ont rien donné **2.** [stone-like - texture, feel] pierreux **3.** [unfeeling] insensible ▪ [look, silence] glacial ▪ **a ~ heart** un cœur de pierre.

stony-broke *adj UK inf* fauché (comme les blés), à sec.

stony-faced *adj* au visage impassible.

stood [stʊd] *pt* & *pp* ▷ **stand**.

stooge [stuːdʒ] *n* **1.** *inf pej* larbin *m*, laquais *m* **2.** THEAT [straight man] faire-valoir *m inv*.

stook [stʊk] ◇ *n* moyette *f*.
◇ *vt* moyetter.

stool [stuːl] *n* **1.** [seat] tabouret *m* ▪ **to fall between two ~s** *UK* être assis entre deux chaises **2.** MED selle *f* **3.** HORT [tree stump] souche *f* ▪ [shoot] rejet *m* de souche ▪ [base of plant] pied *m* de plante **4.** *US* [windowsill] rebord *m* de fenêtre.

stoolpigeon ['stuːl,pɪdʒn] *n inf* indicateur *m*, - trice *f*, indic *mf*, mouchard *m*, - e *f*.

stoop [stuːp] ◇ *vi* **1.** [bend down] se baisser, se pencher ▪ **she ~ed to pick up her pen** elle se baissa *OR* se pencha pour ramasser son stylo **2.** [stand, walk with a stoop] avoir le dos voûté **3.** [abase o.s.] s'abaisser ▪ **she would ~ to anything** elle est prête à toutes les bassesses ▶ **'She Stoops to Conquer'** ***Goldsmith*** 'Elle s'abaisse pour triompher' **4.** [condescend] daigner ▪ **she wouldn't ~ to doing the dirty work herself** elle ne s'abaisserait pas à faire elle-même le sale travail **5.** [bird of prey] fondre, plonger.

◇ *vt* baisser, pencher, incliner.
◇ *n* **1.** [of person] : **to walk with** *OR* **to have a ~** avoir le dos voûté **2.** [by bird of prey] attaque *f* en piqué **3.** *US* [veranda] véranda *f*, porche *m*.

stooping ['stu:pɪŋ] *adj* [back, shoulders, figure] voûté.

stop [stɒp] (*pret & pp* **stopped**, *cont* **stopping**) ◇ *vt* **1.** [cease, finish] arrêter, cesser ▪ **it hasn't stopped raining all day** il n'a pas arrêté de pleuvoir toute la journée ▪ **I wish they'd ~ that noise!** j'aimerais qu'ils arrêtent ce bruit! ▪ **~ it, that hurts!** arrête, ça fait mal!
2. [prevent] empêcher ▪ **to ~ sb (from) doing sthg** empêcher qqn de faire qqch ▪ **it's too late to ~ the meeting from taking place** il est trop tard pour empêcher la réunion d'avoir lieu ▪ **she's made up her mind and there's nothing we can do to ~ her** elle a pris sa décision et nous ne pouvons rien faire pour l'arrêter
3. [cause to halt] arrêter ▪ **I managed to ~ the car** j'ai réussi à arrêter la voiture ▪ **a woman stopped me to ask the way to the station** une femme m'a arrêté pour me demander le chemin de la gare ▪ **the sound of voices stopped him short** *OR* **stopped him in his tracks** un bruit de voix le fit s'arrêter net ➡ **to ~ a bullet** *inf* se prendre une balle ▪ **~ thief!** au voleur!
4. [arrest] arrêter
5. *UK* [withhold - sum of money, salary] retenir ▪ **the money will be stopped out of your wages** la somme sera retenue sur votre salaire
6. [interrupt] interrompre, arrêter ▪ [suspend] suspendre, arrêter ▪ [cut off] couper ▪ **once he starts talking about the war there's no stopping him** une fois qu'il commence à parler de la guerre, on ne peut plus l'arrêter ▪ **his father threatened to ~ his allowance** son père menaça de lui couper les vivres ▪ **to ~ a cheque** faire opposition à un chèque
7. [block - hole, gap] boucher ▪ **to ~ one's ears** se boucher les oreilles
8. [fill - tooth] plomber
9. MUS [string] presser ▪ [wind instrument] boucher.
◇ *vi* **1.** [halt, pause - person, vehicle, machine] arrêter, s'arrêter ▪ **go on, don't ~** continue, ne t'arrête pas ▪ **my watch has stopped** ma montre s'est *OR* est arrêtée ▪ **does the bus ~ near the church?** le bus s'arrête-t-il près de l'église? ▪ **we can ~ for tea on the way** nous pouvons nous arrêter en chemin pour prendre le thé ▪ **we drove from London to Edinburgh without stopping** nous avons roulé de Londres à Édimbourg d'une traite ▪ **the bus kept stopping and starting** le bus a fait beaucoup d'arrêts en cours de route ▪ **to ~ dead in one's tracks** s'arrêter net ▪ **I used to play football but I stopped last year** je jouais au football mais j'ai arrêté l'année dernière ▪ *fig* **she doesn't know where** *OR* **when to ~** elle ne sait pas s'arrêter ▪ **they'll ~ at nothing to get what they want** ils ne reculeront devant rien pour obtenir ce qu'ils veulent ▪ **if you stopped to consider, you'd never do anything** si on prenait le temps de réfléchir, on ne ferait jamais rien ▪ **they stopped short of actually harming him** ils ne lui ont pas fait de mal, mais il s'en est fallu de peu ▪ **she began talking then stopped short** elle commença à parler puis s'arrêta net *OR* brusquement
2. [come to an end] cesser, s'arrêter, se terminer ▪ **the rain has stopped** la pluie s'est arrêtée
3. [stay] rester ▪ [reside] loger ▪ **I'm late, I can't ~** je suis en retard, je ne peux pas rester ▪ **we've got friends stopping with us** nous avons des amis qui séjournent chez nous en ce moment ▪ **which hotel did you ~ at?** dans quel hôtel êtes-vous descendus?
◇ *n* **1.** [stopping place - for buses] arrêt *m* ; [- for trains] station *f*
2. [break - in journey, process] arrêt *m*, halte *f* ; [- in work] pause *f* ▪ **we made several ~s to pick up passengers** nous nous sommes arrêtés à plusieurs reprises pour prendre des passagers ▪ **our first ~ was Brussels** nous avons fait une première halte à Bruxelles ▪ **my whole career has been full of ~s and starts** ma carrière entière est faite de hauts et de bas
3. [standstill] arrêt *m* ▪ **to come to a ~** s'arrêter ▪ **she brought the bus to a ~** elle arrêta le bus
4. [end] : **to put a ~ to sthg** mettre fin *OR* un terme à qqch
5. *UK* [full stop] point *m* ▪ [in telegrams] stop *m*
6. [on organ] jeu *m* (d'orgue) ▪ **to pull out all the ~s (to do sthg)** remuer ciel et terre (pour faire qqch)
7. [plug, stopper] bouchon *m*
8. [blocking device] arrêt *m*
9. PHOT diaphragme *m*
10. LING occlusive *f*
11. [in bridge] contrôle *m*.
◇ *comp* [button, mechanism, signal] d'arrêt.
◆ **stop around** *US inf* = **stop by**.
◆ **stop away** *vi insep UK inf* rester absent.
◆ **stop by** *vi insep inf* passer ▪ **you must ~ by and see us next time you're in London** il faut que vous passiez nous voir la prochaine fois que vous venez à Londres ▪ **I'll ~ by at the chemist's on my way home** je passerai à la pharmacie en rentrant.
◆ **stop down** ◇ *vi insep* **1.** *UK* [gen] rester en bas ▪ **to ~ down a year** SCH redoubler une année
2. PHOT diaphragmer.
◇ *vt sep* PHOT diaphragmer.
◆ **stop in** *vi insep UK inf* **1.** [stay at home] ne pas sortir, rester à la maison
2. = **stop by**.
◆ **stop off** *vi insep* s'arrêter, faire une halte.
◆ **stop out** *vi insep UK inf* ne pas rentrer.
◆ **stop over** *vi insep* [gen] s'arrêter, faire une halte ▪ TRANSP [on flight, cruise] faire escale.
◆ **stop round** *US inf* = **stop by**.
◆ **stop up** *vi insep UK inf* ne pas se coucher, veiller.

stop-and-go *US* = **stop-go**.

stopcock ['stɒpkɒk] *n UK* robinet *m* d'arrêt.

stopgap ['stɒpgæp] ◇ *n* bouche-trou *m*.
◇ *adj* de remplacement ▪ **a ~ measure** un palliatif.

stop-go *adj* ECON : **~ policy** politique *f* économique en dents de scie *(alternant arrêt de la croissance et mesures de relance), politique f du stop-and-go.*

stoplight ['stɒplaɪt] *n* **1.** [traffic light] feu *m* rouge **2.** *UK* [brake-light] stop *m*.

stop-off *n* halte *f*, courte halte *f*.

stopover ['stɒp,əʊvər] *n* [gen] halte *f* ▪ [on flight] escale *f*.

stoppage ['stɒpɪdʒ] *n* **1.** [strike] grève *f*, arrêt *m* de travail **2.** *UK* [sum deducted] retenue *f* **3.** [halting, stopping] arrêt *m*, interruption *f* ▪ FTBL arrêt *m* de jeu **4.** [blockage] obstruction *f* ▪ MED occlusion *f*.

stopper ['stɒpər] ◇ *n* **1.** [for bottle, jar] bouchon *m* ▪ [for sink] bouchon *m*, bonde *f* ▪ [for pipe] obturateur *m* ▪ [on syringe] embout *m* de piston **2.** FTBL stoppeur *m* **3.** [in bridge] arrêt *m*.
◇ *vt* boucher, fermer.

stopping ['stɒpɪŋ] ◇ *n* **1.** [coming or bringing to a halt] arrêt *m* ▪ **~ distance** AUT distance *f* d'arrêt **2.** [blocking] obturation *f* ▪ **the ~ (up) of a leak** le colmatage d'une fuite **3.** [cancellation - of payment, leave etc] suspension *f* ; [- of service] suppression *f* ; [- of cheque] opposition *f*.
◇ *adj* [place] où l'on s'arrête.

stopping train *n UK* omnibus *m*.

stop press *n* nouvelles *fpl* de dernière minute ▪ **'~!'** 'dernière minute'.

stop sign *n* (signal *m* de) stop *m*.

stop valve *n* soupape *f* *OR* robinet *m* d'arrêt.

stopwatch ['stɒpwɒtʃ] *n* chronomètre *m*.

storage ['stɔ:rɪdʒ] ◇ *n* **1.** [putting into store] entreposage *m*, emmagasinage *m* ▪ [keeping, conservation] stockage *m* ▪ **our furniture is in ~** nos meubles sont au garde-meubles **2.** COMPUT (mise *f* en) mémoire *f*.
◇ *comp* **1.** [charges] de stockage, d'emmagasinage **2.** COMPUT de mémoire.

storage battery *n* accumulateur *m*, batterie *f* secondaire.

storage cell = **storage battery**.

storage heater, storage radiator *n* radiateur *m* à accumulation.

storage space *n* espace *m* de rangement.

storage tank *n* [for fuel] réservoir *m* (de stockage) ▪ [for rainwater] citerne *f*.

store [stɔːʳ] ◇ *n* **1.** [large shop] grand magasin *m* ■ *US* [shop] magasin *m* **2.** [stock - of goods] stock *m*, réserve *f*, provision *f* ; [- of food] provision *f* ; [- of facts, jokes, patience, knowledge] réserve *f* ; [- of wisdom] fonds *m* ■ **we should get in** *OR* **lay in a ~ of coal** nous devrions faire provision de charbon **3.** [place - warehouse] entrepôt *m*, dépôt *m* ; [- in office, home, shop] réserve *f* ; [- in factory] magasin *m*, réserve *f* ■ **furniture ~** garde-meubles *m inv* **4.** COMPUT [memory] mémoire *f* **5.** [value] : **to lay** *OR* **to put** *OR* **to set great ~ by sthg** faire grand cas de qqch.
◇ *comp* **1.** *US* [store-bought - gen] de commerce ; [- clothes] de confection **2.** [for storage] : **~ cupboard** placard *m* de rangement.
◇ *vt* **1.** [put away, put in store - goods, food] emmagasiner, entreposer ; [- grain, crop] engranger ; [- heat] accumuler, emmagasiner ; [- electricity] accumuler ; [- files, documents] classer ; [- facts, ideas] engranger, enregistrer dans sa mémoire ■ **we ~d our furniture at my mother's house** nous avons laissé *OR* mis nos meubles chez ma mère **2.** [keep] conserver, stocker ■ **'~ in a cool place'** 'à conserver au frais' **3.** [fill with provisions] approvisionner **4.** COMPUT stocker.
◆ **stores** *npl* [provisions] provisions *fpl*.
◆ **in store** *adv phr* : **they had a surprise in ~ for her** ils lui avaient réservé une surprise ■ **who knows what the future has in ~?** qui sait ce que l'avenir nous réserve? ■ **if only we'd realised all the problems that were in ~ for us** si seulement nous nous étions rendu compte de tous les problèmes qui nous attendaient.
◆ **store away, store up** *vt sep* garder en réserve ■ **he ~d (away) the anecdote for future use** il a noté l'anecdote en se disant qu'il la replacerait ■ **he's just storing up trouble for himself by keeping silent** en ne disant rien, il ne fait que se préparer des ennuis.

store-bought *adj* [gen] de commerce ■ [clothes] de confection ■ **a ~ cake** un gâteau acheté en pâtisserie.

store card *n* carte *f* de crédit *(d'un grand magasin)*.

store detective *n* vigile *m (dans un magasin)*.

storefront ['stɔːfrʌnt] *n US* devanture *f* de magasin.

storehouse ['stɔːhaʊs] (*pl* [-haʊzɪz]) *n* **1.** *liter* magasin *m*, entrepôt *m*, dépôt *m* **2.** *fig* [of information, memories] mine *f*.

storekeeper ['stɔːˌkiːpəʳ] *n* **1.** [in warehouse] magasinier *m*, - ère *f* **2.** *US* [shopkeeper] commerçant *m*, - e *f*.

storeman ['stɔːmən] (*pl* **storemen** [-mən]) *n UK* manutentionnaire *m*.

storeroom ['stɔːrʊm] *n* **1.** [in office, shop] réserve *f* ■ [in factory] magasin *m*, réserve *f* ■ [in home] débarras *m* **2.** NAUT soute *f*, magasin *m*.

storey *UK* (*pl* **storeys**), **story** *US* (*pl* **stories**) ['stɔːrɪ] *n* étage *m*.

-storey(ed) *UK*, **-storied** *US* ['stɔːrɪ(d)] *in cpds* : **a single-/five- building** un bâtiment à un étage/à cinq étages.

stork [stɔːk] *n* cigogne *f*.

storm [stɔːm] ◇ *n* **1.** METEOR tempête *f* ■ [thunderstorm] orage *m* ■ [on Beaufort scale] tempête *f* ■ **it was a ~ in a teacup** *UK* ce fut une tempête dans un verre d'eau **2.** *fig* [furore] tempête *f*, ouragan *m* ■ **the arms deal caused a political ~** la vente d'armes a déclenché un véritable scandale politique ■ **a ~ of protest** une déferlante de critiques ■ **a ~ of criticism** une marée de condamnations **3.** MIL : **to take by ~** prendre d'assaut ■ **the show took Broadway by ~** *fig* le spectacle a connu un succès foudroyant à Broadway.
◇ *vi* **1.** [go angrily] : **to ~ in/out** entrer/sortir comme un ouragan ■ **she ~ed off without saying a word** elle est partie furieuse, sans dire un mot **2.** [be angry] tempêter, fulminer **3.** [rain] tomber à verse ■ [wind] souffler violemment ■ [snow] faire rage.
◇ *vt* emporter, enlever d'assaut.

storm cellar *n US* abri *m* contre les cyclones.

storm cloud *n* **1.** METEOR nuage *m* d'orage **2.** *fig* nuage *m* menaçant.

storm cone *n* cône *m* de tempête.

storm door *n US* porte *f* extérieure *(qui double la porte de la maison pour éviter les courants d'air)*.

storming ['stɔːmɪŋ] *n* [attack] assaut *m* ■ [capture] prise *f* (d'assaut) ■ **the ~ of the Bastille** HIST la prise de la Bastille.

storm lantern *n* lampe *f* tempête.

stormproof ['stɔːmpruːf] *adj* à l'épreuve de la tempête.

storm trooper *n* membre *m* des troupes d'assaut ■ **the ~s** les troupes *fpl* d'assaut.
◆ **stormtrooper** *adj* [tactics] brutal, impitoyable.

storm troops *npl* troupes *fpl* d'assaut.

storm window *n* contre-fenêtre *f*.

stormy ['stɔːmɪ] (*comp* **stormier**, *superl* **stormiest**) *adj* **1.** [weather] orageux, d'orage ■ [sea] houleux, démonté ■ **it was a ~ day** il faisait un temps orageux **2.** *fig* [relationship] orageux ■ [debate] houleux ■ [look] furieux ■ [career, life] tumultueux, mouvementé.

story ['stɔːrɪ] (*pl* **stories**) *n* **1.** [tale, work of fiction - spoken] histoire *f* ; [- written] histoire *f*, conte *m* ■ **to tell sb a ~** raconter une histoire à qqn ■ **this is a true ~** c'est une histoire vraie ■ **a collection of her poems and stories** un recueil de ses poèmes et nouvelles ■ **it's always the same old ~** *fig* c'est toujours la même histoire
2. [plot - story line] intrigue *f*, scénario *m*
3. [account] histoire *f* ■ **I got the inside ~ from his wife** j'ai appris la vérité sur cette histoire par sa femme ■ **well, that's my ~ and I'm sticking to it** *hum* c'est la version officielle ■ **the witness changed his ~** le témoin est revenu sur sa version des faits ■ **but that's another ~** mais ça, c'est une autre histoire ■ **that's not the whole ~, that's only part of the ~** mais ce n'est pas tout ■ **we'll probably never know the whole** *OR* **full ~** nous ne saurons peut-être jamais le fin mot de l'histoire ■ **to cut** *UK OR* **make** *US* **a long ~ short** enfin bref
4. [history] histoire *f* ■ **his life ~** l'histoire de sa vie ■ **that's the ~ of my life!** *hum* ça m'arrive tout le temps!
5. *euph* [lie] histoire *f*
6. [rumour] rumeur *f*, bruit *m* ■ **there's a ~ going about that they're getting divorced** le bruit court qu'ils vont divorcer ■ **or so the ~ goes** c'est du moins ce que l'on raconte
7. PRESS [article] article *m* ■ **there's a front-page ~ about** *OR* **on the riots** il y a un article en première page sur les émeutes ■ **all the papers ran** *OR* **carried the ~** tous les journaux en ont parlé ‖ [event, affair] affaire *f* ■ **what's the ~?** quelle nouvelle? ■ **the ~ broke just after the morning papers had gone to press** on a appris la nouvelle juste après la mise sous presse des journaux du matin
8. *US* = storey.

storyboard ['stɔːrɪbɔːd] *n* story-board *m*.

storybook ['stɔːrɪbʊk] ◇ *n* livre *m* de contes.
◇ *adj* : **a ~ ending** une fin romanesque ■ **a ~ romance** une idylle de conte de fées.

story line *n* intrigue *f*, scénario *m*.

storyteller ['stɔːrɪˌteləʳ] *n* **1.** conteur *m*, - euse *f* **2.** *euph* [liar] menteur *m*, - euse *f*.

stout [staʊt] ◇ *adj* **1.** [corpulent] gros, grosse *f*, corpulent, fort **2.** [strong - stick] solide ; [- structure, material] solide, robuste **3.** [brave] vaillant, courageux ■ [firm, resolute - resistance, opposition, enemy] acharné ; [- support, supporter] fidèle, loyal.
◇ *n* stout *m*, bière *f* brune forte.

stouthearted [ˌstaʊt'hɑːtɪd] *adj lit* vaillant, courageux.

stoutly ['staʊtlɪ] *adv* **1.** [solidly] solidement, robustement **2.** [bravely] vaillamment, courageusement ■ [firmly, resolutely - resist, defend, oppose] avec acharnement ; [- support] fidèlement, loyalement.

stove [stəʊv] ◇ *pt & pp* ▷ **stave**.
◇ *n* **1.** [for heating] poêle *m* **2.** [cooker - gen] cuisinière *f* ; [- portable] réchaud *m* ■ [kitchen range] fourneau *m* **3.** INDUST [kiln] four *m*, étuve *f*.

stove-in *adj US* défoncé, enfoncé.

stovepipe ['stəʊvpaɪp] *n* **1.** *liter* tuyau *m* de poêle **2.** *inf* **~ (hat)** tuyau *m* de poêle.

stow [stəʊ] *vt* **1.** [store] ranger, stocker ■ [in warehouse] emmagasiner ■ NAUT [cargo] arrimer ■ [equipment, sails] ranger ■ **he ~ed the keys behind the clock** [hid] il a caché les clés derrière la pendule ; [hurriedly] il a fait disparaître les clés derrière la pendule **2.** [pack, fill] remplir.
◆ **stow away** ◇ *vi insep* [on ship, plane] s'embarquer clandestinement, être un passager clandestin.
◇ *vt sep* **1.** = **stow** *(sense 1)* **2.** *UK inf* [food] enfourner.

stowage ['stəʊɪdʒ] *n* **1.** [of goods - in warehouse] emmagasinage *m* ; [- on ship] arrimage *m* **2.** [capacity - gen] espace *m* utile *OR* de rangement ; [- in warehouse] espace *m* d'emmagasinage ; [- on ship] espace *m* d'arrimage.

stowaway ['stəʊəweɪ] *n* passager *m* clandestin, passagère *f* clandestine.

straddle ['strædl] ◇ *vt* **1.** [sit astride of - horse, bicycle, chair, wall] chevaucher ■ [mount - horse, bicycle] enfourcher ■ [step over - ditch, obstacle] enjamber **2.** [span, spread over] enjamber ■ **the park ~s the state line** le parc est à cheval sur la frontière entre les États **3.** MIL [target] encadrer **4.** *US inf* **to ~ the fence** [be noncommittal] ne pas prendre position.
◇ *vi inf US inf fig* [sit on the fence] ne pas prendre position.

strafe [strɑːf] *vt* [with machine guns] mitrailler (au sol) ■ [with bombs] bombarder.

straggle ['strægl] ◇ *vi* **1.** [spread in long line - roots, creeper, branches] pousser de façon désordonnée ■ [be scattered - trees, houses] être disséminé ■ **the suburbs ~d on for miles along the railway line** la banlieue s'étendait sur des kilomètres le long de la voie ferrée ■ [hang untidily - hair] pendre (lamentablement) **2.** [linger] traîner, traînasser.
◇ *n* : **there was a constant ~ of visitors** il y a eu un défilé ininterrompu de visiteurs ■ **all I saw was a ~ of houses/trees on the hillside** je n'ai aperçu que quelques maisons disséminées/ quelques arbres disséminés sur la colline ■ **a ~ of islands** un long chapelet d'îles.

straggler ['stræglər] *n* **1.** [lingerer] traînard *m*, - e *f* ■ [in race] retardataire *mf* **2.** BOT gourmand *m*.

straggling ['stræglɪŋ] *adj* [vine, plant] maigre, (qui pousse) tout en longueur ■ [houses, trees] disséminé ■ [village, street] tout en longueur ■ [beard] épars.

straggly ['stræglɪ] *adj* [hair] maigre ■ [beard] épars, hirsute ■ [roots] long et mince.

straight [streɪt] ◇ *adj* **1.** [not curved - line, road, nose] droit ; [- hair] raide ■ **keep your back ~** tiens-toi droit, redresse-toi **2.** [level, upright] droit ■ **the picture isn't ~** le tableau n'est pas droit *OR* est de travers ■ **to put** *OR* **to set ~** [picture] remettre d'aplomb, redresser ; [hat, tie] ajuster ■ **hold** *OR* **keep the tray ~** tenez le plateau bien droit
3. [honest, frank] franc, franche *f*, droit ■ **to be ~ with sb** être franc avec qqn ■ **to give sb a ~ answer** répondre franchement à qqn ■ **he's always been ~ in his dealings with me** il a toujours été honnête avec moi ■ **to do some ~ talking** parler franchement ■ **at the meeting he did some ~ talking** il n'a pas mâché ses mots à la réunion ■ **are you being ~ with me?** est-ce que tu joues franc jeu avec moi?
4. [correct, clear] clair ■ **to put** *OR* **to set the record ~** mettre les choses au clair ■ **just to set the record ~** pour que ce soit bien clair ■ **let's get this ~** entendons-nous bien sur ce point ■ **have you put her ~?** as-tu mis les choses au point avec elle? ■ **now just you get this ~!** mets-toi bien ceci dans la tête!, qu'on se mette bien d'accord sur ce point!
5. [tidy, in order - room, desk, accounts] en ordre ■ **to put** *OR* **to set ~** [room, house] mettre en ordre, mettre de l'ordre dans ; [affairs] mettre de l'ordre dans
6. [quits] quitte
7. [direct] droit, direct ■ **he hit him a ~ left** il lui a porté un direct du gauche | POL : **~ fight** *une élection où ne se présentent que deux candidats* ▶ **to vote a~ ticket** *US* voter pour une liste sans panachage
8. [pure, utter] pur ■ **it's just ~ propaganda** c'est de la propagande pure et simple
9. [consecutive] consécutif, de suite ■ **to have three ~ wins** gagner trois fois de suite *OR* d'affilée ■ **a ~ flush** CARDS une quinte flush
10. [neat - whisky, vodka] sec, sèche *f*
11. [serious] sérieux ■ **to keep a ~ face** garder son sérieux ■ **it's the first ~ role she's played in years** c'est son premier rôle sérieux depuis des années
12. *inf* [conventional] vieux jeu *(inv)* ■ [heterosexual] hétéro ■ [not a drug user] qui ne se drogue pas
13. AUT [cylinders] en ligne ■ **a ~ eight engine** un moteur huit cylindres en ligne
14. GEOM [angle] plat
15. *US* SCH : **he got ~ As all term** il n'a eu que de très bonnes notes tout le semestre ■ **a ~ A student** un étudiant brillant.
◇ *adv* **1.** [in a straight line] droit, en ligne droite ■ **the rocket shot ~ up** la fusée est montée à la verticale *OR* en ligne droite ■ **to shoot ~** viser juste | *fig* **I can't see ~** je ne vois pas bien ■ **I can't think ~** je n'ai pas les idées claires ▶ **to go ~** *inf* [criminal] revenir dans le droit chemin
2. [upright - walk, sit, stand] (bien) droit ■ **sit up ~!** tiens-toi droit *OR* redresse-toi (sur ta chaise)!
3. [directly] (tout) droit, directement ■ **he looked me ~ in the eye** il me regarda droit dans les yeux ■ **it's ~ across the road** c'est juste en face ■ **the car came ~ at me** la voiture a foncé droit sur moi ■ **go ~ to bed!** va tout de suite te coucher! ■ **the ball went ~ through the window** la balle est passée par la fenêtre ■ **they mostly go ~ from school to university** pour la plupart, ils passent directement du lycée à l'université ■ **to come ~ to the point** aller droit au fait ■ **~ ahead** tout droit ■ **he looked ~ ahead** il regarda droit devant lui ■ **~ off** *inf* sur-le-champ, tout de suite ■ **~ on** tout droit ■ **go ~ on till you come to a roundabout** continuez tout droit jusqu'à ce que vous arriviez à un rond-point
4. [frankly] franchement, carrément, tout droit ■ **I told him ~ (out) what I thought of him** je lui ai dit franchement ce que je pensais de lui ▶ **~ up** *UK inf* [honestly] sans blague
5. [neat, unmixed] : **to drink whisky ~** boire son whisky sec.
◇ *n* **1.** [on racecourse, railway track] ligne *f* droite ■ **the final** *OR* **home ~** la dernière ligne droite ▶ **to keep to the ~ and narrow** rester dans le droit chemin
2. [level] : **to be out of ~** *UK* être de biais *OR* de travers ■ **on the ~** TEX de droit fil
3. *inf* [person] : **he's a ~** [conventional person] il est conventionnel, c'est quelqu'un de conventionnel ; [heterosexual] il est hétéro, c'est un hétéro.

straightaway [ˌstreɪtə'weɪ] ◇ *adv* tout de suite, sur-le-champ.
◇ *adj US* droit.
◇ *n US* ligne *f* droite.

straighten ['streɪtn] ◇ *vt* **1.** [remove bend or twist from - line, wire] redresser ; [- nail] redresser, défausser ; [- wheel] redresser, dévoiler ; [- hair] décrêper **2.** [adjust - picture] redresser, remettre d'aplomb ; [- tie, hat] redresser, ajuster ; [- hem] arrondir, rectifier ■ **she ~ed her back** *OR* **shoulders** elle se redressa ■ **he had his nose ~ed** il s'est fait redresser le nez **3.** [tidy - room, papers] ranger, mettre de l'ordre dans ■ [organize - affairs, accounts] mettre en ordre, mettre de l'ordre dans.
◇ *vi* [person] se dresser, se redresser ■ [plant] pousser droit ■ [hair] devenir raide ■ [road] devenir droit.
◆ **straighten out** ◇ *vt sep* **1.** [nail, wire] redresser **2.** [situation] débrouiller, arranger ■ [problem] résoudre ■ [mess, confusion] mettre de l'ordre dans, débrouiller ■ **don't worry, things will ~ themselves out** ne t'en fais pas, les choses vont s'arranger **3.** : **to ~ sb out** *inf* [help] remettre qqn dans la bonne voie ; [punish] remettre qqn à sa place ■ **I'll soon ~ her out!** je vais lui apprendre!
◇ *vi insep* [road] devenir droit ■ [plant] pousser droit ■ [hair] devenir raide.
◆ **straighten up** ◇ *vi insep* [person] se dresser, se redresser ■ [plant] pousser droit.
◇ *vt sep* [room, papers] ranger, mettre de l'ordre dans ■ [affairs] mettre de l'ordre dans, mettre en ordre.

straight-faced *adj* qui garde son sérieux, impassible.

straightforward [ˌstreɪt'fɔːwəd] *adj* **1.** [direct - person] direct ; [- explanation] franc, franche *f* ; [- account] très clair ■ **it's impossible to get a ~ answer out of her** il est impossible d'obtenir d'elle une réponse nette et précise **2.** [easy, simple - task, problem] simple, facile ; [- instructions] clair ■ **it was all quite ~** ce n'était pas compliqué du tout **3.** [pure, utter] pur.

straightforwardly [ˌstreɪtˈfɔːwədlɪ] *adv* **1.** [honestly - act, behave] avec franchise ; [- answer] franchement, sans détour **2.** [without complications] simplement, sans anicroche.

straightjacket [ˈstreɪtˌdʒækɪt] = **straitjacket.**

straightlaced [ˌstreɪtˈleɪst] = **straitlaced.**

straight man *n* faire-valoir *m inv.*

straight-out *adj* US *inf* **1.** [forthright - answer] net ; [- refusal] catégorique **2.** [utter - liar, hypocrite] fieffé ; [- lie, dishonesty] pur ; [- opponent, supporter] inconditionnel.

straight razor *n* US rasoir *m* à main.

strain [streɪn] ◇ *n* **1.** [on rope, girder - pressure] pression *f* ; [- tension] tension *f* ; [- pull] traction *f* ; [- weight] poids *m* ▪ **the rope snapped under the ~** la corde a rompu sous la tension ▪ **the weight put too much ~ on the rope** le poids a exercé une trop forte tension sur la corde ▪ **to collapse under the ~** [bridge, animal] s'effondrer sous le poids ▪ **I took most of the ~** c'est moi qui ai fourni le plus gros effort ▪ **the buttress takes the ~ off the wall** le contrefort réduit la pression qui s'exerce sur le mur ▪ **the girder can't take the ~** la poutre ne peut pas supporter cette pression OR sollicitation ▪ **the war is putting a great ~ on the country's resources** la guerre pèse lourd sur OR grève sérieusement les ressources du pays
2. [mental or physical effort] (grand) effort *m* ▪ [overwork] surmenage *m* ▪ [tiredness] (grande) fatigue *f* ▪ **he's beginning to feel/show the ~** il commence à sentir la fatigue/à donner des signes de fatigue ▪ **I've been under great physical ~** je me suis surmené ▪ **the ~ of making polite conversation** l'effort que ça demande de faire la conversation à quelqu'un | [stress] stress *m*, tension *f* OR fatigue *f* nerveuse ▪ **the situation has put our family under a great deal of ~** la situation a mis notre famille à rude épreuve ▪ **he can't take the ~ anymore** il ne peut plus supporter cette situation stressante ▪ **it's a terrible ~ on her nerves** elle trouve ça difficile à supporter nerveusement ▪ **the arrival of a new secretary took the immediate ~ off me** avec l'arrivée d'une nouvelle secrétaire, j'ai été immédiatement soulagée d'une partie de mon travail ▪ **I couldn't stand the ~ of commuting** je trouvais trop épuisant de prendre les transports en commun tous les matins
3. MED [of muscle] froissement *m* ▪ [sprain - of ankle, wrist] entorse *f* ▪ **to give one's back a ~** se donner un tour de reins
4. [breed, variety - of animals] lignée *f*, race *f* ▪ [of plant, virus etc] souche *f*
5. [style] genre *m*, style *m*
6. [streak, touch] fond *m*, tendance *f* ▪ **there is a ~ of madness in the family** il y a une prédisposition à la folie dans la famille.
◇ *vt* **1.** [rope, cable, girder] tendre (fortement) ▪ **to be ~ed to breaking point** être tendu au point de se rompre | [resources, economy, budget] grever
2. [force - voice] forcer ▪ **he ~ed his ears to hear what they were saying** il tendit l'oreille pour entendre ce qu'ils disaient ▪ **to ~ every nerve OR sinew to do sthg** s'efforcer de faire qqch
3. [hurt, damage - muscle] froisser ; [- eyes] fatiguer ▪ **you'll ~ your eyes** tu vas te fatiguer les yeux ▪ **to ~ one's back** se donner un tour de reins ▪ **I've ~ed my arm** je me suis froissé un muscle du bras ▪ **to ~ o.s.** [by gymnastics, lifting] se froisser un muscle ; [by overwork] se surmener ▪ **mind you don't ~ yourself lifting that typewriter** attention de ne pas te faire mal en soulevant cette machine à écrire ▪ *hum* **don't ~ yourself!** surtout ne te fatigue pas!
4. [force - meaning] forcer ; [- word] forcer le sens de
5. [test - patience] mettre à l'épreuve, abuser de ; [- friendship, relationship] mettre à l'épreuve, mettre à rude épreuve
6. CULIN [soup, milk] passer ▪ [vegetables] (faire) égoutter
7. *lit* [press - child, lover] serrer.
◇ *vi* **1.** [pull] tirer fort ▪ [push] pousser fort ▪ **she was ~ing at the door** [pull] elle tirait sur la porte de toutes ses forces ; [push] elle poussait (sur) la porte de toutes ses forces ▪ **the dog ~ed at the leash** le chien tirait sur sa laisse ▪ **to be ~ing at the leash** *fig* piaffer d'impatience ▪ **she ~ed under the weight** elle ployait sous la charge
2. [strive] s'efforcer, faire beaucoup d'efforts ▪ **to ~ to do sthg** s'efforcer de faire qqch
3. [rope, cable] se tendre.
◆ **strains** *npl* [in music] accents *mpl*, accords *mpl* ▪ [in verse] accents *mpl*.
◆ **strain off** *vt sep* [liquid] vider, égoutter.

strained [streɪnd] *adj* **1.** [forced - manner, laugh] forcé, contraint ; [- voice] forcé ; [- language, style etc] forcé, exagéré **2.** [tense - atmosphere, relations, person] tendu **3.** [sprained - ankle, limb] foulé ; [- muscle] froissé ▪ **to have a ~ shoulder** s'être froissé un muscle à l'épaule ▪ **to have a ~ neck** avoir un torticolis ▪ [tired - eyes] fatigué **4.** CULIN [liquid] filtré ▪ [soup] passé ▪ [vegetables] égoutté ▪ [baby food] en purée.

strainer [ˈstreɪnəʳ] *n* passoire *f.*

strait [streɪt] *n* GEOG : **~, ~s** détroit *m.*
◆ **straits** *npl* [difficulties] gêne *f*, situation *f* fâcheuse ▪ **to be in financial ~s** avoir des ennuis financiers OR des problèmes d'argent.

STRAITS

the Straits of Dover le pas de Calais ;
the Strait of Gibraltar le détroit de Gibraltar ;
the Strait of Hormuz or Ormuz le détroit d'Hormuz ou d'Ormuz ;
the Strait of Magellan le détroit de Magellan ;
the Strait of Malacca le détroit de Malacca.

straitened [ˈstreɪtnd] *adj* : **in ~ circumstances** dans le besoin OR la gêne.

straitjacket [ˈstreɪtˌdʒækɪt] *n* camisole *f* de force.

straitlaced [ˌstreɪtˈleɪst] *adj* collet monté *(inv)* ▪ **he was always very proper and ~** il était toujours très digne et très guindé.

strand [strænd] ◇ *n* **1.** [of thread, string, wire] brin *m*, toron *m* ▪ **a ~ of hair** une mèche de cheveux **2.** [in argument, plot, sequence] fil *m* ▪ **the main ~ of the narrative** le fil conducteur (du récit) **3.** *lit* [beach] plage *f* ▪ [shore] grève *f*, rivage *m.*
◇ *vt* **1.** [ship, whale] échouer ▪ **the ship was ~ed on a mudbank** le bateau s'est échoué sur un banc de vase **2.** *(usu passive)* **to be ~ed** [person, vehicle] rester en plan OR coincé ▪ **she was ~ed in Seville with no money** elle s'est retrouvée coincée à Séville sans un sou vaillant.
◆ **Strand** *pr n* : **the Strand** *quartier du centre de Londres célèbre pour ses théâtres.*

stranded [ˈstrændɪd] *adj* **1.** [person, car] bloqué ▪ **the ~ holidaymakers camped out in the airport** les vacanciers, ne pouvant pas partir, campèrent à l'aéroport **2.** BIOL & CHEM [molecule, sequence] torsadé.

strange [streɪndʒ] *adj* **1.** [odd] étrange, bizarre ▪ [peculiar] singulier, insolite ▪ **it's ~ that he should be so late** c'est bizarre OR étrange qu'il ait tant de retard ▪ **she has some ~ ideas** elle a des idées bizarres OR de drôles d'idées ▪ **~ to say, I've never been there** chose curieuse OR étrange, je n'y suis jamais allé ▪ **~ as it may seem** aussi étrange que cela paraisse OR puisse paraître ▪ **truth is ~r than fiction** la vérité dépasse la fiction **2.** [unfamiliar] inconnu ▪ **to find o.s. in ~ surroundings** se trouver dans un endroit inconnu ▪ **I woke up to find a ~ man in my room** lorsque je me suis réveillé il y avait un inconnu dans ma chambre **3.** [unaccustomed] : **he is still ~ to city life** il n'est pas encore accoutumé à OR il n'a pas encore l'habitude de la vie citadine **4.** [unwell] bizarre ▪ **to look/to feel ~** avoir l'air/se sentir bizarre **5.** PHYS [matter, particle] étrange.

strangely [ˈstreɪndʒlɪ] *adv* étrangement, bizarrement ▪ **~ enough, I never saw him again** chose curieuse OR chose étrange, je ne l'ai jamais revu ▪ **her face was ~ familiar to him** son visage lui était singulièrement familier ▪ **he spoke in a ~ calm voice** il parla d'une voix étonnamment calme.

strangeness [ˈstreɪndʒnɪs] *n* **1.** [of person, situation] étrangeté *f*, bizarrerie *f*, singularité *f* **2.** PHYS étrangeté *f.*

stranger [ˈstreɪndʒəʳ] *n* **1.** [unknown person] inconnu *m*, - e *f* ▪ **never talk to ~s** ne parle jamais à des inconnus ▪ **we are complete ~s** nous ne nous sommes jamais rencontrés ▪ **we were ~s until yesterday** nous ne nous connaissons que depuis hier ▪ **a perfect ~** un parfait inconnu ▪ **hello ~!** *hum* tiens, un revenant! **2.** [person from elsewhere] étranger *m*, - ère *f* ▪ **I'm a ~ here myself** je ne suis pas d'ici non plus **3.** [novice] novice *m* ▪ **I am not exactly a ~ to jazz** je ne suis pas complètement ignorant en matière de jazz ▪ **he is no ~ to loneliness/misfortune** il sait ce qu'est la solitude/le malheur.

strangle ['stræŋgl] *vt* **1.** *liter* étrangler **2.** *fig* [opposition, growth, originality] étrangler, étouffer.

strangled ['stræŋgld] *adj* [cry, sob] étranglé, étouffé ■ [voice] étranglé.

stranglehold ['stræŋglhəʊld] *n* [grip around throat] étranglement *m*, étouffement *m*, strangulation *f* ■ [in wrestling] étranglement *m* ■ **to have a ~ on sb** *liter & fig* tenir qqn à la gorge ■ **to have a ~ on sthg** *fig* tenir qqch à la gorge ■ **superstition still retains a ~ on the country** l'emprise des superstitions sur le pays est toujours très forte ■ **to have a ~ on the market/economy** jouir d'un monopole sur le marché/l'économie.

strangler ['stræŋglər] *n* étrangleur *m*, - euse *f*.

strangling ['stræŋglɪŋ] *n* **1.** [killing] étranglement *m*, strangulation *f* ■ *fig* [of opposition, protest, originality] étranglement *m*, étouffement *m* **2.** [case] : **that brings to five the number of ~s** cela porte à cinq le nombre de personnes étranglées.

strangulate ['stræŋgjuleɪt] *vt* **1.** MED étrangler **2.** = **strangle**.

strangulation [ˌstræŋgju'leɪʃn] *n* strangulation *f* ■ **the victim died of ~** la victime est morte étranglée.

strap [stræp] (*pret & pp* **strapped**, *cont* **strapping**) ◇ *n* **1.** [belt - of leather] courroie *f*, sangle *f*, lanière *f* ; [- of cloth, metal] sangle *f*, bande *f* **2.** [support - for bag, camera, on harness] sangle *f* ■ [fastening - for dress, bra] bretelle *f* ; [- for hat, bonnet] bride *f* ; [- for helmet] attache *f* ; [- for sandal] lanière *f* ; [- under trouser leg] sous-pied *m* ; [- for watch] bracelet *m* **3.** [as punishment] : **to give sb/to get the ~** administrer/recevoir une correction (à coups de ceinture) **4.** [on bus, underground] poignée *f* **5.** = **strop 6.** TECH lien *m*.
◇ *vt* sangler, attacher.
◆ **strap down** *vt sep* sangler, attacher avec une sangle OR une courroie.
◆ **strap in** *vt sep* [in car] attacher la ceinture (de sécurité) de ■ [child - in high chair, pram] attacher avec un harnais OR avec une ceinture ■ **he strapped himself into the driving seat** il s'est installé au volant et a attaché sa ceinture de sécurité ■ **are you strapped in?** as-tu mis ta ceinture?
◆ **strap on** *vt sep* [bag, watch] attacher.
◆ **strap up** *vt sep* [suitcase, parcel] sangler ■ [limbs, ribs] mettre un bandage à, bander.

straphang ['stræphæŋ] *vi UK inf* voyager debout *(dans les transports en commun)*.

straphanger ['stræphæŋər] *n UK inf* voyageur *m*, - euse *f* debout *(dans les transports en commun)*.

strapless ['stræplɪs] *adj* [dress, bra etc] sans bretelles.

strapped [stræpt] *adj inf* **to be ~ for cash** être fauché.

strapping ['stræpɪŋ] *adj inf* costaud ■ **a fine ~ girl** un beau brin de fille.

Strasbourg ['stræzbɜ:g] *pr n* Strasbourg.

strata ['strɑ:tə] *pl* ▷ **stratum**.

stratagem ['strætədʒəm] *n* stratagème *m*.

strategic [strə'ti:dʒɪk] *adj* stratégique.

strategically [strə'ti:dʒɪklɪ] *adv* stratégiquement, du point de vue de la stratégie.

strategist ['strætɪdʒɪst] *n* stratège *m*.

strategy ['strætɪdʒɪ] (*pl* **strategies**) *n* [gen - MIL] stratégie *f* ■ **marketing strategies** stratégies de marketing.

stratification [ˌstrætɪfɪ'keɪʃn] *n* stratification *f*.

stratified ['strætɪfaɪd] *adj* stratifié, en couches.

stratify ['strætɪfaɪ] (*pret & pp* **stratified**) ◇ *vt* stratifier.
◇ *vi* se stratifier.

stratocumulus [ˌstrætəʊ'kju:mjʊləs] (*pl* **stratocumuli** [-laɪ]) *n* stratocumulus *m*.

stratosphere ['strætəˌsfɪər] *n* stratosphère *f*.

stratum ['strɑ:təm] (*pl* **strata** ['strɑ:tə]) *n* **1.** GEOL strate *f*, couche *f* **2.** *fig* couche *f*.

Stravinsky [strə'vɪnskɪ] *pr n* Stravinski.

straw [strɔ:] ◇ *n* **1.** AGRIC paille *f* ■ **man of ~** *UK*, **~ man** *US* homme *m* de paille **2.** [for drinking] paille *f* ■ **to drink sthg through a ~** boire qqch avec une paille **3.** *phr* **to catch** OR **to clutch at a ~** OR **at ~s** se raccrocher désespérément à la moindre lueur d'espoir ■ **to draw** OR **to get the short ~** être tiré au sort, être de corvée ■ **that's the last ~** OR **the ~ that breaks the camel's back** c'est la goutte d'eau qui fait déborder le vase ■ **I don't care a ~** OR **two ~s!** *UK inf* je m'en fiche! ■ **it's not worth a ~** *inf* ça ne vaut pas un clou.
◇ *comp* [gen] de OR en paille ■ [roof] en paille, en chaume.

strawberry ['strɔ:bərɪ] (*pl* **strawberries**) ◇ *n* [fruit] fraise *f* ■ [plant] fraisier *m*.
◇ *comp* [jam] de fraises ■ [tart] aux fraises ■ [ice cream] à la fraise.

STRAWBERRIES AND CREAM

En Grande-Bretagne, on déguste traditionnellement des fraises à la crème lors de manifestations en plein air, notamment pendant les tournois de tennis à Wimbledon.

strawberry blonde ◇ *adj* blond vénitien *(inv)*.
◇ *n* blonde *f* qui tire sur le roux.

strawberry mark *n* tache *f* de vin, envie *f*.

straw-coloured *adj* (couleur) paille *(inv)*.

straw hat *n* chapeau *m* de paille.

straw mattress *n* paillasse *f*.

straw poll *n* [vote] vote *m* blanc ■ [opinion poll] sondage *m* d'opinion.

straw vote *US* = **straw poll**.

stray [streɪ] ◇ *vi* **1.** [child, animal] errer ■ **some sheep had ~ed onto the railway line** des moutons s'étaient aventurés sur la ligne de chemin de fer ■ **to ~ away** [get lost] s'égarer ; [go away] s'en aller ■ **the children ~ed (away) from the rest of the group** les enfants se sont écartés du groupe ■ **to ~ from the fold** *liter & fig* s'écarter du troupeau ■ **to ~ (away) from the right path** *liter & fig* faire fausse route **2.** [speaker, writer] s'éloigner du sujet ■ **but I am ~ing from the point** mais je m'écarte du sujet **3.** [thoughts] errer, vagabonder ■ **her thoughts ~ed (back) to her days in Japan** elle se mit à penser à sa vie au Japon.
◇ *n* [dog] chien *m* errant OR perdu ■ [cat] chat *m* errant OR perdu ■ [cow, sheep] animal *m* égaré ■ [child] enfant *m* perdu OR abandonné.
◇ *adj* **1.** [lost - dog, cat] perdu, errant ; [- cow, sheep] égaré ; [- child] perdu, abandonné **2.** [random - bullet] perdu ; [- thought] vagabond ; [- memory] fugitif ■ **she pushed back a few ~ curls** elle repoussa quelques mèches folles OR rebelles **3.** [occasional - car, boat] isolé, rare.
◆ **strays** *npl* RADIO & TELEC parasites *mpl*, friture *f*.

streak [stri:k] ◇ *n* **1.** [smear - of blood, dirt] filet *m* ; [- of ink, paint] traînée *f* ■ **the tears had left grubby ~s down her face** les larmes avaient laissé des traînées sales sur ses joues ■ [line, stripe - of light] trait *m*, rai *m* ; [- of ore] filon *m*, veine *f* ; [- in marble] veine *f* ■ **the carpet has green ~s** la moquette est striée de vert ■ **her hair has grey ~s in it** elle a les cheveux gris ■ **to have blond ~s put in one's hair** se faire faire des mèches blondes ■ **~s of lightning lit up the sky** des éclairs zébraient le ciel ■ **they drove past like a ~ of lightning** leur voiture est passée comme un éclair
2. [of luck] période *f* ■ **I've had a ~ of (good) luck** je viens de traverser une période faste ■ **he's hit a winning ~** [in gambling] la chance lui a souri ; [good deal] il tient un bon filon ■ **he's just had a ~ of bad luck lately** il vient d'essuyer toute une série de revers
3. [tendency] : **he has a mean ~** OR **a ~ of meanness in him** il est un peu mesquin ■ **there has always been a ~ of madness in the family** il y a toujours eu une prédisposition à la folie dans la famille ■ [trace] trace *f*
4. *inf* [naked dash] : **to do a ~** *traverser un lieu public nu en courant*.
◇ *vt* [smear] tacher ■ **the wall was ~ed with paint** il y avait des traînées de peinture sur le mur ■ **her hands were ~ed with blue ink** elle avait des taches d'encre bleue sur les mains

■ [stripe] strier, zébrer ■ **her hair is ~ed with grey** [natural] elle a des cheveux gris ; [artificial] elle s'est fait des mèches grises ■ **she's had her hair ~ed** elle s'est fait faire des mèches.
<> *vi* **1.** [go quickly] : **to ~ in/out** entrer/sortir comme un éclair ■ **to ~ past** passer en courant d'air
2. [run naked] faire du streaking *(traverser un lieu public nu en courant).*

streaker ['stri:kər] *n* streaker *mf (personne nue qui traverse un lieu public en courant).*

streaky ['stri:kɪ] (*comp* **streakier**, *superl* **streakiest**) *adj* **1.** [colour, surface] marbré, jaspé, zébré ■ [rock, marble] veiné **2.** CULIN [meat] entrelardé, persillé ■ **~ bacon** bacon *m* entrelardé.

stream [stri:m] <> *n* **1.** [brook] ruisseau *m*
2. [current] courant *m* ■ **to go with the ~** *liter* aller au fil de l'eau ; *fig* suivre le courant *OR* le mouvement ■ **to go against the ~** *liter & fig* aller à contre-courant
3. [flow - of liquid] flot *m*, jet *m* ; [- of air] courant *m* ; [- of blood, lava] ruisseau *m*, flot *m*, cascade *f*, torrent *m* ; [- of people, traffic] flot *m*, défilé *m* (continu) ; [- of tears] ruisseau *m*, torrent *m* ■ **a red hot ~ of lava flowed down the mountain** une coulée de lave incandescente descendait le flanc de la montagne ■ **we've received a steady ~ of applications** nous avons reçu un flot incessant de candidatures ■ **she unleashed a ~ of insults** elle lâcha un torrent d'injures ➊ **~ of consciousness** monologue *m* intérieur
4. INDUST & TECH : **to be on/off ~** être en service/hors service ■ **to come on ~** être mis en service
5. *UK* SCH classe *f* de niveau ■ **we're in the top ~** nous sommes dans la section forte.
<> *vi* **1.** [flow - water, tears] ruisseler, couler à flots ; [- blood] ruisseler ■ **tears ~ed down her face** des larmes ruisselaient sur son visage ■ **sunlight ~ed into the room** le soleil entra à flots dans la pièce
2. [flutter] flotter, voleter ■ **flags were ~ing in the wind** des drapeaux flottaient au vent
3. [people, traffic] : **to ~ in/out** entrer/sortir à flots ■ **cars ~ed out of the city in their thousands** des milliers de voitures sortaient de la ville en un flot ininterrompu ■ **I watched as the demonstrators ~ed past** je regardai passer les flots de manifestants.
<> *vt* **1.** [flow with] : **to ~ blood/tears** ruisseler de sang/de larmes
2. *UK* SCH répartir en classes de niveau.

streamer ['stri:mər] *n* **1.** [decoration] serpentin *m* **2.** [banner] banderole *f* ■ [pennant] flamme *f* **3.** ASTRON flèche *f* lumineuse **4.** PRESS manchette *f*.

streaming ['stri:mɪŋ] <> *n UK* SCH répartition *f* en classes de niveau.
<> *adj* [surface, window, windscreen] ruisselant ■ **I've got a ~ cold** *UK* j'ai attrapé un gros rhume.

streamline ['stri:mlaɪn] <> *vt* **1.** AUT & AERON donner un profil aérodynamique à, profiler, caréner **2.** ECON & INDUST [company, production] rationaliser ■ [industry] dégraisser, restructurer.
<> *n* **1.** AUT & AERON ligne *f* aérodynamique, forme *f* profilée *OR* carénée **2.** PHYS écoulement *m* non perturbé.

streamlined ['stri:mlaɪnd] *adj* **1.** AUT & AERON aérodynamique, profilé, caréné **2.** *fig* [building] aux contours harmonieux ■ [figure] svelte **3.** ECON & INDUST [company, production] rationalisé ■ [industry] dégraissé, restructuré.

streamlining ['stri:mlaɪnɪŋ] *n* **1.** AUT & AERON carénage *m* **2.** ECON & INDUST [of business, organization] rationalisation *f* ■ [of industry] dégraissage *m*, restructuration *f*.

street [stri:t] <> *n* rue *f* ■ **in** *UK OR* **on** *US* **a ~** dans une rue ■ **a ~ of houses** une rue résidentielle ■ **to put** *OR* **to turn sb out into the ~** mettre qqn à la rue ■ **to be on the ~** *OR* **~s** [as prostitute] *inf* faire le trottoir ; [homeless person] être à la rue *OR* sur le pavé ■ **to take to the ~s** [protestors] descendre dans la rue ■ **to walk the ~s** [as prostitute] *inf* faire le trottoir ; [from idleness] battre le pavé, flâner dans les rues ; [in search] faire les rues ➊ **that's right up his ~!** *inf* [competence] c'est tout à fait son rayon *OR* dans ses cordes! ; [interest] c'est tout à fait son truc!
<> *comp* [noises] de la rue ■ [musician] des rues.

◆ **streets** *adv inf* **to be ~s ahead of sb** dépasser qqn de loin ■ **they're ~s apart in the way they think** ils ne partagent pas du tout les mêmes opinions.

street café *n UK* café *m* avec terrasse.

streetcar ['stri:tkɑ:r] *n US* tramway *m*.

street cleaner = **street sweeper**.

street cred [-kred] *inf*, **street credibility** *n* ≃ image *f* cool *inf OR* branchée *inf*.

street door *n* porte *f* (qui donne) sur la rue, porte *f* d'entrée.

street guide *n* plan *m* de la ville, répertoire *m* des rues.

streetlamp ['stri:tlæmp], **streetlight** ['stri:tlaɪt] *n* réverbère *m*.

street lighting *n* éclairage *m* public.

street map *n* plan *m* de la ville.

street market *n* marché *m* en plein air *OR* à ciel ouvert.

street party *n fête de rue organisée en l'honneur d'un événement national.*

street person *n* SDF *mf*.

street plan = **street map**.

street sweeper *n* [person] balayeur *m*, - euse *f* ■ [machine] balayeuse *f*.

street theatre *n* théâtre *m* de rue *OR* de foire.

street trader *n* marchand *m* ambulant, marchande *f* ambulante.

street urchin *n* gamin *m*, - e *f OR* gosse *mf* des rues.

street value *n* [of drugs] valeur *f* marchande.

street vendor *US* = **street trader**.

streetwalker ['stri:t,wɔ:kər] *n dated* fille *f* de joie.

streetwise ['stri:twaɪz] *adj inf qui connaît la vie de la rue, ses dangers et ses codes.*

strength [streŋθ] *n* **1.** *(U)* [physical power - of person, animal, muscle] force *f*, puissance *f* ■ **she doesn't know her own ~** elle ne connaît pas sa force ■ **his ~ failed him** ses forces l'ont trahi *OR* abandonné ■ **I haven't the ~ to lift these boxes** je n'ai pas assez de force *OR* je ne suis pas assez fort pour soulever ces cartons ■ **to lose ~** perdre des forces, s'affaiblir ■ **by sheer ~** de force ■ **with all my ~** de toutes mes forces ■ [health] forces *fpl* ■ **to get one's ~ back** reprendre des *OR* recouvrer ses forces ➊ **to go from ~ to ~** *liter* [sick person] aller de mieux en mieux ; *fig* [business] être en plein essor
2. [of faith, opinion, resolution] force *f*, fermeté *f* ■ [of emotion, feeling] force *f* ■ [of music, art] force *f* ■ **~ of character** force de caractère ■ **~ of purpose** résolution *f* ■ **they have no ~ of purpose** ils n'ont aucune détermination ■ **~ of will** volonté *f* ➊ **give me ~!** pitié!
3. [intensity - of earthquake, wind] force *f*, intensité *f* ; [- of current, light] intensité *f* ; [- of sound, voice, lens, magnet] force *f*, puissance *f*
4. [strong point, asset] force *f*, point *m* fort ■ **her ambition is her main ~** son ambition fait l'essentiel de sa force
5. [solidity] solidité *f* ■ *fig* [of claim, position, relationship] solidité *f* ■ [vigour - of argument, protest] force *f*, vigueur *f* ■ **to argue from a position of ~** être en position de force ■ FIN [of currency, economy] solidité *f* ■ **the dollar has gained/fallen in ~** le dollar s'est consolidé/a chuté
6. [of alcohol] teneur *f* en alcool ■ [of solution] titre *m* ■ [of coffee, tobacco] force *f*
7. *(U)* [numbers] effectif *m*, effectifs *mpl* ■ **we're at full ~** nos effectifs sont au complet ■ **the staff must be brought up to ~** il faut engager du personnel ■ **the protestors turned up in ~** les manifestants sont venus en force *OR* en grand nombre.

◆ **on the strength of** *prep phr* en vertu de, sur la foi de ■ **he was accepted on the ~ of his excellent record** il a été accepté grâce à ses excellents antécédents.

strengthen ['streŋθn] <> *vt* **1.** [physically - body, muscle] fortifier, raffermir ; [- person] fortifier, tonifier ; [- voice] renforcer ■ [improve - eyesight, hearing] améliorer ■ **to ~ one's grip** *OR* **hold on sthg** *liter & fig* resserrer son emprise sur qqch

2. [reinforce - firm, nation] renforcer ; [- fear, emotion, effect] renforcer, intensifier ; [- belief, argument] renforcer ; [- link, friendship] renforcer, fortifier ■ **the decision ~ed my resolve** la décision n'a fait que renforcer ma détermination ■ [morally - person] fortifier ■ **I felt ~ed by the experience** je suis sorti plus fort de cette expérience **3.** [foundation, structure] renforcer, consolider ■ [material] renforcer **4.** FIN [currency, economy] consolider.
◇ *vi* **1.** [physically - body] se fortifier, se raffermir ; [- voice] devenir plus fort ; [- grip] se resserrer **2.** [increase - influence, effect, desire] augmenter, s'intensifier ; [- wind] forcir ; [- current] augmenter, se renforcer ; [- friendship, character, resolve] se renforcer, se fortifier **3.** FIN [prices, market] se consolider, se raffermir.

strengthening ['streŋθənɪŋ] ◇ *n* **1.** [physical - of body, muscle] raffermissement *m* ; [- of voice] renforcement *m* ; [- of hold, grip] resserrement *m* **2.** [increase - of emotion, effect, desire] renforcement *m*, augmentation *f*, intensification *f* ■ [reinforcement - of character, friendship, position] renforcement *m* ; [- of wind, current] renforcement *m* **3.** [of structure, building] renforcement *m*, consolidation *f* **4.** FIN consolidation *f*.
◇ *adj* fortifiant, remontant ■ MED tonifiant.

strenuous ['strenjʊəs] *adj* **1.** [physically - activity, exercise, sport] ardu ■ **I'm not allowed to do anything ~** je ne dois pas me fatiguer ■ **avoid very ~ games like squash** évitez les sports comme le squash qui demandent une grande dépense d'énergie **2.** [vigorous - opposition, support] acharné, énergique ; [- protest] vigoureux, énergique ; [- opponent, supporter] zélé, très actif ■ **to make ~ efforts to do sthg** faire des efforts considérables pour faire qqch.

strenuously ['strenjʊəslɪ] *adv* **1.** [play, swim, work] en se dépensant beaucoup, en faisant de gros efforts **2.** [fight, oppose, resist] avec acharnement, énergiquement.

streptococcus [ˌstreptə'kɒkəs] (*pl* **streptococci** [-'kɒksaɪ]) *n* streptocoque *m*.

stress [stres] ◇ *n* **1.** [nervous tension] stress *m*, tension *f* nerveuse ■ **to suffer from ~** être stressé ■ **to be under ~** [person] être stressé ; [relationship] être tendu ■ **she's been under a lot of ~ lately** elle a été très stressée ces derniers temps ■ **the ~es and strains of being a parent** les angoisses qu'on éprouve lorsqu'on a des enfants ■ **she copes well in times of ~** elle sait faire face dans les moments difficiles ‖ [pressure] pression *f* ■ **I always work better under ~** je travaille toujours mieux quand je suis sous pression
2. CONSTR & TECH contrainte *f*, tension *f* ■ **to be in ~** [beam, girder] être sous contrainte ■ **there is too much ~ on the foundations** la contrainte que subissent les fondations est trop forte ■ **can the girders take the ~?** est-ce que les poutres peuvent soutenir la charge OR la tension?
3. [emphasis] insistance *f* ■ **to lay ~ on sthg** [fact, point, detail] insister sur, souligner ; [qualities, values, manners] insister sur, mettre l'accent sur
4. LING [gen] accentuation *f* ■ [on syllable] accent *m* ■ **the ~ is OR falls on the third syllable** l'accent tombe sur la troisième syllabe ‖ [accented syllable] syllabe *f* accentuée
5. MUS accent *m*.
◇ *vt* **1.** [emphasize - fact, point, detail] insister sur, faire ressortir, souligner ; [- value, qualities] insister sur, mettre l'accent sur ■ **this point cannot be ~ed enough** on ne saurait trop insister sur ce point
2. [in phonetics, poetry, music] accentuer
3. CONSTR & TECH [structure, foundation] mettre sous tension OR en charge ■ [concrete, metal] solliciter.
◇ *vi inf* stresser.
◆ **stress out** *vt inf* stresser.

stress-buster *n inf* éliminateur *m* de stress.

stressed [strest] *adj* **1.** [person] stressé, tendu ■ [relationship] tendu **2.** [syllable, word] accentué.

stressed-out *adj inf* stressé.

stressful ['stresfʊl] *adj* [lifestyle, job, conditions] stressant ■ [moments] de stress.

stress management *n* gestion *f* du stress.

stress mark *n* LING marque *f* d'accent.

stress-timed *adj* : ~ **language** *langue dont le rythme est fonction des syllabes accentuées.*

stretch [stretʃ] ◇ *vt* **1.** [pull tight] tendre ■ **~ the rope tight** tendez bien la corde
2. [pull longer or wider - elastic] étirer ; [- garment, shoes] élargir ■ **to ~ sthg out of shape** déformer qqch
3. [extend, reach to full length] étendre ■ **~ your arms upwards** tendez les bras vers le haut ■ **if I ~ up my hand I can reach the ceiling** si je tends la main je peux toucher le plafond ■ **to ~ o.s.** s'étirer ■ **to ~ one's legs** se dégourdir les jambes ■ **the bird ~ed its wings** l'oiseau déploya ses ailes
4. [force, strain, bend - meaning, truth] forcer, exagérer ; [- rules] tourner, contourner, faire une entorse à ; [- principle] faire une entorse à ; [- imagination] faire un gros effort de ■ **you're really ~ing my patience** ma patience a des limites ■ **that's ~ing it a bit (far)!** là vous exagérez!, là vous allez un peu loin! ■ **it would be ~ing a point to call him a diplomat** dire qu'il est diplomate serait exagérer OR aller un peu loin ■ **I suppose we could ~ a point and let him stay** je suppose qu'on pourrait faire une entorse au règlement et lui permettre de rester
5. [budget, income, resources, supplies - get the most from] tirer le maximum de ; [- overload] surcharger, mettre à rude épreuve ■ **our resources are ~ed to the limit** nos ressources sont exploitées OR utilisées au maximum ■ **our staff are really ~ed today** le personnel travaille à la limite de ses possibilités aujourd'hui ■ **to be fully ~ed** [machine, engine] tourner à plein régime ; [factory, economy] fonctionner à plein régime ; [person, staff] faire son maximum ■ [person - use one's talents] : **the job won't ~ you enough** le travail ne sera pas assez stimulant pour vous
6. MED [ligament, muscle] étirer.
◇ *vi* **1.** [be elastic] s'étirer ■ [become longer] s'allonger ■ [become wider] s'élargir ■ **the shoes will ~ with wear** vos chaussures vont se faire OR s'élargir à l'usage ■ **my pullover has ~ed out of shape** mon pull s'est déformé
2. [person, animal - from tiredness] s'étirer ; [- on ground, bed] s'étendre, s'allonger ; [- to reach something] tendre la main ■ **he had to ~ to reach it** [reach out] il a dû tendre le bras pour l'atteindre ; [stand on tiptoe] il a dû se mettre sur la pointe des pieds pour l'atteindre ■ **she ~ed across me to get the salt** elle a passé le bras devant moi pour attraper le sel ■ **he ~ed up to touch the cupboard** il s'est mis sur la pointe des pieds pour atteindre le placard
3. [spread, extend - in space, time] s'étendre ■ **the forest ~es as far as the eye can see** la forêt s'étend à perte de vue ■ **the road ~ed across 500 miles of desert** la route parcourait 800 km de désert ■ **my salary won't ~ to a new car** mon salaire ne me permet pas d'acheter une nouvelle voiture.
◇ *n* **1.** [expanse - of land, water] étendue *f* ■ **this ~ of the road is particularly dangerous in the winter** cette partie de la route est très dangereuse en hiver ■ **a new ~ of road/motorway** un nouveau tronçon de route/d'autoroute ■ **it's a lovely ~ of river/scenery** cette partie de la rivière/du paysage est magnifique ■ [on racetrack] ligne *f* droite ■ **to go into the final OR finishing ~** entamer la dernière ligne droite
2. [period of time] laps *m* de temps ■ **for long ~es at a time there was nothing to do** il n'y avait rien à faire pendant de longues périodes ■ **to do a ~ of ten years in the army** passer dix ans dans l'armée ■ **he did a ~ in Dartmoor** *inf* il a fait de la taule à Dartmoor
3. [act of stretching] étirement *m* ■ **he stood up, yawned and had a ~** il se leva, bâilla et s'étira ■ **to give one's legs a ~** se dégourdir les jambes ■ **by no ~ of the imagination** même en faisant un gros effort d'imagination ▶ **by a long ~ : he's the better writer by a long ~** c'est lui de loin le meilleur écrivain ■ **not by a long ~!** loin de là!
4. [elasticity] élasticité *f* ■ **there's a lot of ~ in these stockings** ces bas sont très élastiques OR s'étirent facilement
5. SPORT [exercise] étirement *m* ■ **do a couple of ~es before breakfast** faites quelques exercices d'assouplissement avant le petit déjeuner.
◇ *adj* TEX [material] élastique, stretch *(inv)* ■ [cover] extensible.
◆ **at a stretch** *adv phr* d'affilée.
◆ **at full stretch** *adv phr* : **to be at full ~** [factory, machine] fonctionner à plein régime OR à plein rendement ; [person] se donner à fond, faire son maximum ■ **we were working at full ~** nous travaillions d'arrache-pied.

◆ **stretch out** ◇ *vt sep* **1.** [pull tight] tendre ■ **the sheets had been ~ed out on the line to dry** on avait étendu les draps sur le fil à linge pour qu'ils sèchent ■ **the plastic sheet was ~ed out on the lawn** la bâche en plastique était étalée sur la pelouse
2. [extend, spread - arms, legs] allonger, étendre ; [- hand] tendre ; [- wings] déployer ■ **she ~ed out her hand towards him/for the cup** elle tendit la main vers lui/pour prendre la tasse ■ **she lay ~ed out in front of the television** elle était allongée par terre devant la télévision
3. [prolong - interview, meeting] prolonger, faire durer ; [- account] allonger
4. [make last - supplies, income] faire durer.
◇ *vi insep* **1.** [person, animal] s'étendre, s'allonger ■ **they ~ed out on the lawn in the sun** ils se sont allongés au soleil sur la pelouse
2. [forest, countryside] s'étendre ■ [prospects, season] s'étendre, s'étaler ■ **a nice long holiday ~ed out before them** ils avaient de longues vacances devant eux.

stretcher ['stretʃər] *n* **1.** MED brancard *m*, civière *f* **2.** [for shoes] tendeur *m*, forme *f* ■ [for gloves] ouvre-gants *m inv* ■ [in umbrella] baleine *f* ■ ART & SEW [for canvas] cadre *m*, châssis *m* **3.** CONSTR [brick, stone] panneresse *f*, carreau *m* **4.** [crossbar - in structure] traverse *f* ; [- on chair] barreau *m*, bâton *m*.

stretcher-bearer *n* brancardier *m*.

stretcher case *n blessé ou malade ayant besoin d'être porté sur un brancard* ■ **I was practically a ~ by the time the parents got home** *hum* je ne tenais plus debout *OR* j'étais bon pour l'hôpital quand les parents sont rentrés.

stretch fabric *n* stretch *m*.

stretchmarks ['stretʃmɑːks] *npl* vergetures *fpl*.

stretchy ['stretʃɪ] (*comp* **stretchier**, *superl* **stretchiest**) *adj* élastique, extensible.

strew [struː] (*pret* **strewed**, *pp* **strewn** [struːn] *OR* **strewed**) *vt lit* **1.** [scatter - seeds, flowers, leaves] répandre, éparpiller ■ [throw - toys, papers] éparpiller, jeter ; [- debris] éparpiller, disséminer ■ **the guests ~ed confetti over the bride** les invités ont lancé des confettis sur la mariée ■ **wreckage was strewn all over the road** il y avait des débris partout sur la route ■ **their conversation was strewn with four-letter words** leur conversation était truffée de gros mots **2.** [cover - ground, floor, path] joncher, parsemer ; [- table] joncher ■ **the path was strewn with leaves/litter** l'allée était jonchée de feuilles/de détritus.

strewth [struːθ] *interj UK inf dated* ~! mon Dieu!, bon sang!

striation [straɪ'eɪʃn] *n* striation *f*.

stricken ['strɪkn] *adj fml* **1.** [ill] malade ■ [wounded] blessé ■ [damaged, troubled] ravagé, dévasté ■ **to be ~ in years** être âgé et infirme **2.** [afflicted] frappé, atteint ■ **~ by** *OR* **with blindness** frappé de cécité ■ **they were ~ with grief/fear** ils étaient accablés de chagrin/transis de peur.

-stricken *in cpds* : **grief~** accablé de chagrin ■ **terror~** saisi d'épouvante.

strict [strɪkt] *adj* **1.** [severe, stern - person, discipline] strict, sévère ■ [inflexible - principles] strict, rigoureux ; [- belief, code, rules] strict, rigide ■ **she's a ~ vegetarian** c'est une végétarienne pure et dure ■ **I gave ~ orders not to be disturbed** j'ai formellement ordonné qu'on ne me dérange pas ■ **I'm on a ~ diet** je suis un régime très strict **2.** [exact, precise - meaning, interpretation] strict ■ **in the ~ sense of the word** au sens strict du terme ■ **it's a ~ translation from the Hebrew** c'est une traduction exacte *OR* fidèle de l'hébreu ➤ **~ construction** *US* LAW interprétation *f* stricte de la constitution **3.** [absolute - accuracy, hygiene] strict, absolu ■ **he told me in the ~est confidence** il me l'a dit à titre strictement confidentiel ■ **in ~ secrecy** dans le plus grand secret.

strictly ['strɪktlɪ] *adv* **1.** [severely - act, treat] strictement, avec sévérité ■ **the children were very ~ brought up** les enfants ont reçu une éducation extrêmement stricte **2.** [exactly - interpret, translate] fidèlement, exactement ■ **~ speaking** à strictement *OR* à proprement parler **3.** [absolutely, rigorously] strictement, absolument ■ **what you say is not ~ accurate** ce que vous dites n'est pas tout à fait exact ■ **to adhere ~ to one's principles** adhérer rigoureusement à ses principes ■ **to adhere ~ to one's diet** suivre scrupuleusement son régime ■ **~ forbidden** *OR* **prohibited** formellement interdit ■ **'smoking ~ forbidden'** 'défense absolue de fumer'.

stricture ['strɪktʃər] *n fml* **1.** [criticism] critique *f* sévère ■ **to pass ~ on sb/sthg** critiquer qqn/qqch sévèrement **2.** [restriction] restriction *f* **3.** MED striction *f*, sténose *f*.

stride [straɪd] (*pret* **strode** [strəʊd], *pp* **stridden** ['strɪdn]) ◇ *n* **1.** [step] grand pas *m*, enjambée *f* SPORT foulée *f* ■ **to take big** *OR* **long ~s** faire de grandes enjambées ■ **with giant ~s** à pas de géant ■ **he crossed the threshold in** *OR* **with one ~** il a franchi le seuil d'une seule enjambée ■ **she recognized him by his purposeful ~** elle l'a reconnu à son pas décidé ➤ **to get** *OR* **to hit** *US* **into one's ~** trouver son rythme ■ **to be caught off ~** *US* être pris au dépourvu ■ **to take sthg in one's ~** ne pas se laisser démonter *OR* abattre ■ **to put sb off their ~** faire perdre le rythme à qqn **2.** *fig* [progress] : **to make great ~s** faire de grands progrès, avancer à pas de géant ■ **he is making great ~s in German** il fait de grands progrès en allemand.
◇ *vi* marcher à grands pas *OR* à grandes enjambées ■ **to ~ away/in/out** s'éloigner/entrer/sortir à grands pas ■ **he strode up and down the street** il faisait les cent pas dans la rue ■ **he strode up and down the room** il arpentait la pièce.
◇ *vt* [streets, fields, deck] arpenter.
◆ **strides** *npl UK* & *Australia inf* [trousers] pantalon *m*.

stridency ['straɪdənsɪ] *n* stridence *f*.

strident ['straɪdnt] *adj* strident ■ **~ demands** des revendications véhémentes.

stridently ['straɪdəntlɪ] *adv* [call, cry, sing] d'une voix stridente ■ [sound, ring] en faisant un bruit strident ■ [demand] avec véhémence, à grands cris.

strife [straɪf] *n (U) fml* [conflict] dissensions *fpl* ■ [struggles] luttes *fpl* ■ [quarrels] querelles *fpl* ■ **industrial ~** conflits sociaux.

strife-torn *adj* déchiré par les conflits.

strike [straɪk] (*pret* & *pp* **struck** [strʌk], *cont* **striking**) ◇ *n* **1.** [by workers] grève *f* ■ **to go on ~** se mettre en *OR* faire grève ■ **to be (out) on ~** être en grève ■ **the Italian air ~** la grève des transports aériens en Italie ■ **railway ~** grève des chemins de fer ■ **coal** *OR* **miners' ~** grève des mineurs ■ **postal** *OR* **post office ~** grève des postes ■ **rent ~** grève des loyers ➤ **the General Strike** *UK* HIST la grande grève
2. MIL raid *m*, attaque *f* ■ **to carry out air ~s against** *OR* **on enemy bases** lancer des raids aériens contre des bases ennemies ■ **retaliatory ~** raid de représailles ‖ [nuclear] deuxième frappe *f* ■ [by bird of prey, snake] attaque *f*
3. AERON & MIL [planes] escadre *f (d'avions participant à un raid)*
4. PETR & MIN [discovery] découverte *f* ■ **a gold ~** la découverte d'un gisement d'or ■ **the recent oil ~s in the North Sea** la découverte récente de gisements de pétrole en mer du Nord ➤ **it was a lucky ~** c'était un coup de chance
5. [of clock - chime, mechanism] sonnerie *f* ■ **life was regulated by the ~ of the church clock** la vie était rythmée par la cloche de l'église
6. [act or instance of hitting] coup *m* ■ [sound] bruit *m*
7. [in baseball] strike *m* ■ *US fig* [black mark] mauvais point *m* ■ **he has two ~s against him** *fig* il est mal parti
8. [in bowling] honneur *m* double ■ **to get** *OR* **to score a ~** réussir un honneur double
9. FISHING [by fisherman] ferrage *m* ■ [by fish] touche *f*.
◇ *comp* **1.** [committee, movement] de grève ■ **to threaten ~ action** menacer de faire *OR* de se mettre en grève
2. MIL [aircraft, mission] d'intervention, d'attaque.
◇ *vt* **1.** [hit] frapper ■ **he struck me with his fist** il m'a donné un coup de poing ■ **the chairman struck the table with his gavel** le président donna un coup de marteau sur la table ■ **she took the vase and struck him on** *OR* **over the head** elle saisit le vase et lui donna un coup sur la tête ■ **she struck him across the face** elle lui a donné une gifle ■ **a light breeze struck the sails** une légère brise gonfla les voiles ■ **a wave struck the side of the boat** une vague a heurté le côté du bateau ‖ [inflict, deliver - blow] donner ■ **who struck the first blow?** qui a porté le premier coup?, qui a frappé le premier? ■ **he struck the tree a mighty blow with the axe** il a donné un grand coup de hache dans l'arbre ■ **the trailer struck the post a glancing blow** la

remorque a percuté le poteau en passant ■ **to ~ a blow for democracy/women's rights** *fig* [law, event] faire progresser la démocratie/les droits de la femme ; [person, group] marquer des points en faveur de la démocratie/des droits des femmes
2. [bump into, collide with] heurter, cogner ■ **his foot struck the bar on his first jump** son pied a heurté la barre lors de son premier saut ■ **she fell and struck her head on** *OR* **against the kerb** elle s'est cogné la tête contre le bord du trottoir en tombant ■ **we've struck ground!** NAUT nous avons touché (le fond)!
3. [assail, attain - subj: bullet, torpedo, bomb] toucher, atteindre ; [- subj: lightning] frapper ■ **he was struck by a piece of shrapnel** il a été touché par *OR* il a reçu un éclat de grenade ■ **to be struck by lightning** être frappé par la foudre, être foudroyé ■ [afflict - subj: drought, disease, worry, regret] frapper ; [- subj: storm, hurricane, disaster, wave of violence] s'abattre sur, frapper ■ **an earthquake struck the city** un tremblement de terre a frappé la ville ■ **the pain struck her as she tried to get up** la douleur l'a saisie au moment où elle essayait de se lever ■ **I was struck by** *OR* **with doubts** j'ai été pris de doute(s), le doute s'est emparé de moi
4. [occur to] frapper ■ **only later did it ~ me as unusual** ce n'est que plus tard que j'ai trouvé ça *OR* que cela m'a paru bizarre ■ **it suddenly struck him how little had changed** il a soudain pris conscience du fait que peu de choses avaient changé ■ **a terrible thought struck her** une idée affreuse lui vint à l'esprit ■ **it doesn't ~ me as being the best course of action** il ne me semble pas que ce soit la meilleure voie à suivre
5. [impress] frapper, impressionner ■ **what ~s you is the silence** ce qui (vous) frappe, c'est le silence ■ **how did she ~ you?** quelle impression vous a-t-elle faite?, quel effet vous a-t-elle fait? ■ **how did Tokyo/the film ~ you?** comment avez-vous trouvé Tokyo/le film? ■ **we can eat here and meet them later, how does that ~ you?** on peut manger ici et les retrouver plus tard, qu'en penses-tu? ■ **I was very struck with** *UK OR* **by** *US* **the flat** l'appartement m'a plu énormément ■ **I wasn't very struck with** *UK OR* **by** *US* **his colleague** son collègue ne m'a pas fait une grande impression
6. [chime] sonner ■ **it was striking midnight as we left** minuit sonnait quand nous partîmes
7. [play - note, chord] jouer ■ **to ~ a false note** MUS faire une fausse note ; [speech] sonner faux ■ **his presence/his words struck a gloomy note** sa présence a/ses paroles ont mis une note de tristesse ■ **the report ~s an optimistic note/a note of warning for the future** le rapport est très optimiste/très alarmant pour l'avenir ◐ **to ~ a chord : does it ~ a chord?** est-ce que cela te rappelle *OR* dit quelque chose? ■ **to ~ a chord with the audience** faire vibrer la foule ■ **her description of company life will ~ a chord with many managers** beaucoup de cadres se reconnaîtront dans sa description de la vie en entreprise
8. [arrive at, reach - deal, treaty, agreement] conclure ■ **I'll ~ a bargain with you** je te propose un marché ■ **it's not easy to ~ a balance between too much and too little freedom** il n'est pas facile de trouver un équilibre *OR* de trouver le juste milieu entre trop et pas assez de liberté
9. [cause a feeling of] : **to ~ fear** *OR* **terror into sb** remplir qqn d'effroi
10. [cause to become] rendre ■ **to ~ sb blind/dumb** rendre qqn aveugle/muet ■ **I was struck dumb by the sheer cheek of the man!** je suis resté muet devant le culot de cet homme! ■ **a stray bullet struck him dead** il a été tué par une balle perdue
11. [ignite - match] frotter, allumer ; [- sparks] faire jaillir
12. [discover - gold] découvrir ; [- oil, water] trouver ■ **to ~ it lucky** *UK inf* [material gain] trouver le filon ; [be lucky] avoir de la veine ■ **to ~ it rich** *inf* trouver le filon, faire fortune
13. [adopt - attitude] adopter
14. [mint - coin, medal] frapper
15. [take down - tent] démonter ■ NAUT [- sail] amener, baisser ■ **to ~ camp** lever le camp ■ **to ~ the flag** *OR* **the colours** NAUT amener les couleurs
16. [delete - name, remark, person] rayer ; [- from professional register] radier
17. [attack] attaquer
18. *US* [go on strike at] : **the union is striking four of the company's plants** le syndicat a déclenché des grèves dans quatre des usines de la société
19. BOT : **to ~ roots** prendre racine.

◇ *vi* **1.** [hit] frapper ■ **she struck at me with her umbrella** elle essaya de me frapper avec son parapluie ■ **to ~ home** [blow] porter ; [missile, remark] faire mouche ◐ **to ~ lucky** *inf* avoir de la veine ■ **~ while the iron is hot** *prov* il faut battre le fer pendant qu'il est chaud *prov*
2. [stop working] faire grève ■ **they're striking for more pay** ils font grève pour obtenir une augmentation de salaire
3. [attack - gen] attaquer ; [- snake] mordre ; [- wild animal] sauter *OR* bondir sur sa proie ; [- bird of prey] fondre *OR* s'abattre sur sa proie ■ **the murderer has struck again** l'assassin a encore frappé ■ **these are measures which ~ at the root/heart of the problem** voici des mesures qui attaquent le problème à la racine/qui s'attaquent au cœur du problème ■ **this latest incident ~s right at the heart of government policy** ce dernier incident remet complètement en cause la politique gouvernementale
4. [chime] sonner
5. [happen suddenly - illness, disaster, earthquake] survenir, se produire, arriver ■ **we were travelling quietly along when disaster struck** nous roulions tranquillement lorsque la catastrophe s'est produite
6. FISHING [fisherman] ferrer ■ [fish] mordre (à l'hameçon).

◆ **strike back** *vi insep* se venger ■ MIL contre-attaquer.
◆ **strike down** *vt sep* foudroyer, terrasser.
◆ **strike off** ◇ *vt sep* **1.** [delete, remove - from list] rayer, barrer ; [- from professional register] radier
2. [sever] couper
3. TYPO tirer.
◇ *vi insep* [go] : **we struck off into the forest** nous sommes entrés *OR* avons pénétré dans la forêt.
◆ **strike on** *vt insep UK* [solution, right answer] trouver (par hasard), tomber sur ■ [plan] trouver ■ [idea] avoir.
◆ **strike out** ◇ *vi insep* **1.** [set up on one's own] s'établir à son compte ■ [launch out] se lancer ■ **they decided to ~ out into a new field** ils ont décidé de se lancer dans un nouveau domaine
2. [go] : **she struck out across the fields** elle prit à travers champs
3. [swim] : **we struck out for the shore** nous avons commencé à nager en direction de la côte
4. [aim a blow] : **he struck out at me** il essaya de me frapper ■ **they struck out in all directions with their truncheons** ils distribuaient des coups de matraque à droite et à gauche
5. [in baseball] s'éliminer.
◇ *vt sep* **1.** [cross out] rayer, barrer
2. [in baseball] éliminer.
◆ **strike through** *vt sep UK* [cross out] rayer, barrer.
◆ **strike up** ◇ *vt insep* **1.** [start] : **to ~ up a conversation with sb** engager la conversation avec qqn ■ **to ~ up an acquaintance/a friendship with sb** lier connaissance/se lier d'amitié avec qqn
2. MUS [start playing] commencer à jouer.
◇ *vi insep* [musician, orchestra] commencer à jouer ■ [music] commencer.
◆ **strike upon** *UK* = **strike on**.

THE GENERAL STRIKE

Grève générale sans précédent qui paralysa l'Angleterre pendant neuf jours en 1926. Elle éclata dans le secteur minier et s'étendit rapidement à toute l'industrie. La grève des mineurs dura six mois.

strikebound ['straɪkbaʊnd] *adj* [factory, department] bloqué par une *OR* la grève ■ [industry, country] bloqué par des grèves.

strikebreaker ['straɪk,breɪkər] *n* briseur *m*, -euse *f* de grève.

strike force *n* **1.** [nuclear capacity] force *f* de frappe **2.** [of police, soldiers - squad] détachement *m* *OR* brigade *f* d'intervention ; [- larger force] force *f* d'intervention.

strike pay *n* salaire *m* de gréviste *(versé par le syndicat ou par un fonds de solidarité).*

striker ['straɪkər] *n* **1.** INDUST gréviste *mf* **2.** FTBL buteur *m* **3.** [device - on clock] marteau *m* ; [- in gun] percuteur *m*.

striking ['straɪkɪŋ] <> *adj* **1.** [remarkable - contrast, resemblance, beauty] frappant, saisissant **2.** [clock] qui sonne les heures ▪ **~ mechanism** sonnerie *f* (des heures) **3.** MIL [force] d'intervention **4.** INDUST en grève **5.** *phr* **within ~ distance** à proximité ▪ **she lives within ~ distance of London** elle habite tout près de Londres.
<> *n* **1.** [of clock] sonnerie *f* (des heures) **2.** [of coins] frappe *f*.

strikingly ['straɪkɪŋlɪ] *adv* remarquablement ▪ **a ~ beautiful woman** une femme d'une beauté saisissante.

string [strɪŋ] (*pret & pp* **strung** [strʌŋ]) <> *n* **1.** [gen - for parcel] ficelle *f* ; [- on apron, pyjamas] cordon *m* ▪ **a piece of ~** un bout *OR* un morceau de ficelle ▪ [for puppet] ficelle *f*, fil *m* ➊ **to have sb on a ~** *inf* mener qqn par le bout du nez ▪ **he pulls the ~s** c'est lui qui tire les ficelles ▪ **to pull ~s for sb** *inf* [obtain favours] user de son influence *OR* faire jouer ses relations pour aider qqn ; [get job, promotion] pistonner qqn ▪ **no ~s attached** *inf* sans condition *OR* conditions ▪ **there are no ~s attached** cela n'engage à rien
2. [for bow, tennis racket, musical instrument] corde *f* ▪ **the ~s** MUS les cordes ➊ **to have more than one/a second ~ to one's bow** avoir plus d'une/une seconde corde à son arc
3. [row, chain - of beads, pearls] rang *m*, collier *m* ; [- of onions, sausages] chapelet *m* ; [- of visitors, cars] file *f* ▪ **a ~ of islands** un chapelet d'îles ▪ **a ~ of fairy lights** une guirlande (électrique) ▪ **she owns a ~ of shops** elle est propriétaire d'une chaîne de magasins ▪ **a ~ of race horses** une écurie de course
4. [series - of successes, defeats] série *f* ; [- of lies, insults] kyrielle *f*, chapelet *m* ▪ **he has a whole ~ of letters after his name** il a toute une kyrielle de diplômes
5. COMPUT & LING chaîne *f* ▪ MATHS séquence *f*.
<> *comp* **1.** MUS [band, instrument, orchestra] à cordes ▪ **~ player** musicien *m*, - enne *f* qui joue d'un instrument à cordes ▪ **the ~ section** les cordes *fpl* ▪ **~ quartet** quatuor *m* à cordes
2. [made of string] de *OR* en ficelle ▪ **~ bag** filet *m* à provisions ▪ **~ vest** tricot *m* de corps à grosses mailles.
<> *vt* **1.** [guitar, violin] monter, mettre des cordes à ▪ [racket] corder ▪ [bow] mettre une corde à
2. [beads, pearls] enfiler
3. [hang] suspendre ▪ [stretch] tendre ▪ **Christmas lights had been strung across the street** des décorations de Noël avaient été suspendues en travers de la rue
4. CULIN [beans] enlever les fils de.

◆ **string along** *inf* <> *vi insep* **1.** [tag along] suivre (les autres) ▪ **do you mind if I ~ along?** est-ce que ça vous gêne si je viens avec vous *OR* si je vous accompagne?
2. [agree] : **to ~ along with sb** se ranger à l'avis de qqn.
<> *vt sep* [person] faire marcher.

◆ **string out** *vt sep* [washing, lamps] suspendre (sur une corde) ▪ **lights were strung out along the runway** des lumières s'échelonnaient le long de la piste.

◆ **string together** *vt sep* **1.** [beads] enfiler ▪ [words, sentences] enchaîner ▪ **she can barely ~ two words together in French** c'est à peine si elle peut faire une phrase en français **2.** [improvise - story] monter, improviser.

◆ **string up** *vt sep* **1.** [lights] suspendre ▪ [washing] étendre **2.** *inf* [hang - person] pendre.

string bean *n* **1.** [vegetable] haricot *m* vert **2.** *inf* [person] grande perche *f*.

stringboard ['strɪŋbɔːd] *n* limon *m* (d'escalier).

stringed [strɪŋd] *adj* [instrument] à cordes.

-stringed *in cpds* : **five-** à cinq cordes.

stringency ['strɪndʒənsɪ] *n* **1.** [severity] rigueur *f*, sévérité *f* **2.** ECON & FIN austérité *f*.

stringent ['strɪndʒənt] *n* **1.** [rules] rigoureux, strict, sévère ▪ [measures, conditions] rigoureux, draconien **2.** ECON & FIN [market] tendu.

string-pulling [-ˌpʊlɪŋ] *n* piston *m* ▪ **he got the job through ~** il a décroché ce poste grâce à ses relations.

string variable *n* COMPUT variable *f* alphanumérique.

stringy ['strɪŋɪ] (*comp* **stringier**, *superl* **stringiest**) *adj* **1.** [meat, vegetable] filandreux, fibreux ▪ [cooked cheese] qui file **2.** [long - plant] (qui pousse) tout en longueur ; [- build, limbs] filiforme.

strip [strɪp] (*pret & pp* **stripped**) <> *n* **1.** [of paper, carpet] bande *f* ▪ [of metal] bande *f*, ruban *m* ▪ [of land] bande *f*, langue *f* ▪ **there was a thin ~ of light under the door** il y avait un mince rai de lumière sous la porte ▪ **a narrow ~ of water** [sea] un étroit bras de mer ; [river] un étroit ruban de rivière ▪ **can you cut off a ~ of material?** pouvez-vous couper une bande de tissu? ▪ **she cut the dough/material into ~s** elle coupa la pâte en lamelles/le tissu en bandes ▪ **to tear sthg into ~s** déchirer qqch en bandes
2. *US* [street with businesses] avenue *f* commerçante ➊ **the Strip, Sunset Strip** *artère de Las Vegas où se trouvent tous les casinos*
3. AERON piste *f*
4. [light] : **neon ~** tube *m* néon
5. SPORT tenue *f*
6. [striptease] strip-tease *m*.
<> *vt* **1.** [undress] déshabiller, dévêtir ▪ **they were stripped to the waist** ils étaient torse nu, ils étaient nus jusqu'à la ceinture ▪ **to ~ sb naked** déshabiller qqn (complètement)
2. [make bare - tree] dépouiller, dénuder ; [- door, furniture] décaper ; [- wire] dénuder ▪ **the walls need to be stripped first** [of wallpaper] il faut d'abord enlever *OR* arracher le papier peint ; [of paint] il faut d'abord décaper les murs
3. [remove cover from] découvrir ▪ [take contents from] vider ▪ **to ~ a bed** défaire un lit ▪ **the windows had been stripped of their curtains** on avait enlevé les rideaux des fenêtres ▪ **the liner is to be completely stripped and refitted** le paquebot doit être refait de fond en comble
4. [remove - gen] enlever ; [- paint] décaper ▪ **we stripped the wallpaper from the walls** nous avons arraché le papier peint des murs ▪ **the birds have stripped the cherries from the trees** les oiseaux ont fait des ravages dans les cerisiers
5. [deprive] dépouiller, démunir ▪ **to ~ sb of his/her privileges/possessions** dépouiller qqn de ses privilèges/biens ▪ **he was stripped of his rank** il a été dégradé
6. [dismantle - engine, gun] démonter
7. TECH [screw, bolt] arracher le filet de ▪ [gear] arracher les dents de.
<> *vi* **1.** [undress] se déshabiller, se dévêtir ▪ **to ~ to the waist** se dévêtir jusqu'à la ceinture, se mettre torse nu
2. [do a striptease] faire un strip-tease.

◆ **strip down** <> *vt sep* **1.** [bed] défaire (complètement) ▪ [wallpaper] arracher, enlever ▪ [door, furniture] décaper ▪ **the text has been stripped down to its bare essentials** *fig* le texte a été réduit à l'essentiel
2. [dismantle - engine, mechanism] démonter.
<> *vi insep* se déshabiller ▪ **he stripped down to his underpants** il s'est déshabillé, ne gardant que son slip.

◆ **strip off** <> *vt sep* [gen] enlever, arracher ▪ [clothes, shirt] enlever ▪ [paint] décaper ▪ **to ~ the leaves off a tree** dépouiller un arbre de ses feuilles.
<> *vi insep* se déshabiller, se mettre nu.

◆ **strip out** *vt sep* [engine, mechanism] démonter, démanteler.

strip cartoon *n UK* bande *f* dessinée.

strip club *n* boîte *f* de strip-tease.

strip cropping [-ˌkrɒpɪŋ] *n (U)* culture *f* en bande *(pour limiter l'érosion)*.

stripe [straɪp] <> *n* **1.** [on animal] zébrure *f* ▪ [on material, shirt] raie *f*, rayure *f* ▪ [on car] filet *m* **2.** MIL galon *m*, chevron *m* ▪ **to get/to lose one's ~s** gagner/perdre ses galons **3.** [kind] genre *m* **4.** [lash] coup *m* de fouet ▪ [mark] marque *f* d'un coup de fouet.
<> *vt* rayer, marquer de rayures.

striped [straɪpt] *adj* [animal] tigré, zébré ▪ [material, shirt, pattern] rayé, à rayures ▪ **~ with blue** avec des rayures bleues.

stripey ['straɪpɪ] = **stripy**.

strip farming *n* **1.** HIST système *m* des openfields **2.** = **strip cropping**.

strip light *n* (tube *m*) néon *m*.

strip lighting *n* éclairage *m* fluorescent *OR* au néon.

stripling ['strɪplɪŋ] *n lit & hum* tout jeune homme *m*.

strip mining *n esp US* extraction *f* à ciel ouvert.

stripped [strɪpt] *adj* [wood] décapé ▪ **~ pine furniture** meubles *mpl* en pin naturel.

stripper ['strɪpəʳ] *n* **1.** [in strip club] strip-teaseuse *f* ▪ **the club had two male ~s** le club avait deux strip-teaseurs **2.** [for paint] décapant *m*.

strip poker *n* strip-poker *m*.

strip search *n* fouille *f* corporelle *(la personne fouillée devant se déshabiller)*.
◆ **strip-search** *vt* : **to ~ sb** fouiller qqn après l'avoir fait déshabiller.

strip show *n* (spectacle *m* de) strip-tease *m*.

striptease ['strɪpti:z] *n* strip-tease *m* ▪ **~ artist** strip-teaseur *m*, - euse *f*.

stripy ['straɪpɪ] (*comp* **stripier**, *superl* **stripiest**) *adj* [material, shirt, pattern] rayé, à rayures ▪ ZOOL tigré, zébré.

strive [straɪv] (*pret* **strove** [strəʊv], *pp* **striven** ['strɪvn]) *vt fml & lit* **1.** [attempt] : **to ~ to do sthg** s'évertuer à *OR* s'acharner à faire qqch ▪ **to ~ after** *OR* **for sthg** faire tout son possible pour obtenir qqch, s'efforcer d'obtenir qqch ▪ **to ~ for effect** chercher à se faire remarquer à tout prix **2.** [struggle] lutter, se battre ▪ **all her life she strove for success/recognition** toute sa vie, elle s'est battue pour réussir/être reconnue.

strobe [strəʊb] *n* **1.** : **~ (lighting)** lumière *f* stroboscopique **2.** = **stroboscope**.

stroboscope ['strəʊbəskəʊp] *n* stroboscope *m*.

strode [strəʊd] *pt* ▷ **stride**.

stroke [strəʊk] ◇ *n* **1.** [blow, flick] coup *m* ▪ **with a ~ of the brush** d'un coup de pinceau ▪ **with a ~ of the pen** d'un trait de plume ▪ **they were given 50 ~s** ils ont reçu 50 coups de fouet
2. SPORT [in golf, tennis, cricket, billiards] coup *m* ▪ [in swimming - movement] mouvement *m* des bras ; [- style] nage *f* ▪ [in rowing - movement] coup *m* d'aviron ; [- technique] nage *f* ▪ **she swam across the river with quick ~s** elle traversa rapidement la rivière à la nage ▪ **to keep ~** garder la cadence ▶ **to set the ~** *liter & fig* donner la cadence ▪ **to put sb off his ~** *liter* [in rowing] faire perdre sa cadence *OR* son rythme à qqn ; [in golf] faire manquer son coup à ; *fig* faire perdre tous ses moyens à qqn ▪ **to be off one's ~** ne pas être au mieux de sa forme
3. [mark - from pen, pencil] trait *m* ▪ [from brush] trait *m*, touche *f* ▪ [on letters, figures] barre *f* ▪ **written with thick/thin ~s** écrit d'une écriture appuyée/fine ▮ TYPO [oblique dash] barre *f* oblique ▪ **225 ~ 62** *UK* 225 barre oblique 62
4. [piece, example - of luck] coup *m* ; [- of genius] trait *m* ▪ **it was a ~ of brilliance!** c'était un coup de génie! ▪ **she didn't do a ~ (of work) all day** *UK* elle n'a rien fait de la journée
5. [of clock, bell] coup *m* ▪ **on the ~ of midnight** sur le coup de minuit ▪ **on the ~ of 6** à 6 h sonnantes *OR* tapantes ▪ **he arrived on the ~** il est arrivé à l'heure exacte *OR* précise ▪ **at the third ~ it will be 6:32 precisely** *UK* TELEC au troisième top, il sera exactement 6 h 32
6. MED attaque *f* (d'apoplexie) ▪ **to have a ~** avoir une attaque
7. NAUT [oarsman] chef *m* de nage
8. TECH [of piston] course *f* ▪ **two-/four-~ engine** un moteur à deux/quatre temps
9. [caress] caresse *f* ▪ **she gave the cat a ~** elle a caressé le chat.
◇ *vt* **1.** [caress] caresser ▪ **he ~d her hand** il lui caressait la main ▪ **to ~ sb's ego** caresser qqn dans le sens du poil
2. [in rowing] : **to ~ a boat** être chef de nage, donner la nage
3. SPORT [ball] frapper.
◇ *vi* [in rowing] être chef de nage, donner la nage.
◆ **at a stroke, at one stroke** *adv phr* d'un seul coup.

stroll [strəʊl] ◇ *vi* se balader, flâner ▪ **to ~ in/out/past** entrer/sortir/passer sans se presser ▪ **we ~ed round the shops** nous avons fait un petit tour dans les magasins.
◇ *vt* : **to ~ the streets** se promener dans les rues.
◇ *n* petit tour *m*, petite promenade *f* ▪ **to go for a ~** aller faire un tour *OR* une petite promenade.

stroller ['strəʊləʳ] *n* **1.** [walker] promeneur *m*, - euse *f* **2.** *US* [pushchair] poussette *f*.

strolling ['strəʊlɪŋ] *adj* [player, musician] ambulant.

strong [strɒŋ] (*comp* **stronger** ['strɒŋgəʳ], *superl* **strongest** ['strɒŋgɪst]) ◇ *adj* **1.** [sturdy - person, animal, constitution, arms] fort, robuste ; [- building] solide ; [- cloth, material] solide, résistant ; [- shoes, table] solide, robuste ▪ **you need a ~ stomach to eat this junk** *inf* il faut avoir un estomac en béton pour manger des cochonneries pareilles ▪ **you'd need a ~ stomach to go and watch that film** il faut avoir l'estomac bien accroché pour aller voir ce film ▪ [in health - person] en bonne santé ; [- heart] solide, robuste ; [- eyesight] bon ▪ **he'll be able to go out once he's ~ again** il pourra sortir quand il aura repris des forces ▶ **to be as ~ as a horse** [powerful] être fort comme un turc *OR* un bœuf ; [in good health] avoir une santé de fer
2. [in degree, force - sea current, wind, light, lens, voice] fort, puissant ; [- magnet] puissant ▪ ELEC [- current] intense ▪ MUS [- beat] fort ▪ **there is a ~ element of suspense in the story** il y a beaucoup de suspense dans cette histoire ▪ **it's my ~ suit** [in cards] c'est ma couleur forte ; *fig* c'est mon fort ▪ **tact isn't her ~ suit** *OR* **point** *fig* le tact n'est pas son (point) fort ▪ **what are his ~ points?** quels sont ses points forts? ▪ [firm - conviction, belief] ferme, fort, profond ; [- protest, support] énergique, vigoureux ; [- measures] énergique, draconien ▪ **he is a ~ believer in discipline** il est de ceux qui croient fermement à la discipline ▪ **she is a ~ supporter of the government** elle soutient le gouvernement avec ferveur ▪ **she is a ~ supporter of Sunday trading** c'est une ardente partisane de l'ouverture des commerces le dimanche ▪ [intense, vivid - desire, imagination, interest] vif ; [- colour] vif, fort ▪ **to exert a ~ influence on sb** exercer beaucoup d'influence *OR* une forte influence sur qqn ▪ [emotionally, morally - character] fort, bien trempé ; [- feelings] intense, fort ; [- nerves] solide ▪ **I have ~ feelings on** *OR* **about the death penalty** [against] je suis tout à fait contre la peine de mort ; [for] je suis tout à fait pour la peine de mort ▪ **I have no ~ feelings** *OR* **views one way or the other** cela m'est égal ▪ **he had a ~ sense of guilt** il éprouvait un fort sentiment de culpabilité ▪ **to have a ~ will** avoir de la volonté ▪ **you'll have to be ~ now** [when consoling or encouraging] il va falloir être courageux maintenant
3. [striking - contrast, impression] fort, frappant, marquant ; [- accent] fort ▪ **to bear a ~ resemblance to sb** ressembler beaucoup *OR* fortement à qqn ▪ **his speech made a ~ impression on them** son discours les a fortement impressionnés *OR* a eu un profond effet sur eux ▪ **there is a ~ chance** *OR* **probability that he will win** il y a de fortes chances pour qu'il gagne
4. [solid - argument, evidence] solide, sérieux ▪ **we have ~ reasons to believe them innocent** nous avons de bonnes *OR* sérieuses raisons de croire qu'ils sont innocents ▪ **they have a ~ case** ils ont de bons arguments ▪ **we're in a ~ bargaining position** nous sommes bien placés *OR* en position de force pour négocier
5. [in taste, smell] fort ▪ **I like ~ coffee** j'aime le café fort *OR* corsé ▪ **this whisky is ~ stuff** ce whisky est fort ▪ **there's a ~ smell of gas in here** il y a une forte odeur de gaz ici
6. [in ability - student, team] fort ; [- candidate, contender] sérieux ▪ **he is a ~ contender for the presidency** il a de fortes chances de remporter l'élection présidentielle ▪ **she is particularly ~ in science subjects** elle est particulièrement forte dans les matières scientifiques ▪ **in very ~ form** en très grande forme ▪ **the film was ~ on style but weak on content** le film était très bon du point de vue de la forme mais pas du tout du point de vue du contenu
7. [tough, harsh - words] grossier ▪ **to use ~ language** dire des grossièretés, tenir des propos grossiers ▪ **she gave us her opinion in ~ terms** elle nous a dit ce qu'elle pensait sans mâcher ses mots ▪ **his latest film is ~ stuff** son dernier film est vraiment dur
8. [in number] : **an army 5,000 ~** une armée forte de 5 000 hommes ▪ **the marchers were 400 ~** les manifestants étaient au nombre de 400
9. COMM & ECON [currency, price] solide ▪ [market] ferme ▪ **the dollar has got ~er** le dollar s'est consolidé
10. GRAM [verb, form] fort.
◇ *adv inf* **to be going ~** [person] être toujours solide *OR* toujours d'attaque ; [party] battre son plein ; [machine, car] fonctionner toujours bien ; [business, economy] être florissant, prospérer ▪ **he's 80 years of age and still going ~** il a 80 ans et toujours bon pied bon œil ▪ **to come on ~** [insist] insister lourdement ; [make a pass] faire des avances ▪ **that's (coming it) a bit ~!** vous y allez un peu fort!, vous exagérez!

strongarm ['strɒŋɑ:m] *adj inf* [methods] brutal, violent ■ **to use ~ tactics** employer la manière forte.
◆ **strong-arm** *vt inf* faire violence à ■ **to strong-arm sb into doing sthg** forcer la main à qqn pour qu'il fasse qqch.

strongbox ['strɒŋbɒks] *n* coffre-fort *m*.

stronghold ['strɒŋhəʊld] *n* **1.** MIL forteresse *f*, fort *m* **2.** *fig* bastion *m*.

strongly ['strɒŋlɪ] *adv* **1.** [greatly - regret] vivement, profondément ; [- impress, attract] fortement, vivement ■ **the kitchen smelt ~ of bleach** il y avait une forte odeur de Javel dans la cuisine ■ **I am ~ tempted to say yes** j'ai très envie de dire oui ■ **I ~ disagree with you** je ne suis pas du tout d'accord avec vous ■ **the report was ~ critical of the hospital** le rapport était extrêmement critique à l'égard de l'hôpital **2.** [firmly - believe, support] fermement ■ [forcefully - attack, defend, protest] énergiquement, vigoureusement, avec force ; [- emphasize] fortement ■ **a ~ worded protest** une violente protestation ■ **I feel very ~ about the matter** c'est un sujet *OR* une affaire qui me tient beaucoup à cœur **3.** [sturdily - constructed] solidement ■ **~ built** [person] costaud, bien bâti ; [wall, structure] solide, bien construit.

strongman ['strɒŋmæn] (*pl* **strongmen** [-men]) *n* hercule *m* (de foire).

strong-minded *adj* résolu, déterminé.

strongroom ['strɒŋru:m] *n UK* [in castle, house] chambre *f* forte ■ [in bank] chambre *f* forte, salle *f* des coffres.

strong-willed [-'wɪld] *adj* volontaire, résolu, tenace.

strontium ['strɒntɪəm] *n* strontium *m*.

strop [strɒp] (*pret & pp* **stropped**, *cont* **stropping**) ◇ *n* cuir *m* (à rasoir).
◇ *vt* [razor] repasser sur le cuir.

stroppy ['strɒpɪ] (*comp* **stroppier**, *superl* **stroppiest**) *adj UK inf* **there's no need to get ~!** tu n'as pas besoin de monter sur tes grands chevaux!

strove [strəʊv] *pt* ▷ **strive**.

struck [strʌk] ◇ *pt & pp* ▷ **strike**.
◇ *adj US* [industry] bloqué pour cause de grève ■ [factory] fermé pour cause de grève.

structural ['strʌktʃərəl] *adj* **1.** [gen] structural ■ [change, problem] structurel, de structure ■ [unemployment] structurel ■ LING [analysis] structural, structurel ■ **~ linguistics/psychology** linguistique *f* /psychologie *f* structurale **2.** CONSTR [fault, steel] de construction ■ [damage, alterations] structural ■ **~ engineering** génie *m* civil.

structuralism ['strʌktʃərəlɪzm] *n* structuralisme *m*.

structuralist ['strʌktʃərəlɪst] ◇ *n* structuraliste *mf*.
◇ *adj* structuraliste.

structurally ['strʌktʃərəlɪ] *adv* **1.** [gen] du point de vue de la structure **2.** CONSTR du point de vue de la construction ■ **the building is ~ sound** le bâtiment est solidement construit.

structure ['strʌktʃər] ◇ *n* **1.** [composition, framework] structure *f* ■ [of building] structure *f*, ossature *f*, armature *f* **2.** [building] construction *f*, bâtisse *f*.
◇ *vt* structurer.

structured ['strʌktʃəd] *adj* structuré.

struggle ['strʌgl] ◇ *n* [gen] lutte *f* ■ [physical fight] bagarre *f*, lutte *f* ■ **power ~** lutte pour le pouvoir ■ **there was evidence of a ~** il y avait des traces de lutte ■ **the rebels put up a fierce ~** les rebelles ont opposé une vive résistance ■ **they surrendered without a ~** ils se sont rendus sans opposer de résistance ■ **I finally succeeded but not without a ~** j'y suis finalement parvenu, non sans peine ■ **it was a ~ to convince him** on a eu du mal à le convaincre ■ **power ~** lutte pour le pouvoir ■ **there was a bitter ~ for leadership of the party** les candidats à la direction du parti se sont livré une lutte acharnée ■ **bringing up the children on her own was an uphill ~** *UK* élever ses enfants seule n'a pas été facile ■ **it was a ~ for him to climb the ten flights of stairs** il a eu de la peine à monter les dix étages à pied.
◇ *vi* **1.** [fight] lutter, se battre ■ **she ~d with her attacker** elle a lutté contre *OR* s'est battue avec son agresseur ■ **to ~ with one's conscience** se débattre avec sa conscience **2.** [try hard, strive] lutter, s'efforcer, se démener ■ **I ~d to open the door** je me suis démené pour ouvrir la porte ■ **he ~d with the lock** il s'est battu avec la serrure ■ **she ~d to control her temper** elle avait du mal à garder son calme ■ **she had to ~ to make ends meet** elle a eu bien du mal à joindre les deux bouts ■ **I left him struggling through a Latin translation** je l'ai laissé aux prises avec une traduction latine **3.** [expressing movement] **: he ~d back up onto the ledge** il remonta avec peine *OR* avec difficulté sur la corniche ■ **he ~d into his clothes** il enfila ses habits avec peine ■ **to ~ to one's feet** [old person] se lever avec difficulté *OR* avec peine ; [in fight] se relever péniblement ■ **to ~ up a hill** [person] gravir péniblement une colline ; [car] peiner dans une côte.
◆ **struggle along** *vi insep liter* peiner, avancer avec peine ■ *fig* subsister avec difficulté.
◆ **struggle on** *vi insep* **1.** = **struggle along 2.** [keep trying] continuer à se battre.
◆ **struggle through** *vi insep* [in difficult situation] s'en sortir tant bien que mal.

struggling ['strʌglɪŋ] *adj* [hard up - painter, writer etc] qui tire le diable par la queue, qui a du mal à joindre les deux bouts.

strum [strʌm] (*pret & pp* **strummed**, *cont* **strumming**) ◇ *vt* [guitar] gratter sur ■ **to ~ a tune on the guitar** jouer un petit air à la guitare.
◇ *vi* [guitarist] gratter ■ **she started strumming on her guitar** elle commença à gratter sa guitare.
◇ *n* [on guitar] raclement *m* ■ **he gave the guitar a ~** il a gratté les cordes de la guitare.

strumpet ['strʌmpɪt] *n arch & hum* femme *f* de petite vertu.

strung [strʌŋ] ◇ *pt & pp* ▷ **string**.
◇ *adj* [guitar, piano] muni de cordes, monté ■ [tennis racket] cordé.

strung-out△ *adj* **1.** *drugs sl* **to be ~** [addicted] être accroché *OR* accro ; [high] être shooté△, planer ; [suffering withdrawal symptoms] être en manque **2.** [uptight] crispé, tendu.

strung-up *adj inf* tendu, nerveux.

strut [strʌt] (*pret & pp* **strutted**, *cont* **strutting**) ◇ *n* **1.** [support - for roof, wall] étrésillon *m*, étançon *m*, contrefiche *f* ; [- for building] étai *m*, support *m* ; [- between uprights] entretoise *f*, traverse *f* ; [- for beam] jambe *f* de force ; [- in plane wing, model] support *m* **2.** [crossbar - of chair, ladder] barreau *m* **3.** [gait] démarche *f* fière.
◇ *vi* **: to ~ (about)** *OR* **around** plastronner, se pavaner.
◇ *vt US* **to ~ one's stuff** *inf* se montrer en spectacle.

strychnine ['strɪkni:n] *n* strychnine *f*.

stub [stʌb] (*pret & pp* **stubbed**, *cont* **stubbing**) ◇ *n* **1.** [stump - of tree] chicot *m*, souche *f* ; [- of pencil] bout *m* ; [- of tail] moignon *m* ; [- of cigarette] mégot *m* **2.** [counterfoil - of cheque] souche *f*, talon *m* ; [- of ticket] talon *m*.
◇ *vt* **: to ~ one's toe/foot** se cogner le doigt de pied/le pied ■ **he stubbed his toe against the kerb** il a buté contre le bord du trottoir.
◆ **stub out** *vt sep* [cigarette] écraser.

stubble ['stʌbl] *n* **1.** AGRIC chaume *m* **2.** [on chin] barbe *f* de plusieurs jours.

stubbly ['stʌblɪ] (*comp* **stubblier**, *superl* **stubbliest**) *adj* **1.** [chin, face] mal rasé ■ [beard] de plusieurs jours ■ [hair] en brosse **2.** [field] couvert de chaume.

stubborn ['stʌbən] *adj* **1.** [determined - person] têtu, obstiné ; [- animal] rétif, récalcitrant ; [- opposition] obstiné, acharné ; [- refusal, insistence] obstiné ■ **she maintained a ~ silence** elle garda obstinément le silence *OR* s'obstina à ne rien dire **2.** [resistant - cold, cough, symptoms] persistant, opiniâtre ; [- stain] récalcitrant, rebelle.

stubbornly ['stʌbənlɪ] *adv* obstinément, opiniâtrement ■ **he ~ insisted on doing it himself** il s'obstina à le faire lui-même.

stubbornness ['stʌbənnɪs] *n* [of person] entêtement *m*, obstination *f*, opiniâtreté *f* ▪ [of resistance] acharnement *m*.

stubby ['stʌbɪ] (*comp* **stubbier**, *superl* **stubbiest**) ◇ *adj* [finger] boudiné, court et épais ▪ [tail] très court, tronqué ▪ [person] trapu.
◇ *n Australia inf* petite canette *f* de bière.

stucco ['stʌkəʊ] (*pl* **stuccos** *OR pl* **stuccoes**) ◇ *n* stuc *m*.
◇ *comp* [ceiling, wall, façade] de *OR* en stuc, stuqué.
◇ *vt* stuquer.

stuck [stʌk] ◇ *pt* & *pp* ▷ **stick**.
◇ *adj* **1.** [jammed - window, mechanism] coincé, bloqué ; [- vehicle, lift] bloqué ▪ **he got his hand ~ inside the jar** il s'est pris *OR* coincé la main dans le pot ▪ **to get ~ in the mud** s'embourber ▪ **to get ~ in the sand** s'enliser ▪ **to be** *OR* **to get ~ in traffic** être coincé *OR* bloqué dans les embouteillages ▪ [stranded] coincé, bloqué ▪ **they were** *OR* **they got ~ at the airport overnight** ils sont restés bloqués *OR* ils ont dû passer toute la nuit à l'aéroport
2. [in difficulty] : **if you get ~ go on to the next question** si tu sèches, passe à la question suivante ▪ **he's never ~ for an answer** il a toujours réponse à tout ▪ **to be ~ for money** être à court d'argent
3. [in an unpleasant situation, trapped] coincé ▪ **to be ~ in a boring/dead-end job** avoir un boulot ennuyeux/sans avenir
4. *inf* [lumbered] : **to get** *OR* **to be ~ with sthg** se retrouver avec qqch sur les bras ▪ **as usual I got ~ with (doing) the washing-up** comme d'habitude, c'est moi qui me suis tapé la vaisselle ▪ **he was ~ with the nickname "Teddy"** le surnom "de Teddy" lui est resté ▪ **it's not a very good car but we're ~ with it** ce n'est pas génial comme voiture, mais on n'a pas le choix
5. *inf* [fond, keen] : **to be ~ on sb** en pincer pour qqn
6. *UK inf phr* **he got ~ into his work** il s'est mis au travail ▪ **get ~ in!** allez-y!

stuck-up *adj inf* bêcheur, snob.

stud [stʌd] (*pret* & *pp* **studded**, *cont* **studding**) ◇ *n* **1.** [nail, spike] clou *m* (*à grosse tête*) ▪ [decorative] clou *m* (*décoratif*) ▪ [on shoe] clou *m* (*à souliers*), caboche *f* ▪ [on belt] clou *m* ▪ [on football boots, track shoes] crampon *m* ▪ [on tyre] clou *m* **2.** [earring] = **stud earring 3.** [on roadway] catadioptre *m* **4.** [on shirt] agrafe *f* (*servant à fermer un col, un plastron etc*) **5.** TECH [screw] goujon *m* ▪ [pin, pivot] tourillon *m* ▪ [lug] ergot *m* **6.** CONSTR montant *m* **7.** [on chain] étai *m* **8.** [reproduction] monte *f* ▪ **to put a stallion (out) to ~** mener un étalon à la monte ▪ **to be at ~** saillir **9.** [stud farm] haras *m* **10.** [stallion] étalon *m* **11.**△ [man - gen] mec△ *m* ▪ [promiscuous man] tombeur *m* ▪ [lover] jules△ *m*.
◇ *vt* [shoes, belt] clouter ▪ [door, chest] clouter, garnir de clous.

studded ['stʌdɪd] *adj* **1.** [tyre, belt, jacket] clouté **2.** [spangled] : **~ with** émaillé *OR* parsemé de.

-studded *in cpds*: **diamond~** émaillé de diamants ▪ **star~** [sky] parsemé d'étoiles ; [show] plein de vedettes.

stud earring *n* clou *m* d'oreille.

student ['stju:dnt] ◇ *n* UNIV étudiant *m*, - e *f* ▪ SCH élève *mf*, lycéen *m*, - enne *f* ▪ **she's a biology ~** *OR* **a ~ of biology** elle étudie la biologie *OR* est étudiante en biologie.
◇ *comp* [life] d'étudiant, estudiantin ▪ [hall of residence, canteen] universitaire ▪ [participation - UNIV] étudiant ▪ SCH des élèves ▪ [power, union] étudiant ▪ [protest - UNIV] d'étudiants, étudiant ▪ SCH d'élèves, de lycéens ▪ [attitudes - UNIV] des étudiants ▪ SCH des élèves.

student card *n* carte *f* d'étudiant.

student grant *n* bourse *f* (d'études).

student hostel *n* résidence *f* universitaire.

student loan *n prêt bancaire pour étudiants*.

student nurse *n* élève *m* infirmier, élève *f* infirmière.

studentship ['stju:dntʃɪp] *n UK* bourse *f* (d'études).

students' union *n* **1.** [trade union] syndicat *m* *OR* union *f* des étudiants **2.** [premises] ≃ foyer *m* des étudiants.

STUDENTS' UNION

Dans les universités britanniques et américaines, on appelle *students' union* à la fois le syndicat des étudiants et le local lui-même. Les syndicats défendent les intérêts des étudiants et leur offrent différents services.

student teacher *n* [in primary school] instituteur *m*, - trice *f* stagiaire ▪ [in secondary school] professeur *m* stagiaire.

stud farm *n* haras *m*.

studied ['stʌdɪd] *adj* [ease, politeness, indifference] étudié ▪ [insult, rudeness, negligence] délibéré ▪ [elegance] recherché ▪ [manner, pose] étudié, affecté ▪ **he wore a look of ~ boredom** il affichait l'ennui.

studio ['stju:dɪəʊ] (*pl* **studios**) *n* [gen - CIN] & RADIO studio *m*.

studio apartment *n US* studio *m*.

studio audience *n* public *m* (*présent lors de la diffusion ou de l'enregistrement d'une émission*).

studio couch *n* canapé-lit *m*, canapé *m* convertible.

studio flat *n UK* studio *m*.

studious ['stju:djəs] *adj* **1.** [diligent - person] studieux, appliqué ▪ [painstaking - attention, effort] soutenu ; [- piece of work] soigné, sérieux **2.** [deliberate - indifference] délibéré, voulu.

studiously ['stju:djəslɪ] *adv* **1.** [diligently - prepare, work, examine] minutieusement, soigneusement **2.** [deliberately] d'une manière calculée *OR* délibérée ▪ **~ indifferent** d'une indifférence feinte ▪ **she ~ ignored him** elle s'ingéniait à ignorer sa présence.

study ['stʌdɪ] ◇ *vt* (*pl* **studies**) **1.** [gen - SCH] & UNIV étudier ▪ **she's studying medicine/history** elle fait des études de médecine/d'histoire, elle est étudiante en médecine/histoire **2.** [examine - plan, evidence, situation] étudier, examiner ▪ [observe - expression, reactions] étudier, observer attentivement ; [- stars] observer.
◇ *vi* (*pret* & *pp* **studied**) [gen] étudier ▪ SCH & UNIV étudier, faire ses études ▪ **she's ~ing to be an architect** elle fait des études pour devenir architecte *OR* des études d'architecture ▪ **he's ~ing for a degree in history** il étudie dans le but d'obtenir un diplôme d'histoire ▪ **to ~ for an exam** préparer un examen ▪ **I studied under her at university** je suivais ses cours à l'université.
◇ *n* (*pl* **studies**) **1.** [gen] étude *f* ▪ **he sets aside one day a week for ~** il consacre un jour par semaine à ses études ▪ **the plan is under ~** le projet est à l'étude ▪ **her thesis is a ~ of multi-racial communities** sa thèse est une étude des communautés *OR* sur les communautés multiraciales **2.** [room] bureau *m*, cabinet *m* de travail **3.** ART, MUS & PHOT étude *f*.
◇ *comp* [hour, period, room] d'étude ▪ **~ tour** voyage *m* d'étude.
◆ **studies** *npl* SCH & UNIV études *fpl* ▪ **the School of Oriental Studies** l'Institut des études orientales.

study group *n* groupe *m* de travail *OR* d'étude.

study hall *n US* [place] salle *f* de permanence *OR* d'études ▪ [period] heure *f* de permanence *OR* d'étude.

stuff [stʌf] ◇ *n* (*U*) **1.** *inf* [indefinite sense - things] choses *fpl*, trucs *mpl* ; [- substance] substance *f*, matière *f* ▪ **he writes some good ~** il écrit de bons trucs ▪ **what's that sticky ~ in the sink?** qu'est-ce que c'est que ce truc gluant dans l'évier? ▪ **they go climbing and sailing and ~ like that** ils font de l'escalade, de la voile et des trucs du même genre ▪ **I used to drink whisky but now I never touch the ~** avant, je buvais du whisky, mais maintenant je n'y touche plus ▪ **no thanks, I can't stand the ~** non merci, j'ai horreur de ça ▪ **this mustard is strong ~** cette moutarde est forte ▪ **the book is strong ~** [sexually explicit] ce livre n'est pas à mettre entre toutes les mains ; [depressing] ce livre est dur ▪ **she's a nice bit of ~!** c'est un canon!
2. *inf pej* [rubbish, nonsense] bêtises *fpl*, sottises *fpl* ▪ **don't give me all that ~ about the British Empire!** passe-moi le topo débile sur l'empire britannique! ▪ **do you call that ~ art/music?** vous appelez ça de l'art/de la musique?
3. *inf* [possessions] affaires *fpl* ▪ **clear all that ~ off the table!** enlève tout ce bazar de sur la table! ▪ **have you packed all your**

~? est-ce que tu as fini de faire tes bagages? ■ [equipment] affaires *fpl*, matériel *m* ■ **where's my shaving/fishing ~?** où est mon matériel de rasage/de pêche?
4. *inf phr* **to do one's ~** faire ce qu'on a à faire ■ **that's the ~!** c'est ça!, allez-y! ■ **to know one's ~** connaître son affaire
5. *lit* [essence] étoffe *f* ■ **he's the ~ that heroes are made of** il est de l'étoffe dont sont faits les héros
6.△ *drug sl* came△ *f*
7. *arch* [fabric] étoffe *f* (de laine).
◇ *vt* **1.** *inf* [shove] fourrer ■ [expressing anger, rejection etc] : **he told me I could ~ my report**△ il m'a dit qu'il se foutait pas mal de mon rapport△ ■ **you can ~ that idea!**△ tu sais où tu peux te la mettre, ton idée!△ ■ **get ~ed!**△ va te faire voir!△ ■ **~ him!**△ il peut aller se faire voir!△
2. *inf* [cram, pack full] bourrer ■ **their house is ~ed with souvenirs from India** leur maison est bourrée de souvenirs d'Inde ■ **her head is ~ed with useless information** elle a la tête farcie de renseignements inutiles
3. [plug - gap] boucher
4. [cushion, armchair] rembourrer ■ **~ed with foam** rembourré de mousse
5. CULIN farcir ■ **~ed with sausagemeat** farci de chair à saucisse
6. [in taxidermy - animal, bird] empailler
7. *inf* [with food] : **to ~ o.s.** *OR* **one's face**△ bâfrer, s'empiffrer ■ **to ~ o.s. with cake** s'empiffrer de gâteau ■ **I'm ~ed** je n'ai plus faim
8. *US* POL [ballot box] remplir de bulletins de votes truqués.
◆ **stuff up** *vt sep* [block] boucher ■ **my nose is all ~ed up** j'ai le nez complètement bouché.

stuffed [stʌft] *adj* **1.** CULIN farci **2.** [chair, cushion] rembourré.

stuffed animal *n UK* [mounted] animal *m* empaillé ■ *US* [toy] peluche *f*.

stuffed shirt *n* prétentieux *m*, - euse *f*.

stuffily ['stʌfɪlɪ] *adv* [say, reply] d'un ton désapprobateur.

stuffiness ['stʌfɪnɪs] *n* **1.** [of room] manque *m* d'air **2.** [of person] esprit *m* collet monté *OR* vieux jeu, pruderie *f*.

stuffing ['stʌfɪŋ] *n* **1.** [for furniture, toys] rembourrage *m*, bourre *f* ■ [for clothes] rembourrage *m* ■ [in taxidermy] paille *f* ■ **to knock the ~ out of sb** *inf* [in fight] casser la figure à qqn ■ **the news of his death really knocked the ~ out of me** ça m'a fait un sacré coup d'apprendre qu'il était mort **2.** CULIN farce *f*.

stuffy ['stʌfɪ] (*comp* **stuffier**, *superl* **stuffiest**) *adj* **1.** [room] mal aéré, mal ventilé, qui sent le renfermé ■ **it's terribly ~ in here** [stale] ça sent terriblement le renfermé ici ; [stifling] on manque d'air *OR* on étouffe ici **2.** *pej* [person - prim] collet monté *(inv)* ; [- old-fashioned] vieux jeu *(inv)* ■ [atmosphere, reception] guindé **3.** [dull - book, subject, lecture] ennuyeux **4.** [nose] bouché.

stultify ['stʌltɪfaɪ] (*pret & pp* **stultified**) *vt* [make stupid] abrutir ■ [stifle - creativity, talent] étouffer.

stultifying ['stʌltɪfaɪɪŋ] *adj* [work] abrutissant, assommant ■ [atmosphere] abrutissant, débilitant.

stumble ['stʌmbl] ◇ *vi* **1.** [person] trébucher, faire un faux pas ■ [horse] broncher, faire un faux pas ■ **he ~d over the toys in the hall** il a trébuché sur les jouets dans le couloir ■ **to ~ along/in/out** avancer/entrer/sortir en trébuchant ■ **he was stumbling about in the dark** il avançait en trébuchant dans le noir ■ **they ~d out into the bright light** ils sortirent en chancelant sous la lumière aveuglante **2.** [in speech] trébucher ■ **to ~ over a long word** trébucher sur un mot long ■ **he managed to ~ through his lecture** c'est d'une voix mal assurée qu'il a finalement prononcé son cours.
◇ *n* **1.** [in walking] faux pas *m* **2.** [in speech] : **she read the poem without a ~** elle a lu le poème sans se tromper *OR* sans se reprendre une seule fois.
◆ **stumble across, stumble on, stumble upon** *vt insep* **1.** [meet] rencontrer par hasard, tomber sur **2.** [discover] trouver par hasard, tomber sur.

stumbling block ['stʌmblɪŋ-] *n* pierre *f* d'achoppement.

stump [stʌmp] ◇ *n* **1.** [of tree] chicot *m*, souche *f* **2.** [of limb, tail] moignon *m* ■ [of tooth] chicot *m* ■ [of pencil, blade] (petit) bout *m* **3.** *US* POL estrade *f (d'un orateur politique)* ■ **to be** *OR* **to go on the ~** faire une tournée électorale.
◇ *vt* **1.** *inf* [bewilder] laisser perplexe ■ [with question] coller ■ **I'm ~ed** [don't know answer] je sèche ; [don't know what to do] je ne sais pas quoi faire ■ **the question had them ~ed** la question les a laissés sans voix ■ **she's ~ed for an answer** [in quiz] elle ne connaît pas la réponse ; [for solution] elle ne trouve pas de solution **2.** *US* POL [constituency, state] faire une tournée électorale dans.
◇ *vi* **1.** [walk heavily] marcher d'un pas lourd ■ **to ~ in/out** [heavily] entrer/sortir d'un pas lourd **2.** *US* POL faire une tournée électorale.
◆ **stumps** *npl inf* [legs] quilles *fpl*.
◆ **stump up** *UK inf* ◇ *vi insep* casquer.
◇ *vt sep* [money] cracher, aligner ■ [deposit] payer.

stumpy ['stʌmpɪ] (*comp* **stumpier**, *superl* **stumpiest**) *adj* [person] boulot, courtaud ■ [arms, legs] court et épais ■ [tail] tronqué.

stun [stʌn] (*pret & pp* **stunned**, *cont* **stunning**) *vt* **1.** [knock out] assommer **2.** *fig* [astonish] abasourdir, stupéfier.

stung [stʌŋ] *pt & pp* ▻ **sting**.

stun gun *n* fusil *m* paralysant.

stunk [stʌŋk] *pp* ▻ **stink**.

stunned [stʌnd] *adj* **1.** [knocked out] assommé **2.** *fig* abasourdi, stupéfait ■ **she was ~ by the news** la nouvelle l'a abasourdi.

stunner ['stʌnər] *n inf* [woman] fille *f* superbe ■ [car] voiture *f* fantastique.

stunning ['stʌnɪŋ] *adj* **1.** [blow] étourdissant **2.** [astounding - news, event] stupéfiant, renversant ■ [beautiful - dress, car] fantastique ; [- woman, figure] superbe.

stunningly ['stʌnɪŋlɪ] *adv* remarquablement, incroyablement ■ **~ beautiful** d'une beauté éblouissante.

stunt [stʌnt] ◇ *n* **1.** [feat] tour *m* de force, exploit *m* spectaculaire ■ [in plane] acrobatie *f* (aérienne) ■ **it was quite a ~!** il fallait le faire! **2.** [by stunt man] cascade *f* ■ **to do a ~** [in plane] faire des acrobaties ; [stunt man] faire une cascade **3.** [trick] truc *m* ■ [hoax] farce *f*, canular *m* ■ **to pull a ~** faire un canular *OR* une farce **4.** [plant] plante *f* chétive *OR* rabougrie ■ [animal] animal *m* dont la croissance a été freinée.
◇ *comp* : **~ driver** conducteur *m* cascadeur, conductrice *f* cascadeuse ■ **~ pilot** aviateur *m*, - trice *f* qui fait des cascades, spécialiste *mf* de l'acrobatie aérienne.
◇ *vi* **1.** AERON faire des acrobaties **2.** CIN & TV faire des cascades.
◇ *vt* [impede - growth, development] retarder ; [- person] freiner *OR* retarder la croissance de ; [- intelligence] freiner le développement de.

stunted ['stʌntɪd] *adj* [person] chétif ■ [plant] chétif, rabougri ■ [growth, intelligence] retardé.

stunt man *n* cascadeur *m*.

stunt woman *n* cascadeuse *f*.

stupefaction [,stju:pɪ'fækʃn] *n* stupéfaction *f*, stupeur *f*.

stupefied ['stju:pɪfaɪd] *adj* stupéfait.

stupefy ['stju:pɪfaɪ] (*pret & pp* **stupefied**) *vt* **1.** [subj: alcohol, drugs, tiredness] abrutir ■ [subj: blow] assommer, étourdir **2.** [astound] stupéfier, abasourdir.

stupefying ['stju:pɪfaɪɪŋ] *adj* stupéfiant.

stupendous [stju:'pendəs] *adj* [amount, achievement, talent] extraordinaire, prodigieux ■ [event] prodigieux, extraordinaire ■ [book, film] extraordinaire.

stupid ['stju:pɪd] ◇ *adj* **1.** [foolish] stupide, bête ■ **he's always saying/doing ~ things** il dit/faitsans arrêt des bêtises ■ **stop being so ~!** arrête de faire l'idiot *OR* l'imbécile! **2.** *lit* [from alcohol, drugs, sleep] abruti, hébété ■ [from blow] étourdi ■ **to drink o.s. ~** s'abrutir d'alcool **3.** *inf* [wretched, confounded] maudit, fichu.
◇ *n inf* bêta *m*, - asse *f*, idiot *m*, - e *f*.

stupidity [stju:'pɪdətɪ] (*pl* **stupidities**) *n* stupidité *f*, bêtise *f*, sottise *f*.

stupidly ['stju:pɪdlɪ] *adv* stupidement, bêtement ■ **I ~ forgot to phone them** je suis bête, j'ai oublié de leur téléphoner.

stupor ['stju:pəʳ] *n* stupeur *f*, abrutissement *m* ■ **to be in a drunken ~** être abruti par l'alcool.

sturdily ['stɜ:dɪlɪ] *adv* **1.** [solidly] solidement, robustement ■ **to be ~ built** [person] être costaud *OR* bien bâti ; [toys, furniture, equipment] être solide ; [house] être de construction solide, être robuste **2.** [firmly - deny, refuse, oppose] énergiquement, vigoureusement.

sturdiness ['stɜ:dɪnɪs] *n* **1.** [solidity] solidité *f*, robustesse *f* **2.** [firmness] fermeté *f*.

sturdy ['stɜ:dɪ] (*comp* **sturdier**, *superl* **sturdiest**) *adj* **1.** [robust - person] robuste, vigoureux ; [- limbs] robuste ; [- table, tree, shoes] robuste, solide **2.** [firm - denial, defence, opposition, support] énergique, vigoureux ; [- voice] ferme.

sturgeon ['stɜ:dʒən] (*pl inv*) *n* esturgeon *m*.

stutter ['stʌtəʳ] ◇ *n* bégaiement *m* ■ **to speak with a** *OR* **to have a ~** bégayer, être bègue.
◇ *vi* bégayer.
◇ *vt* : **to ~ (out)** bégayer, bredouiller.

stutterer ['stʌtərəʳ] *n* bègue *mf*.

stuttering ['stʌtərɪŋ] ◇ *n* bégaiement *m*.
◇ *adj* bègue, qui bégaie.

sty [staɪ] (*pl* **sties**) *n* **1.** [for pigs] porcherie *f* **2.** = **stye**.

stye [staɪ] *n* orgelet *m*, compère-loriot *m*.

stygian ['stɪdʒɪən] *adj liter* glauque.

style [staɪl] ◇ *n* **1.** [manner] style *m*, manière *f* ■ ART, LIT & MUS style *m* ■ **~ of life** mode *m* de vie ■ **I don't like his ~ of dressing** je n'aime pas sa façon de s'habiller ■ **they've adopted a new management ~** [approach] ils ont adopté un nouveau style de gestion ■ **they danced the charleston, 1920s ~** ils ont dansé le charleston comme on le dansait dans les années vingt **2.** [fashion - in clothes] mode *f* ■ **to be dressed in the latest ~** être habillé à la dernière mode ■ [model, design] modèle *m* ■ **all the latest ~s** tous les derniers modèles
3. [elegance - of person] allure *f*, chic *m* ; [- of dress, picture, building, film] style *m* ■ **she's got real ~** elle a vraiment de l'allure *OR* du chic ■ **to live in ~** mener grand train, vivre dans le luxe ■ **he likes to do things in ~** il aime faire bien les choses ■ **they made their entrance in great ~** ils ont fait une entrée très remarquée ■ **they drove off in ~ in a fleet of limousines** ils sont partis en grande pompe dans un cortège de limousines
4. [type] genre *m* ■ **I wouldn't have thought cheating was your ~** je n'aurais jamais pensé que c'était ton genre de tricher ■ **that's the ~!** c'est ça!, bravo!
5. TYPO [in editing] style *m* ■ **house ~** style de la maison
6. *UK fml* [title] titre *m*
7. BOT style *m*
8. = **stile**.
◇ *vt* **1.** [call] appeler, désigner ■ **she ~s herself "countess"** elle se fait appeler "comtesse"
2. [design - dress, jewel, house] créer, dessiner ■ **to ~ sb's hair** coiffer qqn ■ **~d for comfort and elegance** conçu pour le confort et l'élégance
3. PRESS & TYPO [manuscript] mettre au point *(selon les précisions stylistiques de l'éditeur)*.

-style *in cpds* dans le style de ■ **baroque~ architecture** architecture *f* de style baroque, baroque *m*.

style sheet *n* COMPUT feuille *f* de style.

styli ['staɪlaɪ] *pl* ▷ **stylus**.

styling ['staɪlɪŋ] *n* [of dress] forme *f*, ligne *f* ■ [of hair] coupe *f* ■ [of car] ligne *f* ■ **~ gel** gel *m* coiffant ■ **~ mousse** mousse *f* coiffante.

stylish ['staɪlɪʃ] *adj* [person] élégant, chic *(inv)* ■ [clothes, hotel, neighbourhood] élégant, chic *(inv)* ■ [book, film] qui a du style.

stylishly ['staɪlɪʃlɪ] *adv* [dress] avec chic, avec allure, élégamment ■ [live] élégamment ■ [travel] dans le luxe ■ [write] avec style *OR* élégance.

stylishness ['staɪlɪʃnɪs] *n* chic *m*, élégance *f*.

stylist ['staɪlɪst] *n* **1.** [designer - for clothes] styliste *mf* (de mode), modéliste *mf* ; [- for cars, furniture] styliste *mf* ■ **(hair) ~** coiffeur *m*, - euse *f* **2.** ART & LIT styliste *mf*.

stylistic [staɪ'lɪstɪk] *adj* ART, LIT & LING stylistique.

stylistically [staɪ'lɪstɪklɪ] *adv* d'un point de vue stylistique.

stylistics [staɪ'lɪstɪks] *n (U)* stylistique *f*.

stylize, ise ['staɪlaɪz] *vt* styliser.

stylized ['staɪlaɪzd] *adj* stylisé.

stylus ['staɪləs] (*pl* **styluses** *OR pl* **styli** ['staɪlaɪ]) *n* [on record player] saphir *m* ■ [tool] style *m*, stylet *m*.

stymie ['staɪmɪ] ◇ *vt* **1.** [in golf] barrer le trou à **2.** *inf fig* [person] coincer ■ [plan] ficher en l'air.
◇ *n* [in golf] trou *m* barré ■ *fig* obstacle *m*, entrave *f*.

styptic ['stɪptɪk] ◇ *adj* styptique.
◇ *n* styptique *m*.

styptic pencil *n* crayon *m* hémostatique.

Styria ['stɪrɪə] *pr n* Styrie *f*.

Styrofoam® ['staɪrəfəʊm] *n* polystyrène *m* expansé.

Styx [stɪks] *pr n* : **the (River) ~** le Styx.

suave [swɑ:v] *adj* **1.** [polite, charming] poli ■ *pej* [smooth] doucereux, mielleux, onctueux **2.** [elegant] élégant, chic.

suavely ['swɑ:vlɪ] *adv* **1.** [politely, charmingly] poliment ■ *pej* [smoothly] mielleusement **2.** [elegantly] avec élégance.

suaveness ['swɑ:vnɪs], **suavity** ['swɑ:vətɪ] *n* **1.** [politeness, charm] politesse *f* ■ *pej* manières *fpl* doucereuses **2.** [elegance] élégance *f*.

sub [sʌb] (*pret & pp* **subbed**, *cont* **subbing**) ◇ *n* **1.** = **submarine 2.** = **subeditor 3.** = **subscription 4.** = **substitute**.
◇ *vi & vt* **1.** = **subcontract 2.** = **subedit**.

sub- *in cpds* sub-, sous ■ **to run a ~four minute mile** courir le mile en moins de quatre minutes.

subalpine [,sʌb'ælpaɪn] *adj* subalpin.

subaltern ['sʌbltən] ◇ *n* **1.** *UK* MIL *officier de l'armée de terre d'un rang inférieur à celui de capitaine* **2.** [subordinate - gen] subalterne *mf*, subordonné *m*, - e *f*.
◇ *adj* subalterne.

sub-aqua [-'ækwə] *adj* sous-marin, subaquatique.

subaquatic [,sʌbə'kwætɪk] *adj* subaquatique.

subarctic [,sʌb'ɑ:ktɪk] ◇ *adj* **1.** GEOG subarctique **2.** [very cold - weather] glacial, arctique.
◇ *n* zone *f* subarctique.

subatomic [,sʌbə'tɒmɪk] *adj* subatomique.

subcategory ['sʌb,kætəgərɪ] (*pl* **subcategories**) *n* sous-catégorie *f*.

subclass ['sʌbklɑ:s] *n* sous-classe *f*.

subclinical [,sʌb'klɪnɪkl] *adj* infraclinique.

subcommittee ['sʌbkə,mɪtɪ] *n* sous-comité *m*, sous-commission *f*.

subcompact [,sʌbkəm'pækt] *n US* (très) petite voiture *f*.

subconscious [,sʌb'kɒnʃəs] ◇ *adj* subconscient ■ **the ~ mind** le subconscient.
◇ *n* subconscient *m*.

subconsciously [,sʌb'kɒnʃəslɪ] *adv* d'une manière subconsciente, inconsciemment.

subcontinent [,sʌb'kɒntɪnənt] *n* sous-continent *m* ■ **the (Indian) Subcontinent** le sous-continent indien.

subcontract ◇ *vt* [,sʌbkən'trækt] [pass on] (faire) sous-traiter ■ **they ~ some of the work (out) to local firms** ils sous-traitent une partie du travail à des entreprises locales.
◇ *vi* [,sʌbkən'trækt] travailler en sous-traitance.
◇ *n* [sʌb'kɒntrækt] (contrat *m* de) sous-traitance *f*.

subcontracting [,sʌbkən'træktɪŋ] *adj* sous-traitant.

subcontractor [,sʌbkən'træktəʳ] *n* sous-traitant *m*, sous-traitante *f*.

subcortex [ˌsʌb'kɔ:teks] *n* zone *f* (cérébrale) sous-corticale.

subculture ['sʌbˌkʌltʃər] *n* **1.** [gen, - SOCIOL] subculture *f* **2.** BIOL culture *f* repiquée *OR* secondaire.

subcutaneous [ˌsʌbkju:'teɪnjəs] *adj* sous-cutané.

subcutaneously [ˌsʌbkju:'teɪnjəslɪ] *adv* de manière sous-cutanée.

subdivide [ˌsʌbdɪ'vaɪd] <> *vt* subdiviser.
<> *vi* se subdiviser.

subdivision [ˌsʌbdɪ'vɪʒn] *n* subdivision *f*.

subdominant [ˌsʌb'dɒmɪnənt] *n* BIOL & MUS sous-dominante *f*.

subdue [səb'dju:] *vt* **1.** [country, tribe] assujettir, soumettre ▪ [rebels] soumettre ▪ [rebellion] réprimer **2.** [feelings, passions] refréner, maîtriser ▪ [fears, anxiety] apaiser.

subdued [səb'dju:d] *adj* **1.** [person] silencieux ▪ [mood] sombre ▪ [emotion, feeling] contenu ▪ [audience] peu enthousiaste ▪ **it was rather a ~ gathering** ce fut un rassemblement plutôt sombre **2.** [voice, sound] bas ▪ [conversation] à voix basse **3.** [light, lighting] tamisé, atténué ▪ [colours] sobre.

subedit [ˌsʌb'edɪt] <> *vt* corriger, préparer pour l'impression.
<> *vi* travailler comme secrétaire de rédaction.

subeditor [ˌsʌb'edɪtər] *n* secrétaire *mf* de rédaction.

subentry [ˌsʌb'entrɪ] (*pl* **subentries**) *n* sous-entrée *f*.

subequatorial ['sʌbˌekwə'tɔ:rɪəl] *adj* subéquatorial.

subgroup ['sʌbgru:p] *n* sous-groupe *m*.

subhead ['sʌbhed], **subheading** ['sʌbˌhedɪŋ] *n* [title] sous-titre *m* ▪ [division] paragraphe *m*.

subhuman [ˌsʌb'hju:mən] <> *adj* [intelligence] limité ▪ [crime] brutal, bestial ▪ **to live in ~ conditions** vivre dans des conditions terribles *OR* inhumaines.
<> *n* sous-homme *m*.

subject <> *n* ['sʌbdʒekt] **1.** [topic] sujet *m* ▪ **on the ~ of** au sujet de, à propos de ▪ **let's come** *OR* **get back to the ~** revenons à nos moutons ▪ **don't try and change the ~** n'essaie pas de changer de conversation *OR* de sujet ▪ **let's drop the ~** parlons d'autre chose ▪ **while we're on the ~** à (ce) propos ▪ **while we're on the ~ of holidays** puisque nous parlons de vacances
2. [in letters and memos] : **~: recruitment of new staff** objet: recrutement de personnel
3. ART, LIT & PHOT sujet *m*
4. GRAM & PHILOS sujet *m*
5. SCH & UNIV matière *f*, discipline *f* ▪ [field] domaine *m* ▪ **I was always better at science ~s** j'ai toujours été plus fort en sciences ▪ **it's not really my ~** ce n'est pas vraiment mon domaine
6. POL sujet *m*, - ette *f* ▪ **she is a British ~** c'est une ressortissante britannique ▪ **foreign ~s** ressortissants *mpl* étrangers
7. MED & PSYCHOL [of test] sujet *m*
8. [cause] sujet *m*, motif *m*, raison *f* ▪ **he was the ~ of much comment** il a été l'objet de nombreux commentaires.
<> *adj* ['sʌbdʒekt] **1.** [subordinate] dépendant ▪ **they are ~ to my authority** ils sont placés sous mon autorité, ils dépendent de moi ▪ **we are all ~ to the rule of law** nous sommes tous soumis à la loi
2. [liable, prone] : **~ to** sujet à ▪ **~ to attack** exposé à l'attaque ▪ **the terms are ~ to alteration without notice** les termes peuvent être modifiés sans préavis ▪ **~ to tax** imposable ▪ **the price is ~ to a handling charge** les frais de manutention sont en sus.
<> *vt* [səb'dʒekt] **1.** [country, people] soumettre, assujettir
2. [expose] : **to ~ to** soumettre à ▪ **they ~ all applicants to lengthy testing procedures** ils font passer de longs examens à tous les candidats ▪ **the material was ~ed to intense heat** le matériau a été soumis *OR* exposé à une température très élevée ▪ **I refuse to ~ anyone to such indignities** je refuse de faire subir de tels affronts à qui que ce soit.
◆ **subject to** *prep phr* ['sʌbdʒekt] [save for] sous réserve de, sauf ▪ [conditional upon] à condition de ▪ **these are the rules, ~ to revision** voici le règlement, sous réserve de modification ▪ **~ to your passing the exam** à condition de réussir *OR* à condition que vous réussissiez l'examen.
Voir module d'usage

subject catalogue *n* fichier *m* par matières.

subject index *n* index *m* des matières.

subjection [səb'dʒekʃn] *n* **1.** [act of subjecting] assujettissement *m* **2.** [state of being subjected] sujétion *f*, assujettissement *m*, soumission *f*.

subjective [səb'dʒektɪv] <> *adj* **1.** [viewpoint, argument, criticism] subjectif **2.** GRAM [pronoun, case] sujet ▪ [genitive] subjectif **3.** MED [symptom] subjectif.
<> *n* GRAM (cas *m*) sujet *m*, nominatif *m*.

subjectively [səb'dʒektɪvlɪ] *adv* subjectivement.

subjectivism [səb'dʒektɪvɪzm] *n* subjectivisme *m*.

subjectivity [ˌsʌbdʒek'tɪvətɪ] *n* subjectivité *f*.

subject matter *n* [topic] sujet *m*, thème *m* ▪ [substance] substance *f*, contenu *m*.

sub judice [-'dʒu:dɪsɪ] *adj* en instance, pendant.

subjugate ['sʌbdʒʊgeɪt] *vt* **1.** [people, tribe, country] assujettir, soumettre ▪ [rebels] soumettre **2.** [feelings] dompter ▪ [reaction] réprimer.

subjugation [ˌsʌbdʒʊ'geɪʃn] *n* soumission *f*, assujettissement *m*.

subjunctive [səb'dʒʌŋktɪv] <> *adj* subjonctif ▪ **~ mood** mode *m* subjonctif.
<> *n* subjonctif *m* ▪ **in the ~** au subjonctif.

sublease [ˌsʌb'li:s] <> *n* sous-location *f*.
<> *vt* sous-louer.

sublet [ˌsʌb'let] (*pret & pp* **sublet**, *cont* **subletting**) <> *vt* sous-louer.
<> *n* sous-location *f*.

sublieutenant [ˌsʌblef'tenənt] *n UK* ≃ enseigne *m* de vaisseau deuxième classe.

CHANGING THE SUBJECT

Au fait, tu as des nouvelles de Jean-Pierre ? By the way, have you heard from Jean-Pierre?

Puisqu'on parle d'argent *OU* **En parlant d'argent, tu n'oublies pas que tu me dois 10 euros ?** Talking of money, you haven't forgotten that you owe me 10 euros, have you?

À propos de livres, ce n'est pas à toi que j'aurais prêté « Germinal », par hasard ? While we're on the subject of books, it wasn't you that I lent "Germinal" to, was it?

Ah, tant que j'y pense *OU* **avant que j'oublie, ta mère a appelé.** Oh, before I forget, your mother called.

Oui, comme je disais tout à l'heure... Yes, as I was just saying...

Tout ça c'est très bien, mais on n'a toujours pas parlé du cadeau d'Annick. That's all well and good, but we still haven't discussed Annick's present.

Bon, changeons de sujet ! Right, let's change the subject!

Et si on parlait d'autre chose ? Let's talk about something else!

sublimate <> *vt* ['sʌblɪmeɪt] [gen, - CHEM] [PSYCH] sublimer.
<> *n* ['sʌblɪmət] CHEM sublimé *m*.

sublimation [ˌsʌblɪ'meɪʃn] *n* sublimation *f*.

sublime [sə'blaɪm] <> *adj* **1.** [noble, inspiring] sublime **2.** *inf* [very good] génial, sensationnel **3.** [utter - disregard, contempt, ignorance] suprême, souverain.
<> *n* : **the ~** le sublime ■ **from the ~ to the ridiculous** du sublime au grotesque.
<> *vt* sublimer.

sublimely [sə'blaɪmlɪ] *adv* complètement, totalement.

subliminal [ˌsʌb'lɪmɪnl] *adj* infraliminaire, subliminaire, subliminal ■ **~ advertising** publicité *f* subliminale *OR* invisible.

submachine gun [ˌsʌbmə'ʃi:n-] *n* mitraillette *f*.

submarine [ˌsʌbmə'ri:n] <> *n* sous-marin *m*.
<> *adj* sous-marin.

submariner [sʌb'mærɪnəʳ] *n* sous-marinier *m*.

submediant [ˌsʌb'mi:djənt] *n* sus-dominante *f*, sixte *f*.

submenu ['sʌbˌmenju:] *n* COMPUT sous-menu *m*.

submerge [səb'mɜ:dʒ] <> *vt* **1.** [plunge] submerger, immerger ■ **to ~ o.s. in work** *fig* se plonger dans le travail **2.** [flood] submerger, inonder.
<> *vi* [submarine] plonger.

submerged [səb'mɜ:dʒd] *adj* submergé ■ **a ~ volcano** un volcan sous-marin.

submersible [səb'mɜ:səbl] <> *adj* submersible.
<> *n* submersible *m*.

submersion [səb'mɜ:ʃn] *n* **1.** [in liquid] immersion *f* ■ [of submarine] plongée *f* **2.** [flooding] inondation *f*.

submission [səb'mɪʃn] *n* **1.** [yielding] soumission *f* ■ **their total ~ to fate** leur fatalisme ■ **to beat sb into ~** réduire qqn par la violence **2.** [submissiveness] soumission *f*, docilité *f* **3.** [referral - gen] soumission *f* ■ LAW [of case] renvoi *m* **4.** [proposition, argument - gen] thèse *f* ■ LAW plaidoirie *f* ■ **her ~ is that...** elle soutient que... **5.** [in wrestling] soumission *f*.

submissive [səb'mɪsɪv] *adj* soumis.

submissively [səb'mɪsɪvlɪ] *adv* [behave, confess, accept] docilement ■ [yield, react] avec résignation.

submissiveness [səb'mɪsɪvnɪs] *n* soumission *f*, docilité *f*.

submit [səb'mɪt] (*pret & pp* **submitted**, *cont* **submitting**)
<> *vi* **1.** *liter* se rendre, se soumettre **2.** *fig* se soumettre, se plier ■ **we shall never ~ to such demands** nous n'accéderons jamais à de telles exigences ■ **to ~ to one's fate** accepter son destin.
<> *vt* **1.** [propose] soumettre ■ **I ~ that...** LAW je soutiens *OR* je maintiens que... **2.** [yield] : **to ~ o.s. to sb/sthg** se soumettre à qqn/qqch.

subnormal [ˌsʌb'nɔ:ml] *adj* **1.** [person] arriéré ■ **educationally ~ children** des enfants arriérés *(du point de vue scolaire)* **2.** [temperatures] au-dessous de la normale.

suborder ['sʌbˌɔ:dəʳ] *n* BIOL sous-ordre *m*.

subordinate <> *n* [sə'bɔ:dɪnət] subordonné *m*, - e *f*, subalterne *mf*.
<> *adj* **1.** [in rank, hierarchy] subordonné, subalterne ■ **he is ~ to the duty officer** son grade est inférieur à celui de l'officier de permanence **2.** [secondary] subordonné, accessoire ■ **but that is ~ to the main problem** mais c'est secondaire par rapport au problème principal **3.** GRAM subordonné.
<> *vt* [sə'bɔ:dɪneɪt] subordonner.

subordinate clause [sə'bɔ:dɪnət-] *n* GRAM (proposition *f*) subordonnée *f*.

subordinating conjunction [sə'bɔ:dɪneɪtɪŋ-] *n* GRAM conjonction *f* de subordination.

subordination [səˌbɔ:dɪ'neɪʃn] *n* subordination *f*.

suborn [sʌ'bɔ:n] *vt* suborner.

subplot ['sʌbˌplɒt] *n* intrigue *f* secondaire.

subpoena [sə'pi:nə] <> *n* citation *f (à comparaître en qualité de témoin)*, assignation *f*.
<> *vt* citer *(à comparaître en qualité de témoin)*.

sub-postmaster *n* UK receveur *m (dans un petit bureau de poste local)*.

sub-postmistress *n* UK receveuse *f (dans un petit bureau de poste local)*.

sub-post office *n* UK petit bureau *m* de poste local.

subprogram ['sʌbˌprəʊgræm] *n* COMPUT sous-programme *m*.

subrogate ['sʌbrəgeɪt] *vt* subroger.

sub rosa [-'rəʊzə] *adv* confidentiellement, sous le sceau du secret.

subroutine ['sʌbru:ˌti:n] *n* COMPUT sous-programme *m*.

sub-Saharan Africa *pr n* Afrique *f* subsaharienne.

subscribe [səb'skraɪb] <> *vi* **1.** [to magazine, service] s'abonner, être abonné ■ **we ~ to several publications** nous sommes abonnés à plusieurs publications **2.** [to loan, fund, campaign, share issue] souscrire ■ **to ~ to a charity** faire des dons à une œuvre de charité **3.** : **to ~ to** [opinion, belief] souscrire à.
<> *vt* **1.** [donate] donner, faire don de **2.** *fml* [write - one's name, signature] apposer ■ [sign - document] signer.

subscriber [səb'skraɪbəʳ] *n* **1.** [to newspaper, service, telephone system] abonné *m*, - e *f* **2.** [to fund, campaign, share issue] souscripteur *m*, - trice *f* **3.** [to opinion, belief] partisan *m*, adepte *mf*.

subscriber trunk dialling *n* UK automatique *m*.

subscript ['sʌbskrɪpt] <> *n* COMPUT, MATHS & TYPO indice *m*.
<> *adj* en indice.

subscription [səb'skrɪpʃn] *n* **1.** [to newspaper, magazine] abonnement *m* ■ **to take out a ~ to a magazine** s'abonner à un magazine **2.** [to fund, campaign, share issue] souscription *f* ■ [to club, organization] cotisation *f* **3.** [to opinion, belief] adhésion *f*.

subsection ['sʌbˌsekʃn] *n* [of text, contract etc] article *m*, paragraphe *m*.

subsequent ['sʌbsɪkwənt] *adj* **1.** [next] suivant, subséquent *fml* ■ **to await ~ events** attendre de connaître la suite des événements ■ **~ to 1880** après 1880 ■ **~ to this** par la suite **2.** [consequent] conséquent, consécutif.

subsequently ['sʌbsɪkwəntlɪ] *adv* par la suite, subséquemment *fml*.

subservience [səb'sɜ:vjəns] *n* **1.** [servility] servilité *f* **2.** [subjugation] asservissement *m*.

subservient [səb'sɜ:vjənt] *adj* **1.** [servile] servile, obséquieux *pej* **2.** [subjugated] asservi **3.** [secondary] secondaire, accessoire.

subset ['sʌbset] *n* sous-ensemble *m*.

subside [səb'saɪd] *vi* **1.** [abate - shooting, laughter] cesser ; [- storm, rage, pain] se calmer ■ [recede - water] se retirer, baisser ; [- danger] s'éloigner **2.** [sink - house, land] s'abaisser ; [- wall, foundations] se tasser ■ [settle - sediment] se déposer.

subsidence [səb'saɪdns, 'sʌbsɪdns] *n* [of house, land] affaissement *m* ■ [of wall, foundations] tassement *m* ■ **'road liable to ~'** 'chaussée déformée'.

subsidiarity [sʌbˌsɪdɪ'ærɪtɪ] *n* subsidiarité *f*.

subsidiary [səb'sɪdjərɪ] (*pl* **subsidiaries**) <> *adj* [supplementary] supplémentaire, complémentaire ■ [secondary - question, reason] subsidiaire ; [- idea, action] accessoire ■ **~ company** filiale *f*.
<> *n* COMM filiale *f*.

subsidize, ise ['sʌbsɪdaɪz] *vt* subventionner.

subsidy ['sʌbsɪdɪ] (*pl* **subsidies**) *n* subvention *f* ■ **government ~** subvention de l'État ■ **export subsidies** primes *fpl* à l'exportation.

subsist [səb'sɪst] *vi* subsister ■ **they ~ on fish and rice** ils vivent de poisson et de riz.

subsistence [səb'sɪstəns] <> *n* subsistance *f*, existence *f*.
<> *comp* [wage] à peine suffisant pour vivre ▪ [economy, farming] d'autoconsommation ▪ **to live at ~ level** avoir tout juste de quoi vivre.

subsistence allowance *n* UK [advance] acompte *m* (*perçu avant l'engagement définitif*) ▪ [expenses] frais *mpl* (de subsistance).

subsoil ['sʌbsɔɪl] *n* GEOL sous-sol *m*.

subspecies ['sʌb,spi:ʃi:z] (*pl inv*) *n* sous-espèce *f*.

substance ['sʌbstəns] *n* **1.** [matter] substance *f* ▪ **illegal ~s** stupéfiants *mpl* **2.** [solidity] solidité *f* **3.** [essential part, gist] essentiel *m*, substance *f* ▪ [basis] fond *m* **4.** [significance, weight] étoffe *f*, poids *m* ▪ **their claim lacks ~** leur revendication est sans fondement OR n'est pas fondée **5.** [wealth] richesses *fpl* ▪ [power] pouvoir *m* ▪ [influence] influence *f* ▪ **a woman of ~** [rich] une femme riche OR aisée ; [powerful] une femme puissante ; [influential] une femme influente.
◆ **in substance** *adv phr* [generally] en gros, en substance ▪ [basically] à la base, au fond ▪ [in brief] en substance, en somme.

substance abuse *n fml* abus *m* de stupéfiants.

substandard [,sʌb'stændəd] *adj* **1.** [work, output] médiocre, en dessous des niveaux requis ▪ [meal, merchandise] de qualité inférieure ▪ **~ housing** *logements ne respectant pas les normes requises* ▪ **they live in ~ housing** ils habitent des logements insalubres **2.** LING non conforme à la norme.

substantial [səb'stænʃl] *adj* **1.** [large] considérable, important ▪ LAW [damages] élevé **2.** [nourishing - food] nourrissant ; [- meal] solide, copieux, substantiel **3.** [convincing - argument, evidence] solide, convaincant **4.** [real, tangible] réel, substantiel ▪ PHILOS substantiel **5.** [solidly built] solide **6.** [rich] riche, aisé ▪ [powerful] puissant ▪ [influential] influent ▪ [well-established] solide, bien établi ▪ **a ~ company** une société solidement implantée.

substantially [səb'stænʃəlɪ] *adv* **1.** [considerably] considérablement **2.** [generally] en gros, en grande partie ▪ [fundamentally] fondamentalement, au fond **3.** [solidly] solidement ▪ **~ built** solide **4.** PHILOS [as for the substance] substantiellement.

substantiate [səb'stænʃɪeɪt] *vt* confirmer, apporter OR fournir des preuves à l'appui de.

substantiation [səb,stænʃɪ'eɪʃn] *n* (*U*) [proof] preuve *f* ▪ [reason] bien-fondé *m*, justification *f*.

substantival [,sʌbstən'taɪvl] *adj* GRAM substantif.

substantive <> *adj* [sʌb'stæntɪv] **1.** [real, important] substantiel ▪ [permanent - rank] permanent ▪ [independent - means, resources] indépendant **2.** GRAM nominal.
<> *n* ['sʌbstəntɪv] GRAM substantif *m*.

substation ['sʌb,steɪʃn] *n* sous-station *f*.

substitute ['sʌbstɪtju:t] <> *n* **1.** [person] remplaçant *m*, - e *f* **2.** [thing] produit *m* de remplacement OR de substitution ▪ **we'll have to find a ~ for it** il faut que nous trouvions quelque chose pour le remplacer ▪ **use a low-fat ~ instead of butter** utilisez un produit à faible teneur en matière grasse à la place du beurre ▪ **sugar ~** édulcorant *m* de synthèse ▪ **there's no ~ for real coffee** rien ne vaut le vrai café **3.** GRAM terme *m* suppléant.
<> *adj* remplaçant ▪ **it'll do as a ~ cork** ça fera office de bouchon ▪ **~ teacher** US suppléant *m*, - e *f*.
<> *vt* [gen] substituer, remplacer ▪ SPORT remplacer ▪ **to ~ sthg for sthg** substituer qqch à qqch ▪ **margarine may be ~d for butter** on peut remplacer le beurre par de la margarine, on peut utiliser de la margarine au lieu du beurre.
<> *vi* : **to ~ for sb/sthg** remplacer qqn/qqch.

substitution [,sʌbstɪ'tju:ʃn] *n* [gen] remplacement *m*, substitution *f* ▪ SPORT remplacement *m*.

substrata [,sʌb'strɑ:tə] *pl* ▷ **substratum**.

substrate ['sʌbstreɪt] *n* [gen, - CHEM] [ELECTRON] substrat *m*.

substratum [,sʌb'strɑ:təm] (*pl* **substrata** [,sʌb'strɑ:tə]) *n* **1.** [infrastructure, base] fond *m* **2.** GEOL [underlying formation] substratum *m* ▪ [subsoil] sous-sol *m* **3.** LING substrat *m* **4.** PHOT substratum *m*.

substructure ['sʌb,strʌktʃər] *n* CONSTR infrastructure *f* ▪ **various ~s make up the organization** l'organisation se compose de plusieurs services distincts.

subsume [səb'sju:m] *vt* subsumer.

subtenant [,sʌb'tenənt] *n* sous-locataire *mf*.

subtend [səb'tend] *vt* sous-tendre.

subterfuge ['sʌbtəfju:dʒ] *n* subterfuge *m*.

subterranean [,sʌbtə'reɪnjən] *adj* souterrain.

subtitle ['sʌb,taɪtl] <> *n* CIN, LIT & PRESS sous-titre *m*.
<> *vt* sous-titrer.

subtitled ['sʌb,taɪtld] *adj* sous-titré, avec sous-titrage.

subtitling ['sʌb,taɪtlɪŋ] *n* sous-titrage *m*.

subtle ['sʌtl] *adj* subtil ▪ **there's a very ~ difference between them** il y a une très légère différence entre eux ▪ **you're not very ~, are you?** la subtilité n'est vraiment pas ton fort!

subtlety ['sʌtltɪ] (*pl* **subtleties**) *n* **1.** [subtle nature] subtilité *f* ▪ **~ is not one of his strong points** la subtilité n'est pas son fort **2.** [detail, distinction] subtilité *f*.

subtly ['sʌtlɪ] *adv* subtilement.

subtonic [,sʌb'tɒnɪk] *n* sous-tonique *f*.

subtotal ['sʌb,təʊtl] *n* total *m* partiel.

subtract [səb'trækt] *vt* soustraire, déduire ▪ **~ 52 from 110** ôtez OR retranchez 52 de 110.

subtraction [səb'trækʃn] *n* soustraction *f*.

subtropical [,sʌb'trɒpɪkl] *adj* subtropical.

suburb ['sʌbɜ:b] *n* banlieue *f*, faubourg *m* ▪ **the London ~ of Barking** Barking, dans la banlieue de Londres ▪ **in the ~s** en banlieue ▪ **the outer ~s** la grande banlieue.

SUBURB

À la différence du mot « banlieue » qui en est souvent la traduction, le mot « suburbs » ne désigne que rarement les quartiers en difficultés. Elle évoque plutôt des cités tranquilles, bourgeoises, confortables. Sur le plan social, en faisant la part des différences urbanistiques, les équivalents les plus proches des « banlieues en difficultés » françaises sont, en Grande-Bretagne, les *inner cities* (les centres urbains) et, aux États-Unis, les *housing projects* (proches des cités HLM).

suburban [sə'bɜ:bn] *adj* **1.** [street, railway, dweller] de banlieue ▪ [population, growth] de banlieue, suburbain **2.** *pej* [mentality, outlook] de petit-bourgeois.

suburbanite [sə'bɜ:bənaɪt] *n* banlieusard *m*, - e *f*.

suburbia [sə'bɜ:bɪə] *n* la banlieue ▪ **in ~** en banlieue.

subversion [səb'vɜ:ʃn] *n* subversion *f*.

subversive [səb'vɜ:sɪv] <> *adj* subversif.
<> *n* élément *m* subversif.

subvert [səb'vɜ:t] *vt* **1.** [undermine - society, state, institution] subvertir *lit*, renverser **2.** [corrupt - individual] corrompre.

subway ['sʌbweɪ] *n* **1.** UK [pedestrian underpass] passage *m* souterrain **2.** US [railway] métro *m*.

sub-zero *adj* au-dessous de zéro.

succeed [sək'si:d] <> *vi* **1.** [manage successfully] réussir ▪ **to ~ in doing sthg** réussir OR parvenir OR arriver à faire qqch ◐ **if at first you don't ~, try again** *prov* si vous ne réussissez pas du premier coup, recommencez **2.** [work out] réussir ▪ **the first attack did not ~** la première offensive a échoué **3.** [do well] réussir, avoir du succès ▪ **to ~ in business/in publishing** réussir dans les affaires/l'édition ◐ **nothing ~s like success** *prov* un succès en entraîne un autre **4.** [follow on] succéder ▪ **to ~ to the throne** monter sur le trône.

◇ *vt* [subj: person] succéder à, prendre la suite de ■ **I ~ed him as editor** je lui ai succédé au poste de rédacteur ▌[subj: event, thing] succéder à, suivre ■ **as month ~ed month** au fur et à mesure que les mois passaient.

succeeding [sək'si:dɪŋ] *adj* **1.** [subsequent] suivant, qui suit ■ **each ~ year** chaque année qui passe **2.** [future] futur, à venir.

success [sək'ses] ◇ *n* réussite *f*, succès *m* ■ **her ~ in the elections** sa victoire aux élections ■ **his ~ in the exam** son succès à l'examen ■ **to meet with** *OR* **to achieve ~** réussir ■ **I wish you every ~** je vous souhaite beaucoup de succès ■ **I had no ~ in trying to persuade them** je n'ai pas réussi à les convaincre ■ **I tried to convince them, but without ~** j'ai essayé de les convaincre, mais sans succès ■ **to make a ~ of sthg** mener qqch à bien ■ **I haven't had much ~ in finding work** mes recherches pour un emploi n'ont pas donné grand-chose ■ **their record was a great ~** leur disque a eu un succès fou ■ **the evening was a ~** la soirée a été réussie *OR* a été une réussite.
◇ *comp* [rate] de réussite, de succès.

successful [sək'sesful] *adj* **1.** [resulting in success - attempt, effort, plan] qui réussit ; [- negotiations] fructueux ; [- outcome] heureux ; [- performance, mission, partnership] réussi ■ **his efforts were supremely ~** ses efforts ont été couronnés de succès ■ **she was not ~ in her application for the post** sa candidature à ce poste n'a pas été retenue ■ **I was ~ in convincing them** j'ai réussi *OR* je suis arrivé *OR* je suis parvenu à les convaincre ■ **she brought the project to a ~ conclusion** elle a mené le projet à bien **2.** [thriving - singer, record, author, book, play] à succès ; [- businessman] qui a réussi ; [- life, career] réussi ■ **their first record was very ~** leur premier disque a eu un succès fou ■ **she's a ~ businesswoman** elle a réussi dans les affaires.

successfully [sək'sesfʊlɪ] *adv* avec succès ■ **to do sthg ~** réussir à faire qqch.

succession [sək'seʃn] *n* **1.** [series] succession *f*, suite *f* ■ **she made three phone calls in ~** elle a passé trois coups de fil de suite ■ **the fireworks went off in quick** *OR* **rapid ~** les feux d'artifice sont partis les uns après les autres **2.** [ascension to power] succession *f* ■ **his ~ to the post** sa succession au poste **3.** LAW [descendants] descendance *f* ■ [heirs] héritiers *mpl*.

successive [sək'sesɪv] *adj* [attempts, generations] successif ■ [days, years] consécutif.

successively [sək'sesɪvlɪ] *adv* [in turn] successivement, tour à tour, l'un/l'une après l'autre.

successor [sək'sesər] *n* **1.** [replacement] successeur *m* ■ **I'm to be his ~** c'est moi qui dois lui succéder ■ **she's the ~ to the throne** c'est l'héritière de la couronne **2.** [heir] héritier *m*, - ère *f*.

success story *n* réussite *f*.

succinct [sək'sɪŋkt] *adj* succinct, concis.

succinctly [sək'sɪŋktlɪ] *adv* succinctement, avec concision.

succor *US* = **succour**.

succour *UK*, **succor** *US* ['sʌkər] ◇ *n* secours *m*, aide *f*.
◇ *vt* secourir, aider.

succubus ['sʌkjʊbəs] (*pl* **succubi** [-baɪ]) *n* succube *m*.

succulence ['sʌkjʊləns] *n* succulence *f*.

succulent ['sʌkjʊlənt] ◇ *adj* **1.** [tasty] succulent **2.** BOT succulent.
◇ *n* plante *f* grasse.

succumb [sə'kʌm] *vi* **1.** [yield] succomber, céder ■ **he ~ed to her charm** il a succombé à son charme **2.** [die] succomber, mourir.

such [sʌtʃ] ◇ *det* & *predet* **1.** [of the same specified kind] tel, pareil ■ **~ a song** une telle chanson, une chanson pareille *OR* de ce genre ■ **~ songs** de telles chansons, des chansons pareilles *OR* de ce genre ■ **~ weather** un temps pareil *OR* comme ça ■ **no ~ place exists** un tel endroit n'existe pas ■ **have you ever heard ~ a thing?** avez-vous jamais entendu une chose pareille? ■ **~ a thing is unheard-of** ce genre de chose est sans précédent ■ **I said no ~ thing!** je n'ai rien dit de tel *OR* de la sorte! ■ **you'll do no ~ thing!** il n'en est pas question! ▌[followed by 'as'] : **there is no ~ thing as magic** la magie n'existe pas ■ **we will take ~ steps as are considered necessary** nous prendrons toutes les mesures nécessaires ■ **I'm not ~ a fool as to believe him!** je ne suis pas assez bête pour le croire! ■ **~ money as we have** le peu d'argent que nous avons ▌[followed by 'that'] : **their timetable is ~ that we never see them** leur emploi du temps est tel que nous ne les voyons jamais **2.** [as intensifier] tel ■ **my accounts are in ~ a mess!** mes comptes sont dans un de ces états! ■ **she has ~ courage!** elle a un de ces courages! ■ **it's ~ a pity you can't come!** c'est tellement dommage que vous ne puissiez pas venir! ■ **you gave me ~ a scare!** tu m'as fait une de ces peurs! ■ **~ tall buildings** des immeubles aussi hauts ■ **~ a handsome man** un si bel homme ■ **I didn't realize it was ~ a long way** je ne me rendais pas compte que c'était si loin ■ **I've never read ~ beautiful poetry** je n'ai jamais lu de si belle poésie ▌[followed by 'that'] : **he was in ~ pain that he fainted** il souffrait tellement qu'il s'est évanoui.
◇ *pron* : **~ is the power of the media** voilà ce que peuvent faire les médias ■ **~ were my thoughts last night** voilà où j'en étais hier soir ■ **~ is life!** c'est la vie!

➤ **and such** *adv phr* et d'autres choses de ce genre *OR* de la sorte.

➤ **as such** *adv phr* [strictly speaking] en soi ■ [in that capacity] en tant que tel, à ce titre ■ **she doesn't get a salary as ~** elle n'a pas de véritable salaire *OR* pas de salaire à proprement parler ■ **have they offered you more money? – well, not as ~** vous ont-ils proposé plus d'argent? – pas véritablement ■ **she's an adult and as ~ she has rights** elle est majeure et en tant que telle elle a des droits.

➤ **such and such** *predet phr* tel.

➤ **such as** *prep phr* tel que, comme ■ **I can think of lots of reasons – ~ as?** je vois beaucoup de raisons – comme quoi par exemple?

➤ **such as it is, such as they are** *adv phr* : **and this is my study, ~ as it is** et voici ce que j'appelle mon bureau ■ **I'll give you my opinion, ~ as it is** je vais vous donner mon avis, prenez-le pour ce qu'il vaut ■ **you're welcome to use my notes, ~ as they are** je te prêterai mes notes avec plaisir, elles valent ce qu'elles valent.

suchlike ['sʌtʃlaɪk] ◇ *adj* semblable, pareil.
◇ *pron* : **frogs, toads and ~** les grenouilles, les crapauds et autres animaux (du même genre).

suck [sʌk] ◇ *vt* **1.** [with mouth] sucer ■ **she was ~ing orange juice through a straw** elle sirotait du jus d'orange avec une paille ■ **~ the poison out** aspirez le poison ➤ **to ~ sb dry** prendre jusqu'à son dernier sou à qqn **2.** [pull] aspirer ■ **we found ourselves ~ed into an argument** *fig* nous nous sommes trouvés entraînés dans une dispute.
◇ *vi* **1.** [with mouth] : **to ~ at** *OR* **on sthg** sucer *OR* suçoter qqch ■ **the child was ~ing at her breast** l'enfant tétait son sein **2.**△ *US* [be disgusting] : **this town ~s!** cette ville est dégueulasse!△ **3.**△ *dated* & *phr* **(ya boo) ~s to you!** va te faire voir!△.
◇ *n* **1.** [act of sucking - gen] : **to have a ~ at sthg** sucer *OR* suçoter qqch ■ **he took a long ~ on his cigar** il tira longuement sur son cigare ■ [at breast] tétée *f* ■ **to give ~** donner le sein, allaiter **2.** [force] aspiration *f*.

➤ **suck down** *vt sep* [subj: sea, quicksand, whirlpool] engloutir.

➤ **suck off**▲ *vt sep* sucer▲, tailler une pipe à▲.

➤ **suck up** ◇ *vt sep* [subj: person] aspirer, sucer ■ [subj: vacuum cleaner, pump] aspirer ■ [subj: porous surface] absorber.
◇ *vi insep inf* **to ~ up to sb** lécher les bottes à qqn.

sucker ['sʌkər] ◇ *n* **1.** *inf* [dupe] pigeon *m*, gogo *m* ■ **I'm a ~ for chocolate** je raffole du chocolat ■ **you've been played for a ~** *US* vous vous êtes fait rouler *OR* pigeonner ■ **OK, ~, you asked for it** OK, mec, tu l'auras voulu **2.** *UK* [suction cup or pad] ventouse *f* **3.** ZOOL [of insect] suçoir *m* ■ [of octopus, leech] ventouse *f* **4.** BOT drageon *m* **5.** *US* [lollipop] sucette *f*.
◇ *vt* **1.** HORT enlever les drageons de **2.** △ *US* [dupe] refaire, pigeonner.
◇ *vi* BOT [plant] drageonner.

sucking pig ['sʌkɪŋ-] *n* cochon *m* de lait.

suckle ['sʌkl] ◇ *vt* **1.** [child] allaiter, donner le sein à ■ [animal] allaiter **2.** *fig* [raise] élever.
◇ *vi* téter.

suckling ['sʌklɪŋ] *n* **1.** [child] nourrisson *m*, enfant *m* encore au sein ■ [animal] animal *m* qui tète **2.** [act] allaitement *m*.

sucrose ['su:krəʊz] *n* saccharose *f*.

suction ['sʌkʃn] *n* succion *f*, aspiration *f* ■ **it adheres by ~** ça fait ventouse.

suction cup, suction pad *n* ventouse *f*.

suction pump *n* pompe *f* aspirante.

suction valve *n* clapet *m* OR soupape *f* d'aspiration.

Sudan [su:'dɑ:n] *pr n* Soudan *m* ■ **in ~, in the ~** au Soudan.

Sudanese [,su:də'ni:z] (*pl inv*) ◇ *n* Soudanais *m*, - e *f*.
◇ *adj* soudanais.

sudden ['sʌdn] *adj* soudain, subit ■ **there was a ~ bend in the road** il y avait un virage soudain ■ **she had a ~ change of heart** elle a soudainement OR subitement changé d'avis ■ **this is all very ~!** c'est plutôt inattendu! ■ **~ death** *liter* mort *f* subite ; GAMES & SPORT *jeu pour partager les ex aequo (où le premier point perdu, le premier but concédé etc, entraîne l'élimination immédiate)*.

◆ **all of a sudden** *adv phr* soudain, subitement, tout d'un coup.

sudden infant death syndrome *n* mort *f* subite du nourrisson.

suddenly ['sʌdnlɪ] *adv* soudainement, subitement, tout à coup.

suddenness ['sʌdnnɪs] *n* soudaineté *f*, caractère *m* subit OR imprévu.

sudoku ['su:dəʊku:] *n* sudoku *m*.

suds [sʌdz] *npl* [foam] mousse *f* ■ [soapy water] eau *f* savonneuse.

sue [su:] ◇ *vt* poursuivre en justice, intenter un procès à ■ **to ~ sb for** OR **over sthg** poursuivre qqn en justice pour qqch ■ **to be ~d for damages/libel** être poursuivi en dommages-intérêts/en diffamation ■ **she's suing him for divorce** elle a entamé une procédure de divorce.
◇ *vi* **1.** LAW intenter un procès, engager des poursuites ■ **she threatened to ~ for libel** elle a menacé d'intenter un procès en diffamation ■ **he's suing for divorce** il a entamé une procédure de divorce **2.** *fml* [solicit] : **to ~ for** solliciter.

suede [sweɪd] ◇ *n* daim *m*, suède *m spec*.
◇ *comp* [jacket, purse, shoes] en OR de daim ■ [leather] suédé.

suet ['sʊɪt] *n* graisse *f* de rognon.

suet pudding *n sorte de pudding sucré ou salé à base de farine et de graisse de bœuf.*

Suez ['sʊɪz] *pr n* Suez ■ **the ~ Canal** le canal de Suez ■ **the ~ crisis** l'affaire du canal de Suez.

suffer ['sʌfər] ◇ *vi* **1.** [feel pain] souffrir ■ **I'll make you ~ for this!** *fig* tu vas me payer ça!, je te revaudrai ça!
2. [be ill, afflicted] souffrir ■ **to ~ from** [serious disease] souffrir de ; [cold, headache] avoir ■ **to ~ from diabetes** être diabétique ■ **he's still ~ing from the effects of the anaesthetic** il ne s'est pas encore tout à fait remis des suites de l'anesthésie ■ **they're still ~ing from shock** ils sont encore sous le choc ■ **she ~s from an inferiority complex** elle fait un complexe d'infériorité
3. [be affected] : **it's the children who ~ in a marriage break-up** ce sont les enfants qui souffrent lors d'une séparation ■ **the low-paid will be the first to ~** les petits salaires seront les premiers touchés ■ **the schools ~ from a lack of funding** les établissements scolaires manquent de crédits
4. [deteriorate] souffrir, se détériorer ■ **her health is ~ing under all this stress** sa santé se ressent de tout ce stress.
◇ *vt* **1.** [experience - pain, thirst] souffrir de ; [- hardship] souffrir, subir ■ **she ~ed a lot of pain** elle a beaucoup souffert ■ **I ~ed agonies!** *inf* j'ai souffert le martyre! ■ **our scheme has ~ed a serious setback** notre projet a subi OR essuyé un grave revers ■ **you'll have to ~ the consequences** vous devrez en subir les conséquences
2. [stand, put up with] tolérer, supporter ■ **he doesn't ~ fools gladly** il ne tolère pas les imbéciles
3. *lit* [allow] permettre, souffrir *lit* ■ **~ the little children to come unto me** BIBLE laissez venir à moi les petits enfants.

sufferance ['sʌfrəns] *n* **1.** [tolerance] tolérance *f* ■ **on ~** par tolérance ■ **remember you are only here on ~** n'oubliez pas que votre présence ici n'est que tolérée OR est tout juste tolérée **2.** [endurance] endurance *f*, résistance *f* **3.** [suffering] souffrance *f*.

sufferer ['sʌfrər] *n* malade *mf*, victime *f* ■ **~s from heart disease** les personnes cardiaques ■ **a polio ~** un polio ■ **good news for arthritis ~s** une bonne nouvelle pour les personnes sujettes à l'arthrite OR qui souffrent d'arthrite.

suffering ['sʌfrɪŋ] ◇ *n* souffrance *f*, souffrances *fpl*.
◇ *adj* souffrant, qui souffre.

suffice [sə'faɪs] ◇ *vi fml* suffire, être suffisant ■ **~ it to say (that) she's overjoyed** inutile de dire qu'elle est ravie.
◇ *vt* suffire à, satisfaire ■ **empty promises will not ~ him** il ne se contentera pas de vaines promesses.

sufficiency [sə'fɪʃnsɪ] (*pl* **sufficiencies**) *n* quantité *f* suffisante ■ **the country already had a ~ of oil** le pays avait déjà suffisamment de pétrole OR du pétrole en quantité suffisante.

sufficient [sə'fɪʃnt] *adj* **1.** [gen] suffisant ■ **there's ~ food for everyone** il y a assez OR suffisamment à manger pour tout le monde ■ **have you had ~ to eat?** avez-vous mangé à votre faim? ■ **three will be quite ~ for our needs** trois nous suffiront amplement ■ **we don't have ~ evidence to convict them** nous ne disposons pas d'assez de preuves pour les inculper **2.** PHILOS suffisant.

sufficiently [sə'fɪʃntlɪ] *adv* suffisamment, assez ■ **a ~ large quantity** une quantité suffisante.

suffix ['sʌfɪks] ◇ *n* suffixe *m*.
◇ *vt* suffixer.

suffocate ['sʌfəkeɪt] ◇ *vi* **1.** [die] suffoquer, étouffer, s'asphyxier **2.** [be hot, lack fresh air] suffoquer, étouffer **3.** *fig* [with anger, emotion etc] s'étouffer, suffoquer.
◇ *vt* **1.** [kill] suffoquer, étouffer, asphyxier **2.** *fig* [repress, inhibit] étouffer, suffoquer.

suffocating ['sʌfəkeɪtɪŋ] *adj* **1.** [heat, room] suffocant, étouffant ■ [smoke, fumes] asphyxiant, suffocant **2.** *fig* étouffant.

suffocation [,sʌfə'keɪʃn] *n* suffocation *f*, étouffement *m*, asphyxie *f* ■ **to die from ~** mourir asphyxié.

suffrage ['sʌfrɪdʒ] *n* **1.** [right to vote] droit *m* de suffrage OR de vote ■ **universal ~** suffrage *m* universel ■ **women's ~** le droit de vote pour les femmes **2.** *fml* [vote] suffrage *m*, vote *m*.

suffragette [,sʌfrə'dʒet] *n* suffragette *f*.

THE SUFFRAGETTES

Militantes britanniques luttant pour le droit de vote des femmes au début du XXe siècle. Menées par Emmeline Pankhurst, elles mirent en œuvre différents moyens d'action (manifestations, interruptions de meetings, attentats, incendies criminels, grèves de la faim) qui eurent finalement raison du Premier ministre Asquith, lequel fit adopter par le Parlement, en 1918, un projet de loi accordant le droit de vote à certaines catégories de femmes (femmes mariées, femmes au foyer et femmes diplômées âgées d'au moins 30 ans). En 1928, une nouvelle loi étendit ce droit à toutes les femmes.

suffuse [sə'fju:z] *vt* (*usu passive*) se répandre sur, baigner ■ **~d with light** inondé de lumière ■ **the sky was ~d with red** le ciel était tout empourpré.

Sufi ['su:fɪ] *n* soufi *m*, çoufi *m*.

sugar ['ʃʊgər] ◇ *n* **1.** [gen, - CHEM] sucre *m* ■ **how many ~s?** combien de sucres? **2.** *US inf* [to a man] mon chéri ■ [to a woman] ma chérie.
◇ *vt* sucrer.
◇ *interj inf* : **oh ~!** mince alors!

sugar basin *n UK* sucrier *m*.

sugar beet *n* betterave *f* sucrière OR à sucre.

sugar bowl *n* sucrier *m* ■ **the Sugar Bowl** *US* SPORT *tournoi de football américain de La Nouvelle-Orléans.*

sugar candy *n* sucre *m* candi.

sugarcane ['ʃʊgəkeɪn] *n* canne *f* à sucre.

sugar-coated [-ˌkəʊtɪd] *adj* dragéifié ■ **~ almonds** dragées *fpl*.

sugar cube *n* morceau *m* de sucre.

sugar daddy *n inf* vieux protecteur *m*.

sugared ['ʃʊgəd] *adj* **1.** *liter* sucré **2.** *fig* mielleux, doucereux.

sugared almond *n* dragée *f*.

sugar-free *adj* sans sucre.

sugar lump *n* morceau *m* de sucre.

sugar maple *n* érable *m* à sucre.

sugar pea *n* mange-tout *m inv*.

sugarplum ['ʃʊgəplʌm] *n* [candied plum] prune *f* confite ■ [boiled sweet] bonbon *m*.

sugarsnap peas *npl* CULIN pois *mpl* gourmands.

sugar syrup *n* CULIN sirop *m* de sucre.

sugary ['ʃʊgərɪ] *adj* **1.** [drink, food] (très) sucré ■ [taste] sucré **2.** [manner, tone] mielleux, doucereux.

suggest [sə'dʒest] *vt* **1.** [propose, put forward] suggérer, proposer ■ **I ~ (that) we do nothing for the moment** je suggère *OR* je propose que nous ne fassions rien pour l'instant ■ **he ~ed that the meeting be held next Tuesday** il a proposé de fixer la réunion à mardi prochain ■ **a new plan ~ed itself** un nouveau plan s'est dessiné **2.** [recommend] proposer, conseiller, recommander **3.** [imply, insinuate] suggérer ■ **just what are you ~ing?** que voulez-vous dire par là?, qu'allez-vous insinuer là? **4.** [indicate, point to] suggérer, laisser supposer ■ **recent studies ~ that radiation may be the cause** des études récentes semblent indiquer que le problème est dû à des radiations **5.** [evoke] suggérer, évoquer.

suggestion [sə'dʒestʃn] *n* **1.** [proposal] suggestion *f*, proposition *f* ■ **may I make a ~?** puis-je faire une suggestion? ■ **if nobody has any other ~s, we'll move on** si personne n'a rien d'autre à suggérer *OR* à proposer, nous allons passer à autre chose ■ **we are always open to ~s** toute suggestion est la bienvenue ➲ **'serving ~'** 'suggestion de présentation' **2.** [recommendation] conseil *m*, recommandation *f* ■ **their ~ is that we stop work immediately** ils proposent que nous arrêtions le travail immédiatement **3.** [indication] indication *f* **4.** [trace, hint] soupçon *m*, trace *f* **5.** [implication] suggestion *f*, implication *f* ■ **there is no ~ of negligence on their part** rien ne laisse penser qu'il y ait eu négligence de leur part **6.** PSYCHOL suggestion *f*.
Voir module d'usage

suggestive [sə'dʒestɪv] *adj* **1.** [indicative, evocative] suggestif **2.** [erotic] suggestif.

suggestively [sə'dʒestɪvlɪ] *adv* de façon suggestive.

suicidal [su:ɪ'saɪdl] *adj* suicidaire ■ **I was feeling ~** j'avais envie de me tuer ■ **to stop now would be ~** ce serait un suicide de s'arrêter maintenant.

suicide ['su:ɪsaɪd] ◇ *n* [act] suicide *m* ■ **to commit ~** se suicider ■ **privatization would be financial ~** la privatisation représenterait un véritable suicide financier.
◇ *comp* [mission, plane, squad] suicide ■ [attempt, bid, pact] de suicide.

suit [su:t] ◇ *n* **1.** [outfit - for men] costume *m*, complet *m* ; [- for women] tailleur *m* ; [- for particular activity] combinaison *f* ■ **he came in a ~ and tie** il est venu en costume-cravate ■ **~ of clothes** tenue *f* ■ **~ of armour** armure *f* complète **2.** [complete set] jeu *m* **3.** [in card games] couleur *f* ■ **long** *OR* **strong ~** couleur forte ■ **generosity is not his strong ~** *fig* la générosité n'est pas vraiment son (point) fort **4.** LAW [lawsuit] action *f*, procès *m* ■ **to bring** *OR* **to file a ~ against sb** intenter un procès à qqn, poursuivre qqn en justice ■ **criminal ~** action au pénal **5.** *fml* [appeal] requête *f*, pétition *f* ■ *lit* [courtship] cour *f* ■ **to pay ~ to sb** faire la cour à qqn.
◇ *vt* **1.** [be becoming to - subj: clothes, colour] aller à ■ **black really ~s her** le noir lui va à merveille **2.** [be satisfactory or convenient to] convenir à, arranger ■ **Tuesday ~s me best** c'est mardi qui me convient *OR* qui m'arrange le mieux ➲ **~ yourself!** *inf* faites ce qui vous chante! **3.** [agree with] convenir à, aller à, réussir à **4.** [be appropriate] convenir à, aller à, être fait pour ■ **clothes to ~ all tastes** des vêtements pour tous les goûts ■ **the role ~s her perfectly** le rôle lui va comme un gant **5.** [adapt] adapter, approprier ■ **to ~ the action to the word** joindre le geste à la parole.
◇ *vi* [be satisfactory] convenir, aller ■ **will that date ~?** cette date vous convient-elle *OR* est-elle à votre convenance?
◆ **suit up** *vi insep* [dress - diver, pilot, astronaut etc] mettre sa combinaison.

suitability [ˌsu:tə'bɪlətɪ] *n* [of clothing] caractère *m* approprié ■ [of behaviour, arrangements] caractère *m* convenable ■ [of act, remark] à-propos *m*, pertinence *f* ■ [of time, place] opportunité *f* ■ **they doubt his ~ for the post** ils ne sont pas sûrs qu'il soit fait pour ce poste ■ **they're worried about the film's ~ for younger audiences** ils ont peur que le film ne convienne pas à un public jeune.

suitable ['su:təbl] *adj* **1.** [convenient] approprié, adéquat ■ **will that day be ~ for you?** cette date-là vous convient-elle? **2.** [appropriate - gen] qui convient ; [- clothing] approprié, adéquat ; [- behaviour] convenable ; [- act, remark] approprié, pertinent ; [- time, place] propice ■ **~ for all occasions** qui convient dans toutes les occasions ■ **'not ~ for children'** 'réservé aux adultes' ■ **this is hardly a ~ time for a heart to heart** ce n'est pas vraiment le bon moment pour se parler à cœur ouvert ■ **the most ~ candidate for the post** le candidat le plus apte à occuper ce poste ■ **the house is not ~ for a large family** la maison ne conviendrait pas à une famille nombreuse.

suitably ['su:təblɪ] *adv* [dress] de façon appropriée ■ [behave] convenablement, comme il faut ■ **I tried to look ~ surprised** j'ai essayé d'adopter une expression de surprise ■ [as intensifier] : **he was ~ impressed** il a été plutôt impressionné.

suitcase ['su:tkeɪs] *n* valise *f* ■ **I've been living out of a ~ for weeks** ça fait des semaines que je n'ai pas défait mes valises.

SUGGESTIONS

J'aimerais faire une proposition. I'd like to make a suggestion.

Et si on allait au restaurant ? Why don't we go to a restaurant?

Allons voir une exposition. Let's go to an exhibition.

Qu'est-ce que vous diriez d'une partie de cartes ? How about a game of cards?

Une petite balade, ça te dit *OU* **ça te dirait?** How about going for a walk?

Tu ne veux pas qu'on aille au cinéma ? Why don't we go to the cinema?

Tu pourrais essayer de le contacter. You could try getting in touch with him.

On pourrait peut-être lui offrir un livre. Maybe we could buy him a book.

Pourquoi ne lui en parlerais-tu pas ? Why don't you talk to him about it?

Je suggère *OU* **propose que nous en reparlions demain.** I suggest we talk about this again tomorrow.

suite [swi:t] *n* **1.** [rooms] suite *f*, appartement *m* ▪ **a ~ of rooms** une enfilade de pièces **2.** [furniture] mobilier *m* ▪ **bedroom ~** chambre *f* à coucher **3.** MUS suite *f* ▪ **a cello ~** une suite pour violoncelle **4.** [staff, followers] suite *f* **5.** COMPUT ensemble *m* (de programmes), progiciel *m*.

suited ['su:tɪd] *adj* **1.** [appropriate] approprié ▪ **he's not ~ to teaching** il n'est pas fait pour l'enseignement ▪ **she's ideally ~ for the job** ce travail lui convient tout à fait **2.** [matched] assorti ▪ **they are well ~ (to each other)** ils sont faits l'un pour l'autre, ils sont bien assortis.

suiting ['su:tɪŋ] *n* tissu *m* de confection.

suitor ['su:tər] *n* **1.** *dated* [wooer] amoureux *m*, soupirant *m* **2.** LAW plaignant *m*, - e *f*.

sulfate *US* = **sulphate**.

sulfide *US* = **sulphide**.

sulfur *etc US* = **sulphur**.

sulk [sʌlk] <> *vi* bouder, faire la tête.
<> *n* bouderie *f* ▪ **to have a ~** *OR* **(a fit of) the ~s** faire la tête.

sulkily ['sʌlkɪlɪ] *adv* [act] en boudant, d'un air maussade ▪ [answer] d'un ton maussade.

sulky ['sʌlkɪ] (*comp* **sulkier**, *superl* **sulkiest**, *pl* **sulkies**) <> *adj* [person, mood] boudeur, maussade.
<> *n* sulky *m*.

sullen ['sʌlən] *adj* **1.** [person, behaviour, appearance, remark] maussade, renfrogné **2.** [clouds] menaçant.

sullenly ['sʌlənlɪ] *adv* [behave] d'un air maussade *OR* renfrogné ▪ [answer, say, refuse] d'un ton maussade ▪ [agree, obey] de mauvaise grâce, à contre-cœur.

sullenness ['sʌlənnɪs] *n* [temperament] humeur *f* maussade ▪ [of appearance] air *m* renfrogné.

sully ['sʌlɪ] (*pret & pp* **sullied**) *vt* **1.** [dirty] souiller **2.** *fig* [reputation] ternir.

sulphate *UK*, **sulfate** *US* ['sʌlfeɪt] *n* sulfate *m* ▪ **copper/zinc ~** sulfate *m* de cuivre/de zinc.

sulphide *UK*, **sulfide** *US* ['sʌlfaɪd] *n* sulfure *m*.

sulphite *UK*, **sulfite** *US* ['sʌlfaɪt] *n* sulfite *m*.

sulphur *UK*, **sulfur** *US* ['sʌlfər] *n* soufre *m*.

sulphuric *UK*, **sulfuric** *US* [sʌl'fjʊərɪk] *adj* sulfurique ▪ **~ acid** acide *m* sulfurique.

sulphurous *UK*, **sulfurous** *US* ['sʌlfərəs] *adj liter & fig* sulfureux.

sultan ['sʌltən] *n* sultan *m*.

sultana [səl'tɑ:nə] *n* **1.** *UK* [raisin] raisin *m* de Smyrne **2.** [woman] sultane *f*.

sultanate ['sʌltənət] *n* sultanat *m*.

sultriness ['sʌltrɪnɪs] *n* **1.** [of weather] chaleur *f* étouffante **2.** [sensuality] sensualité *f*.

sultry ['sʌltrɪ] (*comp* **sultrier**, *superl* **sultriest**) *adj* **1.** [weather] lourd ▪ [heat] étouffant, suffocant **2.** [person, look, smile] sensuel ▪ [voice] chaud, sensuel.

sum [sʌm] (*pret & pp* **summed**, *cont* **summing**) <> *n* **1.** [amount of money] somme *f* ▪ **it's going to cost us a considerable ~ (of money)** ça va nous coûter beaucoup d'argent *OR* très cher **2.** [total] total *m*, somme *f* **3.** [arithmetical operation] calcul *m* ▪ **to do ~s** *UK* faire du calcul ▪ **they've really got their ~s right** *fig* ils ont bien calculé leur coup **4.** [gist] somme *f* ▪ **in ~** en somme, somme toute.
<> *vt* [add] additionner, faire le total de ▪ [calculate] calculer.
◆ **sum up** <> *vt sep* **1.** [summarize] résumer, récapituler ▪ **one word ~s the matter up** un mot suffit à résumer la question **2.** [size up] jauger ▪ **he summed us up immediately** il nous a jaugés *OR* classés sur-le-champ.
<> *vi insep* [gen] récapituler, faire un résumé ▪ LAW [judge] résumer.

Sumatra [sʊ'mɑ:trə] *pr n* Sumatra ▪ **in ~** à Sumatra.

Sumatran [sʊ'mɑ:trən] <> *n* Sumatranais *m*, - e *f*.
<> *adj* sumatranais.

summa cum laude ['sʌmə,kʊm'laʊdeɪ] *adj & adv US* avec les plus grands honneurs ▪ **to graduate ~** obtenir un diplôme avec mention très honorable.

summarily ['sʌmərəlɪ] *adv* sommairement.

summarize, ise ['sʌməraɪz] *vt* résumer.
Voir module d'usage

summary ['sʌmərɪ] (*pl* **summaries**) <> *n* **1.** [synopsis - of argument, situation] résumé *m*, récapitulation *f* ; [- of book, film] résumé *m* ▪ **there is a news ~ every hour** il y a un court bulletin d'information toutes les heures **2.** [written list] sommaire *m*, résumé *m* ▪ FIN [of accounts] relevé *m*.
<> *adj* [gen, - LAW] sommaire.

summation [sʌ'meɪʃn] *n* **1.** [addition] addition *f* ▪ [sum] somme *f*, total *m* **2.** [summary] récapitulation *f*, résumé *m*.

summer ['sʌmər] <> *n* [season] été *m* ▪ **in (the) ~** en été ▪ **in the ~ of 1942** pendant *OR* au cours de l'été 1942 ▪ **we've had a good ~** [good weather] on a eu un bel été ; [profitable tourist season] la saison était bonne.
<> *comp* [clothes, residence, day, holidays] d'été ▪ [heat, sports] estival ▪ **~ house** *US* maison *f* de campagne.
<> *vi* passer l'été.
<> *vt* [cattle, sheep] estiver.

summer camp *n US* colonie *f* de vacances.

summerhouse ['sʌməhaʊs] (*pl* [-haʊzɪz]) *n UK* pavillon *m* (de jardin).

summersault ['sʌməsɔ:lt] = **somersault**.

summer school *n* stage *m* d'été.

summer solstice *n* solstice *m* d'été.

summer squash *n US* courgette *f* jaune.

summer term *n* troisième trimestre *m*.

summertime ['sʌmətaɪm] *n* [season] été *m* ▪ **in the ~** en été.
◆ **summer time** *n* heure *f* d'été.

summerweight ['sʌməweɪt] *adj* léger, d'été.

summery ['sʌmərɪ] *adj* d'été.

SUMMARIZING

Finalement, ça n'était pas si mal. It wasn't that bad in the end.

Après tout, ce n'est pas mon problème. After all, it isn't my problem.

Tout compte fait, il est aimable. All things considered, he's quite nice.

En fin de compte, je me suis bien amusé. I had a good time in the end.

En gros, ça veut dire qu'ils refusent de nous aider. So basically, they are refusing to help us.

En un mot, c'est non. In a word, no.

Bref, elle a décidé de venir plutôt la semaine prochaine. To cut a long story short, she's decided to come next week instead.

Pour résumer *OU* **récapituler, ils ont l'intention de porter plainte.** To sum up, they intend to press charges.

summing-up [ˌsʌmɪŋ-] (*pl* **summings-up**) *n* [gen] résumé *m*, récapitulation *f* ▪ LAW résumé *m*.

summit ['sʌmɪt] ◇ *n* **1.** [peak - of mountain] sommet *m*, cime *f* ; [- of glory, happiness, power] apogée *m*, summum *m* **2.** POL [meeting] sommet *m*.
◇ *comp* [talks, agreement] au sommet.

summit conference *n* (conférence *f* au) sommet *m*.

summon ['sʌmən] *vt* **1.** [send for - person] appeler, faire venir ; [- help] appeler à, requérir ▪ **we were ~ed to his presence** nous fûmes appelés auprès de lui **2.** [convene] convoquer **3.** LAW citer, assigner ▪ **to ~ sb to appear in court** citer qqn en justice ▪ **the court ~ed her as a witness** la cour l'a citée comme témoin **4.** [muster - courage, strength] rassembler, faire appel à ▪ **he couldn't ~ enough courage to ask her out** il n'a pas trouvé le courage nécessaire pour lui demander de sortir avec lui **5.** *fml* [order] sommer, ordonner à ▪ **she ~ed us in/up** elle nous a sommés OR ordonné d'entrer/de monter.
◆ **summon up** *vt sep* **1.** [courage, strength] rassembler, faire appel à ▪ **she ~ed up her courage to ask him** elle a pris son courage à deux mains pour lui poser la question **2.** [help, support] réunir, faire appel à ▪ **I can't ~ up much interest in this plan** je n'arrive pas à m'intéresser beaucoup à ce projet **3.** [memories, thoughts] évoquer **4.** [spirits] invoquer.

summons ['sʌmənz] (*pl* **summonses**) ◇ *n* **1.** LAW citation *f*, assignation *f* ▪ **he received** OR **got a ~ for speeding** il a reçu une citation à comparaître en justice pour excès de vitesse ▪ **to take out a ~ against sb** faire assigner qqn en justice **2.** [gen] convocation *f* **3.** MIL sommation *f*.
◇ *vt* LAW citer OR assigner (à comparaître) ▪ **she was ~ed to testify** elle a été citée à comparaître en tant que témoin.

sumo ['su:məʊ] ◇ *n* sumo *m*.
◇ *comp* : **~ wrestler** lutteur *m* de sumo ▪ **~ wrestling** sumo *m*.

sump [sʌmp] *n* **1.** TECH puisard *m* ▪ *UK* AUT carter *m* **2.** [cesspool] fosse *f* d'aisances.

sump oil *n UK* huile *f* de carter.

sumptuous ['sʌmptʃʊəs] *adj* somptueux.

sumptuously ['sʌmptʃʊəslɪ] *adv* somptueusement.

sum total *n* totalité *f*, somme *f* totale ▪ **the report contains the ~ of research in the field** ce rapport contient tous les résultats de la recherche en ce domaine ▪ **that is the ~ of our knowledge** voilà à quoi se résume tout ce que nous savons.

sun [sʌn] (*pret & pp* **sunned**, *cont* **sunning**) ◇ *n* soleil *m* ▪ **the ~ is shining** le soleil brille, il y a du soleil ▪ **the ~ is in my eyes** j'ai le soleil dans les yeux ▪ **I can't stay in the ~ for very long** je ne peux pas rester très longtemps au soleil ▪ **she's caught the ~** elle a attrapé un coup de soleil ▪ **the living room gets the ~ in the afternoon** le salon est ensoleillé l'après-midi ▪ **to take a photograph into the ~** prendre une photo à contre-jour ➊ **a place in the ~** une place au soleil ▪ **under the ~ : I've tried everything under the ~** j'ai tout essayé ▪ **she called him all the names under the ~** elle l'a traité de tous les noms ▪ **there's nothing new under the ~** il n'y a rien de nouveau sous le soleil ▪ **The Sun** PRESS *quotidien britannique à sensation, see also* **tabloid**.
◇ *vt* : **to ~ o.s.** [person] prendre le soleil, se faire bronzer ; [animal] se chauffer au soleil.

Sun. (*written abbrev of* **Sunday**) dim.

sunbaked ['sʌnbeɪkt] *adj* desséché par le soleil.

sunbath ['sʌnbɑ:θ] (*pl* [-bɑ:ðz]) *n* bain *m* de soleil.

sunbathe ['sʌnbeɪð] ◇ *vi* prendre un bain de soleil, se faire bronzer.
◇ *n UK* bain *m* de soleil.

sunbather ['sʌnbeɪðəʳ] *n personne qui prend un bain de soleil.*

sunbathing ['sʌnbeɪðɪŋ] *n (U)* bains *mpl* de soleil.

sunbeam ['sʌnbi:m] *n* rayon *m* de soleil.

sunbed ['sʌnbed] *n* [in garden, on beach] lit *m* pliant ▪ [with tanning lamps] lit *m* à ultraviolets.

sunbelt ['sʌnbelt] *n US* **the ~** OR **Sunbelt** les États du sud et de l'ouest des États-Unis.

sunblind ['sʌnblaɪnd] *n UK* store *m*.

sun block *n* écran *m* total.

sunbonnet ['sʌnˌbɒnɪt] *n* capeline *f*.

sunburn ['sʌnbɜ:n] *n* coup *m* de soleil.

sunburnt ['sʌnbɜ:nt], **sunburned** ['sʌnbɜ:nd] *adj* brûlé par le soleil ▪ **I get ~ easily** j'attrape facilement des coups de soleil.

sunburst ['sʌnbɜ:st] *n* **1.** [through clouds] rayon *m* de soleil **2.** [pattern] soleil *m* ▪ [brooch] broche *f* en forme de soleil ▪ **a ~ clock** une pendule soleil.

sun cream *n* crème *f* solaire.

sundae ['sʌndeɪ] *n coupe de glace aux fruits et à la crème chantilly.*

Sunday ['sʌndeɪ] ◇ *n* **1.** [day] dimanche *m* **2.** *UK* [newspaper] : **the ~s** les journaux *mpl* du dimanche.
◇ *comp* [clothes, newspaper, driver, painter] du dimanche ▪ [peace, rest, mass] dominical ▪ **the ~ roast** OR **joint** le rôti du dimanche.

SUNDAY PAPERS

Les principaux hebdomadaires britanniques paraissant le dimanche sont :
The Independent on Sunday ;
The Mail on Sunday (tendance conservatrice) ;
The News of the World (journal à sensation) ;
The Observer (tendance centre gauche) ;
The People (journal à sensation) ;
The Sunday Express ;
The Sunday Mirror (tendance centre gauche) ;
The Sunday Telegraph (tendance conservatrice) ;
The Sunday Times (tendance conservatrice).

Sunday best *n* vêtements *mpl* du dimanche ▪ **they were dressed in their ~** ils étaient tout endimanchés, ils avaient mis leurs vêtements du dimanche.

Sunday opening *n* = **Sunday trading**.

Sunday school *n* ≃ catéchisme *m*.

Sunday trading *n ouverture des magasins le dimanche* ▪ **~ laws** *lois réglementant l'ouverture des magasins le dimanche.*

sun deck *n* [of house] véranda *f*, terrasse *f* ▪ NAUT pont *m* supérieur OR promenade.

sundial ['sʌndaɪəl] *n* cadran *m* solaire.

sundown ['sʌndaʊn] *n* coucher *m* du soleil.

sundrenched ['sʌndrentʃt] *adj* inondé de soleil.

sundress ['sʌndres] *n* bain *m* de soleil *(robe)*.

sun-dried *adj* séché au soleil.

sundry ['sʌndrɪ] ◇ *adj* divers, différent.
◇ *pron* : **she told all and ~ about it** elle l'a raconté à qui voulait l'entendre.
◆ **sundries** *npl* articles *mpl* divers.

sunflower ['sʌnˌflaʊəʳ] ◇ *n* tournesol *m*, soleil *m* ▪ **the Sunflower State** le Kansas.
◇ *comp* [oil, seed] de tournesol.

sung [sʌŋ] ◇ *pp* ▻ **sing**.
◇ *adj* : **~ mass** messe *f* chantée.

sunglasses ['sʌnˌglɑ:sɪz] *npl* lunettes *fpl* de soleil.

sun god *n* dieu *m* solaire, dieu-soleil *m*.

sunhat ['sʌnhæt] *n* chapeau *m* de soleil.

sunk [sʌŋk] ◇ *pp* ▻ **sink**.
◇ *adj inf* fichu.

sunken ['sʌŋkən] *adj* **1.** [boat, rock] submergé ▪ [garden] en contrebas ▪ [bathtub] encastré (au ras du sol) **2.** [hollow - cheeks] creux, affaissé ; [- eyes] creux.

sunlamp ['sʌnlæmp] *n* lampe *f* à rayons ultraviolets OR à bronzer.

sunlight ['sʌnlaɪt] *n* (lumière *f* du) soleil *m* ■ **in the ~** au soleil.

sunlit ['sʌnlɪt] *adj* ensoleillé.

sun lotion *n* lait *m* solaire.

sun lounge *n* *UK* solarium *m*.

sunlounger ['sʌn,laʊndʒəʳ] *n* *UK* chaise *f* longue *(où l'on s'allonge pour bronzer)*.

Sunni ['sʌnɪ] *n* **1.** [religion] sunnisme *m* **2.** [person] sunnite *mf*.

Sunnite ['sʌnaɪt] <> *adj* sunnite.
<> *n* sunnite *mf*.

sunny ['sʌnɪ] (*comp* **sunnier**, *superl* **sunniest**) *adj* **1.** [day, place etc] ensoleillé ■ **it's a ~ day, it's ~** il fait (du) soleil *OR* beau ■ **~ intervals** *OR* **periods** METEOR éclaircies *fpl* **2.** *fig* [cheerful - disposition] heureux ; [- smile] radieux, rayonnant ■ **to look on the ~ side** voir le bon côté des choses ■ **he's on the ~ side of sixty** *UK* il n'a pas encore la soixantaine.

sunny-side up *adj* : **eggs ~** œufs *mpl* sur le plat.

sunray lamp ['sʌnreɪ-] = **sunlamp**.

sunray treatment *n* héliothérapie *f*.

sunrise ['sʌnraɪz] *n* lever *m* du soleil ■ **at ~** au lever du soleil ■ **~ is about 6 o'clock** le soleil se lève vers 6 h.

sunrise industry *n* industrie *f* de pointe.

sunroof ['sʌnru:f] *n* toit *m* ouvrant.

sunscreen ['sʌnskri:n] *n* [suntan lotion] écran *m* *OR* filtre *m* solaire.

sunset ['sʌnset] *n* coucher *m* du soleil ■ **at ~** au coucher du soleil ■ **~ is about 6 o'clock** le soleil se couche vers 18 h.

sunshade ['sʌnʃeɪd] *n* [lady's parasol] ombrelle *f* ■ [for table] parasol *m* ■ [on cap] visière *f*.

sunshine ['sʌnʃaɪn] *n* **1.** [sunlight] (lumière *f* du) soleil *m* ■ **in the ~** au soleil ■ **we generally get at least 150 hours of ~ in July** en général, nous avons au moins 150 heures d'ensoleillement en juillet ■ **his visit brought a little ~ into our lives** *fig* sa visite a apporté un peu de soleil dans notre vie ■ **the Sunshine State** la Floride **2.** *inf* [term of address] : **hello ~!** salut ma jolie!, salut mon mignon!

sunspecs ['sʌnspeks] *npl* *inf* lunettes *fpl* noires.

sunspot ['sʌnspɒt] *n* tache *f* solaire.

sunstroke ['sʌnstrəʊk] *n (U)* insolation *f* ■ **to have/to get ~** avoir/attraper une insolation.

suntan ['sʌntæn] <> *n* bronzage *m* ■ **to have a ~** être bronzé ■ **to get a ~** se faire bronzer, bronzer.
<> *comp* [cream, lotion, oil] solaire, de bronzage.

suntanned ['sʌntænd] *adj* bronzé.

suntrap ['sʌntræp] *n* coin *m* abrité et très ensoleillé ■ **the garden is a real ~** le jardin est toujours très ensoleillé.

sun-up ['sʌnʌp] *n* lever *m* du soleil ■ **at ~** au lever du soleil.

sun visor *n* [on cap, for eyes] visière *f* ■ AUT pare-soleil *m*.

sun-worship *n* culte *m* du Soleil.

sun-worshipper *n* **1.** RELIG adorateur *m*, - trice *f* du Soleil **2.** *fig* adepte *mf* *OR* fanatique *mf* du bronzage.

sup [sʌp] (*pret & pp* **supped**, *cont* **supping**) <> *vi* *arch* [have supper] souper.
<> *vt* boire à petites gorgées.
<> *n* petite gorgée *f*.

super ['su:pəʳ] <> *adj* **1.** *inf* [wonderful] super *(inv)*, terrible, génial ■ **it was a ~ party!** c'était génial comme fête! **2.** [superior] supérieur, super-.
<> *interj* *inf* super, formidable.

superable ['su:pərəbl] *adj* surmontable.

superabundance [,su:pərə'bʌndəns] *n* surabondance *f*.

superabundant [,su:pərə'bʌndənt] *adj* surabondant.

superannuated [,su:pə'rænjʊeɪtɪd] *adj* **1.** [person] à la retraite, retraité **2.** [object] suranné, désuet, - ète *f*.

superannuation ['su:pə,rænjʊ'eɪʃn] *n* **1.** [act of retiring] mise *f* à la retraite **2.** [pension] pension *f* de retraite **3.** [contribution] versement *m* *OR* cotisation *f* pour la retraite ■ **~ fund** caisse *f* de retraite.

superb [su:'pɜ:b] *adj* superbe, magnifique.

superbly [su:'pɜ:blɪ] *adv* superbement, magnifiquement.

Super Bowl *pr n* *US* Superbowl *m (finale du championnat des États-Unis de football américain)*.

superbug ['su:pəbʌg] *n* *germe résistant aux traitements antibiotiques*.

supercharged ['su:pətʃɑ:dʒd] *adj* TECH [engine] surcomprimé.

supercharger ['su:pətʃɑ:dʒəʳ] *n* compresseur *m*.

supercilious [,su:pə'sɪlɪəs] *adj* hautain, arrogant, dédaigneux.

superciliously [,su:pə'sɪlɪəslɪ] *adv* [act] d'un air hautain, avec arrogance *OR* dédain ■ [speak] d'un ton hautain, avec arrogance *OR* dédain.

supercomputer [,su:pəkəm'pju:təʳ] *n* supercalculateur *m*, superordinateur *m*.

superconductor [,su:pəkən'dʌktəʳ] *n* supraconducteur *m*.

super-duper [-'du:pəʳ] *adj* *inf* super, superchouette.

superego [,su:pər'i:gəʊ] (*pl* **superegos**) *n* surmoi *m*.

superficial [,su:pə'fɪʃl] *adj* [knowledge] superficiel ■ [differences] superficiel, insignifiant ■ [person] superficiel, frivole, léger ■ [wound] superficiel, léger.

superficiality ['su:pə,fɪʃɪ'ælətɪ] *n* caractère *m* superficiel, manque *m* de profondeur.

superficially [,su:pə'fɪʃəlɪ] *adv* superficiellement.

superfine ['su:pəfaɪn] *adj* [quality, product] extrafin, superfin, surfin ■ [analysis] très fin ■ [distinction, detail] subtil.

superfluity [,su:pə'flʊətɪ] *n* **1.** [superfluousness] caractère *m* superflu **2.** [excess] surabondance *f*.

superfluous [su:'pɜ:flʊəs] *adj* superflu ■ **it is ~ to say...** (il est) inutile de *OR* il va sans dire... ■ **I felt ~** je me sentais de trop.

superfluously [su:'pɜ:flʊəslɪ] *adv* de manière superflue, inutilement.

superglue ['su:pəglu:] *n* superglu *f*.

supergrass ['su:pəgrɑ:s] *n* *indicateur de police très bien placé dans les milieux criminels*.

supergroup ['su:pəgru:p] *n* *groupe de rock dont chaque membre est déjà célèbre pour avoir appartenu à un autre groupe*.

superhero ['su:pə,hɪərəʊ] (*pl* **superheroes**) *n* superman *m*, surhomme *m*.

superhighway ['su:pə,haɪweɪ] *n* **1.** *US* AUT autoroute *f* **2.** COMPUT autoroute *f*.

superhuman [,su:pə'hju:mən] *adj* surhumain.

superimpose [,su:pərɪm'pəʊz] *vt* superposer ■ **to ~ sthg on sthg** superposer qqch à qqch ■ **~d photos** des photos en surimpression.

superintend [,su:pərɪn'tend] *vt* **1.** [oversee - activity] surveiller ; [- person] surveiller, avoir l'œil sur **2.** [run - office, institution] diriger.

superintendent [,su:pərɪn'tendənt] *n* **1.** [of institution] directeur *m*, - trice *f* ■ [of department, office] chef *m* **2.** [of police] ≃ commissaire *m* (de police) **3.** *US* [of apartment building] gardien *m*, - enne *f*, concierge *mf*.

superior [su:'pɪərɪəʳ] <> *adj* **1.** [better, greater] supérieur ■ **a ~ wine** un vin de qualité supérieure ■ **~ to** supérieur à ■ **the book is vastly ~ to the film** le livre est bien meilleur que le film ■ **~ in number to** supérieur en nombre à, numériquement supérieur à **2.** [senior - officer, position] supérieur

■ ~ **to** supérieur à, au-dessus de **3.** *pej* [supercilious] suffisant, hautain **4.** [upper] supérieur ■ **the ~ limbs** les membres *mpl* supérieurs **5.** TYPO : ~ **letter** lettre *f* supérieure *OR* suscrite **6.** BIOL supérieur.
◇ *n* supérieur *m*, - e *f*.
◆ **Superior** *pr n* : **Lake Superior** le lac Supérieur.

superiority [su:ˌpɪərɪ'ɒrətɪ] *n* **1.** [higher amount, worth] supériorité *f* ■ **their ~ in numbers** leur supériorité numérique ■ **the ~ of this brand to** *OR* **over all the others** la supériorité de cette marque par rapport à toutes les autres **2.** *pej* [arrogance] supériorité *f*, arrogance *f*.

superiority complex *n* complexe *m* de supériorité.

superlative [su:'pɜ:lətɪv] ◇ *adj* **1.** [outstanding - quality, skill, performance] sans pareil ; [- performer, athlete] sans pareil, inégalé **2.** [overwhelming - indifference, ignorance, joy] suprême **3.** GRAM superlatif.
◇ *n* superlatif *m* ■ **in the ~** au superlatif ■ **she always speaks in ~s** elle a tendance à tout exagérer.

superlatively [su:'pɜ:lətɪvlɪ] *adv* au plus haut degré, exceptionnellement ■ **a ~ good candidate** un candidat exceptionnel ■ **she is ~ efficient** elle est on ne peut plus efficace.

superman ['su:pəmæn] (*pl* **supermen** [-men]) *n* PHILOS [gen] surhomme *m* ■ [gen] superman *m*.
◆ **Superman** *pr n* [comic book hero] Superman *m*.

supermarket ['su:pəˌmɑ:kɪt] *n* supermarché *m*.

supernatural [ˌsu:pə'nætʃrəl] ◇ *adj* surnaturel.
◇ *n* surnaturel *m*.

supernova [ˌsu:pə'nəʊvə] (*pl* **supernovas** *OR pl* **supernovae** [-vi:]) *n* supernova *f*.

supernumerary [ˌsu:pə'nju:mərərɪ] (*pl* **supernumeraries**) ◇ *adj* [extra] surnuméraire ■ [superfluous] superflu.
◇ *n* [gen, - ADMIN] surnuméraire *m* ■ CIN & TV figurant *m*, - e *f*.

superpose [ˌsu:pə'pəʊz] *vt* superposer ■ **to ~ sthg on sthg** superposer qqch à qqch.

superpower ['su:pəˌpaʊəʳ] *n* superpuissance *f*, super-grand *m*.

supersaturated [ˌsu:pə'sætʃəreɪtɪd] *adj* [liquid] sursaturé ■ [vapour] sursaturant.

superscript ['su:pəskrɪpt] ◇ *n* exposant *m*.
◇ *adj* en exposant.

supersede [ˌsu:pə'si:d] *vt* [person - get rid of] supplanter, détrôner ; [- replace] succéder à, remplacer ■ [object] remplacer ■ **~d methods** méthodes périmées.

supersonic [ˌsu:pə'sɒnɪk] *adj* supersonique ■ **~ bang** *OR* **boom** bang *m* (supersonique).

superstar ['su:pəstɑ:ʳ] *n* superstar *f*.

superstition [ˌsu:pə'stɪʃn] *n* superstition *f*.

superstitious [ˌsu:pə'stɪʃəs] *adj* superstitieux ■ **to be ~ about sthg** être superstitieux au sujet de qqch.

superstitiously [ˌsu:pə'stɪʃəslɪ] *adv* superstitieusement.

superstore ['su:pəstɔ:ʳ] *n* hypermarché *m*.

superstructure ['su:pəˌstrʌktʃəʳ] *n* superstructure *f*.

supertanker ['su:pəˌtæŋkəʳ] *n* supertanker *m*, superpétrolier *m*.

supertax ['su:pətæks] *n* ≃ impôt *m* sur les grandes fortunes.

supertonic [ˌsu:pə'tɒnɪk] *n* sus-tonique *f*.

supervise ['su:pəvaɪz] ◇ *vt* **1.** [oversee - activity, exam] surveiller ; [- child, staff] surveiller, avoir l'œil sur **2.** [run - office, workshop] diriger.
◇ *vi* surveiller.

supervision [ˌsu:pə'vɪʒn] *n* **1.** [of person, activity] surveillance *f*, contrôle *m* ■ **the children must be under the ~ of qualified staff at all times** les enfants doivent être sous la surveillance de personnel qualifié à tout moment ■ **translated under the ~ of the author** traduit sous la direction de l'auteur **2.** [of office] direction *f*.

supervision order *n* LAW *nomination par un tribunal pour enfants d'un travailleur social chargé d'assurer la tutelle d'un enfant.*

supervisor ['su:pəvaɪzəʳ] *n* [gen] surveillant *m*, - e *f* ■ COMM [of department] chef *m* de rayon ■ SCH & UNIV [at exam] surveillant *m*, - e *f* ■ UNIV [of thesis] directeur *m*, - trice *f* de thèse ■ [of research] directeur *m*, - trice *f* de recherches.

supervisory ['su:pəvaɪzərɪ] *adj* de surveillance ■ **in a ~ role** *OR* **capacity** à titre de surveillant.

superwoman ['su:pəˌwʊmən] (*pl* **superwomen** [-ˌwɪmɪn]) *n* superwoman *f*.

supine ['su:paɪn] *adj* **1.** *lit* [on one's back] couché *OR* étendu sur le dos **2.** *fig* [passive] indolent, mou *(before vowel or silent 'h'* **mol***)*, molle *f*, passif.

supper ['sʌpəʳ] *n* [evening meal] dîner *m* ■ [late-night meal] souper *m* ■ **to have** *OR* **to eat ~** dîner, souper ■ **we had steak for ~** nous avons mangé du steak au dîner *OR* au souper ▶ **I'll raise his salary but I intend to make him sing for his ~!** je vais lui accorder une augmentation, mais c'est donnant donnant!

supper club *n* US *boîte de nuit qui fait aussi restaurant.*

suppertime ['sʌpətaɪm] *n* [in evening] heure *f* du *OR* de dîner ■ [later at night] heure *f* du *OR* de souper.

supplant [sə'plɑ:nt] *vt* [person] supplanter, évincer ■ [thing] supplanter, remplacer.

supple ['sʌpl] *adj* souple ■ **to become ~** s'assouplir.

supplement ◇ *n* ['sʌplɪmənt] **1.** [additional amount - paid] supplément *m* ; [- received] complément *m* ■ **a ~ is charged for occupying a single room** il y a un supplément à payer pour les chambres à un lit ▶ **food~** complément *m* alimentaire **2.** PRESS supplément *m* **3.** UK ADMIN [allowance] allocation *f*.
◇ *vt* ['sʌplɪment] [increase] augmenter ■ [complete] compléter ■ **I work nights to ~ my income** j'augmente mes revenus en travaillant la nuit ■ **he ~s his diet with vitamins** il complète son régime en prenant des vitamines.

supplementary [ˌsʌplɪ'mentərɪ] *adj* **1.** [gen] complémentaire, additionnel ■ **~ to** en plus de ▶ **~ income** revenus *mpl* annexes **2.** GEOM [angle] supplémentaire.

supplementary benefit *n ancien nom pour 'income support'.*

suppleness ['sʌplnɪs] *n* souplesse *f*.

suppletion [sə'pli:ʃn] *n* LING suppléance *f*.

suppletive [sə'pli:tɪv] *adj* LING supplétif.

supplicant ['sʌplɪkənt] *n* suppliant *m*, - e *f*.

supplication [ˌsʌplɪ'keɪʃn] *n* supplication *f* ■ **he knelt in ~** il supplia à genoux.

supplier [sə'plaɪəʳ] *n* COMM fournisseur *m*, - euse *f*.

supply[1] [sə'plaɪ] (*pret & pp* **supplied**, *pl* **supplies**) ◇ *vt*
1. [provide - goods, services] fournir ■ **to ~ sthg to sb** fournir qqch à qqn ■ **to ~ electricity/water to a town** alimenter une ville en électricité/eau
2. [provide sthg to - person, institution, city] fournir, approvisionner ■ MIL ravitailler, approvisionner ■ **to ~ sb with sthg** fournir qqch à qqn, approvisionner qqn en qqch ■ **the farm keeps us supplied with eggs and milk** grâce à la ferme nous avons toujours des œufs et du lait ■ **I supplied him with the details/the information** je lui ai fourni les détails/les informations
3. [equip] munir ■ **all toys are supplied with batteries** des piles sont fournies avec tous les jouets
4. [make good - deficiency] suppléer à ; [- omission] réparer, compenser ■ [satisfy - need] répondre à.
◇ *n* **1.** [stock] provision *f*, réserve *f* ■ **the nation's ~ of oil** les réserves nationales de pétrole ■ **we're getting in** *OR* **laying in a ~ of coal** nous faisons des provisions de charbon, nous nous approvisionnons en charbon ■ **water is in short ~ in the southeast** on manque d'eau dans le sud-est
2. [provision - of goods, equipment] fourniture *f* ; [- of fuel] alimentation *f* ■ MIL ravitaillement *m*, approvisionnement *m* ■ **the domestic hot water ~** l'alimentation domestique en eau chaude
3. ECON offre *f*

4. *UK* [clergyman, secretary, teacher] remplaçant *m*, - e *f*, suppléant *m*, - e *f* ▪ **to be on ~** faire des remplacements *OR* des suppléances
5. *(usu pl)* POL [money] crédits *mpl*.
◇ *comp* **1.** [convoy, train, truck, route] de ravitaillement ▪ **~ ship** ravitailleur *m*
2. [secretary] intérimaire ▪ [clergyman] suppléant.
◆ **supplies** *npl* [gen] provisions *fpl* ▪ [of food] vivres *mpl* ▪ MIL subsistances *fpl*, approvisionnements *mpl* ▪ **office supplies** fournitures *fpl* de bureau.

supply[2] ['sʌplɪ] *adv* souplement, avec souplesse.

supply-side economics [sə'plaɪ-] *n* économie *f* de l'offre.

supply teacher [sə'plaɪ-] *n UK* remplaçant *m*, - e *f*.

support [sə'pɔːt] ◇ *vt* **1.** [back - action, campaign, person] soutenir, appuyer ; [- cause, idea] défendre, soutenir ▪ **she ~s the Labour Party** elle est pour *OR* elle soutient le parti travailliste ▪ **I can't ~ their action** je ne peux pas approuver leur action ▪ **we ~ her in her decision** nous approuvons sa décision ▪ **the Democrats will ~ the bill** les Démocrates seront pour *OR* appuieront le projet de loi ▪ SPORT être supporter de, supporter ▪ **he ~s Tottenham** c'est un supporter de Tottenham
2. [assist] soutenir, aider ▪ CIN & THEAT : **~ed by a superb cast** avec une distribution superbe
3. [hold up] supporter, soutenir ▪ **her legs were too weak to ~ her** ses jambes étaient trop faibles pour la porter ▪ **she held on to the table to ~ herself** elle s'agrippa à la table pour ne pas tomber
4. [provide for financially - person] subvenir aux besoins de ; [- campaign, project] aider financièrement ▪ **she has three children to ~** elle a trois enfants à charge ▪ **she earns enough to ~ herself** elle gagne assez pour subvenir à ses propres besoins ▪ **he ~s himself by teaching** il gagne sa vie en enseignant ▪ **the theatre is ~ed by contributions** le théâtre est financé par des contributions
5. [sustain] faire vivre ▪ **the land has ~ed four generations of tribespeople** cette terre a fait vivre la tribu pendant quatre générations
6. [substantiate, give weight to] appuyer, confirmer, donner du poids à ▪ **there is no evidence to ~ his claim** il n'y a aucune preuve pour appuyer ses dires
7. [endure] supporter, tolérer
8. FIN [price, currency] maintenir.
◇ *n* **1.** [backing] soutien *m*, appui *m* ▪ **~ for the Socialist Party is declining** le nombre de ceux qui soutiennent le parti socialiste est en baisse ▪ **he's trying to drum up** *OR* **to mobilize ~ for his scheme** il essaie d'obtenir du soutien pour son projet ▪ **to give** *OR* **to lend one's ~ to sthg** accorder *OR* prêter son appui à qqch ▪ **she gave us her full ~** elle nous a pleinement appuyés ▪ **you have my full ~ on this** je vous soutiens à cent pour cent, vous pouvez compter sur mon soutien inconditionnel ▪ **to speak in ~ of a motion** appuyer une motion ▪ **they are striking in ~ of the miners** ils font grève par solidarité avec les mineurs
2. [assistance, encouragement] appui *m*, aide *f* ▪ **a mutual ~ scheme** un système d'entraide ▪ **she gave me the emotional ~ I needed** elle m'a apporté le soutien affectif dont j'avais besoin
3. [person who offers assistance, encouragement] soutien *m* ▪ **she's been a great ~ to me** elle m'a été d'un grand soutien
4. [holding up] soutien *m* ▪ **I was holding his arm for ~** je m'appuyais sur son bras ▪ **this bra gives good ~** ce soutien-gorge maintient bien la poitrine
5. [supporting structure, prop] appui *m* ▪ CONSTR & TECH soutien *m*, support *m*
6. [funding] soutien *m* ▪ **they depend on the government for financial ~** ils sont subventionnés par le gouvernement ▪ **what are your means of ~?** quelles sont vos sources de revenus? ▪ **she is their only means of ~** ils n'ont qu'elle pour les faire vivre
7. [substantiation, corroboration] corroboration *f* ▪ **in ~ of her theory** à l'appui de *OR* pour corroborer sa théorie
8. *US* ECON [subsidy] subvention *f*
9. COMPUT assistance *f*
10. MUS = **support band**.
◇ *comp* **1.** [troops, unit] de soutien
2. [hose, stockings] de maintien ▪ [bandage] de soutien
3. CONSTR & TECH [structure, device, frame] de soutien
4. ADMIN : **~ services** services *mpl* d'assistance technique.

supportable [sə'pɔːtəbl] *adj fml* supportable.

support band *n* groupe *m* en première partie ▪ **who was the ~?** qui est-ce qu'il y avait en première partie?

supporter [sə'pɔːtər] *n* **1.** CONSTR & TECH [device] soutien *m*, support *m* **2.** [advocate, follower - of cause, opinion] adepte *mf*, partisan *m* ; [- of political party] partisan *m* ▪ SPORT supporter *m*, supporteur *m*, - trice *f* **3.** HERALD tenant *m*.

support group *n* groupe *m* d'entraide.

supporting [sə'pɔːtɪŋ] *adj* **1.** CONSTR & TECH [pillar, structure] d'appui, de soutènement ▪ [wall] porteur ▪ **~ beam** CONSTR sommier *m* **2.** CIN & THEAT [role] secondaire, de second plan ▪ [actor] qui a un rôle secondaire *OR* de second plan ▪ **with a ~ cast of thousands** avec des milliers de figurants **3.** [substantiating] qui confirme, qui soutient ▪ **do you have any ~ evidence?** avez-vous des preuves à l'appui?

supportive [sə'pɔːtɪv] *adj* [person] qui est d'un grand soutien ▪ [attitude] de soutien ▪ **my parents have always been very ~** mes parents m'ont toujours été d'un grand soutien ▪ **~ therapy** MED thérapie *f* de soutien.

suppose [sə'pəʊz] ◇ *vt* **1.** [assume] supposer ▪ **I ~ it's too far to go and see them now** je suppose que c'est trop loin pour qu'on aille les voir maintenant ▪ **~ x equals y** MATHS soit x égal à y ▪ **I ~ you think that's funny!** je suppose que vous trouvez ça drôle! **2.** [think, believe] penser, croire ▪ **do you ~ he'll do it?** pensez-vous *OR* croyez-vous qu'il le fera? ▪ **I ~ so** [affirmative response] je suppose que oui ; [expressing reluctance] oui, peut-être ▪ **I ~ not, I don't ~ so** je ne (le) pense pas ▪ **I don't ~ he'll agree** ça m'étonnerait qu'il soit d'accord, je ne pense pas qu'il sera d'accord ▪ **and who do you ~ I met in the shop?** et devine qui j'ai rencontré dans le magasin! **3.** [imply] supposer.
◇ *vi* supposer, imaginer ▪ **he's gone, I ~?** il est parti, je suppose *OR* j'imagine ? ▪ **there were, I ~, about 50 people there** il y avait, je dirais, une cinquantaine de personnes.
◇ *conj* si ▪ **~ they see you?** et s'ils vous voyaient? ▪ **~ we wait and see** et si on attendait pour voir? ▪ **~ I'm right and she does come?** mettons *OR* supposons que j'aie raison et qu'elle vienne?

SUPPOSITIONS

Supposons qu'il ait raison et qu'elle démissionne. Supposing he's right and she does resign.

En admettant qu'on commence demain, est-ce que nous tiendrons les délais ? Assuming we start tomorrow, will we meet the deadline?

Et s'il décidait de ne plus vendre ? What if he decided not to sell?

Et à supposer qu'il ne puisse pas être présent ? Supposing he can't be there?

J'imagine qu'il a eu un empêchement. I guess something came up.

supposed [sə'pəʊzd] *adj* **1.** [presumed] présumé, supposé ▪ [alleged] prétendu ▪ **all these ~ experts** *pej* tous ces prétendus experts **2.** *phr* **to be ~ to : to be ~ to do sthg** être censé faire qqch ▪ **she was ~ to be at work** elle était censée être à son travail ▪ **what's that switch ~ to do?** à quoi sert cet interrupteur? ▪ **how am I ~ to know?** comment est-ce que je saurais *OR* suis censé savoir, moi? ▪ **I'm not ~ to know** je ne suis pas censé savoir ▪ **you're not ~ to do that!** tu ne devrais pas faire ça! ▪ **what's that ~ to mean?** qu'est-ce que tu veux dire par là? ▪ **we're not ~ to use dictionaries** nous n'avons pas le droit de nous servir de dictionnaires ▪ **this restaurant is ~ to be very good** il paraît que ce restaurant est excellent.

supposedly [sə'pəʊzɪdlɪ] *adv* soi-disant *(adv)* ▪ **he's ~ too sick to walk** il est soi-disant trop malade pour marcher.

supposing [sə'pəʊzɪŋ] *conj* si, à supposer que ▪ **~ he still wants to go** et s'il veut encore y aller? ▪ **~ you are right** admettons *OR* mettons que vous ayez raison ▪ **always ~ I can do it** en supposant *OR* en admettant que je puisse le faire.

supposition [,sʌpə'zɪʃn] *n* supposition *f*, hypothèse *f* ▪ **his theory was pure ~** sa théorie n'était qu'une hypothèse ▪ **on the ~ that your mother agrees** dans l'hypothèse où votre mère serait d'accord, à supposer que votre mère soit d'accord.
Voir module d'usage

suppository [sə'pɒzɪtrɪ] (*pl* **suppositories**) *n* suppositoire *m*.

suppress [sə'pres] *vt* **1.** [put an end to] supprimer, mettre fin à ▪ **the new régime ~ed all forms of dissent** le nouveau régime a mis fin *OR* un terme à toute forme de dissidence **2.** [withhold] supprimer, faire disparaître ▪ **to ~ evidence** faire disparaître des preuves ▮ [conceal] supprimer, cacher ▪ **to ~ the truth/a scandal** étouffer la vérité/un scandale **3.** [withdraw from publication] supprimer, interdire ▪ **the government has ~ed the report** le gouvernement a interdit la parution du rapport **4.** [delete] supprimer, retrancher **5.** [inhibit - growth, weeds] supprimer, empêcher **6.** [hold back, repress - anger, yawn, smile] réprimer ; [- tears] retenir, refouler ; [- feelings, desires] étouffer, refouler ▪ **to ~ a cough** réprimer *OR* retenir son envie de tousser ▪ **to ~ a sneeze** se retenir pour ne pas éternuer **7.** PSYCHOL refouler **8.** ELECTRON & RADIO antiparasiter.

suppression [sə'preʃn] *n* **1.** [ending - of rebellion, demonstration] suppression *f*, répression *f* ; [- of rights] suppression *f*, abolition *f* ; [- of a law, decree] abrogation *f* **2.** [concealment - of evidence, information] suppression *f*, dissimulation *f* ; [- of scandal] étouffement *m* **3.** [non-publication - of document, report] suppression *f*, interdiction *f* ; [- of part of text] suppression *f* **4.** [holding back - of feelings, thoughts] refoulement *m* **5.** PSYCHOL refoulement *m* **6.** ELECTRON & RADIO antiparasitage *m*.

suppressive [sə'presɪv] *adj* répressif.

suppressor [sə'presər] *n* ELEC dispositif *m* antiparasite.

suppurate ['sʌpjʊreɪt] *vi* suppurer.

supra ['su:prə] *adv* supra.

supremacist [sʊ'preməsɪst] *n personne qui croit en la suprématie d'un groupe* ▪ **they are white ~s** ils croient en la suprématie de la race blanche.

supremacy [sʊ'preməsɪ] *n* **1.** [dominance] suprématie *f*, domination *f* ▪ **each nation tried to gain ~ over the other** chaque nation essayait d'avoir la suprématie sur l'autre **2.** [superiority] suprématie *f*.

supreme [sʊ'pri:m] *adj* **1.** [highest in rank, authority] suprême ▪ **the Supreme Court of Judicature** HIST la Cour souveraine de justice **2.** [great, outstanding] extrême ▪ **a ~ effort** un effort suprême ▪ **she handles politicians with ~ skill** elle sait parfaitement s'y prendre avec les hommes politiques ▪ **to make the ~ sacrifice** sacrifier sa vie, faire le sacrifice de sa vie.

Supreme Court *pr n* : **the ~** la Cour suprême *(des États-Unis)*.

SUPREME COURT

La Cour suprême est l'organe supérieur du pouvoir judiciaire américain. Composée de membres nommés par le président des États-Unis, elle détient l'ultime pouvoir de décision et a le droit d'interpréter la Constitution.

supremely [sʊ'pri:mlɪ] *adv* suprêmement, extrêmement.

Supreme Soviet *pr n* Soviet *m* suprême.

supremo [sʊ'pri:məʊ] (*pl* **supremos**) *n UK inf* (grand) chef *m*.

Supt. *written abbr of* **superintendent**.

surcharge ['sɜ:tʃɑ:dʒ] ◇ *n* **1.** [extra duty, tax] surtaxe *f* **2.** [extra cost] supplément *m* **3.** [overprinting - on postage stamp] surcharge *f*.
◇ *vt* **1.** [charge extra duty or tax on] surtaxer **2.** [charge a supplement to] faire payer un supplément à **3.** [overprint - postage stamp] surcharger.

surd [sɜ:d] ◇ *n* **1.** LING sourde *f* **2.** MATHS équation *f* irrationnelle.
◇ *adj* **1.** LING sourd **2.** MATHS irrationnel.

sure [ʒʊər] ◇ *adj* **1.** [convinced, positive] sûr, certain ▪ **are you ~ of the facts?** êtes-vous sûr *OR* certain des faits? ▪ **I'm not ~ you're right** je ne suis pas sûr *OR* certain que vous ayez raison ▪ **he's not ~ whether he's going to come or not** il n'est pas sûr de venir ▪ **she isn't ~ of** *OR* **about her feelings for him** elle n'est pas sûre de ses sentiments pour lui ▪ **you seem convinced, but I'm not so ~** tu sembles convaincu, mais moi j'ai des doutes ▪ **he'll win, I'm ~** il gagnera, j'en suis sûr ▪ **I'm ~ I've been here before** je suis sûr d'être déjà venu ici ▪ **what makes you so ~?, how can you be so ~?** qu'est-ce qui te fait dire ça?
2. [confident, assured] sûr ▪ **you can be ~ of good service in this restaurant** dans ce restaurant, vous êtes sûr d'être bien servi ▪ **to be ~ of o.s.** être sûr de soi, avoir confiance en soi
3. [certain - to happen] sûr, certain ▪ **one thing is ~, he won't be back in a hurry!** une chose est sûre *OR* certaine, il ne va pas revenir de sitôt! ▪ **we're ~ to meet again** nous nous reverrons sûrement ▪ **they're ~ to get caught** ils vont sûrement se faire prendre ▪ **the play is ~ to be a success** la pièce va certainement avoir du succès ▪ **it's a ~ bet he'll be late** il y a tout à parier qu'il sera en retard ▪ **~ thing!** *inf* bien sûr (que oui)!, pour sûr! ▪ **it's a ~ thing** [it's a certainty] c'est dans la poche ▪ **be ~ to : be ~ to be on time tomorrow** il faut que vous soyez à l'heure demain ▪ **to make ~ (that) : we made ~ that no one was listening** nous nous sommes assurés *OR* nous avons vérifié que personne n'écoutait ▪ **it is his job to make ~ that everyone is satisfied** c'est lui qui veille à ce que tout le monde soit satisfait ▪ **make ~ you don't lose your ticket** prends garde à ne pas perdre ton billet ▪ **make ~ you've turned off the gas** vérifie que tu as éteint le gaz
4. [firm, steady] sûr ▪ **with a ~ hand** d'une main sûre ▪ **a ~ grasp of the subject** *fig* des connaissances solides en la matière
5. [reliable, irrefutable] sûr ▪ **insomnia is a ~ sign of depression** l'insomnie est un signe incontestable de dépression.
◇ *adv* **1.** *inf* [of course] bien sûr, pour sûr ▪ **can I borrow your car? – ~ (you can)!** (est-ce que) je peux emprunter ta voiture? – bien sûr (que oui)!
2. *US inf* [really] drôlement, rudement ▪ **are you hungry? – I ~ am!** as-tu faim? – plutôt! *OR* et comment!
3. [as intensifier] : **(as) ~ as** aussi sûr que ▪ **as ~ as my name is Jones** aussi sûr que je m'appelle Jones ▪ **as ~ as I'm standing here (today)** aussi sûr que deux et deux font quatre.
◆ **for sure** *adv phr* : **I'll give it to you tomorrow for ~** je te le donnerai demain sans faute ▪ **one thing is for ~, I'm not staying here!** une chose est sûre, je ne reste pas ici! ▪ **I think he's single but I can't say for ~** je crois qu'il est célibataire, mais je ne peux pas l'affirmer.
◆ **sure enough** *adv phr* effectivement, en effet ▪ **she said she'd ring and ~ enough she did** elle a dit qu'elle appellerait, et c'est ce qu'elle a fait.
◆ **to be sure** *adv phr* : **to be ~, his offer is well-intentioned** ce qui est certain, c'est que son offre est bien intentionnée.

surefire ['ʃʊəfaɪər] *adj inf* infaillible, sûr.

surefooted ['ʃʊə,fʊtɪd] *adj* au pied sûr.

surely ['ʃʊəlɪ] *adv* **1.** [used to express surprise, incredulity, to contradict] quand même, tout de même ▪ **they ~ can't have forgotten** ils n'ont pas pu oublier, quand même ▪ **you're ~ not suggesting it was my fault?** vous n'insinuez tout de même pas que c'était de ma faute? ▪ **~ you must be joking!** vous plaisantez, j'espère? ▪ **the real figures are a lot higher, ~?** mais les chiffres sont en fait beaucoup plus élevés, non? ▪ **~ to**

goodness *OR* **to God they must know by now** *UK* ce n'est pas possible qu'ils ne soient pas au courant à l'heure qu'il est **2.** [undoubtedly, assuredly] sûrement, sans (aucun) doute **3.** [steadily] sûrement ▪ **things are improving slowly but ~** les choses s'améliorent lentement mais sûrement **4.** *US* [of course] bien sûr, certainement.

sureness ['ʃʊənɪs] *n* **1.** [certainty] certitude *f* **2.** [assurance] assurance *f* **3.** [steadiness] sûreté *f* ▪ [accuracy] justesse *f*, précision *f*.

surety ['ʃʊərətɪ] (*pl* **sureties**) *n* **1.** [guarantor] garant *m*, - e *f*, caution *f* ▪ **to act as** *OR* **to stand ~ (for sb)** se porter garant (de qqn) **2.** [collateral] caution *f*, sûreté *f*.

surf [sɜ:f] ◇ *n (U)* **1.** [waves] vagues *fpl* (déferlantes), ressac *m* ▪ **to ride the ~** faire du surf **2.** [foam] écume *f*.
◇ *vt* : **to ~ the Net** *OR* **Web** surfer *OR* naviguer sur le Net *OR* Web.
◇ *vi* surfer, faire du surf ▪ COMPUT surfer (sur le Net).

surface ['sɜ:fɪs] ◇ *n* **1.** [exterior, top] surface *f* ▪ **the submarine/diver came to the ~** le sous-marin/plongeur fit surface ▪ **all the old tensions came** *OR* **rose to the ~ when they met** *fig* toutes les vieilles discordes ont refait surface quand ils se sont revus **2.** [flat area] surface *f* **3.** [covering layer] revêtement *m* ▪ **road ~** revêtement *m* **4.** [outward appearance] surface *f*, extérieur *m*, dehors *m* ▪ **on the ~ she seems nice enough** au premier abord elle paraît assez sympathique ▪ **there was a feeling of anxiety lying beneath** *OR* **below the ~** on sentait une angoisse sous-jacente ▪ **the discussion hardly scratched the ~ of the problem** le problème a à peine été abordé dans la discussion **5.** GEOM [area] surface *f*, superficie *f*.
◇ *vi* **1.** [submarine, diver, whale] faire surface, monter à la surface ▪ **to ~ again** refaire surface, remonter à la surface **2.** [become manifest] apparaître, se manifester ▪ **he ~d again after many years of obscurity** il a réapparu après être resté dans l'ombre pendant de nombreuses années ▪ **rumours like this tend to ~ every so often** ce type de rumeur a tendance à refaire surface de temps à autre **3.** *inf* [get up] se lever, émerger.
◇ *vt* [put a surface on - road] revêtir ; [- paper] calandrer.
◇ *adj* **1.** [superficial] superficiel **2.** [exterior] de surface ▪ **~ measurements** superficie *f* **3.** MIN [workers] de surface, au jour ▪ [work] à la surface, au jour ▪ MIL [forces] au sol ▪ [fleet] de surface.

surface area *n* surface *f*, superficie *f*.

surface mail *n* [by land] courrier *m* par voie de terre ▪ [by sea] courrier *m* par voie maritime.

surface tension *n* tension *f* superficielle.

surface-to-air *adj* sol-air *(inv)*.

surface-to-surface *adj* sol-sol *(inv)*.

surfboard ['sɜ:fbɔ:d] *n* (planche *f* de) surf *m*.

surfboarding ['sɜ:fbɔ:dɪŋ] *n* surf *m*.

surfcasting ['sɜ:fkɑ:stɪŋ] *n pêche à la ligne dans le ressac.*

surfeit ['sɜ:fɪt] ◇ *n fml* [excess] excès *m*, surabondance *f*.
◇ *vt* rassasier.

surfer ['sɜ:fər] *n* SPORT surfeur *m*, - euse *f* ▪ COMPUT internaute *mf*.

surfing ['sɜ:fɪŋ] *n* surf *m*.

surge [sɜ:dʒ] ◇ *n* **1.** [increase - of activity] augmentation *f*, poussée *f* ; [- of emotion] vague *f*, accès *m* ▪ ELEC [- of voltage, current] pointe *f* ▪ **a big ~ in demand** une forte augmentation de la demande ▪ **a ~ of pain/pity** un accès de douleur/de pitié ▪ **he felt a ~ of pride at the sight of his son** la fierté l'envahit en regardant son fils ▪ **I felt a ~ of hatred** j'ai senti la haine monter en moi **2.** [rush, stampede] ruée *f* ▪ **there was a sudden ~ for the exit** tout à coup les gens se sont rués vers la sortie ▪ **a ~ of spectators carried him forward** il fut emporté par le flot des spectateurs **3.** NAUT houle *f*.
◇ *vi* **1.** [well up - emotion] monter **2.** [rush - crowd] se ruer, déferler ; [- water] couler à flots *OR* à torrents ; [- waves] déferler ▪ **the gates of the stadium opened and the fans ~d in/out** les portes du stade s'ouvrirent et des flots de spectateurs s'y engouffrèrent/en sortirent ▪ **the truck ~d forward** le camion a bondi en avant ▪ **blood ~d to her cheeks** le sang lui est monté au visage **3.** ELEC subir une brusque pointe de tension.
➜ **surge up** *vi insep* = **surge** *(vi sense 1)*.

surgeon ['sɜ:dʒən] *n* chirurgien *m*, - enne *f* ▪ **a woman ~** une chirurgienne, une femme chirurgien.

surgeon general (*pl* **surgeons general**) *n* **1.** MIL médecin-général *m* **2.** *US* ADMIN chef *m* des services de santé.

surgery ['sɜ:dʒərɪ] (*pl* **surgeries**) *n* **1.** [field of medicine] chirurgie *f* **2.** *(U)* [surgical treatment] intervention *f* chirurgicale, interventions *fpl* chirurgicales ▪ **minor/major ~ might be necessary** une intervention chirurgicale mineure/importante pourrait s'avérer nécessaire ▪ **to perform ~ on sb** opérer qqn ▪ **to have brain/heart ~** se faire opérer du cerveau/du cœur ▪ **the patient is undergoing ~** le malade est au bloc opératoire **3.** *UK* [consulting room] cabinet *m* médical *OR* de consultation ▪ [building] centre *m* médical ▪ [consultation] consultation *f* ▪ **Doctor Jones doesn't take ~ on Fridays** le docteur Jones ne consulte pas le vendredi ▪ **~ hours** heures *fpl* de consultation **4.** *UK* POL permanence *f* ▪ **our MP holds a ~ on Saturdays** notre député tient une permanence le samedi.

surgical ['sɜ:dʒɪkl] *adj* **1.** [operation, treatment] chirurgical ▪ [manual, treatise] de chirurgie ▪ [instrument, mask] chirurgical, de chirurgien ▪ [methods, shock] opératoire **2.** [appliance, boot, stocking] orthopédique **3.** MIL : **~ strike** offensive *f* "chirurgicale".

surgical dressing *n* pansement *m*.

surgically ['sɜ:dʒɪklɪ] *adv* par intervention chirurgicale.

surgical spirit *n UK* alcool *m* à 90 (degrés).

surging ['sɜ:dʒɪŋ] *adj* [crowd, waves] déferlant ▪ [water] qui coule à flots *OR* à torrents.

Surinam [,sʊərɪ'næm] *pr n* Surinam *m*, Suriname *m* ▪ **in ~** au Surinam.

Surinamese [,sʊərɪnæ'mi:z] ◇ *n* Surinamien *m*, - enne *f* ▪ **the ~** les Surinamiens.
◇ *adj* surinamien.

surly ['sɜ:lɪ] (*comp* **surlier**, *superl* **surliest**) *adj* [ill-tempered] hargneux, grincheux ▪ [gloomy] maussade, renfrogné.

surmise [sɜ:'maɪz] ◇ *vt* conjecturer, présumer ▪ **I can only ~ what the circumstances were** je ne puis que conjecturer quelles étaient les circonstances ▪ **I ~d that he was lying** je me suis douté qu'il mentait.
◇ *n fml* conjecture *f*, supposition *f* ▪ **your conclusion is pure ~** votre conclusion est entièrement hypothétique.

surmount [sɜ:'maʊnt] *vt* **1.** [triumph over] surmonter, vaincre **2.** *fml* [cap, top] surmonter.

surname ['sɜ:neɪm] *n UK* nom *m* (de famille).

surpass [sə'pɑ:s] *vt* **1.** [outdo, outshine] surpasser ▪ **you have ~ed yourselves** vous vous êtes surpassés **2.** [go beyond] surpasser, dépasser ▪ **that kind of behaviour ~es my understanding** ce genre de comportement me dépasse.

surpassing [sə'pɑ:sɪŋ] *adj lit* sans égal.

surplice ['sɜ:plɪs] *n* surplis *m*.

surplus ['sɜ:pləs] ◇ *n* **1.** [overabundance] surplus *m*, excédent *m* ▪ **Japan's trade ~** l'excédent commercial du Japon **2.** *(U)* [old military clothes] surplus *mpl* ▪ **an army ~ store** un magasin de surplus de l'armée **3.** FIN [in accounting] boni *m*.
◇ *adj* **1.** [gen] en surplus, en trop ▪ **pour off any ~ liquid** enlevez tout excédent de liquide ▪ **to be ~ to requirements** excéder les besoins **2.** COMM & ECON en surplus, excédentaire ▪ **~ production** production *f* excédentaire.

surprise [sə'praɪz] ◇ *n* **1.** [unexpected event, experience etc] surprise *f* ▪ **it was a ~ to me** cela a été une surprise pour moi, cela m'a surpris ▪ **what a lovely ~!** quelle merveilleuse surprise ! ▪ **her death came as no ~** sa mort n'a surpris personne ▪ **his resignation came as a ~ to everyone** sa démission a surpris tout le monde ▪ **to give sb a ~** faire une surprise à qqn ▪ **you're in for (a bit of) a ~** tu vas être surpris !, tu vas avoir une (sacrée) surprise ! **2.** [astonishment] surprise *f*, étonnement *m* ▪ **much to my ~, she agreed** à ma grande surprise *OR*

à mon grand étonnement, elle accepta ■ **he looked at me in ~** il me regarda d'un air surpris *OR* étonné **3.** [catching unawares] surprise *f* ■ **the element of ~ is on our side** nous avons l'effet de surprise pour nous ■ **their arrival took me by ~** leur arrivée m'a pris au dépourvu ■ **the soldiers took the enemy by ~** les soldats ont pris l'ennemi par surprise.
<> *comp* [attack, present, victory] surprise ■ [announcement] inattendu ■ **the Prime Minister made a ~ visit to Ireland** le Premier ministre a fait une visite surprise en Irlande ◆ **~ party** *fête organisée pour quelqu'un sans qu'il ou elle le sache.*
<> *vt* **1.** [amaze] surprendre, étonner ■ **it ~d me that they didn't give her the job** j'ai été surpris *OR* étonné qu'ils ne l'aient pas embauchée ■ **shall we ~ her?** si on lui faisait une surprise ? ■ **it wouldn't ~ me if they lost** ça ne m'étonnerait pas *OR* je ne serais pas surpris qu'ils perdent ■ **go on, ~ me!** *iron* vas-y, annonce ! **2.** [catch unawares] surprendre ■ **the burglar was ~d by the police** le cambrioleur fut surpris par la police.
Voir module d'usage

surprised [sə'praɪzd] *adj* surpris, étonné ■ **she was ~ to learn that she had got the job** elle a été surprise d'apprendre qu'on allait l'embaucher ■ **don't be ~ if she doesn't come** ne vous étonnez pas si elle ne vient pas ■ **I wouldn't *OR* I shoudn't be ~ if they'd forgotten** cela ne m'étonnerait pas qu'ils aient oublié ■ **I'm ~ by *OR* at his reaction** sa réaction me surprend *OR* m'étonne ■ **it looks easy but you'd be ~** ça semble facile mais ne vous y fiez pas.

surprising [sə'praɪzɪŋ] *adj* surprenant, étonnant ■ **it's not at all *OR* not in the least ~** cela n'a rien d'étonnant.

surprisingly [sə'praɪzɪŋlɪ] *adv* étonnamment ■ **for a ten-year-old, she's ~ mature** elle est vraiment très mûre pour une fille de dix ans ■ **~, he managed to win** chose suprenante *OR* étonnante, il a quand même gagné ■ **he apologized, ~ enough** chose surprenante *OR* étonnante, il s'est excusé ■ **not ~, the play sold out** toutes les places ont été louées, ce qui n'a rien d'étonnant.

surreal [sə'rɪəl] <> *adj* **1.** [strange, dreamlike] étrange, onirique **2.** [surrealist] surréaliste.
<> *n* : **the ~** le surréel.

surrealism [sə'rɪəlɪzm] *n* ART & LIT surréalisme *m.*

surrealist [sə'rɪəlɪst] ART & LIT <> *adj* surréaliste.
<> *n* surréaliste *mf.*

surrealistic [sə,rɪəl'ɪstɪk] *adj* **1.** ART & LIT surréaliste **2.** *fig* surréel, surréaliste.

surrender [sə'rendəʳ] <> *vi* **1.** MIL [capitulate] se rendre, capituler ■ **they ~ed to the enemy** ils se rendirent à *OR* ils capitulèrent devant l'ennemi **2.** [give o.s. up] se livrer **3.** *fig* [abandon o.s.] se livrer, s'abandonner ■ **to ~ to temptation** se livrer *OR* s'abandonner à la tentation.
<> *vt* **1.** [city, position] livrer ■ [relinquish - possessions, territory] céder, rendre ; [- one's seat] céder, laisser ; [- arms] rendre, livrer ; [- claim, authority, freedom, rights] renoncer à ; [- hopes] abandonner ■ **to ~ o.s. to sthg** se livrer *OR* s'abandonner à qqch **2.** [hand in - ticket, coupon] remettre.
<> *n* **1.** [capitulation] reddition *f*, capitulation *f* ■ **the government's ~ to the unions** la capitulation du gouvernement devant les syndicats **2.** [relinquishing - of possessions, territory] cession *f* ; [- of arms] remise *f* ; [- of claim, authority, freedom, rights] renonciation *f*, abdication *f* ; [- of hopes] abandon *m.*

surreptitious [,sʌrəp'tɪʃəs] *adj* subreptice *lit*, furtif, clandestin.

surreptitiously [,sʌrəp'tɪʃəslɪ] *adv* subrepticement *lit*, furtivement, à la dérobée.

surrey ['sʌrɪ] *n voiture hippomobile à deux places.*

surrogacy ['sʌrəgəsɪ] *n* maternité *f* de remplacement *OR* de substitution.

surrogate ['sʌrəgeɪt] <> *n* **1.** *fml* [substitute - person] remplaçant *m*, - e *f*, substitut *m* ; [- mother] mère *f* porteuse ; [- thing] succédané *m* **2.** PSYCHOL substitut *m* **3.** *US* LAW magistrat *m* de droit civil *(juridiction locale)* **4.** *UK* RELIG évêque *m* auxiliaire.
<> *adj* de substitution, de remplacement ■ **they served as ~ parents to her** ils ont en quelque sorte remplacé ses parents.

surrogate mother *n* PSYCHOL substitut *m* maternel ■ MED mère *f* porteuse.

surround [sə'raʊnd] <> *vt* **1.** [gen] entourer ■ **the garden is ~ed by a brick wall** le jardin est entouré d'un mur en briques ■ **there is a great deal of controversy ~ing the budget cuts** il y a une vive controverse autour des réductions budgétaires **2.** [subj: troops, police, enemy] encercler, cerner ■ **~ed by enemy soldiers** encerclé *OR* cerné par des troupes ennemies.
<> *n UK* [border, edging] bordure *f.*

surrounding [sə'raʊndɪŋ] *adj* environnant ■ **there's a lovely view of the ~ countryside** il y a une belle vue sur le paysage alentour.
◆ **surroundings** *npl* **1.** [of town, city] alentours *mpl*, environs *mpl* **2.** [setting] cadre *m*, décor *m* **3.** [environment] environnement *m*, milieu *m.*

surtax ['sɜ:tæks] *n impôt supplémentaire qui s'applique au-delà d'une certaine tranche de revenus.*

surveillance [sɜ:'veɪləns] *n* surveillance *f* ■ **to keep sb under constant ~** garder qqn sous surveillance continue ■ **the house is under police ~** la maison est surveillée par la police.

survey <> *vt* [sə'veɪ] **1.** [contemplate] contempler ■ [inspect] inspecter, examiner ■ [review] passer en revue **2.** [make a study of] dresser le bilan de, étudier **3.** [poll] sonder ■ **65% of women ~ed were opposed to the measure** 65 % des femmes interrogées sont contre cette mesure **4.** [land] arpenter, relever, faire un relèvement de ■ *UK* [house] expertiser, faire une expertise de.

SURPRISE

Eh bien, pour une surprise c'est une surprise ! This certainly is a surprise!

Quelle bonne surprise ! What a nice surprise !

À ma grande surprise, elle a accepté. Much to my surprise, she accepted.

Oh mon Dieu ! Oh my God!

Ça alors ! Well I never!

Je n'en croyais pas mes yeux ! I couldn't believe my eyes!

C'est une plaisanterie ! You can't be serious!

Non ! Never!

(C'est) incroyable ! (That's) amazing!

Alors ça, c'est la meilleure ! *inf* I've never heard anything like it!

C'est pas vrai ! *inf* I don't believe it!

Tu ne devineras jamais ce qu'elle m'a dit ! You'll never guess what she said to me!

Pas possible ! *inf* I don't believe it!

J'étais sidéré *OU* stupéfait. I was stunned.

Il faut le voir pour le croire. It has to be seen to be believed.

Je n'en reviens toujours pas. I still can't get over it.

Tu m'en bouches un coin. *inf* You amaze me.

J'en suis resté baba. *inf* I was gobsmacked *UK.*

Ça m'a fait un de ces chocs ! *inf* I got one hell of a shock!

Tu aurais vu sa tête ! *inf* You should have seen his face!

◇ *n* ['sɜ:veɪ] **1.** [study, investigation] étude *f*, enquête *f* ▪ **they carried out a ~ of retail prices** ils ont fait une enquête sur les prix au détail **2.** [overview] vue *f* d'ensemble **3.** [poll] sondage *m* **4.** [of land] relèvement *m*, levé *m* ▪ **aerial ~** levé aérien ▪ *UK* [of house] expertise *f* ▪ **to have a ~ done** faire faire une expertise.

surveying [sə'veɪɪŋ] *n* [measuring - of land] arpentage *m*, levé *m* ▪ *UK* [examination - of buildings] examen *m*.

surveyor [sə'veɪəʳ] *n* **1.** [of land] arpenteur *m*, géomètre *m* **2.** *UK* [of buildings] géomètre-expert *m*.

survival [sə'vaɪvl] ◇ *n* **1.** [remaining alive] survie *f* ▪ **what are their chances of ~?** quelles sont leurs chances de survie? ▪ **the ~ of the fittest** la survie du plus apte **2.** [relic, remnant] survivance *f*, vestige *m* ▪ **the custom is a ~ from the Victorian era** cette coutume remonte à l'époque victorienne.
◇ *comp* [course, kit] de survie.

survive [sə'vaɪv] ◇ *vi* **1.** [remain alive] survivre **2.** [cope, pull through] : **don't worry, I'll ~!** *inf* ne t'inquiète pas, je n'en mourrai pas! ▪ **how can they ~ on such low wages?** comment font-ils pour vivre *OR* pour subsister avec des salaires si bas? ▪ **he earned just enough to ~ on** il gagnait tout juste de quoi survivre **3.** [remain, be left] subsister ▪ **only a dozen of his letters have ~d** il ne subsiste *OR* reste qu'une douzaine de ses lettres.
◇ *vt* **1.** [live through] survivre à, réchapper à *OR* de ▪ **few of the soldiers ~d the battle** peu de soldats ont survécu à la bataille ▪ **we thought he'd never ~ the shock** nous pensions qu'il ne se remettrait jamais du choc **2.** [cope with, get through] supporter ▪ **I never thought I'd ~ the evening!** jamais je n'aurais cru que je tiendrais jusqu'à la fin de la soirée! **3.** [outlive, outlast] survivre à ▪ **she ~d her husband by 20 years** elle a survécu 20 ans à son mari ▪ **she is ~d by two daughters** elle laisse deux filles **4.** [withstand] survivre à, résister à.

surviving [sə'vaɪvɪŋ] *adj* survivant ▪ **his only ~ son** son seul fils encore en vie.

survivor [sə'vaɪvəʳ] *n* **1.** [of an accident, attack] survivant *m*, - e *f*, rescapé *m*, - e *f* ▪ **there are no reports of any ~s** aucun survivant n'a été signalé ▪ **she'll be all right, she's a born ~** elle s'en sortira, elle est solide **2.** LAW survivant *m*, - e *f*.

susceptibility [sə,septə'bɪlətɪ] (*pl* **susceptibilities**) *n* **1.** [predisposition - to an illness] prédisposition *f* **2.** [vulnerability] sensibilité *f* ▪ **his ~ to flattery** sa sensibilité à la flatterie **3.** [sensitivity] sensibilité *f*, émotivité *f* **4.** PHYS susceptibilité *f*.

susceptible [sə'septəbl] *adj* **1.** [prone - to illness] prédisposé ▪ **I'm very ~ to colds** je m'enrhume très facilement **2.** [responsive] sensible ▪ **~ to flattery** sensible à la flatterie **3.** [sensitive, emotional] sensible, émotif **4.** *fml* [capable] susceptible.

sushi ['su:ʃɪ] *n* sushi *m* ▪ **~ bar** sushi-bar *m*.

suspect ◇ *vt* [sə'spekt] **1.** [presume, imagine] soupçonner, se douter de ▪ **to ~ foul play** soupçonner quelque chose de louche ▪ **I ~ed there would be trouble** je me doutais qu'il y aurait des problèmes ▪ **I ~ed as much!** je m'en doutais! ▪ **what happened, I ~, is that they had an argument** ce qui s'est passé, j'imagine, c'est qu'ils se sont disputés **2.** [mistrust] douter de, se méfier de ▪ **to ~ sb's motives** avoir des doutes sur les intentions de qqn **3.** [person - of wrongdoing] soupçonner, suspecter ▪ **to be ~ed of sthg** être soupçonné de qqch ▪ **to ~ sb of sthg** *OR* **of doing sthg** soupçonner qqn de qqch *OR* d'avoir fait qqch.
◇ *n* ['sʌspekt] suspect *m*, - e *f*.
◇ *adj* ['sʌspekt] suspect ▪ **his views on apartheid are rather ~** ses vues sur l'apartheid sont plutôt douteuses.

suspected [sə'spektɪd] *adj* présumé ▪ **he's undergoing tests for a ~ tumour** on est en train de lui faire des analyses pour s'assurer qu'il ne s'agit pas d'une tumeur.

suspend [sə'spend] *vt* **1.** [hang] suspendre ▪ **~ed from the ceiling** suspendu au plafond **2.** [discontinue] suspendre ▪ [withdraw - permit, licence] retirer (provisoirement), suspendre ▪ **bus services have been ~ed** le service des autobus a été suspendu *OR* interrompu **3.** [defer] suspendre, reporter ▪ **to ~ judgment** suspendre son jugement ▪ **the commission decided to ~ its decision** la commission décida de surseoir à sa décision ▪ **to ~ one's disbelief** faire taire son incrédulité **4.** [exclude temporarily - official, member, sportsman] suspendre ; [- worker] suspendre, mettre à pied ; [- pupil, student] exclure provisoirement ▪ **two pupils have been ~ed from school for smoking** deux élèves surpris à fumer font l'objet d'un renvoi provisoire.

suspended animation [sə'spendɪd-] *n* [natural state] hibernation *f* ▪ [induced state] hibernation *f* artificielle.

suspended sentence *n* LAW condamnation *f* avec sursis ▪ **she got a three-month ~** elle a été condamnée à trois mois de prison avec sursis.

suspender [sə'spendəʳ] *n* *UK* [for stockings] jarretelle *f* ▪ [for socks] fixe-chaussette *m*.
◆ **suspenders** *npl* *US* [for trousers] bretelles *fpl*.

suspender belt *n* *UK* porte-jarretelles *m inv*.

suspense [sə'spens] *n* **1.** [anticipation] incertitude *f* ▪ **to keep** *OR* **to leave sb in ~** laisser qqn dans l'incertitude ▪ **to break the ~** mettre fin à l'incertitude ▪ **the ~ is killing me!** *inf* quel suspense! ▪ [in films, literature] suspense *m* ▪ **she manages to maintain the ~ throughout the book** elle réussit à maintenir *OR* faire durer le suspense jusqu'à la fin du livre **2.** ADMIN & LAW : **in ~** en suspens.

suspense account *n* compte *m* d'ordre.

suspension [sə'spenʃn] *n* **1.** [interruption] suspension *f* ▪ [withdrawal] suspension *f*, retrait *m* (provisoire) **2.** [temporary dismissal - from office, political party, club, team] suspension *f* ; [- from job] suspension *f*, mise *f* à pied ; [- from school, university] exclusion *f* provisoire **3.** AUT & TECH suspension *f* **4.** CHEM suspension *f* ▪ **in ~** en suspension.

suspension bridge *n* pont *m* suspendu.

suspicion [sə'spɪʃn] *n* **1.** [presumption of guilt, mistrust] soupçon *m*, suspicion *f* ▪ **her neighbours' strange behaviour aroused her ~** *OR* **~s** le comportement étrange de ses voisins éveilla ses soupçons ▪ **to be above** *OR* **beyond ~** être au-dessus de tout soupçon ▪ **I have my ~s about this fellow** j'ai des doutes sur cet individu ▪ **the new boss was regarded with ~** on considérait le nouveau patron avec méfiance ▪ **to be under ~** être soupçonné ▪ **he was arrested on ~ of drug trafficking** LAW il a été arrêté parce qu'on le soupçonnait de trafic de drogue **2.** [notion, feeling] soupçon *m* ▪ **I had a growing ~ that he wasn't telling the truth** je soupçonnais de plus en plus qu'il ne disait pas la vérité ▪ **I had a (sneaking) ~ you'd be here** j'avais comme un pressentiment que tu serais là **3.** [trace, hint] soupçon *m*, pointe *f*.

suspicious [sə'spɪʃəs] *adj* **1.** [distrustful] méfiant, soupçonneux ▪ **his strange behaviour made us ~** son comportement étrange a éveillé nos soupçons *OR* notre méfiance ▪ **she became ~ when he refused to give his name** elle a commencé à se méfier quand il a refusé de donner son nom **2.** [suspect] suspect ▪ **there are a lot of ~-looking characters in this pub** il y a beaucoup d'individus suspects dans ce pub ▪ **it is ~ that she didn't phone the police** le fait qu'elle n'a pas téléphoné à la police est suspect.

suspiciously [sə'spɪʃəslɪ] *adv* **1.** [distrustfully] avec méfiance, soupçonneusement **2.** [strangely] de façon suspecte ▪ **she was ~ keen to leave** son empressement à partir était suspect ▪ **it looks ~ like malaria** ça ressemble étrangement au paludisme.

suss [sʌs] *vt* *UK inf* flairer ▪ **she ~ed what he was after** elle a compris où il voulait en venir.
◆ **suss out** *vt sep* *UK inf* **1.** [device, situation] piger ▪ **I can't ~ out this computer program** je n'arrive pas à piger (comment marche) ce nouveau logiciel **2.** [person] saisir le caractère de ▪ **I've got him ~ed out** je sais à qui j'ai affaire.

sustain [sə'steɪn] *vt* **1.** [maintain, keep up - conversation] entretenir ; [- effort, attack, pressure] soutenir, maintenir ; [- sb's interest] maintenir **2.** [support physically] soutenir, supporter **3.** [support morally] soutenir **4.** MUS [note] tenir, soutenir **5.** [nourish] nourrir ▪ **they had only dried fruit and water to ~ them** ils n'avaient que des fruits secs et de l'eau pour subsister ▪ **a planet capable of ~ing life** une planète capable de maintenir la vie **6.** [suffer - damage] subir ; [- defeat, loss] subir, essuyer ; [- injury] recevoir ▪ **the man ~ed a serious blow to the**

head l'homme a été grièvement atteint à la tête ▪ [withstand] supporter **7.** LAW [accept as valid] admettre ▪ **objection ~ed** objection admise ▪ **the court ~ed her claim** le tribunal lui accorda gain de cause **8.** [corroborate - assertion, theory, charge] corroborer **9.** THEAT [role] tenir.

sustainable [səs'teɪnəbl] *adj* [development, agriculture, politics] viable, durable.

sustained [sə'steɪnd] *adj* [effort, attack] soutenu ▪ [discussion] prolongé.

sustaining [sə'steɪnɪŋ] *adj* nourrissant, nutritif.

sustenance ['sʌstɪnəns] *n* **1.** [nourishment] valeur *f* nutritive ▪ **stale bread provided her only form of ~** elle se nourrissait uniquement de pain rassis ▪ **his neighbours provided moral ~ during the crisis** *fig* ses voisins l'ont soutenu moralement pendant la crise **2.** [means of subsistence] subsistance *f* ▪ **they could not derive ~ from the land** ils ne pouvaient pas vivre de la terre.

suture ['su:tʃəʳ] ◇ *n* **1.** MED point *m* de suture **2.** ANAT & BOT suture *f*.
◇ *vt* MED suturer.

SUV (*abbrev of* **sport utility vehicle**) *n* AUTO 4 x 4 *m*.

suzerain ['su:zəreɪn] ◇ *n* **1.** HIST suzerain *m*, - e *f* **2.** POL [state] État *m* dominant.
◇ *adj* **1.** HIST suzerain **2.** POL [state, power] dominant.

svelte [svelt] *adj* svelte.

Svengali [ˌsveŋ'gɑ:lɪ] *n* manipulateur *m*.

SW 1. (*written abbrev of* **short wave**) OC **2.** (*written abbrev of* **south-west**) S-O.

swab [swɒb] (*pret & pp* **swabbed**, *cont* **swabbing**) ◇ *n* **1.** MED [cotton] tampon *m* ▪ [specimen] prélèvement *m* **2.** [mop] serpillière *f*.
◇ *vt* **1.** MED [clean] nettoyer (avec un tampon) **2.** [mop] laver ▪ **to ~ down the decks** laver le pont.

Swabia ['sweɪbjə] *pr n* Souabe *f* ▪ **in ~** en Souabe.

swaddle ['swɒdl] *vt* [wrap] envelopper, emmitoufler ▪ **~d in blankets** enveloppé *OR* emmitouflé dans des couvertures.

swaddling clothes *npl arch* & BIBLE maillot *m*, langes *mpl* ▪ **the infant was wrapped in ~** le nourrisson était emmailloté.

swag [swæg] *inf n UK* [booty] butin *m*.

swagger ['swægəʳ] ◇ *vi* **1.** [strut] se pavaner ▪ **he ~ed into/out of the room** il entra dans/sortit de la pièce en se pavanant **2.** [boast] se vanter, fanfaronner, plastronner.
◇ *n* [manner] air *m* arrogant ▪ [walk] démarche *f* arrogante ▪ **he entered the room with a ~** il entra dans la pièce en se pavanant.

swaggering ['swægərɪŋ] ◇ *adj* [gait, attitude] arrogant ▪ [person] fanfaron, bravache.
◇ *n* [proud gait] démarche *f OR* allure *f* arrogante ▪ [boasting] vantardise *f*.

swagger stick *n* [gen] badine *f*, canne *f* ▪ MIL bâton *m* (d'officier).

Swahili [swɑ:'hi:lɪ] ◇ *n* **1.** LING swahili *m*, souahéli *m* **2.** [person] Swahili *m*, - e *f*, Souahéli *m*, - e *f*.
◇ *adj* swahili, souahéli.

swallow ['swɒləʊ] ◇ *vt* **1.** [food, drink, medicine] avaler **2.** *inf* [believe] avaler, croire ▪ **he'll ~ anything** il avalerait n'importe quoi **3.** [accept unprotestingly] avaler, accepter ▪ **I find it hard to ~** je trouve ça un peu raide ▪ **I'm not going to ~ that sort of treatment** pas question que j'accepte d'être traité de cette façon **4.** [repress] ravaler ▪ **he had to ~ his pride** il a dû ravaler sa fierté **5.** [retract] : **to ~ one's words** ravaler ses paroles **6.** [absorb] engloutir.
◇ *vi* avaler, déglutir ▪ **it hurts when I ~** j'ai mal quand j'avale ▪ **she ~ed hard and continued her speech** elle avala sa salive et poursuivit son discours.
◇ *n* **1.** [action] gorgée *f* ▪ **he finished his drink with one ~** il finit sa boisson d'un trait *OR* d'un seul coup **2.** ORNITH hirondelle *f* ▪ **one ~ doesn't make a summer** *prov* une hirondelle ne fait pas le printemps *prov*.

◆ **swallow up** *vt sep* engloutir ▪ **the Baltic States were ~ed up by the Soviet Union** les pays baltes ont été engloutis par l'Union soviétique ▪ **I wished the ground would open and ~ me up** j'aurais voulu être à six pieds sous terre ▪ **they were ~ed up in the crowd** ils ont disparu dans la foule.

swallow dive *n UK* SPORT saut *m* de l'ange.

swallow hole *n UK* gouffre *m*, aven *m*.

swallowtail ['swɒləʊteɪl] *n* machaon *m*.

swallow-tailed coat *n* queue-de-pie *f*.

swam [swæm] *pt* ⊳ **swim**.

swamp [swɒmp] ◇ *n* marais *m*, marécage *m*.
◇ *vt* **1.** [flood] inonder ▪ [cause to sink] submerger **2.** [overwhelm] inonder, submerger ▪ **she was ~ed with calls** elle a été submergée d'appels ▪ **we're ~ed (with work) at the office at the moment** nous sommes débordés de travail au bureau en ce moment.

swampland ['swɒmplænd] *n (U)* marécages *mpl*, terrain *m* marécageux.

swampy ['swɒmpɪ] (*comp* **swampier**, *superl* **swampiest**) *adj* marécageux.

swan [swɒn] (*pret & pp* **swanned**, *cont* **swanning**) ◇ *n* cygne *m* ▪ **the Swan of Avon** Shakespeare ▪ **'Swan Lake'** ***Tchaikovsky*** 'le Lac des cygnes'.
◇ *vi inf UK* **they spent a year swanning round Europe** ils ont passé une année à se balader en Europe ▪ **he came swanning into the office at 10:30** il est arrivé au bureau comme si de rien n'était à 10 h 30.

swan dive *n US* SPORT saut *m* de l'ange.

swank [swæŋk] *inf* ◇ *vi* se vanter, frimer.
◇ *n UK* **1.** [boasting] frime *f* **2.** [boastful person] frimeur *m*, - euse *f* **3.** *US* [luxury] luxe *m*, chic *m*.
◇ *adj* = **swanky**.

swanky ['swæŋkɪ] (*comp* **swankier**, *superl* **swankiest**) *adj inf* [gen] chic ▪ [club, school] chic.

swan neck *n* col-de-cygne *m*.

swansdown ['swɒnzdaʊn] *n* **1.** [feathers] duvet *m* de cygne **2.** TEX molleton *m*.

swansong ['swɒnsɒŋ] *n* chant *m* du cygne.

swap [swɒp] (*pret & pp* **swapped**, *cont* **swapping**) ◇ *vt* **1.** [possessions, places] échanger ▪ **to ~ sthg for sthg** échanger qqch contre qqch ▪ **I'll ~ my coat for yours, I'll ~ coats with you** échangeons nos manteaux ▪ **they've swapped places** ils ont échangé leurs places ▪ **he swapped places with his sister** il a échangé sa place contre celle de sa sœur ▪ **I wouldn't ~ places with him for love nor money** je ne voudrais être à sa place pour rien au monde **2.** [ideas, opinions] échanger ▪ **they swapped insults over the garden fence** ils échangèrent des insultes par-dessus la clôture du jardin.
◇ *vi* échanger, faire un échange *OR* un troc ▪ **I'll ~ with you** on échangera, on fera un échange.
◇ *n* **1.** [exchange] troc *m*, échange *m* ▪ **to do a ~** faire un troc *OR* un échange **2.** [duplicate - stamp in collection etc] double *m*.

◆ **swap over, swap round** ◇ *vt sep* échanger, intervertir.
◇ *vi insep* : **do you mind swapping over** *OR* **round so I can sit next to Max?** est-ce que ça te dérange qu'on échange nos places pour que je puisse m'asseoir à côté de Max?

swap meet *n US* foire *f* au troc.

swap shop *n* foire *f* au troc, magasin *m* de troc.

swarm [swɔ:m] ◇ *n* **1.** [of bees] essaim *m* ▪ [of ants] colonie *f* **2.** *fig* [of people] essaim *m*, nuée *f*, masse *f*.
◇ *vi* **1.** ENTOM essaimer **2.** *fig* [place] fourmiller, grouiller ▪ **the streets were ~ing with people** les rues grouillaient de monde **3.** *fig* [people] affluer ▪ **the crowd ~ed in/out** la foule s'est engouffrée à l'intérieur/est sortie en masse ▪ **children were ~ing round the ice-cream van** les enfants s'agglutinaient autour du camion du marchand de glaces **4.** [climb] grimper (lestement).

swarthy ['swɔ:ðɪ] (*comp* **swarthier**, *superl* **swarthiest**) *adj* basané.

swashbuckler ['swɒʃ,bʌklər] *n* **1.** [adventurer] aventurier *m*, - ère *f* ▪ [swaggerer] fier-à-bras *m*, matamore *m* **2.** [film] film *m* de cape et d'épée ▪ [novel] roman *m* de cape et d'épée.

swashbuckling ['swɒʃ,bʌklɪŋ] *adj* [person] fanfaron ▪ [film, story] de cape et d'épée.

swastika ['swɒstɪkə] *n* ANTIQ svastika *m* ▪ [Nazi] croix *f* gammée.

swat [swɒt] (*pret & pp* **swatted**, *cont* **swatting**) ◇ *vt* **1.** [insect] écraser **2.** *inf* [slap] frapper.
◇ *n* **1.** [device] tapette *f* **2.** [swipe] : **he took a ~ at the mosquito** il essaya d'écraser le moustique **3.** *inf* = **swot**.

swatch [swɒtʃ] *n* échantillon *m* de tissu.

swathe [sweɪð] ◇ *vt* **1.** [bind] envelopper, emmailloter ▪ **his head was ~d in bandages** sa tête était enveloppée de pansements **2.** [envelop] envelopper ▪ **~d in mist** enveloppé de brume.
◇ *n* **1.** AGRIC andain *m* **2.** [strip of land] bande *f* de terre ▪ **the army cut a ~ through the town** l'armée a tout détruit sur son passage dans la ville ▪ **the new motorway cuts a ~ through the countryside** la nouvelle autoroute coupe à travers la campagne **3.** [strip of cloth] lanière *f*.

swatter ['swɒtər] *n* tapette *f*.

sway [sweɪ] ◇ *vi* **1.** [pylon, bridge] se balancer, osciller ▪ [tree] s'agiter ▪ [bus, train] pencher ▪ [boat] rouler ▪ [person - deliberately] se balancer ; [- from tiredness, drink] chanceler, tituber ▪ **the poplars ~ed in the wind** les peupliers étaient agités par le vent ▪ **to ~ from side to side/to and fro** se balancer de droite à gauche/d'avant en arrière **2.** [vacillate] vaciller, hésiter ▪ [incline, tend] pencher ▪ **to ~ towards conservatism** pencher vers le conservatisme.
◇ *vt* **1.** [pylon] (faire) balancer, faire osciller ▪ [tree] agiter ▪ [hips] rouler, balancer **2.** [influence] influencer ▪ **don't be ~ed by his charm** ne te laisse pas influencer par son charme **3.** *arch* [rule] régner sur.
◇ *n* **1.** [rocking - gen] balancement *m* ; [- of a boat] roulis *m* **2.** [influence] influence *f*, emprise *f*, empire *m* ▪ **to hold ~ over sb/sthg** avoir de l'influence OR de l' emprise sur qqn/qqch ▪ **the economic theories that hold ~ today** les théories économiques qui ont cours aujourd'hui.

Swazi ['swɑːzɪ] *n* Swazi *mf*.

Swaziland ['swɑːzɪlænd] *pr n* Swaziland *m* ▪ **in ~** au Swaziland.

swear [sweər] (*pret* **swore** [swɔːr], *pp* **sworn** [swɔːn]) ◇ *vi* **1.** [curse] jurer ▪ **to ~ at sb** injurier qqn ▪ **they started ~ing at each other** ils ont commencé à se traiter de tous les noms OR à s'injurier ▪ **don't ~ in front of the children** ne dis pas de gros mots devant les enfants ▶ **to ~ like a trooper** jurer comme un charretier **2.** [vow, take an oath] jurer ▪ **she swore on her honour/on her mother's grave** elle jura sur l'honneur/sur la tombe de sa mère ▪ **I can't ~ to its authenticity** je ne peux pas jurer de son authenticité ▪ **I wouldn't ~ to it, but I think it was him** je n'en jurerais pas, mais je crois que c'était lui ▪ **I ~ I'll never do it again!** je jure de ne plus jamais recommencer! ▪ **he ~s he's never seen her before** il jure qu'il ne l'a jamais vue.
◇ *vt* **1.** [pledge, vow] : **to ~ an oath** prêter serment ▪ **to ~ allegiance to the Crown** jurer allégeance à la couronne ▪ **to ~ a charge against sb** LAW faire une déposition sous serment contre qqn **2.** [make sb pledge] : **to ~ sb to secrecy** faire jurer à qqn de garder le secret.
◆ **swear by** *vt insep* : **she ~s by that old sewing machine of hers** elle ne jure que par sa vieille machine à coudre.
◆ **swear in** *vt sep* [witness, president] faire prêter serment à, assermenter *fml*.
◆ **swear off** *vt insep inf* renoncer à.

swearword ['sweəwɜːd] *n* grossièreté *f*, juron *m*, gros mot *m*.

sweat [swet] (*UK pret & pp* **sweated**) (*US pret & pp* **sweat** OR **sweated**) ◇ *n* **1.** [perspiration] sueur *f*, transpiration *f* ▪ **~ was dripping from his forehead** son front était ruisselant de sueur ▪ **I woke up covered in ~** je me suis réveillé en nage OR couvert de sueur OR tout en sueur ▪ **to break into** OR **to come out in a cold ~** avoir des sueurs froides ▪ **she earned it by the ~ of her brow** elle l'a gagné à la sueur de son front **2.** *inf* [unpleasant task] corvée *f* ▶ **can you give me a hand? – no ~!** peux-tu me donner un coup de main? – pas de problème! **3.** *UK inf* [anxious state] : **there's no need to get into a ~ about it!** pas la peine de te mettre dans des états pareils! **4.** *inf* [person] : **(old) ~** *UK* [old soldier] vieux soldat *m* ; [experienced worker] vieux routier *m*.
◇ *vi* **1.** [perspire] suer, transpirer ▪ **the effort made him ~** l'effort l'a mis en sueur ▪ **she was ~ ing profusely** elle suait à grosses gouttes ▶ **to ~ like a pig** *inf* suer comme un bœuf **2.** *fig* [work hard, suffer] suer ▪ **I'll make them ~ for this!** ils vont me le payer! ▪ **she's ~ing over her homework** elle est en train de suer sur ses devoirs **3.** [ooze - walls] suer, suinter ; [- cheese] suer.
◇ *vt* **1.** [cause to perspire] faire suer OR transpirer ▪ [exude] : **to ~ blood** *fig* suer sang et eau ▪ **he ~ed blood over this article** il a sué sang et eau sur cet article ▪ **to ~ buckets** *inf* suer comme un bœuf **2.** *US inf* [extort] : **we ~ed the information out of him** on lui a fait cracher le morceau **3.** *US phr* **don't ~ it!** *inf* pas de panique! **4.** CULIN cuire à l'étouffée.
◆ **sweat off** *vt sep* éliminer.
◆ **sweat out** *vt sep* **1.** [illness] : **stay in bed and try to ~ out the cold** restez au chaud dans votre lit et votre rhume partira **2.** *phr* **leave him to ~ it out** laissez-le se débrouiller tout seul.

sweatband ['swetbænd] *n* **1.** SPORT [headband] bandeau *m* ▪ [wristband] poignet *m* **2.** [in a hat] cuir *m* intérieur.

sweated ['swetɪd] *adj* : **~ labour** [staff] main-d'œuvre *f* exploitée ; [work] exploitation *f*.

sweater ['swetər] *n* pull-over *m*, pull *m*.

sweat gland *n* glande *f* sudoripare.

sweating ['swetɪŋ] *n* transpiration *f*, sudation *f spec*.

sweatpants ['swetpænts] *npl US* pantalon *m* de survêtement.

sweatshirt ['swetʃɜːt] *n* sweat-shirt *m*.

sweatshop ['swetʃɒp] *n* ≃ atelier *m* clandestin.

sweat suit *n* survêtement *m*.

sweaty ['swetɪ] (*comp* **sweatier**, *superl* **sweatiest**) *adj* **1.** [person] (tout) en sueur ▪ [hands] moite ▪ [feet] qui transpire ▪ [clothing] trempé de sueur ▪ **he's got ~ feet** il transpire des pieds ▪ **his uniform smelt ~** son uniforme sentait la sueur **2.** [weather, place] d'une chaleur humide OR moite **3.** [activity] qui fait transpirer.

swede [swiːd] *n UK* rutabaga *m*, chou-navet *m*.

Swede [swiːd] *n* Suédois *m*, - e *f*.

Sweden ['swiːdn] *pr n* Suède *f* ▪ **in ~** en Suède.

Swedish ['swiːdɪʃ] ◇ *npl* : **the ~** les Suédois *mpl*.
◇ *n* LING suédois *m*.
◇ *adj* suédois.

sweep [swiːp] (*pret & pp* **swept** [swept]) ◇ *vt* **1.** [with a brush - room, street, dust, leaves] balayer ; [- chimney] ramoner ▪ **to ~ the floor** balayer le sol ▪ **I swept the broken glass into the dustpan** j'ai poussé le verre cassé dans la pelle avec le balai ▶ **to ~ sthg under the carpet** OR **the rug** tirer le rideau sur qqch
2. [with hand] : **she swept the coins off the table into her handbag** elle a fait glisser les pièces de la table dans son sac à main **3.** [subj: wind, tide, crowd etc] : **the wind swept his hat into the river** le vent a fait tomber son chapeau dans la rivière ▪ **the small boat was swept out to sea** le petit bateau a été emporté vers le large ▪ **three fishermen were swept overboard** un paquet de mer emporta trois pêcheurs ▪ **to ~ everything before one** *fig* faire des ravages ▪ **the incident swept all other thoughts from her mind** l'incident lui fit oublier tout le reste ▪ **he was swept to power on a wave of popular discontent** il a été porté au pouvoir par une vague de mécontentement

populaire ▶ **to be swept off one's feet (by sb)** [fall in love] tomber fou amoureux (de qqn) ; [be filled with enthusiam] être enthousiasmé (par qqn)
4. [spread through - subj: fire, epidemic, rumour, belief] gagner ■ **a new craze is ~ing America** une nouvelle mode fait fureur aux États-Unis ■ **the flu epidemic which swept Europe in 1919** l'épidémie de grippe qui sévit en Europe en 1919
5. [scan, survey] parcourir ■ **searchlights continually ~ the open ground outside the prison camp** des projecteurs parcourent *OR* balayent sans cesse le terrain qui entoure la prison
6. [win easily] gagner *OR* remporter haut la main ■ **the Popular Democratic Party swept the polls** le parti démocratique populaire a fait un raz-de-marée aux élections ▶ **to ~ the board** remporter tous les prix
7. NAUT [mines, sea, channel] draguer ■ **the port has been swept for mines** le port a été dragué.
◇ *vi* **1.** [with a brush] balayer
2. [move quickly, powerfully] : **harsh winds swept across the bleak steppes** un vent violent balayait les mornes steppes ■ **I watched storm clouds ~ing across the sky** je regardais des nuages orageux filer dans le ciel ■ **the Barbarians who swept into the Roman Empire** les Barbares qui déferlèrent sur l'Empire romain ■ **nationalism swept through the country** une vague de nationalisme a submergé le pays ■ **the fire swept through the forest** l'incendie a ravagé la forêt
3. [move confidently, proudly] : **he swept into/out of the room** il entra/sortit majestueusement de la pièce
4. [stretch - land] s'étendre ■ **the fields ~ down to the lake** les prairies descendent en pente douce jusqu'au lac ■ **the river ~s round in a wide curve** le fleuve décrit une large courbe
5. NAUT : **to ~ for mines** draguer, déminer.
◇ *n* **1.** [with a brush] coup *m* de balai
2. [movement] : **with a ~ of her arm** d'un geste large ■ **in** *OR* **at one ~** d'un seul coup
3. [curved line, area] (grande) courbe *f*, étendue *f*
4. [range] gamme *f* ■ **the members of the commission represent a broad ~ of opinion** les membres de la commission représentent un large éventail d'opinions
5. [scan, survey] : **her eyes made a ~ of the room** elle parcourut la pièce des yeux ■ **they jumped over the wall between two ~s of the searchlight** ils sautèrent par-dessus le mur entre deux passages du projecteur
6. ELECTRON [by electron beam] balayage *m*
7. [search] fouille *f*
8. [gen, - MIL] [- attack] attaque *f* ; [- reconnaissance] reconnaissance *f* ■ **the rescue party made a ~ of the area** l'équipe de secours a ratissé les environs
9. [chimney sweep] ramoneur *m*
10. *inf* [sweepstake] sweepstake *m*
11. AERON flèche *f*.
◆ **sweep along** *vt sep* [subj: wind, tide, crowd] emporter, entraîner.
◆ **sweep aside** *vt sep* **1.** [object, person] écarter
2. [advice, objection] repousser, rejeter ■ [obstacle] écarter.
◆ **sweep away** *vt sep* **1.** [dust, snow] balayer
2. [subj: wind, tide, crowd] emporter, entraîner.
◆ **sweep by** *vi insep* [car] passer à toute vitesse ■ [person - majestically] passer majestueusement ; [- disdainfully] passer dédaigneusement.
◆ **sweep down** *vi insep* [steps] descendre.
◆ **sweep past** = **sweep by**.
◆ **sweep up** ◇ *vt sep* [dust, leaves] balayer.
◇ *vi insep* balayer.

sweeper ['swi:pər] *n* **1.** [person] balayeur *m*, - euse *f* **2.** [device - for streets] balayeuse *f* ; [- for carpets] balai *m* mécanique **3.** FTBL libero *m*.

sweeping ['swi:pɪŋ] *adj* **1.** [wide - movement, curve] large ■ **with a ~ gesture** d'un geste large, d'un grand geste ■ **a ~ view** une vue panoramique **2.** [indiscriminate] : **a ~ generalization** *OR* **statement** une généralisation excessive ■ **that's rather a ~ generalization** là, vous généralisez un peu trop **3.** [significant, large - amount] considérable ■ **~ budget cuts** des coupes sombres dans le budget **4.** [far-reaching - measure, change] de grande portée, de grande envergure ■ **~ reforms** des réformes de grande envergure.
◆ **sweepings** *npl* balayures *fpl*.

sweepstake ['swi:psteɪk] *n* sweepstake *m*.

sweet [swi:t] ◇ *adj* **1.** [tea, coffee, taste] sucré ■ [fruit, honey] doux, douce *f*, sucré ■ [wine] moelleux **2.** [fresh, clean - air] doux, douce *f* ; [- breath] frais, fraîche *f* ; [- water] pur **3.** [fragrant - smell] agréable, suave ■ **the roses smell so ~!** les roses sentent si bon! **4.** [musical - sound, voice] mélodieux ; [- words] doux, douce *f* ■ **to whisper ~ nothings in sb's ear** murmurer des mots d'amour à l'oreille de qqn, conter fleurette à qqn **5.** [pleasant, satisfactory - emotion, feeling, success] doux, douce *f* ■ **revenge is ~** la vengeance est douce **6.** [kind, generous] gentil ■ **it was very ~ of you** c'était gentil de votre part ▶ **to keep sb ~** *inf UK* cultiver les bonnes grâces de qqn **7.** [cute] mignon, adorable **8.** *inf* [in love] : **to be ~ on sb** *UK* avoir le béguin pour qqn **9.** *inf* [as intensifier] : **he'll please his own ~ self, he'll go his own ~ way** il n'en fera qu'à sa tête ■ **she'll come in her own ~ time** elle viendra quand ça lui plaira ▶ **~ FA**△ *UK* rien du tout, que dalle△.
◇ *n* **1.** *UK* [confectionery] bonbon *m* **2.** *UK* [dessert] dessert *m* **3.** [term of address] : **my ~** mon chéri *m*, ma chérie *f*.

sweet-and-sour *adj* aigre-doux, - douce *f* ■ **~ pork** porc *m* à la sauce aigre-douce.

sweetbread ['swi:tbred] *n* [thymus] ris *m* ■ [pancreas] pancréas *m*.

sweetbrier [,swi:t'braɪər] *n* églantier *m* odorant.

sweet chestnut *n* marron *m*.

sweet cider *n UK* cidre *m* doux.

sweet corn *n* maïs *m* doux.

sweeten ['swi:tn] *vt* **1.** [food, drink] sucrer ■ **~ed with honey** sucré avec du miel **2.** [mollify, soften] : **to ~ (up)** amadouer, enjôler **3.** *inf* [bribe] graisser la patte à **4.** [make more attractive - task] adoucir ; [- offer] améliorer **5.** [improve the odour of] parfumer, embaumer.

sweetener ['swi:tnər] *n* **1.** [for food, drink] édulcorant *m*, sucrette *f* ■ **artificial ~s** édulcorants artificiels **2.** *UK inf* [present] cadeau *m* ■ [bribe] pot-de-vin *m*.

sweetening ['swi:tnɪŋ] *n* **1.** [substance] édulcorant *m*, édulcorants *mpl* **2.** [process - of wine] sucrage *m* ; [- of water] adoucissement *m*.

sweetheart ['swi:thɑ:t] *n* **1.** [lover] petit ami *m*, petite amie *f* ■ **they're ~s** ils sont amoureux ■ **they were childhood ~s** ils s'aimaient *OR* ils étaient amoureux quand ils étaient enfants **2.** [term of address] (mon) chéri *m*, (ma) chérie *f*.

sweetie ['swi:tɪ] *n inf* **1.** [darling] chéri *m*, - e *f*, chou *m* ■ **he's a real ~** il est vraiment adorable **2.** *UK baby* [sweet] bonbon *m*.

sweetiepie ['swi:tɪpaɪ] *inf* = **sweetie** *(sense 1)*.

sweetly ['swi:tlɪ] *adv* **1.** [pleasantly, kindly] gentiment ■ [cutely] d'un air mignon ■ **she smiled at him ~** elle lui sourit gentiment ■ **he was whispering ~ in her ear** il lui chuchotait tendrement à l'oreille **2.** [smoothly] sans à-coups ■ [accurately] avec précision **3.** [musically] harmonieusement, mélodieusement ■ **she sings very ~** elle a une voix très mélodieuse.

sweetness ['swi:tnɪs] *n* **1.** [of food, tea, coffee] goût *m* sucré ■ [of wine] (goût *m*) mœlleux *m* **2.** [freshness - of air] douceur *f* ; [- of breath] fraîcheur *f* ; [- of water] pureté *f* **3.** [fragrance] parfum *m* **4.** [musicality - of sound] son *m* mélodieux ; [- of voice, words] douceur *f* **5.** [pleasure, satisfaction] douceur *f* **6.** [kindness, generosity] gentillesse *f* ■ **she's all ~ and light** elle est on ne peut plus gentille.

sweet pea *n* pois *m* de senteur.

sweet potato *n* patate *f* douce.

sweet shop *n UK* confiserie *f*.

sweet talk *n (U) inf* flatteries *fpl*, paroles *fpl* mielleuses.
◆ **sweet-talk** *vt inf* embobiner ■ **she sweet-talked him into doing it** elle l'a si bien embobiné qu'il a fini par le faire.

sweet tooth *n* : **to have a ~** adorer les *OR* être friand de sucreries.

sweet william *n* œillet *m* de poète.

swell [swel] (*pret* **swelled**, *pp* **swelled** *OR* **swollen** ['swəʊln]) ◇ *vi* **1.** [distend - wood, pulses etc] gonfler ; [- part of body] enfler, gonfler ■ **her heart ~ed with joy/pride** *fig* son cœur s'est gonflé de joie/d'orgueil **2.** [increase] augmenter ■ **the crowd ~ed to nearly two hundred** la foule grossit et il y eut bientôt près de 200 personnes **3.** [well up - emotion] monter, surgir ■ **I felt anger ~ in me** je sentais la colère monter en moi **4.** [rise - sea, tide] monter ; [- river] se gonfler, grossir **5.** [grow louder] s'enfler ■ **the music ~ed to its climax** la musique atteignit alors son point culminant.

◇ *vt* **1.** [distend] gonfler ■ **her eyes were swollen with tears** ses yeux étaient pleins de larmes **2.** [increase] augmenter, grossir ■ **to ~ the ranks of the unemployed** venir grossir les rangs des chômeurs **3.** [cause to rise] gonfler, grossir.

◇ *n* **1.** NAUT houle *f* **2.** [bulge] gonflement *m* **3.** [increase] augmentation *f* **4.** MUS crescendo *m*.

◇ *adj US inf dated* [great] super, chouette ■ **we had a ~ time** on s'est super bien amusés.

◇ *interj US inf dated* super.

◆ **swell up** = swell *(vi sense 1)*.

swelling ['swelɪŋ] ◇ *n* **1.** MED enflure *f*, gonflement *m* ■ **there was some ~ around the ankle** la cheville était un peu enflée **2.** [increase] augmentation *f*, grossissement *m*.

◇ *adj* [increasing] croissant.

swelter ['sweltəʳ] *vi* [feel too hot] étouffer de chaleur ■ [sweat] suer à grosses gouttes, être en nage.

sweltering ['sweltərɪŋ] *adj* [day, heat] étouffant, oppressant ■ **it was simply ~ in the kitchen** il faisait une chaleur vraiment étouffante dans la cuisine.

swept [swept] *pt* & *pp* ▷ **sweep**.

swept-back *adj* **1.** AERON [wings] en flèche (arrière) **2.** [hair] ramené en arrière.

swept-wing *adj* [aircraft] aux ailes en flèche.

swerve [swɜːv] ◇ *vi* **1.** [car, driver, ship] faire une embardée ■ [ball] dévier ■ [aeroplane, bird, runner] virer ■ **the car ~d to the left/towards us/round the corner/off the road** la voiture fit une embardée vers la gauche/vira pour foncer droit vers nous/prit le virage brusquement/fit une embardée et quitta la chaussée **2.** *fig* [budge, deviate] dévier.

◇ *vt* **1.** [vehicle] faire virer ■ [ball] faire dévier ■ **she ~d the car to the left** elle donna un coup de volant vers la gauche **2.** *fig* [person] détourner, faire dévier.

◇ *n* [by car, driver, ship] embardée *f* ■ [by aeroplane, bird, runner, ball] déviation *f*.

swift [swɪft] ◇ *adj* **1.** [fast] rapide **2.** [prompt] prompt, rapide ■ **~ to react** prompt à réagir ■ **she received a ~ reply** elle reçut une réponse immédiate ■ **she took ~ revenge** elle n'a pas tardé à se venger.

◇ *adv* : **~-moving** rapide ■ **~-flowing** [river, stream] au cours rapide.

◇ *n* ORNITH martinet *m*.

swift-footed *adj lit* leste, véloce *lit*.

swiftly ['swɪftlɪ] *adv* **1.** [quickly] rapidement, vite **2.** [promptly] promptement, rapidement.

swiftness ['swɪftnɪs] *n* **1.** [speed] rapidité *f*, célérité *f lit* **2.** [promptness] promptitude *f*, rapidité *f*.

swig [swɪg] ◇ *vt* (*pret* & *pp* **swigged**, *cont* **swigging**) lamper, siffler.

◇ *n* lampée *f*, coup *m* ■ **have a ~ of this** bois un coup de ça ■ **he took a long ~ at his bottle** il porta sa bouteille à sa bouche et but un grand coup.

◆ **swig down** *vt sep inf* vider d'un trait, siffler.

swill [swɪl] ◇ *vt* **1.** *UK* [wash] laver à grande eau ■ **go and ~ the glass (out) under the tap** va passer le verre sous le robinet **2.** *inf* [drink] écluser.

◇ *n* **1.** [for pigs] pâtée *f* **2.** [wash] : **to give sthg a ~** laver qqch.

swim [swɪm] (*pret* **swam** [swæm], *pp* **swum** [swʌm], *cont* **swimming**) ◇ *vi* **1.** [fish, animal] nager ■ [person - gen] nager ; [- for amusement] nager, se baigner ; [- for sport] nager, faire de la natation ■ **to go swimming** [gen] (aller) se baigner ; [in swimming pool] aller à la piscine ■ **she's learning to ~** elle apprend à nager ■ **I can't ~!** je ne sais pas nager! ■ **the lake was too cold to ~ in** le lac était trop froid pour qu'on s'y baigne ■ **to ~ across a river** traverser une rivière à la nage ■ **to ~ upstream/downstream** monter/descendre le courant à la nage ■ **he managed to ~ to safety** il a réussi à se sauver en nageant ■ **the raft sank and they had to ~ for it** le radeau a coulé et ils ont été obligés de nager ▶ **to ~ against the tide** *liter* & *fig* nager à contre-courant **2.** [be soaked] nager, baigner ■ **the salad was swimming in oil** la salade baignait dans l'huile **3.** [spin] : **my head is swimming** j'ai la tête qui tourne ■ **that awful feeling when the room starts to ~** cette impression horrible quand la pièce se met à tourner.

◇ *vt* **1.** [river, lake etc] traverser à la nage ■ **she swam the (English) Channel** elle a traversé la Manche à la nage **2.** [a stroke] nager ■ **can you ~ butterfly?** est-ce que tu sais nager le papillon? **3.** [distance] nager ■ **she swam ten lengths** elle a fait dix longueurs **4.** [animal] : **they swam their horses across the river** ils ont fait traverser la rivière à leurs chevaux (à la nage).

◇ *n* : **to go for a ~** [gen] (aller) se baigner ; [in swimming pool] aller à la piscine ■ **he had his morning ~** il s'est baigné comme tous les matins ■ **I feel like a ~** j'ai envie d'aller me baigner ■ **did you have a nice ~?** est-ce que la baignade a été agréable? ■ **it's a good 20-minute ~ out to the island** il faut 20 bonnes minutes pour atteindre l'île à la nage.

swimmer ['swɪməʳ] *n* [one who swims] nageur *m*, - euse *f* ■ [bather] baigneur *m*, - euse *f*.

swimming ['swɪmɪŋ] ◇ *n* [gen] nage *f* ■ SPORT natation *f*.

◇ *comp* [lesson, classes] de natation.

swimming bath, swimming baths *(npl) n UK* piscine *f*.

swimming cap *n* bonnet *m* de bain.

swimming costume *n UK* maillot *m* de bain.

swimming instructor *n* maître-nageur *m*.

swimmingly ['swɪmɪŋlɪ] *adv UK inf* à merveille ■ **everything's going ~** tout marche comme sur des roulettes.

swimming pool *n* piscine *f*.

swimming trunks *npl* maillot *m* OR slip *m* de bain.

swimsuit ['swɪmsuːt] *n* maillot *m* de bain.

swimwear ['swɪmweəʳ] *n (U)* maillots *mpl* de bain.

swindle ['swɪndl] ◇ *vt* escroquer ■ **they were ~d out of all their savings** on leur a escroqué toutes leurs économies.

◇ *n* escroquerie *f*, vol *m* ■ **it's a real ~** c'est une véritable escroquerie.

swindler ['swɪndləʳ] *n* escroc *m*.

swine [swaɪn] (*pl* **swine** OR *pl* **swines**) *n* **1.** (*pl* swine) *lit* [pig] porc *m*, pourceau *m lit* **2.** *inf* [unpleasant person] fumier *m*, ordure *f* ■ **you (filthy) ~!** espèce de fumier! ■ **it's a ~ of a job** c'est un sale boulot.

swineherd ['swaɪnhɜːd] *n* porcher *m*, - ère *f*.

swing [swɪŋ] (*pret* & *pp* **swung** [swʌŋ]) ◇ *vi* **1.** [sway, move to and fro - gen] se balancer ; [- pendulum] osciller ■ [hang, be suspended] pendre, être suspendu ■ **he walked along with his arms ~ing** il marchait en balançant les bras ■ **a basket swung from her arm** un panier se balançait à son bras ■ **~ing from a cord** suspendu à une corde ▶ **to ~ both ways** *inf* marcher à voile et à vapeur

2. [move from one place to another] : **to ~ from tree to tree** se balancer d'arbre en arbre ■ **to ~ into action** *fig* passer à l'action

3. [make a turn] virer ■ **the lorry swung through the gate** le camion vira pour franchir le portail ■ **the car in front swung out to overtake** la voiture de devant a déboîté pour doubler ■ **the door swung open/shut** la porte s'est ouverte/s'est refermée ■ **the gate swung back in my face** le portail s'est refermé devant moi

4. *fig* [change direction] virer ■ **her mood ~s between depression and elation** elle passe de la dépression à l'exultation

5. *inf* [be hanged] être pendu

6. [hit out, aim a blow] essayer de frapper ■ **he swung at them with the hammer** il a essayé de les frapper avec le marteau ■ **I swung at him** je lui ai décoché un coup de poing

7. *inf* [musician] swinguer ■ [music] swinguer, avoir du swing

8. *inf dated* [be modern, fashionable] être dans le vent OR in ■ **he was there in the sixties, when London was really ~ing** il était là dans les années soixante, quand ça bougeait à Londres

9. *inf* [be lively] chauffer ▪ **the party was beginning to ~** la fête commençait à être très animée
10. *inf* [try hard] : **I'm in there ~ing for you** je fais tout ce que je peux pour toi.
◇ *vt* **1.** [cause to sway] balancer ▪ **he walked along ~ing his arms** il marchait en balançant les bras ▪ **to ~ one's hips** balancer les *OR* rouler des hanches
2. [move from one place to another] : **she swung her bag onto the back seat** elle jeta son sac sur le siège arrière ▪ **he swung a rope over a branch** il lança une corde par-dessus une branche ▪ **I swung myself (up) into the saddle** je me suis hissé sur la selle, j'ai sauté en selle
3. [turn - steering wheel] (faire) tourner ; [- vehicle] faire virer ▪ **the accident swung public opinion against the company** *fig* l'accident a provoqué un revirement de l'opinion contre la compagnie
4. [aim] : **she swung the bat at the ball** elle essaya de frapper la balle avec sa batte
5. *inf* [manage, pull off] : **to ~ sthg** réussir *OR* arriver à faire qqch ▪ **I think I should be able to ~ it** je crois pouvoir me débrouiller
6. *inf* **to ~ it** avoir le swing.
◇ *n* **1.** [to-and-fro movement, sway - gen] balancement *m* ; [- of pendulum] oscillation *f* ▪ **with a ~ of his arm** en balançant son bras
2. [arc described] arc *m*, courbe *f*
3. [swipe, attempt to hit] (grand) coup *m* ▪ **I took a ~ at him** je lui ai décoché un coup de poing ▪ **he took a ~ at the ball** il donna un coup pour frapper la balle
4. [hanging seat] balançoire *f* ▶ **what you lose on the ~s you gain on the roundabouts** ce que l'on perd d'un côté, on le récupère de l'autre ▪ **it's ~s and roundabouts really** en fait, on perd d'un côté ce qu'on gagne de l'autre
5. [change, shift] changement *m* ▪ **his mood ~s are very unpredictable** ses sautes d'humeur sont très imprévisibles ▪ **seasonal ~s** COMM fluctuations *fpl* saisonnières ▪ **the upward/downward ~ of the market** ST. EX la fluctuation du marché vers le haut/le bas ‖ POL revirement *m* ▪ **America experienced a major ~ towards conservatism** les États-Unis ont connu un important revirement vers le conservatisme
6. [in boxing, golf] swing *m*
7. [rhythm - gen] rythme *m* ▪ [jazz rhythm, style of jazz] swing *m* ▪ **a ~ band** un orchestre de swing
8. *US* POL [tour] tournée *f*
9. *phr* **to get into the ~ of things** *inf* : **I'm beginning to get into the ~ of things** je commence à être dans le bain ▪ **to go with a ~** *inf* [music] être très rythmé *OR* entraînant ; [party] swinguer ; [business] marcher très bien.

◆ **in full swing** *adj phr* : **the party was in full ~** la fête battait son plein ▪ **production is in full ~** on produit à plein rendement ▪ **the town's packed when the season's in full ~** en pleine saison, il y a foule en ville ▪ **once it's in full ~, the project will require more people** une fois lancé, il faudra plus de gens sur le projet.

◆ **swing round** ◇ *vt sep* [vehicle] faire virer ▪ [person] faire tourner ▪ **he swung the car round the corner** il a tourné au coin.
◇ *vi insep* [turn round - person] se retourner, pivoter ; [- crane] tourner, pivoter.

◆ **swing to** *vi insep* [door, gate] se refermer.

swingboat ['swɪŋbəʊt] *n* nacelle *f (balançoire de champ de foire)*.

swing bridge *n* pont *m* tournant.

swing door *n* porte *f* battante.

swingeing ['swɪndʒɪŋ] *adj UK* [increase, drop] énorme ▪ [cuts] draconien ▪ [blow] violent ▪ [criticism, condemnation] sévère ▪ [victory, defeat] écrasant.

swinger ['swɪŋəʳ] *n inf dated* **1.** [fashionable person] branché *m*, - e *f* ▪ [pleasure-seeker] noceur *m*, - euse *f* **2.** [promiscuous person] débauché *m*, - e *f*.

swinging ['swɪŋɪŋ] *adj* **1.** [swaying] balançant ▪ [pivoting] tournant, pivotant **2.** [rhythmic - gen] rythmé, cadencé ; [- jazz, jazz musician] swinguant **3.** *inf dated* [trendy] in ▪ **the ~ sixties** les folles années soixante.

swing-wing ◇ *adj* à géométrie variable.
◇ *n* avion *m* à géométrie variable.

swinish ['swaɪnɪʃ] *adj inf* sale, pas sympa.

swipe [swaɪp] ◇ *vi* : **to ~ at** : **he ~d at the fly with his newspaper** il donna un grand coup de journal pour frapper la mouche.
◇ *vt* **1.** [hit] donner un coup à **2.** *inf* [steal] piquer, faucher **3.** [credit card] passer.
◇ *n* (grand) coup *m* ▪ **to take a ~ at sthg** *liter* donner un grand coup pour frapper qqch ; *fig* [criticize] tirer à boulets rouges sur qqch.

swipe card *n* carte *f* magnétique.

swirl [swɜːl] ◇ *vi* tourbillonner, tournoyer.
◇ *vt* faire tourbillonner *OR* tournoyer ▪ **a sudden wind ~ed the leaves around** une brusque bourrasque fit tournoyer *OR* tourbillonner les feuilles ▪ **the raft was ~ed downstream** le radeau a été emporté dans le tourbillon du courant ▪ **he ~ed her round the dance floor** il la fit tournoyer autour de la piste (de danse).
◇ *n* tourbillon *m*.

swish [swɪʃ] ◇ *vi* [whip] siffler ▪ [leaves, wind] chuinter, bruire *lit* ▪ [fabric, skirt] froufrouter ▪ [water] murmurer ▪ **the curtains ~ed open/shut** les rideaux s'ouvrirent/se refermèrent en froufroutant.
◇ *vt* : **the horse ~ed its tail** le cheval donna un coup de queue.
◇ *n* **1.** [sound - of fabric, skirt] froufroutement *m*, froissement *m* ; [- of leaves, wind] bruissement *m* ; [- of water] murmure *m* **2.** [movement] : **the cow flicked the flies away with a ~ of its tail** la vache chassa les mouches d'un coup de queue.
◇ *adj UK inf* [smart] chic.

Swiss [swɪs] (*pl inv*) ◇ *n* Suisse *m*, Suissesse *f* ▪ **the ~** les Suisses *mpl*.
◇ *adj* [gen] suisse ▪ [confederation, government] helvétique ▪ **~ bank account** compte *m* en Suisse.

Swiss cheese *n* emmental *m*.

Swiss-French ◇ *n* **1.** LING suisse *m* romand **2.** [person] Suisse *m* romand, Suisse *f* romande.
◇ *adj* suisse romand.

Swiss-German ◇ *n* **1.** LING suisse *m* allemand *OR* alémanique **2.** [person] Suisse *m* allemand, Suisse *f* allemande.
◇ *adj* suisse allemand *OR* alémanique.

Swiss Guard *n* **1.** [papal bodyguard] garde *f* (pontificale) suisse **2.** HIST [in France] membre *m* des troupes suisses ▪ **the ~** les troupes *fpl* suisses.

swiss roll *n* (gâteau *m*) roulé *m*.

switch [swɪtʃ] ◇ *n* **1.** ELEC [for light] interrupteur *m* ▪ [on radio, television] bouton *m* ▪ TECH & TELEC commutateur *m* ▪ **is the ~ on/off?** est-ce que c'est allumé/éteint? ▪ **to flick** *OR* **to throw a ~** actionner un commutateur ▪ **two-way ~** (interrupteur *m*) va-et-vient *m* **2.** [change - gen] changement *m* ; [- of opinion, attitude] changement *m*, revirement *m* ▪ **the ~ to the new equipment went very smoothly** on s'est très bien adaptés au nouveau matériel **3.** [swap, trade] échange *m* **4.** *US* RAIL : **~es** [points] aiguillage *m* **5.** [stick] baguette *f*, badine *f* ▪ [riding crop] cravache *f* **6.** [hairpiece] postiche *m* **7.** ZOOL [hair on tail] fouet *m* de la queue.
◇ *vt* **1.** [change, exchange] changer de ▪ **to ~ places with sb** échanger sa place avec qqn ▪ **she offered to ~ jobs with me** elle a offert d'échanger son poste contre le mien **2.** [transfer - allegiance, attention] transférer ▪ **she ~ed her attention back to the speaker** elle reporta son attention sur le conférencier ▪ [divert - conversation] orienter, détourner ▪ **I tried to ~ the discussion to something less controversial** j'ai essayé d'orienter la discussion vers un sujet moins épineux **3.** ELEC, RADIO & TV [circuit] commuter ▪ **to ~ channels/frequencies** changer de chaîne/de fréquence **4.** *US* RAIL aiguiller.
◇ *vi* changer ▪ **she started studying medicine but ~ed to architecture** elle a commencé par étudier la médecine, mais elle a changé pour faire architecture ▪ **I'd like to ~ to another topic** j'aimerais changer de sujet ▪ **can I ~ to another channel?** est-ce que je peux changer de chaîne? ▪ **the committee ~ed to the problem of recruitment** le comité passa au problème du recrutement ▪ **they've ~ed to American equipment** ils ont

adopté du matériel américain ■ **he ~es effortlessly from one language to another** il passe d'une langue à une autre avec une grande aisance.

◆ **switch around** = **switch round**.

◆ **switch off** ◇ *vt sep* [light] éteindre ■ [electrical appliance] éteindre, arrêter ■ **don't forget to ~ the lights off when you leave** n'oublie pas d'éteindre la lumière en partant ■ **the radio ~es itself off** la radio s'éteint *OR* s'arrête automatiquement ■ **they've ~ed off the power** ils ont coupé le courant ■ **to ~ off the engine** AUT couper le contact, arrêter le moteur.
◇ *vi insep* **1.** [go off - light] s'éteindre ; [- electrical appliance] s'éteindre, s'arrêter ■ **how do you get the oven to ~ off?** comment tu éteins le four? **2.** [TV viewer, radio listener] éteindre le poste ■ **don't ~ off!** restez à l'écoute! **3.** *inf* [stop paying attention] décrocher.

◆ **switch on** ◇ *vt sep* **1.** ELEC [light, heating, oven, TV, radio] allumer ■ [engine, washing machine, vacuum cleaner] mettre en marche ■ **the power isn't ~ed on** il n'y a pas de courant ■ **to ~ on the ignition** AUT mettre le contact **2.** *fig* & *pej* **to ~ on the charm/tears** sourire/pleurer sur commande.
◇ *vi insep* **1.** ELEC [light, heating, oven, TV, radio] s'allumer ■ [engine, washing machine, vacuum cleaner] se mettre en marche **2.** [TV viewer, radio listener] allumer le poste.

◆ **switch over** *vi insep* **1.** = **switch** *(vi)* **2.** TV changer de chaîne ■ RADIO changer de station.

◆ **switch round** ◇ *vt sep* changer de place, déplacer ■ **he ~ed the glasses round when she wasn't looking** il échangea les verres pendant qu'elle ne regardait pas ■ **the manager has ~ed the team round again** l'entraîneur a encore changé l'équipe.
◇ *vi insep* [two people] changer de place.

Switch® [swɪtʃ] *n* carte *f* Switch (de débit).

switchback ['swɪtʃbæk] ◇ *n* **1.** [road] route *f* accidentée et sinueuse **2.** *UK* [roller coaster] montagnes *fpl* russes.
◇ *adj* : **a ~ road** une route accidentée et sinueuse.

switchblade ['swɪtʃbleɪd] *n US* (couteau *m* à) cran d'arrêt *m*.

switchboard ['swɪtʃbɔ:d] *n* **1.** TELEC standard *m* **2.** ELEC tableau *m*.

switchboard operator *n* standardiste *mf*.

switched-on [ˌswɪtʃt-] *adj UK inf dated* [fashionable] dans le vent, in.

switchgear ['swɪtʃgɪəʳ] *n* appareillage *m* de commutation.

switch-hitter *n US* **1.** SPORT batteur *m* ambidextre **2.**△ [bisexual] bi *mf*.

switching ['swɪtʃɪŋ] *n* COMPUT, ELEC & TELEC commutation *f* ■ **data ~** COMPUT commutation de données.

switchover ['swɪtʃˌəʊvəʳ] *n* [to another method, system] passage *m*, conversion *f*.

Switzerland ['swɪtsələnd] *pr n* Suisse *f* ■ **in ~** en Suisse ■ **French-/Italian-speaking ~** la Suisse romande/italienne ■ **German-speaking ~** la Suisse allemande *OR* alémanique.

swivel ['swɪvl] (*UK pret & pp* **swivelled**, *cont* **swivelling**) (*US pret & pp* **swiveled**, *cont* **swiveling**) ◇ *n* [gen] pivot *m* ■ [for gun] tourillon *m*.
◇ *comp* [lamp, joint etc] pivotant, tournant.
◇ *vi* : **to ~ (round)** pivoter, tourner ■ **she swivelled round in her chair** elle pivota sur sa chaise.
◇ *vt* : **to ~ (round)** [chair, wheel etc] faire pivoter.

swivel chair *n* chaise *f* pivotante ■ [with arms] fauteuil *m* pivotant.

swiz(z) [swɪz] *n UK inf* escroquerie *f*, vol *m* ■ **what a ~!** c'est du vol!

swizzle ['swɪzl] *n* **1.** *UK inf* = **swiz(z) 2.** *US* [cocktail] cocktail *m* *(préparé dans un verre mélangeur)*.

swizzle stick *n* fouet *m*.

swollen ['swəʊln] ◇ *pp* ▷ **swell**.
◇ *adj* **1.** [part of body] enflé, gonflé ■ **her ankle was badly ~** sa cheville était très enflée ■ **his face was ~** il avait le visage enflé *OR* bouffi ■ **starving children with ~ abdomens** des enfants affamés au ventre ballonné ■ **her eyes were red and ~ with crying** elle avait les yeux rouges et gonflés à force de pleurer **2.** [sails] bombé, gonflé ■ [lake, river] en crue.

swollen-headed *adj inf* qui a la grosse tête.

swoon [swu:n] ◇ *vi* **1.** [become ecstatic] se pâmer, tomber en pâmoison **2.** *dated* [faint] s'évanouir, se pâmer *lit*.
◇ *n* pâmoison *f* ■ **to fall to the ground in a ~** tomber par terre en pâmoison ■ **she was (all) in a ~ over meeting her idol** elle était tout en émoi après avoir rencontré son idole.

swoop [swu:p] ◇ *vi* **1.** [dive - bird] s'abattre, fondre ; [- aircraft] piquer, descendre en piqué ■ **the gulls ~ed down on the rocks** les mouettes s'abattirent sur *OR* fondirent sur les rochers **2.** [make a raid - police, troops etc] faire une descente.
◇ *n* **1.** [dive - by bird, aircraft] descente *f* en piqué **2.** [raid - by police, troops etc] descente *f* ■ **fifteen arrested in drugs ~** quinze personnes arrêtées dans une opération antidrogue **3.** *phr* **in one fell ~** d'un seul coup.

swoosh [swʊʃ] *inf* ◇ *vi* [water] murmurer ■ [vehicle, tyres] siffler, chuinter ■ **the express train ~ed past** le rapide est passé à toute vitesse.
◇ *n* bruissement *m*, chuintement *m*, sifflement *m*.

swop [swɒp] (*pret & pp* **swopped**, *cont* **swopping**) = **swap**.

sword [sɔ:d] ◇ *n* épée *f* ■ **they fought with ~s** ils se sont battus à l'épée ■ **all the prisoners were put to the ~** tous les prisonniers furent passés au fil de l'épée ■ **the ~ of justice** le glaive de la justice ■ **he lived by the ~ and died by the ~** il a vécu par l'épée, il a péri par l'épée.
◇ *comp* [blow, handle, wound] d'épée.

sword dance *n* danse *f* du sabre.

sword-fight *n* [between two people] duel *m* (à l'épée) ■ [between several people] bataille *f* à l'épée.

swordfish ['sɔ:dfɪʃ] (*pl inv OR pl* **swordfishes**) *n* espadon *m*, poisson-épée *m*.

swordplay ['sɔ:dpleɪ] *n* [skill] maniement *m* de l'épée ■ **they were taught riding and ~** on leur apprenait à monter à cheval et à manier l'épée ■ [activity] : **the last scene consisted of ~** la dernière scène était une scène de combats à l'épée.

swordsman ['sɔ:dzmən] (*pl* **swordsmen** [-mən]) *n* épéiste *m*, lame *f (personne)*.

swordsmanship ['sɔ:dzmənʃɪp] *n* maniement *m* de l'épée ■ **we admired her ~** nous admirâmes sa façon de manier l'épée.

swordstick ['sɔ:dstɪk] *n* canne-épée *f*, canne *f* armée.

sword-swallower *n* avaleur *m*, - euse *f* de sabres.

swore [swɔ:ʳ] *pt* ▷ **swear**.

sworn [swɔ:n] ◇ *pp* ▷ **swear**.
◇ *adj* **1.** LAW [declaration] fait sous serment ■ [evidence] donné sous serment **2.** [committed - enemy] juré ; [- friend] indéfectible.

swot [swɒt] (*pret & pp* **swotted**, *cont* **swotting**) *UK inf* ◇ *vi* bûcher, potasser ■ **to ~ for an exam** bûcher *OR* potasser un examen.
◇ *n pej* bûcheur *m*, -euse *f*.

◆ **swot up** *UK inf* ◇ *vi insep* bûcher, potasser ■ **to ~ up on sthg** bûcher *OR* potasser qqch.
◇ *vt sep* bûcher, potasser.

swum [swʌm] *pp* ▷ **swim**.

swung [swʌŋ] *pt & pp* ▷ **swing**.

swung dash *n* tilde *m*.

sycamore ['sɪkəmɔ:ʳ] *n* **1.** *UK* sycomore *m*, faux platane *m* **2.** *US* platane *m*.

sycophancy ['sɪkəfənsɪ] *n* flagornerie *f*.

sycophant ['sɪkəfænt] *n* flagorneur *m*, - euse *f*.

sycophantic [ˌsɪkə'fæntɪk] *adj* [person] flatteur, flagorneur ■ [behaviour] de flagorneur ■ [approval, praise] obséquieux.

syllabi ['sɪləbaɪ] *pl* ▷ **syllabus**.

syllabic [sɪ'læbɪk] *adj* syllabique.

syllabify [sɪ'læbɪfaɪ] (*pret & pp* **syllabified**) *vt* décomposer en syllabes.

syllable ['sɪləbl] *n* syllabe *f* ▪ **I had to explain it to him in words of one ~** j'ai dû le lui expliquer en termes simples.

syllabub ['sɪləbʌb] *n* UK [dessert] (crème *f*) sabayon *m*.

syllabus ['sɪləbəs] (*pl* **syllabuses** OR *pl* **syllabi** ['sɪləbaɪ]) *n* SCH & UNIV programme *m* (d'enseignement) ▪ **do you know what's on the ~?** savez-vous ce qu'il y a au programme?

syllogism ['sɪlədʒɪzm] *n* syllogisme *m*.

sylph [sɪlf] *n* **1.** [mythical being] sylphe *m* **2.** *lit* [girl, woman] sylphide *f*.

sylphlike ['sɪlflaɪk] *adj lit* [figure] gracile, de sylphe ▪ [woman] gracieuse.

sylvan ['sɪlvən] *adj lit* sylvestre.

Sylvester [sɪl'vestəʳ] *pr n* : **Saint ~** saint Sylvestre.

symbiosis [,sɪmbaɪ'əʊsɪs] *n liter & fig* symbiose *f* ▪ **in ~** en symbiose.

symbiotic [,sɪmbaɪ'ɒtɪk] *adj liter & fig* symbiotique.

symbol ['sɪmbl] *n* symbole *m*.

symbolic [sɪm'bɒlɪk] *adj* symbolique.

symbolically [sɪm'bɒlɪklɪ] *adv* symboliquement.

symbolism ['sɪmbəlɪzm] *n* symbolisme *m*.

symbolist ['sɪmbəlɪst] ◇ *adj* symboliste.
◇ *n* symboliste *mf*.

symbolization [,sɪmbəlaɪ'zeɪʃn] *n* symbolisation *f*.

symbolize, ise ['sɪmbəlaɪz] *vt* symboliser.

symmetric [sɪ'metrɪk] *adj* LOGIC & MATHS symétrique.

symmetrical [sɪ'metrɪkl] *adj* symétrique.

symmetrically [sɪ'metrɪklɪ] *adv* symétriquement.

symmetry ['sɪmətrɪ] *n* symétrie *f*.

sympathetic [,sɪmpə'θetɪk] *adj* **1.** [compassionate] compatissant ▪ **~ words** des paroles compatissantes OR de sympathie **2.** [well-disposed] bien disposé ▪ [understanding] compréhensif ▪ **the public is generally ~ to** OR **towards the strikers** l'opinion publique est dans l'ensemble bien disposée envers les grévistes ▪ **she spoke to a ~ audience** elle s'adressa à un auditoire bienveillant ▪ **the town council was ~ to our grievances** la municipalité a accueilli nos revendications avec compréhension **3.** [congenial, likeable] sympathique, agréable **4.** ANAT sympathique **5.** MUS : **~ string** corde *f* qui vibre par résonance.

sympathetically [,sɪmpə'θetɪklɪ] *adv* **1.** [compassionately] avec compassion **2.** [with approval] avec bienveillance **3.** ANAT par sympathie.

sympathize, ise ['sɪmpəθaɪz] *vi* **1.** [feel compassion] sympathiser, compatir ▪ **we all ~d with him when his wife left** nous avons tous compati à son malheur quand sa femme est partie ▪ **poor Emma, I really ~ with her!** cette pauvre Emma, je la plains vraiment! **2.** [feel understanding] : **he could not ~ with their feelings** il ne pouvait pas comprendre leurs sentiments ▪ **we understand and ~ with their point of view** nous comprenons et partageons leur point de vue **3.** [favour, support] sympathiser ▪ **certain heads of state openly ~d with the terrorists** certains chefs d'État sympathisaient ouvertement avec les terroristes.

sympathizer ['sɪmpəθaɪzəʳ] *n* **1.** [comforter] : **she received many cards from ~s after her husband's death** elle a reçu de nombreuses cartes de condoléances après la mort de son mari **2.** [supporter] sympathisant *m*, - e *f* ▪ **she was suspected of being a communist ~** elle était soupçonnée d'être sympathisante communiste.

sympathy ['sɪmpəθɪ] (*pl* **sympathies**) *n* **1.** [compassion] compassion *f* ▪ **to have** OR **to feel ~ for sb** éprouver de la compassion envers qqn ▪ **her tears were only a means of gaining ~** elle ne pleurait que pour qu'on s'attendrisse sur elle ▪ **you have my deepest sympathies** toutes mes condoléances **2.** [approval, support] soutien *m* ▪ **the audience was clearly not in ~ with the speaker** il était évident que le public ne partageait pas les sentiments de l'orateur ▪ **she has strong left-wing sympathies** elle est très à gauche ▪ **I have no ~ for** OR **with terrorism** je désapprouve tout à fait le terrorisme ▪ **his sympathies did not lie with his own class** il ne partageait pas les valeurs de sa propre classe ▪ **to come out in ~ (with sb)** faire grève par solidarité (avec qqn) **3.** [affinity] sympathie *f*.
Voir module d'usage

sympathy strike *n* grève *f* de solidarité.

symphonic [sɪm'fɒnɪk] *adj* symphonique.

symphony ['sɪmfənɪ] (*pl* **symphonies**) ◇ *n* symphonie *f*.
◇ *comp* [concert, orchestra] symphonique.

symposium [sɪm'pəʊzjəm] (*pl* **symposiums** OR *pl* **symposia** [-zjə]) *n* symposium *m*, colloque *m* ▪ **'The Symposium'** *Plato* 'le Banquet'.

symptom ['sɪmptəm] *n* MED & *fig* symptôme *m* ▪ **to show ~s of fatigue** donner des signes de fatigue.

symptomatic [,sɪmptə'mætɪk] *adj* MED & *fig* symptomatique.

synaeresis [sɪ'nɪərəsɪs] (*pl* **synaereses** [-si:z]) = **syneresis**.

synagogue ['sɪnəgɒg] *n* synagogue *f*.

synapse ['saɪnæps] *n* synapse *f*.

sync(h) [sɪŋk] *inf* ◇ *n* (*abbrev of* **synchronization**) synchronisation *f* ▪ **to be in/out of ~** être/ne pas être synchro.
◇ *vt* = **synchronize**.

synchromesh ['sɪŋkrəʊmeʃ] ◇ *adj* : **~ gearbox** boîte *f* de vitesses avec synchroniseur.
◇ *n* synchroniseur *m*.

synchronic [sɪŋ'krɒnɪk] *adj* synchronique.

synchronization [,sɪŋkrənaɪ'zeɪʃn] *n* synchronisation *f*.

synchronize, ise ['sɪŋkrənaɪz] ◇ *vt* synchroniser.
◇ *vi* être synchronisé.

synchronized swimming ['sɪŋkrənɪzd-] *n* natation *f* synchronisée.

SYMPATHY

Je suis vraiment désolé. I'm so sorry.

C'est vraiment triste/terrible/affreux ! That's so sad/dreadful/awful!

Si je peux vous aider en quoi que ce soit, surtout n'hésitez pas. You know where I am if there's anything I can do to help.

Tu n'as vraiment pas de chance OU **de bol !** *inf* Bad luck!

Mon/Ma pauvre ! You poor thing!

Je compatis. I sympathize.

Je suis de tout cœur avec vous. My thoughts are with you.

Sincères condoléances. Please accept my condolences.

Ça m'a fait beaucoup de peine d'apprendre la disparition de ton père. I was so sorry to hear about the death of your father.

Je vous souhaite un prompt rétablissement ! Hope you're feeling better soon!

Remets-toi vite ! Get well soon!

syncline ['sɪŋklaɪn] *n* synclinal *m*.

syncopate ['sɪŋkəpeɪt] *vt* syncoper.

syncopation [,sɪŋkə'peɪʃn] *n* MUS syncope *f*.

syncretism ['sɪŋkrɪtɪzm] *n* syncrétisme *m*.

syndicalism ['sɪndɪkəlɪzm] *n* [doctrine] syndicalisme *m* révolutionnaire.

syndicalist ['sɪndɪkəlɪst] <> *n* syndicaliste *mf* révolutionnaire.
<> *adj* de syndicalisme révolutionnaire.

syndicate <> *n* ['sɪndɪkət] **1.** COMM & FIN groupement *m*, syndicat *m* ▪ **the loan was underwritten by a ~ of banks** le prêt était garanti par un consortium bancaire **2.** [of organized crime] association *f* ▪ **crime ~s** associations de grand banditisme ▪ **the Syndicate** la Mafia **3.** PRESS agence *f* de presse *(qui vend des articles, des photos etc à plusieurs journaux pour publication simultanée)*.
<> *vt* ['sɪndɪkeɪt] **1.** COMM & FIN [loan] syndiquer **2.** PRESS publier simultanément dans plusieurs journaux ▪ *US* RADIO vendre à plusieurs stations ▪ *US* TV vendre à plusieurs chaînes ▪ **she writes a ~d column** elle écrit une chronique qui est publiée dans plusieurs journaux.
<> *vi* [form a syndicate] former un groupement *OR* syndicat.

syndrome ['sɪndrəʊm] *n* syndrome *m*.

synecdoche [sɪn'ekdəkɪ] *n* synecdoque *f*.

syneresis [sɪ'nɪərəsɪs] (*pl* **synereses** [-si:z]) *n* synérèse *f*.

synergy ['sɪnədʒɪ] (*pl* **synergies**) *n* synergie *f*.

synod ['sɪnəd] *n* synode *m*.

synonym ['sɪnənɪm] *n* synonyme *m*.

synonymous [sɪ'nɒnɪməs] *adj liter* & *fig* synonyme ▪ **success is not always ~ with merit** le succès n'est pas toujours synonyme de mérite.

synonymy [sɪ'nɒnɪmɪ] *n* synonymie *f*.

synopsis [sɪ'nɒpsɪs] (*pl* **synopses** [-si:z]) *n* [gen] résumé *m* ▪ [of a film] synopsis *m*.

synopsize, ise [sɪ'nɒpsaɪz] *vt US* [summarize] résumer, faire un résumé de.

synoptic [sɪ'nɒptɪk] *adj* synoptique.

syntactic [sɪn'tæktɪk] *adj* syntaxique.

syntactically [sɪn'tæktɪklɪ] *adv* du point de vue syntaxique.

syntactics [sɪn'tæktɪks] *n (U)* syntactique *f*.

syntagm ['sɪntæm] *n* syntagme *m*.

syntax ['sɪntæks] *n* syntaxe *f*.

synthesis ['sɪnθəsɪs] (*pl* **syntheses** [-si:z]) *n* synthèse *f*.

synthesize, ise ['sɪnθəsaɪz] *vt* **1.** BIOL & CHEM [produce by synthesis] synthétiser **2.** [amalgamate, fuse] synthétiser **3.** MUS synthétiser.

synthesizer ['sɪnθəsaɪzə^r] *n* synthétiseur *m* ▪ **voice ~** synthétiseur *m* de voix.

synthetic [sɪn'θetɪk] <> *adj* **1.** [artificial, electronically produced] synthétique ▪ **~ image** image *f* de synthèse **2.** *fig* & *pej* [food] qui a un goût chimique **3.** LING synthétique **4.** PHILOS [reasoning, proposition] synthétique.
<> *n* produit *m* synthétique.
◆ **synthetics** *npl* fibres *fpl* synthétiques.

synthetically [sɪn'θetɪklɪ] *adv* synthétiquement.

syphilis ['sɪfɪlɪs] *n (U)* syphilis *f*.

syphilitic [,sɪfɪ'lɪtɪk] <> *adj* syphilitique.
<> *n* syphilitique *mf*.

syphon ['saɪfn] = **siphon**.

Syria ['sɪrɪə] *pr n* Syrie *f* ▪ **in ~** en Syrie.

Syrian ['sɪrɪən] <> *n* Syrien *m*, - enne *f*.
<> *adj* syrien ▪ **the ~ Desert** le désert de Syrie.

syringe [sɪ'rɪndʒ] <> *n* seringue *f*.
<> *vt* seringuer.

syrup ['sɪrəp] *n* **1.** [sweetened liquid] sirop *m* ▪ **peaches in ~** pêches *fpl* au sirop ▪ **~ of figs** sirop de figues **2.** [treacle] mélasse *f* **3.** MED sirop *m*.

syrupy ['sɪrəpɪ] *adj* **1.** [viscous] sirupeux **2.** *pej* [sentimental] sirupeux, à l'eau de rose.

system ['sɪstəm] *n* **1.** [organization, structure] système *m* ▪ **the Social Security ~** le système des prestations sociales **2.** [method] système *m* ▪ **a new ~ of sorting mail** un nouveau système pour trier le courrier **3.** ANAT système *m* ▪ **the muscular ~** le système musculaire **4.** [orderliness] méthode *f* ▪ **you need some ~ in the way you work** vous devriez être plus systématique *OR* méthodique dans votre travail **5.** [human body] organisme *m* ▪ **bad for the ~** nuisible à l'organisme ▮ *fig* **to get sthg out of one's ~** se débarrasser de qqch ▪ **go on, get it out of your ~!** vas-y, défoule-toi! ▪ **she can't get him out of her ~** elle n'arrive pas à l'oublier **6.** [equipment, device, devices] : **the electrical ~ needs to be replaced** l'installation électrique a besoin d'être remplacée ▪ **a fault in the cooling ~** un défaut dans le circuit de refroidissement **7.** [network] réseau *m* ▪ **the rail/river/road ~** le réseau ferroviaire/fluvial/routier **8.** COMPUT système *m* **9.** [established order] : **the ~** le système ▪ **you can't beat** *OR* **buck the ~** *inf* on ne peut rien contre le système **10.** GEOL système *m*.

systematic [,sɪstə'mætɪk] *adj* systématique.

systematically [,sɪstə'mætɪklɪ] *adv* systématiquement.

systematization [,sɪstɪmətaɪ'zeɪʃn] *n* systématisation *f*.

systematize, ise ['sɪstəmətaɪz] *vt* systématiser.

system error *n* COMPUT erreur *f* système.

systemic [sɪs'temɪk] *adj* systémique.

systems analysis ['sɪstəmz-] *n* analyse *f* fonctionnelle.

systems analyst ['sɪstəmz-] *n* analyste *m* fonctionnel, analyste *f* fonctionnelle.

systems disk *n* COMPUT disque *m* système.

systems engineer ['sɪstəmz-] *n* ingénieur *m* système.

systems engineering ['sɪstəmz-] *n* assistance *f* technico-commerciale.

systems software *n* COMPUT logiciel *m* de base.

systole ['sɪstəlɪ] *n* systole *f*.

T

t (*pl* **t's** *OR pl* **ts**), **T** (*pl* **T's** *OR pl* **Ts**) [tiː] *n* [letter] t *m*, T *m* ▪ **T for Tommy** ≃ T comme Thérèse ▪ **to a T** parfaitement, à merveille ▪ **that's her to a T** c'est tout à fait elle ▪ **the jacket fits** *OR* **suits her to a T** la veste lui va à merveille, *see also* **f**.

ta [tɑː] *interj UK inf* merci.

TA *n* = **Territorial Army**.

tab [tæb] *n* **1.** [on garment - flap] patte *f* ; [- loop] attache *f* ▪ [over ear] oreillette *f* ▪ [on shoelaces] ferret *m* **2.** [tag - on clothing, luggage] étiquette *f* ; [- on file, dictionary] onglet *m* ▪ *fig* **to keep ~s on sb** avoir qqn à l'œil, avoir l'œil sur qqn ▪ **I'll keep ~s on how the case progresses** je vais surveiller l'évolution de cette affaire **3.** [bill] addition *f*, note *f* ▪ **to pick up the ~** *liter* payer (la note) ; *fig* payer l'addition **4.** AERON compensateur *m* automatique à ressort.

Tabasco® [tə'bæskəʊ] *n* Tabasco® *m*.

tabbouleh [tə'buːlɪ] *n (U)* taboulé *m*.

tabby ['tæbɪ] (*pl* **tabbies**) <> *n* : **~ (cat)** chat *m* tigré, chatte *f* tigrée.
<> *adj* tigré.

tabernacle ['tæbənækl] *n* **1.** BIBLE & RELIG tabernacle *m* **2.** [place of worship] temple *m*.

tab key *n* touche *f* de tabulation.

table ['teɪbl] <> *n* **1.** [furniture] table *f* ▪ **to get round the negotiating ~** s'asseoir à la table des négociations ‖ [for meals] table *f* ▪ **to be at ~** être à table ▪ **may I leave the ~?** puis-je sortir de table *OR* quitter la table?
2. [people seated] table *f*, tablée *f*
3. *fml* [food] : **she keeps an excellent ~** elle a une excellente table
4. TECH [of machine] table *f* ▪ MUS [of violin] table *f* d'harmonie
5. [list] liste *f* ▪ [chart] table *f*, tableau *m* ▪ [of fares, prices] tableau *m*, barème *m* ▪ SPORT classement *m* ▪ **our team came bottom in the ~** notre équipe s'est classée dernière *OR* était dernière au classement ‖ SCH : **(multiplication) ~** table *f* (de multiplication) ▪ **we have to learn our 4 times ~** il faut qu'on apprenne la table de 4 ➋ **~ of contents** table *f* des matières
6. [slab - of stone, marble] plaque *f* ▪ **the Tables of the Law** BIBLE les Tables de la Loi
7. GEOG plateau *m*
8. ANAT [of cranium] table *f*
9. *phr* **to put** *OR* **to lay sthg on the ~** mettre qqch sur la table ▪ **under the ~** [drunk] : **to be under the ~** rouler sous la table, être ivre mort ▪ **he can drink me under the ~** il peut boire beaucoup plus que moi ▪ **the man offered me £100 under the ~** l'homme m'a offert 100 livres en dessous-de-table.
<> *comp* [lamp, leg, linen] de table.
<> *vt* **1.** *UK* [submit - bill, motion] présenter
2. *US* [postpone] ajourner, reporter
3. [tabulate] présenter sous forme de tableau ▪ [classify] classifier
4. [schedule] prévoir, fixer ▪ **the discussion is ~d for 4 o'clock** la discussion est prévue *OR* a été fixée à 16 h.

table dancer *n* danseuse *f* de bar.

tableau ['tæbləʊ] (*pl* **tableaus** *OR pl* **tableaux** [-bləʊz]) *n* tableau *m*.

tablecloth ['teɪblklɒθ] *n* nappe *f*.

table d'hôte ['tɑːbl,dəʊt] *n* : **the ~** le menu à prix fixe.

table lamp *n* lampe *f* (de table).

table manners *npl* manière *f* de se tenir à table ▪ **he has terrible/excellent ~** il se tient très mal/très bien à table.

tablemat ['teɪblmæt] *n* set *m* de table.

Table Mountain *pr n* la Montagne de la Table.

table salt *n* sel *m* de table, sel *m* fin.

tablespoon ['teɪblspuːn] *n* [for serving] grande cuillère *f*, cuillère *f* à soupe ▪ [as measure] grande cuillerée *f*, cuillerée *f* à soupe.

tablespoonful ['teɪbl,spuːnfʊl] *n* grande cuillerée *f*, cuillerée *f* à soupe.

tablet ['tæblɪt] *n* **1.** [for writing - stone, wax etc] tablette *f* ; [- pad] bloc-notes *m* **2.** [pill] comprimé *m*, cachet *m* **3.** [of chocolate] tablette *f* ▪ [of soap] savonnette *f* **4.** [plaque] plaque *f* (commémorative) **5.** COMPUT tablette *f*.

table tennis *n* tennis *m* de table, ping-pong *m*.

table top *n* dessus *m* de table, plateau *m* (de table).

tableware ['teɪblweəʳ] *n* vaisselle *f*.

table wine *n* vin *m* de table.

tabloid ['tæblɔɪd] <> *n* : **~ (newspaper)** tabloïde *m* ▪ **it's front-page news in all the ~s** c'est à la une de tous les journaux à sensation.
<> *adj* : **the ~ press** la presse à sensation.

TABLOID

Dans les pays anglo-saxons, le format tabloïde, c'est-à-dire un format réduit par rapport à celui des autres journaux, est caractéristique des journaux populaires. Les tabloïdes les plus populaires, qui traitent notamment de sexe et de célébrité, sont souvent tournés en dérision par les milieux intellectuels. Les principaux tabloïdes britanniques sont : *The Daily Express, The Daily Mail, The Daily Mirror, The Star, The Sun* et *The Daily Sport*.

taboo [tə'buː] <> *adj* [subject, word] tabou.
<> *n* tabou *m*.
<> *vt* proscrire, interdire.

tabular ['tæbjʊlə^r] *adj* **1.** [statistics, figures] tabulaire ■ **in ~ form** sous forme de tableaux **2.** [crystal] tabulaire.

tabula rasa ['tæbjʊlə'rɑːzə] (*pl* **tabulae rasae** ['tæbjʊliː'rɑːziː]) *n* table *f* rase.

tabulate ['tæbjʊleɪt] *vt* **1.** [in table form] mettre sous forme de table *OR* tableau ■ [in columns] mettre en colonnes **2.** [classify] classifier.

tabulator ['tæbjʊleɪtə^r] *n* tabulateur *m*.

tachograph ['tækəgrɑːf] *n* tachygraphe *m*.

tachometer [tæ'kɒmɪtə^r] *n* tachymètre *m*.

tachymeter [tæ'kɪmɪtə^r] *n* tachéomètre *m*.

tacit ['tæsɪt] *adj* tacite, implicite.

tacitly ['tæsɪtlɪ] *adv* tacitement.

taciturn ['tæsɪtɜːn] *adj* taciturne, qui parle peu.

tack [tæk] ◇ *n* **1.** [nail] pointe *f* ■ [for carpeting, upholstery] semence *f* ■ **~, thumb-~** punaise *f* **2.** *UK* SEW point *m* de bâti **3.** NAUT [course] bordée *f*, bord *m* ■ **to make** *OR* **to set a ~** courir *OR* tirer une bordée ■ **to be on a starboard/port ~** être tribord/bâbord amures | *fig* **to be on the right ~** être sur la bonne voie ■ **to be on the wrong ~** faire fausse route ■ **he went off on a quite different ~** il est parti sur une toute autre piste *fig* ■ **she changed ~ in mid-conversation** elle changea de sujet en pleine conversation **4.** *inf* [food] bouffe *f* **5.** [harness] sellerie *f*.
◇ *vt* **1.** [carpet] clouer **2.** SEW faufiler, bâtir.
◇ *vi* NAUT faire *OR* courir *OR* tirer une bordée, louvoyer.
◆ **tack down** *vt sep* **1.** [carpet, board] clouer **2.** SEW maintenir en place au point de bâti.
◆ **tack on** *vt sep* **1.** [with nails] fixer avec des clous **2.** SEW bâtir **3.** *fig* ajouter, rajouter ■ **the conclusion seems ~ed on** la conclusion semble avoir été ajoutée après coup.

tackily ['tækɪlɪ] *adv* [shoddily] minablement ■ [in bad taste] avec mauvais goût.

tacking ['tækɪŋ] *n* SEW bâti *m*, faufilage *m*.

tacking stitch *n* point *m* de bâti.

tackle ['tækl] ◇ *vt* **1.** SPORT tacler ■ *fig* [assailant, bank robber] saisir, empoigner **2.** [task, problem] s'attaquer à ■ [question, subject] s'attaquer à, aborder ■ **to ~ a job** se mettre au travail, s'atteler à la tâche | [confront] interroger ■ **I ~d him on** *OR* **about his stand on abortion** je l'ai interrogé sur sa prise de position sur l'avortement.
◇ *vi* SPORT tacler.
◇ *n* **1.** [equipment] attirail *m*, matériel *m* ■ **fishing ~** matériel *m OR* articles *mpl* de pêche **2.** [ropes and pulleys] appareil *m OR* appareils *mpl* de levage ■ [hoist] palan *m* **3.** SPORT [gen] tacle *m* ■ **good ~!** bien taclé! **4.** [in American football - player] plaqueur *m* **5.** NAUT [rigging] gréement *m*.

tackling ['tæklɪŋ] *n* **1.** SPORT tacle *m* **2.** [of problem, job] manière *f* d'aborder.

tacky ['tækɪ] (*comp* **tackier**, *superl* **tackiest**) *adj* **1.** [sticky] collant, poisseux ■ [of paint] pas encore sec **2.** *inf* [shoddy] minable, moche **3.** *inf* [vulgar] de mauvais goût, vulgaire ■ *US* [person] beauf, vulgaire.

taco ['tækəʊ] (*pl* **tacos**) *n* taco *m* (*crêpe mexicaine farcie*).

tact [tækt] *n* tact *m*, diplomatie *f*, doigté *m*.

tactful ['tæktfʊl] *adj* [person] plein de tact, qui fait preuve de tact ■ [remark, suggestion] plein de tact ■ [inquiry] discret, - ète *f* ■ [behaviour] qui fait preuve de tact *OR* de délicatesse ■ **that wasn't a very ~ thing to say** ce n'était pas très diplomatique de dire ça ■ **try to be more ~** essaie de faire preuve de plus de tact ■ **they gave us a ~ hint** ils nous ont fait discrètement comprendre.

tactfully ['tæktfʊlɪ] *adv* avec tact *OR* délicatesse.

tactic ['tæktɪk] *n* tactique *f* ■ MIL tactique *f*.

tactical ['tæktɪkl] *adj* **1.** MIL tactique **2.** [shrewd] adroit ■ **a purely ~ manoeuvre** une manœuvre purement diplomatique ■ **~ voting** (*U*) **: there has been a lot of ~ voting** beaucoup de gens ont voté utile.

tactically ['tæktɪklɪ] *adv* du point de vue tactique ■ **to vote ~** voter utile.

tactician [tæk'tɪʃn] *n* tacticien *m*, - enne *f*.

tactics ['tæktɪks] *n* (*U*) MIL & SPORT tactique *f*.

tactile ['tæktaɪl] *adj* tactile.

tactless ['tæktlɪs] *adj* [person] dépourvu de tact, qui manque de doigté ■ [answer] indiscret, - ète *f*, peu diplomatique ■ **what a ~ thing to say/to do!** il faut vraiment manquer de tact pour dire/faire une chose pareille! ■ **how ~ of him!** quel manque de tact de sa part!

tactlessly ['tæktlɪslɪ] *adv* sans tact.

tactlessness ['tæktlɪsnɪs] *n* manque *m* de tact, indélicatesse *f*.

tad [tæd] *n inf* [small bit] **: a ~** un peu ■ **the coat is a ~ expensive** le manteau est un chouia trop cher.

tadpole ['tædpəʊl] *n* ZOOL têtard *m*.

Tadzhik [tɑː'dʒiːk] *n* Tadjik *mf*.

Tadzhiki [tɑː'dʒiːkɪ] ◇ *n* tadjik *m*.
◇ *adj* tadjik.

taffeta ['tæfɪtə] ◇ *n* taffetas *m*.
◇ *adj* [dress] en taffetas.

taffy ['tæfɪ] (*pl* **taffies**) *n US* bonbon *m* au caramel.

Taffy ['tæfɪ] (*pl* **Taffies**) *n inf nom péjoratif ou humoristique désignant un Gallois*.

tag [tæg] (*pret & pp* **tagged**, *cont* **tagging**) ◇ *n* **1.** [label - on clothes, suitcase] étiquette *f* ; [- on file] onglet *m* ■ **(price) ~** étiquette *f* de prix ■ **(name) ~** [gen] étiquette *f* (où est marqué le nom) ; [for dog, soldier] plaque *f* d'identité **2.** [on shoelace] ferret *m* **3.** [on jacket, coat - for hanging] patte *f* **4.** [graffiti] tag *m* **5.** *US* [licence plate] plaque *f* minéralogique **6.** [quotation] citation *f* ■ [cliché] cliché *m*, lieu *m* commun ■ [catchword] slogan *m* **7.** GRAM **: ~ (question)** question-tag *f* **8.** GAMES chat *m*.
◇ *vt* **1.** [label - package, article, garment] étiqueter ; [- animal] marquer ; [- file] mettre un onglet à ; [- criminal] pincer, épingler ■ *fig* [- person] étiqueter **2.** *US* [follow] suivre ■ [subj: detective] filer **3.** [leave graffiti on] faire des graffiti sur.
◆ **tag along** *vi insep* suivre ■ **to ~ along with sb** [follow] suivre qqn ; [accompany] aller *OR* venir avec qqn ■ **do you mind if I ~ along?** ça vous gêne si je viens?
◆ **tag on** ◇ *vt sep* ajouter.
◇ *vi insep inf* **to ~ on to sb** suivre qqn partout ■ **to ~ on behind sb** traîner derrière qqn.

Tagalog [tə'gɑːlɒg] *n* [person] Tagal *mf*.

tagmemics [tæg'miːmɪks] *n* (*U*) tagmémique *f*.

tahini [tə'hiːnɪ] *n* CULIN tahini *m*.

Tahiti [tɑː'hiːtɪ] *pr n* Tahiti ■ **in ~** à Tahiti.

Tahitian [tɑː'hiːʃn] ◇ *n* Tahitien *m*, - enne *f*.
◇ *adj* tahitien.

tai chi [taɪ'tʃiː] *n* tai chi *m*.

tail [teɪl] ◇ *n* **1.** [of animal] queue *f* ■ **with one's ~ between one's legs** *fig* la queue basse ■ **it's a case of the ~ wagging the dog** c'est le monde à l'envers ■ **the detective was still on his ~** *fig* le détective le filait toujours | [of vehicle] *inf* **the car was right on my ~** *fig* la voiture me collait au derrière *OR* aux fesses ■ **to turn ~ and run** prendre ses jambes à son cou **2.** [of kite, comet, aircraft] queue *f* ■ [of musical note] queue *f* **3.** [of coat] basque *f* ■ [of dress] traîne *f* ■ [of shirt] pan *m* **4.** [end - of storm] queue *f* ; [- of procession] fin *f*, queue *f* ; [- of queue] bout *m* **5.** *inf* [follower - police officer, detective] *personne qui file* ■ **to put a ~ on sb** faire filer qqn **6.** *US inf* [bottom] fesses *fpl* ■ **he worked his ~ off** il s'est vraiment décarcassé.
◇ *vt* **1.** *inf* [follow] suivre, filer **2.** [animal] couper la queue à.
◆ **tails** ◇ *npl inf* [tailcoat] queue *f* de pie.
◇ *adv* [of coin] **: it's ~s!** (c'est) pile!
◆ **tail along** *vi insep* suivre ■ **she ~ed along behind** *OR* **after us** elle traînait derrière nous.

◆ **tail away** *vi insep* [sound] s'affaiblir, décroître ▪ [interest] diminuer petit à petit ▪ [book] se terminer en queue de poisson ▪ [competitors in race] s'espacer.

◆ **tail back** *vi insep* [traffic] être arrêté, former un bouchon ▪ [demonstration, runners] s'égrener, s'espacer ▪ **the line of cars ~ed back for 10 miles** la file de voitures s'étendait sur 16 km.

◆ **tail off** *vi insep* [quality] baisser ▪ [numbers] diminuer, baisser ▪ [voice] devenir inaudible ▪ [story] se terminer en queue de poisson.

tail assembly *n* AERON dérive *f*.

tailback ['teɪlbæk] *n* bouchon *m* (de circulation).

tailboard ['teɪlbɔːd] *n* hayon *m (de camion)*.

tailcoat [ˌteɪl'kəʊt] *n* queue *f* de pie.

tail end *n* [of storm] fin *f* ▪ [of cloth] bout *m* ▪ [of procession] queue *f*, fin *f* ▪ [of story] chute *f*.

tailender [teɪl'endəʳ] *n* [in race] dernier *m*, - ère *f*.

tail feather *n* penne *f*.

tailfin ['teɪlfɪn] *n* **1.** [fish] nageoire *f* caudale **2.** NAUT dérive *f*.

tailgate ['teɪlgeɪt] ◇ *n* AUT hayon *m*.
◇ *vt* coller au pare-chocs de.

tail lamp, taillight ['teɪllaɪt] *n* feu *m* arrière.

tailor ['teɪləʳ] ◇ *n* tailleur *m*.
◇ *vt* [garment] faire sur mesure ▪ [equipment] adapter à un besoin particulier, concevoir en fonction d'un usage particulier ▪ **the kitchen was ~ed to our needs** la cuisine a été faite spécialement pour nous *OR* conçue en fonction de nos besoins.

tailored ['teɪləd] *adj* [clothes, equipment] (fait) sur mesure ▪ [skirt] ajusté.

tailor-made *adj* [specially made - clothes, equipment] (fait) sur mesure ▪ [very suitable] (comme) fait exprès ▪ **the job could have been ~ for her** on dirait que le poste est taillé pour elle.

tailpiece ['teɪlpiːs] *n* **1.** [addition - to speech] ajout *m* ; [- to document] appendice *m* ; [- to letter] post-scriptum *m inv* **2.** MUS cordier *m (d'un violon)* **3.** TYPO cul-de-lampe *m*.

tail pipe *n* *US* tuyau *m* d'échappement.

tailplane ['teɪlpleɪn] *n* AERON stabilisateur *m*.

tail section *n* AERON arrière *m*.

tailspin ['teɪlspɪn] *n* vrille *f* ▪ **to be in a ~** AERON vriller ; *fig* être en dégringolade.

tailwind ['teɪlwɪnd] *n* vent *m* arrière.

taint [teɪnt] ◇ *vt* **1.** [minds, morals] corrompre, souiller ▪ [person] salir la réputation de ▪ [reputation] salir **2.** [food] gâter ▪ [air] polluer, vicier ▪ [water] polluer, infecter.
◇ *n* **1.** [infection] infection *f* ▪ [contamination] contamination *f* ▪ [decay] décomposition *f* **2.** *fig* [of sin, corruption] tache *f*, souillure *f*.

tainted ['teɪntɪd] *adj* **1.** [morals] corrompu, dépravé ▪ [reputation] terni, sali ▪ [politician] dont la réputation est ternie *OR* salie ▪ [money] sale **2.** [food] gâté ▪ [meat] avarié ▪ [air] vicié, pollué ▪ [water] infecté, pollué ▪ [blood] impur.

Taiwan [ˌtaɪ'wɑːn] *pr n* Taïwan ▪ **in ~** à Taïwan.

Taiwanese [ˌtaɪwə'niːz] ◇ *n* Taïwanais *m*, - e *f*.
◇ *adj* taïwanais.

Tajikistan, Tadjikistan, Tadzhikistan [təˌdʒɪkɪ'stɑːn] *pr n* Tadjikistan *m* ▪ **in ~** au Tadjikistan.

Taj Mahal [ˌtɑːdʒmə'hɑːl] *pr n* : **the ~** le Tadj Mahall, le Taj Mahal.

take [teɪk] (*pret* **took** [tʊk], *pp* **taken** ['teɪkən]) ◇ *vt*

A.

1. [get hold of] prendre ▪ [seize] prendre, saisir ▪ **let me ~ your coat** donnez-moi votre manteau ▪ **she took the book from him** elle lui a pris le livre ▪ **to ~ sb's hand** prendre qqn par la main ▪ **she took his arm** elle lui a pris le bras
2. [get control of, capture - person] prendre, capturer ; [- fish, game] prendre, attraper ▪ MIL prendre, s'emparer de ▪ **to ~ sb prisoner** faire qqn prisonnier ▪ **to ~ control of a situation** prendre une situation en main ▪ **to ~ the lead in sthg** [in competition] prendre la tête de qqch ; [set example] être le premier à faire qqch

B.

1. [carry from one place to another] porter, apporter ▪ [carry along, have in one's possession] prendre, emporter ▪ **she took her mother a cup of tea** elle a apporté une tasse de thé à sa mère ▪ **he took the map with him** il a emporté la carte ▪ **she took some towels upstairs** elle a monté des serviettes ▪ **the committee wanted to ~ the matter further** *fig* le comité voulait mener l'affaire plus loin ▶ **the devil ~ it!** que le diable l'emporte!
2. [person - lead] mener, emmener ; [- accompany] accompagner ▪ **her father ~s her to school** son père l'emmène à l'école ▪ **could you ~ me home?** pourriez-vous me ramener *OR* me raccompagner? ▪ **he offered to ~ them to work in the car** il leur a proposé de les emmener au bureau en voiture *OR* de les conduire au bureau ▪ **please ~ me with you** emmène-moi, s'il te plaît ▪ **I don't want to ~ you out of your way** je ne veux pas vous faire faire un détour ▪ **her job took her all over Africa** son travail l'a fait voyager dans toute l'Afrique ▪ **that's what first took me to Portugal** c'est ce qui m'a amené au Portugal
3. [obtain from specified place] prendre, tirer ▪ [remove from specified place] prendre, enlever ▪ **she took a handkerchief from her pocket** elle a sorti un mouchoir de sa poche ▪ **I took a chocolate from the box** j'ai pris un chocolat dans la boîte ▪ **~ your feet off the table** enlève tes pieds de la table
4. [appropriate, steal] prendre, voler ▪ **to ~ sthg from sb** prendre qqch à qqn ▪ **his article is taken directly from my book** le texte de son article est tiré directement de mon livre
5. [draw, derive] prendre, tirer ▪ **a passage taken from a book** un passage extrait d'un livre ▪ **a phrase taken from Latin** une expression empruntée au latin

C.

1. [subj: bus, car, train etc] conduire, transporter ▪ **the ambulance took him to hospital** l'ambulance l'a transporté à l'hôpital ▪ **this bus will ~ you to the theatre** ce bus vous conduira au théâtre
2. [obj: bus, car, plane, train] prendre ▪ [obj: road] prendre, suivre ▪ **~ a right** *US* prenez à droite

D.

1. [have - attitude, bath, holiday] prendre ▪ [make - nap, trip, walk] faire ; [- decision] prendre ▪ **she took a quick look at him** elle a jeté un rapide coup d'œil sur lui ▪ **let's ~ five** *US inf* soufflons cinq minutes
2. PHOT : **to ~ a picture** prendre une photo ▪ **she took his picture** *OR* **a picture of him** elle l'a pris en photo ▪ **we had our picture taken** nous nous sommes fait photographier *OR* prendre en photo
3. [receive, get] recevoir ▪ **he took the blow on his arm** il a pris le coup sur le bras ▪ **you can ~ the call in my office** vous pouvez prendre l'appel dans mon bureau ▮ [earn, win - prize] remporter, obtenir ; [- degree, diploma] obtenir, avoir ▪ **the bookstore ~s about $3,000 a day** la librairie fait à peu près 3 000 dollars (de recette) par jour ▪ **how much does he ~ home a month?** quel est son salaire mensuel net?

E.

1. [assume, undertake] prendre ▪ **to ~ the blame for sthg** prendre la responsabilité de qqch ▪ **I ~ responsibility for their safety** je me charge de leur sécurité
2. [commit oneself to] : **he took my side in the argument** il a pris parti pour moi dans la dispute ▪ **to ~ the Fifth (Amendment)** *US* invoquer le Cinquième Amendement *(pour refuser de répondre)*
3. [allow oneself] : **may I ~ the liberty of inviting you to dinner?** puis-je me permettre de vous inviter à dîner? ▪ **he took the opportunity to thank them** *OR* **of thanking them** il a profité de l'occasion pour les remercier

F.

1. [accept - job, gift, payment] prendre, accepter ; [- bet] accepter ▪ **the owner won't ~ less than $100 for it** le propriétaire en veut au moins 100 dollars ▪ **I won't ~ "no" for an answer** pas

question de refuser ▪ **it's my last offer, (you can) ~ it or leave it** c'est ma dernière offre, c'est à prendre ou à laisser ▪ **I'll ~ it from here** je prends la suite
2. [accept as valid] croire ▪ **to ~ sb's advice** suivre les conseils de qqn ▪ **~ it from me, he's a crook** croyez-moi, c'est un escroc
3. [deal with] : **let's ~ things one at a time** prenons les choses une par une ▪ **how did she ~ the questioning?** comment a-t-elle réagi à *OR* pris l'interrogatoire? ▪ **to ~ sthg badly** prendre mal qqch ➤ **to ~ things easy** *inf* *OR* **it easy** *inf* se la couler douce ▪ **~ it easy!** [don't get angry] du calme!
4. [bear, endure - pain] supporter ; [- damage, loss] subir ▪ **don't ~ any nonsense!** ne te laisse pas faire! ▪ **your father won't ~ any nonsense** ton père ne plaisante pas avec ce genre de choses ▪ **she can ~ it** elle tiendra le coup ▪ **we couldn't ~ any more** on n'en pouvait plus ▪ **I find his constant sarcasm rather hard to ~** je trouve ses sarcasmes perpétuels difficiles à supporter ▪ **don't expect me to ~ this lying down** ne comptez pas sur moi pour accepter ça sans rien dire ▪ **those shoes have taken a lot of punishment** ces chaussures en ont vu de toutes les couleurs
5. [experience, feel] : **to ~ fright** prendre peur ▪ **don't ~ offence** ne vous vexez pas, ne vous offensez pas ▪ **she ~s pride in her work** elle est fière de ce qu'elle fait

G.
1. [consider, look at] prendre, considérer ▪ **~ Einstein (for example)** prenons (l'exemple d')Einstein ▪ **taking everything into consideration** tout bien considéré ▪ **to ~ sthg/sb seriously** prendre qqch/qqn au sérieux ‖ [consider as] : **what do you ~ me for?** pour qui me prenez-vous? ▪ **he took me for somebody else** il m'a pris pour quelqu'un d'autre
2. [suppose, presume] supposer, présumer ▪ **he's never been to Madrid, I ~ it** si je comprends bien, il n'a jamais été à Madrid ▪ **I ~ it you're his mother** je suppose que vous êtes sa mère
3. [interpret, understand] prendre, comprendre ▪ **don't ~ that literally** ne le prenez pas au pied de la lettre

H.
[require] prendre, demander ▪ **how long will it ~ to get there?** combien de temps faudra-t-il pour y aller? ▪ **the flight ~s three hours** le vol dure trois heures ▪ **it will ~ you ten minutes** vous en avez pour dix minutes ▪ **it took him a minute to understand** il a mis une minute avant de comprendre ▪ **it ~s time to learn a language** il faut du temps pour apprendre une langue ▪ **what kind of batteries does it ~?** quelle sorte de piles faut-il? ▪ **it took four people to stop the brawl** ils ont dû se mettre à quatre pour arrêter la bagarre ▪ **it ~s patience to work with children** il faut de la patience *OR* il faut être patient pour travailler avec les enfants ▪ **one glance was all it took** un regard a suffi ▪ **her story ~s some believing** *inf* son histoire n'est pas facile à croire ‖ GRAM : **"falloir" ~s the subjunctive** "falloir" est suivi du subjonctif ➤ **to have what it ~s to do/to be sthg** avoir les qualités nécessaires pour faire/être qqch ▪ **he's so lazy – it ~s one to know one!** *inf* il est vraiment paresseux – tu peux parler! ▪ **it ~s two to tango** *inf hum* il faut être deux pour faire ça

I.
1. [food, drink etc] prendre ▪ **do you ~ milk in your coffee?** prenez-vous du lait dans votre café? ▪ **she refused to ~ any food** elle a refusé de manger (quoi que ce soit) ▪ **'not to be taken internally'** [on bottle] '(à) usage externe' ▪ **to ~ the air** prendre l'air
2. [wear] faire, porter ▪ **she ~s a size 10** elle prend du 38 ▪ **what size shoe do you ~?** quelle est votre pointure?
3. [pick out, choose] prendre, choisir ▪ [buy] prendre, acheter ▪ [rent] prendre, louer ▪ **I'll ~ it** je le prends ▪ **what newspaper do you ~?** quel journal prenez-vous?
4. [occupy - chair, seat] prendre, s'asseoir sur ▪ **~ a seat** asseyez-vous ▪ **is this seat taken?** cette place est-elle occupée *OR* prise?
5. [ascertain, find out] prendre ▪ **to ~ a reading from a meter** lire *OR* relever un compteur
6. [write down - notes, letter] prendre ▪ **he took a note of her address** il a noté son adresse
7. [subtract] soustraire, déduire ▪ **they took 10% off the price** ils ont baissé le prix de 10 % ▪ **~ 4 from 9 and you have 5** ôtez 4 de 9, il reste 5
8. SCH & UNIV [exam] passer, se présenter à ▪ [course] prendre, suivre ▪ **I took Latin and Greek at A level** ≃ j'ai pris latin et grec au bac ▪ **she ~s us for maths** on l'a en maths
9. [contract, develop] : **to ~ sick** tomber malade ▪ **she took an instant dislike to him** elle l'a tout de suite pris en aversion
10. [direct, aim] : **she took a swipe at him** elle a voulu le gifler
11. [refer] : **she ~s all her problems to her sister** elle raconte tous ses problèmes à sa sœur ▪ **he took the matter to his boss** il a soumis la question à son patron ▪ **they intend to ~ the case to the High Court** LAW ils ont l'intention d'en appeler à la Cour suprême
12. [have recourse to] : **he took an axe to the door** il a donné des coups de hache dans la porte ▪ **they took legal proceedings against him** LAW ils lui ont intenté un procès
13. [catch unawares] prendre, surprendre ▪ **to ~ sb by surprise** *OR* **off guard** surprendre qqn, prendre qqn au dépourvu ▪ **his death took us by surprise** sa mort nous a surpris
14. [negotiate - obstacle] franchir, sauter ; [- bend in road] prendre, négocier
15. *inf* [deceive, cheat] avoir, rouler ▪ **they took him for every penny (he was worth)** ils lui ont pris jusqu'à son dernier sou.
◇ *vi* **1.** [work, have desired effect] prendre ▪ **did the dye ~?** est-ce que la teinture a pris? ▪ **it was too cold for the seeds to ~** il faisait trop froid pour que les graines germent **2.** [become popular] prendre, avoir du succès **3.** [fish] prendre, mordre.
◇ *n* **1.** [capture] prise *f* **2.** CIN, PHOT & TV prise *f* de vue ▪ RADIO enregistrement *m*, prise *f* de son **3.** *US* [interpretation] interprétation *f* ▪ **what's your ~ on her attitude?** comment est-ce que tu interprètes son attitude? **4.** *US inf* [takings] recette *f* ▪ [share] part *f* ▪ **to be on the ~** toucher des pots-de-vin.

◆ **take aback** *vt sep* [astonish] étonner, ébahir ▪ [disconcert] déconcerter.

◆ **take after** *vt insep* ressembler à, tenir de.

◆ **take apart** *vt sep* **1.** [dismantle] démonter ▪ **they took the room apart looking for evidence** *fig* ils ont mis la pièce sens dessus dessous pour trouver des preuves **2.** [criticize] critiquer.

◆ **take aside** *vt sep* prendre à part, emmener à l'écart.

◆ **take away** *vt sep* **1.** [remove] enlever, retirer ▪ **~ that knife away from him** enlevez-lui ce couteau ▪ **they took away his pension** ils lui ont retiré sa pension **2.** [carry away - object] emporter ; [- person] emmener ▪ **'sandwiches to ~ away'** *UK* 'sandwiches à emporter' ▪ **'not to be taken away'** [in library] 'à consulter sur place' **3.** MATHS soustraire, retrancher ▪ **nine ~ away six is three** neuf moins six font trois.

◆ **take away from** *vt insep* [detract from] : **that doesn't ~ away from his achievements as an athlete** ça n'enlève rien à ses exploits d'athlète.

◆ **take back** *vt sep* **1.** [after absence, departure] reprendre ▪ **she took her husband back** elle a accepté que son mari revienne vivre avec elle **2.** [return] rapporter ▪ [accompany] raccompagner ▪ **~ it back to the shop** rapporte-le au magasin ▪ **he took her back home** il l'a raccompagnée *OR* ramenée chez elle **3.** [retract, withdraw] retirer, reprendre ▪ **I ~ back everything I said** je retire tout ce que j'ai dit ▪ **all right, I ~ it back!** d'accord, je n'ai rien dit! **4.** [remind of the past] : **that ~s me back to my childhood** ça me rappelle mon enfance ▪ **that song ~s me back forty years** cette chanson me ramène quarante ans en arrière **5.** TYPO transférer à la ligne précédente.

◆ **take down** ◇ *vt sep* **1.** [lower] descendre ▪ **she took the book down from the shelf** elle a pris le livre sur l'étagère ▪ **can you help me ~ the curtains down?** peux-tu m'aider à décrocher les rideaux? ▪ **she took his picture down from the wall** elle a enlevé sa photo du mur ▪ **he took his trousers down** il a baissé son pantalon **2.** [note] prendre, noter ▪ **he took down the registration number** il a relevé le numéro d'immatriculation.
◇ *vi insep* se démonter.

◆ **take in** *vt sep* **1.** [bring into one's home - person] héberger ; [- boarder] prendre ; [- orphan, stray animal] recueillir ▪ **she ~s in ironing** elle fait du repassage à domicile ▪ [place in custody] : **the police took him in** la police l'a mis *OR* placé en garde à vue **2.** [air, water, food etc] : **whales ~ in air through their blowhole** les baleines respirent par l'évent **3.** [understand, perceive] saisir, comprendre ▪ **he was sitting taking it all in** il était là, assis, écoutant tout ce qui se disait ▪ **I can't ~ in the fact that I've won** je n'arrive pas à croire que j'ai gagné ▪ **she took in the situation at a glance** elle a compris la situation en un clin d'œil

4. [make smaller - garment] reprendre ; [- in knitting] diminuer ▪ **to ~ in a sail** NAUT carguer *OR* serrer une voile **5.** [attend, go to] aller à ▪ **to ~ in a show** aller au théâtre ▪ **she took in the castle while in Blois** elle a visité le château pendant qu'elle était à Blois **6.** *inf (usu passive) inf* [cheat, deceive] tromper, rouler ▪ **don't be taken in by him** ne vous laissez pas rouler par lui ▪ **I'm not going to be taken in by your lies** je ne suis pas dupe de tes mensonges.

◆ **take off** ◇ *vt sep* **1.** [remove - clothing, lid, make-up, tag] enlever ▪ **he often ~s the phone off the hook** il laisse souvent le téléphone décroché ▪ **to ~ off the brake** AUT desserrer le frein (à main) ▪ *fig* **he didn't ~ his eyes off her all night** il ne l'a pas quittée des yeux de la soirée ▪ **I tried to ~ her mind off her troubles** j'ai essayé de lui changer les idées *OR* de la distraire de ses ennuis ▪ **his retirement has taken ten years off him** *inf* sa retraite l'a rajeuni de dix ans **2.** [deduct] déduire, rabattre ▪ **the manager took 10% off the price** le directeur a baissé le prix de 10 % **3.** [lead away] emmener ▪ **she was taken off to hospital** on l'a transportée à l'hôpital ▪ **she took herself off to Italy** elle est partie en Italie **4.** [time] : **~ a few days off** prenez quelques jours (de vacances *OR* de congé) ▪ **she ~s Thursdays off** elle ne travaille pas le jeudi **5.** *inf* [copy] imiter ▪ [mimic] imiter, singer **6.** THEAT annuler.
◇ *vi insep* **1.** [aeroplane] décoller ▪ **they took off for** *OR* **to Heathrow** ils se sont envolés pour Heathrow **2.** [person - depart] partir **3.** *inf* [become successful] décoller.

◆ **take on** ◇ *vt sep* **1.** [accept, undertake] prendre, accepter ▪ **to ~ on the responsibility for sthg** se charger de qqch ▪ **don't ~ on more than you can handle** ne vous surchargez pas ▪ **she took it on herself to tell him** elle a pris sur elle de le lui dire ▪ **he took the job on** [position] il a accepté le poste ; [task] il s'est mis au travail **2.** [contend with, fight against] lutter *OR* se battre contre ▪ [compete against] jouer contre ▪ **the unions took on the government** les syndicats se sont attaqués *OR* s'en sont pris au gouvernement ▪ **he took us on at poker** il nous a défiés au poker **3.** [acquire, assume] prendre, revêtir ▪ **her face took on a worried look** elle a pris un air inquiet **4.** [load] prendre, embarquer **5.** [hire] embaucher, engager.
◇ *vi insep inf* [fret, carry on] s'en faire ▪ **don't ~ on so!** ne t'en fais pas!

◆ **take out** *vt sep* **1.** [remove - object] prendre, sortir ; [- stain] ôter, enlever ▪ [extract - tooth] arracher ▪ **he took the knife out of his pocket** il a sorti le couteau de sa poche ▪ **~ your hands out of your pockets** enlève les mains de tes poches ▪ **to ~ out sb's appendix/tonsils** MED enlever l'appendice/les amygdales à qqn **2.** [carry, lead outside - object] sortir ; [- person] faire sortir ▪ [escort] emmener ▪ **to ~ sb out to dinner/to the movies** emmener qqn dîner/au cinéma ▪ **would you ~ the dog out?** tu veux bien sortir le chien *OR* aller promener le chien? **3.** [food] emporter ▪ **'sandwiches to ~ out'** *US* 'sandwiches à emporter' **4.** [obtain - subscription] prendre ; [- insurance policy] souscrire à, prendre ; [- licence] se procurer ▪ COMM [- patent] prendre ▪ **to ~ out a mortgage** faire un emprunt-logement **5.** *inf* [destroy - factory, town] détruire ; [- person] supprimer, liquider **6.** *phr* **to ~ sb out of himself/herself** changer les idées à qqn ▪ **working as an interpreter ~s a lot out of you** *inf* le travail d'interprète est épuisant ▪ **the operation really took it out of him** *inf* l'opération l'a mis à plat ▪ **to ~ it out on sb** s'en prendre à qqn ▪ **he took his anger out on his wife** *inf* il a passé sa colère sur sa femme.

◆ **take over** ◇ *vt sep* **1.** [assume responsibility of] reprendre ▪ **will you be taking over his job?** est-ce que vous allez le remplacer (dans ses fonctions)? **2.** [gain control of, invade] s'emparer de ▪ **the military took over the country** l'armée a pris le pouvoir ▪ **fast-food restaurants have taken over Paris** les fast-foods ont envahi Paris **3.** FIN [buy out] absorber, racheter **4.** [carry across] apporter ▪ [escort across] emmener.
◇ *vi insep* **1.** [as replacement] : **who will ~ over now that the mayor has stepped down?** qui va prendre la relève maintenant que le maire a donné sa démission? ▪ **I'll ~ over when he leaves** je le remplacerai quand il partira ▪ **compact discs have taken over from records** le (disque) compact a remplacé le (disque) vinyle **2.** [army, dictator] prendre le pouvoir.

◆ **take to** *vt insep* **1.** [have a liking for - person] se prendre d'amitié *OR* de sympathie pour, prendre en amitié ; [- activity, game] prendre goût à ▪ **I think he took to you** je crois que vous lui avez plu ▪ **we took to one another at once** nous avons tout de suite sympathisé **2.** [acquire as a habit] se mettre à ▪ **to ~ to drink** *OR* **to the bottle** se mettre à boire ▪ **to ~ to doing sthg** se mettre à faire qqch **3.** [make for, head for] : **he's taken to his bed with the flu** il est alité avec la grippe ▪ **the rebels took to the hills** les insurgés se sont réfugiés dans les collines.

◆ **take up** ◇ *vt sep* **1.** [carry, lead upstairs - object] monter ; [- person] faire monter **2.** [pick up - object] ramasser, prendre ; [- passenger] prendre ▪ **they're taking up the street** la rue est en travaux ▪ **we finally took up the carpet** nous avons enfin enlevé la moquette **3.** [absorb] absorber **4.** [shorten] raccourcir ▪ **you'd better ~ up the slack in that rope** tu ferais mieux de retendre *OR* tendre cette corde **5.** [fill, occupy - space] prendre, tenir ; [- time] prendre, demander ▪ **this table ~s up too much room** cette table prend trop de place *OR* est trop encombrante ▪ **moving took up the whole day** le déménagement a pris toute la journée ▪ **her work ~s up all her attention** son travail l'absorbe complètement **6.** [begin, become interested in - activity, hobby] se mettre à ; [- job] prendre ; [- career] commencer, embrasser **7.** [continue, resume] reprendre, continuer ▪ **I took up the tale where Susan had left off** j'ai repris l'histoire là où Susan l'avait laissée **8.** [adopt - attitude] prendre, adopter ; [- method] adopter ; [- place, position] prendre ; [- idea] adopter ▪ **they took up residence in town** ils se sont installés en ville **9.** [accept - offer] accepter ; [- advice, suggestion] suivre ; [- challenge] relever **10.** [discuss] discuter, parler de ▪ [bring up] aborder ▪ **~ it up with the boss** parlez-en au patron.
◇ *vi insep* reprendre, continuer.

◆ **take upon** *vt sep* : **he took it upon himself to organize the meeting** il s'est chargé d'organiser la réunion.

◆ **take up on** *vt sep* **1.** [accept offer, advice of] : **he might ~ you up on that someday!** il risque de vous prendre au mot un jour! ▪ **she took him up on his promise** elle a mis sa parole à l'épreuve **2.** [ask to explain] : **I'd like to ~ you up on that point** j'aimerais revenir sur ce point avec vous.

◆ **take up with** *vt insep* **1.** [befriend] : **to ~ up with sb** se lier d'amitié avec qqn, prendre qqn en amitié **2.** [preoccupy] : **to be taken up with doing sthg** être occupé à faire qqch ▪ **she's taken up with her business** elle est très prise par ses affaires ▪ **meetings were taken up with talk about the economy** on passait les réunions à parler de l'économie.

takeaway ['teɪkə,weɪ] ◇ *n* **UK & New Zealand** [shop] *boutique de plats à emporter* ▪ [food] plat *m* à emporter ▪ **Chinese ~** [shop] traiteur *m* chinois ; [meal] repas *m* chinois à emporter.
◇ *adj* : **~ food** plats *mpl* à emporter.

take-home pay *n* salaire *m* net *(après impôts et déductions sociales).*

taken ['teɪkən] ◇ *pp* ▷ **take.**
◇ *adj* **1.** [seat] pris, occupé **2.** : **to be ~ with sthg/sb** [impressed] être impressionné par qqch/qqn ; [interested] s'intéresser à qqch/qqn ▪ **they were quite ~ with the performance** l'interprétation leur a beaucoup plu.

takeoff ['teɪkɒf] *n* **1.** AERON décollage *m* **2.** [imitation] imitation *f*, caricature *f* **3.** ECON décollage *m* économique.

takeover ['teɪk,əʊvər] *n* [of power, of government] prise *f* de pouvoir ▪ [of company] prise *f* de contrôle.

takeover bid *n* offre *f* publique d'achat, OPA *f*.

taker ['teɪkər] *n* **1.** [buyer] acheteur *m*, - euse *f*, preneur *m*, - euse *f* ▪ [of suggestion, offer] preneur *m*, - euse *f* ▪ **there were no ~s** personne n'en voulait ▪ **any ~s?** y a-t-il des preneurs? **2.** [user] : **~s of drugs are at highest risk** ce sont les toxicomanes qui courent les plus grands risques.

takeup ['teɪkʌp] *n* [of benefits] réclamation *f* ▪ **there has been a 75% ~ rate for the new benefit** 75 % des gens concernés par la nouvelle allocation l'ont effectivement demandée.

taking ['teɪkɪŋ] ◇ *adj* engageant, séduisant.
◇ *n* [of city, power] prise *f* ▪ [of criminal] arrestation *f* ▪ [of blood, sample] prélèvement *m* ▪ **the apples are there for the ~** prenez (donc) une pomme, elles sont là pour ça.

◆ **takings** *npl* COMM recette *f*.

talc [tælk] ◇ *n* talc *m*.
◇ *vt* talquer ▪ **to ~ o.s.** se mettre du talc, se talquer.

talcum powder ['tælkəm-] *n* talc *m*.

tale [teɪl] *n* **1.** [story] conte *m*, histoire *f* ■ [legend] histoire *f*, légende *f* ■ [account] récit *m* ■ **to tell a ~** raconter une histoire ■ **the astronaut lived/didn't live to tell the ~** l'astronaute a survécu/n'a pas survécu pour raconter ce qui s'est passé ▶ **and thereby hangs a ~** *hum* et là-dessus il y en aurait ■ **'A Tale of Two Cities'** *Dickens* 'le Conte des deux villes' **2.** [gossip] histoires *fpl* ■ **to tell ~s on sb** raconter des histoires sur le compte de qqn ■ **you shouldn't tell ~s** [denounce] il ne faut pas rapporter ; [lie] il ne faut pas raconter des histoires.

talent ['tælənt] *n* **1.** [gift] talent *m*, don *m* ■ **she has great musical ~** elle est très douée pour la musique, elle a un grand don pour la musique ■ **you have a ~ for saying the wrong thing** tu as le don pour dire ce qu'il ne faut pas **2.** [talented person] talent *m* **3.** *inf* [opposite sex - girls] jolies filles *fpl*, minettes *fpl* ; [- boys] beaux mecs *mpl* **4.** [coin] talent *m*.

talented ['tæləntɪd] *adj* talentueux, doué ■ **she's a ~ musician** c'est une musicienne de talent ■ **she's really ~** elle a beaucoup de talent.

talent scout, talent-spotter *n* [for films] dénicheur *m*, - euse *f* de vedettes ■ [for sport] dénicheur *m*, - euse *f* de futurs grands joueurs.

tale-telling *n* rapportage *m*.

talisman ['tælɪzmən] (*pl* **talismans**) *n* talisman *m*.

talk [tɔːk] ◇ *vi* **1.** [speak] parler ■ [discuss] discuter ■ [confer] s'entretenir ■ **to ~ to sb** parler à qqn ■ **to ~ with sb** parler OR s'entretenir avec qqn ■ **to ~ of** OR **about sthg** parler de qqch ■ **we sat ~ing together** nous sommes restés à discuter OR à bavarder ■ **to ~ in signs/riddles** parler par signes/par énigmes ■ **they were ~ing in Chinese** ils parlaient en chinois ■ **to ~ for the sake of ~ing** parler pour ne rien dire ■ **that's no way to ~!** en voilà des façons de parler! ■ **they no longer ~ to each other** ils ne se parlent plus, ils ne s'adressent plus la parole ■ **don't you ~ to me like that!** je t'interdis de me parler sur ce ton! ■ **to ~ to o.s.** parler tout seul ■ **I'll ~ to you about it tomorrow morning** [converse] je vous en parlerai demain matin ; [as threat] j'aurai deux mots à vous dire à ce sujet demain matin ■ **it's no use ~ing to him, he never listens!** on perd son temps avec lui, il n'écoute jamais! ■ **to ~ of this and that** parler de la pluie et du beau temps OR de choses et d'autres ■ **~ing of Switzerland, have you ever been skiing?** à propos de la Suisse, vous avez déjà fait du ski? ■ **now you're ~ing!** voilà qui s'appelle parler! ■ **you can ~!, look who's ~ing!, you're a fine one to ~!** tu peux parler, toi! ■ **it's easy for you to ~, you've never had a gun in your back!** c'est facile à dire OR tu as beau jeu de dire ça, on ne t'a jamais braqué un pistolet dans le dos! ■ **~ about luck!** [admiring] qu'est-ce qu'il a comme chance!, quel veinard! ; [complaining] tu parles d'une veine! ▶ **to ~ through one's hat** OR **the back of one's neck** OR **one's backside** *inf* OR **one's arse** ▲ dire des bêtises OR ; n'importe quo i
2. [chat] causer, bavarder ■ [gossip] jaser
3. [reveal secrets, esp unwillingly] parler ■ **to make sb ~** faire parler qqn ■ **we have ways of making people ~** on a les moyens de faire parler les gens.
◇ *vt* **1.** [language] parler ■ **to ~ slang** parler argot ■ **~ sense!** ne dis pas de sottises!, ne dis pas n'importe quoi! ■ **now you're ~ing sense** vous dites enfin des choses sensées ■ **stop ~ing rubbish!** *inf* OR **nonsense!** arrête de dire des bêtises! ▶ **to ~ turkey** *US inf* parler franc
2. [discuss] parler ■ **to ~ business/politics** parler affaires/politique.
◇ *n* **1.** [conversation] conversation *f* ■ [discussion] discussion *f* ■ [chat] causette *f*, causerie *f* ■ [formal] entretien *m* ■ **to have a ~ with sb about sthg** parler de qqch avec qqn, s'entretenir avec qqn de qqch ■ **that's fighting ~!** c'est un défi!
2. [speech, lecture] exposé *m* ■ **to give a ~ on** OR **about sthg** faire un exposé sur qqch ■ **there was a series of radio ~s on modern Japan** il y a eu à la radio une série d'émissions où des gens venaient parler du Japon moderne
3. *(U)* [noise of talking] paroles *fpl*, propos *mpl* ■ **there is a lot of ~ in the background** il y a beaucoup de bruit OR de gens qui parlent
4. [speculative] discussion *f*, rumeur *f* ■ **most of the ~ was about the new road** il a surtout été question de OR on a surtout parlé de la nouvelle route ■ **there's some ~ of building a concert hall** [discussion] il est question OR on parle de construire une salle de concert ; [rumour] le bruit court qu'on va construire une salle de concert ■ **enough of this idle ~!** assez parlé! ■ **he's all ~** tout ce qu'il dit, c'est du vent
5. *(U)* [gossip] racontars *mpl*, bavardage *m*, bavardages *mpl*, potins *mpl* ■ **it's the ~ of the town** on ne parle que de ça.

◆ **talks** *npl* [negotiations] négociations *fpl*, pourparlers *mpl* ■ [conference] conférence *f* ■ **official peace ~s** des pourparlers officiels sur la paix ■ **so far there have only been ~s about ~s** jusqu'ici il n'y a eu que des négociations préliminaires.

◆ **talk about** *vt insep* **1.** [discuss] parler de ■ **to ~ to sb about sthg** parler de qqch à qqn ■ **what are you ~ing about?** [I don't understand] de quoi parles-tu? ; [annoyed] qu'est-ce que tu racontes? ■ **it gives them something to ~ about** ça leur fait un sujet de conversation ■ **they were ~ing about going away for the weekend** ils parlaient OR envisageaient de partir pour le week-end
2. [mean] : **we're not ~ing about that!** il ne s'agit pas de cela! ■ **when it comes to hardship, he knows what he's ~ing about** pour ce qui est de souffrir, il sait de quoi il parle ■ **you don't know what you're ~ing about!** tu ne sais pas ce que tu dis!

◆ **talk at** *vt insep* : **to ~ at sb : I hate people who ~ at me not to me** je ne supporte pas les gens qui parlent sans se soucier de ce que j'ai à dire.

◆ **talk away** *vi insep* passer le temps à parler, parler sans arrêt ■ **they were still ~ing away at 3 a.m.** ils étaient encore en grande conversation à 3 h du matin.

◆ **talk back** *vi insep* [insolently] répondre ■ **to ~ back to sb** répondre (insolemment) à qqn.

◆ **talk down** ◇ *vt sep* **1.** [silence] : **to ~ sb down** réduire qqn au silence (en parlant plus fort que lui)
2. [aircraft] faire atterrir par radio-contrôle
3. [would-be suicide] : **the police managed to ~ him down from the roof** la police a réussi à le convaincre de redescendre du toit.
◇ *vi insep* : **to ~ down to sb** parler à qqn comme à un enfant.

◆ **talk into** *vt sep* : **to ~ sb into doing sthg** persuader qqn de faire qqch ■ **she allowed herself to be ~ed into going** elle s'est laissé convaincre d'y aller.

◆ **talk out** *vt sep* **1.** [problem, disagreement] débattre de, discuter de ■ **they managed to ~ out the problem** à force de discussions, ils sont arrivés à trouver une solution au problème
2. POL : **to ~ out a bill** *prolonger la discussion d'un projet de loi jusqu'à ce qu'il soit trop tard pour le voter avant la clôture de la séance.*

◆ **talk out of** *vt sep* dissuader ■ **to ~ sb out of doing sthg** dissuader qqn de faire qqch.

◆ **talk over** *vt sep* discuter OR débattre de ■ **let's ~ it over** discutons-en, parlons-en.

◆ **talk round** ◇ *vt sep* [convince] persuader, convaincre ■ **to ~ sb round to one's way of thinking** amener qqn à sa façon de penser OR à son point de vue.
◇ *vt insep* [problem] tourner autour de.

◆ **talk up** *vt sep* vanter les mérites de, faire de la publicité pour.

talkative ['tɔːkətɪv] *adj* bavard, loquace.

talk-back *n* TV & RADIO émetteur-récepteur *m*.

talk time *n (U)* crédit *m* de communication.

talker ['tɔːkəʳ] *n* **1.** [speaker] causeur *m*, - euse *f*, bavard *m*, - e *f* ■ **he's a fast ~** [gen] il parle vite ; COMM il a du bagout **2.** [talking bird] oiseau *m* qui parle.

talkie ['tɔːkɪ] *n inf* film *m* parlant.

talking ['tɔːkɪŋ] ◇ *n (U)* conversation *f*, propos *mpl* ■ **he did all the ~** il était le seul à parler.
◇ *adj* [film] parlant ■ [bird] qui parle.

talking book *n* lecture *f* enregistrée d'un livre *(généralement à l'usage des aveugles)*.

talking head *n* TV présentateur *m*, - trice *f (dont on ne voit que la tête et les épaules)*.

talking point *n* sujet *m* de conversation OR de discussion.

talking-to *n inf* attrapade *f*, réprimande *f* ■ **he needs a good ~** il a besoin qu'on lui passe un bon savon.

talk show *n* causerie *f* (radiodiffusée *OR* télévisée), talk-show *m*.

tall [tɔ:l] *adj* **1.** [person] grand, de grande taille ■ **how ~ are you?** combien mesurez-vous? ■ **I'm 6 feet ~** je mesure *OR* fais 1 m 80 ■ **she's grown a lot ~er in the past year** elle a beaucoup grandi depuis un an ❙ [building] haut, élevé ■ [tree, glass] grand, haut ■ **how ~ is that tree?** quelle est la hauteur de cet arbre? ■ **it's at least 80 feet ~** il fait au moins 25 mètres de haut ■ **it's a very ~ tree** c'est un très grand arbre **2.** *phr* **a ~ story** une histoire invraisemblable *OR* abracadabrante, une histoire à dormir debout ■ **that's a ~ order** c'est beaucoup demander.

tallboy ['tɔ:lbɔɪ] *n* [furniture] (grande) commode *f*.

tallness ['tɔ:lnɪs] *n* [of person] (grande) taille *f* ■ [of tree, building] hauteur *f*.

tallow ['tæləʊ] *n* suif *m* ■ **~ candle** chandelle *f*.

tall ship *n* voilier *m* gréé en carré.

tally ['tælɪ] <> *n* (*pl* **tallies**) **1.** [record] compte *m*, enregistrement *m* ■ COMM pointage *m* ■ *US* SPORT [score] score *m* ■ **to keep a ~ of names** pointer des noms sur une liste ■ **to keep a ~ of the score** compter les points **2.** HIST [stick] taille *f*, baguette *f* à encoches ■ [mark] encoche *f* **3.** [label] étiquette *f* **4.** [counterfoil - of cheque, ticket] talon *m* ■ [duplicate] contrepartie *f*, double *m*.

<> *vt* (*pret & pp* **tallied**) **1.** [record] pointer **2.** [count up] compter.

<> *vi* (*pret & pp* **tallied**) correspondre ■ **I couldn't make the figures ~** je ne pouvais faire concorder les chiffres ■ **your story must ~ with mine** il faut que ta version des faits concorde avec la mienne.

tallyho [,tælɪ'həʊ] (*pl* **tallyhos**) <> *interj* taïaut, tayaut.

<> *n* cri *m* de taïaut.

Talmud ['tælmʊd] *n* Talmud *m*.

talon ['tælən] *n* **1.** [of hawk, eagle] serre *f* ■ [of tiger, lion] griffe *f* **2.** CARDS talon *m*.

tamable ['teɪməbl] = **tameable**.

tamarind ['tæmərɪnd] *n* [fruit] tamarin *m* ■ [tree] tamarinier *m*.

tamarisk ['tæmərɪsk] *n* tamaris *m*, tamarix *m*.

tambourine [,tæmbə'ri:n] *n* tambour *m* de basque, tambourin *m*.

tame [teɪm] <> *adj* **1.** [as pet - hamster, rabbit] apprivoisé, domestiqué ■ [normally wild - bear, hawk] apprivoisé ■ [esp in circus - lion, tiger] dompté ■ **the deer had become very ~** les cerfs n'étaient plus du tout farouches ■ **I'll ask our ~ Frenchman if he knows what it means** *hum* je vais demander à notre Français de service s'il sait ce que cela veut dire **2.** [insipid, weak] fade, insipide ■ **the book has a very ~ ending** le livre finit de manière très banale.

<> *vt* **1.** [as pet - hamster, rabbit] apprivoiser, domestiquer ■ [normally wild - bear, hawk] apprivoiser ■ [in circus - lion, tiger] dompter **2.** [person] mater, soumettre ■ [natural forces] apprivoiser ■ [passions] dominer.

tameable ['teɪməbl] *adj* [hawk, bear, rabbit] apprivoisable ■ [lion, tiger] domptable.

tamely ['teɪmlɪ] *adv* [submit] docilement, sans résistance ■ [end] platement, de manière insipide ■ [write] de manière fade, platement.

tameness ['teɪmnɪs] *n* **1.** [of bird, hamster] nature *f* apprivoisée ■ [of lion, tiger] nature *f* domptée **2.** [of person] docilité *f* **3.** [of ending, style] fadeur *f*, insipidité *f* ■ [of party, film] manque *m* d'intérêt, banalité *f*.

tamer ['teɪmə^r] *n* dresseur *m*, -euse *f*.

Tamil ['tæmɪl] <> *n* **1.** [person] Tamoul *m*, - e *f* **2.** LING tamoul *m*.

<> *adj* tamoul.

taming ['teɪmɪŋ] *n* [of animal] apprivoisement *m* ■ [of lions, tigers] domptage *m*, dressage *m* ■ **'The Taming of the Shrew'** ***Shakespeare*** 'la Mégère apprivoisée'.

Tammany ['tæmənɪ] *n* *US* POL *organisation centrale du parti démocrate de New York (souvent impliquée dans des affaires de corruption)* ■ **~ Hall** *siège du parti démocrate new-yorkais aux XVIIIe et XIXe siècles.*

tam-o'-shanter [,tæmə'ʃæntə^r] *n* béret *m* écossais.

tamp [tæmp] *vt* tasser, damer ■ [for blasting - drill hole] bourrer (à l'argile *OR* au sable).

◆ **tamp down** *vt sep* [earth] tasser, damer ■ [gunpowder, tobacco] tasser.

tamper ['tæmpə^r] ◆ **tamper with** *vt insep* **1.** [meddle with - brakes, machinery] trafiquer ■ [lock] essayer de forcer *OR* crocheter, fausser ■ [possessions] toucher à ■ [falsify - records, accounts, evidence] falsifier, altérer ■ **the TV has been ~ed with** quelqu'un a déréglé la télévision **2.** *US* LAW [witness] suborner ■ [jury] soudoyer.

tamperproof ['tæmpə,pru:f] *adj* scellé.

tampon ['tæmpɒn] *n* MED tampon *m* ■ [for feminine use] tampon *m* périodique *OR* hygiénique.

tan [tæn] (*pret & pp* **tanned**, *cont* **tanning**) <> *n* **1.** [from sun] bronzage *m* ■ **I got a good ~ in the mountains** j'ai bien bronzé à la montagne **2.** MATHS tangente *f*.

<> *vt* **1.** [leather, skins] tanner ■ **to ~ sb's hide** *inf fig* rosser qqn **2.** [from sun] bronzer, brunir.

<> *vi* bronzer.

<> *adj* [colour] brun roux, brun clair ■ [leather] jaune ■ *US* [tanned] bronzé.

tandem ['tændəm] <> *n* **1.** [carriage] tandem *m* ■ **to harness two horses in ~** atteler deux chevaux en tandem *OR* en flèche ■ **to work in ~** *fig* travailler en tandem *OR* en collaboration **2.** [bike] tandem *m*.

<> *adv*: **to ride ~** rouler en tandem.

<> *adj* double ■ **~ exchange** TELEC central *m* tandem.

tandoori [tæn'dʊərɪ] <> *n* cuisine *f* tandoori.

<> *adj* tandoori *(inv)*.

tang [tæŋ] *n* **1.** [taste] goût *m* (fort) **2.** [smell] odeur *f* forte **3.** [hint - of irony] pointe *f* **4.** [of knife, sword] soie *f*.

tangent ['tændʒənt] *n* MATHS tangente *f* ■ **to be at a ~** former une tangente ■ **to go off at** *OR* **on a ~** *fig* partir dans une digression.

tangential [tæn'dʒenʃl] *adj* tangentiel.

tangerine [,tændʒə'ri:n] <> *n* **1.** [fruit] : **~ (orange)** mandarine *f* ■ **~ (tree)** mandarinier *m* **2.** [colour] mandarine *f*.

<> *adj* [in colour] mandarine *(inv)*.

tangibility [,tændʒə'bɪlətɪ] *n* tangibilité *f*.

tangible ['tændʒəbl] *adj* **1.** [palpable] tangible ■ [real, substantial] tangible, réel ■ **the ~ world** le monde sensible ■ **it made no ~ difference** ça n'a pas changé grand-chose **2.** LAW [assets] réel, matériel ■ [property] corporel.

tangibly ['tændʒəblɪ] *adv* tangiblement, manifestement, de manière tangible.

Tangier [tæn'dʒɪə^r] *pr n* Tanger.

tangle ['tæŋgl] <> *n* **1.** [of wire, string, hair] enchevêtrement *m* ■ [of branches, weeds] fouillis *m*, enchevêtrement *m* ■ **this string is in an awful ~** cette ficelle est tout embrouillée ■ **to get into a ~** [wires, string] s'embrouiller, s'emmêler ; [hair] s'emmêler **2.** [muddle] fouillis *m*, confusion *f* ■ **a legal ~** une affaire compliquée *OR* embrouillée du point de vue juridique ■ **to get into a ~** [person] s'empêtrer, s'embrouiller ; [records, figures] s'embrouiller **3.** [disagreement] accrochage *m*, différend *m* ■ **I had a ~ with the social security officials** j'ai eu des mots *OR* maille à partir avec les employés de la sécurité sociale.

<> *vt* [wire, wool] emmêler, enchevêtrer ■ [figures] embrouiller ■ **to get ~d** [string] s'emmêler ; [situation] s'embrouiller.

◇ *vi* **1.** [wires, hair] s'emmêler **2.** *inf* [disagree] avoir un différend *OR* un accrochage ▪ **you'd better not ~ with her** il vaut mieux éviter de se frotter à elle.
◆ **tangle up** *vt sep* [string, wire] emmêler, enchevêtrer ▪ **to get ~d up** s'emmêler.

tangled ['tæŋgld] *adj* **1.** [string, creepers] emmêlé, enchevêtré ▪ [undergrowth] touffu ▪ [hair] emmêlé **2.** [complex - story, excuse] embrouillé ; [- love life] complexe.

tango ['tæŋgəʊ] (*pl* **tangos**) ◇ *n* tango *m*.
◇ *vi* danser le tango.

tangy ['tæŋɪ] (*comp* **tangier**, *superl* **tangiest**) *adj* [in taste] qui a un goût fort ▪ [in smell] qui a une odeur forte.

tank [tæŋk] ◇ *n* **1.** [container - for liquid, gas] réservoir *m*, cuve *f*, citerne *f* ; [- for rainwater] citerne *f*, bac *m* ; [- for processing] cuve *f* ; [- for transport] réservoir *m*, citerne *f* ▪ [barrel] tonneau *m*, cuve *f* ▪ **(petrol)** *UK OR* **fuel() ~** AUT réservoir *m* (d'essence) ▪ **(domestic) hot water ~** ballon *m* d'eau chaude ▪ **(fish) ~** aquarium *m* **2.** MIL tank *m*, char *m* d'assaut ▪ **armoured ~** blindé *m*.
◇ *comp* de char *OR* chars d'assaut ▪ **~ regiment** régiment *m* de chars (d'assaut).
◇ *vt* mettre en cuve *OR* en réservoir.
◆ **tank up** *UK* ◇ *vi insep* AUT faire le plein (d'essence).
◇ *vt sep inf* **to get ~ed up** se soûler.

tankard ['tæŋkəd] *n* chope *f*.

tanker ['tæŋkər] *n* [lorry] camion-citerne *m* ▪ [ship] bateau-citerne *m*, navire-citerne *m* ▪ [plane] avion-ravitailleur *m* ▪ **(oil) ~** NAUT pétrolier *m*.

tankful ['tæŋkfʊl] *n* [of petrol] réservoir *m* (plein) ▪ [of water] citerne *f* (pleine).

tank top *n* débardeur *m*.

tank trap *n* piège *m* à chars.

tanned [tænd] *adj* **1.** [person] hâlé, bronzé **2.** [leather] tanné.

tanner ['tænər] *n* **1.** [of leather] tanneur *m*, - euse *f* **2.** *UK inf* *ancienne pièce de six pence*.

tannery ['tænərɪ] (*pl* **tanneries**) *n* tannerie *f* *(countable)*.

tannic ['tænɪk] *adj* tannique.

tannin ['tænɪn] *n* tanin *m*, tannin *m*.

tanning ['tænɪŋ] *n* **1.** [of skin] bronzage *m* **2.** [of hides] tannage *m* ▪ *fig* raclée *f* ▪ **to give sb a ~** *inf* rosser qqn.

Tannoy® ['tænɔɪ] *n UK* système *m* de haut-parleurs ▪ **the delay was announced over the ~** le retard fut annoncé par haut-parleur.

tantalize, ise ['tæntəlaɪz] *vt* tourmenter, taquiner.

tantalizing ['tæntəlaɪzɪŋ] *adj* [woman] provocant, aguichant ▪ [smell] alléchant, appétissant ▪ [hint, possibility] tentant.

tantalizingly ['tæntəlaɪzɪŋlɪ] *adv* cruellement ▪ **victory was ~ close** nous étions si près de la victoire que c'en était frustrant ▪ **~ slow** d'une lenteur désespérante.

Tantalus ['tæntələs] *pr n* Tantale.

tantamount ['tæntəmaʊnt] ◆ **tantamount to** *prep phr* équivalent à ▪ **his statement was ~ to an admission of guilt** sa déclaration équivalait à un aveu.

tantric sex *n* sexe *m* tantrique.

tantrum ['tæntrəm] *n* crise *f* de colère *OR* de rage ▪ **to have** *OR* **to throw a ~** piquer une crise.

Tanzania [ˌtænzə'nɪə] *pr n* Tanzanie *f* ▪ **in ~** en Tanzanie.

Tanzanian [ˌtænzə'nɪən] ◇ *n* Tanzanien *m*, - enne *f*.
◇ *adj* tanzanien.

Taoiseach ['ti:ʃək] *n titre du Premier ministre de la République d'Irlande*.

Taoism ['tɑ:əʊɪzm] *n* taoïsme *m*.

Taoist ['tɑ:əʊɪst] ◇ *adj* taoïste.
◇ *n* taoïste *mf*.

tap [tæp] (*pret & pp* **tapped**, *cont* **tapping**) ◇ *vt* **1.** [strike] taper légèrement, tapoter ▪ **someone tapped me on the shoulder** quelqu'un m'a tapé sur l'épaule ▪ **she was tapping her fingers on the table** elle pianotait *OR* tapotait sur la table ▪ **he tapped his feet to the rhythm** il marquait le rythme en tapant du pied
2. [barrel, cask] mettre en perce, percer ▪ [gas, water main] faire un branchement sur ▪ [current] capter ▪ [tree] inciser ▪ [pine] gemmer
3. [exploit - resources, market] exploiter ; [- talent, service] faire appel à, tirer profit de ; [- capital] drainer ▪ **to ~ sb for information** soutirer des informations à qqn ▪ **to ~ sb for a loan** *inf* taper qqn
4. TELEC [conversation] capter ▪ **to ~ sb's line** *OR* **phone** mettre qqn sur (table d')écoute
5. TECH [screw] tarauder, fileter
6. ELEC faire une dérivation sur
7. MED poser un drain sur.
◇ *vi* **1.** [knock] tapoter, taper légèrement ▪ **to ~ at the door** frapper doucement à la porte ▪ **the woodpeckers are tapping on the bark** les piverts donnent des coups de bec sur l'écorce
2. [dance] faire des claquettes.
◇ *n* **1.** [for water, gas] robinet *m* ▪ [on barrel] robinet *m*, chantepleure *f* ▪ [plug] bonde *f* ▪ **to turn a ~ on/off** ouvrir/fermer un robinet ▪ **to leave the ~ running** laisser le robinet ouvert ▪ **on ~** [beer] en fût ; *inf figinf* [money, person, supply] disponible
2. [blow] petit coup *m*, petite tape *f* ▪ **to give sb a ~ on the shoulder** donner une petite tape sur l'épaule à qqn
3. [on shoe] fer *m*
4. [dancing] claquettes *fpl* ▪ **to dance ~** faire des claquettes ▪ **~ shoes** claquettes *fpl (chaussures)*
5. TECH : **(screw) ~** taraud *m*
6. ELEC dérivation *f*, branchement *f*
7. TELEC : **to put a ~ on sb's phone** mettre (le téléphone de) qqn sur table d'écoute
8. MED drain *m*.
◆ **tap in** *vt sep* **1.** [plug] enfoncer à petits coups
2. COMPUT taper.
◆ **tap out** *vt sep* **1.** [plug] sortir à petits coups ▪ [pipe] vider, débourrer
2. [code, rhythm] taper.

tap dance *n* claquettes *fpl (danse)*.
◆ **tap-dance** *vi* faire des claquettes.

tap dancing *n (U)* claquettes *fpl (danse)*.

tape [teɪp] ◇ *n* **1.** [strip] bande *f*, ruban *m* ▪ SEW ruban *m*, ganse *f* ▪ MED sparadrap *m* ▪ **name ~** ruban *m* de noms tissés **2.** [for recording] bande *f* (magnétique) ▪ COMPUT bande *f* ▪ [for video, audio] cassette *f* ▪ [recording] enregistrement *m* ▪ **on ~** sur bande, enregistré **3.** SPORT fil *m* d'arrivée **4.** [for measuring] : **~ (measure)** mètre *m* (à ruban).
◇ *vt* **1.** [record] enregistrer **2.** [fasten - package] attacher avec du ruban adhésif ▪ [stick] scotcher **3.** *US* [bandage] bander **4.** *phr* **she's got him ~d** *UK inf* elle sait ce qu'il vaut ▪ **we have the situation ~d** on a la situation bien en main.
◆ **tape together** *vt sep* [fasten] attacher ensemble avec du ruban adhésif ▪ [stick] coller (avec du ruban adhésif).
◆ **tape up** *vt sep* [fasten - parcel] attacher avec du ruban adhésif ▪ [close - letterbox, hole] fermer avec du ruban adhésif ▪ *US* [bandage up] bander.

tape cleaner *n* nettoyeur *m* de tête, produit *m* de nettoyage de tête.

tape deck *n* platine *f* de magnétophone.

tape drive *n* dérouleur *m* de bande (magnétique), lecteur *m* de bande (magnétique).

tape head *n* tête *f* de lecture.

tape measure *n* mètre *m* (ruban), centimètre *m*.

taper ['teɪpər] ◇ *vt* [column, trouser leg, plane wing] fuseler ▪ [stick, table leg] effiler, tailler en pointe.
◇ *vi* [column, trouser leg, plane wing] être fuselé ▪ [stick, shape, table leg] se terminer en pointe, s'effiler ▪ [finger] être effilé.
◇ *n longue bougie fine* ▪ RELIG cierge *m*.

◆ **taper off** *vi insep* **1.** [shape] se terminer en fuseau *OR* en pointe **2.** [noise] diminuer progressivement, décroître, s'affaiblir ▪ [conversation] tomber ▪ [level of interest, activity] décroître progressivement.

tape reader *n* COMPUT lecteur *m* de bande.

tape-record [-rɪˌkɔ:d] *vt* enregistrer (sur bande magnétique).

tape recorder *n* magnétophone *m*, lecteur *m* de cassettes.

tape recording *n* enregistrement *m* (sur bande magnétique).

tapered ['teɪpəd], **tapering** ['teɪpərɪŋ] *adj* [trousers] en fuseau ▪ [stick, candle] en pointe, pointu ▪ [table leg] fuselé ▪ **~ fingers** des doigts effilés *OR* fuselés.

tape streamer *n* COMPUT streamer *m*.

tapestry ['tæpɪstrɪ] (*pl* **tapestries**) *n* tapisserie *f*.

tapeworm ['teɪpwɜ:m] *n* ténia *m*, ver *m* solitaire.

tapioca [ˌtæpɪ'əʊkə] *n* tapioca *m*.

tapir ['teɪpəʳ] (*pl inv OR pl* **tapirs**) *n* tapir *m*.

tappet ['tæpɪt] *n* TECH : **(valve) ~** poussoir *m* (de soupape), taquet *m*.

taproom ['tæprʊm] *n UK* salle *f* (*d'un café*), bar *m*.

tap water *n* eau *f* du robinet.

tar [tɑ:ʳ] (*pret & pp* **tarred**, *cont* **tarring**) ◇ *n* **1.** goudron *m* ▪ [on road] goudron *m*, bitume *m* ▪ **to beat the ~ out of sb** *US inf* flanquer une rouste à qqn **2.** *inf* [sailor] matelot *m*, loup *m* de mer.
◇ *vt* goudronner ▪ [road] goudronner, bitumer ▪ NAUT goudronner ▪ **to ~ and feather sb** couvrir qqn de goudron et de plumes ➲ **to be tarred with the same brush** être à mettre dans le même panier *OR* sac.

taramasalata [ˌtærəməsə'lɑ:tə] *n* tarama *m*.

tarantula [tə'ræntjʊlə] (*pl* **tarantulas** *OR pl* **tarantulae** [-li:]) *n* tarentule *f*.

tardiness ['tɑ:dɪnɪs] *n fml & lit* **1.** [lateness] retard *m* **2.** [slowness] lenteur *f*.

tardy ['tɑ:dɪ] (*comp* **tardier**, *superl* **tardiest**) *adj* **1.** *US* SCH en retard **2.** *fml & lit* [late] tardif **3.** *fml & lit* [slow] lent, nonchalant.

tare [teəʳ] *n* **1.** [weight] tare *f*, poids *m* à vide **2.** BOT vesce *f*.

target ['tɑ:gɪt] (*pret & pp* **targeted**, *cont* **targeting**) ◇ *n* **1.** [for archery, shooting] cible *f* ▪ MIL cible *f*, but *m* ▪ [objective] cible *f*, objectif *m* ▪ **the ~ of criticism/jokes** la cible de critiques/plaisanteries ▪ **to be on ~** [missile] suivre la trajectoire prévue ; [plans] se dérouler comme prévu ; [productivity] atteindre les objectifs prévus ▪ **to meet production ~s** atteindre les objectifs de production ➲ **moving ~** MIL & *fig* cible *f* mobile **2.** ELECTRON & PHYS cible *f* **3.** [in surveying] mire *f* **4.** CULIN [joint] épaule *f* de mouton.
◇ *comp* **1.** [date, amount] prévu ▪ **my ~ weight is 10 stone** je me suis fixé le poids idéal de 63 kg, mon poids idéal est (de) 63 kg **2.** MIL : **~ area** zone *f* cible **3.** COMM : **~ audience/reader/user** public-/lecteur-/usager-cible **4.** COMPUT : **~ disk/drive** disquette/unité de destination.
◇ *vt* **1.** [make objective of - enemy troops, city etc] prendre pour cible, viser **2.** [aim - missile] diriger ▪ [subj: benefits] être destiné à ▪ [subj: advertisement] viser, s'adresser à.

target language *n* langue *f* cible.

target practice *n (U)* MIL [gen] exercices *mpl* de tir.

tarheel ['tɑ:hi:l] *n US* habitant *m*, - e *f* de Caroline du Nord ▪ **the Tarheel State** la Caroline du Nord.

tariff ['tærɪf] ◇ *n* **1.** [customs] tarif *m* douanier ▪ [list of prices] tarif *m*, tableau *m* des prix ▪ **~ reform** réforme *f* des tarifs douaniers **2.** *UK* [menu] menu *m* **3.** *UK* [rate - of gas, electricity] tarif *m*.
◇ *adj* tarifaire.

Tarmac® ['tɑ:mæk] (*pret & pp* **tarmacked**, *cont* **tarmacking**) *n UK* **1.** [on road] tarmacadam *m*, macadam *m* **2.** [at airport - runway] piste *f* ; [- apron] aire *f* de stationnement, piste *f* d'envol.
◆ **tarmac** *vt* macadamiser, goudronner.

Tarmacadam® [ˌtɑ:mə'kædəm] = **Tarmac**® *(n)*.

tarn [tɑ:n] *n* petit lac *m* de montagne.

tarnish ['tɑ:nɪʃ] ◇ *vt* **1.** [metal] ternir ▪ [mirror] ternir, désargenter **2.** [reputation] ternir, salir.
◇ *vi* se ternir.
◇ *n* ternissure *f*.

tarnished ['tɑ:nɪʃt] *adj liter & fig* terni.

tarot ['tærəʊ] *n (U)* tarot *m*, tarots *mpl* ▪ **~ card** carte *f* de tarot.

tarp [tɑ:p] *n US inf* toile *f* goudronnée.

tarpaulin [tɑ:'pɔ:lɪn] *n* bâche *f* ▪ NAUT prélart *m*.

tarragon ['tærəgən] *n* estragon *m* ▪ **~ vinegar/sauce** vinaigre *m* /sauce *f* à l'estragon.

tarry¹ ['tærɪ] (*pret & pp* **tarried**) *vi lit* [delay] s'attarder, tarder ▪ [remain] rester, demeurer.

tarry² ['tɑ:rɪ] *adj* goudronneux ▪ [fingers, shoes] plein *OR* couvert de goudron.

tarsus ['tɑ:səs] (*pl* **tarsi** [-saɪ]) *n* tarse *m*.

tart [tɑ:t] ◇ *n* **1.** CULIN tarte *f* ▪ [small] tartelette *f* **2.** △ *UK* [girl] gonzesse△ *f* ▪ [prostitute] grue△ *f*.
◇ *adj* **1.** [sour - fruit] acide ; [- taste] aigre, acide **2.** [remark] acerbe, caustique.
◆ **tart up** *vt sep UK inf* [house, restaurant etc] retaper, rénover ▪ **to ~ o.s. up, to get ~ed up** se pomponner.

tartan ['tɑ:tn] ◇ *n* [design] tartan *m* ▪ [fabric] tartan *m*, tissu *m* écossais.
◇ *comp* [skirt, trousers] en tissu écossais ▪ [pattern] tartan.

tartar ['tɑ:təʳ] *n* **1.** [on teeth] tartre *m* **2.** *UK* [fearsome person] tyran *m*.
◆ **Tartar** *n* = **Tatar**.

tartar(e) sauce ['tɑ:tə-] *n* sauce *f* tartare.

Tartary ['tɑ:tərɪ] = **Tatary**.

tartlet ['tɑ:tlɪt] *n UK* tartelette *f*.

tartly ['tɑ:tlɪ] *adv* avec aigreur, de manière acerbe.

tartrazine ['tɑ:trəzi:n] *n* tartrazine *f*.

tarty△ ['tɑ:tɪ] (*comp* **tartier**, *superl* **tartiest**) *adj UK* vulgaire.

Tarzan ['tɑ:zn] *pr n* Tarzan.

task [tɑ:sk] ◇ *n* [chore] tâche *f*, besogne *f* ▪ [job] tâche *f*, travail *m* ▪ SCH devoir *m* ▪ **to set sb a ~** imposer une tâche à qqn ▪ **convincing them will be no easy ~** les convaincre ne sera pas chose facile ➲ **to take sb to ~** réprimander qqn, prendre qqn à partie.
◇ *vt* = **tax** *(vt sense 3)*.

task force *n* MIL corps *m* expéditionnaire ▪ [gen] groupe *m* de travail, mission *f*.

taskmaster ['tɑ:skˌmɑ:stəʳ] *n* tyran *m* ▪ **he's a hard ~** il mène la vie dure à ses subordonnés, c'est un véritable négrier.

task work *n* travail *m* à la tâche *OR* aux pièces.

Tasmania [tæz'meɪnjə] *pr n* Tasmanie *f* ▪ **in ~** en Tasmanie.

Tasmanian [tæz'meɪnjən] ◇ *n* Tasmanien *m*, - enne *f*.
◇ *adj* tasmanien.

tassel ['tæsl] (*UK pret & pp* **tasselled**, *cont* **tasselling**) (*US pret & pp* **tasseled**, *cont* **tasseling**) ◇ *n* **1.** [on clothing, furnishing] gland *m* **2.** BOT épillets *mpl*, panicule *f*, inflorescence *f* mâle.
◇ *vt* garnir de glands.

taste [teɪst] ◇ *n* **1.** [sense] goût *m* ▪ **to lose one's sense of ~** perdre le goût, être atteint d'agueusie ▪ **to be sweet/salty to the ~** avoir un goût sucré/salé
2. [flavour] goût *m*, saveur *f* ▪ **this cheese doesn't have much ~** ce fromage n'a pas beaucoup de goût *OR* est assez fade

■ **add sugar to ~** CULIN ajouter du sucre à volonté ▶ **to leave a bad ~ in the mouth** [food] laisser un mauvais goût dans la bouche ; *fig* laisser un mauvais souvenir *OR* un goût amer **3.** [small amount - of food] bouchée *f* ; [- of drink] goutte *f* ■ **can I have a ~ of the chocolate cake?** est-ce que je peux goûter au gâteau au chocolat?
4. [liking, preference] goût *m*, penchant *m* ■ **to have expensive/simple ~s** avoir des goûts de luxe/simples ■ **to develop a ~ for sthg** prendre goût à qqch ■ **to have a ~ for sthg** avoir un penchant *OR* un faible pour qqch ■ **it's a matter of ~** c'est (une) affaire de goût ■ **I don't share his ~ in music** je ne partage pas ses goûts en (matière de) musique, nous n'avons pas les mêmes goûts en (matière de) musique ■ **is it to your ~?** est-ce à votre goût?, est-ce que cela vous convient?, cela vous plaît?
5. [discernment] goût *m* ■ **to have good ~** avoir du goût, avoir bon goût ■ **they have no ~** ils n'ont aucun goût ■ **she has good ~ in clothes** elle s'habille avec goût ■ **the joke was in extremely bad ~** la plaisanterie était de très mauvais goût
6. [experience] aperçu *m* ■ [sample] échantillon *m* ■ **the sweet ~ of success** les joies *OR* les délices de la réussite ■ **he's already had a ~ of prison life** il a déjà tâté *OR* goûté de la prison ■ **the experience gave me a ~ of life in the army** l'expérience m'a donné un aperçu de la vie militaire ■ **a ~ of things to come** un avant-goût de l'avenir.
◇ *vt* **1.** [flavour, ingredient] sentir (le goût de) ■ **can you ~ the brandy in it?** est-ce que vous sentez le (goût du) cognac?
2. [sample, try] goûter à ■ [for quality] goûter ■ **to ~ (the) wine** [in restaurant] goûter le vin ; [in vineyard] déguster le vin ‖ [eat] manger ■ [drink] boire
3. [experience - happiness, success] goûter, connaître.
◇ *vi* [food] : **to ~ good/bad** avoir bon/mauvais goût ■ **to ~ salty** avoir un goût salé ■ **to ~ of sthg** avoir le *OR* un goût de qqch.

taste bud *n* papille *f* gustative.

tasteful [ˈteɪstfʊl] *adj* [decoration] raffiné, de bon goût ■ [work of art] de bon goût ■ [clothing] de bon goût, élégant.

tastefully [ˈteɪstfʊlɪ] *adv* avec goût.

tasteless [ˈteɪstlɪs] *adj* **1.** [food] fade, insipide, sans goût **2.** [remark] de mauvais goût ■ [decoration, outfit, person] qui manque de goût, de mauvais goût.

tastelessly [ˈteɪstlɪslɪ] *adv* [decorated, dressed] sans goût.

taster [ˈteɪstəʳ] *n* dégustateur *m*, -trice *f*.

tasty [ˈteɪstɪ] (*comp* **tastier**, *superl* **tastiest**) *adj* **1.** [flavour] savoureux, délicieux ■ [spicy] relevé, bien assaisonné ■ [dish] qui a bon goût **2.** *inf* [attractive] séduisant.

tat [tæt] (*pret & pp* **tatted**, *cont* **tatting**) ◇ *vi* [make lace] faire de la frivolité.
◇ *n inf (U) UK inf pej* [clothes] fripes *fpl* ■ [goods] camelote *f*.

Tatar [ˈtɑːtəʳ] ◇ *n* [person] Tatar *m*, - e *f*.
◇ *adj* tatar.

Tatary [ˈtɑːtərɪ] *pr n* Tatarie *f* ■ **in ~** en Tatarie.

tattered [ˈtætəd] *adj* [clothes] en lambeaux, en loques ■ [page, book] en lambeaux, en morceaux, tout déchiré ■ [person] en haillons, loqueteux ■ [reputation] en miettes, ruiné.

tatters [ˈtætəz] *npl* : **to be in ~** *liter* être en lambeaux *OR* en loques ■ **her reputation is in ~** *fig* sa réputation est ruinée.

tattle [ˈtætl] *inf* ◇ *vi* [chatter] jaser, cancaner ■ [tell secrets] rapporter.
◇ *n (U)* [gossiping] commérages *mpl*, cancans *mpl*.

tattle-tale *n* = telltale *(n)*.

tattoo [təˈtuː] (*pl* **tattoos**) ◇ *n* **1.** [on skin] tatouage *m* ■ **he had ~s across his chest** il avait la poitrine tatouée **2.** MIL [signal] retraite *f* ■ [ceremony, parade] parade *f* militaire **3.** [on drums] battements *mpl* ■ **to beat a ~ on the drums** battre le tambour ‖ *fig* [on door, table] : **he beat a furious ~ on the door with his fists** il tambourinait violemment sur *OR* contre la porte avec ses poings.
◇ *vi & vt* tatouer.

tattooist [təˈtuːɪst] *n* tatoueur *m*.

tatty [ˈtætɪ] (*comp* **tattier**, *superl* **tattiest**) *adj UK inf* [clothes] fatigué, défraîchi ■ [person] défraîchi, miteux ■ [house] délabré, en mauvais état ■ [book] écorné, en mauvais état.

taught [tɔːt] *pt & pp* ▷ **teach**.

taunt [tɔːnt] ◇ *vt* railler, tourner en ridicule, persifler.
◇ *n* raillerie *f*, sarcasme *m*.

taunting [ˈtɔːntɪŋ] ◇ *n (U)* railleries *fpl*, sarcasmes *mpl*.
◇ *adj* railleur, sarcastique.

Taurus [ˈtɔːrəs] *pr n* ASTROL & ASTRON Taureau *m* ■ **he's a ~** il est (du signe du) Taureau.

taut [tɔːt] *adj* [rope, cable] tendu, raide ■ [situation] tendu.

tauten [ˈtɔːtn] ◇ *vt* [rope, cable etc] tendre, raidir.
◇ *vi* se tendre.

tautological [ˌtɔːtəˈlɒdʒɪkl] *adj* tautologique, pléonastique.

tautology [tɔːˈtɒlədʒɪ] (*pl* **tautologies**) *n* tautologie *f*, pléonasme *m*.

tavern [ˈtævn] *n* auberge *f*, taverne *f*.

tawdry [ˈtɔːdrɪ] (*comp* **tawdrier**, *superl* **tawdriest**) *adj* [clothes] voyant, tapageur, de mauvaise qualité ■ [jewellery] clinquant ■ [goods] de mauvaise qualité ■ [motives, situation] bas, indigne.

tawny [ˈtɔːnɪ] (*comp* **tawnier**, *superl* **tawniest**) *adj* [colour] fauve.

tawny owl *n* chouette *f* hulotte.

tax [tæks] ◇ *n* **1.** [on income] contributions *fpl* ■ ADMIN impôt *m* ■ **to levy** *OR* **to collect ~es** lever *OR* percevoir des impôts ■ **most of my income goes in ~** la plus grande partie de mes revenus va aux impôts ■ **I don't pay much ~** je ne paie pas beaucoup d'impôts ■ **after ~** net (d'impôt) **2.** [on goods, services, imports] taxe *f* ■ **to levy** *OR* **to put a 10% ~ on sthg** frapper qqch d'une taxe de 10 %, imposer *OR* taxer qqch à 10 % ■ **baby food is free of ~** les aliments pour bébés sont exempts *OR* exonérés de taxe ■ **a ~ on books/knowledge** une taxe sur les livres/le savoir **3.** *fig* [strain - on patience, nerves] épreuve *f* ; [- on strength, resources] mise *f* à l'épreuve.
◇ *comp* [burden] fiscal ■ [assessment] de l'impôt ■ [liability] à l'impôt ■ **~ dollars** *US* l'argent *m* du contribuable ■ **~ expert** fiscaliste *mf*.
◇ *vt* **1.** [person, company] imposer, frapper d'un impôt ■ [goods] taxer, frapper d'une taxe ■ **the rich will be more heavily ~ed** les riches seront plus lourdement imposés *OR* payeront plus d'impôts **2.** *UK* **to ~ one's car** acheter la vignette (automobile) **3.** *fig* [strain - patience, resources] mettre à l'épreuve ; [- strength, nerves] éprouver **4.** [accuse] : **to ~ sb with sthg** accuser *OR* taxer qqn de qqch.

taxable [ˈtæksəbl] *adj* [income, goods, land] imposable.

tax adjustment *n* redressement *m* fiscal *OR* d'impôt.

tax allowance *n* abattement *m* fiscal.

taxation [tækˈseɪʃn] ◇ *n (U)* **1.** [of goods] taxation *f* ■ [of companies, people] imposition *f* **2.** [taxes] impôts *mpl*, contributions *fpl*.
◇ *comp* [system] fiscal ■ **~ authorities** administration *f* fiscale, fisc *m* ■ **~ year** année *f* fiscale d'imposition, exercice *m* fiscal.

tax avoidance *n* moyen *m* (légal) pour payer moins d'impôts.

tax bracket *n* tranche *f* d'imposition.

tax break *n* réduction *f* d'impôt.

tax code *n* barème *m* fiscal.

tax collector *n* percepteur *m*.

tax cut *n* baisse *f* de l'impôt.

tax-deductible *adj* déductible des impôts, sujet à un dégrèvement d'impôts.

tax disc *n UK* vignette *f* automobile.

tax evasion *n* fraude *f* fiscale.

tax-exempt *US* = **tax-free**.

tax-exemption *n* exonération *f* d'impôt.

tax exile *n personne qui s'expatrie pour des raisons fiscales.*

tax form *n* feuille *f* OR déclaration *f* d'impôts.

tax-free *adj* [goods] exonéré de taxes, non taxé ▪ [interest] exonéré d'impôts, exempt d'impôts.

tax haven *n* paradis *m* fiscal.

taxi ['tæksɪ] <> *n* (*pl* **taxis** OR *pl* **taxies**) taxi *m* ▪ **to get** OR **to take a ~** prendre un taxi ▪ **to hail a ~** héler un taxi.
<> *vi* (*pret & pp* **taxied**, *cont* **taxying**) [aircraft] se déplacer au sol ▪ **the plane taxied across the tarmac** l'avion traversa lentement l'aire de stationnement.
<> *vt* (*pret & pp* **taxied**, *cont* **taxying**) [carry passengers] transporter en taxi.

taxicab ['tæksɪkæb] *n* taxi *m*.

taxidermist ['tæksɪdɜːmɪst] *n* empailleur *m*, - euse *f*, taxidermiste *mf*, naturaliste *mf*.

taxidermy ['tæksɪdɜːmɪ] *n* empaillage *m*, taxidermie *f*, naturalisation *f* des animaux.

taxi driver *n* chauffeur *m* de taxi.

taximeter ['tæksɪˌmiːtər] *n* taximètre *m*, compteur *m* (de taxi).

tax incentive *n* incitation *f* fiscale.

taxing ['tæksɪŋ] *adj* [problem, time] difficile ▪ [climb] ardu.

tax inspector *n* inspecteur *m*, -trice *f* des impôts.

taxiplane ['tæksɪpleɪn] *n* avion-taxi *m*.

taxi rank *UK*, **taxi stand** *US n* station *f* de taxis.

taxiway ['tæksɪweɪ] *n* AERON taxiway *m*, chemin *m* de roulement.

taxman ['tæksmæn] (*pl* **taxmen** [-men]) *n* **1.** [person] percepteur *m* (du fisc) **2.** *UK inf* [Inland Revenue] : **the ~** le fisc.

taxonomy [tæk'sɒnəmɪ] (*pl* **taxonomies**) *n* taxinomie *f*, taxonomie *f*.

taxpayer ['tæksˌpeɪər] *n* contribuable *mf*.

tax rebate *n* dégrèvement *m* d'impôts.

tax relief *n (U)* dégrèvement *m* fiscal ▪ **to get ~ on sthg** obtenir un dégrèvement OR allégement fiscal sur qqch.

tax return *n* déclaration *f* de revenus OR d'impôts.

tax shelter *n* avantage *m* fiscal.

tax year *n* année *f* fiscale *(qui commence en avril en Grande-Bretagne).*

TB *n* = **tuberculosis**.

T-bar *n* **1.** [for skiers] téléski *m*, remonte-pente *m* **2.** [wrench] clé *f* à pipe en forme de T ▪ [bar] profilé *m* OR fer *m* en T.

T-bill *n US* [treasury bill] bon *m* du Trésor.

T-bone (steak) *n* steak *m* dans l'aloyau *(sur l'os).*

tbs., tbsp. (*written abbrev of* **tablespoon(ful)**) cs.

T-cell *n* lymphocyte *m* T.

Tchaikovsky [tʃaɪ'kɒfskɪ] *pr n* Tchaïkovski.

TCP® (*abbrev of* **trichlorophonoxyacetic acid**) *n UK désinfectant utilisé pour nettoyer des petites plaies ou pour se gargariser.*

te [tiː] *n* MUS si *m*.

tea [tiː] *n* **1.** [drink, plant] thé *m* ▪ **a cup of ~** une tasse de thé ▪ **more ~?** encore un peu de thé? ➊ **~ service** service *m* à thé ▪ **I wouldn't do it for all the ~ in China** je ne le ferais à aucun prix OR pour rien au monde **2.** [afternoon snack] thé *m* ▪ [evening meal] repas *m* du soir ▪ **to ask sb to ~** inviter qqn à prendre le thé **3.** [infusion] infusion *f*, tisane *f*.

TEA

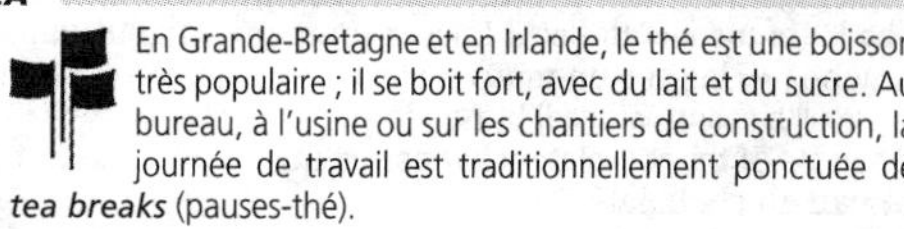

En Grande-Bretagne et en Irlande, le thé est une boisson très populaire ; il se boit fort, avec du lait et du sucre. Au bureau, à l'usine ou sur les chantiers de construction, la journée de travail est traditionnellement ponctuée de *tea breaks* (pauses-thé).

teabag ['tiːbæg] *n* sachet *m* de thé.

tea break *n* pause *f* pour prendre le thé, ≃ pause-café *f*.

tea caddy *n* boîte *f* à thé.

teacake ['tiːkeɪk] *n petite brioche.*

teach [tiːtʃ] (*pret & pp* **taught** [tɔːt]) <> *vt* **1.** [gen] apprendre ▪ **to ~ sb sthg** OR **sthg to sb** apprendre qqch à qqn ▪ **she taught herself knitting/French** elle a appris à tricoter/elle a appris le français toute seule ▪ **you can't ~ them anything!** ils savent tout!, ils n'ont plus rien à apprendre! ▪ **to ~ sb (how) to do sthg** apprendre à qqn à faire qqch ▪ **didn't anyone ever ~ you not to interrupt people?** on ne t'a jamais dit OR appris qu'il ne faut pas couper la parole aux gens? ▮ [as threat] : **I'll ~ you to be rude to your elders!** je vais t'apprendre à être insolent envers les aînés! ▪ **that'll ~ you (not) to go off on your own** ça t'apprendra à t'en aller toute seule ▪ **that'll ~ you (a lesson)!** ça t'apprendra!, c'est bien fait pour toi! ▪ **that taught them a lesson they won't forget** cela leur a donné une leçon dont ils se souviendront ➊ **you can't ~ your grandmother to suck eggs** *inf* on n'apprend pas à un vieux singe à faire la grimace *prov* **2.** SCH [physics, history etc] enseigner, être professeur de ▪ [pupils, class] faire cours à ▪ **she taught us (to speak) French** elle nous a appris OR enseigné le français ▪ **to ~ school** *US* être enseignant.
<> *vi* [as profession] être enseignant, enseigner ▪ [give lessons] faire cours.

teachable ['tiːtʃəbl] *adj* **1.** [subject] que l'on peut enseigner, susceptible d'être enseigné ▪ [children] à qui on peut apprendre quelque chose **2.** *US* ADMIN scolarisable.

teacher ['tiːtʃər] *n* [in primary school] instituteur *m*, - trice *f*, maître *m*, maîtresse *f* ▪ [in secondary school] professeur *mf*, enseignant *m*, - e *f* ▪ [in special school] éducateur *m*, - trice *f* ▪ **French/history ~** professeur de français/d'histoire ➊ **~ pupil ratio** taux *m* d'encadrement.

teacher's aide *n US* assistant *m*, - e *f* pédagogique.

teacher's college *US* = **teacher training college**.

teacher's pet *n* chouchou *m*, - oute *f* du professeur.

teacher training *n UK* formation *f* pédagogique des enseignants ▪ **~ certificate** diplôme *m* d'enseignement.

teacher training college *n* centre *m* de formation pédagogique, ≃ école *f* normale.

tea chest *n* caisse *f* (à thé).

teaching ['tiːtʃɪŋ] <> *n* **1.** [career] enseignement *m* **2.** [of subject] enseignement *m* ▪ **EFL ~** l'enseignement de l'anglais (comme) langue étrangère **3.** *(U)* [hours taught] heures *fpl* d'enseignement, (heures *fpl* de) cours *mpl*.
<> *comp* [profession, staff] enseignant.
◆ **teachings** *npl* [of leader, church] enseignements *mpl*.

teaching aid *n* matériel *m* pédagogique.

teaching diploma *n* diplôme *m* d'enseignement.

teaching hospital *n* centre *m* hospitalo-universitaire, CHU *m*.

teaching practice *n (U)* stage *m* pédagogique *(pour futurs enseignants).*

tea cloth *UK* = **tea towel**.

tea cosy *n* cosy *m*.

teacup ['tiːkʌp] *n* tasse *f* à thé.

tea dance *n* thé *m* dansant.

tea-drinker *n* buveur *m*, - euse *f* de thé.

tea garden *n* [garden] *jardin de restaurant qui fait salon de thé.*

teak [ti:k] <> *n* : **~ (wood)** teck *m*, tek *m*.
<> *comp* en teck.

teakettle ['ti:,ketl] *n* bouilloire *f*.

teal [ti:l] (*pl inv* OR *pl* **teals**) *n* sarcelle *f*.

tea lady *n* UK *dame qui prépare ou sert le thé pour les employés d'une entreprise.*

tealeaf ['ti:li:f] (*pl* **tealeaves** [-li:vz]) *n* **1.** feuille *f* de thé ▪ **to read the tealeaves** ≃ lire dans le marc de café **2.** △ UK *hum* [thief] voleur *m*, -euse *f*.

team [ti:m] <> *n* **1.** SPORT [gen] équipe *f* **2.** [of horses, oxen etc] attelage *m*.
<> *vt* **1.** [workers, players] mettre en équipe ▪ [horses, oxen etc] atteler ▪ **I was ~ed with my brother** j'ai fait équipe avec mon frère **2.** [colours, garments] assortir, harmoniser.
◆ **team up** <> *vt sep* **1.** [workers, players] mettre en équipe ▪ [horses, oxen etc] atteler **2.** [colours, clothes] assortir, harmoniser.
<> *vi insep* **1.** [workers] faire équipe, travailler en collaboration ▪ **to ~ up with sb** faire équipe avec qqn ▪ **the two villages ~ed up to put on the show** les deux villages ont collaboré pour monter le spectacle **2.** [colours, clothes] être assorti, s'harmoniser.

team game *n* jeu *m* d'équipe.

team mate *n* coéquipier *m*, - ère *f*.

team member *n* équipier *m*, - ère *f*.

team player *n* : **to be a (good) ~** avoir l'esprit d'équipe.

team spirit *n* esprit *m* d'équipe.

teamster ['ti:mstər] *n* US routier *m*, camionneur *m*.
◆ **Teamster** *n* US *membre du syndicat américain des camionneurs.*

Teamsters' Union *pr n syndicat américain des camionneurs.*

teamwork ['ti:mw3:k] *n* travail *m* d'équipe.

tea party *n* [for adults] thé *m* ▪ [for children] goûter *m* ▪ **I'm having a little ~ on Sunday** j'ai invité quelques amis à prendre le thé dimanche.

tea plant *n* arbre *m* à thé, théier *m*.

tea plate *n* UK petite assiette *f*, assiette *f* à dessert.

teapot ['ti:pɒt] *n* théière *f*.

tear[1] [teər] (*pret* **tore** [tɔ:r], *pp* **torn** [tɔ:n]) <> *vt* **1.** [rip - page, material] déchirer ; [- clothes] déchirer, faire un accroc à ; [- flesh] déchirer, arracher ▪ **I tore my jacket on a nail** j'ai fait un accroc à ma veste avec un clou ▪ **he tore a hole in the paper** il a fait un trou dans le papier ▪ **'~ along the dotted line'** 'détacher suivant le pointillé' ▪ **the dog was ~ing the meat from a bone** le chien déchiquetait la viande d'un os ▪ **her heart was torn by grief/remorse** elle était déchirée par la douleur/le remords ▪ **she tore open the letter** elle ouvrit l'enveloppe en la déchirant, elle déchira l'enveloppe ▪ **to ~ sthg in two** OR **in half** déchirer qqch en deux ▪ **you can ~ a piece off this cloth** vous pouvez déchirer un morceau de ce tissu ▪ **to ~ sthg to shreds** mettre qqch en lambeaux ▪ **the critics tore the film to shreds** *fig* les critiques ont éreinté le film
2. [muscle, ligament] froisser, déchirer
3. [grab, snatch] arracher ▪ **he tore the cheque from** OR **out of my hand** il m'a arraché le chèque des mains
4. *fig* [divide] tirailler, déchirer ▪ **I'm torn between going and staying** je suis tiraillé entre le désir de partir et celui de rester, j'hésite entre partir et rester ▪ **the country had been torn by civil war for 30 years** ça faisait 30 ans que le pays était déchiré par la guerre civile
5. *fig* [separate] arracher ▪ **sorry to ~ you from your reading, but I need your help** je regrette de vous arracher à votre lecture, mais j'ai besoin de votre aide ▪ **that's torn it** UK *inf*, **that ~s it** US *inf* c'est le bouquet, il ne manquait plus que cela.
<> *vi* **1.** [paper, cloth] se déchirer
2. [as verb of movement] : **to ~ after sb** se précipiter OR se lancer à la poursuite de qqn ▪ **to ~ along** [runner] courir à toute allure ; [car] filer à toute allure ▪ **to ~ up/down the stairs** monter/descendre l'escalier quatre à quatre ▪ **the cyclists came ~ing past** les cyclistes sont passés à toute allure OR vitesse
3. [hurry] : **he tore through the book/the report** il a lu le livre/le rapport très rapidement.
<> *n* [in paper, cloth] déchirure *f* ▪ [in clothes] déchirure *f*, accroc *m* ▪ **this page has a ~ in it** cette page est déchirée ▪ **who's responsible for the ~s in the curtains?** qui a déchiré les rideaux?
◆ **tear apart** *vt sep* **1.** [rip to pieces] déchirer
2. [divide] : **no-one can ~ them apart** [friends] on ne peut pas les séparer, ils sont inséparables ; [fighters] on n'arrive pas à les séparer ▪ **the party was being torn apart by internal strife** le parti était déchiré OR divisé par des luttes intestines.
◆ **tear at** *vt insep* : **to ~ at sthg** déchirer OR arracher qqch.
◆ **tear away** *vt sep* **1.** [remove - wallpaper] arracher, enlever ▪ *fig* [- gloss, façade] enlever
2. [from activity] arracher ▪ **to ~ sb away from sthg** arracher qqn à qqch ▪ **I just couldn't ~ myself away** je ne pouvais tout simplement pas me décider à partir ▪ **surely you can ~ yourself away from your work for ten minutes?** tu ne vas pas me dire que tu ne peux pas t'éloigner de ton travail pendant dix minutes?, tu peux quand même laisser ton travail dix minutes!
◆ **tear down** *vt sep* **1.** [remove - poster] arracher
2. [demolish - building] démolir ▪ *fig* [- argument] démolir, mettre par terre.
◆ **tear into** *vt insep* **1.** [attack, rush at] se précipiter sur ▪ **the boxers tore into each other** les boxeurs se sont jetés l'un sur l'autre
2. *inf* [reprimand] enguirlander, passer un savon à ▪ [criticize] taper sur, descendre (en flèche)
3. [bite into - subj: teeth, knife] s'enfoncer dans
4. [run] : **she came ~ing into the garden** elle a déboulé dans le jardin à toute allure, elle s'est précipitée dans le jardin.
◆ **tear off** *vt sep* **1.** [tape, wrapper] arracher, enlever en arrachant ▪ [along perforations] détacher ▪ [clothing] retirer OR enlever rapidement ⊃ **to ~ sb off a strip** *inf*, **to ~ a strip off sb** UK *inf* passer un savon à qqn, enguirlander qqn
2. *inf* [report, essay etc - do hurriedly] écrire à toute vitesse ; [- do badly] bâcler, torcher.
◆ **tear out** *vt sep* [page] arracher ▪ [coupon, cheque] détacher ▪ **to ~ one's hair (out)** *liter* & *fig* s'arracher les cheveux.
◆ **tear up** *vt sep* **1.** [paper, letter] déchirer (en morceaux) ▪ *fig* [agreement, contract] déchirer
2. [pull up - fence, weeds, surface] arracher ; [- tree] déraciner.

tear[2] [tɪər] *n* larme *f* ▪ **to be in ~s** être en larmes ▪ **to burst into ~s** fondre en larmes ▪ **to shed ~s** verser des larmes ▪ **I shed no ~s over her resignation** sa démission ne m'a pas ému outre mesure OR ne m'a pas arraché de larmes ▪ **to shed ~s of joy** pleurer de joie, verser des larmes de joie ▪ **he had ~s** OR **there were ~s in his eyes** il avait les larmes aux yeux ▪ **to be on the verge of ~s, to be near to ~s** être au bord des larmes ▪ **to be moved to ~s** être ému aux larmes ▪ **to be bored to ~s** *fig* s'ennuyer à mourir.

tearaway ['teərə,weɪ] *n* UK casse-cou *mf inv*.

teardrop ['tɪədrɒp] *n* larme *f*.

tear duct [tɪər-] *n* canal *m* lacrymal.

tearful ['tɪəfʊl] *adj* **1.** [emotional - departure, occasion] larmoyant ; [- story, account] larmoyant, à faire pleurer **2.** [person] en larmes, qui pleure ▪ [face] en larmes ▪ [voice] larmoyant ▪ **I'm feeling a bit ~** j'ai envie de pleurer.

tearfully ['tɪəfʊlɪ] *adv* en pleurant, les larmes aux yeux.

tear gas [tɪər-] *n* gaz *m* lacrymogène.

tearing ['teərɪŋ] <> *n* déchirement *m*.
<> *adj* **1.** *liter* **a ~ sound** [from paper] un bruit de déchirement ; [from stitching] un (bruit de) craquement **2.** UK [as intensifier] : **to be in a ~ hurry** être terriblement pressé.

tearjerker ['tɪə,dʒ3:kər] *n inf* **the film/the book is a real ~** c'est un film/un livre à faire pleurer.

tearoom ['ti:rʊm] *n* salon *m* de thé.

tearstained ['tɪəsteɪnd] *adj* barbouillé de larmes.

tease [ti:z] ◇ *vt* **1.** [person] taquiner ■ [animal] tourmenter **2.** [fabric] peigner ■ [wool] peigner, carder **3.** *US* [hair] crêper.
◇ *vi* faire des taquineries ■ **I'm only teasing** c'est pour rire.
◇ *n inf* **1.** [person] taquin *m*, - e *f* ■ [sexually] allumeuse *f* **2.** [behaviour] taquinerie *f*.
◆ **tease out** *vt sep* **1.** [wool, hair] démêler **2.** [information, facts] faire ressortir ■ **to ~ out a problem** débrouiller *OR* démêler un problème, tirer un problème au clair.

teasel ['ti:zl] (*UK pret & pp* **teaselled**, *cont* **teaselling**) (*US pret & pp* **teaseled**, *cont* **teaseling**) ◇ *n* **1.** BOT cardère *f* **2.** TEX carde *f*.
◇ *vt* [cloth] peigner, démêler.

teaser ['ti:zəʳ] *n inf* **1.** [person] taquin *m*, - e *f* **2.** [problem] problème *m* difficile, colle *f* **3.** [advertisement] aguiche *f*.

tea service, tea set *n* service *m* à thé.

tea shop *n UK* salon *m* de thé.

teasing ['ti:zɪŋ] ◇ *n (U)* **1.** [tormenting] taquineries *fpl* **2.** TEX peignage *m*.
◇ *adj* taquin.

teasingly ['ti:zɪŋlɪ] *adv* pour me/le *etc* taquiner.

Teasmaid® ['ti:zmeɪd] *n UK théière automatique avec horloge incorporée.*

teaspoon ['ti:spu:n] *n* **1.** [spoon] cuiller *f OR* cuillère *f* à café **2.** = **teaspoonful**.

teaspoonful ['ti:spu:n,fʊl] *adj* cuiller *f OR* cuillère *f* à café *(mesure)*.

tea strainer *n* passoire *f* à thé, passe-thé *m inv*.

teat [ti:t] *n* **1.** [on breast] mamelon *m*, bout *m* de sein ■ [of animal] tétine *f*, tette *f* ■ [for milking] trayon *m* **2.** *UK* [on bottle] tétine *f* ■ [dummy] tétine *f*, sucette *f* **3.** TECH téton *m*.

tea table *n* table *f* (mise) pour le thé *OR* à thé.

teatime ['ti:taɪm] *n* l'heure *f* du thé.

tea towel *n UK* torchon *m* (à vaisselle).

tea tray *n* plateau *m* à thé.

tea trolley *n UK* table *f* roulante *(pour servir le thé)*.

tea urn *n* fontaine *f* à thé.

tea wagon *US* = **tea trolley**.

teazel ['ti:zl] (*UK pret & pp* **teazelled**, *cont* **teazelling** *US*, *pret & pp* **teazeled**, *cont* **teazeling**) = **teasel**.

teazle ['ti:zl] = **teasel**.

TEC [tek] (*abbrev of* **Training and Enterprise Council**) *n centre d'emploi et de formation.*

tech [tek] *n inf* = **technical college**.

techie ['tekɪ] *n inf* technicien *m*, - enne *f*.

technical ['teknɪkl] *adj* **1.** [gen - TECH] technique ■ **~ hitch** incident *m* technique **2.** [according to rules] technique ■ **for ~ reasons** pour des raisons d'ordre technique ■ **the judgment was quashed on a ~ point** LAW le jugement a été cassé pour vice de forme *OR* de procédure ■ **it's a purely ~ point** *fig* ce n'est qu'un point de détail ➲ **~ knockout** SPORT knock-out *m inv* technique.

technical college *n* ≃ institut *m* de technologie.

technical drawing *n* dessin *m* industriel.

technical foul *n* SPORT faute *f* technique.

technicality [,teknɪ'kælətɪ] (*pl* **technicalities**) *n* **1.** [technical nature] technicité *f* **2.** [formal detail] détail *m OR* considération *f* (d'ordre) technique ■ [technical term] terme *m* technique ■ **to lose one's case on a ~** LAW perdre un procès pour vice de forme.

technically ['teknɪklɪ] *adv* **1.** [on a technical level] sur un plan technique ■ [in technical terms] en termes techniques ■ **~ advanced** de pointe, sophistiqué, avancé sur le plan technique **2.** [in theory] en théorie, en principe.

technical writing *n* rédaction *f* technique.

technician [tek'nɪʃn] *n* technicien *m*, - enne *f*.

Technicolor® ['teknɪ,kʌləʳ] ◇ *n* Technicolor® *m* ■ **in (glorious) ~** en Technicolor.
◇ *adj* en technicolor.

technique [tek'ni:k] *n* technique *f*.

techno ['teknəʊ] *n* MUS techno *f*.

technobabble ['teknəʊ,bæbl] *n* jargon *m* technique.

technocrat ['teknəkræt] *n* technocrate *mf*.

technological [,teknə'lɒdʒɪkl] *adj* technologique.

technologist [tek'nɒlədʒɪst] *n* technologue *mf*, technologiste *mf*.

technology [tek'nɒlədʒɪ] (*pl* **technologies**) *n* technologie *f*.

technophobe ['teknəfəʊb] *n* technophobe *mf*.

tectonic [tek'tɒnɪk] *adj* tectonique ■ **~ plates** plaques *fpl* tectoniques.

tectonics [tek'tɒnɪks] *n (U)* tectonique *f*.

ted [ted] (*pret & pp* **tedded**, *cont* **tedding**) ◇ *vt* [hay] faner.
◇ *n inf* = **teddy boy**.

teddy ['tedɪ] (*pl* **teddies**) *n* **1.** : **~ (bear)** ours *m* en peluche **2.** [garment] teddy *m*.

teddy boy *n UK* ≃ blouson *m* noir *(personne)*.

tedious ['ti:djəs] *adj* [activity, work] ennuyeux, fastidieux ■ [time] ennuyeux ■ [journey] fatigant, pénible ■ [person] pénible.

tediously ['ti:djəslɪ] *adv* péniblement ■ [monotonously] de façon monotone, fastidieusement.

tediousness ['ti:djəsnɪs] *n* ennui *m*, monotonie *f*.

tedium ['ti:djəm] *n* ennui *m*.

tee [ti:] ◇ *n* [in golf - peg] tee *m* ; [- area] tertre *m OR* point *m* de départ ■ **the 17th ~** le départ du 17ᵉ trou.
◇ *vt* placer sur le tee.
◇ *vi* placer la balle sur le tee.
◆ **tee off** ◇ *vi insep* **1.** [in golf] jouer sa balle *OR* partir du tee *(du tertre de départ)* ■ *fig* commencer, démarrer **2.** *US inf* [get angry] se fâcher, s'emporter.
◇ *vt sep inf US* [annoy] agacer, casser les pieds à ■ **I'm ~d off** j'en ai ras le bol *OR* marre.
◆ **tee up** *vi insep* placer la balle sur le tee.

tee-hee [-'hi:] *interj* hi! hi!

teem [ti:m] *vi* **1.** [be crowded] grouiller, fourmiller ■ **the streets were ~ing (with people)** les rues grouillaient (de monde) ■ **the children came ~ing through the gates** une horde d'enfants a franchi les grilles **2.** [rain] : **it's absolutely ~ing (down *OR* with rain)** il pleut à verse *OR* à torrents.

teeming ['ti:mɪŋ] *adj* **1.** [streets] grouillant de monde ■ [crowds, shoppers] grouillant, fourmillant ■ [ants, insects etc] grouillant **2.** [rain] battant, torrentiel.

teen [ti:n] *adj* [teenage - fashion, magazine] pour adolescents *OR* jeunes ■ **~ idol** idole *f* des jeunes.

teenage ['ti:neɪdʒ] *adj* jeune, adolescent ■ [habits, activities] d'adolescents ■ [fashion, magazine] pour les jeunes ■ **the ~ years** l'adolescence.

teenager ['ti:n,eɪdʒəʳ] *n* jeune *mf (entre 13 et 19 ans)*, adolescent *m*, - e *f*.

teens [ti:nz] *npl* **1.** [age] adolescence *f (entre 13 et 19 ans)* ■ **she's in her ~** c'est une adolescente **2.** [numbers] *les chiffres entre 13 et 19.*

teensy(-weensy) [,ti:nzɪ('wi:nzɪ)] *inf* = **teeny-weeny**.

teeny ['ti:nɪ] *adj inf* tout petit, minuscule.

teenybopper ['ti:nɪ,bɒpəʳ] *n inf jeune qui aime la musique pop.*

teeny-weeny *adj inf* tout petit, minuscule.

teepee ['ti:pi:] = **tepee**.

tee shirt = **T-shirt**.

teeter ['ti:tər] <> *vi* **1.** [person] chanceler ■ [pile, object] vaciller, être sur le point de tomber ■ **to ~ on the brink of sthg** *fig* être au bord de qqch, friser qqch **2.** *US* [see-saw] se balancer, basculer.
<> *n US* jeu *m* de bascule.

teeth [ti:θ] *pl* ⊳ **tooth**.

teethe [ti:ð] *vi* faire OR percer ses premières dents ■ **to be teething** commencer à faire ses dents.

teething ['ti:ðɪŋ] *n* poussée *f* dentaire, dentition *f*.

teething ring *n* anneau *m* de dentition.

teething troubles *npl liter* douleurs *fpl* provoquées par la poussée des dents ■ *fig* difficultés *fpl* initiales OR de départ ■ **we're having ~ with the new computer** nous avons des problèmes de mise en route avec le nouvel ordinateur.

teetotal [ti:'təʊtl] *adj* [person] *qui ne boit jamais d'alcool* ■ [organization] antialcoolique.

teetotaller *UK*, **teetotaler** *US* [ti:'təʊtlər] *n personne qui ne boit jamais d'alcool*.

TEFL ['tefl] (*abbrev of* **Teaching (of) English as a Foreign Language**) *n enseignement de l'anglais langue étrangère*.

Teflon® ['teflɒn] *n* Teflon® *m* ■ **a ~-coated pan** une casserole teflonisée.

tegument ['tegjʊmənt] *n* tégument *m*.

te-hee ['ti:'hi:] = **tee-hee**.

Tehran, Teheran [,teə'rɑ:n] *pr n* Téhéran.

tel. (*written abbrev of* **telephone**) tél.

telebanking ['telɪbæŋkɪŋ] *n* FIN services *mpl* bancaires en ligne, télébanque *f*.

telecast ['telɪkɑ:st] <> *n* émission *f* de télévision, programme *m* télédiffusé.
<> *vt* diffuser, téléviser.

telecom(s) ['telɪkɒm(z)] *n* = **telecommunications**.

telecommunications ['telɪkə,mju:nɪ'keɪʃnz] <> *n (U)* télécommunications *fpl*.
<> *comp* [engineer] des télécommunications ■ [satellite] de télécommunication.

telecommuting [,telɪkə'mju:tɪŋ] *n* télétravail *m*.

teleconference ['telɪ,kɒnfərəns] *n* téléconférence *f*.

teleconferencing [,telɪ'kɒnfərənsɪŋ] *n* téléconférence *f*.

telegram ['telɪgræm] *n* télégramme *m* ■ [in press, diplomacy] dépêche *f* ■ **by ~** par télégramme.

telegraph ['telɪgrɑ:f] <> *n* **1.** [system] télégraphe *m* ■ **the Telegraph** PRESS *nom abrégé du «Daily Telegraph»* ■ **Telegraph reader** *lecteur du «Daily Telegraph» (typiquement conservateur), see also* **broadsheet 2.** [telegram] télégramme *m*.
<> *comp* [service, wire] télégraphique ■ **~ pole** OR **post** poteau *m* télégraphique.
<> *vt* [news] télégraphier ■ [money] télégraphier, envoyer par télégramme.
<> *vi* télégraphier.

telegrapher [tɪ'legrəfər] *n* télégraphiste *mf*.

telegraphic [,telɪ'græfɪk] *adj* télégraphique.

telegraphist [tɪ'legrəfɪst] *n* télégraphiste *mf*.

telegraphy [tɪ'legrəfɪ] *n* télégraphie *f*.

telemarketing ['telɪ,mɑ:kɪtɪŋ] *n* vente *f* par téléphone.

Telemessage® ['telɪ,mesɪdʒ] *n UK* télémessagerie *f*, courrier *m* électronique.

teleology [,telɪ'ɒlədʒɪ] *n* téléologie *f*.

telepathic [,telɪ'pæθɪk] *adj* [person] télépathe ■ [message, means] télépathique.

telepathy [tɪ'lepəθɪ] *n* télépathie *f*, transmission *f* de pensée.

telephone ['telɪfəʊn] <> *n* téléphone *m* ■ **to be on the ~** [talking] être au téléphone, téléphoner ; [subscriber] avoir le téléphone, être abonné au téléphone ■ **the boss is on the ~ for you** le patron te demande au téléphone ■ **you're wanted on the ~** on vous demande au téléphone ■ **to answer the ~** répondre au téléphone ■ **I use the ~ a lot** je téléphone beaucoup.
<> *comp* [line, receiver] de téléphone ■ [call, message] téléphonique ■ [bill, charges] téléphonique, de téléphone ■ [service] des télécommunications.
<> *vt* [person] téléphoner à, appeler (au téléphone) ■ [place] téléphoner à, appeler ■ [news, message, invitation] téléphoner, envoyer par téléphone ■ **to ~ the United States/home** téléphoner aux États-Unis/chez soi.
<> *vi* [call] téléphoner, appeler ■ [be on phone] être au téléphone.

telephone banking *n* FIN banque *f* au téléphone.

telephone book *n* annuaire *m* (téléphonique).

telephone booth, telephone box *n* cabine *f* téléphonique.

telephone directory = **telephone book**.

telephone exchange *n* central *m* téléphonique.

telephone kiosk *UK* = **telephone booth**.

telephone number *n* numéro *m* de téléphone.

telephone-tapping [-'tæpɪŋ] *n* mise *f* sur écoute téléphonique.

telephonic [,telɪ'fɒnɪk] *adj* téléphonique.

telephonist [tɪ'lefənɪst] *n UK* standardiste *mf*, téléphoniste *mf*.

telephony [tɪ'lefənɪ] *n* téléphonie *f*.

telephoto lens [,telɪ'fəʊtəʊ-] *n* téléobjectif *m*.

teleport ['telɪpɔ:t] *vt* téléporter.

teleprinter ['telɪ,prɪntər] *n UK* téléscripteur *m*, téléimprimeur *m*.

Teleprompter® [,telɪ'prɒmptər] *n* prompteur *m*, téléprompteur *m*, télésouffleur *m offic*.

telesales ['telɪseɪlz] *npl* vente *f* par téléphone.

telescope ['telɪskəʊp] <> *n* télescope *m*, longue-vue *f* ■ ASTRON télescope *m*, lunette *f* astronomique.
<> *vt* [shorten, condense - parts, report] condenser, abréger.
<> *vi* **1.** [collapse - parts] s'emboîter **2.** [railway carriages] se télescoper.

telescopic [,telɪ'skɒpɪk] *adj* [aerial] télescopique ■ [umbrella] pliant ■ **~ lens** téléobjectif *m* ■ **~ sight** lunette *f*.

teleshopping [,telɪ'ʃɒpɪŋ] *n* téléachat *m*.

teletex ['telɪteks] *n* Télétex® *m*.

teletext ['telɪtekst] *n* télétexte *m*, vidéographie *f* diffusée.

telethon ['telɪθɒn] *n* Téléthon *m*.

Teletype® ['telɪtaɪp] <> *n* Télétype® *m*.
<> *vt* transmettre parTélétype®.

televangelist [,telɪ'vændʒəlɪst] *n évangéliste qui prêche à la télévision*.

televideo [telɪ'vɪdəʊ] *n* combiné *m* télémagnétoscope.

televiewer ['telɪvju:ər] *n* téléspectateur *m*, - trice *f*.

televise ['telɪvaɪz] *vt* téléviser.

television ['telɪ,vɪʒn] <> *n* **1.** [system, broadcasts] télévision *f* ■ **to watch ~** regarder la télévision ■ **to go on ~** passer à la télévision ■ **to work in ~** travailler à la télévision **2.** [set] téléviseur *m*, (poste *m* de) télévision *f* ■ **I saw her on (the) ~** je l'ai vue à la télévision ■ **to turn the ~ up/down/off/on** monter le son de/baisser le son de/éteindre/allumer la télévision

■ **is there anything good on ~ tonight?** qu'est-ce qu'il y a de bien à la télévision ce soir? ■ **colour/black-and-white ~** télévision *f* (en) couleur/(en) noir et blanc.
<> *comp* [camera, engineer, programme, station, screen] de télévision ■ [picture, news] télévisé ■ [satellite] de télédiffusion ■ **to make a ~ appearance** passer à la télévision ■ **~ film** téléfilm *m*, film *m* pour la télévision ■ **~ lounge** salle *f* de télévision.

television licence *n UK* redevance *f* (de télévision).

television set *n* téléviseur *m*, (poste *m* de) télévision *f*.

telework ['telɪwɜːk] *vi* télétravailler.

teleworker ['telɪwɜːkəʳ] *n* télétravailleur *m*, - euse *f*.

teleworking [,telɪ'wɜːkɪŋ] *n* télétravail *m*.

telex ['teleks] <> *n* télex *m*.
<> *vt* envoyer par télex, télexer.

tell [tel] (*pret & pp* **told** [təʊld]) <> *vt* **1.** [inform of] dire à ■ **to ~ sb sthg** dire qqch à qqn ■ **I told him the answer/what I thought** je lui ai dit la réponse/ce que je pensais ■ **to ~ sb about** *OR* **of** *lit* **sthg** dire qqch à qqn, parler à qqn de qqch ■ **they told me (that) they would be late** ils m'ont dit qu'ils seraient en retard ■ **I'm pleased to ~ you you've won** j'ai le plaisir de vous informer *OR* annoncer que vous avez gagné ■ **let me ~ you how pleased I am** laissez-moi vous dire *OR* permettez-moi de vous dire à quel point je suis heureux ■ **I'm told he's coming tomorrow** j'ai entendu dire *OR* on m'a dit qu'il venait demain ■ **so I've been told** c'est ce qu'on m'a dit ■ **it doesn't ~ us much** cela ne nous en dit pas très long, cela ne nous apprend pas grand-chose ■ **can you ~ me the time?** pouvez-vous me dire l'heure (qu'il est)? ■ **can you ~ me your name/age?** pouvez-vous me dire votre nom/âge? ➔ **a little bird told me!** c'est mon petit doigt qui me l'a dit!
2. [explain to] expliquer à, dire à ■ **this brochure ~s me all I need to know** cette brochure m'explique tout ce que j'ai besoin de savoir ■ **can you ~ me the way to the station/to Oxford?** pouvez-vous m'indiquer le chemin de la gare/la route d'Oxford? ■ **do you want me to ~ you again?** voulez-vous que je vous le redise *OR* répète? ■ **who can ~ me the best way to make omelettes?** qui peut me dire *OR* m'expliquer la meilleure façon de faire des omelettes? ➔ **if I've told you once, I've told you a thousand times!** je te l'ai dit cent fois! ■ **(I'll) ~ you what, let's play cards** j'ai une idée, on n'a qu'à jouer aux cartes
3. [instruct, order] : **to ~ sb to do sthg** dire à qqn de faire qqch ■ **I thought I told you not to run?** je croyais t'avoir interdit *OR* défendu de courir? ■ **he didn't need to be told twice!** il ne s'est pas fait prier!, je n'ai pas eu besoin de lui dire deux fois!
4. [recount - story, joke] raconter ; [- news] annoncer ; [- secret] dire, raconter ■ **to ~ sb about sthg** parler à qqn de qqch, raconter qqch à qqn ■ **~ them about** *OR* **of your life as an explorer** racontez-leur votre vie d'explorateur ■ **could you ~ me a little about yourself?** pourriez-vous me parler un peu de vous-même? ■ **I told myself it didn't matter** je me suis dit que cela n'avait pas d'importance ■ **I could ~ you a thing or two about his role in it** je pourrais vous en dire long sur son rôle dans tout cela ■ **don't ~ me, let me guess!** ne me dites rien, laissez-moi deviner! ■ **~ it like it is!** *inf* n'ayez pas peur de dire la vérité! ➔ **~ that to the marines!** *inf*, **~ me another!** *inf* à d'autres!, mon œil!
5. [utter - truth, lie] dire, raconter ■ **to ~ sb the truth** dire la vérité à qqn ■ **to ~ lies** mentir, dire des mensonges ■ **I ~ a lie!** *fig* je me trompe!
6. [assure] dire, assurer ■ **didn't I ~ you?, I told you so!** je vous l'avais bien dit! ■ **let me ~ you!** [believe me] je vous assure!, croyez-moi! ; [as threat] tenez-vous-le pour dit! ■ **I can ~ you!** c'est moi qui vous le dis! ➔ **you're ~ing me!** *inf*, **~ me about it!** *inf* à qui le dites-vous!
7. [distinguish] distinguer ■ **to ~ right from wrong** distinguer le bien du mal ■ **you can hardly ~ the difference between them** on voit *OR* distingue à peine la différence entre eux ■ **how can you ~ one from another?** comment les distinguez-vous l'un de l'autre? ▮ [see] voir ■ [know] savoir ■ [understand] comprendre ■ **how can you ~ when it's ready?** à quoi voit-on *OR* comment peut-on savoir que c'est prêt? ■ **no one could ~ whether the good weather would last** personne ne pouvait dire si le beau temps allait durer ■ **there's no ~ing what he might do next/how he'll react** (il est) impossible de dire ce qu'il est susceptible de faire ensuite/comment il réagira.
<> *vi* **1.** [reveal] : **that would be ~ing!** ce serait trahir un secret! ■ **I won't ~** je ne dirai rien à personne ■ **time will ~** qui vivra verra, le temps nous le dira ■ **more than words can ~** plus que les mots ne peuvent dire
2. [know] savoir ■ **how can I ~?** comment le saurais-je? ■ **who can ~?** qui peut savoir?, qui sait? ■ **you never can ~** on ne sait jamais
3. [have effect] se faire sentir, avoir de l'influence ■ **breeding ~s** *UK* bon sang ne saurait mentir *prov* ■ **her age is beginning to ~** elle commence à accuser son âge ■ **the strain is beginning to ~** la tension commence à se faire sentir ■ **her aristocratic roots told against her** ses origines aristocratiques lui nuisaient
4. *lit* [story, book] : **to ~ of sthg** raconter qqch ■ **I've heard ~ of phantom ships** j'ai entendu parler de navires fantômes
5. *lit* [bear witness] : **to ~ of** témoigner de ■ **the scars told of his reckless life** ses cicatrices témoignaient de sa vie mouvementée.

◆ **tell apart** *vt sep* distinguer (entre) ■ **I couldn't ~ the twins apart** je ne pouvais pas distinguer les jumeaux l'un de l'autre.

◆ **tell off** *vt sep* **1.** [scold] réprimander, gronder ■ **to ~ sb off for doing sthg** gronder *OR* réprimander qqn pour avoir fait qqch
2. [select] affecter, désigner.

◆ **tell on** *vt insep* **1.** [denounce] dénoncer
2. [have effect on] se faire sentir sur, produire un effet sur ■ **the strain soon began to ~ on her health** la tension ne tarda pas à avoir un effet néfaste sur sa santé.

teller ['teləʳ] *n* **1.** [in bank] : **(bank) ~** caissier *m*, - ère *f*, guichetier *m*, - ère *f* **2.** POL [of votes] scrutateur *m*, - trice *f* **3.** [of story] : **(story) ~** conteur *m*, - euse *f*, narrateur *m*, - trice *f*.

telling ['telɪŋ] <> *adj* **1.** [revealing - smile, figures, evidence] révélateur, éloquent ■ **a ~ look** un regard qui en dit long **2.** [effective - style] efficace ; [- account] saisissant ; [- remark, argument] qui porte ■ **it was a ~ blow** le coup fut bien asséné *OR* porta.
<> *n* récit *m*, narration *f* ■ **the story is long in the ~** l'histoire est longue à raconter.

telling-off (*pl* **tellings-off**) *n* réprimande *f* ■ **to get a good ~** se faire gronder ■ **to give sb a ~** réprimander qqn.

telltale ['telteɪl] <> *n* **1.** [person] rapporteur *m*, - euse *f* **2.** MECH indicateur *m* ■ **~ lamp** lampe *f* témoin.
<> *adj* [marks] révélateur ■ [look, blush, nod] éloquent.

telly ['telɪ] (*pl* **tellies**) *n UK inf* télé *f* ■ **on the ~** à la télé.

temerity [tɪ'merətɪ] *n* témérité *f*, audace *f*.

temp [temp] <> *n* (*abbrev of* **temporary employee**) intérimaire *mf*.
<> *vi* : **she's ~ing** elle fait de l'intérim.

temp. (*written abbrev of* **temperature**) temp.

temper ['tempəʳ] <> *n* **1.** [character] caractère *m*, tempérament *m* ■ **to have an even ~** être d'un tempérament calme *OR* d'humeur égale ■ **to have a quick** *OR* **hot ~** se mettre facilement en colère ■ **he's got a foul** *OR* **an awful ~** il a mauvais caractère ▮ [patience] patience *f* ■ [calm] calme *m*, sang-froid *m inv* ■ **do try and keep** *OR* **hold your ~** essayez donc de garder votre calme *OR* sang-froid, essayez donc de vous maîtriser ■ **to lose one's ~** perdre patience, se mettre en colère ■ **to lose one's ~ with sb** s'emporter contre qqn ■ **don't try my ~** ne m'énerve pas **2.** [mood] humeur *f* ■ **to be in a bad ~** être de mauvaise humeur ▮ [bad mood] (crise *f* de) colère *f*, mauvaise humeur *f* ■ **to be in a ~** être de mauvaise humeur **3.** METALL trempe *f*.
<> *vt* **1.** [moderate - passions] modérer, tempérer ; [- pain, suffering] adoucir ■ **justice ~ed with mercy** la justice tempérée de pitié **2.** METALL tremper.
<> *interj* : **~!** on se calme!, du calme!

temperament ['temprəmənt] *n* [character] tempérament *m*, nature *f* ■ [moodiness] humeur *f* changeante *OR* lunatique.

temperamental [ˌtemprəˈmentl] *adj* **1.** [moody - person] capricieux, lunatique ■ [unpredictable - animal, machine] capricieux **2.** [relating to character] du tempérament, de la personnalité.

temperamentally [ˌtemprəˈmentəlɪ] *adv* de par son caractère.

temperance [ˈtemprəns] ◇ *n* **1.** [moderation] modération *f*, sobriété *f* **2.** [abstinence from alcohol] tempérance *f*.
◇ *comp* [movement] antialcoolique ■ **~ hotel** *hôtel où l'on ne sert pas de boissons alcoolisées.*

temperate [ˈtemprət] *adj* **1.** [climate] tempéré **2.** [moderate - person] modéré, mesuré ; [- character, appetite] modéré ; [- reaction, criticism] modéré, sobre.

Temperate Zone *pr n* zone *f* tempérée.

temperature [ˈtemprətʃəʳ] ◇ *n* **1.** MED température *f* ■ **to have** *OR* **to run a ~** avoir de la température *OR* de la fièvre ■ **she has a ~ of 39°C** elle a 39° de fièvre ■ **to take sb's ~** prendre la température de qqn ■ **to take the ~ of a situation** *fig* prendre le pouls d'une situation ■ **her contribution certainly raised the ~ of the debate** son intervention a sans aucun doute fait monter le ton du débat **2.** METEOR & PHYS température *f* ■ **the ~ fell overnight** la température a baissé du jour au lendemain ■ **~s will be in the low twenties** il fera un peu plus de vingt degrés.
◇ *comp* [change] de température ■ [control] de la température ■ [gradient] thermique ■ **~ chart** feuille *f* de température ■ **~ gauge** indicateur *m* de température.

tempered [ˈtempəd] *adj* **1.** [steel] trempé **2.** MUS [scale] tempéré.

temper tantrum *n* crise *f* de colère ■ **to have** *OR* **to throw a ~** piquer une colère.

tempest [ˈtempɪst] *n lit* tempête *f*, orage *m*.

tempestuous [temˈpestjʊəs] *adj* **1.** [weather] de tempête **2.** [person] impétueux, fougueux ■ [meeting] agité ■ **a ~ love affair** une liaison orageuse *OR* tumultueuse.

tempi [ˈtempiː] *pl* ▷ **tempo**.

Templar [ˈtempləʳ] *n* [in crusades] : **Knight ~** chevalier *m* du Temple, templier *m*.

template [ˈtemplɪt] *n* **1.** TECH gabarit *m*, calibre *m*, patron *m* **2.** [beam] traverse *f* **3.** COMPUT masque *m* de saisie.

temple [ˈtempl] *n* **1.** RELIG temple *m* **2.** ANAT tempe *f*.

Temple Bar *pr n porte ouest de la City de Londres où le maire vient accueillir le souverain.*

tempo [ˈtempəʊ] (*pl* **tempos** *OR pl* **tempi** [ˈtempiː]) *n* tempo *m*.

temporal [ˈtempərəl] *adj* **1.** [gen - GRAM] temporel **2.** [secular] temporel, séculier.

temporarily [*UK* ˈtempərərəlɪ, *US* ˌtempəˈrerəlɪ] *adv* provisoirement, temporairement.

temporary [ˈtempərərɪ] (*pl* **temporaries**) ◇ *adj* [accommodation, solution, powers] temporaire, provisoire ■ [employment] temporaire, intérimaire ■ [improvement] passager, momentané ■ [relief] passager ■ **on a ~ basis** à titre temporaire ■ **a ~ appointment** une nomination temporaire *OR* provisoire ■ **~ teacher** SCH professeur *m* suppléant.
◇ *n* intérimaire *mf*.

temporary restraining order *n US* LAW injonction *f* du tribunal.

temporize, ise [ˈtempəraɪz] *vi fml* [try to gain time] temporiser, chercher à gagner du temps.

tempt [tempt] *vt* [entice] tenter, donner envie à ■ [seduce] tenter, séduire ■ [attract] attirer, tenter ■ **to ~ sb to do sthg** *OR* **into doing sthg** donner à qqn l'envie de faire qqch ■ **did you hit him? – no, but I was sorely ~ed** tu l'as frappé? – non, mais ce n'est pas l'envie qui m'en manquait ■ **I'm ~ed to accept their offer** je suis tenté d'accepter leur proposition ■ **don't ~ me!** *hum* n'essayez pas de me tenter!, ne me tentez pas! ■ **can I ~ you to another sandwich?** je peux vous proposer encore un sandwich?, vous voulez encore un sandwich? ➤ **to ~ fate/providence** tenter le diable/le sort.

temptation [tempˈteɪʃn] *n* tentation *f* ■ **to put ~ in sb's way** exposer qqn à la tentation ■ **it's a great ~** c'est très tentant ■ **to give in to ~** céder *OR* succomber à la tentation.

tempter [ˈtemptəʳ] *n* tentateur *m*.

tempting [ˈtemptɪŋ] *adj* [offer] tentant, attrayant ■ [smell, meal] appétissant.

temptress [ˈtemptrɪs] *n lit & hum* tentatrice *f*.

ten [ten] ◇ *det* dix.
◇ *n* dix *m* ■ **~s of thousands of refugees** des dizaines de milliers de réfugiés ■ **~ to one** [in ratio, bets] dix contre un ■ **~ to one we won't sell anything** je te parie que nous ne vendrons rien.
◇ *pron* dix.
◆ **tens** *npl* MATHS dizaines *fpl* ■ **~s column** colonne *f* des dizaines, *see also* **five**.

tenable [ˈtenəbl] *adj* **1.** [argument, position] défendable, soutenable **2.** [post] que l'on occupe, auquel on est nommé ■ **the appointment is ~ for a five-year period** on est nommé à ce poste pour cinq ans.

tenacious [tɪˈneɪʃəs] *adj* **1.** [stubborn, persistent - person] entêté, opiniâtre ; [- prejudice, opposition] tenace, obstiné **2.** [firm - grip] ferme, solide.

tenaciously [tɪˈneɪʃəslɪ] *adv* avec ténacité, obstinément.

tenacity [tɪˈnæsətɪ] *n* ténacité *f*, opiniâtreté *f*.

tenancy [ˈtenənsɪ] (*pl* **tenancies**) ◇ *n* **1.** [of house, land] location *f* ■ **to take up the ~ on a house** prendre une maison en location **2.** [period] : **(period of) ~** (période *f* de) location *f* ■ **during his ~ of Government House** *fig* pendant qu'il était gouverneur **3.** [property] : **a council ~** un logement appartenant à la municipalité, ≃ une HLM.
◇ *comp* de location.

tenant [ˈtenənt] ◇ *n* locataire *mf*.
◇ *comp* [rights] du locataire.

tenant farmer *n* métayer *m*, - ère *f*.

tenantry [ˈtenəntrɪ] *n* AGRIC ensemble *m* des tenanciers *OR* locataires.

ten-cent store *n US* bazar *m*.

tench [tenʃ] (*pl inv*) *n* tanche *f*.

tend [tend] ◇ *vi* **1.** [be inclined] : **to ~ to** avoir tendance à, tendre à ■ **that does ~ to be the case** c'est souvent le cas **2.** [colour] : **red ~ing to orange** rouge tirant sur l'orange **3.** [go, move] tendre ■ **his writings ~ to** *OR* **towards exoticism** ses écrits tendent vers l'exotisme ■ **in later life, she ~ed more towards a Marxist view of things** vers la fin de sa vie, elle inclina *OR* évolua vers des idées marxistes **4.** [look after] : **she ~ed to his every wish** elle lui a passé tous ses caprices, elle a fait ses quatre volontés ■ **to ~ to one's business/one's guests** s'occuper de ses affaires/ses invités ■ **to ~ to sb's wounds** panser *OR* soigner les blessures de qqn.
◇ *vt* **1.** [take care of - sheep] garder ; [- sick, wounded] soigner ; [- garden] entretenir, s'occuper de **2.** *US* [customer] servir.

tendency [ˈtendənsɪ] (*pl* **tendencies**) *n* **1.** [inclination] tendance *f* ■ **he has a ~ to forget things** il a tendance à tout oublier ■ **she has a natural ~ to** *OR* **towards laziness** elle est d'un naturel paresseux ■ **to have suicidal tendencies** avoir des tendances suicidaires **2.** [trend] tendance *f* ■ **a growing ~ towards conservatism** une tendance de plus en plus marquée vers le conservatisme **3.** POL tendance *f*, groupe *m*.

tendentious [tenˈdenʃəs] *adj* tendancieux.

tender [ˈtendəʳ] ◇ *adj* **1.** [affectionate - person] tendre, affectueux, doux, douce *f* ; [- heart, smile, words] tendre ; [- memories] doux, douce *f* ➤ **~ loving care : to need some ~ loving care** avoir besoin d'être dorloté ■ **with ~ loving care** avec beaucoup de tendresse **2.** [sensitive - skin] délicat, fragile ■ [sore] sensible, douloureux ■ **my knee is still ~** mon genou me fait encore mal ■ **to touch sb on a ~ spot** *fig* toucher le point

sensible de qqn **3.** [meat, vegetables] tendre **4.** *lit* [innocent - age, youth] tendre ▪ **she gave her first concert at the ~ age of six** elle a donné son premier concert alors qu'elle n'avait que six ans.
◇ *vt* **1.** [resignation] donner ▪ [apologies] présenter ▪ [thanks] offrir ▪ [bid, offer] faire **2.** [money, fare] tendre ▪ **to ~ sthg to sb** tendre qqch à qqn.
◇ *vi* faire une soumission ▪ **to ~ for a contract** faire une soumission pour une adjudication, soumissionner une adjudication.
◇ *n* **1.** *UK* [statement of charges] soumission *f* ▪ [bid] offre *f* ▪ **to put in** *OR* **to submit a ~ for a job** soumissionner un travail, faire une soumission pour un travail ▪ **to put a job out to ~, to invite ~s for a job** faire un appel d'offres pour un travail **2.** RAIL tender *m* **3.** NAUT [shuttle] navette *f* ▪ [supply boat] ravitailleur *m* **4.** [supply vehicle] véhicule *m* ravitailleur ▪ **(fire) ~** *UK* voiture *f* de pompier.

tenderfoot ['tendəfʊt] (*pl* **tenderfoots** *OR pl* **tenderfeet** [-fi:t]) *n* **1.** [beginner] novice *mf*, nouveau *m*, nouvelle *f* **2.** *US inf* [newcomer] nouveau venu *m*, nouvelle venue *f*.

tenderhearted [,tendə'hɑ:tɪd] *adj* au cœur tendre, compatissant.

tenderize, ise ['tendəraɪz] *vt* attendrir.

tenderizer ['tendəraɪzər] *n* attendrisseur *m*.

tenderloin ['tendəlɔɪn] *n* **1.** [meat] filet *m* **2.** *US* [district] quartier *m* chaud *(connu pour sa corruption)*.

tenderly ['tendəlɪ] *adv* tendrement, avec tendresse.

tenderness ['tendənɪs] *n* **1.** [of person, feelings] tendresse *f*, affection *f* **2.** [of skin] sensibilité *f* ▪ [of plant] fragilité *f* ▪ [soreness] sensibilité *f* **3.** [of meat, vegetables] tendreté *f*.

tendon ['tendən] *n* tendon *m*.

tendril ['tendrəl] *n* **1.** BOT vrille *f*, cirre *m* **2.** [of hair] boucle *f*.

tenement ['tenəmənt] *n* **1.** [block of flats] immeuble *m* (ancien) **2.** [slum] taudis *m* **3.** [dwelling] logement *m*.

tenement building *n* immeuble *m* (ancien).

tenement house *n* maison *f* divisée en appartements.

Tenerife [,tenə'ri:f] *pr n* Tenerife, Ténériffe ▪ **in ~** à Tenerife.

tenet ['tenɪt] *n* [principle] principe *m*, dogme *m* ▪ [belief] croyance *f*.

tenfold ['tenfəʊld] ◇ *adv* dix fois autant *OR* plus, au décuple ▪ **to increase ~** décupler.
◇ *adj* : **a ~ increase in applications** dix fois plus de demandes.

ten-gallon hat *n* chapeau *m* de cowboy.

tenner ['tenər] *n UK inf* billet *m* de 10 livres.

Tennessee [,tenə'si:] *pr n* Tennessee *m* ▪ **in ~** dans le Tennessee.

tennis ['tenɪs] ◇ *n* tennis *m* ▪ **to have** *OR* **to play a game of ~** faire une partie de tennis.
◇ *comp* [ball, court, player, racket] de tennis.

tennis elbow *n (U)* tennis-elbow *m*, synovite *f* du coude.

tennis shoe *n* (chaussure *f* de) tennis *f*.

tennis whites *npl* tenue *f* de tennis.

tenon ['tenən] ◇ *n* tenon *m*.
◇ *vt* tenonner.

tenor ['tenər] ◇ *n* **1.** [general sense - of conversation] sens *m* général, teneur *f* ; [- of letter] contenu *m*, teneur *f* **2.** [general flow - of events] cours *m*, marche *f* **3.** MUS ténor *m*.
◇ *comp* [part, voice] de ténor ▪ [aria] pour (voix de) ténor ▪ **~ recorder** flûte *f* à bec ▪ **~ saxophone** saxophone *m* ténor.
◇ *adv* : **to sing ~** avoir une voix de *OR* être ténor.

tenpin bowling ['tenpɪn-] *n UK* bowling *m*.

tenpins ['tenpɪnz] *n US* bowling *m*.

tense [tens] ◇ *adj* **1.** [person, situation] tendu ▪ [smile] crispé ▪ **her voice was ~ with emotion** elle avait la voix étranglée par l'émotion ▪ **we spent several ~ hours waiting for news** nous avons passé plusieurs heures à attendre des nouvelles dans un état de tension nerveuse **2.** [muscles, rope, spring] tendu ▪ **to become ~** se tendre **3.** LING [vowel] tendu.
◇ *vt* [muscle] tendre, bander ▪ **to ~ oneself** se raidir.
◇ *n* GRAM temps *m*.
◆ **tense up** ◇ *vi insep* [muscle] se tendre, se raidir ▪ [person] se crisper, devenir tendu ▪ **don't ~ up** détends-toi, décontracte-toi.
◇ *vt sep* [person] rendre nerveux ▪ **she's all ~d up** elle est vraiment tendue.

tensely ['tenslɪ] *adv* [move, react] de façon tendue ▪ [speak] d'une voix tendue ▪ **they waited ~ for the doctor to arrive** ils ont attendu le médecin dans un état de grande tension nerveuse.

tensile ['tensaɪl] *adj* MECH extensible, élastique ▪ **~ stress** force *f* de tension.

tensile strength *n* résistance *f* à la tension, limite *f* élastique à la tension.

tension ['tenʃn] *n* **1.** [of person, situation, voice] tension *f* **2.** [of muscle, rope, spring] tension *f* **3.** ELEC tension *f*, voltage *m* **4.** MECH & TECH tension *f*, (force *f* de) traction *f*.

tension headache *n* mal *m* de tête dû à la tension nerveuse.

tensor ['tensər] *n* ANAT & MATHS tenseur *m*.

ten-spot *n US inf* billet *m* de dix dollars.

tent [tent] ◇ *n* [for camping] tente *f* ▪ **to put up** *OR* **to pitch a ~** monter une tente.
◇ *comp* [peg, pole] de tente.
◇ *vi* camper.

tentacle ['tentəkl] *n* tentacule *m*.

tentative ['tentətɪv] *adj* **1.** [provisional] provisoire ▪ [preliminary] préliminaire ▪ [experimental] expérimental ▪ **our plans are only ~** nos projets ne sont pas définitifs **2.** [uncertain - smile] timide ; [- person] indécis, hésitant ; [- steps] hésitant.

tentatively ['tentətɪvlɪ] *adv* **1.** [suggest] provisoirement ▪ [act] à titre d'essai **2.** [smile] timidement ▪ [walk] d'un pas hésitant.

tenterhooks ['tentəhʊks] *npl* TEX clous *mpl* à crochet ▪ **to be on ~** être sur des charbons ardents.

tenth [tenθ] ◇ *adj* dixième.
◇ *n* **1.** [gen - MATHS] dixième *m* **2.** MUS dixième *f*.
◇ *adv* en dixième place, à la dixième place, *see also* **fifth**.

tenuous ['tenjʊəs] *adj* **1.** [fine - distinction] subtil, ténu ; [- thread] ténu **2.** [flimsy - link, relationship] précaire, fragile ; [- evidence] mince, faible ; [- argument] faible **3.** [precarious - existence] précaire.

tenuously ['tenjʊəslɪ] *adv* de manière ténue *OR* précaire.

tenuousness ['tenjʊəsnɪs] *n* **1.** [of distinction] subtilité *f* ▪ [of thread] ténuité *f* ▪ [of voice] faiblesse *f* **2.** [of link, relationship] fragilité *f*, précarité *f* ▪ [of evidence] minceur *f*, faiblesse *f* ▪ [of argument] faiblesse *f* **3.** [of existence] précarité *f* **4.** PHYS raréfaction *f*.

tenure ['tenjər] *n* **1.** [of land, property] bail *m* **2.** [of post] occupation *f* ▪ **during his ~ as chairman** pendant qu'il occupait le poste de président *OR* était président ▪ **to have ~** *US* UNIV être titulaire.

tenure-tracked *adj US* **he's got a ~ job** son poste est en voie de titularisation.

tepee ['ti:pi:] *n* tipi *m*.

tepid ['tepɪd] *adj* **1.** [water] tiède **2.** [welcome, thanks] tiède, réservé.

tequila [tɪ'ki:lə] *n* tequila *f*.

Ter. *written abbr of* **terrace**.

terbium ['tɜ:bɪəm] *n* terbium *m*.

tercentenary [ˌtɜːsen'tiːnərɪ] (*pl* **tercentenaries**), **tercentennial** [ˌtɜːsen'tenjəl] ◇ *n* tricentenaire *m*.
◇ *adj* du tricentenaire.

Teresa [tə'riːzə] *pr n* : **~ of Avila** sainte Thérèse d'Avila ▪ **Mother ~** Mère Teresa.

term [tɜːm] ◇ *n* **1.** [period, end of period] terme *m* ▪ [of pregnancy] terme *m* ▪ **in the long/short ~** à long/court terme ▪ **to reach (full) ~** arriver *OR* être à terme
2. SCH & UNIV trimestre *m* ▪ **in** *OR* **during ~ (time)** pendant le trimestre
3. LAW & POL [of court, parliament] session *f* ▪ [of elected official] mandat *m* ▪ **the president is elected for a 4-year ~** le président est élu pour (une période *OR* une durée de) 4 ans ▸ **during my ~ of office** [gen] pendant que j'étais en fonction ; POL pendant mon mandat
4. [in prison] peine *f* ▪ **~ of imprisonment** peine de prison ▪ **to serve one's ~** purger sa peine
5. [word, expression] terme *m* ▪ **she spoke of you in very flattering ~s** elle a parlé de vous en (des) termes très flatteurs ▪ **she told him what she thought in no uncertain ~s** elle lui a dit carrément ce qu'elle pensait
6. LOGIC & MATHS terme *m*.
◇ *vt* appeler, nommer ▪ **I wouldn't ~ it a scientific book exactly** je ne dirais pas vraiment que c'est un livre scientifique.
◆ **terms** *npl* **1.** [conditions - of employment] conditions *fpl* ; [- of agreement, contract] termes *mpl* ▪ **under the ~s of the agreement** selon les termes de l'accord ▪ **~s of payment** modalités *fpl* de paiement ▪ **what are the inquiry's ~s of reference?** quelles sont les attributions *OR* quel est le mandat de la commission d'enquête? ▪ **to dictate ~s to sb** imposer des conditions à qqn ▪ **she would only accept on her own ~s** elle n'était disposée à accepter qu'après avoir posé ses conditions ▪ **not on any ~s** à aucun prix, à aucune condition
2. [perspective] : **he refuses to consider the question in international ~s** il refuse d'envisager la question d'un point de vue international ▪ **in personal ~s, it was a disaster** sur le plan personnel, c'était une catastrophe
3. [rates, tariffs] conditions *fpl*, tarifs *mpl* ▪ **we offer easy ~s** nous proposons des facilités de paiement ▮ [in hotel] : **weekly ~s** tarifs à la semaine
4. [relations] : **to be on good ~s with sb** être en bons termes avec qqn ▪ **on equal ~s** d'égal à égal ▪ **they're no longer on speaking ~s** ils ne se parlent plus
5. [agreement] accord *m* ▪ **to make ~s** *OR* **to come to ~s with sb** arriver à *OR* conclure un accord avec qqn ▮ [acceptance] : **to come to ~s with sthg** se résigner à qqch, arriver à accepter qqch.
◆ **in terms of** *prep phr* en ce qui concerne, pour ce qui est de ▪ **in ~s of profits, we're doing well** pour ce qui est des bénéfices, tout va bien ▪ **I was thinking more in ~s of a Jaguar** je pensais plutôt à une Jaguar.

termagant ['tɜːməgənt] *n* mégère *f*, harpie *f*.

terminal ['tɜːmɪnl] ◇ *adj* **1.** [final] terminal ▪ **~ station** RAIL terminus *m* ▪ **~ velocity** vitesse *f* limite **2.** MED [ward] pour malades condamnés *OR* incurables ▪ [patient] en phase terminale ▪ [disease] qui est dans sa phase terminale ▪ **he has ~ cancer** il a un cancer en phase terminale **3.** [termly] trimestriel.
◇ *n* **1.** [for bus, underground] terminus *m* ▪ [at airport] terminal *m*, aérogare *f* ▪ **~ (platform)** PETR terminal **2.** COMPUT terminal *m* **3.** ELEC [of battery] borne *f* **4.** LING terminaison *f*.

terminally ['tɜːmɪnəlɪ] *adv* : **the ~ ill** les malades condamnés *OR* qui sont en phase terminale.

terminate ['tɜːmɪneɪt] ◇ *vt* **1.** [end - project, work] terminer ; [- employment] mettre fin *OR* un terme à ; [- contract] résilier, mettre fin *OR* un terme à ; [- pregnancy] interrompre **2.** *US inf* [employee] virer **3.** *inf* [kill] descendre.
◇ *vi* **1.** [end] se terminer ▪ **the row ~d in** *OR* **with her resignation** la dispute s'est terminée par sa démission **2.** LING se terminer **3.** RAIL : **this train ~s at Cambridge** ce train ne va pas plus loin que Cambridge.

termination [ˌtɜːmɪ'neɪʃn] *n* **1.** [end - gen] fin *f* ; [- of contract] résiliation *f* ▪ **~ of employment** licenciement *m* **2.** [abortion] interruption *f* de grossesse, avortement *m* **3.** LING terminaison *f*, désinence *f*.

termini ['tɜːmɪnaɪ] *pl* ▷ **terminus**.

terminological [ˌtɜːmɪnə'lɒdʒɪkl] *adj* terminologique.

terminologist [ˌtɜːmɪ'nɒlədʒɪst] *n* terminologue *mf*.

terminology [ˌtɜːmɪ'nɒlədʒɪ] (*pl* **terminologies**) *n* terminologie *f*.

term insurance *n* assurance *f* à terme.

terminus ['tɜːmɪnəs] (*pl* **terminuses** *OR pl* **termini** ['tɜːmɪnaɪ]) *n* terminus *m*.

termite ['tɜːmaɪt] *n* termite *m*, fourmi *f* blanche.

termly ['tɜːmlɪ] ◇ *adj* trimestriel.
◇ *adv* trimestriellement, par trimestre.

term paper *n US* SCH & UNIV dissertation *f* trimestrielle.

tern [tɜːn] *n* hirondelle *f* de mer, sterne *f*.

Terr *written abbr of* **terrace**.

terrace ['terəs] *n* **1.** AGRIC & GEOL terrasse *f* **2.** [patio] terrasse *f* **3.** [embankment] terre-plein *m* **4.** *UK* [of houses] rangée *f* **5.** = **terraced house**.
◆ **terraces** *npl* SPORT gradins *mpl* ▪ **on the ~s** dans les gradins.

TERRACE

Ce terme désigne une rangée de maisons mitoyennes à un ou deux étages. À l'origine, les ***terraced houses*** étaient des logements ouvriers, construits à proximité des usines ou des mines de charbon.

terraced ['terəst] *adj* [garden] suspendu, étagé, en terrasses ▪ [hillside] cultivé en terrasses.

terraced house *n UK maison faisant partie d'une "terrace"* ▪ **~s** maisons *fpl* alignées.

terracotta [ˌterə'kɒtə] ◇ *n* [earthenware] terre *f* cuite.
◇ *comp* [pottery] en terre cuite ▪ [colour] rouille *(inv)*.

terra firma [ˌterə'fɜːmə] *n lit* & *hum* terre *f* ferme.

terrain [te'reɪn] *n* terrain *m*.

terrapin ['terəpɪn] *n* tortue *f* d'eau douce.

terrarium [tə'reərɪəm] *n* [for plants] mini-serre *f* ▪ [for reptiles] terrarium *m*.

Terrence Higgins Trust [ˌterəns'hɪgɪnz-] *pr n* : **the ~** *association britannique de lutte contre le sida.*

terrestrial [tə'restrɪəl] ◇ *adj* terrestre.
◇ *n* terrien *m*, - enne *f*.

terrible ['terəbl] *adj* **1.** [severe, serious - cough, pain] affreux, atroce ; [- accident] effroyable, affreux ; [- storm] effroyable ▪ **it caused ~ damage** cela a provoqué d'importants dégâts ▪ **it was a ~ blow** ce fut un coup terrible **2.** [very bad - experience, dream] atroce ; [- food, smell] épouvantable ; [- conditions, poverty] épouvantable, effroyable ▪ **to feel ~** [ill] se sentir très mal ; [morally] s'en vouloir beaucoup, avoir des remords ▪ **I feel ~ about the whole situation** je m'en veux beaucoup pour tout ce qui s'est passé ▪ **I feel ~ about leaving them on their own** cela m'ennuie terriblement de les laisser seuls ▪ **I was always ~ at French** j'ai toujours été nul en français ▪ **the food was a ~ disappointment** on a été terriblement déçus par la nourriture.

terribly ['terəblɪ] *adv* **1.** *inf* [as intensifier] terriblement, extrêmement ▪ **I'm ~ sorry** je suis vraiment désolé ▪ **she's ~ clever** elle est drôlement *OR* rudement intelligente **2.** [very badly] affreusement mal, terriblement mal.

terrier ['terɪəʳ] *n* terrier *m (chien)*.

terrific [tə'rɪfɪk] *adj* **1.** [extreme, intense - noise, crash] épouvantable, effroyable ; [- speed] fou *(before vowel or silent 'h'* **fol**), folle *f* ; [- heat] terrible, épouvantable ; [- appetite] énorme, robuste ■ **these trees grow to a ~ height** ces arbres atteignent une taille énorme **2.** *inf* [superb, great] terrible, super ■ **you look ~ in that dress** cette robe te va super bien.

terrifically [tə'rɪfɪklɪ] *adv inf* **1.** [extremely, enormously] extrêmement, très **2.** [very well] merveilleusement (bien).

terrified ['terɪfaɪd] *adj* terrifié ■ **to be ~ of sthg** avoir une peur bleue *OR* avoir très peur de qqch.

terrify ['terɪfaɪ] (*pret & pp* **terrified**) *vt* terrifier, effrayer.

terrifying ['terɪfaɪɪŋ] *adj* [dream] terrifiant ■ [person] terrible, épouvantable ■ [weaker use] terrifiant, effroyable ■ **what a ~ thought!** rien que d'y penser, je frémis!

terrifyingly ['terɪfaɪɪŋlɪ] *adv* de façon terrifiante *OR* effroyable.

terrine [te'ri:n] *n* terrine *f*.

territorial [ˌterɪ'tɔ:rɪəl] ◇ *adj* territorial.
◇ *n* territorial *m* ■ **the Territorials** l'armée *f* territoriale *OR* la territoriale britannique.

Territorial Army *pr n* (armée *f*) territoriale *f* britannique.

territorialism [ˌterə'tɔ:rɪəlɪzm] *n* territorialisme *m*.

territorial waters *npl* eaux *fpl* territoriales.

territory ['terətrɪ] (*pl* **territories**) *n* [area] territoire *m* ■ [of salesperson] territoire *m*, région *f* ■ [of knowledge] domaine *m*.

terror ['terəʳ] *n* **1.** [fear] terreur *f*, épouvante *f* ■ **to be in a state of ~** être terrorisé *OR* terrifié ■ **to have a ~ of (doing) sthg** avoir extrêmement peur *OR* la terreur de (faire) qqch **2.** [frightening event or aspect] terreur *f* **3.** [terrorism] terreur *f* **4.** *inf* [person] terreur *f*.
◆ **Terror** *n* : **the Terror** HIST la Terreur.

terrorism ['terərɪzm] *n* terrorisme *m*.

terrorist ['terərɪst] ◇ *n* terroriste *mf*.
◇ *adj* [bomb] de terroriste ■ [campaign, attack, group] terroriste.

terrorize, ise ['terəraɪz] *vt* terroriser.

terror-stricken, terror-struck *adj* épouvanté, saisi de terreur.

terry (towelling) ['terɪ-] *n* : **~ (cloth)** tissu-éponge *m*.

terse [tɜ:s] *adj* [concise] concis, succinct ■ [laconic] laconique ■ [abrupt] brusque, sec, sèche *f*.

tersely ['tɜ:slɪ] *adv* [concisely] avec concision ■ [laconically] laconiquement ■ [abruptly] brusquement, sèchement.

terseness ['tɜ:snɪs] *n* [concision] concision *f* ■ [laconicism] laconisme *m* ■ [abruptness] brusquerie *f*.

tertiary ['tɜ:ʃərɪ] *adj* [gen - INDUST] tertiaire ■ [education] postscolaire.
◆ **Tertiary** ◇ *adj* GEOL tertiaire.
◇ *n* : **the Tertiary** GEOL le tertiaire.

Terylene® ['terəli:n] ◇ *n* Térylène® *m*, ≃ Tergal® *m*.
◇ *adj* en Tergal®.

TESL ['tesl] (*abbrev of* **Teaching (of) English as a Second Language**) *n* enseignement *m* de l'anglais langue seconde.

TESSA ['tesə] (*abbrev of* **tax-exempt special savings account**) *n en Grande-Bretagne, plan d'épargne exonéré d'impôt.*

tessellated ['tesəleɪtɪd] *adj* en mosaïque.

tessitura [ˌtesɪ'tʊərə] *n* tessiture *f*.

test [test] ◇ *n* **1.** [examination - gen] test *m* ■ SCH contrôle *m*, interrogation *f* ■ **to pass a ~** réussir à un examen ■ **biology ~** interrogation de biologie ■ **to sit** *OR* **to take a ~** passer un examen ▶ **I'm taking my (driving) ~ tomorrow** je passe mon permis (de conduire) demain ■ **did you pass your (driving) ~?** avez-vous été reçu au permis (de conduire)?
2. MED [of blood, urine] test *m*, analyse *f* ■ [of eyes, hearing] examen *m* ■ **to have a blood ~** faire faire une analyse de sang ■ **to have an eye ~** se faire examiner la vue ■ **the lab did a ~ for salmonella** le laboratoire a fait une analyse pour détecter la présence de salmonelles
3. [trial - of equipment, machine] test *m*, essai *m*, épreuve *f* ; [- of quality] contrôle *m* ■ **to carry out ~s on sthg** effectuer des tests sur qqch ■ **all new drugs undergo clinical ~s** tous les nouveaux médicaments subissent des tests cliniques ■ **to be on ~** être testé *OR* à l'essai ■ **to put sthg to the ~** tester qqch, faire l'essai de qqch
4. [of character, endurance, resolve] test *m* ■ **to put sb to the ~** éprouver qqn, mettre qqn à l'épreuve ■ **his courage was really put to the ~** son courage fut sérieusement mis à l'épreuve *OR* éprouvé ■ **to stand the ~** se montrer à la hauteur ▶ **~ of strength** *liter & fig* épreuve *f* de force ■ **to stand the ~ of time** durer, résister à l'épreuve du temps ■ **her books have certainly stood the ~ of time** ses livres n'ont pas pris une ride
5. [measure] test *m* ■ **it's a ~ of union solidarity** c'est un test de la solidarité syndicale
6. *UK* SPORT test-match *m*.
◇ *comp* [flight, strip etc] d'essai.
◇ *vt* **1.** [examine - ability, knowledge, intelligence] tester, mesurer ■ SCH [pupils] tester, contrôler les connaissances de ■ **we were ~ed in geography** nous avons eu un contrôle de géographie ■ **she was ~ed on her knowledge of plants** on a testé *OR* vérifié ses connaissances botaniques
2. MED [blood, urine] analyser, faire une analyse de ■ [sight, hearing] examiner ■ **to have one's eyes ~ed** se faire examiner la vue ■ **you need your eyes ~ing!** *UK OR* **~ed!** *US fig* il faut mettre des lunettes!
3. [try out - prototype, car] essayer, faire l'essai de ; [- weapon] tester ; [- drug] tester, expérimenter ■ **none of our products are ~ed on animals** nos produits ne sont pas testés sur les animaux
4. [check - batteries, pressure, suspension] vérifier, contrôler
5. [measure - reaction, popularity] mesurer, évaluer
6. [analyse - soil] analyser, faire des prélèvements dans ; [- water] analyser ■ **to ~ food for starch** rechercher la présence d'amidon dans les aliments ▶ **to ~ the water** tâter le terrain
7. [tax - machinery, driver, patience] éprouver, mettre à l'épreuve ■ **to ~ sb to the limit** pousser qqn à bout *OR* à la dernière extrémité ■ **to ~ sb's patience to the limit** mettre la patience de qqn à rude épreuve.
◇ *vi* **1.** [make examination] : **to ~ for salmonella** faire une recherche de salmonelles ■ **to ~ for the presence of gas** rechercher la présence de gaz
2. RADIO & TELEC : **~ ing, ~ing!** un, deux, trois!
◆ **test out** *vt sep* **1.** [idea, theory] tester
2. [prototype, product] essayer, mettre à l'essai ■ **these products are ~ed out on animals** ces produits sont testés sur les animaux.

testament ['testəmənt] *n* **1.** LAW testament *m* **2.** BIBLE testament *m* ■ **the New Testament** le Nouveau Testament ■ **the Old Testament** l'Ancien Testament.

testate ['testeɪt] *adj* : **to die ~** mourir en ayant laissé un testament *OR* testé.

test ban *n* interdiction *f* des essais nucléaires.

test-bed *n* banc *m* d'essai *OR* d'épreuve.

test card *n UK* TV mire *f*.

test case *n* LAW précédent *m*, affaire *f* qui fait jurisprudence.

test drive (*pret* **test-drove**, *pp* **test-driven**) *n* essai *m* sur route.
◆ **test-drive** *vt* [car] essayer.

tester ['testəʳ] *n* **1.** [person] contrôleur *m*, - euse *f*, vérificateur *m*, - trice *f* **2.** [machine] appareil *m* de contrôle *OR* de vérification **3.** [sample - of make-up, perfume] échantillon *m* **4.** [over bed] baldaquin *m*, ciel *m*.

testicle ['testɪkl] *n* testicule *m*.

testify ['testɪfaɪ] (*pret & pp* **testified**) ◇ *vt* déclarer, affirmer ■ **I can ~ that she remained at home** je peux attester qu'elle est restée à la maison.

<> *vi* [be witness] porter témoignage, servir de témoin ■ [make statement] déposer, faire une déposition ■ **to ~ for/against sb** déposer en faveur de/contre qqn ■ **I can ~ to her honesty** je peux attester OR témoigner de son honnêteté ■ **his behaviour testified to his guilt** son comportement témoignait de sa culpabilité.

testimonial [ˌtestɪˈməʊnjəl] <> *n* **1.** [certificate] attestation *f* ■ [reference] recommandation *f*, attestation *f* **2.** [tribute] témoignage *m*.
<> *comp* qui porte témoignage ■ **~ match** UK jubilé *m*.

testimony [UK ˈtestɪmənɪ, US ˈtestəməʊnɪ] (*pl* **testimonies**) *n* **1.** [statement] déclaration *f* ■ LAW témoignage *m*, déposition *f* **2.** [sign, proof] témoignage *m* ■ **to bear ~ to the truth** porter OR rendre témoignage de la vérité ■ **the monument is a lasting ~ to** OR **of his genius** ce monument est le témoignage vivant de son génie.

testing [ˈtestɪŋ] <> *adj* [difficult] difficile, éprouvant.
<> *n* **1.** [of product, machine, vehicle] (mise *f* à l')essai *m* **2.** MED [of sight, hearing] examen *m* ■ [of blood, urine] analyse *f* ■ [of reaction] mesure *f* **3.** [of intelligence, knowledge, skills] évaluation *f* ■ [of candidate] évaluation *f*, examen *m*.

testing bench *n* banc *m* d'essai.

testing ground *n* terrain *m* d'essai.

test match *n* UK match *m* international, test-match *m*.

testosterone [teˈstɒstərəʊn] *n* testostérone *f*.

test paper *n* **1.** CHEM papier *m* réactif **2.** UK SCH interrogation *f* écrite.

test pattern *n* US mire *f*.

test piece *n* MUS morceau *m* imposé OR de concours.

test pilot *n* pilote *m* d'essai.

test run *n* essai *m* ■ **to go for a ~** faire un essai.

test tube *n* éprouvette *f*.
◆ **test-tube** *adj* de laboratoire.

test-tube baby *n* bébé-éprouvette *m*.

testy [ˈtestɪ] (*comp* **testier**, *superl* **testiest**) *adj* irritable, grincheux.

tetanus [ˈtetənəs] <> *n* tétanos *m*.
<> *comp* [vaccination, injection] antitétanique.

tetchily [ˈtetʃɪlɪ] *adv* d'un ton irrité.

tetchy [ˈtetʃɪ] (*comp* **tetchier**, *superl* **tetchiest**) *adj* UK grincheux, irascible.

tête-à-tête [ˌteɪtɑːˈteɪt] <> *n* (conversation *f* en) tête-à-tête *m inv*.
<> *adj* en tête-à-tête.

tether [ˈteðəʳ] <> *n* [for horse] longe *f*, attache *f* ■ **to be at the end of one's ~** [depressed] être au bout du rouleau ; [exasperated] être à bout de patience.
<> *vt* [horse] attacher.

Teutonic [tjuːˈtɒnɪk] *adj* teuton.

Tex *n* **1.** *written abbr of* **Texan** **2.** *written abbr of* **Texas**.

Texan [ˈteksn] <> *n* Texan *m*, - e *f*.
<> *adj* texan.

Texas [ˈteksəs] *pr n* Texas *m* ■ **in ~** au Texas.

Tex-Mex [ˌteksˈmeks] *n* **1.** CULIN *cuisine mexicaine adaptée aux goûts américains* **2.** [music] musique *f* mexico-américaine.

text [tekst] <> *n* **1.** [gen - COMPUT] texte *m* **2.** TELEC mini-message *m*.
<> *comp* **1.** COMPUT : **~ mode** mode *m* texte ■ **~ processing** traitement *m* automatique de texte sur ordinateur **2.** TELEC : **~-message** mini-message *m* ■ **~-messaging** *(U)* TELEC service *m* de mini-messages.
<> *vi* TELEC envoyer un mini-message (à qqn).

TEXT MESSAGING

Comme partout ailleurs, la messagerie électronique sur téléphones portables est très en vogue dans les pays anglo-saxons. Pour la rendre plus rapide, on a l'habitude d'employer de simples lettres ou chiffres pour représenter des mots ou des syllabes qui ont le même son. Par exemple, « u » = « you » (donc « urs » = « yours », etc), « 2 » = « to » ou « too », « 4 » = « for », « b4 » = « before », « w8 » = « wait ».

textbook [ˈtekstbʊk] <> *n* SCH [gen] manuel *m*.
<> *comp* [typical] typique ■ [ideal] parfait, idéal ■ **it's a ~ case** c'est un exemple classique OR typique.

textile [ˈtekstaɪl] <> *n* textile *m*.
<> *comp* [industry] textile.

texting [ˈtekstɪŋ] *n (U)* TELEC service *m* de mini-messages.

textual [ˈtekstjʊəl] *adj* textuel, de texte ■ **~ analysis** analyse *f* de texte ■ **~ criticism** critique *f* littéraire d'un texte.

textually [ˈtekstjʊəlɪ] *adv* textuellement, mot à mot.

texture [ˈtekstʃəʳ] *n* **1.** [of fabric] texture *f* ■ [of leather, wood, paper, skin, stone] grain *m* **2.** [of food, soil] texture *f*, consistance *f* ■ [of writing] structure *f*, texture *f*.

TFT [ˌtiːefˈtiː] (*abbrev of* **thin-film transistor**) *adj* TFT ■ **TFT screen** écran *m* TFT.

TGWU (*abbrev of* **Transport and General Workers' Union**) *pr n le plus grand syndicat interprofessionnel britannique*.

Thai [taɪ] (*pl inv* OR *pl* **Thais**) <> *n* **1.** [person] Thaï *mf*, Thaïlandais *m*, - e *f* **2.** LING thaï *m*, thaïlandais *m*.
<> *adj* thaï, thaïlandais ■ **~ boxing** boxe *f* thaïlandaise.

Thailand [ˈtaɪlænd] *pr n* Thaïlande *f* ■ **in ~** en Thaïlande.

thalidomide [θəˈlɪdəmaɪd] *n* thalidomide *f*.

thalidomide baby *n bébé victime de la thalidomide*.

Thames [temz] *pr n* : **the (River) ~** la Tamise.

than (*weak form* [ðən], *strong form* [ðæn]) <> *conj* **1.** [after comparative adj, adv] que ■ **he plays tennis better ~ I do** il joue au tennis mieux que moi ■ **it's quicker by train ~ by bus** ça va plus vite en train qu'en bus **2.** [following negative clause] : **nothing is worse ~ to spend** OR **spending the holidays on your own** rien n'est pire que de passer les vacances tout seul **3.** [with 'rather', 'sooner'] : **I'd do anything rather ~ have to see him** je ferais n'importe quoi plutôt que d'être obligé de le voir ■ **I'd prefer to stay here rather ~ go out, I'd rather** OR **sooner stay here ~ go out** je préférerais rester ici que de sortir **4.** [after 'different'] : **he is different ~ he used to be** il n'est plus le même.
<> *prep* **1.** [after comparative adj, adv] que ■ **the cedars are older ~ the oaks** les cèdres sont plus vieux que les chênes **2.** [indicating quantity, number] : **more ~ 15 people** plus de 15 personnes ■ **less** OR **fewer ~ 15 people** moins de 15 personnes ■ **there are more policemen ~ demonstrators** il y a plus de policiers que de manifestants **3.** [after 'other' in negative clauses] : **we have no sizes other ~ 40 or 42** nous n'avons pas d'autres tailles que 40 ou 42 ■ **it was none other ~ the Prime Minister who launched the appeal** c'est le Premier ministre en personne qui a lancé l'appel **4.** [after 'different'] : **she seems different ~ before** elle semble avoir changé ■ **she has different tastes ~ yours** elle a des goûts différents des vôtres.

thane [θeɪn] *n* HIST thane *m*, ≃ baron *m*.

thank [θæŋk] *vt* **1.** remercier ■ **to ~ sb for sthg** remercier qqn de OR pour qqch ■ **Mary Edwards ~s Mr. Wilson for his kind invitation** *fml* Mary Edwards remercie M. Wilson de son invitation ■ **to ~ sb for doing sthg** remercier qqn d'avoir fait qqch ■ **I can't ~ you enough for what you've done** je ne sais comment vous remercier pour ce que vous avez fait pour moi ■ **you have him to ~ for that** tu peux lui dire merci ■ **you won't ~ me for it** vous allez m'en vouloir ■ **you only have yourself to ~ for that!** c'est à toi seul qu'il faut t'en prendre! ■ **~ God** OR **goodness!** Dieu merci! **2.** [as request] : **I'll ~ you to keep quiet about it** je vous prierai de ne pas en parler.
◆ **thanks** <> *npl* **1.** remerciements *mpl* ■ **give her my ~s for the flowers** remerciez-la de ma part pour les fleurs

■ **(many) ~s for all your help** merci (beaucoup) pour toute votre aide ■ **received with ~s** ADMIN pour acquit **2.** RELIG louange *f*, grâce *f* ■ **~s be to God** rendons grâce à Dieu.
◇ *interj* merci ■ **~s a lot, ~s very much** merci beaucoup, merci bien ■ **~s a million** merci mille fois ■ **~s for coming** merci d'être venu ■ **no ~s!** (non) merci! ■ **~s for nothing!** je te remercie! *iron.*
◆ **thanks to** *prep phr* grâce à ■ **~s to you, we lost the contract** à cause de vous, nous avons perdu le contrat ■ **no ~s to you!** ce n'est sûrement pas grâce à vous!
Voir module d'usage

thankful ['θæŋkful] *adj* reconnaissant, content ■ **I'm ~ for all their help** je leur suis reconnaissant de toute leur aide ■ **she was just ~ (that) no one recognized her** elle s'estimait surtout heureuse que personne ne l'ait reconnue ■ **I'm only ~ everything went off all right** je me félicite que tout se soit bien passé.

thankfully ['θæŋkfulı] *adv* **1.** [with gratitude] avec reconnaissance *OR* gratitude **2.** [with relief] avec soulagement **3.** [fortunately] heureusement.

thankfulness ['θæŋkfulnıs] *n* gratitude *f*, reconnaissance *f*.

thankless ['θæŋklıs] *adj* [task, person] ingrat.

thanksgiving ['θæŋks,gıvıŋ] *n* action *f* de grâce.

Thanksgiving (Day) *n fête nationale américaine célébrée le 4e jeudi de novembre.*

THANKSGIVING

Jour d'action de grâce, célébré aux États-Unis le quatrième jeudi du mois de novembre pour remercier Dieu de la récolte et de toutes les bonnes choses qui ont pu arriver dans l'année. L'origine de cette fête fédérale remonte à 1621, alors que les *Pilgrims* (colons britanniques) récoltaient leur première moisson. Le dîner familial qui a lieu en cette occasion est traditionnellement composé d'une dinde aux airelles accompagnée de patates douces et se termine par une tarte au potiron.

thanks offering *n fml* action *f* de grâce.

thank you *interj* merci ■ **to say ~** dire merci ■ **~ very** *OR* **so much** merci beaucoup *OR* bien ■ **~ for coming** merci d'être venu.
◆ **thank you** *n* merci *m*, remerciement *m* ■ **without so much as a thank you** sans même dire merci.

thank-you letter ['θæŋkju:-] *n* lettre *f* de remerciement.

that [ðæt (*weak form of rel pron and conj* [ðət])] (*pl* **those** [ðəuz]) ◇ *demonstrative pronoun* **1.** [thing indicated] cela, ce, ça ■ **after/before ~** après/avant cela ■ **what's ~?** qu'est-ce que c'est que ça? ■ **who's ~?** [gen] qui est-ce? ; [on phone] qui est à l'appareil? ■ **is ~ you Susan?** c'est toi Susan? ■ **what did she mean by ~?** qu'est-ce qu'elle voulait dire par là? ■ **those are my parents** voilà mes parents ■ **~ is where I live** c'est là que j'habite ■ **~ was three months ago** il y a trois mois de cela ■ **I've only got one coat and ~'s old** je n'ai qu'un manteau et encore, il est vieux ■ **so THAT'S how it works!** c'est donc comme ça que ça marche! ■ **~'s as may be** peut-être bien ▶ **it's not as hot as (all) ~!** *inf* il ne fait pas si chaud que ça! ■ **so it's come to ~** voilà donc où nous en sommes (arrivés) ■ **if it comes to ~, you can always leave** si ça en arrive là, vous pouvez toujours partir ■ **~'s a good boy!** en voilà un gentil petit garçon! ■ **~'s all we need!** il ne manquait plus que ça! ■ **~'s enough (of ~)!** ça suffit! ■ **~'s it!** [finished] c'est fini! ; [correct] c'est ça! ■ **~'s more like it!** voilà qui est déjà mieux! ■ **well, ~'s ~!** eh bien voilà! ■ **I said "no" and ~'s ~!** j'ai dit "non", un point c'est tout! ■ **~'s the government all over** *OR* **for you!** c'est bien l'administration ça! ■ **is she intelligent? – ~ she is!** elle est intelligente? – ça oui *OR* pour sûr!
2. [in contrast to 'this'] celui-là *m*, celle-là *f* ■ **those** ceux-là *mpl*, celles-là *f* ■ **this is an ash, ~ is an oak** ceci est un frêne et ça, c'est un chêne ■ **which book do you prefer, this or ~?** quel livre préférez-vous, celui-ci ou celui-là?
3. [used when giving further information] celui *m*, celle *f* ■ **those** ceux *mpl*, celles *f* ■ **there are those who believe that...** il y a des gens qui croient que... ■ **a sound like ~ of a baby crying** un bruit comme celui que fait un bébé qui pleure ■ **all those interested should contact the club secretary** tous ceux qui sont intéressés doivent contacter le secrétaire du club.
◇ *det* **1.** [the one indicated] ce *m*, cet *m* (*before vowel or silent 'h'*), cette *f* ■ **those** ces *mf pl* ■ **~ man** homme ■ **at ~ moment** à ce moment-là ■ **it was raining ~ day** il pleuvait ce jour-là ■ **we all agree on ~ point** nous sommes tous d'accord là-dessus ■ **I like ~ idea of his** j'aime son idée ■ **how's ~ son of yours?** comment va ton fils? ■ **if I get hold of ~ son of yours** *pej* si je mets la main sur ton sacré fils!
2. [in contrast to 'this'] ce...-là *m*, cet...-là *m* (*before vowel or silent 'h'*), cette...-là *f* ■ **those** ces...-là *mf pl* ■ **~ house over there is for sale** cette *OR* la maison là-bas est à vendre ■ **~ one** celui-là *m*, celle-là *f*.
◇ *adv* **1.** [so] si, aussi ■ **can you run ~ fast?** pouvez-vous courir aussi vite que ça? ■ **he's not (all) ~ good-looking** il n'est pas si beau que ça ■ **there's a pile of papers on my desk ~ high!** il y a une pile de papiers haute comme ça sur mon bureau!
2. *inf* [with result clause] si, tellement ■ **I could have cried, I was ~ angry** j'en aurais pleuré tellement j'étais en colère.
◇ *rel pron* **1.** [subject of verb] qui ■ **the conclusions ~ emerge from this** les conclusions qui en ressortent ■ **nothing ~ matters** rien d'important
2. [object or complement of verb] que ■ **the house ~ Jack built** la maison que Jack a construite ■ **is this the best ~ you can do?** est-ce que c'est ce que vous pouvez faire de mieux? ■ **fool ~ I am, I agreed** imbécile que je suis, j'ai accepté ■ **pessimist/optimist ~ he is** pessimiste/optimiste comme il est
3. [object of preposition] lequel *m*, laquelle *f*, lesquels *mpl*, lesquelles *f* ■ **the box ~ I put it in/on** le carton dans lequel/sur lequel je l'ai mis ■ **the songs ~ I was thinking of** *OR* **about** les

THANKS

Saying thank you

Merci beaucoup. Thank you very much.

Je vous remercie. Thank you.

Merci mille fois *OU* **infiniment.** Many thanks.

Merci, c'est très gentil à vous. Thanks, that's very kind of you.

Je ne sais comment vous remercier. I can't thank you enough.

Je vous remercie de *OU* **pour votre aide.** Thank you for your help.

Je voulais vous remercier de m'avoir encouragé. I wanted to thank you for encouraging me.

Merci (beaucoup) de m'avoir dépanné l'autre jour. Thanks (a lot) for helping me out the other day.

Je vous suis très reconnaissant de votre soutien. I'm very grateful for your support.

Responding to thanks

De rien. Don't mention it.

Je t'en prie/Je vous en prie. You're welcome.

Ce n'est rien. Don't mention it.

Il n'y a pas de quoi. Not at all.

Tout le plaisir est pour moi. My pleasure.

Oh de rien, n'hésitez pas... Any time!

chansons auxquelles je pensais ▪ **the woman/the film ~ we're talking about** la femme/le film dont nous parlons ▪ **not ~ I know of** pas que je sache
4. [when] où ▪ **during the months ~ we were in Chicago** pendant les mois que nous avons passés *OR* où nous étions à Chicago.
◇ *conj* **1.** [gen] que ▪ **I said ~ I had read it** j'ai dit que je l'avais lu ▪ **it's not ~ she isn't friendly** ce n'est pas qu'elle ne soit pas amicale ▪ **~ he is capable has already been proven** *fml* il a déjà prouvé qu'il était capable ▪ **~ I should live to see the day when...** *fml* [expressing incredulity] je n'aurais jamais cru qu'un jour... ▪ **oh, ~ it were possible!** si seulement c'était possible! **2.** *arch* & *lit* [in order that] afin que, pour que.
◆ **and (all) that** *adv phr inf* [and so on] et tout le bastringue.
◆ **at that** *adv phr* **1.** [what's more] en plus ▪ **it's a forgery and a pretty poor one at ~** c'est une copie et une mauvaise en plus **2.** *inf* [indicating agreement] en fait ▪ **perhaps we're not so badly off at ~** en fait, on n'est peut-être pas tellement à plaindre **3.** [then] à ce moment-là.
◆ **like that** *inf* ◇ *adj phr* **1.** [indicating character or attitude] comme ça
2. [close, intimate] comme les deux doigts de la main ▪ **he's like ~ with the boss** il est au mieux avec le patron.
◇ *adv phr* [in that way] comme ça.
◆ **not that** *conj phr* : **if he refuses, not ~ he will, is there an alternative?** s'il refuse, même si cela est peu probable, est-ce qu'il y a une autre solution? ▪ **he's already left, not ~ it matters** il est déjà parti, encore que ce soit sans importance.
◆ **that is (to say)** *adv phr* enfin ▪ **I'd like to ask you something, ~ is, if you've got a minute** j'aimerais vous poser une question, enfin, si vous avez un instant.
◆ **that way** *adv phr* **1.** [in that manner] de cette façon ▪ **what makes him act ~ way?** qu'est-ce qui le pousse à agir comme ça?
2. *inf* [in that respect] : **she's funny ~ way** c'est son côté bizarre ▪ **I didn't know he was ~ way inclined** je ne connaissais pas ce côté-là de lui.
◆ **with that** *adv phr* là-dessus.

thatch [θætʃ] ◇ *n* **1.** CONSTR chaume *m* **2.** *UK inf fig* [hair] tignasse *f*.
◇ *comp* [roof] de *OR* en chaume.
◇ *vt* [roof] couvrir de chaume.

thatched [θætʃt] *adj* [roof] en chaume ▪ [house] qui a un toit en chaume ▪ **~ cottage** chaumière *f*.

thatcher ['θætʃər] *n* couvreur *m* en chaume.

Thatcherism ['θætʃərɪzm] *n* POL thatchérisme *m (politique de Margaret Thatcher)*.

Thatcherite ['θætʃəraɪt] ◇ *n* partisan *m* du thatchérisme.
◇ *adj* [policy, view] thatchérien.

that's = that is.

thaw [θɔ:] ◇ *vi* **1.** [ice, snow] fondre ▪ **it's beginning to ~** il commence à dégeler **2.** [frozen food] dégeler, se décongeler **3.** [hands, feet] se réchauffer **4.** *fig* [person, relations] se dégeler, être plus détendu ▪ **she seems at last to be ~ing towards me** elle semble enfin perdre sa réserve *OR* sa froideur à mon égard.
◇ *vt* **1.** [ice, snow] faire dégeler *OR* fondre **2.** [frozen food] dégeler, décongeler.
◇ *n* **1.** METEOR dégel *m* **2.** POL détente *f*, dégel *m*.
◆ **thaw out** ◇ *vt sep* **1.** [frozen food] décongeler, dégeler **2.** [feet, hands] réchauffer **3.** *fig* [make relaxed - person] dégeler, mettre à l'aise.
◇ *vi insep* **1.** [frozen food] décongeler, dégeler **2.** [hands, feet] se réchauffer **3.** *fig* [become relaxed] se dégeler, perdre sa froideur *OR* réserve.

the *(weak form* [ðə], *before vowel* [ðɪ], *strong form* [ði:]*) det* **1.** [with noun, adj] le *m*, la *f*, l' *mf (before vowel or silent 'h')*, les *mf pl* ▪ **~ blue dress is ~ prettiest** la robe bleue est la plus jolie ▪ **translated from ~ Latin** traduit du latin **2.** [with names, titles] : **~ Smiths/Martins** les Smith/Martin **3.** [with numbers, dates] : **Monday June ~ tenth** *OR* **~ tenth of June** le lundi 10 juin ▪ **~ 80s** les années 80 ▪ **~ 1820s** les années 1820 à 1830 **4.** [in prices, quantities] : **tomatoes are 40p ~ pound** les tomates sont à 40 pence la livre ▪ **the car does 40 miles to ~ gallon** la voiture consomme 7 litres aux 100 **5.** [with comparatives] : **~ more ~ better** plus il y en a, mieux c'est ▪ **~ less said ~ better** moins on en parlera, mieux cela vaudra **6.** [stressed form] : **for him Bach is THE composer** pour lui, Bach est le compositeur par excellence ▪ **do you mean THE John Irving?** vous voulez dire le célèbre John Irving? **7.** [enough] le *m*, la *f*, l' *mf (before vowel or silent 'h')*, les *mf pl* ▪ **I haven't ~ time/money to do it** je n'ai pas le temps de/l'argent pour le faire **8.** [instead of 'your', 'my' etc] : **how's ~ wife?** *inf* comment va ta femme? ▪ **I've brought ~ family along** j'ai emmené la famille.

theatre *UK*, **theater** *US* ['θɪətər] ◇ *n* **1.** [building] théâtre *m* ▪ **to go to the ~** aller au théâtre ▪ **movie ~** *US* cinéma *m* **2.** [form] théâtre *m*, art *m* dramatique ▪ [plays in general] théâtre *m* ▪ [profession] théâtre *m* ▪ **Greek/modern ~** le théâtre antique/moderne ▪ **I've been in the ~ for over 30 years** je fais du théâtre depuis plus de 30 ans **3.** [hall] salle *f* de spectacle ▪ [for lectures] salle *f* de conférences ▪ UNIV amphithéâtre *m* **4.** MED : **(operating) ~** salle *f* d'opération ▪ **she's in (the) ~** [doctor] elle est en salle d'opération ; [patient] elle est sur la table d'opération **5.** *fig* [for important event] théâtre *m* ▪ **~ of war** MIL théâtre des hostilités.
◇ *comp* **1.** [programme, tickets] de théâtre ▪ [manager] du théâtre ▪ **~ company** troupe de théâtre, compagnie théâtrale ▪ **~ workshop** atelier *m* de théâtre **2.** MED [staff, nurse] de salle d'opération ▪ [routine, job] dans la salle d'opération.

theatregoer ['θɪətə,gəʊər] *n* amateur *m* de théâtre.

theatre in the round *n* théâtre *m* en rond.

theatreland ['θɪətəlænd] *n UK* quartier *m* des théâtres.

theatrical [θɪ'ætrɪkl] *adj* **1.** THEAT [performance, season] théâtral **2.** *fig* [exaggerated - gesture, behaviour] théâtral, affecté.
◆ **theatricals** *npl* **1.** THEAT théâtre *m* d'amateur **2.** *fig* comédie *f*.

thee [ði:] *pron* BIBLE & *arch* te, t' *(before vowel or silent 'h')* ▪ [after prep] toi.

theft [θeft] *n* vol *m*.

their *(weak form* [ðər], *strong form* [ðeər]*) det* leur *(sg)*, leurs *(pl)* ▪ **~ clothes** leurs vêtements ▪ **somebody's left ~ umbrella behind** quelqu'un a oublié son parapluie ▪ **a house of ~ own** leur propre maison, une maison à eux ▪ **everyone must bring ~ own book** chacun doit apporter son livre.

theirs [ðeəz] *pron* le leur *m*, la leur *f*, les leurs *mf pl* ▪ **our car is sturdier than ~** notre voiture est plus solide que la leur ▪ **I like that painting of ~** j'aime leur tableau ▪ **a friend of ~** un de leurs amis ▪ **is this yours or ~?** est-ce que ceci est à vous ou à eux? ▪ **it is not ~ to choose** ce n'est pas à eux de choisir, le choix ne leur appartient pas.

theism ['θi:ɪzm] *n* RELIG théisme *m*.

theist ['θi:ɪst] ◇ *adj* théiste.
◇ *n* théiste *mf*.

them *(weak form* [ðəm], *strong form* [ðem]*) pron* **1.** [direct obj] les ▪ **I met ~ last week** je les ai rencontrés la semaine dernière **2.** [indirect obj] leur ▪ **we bought/gave ~ some flowers** nous leur avons acheté/donné des fleurs **3.** [after preposition] : **it's for ~** c'est pour eux ▪ **both of ~ are wool** ils sont tous les deux en laine ▪ **neither of ~ is happy** ils ne sont heureux ni l'un ni l'autre ▪ **I don't want any of ~** je n'en veux aucun ▪ **a few of ~ seemed genuinely interested** quelques-uns d'entre eux semblaient vraiment intéressés.

thematic [θɪ'mætɪk] *adj* thématique.

theme [θi:m] *n* **1.** [subject, topic] thème *m*, sujet *m* **2.** MUS thème *m* **3.** GRAM & LING thème *m*.

theme park *n* parc *m* à thème.

theme pub *n UK* pub *m* à thème.

theme song *n* **1.** [from film] chanson *f* (de film) **2.** *US* [signature tune] indicatif *m*.

theme tune *n* **1.** [from film] musique *f* (de film) **2.** *UK* [signature tune] indicatif *m*.

themselves [ðəm'selvz] *pron* **1.** [reflexive use] : **they hurt ~** ils se sont fait mal ▪ **the girls enjoyed ~** les filles se sont bien amusées **2.** [emphatic use] eux-mêmes *mpl*, elles-mêmes *f* ▪ **they had to come ~** ils ont dû venir eux-mêmes *OR* en personne ▪ **they came by ~** ils sont venus tout seuls **3.** [referring to things] eux-mêmes *mpl*, elles-mêmes *f* ▪ **the details in ~ are not important** ce ne sont pas les détails en eux-mêmes qui sont importants.

then [ðen] ◇ *adv* **1.** [at a particular time] alors, à ce moment-là ▪ [in distant past] à l'époque, à cette époque, à cette époque-là ▪ **we can talk about it ~** nous pourrons en parler à ce moment-là ▪ **Marilyn, or Norma Jean as she ~ was known** Marilyn, ou Norma Jean comme elle s'appelait alors ▪ **by ~** [in future] d'ici là ; [in past] entre-temps ▪ **from ~ on** à partir de ce moment-là ▪ **since ~** depuis (lors) ▪ **until ~** [in future] jusque-là ; [in past] jusqu'alors, jusqu'à ce moment-là
2. [afterwards, next] puis, ensuite ▪ **do your homework first, ~ you can watch TV** fais d'abord tes devoirs, et ensuite tu pourras regarder la télé
3. [so, in that case] donc, alors ▪ **you were right ~!** mais alors, vous aviez raison! ▪ **I'll see you at 6 ~** bon, je te retrouve à 6 h alors ▪ **if x equals 10 ~ y...** si x égale 10 alors y... ▪ **if it's not in my bag, ~ look in the cupboard** si ce n'est pas dans mon sac, regarde dans le placard
4. [also] et puis ▪ **~ there's Peter to invite** et puis il faut inviter Peter
5. [therefore] donc ▪ **these ~ are the main problems** voici donc les principaux problèmes.
◇ *adj* d'alors, de l'époque.
◆ **then again** *adv phr* : **and ~ again, you may prefer to forget it** mais enfin peut-être que vous préférez ne plus y penser ▪ **but ~ again, no one can be sure** mais après tout, on ne sait jamais.

thence [ðens] *adv lit & fml* **1.** [from that place] de là, de ce lieu, de ce lieu-là **2.** [from that time] depuis lors **3.** [therefore] par conséquent.

thenceforth [,ðens'fɔ:θ], **thenceforward** [,ðens'fɔ:wəd] *adv lit & fml* dès lors, désormais.

theocracy [θɪ'ɒkrəsɪ] (*pl* **theocracies**) *n* théocratie *f*.

theodolite [θɪ'ɒdəlaɪt] *n* théodolite *m*.

theologian [θɪə'ləʊdʒən] *n* théologien *m*, - enne *f*.

theological [θɪə'lɒdʒɪkl] *adj* théologique ▪ **~ college** séminaire *m*.

theology [θɪ'ɒlədʒɪ] *n* théologie *f*.

theorem ['θɪərəm] *n* théorème *m*.

theoretical [θɪə'retɪkl] *adj* théorique.

theoretically [θɪə'retɪklɪ] *adv* théoriquement, en principe.

theoretician [,θɪərə'tɪʃn] *n* théoricien *m*, - enne *f*.

theorist ['θɪərɪst] *n* théoricien *m*, - enne *f*.

theorize, ise ['θɪəraɪz] ◇ *vi* **1.** [speculate] théoriser, faire des théories **2.** [scientist] élaborer des théories.
◇ *vt* : **scientists ~d that the space probe would disintegrate** les scientifiques émirent l'hypothèse que la sonde spatiale se désintégrerait.

theory ['θɪərɪ] (*pl* **theories**) *n* **1.** [hypothesis] théorie *f* ▪ **I have a ~ about his disappearance** j'ai mon idée sur sa disparition **2.** [principles, rules] théorie *f*.
◆ **in theory** *adv phr* en théorie, théoriquement, en principe.

theosophy [θɪ'ɒsəfɪ] *n* théosophie *f*.

therapeutic [,θerə'pju:tɪk] *adj* thérapeutique.

therapeutic cloning *n* clonage *m* thérapeutique.

therapeutically [,θerə'pju:tɪklɪ] *adv* : **used ~** utilisé comme thérapeutique.

therapist ['θerəpɪst] *n* thérapeute *mf*.

therapy ['θerəpɪ] (*pl* **therapies**) *n* thérapie *f* ▪ **to go for *OR* to be in ~** suivre une thérapie.

there [(*weak form* [ðər], *strong form* [ðeər])] ◇ *adv* **1.** [in o to a particular place] là, y ▪ **they aren't ~** ils ne sont pas là, ils n'y sont pas ▪ **who's ~?** qui est là? ▪ **see that woman ~? that's Mar got** tu vois cette femme là-bas? c'est Margot ▪ **so ~ we were I was** donc, on était/j'étais là ▪ **she got ~ in the end** [reached place] elle a fini par arriver ; [completed a task] elle a fini pa y arriver ▪ **she just sat/stood ~** elle était assise/debout là ▪ **here and ~** çà et là ▪ **~ it is** le voilà ▪ **it's around ~ somewhere** c'est quelque part par là ▪ **back ~** là-bas ▪ **in ~** là-dedans ▪ **o ~** là-dessus ▪ **over ~** là-bas ▪ **under ~** là-dessous ▪ **that car ~** cette voiture-là
2. [available] là
3. [in existence] là
4. [on or at a particular point] là ▪ **we disagree ~, ~ we disagree** nous ne sommes pas d'accord là-dessus ▪ **~ you're wrong** là vous vous trompez ▪ **let's leave it ~** restons-en là ▪ **could I jus stop you ~?** puis-je vous interrompre ici? ▪ **as for the food, I've no complaints ~** pour ce qui est de la nourriture, là je n'ai pa à me plaindre ▪ **you've got me ~!** *inf* là, je ne sais pas quo vous répondre *OR* dire!
5. [drawing attention to someone or something] : **hello *OR* hi ~!** salut! ▪ **hey ~!** hep, vous là-bas! ▪ **~ they are!** les voilà! ▪ **~ yo go again!** ça y est, vous recommencez! ▪ **~'s the bell, I must be going** tiens ça sonne, je dois partir ▪ **~'s gratitude for you** *iro* c'est beau la reconnaissance! *iron* ▪ **now finish your homework, ~'s a good boy** maintenant sois un grand garçon et finis tes devoirs
6. *phr* **he's not all *OR* not quite ~** [stupid] il n'a pas toute sa tête [senile] il n'a plus toute sa tête.
◇ *pron* : **~ is** *(before singular noun)* il y a ▪ **~ are** *(before plural noun)* il y a ▪ **~'s a bus coming** il y a un bus qui arrive ▪ **what happens if ~'s a change of plan?** qu'est-ce qui se passe si on change d'idée? ▪ **~ must have been a mistake** il a dû y avoir une erreur ▪ **~ were some pieces missing** il manquait des pièces ▪ **~'s no knowing what he'll do next** il est impossible de prévoir ce qu'il fera ensuite ▪ **~ was no denying it** c'était indéniable ▪ **~ comes a time when you have to slow down** il arrive un moment où il faut ralentir le rythme.
◇ *interj* **1.** [soothing] : **~ now, don't cry!** allons! *OR* là! ne pleure pas! ▪ **~, ~!** allez!
2. [aggressive] : **~ now, what did I say?** voilà, qu'est-ce que je t'avais dit?
3. [after all] : **but, ~, it's not surprising** mais enfin, ce n'est pas surprenant.
◆ **so there** *adv phr* voilà.
◆ **there again** *adv phr* après tout ▪ **but ~ again, no one really knows** mais après tout, personne ne sait vraiment.
◆ **there and back** *adv phr* : **we did the trip ~ and back in three hours** nous avons fait l'aller retour en trois heures.
◆ **there and then, then and there** *adv phr* sur-le-champ.
◆ **there you are, there you go** *adv phr* **1.** [never mind] : **it wasn't the ideal solution, but ~ you are *OR* go** ce n'était pas l'idéal, mais enfin *OR* mais qu'est-ce que vous voulez
2. [I told you so] voilà, ça y est
3. [here you are] tenez, voilà.

thereabout ['ðeərəbaʊt] *US* = **thereabouts**.

thereabouts ['ðeərəbaʊts] *adv* **1.** [indicating place] par là, dans les environs, pas loin ▪ **somewhere ~** quelque part par là **2.** [indicating quantity, weight] à peu près, environ **3.** [indicating price] environ ▪ **£10 or ~** 10 livres environ **4.** [indicating time] aux alentours de ▪ **at 10 p.m. or ~** aux alentours de 22 h, vers 10 h du soir.

thereafter [,ðeər'ɑ:ftər] *adv fml* **1.** [subsequently] par la suite **2.** [below] ci-dessous.

thereby [,ðeər'baɪ] *adv* **1.** *fml* de ce fait, ainsi **2.** *phr* **~ hangs a tale!** c'est une longue histoire!

therefore ['ðeəfɔ:r] *adv* donc, par conséquent.

therein [,ðeər'ɪn] *adv* LAW & *fml* **1.** [within] à l'intérieur ▪ **the box and all that is contained ~** la boîte et son contenu **2.** [in that respect] là ▪ **~ lies the difficulty** là est la difficulté.

thereof [,ðeər'ɒv] *adv arch & fml* de cela, en ▪ **all citizens of the republic are subject to the laws ~** tous les citoyens de la république doivent se soumettre aux lois de celle-ci.

thereon [ˌðeərˈɒn] *adv arch & fml* **1.** [on that subject] là-dessus **2.** = **thereupon** *(sense 1).*

there's = **there is.**

thereto [ˌðeəˈtuː] *adv* LAW & *fml* **the letter attached ~** la lettre ci-jointe ■ **a copy of the Bill and the amendments ~** une copie du projet de loi et de ses amendements.

theretofore [ˌðeətuːˈfɔːʳ] *adv* LAW & *fml* jusqu'alors, avant cela.

thereunder [ðeərˈʌndəʳ] *adv* LAW & *fml* là-dessous, en dessous.

thereupon [ˌðeərəˈpɒn] *adv fml* **1.** [then] sur ce **2.** LAW [on that subject] à ce sujet, là-dessus.

therewith [ˌðeəˈwɪð] *adv* **1.** LAW [with] avec cela ■ [in addition] en outre **2.** *arch* = **thereupon** *(sense 1).*

therm [θɜːm] *n UK* ≃ 1,055 x 10 exposant 8 joules *(unité de chaleur),* ≃.

thermal [ˈθɜːml] ◇ *adj* **1.** PHYS [energy, insulation] thermique ■ [conductor, unit] thermique, de chaleur **2.** [spring, stream] thermal ■ **~ baths** thermes *mpl* **3.** [underwear] en chlorofibres, en Rhovyl® *OR* Thermolactyl®.
◇ *n* AERON & METEOR thermique *m*, ascendance *f* thermique.
◆ **thermals** *npl* [thermal underwear] sous-vêtements *mpl* en chlorofibres.

thermal printer *n* imprimante *f* thermique.

thermal reactor *n* réacteur *m* thermique.

thermic [ˈθɜːmɪk] *adj* PHYS thermique.

thermocouple [ˈθɜːməʊkʌpl] *n* thermocouple *m*.

thermodynamic [ˌθɜːməʊdaɪˈnæmɪk] *adj* thermodynamique.

thermodynamics [ˌθɜːməʊdaɪˈnæmɪks] *n (U)* thermodynamique *f*.

thermoelectric(al) [ˌθɜːməʊɪˈlektrɪk(l)] *adj* thermoélectrique.

thermometer [θəˈmɒmɪtəʳ] *n* thermomètre *m*.

thermonuclear [ˌθɜːməʊˈnjuːklɪəʳ] *adj* thermonucléaire.

thermoplastic [ˌθɜːməʊˈplæstɪk] ◇ *adj* thermoplastique.
◇ *n* thermoplastique *m*.

Thermos® [ˈθɜːmɒs] *n* : **~ (flask)** Thermos® *f*.

thermostat [ˈθɜːməstæt] *n* thermostat *m*.

thermostatic [ˌθɜːməˈstætɪk] *adj* thermostatique.

thermostatically [ˌθɜːməˈstætɪklɪ] *adv* : **~ controlled** contrôlé par thermostat.

thesaurus [θɪˈsɔːrəs] *(pl* **thesauri** [-raɪ] *OR pl* **thesauruses** [-sɪz]) *n* **1.** [book of synonyms] ≃ dictionnaire *m* analogique **2.** COMPUT thésaurus *m*.

these [ðiːz] *pl* ⊳ **this.**

Theseus [ˈθiːsjuːs] *pr n* Thésée.

thesis [ˈθiːsɪs] *(pl* **theses** [-siːz]) *n* [gen - UNIV] thèse *f*.

thespian [ˈθespɪən] *fml & hum* ◇ *adj* dramatique, de théâtre.
◇ *n* acteur *m*, - trice *f*.

Thessalonians [ˌθesəˈləʊnjənz] *npl* Thessaloniciens *mpl*.

they [ðeɪ] *pron* ils *mpl*, elles *f* ■ [stressed form] eux *mpl*, elles *fpl* ■ **~'ve left** ils sont partis ■ **they bought the flowers** ce sont eux qui ont acheté les fleurs ■ **oh, there ~ are!** ah, les voilà! ■ **~ say that...** on prétend que...

they'd [ðeɪd] **1.** = **they had 2.** = **they would.**

they'll [ðeɪl] = **they will.**

they're [ðeəʳ] = **they are.**

they've [ðeɪv] = **they have.**

thick [θɪk] ◇ *adj* **1.** [wall, slice, writing] épais, - aisse *f*, gros, grosse *f* ■ [print] gras, grasse *f* ■ [lips] épais, charnu ■ [shoes, boots] gros, grosse *f* ■ **the snow was ~ on the ground** il y avait une épaisse couche de neige sur le sol ■ **the boards are 20 cm ~** les planches ont une épaisseur de 20 cm, les planches font 20 cm d'épaisseur ▸ **to give sb a ~ ear** *UK* donner une gifle à qqn
2. [beard, eyebrows, hair] épais, touffu ■ [grass, forest, crowd] épais, - aisse *f*, dense ■ **pubs are not very ~ on the ground round here** les pubs sont plutôt rares par ici
3. [soup, cream, sauce] épais
4. [fog, smoke] épais, dense ■ [clouds] épais ■ [darkness, night] profond ▸ **my head feels a bit ~ this morning** *inf* j'ai un peu mal au crâne ce matin
5. : **~ with: the shelves were ~ with dust** les étagères étaient recouvertes d'une épaisse couche de poussière ■ **the air was ~ with smoke** [from smokers] la pièce était enfumée ; [from fire, guns] l'air était empli d'une épaisse fumée ■ **the streets were ~ with police** les rues étaient pleines de policiers
6. [voice - with emotion] voilé ; [- after late night, drinking] pâteux
7. [accent] fort, prononcé
8. *inf* [intimate] intime, très lié ■ **he's very ~ with the boss** il est très bien avec le chef, lui et le chef sont comme les deux doigts de la main ▸ **those two are as ~ as thieves** ces deux-là s'entendent comme larrons en foire
9. *inf* [stupid] obtus, bouché ■ **he's as ~ as two short planks** *OR* **as a brick** il est bête comme ses pieds
10. *UK inf* [unreasonable] : **that's** *OR* **it's a bit ~** ça, c'est un peu dur à avaler *OR* fort *OR* raide.
◇ *adv* [spread] en couche épaisse ■ [cut] en tranches épaisses, en grosses tranches ■ **the snow lay ~ on the ground** il y avait une épaisse couche de neige sur le sol ■ **the grass grows ~ at the bottom of the hill** l'herbe pousse dru en bas de la colline ▸ **~ and fast : arrows started falling ~ and fast around them** les flèches pleuvaient autour d'eux ■ **invitations/phone calls began to come in ~ and fast** il y eut une avalanche d'invitations/de coups de téléphone ■ **to lay it on ~** en rajouter.
◇ *n phr* : **to stick** *OR* **to stay with sb through ~ and thin** rester fidèle à qqn contre vents et marées *OR* quoi qu'il arrive.
◆ **in the thick of** *prep phr* au milieu *OR* cœur de, en plein, en plein milieu de ■ **in the ~ of the discussion** en pleine discussion ■ **he's really in the ~ of it** [dispute, activity] il est vraiment dans le feu de l'action.

thicken [ˈθɪkn] ◇ *vi* **1.** [fog, clouds, smoke] s'épaissir, devenir plus épais ■ [bushes, forest] s'épaissir **2.** [sauce] épaissir ■ [jam, custard] durcir **3.** [crowd] grossir **4.** [mystery] s'épaissir ■ **the plot ~s** les choses se compliquent *OR* se corsent, l'histoire se corse.
◇ *vt* [sauce, soup] épaissir.

thickener [ˈθɪknəʳ] *n* [for sauce, soup] liant *m* ■ [for oil, paint] épaississant *m*.

thickening [ˈθɪknɪŋ] ◇ *n* **1.** [of fog, clouds, smoke] épaississement *m* ■ [of sauce] liaison *f* **2.** CULIN [thickener] liant *m*.
◇ *adj* [agent] épaississant ■ [process] d'épaississement.

thicket [ˈθɪkɪt] *n* fourré *m*.

thickhead [ˈθɪkhed] *n inf* bêta *m*, - asse *f*, imbécile *mf*, andouille *f*.

thickheaded [ˌθɪkˈhedɪd] *adj inf* obtus, bouché.

thickie [ˈθɪkɪ] *(pl* **thickies**) *n UK inf* bêta *m*, - asse *f*, imbécile *mf*, andouille *f*.

thickly [ˈθɪklɪ] *adv* **1.** [spread] en couche épaisse ■ [cut] en tranches épaisses **2.** [densely] dru ■ **~ populated** très peuplé, à forte densité de population **3.** [speak] d'une voix rauque *OR* pâteuse.

thickness [ˈθɪknɪs] *n* **1.** [of wall, snow, layer] épaisseur *f* ■ [of string, bolt] épaisseur *f*, grosseur *f* **2.** [of beard, hair] épaisseur *f*, abondance *f* **3.** [of fog, smoke, forest] épaisseur *f*, densité *f*.

thickset [ˌθɪkˈset] *adj* trapu, costaud.

thick-skinned [-ˈskɪnd] *adj* peu sensible, qui a la peau dure.

thicky [ˈθɪkɪ] *(pl* **thickies**) *UK inf* = **thickie.**

thief [θi:f] (*pl* **thieves** [θi:vz]) *n* voleur *m*, - euse *f* ▪ **stop ~!** au voleur! ◗ **thieves' kitchen** repaire *m* de brigands.

thieve [θi:v] *vi* & *vt* *inf* voler.

thieves [θi:vz] *pl* ▷ **thief**.

thieving ['θi:vɪŋ] *inf* ◇ *adj* voleur ▪ **keep your ~ hands off!** pas touche!, bas les pattes!
◇ *n (U)* vol *m*, vols *mpl*.

thigh [θaɪ] *n* cuisse *f*.

thighbone ['θaɪbəʊn] *n* fémur *m*.

thigh boots, thigh-high boots *npl* cuissardes *fpl*.

thimble ['θɪmbl] *n* dé *m* à coudre.

thimbleful ['θɪmblfʊl] *n* *fig* [of liquid] doigt *m*, goutte *f*.

thin [θɪn] ◇ *adj* (*comp* **thinner**, *superl* **thinnest**) **1.** [layer, wall, wire etc] mince, fin ▪ [person, leg, neck] mince, maigre ▪ [clothing, blanket] léger, fin ▪ [carpet] ras ▪ [crowd] peu nombreux, épars ▪ **to become** *OR* **to get** *OR* **to grow ~** [person] maigrir ◗ **he's as ~ as a rake** *UK* *OR* **as a rail** *US* il est maigre comme un clou ▪ **it's the ~ end of the wedge** cela ne présage rien de bon ▪ **cheap hotels are ~ on the ground** les hôtels bon marché sont rares **2.** [beard, hair] clairsemé ▪ **he's getting a bit ~ on top** il commence à perdre ses cheveux, il se dégarnit **3.** [soup, sauce] clair ▪ [cream] liquide ▪ [paint, ink] délayé, dilué ▪ [blood] appauvri, anémié **4.** [smoke, clouds, mist] léger ▪ [air] raréfié ▪ **she seemed to vanish into ~ air** elle semblait s'être volatilisée **5.** [excuse, argument] mince, peu convaincant ▪ **the report is rather ~ on facts** le rapport ne présente pas beaucoup de faits concrets **6.** [profits] maigre **7.** [voice] grêle.
◇ *adv* [spread] en fine couche, en couche mince ▪ [cut] en tranches minces *OR* fines.
◇ *vt* (*pret* & *pp* **thinned**, *cont* **thinning**) [sauce, soup] allonger, délayer, éclaircir.
◇ *vi* (*pret* & *pp* **thinned**, *cont* **thinning**) [crowd] s'éclaircir, se disperser ▪ [fog] se lever, devenir moins dense *OR* épais ▪ [smoke] devenir moins dense *OR* épais ▪ [population] se réduire ▪ **his hair is thinning** il perd ses cheveux.
◆ **thin out** ◇ *vt sep* [plants] éclaircir.
◇ *vi insep* [crowd] se disperser ▪ [population] se réduire, diminuer ▪ [fog] se lever.

thine [ðaɪn] BIBLE & *arch* ◇ *poss adj* ton *m*, ta *f*, tes *mf pl*.
◇ *pron* le tien *m*, la tienne *f*, les tiens *mpl*, les tiennes *f*.

thing [θɪŋ] *n*

A.

1. [object, item] chose *f*, objet *m* ▪ **what's that yellow ~ on the floor?** qu'est-ce que c'est que ce truc jaune par terre? ▪ **what's that ~ for?** à quoi ça sert, ça? ▪ **where's my hat? I can't find the ~ anywhere** où est mon chapeau? je ne le trouve nulle part ▪ **I had to rewrite the whole ~** j'ai dû tout réécrire ▪ **the ~ he loves most is his pipe** ce qu'il aime le plus, c'est sa pipe ▪ **I need a few ~s from the shop** j'ai besoin de faire quelques courses ▪ **she loves books and posters and ~s** elle aime les livres, les posters, ce genre de choses ▪ **I must be seeing ~s** je dois avoir des visions ▪ **I must be hearing ~s** je dois rêver, j'entends des voix
2. [activity, event] chose *f* ▪ **she's still into this art ~ in a big way** *inf* elle est encore très branchée art ▪ **the ~ to do is to pretend you're asleep** vous n'avez qu'à faire semblant de dormir ▪ **the next ~ on the agenda** le point suivant à l'ordre du jour ▪ **it's the best ~ to do** c'est ce qu'il y a de mieux à faire ▪ **that was a silly ~ to do!** ce n'était pas la chose à faire! ▪ **she certainly gets ~s done** avec elle, ça ne traîne pas
3. [in negative clauses] : **I don't know a ~ about what happened** j'ignore tout de ce qui s'est passé ▪ **not a ~ was overlooked** pas un détail n'a été négligé ▪ **I didn't understand a ~ she said** je n'ai rien compris à ce qu'elle disait, je n'ai pas compris un mot de ce qu'elle disait ▪ **we couldn't do a ~ about it** nous n'y pouvions absolument rien ▪ **she hadn't got a ~ on** elle était entièrement nue ▪ **I haven't got a ~ to wear** je n'ai rien à me mettre sur le dos
4. [creature, being] créature *f*, être *m* ▪ **what a sweet little ~!** quel amour! ▪ **poor ~!** [said about somebody] le/la pauvre! ; [said to somebody] mon/ma pauvre! ; [animal] (la) pauvre bête!
5. [monster] : **the ~ from outer space** le monstre de l'espace

B.

1. [idea, notion] idée *f*, chose *f* ▪ **the best ~ would be to ask them** le mieux serait de leur demander ▪ **it would be a good ~ if we all went together** ce serait une bonne chose que nous y allions tous ensemble ▪ **to be on to a good ~** être sur une bonne affaire ◗ **to know a ~ or two about sthg** s'y connaître en qqch ▪ **I could show him a ~ or two about hang gliding** je pourrais lui apprendre une ou deux petites choses en deltaplane
2. [matter, question] chose *f*, question *f* ▪ **the ~ is, we can't really afford it** le problème, c'est qu'on n'a pas vraiment les moyens ▪ **the main ~ is to succeed** ce qui importe, c'est de réussir ▪ **the important ~ is not to stop** ce qui compte, c'est de ne pas arrêter ◗ **it's one ~ to talk but quite another to act** parler est une chose, agir en est une autre ▪ **what with one ~ and another, I haven't had time** avec tout ce qu'il y avait à faire, je n'ai pas eu le temps ▪ **if it's not one ~, it's another** ça ne s'arrête jamais
3. [remark] : **that's not a very nice ~ to say** ce n'est pas très gentil de dire ça ▪ **she said some nasty ~s about him** elle a dit des méchancetés sur lui ▪ **how can you say such a ~?** comment pouvez-vous dire une chose pareille? ▪ **I said no such ~!** je n'ai rien dit de tel!
4. [quality, characteristic] chose *f* ▪ **one of the ~s I like about her is her sense of humour** une des choses que j'aime chez elle, c'est son sens de l'humour ▪ **the town has a lot of ~s going for it** la ville a beaucoup de bons côtés

C.

1. *inf* [strong feeling] : **to have a ~ about sthg** [like] aimer qqch ; [dislike] ne pas aimer qqch ▪ **I have a ~ about jazz** [like] j'aime vraiment le jazz ; [dislike] je n'aime vraiment pas le jazz ▪ **it's a bit of a ~ with me** [like] j'aime assez ça ; [dislike] c'est ma bête noire
2. [interest] : **it's not really my ~** ce n'est pas vraiment mon truc ▪ **to do one's own ~ : he went off to the States to do his own ~** il est parti aux États-Unis vivre sa vie
3. [what is needed, required] idéal *m* ▪ **hot cocoa is just the ~ on a winter's night** un chocolat chaud c'est l'idéal les soirs d'hiver ▪ **that's the very ~ for my bad back!** c'est juste ce dont j'avais besoin pour mon mal de dos!
4. [fashion] mode *f* ▪ **it's quite the ~** c'est très à la mode ▪ **a ~ of the past** une chose du passé
5. [fuss] : **to make a big ~ about sthg** faire (tout) un plat de qqch
6. *inf* [relationship] : **to have a ~ with sb** avoir une liaison avec qqn.
◆ **things** *npl* **1.** [belongings] effets *mpl*, affaires *fpl* ▪ [clothes] affaires *fpl* ▪ [equipment] affaires *fpl*, attirail *m* ▪ [tools] outils *mpl*, ustensiles *mpl* ▪ **put your ~s away** ramassez vos affaires ▪ **you can take your ~s off in the bedroom** vous pouvez vous déshabiller dans la chambre ▪ **to take the tea ~s away** desservir la table (après le thé) **2.** [situation, circumstances] choses *fpl* ▪ **how's** *inf* *OR* **how are ~s?** comment ça va? ▪ **~s are getting better** les choses vont mieux ▪ **I feel rather out of ~s** je n'ai pas l'impression d'être vraiment dans le bain ▪ **I need time to think ~s over** j'ai besoin de temps pour réfléchir ▪ **as ~s are** *OR* **stand, ~s being what they are** dans l'état actuel des choses, les choses étant ce qu'elles sont ◗ **it's just one of those ~s** ce sont des choses qui arrivent **3.** [specific aspect of life] choses *fpl* ▪ **she's interested in all ~s French** elle s'intéresse à tout ce qui est français ▪ **moderation in all ~s** de la modération en tout ▪ **she wants to be an airline pilot of all ~s!** elle veut être pilote de ligne, non mais vraiment! **4.** [facts, actions etc] choses *fpl* ▪ **I've heard good ~s about his work** on dit du bien de son travail **5.** LAW [property] biens *mpl*.
◆ **for one thing** *adv phr* (tout) d'abord ▪ **for one ~... and for another** (tout) d'abord... et puis.

thingamabob ['θɪŋəmə͵bɒb], **thingamajig, thingumajig** ['θɪŋəmədʒɪg], **thingummy** ['θɪŋəmɪ] *n* *inf* machin *m*, truc *m*, bidule *m*.

thingy ['θɪŋɪ] *n* *inf* [object] truc *m*, bidule *m*, machin *m*, bitoniau *m* ▪ [person] Machin-Chose, Trucmuche.

think [θɪŋk] (*pret* & *pp* **thought** [θɔ:t]) ◇ *vi* **1.** [reason] penser, raisonner ▪ **to ~ for oneself** se faire ses propres opinions ▪ **sorry, I wasn't ~ing clearly** désolé, je n'avais pas les idées claires ▪ **to ~ aloud** penser tout haut ▪ **to ~ big** *inf* voir les choses en grand ■ ~ **big!** sois ambitieux! ▶ **to ~ on one's feet** réfléchir vite ■ **you couldn't hear yourself ~** il n'était pas possible de se concentrer ■ **I can't ~ straight with this headache** ce mal de tête m'embrouille les idées

2. [ponder, reflect] penser, réfléchir ■ **he thought for a moment** il a réfléchi un instant ■ **~ again!** [reconsider] repensez-y! ; [guess] vous n'y êtes pas, réfléchissez donc! ■ **let me ~** laisse-moi réfléchir ■ **I thought hard** j'ai beaucoup réfléchi ■ **that's what set me ~ing** c'est ce qui m'a fait réfléchir

3. [imagine] (s')imaginer ■ **if you ~ I'd lend you my car again...** si tu t'imagines que je te prêterai encore ma voiture... ■ **just ~!** imaginez (-vous) un peu!

4. [believe, have as opinion] penser, croire ■ **to her way of ~ing** à son avis ■ **it's a lot harder than I thought** c'est beaucoup plus difficile que je ne croyais ▶ **oh, he's so honest, I don't ~!** honnête, mon œil, oui!

◇ *vt* **1.** [ponder, reflect on] penser à, réfléchir à ■ **he was ~ing what they could do next** il se demandait ce qu'ils allaient pouvoir faire ensuite ■ **I was just ~ing how ironic it all is** je pensais simplement à l'ironie de la chose ■ **I kept ~ing "why me?"** je n'arrêtais pas de me dire: pourquoi moi? ■ **I'm happy to ~ she's not all alone** je suis content de savoir qu'elle n'est pas toute seule ■ **to ~ deep/evil thoughts** avoir des pensées profondes/de mauvaises pensées

2. [believe] penser, croire ■ **I ~ so** je crois ■ **I ~ not** je ne crois pas ■ **he's a crook – I thought so** *OR* **I thought as much** c'est un escroc – je m'en doutais ■ **more tea? – I don't ~ I will, thank you** encore un peu de thé? – non merci, je ne pense pas ■ **they asked me what I thought** ils m'ont demandé mon avis ■ **he wants cream walls – what do you ~?** il veut des murs crème – qu'est-ce que tu en penses? ■ **I thought I heard a noise** j'ai cru *OR* il m'a semblé entendre un bruit ■ **it's expensive, don't you ~?** c'est cher, tu ne trouves pas? ■ **she ~s she's talented** elle se croit *OR* se trouve douée ■ **that's what you ~!** tu te fais des illusions! ■ **what will people ~?** qu'en dira-t-on?, qu'est-ce que les gens vont penser? ■ **anyone would ~ he owned the place** on croirait que c'est lui le propriétaire ■ **anybody would ~ it was Sunday** on dirait un dimanche ■ **(just) who does he ~ he is?** (mais) pour qui se prend-il? ■ **you always ~ the best/ the worst of everyone** vous avez toujours une très bonne/ mauvaise opinion de tout le monde

3. [judge, consider] juger, considérer ■ **you must ~ me very nosy** vous devez me trouver très curieux ■ **if you ~ it necessary** si vous le jugez nécessaire

4. [imagine] (s')imaginer ■ **I can't ~ why he refused** je ne vois vraiment pas pourquoi il a refusé ■ **you'd ~ she'd be pleased** elle devrait être contente ■ **who'd have thought she'd become president!** qui aurait dit qu'elle serait un jour président! ■ **who'd have thought it!** qui l'eût cru! ■ **just ~ what we can do with all that money!** imaginez ce qu'on peut faire avec tout cet argent! ■ **and to ~ she did it all by herself** et dire *OR* quand on pense qu'elle a fait cela toute seule

5. [remember] penser à, se rappeler ■ **I can't ~ what his name is** je n'arrive pas à me rappeler son nom, son nom m'échappe ■ **to ~ to do sthg** penser à faire qqch ■ **did you ~ to buy some bread?** as-tu pensé à acheter du pain?

6. [expect] penser, s'attendre à ■ **I don't ~ she'll come** je ne pense pas qu'elle viendra *OR* vienne ■ **I didn't ~ to find you here** je ne m'attendais pas à vous trouver ici

7. [have as intention] : **I ~ I'll go for a walk** je crois que je vais aller me promener

8. [in requests] : **do you ~ you could help me?** pourriez-vous m'aider?

◇ *n* : **we've had a ~ about it** nous y avons réfléchi ▶ **you've got another ~ coming!** *inf* tu te fais des illusions!

◆ **think about** *vt insep* **1.** [ponder, reflect on] : **to ~ about sthg/doing sthg** penser à qqch/à faire qqch ■ **what are you ~ing about?** à quoi pensez-vous? ■ **it's not a bad idea, if you ~ about it** ce n'est pas une mauvaise idée, si tu réfléchis bien ■ **she's ~ing about starting a business** elle pense à *OR* envisage de monter une affaire ■ **we'll ~ about it** nous allons y penser *OR* réfléchir ■ **she has a lot to ~ about just now** elle est très préoccupée en ce moment ■ **there's so much to ~ about when you buy a house** il y a tant de choses à prendre en considération quand on achète une maison ■ **the conference gave us much to ~ about** la conférence nous a donné matière à réflexion

2. [consider seriously] penser ■ **all he ~s about is money** il n'y a que l'argent qui l'intéresse.

◆ **think ahead** *vi insep* prévoir.

◆ **think back** *vi insep* : **to ~ back to sthg** se rappeler qqch.

◆ **think of** *vt insep* **1.** [have as tentative plan] penser à, envisager de

2. [have in mind] : **whatever were you ~ing of?** où avais-tu la tête? ▶ **come to ~ of it, that's not a bad idea** à la réflexion, ce n'est pas une mauvaise idée

3. [remember] penser à, se rappeler ■ **he couldn't ~ of the name** il ne se rappelait pas le nom, le nom ne lui venait pas

4. [come up with - idea, solution] : **she's the one who thought of double-checking it** c'est elle qui a eu l'idée de le vérifier ■ **it's the only way they could ~ of doing it** ils ne voyaient pas d'autre façon de s'y prendre ■ **I thought of the answer** j'ai trouvé la réponse ■ **I've just thought of something, she'll be out** j'avais oublié *OR* je viens de me rappeler, elle ne sera pas là ■ **I've just thought of something else** il y a autre chose *OR* c'est pas tout ■ **I'd never have thought of that** je n'y aurais jamais pensé ■ **whatever will they ~ of next?** qu'est-ce qu'ils vont bien pouvoir trouver ensuite? ■ **I thought better of it** je me suis ravisé ■ **he thought nothing of leaving the baby alone for hours at a time** il trouvait (ça) normal de laisser le bébé seul pendant des heures ■ **thank you – ~ nothing of it!** merci – mais je vous en prie *OR* mais c'est tout naturel!

5. [judge, have as opinion] estimer ■ **what do you ~ of the new teacher?** comment trouvez-vous le *OR* que pensez-vous du nouveau professeur? ■ **she ~s very highly of** *OR* **very well of him** elle a une très haute opinion de lui ■ **he ~s of himself as an artist** il se prend pour un artiste ■ **as a doctor she is very well thought of** elle est très respectée en tant que médecin ■ **I hope you won't ~ badly of me if I refuse** j'espère que vous ne m'en voudrez pas si je refuse ■ **I don't ~ much of that idea** cette idée ne me dit pas grand-chose

6. [imagine] penser à, imaginer ■ **just ~ of it, me as president!** imaginez un peu: moi président!, vous m'imaginez président?

7. [take into consideration] penser à, considérer ■ **I have my family to ~ of** il faut que je pense à ma famille ■ **he never ~s of her** il n'a aucun égard *OR* aucune considération pour elle ■ **you can't ~ of everything** on ne peut pas penser à tout.

◆ **think out** *vt sep* [plan] élaborer, préparer ■ [problem] bien étudier *OR* examiner ■ [solution] bien étudier ■ **a carefully thought-out answer** une réponse bien pesée ■ **a well-thought-out plan** un projet bien conçu *OR* ficelé.

◆ **think over** *vt sep* bien examiner, bien réfléchir à ■ **we'll have to ~ it over** il va falloir que nous y réfléchissions ■ **on ~ing things over we've decided not to sell the house** réflexion faite, on a décidé de ne pas vendre la maison ■ **I need some time to ~ things over** j'ai besoin de temps pour réfléchir.

◆ **think up** *vt sep* [excuse, plan] trouver.

thinkable ['θɪŋkəbl] *adj* pensable, concevable, imaginable.

thinker ['θɪŋkər] *n* penseur *m*, - euse *f*.

thinking ['θɪŋkɪŋ] ◇ *adj* [person] pensant, rationnel, qui réfléchit ■ **it's the ~ man's answer to pulp fiction** c'est un roman de hall de gare en plus intelligent.

◇ *n* **1.** [act] pensée *f*, pensées *fpl*, réflexion *f* ■ **I've done some serious ~ about the situation** j'ai bien *OR* sérieusement *OR* mûrement réfléchi à la situation **2.** [opinion, judgment] point *m* de vue, opinion *f*, opinions *fpl* ■ **she finally came round to my way of ~** elle s'est finalement ralliée à mon point de vue.

thinking cap *n* : **to put on one's ~** *inf fig* se mettre à réfléchir, cogiter.

think tank *n* groupe *m* d'experts.

thin-lipped *adj* aux lèvres minces *OR* fines.

thinly ['θɪnlɪ] *adv* [spread] en couche mince ■ [cut] en fines tranches ■ **a ~ disguised insult** une insulte à peine voilée ■ **the area is ~ populated** la région n'est pas très peuplée.

thinner ['θɪnər] ◇ *compar* ▷ **thin**.
◇ *n* [solvent] diluant *m*.

thinness ['θɪnnɪs] *n* **1.** [of layer, wall] minceur *f*, finesse *f* ■ [of person] minceur *f*, maigreur *f* ■ [of wire] finesse *f* ■ [of clothing, blanket, carpet] légèreté *f*, finesse *f* **2.** [of beard, hair] finesse *f*, rareté *f* **3.** [of excuse] faiblesse *f*, insuffisance *f*.

third [θɜ:d] <> *det* troisième ■ **~ finger** annulaire *m* ■ **~ person** GRAM troisième personne *f* ■ **in the ~ person** à la troisième personne ■ **~ time lucky** la troisième fois sera la bonne.
<> *n* **1.** [gen] troisième *mf* **2.** [fraction] tiers *m* **3.** MUS tierce *f* **4.** AUT : **~ (gear)** troisième *f* ■ **in ~ (gear)** en troisième **5.** *UK* UNIV ≃ licence *f* sans mention.
<> *adv* en troisième place *f* *OR* position *f*, *see also* **fifth**.

third class <> *n* **1.** [for travel] troisième classe *f* ■ [for accommodation] troisième catégorie *f* **2.** *US* [for mail] ≃ tarif *m* "imprimés", ≃ tarif *m* lent.
<> *adv* **1.** [travel] en troisième classe **2.** *US* **to mail a package ~** ≃ envoyer un colis au tarif lent.
◆ **third-class** *adj* **1.** [ticket, compartment] de troisième classe ■ [hotel, accommodation] de troisième catégorie **2.** [inferior - merchandise] de qualité inférieure, de pacotille ; [- restaurant] de qualité inférieure **3.** *UK* UNIV : **third-class degree** ≃ licence *f* sans mention **4.** *US* [mail] au tarif "imprimés", au tarif lent.

third degree *n inf* **to give sb the ~** [torture] passer qqn à tabac ; [interrogate] cuisiner qqn.

third-degree burn *n* brûlure *f* au troisième degré.

Third Estate *n* HIST : **the ~** le Tiers état.

thirdly ['θɜ:dlɪ] *adv* troisièmement, en troisième lieu, tertio.

third party *n* tierce personne *f*, tiers *m*.
◆ **third-party** *adj* : **third-party insurance** assurance *f* au tiers.

third-rate *adj* de qualité inférieure.

third reading *n* [of a bill] *dernière lecture*.

Third World *n* : **the ~** le tiers-monde.
◆ **Third-World** *comp* du tiers-monde.

thirst [θɜ:st] <> *n liter & fig* soif *f* ■ **all that hard work has given me a ~** ça m'a donné soif de travailler dur comme ça ■ **he has a ~ for adventure** *fig* il a soif d'aventure.
<> *vi* : **to ~ for sthg** avoir soif de qqch ■ **a jealous husband ~ing for revenge** *fig* un mari jaloux assoiffé de vengeance ■ **to ~ for knowledge** *fig* être avide de connaissances.

thirsty ['θɜ:stɪ] (*comp* **thirstier**, *superl* **thirstiest**) *adj* **1.** : **to be ~** avoir soif ■ **I feel very ~** j'ai très soif ■ **salted peanuts make you ~** les cacahuètes salées donnent soif ■ **it's ~ work** ça donne soif **2.** *fig* [for knowledge, adventure] assoiffé ■ **she was ~ for revenge** elle était assoiffée de vengeance **3.** [plant] qui a besoin de beaucoup d'eau ■ [soil] desséché.

thirteen [,θɜ:'ti:n] <> *det* treize.
<> *n* treize *m inv*.
<> *pron* treize, *see also* **five**.

thirteenth [,θɜ:'ti:nθ] <> *det* treizième.
<> *n* treizième *mf*, *see also* **fifth**.

thirtieth ['θɜ:tɪəθ] <> *det* trentième.
<> *n* trentième *mf*, *see also* **fifth**.

thirty ['θɜ:tɪ] (*pl* **thirties**) <> *n* trente *m inv*.
<> *det* trente ■ **the Thirty Years' War** HIST la guerre de Trente Ans.
<> *pron* trente, *see also* **fifty**.

thirty-three *n* [record] trente-trois tours *m inv*.

this [ðɪs] (*pl* **these** [ði:z]) <> *demonstrative pronoun* **1.** [person, situation, statement, thing indicated] ceci, ce ■ **what's ~?** qu'est-ce que c'est (que ça) ? ■ **who's ~?** [gen] qui est-ce? ; [on phone] qui est à l'appareil? ■ **~ is for you** tiens, c'est pour toi ■ **~ is Mr Smith speaking** [on phone] M. Smith à l'appareil, c'est M. Smith ■ **~ is my mother** [in introduction] je vous présente ma mère ; [in picture] c'est ma mère ■ **~ is what he told me** voici ce qu'il m'a dit ■ **~ is where I live** c'est ici que j'habite ■ **what's ~ I hear about your leaving?** on me dit que vous partez? ■ **it was like ~** voici comment les choses se sont passées ■ **do it like ~** voici comment il faut faire ■ **I didn't want it to end like ~** je ne voulais pas que ça finisse *OR* se termine comme ça ■ **that it should come to ~** qu'on en arrive là ■ **and there's no way she could live with you? – well, ~ is it** et elle ne pourrait pas vivre avec toi? – non, justement ■ **~ is it, wish me luck** voilà, souhaite-moi bonne chance ■ **I'll tell you ~...** je vais te dire une chose... ■ **after/before ~** après/avant ça ■ **at** *OR* **with ~, he left the room** là-dessus *OR* sur ce, il a quitté la pièce ◗ **they sat chatting about ~, that and the other** ils étaient là, assis, à bavarder de choses et d'autres ■ **it's always John ~ and John that** c'est John par-ci, John par-là **2.** [contrasted with 'that'] celui-ci *m*, celle-ci *f* ■ **these** ceux-ci *mpl*, celles-ci *f* ■ **~ is a rose, that is a peony** ceci est une rose, ça c'est une pivoine ■ **I want these, not those!** je veux ceux-ci, pas ceux-là!
<> *det* **1.** [referring to a particular person, idea, time or thing] ce *m*, cet *m (before vowel or silent 'h')*, cette *f* ■ **these** ces *mf pl* ■ **~ plan of yours won't work** votre projet ne marchera pas ■ **~ way please** par ici s'il vous plaît ■ **~ funny little man came up to me** un petit bonhomme à l'air bizarre est venu vers moi ■ **by ~ time tomorrow he'll be gone** demain à cette heure-ci, il sera parti ■ **~ time last week** la semaine dernière à la même heure ■ **~ coming week** la semaine prochaine *OR* qui vient ■ **saving money isn't easy these days** faire des économies n'est pas facile aujourd'hui *OR* de nos jours ■ **I've been watching you ~ past hour** ça fait une heure *OR* voici une heure que je vous regarde ■ **what are you doing ~ Christmas?** qu'est-ce que vous faites pour Noël cette année? **2.** [contrasted with 'that'] ce... -ci *m*, cet... -ci *m (before vowel or silent 'h')*, cette... -ci *f* ■ **these** ces... -ci *mf pl* ■ **which do you prefer, ~ one or that one?** lequel tu préfères, celui-ci ou celui-là? ■ **people ran ~ way and that** les gens couraient dans tous les sens.
<> *adv* aussi, si ■ **it was ~ high** c'était haut comme ça ■ **we've come ~ far, we might as well go on** [on journey] nous sommes venus jusqu'ici, alors autant continuer ; [on project] maintenant que nous en sommes là, autant continuer.

thistle ['θɪsl] *n* chardon *m*.

THISTLE

Le chardon est l'emblème de l'Écosse.

thistledown ['θɪsəldaʊn] *n* duvet *m* de chardon.

thistly ['θɪslɪ] *adj* couvert de chardons.

tho, tho' [ðəʊ] = **though**.

Thomas ['tɒməs] *pr n* : **Saint ~** saint Thomas.

thong [θɒŋ] *n* **1.** [strip - of leather, rubber] lanière *f* **2.** [G-string] cache-sexe *m*.
◆ **thongs** *npl US* tongs *fpl*.

thoracic [θɔ:'ræsɪk] *adj* thoracique.

thorax ['θɔ:ræks] (*pl* **thoraxes** *OR pl* **thoraces** ['θɔ:rəsi:z]) *n* thorax *m*.

thorn [θɔ:n] *n* **1.** [prickle] épine *f* ■ **it's a ~ in his side** *OR* **flesh** c'est une source d'irritation constante pour lui, c'est sa bête noire **2.** [tree, shrub] arbuste *m* épineux ■ [hawthorn] aubépine *f*.

thornbush ['θɔ:nbʊʃ] *n* buisson *m* épineux.

thorny ['θɔ:nɪ] (*comp* **thornier**, *superl* **thorniest**) *adj liter & fig* épineux.

thorough ['θʌrə] *adj* **1.** [complete - inspection, research] minutieux, approfondi ■ **to give sthg a ~ cleaning/dusting** nettoyer/épousseter qqch à fond ■ **she has a ~ knowledge of her subject** elle a une connaissance parfaite de son sujet, elle connaît son sujet à fond *OR* sur le bout des doigts **2.** [conscientious - work, worker] consciencieux, sérieux **3.** [as intensifier] absolu, complet, - ète *f* ■ **what a ~ bore this book is!** qu'est-ce qu'il est ennuyeux, ce livre! ■ **the man is a ~ scoundrel!** ce type est une crapule finie! ■ **it's a ~ nuisance!** c'est vraiment très embêtant!

thoroughbred ['θʌrəbred] <> *adj* [horse] pur-sang *(inv)* ■ [animal - gen] de race.
<> *n* **1.** [horse] pur-sang *m inv* ■ [animal - gen] bête *f* de race **2.** [person] : **she's a ~** elle a de la classe, elle est racée.

thoroughfare ['θʌrəfeəʳ] *n* voie *f* de communication ■ **the main ~** la rue *OR* l'artère *f* principale ■ **'no ~'** [no entry] 'passage interdit' ; [cul-de-sac] 'voie sans issue' ◗ **public ~** voie publique.

thoroughly ['θʌrəlɪ] *adv* **1.** [minutely, in detail - search] à fond, de fond en comble ; [- examine] à fond, minutieusement ▪ **read all the questions ~** lisez très attentivement toutes les questions **2.** [as intensifier] tout à fait, absolument.

thoroughness ['θʌrənɪs] *n* minutie *f.*

those [ðəuz] *pl* ▻ **that.**

thou[1] [ðaʊ] *pron* BIBLE & *dial* tu ▪ [stressed form] toi.

thou[2] [θaʊ] (*pl inv* OR *pl* **thous**) *n* **1.** = **thousand 2.** = **thousandth of an inch.**

though [ðəʊ] <> *conj* bien que, quoique ▪ **~ young, she's very mature** bien qu'elle soit jeune OR quoique jeune, elle est très mûre ▪ **he enjoyed the company ~ not the food** il appréciait les gens avec qui il était mais pas ce qu'il mangeait ▪ **kind ~ she was, we never really got on** malgré sa gentillesse, nous ne nous sommes jamais très bien entendus ▪ **it's an excellent book, ~ I say so myself** c'est un très bon livre, sans fausse modestie ▪ **strange ~ it may seem** aussi étrange que cela puisse paraître.
<> *adv* pourtant ▪ **he's a difficult man; I like him ~** il n'est pas facile à vivre ; pourtant je l'aime bien.

thought [θɔ:t] <> *pt* & *pp* ▻ **think.**
<> *n* **1.** *(U)* [reflection] pensée *f*, réflexion *f* ▪ **to give a problem much** OR **a lot of ~** bien réfléchir à un problème ▪ **after much ~** après mûre réflexion, après avoir mûrement réfléchi ▪ **we gave some ~ to the matter** nous avons réfléchi à la question ▪ **she was lost** OR **deep in ~** elle était absorbée par ses pensées OR plongée dans ses pensées
2. *(countable)* [consideration] considération *f*, pensée *f* ▪ **I haven't given it a ~** je n'y ai pas pensé ▪ **don't give it another ~** n'y pensez plus ▪ **to collect one's ~s** rassembler ses esprits ▪ **my ~s were elsewhere** j'avais l'esprit ailleurs ▪ **my ~s went back to the time I had spent in Tunisia** j'ai repensé au temps où j'étais en Tunisie ▪ **she accepted the job with no ~ of her family** elle a accepté le travail sans tenir compte de sa famille ▪ **he had no ~ for his own safety** il ne pensait pas à sa propre sécurité ▪ **our ~s are with you** nos pensées vous accompagnent
3. [idea, notion] idée *f*, pensée *f* ▪ **the ~ occurred to me that you might like to come** l'idée m'est venue OR je me suis dit que cela vous ferait peut-être plaisir de venir ▪ **I had to give up all ~** OR **~s of finishing on time** j'ai dû finalement renoncer à l'idée de terminer à temps ▪ **the mere ~ of it makes me feel ill** rien que d'y penser, ça me rend malade ▪ **that's a ~!** ça, c'est une idée! ▪ **what an awful ~!** quelle horreur!
4. [intention] idée *f*, intention *f* ▪ **her one ~ was to reach the top** sa seule idée était d'atteindre le sommet ▪ **it's the ~ that counts** c'est l'intention qui compte
5. [opinion] opinion *f*, avis *m* ▪ **we'd like your ~s on the matter** nous aimerions savoir ce que vous en pensez
6. *(U)* [doctrine, ideology] pensée *f* ▪ **contemporary political ~** la pensée politique contemporaine.

thoughtful ['θɔ:tfʊl] *adj* **1.** [considerate, kind] prévenant, gentil, attentionné ▪ **it was a ~ gesture** c'était un geste plein d'attention ▪ **be more ~ next time** pensez un peu plus aux autres la prochaine fois ▪ **it was very ~ of them to send the flowers** c'était très aimable à eux OR gentil de leur part d'envoyer les fleurs **2.** [pensive] pensif **3.** [reasoned - decision, remark, essay] réfléchi ; [- study] sérieux.

thoughtfully ['θɔ:tfʊlɪ] *adv* **1.** [considerately, kindly] avec prévenance OR délicatesse, gentiment **2.** [pensively] pensivement **3.** [with careful thought] d'une manière réfléchie.

thoughtfulness ['θɔ:tfʊlnɪs] *n* **1.** [kindness] prévenance *f*, délicatesse *f*, gentillesse *f* **2.** [pensiveness] air *m* pensif.

thoughtless ['θɔ:tlɪs] *adj* **1.** [inconsiderate - person, act, behaviour] inconsidéré, irréfléchi, qui manque de délicatesse ; [- remark] irréfléchi ▪ **it was ~ of me** ce n'était pas très délicat de ma part ▪ **what a ~ thing to do!** quel manque de délicatesse! **2.** [hasty, rash - decision, action] irréfléchi, hâtif ; [- person] irréfléchi, léger.

thoughtlessly ['θɔ:tlɪslɪ] *adv* **1.** [inconsiderately] sans aucun égard, sans aucune considération **2.** [hastily] hâtivement, sans réfléchir.

thoughtlessness ['θɔ:tlɪsnɪs] *n (U)* manque *m* d'égards OR de prévenance.

thought-provoking *adj* qui pousse à la réflexion, stimulant.

thousand ['θaʊznd] <> *det* mille ▪ **a ~ years** mille ans, un millénaire ▪ **five ~ people** cinq mille personnes ▪ **I've already told you a ~ times** je te l'ai déjà dit mille fois ▶ **'The Thousand and One Nights'** 'les Mille et une nuits'.
<> *n* mille *m inv* ▪ **in the year two ~** en l'an deux mille ▪ **there were ~s of people** il y avait des milliers de personnes.

Thousand Island dressing *n sauce à base de mayonnaise, de ketchup et de cornichons hachés.*

thousandth ['θaʊzntθ] <> *det* millième.
<> *n* millième *m.*

thrall [θrɔ:l] *n fml* **1.** [state] servitude *f*, esclavage *m* ▪ **to be in ~ to sb** être l'esclave de qqn **2.** [person] esclave *mf.*

thrash [θræʃ] <> *vt* **1.** [in punishment] battre ▪ **the horse reared and ~ed the air with its hooves** le cheval se cabra et fouetta l'air de ses sabots **2.** SPORT [defeat] battre à plate couture OR à plates coutures **3.** [move vigorously] : **to ~ one's arms/legs (about)** battre des bras/jambes **4.** [thresh - corn] battre.
<> *vi* [move violently] se débattre.
<> *n* **1.** [stroke] battement *m* **2.** *UK inf* [party] sauterie *f.*
◆ **thrash about, thrash around** <> *vi insep* [person, fish] se débattre.
<> *vt sep* [arms, legs, tail] battre de ▪ [stick] agiter.
◆ **thrash out** *vt sep* [problem] débattre de ▪ [agreement] finir par trouver ▪ **we'll ~ it out over lunch** on démêlera OR éclaircira cette affaire pendant le repas.

thrashing ['θræʃɪŋ] *n* **1.** [punishment] raclée *f*, correction *f* ▪ **I gave him a good ~** je lui ai donné une bonne correction **2.** SPORT : **to get a ~** se faire battre à plates coutures ▪ **we gave the team a ~** on a battu l'équipe à plates coutures **3.** [of corn] battage *m.*

THREATS

Si vous n'arrêtez pas ce vacarme, j'appelle la police ! If you don't stop that noise, I'll call the police!

Sortez d'ici ou j'appelle la police ! Get out or I'll call the police!

Pose ça tout de suite, sinon c'est la fessée ! Put that down now or you'll get a smack!

Je te préviens, tu n'as pas intérêt à lui répéter ce que je viens de te dire. I'm warning you, you'd better not tell him what I've just said.

Donne-moi ça tout de suite, sinon... Give it to me right now, or else...

Je t'aurai prévenu... I'm warning you...

Ma patience a des limites... Don't try my patience...

Tu veux une claque ? *inf* Do you want a slap?

Si jamais tu recommences... If I you ever do that again...

Arrête ou il va t'arriver des bricoles ! *inf* Stop that or there'll be trouble!

thread [θred] <> *n* **1.** SEW & MED fil *m* ▪ **his life hung by a ~ *fig*** sa vie ne tenait qu'à un fil **2.** *fig* [of water, smoke] filet *m* ▪ [of light] mince rayon *m* ▪ [of story, argument] fil *m* **3.** TECH [of screw] pas *m*, filetage *m*.
<> *vt* **1.** [needle, beads, cotton] enfiler ▪ **she ~ed black cotton through the needle** elle a enfilé une aiguillée de coton noir ▪ **she quickly ~ed the film into the projector** elle a vite monté le film sur le projecteur ▪ **she ~ed her way through the crowd/market *fig*** elle s'est faufilée parmi la foule/à travers le marché **2.** TECH [screw] tarauder, fileter.
<> *vi* [needle, cotton] s'enfiler ▪ **the tape ~s through the slot** la bande passe dans la fente.

threadbare ['θredbeə^r^] *adj* **1.** [carpet, clothing] usé, râpé ▪ **he lived a ~ existence** il menait une existence miséreuse **2.** [joke, excuse, argument] usé, rebattu.

threat [θret] *n liter & fig* menace *f* ▪ **to make ~s against sb** proférer des menaces contre qqn ▪ **he's a ~ to our security** il constitue une menace pour notre sécurité ▪ **the country lives under (the) ~ of war** le pays vit sous la menace de la guerre.
Voir module d'usage page précédente

threaten ['θretn] <> *vt* **1.** [make threats against - person] menacer ▪ **to ~ to do sthg** menacer de faire qqch ▪ **he ~ed her with a gun** il l'a menacée avec un pistolet ▪ **we were ~ed with the sack** on nous a menacés de licenciement ▪ **to ~ proceedings against sb, to ~ sb with proceedings** LAW menacer de poursuivre qqn, menacer qqn de poursuites **2.** [subj: danger, unpleasant event] menacer ▪ **the species is ~ed with extinction** l'espèce est menacée *OR* en voie de disparition ▪ **our jobs are ~ed** nos emplois sont menacés **3.** [be a danger for - society, tranquillity] menacer, être une menace pour.
<> *vi* [danger, storm] menacer.

threatening ['θretnɪŋ] *adj* [danger, sky, storm, person] menaçant ▪ [letter] de menaces ▪ [gesture] menaçant, de menace ▪ **to use ~ language** prononcer des paroles menaçantes.

threateningly ['θretnɪŋlɪ] *adv* [behave, move] de manière menaçante, d'un air menaçant ▪ [say] d'un ton *OR* sur un ton menaçant.

three [θri:] <> *det* trois.
<> *n* trois *m*.
<> *pron* trois, *see also* **five**.

three-cornered *adj* triangulaire ▪ **~ discussion** débat *m* à trois ▪ **~ hat** tricorne *m*.

three-D, three-dimensional [-dɪ'menʃənl] *adj* **1.** [object] à trois dimensions, tridimensionnel ▪ [film] en relief ▪ [image] en trois dimensions **2.** [character - in book, play etc] qui semble réel.

three-day event *n* EQUIT concours *m* hippique sur trois jours.

threefold ['θri:fəʊld] <> *adj* triple.
<> *adv* trois fois autant.

three-legged [-'legɪd] *adj* [stool, table] à trois pieds ▪ [animal] à trois pattes.

three-legged race [-'legɪd-] *n course où les participants courent par deux, la jambe gauche de l'un attachée à la droite de l'autre.*

Three Mile Island *pr n* Three Mile Island *(théâtre d'un accident dans une centrale nucléaire aux États-Unis en 1979).*

threepenny ['θrepənɪ] *UK* <> *n* : **~ (bit *OR* piece)** *ancienne pièce de trois pence.*
<> *adj* à trois pence, coûtant trois pence ▪ **'The Threepenny Opera' *Brecht*** 'l'Opéra de quat' sous'.

three-piece *adj* : **~ suite *UK*, ~ set *US*** *salon comprenant un canapé et deux fauteuils assortis* ▪ **~ (suit)** (costume *m*) trois-pièces *m inv*.

three-point turn *n* AUT demi-tour *m* en trois manœuvres.

three-quarter <> *adj* [sleeve] trois-quarts *(inv)* ▪ [portrait] de trois-quarts ▪ **~ (length) jacket** veste *f* trois-quarts.
<> *n* [in rugby] : **~ (back)** trois-quart *m inv*.

three-quarters <> *npl* trois quarts *mpl*.
<> *adv* aux trois quarts.

three-ring circus *n US* cirque *m* à trois pistes ▪ **it's a real ~ *fig*** c'est un véritable cirque.

threescore [,θri:'skɔ:^r^] *lit* <> *adj* soixante.
<> *n* soixante *m*.

three-sided *adj* [shape] à trois côtés *OR* faces ▪ [discussion] à trois.

threesome ['θri:səm] *n* **1.** [group] groupe *m* de trois personnes ▪ **we went as a ~** nous y sommes allés à trois **2.** [in cards, golf] partie *f OR* jeu *m* à trois ▪ **she came along to make up a ~** elle est venue pour que nous soyons trois (joueurs).

three-star *adj* trois étoiles.

three-way *adj* [discussion, conversation] à trois ▪ [division] en trois ▪ [switch] à trois voies *OR* directions.

three-wheeler *n* [tricycle] tricycle *m* ▪ [car] voiture *f* à trois roues.

thresh [θreʃ] *vt* [corn, wheat] battre.

thresher ['θreʃə^r^] *n* AGRIC **1.** [person] batteur *m*, -euse *f* **2.** [machine] batteuse *f*.

threshing machine *n* batteuse *f*.

threshold ['θreʃhəʊld] <> *n* **1.** [doorway] seuil *m*, pas *m* de la porte ▪ **to cross the ~** franchir le seuil **2.** *fig* seuil *m*, début *m* ▪ **we are on the ~ of new discoveries** nous sommes sur le point de faire de nouvelles découvertes **3.** ECON & FIN niveau *m*, limite *f* **4.** ANAT & PSYCHOL seuil *m*.
<> *comp* **1.** *UK* ECON : **~ (wage) agreement/policy** accord *m* /politique *f* d'indexation des salaires sur les prix **2.** ELEC [current, voltage] de seuil **3.** LING : **~ level** niveau *m* seuil.

threw [θru:] *pt* ▻ **throw**.

thrice [θraɪs] *adv lit & arch* trois fois.

thrift [θrɪft] *n* **1.** [care with money] économie *f*, esprit *m* d'économie **2.** *US* [savings bank] : **~ (institution)** caisse *f* d'épargne.

thriftiness ['θrɪftɪnɪs] *n* sens *m* de l'économie.

thrift shop *n magasin vendant des articles d'occasion au profit d'œuvres charitables.*

thrifty ['θrɪftɪ] (*comp* **thriftier**, *superl* **thriftiest**) *adj* économe, peu dépensier.

thrill [θrɪl] <> *n* [feeling of excitement] frisson *m* ▪ [exciting experience, event] sensation *f*, émotion *f* ▪ **with a ~ of anticipation/pleasure** en frissonnant d'avance/de plaisir ▪ **it was a real ~ to meet the president** j'ai ressenti une grande émotion à rencontrer le président ▪ **they got quite a ~ out of the experience** ils ont été ravis *OR* enchantés de l'expérience.
<> *vt* transporter, électriser ▪ **the sight of the pyramids ~ed us** le spectacle des pyramides nous a procuré une vive émotion.
<> *vi* [with joy] tressaillir, frissonner.

thrilled [θrɪld] *adj* ravi ▪ **she was ~ to be chosen** elle était ravie d'avoir été choisie ▪ **I was ~ with the new chairs** j'étais très content des nouvelles chaises ▶ **to be ~ to bits *inf*** être aux anges.

thriller ['θrɪlə^r^] *n* [film, book] thriller *m*.

thrilling ['θrɪlɪŋ] *adj* [adventure, film, story] palpitant, saisissant, excitant ▪ [speech] passionnant.

thrive [θraɪv] (*pret* **thrived** *OR* **throve** [θrəʊv], *pp* **thrived** *OR* **thriven** ['θrɪvn]) *vi* **1.** [plant] pousser (bien) ▪ [child] grandir, se développer ▪ [adult] se porter bien, respirer la santé ▪ **she ~d on the mountain air** l'air des montagnes lui réussissait très bien ▪ **he ~s on hard work** il aime bien travailler dur **2.** [business, company] prospérer, être florissant ▪ [businessman] prospérer, réussir.

thriving ['θraɪvɪŋ] *adj* **1.** [person] florissant de santé, vigoureux ▪ [animal] vigoureux ▪ [plant] robuste, vigoureux **2.** [business, company] prospère, florissant ▪ [businessman] prospère.

thro' [θru:] *lit* = **through**.

throat [θrəʊt] *n* gorge *f* ▪ **get this drink/medicine down your ~!** *hum* avalez-moi cette boisson/ce médicament! ▪ **he grabbed him by the ~** il l'a pris à la gorge ▪ **to clear one's ~** s'éclaircir la voix ◆ **the two brothers are always at each other's ~s** les deux frères sont toujours en train de se battre ▪ **she's always jumping down my ~** *inf* elle est toujours à me crier dessus ▪ **he never misses the chance to ram** *OR* **to shove his success down my ~** *inf* il ne manque jamais une occasion de me rebattre les oreilles avec sa réussite.

throaty ['θrəʊtɪ] (*comp* **throatier**, *superl* **throatiest**) *adj* [voice, laugh etc] guttural, rauque.

throb [θrɒb] (*pret & pp* **throbbed**, *cont* **throbbing**) ◇ *vi* **1.** [music] vibrer ▪ [drums] battre (rythmiquement) ▪ [engine, machine] vrombir, vibrer ▪ **the place was throbbing (with life)** *fig* l'endroit grouillait de vie **2.** [heart] battre fort, palpiter **3.** [pain] lanciner ▪ **my head is throbbing** j'ai très mal à la tête ▪ **my finger still ~s where I hit it** j'ai encore des élancements dans le doigt là où je l'ai cogné.
◇ *n* **1.** [of music, drums] rythme *m*, battement *m* rythmique, battements *mpl* rythmiques ▪ [of engine, machine] vibration *f*, vibrations *fpl*, vrombissement *m*, vrombissements *mpl* **2.** [of heart] battement *m*, battements *mpl*, pulsation *f*, pulsations *fpl* **3.** [of pain] élancement *m*.

throbbing ['θrɒbɪŋ] *adj* **1.** [rhythm] battant ▪ [drum] qui bat rythmiquement ▪ [engine, machine] vibrant, vrombissant **2.** [heart] battant, palpitant **3.** [pain] lancinant.

throes *npl* ▭ **death throes**.
◆ **in the throes of** *prep phr* : **in the ~ of war/illness** en proie à la guerre/la maladie ▪ **to be in the ~ of doing sthg** être en train de faire qqch.

thrombosis [θrɒm'bəʊsɪs] (*pl* **thromboses** [-si:z]) *n* thrombose *f*, thromboses *fpl*.

throne [θrəʊn] ◇ *n* trône *m* ▪ **to come to the ~** monter sur le trône ▪ **on the ~** sur le trône.
◇ *vt* [monarch] mettre sur le trône ▪ [bishop] introniser.

throne room *n* salle *f* du trône.

throng [θrɒŋ] ◇ *n* foule *f*, multitude *f*.
◇ *vt* : **demonstrators ~ed the streets** des manifestants se pressaient dans les rues ▪ **the shops were ~ed with people** les magasins grouillaient de monde *OR* étaient bondés.
◇ *vi* affluer, se presser ▪ **crowds of people ~ed towards the stadium** les gens se dirigeaient en masse vers le stade ▪ **people ~ed into the square to get a glimpse of the president** les gens se sont pressés sur la place pour apercevoir le président.

throttle ['θrɒtl] ◇ *n* [of car] accélérateur *m* ▪ [of motorcycle] poignée *f* d'accélération *OR* des gaz ▪ [of aircraft] commande *f* des gaz ▪ **to open/to close the ~** mettre/réduire les gaz ▪ **at full ~** (à) pleins gaz.
◇ *comp* [controls] : **~ valve** papillon *m* des gaz, soupape *f* d'étranglement.
◇ *vt* [strangle] étrangler.
◆ **throttle down, throttle back** *vt sep* mettre au ralenti.

through [θru:] ◇ *prep* **1.** [from one end or side to the other] à travers ▪ **to walk ~ the streets** se promener dans *OR* à travers les rues ▪ **we travelled ~ America** nous avons parcouru les États-Unis ▪ **the river flows ~ a deep valley** le fleuve traverse une vallée profonde ▪ **the bullet went straight ~ his shoulder** la balle lui a traversé l'épaule de part en part ▪ **we went ~ a door** nous avons passé une porte ▪ **he could see her ~ the window** il pouvait la voir par la fenêtre ▪ **can you see ~ it?** est-ce que tu peux voir au travers? ▪ **a shiver ran ~ him** il fut parcouru d'un frisson ▪ **he drove ~ a red light** il a brûlé un feu rouge ▪ **to slip ~ the net** *liter & fig* passer à travers les mailles du filet ▪ **he goes ~ his money very quickly** l'argent lui brûle les doigts ▪ **she ate her way ~ a whole box of chocolates** elle a mangé toute une boîte de chocolats
2. [in] dans, à travers ▪ **he got a bullet ~ the leg** une balle lui a traversé la jambe ▪ **the bull had a ring ~ its nose** le taureau avait un anneau dans le nez
3. [from beginning to end of] à travers ▪ **~ the ages** à travers les âges ▪ **halfway ~ the performance** à la moitié *OR* au milieu de la représentation ▪ **she has lived ~ some difficult times** elle a connu *OR* traversé des moments difficiles ▪ **we had to sit ~ a boring lecture** nous avons dû rester à écouter une conférence ennuyeuse ▪ **I slept ~ the storm** l'orage ne m'a pas réveillé ▪ **she maintained her dignity ~ it all** elle a toujours gardé sa dignité
4. *US* [to, until] : **80 ~ 100** de 80 à 100 ▪ **April ~ July** d'avril jusqu'en juillet, d'avril à juillet
5. [by means of] par, grâce à ▪ **I sent it ~ the post** je l'ai envoyé par la poste ▪ **it was only ~ his intervention that we were allowed out** c'est uniquement grâce à son intervention qu'on nous a laissés sortir ▪ **I met a lot of people ~ him** il m'a fait rencontrer beaucoup de gens ▪ **she was interviewed ~ an interpreter** on l'a interviewée par l'intermédiaire d'un interprète
6. [because of] à cause de ▪ **~ no fault of his own, he lost his job** il a perdu son emploi sans que ce soit de sa faute.
◇ *adv* **1.** [from one side to the other] : **please go ~ into the lounge** passez dans le salon, s'il vous plaît ▪ **I couldn't get ~** je ne pouvais pas passer ▪ **we shoved our way ~** nous nous sommes frayé un chemin en poussant ▪ **the nail had gone right ~** le clou était passé au travers
2. [from beginning to end] : **I slept ~ until 8** j'ai dormi (sans me réveiller) jusqu'à 8 h ▪ **I read the letter ~** j'ai lu la lettre jusqu'au bout ▪ **I left halfway ~** je suis parti au milieu
3. [directly] : **the train goes ~ to Paris without stopping** le train va directement à Paris *OR* est sans arrêt jusqu'à Paris
4. [completely] : **to be wet ~** être complètement trempé ▪ **she's an aristocrat ~ and ~** c'est une aristocrate jusqu'au bout des ongles
5. TELEC : **can you put me ~ to Elaine/to extension 363?** pouvez-vous me passer Elaine/le poste 363? ▪ **I tried ringing him, but I couldn't get ~** j'ai essayé de l'appeler mais je n'ai pas réussi à l'avoir ▪ **you're ~ now** vous êtes en ligne.
◇ *adj* **1.** [direct - train, ticket] direct ▪ [traffic] en transit, de passage ▪ **'no ~ road** *UK*, **not a ~ street** *US*' 'voie sans issue'
2. [finished] : **are you ~?** avez-vous fini?, c'est fini? ▪ **he's ~ with his work at last** il a enfin terminé tout son travail ▪ **I'll be ~ reading the newspaper in a minute** j'aurai fini de lire le journal dans un instant ▪ **I'm ~ with smoking** la cigarette, c'est fini ▪ **she's ~ with him** elle en a eu assez de lui.

throughout [θru:'aʊt] ◇ *prep* **1.** [in space] partout dans ▪ **~ the world** dans le monde entier, partout dans le monde ▪ **~ Europe** à travers *OR* dans toute l'Europe, partout en Europe **2.** [in time] : **~ the year** pendant toute l'année ▪ **~ my life** (durant) toute ma vie.
◇ *adv* **1.** [everywhere] partout ▪ **the house has been repainted ~** la maison a été entièrement repeinte **2.** [all the time] (pendant) tout le temps ▪ **she remained silent ~** elle est restée silencieuse du début jusqu'à la fin.

throughput ['θru:pʊt] *n* COMPUT débit *m*.

throughway ['θru:weɪ] = **thruway**.

throve [θrəʊv] *pt* ▭ **thrive**.

throw [θrəʊ] (*pret* **threw** [θru:], *pp* **thrown** [θrəʊn]) ◇ *vt* **1.** [stone] lancer, jeter ▪ [ball] lancer ▪ [coal onto fire] mettre ▪ **~ me the ball, ~ the ball to me** lance-moi le ballon ▪ **could you ~ me my lighter?** peux-tu me lancer mon briquet? ▪ **she threw the serviette into the bin** elle a jeté la serviette à la poubelle ▪ **he threw his jacket over a chair** il a jeté sa veste sur une chaise ▪ **she threw a few clothes into a suitcase** elle a jeté quelques affaires dans une valise ▪ **I threw some cold water on my face** je me suis aspergé la figure avec de l'eau froide ▪ **a group of rioters threw stones at the police** un groupe de manifestants a lancé *OR* jeté des pierres sur les policiers ▪ **he threw two sixes** [in dice] il a jeté deux six ▪ **to ~ sb into prison** *OR* **jail** jeter qqn en prison
2. [opponent, rider] jeter (par terre) ▪ **the horse threw him** le cheval le désarçonna *OR* le jeta à terre
3. [with force, violence] projeter ▪ **she was ~n clear** [in car accident] elle a été éjectée ▪ **to ~ open** ouvrir en grand *OR* tout grand ▪ **she threw herself into an armchair** elle s'est jetée dans

un fauteuil ■ **he threw himself at her feet** il s'est jeté à ses pieds ■ **she threw herself at him** [attacked] elle s'est jetée *OR* s'est ruée sur lui ; [as lover] elle s'est jetée sur lui *OR* à sa tête ■ **he threw himself on the mercy of the king** *fig* il s'en est remis au bon vouloir du roi

4. [plunge] plonger ■ **the news threw them into confusion/a panic** les nouvelles les ont plongés dans l'embarras/les ont affolés ■ **to ~ o.s. into one's work** se plonger dans son travail ■ **she threw herself into the job of organizing the wedding** elle s'est plongée avec enthousiasme dans l'organisation du mariage

5. [direct, aim - look, glance] jeter, lancer ; [- accusation, reproach] lancer, envoyer ; [- punch] lancer, porter ■ [cast - light, shadows] projeter ■ **don't ~ that one at me!** ne me faites pas ce reproche!, ne me jetez pas ça à la figure! ■ **to ~ one's voice** THEAT projeter sa voix ■ **to ~ a bridge over a river** CONSTR jeter un pont sur une rivière

6. [confuse] désarçonner, dérouter, déconcerter ■ **that question really threw me!** cette question m'a vraiment désarçonné!, je ne savais vraiment pas quoi répondre à cette question! ■ **I was completely ~n for a few seconds** je suis resté tout interdit pendant quelques secondes

7. [activate - switch, lever, clutch] actionner

8. SPORT [race, match] perdre délibérément

9. [silk] tordre ■ [subj: potter] : **to ~ a pot** tourner un vase

10. VET [subj: cat, pig] : **to ~ a litter** mettre bas.

◇ *n* **1.** [of ball, javelin] jet *m*, lancer *m* ■ [of dice] lancer *m* ■ **his whole fortune depended on a single ~ of the dice** toute sa fortune dépendait d'un seul coup de dés ■ **a free ~** SPORT un lancer franc ■ **that was a good ~!** vous avez bien visé!

2. *inf* [go, turn] coup *m*, tour *m* ■ **10p a ~** 10 pence le coup ■ **at £20 a ~ I can't afford it** à 20 livres chaque fois, je ne peux pas me l'offrir ■ **it's your ~** à toi

3. [cover] couverture *f* ■ [piece of fabric] jeté *m* de fauteuil *OR* de canapé.

◆ **throw about** *UK*, **throw around** *vt sep* **1.** [toss] lancer ■ [scatter] jeter, éparpiller ■ **the boys were ~ing a ball about** les garçons jouaient à la balle ■ **to be ~n about** être ballotté

2. [move violently] : **to ~ o.s. about** s'agiter, se débattre ■ **she was ~ing her arms about wildly** elle agitait frénétiquement les bras.

◆ **throw aside** *vt sep* [unwanted object] rejeter, laisser de côté ■ [friend, work] laisser tomber, laisser de côté ■ [idea, suggestion] rejeter, repousser.

◆ **throw away** ◇ *vt sep* **1.** [old clothes, rubbish] jeter

2. *fig* [waste - advantage, opportunity, talents] gaspiller, gâcher ; [- affection, friendship] perdre ■ **don't ~ your money away on expensive toys** ne gaspille pas ton argent à acheter des jouets coûteux ■ **you're ~ing away your only chance of happiness** vous êtes en train de gâcher votre seule chance de bonheur

3. THEAT [line, remark] laisser tomber.

◇ *vi insep* [in cards] se défausser.

◆ **throw back** *vt sep* **1.** [gen] relancer, renvoyer ■ [fish] rejeter (à l'eau) ■ *fig* [image, light] réfléchir, renvoyer

2. [hair, head] rejeter en arrière ■ [shoulders] redresser, jeter en arrière

3. [curtains] ouvrir ■ [shutters] repousser, ouvrir tout grand ■ [bedclothes] repousser

4. *phr* [force to rely on] : **we were ~n back on our own resources** on a dû se rabattre sur nos propres ressources.

◆ **throw down** *vt sep* **1.** [to lower level] jeter ■ **can you ~ the towel down to me?** pouvez-vous me lancer la serviette? ■ **she threw her bag down on the floor** elle a jeté son sac par terre ■ **to ~ o.s. down on the ground/on one's knees** se jeter par terre/à genoux ■ **he threw his cards down on the table** il a jeté ses cartes sur la table

2. [weapons] jeter, déposer ■ **they threw down their arms** ils ont déposé les armes

3. *fig* [challenge] lancer.

◆ **throw in** ◇ *vt sep* **1.** [into box, cupboard etc] jeter ■ [through window] jeter, lancer ■ **to ~ in the towel** *fig* & SPORT jeter l'éponge ■ **to ~ in one's hand** abandonner la partie, s'avouer vaincu

2. [interject - remark, suggestion] placer ■ [include] : **breakfast is ~n in** le petit déjeuner est compris ■ **the salesman said he'd ~ in a free door if we bought new windows** le vendeur nous a promis une porte gratuite pour l'achat de fenêtres neuve ■ **with a special trip to Stockholm ~n in** avec en prime une excursion à Stockholm

3. SPORT [ball] remettre en jeu.

◇ *vi insep US* **to ~ in with sb** s'associer à *OR* avec qqn.

◆ **throw off** *vt sep* **1.** [discard - clothes] enlever *OR* ôter (à la hâte) ; [- mask, disguise] jeter

2. [get rid of - habit, inhibition] se défaire de, se débarrasse de ; [- burden] se libérer de, se débarrasser de ; [- cold, infection] se débarrasser de

3. [elude - pursuer] perdre, semer ■ **he managed to ~ the dog off the trail** il a réussi à dépister les chiens.

◆ **throw on** *vt sep* [clothes] enfiler *OR* passer (à la hâte).

◆ **throw out** *vt sep* **1.** [rubbish, unwanted items] jeter, mettr au rebut

2. [eject - from building] mettre à la porte, jeter dehors ; [- from night club] jeter dehors, vider ■ [evict - from accommodation] expulser ■ [expel - from school, army] renvoyer, expulser

3. [reject - bill, proposal] rejeter, repousser

4. [extend - arms, leg] tendre, étendre ■ **to ~ out one's ches** bomber le torse

5. [make - remark, suggestion] émettre, laisser tomber ■ **to ~ out a challenge** lancer un défi

6. [disturb - person] déconcerter, désorienter ■ [upset - calculation, results] fausser

7. [emit - light] émettre, diffuser ; [- smoke, heat] émettre, répandre.

◆ **throw over** *vt sep inf* [girlfriend, boyfriend] quitter, laisse tomber ■ [plan] abandonner, renoncer à.

◆ **throw together** *vt sep* **1.** *inf* [make quickly - equipment, table] fabriquer à la hâte, bricoler ■ **he managed to ~ a mea together** il a réussi à improviser un repas

2. [gather] rassembler à la hâte ■ **she threw a few things together and rang for a taxi** elle a jeté quelques affaires dans un sac et a appelé un taxi

3. [by accident] réunir par hasard.

◆ **throw up** ◇ *vt sep* **1.** [above one's head] jeter *OR* lancer en l'air ■ **can you ~ me up my towel?** peux-tu me lancer ma serviette? ■ **she threw up her hands in horror** elle a levé les bras en signe d'horreur

2. [produce - problem] produire, créer ; [- evidence] mettre à jour ; [- dust, dirt] soulever ; [- artist] produire

3. [abandon - career, studies] abandonner, laisser tomber ; [- chance, opportunity] laisser passer, gaspiller

4. *pej* [construct - building] construire *OR* bâtir en moins de deux

5. *inf* [vomit] vomir.

◇ *vi insep inf* vomir, rendre.

throwaway ['θrəʊə,weɪ] ◇ *adj* [line, remark] fait comme par hasard *OR* comme si de rien n'était.

◇ *comp* [bottle, carton etc] jetable, à jeter, à usage unique.

throwback ['θrəʊbæk] *n* **1.** ANTHR & BIOL régression *f* atavique **2.** [of fashion, custom] : **those new hats are a ~ to the 1930s** ces nouveaux chapeaux marquent un retour aux années 30 *OR* sont inspirés des années 30.

thrower ['θrəʊər] *n* lanceur *m*, - euse *f*.

throw-in *n* FTBL rentrée *f* en touche.

thrown [θrəʊn] *pp* ➢ **throw**.

thru [θru:] *US* = **through**.

thrum [θrʌm] *vi* [engine, machine] vibrer, vrombir ■ [rain] tambouriner.

thrush [θrʌʃ] *n* **1.** [bird] grive *f* **2.** *(U)* MED [oral] muguet *m* ■ [vaginal] mycose *f*, candidose *f*.

thrust [θrʌst] (*pret & pp* **thrust**) ◇ *vt* **1.** [push, shove] enfoncer, fourrer, plonger ■ **he ~ his finger/elbow into my ribs** il m'a enfoncé le doigt/le coude dans les côtes ■ **he ~ his sword into its scabbard** il a glissé son épée dans son fourreau ■ **to ~ one's hands into one's pockets** enfoncer *OR* fourrer les mains dans ses poches ■ **he ~ her into the cell** il l'a poussée violemment dans la cellule ■ **she ~ the money into his hands/into his bag** elle lui a fourré l'argent dans les mains/dans le sac ■ **to ~ one's way through the crowd/to the front** se frayer un chemin à travers la foule/pour être devant **2.** [force - responsibility, fame] imposer ■ **the job was ~ upon me** on m'a imposé ce travail

▪ **fame was ~ upon her overnight** la gloire lui est tombée dessus du jour au lendemain ▪ **he was ~ into the limelight** il a été mis en vedette ▪ **to ~ o.s. on** *OR* **upon sb** imposer sa présence à qqn, s'imposer à qqn.

◇ *vi* **1.** [push] : **he ~ past her** [rudely] il l'a bousculée en passant devant elle ; [quickly] il est passé devant elle comme une flèche ▪ **towers ~ing upwards into the sky** *fig* des tours qui s'élancent vers le ciel **2.** FENCING allonger *OR* porter une botte ▪ **he ~ at him with a knife** il a essayé de lui donner un coup de couteau.

◇ *n* **1.** [lunge] poussée *f* ▪ [stab] coup *m* **2.** *fig* [remark] pointe *f* **3.** *(U)* [force - of engine] poussée *f* ▪ *fig* [drive] dynamisme *m*, élan *m* **4.** [of argument, story] sens *m*, idée *f* ▪ [of policy] idée *f* directrice ▪ [of research] aspect *m* principal ▪ **the main ~ of her argument** l'idée maîtresse de son argument **5.** *(U)* ARCHIT & GEOL poussée *f*.

◆ **thrust aside** *vt sep* [person, thing] écarter brusquement ▪ [suggestion] écarter *OR* rejeter brusquement.

◆ **thrust away** *vt sep* repousser.

◆ **thrust forward** *vt sep* pousser en avant brusquement ▪ **to ~ o.s. forward** *liter* se frayer un chemin ; *fig* se mettre en avant.

◆ **thrust in** ◇ *vi insep* [physically] s'introduire de force.

◇ *vt sep* [finger, pointed object] enfoncer ▪ **she ~ her hand in** elle a brusquement mis la main dedans ▪ **to ~ one's way in** se frayer un passage pour entrer.

◆ **thrust out** *vt sep* **1.** [arm, leg] allonger brusquement ▪ [hand] tendre brusquement ▪ [chin] projeter en avant ▪ **she ~ her head out of the window** elle a brusquement passé la tête par la fenêtre ▪ **to ~ out one's chest** bomber la poitrine **2.** [eject] pousser dehors.

thrusting ['θrʌstɪŋ] *adj* [dynamic] dynamique, entreprenant, plein d'entrain ▪ *pej* qui se fait valoir, qui se met en avant.

thruway ['θru:weɪ] *n US* ≃ autoroute *f (à cinq ou six voies)*.

thud [θʌd] *(pret & pp* **thudded**, *cont* **thudding**) ◇ *vi* **1.** faire un bruit sourd ▪ [falling object] tomber en faisant un bruit sourd **2.** [walk or run heavily] : **to ~ across/in/past** traverser/entrer/passer à pas pesants ▪ **we could hear people thudding about in the flat above** on entendait les gens du dessus marcher à pas lourds **3.** [heart] battre fort.

◇ *n* bruit *m* sourd.

thug [θʌg] *n* voyou *m*.

thuggery ['θʌgərɪ] *n* brutalité *f*, violence *f*.

thumb [θʌm] ◇ *n* pouce *m* ▪ **to be under sb's ~** être sous la coupe de qqn ▪ **his mother's really got him under her ~** sa mère a vraiment de l'emprise sur lui *OR* en fait vraiment ce qu'elle veut ▪ **to be all (fingers and) ~s** être maladroit ▶ **to stick out like a sore ~** [be obvious] crever les yeux ; [be obtrusive] : **that factory sticks out like a sore ~** cette usine gâche le paysage.

◇ *vt* **1.** [book, magazine] feuilleter, tourner les pages de ▪ [pages] tourner ▪ **the catalogue has been well ~ed** les pages du catalogue sont bien écornées **2.** [hitch] : **to ~ a lift** *UK OR* **ride** *US* faire du stop *OR* de l'auto-stop ▪ **they ~ed a lift to Exeter** ils sont allés à Exeter en stop ▪ **she ~ed a lift from a passing motorist** elle a réussi à se faire prendre en stop par une voiture qui passait **3.** *phr* **to ~ one's nose at sb** faire un pied de nez à qqn.

◇ *vi US inf* faire du stop *OR* de l'auto-stop.

◆ **thumb through** *vt insep* [book, magazine] feuilleter ▪ [files] consulter rapidement ▪ [pages] tourner.

thumb index *n* répertoire *m* à onglets.

thumbnail ['θʌmneɪl] *n* ongle *m* du pouce ▪ **~ sketch** [of plan] aperçu *m*, croquis *m* rapide ; [of personality] bref portrait *m*.

thumbscrew ['θʌmskru:] *n* **1.** TECH vis *f* à papillon *OR* à ailettes **2.** [instrument of torture] poucettes *fpl*.

thumbs-down *n* : **he gave her the ~ as he came out** en sortant, il lui a fait signe que cela avait mal marché ▪ **my proposal was given the ~** ma proposition a été rejetée.

thumbs-up *n* : **to give sb the ~** [all OK] faire signe à qqn que tout va bien ; [in encouragement] faire signe à qqn pour l'encourager ▪ **they've given me the ~ for my thesis** ils m'ont donné le feu vert pour ma thèse.

thumbtack ['θʌmtæk] *n US* punaise *f*.

thump [θʌmp] ◇ *vt* donner un coup de poing à, frapper d'un coup de poing ▪ **he ~ed me in the stomach/on the head** il m'a donné un coup de poing à l'estomac/à la tête ▪ **to ~ sb on the back** donner une grande tape dans le dos à qqn ▪ **he ~ed his fist on the table** il a frappé du poing sur la table.

◇ *vi* **1.** [bang] cogner ▪ **he ~ed on the door/wall** il a cogné à la porte/contre le mur ▪ **my heart was ~ing with fear/excitement** la peur/l'émotion me faisait battre le cœur **2.** [run or walk heavily] : **to ~ in/out/past** entrer/sortir/passer à pas lourds.

◇ *n* **1.** [blow - gen] coup *m* ; [- with fist] coup *m* de poing ; [- with stick] coup *m* de bâton ▪ **to give sb a ~** assener un coup de poing à qqn ▪ **he got a ~ in the stomach** il a reçu un coup de poing à l'estomac **2.** [sound] bruit *m* sourd.

◇ *adv* : **to go ~** *inf* faire boum.

◆ **thump out** *vt sep* : **to ~ out a tune on the piano** marteler un air au piano.

thumping ['θʌmpɪŋ] *UK inf* ◇ *adj* [success] énorme, immense, phénoménal ▪ [difference] énorme.

◇ *adv dated* [as intensifier] : **a ~ great meal** un repas énorme.

thunder ['θʌndər] ◇ *n* **1.** METEOR tonnerre *m* ▪ **there's ~ in the air** le temps est à l'orage ▶ **to be as black as ~** [angry] être dans une colère noire **2.** [of applause, guns] tonnerre *m* ▪ [of engine, traffic] bruit *m* de tonnerre ▪ [of hooves] fracas *m* **3.** *UK dated* **by ~!** tonnerre!

◇ *vi* **1.** METEOR tonner ▪ **it's ~ing** il tonne, ça tonne **2.** [guns, waves] tonner, gronder ▪ [hooves] retentir ▪ **a train ~ed past** le train est passé dans un grondement de tonnerre **3.** [shout] : **to ~ at sb/against sthg** tonner contre qqn/contre qqch.

◇ *vt* [order, threat, applause] lancer d'une voix tonitruante *OR* tonnante.

thunderbolt ['θʌndəbəʊlt] *n* METEOR éclair *m* ▪ *fig* coup *m* de tonnerre.

thunderclap ['θʌndəklæp] *n* coup *m* de tonnerre.

thundercloud ['θʌndəklaʊd] *n* METEOR nuage *m* orageux ▪ *fig* nuage *m* noir.

thunderhead ['θʌndəhed] *n esp US* cumulo-nimbus *m*.

thundering ['θʌndərɪŋ] *UK inf dated* ◇ *adj* **1.** [terrible] : **to be in a ~ temper** *OR* **rage** être dans une colère noire *OR* hors de soi ▪ **it's a ~ nuisance!** quelle barbe! **2.** [superb - success] foudroyant, phénoménal.

◇ *adv* : **it's a ~ good read** c'est un livre formidable.

thunderous ['θʌndərəs] *adj* [shouts, noise] retentissant ▪ **there was ~ applause** il y eut un tonnerre d'applaudissements.

thunderstorm ['θʌndəstɔ:m] *n* orage *m*.

thunderstruck ['θʌndəstrʌk] *adj* foudroyé, abasourdi ▪ **she was ~ by the news** la nouvelle la foudroya.

thundery ['θʌndərɪ] *adj* METEOR orageux.

Thur, Thurs *(written abbrev of* **Thursday**) jeu.

Thursday ['θɜ:zdeɪ] *n* jeudi *m* ▪ **Black ~** Jeudi noir *(jour du krach de Wall Street qui déclencha la crise de 1929)*, *see also* **Friday**.

thus [ðʌs] *adv* [so] ainsi, donc ▪ [as a result] ainsi, par conséquent ▪ [in this way] ainsi ▪ **~ far** [in present] jusqu'ici ; [in past] jusque-là.

thwack [θwæk] ◇ *n* **1.** [blow] grand coup *m* ▪ [slap] claque *f* **2.** [sound] claquement *m*, coup *m* sec.

◇ *vt* donner un coup sec à ▪ [slap - person] gifler.

thwart [θwɔ:t] *vt* [plan] contrecarrer, contrarier ▪ [person - in efforts] contrarier les efforts de ; [- in plans] contrarier les projets de ; [- in attempts] contrecarrer les tentatives de ▪ **I was ~ed in my attempts to leave the country** mes tentatives de quitter le pays ont été contrecarrées.

thy [ðaɪ] *poss adj* BIBLE & *dial* & *lit* ton *m*, ta *f*, tes *mf pl*.

thyme [taɪm] *n (U)* thym *m*.

thyroid ['θaɪrɔɪd] ◇ *n* thyroïde *f*.
◇ *adj* thyroïde.

thyself [ðaɪ'self] *pers pron* BIBLE & *dial* & *lit (reflexive)* te ▪ *(intensifier)* toi-même.

ti [tiː] = **te**.

Tiananmen Square ['tjænənmen-] *pr n* la place Tian'anmen.

tiara [tɪ'ɑːrə] *n* [gen] diadème *m* ▪ RELIG tiare *f*.

Tiber ['taɪbəʳ] *pr n* : **the (River)** ~ le Tibre.

Tiberias [taɪ'bɪərɪæs] *pr n* : **Lake** ~ le lac de Tibériade.

Tiberius [taɪ'bɪərɪəs] *pr n* Tibère.

Tibet [tɪ'bet] *pr n* Tibet *m* ▪ **in** ~ au Tibet.

Tibetan [tɪ'betn] ◇ *n* **1.** [person] Tibétain *m*, - e *f* **2.** LING tibétain *m*.
◇ *adj* tibétain.

tibia ['tɪbɪə] (*pl* **tibias** *OR pl* **tibiae** [-biː]) *n* tibia *m*.

tic [tɪk] *n* : **(nervous)** ~ tic *m* (nerveux).

tich [tɪtʃ] *n UK inf* microbe *m*.

tichy ['tɪtʃɪ] *adj UK inf* minuscule, tout petit.

Ticino [tɪ'tʃiːnəʊ] *pr n* Tessin *m*.

tick [tɪk] ◇ *vi* [clock, time-bomb] faire tic-tac ▪ [motivation] : **I wonder what makes him** ~ je me demande ce qui le motive.
◇ *vt UK* [mark - name, item] cocher, pointer ; [- box, answer] cocher ▪ SCH [- as correct] marquer juste.
◇ *n* **1.** [of clock] tic-tac *m* **2.** *UK inf* [moment] instant *m* ▪ **I'll only be a** ~ j'en ai pour une seconde **3.** *UK* [mark] coche *f* ▪ **to put a** ~ **against sthg** cocher qqch **4.** ZOOL tique *f* **5.** *UK inf* [credit] crédit *m* ▪ **to buy sthg on** ~ acheter qqch à crédit **6.** TEX [ticking] toile *f* à matelas ▪ [covering - for mattress] housse *f* (de matelas) ; [- for pillow] housse *f* (d'oreiller), taie *f*.
◆ **tick away** *vi insep* **1.** [clock] faire tic-tac ▪ [taximeter] tourner **2.** [time] passer.
◆ **tick off** *vt sep* **1.** [name, item] cocher, pointer **2.** *fig* [count - reasons, chapters] compter, énumérer ▪ **he ~ed off the EU countries on his fingers** il compta les pays de l'UE sur ses doigts **3.** *UK inf* [scold] attraper, passer un savon à ▪ **she got ~ed off for being late** elle s'est fait attraper pour être arrivée en retard **4.** *US inf* [annoy] agacer, taper sur le système à.
◆ **tick over** *vi insep* **1.** *UK* [car engine] tourner au ralenti ▪ [taximeter] tourner **2.** *fig* [business, production] tourner normalement.

ticked [tɪkt] *adj US inf* en rogne.

ticker ['tɪkəʳ] *n* **1.** *US* [printer] téléscripteur *m*, téléimprimeur *m* **2.** *inf* [heart] palpitant *m*, cœur *m* **3.** *inf* [watch] tocante *f*, toquante *f*.

tickertape ['tɪkəteɪp] *n* **1.** [tape] bande *f* de téléscripteur *OR* de téléimprimeur **2.** *US fig* **to get a ~ reception** *OR* **welcome** recevoir un accueil triomphal.

tickertape parade *n aux États-Unis, défilé où l'on accueille un héros national sous une pluie de serpentins.*

ticket ['tɪkɪt] ◇ *n* **1.** [for travel - on coach, plane, train] billet *m* ; [- on bus, underground] billet *m*, ticket *m* ▪ [for entry - to cinema, theatre, match] billet *m* ; [- to car park] ticket *m* (de parking) ▪ [for membership - of library] carte *f* ▶ **this play's the hottest ~ in town** c'est le spectacle dont tout le monde parle en ce moment **2.** [receipt - in shop] ticket *m* (de caisse), reçu *m* ; [- for left-luggage, cloakroom] ticket *m* (de consigne) ; [- from pawnshop] reconnaissance *f* **3.** [label] étiquette *f* **4.** AUT [fine] P-V *m*, contravention *f*, amende *f* ▪ **to get a** ~ avoir un P-V **5.** *US* POL [set of principles] : **he fought the election on a Democratic** ~ il a basé son programme électoral sur les principes du Parti démocrate **6.** *inf* AERON & NAUT [certificate] brevet *m* **7.**△ *UK mil sl* **to get one's** ~ être libéré des obligations militaires **8.** *phr* **that's (just) the ~ !** *inf* voilà exactement ce qu'il faut!
◇ *vt* **1.** [label] étiqueter **2.** [earmark] désigner, destiner **3.** *US* [issue with a ticket] donner un billet à **4.** *US* [issue with a parking ticket] mettre un P-V à.

ticket agency *n* **1.** THEAT agence *f* de spectacles **2.** RAIL agence *f* de voyages.

ticket collector *n* RAIL contrôleur *m*, - euse *f*.

ticket holder *n* personne *f* munie d'un billet.

ticket inspector = **ticket collector**.

ticket machine *n* distributeur *m* de tickets, billetterie *f* automatique.

ticket office *n* bureau *m* de vente des billets, guichet *m*.

ticket taker *n US* contrôleur *m*, - euse *f*.

ticket tout *n UK* revendeur *m*, - euse *f* de billets *(sur le marché noir)*.

ticking ['tɪkɪŋ] *n* **1.** [of clock] tic-tac *m* **2.** TEX toile *f* (à matelas).

ticking off (*pl* **tickings off**) *n UK inf* **to give sb a** ~ enguirlander qqn, tirer les oreilles à qqn ▪ **she got a ~ for being late** elle s'est fait enguirlander parce qu'elle était en retard.

tickle ['tɪkl] ◇ *vt* **1.** *liter* [by touching] chatouiller ▪ **to ~ sb in the ribs/under the chin** chatouiller les côtes/le menton à qqn **2.** *fig* [curiosity, vanity] chatouiller **3.** *fig* [amuse] amuser, faire rire ▪ [please] faire plaisir à ▶ **to be ~d pink** *OR* **to death** être ravi *OR* aux anges.
◇ *vi* [person, blanket] chatouiller ▪ [beard] piquer ▪ **don't ~!** ne me chatouille pas!
◇ *n* [on body] chatouillement *m* ▪ [in throat] picotement *m* ▪ **I've got an awful ~ in my throat** j'ai la gorge qui picote atrocement.

tickling ['tɪklɪŋ] ◇ *n (U)* [of person] chatouilles *fpl* ▪ [of blanket] picotement *m*.
◇ *adj* [throat] qui grattouille *OR* picote ▪ [cough] d'irritation, qui gratte la gorge ▪ **you get a ~ sensation in your feet** on a une sensation de picotement dans les pieds.

ticklish ['tɪklɪʃ] *adj* **1.** [person, feet] chatouilleux ▪ [sensation] de chatouillement **2.** *inf* [touchy] chatouilleux **3.** *inf* [delicate - situation, topic] délicat, épineux ; [- moment] crucial ; [- negotiations] délicat.

tickly ['tɪklɪ] *adj inf* [sensation] de chatouillis ▪ [blanket] qui chatouille ▪ [beard] qui pique.

ticktack ['tɪk,tæk] = **tic tac**.

ticktock ['tɪktɒk] *n* [of clock] tic-tac *m*.

tic tac ['tɪk,tæk] *n* **1.** *UK* gestuelle *f* des bookmakers *(pour indiquer la cote)* **2.** *US* tic-tac *m*.

tidal ['taɪdl] *adj* [estuary, river] qui a des marées ▪ [current, cycle, force] de la marée ▪ [ferry] dont les horaires sont fonction de la marée ▪ [energy] marémoteur.

tidal wave *n* raz-de-marée *m inv* ▪ *fig* [of sympathy] élan *m*.

tidbit ['tɪdbɪt] *US* = **titbit**.

tiddledywinks ['tɪdldɪwɪŋks] *n US* = **tiddlywinks**.

tiddler ['tɪdləʳ] *n inf* **1.** [fish] petit poisson *m* ▪ [minnow] fretin *m* ▪ [stickleback] épinoche *f* **2.** *UK* [child] mioche *m*.

tiddly ['tɪdlɪ] (*comp* **tiddlier**, *superl* **tiddliest**) *adj UK inf* **1.** [tiny] tout petit, minuscule **2.** [tipsy] éméché, paf.

tiddlywink ['tɪdlɪwɪŋk] *n* pion *m* (du jeu de puce).
◆ **tiddlywinks** *n (U)* jeu *m* de puce.

tide [taɪd] *n* **1.** [of sea] marée *f* ▪ **at high/low ~** à marée haute/basse ▪ **high ~ is at 17.29** la mer est haute à 17 h 29, la marée haute est à 17 h 29 **2.** [of opinion] courant *m* ▪ [of discontent, indignation] vague *f* ▪ [of events] cours *m*, marche *f* ▪ **the ~ has turned** la chance a tourné ▪ **there is a rising ~ of unrest amongst the workforce** il y a une agitation grandissante parmi le personnel.
◆ **tide over** *vt sep* dépanner.

tidemark ['taɪdmɑːk] *n* **1.** [on shore] laisse *f* de haute mer **2.** *fig & hum* [round bath, neck] marque *f* de crasse.

tideway ['taɪdweɪ] *n* [channel] lit *m* de la marée ▪ [part of river] estuaire *m*, aber *m*.

tidily ['taɪdɪlɪ] *adv* [pack, fold] soigneusement, avec soin ▪ **~ dressed** [adult] bien habillé *OR* mis ; [child] habillé proprement ▪ **put your books/clothes away ~** range bien tes livres/habits.

tidiness ['taɪdɪnɪs] *n* **1.** [of drawer, desk, room] ordre *m* **2.** [of appearance] netteté *f* **3.** [of work, exercise book] propreté *f*, netteté *f* ▪ [of writing] netteté *f*.

tidings ['taɪdɪŋz] *npl arch & lit* nouvelles *fpl*.

tidy ['taɪdɪ] (*comp* **tidier**, *superl* **tidiest**, *pl* **tidies**, *pret & pp* **tidied**) ◇ *adj* **1.** [room, house, desk] rangé, ordonné, en ordre ▪ [garden, town] propre ▪ **neat and ~** propre et net ▪ **he keeps his flat very ~** il tient son appartement bien rangé **2.** [in appearance - person] soigné ; [- clothes, hair] soigné, net **3.** [work, writing] soigné, net **4.** [in character - person] ordonné, méthodique **5.** *inf* [sum, profit] joli, coquet.
◇ *n* **1.** [receptacle] vide-poches *m inv* **2.** *US* [on chair] têtière *f*.
◇ *vt* [room] ranger, mettre de l'ordre dans ▪ [desk, clothes, objects] ranger ▪ **to ~ one's hair** se recoiffer.
➡ **tidy away** *vt sep* ranger, ramasser.
➡ **tidy up** ◇ *vi insep* **1.** [in room] tout ranger **2.** [in appearance] s'arranger.
◇ *vt sep* [room, clothes] ranger, mettre de l'ordre dans ▪ [desk] ranger ▪ **to ~ o.s. up** s'arranger ▪ **~ your things up** [make tidy] range tes affaires ; [put away] range *OR* ramasse tes affaires.

tidy-out *n inf* **to have a ~** [make tidy] faire du (grand) rangement ; [clear out] faire du rangement par le vide.

tidy-up *n inf* **to have a ~** faire du rangement ▪ **we'll have to give the place a ~ before the guests arrive** il va falloir mettre de l'ordre *OR* faire du rangement dans la maison avant l'arrivée des invités.

tie [taɪ] ◇ *n* **1.** [necktie] cravate *f*
2. [fastener - gen] attache *f* ; [- on apron] cordon *m* ; [- for curtain] embrasse *f* ; [- on shoes] lacet *m*
3. [bond, link] lien *m*, attache *f* ▪ **family ~s** liens de parenté *OR* familiaux ▪ **there are strong ~s between the two countries** les deux pays entretiennent d'étroites relations
4. [restriction] entrave *f*
5. SPORT [draw] égalité *f* ▪ [drawn match] match *m* nul ▪ **the match ended in a ~** les deux équipes ont fait match nul ▮ [in competition] *compétition dont les gagnants sont ex aequo* ▪ **it was a ~ for first/second place** il y avait deux premiers/seconds ex aequo ▮ POL égalité *f* de voix ▪ **the election resulted in a ~** les candidats ont obtenu le même nombre de voix *OR* étaient à égalité des voix
6. FTBL [match] match *m* ▪ **a championship ~** un match de championnat
7. MUS liaison *f*
8. *US* RAIL traverse *f*
9. CONSTR tirant *m*.
◇ *vt* **1.** [with string, rope - parcel] attacher, ficeler ▪ **they ~d him to a tree** il l'ont attaché *OR* ligoté à un arbre ▪ **his hands and feet were ~d** ses mains et ses pieds étaient ligotés
2. [necktie, scarf, shoelaces] attacher, nouer ▪ **why not ~ some string to the handle?** pourquoi ne pas attacher une ficelle à la poignée? ▪ **she ~d a bow/a ribbon in her hair** elle s'est mis un nœud/un ruban dans les cheveux ▪ **to ~ a knot in sthg, to ~ sthg in a knot** faire un nœud à qqch ⊳ **he's still ~d to his mother's apron strings** il n'a pas encore quitté les jupes de sa mère
3. [confine - subj: responsibility, job etc] **: she's ~d to the house** [unable to get out] elle est clouée à la maison ; [kept busy] la maison l'accapare beaucoup ▪ **the job keeps me very much ~d to my desk** mon travail m'oblige à passer beaucoup de temps devant mon bureau ▪ **they're ~d to *OR* by the conditions of the contract** ils sont liés par les conditions du contrat
4. MUS lier.
◇ *vi* **1.** [apron, shoelace etc] s'attacher, se nouer
2. [draw - players] être à égalité ; [- in match] faire match nul ; [- in exam, competition] être ex aequo ; [- in election] obtenir le même score *OR* nombre de voix ▪ **they ~d for third place in the competition** ils étaient troisième ex aequo au concours.

➡ **tie back** *vt sep* [hair] attacher (en arrière) ▪ [curtains, plant] attacher ▪ **her hair was ~d back in a bun** ses cheveux étaient ramassés en chignon.
➡ **tie down** *vt sep* **1.** [with string, rope - person, object] attacher
2. *fig* [restrict] accaparer ▪ **she doesn't want to feel ~d down** elle ne veut pas perdre sa liberté ▪ **I'd rather not be ~d down to a specific time** je préférerais qu'on ne fixe pas une heure précise ▪ **we must ~ them down to the terms of the contract** il faut les obliger à respecter les termes du contrat.
➡ **tie in** ◇ *vi insep* **1.** [be connected] être lié *OR* en rapport ▪ **this ~s in with what I said before** cela rejoint ce que j'ai dit avant
2. [correspond] correspondre, concorder ▪ **the evidence doesn't ~ in with the facts** les indices dont nous disposons ne correspondent pas aux faits *OR* ne cadrent pas avec les faits.
◇ *vt sep* **: how is this ~d in with your previous experiments?** quel est le lien *OR* le rapport avec vos expériences antérieures? ▪ **she's trying to ~ her work experience in with her research** elle essaie de faire coïncider son expérience professionnelle et ses recherches.
➡ **tie on** *vt sep* attacher, nouer.
➡ **tie together** ◇ *vi insep* **: it all ~s together** tout se tient.
◇ *vt sep* [papers, sticks] attacher (ensemble) ▪ **to ~ sb's hands/feet together** attacher les mains/les pieds de qqn.
➡ **tie up** ◇ *vt sep* **1.** [parcel, papers] ficeler ▪ [plant, animal] attacher ▪ [prisoner] attacher, ligoter ▪ [boat] attacher, amarrer ▪ [shoelace] nouer, attacher ▪ **the letters were ~d up in bundles** les lettres étaient ficelées en liasses
2. (*usu passive*) [money, supplies] immobiliser ▪ **their money is all ~d up in shares** leur argent est entièrement investi dans des actions ▪ **her inheritance is ~d up until her 21st birthday** elle ne peut toucher à son héritage avant son 21e anniversaire
3. [connect - company, organization] lier par des accords
4. [complete, finalize - deal] conclure ; [- terms of contract] fixer ▪ **there are still a few loose ends to ~ up** il y a encore quelques points de détail à régler
5. [impede - traffic] bloquer ; [- progress, production] freiner, entraver.
◇ *vi insep* **1.** [be connected] être lié ▪ **how does this ~ up with the Chicago gang killings?** quel est le rapport avec les assassinats du gang de Chicago?
2. NAUT accoster.

tieback ['taɪbæk] *n* [cord] embrasse *f* (de rideaux) ▪ [curtain] rideau *m* (*retenu par une embrasse*).

tie beam *n* CONSTR longrine *f*.

tiebreak(er) ['taɪbreɪk(əʳ)] *n* TENNIS tie-break *m* ▪ [in game, contest] épreuve *f* subsidiaire ▪ [in quiz] question *f* subsidiaire.

tie clasp, tie clip *n* fixe-cravate *m*.

tied [taɪd] *adj* **1.** SPORT **: to be ~** [players] être à égalité ; [game] être nul **2.** [person - by obligation, duties] pris, occupé ▪ **he doesn't want to feel ~** il ne veut pas s'engager ▪ **she isn't ~ by any family obligations** elle n'a *OR* elle n'est tenue par aucune obligation familiale **3.** MUS [note] lié.

tied cottage *n UK logement attaché à une ferme et occupé par un employé agricole*.

tied house *n* [pub] *pub lié par contrat à une brasserie qui l'approvisionne* ▪ [house] logement *m* de fonction.

tied up *adj* [busy] **: to be ~** être occupé *OR* pris ▪ **she's ~ with the children every Wednesday** elle est prise par les enfants tous les mercredis ▪ **he's ~ in a meeting until 5** il est en réunion jusqu'à 17 h.

tie-dye *vt* teindre en nouant (*pour obtenir une teinture non uniforme*).

tie-in *n* **1.** [connection] lien *m*, rapport *m* **2.** *US* COMM [sale] vente *f* par lots ▪ [items] lot *m* **3.** [in publishing] *livre, cassette etc lié à un film ou une émission*.

tie line *n* TELEC ligne *f* interautomatique.

tiepin ['taɪpɪn] *n* épingle *f* de cravate.

tier [tɪəʳ] ◇ *n* **1.** [row of seats - in theatre, stadium] gradin *m*, rangée *f* ■ [level] étage *m* **2.** ADMIN échelon *m*, niveau *m* ■ **a five-~ system** un système à cinq niveaux **3.** [of cake] étage *m*.
◇ *vt* [seating] disposer en gradins.

tiered ['tɪəd] *adj* [seating] en gradins ■ [system] à plusieurs niveaux.

tie-rod *n* AUT tirant *m*.

Tierra del Fuego [tɪˌerədel'fweɪgəʊ] *pr n* Terre de Feu *f* ■ **in ~** en Terre de Feu.

tie-tack *n* *US* fixe-cravate *m*.

tiff [tɪf] *n* *UK inf* prise *f* de bec ■ **they've had a bit of a ~** ils se sont un peu disputés ■ **a lover's ~** une dispute d'amoureux.

tig [tɪg] *n* (jeu *m* du) chat *m*.

tiger ['taɪgəʳ] *n* tigre *m* ■ **to hunt ~** aller à la chasse au tigre ▶ **to get off the ~** *OR* **the ~'s back** se tirer d'embarras ■ **to have a ~ by the tail** se trouver pris dans une situation dont on n'est plus maître.

tiger cub *n* petit *m* du tigre.

tiger lily *n* lis *m* tigré.

tiger moth *n* ENTOM écaille *f*.

tight [taɪt] ◇ *adj* **1.** [garment, footwear] serré, étroit ■ **it's a ~ fit** c'est trop serré *OR* juste ■ **~ jeans** [too small] un jean trop serré ; [close-fitting] un jean moulant ■ **a ~ skirt** [too small] une jupe trop serrée ; [close-fitting] une jupe moulante
2. [stiff - drawer, door] dur à ouvrir ; [- tap] dur à tourner ; [- lid] dur à enlever ; [- screw] serré ■ [constricted] pesant ■ **I've got a ~ feeling across my chest** j'ai comme un poids sur la poitrine ■ **it was a ~ squeeze but we got everyone in** on a eu du mal mais on a réussi à faire entrer tout le monde ▶ **to be in a ~ corner** *OR* **spot** être dans une situation difficile
3. [taut - rope] raide, tendu ; [- bow] tendu ; [- net, knitting, knot] serré ; [- skin] tiré ; [- group] serré ■ **her face looked ~ and drawn** elle avait les traits tirés ■ [firm] : **to keep (a) ~ hold** *OR* **grasp on sthg** bien tenir qqch ■ **she kept a ~ hold on the rail** elle s'agrippait à la balustrade ■ **she kept a ~ hold on the expenses** *fig* elle surveillait les dépenses de près ■ **you should keep a ~er rein on the children/your emotions** *fig* il faudrait surveiller les enfants de plus près/mieux maîtriser vos émotions
4. [sharp - bend, turn] brusque
5. [strict - control, restrictions] strict, sévère ; [- security] strict ■ **to run a ~ ship** mener son monde à la baguette
6. [limited - budget, credit] serré, resserré ■ **money is a bit ~** *OR* **things are a bit ~ at the moment** l'argent manque un peu en ce moment
7. [close - competition] serré
8. [busy - schedule] serré, chargé ■ **it was ~ but I made it in time** c'était juste, mais je suis arrivé à temps
9. *inf* [mean] radin, pingre
10. *inf* [drunk] soûl, rond.
◇ *adv* [close, fasten] bien ■ **packed ~** [bag] bien rempli *OR* plein ; [pub, room] bondé ■ **hold ~!** tenez-vous bien!, accrochez-vous bien! ■ **she held the rabbit ~ in her arms** elle serrait le lapin dans ses bras ■ **pull the thread ~** tirez *OR* tendez bien le fil ■ **it needs to be turned/screwed ~** il faut le serrer/le visser à fond.
➤ **tights** *npl* : **(pair of) ~s** collant *m*, collants *mpl*.

tight-arsed▲ *UK* [-ɑːst], **tight-assed**▲ *US* [-æst] *adj* coincé, constipé.

tighten ['taɪtn] ◇ *vt* **1.** [belt, strap] resserrer ■ **he ~ed his grasp on the rail** il agrippa plus fermement la balustrade ▶ **to ~ one's belt** *liter* resserrer sa ceinture ; *fig* se serrer la ceinture **2.** [nut, screw] serrer, bien visser ■ [knot] serrer ■ [cable, rope] serrer, tendre **3.** [control, security, regulations] renforcer ■ [credit] resserrer.
◇ *vi* **1.** [grip] : **his finger ~ed on the trigger** son doigt se serra sur la gâchette **2.** [nut, screw, knot] se resserrer ■ [cable, rope] se raidir, se tendre **3.** [control, security, regulation] être renforcé ■ [credit] se resserrer **4.** [throat, stomach] se nouer.
➤ **tighten up** *vt sep* **1.** [nut, screw] serrer **2.** [control, security, regulation] renforcer.
➤ **tighten up on** *vt insep* : **to ~ up on discipline/security** renforcer la discipline/la sécurité ■ **the government are ~ing up on drug pushers/tax evasion** le gouvernement renforce la lutte contre les revendeurs de drogue/la fraude fiscale.

tightening ['taɪtnɪŋ] *n* [of screw, credit] resserrement *m* ■ [of control, regulation] renforcement *m* ■ **he felt a ~ in his throat** il sentit sa gorge se nouer.

tightfisted [ˌtaɪt'fɪstɪd] *adj pej* avare, pingre.

tight-fitting *adj* [skirt, trousers] moulant ■ [lid] qui ferme bien.

tight-knit [-'nɪt] *adj* [community, family] (très) uni.

tight-lipped [-'lɪpt] *adj* : **he sat ~ and pale** il était assis, pâle et muet.

tightly ['taɪtlɪ] *adv* **1.** [firmly - hold, fit, screw] (bien) serré ■ **he held his daughter ~ to him** il serrait sa fille tout contre lui ■ **hold on ~** tenez-vous *OR* accrochez-vous bien ■ **we held on ~ to the rail** nous nous sommes agrippés fermement à la balustrade ■ **the cases were ~ sealed** les caisses étaient bien scellées ■ **her eyes were ~ shut** elle avait les yeux bien fermés ■ **news is ~ controlled** les informations sont soumises à un contrôle rigoureux ■ **~ curled hair** des cheveux frisés **2.** [densely] : **the lecture hall was ~ packed** l'amphithéâtre était bondé *OR* plein à craquer.

tightness ['taɪtnɪs] *n* **1.** [of garment, shoes] étroitesse *f* **2.** [stiffness - of drawer, screw, tap] dureté *f* **3.** [tautness - of bow, rope] raideur *f* ■ **he felt a sudden ~ in his throat** il sentit soudain sa gorge se nouer **4.** [strictness - of control, regulation] rigueur *f*, sévérité *f* ; [- of security] rigueur *f*.

tightrope ['taɪtrəʊp] *n* corde *f* raide ■ **to walk the ~** marcher sur la corde raide ■ **she's walking a political ~** *fig* elle s'est aventurée sur un terrain politique glissant *OR* dangereux.

tightrope walker *n* funambule *mf*.

Tigré ['tiːgreɪ] *pr n* Tigré *m* ■ **in ~** dans le Tigré.

tigress ['taɪgrɪs] *n* ZOOL & *fig* tigresse *f*.

tilde ['tɪldə] *n* tilde *m*.

tile [taɪl] ◇ *n* [for roof] tuile *f* ■ [for wall, floor] carreau *m* ■ **to have a night (out) on the ~s** *inf* faire la noce.
◇ *vt* [roof] couvrir de tuiles ■ [floor, wall] carreler.

tiled [taɪld] *adj* [floor, wall] carrelé ■ **~ floor** sol *m* carrelé ■ **~ roof** toit *m* de tuiles.

tiler ['taɪləʳ] *n* [of roof] couvreur *m* *(de toits en tuiles)* ■ [of floor, wall] carreleur *m*, -euse *f*.

tiling ['taɪlɪŋ] *n* *(U)* **1.** [putting on tiles - on roof] pose *f* des tuiles ; [- on floor, in bathroom] carrelage *m* **2.** [tiles - on roof] tuiles *fpl* ; [- on floor, wall] carrelage *m*, carreaux *mpl*.

till [tɪl] ◇ *conj* & *prep* = **until**.
◇ *n* **1.** [cash register] caisse *f* (enregistreuse) ■ [drawer] tiroir-caisse *m* ■ **to be caught with one's fingers** *OR* **hands in the ~** être pris en flagrant délit *OR* la main dans le sac **2.** [money] caisse *f*.
◇ *vt* AGRIC labourer.

tiller ['tɪləʳ] *n* **1.** NAUT barre *f*, gouvernail *m* **2.** BOT pousse *f*, talle *f*.

tilt [tɪlt] ◇ *vt* **1.** [lean] pencher, incliner ■ **to ~ one's chair (back)** se balancer sur sa chaise ■ **to ~ one's head back** renverser la tête en arrière ■ **this may ~ the odds in our favour** *fig* cela peut faire pencher la balance de notre côté **2.** [cover - gen] bâcher ■ NAUT tauder.
◇ *vi* **1.** [lean] se pencher, s'incliner ■ **to ~ backwards/forwards** se pencher en arrière/en avant ■ **don't ~ back on your chair** ne te balance pas sur ta chaise **2.** HIST [joust] jouter ■ **to ~ at sb** HIST diriger un coup de lance contre qqn ; *fig* lancer des piques à qqn ▶ **to ~ at windmills** se battre contre des moulins à vent.
◇ *n* **1.** [angle] inclinaison *f* ■ [slope] pente *f* ■ **she wore her hat at a ~** elle portait son chapeau incliné **2.** HIST [joust] joute *f*

■ [thrust] coup *m* de lance ■ *fig* **to have a ~ at sb** s'en prendre à qqn, décocher des pointes à qqn **3.** [awning] store *m* (de toile), bâche *f* ■ NAUT taud *m*.

◆ **full tilt** *adv phr* : **he ran full ~ into her** il lui est rentré en plein dedans ■ **he ran full ~ into the door** il est rentré en plein dans la porte.

◆ **tilt over** *vi insep* **1.** [slant] pencher **2.** [overturn] se renverser, basculer.

timber ['tɪmbəʳ] ◇ *n* **1.** [wood] bois *m* de charpente *OR* de construction *OR* d'œuvre **2.** *(U)* [trees] arbres *mpl*, bois *m* ■ **land under ~** terre *f* boisée ■ **standing ~** bois sur pied **3.** [beam] madrier *m*, poutre *f* ■ [on ship] membrure *f*.
◇ *comp* [roof, fence] en bois.
◇ *vt* [tunnel] boiser.
◇ *interj* : **~!** attention!

timbered ['tɪmbəd] *adj* [region, land] boisé ■ [house] en bois.

timbering ['tɪmbərɪŋ] *n* boisage *m*.

timber merchant *n* marchand *m* de bois.

timberwork ['tɪmbəwɜːk] *n* structure *f* en bois.

timberyard ['tɪmbəjɑːd] *n* chantier *m* de bois.

timbre ['tæmbrə, 'tɪmbəʳ] *n* LING & MUS timbre *m*.

Timbuktu [ˌtɪmbʌk'tuː] *pr n* Tombouctou.

time [taɪm] ◇ *n* **1.** [continuous stretch of time] temps *m* ■ **as ~ goes by** avec le temps ■ **the price has gone up over ~** le prix a augmenté avec le temps ■ **these things take ~** cela ne se fait pas du jour au lendemain ■ **to have ~ on one's hands** *OR* **~ to spare** avoir du temps ■ **since the dawn of ~** depuis la nuit des temps ■ **doesn't ~ fly!** comme le temps passe vite! ■ **~ heals all wounds** le temps guérit tout ■ **only ~ will tell** seul l'avenir nous le dira ■ **~ will prove me right** l'avenir me donnera raison ■ **it's a race against ~** c'est une course contre la montre ■ **~ is on our side** le temps joue en notre faveur ▶ **~ is money** *prov* le temps, c'est de l'argent *prov* ■ **~ and tide wait for no man** *prov* les événements n'attendent personne
2. [period of time spent on particular activity] temps *m* ■ **there's no ~ to lose** il n'y a pas de temps à perdre ■ **he lost no ~ in telling me** il s'est empressé de me le dire ■ **to make up for lost ~** rattraper le temps perdu ■ **to make good/poor ~ doing sthg** mettre peu de temps/longtemps à faire qqch ■ **I passed the ~ reading** j'ai passé mon temps à lire ■ **take your ~ over it** prenez le temps qu'il faudra ■ **you took your ~ about it!** tu en as mis du temps! ■ **she made the ~ to read the report** elle a pris le temps de lire le rapport ■ **half the ~ he doesn't know what he's doing** la moitié du temps il ne sait pas ce qu'il fait ■ **most of the ~** la plupart du temps ■ **it rained part** *OR* **some of the ~** il a plu par moments ■ **we spend the better part of our ~ working** nous passons le plus clair de notre temps à travailler ■ **I start in three weeks' ~** je commence dans trois semaines ▶ **all in good ~!** chaque chose en son temps! ■ **I'll finish it in my own good ~** je le finirai quand bon me semblera
3. [available period of time] temps *m* ■ **I haven't (the) ~ to do the shopping** je n'ai pas le temps de faire les courses ■ **I've no ~ for gossip** *liter* je n'ai pas le temps de papoter ; *fig* je n'ai pas de temps à perdre en bavardages ■ **my ~ is my own** mon temps m'appartient ■ **my ~ is not my own** je ne suis pas libre de mon temps ■ **we've just got ~ to catch the train** on a juste le temps d'attraper le train ■ **you have plenty of ~ to finish it** vous avez largement le temps de le finir ■ **we've got plenty of ~** *OR* **all the ~ in the world** nous avons tout le temps
4. [while] temps *m* ■ **after a ~** après un (certain) temps ■ **a long ~ ago** il y a longtemps ■ **it's a long ~ since we've been out for a meal together** ça fait longtemps que nous ne sommes pas sortis dîner ensemble ■ **he waited for a long ~** il a attendu longtemps ■ **it'll be a long ~ before I do that again** je ne suis pas près de recommencer, je ne recommencerai pas de si tôt *OR* de sitôt ■ **you took a long ~!** tu en as mis du temps!, il t'en a fallu du temps! ■ **long ~ no see!** *inf* ça faisait longtemps! ■ **a short ~** peu de temps ■ **she's going to stay with us for a short ~** elle va rester avec nous pendant quelque temps ■ **in the shortest possible ~** dans les plus brefs délais, le plus vite *OR* tôt possible ■ **after some ~** au bout de quelque temps, après un certain temps ■ **some ~ ago** il y a quelque temps ■ **it's the best film I've seen for some ~** c'est le meilleur film que j'aie vu depuis un moment ■ **it will take (quite) some ~ to repair** il va falloir pas mal de temps pour le réparer
5. [time taken or required to do something] temps *m*, durée *f* ■ **the flying ~ to Madrid is two hours** la durée du vol pour Madrid est de deux heures ■ **she finished in half the ~ it took me to finish** elle a mis deux fois moins de temps que moi pour finir
6. [by clock] heure *f* ■ **what ~ is it?, what's the ~?** quelle heure est-il? ■ **what ~ do you make it?** quelle heure avez-vous? ■ **have you got the right ~ on you?** avez-vous l'heure juste? ■ **the ~ is twenty past three** il est trois heures vingt ■ **what ~ are we leaving?** à quelle heure partons-nous? ■ **do you know how to tell the ~?** est-ce que tu sais lire l'heure? ■ **could you tell me the ~?** pourriez-vous me dire l'heure (qu'il est)? ■ **have you seen the ~?** avez-vous vu l'heure? ■ **this old watch still keeps good ~** cette vieille montre est toujours à l'heure *OR* exacte ■ **we'll have to keep an eye on the ~** il faudra surveiller l'heure ■ **it is almost ~ to leave/for my bus** il est presque l'heure de partir/de mon bus ■ **it's ~ I was going** il est temps que je parte ■ **it's dinner ~, it's ~ for dinner** c'est l'heure de dîner ■ **there you are, it's about ~!** te voilà, ce n'est pas trop tôt! ▶ **I wouldn't give him the ~ of day** je ne lui dirais même pas bonjour ■ **to pass the ~ of day with sb** échanger quelques mots avec qqn
7. [system] : **local ~** heure *f* locale ■ **it's 5 o'clock Tokyo ~** il est 5 h, heure de Tokyo
8. [schedule] : **is the bus running to ~?** est-ce que le bus est à l'heure? ■ **within the required ~** dans les délais requis
9. [particular point in time] moment *m* ■ **at that ~ I was in Madrid** à ce moment-là j'étais *OR* j'étais alors à Madrid ■ **I worked for her at one ~** à un moment donné j'ai travaillé pour elle ■ **at the present ~** en ce moment, à présent ■ **at a later ~** plus tard ■ **at a given ~** à un moment donné ■ **at any one ~** à la fois ■ **an inconvenient ~** un moment inopportun ■ **at the best of ~s** même quand tout va bien ■ **even at the best of ~s he is not that patient** même dans ses bons moments il n'est pas particulièrement patient ■ **at no ~ did I agree to that** je n'ai jamais donné mon accord pour cela ■ **by the ~ you get this...** le temps que tu reçoives ceci..., quand tu auras reçu ceci... ■ **by that ~ it will be too late** à ce moment-là il sera trop tard ■ **by that ~ we'll all be dead** d'ici là nous serons tous morts ■ **by this ~ next week** d'ici une semaine, dans une semaine ■ **this ~ next week** la semaine prochaine à cette heure-ci ■ **this ~ last week** il y a exactement une semaine ■ **from that ~ on we had nothing to do with them** à partir de ce moment-là, nous avons refusé d'avoir affaire à eux ■ **in between ~s** entre-temps ■ **until such ~ as I hear from them** jusqu'à ce que *OR* en attendant que j'aie de leurs nouvelles
10. [suitable moment] moment *m* ■ **now is the ~ to invest** c'est maintenant qu'il faut investir ■ **when the ~ comes** (quand) le moment (sera) venu ■ **we'll talk about that when the ~ comes** nous en parlerons en temps utile ■ **the ~ has come to make a stand** c'est le moment d'avoir le courage de ses opinions ■ **it's about ~ we taught her a lesson** il est grand temps que nous lui donnions une bonne leçon ■ **there's no ~ like the present** [let's do it now] faisons-le maintenant ■ **there's a ~ and a place for everything** il y a un temps et un lieu pour *OR* à tout
11. [occasion, instance] fois *f* ■ **I'll forgive you this ~** je vous pardonne cette fois-ci *OR* pour cette fois ■ **each** *OR* **every ~** chaque fois ■ **she succeeds every ~** elle réussit à chaque fois ■ **the last ~ he came** la dernière fois qu'il est venu ■ **another** *OR* **some other ~** une autre fois ■ **many ~s** bien des fois, très souvent ■ **many a ~ I've wondered...** je me suis demandé plus d'une *OR* bien des fois... ■ **it costs 15 cents a ~** ça coûte 15 cents à chaque fois ■ **the one ~ I'm winning, he wants to stop playing** pour une fois que je gagne, il veut arrêter de jouer ■ **nine ~s out of ten the machine doesn't work** neuf fois sur dix la machine ne marche pas ■ **we'll have to decide some ~ or other** tôt ou tard *OR* un jour ou l'autre il va falloir nous décider ■ **do you remember that ~ we went to Germany?** tu te rappelles la fois où nous sommes allés en Allemagne? ■ **there's always a first ~** il y a un début à tout ■ **give me a good detective story every ~!** rien ne vaut un bon roman policier!
12. [experience] : **to have a good ~** bien s'amuser ■ **she's had a terrible ~ of it** elle a beaucoup souffert ■ **I had the ~ of my life** jamais je ne me suis si bien *OR* autant amusé ■ **we had an awful ~ at the picnic** nous nous sommes ennuyés à mourir au pique-nique ■ **it was a difficult ~ for all of us** c'était une période difficile pour nous tous ■ **she had a hard ~ bringing up five children alone** ça a été difficile pour elle d'élever cinq enfants seule

13. [hours of work] : **to work part/full ~** travailler à temps partiel/à plein temps ▪ **in company ~** *UK*, **on company ~** *US* pendant les heures de travail ▪ **in your own ~** *UK*, **on your own ~** *US* pendant votre temps libre, en dehors des heures de travail ▪ **~ off** temps *m* libre
14. [hourly wages] : **we pay ~ and a half on weekends** nous payons les heures du week-end une fois et demie le tarif normal ▪ **overtime is paid at double ~** les heures supplémentaires sont payées *OR* comptées double
15. *(usu pl)* [era] époque *f*, temps *m* ▪ **in Victorian ~s** à l'époque victorienne ▪ **in the ~ of Henry IV** à l'époque d'Henri IV, du temps d'Henri IV ▪ **in ~s past, in former ~s** autrefois, jadis ▪ **in ~s to come** à l'avenir ▪ **at one ~, things were different** autrefois *OR* dans le temps les choses étaient différentes ▪ **in ~ (s) of need/war** en temps de pénurie/de guerre ▪ **~ was when doctors made house calls** il fut un temps où les médecins faisaient des visites à domicile ▪ **those were happy ~s!** c'était le bon (vieux) temps! ▪ **in our ~** de nos jours ▪ **the ~s we live in** l'époque où nous vivons ▪ **in my ~ children didn't talk back** de mon temps les enfants ne répondaient pas ➲ **to be ahead of** *OR* **before one's ~** être en avance sur son époque *OR* sur son temps ▪ **to be behind the ~s** être en retard sur son époque *OR* sur son temps ▪ **to keep up with the ~s** vivre avec son temps ▪ **to move with the ~s** évoluer avec son temps ▪ **~s have changed** autres temps, autres mœurs *prov*
16. [lifetime] : **I've heard some odd things in my ~!** j'en ai entendu, des choses, dans ma vie! ▪ **at my ~ of life** à mon âge ▪ **that was before your ~** [birth] vous n'étiez pas encore né ; [arrival] vous n'étiez pas encore là ▪ **her ~ has come** [childbirth] elle arrive à son terme ; [death] son heure est venue *OR* a sonné ; [success] son heure est venue ▪ **he died before his ~** il est mort avant l'âge
17. [season] : **it's hot for the ~ of year** il fait chaud pour la saison
18. [end of period] fin *f* ▪ **~'s up** [on exam, visit] c'est l'heure ; [on meter, telephone] le temps est écoulé ▪ **~, (gentlemen) please!** [in pub] *UK* on ferme! ▪ **the referee called ~** SPORT l'arbitre a sifflé la fin du match
19. *US* COMM : **to buy sthg on ~** acheter qqch à tempérament *OR* à terme *OR* à crédit
20.△ [in prison] : **to do ~** faire de la taule△ ▪ **he's serving ~ for murder** il est en taule pour meurtre△
21. MUS mesure *f* ▪ **in triple** *OR* **three-part ~** à trois temps ▪ **~ (value)** valeur *f (d'une note)*
22. RADIO & TV espace *m* ▪ **to buy/to sell ~ on television** acheter/vendre de l'espace publicitaire à la télévision.
◇ *vt* **1.** [on clock - runner, worker] chronométrer ▪ **~ how long she takes to finish** regardez combien de temps elle met pour finir ▪ **he ~d his speech to last 20 minutes** il a fait en sorte que son discours dure 20 minutes ▪ **to ~ an egg** minuter le temps de cuisson d'un œuf
2. [schedule] fixer *OR* prévoir (l'heure de) ▪ **they ~d the attack for 6 o'clock** l'attaque était prévue pour 6 h
3. [choose right moment for] choisir *OR* calculer le moment de ▪ **he ~d the blow perfectly** il a frappé au bon moment ▪ **your remark was perfectly/badly ~d** votre observation est venue au bon/au mauvais moment
4. [synchronize] régler, ajuster.
◆ **times** ◇ *npl* [indicating degree] fois *f* ▪ **she's ten ~s cleverer than he is** elle est dix fois plus intelligente que lui.
◇ *prep* MATHS : **3 ~s 2 is 6** 3 fois 2 font *OR* égalent 6.
◆ **ahead of time** *adv phr* en avance ▪ **I'm ten minutes ahead of ~** j'ai dix minutes d'avance.
◆ **all the time** *adv phr* : **he talked all the ~ we were at lunch** il a parlé pendant tout le déjeuner ▪ **he's been watching us all the ~** il n'a pas cessé de nous regarder ▪ **I knew it all the ~** je le savais depuis le début.
◆ **any time** *adv phr* n'importe quand ▪ **come over any ~** venez quand vous voulez ▪ **thanks for all your help – any ~** merci de votre aide – de rien.
◆ **at a time** *adv phr* : **for days at a ~** pendant des journées entières, des journées durant ▪ **take one book at a ~** prenez les livres un par un *OR* un (seul) livre à la fois ▪ **she ran up the stairs two at a ~** elle a monté les marches quatre à quatre.
◆ **at all times** *adv phr* à tous moments.
◆ **at any time** *adv phr* à toute heure ▪ **at any ~ of day or night** à n'importe quelle heure du jour ou de la nuit ▪ **at any ~ during office hours** n'importe quand pendant les heures de bureau ▪ **he could die at any ~** il peut mourir d'un moment à l'autre.
◆ **at the same time** *adv phr* **1.** [simultaneously] en même temps
2. [yet] en même temps
3. [nevertheless] pourtant, cependant.
◆ **at the time** *adv phr* : **at the ~ of their wedding** au moment de leur mariage ▪ **I didn't pay much attention at the ~** sur le moment je n'ai pas fait vraiment attention.
◆ **at times** *adv phr* parfois, par moments.
◆ **behind time** *adv phr* en retard ▪ **the project was running behind ~** le projet avait du retard.
◆ **for a time** *adv phr* pendant un (certain) temps.
◆ **for all time** *adv phr* pour toujours.
◆ **for the time being** *adv phr* pour le moment.
◆ **from time to time** *adv phr* de temps en temps, de temps à autre.
◆ **in time** *adv phr* **1.** [eventually] : **he'll forget about it in (the course of) ~** il finira par l'oublier (avec le temps)
2. [not too late] : **let me know in (good) ~** prévenez-moi (bien) à l'avance ▪ **she arrived in ~ for the play** elle est arrivée à l'heure pour la pièce ▪ **you're just in ~ to greet our guests** tu arrives juste à temps pour accueillir nos invités ▪ **I'll be back in ~ for the film** je serai de retour à temps pour le film
3. MUS en mesure ▪ **to be** *OR* **keep in ~ (with the music)** être en mesure (avec la musique).
◆ **in (next to) no time, in no time at all** *adv phr* en un rien de temps.
◆ **of all time** *adv phr* de tous les temps.
◆ **of all times** *adv phr* : **why now of all ~s?** pourquoi faut-il que ce soit juste maintenant?
◆ **on time** *adv phr* à l'heure.
◆ **out of time** *adv phr* : **he got out of ~** il a perdu la mesure.
◆ **time after time, time and (time) again** *adv phr* maintes et maintes fois.

time-and-motion *n* : **~ study** étude *f* de productivité *(qui se concentre sur l'efficacité des employés)*.

time bomb *n liter & fig* bombe *f* à retardement ▪ **they're sitting on a ~** *fig* ils dansent sur un volcan.

time capsule *n* capsule *f* témoin *(qui doit servir de témoignage historique aux générations futures)*.

time card *n* INDUST carte *f OR* fiche *f* de pointage.

time chart *n* **1.** [showing time zones] carte *f* des fuseaux horaires **2.** [showing events] table *f* d'événements historiques **3.** [showing planning] calendrier *m*, planning *m*.

time check *n* [on radio] rappel *m* de l'heure.

time clock *n* INDUST pointeuse *f*.

time-consuming *adj* [work] qui prend beaucoup de temps, prenant ▪ [tactics] dilatoire.

time-critical *adj* critique en termes de temps.

time deposit *n US* FIN dépôt *m* à terme.

time difference *n* décalage *m* horaire.

time-expired *adj* périmé, obsolète.

time exposure *n* **1.** [of film] pose *f* **2.** [photograph] photo *f* prise en pose.

time-filler *n* : **I'm just doing this job as a ~** je fais ce travail uniquement pour tuer le temps.

time frame *n* délai *m* ▪ **what's our ~?** de combien de temps disposons-nous?

time fuse *n* détonateur *m OR* fusée *f* à retardement.

time-honoured [-ˌɒnəd] *adj* consacré (par l'usage).

timekeeper [ˈtaɪmˌkiːpəʳ] *n* **1.** [watch] montre *f* ▪ [clock] horloge *f* ▪ [stopwatch] chronomètre *m* **2.** [supervisor] pointeau *m* **3.** [employee, friend] : **he's a good ~** il est toujours à l'heure, il est toujours très ponctuel **4.** SPORT chronométreur *m* (officiel), chronométreuse *f* (officielle).

timekeeping [ˈtaɪmˌkiːpɪŋ] *n* [of employee] ponctualité *f*.

time lag *n* **1.** [delay] décalage *m* dans le temps **2.** [in time zones] décalage *m* horaire.

time lapse *n* décalage *m* horaire.

timeless ['taɪmlɪs] *adj* éternel, hors du temps, intemporel.

time limit *n* [gen] délai *m*, date *f* limite ■ LAW délai *m* de forclusion ■ **the work must be completed within the ~** le travail doit être terminé avant la date limite.

timeliness ['taɪmlɪnɪs] *n* [of remark] à-propos *m*, opportunité *f* ■ [of visit] opportunité *f*.

timely ['taɪmlɪ] *adj* [remark, intervention, warning] qui tombe à point nommé, opportun ■ [visit] opportun ■ **he made a ~ escape** il s'est échappé juste à temps.

time machine *n* machine *f* à voyager dans le temps.

time off *n* temps *m* libre.

time out *n* **1.** SPORT temps *m* mort ■ [in chess match] temps *m* de repos **2.** [break] : **I took ~ to travel** [from work] je me suis mis en congé pour voyager ; [from studies] j'ai interrompu mes études pour voyager.

timepiece ['taɪmpi:s] *n* *fml* & *dated* [watch] montre *f* ■ [clock] horloge *f*, pendule *f*.

timer ['taɪməʳ] *n* **1.** CULIN minuteur *m* ■ **(egg) ~** sablier *m*, compte-minutes *m inv* **2.** [counter] compteur *m* **3.** [for lighting] minuterie *f* **4.** [stopwatch] chronomètre *m* **5.** SPORT [timekeeper] chronométreur *m*, -euse *f* **6.** AUT distributeur *m* (d'allumage).

time-saver *n* : **a dishwasher is a great ~** on gagne beaucoup de temps avec un lave-vaisselle, un lave-vaisselle permet de gagner beaucoup de temps.

time-saving ◇ *adj* qui économise OR fait gagner du temps.
◇ *n* gain *m* de temps.

time scale *n* échelle *f* dans le temps.

timeserver ['taɪm,sɜ:vəʳ] *n* **1.** [opportunist] opportuniste *mf* **2.** [employee] tire-au-flanc *m inv*.

time-serving ◇ *adj* opportuniste.
◇ *n* opportunisme *m*.

time-share ◇ *n* : **to buy a ~ in a flat** acheter un appartement en multipropriété.
◇ *adj* [flat] en multipropriété ■ [computer] en temps partagé.

time-sharing *n* **1.** [of flat, villa] multipropriété *f* **2.** COMPUT (travail *m*) en temps *m* partagé.

time sheet *n* fiche *f* horaire.

time signal *n* RADIO signal *m* OR top *m* horaire.

time signature *n* MUS indication *f* de la mesure.

time slice *n* COMPUT tranche *f* de temps.

time switch *n* [for oven, heating] minuteur *m* ■ [for lighting] minuterie *f*.

timetable ['taɪm,teɪbl] ◇ *n* **1.** [for transport] horaire *m* ■ **bus ~** indicateur *m* OR horaire des autobus **2.** [schedule] emploi *m* du temps **3.** [calendar] calendrier *m* ■ **exam ~** dates *fpl* OR calendrier des examens.
◇ *vt* [meeting - during day] fixer une heure pour ; [- during week, month] fixer une date pour ■ SCH [classes, course] établir un emploi du temps pour ■ **the train is ~d to arrive at six o'clock** l'arrivée du train est prévue à 6 h ■ **her visit is ~d to coincide with the celebrations** sa visite devrait coïncider avec les festivités.

time travel *n* voyage *m* dans le temps.

time trial *n* SPORT course *f* contre la montre.

time warp *n* : **it's like living in a ~** c'est comme si on vivait hors du temps.

timewasting ['taɪmweɪstɪŋ] *n* perte *f* de temps ■ **the team was accused of ~** on a reproché à l'équipe d'avoir joué la montre.

timework ['taɪmwɜ:k] *n* [hourly] travail *m* payé à l'heure ■ [daily] travail *m* payé à la journée.

timeworn ['taɪmwɔ:n] *adj* [object] usé par le temps, vétuste ■ *fig* [idea, phrase] rebattu, éculé.

time zone *n* fuseau *m* horaire.

timid ['tɪmɪd] *adj* timide.

timidity [tɪ'mɪdətɪ] *n* timidité *f*.

timidly ['tɪmɪdlɪ] *adv* timidement.

timidness ['tɪmɪdnɪs] *n* timidité *f*.

timing ['taɪmɪŋ] *n* **1.** [of actor] minutage *m* (du débit) ■ [of musician] sens *m* du rythme ■ [of tennis player] timing *m* ■ [of stunt driver] synchronisation *f* ■ **you need a good sense of ~** il faut savoir choisir le bon moment ■ **cooking such a big meal requires careful ~** pour préparer un si grand repas, il faut organiser son temps avec soin ■ **that was good ~!** voilà qui était bien calculé! **2.** [chosen moment - of operation, visit] moment *m* choisi ■ **the ~ of the statement was unfortunate** cette déclaration est vraiment tombée à un très mauvais moment **3.** SPORT chronométrage *m* **4.** AUT réglage *m* de l'allumage.

timing mechanism *n* [for bomb, in clock] mécanisme *m* d'horlogerie.

timorous ['tɪmərəs] *adj* timoré, craintif.

Timothy ['tɪməθɪ] *pr n* Timothée.

timpani ['tɪmpənɪ] *npl* MUS timbales *fpl*.

tin [tɪn] (*pret* & *pp* **tinned**, *cont* **tinning**) ◇ *n* **1.** [metal] étain *m* ■ **~ (plate)** fer-blanc *m* **2.** *UK* [can] boîte *f* (en fer-blanc) ■ **a ~ of paint** un pot de peinture **3.** [for storing] boîte *f* en fer ■ **biscuit ~** [empty] boîte *f* à biscuits ; [full] boîte *f* de biscuits **4.** [for cooking meat] plat *m* ■ [for cooking bread, cakes, etc] moule *m*.
◇ *comp* [made of tin] en étain ■ [made of tinplate] en fer-blanc ■ [box] en fer ■ [roof] en tôle ■ **'The Tin Drum'** *Grass* 'le Tambour'.
◇ *vt* **1.** *UK* [food] mettre en conserve OR en boîte **2.** [plate] étamer.

tin can *n* boîte *f* (en fer-blanc).

tincture ['tɪŋktʃəʳ] ◇ *n* **1.** CHEM & PHARM teinture *f* **2.** [colour, tint] teinte *f*, nuance *f* **3.** *lit* [trace, hint] teinte *f*, touche *f*.
◇ *vt* *liter* & *fig* teinter.

tinder ['tɪndəʳ] *n (U)* [in tinderbox] amadou *m* ■ [dry wood] petit bois *m* ■ [dry grass] herbes *fpl* sèches.

tinderbox ['tɪndəbɒks] *n* **1.** [lighter] briquet *m* à amadou **2.** [dry place] endroit *m* sec **3.** *fig* [explosive situation] poudrière *f*, situation *f* explosive.

tine [taɪn] *n* [of fork] dent *f* ■ [of antler] andouiller *m*.

tinfoil ['tɪnfɔɪl] *n* papier *m* d'aluminium.

ting [tɪŋ] ◇ *onom* ding.
◇ *vi* tinter.
◇ *vt* faire tinter.

ting-a-ling ◇ *onom* [of phone, doorbell, bike] dring-dring.
◇ *n* dring-dring *m*.

tinge [tɪndʒ] ◇ *n* teinte *f*, nuance *f*.
◇ *vt* teinter ■ **her smile was ~d with sadness** *fig* son sourire était empreint de tristesse.

tingle ['tɪŋgl] ◇ *vi* **1.** [with heat, cold - ears, cheeks, hands] fourmiller, picoter ■ **the cold wind made my face ~** le vent froid me piquait le visage ■ **his cheeks were tingling** les joues lui picotaient ■ **it makes my tongue ~** ça me pique la langue **2.** [with excitement, pleasure] frissonner, frémir.
◇ *n* **1.** [stinging] picotements *mpl*, fourmillements *mpl* **2.** [thrill] frisson *m*, frémissement *m*.

tingling ['tɪŋglɪŋ] ◇ *n* [stinging] picotement *m*, fourmillement *m* ■ [from excitement] frisson *m*, frémissement *m*.
◇ *adj* [sensation] de picotement, de fourmillement.

tingly ['tɪŋglɪ] *adj* [sensation] de picotement, de fourmillement.

tin god *n* demi-dieu *m*.

tin hat *n* casque *m* (militaire).

tinker ['tɪŋkəʳ] ◇ *n* **1.** [pot mender] rétameur *m* ▪ [gipsy] romanichel *m*, - elle *f* ▶ **I don't give a ~'s cuss** *OR* **damn!** *inf* je m'en fiche comme de ma première chemise! ▪ **it's not worth a ~'s cuss** *inf* ça vaut des clopinettes ▪ **~, tailor, soldier, sailor...** [child's rhyme] ≃ il m'aime un peu, beaucoup, passionnément... **2.** *UK inf* [child] voyou *m*, garnement *m* **3.** [act of tinkering] bricolage *m*.
◇ *vi* : **he spends hours ~ing with that car** il passe des heures à bricoler cette voiture ▪ **someone has ~ed with this report** quelqu'un a trafiqué ce rapport.

tinkle ['tɪŋkl] ◇ *vi* [bell] tinter.
◇ *vt* faire tinter.
◇ *n* **1.** [ring] tintement *m* **2.** *UK* [phone call] : **to give sb a ~** *inf* donner *OR* passer un coup de fil à qqn **3.** *inf* [act of urinating] : **to go for a ~** aller faire pipi.

tinkling ['tɪŋklɪŋ] ◇ *n* tintement *m*.
◇ *adj* [bell] qui tinte ▪ [water] qui murmure.

tin mine *n* mine *f* d'étain.

tinned [tɪnd] *adj UK* [sardines, fruit etc] en boîte, en conserve ▪ **~ food** conserves *fpl*.

tinnitus [tɪ'naɪtəs] *n (U)* MED acouphène *m*.

tinny ['tɪnɪ] (*comp* **tinnier**, *superl* **tinniest**) *adj* **1.** [sound] métallique, de casserole ▪ [taste] métallique **2.** *inf* [poor quality] de quatre sous **3.** *especially Australia* canette *f* de bière *inf*.

tin opener *n UK* ouvre-boîte *m*, ouvre-boîtes *m inv*.

Tin Pan Alley *n* : **he works in ~** il travaille dans la musique pop.

tinplate ['tɪnpleɪt] *n* fer-blanc *m*.

tin-pot *adj UK* **1.** [worthless - car, machine] qui ne vaut rien **2.** [insignificant, hopeless] médiocre ▪ **a ~ regime/dictator** un régime/un dictateur fantoche.

tinsel ['tɪnsl] (*UK pret & pp* **tinselled**, *cont* **tinselling**) (*US pret & pp* **tinseled**, *cont* **tinseling**) ◇ *n (U)* **1.** [for Christmas tree] guirlandes *fpl* de Noël ▪ [in fine strands] cheveux *mpl* d'ange **2.** *fig* clinquant *m* ▪ **Tinsel Town** *hum & pej nom donné à Hollywood.*
◇ *vt* [tree] orner *OR* décorer de guirlandes.

tinsmith ['tɪnsmɪθ] *n* étameur *m*, ferblantier *m*.

tin soldier *n* soldat *m* de plomb.

tint [tɪnt] ◇ *n* **1.** [colour, shade] teinte *f*, nuance *f* **2.** [hair dye] shampooing *m* colorant **3.** [in engraving, printing] hachure *f*, hachures *fpl*.
◇ *vt* teinter ▪ **~ed lenses** verres *mpl* teintés ▪ **she ~s her hair** elle se teint les cheveux.

Tintoretto [ˌtɪntə'retəʊ] *pr n* le Tintoret.

tin whistle *n* flûtiau *m*, pipeau *m*.

tiny ['taɪnɪ] (*comp* **tinier**, *superl* **tiniest**) *adj* tout petit, minuscule ▪ **a ~ bit** un tout petit peu ▪ **the meat is a ~ bit overdone** la viande est un tantinet trop cuite.

tip [tɪp] (*pret & pp* **tipped**, *cont* **tipping**) ◇ *n* **1.** [extremity - of ear, finger, nose] bout *m* ; [- of tongue] bout *m*, pointe *f* ; [- of cigarette, wing] bout *m* ; [- of blade, knife, fork] pointe *f* ▪ **stand on the ~s of your toes** mettez-vous sur la pointe des pieds ▶ **his name is on the ~ of my tongue** j'ai son nom sur le bout de la langue
2. [of island, peninsula] extrémité *f*, pointe *f* ▪ **it's just the ~ of the iceberg** *fig* ce n'est que la partie émergée de l'iceberg
3. [cap - on walking stick, umbrella] embout *m* ; [- on snooker cue] procédé *m*
4. *UK* [dump - for rubbish] dépotoir *m*, dépôt *m* d'ordures ; [- for coal] terril *m* ▪ *fig* **your room is a real ~** *inf* ! quel bazar, ta chambre! ▪ **the house is a bit of a ~** *inf* la maison est un peu en désordre
5. [hint - for stock market, race] tuyau *m* ▪ [advice] conseil *m* ▪ **to give sb a ~** [for race] donner un tuyau à qqn ; [for repairs, procedure] donner un tuyau *OR* un conseil à qqn
6. [money] pourboire *m* ▪ **to give sb a ~** donner un pourboire à qqn.
◇ *vt* **1.** [cane] mettre un embout à ▪ [snooker cue] mettre un procédé à ▪ **an ivory-tipped cane** une canne à pommeau d'ivoire ▪ **arrows tipped with poison** des flèches empoisonnées
2. [tilt, lean] incliner, pencher ▪ **to ~ one's hat to sb** saluer qqn d'un coup de chapeau ▪ **the boxer tipped the scales at 80 kg** le boxeur pesait 80 kg ▪ **to ~ the scales in sb's favour** *fig* faire pencher la balance en faveur de qqn
3. [upset, overturn] renverser, faire chavirer ▪ **I was tipped off my stool/into the water** on m'a fait tomber de mon tabouret/dans l'eau
4. *UK* [empty, pour] verser ▪ [unload] déverser, décharger
5. [winning horse] pronostiquer ▪ **Orlando is tipped for the 2.30** *OR* **to win the 2.30** Orlando est donné gagnant dans la course de 14 h 30 ▪ **you've tipped a winner there** *fig* vous avez trouvé un bon filon ▪ **he's tipped to be the next president** *OR* **as the next president** on pronostique qu'il sera le prochain président ▶ **to ~ sb the wink** *inf* avertir *OR* prévenir qqn
6. [porter, waiter] donner un pourboire à ▪ **she tipped him £1** elle lui a donné une livre de pourboire.
◇ *vi* **1.** *UK* [tilt] incliner, pencher
2. *UK* [overturn] basculer, se renverser
3. *UK* [rubbish] : **'no tipping'** 'défense de déposer des ordures'
4. [give money] laisser un pourboire.
◆ **tip back** ◇ *vi insep* se rabattre en arrière, s'incliner en arrière ▪ **don't ~ back on your chair** ne te balance pas sur ta chaise.
◇ *vt sep* faire basculer (en arrière) ▪ **don't ~ your chair back too far** ne te penche pas trop en arrière sur ta chaise.
◆ **tip down** *UK inf* ◇ *vi insep* : **the rain is tipping down, it's tipping down (with rain)** il pleut des cordes.
◇ *vt sep phr* : **it's tipping it down** il pleut des cordes.
◆ **tip off** *vt sep* avertir, prévenir.
◆ **tip out** *vt sep UK* **1.** [empty - liquid, small objects] vider, verser ; [- rubbish, larger objects] déverser, décharger
2. [overturn, toss] faire basculer.
◆ **tip over** ◇ *vi insep* **1.** [tilt] pencher
2. [overturn - boat] chavirer, se renverser.
◇ *vt sep* faire basculer, renverser.
◆ **tip up** ◇ *vi insep* **1.** [cinema seat] se rabattre ▪ [bunk, plank, cart] basculer
2. [bucket, cup, vase] se renverser.
◇ *vt sep* **1.** [seat, table] faire basculer, rabattre
2. [upside down - bottle, barrel] renverser.

tip-off *n inf* **to give sb a ~** [hint] filer un tuyau à qqn ; [warning] avertir *OR* prévenir qqn.

tipped ['tɪpt] *adj* : **~ with felt/steel** à bout feutré/ferré ▮ [cigarettes] (à) bout filtre *(inv)*.

-tipped *in cpds* à bout... ▪ **steel/felt~** à bout ferré/feutré ▪ **a felt~ pen** un crayon-feutre, un feutre.

tipper ['tɪpəʳ] *n* **1.** = **tipper truck 2.** [tipping device] benne *f* (basculante) **3.** [customer] : **he's a generous ~** il laisse toujours de bons pourboires.

tipper truck *n* camion *m* à benne (basculante).

Tipp-Ex® ['tɪpeks] *n* correcteur *m* liquide, Tipp-Ex® *m*.
◆ **tippex out** *vt sep* : **to ~ sthg out** effacer qqch (avec du Tipp-Ex®).

tipple ['tɪpl] ◇ *vi inf* picoler.
◇ *n* **1.** *inf* [drink] : **he likes a ~ now and then** il aime boire un coup de temps à autre **2.** MIN [device] culbuteur *m* ▪ [place - for loading] aire *f* de chargement ; [- for unloading] aire *f* de déchargement.

tippler ['tɪpləʳ] *n inf* picoleur *m*, - euse *f*.

tipster ['tɪpstəʳ] *n* : **(racing) ~** pronostiqueur *m*, - euse *f*.

tipsy ['tɪpsɪ] (*comp* **tipsier**, *superl* **tipsiest**) *adj inf* pompette, rond ▪ **to get ~** se griser ▪ **white wine makes me ~** le vin blanc me monte à la tête.

tiptoe ['tɪptəʊ] ◇ *n* : **on ~** sur la pointe des pieds.
◇ *vi* marcher sur la pointe des pieds ▪ **to ~ in/out** entrer/sortir sur la pointe des pieds.

tip-top *adj inf* de premier ordre, de toute première qualité ▪ **in ~ condition** en excellent état.

tip-up *adj* : **~ seat** [in cinema, theatre] siège *m* rabattable, strapontin *m* ; [in metro] strapontin *m* ■ **~ truck** *UK* camion *m* à benne (basculante).

tirade [taɪ'reɪd] *n* diatribe *f* ■ **a ~ of abuse** une bordée d'injures.

tiramisu [,tɪrəmɪ'su:] *n* CULIN tiramisu *m*.

tire ['taɪəʳ] ◇ *vi* **1.** [become exhausted] se fatiguer ■ **she ~s easily** elle est vite fatiguée **2.** [become bored] se fatiguer, se lasser ■ **he soon ~d of her/of her company** il se lassa vite d'elle/de sa compagnie.
◇ *vt* **1.** [exhaust] fatiguer **2.** [bore] fatiguer, lasser.
◇ *n US* = **tyre**.
◆ **tire out** *vt sep* épuiser, éreinter ■ **you'll ~ yourself out moving all those boxes** vous allez vous épuiser à déplacer toutes ces caisses.

tired ['taɪəd] *adj* **1.** [exhausted] fatigué ■ **to feel ~** se sentir fatigué ■ **to get ~** se fatiguer ■ **the walk made me ~** la marche m'a fatigué ■ **I'm so ~ I could drop** je tombe de sommeil ■ **my eyes are ~** j'ai les yeux fatigués ■ **in a ~ voice** d'une voix lasse **2.** [fed up] fatigué, las, lasse *f* ■ **to be ~ of sthg/sb** en avoir assez de qqch/qqn ■ **she soon got ~ of him** elle se fatigua *OR* se lassa vite de lui **3.** [hackneyed] rebattu **4.** *fig* [old - skin] desséché ; [- vegetable] défraîchi, flétri ; [- upholstery, springs, car] fatigué.

tiredly ['taɪədlɪ] *adv* [say] d'une voix lasse ■ [move, walk] avec lassitude.

tiredness ['taɪədnɪs] *n* **1.** [exhaustion] fatigue *f* **2.** [tedium] fatigue *f*, lassitude *f*.

tireless ['taɪəlɪs] *adj* [effort] infatigable, inlassable ■ [energy] inépuisable.

tirelessly ['taɪəlɪslɪ] *adv* infatigablement, inlassablement, sans ménager ses efforts.

tiresome ['taɪəsəm] *adj* [irritating] agaçant, ennuyeux ■ [boring] assommant, ennuyeux.

tiring ['taɪərɪŋ] *adj* fatigant.

tiro ['taɪrəʊ] = **tyro**.

Tirol [tɪ'rəʊl] = **Tyrol**.

'tis [tɪz] *dial & lit* = **it is**.

tissue ['tɪʃu:] *n* **1.** ANAT & BOT tissu *m* **2.** TEX tissu *m*, étoffe *f* ■ **a ~ of lies** *fig* un tissu de mensonges **3.** [paper handkerchief] mouchoir *m* en papier, Kleenex® *m* ■ [toilet paper] papier *m* hygiénique.

tissue paper *n* papier *m* de soie.

tit [tɪt] *n* **1.** ORNITH mésange *f* **2.**△ [breast] nichon△ *m* **3.**△ *pej* imbécile *mf* **4.** *phr* **it's ~ for tat!** c'est un prêté pour un rendu!

Titan ['taɪtn] *n* ASTRON Titan ■ MYTH Titan *m*.

titanic [taɪ'tænɪk] *adj* **1.** [huge] titanesque, colossal **2.** CHEM au titane ■ **~ acid** acide *m* de titane.

titanium [taɪ'teɪnɪəm] *n* titane *m*.

titbit ['tɪtbɪt] *n* **1.** CULIN bon morceau *m*, morceau *m* de choix **2.** [of information, of scandal] détail *m* croustillant ■ **~ of gossip** potin *m*, racontar *m*.

titch [tɪtʃ] = **tich**.

titchy ['tɪtʃɪ] = **tichy**.

tithe [taɪð] ◇ *n* HIST dîme *f* ■ **to pay ~s** payer la dîme.
◇ *vt* lever la dîme sur.

Titian ['tɪʃn] *pr n* (le) Titien.

Titicaca [tɪtɪ'kɑ:kɑ:] *pr n* : **Lake ~** le lac Titicaca.

titillate ['tɪtɪleɪt] *vt* titiller.

titillation [,tɪtɪ'leɪʃn] *n* titillation *f*.

titivate ['tɪtɪveɪt] *inf hum* ◇ *vi* se bichonner, se pomponner.
◇ *vt* bichonner.

titivation [,tɪtɪ'veɪʃn] *n inf* bichonnage *m*.

title ['taɪtl] ◇ *n* **1.** [indicating rank, status] titre *m* ■ **he was given a ~ for services to industry** [sir] on lui a conféré un titre pour services rendus à l'industrie ; [lord] on l'a anobli pour services rendus à l'industrie ■ **the monarch bears the ~ of Defender of the Faith** le monarque porte le titre de défenseur de la foi ‖ [nickname] surnom *m* ■ **she earned the ~ "Iron Lady"** on l'a surnommée "la Dame de Fer" **2.** [of book, film, play, song] titre *m* ■ [of newspaper article] titre *m*, intitulé *m* **3.** PRINT titre *m* **4.** SPORT titre *m* ■ **to win the ~** remporter le titre ■ **he holds the world heavyweight boxing ~** il détient le titre de champion du monde de boxe des poids lourds **5.** LAW droit *m*, titre *m*.
◇ *comp* [music] du générique.
◇ *vt* [book, chapter, film] intituler.
◆ **titles** *npl* CIN & TV [credits] générique *m*.

titled ['taɪtld] *adj* [person, family] titré.

title deed *n* titre *m* de propriété.

titleholder ['taɪtl,həʊldəʳ] *n* détenteur *m*, - trice *f* du titre, tenant *m*, - e *f* du titre.

title page *n* page *f* de titre.

title role *n* rôle-titre *m*.

title track *n* morceau *m* qui donne son titre à l'album.

titmouse ['tɪtmaʊs] (*pl* **titmice** [-maɪs]) *n* ORNITH mésange *f*.

titter ['tɪtəʳ] ◇ *vi* rire bêtement *OR* sottement, glousser.
◇ *n* petit rire *m* bête *OR* sot, gloussement *m*.

tittle ['tɪtl] *n* TYPO signe *m* diacritique, iota *m*.

tittle-tattle [-,tætl] ◇ *n (U)* potins *mpl*, cancans *mpl*.
◇ *vi* jaser, cancaner.

titular ['tɪtjʊləʳ], **titulary** ['tɪtjʊlərɪ] *adj* nominal.

Titus ['taɪtəs] *pr n* Tite.

tizzy ['tɪzɪ] *n inf* panique *f* ■ **to be in a ~** paniquer ■ **don't get into a ~ about it** ne t'affole pas pour ça.

T-junction *n* intersection *f* en T.

TLC *n* = **tender loving care**.

TN *written abbr of* **Tennessee**.

TNT (*abbrev of* **trinitrotoluene**) *n* TNT *m*.

to (*strong form* [tu:], *weak form before vowel* [tʊ], *weak form before consonant* [tə]) ◇ *prep*

A.

1. [indicating direction] : **to go to school/the cinema** aller à l'école/au cinéma ■ **let's go to town** allons en ville ■ **he climbed to the top** il est monté jusqu'au sommet *OR* jusqu'en haut ■ **we've been to it before** nous y sommes déjà allés ■ **the vase fell to the ground** le vase est tombé par *OR* à terre ■ **I invited them to dinner** je les ai invités à dîner ■ **let's go to Susan's** allons chez Susan ■ **to go to the doctor** *OR* **doctor's** aller chez le médecin ■ **the road to the south** la route du sud ■ **our house is a mile to the south** notre maison est à un mille au sud ■ **it's 12 miles to the nearest town** [from here] nous sommes à 12 miles de la ville la plus proche ; [from there] c'est à 12 miles de la ville la plus proche ■ **what's the best way to the station?** quel est le meilleur chemin pour aller à la gare? ■ **I sat with my back to her** j'étais assis lui tournant le dos ■ **tell her to her face** dites-le-lui en face

2. [indicating location, position] à ■ **she lives next door to us** elle habite à côté de chez nous ■ **to one side** d'un côté ■ **to the left/right** à gauche/droite

3. [with geographical names] : **to Madrid** à Madrid ■ **to Le Havre** au Havre ■ **to France** en France ■ **to the United States** aux États-Unis ■ **I'm off to Paris** je pars à *OR* pour Paris ■ **the road to Chicago** la route de Chicago ■ **planes to and from Europe** les vols à destination et en provenance de l'Europe

4. [indicating age, amount or level reached] jusqu'à ■ **the snow came (up) to her knees** la neige lui arrivait aux genoux ■ **it's accurate to the millimetre** c'est exact au millimètre près ■ **it weighs 8 to 9 pounds** ça pèse entre 8 et 9 livres ■ **moderate to cool temperatures** des températures douces ou fraîches

5. [so as to make contact with] à, contre ■ **she pinned the brooch to her dress** elle a épinglé la broche sur sa robe ■ **they danced cheek to cheek** ils dansaient joue contre joue

B.

1. [before the specified hour or date] : **it's ten minutes to three** il est trois heures moins dix ■ **it's twenty to** il est moins vingt ■ **how long is it to dinner?** on dîne dans combien de temps? ■ **there's only two weeks to Christmas** il ne reste que deux semaines avant Noël
2. [up to and including] (jusqu')à ■ **from March to June** de mars (jusqu')à juin ■ **from day to day** de jour en jour ■ **I do everything from scrubbing the floor to keeping the books** je fais absolument tout, depuis le ménage jusqu'à la comptabilité

C.

1. [before infinitive] : **to talk** parler
2. [after verb] : **she lived to be 100** elle a vécu jusqu'à 100 ans ■ **we are to complete the work by Monday** nous devons finir le travail pour lundi ■ **she went on to become a brilliant guitarist** elle est ensuite devenue une excellente guitariste ■ **you can leave if you want to** vous pouvez partir si vous voulez ■ **why? – because I told you to** pourquoi? – parce que je t'ai dit de le faire ■ **would you like to come? – we'd love to** voulez-vous venir? – avec plaisir *fml* OR oh, oui!
3. [after noun] : **I have a lot to do** j'ai beaucoup à faire ■ **that's no reason to leave** ce n'est pas une raison pour partir ■ **the first to complain** le premier à se plaindre ■ **that's the way to do it** voilà comment il faut faire
4. [after adjective] : **I'm happy/sad to see her go** je suis content/triste de la voir partir ■ **difficult/easy to do** difficile/facile à faire ■ **she's too proud to apologize** elle est trop fière pour s'excuser
5. [after 'how', 'which', 'where' etc] : **do you know where to go?** savez-vous où aller? ■ **he told me how to get there** il m'a dit comment y aller
6. [indicating purpose] pour ■ **I did it to annoy her** je l'ai fait exprès pour l'énerver
7. [introducing statement] pour ■ **to put it another way** en d'autres termes
8. [in exclamations] : **oh, to be in England!** ah, si je pouvais être en Angleterre! ■ **and to think I nearly married him!** quand je pense que j'ai failli l'épouser!
9. [in headlines] : **unions to strike** les syndicats s'apprêtent à déclencher la grève

D.

1. [indicating intended recipient, owner] à ■ **I showed the picture to her** je lui ai montré la photo ■ **show it to her** montrez-le-lui ■ **that book belongs to her** ce livre lui appartient ■ **be kind to him/to animals** soyez gentil avec lui/bon envers les animaux ■ **what's it to him?** qu'est-ce que cela peut lui faire?
2. [in the opinion of] pour ■ **it sounds suspicious to me** cela me semble bizarre ■ **it didn't make sense to him** ça n'avait aucun sens pour lui
3. [indicating intention] : **with a view to clarifying matters** dans l'intention d'éclaircir la situation ■ **it's all to no purpose** tout cela ne sert à rien OR est en vain
4. [indicating resulting state] : **the light changed to red** le feu est passé au rouge ■ **the noise drove him to distraction** le bruit le rendait fou ■ **the rain turned to snow** la pluie avait fait place à la neige ■ **(much) to my relief/surprise/delight** à mon grand soulagement/mon grand étonnement/ma grande joie ■ **smashed to pieces** brisé en mille morceaux ■ **he was beaten to death** il a été battu à mort ■ **they starved to death** ils sont morts de faim ■ **she sang the baby to sleep** elle a chanté jusqu'à ce que le bébé s'endorme
5. [as regards] : **the answer to your question** la réponse à votre question ■ **no one was sympathetic to his ideas** ses idées ne plaisaient à personne ■ **what would you say to a game of bridge?** que diriez-vous d'un bridge?, si on faisait un bridge? ■ **that's all there is to it** c'est aussi simple que ça ■ **there's nothing to it** il n'y a rien de plus simple ■ **'to translating annual report: $300'** COMM [on bill] 'traduction du rapport annuel: 300 dollars' ■ **'to services rendered'** 'pour services rendus'
6. [indicating composition or proportion] : **there are 16 ounces to a pound** il y a 16 onces dans une livre ■ **there are 6 francs to the dollar** un dollar vaut 6 francs ■ **one cup of sugar to every three cups of fruit** une tasse de sucre pour trois tasses de fruits ■ **Milan beat Madrid by 4 (points) to 3** Milan a battu Madrid 4 (points) à 3 ■ **I'll bet 100 to 1** je parierais 100 contre 1 ■ **the odds are 1000 to 1 against it happening again** il y a 1 chance sur 1000 que cela se produise à nouveau ■ **the vote was 6 to 3** il y avait 6 voix contre 3
7. [per] : **how many miles do you get to the gallon?** ≃ vous faites combien de litres au cent?
8. [indicating comparison] : **inferior to** inférieur à ■ **they compare her to Callas** on la compare à (la) Callas ■ **inflation is nothing (compared) to last year** l'inflation n'est rien à côté de OR en comparaison de l'année dernière
9. [of] de ■ **the key to this door** la clé de cette porte ■ **he's secretary to the director/to the committee** c'est le secrétaire du directeur/du comité ■ **the French ambassador to Algeria** l'ambassadeur français en Algérie ■ **ambassador to the King of Thailand** ambassadeur auprès du roi de Thaïlande ■ **she's interpreter to the president** c'est l'interprète du président
10. [in accordance with] : **to his way of thinking, to his mind** à son avis ■ **to hear him talk, you'd think he was an expert** à l'entendre parler, on croirait que c'est un expert ■ **the climate is not to my liking** le climat ne me plaît pas ■ **add salt to taste** salez selon votre goût OR à volonté ■ **she made out a cheque to the amount of £15** elle a fait un chèque de 15 livres
11. [indicating accompaniment, simultaneity] : **we danced to live music** nous avons dansé sur la musique d'un orchestre
12. [in honour of] à ■ **(here's) to your health!** à la vôtre! ■ **to my family** [in dedication] à ma famille ■ **a monument to the war dead** un monument aux morts

E.

1. [indicating addition] : **add flour to the list** ajoutez de la farine sur la liste ■ **add 3 to 6** additionnez 3 et 6, ajoutez 3 à 6 ■ **in addition to Charles, there were three women** en plus de Charles, il y avait trois femmes
2. MATHS : **2 to the 3rd power, 2 to the 3rd** 2 (à la) puissance 3.
◇ *adv* **1.** [closed] fermé ■ **the wind blew the door to** un coup de vent a fermé la porte **2.** [back to consciousness] : **to come to** revenir à soi, reprendre connaissance **3.** NAUT : **to bring a ship to** mettre un bateau en panne.

toad [təʊd] *n* **1.** ZOOL crapaud *m* **2.** *inf fig* [person] rat *m*.

toad-in-the-hole *n* UK CULIN *plat composé de saucisses cuites au four dans une sorte de pâte à crêpes.*

toadstool ['təʊdstu:l] *n* champignon *m* (vénéneux).

toady ['təʊdɪ] (*pl* **toadies**, *pret & pp* **toadied**) *pej* ◇ *n* flatteur *m*, - euse *f*.
◇ *vi* être flatteur ■ **to ~ to sb** passer de la pommade à qqn.

to and fro *adv phr* : **to go ~** aller et venir, se promener de long en large ■ **to swing ~** se balancer d'avant en arrière.
▸ **to-and-fro** *adj* : **a to-and-fro movement** un mouvement de va-et-vient.

toast [təʊst] ◇ *n* **1.** [bread] pain *m* grillé ■ **a piece** OR **slice of ~** une tartine grillée, un toast ■ **don't burn the ~** ne brûle pas le pain ■ **cheese/sardines on ~** fromage fondu/sardines sur du pain grillé **2.** [drink] toast *m* ■ **to drink a ~ to sb** porter un toast à qqn, boire à la santé de qqn ■ **we drank a ~ to their success/future happiness** on a bu à leur succès/bonheur futur ■ **to propose a ~ to sb** porter un toast à qqn ■ **she was the ~ of the town** elle était la coqueluche de la ville.
◇ *vt* **1.** [grill] griller ■ **he was ~ing himself/his toes by the fire** *fig* il se chauffait/il se rôtissait les orteils devant la cheminée **2.** [drink to - person] porter un toast à, boire à la santé de ; [- success, win] arroser ■ **they ~ed her victory in champagne** ils ont arrosé sa victoire au champagne.

toasted ['təʊstɪd] *adj* : **~ sandwich** sandwich *m* grillé ■ **~ cheese** fromage *m* fondu.

toaster ['təʊstə^r] *n* grille-pain *m inv* (électrique), toaster *m*.

toasting fork ['təʊstɪŋ] *n* fourchette *f* à griller le pain.

toastmaster ['təʊst,mɑ:stə^r] *n* animateur *m (qui annonce les toasts ou les discours lors d'une réception).*

toast rack *n* porte-toasts *m inv*.

tobacco [tə'bækəʊ] (*pl* **tobaccos**) ◇ *n* **1.** tabac *m* ■ **chewing ~** tabac *m* à chiquer **2.** BOT : **~ (plant)** (pied *m* de) tabac *m*.
◇ *comp* [leaf, plantation, smoke] de tabac ■ [industry] du tabac.

tobacconist [tə'bækənɪst] *n* marchand *m*, - e *f* de tabac, buraliste *mf* ▪ **~'s (shop)** (bureau *m* de) tabac *m*.

tobacco pouch *n* blague *f* à tabac.

Tobago [tə'beɪgəu] ⊳ **Trinidad and Tobago**.

-to-be *in cpds* : **mother~** future mère *f*.

toboggan [tə'bɒgən] <> *n* luge *f*.
<> *comp* [race] de luge.
<> *vi* **1.** SPORT : **to ~** *OR* **go ~ing** faire de la luge ▪ **they ~ed down the slope** ils ont descendu la pente en luge **2.** *US* [prices, sales] dégringoler.

toboggan run *n* piste *f* de luge.

tod [tɒd] *n UK phr* **to be on one's ~** *inf* être tout seul.

today [tə'deɪ] <> *adv* aujourd'hui ▪ **a week ~** [past] il y a huit jours aujourd'hui ; [future] dans huit jours aujourd'hui ▪ **they arrived a week ago ~** ils sont arrivés il y a huit jours ▪ **he died 5 years ago ~** cela fait 5 ans aujourd'hui qu'il est mort ➋ **here ~ and gone tomorrow** ça va ça vient.
<> *n* aujourd'hui *m* ▪ **what's ~'s date?** quelle est la date d'aujourd'hui? ▪ **what day is it ~?** quel jour est-on (aujourd'hui)? ▪ **~ is March 17th** aujourd'hui, on est le 17 mars ▪ **it's Monday ~** on est lundi aujourd'hui ▪ **a week from ~** dans une semaine aujourd'hui ▪ **three weeks from ~** dans trois semaines ▪ **as from ~** à partir d'aujourd'hui ▪ **the youth of ~, ~'s youth** la jeunesse d'aujourd'hui ➋ **~'s the day!** c'est le grand jour!, *see also* **tabloid**.

toddle ['tɒdl] *vi* **1.** [start to walk - child] faire ses premiers pas ▪ [walk unsteadily] marcher d'un pas chancelant **2.** *inf* [go] aller ▪ [stroll] se balader ▪ [go away] s'en aller, partir ▪ **she ~d along after him** elle trottinait derrière lui.
◆ **toddle off** *vi insep inf* [go] aller ▪ [go away] s'en aller, partir bien gentiment.

toddler ['tɒdlə^r] *n* tout petit *m* /toute petite *f (qui fait ses premiers pas)* ▪ **their children are still ~s** leurs enfants sont tout juste en âge de marcher.

toddy ['tɒdɪ] (*pl* **toddies**) *n* **1.** [drink] : **(hot) ~** ≃ grog *m* **2.** [sap] sève *f* de palmier *(utilisée comme boisson)*.

to-die-for *adj inf* de rêve.

to-do *n inf* **1.** [fuss] remue-ménage *m inv*, tohu-bohu *m inv* ▪ **she made a great ~ about it** elle en a fait tout un plat ▪ **there was a great ~ over her wedding** son mariage a fait grand bruit ▪ **what a ~!** quelle affaire!, quelle histoire! **2.** *US* [party] bringue *f*.

toe [təu] <> *n* **1.** ANAT orteil *m*, doigt *m* de pied ▪ **big/little ~** gros/petit orteil ➋ **to step** *OR* **to tread on sb's ~s** *liter & fig* marcher sur les pieds de qqn ▪ **she kept us on our ~s** elle ne nous laissait aucun répit **2.** [of sock, shoe] bout *m* ▪ **the ~ of Italy** *fig* la pointe de l'Italie.
<> *vt* **1.** [ball] toucher du bout du pied **2.** *phr* **to ~ the line** *OR US* **mark** se mettre au pas, obtempérer ▪ **to ~ the party line** POL s'aligner sur le *OR* suivre la ligne du parti.

toe cap *n* bout *m* renforcé *(de soulier)* ▪ **steel ~** bout *m* ferré.

toe clip *n* cale-pied *m*.

TOEFL (*abbrev of* **Test of English as a Foreign Language**) *n test d'anglais passé par les étudiants étrangers désirant faire des études dans une université américaine*.

toehold ['təuhəuld] *n* prise *f* de pied ▪ **to get** *OR* **to gain a ~** [climber] trouver une prise (pour le pied) ; *fig* prendre pied, s'implanter.

toeless ['təulɪs] *adj* **1.** ANAT sans orteil *OR* orteils **2.** [sock, shoe] (à bout) ouvert.

toenail ['təuneɪl] *n* ongle *m* de pied.

toe-piece *n* [of ski] butée *f*.

toerag^△ ['təuræg] *n UK pej* ordure^△ *f*.

toff [tɒf] *n UK inf* aristo *m*.

toffee ['tɒfɪ] *n UK* caramel *m* (au beurre) ▪ **I can't speak Italian for ~** *inf* je suis incapable de parler italien.

toffee apple *n* pomme *f* d'amour *(confiserie)*.

toffee-nosed *adj UK inf* bêcheur, snob.

tofu ['təufu:] *n* tofu *m inv*.

tog [tɒg] (*pret & pp* **togged**, *cont* **togging**) *n* [measurement of warmth] pouvoir *m* adiathermique, PA *m* ▪ **~ number** indice *m* de PA.
◆ **togs** *npl inf* [clothes] fringues *fpl* ▪ SPORT affaires *fpl*.
◆ **tog out, tog up** *vt sep inf* nipper, fringuer ▪ **she was all togged up in her best clothes** elle était super sapée ▪ **they were all togged out for the match** ils s'étaient tous mis en tenue pour le match.

toga ['təugə] *n* toge *f*.

together [tə'geðə^r] <> *adv* **1.** [with each other] ensemble ▪ **they get on well ~** ils s'entendent bien ▪ **we're all in this ~!** on est tous logés à la même enseigne! **2.** [jointly] : **she's cleverer than both of them put ~** elle est plus intelligente qu'eux deux réunis ▪ **even taken ~, their efforts don't amount to much** même si on les considère dans leur ensemble, leurs efforts ne représentent pas grand-chose **3.** [indicating proximity] : **tie the two ribbons ~** attachez les deux rubans l'un à l'autre ▪ **she tried to bring the two sides ~** elle a essayé de rapprocher les deux camps ▪ **we were crowded ~ into the room** on nous a tous entassés dans la pièce **4.** [at the same time] à la fois, en même temps, ensemble ▪ **all ~ now!** [pull] tous ensemble!, ho hisse! ; [sing, recite] tous ensemble *OR* en chœur! **5.** [consecutively] : **for 12 hours ~** pendant 12 heures d'affilée *OR* de suite.
<> *adj inf* [person] équilibré, bien dans sa peau.
◆ **together with** *conj phr* ainsi que, en même temps que.

togetherness [tə'geðənɪs] *n* [unity] unité *f* ▪ [solidarity] solidarité *f* ▪ [comradeship] camaraderie *f*.

toggle ['tɒgl] <> *n* **1.** [peg] cheville *f* **2.** SEW bouton *m* de duffle-coat **3.** NAUT cabillot *m*.
<> *vt* NAUT attacher avec un cabillot.
<> *vi* COMPUT basculer ▪ **to ~ between** alterner entre.

toggle switch *n* ELEC interrupteur *m* à bascule ▪ COMPUT bascule *f OR* interrupteur *m* de changement de mode.

Togo ['təugəu] *pr n* Togo *m* ▪ **in ~** au Togo.

Togolese [,təugə'li:z] (*pl inv*) <> *n* Togolais *m*, - e *f*.
<> *adj* togolais.

toil [tɔɪl] <> *vi* **1.** [labour] travailler dur, peiner ▪ **he ~ed over his essay for weeks** il a peiné *OR* il a sué sur sa dissertation pendant des semaines **2.** [as verb of movement] avancer péniblement ▪ **they ~ed up the hill on their bikes/on foot** ils montèrent péniblement la colline à vélo/à pied.
<> *n* labeur *m lit*, travail *m* (pénible).
◆ **toil away** *vi insep* travailler dur, peiner.

toilet ['tɔɪlɪt] *n* **1.** [lavatory] toilettes *fpl* ▪ **to go to the ~** aller aux toilettes *OR* aux cabinets ▪ **the ~ won't flush** la chasse d'eau ne marche pas ▪ **he threw it down the ~** il l'a jeté dans les toilettes ▪ **'Public Toilets'** 'Toilettes, W-C Publics' **2.** = **toilette**.

toilet bag *n* trousse *f* de toilette.

toilet humour *n* humour *m* scatologique.

toilet paper *n* papier *m* hygiénique.

toiletries ['tɔɪlɪtrɪz] *npl* articles *mpl* de toilette.

toilet roll *n* rouleau *m* de papier hygiénique.

toilet seat *n* siège *m* des cabinets *OR* W-C *OR* toilettes.

toilet soap *n* savon *m* de toilette.

toilette [twɑ:'let] *n dated & fml* toilette *f (action de se laver)*.

toilet tissue = **toilet paper**.

toilet-train *vt* : **to ~ a child** apprendre à un enfant à être propre.

toilet-trained [-,treɪnd] *adj* propre.

toilet water *n* eau *f* de toilette.

toils [tɔɪlz] *npl lit* rets *mpl lit*, filets *mpl*.

to-ing and fro-ing [,tu:ɪŋən'frəuɪŋ] *n (U) inf* allées et venues *fpl*.

token ['təʊkn] <> *n* **1.** [of affection, appreciation, esteem etc] marque *f*, témoignage *m* ▪ **as a ~ of** *OR* **in ~ of my gratitude** en témoignage *OR* en gage de ma reconnaissance ▪ **a love ~** un gage d'amour **2.** [indication] signe *m* **3.** [souvenir, gift] souvenir *m* **4.** [for machine] jeton *m* **5.** [voucher] bon *m* **6.** LING occurrence *f*.
<> *adj* [gesture, effort] symbolique, pour la forme ▪ [increase, protest] symbolique, de pure forme.
◆ **by the same token** *adv phr* de même, pareillement.

token payment *n* paiement *m* symbolique (d'intérêts).

Tokyo ['təʊkjəʊ] *pr n* Tokyo.

told [təʊld] *pt & pp* ▷ **tell**.

Toledo [tɒ'leɪdəʊ] *pr n* Tolède.

tolerable ['tɒlərəbl] *adj* **1.** [pain, situation, behaviour] tolérable ▪ [standard] admissible **2.** [not too bad] pas trop mal, passable.

tolerably ['tɒlərəblɪ] *adv* passablement ▪ **she performed ~ (well)** elle n'a pas trop mal joué ▪ **they were ~ pleased with the results** ils étaient assez contents des résultats.

tolerance ['tɒlərəns] *n* tolérance *f* ▪ **they showed great ~** ils ont fait preuve de beaucoup de tolérance, ils ont été très tolérants ▪ **to develop (a) ~ to a drug** développer une accoutumance à un médicament ▪ **they have little ~ to cold** ils ont peu de résistance au froid.

tolerant ['tɒlərənt] *adj* tolérant ▪ **he's not very ~ of others** il n'est pas très tolérant envers les autres ▪ **she's not very ~ of criticism** elle ne supporte pas bien les critiques ▪ **~ to heat/cold** PHYS résistant à la chaleur/au froid.

tolerantly ['tɒlərəntlɪ] *adv* avec tolérance.

tolerate ['tɒləreɪt] *vt* tolérer.

toleration [,tɒlə'reɪʃn] *n* tolérance *f*.

toll [təʊl] <> *n* **1.** [on bridge, road] péage *m* **2.** [of victims] nombre *m* de victimes ▪ [of casualties] nombre *m* de blessés ▪ [of deaths] nombre *m* de morts ▪ **the epidemic took a heavy ~ of** *OR* **among the population** l'épidémie a fait beaucoup de morts *OR* de victimes parmi la population ▪ **the years have taken their ~** les années ont laissé leurs traces ▪ **her illness took its ~ on her family** sa maladie a ébranlé sa famille **3.** [of bell] sonnerie *f*.
<> *vt vi* [bell] sonner.

tollbooth ['təʊlbu:θ] *n* (poste *m* de) péage *m*.

toll bridge *n* pont *m* à péage.

toll-free *US* <> *adj* : **~ number** numéro *m* vert.
<> *adv* : **to call ~** appeler un numéro vert.

tollgate ['təʊlgeɪt] *n* (barrière *f* de) péage *m*.

tollhouse ['təʊlhaʊs] (*pl* [-haʊzɪz]) *n* (bureau *m* de) péage *m*.

tollroad ['təʊlrəʊd] *n* route *f* à péage.

Tolstoy ['tɒlstɔɪ] *pr n* : **Leon ~** Léon Tolstoï.

tom [tɒm] *n* [cat] matou *m*.

Tom [tɒm] *pr n* [dimin of Thomas] : **any** *OR* **every ~, Dick or Harry** n'importe qui, le premier venu ▪ **'~ Thumb'** 'Tom Pouce'.

tomahawk ['tɒməhɔ:k] *n* tomahawk *m*.

tomato [*UK* tə'mɑ:təʊ, *US* tə'meɪtəʊ] (*pl* **tomatoes**) <> *n* tomate *f*.
<> *comp* [juice, salad, soup] de tomates ▪ **~ ketchup** ketchup *m* ▪ **~ plant** (pied *m* de) tomate *f* ▪ **~ sauce** sauce *f* tomate.

tomb [tu:m] *n* tombeau *m*, tombe *f*.

tombola [tɒm'bəʊlə] *n UK* tombola *f*.

tomboy ['tɒmbɔɪ] *n* garçon *m* manqué.

tombstone ['tu:mstəʊn] *n* pierre *f* tombale.

tomcat ['tɒmkæt] *n* chat *m*, matou *m*.

tome [təʊm] *n* gros volume *m*.

tomfool [,tɒm'fu:l] *inf* <> *n* idiot *m*, - e *f*, imbécile *mf*.
<> *adj* idiot, imbécile.

tomfoolery [tɒm'fu:lərɪ] *n (U) inf* [foolish words] absurdités *fpl*, idioties *fpl*, bêtises *fpl* ▪ [foolish behaviour] bêtises *fpl*.

Tommy ['tɒmɪ] (*pl* **Tommies**) *pr n dated surnom donné autrefois aux soldats britanniques.*

tommy gun *n inf* mitraillette *f*.

tomorrow [tə'mɒrəʊ] <> *adv* demain ▪ **~ morning/evening** demain matin/soir ▪ **see you ~!** à demain! ▪ **a week ~** [past] cela fera huit jours demain ; [future] dans une semaine de main.
<> *n* **1.** *liter* demain *m* ▪ **what's ~'s date?** le combien serons-nous demain? ▪ **what day is it** *OR* **will it be ~?** quel jour serons-nous demain? ▪ **~ is** *OR* **will be March 17th** demain, on sera le 17 mars ▪ **~ is Monday** demain, c'est lundi ▪ **a week from ~** dans une semaine demain ▪ **the day after ~** après-demain dans deux jours ▪ **~ may never come** qui sait où nous serons demain ▪ **~ never comes** demain n'arrive jamais ▪ **~ is another day** demain il fera jour ▶ **never put off till ~ what you can do today** *prov* il ne faut jamais remettre au lendemain ce que l'on peut faire le jour même *prov* **2.** *fig* [future] demain *m*, lendemain *m* ▪ **we look forward to a bright ~** nous espérons des lendemains qui chantent ▪ **~'s world** le monde de demain ▶ **he spends money like there was no ~** *inf* il dépense (son argent) comme si demain n'existait pas.

tomtit ['tɒmtɪt] *n* mésange *f*.

tom-tom *n* tam-tam *m*.

ton [tʌn] *n* **1.** [weight] tonne *f* ▪ **a 35-- lorry** un 35 tonnes ▪ *fig* **this suitcase weighs a ~!** cette valise pèse une tonne! ▶ **(register) ~** NAUT tonneau *m* **2.** *inf* [speed] : **to do a ~** rouler à plus de 150.
◆ **tons** *npl inf* [lots] : **~s of money** des tas *OR* des tonnes d'argent ▪ **~s of people** des tas de gens ▪ **~s better** beaucoup mieux.

tonal ['təʊnl] *adj* tonal.

tonality [tə'nælətɪ] (*pl* **tonalities**) *n* MUS tonalité *f*.

tone [təʊn] <> *n* **1.** [of voice] ton *m* (de la voix) ▪ **don't (you) speak to me in that ~ (of voice)!** ne me parle pas sur ce ton! ▪ **I didn't much like the ~ of her remarks** je n'ai pas beaucoup aimé le ton de ses remarques ▪ **to raise/to lower the ~ of one's voice** hausser/baisser le ton ▪ **he spoke to me in soft ~s** *OR* **in a soft ~** il m'a parlé d'une voix douce **2.** [sound - of voice, musical instrument] sonorité *f* ▪ [of singer] timbre *m* (de la voix) ▪ **the rich bass ~s of his voice** la richesse de sa voix dans les tons graves ▪ **I thought I recognized those dulcet ~s** *hum* j'ai cru reconnaître cette douce voix **3.** MUS ton *m* **4.** LING ton *m* ▪ **rising/falling ~** ton ascendant/descendant **5.** TELEC tonalité *f* ▪ **please speak after the ~** veuillez parler après le signal sonore **6.** [control - of amplifier, radio] tonalité *f* **7.** [shade] ton *m* ▪ **soft blue ~s** des tons bleu pastel ▪ **a two-- colour scheme** une palette de couleurs à deux tons **8.** [style, atmosphere - of poem, article] ton *m* ▪ **to set the ~** donner le ton **9.** [classiness] chic *m*, classe *f* ▪ **to give/to lend ~ to sthg** donner de la classe/apporter un plus à qqch ▪ **it lowers/raises the ~ of the neighbourhood** cela rabaisse/rehausse le standing du quartier **10.** FIN [of market] tenue *f* **11.** PHYSIOL [of muscle, nerves] tonus *m* **12.** *US* [single musical sound] note *f*.
<> *vi* [colour] s'harmoniser.
<> *vt* = **tone up**.
◆ **tone down** *vt sep* **1.** [colour, contrast] adoucir **2.** [sound, voice] atténuer, baisser **3.** [moderate - language, statement, views] tempérer, modérer ; [- effect] adoucir, atténuer ▪ **his article had to be ~d down for publication** son article a dû être édulcoré avant d'être publié.
◆ **tone in** *vi insep* s'harmoniser, s'assortir.
◆ **tone up** *vt sep* [body, muscles] tonifier.

tone arm *n* bras *m* de lecture.

tone-deaf *adj* : **to be ~** ne pas avoir d'oreille.

tone language *n* LING langue *f* à tons.

toneless ['təʊnlɪs] *adj* [voice] blanc, blanche *f*, sans timbre ▪ [colour] terne.

tone poem *n* poème *m* symphonique.

toner ['təʊnəʳ] *n* [for hair] colorant *m* ▪ [for skin] lotion *f* tonique ▪ PHOT toner *m*, encre *f*.

Tonga ['tɒŋgə] *pr n* Tonga ▪ **in ~** à Tonga.

Tongan ['tɒŋgən] ◇ *n* **1.** [person] Tongan *m*, - e *f* **2.** LING tongan *m*.
◇ *adj* tongan.

tongs [tɒŋz] *npl* : **(pair of) ~** pinces *fpl* ▪ **fire ~** pincettes *fpl* ▪ **(sugar) ~** pince *f* (à sucre).

tongue [tʌŋ] ◇ *n* **1.** ANAT langue *f* ▪ **to put** *OR* **to stick one's ~ out (at sb)** tirer la langue (à qqn) ▪ **his ~ was practically hanging out** *fig* [very eager] il en salivait littéralement ; [very thirsty] il était pratiquement mort de soif **2.** *fig* [for speech] langue *f* ▪ **to lose/to find one's ~** perdre/retrouver sa langue ▪ **hold your ~!** tenez votre langue!, taisez-vous! ▪ **try to keep a civil ~ in your head!** essayez de rester courtois *OR* correct! ▪ **I can't get my ~ round his name** *UK* je n'arrive pas à prononcer correctement son nom ▪ **to have a sharp ~** avoir la langue acérée ▪ **she has a quick ~** elle n'a pas sa langue dans sa poche ▪ **~s will wag** les langues iront bon train, ça va jaser ▶ **~ in cheek** ironiquement ▪ **she said it (with) ~ in cheek** elle l'a dit avec une ironie voilée, il ne faut pas prendre au sérieux ce qu'elle a dit ▪ **a ~-in-cheek remark** une réflexion ironique **3.** [language] *fml* & *lit* langue *f* ▪ **to speak in ~s** RELIG avoir le don des langues **4.** *(U)* CULIN langue *f* (de bœuf) **5.** [of shoe] languette *f* ▪ [of bell] battant *m* ▪ [of buckle] ardillon *m* ▪ TECH languette *f*, languette *f* **6.** [of flame, land, sea] langue *f*.
◇ *vt* **1.** MUS [note] détacher ▪ [phrase] détacher les notes de **2.** [in woodworking] langueter.

tongue-in-cheek ▷ **tongue** *(n sense 2)*.

tongue-lashing *n inf* **to give sb a ~** sonner les cloches à qqn.

tongue-tied *adj* muet *fig*, trop timide (pour parler) ▪ **she was completely ~** elle semblait avoir perdu sa langue.

tongue-twister *n mot ou phrase très difficile à prononcer.*

tonguing ['tʌŋɪŋ] *n* MUS coup *m* de langue.

tonic ['tɒnɪk] ◇ *n* **1.** MED tonique *m*, fortifiant *m* ▪ *fig* **the news was a ~ to us all** la nouvelle nous a remonté le moral à tous **2.** [cosmetic] lotion *f* tonique ▪ **hair ~** lotion *f* capillaire **3.** [drink] tonic *m* **4.** MUS tonique *f* **5.** LING syllabe *f* tonique *OR* accentuée.
◇ *adj* tonique ▪ **~ syllable/stress** LING syllabe *f* /accent *m* tonique.

tonic sol-fa *n* solfège *m*.

tonic water *n* tonic *m*, ≃ Schweppes® *m*.

tonight [tə'naɪt] ◇ *n* [this evening] ce soir ▪ [this night] cette nuit ▪ **in ~'s newspaper** dans le journal de ce soir ▪ **~'s the night** c'est le grand soir.
◇ *adv* [this evening] ce soir ▪ [this night] cette nuit *f*.

tonnage ['tʌnɪdʒ] *n* **1.** [total weight] poids *m* total d'une chose **2.** [capacity - of a ship] tonnage *m*, jauge *f* ▪ [of a port] tonnage *m*.

tonne [tʌn] *n* tonne *f* (métrique).

tonsil ['tɒnsl] *n (usu pl)* amygdale *f* ▪ **to have one's ~s out** se faire opérer des amygdales.

tonsillitis [,tɒnsɪ'laɪtɪs] *n (U)* angine *f*, amygdalite *f spec* ▪ **to have ~** avoir une angine.

tonsure ['tɒnʃəʳ] ◇ *n* tonsure *f*.
◇ *vt* tonsurer.

Tony (Award) *n US* Tony *m (Oscar du théâtre)*.

too [tu:] *adv* **1.** [as well] aussi, également ▪ **I like jazz – I do ~** *OR* **me ~** j'aime le jazz – moi aussi ▪ **he's a professor ~** [as well as sthg else] il est également professeur ; [as well as sb else] lui aussi est professeur
2. [excessively] trop ▪ **she works ~ hard** elle travaille trop ▪ **I have one apple ~ many** j'ai une pomme de trop ▪ **that's ~ bad** c'est vraiment dommage ; *iron* tant pis! ▪ **~ little money** trop peu d'argent ▪ **~ few people** trop peu de gens ▪ **all ~ soon we had to go home** très vite, nous avons dû rentrer ▪ **you're going ~ far** *fig* tu exagères, tu vas trop loin
3. [with negatives] trop ▪ **I wasn't ~ happy about it** ça ne me réjouissait pas trop
4. [moreover] en outre, en plus
5. [for emphasis] : **and quite right ~!** tu as/il a *etc* bien fait ▪ **about time ~!** ce n'est pas trop tôt! ▪ **I should think so ~!** j'espère bien! ▪ **~ true!** ça, c'est vrai!
6. *US* [indeed] : **you didn't do your homework – I did ~!** tu n'as pas fait tes devoirs – si!

toodle-oo [,tu:dl'u:], **toodle-pip** *interj UK inf dated* salut.

took [tʊk] *pt* ▷ **take**.

tool [tu:l] ◇ *n* **1.** [instrument] outil *m* ▪ **set of ~s** outillage *m* ▪ **the ~s of the trade** les instruments de travail ▶ **to down ~s** cesser le travail, se mettre en grève, débrayer **2.** TYPO fer *m* de reliure **3.** [dupe] : **he was nothing but a ~ of the government** il n'était que le jouet *OR* l'instrument du gouvernement **4.**△ [penis] engin△ *m* **5.**△ *UK crime sl* [gun] arme *f*.
◇ *vt* [decorate - wood] travailler, façonner ; [- stone] sculpter ; [- book cover] ciseler ▪ **~ed leather** cuir *m* repoussé.
◇ *vi inf* rouler *(en voiture)*.
◆ **tool up** ◇ *vi insep* s'équiper.
◇ *vt sep* outiller, équiper.

toolbag ['tu:lbæg] *n* trousse *f* à outils.

tool bar *n* COMPUT barre *f* d'outils.

toolbox ['tu:lbɒks] *(pl* **toolboxes***)* *n* boîte *f* à outils.

toolchest ['tu:ltʃest] *n* coffre *m* à outils.

tooling ['tu:lɪŋ] *n* **1.** [decoration] façonnage *m* ▪ [on leather] repoussé *m* ▪ [in stone] ciselure *f* **2.** [equipment] outillage *m*.

toolkit ['tu:lkɪt] *n* jeu *m* d'outils.

toolmaker ['tu:l,meɪkəʳ] *n* outilleur *m*.

toolshed ['tu:lʃed] *n* remise *f*, resserre *f*.

toot [tu:t] ◇ *vi* [car] klaxonner ▪ [train] siffler.
◇ *vt* : **he ~ed his horn** AUT il a klaxonné *OR* donné un coup de klaxon.
◇ *n* [sound] appel *m* ▪ **the tugboat gave a ~** le remorqueur a donné un coup de sirène ▪ **a ~ of the horn** AUT un coup de klaxon.

tooth [tu:θ] *(pl* **teeth***)* ◇ *n* **1.** ANAT dent *f* ▪ **a set of teeth** une denture, une dentition ▪ **a false ~** une fausse dent ▪ **a set of false teeth** un dentier ▪ **to have a ~ out** se faire arracher une dent ▪ **to bare** *OR* **to show one's teeth** montrer les dents ▶ **baby teeth** dents *fpl* de lait ▪ **to have no teeth** *liter* être édenté ; *fig* manquer de force **2.** [of comb, file, cog, saw] dent *f* **3.** *phr* **to be fed up** *OR* **sick to the back teeth** *inf* en avoir plein le dos *OR* ras le bol ▪ **to fight ~ and nail** se battre bec et ongles ▪ **to get one's teeth into sthg** se mettre à fond à qqch ▪ **she needs something to get her teeth into** elle a besoin de quelque chose qui la mobilise ▪ **the play gives you nothing to get your teeth into** la pièce manque de substance ▪ **it was a real kick in the teeth** *inf* ça m'a fichu un sacré coup ▪ **it's better than a kick in the teeth** c'est mieux que rien ▪ **to set sb's teeth on edge** faire grincer qqn des dents ▪ **she's a bit long in the ~** elle n'est plus toute jeune.
◇ *vi* [cogwheels] s'engrener.
◆ **in the teeth of** *prep phr* malgré.

toothache ['tu:θeɪk] *n* mal *m* de dents ▪ **to have ~** *OR US* **a ~** avoir mal aux dents.

toothbrush ['tu:θbrʌʃ] *(pl* **toothbrushes***)* *n* brosse *f* à dents.

toothcomb ['tu:θkəʊm] ▷ **fine-tooth comb**.

toothed [tu:θt] *adj* [wheel] denté.

toothless ['tu:θlɪs] *adj* **1.** *liter* édenté, sans dents **2.** *fig* sans pouvoir *OR* influence.

tooth mug *n* verre *m* à dents.

toothpaste ['tu:θpeɪst] *n* dentifrice *m*, pâte *f* dentifrice.

toothpick ['tu:θpɪk] *n* cure-dents *m inv*.

toothsome ['tu:θsəm] *adj lit & hum* **1.** [food] appétissant **2.** [person] séduisant.

toothy ['tu:θɪ] (*comp* **toothier**, *superl* **toothiest**) *adj inf* **a ~ grin** un sourire tout en dents.

tootle ['tu:tl] *inf* <> *vi* **1.** [on musical instrument] jouer un petit air **2.** *UK* [drive] : **we were tootling along quite nicely until the tyre burst** nous suivions notre petit bonhomme de chemin lorsque le pneu a éclaté.
<> *n* **1.** [on musical instrument] petit air *m* **2.** [drive] petit tour *m* en voiture.

toots [tʊts] (*pl* **tootses**) *inf* = **tootsie** *(sense 2)*.

tootsie, tootsy ['tʊtsɪ] (*pl* **tootsies**) *n inf* **1.** *baby* [foot] pied *m*, peton *m* ▪ [toe] doigt *m* de pied, orteil *m* **2.** *US* [term of address] chéri *m*, - e *f*, mon petit chou *m*.

top [tɒp] (*pret & pp* **topped**, *cont* **topping**) <> *n* **1.** [highest point] haut *m*, sommet *m* ▪ [of tree] sommet *m*, cime *f* ▪ **carrot ~s** fanes *fpl* de carottes ▪ **at the ~ of the stairs** en haut de l'escalier ▪ **he searched the house from ~ to bottom** il a fouillé la maison de fond en comble ▪ **she filled the jar right to the ~** elle a rempli le bocal à ras bord ▪ **the page number is at the ~ of the page** la numérotation se trouve en haut de la page ▮ [surface] dessus *m*, surface *f* ▪ [end] : **at the ~ of the street** au bout de la rue ▪ **at the ~ of the garden** au fond du jardin ▶ **to blow one's ~** *inf* piquer une crise, exploser ▪ **from ~ to toe** *UK* de la tête aux pieds ▪ **he's getting thin on ~** il commence à se dégarnir ▪ **to come out on ~** avoir le dessus ▪ **he doesn't have much up ~** *UK inf* il n'est pas très futé ▪ **over the ~ : the soldiers went over the ~** *liter* les soldats sont montés à l'assaut ▪ **I think he went a bit over the ~** *UK inf fig* à mon avis, il est allé trop loin ▪ **he's a bit over the ~** il en fait un peu trop
2. [cap, lid] couvercle *m* ▪ **where's the ~ to my pen?** où est le capuchon de mon stylo? ▪ **bottle ~** [screw-on] bouchon *m* (de bouteille) ; [on beer bottle] capsule *f* (de bouteille)
3. [highest degree] : **he is at the ~ of his form** il est au meilleur de sa forme ▪ **at the ~ of one's voice** à tue-tête
4. [most important position] : **at the ~ of the table** *UK* à la place d'honneur ▪ **she's ~ of her class** elle est première de sa classe ▪ **someone who has reached the ~ in their profession** quelqu'un qui est arrivé en haut de l'échelle dans sa profession ▪ **to be (at the) ~ of the bill** THEAT être en tête d'affiche ▪ **to reach the ~ of the tree** arriver en haut de l'échelle ▪ **it's tough at the ~!** c'est la rançon de la gloire! ▪ **this car is the ~ of the range** c'est une voiture haut de gamme
5. *UK* AUT : **she changed into ~** elle a enclenché la quatrième *OR* la cinquième
6. [garment] haut *m*
7. [beginning] : **play it again from the ~** reprends au début ▪ **let's take it from the ~** commençons par le commencement
8. [toy] toupie *f* ▪ **to spin a ~** lancer *OR* fouetter une toupie ▶ **to sleep like a ~** *UK* dormir comme un loir.
<> *vt* **1.** [form top of] couvrir ▪ **a cake topped with chocolate** un gâteau recouvert de chocolat
2. *UK* [trim] écimer, étêter ▪ **to ~ and tail gooseberries** équeuter des groseilles
3. [exceed] dépasser ▪ **he topped her offer** il a renchéri sur son offre ▪ **his score ~s the world record** avec ce score, il bat le record du monde ▪ **that ~s the lot!** *UK* ça, c'est le bouquet!
4. [be at the top of] : **the book topped the best-seller list** ce livre est arrivé en tête des best-sellers
5.△ *UK* [kill] faire la peau à ▪ **to ~ o.s.** faire hara-kiri.
<> *adj* : **the ~ floor** *OR* **storey** le dernier étage ▪ **the ~ shelf** l'étagère du haut ▪ **the ~ button of her dress** le premier bouton de sa robe ▪ **in the ~ right-hand corner** dans le coin en haut à droite ▪ **~ management** la direction générale ▪ **the ~ banks in the country** les grandes banques du pays ▪ **the ~ speed of this car is 150 mph** la vitesse maximum de cette voiture est de 240 km/h ▪ **to be on ~ form** être en pleine forme ▶ **the ~ brass** *UK inf* MIL les officiers *mpl* supérieurs, les gros bonnets *mpl* ▪ **to pay ~ whack for sthg** *UK inf* payer qqch au prix fort ▪ **I can offer you £20 ~ whack** *inf* je vous en donne 20 livres, c'est mon dernier prix.
◆ **on top of** *prep phr* : **suddenly the lorry was on ~ of him** d'un seul coup, il a réalisé que le camion lui arrivait dessus ▪ **we're living on ~ of each other** nous vivons les uns sur les autres ▶ **on ~ of everything else** pour couronner le tout ▪ **it's just one thing on ~ of another** ça n'arrête pas ▪ **don't worry, I'm on ~ of things** ne t'inquiète pas, je m'en sors très bien ▪ **it's all getting on ~ of him** il est dépassé par les événements ▪ **to feel on ~ of the world** avoir la forme.
◆ **top off** *vt sep* **1.** *UK* [conclude] terminer, couronner **2.** *US* [fill to top] remplir.
◆ **top out** *vt insep* [building] fêter l'achèvement de.
◆ **top up** *vt sep UK* [fill up] remplir ▪ **can I ~ up your drink** ? ▪ **~ you up?** encore une goutte? ▪ **to ~ up the battery** AUT ajouter de l'eau dans la batterie.

topaz ['təʊpæz] *n* topaze *f*.

topcoat ['tɒpkəʊt] *n* **1.** [clothing] pardessus *m*, manteau *m* **2.** [paint] couche *f* de finition.

top dog *n inf* chef *m*.

top-down *adj* hiérarchisé.

top drawer *n UK inf* **a family right out of the ~** une famille de la haute.
◆ **top-drawer** *adj UK inf* de tout premier rang.

top-dressing *n* AGRIC fumure *f* en surface.

top-flight *adj* de premier ordre.

top gear *n* vitesse *f* supérieure.

top hat *n* (chapeau *m*) haut-de-forme *m*.

top-heavy *adj* **1.** [unbalanced] trop lourd du haut, déséquilibré ▪ **a ~ bureaucracy** *fig* une bureaucratie à structure dirigeante trop lourde **2.** FIN surcapitalisé.

top-hole *adj UK inf dated* épatant, formidable.

topiary ['təʊpjərɪ] <> *n* art *m* de tailler les arbres, topiaire *f spec*.
<> *adj* topiaire.

topic ['tɒpɪk] *n* [theme] sujet *m*, thème *m* ▪ **tonight's ~ for debate is unemployment** le débat de ce soir porte sur le chômage.

topical ['tɒpɪkl] *adj* **1.** [current] actuel ▪ **a ~ question** une question d'actualité **2.** MED topique, à usage local.

topicality [,tɒpɪ'kælətɪ] (*pl* **topicalities**) *n* actualité *f*.

topknot ['tɒpnɒt] *n* **1.** [of hair] chignon *m* ▪ [of ribbons] ornement *m* fait de rubans ▪ [of feathers] aigrette *f* **2.** ZOOL pleuronectidé *m*.

topless ['tɒplɪs] *adj* [sunbather] aux seins nus ▪ **to go ~** ne pas porter de haut ▪ **~ bar** bar *m* topless.

top-level *adj* de très haut niveau.

topmast ['tɒpmɑ:st] *n* mât *m* de hune.

topmost ['tɒpməʊst] *adj* le plus haut, le plus élevé.

top-notch ['tɒp'nɒtʃ] *adj inf* excellent.

top-of-the-range *adj* haut de gamme *inv*.

topographical [,tɒpə'græfɪkl] *adj* topographique.

topography [tə'pɒgrəfɪ] *n* topographie *f*.

topology [tə'pɒlədʒɪ] *n* topologie *f*.

toponym ['tɒpənɪm] *n* toponyme *m*.

topper ['tɒpə^r] *n UK inf* [top hat] (chapeau *m*) haut-de-forme *m*.

topping ['tɒpɪŋ] *n* dessus *m* ▪ CULIN garniture *f* ▪ **a cake with a chocolate ~** un gâteau recouvert de chocolat.

topple ['tɒpl] <> *vi* [fall] basculer ▪ [totter] vaciller ▪ **the whole pile ~d over** toute la pile s'est effondrée ▪ **he ~d over backwards** il a perdu l'équilibre et est tombé en arrière.
<> *vt* **1.** [cause to fall] faire tomber, faire basculer **2.** *fig* renverser ▪ **the scandal almost ~d the government** ce scandale a failli faire tomber le gouvernement.

top-ranking *adj* de premier rang, haut placé.

tops [tɒps] *n inf dated* **it's the ~!** c'est bath!

topsail ['tɒpsl, 'tɒpseɪl] *n* hunier *m*.

top-secret *adj* top secret *(inv)*, ultraconfidentiel.

top-security *adj* de haute sécurité ▪ **~ prison** ≃ quartier *m* de haute sécurité.

topside ['tɒpsaɪd] *n UK* [of beef] tende-de-tranche *m*.

topsoil ['tɒpsɔɪl] *n* terre *f* superficielle, couche *f* arable.

topspin ['tɒpspɪn] *n* : **to put ~ on a ball** donner de l'effet à une balle.

topsy-turvy [,tɒpsɪ'tɜ:vɪ] *adj & adv* sens dessus dessous ▪ **a ~ world** le monde à l'envers.

top ten *n hit parade des dix meilleures ventes de disques pop et rock*.

top-up *n UK* **can I give you a ~?** je vous ressers?, encore une goutte?

top-up card *n* TELEC recharge *f* de téléphone mobile.

tor [tɔ:ʳ] *n* colline *f* rocailleuse *(notamment dans le sud-ouest de l'Angleterre)*.

Torah ['tɔ:rə] *pr n* Torah *f*.

torch [tɔ:tʃ] *(pl* **torches***)* <> *n* **1.** *UK* [electric] lampe *f* de poche **2.** [flaming stick] torche *f*, flambeau *m* ▪ **to put a ~ to sthg** mettre le feu à qqch ➊ **to carry a ~ for sb** en pincer pour qqn **3.** TECH [for welding, soldering etc] chalumeau *m*.
<> *vt* mettre le feu à.

torchbearer ['tɔ:tʃ,beərəʳ] *n* porteur *m* de flambeau.

torchlight ['tɔ:tʃlaɪt] <> *n* lumière *f* de flambeau *OR* de torche ▪ **by ~** à la lueur des flambeaux.
<> *comp* : **a ~ procession** une retraite aux flambeaux.

torch song *n* chanson *f* d'amour populaire.

tore [tɔ:ʳ] *pt* ▻ **tear**.

toreador ['tɒrɪədɔ:ʳ] *n* torero *m*, toréador *m*.

torment <> *n* ['tɔ:ment] **1.** [suffering] supplice *m* ▪ *lit* tourment *m* ▪ **to be in ~** être au supplice ▪ **to suffer ~** souffrir le martyre **2.** [ordeal] rude épreuve *f* **3.** [pest] démon *m*.
<> *vt* [tɔ:'ment] **1.** [cause pain to] torturer ▪ **~ed by doubt** harcelé de doutes **2.** [harass] tourmenter, harceler.

tormenter, tormentor [tɔ:'mentəʳ] *n* persécuteur *m*, -trice *f*, bourreau *m*.

torn [tɔ:n] *pp* ▻ **tear**.

tornado [tɔ:'neɪdəʊ] *(pl* **tornados** *OR pl* **tornadoes***)* *n* [storm] tornade *f* ▪ *fig* [person, thing] ouragan *m*.

torpedo [tɔ:'pi:dəʊ] *(pl* **torpedoes**, *pret & pp* **torpedoed***)*
<> *n* **1.** MIL torpille *f* **2.** *US* [firework] pétard *m*.
<> *vt* **1.** MIL torpiller **2.** *fig* [destroy - plan] faire échouer, torpiller.

torpedo boat *n* torpilleur *m*, vedette *f* lance-torpilles.

torpedo tube *n* tube *m* lance-torpilles.

torpid ['tɔ:pɪd] *adj fml* léthargique.

torpor ['tɔ:pəʳ] *n fml* torpeur *f*, léthargie *f*, engourdissement *m*.

torque [tɔ:k] *n* **1.** [rotational force] moment *m* de torsion ▪ AUT couple *m* moteur **2.** HIST [collar] torque *m*.

torque wrench *n* clef *f* dynamométrique.

torrent ['tɒrənt] *n* **1.** [of liquid] torrent *m* ▪ **the rain came down in ~s** il pleuvait à torrents *OR* à verse **2.** [of emotion, abuse etc] torrent *m* ▪ **a ~ of insults** un torrent *OR* flot d'injures.

torrential [tə'renʃl] *adj* torrentiel.

torrid ['tɒrɪd] *adj* **1.** [hot] torride ▪ **the ~ zone** la zone intertropicale **2.** [passionate] passionné, ardent.

torsion ['tɔ:ʃn] *n* torsion *f*.

torsion bar *n* barre *f* de torsion.

torso ['tɔ:səʊ] *(pl* **torsos***)* *n* [human] torse *m* ▪ [sculpture] buste *m*.

tort [tɔ:t] *n* LAW délit *m*, préjudice *m* ▪ **~s lawyer** *US* avocat *m* spécialisé en responsabilité délictuelle.

tortilla [tɔ:'ti:lə] *n* tortilla *f (galette de maïs)*.

tortoise ['tɔ:təs] *n* tortue *f*.

tortoiseshell ['tɔ:təsʃel] <> *n* **1.** [substance] écaille *f* (de tortue) **2.** [cat] chat *m* roux tigré **3.** [butterfly] vanesse *f*.
<> *adj* **1.** [comb, ornament] en écaille **2.** [cat] roux tigré.

tortuous ['tɔ:tjʊəs] *adj* **1.** [path] tortueux, sinueux **2.** [argument, piece of writing] contourné, tarabiscoté ▪ [mind] retors.

tortuously ['tɔ:tjʊəslɪ] *adv* tortueusement, de manière tortueuse.

torture ['tɔ:tʃəʳ] <> *n* **1.** [cruelty] torture *f*, supplice *m* **2.** *fig* torture *f*, tourment *m*.
<> *vt* **1.** [inflict pain on] torturer **2.** [torment] torturer ▪ **~d by remorse** tenaillé par le remords **3.** [distort] : **she ~s the Spanish language** elle écorche la langue espagnole.

torture chamber *n* chambre *f* de torture.

torturer ['tɔ:tʃərəʳ] *n* tortionnaire *mf*, bourreau *m*.

Tory ['tɔ:rɪ] *(pl* **Tories***)* <> *n* POL tory *m*, membre *m* du parti conservateur.
<> *adj* [party, MP] tory, conservateur.

Toryism ['tɔ:rɪɪzm] *n* POL torysme *m*.

toss [tɒs] <> *vt* **1.** [throw] lancer, jeter ▪ **she ~ed him the ball** elle lui a lancé la balle ▪ **the horse nearly ~ed its rider into the ditch** le cheval a failli faire tomber son cavalier dans le fossé ▪ **he was ~ed by the bull** le taureau l'a projeté en l'air ▪ **to ~ pancakes** *UK* faire sauter des crêpes ▪ **to ~ a coin** jouer à pile ou face ▪ **she ~ed back her head with a laugh** elle rejeta la tête en arrière en riant **2.** CULIN mélanger ▪ **to ~ the salad** remuer *OR* retourner la salade ▪ **~ the carrots in butter** ajoutez du beurre et mélangez aux carottes.
<> *vi* s'agiter ▪ **to ~ and turn in bed** avoir le sommeil agité ▪ **to pitch and ~** [boat] tanguer ▪ **shall we ~ for it?** on joue à pile ou face?
<> *n* **1.** [throw - gen] lancer *m*, lancement *m* ; [- of a coin] coup *m* de pile ou face ▪ SPORT tirage *m* au sort ▪ **to win/to lose the ~** gagner/perdre à pile ou face ▪ **our team won the ~** notre équipe a gagné au tirage au sort ➊ **to argue the ~** *UK* ergoter, chicaner ▪ **I don't give a ~** *UK inf* je m'en fiche **2.** [of head] mouvement *m* brusque **3.** [fall from horse] chute *f* ▪ **to take a ~** [from horse] être désarçonné, faire une chute.

◆ **toss about** *UK*, **toss around** <> *vt sep* **1.** [rock, buffet] ballotter, secouer **2.** *fig* **figures of £5,000 were being ~ed around** on avançait allègrement des chiffres de l'ordre de 5000 livres.
<> *vi insep* s'agiter.

◆ **toss off** <> *vt sep* **1.** [do hastily] expédier ▪ **to ~ off a letter** écrire une lettre au pied levé **2.** [drink quickly] boire d'un coup, lamper.
<> *vi insep*▲ *UK* [masturbate] se branler▲.

◆ **toss up** <> *vt sep* lancer, jeter.
<> *vi insep* jouer à pile ou face.

toss-up *n* coup *m* de pile ou face ▪ **it's a ~ whether he'll get the job or not** *fig* s'il obtient le poste, ça se jouera vraiment à pile ou face.

tot [tɒt] *(pret & pp* **totted**, *cont* **totting***)* *n* **1.** *inf* [child] petit enfant *m* ▪ **tiny ~s** les tout petits *mpl* **2.** *UK* [of alcohol] goutte *f*.

◆ **tot up** *UK* <> *vt sep* additionner ▪ **I'll ~ up your bill** je vais vous faire l'addition.
<> *vi insep* : **that ~s up to £3** ça fait 3 livres en tout.

total ['təʊtl] *(UK pret & pp* **totalled**, *cont* **totalling***)* *(US pret & pp* **totaled**, *cont* **totaling***)* <> *adj* **1.** [amount, number] total ▪ **the ~ gains/losses** le total des profits/pertes **2.** [as intensifier] complet, -ète *f* ▪ **~ silence** un silence absolu ▪ **that's ~ nonsense!** c'est complètement absurde! ▪ **he was a ~ stranger to me** je ne le connaissais ni d'Ève ni d'Adam.
<> *n* total *m* ▪ **she wrote a ~ of ten books** elle a écrit dix livres en tout.
<> *vt* **1.** [add up] additionner, faire le total de **2.** [amount to] s'élever à ▪ **the collection totalled 50 cars** cette collection comptait 50 voitures en tout **3.** *US inf* [wreck] démolir.

◆ **in total** *adv phr* au total.

totalitarian [,təʊtælɪ'teərɪən] *adj* totalitaire.

totalitarianism [ˌtəutælɪ'teərɪənɪzm] *n* totalitarisme *m*.

totality [təu'tælətɪ] (*pl* **totalities**) *n* **1.** totalité *f* **2.** ASTRON occultation *f* totale.

totalizator ['təutəlaɪzeɪtəʳ] *n* **1.** [adding machine] totalisateur *m*, machine *f* totalisatrice **2.** *UK* [in betting] pari *m* mutuel.

totalizer ['təutəlaɪzəʳ] = **totalizator**.

totally ['təutəlɪ] *adv* [completely] totalement, entièrement, complètement ▪ **do you agree? - yes, ~** êtes-vous d'accord? - oui, tout à fait.

total quality management *n* qualité *f* totale.

tote [təut] <> *n* (*abbrev of* **totalizator**) pari *m* mutuel ▪ **~ board** tableau *m* électronique.
<> *vt inf* porter.

tote bag *n* grand sac *m*, fourre-tout *m inv*.

totem ['təutəm] *n* totem *m*.

totemism ['təutəmɪzm] *n* totémisme *m*.

totem pole *n* mât *m* totémique.

toto ['təutəu] ◆ **in toto** *adv phr fml* entièrement, complètement.

totter ['tɒtəʳ] <> *vi* **1.** *liter* [person] chanceler, tituber ▪ [pile, vase] chanceler ▪ **he ~ed down the stairs** il descendit les escaliers en chancelant **2.** *fig* [government, company etc] chanceler, être dans une mauvaise passe.
<> *n* vacillement *m* ▪ [gait] démarche *f* titubante *OR* chancelante.

tottering ['tɒtərɪŋ], **tottery** ['tɒtərɪ] *adj* chancelant ▪ [building] branlant ▪ [government] chancelant, déstabilisé ▪ **with ~ steps** en titubant.

toucan ['tu:kən] *n* toucan *m*.

toucan crossing *n UK* passage *m* mixte piétons-cyclistes.

touch [tʌtʃ] (*pl* **touches**) <> *n* **1.** [sense] toucher *m* ▪ **sense of ~** sens *m* du toucher ▪ **soft to the ~** doux au toucher
2. [physical contact] toucher *m*, contact *m* ▪ [light brushing] effleurement *m*, frôlement *m* ▪ **the machine works at the ~ of a button** il suffit de toucher un bouton pour mettre en marche cet appareil
3. [style] touche *f* ▪ *fig* **to give sthg a personal ~** ajouter une note personnelle à qqch ▪ **to have the right ~ with sthg/sb** savoir s'y prendre avec qqch/qqn ▪ **the house needed a woman's ~** il manquait dans cette maison une présence féminine ▪ **the cook has lost his ~** le cuisinier a perdu la main
4. [detail] : **to put the final** *OR* **finishing ~es to sthg** apporter la touche finale à qqch ▪ **that logo in the bottom corner is a nice ~** c'est une bonne idée d'avoir mis ce logo dans le coin en bas ▮ [slight mark] coup *m* ▪ **with a ~ of the pen** d'un coup de stylo
5. [small amount, hint] note *f*, pointe *f* ▪ **there's a ~ of spring in the air** ça sent le printemps ▪ **he answered with a ~ of bitterness** il a répondu avec une pointe d'amertume ▪ **I got a ~ of sunstroke** j'ai eu une petite insolation ▪ **I've got a ~ of flu** je suis un peu grippé, j'ai une petite grippe ▪ **to add a ~ of class to sthg** rendre qqch plus distingué
6. [contact] : **to be/to keep in ~ with sb** être/rester en contact avec qqn ▪ **I'll be in ~!** je te contacterai! ▪ **keep** *OR* **stay in ~!** donne-nous de tes nouvelles! ▪ **to get in ~ with sb** contacter qqn ▪ **he put me in ~ with the director** il m'a mis en relation avec le directeur ▪ **she is** *OR* **keeps in ~ with current events** elle se tient au courant de l'actualité ▪ **she is out of ~ with politics** elle ne suit plus l'actualité politique ▪ **they lost ~ long ago** ils se sont perdus de vue il y a longtemps ▪ **he has lost ~ with reality** il a perdu le sens des réalités
7. [of an instrument] toucher *m* ▪ [of a typewriter] frappe *f*
8. SPORT touche *f* ▪ **to kick the ball into ~** mettre le ballon en touche ▪ **to kick sthg into ~** *fig* mettre qqch au rencart ▪ **to kick sb into ~** *UK inf fig* mettre qqn sur la touche
9. *phr* **to be an easy** *OR* **soft ~** *inf* se laisser taper trop facilement.
<> *vt* **1.** [make contact with] toucher ▪ **to ~ lightly** frôler, effleurer ▪ **she ~ed it with her foot** elle l'a touché du pied ▪ **he ~ed his hat to her** il a porté la main à son chapeau pour la saluer ▪ **since they met, her feet haven't ~ed the ground** depuis leur rencontre, elle est sur un nuage ▪ **can you ~ the bottom?** as-tu pied? ▪ **the law can't ~ him** la loi ne peut rien contre lui
2. [handle] toucher à ▪ **don't ~ her things** ne dérangez pas ses affaires ▪ **don't ~ anything until I get home** ne touchez à rien avant mon retour ▪ **he swears he never ~ed her** il jure qu'il ne l'a jamais touchée ▪ **I didn't ~ him!** je n'ai pas touché à un cheveu de sa tête!
3. [adjoin] jouxter
4. (*usu neg*) [eat, drink] toucher à ▪ **I never ~ meat** je ne mange jamais de viande ▪ **she didn't ~ her vegetables** elle n'a pas touché aux légumes
5. [move emotionally] émouvoir, toucher ▪ **his remark ~ed a (raw) nerve** sa réflexion a touché un point sensible ▪ **to ~ sb to the quick** *UK* toucher qqn au vif
6. [damage] : **the fire didn't ~ the pictures** l'incendie a épargné les tableaux ▪ **the war didn't ~ this area** cette région a été épargnée par la guerre
7. [concern] concerner, toucher
8. (*usu neg*) *inf* [rival] valoir, égaler ▪ **nothing can ~ butter for cooking** rien ne vaut la cuisine au beurre
9. *US* [dial] : **~ 645** faites le 645
10. *phr* **to ~ sb for a loan** *inf* taper qqn.
<> *vi* **1.** [be in contact] se toucher
2. [adjoin - properties, areas] se toucher, être contigus
3. [handle] : **'do not ~!'** 'défense de toucher'.
◆ **a touch** *adv phr* : **there was a ~ too much pepper in the soup** le potage était un petit peu trop poivré.
◆ **touch down** <> *vi insep* **1.** [aeroplane, spacecraft - on land] atterrir ; [- on sea] amerrir
2. RUGBY marquer un essai.
<> *vt sep* RUGBY : **to ~ the ball down** marquer un essai.
◆ **touch off** *vt sep* [explosive] faire exploser, faire détoner ▪ *fig* déclencher, provoquer.
◆ **touch on** *vt insep* aborder ▪ **his speech barely ~ed on the problem of unemployment** son discours a à peine effleuré le problème du chômage.
◆ **touch up** *vt sep* **1.** [painting, photograph] faire des retouches à, retoucher ▪ [paintwork] refaire
2.△ *UK* [sexually] peloter.

touch-and-go *adj* : **a ~ situation** une situation dont l'issue est incertaine ▪ **it was ~ whether we'd make it in time** nous avons bien failli ne pas arriver à temps.

touchdown ['tʌtʃdaun] *n* **1.** [on land] atterrissage *m* ▪ [on sea] amerrissage *m* **2.** [in American football] but *m*.

touché ['tu:ʃeɪ] *interj* **1.** [fencing] touché **2.** *fig* très juste.

touched [tʌtʃt] *adj* **1.** [with gratitude] touché ▪ **she was ~ by his thoughtfulness** elle était touchée par sa délicatesse **2.** *UK inf* [mad] toqué, timbré.

touch football *n US sorte de football sans "tackling"*.

touching ['tʌtʃɪŋ] <> *adj* touchant, émouvant.
<> *prep lit* touchant.

touchingly ['tʌtʃɪŋlɪ] *adv* d'une manière touchante.

touch-in goal *n* RUGBY en-but *m*.

touch judge *n* RUGBY juge *m* de touche.

touch kick *n* RUGBY coup *m* de pied en touche.

touchline ['tʌtʃlaɪn] *n* SPORT ligne *f* de touche.

touchpaper ['tʌtʃˌpeɪpəʳ] *n* papier *m* nitraté.

touch rugby *n sorte de rugby sans "tackling"*.

touch screen *n* COMPUT écran *m* tactile.

touchstone ['tʌtʃstəun] *n* MINER & *fig* pierre *f* de touche.

touch-tone *adj* : **~ telephone** téléphone *m* à touches.

touch-type *vi* taper sans regarder le clavier.

touch-typing [-ˌtaɪpɪŋ] *n* dactylographie *f* (sans regarder le clavier).

touchy ['tʌtʃɪ] (*comp* **touchier**, *superl* **touchiest**) *adj* **1.** [oversensitive] susceptible, ombrageux ▪ **she's ~ about her weight** elle est susceptible *OR* chatouilleuse sur la question de son poids ▪ **he's very ~** il se froisse *OR* vexe pour un rien **2.** [matter, situation] délicat, épineux.

tough [tʌf] ◇ *adj* **1.** [resilient - person] solide, résistant, robuste ; [- meat] dur, coriace ; [- animal, plant] résistant, robuste ; [- substance, fabric] solide, résistant ▪ **she's ~ enough to win** elle a assez d'endurance pour gagner ▶ **he's as ~ as old boots** *UK* il est coriace ▪ **this steak is as ~ as old boots** ce n'est pas du bifteck, c'est de la semelle
2. [difficult] dur, pénible ▪ **a ~ problem** un problème épineux ▪ **it's ~ on him** c'est un coup dur pour lui ▪ **she made it ~ for him** elle lui a mené la vie dure ▪ **that's a ~ act to follow** c'est difficile de faire mieux ▪ **I gave them a ~ time** je leur en ai fait voir de toutes les couleurs ▪ **she had a ~ life** elle n'a pas eu une vie facile
3. [severe] sévère ▪ **to get ~ with sb** se montrer dur avec qqn ▪ **the boss takes a ~ line with people who are late** le patron ne plaisante pas avec les retardataires ▮ [resolute] dur, inflexible ▪ **she's a ~ person to deal with** elle ne fait pas de concessions ▶ **he's a ~ cookie** *US inf* il n'est pas commode ▪ **they're ~ customers** ce sont des durs à cuire
4. [rough, hardened] dur
5. *inf* [unfortunate] malheureux ▪ **that's your ~ luck!** tant pis pour vous!
◇ *adv inf* **to talk ~, to act ~** jouer au dur.
◇ *vt phr* **to ~ it out** *inf* tenir bon.
◇ *n inf* dur *m*, - e *f*.

toughen ['tʌfn] ◇ *vt* [metal, leather] rendre plus solide, renforcer ▪ [person] endurcir ▪ [conditions] rendre plus sévère ▪ **~ed glass** verre *m* trempé.
◇ *vi* [metal, glass, leather] durcir ▪ [person] s'endurcir.
◆ **toughen up** *vt sep* & *vi insep* = **toughen**.

toughened ['tʌfnd] *adj* [glass] trempé.

toughie ['tʌfɪ] *n inf* [person] dur *m*, - e *f* ▪ [problem] casse-tête *m*, cactus *m*.

toughly ['tʌflɪ] *adv* [fight] avec acharnement, âprement ▪ [speak] durement, sans ménagement.

toughness ['tʌfnɪs] *n* **1.** [of fabric, glass, leather] solidité *f* ▪ [of meat] dureté *f* ▪ [of metal] ténacité *f*, résistance *f* **2.** [of job] difficulté *f* ▪ [of struggle] acharnement *m*, âpreté *f* **3.** [of character - strength] force *f*, résistance *f* ; [- hardness] dureté *f* ; [- severity] inflexibilité *f*, sévérité *f*.

toupee ['tu:peɪ] *n* postiche *m*.

tour [tʊə^r] ◇ *n* **1.** [trip] voyage *m* ▪ **we're going on a ~ of Eastern Europe** nous allons visiter les pays de l'Est ▶ **she's on a walking ~in Wales** elle fait une randonnée à pied dans le pays de Galles ▪ **they're off on a world ~** ils sont partis faire le tour du monde **2.** [of a building] visite *f* ▪ **we went on a ~ of the factory** nous avons visité l'usine **3.** [official journey] tournée *f* ▪ **the dance company is on ~** la troupe de danseurs est en tournée ▪ **to go on ~** faire une tournée ▶ **~ of duty** MIL service *m* ▪ **~ of inspection** tournée *f* d'inspection.
◇ *vt* **1.** [visit] visiter **2.** SPORT & THEAT : **the orchestra is ~ing the provinces** l'orchestre est en tournée en province.
◇ *vi* voyager, faire du tourisme.

tourer ['tʊərə^r] *n* voiture *f* de tourisme.

Tourette's Syndrome, Tourette syndrome *n* MED syndrome *m* Gilles de la Tourette.

tour guide *n* [person] guide *m* ▪ [book] guide *m* touristique.

touring ['tʊərɪŋ] ◇ *adj* : **~ bicycle** vélo *m* de randonnée ▪ **~ company** THEAT [permanently] troupe *f* ambulante ; [temporarily] troupe *f* en tournée ▪ **~ party** SPORT équipe *f* en tournée.
◇ *n (U)* tourisme *m*, voyages *mpl* touristiques.

tourism ['tʊərɪzm] *n* tourisme *m*.

tourist ['tʊərɪst] ◇ *n* touriste *mf* ▪ **the ~s** SPORT les visiteurs *mpl*.
◇ *comp* [agency, centre] de tourisme ▪ [attraction, information, ticket] touristique ▪ **~ (information) office** office *m* de tourisme, syndicat *m* d'initiative.

tourist class *n UK* classe *f* touriste.

tourist trade *n* tourisme *m*.

tourist trap *n* attrape-touristes *m inv*.

touristy ['tʊərɪstɪ] *adj inf pej* trop touristique.

tournament ['tɔ:nəmənt] *n* tournoi *m*.

tourniquet ['tʊənɪkeɪ] *n* garrot *m*.

tour operator *n* [travel agency] tour-opérateur *m*, voyagiste *m* ▪ [bus company] compagnie *f* de cars *(qui organise des voyages)*.

tousle ['taʊzl] *vt* [hair] ébouriffer ▪ [clothes] friper, froisser.

tousled ['taʊzld] *adj* [hair] ébouriffé ▪ [clothes] fripé, froissé ▪ **his ~ appearance** son aspect débraillé.

tout [taʊt] *UK* ◇ *n* **1.** : **(ticket) ~** revendeur *m*, - euse *f* de billets *(au marché noir)* **2.** [in racing] pronostiqueur *m*, - euse *f*.
◇ *vt* **1.** [peddle - tickets] revendre *(au marché noir)* ; [- goods] vendre *(en vantant sa marchandise)* ▪ **the cries of the market traders ~ing their wares** les cris des marchands essayant de raccrocher les clients **2.** [promote] : **he is being ~ed as a future prime minister** on veut faire de lui un futur premier ministre.
◇ *vi* **1.** : **salesmen ~ing for custom** des vendeurs qui essaient d'attirer les clients ▪ **they've been ~ing around for work/business** ils essayaient de trouver du travail/de se constituer une clientèle **2.** [racing] vendre des pronostics.

tow [təʊ] ◇ *vt* tirer ▪ [boat, car] remorquer ▪ [barge] haler ▪ **the police ~ed my car away** la police a emmené ma voiture à la fourrière.
◇ *n* **1.** [action] remorquage *m* ▪ [vehicle] véhicule *m* en remorque ▪ **to be on ~** être en remorque ▪ **can you give me a ~?** pourriez-vous remorquer ma voiture? ▪ **they arrived with all the kids in ~** *fig* ils sont arrivés avec tous leurs enfants **2.** [line] câble *m* de remorquage **3.** TEX filasse *f*, étoupe *f*.

towards [tə'wɔ:dz], **toward** [tə'wɔ:d] *US prep* **1.** [in the direction of] dans la direction de, vers ▪ **he turned ~ her** il s'est tourné vers elle ▪ **we headed ~ Chicago** nous avons pris la direction de Chicago ▪ **she was standing with her back ~ him** elle lui tournait le dos ▪ **the negotiations are a first step ~ peace** *fig* les négociations sont un premier pas sur le chemin de la paix ▪ **they are working ~ a solution** *fig* ils cherchent une solution **2.** [indicating attitude] envers ▪ **she's very hostile ~ me** elle est très hostile à mon égard ▪ **the public's attitude ~ crime** l'attitude de l'opinion publique face à la criminalité ▪ **his feelings ~ her** ses sentiments pour elle, les sentiments qu'il éprouve pour elle **3.** [as contribution to] pour ▪ **the money is going ~ a new car** l'argent contribuera à l'achat d'une nouvelle voiture ▪ **I'll give you something ~ your expenses** je vous donnerai quelque chose pour payer une partie de vos frais **4.** [near - in time] vers ; [- in space] près de ▪ **~ the end of his life** vers *OR* sur la fin de sa vie ▪ **~ the middle** vers le milieu.

tow-away zone ['təʊəweɪ-] *n US zone de ramassage des véhicules en infraction.*

towbar ['təʊbɑ:^r] *n* barre *f* de remorquage.

towel ['taʊəl] (*UK pret & pp* **towelled**, *cont* **towelling**) (*US pret & pp* **toweled** *OR* **towelled**, *cont* **toweling** *OR* **towelling**) ◇ *n* serviette *f* (de toilette) ▪ [for hands] essuie-mains *m inv* ▪ [for glasses] essuie-verres *m inv* ▪ **(dish) ~** torchon *m* à vaisselle ▪ **~ rack** *OR* **rail** *OR* **ring** porte-serviettes *m inv*.
◇ *vt* frotter avec une serviette ▪ **to ~ o.s. dry** *OR* **down** s'essuyer *OR* se sécher avec une serviette.

towelling *UK*, **toweling** *US* ['taʊəlɪŋ] ◇ *n* [material] tissu *m* éponge.
◇ *comp* [robe, shirt] en tissu éponge.

tower ['taʊə^r] ◇ *n* tour *f* ▪ **church ~** clocher *m* ▪ **he's a ~ of strength** c'est un roc.
◇ *vi* : **the skyscraper ~s above** *OR* **over the city** le gratte-ciel domine la ville ▪ **he ~ed above** *OR* **over me** j'étais tout petit à côté de lui ▪ **she ~s above** *OR* **over her contemporaries** *fig* elle domine de loin ses contemporains.

tower block *n UK* tour *f* (d'habitation), gratte-ciel *m*.

towering ['taʊərɪŋ] *adj* **1.** [very high - skyscraper, tree, statue] très haut, imposant **2.** [excessive] démesuré ▪ **in a ~ rage** dans une colère noire.

towline ['təʊlaɪn] = **towrope**.

town [taʊn] *n* ville *f* ▪ **a country ~** une ville de province ▪ **I work in ~** je travaille en ville ▪ **she's going into ~** elle va en ville ▪ **he's out of ~ this week** il n'est pas là *OR* il est en déplacement cette semaine ▪ **we're from out of ~** *US* nous ne sommes pas d'ici ◗ **~ gas** gaz *m* de ville ▪ **it's the talk of the ~** toute la ville en parle ▪ **they went out on the ~ last night** *inf* hier soir, ils ont fait une virée en ville ▪ **they really went to ~ on the stadium** *inf* pour le stade ils n'ont pas fait les choses à moitié *OR* ils ont vraiment mis le paquet.

town centre *n* centre-ville *m*.

town clerk *n* secrétaire *mf* de mairie.

town council *n* conseil *m* municipal.

town councillor *n* conseiller *m* municipal, conseillère *f* municipale.

town crier *n* garde champêtre *m*.

town dweller *n* citadin *m*, - e *f*.

townee *UK*, **townie** *US* [taʊ'ni:] *n inf* citadin *m*, - e *f*.

town hall *n* hôtel de ville *m*, mairie *f*.

town house *n* **1.** [gen] maison *f* en ville ▪ [more imposing] ≃ hôtel *m* particulier **2.** *US* maison *f* mitoyenne (en ville).

town meeting *n US assemblée générale des habitants d'une ville.*

town planner *n* urbaniste *mf*.

town planning *n* urbanisme *m*.

townscape ['taʊnskeɪp] *n* paysage *m* urbain.

townsfolk ['taʊnzfəʊk] *npl* citadins *mpl*.

township ['taʊnʃɪp] *n* **1.** [gen] commune *f* ▪ *US* canton *m* **2.** *South Africa* township *f* ▪ **~ violence** la violence dans les ghettos noirs.

townsman ['taʊnzmən] (*pl* **townsmen** [-mən]) *n* citadin *m*.

townspeople ['taʊnz,pi:pl] *npl* citadins *mpl*.

towpath ['təʊpɑ:θ] (*pl* [-pɑ:ðz]) *n* chemin *m* de halage.

towrope ['təʊrəʊp] *n* câble *m* de remorque ▪ [to towpath] câble *m* de halage.

tow-start *n* AUT : **to give sb a ~** faire démarrer qqn en remorque.

tow truck *US* = **breakdown lorry**.

toxaemia *UK*, **toxemia** *US* [tɒk'si:mɪə] *n* toxémie *f*.

toxic ['tɒksɪk] *adj* toxique.

toxicity [tɒk'sɪsətɪ] *n* toxicité *f*.

toxic shock syndrome *n* syndrome *m* du choc toxique.

toxin ['tɒksɪn] *n* toxine *f*.

toy [tɔɪ] (*pl* **toys**) <> *n* jouet *m*.
<> *comp* **1.** [car, train] miniature ▪ **~ soldier** soldat *m* de plomb ▪ **~ theatre** théâtre *m* de marionnettes ▪ **~ trumpet** trompette *f* d'enfant **2.** [box, chest, drawer] à jouets **3.** [dog] nain.
◆ **toy with** *vt insep* jouer avec ▪ **to ~ with one's food** manger du bout des dents ▪ **she ~ed with the idea of going home** elle jouait avec l'idée de rentrer chez elle.

toy boy *n inf pej jeune homme sortant avec une femme mûre.*

toymaker ['tɔɪ,meɪkəʳ] *n* fabricant *m* de jouets.

toy shop *n* magasin *m* de jouets.

trace [treɪs] <> *n* **1.** [sign] trace *f* ▪ **to disappear** *OR* **to sink without ~** disparaître sans laisser de traces ▪ **there is no ~ of it now** il n'en reste plus aucune trace ▪ **we've lost all ~ of her** nous ignorons ce qu'elle est devenue ▪ **~s of cocaine were found in his blood** l'analyse de son sang a révélé des traces de cocaïne ▪ **a ~ of a smile** un sourire à peine esquissé ▪ **without a ~ of fear** sans la moindre peur
2. [trail] trace *f* de pas, piste *f* ▪ *US* [path] piste *f*, sentier *m*
3. [drawing] tracé *m*
4. TECH : **a radar ~** la trace d'un spot
5. [harness] trait *m*.
<> *vt* **1.** [follow trail of] suivre la trace de ▪ [track down - object] retrouver ▪ **she ~d him as far as New York** elle a suivi sa piste jusqu'à New York ▪ **they ~d the murder to him** ils ont finalement établi qu'il était le meurtrier ▪ **we eventually ~d the problem to a computer error** nous avons finalement découvert que le problème était dû à une erreur de l'ordinateur
2. [follow development of] suivre ▪ **the film ~s the rise to power of a gangland boss** ce film relate l'ascension d'un chef de gang
3. [mark outline of] tracer, dessiner ▪ [with tracing paper] décalquer.
◆ **trace back** <> *vt sep* : **to ~ sthg back to its source** retrouver l'origine de qqch ▪ **she can ~ her ancestry back to the 15th century** sa famille remonte au XVe siècle ▪ **the cause of the epidemic was ~d back to an infected water supply** on a découvert que l'épidémie était due à la contamination de l'alimentation en eau.
<> *vi insep US* **1.** [go back] : **to ~ back to** remonter à
2. [be due to] être dû à.

traceable ['treɪsəbl] *adj* [object] retrouvable, qui peut être retrouvé.

trace element *n* oligoélément *m*.

tracer ['treɪsəʳ] *n* **1.** [person] traceur *m*, - euse *f* ▪ [device] traçoir *m* **2.** CHEM traceur *m*.

tracer bullet *n* balle *f* traçante.

tracery ['treɪsərɪ] (*pl* **traceries**) *n* filigrane *m*, dentelles *fpl* ▪ [on leaf, insect wing] nervures *fpl* ▪ ARCHIT réseau *m*.

trachea [trə'ki:ə] (*pl* **tracheae** [-'ki:i:] *OR pl* **tracheas**) *n* trachée *f*.

tracheotomy [,trækɪ'ɒtəmɪ] (*pl* **tracheotomies**) *n* trachéotomie *f*.

trachoma [trə'kəʊmə] *n* trachome *m*.

tracing ['treɪsɪŋ] *n* [process] calquage *m* ▪ [result] calque *m*.

tracing paper *n* papier-calque *m inv*, papier *m* à décalquer.

track [træk] <> *n* **1.** [path, route] chemin *m*, sentier *m* ▪ [of planet, star, aeroplane] trajectoire *f* ▪ **a mountain ~** un sentier de montagne ▪ **a farm ~** un chemin de campagne ▮ *fig* **to be on the right ~** être sur la bonne voie ▪ **he's on the wrong ~** il fait fausse route ▪ **you're way off ~!** *inf* tu es complètement à côté de la plaque!
2. SPORT : **motor-racing ~** *UK* autodrome *m* ▪ **~ and field** athlétisme *m* ▪ **~ and field events** épreuves *fpl* d'athlétisme
3. RAIL voie *f*, rails *mpl* ▪ **the train jumped the ~s** le train a déraillé *OR* a quitté les rails
4. [mark, trail] trace *f*, piste *f* ▪ [of animal, person] piste *f* ▪ [of boat] sillage *m* ▪ **to be on sb's ~** *OR* **~s** être sur la piste de qqn ▪ **the terrorists had covered their ~s well** les terroristes n'avaient pas laissé de traces ▪ **that should throw them off my ~** avec ça, je devrais arriver à les semer ▪ **to keep ~ of** suivre ▪ **it's hard to keep ~ of her, she moves around so much** il est difficile de rester en contact avec elle, elle bouge tout le temps ▪ **we like to keep ~ of current events** nous aimons nous tenir au courant de l'actualité ▪ **we'll have to keep ~ of the time!** il ne faudra pas oublier l'heure! ▪ **to lose ~ of** : **don't lose ~ of those files** n'égarez pas ces dossiers ▪ **I lost ~ of them years ago** j'ai perdu le contact avec eux *OR* je les ai perdus de vue il y a des années ▪ **she lost all ~ of time** elle a perdu toute notion du temps ▪ **he lost ~ of what he was saying** il a perdu le fil de ce qu'il disait ◗ **to make ~s** *inf* mettre les voiles
5. [on LP, tape] plage *f* ▪ COMPUT piste *f*
6. AUT [tyre tread] chape *f* ▪ [space between wheels] écartement *m*
7. *US* SCH classe *f* de niveau ▪ **~ system** *répartition des élèves en sections selon leurs aptitudes.*
<> *vt* **1.** [follow - animal] suivre à la trace, filer ; [- rocket] suivre la trajectoire de ▪ [criminal] traquer
2. *US* **don't ~ mud into the house!** ne traîne pas de boue dans la maison!
<> *vi* **1.** [stylus] suivre le sillon
2. [with camera] faire un traveling *OR* travelling.
◆ **track down** *vt sep* retrouver, localiser ▪ [animal, criminal] traquer et capturer.

trackball ['trækbɔ:l] *n* COMPUT boule *f* de commande, trackball *m*.

tracked [trækt] *adj* chenillé, à chenilles.

tracker ['trækər] *n* **1.** [person - gen] poursuivant *m*, - e *f* ; [- in hunting] traqueur *m*, - euse *f* **2.** [device] appareil *m* de poursuite.

tracker dog *n* chien *m* policier.

track event *n* épreuve *f* sur piste.

tracking ['trækɪŋ] <> *n* **1.** poursuite *f* ▪ [of missile] repérage *m* **2.** US SCH *répartition des élèves en sections selon leurs aptitudes.*
<> *comp* [radar, satellite] de poursuite.

tracking shot *n* CIN traveling *m*, travelling *m*.

track meet *n* US rencontre *f* d'athlétisme.

track record *n* SPORT & *fig* dossier *m*, carrière *f* ▪ **she has a good ~** elle a fait ses preuves ▪ **given his ~** vu ce qu'il a déjà accompli.

track rod *n* UK biellette *f* de connexion.

track shoe *n* chaussure *f* d'athlétisme.

tracksuit ['træk,su:t] *n* survêtement *m*.

tract [trækt] *n* **1.** [pamphlet] tract *m* **2.** [large area] étendue *f* ▪ US [housing estate] lotissement *m* ▪ [mining] gisement *m* ▪ **a ~ house** un pavillon **3.** ANAT : **digestive/respiratory ~** appareil *m* digestif/respiratoire.

tractable ['træktəbl] *adj* [person, animal] accommodant ▪ [material] malléable ▪ [problem] soluble, facile à résoudre.

traction ['trækʃn] *n* **1.** MECH traction *f* **2.** MED : **to be in ~** être en extension ▪ **~ splint** attelle *f* d'extension.

traction engine *n* locomotive *f*.

tractor ['træktər] *n* [on farm] tracteur *m* ▪ TECH locomobile *f*.

tractorfeed ['træktəfi:d] *n* COMPUT dispositif *m* d'entraînement à picots.

tractor-trailer *n* US semi-remorque *m*.

trad [træd] *inf* <> *adj* MUS traditionnel.
<> *n* : **~ (jazz)** jazz traditionnel des années 30.

trade [treɪd] <> *n* **1.** *(U)* COMM commerce *m*, affaires *fpl* ▪ **the clothing ~** la confection, l'industrie *f* de la confection ▪ **she is in the tea ~** elle est dans le commerce du thé, elle est négociante en thé ▪ **~ is brisk** les affaires vont bien ▪ **to do a good** *OR* **roaring ~** faire des affaires en or ▪ **domestic/foreign ~** commerce intérieur/extérieur ▪ **retail/wholesale ~** commerce de détail/de gros ▪ **Minister of Trade** UK, **Secretary of Trade** US ministre *m* du Commerce
2. [illicit dealings] trafic *m* ▪ **the drug ~** le trafic de drogue
3. [vocation, occupation] métier *m* ▪ **she is an electrician by ~** elle est électricienne de son métier *OR* de son état ▪ **to be in the ~** être du métier ▪ **as we say in the ~** comme on dit dans le métier
4. [exchange] échange *m* ▪ **fair ~** échange équitable
5. [regular customers] clientèle *f*
6. US [transaction] transaction *f* commerciale.
<> *comp* **1.** COMM [agreement, balance] commercial ▪ **~ deficit** balance *f* commerciale déficitaire, déficit *m* extérieur ▪ **~ figures** résultats *mpl* financiers
2. [publication] spécialisé.
<> *vt* [exchange] échanger, troquer ▪ **he ~d a marble for a toffee** il a échangé *OR* troqué une bille contre un caramel.
<> *vi* **1.** [businessman, country] faire du commerce ▪ **he ~s in clothing** il est négociant en confection, il est dans la confection ▪ **to ~ at a loss** vendre à perte ▪ **to ~ with sb** avoir *OR* entretenir des relations commerciales avec qqn ▪ **they stopped trading with Iran** ils ont arrêté toute relation commerciale avec l'Iran
2. US [private individual] faire ses achats ▪ **to ~ at** *OR* **with** faire ses courses à *OR* chez
3. ST. EX [currency, commodity] : **corn is trading at £25** le maïs se négocie à 25 livres.
◆ **trades** *npl* [winds] alizés *mpl*.
◆ **trade in** *vt sep* faire reprendre ▪ **I ~d my television in for a new one** ils ont repris mon vieux téléviseur quand j'ai acheté le nouveau.
◆ **trade off** *vt sep* échanger, troquer ▪ [as a compromise] accepter en compensation ▪ **to ~ sthg off against sthg** laisser *OR* abandonner qqch pour qqch.
◆ **trade on** *vt insep* exploiter, profiter de ▪ **I'd hate to ~ on** *OR* **upon your kindness** je ne voudrais pas abuser de votre gentillesse.

trade association *n* association *f* professionnelle.

trade barriers *npl* barrières *fpl* douanières.

Trade Descriptions Act *pr n loi britannique contre la publicité mensongère.*

trade discount *n* remise *f* professionnelle *OR* au détaillant.

trade fair *n* foire *f OR* exposition *f* commerciale.

trade-in *n* reprise *f* ▪ **they took my old refrigerator as a ~** ils ont repris mon vieux réfrigérateur.

trademark ['treɪdmɑ:k] <> *n* marque *f* (de fabrique) ▪ *fig* signe *m* caractéristique.
<> *vt* [label a product] apposer une marque sur ▪ [register a product] déposer.

trade name *n* [of product] nom *m* de marque ▪ [of firm] raison *f* commerciale.

trade-off *n* échange *m* ▪ [compromise] compromis *m*.

trade paper *n* revue *f* spécialisée.

trade price *n* prix *m* de gros.

trader ['treɪdər] *n* **1.** [gen] commerçant *m*, - e *f*, marchand *m*, - e *f* ▪ [on large scale] négociant *m*, - e *f* **2.** [ship] navire *m* marchand *OR* de commerce **3.** US ST. EX contrepartiste *m*.

trade route *n* route *f* commerciale.

trade secret *n* secret *m* de fabrication.

trade show *n* salon *m* (professionnel).

tradesman ['treɪdzmən] (*pl* **tradesmen** [-mən]) *n* **1.** [trader] commerçant *m*, marchand *m* ▪ **~'s entrance** entrée *f* de service *OR* des fournisseurs **2.** [skilled workman] ouvrier *m* qualifié.

Trades Union Congress *n confédération des syndicats britanniques.*

trade(s) union *n* syndicat *m* ▪ **to join a ~** se syndiquer.

trade unionism *n* syndicalisme *m*.

trade(s) unionist *n* syndicaliste *mf*.

trade wind *n* alizé *m*.

trading ['treɪdɪŋ] <> *n* commerce *m*, négoce *m* ▪ [illicit dealing] trafic *m* ▪ **~ on the Stock Exchange was heavy** le volume de transactions à la Bourse était important ▪ **~ losses for the past year were heavy** les pertes subies pour l'exercice de l'année écoulée ont été lourdes.
<> *comp* [company, partner] commercial ▪ **~ nation** nation *f* commerçante ▪ **~ standards** normes *fpl* de conformité ▪ **~ standards office** ≃ Direction *f* de la consommation et de la répression des fraudes ▪ **~ year** COMM année *f* d'exploitation, exercice *m*.

trading estate *n* UK zone *f* artisanale et commerciale.

trading floor *n* ST. EX corbeille *f*.

trading post *n* US comptoir *m* commercial.

trading profit *n* bénéfice(s) *mpl* d'exploitation.

trading stamp *n* timbre-prime *m*, vignette-épargne *f*.

trading standards officer *n* fonctionnaire *m* du service de la répression des fraudes.

tradition [trə'dɪʃn] *n* tradition *f*, coutume *f* ▪ **it's in the best ~ of New Year's Eve parties** c'est dans la plus pure tradition des réveillons du Nouvel An ▪ **~ has it that...** la tradition veut que... ■ **the ~ that...** la tradition selon laquelle... *OR* qui veut que... ■ **a comedian in the ~ of Chaplin** un comédien dans la lignée de Chaplin ■ **to break with ~** rompre avec la tradition.

traditional [trə'dɪʃənl] *adj* traditionnel ■ **it is ~ to sing Auld Lang Syne at New Year** il est de tradition de chanter Auld Lang Syne au Nouvel An.

traditionalist [trə'dɪʃnəlɪst] ◇ *n* traditionaliste *mf.*
◇ *adj* traditionaliste.

traditionally [trə'dɪʃnəlɪ] *adv* traditionnellement.

traffic ['træfɪk] (*pret & pp* **trafficked**, *cont* **trafficking**) ◇ *n* **1.** [on roads] circulation *f* ■ [rail, air, maritime] trafic *m* ■ **holiday ~** [outward] la circulation des grands départs ; [homeward] la circulation des grands retours ■ **the ~ is heavy/light** la circulation est dense/fluide ■ **there is a great deal of ~ on the roads** les routes sont encombrées ■ **~ in and out of the city** circulation à destination et en provenance de la ville ■ **road closed to heavy ~** route interdite aux poids lourds ■ **eastbound ~** circulation ouest-est ■ **the cyclist weaved through the ~** le cycliste se faufila entre les voitures ➊ **~ calming** *mesures visant à ralentir la circulation* **2.** COMM commerce *m* ■ [illicit] trafic *m* ■ *US* [customers] clientèle *f* ■ **the ~ in arms/drugs** le trafic des armes/de drogue **3.** *UK* [dealings] échange *m.*
◇ *vi* : **to ~ in** faire le commerce de.

traffic circle *n US* rond-point *m*, sens *m* giratoire.

traffic control *n* régulation *f* de la circulation ■ AERON, NAUT & RAIL contrôle *m* du trafic ■ **~ tower** tour *f* de contrôle.

traffic controller *n* contrôleur *m*, - euse *f* de la navigation aérienne, aiguilleur *m* du ciel.

traffic island *n* TRANSP refuge *m.*

traffic jam *n UK* embouteillage *m*, bouchon *m.*

trafficker ['træfɪkəʳ] *n* trafiquant *m*, - e *f* ■ **drug ~** trafiquant *m* de drogue.

traffic lights *npl* feu *m* de signalisation ■ **the ~ are (on) green** le feu est (au) vert ■ **carry on to the next set of ~** continuez jusqu'aux prochains feux.

traffic offence *n* infraction *f* au code de la route.

traffic police *n* [speeding, safety] police *f* de la route ■ [point duty] police *f* de la circulation.

traffic policeman *n* agent *m* de police ■ [on point duty] agent *m* de la circulation.

traffic signal *n* feu *m* de signalisation.

traffic violation *US* = **traffic offence**.

traffic warden *n UK* contractuel *m*, - elle *f.*

TRAFFIC WARDEN

En Grande-Bretagne, les contractuels sont non seulement habilités à dresser les procès-verbaux mais aussi à régler la circulation.

tragedian [trə'dʒiːdɪən] *n* [author] auteur *m* tragique ■ [actor] tragédien *m.*

tragedy ['trædʒədɪ] (*pl* **tragedies**) *n* [gen - THEAT] tragédie *f* ■ **it's a ~ that this should happen to her** c'est tragique que ça lui arrive à elle.

tragic ['trædʒɪk] *adj* tragique.

tragically ['trædʒɪklɪ] *adv* tragiquement ■ **the trip went ~ wrong** le voyage a tourné au drame.

tragic irony *n* ironie *f* tragique.

tragicomedy [,trædʒɪ'kɒmədɪ] (*pl* **tragicomedies**) *n* tragi-comédie *f.*

tragicomic [,trædʒɪ'kɒmɪk] *adj* tragi-comique.

trail [treɪl] ◇ *n* **1.** [path] sentier *m*, chemin *m* ■ [through jungle] piste *f* ■ **to break a ~** faire la trace, tracer ■ **he hit the campaign ~** *fig* il est parti en campagne (électorale) ■ **the end of the ~** *US* le bout de la piste *(nom donné à la Californie par les pionniers américains)* ■ **the ~ of tears** *US* HIST le chemin des larmes **2.** [traces of passage] piste *f*, trace *f* ■ **to be on the ~ of sb/sthg** être sur la piste de qqn/qqch ■ **a false ~** une fausse piste ■ **the storm left a ~ of destruction** l'orage a tout détruit sur son passage **3.** [of blood, smoke] traînée *f* ■ [of comet] queue *f* **4.** [of gun] crosse *f* *OR* flèche *f* d'affût.
◇ *vt* **1.** [follow] suivre, filer ■ [track] suivre la piste de ■ [animal, criminal] traquer **2.** [drag behind, tow] traîner ■ [boat, trailer] tirer, remorquer ■ **she ~ed her hand in the water** elle laissait traîner sa main dans l'eau **3.** [lag behind] être en arrière par rapport à **4.** [gun] porter à la main **5.** [advertise] diffuser (une bande-annonce).
◇ *vi* **1.** [long garment] traîner ■ [plant] ramper ■ **smoke ~ed from the chimney** de la fumée sortait de la cheminée **2.** [move slowly] traîner ■ **he ~ed along at a snail's pace** il avançait comme un escargot **3.** [lag behind in contest] être à la traîne ■ **he's ~ing in the polls** il est à la traîne dans les sondages **4.** [follow] suivre, filer ■ **with five children ~ing behind her** avec cinq enfants dans son sillage.

◆ **trail away** *vi insep* s'estomper ■ **his voice ~ed away to a whisper** sa voix ne fut plus qu'un murmure.

◆ **trail off** *vi insep* s'estomper ■ **he ~ed off in mid sentence** il n'a pas terminé sa phrase.

THE TRAIL OF TEARS

Nom donné au trajet que les Indiens d'Amérique parcoururent sous la contrainte en 1938 pour rejoindre les réserves situées à l'ouest du Mississippi où ils devaient vivre. Un grand nombre d'entre eux succombèrent à la maladie et aux mauvais traitements.

trailblazer ['treɪl,bleɪzəʳ] *n fig* pionnier *m*, - ère *f.*

trailblazing ['treɪl,bleɪzɪŋ] *adj* de pionnier.

trailer ['treɪləʳ] *n* **1.** AUT remorque *f* ■ *US* camping-car *m* ■ **~ court, ~ park** *US terrain aménagé pour les camping-cars* ■ **~ home** caravane *f* ■ **~ tent** tente *f* remorque **2.** CIN & TV bande-annonce *f* **3.** [end of film roll] amorce *f.*

trailer-truck *n US* semi-remorque *m.*

trailing ['treɪlɪŋ] *adj* traînant ■ [plant] rampant ■ **~ edge** AERON bord *m* de fuite.

train [treɪn] ◇ *n* **1.** [railway] train *m* ■ [underground] métro *m*, rame *f* ■ **to go by ~** prendre le train, aller en train ■ **I met a friend on the ~** j'ai rencontré un ami dans le train ■ **to transport goods by ~** transporter des marchandises par voie ferrée *OR* rail ■ **'to the ~s'** 'accès aux quais'
2. [procession - of vehicles] file *f*, cortège *m* ; [- of mules] file *f* ; [- of camels] caravane *f* ■ MIL convoi *m* ■ [retinue] suite *f*, équipage *m* ■ MIL équipage *m* ■ **the famine brought disease in its ~** la maladie succéda à la famine
3. [of dress] traîne *f*
4. [connected sequence] suite *f*, série *f* ■ **in an unbroken ~** en succession ininterrompue ■ **a ~ of thought** un enchaînement d'idées ■ **my remark interrupted her ~ of thought** ma remarque a interrompu le fil de sa pensée *OR* ses pensées ■ **to follow sb's ~ of thought** suivre le raisonnement de qqn
5. MECH train *m* ■ **~ of gears** train d'engrenage
6. *fml* [progress] : **in ~** en marche
7. [fuse] amorce *f* ■ [of gunpowder] traînée *f* (de poudre).
◇ *comp* [dispute, strike] des cheminots, des chemins de fer ■ [reservation, ticket] de train ■ **there is a good ~ service to the city** la ville est bien desservie par le train ■ **~ station** gare *f (de chemin de fer).*
◇ *vt* **1.** [employee, soldier] former ■ [voice] travailler ■ [animal] dresser ■ [mind] former ■ SPORT entraîner ■ [plant - by pruning] tailler ; [- by tying] palisser ■ [climbing plant] diriger, faire grimper ■ **he is ~ing sb to take over from him** il forme son successeur ■ **she was ~ed in economics** elle a reçu une formation d'économiste ■ **to ~ sb to use sthg** apprendre à qqn à utiliser qqch ■ **to ~ sb up** former *OR* préparer qqn ■ **the dogs have been ~ed to detect explosives** les chiens ont été dressés pour détecter les explosifs
2. [direct, aim] viser ■ **he ~ed his gun on us** il a braqué son arme sur nous.
◇ *vi* **1.** recevoir une formation ■ **I ~ed as a translator** j'ai reçu une formation de traducteur ■ **she's ~ing as a teacher** elle suit une formation pédagogique
2. SPORT s'entraîner, se préparer.

trainbearer ['treɪn,beərəʳ] *n personne qui porte la traîne d'un dignitaire* ▪ [at wedding] demoiselle *f* OR dame *f* d'honneur ▪ [boy] page *m*.

trained [treɪnd] *adj* compétent, qualifié ▪ [engineer] breveté, diplômé ▪ [nurse, translator] diplômé, qualifié ▪ **he's not ~ for this job** il n'est pas qualifié OR n'a pas la formation requise pour ce poste ▪ **she has her boss well ~!** *hum* elle a bien dressé son patron! ▪ **a ~ eye** un œil exercé ▪ **he has a ~ voice** il a travaillé sa voix ▮ [animal] dressé ▪ **a ~ parrot** un perroquet savant.

trainee [treɪ'ni:] <> *n* stagiaire *mf* ▪ **sales ~** stagiaire de vente.
<> *comp* stagiaire, en stage ▪ [in trades] en apprentissage ▪ **~ computer programmer** élève *mf* programmeur.

trainer ['treɪnəʳ] *n* **1.** SPORT entraîneur *m* **2.** [of animal] dresseur *m*, - euse *f* ▪ [of racehorses] entraîneur *m* ▪ [of lion] dompteur *m*, - euse *f* **3.** AERON [simulator] simulateur *m* ▪ **~ (aircraft)** avion-école *m* **4.** *UK* [shoe] chaussure *f* de sport.

training ['treɪnɪŋ] <> *n* **1.** formation *f* ▪ [of soldier] instruction *f* ▪ [of animal] dressage *m* ▪ **further ~** perfectionnement *m* ➜ **to do one's basic ~** MIL faire ses classes **2.** SPORT entraînement *m*, préparation *f* ▪ **to be in ~** être en cours d'entraînement OR de préparation ▪ **I'm out of ~** j'ai perdu la forme ▪ **to be in ~ for sthg** s'entraîner pour OR se préparer à qqch.
<> *comp* [centre, programme, scheme] de formation ▪ **~ manual** manuel *m* d'instruction.

Training Agency *pr n* : **the ~** *organisme britannique créé en 1989, qui propose des stages de formation et de recyclage.*

training camp *n* camp *m* d'entraînement ▪ MIL base *f* école.

training college *n* école *f* spécialisée OR profession nelle.

training course *n* stage *m* de formation.

training shoes *npl* chaussures *fpl* de sport.

train set *n* train *m* électrique.

trainspotter *n UK amateur de trains dont la passion consiste à relever les numéros d'immatriculation des locomotives* ▪ [nerd] crétin *m*, - e *f*.

trainspotting [-'spɒtɪŋ] *n* : **to go ~** observer les trains.

traipse [treɪps] *inf* <> *vi* : **we all ~d off to the shops** nous sommes tous partis traîner dans les magasins ▪ **to ~ about** OR **around** se balader, vadrouiller.
<> *n* longue promenade.

trait [treɪ, treɪt] *n* trait *m*.

traitor ['treɪtəʳ] *n* traître *m* ▪ **you're a ~ to your country/to the cause** vous trahissez votre pays/la cause ▪ **he turned ~** [gen] il s'est mis à trahir ; [soldier, spy] il est passé OR s'est vendu à l'ennemi.

traitress ['treɪtrɪs] *n* traîtresse *f*.

trajectory [trə'dʒektərɪ] (*pl* **trajectories**) *n* trajectoire *f*.

tra-la(-la) [trɑ:'lɑ:, ,trɑ:lɑ:'lɑ:] *onom refrain de chanson sans sens particulier.*

tram [træm] *n UK* tram *m*, tramway *m* ▪ MIN berline *f*, benne *f* roulante ▪ **to go by ~** prendre le tram.

tramcar ['træmkɑ:ʳ] *n UK* tram *m*, tramway *m*.

tramline ['træmlaɪn] *n UK* [rails] voie *f* de tramway ▪ [route] ligne *f* de tramway.
◆ **tramlines** *npl* [in tennis, badminton] lignes *fpl* de côté.

tramp [træmp] <> *n* **1.** [vagabond] clochard *m*, - e *f*, chemineau *m* *dated* ▪ **'The Tramp'** ***Chaplin*** 'le Vagabond' **2.** [sound] bruit *m* de pas ▪ **I could hear the ~ of soldiers' feet** j'entendais le pas lourd des soldats **3.** [long walk] randonnée *f* (à pied), promenade *f* **4.** [ship] : **~ (steamer)** tramp *m* **5.** *US inf pej* traînée.
<> *vi* [hike] marcher, se promener ▪ [walk heavily] marcher d'un pas lourd ▪ **to ~ up and down** faire les cent pas.
<> *vt* parcourir ▪ **he ~ed the streets in search of work** il a battu le pavé pour trouver du travail.

trample ['træmpl] <> *vt* piétiner, fouler aux pieds ▪ **the crowd ~d the man to death** l'homme est mort piétiné par la foule ▮ [sb's feelings] bafouer.
<> *vi* marcher d'un pas lourd.
<> *n* [action] piétinement *m* ▪ [sound] bruit *m* de pas.
◆ **trample on, trample over** *vt insep* piétiner ▪ *fig* [sb's feelings] bafouer ▪ [objections] passer outre à.

trampoline ['træmpəli:n] <> *n* trampoline *m*.
<> *vi* : **to ~, to go trampolining** faire du trampoline.

tramway ['træmweɪ] (*pl* **tramways**) *n UK* [rails] voie *f* de tramway ▪ [route] ligne *f* de tramway.

trance [trɑ:ns] *n* transe *f* ▪ MED catalepsie *f* ▪ **to go** OR **to fall into a ~** entrer en transe ; MED tomber en catalepsie ▪ **he put me into a ~** il m'a hypnotisé, il m'a fait entrer en transe.

trannie, tranny ['trænɪ] (*pl* **trannies**) *n UK inf* [transistor radio] transistor *m*.

tranquil ['træŋkwɪl] *adj* tranquille, paisible.

tranquillity *UK*, **tranquility** *US* [træŋ'kwɪlɪtɪ] *n* tranquillité *f*, calme *m*.

tranquillize, ise *UK*, **tranquilize** *US* ['træŋkwɪlaɪz] *vt* calmer, apaiser ▪ MED mettre sous tranquillisants.

tranquillizer *UK*, **tranquilizer** *US* ['træŋkwɪlaɪzəʳ] *n* tranquillisant *m*, calmant *m*.

transact [træn'zækt] *vt* traiter, régler.

transaction [træn'zækʃn] *n* **1.** [gen - BANK] opération *f*, affaire *f* ▪ **cash ~** opération *f* au comptant ▮ ECON, FIN & ST. EX transaction *f* ▪ **Stock Exchange ~s** opérations *fpl* de Bourse **2.** [act of transacting] conduite *f*, gestion *f* **3.** COMPUT mouvement *m*.
◆ **transactions** *npl* [proceedings of an organization] travaux *mpl* ▪ [minutes] actes *mpl*.

transalpine [,trænz'ælpaɪn] *adj* transalpin.

transatlantic [,trænzət'læntɪk] *adj* transatlantique.

transceiver [træn'si:vəʳ] *n* émetteur-récepteur *m*.

transcend [træn'send] *vt* **1.** [go beyond] transcender, dépasser ▪ PHILOS & RELIG transcender **2.** [surpass] surpasser.

transcendent [træn'sendənt] *adj* transcendant.

transcendental [,trænsen'dentl] *adj* transcendantal.

transcendental meditation *n* méditation *f* transcendantale.

transcontinental ['trænz,kɒntɪ'nentl] *adj* transcontinental ▪ **the Transcontinental Railroad** la Transcontinentale.

THE TRANSCONTINENTAL RAILROAD

Voie de chemin de fer traversant les États-Unis d'est en ouest. Achevée en 1869, elle fut construite par deux compagnies : la *Union Pacific* et la *Central Pacific*, qui, parties respectivement de la côte est et de la côte ouest, se rejoignirent dans l'Utah.

transcribe [træn'skraɪb] *vt* transcrire.

transcript ['trænskrɪpt] *n* transcription *f* ▪ *US* SCH & UNIV *dossier complet de la scolarité.*

transcription [træn'skrɪpʃn] *n* transcription *f*.

transducer [trænz'dju:səʳ] *n* transducteur *m*.

transect [træn'sekt] *vt* sectionner transversalement.

transept ['trænsept] *n* transept *m*.

trans fat ['trænz-] *n* BIOL & CHEM acide *m* gras trans.

transfer <> *vt* [træns'fɜ:ʳ] **1.** [move] transférer ▪ [employee, civil servant] transférer, muter ▪ [soldier] muter ▪ [player] transférer ▪ [passenger] transférer, transborder ▪ [object, goods] transférer, transporter ▪ [money] virer ▪ **can this ticket be transferred to another airline?** peut-on utiliser ce billet d'avion sur une autre compagnie? ▪ **I transferred the funds to my bank account** j'ai fait virer l'argent sur mon compte bancaire **2.** [convey - property, ownership] transmettre, transférer ; [- power, responsibility] passer ▪ LAW faire cession de, céder

3. TELEC : **I'd like to ~ the charges** *UK* je voudrais téléphoner en PCV ▪ **I'm transferring you now** [operator] je vous mets en communication ▶ **transferred charge call** *UK* communication *f* en PCV **4.** [displace - design, picture] reporter, décalquer ▪ **to ~ a design from one surface to another** décalquer un dessin d'un support sur un autre ▪ **she transferred her affection/allegiance to him** *fig* elle a reporté son affection/sa fidélité sur lui.
◇ *vi* [træns'fɜːʳ] **1.** [move] être transféré ▪ [employee, civil servant] être muté *OR* transféré ▪ [soldier] être muté ▪ SPORT [player] être transféré ▪ **I'm transferring to history** je me réoriente en histoire **2.** [change mode of transport] être transféré *OR* transbordé.
◇ *n* ['trænsfɜːʳ] **1.** [gen] transfert *m* ▪ [of employee, civil servant] mutation *f* ▪ [of passenger] transfert *m*, transbordement *m* ▪ [of player] transfert *m* ▪ [of goods, objects] transfert *m*, transport *m* ▪ [of money] virement *m* ▪ **~ of a debt** cession *f OR* revirement *m* d'une créance ▪ **bank ~** virement *m* bancaire **2.** LAW transmission *f*, cession *f* ▪ **~ of ownership from sb to sb** transfert *m OR* translation *f* de propriété de qqn à qqn **3.** POL : **~ of power** passation *f* de pouvoir **4.** [design, picture] décalcomanie *f* ▪ [rub-on] autocollant *m* ▪ [sew-on] décalque *m* **5.** [change of mode of travel] transfert *m* ▪ [at airport, train station] correspondance *f*.

transferable [træns'fɜːrəbl] *adj* transmissible ▪ LAW cessible ▪ **this ticket is not ~** ce billet est strictement personnel ▪ **~ securities** FIN valeurs *fpl* négociables.

transference ['trænsfərəns] *n* [gen - PSYCHOL] transfert *m* ▪ [of employee, civil servant] mutation *f* ▪ [of money] virement *m* ▪ [of power] passation *f* ▪ [of ownership] transfert *m OR* translation *f* de propriété.

transfer list *n UK* liste *f* des joueurs transférables.

transfer passenger *n* [between flights] voyageur *m*, - euse *f* en transit.

transfigure [træns'fɪgəʳ] *vt* transfigurer.

transfix [træns'fɪks] *vt liter* transpercer ▪ *fig* pétrifier ▪ **to be ~ed with fear** être paralysé par la peur ▪ **she stood ~ed** elle est restée clouée sur place.

transform [træns'fɔːm] ◇ *vt* **1.** [change - gen] transformer, métamorphoser ▪ **to ~ sthg into sthg** transformer qqch en qqch **2.** ELEC transformer ▪ CHEM, MATHS & PHYS transformer, convertir **3.** GRAM transformer.
◇ *n* **1.** LING transformation *f* **2.** MATHS transformée *f*.

transformation [ˌtrænsfə'meɪʃn] *n* transformation *f*, métamorphose *f* ▪ ELEC & MATHS transformation *f* ▪ CHEM & PHYS conversion *f* ▪ LING transformation *f*.

transformational grammar [ˌtrænsfə'meɪʃənl-] *n* grammaire *f* transformationnelle.

transformer [træns'fɔːməʳ] ◇ *n* transformateur *m*.
◇ *comp* : **~ station** station *f* de transformation.

transfusion [træns'fjuːʒn] *n* [gen - MED] transfusion *f* ▪ **they gave him a ~** ils lui ont fait une transfusion.

transgenic [trænz'dʒenɪk] *adj* transgénique.

transgress [træns'gres] *fml* ◇ *vt* transgresser, enfreindre.
◇ *vi* pécher.

transgression [træns'greʃn] *n fml* **1.** [overstepping] transgression *f* **2.** [crime] faute *f*, violation *f (d'une loi)* ▪ RELIG péché *m*.

transgressor [træns'gresəʳ] *n* [gen - LAW] transgresseur *m* ▪ RELIG pécheur *m*, - eresse *f*.

tranship [træns'ʃɪp] = **transship**.

transience ['trænzɪəns] *n* caractère *m* éphémère *OR* transitoire.

transient ['trænzɪənt] ◇ *adj* [temporary] transitoire, passager ▪ [fleeting] éphémère.
◇ *n* **1.** [person] voyageur *m*, - euse *f* en transit **2.** [goods] marchandise *f* en transit.

transistor [træn'zɪstəʳ] *n* transistor *m*.

transistorize, ise [træn'zɪstəraɪz] *vt* transistoriser ▪ **~d circuit** circuit *m* à transistors.

transistor radio *n* transistor *m*.

transit ['trænsɪt] ◇ *n* [of goods, passengers] transit *m* ▪ ASTRON passage *m* ▪ **in ~** en transit ▪ **goods lost in ~** marchandises égarées pendant le transport.
◇ *comp* [goods, passengers] en transit ▪ [documents, port] de transit ▪ **~ authority** *US* régie *f* des transports (en commun) ▪ **~ lounge** salle *f* de transit.
◇ *vt* [goods, passengers] transiter ▪ ASTRON passer sur.

transit camp *n* camp *m* de transit.

transition [træn'zɪʃn] ◇ *n* transition *f*, passage *m*.
◇ *comp* [period] de transition.

transitional [træn'zɪʃənl] *adj* de transition, transitoire.

transitive ['trænzɪtɪv] *adj* transitif.

transitively ['trænzɪtɪvlɪ] *adv* transitivement.

transitory ['trænzɪtrɪ] *adj* transitoire, passager.

translatable [træns'leɪtəbl] *adj* traduisible.

translate [træns'leɪt] ◇ *vt* **1.** traduire ▪ **to ~ sthg from Spanish into English** traduire qqch de l'espagnol en anglais ▪ **it can be ~d as...** on peut le traduire par... ▪ **~d into Fahrenheit** exprimé *OR* converti en Fahrenheit **2.** RELIG [transfer - cleric, relics] transférer ▪ [convey to heaven] ravir.
◇ *vi* **1.** [words] se traduire ▪ **it doesn't ~** c'est intraduisible **2.** [person] traduire.

translation [træns'leɪʃn] *n* **1.** traduction *f* ▪ SCH version *f* ▪ **the book is a ~ from (the) Chinese** le livre est traduit du chinois ▪ **the text loses something in the ~** le texte perd quelque chose à la traduction **2.** RELIG [of cleric, relics] translation *f* ▪ [conveying to heaven] ravissement *m*.

translator [træns'leɪtəʳ] *n* traducteur *m*, - trice *f*.

transliterate [trænz'lɪtəreɪt] *vt* translitérer, translittérer.

transliteration [ˌtrænzlɪtə'reɪʃn] *n* translitération *f*, translittération *f*, transcription *f*.

translucent [trænz'luːsnt] *adj* translucide, diaphane.

transmigration [ˌtrænzmaɪ'greɪʃn] *n* [of souls] transmigration *f* ▪ [of people] émigration *f*.

transmission [trænz'mɪʃn] *n* **1.** transmission *f* ▪ [broadcast] retransmission *f* **2.** AUT transmission *f* ▪ *US* boîte *f* de vitesses.

transmit [trænz'mɪt] (*pret & pp* **transmitted**, *cont* **transmitting**) ◇ *vt* transmettre ▪ TELEC émettre, diffuser.
◇ *vi* RADIO, TELEC & TV émettre, diffuser.

transmitter [trænz'mɪtəʳ] *n* transmetteur *m* ▪ RADIO & TV émetteur *m* ▪ [in telephone] microphone *m* (téléphonique).

transmitting [trænz'mɪtɪŋ] ◇ *adj* TELEC émetteur *m*.
◇ *n* transmission *f*.

transmute [trænz'mjuːt] *vt* transmuer, transmuter.

transnational [ˌtrænz'næʃənl] *adj* transnational.

transom ['trænsəm] *n* **1.** [in window] petit bois *m* horizontal ▪ [above door] traverse *f* d'imposte **2.** *US* [fanlight] : **~ (window)** imposte *f* (semi-circulaire).

transparency [træns'pærənsɪ] (*pl* **transparencies**) *n* **1.** [gen - PHYS] transparence *f* **2.** [for overhead projector] transparent *m* ▪ *esp UK* [slide] diapositive *f*.

transparent [træns'pærənt] *adj* [gen - PHYS] transparent.

transpiration [ˌtrænspɪ'reɪʃn] *n* BOT & PHYSIOL transpiration *f*.

transpire [træn'spaɪəʳ] ◇ *vi* **1.** [be discovered, turn out] apparaître ▪ **it ~d that he had been embezzling funds** on a appris *OR* on s'est aperçu qu'il avait détourné des fonds **2.** [happen] se passer, arriver **3.** BOT & PHYSIOL transpirer.
◇ *vt* BOT & PHYSIOL transpirer.

transplant ◇ *vt* [træns'plɑ:nt] **1.** BOT [plant] transplanter ■ [seedling] repiquer **2.** MED [organ] greffer, transplanter ■ [tissue] greffer **3.** [population] transplanter.
◇ *n* ['træns,plɑ:nt] MED [organ] transplant *m* ■ [tissue] greffe *f* ■ [operation] greffe *f* ■ **she's had a kidney ~** on lui a fait une greffe du rein ■ **she's had a heart ~** on lui a greffé un cœur.

transplantation [,trænsplɑ:n'teɪʃn] *n* **1.** BOT [of seedling] repiquage *m* ■ [of plant] transplantation *f* **2.** *fig* [of people] transplantation *f*.

transport ◇ *n* ['trænspɔ:t] **1.** *(U)* UK [system] transport *m*, transports *mpl* **2.** [means] moyen *m* de transport OR de locomotion ▶ **~ plane** avion *m* de transport ■ **~ ship** navire *m* de transport ■ **troop ~** MIL transport *m* de troupes **3.** [of goods] transport *m* **4.** *lit* [of joy] transport *m* ■ [of anger] accès *m*.
◇ *vt* [træn'spɔ:t] transporter.

transportable [træn'spɔ:təbl] *adj* transportable.

transportation [,trænspɔ:'teɪʃn] *n* **1.** US [transport] transport *m* ■ **public ~** transports publics ■ **~ system** système *m* des transports **2.** [of criminals] transportation *f*.

transport café *n* UK ≃ routier *m (restaurant)*.

transporter [træn'spɔ:tə^r] *n* **1.** MIL [for troops - lorry] camion *m* de transport ; [- ship] navire *m* de transport ■ [for tanks] camion *m* porte-char **2.** [for cars - lorry] camion *m* pour transport d'automobiles ; [- train] wagon *m* pour transport d'automobiles.

transpose [træns'pəʊz] *vt* transposer.

transposition [,trænspə'zɪʃn] *n* transposition *f*.

transputer [træns'pju:tə^r] *n* COMPUT transputer *m*.

transsexual [træns'sekʃʊəl] *n* transsexuel *m*, - elle *f*.

transship [træns'ʃɪp] *(pret & pp* **transshipped**, *cont* **transshipping**) *vt* transborder.

Trans-Siberian ['trænz-] *adj* : **the ~ (Railway)** le Transsibérien.

transubstantiation ['trænsəb,stænʃɪ'eɪʃn] *n* transsubstantiation *f*.

transverse ['trænzvɜ:s] ◇ *adj* [beam, line] transversal ■ ANAT transverse.
◇ *n* [gen] partie *f* transversale ■ GEOM axe *m* transversal *(d'une hyperbole)*.

transvestism [trænz'vestɪzm] *n* travestisme *m*, transvestisme *m*.

transvestite [trænz'vestaɪt] *n* travesti *m*.

Transylvania [,trænsɪl'veɪnjə] *pr n* Transylvanie *f* ■ **in ~** en Transylvanie.

Transylvanian [,trænsɪl'veɪnjən] ◇ *n* Transylvanien *m*, - enne *f*.
◇ *adj* transylvanien.

trap [træp] *(pret & pp* **trapped**, *cont* **trapping**) ◇ *n* **1.** [snare] piège *m* ■ [dug in ground] trappe *f* ■ [gintrap] collet *m* ■ **to set** OR **to lay a ~ for hares** dresser OR tendre un piège pour les lièvres **2.** *fig* piège *m*, traquenard *m* ■ **to set** OR **to lay a ~ for sb** tendre un piège à qqn ■ **the poverty ~** le piège de la pauvreté **3.** [in drain] siphon *m* **4.** SPORT [in dog racing] box *m* de départ ■ [for shooting] ball-trap *m* **5.** [carriage] cabriolet *m*, charrette *f* anglaise **6.** [trapdoor] trappe *f* **7.** △ [mouth] gueule *f* △.
◇ *vt* **1.** [animal] prendre au piège, piéger **2.** *fig* [opponent] piéger ■ **he trapped me into thinking I was safe** il m'a piégé en me faisant croire que j'étais hors de danger **3.** [immobilize, catch] bloquer, immobiliser ■ **I trapped my leg** OR **my leg got trapped under the table** je me suis coincé la jambe OR j'avais la jambe coincée sous la table ■ **she trapped her fingers in the door** elle s'est pris les doigts dans la porte ■ **they were trapped in the rubble** ils étaient coincés OR immobilisés sous les décombres **4.** [hold back - water, gas] retenir.

trapdoor [,træp'dɔ:^r] *n* trappe *f*.

trapes [treɪps] *inf* = **traipse**.

trapeze [trə'pi:z] *n* trapèze *m (de cirque)* ■ **~ artist** trapéziste *mf*.

trapezium [trə'pi:zjəm] *(pl* **trapeziums** OR *pl* **trapezia** [-zjə]) *n* **1.** GEOM UK trapèze *m* ■ US quadrilatère *m* trapézoïdal **2.** ANAT trapèze *m*.

trapezoid ['træpɪzɔɪd] ◇ *n* **1.** GEOM UK quadrilatère *m* trapézoïdal ■ US trapèze *m* **2.** ANAT trapézoïde *m*.
◇ *adj* trapézoïde.

trapper ['træpə^r] *n* trappeur *m*.

trappings ['træpɪŋz] *npl* **1.** [accessories] ornements *mpl* ■ **the ~ of power** les signes extérieurs du pouvoir **2.** [harness] harnachement *m*, caparaçon *m*.

Trappist ['træpɪst] ◇ *n* trappiste *m*.
◇ *comp* [monk, monastery] de la Trappe.

traps [træps] *npl* [luggage] bagages *mpl*, affaires *fpl*.

trapshooting ['træp,ʃu:tɪŋ] *n* ball-trap *m*.

trash [træʃ] ◇ *n (U)* **1.** [nonsense] bêtises *fpl*, âneries *fpl* ■ **he talks/writes a lot of ~** il dit/écrit beaucoup d'âneries ■ **what utter ~!** c'est vraiment n'importe quoi! **2.** [goods] camelote *f* ■ **they sell a lot of ~** ils vendent beaucoup de camelote **3.** US [waste] ordures *fpl* ■ **to put something in the ~** mettre qqch à la poubelle **4.** *inf* [people] racaille *f*.
◇ *vt inf* **1.** [reject] jeter, bazarder **2.** [criticize] débiner, éreinter **3.** [vandalize] vandaliser, saccager **4.** US SPORT [opponent] démolir.

trashcan ['træʃkæn] *n* US poubelle *f*.

trashman ['træʃmæn] *(pl* **trashmen** [-men]) *n* US éboueur *m*.

trashy ['træʃɪ] *(comp* **trashier**, *superl* **trashiest**) *adj* [goods] de pacotille ■ [magazine, book] de quatre sous ■ [idea, article] qui ne vaut rien ■ [programme] lamentable, au-dessous de tout.

trauma [UK 'trɔ:mə, US 'traʊmə] *(pl* **traumas** OR *pl* **traumata** [-mətə]) *n* [gen - PSYCHOL] trauma *m spec*, traumatisme *m* ■ MED traumatisme *m*.

traumatic [trɔ:'mætɪk] *adj* [gen - PSYCHOL] traumatisant ■ MED traumatique.

traumatism [UK 'trɔ:mətɪzm, US 'traʊmətɪzm] *n* traumatisme *m*.

traumatize, ise [UK 'trɔ:mətaɪz, US 'traʊmətaɪz] *vt* traumatiser.

travel ['trævl] (UK *pret & pp* **travelled**, *cont* **travelling**) (US *pret & pp* **traveled**, *cont* **traveling**) ◇ *vi* **1.** [journey - traveller] voyager ■ **to ~ by air/car** voyager en avion/en voiture ■ **they travelled to Greece by boat** ils sont allés en Grèce en bateau ■ **to ~ round the world** faire le tour du monde ■ **she's travelling (about** OR **around) somewhere in Asia** elle est en voyage quelque part en Asie ■ **we travelled across France by train** nous avons traversé la France en train ■ **to ~ light** voyager avec peu de bagages ■ **to ~ back** revenir, rentrer ■ **let's ~ back in time to 1940** retournons en 1940 **2.** COMM être voyageur OR représentant de commerce **3.** [go, move - person] aller ; [- vehicle, train] aller, rouler ; [- piston, shuttle] se déplacer ; [- light, sound] se propager ■ **we were travelling at an average speed of 60 m.p.h.** on faisait du 90 km/h de moyenne ■ **the components ~ along a conveyor belt** les pièces détachées sont transportées sur un tapis roulant **4.** *inf* [go very fast] rouler (très) vite **5.** *fig* [thoughts, mind] : **my mind travelled back to last June** mes pensées m'ont ramené au mois de juin dernier **6.** [news, rumour] se répandre, se propager, circuler ■ **news ~s fast** les nouvelles vont vite **7.** [food] supporter le voyage.
◇ *vt* **1.** [distance] faire, parcourir ■ **I travelled 50 miles to get here** j'ai fait 80 km pour venir ici **2.** [area, road] parcourir.
◇ *n (U)* [journeys] voyage *m*, voyages *mpl* ■ **~ broadens the mind** les voyages ouvrent l'esprit.
◇ *comp* [book] de voyages ■ [guide, brochure] touristique ■ [writer] qui écrit des récits de voyage.
◆ **travels** *npl* [journeys] voyages *mpl* ■ [comings and goings] allées et venues *fpl* ■ **I met them on my ~s in China** je les ai rencontrés au cours de mes voyages en Chine.

travel agency *n* agence *f* de voyages.

travel agent *n* agent *m* de voyages ■ **~'s** agence *f* de voyages.

travelator ['trævəleɪtər] = **travolator**.

travel book *n* récit *m* de voyages.

travel brochure *n* dépliant *m* touristique.

travel bureau *n* agence *f* de voyages.

Travelcard ['trævlkɑːd] *n* carte *f* d'abonnement *(pour les transports en commun à Londres)*.

traveled ['trævld] *US* = **travelled**.

traveler ['trævlər] *US* = **traveller**.

travel insurance *n (U)* **to take out ~** prendre une assurance-voyage.

travelled *UK*, **traveled** *US* ['trævld] *adj* **1.** [person] qui a beaucoup voyagé ■ **he's a well-~ man** il a beaucoup voyagé **2.** [road, path] fréquenté.

traveller *UK*, **traveler** *US* ['trævlər] *n* **1.** [gen] voyageur *m*, - euse *f* ■ **I'm not a good ~** je supporte mal les voyages **2.** [salesman] voyageur *m*, - euse *f* de commerce **3.** [gipsy] bohémien *m*, - enne *f* **4.** [lifestyle] nomade *mf* New Age.

traveller's cheque *n* chèque *m* de voyage, traveller's cheque *m*.

travelling *UK*, **traveling** *US* ['trævlɪŋ] <> *n (U)* voyage *m*, voyages *mpl*.
<> *adj* [companion, bag] de voyage ■ [preacher, musician] itinérant ■ [crane] mobile.

travelling clock *n* réveil *m* de voyage.

travelling expenses *npl* frais *mpl* de déplacement.

travelling library *n* ≃ bibliobus *m*.

travelling people *npl* gens *mpl* du voyage.

travelling salesman *n* représentant *m* OR voyageur *m* de commerce.

travelogue *UK*, **travelog** *US* ['trævəlɒg] *n* [lecture, book] récit *m* de voyage ■ [film] film *m* de voyage.

travel-sick *adj UK* **to be ~** [in car] avoir mal au cœur en voiture, avoir le mal de la route ; [in boat] avoir le mal de mer ; [in plane] avoir le mal de l'air.

travel sickness *n* mal *m* de la route.

traverse ['trævəs, ˌtrə'vɜːs] <> *vt fml* traverser.
<> *vi* [in climbing, skiing] faire une traversée, traverser.
<> *n* **1.** [beam] traverse *f* **2.** [gallery] galerie *f* transversale.

travesty ['trævəstɪ] <> *n (pl* **travesties***)* [parody] parodie *f*, pastiche *m* ■ *pej* [mockery, pretence] simulacre *m*, travestissement *m* ■ **the trial was a ~ of justice** le procès n'était qu'un simulacre de justice.
<> *vt (pret & pp* **travestied***)* [justice] bafouer.

travolator ['trævəleɪtər] *n* tapis *m* OR trottoir *m* roulant.

trawl [trɔːl] <> *n* **1.** FISHING : **~ (net)** chalut *m* ■ **~ line** palangre *f* **2.** [search] recherche *f*.
<> *vi* **1.** FISHING pêcher au chalut ■ **to ~ for mackerel** pêcher le maquereau au chalut **2.** [search] chercher ■ **to ~ for information** chercher des renseignements, aller à la pêche (aux renseignements).
<> *vt* [net] traîner, tirer ■ [sea] pêcher dans.

trawler ['trɔːlər] *n* [boat, fisherman] chalutier *m*.

tray [treɪ] *n* **1.** [for carrying] plateau *m* **2.** [for papers] casier *m* (de rangement) ■ [for mail] corbeille *f* ■ **in/out ~** corbeille arrivée/départ.

traycloth ['treɪklɒθ] *n* napperon *m* (de plateau).

treacherous ['tretʃərəs] *adj* **1.** [disloyal - ally] traître, perfide ■ *fig* [memory] infidèle **2.** [dangerous - water, current, ice] traître ■ **the roads are ~** les routes sont très glissantes.

treachery ['tretʃərɪ] *(pl* **treacheries***)* *n* perfidie *f*, traîtrise *f*.

treacle ['triːkl] *n UK* [molasses] mélasse *f* ■ [golden syrup] mélasse *f* raffinée.

treacle pudding *n UK* pudding *m* à la mélasse.

treacle tart *n UK* tarte *f* à la mélasse.

treacly ['triːklɪ] *adj* [sweet] sirupeux ■ *fig* [sentimental] mièvre, sirupeux.

tread [tred] *(pret* **trod** [trɒd], *pp* **trod** OR **trodden** ['trɒdn]) <> *vt* **1.** [walk] : **a path had been trodden through the grass** les pas des marcheurs avaient tracé un chemin dans l'herbe ■ **she trod the streets looking for him** elle a battu le pavé OR parcouru la ville à sa recherche ■ **the path had been trodden by generations of hikers** des générations de randonneurs avaient foulé ce chemin ◐ **to ~ the boards** monter sur les planches **2.** [trample] fouler ■ **to ~ grapes** fouler du raisin ■ **to ~ sthg underfoot** fouler qqch aux pieds, piétiner qqch ◐ **to ~ water** nager sur place **3.** [stamp] enfoncer, écraser ■ **she trod the cigarette into the sand** elle a écrasé du pied le mégot dans le sable.
<> *vi* **1.** [walk] marcher ■ **to ~ lightly** marcher d'un pas léger ■ **to ~ carefully** OR **warily** *fig* y aller doucement OR avec précaution **2.** [step] : **to ~ on sthg** [accidentally] marcher sur qqch ; [deliberately] marcher (exprès) sur qqch ■ **he trod on my foot** il m'a marché sur le pied ◐ **to ~ on sb's toes** marcher sur les pieds de qqn.
<> *n* **1.** [footstep] pas *m* ■ **to walk with a heavy ~** marcher d'un pas lourd ‖ [sound of steps] bruit *m* de pas **2.** [of stairs] marche *f*, giron *m spec* **3.** [of shoe] semelle *f* ■ [of tyre - depth] bande *f* de roulement ; [- pattern] sculptures *fpl* ■ **there's no ~ left** [on shoe] la semelle est usée ; [on tyre] le pneu est lisse.
◆ **tread down** *vt sep* tasser (du pied).
◆ **tread in** *vt sep* [plant] tasser la terre autour de.

treadle ['tredl] <> *n* pédale *f (sur un tour ou sur une machine à coudre)*.
<> *vi* actionner la pédale.

treadmill ['tredmɪl] *n* [machine] manège *m* ■ HIST *roue ou manège mus par un homme ou un animal et actionnant une machine*.

treas. *(written abbrev of* **treasurer***)* trés.

treason ['triːzn] *n* trahison *f*.

treasonable ['triːznəbl] *adj* [action, statement] qui constitue une trahison.

treasure ['treʒər] <> *n* **1.** [valuables] trésor *m* ■ **the Treasure State** le Montana **2.** [art] joyau *m*, trésor *m* **3.** *inf* [person] trésor *m*, ange *m*.
<> *vt* **1.** [friendship, possession] tenir beaucoup à **2.** [gift] garder précieusement, être très attaché à ■ [memory] conserver précieusement, chérir *fml* ■ [moment] chérir *fml*.

treasure house *n* **1.** [museum] trésor *m (lieu)* **2.** [room, library] mine *f*, trésor *m* **3.** *fig* [person] : **she's a ~ of information** c'est un puits de science OR une mine de renseignements.

treasure hunt *n* chasse *f* au trésor.

treasurer ['treʒərər] *n* **1.** [of club] trésorier *m*, - ère *f* **2.** *US* [of company] directeur *m* financier.

treasure trove *n* trésor *m*.

treasury ['treʒərɪ] *(pl* **treasuries***)* *n* **1.** [building] trésorerie *f* **2.** *fig* [of information] mine *f* ■ [of poems] recueil *m* **3.** ADMIN : **the Treasury** la Trésorerie ■ ≃ le ministère des Finances ■ **Secretary/Department of the Treasury** *US* ≃ ministre *m* /ministère *m* des Finances.

treat [triːt] <> *vt* **1.** [deal with] traiter ■ **he ~s them with contempt** il est méprisant envers eux ■ **teachers expect to be ~ed with respect by their pupils** les professeurs exigent que leurs élèves se conduisent respectueusement envers eux ■ **you shouldn't ~ them like children** vous ne devriez pas les traiter comme des enfants **2.** [handle - substance, object] utiliser, se servir de ■ [claim, request] traiter **3.** [consider - problem, question] traiter, considérer ■ **the whole episode was ~ed as a joke** on a pris OR on a considéré tout cet épisode comme une plaisanterie **4.** MED [patient] soigner ■ [illness] traiter ■ **she's being ~ed for cancer** on la soigne pour un cancer **5.** [fruit, timber, crops] traiter ■ **the land has been ~ed with fertilizer** la terre a été traitée aux engrais **6.** [buy] : **to ~ sb to sthg** offrir OR payer

qqch à qqn ■ **I ~ed myself to a new coat** je me suis offert *OR* payé un manteau neuf ■ **go on, ~ yourself!** vas-y, gâte-toi *OR* fais-toi plaisir!
◇ *vi fml* **1.** : **to ~ of** [deal with] traiter de **2.** [negotiate] : **to ~ with sb** traiter avec qqn.
◇ *n* **1.** [on special occasion - enjoyment] gâterie *f*, (petit) plaisir *m* ; [- surprise] surprise *f* ; [- present] cadeau *m* ; [- outing] sortie *f* ■ **as a special ~ we went to the planetarium** on nous a offert tout spécialement une visite au planétarium ■ **let's give her a ~** faisons-lui un petit plaisir ■ **this is my ~** c'est moi qui offre ■ **you've got a ~ in store** on te réserve une surprise, attends-toi à une surprise **2.** [pleasure] plaisir *m*.
➡ **a treat** *adv phr UK inf* à merveille ■ **he's coming on a ~** il fait de sacrés progrès.

treatise ['tri:tɪs] *n* traité *m*.

treatment ['tri:tmənt] *n* **1.** [of person] traitement *m* ■ **we complained of ill ~** nous nous sommes plaints d'avoir été mal traités ■ **they gave him preferential ~** ils lui ont accordé un traitement préférentiel *OR* de faveur ■ **to give sb the (full) ~** traiter qqn avec tous les égards **2.** *(U)* MED soins *mpl*, traitement *m* ■ **a course of ~** un traitement ■ **she was sent to Madrid for ~** on l'a envoyée se faire soigner à Madrid ■ **to receive/to undergo ~** recevoir/suivre un traitement ■ **cancer ~** traitement du cancer ■ **X-ray ~** traitement par rayons X **3.** [of subject] traitement *m*, façon *f* de traiter **4.** [of crops, timber] traitement *m* **5.** [chemical] produit *m* chimique **6.** CIN traitement *m*.

treaty ['tri:tɪ] (*pl* **treaties**) *n* **1.** POL traité *m* ■ **to sign a ~ (with sb)** signer *OR* conclure un traité (avec qqn) ■ **Amsterdam/Maastricht/Rome ~** traité d'Amsterdam/de Maastricht/de Rome **2.** LAW : **they sold the property by private ~** ils ont vendu la propriété par accord privé.

treble ['trebl] ◇ *adj* **1.** [triple] triple ■ **my phone number is 70 ~ 4** *UK* mon numéro de téléphone est le soixante-dix, quatre cent quarante-quatre **2.** MUS [voice] de soprano ■ [part] pour voix de soprano.
◇ *n* **1.** MUS [part, singer] soprano *m* **2.** *(U)* [in hi-fi] aigus *mpl*.
◇ *vt* & *vi* tripler.
◇ *adv* : **to sing ~** chanter dans un registre de soprano.

treble clef *n* clef *f* de sol.

trebly ['treblɪ] *adv* triplement, trois fois plus.

tree [tri:] ◇ *n* **1.** BOT arbre *m* ■ **the Tree of Knowledge/Life** BIBLE l'arbre de la science du bien et du mal/de vie ➤ **to be up a ~** *US* être dans une impasse **2.** [diagram] : **~ (diagram)** représentation *f* en arbre *OR* arborescente, arborescence *f* **3.** [for shoes] embauchoir *m*, forme *f* **4.** [of saddle] arçon *m*.
◇ *vt* [hunter, animal] forcer *OR* obliger à se réfugier dans un arbre.

tree fern *n* fougère *f* arborescente.

treehouse ['tri:haʊs] (*pl* [-haʊzɪz]) *n cabane construite dans un arbre.*

tree-hugger *n inf pej* écolo *mf*.

tree-lined *adj* bordé d'arbres.

tree surgeon *n* arboriculteur *m*, - trice *f (qui s'occupe de soigner et d'élaguer les arbres)*.

treetop ['tri:tɒp] *n* cime *f OR* haut *m OR* faîte *m* d'un arbre ■ **in the ~s** au faîte *OR* au sommet des arbres.

tree trunk *n* tronc *m* d'arbre.

trefoil ['trefɔɪl] *n* ARCHIT & BOT trèfle *m*.

trek [trek] (*pret & pp* **trekked**, *cont* **trekking**) ◇ *n* [walk] marche *f* ■ [hike] randonnée *f* ■ **to go on a ~** faire une marche *OR* une randonnée ‖ [arduous trip] marche *f* pénible ■ **it was a real ~ to get here** ça a été une véritable expédition pour arriver ici ■ **it's a bit of a ~ to the shops** il y a un bout de chemin jusqu'aux magasins.
◇ *vi* [walk] avancer avec peine ■ [hike] faire de la randonnée ■ **we had to ~ across fields to get here** il a fallu passer à travers champs pour arriver ici ‖ [drag o.s.] se traîner ■ **they trekked all the way out here to see us** ils ont fait tout ce chemin pour venir nous voir.

trellis ['trelɪs] ◇ *n* treillage *m*, treillis *m*.
◇ *vt* [wood strips] faire un treillage de ■ [plant] treillager.

tremble ['trembl] ◇ *vi* **1.** [person - with cold] trembler, frissonner ; [- from fear, excitement, rage] trembler, frémir ■ [hands] trembler ■ **to ~ with fear** trembler de peur **2.** [voice - from emotion] trembler, vibrer ; [- from fear] trembler ; [- from old age] trembler, chevroter ■ **her voice ~d with emotion** sa voix tremblait d'émotion **3.** [bridge, house, ground] trembler ■ [engine] vibrer **4.** *fig* [be anxious] frémir ■ **she ~d at the thought** elle frémissait à cette seule pensée.
◇ *n* **1.** [from fear] tremblement *m* ■ [from excitement, rage] frémissement *m* ■ [from cold] frissonnement *m* **2.** [in voice] frémissement *m*, frisson *m*.

trembling ['tremblɪŋ] ◇ *adj* **1.** [body - with cold] frissonnant, grelottant ; [- in fear, excitement] frémissant, tremblant ■ [hands] tremblant **2.** [voice - with emotion] vibrant ; [- with fear] tremblant ; [- because of old age] chevrotant ■ **with a ~ voice** [speaker] d'une *OR* la voix tremblante ; [singer] d'une *OR* la voix chevrotante.
◇ *n* [from cold] tremblement *m*, frissonnement *m* ■ [from fear] tremblement *m*, frémissement *m*.

tremendous [trɪ'mendəs] *adj* **1.** [number, amount] énorme, très grand ■ [cost, speed] très élevé, vertigineux ■ [building, arch] énorme ■ [height] vertigineux, très grand ■ [undertaking] énorme, monumental ■ [admiration, disappointment, pride] très grand, extrême ■ [crash, noise] terrible, épouvantable ■ **there's been a ~ improvement in her work** son travail s'est énormément amélioré ■ **you've been a ~ help** vous m'avez été d'une aide précieuse **2.** [wonderful] sensationnel, formidable ■ **I had a ~ time** je me suis amusé comme un fou ■ **she looks ~ in black** elle a beaucoup d'allure en noir.

tremendously [trɪ'mendəslɪ] *adv* [as intensifier] extrêmement ■ **we heard a ~ loud explosion** on a entendu une formidable explosion ■ **we enjoyed it ~** cela nous a énormément plu.

tremolo ['tremələʊ] (*pl* **tremolos**) *n* MUS trémolo *m* ■ **~ arm** *levier sur une guitare électrique qui sert à varier le ton d'une note.*

tremor ['tremər] *n* **1.** GEOL secousse *f* (sismique) **2.** [in voice] frémissement *m*, frisson *m*, tremblement *m* **3.** [of fear, thrill] frisson *m* ■ **a ~ of anticipation ran through the audience** à l'idée de ce qui allait suivre, la salle fut parcourue d'un frisson.

tremulous ['tremjʊləs] *adj lit* **1.** [with fear] tremblant ■ [with excitement, nervousness] frémissant ■ [handwriting] tremblé ■ **he was ~ with emotion/fear** il tremblait d'émotion/de peur **2.** [timid - person, manner] timide, craintif ; [- animal] craintif, effarouché ; [- smile] timide.

trench [trentʃ] ◇ *n* [gen - CONSTR] & MIL tranchée *f* ■ [ditch] fossé *m*.
◇ *vt* [field] creuser une tranchée *OR* des tranchées dans ■ MIL retrancher.
◇ *vi* creuser une tranchée *OR* des tranchées.

trenchant ['trentʃənt] *adj* incisif, tranchant.

trench coat *n* trench-coat *m*.

trench warfare *n* guerre *f* de tranchées.

trend [trend] ◇ *n* [tendency] tendance *f* ■ [fashion] mode *f* ■ **the ~ is towards shorter skirts** la tendance est aux jupes plus courtes ■ **house prices are on an upward ~ again** le prix des maisons est de nouveau à la hausse ■ **the latest ~s** la dernière mode ■ **to set a/the ~** [style] donner un/le ton ; [fashion] lancer une/la mode.
◇ *vi* [extend - mountain range] s'étendre ■ [veer - coastline] s'incliner ■ [turn - prices, opinion] s'orienter.

trendily ['trendɪlɪ] *adv inf* [dress] branché *(adv)*.

trendsetter ['trend,setər] *n* [person - in style] personne *f* qui donne le ton ; [- in fashion] personne *f* qui lance une mode.

trendsetting ['trend,setɪŋ] ◇ *adj* [person] qui lance une mode ■ [idea, garment] d'avant-garde.
◇ *n* lancement *m* d'une mode.

trendy ['trendɪ] (*comp* **trendier**, *superl* **trendiest**, *pl* **trendies**) *inf* ◇ *adj* [music, appearance] branché ■ [ideas] à la mode, branché ■ [clothes] branché ■ [place, resort] à la mode, branché.
◇ *n pej* branché *m*, - e *f*.

trepan [trɪ'pæn] (*pret & pp* **trepanned**, *cont* **trepanning**) ◇ *vt* **1.** MIN forer **2.** MED trépaner.
◇ *n* **1.** MIN foreuse *f* ■ [for metal, plastic] foret *m* **2.** MED trépan *m*.

trepidation [ˌtrepɪ'deɪʃn] *n* **1.** [alarm] inquiétude *f* ■ **with great ~** avec une vive inquiétude **2.** [excitement] agitation *f*.

trespass ['trespəs] ◇ *vi* **1.** LAW s'introduire dans une propriété privée ■ **you're ~ing** vous êtes sur une propriété privée ■ **to ~ on sb's land** s'introduire OR entrer sans autorisation dans une propriété privée ■ **'no ~ing'** 'défense d'entrer, propriété privée' **2.** *fig* [encroach] : **I don't want to ~ on your time/hospitality** je ne veux pas abuser de votre temps/hospitalité ■ **he's ~ing on my area of responsibility** il empiète sur mon terrain **3.** BIBLE : **to ~ against sb** offenser qqn ■ **to ~ against the law** enfreindre la loi (divine).
◇ *n* **1.** *(U)* LAW entrée *f* non autorisée ■ **to commit ~** s'introduire dans une propriété privée **2.** BIBLE péché *m* ■ **forgive us our ~es** pardonne-nous nos offenses.

trespasser ['trespəsəʳ] *n* **1.** LAW intrus *m*, - e *f* *(dans une propriété privée)* ■ **'~s will be prosecuted'** 'défense d'entrer sous peine de poursuites' **2.** BIBLE pécheur *m*, - eresse *f*.

tress [tres] *n lit* **a ~ (of hair)** une mèche OR une boucle de cheveux ■ **her golden ~es** sa blonde chevelure.

trestle ['tresl] *n* **1.** [for table] tréteau *m* **2.** CONSTR chevalet *m*.

trestle table *n* table *f* à tréteaux.

triad ['traɪæd] *n* [gen] triade *f* ■ MUS accord *m* parfait.

triage ['tri:ɑ:ʒ] *n* MED triage *m (des malades, des blessés)*.

trial ['traɪəl] ◇ *n* **1.** LAW procès *m* ■ **he pleaded guilty at the ~** il a plaidé coupable à son procès OR devant le tribunal ■ **to be** OR **to go on ~ for sthg, to stand ~ for sthg** passer en jugement OR en justice pour qqch ■ **he was put on** OR **sent for ~ for murder** il a été jugé pour meurtre ■ **to bring sb to ~** faire passer OR traduire qqn en justice ■ **his case comes up for ~ in September** son affaire passe en jugement en septembre ■ **~ by jury** jugement *m* par jury **2.** [test] essai *m* ■ **to give sthg a ~** mettre qqch à l'essai, essayer qqch ■ **to be on ~** être à l'essai ■ **it was a ~ of strength** c'était une épreuve de force ▶ **by ~ and error** par tâtonnements, par essais et erreurs ■ **it was just ~ and error** ce n'était qu'une suite d'approximations **3.** [hardship, adversity] épreuve *f* ■ **the ~s of married life** les vicissitudes de la vie conjugale ■ **~s and tribulations** tribulations *fpl* ‖ [person] : **he's always been a ~ to his parents** il a toujours donné du souci à ses parents.
◇ *adj* **1.** [test - flight] d'essai ; [- marriage] à l'essai ■ **on a ~ basis** à titre d'essai ■ **for a ~ period** pendant une période d'essai ▶ **~ balloon** *liter & fig* ballon *m* d'essai **2.** *US* LAW : **~ attorney** OR **lawyer** avocat *m* ■ **~ court** tribunal *m* de première instance ■ **~ judge** ≃ juge *m* d'instance ■ **~ jury** jury *m*.
◆ **trials** *npl* [competition] concours *m* ■ [for selection - match] match *m* de sélection ; [- race] épreuve *f* de sélection.

trial balance *n* FIN balance *f* d'inventaire.

trial run *n* essai *m* ■ **to give sthg a ~** essayer qqch, faire un essai avec qqch.

trial-size(d) *adj* [pack, box] d'essai.

triangle ['traɪæŋgl] *n* **1.** GEOM triangle *m* ■ *US* [set square] équerre *f* **2.** MUS triangle *m*.

triangular [traɪ'æŋgjʊləʳ] *adj* triangulaire.

triangulate [traɪ'æŋgjʊleɪt] *vt* **1.** GEOM diviser en triangles **2.** GEOG [region] trianguler.

triangulation station *n* point *m* géodésique.

Triassic [traɪ'æsɪk] ◇ *n* trias *m*.
◇ *adj* triasique.

triathlon [traɪ'æθlɒn] *n* triathlon *m*.

tribal ['traɪbl] *adj* [games, rites, warfare] tribal ■ [loyalty] à la tribu.

tribalism ['traɪbəlɪzm] *n* tribalisme *m*.

tribe [traɪb] *n* **1.** HIST, SOCIOL & ZOOL tribu *f* **2.** *inf fig* tribu *f*, smala *f*.

tribesman ['traɪbzmən] (*pl* **tribesmen** [-mən]) *n* membre *m* d'une tribu ■ [of particular tribe] membre *m* de la tribu.

triboelectricity ['traɪbəʊɪlek'trɪsətɪ] *n* tribo-électricité *f*.

tribrach ['trɪbræk] *n* LIT tribraque *m*.

tribulation [ˌtrɪbjʊ'leɪʃn] *n lit* affliction *f lit*, malheur *m*.

tribunal [traɪ'bju:nl] *n* [gen - LAW] tribunal *m* ▶ **~ of inquiry** commission *f* d'enquête ■ **military ~** tribunal militaire.

tribune ['trɪbju:n] *n* **1.** ANTIQ tribun *m* **2.** [platform] tribune *f* **3.** [defender] tribun *m*.

tributary ['trɪbjʊtrɪ] (*pl* **tributaries**) ◇ *n* **1.** [ruler, state] tributaire *m* **2.** GEOG [stream] affluent *m*.
◇ *adj* tributaire.

tribute ['trɪbju:t] *n* **1.** [mark of respect] hommage *m* ■ **to pay ~ to sb** rendre hommage à qqn **2.** [indication of efficiency] témoignage *m* ■ **it is a ~ to their organizational skills that everything went so smoothly** si tout a si bien marché, c'est grâce à leurs qualités d'organisateurs **3.** HIST & POL tribut *m*.

trice [traɪs] ◇ *n* [moment] : **in a ~** en un clin d'œil, en un rien de temps.
◇ *vt* NAUT [sail] hisser.

tricentennial [ˌtraɪsen'tenjəl] ◇ *n* tricentenaire *m*.
◇ *adj* tricentenaire ■ [celebrations] du tricentenaire.

triceps ['traɪseps] (*pl* **tricepses** [-sɪz]) *n* triceps *m*.

trichloride [traɪ'klɔ:raɪd] *n* trichlorure *m*.

trichology [trɪ'kɒlədʒɪ] *n* trichologie *f*.

trichromatic [ˌtraɪkrəʊ'mætɪk] *adj* trichrome.

trick [trɪk] ◇ *n* **1.** [deception, ruse] ruse *f*, astuce *f* ■ [stratagem] stratagème *m* ■ **a ~ of the light** un effet d'optique
2. [joke, prank] tour *m*, farce *f*, blague *f* ■ **to play a ~ on sb** faire une farce OR jouer un tour à qqn ■ **what a dirty** OR **mean** OR **nasty ~ to play!** quel sale tour! ▶ **"~ or treat"** "des bonbons ou une farce" *(phrase rituelle des enfants déguisés qui font la quête la veille de la fête de Halloween)*
3. *(usu pl)* [silly behaviour] bêtise *f* ■ **he's up to his old ~s again** il fait encore des siennes
4. [knack] truc *m*, astuce *f* ■ [in conjuring, performance] tour *m* ■ **there, that should do the ~** voilà, ça fera l'affaire ■ **he knows a ~ or two** il a plus d'un tour dans son sac, c'est un malin ▶ **it's one of the ~s of the trade** c'est une vieille ficelle OR un truc du métier
5. [habit] habitude *f*, manie *f* ■ [particularity] particularité *f* ■ [gift] don *m* ■ [mannerism] manie *f*, tic *m*
6. [in card games] pli *m*, levée *f* ■ **to make** OR **to take a ~** faire un pli OR une levée
7. △ *US* [prostitute's client] micheton△ *m*
8. NAUT tour *m* de barre
9. *phr* **how's ~ s?** *inf* comment va?, quoi de neuf ?
◇ *adj* **1.** [for jokes] d'attrape, faux, fausse *f*, de farces et attrapes
2. [deceptive - lighting] truqué ■ **~ photograph** photo *f* truquée ■ **~ photography** truquage *m* photographique ■ **~ question** question-piège *f*
3. *US* [weak - knee] faible ; [- leg] boîteux.
◇ *vt* [deceive] tromper, rouler ■ [swindle] escroquer ■ [catch out] attraper ■ **you've been ~ed!** vous vous êtes fait rouler! ■ **I was ~ed into leaving** on a manœuvré pour me faire partir ■ **she was ~ed out of her inheritance** on lui a escroqué son héritage.
◆ **trick out, trick up** *vt sep lit* parer.

trick cyclist *n* **1.** [in circus] cycliste *m* acrobate **2.**△ *UK pej* [psychiatrist] psy *mf*.

trickery ['trɪkərɪ] *n* ruse *f*, supercherie *f* ■ **through** OR **by ~** par la ruse.

trickle ['trɪkl] <> *vi* **1.** [liquid] dégoutter, tomber en un (mince) filet ▪ **rainwater ~d from the gutters** l'eau de pluie coulait peu à peu des gouttières ▪ **tears ~d down his face** les larmes coulaient *OR* dégoulinaient sur son visage **2.** *fig* **information began to ~ out from behind enemy lines** l'information commença à filtrer depuis l'arrière des lignes ennemies ▪ **cars began to ~ over the border** la circulation a repris progressivement à la frontière ▪ **the ball ~d into the goal** le ballon roula tranquillement dans les buts.
<> *vt* **1.** [liquid] faire couler goutte à goutte ▪ **he ~d a few drops of milk into the flour** il a versé quelques gouttes de lait dans la farine **2.** [sand, salt] faire glisser *OR* couler.
<> *n* **1.** [liquid] filet *m* ▪ **there was only a ~ of water from the tap** un maigre filet d'eau coulait du robinet **2.** *fig* **a ~ of applications began to come in** les candidatures commencèrent à arriver au compte-gouttes ▪ **there was only a ~ of visitors** il n'y avait que quelques rares visiteurs, les visiteurs étaient rares.
◆ **trickle away** *vi insep* **1.** [liquid] s'écouler lentement **2.** *fig* [money, savings] disparaître petit à petit ▪ [crowd] se disperser petit à petit ▪ [people] s'en aller progressivement.
◆ **trickle in** *vi insep* **1.** [rain] entrer goutte à goutte **2.** [spectators] entrer par petits groupes **3.** *fig* **offers of help began to ~ in** quelques offres d'aide commençaient à arriver ▪ **information on the disaster only ~d in at first** au début les informations sur le désastre arrivaient au compte-gouttes.

trickle charger *n* chargeur *m* à régime lent.

trickle-down *adj* : **~ economics** *théorie selon laquelle le bien-être des riches finit par profiter aux classes sociales défavorisées.*

trickster ['trɪkstəʳ] *n* [swindler] filou *m*, escroc *m*.

tricksy ['trɪksɪ] (*comp* **tricksier**, *superl* **tricksiest**) *adj* **1.** [mischievous] espiègle **2.** [sly] malin, - igne *f*, rusé.

tricky ['trɪkɪ] (*comp* **trickier**, *superl* **trickiest**) *adj* **1.** [complex, delicate - job, situation, negotiations] difficile, délicat ; [- problem] épineux, difficile ▪ **the path is ~ in places** le chemin est difficile *OR* peu praticable par endroits **2.** [sly - person] rusé, fourbe.

tricolour *UK*, **tricolor** *US* ['trɪkələʳ] *n* drapeau *m* tricolore.

tricorn ['traɪkɔːn] <> *adj* à trois cornes.
<> *n* tricorne *m*.

tricuspid [traɪ'kʌspɪd] *adj* tricuspide.

tricycle ['traɪsɪkl] <> *n* tricycle *m*.
<> *vi* faire du tricycle.

trident ['traɪdnt] *n* trident *m*.

tried [traɪd] *pt* & *pp* ▻ **try**.

tried-and-tested *adj* qui a fait ses preuves.

triennial [traɪ'enjəl] <> *adj* triennal ▪ BOT trisannuel.
<> *n* **1.** [anniversary] troisième anniversaire *m* **2.** [period] période *f* de trois ans **3.** BOT plante *f* trisannuelle.

trier ['traɪəʳ] *n* : **he's a real ~** il ne se laisse jamais décourager.

Trier ['trɪəʳ] *pr n* Trèves.

trifle ['traɪfl] *n* **1.** [unimportant thing, small amount] bagatelle *f*, broutille *f*, rien *m* ▪ **they quarrel over ~s** il se disputent pour un oui pour un non *OR* pour un rien ▪ **£100 is a mere ~ to them** 100 livres, c'est peu de chose pour eux **2.** CULIN ≃ charlotte *f*.
◆ **a trifle** *adv phr* un peu, un tantinet ▪ **it's a ~ easier than it was** c'est un peu *OR* un rien plus facile qu'avant.
◆ **trifle with** *vt insep* : **to ~ with sb's affections** jouer avec les sentiments de qqn ▪ **he's not a man to be ~d with** avec lui, on ne plaisante pas.

trifling ['traɪflɪŋ] *adj* insignifiant.

trifocal [traɪ'fəʊkl] <> *adj* [lens] à triple foyer.
<> *n* [lens] lentille *f* à triple foyer.

trifoliate [traɪ'fəʊlɪɪt] *adj* à trois feuilles ▪ BOT trifolié.

triforium [traɪ'fɔːrɪəm] (*pl* **triforia** [-rɪə]) *n* triforium *m*.

triform ['traɪfɔːm] *adj* en *OR* à trois parties.

trigger ['trɪgəʳ] <> *n* **1.** [in gun] gâchette *f*, détente *f* ▪ **to pull** *OR* **to squeeze the ~** appuyer sur la gâchette ▪ **he's fast** *OR* **quick on the ~** *liter* il tire vite ; *fig* il réagit vite **2.** *fig* [initiator] déclenchement *m* ▪ **the strike was the ~ for nationwide protests** la grève a donné le signal d'un mouvement de contestation dans tout le pays.
<> *vt* [mechanism, explosion, reaction] déclencher ▪ [revolution, protest] déclencher, provoquer, soulever.
◆ **trigger off** *vt sep* = **trigger** (*vt*).

trigger finger *n* index *m (avec lequel on appuie sur la gâchette).*

trigger-happy *adj inf* [individual] qui a la gâchette facile ▪ [country] prêt à déclencher la guerre pour un rien, belliqueux.

trigonometry [ˌtrɪgə'nɒmətrɪ] *n* trigonométrie *f*.

trig point *n* station *f* géodésique.

trike [traɪk] *n inf* tricycle *m*.

trilby ['trɪlbɪ] *n UK* **~ (hat)** (chapeau *m* en) feutre *m*.

trilingual [traɪ'lɪŋgwəl] *adj* trilingue.

trill [trɪl] <> *n* MUS & ORNITH trille *m* ▪ LING consonne *f* roulée.
<> *vi* triller, faire des trilles.
<> *vt* **1.** [note, word] triller **2.** [consonant] rouler.

trillion ['trɪljən] *n UK* trillion *m* ▪ *US* billion *m*.

trilogy ['trɪlədʒɪ] (*pl* **trilogies**) *n* trilogie *f*.

trim [trɪm] <> *adj* (*comp* **trimmer**, *superl* **trimmest**) **1.** [neat - appearance] net, soigné ; [- person] d'apparence soignée ; [- garden, flowerbed] bien tenu, bien entretenu ; [- ship] en bon ordre **2.** [svelte - figure] svelte, mince **3.** [fit] en bonne santé, en forme.
<> *vt* (*pret* & *pp* **trimmed**, *cont* **trimming**) **1.** [cut - roses] tailler, couper ; [- hair, nails] couper ; [- beard] tailler ; [- candle wick] tailler, moucher ; [- paper, photo] rogner ▪ **I had my hair trimmed** je me suis fait raccourcir les cheveux **2.** [edge] orner, garnir ▪ **the collar was trimmed with lace** le col était bordé *OR* garni de dentelle ▪ [decorate] : **we trimmed the Christmas tree with tinsel** on a décoré le sapin de Noël avec des guirlandes **3.** AERON & NAUT [plane, ship] équilibrer ▪ [sails] régler ▪ **to ~ one's sails** *fig* réviser son jugement **4.** [cut back - budget, costs] réduire, limiter.
<> *n* **1.** [neat state] ordre *m*, bon état *m* ▪ **to be in good ~** être en bon état *OR* ordre **2.** [fitness] forme *f* ▪ **to get in** *OR* **into ~** se remettre en forme **3.** [cut] coupe *f*, taille *f* ▪ **she gave the hedge a ~** elle a taillé la haie ▪ **to have a ~** [at hairdresser's] se faire raccourcir les cheveux ▪ **just a ~, please** simplement rafraîchi, s'il vous plaît **4.** (*U*) [moulding, decoration] moulures *fpl* ▪ [on car] aménagement *m* intérieur, finitions *fpl* intérieures ▪ [on dress] garniture *f* ▪ *US* [in shop window] composition *f* d'étalage **5.** NAUT [of sails] orientation *f*, réglage *m* **6.** CIN coupe *f*.
◆ **trim down** *vt sep* **1.** [wick] tailler, moucher **2.** [budget, costs] réduire.
◆ **trim off** *vt sep* [edge] enlever, couper ▪ [hair] couper ▪ [branch] tailler ▪ [jagged edges] ébarber.

trimaran ['traɪməræn] *n* trimaran *m*.

trimester [traɪ'mestəʳ] *n* **1.** *US* trimestre *m* **2.** [gen] trois mois *mpl*.

trimmer ['trɪməʳ] *n* **1.** CONSTR linçoir *m*, linsoir *m* **2.** [for timber] trancheuse *f (pour le bois)* ▪ **(hedge) ~** taille-haie *m* **3.** ELECTRON trimmer *m*, condensateur *m* ajustable **4.** *pej* [person] opportuniste *mf*.

trimming ['trɪmɪŋ] *n* **1.** SEW parement *m* ▪ [lace, ribbon] passement *m* **2.** CULIN garniture *f*, accompagnement *m* **3.** [accessory] accessoire *m*.
◆ **trimmings** *npl* [scraps] chutes *fpl*, rognures *fpl*.

Trinidad ['trɪnɪdæd] *pr n* (l'île *f* de) la Trinité ▪ **in ~** à la Trinité.

Trinidad and Tobago [-tə'beɪgəʊ] *pr n* Trinité-et-Tobago ▪ **in ~** à Trinité-et-Tobago.

Trinidadian [ˌtrɪnɪ'dædɪən] ◇ *n* Trinidadien *m*, - enne *f*, habitant *m*, - e *f* de la Trinité.
◇ *adj* trinidadien, de la Trinité.

trinitroglycerin [traɪˌnaɪtrəʊ'glɪsərɪ:n] *n* nitroglycérine *f*.

trinity ['trɪnɪtɪ] (*pl* **trinities**) *n* **fml** & **lit** trio *m*, groupe *m* de trois.
◆ **Trinity** *n* RELIG **1.** [union] : **the Trinity** la Trinité **2.** [feast] : **Trinity (Sunday)** (la fête de) la Trinité.

trinket ['trɪŋkɪt] *n* [bauble] bibelot *m*, babiole *f* ■ [jewel] colifichet *m* ■ [on bracelet] breloque *f*.

trio ['tri:əʊ] (*pl* **trios**) *n* **1.** MUS trio *m* (*morceau*) **2.** [group] trio *m*, groupe *m* de trois ■ MUS trio (*joueurs*).

trip [trɪp] (*pret* & *pp* **tripped**, *cont* **tripping**) ◇ *n* **1.** [journey] voyage *m* ■ **to go on a ~** partir OR aller en voyage ■ **we went on a long bus ~** on a fait un long voyage en bus ■ **I had to make three ~s into town** j'ai dû aller trois fois en ville OR faire trois voyages en ville ■ **to make a ~ to the dentist's** aller chez le dentiste **2.** [excursion] promenade *f*, excursion *f* ■ **she took the children on a ~ to the seaside** elle a emmené les enfants en promenade au bord de la mer ■ [outing] promenade *f*, sortie *f* ■ **school ~** sortie scolaire **3.**△ *drug sl* trip△ *m* ■ **to have a bad ~** faire un mauvais trip OR voyage ■ *fig* [experience] : **he seems to be on some kind of nostalgia ~** il semble être en pleine crise de nostalgie.
◇ *vt* **1.** [person - make stumble] faire trébucher ; [- make fall] faire tomber ■ [intentionally] faire un croche-pied OR un croc-en-jambe à **2.** [switch, alarm] déclencher **3.** *phr* **to ~ the light fantastic** *hum* danser.
◇ *vi* **1.** [stumble] trébucher ■ **she tripped on** OR **over the wire** elle s'est pris le pied dans le fil ■ **I tripped on a pile of books** j'ai buté contre OR trébuché sur une pile de livres **2.** [step lightly] : **to ~ in/out** entrer/sortir en sautillant ■ **her name doesn't exactly ~ off the tongue** *fig* son nom n'est pas très facile à prononcer **3.**△ *drug sl* faire un trip ■ **to ~ on acid** faire un trip à l'acide.
◆ **trip over** ◇ *vi insep* trébucher, faire un faux pas.
◇ *vt insep* buter sur OR contre, trébucher sur OR contre.
◆ **trip up** ◇ *vt sep* **1.** [cause to fall] faire trébucher ■ [deliberately] faire un croche-pied à **2.** [trap] désarçonner.
◇ *vi insep* **1.** [fall] trébucher ■ **I tripped up on a stone** j'ai trébuché OR buté contre une pierre **2.** [make a mistake] gaffer, faire une gaffe ■ **I tripped up badly there** là-dessus, j'ai fait une grosse gaffe.

tripartite [ˌtraɪ'pɑ:taɪt] *adj* [division, agreement] tripartite, triparti.

tripe [traɪp] *n* (*U*) **1.** CULIN tripes *fpl* **2.** *UK inf* [nonsense] foutaises *fpl*, bêtises *fpl* ■ **what a load of ~!** quelles foutaises! ■ **the film is utter ~** le film est vraiment nul.

triphammer ['trɪpˌhæmər] *n* marteau *m* à bascule.

triphase ['traɪfeɪz] *adj* ELEC triphasé.

triphthong ['trɪfθɒŋ] *n* triphtongue *f*.

triplane ['traɪpleɪn] *n* triplan *m*.

triple ['trɪpl] ◇ *adj* **1.** [in three parts] triple ■ **the organization serves a ~ purpose** le but de l'organisation est triple **2.** [treble] triple ■ **~ the usual amount** trois fois la dose habituelle.
◇ *n* triple *m*.
◇ *vi* & *vt* tripler.

Triple Alliance *pr n* HIST : **the ~** [1668] la Triple Alliance ; [1882-1914] la Triple-Alliance, la Triplice.

triple jump *n* triple saut *m*.

triplet ['trɪplɪt] *n* **1.** [child] triplé *m*, - e *f* **2.** MUS triolet *m* ■ LIT tercet *m*.

triple time *n* : **in ~** à trois temps.

triplex ['trɪpleks] ◇ *adj* [triple] triple.
◇ *n US* [apartment] triplex *m*.

Triplex® ['trɪpleks] *n UK* **~ (glass)** Triplex® *m*, (verre *m*) Sécurit® *m*.

triplicate ◇ *adj* ['trɪplɪkət] en trois exemplaires, en triple exemplaire.
◇ *n* ['trɪplɪkət] **1.** [document] : **in ~** en trois exemplaires, en triple exemplaire **2.** [third copy] triplicata *m*.
◇ *vt* ['trɪplɪkeɪt] multiplier par trois, tripler.

triply ['trɪplɪ] *adv* triplement.

tripod ['traɪpɒd] *n* trépied *m*.

tripos ['traɪpɒs] *n examen de licence (BA) à l'université de Cambridge*.

tripper ['trɪpər] *n UK* [on day trip] excursionniste *mf* ■ [on holiday] vacancier *m*, - ère *f*.

trip recorder *n* AUT compteur *m* journalier, totalisateur *m* partiel.

trip switch *n* interrupteur *m*.

triptych ['trɪptɪk] *n* triptyque *m*.

tripwire ['trɪpwaɪər] *n* fil *m* de détente.

trireme ['traɪri:m] *n* trirème *f*, trière *f*.

trisect [traɪ'sekt] *vt* diviser en trois parties égales.

trite [traɪt] *adj* [theme, picture] banal ■ **he made a ~ remark** il a dit une banalité.

tritium ['trɪtɪəm] *n* tritium *m*.

triton *n* **1.** ['traɪtn] ZOOL triton *m* **2.** ['traɪtɒn] PHYS triton *m*.
◆ **Triton** *pr n* MYTH Triton.

triturate ['trɪtjʊreɪt] *vt* triturer.

triumph ['traɪəmf] ◇ *n* **1.** [jubilation] (sentiment *m* de) triomphe *m* ■ **to return in ~** rentrer triomphalement ■ **she had a look of ~ on her face** elle avait une expression triomphante **2.** [victory] victoire *f*, triomphe *m* ■ [success] triomphe *m*, (grande) réussite *f* ■ **the musical was an absolute ~** la comédie musicale a été OR a fait un véritable triomphe **3.** [in ancient Rome] triomphe *m*.
◇ *vi* triompher ■ **to ~ over difficulties/a disability** triompher des difficultés/d'une infirmité, vaincre les difficultés/une infirmité.

triumphal [traɪ'ʌmfl] *adj* triomphal.

triumphalist [traɪ'ʌmfəlɪst] *adj* triomphaliste.

triumphant [traɪ'ʌmfənt] *adj* [team] victorieux, triomphant ■ [return] triomphal ■ [cheer, smile] de triomphe, triomphant ■ [success] triomphal.

triumphantly [traɪ'ʌmfəntlɪ] *adv* [march] en triomphe, triomphalement ■ [cheer, smile] triomphalement ■ [announce] d'un ton triomphant, triomphalement ■ [look] d'un air triomphant, triomphalement.

triumvirate [traɪ'ʌmvɪrət] *n* triumvirat *m*.

triune ['traɪju:n] *adj* RELIG trin.

trivet ['trɪvɪt] *n* [when cooking] trépied *m*, chevrette *f* ■ [for table] dessous-de-plat *m inv*.

trivia ['trɪvɪə] *npl* [trifles] bagatelles *fpl*, futilités *fpl* ■ [details] détails *mpl*.

trivial ['trɪvɪəl] *adj* **1.** [insignificant - sum, reason] insignifiant, dérisoire ■ **it's only a ~ offence** ce n'est qu'une peccadille, c'est sans gravité **2.** [pointless - discussion, question] sans intérêt, futile **3.** [banal - story] banal.

triviality [ˌtrɪvɪ'ælətɪ] (*pl* **trivialities**) *n* **1.** [of sum] insignifiance *f*, caractère *m* insignifiant ■ [of discussion] insignifiance *f*, caractère *m* oiseux ■ [of film] banalité *f* **2.** [trifle] futilité *f*, bagatelle *f*.

trivialize, ise ['trɪvɪəlaɪz] *vt* [make insignificant] banaliser, dévaloriser.

trochee ['trəʊki:] *n* trochée *m*.

trod [trɒd] *pt* & *pp* ▷ **tread**.

trodden ['trɒdn] *pp* ▷ **tread**.

troglodyte ['trɒglədaɪt] ◇ *n* troglodyte *m*.
◇ *adj* troglodytique.

troilism ['trɔɪlɪzm] *n* triolisme *m*.

Trojan ['trəʊdʒən] ◇ *adj* troyen ▪ **~ work** travail *m* de titan. ◇ *n* Troyen *m*, - enne *f* ▪ **to work like a ~** travailler comme un forçat.

Trojan Horse *n* HIST & *fig* cheval *m* de Troie.

Trojan War *pr n* guerre *f* de Troie.

troll [trəʊl] ◇ *n* [goblin] troll *m*.
◇ *vi* **1.** FISHING pêcher à la traîne **2.** *UK inf* [stroll] se balader.

trolley ['trɒlɪ] (*pl* **trolleys**) *n* **1.** *UK* [handcart] chariot *m* ▪ [two-wheeled] diable *m* ▪ [for child] poussette *f* ▪ [in supermarket] chariot *m*, Caddie® *m* ▪ [in restaurant] chariot *m* ▪ **to be off one's ~** *inf* être cinglé **2.** *UK* [on rails - in mine] wagonnet *m*, benne *f* **3.** [for tram] trolley *m (électrique)* **4.** *US* [tram] tramway *m*, tram *m*.

trolleybus ['trɒlɪbʌs] *n* trolleybus *m*, trolley *m*.

trolley car *n US* tramway *m*, tram *m*.

trolley case *n UK* valise *f* à roulettes.

trollop ['trɒləp] *n dated* & *pej* [prostitute] putain *f* ▪ [slut] souillon *f*.

trombone [trɒm'bəʊn] *n* trombone *m (instrument)*.

trombonist [trɒm'bəʊnɪst] *n* tromboniste *mf*, trombone *m (musicien)*.

troop [tru:p] ◇ *n* [band - of schoolchildren] bande *f*, groupe *m* ; [- of scouts] troupe *f* ; [- of animals] troupe *f* ▪ MIL [of cavalry, artillery] escadron *m*.
◇ *vi* : **to ~ by** *OR* **past** passer en troupe ▪ **to ~ in/out** entrer/sortir en troupe.
◇ *vt UK* MIL : **to ~ the colour** faire le salut au drapeau.
◆ **troops** *npl* [gen - MIL] troupes *fpl*.

troop carrier *n* [ship] transport *m* de troupes ▪ [plane] avion *m* de transport militaire.

trooper ['tru:pər] *n* **1.** [soldier] soldat *m* de cavalerie **2.** *US* & *Australia* [mounted policeman] membre *m* de la police montée ▪ **(state) ~** ≃ gendarme *m* **3.** *UK* MIL [ship] transport *m* de troupes.

trooping ['tru:pɪŋ] *n UK* **~ (of) the colour** salut *m* au drapeau ▪ **Trooping the Colour** *défilé de régiments ayant lieu chaque année le jour officiel de l'anniversaire de la reine d'Angleterre.*

troopship ['tru:pʃɪp] *n* navire *m* de transport.

trophy ['trəʊfɪ] (*pl* **trophies**) *n* trophée *m*.

tropic ['trɒpɪk] ◇ *n* tropique *m* ▪ **the Tropic of Capricorn/Cancer** le tropique du Capricorne/du Cancer.
◇ *adj lit* = **tropical**.
◆ **tropics** *npl* : **the ~s** les tropiques ▪ **in the ~s** sous les tropiques.

tropical ['trɒpɪkl] *adj* [region] des tropiques, tropical ▪ [weather, forest, medicine] tropical.

trot [trɒt] (*pret* & *pp* **trotted**, *cont* **trotting**) ◇ *n* **1.** [of horse] trot *m* ▪ **to go at a ~** aller au trot, trotter ▪ [of person] : **he went off at a ~** il est parti au pas de course **2.** [ride] promenade *f* à cheval ▪ [run] *inf* petite course *f* ▶ **on the ~** *UK inf* [busy] affairé ; [in succession] d'affilée, de suite.
◇ *vi* **1.** [horse, rider] trotter ▪ **he trotted up to us** il est venu vers nous au trot **2.** [on foot] : **to ~ in/out/past** entrer/sortir/passer en courant.
◇ *vt* [horse] faire trotter.
◆ **trot along** *vi insep* **1.** [horse] trotter, aller au trot **2.** *inf* [person] partir ▪ **~ along now** sauve-toi maintenant.
◆ **trot away** *vi insep* **1.** [horse] partir au trot **2.** *inf* [person] partir au pas de course.
◆ **trot out** *vt sep UK inf* [excuse, information] débiter *pej* ▪ [story, list] débiter *pej*, réciter *pej*.
◆ **trots** *npl UK inf* diarrhée *f* ▪ **to have the ~s** avoir la courante.

troth [trəʊθ] *n arch* **by my ~!** ma foi!, pardieu! *arch*.

Trotsky ['trɒtskɪ] *pr n* Trotski.

Trotskyist ['trɒtskɪɪst] ◇ *adj* trotskiste.
◇ *n* trotskiste *mf*.

Trotskyite ['trɒtskɪaɪt] ◇ *adj* trotskiste.
◇ *n* trotskiste *mf*.

trotter ['trɒtər] *n* **1.** [horse] trotteur *m*, - euse *f* **2.** CULIN : **pig's/sheep's ~s** pieds *mpl* de porc/de mouton.

troubadour ['tru:bədɔ:r] *n* troubadour *m*.

trouble ['trʌbl] ◇ *n* **1.** *(U)* [conflict - esp with authority] ennuis *mpl*, problèmes *mpl* ▪ [discord] discorde *f* ▪ **to be in ~** avoir des ennuis ▪ **you're really in ~ now!** tu es dans de beaux draps *OR* te voilà bien maintenant! ▪ **I've never been in ~ with the police** je n'ai jamais eu d'ennuis *OR* d'histoires avec la police ▪ **to get into ~** s'attirer des ennuis, se faire attraper ▪ **he got into ~ for stealing apples** il s'est fait attraper pour avoir volé des pommes ▪ **he got his friends into ~** il a causé des ennuis à ses amis ▪ **to get sb out of ~** tirer qqn d'affaire ▪ **he's just looking** *OR* **asking for ~** il cherche les ennuis ▪ **there's ~ brewing** ça sent le roussi ▪ **she caused a lot of ~ between them** elle a semé la discorde entre eux ▪ **this means ~** ça va mal se passer
2. *(U)* [difficulties, problems] difficultés *fpl*, ennuis *mpl*, mal *m* ▪ **to make** *OR* **to create ~ for sb** causer des ennuis à qqn ▪ **he's given his parents a lot of ~** [hard time] il a donné du fil à retordre à ses parents ; [worry] il a donné beaucoup de soucis à ses parents ▪ **the baby hardly gives me any ~** le bébé ne me donne pratiquement aucun mal ▪ **to have ~ (in) doing sthg** avoir du mal *OR* des difficultés à faire qqch ▪ **to be in/to get into ~** [climber, swimmer, business] être/se trouver en difficulté ▶ **to get a girl into ~** *UK euph* mettre une fille dans une position intéressante
3. [inconvenience, bother] mal *m*, peine *f* ▪ **to go to a lot of ~ to do** *OR* **doing sthg** se donner beaucoup de mal *OR* de peine pour faire qqch ▪ **you shouldn't have gone to all this ~** il ne fallait pas vous donner tout ce mal *OR* tant de peine ▪ **to put sb to ~** donner du mal à qqn, déranger qqn ▪ **he didn't even take the ~ to read the instructions** il ne s'est même pas donné *OR* il n'a même pas pris la peine de lire les instructions ▪ **I don't want to be any ~** je ne veux pas vous déranger ▪ **it's no ~ (at all)** cela ne me dérange pas (du tout) ▪ **nothing is too much ~ for her** elle se donne vraiment beaucoup de mal ▪ **it's not worth the ~, it's more ~ than it's worth** cela n'en vaut pas la peine, le jeu n'en vaut pas la chandelle
4. [drawback] problème *m*, défaut *m* ▪ **the ~ with him is that he's too proud** le problème avec lui, c'est qu'il est trop fier ▪ **that's the ~** c'est ça l'ennui
5. *(U)* [mechanical failure] ennuis *mpl*, problèmes *mpl* ▪ **I'm having a bit of engine ~** j'ai des problèmes de moteur ▪ **have you found out what the ~ is?** avez-vous trouvé d'où vient la panne? ▪ **what seems to be the ~?** qu'est-ce qui ne va pas?
6. [worry, woe] ennui *m*, souci *m*, problème *m* ▪ **money ~s** ennuis d'argent ▪ **at last your ~s are over** enfin vos soucis sont terminés ▶ **here comes ~!** *inf* tiens, voilà les ennuis qui arrivent!
7. *(U)* [friction] troubles *mpl*, conflits *mpl* ▪ [disorder, disturbance] troubles *mpl*, désordres *mpl* ▪ **the ~ began when the police arrived** l'agitation a commencé quand la police est arrivée ▪ **industrial** *OR* **labour ~s** conflits sociaux
8. *(U)* MED ennuis *mpl*, problèmes *mpl* ▪ **I have kidney/back ~** j'ai des ennuis rénaux/des problèmes de dos.
◇ *vt* **1.** [worry] inquiéter ▪ [upset] troubler ▪ **what ~s me is that we've had no news** ce qui m'inquiète, c'est que nous n'avons pas eu de nouvelles ▪ **he didn't want to ~ her with bad news** il ne voulait pas l'inquiéter en lui annonçant de mauvaises nouvelles ▪ **nothing seems to ~ him** il ne s'en fait jamais, il ne se fait jamais de souci
2. [cause pain to] gêner ▪ **his back is troubling him** il a des problèmes de dos
3. [bother, disturb] déranger ▪ **I won't ~ you with the details just now** je vous ferai grâce des *OR* épargnerai les détails pour l'instant ▪ **he didn't even ~ himself to phone** il ne s'est même pas donné la peine de téléphoner ▪ **don't ~ yourself!** *liter* ne vous dérangez *OR* tracassez pas! ; *iron* ne vous dérangez surtout pas!
4. [in polite phrases] déranger ▪ **can I ~ you to open the window?** est-ce que je peux vous demander d'ouvrir la fenêtre? ▪ **may I ~ you for a light/the salt?** puis-je vous demander du feu/le sel? ▪ **I'll ~ you to be more polite next time!** *UK* [in reproach] vous allez me faire le plaisir d'être plus poli la prochaine fois!
5. *lit* [disturb - water] troubler.

◇ *vi* **1.** [bother] se déranger
2. [worry] se faire du souci, s'en faire.
◆ **Troubles** *npl* HIST : **the Troubles** *le conflit politique en Irlande du Nord.*

troubled ['trʌbld] *adj* **1.** [worried - mind, look] inquiet, - ète *f*, préoccupé ▪ **he seems ~ about something** il semble préoccupé par quelque chose **2.** [disturbed - sleep, night, breathing] agité ; [- water] troublé ▪ [turbulent - marriage, life] agité, mouvementé ▪ **we live in ~ times** nous vivons une époque troublée *OR* agitée.

trouble-free *adj* [journey, equipment] sans problème, sans histoires ▪ [period of time, visit] sans histoires ▪ [life] sans soucis, sans histoires ▪ [industry] sans grèves.

troublemaker ['trʌbl,meɪkəʳ] *n* provocateur *m*, - trice *f*.

troubleshoot ['trʌbl,ʃu:t] *vi* **1.** [overseer, envoy] régler un problème **2.** [mechanic] localiser une panne.

troubleshooter ['trʌbl,ʃu:təʳ] *n* **1.** [in crisis] expert *m (appelé en cas de crise)* ▪ INDUST & POL [in conflict] médiateur *m*, - trice *f* **2.** [mechanic] dépanneur *m*, - euse *f*.

troublesome ['trʌblsəm] *adj* **1.** [annoying - person, cough] gênant, pénible **2.** [difficult - situation] difficile ; [- request] gênant, embarrassant ; [- job] difficile, pénible.

trouble spot *n* point *m* chaud, zone *f* de conflit.

trough [trɒf] *n* **1.** [for animals - drinking] abreuvoir *m* ; [- eating] auge *f* **2.** [depression - in land] dépression *f* ; [- between waves] creux *m* **3.** METEOR dépression *f*, zone *f* dépressionnaire **4.** [on graph, in cycle] creux *m* ▪ FIN creux *m*, dépression *f* **5.** [gutter] gouttière *f* ▪ [channel] chenal *m*.

trounce [traʊns] *vt* [defeat] écraser, battre à plate couture *OR* plates coutures.

trouncing ['traʊnsɪŋ] *n* : **we gave Rovers a real ~** SPORT nous avons écrasé les Rovers.

troupe [tru:p] *n* THEAT troupe *f*.

trouper ['tru:pəʳ] *n* acteur *m*, - trice *f (de théâtre)* ▪ **he's a real ~** *inf fig* c'est un vieux de la vieille.

trouser ['traʊzəʳ] *comp UK* de pantalon.

trouser press *n UK* presse *f* à pantalons.

trousers ['traʊzəz] *npl UK* pantalon *m* ▪ **(a pair of) ~** un pantalon ▪ **she wears the ~** *fig* c'est elle qui porte la culotte.

trouser suit *n UK* tailleur-pantalon *m*.

trousseau ['tru:səʊ] (*pl* **trousseaus** *OR pl* **trousseaux** [-əʊz]) *n* trousseau *m (de jeune mariée)*.

trout [traʊt] (*pl inv OR pl* **trouts**) *n* truite *f* ▪ **~ fishing** la pêche à la truite.

trove [trəʊv] ▷ **treasure trove**.

trowel ['traʊəl] *n* [for garden] déplantoir *m* ▪ [for cement, plaster] truelle *f*.

troy [trɔɪ] *n* : **~ (weight)** troy *m*, troy-weight *m*.

Troy [trɔɪ] *pr n* Troie.

truancy ['tru:ənsɪ] *n* absentéisme *m* (scolaire).

truant ['tru:ənt] ◇ *n* élève *mf* absentéiste ▪ **to play ~** faire l'école buissonnière.
◇ *vi* ADMIN manquer les cours.

truce [tru:s] *n* trêve *f* ▪ **to call a ~** *liter* conclure *OR* établir une trêve ; *fig* faire la paix.

truck [trʌk] ◇ *n* **1.** *esp US* [lorry] camion *m* **2.** *UK* [open lorry] camion *m* à plate-forme ▪ [van] camionnette *f* **3.** *UK* RAIL wagon *m* ouvert, truck *m* **4.** *(U)* [dealings] : **to have no ~ with sb/sthg** refuser d'avoir quoi que ce soit à voir avec qqn/qqch ▪ **they refused to have any ~ with him** ils ont refusé d'avoir affaire à lui **5.** *(U) US* [produce] produits *mpl* maraîchers **6.** [barter] troc *m*, échange *m* **7.** *UK* [payment] paiement *m* en nature.
◇ *vt US* [goods, animals] camionner, transporter par camion.
◇ *vi US* aller *OR* rouler en camion.

truckage ['trʌkɪdʒ] *n US* camionnage *m*.

truck driver *n esp US* camionneur *m*, (chauffeur *m*) routier *m*, -ère *f*.

trucker ['trʌkəʳ] *n US* **1.** [driver] (chauffeur *m*) routier *m*, camionneur *m* **2.** AGRIC maraîcher *m*, - ère *f*.

truck farm *n US* jardin *m* maraîcher.

trucking ['trʌkɪŋ] *n US* camionnage *m*, transport *m* par camion.

truckload ['trʌkləʊd] *n* **1.** *esp US* [lorryload] cargaison *f (d'un camion)* ▪ **a ~ of soldiers** un camion de soldats ▪ **medical aid arrived by the ~** l'aide médicale arriva par camions entiers **2.** *US inf fig* **a ~ of** un tas de.

truck stop *n US* (relais *m*) routier *m*.

truculence ['trʌkjʊləns] *n* agressivité *f*, brutalité *f*.

truculent ['trʌkjʊlənt] *adj* belliqueux, agressif.

truculently ['trʌkjʊləntlɪ] *adv* agressivement.

trudge [trʌdʒ] ◇ *vi* marcher péniblement *OR* en traînant les pieds ▪ **we ~d wearily along the path** nous avons marché *OR* avancé péniblement le long du chemin ▪ **we ~d from shop to shop** nous nous sommes traînés de magasin en magasin.
◇ *vt* : **to ~ the streets** se traîner de rue en rue.
◇ *n* marche *f* pénible ▪ **they began the long ~ up the hill** ils ont entrepris la longue ascension de la colline.

true [tru:] ◇ *adj* **1.** [factual - statement, story] vrai, véridique ; [- account, description] exact, véridique ▪ **is it ~ that they were lovers?** c'est vrai qu'ils étaient amants? ▪ **can it be ~?** est-ce possible? ▪ **the same is *OR* holds ~ for many people** il en va de même pour *OR* c'est vrai aussi pour beaucoup de gens ▪ **to come ~** [dream] se réaliser ; [prophecy] se réaliser, se vérifier ▸ **too ~!** c'est vrai ce que vous dites!, ah oui alors! ▪ **he's so stingy, it's not ~!** *inf* ce n'est pas possible d'être aussi radin!
2. [precise, exact - measurement] exact, juste ▪ MUS [- note] juste ; [- copy] conforme ▪ **he's not a genius in the ~ sense of the word** ce n'est pas un génie au vrai sens du terme ▪ **his aim is ~** *liter & fig* il vise juste
3. [genuine - friendship, feelings] vrai, véritable, authentique ; [- friend, love] vrai, véritable ▪ [real, actual - nature, motive] réel, véritable ▪ **she was a ~ democrat** c'était une démocrate dans l'âme ▪ **a story of ~ love** l'histoire d'un grand amour ▪ **it's not a ~ amphibian** ce n'est pas vraiment un amphibie ▪ **spoken like a ~ soldier!** voilà qui est bien dit!
4. [faithful - lover] fidèle ; [- portrait] fidèle, exact ▪ **to be ~ to sb** être fidèle à *OR* loyal envers qqn ▪ **to be ~ to one's ideals** être fidèle à ses idéaux ▪ **she was ~ to her word** elle a tenu parole ▪ **the painting is very ~ to life** le tableau est très ressemblant ▪ **to be *OR* to run ~ to type** être typique ▪ **~ to form, he arrived half an hour late** fidèle à son habitude *OR* comme à son habitude, il est arrivé avec une demi-heure de retard.
◇ *adv* **1.** [aim, shoot, sing] juste ▪ **to breed ~** BIOL se reproduire dans la conformité de l'espèce ▪ **it doesn't ring ~** cela sonne faux
2. *lit* [truly] : **tell me ~** dites-moi la vérité.
◆ **out of true** *adj phr UK* [wall] hors d'aplomb ▪ [beam] tordu ▪ [wheel] voilé ▪ [axle] faussé ▪ [painting] de travers.
◆ **true up** *vt sep* aligner, ajuster.

true-blue *adj* **1.** [loyal] loyal **2.** *esp UK* POL conservateur, tory ▪ **~ Tories** des fidèles du parti conservateur.

trueborn ['tru:,bɔ:n] *adj* véritable, authentique.

truebred ['tru:,bred] *adj* de race pure.

true-life *adj* vrai, vécu.

truelove ['tru:lʌv] *n lit* bien-aimé *m*, - e *f*.

true north *n* vrai nord *m*, nord géographique.

truffle ['trʌfl] *n* truffe *f*.

truism ['tru:ɪzm] *n* truisme *m*, lapalissade *f*.

truly ['tru:lɪ] *adv* **1.** *fml* [really] vraiment, réellement ▪ **I'm ~ sorry for what I've done** je suis vraiment navré de ce que j'ai fait ▪ **~ it was the last thing on my mind** je vous assure que j'étais loin de penser à ça **2.** [as intensifier] vraiment, absolument ▪ **it was a ~ awful film** c'était absolument épouvantable comme film **3.** [in letterwriting] : **yours ~, Kathryn Schmidt** *US* je vous prie d'agréer, Monsieur *OR* Madame, l'expression de mes sentiments respectueux, Kathryn Schmidt ‖ [myself] : **yours ~** *inf hum* votre humble serviteur.

trump [trʌmp] <> *n* **1.** [in cards] atout *m* ▪ *fig* atout *m*, carte *f* maîtresse ▪ **what's ~s?** quel est l'atout? ▪ **diamonds are ~s** (c'est) atout carreau ➊ **to hold all the ~s** avoir tous les atouts dans son jeu *OR* en main ▪ **to turn up** *OR* **to come up ~s** *UK* sauver la mise **2.** BIBLE [trumpet] trompette *f*.
<> *vt* **1.** [card] couper, jouer atout sur ▪ [trick] remporter avec un atout **2.** [outdo - remark, action] renchérir sur.

trump card *n liter* & *fig* atout *m* ▪ **to play one's ~** *fig* jouer ses atouts.

trumped-up [trʌmpt-] *adj* [story, charge] inventé de toutes pièces.

trumpery ['trʌmpərɪ] (*pl* **trumperies**) *lit* <> *n* **1.** [nonsense] bêtises *fpl* **2.** [trinkets] pacotille *f*.
<> *adj* **1.** [flashy] tapageur, criard **2.** [worthless] sans valeur, insignifiant.

trumpet ['trʌmpɪt] <> *n* **1.** [instrument] trompette *f* ▪ **Armstrong is on ~** Armstrong est à la trompette **2.** [trumpeter] trompettiste *mf* ▪ [in military band] trompette *f* **3.** [of elephant] barrissement *m* **4.** [hearing aid] : **(ear) ~** cornet *m* acoustique.
<> *vi* [elephant] barrir.
<> *vt* [secret, news] claironner ▪ **there's no need to ~ it abroad** il n'est pas nécessaire de le crier sur les toits ▪ **the government's much ~ed land reforms** le battage fait par le gouvernement autour de la réforme agraire.

trumpeter ['trʌmpɪtər] *n* trompettiste *mf* ▪ [in orchestra] trompette *m*.

trumpeting ['trʌmpɪtɪŋ] *n* **1.** [of elephant] barrissement *m*, barrissements *mpl* **2.** MUS coup *m* *OR* coups *mpl* de trompette.

truncate [trʌŋ'keɪt] *vt* [gen - COMPUT] tronquer.

truncated [trʌŋ'keɪtɪd] *adj* tronqué.

truncheon ['trʌntʃən] <> *n* matraque *f*.
<> *vt* matraquer.

trundle ['trʌndl] <> *vi* [heavy equipment, wheelbarrow] avancer *OR* rouler lentement ▪ [person] aller *OR* avancer tranquillement ▪ **to ~ in/out/past** entrer/sortir/passer tranquillement ▪ **I could hear the wheelbarrow trundling down the path** j'entendais quelqu'un pousser bruyamment la brouette sur le chemin.
<> *vt* [push] pousser (avec effort) ▪ [pull] traîner (avec effort) ▪ [wheel] faire rouler bruyamment.
<> *n inf hum* [walk] balade *f*.

trunk [trʌŋk] *n* **1.** [of tree, body] tronc *m* **2.** [of elephant] trompe *f* **3.** [case] malle *f* ▪ [metal] cantine *f* **4.** *US* AUT coffre *m*.
◆ **trunks** *npl* [underwear] slip *m* (d'homme) ▪ **a pair of ~s** [underwear] un slip ; [for swimming] un slip de bain ▪ **(swimming) ~s** maillot *m* *OR* slip de bain.

trunk call *n UK dated* appel *m* interurbain.

trunk line *n* **1.** TELEC inter *m* *dated*, interurbain *m* **2.** RAIL grande ligne *f*.

trunk road *n UK* (route *f*) nationale *f*.

truss [trʌs] <> *vt* **1.** [prisoner, animal] ligoter ▪ [poultry] trousser ▪ [hay] botteler **2.** CONSTR armer, renforcer.
<> *n* **1.** [of hay] botte *f* ▪ [of fruit] grappe *f* **2.** CONSTR ferme *f* **3.** MED bandage *m* herniaire.
◆ **truss up** *vt sep* [prisoner] ligoter ▪ [poultry] trousser.

trust [trʌst] <> *vt* **1.** [have confidence in - person] faire confiance à, avoir confiance en ; [- method, feelings, intuition] faire confiance à, se fier à ; [- judgment, memory] se fier à ▪ **to ~ sb to do sthg** faire confiance à qqn *OR* compter sur qqn pour faire qqch ▪ **I can't ~ him to do the job properly** je ne peux pas compter sur lui pour faire le travail correctement ▪ **~ Mark to put his foot in it!** *hum* pour mettre les pieds dans le plat, on peut faire confiance à Mark! ▪ **~ you!** cela ne m'étonne pas de toi! ➊ **I wouldn't ~ her as far as I could throw her!** je ne lui ferais absolument pas confiance!
2. [entrust] confier ▪ **I certainly wouldn't ~ him with any of my personal secrets** je ne lui confierais certainement pas un secret
3. *fml* [suppose] supposer ▪ [hope] espérer ▪ **I ~ not** j'espère que non.
<> *vi* **1.** [believe] : **to ~ in God** croire en Dieu
2. [have confidence] : **to ~ to luck** s'en remettre à la chance ▪ **we'll just have to ~ to luck that it doesn't rain** espérons qu'avec un peu de chance il ne pleuvra pas.
<> *n* **1.** [confidence, faith] confiance *f*, foi *f* ▪ **to betray sb's ~** trahir la confiance de qqn ▪ **to place one's ~ in sb/sthg** avoir confiance en qqn/qqch, se fier à qqn/qqch ▪ **to take sthg on ~** prendre *OR* accepter qqch en toute confiance *OR* les yeux fermés ▪ **you can't take everything he says on ~** on ne peut pas croire sur parole tout ce qu'il dit
2. [responsibility] responsabilité *f* ▪ **he has a position of ~** il a un poste de confiance *OR* à responsabilités
3. [care] charge *f* ▪ **to give** *OR* **to place sthg into sb's ~** confier qqch aux soins de qqn
4. *(countable)* FIN & LAW [group of trustees] administrateurs *mpl* ▪ **the scholarship is run by a ~** la gestion de la bourse (d'études) a été confiée à un groupe d'administrateurs ‖ [investment] fidéicommis *m* ▪ **to set up a ~ for sb** instituer un fidéicommis pour qqn ▪ **to leave money in ~ for sb** faire administrer un legs par fidéicommis pour qqn
5. [cartel] trust *m*.

trust company *n* société *f* fiduciaire.

trusted ['trʌstɪd] *adj* [method] éprouvé ▪ [figures] fiable ▪ **he's a ~ friend** c'est un ami en qui j'ai entièrement confiance.

trustee [trʌs'ti:] *n* **1.** FIN & LAW fidéicommissaire *m* ▪ [for minor] curateur *m* ▪ [in bankruptcy] syndic *m* **2.** ADMIN administrateur *m*, - trice *f* ▪ **board of ~s** conseil *m* d'administration.

trusteeship [,trʌs'ti:ʃɪp] *n* **1.** FIN & LAW fidéicommis *m* ▪ [for minor] curatelle *f* **2.** ADMIN poste *m* d'administrateur.

trustful ['trʌstfʊl] = **trusting**.

trustfully ['trʌstfʊlɪ] *adv* avec confiance.

trust fund *n* fonds *m* en fidéicommis.

trust hospital *n hôpital britannique ayant opté pour l'autogestion mais qui reçoit toujours son budget de l'État.*

trusting ['trʌstɪŋ] *adj* [nature, person] qui a confiance ▪ [look] confiant ▪ **he's too ~ of people** il fait trop confiance aux gens.

trustingly ['trʌstɪŋlɪ] *adv* en toute confiance.

trust territory *n* territoire *m* sous tutelle.

trustworthiness ['trʌst,wɜ:ðɪnɪs] *n* **1.** [reliability - of person] loyauté *f*, sérieux *m* ; [- of information, source] fiabilité *f* **2.** [accuracy - of report, figures] fiabilité *f*, justesse *f* **3.** [honesty] honnêteté *f*.

trustworthy ['trʌst,wɜ:ðɪ] *adj* **1.** [reliable - person] sur qui on peut compter, à qui on peut faire confiance ; [- information, source] sûr, fiable **2.** [accurate - report, figures] fidèle, précis **3.** [honest] honnête.

trusty ['trʌstɪ] (*comp* **trustier**, *superl* **trustiest**, *pl* **trusties**)
<> *adj arch* & *hum* [steed, sword] loyal, fidèle.
<> *n* [prisoner] *détenu bénéficiant d'un régime de faveur.*

truth [tru:θ] (*pl* **truths** [tru:ðz]) *n* **1.** [true facts] vérité *f* ▪ **I then discovered the ~ about Neil** j'ai alors découvert la vérité sur Neil ▪ **there isn't a grain** *OR* **an ounce of ~ in what he says** il n'y a pas une once de vérité dans ce qu'il dit ▪ **there's some ~ in what he says** il y a du vrai dans ce qu'il dit ▪ **the ~ of the matter is I really don't care any more** la vérité c'est que maintenant je m'en fiche vraiment ▪ **to tell the ~** dire la vérité ➊ **to tell (you) the ~** à vrai dire, à dire vrai ▪ **(the) ~ will out** *prov* la vérité finit toujours par se savoir **2.** [fact, piece of information] vérité *f* ▪ **he learned some important ~s about himself** on lui a dit ses quatre vérités.
◆ **in truth** *adv phr* en vérité.

truth-condition *n* LOGIC & PHILOS condition *f* nécessaire et préalable.

truthful ['tru:θfʊl] *adj* [person] qui dit la vérité ▪ [character] honnête ▪ [article, statement] fidèle à la réalité, vrai ▪ [story] véridique, vrai ▪ [portrait] fidèle.

truthfully ['tru:θfʊlɪ] *adv* [answer, speak] honnêtement, sans mentir ▪ [sincerely] sincèrement, vraiment.

truthfulness ['tru:θfʊlnɪs] *n* [of person] honnêteté *f* ▪ [of portrait] fidélité *f* ▪ [of story, statement] véracité *f*.

truth-function *n* LOGIC fonction *f* vériconditionnelle.

truth set *n* LOGIC & MATHS *ensemble qui n'a pas de solution unique.*

truth-value *n* LOGIC & PHILOS valeur *f* de vérité.

try [traɪ] ◇ *vt* (*pl* **tries**) **1.** [attempt] essayer ▪ **to ~ to do** *OR* **doing sthg** essayer *OR* tâcher de faire qqch, chercher à faire qqch ▪ **she tried not to think about it** elle essaya de ne pas y penser *OR* d'éviter d'y penser ▪ **I tried hard to understand** j'ai tout fait pour essayer de comprendre, j'ai vraiment cherché à comprendre ▪ **to ~ one's best** *OR* **hardest** faire de son mieux ▪ **he tried his best to explain** il a essayé d'expliquer de son mieux ▪ **I'm willing to ~ anything once!** je suis prêt à tout essayer au moins une fois! ▪ **and don't ~ any funny business!** *inf* et pas d'entourloupe! ▪ **just you ~ it!** [as threat] essaie un peu pour voir!
2. [test - method, approach, car] essayer ▪ **the method has been tried and tested** la méthode a fait ses preuves ▪ **(just) ~ me!** *inf* essaie toujours! ▪ **to ~ one's strength against sb** se mesurer à qqn ▪ **to ~ one's luck (at sthg)** tenter sa chance (à qqch)
3. [sample - recipe, wine] essayer, goûter à ; [- clothes] essayer ▪ **~ it, you'll like it** essayez *OR* goûtez-y donc, vous aimerez ▪ **~ this for size** *liter* [garment] essayez ceci pour voir la taille ; [shoe] essayez ceci pour voir la pointure ; *fig* essayez ceci pour voir si ça va
4. [attempt to open - door, window] essayer
5. TELEC essayer ▪ **~ the number again** refaites le numéro ▪ **~ him later** *inf* essayez de le rappeler plus tard
6. [visit] essayer ▪ **I've tried six shops already** j'ai déjà essayé six magasins
7. LAW [person, case] juger ▪ **he was tried for murder** il a été jugé pour meurtre
8. [tax, strain - patience] éprouver, mettre à l'épreuve ▪ **these things are sent to ~ us!** c'est le ciel qui nous envoie ces épreuves! ▪ **it's enough to ~ the patience of a saint** même un ange n'aurait pas la patience ▪ **to be sorely tried** *lit* & *hum* être durement éprouvé.
◇ *vi* (*pret* & *pp* **tried**) essayer ▪ **to ~ and do sthg** essayer de faire qqch ▪ **~ again** refaites un essai, recommencez ▪ **~ later** essayez plus tard ▪ **we can but ~** on peut toujours essayer ▪ **you can do it if you ~** quand on veut, on peut ▪ **just (you) ~!** essaie donc un peu! ▪ **to ~ for sthg** essayer d'obtenir qqch ▪ **she's ~ing for a place at Oxford** elle essaie d'être admise à l'université d'Oxford ▪ **why don't you at least ~ for the job?** pourquoi ne pas au moins vous présenter pour le poste?
◇ *n* (*pl* **tries**) **1.** [attempt] essai *m*, tentative *f* ▪ **to have a ~ at sthg/at doing sthg** essayer qqch/de faire qqch ▪ **good ~!** bien essayé! ▪ **it's worth a ~** cela vaut la peine d'essayer ▪ **I managed it at the first ~** j'ai réussi du premier coup
2. [test, turn] essai *m* ▪ **to give sthg a ~** essayer qqch
3. SPORT [in rugby] essai *m* ▪ **to score a ~** marquer un essai.
◆ **try on** *vt sep* **1.** [garment] essayer ▪ **~ it on for size** essayez-le pour voir la taille
2. *phr* **to ~it on with sb** *UK inf* essayer de voir jusqu'où on peut pousser qqn ; [flirt] essayer de flirter avec qqn ▪ **don't you ~ anything on with me!** [gen] ne fais pas le malin avec moi! ; [flirt] n'essaie pas de flirter avec moi!
◆ **try out** ◇ *vt sep* [new car, bicycle] essayer, faire un essai avec, faire l'essai de ▪ [method, chemical, recipe] essayer ▪ [employee] mettre à l'essai.
◇ *vi insep US* **to ~ out for a team** faire un essai pour se faire engager dans une équipe.

trying ['traɪɪŋ] *adj* [experience] pénible, douloureux, éprouvant ▪ [journey, job] ennuyeux, pénible ▪ [person] fatigant, pénible ▪ **he had a very ~ time** [moment] il a passé un moment très difficile ; [period] il a vécu une période très difficile ; [experience] il a vécu une expérience très difficile *OR* éprouvante.

try-on *n UK inf* **it's a ~** c'est du bluff.

try-out *n* essai *m*.

tryst [trɪst] *n lit* rendez-vous *m* (d'amour).

tsar [zɑ:ʳ] *n* tsar *m*, tzar *m*, czar *m*.

tsarina [zɑ:'ri:nə] *n* tsarine *f*, tzarine *f*.

tsarist ['zɑ:rɪst] ◇ *adj* tsariste.
◇ *n* tsariste *mf*.

T-section *n* profil *m* en T.

tsetse fly ['tsetsɪ-] *n* mouche *f* tsé-tsé.

T-shaped *adj* en forme de T.

T-shirt *n* tee-shirt *m*, t-shirt *m*.

tsp. (*written abbrev of* **teaspoon**) cc.

T-square *n* équerre *f* en T, té *m*, T *m (règle)*.

T-stop *n* PHOT diaphragme *m*.

TT *pr n* (*abbrev of* **Tourist Trophy**) ▪ **~ races** *courses de moto sur l'île de Man.*

Tuareg ['twɑ:reg] (*pl inv OR pl* **Tuaregs**) ◇ *n* **1.** [person] Touareg *m*, - ègue *f* **2.** LING touareg *m*.
◇ *adj* touareg.

tub [tʌb] *n* **1.** [container - for liquid] cuve *f*, bac *m* ; [- for flowers] bac *m* ; [- for washing clothes] baquet *m* ; [- in washing machine] cuve *f* **2.** [contents - of washing powder] baril *m* ; [- of wine, beer] tonneau *m* ; [- of ice cream, yoghurt] pot *m* **3.** *inf* [bath] **: he's in the ~** il prend un bain **4.** *inf* [boat] rafiot *m*.

tuba ['tju:bə] *n* tuba *m*.

tubby ['tʌbɪ] (*comp* **tubbier**, *superl* **tubbiest**) *adj inf* dodu, rondelet.

tube [tju:b] ◇ *n* **1.** [pipe] tube *m* ▪ **he was fed through a ~** on l'a nourri à la sonde **2.** ANAT tube *m*, canal *m* **3.** [of glue, toothpaste] tube *m* **4.** [in tyre] **: (inner) ~** chambre *f* à air **5.** TV **: what's on the ~ tonight?** *inf* qu'est-ce qu'il y a à la télé ce soir? ▪ **(cathode-ray) ~** tube *m* (cathodique) **6.** *UK* [underground] **: the ~** *le métro londonien* ▪ **to go by ~, to take the ~** aller en métro, prendre le métro **7.** *phr* **to go down the ~ s** *inf* tomber à l'eau.
◇ *comp* [map, station] de métro.

tube-feed *vt* nourrir à la sonde.

tubeless ['tju:blɪs] *adj UK* **~ tyre** pneu *m* sans chambre (à air).

tuber ['tju:bəʳ] *n* ANAT & BOT tubercule *m*.

tubercle ['tju:bəkl] *n* tubercule *m*.

tubercular [tju:'bɜ:kjʊləʳ] *adj* tuberculeux.

tuberculin [tju:'bɜ:kjʊlɪn] *n* tuberculine *f*.

tuberculin-tested [-'testɪd] *adj* [cow] tuberculinisé, tuberculiné ▪ **~ milk** ≃ lait *m* certifié.

tuberculosis [tju:ˌbɜ:kjʊ'ləʊsɪs] *n (U)* tuberculose *f* ▪ **he has ~** il a la tuberculose, il est tuberculeux.

tubing ['tju:bɪŋ] *n (U)* tubes *mpl*, tuyaux *mpl* ▪ **a piece of plastic ~** un tube en plastique.

Tubuai Islands [ˌtu:bu:'aɪ-] *pr npl*: **the ~** les îles *fpl* Australes.

tubular ['tju:bjʊləʳ] *adj* [furniture, shape] tubulaire ▪ **~ bells** MUS carillon *m* d'orchestre.

TUC (*abbrev of* **Trades Union Congress**) *pr n la Confédération des syndicats britanniques.*

tuck [tʌk] ◇ *vt* **1.** [shirt] rentrer ▪ [sheet] rentrer, border ▪ **he ~ed his shirt into his trousers** il rentra sa chemise dans son pantalon ▪ **she ~ed the sheets under the mattress** elle borda le lit **2.** [put] mettre ▪ [slip] glisser ▪ **he had a newspaper ~ed under his arm** il avait un journal sous le bras ▪ **she ~ed her hair**

behind her ears elle ramena ses cheveux derrière ses oreilles ■ **his mother came to ~ him into bed** sa mère est venue le border dans son lit.
◇ *n* **1.** SEW rempli *m* ■ **to put** *OR* **to make a ~ in sthg** faire un rempli dans qqch **2.** [in diving] plongeon *m* groupé **3.** *UK inf* SCH boustifaille *f*.
◆ **tuck away** *vt sep* **1.** [hide] cacher ■ [put] mettre, ranger **2.** *inf* [food] s'enfiler, avaler.
◆ **tuck in** ◇ *vt sep* **1.** [shirt, stomach] rentrer **2.** [child] border.
◇ *vi insep inf* [eat] : **we ~ed in to a lovely meal** nous avons attaqué un excellent repas.
◆ **tuck up** *vt sep* **1.** [person] border (dans son lit) ■ **all the children were safely ~ed up in bed** les enfants étaient tous bien bordés dans leurs lits **2.** [skirt, sleeves] remonter ■ [hair] rentrer **3.** [legs] replier, rentrer.

tuck box *n UK* SCH gamelle *f (d'écolier)*.

tucker ['tʌkəʳ] ◇ *n* **1.** [on dress] fichu *m* **2.** *inf Australia & New Zealand inf* [food] bouffe *f*.
◇ *vt inf US inf* [exhaust] crever.

tuck shop *n UK* SCH *petite boutique où les écoliers achètent bonbons, gâteaux etc.*

Tudor ['tju:dəʳ] ◇ *adj* [family, period] des Tudor ■ [king, architecture] Tudor *(inv)*.
◇ *n* Tudor *m inv*, membre *m* de la famille des Tudor.

Tue., Tues. *(written abbrev of* **Tuesday***)* mar.

Tuesday ['tju:zdeɪ] *n* mardi *m*, *see also* **Friday**.

tufa ['tju:fə] *n* tuf *m* calcaire.

tuft [tʌft] *n* **1.** [of hair, grass] touffe *f* **2.** ORNITH : **~ (of feathers)** huppe *f*, aigrette *f*.

tufted ['tʌftɪd] *adj* **1.** [bird] huppé **2.** [grass] en touffe *OR* touffes **3.** [carpet] tufté.

tug [tʌg] *(pret & pp* **tugged**, *cont* **tugging***)* ◇ *n* **1.** [pull] petit coup *m* ■ **he felt a ~ at his sleeve** il sentit qu'on le tirait par la manche **2.** NAUT remorqueur *m*.
◇ *vt* **1.** [handle, sleeve] tirer sur ■ [load] tirer, traîner **2.** NAUT remorquer.
◇ *vi* : **to ~ at** *OR* **on sthg** tirer sur qqch ■ **the music tugged at her heartstrings** *fig* cette musique l'émouvait.

tugboat ['tʌgbəʊt] *n* remorqueur *m*.

tug-of-love *n UK inf conflit entre des parents en instance de divorce pour avoir la garde d'un enfant.*

tug-of-war *n* SPORT tir *m* à la corde ■ *fig* lutte *f* acharnée.

tuition [tju:'ɪʃn] *n (U)* **1.** *UK* [instruction] cours *mpl* **2.** UNIV : **~ (fees)** frais *mpl* de scolarité.

tulip ['tju:lɪp] *n* tulipe *f*.

tulle [tju:l] *n* tulle *m*.

tum [tʌm] *n UK inf* ventre *m*.

tumble ['tʌmbl] ◇ *vi* **1.** [fall - person] faire une chute, dégringoler ; [- ball, objects] dégringoler ■ **he ~d down the stairs** il a fait une culbute dans *OR* il a dégringolé (dans) l'escalier ■ **to ~ head over heels** faire une culbute *OR* un roulé-boulé ■ **the bottles came tumbling off the shelf** les bouteilles ont dégringolé de l'étagère **2.** [collapse - prices] dégringoler, s'effondrer ■ **the Chancellor's resignation sent share prices tumbling** la démission du ministre des Finances a fait dégringoler le prix des actions **3.** [rush] se précipiter **4.** [perform somersaults] faire des sauts périlleux.
◇ *vt* [knock, push - person] renverser, faire tomber *OR* dégringoler.
◇ *n* [fall] chute *f*, culbute *f*, roulé-boulé *m* ■ [somersault] culbute *f*, cabrioles *fpl* ■ **to take a ~** faire une chute *OR* une culbute ■ **share prices took a ~ today** le prix des actions s'est effondré aujourd'hui.
◆ **tumble about** ◇ *vi insep* [children] gambader, batifoler ■ [acrobat] faire des cabrioles ■ [swimmer] s'ébattre ■ [water] clapoter.
◇ *vt sep* mettre en désordre.
◆ **tumble down** *vi insep* [person] faire une culbute, dégringoler ■ [pile] dégringoler ■ [wall, building] s'effondrer.
◆ **tumble out** ◇ *vi insep* **1.** [person - from tree, loft] faire une culbute, dégringoler ; [- from bus, car] se jeter, sauter ■ [possessions, contents] tomber (en vrac) ■ **the apples ~d out of her basket** les pommes ont roulé de son panier ■ **he ~d out of bed at midday** il est tombé du lit à midi *hum* **2.** [news, confession] s'échapper.
◇ *vt sep* faire tomber en vrac *OR* en tas.
◆ **tumble over** ◇ *vi insep* [person] culbuter, faire une culbute ■ [pile, vase] se renverser.
◇ *vt sep* renverser, faire tomber.
◆ **tumble to** *vt insep UK inf* [fact, secret, joke] piger, saisir, comprendre.

tumbledown ['tʌmbldaʊn] *adj* en ruines, délabré.

tumble-drier *n* sèche-linge *m inv*.

tumble-dry *vt* faire sécher dans le sèche-linge.

tumbler ['tʌmbləʳ] *n* **1.** [glass] verre *m* (droit) ■ [beaker] gobelet *m*, timbale *f* **2.** [acrobat] acrobate *mf* **3.** [in lock] gorge *f* (de serrure) **4.** = **tumble-drier 5.** [pigeon] pigeon *m* culbutant.

tumbler switch *n* interrupteur *m* à bascule.

tumbleweed ['tʌmblwi:d] *n* amarante *f*.

tumbrel ['tʌmbrəl], **tumbril** ['tʌmbrɪl] *n* tombereau *m*.

tumescent [,tju:'mesnt] *adj* tumescent.

tumid ['tju:mɪd] *adj* **1.** MED tuméfié **2.** *lit* [style] ampoulé, boursouflé.

tummy ['tʌmɪ] *inf* ◇ *n* ventre *m*.
◇ *comp* : **to have (a) ~ ache** avoir mal au ventre ■ **~ button** nombril *m*.

tumour *UK*, **tumor** *US* ['tju:məʳ] *n* tumeur *f*.

tumuli ['tju:mjʊlaɪ] *pl* ▷ **tumulus**.

tumult ['tju:mʌlt] *n* **1.** [noise] tumulte *m* ■ [agitation] tumulte *m*, agitation *f* ■ **in (a) ~** dans le tumulte **2.** *fml & lit* [of feelings] émoi *m*.

tumultuous ['tju:mʌltjʊəs] *adj* [crowd, noise] tumultueux ■ [applause] frénétique ■ [period] tumultueux, agité ■ **he got a ~ welcome** il a reçu un accueil enthousiaste.

tumulus ['tju:mjʊləs] *(pl* **tumuli** ['tju:mjʊlaɪ]*)* *n* tumulus *m*.

tun [tʌn] *n* fût *m*, tonneau *m*.

tuna [*UK* 'tju:nə, *US* 'tu:nə] *n* : **~ (fish)** thon *m*.

tundra ['tʌndrə] *n* toundra *f*.

tune [tju:n] ◇ *n* [melody] air *m*, mélodie *f* ■ **give us a ~ on the mouth organ** joue-nous un petit air d'harmonica ■ **they marched to the ~ of Rule Britannia** ils marchèrent sur l'air de *OR* aux accents de Rule Britannia ▶ **to call the ~** *UK inf* faire la loi.
◇ *vt* **1.** [musical instrument] accorder ■ **the strings are ~d to the key of G** les cordes sont en sol **2.** [regulate - engine, machine] mettre au point, régler **3.** [radio, television] régler ■ **the radio is ~d to Voice of America** la radio est réglée sur la Voix de l'Amérique ■ **we can't ~ our TV to Channel 5** nous ne pouvons pas capter la chaîne 5 sur notre télé ■ **stay ~d!** restez à l'écoute! **4.** [adapt] : **politicians always ~ their remarks to suit their audience** les hommes politiques se mettent toujours au diapason de leur auditoire, les hommes politiques adaptent toujours leurs commentaires à leur auditoire.
◆ **in tune** ◇ *adj phr* [instrument] accordé, juste ■ [singer] qui chante juste ■ **the violins are not in ~ with the piano** les violons ne sont pas accordés avec le piano ■ **to be in ~ with** *fig* être en accord avec.
◇ *adv phr* juste.
◆ **out of tune** ◇ *adj phr* [instrument] faux, fausse *f*, désaccordé ■ [singer] qui chante faux ■ **to be out of ~ with** *fig* être en désaccord avec ■ **the MP was out of ~ with the rest of his party** le député n'était pas sur la même longueur d'onde que les autres membres de son parti *OR* était en désaccord avec les autres membres de son parti.
◇ *adv phr* faux.
◆ **to the tune of** *prep phr* : **they were given grants to the ~ of £100,000** on leur a accordé des subventions qui s'élevaient à 100 000 livres.

◆ **tune in** <> *vi insep* RADIO & TV se mettre à l'écoute ▪ ~ **in to this channel next week** soyez à l'écoute de cette chaîne la semaine prochaine.
<> *vt sep* **1.** [radio, television] régler sur **2.** *inf fig* **to be ~d in to sthg** être branché sur qqch.
◆ **tune out** *US* <> *vi insep* [refuse to listen] faire la sourde oreille ▪ [stop listening] décrocher.
<> *vt sep* **1.** [remark] ignorer **2.** [radio] éteindre.
◆ **tune up** <> *vi insep* MUS [player] accorder son instrument ▪ [orchestra] accorder ses instruments.
<> *vt sep* **1.** MUS accorder **2.** AUT mettre au point, régler.

tuned-in [tju:nd-] *adj inf* branché.

tuneful ['tju:nfʊl] *adj* [song, voice] mélodieux ▪ [singer] à la voix mélodieuse.

tunefully ['tju:nfʊlɪ] *adv* mélodieusement.

tuneless ['tju:nlɪs] *adj* peu mélodieux, discordant.

tunelessly ['tju:nlɪslɪ] *adv* [with no tune] de manière peu mélodieuse ▪ [out of tune] faux *(adv).*

tuner ['tju:nəʳ] *n* **1.** [of piano] accordeur *m* **2.** RADIO & TV tuner *m*, syntonisateur *m spec.*

tuner amplifier *n* ampli-tuner *m.*

tune-up *n* AUT réglage *m*, mise *f* au point.

tungsten ['tʌŋstən] *n* tungstène *m.*

tungsten carbide *n* carbure *m* de tungstène.

tungsten lamp *n* lampe *f* au tungstène.

tungsten steel *n* acier *m* au tungstène.

tunic ['tju:nɪk] *n* [gen - BOT] tunique *f.*

tuning ['tju:nɪŋ] *n* **1.** MUS accord *m* **2.** RADIO & TV réglage *m* **3.** AUT réglage *m*, mise *f* au point.

tuning fork *n* diapason *m.*

Tunisia [tju:'nɪzɪə] *pr n* Tunisie *f* ▪ **in ~** en Tunisie.

Tunisian [tju:'nɪzɪən] <> *n* Tunisien *m*, - enne *f.*
<> *adj* tunisien.

tunnel ['tʌnl] (*UK pret & pp* **tunnelled**, *cont* **tunnelling**) (*US pret & pp* **tunneled**, *cont* **tunneling**) <> *n* [gen - RAIL] tunnel *m* ▪ MIN galerie *f* ▪ [of mole, badger] galerie *f* ▪ **to make** *OR* **to dig a ~** [gen] percer *OR* creuser un tunnel ; MIN percer *OR* creuser une galerie.
<> *vt* [hole, passage] creuser, percer ▪ **to ~ one's way through the earth** CONSTR creuser un tunnel dans la terre ; [mole] creuser une galerie dans la terre.
<> *vi* [person] creuser *OR* percer un tunnel *OR* des tunnels ▪ [badger, mole] creuser une galerie *OR* des galeries.

tunnelling machine ['tʌnlɪŋ-] *n* foreuse *f.*

tunnel vision *n* **1.** OPT rétrécissement *m* du champ visuel **2.** *fig* esprit *m* borné ▪ **to have ~** avoir des vues étroites, voir les choses par le petit bout de la lorgnette.

tunny ['tʌnɪ] = **tuna**.

tuppence ['tʌpəns] *n UK* deux pence *mpl* ▪ **I don't care ~ for your opinion** *inf* je me fiche pas mal de votre opinion *OR* de ce que vous pensez.

tuppenny ['tʌpnɪ] *adj UK* de *OR* à deux pence.

tuppenny-ha'penny ['tʌpnɪ,heɪpnɪ] *adj UK inf* de rien du tout, de quatre sous.

Tupperware® ['tʌpəweəʳ] <> *n* Tupperware® *m* ▪ **~ party** réunion *f* Tupperware®.
<> *comp* en Tupperware®.

turban ['tɜ:bən] *n* turban *m.*

turbaned ['tɜ:bənd] *adj* [person] en turban ▪ [head] coiffé d'un turban, enturbanné.

turbid ['tɜ:bɪd] *adj* trouble.

turbine ['tɜ:baɪn] *n* turbine *f* ▪ **gas/steam ~** turbine *f* à gaz/à vapeur.

turbo ['tɜ:bəʊ] (*pl* **turbos**) *n* **1.** AUT turbo *m* **2.** [turbine] turbine *f.*

turbocharged ['tɜ:bəʊtʃɑ:dʒd] *adj* turbo.

turbocharger ['tɜ:bəʊtʃɑ:dʒəʳ] *n* turbocompresseur *m.*

turbodiesel [,tɜ:bəʊ'di:zl] *n* turbodiesel *m.*

turbojet [,tɜ:bəʊ'dʒet] *n* [engine] turboréacteur *m* ▪ [plane] avion *m* à turboréacteur.

turboprop [,tɜ:bəʊ'prɒp] *n* [engine] turbopropulseur *m* ▪ [plane] avion *m* à turbopropulseur.

turbot ['tɜ:bət] (*pl inv OR pl* **turbots**) *n* turbot *m.*

turbulence ['tɜ:bjʊləns] *n* **1.** [unrest] turbulence *f*, agitation *f* **2.** [in air] turbulence *f* ▪ [in sea] agitation *f* **3.** PHYS turbulence *f.*

turbulent ['tɜ:bjʊlənt] *adj* [crowd, period, emotions] tumultueux ▪ [sea] agité ▪ [meeting] houleux.

turd△ [tɜ:d] *n* **1.** [excrement] merde△ *f* **2.** *pej* [person] con△ *m*, salaud△ *m.*

tureen [tə'ri:n] *n* soupière *f.*

turf [tɜ:f] (*pl* **turfs** *OR pl* **turves** [tɜ:vz]) <> *n* **1.** [grass] gazon *m* **2.** [sod] motte *f* de gazon **3.** SPORT turf *m* **4.** [peat] tourbe *f* **5.**△ *US* [of gang] territoire *m* réservé, chasse *f* gardée.
<> *vt* **1.** [with grass] : **~ (over)** gazonner **2.** *UK inf* [throw] balancer, flanquer, jeter.
◆ **turf out** *vt sep UK inf* [eject, evict - person] vider, flanquer à la porte ▪ [remove - furniture, possessions] sortir, enlever ▪ [throw away - rubbish] bazarder ▪ **he was ~ed out of the club** il s'est fait virer *OR* vider du club.

turf accountant *n UK fml* bookmaker *m.*

Turgenev [tɜ:'geɪnjev] *pr n* Tourgueniev.

turgid ['tɜ:dʒɪd] *adj* **1.** [style, prose] ampoulé, boursouflé **2.** MED enflé, gonflé.

Turin Shroud *pr n* : **the ~** le saint suaire.

Turk [tɜ:k] *n* Turc *m*, Turque *f.*

Turkestan, Turkistan [,tɜ:kɪ'stɑ:n] *pr n* Turkistan *m* ▪ **in ~** au Turkistan.

turkey ['tɜ:kɪ] (*pl inv OR pl* **turkeys**) *n* **1.** [bird - cock] dindon *m* ; [- hen] dinde *f* ▪ *fig* **it was a real ~ shoot** *US* c'était gagné d'avance **2.** CULIN dinde *f* **3.** *US inf* [fool] idiot *m*, - e *f*, imbécile *mf* **4.** *US inf* [flop] bide *m* ▪ THEAT four *m.*

Turkey ['tɜ:kɪ] *pr n* Turquie *f* ▪ **in ~** en Turquie.

turkey buzzard *n* vautour *m* aura.

turkey cock *n* dindon *m* ▪ *inf fig*inf crâneur *m*, - euse *f.*

Turkish ['tɜ:kɪʃ] <> *n* LING turc *m.*
<> *adj* turc.

Turkish bath *n* bain *m* turc.

Turkish coffee *n* café *m* turc.

Turkish delight *n* loukoum *m.*

Turkistan = **Turkestan**.

Turkman ['tɜ:kmən] (*pl* **Turkmans** *OR pl* **Turkmen** [-men]) <> *n* Turkmène *mf.*
<> *adj* turkmène.

Turkmen [-men] *n* LING turkmène *m.*

Turkmenia = **Turkmenistan**.

Turkmenistan [,tɜ:k'menɪən] *adj* turkmène.

Turkmenistan [,tɜ:kmenɪ'stɑ:n], **Turkmenia** [tɜ:k'mi:nɪə] *pr n* Turkménistan *m* ▪ **in ~** au Turkménistan.

turmeric ['tɜ:mərɪk] *n* curcuma *m*, safran *m* des Indes.

turmoil ['tɜ:mɔɪl] *n* **1.** [confusion] agitation *f*, trouble *m*, chaos *m* ▪ **the country was in ~** le pays était en ébullition *OR* en effervescence **2.** [emotional] trouble *m*, émoi *m* ▪ **her mind was in (a) ~** elle avait l'esprit troublé, elle était en émoi.

turn [tɜːn] ◇ *vt*

A.

1. [cause to rotate, move round] tourner ▪ [shaft, axle] faire tourner, faire pivoter ▪ [direct] diriger ▪ **she ~ed the key in the lock** [to lock] elle a donné un tour de clé (à la porte), elle a fermé la porte à clé ; [to unlock] elle a ouvert la porte avec la clé ▪ **~ the wheel all the way round** faites faire un tour complet à la roue ▪ **~ the knob to the right** tournez le bouton vers la droite ▪ **she ~ed the oven to its highest setting** elle a allumé *OR* mis le four à la température maximum ▪ **he ~ed the car into the drive** il a engagé la voiture dans l'allée ▪ **~ your head this way** tournez la tête de ce côté
2. *fig* [change orientation of] : **she ~ed the conversation to sport** elle a orienté la conversation vers le sport ▪ **their votes could ~ the election in his favour** leurs voix pourraient faire basculer les élections en sa faveur ▪ **nothing would ~ the rebels from their cause** rien ne pourrait détourner les rebelles de leur cause ▪ **you've ~ed my whole family against me** vous avez monté toute ma famille contre moi ▪ **she ~ed her attention to the problem** elle s'est concentrée sur le problème ▪ **how can we ~ this policy to our advantage** *OR* **account?** comment tirer parti de cette politique?, comment tourner cette politique à notre avantage? ➔ **to ~ one's back on sb** *liter* tourner le dos à qqn ▪ **she looked at the letter the minute his back was ~ed** dès qu'il a eu le dos tourné, elle a jeté un coup d'œil à la lettre ▪ **how can you ~ your back on your own family?** comment peux-tu abandonner ta famille? ▪ **she was so pretty that she ~ed heads wherever she went** elle était si jolie que tout le monde se retournait sur son passage ▪ **success had not ~ed his head** la réussite ne lui avait pas tourné la tête, il ne s'était pas laissé griser par la réussite ▪ **to ~ the tables on sb** reprendre l'avantage sur qqn ▪ **now the tables are ~ed** maintenant les rôles sont renversés, tel est pris qui croyait prendre *prov*

B.

1. [flip over - page] tourner ; [- collar, mattress, sausages, soil] retourner ▪ **the very thought of food ~s my stomach** l'idée même de manger me soulève le cœur ▪ **to ~ sthg on its head** bouleverser qqch, mettre qqch sens dessus dessous
2. [send away] : **he ~ed the beggar from his door** il a chassé le mendiant
3. [release, let loose] : **he ~ed the cattle into the field** il a fait rentrer le bétail dans le champ
4. [go round - corner] tourner
5. [reach - in age, time] passer, franchir ▪ **I had just ~ed twenty** je venais d'avoir vingt ans ▪ **she's ~ed thirty** elle a trente ans passés, elle a dépassé le cap de la trentaine ▪ **it has only just ~ed four o'clock** il est quatre heures passées de quelques secondes
6. [do, perform] faire ▪ **to ~ a cartwheel** faire la roue
7. [ankle] tordre ▪ **I've ~ed my ankle** je me suis tordu la cheville

C.

1. [transform, change] changer, transformer ▪ [make] faire devenir, rendre ▪ **to ~ sthg into sthg** transformer *OR* changer qqch en qqch ▪ **she ~ed the remark into a joke** elle a tourné la remarque en plaisanterie ▪ **they're ~ing the book into a film** ils adaptent le livre pour l'écran ‖ [in colour] : **time had ~ed the pages yellow** le temps avait jauni les pages
2. [make bad, affect] : **the lemon juice ~ed the milk (sour)** le jus de citron a fait tourner le lait
3. *US* COMM [goods] promouvoir la vente de ▪ [money] gagner ▪ **to ~ a good profit** faire de gros bénéfices
4. TECH [shape] tourner, façonner au tour ▪ **a well ~ed leg** une jambe bien faite ▪ **to ~ a phrase** *fig* faire des phrases.

◇ *vi* **1.** [move round - handle, key, wheel] tourner ; [- shaft] tourner, pivoter ; [- person] se tourner ▪ **to ~ on an axis** tourner autour d'un axe ▪ **the crane ~ed (through) 180°** la grue a pivoté de 180° ▪ **he ~ed right round** il a fait volte-face ▪ **they ~ed towards me** ils se sont tournés vers moi *OR* de mon côté ▪ **they ~ed from the gruesome sight** ils se sont détournés de cet horrible spectacle
2. [flip over - page] tourner ; [- car, person, ship] se retourner
3. [change direction - person] tourner ; [- vehicle] tourner, virer ; [- luck, wind] tourner, changer ; [- river, road] faire un coude ; [- tide] changer de direction ▪ **~ (to the) right** [walking] tournez à droite ; [driving] tournez *OR* prenez à droite ▪ **he ~ed (round) and went back** il a fait demi-tour et est revenu sur ses pas ▪ **the car ~ed into our street** la voiture a tourné dans notre rue ▪ **we ~ed onto the main road** nous nous sommes engagés dans *OR* nous avons pris la grand-route ▪ **the market ~ed downwards/upwards** ST. EX le marché était à la baisse/à la hausse ▪ **I don't know where** *OR* **which way to ~** *fig* je ne sais plus quoi faire
4. *(with adj or noun complement)* [become] devenir ▪ **the weather's ~ed bad** le temps s'est gâté ▪ **the argument ~ed nasty** la dispute s'est envenimée ▪ **a lawyer ~ed politician** un avocat devenu homme politique ▪ **to ~ professional** passer *OR* devenir professionnel
5. [transform] se changer, se transformer ▪ **the rain ~ed to snow** la pluie s'est transformée en neige ▪ **the little girl had ~ed into a young woman** la petite fille était devenue une jeune femme ▪ **their love ~ed to hate** leur amour se changea en haine *OR* fit place à la haine
6. [leaf] tourner, jaunir ▪ [milk] tourner ▪ **the weather has ~ed** le temps a changé.

◇ *n* **1.** [revolution, rotation] tour *m* ▪ **he gave the handle a ~** il a tourné la poignée ▪ **give the screw another ~** donnez un autre tour de vis
2. [change of course, direction] tournant *m* ▪ [in skiing] virage *m* ▪ **to make a right ~** [walking] tourner à droite ; [driving] tourner *OR* prendre à droite ▪ **'no right ~'** 'défense de tourner à droite' ‖ *fig* **at every ~** à tout instant, à tout bout de champ
3. [bend, curve in road] virage *m*, tournant *m* ▪ **there is a sharp ~ to the left** la route fait un brusque virage *OR* tourne brusquement à gauche
4. [change in state, nature] tour *m*, tournure *f* ▪ **the conversation took a new ~** la conversation a pris une nouvelle tournure ▪ **it was an unexpected ~ of events** les événements ont pris une tournure imprévue ▪ **things took a ~ for the worse/better** les choses se sont aggravées/améliorées ▪ **the situation took a tragic ~** la situation a tourné au tragique
5. [time of change] : **at the ~ of the century** au tournant du siècle
6. [in game, order, queue] tour *m* ▪ **it's my ~** c'est à moi, c'est mon tour ▪ **whose ~ is it?** [in queue] (c'est) à qui le tour? ; [in game] c'est à qui de jouer? ▪ **it's his ~ to do the dishes** c'est à lui *OR* c'est son tour de faire la vaisselle ▪ **you'll have to wait your ~** il faudra attendre ton tour ▪ **they laughed and cried by ~s** ils passaient tour à tour du rire aux larmes ▪ **to take it in ~s to do sthg** faire qqch à tour de rôle ▪ **let's take it in ~s to drive** relayons-nous au volant ▪ **we took ~s sleeping on the floor** nous avons dormi par terre à tour de rôle ‖ [shift] : **~ of duty** [gen] tour *m* de service ; MIL tour *m* de garde
7. [action, deed] : **to do sb a good/bad ~** rendre service/jouer un mauvais tour à qqn ▪ **I've done my good ~ for the day** j'ai fait ma bonne action de la journée ➔ **one good ~ deserves another** *prov* un service en vaut un autre, un service rendu en appelle un autre
8. *inf* [attack of illness] crise *f*, attaque *f* ▪ **she had one of her (funny) ~s this morning** elle a eu une de ses crises ce matin
9. *inf* [shock] : **you gave me quite a ~!** tu m'as fait une sacrée peur!, tu m'as fait une de ces peurs!
10. *dated* [short trip, ride, walk] tour *m* ▪ **let's go for** *OR* **take a ~ in the garden** allons faire un tour dans le jardin
11. [tendency, style] : **to have an optimistic ~ of mind** être optimiste de nature *OR* d'un naturel optimiste ▪ **to have a good ~ of speed** rouler vite ▪ **~ of phrase** tournure *f* *OR* tour *m* de phrase ▪ **she has a witty ~ of phrase** elle est très spirituelle *OR* pleine d'esprit
12. [purpose, requirement] exigence *f*, besoin *m* ▪ **this book has served its ~** ce livre a fait son temps
13. MUS doublé *m*
14. ST. EX [transaction] transaction *f (qui comprend l'achat et la vente)* ▪ *UK* [difference in price] écart *m* entre le prix d'achat et le prix de vente
15. *UK* THEAT numéro *m*
16. *UK phr* **done to a ~** *inf* CULIN : **the chicken was done to a ~** le poulet était cuit à point.

◆ **in turn** *adv phr* : **she interviewed each of us in ~** elle a eu un entretien avec chacun de nous l'un après l'autre ▪ **I told Sarah and she in ~ told Paul** je l'ai dit à Sarah qui, à son tour, l'a dit à Paul ▪ **I worked in ~ as a waiter, an actor and a teacher** j'ai travaillé successivement *OR* tour à tour comme serveur, acteur et enseignant.

◆ **on the turn** *adj phr* : **the tide is on the ~** *liter* c'est le changement de marée ; *fig* le vent tourne ■ **the milk is on the ~** le lait commence à tourner.

◆ **out of turn** *adv phr* : **don't play out of ~** attends ton tour pour jouer ■ **to speak out of ~** *fig* faire des remarques déplacées, parler mal à propos.

◆ **turn against** *vt insep* se retourner contre, s'en prendre à.

◆ **turn around** = **turn round**.

◆ **turn aside** ◇ *vi insep* [move to one side] s'écarter ■ *liter* & *fig* [move away] se détourner.

◇ *vt sep liter* & *fig* écarter, détourner.

◆ **turn away** ◇ *vt sep* **1.** [avert] détourner ■ **she ~ed her head away from him** elle s'est détournée de lui **2.** [reject - person] renvoyer ■ [stronger] chasser ■ **the college ~ed away hundreds of applicants** l'université a refusé des centaines de candidats.

◇ *vi insep* se détourner ■ **he ~ed away from them in anger** en *OR* de colère, il leur a tourné le dos.

◆ **turn back** ◇ *vi insep* **1.** [return - person] revenir, rebrousser chemin ; [- vehicle] faire demi-tour ■ **it was getting dark so we decided to ~ back** comme il commençait à faire nuit, nous avons décidé de faire demi-tour ■ **my mind is made up, there is no ~ing back** ma décision est prise, je n'y reviendrai pas **2.** [go back in book] : **~ back to chapter one** revenez *OR* retournez au premier chapitre.

◇ *vt sep* **1.** [force to return] faire faire demi-tour à ■ [refugee] refouler **2.** [fold - collar, sheet] rabattre ; [- sleeves] remonter, retrousser ; [- corner of page] corner **3.** *phr* **to ~ the clock back** remonter dans le temps, revenir en arrière.

◆ **turn down** ◇ *vt sep* **1.** [heating, lighting, sound] baisser **2.** [fold - sheet] rabattre, retourner ; [- collar] rabattre **3.** [reject - offer, request, suitor] rejeter, repousser ; [- candidate, job] refuser ■ **she ~ed me down flat** *inf* elle m'a envoyé balader.

◇ *vi insep* [move downwards] tourner vers le bas.

◆ **turn in** ◇ *vt sep* **1.** [return, give in - borrowed article, equipment, piece of work] rendre, rapporter ; [- criminal] livrer à la police **2.** [fold in] : **~ in the edges** rentrez les bords **3.** [produce] : **the actor ~ed in a good performance** l'acteur a très bien joué ■ **the company ~ed in record profits** l'entreprise a fait des bénéfices record.

◇ *vi insep* **1.** [feet, toes] : **my toes ~ in** j'ai les pieds en dedans **2.** *inf* [go to bed] se coucher **3.** *phr* **to ~ in on o.s.** se replier sur soi-même.

◆ **turn off** ◇ *vt sep* **1.** [switch off - light] éteindre ; [- heater, radio, television] éteindre, fermer ■ [cut off at mains] couper ■ [tap] fermer ■ **she ~ed the ignition/engine off** elle a coupé le contact/arrêté le moteur **2.** *inf* [fail to interest] rebuter ■ [sexually] couper l'envie à.

◇ *vi insep* **1.** [leave road] tourner ■ **we ~ed off at junction 5** nous avons pris la sortie d'autoroute 5 **2.** [switch off] s'éteindre.

◆ **turn on** ◇ *vt sep* **1.** [switch on - electricity, heating, light, radio, television] allumer ; [- engine] mettre en marche ; [- water] faire couler ; [- tap] ouvrir ■ [open at mains] ouvrir ■ **she can ~ on the charm/the tears whenever necessary** *inf fig* elle sait faire du charme/pleurer quand il le faut **2.** *inf* [person - interest] intéresser ; [- sexually] exciter ; [- introduce to drugs] initier à la drogue ■ **the movie didn't ~ me on at all** le film ne m'a vraiment pas emballé.

◇ *vt insep* [attack] attaquer ■ **his colleagues ~ed on him and accused him of stealing** ses collègues s'en sont pris à lui et l'ont accusé de vol.

◇ *vi insep* **1.** [switch on] s'allumer **2.** [depend, hinge on] dépendre de, reposer sur ■ **everything ~s on whether he continues as president** tout dépend s'il reste président ou non.

◆ **turn out** ◇ *vt sep* **1.** [switch off - light] éteindre ; [- gas] éteindre, couper **2.** [point outwards] : **she ~s her toes out when she walks** elle marche en canard **3.** [dismiss, expel] mettre à la porte ■ [tenant] expulser, déloger ■ **he ~ed his daughter out of the house** il a mis sa fille à la porte *OR* a chassé sa fille de la maison **4.** [empty - container, pockets] retourner, vider ; [- contents] vider ; [- jelly] verser ■ **~ the cake out onto a plate** démoulez le gâteau sur une assiette **5.** *UK* [clean] nettoyer à fond **6.** [produce] produire, fabriquer ■ **he ~s out a book a year** il écrit un livre par an ■ **few schools ~ out the kind of people we need** peu d'écoles forment le type de gens qu'il nous faut **7.** [police, troops] envoyer **8.** *(usu passive)* [dress] habiller ■ **nicely** *OR* **smartly ~ed out** élégant.

◇ *vi insep* **1.** [show up] venir, arriver ■ MIL [guard] (aller) prendre la faction ■ [troops] aller au rassemblement ■ **thousands ~ed out for the concert** des milliers de gens sont venus *OR* ont assisté au concert **2.** [car, person] sortir, partir **3.** [point outwards] : **my feet ~ out** j'ai les pieds en canard *OR* en dehors **4.** [prove] se révéler, s'avérer ■ **his statement ~ed out to be false** sa déclaration s'est révélée fausse ■ **he ~ed out to be a scoundrel** il s'est révélé être un vaurien, on s'est rendu compte que c'était un vaurien ■ [end up] : **I don't know how it ~ed out** je ne sais pas comment cela a fini ■ **the story ~ed out happily** l'histoire s'est bien terminée *OR* a bien fini ■ **the evening ~ed out badly** la soirée a mal tourné ■ **everything will ~ out fine** tout va s'arranger *OR* ira bien ■ **as it ~s out, he needn't have worried** en l'occurrence *OR* en fin de compte, ce n'était pas la peine de se faire du souci.

◆ **turn over** ◇ *vt sep* **1.** [playing card, mattress, person, stone] retourner ■ [page] tourner ■ [vehicle] retourner ■ [boat] faire chavirer ■ **I was ~ing over the pages of the magazine** je feuilletais la revue ▶ **to ~ over a new leaf** s'acheter une conduite **2.** [consider] réfléchir à *OR* sur ■ **I was ~ing the idea over in my mind** je tournais et retournais *OR* ruminais l'idée dans ma tête **3.** [hand over, transfer] rendre, remettre ■ **to ~ sb over to the authorities** livrer qqn aux autorités **4.** [change] transformer, changer **5.** COMM : **the store ~s over £1,000 a week** la boutique fait un chiffre d'affaires de 1 000 livres par semaine **6.** [search through] fouiller **7.** *UK inf* [rob - person] voler, dévaliser ; [- store] dévaliser ; [- house] cambrioler.

◇ *vi insep* **1.** [roll over - person] se retourner ; [- vehicle] se retourner, faire un tonneau ; [- boat] se retourner, chavirer **2.** [engine] commencer à tourner **3.** [when reading] tourner ■ **please ~ over** [in letter] = PTO **4.** COMM [merchandise] s'écouler, se vendre.

◆ **turn round** ◇ *vi insep UK* **1.** [rotate - person] se retourner ; [- object] tourner ■ **the dancers ~ed round and round** les danseurs tournaient *OR* tournoyaient (sur eux-mêmes) **2.** [face opposite direction - person] faire volte-face, faire demi-tour ; [- vehicle] faire demi-tour ■ **she ~ed round and accused us of stealing** *fig* elle s'est retournée contre nous et nous a accusés de vol.

◇ *vt sep* **1.** [rotate - head] tourner ; [- object, person] tourner, retourner ; [- vehicle] faire faire demi-tour à ■ **could you ~ the car round please?** tu peux faire demi-tour, s'il te plaît? **2.** [quantity of work] traiter **3.** [change nature of] : **to ~ a situation round** renverser une situation ■ **to ~ a company round** COMM faire prospérer une entreprise qui périclitait, sauver une entreprise de la faillite **4.** [sentence, idea] retourner.

◆ **turn to** *vt insep* **1.** *liter* [person] se tourner vers ■ [page] aller à ■ **~ to chapter one** allez au premier chapitre **2.** [seek help from] s'adresser à, se tourner vers ■ **to ~ to sb for advice** consulter qqn, demander conseil à qqn ■ **I don't know who to ~ to** je ne sais pas à qui m'adresser *OR* qui aller trouver **3.** *fig* [shift, move on to] : **her thoughts ~ed to her sister** elle se mit à penser à sa sœur ■ **the discussion ~ed to the war** on se mit à discuter de la guerre ■ [address - subject, issue etc] aborder, traiter ■ **let us ~ to another topic** passons à un autre sujet.

◆ **turn up** ◇ *vt sep* **1.** [heat, lighting, radio, TV] mettre plus fort ■ **to ~ the sound up** augmenter *OR* monter le volume **2.** [find, unearth] découvrir, dénicher ■ [buried object] déterrer ■ **her research ~ed up some interesting new facts** sa recherche a révélé de nouveaux détails intéressants **3.** [point upwards] remonter, relever ■ **she has a ~ed-up nose** elle a le nez retroussé **4.** [collar] relever ■ [trousers] remonter ■ [sleeve] retrousser, remonter.

◇ *vi insep* **1.** [appear] apparaître ■ [arrive] arriver ■ **she ~ed up at my office this morning** elle s'est présentée à mon bureau ce matin ■ **I'll take the first job that ~s up** je prendrai le premier poste qui se présentera ▶ **he ~s up like a bad penny** il arrive (toujours) au mauvais moment *OR* mal **2.** [be found] être trouvé *OR* retrouvé ■ **her bag ~ed up eventually** elle a fini par retrouver son sac **3.** [happen] se passer, arriver ■ **don't worry, something will ~ up** ne t'en fais pas, tu finiras par trouver quelque chose ■ **until something better ~s up** en attendant mieux.

turnabout ['tɜ:nəbaʊt] *n* volte-face *f inv*.

turnaround ['tɜ:nəraʊnd] *US* = **turnround**.

turncoat ['tɜ:nkəʊt] *n* renégat *m*, - e *f*, transfuge *mf*.

turndown ['tɜ:ndaʊn] <> *n* **1.** [rejection] refus *m* **2.** [in prices] tendance *f* à la baisse ▪ [in the economy] (tendance à la) baisse *f*.
<> *adj* [collar] rabattu ▪ [edge] à rabattre.

turned [tɜ:nd] *adj* **1.** [milk] tourné **2.** TYPO : **~ comma** ≃ guillemet *m* ▪ **~ period** point *m* décimal ▪ ≃ virgule *f*.

turned-on *adj inf* **1.** [up-to-date] branché, câblé **2.** [aroused] excité ▪ **to get ~** s'exciter.

turner ['tɜ:nəʳ] *n* **1.** [lathe operator] tourneur *m* **2.** *US* [gymnast] gymnaste *mf*.

turning ['tɜ:nɪŋ] *n* **1.** *UK* [side road] route *f* transversale ▪ [side street] rue *f* transversale, petite rue ▪ **take the third ~ on the right** prenez la troisième à droite **2.** *UK* [bend - in river] coude *m* ; [- in road] virage *m* ▪ [fork] embranchement *m*, carrefour *m* **3.** INDUST tournage *m*.

turning circle *n UK* AUT rayon *m* de braquage.

turning point *n* [decisive moment] moment *m* décisif ▪ [change] tournant *m* ▪ **1989 marked a ~ in my career** l'année 1989 marqua un tournant dans ma carrière.

turning radius *US* = **turning circle**.

turnip ['tɜ:nɪp] *n* navet *m*.

turnkey ['tɜ:nki:] <> *n* [jailer] geôlier *m*, - ère *f*.
<> *adj* CONSTR [project] clés en main.

turn-off *n* **1.** [road] sortie *f* (de route), route *f* transversale, embranchement *m* **2.** *inf* [loss of interest] : **it's a real ~** [gen] c'est vraiment à vous dégoûter ; [sexual] ça vous coupe vraiment l'envie.

turn-on *n inf* **he finds leather a ~** il trouve le cuir excitant, le cuir l'excite.

turnout ['tɜ:naʊt] *n* **1.** [attendance - at meeting, concert] assistance *f* ▪ POL [at election] (taux *m* de) participation *f* ▪ **there was a good ~** [gen] il y avait beaucoup de monde, beaucoup de gens sont venus ; POL il y avait un fort taux de participation **2.** [dress] mise *f*, tenue *f* **3.** *UK* [clearout] : **I had a ~ of my old clothes for the jumble sale** j'ai trié mes vieux vêtements pour la vente de charité **4.** *US* AUT refuge *m (pour se laisser doubler)*.

turnover ['tɜ:nˌəʊvəʳ] *n* **1.** *UK* FIN chiffre *m* d'affaires **2.** [of staff, tenants] renouvellement *m* ▪ **there is a high ~ of tenants** les locataires changent souvent **3.** *US* [of stock] vitesse *f* de rotation ▪ [of shares] mouvement *m* ▪ **computer magazines have a high ~** les revues d'informatique se vendent bien **4.** CULIN : **apple ~** chausson *m* aux pommes.

turnpike ['tɜ:npaɪk] *n* **1.** [barrier] barrière *f* de péage **2.** *US* [road] autoroute *f* à péage.

turnround ['tɜ:nraʊnd] *n* **1.** : **~ (time)** [of passenger ship, plane] temps *m* nécessaire entre deux voyages ; [for freight] temps nécessaire pour le déchargement ; NAUT estarie *f*, starie *f* ; COMPUT temps de retournement, délai *m* d'exécution **2.** [reversal - of fortunes] retournement *m*, renversement *m* ; [- of opinions] revirement *m*, volte-face *f inv*.

turnstile ['tɜ:nstaɪl] *n* tourniquet *m (barrière)*.

turntable ['tɜ:nˌteɪbl] *n* **1.** [on record player] platine *f* **2.** RAIL plaque *f* tournante **3.** [on microscope] platine *f*.

turntable ladder *n* échelle *f* pivotante *(des pompiers)*.

turn-up *n UK* **1.** [on trousers] revers *m* **2.** *inf* [surprise] surprise *f* ▪ **that's a ~ for the book** *OR* **books** c'est une sacrée surprise.

turpentine ['tɜ:pəntaɪn] *n UK* (essence *f* de) térébenthine *f*.

turpitude ['tɜ:pɪtju:d] *n* turpitude *f*.

turps [tɜ:ps] *(U) UK* = **turpentine**.

turquoise ['tɜ:kwɔɪz] <> *n* **1.** [gem] turquoise *f* **2.** [colour] turquoise *m inv*.
<> *adj* **1.** [bracelet, ring] de *OR* en turquoise **2.** [in colour] turquoise *(inv)*.

turret ['tʌrɪt] *n* tourelle *f*.

turtle ['tɜ:tl] *n* **1.** [in sea] tortue *f* marine ▪ *US* [on land] tortue *f* **2.** *phr* **to turn ~** se renverser.

turtledove ['tɜ:tldʌv] *n* tourterelle *f*.

turtleneck ['tɜ:tlnek] <> *adj* [sweater, dress] à col montant, à encolure montante ▪ *US* à col roulé.
<> *n* col *m* montant, encolure *f* montante ▪ *US* (pull *m* à) col *m* roulé.

turves [tɜ:vz] *pl* ▷ **turf**.

Tuscan ['tʌskən] <> *n* **1.** [person] Toscan *m*, - e *f* **2.** LING toscan *m*.
<> *adj* toscan.

Tuscany ['tʌskənɪ] *pr n* Toscane *f* ▪ **in ~** en Toscane.

tush [tʌʃ] *n US inf* [buttocks] fesses *fpl*.

tusk [tʌsk] *n* [of elephant, boar] défense *f*.

tussle ['tʌsl] <> *n* **1.** [scuffle] mêlée *f*, bagarre *f* ▪ **to have a ~ with sb** se battre contre qqn, en venir aux mains avec qqn **2.** [struggle] lutte *f* **3.** [quarrel] dispute *f*.
<> *vi* [scuffle, fight] se battre ▪ **I ~d with her for the ball** je me suis battu avec elle pour avoir la balle, on s'est disputé la balle.

tut [tʌt] *(pret & pp* **tutted**, *cont* **tutting)** <> *interj* : **tut!, tut-tut!** [in disapproval] allons donc! ; [in annoyance] zut!
<> *vi* [in disapproval] pousser une exclamation désapprobatrice ▪ [in annoyance] exprimer son mécontentement.

Tutankhamen [ˌtu:təŋ'kɑ:mən], **Tutankhamun** [ˌtu:təŋkɑ:'mu:n] *pr n* Toutankhamon.

tutelage ['tju:tɪlɪdʒ] *n fml* tutelle *f* ▪ **under his ~** sous sa tutelle.

tutor ['tju:təʳ] <> *n* **1.** [teacher] professeur *m* particulier ▪ [full-time] précepteur *m*, - trice *f* ▪ **piano ~** professeur de piano **2.** *UK* UNIV [teacher] professeur *m (qui dirige et supervise les travaux d'un groupe d'étudiants)* ▪ *UK* SCH professeur *m* principal *(surtout dans les écoles privées)* **3.** *Scotland* LAW [guardian] tuteur *m*, - trice *f*.
<> *vt* **1.** [instruct] donner des cours (particuliers) à **2.** *UK* UNIV diriger les études de **3.** *Scotland* LAW être le tuteur de.
<> *vi* **1.** [pupil] suivre des cours particuliers **2.** [teacher] donner des cours particuliers.

tutorial [tju:'tɔ:rɪəl] UNIV <> *n* (séance *f* de) travaux *mpl* dirigés, TD *mpl*.
<> *adj* [work] de travaux dirigés ▪ [duties] de directeur d'études.

tutti frutti [ˌtu:tɪ'fru:tɪ] *(pl* **tutti fruttis)** <> *n* plombières *f*, tutti-frutti *m*.
<> *adj* [ice cream, flavour] tutti-frutti.

tut-tut = **tut**.

tutu ['tu:tu:] *n* tutu *m*.

Tuvalu [tu:'vɑ:lu:] *n* Tuvalu *m*.

tu-whit tu-whoo [tə'wɪttə'wu:] *onom* hou-hou.

tux [tʌks] *n inf* = **tuxedo**.

tuxedo [tʌk'si:dəʊ] *(pl* **tuxedos)** *n US* smoking *m*.

TV <> *n (abbrev of* **television)** TV *f*.
<> *comp* [programme, set, star] de télé ▪ **~ dinner** plateau-repas *m*, repas *m* tout prêt *OR* prêt à consommer *(que l'on mange devant la télé)*.

TV movie *n* téléfilm *m*, film *m* de télévision.

twaddle ['twɒdl] *n (U) UK inf* bêtises *fpl*, âneries *fpl*, imbécillités *fpl* ▪ **what a load of ~!** quelles âneries!

twain [tweɪn] *n lit* **never the ~ shall meet** les deux sont inconciliables, les deux ne pourront jamais se mettre d'accord.

twang [twæŋ] <> *n* **1.** [of wire, guitar] son *m* de corde pincée **2.** [in voice] ton *m* nasillard ▪ **she speaks with a ~** elle parle du nez, elle nasille **3.** [accent] accent *m* ▪ **he has a slight Australian ~** il a un léger accent australien.
<> *vt* [string instrument] pincer les cordes de.
<> *vi* [arrow, bow, wire] vibrer.

'twas [twɒz] *lit & dial* = **it was**.

twat▲ [twæt, twɒt] *n* **1.** [female genitals] chatte△ *f* **2.** [fool] con△ *m*.

tweak [twi:k] ◇ *vt* **1.** [twist - ear, nose] tordre (doucement), pincer ▪ [pull] tirer (sur) **2.** AUT mettre au point ▪ *fig* & COMPUT peaufiner, mettre au point.
◇ *n* (petit) coup *m* sec ▪ **he gave my ear a ~** il m'a tiré l'oreille.

twee [twi:] *adj UK inf* [person] chichiteux ▪ [idea, sentiment] mièvre ▪ [decor] cucul *(inv)*.

tweed [twi:d] ◇ *n* [cloth] tweed *m*.
◇ *comp* [jacket, skirt] de tweed, en tweed.
◆ **tweeds** *npl* [clothes] vêtements *mpl* de tweed ▪ [suit] costume *m* de tweed.

tweedy ['twi:dɪ] (*comp* **tweedier**, *superl* **tweediest**) *adj* **1.** [fabric] qui ressemble au tweed **2.** *pej* [man] qui a le genre gentleman-farmer ▪ [woman] qui fait bourgeoise de campagne.

tweenage ['twi:neɪdʒ] *adj inf* préadolescence *f*.

tweenager ['twi:neɪdʒəʳ] *n inf* préado *mf*, préadolescent *m*, - e *f*.

tweet [twi:t] ◇ *n* pépiement *m*.
◇ *onom* cui-cui.
◇ *vi* pépier.

tweeter ['twi:təʳ] *n* tweeter *m*, haut-parleur *m* d'aigus.

tweezers ['twi:zəz] *npl* : **(pair of) ~** pince *f* à épiler.

twelfth [twelfθ] ◇ *det* douzième.
◇ *n* **1.** [ordinal] douzième *mf* **2.** [fraction] douzième *m*, *see also* **fifth**.

Twelfth Night *n* la fête des Rois.

twelve [twelv] ◇ *det* douze *(inv)*.
◇ *n* douze *m inv*.
◇ *pron* douze, *see also* **five**.

twelve-tone *adj* MUS dodécaphonique ▪ **~ system** dodécaphonisme *m*.

twentieth ['twentɪəθ] ◇ *det* vingtième.
◇ *n* **1.** [ordinal] vingtième *mf* **2.** [fraction] vingtième *m*, *see also* **fiftieth**.

twenty ['twentɪ] ◇ *det* vingt *(inv)* ▪ **to smoke ~ a day** fumer un paquet par jour.
◇ *n* vingt *m*.
◇ *pron* vingt, *see also* **fifty**.

twenty-first *n* [birthday] vingt-et-unième anniversaire *m*.

twenty-four *adj* : **~-hour service** service *m* vingt-quatre heures sur vingt-quatre OR jour et nuit ▪ **open ~ hours a day** ouvert vingt-quatre heures sur vingt-quatre.

twenty-one *n* [pontoon] vingt-et-un *m inv (jeu)*.

twenty-twenty vision *n* : **to have ~** avoir dix dixièmes à chaque œil.

'twere [twɜ:ʳ] *lit & dial* = **it were**.

twerp [twɜ:p] *n inf* andouille *f*, crétin *m*, - e *f*.

twice [twaɪs] ◇ *adv* **1.** [with noun] deux fois ▪ **~ 3 is 6** deux fois 3 font 6 **2.** [with verb] deux fois ▪ **they didn't need to be asked** OR **told ~** ils ne se sont pas fait prier, ils ne se le sont pas fait dire deux fois **3.** [with adj or adv] : **~ weekly/daily** deux fois par semaine/jour ▪ **she can run ~ as fast as me** elle court deux fois plus vite que moi ▪ **it's ~ as good** c'est deux fois mieux ▪ **~ as much time/as many apples** deux fois plus de temps/de pommes.
◇ *predet* deux fois ▪ **~ a day** deux fois par jour ▪ **~ the price** deux fois plus cher ▪ **he's almost ~ your height** il est presque deux fois plus grand que vous ▪ **since the operation he is ~ the man he was** depuis son opération il est transformé OR en pleine forme ▪ **he's ~ the man you are!** il vaut deux fois mieux que toi!

twiddle ['twɪdl] ◇ *vt* [knob, dial] tourner, manier ▪ [moustache] tripoter, jouer avec ▪ **to ~ one's thumbs** *liter & fig* se tourner les pouces.
◇ *vi* : **to ~ with the knob** tourner le bouton.
◇ *n* : **give the knob a ~** tournez le bouton.

twig [twɪg] (*pret & pp* **twigged**, *cont* **twigging**) ◇ *vi & vt UK inf* [understand] piger.
◇ *n* [for fire] brindille *f* ▪ [on tree] petite branche *f*.

twilight ['twaɪlaɪt] ◇ *n* **1.** [in evening] crépuscule *m* ▪ [in morning] aube *f* ▪ **at ~** [evening] au crépuscule ; [morning] à l'aube **2.** [half-light] pénombre *f*, obscurité *f*, demi-jour *m* **3.** *fig* [last stages, end] crépuscule *m* ▪ **in the ~ of his life** au crépuscule de sa vie.
◇ *comp* : **a ~ world** un monde nébuleux ▪ **his ~ years** les dernières années de sa vie ▪ **~ sleep** MED demi-sommeil *m* provoqué.

twill [twɪl] *n* sergé *m*.

'twill [twɪl] *lit & dial* = **it will**.

twin [twɪn] (*pret & pp* **twinned**, *cont* **twinning**) ◇ *n* jumeau *m*, - elle *f*.
◇ *adj* **1.** [child, sibling] : **they have ~ boys/girls** ils ont des jumeaux/des jumelles ▪ **my ~ sister** ma sœur jumelle **2.** [dual - spires, hills] double, jumeau ; [- aims] double.
◇ *vt* [town] jumeler ▪ **our town is twinned with Hamburg** notre ville est jumelée avec Hambourg.

twin-bedded [-'bedɪd] *adj* [room] à deux lits.

twin beds *npl* lits *m* jumeaux.

twin carburettor *n* carburateur *m* double-corps.

twin cylinder ◇ *n* moteur *m* à deux cylindres.
◇ *adj* à deux cylindres.

twine [twaɪn] ◇ *vt* **1.** [wind - hair, string] entortiller, enrouler **2.** [weave] tresser.
◇ *vi* **1.** [stem, ivy] s'enrouler ▪ **the honeysuckle had ~d around the tree** le chèvrefeuille s'était enroulé autour de l'arbre **2.** [path, river] serpenter.
◇ *n (U)* (grosse) ficelle *f*.

twin-engined [-'endʒɪnd] *adj* bimoteur.

twinge [twɪndʒ] *n* **1.** [of guilt, shame] sentiment *m* ▪ **to have** OR **to feel a ~ of remorse** ressentir un certain remords ▪ **he watched her leave with a ~ of sadness** il la regarda partir avec (une certaine) tristesse **2.** [of pain] élancement *m*, tiraillement *m* ▪ **she felt a ~ in her back** elle sentit une petite douleur dans le dos.

twining ['twaɪnɪŋ] *adj* [plant] volubile.

twinjet [twɪn'dʒet] *n* biréacteur *m*.

twinkle ['twɪŋkl] ◇ *vi* **1.** [star, diamond] briller, scintiller **2.** [eyes] briller, pétiller ▪ **her eyes ~d with excitement** ses yeux brillaient d'excitation.
◇ *n* **1.** [of star, diamond, light] scintillement *m* **2.** [in eye] pétillement *m* ▪ **he had a ~ in his eye** il avait les yeux pétillants ▪ **when you were just a ~ in your father's eye** *hum* bien avant que tu ne fasses ton entrée dans le monde.

twinkling ['twɪŋklɪŋ] ◇ *adj* **1.** [star, gem, sea] scintillant, brillant **2.** [eyes] pétillant, brillant **3.** *fig* [feet] agile.
◇ *n (U)* **1.** [of star, light, gem] scintillement *m* **2.** [in eyes] pétillement *m* ▪ **in the ~ of an eye** en un clin d'œil.

twinning ['twɪnɪŋ] *n* jumelage *m* (de villes).

twin room *n* chambre *f* à deux lits.

twin-screw *adj* [boat] à deux hélices.

twinset ['twɪn,set] *n* twin set *m*.

twin town *n* ville *f* jumelée OR jumelle.

twin tub *n* machine *f* à laver à deux tambours.

twirl [twɜ:l] ◇ *vt* **1.** [spin - stick, parasol, handle] faire tournoyer ; [- lasso] faire tourner ▪ **she ~ed the stick (round) in the air** elle jeta le bâton en l'air en le faisant tournoyer **2.** [twist - moustache, hair] tortiller, friser.
◇ *vi* [dancer, lasso, handle] tournoyer ▪ **she ~ed round to face us** elle se tourna pour nous faire face, elle fit volte-face vers nous.
◇ *n* **1.** [whirl - of body, stick] tournoiement *m* ▪ [pirouette] pirouette *f* ▪ **to do a ~** tourner sur soi-même, faire une pirouette **2.** [written flourish] fioriture *f*.

twist [twɪst] ◇ *vt* **1.** [turn - round and round] tourner ; [- round axis] tourner, visser ; [- tightly] tordre ■ **try ~ing the dial to the left** essaie de tourner le cadran vers la gauche ■ **you have to ~ the lid clockwise** il faut visser le couvercle dans le sens des aiguilles d'une montre ■ **the railings were ~ed out of shape** les grilles étaient toutes tordues
2. [twine] tresser, entortiller ■ [wind] enrouler, tourner ■ **the seat-belt got ~ed** la ceinture (de sécurité) s'est entortillée ■ **he ~ed the threads into a rope** il a tressé *OR* torsadé les fils pour en faire une corde
3. [body, part of body] tourner ■ **I ~ed my head (round) to the left** j'ai tourné la tête vers la gauche ■ **he ~ed himself free** il s'est dégagé en se tortillant ■ **her face was ~ed with pain** *fig* ses traits étaient tordus par la douleur, la douleur lui tordait le visage ▶ **to ~ sb's arm** *liter* tordre le bras à qqn ; *fig* forcer la main à qqn ■ **if you ~ his arm, he'll agree to go** si tu insistes un peu, il voudra bien y aller
4. [sprain - ankle, wrist] tordre, fouler ■ **I've ~ed my ankle** je me suis tordu *OR* foulé la cheville ■ **I seem to have ~ed my neck** je crois que j'ai attrapé un torticolis
5. [distort - words] déformer ; [- argument] déformer, fausser
6. *UK inf* [cheat, swindle] arnaquer.
◇ *vi* **1.** [road, stream] serpenter ■ **the path ~ed and turned through the forest** le chemin zigzaguait à travers la forêt
2. [become twined] s'enrouler ■ **the ivy ~ed round the tree** le lierre s'enroulait autour de l'arbre
3. [body, part of body] se tortiller ■ **the dog ~ed out of my arms** le chien s'est dégagé de mes bras en se tortillant ■ **his mouth ~ed into a smile** il eut un rictus
4. [be sprained - ankle] se tordre, se fouler ; [- knee] se tordre
5. [dance] twister
6. [in pontoon] : **~!** encore une carte!
◇ *n* **1.** [turn, twirl] tour *m*, torsion *f* ■ **to give sthg a ~** [dial, handle, lid] (faire) tourner qqch ; [wire] tordre qqch ■ **there's a ~ in the tape** la bande est entortillée ■ **to get (o.s.) into a ~ about sthg** [get angry] se fâcher *OR* s'énerver au sujet de qqch ; [get upset] prendre qqch au tragique, se mettre dans tous ses états
2. [in road] tournant *m*, virage *m* ■ [in river] coude *m* ■ [in staircase] tournant *m* ■ *fig* [in thinking] détour *m* ■ **it's difficult to follow the ~s and turns of his argument/of government policy** il est difficile de suivre les méandres de son argumentation/de la politique gouvernementale
3. [coil - of tobacco] rouleau *m* ; [- of paper] tortillon *m*
4. CULIN : **a ~ of lemon** un zeste de citron
5. [in story, plot] tour *m* ■ **the film has an exciting ~ at the end** le film se termine par un coup de théâtre passionnant ■ **the book gives a new ~ to the old story** le livre donne une nouvelle tournure *OR* un tour nouveau à cette vieille histoire ■ **by a strange ~ of fate, we met again years later in Zimbabwe** par un hasard extraordinaire *OR* un caprice du destin, nous nous sommes retrouvés au Zimbabwe des années après
6. [dance] twist *m* ■ **to do** *OR* **to dance the ~** twister
7. *UK inf* [cheat] arnaque *f*
8. *UK inf phr* **to be completely round the ~** être complètement dingue *OR* cinglé ■ **they're driving me round the ~!** ils me rendent dingue!

◆ **twist about** *UK*, **twist around** *vi insep* **1.** [wire, rope] s'entortiller, s'emmêler
2. [road] serpenter, zigzaguer.

◆ **twist off** ◇ *vt sep* [lid] dévisser ■ [cork] enlever en tournant ■ [branch] enlever *OR* arracher en tordant.
◇ *vi insep* [cap, lid] se dévisser.

◆ **twist round** *UK* ◇ *vt sep* [rope, tape] enrouler ■ [lid] tourner, visser ■ [handle] (faire) tourner ■ [swivel chair] faire tourner *OR* pivoter ■ [hat] tourner ■ [head] tourner ■ **I ~ed myself round on my chair** je me suis retourné sur ma chaise.
◇ *vi insep* **1.** [person] se retourner
2. [strap, rope] se tortiller ■ [swivel chair] se tourner, pivoter
3. [path] serpenter, zigzaguer.

◆ **twist together** *vt sep* [threads] tresser, enrouler ■ [wires] enrouler.

◆ **twist up** ◇ *vt sep* [threads, wires] enrouler, emmêler.
◇ *vi insep* **1.** [threads, wires] s'emmêler, s'enchevêtrer
2. [smoke] monter en volutes.

twisted ['twɪstɪd] *adj* **1.** [personality, smile] tordu ■ [mind] tordu, mal tourné **2.** [logic, argument] faux, fausse *f*, tordu **3.** [dishonest] malhonnête ■ [politician, lawyer, businessman] malhonnête, véreux **4.** *inf* [crazy] tordu.

twister ['twɪstər] *n inf* **1.** *UK* [crook] escroc *m* **2.** *US* [tornado] tornade *f*.

twit [twɪt] *n inf UK inf* [idiot] crétin *m*, - e *f*, imbécile *mf*.

twitch [twɪtʃ] ◇ *vi* **1.** [jerk - once] avoir un mouvement convulsif ; [- habitually] avoir un tic ■ [muscle] se contracter convulsivement ■ **his hands ~ed nervously** ses mains se contractaient nerveusement ■ **his right eye ~es** il a un tic à l'œil droit ■ **the rabbit's nose ~ed** le lapin a remué le nez **2.** [wriggle] s'agiter, se remuer.
◇ *vt* [ears, nose] remuer, bouger ■ [curtain, rope] tirer d'un coup sec, donner un coup sec à.
◇ *n* **1.** [nervous tic] tic *m* ■ [muscular spasm] spasme *m* ■ **to have a (nervous) ~** avoir un tic (nerveux) ■ **the rabbit's ears gave a ~** le lapin a remué les oreilles **2.** [tweak, pull - on hair, rope] coup *m* sec, saccade *f*.

twitchy ['twɪtʃɪ] *adj* [person] agité, nerveux.

twitter ['twɪtər] ◇ *vi* **1.** [bird] gazouiller, pépier **2.** [person - chatter] jacasser ■ **she's always ~ing (on) about her daughter** elle ne parle que de sa fille.
◇ *n* **1.** [of bird] gazouillement *m*, pépiement *m* **2.** [of person] bavardage *m* **3.** *inf* [agitation] état *m* d'agitation ■ **to be all of a** *OR* **in a ~ about sthg** être dans tous ses états *OR* sens dessus dessous à cause de qqch.

'twixt [twɪkst] *lit* = **betwixt**.

two [tu:] (*pl* **twos**) ◇ *det* deux *(inv)*.
◇ *n* **1.** deux *m inv* ■ **to cut sthg in ~** couper qqch en deux ■ **in ~s, ~ by ~** deux par deux ■ **in ~s and threes** par (groupes de) deux ou trois ■ **~ at a time** deux à la fois **2.** *phr* **to put ~ and ~ together** faire le rapport (entre deux choses) et tirer ses conclusions ■ **she put ~ and ~ together, and made five** elle en a tiré des conclusions erronées ■ **they're ~ of a kind** ils sont du même genre, ils se ressemblent tous les deux ■ **that makes ~ of us** vous n'êtes pas le seul, moi c'est pareil ■ **~'s company, three's a crowd** deux ça va, trois c'est trop.
◇ *pron* deux *mf pl* ■ **there are ~ (of them)** il y en a deux, ils sont deux, *see also* **five**.

two-bit *adj US inf pej* de pacotille.

two-chamber system *n* POL système *m* bicaméral.

two-dimensional *adj* **1.** [figure, drawing] à deux dimensions **2.** [simplistic - character] sans profondeur, simpliste.

two-door *adj* [car] à deux portes.

two-edged *adj* [sword, policy, argument] à double tranchant.

two-faced *adj* hypocrite.

twofold ['tu:fəʊld] ◇ *adj* double ■ **their aims are ~** ils ont deux objectifs *OR* un objectif double ■ **there has been a ~ increase in attendance** l'assistance a doublé.
◇ *adv* [increase] au double ■ **prices have risen ~** les prix ont doublé.

two-four time *n* MUS mesure *f* à deux temps, deux-quatre *m inv*.

two-handed *adj* [tool] à deux poignées ■ [saw] à deux mains, forestière ■ [sword] à deux mains ■ [game] qui se joue à deux, pour deux joueurs ■ **a ~ backhand** [in tennis] un revers à deux mains.

two-lane *adj US* [highway] à deux voies.

two-legged [-'legɪd] *adj* bipède.

two-party *adj* [coalition, system] biparti, bipartite.

twopence ['tʌpəns] *n UK* deux pence *mpl*.

twopenny ['tʌpnɪ] *adj UK inf* à *OR* de deux pence.

two-piece ◇ *adj* en deux parties ■ **~ swimming costume** (maillot *m* de bain) deux-pièces *m* ■ **~ suit** [man's] costume *m* deux-pièces ; [woman's] tailleur *m*.
◇ *n* [bikini] deux-pièces *m* ■ [man's suit] costume *m* deux-pièces ■ [woman's suit] tailleur *m*.

two-ply *adj* [wool] à deux fils ■ [rope] à deux brins ■ [tissue] double, à double épaisseur ■ [wood] à deux épaisseurs.

two-seater ◇ *adj* à deux places.
◇ *n* [plane] avion *m* à deux places ■ [car] voiture *f* à deux places.

two-sided *adj* [problem] qui a deux aspects ■ [argument] discutable, qui comporte deux points de vue.

twosome ['tu:səm] *n* **1.** [couple] couple *m* **2.** [match] partie *f* à deux.

two-star ◇ *adj* **1.** [restaurant, hotel] deux étoiles **2.** *UK* [petrol] ordinaire.
◇ *n UK* [petrol] (essence *f*) ordinaire *m*.

two-step *n* [dance, music] pas *m* de deux.

two-storey *adj* à deux étages.

two-stroke *adj* [engine] à deux temps.

two-tier *adj* [cake, management] à deux étages.

two-time *vt inf* [lover] tromper, être infidèle à.

two-timer *n inf* [lover] amant *m*, maîtresse *f* infidèle.

two-tone *adj* [in colour] à deux tons ■ [in sound] de deux tons.

two-way *adj* [traffic] dans les deux sens ■ [street] à double sens ■ [agreement, process] bilatéral ■ **~ mirror** glace *f* sans tain ■ **~ radio** TELEC émetteur-récepteur *m* ■ **~ switch** ELEC va-et-vient *m inv*.

two-way street *n* rue *f* à double sens ■ *phr* ça doit fonctionner dans les deux sens.

two-wheeler *n* [motorbike] deux-roues *m* ■ [bicycle] bicyclette *f*, deux-roues *m*.

TX *written abbr of* **Texas**.

tycoon [taɪ'ku:n] *n* homme *m* d'affaires important, magnat *m* ■ **oil/newspaper ~** magnat du pétrole/de la presse.

tyke [taɪk] *n* **1.** [dog] chien *m* bâtard **2.** *inf* [child] sale gosse *mf*.

tympani ['tɪmpənɪ] = **timpani**.

tympanum ['tɪmpənəm] (*pl* **tympana** [-nə] *OR pl* **tympanums**) *n* **1.** ANAT, ARCHIT & ZOOL tympan *m* **2.** MUS timbale *f*.

type [taɪp] ◇ *n* **1.** [gen - BIOL] : **blood/hair ~** type *m* sanguin/de cheveux **2.** [sort, kind] sorte *f*, genre *m*, espèce *f* ■ [make - of coffee, shampoo etc] marque *f* ■ [model - of car, plane, equipment etc] modèle *m* ■ **what ~ of car do you drive?** qu'est-ce que vous avez comme voiture?, quel modèle de voiture avez-vous? **3.** [referring to person] genre *m*, type *m* ■ **she's not that ~ (of person)** ce n'est pas son genre ■ **he's not my ~** ce n'est pas mon type (d'homme) ■ **I know his/their ~** je connais les gens de son espèce/de cette espèce ■ **she's one of those sporty ~s** elle est du genre sportif **4.** [typical example] type *m*, exemple *m* **5.** *(U)* TYPO [single character] caractère *m* ■ [block of print] caractères *mpl* (d'imprimerie) ■ **to set ~** composer.
◇ *vt* **1.** [subj: typist] taper (à la machine) ■ **to ~ sthg into a computer** saisir qqch à l'ordinateur ■ **to ~ a letter** taper une lettre **2.** MED [blood sample] classifier, déterminer le type de.
◇ *vi* [typist] taper (à la machine) ■ **I can only ~ with two fingers** je ne tape qu'avec deux doigts.
◆ **type out** *vt sep* **1.** [letter] taper (à la machine) **2.** [error] effacer (à la machine).
◆ **type over** *vt insep* COMPUT écraser.
◆ **type up** *vt sep* [report, notes] taper (à la machine).

-type *in cpds* du type, genre.

typecast ['taɪpkɑ:st] (*pret & pp* **typecast**) *vt* [actor] enfermer dans le rôle de ■ **he is always ~ as a villain** on lui fait toujours jouer des rôles de bandit.

typeface ['taɪpfeɪs] *n* œil *m* du caractère.

typeover ['taɪp,əuvər] *n* : **'typeover'** '(mode) écraser'.

typescript ['taɪpskrɪpt] *n* texte *m* dactylographié, tapuscrit *m*.

typeset ['taɪpset] (*pret & pp* **typeset**, *cont* **typesetting**) *vt* PRINT composer.

typesetter ['taɪp,setər] *n* [worker] compositeur *m*, - trice *f* ■ [machine] linotype *f*.

typesetting ['taɪp,setɪŋ] *n* PRINT composition *f*.

typewriter ['taɪp,raɪtər] *n* machine *f* à écrire.

typewritten ['taɪp,rɪtn] *adj* dactylographié, tapé à la machine.

typhoid ['taɪfɔɪd] ◇ *n (U)* typhoïde *f*.
◇ *comp* [injection] antityphoïdique ■ [symptoms] de la typhoïde ■ **~ fever** (fièvre *f*) typhoïde *f*.

typhoon [taɪ'fu:n] *n* typhon *m*.

typhus ['taɪfəs] *n* typhus *m*.

typical ['tɪpɪkl] *adj* typique, caractéristique ■ **it's a ~ example of Aztec pottery** c'est un exemple type de poterie aztèque ■ **the ~ American** l'Américain typique *OR* type ■ **that's ~ of her!** *pej* c'est bien d'elle! ■ **he said with ~ self-deprecation** il dit avec son humilité habituelle ■ **~ man!** c'est bien un homme!

typically ['tɪpɪklɪ] *adv* **1.** [normally] d'habitude **2.** [characteristically] typiquement ■ **it's a ~ French scene** c'est une scène bien française *OR* typiquement française ■ **~, she changed her mind at the last minute** comme à son habitude, elle a changé d'avis au dernier moment.

typify ['tɪpɪfaɪ] (*pret & pp* **typified**) *vt* **1.** [be typical of] être typique *OR* caractéristique de **2.** [embody, symbolize] symboliser, être le type même de.

typing ['taɪpɪŋ] *n* **1.** [typing work] : **he had 10 pages of ~ to do** il avait 10 pages à taper *OR* dactylographier **2.** [typescript] tapuscrit *m*, texte *m* dactylographié **3.** [skill] dactylo *f*, dactylographie *f*.

typing error *n* faute *f* de frappe.

typing pool *n* bureau *m OR* pool *m* des dactylos.

typing speed *n* vitesse *f* de frappe ■ **I have a ~ of 30 words a minute** je tape 30 mots à la minute.

typist ['taɪpɪst] *n* dactylo *mf*, dactylographe *mf*.

typo ['taɪpəu] (*pl* **typos**) *n inf* [in typescript] faute *f* de frappe ■ [in printed text] coquille *f*.

typographer [taɪ'pɒgrəfər] *n* typographe *mf*.

typographic [,taɪpə'græfɪk] *adj* typographique.

typography [taɪ'pɒgrəfɪ] *n* typographie *f*.

typology [taɪ'pɒlədʒɪ] *n* typologie *f*.

tyrannical [tɪ'rænɪkl] *adj* tyrannique.

tyrannicide [tɪ'rænɪsaɪd] *n* **1.** [person] tyrannicide *mf* **2.** [act] tyrannicide *m*.

tyrannize, ise ['tɪrənaɪz] ◇ *vt* tyranniser.
◇ *vi* : **to ~ over sb** tyranniser qqn.

tyrannosaur [tɪ'rænəsɔ:r], **tyrannosaurus** [tɪ,rænə'sɔ:rəs] *n* tyrannosaure *m*.

tyranny ['tɪrənɪ] (*pl* **tyrannies**) *n* tyrannie *f*.

tyrant ['taɪrənt] *n* tyran *m*.

tyre *UK*, **tire** *US* ['taɪər] *n* pneu *m*.

tyre gauge *n* manomètre *m (pour pneus)*.

tyre iron, tyre lever *n* démonte-pneu *m*.

tyre pressure *n* pression *f* des pneus.

tyro ['taɪrəu] (*pl* **tyros**) *n fml* débutant *m*, - e *f*, novice *mf*.

Tyrol [tɪ'rəul] *pr n* Tyrol *m* ■ **in the ~** dans le Tyrol.

Tyrolean [tɪrə'lɪən], **Tyrolese** [,tɪrə'li:z] ◇ *n* Tyrolien *m*, - enne *f*.
◇ *adj* tyrolien.

Tyrrhenian Sea [tɪ'ri:nɪən-] *pr n* : **the ~** la mer Tyrrhénienne.

tzar *etc* [zɑ:r] = **tsar**.

tzetze fly ['tsetsɪ-] = **tsetse fly**.

U

u (*pl* **u's** *OR pl* **us**), **U** (*pl* **U's** *OR pl* **Us**) [juː] *n* [letter] u *m*, U *m*, *see also* **f**.

U ◇ *n* (*abbrev of* **universal**) *désigne un film tous publics en Grande-Bretagne*.
◇ *adj* *UK inf* [upper-class - expression, activity] ≃ distingué ■ **U/non-U language** langage *m* distingué/vulgaire.

UAE (*abbrev of* **United Arab Emirates**) *pr n* EAU *mpl*.

UAW (*abbrev of* **United Automobile Workers**) *pr n syndicat américain de l'industrie automobile*.

UB40 (*abbrev of* **unemployment benefit form 40**) *n* **1.** [card] *en Grande-Bretagne, carte de pointage pour bénéficier de l'allocation de chômage* **2.** *inf* [person] chômeur *m*, - euse *f*.

U-bend *n* [in pipe] coude *m* ■ [under sink] siphon *m*.

ubiquitous [juː'bɪkwɪtəs] *adj* [gen] omniprésent, que l'on trouve partout ■ [person] doué d'ubiquité, omniprésent.

ubiquity [juː'bɪkwətɪ] *n* ubiquité *f*, omniprésence *f*.

U-boat *n* sous-marin *m* allemand.

UCAS ['juːkæs] (*abbrev of* **Universities and Colleges Admissions Service**) *n* UNIV & SCH service *m* des admissions dans les universités.

UCATT ['juːkæt] (*abbrev of* **Union of Construction, Allied Trades and Technicians**) *pr n syndicat britannique des employés du bâtiment*.

UCCA ['ʌkə] (*abbrev of* **Universities Central Council on Admissions**) *pr n organisme centralisant les demandes d'inscription dans les universités britanniques*.

UCL (*abbrev of* **University College, London**) *pr n l'une des facultés de l'Université de Londres*.

UCW (*abbrev of* **Union of Communication Workers**) *pr n syndicat britannique des communications*.

UDA (*abbrev of* **Ulster Defence Association**) *pr n organisation paramilitaire protestante en Irlande du Nord déclarée hors la loi en 1992*.

UDC (*abbrev of* **Urban District Council**) *n* *UK conseil d'une communauté urbaine*.

udder ['ʌdər] *n* mamelle *f*, pis *m*.

UDM (*abbrev of* **Union of Democratic Mineworkers**) *pr n syndicat britannique de mineurs*.

UEFA [juː'eɪfə] (*abbrev of* **Union of European Football Associations**) *pr n* UEFA *f*.

UFC (*abbrev of* **Universities Funding Council**) *pr n organisme répartissant les crédits entre les universités en Grande-Bretagne*.

UFO [ˌjuːef'əʊ, 'juːfəʊ] (*abbrev of* **unidentified flying object**) *n* OVNI *m*, ovni *m*.

Uganda [juː'gændə] *pr n* Ouganda *m* ■ **in ~** en Ouganda.

Ugandan [juː'gændən] ◇ *n* Ougandais *m*, - e *f*.
◇ *adj* ougandais.

ugh [ʌg] *interj* : **~!** beurk!, berk!, pouah!

Ugli® ['ʌglɪ] (*pl* **Uglis** *OR pl* **Uglies**) *n* tangelo *m*.

ugliness ['ʌglɪnɪs] *n* laideur *f*.

ugly ['ʌglɪ] (*comp* **uglier**, *superl* **ugliest**) *adj* **1.** [in appearance - person, face, building] laid, vilain ■ **it was an ~ sight** ce n'était pas beau à voir ■ **as ~ as sin** laid à faire peur **2.** [unpleasant, nasty - habit] sale, désagréable ; [- behaviour] répugnant ; [- quarrel] mauvais ; [- clouds, weather] vilain, sale ; [- rumour, word] vilain ; [- situation] fâcheux, mauvais ■ **there were some ~ scenes** il y a eu du vilain ■ **the ~ truth is...** la vérité, dans toute son horreur, c'est que... ■ **he was in an ~ mood** il était d'une humeur massacrante, il était de fort méchante humeur ■ **he's an ~ customer** c'est un sale individu, il n'est pas commode ■ **to turn** *OR* **to get ~** [person] devenir *OR* se faire menaçant ; [situation] prendre mauvaise tournure *OR* une sale tournure.

ugly duckling *n* vilain petit canard *m*.

UHF (*abbrev of* **ultra-high frequency**) *n* UHF *f*.

uh-huh [ʌ'hʌ] *interj* *inf* **~!** [as conversation filler] ah ah! ; [in assent] oui oui!, OK!

UHT (*abbrev of* **ultra heat treated**) *adj* UHT.

uh-uh ['ʌʌ] *interj* *inf* [no] non non! ■ [in warning] hé!, hein!

UK ◇ *pr n* (*abbrev of* **United Kingdom**) Royaume-Uni *m* ■ **in the ~** au Royaume-Uni.
◇ *comp* du Royaume-Uni.

ukelele [ˌjuːkə'leɪlɪ] = **ukulele**.

Ukraine [juː'kreɪn] *pr n* Ukraine *f* ■ **in ~** en Ukraine.

Ukrainian [juː'kreɪnjən] ◇ *n* **1.** [person] Ukrainien *m*, - enne *f* **2.** LING ukrainien *m*.
◇ *adj* ukrainien.

ukulele [ˌjuːkə'leɪlɪ] *n* guitare *f* hawaïenne, ukulélé *m*.

ulcer ['ʌlsər] *n* **1.** MED [in stomach] ulcère *m* ■ [in mouth] aphte *m* **2.** *fig* plaie *f*.

ulcerated ['ʌlsəreɪtɪd] *adj* ulcéreux.

ulceration [ˌʌlsə'reɪʃn] *n* ulcération *f*.

ulcerous ['ʌlsərəs] *adj* **1.** [ulcerated] ulcéreux **2.** [causing ulcers] ulcératif.

ulna ['ʌlnə] (*pl* **ulnae** [-niː] *OR* **ulnas**) *n* cubitus *m*.

Ulster ['ʌlstəʳ] *pr n* **1.** [province] Ulster *m* ■ **in ~** dans l'Ulster **2.** [N.Ireland] Irlande *f* du Nord, Ulster *m*.

Ulster Democratic Unionist Party *pr n parti politique essentiellement protestant exigeant le maintien de l'Ulster au sein du Royaume-Uni.*

Ulsterman ['ʌlstəmən] (*pl* **Ulstermen** [-mən]) *n* Ulstérien *m*, habitant *m* de l'Irlande du Nord.

Ulsterwoman ['ʌlstə,wʊmən] (*pl* **Ulsterwomen** [-,wɪmɪn]) *n* Ulstérienne *f*, habitante *f* de l'Irlande du Nord.

ulterior [ʌl'tɪərɪəʳ] *adj* [hidden, secret] secret, - ète *f*, dissimulé ■ **~ motive** arrière-pensée *f*.

ultima ['ʌltɪmə] *n* dernière syllabe *f* d'un mot.

ultimata [,ʌltɪ'meɪtə] *pl* ⊳ **ultimatum**.

ultimate ['ʌltɪmət] <> *adj* **1.** [eventual, final - ambition, power, responsibility] ultime ; [- cost, destination, objective] ultime, final ; [- solution, decision, answer] final, définitif ■ **they regard nuclear weapons as the ~ deterrent** ils considèrent les armes nucléaires comme l'ultime moyen de dissuasion **2.** [basic, fundamental - cause] fondamental, premier ; [- truth] fondamental, élémentaire **3.** [extreme, supreme - authority, insult] suprême ; [- cruelty, stupidity] suprême, extrême ■ **it's their idea of the ~ holiday** c'est leur conception des vacances idéales **4.** [furthest] le plus éloigné ■ **the ~ origins of mankind** les origines premières de l'homme.
<> *n* comble *m*, summum *m* ■ **the ~ in comfort** le summum du confort ■ **the ~ in hi-fi** le nec plus ultra de la hi-fi.

ultimately ['ʌltɪmətlɪ] *adv* **1.** [eventually, finally] finalement, en fin de compte, à la fin ■ [later] par la suite ■ **a solution will ~ be found** on finira bien par trouver une solution ■ **~ there will be peace** tôt ou tard, il y aura la paix **2.** [basically] en dernière analyse, en fin de compte.

ultimatum [,ʌltɪ'meɪtəm] (*pl* **ultimatums** OR *pl* **ultimata** [,ʌltɪ'meɪtə]) *n* ultimatum *m* ■ **to give** OR **to issue** OR **to deliver an ~ to sb** adresser un ultimatum à qqn.

ultimo ['ʌltɪməʊ] *adv fml* du mois dernier.

ultra- *in cpds* ultra-, hyper- ■ **~right-wing** d'extrême droite.

ultrahigh frequency [,ʌltrə'haɪ-] *n* ultra haute fréquence *f*.

ultra-low-sulphur petrol *n* AUT essence *f* à très basse teneur en soufre.

ultramarine [,ʌltrəmə'ri:n] *adj* bleu outremer *(inv)*.

ultramodern [,ʌltrə'mɒdən] *adj* ultramoderne.

ultrasonic [,ʌltrə'sɒnɪk] *adj* ultrasonique.
◆ **ultrasonics** *n (U)* science *f* des ultrasons.

ultrasound ['ʌltrəsaʊnd] *n* ultrason *m*.

ultrasound scan *n* échographie *f*.

ultraviolet [,ʌltrə'vaɪələt] <> *adj* ultraviolet.
<> *n* ultraviolet *m*.

ululate ['ju:ljʊleɪt] *vi fml* [owl] ululer, hululer ■ [dog] hurler.

Ulysses [ju:'lɪsi:z] *pr n* Ulysse.

um [ʌm] *inf* <> *interj* euh.
<> *vi* (*pret & pp* **ummed**, *cont* **umming**) dire euh ■ **to ~ and ah** tergiverser, hésiter ■ **he's always umming and ahing** il n'arrive jamais à se décider.

umber ['ʌmbəʳ] <> *adj* [colour, paint] terre d'ombre *(inv)*.
<> *n* [clay] terre *f* d'ombre OR de Sienne.

umbilical [ʌm'bɪlɪkl] *adj* ombilical.

umbilical cord *n* cordon *m* ombilical.

umbilicus [ʌm'bɪlɪkəs] (*pl* **umbilici** [-saɪ]) *n* MED ombilic *m*, nombril *m*.

umbrage ['ʌmbrɪdʒ] *n* [offence] : **to take ~ at sthg** prendre ombrage de qqch, s'offenser de qqch.

umbrella [ʌm'brelə] <> *n* **1.** parapluie *m* ■ **to put up/down an ~** ouvrir/fermer un parapluie **2.** *fig* [protection, cover] protection *f* ■ MIL écran *m* OR rideau *m* de protection **3.** [of jellyfish] ombrelle *f*.
<> *comp* [term] général ■ [organization] qui en recouvre OR chapeaute plusieurs autres.

umbrella stand *n* porte-parapluies *m inv*.

umlaut ['ʊmlaʊt] *n* [in German] umlaut *m*, inflexion *f* vocalique ■ [diaeresis] tréma *m*.

umpire ['ʌmpaɪəʳ] <> *n* arbitre *mf*.
<> *vt* [match, contest] arbitrer.
<> *vi* servir d'arbitre, être arbitre.

umpteen [,ʌmp'ti:n] *inf* <> *adj* je ne sais combien de, des tas de ■ **I've told you ~ times** je te l'ai dit trente-six fois OR cent fois.
<> *pron* : **there were ~ of them** il y en avait des quantités OR je ne sais combien.

umpteenth [,ʌmp'ti:nθ] *adj inf* énième, nième.

UMW (*abbrev of* **United Mineworkers of America**) *pr n syndicat américain de mineurs.*

'un [ʌn] *pron inf* **the little ~s** les petiots *mpl* ■ **the young ~s** les jeunots *mpl*.

UN (*abbrev of* **United Nations**) <> *pr n* : **the ~** l'ONU *f*, l'Onu *f*.
<> *comp* de l'ONU.

unabashed [,ʌnə'bæʃt] *adj* **1.** [undeterred] nullement décontenancé OR déconcerté, imperturbable ■ **she was quite ~ by the criticism** elle ne se laissa pas intimider OR elle ne fut nullement décontenancée par les critiques **2.** [unashamed] sans honte, qui n'a pas honte.

unabated [,ʌnə'beɪtɪd] <> *adv* [undiminished] sans diminuer ■ **the storm/the noise continued ~ for most of the night** la tempête/le bruit a continué sans répit pendant une grande partie de la nuit.
<> *adj* non diminué ■ **their enthusiasm was ~** leur enthousiasme ne diminuait pas, ils montraient toujours autant d'enthousiasme.

unabbreviated [,ʌnə'bri:vɪeɪtɪd] *adj* [word] sans abréviation ■ **in its ~ form** sous sa forme non abrégée, en toutes lettres.

unable [ʌn'eɪbl] *adj* : **to be ~ to do sthg** [gen] ne pas pouvoir faire qqch ; [not know how to] ne pas savoir faire qqch ; [be incapable of] être incapable de faire qqch ; [not be in a position to] ne pas être en mesure de faire qqch ; [be prevented from] être dans l'impossibilité de faire qqch ■ **unfortunately I'm ~ to come** malheureusement, je ne peux pas venir OR il m'est impossible de venir.

unabridged [,ʌnə'brɪdʒd] *adj* [text, version, edition] intégral ■ **the film is ~** le film est dans sa version intégrale.

unacceptable [,ʌnək'septəbl] *adj* **1.** [intolerable - violence, behaviour] inadmissible, intolérable ; [- language] inacceptable ■ **it is ~ that anyone should have to** OR **for anyone to have to sleep rough** il est inadmissible que des gens soient obligés de coucher dehors ■ **the ~ face of capitalism** *allusion Edward Heath* la face honteuse du capitalisme **2.** [gift, proposal] inacceptable.

unacceptably [,ʌnək'septəblɪ] *adv* [noisy, rude] à un point inacceptable OR inadmissible.

unaccompanied [,ʌnə'kʌmpənɪd] *adj* **1.** [child, traveller] non accompagné, seul **2.** MUS [singing] sans accompagnement, a capella ■ [singer] non accompagné, a capella ■ [song] sans accompagnement ■ [choir] a capella ■ **for ~ violin** pour violon seul.

unaccomplished [,ʌnə'kʌmplɪʃt] *adj* **1.** [incomplete - task] inachevé, inaccompli **2.** [unfulfilled - wish, plan] non réalisé, non accompli **3.** [untalented - actor, player] sans grand talent, médiocre ; [- performance] médiocre.

unaccountable [ˌʌnəˈkaʊntəbl] *adj* **1.** [inexplicable - disappearance, reason] inexplicable **2.** [to electors, public etc] : **representatives who are ~ to the general public** les représentants qui ne sont pas responsables envers le grand public.

unaccountably [ˌʌnəˈkaʊntəblɪ] *adv* inexplicablement, de manière inexplicable ■ **she was ~ delayed** elle a été retardée sans que l'on sache (trop) pourquoi.

unaccounted [ˌʌnəˈkaʊntɪd] ◆ **unaccounted for** *adj phr* **1.** [money] qui manque ■ **there is still a lot of money ~ for** il manque encore beaucoup d'argent **2.** [person] qui manque, qui a disparu ■ [plane] qui n'est pas rentré ■ **by nightfall, two children were still ~ for** à la tombée de la nuit, il manquait encore deux enfants.

unaccustomed [ˌʌnəˈkʌstəmd] *adj* **1.** [not used to - person] : **he is ~ to wearing a tie** il n'a pas l'habitude de mettre des cravates ■ **~ as I am to public speaking** bien que je n'aie guère l'habitude de prendre la parole en public **2.** [unusual, uncharacteristic - rudeness, light-heartedness] inhabituel, inaccoutumé.

unacknowledged [ˌʌnəkˈnɒlɪdʒd] *adj* **1.** [unrecognized - truth, fact] non reconnu ; [- qualities, discovery] non reconnu, méconnu **2.** [ignored - letter] resté sans réponse.

unacquainted [ˌʌnəˈkweɪntɪd] *adj* **1.** [ignorant] : **to be ~ with sthg** ne pas être au courant de qqch **2.** [two people] : **I am ~ with her** je ne la connais pas, je n'ai pas fait sa connaissance.

unadopted [ˌʌnəˈdɒptɪd] *adj* **1.** *UK* [road] non pris en charge *OR* entretenu par la commune **2.** [resolution, bill] non adopté, rejeté **3.** [child] qui n'est pas adopté.

unadorned [ˌʌnəˈdɔːnd] *adj* [undecorated] sans ornement, naturel, simple.

unadulterated [ˌʌnəˈdʌltəreɪtɪd] *adj* **1.** [milk, flour] pur, naturel ■ [wine] non frelaté **2.** [pleasure, joy] pur (et simple), parfait.

unadventurous [ˌʌnədˈventʃərəs] *adj* [person] qui ne prend pas de risques, qui manque d'audace ■ [lifestyle] conventionnel, banal ■ [performance] terne ■ [holiday] banal.

unadvertised [ˌʌnˈædvətaɪzd] *adj* [job] non affiché, pour lequel il n'y a pas eu d'annonce ■ [meeting, visit] discret(ète), sans publicité.

unadvisable [ˌʌnədˈvaɪzəbl] *adj* imprudent, à déconseiller ■ **it is ~ for her to travel** les voyages lui sont déconseillés, il vaut mieux qu'elle évite de voyager.

unaffected [ˌʌnəˈfektɪd] *adj* **1.** [resistant] non affecté, qui résiste ■ **~ by cold** qui n'est pas affecté par le *OR* qui résiste au froid **2.** [unchanged, unaltered] qui n'est pas touché *OR* affecté **3.** [indifferent] indifférent, insensible ■ **he seems quite ~ by his loss** sa perte ne semble pas l'émouvoir, sa perte n'a pas du tout l'air de le toucher **4.** [natural - person, manners, character] simple, naturel, sans affectation ; [- style] simple, sans recherche.

unaffiliated [ˌʌnəˈfɪlɪeɪtɪd] *adj* [unions] indépendant.

unafraid [ˌʌnəˈfreɪd] *adj* sans peur, qui n'a pas peur ■ **he was quite ~** il n'avait pas du tout peur.

unaided [ˌʌnˈeɪdɪd] ◇ *adj* sans aide (extérieure) ■ **it is his own ~ work** c'est un travail qu'il a fait tout seul *OR* sans l'aide de personne.
◇ *adv* [work] tout seul, sans être aidé.

unaligned [ˌʌnəˈlaɪnd] *adj* **1.** [wheels, posts] non aligné, qui n'est pas aligné **2.** POL non-aligné.

unalike [ˌʌnəˈlaɪk] *adj* différent, peu ressemblant ■ **they look *OR* seem quite ~** ils ne se ressemblent absolument pas.

unalloyed [ˌʌnəˈlɔɪd] *adj* **1.** [joy, enthusiasm] sans mélange, parfait **2.** [metal] pur, sans alliage.

unalterable [ʌnˈɔːltərəbl] *adj* [fact] immuable ■ [decision] irrévocable ■ [truth] certain, immuable.

unaltered [ˌʌnˈɔːltəd] *adj* inchangé, non modifié ■ **the original building remains ~** le bâtiment d'origine reste tel quel *OR* n'a pas subi de modifications.

unambiguous [ˌʌnæmˈbɪgjʊəs] *adj* [wording, rule] non ambigu, non équivoque ■ [thinking] clair.

unambiguously [ˌʌnæmˈbɪgjʊəslɪ] *adv* sans ambiguïté, sans équivoque.

unambitious [ˌʌnæmˈbɪʃəs] *adj* sans ambition, peu ambitieux.

un-American *adj* **1.** [uncharacteristic] peu américain **2.** [anti-American] antiaméricain.

unanimity [ˌjuːnəˈnɪmətɪ] *n* unanimité *f*.

unanimous [juːˈnænɪməs] *adj* unanime ■ **passed by a ~ vote** voté à l'unanimité ■ **the audience was ~ in its approval** le public a approuvé à l'unanimité.

unanimously [juːˈnænɪməslɪ] *adv* [decide, agree] à l'unanimité, unanimement ■ [vote] à l'unanimité.

unannounced [ˌʌnəˈnaʊnst] ◇ *adj* [arrival, event] inattendu.
◇ *adv* [unexpectedly] de manière inattendue, sans se faire annoncer ■ [suddenly] subitement ■ **he turned up ~** il est arrivé à l'improviste.

unanswerable [ˌʌnˈɑːnsərəbl] *adj* **1.** [impossible - question, problem] auquel il est impossible de répondre **2.** [irrefutable - argument, logic] irréfutable, incontestable.

unanswered [ˌʌnˈɑːnsəd] *adj* **1.** [question] qui reste sans réponse ■ [prayer] inexaucé ■ **my main argument was left ~** on n'a toujours pas réfuté mon argument principal **2.** [unsolved - mystery, puzzle] non résolu **3.** [letter] (resté) sans réponse.

unanticipated [ˌʌnænˈtɪsɪpeɪtɪd] *adj* [success, arrival] inattendu ■ [situation, event, result, outcome] imprévu, inattendu ■ [announcement] inattendu, surprenant.

unappetizing, ising [ˌʌnˈæpɪtaɪzɪŋ] *adj* peu appétissant.

unappreciated [ˌʌnəˈpriːʃɪeɪtɪd] *adj* [person, talents] méconnu, incompris ■ [efforts, kindness] non apprécié, qui n'est pas apprécié.

unappreciative [ˌʌnəˈpriːʃɪətɪv] *adj* [audience] froid, indifférent ■ **to be ~ of sthg** être indifférent à qqch.

unapproachable [ˌʌnəˈprəʊtʃəbl] *adj* **1.** [person] inabordable, d'un abord difficile **2.** [place] inaccessible, inabordable.

unarguable [ʌnˈɑːgjʊəbl] *adj* incontestable.

unarguably [ʌnˈɑːgjʊəblɪ] *adv* incontestablement.

unarmed [ˌʌnˈɑːmd] *adj* **1.** [person, vehicle] sans armes, non armé **2.** BOT sans épines.

unarmed combat *n* combat *m* à mains nues.

unashamed [ˌʌnəˈʃeɪmd] *adj* [curiosity, gaze] sans gêne ■ [greed, lie, hypocrisy] effronté, sans scrupule ■ [person] sans honte.

unashamedly [ˌʌnəˈʃeɪmɪdlɪ] *adv* [brazenly] sans honte, sans scrupule ■ [openly] sans honte, sans se cacher ■ **she lied quite ~** elle mentait absolument sans vergogne, c'était une menteuse tout à fait éhontée ■ **he is ~ greedy** il est d'une gourmandise éhontée.

unasked [ˌʌnˈɑːskt] ◇ *adj* [question] que l'on n'a pas posé ■ **the central question is still ~** la question essentielle reste à poser.
◇ *adv* : **he came ~** il est venu sans avoir été invité.

unassailable [ˌʌnəˈseɪləbl] *adj* [fort, city] imprenable, inébranlable ■ [certainty, belief] inébranlable ■ [reputation] inattaquable ■ [argument, reason] inattaquable, irréfutable.

unassigned [ˌʌnəˈsaɪnd] *adj* [office, room - for person] non attribué ; [- for purpose] non affecté ■ [task] non assigné.

unassisted [ˌʌnəˈsɪstɪd] ◇ *adv* sans aide, tout seul. ◇ *adj* sans aide.

unassuming [ˌʌnəˈsjuːmɪŋ] *adj* modeste, sans prétentions.

unassumingly [ˌʌnəˈsjuːmɪŋlɪ] *adv* modestement, sans prétention.

unattached [ˌʌnəˈtætʃt] *adj* **1.** [unconnected - building, part, group] indépendant **2.** [not married] libre, sans attaches.

unattainable [ˌʌnəˈteɪnəbl] *adj* [goal, place] inaccessible.

unattended [ˌʌnəˈtendɪd] *adj* **1.** [vehicle, luggage] laissé sans surveillance **2.** [person] sans escorte, seul.

unattractive [ˌʌnəˈtræktɪv] *adj* [face, room, wallpaper] peu attrayant, assez laid ▪ [habit] peu attrayant, désagréable ▪ [personality] déplaisant, peu sympathique ▪ [prospect] désagréable, peu attrayant, peu agréable.

unauthorized, ised [ˌʌnˈɔːθəraɪzd] *adj* [absence, entry] non autorisé, fait sans autorisation.

unavailable [ˌʌnəˈveɪləbl] *adj* [person] indisponible, qui n'est pas libre ▪ [resources] indisponible, qu'on ne peut se procurer ▪ **the book is ~** [in library, bookshop] le livre n'est pas disponible ; [from publisher] le livre est épuisé ▪ **the Minister was ~ for comment** le ministre s'est refusé à tout commentaire.

unavailing [ˌʌnəˈveɪlɪŋ] *adj* [effort, attempt] vain, inutile ▪ [method] inefficace.

unavoidable [ˌʌnəˈvɔɪdəbl] *adj* [accident, delay] inévitable.

unavoidably [ˌʌnəˈvɔɪdəblɪ] *adv* [happen] inévitablement ▪ [detain] malencontreusement ▪ **I was ~ delayed** j'ai été retardé malgré moi *OR* pour des raisons indépendantes de ma volonté.

unaware [ˌʌnəˈweəʳ] *adj* [ignorant] inconscient, qui ignore ▪ **to be ~ of** [facts] ignorer, ne pas être au courant de ; [danger] être inconscient de, ne pas avoir conscience de ▪ **I was ~ that they had arrived** j'ignorais *OR* je ne savais pas qu'ils étaient arrivés.

unawares [ˌʌnəˈweəz] *adv* **1.** [by surprise] au dépourvu, à l'improviste ▪ **to catch** *OR* **to take sb ~** prendre qqn à l'improviste *OR* au dépourvu ▪ **the photographer caught us ~** le photographe nous a pris sans qu'on s'en rende compte *OR* à notre insu **2.** [unknowingly] inconsciemment **3.** [by accident] par mégarde, par inadvertance.

unbalance [ˌʌnˈbæləns] ◇ *vt* déséquilibrer. ◇ *n* déséquilibre *m*.

unbalanced [ˌʌnˈbælənst] *adj* **1.** [load] mal équilibré **2.** [person, mind] déséquilibré, désaxé **3.** [reporting] tendancieux, partial **4.** FIN [economy] déséquilibré ▪ [account] non soldé **5.** ELEC [circuit, load] déséquilibré.

unbearable [ʌnˈbeərəbl] *adj* insupportable ▪ **'The Unbearable Lightness of Being'** ***Kundera*** 'l'Insoutenable légèreté de l'être'.

unbearably [ʌnˈbeərəblɪ] *adv* insupportablement ▪ **he is ~ conceited** il est d'une vanité insupportable.

unbeatable [ˌʌnˈbiːtəbl] *adj* [champion, prices] imbattable.

unbeaten [ˌʌnˈbiːtn] *adj* [fighter, team] invaincu ▪ [record, price] non battu.

unbecoming [ˌʌnbɪˈkʌmɪŋ] *adj* **1.** [dress, colour, hat] peu seyant, qui ne va pas ▪ **that coat is rather ~** ce manteau ne lui/te va pas **2.** [behaviour] malséant.

unbeknown(st) [ˌʌnbɪˈnəʊn(st)] *adv* : **~ to** à l'insu de ▪ **~ to him** à son insu, sans qu'il le sache.

unbelief [ˌʌnbɪˈliːf] *n* **1.** [incredulity] incrédulité *f* **2.** RELIG incroyance *f*.

unbelievable [ˌʌnbɪˈliːvəbl] *adj* **1.** [extraordinary] incroyable ▪ **it's ~ that they should want to marry so young** il est incroyable *OR* je n'arrive pas à croire qu'ils veuillent se marier si jeunes **2.** [implausible] incroyable, invraisemblable.

unbelievably [ˌʌnbɪˈliːvəblɪ] *adv* **1.** [extraordinarily] incroyablement, extraordinairement ▪ **~ beautiful/cruel** d'une beauté/cruauté incroyable *OR* extraordinaire ▪ **~, he agreed** aussi incroyable que cela puisse paraître, il a accepté **2.** [implausibly] invraisemblablement, incroyablement.

unbeliever [ˌʌnbɪˈliːvəʳ] *n* incroyant *m*, - e *f*.

unbelieving [ˌʌnbɪˈliːvɪŋ] *adj* [gen] incrédule, sceptique ▪ RELIG incroyant.

unbending [ˌʌnˈbendɪŋ] *adj* **1.** [will, attitude] intransigeant, inflexible **2.** [pipe, metal] rigide, non flexible.

unbias(s)ed [ˌʌnˈbaɪəst] *adj* impartial.

unbidden [ˌʌnˈbɪdn] *adv* *lit* spontanément, sans que l'on demande.

unbleached [ˌʌnˈbliːtʃt] *adj* [fabric] non traité.

unblemished [ˌʌnˈblemɪʃt] *adj* [purity, skin, colour, reputation] sans tache, sans défaut ▪ **an ~ record** un parcours sans faute.

unblinking [ˌʌnˈblɪŋkɪŋ] *adj* [impassive] impassible ▪ [fearless] impassible, imperturbable ▪ **she stared at me with ~ eyes** elle me regarda fixement sans ciller.

unblock [ˌʌnˈblɒk] *vt* [sink] déboucher ▪ [traffic jam] dégager.

unblushing [ˌʌnˈblʌʃɪŋ] *adj* éhonté.

unbolt [ˌʌnˈbəʊlt] *vt* [door] déverrouiller, tirer le verrou de ▪ [scaffolding] déboulonner.

unborn [ˌʌnˈbɔːn] *adj* [child] qui n'est pas encore né.

unbound [ˌʌnˈbaʊnd] *adj* **1.** [prisoner, hands] non lié **2.** [book, periodical] non relié **3.** LING [morpheme] libre.

unbounded [ˌʌnˈbaʊndɪd] *adj* [gratitude, admiration] illimité, sans borne ▪ [pride, greed] démesuré.

unbowed [ˌʌnˈbaʊd] *adj* insoumis, invaincu.

unbreakable [ˌʌnˈbreɪkəbl] *adj* **1.** [crockery] incassable **2.** [habit] dont on ne peut pas se débarrasser **3.** [promise] sacré ▪ [will, spirit] inébranlable, que l'on ne peut briser.

unbridled [ˌʌnˈbraɪdld] *adj* [horse] débridé, sans bride ▪ [anger, greed] sans retenue, effréné.

unbroken [ˌʌnˈbrəʊkn] *adj* **1.** [line] continu ▪ [surface, expanse] continu, ininterrompu ▪ [sleep, tradition, peace] ininterrompu **2.** [crockery, eggs] intact, non cassé ▪ [fastening, seal] intact, non brisé ▪ [record] non battu **3.** *fig* [promise] tenu, non rompu ▪ **despite all her troubles, her spirit remains ~** malgré tous ses ennuis, elle garde le moral *OR* elle ne se laisse pas abattre **4.** [voice] qui n'a pas (encore) mué **5.** [horse] indompté.

unbuckle [ˌʌnˈbʌkl] *vt* [belt] déboucler, dégrafer ▪ [shoe] défaire la boucle de.

unburden [ˌʌnˈbɜːdn] *vt* **1.** *liter & fml* décharger (d'un fardeau) **2.** *fig* [heart] livrer, épancher, soulager ▪ [grief, guilt] se décharger de ▪ [conscience, soul] soulager ▪ **to ~ o.s. to sb** se confier à qqn, s'épancher auprès de qqn.

unbutton [ˌʌnˈbʌtn] ◇ *vt* [shirt, jacket] déboutonner. ◇ *vi inf fig* se déboutonner.

uncalled-for [ˌʌnˈkɔːld-] *adj* [rudeness, outburst] qui n'est pas nécessaire, injustifié ▪ [remark] mal à propos, déplacé.

uncannily [ʌnˈkænɪlɪ] *adv* [accurate, familiar] étrangement ▪ [quiet] mystérieusement, étrangement.

uncanny [ʌnˈkænɪ] (*comp* **uncannier**, *superl* **uncanniest**) *adj* **1.** [eerie - place] sinistre, qui donne le frisson ; [- noise] mystérieux, sinistre ; [- atmosphere] étrange, sinistre **2.** [strange - accuracy, likeness, ability] troublant, étrange.

uncap [ˌʌnˈkæp] (*pret & pp* **uncapped**, *cont* **uncapping**) *vt* [bottle, jar] décapsuler, déboucher.

uncared-for [ˌʌnˈkeəd-] *adj* [appearance] négligé, peu soigné ▪ [house, bicycle] négligé, (laissé) à l'abandon ▪ [child] laissé à l'abandon, délaissé.

uncaring [ˌʌnˈkeərɪŋ] *adj* [unfeeling] insensible, dur.

unceasing [ˌʌnˈsiːsɪŋ] *adj* incessant, continuel.

unceasingly [ˌʌnˈsiːsɪŋlɪ] *adv* sans cesse, continuellement.

uncelebrated [ˌʌnˈselɪbreɪtɪd] *adj* [birthday, success] non célébré *OR* fêté.

uncensored [ˌʌnˈsensəd] *adj* non censuré.

unceremonious [ˈʌnˌserɪˈməʊnjəs] *adj* **1.** [abrupt] brusque **2.** [without ceremony] sans façon.

unceremoniously [ˈʌnˌserɪˈməʊnjəslɪ] *adv* **1.** [abruptly] avec brusquerie, brusquement **2.** [without ceremony] sans cérémonie ▪ **they were pushed ~ into the back of the police van** on les a poussés brutalement à l'arrière de la voiture cellulaire.

uncertain [ʌnˈsɜːtn] *adj* **1.** [unsure] incertain ▪ **we were ~ whether to continue** *OR* **we should continue** nous ne savions pas trop si nous devions continuer ▪ **to be ~ about sthg** être inquiet au sujet de *OR* incertain de qqch **2.** [unpredictable - result, outcome] incertain, aléatoire ; [- weather] incertain ▪ **it's ~ whether we'll succeed or not** il n'est pas sûr *OR* certain que nous réussissions ▪ **in no ~ terms** en termes on ne peut plus clairs, sans mâcher ses mots **3.** [unknown] inconnu, incertain **4.** [unsteady - voice, steps] hésitant, mal assuré **5.** [undecided - plans] incertain, pas sûr.

uncertainly [ʌnˈsɜːtnlɪ] *adv* avec hésitation, d'une manière hésitante.

uncertainty [ʌnˈsɜːtntɪ] (*pl* **uncertainties**) *n* incertitude *f*, doute *m* ▪ **to be in a state of ~** être dans le doute ▪ **I am in some ~ as to whether I should tell him** je ne sais pas trop *OR* je ne suis pas trop sûre si je dois le lui dire ou non.

uncertified [ˌʌnˈsɜːtɪfaɪd] *adj* [copy] non certifié ▪ [doctor, teacher] non diplômé ▪ **~ teacher** *US* ≃ maître *m* auxiliaire.

unchain [ˌʌnˈtʃeɪn] *vt* [door, dog] enlever *OR* défaire les chaînes de, désenchaîner ▪ [emotions] déchaîner.

unchallenged [ˌʌnˈtʃæləndʒd] ◇ *adj* **1.** [authority, leader] incontesté, indiscuté ▪ [version] non contesté **2.** LAW [witness] non récusé ▪ [evidence] non contesté.
◇ *adv* **1.** [unquestioned] sans discussion, sans protestation ▪ **her decisions always go ~** ses décisions ne sont jamais contestées *OR* discutées ▪ **that remark cannot go ~** on ne peut pas laisser passer cette remarque sans protester **2.** [unchecked] sans rencontrer d'opposition.

unchangeable [ˌʌnˈtʃeɪndʒəbl] *adj* immuable, invariable.

unchanged [ˌʌnˈtʃeɪndʒd] *adj* inchangé.

unchanging [ˌʌnˈtʃeɪndʒɪŋ] *adj* invariable, immuable.

uncharacteristic [ˈʌnˌkærəktəˈrɪstɪk] *adj* peu caractéristique, peu typique ▪ **it's ~ of him** cela ne lui ressemble pas.

uncharacteristically [ˈʌnˌkærəktəˈrɪstɪklɪ] *adv* d'une façon peu caractéristique.

uncharitable [ˌʌnˈtʃærɪtəbl] *adj* [unkind] peu charitable, peu indulgent.

uncharted [ˌʌnˈtʃɑːtɪd] *adj* **1.** [unmapped - region, forest, ocean] dont on n'a pas dressé la carte ▪ [not on map] qui n'est pas sur la carte **2.** *fig* **we're moving into ~ waters** nous faisons un saut dans l'inconnu ▪ **the ~ regions of the mind** les coins inexplorés de l'esprit.

unchecked [ˌʌnˈtʃekt] ◇ *adj* **1.** [unrestricted - growth, expansion, tendency] non maîtrisé ▪ [anger, instinct] non réprimé, auquel on laisse libre cours **2.** [unverified - source, figures] non vérifié ▪ [proofs] non relu.
◇ *adv* **1.** [grow, expand] continuellement, sans arrêt ▪ [continue] impunément, sans opposition ▪ **such rudeness can't go ~** on ne peut pas laisser passer une telle impolitesse *OR* grossièreté ▪ **the growth of industry continued ~** la croissance industrielle s'est poursuivie de façon constante **2.** [advance] sans rencontrer d'opposition.

unchristian [ˌʌnˈkrɪstʃən] *adj* **1.** RELIG peu chrétien **2.** *fig* barbare.

uncivil [ˌʌnˈsɪvl] *adj* impoli, grossier ▪ **to be ~ to sb** être impoli envers *OR* à l'égard de qqn.

uncivilized, ised [ˌʌnˈsɪvɪlaɪzd] *adj* **1.** [people, tribe] non civilisé **2.** [primitive, barbaric - behaviour, conditions] barbare ; [- people] barbare, inculte **3.** *fig* [ridiculous] impossible, extraordinaire.

unclad [ˌʌnˈklæd] *adj lit* sans vêtements, nu.

unclaimed [ˌʌnˈkleɪmd] *adj* [property, reward] non réclamé ▪ [rights] non revendiqué.

unclasp [ˌʌnˈklɑːsp] *vt* [hands] ouvrir ▪ [bracelet] dégrafer, défaire.

unclassified [ˌʌnˈklæsɪfaɪd] *adj* **1.** [not sorted - books, papers] non classé **2.** *UK* [road] non classé **3.** [information] non secret.

uncle [ˈʌŋkl] *n* [relative] oncle *m* ▪ **"hello uncle"** "bonjour mon oncle", "bonjour tonton" ➊ **to cry** *OR* **to say ~** *US inf* s'avouer vaincu, se rendre ▪ **'Uncle Tom's Cabin' *Stowe*** 'la Case de l'oncle Tom'.

unclean [ˌʌnˈkliːn] *adj* **1.** [dirty - water] sale ; [- habits] sale **2.** RELIG impur.

unclear [ˌʌnˈklɪəʳ] *adj* **1.** [confused, ambiguous - thinking, purpose, reason] pas clair, pas évident ▪ **I'm still ~ about what exactly I have to do** je ne sais pas encore très bien ce que je dois faire exactement **2.** [uncertain - future, outcome] incertain ▪ **it is now ~ whether the talks will take place or not** nous ne savons pas bien pour le moment si la conférence va avoir lieu **3.** [indistinct - sound, speech] indistinct, inaudible ; [- outline] flou.

unclench [ˌʌnˈklentʃ] *vt* [fist, teeth] desserrer.

Uncle Sam [-sæm] *pr n* Oncle Sam *(personnage représentant les États-Unis dans la propagande pour l'armée)*.

Uncle Tom△ *n US pej Noir qui se comporte de façon obséquieuse avec les Blancs.*

unclog [ˌʌnˈklɒg] (*pret & pp* **unclogged**, *cont* **unclogging**) *vt* [drain] déboucher ▪ [wheel] débloquer.

unclothed [ˌʌnˈkləʊðd] *adj* dévêtu, nu.

unclouded [ˌʌnˈklaʊdɪd] *adj* **1.** [sky] dégagé, sans nuages ▪ *fig* [thinking] limpide ▪ [mind] clair **2.** [liquid] clair, limpide.

uncluttered [ˌʌnˈklʌtəd] *adj* [room] dépouillé, simple ▪ [style of writing] sobre ▪ [design] dépouillé ▪ [mind, thinking] clair, net.

uncoil [ˌʌnˈkɔɪl] ◇ *vt* dérouler.
◇ *vi* se dérouler.

uncombed [ʌnˈkəʊmd] *adj* [hair] mal peigné, ébouriffé ▪ [wool] non peigné.

uncomfortable [ˌʌnˈkʌmftəbl] *adj* **1.** [physically - chair, bed, clothes] inconfortable, peu confortable ; [- position] inconfortable, peu commode ▪ **I feel most ~ perched on this stool** je ne me sens pas du tout à l'aise perché sur ce tabouret **2.** *fig* [awkward, uneasy - person] mal à l'aise, gêné ▪ [difficult, embarrassing - situation, truth] difficile, gênant ▪ [unpleasant] désagréable ▪ **I feel ~ about the whole thing** je me sens mal à l'aise avec tout ça ▪ **to make sb (feel) ~** mettre qqn mal à l'aise ▪ **to make life** *OR* **things (very) ~ for sb** créer des ennuis à qqn.

uncomfortably [ˌʌnˈkʌmftəblɪ] *adv* **1.** [lie, sit, stand] inconfortablement, peu confortablement ▪ [dressed] mal, inconfortablement **2.** [unpleasantly - heavy, hot] désagréablement ▪ **he came ~ close to discovering the truth** il a été dangereusement près de découvrir la vérité **3.** [uneasily] avec gêne ▪ **he shifted ~ in his seat** il bougeait avec embarras sur son siège.

uncommercial [ˌʌnkəˈmɜːʃl] *adj* peu commercial.

uncommitted [ˌʌnkəˈmɪtɪd] *adj* [person, literature] non engagé ▪ **an ~ relationship** une relation libre.

uncommon [ʌnˈkɒmən] *adj* **1.** [rare, unusual - disease, species] rare, peu commun **2.** *fml* [exceptional] singulier, extraordinaire.

uncommonly [ʌn'kɒmənlɪ] *adv* **1.** [rarely] rarement, inhabituellement **2.** *fig* [exceptionally - clever, cold, polite] singulièrement, exceptionnellement.

uncommunicative [,ʌnkə'mju:nɪkətɪv] *adj* peu communicatif, taciturne ▪ **to be ~ about sthg** se montrer réservé sur qqch.

uncomplaining [,ʌnkəm'pleɪnɪŋ] *adj* qui ne se plaint pas.

uncompleted [,ʌnkəm'pli:tɪd] *adj* inachevé.

uncomplicated [,ʌn'kɒmplɪkeɪtɪd] *adj* peu compliqué, simple.

uncomplimentary ['ʌn,kɒmplɪ'mentərɪ] *adj* peu flatteur ▪ **he was very ~ about you** ce qu'il a dit de vous était loin d'être flatteur.

uncomprehending ['ʌn,kɒmprɪ'hendɪŋ] *adj* qui ne comprend pas.

uncomprehendingly ['ʌn,kɒmprɪ'hendɪŋlɪ] *adv* sans comprendre.

uncompromising [,ʌn'kɒmprəmaɪzɪŋ] *adj* [rigid - attitude, behaviour] rigide, intransigeant, inflexible ▪ [committed - person] convaincu, ardent.

uncompromisingly [,ʌn'kɒmprəmaɪzɪŋlɪ] *adv* sans concession, de manière intransigeante.

unconcealed [,ʌnkən'si:ld] *adj* [joy, anger] évident, non dissimulé.

unconcern [,ʌnkən'sɜ:n] *n* **1.** [indifference] indifférence *f* **2.** [calm] sang-froid *m inv* ▪ **she continued with apparent ~** elle poursuivit avec un sang-froid apparent.

unconcerned [,ʌnkən'sɜ:nd] *adj* **1.** [unworried, calm] qui ne s'inquiète pas, insouciant ▪ **he seemed quite ~ about the exam/her health** il ne semblait pas du tout s'inquiéter de l'examen/de sa santé **2.** [uninterested] indifférent.

unconditional [,ʌnkən'dɪʃənl] *adj* **1.** [support, submission] inconditionnel, sans condition ▪ **~ discharge** LAW libération *f* inconditionnelle ▪ **~ surrender** reddition *f* inconditionnelle **2.** MATHS [equality] sans conditions.

unconditionally [,ʌnkən'dɪʃnəlɪ] *adv* [accept, surrender] inconditionnellement, sans condition.

unconditioned [,ʌnkən'dɪʃənd] *adj* **1.** PSYCHOL [reflex] inconditionnel **2.** PHILOS absolu, inconditionné.

unconfirmed [,ʌnkən'fɜ:md] *adj* non confirmé.

uncongenial [,ʌnkən'dʒi:njəl] *adj* [surroundings] peu agréable ▪ [personality] antipathique.

unconnected [,ʌnkə'nektɪd] *adj* [unrelated - facts, incidents] sans rapport ; [- ideas, thoughts] sans suite, décousu.

unconquerable [,ʌn'kɒŋkərəbl] *adj* [opponent, peak] invincible ▪ [obstacle, problem] insurmontable ▪ [instinct, will] irrépressible.

unconquered [,ʌn'kɒŋkəd] *adj* [nation, territory] qui n'a pas été conquis ▪ [mountain] invaincu.

unconscionable [ʌn'kɒnʃənəbl] *adj fml* **1.** [liar] sans scrupules **2.** [demand] déraisonnable ▪ [time] extraordinaire.

unconscious [ʌn'kɒnʃəs] <> *adj* **1.** [in coma] sans connaissance ▪ **to knock sb ~** assommer qqn ▮ [in faint] évanoui **2.** [unaware] inconscient ▪ **she seemed ~ of all the noise around her** elle semblait ne pas avoir conscience de tout le bruit autour d'elle **3.** [unintentional] inconscient, involontaire **4.** PSYCHOL [motives] inconscient ▪ **the ~ mind** l'inconscient *m*. <> *n* [gen - PSYCHOL] inconscient *m* ▪ **the ~** l'inconscient.

unconsciously [ʌn'kɒnʃəslɪ] *adv* inconsciemment, sans s'en rendre compte.

unconsciousness [ʌn'kɒnʃəsnɪs] *n (U)* **1.** MED [coma] perte *f* de connaissance ▪ [fainting] évanouissement *m* **2.** [lack of awareness] inconscience *f*.

unconsidered [,ʌnkən'sɪdəd] *adj* **1.** [thought, action] irréfléchi **2.** *fml* [object] sans importance.

unconstitutional ['ʌn,kɒnstɪ'tju:ʃənl] *adj* inconstitutionnel.

unconsummated [,ʌn'kɒnsəmeɪtɪd] *adj* [marriage] non consommé.

uncontested [,ʌnkən'testɪd] *adj* [position, authority] non disputé, incontesté ▪ **the seat was ~** POL il n'y avait qu'un candidat pour le siège.

uncontrollable [,ʌnkən'trəʊləbl] *adj* **1.** [fear, desire, urge] irrésistible, irrépressible ▪ [stammer] que l'on ne peut maîtriser *OR* contrôler ▪ **to be seized by ~ laughter/anger** être pris d'un fou rire/d'un accès de colère **2.** [animal] indomptable ▪ [child] impossible à discipliner **3.** [inflation] qui ne peut être freiné, galopant.

uncontrollably [,ʌnkən'trəʊləblɪ] *adv* **1.** [helplessly] irrésistiblement ▪ **he was laughing ~** il avait le fou rire ▪ **I shook ~** je tremblais sans pouvoir m'arrêter **2.** [out of control] **: the boat rocked ~** on n'arrivait pas à maîtriser le tangage du bateau **3.** [fall, increase] irrésistiblement.

uncontrolled [,ʌnkən'trəʊld] *adj* **1.** [unrestricted - fall, rise] effréné, incontrôlé ; [- population growth] non contrôlé ; [- anger, emotion] incontrôlé, non retenu **2.** [unverified - experiment] non contrôlé.

uncontroversial ['ʌn,kɒntrə'vɜ:ʃl] *adj* qui ne prête pas à controverse, incontestable.

unconventional [,ʌnkən'venʃənl] *adj* non conformiste.

unconventionally [,ʌnkən'venʃnəlɪ] *adv* [live, think] d'une manière originale *OR* peu conventionnelle ▪ [dress] d'une manière originale.

unconvinced [,ʌnkən'vɪnst] *adj* incrédule, sceptique ▪ **to be/to remain ~ by sthg** être/rester sceptique à l'égard de qqch.

unconvincing [,ʌnkən'vɪnsɪŋ] *adj* peu convaincant.

unconvincingly [,ʌnkən'vɪnsɪŋlɪ] *adv* [argue, lie] d'un ton *OR* d'une manière peu convaincante, peu vraisemblablement.

uncooked [,ʌn'kʊkt] *adj* non cuit, cru.

uncool [,ʌn'ku:l] *adj inf* pas cool.

uncooperative [,ʌnkəʊ'ɒpərətɪv] *adj* peu coopératif.

uncoordinated [,ʌnkəʊ'ɔ:dɪneɪtɪd] *adj* **1.** [movements] mal coordonné **2.** [clumsy] maladroit **3.** [unorganized - efforts] qui manque de coordination, mal organisé.

uncork [,ʌn'kɔ:k] *vt* [bottle] déboucher ▪ *fig* [emotions] déchaîner.

uncorroborated [,ʌnkə'rɒbəreɪtɪd] *adj* non corroboré.

uncountable [,ʌn'kaʊntəbl] *adj* **1.** [numberless] incalculable, innombrable **2.** GRAM non dénombrable.

uncouple [,ʌn'kʌpl] *vt* [engine] découpler ▪ [carriage] dételer ▪ [cart, trailer] détacher.

uncouth [ʌn'ku:θ] *adj* grossier, fruste.

uncover [ʌn'kʌvər] *vt* découvrir.

uncovered [ʌn'kʌvəd] *adj* **1.** *liter* découvert ▪ **food should not be left ~** la nourriture ne doit pas rester à l'air **2.** FIN sans couverture.

uncritical [,ʌn'krɪtɪkl] *adj* [naïve] dépourvu d'esprit critique, non critique ▪ [unquestioning] inconditionnel.

uncross [,ʌn'krɒs] *vt* décroiser.

uncrowded [,ʌn'kraʊdɪd] *adj* où il n'y a pas beaucoup de monde.

uncrowned [,ʌn'kraʊnd] *adj* sans couronne, non couronné.

UNCTAD (*abbrev of* **United Nations Conference on Trade and Development**) *pr n* CNUCED *f*.

unction [ˈʌŋkʃn] *n* onction *f*.

unctuous [ˈʌŋktjʊəs] *adj fml* mielleux, onctueux.

uncultivated [ˌʌnˈkʌltɪveɪtɪd] *adj* **1.** [land] inculte, en friche **2.** = **uncultured**.

uncultured [ˌʌnˈkʌltʃəd] *adj* [manners, person] inculte ■ [accent, speech] qui manque de raffinement.

uncurl [ˌʌnˈkɜːl] ◇ *vt* [rope] dérouler ■ [body, toes] étirer.
◇ *vi* [leaf] s'ouvrir.

uncut [ˌʌnˈkʌt] *adj* **1.** [hair, nails] non coupé ■ [hedge, stone] non taillé ■ [diamond] non taillé, brut ■ [corn, wheat] non récolté, sur pied ■ [pages] non rogné ■ [drugs] pur **2.** [uncensored - film, text] intégral, sans coupures.

undamaged [ˌʌnˈdæmɪdʒd] *adj* **1.** [car, contents, merchandise, building, roof] indemne, intact, non endommagé **2.** *fig* [reputation] intact.

undamped [ˌʌnˈdæmpt] *adj* [enthusiasm, feelings] intact, non affaibli.

undated [ˌʌnˈdeɪtɪd] *adj* non daté, sans date.

undaunted [ˌʌnˈdɔːntɪd] *adj* **1.** [not discouraged] qui ne se laisse pas décourager *OR* démonter ■ **she was ~ by their criticism** leurs critiques ne la décourageaient pas ■ **he carried on ~** il a continué sans se laisser décourager **2.** [fearless] sans peur.

undecided [ˌʌndɪˈsaɪdɪd] *adj* [person, issue] indécis ■ [outcome] incertain ■ **he is ~ whether to stay or go** il n'a pas décidé s'il restera ou s'il partira ■ **the matter is still ~** la question n'a pas encore été résolue.

undecipherable [ˌʌndɪˈsaɪfərəbl] *adj* [writing] indéchiffrable, illisible ■ [code] indéchiffrable.

undeclared [ˌʌndɪˈkleəd] *adj* [goods] non déclaré ■ [love] non avoué.

undefeated [ˌʌndɪˈfiːtɪd] *adj* invaincu.

undefended [ˌʌndɪˈfendɪd] *adj* **1.** MIL [fort, town] sans défense **2.** LAW [lawsuit] où on ne présente pas de défense.

undefinable [ˌʌndɪˈfaɪnəbl] *adj* indéfinissable, impossible à définir.

undelivered [ˌʌndɪˈlɪvəd] *adj* [letter] non remis, non distribué ■ **if ~ please return to sender** en cas de non-distribution, prière de retourner à l'expéditeur.

undemanding [ˌʌndɪˈmɑːndɪŋ] *adj* [person] facile à vivre, qui n'est pas exigeant ■ [work] simple, qui n'est pas astreignant.

undemocratic [ˈʌnˌdeməʊˈkrætɪk] *adj* antidémocratique, peu démocratique.

undemonstrative [ˌʌndɪˈmɒnstrətɪv] *adj* réservé, peu démonstratif.

undeniable [ˌʌndɪˈnaɪəbl] *adj* indéniable, incontestable.

undeniably [ˌʌndɪˈnaɪəblɪ] *adv* [true] incontestablement, indiscutablement.

under [ˈʌndər] ◇ *prep* **1.** [beneath, below] sous ■ **the newspaper was ~ the chair/cushion** le journal était sous la chaise/le coussin ■ **I can't see anything ~ it** je ne vois rien (en-)dessous ■ **he wore a white shirt ~ his jacket** il portait une chemise blanche sous sa veste ■ **we took shelter ~ a tree** nous nous sommes abrités sous un arbre ■ **it can only be seen ~ a microscope** on ne peut le voir qu'au microscope ■ [with verbs of movement] : **we had to crawl ~ the barbed wire** on a dû passer sous les barbelés en rampant ■ **she was swimming ~ water/~ the bridge** elle nageait sous l'eau/sous le pont
2. [less than] moins de, au-dessous de ■ **everything is ~ £5** tout est à moins de 5 livres ■ **is she ~ 16?** est-ce qu'elle a moins de 16 ans?
3. [weighed down by] sous le poids de ■ **to sink ~ the weight of one's debts** *fig* sombrer sous le poids de ses dettes
4. [indicating conditions or circumstances] sous, dans ■ **we had to work ~ appalling conditions** on a dû travailler dans des conditions épouvantables ■ [subject to] sous ■ **~ duress/threat** sous la contrainte/la menace ■ MED sous ■ **~ sedation/treatment** sous calmants/traitement
5. [directed, governed by] sous (la direction de) ■ **he studied ~ Fox** il a été l'élève de Fox ■ **she has two assistants ~ her** elle a deux assistants sous ses ordres ■ **the book describes Uganda ~ Amin** le livre décrit l'Ouganda sous (le régime d')Amin Dada
6. [according to] conformément à, en vertu de, selon ■ **~ the new law, all this will change** avec la nouvelle loi, tout ceci va changer ■ **~ the new law, elections will be held every four years** en vertu de *OR* selon la nouvelle loi, les élections auront lieu tous les quatre ans ■ **~ the Emergency Powers Act** conformément à la loi instituant l'état d'urgence ■ **~ (the terms of) his will/the agreement** selon (les termes de) son testament/l'accord
7. [in the process of] en cours de ■ **the matter is ~ consideration/discussion** on est en train d'étudier/de discuter la question
8. AGRIC : **~ wheat/barley** en blé/orge
9. [in classification] : **you'll find the book ~ philosophy** vous trouverez le livre sous la rubrique philosophie ■ **she writes ~ the name of Heidi Croft** elle écrit sous le nom de Heidi Croft ■ **few singers perform ~ their own name** peu de chanteurs gardent leur vrai nom.
◇ *adv* **1.** *(with verbs)* [below ground, water, door etc] : **to slide** *OR* **to slip ~** se glisser dessous ■ **to stay ~** [under water] rester sous l'eau
2. MED [anaesthetized] sous l'effet de l'anesthésie
3. [less - in age, price] : **you have to be 16 or ~ to enter** il faut avoir 16 ans ou moins pour se présenter ■ **items at £20 and ~** des articles à 20 livres et au-dessous.

under- *in cpds* **1.** [below] sous- ■ **holidays for the ~30s** vacances pour les moins de 30 ans **2.** [junior] sous-.

under-18 *n (usu pl)* personne *f* de moins de 18 ans, mineur *m*, - e *f*.

underachieve [ˌʌndərəˈtʃiːv] *vi* ne pas obtenir les résultats attendus.

underachiever [ˌʌndərəˈtʃiːvər] *n* [gen] *personne ou élève qui n'obtient pas les résultats escomptés.*

underage [ˌʌndərˈeɪdʒ] *adj* [person] mineur ■ **~ drinking** consommation *f* d'alcool par les mineurs ■ **~ sex** rapports *mpl* sexuels avant l'âge légal.

underarm [ˈʌndərɑːm] ◇ *adv* SPORT [bowl, hit] (par) en dessous.
◇ *adj* [deodorant] pour les aisselles ■ [hair] sous les bras *OR* les aisselles ■ SPORT [bowling, throw] par en dessous.

underbelly [ˈʌndəˌbelɪ] (*pl* **underbellies**) *n* **1.** *liter* bas-ventre *m* **2.** *fig* point *m* faible.

underblanket [ˈʌndəˌblæŋkɪt] *n* alaise *f*.

underbody [ˈʌndəˌbɒdɪ] *n* AUT dessous *m* de caisse.

underbrush [ˈʌndəbrʌʃ] *n (U) US* sous-bois *m*, broussailles *fpl*.

undercarriage [ˈʌndəˌkærɪdʒ] *n* [of aeroplane] train *m* d'atterrissage ■ [of vehicle] châssis *m*.

undercharge [ˌʌndəˈtʃɑːdʒ] *vt* [customer] faire payer insuffisamment *OR* moins cher à ■ **she ~d him by £6** elle lui a fait payer 6 livres de moins que le prix.

underclass [ˌʌndəˈklɑːs] *n* : **the ~** les exclus, le quart-monde.

underclothes [ˈʌndəkləʊðz] *npl* sous-vêtements *mpl* ■ [for women] lingerie *f*, dessous *mpl*.

underclothing [ˈʌndəˌkləʊðɪŋ] *n (U)* = **underclothes**.

undercoat [ˈʌndəkəʊt] *n* [of paint] sous-couche *f* ■ [of antirust] couche *f* d'antirouille.

undercook [ˌʌndəˈkʊk] *vt* ne pas assez cuire.

undercover [ˈʌndəˌkʌvəʳ] *adj* [methods, work] secret, - ète *f*, clandestin ■ **~ agent** agent *m* secret.

undercurrent [ˈʌndəˌkʌrənt] *n* **1.** [in sea] courant *m* sous-marin ■ [in river] courant *m* **2.** *fig* [feeling] sentiment *m* sous-jacent.

undercut [ˌʌndəˈkʌt] ◇ *vt* (*pret & pp* **undercut**, *cont* **undercutting**) **1.** COMM [competitor] vendre moins cher que ■ [prices] casser **2.** [undermine - efforts, principle] amoindrir **3.** SPORT [ball] lifter.
◇ *n* **1.** SPORT lift *m* **2.** CULIN [meat] (morceau *m* de) filet *m*.

underdeveloped [ˌʌndədɪˈveləpt] *adj* **1.** [country, society] en voie de développement **2.** [stunted - foetus, plant] qui n'est pas complètement développé OR formé **3.** *fig* [argument, idea] insuffisamment développé OR exposé **4.** PHOT [film, print] insuffisamment développé.

underdog [ˈʌndədɒg] *n* : **the ~** [in fight, contest] celui *m* /celle *f* qui risque de perdre OR qui part perdant ; [in society] le laissé-pour-compte *m*, la laissée-pour-compte *f*, opprimé *m*, - e *f*.

underdone [ˌʌndəˈdʌn] *adj* [accidentally] pas assez cuit ■ [deliberately - meat] saignant ; [- vegetable, cake] pas trop cuit.

underdressed [ˌʌndəˈdrest] *adj* [lightly clad] trop légèrement vêtu ■ [informally dressed] habillé trop sport.

underemployed [ˌʌndərɪmˈplɔɪd] *adj* [worker, equipment] sous-employé ■ [resources] sous-exploité.

underestimate ◇ *vt* [ˌʌndərˈestɪmeɪt] [size, strength] sous-estimer ■ [person, value] sous-estimer, mésestimer.
◇ *n* [ˌʌndərˈestɪmət] sous-estimation *f*.

underestimation [ˈʌndərˌestɪˈmeɪʃn] *n* sous-estimation *f*.

underexpose [ˌʌndərɪkˈspəʊz] *vt* **1.** PHOT [print, film] sous-exposer **2.** [person] faire insuffisamment la publicité de.

underexposure [ˌʌndərɪkˈspəʊʒəʳ] *n* **1.** PHOT [lack of exposure] sous-exposition *f* ■ [photo, print] photo *f* sous-exposée **2.** [to publicity] manque *m* de publicité ■ [social] : **~ to other children may inhibit development** le manque de contact avec d'autres enfants freine le développement.

underfed [ˌʌndəˈfed] ◇ *pt & pp* ▷ **underfeed**.
◇ *adj* [person] sous-alimenté.

underfeed [ˌʌndəˈfiːd] (*pret & pp* **underfed** [ˌʌndəˈfed]) *vt* sous-alimenter.

underfelt [ˈʌndəfelt] *n* thibaude *f*.

underfinanced [ˌʌndəˈfaɪnænst] *adj* [business, scheme, school] qui manque de fonds.

underfloor [ˈʌndəflɔːʳ] *adj* [pipes, wiring] qui se trouve sous le plancher ■ **~ heating** chauffage *m* par le sol.

underfoot [ˌʌndəˈfʊt] *adv* sous les pieds ■ **the grass is wet ~** l'herbe est humide ■ **to trample sb/sthg ~** *liter & fig* [person] fouler qqn/qqch aux pieds ; [animal] piétiner qqn/qqch.

undergarment [ˈʌndəˌgɑːmənt] *n* sous-vêtement *m*.

underglaze [ˈʌndəgleɪz] *n* sous-couche *f*.

undergo [ˌʌndəˈgəʊ] (*pret* **underwent** [-ˈwent], *pp* **undergone** [-ˈgɒn]) *vt* **1.** [experience - change] subir ; [- hardship] subir, éprouver **2.** [test, trials] subir, passer ■ [training] suivre **3.** [be subject to] subir ■ **the building/the system is ~ing modernization** l'immeuble/le système est en cours de modernisation **4.** MED : **to ~ an operation** subir une intervention chirurgicale ■ **to ~ treatment** suivre un traitement.

undergrad [ˈʌndəgræd] *n inf* étudiant *m*, - e *f (qui prépare une licence)*.

undergraduate [ˌʌndəˈgrædʒʊət] ◇ *n* étudiant *m*, - e *f (qui prépare une licence)* ■ **she was an ~ at Manchester** elle était en licence à Manchester.
◇ *adj* [circles, life] estudiantin, étudiant ■ [course] pour les étudiants de licence ■ [accommodation, grant] pour étudiants ■ [humour] d'étudiant.

underground ◇ *adj* [ˈʌndəgraʊnd] **1.** [subterranean - explosion] souterrain ; [- car park] en sous-sol, souterrain ■ **~ railway** métro *m* **2.** [secret] secret, - ète *f*, clandestin ■ **the Underground Railroad** HIST *réseau clandestin qui permettait aux fugitifs noirs des États esclavagistes de rejoindre le nord des États-Unis ou le Canada* **3.** [unofficial - literature, theatre] d'avant-garde, underground *(inv)* ; [- institutions] parallèle **4.** [illegal - methods] illégal.
◇ *n* [ˈʌndəgraʊnd] **1.** MIL & POL [resistance] résistance *f* ■ [secret army] armée *f* secrète **2.** ART, MUS & THEAT avant-garde *f*, underground *m inv* **3.** *UK* [railway] métro *m* ■ **to go by ~** aller en métro.
◇ *adv* [ˌʌndəˈgraʊnd] **1.** [below surface] sous (la) terre **2.** [in hiding] : **to go ~** passer dans la clandestinité, prendre le maquis.

undergrowth [ˈʌndəgrəʊθ] *n (U)* sous-bois *m* ■ [scrub] broussailles *fpl*.

underhand [ˌʌndəˈhænd] ◇ *adj* **1.** [action] en dessous, en sous-main ■ [person] sournois ■ **in an ~ way** sournoisement **2.** SPORT par en dessous.
◇ *adv* sournoisement.

underhanded [ˌʌndəˈhændɪd] *adj* **1.** = **underhand 2.** [short-handed] qui manque de personnel.

underinsure [ˌʌndərɪnˈʃɔːʳ] *vt* sous-assurer.

underlain [ˌʌndəˈleɪn] *pp* ▷ **underlie**.

underlay ◇ *pt* ▷ **underlie**.
◇ *vt* [ˌʌndəˈleɪ] (*pret & pp* **underlaid** [-ˈleɪd]) [carpet] doubler.
◇ *n* [ˈʌndəleɪ] [felt] thibaude *f* ■ [foam] doublure *f*.

underlie [ˌʌndəˈlaɪ] (*pret* **underlay** [ˌʌndəˈleɪ], *pp* **underlain** [ˌʌndəˈleɪn]) *vt* sous-tendre, être à la base de.

underline [ˌʌndəˈlaɪn] *vt liter & fig* souligner.

underling [ˈʌndəlɪŋ] *n pej* subalterne *mf*, sous-fifre *m*.

underlining [ˌʌndəˈlaɪnɪŋ] *n* soulignage *m*, soulignement *m*.

underlying [ˌʌndəˈlaɪɪŋ] *adj* sous-jacent.

undermanned [ˌʌndəˈmænd] *adj* à court de personnel ■ NAUT à équipage incomplet.

undermentioned [ˌʌndəˈmenʃnd] *adj fml* & ADMIN ci-dessous (mentionné).

undermine [ˌʌndəˈmaɪn] *vt* [cliff] miner, saper ■ [authority, person] saper ■ [health] user ■ [confidence] ébranler.

undermost [ˈʌndəməʊst] ◇ *adj* [in heap] le dernier, le plus bas ■ [in depth] le plus profond OR bas.
◇ *adv* tout en bas.

undernamed [ˌʌndəˈneɪmd] (*pl inv*) ◇ *n* personne *f* nommée ci-dessous OR dont le nom suit.
◇ *adj* nommé ci-dessous.

underneath [ˌʌndəˈniːθ] ◇ *prep* sous, au-dessous de, en dessous de ■ **she was wearing two pullovers ~ her coat** elle portait deux pull-overs sous son manteau.
◇ *adv* **1.** [in space] (en) dessous, au-dessous ■ **I've got a pullover on ~** j'ai un pull dessous **2.** [within oneself] : **he smiled, but ~ he felt afraid/helpless** il a souri, mais dans le fond il avait peur/il se sentait impuissant.
◇ *n* dessous *m*.
◇ *adj* de dessous, d'en dessous.

undernourished [ˌʌndəˈnʌrɪʃt] *adj* sous-alimenté.

undernourishment [ˌʌndəˈnʌrɪʃmənt] *n* sous-alimentation *f*.

underpaid ◇ *adj* [ˈʌndəpeɪd] sous-payé.
◇ *pt & pp* [ˌʌndəˈpeɪd] ▷ **underpay**.

underpants [ˈʌndəpænts] *npl* **1.** [for men] slip *m (d'homme)* ■ **a pair of ~** un caleçon **2.** *US* [for women] culotte *f*.

underpass [ˈʌndəpɑːs] *n* **1.** [subway] passage *m* souterrain **2.** [road] route *f* inférieure.

underpay [ˌʌndəˈpeɪ] (*pret & pp* **underpaid** [ˌʌndəˈpeɪd]) *vt* sous-payer.

underperform [ˌʌndəpəˈfɔːm] *vi* rester en deçà de ses possibilités.

underpin [ˌʌndəˈpɪn] (*pret & pp* **underpinned**, *cont* **underpinning**) *vt liter & fig* soutenir, étayer.

underplay [ˌʌndəˈpleɪ] ◇ *vt* **1.** [minimize - importance] minimiser ; [- event] réduire OR minimiser l'importance de **2.** THEAT [role] jouer avec retenue.
◇ *vi* [in cards] jouer volontairement une petite carte.

underpopulated [ˌʌndəˈpɒpjʊleɪtɪd] *adj* sous-peuplé.

underpowered [ˌʌndəˈpaʊəd] *adj* qui manque de puissance.

underprice [ˌʌndəˈpraɪs] *vt* **1.** [for sale] vendre au-dessous de sa valeur **2.** [for estimate] sous-évaluer.

underprivileged [ˌʌndəˈprɪvɪlɪdʒd] ◇ *adj* [person, social class] défavorisé, déshérité.
◇ *npl* : **the ~** les économiquement faibles *mpl*.

underproduce [ˌʌndəprəˈdjuːs] ◇ *vt* produire insuffisamment de.
◇ *vi* produire insuffisamment.

underquote [ˌʌndəˈkwəʊt] *vt* **1.** [goods, securities, services] *proposer à un prix inférieur à celui du marché* **2.** [competitor] vendre moins cher que.

underrate [ˌʌndəˈreɪt] *vt* sous-estimer.

underrated [ˌʌndəˈreɪtɪd] *adj* [person] méconnu ▪ [book, film] sous-estimé.

underrehearsed [ˌʌndərɪˈhɜːst] *adj* MUS & THEAT insuffisamment répété.

underripe [ˌʌndəˈraɪp] *adj* pas mûr.

underscore [ˌʌndəˈskɔːr] ◇ *vt* souligner.
◇ *n* soulignage *m*, soulignement *m*.

undersea [ˈʌndəsiː] ◇ *adj* sous-marin.
◇ *adv* sous la mer.

underseal [ˈʌndəsiːl] *UK* AUT ◇ *n* **1.** [product] produit *m* antirouille **2.** [act, result] couche *f* antirouille.
◇ *vt* faire un traitement antirouille.

underseas [ˌʌndəˈsiːz] = **undersea** *(adv)*.

undersecretary [ˌʌndəˈsekrətərɪ] (*pl* **undersecretaries**) *n* POL **1.** *UK* [in department] chef *m* de cabinet **2.** [politician] sous-secrétaire *m* ▪ **~ of state** sous-secrétaire d'État.

undersell [ˌʌndəˈsel] (*pret & pp* **undersold** [ˌʌndəˈsəʊld]) ◇ *vt* [competitor] vendre moins cher que ▪ [goods] vendre au rabais ▪ **to ~ o.s.** *fig* se sous-estimer.
◇ *vi* [goods] se vendre mal.

undersexed [ˌʌndəˈsekst] *adj* qui manque de libido.

undershirt [ˈʌndəʃɜːt] *n US* maillot *m* OR tricot *m* de corps.

undershorts [ˈʌndəʃɔːts] *npl US* caleçon *m*, slip *m*.

underside [ˈʌndəsaɪd] *n* : **the ~** le dessous, la face inférieure.

undersigned [ˈʌndəsaɪnd] (*pl inv*) *fml* ◇ *n* : **the ~** le soussigné, la soussignée.
◇ *adj* soussigné.

undersize(d) [ˌʌndəˈsaɪz(d)] *adj* trop petit.

underskirt [ˈʌndəskɜːt] *n* jupon *m*.

undersoil [ˈʌndəsɔɪl] *n* AGRIC sous-sol *m*.

undersold [ˌʌndəˈsəʊld] *pt & pp* ▷ **undersell**.

understaffed [ˌʌndəˈstɑːft] *adj* qui manque de personnel.

understand [ˌʌndəˈstænd] (*pret & pp* **understood** [-ˈstʊd])
◇ *vt* **1.** [meaning] comprendre ▪ **is that understood?** est-ce compris? ▪ **to make o.s. understood** se faire comprendre ▪ **I can't ~ it!** je ne comprends pas!, cela me dépasse!
2. [subject, theory] comprendre, entendre ▪ **I don't ~ a thing about economics** je ne comprends rien à l'économie
3. [character, person] comprendre ▪ **I ~ your need to be independent** je comprends bien que vous ayez besoin d'être indépendant
4. [believe] comprendre, croire ▪ **I ~ you need a loan** j'ai cru comprendre que OR si j'ai bien compris, vous avez besoin d'un prêt ▪ **they are understood to have fled the country** il paraît qu'ils ont fui le pays ▪ **we were given to ~ that he was very ill** on nous a fait comprendre OR donné à entendre qu'il était très malade ▪ **so I ~** c'est ce que j'ai compris
5. [interpret] entendre ▪ **what do you ~ by "soon"?** qu'est-ce que vous entendez par "bientôt"? ▪ **as I ~ it, there's nothing to pay** d'après ce que j'ai compris, il n'y a rien à payer
6. [leave implicit] entendre, sous-entendre ▪ **she let it be understood that she preferred to be alone** elle a laissé entendre OR donné à entendre qu'elle préférait être seule ▪ **the object of the sentence is understood** GRAM l'objet de la phrase est sous-entendu.
◇ *vi* comprendre ▪ **if you do that once more you're out, ~?** faites ça encore une fois et vous êtes viré, compris? ▪ **they ~ about international finance** ils comprennent la OR ils s'y connaissent en finance internationale.

understandable [ˌʌndəˈstændəbl] *adj* compréhensible ▪ **that's perfectly ~** cela se comprend parfaitement.

understandably [ˌʌndəˈstændəblɪ] *adv* **1.** [naturally] naturellement ▪ **they were, ~ (enough), deeply embarrassed** ils étaient profondément gênés, ce qui se comprend parfaitement **2.** [speak, write] de manière compréhensible.

understanding [ˌʌndəˈstændɪŋ] ◇ *n* **1.** *(U)* [comprehension] compréhension *f* ▪ [intelligence] intelligence *f* ▪ [knowledge] connaissance *f*, connaissances *fpl* ▪ **it is our ~ that they have now left the country** d'après ce que nous avons compris, ils ont quitté le pays à présent ▪ **they have little ~ of what the decision involves** ils ne comprennent pas très bien ce que la décision entraînera ▪ **it's beyond all ~!** cela dépasse l'entendement!, c'est à n'y rien comprendre! **2.** [agreement] accord *m*, arrangement *m* ▪ **to come to an ~ about sthg (with sb)** s'entendre (avec qqn) sur qqch **3.** [interpretation] compréhension *f*, interprétation *f* ▪ [conception] conception *f* **4.** [relationship - between people] bonne intelligence *f*, entente *f* ; [- between nations] entente *f* **5.** [sympathy] : **he showed great ~** il a fait preuve de beaucoup de compréhension **6.** [condition] condition *f*.
◇ *adj* compréhensif, bienveillant.
◆ **on the understanding that** *conj phr* à condition que ▪ **on the ~ that the money is given to charity** à condition que l'argent soit donné à des bonnes œuvres.

understandingly [ˌʌndəˈstændɪŋlɪ] *adv* avec compréhension, avec bienveillance.

understate [ˌʌndəˈsteɪt] *vt* **1.** [minimize] minimiser (l'importance de) **2.** [state with restraint] dire avec retenue, modérer l'expression de.

understated [ˌʌndəˈsteɪtɪd] *adj* discret, - ète *f*.

understatement [ˌʌndəˈsteɪtmənt] *n* **1.** affirmation *f* en dessous de la vérité ▪ **that's a bit of an ~!** c'est peu dire! ▪ **that's the ~ of the year!** *hum* c'est le moins qu'on puisse dire! **2.** LING & LIT litote *f*.

understood [-ˈstʊd] *pt & pp* ▷ **understand**.

understudy [ˈʌndəˌstʌdɪ] ◇ *n* (*pl* **understudies**) THEAT doublure *f*.
◇ *vt* (*pret & pp* **understudied**) [role] apprendre un rôle en tant que doublure ▪ [actor] doubler.

undertake [ˌʌndəˈteɪk] (*pret* **undertook** [-ˈtʊk], *pp* **undertaken** [-ˈteɪkn]) *vt fml* **1.** [take up - job, project] entreprendre ; [- experiment] entreprendre, se lancer dans ; [- responsibility] assumer, se charger de ; [- change] entreprendre, mettre en œuvre **2.** [agree, promise] s'engager à.

undertaker [ˈʌndəˌteɪkər] *n* ordonnateur *m* des pompes funèbres.

undertaking [ˌʌndəˈteɪkɪŋ] *n* **1.** [promise] engagement *m* ▪ **to give a (written) ~ to do sthg** s'engager (par écrit) à faire qqch ▪ **she gave an ~ that she wouldn't intervene** elle a promis de ne pas intervenir **2.** [enterprise] entreprise *f.*

under-the-counter *inf* ◇ *adj* [agreement, offer, sale] en douce, clandestin ▪ **an ~ payment** un dessous-de-table.
◇ *adv* clandestinement, sous le manteau.

undertone [ˈʌndətəʊn] *n* **1.** [in speech] voix *f* basse ▪ **to speak in an ~** parler à voix basse *OR* à mi-voix **2.** [of feeling] nuance *f* ▪ **all her poetry has a tragic ~** toute sa poésie a un fond de tragique.

undertook [-ˈtʊk] *pt* ▷ **undertake**.

undertow [ˈʌndətəʊ] *n* courant *m* de retour.

underuse [ˌʌndəˈju:z] *vt* sous-utiliser.

undervalue [ˌʌndəˈvælju:] *vt* [object] sous-évaluer, sous-estimer ▪ [person, help] sous-estimer.

underwater [ˌʌndəˈwɔ:tə^r] ◇ *adj* sous-marin.
◇ *adv* sous l'eau.

underwear [ˈʌndəweə^r] *n (U)* sous-vêtements *mpl.*

underweight [ˌʌndəˈweɪt] *adj* **1.** [person] qui ne pèse pas assez, trop maigre ▪ **to be ~** être en dessous de son poids normal **2.** [goods] d'un poids insuffisant ▪ **all the packets are 20 grams ~** il manque 20 grammes à chaque paquet.

underwent [-ˈwent] *pt* ▷ **undergo**.

underwhelm [ˌʌndəˈwelm] *vt hum* décevoir, désappointer.

underwired [ˈʌndəˌwaɪəd] *adj* : **~ bra** soutien-gorge *m* avec armature.

underworld [ˈʌndəˌwɜ:ld] ◇ *n* **1.** [of criminals] pègre *f*, milieu *m* **2.** MYTH : **the ~** les Enfers *mpl.*
◇ *comp* [activity] du milieu ▪ [contact] dans *OR* avec le milieu.

underwrite [ˈʌndəraɪt] (*pret* **underwrote** [-ˈrəʊt], *pp* **underwritten** [-ˈrɪtn]) *vt* **1.** [for insurance - policy] garantir ; [- risk] garantir, assurer contre **2.** ST. EX [shares] garantir **3.** [support - financially] soutenir *OR* appuyer financièrement ; [- by agreement] soutenir, souscrire à.

underwriter [ˈʌndəˌraɪtə^r] *n* **1.** [of insurance] assureur *m* **2.** ST. EX syndicataire *mf.*

underwritten [-ˈrɪtn] *pp* ▷ **underwrite**.

underwrote [-ˈrəʊt] *pt* ▷ **underwrite**.

undeserved [ˌʌndɪˈzɜ:vd] *adj* immérité, injuste.

undeservedly [ˌʌndɪˈzɜ:vɪdlɪ] *adv* injustement, indûment.

undeserving [ˌʌndɪˈzɜ:vɪŋ] *adj* [person] peu méritant ▪ [cause] peu méritoire ▪ **he is quite ~ of such praise** il est parfaitement indigne de *OR* il ne mérite pas du tout de telles louanges.

undesirable [ˌʌndɪˈzaɪərəbl] ◇ *adj* indésirable ▪ **highly ~** tout à fait inopportun.
◇ *n* indésirable *mf.*

undetected [ˌʌndɪˈtektɪd] *adj* [error] non détecté, non décelé ▪ [disease] non détecté, non dépisté ▪ **to go ~** passer inaperçu.

undetermined [ˌʌndɪˈtɜ:mɪnd] *adj* **1.** [unknown] inconnu, indéterminé **2.** [hesitant] irrésolu, indécis.

undeterred [ˌʌndɪˈtɜ:d] *adj* sans se laisser décourager ▪ **she was ~ by this setback** elle ne s'est pas laissé décourager par ce revers.

undeveloped [ˌʌndɪˈveləpt] *adj* **1.** non développé ▪ [country] en développement ▪ [muscles, organs] non formé ▪ [land, resources] non exploité **2.** [immature] immature.

undid [ˌʌnˈdɪd] *pt* ▷ **undo**.

undies [ˈʌndɪz] *npl inf* dessous *mpl.*

undigested [ˌʌndɪˈdʒestɪd] *adj* mal digéré, non digéré.

undignified [ʌnˈdɪgnɪfaɪd] *adj* [behaviour, person] qui manque de dignité.

undiluted [ˌʌndaɪˈlju:tɪd] *adj* **1.** [juice] non dilué **2.** *fig* [emo-tion] sans mélange, parfait.

undiminished [ˌʌndɪˈmɪnɪʃt] *adj* intact, non diminué.

undimmed [ˌʌnˈdɪmd] *adj lit* **1.** [light, faculty] non diminu- **2.** *fig* [fame, lustre] non terni ▪ [memory] intact.

undiplomatic [ˌʌndɪpləˈmætɪk] *adj* [action] peu diplomat-que ▪ [person] peu diplomate, qui manque de diplomatie.

undisciplined [ʌnˈdɪsɪplɪnd] *adj* indiscipliné.

undisclosed [ˌʌndɪsˈkləʊzd] *adj* non divulgué ▪ **for an ~ sur** pour une somme dont le montant n'a pas été révélé.

undiscovered [ˌʌndɪˈskʌvəd] *adj* non découvert ▪ **th- manuscript lay ~ for centuries** le manuscrit est resté inconn- des siècles durant.

undiscriminating [ˌʌndɪsˈkrɪmɪneɪtɪŋ] *adj* qui manqu de discernement.

undisguised [ˌʌndɪsˈgaɪzd] *adj* non déguisé, non dissi-mulé.

undismayed [ˌʌndɪsˈmeɪd] *adj* qui ne se laisse pas décou-rager ▪ **he seemed quite ~ by his defeat** sa défaite ne semblai- pas du tout l'avoir découragé.

undisputed [ˌʌndɪˈspju:tɪd] *adj* incontesté.

undistinguished [ˌʌndɪˈstɪŋgwɪʃt] *adj* **1.** [person] peu dis-tingué, sans distinction **2.** [style, taste] banal, quelconque.

undisturbed [ˌʌndɪˈstɜ:bd] *adj* **1.** [in peace] tranquill- **2.** [unchanged, untroubled] inchangé, tranquille **3.** [untouched body, ground, papers] non dérangé, non déplacé.

undivided [ˌʌndɪˈvaɪdɪd] *adj* **1.** [whole] entier ▪ **you have m- ~ love** vous avez tout mon amour **2.** [unanimous] unanime.

undo [ˌʌnˈdu:] (*pret* **undid** [-dɪd], *pp* **undone** [-ˈdʌn]) ◇ *v-* **1.** [bow, knot] défaire ▪ **to come undone** se défaire **2.** [ruin work] détruire ; [- effect] annuler ; [- plan] mettre en éche- **3.** [repair - wrong] réparer.
◇ *vt & vi* COMPUT annuler.

undocumented [ˌʌnˈdɒkjʊmentɪd] *adj* non documenté.

undoing [ˌʌnˈdu:ɪŋ] *n* (cause *f* de) perte *f* ▪ **his indecisio- proved to be his ~** son indécision aura causé sa perte.

undone [-ˈdʌn] ◇ *pp* ▷ **undo**.
◇ *adj* **1.** [button, clothes, hair] défait **2.** [task] non accompl- **3.** *arch* [hope, plan] ruiné, anéanti ▪ **we are ~!** *arch & hum* nou- sommes perdus!

undoubted [ʌnˈdaʊtɪd] *adj* indubitable.

undoubtedly [ʌnˈdaʊtɪdlɪ] *adv* indubitablement.

undreamed-of [ʌnˈdri:mdɒv], **undreamt-of** [ʌnˈdremt-ɒv] *adj* inconcevable, impensable, auquel on ne songe pas.

undress [ˌʌnˈdres] ◇ *vt* déshabiller.
◇ *vi* se déshabiller.

undressed [ˌʌnˈdrest] *adj* **1.** [person] déshabillé ▪ **to get ~** se déshabiller **2.** [wound] non pansé **3.** [salad] non assaisonné.

undrinkable [ˌʌnˈdrɪŋkəbl] *adj* **1.** [bad-tasting] imbuvable **2.** [unfit for drinking] non potable.

undue [ˌʌnˈdju:] *adj* excessif.

undulate [ˈʌndjʊleɪt] *vi* onduler.

undulating [ˈʌndjʊleɪtɪŋ] *adj* [curves, hills] onduleux.

undulation [ˌʌndjʊˈleɪʃn] *n* ondulation *f.*

unduly [ˌʌnˈdju:lɪ] *adv* excessivement, trop.

undying [ʌnˈdaɪɪŋ] *adj* [faith] éternel ▪ **to swear one's ~ love (for sb)** jurer un amour éternel (à qqn).

unearned [ˌʌnˈɜ:nd] *adj* **1.** [undeserved - fame, privilege] non mérité, immérité **2.** ECON non gagné en travaillant *OR* par le travail ▪ **~ increment** plus-value *f.*

unearned income *n (U)* revenus *mpl* non professionnels, rentes *fpl.*

unearth [ˌʌn'ɜːθ] *vt* **1.** [dig up] déterrer **2.** *fig* [find - equipment, fact] dénicher ; [- old ideas] ressortir, ressusciter.

unearthly [ʌn'ɜːθlɪ] *adj* **1.** [weird] étrange ■ [unnatural] surnaturel ■ [mysterious] mystérieux ■ [sinister] sinistre **2.** *fig* **at an ~ hour** à une heure indue.

unease [ʌn'iːz] *n lit* **1.** [of mind] inquiétude *f*, malaise *m* ■ [embarrassment] malaise *m*, gêne *f* **2.** POL [unrest] troubles *mpl* ■ [tension] tension *f*.

uneasily [ʌn'iːzɪlɪ] *adv* **1.** [anxiously - wait, watch] anxieusement, avec inquiétude ; [- sleep] d'un sommeil agité **2.** [with embarrassment] avec gêne, mal à l'aise.

uneasy [ʌn'iːzɪ] (*comp* **uneasier**, *superl* **uneasiest**) *adj* **1.** [troubled - person] inquiet, - ète *f* ; [- sleep] agité ■ **I had the ~ feeling we were being followed** j'avais la désagréable impression que l'on nous suivait ■ **to feel ~ about (doing) sthg** se sentir inquiet à l'idée de (faire) qqch ■ **I had an ~ conscience about it** je n'avais pas la conscience tranquille à ce sujet **2.** [embarrassed - person] mal à l'aise, gêné ; [- silence] gêné **3.** [uncertain - peace, situation] précaire.

uneaten [ˌʌn'iːtn] *adj* qui n'a pas été mangé ■ **he left his meal ~** il n'a pas touché à son repas.

uneconomic ['ʌnˌiːkə'nɒmɪk] *adj* **1.** [expensive] peu économique ■ [unproductive] non rentable **2.** = **uneconomical**.

uneconomical ['ʌnˌiːkə'nɒmɪkl] *adj* [wasteful] peu rentable.

unedited [ˌʌn'edɪtɪd] *adj* CIN & TV non monté ■ [speech, text] non édité, non révisé.

uneducated [ˌʌn'edjʊkeɪtɪd] *adj* **1.** [person] sans instruction **2.** [behaviour, manners] sans éducation, inculte ■ [writing] informe ■ [speech] populaire.

UNEF (*abbrev of* **United Nations Emergency Force**) *pr n* FUNU *f*.

unelectable [ˌʌnɪ'lektəbl] *adj* [person] inéligible ■ [party] incapable de remporter des élections.

unemotional [ˌʌnɪ'məʊʃənl] *adj* [person] impassible ■ [behaviour, reaction] qui ne trahit aucune émotion ■ [voice] neutre ■ [account, style] sans passion, neutre.

unemployable [ˌʌnɪm'plɔɪəbl] *adj* [person] inapte au travail, que l'on ne peut pas embaucher.

unemployed [ˌʌnɪm'plɔɪd] ◇ *npl* : **the ~** les chômeurs *mpl*, les demandeurs *mpl* d'emploi.
◇ *adj* au chômage.

unemployment [ˌʌnɪm'plɔɪmənt] ◇ *n* chômage *m*.
◇ *comp* [compensation, rate] de chômage ■ **~ figures** les chiffres *mpl* du chômage ■ **~ insurance** assurance *f* chômage.

unemployment benefit *n UK* allocation *f* de chômage.

unencumbered [ˌʌnɪn'kʌmbəd] *adj* [passage] dégagé, non encombré ■ [person] non encombré.

unending [ʌn'endɪŋ] *adj* sans fin, interminable.

unendurable [ˌʌnɪn'djʊərəbl] *adj* intolérable.

unenlightened [ˌʌnɪn'laɪtnd] *adj* [person] ignorant, peu éclairé ■ [practice] arriéré.

unenterprising [ˌʌn'entəpraɪzɪŋ] *adj* [person] peu entreprenant ■ [measure] timoré.

unenthusiastic [ʌnɪnˌθjuːzɪ'æstɪk] *adj* peu enthousiaste.

unenthusiastically [ˌʌnɪnθjuːzɪ'æstɪklɪ] *adv* [say] sans enthousiasme ■ [welcome] tièdement.

unenviable [ˌʌn'envɪəbl] *adj* [conditions, situation, task] peu enviable.

unequal [ˌʌn'iːkwəl] *adj* **1.** [amount, number, result] inégal **2.** [contest, struggle] inégal, non équilibré **3.** *fml* [incapable] : **to be ~ to a job/to a task** ne pas être à la hauteur d'un travail/d'une tâche.

unequalled *UK*, **unequaled** *US* [ˌʌn'iːkwəld] *adj* inégalé, sans pareil.

unequivocal [ˌʌnɪ'kwɪvəkl] *adj* sans équivoque.

unequivocally [ˌʌnɪ'kwɪvəklɪ] *adv* sans équivoque, clairement.

unerring [ˌʌn'ɜːrɪŋ] *adj* infaillible, sûr ■ [accuracy, judgement] infaillible, sûr ■ [aim] sûr.

UNESCO [juː'neskəʊ] (*abbrev of* **United Nations Educational, Scientific and Cultural Organization**) *pr n* Unesco *f*.

unescorted [ˌʌn'ɪskɔːtɪd] *adj* non accompagné.

unessential [ˌʌnɪ'senʃl] = **inessential**.

unethical [ʌn'eθɪkl] *adj* contraire à l'éthique.

uneven [ˌʌn'iːvn] *adj* **1.** [line] irrégulier, qui n'est pas droit ■ [surface] irrégulier, rugueux ■ [ground] raboteux, accidenté ■ [edge] inégal **2.** [unequal - contest, quality, distribution] inégal ■ **his performance was very ~** *fig* il a joué de façon très inégale **3.** [number] impair.

unevenly [ˌʌn'iːvnlɪ] *adv* **1.** [divide, spread] inégalement ■ **the contestants are ~ matched** les adversaires ne sont pas de force égale **2.** [cut, draw] irrégulièrement.

unevenness [ˌʌn'iːvnnɪs] *n* **1.** [of edge, ground, line, surface] irrégularité *f* **2.** [of contest, distribution, quality] inégalité *f*.

uneventful [ˌʌnɪ'ventfʊl] *adj* [day] sans événement marquant, sans histoires.

uneventfully [ˌʌnɪ'ventfʊlɪ] *adv* sans incidents.

unexceptionable [ˌʌnɪk'sepʃnəbl] *adj fml* irréprochable.

unexciting [ˌʌnɪk'saɪtɪŋ] *adj* [life] peu passionnant ■ [film] sans grand intérêt ■ [food] quelconque.

unexpected [ˌʌnɪk'spektɪd] *adj* inattendu, imprévu.

unexpectedly [ˌʌnɪk'spektɪdlɪ] *adv* **1.** [arrive] à l'improviste, de manière imprévue ■ [fail, succeed] contre toute attente, de manière inattendue **2.** [surprisingly] étonnamment.

unexplained [ˌʌnɪk'spleɪnd] *adj* [mystery, reason] inexpliqué.

unexploded [ˌʌnɪk'spləʊdɪd] *adj* non explosé.

unexplored [ˌʌnɪk'splɔːd] *adj* inexploré, inconnu ■ [solution, possibility] inexploré.

unexpressed [ˌʌnɪk'sprest] *adj* inexprimé.

unexpurgated [ˌʌn'ekspəgeɪtɪd] *adj* non expurgé, intégral.

unfailing [ʌn'feɪlɪŋ] *adj* [loyalty, support] sûr, à toute épreuve ■ [courage] inébranlable, à toute épreuve ■ [energy, supply] intarissable, inépuisable ■ [good mood, interest] constant, inaltérable.

unfailingly [ʌn'feɪlɪŋlɪ] *adv* inlassablement, toujours.

unfair [ˌʌn'feəʳ] *adj* [advantage, decision, treatment] injuste ■ [system] injuste, inique ■ [judgement] inique ■ [competition, play] déloyal ■ **to be ~ to sb** se montrer injuste envers qqn.

unfair dismissal *n* INDUST licenciement *m* abusif.

unfairly [ˌʌn'feəlɪ] *adv* [treat] inéquitablement, injustement ■ [compete] déloyalement ■ **to be ~ dismissed** INDUST être victime d'un licenciement abusif.

unfairness [ˌʌn'feənɪs] *n (U)* injustice *f*.

unfaithful [ˌʌn'feɪθfʊl] *adj* infidèle ■ **to be ~ to sb** être infidèle à qqn.

unfaithfully [ˌʌn'feɪθfʊlɪ] *adv* infidèlement.

unfaltering [ʌn'fɔːltərɪŋ] *adj* [speech, steps] ferme, assuré.

unfamiliar [ˌʌnfə'mɪljəʳ] *adj* [face, person, surroundings] inconnu ■ [ideas] peu familier, que l'on connaît mal ■ **I'm ~ with his writings** je connais mal ses écrits.

unfamiliarity [ˈʌnfəˌmɪlɪˈærətɪ] *n* [strangeness - of faces, ideas, surroundings] aspect *m* peu familier, étrangeté *f* ▪ [newness] nouveauté *f*.

unfashionable [ˌʌnˈfæʃnəbl] *adj* **1.** [clothes, ideas] démodé **2.** [area] peu chic.

unfasten [ˌʌnˈfɑːsn] *vt* [button, lace] défaire ▪ [gate] ouvrir ▪ [belt, bonds, rope] détacher.

unfathomable [ʌnˈfæðəməbl] *adj* insondable.

unfavourable *UK*, **unfavorable** *US* [ˌʌnˈfeɪvrəbl] *adj* défavorable.

unfavourably *UK*, **unfavorably** *US* [ˌʌnˈfeɪvrəblɪ] *adv* défavorablement.

unfazed [ʌnˈfeɪzd] *adj inf* imperturbable, impassible.

unfeeling [ʌnˈfiːlɪŋ] *adj* insensible, dur.

unfeminine [ˌʌnˈfemɪnɪn] *adj* qui manque de féminité, peu féminin.

unfettered [ˌʌnˈfetəd] *adj fml* [action] sans contrainte, sans entrave ▪ [imagination, violence] débridé ▪ **~ by moral constraints** libre de toute contrainte morale.

unfinished [ˌʌnˈfɪnɪʃt] *adj* **1.** [incomplete] incomplet, - ète *f*, inachevé ▶ **~ business** *liter* affaires *fpl* à régler ; *fig* questions *fpl* à régler **2.** [rough - furniture] brut, non fini ▪ TEX sans apprêt.

unfit [ˌʌnˈfɪt] <> *adj* **1.** [unsuited - permanently] inapte ; [- temporarily] qui n'est pas en état ▪ **~ for human consumption** impropre à la consommation ▪ **he's still ~ for work** il n'est toujours pas en état de reprendre le travail **2.** [unhealthy - person] qui n'est pas en forme, qui est en mauvaise forme ; [- condition] mauvais.
<> *vt* (*pret & pp* **unfitted**, *cont* **unfitting**) *fml* rendre inapte.

unfitness [ˌʌnˈfɪtnɪs] *n* **1.** [unsuitability] inaptitude *f*, incapacité *f* **2.** [lack of health, physical fitness] mauvaise forme *f*.

unfitted [ˌʌnˈfɪtɪd] *adj fml* [unprepared] mal préparé ▪ [unsuitable] inapte ▪ **to be ~ to do sthg** être inapte à faire qqch ▪ **~ for** inapte.

unfitting [ˌʌnˈfɪtɪŋ] *adj* [remarks] déplacé, inconvenant ▪ [behaviour] inconvenant.

unfix [ˌʌnˈfɪks] *vt* [bayonet] remettre.

unflagging [ˌʌnˈflægɪŋ] *adj* [courage] infatigable, inlassable ▪ [enthusiasm] inépuisable.

unflappable [ˌʌnˈflæpəbl] *adj UK inf* imperturbable, qui ne se laisse pas démonter.

unflattering [ˌʌnˈflætərɪŋ] *adj* peu flatteur.

unflinching [ʌnˈflɪntʃɪŋ] *adj* intrépide, qui ne bronche pas.

unfocus(s)ed [ˌʌnˈfəʊkəst] *adj* [gaze, photo] flou ▪ **~ energy** *fig* énergie sans but.

unfold [ʌnˈfəʊld] <> *vt* **1.** [spread out - cloth, map] déplier **2.** [reveal - intentions, plans] exposer, révéler ; [- story] raconter, dévoiler ; [- secret] dévoiler ; [- reasons] faire connaître.
<> *vi* **1.** [cloth, map] se déplier ▪ [wings] se déployer **2.** [plan, story] se dévoiler, se développer ▪ [view] se dérouler, s'étendre ▪ **the drama ~ed before our eyes** le drame se déroulait devant nos yeux.

unforeseeable [ˌʌnfɔːˈsiːəbl] *adj* imprévisible.

unforeseen [ˌʌnfɔːˈsiːn] *adj* imprévu, inattendu.

unforgettable [ˌʌnfəˈgetəbl] *adj* inoubliable.

unforgivable [ˌʌnfəˈgɪvəbl] *adj* impardonnable.

unforgivably [ˌʌnfəˈgɪvəblɪ] *adv* impardonnablement.

unforgiving [ˌʌnfəˈgɪvɪŋ] *adj* implacable, impitoyable, sans merci.

unforgotten [ˌʌnfəˈgɒtn] *adj* inoublié.

unformatted [ˌʌnˈfɔːmætɪd] *adj* COMPUT non formaté.

unformed [ˌʌnˈfɔːmd] *adj* **1.** [undeveloped] non form **2.** [shapeless] informe, sans forme.

unforthcoming [ʌnˌfɔːθˈkʌmɪŋ] *adj* : **he was very ~ abo the date of the elections** il s'est montré très discret sur la da des élections.

unfortunate [ʌnˈfɔːtʃnət] <> *adj* **1.** [unlucky] malheureu malchanceux **2.** [regrettable - incident, situation] fâcheux, re grettable ; [- joke, remark] malencontreux ▪ **it's just ~ thing turned out this way** il est malheureux *OR* regrettable que le choses se soient passées ainsi.
<> *n euph & fml* malheureux *m*, - euse *f*.

unfortunately [ʌnˈfɔːtʃnətlɪ] *adv* malheureusement.

unfounded [ˌʌnˈfaʊndɪd] *adj* infondé, dénué de fonde ment.

unframed [ˌʌnˈfreɪmd] *adj* sans cadre.

unfreeze [ˌʌnˈfriːz] (*pret* **unfroze** [-ˈfrəʊz], *pp* **unfroze** [-ˈfrəʊzn]) <> *vt* **1.** [de-ice] dégeler **2.** FIN [credit, rent] déblo quer, dégeler.
<> *vi* (se) dégeler.

unfriendly [ˌʌnˈfrendlɪ] (*comp* **unfriendlier**, *superl* **ur friendliest**) *adj* inamical, froid.

unfrock [ˌʌnˈfrɒk] *vt* défroquer.

unfroze [-ˈfrəʊz] *pt* ▷ **unfreeze**.

unfrozen [-ˈfrəʊzn] *pp* ▷ **unfreeze**.

unfruitful [ˌʌnˈfruːtfʊl] *adj* **1.** [barren] stérile, improduct **2.** *fig* [efforts, search] infructueux, vain.

unfulfilled [ˌʌnfʊlˈfɪld] *adj* [person] insatisfait, frustr ▪ [dream] non réalisé ▪ [ambition, hopes] inaccompli ▪ [promise non tenu ▪ **to feel ~** éprouver un sentiment d'insatisfactio

unfunded [ˌʌnˈfʌndɪd] *adj* sans subvention ▪ **~ debt** FI dette *f* non provisionnée.

unfunny [ˌʌnˈfʌnɪ] *adj* [experience, joke, situation] qui n'a rie d'amusant.

unfurl [ˌʌnˈfɜːl] <> *vt* [flag, sail] déferler, déployer.
<> *vi* se déployer.

unfurnished [ˌʌnˈfɜːnɪʃt] *adj* [flat, room] non meublé.

unfussy [ˌʌnˈfʌsɪ] *adj* [clothes, manners, person] simple, pa compliqué ▪ [design, furniture] simple.

ungainly [ʌnˈgeɪnlɪ] (*comp* **ungainlier**, *superl* **ungainliest** *adj* [in movement] maladroit, gauche ▪ [in appearance] dégin gandé, disgracieux.

ungallant [ʌnˈgælənt] = **ungentlemanly**.

ungentlemanly [ʌnˈdʒentlmənlɪ] *adj* [attitude, conduct, re mark] peu courtois, peu galant.

ungodly [ˌʌnˈgɒdlɪ] *adj* **1.** *lit* irréligieux, impie **2.** *hum & fi* [noise] infernal ▪ **at an ~ hour** à une heure impossible o indue.

ungovernable [ˌʌnˈgʌvənəbl] *adj* **1.** [feelings, temper] irré pressible **2.** [country] ingouvernable.

ungracious [ˌʌnˈgreɪʃəs] *adj* désagréable.

ungrammatical [ˌʌngrəˈmætɪkl] *adj* agrammatical, non grammatical.

ungrateful [ʌnˈgreɪtfʊl] *adj* **1.** [person] ingrat ▪ **to be ~ to sb** manquer de reconnaissance envers qqn **2.** *fml & lit* [task] ingrat.

ungratefully [ʌnˈgreɪtfʊlɪ] *adv* de manière ingrate, avec ingratitude.

ungratefulness [ʌnˈgreɪtfʊlnɪs] *n* ingratitude *f*.

unguarded [ˌʌnˈgɑːdɪd] *adj* **1.** [house] non surveillé, non gardé ▪ [suitcase] sans surveillance, non surveillé **2.** [fire] sans pare-feu **3.** [remark] irréfléchi ▪ **in an ~ moment** dans un moment d'inattention **4.** [feelings] franc, franche *f*.

unguent [ˈʌŋgwənt] *n lit* onguent *m*, pommade *f*.

ungulate ['ʌŋgjʊleɪt] ◇ *adj* ongulé.
◇ *n* ongulé *m*.

unhampered [ˌʌn'hæmpəd] *adj* non entravé, libre.

unhand [ˌʌn'hænd] *vt* ***arch*** & ***hum*** lâcher.

unhappily [ʌn'hæpɪlɪ] *adv* **1.** [sadly] tristement **2.** ***fml*** [unfortunately] malheureusement.

unhappiness [ʌn'hæpɪnɪs] *n* chagrin *m*, peine *f*.

unhappy [ʌn'hæpɪ] (*comp* **unhappier**, *superl* **unhappiest**) *adj* **1.** [sad] triste, malheureux ■ **to make sb ~** rendre qqn malheureux **2.** ***fml*** [unfortunate - coincidence] malheureux, regrettable ; [- remark] malheureux, malencontreux **3.** [displeased] mécontent ■ [worried] inquiet, - ète *f* ■ **to be ~ about** *OR* **with sthg** être mécontent de qqch ■ **she was ~ about me spending so much money** [displeased] elle n'aimait pas que je dépense tant d'argent ; [worried] cela l'inquiétait que je dépense tant d'argent.

unharmed [ˌʌn'hɑːmd] *adj* **1.** [person] sain et sauf, indemne ■ **to escape ~** s'en sortir indemne **2.** [vase] intact ■ [house, paintwork] non endommagé.

unharness [ˌʌn'hɑːnɪs] *vt* [remove harness from] déharnacher ■ [unhitch] dételer.

UNHCR (*abbrev of* **United Nations High Commission for Refugees**) *pr n* HCR *m*.

unhealthily [ʌn'helθɪlɪ] *adv* d'une manière malsaine.

unhealthy [ʌn'helθɪ] (*comp* **unhealthier**, *superl* **unhealthiest**) *adj* **1.** [person] malade ■ [complexion] maladif **2.** [air, place] malsain, insalubre **3.** ***fig*** [curiosity, interest] malsain, morbide.

unheard [ˌʌn'hɜːd] *adj* non entendu ■ **his cries for help went ~** personne n'a entendu ses appels à l'aide ‖ LAW [case] non jugé ■ **to be judged ~** être jugé sans être entendu.

unheard-of *adj* **1.** [extraordinary] inouï, sans précédent **2.** [unprecedented] inconnu, sans précédent **3.** [unknown] inconnu, ignoré.

unheated [ˌʌn'hiːtɪd] *adj* sans chauffage.

unheeded [ˌʌn'hiːdɪd] *adj* [ignored - message, warning] ignoré, dont on ne tient pas compte ■ **his instructions went** *OR* **were ~** ses instructions n'ont pas été suivies ■ [unnoticed] inaperçu ■ **the announcement went ~** on n'a pas tenu compte de l'annonce.

unheeding [ˌʌn'hiːdɪŋ] *adj* **1.** [unconcerned] insouciant, indifférent **2.** [inattentive] inattentif.

unhelpful [ˌʌn'helpfʊl] *adj* [person] peu secourable *OR* serviable ■ [instructions, map] qui n'est d'aucun secours ■ [advice] inutile ■ **you're being deliberately ~** vous faites exprès de ne pas nous aider.

unhelpfully [ˌʌn'helpfʊlɪ] *adv* **1.** [act] sans aider, sans coopérer **2.** [advise, say, suggest] inutilement.

unhelpfulness [ˌʌn'helpfʊlnɪs] *n* inutilité *f* ■ [of person] manque *m* d'obligeance.

unheralded [ˌʌn'herəldɪd] *adj* [unannounced] non annoncé ■ [unexpected] inattendu.

unhesitating [ʌn'hezɪteɪtɪŋ] *adj* [reply] immédiat, spontané ■ [belief] résolu, ferme ■ [person] résolu, qui n'hésite pas.

unhindered [ʌn'hɪndəd] *adj* sans entrave *OR* obstacle.

unhinge [ˌʌn'hɪndʒ] *vt* **1.** [door, window] démonter, enlever de ses gonds **2.** ***fig*** [mind, person] déséquilibrer, déranger.

unhinged [ˌʌn'hɪndʒd] *adj* déséquilibré.

unhitch [ˌʌn'hɪtʃ] *vt* **1.** [rope] détacher, décrocher **2.** [horse, ox] dételer.

unholy [ˌʌn'həʊlɪ] (*comp* **unholier**, *superl* **unholiest**) *adj* **1.** RELIG profane, impie ■ **an ~ alliance** ***fig*** une alliance *f* contre nature **2.** ***inf*** [awful - noise, mess] impossible, invraisemblable ■ **at an ~ hour** à une heure impossible *OR* indue.

unhook [ˌʌn'hʊk] ◇ *vt* **1.** [remove, take down] décrocher **2.** [bra, dress] dégrafer, défaire.
◇ *vi* [bra, dress] se dégrafer.

unhoped-for [ʌn'həʊpt-] *adj* inespéré.

unhopeful [ʌn'həʊpfʊl] *adj* **1.** [person] pessimiste, sans illusion **2.** [situation] décourageant.

unhorse [ˌʌn'hɔːs] *vt* **1.** EQUIT démonter, désarçonner **2.** ***fig*** [from power] faire tomber, renverser.

unhurried [ʌn'hʌrɪd] *adj* [person] qui ne se presse pas ■ [manner] tranquille, serein ■ **we enjoyed an ~ lunch** nous avons pris plaisir à déjeuner sans nous presser.

unhurt [ˌʌn'hɜːt] *adj* indemne, sans blessure.

unhygienic [ˌʌnhaɪ'dʒiːnɪk] *adj* antihygiénique, non hygiénique.

uni ['juːnɪ] (*abbrev of* **university**) *n* ***inf*** fac *f*.

UNICEF ['juːnɪˌsef] (*abbrev of* **United Nations International Children's Emergency Fund**) *pr n* Unicef *m*.

unicorn ['juːnɪkɔːn] *n* MYTH licorne *f*.

unicycle ['juːnɪsaɪkl] *n* monocycle *m*.

unidentifiable [ˌʌnaɪ'dentɪfaɪəbl] *adj* non identifiable.

unidentified [ˌʌnaɪ'dentɪfaɪd] *adj* non identifié.

unidentified flying object *n* objet *m* volant non identifié.

UNIDO (*abbrev of* **United Nations Industrial Development Organization**) *pr n* ONUDI *f*.

unification [ˌjuːnɪfɪ'keɪʃn] *n* unification *f*.

uniform ['juːnɪfɔːm] ◇ *n* uniforme *m* ■ **in ~** [gen] en uniforme ; MIL sous les drapeaux ■ **to wear ~** porter l'uniforme.
◇ *adj* [identical] identique, pareil ■ [constant] constant ■ [unified] uniforme.

uniform business rate *n* [in UK] ≃ taxe *f* professionnelle.

uniformed ['juːnɪfɔːmd] *adj* [gen] en uniforme ■ [policeman, soldier] en tenue.

uniformity [ˌjuːnɪ'fɔːmətɪ] (*pl* **uniformities**) *n* uniformité *f*.

uniformly ['juːnɪfɔːmlɪ] *adv* uniformément.

unify ['juːnɪfaɪ] (*pret & pp* **unified**) *vt* **1.** [unite - country] unifier **2.** [make uniform - legislation, prices] uniformiser.

unifying ['juːnɪfaɪɪŋ] *adj* unificateur.

unilateral [ˌjuːnɪ'lætərəl] *adj* **1.** [action, decision] unilatéral **2.** MED [paralysis] hémiplégique.

unilateralism [ˌjuːnɪ'lætərəlɪzm] *n* doctrine *f* du désarmement unilatéral.

unilateralist [ˌjuːnɪ'lætərəlɪst] *n* partisan *m* du désarmement unilatéral.

unilaterally [ˌjuːnɪ'lætərəlɪ] *adv* **1.** [act, decide] unilatéralement **2.** MED : **to be paralysed ~** être paralysé d'un seul côté, être hémiplégique.

unimaginable [ˌʌnɪ'mædʒɪnəbl] *adj* inimaginable, inconcevable.

unimaginably [ˌʌnɪ'mædʒɪnəblɪ] *adv* incroyablement, invraisemblablement.

unimaginative [ˌʌnɪ'mædʒɪnətɪv] *adj* manquant d'imagination, peu imaginatif.

unimaginatively [ˌʌnɪ'mædʒɪnətɪvlɪ] *adv* sans imagination.

unimpaired [ˌʌnɪm'peəd] *adj* [faculty, strength] intact ■ [health] non altéré.

unimpeachable [ˌʌnɪm'piːtʃəbl] *adj* ***fml*** [source, evidence] incontestable ■ [reputation, honesty] irréprochable.

unimpeded [ˌʌnɪm'piːdɪd] *adj* sans obstacle, libre.

unimportant [ˌʌnɪm'pɔːtənt] *adj* **1.** [detail, matter, question] sans importance, insignifiant **2.** [person] sans influence, sans importance.

unimposing [ˌʌnɪm'pəʊzɪŋ] *adj* **1.** [unimpressive] peu imposant OR impressionnant **2.** [insignificant] insignifiant.

unimpressed [ˌʌnɪm'prest] *adj* non impressionné ■ **I was ~ by her** elle ne m'a pas fait une grosse impression ■ **they were ~ by your threats** ils n'étaient pas impressionnés par vos menaces.

unimpressive [ˌʌnɪm'presɪv] *adj* guère impressionnant.

uninformative [ˌʌnɪn'fɔːmətɪv] *adj* [book, leaflet, person] qui n'apprend rien ■ [conversation] qui n'est pas très instructif.

uninformed [ˌʌnɪn'fɔːmd] *adj* [person] non informé ■ [opinion] mal informé ■ [reader] non averti ■ **to make an ~ guess** deviner au hasard.

uninhabitable [ˌʌnɪn'hæbɪtəbl] *adj* inhabitable.

uninhabited [ˌʌnɪn'hæbɪtɪd] *adj* inhabité.

uninhibited [ˌʌnɪn'hɪbɪtɪd] *adj* [person] sans inhibition OR inhibitions ■ [behaviour, reaction] non réfréné, non réprimé ■ [laughter] franc et massif, sans retenue.

uninitiated [ˌʌnɪ'nɪʃɪeɪtɪd] ◇ *npl* : **the ~** les profanes *mpl*, les non-initiés *mpl*, les non-initiées *fpl* ■ **to** OR **for the ~** pour le profane.
◇ *adj* non initié.

uninjured [ˌʌn'ɪndʒəd] *adj* [person] indemne, sain et sauf.

uninspired [ˌʌnɪn'spaɪəd] *adj* qui manque d'inspiration.

uninspiring [ˌʌnɪn'spaɪrɪŋ] *adj* [dull] qui n'inspire pas ■ [mediocre] médiocre ■ [unexciting] qui n'est pas passionnant ■ [uninteresting] sans intérêt.

uninstall [ˌʌnɪn'stɔːl] *vt* COMPUT désinstaller.

unintelligent [ˌʌnɪn'telɪdʒənt] *adj* inintelligent, qui manque d'intelligence.

unintelligible [ˌʌnɪn'telɪdʒəbl] *adj* inintelligible ■ [writing] illisible.

unintended [ˌʌnɪn'tendɪd] *adj* non intentionnel, accidentel, fortuit.

unintentional [ˌʌnɪn'tenʃənl] *adj* involontaire, non intentionnel.

unintentionally [ˌʌnɪn'tenʃnəlɪ] *adv* sans le vouloir, involontairement.

uninterested [ˌʌn'ɪntrəstɪd] *adj* [indifferent] indifférent.

uninteresting [ˌʌn'ɪntrəstɪŋ] *adj* [subject] inintéressant, sans intérêt ■ [book] inintéressant, ennuyeux ■ [person] ennuyeux.

uninterrupted ['ʌnˌɪntə'rʌptɪd] *adj* continu, ininterrompu.

uninterruptedly ['ʌnˌɪntə'rʌptɪdlɪ] *adv* de façon ininterrompue, sans interruption.

uninvited [ˌʌnɪn'vaɪtɪd] *adj* **1.** [person] qu'on n'a pas invité ■ **an ~ guest** un invité inattendu ■ **he turned up ~ at the party** il a débarqué à la soirée sans y avoir été invité **2.** [comment] non sollicité.

uninviting [ˌʌnɪn'vaɪtɪŋ] *adj* [place] peu accueillant ■ [prospect] peu attrayant ■ [smell] peu attirant.

union ['juːnjən] ◇ *n* **1.** [act of linking, uniting] union *f* ■ COMM regroupement *m*, fusion *f* **2.** INDUST syndicat *m* **3.** [association] association *f*, union *f* **4.** [marriage] union *f*, mariage *m* **5.** MATHS union *f*.
◇ *comp* [dues, leader, meeting] syndical ■ [member] d'un OR du syndicat ■ **~ shop** US atelier *m* d'ouvriers syndiqués, union shop *m*.
◆ **Union** *n* **1.** POL [country] : **the Union of South Africa** la République d'Afrique du Sud **2.** HIST : **the Union** UK [with Scotland] l'Union *f* de l'Angleterre et de l'Écosse ; [with Northern Ireland] l'Union de l'Angleterre et de l'Irlande du Nord ; US les États *mpl* de l'Union.

Union Flag = **Union Jack**.

unionism ['juːnjənɪzm] *n* **1.** INDUST syndicalisme *m* **2.** P(unionisme *m*.

unionist ['juːnjənɪst] ◇ *adj* INDUST syndicaliste.
◇ *n* **1.** INDUST syndicaliste *mf* **2.** POL unioniste *mf* ■ [in America Civil War] nordiste *mf*.

unionize, ise ['juːnjənaɪz] ◇ *vi* se syndicaliser, se synd quer.
◇ *vt* syndicaliser, syndiquer.

Union Jack *n* Union Jack *m (drapeau officiel du Royaum Uni)*.

THE UNION JACK

Le drapeau du Royaume-Uni est composé de trois éléments. Il rassemble en effet la croix de Saint-Georges anglaise (rouge sur fond blanc), la croix de Saint-André écossaise (blanche sur fond bleu) et la croix de Saint-Patrick irlandaise (rouge). Le drapeau gallois (dragon rouge sur fond vert) ne fait pas partie de l'Union Jack. À strictement parler, le terme *Union Jack* ne désigne ce drapeau que lorsqu'il est arboré par un navire de la *Royal Navy* ; autrement on devrait dire *Union Flag*. Mais le public ne fait généralement pas la distinction.

unique [juː'niːk] *adj* **1.** [sole, single] unique ■ [particular] pa ticulier, propre ■ **a problem ~ to this region** un problème pr pre à cette région **2.** [exceptional] exceptionnel, remarqua ble.

uniquely [juː'niːklɪ] *adv* [particularly] particulièrement ■ [r markably] exceptionnellement, remarquablement.

uniqueness [juː'niːknɪs] *n* originalité *f*.

unironed [ʌn'aɪənd] *adj* non repassé.

unisex ['juːnɪseks] *adj* unisexe.

unison ['juːnɪzn] *n* unisson *m* ■ **in ~** à l'unisson.

UNISON ['juːnɪzən] *pr n "super-syndicat" de la fonction pu blique en Grande-Bretagne.*

unit ['juːnɪt] ◇ *n* **1.** [constituent, component] unité *f* **2.** [grou unité *f* ■ [team] équipe *f*, unité *f* ■ **army ~** unité de l'armé ■ **family ~** cellule *f* familiale ■ **production ~** unité de produc tion **3.** [department] service *m* ■ [centre] centre *m* ■ [building locaux *mpl* ■ [offices] bureaux *mpl* ■ **child care ~** service de pé diatrie ■ **operating ~** bloc *m* opératoire **4.** [in amounts, meas urement] unité *f* ■ **~ of currency** unité monétaire **5.** [part - o furniture] élément *m* ; [- of mechanism, system] bloc *m*, élémen *m* ■ **transformer ~** bloc transformateur **6.** SCH [lesson] unité ■ **~ 5** unité 5.
◇ *comp* [furniture] par éléments, modulaire.
◆ **units** *npl* MATHS : **the ~s** les unités *fpl*.

unitary ['juːnɪtrɪ] *adj* **1.** [united, single] unitaire **2.** [govern ment] centralisé.

unit charge *n* TELEC taxe *f* unitaire.

unit cost *n* COMM coût *m* unitaire.

unite [juː'naɪt] ◇ *vt* **1.** [join, link - forces] unir, rassemble **2.** [unify - country, party] unifier, unir **3.** [bring together - people relatives] réunir.
◇ *vi* s'unir ■ **they ~d in their efforts to defeat the enemy** ils on conjugué leurs efforts pour vaincre l'ennemi.

united [juː'naɪtɪd] *adj* [family] uni ■ [efforts] conjugué ■ [coun try, party] uni, unifié ■ **to present a ~ front** montrer un front un ■ **to be ~ against sb/sthg** être uni contre qqn/qqch ■ **we are ~ in our aims** nous sommes d'accord dans nos objectifs, nous partageons les mêmes objectifs ▶ **~ we stand, divided we fall** *prov* l'union fait la force *prov*.

United Arab Emirates *pr npl* : **the ~** les Émirats *mp* arabes unis ■ **in the ~** dans les Émirats arabes unis.

United Arab Republic *pr n* République *f* arabe unie ■ **in the ~** dans la République arabe unie.

United Kingdom *pr n* Royaume-Uni *m* ■ **in the ~** au Royaume-Uni.

United Nations *pr n* Nations *fpl* unies.

United States *pr n* États-Unis *mpl* ■ **in the ~** aux États-Unis ■ **the ~ of America** les États-Unis d'Amérique.

nit price *n* prix *m* unitaire *OR* à l'unité.

nit trust *n UK* FIN ≃ SICAV *f*.

nity ['ju:nətɪ] (*pl* **unities**) *n* **1.** [union] unité *f*, union *f* ▪ **strength lies in ~** l'union fait la force **2.** [identity - of purpose] identité *f* ; [- of views] unité *f* **3.** [harmony] harmonie *f* **4.** THEAT unité *f* **5.** MATHS unité *f*.

niv. *written abbr of* **university**.

niversal [ˌju:nɪ'vɜ:sl] ◇ *adj* [belief, education, language] universel ▪ **topics of ~ interest** sujets qui intéressent tout le monde ➊ **~ product code** *US* code *m* barres.
◇ *n* **1.** [truth] vérité *f* universelle ▪ [proposition] proposition *f* universelle **2.** LING & PHILOS : **~ s** universaux *mpl*.

niversal grammar *n* grammaire *f* universelle.

niversality [ˌju:nɪvɜ:'sælətɪ] *n* universalité *f*.

niversal joint *n* (joint *m* de) cardan *m*.

niversally [ˌju:nɪ'vɜ:səlɪ] *adv* universellement ▪ **a ~ held opinion** une opinion qui prévaut partout ▪ **he is ~ liked/admired** tout le monde l'aime bien/l'admire.

niverse ['ju:nɪvɜ:s] *n* univers *m*.

niversity [ˌju:nɪ'vɜ:sətɪ] (*pl* **universities**) ◇ *n* université *f* ▪ **to go to ~** aller à l'université, faire des études universitaires ▪ **to be at ~** être à l'université *OR* en faculté.
◇ *comp* [building, campus, team] universitaire ▪ [professor, staff] d'université ▪ [education, studies] supérieur, universitaire ▪ **~ fees** frais *mpl* d'inscription à l'université.

NIVERSITY

Les universités britanniques se divisent en deux catégories : les *old universities* et les *new universities*. La première catégorie recouvre non seulement les vieilles universités à traditions historiques (Oxford, Cambridge, Durham…) mais aussi celles qui furent établies au cours de la période d'expansion suivant la Deuxième Guerre Mondiale (les *redbrick universities*). La plupart des *new universities* sont d'anciens *polytechnics*, qui sont l'équivalent des IUT et étaient orientés plutôt vers la technologie et la formation professionnelle.
Aujourd'hui, même si des différences importantes demeurent, la distinction entre les deux types d'institution est officiellement abolie et toutes se font concurrence pour attirer des étudiants et des fonds de recherche. Toutes les universités, *old* et *new*, se trouvent dans la nécessité de s'adapter à la montée en flèche du nombre d'inscriptions, qui est allé de 7% des jeunes dans les années 70 à plus de 30% aujourd'hui.

nivocal [ˌju:nɪ'veʊkl] ◇ *adj* [message, term, text] univoque.
◇ *n* LING mot *m* univoque.

njust [ˌʌn'dʒʌst] *adj* injuste.

njustifiable [ʌn'dʒʌstɪfaɪəbl] *adj* [behaviour] injustifiable, inexcusable ▪ [claim] que l'on ne peut justifier ▪ [error] injustifié.

njustifiably [ʌn'dʒʌstɪfaɪəblɪ] *adv* sans justification.

njustified [ʌn'dʒʌstɪfaɪd] *adj* [unwarranted] injustifié ▪ **~ absences** absences sans motif valable ▪ **such accusations are ~** de telles plaintes sont sans fondement *OR* sont injustifiées.

njustly [ˌʌn'dʒʌstlɪ] *adv* injustement, à tort.

nkempt [ˌʌn'kempt] *adj* [hair] mal peigné, en bataille ▪ [beard] hirsute ▪ [appearance, person] négligé, débraillé ▪ [garden] mal entretenu, en friche.

nkind [ʌn'kaɪnd] *adj* **1.** [person] peu aimable, qui n'est pas gentil ▪ [manner] peu aimable ▪ [thought] vilain, méchant ▪ [remark] désobligeant, méchant ▪ **he was rather ~ to me** il n'a pas été très gentil à mon égard *OR* avec moi **2.** [climate] rigoureux, rude.

nkindly [ʌn'kaɪndlɪ] ◇ *adv* [cruelly] méchamment, cruellement ▪ [roughly] sans ménagement ▪ **I hope you won't take it ~ but I'll have to decline your invitation** j'espère que vous ne serez pas offensé mais je dois décliner votre invitation ▪ **she didn't mean it ~** elle n'a voulu blesser *OR* offenser personne.
◇ *adj lit* [person] peu aimable *OR* gentil ▪ [action] vilain ▪ [remark] désobligeant.

unknowable [ˌʌn'nəʊəbl] ◇ *adj* inconnaissable.
◇ *n* inconnaissable *m*.

unknowing [ˌʌn'nəʊɪŋ] *adj* inconscient ▪ **they went, all ~, to their deaths** ils allaient, sans le savoir, au-devant de leur mort.

unknowingly [ˌʌn'nəʊɪŋlɪ] *adv* à mon/son *etc* insu, sans m'en/s'en *etc* apercevoir.

unknown [ˌʌn'nəʊn] ◇ *adj* **1.** [not known] inconnu ▪ **for reasons ~ to us** pour des raisons que nous ignorons *OR* qui nous sont inconnues ▪ **~ to his son, he sold the house** à l'insu de son fils *OR* sans que son fils le sache, il a vendu la maison ▪ **these drugs are ~ to most family doctors** ces médicaments sont inconnus de la plupart des généralistes ➊ **~ quantity** MATHS & *fig* inconnue *f* **2.** [obscure - cause] inconnu, mystérieux ; [- place] inconnu **3.** [obscure - actor, writer] inconnu, méconnu.
◇ *n* **1.** [person] inconnu *m*, - e *f* **2.** [place, situation] inconnu *m* **3.** MATHS & LOGIC inconnue *f*.

Unknown Soldier, Unknown Warrior *n* : **the ~** le Soldat *m* inconnu.

unlace [ˌʌn'leɪs] *vt* [bodice, shoe] délacer, défaire le lacet *OR* les lacets de.

unladen [ˌʌn'leɪdn] *adj* **1.** [goods] déchargé **2.** [lorry, ship] à vide ▪ **~ weight** poids *m* à vide.

unladylike [ˌʌn'leɪdɪlaɪk] *adj* [girl] mal élevé ▪ [behaviour, posture] peu distingué ▪ **it's ~ to whistle** une jeune fille bien élevée ne siffle pas.

unlamented [ˌʌnlə'mentɪd] *adj* regretté de personne.

unlatch [ˌʌn'lætʃ] ◇ *vt* [door] soulever le loquet de, ouvrir.
◇ *vi* [door] s'ouvrir.

unlawful [ˌʌn'lɔ:fʊl] *adj* illicite, illégal ▪ **their marriage was deemed ~** leur mariage fut jugé illégitime ➊ **~ assembly** LAW réunion *f* illégale, attroupement *m* illégal ▪ **~ killing** meurtre *m*.

unlawfully [ˌʌn'lɔ:fʊlɪ] *adv* illicitement, illégalement.

unleaded [ˌʌn'ledɪd] ◇ *adj* [petrol] sans plomb.
◇ *n inf* [petrol] sans-plomb *m inv*.

unlearn [ˌʌn'lɜ:n] (*pret & pp* **unlearned** *OR* **unlearnt** [-'lɜ:nt]) *vt* désapprendre.

unlearnt [-'lɜ:nt] *adj* [lesson] non appris ▪ [reflex] inné, non acquis.

unleash [ˌʌn'li:ʃ] *vt* **1.** [dog] lâcher **2.** *fig* [anger, violence] déchaîner ▪ **she ~ed a stream of invective** elle lâcha une bordée d'injures.

unleavened [ˌʌn'levnd] *adj* [bread - CULIN] sans levain ▪ RELIG azyme.

unless [ən'les] *conj* à moins que *(+ subjunctive)*, à moins de *(+ infinitive)* ▪ **I'll go ~ he phones first** j'irai, à moins qu'il téléphone d'abord ▪ **~ I'm very much mistaken** à moins que je ne me trompe ▪ **~ he pays me tomorrow, I'm leaving** s'il ne m'a pas payé demain, je m'en vais ▪ **you won't win ~ you practise** vous ne gagnerez pas si vous ne vous entraînez pas ▪ **don't speak ~ spoken to** ne parle que lorsqu'on t'adresse la parole ▪ **~ I hear otherwise** *OR* **to the contrary** sauf avis contraire, sauf contrordre.

unliberated [ˌʌn'lɪbəreɪtɪd] *adj* non libéré.

unlicensed [ˌʌn'laɪsənst] *adj* [parking, sale] illicite, non autorisé ▪ [fishing, hunting] sans permis, illicite ▪ [car] sans vignette ▪ [premises] qui n'a pas de licence de débit de boissons.

unlikable [ˌʌn'laɪkəbl] *adj* [person] peu sympathique ▪ [place, thing] peu agréable.

unlike [ˌʌn'laɪk] ◇ *adj* [dissimilar] dissemblable ▪ [different] différent ▪ [showing no likeness] peu ressemblant ▪ [unequal] inégal ▪ **the two sisters are quite ~ each other** les deux sœurs ne se ressemblent pas du tout.
◇ *prep* **1.** [different from] différent de, qui ne ressemble pas à ▪ **she is not ~ your sister in looks** elle n'est pas sans ressem-

bler à votre sœur **2.** [uncharacteristic of] : **that's (very) ~ him!** cela ne lui ressemble pas (du tout)! **3.** [in contrast to] à la différence de, contrairement à.

unlikeable [ˌʌn'laɪkəbl] = **unlikable.**

unlikelihood [ʌn'laɪklɪhʊd] *n* improbabilité *f.*

unlikely [ʌn'laɪklɪ] *adj* **1.** [improbable - event, outcome] improbable, peu probable ■ **it is very** *OR* **most ~ that it will rain** il est très peu probable qu'il pleuve, il y a peu de chances pour qu'il pleuve ■ **in the ~ event of my winning** au cas improbable où je gagnerais **2.** [person] peu susceptible, qui a peu de chances ■ **he is ~ to come/to fail** il est peu probable qu'il vienne/échoue, il est peu susceptible de venir/d'échouer ■ **she is ~ to choose him** elle a peu de chances de le choisir, il y a peu de chances pour qu'elle le choisisse **3.** [implausible - excuse, story] invraisemblable **4.** [unexpected - situation, undertaking, costume etc] extravagant, invraisemblable ; [- person] peu indiqué ■ **the manager chose the most ~ person to run the department** le directeur a choisi la personne la moins indiquée au monde pour diriger le service ■ **he seems an ~ choice** il semble un choix peu judicieux.

unlimited [ʌn'lɪmɪtɪd] *adj* **1.** [possibilities, space] illimité, sans limites ■ [power] illimité, sans bornes ■ [time] infini, illimité **2.** *UK* FIN : **~ liability** responsabilité *f* illimitée.

unlined [ˌʌn'laɪnd] *adj* **1.** [paper] non réglé, uni **2.** [curtain, clothes] sans doublure **3.** [face] sans rides.

unlisted [ʌn'lɪstɪd] *adj* **1.** [not on list - name] qui ne paraît pas sur la liste **2.** *US* TELEC qui est sur la liste rouge **3.** ST. EX non coté (en Bourse).

unlit [ˌʌn'lɪt] *adj* **1.** [candle, fire] non allumé **2.** [room, street] non éclairé.

unload [ˌʌn'ləʊd] ◇ *vt* **1.** [remove load from - gun, ship, truck] décharger **2.** [remove - cargo, furniture] décharger ; [- film] enlever **3.** *inf* [get rid of] se débarrasser de, se défaire de ■ **to ~ sthg onto sb** se décharger de qqch sur qqn **4.** *fig* [responsibility, worries] décharger.
◇ *vi* [ship, truck] décharger.

unlock [ˌʌn'lɒk] ◇ *vt* **1.** [door] ouvrir **2.** *fig* [mystery, puzzle] résoudre, donner la clé de ■ [secret] dévoiler.
◇ *vi* s'ouvrir.

unlooked-for [ˌʌn'lʊkt-] *adj* inattendu, imprévu.

unloose(n) [ˌʌn'lu:s(n)] *vt* [belt, grip] relâcher, desserrer.

unloose [ˌʌn'lu:s] = **unleash.**

unlovable [ˌʌn'lʌvəbl] *adj* peu attachant.

unloved [ˌʌn'lʌvd] *adj* privé d'affection, aimé de personne ■ **to feel ~** se sentir mal aimé.

unloving [ˌʌn'lʌvɪŋ] *adj* peu affectueux.

unluckily [ʌn'lʌkɪlɪ] *adv* malheureusement.

unlucky [ʌn'lʌkɪ] (*comp* **unluckier**, *superl* **unluckiest**) *adj* **1.** [person] malchanceux ■ [day] de malchance ■ **we were ~ enough to get caught in a jam** nous avons eu la malchance d'être pris dans un embouteillage ■ **to be ~ in love** être malheureux en amour **2.** [colour, number] qui porte malheur ■ [omen] funeste, mauvais ■ **it's supposed to be ~ to break a mirror** c'est censé porter malheur de casser un miroir.

unmade [ˌʌn'meɪd] *adj* **1.** [bed] défait **2.** *UK* [road] non goudronné.

unman [ˌʌn'mæn] (*pret & pp* **unmanned**, *cont* **unmanning**) *vt* **1.** NAUT renvoyer l'équipage de **2.** *lit* [person] faire perdre courage à.

unmanageable [ʌn'mænɪdʒəbl] *adj* **1.** [vehicle] peu maniable ■ [object] peu maniable, difficile à manier **2.** [animal] difficile, indocile ■ [children] difficile, impossible **3.** [situation] difficile à gérer **4.** [hair] difficile à coiffer, rebelle.

unmanly [ˌʌn'mænlɪ] *adj* **1.** [effeminate] efféminé, peu viril **2.** [cowardly] lâche.

unmanned [ˌʌn'mænd] *adj* [without crew - plane, ship] sans équipage ; [- spacecraft, flight] inhabité ■ RAIL [- station] sans personnel ; [- level crossing] non gardé, automatique ■ **the border post/switchboard was ~** il n'y avait personne au pos frontière/au standard ■ **the control centre was left ~** le cent de contrôle est resté sans surveillance.

unmannerly [ʌn'mænəlɪ] *adj fml* [person] discourtois, m élevé ■ [behaviour] mal élevé.

unmapped [ˌʌn'mæpt] *adj* [area] pour lequel il n'existe p de carte, dont on n'a pas dressé la carte.

unmarked [ˌʌn'mɑ:kt] *adj* **1.** [face, furniture, page] sans ma que, sans tache **2.** [without identifying features] : **the radioacti waste was carried in ~ drums** les déchets radioactifs étaie transportés dans des barils non identifiés ■ **an ~ police c** une voiture de police banalisée **3.** [without name tag, lab sans nom, non marqué **4.** [essay] non corrigé **5.** LING nc marqué **6.** SPORT [player] démarqué.

unmarketable [ˌʌn'mɑ:kɪtəbl] *adj* invendable.

unmarred [ˌʌn'mɑ:d] *adj lit* non abîmé ■ [reputation] sa tache, entier.

unmarriageable [ˌʌn'mærɪdʒəbl] *adj* immariable.

unmarried [ˌʌn'mærɪd] *adj* non marié, célibatai ■ **~ mother** mère *f* célibataire.

unmask [ˌʌn'mɑ:sk] *vt* démasquer.

unmatched [ˌʌn'mætʃt] *adj* inégalé, sans égal *OR* pareil.

unmentionable [ʌn'menʃnəbl] *adj* [subject] dont il ne fa pas parler, interdit ■ [word] qu'il ne faut pas prononcer, i terdit.

◆ **unmentionables** *npl euph & hum* [underwear] dessou *mpl*, sous-vêtements *mpl.*

unmerciful [ʌn'mɜ:sɪfʊl] *adj* impitoyable, sans pitié ■ **to b ~ to** *OR* **towards sb** être sans pitié pour qqn.

unmerited [ˌʌn'merɪtɪd] *adj* [undeserved] immérité ■ [unjus injuste.

unmetered [ʌn'mi:təd] *adj* illimité.

unmindful [ʌn'maɪndfʊl] *adj fml* [uncaring] peu soucieu ■ [forgetful] oublieux ■ [inattentive] inattentif.

unmistakable [ˌʌnmɪ'steɪkəbl] *adj* [not mistakeable] facil ment reconnaissable ■ [clear, obvious] indubitable, man feste, évident.

unmistakably [ˌʌnmɪ'steɪkəblɪ] *adv* **1.** [undeniably] ind niablement, sans erreur possible **2.** [visibly] visiblemen manifestement.

unmistakeable [ˌʌnmɪ'steɪkəbl] = **unmistakable.**

unmitigated [ʌn'mɪtɪgeɪtɪd] *adj* **1.** [total - disaster, chao total ; [- stupidity] pur, total **2.** [undiminished] non mitigé.

unmourned [ˌʌn'mɔ:nd] *adj* : **he died ~** personne ne l' pleuré.

unmoved [ˌʌn'mu:vd] *adj* indifférent, insensible ■ **to be ~ b sthg** rester insensible à qqch ■ **the music left me ~** la musiqu ne m'a pas ému ■ **he remained ~** il a continué, imperturbabl *OR* impassible.

unmusical [ˌʌn'mju:zɪkl] *adj* **1.** [sound] peu musica **2.** [person] peu musicien.

unnameable [ˌʌn'neɪməbl] *adj* innommable, sans nom.

unnamed [ˌʌn'neɪmd] *adj* **1.** [anonymous] anonyme ■ [unspe cified] non précisé **2.** [having no name - child] sans nom, qui n' pas reçu de nom ; [- desire, fear] inavoué.

unnatural [ʌn'nætʃrəl] *adj* **1.** [affected - behaviour, manne tone] affecté, peu naturel ; [- laughter] peu naturel, forc **2.** [odd, abnormal - circumstances, state] anormal ; [- phenomenon surnaturel **3.** [perverse - love, passion] contre nature.

unnaturally [ʌn'nætʃrəlɪ] *adv* [behave, laugh, walk] bizarre ment, de façon peu naturelle.

unnecessarily [*UK* ʌn'nesəsərɪlɪ, *US* ˌʌnnesə'serəlɪ] *adv* san nécessité *OR* raison.

unnecessary [ʌn'nesəsərɪ] *adj* superflu, inutile ▪ **it's quite ~ for you all to attend** il n'est vraiment pas nécessaire *OR* utile que vous y alliez tous ▪ **it's a lot of ~ fuss** c'est beaucoup d'agitation pour rien.

unnerve [,ʌn'nɜ:v] *vt* démonter, déconcerter.

unnerving [,ʌn'nɜ:vɪŋ] *adj* [event, experience] déconcertant, perturbant.

unnoticed [,ʌn'nəʊtɪst] *adj* inaperçu ▪ **to pass ~** passer inaperçu.

UNO (*abbrev of* **United Nations Organization**) *pr n* ONU *f.*

unobjectionable [,ʌnəb'dʒekʃnəbl] *adj* [idea, activity] acceptable ▪ [behaviour, person] qui ne peut être critiqué.

unobservant [,ʌnəb'zɜ:vənt] *adj* peu observateur.

unobserved [,ʌnəb'zɜ:vd] *adj* inaperçu ▪ **she crept past ~** elle s'est faufilée sans se faire remarquer.

unobstructed [,ʌnəb'strʌktɪd] *adj* **1.** [entry, passage, view] non obstrué, libre **2.** [activity, progress] sans obstacle.

unobtainable [,ʌnəb'teɪnəbl] *adj* impossible à obtenir.

unobtrusive [,ʌnəb'tru:sɪv] *adj* [person] discret, - ète *f*, effacé ▪ [object] discret, - ète *f*, pas trop visible ▪ [smell] discret, - ète *f.*

unoccupied [,ʌn'ɒkjʊpaɪd] *adj* **1.** [person] qui ne fait rien, oisif **2.** [house] inoccupé, vide ▪ [seat] libre **3.** MIL [zone, territory] non occupé, libre.

unofficial [,ʌnə'fɪʃl] *adj* **1.** [unconfirmed - report] officieux, non officiel **2.** [informal - appointment] non officiel, privé **3.** INDUST : **~ strike** grève *f* sauvage.

unofficially [,ʌnə'fɪʃəlɪ] *adv* [informally] officieusement ▪ [in private] en privé.

unopened [,ʌn'əʊpənd] *adj* **1.** [letter, bottle] fermé **2.** BOT non éclos.

unopposed [,ʌnə'pəʊzd] *adj* : **she was elected ~** elle était la seule candidate (et elle a été élue).

unorganized, ised [,ʌn'ɔ:gənaɪzd] *adj* inorganisé, non organisé.

unoriginal [,ʌnə'rɪdʒənl] *adj* sans originalité.

unorthodox [,ʌn'ɔ:θədɒks] *adj* non orthodoxe, pas très orthodoxe ▪ RELIG hétérodoxe.

unpack [,ʌn'pæk] ◇ *vt* **1.** [bag, suitcase] défaire ▪ [books, clothes, shopping] déballer ▪ **to get ~ed** défaire ses bagages **2.** COMPUT décompresser.
◇ *vi* défaire ses bagages.

unpaid [,ʌn'peɪd] *adj* **1.** [helper, job] bénévole, non rémunéré **2.** [bill, salary] impayé ▪ [employee] non payé ▪ **~ holiday** congé *m* sans solde.

unpalatable [ʌn'pælətəbl] *adj* [food] immangeable ▪ *fig* [idea] dérangeant ▪ [truth] désagréable à entendre.

unparalleled [ʌn'pærəleld] *adj* [unequalled] sans pareil ▪ [unprecedented] sans précédent.

unpardonable [ʌn'pɑ:dnəbl] *adj* impardonnable, inexcusable.

unparliamentary ['ʌn,pɑ:lə'mentərɪ] *adj* [behaviour] peu courtois ▪ **~ language** *UK* POL langage *m* grossier.

unpatriotic ['ʌn,pætrɪ'ɒtɪk] *adj* [person] peu patriote ▪ [sentiment, song] peu patriotique.

unpaved [,ʌn'peɪvd] *adj* [street] non pavé.

unperturbed [,ʌnpə'tɜ:bd] *adj* imperturbable, impassible ▪ **to be ~ by sthg** rester imperturbable face à qqch.

unpick [,ʌn'pɪk] *vt* découdre.

unpin [,ʌn'pɪn] (*pret & pp* **unpinned**, *cont* **unpinning**) *vt* [seam] enlever les épingles de.

unplaced [,ʌn'pleɪst] *adj* [horse, competitor] non placé.

unplanned [,ʌn'plænd] *adj* [visit, activity] imprévu.

unplayable [,ʌn'pleɪəbl] *adj* [pitch] impraticable ▪ [ball, shot - in tennis, squash etc] qu'on ne peut rattraper ; [- in golf] impossible à jouer.

unpleasant [ʌn'pleznt] *adj* [person] désagréable ▪ [smell, weather] désagréable, mauvais ▪ [remark] désagréable, désobligeant ▪ [memory] pénible ▪ **the boss was most ~ to her** le patron était très désagréable avec elle.

unpleasantly [ʌn'plezntlɪ] *adv* désagréablement, de façon déplaisante.

unpleasantness [ʌn'plezntnɪs] *n* **1.** [of person] côté *m* désagréable ▪ [of experience, weather] désagrément *m* **2.** [discord] friction *f*, dissension *f.*

unplug [ʌn'plʌg] (*pret & pp* **unplugged**, *cont* **unplugging**) *vt* ELEC débrancher.

unplumbed [,ʌn'plʌmd] *adj* [depths, area of knowledge] insondé.

unpolished [,ʌn'pɒlɪʃt] *adj* **1.** [furniture, brass] non poli ▪ [floor, shoes] non ciré **2.** *fig* [person] qui manque de savoir-vivre ▪ [manners, style] peu raffiné, peu élégant.

unpolluted [,ʌnpə'lu:tɪd] *adj* non pollué.

unpopular [,ʌn'pɒpjʊlər] *adj* impopulaire, peu populaire ▪ **I'm rather ~ with the bosses** je ne suis pas très bien vu des patrons ▪ **to make o.s. ~** se rendre impopulaire.

unpopularity ['ʌn,pɒpjʊ'lærətɪ] *n* impopularité *f.*

unpractised *UK*, **unpracticed** *US* [ʌn'præktɪst] *adj* inexpérimenté.

unprecedented [ʌn'presɪdəntɪd] *adj* sans précédent.

unpredictable [,ʌnprɪ'dɪktəbl] *adj* imprévisible.

unpredictably [,ʌnprɪ'dɪktəblɪ] *adv* de façon imprévisible.

unprejudiced [,ʌn'predʒʊdɪst] *adj* impartial, sans parti pris.

unprepared [,ʌnprɪ'peəd] *adj* mal préparé ▪ **I was ~ for what happened** je n'étais pas préparés à ce qui s'est passé.

unprepossessing ['ʌn,pri:pə'zesɪŋ] *adj* [place] peu attrayant ▪ [person, smile] peu avenant *OR* engageant.

unpretentious [,ʌnprɪ'tenʃəs] *adj* sans prétention.

unprincipled [ʌn'prɪnsəpld] *adj* [person, behaviour] sans scrupules.

unprintable [,ʌn'prɪntəbl] *adj* [language] grossier.

unprocessed [ʌn'prəʊsest] *adj* **1.** [food, wool] non traité, naturel **2.** PHOT [film] non développé **3.** [data] brut.

unproductive [,ʌnprə'dʌktɪv] *adj* [land] improductif, stérile ▪ [discussion, weekend] improductif.

unprofessional [,ʌnprə'feʃənl] *adj* [attitude, conduct] peu professionnel.

unprofitable [,ʌn'prɒfɪtəbl] *adj* **1.** [business] peu rentable **2.** [discussions] peu profitable ▪ [action] inutile.

Unprofor ['ʌnprəfɔ:] (*abbrev of* **United Nations Protection Force**) *n* FORPRONU *f.*

unprompted [,ʌn'prɒmptɪd] *adj* [action, words] spontané.

unpronounceable [,ʌnprə'naʊnsəbl] *adj* imprononçable.

unprotected [,ʌnprə'tektɪd] *adj* **1.** [person] sans protection, non défendu ▪ **~ sex** rapports *mpl* non protégés **2.** [machinery] sans protection, non protégé **3.** [wood] non traité **4.** [exposed] exposé (aux intempéries).

unprovoked [,ʌnprə'vəʊkt] *adj* [attack, insult] injustifié.

unpublishable [,ʌn'pʌblɪʃəbl] *adj* impubliable.

unpublished [,ʌn'pʌblɪʃt] *adj* [manuscript, book] inédit, non publié.

unpunctual [,ʌn'pʌŋktʃʊəl] *adj* peu ponctuel, souvent en retard.

unpunished [,ʌn'pʌnɪʃt] *adj* impuni ▪ **he can't be allowed to go ~** il ne peut pas rester impuni.

unputdownable [ˌʌnpʊtˈdaʊnəbl] *adj* ***UK inf*** [book, novel] passionnant, dont on a du mal à s'arracher.

unqualified [ˌʌnˈkwɒlɪfaɪd] *adj* **1.** [unskilled] non qualifié ▪ [without diploma] qui n'a pas les diplômes requis ▪ [unsuitable] qui n'a pas les qualités requises **2.** [not competent] non qualifié *OR* compétent ▪ **she is ~ to decide** elle n'est pas qualifiée pour décider **3.** [unrestricted - admiration, approval] inconditionnel, sans réserve ; [- success] complet, - ète *f*.

unquenchable [ˌʌnˈkwentʃəbl] *adj* ***lit*** [curiosity, desire, thirst] insatiable.

unquestionable [ʌnˈkwestʃənəbl] *adj* **1.** [undeniable] incontestable, indubitable **2.** [above suspicion] qui ne peut être mis en question.

unquestionably [ʌnˈkwestʃənəblɪ] *adv* indéniablement, incontestablement.

unquestioned [ʌnˈkwestʃənd] *adj* [decision, leader, principle] indiscuté, incontesté.

unquestioning [ʌnˈkwestʃənɪŋ] *adj* [faith, love, obedience, belief] absolu, aveugle.

unquote [ˌʌnˈkwəʊt] *adv* fin de citation ▪ [in dictation] fermez les guillemets.

unravel [ʌnˈrævl] (***UK** pret & pp* **unravelled**, *cont* **unravelling** ***US**, pret & pp* **unraveled**, *cont* **unraveling**) ◇ *vt* **1.** [knitting] défaire ▪ [textile] effiler, effilocher **2.** [untangle - knots, string] démêler ▪ ***fig*** [mystery] débrouiller, éclaircir.
◇ *vi* [knitting] se défaire ▪ [textile] s'effilocher.

unread [ˌʌnˈred] *adj* **1.** [person] qui a peu lu **2.** [book, report] qui n'a pas été lu.

unreadable [ˌʌnˈriːdəbl] *adj* **1.** [handwriting, signature] illisible **2.** [book, report] illisible, ennuyeux.

unready [ˌʌnˈredɪ] *adj* **1.** [unprepared] non préparé, qui n'est pas prêt **2.** [unwilling] peu disposé.

unreal [ˌʌnˈrɪəl] *adj* **1.** [appearance, feeling] : **it all seems so ~** tout paraît si irréel ▪ **an ~ situation** une situation artificielle **2.** △ [very good] incroyable.

unrealistic [ˌʌnrɪəˈlɪstɪk] *adj* irréaliste, peu réaliste.

unrealistically [ˌʌnrɪəˈlɪstɪklɪ] *adv* : **his hopes were ~ high** ses espoirs étaient trop grands pour être réalistes.

unreality [ˌʌnrɪˈælətɪ] *n* irréalité *f*.

unrealizable, isable [ˌʌnˈrɪəlaɪzəbl] *adj* [aim, dream] irréalisable ▪ [fact, situation, state] inconcevable.

unreason [ˌʌnˈriːzn] *n* ***fml*** déraison *f* ***fml***, folie *f*.

unreasonable [ʌnˈriːznəbl] *adj* **1.** [absurd, preposterous] déraisonnable ▪ **you're being ~** vous n'êtes pas raisonnable **2.** [excessive] excessif, déraisonnable.

unreasonably [ʌnˈriːznəblɪ] *adv* déraisonnablement.

unreasoning [ʌnˈriːznɪŋ] *adj* irrationnel.

unrecognizable, isable [ˌʌnˈrekəgnaɪzəbl] *adj* méconnaissable.

unrecognized, ised [ˌʌnˈrekəgnaɪzd] *adj* **1.** [without being recognized] : **he slipped out ~** il s'est glissé vers la sortie sans être reconnu **2.** [not acknowledged - talent, achievement] méconnu.

unreconstructed [ˌʌnriːkənˈstrʌktɪd] *adj* [person, ideas] rétrograde.

unrefined [ˌʌnrɪˈfaɪnd] *adj* **1.** [petrol] brut, non raffiné ▪ [sugar] non raffiné ▪ [flour] non bluté **2.** [person, manners] peu raffiné, fruste.

unregistered [ˌʌnˈredʒɪstəd] *adj* **1.** [luggage, complaint] non enregistré **2.** [mail] non recommandé **3.** [car] non immatriculé **4.** [voter, student] non inscrit ▪ [birth] non déclaré.

unrehearsed [ˌʌnrɪˈhɜːst] *adj* **1.** [improvised] improvisé, spontané **2.** MUS & THEAT qui n'a pas été répété.

unrelated [ˌʌnrɪˈleɪtɪd] *adj* **1.** [unconnected] sans rapport ▪ **the two incidents are ~** les deux incidents sont sans rapport l'un avec l'autre ▪ **his answer was completely ~ to the question** sa réponse n'avait absolument aucun rapport *OR* absolument rien à voir avec la question **2.** [people] sans lien de parenté.

unrelenting [ˌʌnrɪˈlentɪŋ] *adj* **1.** [activity, effort] soutenu, continuel **2.** [person] tenace, obstiné.

unreliability [ˈʌnrɪˌlaɪəˈbɪlətɪ] *n* **1.** [of person] manque *m* de sérieux **2.** [of method, machine] manque *m* de fiabilité.

unreliable [ˌʌnrɪˈlaɪəbl] *adj* **1.** [person] peu fiable, sur qui on ne peut pas compter **2.** [car, machinery] peu fiable **3.** [service] peu fiable, peu sûr ▪ [business, company] qui n'inspire pas confiance **4.** [information, memory] peu fiable.

unrelieved [ˌʌnrɪˈliːvd] *adj* [pain] constant, non soulagé ▪ [gloom, misery] constant, permanent ▪ [boredom] mortel ▪ [landscape, routine] monotone.

unremarkable [ˌʌnrɪˈmɑːkəbl] *adj* peu remarquable, quelconque.

unremarked [ˌʌnrɪˈmɑːkt] *adj* inaperçu.

unremitting [ˌʌnrɪˈmɪtɪŋ] *adj* [activity, rain] incessant, ininterrompu ▪ [demands, efforts] inlassable, infatigable ▪ [opposition] implacable, opiniâtre ▪ **they were ~ in their efforts to find a solution** ils se sont efforcés avec assiduité de trouver une solution.

unrepeatable [ˌʌnrɪˈpiːtəbl] *adj* [remark] qu'on n'ose pas répéter, trop grossier pour être répété ▪ [offer, performance] exceptionnel, unique.

unrepentant [ˌʌnrɪˈpentənt] *adj* impénitent.

unreported [ˌʌnrɪˈpɔːtɪd] *adj* non signalé *OR* mentionné.

unrepresentative [ˌʌnreprɪˈzentətɪv] *adj* non représentatif ▪ **his opinions are ~ of the group** ses opinions ne représentent pas celles du groupe.

unrequited [ˌʌnrɪˈkwaɪtɪd] *adj* ***lit*** non réciproque, non partagé.

unreserved [ˌʌnrɪˈzɜːvd] *adj* **1.** [place] non réservé **2.** [unqualified] sans réserve, entier.

unreservedly [ˌʌnrɪˈzɜːvɪdlɪ] *adv* **1.** [without qualification] sans réserve, entièrement **2.** [frankly] sans réserve, franchement.

unresolved [ˌʌnrɪˈzɒlvd] *adj* [issue, problem] non résolu.

unresponsive [ˌʌnrɪˈspɒnsɪv] *adj* [without reaction] qui ne réagit pas ▪ [unaffected] insensible ▪ [audience] passif.

unrest [ˌʌnˈrest] *n (U)* agitation *f*, troubles *mpl*.

unrestrained [ˌʌnrɪˈstreɪnd] *adj* [anger, growth, joy] non contenu ▪ **the ~ use of force** l'usage sans limites de la force.

unrestricted [ˌʌnrɪˈstrɪktɪd] *adj* [access, parking] libre ▪ [number, time] illimité ▪ [power] absolu.

unrewarded [ˌʌnrɪˈwɔːdɪd] *adj* [person] non récompensé ▪ [effort, search] vain, infructueux ▪ **our efforts went ~** nos efforts sont restés sans récompense.

unrewarding [ˌʌnrɪˈwɔːdɪŋ] *adj* **1.** [financially] pas très intéressant financièrement **2.** ***fig*** [work, experience] ingrat.

unripe [ˌʌnˈraɪp] *adj* vert.

unrivalled ***UK***, **unrivaled** ***US*** [ʌnˈraɪvld] *adj* sans égal *OR* pareil, incomparable.

unroll [ˌʌnˈrəʊl] *vt* dérouler.

unromantic [ˌʌnrəˈmæntɪk] *adj* [person - unsentimental] peu romantique ; [- down-to-earth] prosaïque, terre à terre *(inv)* ▪ [ideas, place] peu romantique.

unruffled [ˌʌnˈrʌfld] *adj* **1.** [person] imperturbable, qui ne perd pas son calme ▪ **she remained completely ~** elle n'a pas sourcillé *OR* bronché **2.** [hair] lisse ▪ [water] calme, lisse.

unruled [ʌnˈruːld] *adj* blanc, blanche *f*, non réglé.

unruly [ʌnˈruːlɪ] *adj* **1.** [children] indiscipliné, turbulent ▪ [mob] incontrôlé **2.** [hair] indiscipliné.

unsaddle [ˌʌnˈsædl] *vt* [horse] desseller ▪ [rider] désarçonner.

unsafe [ˌʌn'seɪf] *adj* **1.** [dangerous - machine, neighbourhood] peu sûr, dangereux ; [- building, bridge] peu solide, dangereux ■ **~ sex** rapports *mpl* non protégés **2.** [endangered] en danger ■ **I feel very ~ here** je ne me sens pas du tout en sécurité ici.

unsaid [ˌʌn'sed] *adj* non dit, inexprimé ■ **a lot was left ~** beaucoup de choses ont été passées sous silence.

unsal(e)able [ˌʌn'seɪləbl] *adj* invendable.

unsatisfactory ['ʌnˌsætɪs'fæktərɪ] *adj* peu satisfaisant, qui laisse à désirer.

unsatisfied [ˌʌn'sætɪsfaɪd] *adj* **1.** [person - unhappy] insatisfait, mécontent ; [- unconvinced] non convaincu **2.** [desire] insatisfait, inassouvi.

unsatisfying [ˌʌn'sætɪsfaɪɪŋ] *adj* **1.** [activity, task] peu gratifiant, ingrat **2.** [unconvincing] peu convaincant **3.** [meal - insufficient] insuffisant, peu nourrissant ; [- disappointing] décevant.

unsaturated [ˌʌn'sætʃəreɪtɪd] *adj* non saturé.

unsavoury *UK*, **unsavory** *US* [ˌʌn'seɪvərɪ] *adj* **1.** [behaviour, habits] répugnant, très déplaisant ■ [person] peu recommandable ■ [place] louche ■ [reputation] douteux **2.** [smell] fétide, nauséabond.

unsay [ˌʌn'seɪ] (*pret & pp* **unsaid** [ˌʌn'sed]) *vt* retirer, revenir sur.

unscathed [ˌʌn'skeɪðd] *adj* [physically] indemne, sain et sauf ■ [psychologically] non affecté.

unscheduled [*UK* ˌʌn'ʃedju:ld, *US* ˌʌn'skedʒʊld] *adj* imprévu.

unschooled [ˌʌn'sku:ld] *adj fml* **1.** [person] qui n'a pas d'instruction **2.** [talent] inné, naturel.

unscientific ['ʌnˌsaɪən'tɪfɪk] *adj* non *OR* peu scientifique.

unscramble [ˌʌn'skræmbl] *vt* [code, message] déchiffrer ■ *fig* [problem] résoudre.

unscrew [ˌʌn'skru:] ◇ *vt* dévisser.
◇ *vi* se dévisser.

unscripted [ˌʌn'skrɪptɪd] *adj* [play, speech] improvisé ■ [item, subject] non programmé.

unscrupulous [ʌn'skru:pjʊləs] *adj* [person] sans scrupules, peu scrupuleux ■ [behaviour, methods] malhonnête, peu scrupuleux.

unscrupulously [ʌn'skru:pjʊləslɪ] *adv* sans scrupules, peu scrupuleusement.

unseal [ˌʌn'si:l] *vt* [open - letter] ouvrir, décacheter ; [- deed, testament] desceller.

unsealed [ˌʌn'si:ld] *adj* [letter] ouvert, décacheté ■ [deed, testament] descellé.

unseasonably [ʌn'si:znəblɪ] *adv* : **an ~ cold night** une nuit fraîche pour la saison.

unseasoned [ˌʌn'si:znd] *adj* **1.** [food] non assaisonné **2.** [wood] vert.

unseat [ˌʌn'si:t] *vt* [rider] désarçonner ■ [government, king] faire tomber.

unsecured [ˌʌnsɪ'kjʊəd] *adj* **1.** [door, window - unlocked] qui n'est pas fermé à clé ; [- open] mal fermé **2.** FIN [creditor, loan] sans garantie.

unseeded [ˌʌn'si:dɪd] *adj* SPORT non classé.

unseemly [ʌn'si:mlɪ] *adj lit* [improper - behaviour] inconvenant, déplacé ; [- dress] inconvenant, peu convenable ■ [rude] indécent, grossier.

unseen [ˌʌn'si:n] ◇ *adj* **1.** [invisible] invisible ■ [unnoticed] inaperçu **2.** [not seen previously] : **to buy sthg sight ~** acheter qqch sans l'avoir vu ■ **an ~ translation** *UK* SCH & UNIV une traduction sans préparation *OR* à vue.
◇ *n UK* SCH & UNIV traduction *f* sans préparation *OR* à vue.

unsegregated [ˌʌn'segrɪˌgeɪtɪd] *adj* où la ségrégation n'est pas appliquée.

unselfconscious [ˌʌnself'kɒnʃəs] *adj* naturel ■ **she's quite ~ about speaking up** elle n'a vraiment pas peur de dire ce qu'elle pense, elle dit ce qu'elle pense sans la moindre gêne.

unselfish [ˌʌn'selfɪʃ] *adj* [person, act] généreux, désintéressé.

unselfishly [ˌʌn'selfɪʃlɪ] *adv* généreusement, sans penser à soi.

unsettle [ˌʌn'setl] *vt* **1.** [person] inquiéter, troubler **2.** [stomach] déranger.

unsettled [ˌʌn'setld] *adj* **1.** [unstable - conditions, situation] instable, incertain ; [- person] troublé, perturbé, inquiet, - ète *f* ; [- stomach] dérangé ; [- weather] incertain, changeant **2.** [unfinished - issue, argument, dispute] qui n'a pas été réglé **3.** [account, bill] non réglé, impayé **4.** [area, region] inhabité, sans habitants.

unsettling [ˌʌn'setlɪŋ] *adj* [disturbing] troublant, perturbateur.

unshakeable [ʌn'ʃeɪkəbl] *adj* [conviction, faith] inébranlable ■ [decision] ferme.

unshaken [ˌʌn'ʃeɪkən] *adj* inébranlable.

unshaven [ˌʌn'ʃeɪvn] *adj* non rasé.

unsheathe [ˌʌn'ʃi:ð] *vt* dégainer.

unshockable [ˌʌn'ʃɒkəbl] *adj* imperturbable, impassible.

unshod [ˌʌn'ʃɒd] *adj* [horse] qui n'est pas ferré.

unsightly [ʌn'saɪtlɪ] *adj* disgracieux, laid.

unsigned [ˌʌn'saɪnd] *adj* non signé, sans signature.

unsinkable [ˌʌn'sɪŋkəbl] *adj* [boat] insubmersible ■ *fig* [person] qui ne se démonte pas facilement.

unskilful *UK*, **unskillful** *US* [ˌʌn'skɪlfʊl] *adj* [lacking skill] inexpert, malhabile ■ [clumsy] maladroit.

unskilled [ˌʌn'skɪld] *adj* **1.** [worker] sans formation professionnelle, non spécialisé, non qualifié **2.** [job, work] qui ne nécessite pas de connaissances professionnelles.

unskillful *US* = **unskilful**.

unsmiling [ˌʌn'smaɪlɪŋ] *adj* [person, face] austère, sérieux.

unsociable [ʌn'səʊʃəbl] *adj* [person] sauvage, peu sociable ■ [place] peu accueillant.

unsocial [ˌʌn'səʊʃl] *adj* : **she works ~ hours** elle travaille en dehors des heures normales.

unsolicited [ˌʌnsə'lɪsɪtɪd] *adj* non sollicité.

unsolved [ˌʌn'sɒlvd] *adj* [mystery] non résolu, inexpliqué ■ [problem] non résolu.

unsophisticated [ˌʌnsə'fɪstɪkeɪtɪd] *adj* **1.** [person - in dress, tastes] simple ; [- in attitude] simple, naturel **2.** [dress, style] simple, qui n'est pas sophistiqué **3.** [device, machine] (de conception) simple ■ [approach, method] rudimentaire, simpliste *pej*.

unsought [ˌʌn'sɔ:t] *adj* [advice, compliment] non sollicité, non recherché.

unsound [ˌʌn'saʊnd] *adj* **1.** [argument, conclusion, reasoning] mal fondé, peu pertinent ■ [advice, decision] peu judicieux, peu sensé ■ [enterprise, investment] peu sûr, risqué ■ [business] peu sûr, précaire ■ **the project is economically ~** le projet n'est pas sain *OR* viable sur le plan économique **2.** [building, bridge] peu solide, dangereux **3.** *phr* **to be of ~ mind** ne pas jouir de toutes ses facultés mentales.

unsparing [ʌn'speərɪŋ] *adj* **1.** [generous] généreux, prodigue ■ **they were ~ in their efforts to help us** ils n'ont pas ménagé leurs efforts pour nous aider **2.** [harsh] sévère.

unspeakable [ʌn'spi:kəbl] *adj* **1.** [crime, pain] épouvantable, atroce **2.** [beauty, joy] indicible, ineffable.

unspeakably [ʌn'spi:kəblɪ] *adv* [cruel, rude] épouvantablement, atrocement ■ [beautiful] indiciblement, ineffablement.

unspecified [ˌʌn'spesɪfaɪd] *adj* non spécifié.

unspoiled [ˌʌn'spɔɪld], **unspoilt** [ˌʌn'spɔɪlt] *adj* **1.** [person] (qui est resté) naturel **2.** [beauty, town] qui n'est pas gâté *OR* défiguré **3.** [flavour] naturel.

unspoken [ˌʌn'spəʊkən] *adj* **1.** [agreement] tacite **2.** [thought, wish] inexprimé ▪ [word] non prononcé.

unsporting [ˌʌn'spɔ:tɪŋ], **unsportsmanlike** [ʌn'spɔ:tsmənlaɪk] *adj* déloyal ▪ **it was ~ of him just to quit like that** ce n'était pas fair-play de sa part d'abandonner comme ça.

unstable [ˌʌn'steɪbl] *adj* **1.** [chair, government, price, situation] instable **2.** [marriage] peu solide **3.** [person] déséquilibré, instable.

unstated [ˌʌn'steɪtɪd] *adj* **1.** [agreement] tacite **2.** [desire] inexprimé.

unstatesmanlike [ˌʌn'steɪtsmənlaɪk] *adj* peu digne.

unsteadily [ˌʌn'stedɪlɪ] *adv* [walk] d'un pas chancelant *OR* incertain, en titubant ▪ [speak] d'une voix mal assurée ▪ [hold, write] d'une main tremblante.

unsteady [ˌʌn'stedɪ] (*comp* **unsteadier**, *superl* **unsteadiest**) *adj* **1.** [chair, ladder] instable, branlant **2.** [step, voice] mal assuré, chancelant ▪ [hand] tremblant ▪ **to be ~ on one's feet** [from illness, tiredness] ne pas être très solide sur ses jambes ; [from drink] tituber **3.** [rhythm, speed, temperature] irrégulier ▪ [flame] vacillant.

unstick [ˌʌn'stɪk] (*pret & pp* **unstuck** [ˌʌn'stʌk]) ◇ *vt* décoller.
◇ *vi* se décoller.

unstinting [ˌʌn'stɪntɪŋ] *adj* [care] infini ▪ [help] généreux ▪ [efforts] incessant, illimité ▪ [support] sans réserve, inconditionnel ▪ [person] généreux, prodigue ▪ **the firm has been ~ in its efforts to help us** l'entreprise ne ménage pas ses efforts pour nous aider.

unstop [ˌʌn'stɒp] (*pret & pp* **unstopped**, *cont* **unstopping**) *vt* [drain, sink] déboucher.

unstoppable [ˌʌn'stɒpəbl] *adj* qu'on ne peut pas arrêter.

unstrap [ˌʌn'stræp] (*cont* **unstrapping**, *pret & pp* **unstrapped**) *vt* défaire les sangles de ▪ **to ~ sthg from sthg** détacher qqch de qqch.

unstressed [ˌʌn'strest] *adj* LING inaccentué, atone.

unstructured [ˌʌn'strʌktʃəd] *adj* [activity] non structuré ▪ [group] non organisé.

unstuck [ˌʌn'stʌk] ◇ *pt & pp* ▷ **unstick**.
◇ *adj* [envelope, label] décollé ▪ **to come ~** *liter* se décoller ; *fig* [plan, system] tomber à l'eau ; [person] échouer.

unstudied [ˌʌn'stʌdɪd] *adj* [natural] naturel ▪ [spontaneous] spontané.

unsubstantiated [ˌʌnsəb'stænʃɪeɪtɪd] *adj* [report, story] non confirmé ▪ [accusation] non fondé.

unsubscribe [ˌʌnsəb'skraɪb] *vi* se désinscrire (de) ▪ **to unsubscribe (from sth)** se désinscrire (de qqch).

unsubtle [ˌʌn'sʌtl] *adj* [person, remark] peu subtil, sans finesse ▪ [joke] gros, grosse *f*.

unsuccessful [ˌʌnsək'sesfʊl] *adj* [plan, project] qui est un échec, qui n'a pas réussi ▪ [attempt] vain, infructueux ▪ [person] qui n'a pas de succès ▪ [application, demand] refusé, rejeté ▪ [marriage] malheureux ▪ **to be ~** échouer ▪ **I was ~ in my attempts to find her** je n'ai pas réussi *OR* je ne suis pas arrivé à la trouver, je l'ai cherchée en vain *OR* sans succès.

unsuccessfully [ˌʌnsək'sesfʊlɪ] *adv* en vain, sans succès.

unsuitable [ˌʌn'su:təbl] *adj* [arrangement, candidate, qualities] qui ne convient pas ▪ [behaviour, language] inconvenant ▪ [moment, time] inopportun ▪ [clothing] peu approprié, inadéquat ▪ **he chose an ~ time to call** il a mal choisi le moment pour appeler ▪ **'~ for children'** 'ne convient pas aux enfants'.

unsuitably [ˌʌn'su:təblɪ] *adv* [behave] de façon inconvenante ▪ [dress] d'une manière inadéquate.

unsuited [ˌʌn'su:tɪd] *adj* [person] inapte ▪ [machine, tool] mal adapté, impropre ▪ **he is ~ to politics** il n'est pas fait pour la politique ▪ **as a couple they seem totally ~** ils forment un couple mal assorti, ils ne vont pas du tout ensemble.

unsung [ˌʌn'sʌŋ] *adj lit* [deed, hero] méconnu.

unsupported [ˌʌnsə'pɔ:tɪd] *adj* **1.** [argument, theory] non vérifié ▪ [accusation, statement] non fondé **2.** [wall, aperture] sans support **3.** *fig* [person - financially, emotionally] : **to be ~** n'avoir aucun soutien.

unsure [ˌʌn'ʃɔ:ʳ] *adj* [lacking self-confidence] qui manque d'assurance, qui n'est pas sûr de soi ▪ [hesitant] incertain ▪ **to be ~ of o.s.** manquer d'assurance ▪ **they were ~ of his reaction** ils ignoraient quelle serait sa réaction.

unsurpassed [ˌʌnsə'pɑ:st] *adj* sans égal *OR* pareil.

unsurprisingly [ˌʌnsə'praɪzɪŋlɪ] *adv* bien entendu, évidemment.

unsuspected [ˌʌnsə'spektɪd] *adj* insoupçonné.

unsuspecting [ˌʌnsə'spektɪŋ] *adj* qui ne soupçonne rien, qui ne se doute de rien.

unsuspectingly [ˌʌnsə'spektɪŋlɪ] *adv* sans se douter de rien, sans se méfier.

unsweetened [ˌʌn'swi:tnd] *adj* sans sucre, non sucré.

unswerving [ʌn'swɜ:vɪŋ] *adj* [devotion, loyalty] indéfectible, à toute épreuve ▪ [determination] inébranlable.

unsympathetic ['ʌnˌsɪmpə'θetɪk] *adj* **1.** [unfeeling] insensible, incompréhensif ▪ **to be ~ to a cause** être opposé *OR* hostile à une cause **2.** [unlikeable] antipathique.

unsympathetically ['ʌnˌsɪmpə'θetɪklɪ] *adv* [speak, behave] sans montrer la moindre sympathie.

unsystematic [ˌʌnsɪstə'mætɪk] *adj* non systématique, non méthodique.

untainted [ˌʌn'teɪntɪd] *adj* [water] pur ▪ *fig* [reputation] sans tache.

untangle [ˌʌn'tæŋgl] *vt* [hair, necklace, rope] démêler ▪ *fig* [mystery] débrouiller, éclaircir.

untapped [ˌʌn'tæpt] *adj* inexploité.

untarnished [ˌʌn'tɑ:nɪʃt] *adj* [silver] non terni ▪ *fig* [reputation] non terni, sans tache.

untenable [ˌʌn'tenəbl] *adj* [argument, theory] indéfendable ▪ [position] intenable.

untested [ˌʌn'testɪd] *adj* [employee, method, theory] qui n'a pas été mis à l'épreuve ▪ [invention, machine, product] qui n'a pas été essayé ▪ [drug] non encore expérimenté.

unthinkable [ʌn'θɪŋkəbl] *adj* impensable, inconcevable.

unthinking [ʌn'θɪŋkɪŋ] *adj* [action, remark] irréfléchi, inconsidéré ▪ [person] irréfléchi, étourdi.

untidily [ʌn'taɪdɪlɪ] *adv* sans soin, d'une manière négligée.

untidiness [ʌn'taɪdɪnɪs] *n* [of dress] manque *m* de soin, débraillé *m* ▪ [of person] manque *m* d'ordre ▪ [of room] désordre *m*.

untidy [ʌn'taɪdɪ] (*comp* **untidier**, *superl* **untidiest**) *adj* [cupboard, desk, room] mal rangé, en désordre ▪ [appearance] négligé, débraillé ▪ [person] désordonné.

untie [ˌʌn'taɪ] *vt* [string] dénouer ▪ [knot] défaire ▪ [bonds] défaire, détacher ▪ [package] défaire, ouvrir ▪ [prisoner] détacher, délier.

until [ən'tɪl] ◇ *prep* **1.** [up to] jusqu'à ▪ **~ midnight/Monday** jusqu'à minuit/lundi ▪ **~ such time as you are ready** jusqu'à ce que *OR* en attendant que vous soyez prêt ▪ **she was here (up) ~ February** elle était ici jusqu'en février ▪ **(up) ~ now** jusqu'ici, jusqu'à présent ▪ **(up) ~ then** jusque-là **2.** *(with negative)* [before] : **they didn't arrive ~ 8 o'clock** ils ne sont arrivés qu'à 8 h ▪ **your car won't be ready ~ next week** votre voiture ne sera pas prête avant la semaine prochaine.
◇ *conj* [up to the specified moment - in present] jusqu'à ce que ; [- in past] avant que, jusqu'à ce que ▪ **I'll wait here ~ you come back** j'attendrai ici jusqu'à ce que tu reviennes ▪ **wait ~ she**

says hello attendez qu'elle dise bonjour ■ **I laughed ~ I cried** j'ai ri aux larmes ■ [with negative main clause] : **~ she spoke I didn't realize she was Spanish** jusqu'à ce qu'elle commence à parler, je ne m'étais pas rendu compte qu'elle était espagnole ■ **she won't go to sleep ~ her mother comes home** elle ne s'endormira pas avant que sa mère (ne) soit rentrée *OR* tant que sa mère n'est pas rentrée ■ **don't sign anything ~ the boss gets there** ne signez rien avant que le patron n'arrive, attendez le patron pour signer quoi que ce soit ■ **the play didn't start ~ everyone was seated** la pièce n'a commencé qu'une fois que tout le monde a été assis.

untimely [ʌn'taɪmlɪ] *adj* **1.** [premature] prématuré, précoce **2.** [inopportune - remark] inopportun, déplacé ; [- moment] inopportun, mal choisi ; [- visit] intempestif.

untiring [ʌn'taɪərɪŋ] *adj* [efforts] inlassable, infatigable.

untiringly [ʌn'taɪərɪŋlɪ] *adv* inlassablement, infatigablement.

untitled [ˌʌn'taɪtld] *adj* [painting] sans titre ■ [person] non titré.

unto ['ʌntu:] *prep arch* & *lit* **1.** *(indicating dative)* [to] à ■ **do ~ others as you would have them do ~ you** ne faites pas à autrui ce que vous ne voudriez pas qu'il vous fît **2.** [until] jusqu'à.

untogether [ˌʌntə'geðə^r] *adj inf* **he's very ~** [in work] il est très mal organisé ; [emotionally] il est vraiment mal dans sa peau.

untold [ˌʌn'təʊld] *adj* **1.** [tale] jamais raconté ■ [secret] jamais dévoilé **2.** [great - joy, suffering] indicible, indescriptible ; [- amount, number] incalculable.

untouchable [ˌʌn'tʌtʃəbl] ◇ *adj* intouchable.
◇ *n* [in India] intouchable *mf* ■ *fig* paria *m*.

untouched [ˌʌn'tʌtʃt] *adj* **1.** [not changed] auquel on n'a pas touché, intact **2.** [unharmed - person] indemne, sain et sauf ; [- thing] indemne, intact.

untoward [ˌʌntə'wɔ:d] *adj fml* [unfortunate - circumstances] fâcheux, malencontreux ; [- effect] fâcheux, défavorable.

untrained [ˌʌn'treɪnd] *adj* [person] sans formation ■ [ear] inexercé ■ [mind] non formé ■ [voice] non travaillé ■ [dog, horse] non dressé ■ **to the ~ eye** pour un œil inexercé.

untrammelled *UK*, **untrammeled** *US* [ʌn'træməld] *adj lit* sans contrainte, sans entraves.

untranslatable [ˌʌntræns'leɪtəbl] *adj* intraduisible.

untreated [ˌʌn'tri:tɪd] *adj* **1.** [unprocessed - food, wood] non traité ; [- sewage] brut **2.** [infection, tumour] non traité, non soigné.

untried [ˌʌn'traɪd] *adj* [method, recruit, theory] qui n'a pas été mis à l'épreuve ■ [invention, product] qui n'a pas été essayé.

untroubled [ˌʌn'trʌbld] *adj* tranquille, paisible ■ **they seemed ~ by the situation** ils ne semblaient pas (être) affectés par la situation.

untrue [ˌʌn'tru:] *adj* **1.** [incorrect - belief, statement] faux, fausse *f*, erroné ; [- measurement, reading] erroné, inexact **2.** [disloyal] : **to be ~ to sb** être déloyal envers *OR* infidèle à qqn.

untrustworthy [ˌʌn'trʌstˌwɜ:ðɪ] *adj* [person] qui n'est pas digne de confiance.

untruth [ˌʌn'tru:θ] *n euph* & *fml* [lie] mensonge *m*, invention *f*.

untruthful [ˌʌn'tru:θfʊl] *adj* [statement] mensonger ■ [person] menteur ■ **to say ~ things** mentir, dire des mensonges.

untutored [ˌʌn'tju:təd] *adj* **1.** [person] sans instruction ■ [eye, ear] inexercé ■ [voice] non travaillé ■ [mind] non formé **2.** [skill, talent] inné, naturel.

unusable [ˌʌn'ju:zəbl] *adj* inutilisable.

unused *adj* **1.** [ˌʌn'ju:zd] [not in use] inutilisé ■ [new - machine, material] neuf, qui n'a pas servi ; [- clothing, shoes] neuf, qui n'a pas été porté **2.** [ʌn'ju:st] [unaccustomed] : **to be ~ to sthg** ne pas avoir l'habitude de qqch, ne pas être habitué à qqch.

unusual [ʌn'ju:ʒl] *adj* [uncommon] peu commun, inhabituel ■ [odd] étrange, bizarre ■ **it's ~ for her to be so brusque** il est rare qu'elle soit si brusque, ça ne lui ressemble pas *OR* ce n'est pas son genre d'être aussi brusque.

unusually [ʌn'ju:ʒəlɪ] *adv* [exceptionally] exceptionnellement, extraordinairement ■ **she is ~ intelligent** elle est d'une intelligence exceptionnelle ■ [abnormally] exceptionnellement, anormalement ■ **~, it wasn't raining** chose rare, il ne pleuvait pas.

unutterable [ʌn'ʌtərəbl] *adj fml* [misery, pain] indicible, indescriptible ■ [boredom] mortel ■ [joy] inexprimable.

unutterably [ʌn'ʌtərəblɪ] *adv fml* [miserable, tired] terriblement, horriblement ■ [happy] extraordinairement.

unvarnished [ˌʌn'vɑ:nɪʃt] *adj* **1.** [furniture] non verni **2.** *fig* [plain, simple] simple, sans fard.

unvarying [ʌn'veərɪɪŋ] *adj* invariable, uniforme.

unveil [ˌʌn'veɪl] *vt* [painting] dévoiler, inaugurer ■ *fig* [secret] dévoiler, révéler.

unveiling [ˌʌn'veɪlɪŋ] *n* [of painting, sculpture] dévoilement *m*, inauguration *f* ■ [of secret] dévoilement *m*, révélation *f*.

unverified [ˌʌn'verɪfaɪd] *adj* non vérifié.

unversed [ˌʌn'vɜ:st] *adj fml* peu versé ■ **to be ~ in sthg** être peu versé dans qqch.

unvoiced [ˌʌn'vɔɪst] *adj* **1.** [desire, objection] inexprimé **2.** PHON non voisé, sourd.

unwaged [ˌʌn'weɪdʒd] ◇ *adj* [unsalaried] non salarié ■ [unemployed] sans emploi, au chômage.
◇ *npl* : **the ~** les sans-emploi *mpl*.

unwanted [ˌʌn'wɒntɪd] *adj* [child, pregnancy] non désiré, non souhaité ■ [books, clothing] dont on n'a plus besoin, dont on veut se séparer ■ [hair] superflu ■ **I felt ~ as a child** j'ai été privé d'affection dans mon enfance.

unwarranted [ʌn'wɒrəntɪd] *adj* [concern, criticism] injustifié ■ [remark, interference] déplacé.

unwary [ʌn'weərɪ] *adj* [person, animal] qui n'est pas méfiant *OR* sur ses gardes.

unwashed [ˌʌn'wɒʃt] ◇ *adj* [dishes, feet, floor] non lavé ■ [person] qui ne s'est pas lavé.
◇ *npl* : **the great ~** *UK hum* & *pej* la populace.

unwavering [ʌn'weɪvərɪŋ] *adj* [devotion, support] indéfectible, à toute épreuve ■ [look] fixe ■ [person] inébranlable, ferme.

unwed [ˌʌn'wed] *adj* célibataire.

unwelcome [ʌn'welkəm] *adj* [advances, attention] importun ■ [advice] non sollicité ■ [visit] inopportun ■ [visitor] importun, gênant ■ [news, situation] fâcheux ■ **he made his mother feel ~** il a donné l'impression à sa mère qu'elle gênait.

unwelcoming [ʌn'welkəmɪŋ] *adj* [person, look] hostile, froid ■ [place] peu accueillant.

unwell [ˌʌn'wel] *adj* [indisposed] souffrant, indisposé *fml* ■ [ill] malade.

unwholesome [ˌʌn'həʊlsəm] *adj* [climate] malsain, insalubre ■ [activity, habits, thoughts] malsain, pernicieux ■ [fascination, interest] malsain, morbide ■ [drink, food] peu sain, nocif.

unwieldy [ʌn'wi:ldɪ] *adj* **1.** [chair, package] peu maniable, encombrant **2.** [argument, method] maladroit ■ [bureaucracy, system] lourd.

unwilling [ˌʌn'wɪlɪŋ] *adj* [helper, student] réticent, peu enthousiaste ■ **he was ~ to cooperate** il n'était pas vraiment disposé à coopérer ■ **I was their ~ accomplice** j'étais leur complice malgré moi *OR* à mon corps défendant.

unwillingly [ʌn'wɪlɪŋlɪ] *adv* à contrecœur, contre son gré.

unwillingness [ʌn'wɪlɪŋnɪs] *n* manque *m* d'enthousiasme, réticence *f*.

unwind [ˌʌn'waɪnd] (*pret* & *pp* **unwound** [ˌʌn'waʊnd]) ◇ *vt* dérouler.

◇ *vi* **1.** [bail of yarn, cord] se dérouler **2.** *fig* [relax] se détendre, se relaxer.

unwise [,ʌn'waɪz] *adj* [action, decision] peu judicieux, imprudent.

unwisely [,ʌn'waɪzlɪ] *adv* imprudemment.

unwitting [ʌn'wɪtɪŋ] *adj fml* [accomplice] involontaire, malgré soi ▪ [insult] non intentionnel, involontaire.

unwittingly [ʌn'wɪtɪŋlɪ] *adv* involontairement, sans (le) faire exprès.

unworkable [,ʌn'wɜ:kəbl] *adj* [idea, plan] impraticable, impossible à réaliser ▪ **your project is ~** votre projet ne marchera pas *OR* est infaisable.

unworldly [,ʌn'wɜ:ldlɪ] *adj* **1.** [spiritual] spirituel, détaché de ce monde ▪ [ascetic] d'ascète, ascétique **2.** [naive] naïf, ingénu.

unworn [,ʌn'wɔ:n] *adj* [clothing] qui n'a pas été porté, (comme) neuf ▪ [carpet] qui n'est pas usé.

unworthiness [ʌn'wɜ:ðɪnɪs] *n* [of person] indignité *f*, manque *m* de mérite ▪ [of action] indignité *f*.

unworthy [ʌn'wɜ:ðɪ] *adj* [unbefitting] indigne ▪ [undeserving] indigne, peu méritant ▪ **he felt ~ of such praise** il se croyait indigne de *OR* il ne croyait pas mériter de telles louanges ▪ **such details are ~ of her attention** de tels détails ne méritent pas son attention.

unwound [,ʌn'waʊnd] ◇ *pt & pp* ▷ **unwind**.
◇ *adj* : **to come ~** se dérouler.

unwounded [,ʌn'wu:ndɪd] *adj* non blessé, indemne.

unwrap [,ʌn'ræp] (*pret & pp* **unwrapped**, *cont* **unwrapping**) *vt* déballer, ouvrir.

unwritten [,ʌn'rɪtn] *adj* [legend, story] non écrit ▪ [agreement] verbal, tacite ▪ **an ~ rule** une règle tacitement admise ▪ **~ law** droit *m* coutumier.

unyielding [ʌn'ji:ldɪŋ] *adj* [ground, material] très dur ▪ [person] inflexible, intransigeant ▪ [determination, principles] inébranlable.

unzip [,ʌn'zɪp] (*pret & pp* **unzipped**, *cont* **unzipping**) ◇ *vt* ouvrir *OR* défaire (la fermeture Éclair® de) ▪ COMPUT dézipper.
◇ *vi* se dégrafer.

up [ʌp] ◇ *adv*

A.

1. [towards a higher position or level] en haut ▪ **he's on his way up** il monte ▪ **they had coffee sent up** ils ont fait monter du café ▪ **hang it higher up** accrochez-le plus haut ▪ **wait till the moon comes up** attends que la lune se lève

2. [in a higher position, at a higher level] : **she wears her hair up** elle porte ses cheveux relevés ▪ **heads up!** attention! ▮ [in a high place or position] : **up above** au-dessus ▪ **up in the air** en l'air ▪ **look at the kite up in the sky** regardez le cerf-volant (là-haut) dans le ciel ▪ **I live eight floors up** j'habite au huitième (étage) ▪ **she lives three floors up from us** elle habite trois étages au-dessus de chez nous ▪ **she's up in her room** elle est en haut dans sa chambre ▪ **from up on the mountain** du haut de la montagne ▪ **do you see her up on that hill?** la voyez-vous en haut de *OR* sur cette colline? ▪ **what are you doing up there?** qu'est-ce que vous faites là-haut? ▪ **have you ever been up in a plane?** avez-vous déjà pris l'avion? ▪ **up the top** tout en haut ▪ **she's up there with the best (of them)** *fig* elle est parmi *OR* dans les meilleurs

3. [in a raised position] levé ▪ **Charles has his hand up** Charles a la main levée ▪ **wind the window up** [in car] remontez la vitre ▪ **she turned her collar up** elle a relevé son col

4. [into an upright position] debout ▪ **up you get!** debout! ▪ **he helped me up** il m'a aidé à me lever *OR* à me mettre debout ▪ **the trunk was standing up on end** la malle était debout ⊳ **up and at them!** *inf* grouillez-vous!△

5. [out of bed] : **she's always up and doing** elle n'arrête jamais

6. [facing upwards] : **the body was lying face up** le corps était couché sur le dos ▪ **he turned his hand palm up** il a tourné la main paume vers le haut ▪ **'fragile – this way up'** 'fragile haut' ▪ **I don't know which end is up anymore** *fig* je suis complètement déboussolé

7. [erected, installed] : **they're putting up a new hotel there** il construisent un nouvel hôtel là-bas ▪ **help me get the cutains/the pictures up** aide-moi à accrocher les rideaux/les tableaux

8. [on wall] : **up on the blackboard** au tableau ▪ **I saw an announcement up about it** je l'ai vu sur une affiche

B.

1. [towards north] : **it's cold up here** il fait froid ici ▪ **up there** là-bas ▪ **up north** dans le nord

2. [in, to or from a larger place] : **she's up in Maine for the wee** elle passe une semaine dans le Maine ▪ **we're up from Munich** nous venons *OR* arrivons de Munich ▪ **he was on his wa up to town** il allait en ville

3. *UK* [at university] : **he's up at Oxford** il est à Oxford

4. [further] : **there's a café up ahead** il y a un café plus loin ▪ **th sign up ahead says 10 miles** la pancarte là-bas indique 10 miles

5. [in phrasal verbs] : **the clerk came up to him** le vendeur s'es approché de lui *OR* est venu vers lui ▪ **up came a small, blond child** (alors,) un petit enfant blond s'est approché

6. [close to] : **up close** de près ▪ **I like to sit up front** j'aime bie m'asseoir devant ▪ **when you get right up to her** quand vou la voyez de près

C.

1. [towards a higher level] : **prices have gone up by 10 per cent** le prix ont augmenté *OR* monté de 10 pour cent ▪ **the temperature soared up into the thirties** la température est montée au dessus de trente degrés ▪ **they can cost anything from £750 u** ils coûtent au moins 750 livres, on en trouve à partir de 75 livres

2. [more loudly, intensely] plus fort ▪ **speak up** parlez plus fort

D.

1. *inf* [indicating completion] : **drink up!** finissez vos verres! ▪ **ea up your greens** mange tes légumes

2. [into small pieces] : **he ripped the shirt up** il a mis la chemise en lambeaux

3. [together] : **add these figures up** additionnez ces chiffres ▪ **the teacher gathered up his notes** le professeur a ramassé ses notes

E.

1. [before an authority] : **he came up before the judge for rape** il a comparu devant le juge pour viol

2. *inf* [indicating support] : **up (with) the Revolution!** vive la Révolution! ▪ **up the Lakers!** SPORT allez les Lakers!

◇ *adj*

A.

1. [at or moving towards higher level] haut ▪ **the river is up** le fleuve est en crue ▪ **the tide is up** la marée est haute ▪ **prices are up on last year** les prix ont augmenté par rapport à l'année dernière ▪ **the temperature is up in the twenties** la température a dépassé les vingt degrés

2. [in a raised position] levé ▪ **keep the windows up** [in car] n'ouvrez pas les fenêtres ▪ **her hair was up (in a bun)** elle avait un chignon ▪ **her hood was up so I couldn't see her face** sa capuche était relevée, si bien que je ne voyais pas sa figure ▪ **his defences were up** *fig* il était sur ses gardes

3. [in an upwards direction] : **the up escalator** l'escalier roulant ascendant

4. [out of bed] : **is she up yet?** est-elle déjà levée *OR* debout? ▪ **she was up late last night** elle s'est couchée *OR* elle a veillé tard hier soir ▪ **they were up all night** ils ne se sont pas couchés de la nuit, ils ont passé une nuit blanche

5. [in tennis] : **was the ball up?** la balle était-elle bonne?

B.

1. [road] en travaux ▪ **'road up'** 'travaux'

2. [erected, installed] : **these buildings haven't been up long** ça ne fait pas longtemps que ces immeubles ont été construits ▪ **are the new curtains up yet?** les nouveaux rideaux ont-ils été posés?

1. [finished, at an end] terminé ▪ **time is up!** [on exam, visit] c'est l'heure! ; [in game, on meter] le temps est écoulé! ▪ **when the month was up he left** à la fin du mois, il est parti
2. [ahead] : **I'm $50 up on you** *inf* j'ai 50 dollars de plus que vous ▪ **Madrid was two goals up** SPORT Madrid menait de deux buts ➤ **to be one up on sb** *inf* avoir un avantage sur qqn
3. *inf* [ready] prêt ▪ **dinner's up** le dîner est prêt
4. [in operation] : **the computer's up again** l'ordinateur fonctionne à nouveau

1. *inf* [cheerful] gai ▪ **he seemed very up when I saw him** il avait l'air en pleine forme quand je l'ai vu
2. *inf* [well-informed] : **he's really up on history** il est fort *OR* calé en histoire ▪ **she's always up with the latest trends** elle est toujours au courant de la dernière mode

1. [before an authority] comparaître ▪ **to be up before a court/a judge** comparaître devant un tribunal/un juge ▪ **she's up before the board tomorrow** elle comparaît devant le conseil demain
2. *inf phr* **something's up** [happening] il se passe quelque chose ; [wrong] quelque chose ne va pas ▪ **what's up?** [happening] qu'est-ce qui se passe? ; [wrong] qu'est-ce qu'il y a? ; *US* [as greeting] quoi de neuf? ▪ **what's up with you?** [happening] quoi de neuf? ; [wrong] qu'est-ce que tu as? ▪ **something's up with Mum** il y a quelque chose qui ne va pas chez maman, maman a quelque chose.
◇ *prep* **1.** [indicating motion to a higher place or level] : **we carried our suitcases up the stairs** nous avons monté nos valises ▪ **I climbed up the ladder** je suis monté à l'échelle ▪ **the cat climbed up the tree** le chat a grimpé dans l'arbre ▪ **further up the wall** plus haut sur le mur ➤ **up hill and down dale** *lit* par monts et par vaux **2.** [at or to the far end of] : **her flat is up those stairs** son appartement est en haut de cet escalier ▪ **we walked up the street** nous avons monté la rue ▪ **she pointed up the street** elle a montré le haut de la rue ▪ **the café is just up the road** le café se trouve plus loin *OR* plus haut dans la rue **3.** [towards the source of] : **up the river** en amont ▪ **a voyage up the Amazon** une remontée de l'Amazone **4.** △ *UK* [out at] à ▪ **he's up the pub** il est au pub **5.** *phr* **up yours!**△ va te faire voir!△.
◇ *vt* (*pret & pp* **upped**, *cont* **upping**) **1.** [increase] augmenter **2.** [promote] lever, relever ▪ **the boss upped him to district manager** le patron l'a bombardé directeur régional.
◇ *vi* (*pret & pp* **upped**, *cont* **upping**) *inf* **she upped and left** elle a fichu le camp ▪ **he upped and married her** en moins de deux, il l'a épousée.
◇ *n* **1.** [high point] haut *m* ▪ **ups and downs** [in land, road] accidents *mpl* ; [of market] fluctuations *fpl* ▮ [in life] : **we all have our ups and downs** nous avons tous des hauts et des bas **2.** [increase] : **prices are on the up** les prix sont en train d'augmenter.
➡ **up against** *prep phr* **1.** [touching] contre **2.** [in competition or conflict with] : **you're up against some good candidates** vous êtes en compétition avec de bons candidats ▪ **they don't know what they're up against!** ils ne se rendent pas compte de ce qui les attend! ➤ **to be up against it** *inf* être dans le pétrin.
➡ **up and about, up and around** *adj phr* [gen] : **I've been up and about since 7 o'clock** je suis levé depuis 7 h ▮ [after illness] : **so you're up and about again?** alors tu n'es plus alité?
➡ **up and down** ◇ *adv phr* **1.** [upwards and downwards] : **he was jumping up and down** il sautait sur place ▪ **she looked us up and down** elle nous a regardé de haut en bas ▪ **the bottle bobbed up and down on the waves** la bouteille montait et descendait sur les vagues **2.** [to and fro] de long en large ▪ **I could hear him walking up and down** je l'entendais faire les cent pas *OR* marcher de long en large **3.** [in all parts of] : **up and down the country** dans tout le pays.
◇ *adj phr* : **she's been very up and down lately** elle a eu beaucoup de hauts et de bas ces derniers temps.
➡ **up for** *prep phr* **1.** [under consideration, about to undergo] à ▪ **the house is up for sale** la maison est à vendre ▪ **the project is up for discussion** on va discuter du projet ▪ **she's up for election** elle est candidate *OR* elle se présente aux élections **2.** [due to be tried for] être jugé ▪ **he's up for murder/speeding** il va être jugé pour meurtre/excès de vitesse **3.** *inf* [interested in, ready for] : **are you still up for supper tonight?** tu veux toujours qu'on dîne ensemble ce soir? ▪ **he's up for anything** il est toujours partant.
➡ **up to** *prep phr* **1.** [as far as] jusqu'à ▪ **he can count up to 100** il sait compter jusqu'à 100 ▪ **I'm up to page 120** j'en suis à la page 120 ▪ **up to and including Saturday** jusqu'à samedi inclus ▪ **up to** *OR* **up until now** jusqu'à maintenant, jusqu'ici ▪ **up to** *OR* **up until then** jusqu'alors, jusque-là ▪ **we were up to our knees in mud** nous avions de la boue jusqu'aux genoux **2.** [the responsibility of] : **which film do you fancy? – it's up to you** quel film est-ce que tu veux voir? – c'est comme tu veux ▪ **if it were up to me...** si c'était moi qui décidais *OR* à moi de décider... ▪ **it's up to them to pay damages** c'est à eux *OR* il leur appartient de payer les dégâts **3.** [capable of] : **to be up to doing sthg** être capable de faire qqch ▪ **my German is not up to translating novels** mon niveau d'allemand ne me permet pas de traduire des romans ▪ **are you going out tonight? – no, I don't feel up to it** tu sors ce soir? – non, je n'en ai pas tellement envie ▪ **I'm not up to going back to work** je ne suis pas encore en état de reprendre le travail ➤ **the football team isn't up to much** *inf* l'équipe de foot ne vaut pas grand-chose **4.** [as good as] : **his work is not up to his normal standard** son travail n'est pas aussi bon que d'habitude ▪ **the levels are up to standard** les niveaux sont conformes aux normes ▪ **I don't feel up to par** je ne me sens pas en forme **5.** [engaged in, busy with] : **let's see what she's up to** allons voir ce qu'elle fait *OR* fabrique ▪ **what have you been up to lately?** qu'est-ce que tu deviens? ▪ **they're up to something** ils manigancent quelque chose ▪ **she's up to no good** elle prépare un mauvais coup ▪ **the things we got up to in our youth!** qu'est-ce qu'on *OR* ce qu'on ne faisait pas quand on était jeunes!

up-and-coming *adj* plein d'avenir, qui promet, qui monte.

up-and-under *n* [in rugby] chandelle *f*.

up-and-up *n phr* **to be on the ~** *UK* [improving] aller de mieux en mieux ; *US* [honest] être honnête.

upbeat ['ʌpbi:t] ◇ *adj* [mood, person] optimiste ▪ [music] entraînant.
◇ *n* MUS levé *m*.

upbraid [ʌp'breɪd] *vt fml* réprimander.

upbringing ['ʌp,brɪŋɪŋ] *n* éducation *f*.

upcoming ['ʌp,kʌmɪŋ] *adj* [event] à venir, prochain ▪ [book] à paraître, qui va paraître ▪ [film] qui va sortir ▪ **'~ attractions'** 'prochainement'.

update ◇ *vt* [,ʌp'deɪt] [information, record] mettre à jour, actualiser ▪ [army, system] moderniser.
◇ *n* ['ʌpdeɪt] [of information, record] mise *f* à jour, actualisation *f* ▪ [of army, system] modernisation *f* ▪ **an ~ on the situation** une mise au point sur la situation.

updated [,ʌp'deɪtɪd] *adj* [records] mis à jour ▪ [army, system] modernisé.

upend [ʌp'end] *vt* **1.** *liter* [object] mettre debout ▪ [person] mettre la tête en bas **2.** *fig* [upset] bouleverser.

upfront [,ʌp'frʌnt] *adj inf* **1.** [frank - person] franc, franche *f*, ouvert ; [- remark] franc, franche *f*, direct **2.** [payment] d'avance.
➡ **up front** *adv* [pay] d'avance.

upgradable [ʌp'greɪdəbl] *adj* COMPUT extensible.

upgrade ◇ *vt* [,ʌp'greɪd] **1.** [improve] améliorer ▪ [increase] augmenter ▪ [modernize - computer system] moderniser, actualiser ▪ **I was ~d to business class** [on plane] on m'a mis en classe affaires **2.** [job] revaloriser ▪ [employee] promouvoir ▪ **I was ~d** je suis monté en grade ▪ **she was ~d to sales manager** elle a été promue directrice des ventes.

◇ *vi* [ˌʌp'greɪd] : **we've ~d to a more powerful system** on est passés à un système plus puissant.
◇ *n* ['ʌpgreɪd] **1.** *phr* **to be on the ~** [price, salary] augmenter, être en hausse ; [business, venture] progresser, être en bonne voie ; [sick person] être en voie de guérison **2.** *US* [slope] montée *f* **3.** COMPUT [of software] actualisation *f* ■ [of system] extension *f*.

upheaval [ʌp'hi:vl] *n* [emotional, political etc] bouleversement *m* ■ [social unrest] agitation *f*, perturbations *fpl*.

upheld [ʌp'held] *pt* & *pp* ▷ **uphold**.

uphill [ˌʌp'hɪl] ◇ *adj* **1.** [road, slope] qui monte **2.** *fig* [task] ardu, pénible ■ [battle] rude, acharné ■ **it was an ~ struggle convincing him** j'ai eu beaucoup de mal à le convaincre.
◇ *adv* : **to go ~** [car, person] monter (la côte) ; [road] monter.

uphold [ʌp'həʊld] (*pret* & *pp* **upheld** [ʌp'held]) *vt* **1.** [right] défendre, faire respecter ■ [law, rule] faire respecter *OR* observer **2.** LAW [conviction, decision] maintenir, confirmer.

upholster [ʌp'həʊlstəʳ] *vt* recouvrir, tapisser ■ **~ed in leather** recouvert *OR* tapissé de cuir.

upholstery [ʌp'həʊlstərɪ] *n (U)* **1.** [covering - fabric] tissu *m* d'ameublement ; [- leather] cuir *m* ; [- in car] garniture *f* **2.** [trade] tapisserie *f*.

upkeep ['ʌpki:p] *n (U)* [maintenance] entretien *m* ■ [cost] frais *mpl* d'entretien.

uplift ◇ *vt* [ʌp'lɪft] [person - spiritually] élever (l'esprit de) ; [- morally] encourager ■ **he felt ~ed by the news** la nouvelle lui a redonné courage.
◇ *comp* ['ʌplɪft] : **~ bra** soutien-gorge *m* de maintien.

uplifting [ʌp'lɪftɪŋ] *adj* édifiant.

uplighter ['ʌplaɪtəʳ] *n applique ou lampadaire diffusant la lumière vers le haut.*

upload ['ʌpləʊd] *vt* COMPUT télécharger *(vers un gros ordinateur)*.

up-market ◇ *adj* [goods, service, area] haut de gamme, de première qualité ■ [newspaper, television programme] qui vise un public cultivé ■ [audience] cultivé.
◇ *adv* : **she's moved ~** elle fait dans le haut de gamme maintenant.

upmost ['ʌpməʊst] = **uppermost**.

upon [ə'pɒn] *prep* **1.** *fml* [indicating position or place] : **~ the grass/the table** sur la pelouse/la table ■ **she had a sad look ~ her face** elle avait l'air triste ■ **the ring ~ her finger** la bague à son doigt
2. *fml* [indicating person or thing affected] : **attacks ~ old people are on the increase** les attaques contre les personnes âgées sont de plus en plus fréquentes
3. *fml* [immediately after] à ■ **~ our arrival in Rome** à notre arrivée à Rome ■ **~ hearing the news, he rang home** lorsqu'il a appris la nouvelle, il a appelé chez lui ■ **~ request** sur simple demande
4. [indicating large amount] et ■ **we receive thousands ~ thousands of offers each year** nous recevons plusieurs milliers de propositions chaque année
5. [indicating imminence] : **the holidays are nearly ~ us** les vacances approchent
6. *phr* **~ my word!** *dated* ma parole!

upper ['ʌpəʳ] ◇ *adj* **1.** [physically higher] supérieur, plus haut *OR* élevé ■ [top] du dessus, du haut ■ **~ lip** lèvre supérieure ■ **temperatures are in the ~ 30s** la température dépasse 30 degrés ➤ **to have the ~ hand** avoir le dessus ■ **to get** *OR* **to gain the ~ hand** prendre le dessus *OR* l'avantage **2.** [higher in order, rank] supérieur ■ **the Upper House** [gen] la Chambre haute ; [in England] la Chambre des lords **3.** GEOG [inland] haut.
◇ *n* **1.** [of shoe] empeigne *f* ■ **to be on one's ~s** *UK inf* manger de la vache enragée, être fauché **2.** △ *drug sl* excitant *m*, stimulant *m*.

upper case *n* TYPO haut *m* de casse.
◆ **upper-case** *adj* : **an upper-case letter** une majuscule.

upper class *n* : **the ~, the ~es** *l'aristocratie et la haute bou*
geoisie.
◆ **upper-class** *adj* **1.** [accent, family] aristocratique **2.**
UNIV [student] *de troisième ou quatrième année.*

upper-crust *adj inf* aristocratique.

upper middle class *n* : **the ~** *classe sociale réunissant l professions libérales et universitaires, les cadres de l'indu trie et les hauts fonctionnaires.*

uppermost ['ʌpəməʊst] ◇ *adj* **1.** [part, side] le plus ha *OR* élevé ■ [drawer, storey] du haut, du dessus **2.** [most prom nent] le plus important ■ **it's not ~ in my mind** ce n'est pas m préoccupation essentielle en ce moment.
◇ *adv* [most prominently] : **the question that comes ~ in my mi** la question que je me pose en premier *OR* avant toute a tre.

upper sixth *n UK* SCH (classe *f*) terminale *f*.

Upper Volta [-'vɒltə] *pr n* Haute-Volta *f* ■ **in ~** en Haut Volta.

uppity ['ʌpətɪ] *adj inf* [arrogant] arrogant, suffisant ■ [snobbis snob *(inv)*.

upraised [ʌp'reɪzd] *adj* levé.

upright ['ʌpraɪt] ◇ *adj* **1.** [erect] droit ■ **~ piano** piano droit ■ **~ vacuum cleaner** aspirateur-balai *m* **2.** [honest] dro
◇ *adv* **1.** [sit, stand] droit ■ **he sat bolt ~** il se redressa (sur so siège) **2.** [put] droit, debout.
◇ *n* **1.** [of door, bookshelf] montant *m*, portant *m* ■ [of goal pos montant *m* du but ■ ARCHIT pied-droit *m* **2.** [piano] piano droit **3.** [vacuum cleaner] aspirateur-balai *m*.

uprising ['ʌpˌraɪzɪŋ] *n* soulèvement *m*, révolte *f*.

upriver [ˌʌp'rɪvəʳ] ◇ *adj* (situé) en amont, d'amont.
◇ *adv* [be] en amont ■ [move] vers l'amont ■ [row, swim] contr le courant.

uproar ['ʌprɔ:ʳ] *n* [noise] tumulte *m*, vacarme *m* ■ [protes protestations *fpl*, tollé *m* ■ **his speech caused quite an ~** [pr tests] son discours a mis le feu aux poudres ; [shouting] so discours a déclenché le tumulte ■ **the town was in (an) ~ ov the new taxes** la ville entière s'est élevée contre le nouv impôt.

uproarious [ʌp'rɔ:rɪəs] *adj* [crowd, group] hilare ■ [film, jok hilarant, désopilant ■ [laughter] tonitruant.

uproot [ʌp'ru:t] *vt liter* & *fig* déraciner.

upscale ['ʌpskeɪl] *adj US* haut de gamme.

upset ◇ *vt* (*pret* & *pp* **upset**, *cont* **upsetting**) [ʌp'set] **1.** [ove turn - chair, pan] renverser ; [- milk, paint] renverser, répa dre ; [- boat] faire chavirer **2.** [disturb - plans, routine] boule verser, déranger ; [- procedure] bouleverser ; [- calculation results] fausser ; [- balance] rompre, fausser **3.** [person - anno contrarier, ennuyer ; [- offend] fâcher, vexer ; [- worry] inquié ter, tracasser ■ **it's not worth upsetting yourself over** ce n'e pas la peine de vous en faire **4.** [make ill - stomach] dérange [- person] rendre malade.
◇ *adj* [ʌp'set] **1.** [annoyed] ennuyé, contrarié ■ [offended] fâ ché, vexé ■ [worried] inquiet, - ète *f* ■ **there's no reason to g so ~** il n'y a pas de quoi en faire un drame *OR* te fâcher ■ **he ~ about losing the deal** cela l'ennuie d'avoir perdu l'affair ■ **I was most ~ that she left** j'étais très ennuyé qu'elle soit pa tie ■ **why is she so ~?** qu'est-ce qu'elle a? **2.** [stomach] dérang ■ **to have an ~ stomach** avoir une indigestion.
◇ *n* ['ʌpset] **1.** [in plans] bouleversement *m* ■ [of governmen renversement *m* ■ [of team] défaite *f* ■ **the result caused a ma jor political ~** le résultat a entraîné de grands bouleverse ments politiques **2.** [emotional] bouleversement *m* **3.** [stomach] indigestion *f*.

upsetting [ʌp'setɪŋ] *adj* [annoying] ennuyeux, contrarian ■ [offensive] vexant ■ [saddening] attristant, triste ■ [worryin inquiétant.

upshot ['ʌpʃɒt] *n* résultat *m*, conséquence *f*.

upside ['ʌpsaɪd] *n* **1.** [surface] dessus *m* **2.** [of situation] avan tage *m*, bon côté *m*.

upside down <> *adj* **1.** [cup, glass] à l'envers, retourné ▪ **upside-down cake** gâteau *m* renversé **2.** [room, house] sens dessus dessous.
<> *adv* **1.** [in inverted fashion] à l'envers ▪ **she hung ~ from the bar** elle s'est suspendue à la barre la tête en bas **2.** [in disorderly fashion] sens dessus dessous ▪ **we turned the house ~ looking for the keys** nous avons mis la maison sens dessus dessous en cherchant les clés ▪ **the news turned our world ~** la nouvelle a bouleversé notre univers.

upstage [ˌʌp'steɪdʒ] <> *adv* [move] vers le fond de la scène ▪ [enter, exit] par le fond de la scène ▪ [stand] au fond de la scène.
<> *vt fig* éclipser, voler la vedette à.

upstairs [ˌʌp'steəz] <> *adv* en haut, à l'étage ▪ **to go ~** monter (à l'étage) ▪ **I'll take your bags ~** je monterai vos bagages ▪ **let me show you ~** permettez que je vous fasse monter.
<> *adj* [room, window] du haut, (situé) à l'étage ▪ [flat, neighbour] du dessus.
<> *n* étage *m*.

upstanding [ˌʌp'stændɪŋ] *adj* **1.** [in character] intègre, droit ▪ [in build] bien bâti **2.** *fml* [on one's feet] : **be ~** levez-vous.

upstart ['ʌpstɑ:t] *n pej* parvenu *m*, - e *f*.

upstate [ˌʌp'steɪt] *US* <> *adv* [live] dans le nord (de l'État) ▪ [move] vers le nord (de l'État).
<> *adj* au nord (de l'État).

upstream [ˌʌp'stri:m] <> *adv* **1.** [live] en amont ▪ [move] vers l'amont ▪ [row, swim] contre le courant **2.** ECON en amont.
<> *adj* **1.** [gen] d'amont, (situé) en amont **2.** ECON en amont.

upsurge ['ʌpsɜ:dʒ] *n* [gen] mouvement *m* vif ▪ [of anger, enthusiasm] vague *f*, montée *f* ▪ [of interest] renaissance *f*, regain *m* ▪ [in production, sales] montée *f*, augmentation *f*.

upswing ['ʌpswɪŋ] *n* **1.** [movement] mouvement *m* ascendant, montée *f* **2.** [improvement] amélioration *f* ▪ **there's been an ~ in sales** il y a eu une progression des ventes.

uptake ['ʌpteɪk] *n* **1.** [of air] admission *f* ▪ [of water] prise *f*, adduction *f* **2.** *phr* **to be quick on the ~** avoir l'esprit vif *OR* rapide, comprendre vite ▪ **to be slow on the ~** être lent à comprendre *OR* à saisir **3.** [of offer, allowance] : **a campaign to improve the ~ of child benefit** une campagne pour inciter les gens à réclamer leurs allocations familiales.

upthrust ['ʌpθrʌst] *n* [of piston] poussée *f* ascendante ▪ GEOL soulèvement *m*.

uptight [ʌp'taɪt] *adj inf* **1.** [tense] tendu, crispé ▪ [irritable] irritable, énervé ▪ [nervous] nerveux, inquiet, - ète *f* ▪ **he gets so ~ whenever I mention it** [tense] il se crispe chaque fois que j'en parle ; [annoyed] il s'énerve chaque fois que j'en parle **2.** [prudish] coincé, collet monté *(inv)*.

uptime ['ʌptaɪm] *n* COMPUT temps *m* de bon fonctionnement.

up-to-date *adj* **1.** [information, report - updated] à jour ; [- most current] le plus récent ▪ **I try to keep ~ on the news** j'essaie de me tenir au courant de l'actualité ▪ **to bring sb ~ on sthg** mettre qqn au courant de qqch ▪ **they brought the reports ~** ils ont mis les rapports à jour **2.** [modern - machinery, methods] moderne.

up-to-the-minute *adj* le plus récent ▪ **~ news reporting** bulletins *mpl* (d'information) de dernière minute.

uptown [ˌʌp'taʊn] *US* <> *adj* des quartiers résidentiels.
<> *adv* [be, live] dans les quartiers résidentiels ▪ [move] vers les quartiers résidentiels.
<> *n* les quartiers *mpl* résidentiels.

upturn <> *n* ['ʌptɜ:n] [in economy, situation] amélioration *f* ▪ [in production, sales] progression *f*, reprise *f* ▪ **there's been an ~ in the market** il y a eu une progression du marché.
<> *vt* [ʌp'tɜ:n] [turn over] retourner ▪ [turn upside down] mettre à l'envers ▪ [overturn] renverser.

upturned [ʌp'tɜ:nd] *adj* **1.** [nose] retroussé ▪ **~ faces** visages tournés vers le haut **2.** [upside down] retourné, renversé.

upward ['ʌpwəd] <> *adj* [movement] ascendant ▪ [trend] à la hausse.
<> *adv US* = **upwards**.

upwardly mobile ['ʌpwədlɪ-] *adj* susceptible de promotion sociale.

upward mobility *n* ascension *f* sociale.

upwards ['ʌpwədz] *adv* **1.** [move, climb] vers le haut ▪ **to slope ~** monter ▪ **if you look ~ you can see...** si vous levez la tête *OR* les yeux, vous voyez... ▪ **prices are moving ~** les prix sont à la hausse **2.** [facing up] : **she placed the photos (face) ~ on the table** elle a posé les photos sur la table face vers le haut ▪ **he lay on the floor face ~** il était allongé par terre sur le dos **3.** [onwards] : **from 15 years ~** à partir de 15 ans.
◆ **upwards of** *prep phr* : **~ of 100 candidates applied** plus de 100 candidats se sont présentés ▪ **they can cost ~ of £150** ils peuvent coûter 150 livres et plus.

upwind [ˌʌp'wɪnd] <> *adv* du côté du vent, contre le vent.
<> *adj* dans le vent, au vent ▪ **to be ~ of sthg** être dans le vent *OR* au vent par rapport à qqch.

Ural ['jʊərəl] *adj* : **the ~ Mountains** les monts *mpl* Oural, l'Oural *m*.

Urals ['jʊərəlz] *pr npl* : **the ~** l'Oural *m*.

uranium [jʊ'reɪnjəm] *n* uranium *m* ▪ **~ series** série *f* uranique.

Uranus ['jʊərənəs] *pr n* ASTRON & MYTH Uranus.

urban ['ɜ:bən] *adj* urbain ▪ **~ area** zone *f* urbaine, agglomération *f* ▪ **~ blight** *OR* **decay** dégradation *f* urbaine ▪ **~ district** *UK* ADMIN district *m* urbain ▪ **~ guerrilla** personne *f* qui pratique la guérilla urbaine ▪ **the ~ jungle** la jungle de la ville ▪ **~ renewal** rénovations *fpl* urbaines.

urbane [ɜ:'beɪn] *adj* [person] poli, qui a du savoir-vivre ▪ [manner] poli, raffiné.

urbanite ['ɜ:bənaɪt] *n* citadin *m*, - e *f*.

urbanity [ɜ:'bænətɪ] *n* urbanité *f fml*, savoir-vivre *m*.

urbanize, ise ['ɜ:bənaɪz] *vt* urbaniser.

urchin ['ɜ:tʃɪn] *n* galopin *m*, polisson *m*, - onne *f*.

Urdu ['ʊədu:] *n* ourdou *m*, urdu *m*.

ureter [ˌjʊə'ri:tə] *n* uretère *m*.

urethra [ˌjʊə'ri:θrə] *n* urètre *m*.

urge [ɜ:dʒ] <> *n* forte envie *f*, désir *m* ▪ **I felt** *OR* **I had a sudden ~ to tell her** j'avais tout à coup très envie de lui dire ▪ **the sexual ~** les pulsions *fpl* sexuelles.
<> *vt* **1.** [person - incite] exhorter, presser ▪ **I ~ you to reconsider** je vous conseille vivement de reconsidérer votre position ▪ **she ~d us not to sell the house** elle nous a vivement déconseillé de vendre la maison ▪ **he ~d them to revolt** il les a incités à la révolte *OR* à se révolter **2.** [course of action] conseiller vivement, préconiser ▪ [need, point] insister sur.
◆ **urge on** *vt sep* talonner, presser ▪ [person, troops] faire avancer ▪ **to ~ sb on to do sthg** inciter qqn à faire qqch.

urgency ['ɜ:dʒənsɪ] *n* urgence *f* ▪ **it's a matter of great ~** c'est une affaire très urgente ▪ **there's no great ~** cela n'est pas urgent *OR* ne presse pas ▪ **there was a note of ~ in her voice** il y avait de l'insistance dans sa voix.

urgent ['ɜ:dʒənt] *adj* **1.** [matter, need] urgent, pressant ▪ [message] urgent ▪ **it's not ~** ce n'est pas urgent, ça ne presse pas ▪ **the roof is in ~ need of repair** le toit a un besoin urgent d'être réparé **2.** [manner, voice] insistant ▪ **he was ~ in his demands for help** il a insisté pour qu'on lui vienne en aide.

urgently ['ɜ:dʒəntlɪ] *adv* d'urgence, de toute urgence ▪ **they appealed ~ for help** ils ont demandé du secours avec insistance ▪ **supplies are ~ needed** un ravitaillement est absolument nécessaire.

urinal ['jʊərɪnl] *n* [fitting] urinal *m* ▪ [building] urinoir *m*.

urinate ['jʊərɪneɪt] *vi* uriner.

urine ['jʊərɪn] *n* urine *f*.

URL (*abbrev of* **uniform resource locator**) *n* URL *m*, adresse *f* sur la toile *offic*.

urn [ɜ:n] *n* **1.** [container - gen] urne *f* **2.** [for ashes] urne *f* (funéraire) **3.** [for coffee, tea] fontaine *f*.

urology [jʊəˈrɒlədʒɪ] *n* urologie *f*.

Ursa [ˈɜːsə] *pr n* : **~ Major/Minor** la Grande/Petite Ourse.

Uruguay [ˈjʊərəgwaɪ] *pr n* Uruguay *m* ■ **in ~** en Uruguay.

Uruguayan [ˌjʊərʊˈgwaɪən] ◇ *n* Uruguayen *m*, - enne *f*. ◇ *adj* uruguayen.

us [ʌs] *pron* **1.** [object form of 'we'] nous ■ **tell us the truth** dites-nous la vérité ■ **it's us!** c'est nous! ■ **most of us are students** nous sommes presque tous des étudiants ■ **all four of us went** nous y sommes allés tous les quatre ■ **there are three of us** nous sommes trois **2.** *inf* [me - direct object] me ; [- indirect object] me, moi ■ **give us a kiss!** embrasse-moi!

US ◇ *pr n* (*abbrev of* **United States**) ■ **the ~** les USA *mpl* ■ **in the ~** aux USA, aux États-Unis.
◇ *comp* des États-Unis, américain.

USA *pr n* **1.** (*abbrev of* **United States of America**) ■ **the ~** les USA *mpl* ■ **in the ~** aux USA, aux États-Unis **2.** (*abbrev of* **United States Army**) *armée des États-Unis*.

USB [ˌjuːesˈbiː] (*abbrev of* **universal serial bus**) *n* COMPUT USB *m*.

usable [ˈjuːzəbl] *adj* utilisable.

USAF (*abbrev of* **United States Air Force**) *pr n armée de l'air des États-Unis*.

usage [ˈjuːzɪdʒ] *n* **1.** [custom, practice] coutume *f*, usage *m* **2.** [of term, word] usage *m* ■ **the term is in common ~** le terme est employé couramment ■ **that phrase has long since dropped out of ~** cette expression n'est plus usitée depuis longtemps **3.** [employment] usage *m*, emploi *m* ■ [treatment - of material, tool] manipulation *f* ; [- of person] traitement *m* ■ **designed for rough ~** conçu pour résister aux chocs.

USDA (*abbrev of* **United States Department of Agriculture**) *pr n ministère américain de l'Agriculture*.

USDI (*abbrev of* **United States Department of the Interior**) *pr n ministère américain de l'Intérieur*.

use[1] [juːs] *n* **1.** [utilization - of materials] utilisation *f*, emploi *m* ■ [consumption - of water, resources etc] consommation *f* ■ [being used, worn etc] usage *m* ■ **to stretch (out) with ~** se détendre à l'usage ■ **to wear out with ~** s'user ■ **the dishes are for everyday ~** c'est la vaisselle de tous les jours ■ **ready for ~** prêt à l'emploi ■ **'directions for ~'** 'mode d'emploi' ■ **'for your personal ~'** pour votre usage personnel ■ **'for customer ~ only'** 'réservé à notre clientèle' ■ **'for external/internal ~ only'** MED 'à usage externe/interne' ■ **'for ~ in case of emergency'** 'à utiliser en cas d'urgence' ■ **the film is for ~ in teaching** le film est destiné à l'enseignement ▶ **in ~** [machine, system] en usage, utilisé ; [lift, cash point] en service ; [phrase, word] usité ■ **in general ~** d'emploi courant, d'utilisation courante ■ **'not in ~', 'out of ~'** 'hors d'usage' ; [lift, cash point] 'hors service' ■ **the phrase is no longer in ~** l'expression est inusitée *OR* ne s'utilise plus ■ **to come into ~** entrer en service ■ **to go out of ~** [machine] être mis au rebut ■ **to make ~ of sthg** se servir de *OR* utiliser qqch ■ **to make good ~ of, to put to go od ~** [machine, money] faire bon usage de ; [opportunity, experience] tirer profit de
2. [ability or right to use] usage *m*, utilisation *f* ■ **we gave them the ~ of our car** nous leur avons laissé l'usage de notre voiture ■ **she lost the ~ of her legs** elle a perdu l'usage de ses jambes ■ **the old man still has the full ~ of his faculties** le vieil homme jouit encore de toutes ses facultés
3. [practical application] usage *m*, emploi *m* ■ **we found a ~ for the old fridge** nous avons trouvé un emploi pour le vieux frigo ▶ **I have my ~s** *hum* il m'arrive de servir à quelque chose
4. [need] besoin *m*, usage *m* ■ **to have no ~ for sthg** *liter* ne pas avoir besoin de qqch ; *fig* n'avoir que faire de qqch ■ **this department has no ~ for slackers** il n'y a pas de place pour les fainéants dans ce service
5. [usefulness] : **to be of ~ (to sb)** être utile (à qqn), servir (à qqn) ■ **were the instructions (of) any ~?** est-ce que le mode d'emploi a servi à quelque chose? ■ **I found his advice to be of little ~, his advice was of little ~ to me** je n'ai pas trouvé ses conseils très utiles ■ **he's not much ~ as a secretary** il n'est pas brillant comme secrétaire ■ **to be (of) no ~** [thing] ne servir à rien ; [person] n'être bon à rien ■ **there's no ~ shouting** ça ne sert à rien de crier, (c'est) inutile de crier ■ **it's no ~, we might as well give up** c'est inutile *OR* ça ne sert à rien, autant abandonner ■ **I tried to convince her but it was no ~** j'ai essayé de la convaincre mais il n'y avait rien à faire ■ **is it any ~ calling her?** est-ce que ça servira à quelque chose de l'appeler? ■ **what's the ~ of waiting?** à quoi bon attendre?, à quoi ça sert d'attendre? ■ **oh, what's the ~?** à quoi bon? ■ **that's a fat lot of ~!** *inf iron* ça nous fait une belle jambe!
6. LING usage *m*.

use[2] [juːz] ◇ *vt* **1.** [put into action - service, tool, skills] se servir de, utiliser ; [- product] utiliser ; [- method, phrase, word] employer ; [- name] utiliser, faire usage de ; [- vehicle, form of transport] prendre ■ **these are the notebooks he ~d** ce sont les cahiers dont il s'est servi *OR* qu'il a utilisés ■ **it's no longer ~d** [machine, tool] ça ne sert plus ■ **I always ~ public transport** je prends toujours les transports en commun ■ **we ~ this room as an office** nous nous servons de cette pièce comme bureau, cette pièce nous sert de bureau ■ **what is this ~d for *OR* as?** à quoi cela sert-il? ■ **it's ~d for identifying the blood type** cela sert à identifier le groupe sanguin ■ **what battery does this radio ~?** quelle pile faut-il pour cette radio? ■ **my car ~s unleaded petrol** ma voiture marche à l'essence sans plomb ■ **may I ~ the phone?** puis-je téléphoner? ■ **he asked to ~ the toilet *UK OR* bathroom *US*** il a demandé à aller aux toilettes ■ **to ~ force/violence** avoir recours à la force/violence ■ **~ your imagination!** utilise ton imagination! ■ **~ your initiative!** fais preuve d'initiative! ■ **~ your head *OR* your brains!** réfléchis un peu! ■ **~ your eyes!** ouvrez l'œil! ▶ **he could certainly ~ some help** *inf* un peu d'aide ne lui ferait pas de mal ■ **we could all ~ a holiday!** *inf* nous aurions tous bien besoin de vacances! **2.** [exploit, take advantage of - opportunity] profiter de ; [- person] se servir de **3.** [consume] consommer, utiliser ■ [finish, use up] finir, épuiser ■ **the car's using a lot of oil** la voiture consomme beaucoup d'huile **4.** *fml* [treat physically] traiter ■ [behave towards] agir envers ■ **I consider I was ill ~d** je considère qu'on ne m'a pas traité comme il faut **5.** △ [drug] prendre.
◇ *modal vb (only in past tense)* : **he ~d to drink a lot** il buvait beaucoup avant ■ **it ~d to be true** c'était vrai autrefois ■ **she can't get about the way she ~d to** elle ne peut plus se déplacer comme avant ■ **we ~d not *OR* we didn't ~ to eat meat** avant, nous ne mangions pas de viande.
◆ **use up** *vt sep* [consume] consommer, prendre ■ [exhaust - paper, soap] finir ; [- patience, energy, supplies] épuiser ■ **she ~d up the leftovers to make the soup** elle a utilisé les restes pour faire un potage ■ **did you ~ up all your money?** as-tu dépensé tout ton argent? ■ **the paper was all ~d up** il ne restait plus de papier.

use-by date *n* date *f* limite de consommation.

used[1] [juːzd] *adj* [book, car] d'occasion ■ [clothing] d'occasion, usagé ■ [glass, linen] sale, qui a déjà servi.

used[2] [juːst] *adj* [accustomed] : **to be ~ to (doing) sthg** avoir l'habitude de *OR* être habitué à (faire) qqch ■ **to be ~ to sb** être habitué à qqn ■ **to get ~ to sthg** s'habituer à qqch ■ **you'll soon get ~ to the idea** tu te feras à l'idée.

useful [ˈjuːsfʊl] *adj* **1.** [handy - book, information, machine] utile, pratique ; [- discussion, experience] utile, profitable ; [- method] utile, efficace ■ **does it serve any ~ purpose?** est-ce utile?, est-ce que cela sert à quelque chose? ■ **you could be ~ to the director** vous pourriez rendre service au directeur ■ **the information was ~ to us in making a decision** les renseignements nous ont aidés à prendre une décision ■ **make yourself ~ and help me tidy up** rends-toi utile et aide-moi à ranger ■ **she's a ~ person to know** c'est une femme qu'il est bon de connaître ■ **he's very ~ around the house** il est très utile *OR* il rend beaucoup de services dans la maison **2.** *inf* [satisfactory - performance, score] honorable ■ **he's a very ~ player** c'est un joueur très compétent.

usefully [ˈjuːsfʊlɪ] *adv* utilement ■ **you could ~ devote a further year's study to the subject** tu pourrais consacrer avec profit une année d'étude supplémentaire au sujet.

usefulness [ˈjuːsfʊlnɪs] *n* utilité *f* ■ **it's outlived its ~** ça a fait son temps, ça ne sert plus à rien.

useless [ˈjuːslɪs] *adj* **1.** [bringing no help - book, information, machine] inutile ; [- discussion, experience] vain, qui n'apporte rien ; [- advice, suggestion] qui n'apporte rien, qui ne vaut rien ; [- attempt, effort] inutile, vain ▪ **the contract is ~ to them** le contrat leur est inutile ▪ **it's ~ trying to reason with him, it's ~ to try and reason with him** ça ne sert à rien *OR* c'est inutile d'essayer de lui faire entendre raison **2.** *inf* [incompetent] nul ▪ **she makes me feel ~** elle me donne l'impression d'être bon à rien ▪ **I'm ~ at history/maths** je suis nul en histoire/math ▪ **she's ~ as a navigator** elle est nulle *OR* elle ne vaut rien en tant que navigateur.

uselessly ['ju:slɪslɪ] *adv* inutilement.

Usenet® ['ju:znet] *n* Usenet® *m*, forum *m* électronique.

user ['ju:zəʳ] ◇ *n* [of computer, machine] utilisateur *m*, - trice *f* ▪ [of airline, public service, road] usager *m*, -ère *f* ▪ [of electricity, gas, oil] usager *m*, -ère *f*, utilisateur *m*, - trice *f* ▪ [of drugs] consommateur *m*, - trice *f*, usager *m*, -ère *f*.
◇ *in cpds* par l'utilisateur ▪ **~-programmable** programmable par l'utilisateur.

user-friendly *adj* [gen - COMPUT] convivial, facile à utiliser.

user-interface *n* COMPUT & *fig* interface *f* utilisateur.

usher ['ʌʃəʳ] ◇ *vt* conduire, accompagner ▪ **he ~ed us into/out of the living room** il nous a fait entrer au/sortir du salon.
◇ *n* **1.** [at concert, theatre, wedding] placeur *m*, - euse *f* **2.** [doorkeeper] portier *m* ▪ LAW huissier *m*.
◆ **usher in** *vt sep fig* inaugurer, marquer le début de.

usherette [,ʌʃə'ret] *n* ouvreuse *f*.

USM *pr n* (*abbrev of* **United States Mint**) ≃ la Monnaie *(aux États-unis)*.

USN (*abbrev of* **United States Navy**) *pr n marine de guerre des États-Unis.*

USS (*abbrev of* **United States Ship**) *initiales précédant le nom des navires américains* ▪ **the ~ Washington** le Washington.

USSR (*abbrev of* **Union of Soviet Socialist Republics**) *pr n* : **the ~** l'URSS *f* ▪ **in the ~** en URSS.

usu. *written abbr of* **usually**.

usual ['ju:ʒəl] ◇ *adj* [customary - activity, place] habituel ; [- practice, price] habituel, courant ; [- expression, word] courant, usité ▪ [doctor] habituel, traitant, de famille ▪ **my ~ diet consists of fish and vegetables** généralement *OR* d'habitude je mange du poisson et des légumes ▪ **let's meet at the ~ time** retrouvons-nous à l'heure habituelle *OR* à la même heure que d'habitude ▪ **6 o'clock is the ~ time he gets home** d'habitude *OR* en général il rentre à 18 h ▪ **later than ~** plus tard que d'habitude ▪ **she was her ~ cheery self** elle était gaie comme d'habitude ▪ **she's her ~ self again** elle est redevenue elle-même ▪ **with her ~ optimism** avec son optimisme habituel, avec l'optimisme qui est le sien *OR* qui la caractérise ▪ **it's not ~ for him to be so bitter** il est rarement si amer, c'est rare qu'il soit si amer ▪ **it's the ~ story** c'est toujours la même histoire ▪ **it's quite ~ to see flooding in the spring** il y a souvent des inondations au printemps ▪ **I believe it's the ~ practice** je crois que c'est ce qui se fait d'habitude ▪ **as is ~ with young mothers** comme d'habitude avec les jeunes mamans.
◇ *n inf* [drink, meal] : **what will you have? – the ~, please** que prends-tu? – comme d'habitude, s'il te plaît.
◆ **as usual, as per usual** *adv phr* comme d'habitude ▪ **life goes on as ~** la vie continue ▪ **'business as ~'** [during building work] 'le magasin reste ouvert pendant la durée des travaux' ▪ **it's business as ~** *fig* il n'y a rien à signaler.

usually ['ju:ʒəlɪ] *adv* généralement, d'habitude, d'ordinaire ▪ **she's not ~ late** il est rare qu'elle soit en retard, elle est rarement en retard ▪ **the roads were more than ~ busy** il y avait encore plus de trafic que d'habitude *OR* d'ordinaire *OR* de coutume sur les routes.

usurer ['ju:ʒərəʳ] *n* usurier *m*, - ère *f*.

usurp [ju:'zɜ:p] *vt* usurper.

usurper [ju:'zɜ:pəʳ] *n* usurpateur *m*, - trice *f*.

usury ['ju:ʒʊrɪ] *n* usure *f (intérêt)*.

UT *written abbr of* **Utah**.

Utah ['ju:tɑ:] *pr n* Utah *m* ▪ **in ~** dans l'Utah.

ute [ju:t] (*abbrev of* **utility vehicle** *OR* **utility truck**) *n inf Australia* camionnette *f*.

utensil [ju:'tensl] *n* ustensile *m*, outil *m* ▪ **cooking ~s** ustensiles de cuisine.

uterine ['ju:tərаɪn] *adj* utérin.

uterus ['ju:tərəs] (*pl* **uteri** [-raɪ] *OR pl* **uteruses**) *n* utérus *m*.

utilitarian [,ju:tɪlɪ'teərɪən] ◇ *adj* **1.** [functional] utilitaire, fonctionnel **2.** PHILOS utilitariste.
◇ *n* utilitariste *mf*.

utilitarianism [,ju:tɪlɪ'teərɪənɪzm] *n* utilitarisme *m*.

utility [ju:'tɪlətɪ] (*pl* **utilities**) ◇ *n* **1.** [usefulness] utilité *f* **2.** [service] service *m* **3.** COMPUT utilitaire *m*, programme *m* utilitaire **4.** *US* [room] = **utility room**.
◇ *adj* [fabric, furniture] utilitaire, fonctionnel ▪ [vehicle] utilitaire.

utility program *n* COMPUT (logiciel *m*) utilitaire *m*.

utility room *n pièce servant à ranger les appareils ménagers, provisions etc.*

utilization [,ju:tɪlaɪ'zeɪʃn] *n* utilisation *f*.

utilize, ise ['ju:tɪlaɪz] *vt* [use] utiliser, se servir de ▪ [make best use of] exploiter ▪ **you could have ~d your time better** vous auriez pu tirer meilleur parti de votre temps *OR* mieux profiter de votre temps.

utmost ['ʌtməʊst] ◇ *adj* **1.** [greatest] le plus grand ▪ **it's a matter of the ~ seriousness** c'est une affaire extrêmement sérieuse ▪ **with the ~ respect, I cannot agree with your conclusions** avec tout le respect que je vous dois, je ne peux pas partager vos conclusions **2.** [farthest] : **to the ~ ends of the earth** au bout du monde.
◇ *n* **1.** [maximum] maximum *m*, plus haut degré *m* ▪ **the ~ in comfort** ce qui se fait de mieux en matière de confort **2.** [best effort] : **we did our ~ to fight the new taxes** nous avons fait tout notre possible *OR* tout ce que nous pouvions pour lutter contre les nouveaux impôts ▪ **she tried her ~** elle a fait de son mieux.

utopia, Utopia [ju:'təʊpjə] *n* utopie *f*.

utopian, Utopian [ju:'təʊpjən] ◇ *adj* utopique.
◇ *n* utopiste *mf*.

utter ['ʌtəʳ] ◇ *vt* **1.** [pronounce - word] prononcer, proférer ; [- cry, groan] pousser ▪ **he didn't ~ a sound** il n'a pas ouvert la bouche, il n'a pas soufflé mot **2.** LAW [libel] publier ▪ [counterfeit money] émettre, mettre en circulation.
◇ *adj* [amazement, bliss] absolu, total ▪ [fool] parfait, fini ▪ **he's talking ~ rubbish** ce qu'il dit n'a aucun sens *OR* est absolument idiot ▪ **it's an ~ scandal** c'est un véritable scandale.

utterance ['ʌtərəns] *n* **1.** [statement] déclaration *f* ▪ LING énoncé *m* **2.** [expression] expression *f*, énonciation *f* ▪ **to give ~ to sthg** exprimer qqch.

utterly ['ʌtəlɪ] *adv* complètement, tout à fait.

uttermost ['ʌtəməʊst] = **utmost**.

U-turn *n* **1.** AUT demi-tour *m* ▪ **to make a ~** faire (un) demi-tour ▪ **'no ~s'** 'défense de faire demi-tour' **2.** *fig* volte-face *f inv*, revirement *m* ▪ **the government were accused of making a ~ on health policy** le gouvernement a été accusé de faire volte-face en matière de politique de santé.

UV (*abbrev of* **ultra-violet**) *n* UV *m*.

uvula ['ju:vjʊlə] (*pl* **uvulas** *OR pl* **uvulae** [-li:]) *n* luette *f*, uvule *f spec*, uvula *f spec*.

uvular ['ju:vjʊləʳ] *adj* uvulaire.

uxorious [ʌk'sɔ:rɪəs] *adj fml* & *lit* excessivement dévoué à sa femme.

Uzbek ['ʊzbek] *n* [person] Ouzbek *mf*.

Uzbekistan [ʊz,bekɪ'stɑ:n] *pr n* Ouzbékistan *m* ▪ **in ~** en Ouzbékistan.

v (*pl* **v's** *OR pl* **vs**), **V** (*pl* **V's** *OR pl* **Vs**) [vi:] *n* [letter] v *m*, V *m* ■ **V for Victor** V comme Victor ■ **V-1 (bomb)** V1 *m* ■ **V-2 (rocket)** V2 *m* ■ **V-8 (engine)** moteur *m* à huit cylindres en V, *see also* **f**.

v 1. (*written abbrev of* **verb**) v **2.** (*written abbrev of* **verse**) v **3.** *written abbrev of* **versus 4.** (*written abbrev of* **vide**) v.

V <> *n* [Roman numeral] V *m*.
<> (*written abbrev of* **volt**) V.

VA *written abbrev of* **Virginia**.

vac [væk] (*abbrev of* **vacation**) *n UK inf* UNIV [recess] vacances *fpl* ■ **the Easter ~** les vacances de Pâques.

vacancy ['veɪkənsɪ] (*pl* **vacancies**) *n* **1.** [emptiness] vide *m* **2.** [lack of intelligence] ineptie *f*, esprit *m* vide **3.** [in hotel] chambre *f* libre ■ **'no vacancies'** 'complet' **4.** [job] poste *m* vacant *OR* libre, vacance *f* ■ **do you have any vacancies?** avez-vous des postes à pourvoir?, est-ce qu'il y a de l'embauche? ■ **we have a ~ for a sales clerk** nous avons un poste de vendeur à pourvoir, nous cherchons un vendeur ■ **'no vacancies'** pas d'embauche ■ **'vacancies for waitresses'** 'cherchons serveuses'.

vacant ['veɪkənt] *adj* **1.** [house, room - to rent] libre, à louer ; [- empty] inoccupé ■ [seat] libre, inoccupé ■ **is this seat ~?** y a-t-il quelqu'un à cette place?, est-ce que cette place est libre? ■ **the room becomes ~ tomorrow** la chambre sera libérée *OR* disponible demain ■ **apartments sold with ~ possession** appartements libres à la vente **2.** [job, position] vacant, libre ■ **there are several ~ places to be filled** il y a plusieurs postes à pourvoir ■ **I found the job through the "situations ~" column** j'ai trouvé le poste grâce à la rubrique des offres d'emploi **3.** [empty - mind, look] vide ■ [stupid - person, look] niais, idiot ■ **I asked a question and she just looked ~** j'ai posé une question et elle a eu l'air de ne pas comprendre **4.** [time] de loisir, perdu ■ [hour] creux, de loisir.

vacant lot *n US* terrain *m* vague.

vacantly ['veɪkəntlɪ] *adv* [expressionlessly] d'un air absent *OR* vague ■ [stupidly] d'un air niais *OR* idiot ■ **she stared ~ into space** elle avait le regard perdu dans le vague.

vacate [və'keɪt] *vt* [hotel room] libérer, quitter ■ [flat, house] quitter, déménager de ■ [job] démissionner de ■ **they ~d the premises yesterday** ils ont quitté *OR* libéré les lieux hier.

vacation [və'keɪʃn] <> *n* **1.** *UK* UNIV [recess] vacances *fpl* ■ LAW vacations *fpl*, vacances *fpl* judiciaires ■ **~ course** UNIV cours *mpl* d'été **2.** *US* [holiday] vacances *fpl* ■ **they went to Italy on ~** ils ont passé leurs vacances en Italie ■ **when are you going on** *OR* **taking ~?** quand est-ce que vous prenez vos vacances?
<> *vi US* prendre *OR* passer des vacances.

vacationer [və'keɪʃənər], **vacationist** [və'keɪʃənɪst] *n US* vacancier *m*, - ère *f*.

vacation resort *n US* camp *m* de vacances.

vaccinate ['væksɪneɪt] *vt* vacciner ■ **have you been ~d against polio?** est-ce que vous êtes vacciné *OR* est-ce que vous vous êtes fait vacciner contre la polio?

vaccination [ˌvæksɪ'neɪʃn] *n* vaccination *f* ■ **polio ~, ~ against polio** vaccination contre la polio.

vaccine [*UK* 'væksi:n, *US* væk'si:n] *n* vaccin *m* ■ **smallpox ~** vaccin contre la variole.

vacillate ['væsəleɪt] *vi* hésiter.

vacillating ['væsəleɪtɪŋ] <> *adj* [behaviour] indécis, irrésolu.
<> *n* indécision *f*.

vacillation [ˌvæsə'leɪʃn] *n* hésitation *f*, indécision *f*.

vacuity [væ'kju:ətɪ] (*pl* **vacuities**) *n fml* **1.** [of person, reasoning] vacuité *f* **2.** [statement] ânerie *f*, niaiserie *f*.

vacuous ['vækjuəs] *adj fml* [eyes, look] vide, sans expression ■ [remark] sot, sotte *f*, niais ■ [film, novel] idiot, dénué de tout intérêt ■ [life] vide de sens.

vacuum ['vækjuəm] (*pl* **vacuums** *OR pl* **vacua** [-juə]) <> *n* **1.** [void] vide *m* **2.** PHYS vacuum *m* **3.** [machine] : **~ (cleaner)** aspirateur *m* ■ **I gave the room a quick ~** j'ai passé l'aspirateur en vitesse dans la pièce.
<> *vt* [carpet] passer l'aspirateur sur ■ [flat, room] passer l'aspirateur dans.

vacuum cleaner *n* aspirateur *m*.

vacuum flask *n UK* (bouteille *f*) Thermos® *f*.

vacuum-packed *adj* emballé sous vide.

vacuum pump *n* pompe *f* à vide.

vacuum tube *n US* tube *m* électronique *OR* à vide.

vagabond ['vægəbɒnd] <> *n* [wanderer] vagabond *m*, - e *f* ■ [tramp] clochard *m*, - e *f*.
<> *adj* vagabond, errant.

vagary ['veɪgərɪ] (*pl* **vagaries**) *n* caprice *m*.

vagina [və'dʒaɪnə] (*pl* **vaginas** *OR pl* **vaginae** [-ni:]) *n* vagin *m*.

vaginal [və'dʒaɪnl] *adj* vaginal ■ **~ discharge** pertes *fpl* blanches ■ **~ smear** frottis *m* vaginal.

vagrancy ['veɪgrənsɪ] *n* [gen - LAW] vagabondage *m*.

vagrant ['veɪgrənt] <> *n* [wanderer] vagabond *m*, - e *f* ■ [tramp] clochard *m*, - e *f* ■ [beggar] mendiant *m*, - e *f*.
<> *adj* vagabond.

vague [veɪg] *adj* **1.** [imprecise - promise, statement] vague, imprécis ; [- person] vague ■ **she had only a ~ idea of what he meant** elle ne comprenait que vaguement ce qu'il voulait dire ■ **his instructions were ~** ses instructions manquaient de précision ■ **they were ~ about their activities** [imprecise] ils n'ont pas précisé la nature de leurs activités ; [evasive] ils sont restés vagues sur la nature de leurs activités ▪ [unsure] : **I'm still ~ about how to get there** je ne comprends toujours pas comment y aller ▪ **I haven't the vaguest idea** je n'en ai pas la moindre idée **2.** [dim - memory, feeling] vague, confus **3.** [indistinct - shape] flou, indistinct **4.** [absent-minded] distrait.

vaguely ['veɪglɪ] *adv* **1.** [not clearly - promise, say] vaguement ; [- remember, understand] vaguement, confusément **2.** [a bit] vaguement ▪ **it tastes ~ like coffee** cela a vaguement un goût de café **3.** [absent-mindedly] distraitement.

vagueness ['veɪgnɪs] *n* **1.** [imprecision - of instructions, statement] imprécision *f*, manque *m* de clarté **2.** [of memory] imprécision *f*, manque *m* de précision ▪ [of feeling] vague *m*, caractère *m* vague *OR* indistinct **3.** [of shape] flou *m*, caractère *m* indistinct **4.** [absent-mindedness] distraction *f*.

vagus ['veɪgəs] (*pl* **vagi** [-dʒaɪ]) *n* nerf *m* vague *OR* pneumogastrique, pneumogastrique *m*.

vain [veɪn] *adj* **1.** [conceited] vaniteux **2.** [unsuccessful - attempt, effort] vain, inutile ; [- hope, plea, search] vain, futile **3.** [idle - promise] vide, en l'air ; [- word] creux, en l'air.

◆ **in vain** *adv phr* [unsuccessfully] en vain, inutilement ▪ **they tried in ~ to free the driver** ils ont essayé sans succès *OR* en vain de libérer le conducteur ▪ **all their efforts were in ~** leurs efforts n'ont servi à rien *OR* étaient vains ▪ **it was all in ~** c'était peine perdue ▪ **to take sb's name in ~** [show disrespect] manquer de respect envers le nom de qqn ; [mention name] parler de qqn en son absence.

vainglorious [,veɪn'glɔːrɪəs] *adj lit* [proud] vaniteux, orgueilleux ▪ [boastful] vantard.

valance ['væləns] *n* [round bed frame] frange *f* de lit ▪ [round shelf, window] lambrequin *m*, frange *f*.

vale [veɪl] *n lit* vallée *f*, val *m lit*.

valediction [,vælɪ'dɪkʃn] *n* [act] adieux *mpl* ▪ [speech] discours *m* d'adieu.

valedictory [,vælɪ'dɪktərɪ] (*pl* **valedictories**) *fml* <> *adj* d'adieu.
<> *n* discours *m* d'adieu.

valence ['veɪləns] *n* **1.** *US* = **valency 2.** [bonding capacity] atomicité *f*.

Valencia [və'lenʃɪə] *pr n* Valence.

valency ['veɪlənsɪ] (*pl* **valencies**) *n* CHEM & LING valence *f*.

valentine ['væləntaɪn] *n* **1.** [card] : **~ (card)** carte *f* de la Saint-Valentin **2.** [person] bien-aimé *m*, - e *f* ▪ **be my ~** c'est toi que j'aime.

Valentine ['væləntaɪn] *pr n* : **Saint ~** Saint Valentin ▪ **(Saint) ~'s Day** la Saint-Valentin ▪ **the Saint ~'s Day Massacre** *US* HIST le massacre de la Saint-Valentin.

THE SAINT VALENTINE'S DAY MASSACRE

Assassinat de cinq membres d'un gang de Chicago par une bande rivale, le 14 février 1929. Bien que sa culpabilité n'ait jamais pu être prouvée, Al Capone fut soupçonné d'en avoir été l'instigateur.

valerian [və'lɪərɪən] *n* valériane *f*.

Valerian [və'lɪərɪən] *pr n* Valérien.

valet <> *n* ['vælɪt, 'væleɪ] **1.** [manservant] valet *m* de chambre ▪ **~ service** le pressing de l'hôtel **2.** [clothing rack] valet *m* **3.** [for cars] : **'~ parking'** 'voiturier'.
<> *vt* [vælɪt] AUT : **to have one's car ~ed** faire faire un lavage-route à sa voiture.

valeting ['vælɪtɪŋ] *n* AUT lavage-toute *m*.

valetudinarian [,vælɪtjuːdɪ'neərɪən] *arch & lit n* valétudinaire *mf*.

Valhalla [væl'hælə] *n* Walhalla *m*.

valiance ['væljəns] *n lit* vaillance *f lit*, bravoure *f*.

valiant ['væljənt] *adj* [person] vaillant, courageux ▪ [behaviour, deed] courageux, brave ▪ **she made a ~ attempt to put out the fire** elle a tenté avec courage *OR* courageusement d'éteindre l'incendie.

valiantly ['væljəntlɪ] *adv* vaillamment, courageusement.

valid ['vælɪd] *adj* **1.** [argument, reasoning] valable, fondé ▪ [excuse] valable **2.** [contract, passport] valide, valable ▪ **my driver's licence is no longer ~** mon permis de conduire est périmé ▪ **~ for two months** [on train ticket] valable deux mois.

validate ['vælɪdeɪt] *vt* **1.** [argument, claim] confirmer, prouver la justesse de **2.** [document] valider.

validation [,vælɪ'deɪʃn] *n* **1.** [of argument, claim] confirmation *f*, preuve *f* **2.** [of document] validation *f*.

validity [və'lɪdətɪ] *n* **1.** [of argument, reasoning] justesse *f*, solidité *f* **2.** [of document] validité *f*.

valise [*UK* və'liːz, *US* və'liːs] *n* mallette *f*.

Valium® ['vælɪəm] (*pl inv*) *n* Valium® *m*.

Valkyrie [væl'kɪərɪ] *n* Walkyrie *f*, Valkyrie *f*.

valley ['vælɪ] *n* vallée *f* ▪ [small] vallon *m* ▪ **the Valleys** *le sud du pays de Galles* ▪ **the Loire/Rhone ~** la vallée de la Loire/du Rhône.

valour *UK*, **valor** *US* ['vælər] *n lit* courage *m*, bravoure *f*, vaillance *f lit*.

valuable ['væljʊəbl] <> *adj* **1.** [of monetary worth] de (grande) valeur **2.** [advice, friendship, time] précieux.
<> *n (usu pl)* **~s** objets *mpl* de valeur.

valuate ['væljʊeɪt] *vt US* estimer, expertiser.

valuation [,væljʊ'eɪʃn] *n* expertise *f*, estimation *f* ▪ **we asked for a ~ of the house** nous avons fait expertiser *OR* estimer la maison ▪ **the ~ of** *OR* **the ~ (put) on the business is £50,000** l'affaire a été estimée *OR* évaluée à 50 000 livres.

valuator ['væljʊeɪtər] *n* expert *m (en expertise de biens)*.

value ['væljuː] <> *n* **1.** [monetary worth] valeur *f* ▪ **they own nothing of ~** ils ne possèdent rien de valeur *OR* rien qui ait de la valeur ▪ **this necklace is of great ~** ce collier vaut cher ▪ **this necklace is of little ~** ce collier ne vaut pas grand-chose *OR* a peu de valeur ▪ **it's of no ~** c'est sans valeur ▪ **it's excellent ~ for money** le rapport qualité-prix est excellent ▪ **it's good ~ at £10** ce n'est pas cher à 10 livres ▪ **we got good ~ for our money** nous en avons eu pour notre argent ▪ **which of the brands gives the best ~?** laquelle des marques est la plus avantageuse? ▪ **property is going up/down in ~** l'immobilier prend/perd de la valeur ▪ **to depreciate in ~** se déprécier ▪ **the increase in ~** la hausse de valeur, l'appréciation ▪ **the loss in ~** la perte de valeur, la dépréciation ▪ **to put a ~ on sthg** évaluer *OR* estimer qqch ▪ **they put a ~ of £50,000 on the house** ils ont estimé *OR* expertisé la maison à 50 000 livres
2. [merit, importance - of method, work] valeur *f* ; [- of person] valeur *f*, mérite *m* ▪ **he had nothing of ~ to add** il n'avait rien d'important *OR* de valable à ajouter ▪ **these books may be of ~ to them** ces livres peuvent leur servir, ils peuvent avoir besoin de ces livres ▪ **they place little/a high ~ on punctuality** ils font peu de cas/grand cas de l'exactitude, ils attachent peu d'importance/beaucoup d'importance à l'exactitude
3. *(usu pl)* [principles] : **~s** valeurs *fpl*
4. [feature] particularité *f*
5. [of colour] valeur *f*
6. LING, LOGIC, MATHS & MUS valeur *f*.
<> *vt* **1.** [assess worth of] expertiser, estimer, évaluer ▪ **they ~d the house at £50,000** ils ont estimé *OR* évalué la maison à 50 000 livres
2. [have high regard for - friendship] apprécier, estimer ; [- honesty, punctuality] faire grand cas de ▪ **if you ~ your freedom/your life you'd better leave** si vous tenez à votre liberté/à la vie, vous feriez mieux de partir ▪ **we greatly ~ your help** nous apprécions beaucoup *OR* nous vous sommes très reconnaissants de votre aide ▪ **does he ~ your opinion?** votre opinion lui importe-t-elle?

value-added tax *n UK* taxe *f* sur la valeur ajoutée.

valued ['væljuːd] *adj* [opinion] estimé ▪ [advice, friend] précieux.

value judgment *n* jugement *m* de valeur.

valueless ['væljʊlɪs] *adj* sans valeur.

valuer ['væljʊəʳ] *n* expert *m (en expertise de biens).*

valve [vælv] *n* **1.** [in pipe, tube, air chamber] valve *f* ▪ [in machine] soupape *f*, valve *f* **2.** ANAT valve *f* ▪ [small] valvule *f* **3.** BOT & ZOOL valve *f* **4.** MUS piston *m*.

valvular ['vælvjʊləʳ] *adj* **1.** [machine] à soupapes *OR* valves **2.** ANAT, BOT & ZOOL valvulaire **3.** MUS [instrument] à pistons.

vamoose [və'mu:s] *vi US inf* filer ▪ **~!** fiche le camp!

vamp [væmp] ◇ *n* **1.** *inf* [woman] vamp *f* **2.** [piecing together] rafistolage *m* **3.** [of story] enjolivement *m* ▪ MUS improvisation *f* **4.** [of shoe] devant *m*.
◇ *vt* **1.** *inf* [seduce] vamper **2.** [repair] rafistoler ▪ [renovate] rénover **3.** [story] enjoliver **4.** MUS [piece, song] improviser des accompagnements à ▪ [accompaniment] improviser.
◇ *vi inf* [woman] jouer la vamp.
◆ **vamp up** *vt sep* = **vamp** *(vt senses 2, 3 & 4).*

vampire ['væmpaɪəʳ] *n* [bat, monster] vampire *m* ▪ [person] vampire *m*, sangsue *f*.

vampire bat *n* vampire *m (chauve-souris).*

vampirism ['væmpaɪərɪzm] *n* vampirisme *m*.

van [væn] *n* **1.** [small vehicle] camionnette *f*, fourgonnette *f* ▪ [large vehicle] camion *m*, fourgon *m* **2.** *UK* RAIL fourgon *m*, wagon *m* **3.** [caravan] caravane *f* **4.** MIL [vanguard] avant-garde *f* ▪ **in the ~** en tête ▪ **in the ~ of abstract art** *fig* à l'avant-garde de l'art abstrait.

V and A *(abbrev of* **Victoria and Albert Museum**) *pr n grand musée londonien des arts décoratifs.*

vandal ['vændl] *n* [hooligan] vandale *mf*.
◆ **Vandal** *n* HIST Vandale *mf*.

vandalism ['vændəlɪzm] *n* vandalisme *m*.

vandalize, ise ['vændəlaɪz] *vt* saccager.

vane [veɪn] *n* **1.** [blade - of propeller] pale *f* ; [- of windmill] aile *f* ; [- of turbine] aube *f* **2.** : **(weather) ~** girouette *f* **3.** ORNITH [of feather] barbe *f*.

vanguard ['vængɑ:d] *n* MIL avant-garde *f* ▪ **in the ~ of the division** en tête de la division ▪ **in the ~ of progress** *fig* à l'avant-garde *OR* à la pointe du progrès.

vanilla [və'nɪlə] *n* [plant] vanillier *m* ▪ [flavour] vanille *f* ▪ **~ ice cream/flavour** glace *f* /parfum *m* à la vanille ▪ **~ essence** extrait *m* de vanille.

vanish ['vænɪʃ] *vi* [object, person, race] disparaître ▪ [hopes, worries] disparaître, se dissiper ▪ **the aeroplane ~ed from sight** l'avion a disparu ▪ **she ~ed into the crowd** elle s'est perdue dans la foule ▪ **entire species have ~ed from the face of the earth** des espèces entières ont disparu de la surface du globe ▪ **just when you need him he ~es!** dès que vous avez besoin de lui, il s'éclipse! ▪ **she did a ~ing act** *fig* elle s'est éclipsée.

vanishing cream ['vænɪʃɪŋ-] *n* crème *f* de beauté.

vanishing point *n* point *m* de fuite.

vanishing trick *n* tour *m* de passe-passe ▪ **he did a ~** *fig* [disappeared] il a disparu.

vanity ['vænətɪ] (*pl* **vanities**) *n* **1.** [conceit] vanité *f*, orgueil *m* ▪ **she refused to use a walking stick out of (sheer) ~** par (pure) vanité elle a refusé d'utiliser une canne ➊ **'Vanity Fair'** *Thackeray* 'la Foire aux vanités' **2.** *fml* & *lit* [futility] futilité *f*, insignifiance *f*, vanité *f lit* **3.** *US* [dressing table] coiffeuse *f*, table *f* de toilette.

vanity bag *n* trousse *f* de toilette *(pour femme).*

vanity case *n* petite valise *f* de toilette, vanity-case *m*.

vanity mirror *n* miroir *m* de courtoisie.

vanity table *n* coiffeuse *f*, table *f* de toilette.

vanquish ['væŋkwɪʃ] *vt* vaincre.

vanquisher ['væŋkwɪʃəʳ] *n* vainqueur *m*.

vantage ['vɑ:ntɪdʒ] *n* **1.** [advantageous situation] avantage *m*, supériorité *f* ▪ **point of ~** point de vue *m* privilégié **2.** [in tennis] avantage *m*.

vantage point *n* point de vue *m* (privilégié).

Vanuatu [væn'wɑ:tu:] *n* Vanuatu *m*.

vapid ['væpɪd] *adj* [conversation, remark] fade, insipide ▪ [style] fade, plat ▪ [person] écervelé.

vapidity [væ'pɪdətɪ] *n* [of conversation] insipidité *f* ▪ [of style] platitude *f*, caractère *m* plat ▪ [of person] frivolité *f*, fadeur *f*.

vapor *US* = **vapour**.

vaporize, ise ['veɪpəraɪz] ◇ *vt* vaporiser.
◇ *vi* se vaporiser.

vaporizer ['veɪpəraɪzəʳ] *n* **1.** [gen] vaporisateur *m* ▪ [for perfume, spray] atomiseur *m*, pulvérisateur *m* **2.** MED [inhaler] inhalateur *m* ▪ [for throat] pulvérisateur *m*.

vaporous ['veɪpərəs] *adj* vaporeux.

vapour *UK*, **vapor** *US* ['veɪpəʳ] ◇ *n* vapeur *f* ▪ [on window] buée *f*.
◇ *vi* **1.** PHYS s'évaporer **2.** *US inf* [brag] se vanter, fanfaronner.

vapour bath *n* bain *m* de vapeur.

vapour trail *n* AERON traînée *f* de condensation.

variability [,veərɪə'bɪlətɪ] *n* variabilité *f*.

variable ['veərɪəbl] ◇ *adj* **1.** [weather] variable, changeant ▪ [quality] variable, inégal ▪ [performance, work] de qualité inégale, inégal **2.** COMPUT & MATHS variable.
◇ *n* variable *f*.

variance ['veərɪəns] *n* **1.** [in statistics] désaccord *m*, divergence *f* ▪ [in law] divergence *f*, différence *f* **2.** CHEM & MATHS variance *f* **3.** *phr* **to be at ~ with sb** être en désaccord avec qqn ▪ **to be at ~ with sthg** ne pas cadrer avec *OR* ne pas concorder avec qqch ▪ **this announcement is at ~ with his previous statements** cette annonce est en contradiction avec *OR* ne s'accorde pas avec ses déclarations antérieures.

variant ['veərɪənt] ◇ *n* [gen - LING] variante *f*.
◇ *adj* **1.** [different] autre, différent ▪ **a ~ spelling** une variante orthographique **2.** [various] varié, divers **3.** LING variant.

variation [,veərɪ'eɪʃn] *n* **1.** [change, modification] variation *f*, modification *f* ▪ **~s in temperature** variations *OR* changements de température ▪ **the level of demand is subject to considerable ~** le niveau de la demande peut varier considérablement **2.** MUS variation *f* ▪ **~s on a theme** variations sur un thème **3.** BIOL variation *f*.

varicoloured *UK*, **varicolored** *US* ['veərɪ,kʌləd] *adj* multicolore, aux couleurs variées, bigarré ▪ *fig* divers.

varicose ['værɪkəʊs] *adj* [ulcer] variqueux ▪ **to have** *OR* **to suffer from ~ veins** avoir des varices.

varied ['veərɪd] *adj* varié, divers.

variegated ['veərɪgeɪtɪd] *adj* **1.** [gen] bigarré **2.** BOT panaché.

variegation [,veərɪ'geɪʃn] *n* bigarrure *f*.

variety [və'raɪətɪ] (*pl* **varieties**) ◇ *n* **1.** [diversity] variété *f*, diversité *f* ▪ **there isn't much ~ in the menu** le menu n'est pas très varié *OR* n'offre pas un grand choix ▪ **he needs more ~ in his diet** il a besoin d'un régime plus varié ➊ **~ is the spice of life** *prov* la diversité est le sel de la vie
2. [number, assortment] nombre *m*, quantité *f* ▪ **for a ~ of reasons** [various] pour diverses raisons ; [many] pour de nombreuses raisons ▪ **in a ~ of ways** de diverses manières ▪ **the dresses come in a ~ of sizes** les robes sont disponibles dans un grand nombre de tailles ▪ **there is a wide ~ of colours/styles to choose from** il y a un grand choix de couleurs/styles
3. [type] espèce *f*, genre *m* ▪ **different varieties of cheese** différentes sortes de fromage, fromages variés
4. BOT & ZOOL [strain] variété *f*
5. *(U)* THEAT & TV variétés *fpl*.
◇ *comp* [artiste, show, theatre] de variétés, de music-hall.

variety store *n US* grand magasin *m*.

variola [və'raɪələ] *n* variole *f*, petite vérole *f*.

variorum [ˌveərɪ'ɔːrəm] ◇ *n* (édition *f*) variorum *m inv*.
◇ *adj* variorum *(inv)*.

various ['veərɪəs] *adj* **1.** [diverse] divers, différent ▪ [several] plusieurs ▪ **at ~ times in his life** à différents moments *OR* à plusieurs reprises dans sa vie **2.** [varied, different] varié.

variously ['veərɪəslɪ] *adv* [in different ways] diversement, de différentes *OR* diverses façons ▪ **he was ~ known as soldier, king and emperor** on le connaissait à la fois comme soldat, roi et empereur.

varnish ['vɑːnɪʃ] ◇ *n liter* & *fig* vernis *m*.
◇ *vt* [nails, painting, wood] vernir ▪ [pottery] vernir, vernisser ▪ **to ~ (over) the truth** *fig* maquiller la vérité.

varnishing ['vɑːnɪʃɪŋ] *n* vernissage *m*.

varsity ['vɑːsətɪ] (*pl* **varsities**) *inf* ◇ *n UK dated* université *f*, fac *f* ▪ **~ match** match *m* interuniversitaire *(entre Oxford et Cambridge)*.
◇ *adj US* SPORT *qui représente l'université au plus haut niveau*.

vary ['veərɪ] ◇ *vi* **1.** [be different] varier ▪ **the students ~ considerably in ability** les étudiants ont des niveaux très différents ▪ **they ~ in size from small to extra large** ils vont de la plus petite taille à la plus grande **2.** [change, alter] changer, se modifier ▪ **his mood varies with the weather** il est très lunatique.
◇ *vt* [diet, menu] varier ▪ [temperature] faire varier.

varying ['veərɪɪŋ] *adj* variable, qui varie ▪ **with ~ degrees of success** avec plus ou moins de succès.

vascular ['væskjʊlər] *adj* vasculaire.

vase [*UK* vɑːz, *US* veɪz] *n* vase *m*.

vasectomy [væ'sektəmɪ] (*pl* **vasectomies**) *n* vasectomie *f* ▪ **to have a ~** subir une vasectomie.

Vaseline® ['væsəliːn] *n* : **~ (jelly)** vaseline *f*.

vassal ['væsl] ◇ *adj* vassal.
◇ *n* vassal *m*.

vast [vɑːst] *adj* vaste, immense, énorme ▪ **~ sums of money** des sommes énormes, énormément d'argent ▪ **it's a ~ improvement on his last performance** c'est infiniment mieux que sa dernière interprétation.

vastly ['vɑːstlɪ] *adv* [wealthy] extrêmement, immensément ▪ [grateful] infiniment ▪ **the show was ~ successful** le spectacle a eu un immense succès.

vastness ['vɑːstnɪs] *n* immensité *f*.

vat [væt] *n* cuve *f*, bac *m*.

VAT [væt, ˌviːeɪ'tiː] (*abbrev of* **value added tax**) *n* TVA *f*.

Vatican ['vætɪkən] ◇ *pr n* : **the ~** le Vatican ▪ **in the ~** au Vatican.
◇ *comp* [edict, bank, policy] du Vatican.

Vatican City *pr n* l'État *m* de la cité du Vatican, le Vatican ▪ **in ~** au Vatican.

Vatican council *n* : **the first/second ~** le premier/deuxième concile du Vatican.

vatman ['vætmæn] (*pl* **vatmen** [-men]) *n UK inf* **the ~** le service de la TVA.

vaudeville ['vɔːdəvɪl] ◇ *n US* vaudeville *m*.
◇ *comp* [artiste, theatre] de vaudeville, de music-hall.

vault [vɔːlt] ◇ *n* **1.** ARCHIT voûte *f* **2.** ANAT voûte *f* **3.** [cellar] cave *f*, cellier *m* ▪ [burial chamber] caveau *m* **4.** [in bank] chambre *f* forte ▪ **a bank ~** les coffres d'une banque, la salle des coffres **5.** [jump] (grand) saut *m* ▪ SPORT saut *m* (à la perche).
◇ *vi* [jump] sauter ▪ SPORT sauter (à la perche) ▪ **he ~ed over the fence** il a sauté par-dessus la clôture.
◇ *vt* **1.** ARCHIT voûter, cintrer **2.** [jump] sauter par-dessus.

vaulted ['vɔːltɪd] *adj* ARCHIT voûté, en voûte.

vaulting ['vɔːltɪŋ] ◇ *n* **1.** ARCHIT voûte *f*, voûtes *fpl* **2.** SPORT saut *m* à la perche.
◇ *adj* **1.** SPORT [pole] de saut **2.** *fig* & *lit* [arrogance] outrecuidant ▪ [ambition] démesuré.

vaulting horse *n* cheval-d'arçons *m inv*.

vaunt [vɔːnt] ◇ *vt lit* vanter, se vanter de.
◇ *vi lit* se vanter.

VC *n* **1.** = **vice-chancellor** **2.** = **vice-chairman**.

VCR (*abbrev of* **video cassette recorder**) *n* magnétoscope *m*.

VD (*abbrev of* **venereal disease**) *n (U)* MST *f*.

VDT *n* = **visual display terminal**.

VDU *n* = **visual display unit**.

veal [viːl] ◇ *n* CULIN veau *m*.
◇ *comp* [cutlet] de veau.

vector ['vektər] ◇ *n* **1.** MATHS & MED vecteur *m* **2.** AERON direction *f*.
◇ *comp* MATHS vectoriel.
◇ *vt* AERON radioguider.

vectorial [vek'tɔːrɪəl] *adj* vectoriel.

VE day (*abbrev of* **Victory in Europe Day**) *n jour de l'armistice du 8 mai 1945*.

vedette [vɪ'det] *n* MUS & NAUT vedette *f*.

vee [viː] *n objet en forme de V*.

veep [viːp] *n US inf* vice-président *m*, - e *f*.

veer [vɪər] ◇ *vi* **1.** [vehicle, road] virer, tourner ▪ [ship] virer de bord ▪ [wind] tourner, changer de direction ▪ **the car ~ed (over) to the left** la voiture a viré vers la *OR* à gauche ▪ **the car ~ed off into the ditch** la voiture a quitté la route et a basculé dans le fossé ▪ **to ~ off course** [car] quitter sa route ; [boat, plane, wind-surfer] quitter sa trajectoire **2.** *fig* **the conversation ~ed round to the elections** la conversation a dévié sur les élections ▪ **her mood ~s between euphoria and black depression** son humeur oscille entre l'euphorie et un profond abattement *OR* va de l'euphorie à un profond abattement.
◇ *vt* **1.** [ship, car] faire virer **2.** [cable] filer.

veg [vedʒ] (*abbrev of* **vegetable/vegetables**) *n inf* légumes *mpl*.

vegan ['viːgən] ◇ *n* végétalien *m*, - enne *f*.
◇ *adj* végétalien.

vegeburger ['vedʒəˌbɜːgər] *n* hamburger *m* végétarien.

vegetable ['vedʒtəbl] ◇ *n* **1.** CULIN & HORT légume *m* ▪ BOT [plant] végétal *m* ▪ **early ~s** primeurs *mpl* ▪ **root ~s** racines *fpl (comestibles)* **2.** *inf fig* [person] légume *m*.
◇ *comp* [matter] végétal ▪ [soup] de légumes.

vegetable butter *n* beurre *m* végétal.

vegetable garden *n* (jardin *m*) potager *m*.

vegetable marrow *n* courge *f*.

vegetable oil *n* huile *f* végétale.

vegetal ['vedʒɪtl] *adj* végétal.

vegetarian [ˌvedʒɪ'teərɪən] ◇ *n* végétarien *m*, - enne *f*.
◇ *adj* végétarien.

vegetarianism [ˌvedʒɪ'teərɪənɪzm] *n* végétarisme *m*.

vegetate ['vedʒɪteɪt] *vi liter* & *fig* végéter.

vegetation [ˌvedʒɪ'teɪʃn] *n* végétation *f*.

vegetative ['vedʒɪtətɪv] *adj liter* & *fig* végétatif.

veggie ['vedʒɪ] *n* & *adj inf* = **vegetarian**.

vehemence ['viːɪməns] *n* [of emotions] ardeur *f*, véhémence *f* ▪ [of actions, gestures] violence *f*, véhémence *f* ▪ [of language] véhémence *f*, passion *f*.

vehement ['viːɪmənt] *adj* [emotions] ardent, passionné, véhément ▪ [actions, gestures] violent, véhément ▪ [language] véhément, passionné.

vehemently ['viːɪməntlɪ] *adv* [speak] avec passion, avec véhémence ▪ [attack] avec violence ▪ [gesticulate] frénétiquement.

vehicle ['viːɪkl] *n* **1.** [gen - AUT] véhicule *m* ▪ **'heavy ~s turning'** 'passage d'engins' ➤ **~ emissions** gaz *mpl* d'échappement **2.** PHARM véhicule *m* **3.** *fig* véhicule *m*.

vehicular [vɪ'hɪkjʊlər] *adj* [gen - AUT] de véhicules, de voitures ■ **~ traffic** circulation automobile ■ **~ access** accès aux véhicules.

veil [veɪl] ◇ *n* **1.** [over face] voile *m* ■ [on hat] voilette *f*, voile *m* ■ **she was wearing a ~** elle était voilée **2.** *fig* voile *m* ■ **to draw a ~ over sthg** mettre un voile sur qqch **3.** RELIG : **to take the ~** prendre le voile.
◇ *vt* **1.** [face] voiler, couvrir d'un voile ■ **to ~ o.s.** se voiler **2.** *fig* [truth, feelings, intentions] voiler, dissimuler, masquer.

veiled [veɪld] *adj* **1.** [wearing a veil] voilé **2.** [hidden, disguised - expression, meaning] voilé, caché ; [- allusion, insult] voilé ; [- hostility] sourd.

vein [veɪn] *n* **1.** ANAT veine *f* **2.** [on insect wing] veine *f* ■ [on leaf] nervure *f* **3.** [in cheese, wood, marble] veine *f* ■ [of ore, mineral] filon *m*, veine *f* ■ **a rich ~ of irony runs through the book** le livre est parcouru d'une ironie sous-jacente **4.** [mood] esprit *m* ■ [style] veine *f*, style *m* ■ **in the same ~** dans le même style *OR* la même veine.

veined [veɪnd] *adj* **1.** [hand, skin] veiné **2.** [leaf] nervuré **3.** [cheese, stone] marbré, veiné ■ **green-~ marble** marbre veiné de vert.

velar ['vi:lər] *adj* ANAT & LING vélaire.

Velcro® ['velkrəʊ] *n* (bande *f*)Velcro® *m*.

veld(t) [velt] *n* veld *m*, veldt *m*.

vellum ['veləm] ◇ *n* vélin *m*.
◇ *adj* de vélin ■ **~ paper** papier *m* vélin.

velocipede [vɪ'lɒsɪpi:d] *n* vélocipède *m*.

velocity [vɪ'lɒsətɪ] (*pl* **velocities**) *n* vélocité *f*.

velodrome ['velədrəʊm] *n* vélodrome *m*.

velour(s) [və'lʊər] (*pl inv*) ◇ *n* velours *m*.
◇ *comp* de *OR* en velours.

velvet ['velvɪt] ◇ *n* velours *m*.
◇ *comp* [curtains, dress] de *OR* en velours ■ *fig* [skin, voice] velouté, de velours ■ **to walk with a ~ tread** marcher à pas de velours *OR* à pas feutrés ■ **an iron hand in a ~ glove** *fig* une main de fer dans un gant de velours.

velveteen [ˌvelvɪ'ti:n] ◇ *n* velvet *m*, velventine *f*, velvantine *f*.
◇ *adj* en *OR* de velventine.

Velvet Revolution *pr n* : **the ~** la Révolution de Velours.

velvety ['velvɪtɪ] *adj* [cloth, complexion, texture] velouteux, velouté ■ *fig* [cream, voice] velouté.

venal ['vi:nl] *adj* vénal.

venality [vi:'nælətɪ] *n* vénalité *f*.

vend [vend] *vt* LAW & *fml* vendre.

vendetta [ven'detə] *n* vendetta *f*.

vending ['vendɪŋ] *n* LAW & *fml* vente *f*.

vending machine *n* distributeur *m* automatique.

vendor ['vendɔ:r] *n* **1.** COMM marchand *m*, - e *f* ■ **ice-cream ~** marchand de glaces **2.** [machine] distributeur *m* automatique **3.** LAW vendeur *m*, - euse *f*.

veneer [və'nɪər] ◇ *n* **1.** [of wood] placage *m* (de bois) ■ **walnut ~** placage noyer **2.** *fig* vernis *m*, masque *m* ■ **a ~ of respectability** un vernis de respectabilité.
◇ *vt* plaquer ■ **~ed in** *OR* **with walnut** plaqué noyer.

venerable ['venərəbl] *adj* [gen - RELIG] vénérable.

venerate ['venəreɪt] *vt* vénérer.

veneration [ˌvenə'reɪʃn] *n* vénération *f*.

venereal [vɪ'nɪərɪəl] *adj* vénérien.

venereal disease *n* maladie *f* vénérienne.

Venetian [vɪ'ni:ʃn] ◇ *n* Vénitien *m*, - enne *f*.
◇ *adj* vénitien, de Venise ■ **~ blind** store *m* vénitien.

Venezuela [ˌvenɪ'zweɪlə] *pr n* Venezuela *m* ■ **in ~** au Venezuela.

Venezuelan [ˌvenɪ'zweɪlən] ◇ *n* Vénézuélien *m*, - enne *f*
◇ *adj* vénézuélien.

vengeance ['vendʒəns] *n* **1.** [revenge] vengeance *f* ■ **to take** *OR* **to wreak ~ on** *OR* **upon sb (for sthg)** se venger sur qqn (de qqch) ■ **to seek ~ for sthg** vouloir tirer vengeance de qqch, chercher à se venger de qqch **2.** *phr* **with a ~** très fort ■ **to work with a ~** travailler d'arrache-pied *OR* à un rythme d'enfer ■ **she's back with a ~** elle fait un retour en force.

vengeful ['vendʒfʊl] *adj* vindicatif.

venial ['vi:njəl] *adj* [gen - RELIG] véniel.

veniality [ˌvi:nɪ'ælətɪ] *n* caractère *m* véniel.

Venice ['venɪs] *pr n* Venise.

venison ['venɪzn] *n* venaison *f*.

venom ['venəm] *n liter* & *fig* venin *m* ■ **with ~** *fig* d'une manière venimeuse.

venomous ['venəməs] *adj liter* venimeux ■ *fig* [remark, insult] venimeux, malveillant ■ [look] haineux, venimeux ■ **he has a ~ tongue** il a une langue de vipère.

venous ['vi:nəs] *adj* veineux.

vent [vent] ◇ *n* **1.** [outlet - for air, gas, liquid] orifice *m*, conduit *m* ; [- in chimney] conduit *m*, tuyau *m* ; [- in volcano] cheminée *f* ; [- in barrel] trou *m* ; [- for ventilation] conduit *m* d'aération **2.** *phr* **to give ~ to sthg** donner *OR* laisser libre cours à qqch ■ **she gave ~ to her anger** elle a laissé échapper sa colère **3.** [in jacket, skirt] fente *f*.
◇ *vt* **1.** [barrel] pratiquer un trou dans, trouer ■ [pipe, radiator] purger **2.** [release - smoke] laisser échapper ; [- gas] évacuer **3.** *fig* [express - anger] décharger ■ **to ~ one's anger/one's spleen on sb** décharger sa colère/sa bile sur qqn.

ventilate ['ventɪleɪt] *vt* **1.** [room] ventiler, aérer ■ **a well/badly ~d room** une pièce bien/mal aérée **2.** *fig* [controversy, question] agiter (au grand jour) ■ [grievance] étaler (au grand jour) **3.** MED [blood] oxygéner.

ventilation [ˌventɪ'leɪʃn] *n* aération *f*, ventilation *f* ■ **a ~ shaft** un conduit d'aération *OR* de ventilation.

ventilator ['ventɪleɪtər] *n* **1.** [in room, building] ventilateur *m* ■ AUT déflecteur *m* **2.** MED respirateur *m* (artificiel).

Ventimiglia [ventɪ'mɪljə] *pr n* Vintimille.

ventricle ['ventrɪkl] *n* ventricule *m*.

ventriloquism [ven'trɪləkwɪzm] *n* ventriloquie *f*.

ventriloquist [ven'trɪləkwɪst] *n* ventriloque *mf*.

ventriloquy [ven'trɪləkwɪ] = **ventriloquism**.

venture ['ventʃər] ◇ *n* **1.** [undertaking] entreprise *f* périlleuse *OR* risquée ■ [adventure] aventure *f* ■ [project] projet *m*, entreprise *f* ■ **it's his first ~ into politics** c'est la première fois qu'il s'aventure dans le domaine politique **2.** COMM & FIN [firm] entreprise *f* ■ **a business ~** une entreprise commerciale, un coup d'essai commercial **3.** *phr* **at a ~** au hasard.
◇ *vt* **1.** [risk - fortune, life] hasarder, risquer ■ **nothing ~d nothing gained** *prov* qui ne risque rien n'a rien *prov* **2.** [proffer - opinion, suggestion] hasarder, avancer, risquer ■ **she didn't dare ~ an opinion on the subject** elle n'a pas osé exprimer sa pensée à ce sujet ■ **if I may ~ a guess/an opinion** si je peux me permettre d'avancer une hypothèse/une opinion **3.** [dare] oser ■ **to ~ to do sthg** s'aventurer *OR* se hasarder à faire qqch.
◇ *vi* **1.** [embark] se lancer ■ **the government has ~d on a new defence policy** le gouvernement s'est lancé dans *OR* a entrepris une nouvelle politique de défense ■ **to ~ into politics** se lancer dans la politique **2.** *(verb of movement)* **I wouldn't ~ out of doors in this weather** je ne me risquerais pas à sortir par ce temps ■ **don't ~ too far across the ice** ne va pas trop loin sur la glace ■ **don't ~ too far from the beach** ne t'éloigne pas trop de la plage.

venture capital *n* capital-risque *m*.

Venture Scout *n UK* éclaireur *m (de grade supérieur)*.

venturesome ['ventʃəsəm] *adj lit* **1.** [daring - nature, person] aventureux, entreprenant **2.** [hazardous - action, journey] hasardeux, risqué.

venue ['venju:] *n* **1.** [setting] lieu *m* (de rendez-vous OR de réunion) ▪ **he hasn't decided on a ~ for the concert** il n'a pas décidé où le concert aura lieu **2.** LAW lieu *m* du procès.

Venus ['vi:nəs] *pr n* ASTRON & MYTH Vénus *f*.

Venus flytrap *n* dionée *f*.

veracious [və'reɪʃəs] *adj* véridique.

veracity [və'ræsətɪ] *n* véracité *f*.

veranda(h) [və'rændə] *n* véranda *f*.

verb [vɜ:b] *n* verbe *m* ▪ **~ phrase** syntagme *m* OR groupe *m* verbal.

verbal ['vɜ:bl] *adj* **1.** [spoken - account, agreement, promise] verbal, oral ; [- confession] oral ▪ **~ memory** mémoire *f* auditive **2.** [related to words] : **~ skills** aptitudes *fpl* à l'oral **3.** [literal - copy, translation] mot à mot, littéral, textuel **4.** GRAM verbal.
◆ **verbals** *npl* LAW aveux *mpl* faits oralement OR de vive voix.

verbalize, ise ['vɜ:bəlaɪz] *vt* [feelings, ideas] verbaliser, exprimer par des mots.

verbally ['vɜ:bəlɪ] *adv* verbalement, oralement ▪ **~ deficient** illettré, analphabète.

verbal noun *n* GRAM nom *m* verbal.

verbatim [vɜ:'beɪtɪm] ◇ *adj* mot pour mot ▪ **~ report** procès-verbal *m (d'une réunion)*.
◇ *adv* textuellement.

verbena [vɜ:'bi:nə] *n* [herb, plant] verveine *f* ▪ [genus] verbénacées *fpl*.

verbiage ['vɜ:bɪɪdʒ] *n* verbiage *m*.

verbose [vɜ:'bəʊs] *adj* verbeux, prolixe.

verbosity [vɜ:'bɒsətɪ] *n* verbosité *f*.

verdant ['vɜ:dənt] *adj lit* verdoyant.

verdict ['vɜ:dɪkt] *n* **1.** LAW verdict *m* ▪ **to reach a ~** arriver à un verdict ▪ **a ~ of guilty/not guilty** un verdict de culpabilité/non-culpabilité ▪ **the jury returned a ~ of not guilty/guilty** le jury a déclaré l'accusé non-coupable/coupable **2.** *fig* [conclusion] verdict *m*, jugement *m* ▪ **to give one's ~ on sthg** donner son verdict sur qqch.

verdigris ['vɜ:dɪgrɪs] ◇ *n* vert-de-gris *m inv*.
◇ *adj* vert-de-grisé.

verdure ['vɜ:dʒə^r] *n lit* verdure *f*.

verge [vɜ:dʒ] ◇ *n* **1.** [edge - of lawn] bord *m* ; [- by roadside] accotement *m*, bas-côté *m* ; [- of forest] orée *f* ▪ **grass ~** [round flowerbed] bordure *f* en gazon ; [by roadside] herbe *f* au bord de la route ; [in park, garden] bande *f* d'herbe **2.** *fig* [brink] bord *m* ▪ [threshold] seuil *m* ▪ **to be on the ~ of bankruptcy/of a nervous breakdown** être au bord de la faillite/de la dépression nerveuse ▪ **to be on the ~ of doing sthg** être sur le point de faire qqch ▪ **he's on the ~ of sixty** il frôle OR frise la soixantaine ▪ **the country has been brought to the ~ of civil war** le pays a été amené au seuil de la guerre civile.
◇ *vt* [road, lawn] border.
◆ **verge on, verge upon** *vt insep* [be close to] côtoyer, s'approcher de ▪ **they are verging on bankruptcy** ils sont au bord de la faillite, la faillite les menace ▪ **his feeling was one of panic verging on hysteria** il ressentait une sorte de panique proche de l'hystérie OR qui frôlait l'hystérie ▪ **green verging on blue** du vert qui tire sur le bleu.

verger ['vɜ:dʒə^r] *n* RELIG bedeau *m*, suisse *m* ▪ [at ceremony] huissier *m* à verge, massier *m*.

Vergil ['vɜ:dʒɪl] = **Virgil**.

verifiable ['verɪfaɪəbl] *adj* vérifiable.

verification [,verɪfɪ'keɪʃn] *n* vérification *f*.

verify ['verɪfaɪ] (*pret* & *pp* **verified**) *vt* [prove - information, rumour] vérifier ▪ [confirm - truth] vérifier, confirmer.

verily ['verəlɪ] *adv arch* vraiment, véritablement.

verisimilitude [,verɪsɪ'mɪlɪtju:d] *n fml* vraisemblance *f*.

veritable ['verɪtəbl] *adj* véritable.

veritably ['verɪtəblɪ] *adv* véritablement.

verity ['verətɪ] (*pl* **verities**) *n fml* vérité *f*.

vermicelli [,vɜ:mɪ'selɪ] *n (U)* vermicelle *m*, vermicelles *mpl*.

vermil(l)ion [və'mɪljən] ◇ *n* vermillon *m*.
◇ *adj* vermillon *(inv)*.

vermin ['vɜ:mɪn] *npl* **1.** [rodents] animaux *mpl* nuisibles ▪ [insects] vermine *f* **2.** *pej* [people] vermine *f*, racaille *f*.

verminous ['vɜ:mɪnəs] *adj* **1.** [place] infesté de vermine OR d'animaux nuisibles, pouilleux ▪ [clothes] pouilleux, couvert de vermine ▪ MED [disease] vermineux **2.** *pej* [person] infect, ignoble.

Vermont [vɜ:'mɒnt] *pr n* Vermont *m* ▪ **in ~** dans le Vermont.

vermouth ['vɜ:məθ] *n* vermouth *m*.

vernacular [və'nækjʊlə^r] ◇ *n* **1.** LING (langue *f*) vernaculaire *m* ▪ **in the ~** LING en langue vernaculaire ; [everyday language] en langage courant **2.** BOT & ZOOL nom *m* vernaculaire **3.** ARCHIT style *m* typique (du pays).
◇ *adj* **1.** BOT, LING & ZOOL vernaculaire **2.** [architecture, style] indigène.

vernal ['vɜ:nl] *adj lit* [flowers, woods, breeze] printanier.

vernal equinox *n* point *m* vernal.

Veronese [,verə'neɪzɪ] *pr n* Véronèse.

verruca [və'ru:kə] (*pl* **verrucas** OR *pl* **verrucae** [-kaɪ]) *n* verrue *f* (plantaire).

versatile ['vɜ:sətaɪl] *adj* **1.** [person] aux talents variés, doué dans tous les domaines ▪ [mind] souple ▪ [tool] polyvalent, à usages multiples **2.** BOT versatile **3.** ZOOL mobile, pivotant.

versatility [,vɜ:sə'tɪlətɪ] *n* **1.** [of person] faculté *f* d'adaptation, variété *f* de talents ▪ [of mind] souplesse *f* ▪ [of tool] polyvalence *f* **2.** BOT & ZOOL versatilité *f*.

verse [vɜ:s] ◇ *n* **1.** [stanza - of poem] strophe *f* ; [- of song] couplet *m* ; [- in bible] verset *m* **2.** *(U)* [poetry] vers *mpl*, poésie *f* ▪ **in ~** en vers.
◇ *comp* [line, epic] en vers.

versed [vɜ:st] *adj* : **~ in** [knowledgeable] versé dans ; [experienced] rompu à.

versifier ['vɜ:sɪfaɪə^r] *n pej* versificateur *m*, - trice *f*.

versify ['vɜ:sɪfaɪ] (*pret* & *pp* **versified**) ◇ *vt* versifier, mettre en vers.
◇ *vi* rimer, faire des vers.

version ['vɜ:ʃn] *n* **1.** [account of events] version *f* **2.** [form - of book, song] version *f* ▪ **did you see the film in the original ~?** est-ce que vous avez vu le film dans sa version originale? ▪ **the screen** OR **film ~ of the book** l'adaptation cinématographique du livre ▪ **he looks like a younger ~ of his father** *fig* c'est l'image de son père en plus jeune **3.** [model - of car, plane] modèle *m* **4.** [translation] version *f*.

verso ['vɜ:səʊ] (*pl* **versos**) *n* [of page] verso *m* ▪ [of coin, medal] revers *m*.

versus ['vɜ:səs] *prep* **1.** [against] contre ▪ **Italy ~ France** SPORT Italie-France ▪ **Dickens ~ Dickens** LAW Dickens contre Dickens **2.** [compared with] par rapport à, par opposition à.

vertebra ['vɜ:tɪbrə] (*pl* **vertebras** OR *pl* **vertebrae** [-bri:]) *n* vertèbre *f*.

vertebral ['vɜ:tɪbrəl] *adj* vertébral ▪ **~ column** colonne *f* vertébrale.

vertebrate ['vɜ:tɪbreɪt] ◇ *adj* vertébré.
◇ *n* vertébré *m*.

vertex ['vɜ:teks] (*pl* **vertexes** OR *pl* **vertices** [-tɪsi:z]) *n* MATHS sommet *m* ▪ ASTRON apex *m* ▪ ANAT vertex *m*.

vertical ['vɜ:tɪkl] ◇ *adj* **1.** [gen - GEOM] vertical ▪ **a ~ cliff** une falaise à pic OR qui s'élève à la verticale ▪ **a ~ drop** une descente OR une pente verticale **2.** *fig* [structure, organization, integration] vertical.
◇ *n* verticale *f* ▪ **out of the ~** écarté de la verticale, hors d'aplomb.

vertically ['vɜ:tɪklɪ] *adv* verticalement ▪ **to take off ~** AERON décoller à la verticale.

vertical takeoff ◇ *n* décollage *m* vertical.
◇ *comp* : **~ aircraft** avion *m* à décollage vertical.

vertiginous [vɜː'tɪdʒɪnəs] *adj fml* vertigineux.

vertigo ['vɜːtɪgəʊ] *n (U)* vertige *m* ▪ **to suffer from** *OR* **to have ~** avoir le vertige ▶ **'Vertigo'** ***Hitchcock*** 'Sueurs froides'.

verve [vɜːv] *n* verve *f*, brio *m*.

very ['verɪ] (*comp* **verier**, *superl* **veriest**) ◇ *adv* **1.** [with adj or adv] très, bien ▪ **was the pizza good? – ~/not ~** la pizza était-elle bonne? – très/pas très ▪ **be ~ careful** faites très *OR* bien attention ▪ **he was ~ hungry/thirsty** il avait très faim/soif ▪ **I ~ nearly fell** j'ai bien failli tomber ▪ **~ few/little** très peu ▪ **there were ~ few of them** [people] ils étaient très peu nombreux ; [objets] il y en avait très peu ▪ **there weren't ~ many people** il n'y avait pas beaucoup de gens, il n'y avait pas grand monde ▶ **~ good!, ~ well!** [expressing agreement, consent] très bien! ▪ **you can't ~ well ask outright** tu ne peux pas vraiment demander directement ▪ **that's all ~ well but...** tout ça, c'est très bien mais...
2. *(with superlative)* [emphatic use] : **our ~ best wine** notre meilleur vin ▪ **the ~ best of friends** les meilleurs amis du monde ▪ **it's the ~ worst thing that could have happened** c'est bien la pire chose qui pouvait arriver ▪ **the ~ latest designs** les créations les plus récentes ▪ **at the ~ latest** au plus tard ▪ **at the ~ least/most** tout au moins/plus ▪ **the ~ first/last person** la (toute) première/dernière personne ▪ **the ~ next day** le lendemain même, dès le lendemain ▪ **we'll stop at the ~ next town** nous nous arrêterons à la prochaine ville ▪ **it's nice to have your ~ own car** *OR* **a car of your ~ own** c'est agréable d'avoir sa voiture à soi ▪ **it's my ~ own** c'est à moi ▪ **the ~ same day** le jour même ▪ **on the ~ same date** exactement à la même date.
◇ *adj* **1.** [extreme, far] : **at the ~ end** [of street, row etc] tout au bout ; [of story, month etc] tout à la fin ▪ **to the ~ end** [in space] jusqu'au bout ; [in time] jusqu'à la fin ▪ **at the ~ back** tout au fond ▪ **at the ~ bottom of the sea** au plus profond de la mer **2.** [exact] : **at that ~ moment** juste à ce moment-là ▪ **the ~ man I need** juste l'homme qu'il me faut ▪ **those were his ~ words** ce sont ses propos mêmes, c'est exactement ce qu'il a dit **3.** [emphatic use] : **the ~ idea!** quelle idée! ▪ **the ~ thought of it makes me shiver** je frissonne rien que d'y penser ▪ **it happened before my ~ eyes** cela s'est passé sous mes yeux.
◆ **very much** ◇ *adv phr* **1.** [greatly] beaucoup, bien ▪ **I ~ much hope to be able to come** j'espère bien que je pourrai venir ▪ **unless I'm ~ much mistaken** à moins que je ne me trompe ▪ **were you impressed? – ~ much so** ça vous a impressionné? – beaucoup
2. [to a large extent] : **the situation remains ~ much the same** la situation n'a guère évolué ▪ **it's ~ much a question of who to believe** la question est surtout de savoir qui on doit croire.
◇ *det phr* beaucoup de.
◇ *pron phr* beaucoup ▪ **she doesn't say ~ much** elle parle peu, elle ne dit pas grand-chose.

very high frequency ['verɪ-] *n (U)* très haute fréquence *f*, (gamme *f* des) ondes *fpl* métriques.

Very light ['vɪərɪ-] *n* fusée *f* éclairante.

very low frequency ['verɪ-] *n* très basse fréquence *f*.

Very Reverend ['verɪ-] *adj* RELIG : **the ~ Alan Scott** le très révérend Alan Scott.

vespers ['vespəz] *npl* vêpres *fpl*.

vessel ['vesl] *n* **1.** *lit* [container] récipient *m* ▪ **a drinking ~** une timbale, un gobelet **2.** NAUT vaisseau *m* **3.** ANAT & BOT vaisseau *m*.

vest [vest] ◇ *n* **1.** *UK* [singlet - for boy, man] maillot *m* de corps, tricot *m* de peau ; [- for woman] chemise *f* **2.** *US* [waistcoat] gilet *m* (de costume).
◇ *vt fml* investir ▪ **the power ~ed in the government** le pouvoir dont le gouvernement est investi ▪ **the president is ~ed with the power to veto the government** le président est doté du pouvoir d'opposer son veto aux projets du gouvernement.

vestal virgin ['vestl-] *n* vestale *f*.

vested interest ['vestɪd-] *n* : **~s** [rights] droits *mpl* acquis ; [investments] capitaux *mpl* investis ; [advantages] intérêts *mpl* ▪ **there are ~s in industry opposed to trade union reform** ceux qui ont des intérêts dans l'industrie s'opposent à la réforme des syndicats ▪ **there are too many ~s** cela dérange trop de gens influents ▪ **to have a ~ in doing sthg** avoir directement intérêt à faire qqch.

vestibule ['vestɪbjuːl] *n* **1.** [in house, church] vestibule *m* ▪ [in hotel] vestibule *m*, hall *m* d'entrée **2.** ANAT vestibule *m* **3.** *US* RAIL sas *m*.

vestige ['vestɪdʒ] *n* **1.** [remnant] vestige *m* ▪ **he clung on to the last ~s of power** il s'est accroché aux derniers vestiges de son autorité **2.** ANAT & ZOOL organe *m* rudimentaire ▪ **the ~ of a tail** une queue rudimentaire.

vestigial [ve'stɪdʒɪəl] *adj* **1.** [remaining] résiduel **2.** ANAT & ZOOL [organ, tail] rudimentaire, atrophié.

vestment ['vestmənt] *n* habit *m* de cérémonie ▪ RELIG vêtement *m* sacerdotal.

vest-pocket *US* ◇ *n* poche *f* de gilet.
◇ *adj* [book, object] de poche ▪ *fig* minuscule, tout petit.

vestry ['vestrɪ] (*pl* **vestries**) *n* **1.** [room] sacristie *f* **2.** [committee] conseil *m* paroissial.

Vesuvius [vɪ'suːvjəs] *pr n* : **(Mount) ~** le Vésuve.

vet [vet] (*pret & pp* **vetted**, *cont* **vetting**) ◇ *n* **1.** (*abbrev of* **veterinary surgeon/veterinary**) vétérinaire *mf* **2.** *US inf* (*abbrev of* **veteran**) ancien combattant *m*, vétéran *m*.
◇ *vt* **1.** [check - application] examiner minutieusement, passer au crible ; [- claims, facts, figures] vérifier soigneusement, passer au crible ; [- documents] contrôler ; [- person] enquêter sur ▪ **she was thoroughly vetted for the job** ils ont soigneusement examiné sa candidature avant de l'embaucher ▪ **the committee has to ~ any expenditure exceeding £100** le comité doit approuver toute dépense au-delà de 100 livres **2.** VET [examine] examiner ▪ [treat] soigner.

veteran ['vetrən] ◇ *n* **1.** MIL ancien combattant *m*, vétéran *m* ▪ **Veterans Day** *US* fête *f* de l'armistice *(le 11 novembre)* **2.** [experienced person] personne *f* chevronnée *OR* expérimentée, vieux *m* de la vieille **3.** [car] voiture *f* ancienne *OR* d'époque ▪ [machinery] vieille machine *f*.
◇ *adj* [experienced] expérimenté, chevronné ▪ **she's a ~ campaigner for civil rights** c'est un vétéran de la campagne pour les droits civiques.

veteran car *n UK* voiture *f* de collection *(normalement antérieure à 1905)*.

veterinarian [ˌvetərɪ'neərɪən] *n US* vétérinaire *mf*.

veterinary ['vetərɪnrɪ] *adj* [medicine, science] vétérinaire.

veterinary surgeon *n UK* vétérinaire *mf*.

veto ['viːtəʊ] (*pl* **vetoes**) ◇ *n* **1.** *(U)* [power] droit *m* de veto ▪ **to use one's ~** exercer son droit de veto **2.** [refusal] veto *m* ▪ **to put a ~ on sthg** mettre *OR* opposer son veto à qqch.
◇ *vt* POL & *fig* mettre *OR* opposer son veto à.

vetting ['vetɪŋ] *n (U)* enquêtes *fpl* ▪ **security ~** enquêtes de sécurité.

vex [veks] *vt* contrarier, ennuyer.

vexation [vek'seɪʃn] *n fml* **1.** [anger] ennui *m*, agacement *m* **2.** [difficulty, annoyance] ennui *m*, tracasserie *f*.

vexatious [vek'seɪʃəs] *adj fml* contrariant, ennuyeux.

vexed [vekst] *adj fml* **1.** [annoyed] fâché, ennuyé, contrarié ▪ **to become ~** se fâcher ▪ **to be ~ with sb** être fâché contre qqn, en vouloir à qqn ▪ **she was ~ to discover that she had left her purse behind** elle a été contrariée quand elle a réalisé qu'elle avait oublié son porte-monnaie **2.** [controversial] controversé ▪ [question] épineux.

vexing ['veksɪŋ] *adj* **1.** [annoying] contrariant, ennuyeux, fâcheux **2.** [frustrating - issue, riddle] frustrant.

VFD (*abbrev of* **voluntary fire department**) *n pompiers bénévoles aux États-Unis*.

VG (*written abbrev of* **very good**) TB.

VGA [ˌviːdʒiː'eɪ] (*abbrev of* **video graphics array** *OR* **video graphics adapter**) *n* COMPUT VGA *m*.

vgc (*written abbrev of* **very good condition**) tbe.

VHF (*abbrev of* **very high frequency**) *n* VHF *f*.

VHS (*abbrev of* **video home system**) *n* VHS *m*.

via ['vaɪə] *prep* **1.** [by way of] via, par **2.** [by means of] par, au moyen de ■ **contact me ~ this number/~ my secretary** contactez-moi à ce numéro/par l'intermédiaire de ma secrétaire ■ **she sent him the letter ~ her sister** elle lui a envoyé la lettre par l'intermédiaire de sa sœur ■ **the best way to get into films is ~ drama school** le meilleur moyen d'entrer dans le monde du cinéma est de passer par une école d'art dramatique.

viability [,vaɪə'bɪlətɪ] *n (U)* **1.** ECON [of company, state] viabilité *f* **2.** [of plan, programme, scheme] chances *fpl* de réussite, viabilité *f* **3.** MED & BOT viabilité *f*.

viable ['vaɪəbl] *adj* **1.** ECON [company, economy, state] viable **2.** [practicable - plan, programme] viable, qui a des chances de réussir **3.** MED & BOT viable.

viaduct ['vaɪədʌkt] *n* viaduc *m*.

vibes [vaɪbz] *npl inf* **1.** = **vibraphone 2.** (*abbrev of* **vibrations**) atmosphère *f*, ambiance *f* ■ **they give off really good/bad ~** avec eux le courant passe vraiment bien/ne passe vraiment pas ■ **I get really bad ~ from her** je la sens vraiment mal.

vibrancy ['vaɪbrənsɪ] *n* enthousiasme *m*.

vibrant ['vaɪbrənt] <> *adj* **1.** [vigorous, lively - person] vif ; [- programme, atmosphere] vibrant, touchant, émouvant ■ **to be ~ with life** être plein de vie **2.** [resonant - sound, voice] vibrant, résonant **3.** [bright - colour, light] brillant.
<> *n* LING vibrante *f*.

vibraphone ['vaɪbrəfəʊn] *n* vibraphone *m*.

vibrate [vaɪ'breɪt] *vi* **1.** [shake, quiver] vibrer **2.** [sound] vibrer, retentir **3.** PHYS [oscillate] osciller, vibrer.

vibration [vaɪ'breɪʃn] *n* vibration *f*.
◆ **vibrations** *npl inf* [feeling] ambiance *f*.

vibrato [vɪ'brɑːtəʊ] (*pl* **vibratos**) <> *n* MUS vibrato *m*.
<> *adv* avec vibrato.

vibrator [vaɪ'breɪtəʳ] *n* **1.** ELEC vibrateur *m* **2.** [medical or sexual] vibromasseur *m*.

vibratory ['vaɪbrətrɪ] *adj* vibratoire.

vicar ['vɪkəʳ] *n* pasteur *m* ■ **the Vicar of Christ** le vicaire de Jésus-Christ.

vicarage ['vɪkərɪdʒ] *n* presbytère *m*.

vicarious [vɪ'keərɪəs] *adj* **1.** [indirect, second-hand - feeling, pride, enjoyment] indirect, par procuration OR contrecoup **2.** [punishment] (fait) pour autrui ■ [suffering, pain] subi pour autrui **3.** [power, authority] délégué **4.** MED vicariant.

vicariously [vɪ'keərɪəslɪ] *adv* **1.** [experience] indirectement ■ **she lived ~ through her reading** elle vivait par procuration à travers ses lectures **2.** [authorize] par délégation, par procuration.

vice <> *n* [vaɪs] **1.** [depravity] vice *m* **2.** [moral failing] vice *m* ■ [less serious] défaut *m* **3.** TECH étau *m* ■ **he held her in a ~-like grip** il la serrait comme dans un étau **4.** *US* = **vice squad**.
<> *prep* ['vaɪsɪ] *fml* [instead of] à la place de, en remplacement de.

vice- [vaɪs] *in cpds* vice-.

vice-admiral *n* vice-amiral *m* d'escadre.

vice-chairman *n* vice-président *m*, - e *f*.

vice-chancellor *n* **1.** *UK* UNIV président *m*, - e *f* d'université **2.** *US* LAW vice-chancelier *m*.

vice-consul *n* vice-consul *m*.

vice-presidency *n* vice-présidence *f*.

vice-president *n* vice-président *m*, - e *f*.

vice-principal *n* SCH directeur *m* adjoint, directrice *f* adjointe.

viceroy ['vaɪsrɔɪ] *n* vice-roi *m*.

vice squad *n* brigade *f* des mœurs.

vice versa [,vaɪsɪ'vɜːsə] *adv* vice versa, inversement.

Vichy water *n* eau *f* de Vichy.

vicinity [vɪ'sɪnətɪ] (*pl* **vicinities**) *n* **1.** [surrounding area] environs *mpl*, alentours *mpl* ■ [neighbourhood] voisinage *m*, environs *mpl* ■ [proximity] proximité *f* ■ **he's somewhere in the ~** il est quelque part dans les environs OR dans le coin ■ **in the ~ of the town centre** [in the area] dans les environs du centre-ville ; [close] à proximité du centre-ville ■ **in the immediate ~** dans les environs immédiats **2.** [approximate figures, amounts] : **his salary is in the ~ of £18,000** son salaire est aux alentours de OR de l'ordre de 18 000 livres.

vicious ['vɪʃəs] *adj* **1.** [cruel, savage - attack, blow] brutal, violent **2.** [malevolent - criticism, gossip, remarks] méchant, malveillant ■ **he has a ~ tongue** il a une langue de vipère **3.** [dog] méchant ■ [horse] vicieux, rétif **4.** [perverse - behaviour, habits] vicieux, pervers.

vicious circle *n* cercle *m* vicieux.

viciously ['vɪʃəslɪ] *adv* [attack, beat] brutalement, violemment ■ [criticize] avec malveillance, méchamment.

viciousness ['vɪʃəsnɪs] *n* [of attack, beating] brutalité *f*, violence *f* ■ [of criticism, gossip] méchanceté *f*, malveillance *f*.

vicissitude [vɪ'sɪsɪtjuːd] *n fml* vicissitude *f*.

victim ['vɪktɪm] *n* **1.** [physical sufferer] victime *f* ■ **to fall ~ to sthg** devenir la victime de qqch ■ **the fire claimed many ~s** l'incendie a fait de nombreuses victimes ■ **road accident ~s** les victimes OR les accidentés de la route ■ **a fund for ~s of cancer** des fonds pour les cancéreux OR les malades du cancer **2.** *fig* victime *f* ■ **to fall ~ to sb's charms** succomber aux charmes de qqn ■ **many people fall ~ to these fraudulent schemes** beaucoup de gens se font avoir par ces combines frauduleuses ■ **education is always the first ~ of government spending cuts** l'éducation est toujours la première à souffrir des réductions des dépenses publiques.

victimization [,vɪktɪmaɪ'zeɪʃn] *n* [for beliefs, race, differences] fait *m* de prendre pour victime ■ [reprisals] représailles *fpl* ■ **there must be no further ~ of workers** il ne doit pas y avoir d'autres représailles contre les ouvriers.

victimize, ise ['vɪktɪmaɪz] *vt* [make victim of] faire une victime de, prendre pour victime ■ [take reprisals against] exercer des OR user de représailles sur ■ **the strikers feel they are being ~d** les grévistes estiment qu'ils sont victimes de représailles.

victor ['vɪktəʳ] *n* vainqueur *m*.

Victoria [vɪk'tɔːrɪə] *pr n* **1.** [person] : **Queen ~** la reine Victoria **2.** [state] Victoria *m* ■ **in ~** dans le Victoria **3.** [lake] : **Lake ~** le lac Victoria.

Victoria Cross *n* MIL croix *f* de Victoria *(en Grande-Bretagne, décoration militaire très prestigieuse)*.

Victorian [vɪk'tɔːrɪən] <> *adj* victorien.
<> *n* Victorien *m*, - enne *f*.

victorious [vɪk'tɔːrɪəs] *adj* [army, campaign, party] victorieux ■ [army] vainqueur ■ [cry] de victoire ■ **to be ~ over sb** être victorieux de qqn, remporter la victoire sur qqn.

victoriously [vɪk'tɔːrɪəslɪ] *adv* victorieusement.

victory ['vɪktərɪ] (*pl* **victories**) *n* victoire *f* ■ **to gain OR to win a ~ over sb** remporter la victoire sur qqn.

victory roll *n* AERON *looping pour marquer une victoire*.

victory sign *n* V *m* de la victoire.

victual ['vɪtl] (*pret & pp* **victualled**, *cont* **victualling**) *arch*
<> *vt* ravitailler, approvisionner.
<> *vi* se ravitailler, s'approvisionner.
◆ **victuals** *npl arch* victuailles *fpl*.

victualler ['vɪtləʳ] *n* fournisseur *m* (de provisions).

video ['vɪdɪəʊ] (*pl* **videos**) <> *n* **1.** [medium] vidéo *f* ■ **I use ~ a lot in my teaching** j'utilise beaucoup la vidéo pendant mes cours **2.** [VCR] magnétoscope *m* ■ **they recorded the series on ~** ils ont enregistré le feuilleton au magnétoscope **3.** [cassette] vidéocassette *f* ■ [recording] vidéo *f* ■ [for pop-song] clip *m*, vidéoclip *m* ■ **we've got a ~ of the film** on a le film en vidéocassette **4.** *US inf* [television] télé *f*.

◇ *comp* **1.** [film, version] (en) vidéo ▪ [services, equipment, signals] vidéo *(inv)* **2.** *US* [on TV] télévisé.
◇ *vt* enregistrer sur magnétoscope, magnétoscoper.

video camera *n* caméra *f* vidéo.

video cassette *n* vidéocassette *f*.

video cassette recorder *n* magnétoscope *m*.

video clip *n* clip *m*, vidéoclip *m*, clip *m* vidéo.

video conference *n* vidéoconférence *f*, visioconférence *f*.

video conferencing *n* vidéoconférence *f*.

video game *n* jeu *m* vidéo.

video machine = **videorecorder**.

video nasty *n* *UK inf* *film vidéo à caractère violent et souvent pornographique*.

video on demand *n (U)* TV vidéo *f* à la demande.

videophone ['vɪdɪəʊfəʊn] *n* vidéophone *m*.

video player = **videorecorder**.

video-record *vt* enregistrer sur magnétoscope, magnétoscoper.

videorecorder ['vɪdɪəʊrɪ,kɔːdəʳ] *n* magnétoscope *m*.

video recording *n* enregistrement *m* sur magnétoscope.

videotape ['vɪdɪəʊteɪp] ◇ *n* bande *f* vidéo.
◇ *vt* enregistrer sur magnétoscope, magnétoscoper.

video telephone *n* videophone.

videotext ['vɪdɪəʊtekst] *n* vidéotex *m*, vidéographie *f* interactive.

vie [vaɪ] (*pret & pp* **vied**, *cont* **vying**) *vi* rivaliser, lutter ▪ **to ~ with sb for sthg** disputer qqch à qqn ▪ **the two children ~d with each other for attention** les deux enfants rivalisaient l'un avec l'autre pour attirer l'attention ▪ **several companies were vying with each other to sponsor the event** plusieurs firmes se battaient pour parrainer l'événement.

Vienna [vɪ'enə] ◇ *pr n* Vienne.
◇ *comp* viennois, de Vienne.

Viennese [,vɪə'niːz] (*pl inv*) ◇ *n* Viennois *m*, - e *f*.
◇ *adj* viennois.

Vietcong [,vjet'kɒŋ] (*pl inv*) *n* Viêt-cong *mf*.

Vietnam [*UK* ,vjet'næm, *US* ,vjet'nɑːm] *pr n* Viêt Nam *m* ▪ **in ~** au Viêt Nam ▪ **the ~ War** la guerre du Viêt Nam.

THE VIETNAM WAR

Conflit opposant, de 1954 à 1975, le Viêt Nam du Nord, communiste, au Viêt Nam du Sud, soutenu militairement par les États-Unis. Aussitôt critiqué par l'opinion publique nationale, l'effort de guerre américain s'intensifia considérablement au milieu des années 1960, sans parvenir pour autant à faire basculer l'issue du conflit. À partir de 1970, sous la présidence de R. Nixon, un processus de cessez-le-feu fut engagé, aboutissant au retrait des troupes américaines en 1973. Un an plus tard, le sud du pays passa aux mains des communistes. Véritable traumatisme national, la guerre du Viêt Nam est peut-être l'épisode le plus pénible de l'histoire des États-Unis. La longueur du conflit, les atrocités commises de part et d'autre, le nombre très élevé de victimes, mais surtout les interrogations sur la finalité de cette guerre remirent dramatiquement en question la légitimité de l'ingérence américaine et provoquèrent chez les jeunes Américains de l'époque un mouvement antimilitariste d'une ampleur sans précédent.

Vietnamese [,vjetnə'miːz] (*pl inv*) ◇ *n* **1.** [person] Vietnamien *m*, - enne *f* **2.** LING vietnamien *m*.
◇ *adj* vietnamien.

view [vjuː] ◇ *n* **1.** [sight] vue *f* ▪ **to come into ~** apparaître ▪ **he turned the corner and disappeared from ~** il a tourné au coin et on l'a perdu de vue *OR* il a disparu ▪ **it happened in full ~ of the television cameras/police** cela s'est passé juste devant les caméras de télévision/sous les yeux de la police ▪ **to be on ~** [house] être ouvert aux visites ; [picture] être exposé ▪ **the woods are within ~ of the house** de la maison o[n] voit les bois ▪ **to hide sthg from ~** [accidentally] cacher qqch d[e] la vue ; [deliberately] cacher qqch aux regards
2. [prospect] vue *f* ▪ **the house has a good ~ of the sea** la maiso[n] a une belle vue sur la mer ▪ **a room with a ~** une chambr[e] avec vue ▪ **from here we have a side ~ of the cathedral** d'ici nou[s] avons une vue de profil de la cathédrale ▪ **you get a better from here** on voit mieux d'ici ▪ **the man in front of me blocke[d] my ~ of the stage** l'homme devant moi m'empêchait de voi[r] la scène
3. [future perspective] : **in ~** en vue ▪ **what do you have in ~ a[s] regards work?** quelles sont vos intentions en ce qui concern[e] le travail? ▪ **with this end in ~** avec *OR* dans cette intentio[n] ▪ **to take the long ~ of sthg** voir qqch à long terme
4. [aim, purpose] but *m*, intention *f* ▪ **with a ~ to doing sthg** e[n] vue de faire qqch, dans l'intention de faire qqch ▪ **the[y] bought the house with a ~ to their retirement** ils ont acheté l[a] maison en pensant à leur retraite
5. [interpretation] vue *f* ▪ **an overall ~** une vue d'ensemble ▪ **h[e] has** *OR* **takes a gloomy ~ of life** il a une vue pessimiste de l[a] vie, il envisage la vie d'une manière pessimiste
6. [picture, photograph] vue *f* ▪ **an aerial ~ of New York** une vu[e] aérienne de New York
7. [opinion] avis *m*, opinion *f* ▪ **in my ~** à mon avis ▪ **that's th[e] official ~** c'est le point de vue officiel ▪ **everybody has thei[r] own ~ of the situation** chacun comprend la situation à sa fa[ç]on, chacun a sa propre façon de voir la situation ▪ **he take[s] the ~ that they are innocent** il pense *OR* estime *OR* soutien[t] qu'ils sont innocents ▪ **I don't take that ~** je ne partage pa[s] cet avis ▪ **she took a poor** *OR* **dim ~ of his behaviour** elle n'ap[]préciait guère son comportement.
◇ *vt* **1.** [look at] voir, regarder ▪ [film] regarder ▪ **~ed fro[m] above/from afar** vu d'en haut/de loin
2. [examine - slides] visionner ; [- through microscope] regarder [- flat, showhouse] visiter, inspecter
3. *fig* [consider, judge] considérer, envisager ▪ **the committe[e] ~ed his application favourably** la commission a porté un re[]gard favorable sur sa candidature ▪ **how do you ~ this mat[]ter?** quel est votre avis sur cette affaire?
4. HUNT [fox] apercevoir
5. COMPUT visualiser, afficher.
◇ *vi* TV regarder la télévision.
◆ **in view of** *prep phr* étant donné, vu ▪ **in ~ of what ha[s] happened** en raison de *OR* étant donné ce qui s'est passé ▪ **i[n] ~ of this** ceci étant.

Viewdata® ['vjuː,deɪtə] *pr n* vidéotex *m*, vidéographie *f* interactive.

viewer ['vjuːəʳ] *n* **1.** TV téléspectateur *m*, - trice *f* **2.** PHOT [fo[r] slides] visionneuse *f* ▪ [viewfinder] viseur *m*.

viewfinder ['vjuː,faɪndəʳ] *n* PHOT viseur *m*.

viewing ['vjuːɪŋ] ◇ *n (U)* **1.** TV programme *m*, programmes *mpl*, émissions *fpl* ▪ **late-night ~ on BBC 2** émissions de fin de soirée sur BBC 2 ▪ **his latest film makes exciting ~** son dernier film est un spectacle passionnant **2.** [of showhouse, exhibition] visite *f* **3.** ASTRON observation *f*.
◇ *comp* **1.** TV [time, patterns] d'écoute ▪ **a young ~ audience** de jeunes téléspectateurs ▪ **~ figures** taux *m* *OR* indice *m* d'écoute ▪ **at peak ~ hours** aux heures de grande écoute **2.** ASTRON & METEOR [conditions] d'observation.

viewpoint ['vjuːpɔɪnt] *n* **1.** [opinion] point de vue *m* **2.** [viewing place] point de vue *m*, panorama *m*.

vigil ['vɪdʒɪl] *n* **1.** [watch] veille *f* ▪ [in sickroom] veillée *f* ▪ [for dead person] veillée *f* funèbre ▪ **to keep (an all-night) ~ by sb's bedside** veiller (toute la nuit) au chevet de qqn **2.** [demonstration] manifestation *f* silencieuse (nocturne) **3.** RELIG vigile *f*.

vigilance ['vɪdʒɪləns] *n* vigilance *f*.

vigilant ['vɪdʒɪlənt] *adj* vigilant, éveillé.

vigilante [,vɪdʒɪ'læntɪ] *n membre d'un groupe d'autodéfense* ▪ **~ group** groupe *m* d'autodéfense.

vigilantly ['vɪdʒɪləntlɪ] *adv* avec vigilance, attentivement.

vignette [vɪ'njet] *n* [illustration] vignette *f* ▪ ART & PHOT portrait *m* en buste dégradé ▪ LIT portrait *m*.

vigor *US* = **vigour**.

vigorous ['vɪgərəs] *adj* **1.** [robust - person, plant] vigoureux ■ [enthusiastic - person] enthousiaste **2.** [forceful - opposition, campaign, support] vigoureux, énergique **3.** [energetic - exercise] énergique.

vigorously ['vɪgərəslɪ] *adv* vigoureusement, énergiquement.

vigour *UK*, **vigor** *US* ['vɪgər] *n* **1.** [physical vitality] vigueur *f*, énergie *f*, vitalité *f* ■ [mental vitality] vigueur *f*, vivacité *f* **2.** [of attack, style] vigueur *f* ■ [of storm] violence *f* **3.** *US* LAW : **in ~** en vigueur.

Viking ['vaɪkɪŋ] ◇ *adj* viking.
◇ *n* Viking *mf*.

vile [vaɪl] *adj* **1.** [morally wrong - deed, intention, murder] vil, ignoble, infâme **2.** [disgusting - person, habit, food, taste] abominable, exécrable ; [- smell] infect, nauséabond ■ **it smells ~!** ça pue! **3.** [very bad - temper] exécrable, massacrant ; [- weather] exécrable ■ **what ~ weather!** quel sale temps!

vilify ['vɪlɪfaɪ] *vt fml* diffamer, calomnier.

villa ['vɪlə] *n* [in country] maison *f* de campagne ■ [by sea] villa *f* ■ *UK* [in town] villa *f* *OR* pavillon *m* (de banlieue) ■ HIST villa *f*.

village ['vɪlɪdʒ] ◇ *n* village *m* ■ **the global ~** le village planétaire.
◇ *comp* du village.

village green *n pelouse au centre du village.*

VILLAGE GREEN

Souvent situé au centre du village, le *village green* est une grande pelouse publique, accueillant kermesses et manifestations sportives.

village hall *n* salle *f* des fêtes.

village idiot *n* idiot *m* du village.

villager ['vɪlɪdʒər] *n* villageois *m*, - e *f*.

villain ['vɪlən] *n* **1.** [ruffian, scoundrel] scélérat *m*, - e *f*, vaurien *m*, - enne *f* ■ [in film, story] méchant *m*, - e *f*, traître *m*, - esse *f* ■ **the ~ of the piece** THEAT & *fig* le méchant, le coupable **2.** *inf* [rascal] coquin *m*, - e *f*, vilain *m*, - e *f* **3.** △ *crime sl* [criminal] bandit *m*, malfaiteur *m* **4.** HIST = **villein**.

villainous ['vɪlənəs] *adj* **1.** [evil - act, person] vil, ignoble, infâme **2.** [foul - food, weather] abominable, exécrable.

villainy ['vɪlənɪ] (*pl* **villainies**) *n* infamie *f*, bassesse *f*.

villein ['vɪlɪn] *n* HIST [free] vilain *m*, - e *f* ■ [unfree] serf *m*, serve *f*.

vim [vɪm] *n inf* énergie *f*, entrain *m*.

VIN (*abbrev of* **vehicle identification number**) *n* AUT numéro *m* d'immatriculation.

vinaigrette [,vɪnɪ'gret] *n* vinaigrette *f*.

vindaloo [vɪndə'lu:] *n plat indien au curry très épicé.*

vindicate ['vɪndɪkeɪt] *vt* **1.** [justify] justifier ■ **this ~s my faith in him** ceci prouve que j'avais raison d'avoir confiance en lui, ceci prouve que la confiance que j'avais en lui était justifiée **2.** [uphold - claim, right] faire valoir, revendiquer.

vindication [,vɪndɪ'keɪʃn] *n* justification *f* ■ **he spoke in ~ of his behaviour** il s'expliqua pour justifier son comportement.

vindictive [vɪn'dɪktɪv] *adj* vindicatif.

vindictively [vɪn'dɪktɪvlɪ] *adv* vindicativement.

vine [vaɪn] ◇ *n* **1.** [grapevine] vigne *f* **2.** [plant - climbing] plante *f* grimpante ; [- creeping] plante *f* rampante.
◇ *comp* [leaf] de vigne ■ [disease] de la vigne ■ **~ grower** viticulteur *m*, vigneron *m* ■ **~ growing** viticulture *f* ■ **~ harvest** vendange *f*, vendanges *fpl*.

vinegar ['vɪnɪgər] *n* vinaigre *m*.

vineyard ['vɪnjəd] *n* vignoble *m*.

viniculture ['vɪnɪkʌltʃər] *n* viniculture *f*.

vino ['vi:nəʊ] *n inf* pinard *m*.

vintage ['vɪntɪdʒ] ◇ *n* **1.** VINIC [wine] vin *m* de cru ■ [year] cru *m*, millésime *m* ■ **this claret is an excellent ~** ce bordeaux est un très grand cru ■ **a 1983 ~** un vin de 1983 **2.** [crop] récolte *f* ■ [harvesting] vendange *f*, vendanges *fpl* **3.** [period] époque *f*.
◇ *adj* **1.** [old] antique, ancien **2.** [classic, superior] classique ■ **it was ~ Agatha Christie** c'était de l'Agatha Christie du meilleur style *OR* cru **3.** [port, champagne] de cru.

vintage car *n UK* voiture *f* de collection *(normalement construite entre 1919 et 1930).*

vintage wine *n* vin *m* de grand cru, grand vin *m*.

vintage year *n* [for wine] grand cru *m*, grande année *f* ■ [for books, films] très bonne année *f*.

vintner ['vɪntnər] *n* négociant *m* en vins.

vinyl ['vaɪnɪl] ◇ *n* vinyle *m*.
◇ *adj* [wallpaper, tiles, coat] de *OR* en vinyle ■ [paint] vinylique.

viol ['vaɪəl] ◇ *n* viole *f*.
◇ *comp* : **~ player** violiste *mf*.

viola [vɪ'əʊlə] ◇ *n* **1.** MUS alto *m* **2.** BOT [genus] violacée *f* ■ [flower] pensée *f*, violette *f*.
◇ *comp* : **~ player** altiste *mf*.

violate ['vaɪəleɪt] *vt* **1.** [promise, secret, treaty] violer ■ [law] violer, enfreindre ■ [rights] violer, bafouer **2.** [frontier, property] violer **3.** [peace, silence] troubler, rompre ■ **to ~ sb's privacy** déranger qqn dans son intimité *OR* dans sa vie privée **4.** [sanctuary, tomb] violer, profaner **5.** *fml* [rape] violer, violenter.

violation [,vaɪə'leɪʃn] *n* **1.** [of promise, rights, secret] violation *f* ■ [of law] violation *f*, infraction *f* ■ SPORT faute *f* ■ **they acted in ~ of the treaty** ils ont contrevenu au traité **2.** [of frontier, property] violation *f* ■ **it's a ~ of my privacy** c'est une atteinte à ma vie privée **3.** ADMIN : **~ of the peace** trouble *m* de l'ordre public **4.** [of sanctuary, tomb] violation *f*, profanation *f* **5.** *US* LAW infraction *f* **6.** *fml* [rape] viol *m*.

violator ['vaɪəleɪtər] *n* **1.** [gen] violateur *m* **2.** *US* LAW contrevenant *m*.

violence ['vaɪələns] *n (U)* **1.** [physical] violence *f* ■ **the men of ~** [terrorists] les terroristes *mpl* ■ **~ broke out in the streets** il y a eu de violents incidents *OR* des bagarres ont éclaté dans les rues **2.** LAW violences *fpl* ■ **robbery with ~** vol avec coups et blessures **3.** [of language, passion, storm] violence *f* **4.** *phr* **to do ~ to** faire violence à.

violent ['vaɪələnt] *adj* **1.** [attack, crime, person] violent ■ **by ~ means** par la violence ■ **to be ~ with sb** se montrer *OR* être violent avec qqn ■ **he gave the door a ~ kick** il a donné un violent coup de pied dans la porte ■ **to die a ~ death** mourir de mort violente **2.** [intense - pain] violent, aigu, - uë *f* ■ [furious - temper] violent ■ [strong, great - contrast, change] violent, brutal ; [- explosion] violent ■ **she took a ~ dislike to him** elle s'est prise d'une vive aversion à son égard **3.** [forceful, impassioned - argument, language, emotions] violent **4.** [wind, weather] violent **5.** [colour] criard, voyant.

violently ['vaɪələntlɪ] *adv* [attack, shake, struggle] violemment ■ [act, react] violemment, avec violence ■ **he was ~ sick** il fut pris de vomissements violents.

violet ['vaɪələt] ◇ *n* **1.** BOT violette *f* **2.** [colour] violet *m*.
◇ *adj* violet.

violin [,vaɪə'lɪn] ◇ *n* violon *m*.
◇ *comp* [concerto] pour violon ■ [lesson] de violon ■ **~ maker** luthier *m*.

violinist [,vaɪə'lɪnɪst] *n* violoniste *mf*.

violoncello [,vaɪələn'tʃeləʊ] *n* violoncelle *m*.

VIP (*abbrev of* **very important person**) ◇ *n* VIP *mf*, personnalité *f*, personnage *m* de marque.
◇ *comp* [guests, visitors] de marque, éminent, très important ■ **to give sb the ~ treatment** traiter qqn comme un personnage de marque ■ **we got ~ treatment** on nous a réservé un accueil princier, on nous a traités comme des rois.

viper ['vaɪpər] *n* ZOOL & *fig* vipère *f* ■ **a ~s' nest** *fig* un nœud de vipères.

virago [vɪ'rɑ:gəʊ] (*pl* **viragoes** *OR pl* **viragos**) *n* mégère *f*, virago *f*.

viral ['vaɪrəl] *adj* viral.

Virgil ['vɜ:dʒɪl] *pr n* Virgile.

virgin ['vɜ:dʒɪn] ◇ *n* [girl] vierge *f*, pucelle *f* ■ [boy] puceau *m*.
◇ *adj* **1.** [sexually] vierge **2.** [forest, soil, olive oil] vierge ■ [fresh] virginal ■ **~ snow** neige *f* fraîche.
◆ **Virgin** *pr n* RELIG : **the Virgin** la Vierge.

virginal ['vɜ:dʒɪnl] ◇ *n* MUS : **~s** virginal *m*.
◇ *adj* virginal.

Virgin birth *n* : **the ~** l'Immaculée Conception *f*.

Virginia [və'dʒɪnjə] *pr n* Virginie *f* ■ **in ~** en Virginie.

Virginia creeper *n* vigne *f* vierge.

Virginian [və'dʒɪnjən] ◇ *n* Virginien *m*, - enne *f*.
◇ *adj* virginien.

Virginia stock *n* malcolmia *m*.

Virginia tobacco *n* virginie *m*, tabac *m* de Virginie.

Virgin Islands *pr npl* : **the ~** les îles *fpl* Vierges.

virginity [və'dʒɪnətɪ] *n* virginité *f*.

Virgin Mary *pr n* : **the ~** la Vierge Marie.

Virgo ['vɜ:gəʊ] *pr n* ASTROL & ASTRON Vierge *f* ■ **he's a ~** il est (du signe de la) Vierge.

virile ['vɪraɪl] *adj* viril.

virility [vɪ'rɪlətɪ] *n* virilité *f*.

virology [ˌvaɪ'rɒlədʒɪ] *n* virologie *f*.

virtual ['vɜ:tʃʊəl] *adj* **1.** [near, as good as] : **the country is in a state of ~ anarchy** c'est pratiquement l'anarchie dans le pays ■ **the strike led to a ~ halt in production** la grève a provoqué une interruption quasi totale de la production ■ **it's a ~ impossibility/dictatorship** c'est une quasi-impossibilité/une quasi-dictature **2.** [actual, effective] : **they are the ~ rulers of the country** en fait ce sont eux qui dirigent le pays, ce sont eux les dirigeants de fait du pays **3.** COMPUT & PHYS virtuel.

virtual image *n* image *f* virtuelle.

virtually ['vɜ:tʃʊəlɪ] *adv* **1.** [almost] pratiquement, quasiment, virtuellement **2.** [actually, in effect] en fait.

virtual memory *n* COMPUT mémoire *f* virtuelle.

virtual reality *n* réalité *f* virtuelle.

virtual storage = **virtual memory**.

virtue ['vɜ:tju:] *n* **1.** [goodness] vertu *f* ■ **to make a ~ of necessity** faire de nécessité vertu ■ **a woman of easy ~** une femme de petite vertu ▶ **~ is its own reward** *prov* la vertu est sa propre récompense **2.** [merit] mérite *m*, avantage *m*.
◆ **by virtue of** *prep phr* en vertu *OR* en raison de.

virtuosity [ˌvɜ:tjʊ'ɒsɪtɪ] *n* virtuosité *f*.

virtuoso [ˌvɜ:tjʊ'əʊzəʊ] (*pl* **virtuosos** *OR pl* **virtuosi** [-si:]) ◇ *n* [gen - MUS] virtuose *mf*.
◇ *adj* de virtuose.

virtuous ['vɜ:tʃʊəs] *adj* vertueux.

virtuously ['vɜ:tʃʊəslɪ] *adv* vertueusement.

virulence ['vɪrʊləns] *n* virulence *f*.

virulent ['vɪrʊlənt] *adj* virulent.

virus ['vaɪrəs] ◇ *n* MED & COMPUT virus *m* ■ **the flu ~** le virus de la grippe.
◇ *comp* MED : **a ~ infection** une infection virale ‖ COMPUT : **~ detector** détecteur *m* de virus.

visa ['vi:zə] ◇ *n* visa *m*.
◇ *vt* ADMIN viser.

visage ['vɪzɪdʒ] *n lit* visage *m*, figure *f*.

vis-à-vis [ˌvi:zɑ:'vi:] (*pl inv*) ◇ *prep* **1.** [in relation to] par rapport à **2.** [opposite] vis-à-vis de.
◇ *adv* vis-à-vis.
◇ *n* **1.** [person or thing opposite] vis-à-vis *m inv* **2.** [counterpart] homologue *mf*.

viscera ['vɪsərə] *npl* viscères *mpl*.

visceral ['vɪsərəl] *adj* viscéral.

viscose ['vɪskəʊs] ◇ *n* viscose *f*.
◇ *adj* visqueux.

viscount ['vaɪkaʊnt] *n* vicomte *m*.

viscountess ['vaɪkaʊntɪs] *n* vicomtesse *f*.

viscous ['vɪskəs] *adj* visqueux, gluant.

vise [vaɪs] *US* = **vice** *(sense 4)*.

visibility [ˌvɪzɪ'bɪlətɪ] *n* visibilité *f* ■ **~ is down to a few yard[s]** la visibilité est réduite à quelques mètres.

visible ['vɪzəbl] *adj* **1.** [gen - OPT] visible ■ **clearly ~ to the nake[d] eye** clairement visible à l'œil nu **2.** [evident] visible, appa[-]rent, manifeste ■ **it serves no ~ purpose** on n'en voit pas vrai[-]ment l'utilité, on ne voit pas vraiment à quoi cela sert ■ **wit[h] no ~ means of support** ADMIN sans ressources apparentes **3.** *ir[...]* ECON visible.

visibly ['vɪzəblɪ] *adv* visiblement.

Visigoth ['vɪzɪˌgɒθ] *pr n* Visigoth *m*, - e *f*, Wisigoth *m*, - e *f*

Visigothic [ˌvɪzɪ'gɒθɪk] *adj* visigoth, wisigoth.

vision ['vɪʒn] *n* **1.** *(U)* OPT [sight] vision *f*, vue *f* ■ **to suffer fro[m] defective ~** avoir une vision défectueuse ■ **outside/withi[n] one's field of ~** hors de/en vue **2.** [insight] vision *f*, clair[-]voyance *f* ■ **a man of ~** un homme clairvoyant ■ **we nee[d] people with ~ and imagination** nous avons besoin de gens ins[-]pirés et imaginatifs **3.** [dream, fantasy] vision *f* ■ **to have ~s** ME[D] & PSYCHOL avoir des visions ■ **he has ~s of being rich and famou[s]** il se voit riche et célèbre ■ **I had ~s of you lying in a hospita[l] bed** je vous voyais couché dans un lit d'hôpital **4.** [concep[-]tion] vision *f*, conception *f* **5.** [apparition] vision *f*, apparitio[n] *f* ■ [lovely sight] magnifique spectacle *m* ■ **she was a ~ in whit[e] lace** elle était ravissante en dentelle blanche **6.** TV image *f*

visionary ['vɪʒənrɪ] (*pl* **visionaries**) ◇ *adj* visionnaire.
◇ *n* visionnaire *mf*.

vision mixer *n* TV **1.** [equipment] mixeur *m*, mélangeur *m* de signaux **2.** [person] opérateur *m* de mixage.

visit ['vɪzɪt] ◇ *n* **1.** [call] visite *f* ■ **to pay sb a ~** rendre visite à qqn ■ **I haven't paid a ~ to the cathedral yet** je n'ai pas encore visité *OR* je ne suis pas encore allé voir la cathédrale ■ **she met him on a return ~ to her home town** elle l'a rencontré quand elle est retournée en visite dans sa ville natale ▶ **to pay a ~** *UK inf euph* aller au petit coin **2.** [stay] visite *f*, séjour *m* ■ [trip] voyage *m*, séjour *m* ■ **she's on a ~ to her aunt's** elle est en visite chez sa tante ■ **she's on a ~ to Amsterdam** elle fait un séjour à Amsterdam ■ **the President is on an official ~ to Australia** le président est en visite officielle en Australie **3.** *US* [chat] causette *f*, bavardage *m* **4.** [Internet] visite *f* (d'un site).
◇ *vt* **1.** [person - go to see] rendre visite à, aller voir ; [- stay with] rendre visite à, séjourner chez ■ **to ~ the sick** visiter les malades **2.** [museum, town] visiter, aller voir **3.** [inspect - place, premises] visiter, inspecter, faire une visite d'inspection à ■ **to ~ the scene of the crime** LAW se rendre sur les lieux du crime **4.** *lit* [inflict] : **to ~ a punishment on sb** punir qqn ■ **the city was ~ed by the plague in the 17th century** la ville a été atteinte par la peste au 17e siècle **5.** [Internet] : visiter (un site).
◇ *vi* visiter ■ **we're just ~ing** nous sommes simplement en visite *OR* de passage.
◆ **visit with** *vt insep US* [call on] passer voir ■ [talk with] bavarder avec.

visitation [ˌvɪzɪ'teɪʃn] *n* **1.** [official visit, inspection] visite *f OR* tour *m* d'inspection ■ RELIG visite *f* épiscopale *OR* pastorale **2.** [social visit] visite *f* **3.** *fml* [affliction] punition *f* du ciel ■ [reward] récompense *f* divine.
◆ **Visitation** *n* RELIG : **the Visitation** la Visitation.

visiting ['vɪzɪtɪŋ] *adj* [circus, performers] de passage ■ [lecturer] invité ■ [birds] de passage, migrateur ■ **the ~ team** SPORT les visiteurs.

visiting card *n UK* carte *f* de visite.

visiting hours *npl* heures *fpl* de visite.

visiting nurse *n US* infirmier *m*, - ère *f* à domicile.

visiting professor *n* UNIV professeur *m* associé *OR* invité.

visiting time = **visiting hours**.

visitor ['vɪzɪtəʳ] *n* **1.** [caller - at hospital, house, prison] visiteur *m*, - euse *f* ▪ **you have a ~** vous avez de la visite ▪ **they are not allowed any ~s after 10 p.m.** ils n'ont pas le droit de recevoir des visiteurs *OR* des visites après 22 h **2.** [guest - at private house] visiteur *m*, - euse *f*, invité *m*, - e *f* ; [- at hotel] client *m*, - e *f* ▪ **we have ~s** on a du monde *OR* des invités **3.** [tourist] visiteur *m*, - euse *f*, touriste *mf* ▪ **~s to the exhibition are requested not to smoke** il est demandé aux personnes visitant l'exposition de ne pas fumer **4.** ORNITH oiseau *m* passager ▪ **this bird is a ~ to these shores** cet oiseau est seulement de passage sur ces côtes.

visitors' book *n* [in house, museum] livre *m* d'or ▪ [in hotel] registre *m*.

visitors' gallery *n* tribune *f* du public.

visitor's passport *n* passeport *m* temporaire.

visor, vizor ['vaɪzəʳ] *n* [on hat] visière *f*.

vista ['vɪstə] *n* **1.** [view] vue *f*, perspective *f* ▪ **a mountain ~** une vue sur les montagnes, une perspective de montagnes **2.** *fig* [perspective] perspective *f*, horizon *m* ▪ [image - of past] vue *f*, vision *f* ; [- of future] perspective *f*, vision *f*.

visual ['vɪʒʊəl] *adj* **1.** [image, impression, faculty] visuel **2.** AERON [landing, navigation] à vue.
◆ **visuals** *npl* supports *mpl* visuels.

visual aid *n* support *m* visuel.

visual arts *npl* arts *mpl* plastiques.

visual display terminal, visual display unit *n* écran *m* (de visualisation), moniteur *m*.

visual field *n* champ *m* visuel.

visual handicap *n* handicap *m* visuel.

visualize, ise ['vɪʒʊəlaɪz] *vt* **1.** [call to mind - scene] se représenter, évoquer ▪ [imagine] s'imaginer, visualiser, se représenter ▪ **he tried to ~ what it would be like** il essaya de s'imaginer comment ce serait **2.** [foresee] envisager, prévoir **3.** TECH [make visible] visualiser ▪ MED rendre visible par radiographie.

visually ['vɪʒʊəlɪ] *adv* visuellement.

visually handicapped, visually impaired
◇ *adj* malvoyant, amblyope *spec*.
◇ *npl* : **the ~** les malvoyants *mpl*.

vital ['vaɪtl] *adj* **1.** [essential - information, services, supplies] vital, essentiel, indispensable ▪ **of ~ importance** d'une importance capitale ▪ **this drug is ~ to the success of the operation** ce médicament est indispensable au succès de l'opération ▪ **it's ~ that I know the truth** il est indispensable que je sache la vérité **2.** [very important - decision, matter] vital, fondamental ▪ **tonight's match is ~** le match de ce soir est décisif **3.** BIOL [function, organ] vital ▪ **a ~ force** une force vitale **4.** [energetic] plein d'entrain, dynamique.
◆ **vitals** *npl* **1.** *hum* & ANAT organes *mpl* vitaux **2.** [essential elements] parties *fpl* essentielles.

vitality [vaɪ'tælətɪ] *n* vitalité *f*.

vitally ['vaɪtəlɪ] *adv* absolument ▪ **it's ~ important that you attend this meeting** il est extrêmement important *OR* il est essentiel que vous assistiez à cette réunion ▪ **this question is ~ important** cette question est d'une importance capitale.

vital statistics *npl* **1.** [demographic] statistiques *fpl* démographiques **2.** *hum* [of woman] mensurations *fpl*.

vitamin [*UK* 'vɪtəmɪn, *US* 'vaɪtəmɪn] *n* vitamine *f* ▪ **~ C/E** vitamine C/E ▪ **with added ~s** vitaminé.

vitamin deficiency *n* carence *f* vitaminique.

vitamin pill *n* comprimé *m* de vitamines.

vitiate ['vɪʃɪeɪt] *vt fml* vicier.

viticulture ['vɪtɪkʌltʃəʳ] *n* viticulture *f*.

vitreous ['vɪtrɪəs] *adj* **1.** [china, rock] vitreux ▪ [enamel] vitrifié **2.** ANAT vitré.

vitrify ['vɪtrɪfaɪ] (*pret & pp* **vitrified**) ◇ *vt* vitrifier.
◇ *vi* se vitrifier.

vitriolic [,vɪtrɪ'ɒlɪk] *adj* **1.** CHEM de vitriol **2.** [attack, description, portrait] au vitriol ▪ [tone] venimeux.

vituperate [vɪ'tju:pəreɪt] *lit* ◇ *vt* vitupérer (contre), vilipender.
◇ *vi* vitupérer.

vituperation [vɪ,tju:pə'reɪʃn] *n (U)* vitupérations *fpl*.

viva[1] ['vi:və] ◇ *interj* : **~!** vive!
◇ *n* vivat *m*.

viva[2] ['vaɪvə] = **viva voce** *(n)*.

vivacious [vɪ'veɪʃəs] *adj* **1.** [manner, person] enjoué, exubérant **2.** BOT vivace.

vivaciously [vɪ'veɪʃəslɪ] *adv* avec vivacité.

vivacity [vɪ'væsətɪ] *n* [in action] vivacité *f* ▪ [in speech] verve *f*.

Vivaldi [vɪ'vældɪ] *pr n* Vivaldi.

vivarium [vaɪ'veərɪəm] (*pl* **vivariums** *OR pl* **vivaria** [-rɪə]) *n* vivarium *m*.

viva voce [,vaɪvə'vəʊsɪ] ◇ *n UK* UNIV [gen] épreuve *f* orale, oral *m* ▪ [for thesis] soutenance *f* de thèse.
◇ *adj* oral.
◇ *adv* de vive voix, oralement.

vivid ['vɪvɪd] *adj* **1.** [bright - colour, light] vif, éclatant ; [- clothes] voyant ▪ **~ green paint** peinture d'un vert éclatant **2.** [intense - feeling] vif **3.** [lively - personality] vif, vivant ; [- imagination] vif ; [- language] coloré ▪ **it was a very ~ performance** c'était une interprétation pleine de verve **4.** [graphic - account, description] vivant ; [- memory] vif, net ; [- example] frappant.

vividly ['vɪvɪdlɪ] *adv* **1.** [coloured] de façon éclatante ▪ [painted, decorated] avec éclat, de façon éclatante **2.** [describe] de façon frappante *OR* vivante ▪ **I can ~ remember the day we first met** j'ai un vif souvenir du jour où nous nous sommes rencontrés.

vividness ['vɪvɪdnɪs] *n* **1.** [of colour, light] éclat *m*, vivacité *f* **2.** [of description, language] vivacité *f* ▪ [of memory] clarté *f*.

viviparous [vɪ'vɪpərəs] *adj* vivipare.

vivisection [,vɪvɪ'sekʃn] *n* vivisection *f*.

vivisectionist [,vɪvɪ'sekʃənɪst] *n* **1.** [practitioner] vivisecteur *m* **2.** [advocate] partisan *m*, - e *f* de la vivisection.

vixen ['vɪksn] *n* **1.** ZOOL renarde *f* **2.** *pej* [woman] mégère *f*.

Viyella® [vaɪ'elə] *n tissu mélangé (laine et coton).*

viz [vɪz] (*abbrev of* **videlicet**) c-à-d.

vizier [vɪ'zɪəʳ] *n* vizir *m*.

vizor ['vaɪzəʳ] = **visor**.

V-neck ◇ *n* encolure *f* en V.
◇ *adj* = **V-necked**.

V-necked *adj* [pullover] à encolure *OR* col en V.

VOA (*abbrev of* **Voice of America**) *pr n station de radio américaine émettant dans le monde entier.*

vocab ['vəʊkæb] *n inf* = **vocabulary**.

vocabulary [və'kæbjʊlərɪ] (*pl* **vocabularies**) *n* vocabulaire *m* ▪ LING vocabulaire *m*, lexique *m*.

vocal ['vəʊkl] ◇ *adj* **1.** ANAT vocal **2.** [oral - communication] oral, verbal **3.** [outspoken - person, minority] qui se fait bien entendre **4.** [noisy - assembly, meeting] bruyant **5.** MUS vocal **6.** LING [sound] vocalique ▪ [consonant] voisé.
◇ *n* LING son *m* vocalique.
◆ **vocals** *npl* MUS chant *m*, musique *f* vocale.

vocal cords *npl* cordes *fpl* vocales.

vocalic [və'kælɪk] *adj* vocalique.

vocalist ['vəʊkəlɪst] *n* chanteur *m*, - euse *f (dans un groupe pop).*

vocalize, ise ['vəʊkəlaɪz] ◇ *vt* **1.** [gen - articulate] exprimer **2.** LING [sound] vocaliser.
◇ *vi* MUS vocaliser, faire des vocalises.

vocal score *n* partition *f* chorale.

vocation [vəʊ'keɪʃn] *n* [gen - RELIG] vocation *f*.

vocational [vəʊ'keɪʃənl] *adj* professionnel ■ **~ course** [short] stage *m* de formation professionnelle ; [longer] enseignement *m* professionnel ■ **~ training** formation *f* professionnelle.

vocationally [vəʊ'keɪʃnəlɪ] *adv* : **~ oriented** à vocation professionnelle ■ **~ relevant subjects** des matières à vocation professionnelle.

vocative ['vɒkətɪv] ◇ *n* GRAM vocatif *m* ■ **in the ~** au vocatif.
◇ *adj* : **the ~ case** le vocatif.

vociferate [və'sɪfəreɪt] *vi* vociférer, hurler.

vociferous [və'sɪfərəs] *adj* bruyant, vociférateur.

vociferously [və'sɪfərəslɪ] *adv* bruyamment, en vociférant.

vodka ['vɒdkə] *n* vodka *f*.

vogue [vəʊg] ◇ *n* [fashion] vogue *f*, mode *f* ■ **to come into ~** devenir à la mode ■ **the ~ for long hair is on the way out** les cheveux longs passent de mode ■ **mini skirts are back in ~** les minijupes sont de nouveau à la mode.
◇ *adj* [style, word] en vogue, à la mode.

voice [vɔɪs] ◇ *n* **1.** [speech] voix *f* ■ **in a low ~** à voix basse ■ **in a loud ~** d'une voix forte ■ **we heard the sound of ~s** on entendait des gens parler ■ **he likes the sound of his own ~** [talkative] il parle beaucoup ; [conceited] il s'écoute parler ■ **to shout at the top of one's ~** crier à tue-tête ■ **to give ~ to sthg** exprimer qqch ■ **keep your ~s down** ne parlez pas si fort ■ **to raise one's ~** [speak louder] parler plus fort ; [get angry] hausser le ton ■ **don't you raise your ~ at** *OR* **to me!** ne prenez pas ce ton-là avec moi! ■ **several ~s were raised in protest** plusieurs voix se sont élevées pour protester ■ **with one ~** d'une seule voix **2.** [of singer] voix *f* ■ **to have a good (singing) ~** avoir une belle voix ■ **to be in good ~** être bien en voix **3.** [say] voix *f* **4.** GRAM voix *f* ■ **in the active/passive ~** à la voix active/passive.
◇ *vt* **1.** [express - feelings] exprimer, formuler ; [- opposition, support] exprimer **2.** LING [consonant] voiser **3.** MUS [organ] harmoniser.

voice box *n* larynx *m*.

voiced [vɔɪst] *adj* LING [consonant] sonore, voisé.

voice-driven *adj* à commande vocale.

voice input *n* COMPUT entrée *f* vocale.

voiceless ['vɔɪslɪs] *adj* **1.** MED aphone **2.** [with no say] sans voix **3.** LING [consonant] non-voisé, sourd.

voice mail *n* [device] boîte *f* vocale ■ [system] messagerie *f* vocale ■ **to check one's ~** consulter sa boîte vocale.

voice-over *n* CIN & TV voix *f* off.

voice recognition *n* COMPUT reconnaissance *f* de la parole.

voice vote *n US* POL vote *m* par acclamation.

void [vɔɪd] ◇ *n* **1.** PHYS & ASTRON vide *m* **2.** [chasm] vide *m* **3.** [emptiness] vide *m*.
◇ *adj* **1.** [empty] vide ■ **~ of interest** dépourvu d'intérêt, sans aucun intérêt **2.** LAW nul **3.** [vacant - position] vacant.
◇ *vt* **1.** *fml* [empty] vider ■ [discharge - bowels] évacuer **2.** LAW annuler, rendre nul.

voidance ['vɔɪdəns] *n* LAW résiliation *f*.

vol. (*written abbrev of* **volume**) vol.

volatile [*UK* 'vɒlətaɪl, *US* 'vɒlətl] ◇ *adj* **1.** CHEM volatil **2.** [person - changeable] versatile, inconstant ; [- temperamental] lunatique **3.** [unstable - situation] explosif, instable ; [- market] instable **4.** *lit* [transitory] fugace **5.** COMPUT [memory] volatil.
◇ *n* CHEM substance *f* volatile.

volatility [,vɒlə'tɪlətɪ] *n* **1.** CHEM volatilité *f* **2.** [of person - changeability] versatilité *f*, inconstance *f* **3.** [of situation, market] instabilité *f*.

volcanic [vɒl'kænɪk] *adj* volcanique.

volcano [vɒl'keɪnəʊ] (*pl* **volcanoes** *OR pl* **volcanos**) *n* volcan *m*.

vole [vəʊl] *n* ZOOL campagnol *m*.

Volga ['vɒlgə] *pr n* : **the (River) ~** la Volga.

volition [və'lɪʃn] *n* [gen - PHILOS] volition *f*, volonté *f* ■ **of one's own ~** de son propre gré.

volley ['vɒlɪ] ◇ *n* **1.** [of gunshots] volée *f*, salve *f* ■ [of arrows, missiles, stones] volée *f*, grêle *f* ■ [of blows] volée *f* **2.** [of insults] grêle *f*, bordée *f*, torrent *m* ■ [of curses] bordée *f*, torrent *m* ■ [of questions] feu *m* roulant ■ [of applause] salve *f* **3.** SPORT volée *f*.
◇ *vt* **1.** [missile, shot] tirer une volée *OR* une salve de **2.** [curses, insults] lâcher une bordée *OR* un torrent de **3.** SPORT reprendre de volée.
◇ *vi* **1.** MIL tirer par salves **2.** SPORT [in tennis] volleyer ■ [in football] reprendre le ballon de volée.

volleyball ['vɒlɪbɔːl] *n* volley-ball *m*, volley *m* ■ **~ player** volleyeur *m*, - euse *f*.

volt [vəʊlt] *n* volt *m*.

Volta ['vɒltə] *pr n* Volta *f* ■ **the Black ~** la Volta Noire ■ **the White ~** la Volta Blanche.

voltage ['vəʊltɪdʒ] *n* voltage *m*, tension *f spec*.

voltaic [vɒl'teɪɪk] *adj* voltaïque.

volte-face [,vɒlt'fɑːs] *n* volte-face *f inv* ■ **the speech represents a complete ~** ce discours marque un revirement complet.

voltmeter ['vəʊlt,miːtə^r] *n* voltmètre *m*.

voluble ['vɒljʊbl] *adj* volubile, loquace.

volume ['vɒljuːm] *n* **1.** [gen - PHYS] volume *m* ■ [capacity] volume *m*, capacité *f* ■ [amount] volume *m*, quantité *f* **2.** ACOUS volume *m* **3.** [book] volume *m*, tome *m* ■ **a rare ~** un exemplaire *OR* un livre rare **4.** [in hairstyle] volume *m*.

volume control *n* RADIO & TV bouton *m* de réglage du volume.

volumetric [,vɒljʊ'metrɪk] *adj* volumétrique.

voluminous [və'luːmɪnəs] *adj* volumineux.

voluntarily [*UK* 'vɒləntrɪlɪ, *US* ,vɒlən'terəlɪ] *adv* **1.** [willingly] volontairement, de son plein gré **2.** [without payment] bénévolement.

voluntary ['vɒləntrɪ] (*pl* **voluntaries**) ◇ *adj* **1.** [freely given - statement, donation, gift] volontaire, spontané **2.** [optional] facultatif **3.** [unpaid - help, service] bénévole ■ **the shop is run on a ~ basis** le personnel du magasin se compose de bénévoles le magasin est tenu par des bénévoles **4.** PHYSIOL volontaire.
◇ *n* **1.** RELIG & MUS morceau *m* d'orgue **2.** [unpaid work] travail *m* bénévole, bénévolat *m*.

voluntary agency, voluntary body *n* organisme *m* bénévole.

voluntary liquidation *n UK* dépôt *m* de bilan ■ **to go into ~** déposer son bilan.

voluntary redundancy *n UK* licenciement *m* consenti ■ **he decided to take ~** il a négocié son licenciement.

Voluntary Service Overseas = VSO.

voluntary work *n* travail *m* bénévole, bénévolat *m*.

voluntary worker *n* bénévole *mf*.

volunteer [,vɒlən'tɪə^r] ◇ *n* **1.** [gen - MIL] volontaire *mf* ■ **the Volunteer State** le Tennessee **2.** [unpaid worker] bénévole *mf*.
◇ *comp* **1.** [army, group] de volontaires **2.** [work, worker] bénévole.
◇ *vt* **1.** [advice, information, statement] donner *OR* fournir spontanément ■ [help, services] donner *OR* proposer volontairement ■ **to ~ to do sthg** se proposer pour *OR* offrir de faire qqch **2.** [say] dire spontanément.
◇ *vi* [gen] se porter volontaire ■ MIL s'engager comme volontaire ■ **to ~ for extra work/guard duty** se porter volontaire pour (faire) du travail supplémentaire/pour être de garde.

voluptuous [və'lʌptʃʊəs] *adj* voluptueux, sensuel.

volute [və'lu:t] *n* volute *f*.

voluted [və'lu:tɪd] *adj* en volute.

vomit ['vɒmɪt] ◇ *n* vomissement *m*, vomi *m*.
◇ *vt liter & fig* vomir ▪ **to ~ blood** vomir du sang.

vomiting ['vɒmɪtɪŋ] *n (U)* vomissements *mpl*.

voodoo ['vu:du:] (*pl* **voodoos**) ◇ *n* vaudou *m*.
◇ *adj* vaudou *(inv)*.
◇ *vt* envoûter, ensorceler.

voracious [və'reɪʃəs] *adj* [appetite, energy, person] vorace ▪ [reader] avide.

voraciously [və'reɪʃəslɪ] *adv* [consume, eat] voracement, avec voracité ▪ [read] avec voracité, avidement.

voracity [vɒ'ræsətɪ] *n* voracité *f*.

vortex ['vɔ:teks] (*pl* **vortexes** *OR pl* **vortices** [-tɪsi:z]) *n* [of water, gas] vortex *m*, tourbillon *m* ▪ *fig* tourbillon *m*, maelström *m*.

votary ['vəʊtərɪ] (*pl* **votaries**) *n* RELIG & *fig* fervent *m*, - e *f*.

vote [vəʊt] ◇ *n* **1.** [ballot] vote *m* ▪ **to have a ~ on sthg** voter sur qqch, mettre qqch au vote ▪ **to put a question to the ~** mettre une question au vote *OR* aux voix ▪ **to take a ~ on sthg** [gen] voter sur qqch ; ADMIN & POL procéder au vote de qqch ▶ **~ of thanks** discours *m* de remerciement
2. [in parliament] vote *m*, scrutin *m* ▪ **the ~ went in the government's favour/against the government** les députés se sont prononcés en faveur du/contre le gouvernement ▶ **~ of confidence** vote *m* de confiance ▪ **~ of no confidence** motion *f* de censure
3. [individual choice] vote *m*, voix *f* ▪ **to count the ~s** [gen] compter les votes *OR* les voix ; POL dépouiller le scrutin ▪ **the candidate got 15,000 ~s** le candidat a recueilli 15 000 voix ▪ **one member, one ~** *système de scrutin "un homme, une voix"*
4. [ballot paper] bulletin *m* de vote
5. [suffrage] droit *m* de vote ▪ **to have the ~** avoir le droit de vote ▪ **to give the ~ to sb** accorder le droit de vote à qqn
6. *(U)* [collectively - voters] vote *m*, voix *fpl* ; [- votes cast] voix *fpl* exprimées ▪ **they won 40% of the ~** ils ont remporté 40 % des voix *OR* des suffrages
7. *UK* POL [grant] vote *m* de crédits.
◇ *vt* **1.** [in election] voter ▪ **~ Malone!** votez Malone! ▪ **to ~ Labour/Republican** voter travailliste/républicain
2. [in parliament, assembly - motion, law, money] voter ▪ **they ~d that the sitting (should) be suspended** ils ont voté la suspension de la séance
3. [elect] élire ▪ [appoint] nommer
4. [declare] proclamer
5. [suggest] proposer.
◇ *vi* voter ▪ **France is voting this weekend** la France va aux urnes ce week-end ▪ **to ~ for/against sb** voter pour/contre qqn ▪ **to ~ in favour of/against sthg** voter pour/contre qqch ▪ **let's ~ on it!** mettons cela aux voix! ▪ **to ~ by a show of hands** voter à main levée ▶ **to ~ with one's feet** *UK* partir en signe de désaccord *OR* pour montrer son désaccord.
◆ **vote down** *vt sep* [bill, proposal] rejeter *(par le vote)*.
◆ **vote in** *vt sep* [person, government] élire ▪ [new law] voter, adopter.
◆ **vote out** *vt sep* [suggestion] rejeter ▪ [minister] relever de ses fonctions.
◆ **vote through** *vt sep* [bill, reform] voter, ratifier.

vote-catcher *n* politique *f* électoraliste.

vote-loser *n* politique *f* qui risque de faire perdre des voix, politique *f* peu populaire.

voter ['vəʊtər] *n* électeur *m*, - trice *f*.

voting ['vəʊtɪŋ] *n* vote *m*, scrutin *m* ▪ **I don't know how the ~ will go** je ne sais pas comment les gens vont voter.

voting booth *n* isoloir *m*.

voting paper *n* bulletin *m* de vote.

votive ['vəʊtɪv] *adj* votif.

vouch [vaʊtʃ] *vi* : **to ~ for sb/sthg** se porter garant de qqn/qqch, répondre de qqn/qqch ▪ **I can ~ for the truth of her story** je peux attester *OR* témoigner de la véracité de sa déclaration.

voucher ['vaʊtʃər] *n* **1.** *UK* [for restaurant, purchase, petrol] bon *m* ▶ **credit ~** bon *m* **2.** [receipt] reçu *m*, récépissé *m* **3.** LAW pièce *f* justificative.

vouchsafe [vaʊtʃ'seɪf] *vt fml* **1.** [grant - help, support] accorder, octroyer ; [- answer] accorder **2.** [undertake] : **to ~ to do sthg** [willingly] accepter gracieusement de faire qqch ; [reluctantly] condescendre à *OR* daigner faire qqch.

vow [vaʊ] ◇ *n* **1.** [promise] serment *m*, promesse *f* ▪ **to make** *OR* **take a ~ to do sthg** promettre *OR* jurer de faire qqch ▪ **I'm under a ~ of silence** j'ai promis de ne rien dire **2.** RELIG vœu *m* ▪ **to take one's ~s** prononcer ses vœux ▪ **to take a ~ of poverty/chastity** faire vœu de pauvreté/de chasteté.
◇ *vt* [swear] jurer ▪ **to ~ to do sthg** jurer de faire qqch.

vowel ['vaʊəl] ◇ *n* voyelle *f*.
◇ *comp* [harmony, pattern, sound] vocalique.

vowel point *n* point-voyelle *m*.

vowel shift *n* mutation *f* vocalique.

vox pop [,vɒks'pɒp] *n UK inf émission de radio ou de TV avec intervention du public.*

voyage ['vɔɪɪdʒ] ◇ *n* voyage *m* ▪ **to go on a ~** partir en voyage ▪ **a ~ to Jupiter** un voyage vers Jupiter.
◇ *vt* NAUT traverser, parcourir.
◇ *vi* **1.** NAUT voyager par mer ▪ **they ~d across the Atlantic/the desert** ils ont traversé l'Atlantique/le désert **2.** *US* AERON voyager par avion.

voyager ['vɔɪədʒər] *n* **1.** [traveller] voyageur *m*, - euse *f* **2.** [explorer] navigateur *m*, - trice *f*.

voyeur [vwɑ:'jɜ:r] *n* voyeur *m*, - euse *f*.

voyeurism [vwɑ:'jɜ:rɪzm] *n* voyeurisme *m*.

vs *written abbr of* **versus**.

V-shaped *adj* en (forme de) V.

V-sign *n* : **to give the ~** [for victory, approval] faire le V de la victoire ▪ **to give sb the ~** *UK* [as insult] ≃ faire un bras d'honneur à qqn.

VSO (*abbrev of* **Voluntary Service Overseas**) *n coopération technique à l'étranger (non rémunérée).*

VSOP (*abbrev of* **very special old pale**) VSOP.

VT *written abbr of* **Vermont**.

VTOL ['vi:tɒl] (*abbrev of* **vertical take off and landing**) *n* [system] décollage *m* et atterrissage *m* vertical ▪ [plane] ADAV *m*, avion *m* à décollage et atterrissage vertical.

VTR *n* = **video tape recorder**.

vulcanite ['vʌlkənaɪt] *n* ébonite *f*.

vulgar ['vʌlgər] *adj* **1.** [rude] vulgaire, grossier **2.** [common - person, taste, decor] vulgaire, commun.

vulgarism ['vʌlgərɪzm] *n* **1.** [uneducated language] vulgarisme *m* ▪ [rude word] grossièreté *f* **2.** = **vulgarity**.

vulgarity [vʌl'gærətɪ] *n* vulgarité *f*.

vulgarize, ise ['vʌlgəraɪz] *vt* **1.** [appearance, language] rendre vulgaire **2.** [popularize] vulgariser, populariser.

Vulgar Latin *n* latin *m* vulgaire.

vulgarly ['vʌlgəlɪ] *adv* **1.** [coarsely] vulgairement, grossièrement **2.** [commonly] vulgairement, communément.

Vulgate ['vʌlgeɪt] *n* Vulgate *f*.

vulnerability [,vʌlnərə'bɪlətɪ] *n* vulnérabilité *f*.

vulnerable ['vʌlnərəbl] *adj* vulnérable ▪ **to be ~ to sthg** être vulnérable à qqch.

vulture ['vʌltʃər] *n* ORNITH & *fig* vautour *m*.

vulva ['vʌlvə] (*pl* **vulvas** *OR pl* **vulvae** [-vi:]) *n* vulve *f*.

vying ['vaɪɪŋ] *n* rivalité *f*.

w (*pl* **w's** *OR pl* **ws**)**, W** (*pl* **W's** *OR pl* **Ws**) ['dʌblju:] *n* [letter] w *m*, W *m*.

W 1. (*written abbrev of* **west**) O **2.** (*written abbrev of* **watt**) w.

WA *written abbr of* **Washington (State)**.

WAAF [wæf] (*abbrev of* **Women's Auxiliary Air Force**) *pr n* *pendant la deuxième guerre mondiale, section féminine auxiliaire de l'armée de l'air britannique.*

wacky ['wækɪ] (*comp* **wackier**, *superl* **wackiest**) *adj inf* farfelu.

wad [wɒd] (*pret & pp* **wadded**, *cont* **wadding**) ◇ *n* **1.** [of cotton wool, paper] tampon *m*, bouchon *m* ■ [of tobacco] chique *f* ■ [of straw] bouchon *m* ■ [of gum] boulette *f* ■ [for cannon, gun] bourre *f* **2.** [of letters, documents] liasse *f*, paquet *m*.
◇ *vt* **1.** [cloth, paper] faire un tampon de ■ [tobacco, chewing gum] faire une boulette de **2.** [hole, aperture] boucher (avec un tampon) ■ MIL [barrel, cannon] bourrer **3.** [quilt, garment] rembourrer ■ **a wadded jacket** une veste ouatée *OR* doublée d'ouate.

wadding ['wɒdɪŋ] *n* **1.** MIL [in gun, cartridge] bourre *f* **2.** [stuffing - for furniture, packing] rembourrage *m*, capitonnage *m* ; [- for clothes] ouate *f*, ouatine *f*.

waddle ['wɒdl] ◇ *vi* [duck, person] se dandiner ■ **to ~ along/in** avancer/entrer en se dandinant.
◇ *n* dandinement *m*.

wade [weɪd] ◇ *vi* patauger, avancer en pataugeant ■ **they ~d across the stream** ils ont traversé le ruisseau en pataugeant ■ **she ~d out to the boat** elle s'avança dans l'eau vers le bateau.
◇ *vt* [river] passer *OR* traverser à gué.
◆ **wade in** *vi insep UK* [in fight, quarrel] s'y mettre.
◆ **wade into** *vt insep UK* [work, task] attaquer, s'atteler à, se mettre à ■ [meal] attaquer, entamer.
◆ **wade through** *vt insep* avancer *OR* marcher péniblement dans ■ *fig* **I'm still wading through "War and Peace"** je suis toujours aux prises avec "Guerre et paix" ■ **it took me a month to ~ through that book** il m'a fallu un mois pour venir à bout de ce livre ■ **she's got a 100-page report to ~ through** elle a un rapport de 100 pages à lire, elle doit se taper un rapport de 100 pages.

wader ['weɪdəʳ] *n* échassier *m*.

waders ['weɪdəz] *npl* cuissardes *fpl (de pêcheur)*.

wading pool *n US* [in swimming pool] petit bassin *m*.

wafer ['weɪfəʳ] ◇ *n* **1.** CULIN gaufrette *f* **2.** RELIG hostie *f* **3.** [seal] cachet *m* (de papier rouge) **4.** COMPUT & TECH tranche *f*.
◇ *vt* **1.** [seal] cacheter (avec du papier rouge) **2.** COMPUT & TECH diviser en tranches.

wafer-thin, wafery ['weɪfərɪ] *adj* mince comme une feuille de papier à cigarette *OR* comme une pelure d'oignon ■ **a ~ majority** une majorité infime.

waffle ['wɒfl] ◇ *n* **1.** CULIN gaufre *f* **2.** *UK inf* [spoken] baratin *m*, bla-bla *m inv* ■ [written] remplissage *m*, baratin *m*.
◇ *vi inf* [in speaking] baratiner, parler pour ne rien dire ■ [in writing] faire du remplissage ■ **to ~ on** *UK* bavarder, faire des laïus ■ **she's always waffling on about her children** elle n'arrête pas de parler de ses enfants.

waffle iron *n* gaufrier *m*.

waffler ['wɒfləʳ] *n UK inf* baratineur *m*, - euse *f*.

waffling ['wɒflɪŋ] *n UK inf* [spoken] baratin *m*, bla-bla *m inv* ■ [written] baratin *m*, remplissage *m*.

waffly ['wɒflɪ] *adj inf* [speech, essay] plein de baratin.

waft [wɑ:ft, wɒft] ◇ *vt* [scent, sound] porter, transporter ■ **the breeze ~ed the curtains gently to and fro** le vent léger faisait ondoyer les rideaux.
◇ *vi* [scent, sound] flotter ■ **a delicious smell ~ed into the room** une délicieuse odeur envahit la pièce ■ **Vanessa ~ed into/out of the room** *fig* Vanessa entra dans/sortit de la pièce d'un pas léger.
◇ *n* [of smoke, air] bouffée *f*.

wag [wæg] (*pret & pp* **wagged**, *cont* **wagging**) ◇ *vt* [tail] agiter, remuer ■ **she wagged her finger at him** elle le menaça du doigt.
◇ *vi* [tail] remuer, frétiller.
◇ *n* **1.** [of tail] remuement *m*, frétillement *m* ■ **with a ~ of its tail** en agitant *OR* en remuant la queue **2.** *UK* [person] plaisantin *m*, farceur *m*, - euse *f*.

wage [weɪdʒ] ◇ *n* **1.** [pay - of worker] salaire *m*, paye *f*, paie *f* ; [- of servant] gages *mpl* ■ **her wage is** *OR* **her ~s are only £100 a week** elle ne gagne que 100 livres par semaine ■ **his employers took it out of his ~s** ses employeurs l'ont prélevé sur sa paie **2.** [reward] salaire *m*, récompense *f*.
◇ *comp* [claim, demand, settlement] salarial ■ [increase, incentive] de salaire ■ **~ differential** écart *m* de salaires.
◇ *vt* : **to ~ war on** *OR* **against** faire la guerre contre ■ **to ~ a campaign for/against sthg** faire campagne pour/contre qqch.

wage bargaining *n (U)* négociations *fpl* salariales.

wage earner *n* salarié *m*, - e *f*.

wage freeze *n* blocage *m* des salaires.

wage packet *n UK* paie *f*, paye *f (surtout en espèces)*.

wager ['weɪdʒəʳ] *fml* ◇ *vt* parier.
◇ *vi* parier, faire un pari.
◇ *n* pari *m* ■ **to make** *OR* **to lay a ~** faire un pari.

wage slip *n* fiche *f* de paie, bulletin *m* de salaire.

waggish ['wægɪʃ] *adj* badin, facétieux.

waggle ['wægl] <> *vt* [tail] agiter, remuer ▪ [pencil] agiter ▪ [loose tooth, screw] faire jouer ▪ [ears, nose] remuer.
<> *vi* [tail] bouger, frétiller ▪ [loose tooth, screw] bouger, branler.
<> *n* : **to give sthg a ~** agiter OR remuer qqch.

waggon *etc* ['wægən] *UK* = **wagon**.

Wagner ['vɑːgnər] *pr n* Wagner.

Wagnerian [vɑːg'nɪərɪən] <> *adj* wagnérien.
<> *n* wagnérien *m*, - enne *f*.

wagon ['wægən] *n* **1.** [horse-drawn] chariot *m* **2.** [truck] camionnette *f*, fourgon *m* ▪ **(patrol) ~** *US* fourgon cellulaire ▪ **(station) ~** *US* break *m* **3.** *UK* RAIL wagon *m* (de marchandises) **4.** *phr* **to be on the ~** *inf* être au régime sec.

wagoner ['wægənər] *n* charretier *m*.

wagonload ['wægənləʊd] *n* AGRIC charretée *f* ▪ RAIL wagon *m*.

wagon train *n* convoi *m* de chariots *(en particulier de colons américains)*.

wagtail ['wægteɪl] *n* hochequeue *m*, bergeronnette *f*.

waif [weɪf] *n* [child - neglected] enfant *m* malheureux, enfant *f* malheureuse ; [- homeless] enfant *m* abandonné, enfant *f* abandonnée ▪ **~s and strays** [animals] animaux errants.

waiflike ['weɪflaɪk] *adj* frêle.

wail [weɪl] <> *vi* **1.** [person - whine, moan] gémir, pousser des gémissements ▪ [baby - cry] hurler ; [- weep] pleurer bruyamment **2.** [wind] gémir ▪ [siren] hurler.
<> *vt* dire en gémissant, gémir.
<> *n* **1.** [of person] gémissement *m* ▪ **"he's gone!" she said with a ~** "il est parti!" dit-elle en gémissant **2.** [of wind] gémissement *m* ▪ [of siren] hurlement *m*.

wailing ['weɪlɪŋ] <> *n (U)* [of person] gémissements *mpl*, plaintes *fpl* ▪ [of wind] gémissements *mpl*, plainte *f* ▪ [of siren] hurlement *m*, hurlements *mpl*.
<> *adj* [person] gémissant ▪ [sound] plaintif.

Wailing Wall *pr n* : **the ~** le mur des Lamentations.

wainscot ['weɪnskət] *n* lambris *m (en bois)*.

waist [weɪst] *n* **1.** [of person, garment] taille *f* ▪ **he put his arm around her ~** il l'a prise par la taille ▪ **he was up to the** OR **his ~ in water** l'eau lui arrivait à la ceinture OR à la taille ▸ **~ measurement, ~ size** tour *m* de taille **2.** [of ship, plane] partie *f* centrale ▪ [of violin] partie *f* resserrée de la table.

waistband ['weɪstbænd] *n* ceinture *f (d'un vêtement)*.

waistcoat ['weɪskəʊt] *n* *UK* gilet *m (de costume)*.

waist-deep *adj* : **he was ~ in water** l'eau lui arrivait à la ceinture OR à la taille.

-waisted ['weɪstɪd] *in cpds* : **a low/high~ dress** une robe à taille basse/haute.

waist-high = **waist-deep**.

waistline ['weɪstlaɪn] *n* taille *f* ▪ **to watch one's ~** surveiller sa ligne.

wait [weɪt] <> *vi* **1.** [person, bus, work] attendre ▪ **just you ~!** [as threat] attends un peu, tu vas voir!, tu ne perds rien pour attendre! ; [you'll see] vous verrez! ▪ **we'll just have to ~ and see** on verra bien ▪ **he didn't ~ to be told twice** il ne se l'est pas fait dire deux fois ▪ **to keep sb ~ing** faire attendre qqn ▪ **they do it while you ~** ils le font devant vous ▪ **'repairs while you ~'** 'réparations minute' ▪ **'keys cut while you ~'** 'clés minute' ▸ **everything comes to him who ~s** *prov* tout vient à point à qui sait attendre *prov*
2. [with 'can'] : **it can ~** cela peut attendre ▪ **he can ~** laisse-le attendre ▪ **I can't ~!** *iron* je brûle d'impatience! ▪ **I can hardly ~ to see them again** j'ai hâte de les revoir ▪ **I can't ~ for the weekend to arrive** j'attends le week-end avec impatience!, vivement le week-end!
3. [with 'until' or 'till'] : **~ until I've finished** attendez que j'aie fini ▪ **can't that ~ until tomorrow?** cela ne peut pas attendre jusqu'à demain? ▪ **just ~ till your parents hear about it** attends un peu que tes parents apprennent cela
4. [serve] servir, faire le service ▪ **to ~ at table** *UK* OR **on table** *US* servir à table, faire le service.
<> *vt* **1.** [period of time] attendre ▪ **I ~ed half an hour** j'ai attendu (pendant) une demi-heure ▪ **I ~ed all day for the repairman to come** j'ai passé toute la journée à attendre le réparateur ▪ **~ a minute!** (attendez) une minute OR un instant! ▪ **~ your turn!** attendez votre tour!
2. *US* [delay] : **don't ~ dinner for me** ne m'attendez pas pour vous mettre à table
3. *US* [serve at] : **to ~ tables** servir à table, faire le service.
<> *n* attente *f* ▪ **we had a long ~** nous avons dû attendre (pendant) longtemps ▪ **she had a half hour** OR **half hour's ~ at Gatwick** il a fallu qu'elle attende une demi-heure OR elle a eu une demi-heure d'attente à Gatwick ▪ **there was an hour's ~ between trains** il y avait une heure de battement OR d'attente entre les trains ▪ **to lie in ~ for** être à l'affût de, guetter.

◆ **waits** *npl* *UK* MUS chanteurs *mpl* de Noël.

◆ **wait about** *vi insep* *UK* traîner, faire le pied de grue ▪ **to ~ about for sb** attendre qqn, faire le pied de grue en attendant qqn ▪ **I can't stand all this ~ing about** cela m'énerve d'être obligé d'attendre OR de traîner comme ça.

◆ **wait around** = **wait about**.

◆ **wait behind** *vi insep* rester ▪ **to ~ behind for sb** rester pour attendre qqn.

◆ **wait for** *vt insep* : **to ~ for sb/sthg** attendre qqn/qqch ▪ **I'm ~ing for the bank to open** j'attends que la banque soit ouverte, j'attends l'ouverture de la banque ▪ **that was worth ~ing for** cela valait la peine d'attendre ▪ **~ for it!** *UK hum* tiens-toi bien! ▸ **'Waiting for Godot'** *Beckett* 'En attendant Godot'.

◆ **wait in** *vi insep* rester à la maison ▪ **I ~ed in all evening for her** je suis resté chez moi toute la soirée à l'attendre.

◆ **wait on** *vt insep* **1.** [serve] : **I'm not here to ~ on you!** [male] je ne suis pas ton serviteur! ; [female] je ne suis pas ta servante OR ta bonne! ▸ **to ~ on sb hand and foot** être aux petits soins pour qqn
2. *US* [in restaurant] : **to ~ on tables** faire le service, servir à table.

◆ **wait out** *vt sep* [concert, film] rester jusqu'à la fin OR jusqu'au bout de, attendre la fin de.

◆ **wait up** *vi insep* **1.** [at night] rester debout, veiller ▪ **her parents always ~ up for her** ses parents ne se couchent jamais avant qu'elle soit rentrée OR attendent toujours qu'elle rentre pour se coucher
2. *US inf* [wait] : **hey, ~ up!** attendez-moi!

◆ **wait upon** = **wait on** *(sense 1)*.

waiter ['weɪtər] *n* serveur *m*, garçon *m* ▪ **~!** s'il vous plaît!, monsieur!

waiting ['weɪtɪŋ] <> *n* attente *f* ▪ **after two hours of ~** après deux heures d'attente, après avoir attendu deux heures ▪ **'no ~'** 'stationnement interdit' ▪ **to be in ~ on sb** être au service de qqn.
<> *adj* **1.** [person, taxi] qui attend **2.** [period] d'attente.

waiting game *n* : **to play a ~** *fig* jouer la montre, attendre son heure ; MIL & POL mener une politique d'attentisme.

waiting list *n* liste *f* d'attente.

waiting room *n* [in office, surgery, airport, station] salle *f* d'attente.

waitress ['weɪtrɪs] *n* serveuse *f* ▪ **~!** s'il vous plaît!, mademoiselle! ▪ **~ service** service *m* à table.

wait state *n* COMPUT état *m* d'attente.

waive [weɪv] *vt* [condition, requirement] ne pas insister sur, abandonner ▪ [law, rule] déroger à ▪ [claim, right] renoncer à, abandonner.

waiver ['weɪvər] *n* [of condition, requirement] abandon *m* ▪ [of law, rule] dérogation *f* ▪ [of claim, right] renonciation *f*, abandon *m* ▪ **full-collision ~** *US* assurance *f* tous risques.

wake [weɪk] *(pret* **woke** [wəʊk] OR **waked**, *pp* **woken** ['wəʊkən] OR **waked**) <> *vi* **1.** [stop sleeping] se réveiller, s'éveiller ▪ **he woke to the news that war had broken out** à son réveil *OR* en se réveillant, il a appris que la guerre avait éclaté ■ **they woke to find themselves famous** du jour au lendemain, ils se sont retrouvés célèbres **2.** = **wake up** *(vi insep sense 2).*

◇ *vt* **1.** [rouse from sleep] réveiller, tirer *OR* sortir du sommeil ■ **the noise was enough to ~ the dead** il y avait un bruit à réveiller les morts **2.** [arouse - curiosity, jealousy] réveiller, éveiller, exciter ; [- memories] réveiller, éveiller, ranimer **3.** [alert] éveiller l'attention de.

◇ *n* **1.** [vigil] veillée *f* (mortuaire) **2.** [of ship] sillage *m*, eaux *fpl* ■ *fig* sillage *m* ■ **famine followed in the ~ of the drought** la famine a suivi la sécheresse ■ **he always brings trouble in his ~** il amène toujours des ennuis (dans son sillage) ■ **in the ~ of the storm** après l'orage.

◆ **wake up** ◇ *vi insep* **1.** [stop sleeping] se réveiller, s'éveiller ■ **~ up!** réveille-toi! ■ **they woke up to find themselves famous** du jour au lendemain, ils se sont retrouvés célèbres **2.** [become alert] se réveiller, prendre conscience ■ **~ up and get down to work!** mais enfin réveille-toi *OR* remue-toi *OR* secoue-toi et mets-toi au travail! ■ **it's time you woke up to the truth** il est temps que tu regardes la vérité en face.

◇ *vt sep* **1.** [rouse from sleep] réveiller, tirer *OR* sortir du sommeil **2.** [alert] réveiller, secouer ■ **the accident woke us up to the dangers of nuclear power** l'accident a attiré *OR* éveillé notre attention sur les dangers de l'énergie nucléaire.

wakeful ['weɪkful] *adj* **1.** [person - unable to sleep] qui ne dort pas, éveillé ; [- alert] vigilant **2.** [night, week] sans sommeil.

waken ['weɪkən] *lit* ◇ *vi* se réveiller, s'éveiller.

◇ *vt* réveiller, tirer *OR* sortir du sommeil.

waking ['weɪkɪŋ] ◇ *adj* [hours] de veille ■ **she spends her ~ hours reading** elle passe tout son temps à lire ■ **a ~ dream** une rêverie, une rêvasserie.

◇ *n* [state] (état *m* de) veille *f*.

Waldorf salad ['wɔːldɔːf-] *n salade composée de pommes, de céleri et de noix, assaisonnée avec de la mayonnaise.*

Wales [weɪlz] *pr n* pays *m* de Galles ■ **in ~** au pays de Galles.

walk [wɔːk] ◇ *vi* **1.** marcher ■ [go for a walk] se promener ■ **~, don't run!** ne cours pas! ■ **he ~ed along the beach** il marchait *OR* se promenait le long de la plage ■ **we ~ed down/up the street** nous avons descendu/monté la rue à pied ■ **he ~ed slowly towards the door** il s'est dirigé lentement vers la porte ■ **she ~ed back and forth** elle marchait de long en large, elle faisait les cent pas ■ **~ with me to the shop** accompagnez-moi au magasin ■ **he ~s in his sleep** il est somnambule ■ **he ~ed downstairs in his sleep** il a descendu l'escalier en dormant ■ **to ~ on one's hands** marcher sur les mains, faire l'arbre fourchu ■ **you have to ~ before you can run** *fig* il faut apprendre petit à petit ➊ **I'm ~ing on air!** je suis aux anges! ■ **he's ~ing tall** *US* il marche la tête haute

2. [as opposed to drive, ride] aller à pied ■ **did you ~ all the way?** avez-vous fait tout le chemin à pied?

◇ *vt* **1.** [cover on foot] faire à pied ■ **you can ~ it in 10 minutes** il faut 10 minutes (pour y aller) à pied ■ **to ~ the streets** [wander] se promener dans les rues ; [looking for something] arpenter les rues, battre le pavé ; [as prostitute] faire le trottoir

2. [escort] accompagner, marcher avec ■ **may I ~ you home?** puis-je vous raccompagner?

3. [take for walk - person] faire marcher ; [- dog] promener ; [- horse] conduire à pied ■ **she ~ed her mother round the garden** elle a fait faire un tour de jardin à sa mère ■ **they ~ed him forcibly to the door** ils l'ont dirigé de force vers la porte ■ **she ~ed the bike up the hill** elle a poussé le vélo dans la côte ➊ **she has ~ed me off my feet** *UK inf* elle m'a fait tellement marcher que je ne tiens plus debout.

◇ *n* **1.** [movement] : **she slowed to a ~** elle a ralenti et s'est mise à marcher ■ **they moved along at a brisk ~** ils marchaient d'un pas rapide

2. [stroll] promenade *f* ■ [long] randonnée *f* ■ **to go for** *OR* **to take a ~** aller se promener, faire une promenade *OR* un tour ■ **I take a 5 km ~ each day** je fais chaque jour une promenade de 5 km ■ **it's a long ~ to the office** ça fait loin pour aller à pied au bureau ■ **the station is a five-minute ~ from here** la gare est à cinq minutes de marche *OR* à cinq minutes à pied d'ici ■ **I took my mother for a ~** j'ai emmené ma mère en promenade *OR* faire un tour ■ **did you take the dog for a ~?** as-tu promené *OR* sorti le chien? ➊ **take a ~!** *US inf* dégage!

3. [gait] démarche *f*, façon *f* de marcher

4. [path] promenade *f* ■ [in garden] allée *f* ■ [in forest] sentier *m*, chemin *m* ■ **a coastal ~** un chemin côtier ■ **the front ~** *US* l'allée *f (de devant la maison)*

5. [occupation] : **I meet people from all ~s** *OR* **from every ~ of life** je rencontre des gens de tous milieux

6. *US* [sidewalk] trottoir *m*.

◆ **walk about** *vi insep UK* se promener, se balader.

◆ **walk across** ◇ *vi insep* traverser (à pied).

◇ *vt sep* faire traverser (à pied).

◆ **walk around** = **walk about**.

◆ **walk away** *vi insep* partir, s'en aller ■ **she ~ed away from the group** elle s'est éloignée du groupe, elle a quitté le groupe ■ **he ~ed away from the accident** il est sorti de l'accident indemne ■ **you can't just ~ away from the situation** tu ne peux pas te désintéresser comme ça de la situation.

◆ **walk away with** *vt insep* : **to ~ away with sthg** *liter* emporter qqch ; *fig* remporter *OR* gagner qqch haut la main ■ **she ~ed away with all the credit** c'est elle qui a reçu tous les honneurs.

◆ **walk back** ◇ *vi insep* [return] revenir *OR* retourner (à pied).

◇ *vt sep* raccompagner (à pied).

◆ **walk in** ◇ *vi insep* entrer ■ **we ~ed in on her as she was getting dressed** nous sommes entrés sans prévenir pendant qu'elle s'habillait.

◇ *vt sep* faire entrer.

◆ **walk into** *vt insep* **1.** [enter - house, room] entrer dans ; [- job] obtenir (sans problème) ; [- situation] se retrouver dans ; [- trap] tomber dans ■ **you ~ed right into that one!** *inf* tu t'es bien fait piéger!

2. [bump into - chair, wall] se cogner à, rentrer dans ; [- person] rentrer dans.

◆ **walk off** ◇ *vi insep* partir, s'en aller.

◇ *vt sep* [get rid of - headache] faire passer en marchant ; [- weight] perdre en faisant de la marche.

◆ **walk off with** *vt insep* : **to ~ off with sthg** [take] emporter qqch ; [steal] voler qqch ■ **he ~ed off with all the prizes** il a remporté *OR* gagné tous les prix (haut la main).

◆ **walk out** *vi insep* **1.** [go out] sortir ■ [leave] partir, s'en aller ■ **we ~ed out of the meeting** nous avons quitté la réunion *OR* nous sommes partis de la réunion (en signe de protestation)

2. [worker] se mettre en grève.

◆ **walk out on** *vt insep* [family, lover] quitter.

◆ **walk over** ◇ *vt insep* [bridge] traverser ■ **don't let them ~ all over you** *fig* ne vous laissez pas avoir, ne vous laissez pas marcher sur les pieds.

◇ *vi insep* aller ■ **the boss ~ed over to congratulate him** le patron s'est approché de lui pour le féliciter.

◆ **walk up** *vi insep* **1.** [go upstairs] monter

2. [come close] s'approcher.

walkabout ['wɔːkəˌbaut] *n* **1.** *UK* **to go on a ~** [actor, politician] prendre un bain de foule **2.** [of an Aborigine] *excursion périodique dans la brousse.*

walkaway ['wɔːkəˌweɪ] *n US inf* **the race was a ~ for him** il a gagné la course haut la main *OR* dans un fauteuil.

walker ['wɔːkəʳ] *n* **1.** [person - stroller] promeneur *m*, - euse *f*, marcheur *m*, - euse *f* ; [- in mountains] randonneur *m*, - euse *f* ■ SPORT marcheur *m*, - euse *f* ■ **she's a fast/slow ~** elle marche vite/lentement **2.** [apparatus - for babies] trotte-bébé *m* ; [- for invalids] déambulateur *m*.

walkie-talkie [ˌwɔːkɪ'tɔːkɪ] *n* (poste *m*) émetteur-récepteur *m* portatif, talkie-walkie *m*.

walk-in *adj* [safe, wardrobe] de plain-pied ■ **~ closet** *OR* **cupboard** [gen] débarras *m* ; [for clothes] dressing *m*.

walking ['wɔːkɪŋ] ◇ *n* **1.** [activity - gen] marche *f* (à pied), promenade *f*, promenades *fpl* ; [- hiking] randonnée *f* ■ SPORT marche *f* (athlétique) **2.** [in basketball] marcher *m*.

◇ *adj* [clothing, shoes] de marche ■ **is it within ~ distance?** est-ce qu'on peut y aller à pied? ■ **a ~ holiday in the Vosges** un séjour de randonnée dans les Vosges ■ **the ~ wounded** les blessés qui peuvent encore marcher ■ **he's a ~ dictionary** *OR* **encyclopedia** *hum* c'est un vrai dictionnaire ambulant.

walking frame *n* déambulateur *m*.

walking papers *npl* *US inf* **to hand** *OR* **to give sb their ~** [employee] renvoyer qqn, mettre *OR* flanquer qqn à la porte ; [lover] plaquer qqn ■ **to get one's ~** se faire mettre à la porte.

walking shoes *n* chaussures *fpl* de marche.

walking stick *n* [cane] canne *f*.

Walkman® ['wɔːkmən] (*pl* **Walkmans**) *n* baladeur *m* *offic*, Walkman® *m*.

walk-on ◇ *n* rôle *m* de figurant.
◇ *comp* : **~ part** rôle *m* de figurant.

walkout ['wɔːkaʊt] *n* [of members, spectators] départ *m* (en signe de protestation) ■ [of workers] grève *f* ■ **to stage a ~** [negotiators, students] partir (en signe de protestation) ; [workers] se mettre en grève.

walkover ['wɔːk,əʊvər] *n* **1.** *UK inf* [victory] victoire *f* dans un fauteuil ■ **the race was a ~ for the German team** l'équipe allemande a gagné la course haut la main *OR* dans un fauteuil **2.** [in horse racing] walk-over *m inv*.

walk-through *n* THEAT répétition *f*.

walk-up *US* ◇ *adj* [apartment] situé dans un immeuble sans ascenseur ■ [building] sans ascenseur.
◇ *n appartement ou bureau situé dans un immeuble sans ascenseur* ■ [building] *immeuble sans ascenseur*.

walkway ['wɔːkweɪ] *n* [path] sentier *m*, chemin *m* ■ [passage] passage *m* *OR* passerelle *f* *(pour piétons, entre deux bâtiments)*.

walky-talky [,wɔːkɪ'tɔːkɪ] (*pl* **walky-talkies**) = **walkie-talkie**.

wall [wɔːl] ◇ *n* **1.** [of building, room] mur *m* ■ [round field, garden] mur *m* de clôture ■ [round castle, city] murs *mpl*, murailles *fpl*, remparts *mpl* ■ **within the city ~s** dans les murs, dans la ville, intra-muros ■ **the Great Wall of China** la Grande Muraille de Chine ■ **a ~ of fire** une muraille de feu ■ **the prisoners went over the ~** les prisonniers ont fait le mur ■ **a ~ of silence** *fig* un mur de silence ➤ **to drive** *OR* **to send sb up the ~** *inf* rendre qqn fou *OR* dingue ■ **to go to the ~** *UK* [business] faire faillite ; [employee] perdre la partie ■ **I'll go up the ~ if I have to work with her** *inf* je vais devenir fou si je dois travailler avec elle ■ **~s have ears** les murs ont des oreilles **2.** [side - of box, cell, vein] paroi *f* ; [- of tyre] flanc *m* **3.** [of mountain] paroi *f*, face *f*.
◇ *vt* [garden, land] clôturer, entourer d'un mur ■ [city] fortifier.
◆ **wall in** *vt sep* [garden] clôturer, entourer d'un mur ■ **she felt ~ed in by social convention** *fig* elle se sentait prisonnière des convenances.
◆ **wall off** *vt sep* séparer par un mur *OR* par une cloison.
◆ **wall up** *vt sep* [door, window] murer, condamner ■ [body, treasure] emmurer.

wallaby ['wɒləbɪ] (*pl* **wallabies**) *n* wallaby *m*.

wall bars *npl* espalier *m* *(pour exercices)*.

wall bracket *n* support *m* mural.

wallchart ['wɔːltʃɑːt] *n* panneau *m* mural.

walled [wɔːld] *adj* [city] fortifié ■ [garden] clos.

wallet ['wɒlɪt] *n* portefeuille *m*.

wallflower ['wɔːl,flaʊər] *n* **1.** BOT giroflée *f* **2.** *inf* [person] : **I'm tired of being a ~** j'en ai assez de faire tapisserie.

wall game *n sorte de football pratiqué à Eton*.

wall hanging *n* tenture *f* murale.

wall lamp, wall light *n* applique *f* *(lampe)*.

Walloon [wɒ'luːn] ◇ *n* [person] Wallon *m*, - onne *f*.
◇ *adj* wallon.

wallop ['wɒləp] *inf* ◇ *vt* **1.** [hit - person] flanquer un coup à, cogner sur ; [- ball] taper sur, donner un grand coup dans **2.** [defeat] écraser, battre à plate couture.
◇ *n* **1.** [blow] beigne *f*, coup *m* ■ **he packs a real ~** il a du punch **2.** [impact] : **she fell down with a ~** et vlan! elle est tombée par terre.

walloping ['wɒləpɪŋ] *inf* ◇ *adj* énorme, phénoménal.
◇ *adv* vachement.
◇ *n* **1.** [beating] raclée *f*, rossée *f* **2.** [defeat] : **they gave our team a ~** ils ont écrasé notre équipe, ils ont battu notre équipe à plate couture.

wallow ['wɒləʊ] ◇ *vi* **1.** [roll about] se vautrer, se rouler **2.** [indulge] se vautrer, se complaire ■ **to ~ in misery** se complaire dans la tristesse ■ **to ~ in self-pity** s'apitoyer sur soi-même.
◇ *n* **1.** [mud] boue *f*, bourbe *f* ■ [place] mare *f* bourbeuse **2.** *inf* [act of wallowing] : **to have a good ~** [in a bath] prendre un bon bain ; [in self-pity] s'apitoyer sur soi-même.

wallpaper ['wɔːl,peɪpər] ◇ *n* papier *m* peint ■ **he downloaded a new ~** COMPUT il a téléchargé un nouveau papier-peint.
◇ *vt* tapisser (de papier peint).

wall socket *n* prise *f* murale.

Wall Street *pr n* FIN Wall Street ■ **the ~ Crash** le krach de Wall Street.

WALL STREET

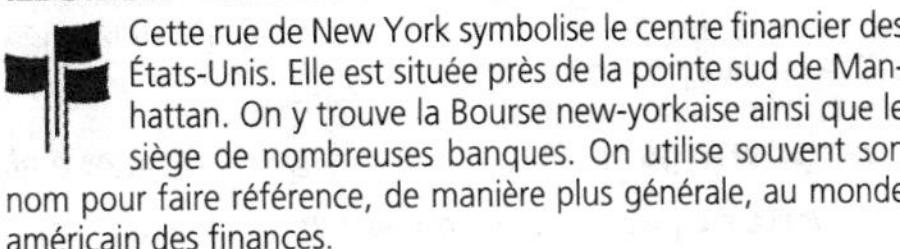

Cette rue de New York symbolise le centre financier des États-Unis. Elle est située près de la pointe sud de Manhattan. On y trouve la Bourse new-yorkaise ainsi que le siège de nombreuses banques. On utilise souvent son nom pour faire référence, de manière plus générale, au monde américain des finances.

THE WALL STREET CRASH

Krach financier à la Bourse de New York, le 24 octobre 1929 (« Jeudi noir »). Il entraîna la ruine de plusieurs milliers d'Américains, acculant certains d'entre eux au suicide. Cet événement est considéré comme le point de départ de la crise économique qu'allaient vivre les États-Unis pendant dix ans (« la grande dépression »).

wall-to-wall *adj* : **~ carpet** *OR* **carpeting** moquette *f* ■ **~ sound** son *m* enveloppant.

wall unit *n* élément *m* mural.

wally ['wɒlɪ] (*pl* **wallies**) *n* *UK inf* imbécile *mf*, andouille *mf*.

walnut ['wɔːlnʌt] ◇ *n* [tree, wood] noyer *m* ■ [fruit] noix *f*.
◇ *comp* [furniture] de *OR* en noyer ■ [oil] de noix ■ [cake] aux noix.

walrus ['wɔːlrəs] (*pl inv OR pl* **walruses**) *n* morse *m* ■ **~ moustache** moustache *f* à la gauloise.

Walter Mitty [wɒltə'mɪtɪ] *adj* : **to lead a ~ existence** vivre dans un monde imaginaire ■ **a ~ character** un rêveur.

waltz [wɔːls] ◇ *n* valse *f*.
◇ *vi* **1.** [dancer] valser, danser une valse **2.** [move] danser ■ **she ~ed in/out of his office** [jauntily] elle est entrée dans/sortie de son bureau d'un pas joyeux ; [brazenly] elle est entrée dans/sortie de son bureau avec effronterie ■ **he ~ed right up to the boss** il s'est approché du patron sans hésitation ■ **to ~ off** partir, s'en aller ■ **they ~ed off with first prize** ils ont remporté le premier prix haut la main.
◇ *vt* **1.** [dance] valser avec, faire valser **2.** [propel] pousser, propulser.

Walworth Road ['wɒlwəθ-] *pr n rue de Londres où se trouve le siège du parti travailliste*.

wan [wɒn] (*comp* **wanner**, *superl* **wannest**) *adj* [person - pale] pâle, blême, blafard ; [- sad] triste ■ [smile] pâle, faible ■ [light, star] pâle.

WAN [wæn] *n* = **wide area network**.

wand [wɒnd] *n* [of fairy, magician] baguette *f* (magique).

wander ['wɒndəʳ] ◇ *vi* **1.** [meander - person] errer, flâner ; [- stream] serpenter, faire des méandres ■ **she ~ed into a café** elle est entrée dans un café d'un pas nonchalant ■ **her eyes ~ed over the crowd** elle a promené son regard sur la foule **2.** [stray - person] s'égarer ■ **he's ~ed off somewhere** il est parti mais il n'en est pas loin ■ **the tourists ~ed into the red light district** les touristes se sont retrouvés par hasard dans le quartier chaud ■ **don't ~ off the path** ne vous écartez pas du chemin **3.** [mind, thoughts] vagabonder, errer ■ **he ~ed off the topic** il s'est écarté du sujet ■ **her attention began to ~** elle commença à être de moins en moins attentive ■ **I can't concentrate, my mind keeps ~ing** je ne peux pas me concentrer, je suis trop distrait ■ **my mind ~ed back to when we first met** mes pensées se sont reportées à l'époque où nous nous sommes connus **4.** [become confused] divaguer, déraisonner.
◇ *vt* errer dans, parcourir (au hasard) ■ **the nomads ~ the desert** les nomades parcourent le désert.
◇ *n* promenade *f*, tour *m* ■ **we went for a ~ round the town** nous sommes allés faire un tour dans la ville.
◆ **wander about** *UK*, **wander around** *vi insep* [without destination] errer, aller sans but ■ [without hurrying] flâner, aller sans se presser.

wanderer ['wɒndərəʳ] *n* vagabond *m*, - e *f* ■ **she's a bit of a ~** *fig* elle n'aime pas trop se fixer.

wandering ['wɒndərɪŋ] ◇ *adj* **1.** [roaming - person] errant, vagabond ; [- tribe] nomade ; [- stream] qui serpente, qui fait des méandres ■ **~ minstrels** ménestrels *mpl* ■ **the Wandering Jew** le Juif errant **2.** [distracted - mind, thoughts, attention] distrait, vagabond **3.** [confused - mind, person] qui divague, qui délire ; [- thoughts] incohérent.
◇ *n* **1.** [trip] = **wanderings 2.** [of mind] délire *m*.
◆ **wanderings** *npl* [trip] vagabondage *m*, voyages *mpl*.

wanderlust ['wɒndəlʌst] *n* envie *f* de voyager.

Wandsworth Prison ['wɒnzwəθ-] *pr n la plus grande prison de Grande-Bretagne.*

wane [weɪn] ◇ *vi* [moon] décroître, décliner ■ [interest, power] diminuer ■ [civilization, empire] décliner, être en déclin.
◇ *n* : **to be on the ~** [moon] décroître, décliner ; [interest, power] diminuer ; [civilization, empire] décliner, être en déclin.

wangle ['wæŋgl] *vt inf* [obtain - through cleverness] se débrouiller pour avoir ; [- through devious means] obtenir par subterfuge, carotter ■ **can you ~ me an invitation?** est-ce que tu peux m'avoir *OR* me dégotter une invitation? ■ **he ~d his way into the job** c'est par combine qu'il a décroché le poste ■ **they ~d their way out of paying the fine** ils se sont débrouillés pour ne pas payer l'amende.

waning ['weɪnɪŋ] ◇ *n* [of moon] décroissement *m* ■ [of interest, power] diminution *f* ■ [of empire] déclin *m*.
◇ *adj* [moon] décroissant, à son déclin ■ [interest, power] qui diminue ■ [empire] sur son déclin, en déclin.

wank▲ [wæŋk] *UK* ◇ *vi* se branler▲.
◇ *n* branlette▲ *f* ■ **to have a ~** se faire une branlette▲.

wanker▲ ['wæŋkəʳ] *n UK* branleur▲ *m*.

wanly ['wɒnlɪ] *adv* **1.** [answer, smile] faiblement, tristement **2.** [shine] faiblement, avec une pâle *OR* faible clarté.

wanna△ ['wɒnə] **1.** = **want to 2.** = **want a**.

wannabe ['wɒnə,biː] *n inf se dit de quelqu'un qui veut être ce qu'il ne peut pas être* ■ **a Michael Jackson ~** un clone de Michael Jackson.

want [wɒnt] ◇ *vt* **1.** [expressing a wish or desire] vouloir, désirer ■ **to ~ sthg badly** avoir très envie de qqch ■ **what do you ~ now?** qu'est-ce que tu veux encore? ■ **all he ~s is to go to bed** tout ce qu'il veut, c'est aller se coucher ■ **to ~ to do sthg** avoir envie de *OR* vouloir faire qqch ■ **she doesn't ~ to** elle n'en a pas envie ■ **he doesn't ~ to know** il ne veut rien savoir ■ **I ~ you to wait here** je veux que tu attendes ici ■ **what do you ~ with her?** qu'est-ce que tu lui veux? ■ **she doesn't ~ much!** *iron* elle n'est pas difficile, elle au moins ■ **now I've got you where I ~ you!** *fig* je te tiens!
2. [desire sexually] désirer, avoir envie de
3. [require to be present] demander, vouloir voir ■ **someone ~s you** *OR* **you're ~ed on the phone** quelqu'un vous demande au téléphone ■ **where do you ~ this wardrobe?** où voulez-vous qu'on mette cette armoire? ■ **you won't be ~ed this afternoon** on n'aura pas besoin de vous cet après-midi ■ **go away, you're not ~ed here** va-t'en, tu n'es pas le bienvenu ici ■ **I know when I'm not ~ed** je sais quand je suis de trop
4. [hunt, look for] chercher, rechercher ■ **to be ~ed by the police** être recherché par la police
5. [need - subj: person] avoir besoin de ; [- subj: task, thing] avoir besoin de, nécessiter ■ **do you have everything you ~?** avez-vous tout ce qu'il vous faut? ■ **I have more than I ~** j'en ai plus qu'il n'en faut ■ **this coat ~s cleaning very badly** ce manteau a besoin d'un bon nettoyage ■ **there are still a couple of things that ~ doing** il y a encore quelques petites choses à faire *OR* qu'il faut faire ■ **what do you ~ with a car that size?** qu'allez-vous faire d'une voiture de cette taille?
6. *inf* [ought] : **you ~ to see a doctor about that leg** vous devez montrer *OR* il faut que vous montriez cette jambe à un médecin ■ **she ~s to watch out, the boss is looking for her** elle devrait faire attention, le patron la cherche
7. *lit* [lack - food, shelter] manquer de.
◇ *vi inf* **the cat ~s in/out** le chat veut entrer/sortir ▌*fig* **he ~s in (on the deal)** il veut une part du gâteau ■ **I ~ out!** je ne suis plus de la partie!
◇ *n* **1.** [desire, wish] désir *m*, envie *f*
2. [requirement] besoin *m* ■ **to have few ~s** avoir peu de besoins, avoir besoin de peu
3. [lack] manque *m* ■ **there's certainly no ~ of goodwill** ce ne sont certainement pas les bonnes volontés qui manquent ■ **to be in ~ of sthg** avoir besoin de qqch
4. [poverty] misère *f*, besoin *m* ■ **to be in ~** être dans le besoin *OR* dans la misère.
◆ **for want of** *prep phr* faute de ■ **I'll take this novel for ~ of anything better** faute de mieux je vais prendre ce roman ■ **for ~ of anything better to do, she went for a walk** n'ayant rien de mieux à faire, elle est allée se promener ■ **if we failed, it wasn't for ~ of trying** nous avons échoué mais ce n'est pas faute d'avoir essayé.
◆ **want for** *vt insep* manquer de ■ **he ~s for nothing** il ne manque de rien.

want ad *n* petite annonce *f*.

wanted ['wɒntɪd] *adj* **1.** [in advertisements] : **'carpenter/cook ~'** 'on recherche (un) charpentier/(un) cuisinier' ■ **'accommodation ~'** 'cherche appartement' **2.** [murderer, thief] recherché ■ **~ notice** avis *m* de recherche.

wanting ['wɒntɪŋ] *adj* **1.** [inadequate] : **to be found ~** [person] ne pas convenir, ne pas faire l'affaire ; [machine] ne pas convenir, ne pas être au point **2.** [lacking] manquant ■ **to be ~ in sthg** manquer de qqch **3.** *euph* [weak-minded] simple d'esprit.

wanton ['wɒntən] ◇ *adj* **1.** [malicious - action, cruelty] gratuit, injustifié ; [- destroyer] vicieux **2.** *fml* [immoral - behaviour, thoughts] licencieux ; [- person] dévergondé.
◇ *n lit* [man] dévergondé *m* ■ [woman] dévergondée *f*, femme *f* légère.

wantonly ['wɒntənlɪ] *adv* **1.** [maliciously] gratuitement, sans justification **2.** *fml* [immorally] licencieusement.

WAP [wæp] (*abbrev of* **wireless application protocol**) *n* TELEC WAP *m* ■ **~ phone** téléphone *m* WAP.

Wapping ['wɒpɪŋ] *pr n quartier de l'Est de Londres où se trouvent les sièges de plusieurs journaux détenus par Rupert Murdoch.*

war [wɔːʳ] (*pret & pp* **warred**, *cont* **warring**) ◇ *n* **1.** [armed conflict] guerre *f* ■ **to be at ~/to go to ~ with sb** être en guerre/entrer en guerre avec qqn ■ **the Allies waged ~ against** *OR* **on the Axis** les Alliés ont fait la guerre aux puissances de l'Axe ■ **he fought in the ~** il a fait la guerre ■ **the troops went off to ~** les troupes sont parties pour *OR* sont allées à la guerre ■ **you've been in the ~s!** *inf hum* on dirait que tu reviens de la guerre!, tu t'es bien arrangé! ■ **the period between the two (World) Wars** l'entre-deux-guerres *m inv* ➲ **~ of attrition** guerre d'usure ■ **~ museum** musée *m* de guerre ■ **the American War of Independence** la guerre d'Indépendance américaine ■ **the War between the States, the War of Secession** la

guerre de Sécession ■ **the Wars of the Roses** la guerre des Deux-Roses ■ **'War and Peace'** ***Tolstoy*** 'Guerre et paix' ■ **'The War of the Worlds'** ***Wells*** 'la Guerre des mondes' **2.** [conflict, struggle] guerre *f*, lutte *f* ■ **to declare** *OR* **to wage ~ on sthg** partir en guerre contre *OR* déclarer la guerre à qqch ■ **the ~ against crime/drugs** la lutte contre le crime/la drogue.
◇ *comp* [criminal, diary, film, hero, pension, wound, zone] de guerre ■ **~ victims** victimes *mpl* de guerre ■ **during the ~ years** pendant la guerre ■ **the ~ effort** l'effort *m* de guerre ■ **~ record** passé *m* militaire ■ **he has a good ~ record** il s'est conduit honorablement pendant la guerre.
◇ *vi* faire la guerre ■ **to ~ with sb** faire la guerre à qqn.

THE WARS OF THE ROSES

Guerres qui, au XVe siècle, opposèrent les deux familles prétendant au trône d'Angleterre : la maison d'York, dont l'emblème était une rose blanche, et la maison de Lancastre, représentée par une rose rouge. Elles prirent fin en 1485 par la victoire d'un Lancastre, le futur Henri VII, qui réconcilia les deux familles en épousant Élisabeth d'York.

THE WAR OF THE WORLDS

Pièce radiophonique adaptée du roman de H.G. Wells et mise en scène par Orson Welles, diffusée le 30 octobre 1938 par une radio new-yorkaise à l'occasion de ***Halloween***. La description très réaliste de l'arrivée sur terre de martiens fut prise au sérieux par les auditeurs, ce qui provoqua une panique générale: désertion des villes, embouteillages gigantesques, mais aussi crises d'hystérie, crises cardiaques et suicides.

War. = Warks.

war baby *n enfant né pendant la guerre.*

warble ['wɔ:bl] ◇ *vi & vt* [subj: bird] gazouiller ■ [subj: person] chanter (avec des trilles).
◇ *n* gazouillis *m*, gazouillement *m*.

warbler ['wɔ:blər] *n* fauvette *f*, pouillot *m*.

warbling ['wɔ:blɪŋ] *n* gazouillis *m*, gazouillement *m*.

war bond *n* titre *m* d'emprunt de guerre *(issu pendant la Deuxième Guerre mondiale)*.

war bride *n* mariée *f* de la guerre.

war cabinet *n* cabinet *m* de guerre.

war chest *n liter* caisse *f* spéciale *(affectée à une guerre)* ■ ***fig*** caisse *f* spéciale *(d'un parti politique, d'hommes d'affaires etc)*.

war clouds *npl* nuages *mpl OR* signes *mpl* précurseurs de guerre ■ **the ~ are gathering** la guerre menace.

war correspondent *n* correspondant *m*, -e *f* de guerre.

war crime *n* crime *m* de guerre.

war cry *n* cri *m* de guerre.

ward [wɔ:d] *n* **1.** [of hospital - room] salle *f* ; [- section] pavillon *m* ■ [of prison] quartier *m* **2.** POL [district] circonscription *f* électorale **3.** LAW [person] pupille *mf* ■ [guardianship] tutelle *f* ■ **she was placed in ~** elle a été placée sous tutelle judiciaire ▶ **~ of court** pupille *mf* sous tutelle judiciaire.
◆ **ward off** *vt sep* [danger, disease] éviter ■ [blow] parer, éviter.

war dance *n* danse *f* de guerre *OR* guerrière.

warden ['wɔ:dn] *n* **1.** [director - of building, institution] directeur *m*, -trice *f* ■ *US* [- of prison] directeur *m*, -trice *f* de prison **2.** [public official - of fortress, town] gouverneur *m* ; [- of park, reserve] gardien *m*, -enne *f* **3.** *UK* UNIV portier *m*.

warder ['wɔ:dər] *n UK* [guard] gardien *m OR* surveillant *m* (de prison).

wardress ['wɔ:drɪs] *n UK* gardienne *f OR* surveillante *f* (de prison).

wardrobe ['wɔ:drəʊb] *n* **1.** [cupboard] armoire *f*, penderie *f* **2.** [clothing] garde-robe *f* ■ THEAT costumes *mpl* ■ **Peter Taylor's ~ by...** CIN & THEAT Peter Taylor est habillé par..., les costumes de Peter Taylor sont de chez...

wardrobe mistress *n* costumière *f*.

wardroom ['wɔ:drum] *n* [quarters] quartiers *mpl* des officiers *(excepté le capitaine)* ■ [officers] officiers *mpl (excepté le capitaine)*.

wardship ['wɔ:dʃɪp] *n* tutelle *f*.

warehouse ◇ *n* [['weəhaʊs], *pl* [-haʊzɪz]] entrepôt *m*, magasin *m*.
◇ *vt* ['weəhaʊz] entreposer, emmagasiner.

warehouseman ['weəhaʊsmən] (*pl* **warehousemen** [-mən]) *n* magasinier *m*.

wares [weəz] *npl* marchandises *fpl*.

warfare ['wɔ:feər] *n* MIL guerre *f* ■ ***fig*** lutte *f*, guerre *f* ■ **class ~** lutte des classes ■ **economic ~** guerre économique.

war game *n (usu pl)* **1.** MIL [simulated battle with maps] kriegspiel *m*, wargame *m* ■ [manoeuvres] manœuvres *fpl* militaires **2.** GAMES wargame *m*.

war grave *n tombeau d'un soldat tombé au champ d'honneur.*

warhead ['wɔ:hed] *n* ogive *f* ■ **nuclear ~** ogive *f OR* tête *f* nucléaire.

warhorse ['wɔ:hɔ:s] *n* [horse] cheval *m* de bataille ■ ***inf fig*** [person] dur *m*, - e *f* à cuire ■ **he's an old ~ of the party** c'est un vétéran du parti.

warily ['weərəlɪ] *adv* [carefully] prudemment, avec prudence *OR* circonspection ■ [distrustfully] avec méfiance.

wariness ['weərɪnɪs] *n* [caution] prudence *f*, circonspection *f* ■ [distrust] méfiance *f*.

Warks *written abbr of* **Warwickshire**.

warlike ['wɔ:laɪk] *adj* guerrier, belliqueux.

warlock ['wɔ:lɒk] *n* sorcier *m*.

warlord ['wɔ:lɔ:d] *n* seigneur *m* de la guerre.

warm [wɔ:m] ◇ *adj* **1.** [moderately hot] chaud ■ **a ~ oven** un four moyen ■ **I can't wait for the ~ weather** j'ai hâte qu'il fasse chaud ■ **will you keep dinner ~ for me?** peux-tu me garder le dîner au chaud? ■ **does that coat keep you ~?** est-ce que ce manteau te tient chaud? ■ **it's a difficult house to keep ~** c'est une maison difficile à chauffer ■ **are you ~ enough?** avez-vous assez chaud? ■ **I can't seem to get ~** je n'arrive pas à me réchauffer ■ **the room is too ~** il fait trop chaud *OR* on étouffe dans cette pièce ■ **the bedroom was nice and ~** il faisait bon *OR* agréablement chaud dans la chambre ▶ **am I right? – you're getting ~er!** est-ce que j'y suis? – tu chauffes! **2.** [clothing] chaud, qui tient chaud **3.** [work] qui donne chaud **4.** [affectionate - feelings] chaud, chaleureux ; [- personality] chaleureux ■ **she has a ~ relationship with her mother** elle a une relation très affectueuse avec sa mère ■ **give my ~est wishes to your wife** toutes mes amitiés à votre femme **5.** [hearty - greeting, welcome] chaleureux, cordial ; [- thanks] vif ; [- admirer, support] ardent, enthousiaste ; [- applause] chaleureux, enthousiaste **6.** [colour, sound] chaud ■ [voice] chaud, chaleureux **7.** [scent, trail] récent.
◇ *vt* **1.** [heat - person, room] réchauffer ; [- food] (faire) chauffer ■ **she ~ed her hands by the fire** elle s'est réchauffé les mains au-dessus du feu ▶ **the sight was enough to ~ the cockles of your heart!** c'était un spectacle à vous chauffer *OR* réchauffer *OR* réjouir le cœur! **2.** [reheat] (faire) réchauffer.
◇ *vi* : **she ~ed to the new neighbours** elle s'est prise de sympathie pour les nouveaux voisins ■ **you'll soon ~ to the idea** tu verras, cette idée finira par te plaire ■ **the speaker began to ~ to his subject** le conférencier s'est laissé entraîner par son sujet.
◇ *n inf* **come into the ~** viens au chaud *OR* où il fait chaud.
◆ **warm over** *vt sep US* [food] (faire) réchauffer ■ ***pej*** [idea] ressasser.

◆ **warm through** *vt sep* (faire) réchauffer complètement.

◆ **warm up** ◇ *vt sep* **1.** [heat - person, room] réchauffer ; [- food] (faire) chauffer ; [- engine, machine] faire chauffer **2.** [reheat] (faire) réchauffer **3.** [animate - audience] mettre en train, chauffer.
◇ *vi insep* **1.** [become hotter - person] se chauffer, se réchauffer ; [- room, engine, food] se réchauffer ; [- weather] devenir plus chaud, se réchauffer **2.** [get ready - athlete, comedian] s'échauffer, se mettre en train ; [- audience] commencer à s'animer **3.** [debate, discussion] s'animer.

war machine *n* machine *f* de guerre.

warm-blooded [-'blʌdɪd] *adj* ZOOL à sang chaud ■ *fig* [ardent] ardent, qui a le sang chaud.

war memorial *n* monument *m* aux morts.

warm-hearted [-'hɑːtɪd] *adj* [kindly] chaleureux, bon ■ [generous] généreux.

warming pan ['wɔːmɪŋ-] *n* bassinoire *f*.

warmly ['wɔːmlɪ] *adv* **1.** [dress] chaudement ■ **the sun shone ~** le soleil chauffait **2.** [greet, smile, welcome] chaleureusement, chaudement ■ [recommend, thank] vivement, chaudement ■ [support] avec enthousiasme, ardemment ■ [applaud] avec enthousiasme, chaleureusement.

warmonger ['wɔːˌmʌŋgəʳ] *n* belliciste *mf*.

warmongering ['wɔːˌmʌŋgərɪŋ] ◇ *n (U)* [activities] activités *fpl* bellicistes ■ [attitude] bellicisme *m* ■ [propaganda] propagande *f* belliciste.
◇ *adj* belliciste.

warmth [wɔːmθ] *n* [of temperature] chaleur *f* ■ [of greeting, welcome] chaleur *f*, cordialité *f* ■ [of recommendation, thanks] chaleur *f*, vivacité *f* ■ [of applause, support] enthousiasme *m* ■ [of colour] chaleur *f*.

warm-up ◇ *n* [gen] préparation *f*, préparations *fpl* ■ [of athlete, singer] échauffement *m* ■ [of audience] mise *f* en train.
◇ *comp* : **~ exercises** exercices *mpl* d'échauffement.

warmups ['wɔːmʌps] *npl* US survêtement *m*.

warn [wɔːn] *vt* **1.** [inform] avertir, prévenir ■ **I ~ed them of the danger** je les ai avertis OR prévenus du danger ■ **~ the police!** alertez la police! ■ **don't say I didn't ~ you!** je t'aurai prévenu! **2.** [advise] conseiller, recommander ■ **he ~ed her about** OR **against travelling at night, he ~ed her not to travel at night** il lui a déconseillé de voyager la nuit, il l'a mise en garde contre les voyages de nuit.

◆ **warn off** *vt sep* décourager ■ **the doctor has ~ed him off alcohol** le médecin lui a vivement déconseillé l'alcool.

warning ['wɔːnɪŋ] ◇ *n* **1.** [caution, notice] avertissement *m* ■ **let that be a ~ to you** que cela vous serve d'avertissement ■ **thanks for the ~** merci de m'avoir prévenu OR m'avoir averti ■ **the boss visited the office without (any) ~** le patron est venu visiter le bureau inopinément OR à l'improviste ■ **he left without any ~** il est parti sans prévenir ■ **they gave us advance ~ of the meeting** ils nous ont prévenus de la réunion ■ **to issue a ~ against sthg** mettre qqn en garde contre qqch **2.** [alarm, signal] alerte *f*, alarme *f* **3.** [advice] conseil *m* ■ **he gave them a stern ~ about the dangers of smoking** il les a sévèrement mis en garde contre les dangers du tabac.
◇ *adj* d'avertissement ■ **they fired a ~ shot** [gen - MIL] ils ont tiré une fois en guise d'avertissement ; NAUT ils ont tiré un coup de semonce ➊ **~ light** voyant *m* (avertisseur), avertisseur *m* lumineux ■ **~ notice** avis *m*, avertissement *m* ■ **~ sign** panneau *m* avertisseur ■ **~ signal** [gen] signal *m* d'alarme OR d'alerte ; AUT signal *m* de détresse ■ **~ triangle** UK AUT triangle *m* de signalisation.

War Office *n ancien nom du ministère de la Défense britannique.*

War On Want *pr n association caritative britannique luttant pour les pays défavorisés.*

warp [wɔːp] ◇ *vt* **1.** [wood] gauchir, voiler ■ [metal, plastic] voiler **2.** *fig* [character, mind] pervertir ■ [thinking] fausser, pervertir.
◇ *vi* [wood] gauchir, se voiler ■ [metal, plastic] se voiler.
◇ *n* **1.** [fault - in wood] gauchissement *m*, voilure *f* ; [- in metal, plastic] voilure *f* **2.** TEX [of yarn] chaîne *f*.

war paint *n* [of Indian] peinture *f* de guerre ■ *fig & hum* [make-up] peinture *f* de guerre *hum*.

warpath ['wɔːpɑːθ] *n* : **to be on the ~** *liter* être sur le sentier de la guerre ■ **be careful, the boss is on the ~** *fig* fais attention, le patron est d'une humeur massacrante.

warped [wɔːpt] *adj* **1.** [wood] gauchi, voilé ■ [metal, plastic] voilé **2.** *fig* [character, person] perverti ■ [thinking, view] faux, fausse *f*, perverti ■ **you've got a ~ mind!, your mind is ~ !** tu as l'esprit tordu! ■ **what a ~ sense of humour!** quel humour morbide!

warplane ['wɔːpleɪn] *n* avion *m* de guerre.

warrant ['wɒrənt] ◇ *n* **1.** LAW [written order] mandat *m* ■ **there's a ~ (out) for his arrest** il y a un mandat d'arrêt contre lui **2.** COMM & FIN [for payment] bon *m* ■ [guarantee] garantie *f* **3.** MIL brevet *m*.
◇ *vt* **1.** [justify] justifier ■ **the situation ~s a new approach** la situation demande que l'on s'y prenne autrement **2.** [declare with certainty] assurer, certifier ■ **I'll ~ (you) that's the last we see of her** c'est la dernière fois qu'on la voit, je vous le garantie.

warrant officer *n* adjudant *m*, -e *f (auxiliaire d'un officier).*

warranty ['wɒrəntɪ] (*pl* **warranties**) *n* **1.** [guarantee] garantie *f* **2.** LAW garantie *f*.

warren ['wɒrən] *n* **1.** [of rabbit] terriers *mpl*, garenne *f* **2.** *fig* [maze of passageways] labyrinthe *m*, dédale *m*.

warring ['wɔːrɪŋ] *adj* [nations, tribes] en guerre ■ *fig* [beliefs] en conflit ■ [interests] contradictoire, contraire.

warrior ['wɒrɪəʳ] *n* guerrier *m*, - ère *f*.

Warsaw ['wɔːsɔː] *pr n* Varsovie.

Warsaw Pact *pr n* : **the ~** le pacte de Varsovie ■ **~ countries** pays *mpl* (membres) du pacte de Varsovie.

warship ['wɔːʃɪp] *n* navire *m* OR bâtiment *m* de guerre.

wart [wɔːt] *n* **1.** MED verrue *f* ■ **she described her family, ~s and all** *fig* elle a fait un portrait sans complaisance de sa famille **2.** BOT excroissance *f*.

wart hog *n* phacochère *m*.

wartime ['wɔːtaɪm] ◇ *n* période *f* de guerre ■ **in ~** en temps de guerre.
◇ *comp* de guerre.

war-torn *adj* déchiré par la guerre.

war-weary *adj* las de la guerre.

war widow *n* veuve *f* de guerre.

wary ['weərɪ] (*comp* **warier**, *superl* **wariest**) *adj* [prudent - person] prudent, sur ses gardes ; [- look] prudent ; [- smile] hésitant ■ [distrustful] méfiant ■ **I'm ~ about promoting these ideas** j'hésite à promouvoir ces idées ■ **the people were ~ of the new regime** les gens se méfiaient du nouveau régime.

was [*weak form* [wəz], *strong form* [wɒz]] *pt* ▷ **be**.

wasabi [wə'sɑːbɪ] *n* wasabi *m*.

wash [wɒʃ] ◇ *vt* **1.** [clean] laver ■ **to ~ o.s.** [person] se laver, faire sa toilette ; [cat, dog] faire sa toilette ■ **go and ~ your hands** va te laver les mains ■ **she ~ed her hair** elle s'est lavé la tête OR les cheveux ■ **to ~ the dishes** faire OR laver la vaisselle ■ **to ~ clothes** faire la lessive ➊ **I ~ my hands of the whole affair** je me lave les mains de toute cette histoire ■ **she ~ed her hands of him** elle s'est désintéressée de lui
2. [subj: current, river, waves - move over] baigner ; [- carry away] emporter, entraîner ■ **the body was ~ed ashore** le cadavre s'est échoué OR a été rejeté sur la côte ■ **the crew was ~ed overboard** l'équipage a été emporté par une vague
3. [coat, cover] badigeonner
4. MIN [gold, ore] laver.
◇ *vi* **1.** [to clean oneself - person] se laver, faire sa toilette

2. [be washable] se laver, être lavable ⮕ **his story just doesn't ~ with me** *UK inf* son histoire ne marche pas avec moi, il ne me fera pas avaler cette histoire.
◇ *n* **1.** [act of cleaning] nettoyage *m* ■ **this floor needs a good ~** ce plancher a bien besoin d'être lavé *OR* nettoyé ■ **your hair needs a ~** il faut que tu te laves la tête ■ **I gave the car a ~** j'ai lavé la voiture ■ **he's having a ~** il se lave, il fait sa toilette ■ **I could do with a quick ~ and brush-up** j'aimerais faire un brin de toilette *OR* me débarbouiller
2. [clothes to be washed] lessive *f*, linge *m* sale ■ **your shirt is in the ~** [laundry basket] ta chemise est au (linge) sale ; [machine] ta chemise est à la lessive ■ **the stain came out in the ~** la tache est partie au lavage ⮕ **it'll all come out in the ~** *UK* [become known] ça finira par se savoir ; [turn out for the best] tout cela finira par s'arranger
3. [movement of water - caused by current] remous *m* ; [- caused by ship] sillage *m*, remous *m* ■ [sound of water] clapotis *m*
4. [of paint] badigeon *m*
5. MED [lotion] solution *f*
6. ART : **~ (drawing)** (dessin *m* au) lavis *m*.
◇ *adj* **US** lavable.
◆ **wash away** *vt sep* [carry off - boat, bridge, house] emporter ; [- river bank, soil] éroder ■ **the rain ~ed away the road** la route s'est effondrée sous l'action de la pluie ■ **to ~ one's sins away** *fig* laver ses péchés.
◆ **wash down** *vt sep* **1.** [clean] laver (à grande eau)
2. [food] arroser ■ [tablet] faire descendre ■ **roast beef ~ed down with Burgundy wine** rosbif arrosé d'un bourgogne.
◆ **wash off** ◇ *vt sep* [remove - with soap] enlever *OR* faire partir au lavage ; [- with water] enlever *OR* faire partir à l'eau.
◇ *vi insep* [disappear - with soap] s'en aller *OR* partir au lavage ; [- with water] s'en aller *OR* partir à l'eau.
◆ **wash out** ◇ *vt sep* **1.** [remove - with soap] enlever *OR* faire partir au lavage ; [- with water] enlever *OR* faire partir à l'eau
2. [clean] laver
3. [carry away - bridge] emporter ; [- road] dégrader
4. [cancel, prevent] : **the game was ~ed out** le match a été annulé à cause de la pluie.
◇ *vi insep* = **wash off**.
◆ **wash up** ◇ *vi insep* **1.** *UK* [wash dishes] faire *OR* laver la vaisselle
2. *US* [wash oneself] se laver, faire sa toilette.
◇ *vt sep* **1.** *UK* [glass, dish] laver ■ **whose turn is it to ~ up the dishes?** à qui le tour de faire *OR* laver la vaisselle?
2. [subj: sea] rejeter ■ **several dolphins were ~ed up on shore** plusieurs dauphins se sont échoués sur la côte.

washable ['wɒʃəbl] *adj* lavable, lessivable.

wash-and-wear *adj* qui ne nécessite aucun repassage.

washbag ['wɒʃ,bæg] *n* trousse *f* de toilette.

washbasin ['wɒʃ,beɪsn] *n* [basin] cuvette *f*, bassine *f* ■ [sink] lavabo *m*.

washboard ['wɒʃ,bɔːd] *n* planche *f* à laver.

washbowl ['wɒʃbəʊl] *US* = **washbasin**.

washcloth ['wɒʃ,klɒθ] *n* [for dishes] lavette *f* ■ *US* [face flannel] ≃ gant *m* de toilette.

washday ['wɒʃ,deɪ] *n* jour *m* de lessive.

washed-out [,wɒʃt-] *adj* **1.** [faded - colour] délavé ; [- curtain, jeans] décoloré, délavé **2.** *inf* [exhausted] épuisé, lessivé.

washed-up *adj inf* fichu.

washer ['wɒʃəʳ] *n* **1.** CONSTR joint *m*, rondelle *f* ■ [in tap] joint *m* **2.** [washing machine] machine *f* à laver, lave-linge *m inv*.

washer-dryer *n* machine *f* à laver séchante.

washer-up (*pl* **washers-up**) *n UK inf* [gen] laveur *m*, - euse *f* de vaisselle ■ [in restaurant] plongeur *m*, - euse *f*.

washerwoman ['wɒʃə,wʊmən] (*pl* **washerwomen** [-,wɪmɪn]) *n* blanchisseuse *f*.

washhouse ['wɒʃhaʊs] (*pl* [-haʊzɪz]) *n* lavoir *m*.

washing ['wɒʃɪŋ] *n* **1.** [act - of car, floors] lavage *m* ; [- of laundry] lessive *f* **2.** [laundry] linge *m*, lessive *f* ■ **to do the ~** faire la lessive, laver le linge ■ **where can I hang the ~?** où puis-je étendre le linge?

washing day = **washday**.

washing line *n* corde *f* à linge.

washing machine *n* machine *f* à laver, lave-linge *m inv*.

washing powder *n* lessive *f OR* détergent *m (en poudre)*.

washing soda *n* cristaux *mpl* de soude.

Washington ['wɒʃɪŋtən] *pr n* **1.** [state] : **~ (State)** l'État *m* de Washington ■ **in ~** dans l'État de Washington **2.** [town] : **~ (DC)** Washington.

washing-up *n UK* vaisselle *f (à laver)* ■ **to do the ~** faire la vaisselle.

washing-up liquid *n UK* produit *m* à vaisselle.

wash-leather *n UK* peau *f* de chamois.

washload ['wɒʃləʊd] *n* [items to be washed] lessive *f*.

washout ['wɒʃaʊt] *n inf* [party, plan] fiasco *m*, échec *m* ■ [person] raté *m*, - e *f*.

washroom ['wɒʃrʊm] *n* **1.** [for laundry] buanderie *f* **2.** *US euph* [lavatory] toilettes *fpl*.

washstand ['wɒʃstænd] *n* table *f* de toilette.

washtub ['wɒʃtʌb] *n* [for laundry] bassine *f*, cuvette *f*.

wasn't [wɒznt] = **was not**.

wasp [wɒsp] *n* guêpe *f* ■ **a ~'s nest** un guêpier.

Wasp, WASP [wɒsp] (*abbrev of* **White Anglo-Saxon Protestant**) *n US Blanc d'origine anglo-saxonne et protestante, appartenant aux classes aisées et influentes.*

waspish ['wɒspɪʃ] *adj* [person - by nature] qui a mauvais caractère ; [- in bad mood] qui est de mauvaise humeur ■ [reply, remark] mordant, méchant.

wassail ['wɒseɪl] *arch* ◇ *n* **1.** [drink - beer] bière *f* épicée ; [- wine] vin *m* chaud **2.** [festivity] beuverie *f*.
◇ *vi* chanter (des chants de Noël).

wast [(*weak form* [wəst], *strong form* [wɒst])] *arch* = **(you) were**.

wastage ['weɪstɪdʒ] *n (U)* **1.** [loss - of materials, money] gaspillage *m*, gâchis *m* ; [- of time] perte *f* ; [- through leakage] fuites *fpl*, pertes *fpl* **2.** [in numbers, workforce] réduction *f* ■ **many students are lost by ~** beaucoup d'étudiants abandonnent en cours de route.

waste [weɪst] ◇ *vt* **1.** [misuse - materials, money] gaspiller ; [- time] perdre ; [- life] gâcher ■ **she ~d no time in telling us about it** elle s'est empressée de nous le raconter ■ **her wit was ~d on them** ils n'ont pas compris *OR* su apprécier son esprit ⮕ **you're wasting your breath!** tu uses ta salive pour rien! ■ **don't ~ your breath trying to convince them** ne te fatigue pas *OR* ne perds pas ton temps à essayer de les convaincre ■ **~ not, want not** *prov* l'économie protège du besoin **2.** [wear away - limb, muscle] atrophier ; [- body, person] décharner ■ **her body was completely ~d by cancer** son corps était complètement miné par le cancer **3.** △ *US* [kill] liquider△.
◇ *n* **1.** [misuse - of materials, money] gaspillage *m*, gâchis *m* ; [- of time] perte *f* ■ **it's a ~ of breath arguing about it** ce n'est pas la peine d'en discuter ■ **that book was a complete ~ of money** ce livre, c'était de l'argent jeté par les fenêtres ■ **it's a ~ of time talking to her** tu perds ton temps à discuter avec elle ■ **what a ~ of time!** que de temps perdu! ■ **it's an enormous ~ of talent** c'est énormément de talent gâché ■ **to go to ~** [gen] se perdre, être gaspillé ; [land] tomber en friche ■ **I'm not going to let the opportunity go to ~** je ne vais pas laisser passer l'occasion **2.** *(U)* [refuse - gen] déchets *mpl* ; [- household] ordures *fpl (ménagères)* ; [- water] eaux *fpl* usées ■ **industrial ~** déchets industriels **3.** [land] terrain *m* vague **4.** *phr* **to lay ~ to sthg, to lay sthg ~** ravager *OR* dévaster qqch.

◇ *adj* **1.** [paper] de rebut ■ [energy] perdu ■ [water] sale, usé ■ [food] qui reste ■ **~ material** déchets *mpl* **2.** [ground] en friche ■ [region] désert, désolé ■ **'The Waste Land'** ***Eliot*** 'la Terre Gaste'.
◆ **wastes** *npl* terres *fpl* désolées, désert *m* ■ **the polar ~s** le désert polaire.
◆ **waste away** *vi insep* dépérir.

wastebasket [ˌweɪst'peɪpə-] *n* ***esp US*** corbeille *f* (à papier).

waste bin *n* ***UK*** [in kitchen] poubelle *f*, boîte *f* à ordures ■ [for paper] corbeille *f* (à papier).

wasted ['weɪstɪd] *adj* **1.** [material, money] gaspillé ■ [energy, opportunity, time] perdu ■ [attempt, effort] inutile, vain ■ [food] inutilisé ■ **a ~ journey** un voyage raté **2.** [figure, person] décharné ■ [limb - emaciated] décharné ; [- enfeebled] atrophié.

waste disposal unit *n* broyeur *m* d'ordures.

wasteful ['weɪstfʊl] *adj* [habits] de gaspillage ■ [person] gaspilleur ■ [procedure] inefficace, peu rentable ■ **a ~ use of natural resources** un gaspillage des ressources naturelles.

wastefully ['weɪstfʊlɪ] *adv* en gaspillant ■ **we spend our time so ~** on gaspille un temps fou.

waste ground *n (U)* **the children were playing on ~** les enfants jouaient sur un terrain vague.

wasteland ['weɪstˌlænd] *n* [land - disused] terrain *m* vague ; [- uncultivated] terres *fpl* en friche *OR* abandonnées ■ [of desert, snow] désert *m* ■ **a cultural ~** ***fig*** un désert culturel.

waste paper *n (U)* papier *m* *OR* papiers *mpl* de rebut.

wastepaper basket [ˌweɪst'peɪpəʳ-] *n* ***UK*** corbeille *f* (à papier).

waste pipe *n* (tuyau *m* de) vidange *f*.

waste product *n* INDUST déchet *m* de production *OR* de fabrication ■ PHYSIOL déchet *m (de l'organisme)*.

waster ['weɪstəʳ] *n* **1.** [gen] gaspilleur *m*, - euse *f* ■ [of money] dépensier *m*, - ère *f* **2.** [good-for-nothing] bon *m* à rien, bonne *f* à rien.

wasting ['weɪstɪŋ] *adj* [disease] qui ronge *OR* mine.

wastrel ['weɪstrəl] = **waster**.

watch [wɒtʃ] ◇ *vt* **1.** [look at, observe - event, film] regarder ; [- animal, person] regarder, observer ■ **they ~ a lot of television** ils regardent beaucoup la télévision ■ **the crowds were ~ing the lions being fed** la foule regardait les lions qu'on était en train de nourrir ■ **we sat outside ~ing the world go by** nous étions assis dehors à regarder les gens passer ■ **~ how I do it** regardez *OR* observez comment je fais ■ **I bet he ignores us, just you ~!** je parie qu'il va nous ignorer, tu vas voir! ▶ **a ~ed pot never boils** ***prov*** inutile de s'inquiéter, ça ne fera pas avancer les choses
2. [spy on - person] surveiller, observer ; [- activities, suspect] surveiller ■ **you'd better ~ him** vous feriez bien de le surveiller *OR* de l'avoir à l'œil
3. [guard, tend - children, pet] surveiller, s'occuper de ; [- belongings, house] surveiller, garder ■ MIL monter la garde devant, garder
4. [pay attention to - health, weight] faire attention à ; [- development, situation] suivre de près ■ **~ where you're going!** regardez devant vous! ■ **~ what you're doing!** faites bien attention (à ce que vous faites)! ■ **~ you don't spill the coffee** fais attention à *OR* prends garde de ne pas renverser le café ■ **can you ~ the milk?** peux-tu surveiller le lait? ■ **we'd better ~ the time** il faut que nous surveillions l'heure ■ **stop ~ing the clock and do some work!** arrêtez de surveiller la pendule et travaillez un peu! ■ **'~ this space'** *annonce d'une publicité ou d'informations à paraître* ■ **~ your head!** attention *OR* gare à votre tête! ■ **~ your language!** surveille ton langage! ▶ **~ it!** [warning] (fais) attention! ; [threat] attention!, gare à vous! ■ **~ your step** ***liter*** & ***fig*** faites attention *OR* regardez où vous mettez les pieds ■ **you should ~ your step** *OR* **~ yourself with the boss** vous feriez bien de vous surveiller quand vous êtes avec le patron.
◇ *vi* **1.** [observe] regarder, observer ■ **I ~ed to see how she would react** j'ai attendu pour voir quelle serait sa réaction
2. [keep vigil] veiller.
◇ *n* **1.** [timepiece] montre *f* ■ **it's 6 o'clock by my ~** il est 6 h à ma montre
2. [lookout] surveillance *f* ■ **be on the ~ for pickpockets** ***UK*** faites attention *OR* prenez garde aux voleurs à la tire ■ **tax inspectors are always on the ~ for fraud** ***UK*** les inspecteurs des impôts sont toujours à l'affût des fraudeurs ■ **a sentry was on ~** *OR* **kept ~** une sentinelle montait la garde ■ **to keep ~ by sb's bed** veiller au chevet de qqn ■ **the police kept a close ~ on the suspect** la police a surveillé le suspect de près ■ **we'll keep ~ on your house during your absence** nous surveillerons votre maison pendant votre absence ■ **we're keeping a ~ on inflation rates** nous surveillons de près les taux d'inflation
3. [person on guard - gen - MIL] sentinelle *f* ■ NAUT homme *m* de quart ■ [group of guards - gen - MIL] garde *f* ■ NAUT quart *m*
4. [period of duty - gen - MIL] garde *f* ■ NAUT quart *m*
5. *lit* [period of the night] **: in the slow ~es of the night** pendant les longues nuits sans sommeil.
◆ **watch for** *vt insep* guetter, surveiller.
◆ **watch out** *vi insep* faire attention, prendre garde ■ **~ out!** [warning] (faites) attention! ■ **to ~ out for sthg** [be on look-out for] guetter qqch ; [be careful of] faire attention *OR* prendre garde à qqch.
◆ **watch over** *vt insep* garder, surveiller ■ **God will ~ over you** Dieu vous protégera.

watchband ['wɒtʃˌbænd] *n* ***US*** bracelet *m* de montre.

watch chain *n* chaîne *f* de montre.

watchdog ['wɒtʃdɒg] ◇ *n* [dog] chien *m*, - enne *f* de garde ■ ***fig*** [person] gardien *m*, - enne *f* ■ **the committee acts as ~ on environmental issues** le comité veille aux problèmes d'environnement.
◇ *comp* [body, committee] de surveillance.

watcher ['wɒtʃəʳ] *n* observateur *m*, - trice *f* ■ [spectator] spectateur *m*, - trice *f* ■ [idle onlooker] curieux *m*, - euse *f*.

watchful ['wɒtʃfʊl] *adj* vigilant, attentif ■ **under the ~ eye of her mother** sous l'œil vigilant de sa mère ■ **to keep a ~ eye on sthg/sb** avoir qqch/qqn à l'œil ■ **she kept a ~ eye on the situation** elle a suivi la situation de près.

watchglass ['wɒtʃglɑːs] *n* verre *m* de montre.

watchmaker ['wɒtʃˌmeɪkəʳ] *n* horloger *m*, - ère *f*.

watchman ['wɒtʃmən] (*pl* **watchmen** [-mən]) *n* gardien *m*.

watch night *n* nuit *f* de la Saint-Sylvestre.

watchstrap ['wɒtʃstræp] *n* bracelet *m* de montre.

watchtower ['wɒtʃˌtaʊəʳ] *n* tour *f* de guet.

watchword ['wɒtʃwɜːd] *n* [password] mot *m* de passe ■ [slogan] mot *m* d'ordre.

water ['wɔːtəʳ] ◇ *n* **1.** [liquid - gen] eau *f* ■ **hot and cold running ~** eau courante chaude et froide ■ **turn on the ~** [at main] ouvre l'eau ; [at tap] ouvre le robinet ■ **they held his head under ~** ils lui ont tenu la tête sous l'eau ■ **the cellar is under 2 metres of ~** il y a 2 mètres d'eau dans la cave ■ **the ~** *OR* **~s of the Seine** l'eau *OR* les eaux de la Seine ■ **the ship was making ~** le bateau prenait l'eau *OR* faisait eau ■ **they're in rough financial ~s** ***fig*** ils sont dans une situation financière difficile ▶ **~ main** conduite *f* *OR* canalisation *f* d'eau ■ **that idea won't hold ~** cette idée ne tient pas debout ■ **you're in hot ~ now** ***inf*** tu vas avoir de gros ennuis, tu es dans de beaux draps ■ **I'm trying to keep my head above ~** *OR* **to stay above ~** ***inf*** j'essaye de me maintenir à flot *OR* de faire face ■ **the wine flowed like ~** le vin coulait à flots ■ **to spend money like ~** jeter l'argent par les fenêtres ■ **they poured** *OR* **threw cold ~ on our suggestion** ils n'ont pas été enthousiasmés par notre suggestion ■ **it's like ~ off a duck's back** ça glisse comme sur les plumes d'un canard ■ **it's ~ under the bridge** c'est du passé ■ **a lot of ~ has passed under the bridge since then** il a coulé beaucoup d'eau sous les ponts depuis **2.** [body of water] eau *f* ■ **she fell in the ~** elle est tombée à l'eau **3.** [tide] marée *f* ■ **at high/low ~** à marée haute/basse **4.** ***euph*** [urine] urine *f* ■ **to make** *OR* **to pass ~** uriner **5.** MED **: ~ on the brain** hydrocéphalie *f* ■ **to have ~ on the knee** avoir un épanchement de synovie **6.** TEX [of cloth] moiré *m*.

<> *vt* **1.** [land, plants] arroser **2.** [animal] donner à boire à, faire boire **3.** [dilute - alcohol] couper (d'eau) **4.** TEX [cloth] moirer.
<> *vi* **1.** [eyes] larmoyer **2.** [mouth] : **the smell made my mouth ~** l'odeur m'a fait venir l'eau à la bouche.
waters *npl* **1.** [territorial] eaux *fpl* ▪ **in Japanese ~s** dans les eaux (territoriales) japonaises **2.** [spa water] : **to take the ~s** prendre les eaux, faire une cure thermale **3.** [of pregnant woman] poche *f* des eaux ▪ **her ~s broke** elle a perdu les eaux, la poche des eaux s'est rompue.
water down *vt sep* [alcohol] couper (d'eau) ▪ *fig* [speech] édulcorer ▪ [complaint, criticism] atténuer.

water bed *n* matelas *m* à eau.
water beetle *n* gyrin *m*, tourniquet *m*.
water bird *n* oiseau *m* aquatique.
water birth *n* accouchement *m* sous l'eau.
water biscuit *n UK* biscuit *m* salé craquant.
water blister *n* ampoule *f*, phlyctène *f spec*.
water boatman *n* ENTOM notonecte *f*.
water bomb *n* bombe *f* à eau.
waterborne ['wɔ:təbɔ:n] *adj* [vehicle] flottant ▪ [commerce, trade] effectué par voie d'eau ▪ [disease] d'origine hydrique.
water bottle *n* [gen] bouteille *f* d'eau ▪ [soldier's, worker's] bidon *m* à eau ▪ [in leather] outre *f*.
water buffalo *n* [India] buffle *m* d'Inde ▪ [Malaysia] karbau *m*, kérabau *m* ▪ [Asia] buffle *m* d'Asie.
water bug *n* nèpe *f*.
water cannon *n* canon *m* à eau.
water carrier *n* **1.** [container] bidon *m* à eau **2.** [person] porteur *m*, - euse *f* d'eau.
Water Carrier *pr n* ASTROL & ASTRON : **the Water Carrier** le Verseau.
water cart *n* [to sprinkle water] arroseuse *f* ▪ [to sell water] voiture *f* de marchand d'eau.
water chestnut *n* châtaigne *f* d'eau.
water chute *n* [in swimming pool] cascade *f*.
water closet *n* W-C *mpl*, toilettes *fpl*, cabinets *mpl*.
watercolour *UK*, **watercolor** *US* ['wɔ:tə,kʌlə^r] <> *n* [paint] couleur *f* pour aquarelle ▪ [painting] aquarelle *f* ▪ **painted in ~** peint à l'aquarelle.
<> *adj* [paint] pour aquarelle, à l'eau ▪ [landscape, portrait] à l'aquarelle.
watercolourist *UK*, **watercolorist** *US* ['wɔ:tə,kʌlərɪst] *n* aquarelliste *mf*.
water-cooled [-,ku:ld] *adj* à refroidissement par eau.
water cooler *n* distributeur *m* d'eau fraîche.
watercourse ['wɔ:təkɔ:s] *n* [river, stream] cours *m* d'eau ▪ [bed] lit *m (d'un cours d'eau)*.
watercress ['wɔ:təkres] *n* cresson *m*.
water-diviner *n* sourcier *m*, - ère *f*, radiesthésiste *mf*.
watered-down [,wɔ:təd-] *adj* [alcohol] coupé (d'eau) ▪ [speech] édulcoré ▪ [complaint, criticism] atténué.
watered silk *n* soie *f* moirée.
waterfall ['wɔ:təfɔ:l] *n* cascade *f*, chute *f* d'eau.
water feature *n* fontaine *f* d'intérieur.
water fountain *n* [for decoration] jet *m* d'eau ▪ [for drinking] distributeur *m* d'eau fraîche.
waterfowl ['wɔ:təfaʊl] (*pl inv* OR *pl* **waterfowls**) *n* [bird] oiseau *m* aquatique ▪ [collectively] gibier *m* d'eau.
waterfront ['wɔ:təfrʌnt] *n* [at harbour] quais *mpl* ▪ [seafront] front *m* de mer ▪ **on the ~** [at harbour] sur les quais ; [on seafront] face à la mer.
Watergate ['wɔ:tə,geɪt] *pr n* Watergate *m*.

WATERGATE

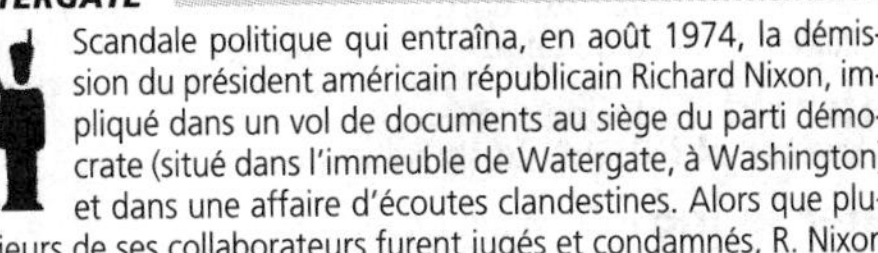
Scandale politique qui entraîna, en août 1974, la démission du président américain républicain Richard Nixon, impliqué dans un vol de documents au siège du parti démocrate (situé dans l'immeuble de Watergate, à Washington) et dans une affaire d'écoutes clandestines. Alors que plusieurs de ses collaborateurs furent jugés et condamnés, R. Nixon démissionna avant sa mise en accusation, ce qui contribua à ébranler la confiance des Américains dans leur gouvernement. Le suffixe ***-gate***, passé dans le langage courant, désigne désormais tout scandale ou toute affaire comparable au Watergate. On l'utilise accolé au nom de la personne ou du lieu associé au scandale : ***Irangate***, ***Dianagate***, ***Monicagate*** etc.

water heater *n* chauffe-eau *m inv*.
water hen *n* poule *f* d'eau.
waterhole ['wɔ:təhəʊl] *n* point *m* d'eau ▪ [in desert] oasis *f*.
water ice *n UK* sorbet *m*.
watering ['wɔ:tərɪŋ] *n* [of garden, plants] arrosage *m* ▪ [of crops, fields] irrigation *f*.
watering can *n* arrosoir *m*.
watering hole *n* [for animals] point *m* d'eau ▪ *inf hum* [pub] ≃ bistrot *m inf*, ≃ bar *m*.
watering place *n* **1.** [waterhole] point *m* d'eau **2.** *UK* [spa] station *f* thermale **3.** *UK* [seaside resort] station *f* balnéaire.
watering pot *n* arrosoir *m*.
water jump *n* brook *m*.
water level *n* [of river, sea] niveau *m* de l'eau ▪ [in tank] niveau *m* d'eau.
water lily *n* nénuphar *m*.
waterline ['wɔ:təlaɪn] *n* **1.** [left by river] ligne *f* des hautes eaux ▪ [left by tide] laisse *f* de haute mer **2.** NAUT [on ship] ligne *f* de flottaison.
waterlogged ['wɔ:təlɒgd] *adj* [land, soil] détrempé ▪ [boat] plein d'eau ▪ [clothing, shoes] imbibé d'eau.
Waterloo [,wɔ:tə'lu:] <> *pr n* Waterloo.
<> *n* : **to meet one's ~** essuyer un revers.
water main *n* conduite *f* d'eau.
watermark ['wɔ:təmɑ:k] <> *n* **1.** = **waterline** *(sense 1)* **2.** [on paper] filigrane *m*.
<> *vt* filigraner.
watermelon ['wɔ:tə,melən] *n* pastèque *f*, melon *m* d'eau.
water meter *n* compteur *m* d'eau.
watermill ['wɔ:təmɪl] *n* moulin *m* à eau.
water nymph *n* naïade *f*.
water ox = **water buffalo**.
water pipe *n* **1.** CONSTR conduite *f* OR canalisation *f* d'eau **2.** [hookah] narguilé *m*.
water pistol *n* pistolet *m* à eau.
water polo *n* water-polo *m*.
water power *n* énergie *f* hydraulique, houille *f* blanche.
waterproof ['wɔ:təpru:f] <> *adj* [clothing, material] imperméable ▪ [container, wall, watch] étanche.
<> *n* imperméable *m*.
<> *vt* [clothing, material] imperméabiliser ▪ [barrel, wall] rendre étanche.
water rat *n* rat *m* d'eau.
water rate *n UK* taxe *f* sur l'eau.
water-resistant *adj* [material] semi-imperméable ▪ [lotion] qui résiste à l'eau ▪ [ink] indélébile, qui résiste à l'eau.
watershed ['wɔ:təʃed] *n* [area of ground] ligne *f* de partage des eaux ▪ *fig* [event] grand tournant *m*.
waterside ['wɔ:təsaɪd] <> *n* bord *m* de l'eau.

◇ *adj* [house, path] au bord de l'eau ▪ [resident] riverain ▪ [flower] du bord de l'eau.

water ski *n* ski *m* nautique.
◆ **water-ski** *vi* faire du ski nautique.

water skiing *n* ski *m* nautique.

water snake *n* serpent *m* d'eau.

water softener *n* adoucisseur *m* d'eau.

water-soluble *adj* soluble dans l'eau.

water sport *n* sport *m* nautique.

water supply *n* [for campers, troops] provision *f* d'eau ▪ [to house] alimentation *f* en eau ▪ [to area, town] distribution *f* des eaux, approvisionnement *m* en eau ▪ **the ~ has been cut off** l'eau a été coupée.

water table *n* surface *f* de la nappe phréatique.

water tank *n* réservoir *m* d'eau, citerne *f*.

watertight ['wɔːtətaɪt] *adj* [box, door] étanche ▪ *fig* [argument, reasoning] inattaquable, indiscutable.

water torture *n* supplice *m* de l'eau.

water tower *n* château *m* d'eau.

water vole *n* rat *m* d'eau.

waterway ['wɔːtəweɪ] *n* cours *m* d'eau, voie *f* navigable.

waterwheel ['wɔːtəwiːl] *n* roue *f* hydraulique.

waterwings ['wɔːtəwɪŋz] *npl* bouée *f* à bras, flotteur *m*.

waterworks ['wɔːtəwɜːks] (*pl inv*) ◇ *n* [establishment] station *f* hydraulique ▪ [system] système *m* hydraulique.
◇ *npl* **1.** [fountain] jet *m* d'eau **2.** *UK inf euph* [urinary system] voies *fpl* urinaires **3.** *inf hum* [tears] : **she turned on the ~** elle s'est mise à pleurer comme une Madeleine.

watery ['wɔːtərɪ] *adj* **1.** [surroundings, world] aquatique ▪ [ground, soil] détrempé, saturé d'eau **2.** [eyes] larmoyant, humide **3.** [coffee, tea] trop léger ▪ [soup] trop liquide, fade ▪ [milk] qui a trop d'eau ▪ [taste] fade, insipide **4.** [light, sun, smile] faible ▪ [colour] délavé, pâle.

watt [wɒt] *n* watt *m*.

wattage ['wɒtɪdʒ] *n* puissance *f* OR consommation *f* (en watts).

wattle ['wɒtl] *n* **1.** [of bird, lizard] caroncule *f* **2.** [sticks] clayonnage *m* ▪ **~ and daub** clayonnage enduit de torchis.

wave [weɪv] ◇ *n* **1.** [in sea] vague *f*, lame *f* ▪ [on lake] vague *f* ▪ **the ~s** les flots *mpl* ▪ **don't make ~s** *fig* ne faites pas de vagues, ne créez pas de remous **2.** [of earthquake, explosion] onde *f* ▪ *fig* [of crime, panic] vague *f* ▪ [of anger] bouffée *f* ▪ [of disgust] vague *f* ▪ **the refugees arrived in ~s** les réfugiés sont arrivés par vagues **3.** [in hair] cran *m*, ondulation *f* **4.** [gesture] geste *m* OR signe *m* de la main ▪ **our neighbour gave us a friendly ~** notre voisin nous a fait un signe amical **5.** RADIO onde *f*.
◇ *vi* **1.** [gesture] faire un signe OR un geste de la main ▪ **his sister ~d at** OR **to him** [greeted] sa sœur l'a salué d'un signe de la main ; [signalled] sa sœur lui a fait signe de la main ▪ **she ~d at** OR **to them to come in** elle leur a fait signe d'entrer **2.** [move - flag] flotter ; [- wheat] onduler, ondoyer ; [- branch] être agité.
◇ *vt* **1.** [brandish - flag] agiter, brandir ; [- pistol, sword] brandir **2.** [gesture] : **his mother ~d him away** sa mère l'a écarté d'un geste de la main ▪ **the guard ~d us back/on** le garde nous a fait signe de reculer/d'avancer ▪ **we ~d goodbye** nous avons fait au revoir de la main ▪ **you can ~ goodbye to your promotion!** *inf fig* tu peux dire adieu à ta promotion! **3.** [hair] onduler.
◆ **wave about** ◇ *vi insep* = **wave** (*vi sense 2*).
◇ *vt sep UK* [flag, sign] agiter, brandir ▪ [pistol, sword] brandir ▪ **he was waving his hands about** il gesticulait.
◆ **wave aside** *vt sep* [person] écarter OR éloigner d'un geste ▪ [protest] écarter ▪ [help, suggestion] refuser, rejeter.
◆ **wave down** *vt sep* : **to ~ sb/a car down** faire signe à qqn/à une voiture de s'arrêter.

wave band *n* bande *f* de fréquences.

wavelength ['weɪvleŋθ] *n* PHYS & RADIO longueur *f* d'onde ▪ **we're just not on the same ~** *fig* nous ne sommes pas sur la même longueur d'onde.

wavelet ['weɪvlɪt] *n* vaguelette *f*.

wave power *n* énergie *f* des vagues.

waver ['weɪvəʳ] *vi* **1.** [person] vaciller, hésiter ▪ [confidence, courage] vaciller, faiblir ▪ **they didn't ~ in their loyalty to the cause** leur attachement à la cause n'a pas faibli **2.** [flame, light] vaciller, osciller ▪ [temperature] osciller **3.** [voice] trembloter, trembler.

waverer ['weɪvərəʳ] *n* irrésolu *m*, - e *f*, indécis *m*, - e *f*.

wavering ['weɪvərɪŋ] ◇ *adj* **1.** [person] irrésolu, indécis ▪ [confidence, courage] vacillant, défaillant **2.** [flame, light] vacillant, oscillant ▪ [steps] vacillant, chancelant ▪ [temperature] oscillant **3.** [voice] tremblotant, tremblant.
◇ *n* **1.** [of person] irrésolution *f*, indécision *f* ▪ [of confidence, courage] défaillance *f* **2.** [of flame, light] vacillement *m*, oscillation *f* ▪ [of temperature] oscillation *f*.

wavy ['weɪvɪ] (*comp* **wavier**, *superl* **waviest**) *adj* **1.** [line] qui ondule, ondulant **2.** [hair] ondulé, qui a des crans.

wavy-haired *adj* aux cheveux ondulés.

wax [wæks] ◇ *n* [for car, floor, furniture] cire *f* ▪ [in ear] cérumen *m* ▪ [for skis] fart *m*.
◇ *comp* [candle, figure] de OR en cire ▪ **~ crayons** crayons *mpl* gras.
◇ *vt* **1.** [floor, table] cirer, encaustiquer ▪ [skis] farter ▪ [car] enduire de cire **2.** [legs] épiler (à la cire).
◇ *vi* **1.** [moon] croître ▪ [influence, power] croître, augmenter ▪ **to ~ and wane** [moon] croître et décroître ; [influence, power] croître et décliner **2.** *arch & hum* [become] devenir ▪ **he ~ed poetic/sentimental** il se fit poète/sentimental.

waxed paper [wækst-] *n* papier *m* paraffiné OR sulfurisé.

waxen ['wæksən] *adj* [candle, figure] de OR en cire ▪ [complexion, face] cireux.

wax museum *n* musée *m* de cire.

wax paper = **waxed paper**.

waxwing ['wækswɪŋ] *n* ORNITH jaseur *m*.

waxwork ['wækswɜːk] *n* [object] objet *m* de OR en cire ▪ [statue of person] statue *f* de cire.

waxworks ['wækswɜːks] (*pl inv*) *n* musée *m* de cire.

waxy ['wæksɪ] (*comp* **waxier**, *superl* **waxiest**) *adj* [complexion, texture] cireux ▪ [colour] cireux, jaunâtre ▪ [potato] ferme, pas farineux.

way [weɪ] ◇ *n*

A.

1. [thoroughfare, path] chemin *m*, voie *f* ▪ [for cars] rue *f*, route *f* ▪ **they live across** OR **over the ~ from the school** ils habitent en face de l'école ➤ **private/public ~** voie privée/publique ▪ **the Way of the Cross** RELIG le chemin de Croix
2. [route leading to a specified place] chemin *m* ▪ **this is the ~ to the library** la bibliothèque est par là ▪ **could you tell me the ~ to the library?** pouvez-vous me dire comment aller à la bibliothèque? ▪ **what's the shortest** OR **quickest ~ to town?** quel est le chemin le plus court pour aller en ville? ▪ **which ~ does this bus go?** par où passe ce bus? ▪ **I had to ask the** OR **my ~** il a fallu que je demande mon chemin ▪ **they went the wrong ~** ils se sont trompés de chemin, ils ont pris le mauvais chemin ➤ **to lose one's ~** *liter* s'égarer, perdre son chemin ; *fig* s'égarer, se fourvoyer ▪ **to know one's ~ around** *liter* savoir s'orienter ; *fig* savoir se débrouiller
3. [route leading in a specified direction] chemin *m*, route *f* ▪ **the ~ back** le chemin OR la route du retour ▪ **he couldn't find the ~ back home** il n'a pas trouvé le chemin pour rentrer (à la maison) ▪ **on our ~ back we stopped for dinner** au retour OR sur le chemin du retour nous nous sommes arrêtés pour dîner ▪ **she showed us the easiest ~ down/up** elle nous a montré le chemin le plus facile pour descendre/monter ▪ **the ~ up is difficult but the ~ down will be easier** la montée est difficile mais la descente sera plus facile ▪ **the ~ in** l'entrée *f* ▪ **the ~ out** la sortie ▪ **I took the back ~ out** je suis sorti par derrière

■ *fig* **miniskirts are on the ~ back in** la minijupe est de retour ■ **miniskirts are on the ~ out** la minijupe n'est plus tellement à la mode ■ **the director is on the ~ out** le directeur ne sera plus là très longtemps ■ **they found a ~ out of the deadlock** ils ont trouvé une solution pour sortir de l'impasse ■ **is there no ~ out of this nightmare?** n'y a-t-il pas moyen de mettre fin à ce cauchemar? ■ **their decision left her no ~ out** leur décision l'a mise dans une impasse ■ **he left himself a ~ out** il s'est ménagé une porte de sortie

4. [direction] direction *f*, sens *m* ■ **come this ~** venez par ici ■ **he went that ~** il est allé par là ■ **'this ~ to the chapel'** 'vers la chapelle' ■ **this ~ and that** de-ci de-là, par-ci par-là ■ **look this ~** regarde par ici ■ **I never looked their ~** je n'ai jamais regardé dans leur direction ■ **to look the other ~** *liter* détourner les yeux ; *fig* fermer les yeux ■ **he didn't know which ~ to look** [embarrassed] il ne savait plus où se mettre ■ **which ~ is the wind blowing?** *liter* d'où vient le vent? ■ **I could tell which ~ the wind was blowing** *fig* je voyais très bien ce qui allait se passer ■ **which ~ do I go from here?** *liter* où est-ce que je vais maintenant? ; *fig* qu'est-ce que je fais maintenant? ■ **get in, I'm going your ~** montez, je vais dans la même direction que vous ■ **we each went our separate ~s** [on road] nous sommes partis chacun de notre côté ; [in life] chacun de nous a suivi son propre chemin ■ **he went the wrong ~** il a pris la mauvaise direction ; [down one-way street] il a pris la rue en sens interdit ▶ **any job that comes my ~** n'importe quel travail qui se présente ■ **everything's going my ~** *inf* tout marche comme je veux en ce moment ■ **the vote went our ~** le vote nous a été favorable ■ **the vote couldn't have gone any other ~** les résultats du vote étaient donnés d'avance ■ **to go one's own ~** n'en faire qu'à sa tête, vivre à sa guise

5. [side] sens *m* ■ **stand the box the other ~ up** posez le carton dans l'autre sens ■ **'this ~ up'** 'haut' ■ **it's the wrong ~ up** c'est dans le mauvais sens ■ **it's the wrong ~ round** c'est dans le mauvais sens ■ **your sweater is the right/wrong ~ out** votre pull est à l'endroit/à l'envers ■ **try it the other ~ round** essayez dans l'autre sens ■ **cats hate having their fur brushed the wrong ~** les chats détestent qu'on les caresse à rebrousse-poil ■ **SHE insulted him? you've got it the wrong ~ round** elle, elle l'a insulté? mais c'est le contraire ■ **he invited her tonight, last time it was the other ~ round** ce soir c'est lui qui l'a invitée, la dernière fois c'était l'inverse

6. [area, vicinity] parages *mpl* ■ **I was out** *OR* **over your ~ yesterday** j'étais près de *OR* du côté de chez vous hier

7. [distance - in space] : **we came part of the ~ by foot** nous avons fait une partie de la route à pied ■ **they were one-third of the ~ through their trip** ils avaient fait un tiers de leur voyage ■ **we've come most of the ~** nous avons fait la plus grande partie du chemin ■ **he can swim quite a ~** il peut nager assez longtemps ■ **a long ~ off** *OR* **away** loin ■ **a little** *OR* **short ~ off** pas très loin, à courte distance ■ **it's a long ~ to Berlin** Berlin est loin ■ **we've come a long ~** [from far away] nous venons de loin ; [made progress] nous avons fait du chemin ■ **we've a long ~ to go** [far to travel] il nous reste beaucoup de route à faire ; [a lot to do] nous avons encore beaucoup à faire ; [a lot to collect, pay] nous sommes encore loin du compte ■ [in time] : **it's a long ~ to Christmas** Noël est encore loin ■ **you have to go back a long ~** il faut remonter loin ■ *fig* **I'm a long ~ from trusting him** je suis loin de lui faire confiance ■ **you're a long ~ off** *OR* **out** [in guessing] vous n'y êtes pas du tout ■ **she'll go a long ~** elle ira loin ■ **the scholarship will go a long ~ towards helping with expenses** la bourse va beaucoup aider à faire face aux dépenses ■ **a little goodwill goes a long ~** un peu de bonne volonté facilite bien les choses ■ **she makes her money go a long ~** elle sait ménager son argent ▶ **a little bit goes a long ~** il en faut très peu

8. [space in front of person, object] : **a tree was in the ~** un arbre bloquait *OR* barrait le passage ■ **I can't see, the cat is in the ~** je ne vois pas, le chat me gêne ■ **put the suitcases under the bed out of the ~** rangez les valises sous le lit, pour qu'elles ne gênent pas ■ **to get out of the ~** s'écarter (du chemin) ■ **we got out of his ~** nous l'avons laissé passer ■ **keep out of the ~!** ne reste pas là! ■ **make ~!** écartez-vous! ■ *fig* **her social life got in the ~ of her studies** ses sorties l'empêchaient d'étudier ■ **I don't want to get in the ~ of your happiness** je ne veux pas entraver votre bonheur ■ **I kept out of the boss's ~** j'ai évité le patron ■ **he wants his boss out of the ~** *inf* il veut se débarrasser de son patron ■ **once the meeting is out of the ~** *inf* dès que nous serons débarrassés de la réunion ■ **they tore down the slums to make ~ for blocks of flats** ils ont démoli les taudis pour pouvoir construire des immeubles ▶ **to clear** *OR* **prepare the ~ for sthg** préparer la voie à qqch ■ **to put difficulties in sb's ~** créer des difficultés à qqn

9. [indicating a progressive action] : **the acid ate its ~ through the metal** l'acide est passé à travers le métal ■ **I fought** *OR* **pushed my ~ through the crowd** je me suis frayé un chemin à travers la foule ■ **we made our ~ towards the train** nous nous sommes dirigés vers le train ■ **I made my ~ back to my seat** je suis retourné à ma place ■ **she made her ~ up through the hierarchy** elle a gravi les échelons de la hiérarchie un par un ■ **she had to make her own ~ in the world** elle a dû faire son chemin toute seule ■ **she talked her ~ out of it** elle s'en est sortie avec de belles paroles ■ **he worked** *OR* **made his ~ through the pile of newspapers** il a lu les journaux un par un ■ **I worked my ~ through college** j'ai travaillé pour payer mes études

B.

1. [means, method] moyen *m*, méthode *f* ■ **in what ~ can I help you?** comment *OR* en quoi puis-je vous être utile? ■ **there are several ~s to go** *OR* **of going about it** il y a plusieurs façons *OR* moyens de s'y prendre ■ **I do it this ~** voilà comment je fais ■ **they thought they would win that ~** ils pensaient pouvoir gagner comme ça ■ **she has her own ~ of cooking fish** elle a sa façon à elle de cuisiner le poisson ■ **you're doing it the right/wrong ~** c'est comme ça/ce n'est pas comme ça qu'il faut (le) faire ■ **do it the usual ~** faites comme d'habitude ■ **there's no ~** *OR* **I can't see any ~ we'll finish on time** nous ne finirons jamais *OR* nous n'avons aucune chance de finir à temps ▶ **love will find a ~** *hum* l'amour finit toujours par triompher ■ **that's the ~ to do it!** c'est comme ça qu'il faut faire!, voilà comment il faut faire! ■ **well done! that's the ~ (to go)!** *US inf* bravo! c'est bien! ■ **what a ~ to go!** [manner of dying] quelle belle mort! ; [congratulations] bravo!

2. [particular manner, fashion] façon *f*, manière *f* ■ **in a friendly ~** gentiment ■ **he spoke in a general ~ about the economy** il a parlé de l'économie d'une façon générale ■ **they see things in the same ~** ils voient les choses de la même façon ■ **in their own (small) ~ they fight racism** à leur façon *OR* dans la limite de leurs moyens, ils luttent contre le racisme ■ **in the same ~, we note that...** de même, on notera que... ■ **that's one ~ to look at it** *OR* **~ of looking at it** c'est une façon *OR* manière de voir les choses ■ **try to see it my ~** mettez-vous à ma place ■ **to her ~ of thinking** à son avis ■ **the ~ she feels about him** les sentiments qu'elle éprouve à son égard ■ **I didn't think you would take it this ~** je ne pensais pas que vous le prendriez comme ça ■ **if that's the ~ you feel about it!** si c'est comme ça que vous le prenez! ▶ **the American ~ of life** la manière de vivre des Américains, le mode de vie américain ■ **yearly strikes have become a ~ of life** les grèves annuelles sont devenues une habitude

3. [custom] coutume *f*, usage *m* ■ [habitual manner of acting] manière *f*, habitude *f* ■ **he knows nothing of their ~s** il les connaît très mal *OR* ne les comprend pas du tout ■ **they're happy in their own ~** ils sont heureux à leur manière ■ **it's not my ~ to criticize** ce n'est pas mon genre *OR* ce n'est pas dans mes habitudes de critiquer ■ **he's not in a bad mood, it's just his ~** il n'est pas de mauvaise humeur, c'est sa façon d'être habituelle ▶ **she got into/out of the ~ of rising early** elle a pris/perdu l'habitude de se lever tôt

4. [facility, knack] : **she has a (certain) ~ with her** elle a le chic ■ **he has a ~ with children** il sait (comment) s'y prendre *OR* il a le chic avec les enfants ■ **she has a ~ with words** elle a le chic pour s'exprimer

5. [indicating a condition, state of affairs] : **let me tell you the ~ it was** laisse-moi te raconter comment ça s'est passé ■ **we can't invite him given the ~ things are** on ne peut pas l'inviter étant donné la situation ■ **we left the flat the ~ it was** nous avons laissé l'appartement tel qu'il était *OR* comme il était ■ **is he going to be staying here? – it looks that ~** est-ce qu'il va loger ici? – on dirait (bien) ■ **it's not the ~ it looks!** ce n'est pas ce que vous pensez! ■ **it's not the ~ it used to be** ce n'est pas comme avant ■ **that's the ~ things are** c'est comme ça ■ **that's the ~ of the world** ainsi va le monde ■ **business is good and we're trying to keep it that ~** les affaires vont bien et nous faisons en sorte que ça dure ■ **life goes on (in) the same old ~** la vie va son train *OR* suit son cours ■ **I don't like the ~ things are going** je n'aime pas la tournure que prennent les choses

■ **we'll never finish the ~ things are going** au train où vont les choses, on n'aura jamais fini ▶ **to be in a bad ~** être en mauvais état ■ **he's in a bad ~** il est dans un triste état ■ **their business is in a bad/good ~** leurs affaires marchent mal/bien
6. [respect, detail] égard *m*, rapport *m* ■ **in what ~?** à quel égard?, sous quel rapport? ■ **in this ~** à cet égard, sous ce rapport ■ **it's important in many ~s** c'est important à bien des égards ■ **in some ~s** à certains égards, par certains côtés ■ **I'll help you in every possible ~** je ferai tout ce que je peux pour vous aider ■ **she studied the problem in every ~ possible** elle a examiné le problème sous tous les angles possibles ■ **useful in more ~s than one** utile à plus d'un égard ■ **these two books, each interesting in its (own) ~** ces deux livres, qui sont intéressants chacun dans son genre ■ **he's clever that ~** sur ce plan-là il est malin ▶ **in a ~ you're right** en un sens vous avez raison ■ **I see what you mean in a ~** d'un certain point de vue *OR* d'une certaine manière, je vois ce que tu veux dire ■ **I am in no ~ responsible** je ne suis absolument pas *OR* aucunement responsable ■ **this in no ~ changes your situation** ceci ne change en rien votre situation
7. [scale] : **to do things in a big ~** faire les choses en grand ■ **she went into politics in a big ~** elle s'est lancée à fond dans la politique ■ **they helped out in a big ~** ils ont beaucoup aidé ■ **it does change the situation in a small ~** ça change quand même un peu la situation
8. *(usu pl)* [part, share] : **we divided the money four ~s** nous avons partagé l'argent en quatre ■ **the committee was split three ~s** le comité était divisé en trois groupes
9. NAUT : **we're gathering/losing ~** nous prenons/perdons de la vitesse ■ **the ship has ~ on** le navire a de l'erre
10. *phr* **she always gets** *OR* **has her ~** elle arrive toujours à ses fins ■ **he only wants it his ~** il n'en fait qu'à sa tête ■ **I'm not going to let you have it all your ~** je refuse de te céder en tout ■ **if I had my ~, he'd be in prison** si cela ne tenait qu'à moi, il serait en prison ■ **I refuse to go – have it your ~** je refuse d'y aller – fais ce que *OR* comme tu veux ■ **no, it was 1789 – have it your ~** non, c'était en 1789 – soit ■ **you can't have it both ~s** il faut choisir ■ **I can stop too, it works both ~s** je peux m'arrêter aussi, ça marche dans les deux sens ■ **there are no two ~s about it** il n'y a pas le choix ■ **no two ~s about it, he was rude** il n'y a pas à dire, il a été grossier ■ **to have one's (wicked) ~ with sb** *hum* coucher avec qqn.

◇ *adv inf* **1.** [far - in space, time] très loin ■ **~ up the mountain** très haut dans la montagne ■ **~ back in the distance** au loin derrière ■ **~ back in the 1930s** déjà dans les années 30 **2.** *fig* **we know each other from ~ back** nous sommes amis depuis très longtemps ■ **you're ~ below the standard** tu es bien en dessous du niveau voulu ■ **he's ~ over forty** il a largement dépassé la quarantaine ■ **she's ~ ahead of her class** elle est très en avance sur sa classe ■ **he's ~ off in his guess** il est loin d'avoir deviné.

◆ **ways** *npl* NAUT [in shipbuilding] cale *f*.

◆ **all the way** *adv phr* : **the baby cried all the ~** le bébé a pleuré tout le long du chemin ■ **don't close the curtains all the ~** ne fermez pas complètement les rideaux ■ **prices go all the ~ from 200 to 1,000 dollars** les prix vont de 200 à 1 000 dollars ■ **I'm with you all the ~** *fig* je vous suis *OR* je vous soutiens jusqu'au bout ▶ **to go all the ~ (with sb)** *inf* aller jusqu'au bout (avec qqn).

◆ **along the way** *adv phr* en route.

◆ **by a long way** *adv phr* : **I prefer chess by a long ~** je préfère de loin *OR* de beaucoup les échecs ■ **he's not as capable as you are by a long ~** il est loin d'être aussi compétent que toi ■ **is your project ready? – not by a long ~!** ton projet est-il prêt? – loin de là!

◆ **by the way** ◇ *adv phr* [incidentally] à propos ■ **I bring up this point by the ~** je signale ce point au passage *OR* en passant.
◇ *adj phr* [incidental] secondaire.

◆ **by way of** *prep phr* **1.** [via] par, via **2.** [as a means of] : **by ~ of illustration** à titre d'exemple ■ **by ~ of introducing himself, he gave us his card** en guise de présentation, il nous a donné sa carte ■ **they receive money by ~ of grants** ils reçoivent de l'argent sous forme de bourses.

◆ **either way** *adv phr* **1.** [in either case] dans les deux cas ■ **shall we take the car or the bus? – it's fine by me** *OR* **I don't mind either ~** tu préfères prendre la voiture ou le bus? – n'importe, ça m'est égal **2.** [more or less] en plus ou en moins **3.** [indicating advantage] : **the match could have gone either ~** le match était ouvert ■ **there's nothing in it either ~** c'est pareil.

◆ **in such a way as to** *conj phr* de façon à ce que.

◆ **in such a way that** *conj phr* de telle façon *OR* manière que.

◆ **in the way of** *prep phr* **1.** [in the form of] : **she receives little in the ~ of salary** son salaire n'est pas bien gros ■ **what is there in the ~ of food?** qu'est-ce qu'il y a à manger? **2.** [within the context of] : **we met in the ~ of business** nous nous sommes rencontrés dans le cadre du travail ▶ **they put me in the ~ of making some money** ils m'ont indiqué un moyen de gagner de l'argent.

◆ **no way** *adv phr inf* pas question.

◆ **on one's way, on the way** *adv & adj phr* **1.** [along the route] : **it's on my ~** c'est sur mon chemin ■ **I'll catch up with you on the ~** je te rattraperai en chemin *OR* en route ‖ [coming, going] : **on the ~ to work** en allant au bureau ■ **I'm on my ~!** j'y vais! ■ **she's on her ~ home** elle rentre chez elle ■ **on his ~ to town he met his father** en allant en ville, il a rencontré son père ▶ **we must be on our ~** il faut que nous y allions ■ **to go one's ~** repartir, reprendre son chemin **2.** *fig* **she has a baby on the ~** elle attend un bébé ■ **her second book is on the ~** [being written] elle a presque fini d'écrire son deuxième livre ; [being published] son deuxième livre est sur le point de paraître ■ **she's on the ~ to success** elle est sur le chemin de la réussite ■ **the patient is on the ~ to recovery** le malade est en voie de guérison ■ **the new school is well on the ~ to being finished** la nouvelle école est presque terminée.

◆ **one way and another** *adv phr* en fin de compte.

◆ **one way or the other, one way or another** *adv phr* **1.** [by whatever means] d'une façon ou d'une autre **2.** [expressing impartiality or indifference] : **I've nothing to say one ~ or the other** je n'ai rien à dire, ni pour ni contre ■ **it doesn't matter to them one ~ or another** ça leur est égal **3.** [more or less] : **a month one ~ or the other** un mois de plus ou de moins.

◆ **out of one's way** *adv phr* : **I don't want to take you out of your ~** je ne veux pas vous faire faire un détour ■ **don't go out of your ~ for me!** *fig* ne vous dérangez pas pour moi! ■ **she went out of her ~ to find me a job** *fig* elle s'est donné du mal pour me trouver du travail.

◆ **under way** *adj & adv phr* : **to be under ~** [person, vehicle] être en route ; *fig* [meeting, talks] être en cours ; [plans, project] être en train ■ **to get under ~** [person, train] se mettre en route, partir ; [car] se mettre en route, démarrer ; *fig* [meeting, plans, talks] démarrer ■ **the meeting was already under ~** la réunion avait déjà commencé ■ **the project is well under ~** le projet est en bonne voie de réalisation ‖ NAUT : **the ship is under ~** le navire est en route ■ **the ship got under ~** le navire a appareillé *OR* a levé l'ancre.

-way *in cpds* : **one~ street** rue *f* à sens unique ■ **a four~ discussion** une discussion à quatre participants ■ **there was a three~ split of the profits** les bénéfices ont été divisés en trois.

waybill ['weɪbɪl] *n* feuille *f* de route, lettre *f* de voiture.

wayfarer ['weɪfeərər] *n* voyageur *m*, - euse *f*.

waylay [,weɪ'leɪ] (*pret & pp* **waylaid** [-'leɪd]) *vt* [attack] attaquer, assaillir ■ [stop] intercepter, arrêter (au passage).

way-out *adj inf* [unusual - film, style] bizarre, curieux ; [- person] excentrique, bizarre.

Ways and Means Committee *pr n commission américaine du budget à la Chambre des représentants.*

wayside ['weɪsaɪd] ◇ *n* bord *m OR* côté *m* de la route.
◇ *adj* au bord de la route.

way station *n US* RAIL petite gare *f* ■ *fig* étape *f*.

wayward ['weɪwəd] *adj* **1.** [person - wilful] entêté, têtu ; [- unpredictable] qui n'en fait qu'à sa tête, imprévisible ■ [behaviour] imprévisible ■ [horse] rétif **2.** [fate] fâcheux, malencontreux.

WBC (*abbrev of* **World Boxing Council**) *pr n* Conseil *m* mondial de la boxe.

WC (*abbrev of* **water closet**) *n* W-C *mpl*.

WCC *pr n* = **World Council of Churches**.

we [wiː] *pron* **1.** [oneself and others] nous ▪ **we, the people** nous, le peuple ▪ **we Democrats believe that...** nous, les démocrates, croyons que... ▪ **as we will see in chapter two** comme nous le verrons *OR* comme on le verra dans le chapitre deux ▪ **we all make mistakes** tout le monde peut se tromper **2.** *fml* [royal] nous ▪ **the royal we** le nous *OR* pluriel de majesté **3.** *inf* [you] : **and how are we today, John?** alors, comment allons-nous aujourd'hui, John ?

weak [wiːk] ◇ *adj* **1.** [physically - animal, person] faible ; [- health] fragile, délicat ; [- eyes, hearing] faible, mauvais ▪ **to become** *OR* **to get** *OR* **to grow ~** *OR* **~er** s'affaiblir ▪ **we were ~ with** *OR* **from hunger** nous étions affaiblis par la faim ▪ **he felt ~ with fear** il avait les jambes molles de peur ▪ **I went ~ at the knees** mes jambes se sont dérobées sous moi, j'avais les jambes en coton ▪ **the ~er sex** le sexe faible
2. [morally, mentally] mou *(before vowel or silent 'h'* **mol**), molle *f*, faible ▪ **in a ~ moment** dans un moment de faiblesse
3. [feeble - argument, excuse] faible, peu convaincant ; [- army, government, institution] faible, impuissant ; [- structure] fragile, peu solide ; [- light, signal, currency, economy, stock market] faible ▪ **she managed a ~ smile** elle a réussi à sourire faiblement ▪ **she answered in a ~ voice** elle répondit d'une voix faible ▪ **he's the ~ link in the chain** c'est lui le maillon faible de la chaîne
4. [deficient, poor - pupil, subject] faible ▪ **I'm ~ in geography, geography is my ~ subject** je suis faible en géographie ▪ **she's rather ~ on discipline** elle est plutôt laxiste
5. [chin] fuyant ▪ [mouth] tombant
6. [acid, solution] faible ▪ [drink, tea] léger ▪ AUT & MECH [mixture] pauvre
7. GRAM & LING [verb] faible, régulier ▪ [syllable] faible, inaccentué.
◇ *npl* : **the ~** les faibles *mpl*.

weaken [ˈwiːkn] ◇ *vt* **1.** [person] affaiblir ▪ [heart] fatiguer ▪ [health] miner **2.** [government, institution, team] affaiblir ▪ FIN [dollar, mark] affaiblir, faire baisser **3.** [argument] enlever du poids *OR* de la force à ▪ [position] affaiblir ▪ [determination] affaiblir, faire fléchir **4.** [structure] affaiblir, rendre moins solide ▪ [foundations, cliff] miner, saper.
◇ *vi* **1.** [person - physically] s'affaiblir, faiblir ; [- morally] faiblir ▪ [voice, health, determination] faiblir ▪ **he finally ~ed and gave in** il s'est finalement laissé fléchir et a cédé **2.** [influence, power] diminuer, baisser **3.** [structure] faiblir, devenir moins solide **4.** FIN [dollar, mark] s'affaiblir ▪ [prices] fléchir, baisser.

weakening [ˈwiːkənɪŋ] *n* [of person, resolve] affaiblissement *m* ▪ [of currency or structure] fléchissement *m*, affaiblissement *m*.

weak-kneed [-niːd] *adj* mou *(before vowel or silent 'h' mol)*, molle *f*, lâche.

weakling [ˈwiːklɪŋ] *n* **1.** [physically] gringalet *m*, petite nature *f* **2.** [morally] faible *mf*, mauviette *f*.

weakly [ˈwɪːklɪ] *adv* [get up, walk] faiblement ▪ [speak] faiblement, mollement.

weak-minded *adj* **1.** [not intelligent] faible *OR* simple d'esprit **2.** [lacking willpower] faible, irrésolu.

weakness [ˈwiːknɪs] *n* **1.** [of person - physical] faiblesse *f* ; [- moral] point *m* faible ▪ **in a moment of ~** dans un moment de faiblesse ▪ **he has a ~ for sports cars** il a un faible pour les voitures de sport **2.** [of government, institution] faiblesse *f*, fragilité *f* **3.** [of structure] fragilité *f* **4.** FIN [of currency] faiblesse *f*.

weak-willed *adj* faible, velléitaire.

weal [wiːl] *n* [mark] marque *f* de coup, zébrure *f*.

Weald [wiːld] *pr n* [region] : **the ~** *région du sud-est de l'Angleterre*.

wealth [welθ] *n (U)* **1.** [richness - of family, person] richesse *f*, richesses *fpl*, fortune *f* ; [- of nation] richesse *f*, prospérité *f* **2.** [large amount - of details, ideas] abondance *f*, profusion *f* ▪ **he showed a ~ of knowledge about Egyptian art** il fit preuve d'une profonde connaissance de l'art égyptien.

wealth tax *n UK* impôt *m* sur la fortune.

wealthy [ˈwelθɪ] (*comp* **wealthier**, *superl* **wealthiest**) ◇ *adj* [person] riche, fortuné ▪ [country] riche.
◇ *npl* : **the ~** les riches *mpl*.

wean [wiːn] *vt* [baby] sevrer ▪ **a generation ~ed on television** une génération qui a grandi avec la télévision.
➡ **wean off** *vt sep* : **to ~ sb off sthg** détourner qqn de qqch ▪ **I've ~ed him off cigarettes** je lui ai fait perdre l'habitude de fumer.

weapon [ˈwepən] *n* **1.** arme *f* ▪ **carrying a ~ is illegal** le port d'armes est illégal **2.** armement *m* ▪ **~s of mass destruction** armes *fpl* de destruction massive.

weaponize [ˈwepənaɪz] *vt* MIL militariser ▪ **~d plutonium** plutonium militaire.

weaponry [ˈwepənrɪ] *n (U)* armes *fpl* ▪ MIL matériel *m* de guerre, armements *mpl*.

weapons-grade *adj* militaire.

wear [weəʳ] (*pret* **wore** [wɔːʳ], *pp* **worn** [wɔːn]) ◇ *vt* **1.** [beard, spectacles, clothing etc] porter ▪ **what shall I ~?** qu'est-ce que je vais mettre? ▪ **I haven't a thing to ~** je n'ai rien à me mettre ▪ **to ~ a seat belt** AUT mettre la ceinture (de sécurité) ▪ **the miniskirt is being worn again this year** la minijupe se porte de nouveau cette année ▪ **he was ~ing slippers/a dressing gown** il était en chaussons/en robe de chambre ▪ **he ~s a beard** il porte la barbe ▪ **she ~s her hair in a bun** elle a un chignon ▪ **do you always ~ make-up?** tu te maquilles tous les jours? ▪ **she wore lipstick** elle s'était mis *OR* elle avait mis du rouge à lèvres ▪ **I often ~ perfume/aftershave** je mets souvent du parfum/de la lotion après-rasage
2. [expression] avoir, afficher ▪ [smile] arborer ▪ **he wore a frown** il fronçait les sourcils
3. [make by rubbing] user ▪ **to ~ holes in sthg** trouer *OR* percer peu à peu qqch ▪ **her shoes were worn thin** ses chaussures étaient complètement usées ▪ **a path had been worn across the lawn** un sentier avait été creusé à travers la pelouse par le passage des gens ▪ **the wheel had worn a groove in the wood** la roue avait creusé le bois
4. *UK inf* [accept - argument, behaviour] supporter, tolérer ▪ **I won't ~ it!** je ne marcherai pas!
5. *phr* **to ~ o.s. to a frazzle** *OR* **a shadow** s'éreinter.
◇ *vi* **1.** [endure, last] durer ▪ **wool ~s better than cotton** la laine résiste mieux à l'usure *OR* fait meilleur usage que le coton ▪ **this coat has worn well** ce manteau a bien servi ▮ *fig* **their friendship has worn well** leur amitié est restée intacte malgré le temps ▪ **she's worn well** *UK inf* elle est bien conservée
2. [be damaged through use] s'user ▪ **this rug has worn badly in the middle** ce tapis est très usé au milieu ▪ **the carpet had worn thin** le tapis était usé *OR* élimé ▪ **the stone had worn smooth** la pierre était polie par le temps ▮ *fig* **her patience was ~ing thin** elle était presque à bout de patience ▪ **his excuses are ~ing a bit thin** ses excuses ne prennent plus ▪ **his jokes are ~ing a bit thin** ses plaisanteries ne sont plus drôles
3. *lit* [time] passer ▪ **as the year wore to its close** comme l'année tirait à sa fin.
◇ *n (U)* **1.** [of clothes] : **for everyday ~** pour porter tous les jours ▪ **clothes suitable for evening ~** tenue de soirée ▪ **a suit for business ~** un costume pour le bureau ➊ **women's ~** vêtements *mpl* pour femmes ▪ **winter ~** vêtements *mpl* d'hiver
2. [use] usage *m* ▪ **these shoes will stand hard ~** ces chaussures feront un bon usage *OR* résisteront bien à l'usure ▪ **there's still plenty of ~ in that dress** cette robe est encore très portable ▪ **to get a lot of ~ from** *OR* **out of sthg** faire durer qqch ▪ **is there any ~ left in them?** feront-ils encore de l'usage?
3. [deterioration] : **~ (and tear)** usure *f* ▪ **living in the big city puts a lot of ~ and tear on people** les grandes villes sont une source de stress pour leurs habitants ▪ **the sheets are beginning to show signs of ~** les draps commencent à être un peu usés *OR* fatigués.
➡ **wear away** ◇ *vt sep* [soles] user ▪ [cliff, land] ronger, éroder ▪ [paint, design] effacer.
◇ *vi insep* [metal] s'user ▪ [land] être rongé *OR* érodé ▪ [grass, topsoil] disparaître *(par usure)* ▪ [design] s'effacer.

◆ **wear down** <> *vt sep* [steps] user ■ *fig* [patience, strength] épuiser petit à petit ■ [courage, resistance] saper, miner ■ **in the end she wore me down** [I gave in to her] elle a fini par me faire céder.
<> *vi insep* [pencil, steps, tyres] s'user ■ [courage] s'épuiser ■ **the heels have worn down** les talons sont usés.
◆ **wear off** <> *vi insep* **1.** [marks, design] s'effacer, disparaître
2. [excitement] s'apaiser, passer ■ [anaesthetic, effects] se dissiper, disparaître ■ [pain] se calmer, passer ■ **the novelty soon wore off** l'attrait de la nouveauté a vite passé.
<> *vt sep* effacer par l'usure, user.
◆ **wear on** *vi insep* [day, season] avancer lentement ■ [battle, discussion] se poursuivre lentement ■ **as time wore on** au fur et à mesure que le temps passait.
◆ **wear out** <> *vt sep* **1.** [clothing, machinery] user
2. [patience, strength, reserves] épuiser ■ **to ~ out one's welcome** abuser de l'hospitalité de ses hôtes
3. [tire] épuiser ■ **to be worn out** être exténué *OR* éreinté ■ **worn out from arguing, he finally accepted their offer** de guerre lasse, il a fini par accepter leur offre.
<> *vi insep* [clothing, shoes] s'user ■ **this material will never ~ out** ce tissu est inusable.
◆ **wear through** <> *vt sep* trouer, percer.
<> *vi insep* se trouer.

wearable ['weərəbl] *adj* portable.

wearily ['wɪərɪlɪ] *adv* avec lassitude ■ **he smiled ~** il sourit d'un air fatigué.

weariness ['wɪərɪnɪs] *n* **1.** [physical] lassitude *f*, fatigue *f* ■ [moral] lassitude *f*, abattement *m* **2.** [boredom] lassitude *f*, ennui *m*.

wearing ['weərɪŋ] *adj* fatigant, épuisant.

wearisome ['wɪərɪsəm] *adj* **1.** [tiring] fatigant, épuisant **2.** [annoying] ennuyeux, lassant.

weary ['wɪərɪ] <> *adj* (*comp* **wearier**, *superl* **weariest**) **1.** [tired - physically, morally] las, lasse *f* *soutenu*, fatigué ■ **she grew ~ of reading** elle s'est lassée de lire ■ **he gave a ~ sigh** il a soupiré d'un air las ■ **I'm ~ of life** j'en ai assez *OR* je suis las de la vie **2.** [tiring - day, journey] fatigant, lassant.
<> *vt* (*pret & pp* **wearied**) [tire] fatiguer, lasser ■ [annoy] lasser, agacer.
<> *vi* (*pret & pp* **wearied**) se lasser.

weasel ['wi:zl] <> *n* belette *f* ■ *pej* [person] fouine *f*.
<> *vi* US ruser ■ [in speaking] parler d'une façon ambiguë.
<> *vt* : **he ~ed his way into the conversation** il s'est insinué dans la conversation.
◆ **weasel out** *vi insep* US *inf* **to ~ out of sthg** se tirer de qqch ■ **he ~ed out of the contract** il s'est débrouillé pour se dégager du contrat ■ **she always ~s out of doing the dishes** elle se débrouille toujours pour échapper à la vaisselle.

weather ['weðər] <> *n* **1.** METEOR temps *m* ■ **what's the ~ (like) today?** quel temps fait-il aujourd'hui? ■ **it's beautiful/terrible ~** il fait beau/mauvais ■ **the ~ is awful** *OR* **foul** il fait un temps de chien ■ **~ permitting** si le temps le permet ■ **surely you're not going out in this ~?** vous n'allez tout de même pas sortir par un temps pareil? ■ **in hot ~** par temps chaud, en période de chaleur ■ **in all ~s** par tous les temps ■ **there was a change in the ~** il y eut un changement de temps, le temps changea **2.** RADIO & TV : **~ (forecast)** (bulletin *m*) météo *f* **3.** *phr* **to feel under the ~** *inf* ne pas être dans son assiette.
<> *comp* [forecast, map] météorologique ■ [conditions] climatique, atmosphérique ■ NAUT [side] du vent ■ **keep your ~ eye open!** *inf* veillez au grain! ■ **I'll keep a ~ eye on the kids** *inf* je vais surveiller les enfants.
<> *vt* **1.** [survive - storm] réchapper à ; [- crisis] survivre à, réchapper à ■ **will he ~ the storm?** *fig* va-t-il se tirer d'affaire *OR* tenir le coup? **2.** [wood] exposer aux intempéries.
<> *vi* [bronze, wood] se patiner ■ [rock] s'éroder ■ **this paint ~s well** cette peinture vieillit bien *OR* résiste bien aux intempéries.

weather balloon *n* ballon-sonde *m*.

weather-beaten *adj* [face, person] buriné ■ [building, stone] dégradé par les intempéries.

weatherboard ['weðəbɔ:d] *n* **1.** *(U)* [on outer walls] planche *f* *OR* planches *fpl* à recouvrement **2.** [on door] planche *f* de recouvrement.

weather bureau *n* US ≃ office *m* national de la météorologie.

weather centre *n* UK ≃ centre *m* météorologique régional.

weathercock ['weðəkɒk] *n* *liter & fig* girouette *f*.

weathered ['weðəd] *adj* [bronze, wood] patiné par le temps ■ [building, stone] érodé par le temps, usé par les intempéries ■ [face] buriné.

weathering ['weðərɪŋ] *n* désagrégation *f*, érosion *f*.

weatherman ['weðəmæn] (*pl* **weathermen** [-men]) *n* : **the ~** le météorologue, le météorologiste ; RADIO & TV le journaliste météo.

weatherproof ['weðəpru:f] <> *adj* [clothing] imperméable ■ [building] étanche.
<> *vt* [clothing] imperméabiliser ■ [building] rendre étanche.

weather report *n* bulletin *m* météorologique.

weather satellite *n* satellite *m* météorologique.

weather ship *n* navire *m* météorologique.

weather station *n* station *f* *OR* observatoire *m* météorologique.

weather strip, weather stripping ['strɪpɪŋ] *n* bourrelet *m* étanche.

weather vane *n* girouette *f*.

weave [wi:v] <> *vt* (*pp* **wove** [wəʊv] *pp* **woven** ['wəʊvn]) **1.** [cloth, web] tisser ■ [basket, garland] tresser ■ **she wove the strands together into a necklace** elle a tressé *OR* entrelacé les fils pour en faire un collier **2.** [story] tramer, bâtir ■ [plot] tisser, tramer ■ [spell] jeter **3.** [introduce] introduire, incorporer **4.** (*pret & pp* **weaved**) [as verb of movement] : **he ~d his way across the room/towards the bar** il s'est frayé un chemin à travers la salle/vers le bar ■ **the cyclist ~d his way through the traffic** le cycliste se faufilait *OR* se glissait à travers la circulation.
<> *vi* (*pp* **wove** [wəʊv] *pp* **woven** ['wəʊvn]) **1.** TEX tisser **2.** [road, river] serpenter **3.** (*pret & pp* **weaved**) [as verb of movement] se faufiler, se glisser ■ **he ~d unsteadily across the street** il a traversé la rue en titubant *OR* en zigzaguant ■ **the boxer ducked and ~d** le boxeur a esquivé tous les coups ■ **come on, get weaving!** *inf* allons, grouillez-vous!
<> *n* tissage *m*.

weaver ['wi:vər] *n* **1.** TEX tisserand *m*, - e *f* **2.** ORNITH tisserin *m*.

weaving ['wi:vɪŋ] <> *n* **1.** [of cloth] tissage *m* ■ [of baskets, garlands] tressage *m* **2.** [of story] récit *m* ■ [of plot] trame *f*.
<> *comp* [industry, mill] de tissage.

web [web] *n* **1.** [of fabric, metal] tissu *m* ■ [of spider] toile *f* ■ *fig* [of lies] tissu *m* ■ [of intrigue] réseau *m* **2.** [on feet - of duck, frog] palmure *f* ; [- of humans] palmature *f*.
◆ **Web** *n* COMPUT : **the Web** le Web, la Toile, le web *m*, la toile *f* mondiale ■ **on the Web** sur le web, sur la toile.

webbed [webd] *adj* palmé ■ **to have ~ feet** *OR* **toes** [duck, frog] avoir les pattes palmées ; [human] avoir une palmature.

webbing ['webɪŋ] *n* *(U)* **1.** TEX [material] toile *f* à sangles ■ [on chair] sangles *fpl* **2.** ANAT [animal] palmure *f* ■ [human] palmature *f*.

web browser *n* COMPUT navigateur *m*.

webcam ['webkæm] *n* webcam *f*.

web designer *n* concepteur *m* de site web.

web-footed [-'fʊtɪd] *adj* [animal] palmipède, qui a les pattes palmées ■ [human] qui a une palmature.

weblog ['weblɒg] *n* COMPUT weblog *m*.

Webmaster ['web,mɑ:stər] *n* webmaster *m*, webmestre *m*.

Web page *n* page *f* Web.

website ['websaɪt] *n* site *m* Web.

wed [wed] (*pret & pp* **wed** *OR* **wedded**, *cont* **wedding**) ◇ *vt lit* **1.** [marry] épouser, se marier avec ▪ **to get ~** se marier **2.** (*usu passive*) [unite] allier ▪ **intelligence wedded to beauty** l'intelligence alliée à la beauté ▪ **he's wedded to the cause** il est véritablement marié à cette cause **3.** [subj: priest] marier.
◇ *vi* [in headline] se marier ▪ **PM's son to ~** le fils du Premier ministre se marie.

we'd [wi:d] **1.** = **we would 2.** = **we had**.

Wed. (*written abbrev of* **Wednesday**) mer.

wedded ['wedɪd] *adj* [person] marié ▪ [bliss, life] conjugal ▪ **her lawful ~ husband** son époux légitime ▪ **the newly ~ couple** les jeunes mariés *mpl*.

wedding ['wedɪŋ] ◇ *n* **1.** [marriage] mariage *m*, noces *fpl* ▪ **to have a church ~** se marier à l'église **2.** [uniting] union *f*.
◇ *comp* [night, trip] de noces ▪ [ceremony, photograph, present] de mariage ▪ **~ cake** gâteau *m* de noces, ≃ pièce *f* montée ▪ **~ invitation** invitation *f* de mariage.

wedding anniversary *n* anniversaire *m* de mariage.

wedding band = **wedding ring**.

wedding day *n* jour *m* du mariage ▪ **on their ~** le jour de leur mariage.

wedding dress *n* robe *f* de mariée.

wedding march *n* marche *f* nuptiale.

wedding reception *n* réception *f* de mariage.

wedding ring *n* alliance *f*, anneau *m* de mariage.

wedge [wedʒ] ◇ *n* **1.** [under door, wheel] cale *f* ▪ **their political differences drove a ~ between the two friends** *fig* les deux amis se sont brouillés à cause de leurs divergences politiques **2.** [for splitting wood] coin *m* **3.** [of cheese, cake, pie] morceau *m*, part *f* **4.** [golf club] cale *f* **5.** [for climber] coin *m*.
◇ *vt* **1.** [make fixed or steady] caler ▪ **I ~d the door open/shut** j'ai maintenu la porte ouverte/fermée par une cale **2.** [squeeze, push] enfoncer ▪ **to ~ sthg apart** fendre *OR* forcer qqch ▪ **he ~d his foot in the door** il a bloqué la porte avec son pied ▪ **she sat ~d between her two aunts** elle était assise coincée entre ses deux tantes ▪ **I found the ring ~d down behind the cushion** j'ai trouvé la bague enfoncée derrière le coussin.
➡ **wedge in** *vt sep* [object] faire rentrer, enfoncer ▪ [person] faire rentrer ▪ **she was ~d in between two Italians** elle était coincée entre deux Italiens.

wedge-heeled [-hi:ld] *adj* à semelle compensée.

wedlock ['wedlɒk] *n fml* mariage *m* ▪ **to be born out of ~** être un enfant naturel, être né hors du mariage.

Wednesday ['wenzdɪ] *n* mercredi *m*, *see also* **Friday**.

wee [wi:] ◇ *adj esp Scotland* tout petit ▪ **in the ~ (small) hours of the morning** au petit matin, aux premières heures du jour.
◇ *vi inf* faire pipi.
◇ *n inf* pipi *m* ▪ **to have a ~** faire pipi.

weed [wi:d] ◇ *n* **1.** [plant] mauvaise herbe *f* ▪ **that plant grows like a ~** cette plante pousse comme du chiendent **2.** *pej* [person] mauviette *f* **3.** *inf* [tobacco] : **the ~** le tabac **4.**[△] *drug sl* herbe *f*.
◇ *vt* désherber, arracher les mauvaises herbes de.
◇ *vi* désherber, arracher les mauvaises herbes.
➡ **weeds** *npl* vêtements *mpl* de deuil.
➡ **weed out** *vt sep* éliminer ▪ [troublemakers] expulser ▪ **to ~ out the bad from the good** faire le tri.

weeding ['wi:dɪŋ] *n* désherbage *m*.

weedkiller ['wi:d,kɪləʳ] *n* herbicide *m*, désherbant *m*.

weedy ['wi:dɪ] (*comp* **weedier**, *superl* **weediest**) *adj* **1.** [ground] couvert *OR* envahi de mauvaises herbes **2.** *inf pej* [person] malingre.

Weejun® ['wi:dʒn] *n US* mocassin *m*.

week [wi:k] *n* semaine *f* ▪ **next/last ~** la semaine prochaine/dernière ▪ **in one ~, in one ~'s time** dans huit jours, d'ici une semaine ▪ **two ~s ago** il y a deux semaines *OR* quinze jours ▪ **within a ~** [gen] dans la semaine, d'ici une semaine ; ADMIN & COMM sous huitaine ▪ **~ ending 25th March** la semaine du 21 mars ▪ **a ~ from today** d'ici huit jours ▪ **a ~ from tomorrow** demain en huit ▪ **yesterday ~, a ~ yesterday** il y a eu une semaine hier ▪ **Monday ~, a ~ on Monday** lundi en huit ▪ **~ in ~ out, ~ after ~, ~ by ~** semaine après semaine ▪ **from ~ to ~** de semaine en semaine ▪ **it rained for ~s on end** il a plu pendant des semaines ▪ **I haven't seen you in *OR* for ~s** ça fait des semaines que je ne t'ai pas vu ▪ **we're taking a ~'s holiday** nous prenons huit jours de congé ▪ **the working ~** la semaine de travail ▪ **a 40-hour/five-day ~** une semaine de 40 heures/cinq jours ▪ **she's paid by the ~** elle est payée à la semaine.

weekday ['wi:k,deɪ] ◇ *n* jour *m* de la semaine ▪ ADMIN & COMM jour *m* ouvrable ▪ **on ~s** en semaine ▪ **'~s only'** 'sauf samedi et dimanche'.
◇ *comp* [activities] de la semaine ▪ **on ~ mornings** le matin en semaine.

weekend [,wi:k'end] ◇ *n* fin *f* de semaine, week-end *m* ▪ **at *UK OR* on *US* the ~** le week-end ▪ **I'll do it at the ~** je le ferai pendant le week-end ▪ **a long ~** un week-end prolongé.
◇ *comp* [schedule, visite] de *OR* du week-end ▪ **~ bag *OR* case** sac *m* de voyage, mallette *f* ▪ **~ break** *séjour d'un week-end*.
◇ *vi* passer le week-end.

weekender [,wi:k'endeʳ] *n personne en voyage pour le week-end* ▪ **most of the cottages belong to ~s** la plupart des maisons sont des résidences secondaires.

weekend return *n UK* RAIL *billet aller-retour valable du vendredi au dimanche soir*.

weekly ['wi:klɪ] ◇ *adj* [visit, meeting] de la semaine, hebdomadaire ▪ [publication, payment, wage] hebdomadaire.
◇ *n* hebdomadaire *m*.
◇ *adv* [once a week] chaque semaine, une fois par semaine ▪ [each week] chaque semaine, tous les huit jours ▪ **twice ~** deux fois par semaine ▪ **he's paid ~** il est payé à la semaine.

weeknight ['wi:k,naɪt] *n* soir *m* de la semaine ▪ **I can't go out on ~s** je ne peux pas sortir le soir en semaine.

weenie ['wi:nɪ] *n US inf* **1.** [frankfurter] saucisse *f* (de Francfort) **2.** [penis] zizi *m* **3.** [person] imbécile *mf*.

weeny ['wi:nɪ] (*comp* **weenier**, *superl* **weeniest**) *adj inf* tout petit, minuscule.

weep [wi:p] (*pret & pp* **wept** [wept]) ◇ *vi* **1.** [person] pleurer, verser des larmes ▪ **to ~ for joy/with vexation** pleurer de joie/de dépit ▪ **she wept for her lost youth** elle pleurait sa jeunesse perdue ▪ **to ~ for sb** pleurer qqn ▪ **the little girl wept over her broken doll** la petite fille pleurait sur sa poupée cassée ▪ **he wept to see her so ill** il a pleuré de la voir si malade ▪ **it's enough to make you ~!** *hum* c'est à faire pleurer! ▪ **I could have wept!** j'en aurais pleuré! **2.** [walls, wound] suinter, suer.
◇ *vt* [tears] verser, pleurer.
◇ *n* : **to have a ~** pleurer, verser quelques larmes.

weeping ['wi:pɪŋ] ◇ *adj* [person] qui pleure ▪ [walls, wound] suintant.
◇ *n (U)* larmes *fpl*, pleurs *mpl*.

weeping willow *n* saule *m* pleureur.

weepy ['wi:pɪ] ◇ *adj* (*comp* **weepier**, *superl* **weepiest**) **1.** [tone, voice] larmoyant ▪ [person] qui pleure ▪ **she is *OR* feels ~** elle a envie de pleurer, elle est au bord des larmes **2.** [film, story] sentimental, larmoyant.
◇ *n* (*pl* weepies) *UK inf* [film] mélo *m*, film *m* sentimental ▪ [book] mélo *m*, roman *m* à l'eau de rose.

weevil ['wi:vl] *n* charançon *m*.

wee-wee *inf baby* ◇ *n* pipi *m*.
◇ *vi* faire pipi.

weft [weft] *n* TEX trame *f*.

weigh [weɪ] ◇ *vt* **1.** [person, thing] peser ▪ **to ~ oneself** se peser ▪ **to ~ sthg in one's hand** soupeser qqch *liter* **2.** [consider] considérer, peser ▪ **let's ~ the evidence** considérons les faits ▪ **she ~ed her words carefully** elle a bien pesé ses mots ▪ **you**

have to ~ the pros and cons il faut peser le pour et le contre ■ **to ~ one thing against another** mettre deux choses en balance **3.** NAUT : **to ~ anchor** lever l'ancre.
<> *vi* **1.** [person, object] peser ■ **how much do you ~?** combien pesez-vous?, quel poids faites-vous? ■ **he doesn't ~ much** il ne pèse pas lourd **2.** [influence] : **his silence began to ~ (heavy)** son silence commençait à devenir pesant ■ **the facts ~ heavily against him** les faits plaident lourdement en sa défaveur.
◆ **weigh down** *vt sep* **1.** *liter* faire plier, courber ■ **she was ~ed down with suitcases** elle pliait sous le poids des valises **2.** *fig* **~ed down with debts/with sorrow** accablé de dettes/de tristesse.
◆ **weigh in** *vi insep* **1.** SPORT se faire peser *(avant une épreuve)* ■ **the boxer ~ed in at 85 kilos** le boxeur faisait 85 kilos avant le match **2.** [join in] intervenir.
◆ **weigh on** *vt insep* peser ■ **his worries ~ed heavily on him** ses soucis lui pesaient beaucoup ■ **the exam ~ed on his mind** l'examen le préoccupait OR tracassait.
◆ **weigh out** *vt sep* peser.
◆ **weigh up** *vt sep* **1.** [consider] examiner, calculer ■ [compare] mettre en balance ■ **to ~ up the situation** peser la situation ■ **I'm ~ing up whether to take the job or not** je me demande si je devrais prendre le poste ■ **to ~ up the pros and cons** peser le pour et le contre **2.** [size up] mesurer.

weighbridge ['weɪbrɪdʒ] *n* pont-bascule *m*.

weigh-in *n* SPORT pesage *m*, pesée *f*.

weighing machine ['weɪɪŋ-] *n* [for people] balance *f* ■ [for loads] bascule *f*.

weight [weɪt] <> *n* **1.** [of person, package, goods] poids *m* ■ **she tested** OR **felt the ~ of the package** elle a soupesé le paquet ■ **my ~ is 50 kg, I'm 50 kilos in ~** je pèse OR je fais 50 kilos ■ **we're the same ~** nous faisons le même poids ■ **he's twice your ~** il pèse deux fois plus lourd que toi ■ **to gain** OR **to put on ~** grossir, prendre du poids ■ **to lose ~** maigrir, perdre du poids ■ **she's watching her ~** elle fait attention à sa ligne ■ **what a ~!** [person] qu'il est lourd! ; [stone, parcel] que c'est lourd! ■ **to sell sthg by ~** vendre qqch au poids ◐ **she's worth her ~ in gold** elle vaut son pesant d'or ■ **take the ~ off your feet** *hum* asseyds-toi un peu
2. [force] poids *m* ■ **he put his full ~ behind the blow** il a frappé de toutes ses forces ◐ **to pull one's ~** faire sa part du travail, y mettre du sien ■ **to throw one's ~ about** OR **around** bousculer les gens
3. [burden] poids *m* ■ **that's a ~ off my mind** je suis vraiment soulagé
4. [importance, influence] poids *m*, influence *f* ■ **their opinion carries quite a lot of ~** leur opinion a un poids OR une autorité considérable ■ **she put** OR **threw all her ~ behind the candidate** elle a apporté tout son soutien au candidat
5. [for scales] poids *m* ■ **~s and measures** poids et mesures ■ **a set of ~s** une série de poids
6. SPORT poids *m* ■ **to lift ~s** soulever des poids OR des haltères
7. PHYS pesanteur *f*, poids *m*.
<> *comp* : **~ allowance** [in aeroplane] poids *m* de bagages autorisé ■ **to have a ~ problem** avoir un problème de poids.
<> *vt* **1.** [put weights on] lester
2. [hold down] retenir OR maintenir avec un poids
3. [bias] : **the system is ~ed in favour of the wealthy** le système est favorable aux riches OR privilégie les riches ■ **the electoral system was ~ed against him** le système électoral lui était défavorable OR jouait contre lui.
◆ **weight down** *vt sep* **1.** [body, net] lester
2. [papers, tarpaulin] maintenir OR retenir avec un poids.

weighted ['weɪtɪd] *adj* **1.** [body, net] lesté **2.** [statistics, average] pondéré.

weighting ['weɪtɪŋ] *n* **1.** [extra salary] indemnité *f*, allocation *f* ■ **London ~** indemnité de résidence à Londres **2.** [of statistics] pondération *f* ■ SCH coefficient *m*.

weightless ['weɪtlɪs] *adj* très léger ■ ASTRONAUT en état d'apesanteur.

weightlessness ['weɪtlɪsnɪs] *n* extrême légèreté *f* ■ ASTRONAUT apesanteur *f*.

weightlifter ['weɪt,lɪftər] *n* haltérophile *mf*.

weightlifting ['weɪt,lɪftɪŋ] *n* haltérophilie *f*.

weight loss *n* perte *f* de poids.

weight training *n* entraînement *m* aux haltères.

weightwatcher ['weɪt,wɒtʃər] *n* [person - on diet] personne *f* qui suit un régime ; [- figure-conscious] personne *f* qui surveille son poids.

weighty ['weɪtɪ] (*comp* **weightier**, *superl* **weightiest**) *adj* **1.** [suitcase, tome] lourd **2.** [responsibility] lourd ■ [problem] important, grave ■ [argument, reasoning] probant, de poids.

weir [wɪər] *n* barrage *m (sur un cours d'eau)*.

weird [wɪəd] *adj* **1.** [mysterious] mystérieux, surnaturel **2.** *inf* [peculiar] bizarre, étrange.

weirdo ['wɪədəʊ] (*pl* **weirdos**) *inf* <> *n* drôle d'oiseau *m* OR de zèbre *m*.
<> *comp* [hairdo] extravagant.

welch [welʃ] = **welsh**.

welcome ['welkəm] <> *vt* **1.** [greet, receive - people] accueillir ■ **I ~d her warmly** je lui ai fait bon accueil OR un accueil chaleureux ■ **they ~d me in** ils m'ont chaleureusement invité à entrer ■ **we ~d him with open arms** nous l'avons accueilli à bras ouverts ■ **would you please ~ Peter Robinson!** [to audience] voulez-vous applaudir Peter Robinson!
2. [accept gladly] être heureux d'avoir, recevoir avec plaisir ■ **I ~d the opportunity to speak to her** j'étais content d'avoir l'occasion de lui parler ■ **he ~d the news** il s'est réjoui de la nouvelle, il a accueilli la nouvelle avec joie ■ **she ~d any comments** elle accueillait volontiers les remarques que l'on pouvait lui faire ■ **we'd ~ a cup of coffee** nous prendrions volontiers une tasse de café.
<> *n* accueil *m* ■ **she said a few words of ~** elle a prononcé quelques mots de bienvenue ■ **we bid them ~** nous leur souhaitons la bienvenue ■ **they gave him a warm ~** ils lui ont fait bon accueil OR réservé un accueil chaleureux ■ **we gave her a big ~ home** nous lui avons fait fête à son retour à la maison ■ **let's give a warm ~ to Louis Armstrong!** [to audience] applaudissons très fort Louis Armstrong! ■ **to overstay** OR **to outstay one's ~** abuser de l'hospitalité de ses hôtes.
<> *adj* **1.** [person] bienvenu ■ **to be ~** être le bienvenu ■ **they made us very ~** ils nous ont fait un très bon accueil ■ **she didn't feel very ~** elle s'est sentie de trop ◐ **to put out the ~ mat (for sb)** faire un accueil chaleureux (à qqn)
2. [pleasant, desirable - arrival] bienvenu ; [- change, interruption, remark] opportun ■ **that's ~ news** nous sommes heureux de l'apprendre ■ **their offer was most ~** leur suggestion m'a fait grand plaisir ■ **this cheque is most ~** ce chèque arrive opportunément OR tombe bien ■ **that's a ~ sight!** c'est un spectacle à réjouir le cœur! ■ **a helping hand is always ~** un coup de main est toujours le bienvenu OR ne fait jamais de mal ■ **the news came as a ~ relief to him** la nouvelle a été un vrai soulagement pour lui, il a été vraiment soulagé d'apprendre la nouvelle
3. [permitted] : **you're ~ to join us** n'hésitez pas à vous joindre à nous ■ **you're ~ to anything you need** servez-vous si vous avez besoin de quelque chose ■ **you're ~ to try** je vous en prie, essayez ■ [grudgingly] : **he's ~ to try!** libre à lui d'essayer! qu'il essaie donc! ■ **I don't need it, she's ~ to it** je n'en ai pas besoin, elle peut bien le prendre OR je le lui donne volontiers ■ **she's ~ to him!** je ne le lui envie pas!
4. [acknowledgment of thanks] : **you're ~!** je vous en prie!, il n'y a pas de quoi!
<> *interj* : **~!** soyez le bienvenu! ■ **~ back** OR **home!** content de vous revoir! ■ **'~ to Wales'** 'bienvenue au pays de Galles'.
◆ **welcome back** *vt sep* accueillir (à son retour).

welcoming ['welkəmɪŋ] *adj* [greeting, smile] accueillant ■ [ceremony, committee] d'accueil.

weld [weld] <> *vt* **1.** MECH & TECH souder ■ **he ~ed the bracket onto the shelf** il a soudé le support à l'étagère **2.** [unite] amalgamer, réunir.
<> *vi* souder.
<> *n* soudure *f*.

welder [weldəʳ] *n* [person] soudeur *m*, - euse *f* ▪ [machine] soudeuse *f*, machine *f* à souder.

welding ['weldɪŋ] *n* soudage *m* ▪ [of groups] union *f*.

welding torch *n* chalumeau *m*.

welfare ['welfeəʳ] <> *n* **1.** [well-being] bien-être *m* ▪ **the ~ of the nation** le bien public ▪ **I am concerned about** *OR* **for her ~** je m'inquiète pour elle ▪ **she's looking after his ~** elle s'occupe de lui **2.** *US* [state aid] assistance *f* publique ▪ **his family is on ~** sa famille touche des prestations sociales *OR* reçoit l'aide sociale ▪ **to live on ~** vivre de l'aide sociale ▪ **people on ~** assistés *mpl* sociaux.
<> *comp* [meals, milk] gratuit ▪ **~ benefits** *US* avantages *mpl* sociaux ▪ **~ check** *US* (chèque *m* d')allocations *fpl* ▪ **~ payments** prestations *fpl* sociales ▪ **~ worker** assistant *m* social, assistante *f* sociale.

welfare centre *n* ≃ centre *m* d'assistance sociale.

Welfare State *n* : **the ~** l'État *m* providence.

well¹ [wel] <> *n* **1.** [for water, oil] puits *m* **2.** [for lift, staircase] cage *f* ▪ [between buildings] puits *m*, cheminée *f* **3.** *UK* LAW barreau *m (au tribunal)*.
<> *vi* = **well up**.
◆ **well out** *vi insep* [water] jaillir.
◆ **well up** *vi insep* [blood, spring, tears] monter, jaillir ▪ **tears ~ed up in her eyes** les larmes lui montèrent aux yeux.

well² [wel] (*comp* **better** [betəʳ], *superl* **best** [best]) <> *adv* **1.** [satisfactorily, successfully] bien ▪ **she speaks French very ~** elle parle très bien (le) français ▪ **it's extremely ~ done** c'est vraiment très bien fait ▪ **the meeting went ~** la réunion s'est bien passée ▶ **to do ~** s'en sortir ▪ **he did very ~ for a beginner** il s'est très bien débrouillé pour un débutant ▪ **to do ~ for o.s.** bien se débrouiller ▪ **to do ~ out of sb/sthg** bien s'en sortir avec qqn/qqch ▪ **that boy will do ~!** ce garçon ira loin! ▪ **the patient is doing ~** le malade se rétablit bien *OR* est en bonne voie de guérison ▪ **we would do ~ to keep quiet** nous ferions bien de nous taire ▪ **~ done!** bravo! ▪ **~ said!** bien dit! ▪ **it was money ~ spent** ce n'était pas de l'argent gaspillé
2. [favourably, kindly] bien ▪ **everyone speaks ~ of you** tout le monde dit du bien de vous ▪ **his action speaks ~ of his courage** son geste montre bien son courage ▪ **she won't take it ~** elle ne va pas apprécier ▪ **she thinks ~ of you** elle a de l'estime pour vous ▪ **he wished her ~** il lui souhaita bonne chance ▶ **to do ~ by sb** traiter qqn comme il se doit
3. [easily, readily] bien ▪ **he could ~ decide to leave** il se pourrait tout à fait qu'il décide de partir ▪ **I couldn't very ~ accept** je ne pouvais guère accepter ▪ **you may ~ be right** il se peut bien que tu aies raison ▪ **I can ~ believe it** je le crois facilement *OR* sans peine ▪ **she was angry, and ~ she might be** elle était furieuse, et à juste titre
4. [to a considerable extent or degree] bien ▪ **she's ~ over** *OR* **past forty** elle a bien plus de quarante ans ▪ **he's ~ on in years** il n'est plus tout jeune ▪ **~ on into the morning** jusque tard dans la matinée ▪ **the fashion lasted ~ into the 1960s** cette mode a duré une bonne partie des années 60 ▪ **it's ~ after midday** il est bien plus de midi ▪ **let me know ~ in advance** prévenez-moi longtemps à l'avance ▪ **the team finished ~ up the league** l'équipe a fini parmi les premières de sa division
5. [thoroughly] bien ▪ **shake/stir ~** bien secouer/agiter ▪ **~ cooked** *OR* **done** bien cuit ▪ **I know only too ~ how hard it is** je ne sais que trop bien à quel point c'est difficile ▪ **how ~ I understand her feelings!** comme je comprends ce qu'elle ressent! ▪ **I bet he was ~ pleased!** *iron* il devait être content! *iron* ▪ **I like him ~ enough** il ne me déplaît pas ▪ **we got ~ and truly soaked** nous nous sommes fait tremper jusqu'aux os ▪ **it's ~ and truly over** c'est bel et bien fini ▪ **it's ~ worth the money** ça vaut largement la dépense ▪ **it's ~ worth trying** ça vaut vraiment la peine d'essayer ▪ **he was ~ annoyed** *inf* il était super-énervé
6. *phr* **to be ~ away** [making good progress] être sur la bonne voie ; [drunk] être complètement parti ▪ **to be ~ in with sb** être bien avec qqn ▪ **to be ~ out of it** s'en sortir à bon compte ▪ **you're ~ out of it** tu as bien fait de partir ▪ **she's ~ rid of him/it!** quel bon débarras pour elle! ▪ **to be ~ up on sthg** s'y connaître en qqch ▪ **to leave** *OR* **let ~ alone** [equipment] ne pas toucher ; [situation] ne pas s'occuper de ; [person] laisser tranquille.
<> *adj* **1.** [good] bien, bon ▪ **all is not ~ with them** il y a quelque chose qui ne va pas chez eux ▪ **it's all very ~ pretending you don't care, but...** c'est bien beau de dire que ça t'est égal, mais... ▶ **all's ~ that ends ~** *prov* tout est bien qui finit bien *prov*
2. [advisable] bien ▪ **it would be ~ to start soon** nous ferions bien de commencer bientôt ▪ **you'd be just as ~ to tell him** *UK* tu ferais mieux de (le) lui dire
3. [in health] : **to be ~** aller *OR* se porter bien ▪ **how are you? – ~, thank you** comment allez-vous? – bien, merci ▪ **he's been ill, but he's better now** il a été malade, mais il va mieux (maintenant) ▪ **to get ~** se remettre, aller mieux ▪ **'get ~ soon'** [on card] 'bon rétablissement' ▪ **I hope you're ~** j'espère que vous allez bien ▪ **you're looking** *OR* **you look ~** vous avez l'air en forme.
<> *interj* **1.** [indicating start or continuation of speech] bon, bien ▪ **~, let me just add that...** alors, laissez-moi simplement ajouter que... ▪ **~, here we are again!** et nous y revoilà!
2. [indicating change of topic or end of conversation] : **~, as I was saying...** donc, je disais que..., je disais donc que... ▪ **right, ~, let's move on to the next subject** bon, alors passons à la question suivante ▪ **~ thank you Mr Alderson, I'll be in touch** eh bien merci M. Alderson, je vous contacterai
3. [softening a statement] : **~, obviously I'd like to come but...** disons que, bien sûr, j'aimerais venir mais... ▪ **he was, ~, rather unpleasant really** il a été, disons, assez désagréable, c'est le mot
4. [expanding on or explaining a statement] : **I've known her for ages, ~ at least three years** ça fait des années que je la connais, enfin au moins trois ans ▪ **you know John? ~ I saw him yesterday** tu connais John? eh bien je l'ai vu hier
5. [expressing hesitation or doubt] ben, eh bien
6. [asking a question] eh bien, alors ▪ **~, what of it?** et alors?
7. [expressing surprise or anger] : **~, look who's here!** ça alors, regardez qui est là! ▪ **~, ~, ~** tiens, tiens ▪ **~, really!** ça alors! ▪ **~ I never!** *inf* ça par exemple!
8. [in relief] eh bien
9. [in resignation] bon ▪ **(oh) ~, it can't be helped** bon tant pis, on n'y peut rien ▪ **(oh) ~, that's life** bon enfin, c'est la vie ▪ **can I come too? – oh, very ~, if you must** je peux venir aussi? – bon allez, si tu y tiens.
<> *npl* : **the ~** ceux *mpl* qui sont en bonne santé.
◆ **all well and good** *adv phr* tout ça, c'est très bien.

we'll [wiːl] **1.** = **we shall 2.** = **we will**.

well-adjusted *adj* [person - psychologically] équilibré ; [- to society, work] bien adapté.

well-advised *adj* sage, prudent ▪ **he would be ~ to leave** il aurait intérêt à partir.

well-aimed [-eɪmd] *adj* [shot] bien ajusté ▪ [criticism, remark] qui porte.

well-appointed [-ə'pɔɪntɪd] *adj UK fml* [house] bien équipé ▪ [hotel] de catégorie supérieure.

well-argued [-'ɑːgjuːd] *adj* bien argumenté.

well-attended [-ə'tendɪd] *adj* : **the meeting was ~** il y avait beaucoup de monde à la réunion.

well-balanced *adj* [person] équilibré, posé ▪ [diet] bien équilibré ▪ [sentence] bien construite.

well-behaved [-bɪ'heɪvd] *adj* [person] bien élevé ▪ [animal] bien dressé.

wellbeing [ˌwel'biːɪŋ] *n* bien-être *m inv* ▪ **for your own ~** pour votre bien.

well-bred *adj* **1.** [well-behaved] bien élevé **2.** [from good family] de bonne famille **3.** [animal] de (bonne) race ▪ [horse] pur-sang *(inv)*.

well-brought-up *adj* bien élevé.

well-built *adj* **1.** [person] bien bâti **2.** [building] bien construit.

well-chosen *adj* [present, words] bien choisi.

well-defined [-dɪ'faɪnd] *adj* **1.** [distinct - colour, contrasts, shape] bien défini, net **2.** [precise - problem] bien défini, précis.

well-deserved [-dɪ'zɜ:vd] *adj* bien mérité.

well-developed *adj* **1.** [person] bien fait ▪ [body, muscles] bien développé **2.** [scheme] bien développé ▪ [idea] bien exposé.

well-disposed [-dɪ'spəuzd] *adj* bien disposé ▪ **to be ~ to** *OR* **towards sb** être bien disposé envers qqn ▪ **to be ~ to** *OR* **towards sthg** voir qqch d'un bon œil.

well-done *adj* [work] bien fait ▪ [meat] bien cuit.

well-dressed *adj* bien habillé.

well-earned [-ɜ:nd] *adj* bien mérité.

well-educated *adj* cultivé, instruit.

well-endowed [-ɪn'daud] *adj euph* **a ~ young man/woman** *fig* un jeune homme bien doté/une jeune femme bien dotée par la nature.

well-equipped [-ɪ'kwɪpt] *adj* [garage, kitchen, person] bien équipé ▪ [with tools] bien outillé ▪ **the vans are ~ to deal with any emergency** les camionnettes sont équipées pour faire face à toute urgence.

well-established *adj* bien établi.

well-fed *adj* [animal, person] bien nourri.

well-founded [-'faundɪd] *adj* [doubt, suspicion] fondé, légitime.

well-heeled [-hi:ld] *adj inf* à l'aise.

well-hung *adj* **1.** [game] bien faisandé **2.**△ [man] bien monté△.

well-informed *adj* [having information] bien informé *OR* renseigné ▪ [knowledgeable] instruit ▪ **he's very ~ about current affairs** il est très au courant de l'actualité.

Wellington ['welɪŋtən] *n UK* **~ (boot)** botte *f* (en caoutchouc).

well-intentioned [-ɪn'tenʃnd] *adj* bien intentionné.

well-kept *adj* **1.** [hands, nails] soigné ▪ [hair] bien coiffé ▪ [house] bien tenu ▪ [garden] bien entretenu **2.** [secret] bien gardé.

well-known *adj* [person] connu, célèbre ▪ [fact] bien connu ▪ **what is less ~ is that she's an accomplished actress** ce qu'on sait moins c'est que c'est une très bonne actrice.

well-made *adj* bien fait.

well-mannered *adj* qui a de bonnes manières, bien élevé.

well-matched *adj* [couple] faits l'un pour l'autre.

well-meaning *adj* bien intentionné.

well-meant *adj* [action, remark] bien intentionné.

well-nigh *adv* presque.

well-off <> *adj* **1.** [financially] aisé **2.** [in a good position] : **they were still ~ for supplies** ils avaient encore largement assez de provisions ▪ **you don't know when you're ~** *fig* vous ne connaissez pas votre bonheur.
<> *npl* : **the ~** les riches *mpl* ▪ **the less ~** ceux qui ont des moyens modestes.

well-oiled *adj* **1.** [machinery] bien graissé ▪ **the operation ran like a ~ machine** l'opération s'est parfaitement déroulée **2.** *inf* [drunk] pompette.

well-padded *adj inf euph* bien enveloppé.

well-paid *adj* bien payé.

well-preserved [-prɪ'zɜ:vd] *adj* [person, building] bien conservé.

well-proportioned [-prə'pɔ:ʃnd] *adj* bien proportionné.

well-read [-red] *adj* cultivé, érudit.

well-rounded *adj* **1.** [complete - education] complet, - ète *f* ; [- life] bien rempli **2.** [figure] rondelet **3.** [style] harmonieux ▪ [sentence] bien tourné.

well-spent *adj* [time] bien utilisé, qui n'est pas perdu ▪ [money] utilement dépensé, que l'on n'a pas gaspillé ▪ **it's money ~** c'est un bon investissement.

well-spoken *adj* [person] qui sait s'exprimer.

wellspring ['welsprɪŋ] *n liter* source *f* ▪ *fig* source *f* intarissable.

well-stacked△ *adj UK* [woman] plantureux.

well-thought-of *adj* bien considéré.

well-thought-out *adj* bien conçu.

well-thumbed [-θʌmd] *adj* [magazine] qui a été beaucoup feuilleté ▪ [book] lu et relu.

well-timed [-'taɪmd] *adj* [arrival, remark] opportun, qui tombe à point ▪ [blow] bien calculé.

well-to-do *inf* <> *adj* aisé, riche.
<> *npl* : **the ~** les nantis *mpl*.

well-tried *adj* éprouvé, qui a fait ses preuves.

well-versed *adj* : **to be ~ in sthg** bien connaître qqch.

well-wisher [-ˌwɪʃər] *n* [gen] personne *f* qui offre son soutien ▪ [of cause, group] sympathisant *m*, - e *f*, partisan *m* ▪ **surrounded by ~s** entouré d'admirateurs.

well-woman clinic *n* centre *m* de santé pour femmes.

well-worn *adj* **1.** [carpet, clothes] usé, usagé **2.** [path] battu **3.** [expression, joke] rebattu ▪ **a ~ phrase** une banalité, un lieu commun.

welly ['welɪ] (*pl* **wellies**) *n UK inf* **1.** [boot] botte *f* (en caoutchouc) **2.** *phr* **give it some ~!** du nerf!

welsh [welʃ] *vi UK inf* partir *OR* décamper sans payer ▪ **to ~ on a promise** ne pas tenir une promesse.

Welsh [welʃ] <> *npl* : **the ~** les Gallois *mpl*.
<> *n* LING gallois *m*.
<> *adj* gallois ▪ **the ~ Guards** *régiment de l'armée britannique* ▪ **the ~ Office** *secrétariat d'État aux affaires galloises.*

THE WELSH ASSEMBLY

L'Assemblée galloise, qui siège à Cardiff, est constituée de 60 membres (*Assembly Members* ou *AMs*) dirigés par le président de l'Assemblée (First Minister). Elle est chargée de voter la plupart des lois en matière de politique intérieure, mais, contrairement au Parlement écossais, elle n'est pas compétente dans le domaine des impôts. La politique étrangère, l'économie, la défense et les affaires européennes demeurent sous le contrôle du gouvernement britannique à Londres.

Welsh dresser *n* vaisselier *m*.

Welshman ['welʃmən] (*pl* **Welshmen** [-mən]) *n* Gallois *m*.

Welsh rabbit, Welsh rarebit *n UK* ≃ toast *m* au fromage.

Welshwoman ['welʃˌwumən] (*pl* **Welshwomen** [-ˌwɪmɪn]) *n* Galloise *f*.

welt [welt] *n* **1.** [on skin] zébrure *f* **2.** [on garment] bordure *f* ▪ [on shoe] trépointe *f*.

welter ['weltər] *n* confusion *f* ▪ **a ~ of detail** une profusion de détails ▪ **a ~ of conflicting information** une avalanche d'informations contradictoires.

welterweight ['weltəweɪt] <> *n* poids *m* welter.
<> *comp* [champion] des poids welter ▪ [fight, title] de poids welter.

Wembley ['wemblɪ] *pr n* : **~ (Stadium)** *stade et salle de concerts à Londres.*

Wenceslas ['wensɪsləs] *pr n* Venceslas.

wench [wentʃ] *n arch & hum* jeune fille *f*, jeune femme *f*.

wend [wend] *vt lit* s'acheminer ▪ **to ~ one's way home** s'acheminer vers chez soi.

Wendy house ['wendɪ-] *n UK* *maison en miniature dans laquelle les jeunes enfants peuvent jouer.*

went [went] *pt* ▷ **go**.

wept [wept] *pt & pp* ▷ **weep**.

were [wɜːʳ] *pt* ▷ **be**.

we're [wɪəʳ] = **we are**.

weren't [wɜːnt] = **were not**.

werewolf ['wɪəwʊlf] (*pl* **werewolves** [-wʊlvz]) *n* loup-garou *m*.

west [west] <> *n* [direction] ouest *m* ■ **the house lies 10 kilometres to the ~ (of the town)** la maison se trouve à 10 kilomètres à l'ouest (de la ville) ■ **a storm is brewing in the ~** un orage couve à l'ouest.
<> *adj* ouest *(inv)* ■ **a ~ wind** un vent d'ouest ■ **in ~ London** dans l'ouest de Londres.
<> *adv* [to the west] vers l'ouest ■ [from the west] de l'ouest ■ **he travelled ~ for three days** pendant trois jours il s'est dirigé en direction de *OR* vers l'ouest ■ **the school lies further ~ of the town hall** l'école se trouve plus à l'ouest de la mairie ■ **drive due ~** roulez droit vers l'ouest ■ **to face ~** [house] être exposé à l'ouest ▶ **to go ~** *liter* aller à *OR* vers l'ouest ■ *inf hum* [person] passer l'arme à gauche ; [thing] tomber à l'eau ■ **there's another job gone ~!** *inf* encore un emploi de perdu!
◄► **West** *n* **1.** POL : **the West** l'Occident *m*, les pays *mpl* occidentaux **2.** [in the U.S.] : **the West** l'Ouest *m*.

West Africa *pr n* Afrique *f* occidentale.

West African <> *n* habitant *m*, - e *f* de l'Afrique occidentale.
<> *adj* [languages, states] de l'Afrique occidentale, ouest-africain.

West Bank <> *pr n* : **the ~** la Cisjordanie ■ **on the ~** en Cisjordanie.
<> *comp* de Cisjordanie.

westbound ['westbaʊnd] *adj* [traffic] en direction de l'ouest ■ [lane, carriageway] de l'ouest ■ [road] vers l'ouest.

West Country *pr n* : **the ~** *le sud-ouest de l'Angleterre (Cornouailles, Devon et Somerset)* ■ **in the ~** dans le sud-ouest de l'Angleterre.

West End <> *pr n* : **the ~** le West End *(centre touristique et commercial de la ville de Londres connu pour ses théâtres)* ■ **in the ~** dans le West End.
<> *comp* qui se situe dans le West End.

westerly ['westəlɪ] (*pl* **westerlies**) <> *adj* [wind] d'ouest ■ [position] à l'ouest, au couchant ■ **to head in a ~ direction** se diriger vers *OR* en direction de l'ouest.
<> *adv* vers l'ouest.
<> *n* vent *m* d'ouest.

western ['westən] <> *adj* **1.** [in direction] ouest, de l'ouest ■ **in ~ Spain** dans l'ouest de l'Espagne ■ **on the ~ side of the state** dans l'ouest de l'État **2.** POL [powers, technology, world] occidental ■ **Western Europe** l'Europe *f* de l'Ouest *OR* occidentale.
<> *n* [film] western *m* ■ [book] roman-western *m*.

Western Australia *pr n* Australie-Occidentale *f* ■ **in ~** en Australie-Occidentale.

Westerner ['westənəʳ] *n* habitant *m*, - e *f* de l'ouest ■ POL Occidental *m*, - e *f*.

westernization [ˌwestənaɪ'zeɪʃn] *n* occidentalisation *f*.

westernize, ise ['westənaɪz] *vt* occidentaliser ■ **Japan is becoming increasingly ~d** le Japon s'occidentalise de plus en plus.

westernmost ['westənməʊst] *adj* le plus à l'ouest.

Western Sahara *pr n* : **the ~** le Sahara occidental ■ **in the ~** au Sahara occidental.

Western Samoa *pr n* Samoa *fpl* occidentales ■ **in ~** dans les Samoa occidentales.

Western Union *pr n compagnie américaine privée des télégraphes.*

West German <> *n* Allemand *m*, - e *f* de l'Ouest.
<> *adj* ouest-allemand.

West Germany *pr n* : **(former) ~** (ex-)Allemagne *f* de l'Ouest ■ **in ~** en Allemagne de l'Ouest.

West Indian <> *n* Antillais *m*, - e *f*.
<> *adj* antillais.

West Indies *pr npl* Antilles *fpl* ■ **in the ~** aux Antilles ■ **the French ~** les Antilles françaises ■ **the Dutch ~** les Antilles néerlandaises.

Westminster ['westmɪnstəʳ] *pr n quartier du centre de Londres où se trouvent le Parlement et le palais de Buckingham.*

WESTMINSTER

C'est dans ce quartier que se trouvent le Parlement et le palais de Buckingham. Le nom de ***Westminster*** est également employé pour désigner le Parlement lui-même.

west-northwest <> *n* ouest-nord-ouest *m*.
<> *adj* à *OR* de l'ouest-nord-ouest ■ **a ~ wind** un vent d'ouest-nord-ouest.
<> *adv* vers l'ouest-nord-ouest.

West Point *pr n importante école militaire américaine.*

west-southwest <> *n* ouest-sud-ouest *m*.
<> *adj* à *OR* de l'ouest-sud-ouest ■ **a ~ wind** un vent d'ouest-sud-ouest.
<> *adv* vers l'ouest-sud-ouest.

West Virginia *pr n* Virginie-Occidentale *f* ■ **in ~** en Virginie-Occidentale.

westward ['westwəd] <> *adj* [to the west] vers l'ouest.
<> *adv* en direction de *OR* vers l'ouest.

westwards ['westwədz] *adv* vers l'ouest.

wet [wet] <> *adj* (*comp* **wetter**, *superl* **wettest**) **1.** [ground, person, umbrella - gen] mouillé ; [- damp] humide ; [- soaked] trempé ■ **to get ~** se faire mouiller ■ **I got my jacket ~** j'ai mouillé ma veste ■ **I got my feet ~** je me suis mouillé les pieds ■ **to be ~ through** [person] être trempé jusqu'aux os *OR* complètement trempé ; [clothes, towel] être complètement trempé ■ **her eyes were ~ with tears** elle avait les yeux baignés de larmes ▶ **to be (still) ~ behind the ears** manquer d'expérience
2. [ink, paint, concrete] frais, fraîche *f* ■ **'~ paint!'** 'peinture fraîche!'
3. [climate, weather - damp] humide ; [- rainy] pluvieux ■ [day] pluvieux, de pluie ■ **it's going to be very ~ all weekend** il va beaucoup pleuvoir tout ce week-end ■ **in ~ weather** par temps de pluie, quand il pleut ■ **the ~ season** la saison des pluies
4. *UK inf* [feeble] : **don't be so ~!** tu es une vraie lavette!
5. *UK inf* POL mou *(before vowel or silent 'h' mol)*, molle *f*, modéré
6. *US* [wrong] : **to be all ~** avoir tort
7. *US* [state, town] *où l'on peut acheter librement des boissons alcoolisées.*
<> *vt* (*pret & pp* **wet** *OR* **wetted**, *cont* **wetting**) [hair, sponge, towel] mouiller ■ **to ~ o.s.** *OR* **one's pants** mouiller sa culotte ■ **to ~ the bed** faire pipi au lit ■ **to ~ one's lips** s'humecter les lèvres ▶ **to ~ o.s.** *inf* [from worry] se faire de la bile ; [from laughter] rire aux larmes ■ **to ~ one's whistle** boire un coup.
<> *n* **1.** *UK* [rain] pluie *f* ■ [damp] humidité *f* ■ **let's get in out of the ~** entrons, ne restons pas sous la pluie
2. *Australia* **the ~** la saison des pluies
3. *UK inf* POL modéré *m*, - e *f OR* mou *m*, molle *f (du parti conservateur)*
4. *UK inf pej* [feeble person] lavette *f*.

wet bar *n US minibar avec un petit évier.*

wet blanket *n inf* rabat-joie *m inv*.

wet dream *n* éjaculation *f OR* pollution *f* nocturne.

wether ['weðəʳ] *n* bélier *m* châtré, mouton *m*.

wet-look <> *adj* brillant ■ **a ~ dress** une robe qui brille.
<> *n* aspect *m* brillant.

wetness ['wetnɪs] *n* humidité *f*.

wet nurse *n* nourrice *f*.
◆ **wet-nurse** *vt* servir de nourrice à, élever au sein.

wet rot *n (U)* moisissure *f* humide.

wet suit *n* combinaison *f OR* ensemble *m* de plongée.

wetting solution ['wetɪŋ-] *n* [for contact lenses] solution *f* de rinçage.

WEU (*abbrev of* **Western European Union**) *pr n* UEO *f*.

we've [wi:v] = **we have**.

whack [wæk] *inf* ◇ *n* **1.** [thump] claque *f*, grand coup *m* ▪ [sound] claquement *m*, coup *m* sec ▪ **to give sb/sthg a ~** donner un grand coup à qqn/qqch **2.** [try] essai *m* ▪ **to have a ~ at sthg** essayer qqch **3.** *UK* [share] part *f* ▪ **she didn't do her fair ~** elle n'a pas fait sa part du travail **4.** *US phr* **out of the ~** déglingué.
◇ *vt* **1.** [thump] donner un coup *OR* des coups à ▪ [spank] donner une claque sur les fesses à **2.** *UK* [defeat] flanquer une dérouillée *OR* raclée à.
◇ *interj* vlan!

whacked [wækt] *adj UK inf* vanné, crevé.

whacking *inf* ['wækɪŋ] ◇ *adj UK* énorme, colossal.
◇ *adv* extrêmement ▪ **a ~ great dog/house** un chien/une maison absolument énorme.
◇ *n* : **to get a ~** [beating] prendre une raclée ; [defeat] prendre une raclée *OR* une déculottée.

whale [weɪl] ◇ *n* **1.** *liter* baleine *f* **2.** *inf phr* **we had a ~ of a time** on s'est drôlement bien amusés.
◇ *vi* **1.** pêcher la baleine **2.** *US inf* **to ~ away at sthg** s'en prendre à qqch.
◇ *vt US inf* **1.** [thump] mettre une raclée à, rosser **2.** SPORT [defeat] mettre une raclée à, battre à plate couture.

whalebone ['weɪlbəʊn] *n* fanon *m* de baleine ▪ [in corset, dress] baleine *f*.

whale oil *n* huile *f* de baleine.

whaler ['weɪlə^r] *n* **1.** [person] pêcheur *m* de baleine **2.** [ship] baleinier *m*.

whale shark *n* requin-baleine *m*.

whaling ['weɪlɪŋ] ◇ *n* **1.** [industry] pêche *f* à la baleine **2.** *US inf* [thrashing] rossée *f*, raclée *f*.
◇ *comp* [industry, port] baleinier ▪ **~ ship** baleinier *m* ▪ **International Whaling Commission** Commission *f* internationale baleinière.

wham [wæm] (*pret & pp* **whammed**, *cont* **whamming**) *inf*
◇ *interj* vlan.
◇ *vt* **1.** [hit - person] donner une raclée à ; [- ball] donner un grand coup dans **2.** [crash - heavy object, vehicle] rentrer dans.

wharf [wɔ:f] (*pl* **wharves** [wɔ:vz] *OR pl* **wharfs**) *n* NAUT quai *m*.

what [wɒt] ◇ *pron* **1.** [in direct questions - as subject] qu'est-ce qui, que ; [- as object] (qu'est-ce) que, quoi ▪ **~ do you want?** qu'est-ce que tu veux?, que veux-tu? ▪ **~'s happening?** qu'est-ce qui se passe?, que se passe-t-il? ▪ **~'s new?** quoi de neuf? ▪ **~'s up?** *inf* qu'est-ce qu'il y a? ; *US* [as greeting] quoi de neuf? ▪ **~'s the matter?, ~ is it?** qu'est-ce qu'il y a? ▪ **~'s it to you?** *inf* qu'est-ce que ça peut te faire? ▪ **~'s that?** qu'est-ce que c'est que ça? ▪ **~'s that building?** qu'est-ce que c'est que ce bâtiment? ▪ **~'s your phone number?** quel est votre numéro de téléphone? ▪ **~'s the Spanish for "light"?** comment dit-on "lumière" en espagnol? ▪ **~'s up with him?** *inf* qu'est-ce qu'il a? ▪ **~ did I tell you?** [gen] qu'est-ce que je vous ai dit? ; [I told you so] je vous l'avais bien dit! ▪ **she must be, ~, 50?** elle doit avoir, quoi, 50 ans? ▪ **Mum? – ~? – can I go out?** Maman? – quoi? – est-ce que je peux sortir? ▪ [with preposition] quoi ▪ **~ are you thinking about?** à quoi pensez-vous? ▪ **~ do you take me for?** pour qui me prenez-vous? ▪ **to ~ do I owe this honour?** *fml & hum* qu'est-ce qui me vaut cet honneur?
2. [in indirect questions - as subject] ce qui ; [- as object] ce que, quoi ▪ **tell us ~ happened** dites-nous ce qui s'est passé ▪ **I asked ~ it was all about** j'ai demandé de quoi il était question ▪ **he didn't understand ~ I said** il n'a pas compris ce que j'ai dit ▪ **I don't know ~ to do to help him** je ne sais pas quoi faire pour l'aider
3. [asking someone to repeat something] comment ▪ **~'s that?** qu'est-ce que tu dis? ▪ **they bought ~?** quoi, qu'est-ce qu'ils ont acheté?
4. [expressing surprise] : **~, another new dress?** quoi, encore une nouvelle robe? ▪ **~, no coffee!** comment *OR* quoi? pas de café? ▪ **I found $350 – you ~!** j'ai trouvé 350 dollars – quoi? ▪ **I told her to leave – you did ~!** je lui ai dit de partir – tu lui as dit quoi?
5. [how much] : **~'s 17 minus 4?** combien *OR* que fait 17 moins 4? ▪ **~ does it cost?** combien est-ce que ça coûte?
6. [that which - as subject] ce qui ; [- as object] ce que, quoi ▪ **~ you need is a hot bath** ce qu'il vous faut, c'est un bon bain chaud ▪ **they spent ~ amounted to a week's salary** ils ont dépensé l'équivalent d'une semaine de salaire ▪ **that's ~ life is all about!** c'est ça la vie! ▪ **education is not ~ it used to be** l'enseignement n'est plus ce qu'il était ▪ **and ~ is worse,...** et ce qui est pire,...
7. [whatever, everything that] : **they rescued ~ they could** ils ont sauvé ce qu'ils ont pu ▪ **say ~ you will** vous pouvez dire *OR* vous direz tout ce que vous voudrez ▪ **say ~ you will, I don't believe you** racontez tout ce que vous voulez, je ne vous crois pas ▪ **come ~ may** advienne que pourra
8. *UK inf dated* [inviting agreement] n'est-ce pas ▪ **an interesting book, ~?** un livre intéressant, n'est-ce pas *OR* pas vrai?
9. *phr* **I'll tell you ~...** écoute! ▪ **you know ~...?** tu sais quoi...? ▪ **I know ~** j'ai une idée ▪ **you'll never guess ~** tu ne devineras jamais (quoi) ▶ **documents, reports and ~ have you** *inf OR* **and ~ not** *inf* des documents, des rapports et je ne sais quoi encore ▪ **and I don't know ~** *inf* et que sais-je encore ▪ **and God knows ~** *inf* et Dieu sait quoi ▪ **look, do you want to come or ~?** alors, tu veux venir ou quoi? ▪ **a trip to Turkey? – ~ next!** un voyage en Turquie? – et puis quoi encore! ▪ **~ have we here?** mais que vois-je? ▪ **we need to find out ~'s ~** *inf* il faut qu'on sache où en sont les choses ▪ **she told me ~ was ~** *inf* elle m'a mis au courant ▪ **they know ~'s ~ in art** *inf* ils s'y connaissent en art ▪ **I'll show him ~'s ~!** *inf* je vais lui montrer de quel bois je me chauffe!
◇ *det* **1.** [in questions] quel *m*, quelle *f*, quels *mpl*, quelles *fpl* ▪ **~ books did you buy?** quels livres avez-vous achetés? ▪ **~ colour/size is it?** de quelle couleur/taille c'est? ▪ **~ day is it?** quel jour sommes-nous?
2. [as many as, as much as] : **I gave her ~ money I had** je lui ai donné le peu d'argent que j'avais ▪ **~ time we had left was spent (in) packing** on a passé le peu de temps qui nous restait à faire les valises ▪ **I gave her ~ comfort I could** je l'ai consolée autant que j'ai pu.
◇ *predet* [expressing an opinion or reaction] : **~ a suggestion!** quelle idée! ▪ **~ a pity!** comme c'est *OR* quel dommage! ▪ **~ an idiot he is!** comme il est bête!, qu'il est bête! ▪ **~ lovely children you have!** quels charmants enfants vous avez! ▪ **you can't imagine ~ a time we had getting here** vous ne pouvez pas vous imaginer le mal qu'on a eu à venir jusqu'ici.
◇ *adv* [in rhetorical questions] : **~ do I care?** qu'est-ce que ça peut me faire? ▪ **~ does it matter?** qu'est-ce que ça peut faire?
◆ **what about** *adv phr* : **~ about lunch?** et si on déjeunait? ▪ **when shall we go? – ~ about Monday?** quand est-ce qu'on y va? – (et si on disait) lundi? ▪ **~ about your promise? – ~ about my promise?** et ta promesse? – ben quoi, ma promesse? ▪ **~ about it?** *inf* et alors? ▪ **do you remember Mary? – ~ about her?** tu te souviens de Mary? – oui, et alors? ▪ **and ~ about you?** et vous donc?
◆ **what for** *adv phr* **1.** [why] : **~ for?** pourquoi? ▪ **~ did you say that for?** pourquoi as-tu dit cela?
2. *phr* **to give sb ~ for** *inf* passer un savon à qqn.
◆ **what if** *conj phr* : **~ if we went to the beach?** et si on allait à la plage? ▪ **he won't come – and ~ if he doesn't?** [supposing] il ne va pas venir – et alors?
◆ **what with** *conj phr* : **~ with work and the children I don't get much sleep** entre le travail et les enfants je ne dors pas beaucoup ▪ **~ with one thing and another I never got there** pour un tas de raisons je n'y suis jamais allé.

whatchamacallit ['wɒtʃəmə,kɔ:lɪt], **what-d'you-call-it** ['wɒtdjʊ,kɔ:lɪt] *n inf* machin *m*, truc *m*.

whatever [wɒt'evər] <> *pron* **1.** [anything, everything] tout ce que ■ I'll do ~ is necessary je ferai le nécessaire ■ ~ you like ce que tu veux
2. [no matter what] quoi que ■ ~ happens, stay calm quoi qu'il arrive, restez calme ■ ~ you do, don't tell her what I said surtout, ne lui répète pas ce que je t'ai dit ■ ~ it may be quoi que ce soit ■ ~ the reason quelle que soit la raison ■ ~ it costs, I want that house je veux cette maison à tout prix ■ I won't do it, ~ you say vous aurez beau dire *OR* vous pouvez dire tout ce que vous voulez, je ne le ferai pas ■ ~ you say, ~ you think best comme tu voudras
3. [indicating surprise] : ~ can that mean? qu'est-ce que ça peut bien vouloir dire? ■ ~ do you want to do that for? et pourquoi donc voulez-vous faire ça? ■ he wants to join the circus – ~ next! il veut travailler dans un cirque – et puis quoi encore! ■ [indicating uncertainty] : it's an urban regeneration area, ~ that means c'est une zone de rénovation urbaine, si tu sais ce qu'ils entendent par là
4. *inf* [some similar thing or things] : I don't want to study English or philosophy or ~ je ne veux étudier ni l'anglais, ni la philosophie, ou que sais-je encore
5. [indicating lack of interest] : shall I take the red or the green? – ~ *inf* je prends le rouge ou le vert? – n'importe.
<> *det* **1.** [any, all] tout, n'importe quel ■ she read ~ books she could find elle lisait tous les livres qui lui tombaient sous la main ■ he gave up ~ ambitions he still had il a abandonné ce qui lui restait d'ambition ■ I'll take ~ fruit you have je prendrai ce que vous avez comme fruits
2. [no matter what] : for ~ reason, he changed his mind pour une raison quelconque, il a changé d'avis ■ she likes all films, ~ subject they have elle aime tous les films quel qu'en soit le sujet.
<> *adv* : choose any topic ~ choisissez n'importe quel sujet ■ I have no doubt ~ je n'ai pas le moindre doute ■ I see no reason ~ to go je ne vois absolument aucune raison d'y aller ■ we have no intention ~ of giving up nous n'avons pas la moindre intention d'abandonner.

whatnot ['wɒtnɒt] *n* **1.** *inf phr* and ~ et ainsi de suite **2.** [furniture] étagère *f*.

what's [wɒts] **1.** = what is **2.** = what has.

whatshername ['wɒtsənem] *n inf* Machine *f*.

whatshisname ['wɒtsɪznem] *n inf* Machin *m*, Machin Chouette *m*.

whatsit ['wɒtsɪt] *n inf* machin *m*, truc *m*.

whatsitsname ['wɒtsɪtsnem] *n inf* machin *m*, truc *m*.

whatsoever [,wɒtsəʊ'evər] *pron* : none ~ aucun ■ he gave us no encouragement ~ il ne nous a pas prodigué le moindre encouragement.

wheat [wi:t] <> *n* blé *m* ■ to separate the ~ from the chaff séparer le bon grain de l'ivraie.
<> *comp* [flour] de blé, de froment ■ [field] de blé.

wheatear ['wi:t,ɪər] *n* traquet *m*, motteux *m*.

wheaten ['wi:tn] *adj* **1.** [bread] de blé *OR* froment **2.** [colour] blond comme les blés.

wheat germ *n* germe *m* de blé.

wheatmeal ['wi:tmi:l] *n* : ~ (flour) farine *f* complète.

wheat rust *n* rouille *f* du blé.

Wheatstone bridge ['wi:tstən-] *n* pont *m* de Wheatstone.

whee [wi:] *interj* : ~! ooooh!

wheedle ['wi:dl] *vt* enjôler ■ to ~ sb into doing sthg convaincre qqn de faire qqch à force de cajoleries ■ to ~ sthg out of sb obtenir qqch de qqn par des cajoleries.

wheedling ['wi:dlɪŋ] <> *n (U)* cajolerie *f*, cajoleries *fpl*.
<> *adj* cajoleur, enjôleur ■ a ~ voice une voix pateline.

wheel [wi:l] <> *n* **1.** [of bicycle, car, train] roue *f* ■ [smaller] roulette *f* ■ [for potter] tour *m* ■ on ~s sur roues *OR* roulettes ■ the ~ has come full circle *fig* la boucle est bouclée ▶ ~ alignment AUT parallélisme *m* des roues ■ the ~ of fortune la roue de la fortune ■ she's a big ~ around here *US* elle est considérée comme une huile par ici **2.** AUT : to be at the ~ *liter* être au volant ; *fig* être aux commandes ■ to get behind *OR* to take the ~ se mettre au *OR* prendre le volant ▶ (steering) ~ volant *m*
3. NAUT barre *f*, gouvernail *m* ■ at the ~ à la barre **4.** [of torture] roue *f*.
<> *vi* **1.** [birds] tournoyer ■ [procession] faire demi-tour ■ MIL [column] effectuer une conversion ■ to ~ to the left tourner sur la gauche ■ to ~ (round) [person] se retourner, faire une volte-face ; [procession] faire demi-tour ; [horse] pirouetter ; [birds] tournoyer **2.** *phr* to ~ and deal *inf* [do business] brasser des affaires ; *pej* magouiller.
<> *vt* [bicycle, trolley] pousser ■ [suitcase] tirer ■ she ~ed the baby around the park elle a promené le bébé dans le parc ■ she ~ed in a trolley full of cakes elle entra en poussant un chariot plein de gâteaux ■ they ~ed on *OR* out the usual celebrities *fig* ils ont ressorti les mêmes célébrités.
◆ **wheels** *npl* **1.** [workings] rouages *mpl* ▶ there are ~s within ~s c'est plus compliqué que ça n'en a l'air **2.** *inf* AUT [car] bagnole *f*.

wheelbarrow ['wi:l,bærəʊ] *n* brouette *f*.

wheelbase ['wi:lbeɪs] *n* AUT empattement *m*.

wheel brace *n* clef *f* en croix.

wheelchair ['wi:l,tʃeər] *n* fauteuil *m* roulant ■ ~ access accès *m* aux handicapés ■ the Wheelchair Olympics les jeux *mpl* Olympiques handisport *OR* pour handicapés.

wheelclamp ['wi:lklæmp] <> *n* sabot *m* de Denver.
<> *vt* : my car was ~ed on a mis un sabot à ma voiture.

wheeled [wi:ld] *adj* à roues, muni de roues.

-wheeled *in cpds* à roues ■ four~ à quatre roues.

wheeler ['wi:lər] *n* **1.** [wheelmaker] charron *m* **2.** [horse] timonier *m*.

wheeler-dealer *n inf pej* affairiste *mf*.

wheelhouse ['wi:lhaʊs] (*pl* [-haʊzɪz]) *n* timonerie *f*.

wheelie bin ['wi:lɪ-] *n* poubelle *f (avec des roues)*.

wheeling and dealing ['wi:lɪŋ-] *n (U) inf* combines *fpl*, manigances *fpl*.

wheelwright ['wi:lraɪt] *n* charron *m*.

wheeze [wi:z] <> *vi* [person] respirer bruyamment *OR* comme un asthmatique ■ [animal] souffler.
<> *vt* dire d'une voix rauque.
<> *n* **1.** [sound of breathing] respiration *f* difficile *OR* sifflante **2.** *UK inf dated* [trick] combine *f* **3.** *UK inf* [joke] blague *f* **4.** *US* [saying] dicton *m*.

wheezy ['wi:zɪ] (*comp* wheezier, *superl* wheeziest) *adj* [person] asthmatique ■ [voice, chest] d'asthmatique ■ [musical instrument, horse] poussif.

whelk [welk] *n* bulot *m*, buccin *m*.

whelp [welp] <> *n* **1.** [animal] petit *m*, - e *f* **2.** *pej* [youth] petit morveux *m*, petite morveuse *f*.
<> *vi* [of animals] mettre bas.

when [wen] <> *adv* quand ■ ~ are we leaving? quand partons-nous? ■ ~ is the next bus? à quelle heure est *OR* quand passe le prochain bus? ■ ~ did the war end? quand la guerre s'est-elle terminée? ■ ~ was the Renaissance? à quand remonte l'époque de la Renaissance? ■ you're open until ~? vous êtes ouvert jusqu'à quand? ■ ~ is the best time to call? quel est le meilleur moment pour appeler?
<> *conj* **1.** [how soon] quand ■ I don't know ~ we'll see you again je ne sais pas quand nous vous reverrons ■ do you remember ~ we met? te souviens-tu du jour où nous nous sommes connus? ■ I wonder ~ the shop opens je me demande à quelle heure ouvre le magasin ■ we don't agree on ~ it should be done nous ne sommes pas d'accord sur le moment où il faudrait le faire
2. [at which time] quand ■ come back next week ~ we'll have more time revenez la semaine prochaine quand nous aurons plus de temps ■ he returned in the autumn, ~ the leaves were beginning to turn il est revenu à l'automne, alors que les feuilles commençaient à jaunir

3. [indicating a specific point in time] quand, lorsque ■ **he turned round ~ she called his name** il s'est retourné quand *OR* lorsqu'elle l'a appelé ■ **~ I was a student** lorsque j'étais *OR* à l'époque où j'étais étudiant ■ **will you still love me ~ I'm old?** m'aimeras-tu encore quand je serai vieux? ■ **she's thinner than ~ I last saw her** elle a maigri depuis la dernière fois que je l'ai vue ■ **on Sunday, ~ I go to the market** [this week] dimanche, quand j'irai au marché ; [every week] le dimanche, quand je vais au marché ■ **I had just walked in the door/he was about to go to bed ~ the phone rang** je venais juste d'arriver/il était sur le point de se coucher quand le téléphone a sonné ■ **we hadn't been gone five minutes ~ Susan wanted to go home** ça ne faisait pas cinq minutes que nous étions partis et Susan voulait déjà rentrer
4. [as soon as] quand, dès que ■ [after] quand, après que ■ **put your pencils down ~ you have finished** posez votre crayon quand vous avez terminé ■ **~ completed, the factory will employ 100 workers** une fois terminée, l'usine emploiera 100 personnes ■ **~ he starts drinking, he can't stop** une fois qu'il a commencé à boire, il ne peut plus s'arrêter ■ **I'll answer any questions ~ the meeting is over** quand la réunion sera terminée, je répondrai à toutes vos questions ■ **~ they had finished dinner, he offered to take her home** quand *OR* après qu'ils eurent dîné, il lui proposa de la ramener ■ **~ she had talked to him, she left** après lui avoir parlé, elle est partie
5. [the time that] : **remember ~ a coffee cost 10 cents?** vous souvenez-vous de l'époque où un café coûtait 10 cents? ■ **that's ~ it snowed so hard** c'est quand il a tant neigé ■ **that's ~ he got up and left** c'est à ce moment-là *OR* c'est alors qu'il s'est levé et est parti ■ **that's ~ the shops close** c'est l'heure où les magasins ferment ■ **now is ~ we should stand up and be counted** c'est le moment d'avoir le courage de nos opinions
6. [whenever] quand, chaque fois que ■ **I try to avoid seeing him ~ possible** j'essaie de l'éviter quand c'est possible
7. [since, given that] quand, étant donné que ■ **what good is it applying ~ I don't qualify for the job?** à quoi bon me porter candidat quand *OR* si je n'ai pas les capacités requises pour faire ce travail? ■ **how can you treat her so badly ~ you know she loves you?** comment pouvez-vous la traiter si mal quand *OR* alors que vous savez qu'elle vous aime?
8. [whereas] alors que ■ **she described him as being lax ~ in fact he's quite strict** elle l'a décrit comme étant négligent alors qu'en réalité il est assez strict.
◇ *rel pron* **1.** [at which time] : **in a period ~ business was bad** à une période où les affaires allaient mal ■ **she was president until 1980, ~ she left the company** elle fut présidente jusqu'en 1980, année où elle a quitté l'entreprise ‖ [which time] : **she started her job in May, since ~ she has had no free time** elle a commencé à travailler en mai et elle n'a pas eu de temps libre depuis ■ **the new office will be ready in January, until ~ we use the old one** le nouveau bureau sera prêt en janvier, jusque là *OR* en attendant, nous utiliserons l'ancien
2. [that] où ■ **do you remember the year ~ we went to Alaska?** tu te rappelles l'année où on est allés en Alaska? ■ **what about the time ~ she didn't show up?** et la fois où elle n'est pas venue? ■ **one day ~ he was out** un jour où il était sorti *OR* qu'il était sorti.

whence [wens] *adv & pron fml* d'où.

whenever [wen'evəʳ] ◇ *conj* **1.** [every time that] quand, chaque fois que ■ **~ we go on a picnic, it rains** chaque fois qu'on part en pique-nique, il pleut ■ **he can come ~ he likes** il peut venir quand il veut ■ **I go to visit her ~ I can** je vais la voir dès que je peux **2.** [at whatever time] quand ■ **you can leave ~ you're ready** vous pouvez partir dès que vous serez prêt ■ **they try to help ~ possible** ils essaient de se rendre utiles quand c'est possible.
◇ *adv* **1.** [expressing surprise] quand ■ **~ did you find the time?** mais quand donc avez-vous trouvé le temps? **2.** [referring to an unknown or unspecified time] : **I'll pick you up at 6 o'clock or ~ is convenient** je te prendrai à 6 heures ou quand ça te convient ➊ **let's assume he started work in April or ~** *inf* supposons qu'il ait commencé à travailler en avril ou quelque chose comme ça ■ **we could have lunch on Thursday or Friday or ~** *inf* on pourrait déjeuner ensemble jeudi ou vendredi ou même un autre jour.

whensoever [,wensəʊ'evəʳ] *lit* = **whenever**.

where [weəʳ] ◇ *adv* **1.** [at, in, to what place] où ■ **~ are yo[u] from?** d'où est-ce que vous venez?, d'où êtes-vous? ■ **~ doe[s] this road lead?** où va cette route?
2. [at what stage, position] : **~ are you in your work/in the book** où en êtes-vous dans votre travail/dans votre lecture? ■ **[~] were we?** où en étions-nous? ■ **~ do you stand on this issue** quelle est votre position *OR* opinion sur cette question? ■ **[~] do you stand with the boss?** quels sont vos rapports avec l[e] patron? ■ **~ do I come into it?** qu'est-ce que j'ai à faire là-de[dans], moi? ■ **~ would I be without you?** que serais-je deven[u] sans toi?
◇ *conj* **1.** [the place at or in which] (là) où ■ **it rains a lot ~ we live** il pleut beaucoup là où nous habitons ■ **she told me ~ to g[o]** [gave me directions] elle m'a dit où (il fallait) aller ; [was rude] elle m'a envoyé promener ■ **there is a factory ~ I used to go t[o] school** il y a une usine là où *OR* à l'endroit où j'allais autre[-]fois à l'école ■ **how did you know ~ to find me?** comment avez[-]vous su où me trouver? ■ **I wonder ~ my keys are** je me de[-]mande où sont mes clés ■ **turn left ~ the two roads mee[t]** tournez à gauche au croisement ‖ *fig* **I just don't know ~ t[o] begin** je ne sais vraiment pas par où commencer
2. [the place that] là que, là où ■ **this is ~ I work** c'est là que j[e] travaille ■ **so that's ~ I left my coat!** voilà où j'ai laissé mo[n] manteau! ■ **he showed me ~ the students live** il m'a montr[é] l'endroit où habitent les étudiants ■ **we can't see well from [~] we're sitting** nous ne voyons pas bien d'où *OR* de là où nou[s] sommes assis ‖ *fig* **I see ~ I went wrong** je vois où je me sui[s] trompé ■ **that's ~ she's mistaken** c'est là qu'elle se trompe[,] voilà son erreur
3. [whenever, wherever] quand, là où ■ **the judge is uncomprom[-]ising ~ drugs are concerned** le juge est intraitable lorsqu'il *o[u]* quand il s'agit de drogue ■ **the situation is hopeless ~ defenc[e] is concerned** pour la défense, la situation est sans espoir ■ **[~] x equals y** MATHS où x égale y ■ **~ possible** là où *OR* quand c'es[t] possible ➊ **~ there's life, there's hope** *prov* tant qu'il y a de l[a] vie, il y a de l'espoir *prov*
4. [whereas, while] là où, alors que ■ **~ others see a horrid bra[t] I see a shy little boy** là où les autres voient un affreux mou[-]tard, je vois un petit garçon timide
5. *inf phr* **~ it's at** là où ça bouge.
◇ *rel pron* **1.** [in which, at which] où ■ **the place ~ we went o[n] holiday** l'endroit où nous sommes allés en vacances ■ **th[e] room ~ he was working** la pièce où *OR* dans laquelle il travail[-]lait ■ **the table ~ they were sitting** la table où *OR* à laquelle il[s] étaient assis ■ **it was the kind of restaurant ~ tourists go** c'étai[t] le genre de restaurant que fréquentent les touristes ‖ *fig* **I'[m] at the part ~ they discover the murder** j'en suis au moment o[ù] ils découvrent le meurtre ■ **it's reached a stage ~ I'm finding i[t] difficult to work** ça en est au point où travailler me devien[t] pénible
2. [in or at which place] : **sign at the bottom, ~ I've put a cross** si[-]gnez en bas, là où j'ai mis une croix.
◇ *n* : **they discussed the ~ and how of his accident** ils ont parl[é] en détail des circonstances de son accident.

whereabouts ◇ *adv* [,weərə'baʊts] où ■ **~ are you from?** d'où êtes-vous? ■ **I used to live in Cumbria – oh, really, ~?** j'ha[-]bitais dans le Cumbria – vraiment? où ça *OR* dans que[l] coin?
◇ *npl* ['weərəbaʊts] : **to know the ~ of sb/sthg** savoir où s[e] trouve qqn/qqch.

whereas [weər'æz] *conj* **1.** [gen] alors que, tandis que **2.** LAW & *fml* attendu que, considérant que.

whereby [weə'baɪ] *rel pron fml* par lequel, au moyen du[-]quel ■ **there's a new system ~ everyone gets one day off a month** il y a un nouveau système qui permet à tout le monde d'avoir un jour de congé par mois.

wherefore ['weəfɔːʳ] ◇ *adv arch & fml* pourquoi, pour quelle raison.
◇ *conj arch & fml* pour cette raison, donc.
◇ *n* ⇨ **why**.

wherein [weər'ɪn] *arch & fml* ◇ *adv & conj* en quoi, dans quoi.
◇ *rel pron* où, dans lequel.

wheresoever [,weəsəʊ'evəʳ] = **wherever**.

whereupon [,weərə'pɒn] ◇ *conj* sur *OR* après quoi, sur ce.
◇ *adv arch* sur quoi.

wherever [weər'evər] ◇ *conj* **1.** [every place] partout où ▪ [no matter what place] où que ▪ **~ you go it's the same thing** où que vous alliez c'est la même chose, c'est partout pareil ▪ **~ we went, he complained about the food** partout où on est allés, il s'est plaint de la nourriture **2.** [anywhere, in whatever place] (là) où ▪ **he can sleep ~ he likes** il peut dormir (là) où il veut ▪ **we can go ~ we please** nous pouvons aller où bon nous semble ▪ **they're from Little Pucklington, ~ that is** ils viennent d'un endroit qui s'appellerait Little Pucklington **3.** [in any situation] quand ▪ **I wish, ~ possible, to avoid job losses** je souhaite éviter toute perte d'emploi quand c'est possible ▪ **grants are given ~ needed** des bourses sont accordées à chaque fois que c'est nécessaire.
◇ *adv inf* **1.** [indicating surprise] mais où donc ▪ **~ have you been?** où étais-tu donc passé? **2.** [indicating unknown or unspecified place] : **they're holidaying in Marbella or Málaga or ~** ils passent leurs vacances à Marbella ou Malaga ou Dieu sait où.

wherewithal ['weəwɪðɔ:l] *n UK* **the ~** les moyens *mpl* ▪ **I don't have the ~ to buy a new coat** je n'ai pas les moyens de me payer un manteau neuf.

whet [wet] (*pret & pp* **whetted**, *cont* **whetting**) *vt* [cutting tool] affûter, aiguiser ▪ [appetite] aiguiser, ouvrir ▪ **to ~ sb's appetite** ouvrir l'appétit à qqn ▪ **her few days in Spain only whetted her appetite for more** *fig* ces quelques jours passés en Espagne n'ont fait que lui donner envie d'y revenir.

whether ['weðər] *conj* **1.** [if] si ▪ **I asked ~ I could come** j'ai demandé si je pouvais venir ▪ **I don't know now ~ it's such a good idea** je ne suis plus sûr que ce soit une tellement *OR* si bonne idée ▪ **the question now is ~ you want the job or not** la question est maintenant de savoir si tu veux cet emploi ou pas **2.** [no matter if] : **~ you want to or not** que tu le veuilles ou non ▪ **~ by accident or design** que ce soit par hasard ou fait exprès.

whetstone ['wetstəʊn] *n* pierre *f* à aiguiser.

whew [fju:] *interj* [relief] ouf ▪ [admiration] oh la la.

whey [weɪ] *n* petit-lait *m*.

which [wɪtʃ] ◇ *det* **1.** [indicating choice] quel *m*, quelle *f*, quels *mpl*, quelles *f* ▪ **~ book did you buy?** quel livre as-tu acheté? ▪ **~ candidate are you voting for?** pour quel candidat allez-vous voter? ▪ **~ one?** lequel?/laquelle? ▪ **~ ones?** lesquels?/lesquelles? ▪ **~ one of you spoke?** lequel de vous a parlé? ▪ **I wonder ~ route would be best** je me demande quel serait le meilleur chemin ▪ **~ way should we go?** par où devrions-nous aller?
2. [referring back to preceding noun or statement] : **he may miss his plane, in ~ case he'll have to wait** il est possible qu'il rate son avion, auquel cas il devra attendre ▪ **she arrives at 5 p.m.at ~ time I'll still be at the office** elle arrive à 17 h, heure à laquelle je serai encore au bureau ▪ **they lived in Madrid for one year, during ~ time their daughter was born** ils ont habité Madrid pendant un an, et c'est à cette époque que leur fille est née.
◇ *pron* **1.** [what one or ones] lequel *m*, laquelle *f*, lesquels *mpl*, lesquelles *f* ▪ **~ of the houses do you live in?** dans quelle maison habitez-vous? ▪ **~ of these books is yours?** lequel de ces livres est le tien? ▪ **~ is the freshest?** quel est le plus frais? ▪ **~ of you saw the accident?** qui de vous a vu l'accident? ▪ **she's from Chicago or Boston, I don't remember ~** elle vient de Chicago ou de Boston, je ne sais plus lequel des deux ▪ **we can play bridge or poker, I don't care ~** on peut jouer au bridge ou au poker, peu m'importe ▪ **I can't tell ~ is ~** je n'arrive pas à les distinguer (l'un de l'autre) ▪ **~ is ~?** lequel est-ce?
2. [the one or ones that - as subject] celui qui *m*, celle qui *f*, ceux qui *mpl*, celles qui *f* ; [- as object] celui que *m*, celle que *f*, ceux que *mpl*, celles que *f* ▪ **show me ~ you prefer** montrez-moi celui que vous préférez ▪ **tell her ~ is yours** dites-lui lequel est le vôtre.
◇ *rel pron* **1.** [adding further information - as subject] qui ; [- as object] que ▪ **the house, ~ is very old, needs urgent repairs** la maison, qui est très vieille, a besoin d'être réparée sans plus attendre ▪ **the vases, each of ~ held white roses, were made of crystal** les vases, qui contenaient chacun des roses blanches, étaient en cristal ▪ **the hand with ~ I write** la main avec laquelle j'écris ▪ **the office in ~ she works** le bureau dans lequel *OR* où elle travaille
2. [commenting on previous statement - as subject] ce qui ; [- as object] ce que ▪ **he looked like a military man, ~ in fact he was** il avait l'air d'un militaire, et en fait c'en était un ▪ **he says it was an accident, ~ I don't believe for an instant** il dit que c'était un accident, ce que je ne crois absolument pas *OR* mais je ne le crois pas un seul instant ▪ **then they arrived, after ~ things got better** puis ils sont arrivés, après quoi tout est allé mieux ▪ **she lied about the letter, from ~ I guessed she was up to something** elle a menti au sujet de la lettre, d'où j'ai deviné qu'elle combinait quelque chose ▪ **he started shouting, upon ~ I left the room** il s'est mis à crier, sur quoi *OR* et sur ce j'ai quitté la pièce.
◆ **Which?** *pr n magazine de l'Union des consommateurs britanniques connu pour ses essais comparatifs.*

whichever [wɪtʃ'evər] ◇ *pron* **1.** [the one that - as subject] celui qui *m*, celle qui *f*, ceux qui *mpl*, celles qui *f* ; [- as object] celui que *m*, celle que *f*, ceux que *mpl*, celles que *f* ▪ **choose ~ most appeals to you** choisissez celui/celle qui vous plaît le plus ▪ **will ~ of you arrives first turn on the heating?** celui d'entre vous qui arrivera le premier pourra-t-il allumer le chauffage? ▪ **shall we go to the cinema or the theatre? – ~ you prefer** on va au cinéma ou au théâtre? – choisis ce que tu préfères ▪ **let's meet at 3.30 or 4, ~ is best for you** donnons-nous rendez-vous à 3 h 30 ou à 4 h, comme cela vous arrange le mieux ▪ **we will reimburse half the value or $1,000, ~ is the greater** nous vous rembourserons la moitié de la valeur ou 1 000 dollars, soit la somme la plus avantageuse **2.** [no matter which one] : **~ of the routes you choose, allow about two hours** quel que soit le chemin que vous choisissiez, comptez environ deux heures ▪ **I'd like to speak either to Mr Brown or Mr Jones, ~ is available** j'aimerais parler à M. Brown ou à M. Jones, celui des deux qui est disponible.
◇ *det* **1.** [indicating the specified choice or preference] : **grants will be given to ~ students most need them** des bourses seront accordées à ceux des étudiants qui en ont le plus besoin ▪ **take ~ seat you like** asseyez-vous où vous voulez ▪ **we'll travel by ~ train is fastest** nous prendrons le train le plus rapide (, peu importe lequel) ▪ **keep ~ one appeals to you most** gardez celui qui vous plaît le plus **2.** [no matter what - as subject] quel que soit... qui ; [- as object] quel que soit... que ▪ **~ job you take, it will mean a lot of travelling** quel que soit le poste que vous preniez, vous serez obligé de beaucoup voyager ▪ **~ way you look at it, it's not fair** peu importe la façon dont on considère la question, c'est vraiment injuste.

whichsoever [,wɪtʃsəʊ'evər] = **whichever**.

whichways ['wɪtʃweɪz] *adv US* où ▪ **she left the papers lying every ~** elle a laissé les papiers traîner partout.

whiff [wɪf] ◇ *n* **1.** [gust, puff] bouffée *f* **2.** [smell] odeur *f* ▪ **he got a sudden ~ of her perfume/of rotten eggs** il sentit soudain l'odeur de son parfum/une odeur d'œufs pourris ▪ **a ~ of scandal** *fig* une odeur de scandale.
◇ *vi inf* sentir mauvais, puer.

whiffy ['wɪfɪ] (*comp* **whiffier**, *superl* **whiffiest**) *adj inf* qui pue.

Whig [wɪg] ◇ *adj* whig.
◇ *n* whig *m*.

while [waɪl] ◇ *conj* **1.** [as] pendant que ▪ **he read the paper ~ he waited** il lisait le journal en attendant ▪ **~ (you're) in London you should visit the British Museum** pendant que vous serez à Londres *OR* pendant votre séjour à Londres, il faut visiter le British Museum ▪ **he cut himself ~ (he was) shaving** il s'est coupé en se rasant ▪ **~ this was going on** pendant ce temps-là ▪ **'heels repaired/keys cut ~ you wait'** 'talons/clés minute' ▪ **~ you're up could you fetch me some water?** puisque tu es debout, peux-tu aller me chercher de l'eau? ▪ **and ~ I'm about** *OR* **at it...** et pendant que j'y suis... **2.** [although] bien que, quoique ▪ **~ I admit it's difficult, it's not impossible** j'admets que c'est difficile, mais ce n'est pas impossible ▪ **~ comprehensive, the report lacked clarity** bien que détaillé le

rapport manquait de clarté **3.** [whereas] alors que, tandis que ▪ **she's left-wing, ~ he's rather conservative** elle est de gauche tandis que lui est plutôt conservateur.
◇ *n* : **to wait a ~** attendre (un peu) ▪ **after a ~** au bout de quelque temps ▪ **for a ~/a long ~ I believed her** pendant un certain temps/pendant assez longtemps je l'ai crue ▪ **I was in the States a short ~ ago** j'étais aux États-Unis il y a peu (de temps) ▪ **she was in the garden a short ~ ago** elle était dans le jardin il y a un instant ▪ **it's been a good ~ since I've seen her** ça fait pas mal de temps que je ne l'ai pas vue ▪ **all the ~** (pendant) tout ce temps ▪ **once in a ~** de temps en temps *OR* à autre.
◆ **while away** *vt sep* faire passer ▪ **she ~d away the hours reading until he returned** elle passa le temps à lire jusqu'à son retour.

whilst [waɪlst] *UK* = **while** *(conj).*

whim [wɪm] *n* caprice *m*, fantaisie *f* ▪ **it's just one of his little ~s** ce n'est qu'une de ses petites lubies ▪ **arrangements are altered at the ~ of the King** les préparatifs sont changés sur un simple caprice du roi ▪ **she indulges his every ~** elle lui passe tous ses caprices ▪ **on a sudden ~ I telephoned her mother** tout à coup l'idée m'a pris de téléphoner à sa mère.

whimper ['wɪmpəʳ] ◇ *vi* [person] gémir, geindre ▪ *pej* pleurnicher ▪ [dog] gémir, pousser des cris plaintifs.
◇ *vt* gémir.
◇ *n* gémissement *m*, geignement *m* ▪ **she did it without a ~** elle l'a fait sans se plaindre.

whimpering ['wɪmpərɪŋ] ◇ *n (U)* gémissements *mpl*, plaintes *fpl* ▪ **stop your ~!** arrête de pleurnicher!
◇ *adj* [voice] larmoyant ▪ [person] qui pleurniche.

whimsical ['wɪmzɪkl] *adj* **1.** [capricious] capricieux, fantasque **2.** [unusual] étrange, insolite.

whimsically ['wɪmzɪklɪ] *adv* étrangement, curieusement.

whimsy ['wɪmsɪ] (*pl* **whimsies**) *n* **1.** [whimsicality] caractère *m* fantasque *OR* fantaisiste **2.** [idea] caprice *m*, fantaisie *f*.

whine [waɪn] ◇ *vi* **1.** [in pain, discomfort - person] gémir, geindre ; [- dog] gémir, pousser des gémissements **2.** [complain] se lamenter, se plaindre ▪ **to ~ about sthg** se plaindre de qqch.
◇ *vt* dire en gémissant ▪ **"I'm hungry," she ~d** "j'ai faim" dit-elle d'une voix plaintive.
◇ *n* **1.** [from pain, discomfort] gémissement *m* **2.** [complaint] plainte *f*.

whiner ['waɪnəʳ] *n inf pej* pleurnichard *m*, - e *f*.

whinge [wɪndʒ] (*cont* **whingeing**) *UK* & *Australia inf pej* ◇ *vi* geindre, pleurnicher ▪ **don't come ~ing to me about your problems** ne venez pas vous plaindre à moi de vos problèmes.
◇ *n* plainte *f*, pleurnicherie *f*.

whingeing ['wɪndʒɪŋ] *UK* & *Australia inf* ◇ *n (U)* gémissement *m* ▪ *pej* pleurnicherie *f*, plainte *f*.
◇ *adj* [person] pleurnicheur ▪ [voice] plaintif.

whining ['waɪnɪŋ] ◇ *n (U)* **1.** [of person] gémissements *mpl* ▪ *pej* pleurnicheries *fpl* ▪ [of dog] gémissements *mpl* **2.** [of machinery, shells] gémissement *m*.
◇ *adj* [person] *pej* geignard, pleurnicheur ▪ [voice] geignard ▪ [dog] qui gémit.

whinny ['wɪnɪ] (*pret* & *pp* **whinnied**, *pl* **whinnies**) ◇ *vi* hennir.
◇ *n* hennissement *m*.

whip [wɪp] (*pret* & *pp* **whipped**, *cont* **whipping**) ◇ *vt* **1.** [person, animal] fouetter ▪ **the cold wind whipped her face** le vent glacial lui fouettait le visage ▪ **the wind whipped her hair about** le vent agitait sa chevelure
2. *inf* [defeat] vaincre, battre
3. CULIN fouetter, battre au fouet ▪ **~ the egg whites** battez les blancs en neige
4. *fig* **his speech whipped them all into a frenzy** son discours les a tous rendus frénétiques ▪ **I'll soon ~ the team into shape** j'aurai bientôt fait de mettre l'équipe en forme ▪ **to ~ sb into line** mettre qqn au pas
5. *UK inf* [steal] faucher, piquer
6. SEW surfiler
7. [cable, rope] surlier.
◇ *vi* **1.** [lash] fouetter ▪ **the rain whipped against the window** la pluie fouettait *OR* cinglait les vitres ▪ **the flags whipped about in the wind** les drapeaux claquaient au vent
2. [move quickly] aller vite, filer ▪ **the car whipped along the road** la voiture filait sur la route ▪ **the ball whipped past him into the net** la balle est passée devant lui comme un éclair pour finir au fond du filet ▪ **can you ~ round to the library for me** pouvez-vous faire un saut à la bibliothèque pour moi?
◇ *n* **1.** [lash] fouet *m* ▪ [for riding] cravache *f*
2. POL [MP] *parlementaire chargé de la discipline de son par[ti] et qui veille à ce que ses députés participent aux votes*
3. *UK* POL [summons] convocation *f*
4. *UK* POL [paper] *calendrier des travaux parlementaires envoy[é] par le "whip" aux députés de son parti*
5. [dessert] : **pineapple ~** crème *f* à l'ananas.
◆ **whip away** *vt sep* [subj: wind] emporter brusquement
◆ **whip in** ◇ *vt sep* **1.** HUNT ramener, rassembler
2. *UK* POL [in parliament] battre le rappel de *(pour voter)*
3. [supporters] rallier.
◇ *vi insep* **1.** [rush in] entrer précipitamment
2. HUNT être piqueur.
◆ **whip off** *vt sep* [take off - jacket, shoes] se débarrasser d[e] ▪ [write quickly - letter, memo] écrire en vitesse.
◆ **whip on** *vt sep* [horse] cravacher.
◆ **whip out** ◇ *vt sep* **1.** [take out] sortir vivement ▪ **h[e] whipped a notebook out of his pocket** il a vite sorti un carne[t] de sa poche
2. [grab] : **someone whipped my bag out of my hand** quelqu'u[n] m'a arraché mon sac des mains.
◇ *vi insep* sortir précipitamment.
◆ **whip round** *vi insep* [person] se retourner vivement[,] faire volte-face.
◆ **whip through** *vt insep inf* [book] parcourir en vitess[e] ▪ [task] expédier, faire en quatrième vitesse.
◆ **whip up** *vt sep* **1.** [curiosity, emotion] attiser ▪ [support] ob[-]tenir
2. [typhoon] susciter, provoquer ▪ [dust] soulever (des nuages de)
3. CULIN battre au fouet, fouetter ▪ **I'll ~ up some lunch** *inf* j[e] vais préparer de quoi déjeuner en vitesse.

whipcord ['wɪpkɔːd] ◇ *n* whipcord *m*.
◇ *comp* en whipcord.

whip hand *n* : **to have the ~** être le maître ▪ **to have the ~ over sb** avoir le dessus sur qqn.

whiplash ['wɪplæʃ] *n* **1.** [stroke of whip] coup *m* de fouet
2. MED : **~ effect** effet *m* du coup du lapin ▪ **~ injury** coup *m* du lapin, syndrome *m* cervical traumatique *spec.*

whipped [wɪpt] *adj* [cream] fouetté.

whipper-in [ˌwɪpəʳ-] (*pl* **whippers-in**) *n* HUNT piqueur *m*.

whippersnapper ['wɪpəˌsnæpəʳ] *n dated* freluquet *m*.

whippet ['wɪpɪt] *n* whippet *m*.

whipping ['wɪpɪŋ] *n* [as punishment - child] correction *f* [- prisoner] coups *mpl* de fouet.

whipping boy *n* bouc *m* émissaire.

whipping cream *n* crème *f* fraîche (à fouetter).

whip-round *n UK inf* collecte *f* ▪ **they had a ~ for her** ils ont fait une collecte pour elle.

whir [wɜːʳ] = **whirr**.

whirl [wɜːl] ◇ *vi* **1.** [person, skater] tourner, tournoyer ▪ **she ~ed round the ice rink** elle a fait le tour de la piste en tourbillonnant **2.** [leaves, smoke] tourbillonner, tournoyer ▪ [dust, water] tourbillonner ▪ [spindle, top] tournoyer ▪ **snowflakes ~ed past the window** des flocons de neige passaient devant la fenêtre en tourbillonnant **3.** [head, ideas] tourner ▪ **my head is ~ing** (j'ai) la tête (qui) me tourne **4.** [move quickly] aller à toute vitesse ▪ **the horses ~ed past us** les chevaux sont passés devant nous à toute allure.

<> *vt* **1.** [dancer, skater] faire tourner **2.** [leaves, smoke] faire tourbillonner *OR* tournoyer ▪ [dust, sand] faire tourbillonner **3.** [take rapidly] : **she ~ed us off on a trip round Europe** elle nous a embarqués pour un tour d'Europe.
<> *n* **1.** [of dancers, leaves, events] tourbillon *m* ▪ *fig* **my head is in a ~** la tête me tourne ▪ **her thoughts were in a ~** tout tourbillonnait dans sa tête ▪ **the mad social ~** *hum* la folle vie mondaine ▪ **the kitchen was a ~ of activity** la cuisine bourdonnait d'activité **2.** [try] : **to give sthg a ~** *inf* s'essayer à qqch **3.** *inf* [trip] promenade *f*, tour *m*.

whirligig ['wɜːlɪgɪg] *n UK* **1.** [top] toupie *f* ▪ [toy windmill] moulin *m* à vent *(jouet)* **2.** [merry-go-round] manège *m* **3.** [of activity, events] tourbillon *m*.

whirlpool ['wɜːlpuːl] *n liter & fig* tourbillon *m*.

whirlpool bath *n* bain *m* à remous.

whirlwind ['wɜːlwɪnd] <> *n* tornade *f*, trombe *f* ▪ **he went through the office accounts like a ~** *fig* il a passé les comptes de la société en revue en un rien de temps.
<> *adj* [trip, romance] éclair *(inv)*.

whirlybird ['wɜːlɪbɜːd] *n inf* hélico *m*.

whirr [wɜːʳ] <> *n* [of wings] bruissement *m* ▪ [of camera, machinery] bruit *m*, ronronnement *m* ▪ [of helicopter, propeller] bruit *m*, vrombissement *m*.
<> *vi* [wings] bruire ▪ [camera, machinery] ronronner ▪ [propeller] vrombir.

whish [wɪʃ] = **swish** *(vi & n)*.

whisk [wɪsk] <> *vt* **1.** [put or take quickly] : **we ~ed the money into the tin/off the counter** nous avons vite fait disparaître l'argent dans la boîte/du comptoir ▪ **the car ~ed us to the embassy** la voiture nous emmena à l'ambassade à toute allure ▪ **she ~ed the children out of the room** elle emmena rapidement les enfants hors de la pièce **2.** CULIN [cream, eggs] battre ▪ [egg whites] battre en neige ▪ **~ in the cream** incorporer la crème avec un fouet **3.** [flick] : **the horse/cow ~ed its tail** le cheval/la vache agitait la queue.
<> *vi* [move quickly] aller vite ▪ **she just ~ed in and out** elle n'a fait qu'entrer et sortir.
<> *n* **1.** [of tail, stick, duster] coup *m* ▪ **the horse gave a ~ of its tail** le cheval agita la queue *OR* donna un coup de queue **2.** [for sweeping] époussette *f* ▪ [for flies] chasse-mouches *m inv* **3.** CULIN fouet *m* ▪ [electric] batteur *m*.
◆ **whisk away** *vt sep* **1.** [dust] enlever, chasser ▪ [dishes, tablecloth] faire disparaître ▪ [flies - with fly swatter] chasser à coups de chasse-mouches ; [- with tail] chasser d'un coup de queue **2.** [take off] : **a car ~ed us away to the embassy** [immediately] une voiture nous emmena sur-le-champ à l'ambassade ; [quickly] une voiture nous emmena à toute allure à l'ambassade.
◆ **whisk off** *vt sep* [quickly] emporter *OR* emmener à vive allure ▪ [suddenly, immediately] conduire sur-le-champ.

whisker ['wɪskəʳ] *n* poil *m* ▪ **she won the contest by a ~** *inf* elle a gagné le concours de justesse ▪ **he came within a ~ of discovering the truth** *inf* il s'en est fallu d'un cheveu *OR* d'un poil qu'il apprenne la vérité.
◆ **whiskers** *npl* [beard] barbe *f* ▪ [moustache] moustache *f* ▪ [on animal] moustaches *fpl*.

whiskered ['wɪskəd] *adj* [bearded] qui a une barbe ▪ [with moustache] qui a une moustache ▪ [animal] qui a des moustaches.

whiskey ['wɪskɪ] *(pl* **whiskeys***)* *US & Ireland* = **whisky**.

whisky *(pl* **whiskies***)* *UK*, **whiskey** *US & Ireland* ['wɪskɪ] *n* whisky *m*, scotch *m* ▪ *US* bourbon *m* ▪ **a ~ and soda** un whisky soda.

whisky sour *n cocktail avec du whisky et du jus de citron.*

whisper ['wɪspəʳ] <> *vi* **1.** [person] chuchoter, parler à voix basse ▪ **to ~ to sb** parler *OR* chuchoter à l'oreille de qqn ▪ **what are you ~ing about?** qu'est-ce que vous avez à chuchoter?
2. [leaves] bruire ▪ [water, wind] murmurer.
<> *vt* **1.** [person] chuchoter, dire à voix basse ▪ **to ~ sthg to sb** chuchoter qqch à qqn ▪ **I ~ed the answer to her** je lui ai soufflé la réponse ▪ **to ~ sweet nothings to sb** susurrer des mots doux à l'oreille de qqn
2. *UK* [rumour] : **it's ~ed that her husband's left her** le bruit court *OR* on dit que son mari l'a quittée.
<> *n* **1.** [of voice] chuchotement *m* ▪ **to speak in a ~** parler tout bas *OR* à voix basse ▪ **we never raised our voices above a ~** nous n'avons fait que murmurer ▪ **not a ~ of this to anyone!** *fig* n'en soufflez mot à personne!
2. [of leaves] bruissement *m* ▪ [of water, wind] murmure *m*
3. *UK* [rumour] rumeur *f*, bruit *m* ▪ **there are ~s of his leaving** le bruit court *OR* on dit qu'il va partir.

whispering ['wɪspərɪŋ] <> *n* **1.** [of voices] chuchotement *m*, chuchotements *mpl* **2.** [of leaves] bruissement *m* ▪ [of water, wind] murmure *m* **3.** *(usu pl) UK* [rumour] rumeur.
<> *adj* **1.** [voice] qui chuchote **2.** [leaves, tree] qui frémit *OR* murmure ▪ [water, wind] qui murmure.

whispering gallery *n* galerie *f* à écho.

whist [wɪst] *n* whist *m*.

whist drive *n* tournoi *m* de whist.

whistle ['wɪsl] <> *vi* **1.** [person - using lips] siffler ; [- using whistle] donner un coup de sifflet, siffler ▪ **to ~ to sb** siffler qqn ▪ **the porter ~d for a taxi** le portier a sifflé un taxi ▶ **you can ~ for it!** *UK inf* tu peux toujours courir *OR* te brosser! ▪ **to ~ in the dark** essayer de se donner du courage **2.** [bird, kettle, train] siffler ▪ **bullets ~d past him** des balles passaient près de lui en sifflant ▪ **the wind ~d through the trees** le vent gémissait dans les arbres.
<> *vt* [tune] siffler, siffloter.
<> *n* **1.** [whistling - through lips] sifflement *m* ; [- from whistle] coup *m* de sifflet ▪ **if you need me, just give a ~** tu n'as qu'à siffler si tu as besoin de moi **2.** [of bird, kettle, train] sifflement *m* **3.** [instrument - of person, on train] sifflet *m* ▪ **to blow a ~** donner un coup de sifflet ▪ **the referee blew his ~ for half-time** l'arbitre a sifflé la mi-temps ▶ **to be as clean as a ~** briller comme un sou neuf ▪ **it's got all the bells and ~s** il a tous les accessoires possibles et imaginables **4.** MUS : **(penny)** *OR* **tin ~** flûtiau *m*, pipeau *m*.
◆ **whistle up** *vt sep UK* **1.** [by whistling] siffler **2.** [find] dénicher, dégoter.

whistle-blower *n inf personne qui vend la mèche.*

whistle-stop <> *n US* RAIL arrêt *m* facultatif ▪ **~ (town)** village *m* perdu.
<> *vi US* POL *faire une tournée électorale en passant par des petites villes.*
<> *adj* : **he made a ~ tour of the West** il a fait une tournée rapide dans l'Ouest.

whit [wɪt] *n lit* petit peu *m* ▪ **he hasn't changed a ~** il n'a absolument pas changé.

Whit [wɪt] <> *n* Pentecôte *f*.
<> *comp* [holidays, week] de Pentecôte ▪ **~ Sunday/Monday** dimanche *m* /lundi *m* de Pentecôte.

white [waɪt] <> *adj* **1.** [colour] blanc, blanche *f* ▪ **she wore a dazzling ~ dress** elle portait une robe d'un blanc éclatant ▪ **his hair has turned ~** ses cheveux ont blanchi ▮ [pale] : **she was ~ with fear/rage** elle était verte de peur/blanche de colère ▪ **his face suddenly went ~** il a blêmi tout d'un coup ▶ **whiter than ~** *liter* plus blanc que blanc ; *fig* sans tache ▪ **you're as ~ as a ghost/sheet** vous êtes pâle comme la mort/un linge ▪ **as ~ as snow** blanc comme neige **2.** [flour, rice] blanc, blanche *f* ▪ **(a loaf of) ~ bread** du pain blanc ▪ **~ wine** vin *m* blanc **3.** [race] blanc, blanche *f* ▪ **a ~ man** un Blanc ▪ **a ~ woman** une Blanche ▪ **an all-~ neighbourhood** un quartier blanc.
<> *n* **1.** [colour] blanc *m* ▪ **the bride wore ~** la mariée était en blanc ▪ **he was dressed all in ~** il était tout en blanc **2.** ANAT [of an eye] blanc *m* ▪ **don't shoot until you see the ~s of their eyes** *fig* ne tirez qu'au dernier moment **3.** CULIN : **(egg) ~** blanc *m* (d'œuf) **4.** [Caucasian] Blanc *m*, Blanche *f* ▪ **'~s only'** 'réservé aux Blancs'.
<> *vi & vt arch* blanchir.
◆ **whites** *npl* [sportswear] tenue *f* de sport blanche *(tennis, cricket)* ▪ [linen] blanc *m*.

◆ **white out** *vt sep* effacer (au correcteur liquide).

whitebait ['waɪtbeɪt] *n* [for fishermen] blanchaille *f* ▪ CULIN petite friture *f*.

white blood cell *n* globule *m* blanc.

whiteboard ['waɪtbɔːd] *n* tableau *m* blanc.

white-collar *adj* : ~ **job** poste *m* d'employé de bureau ▪ ~ **workers** les employés *mpl* de bureau, les cols *mpl* blancs.

whited sepulchre ['waɪtɪd-] *n fml* hypocrite *mf*.

white elephant *n* [useless object] *objet coûteux dont l'utilité ne justifie pas le coût* ▪ **the new submarine has turned out to be a complete ~** le nouveau sous-marin s'est révélé être un luxe tout à fait superflu.

White Ensign *n pavillon de la marine royale britannique*.

white-faced *adj* au visage pâle.

whitefish ['waɪtfɪʃ] (*pl inv* OR *pl* **whitefishes**) *n* corégone *m*.

white fish *n* UK *poissons à chair blanche*.

white flag *n* drapeau *m* blanc.

whitefly ['waɪtflaɪ] (*pl* **whiteflies**) *n* aleurode *m*.

white gold *n* or *m* blanc.

white-haired *adj* [person] aux cheveux blancs ▪ [animal] aux poils blancs.

Whitehall ['waɪthɔːl] *pr n rue du centre de Londres qui réunit de nombreux services gouvernementaux*.

WHITEHALL

Cette rue, dont le nom est souvent employé pour désigner les fonctions administratives du gouvernement, réunit de nombreux services gouvernementaux.

white heat *n* PHYS & *fig* chaleur *f* incandescente ▪ **in the ~ of passion** au plus fort de la passion ▪ **anti-war feelings have reached ~** les sentiments d'hostilité par rapport à la guerre ont atteint un paroxysme.

white hope *n* espoir *m*.

white horses *npl* [waves] moutons *mpl*.

white-hot *adj* PHYS & *fig* chauffé à blanc.

White House *pr n* : **the ~** la Maison-Blanche.

white knight *n fig* sauveur *m*.

white-knuckle *adj* : ~ **ride** tour *m* de manège terrifiant.

white lie *n* pieux mensonge *m*.

white light *n* lumière *f* blanche.

white magic *n* magie *f* blanche.

white meat *n* viande *f* blanche ▪ [of poultry] blanc *m*.

whiten ['waɪtn] *vi* & *vt* blanchir.

whitener ['waɪtnər] *n* agent *m* blanchissant.

whiteness ['waɪtnɪs] *n* blancheur *f* ▪ [of skin] blancheur *f*, pâleur *f*.

whitening ['waɪtnɪŋ] *n* **1.** [substance] blanc *m* **2.** [process - of walls] blanchiment *m* ; [- of linen] blanchissage *m*.

whiteout ['waɪtaʊt] *n* brouillard *m* blanc.

White Out® *n* US correcteur *m* liquide.

white owl *n* harfang *m*, chouette *f* blanche.

white paper *n* UK [government report] livre *m* blanc.

white pepper *n* poivre *m* blanc.

White Russia *pr n* Russie *f* Blanche.

White Russian ◇ *adj* biélorusse.
◇ *n* **1.** [person] Biélorusse *mf* **2.** LING biélorusse *m*.

white sauce *n* sauce *f* blanche, béchamel *f*.

white slavery, white slave trade *n* traite *f* des blanches.

white spirit *n* white-spirit *m*.

white tie *n* [formal clothes] habit *m* ▪ **'white tie'** [on invitation] 'tenue de soirée exigée'.
◆ **white-tie** *adj* habillé.

white trash *n pej* pauvres blancs *mpl*.

whitewall ['waɪtwɔːl] *n* pneu *m* à flanc blanc.

whitewash ['waɪtwɒʃ] ◇ *n* **1.** [substance] lait *m* de chaux **2.** *fig* [cover-up] : **the police report was simply a ~** le rapport de police visait seulement à étouffer l'affaire **3.** SPORT [crushing defeat] défaite *f* cuisante.
◇ *vt* **1.** [building, wall] blanchir à la chaux **2.** *fig* [cover up] blanchir, étouffer **3.** SPORT [defeat] écraser.

white water *n* eau *f* vive.

whitewater rafting ['waɪt,wɔːtər-] *n* descente *f* en eau vive, rafting *m*.

white wedding *n* mariage *m* en blanc.

whiting ['waɪtɪŋ] *n* **1.** ZOOL merlan *m* **2.** [colouring agent] blanc *m*.

whitlow ['wɪtləʊ] *n* panaris *m*.

Whitsun(tide) ['wɪtsn(taɪd)] *n* Pentecôte *f* ▪ **at ~** à la Pentecôte.

whitter ['wɪtər] = **witter**.

whittle ['wɪtl] *vi* & *vt* tailler (au couteau) ▪ **he ~d an arrow from an old stick, he ~d an old stick into an arrow** il a taillé une flèche dans un vieux bâton.
◆ **whittle away** ◇ *vt sep fig* amoindrir, diminuer.
◇ *vi insep* [with a knife] tailler ▪ **their constant teasing ~d away at his patience** *fig* leurs moqueries constantes ont mis sa patience à bout.
◆ **whittle down** *vt sep* [with a knife] tailler (au couteau) ▪ *fig* amenuiser, amoindrir.

whiz(z) [wɪz] (*pret* & *pp* **whizzed**, *cont* **whizzing**) ◇ *vi* **1.** [rush] filer ▪ **a car whizzed past** une voiture est passée à toute allure **2.** [hiss] : **bullets whizzed around** OR **past him** des balles sifflaient tout autour OR passaient près de lui en sifflant.
◇ *n* **1.** [hissing sound] sifflement *m* **2.** *inf* [swift movement] : **I'll just have a (quick) ~ round with the Hoover/duster** je vais juste passer un petit coup d'aspirateur/de chiffon **3.** *inf* [bright person] as *m* ▪ **he's a real computer ~** c'est vraiment un as de l'informatique.

whiz(z) kid *n inf* jeune prodige *m* ▪ **she's a computer ~** c'est un vrai génie de l'informatique.

who [huː] ◇ *pron* [what person or persons - as subject] (qui est-ce) qui ; [- as object] qui est-ce que, qui ▪ **~ are you?** qui êtes-vous? ▪ **~ is it?** [at door] qui est-ce?, qui est là? ▪ **~ is speaking?** [on telephone] qui est à l'appareil? ; [asking for third person] c'est de la part de qui? ▪ **it's Michael – ~?** c'est Michael – qui ça? ▪ **I told him ~ I was** je lui ai dit qui j'étais ▪ **find out ~ they are** voyez qui c'est OR qui sont ces gens ▪ **~ do you think you are?** vous vous prenez pour qui? ▪ **~ do you think you are, giving me orders?** de quel droit est-ce que vous me donnez des ordres? ▪ **~ did you say was coming to the party?** qui avez-vous dit qui viendrait à la soirée? ▪ **you'll have to tell me ~'s ~** il faudra que tu me dises qui est qui ▪ **~ is the film by?** de qui est le film? ▪ **~ is the letter from?** la lettre est de qui?, de qui est la lettre?
◇ *rel pron* qui ▪ **the family ~ lived here moved away** la famille qui habitait ici a déménagé ▪ **those of you ~ were late** ceux d'entre vous qui sont arrivés en retard ▪ **anyone ~ so wishes may leave** ceux qui le souhaitent peuvent partir ▪ **any reader ~ finds the story lacks imagination...** les lecteurs qui trouvent que l'histoire n'est pas très originale... ▪ **Charles, ~ is a policeman, lives upstairs** Charles, qui est policier, vit en haut ▪ **my mother, ~ I believe you've met,...** ma mère, que vous avez déjà rencontrée je crois,...

WHO (*abbrev of* **World Health Organization**) *pr n* OMS *f*.

whoa [wəʊ] *interj* : **~!** ho!, holà!

who'd [huːd] **1.** = **who had 2.** = **who would**.

whodun(n)it [,huː'dʌnɪt] *n inf* série *f* noire ▪ **to read/to write ~s** lire/écrire des romans de série noire.

whoe'er [hu'eəʳ] *pron lit* celui qui, quiconque.

whoever [hu:'evəʳ] *pron* **1.** [any person who] qui ■ **~ wants it can have it** celui qui le veut peut le prendre ■ **I'll give it to ~ needs it** je le donnerai à qui en a besoin ■ **invite ~ you like** invitez qui vous voulez **2.** [the person who] celui qui *m*, celle qui *f*, ceux qui *mpl*, celles qui *f* ■ **~ answered the phone had a nice voice** la personne qui a répondu au téléphone avait une voix agréable ■ **contact ~ found the body** contactez celui qui *OR* la personne qui a trouvé le corps **3.** [no matter who] : **come out, ~ you are!** montrez-vous, qui que vous soyez! ■ **~ gets the job will find it a real challenge** celui qui obtiendra cet emploi n'aura pas la tâche facile ■ **~ you vote for, make sure he's honest** quel que soit celui pour qui vous votez, assurez-vous qu'il est honnête ■ **it's from John Smith, ~ he is** c'est de la part d'un certain John Smith, si ça te dit quelque chose **4.** [emphatic use] qui donc ■ **~ can that be?** qui cela peut-il bien être?

whole [həʊl] ◇ *adj* **1.** *(with sg nouns)* [entire, complete] entier, tout ■ **it took me a ~ day to paint the kitchen** j'ai mis une journée entière *OR* toute une journée pour peindre la cuisine ■ **I've never seen anything like it in my ~ life** je n'ai jamais vu une chose pareille de toute ma vie ■ **that was the ~ point of going there** c'est uniquement pour ça que j'y suis allé ■ **she said nothing the ~ time we were there** elle n'a rien dit tout le temps que nous étions là ■ **he spent the ~ time watching television** il a passé tout son temps à regarder la télévision ■ **the ~ world was watching** le monde entier regardait ■ *(with plural nouns)* entier ■ **there are two ~ months still to go** il reste deux mois entiers ▶ **she won the ~ lot** elle a gagné le tout ■ **the ~ thing** *OR* **business was a farce** ce fut un véritable fiasco ■ **I had to start the ~ thing over again** j'ai dû tout recommencer ■ **forget the ~ thing** n'en parlons plus
2. [as intensifier] tout ■ **he's got a ~ collection of old photographs** il a toute une collection de vieilles photographies ■ **there's a ~ lot of things that need explaining** il y a beaucoup de choses qui doivent être expliquées ■ *(with adj)* **a ~ new way of living** une façon de vivre tout à fait nouvelle
3. [unbroken - china, egg yolk] intact ■ [unhurt - person] indemne, sain et sauf ■ *arch* & BIBLE : **to make ~** sauver
4. CULIN [milk] entier ■ [grain] complet, - ète *f*
5. [brother, sister] : **~ brothers** des frères qui ont les mêmes parents.
◇ *n* **1.** [complete thing, unit] ensemble *m*
2. [as quantifier] : **the ~ of** tout ■ **it will be cold over the ~ of England** il fera froid sur toute l'Angleterre ■ **can you pay the ~ of the amount?** pouvez-vous payer toute la somme *OR* l'intégralité de la somme?
◇ *adv* : **to swallow sthg ~** avaler qqch en entier ■ **he swallowed her story ~** *inf fig* il a gobé tout ce qu'elle lui a dit.
◆ **as a whole** *adv phr* **1.** [as a unit] entièrement ■ **as a ~ or in part** entièrement ou en partie
2. [overall] dans son ensemble ■ **is it true of America as a ~?** est-ce vrai pour toute l'Amérique *OR* l'Amérique en général? ■ **considered as a ~, the festival was a remarkable success** dans son ensemble, le festival a été un vrai succès.
◆ **a whole lot** *adv phr (with comparative adjectives) inf* beaucoup ■ **he's a ~ lot younger than his wife** il est beaucoup plus jeune que sa femme.
◆ **on the whole** *adv phr* dans l'ensemble.

wholefood ['həʊlfu:d] *n* aliment *m* complet ■ **~ shop** magasin *m* diététique.

wholehearted [,həʊl'hɑ:tɪd] *adj* [unreserved] sans réserve ■ **she gave them her ~ support** elle leur a donné un soutien sans réserve *OR* sans faille ■ **he is a ~ supporter of our cause** [devoted] il est dévoué corps et âme à notre cause.

wholeheartedly [,həʊl'hɑ:tɪdlɪ] *adv* [unreservedly] de tout cœur ■ **I agree ~** j'accepte de tout (mon) cœur ■ **he flung himself ~ into his new job** il s'est jeté corps et âme dans son nouveau travail.

wholemeal ['həʊlmi:l] *adj UK* [bread, flour] complet, - ète *f*.

whole note *n US* [semibreve] ronde *f*.

whole number *n* [integer] nombre *m* entier.

whole rest *n US* pause *f*.

wholesale ['həʊlseɪl] ◇ *n* (vente *f* en) gros *m*.
◇ *adj* **1.** COMM [business, price, shop] de gros ■ **~ dealer** *OR* **trader** grossiste *mf* **2.** *fig* [indiscriminate] en masse.
◇ *adv* **1.** COMM en gros ■ **I can get it for you ~** je peux vous le procurer au prix de gros **2.** *fig* [in entirety] : **to reject sthg ~** rejeter qqch en bloc.

wholesaler ['həʊl,seɪləʳ] *n* grossiste *mf*.

wholesome ['həʊlsəm] *adj* [healthy - food, attitude, image, life] sain ; [- air, climate, environment] salubre, salutaire ■ [advice] salutaire ■ **a ~-looking boy** un garçon sain d'aspect.

wholewheat ['həʊlwi:t] *adj US* [bread, flour] complet, - ète *f*.

who'll [hu:l] **1.** = **who will 2.** = **who shall**.

wholly ['həʊlɪ] *adv* entièrement ■ **the firm has two ~-owned subsidiaries** COMM la société a deux filiales à cent pour cent.

whom [hu:m] *fml* ◇ *pron* [in questions] qui ■ **for ~ was the book written?** pour qui le livre a-t-il été écrit?
◇ *rel pron* [as object of verb] que ■ **she is the person ~ I most admire** c'est la personne que j'admire le plus ▮ [after preposition] : **the person to ~ I am writing** la personne à qui *OR* à laquelle j'écris ■ **she saw two men, neither of ~ she recognized** elle a vu deux hommes mais elle n'a reconnu ni l'un ni l'autre.

whomever [hu:m'evəʳ] *fml* & *lit* ◇ *pron* [in questions] : **~ did you get that from?** qui donc vous a donné cela?
◇ *rel pron* : **you may go with ~ you like** vous pouvez y aller avec qui vous voudrez.

whoop [wu:p] ◇ *n* **1.** [yell] cri *m* **2.** MED quinte *f* de toux.
◇ *vi* **1.** [yell] : **she ~ed with joy** elle poussa un cri de joie **2.** MED avoir un accès de toux coquelucheuse.
◆ **whoop up** *vt sep inf* **to ~ it up** [celebrate] faire la noce bruyamment.

whoopee *inf* ◇ *interj* [wʊ'pi:] : **~!** youpi!
◇ *n* ['wʊpi:] : **to make ~** [celebrate] faire la noce bruyamment ; [have sex] faire l'amour.

whoopee cushion *n* coussin-péteur *m*.

whooping cough ['hu:pɪŋ-] *n* MED coqueluche *f*.

whoops [wʊps], **whoops-a-daisy** *interj inf* **~!** houp-là!

whoosh [wʊʃ] *inf* ◇ *n* : **a ~ of air** une bouffée d'air.
◇ *vi* : **fighter planes ~ed by overhead** des avions de combat passèrent en trombe au-dessus de nous ■ **the car ~ed through the puddles** la voiture passa en trombe dans les flaques.
◇ *interj* : **~!** zoum!

whop [wɒp] (*pret* & *pp* **whopped**, *cont* **whopping**) *inf* ◇ *vt* [beat] rosser ■ [defeat] écraser.
◇ *n* [blow] coup.

whopper ['wɒpəʳ] *n inf* **1.** [large object] : **he caught a real ~** [fish] il a attrapé un poisson super géant ■ **that sandwich is a real ~** c'est un énorme sandwich *OR* un sandwich gigantesque **2.** [lie] gros mensonge *m*, mensonge *m* énorme ■ **to tell a ~** dire un mensonge gros comme une maison.

whopping ['wɒpɪŋ] *inf* ◇ *adj* énorme, géant ■ **inflation increased to a ~ 360%** l'inflation a atteint le taux colossal de 360 %.
◇ *adv* : **a ~ great lie** un mensonge énorme.

whore [hɔ:ʳ] *pej* ◇ *n* putain *f* ■ BIBLE [sinner] pécheresse *f*.
◇ *vi* **1.** *liter* **to go whoring** [prostitute o.s.] se prostituer ; [frequent prostitutes] fréquenter les prostituées, courir la gueuse **2.** *fig* **to ~ after sthg** se prostituer pour obtenir qqch.

who're ['hu:əʳ] = **who are**.

whorehouse ['hɔ:haʊs] (*pl* [-haʊzɪz]) *n inf* maison *f* close.

whoremonger ['hɔ:,mʌŋgəʳ] *n arch* & BIBLE vicieux *m*, fornicateur *m arch*.

whorl [wɜ:l] *n* [on a shell] spire *f* ■ [on a finger] sillon *m* ■ BOT verticille *m* ■ **~s of smoke rose from the chimney** la fumée montait en spirale de la cheminée, des volutes de fumée s'échappaient de la cheminée.

whortleberry ['wɜ:tl,berɪ] (*pl* **whortleberries**) *n* myrtille *f*.

who's [hu:z] **1.** = **who is 2.** = **who has.**

whose [hu:z] <> *poss pron* à qui ▪ **~ is it?** à qui est-ce? ▪ **~ could it be?** à qui pourrait-il bien être? ▪ **~ was the winning number?** à qui était le numéro gagnant?
<> *poss adj* **1.** [in a question] à qui, de qui ▪ **~ car was he driving?** à qui était la voiture qu'il conduisait? ▪ **~ child is she?** de qui est-elle l'enfant? ▪ **~ fault is it?** à qui la faute? ▪ **on ~ authority are you acting?** au nom de quelle autorité agissez-vous? **2.** [in a relative clause] dont ▪ **isn't that the man ~ photograph was in the newspaper?** n'est-ce pas l'homme qui était en photo dans le journal? ▪ **the girl, both of ~ parents had died, lived with her aunt** la fille, dont les deux parents étaient morts, vivait avec sa tante ▪ **they had twins neither of ~ names I can remember** ils avaient des jumeaux mais je ne me souviens pas de leurs prénoms.

whosoever [ˌhu:səʊ'evəʳ] *pron fml & lit* celui qui, quiconque.

Who's Who *pr n* ≃ le Bottin mondain.

who've [hu:v] = **who have.**

why [waɪ] <> *adv* pourquoi ▪ **~ am I telling you this?** pourquoi est-ce que je vous dis ça? ▪ **~ is it that he never phones?** pourquoi est-ce qu'il ne téléphone jamais? ▪ **~ continue the war at all?** pourquoi *OR* à quoi bon continuer la guerre? ▪ **~ the sudden panic?** pourquoi toute cette agitation? ▪ **~ not?** pourquoi pas? ▪ **~ not join us?** pourquoi ne pas vous joindre à nous?
<> *conj* pourquoi ▪ **I can't imagine ~ she isn't here** je ne comprends pas pourquoi elle n'est pas ici ▪ **that's ~ he dislikes you** c'est pour ça qu'il *OR* voilà pourquoi il ne vous aime pas ▪ **they've gone, I can't think ~** ils sont partis, je ne sais pas pourquoi.
<> *rel pron* [after 'reason'] : **the reason ~ I lied was that I was scared** j'ai menti parce que j'avais peur ▪ **he didn't tell me the reason ~** il ne m'a pas dit pourquoi ▪ **this is the reason ~ I lied** voilà pourquoi j'ai menti ▪ **there is no (good) reason ~ she shouldn't come** il n'y a pas de raison qu'elle ne vienne pas.
<> *interj* [expressing surprise, indignation etc] : **~, Mr Ricks, how kind of you to call!** M. Ricks! comme c'est gentil à vous de téléphoner! ▪ **~, there's nothing to it!** oh, il n'y a rien de plus simple! ▪ **~, he's an impostor!** mais enfin, c'est un imposteur!
<> *n* : **the ~s and wherefores** le pourquoi et le comment.

WI <> *pr n* = **Women's Institute.**
<> *written abbr of* **Wisconsin.**

Wicca ['wɪkə] *n* Wicca *f*.

Wiccan ['wɪkən] *adj & n* Wiccan *mf*.

wick [wɪk] *n* **1.** [for a candle, lamp] mèche *f* **2.** *UK phr* **to get on sb's ~** *inf* taper sur les nerfs à qqn.

wicked ['wɪkɪd] *adj* **1.** [evil - person, action, thought] mauvais, méchant ▪ [immoral, indecent] vicieux ▪ **it was a ~ thing to do** ce n'était pas gentil ▪ **what a ~ thing to say!** quelle méchanceté! ▪ **it's a ~ waste of natural resources** *fig* c'est un gâchis scandaleux de ressources naturelles ⊙ **~ witch** méchante sorcière *f* ▪ **to have one's ~ way with sb** *hum* séduire qqn **2.** [very bad - weather] épouvantable ; [- temper] mauvais, épouvantable ▪ **there are some ~ bends on those mountain roads** il y a quelques méchants virages sur ces routes de montagne ▪ **prices have gone up something ~** *inf* les prix ont augmenté quelque chose de bien **3.** [mischievous - person] malicieux ; [- smile, look, sense of humour] malicieux, coquin ▪ **you're a ~ little boy** tu es un petit coquin **4.** *inf* [very good] formidable ▪ **she has a ~ forehand** elle a un sacré coup droit ▪ **it's ~!**△ c'est génial! ▪ **~ trainers**△ des baskets d'enfer.

wickedly ['wɪkɪdlɪ] *adv* **1.** [with evil intent] méchamment, avec méchanceté **2.** [mischievously] malicieusement.

wickedness ['wɪkɪdnɪs] *n* **1.** RELIG [sin, evil] iniquité *f*, vilenie *f* ▪ [cruelty - of action, crime] méchanceté *f* ; [- of thought] méchanceté *f*, vilenie *f* **2.** [mischievousness - of look, sense of humour, smile] caractère *m* malicieux *OR* espiègle, malice *f*.

wicker ['wɪkəʳ] <> *n* osier *m* ▪ **made of ~** en osier.
<> *adj* [furniture] en osier.

wickerwork ['wɪkəwɜ:k] <> *n* [material] osier *m* ▪ [objects] vannerie *f*.
<> *comp* [furniture] en osier ▪ [shop] de vannerie.

wicket ['wɪkɪt] *n* **1.** *US* [window] guichet *m* **2.** [gate] (petite) porte *f*, portillon *m* **3.** [in cricket - stumps] guichet *m* ; [- area of grass] terrain *m* (entre les guichets).

wicket keeper *n* gardien *m* de guichet.

wide [waɪd] <> *adj* **1.** [broad] large ▪ **how ~ is it?** cela fait combien (de mètres) de large?, quelle largeur ça fait? ▪ **do you know how ~ it is?** en connaissez-vous la largeur? ▪ **the road is thirty metres ~** la route fait trente mètres de large ▪ **they're making the street wider** ils élargissent la route ▪ **he gave a ~ grin** il a fait un large sourire ▪ **a ~ screen** CIN un grand écran, un écran panoramique ▪ **there are wider issues at stake here** des problèmes plus vastes sont ici en jeu ▪ **we need to see the problem in a wider context** il faut que nous envisagions le problème dans un contexte plus général ▪ **I'm using the word in its widest sense** j'emploie ce mot au sens le plus large ▪ [fully open - eyes] grand ouvert ▪ **she watched with ~ eyes** elle regardait les yeux grands ouverts ▪ **his eyes were ~ with terror** ses yeux étaient agrandis par l'épouvante
2. [extensive, vast] étendu, vaste ▪ **to travel the ~ world** parcourir le vaste monde ▪ **she has ~ experience in this area** elle a une longue *OR* grande expérience dans ce domaine ▪ **he has a ~ knowledge of music** il a de vastes connaissances *OR* des connaissances approfondies en musique ▪ **there are ~ gaps in her knowledge** il y a des lacunes importantes dans ses connaissances ▪ **a ~ range of products** COMM une gamme importante de produits ▪ **a ~ range of views was expressed** des points de vue très différents furent exprimés ▪ **a ~ variety of colours** un grand choix de couleurs
3. [large - difference] : **the gap between rich and poor remains ~** l'écart (existant) entre les riches et les pauvres demeure considérable
4. SPORT : **the shot was ~** le coup est passé à côté ⊙ **to be ~ of the mark** *UK liter* rater *OR* être passé loin de la cible ; *fig* être loin de la vérité *OR* du compte.
<> *adv* **1.** [to full extent] : **open (your mouth) ~** ouvrez grand votre bouche ▪ **she opened the windows ~** elle ouvrit les fenêtres en grand ▪ **he flung his arms ~** il a ouvert grand les bras ▪ **place your feet ~ apart** écartez bien les pieds
2. [away from target] à côté ▪ **the missile went ~** le missile est tombé à côté.

-wide *in cpds* : **state~** à travers tout l'État, dans l'ensemble de l'État ▪ **world~** à travers le monde (entier).

wide-angle lens *n* grand-angle *m*, grand-angulaire *m*.

wide area network *n* réseau *m* étendu.

wide-awake *adj* tout éveillé ▪ *fig* [alert] éveillé, vif.

wide boy *n UK inf pej personnage frimeur, bluffeur et sans scrupule.*

wide-eyed *adj* **1.** [with fear, surprise] les yeux agrandis *OR* écarquillés ▪ **he looked at me in ~ astonishment** il me regarda les yeux écarquillés d'étonnement **2.** [naive] candide, ingénu *lit*.

widely ['waɪdlɪ] *adv* **1.** [broadly] : **to yawn ~** bâiller profondément ▪ **the houses were ~ scattered/spaced** les maisons étaient très dispersées/espacées **2.** [extensively] : **she has travelled ~** elle a beaucoup voyagé ▪ **the drug is now ~ available/used** le médicament est maintenant largement répandu/utilisé ▪ **it was ~ believed that war was inevitable** il était largement *OR* communément admis que la guerre était inévitable ▪ **the truth about the incident is not ~ known** la vérité sur l'incident n'est pas connue du grand public ▪ **~ held beliefs/opinions** des croyances/opinions très répandues ▪ **to be ~ read** [writer, book] être très lu, avoir un grand public ; [person] avoir beaucoup lu, être très cultivé **3.** *fig* [significantly] : **prices vary ~** les prix varient très sensiblement ▪ **the two versions differed ~** les deux versions étaient sensiblement différentes ▪ **the students came from ~ differing backgrounds** les étudiants venaient d'horizons très différents.

widen ['waɪdn] <> *vt* élargir, agrandir ▪ *fig* [experience, influence, knowledge] accroître, étendre ▪ **the tax reform will ~ the gap between rich and poor** la réforme fiscale va accentuer *OR*

agrandir l'écart entre les riches et les pauvres ■ **I've ~ed my study to include recent events** j'ai développé mon étude afin d'y inclure les derniers événements.
◇ *vi* s'élargir ■ [eyes] s'agrandir ■ [smile] s'accentuer.

wide-open *adj* **1.** [extensive] grand ouvert ■ **the ~ spaces of Australia** les grands espaces de l'Australie **2.** [fully open] : **she stood there with her eyes/mouth wide open** elle était là, les yeux écarquillés/bouche bée **3.** *fig* [vulnerable] exposé ■ **he left himself wide open to attack/criticism** il prêtait ainsi le flanc aux attaques/critiques **4.** *US* [town] ouvert.

wide-ranging [-'reɪndʒɪŋ] *adj* **1.** [extensive] large, d'une grande ampleur ■ **she has ~ interests** elle a des intérêts variés ■ **a ~ report/survey** un rapport/une étude de grande envergure **2.** [far-reaching - effect] de grande portée.

widescreen ['waɪdskri:n] ◇ *adj* écran *m* large.
◇ *n* : ~ **(TV)** (TV *f*) écran *m* large.

widespread ['waɪdspred] *adj* **1.** [arms] en croix ■ [wings] déployé **2.** [extensive] (très) répandu ■ **there has been ~ public concern** l'opinion publique se montre extrêmement préoccupée.

wide-wale *adj US* : ~ **corduroy** velours *m* côtelé à côtes épaisses.

widow ['wɪdəʊ] ◇ *n* **1.** [woman] veuve *f* ■ **she's a ~** elle est veuve ■ **a golf ~** *UK inf hum une femme que son mari délaisse pour le golf* ■ **~'s pension** allocation *f* veuvage **2.** TYPO ligne *f* veuve *(dernière ligne d'un paragraphe se trouvant à la première ligne d'une page)*.
◇ *vt (usu passive)* **he was ~ed last year** il a perdu sa femme l'année dernière ■ **she was ~ed last year** elle a perdu son mari l'année dernière ■ **she is recently ~ed** elle est veuve depuis peu, elle a perdu son mari il n'y a pas longtemps ■ **he is twice ~ed** il est deux fois veuf.

widowed ['wɪdəʊd] *adj* : **she supports her ~ mother** elle fait vivre sa mère qui est veuve.

widower ['wɪdəʊə^r] *n* veuf *m*.

widowhood ['wɪdəʊhʊd] *n* veuvage *m*.

widow's peak *n ligne de cheveux sur le front en forme de v.*

width [wɪdθ] *n* **1.** [breadth] largeur *f* ■ **the room was ten metres in ~** la pièce faisait dix mètres de largeur ▮ [of swimming pool] largeur *f* ■ **she swam two ~s** elle a fait deux largeurs de piscine **2.** TEX laize *f*, lé *m*.

widthways ['wɪdθweɪz], **widthwise** ['wɪdθwaɪz] *adv* dans le sens de la largeur.

wield [wi:ld] *vt* **1.** [weapon] brandir ■ [pen, tool] manier **2.** [influence, power] exercer, user de *lit*.

wiener ['wi:nə^r] *n US* saucisse *f* de Francfort.

wife [waɪf] (*pl* **wives** [waɪvz]) *n* **1.** [spouse] femme *f*, épouse *f* ■ ADMIN conjointe *f* ■ **do you take this woman to be your lawful, wedded ~?** *fml* prenez-vous cette femme pour épouse légitime? ■ **the farmer's ~** la fermière **2.** *arch* & *dial* [woman] femme *f*.

wifely ['waɪflɪ] *adj* de bonne épouse.

wife-swapping [-'swɒpɪŋ] *n* échangisme *m*.

WiFi (*abbrev of* **wireless fidelity**) ['waɪfaɪ] *n* COMPUT WiFi *m*.

wig [wɪg] *n* perruque *f* ■ [hairpiece] postiche *m*.

wigging ['wɪgɪŋ] *n UK inf* [scolding] savon *m* ■ **to give sb a (good) ~** passer un savon à qqn.

wiggle ['wɪgl] ◇ *vt* remuer ■ [hips] remuer, tortiller.
◇ *vi* [person] (se) remuer, frétiller ■ [loose object] branler.
◇ *n* **1.** [movement] tortillement *m* ■ **he gave his toes a ~** il remua ses orteils **2.** [wavy line] trait *m* ondulé.

wiggly ['wɪglɪ] *adj* frétillant, qui remue ■ **a ~ line** un trait ondulé.

wigmaker ['wɪg,meɪkə^r] *n* perruquier *m*.

wigwam ['wɪgwæm] *n* wigwam *m*.

wild [waɪld] ◇ *adj* **1.** [undomesticated] sauvage ■ [untamed] farouche ■ **a ~ beast** une bête sauvage ; *fig* une bête féroce ■ **a ~ rabbit** un lapin de garenne ■ **a ~ horse** un cheval sauvage
2. [uncultivated - fruit] sauvage ; [- flower, plant] sauvage, des champs ■ **~ strawberries** fraises *fpl* des bois ■ **many parts of the country are still ~** beaucoup de régions du pays sont encore à l'état sauvage
3. [violent - weather] : **~ weather** du gros temps ■ **a ~ wind** un vent violent *OR* de tempête ■ **a ~ sea** une mer très agitée ■ **it was a ~ night** ce fut une nuit de tempête
4. [mad] fou *(before vowel or silent 'h' **fol**)*, folle *f*, furieux ■ **to be ~ with grief/happiness/jealousy** être fou de douleur/joie/jalousie ■ **he had ~ eyes** *OR* **a ~ look in his eyes** il avait une lueur de folie dans le regard
5. [dishevelled - appearance] débraillé ; [- hair] en bataille, ébouriffé ■ **a ~-looking young man** un jeune homme à l'air farouche
6. [enthusiastic] : **the speaker received ~ applause** l'orateur reçut des applaudissements frénétiques ■ **to be ~ about sb** *inf* être dingue de qqn ■ **to be ~ about sthg** *inf* être dingue de *OR* emballé par qqch
7. [outrageous - idea, imagination] insensé, fantaisiste ; [- promise, talk] insensé ; [- rumour] délirant ; [- plan] extravagant ■ **he has some ~ scheme for getting rich quick** il a un projet farfelu *OR* abracadabrant pour devenir riche en peu de temps ■ **the book's success was beyond his ~est dreams** le succès de son livre dépassait ses rêves les plus fous ■ [reckless] fou *(before vowel or silent 'h' **fol**)*, folle *f* ■ **that was in my ~ youth** c'était au temps de ma folle jeunesse
8. [random] : **to take a ~ swing at sthg** lancer le poing au hasard pour atteindre qqch ■ **at a ~ guess** à vue de nez ■ **aces are ~** CARDS les as sont libres ➋ **to play a ~ card** prendre un risque
9. *inf phr* **~ and woolly** [idea, plan] peu réfléchi ; [place] sauvage, primitif.
◇ *n* : **in the ~** en liberté ■ **the call of the ~** l'appel *m* de la nature ■ **he spent a year living in the ~** *OR* **~s** il a passé un an dans la brousse ■ **the ~s of northern Canada** le fin fond du nord du Canada.
◇ *adv* **1.** [grow, live] en liberté ■ **strawberries grow ~ in the forest** des fraises poussent à l'état sauvage dans la forêt
2. [emotionally] : **to go ~ with joy/rage** devenir fou de joie/colère ■ **when he came on stage the audience went ~** les spectateurs hurlèrent d'enthousiasme quand il arriva sur le plateau
3. [unconstrained] : **to run ~** [animals] courir en liberté ; [children] être déchaîné ■ **they let their children run ~** *liter* ils laissent leurs enfants traîner dans la rue ; *fig* ils ne disciplinent pas du tout leurs enfants ■ **they've left the garden to run ~** ils ont laissé le jardin à l'abandon *OR* revenir à l'état sauvage.

wild boar *n* sanglier *m*.

wild card *n* COMPUT joker *m*.

wildcat ['waɪldkæt] (*pl inv OR pl* **wildcats**) ◇ *n* ZOOL chat *m* sauvage ■ **she's a real ~** *fig* c'est une vraie tigresse.
◇ *adj* [imprudent, ill-considered] aléatoire, hasardeux.

wildcat strike *n* grève *f* sauvage.

wildebeest ['wɪldɪbi:st] (*pl inv OR pl* **wildebeests**) *n* gnou *m*.

wilderness ['wɪldənɪs] ◇ *n* **1.** [uninhabited area] pays *m* désert, région *f* sauvage ■ BIBLE désert *m* ■ **a ~ of snow and ice** une région *OR* une étendue de neige et de glace ▮ *fig* **a cultural ~** *fig* un désert culturel **2.** [overgrown piece of land] jungle *f*.
◇ *adj* [region] reculé ■ **the ~ years** *fig* la traversée du désert.

wild-eyed *adj* **1.** [crazed] au regard fou ■ **she watched in ~ terror** elle regardait, les yeux remplis de terreur **2.** [impractical] extravagant.

wildfire ['waɪld,faɪə^r] *n* : **to spread like ~** se répandre comme une traînée de poudre.

wildfowl ['waɪldfaʊl] *npl* oiseaux *mpl* sauvages ■ HUNT [collectively] sauvagine *f*, gibier *m* à plume.

wild-goose chase *n* : **I was sent on a ~** on m'a envoyé courir au diable pour rien.

wild hyacinth *n* [bluebell] jacinthe *f* des bois.

wildlife ['waɪldlaɪf] <> *n (U)* [wild animals] faune *f* ▪ [wild animals and plants] la faune et la flore.
<> *comp* de la vie sauvage ▪ [photographer] de la nature ▪ [programme] sur la nature *OR* la vie sauvage ▪ [expert, enthusiast] de la faune et de la flore.

wildlife park *n* réserve *f* naturelle.

wildly ['waɪldlɪ] *adv* **1.** [violently] violemment, furieusement **2.** [enthusiastically] : **the crowd applauded ~** la foule applaudissait frénétiquement **3.** [randomly] au hasard ▪ **to swing ~ at sb/sthg** lancer le poing au hasard en direction de qqn/qqch ▪ **exchange rates fluctuated ~** les taux de change fluctuaient de façon aberrante **4.** [extremely] excessivement ▪ **the reports are ~ inaccurate** les comptes rendus sont complètement faux ▪ **~ expensive/funny** follement cher/drôle ▪ **to be ~ jealous/happy** être fou de jalousie/bonheur ▪ **I'm not ~ happy about the decision** cette décision ne m'enchante pas spécialement **5.** [recklessly] avec témérité ▪ **he talked ~ of joining the foreign legion** il parlait avec témérité de s'engager dans la légion étrangère.

wild man *n* [savage] sauvage *m*.

wild oats *npl* : **to sow one's ~** *inf euph* jeter sa gourme.

wild rice *n* zizania *f*.

wild thyme *n* serpolet *m*.

wild west <> *n* : **the ~** le Far West.
<> *comp* : **~ show** *spectacle sur le thème du Far West*.

wiles [waɪlz] *npl* ruses *fpl*.

wilful *etc UK*, **willful** *US* ['wɪlfʊl] *adj* **1.** [action] délibéré ▪ [damage] volontaire, délibéré ▪ **he rebuked her for ~ disobedience** il l'a réprimandée pour avoir désobéi délibérément *OR* à dessein **2.** [person] entêté, obstiné.

wilfully *UK*, **willfully** *US* ['wɪlfʊlɪ] *adv* **1.** [deliberately] délibérément **2.** [obstinately] obstinément, avec entêtement.

wilfulness *UK*, **willfulness** *US* ['wɪlfʊlnɪs] *n* **1.** [of action] caractère *m* délibéré ▪ [of damage] caractère *m* intentionnel **2.** [of character, person] obstination *f*, entêtement *m*.

will¹ [wɪl] *modal vb* **1.** [indicating the future] : **what time ~ you be home tonight?** à quelle heure rentrez-vous ce soir? ▪ **the next meeting ~ be held in July** la prochaine réunion aura lieu en juillet ▪ **I don't think he ~** *OR* **he'll come today** je ne pense pas qu'il vienne *OR* je ne crois pas qu'il viendra aujourd'hui ▪ **do you think she'll marry him? – I'm sure she ~/won't** est-ce que tu crois qu'elle va se marier avec lui? – je suis sûr que oui/non ▪ **he doesn't think he'll be able to fix it** il ne pense pas pouvoir *OR* il ne croit pas qu'il pourra le réparer ▪ **when they come home the children ~ be sleeping** quand ils rentreront, les enfants dormiront *OR* seront endormis
2. [indicating probability] : **that'll be the postman** ça doit être *OR* c'est sans doute le facteur ▪ **she'll be grown up by now** elle doit être grande maintenant ▪ **it won't be ready yet** ce n'est sûrement pas prêt
3. [indicating resolution, determination] : **I'll steal the money if I have to** je volerai l'argent s'il le faut ▪ **I won't have it!** je ne supporterai *OR* n'admettrai pas ça! ▪ **you must come! – I won't!** il faut que vous veniez! – je ne viendrai pas! ▪ **I won't go – oh yes you ~!** je n'irai pas – oh (que) si! ▪ **he can't possibly win – he ~!** il ne peut pas gagner – mais si!
4. [indicating willingness] : **I'll carry your suitcase** je vais porter votre valise ▪ **who'll volunteer? – I ~!** qui se porte volontaire? – moi! ▪ **~ you marry me? – yes, I ~/no, I won't** veux-tu m'épouser? – oui/non ▪ **my secretary ~ answer your questions** ma secrétaire répondra à vos questions ▶ **~ do!** *inf* d'accord!
5. [in requests, invitations] : **~ you please stop smoking?** pouvez-vous éteindre votre cigarette, s'il vous plaît? ▪ **you won't forget, ~ you?** tu n'oublieras pas, n'est-ce pas? ▪ **you WILL remember to lock the door, won't you?** tu n'oublieras pas de fermer à clef, hein? ▪ **won't you join us for lunch?** vous déjeunerez bien avec nous? ▪ **if you ~ come with me** si vous voulez bien venir avec moi ▮ [in orders] : **stop complaining, ~ you!** arrête de te plaindre, tu veux! ▪ **~ you be quiet!** vous allez vous taire!
6. [indicating basic ability, capacity] : **the machine ~ wash up to 5 kilos of laundry** la machine peut laver jusqu'à 5 kilos de linge ▮ [indicating temporary state or capacity] : **the car won't start** la voiture ne veut pas démarrer ▪ **it ~ start, but it dies after a couple of seconds** elle démarre, mais elle s'arrête tout de suite ▪ **the television won't switch on** la télévision ne veut pas s'allumer
7. [indicating habitual action] : **she'll play in her sandpit for hours** elle peut jouer des heures dans son bac à sable ▮ [indicating obstinacy] : **she WILL insist on calling me Uncle Roger** elle insiste pour *OR* elle tient à m'appeler Oncle Roger ▪ **she WILL have the last word** il faut toujours qu'elle ait le dernier mot
8. [used with 'have'] : **another ten years ~ have gone by** dix autres années auront passé ▮ [expressing probability] : **she'll have finished by now** elle doit avoir fini maintenant.

will² [wɪl] <> *n* **1.** [desire, determination] volonté *f* ▪ **he has a weak/strong ~** il a peu/beaucoup de volonté ▪ **a battle of ~** une lutte d'influences ▪ **she no longer has the ~ to live** elle n'a plus envie de vivre ▪ **it is the ~ of the people that...** le peuple veut que... ▶ **to have a ~ of iron** *OR* **an iron ~** avoir une volonté de fer ▪ **to have a ~ of one's own** n'en faire qu'à sa tête, être très indépendant ▪ **with the best ~ in the world** avec la meilleure volonté du monde ▪ **where there's a ~ there's a way** *prov* quand on veut on peut *prov*
2. LAW testament *m* ▪ **last ~ and testament** dernières volontés *fpl* ▪ **did he leave me anything in his ~?** m'a-t-il laissé quelque chose dans son testament?
<> *vt* **1.** [using willpower] : **I was ~ing her to say yes** j'espérais qu'elle allait dire oui ▪ **she ~ed herself to keep walking** elle s'est forcée à poursuivre sa marche ▪ **I could feel the crowd ~ing me on** je sentais que la foule me soutenait
2. [bequeath] léguer ▪ **she ~ed her entire fortune to charity** elle a légué toute sa fortune à des œuvres de charité
3. *lit* [wish, intend] vouloir ▪ **the Lord so ~ed it** le Seigneur a voulu qu'il en soit ainsi.
<> *vi arch & lit* [wish] vouloir.
◆ **against one's will** *adv phr* contre sa volonté ▪ **he left home against his father's ~** il est parti de chez lui contre la volonté de son père.
◆ **at will** *adv phr* à sa guise ▪ **they can come and go at ~ here** ils peuvent aller et venir à leur guise ici ▪ **fire at ~!** feu à volonté!
◆ **with a will** *adv phr* avec ardeur *OR* acharnement ▪ **we set to with a ~** nous nous attelâmes à la tâche avec ardeur.

willful *etc US* = **wilful**.

William ['wɪljəm] *pr n* : **~ of Orange** Guillaume d'Orange ▪ **~ the Conqueror** Guillaume le Conquérant.

willie ['wɪlɪ] *UK* = **willy**.

willies ['wɪlɪz] *npl inf* **he/it gives me the ~** il/ça me fiche la trouille.

willing ['wɪlɪŋ] *adj* **1.** [ready, prepared] : **are you ~ to cooperate with us?** êtes-vous prêt à collaborer avec nous? ▪ **he isn't even ~ to try** il ne veut même pas essayer ▪ **to be ~ and able (to do sthg)** avoir l'envie et les moyens (de faire qqch) ▪ **he's more than ~ to change jobs** il ne demande pas mieux que de changer d'emploi ▪ **~ or not, they must lend a hand** qu'ils le veuillent ou non, ils devront nous aider **2.** [compliant] : **he's a ~ victim** c'est une victime complaisante **3.** [eager, enthusiastic - helper] bien disposé, de bonne volonté **4.** *phr* **to show ~** faire preuve de bonne volonté.

willingly ['wɪlɪŋlɪ] *adv* **1.** [eagerly, gladly] de bon cœur, volontiers ▪ **they ~ gave up their time** ils n'ont pas été avares de leur temps ▪ **I'll do it ~, I'll ~ do it** je le ferai volontiers **2.** [voluntarily] volontairement, de plein gré.

willingness ['wɪlɪŋnɪs] *n* **1.** [enthusiasm] : **he set to with great ~** il s'est attelé à la tâche avec un grand enthousiasme **2.** [readiness] : **he admired her ~ to sacrifice her own happiness** il admirait le fait qu'elle soit prête à sacrifier son propre bonheur.

will-o'-the-wisp [,wɪləðə'wɪsp] *n liter & fig* feu *m* follet.

willow ['wɪləʊ] <> *n* **1.** BOT saule *m* **2.** *inf* CRICKET batte *f*.
<> *comp* de saule ▪ **~ tree** saule *m*.

willow pattern *n motif de céramique chinois très répandu en Grande-Bretagne*.

willowy ['wɪləʊɪ] *adj* [figure, person] élancé, svelte ▪ [object] souple, flexible.

willpower ['wɪl,paʊəʳ] *n* volonté *f* ▪ **he lacks the ~ to diet** il n'a pas suffisamment de volonté pour se mettre au régime ▪ **he gave up smoking through sheer ~** il a arrêté de fumer par la seule force de sa volonté.

willy ['wɪlɪ] (*pl* **willies**) *n UK inf* zizi *m*.

willy-nilly [,wɪlɪ'nɪlɪ] *adv* bon gré mal gré.

wilt[1] [wɪlt] *vb (2nd pers sg) arch & dial* ▷ **will** *(modal vb)*.

wilt[2] [wɪlt] ◇ *vi* [droop - flower, plant] se faner, se flétrir ; [- person] languir, s'alanguir ▪ **he ~ed under her fierce gaze** il perdit contenance sous son regard furieux.
◇ *vt* [cause to droop - flower, plant] faner, flétrir.

Wilts *written abbr of* **Wiltshire**.

wily ['waɪlɪ] (*comp* **wilier**, *superl* **wiliest**) *adj* [person] rusé, malin, - igne *f* ▪ [scheme, trick] habile, astucieux.

wimp [wɪmp] *n inf pej* [person - physically weak] mauviette *f* ; [- morally weak, irresolute] mou *m*, molle *f*, pâte *f* molle.
◆ **wimp out** *vi insep inf* se défiler.

WIMP (*abbrev of* **window, icon, mouse, pull-down menu**) *n* WIMP *m*.

wimpish ['wɪmpɪʃ] *adj inf pej* mollasson.

wimple ['wɪmpl] *n* guimpe *f*.

win [wɪn] (*pret & pp* **won** [wʌn], *cont* **winning**) ◇ *vi* [in competition] gagner ▪ **she always ~s at tennis** elle gagne toujours au tennis ▪ **they're winning three nil** ils gagnent trois à zéro ▪ **he won by only one point** il a gagné d'un point seulement ▪ **who do you think will ~?** à votre avis qui va gagner *OR* l'emporter? ▪ **OK, you ~!** bon, d'accord! ▪ **I (just) can't ~!** j'ai toujours tort! ▶ **to ~ hands down** gagner haut la main.
◇ *vt* **1.** [in competition - award, prize] gagner ; [- scholarship] obtenir ; [- contract] gagner, remporter ▪ **he won first prize** il a gagné *OR* eu le premier prix ▪ **~ yourself a dream holiday!** gagnez des vacances de rêve! ▪ **she won a gold medal in the Olympics** elle a obtenu une médaille d'or aux jeux Olympiques ▪ **his superior finishing speed won him the race** il a gagné la course grâce à sa vitesse supérieure dans la dernière ligne *OR* au finish ▪ **to ~ a place at university** *UK* obtenir une place à l'université ▪ **he has won his place in history** *fig* il s'est fait un nom dans l'histoire ▪ [in war] : **we have won a great victory** nous avons remporté une grande victoire ▪ **this offensive could ~ them the war** cette offensive pourrait leur faire gagner la guerre **2.** [obtain, secure - friendship, love] gagner ; [- sympathy] s'attirer ▪ **to ~ sb's heart** gagner *OR* conquérir le cœur de qqn ▪ **to ~ sb's hand** *arch* obtenir la main de qqn ▪ **his impartiality has won him the respect of his colleagues** son impartialité lui a valu *OR* fait gagner le respect de ses collègues **3.** MIN extraire.
◇ *n* **1.** SPORT victoire *f* ▪ **we haven't had one ~ all season** nous n'avons pas remporté une seule victoire de toute la saison **2.** *US* [in horseracing] : **~, place, show** gagnant, placé et troisième.
◆ **win back** *vt sep* [money, trophy] reprendre, recouvrer ▪ [land] reprendre, reconquérir ▪ [loved one] reconquérir ▪ [esteem, respect, support] retrouver, recouvrer ▪ POL [votes, voters, seats] récupérer, recouvrer.
◆ **win out** *vi insep* triompher ▪ **the need for peace won out over the desire for revenge** le besoin de paix triompha du désir de revanche.
◆ **win over** *vt sep* [convert, convince] rallier ▪ **he has won several of his former opponents over to his ideas** il a rallié plusieurs de ses anciens adversaires à ses idées ▪ **the report won her over to the protesters' cause** le rapport l'a gagnée à la cause des protestataires ▪ **we won him over in the end** nous avons fini par le convaincre.
◆ **win round** *UK* = **win over**.
◆ **win through** *vi insep* remporter ▪ **the striking rail workers won through in the end** les cheminots en grève ont fini par obtenir gain de cause.

wince [wɪns] ◇ *vi* [from pain] crisper le visage, grimacer ▪ **to ~ with pain** grimacer de douleur ▮ *fig* grimacer (de dégoût) ▪ **she winced at the thought** cette pensée l'a fait grimacer de dégoût.
◇ *n* grimace *f*.

winceyette [,wɪnsɪ'et] *UK* ◇ *n* flanelle *f* de coton.
◇ *adj* [nightdress, pyjamas, sheets] en flanelle de coton.

winch [wɪntʃ] ◇ *n* treuil *m*.
◇ *vt* : **to ~ sb/sthg up/down** monter/descendre qqn/qqch au treuil ▪ **the survivors were ~ed to safety** à l'aide d'un treuil on a hissé les rescapés hors de danger.

Winchester disk ['wɪntʃestə-] *n* disque *m* (dur) Winchester.

wind[1] [wɪnd] ◇ *n* **1.** METEOR vent *m* ▪ **the ~ has risen/dropped** le vent s'est levé/est tombé ▪ **the ~ is changing** le vent tourne ▮ NAUT : **into the ~** contre le vent ▪ **off the ~** dans le sens du vent ▪ **before the ~** le vent en poupe ▮ *fig* **the ~s of change are blowing** il y a du changement dans l'air ▪ **the cold ~ of recession** le vent glacial de la récession ▶ **to get ~ of sthg** avoir vent de qqch ▪ **to run like the ~** courir comme le vent ▪ **to be scattered to the four ~s** être éparpillés aux quatre vents ▪ **there's something in the ~** il se prépare quelque chose ▪ **to take the ~ out of sb's sails** couper l'herbe sous le pied à qqn ▪ **let's wait and see which way the ~ is blowing** attendons de voir quelle tournure les événements vont prendre
2. [breath] souffle *m* ▪ **I haven't got my ~ back yet** je n'ai pas encore repris haleine *OR* mon souffle ▪ **to get one's second ~** reprendre haleine *OR* son souffle ▪ **he had the ~ knocked out of him** SPORT on lui a coupé le souffle, on l'a mis hors d'haleine ▶ **to put the ~ up sb** *inf* flanquer la frousse à qqn
3. *inf* [empty talk] vent *m*
4. *(U)* [air in stomach] vents *mpl*, gaz *mpl* ▪ **to break ~** lâcher des vents ▪ **to get a baby's ~ up** faire faire son renvoi à un bébé
5. MUS : **the ~ (section)** les instruments *mpl* à vent, les vents *mpl*.
◇ *vt* **1.** [make breathless] : **to ~ sb** couper le souffle à qqn ▪ **she was quite ~ed by the walk uphill** la montée de la côte l'a essoufflée *OR* lui a coupé le souffle ▪ **don't worry, I'm only ~ed** ne t'inquiète pas, j'ai la respiration coupée, c'est tout
2. [horse] laisser souffler
3. [baby] faire faire son renvoi à
4. HUNT [prey] avoir vent de.

wind[2] [waɪnd] (*pret & pp* **wound** [waʊnd]) ◇ *vi* [bend - procession, road] serpenter ▪ [coil - thread] s'enrouler ▪ **the river ~s through the valley** le fleuve décrit des méandres dans la vallée *OR* traverse la vallée en serpentant.
◇ *vt* **1.** [wrap - bandage, rope] enrouler ▪ **I wound a scarf round my neck** j'ai enroulé une écharpe autour de mon cou ▪ **~ the string into a ball** enrouler la ficelle pour en faire une pelote ▶ **to ~ sb round** *OR* **around one's little finger** mener qqn par le bout du nez **2.** [clock, watch, toy] remonter ▪ [handle] tourner, donner un tour de **3.** *arch & hum* [travel] : **to ~ one's way home** prendre le chemin du retour.
◇ *n* **1.** MECH : **give the clock/watch a ~** remontez l'horloge/la montre ▪ **she gave the handle another ~** elle tourna la manivelle encore une fois, elle donna un tour de manivelle de plus **2.** [bend - of road] tournant *m*, courbe *f* ; [- of river] coude *m*.
◆ **wind back** *vt sep* rembobiner.
◆ **wind down** ◇ *vi insep* **1.** [relax] se détendre, décompresser **2.** MECH [clock, watch] ralentir.
◇ *vt sep* **1.** MECH [lower] faire descendre ▪ [car window] baisser **2.** [bring to an end - business] mener (doucement) vers sa fin.
◆ **wind forward** *vt sep* (faire) avancer.
◆ **wind on** *vt sep* enrouler.
◆ **wind up** ◇ *vt sep* **1.** [conclude - meeting] terminer ; [- account, business] liquider ▪ **the business will be wound up by the end of the year** l'entreprise sera liquidée avant la fin de l'année **2.** [raise] monter, faire monter ▪ [car window] monter, fermer **3.** [string, thread] enrouler ▪ [on a spool] dévider **4.** MECH [clock, watch, toy] remonter ▪ **to be wound up (about sthg)** *inf fig* être à cran(à cause de qqch) **5.** *UK inf* [annoy] asticoter ▪ [tease] faire marcher.

◇ *vi insep inf* [end up] finir ▪ **he wound up in jail** il a fini *OR* s'est retrouvé en prison.

windbag ['wɪndbæg] *n inf pej* moulin *m* à paroles.

windblown ['wɪndbləʊn] *adj* [hair] ébouriffé par le vent ▪ [trees] fouetté *OR* cinglé par le vent.

windbreak ['wɪndbreɪk] *n* abri-vent *m*, coupe-vent *m inv*.

windbreaker® ['wɪnd,breɪkər] *n US* anorak *m*, coupe-vent *m inv*.

windcheater ['wɪnd,tʃi:tər] *n UK* anorak *m*, coupe-vent *m inv*.

windchill factor ['wɪndtʃɪl-] *n* facteur *m* de refroidissement au vent.

winder ['waɪndər] *n* [for clock] remontoir *m* ▪ [for car window] lève-vitre *m*, lève-glace *m* ▪ [for thread, yarn] dévidoir *m*.

windfall ['wɪndfɔ:l] ◇ *n* **1.** [unexpected gain] (bonne) aubaine *f* **2.** [fruit] fruit *m* tombé.
◇ *adj* [fruit] tombé *OR* abattu par le vent ▪ **~ profits/dividends** profits *mpl* /dividendes *mpl* inespérés *OR* inattendus.

windfarm ['wɪndfɑ:m] *n* champ *m* d'éoliennes.

wind gauge [wɪnd-] *n* anémomètre *m*.

winding ['waɪndɪŋ] ◇ *adj* [road, street] tortueux, sinueux ▪ [river] sinueux ▪ [staircase] en hélice, en colimaçon.
◇ *n* **1.** [process] enroulement *m* ▪ ELEC [wire] bobinage *m*, enroulement *m* **2.** [in a river] méandres *mpl*, coudes *mpl* ▪ [in a road] zigzags *mpl*.

winding-up *n* [of account, meeting] clôture *f* ▪ [of business] liquidation *f*.

wind instrument [wɪnd-] *n* instrument *m* à vent.

windjammer ['wɪnd,dʒæmər] *n* **1.** NAUT grand voilier *m* marchand **2.** *UK* [light jacket] anorak *m*, coupe-vent *m inv*.

windlass ['wɪndləs] ◇ *n* treuil *m* ▪ NAUT guindeau *m*.
◇ *vt* [raise] monter au treuil ▪ [haul] tirer au treuil.

windmill ['wɪndmɪl] ◇ *n* **1.** [building] moulin *m* à vent ▪ [toy] moulinet *m* **2.** [wind turbine] aéromoteur *m*, éolienne *f*.
◇ *vi* **1.** [arms] tourner en moulinet **2.** AERON [propeller, rotor] tourner par la force du vent.

window ['wɪndəʊ] ◇ *n* **1.** [in room] fenêtre *f* ▪ [in car] vitre *f*, glace *f* ▪ [in front of shop] vitrine *f*, devanture *f* ▪ [in church] vitrail *m* ▪ [at ticket office] guichet *m* ▪ [on envelope] fenêtre *f* ▪ **she looked out of** *OR* **through the ~** elle regarda par la fenêtre ▪ **he jumped out of the ~** il a sauté par la fenêtre ▪ **to break a ~** casser une vitre *OR* un carreau ▪ **can I try that dress in the ~?** puis-je essayer cette robe (qui est) dans la *OR* en vitrine? ◗ **all our plans have gone out (of) the ~** tous nos projets sont partis en fumée **2.** COMPUT fenêtre *f* **3.** [in diary] créneau *m*, moment *m* libre ▪ **a ~ of opportunity** une possibilité **4.** [insight] : **a ~ on the world of finance** un aperçu des milieux financiers **5.** [opportune time] : **launch ~** ASTRONAUT fenêtre *f OR* créneau *m* de lancement ▪ **weather ~** accalmie *f (permettant de mener à bien des travaux)*.
◇ *comp* de fenêtre ▪ **~ frame** châssis *m* de fenêtre ▪ **~ ledge** rebord *m* de fenêtre.

window box *n* jardinière *f*.

window cleaner *n* [person] laveur *m*, - euse *f* de vitres *OR* carreaux ▪ [substance] nettoyant *m* pour vitres.

window display *n* étalage *m*.

window dresser *n* étalagiste *mf*.

window dressing *n* [merchandise on display] présentation *f* de l'étalage ▪ [activity] : **they need someone to do the ~** ils ont besoin de quelqu'un pour composer *OR* faire l'étalage ▌ *fig* façade *f*.

window envelope *n* enveloppe *f* à fenêtre.

windowpane ['wɪndəʊpeɪn] *n* carreau *m*, vitre *f*.

window seat *n* [in room] banquette *f* sous la fenêtre ▪ [in train, plane] place *f* côté fenêtre.

window shade *n US* store *m*.

window-shopping *n* lèche-vitrines *m inv* ▪ **to go ~** faire du lèche-vitrines.

windowsill ['wɪndəʊsɪl] *n* rebord *m* de fenêtre.

windpipe ['wɪndpaɪp] *n* trachée *f*.

wind power [wɪnd-] *n* énergie *f* du vent *OR* éolienne *spec*.

windproof ['wɪndpru:f] *adj* protégeant du vent.

windscreen ['wɪndskri:n] *n UK* pare-brise *m inv*.

windscreen washer *n UK* lave-glace *m*.

windscreen wiper *n UK* essuie-glace *m*.

windshield ['wɪndʃi:ld] *n US* pare-brise *m inv*.

windshield wiper *n US* essuie-glace *m*.

wind sleeve [wɪnd-], **windsock** ['wɪndsɒk] *n* manche *f* à air.

Windsor ['wɪnʒə-] *pr n* : **~ Castle** le château de Windsor ▪ **the ~s** la famille royale britannique, les Windsor.

wind speed [wɪnd-] *n* vitesse *f* du vent.

windsurf ['wɪndsɜ:f] *vi* faire de la planche à voile.

windsurfer ['wɪnd,sɜ:fər] *n* [board] planche *f* à voile ▪ [person] véliplanchiste *mf*, planchiste *mf*.

windsurfing ['wɪnd,sɜ:fɪŋ] *n* planche *f* à voile ▪ **to go ~** faire de la planche à voile.

windswept ['wɪndswept] *adj* [place] balayé par le vent ▪ [hair] ébouriffé par le vent.

wind tunnel [wɪnd-] *n* tunnel *m* aérodynamique.

wind turbine *n* éolienne *f*.

wind-up [waɪnd-] ◇ *adj* [mechanism] : **a ~ toy/watch** un jouet/une montre à remontoir.
◇ *n UK inf* **is this a ~?** est-ce qu'on veut me faire marcher?

windward ['wɪndwəd] ◇ *adj* NAUT : **on the ~ side** du côté du vent.
◇ *n* côté *m* du vent ▪ **to ~** au vent, contre le vent.

windy ['wɪndɪ] (*comp* **windier**, *superl* **windiest**) *adj* **1.** METEOR : **tomorrow it will be very ~ everywhere** demain il fera du vent *OR* le vent soufflera partout ▪ **a cold, ~ morning** un matin froid et de grand vent ▪ **it's a very wet and ~ place** c'est un endroit très pluvieux et très éventé **2.** *inf* [pompous, verbose] ronflant, pompeux.

wine [waɪn] ◇ *n* vin *m* ▪ **a bottle/glass of ~** une bouteille/un verre de vin ▪ **red/white ~** vin rouge/blanc.
◇ *comp* [bottle, glass] à vin.
◇ *vt* : **to ~ and dine sb** emmener qqn faire un bon dîner bien arrosé.
◇ *vi* : **to go out wining and dining** faire la fête au restaurant.
◇ *adj* [colour] lie-de-vin *(inv)* ▪ **a ~-coloured dress** une robe lie-de-vin.

wine and cheese evening *n petite fête où l'on déguste du vin et du fromage.*

wine bar *n* [drinking establishment] bistrot *m*.

wine cellar *n* cave *f* (à vin), cellier *m*.

wine cooler *n* **1.** [container] seau *m* à rafraîchir (le vin) **2.** *US* [drink] *mélange de vin, de jus de fruit, et d'eau gazeuse.*

wineglass ['waɪnglɑ:s] *n* verre *m* à vin.

winegrower ['waɪn,grəʊər] *n* viticulteur *m*, - trice *f*, vigneron *m*, - onne *f*.

winegrowing ['waɪn,grəʊɪŋ] ◇ *n* viticulture *f*.
◇ *adj* [area, industry] vinicole, viticole.

wine gum *n UK bonbon gélifié aux fruits.*

wine list *n* carte *f* des vins.

wine merchant *n* [shopkeeper] marchand *m*, - e *f* de vin ▪ [wholesaler] négociant *m*, - e *f* en vins.

winepress ['waɪnpres] *n* pressoir *m* à vin.

wine rack *n* casier *m* à vin.

winery ['waɪnərɪ] *n* *US* établissement *m* vinicole.

wine taster *n* [person] dégustateur *m*, - trice *f* ▪ [cup] tâte-vin *m inv*, taste-vin *m inv*.

wine tasting [-,teɪstɪŋ] *n* dégustation *f* (de vins).

wine vinegar *n* vinaigre *m* de vin.

wine waiter *n* sommelier *m*.

wing [wɪŋ] <> *n* **1.** [on bird, insect] aile *f* ▪ **to take ~** *lit* prendre son envol *OR* essor ▪ **to be on the ~** *lit* être en (plein) vol ◐ **~ tip** bout *m* de l'aile ▪ **to take sb under one's ~** prendre qqn sous son aile **2.** AERON aile *f* ▪ [badge] : **to win one's ~s** faire ses preuves, prendre du galon **3.** *UK* AUT aile *f* **4.** POL [section] aile *f* ▪ **the left/right ~** l'aile gauche/droite **5.** ARCHIT aile *f* **6.** [on windmill] aile *f* **7.** SPORT [of field] aile *f* ▪ [player] ailier *m*, -ère *f*.
<> *vt* **1.** [wound - bird] blesser, toucher à l'aile ; [- person] blesser *OR* toucher légèrement **2.** [fly] : **to ~ one's way** *liter & fig* voler **3.** *lit* [cause to fly - arrow] darder, décocher **4.** *phr* **to ~ it** *inf* [improvise] improviser.
◆ **wings** *npl* THEAT coulisse *f*, coulisses *fpl* ▪ **to wait in the ~s** *liter & fig* se tenir dans la coulisse *OR* les coulisses.

wing chair *n* bergère *f* à oreilles.

wing collar *n* col *m* cassé.

wing commander *n* lieutenant-colonel *m*, lieutenante-colonelle *f*.

wingding ['wɪŋdɪŋ] *n* *inf* [party] fête *f*, bringue *f*.

winge [wɪndʒ] (*cont* **wingeing**) *inf* = **whinge**.

winged [wɪŋd] *adj* **1.** [possessing wings] ailé **2.** [wounded - bird, animal] blessé à l'aile ; [- person] blessé légèrement.

-winged *in cpds* : **white~** aux ailes blanches.

winger ['wɪŋər] *n* SPORT ailier *m*, -ère *f*.

wing forward *n* [in rugby] ailier *m*.

wing mirror *n* rétroviseur *m* extérieur.

wing nut *n* papillon *m*, écrou *m* à ailettes.

wingspan ['wɪŋspæn] *n* envergure *f*.

wink [wɪŋk] <> *vi* **1.** [person] faire un clin d'œil ▪ **to ~ at sb** faire un clin d'œil à qqn ▪ **to ~ at sthg** *fig* fermer les yeux sur qqch **2.** *lit* [light, star] clignoter.
<> *vt* : **to ~ an eye at sb** faire un clin d'œil à qqn.
<> *n* clin *m* d'œil ▪ **she gave them a knowing ~** elle leur a fait un clin d'œil entendu ◐ **I didn't get a ~ of sleep** *OR* **sleep a ~ last night** je n'ai pas fermé l'œil de la nuit ▪ **(as) quick as a ~** en un clin d'œil.

winking ['wɪŋkɪŋ] <> *adj* [lights] clignotant.
<> *n* **1.** [of an eye] clins *mpl* d'œil **2.** [of lights, stars] clignotement *m*.

winkle ['wɪŋkl] *n* *UK* bigorneau *m*, vigneau *m*.
◆ **winkle out** *vt sep inf* [information] arracher, extirper ▪ [person] déloger.

winkle-pickers *npl UK inf* chaussures *fpl* pointues.

Winnebago [,wɪnɪ'beɪgəʊ] *n* camping-car *m*, autocaravane *f offic*.

winner ['wɪnər] *n* **1.** [of prize] gagnant *m*, - e *f* ▪ [of battle, war] vainqueur *m* ▪ [of match] vainqueur *m*, gagnant *m* **2.** SPORT [winning point] : **he scored the ~** c'est lui qui a marqué le but décisif ▪ [successful shot] : **he played a ~** il a joué un coup gagnant **3.** [successful person] gagneur *m*, - euse *f* ▪ [successful thing] succès *m* ▪ **her latest book is a sure ~** son dernier livre va faire un vrai tabac ▪ **to be onto a ~** tirer le bon numéro, être parti pour gagner.

Winnie the Pooh [,wɪnɪðə'pu:] *pr n* Winnie l'ourson.

winning ['wɪnɪŋ] *adj* **1.** [successful] gagnant ▪ SPORT [goal, stroke] décisif ▪ **to be on a ~ streak** remporter victoire sur victoire **2.** [charming] engageant, charmant.
◆ **winnings** *npl* gains *mpl*.

winning post *n* poteau *m* d'arrivée.

winnow ['wɪnəʊ] <> *vt* AGRIC vanner ▪ *fig* [separate] démêler, trier.
<> *n* [machine] tarare *m*, vanneuse *f*.

wino ['waɪnəʊ] (*pl* **winos**) *n inf* ivrogne *mf*.

winsome ['wɪnsəm] *adj lit* [person] charmant, gracieux ▪ [smile] engageant, charmeur.

winter ['wɪntər] <> *n* hiver *m* ▪ **it never snows here in (the) ~** il ne neige jamais ici en hiver ▪ **she was born in the ~ of 1913** elle est née pendant l'hiver 1913 ▪ **a cold ~'s day** une froide journée d'hiver ◐ **the ~ of discontent** *l'hiver 1978-1979 en Grande-Bretagne marqué par de graves conflits sociaux.*
<> *comp* d'hiver ▪ **~ resort** station *f* de sports d'hiver.
<> *vi fml* [spend winter] passer l'hiver, hiverner.
<> *vt* [farm animals] hiverner.

THE WINTER OF DISCONTENT

Cette allusion à une citation de Shakespeare fait référence à l'hiver 1978-1979 où, en Grande-Bretagne, éclatèrent de graves conflits sociaux, obligeant le gouvernement travailliste à procéder à un vote qui conduisit les conservateurs au pouvoir. L'expression est utilisée pour désigner des hivers plus récents, perturbés par un climat social difficile.

wintergreen ['wɪntəgri:n] *n* gaulthérie *f* ▪ **oil of ~** essence *f* de wintergreen.

winterize, ise ['wɪntəraɪz] *vt US* aménager pour l'hiver.

winter solstice *n* solstice *m* d'hiver.

winter sports *npl* sports *mpl* d'hiver.

wintertime ['wɪntətaɪm] *n* hiver *m*.

wintry ['wɪntrɪ] *adj* hivernal ▪ *fig* [look, smile] glacial.

wipe [waɪp] <> *vt* **1.** [with cloth] essuyer ▪ **he ~d the plate dry** il a bien essuyé l'assiette ▪ **to ~ one's feet** s'essuyer les pieds ▪ **to ~ one's nose** se moucher ▪ **to ~ one's bottom** s'essuyer ▪ **she ~d the sweat from his brow** elle essuya la sueur de son front ▪ **she ~d her knife clean** elle nettoya son couteau (d'un coup de torchon) ◐ **to ~ the floor with sb** *inf* réduire qqn en miettes ▪ **to ~ the slate clean** passer l'éponge, tout effacer **2.** [delete - from written record, magnetic tape] effacer ▪ **the remark was ~d from the minutes** l'observation fut retirée du compte-rendu.
<> *vi* essuyer ▪ **she ~d round the sink with a wet cloth** elle a essuyé l'évier avec un chiffon humide.
<> *n* **1.** [action of wiping] : **give the table a ~** donne un coup d'éponge sur la table **2.** [cloth] lingette *f* ▪ **antistatic ~** chiffon *m* antistatique.
◆ **wipe away** *vt sep* [blood, tears] essuyer ▪ [dirt, dust] enlever.
◆ **wipe down** *vt sep* [paintwork, walls] lessiver.
◆ **wipe off** *vt sep* **1.** [remove] enlever ▪ **~ that smile** *OR* **grin off your face!** *inf* enlève-moi ce sourire idiot! **2.** [erase] effacer.
◆ **wipe out** *vt sep* **1.** [clean] nettoyer **2.** [erase] effacer ▪ *fig* [insult, disgrace] effacer, laver **3.** [destroy] anéantir, décimer **4.** *inf* [exhaust] crever.
◆ **wipe up** <> *vt sep* éponger, essuyer.
<> *vi insep UK* essuyer (la vaisselle).

wiper ['waɪpər] *n* AUT essuie-glace *m inv*.

wire ['waɪər] <> *n* **1.** [of metal] fil *m* (métallique *OR* de fer) ▪ **a ~ fence** un grillage ▪ **they've cut the telephone ~s** ils ont coupé les fils téléphoniques ◐ **cheese ~** fil *m* à couper ▪ **he got his application in just under the ~** sa candidature est arrivée juste à temps ▪ **we got our ~s crossed** *inf* nous ne nous sommes pas compris, il y a eu un malentendu **2.** [telegram] télégramme *m*.
<> *vt* **1.** [attach] relier avec du fil de fer **2.** ELEC [building, house] mettre l'électricité dans, faire l'installation électrique dans ▪ [connect electrically] brancher ▪ **the lamp is ~d to the switch on the wall** la lampe est branchée sur *OR* reliée à l'interrupteur sur le mur ▪ **the room had been ~d (up) for sound** la pièce avait été sonorisée **3.** TELEC [person] envoyer un télégramme à, télégraphier à ▪ [money, information] envoyer par télégramme, télégraphier.
◆ **wire together** *vt sep* relier avec du fil de fer.

◆ **wire up** *vt sep* **1.** = wire *(vt sense 2)* **2.** *US inf* [make nervous] énerver.

wire brush *n* brosse *f* métallique.

wire cutters *npl* cisaille *f*, pinces *fpl* coupantes.

wired ['waɪəd] *adj* **1.** ELEC [to an alarm] relié à un système d'alarme **2.** [wiretapped] mis sur écoute **3.** [bra] à tiges métalliques **4.** △ [psyched-up] surexcité.

wirefree ['waɪəfriː] *adj* sans fil.

wire-haired *adj* à poils durs.

wireless ['waɪəlɪs] ◇ *n UK dated* TSF *f* ▪ ~ **(set)** poste *m* de TSF ▪ **on the ~** à la TSF.
◇ *comp* [broadcast, waves] de TSF.

wireless operator *n dated* opérateur *m*, - trice *f* de TSF, radiotélégraphiste *mf*.

wire netting, wire mesh *n* grillage *m*.

wire rope *n* câble *m* métallique.

wire service *n US* agence *f* de presse *(envoyant des dépêches télégraphiques)*.

wiretap ['waɪətæp] (*pret & pp* **wiretapped**, *cont* **wiretapping**)
◇ *vt* mettre sur écoute.
◇ *vi* mettre un téléphone sur écoute.
◇ *n* : **they put a ~ on his phone** ils ont mis son téléphone sur écoute.

wire wool *n* éponge *f* métallique.

wiring ['waɪərɪŋ] *n* installation *f* électrique ▪ **the house needs new ~** il faut refaire l'installation électrique *OR* l'électricité dans la maison.

wiry ['waɪərɪ] (*comp* **wirier**, *superl* **wiriest**) *adj* **1.** [person] élancé et robuste ▪ [animal] nerveux, vigoureux **2.** [hair] peu souple, rêche **3.** [grass] élastique, flexible.

Wisconsin [wɪs'kɒnsɪn] *pr n* Wisconsin *m* ▪ **in ~** dans le Wisconsin.

wisdom ['wɪzdəm] *n* **1.** [perspicacity, judgement] sagesse *f* ▪ **I have my doubts about the ~ of moving house this year** j'ai des doutes sur l'opportunité de déménager cette année **2.** [store of knowledge] sagesse *f* ▪ **folk ~** sagesse populaire **3.** [opinion] avis *m* (général), jugement *m* ▪ **(the) received** *OR* **conventional ~** les idées *fpl* reçues ▪ **Donald, in his ~, decided we should cancel** *hum* Donald, toujours prudent, décida que nous devions annuler.

wisdom tooth *n* dent *f* de sagesse.

wise [waɪz] ◇ *adj* **1.** [learned, judicious] sage ▪ **you'd be ~ to take my advice** vous seriez sage de suivre mes conseils ▪ **do you think it's ~ to invite his wife?** crois-tu que ce soit prudent d'inviter sa femme? **2.** [clever, shrewd] habile, astucieux ▪ **the president made a ~ move in dismissing the attorney general** le président a été bien avisé de renvoyer le ministre de la justice ▪ **it's always easy to be ~ after the event** c'est toujours facile d'avoir raison après coup ▶ **the Three Wise Men** les Rois Mages *mpl* ▪ **to be none the wiser** ne pas être plus avancé ▪ **do it while he's out, he'll be none the wiser** fais-le pendant qu'il est sorti et il n'en saura rien ▪ **to be ~ to sthg** *inf* être au courant de qqch ▪ **to get ~ to sthg** *inf* : **you'd better get ~ to what's going on** vous feriez bien d'ouvrir les yeux sur ce qui se passe.
◇ *n fml* **he is in no ~** *OR* **not in any ~ satisfied with his new position** il n'est point *OR* aucunement satisfait de son nouveau poste.

◆ **wise up** *inf* ◇ *vi insep* : **he'd better ~ up!** il ferait bien de se mettre dans le coup! ▪ **she finally ~d up to the fact that she'd never be a great musician** elle a enfin compris qu'elle ne serait jamais une grande musicienne.
◇ *vt sep US* mettre dans le coup.

-wise *in cpds* **1.** [in the direction of] dans le sens de ▪ **length~** dans le sens de la longueur **2.** [in the manner of] à la manière de, comme ▪ **he edged crab~ up to the bar** il s'approcha du bar en marchant de côté comme un crabe **3.** *inf* [as regards] côté ▪ **money~ the job leaves a lot to be desired** le poste laisse beaucoup à désirer côté argent.

wisecrack ['waɪzkræk] *n inf* sarcasme *m*.

wise guy *n inf* malin *m*.

wisely ['waɪzlɪ] *adv* sagement, avec sagesse.

wish [wɪʃ] ◇ *vt* **1.** [expressing something impossible or unlikely] souhaiter ▪ **to ~ sb dead** souhaiter la mort de qqn ▪ **she ~ed herself far away** elle aurait souhaité être loin ▪ **I ~ I were** *OR UK inf* **was somewhere else** j'aimerais bien être ailleurs ▪ **~ you were here** [on postcard] j'aimerais bien que tu sois là ▪ **I ~ you didn't have to leave** j'aimerais que tu ne sois pas *OR* ce serait bien si tu n'étais pas obligé de partir ▪ **I ~ you hadn't said that** tu n'aurais pas dû dire ça ▪ **I ~ I'd never come!** je n'aurais jamais dû venir ▪ **I ~ I'd thought of that before** je regrette de n'y avoir pas pensé plus tôt ▪ **why don't you come with us? – I ~ I could** pourquoi ne venez-vous pas avec nous? – j'aimerais bien ▌[expressing criticism, reproach] : **I ~ you'd be more careful** j'aimerais que vous fassiez plus attention ▪ **I ~ you wouldn't talk so much!** tu ne peux pas te taire un peu?
2. *fml* [want] souhaiter, vouloir ▪ **I don't ~ to appear rude, but...** je ne voudrais pas paraître grossier mais...
3. [in greeting, expressions of goodwill] souhaiter ▪ **he ~ed them success in their future careers** il leur a souhaité de réussir dans leur carrière ▪ **he ~ed us good day** il nous a souhaité le bonjour ▪ **I ~ you well** j'espère que tout ira bien pour vous ▪ **I ~ you (good) luck** je vous souhaite bonne chance ▶ **to ~ sb joy of sthg** souhaiter bien du plaisir à qqn pour qqch.
◇ *vi* **1.** *fml* [want, like] vouloir, souhaiter ▪ **do as you ~** faites comme vous voulez
2. [make a wish] faire un vœu ▪ **to ~ upon a star** *lit* faire un vœu en regardant une étoile.

WISHES

Making wishes

J'espère qu'il n'y aura pas trop de monde. I hope it won't be too busy.

J'aimerais tellement qu'ils viennent avec nous ! I'd love them to come with us!

Ça serait vraiment bien qu'il accepte de rester. It'd be great if he agreed to stay.

Si seulement nous avions une voiture ! If only we had a car!

Si seulement tu avais été plus discret ! If only you'd been a bit more discreet!

Je donnerais n'importe quoi pour être en Grèce. I'd give anything to be in Greece.

Pourvu qu'elle dise oui ! I just hope she says yes!

Wishing somebody something

Joyeux anniversaire ! Happy birthday!

Joyeux Noël ! Happy *OR* Merry Christmas!

Bonne année ! Happy New Year!

Meilleurs vœux ! Best wishes!

Joyeuses Pâques ! Happy Easter!

Bonne continuation ! All the best!

Bonnes vacances ! Enjoy your holiday!

Bon appétit ! Enjoy your meal!

Je te souhaite un bon séjour en Grèce. Enjoy your holiday in Greece.

◇ *n* **1.** [act of wishing, thing wished for] souhait *m*, vœu *m* ▪ **make a ~!** fais un souhait *OR* vœu! ▪ **to grant a ~** exaucer un vœu ▪ **he got his ~, his ~ came true** son vœu s'est réalisé
2. [desire] désir *m* ▪ **to express a ~ for sthg** exprimer le désir de qqch ▪ **it was his last ~** c'était sa dernière volonté ▪ **your ~ is my command** *lit & hum* vos désirs sont des ordres ▪ **she had no great ~ to travel** elle n'avait pas très envie de voyager ▪ **to respect sb's ~es** respecter les vœux de qqn ▪ **she went against my ~es** elle a agi contre ma volonté ▪ **he joined the navy against** *OR* **contrary to my ~es** il s'est engagé dans la marine contre mon gré *OR* ma volonté ➔ **~ list** desiderata *mpl*
3. [regards] : **give your wife my best ~es** transmettez toutes mes amitiés à votre épouse ‖ [in card] : **best ~es for the coming year** meilleurs vœux pour la nouvelle année ▪ **best ~es on your graduation (day)** toutes mes/nos félicitations à l'occasion de l'obtention de votre diplôme ‖ [in letter] : **(with) best ~es** bien amicalement, toutes mes amitiés.

◆ **wish away** *vt sep* : **you can't simply ~ away the things you don't like** on ne peut pas faire comme si les choses qui nous déplaisent n'existaient pas.

◆ **wish for** *vt insep* souhaiter ▪ **what did you ~ for?** quel était ton vœu? ▪ **what more could a man/woman ~ for?** que peut-on souhaiter de plus?

◆ **wish on** *vt sep* **1.** [fate, problem] souhaiter à ▪ **I wouldn't ~ this headache on anyone** je ne souhaite à personne d'avoir un mal de tête pareil
2. [foist on] : **it's a terribly complicated system ~ed on us by head office** c'est un système très compliqué dont nous a fait cadeau la direction.

Voir module d'usage

wishbone ['wɪʃbəʊn] *n* [bone] bréchet *m* ANAT fourchette *f*.

wishful thinking [wɪʃfʊl-] *n* : **I suppose it was just ~** je prenais mes rêves pour la réalité.

wishy-washy ['wɪʃɪ,wɒʃɪ] *adj inf* [behaviour] mou *(before vowel or silent 'h' mol)*, molle *f* ▪ [person] sans personnalité ▪ [colour] délavé ▪ [taste] fadasse.

wisp [wɪsp] *n* [of grass, straw] brin *m* ▪ [of hair] petite mèche *f* ▪ [of smoke, steam] ruban *m* ▪ **a ~ of a girl** *fig* un petit bout de fillette.

wispy ['wɪspɪ] (*comp* **wispier**, *superl* **wispiest**) *adj* [beard] effilé ▪ [hair] épars ▪ [person] (tout) menu.

wisteria [wɪ'stɪərɪə] *n* glycine *f*.

wistful ['wɪstfʊl] *adj* mélancolique, nostalgique.

wistfully ['wɪstfʊlɪ] *adv* d'un air triste et rêveur.

wit [wɪt] *n* **1.** [humour] esprit *m* ▪ **to have a quick/ready ~** avoir de la vivacité d'esprit/beaucoup d'esprit **2.** [humorous person] : **he was a great ~** c'était un homme plein d'esprit **3.** [intelligence] esprit *m*, intelligence *f* ▪ **she has quick ~s** elle a l'esprit fin, elle est très fine ▪ **keep your ~s about you while you're travelling** sois prudent *OR* attentif pendant que tu voyages ▪ **to live by one's ~s** vivre d'expédients ▪ **to collect** *OR* **to gather one's ~s** se ressaisir, reprendre ses esprits ➔ **I was at my ~s' end** je ne savais plus quoi faire ▪ **you frightened me out of my ~s** *OR* **the ~s out of me!** tu m'as fait une de ces peurs!

◆ **to wit** *adv phr fml* à savoir.

witch [wɪtʃ] *n* [sorceress] sorcière *f* ▪ **~es' Sabbath** sabbat *m* (de sorcières).

witchcraft ['wɪtʃkrɑːft] *n (U)* sorcellerie *f*.

witchdoctor ['wɪtʃ,dɒktəʳ] *n* sorcier *m*.

witch-hazel *n* hamamélis *m*.

witch-hunt *n* chasse *f* aux sorcières ▪ *fig* chasse *f* aux sorcières, persécution *f* (politique).

witching hour ['wɪtʃɪŋ-] *n* : **the ~** l'heure *f* fatale.

with [wɪð] *prep* **1.** [by means of] avec ▪ **what did you fix it ~?** avec quoi l'as-tu réparé? ▪ **I've got nothing/I need something to open this can ~** je n'ai rien pour/j'ai besoin de quelque chose pour ouvrir cette boîte ▪ **they fought ~ swords** ils se sont battus à l'épée ▪ **his eyes filled ~ tears** ses yeux se remplirent de larmes ▪ **covered/furnished/lined ~** couvert/meublé/doublé de
2. [describing a feature or attribute] à ▪ **a woman ~ long hair** une femme aux cheveux longs ▪ **which boy? – the one ~ the torn jacket** quel garçon? – celui qui a la veste déchirée ▪ **a man ~ one eye/a hump/a limp** un homme borgne/bossu/boiteux ▪ **a table ~ three legs** une table à trois pieds ▪ **an old woman ~ no teeth** une vieille femme édentée ▪ **she was left ~ nothing to eat or drink** on l'a laissée sans rien à manger ni à boire
3. [accompanied by, in the company of] avec ▪ **can I go ~ you?** puis-je aller avec vous *OR* vous accompagner? ▪ **I have no one to go ~** je n'ai personne avec qui aller ▪ **she stayed ~ him all night** [gen] elle est restée avec lui toute la nuit ; [sick person] elle est restée auprès de lui toute la nuit ▪ **I'll be ~ you in a minute** je suis à vous dans une minute ➔ **are you ~ me?** [supporting] vous êtes avec moi? ; [understanding] vous me suivez? ▪ **I'm ~ you there** là, je suis d'accord avec toi ▪ **I'm ~ you one hundred per cent** *OR* **all the way** je suis complètement d'accord avec vous
4. [in the home of] chez ▪ **I'm (staying) ~ friends** je suis *OR* loge chez des amis ▪ **he stayed ~ a family** il a logé dans une famille ▪ **I live ~ a friend** je vis avec un ami
5. [an employee of] : **she's ~ the UN** elle travaille à l'ONU ▪ **isn't he ~ Ford any more?** ne travaille-t-il plus chez Ford? ‖ [a client of] : **we're ~ the Galena Building Society** nous sommes à la Galena Building Society
6. [indicating joint action] avec ▪ **stop fighting ~ your brother** arrête de te battre avec ton frère ‖ [indicating feelings towards someone else] : **angry/furious/at war ~** fâché/furieux/en guerre contre ▪ **pleased ~** content de
7. [including] : **does the meal come ~ wine?** est-ce que le vin est compris dans le menu? ▪ **the bill came to £16 ~ the tip** l'addition était de 16 livres service compris ▪ **the radio didn't come ~ batteries** la radio était livrée sans piles ‖ CULIN à ▪ **coffee ~ milk** café *m* au lait ▪ **duck ~ orange sauce** canard *m* à l'orange
8. [indicating manner] de, avec ▪ **he knocked the guard out ~ one blow** il assomma le gardien d'un (seul) coup ▪ **he spoke ~ ease** il s'exprima avec aisance
9. [as regards, concerning] : **you never know ~ him** avec lui, on ne sait jamais ▪ **it's an obsession ~ her** c'est une manie chez elle ▪ **what's ~ you?** *inf*, **what's wrong ~ you?** qu'est-ce qui te prend? ▪ **he isn't very good ~ animals** il ne sait pas vraiment s'y prendre avec les bêtes
10. [because of, on account of] de ▪ **sick** *OR* **ill ~ malaria** atteint du paludisme ▪ **~ crime on the increase, more elderly people are afraid to go out** avec l'augmentation du taux de criminalité, de plus en plus de personnes âgées ont peur de sortir ▪ **I can't draw ~ you watching** je ne peux pas dessiner si tu me regardes
11. [in spite of] : **~ all his money he's so stingy** *inf* il a beau avoir beaucoup d'argent, il est vraiment radin.

withal [wɪ'ðɔːl] *adv lit* [as well, besides] de plus, en outre ▪ [nevertheless] néanmoins.

withdraw [wɪð'drɔː] (*pret* **withdrew**, *pp* **withdrawn**) ◇ *vt* **1.** [remove] retirer ▪ **the car has been withdrawn (from sale)** la voiture a été retirée de la vente ▪ **he withdrew his hand from his pocket** il a retiré la main de sa poche **2.** [money] retirer ▪ **I withdrew £500 from my account** j'ai retiré 500 livres de mon compte **3.** [bring out - diplomat] rappeler ; [- troops] retirer **4.** [statement] retirer, rétracter ▪ LAW [charge] retirer ▪ **he withdrew his previous statements** il est revenu sur *OR* il a retiré ses déclarations antérieures.
◇ *vi* **1.** [retire] se retirer ▪ **she has decided to ~ from politics** elle a décidé de se retirer de la politique **2.** [retreat] se retirer ▪ [move back] reculer ▪ **he tends to ~ into himself** il a tendance à se replier sur lui-même ▪ **she often withdrew into a fantasy world** elle se réfugiait souvent dans un monde imaginaire **3.** [back out - candidate, competitor] se retirer, se désister ; [- partner] se rétracter, se dédire **4.** [after sex] se retirer.

withdrawal [wɪð'drɔːəl] ◇ *n* **1.** [removal - of funding, support, troops] retrait *m* ; [- of envoy] rappel *m* ; [- of candidate] retrait *m*, désistement *m* ; [- of love] privation *f* ▪ **I support ~ from NATO** je soutiens notre retrait de l'OTAN **2.** [of statement, remark] rétraction *f* ▪ LAW [of charge] retrait *m*, annulation *f* **3.** PSYCHOL repli *m* sur soi-même, introversion *f* **4.** MED [from drugs] état *m* de manque **5.** [of money] retrait *m* ▪ **to make a ~** faire un retrait.

◇ *comp* : ~ symptoms symptômes *mpl* de manque ■ to have *OR* to suffer from ~ symptoms être en état de manque.

withdrawn [wɪð'drɔːn] ◇ *pp* ▷ withdraw.
◇ *adj* [shy] renfermé, réservé.

withdrew [wɪð'druː] *pt* ▷ withdraw.

wither ['wɪðər] ◇ *vi* 1. [flower, plant] se flétrir, se faner ■ [body - from age] se ratatiner ; [- from sickness] s'atrophier 2. [beauty] se faner ■ [hope, optimism] s'évanouir ■ [memory] s'étioler.
◇ *vt* 1. [plant] flétrir, faner ■ [body - subj: age] ratatiner ; [- subj: sickness] atrophier 2. [beauty] altérer.
◆ **wither away** *vi insep* [flower, plant] se dessécher, se faner ■ [beauty] se faner, s'évanouir ■ [hope, optimism] s'évanouir ■ [memory] disparaître, s'atrophier.

withered ['wɪðəd] *adj* 1. [flower, plant] flétri, fané ■ [face, cheek] fané, flétri ■ he was old and ~ il était vieux et complètement desséché 2. [arm] atrophié.

withering ['wɪðərɪŋ] ◇ *adj* [heat, sun] desséchant ■ [criticism, remark] cinglant, blessant ■ she gave me a ~ look elle m'a lancé un regard méprisant, elle m'a foudroyé du regard.
◇ *n* [of plant] flétrissure *f* ■ [of arm] atrophie *f* ■ [of beauty] déclin *m* ■ [of hope, optimism] évanouissement *m*.

withers ['wɪðəz] *npl* garrot *m* (du cheval).

withhold [wɪð'həʊld] (*pret & pp* withheld [-'held]) *vt* 1. [refuse - love, permission, support] refuser ■ [refuse to pay - rent, tax] refuser de payer ■ to ~ payment refuser de payer 2. [keep back - criticism, news] taire, cacher ■ to ~ the truth from sb cacher la vérité à qqn ■ they ~ 2% of the profits ils retiennent 2 % des bénéfices.

withholding tax [wɪð'həʊldɪŋ-] *n US* retenue *f* à la source.

within [wɪ'ðɪn] ◇ *prep* 1. [inside - place] à l'intérieur de, dans ■ *fig* [- group, system] à l'intérieur de, au sein de ; [- person] en ■ he lived and worked ~ these four walls il a vécu et travaillé entre ces quatre murs ■ a play ~ a play une pièce dans une pièce ■ the man's role ~ the family is changing le rôle de l'homme au sein de la famille est en train de changer ■ a small voice ~ her une petite voix intérieure *OR* au fond d'elle-même 2. [inside the limits of] dans les limites de ■ you must remain ~ the circle tu dois rester dans le *OR* à l'intérieur du cercle ■ to be ~ the law être dans les limites de la loi ■ ~ the framework of the agreement dans le cadre de l'accord ■ it is not ~ the bounds of possibility ça dépasse le cadre du possible ■ to live ~ one's means vivre selon ses moyens ■ the car is well ~ his price range la voiture est tout à fait dans ses prix *OR* ses moyens 3. [before the end of a specified period of time] en moins de ■ I'll let you know ~ a week je vous dirai ce qu'il en est dans le courant de la semaine ■ 'use ~ two days of purchase' 'à consommer dans les deux jours suivant la date d'achat' ■ ~ a week of taking the job, she knew it was a mistake moins d'une semaine après avoir accepté cet emploi, elle sut qu'elle avait fait une erreur 4. [indicating distance, measurement] : they were ~ 10 km of Delhi ils étaient à moins de 10 km de Delhi ■ we are ~ walking distance of the shops nous pouvons aller faire nos courses à pied ■ accurate to ~ 0.1 of a millimetre précis au dixième de millimètre près ■ she came ~ seconds of beating the record elle a failli battre le record à quelques secondes près 5. [during] : enormous changes have taken place ~ a single generation de grands changements ont eu lieu en l'espace d'une seule génération ■ did the accident take place ~ the period covered by the insurance? l'accident a-t-il eu lieu pendant la période couverte par l'assurance?
◇ *adv* dedans, à l'intérieur ■ from ~ de l'intérieur ■ the appointment will be made from ~ la nomination se fera au sein de l'entreprise.

with it *adj inf* 1. [alert] réveillé ■ get ~! réveille-toi!, secoue-toi! 2. *dated* [fashionable] dans le vent.

without [wɪ'ðaʊt] ◇ *prep* sans ■ three nights ~ sleep trois nuits sans dormir ■ ~ milk or sugar sans lait ni sucre ■ to be ~ fear/shame ne pas avoir peur/honte ■ he took it ~ so much as a thank you il l'a pris sans même dire merci ■ (*with present participle*) ~ looking up sans lever les yeux ■ leave the house ~ anybody knowing quittez la maison sans que personne le sache.
◇ *adv lit* au dehors, à l'extérieur ■ a voice from ~ une voix de l'extérieur.
◇ *conj dial* [unless] : ~ they go themselves à moins qu'ils y aillent eux-mêmes.

withstand [wɪð'stænd] (*pret & pp* withstood [-'stʊd]) *vt* [heat, punishment] résister à.

witless ['wɪtlɪs] *adj* sot, sotte *f*, stupide.

witness ['wɪtnɪs] ◇ *n* 1. [onlooker] témoin *m* ■ the police are asking for ~es of *OR* to the accident la police recherche des témoins de l'accident
2. LAW [in court] témoin *m* ■ to call sb as (a) ~ citer qqn comme témoin ■ ~ for the prosecution/defence témoin à charge/décharge ■ [to signature, will] témoin *m* ■ two people must be ~es to my signature/will deux personnes doivent signer comme témoins de ma signature/de mon testament
3. [testimony] : in ~ of sthg en témoignage de qqch ■ to be *OR* to bear ~ to sthg témoigner de qqch ■ to give ~ on behalf of sb témoigner en faveur de qqn
4. RELIG témoignage *m*.
◇ *vt* 1. [see] être témoin de, témoigner de ■ millions ~ed the first moon landing des millions de gens ont vu le premier atterrissage sur la lune
2. [signature] être témoin de ■ [will, document] signer comme témoin
3. [experience - change] voir, connaître.
◇ *vi* [gen - LAW] témoigner, être témoin ■ to ~ to sthg témoigner de qqch ■ to ~ against sb témoigner contre qqn ■ she ~ed to finding the body elle a témoigné avoir découvert le cadavre.

witness box *n UK* barre *f* des témoins ■ in the ~ à la barre.

witness stand *n US* barre *f* des témoins.

witter ['wɪtər] *vi UK inf pej* they were ~ing on about diets ils parlaient interminablement de régimes.

witticism ['wɪtɪsɪzm] *n* bon mot *m*, trait *m* d'esprit.

wittingly ['wɪtɪŋlɪ] *adv fml* en connaissance de cause, sciemment.

witty ['wɪtɪ] (*comp* wittier, *superl* wittiest) *adj* spirituel, plein d'esprit.

wives [waɪvz] *pl* ▷ wife.

wiz [wɪz] *n inf* as *m*, crack *m*.

wizard ['wɪzəd] ◇ *n* 1. [magician] enchanteur *m*, sorcier *m* 2. *fig* [expert] génie *m* ■ she's a real ~ at drawing en dessin, elle est vraiment douée ■ a financial ~ un génie de la finance.
◇ *adj UK inf dated* épatant.
◇ *interj UK inf dated* ~! épatant!

wizardry ['wɪzədrɪ] *n* 1. [magic] magie *f*, sorcellerie *f* 2. *fig* [genius] génie *m* ■ financial ~ le génie de la finance ■ they've installed a new piece of technical ~ in the office ils ont installé une nouvelle merveille de la technique dans le bureau.

wizened ['wɪznd] *adj* [skin, hands] desséché ■ [old person] desséché, ratatiné ■ [face, fruit, vegetables] ratatiné.

wk (*written abbrev of* week) sem.

WMD (*abbrev of* weapons of mass destruction) *npl* ADM *fpl*.

wo [wəʊ] = whoa.

woad [wəʊd] *n* guède *f*.

wobble ['wɒbl] ◇ *vi* 1. [hand, jelly, voice] trembler ■ [chair, table] branler, être branlant *OR* bancal ■ [compass needle] osciller ■ [drunkard] tituber, chanceler ■ [cyclist] aller de travers, aller en zigzag ■ the tightrope walker ~d and almost fell le funambule oscilla et faillit tomber ■ she ~d off/past on her bike elle partit/passa sur son vélo, en équilibre instable 2. *fig* [hesitate, dither] hésiter.
◇ *vt* [table] faire basculer.
◇ *n* : after a few ~s, he finally got going après avoir cherché son équilibre, il se mit enfin en route.

wobbly ['wɒblɪ] (*comp* wobbier, *superl* wobbiest, *pl* wobblies) ◇ *adj* 1. [table, chair] branlant, bancal ■ [pile]

chancelant ■ [jelly] qui tremble **2.** [hand, voice] tremblant ■ **she's rather ~ on her feet** elle flageole un peu *OR* elle ne tient pas très bien sur ses jambes **3.** [line] qui n'est pas droit ■ [handwriting] tremblé.
<> *n UK inf phr* **to throw a ~** *inf* piquer une crise.

wodge [wɒdʒ] *n UK inf* gros bloc *m*, gros morceau *m*.

woe [wəʊ] *lit & hum* <> *n* malheur *m*, infortune *f* ■ **a tale of ~** une histoire pathétique ■ **~ betide anyone who lies to me** malheur à celui qui me raconte des mensonges ■ **a cry of ~** un cri de détresse.
<> *interj* hélas ■ **~ is me!** pauvre de moi!

woebegone ['wəʊbɪ,gɒn] *adj lit & hum* désolé, abattu.

woeful ['wəʊfʊl] *adj* **1.** [sad - person, look, news, situation] malheureux, très triste ; [- scene, tale] affligeant, très triste **2.** [very poor] lamentable, épouvantable, consternant.

woefully ['wəʊfʊlɪ] *adv* **1.** [sadly - look, smile] très tristement **2.** [badly - perform, behave] lamentablement ■ **our funds are ~ inadequate** nous manquons cruellement de fonds.

wog▲ [wɒg] *n UK terme raciste désignant un Noir*, ≃ nègre *m*, négresse *f*.

woggle ['wɒgl] *n UK* bague *f* en cuir *(pour cravate de scout)*.

wok [wɒk] *n* wok *m (poêle chinoise)*.

woke [wəʊk] *pt* ▭ **wake**.

woken ['wəʊkn] *pp* ▭ **wake**.

wold [wəʊld] *n* haute plaine *f*, plateau *m*.

wolf [wʊlf] (*pl* **wolves** [wʊlvz]) <> *n* **1.** ZOOL loup *m* ■ **he is a ~ in sheep's clothing** c'est un loup déguisé en brebis ■ **it helps keep the ~ from the door** c'est un travail purement alimentaire ■ **to throw sb to the wolves** sacrifier qqn **2.** *inf* [seducer] tombeur *m*.
<> *vt* = **wolf down**.
◆ **wolf down** *vt sep inf* [food] engloutir, dévorer.

wolf cub *n* [animal] louveteau *m*.
◆ **Wolf Cub** *n UK inf dated* [scout] louveteau *m*.

wolfhound ['wʊlfhaʊnd] *n* chien-loup *m*.

wolfish ['wʊlfɪʃ] *adj* [appearance] de loup ■ [appetite] vorace.

wolf pack *n* meute *f* de loups.

wolf whistle *n* sifflement *m (au passage d'une femme)*.

wolverine ['wʊlvəri:n] (*pl inv OR pl* **wolverines**) *n* glouton *m*.

wolves [wʊlvz] *pl* ▭ **wolf**.

woman ['wʊmən] (*pl* **women** ['wɪmɪn]) <> *n* **1.** [gen] femme *f* ■ **a young ~** une jeune femme ■ **come here, young ~** venez-là, mademoiselle ■ **she's quite the young ~ now** elle fait très jeune fille maintenant ■ **man's perception of ~** la façon dont les hommes voient les femmes, la vision de la femme qu'a l'homme ■ **what is a ~ supposed to do?** *hum* qu'est-ce qu'on peut faire! ■ **a ~'s work is never done** quand on est une femme, on a toujours quelque chose à faire ■ **I don't even know the ~!** je ne sais même pas qui elle est *OR* qui c'est! ■ **oh, damn the ~!** quelle idiote! ➊ **she's a working/career ~** elle travaille/a une carrière ■ **the women's page** [in newspaper] la page des lectrices ■ **a ~'s** *OR* **women's magazine** un magazine féminin **2.** [employee] femme *f* ■ **the factory women left for work** les ouvrières sont parties travailler ■ **(cleaning) ~** femme de ménage **3.** *inf* [wife] femme *f* ■ [lover] maîtresse *f* ■ **the little ~** ma *OR* la petite femme **4.** *inf* [patronizing term of address] : **my good ~** *dated* ma petite dame ■ **that's enough, ~!** assez, femme!
<> *comp* : **~ doctor** (femme *f*) médecin *m* ■ **~ driver** conductrice *f* ■ **~ friend** amie *f* ■ **~ photographer** photographe *f* ■ **~ police constable** femme *f* agent de police ■ **~ teacher** professeur *m* (femme).

woman-hater *n* misogyne *mf*.

womanhood ['wʊmənhʊd] *n (U)* **1.** [female nature] féminité *f* ■ **to reach ~** devenir une femme **2.** [women collectively] les femmes *fpl*.

womanize, ise ['wʊmənaɪz] *vi* courir les femmes.

womanizer ['wʊmənaɪzər] *n* coureur *m* de jupons.

womankind [,wʊmən'kaɪnd] *n* les femmes *fpl*.

womanly ['wʊmənlɪ] *adj* [virtue, figure] féminin, de femme ■ [act] digne d'une femme, féminin.

womb [wu:m] *n* **1.** ANAT utérus *m* ■ **in his mother's ~** dans le ventre de sa mère **2.** *fig* sein *m*, entrailles *fpl*.

wombat ['wɒmbæt] *n* wombat *m*.

women ['wɪmɪn] *pl* ▭ **woman**.

womenfolk ['wɪmɪnfəʊk] *npl* : **the ~** les femmes *fpl*.

women's group *n* [campaigning organization] groupe *m* féministe ■ [social club] groupe *m* de femmes.

Women's Institute *pr n association britannique des femmes au foyer*.

Women's Lib [-'lɪb] *n* MLF *m*, mouvement *m* de libération de la femme.

Women's Liberation *n* mouvement *m* de libération de la femme, MLF *m*.

Women's Movement *n* mouvement *m* féministe.

women's refuge *n* centre *m* d'accueil pour les femmes.

women's rights *npl* droits *mpl* de la femme.

women's room *n US* toilettes *fpl* des femmes.

women's studies *npl discipline universitaire ayant pour objet la sociologie et l'histoire des femmes, la création littéraire féminine etc.*

won [wʌn] *pt & pp* ▭ **win**.

wonder ['wʌndər] <> *n* **1.** [marvel] merveille *f* ■ **the seven ~s of the world** les sept merveilles du monde ■ **the ~s of science** les miracles de la science ■ **to work** *OR* **to do ~s** [person] faire des merveilles ; [action, event] faire merveille ■ **a hot bath worked ~s for her aching body** un bain chaud la soulagea à merveille de ses douleurs
2. [amazing event or circumstances] : **the ~ (of it) is that he manages to get any work done at all** le plus étonnant dans tout cela, c'est qu'il arrive à travailler ■ **it's a ~ to me that anyone can work in such awful conditions** cela me semble incroyable qu'on puisse travailler dans des conditions aussi épouvantables ■ **it's a ~ that she didn't resign on the spot** c'est étonnant qu'elle n'ait pas démissionné sur-le-champ ■ **no ~ they refused** ce n'est pas étonnant qu'ils aient refusé ■ **no ~!** ce n'est pas étonnant!, cela vous étonne? ■ **is it any ~ that he got lost?** cela vous étonne qu'il se soit perdu? ■ **it's little** *OR* **small ~ no one came** ce n'est guère étonnant que personne ne soit venu ■ **~s will never cease!** *hum* on n'a pas fini d'être étonné!
3. [awe] émerveillement *m* ■ **the children were filled with ~** les enfants étaient émerveillés
4. [prodigy] prodige *m*, génie *m* ■ **a boy ~** un petit prodige *OR* génie.
<> *comp* [drug, detergent] miracle ■ [child] prodige.
<> *vt* **1.** [ask o.s.] se demander ■ **I ~ where she's gone** je me demande où elle est allée ■ **I ~ why** je me demande bien pourquoi ■ **I often ~ that myself** je me pose souvent la question ▮ [in polite requests] : **I was ~ing if you were free tomorrow** est-ce que par hasard vous êtes libre demain? ■ **I ~ if you could help me** pourriez-vous m'aider s'il vous plaît?
2. [be surprised] s'étonner ■ **I ~ that he wasn't hurt** je m'étonne *OR* cela m'étonne qu'il n'ait pas été blessé.
<> *vi* **1.** [think, reflect] penser, réfléchir ■ **it makes you ~** cela donne à penser *OR* réfléchir ■ **I'm ~ing about going tomorrow** je me demande si je ne vais pas y aller demain ■ **I was ~ing about it too** je me posais la même question ■ **the war will be over in a few days – I ~** la guerre sera finie dans quelques jours – je n'en suis pas si sûr
2. [marvel, be surprised] s'étonner, s'émerveiller ■ **to ~ at sthg** s'émerveiller de qqch ■ **the people ~ed at the magnificent sight** les gens s'émerveillaient de ce magnifique spectacle ■ **I don't ~** cela ne m'étonne pas.

wonderful ['wʌndəfʊl] *adj* [enjoyable] merveilleux, formidable ■ [beautiful] superbe, magnifique ■ [delicious] excellent ■ [astonishing] étonnant, surprenant ■ **we had a ~ time/holiday** on a passé des moments/des vacances formidables ■ **what ~ news!** quelle nouvelle formidable! ■ **she has some ~ ideas**

elle a des idées formidables ▪ **that's ~!** c'est merveilleux! ▪ **you've been ~** vous avez été formidable ▪ **you look ~** tu es superbe.

wonderfully ['wʌndəfulɪ] *adv* **1.** *(with adj or adv)* merveilleusement, admirablement ▪ **she was ~ kind** elle était d'une gentillesse merveilleuse **2.** *(with verb)* merveilleusement, à merveille ▪ **she plays ~** elle joue merveilleusement bien.

wondering ['wʌndərɪŋ] *adj* [pensive] songeur, pensif ▪ [surprised] étonné.

wonderland ['wʌndəlænd] *n* pays *m* des merveilles ▪ **a winter ~** un paysage hivernal féerique.

wonderment ['wʌndəmənt] *n* [wonder] émerveillement *m* ▪ [surprise] étonnement *m* ▪ **he looked around in ~** il regarda autour de lui émerveillé.

wonderworker ['wʌndə,wɜ:kər] *n* **: he's a real ~** il accomplit de vrais miracles.

wondrous ['wʌndrəs] *lit* <> *adj* merveilleux.
<> *adv* = **wondrously.**

wondrously ['wʌndrəslɪ] *adv lit* merveilleusement.

wonky ['wɒŋkɪ] (*comp* **wonkier**, *superl* **wonkiest**) *adj UK inf* [table] bancal, branlant ▪ [bicycle] détraqué ▪ [radio, TV] déréglé, détraqué ▪ [line] qui n'est pas bien droit ▪ **your tie is a bit ~** ta cravate est un peu de travers.

wont [wəunt] *lit* <> *n* coutume *f*, habitude *f* ▪ **as was his/her ~** comme de coutume.
<> *adj* **: to be ~ to do sthg** avoir l'habitude *OR* coutume de faire qqch.

won't [wəunt] = **will not.**

woo [wu:] (*pret & pp* **wooed**) *vt* **1.** *dated* [court] courtiser, faire la cour à **2.** [attract - customers, voters] chercher à plaire à, rechercher les faveurs de.

wood [wud] <> *n* **1.** [timber] bois *m* ▪ **the stove burns ~ and coal** le poêle fonctionne au bois et au charbon ➲ **to touch** *UK OR* **knock on** *US* **~** toucher du bois **2.** [forest, copse] bois *m* ➲ **he can't see the ~ for the trees** *fig* les arbres lui cachent la forêt ▪ **we're not out of the ~s yet** *fig* on n'est pas encore sortis de l'auberge, on n'est pas encore tirés d'affaire **3.** VINIC tonneau *m* ▪ **matured in the ~** vieilli au tonneau **4.** SPORT [in bowls] boule *f* ▪ [in golf] bois *m*.
<> *comp* **1.** [wooden - floor, table, house] en bois, de bois **2.** [for burning wood - stove] à bois ; [- fire] de bois.

wood anemone *n* anémone *f* des bois.

woodbine ['wudbaɪn] *n* [honeysuckle] chèvrefeuille *m* ▪ *US* [Virginia creeper] vigne *f* vierge.

woodblock ['wudblɒk] *n* **1.** [for printing] bois *m* de graveur **2.** [for floor] pavé *m* de bois.

wood-burning *adj* [stove, boiler] à bois.

woodcarving ['wud,kɑ:vɪŋ] *n* **1.** [craft] sculpture *f* sur bois **2.** [object] sculpture *f* en bois.

woodchip ['wudtʃɪp] *n* [composite wood] aggloméré *m*.

woodchuck ['wudtʃʌk] *n* marmotte *f* d'Amérique.

woodcock ['wudkɒk] (*pl inv OR pl* **woodcocks**) *n* bécasse *f*.

woodcraft ['wudkrɑ:ft] *n US* **1.** [in woodland] connaissance *f* des bois et forêts **2.** [artistry] art *m* de travailler le bois.

woodcut ['wudkʌt] *n* gravure *f* sur bois.

woodcutter ['wud,kʌtər] *n* bûcheron *m*, - onne *f*.

woodcutting ['wud,kʌtɪŋ] *n* **1.** [in forest] abattage *m* des arbres **2.** [engraving] gravure *f* sur bois.

wooded ['wudɪd] *adj* boisé ▪ **densely ~** très boisé.

wooden ['wudn] *adj* **1.** [made of wood] en bois, de bois ▪ **a ~ leg** une jambe de bois ➲ **to try to sell sb ~ nickels** *US inf* essayer de rouler qqn **2.** [stiff - gesture, manner] crispé, raide ; [- performance, actor] raide, qui manque de naturel.

woodenhead ['wudnhed] *n inf* idiot *m*, - e *f*, imbécile *mf*.

woodenly ['wudnlɪ] *adv* [perform, move, smile, speak] avec raideur.

wooden spoon *n liter* cuillère *f* en bois ▪ **to win the ~** *UK* SPORT gagner la cuillère de bois.

woodland ['wudlənd] <> *n* région *f* boisée.
<> *adj* [fauna] des bois ▪ **~ walks** promenades *fpl* à travers bois.

woodlark ['wudlɑ:k] *n* alouette *f* des bois.

woodlouse ['wudlaus] (*pl* **woodlice** [-laɪs]) *n* cloporte *m*.

wood nymph *n* nymphe *f* des bois, dryade *f*.

woodpecker ['wud,pekər] *n* pic *m*, pivert *m*.

woodpigeon ['wud,pɪdʒn] *n* ramier *m*.

woodpile ['wudpaɪl] *n* tas *m* de bois.

wood pulp *n* pâte *f* à papier.

woodshed ['wudʃed] *n* bûcher *m (abri)*.

woodsman ['wudzmən] (*pl* **woodsmen** [-mən]) *n US* forestier *m*.

woodwind ['wudwɪnd] <> *adj* [music] pour les bois ▪ **~ section** *OR* **instruments** bois *mpl*.
<> *n* **1.** [single instrument] bois *m* **2.** *(U)* [family of instruments] bois *mpl*.

woodwork ['wudwɜ:k] *n (U)* **1.** [craft - carpentry] menuiserie *f* ; [- cabinet-making] ébénisterie *f* **2.** [in building - doors, windows] boiseries *fpl* ; [- beams] charpente *f* ▪ **to come** *OR* **to crawl out of the ~** *inf* sortir d'un peu partout **3.** *inf* FTBL poteaux *mpl*.

woodworm ['wudwɜ:m] *n* [insect] ver *m* de bois ▪ *(U)* [infestation] **: a chair affected** *OR* **damaged by ~** une chaise vermoulue *OR* mangée aux vers ▪ **the sideboard has got ~** le buffet est vermoulu.

woody ['wudɪ] (*comp* **woodier**, *superl* **woodiest**) *adj* **1.** [plant, vegetation] ligneux **2.** [countryside] boisé **3.** [taste] de bois ▪ [smell] boisé.

wooer ['wu:ər] *n dated* prétendant *m*.

woof[1] [wu:f] *n* TEX trame *f*.

woof[2] [wuf] <> *n* [bark] aboiement *m*.
<> *vi* aboyer.
<> *onom* ouah ouah.

woofer ['wufər] *n* haut-parleur *m* de graves, woofer *m*.

wool [wul] <> *n* laine *f* ▪ **pure new ~** pure laine vierge ➲ **all ~ and a yard wide** *US inf* de première classe, de premier ordre ▪ **to pull the ~ over sb's eyes** berner *OR* duper qqn.
<> *adj* [cloth] de laine ▪ [socks, dress] en laine.

woolen *US* = **woollen.**

woollen *UK*, **woolen** *US* ['wulən] *adj* **1.** [fabric] de laine ▪ [jacket, gloves, blanket] en laine **2.** [industry] lainière ▪ [manufacture] de lainages.
◆ **woollens** *UK*, **woolens** *US npl* lainages *mpl*, vêtements *mpl* de laine.

woolly *UK* (*pl* **woollies**), **wooly** *US* (*pl* **woolies**) ['wulɪ] <> *adj* **1.** [socks, hat] en laine **2.** [sheep] laineux **3.** [clouds] cotonneux ▪ [hair] frisé **4.** [vague - thinking, ideas] confus, flou.
<> *n UK inf* [pullover] tricot *m*, lainage *m* ▪ [dress] robe *f* en laine ▪ **winter woollies** lainages *mpl* d'hiver.

woolly-minded *adj* à l'esprit confus.

woolsack ['wulsæk] *n* POL **: the ~** *coussin rouge sur lequel s'assoit le président de la Chambre des lords.*

wooly *US* = **woolly.**

woops [wups] = **whoops.**

woozy ['wu:zɪ] (*comp* **woozier**, *superl* **wooziest**) *adj inf* **1.** [dazed] hébété, dans les vapes **2.** [sick] : **to feel ~** avoir mal au cœur **3.** [from drink] éméché, pompette.

wop△ [wɒp] *n terme injurieux désignant un Italien,* ≃ *macaroni*△ *mf.*

Worcester sauce ['wʊstə-] *n sauce épicée en bouteille.*

Worcs *written abbr of* **Worcestershire**.

word [wɜ:d] ◇ *n* **1.** [gen - LING] [COMPUT - written] mot *m* ; [- spoken] mot *m*, parole *f* ▪ **the ~s of a song** les paroles d'une chanson ▪ **what is the Russian ~ for "head"?, what is the ~ for "head" in Russian?** comment dit-on "tête" en russe? ▪ **the Japanese don't have a ~ for it** les Japonais n'ont pas de mot pour dire cela ▪ **she can't put her ideas/feelings into ~s** elle ne trouve pas les mots pour exprimer ses idées/ce qu'elle ressent ▪ **there are no ~s to describe** *OR* **~s cannot describe how I feel** aucun mot ne peut décrire ce que je ressens ▪ **with these ~s they left** sur ces mots *OR* là-dessus, ils sont partis ▪ **lazy isn't the ~ for it!** paresseux, c'est peu dire! ▪ **idle would be a better ~** oisif serait plus juste ▪ **he doesn't know the meaning of the ~ "generosity"** *fig* il ne sait pas ce que veut dire le mot "générosité" ▪ **he's mad, there's no other ~ for it** il est fou, il n'y a pas d'autre mot ▪ **I don't believe a ~ of it!** je n'en crois pas un mot! ▪ **that's my last** *OR* **final ~ on the matter** c'est mon dernier mot (sur la question) ▪ **those were his dying ~s** ce sont les dernières paroles qu'il a prononcées avant de mourir ▪ **she said a few ~s of welcome** elle a dit quelques mots de bienvenue ▪ **I gave him a few ~s of advice** je lui ai donné quelques conseils ▪ **can I give you a ~ of warning/advice?** puis-je vous mettre en garde/conseiller? ▪ **he didn't say a ~** il n'a rien dit, il n'a pas dit un mot ▪ **and now a ~ from our sponsors** et maintenant, voici un message publicitaire de nos sponsors ▪ **I'm a woman of few ~s** je ne suis pas quelqu'un qui fait de grands discours ▪ **he's a man of few ~s** c'est un homme peu loquace, c'est quelqu'un qui n'aime pas beaucoup parler ▪ **in the ~s of Shelley** comme l'a dit Shelley ▪ **in the ~s of his boss, he's a layabout** à en croire son patron *OR* d'après (ce que dit) son patron, c'est un fainéant ▪ **tell me in your own ~s** dites-le moi à votre façon *OR* avec vos propres mots ▪ **he told me in so many ~s that I was a liar** il m'a dit carrément *OR* sans mâcher ses mots que j'étais menteur ▪ **by** *OR* **through ~ of mouth** oralement ▪ **the news spread by ~ of mouth** la nouvelle se répandit de bouche à oreille ▪ **too stupid for ~s** vraiment trop bête ▪ **~ for ~** [translate] littéralement, mot à mot ; [repeat] mot pour mot ➊ **from the ~ go** dès le départ ▪ **(upon) my ~!** ma parole!, oh la la! ▪ **don't put ~s into my mouth** ne me faites pas dire ce que je n'ai pas dit ▪ **he took the ~s out of my mouth** il a dit exactement ce que j'allais dire ▪ **~s fail me!** j'en perds la parole!, je suis stupéfait! ▪ **he never has a good ~ to say about anyone** personne ne trouve jamais grâce à ses yeux ▪ **to put in a (good) ~ for sb** glisser un mot en faveur de qqn ▪ **to have the last ~** avoir le dernier mot ▪ **it's the last ~ in comfort** *UK* c'est ce qui se fait de mieux en matière de confort

2. [talk] mot *m*, mots *mpl*, parole *f*, paroles *fpl* ▪ **to have a ~ with sb about sthg** toucher un mot *OR* deux mots à qqn au sujet de qqch ▪ **can I have a ~ with you about the meeting?** est-ce que je peux vous dire deux mots à propos de la réunion? ▪ **can I have a ~?** je voudrais vous parler un instant

3. *(U)* [news] nouvelle *f*, nouvelles *fpl* ▪ [message] message *m*, mot *m* ▪ **the ~ got out that there had been a coup** la nouvelle d'un coup d'État a circulé ▪ **~ came from Tokyo that the strike was over** la nouvelle arriva de Tokyo que la grève était terminée ▪ **she brought them ~ of Tom** elle leur a apporté des nouvelles de Tom ▪ **she left ~ for us to follow** elle nous a laissé un message pour dire que nous devions la suivre ▪ **he sent ~ to say he had arrived safely** il a envoyé un mot pour dire qu'il était bien arrivé

4. [promise] parole *f*, promesse *f* ▪ **he gave his ~ that we wouldn't be harmed** il a donné sa parole qu'il ne nous ferait aucun mal ▪ **I give you my ~ on it** je vous en donne ma parole ▪ **to break one's ~** manquer à sa parole ▪ **to go back on one's ~** revenir sur sa parole ▪ **we held** *OR* **kept her to her ~** nous l'avons obligée à tenir sa parole ▪ **he was as good as his ~** il a tenu parole ▪ **I'm a man of my ~** je suis un homme de parole ▪ **~ of honour!** parole d'honneur! ▪ **we only have his ~ for it** il n'y a que lui qui le dit, personne ne peut prouver le contraire ▪ **we'll have to take your ~ for it** nous sommes bien obligés de vous croire ▪ **take my ~ (for it), it's a bargain!** croyez-moi, c'est une affaire! ▪ **I took her at her ~** je l'ai prise au mot ▪ **it's your ~ against mine** c'est votre parole contre la mienne ▪ **my ~ is my bond** je n'ai qu'une parole, je tiens toujours parole

5. [advice] conseil *m* ▪ **a ~ to travellers, watch your luggage!** un petit conseil aux voyageurs, surveillez vos bagages! ▪ **a quick ~ in your ear** je vous glisse un mot à l'oreille ▪ **a ~ to the wise** à bon entendeur, salut

6. [rumour] bruit *m* ▪ **(the) ~ went round that he was dying** le bruit a couru qu'il était sur le point de mourir

7. [order] ordre *m* ▪ **his ~ is law** c'est lui qui fait la loi ▪ **just give** *OR* **say the ~ and we'll be off** vous n'avez qu'à donner le signal et nous partons

8. [watchword] mot *m* d'ordre ▪ [password] mot *m* de passe.

◇ *vt* [letter, document] rédiger, formuler ▪ [contract] rédiger ▪ **they ~ed the petition carefully** ils ont choisi les termes de la pétition avec le plus grand soin ▪ **we sent a strongly ~ed protest** nous avons envoyé une lettre de protestation bien sentie.

◆ **Word** *n* RELIG : **the Word** le Verbe ▪ **the Word of God** la parole de Dieu.

◆ **words** *npl UK inf* [argument] dispute *f* ▪ **to have ~s** se disputer, avoir des mots.

◆ **in a word** *adv phr* en un mot.

◆ **in other words** *adv phr* autrement dit, en d'autres termes.

word association *n* association *f* d'idées par les mots.

word-blind *adj UK* dyslexique.

word-blindness *n UK* dyslexie *f*.

word class *n* LING classe *f* de mots.

word count *n* calcul *m* des mots.

word-for-word *adj* [repetition, imitation] mot pour mot ▪ [translation] littéral.

word game *n jeu de lettres.*

wordiness ['wɜ:dɪnɪs] *n* verbosité *f*.

wording ['wɜ:dɪŋ] *n (U)* **1.** [of letter, speech] termes *mpl*, formulation *f* ▪ [of contract] termes *mpl* ▪ **I think you should change the ~ of the last sentence** je crois que vous devriez reformuler la dernière phrase **2.** ADMIN & LAW rédaction *f*.

wordless ['wɜ:dlɪs] *adj* **1.** *lit* [silent - admiration] muet **2.** [without words - music] sans paroles.

wordlist ['wɜ:dlɪst] *n* [in notebook, textbook] lexique *m*, liste *f* de mots ▪ [in dictionary] nomenclature *f*.

word-of-mouth *adj* [account] oral, verbal.

word order *n* ordre *m* des mots.

word-perfect *adj* [recitation] que l'on connaît parfaitement *OR* sur le bout des doigts ▪ **she rehearsed her speech until she was ~** elle a répété son discours jusqu'à le connaître parfaitement *OR* sur le bout des doigts.

wordplay ['wɜ:dpleɪ] *n (U)* jeu *m* de mots.

word-process ◇ *vi* travailler sur traitement de texte. ◇ *vt* [text] saisir en traitement de texte.

word processing *n* traitement *m* de texte.

word processor *n* machine *f* de traitement de texte.

wordsmith ['wɜ:dsmɪθ] *n* manieur *m* de mots.

wordy ['wɜ:dɪ] (*comp* **wordier**, *superl* **wordiest**) *adj* verbeux.

wore [wɔ:ʳ] *pt* ▷ **wear**.

work [wɜ:k] ◇ *n* **1.** [effort, activity] travail *m*, œuvre *f* ▪ **computers take some of the ~ out of filing** les ordinateurs facilitent le classement ▪ **she's done a lot of ~ for charity** elle a beaucoup travaillé pour des associations caritatives ▪ **keep up the good ~!** continuez comme ça! ▪ **nice ~!** c'est du bon travail! ▪ **~ on the tunnel is to start in March** [existing tunnel] les travaux sur le tunnel doivent commencer en mars ; [new tunnel] la construction du tunnel doit commencer *OR* le tunnel doit être commencé en mars ▪ **~ in progress** ADMIN travail en cours ; [on sign] travaux en cours ▪ **she put a lot of ~ into that book** elle a beaucoup travaillé sur ce livre ▪ **to start ~, to set**

to ~ se mettre au travail ▪ **she set** *OR* **went to ~ on the contract** elle a commencé à travailler sur le contrat ▪ **I set him to ~ (on) painting the kitchen** je lui ai donné la cuisine à peindre ▪ **let's get (down) to ~!** (mettons-nous) au travail! ➤ **all ~ and no play makes Jack a dull boy** *prov* beaucoup de travail et peu de loisirs ne réussissent à personne **2.** [duty, task] travail *m*, besogne *f* ▪ **he's trying to get some ~ done** il essaie de travailler un peu ▪ **it's hard ~** c'est du travail, ce n'est pas facile ▪ **it's thirsty ~** ça donne soif ➤ **to make short** *OR* **light ~ of sthg** expédier qqch ▪ **to make short ~ of sb** *fig* ne faire qu'une bouchée de qqn ▪ **it's nice ~ if you can get it!** *inf* c'est une bonne planque, encore faut-il la trouver! **3.** [paid employment] travail *m*, emploi *m* ▪ **what (kind of) ~ do you do?** qu'est-ce que vous faites dans la vie?, quel travail faites-vous? ▪ **I do translation ~** je suis traducteur, je fais des traductions ▪ **to look for ~** chercher du travail *OR* un emploi ▪ **to be in ~** travailler, avoir un emploi ▪ **to be out of ~** être au chômage *OR* sans travail *OR* sans emploi ▪ **he had a week off ~** [holiday] il a pris une semaine de vacances ; [illness] il n'est pas allé au travail pendant une semaine ▪ **to take time off ~** prendre des congés ▪ **she's off ~ today** elle ne travaille pas aujourd'hui ▪ **to do a full day's ~** faire une journée entière de travail ▪ **people out of ~** [gen] les chômeurs *mpl* ; ADMIN & ECON les inactifs *mpl* **4.** [place of employment] travail *m* ▪ ADMIN lieu *m* de travail ▪ **he's a friend from ~** c'est un collègue ▪ **where is your (place of) ~?** où travaillez-vous?, quel est votre lieu de travail? **5.** [papers, material etc being worked on] travail *m* ▪ **to take ~ home** prendre du travail à la maison **6.** [creation, artefact etc] œuvre *f* ▪ [on smaller scale] ouvrage *m* ▪ SEW ouvrage *m* ▪ **it's all my own ~** j'ai tout fait moi-même ▪ **it's an interesting piece of ~** [gen] c'est un travail intéressant ; ART, LIT & MUS c'est une œuvre intéressante ▪ **the complete ~s of Shakespeare** les œuvres complètes *OR* l'œuvre de Shakespeare ▪ **a ~ of art** une œuvre d'art ▪ **~s of fiction** des ouvrages de fiction **7.** [research] travail *m*, recherches *fpl* ▪ **there hasn't been a lot of ~ done on the subject** peu de travail a été fait *OR* peu de recherches ont été faites sur le sujet **8.** [deed] œuvre *f*, acte *m* ▪ **good ~s** bonnes œuvres ▪ **charitable ~s** actes de charité, actes charitables ▪ **the murder is the ~ of a madman** le meurtre est l'œuvre d'un fou **9.** [effect] effet *m* **10.** PHYS travail *m*.

◇ *vi*

A.

1. [exert effort on a specific task, activity etc] travailler ▪ **we ~ed for hours cleaning the house** nous avons passé des heures à faire le ménage ▪ **to ~ at** *OR* **on sthg : she's ~ing on a novel just now** elle travaille à un roman en ce moment ▪ **he ~s at** *OR* **on keeping himself fit** il fait de l'exercice pour garder la forme ▪ **we have to ~ to a deadline** nous devons respecter des délais dans notre travail ▪ **we have to ~ to a budget** nous devons travailler avec un certain budget

2. [be employed] travailler ▪ **he ~s as a teacher** il a un poste d'enseignant ▪ **I ~ in advertising** je travaille dans la publicité ▪ **I ~ a forty-hour week** je travaille quarante heures par semaine, je fais une semaine de quarante heures ▪ **to ~ for a living** travailler pour gagner sa vie ▪ **to ~ to rule** INDUST faire la grève du zèle

3. [strive for a specific goal or aim] : **to ~ for sthg : they're ~ing for better international relations** ils s'efforcent d'améliorer les relations internationales

4. [study] travailler, étudier

5. [use a specified substance] travailler ▪ **she has always ~ed in** *OR* **with watercolours** elle a toujours travaillé avec de la peinture à l'eau

B.

1. [function, operate - machine, brain, system] fonctionner, marcher ▪ **the lift never ~s** l'ascenseur est toujours en panne ▪ **the radio ~s off batteries** la radio fonctionne avec des piles ▪ **a pump ~ed by hand** une pompe actionnée à la main *OR* manuellement ▪ *fig* **everything ~ed smoothly** tout s'est déroulé comme prévu ▪ **your idea just won't ~** ton idée ne peut pas marcher ▪ **that argument ~s both ways** ce raisonnement est à double tranchant

2. [produce results, succeed] marcher, réussir ▪ **it ~ed brilliantly** ça a très bien marché

3. [drug, medicine] agir, produire *OR* faire son effet

4. [act] agir ▪ **events have ~ed against us/in our favour** les événements ont agi contre nous/en notre faveur ▪ **I'm ~ing on the assumption that they'll sign the contract** je pars du principe qu'ils signeront le contrat

C.

1. [reach a condition or state gradually] : **to ~ loose** se desserrer ▪ **to ~ free** se libérer

2. [face, mouth] se contracter, se crisper

3. [ferment] fermenter.

◇ *vt*

A.

1. [worker, employee] faire travailler ▪ **the boss ~s his staff hard** le patron exige beaucoup de travail de ses employés ▪ **you ~ yourself too hard** tu te surmènes ▪ **to ~ o.s. to death** se tuer à la tâche ➤ **to ~ one's fingers to the bone** s'user au travail

2. [pay for with labour or service] : **I ~ed my way through college** j'ai travaillé pour payer mes études à l'université

3. [carry on activity in] : **he ~s the southern sales area** il travaille pour le service commercial de la région sud ▪ **the candidate ~ed the crowd** *fig* le candidat s'efforçait de soulever l'enthousiasme de la foule ▪ **a real-estate agent who ~s the phones** un agent immobilier qui fait de la prospection par téléphone

4. [achieve, accomplish] : **the story ~ed its magic** *OR* **charm on the public** l'histoire a enchanté le public ▪ **to ~ miracles** faire *OR* accomplir des miracles ▪ **to ~ wonders** faire merveille

5. [make use of, exploit - land] travailler, cultiver ; [- mine, quarry] exploiter, faire valoir

B.

1. [operate] faire marcher, faire fonctionner ▪ **this switch ~s the furnace** ce bouton actionne *OR* commande la chaudière

2. [manoeuvre] : **I ~ed the handle up and down** j'ai remué la poignée de haut en bas ▮ [progress slowly] : **I ~ed my way along the ledge** j'ai longé la saillie avec précaution ▪ **he ~ed his way down/up the cliff** il a descendu/monté la falaise lentement

3. *inf* [contrive] s'arranger ▪ **I ~ed it** *OR* **~ed things so that she's never alone** j'ai fait en sorte qu'elle *OR* je me suis arrangé pour qu'elle ne soit jamais seule

C.

1. [shape - leather, metal, stone] travailler, façonner ; [- clay, dough] travailler, pétrir ; [- object, sculpture] façonner ▪ **she ~ed a figure out of the wood** elle a sculpté une silhouette dans le bois ▪ **~ the putty into the right consistency** travaillez le mastic pour lui donner la consistance voulue

2. [excite, provoke] : **the orator ~ed the audience into a frenzy** l'orateur a enflammé *OR* galvanisé le public ▪ **she ~ed herself into a rage** elle s'est mise dans une colère noire.

➡ **works** ◇ *npl* **1.** [mechanism] mécanisme *m*, rouages *mpl* ▪ [of clock] mouvement *m* ▪ **to foul up** *OR* **to gum up the ~s** *inf* tout foutre en l'air **2.** CIV ENG [construction] travaux *mpl* ▪ [installation] installations *fpl* ▪ **road ~s** travaux ▪ **Minister/Ministry of Works** ministre *m* /ministère *m* des Travaux publics.

◇ *n (with sg vb)* **1.** INDUST [factory] usine *f* ▪ **a printing ~s** une imprimerie ▪ **a gas ~s** une usine à gaz ▪ **price ex ~s** prix *m* sortie usine **2.** *inf* [everything] : **the (whole) ~s** tout le bataclan *OR* le tralala ▪ **to shoot the ~s** *US* jouer le grand jeu ▪ **to give sb the ~s** [special treatment] dérouler le tapis rouge pour qqn *fig* ; [beating] passer qqn à tabac.

➡ **at work** ◇ *adj phr* **1.** [person] : **to be at ~ (on) sthg/doing sthg** travailler (à) qqch/à faire qqch ▪ **they're hard at ~ painting the house** ils sont en plein travail, ils repeignent la maison **2.** [having an effect] : **there are several factors at ~ here** il y a plusieurs facteurs qui entrent en jeu *OR* qui jouent ici ▪ **there are evil forces at ~** des forces mauvaises sont en action.

◇ *adv phr* [at place of work] : **she's at ~** [gen] elle est au travail ; [office] elle est au bureau ; [factory] elle est à l'usine.

➡ **work away** *vi insep* travailler ▪ **we ~ed away all evening** nous avons passé la soirée à travailler.

➡ **work down** *vi insep* glisser ▪ **her socks had ~ed down around her ankles** ses chaussettes étaient tombées sur ses chevilles.

➡ **work in** *vt sep* **1.** [incorporate] incorporer ▪ **~ the ointment in thoroughly** faites bien pénétrer la pommade ▪ **~ the butter into the flour** CULIN incorporez le beurre à la farine **2.** [insert]

faire entrer *OR* introduire petit à petit ▪ **he ~ed in a few sly remarks about the boss** il a réussi à glisser quelques réflexions sournoises sur le patron.

◆ **work off** *vt sep* **1.** [dispose of - fat, weight] se débarrasser de, éliminer ; [- anxiety, frustration] passer, assouvir ▪ **I ~ed off my excess energy chopping wood** j'ai dépensé mon trop-plein d'énergie en cassant du bois **2.** [debt, obligation] : **it took him three months to ~ off his debt** il a dû travailler trois mois pour rembourser son emprunt.

◆ **work on** *vt insep* **1.** [person] essayer de convaincre ▪ **I'll ~ on her** je vais m'occuper d'elle **2.** [task, problem] : **the police are ~ing on who stole the jewels** la police s'efforce de retrouver celui qui a volé les bijoux ▪ **have you got any ideas? – I'm ~ing on it** as-tu des idées? – je cherche.

◆ **work out** ◇ *vt sep* **1.** [discharge fully] acquitter en travaillant ▪ **to ~ out one's notice** faire son préavis **2.** [solve - calculation, problem] résoudre ; [- answer, total] trouver ; [- puzzle] faire, résoudre ; [- code] déchiffrer ▪ **things will ~ themselves out** les choses s'arrangeront toutes seules *OR* d'elles-mêmes **3.** [formulate - idea, plan] élaborer, combiner ; [- agreement, details] mettre au point ▪ **have you ~ed out yet when it's due to start?** est-ce que tu sais quand ça doit commencer? ▪ **she had it all ~ed out** elle avait tout planifié **4.** [figure out] arriver à comprendre ▪ **I finally ~ed out why he was acting so strangely** j'ai enfin découvert *OR* compris pourquoi il se comportait si bizarrement ▪ **I can't ~ her out** je n'arrive pas à la comprendre ▪ **I can't ~ their relationship out** leurs rapports me dépassent **5.** [mine, well] épuiser.

◇ *vi insep* **1.** [happen] se passer ▪ **the trip ~ed out as planned** le voyage s'est déroulé comme prévu ▪ **it all ~ed out for the best** tout a fini par s'arranger pour le mieux **2.** [have a good result - job, plan] réussir ; [- problem, puzzle] se résoudre ▪ **she ~ed out fine as personnel director** elle s'est bien débrouillée comme directeur du personnel ▪ **did the new job ~ out?** ça a marché pour le nouveau boulot? ▪ **it didn't ~ out between them** les choses ont plutôt mal tourné entre eux **3.** [amount to] : **the average price for an apartment ~s out to** *OR* **at $5,000 per square metre** le prix moyen d'un appartement s'élève *OR* revient à 5 000 dollars le mètre carré ▪ **that ~s out at three hours a week** ça fait trois heures par semaine ▪ **electric heating ~s out expensive** le chauffage électrique revient cher **4.** [exercise] faire de l'exercice ▪ [professional athlete] s'entraîner.

◆ **work over** *vt sep* **1.** *US* [revise] revoir, réviser **2.** *inf* [beat up] tabasser, passer à tabac.

◆ **work round** ◇ *vi insep* **1.** [turn] tourner **2.** *fig* [in conversation] : **he finally ~ed round to the subject of housing** il a fini par aborder le sujet du logement ▪ **what's she ~ing round to?** où veut-elle en venir?

◇ *vt sep* [bring round] : **I ~ed the conversation round to my salary** j'ai amené la conversation sur la question de mon salaire.

◆ **work through** ◇ *vt sep* **1.** [insert] faire passer à travers **2.** [progress through] : **we ~ed our way through the crowd** nous nous sommes frayé un chemin à travers la foule ▪ **he ~ed his way through the book** il a lu le livre du début à la fin ▪ **I ~ed the problem through** *fig* j'ai étudié le problème sous tous ses aspects.

◇ *vt insep* **1.** [continue to work] : **she ~ed through lunch** elle a travaillé pendant l'heure du déjeuner **2.** [resolve] : **he ~ed through his emotional problems** il a réussi à assumer ses problèmes affectifs.

◆ **work up** ◇ *vt sep* **1.** [stir up, rouse] exciter, provoquer ▪ **he ~s himself up** *OR* **gets himself ~ed up over nothing** il s'énerve pour rien **2.** [develop] développer ▪ **to ~ up an appetite** se mettre en appétit ▪ **we ~ed up a sweat/thirst playing tennis** jouer au tennis nous a donné chaud/soif ▪ **I can't ~ up any enthusiasm for this work** je n'arrive pas à avoir le moindre enthousiasme pour ce travail **3.** *phr* **to ~ one's way up** faire son chemin ▪ **she ~ed her way up from secretary to managing director** elle a commencé comme secrétaire et elle a fait son chemin jusqu'au poste de P-DG ▪ **I ~ed my way up from nothing** je suis parti de rien.

◇ *vi insep* **1.** [clothing] remonter **2.** [build up] : **the film was ~ing up to a climax** le film approchait de son point culminant ▪ **what are you ~ing up to?** où veux-tu en venir?

workability [ˌwɜːkəˈbɪlətɪ] *n* **1.** [of plan] caractère *m* réalisable **2.** [of mine] caractère *m* exploitable.

workable [ˈwɜːkəbl] *adj* **1.** [plan, proposal] réalisable, faisable **2.** [mine, field] exploitable.

workaday [ˈwɜːkədeɪ] *adj* [clothes, routine] de tous les jours ▪ [man] ordinaire, banal ▪ [incident] courant, banal.

workaholic [ˌwɜːkəˈhɒlɪk] *n inf* bourreau *m* de travail, drogué *m*, - e *f* du travail.

workbag [ˈwɜːkbæg] *n* sac *m* à ouvrage.

workbench [ˈwɜːkbentʃ] *n* établi *m*.

workbook [ˈwɜːkbʊk] *n* **1.** SCH [exercise book] cahier *m* d'exercices ▪ [record book] cahier *m* de classe **2.** [manual] manuel *m*.

work camp *n* **1.** [prison] camp *m* de travail **2.** [voluntary] chantier *m* de travail.

work coat *n US* blouse *f*.

workday [ˈwɜːkdeɪ] ◇ *n* **1.** [day's work] journée *f* de travail **2.** [working day] jour *m* ouvré *OR* où l'on travaille.
◇ *adj* = **workaday**.

worked up [ˌwɜːkt-] *adj* énervé, dans tous ses états ▪ **to get ~** s'énerver, se mettre dans tous ses états.

worker [ˈwɜːkəʳ] *n* **1.** INDUST [- gen] travailleur *m*, - euse *f*, employé *m*, - e *f* ; [- manual] ouvrier *m*, - ère *f*, travailleur *m*, - euse *f* ▪ **he's a fast ~!** il travaille vite! ▪ **she's a hard ~** elle travaille dur **2.** ENTOM ouvrière *f*.

worker ant *n* (fourmi) ouvrière *f*.

worker bee *n* (abeille) ouvrière *f*.

worker director *n ouvrier qui fait partie du conseil d'administration.*

worker-priest *n* prêtre-ouvrier *m*.

work ethic *n exaltation des valeurs liées au travail.*

work experience *n* : **the course includes two months' ~** le programme comprend un stage en entreprise de deux mois.

workfare [ˈwɜːkfeəʳ] *n* POL *principe selon lequel les bénéficiaires de l'allocation de chômage doivent fournir un travail en échange.*

workforce [ˈwɜːkfɔːs] *n* main-d'œuvre *f*, effectifs *mpl*.

workhorse [ˈwɜːkhɔːs] *n* **1.** [horse] cheval *m* de labour **2.** *fig* [worker] bourreau *m* de travail ▪ [machine, vehicle] bonne mécanique *f*.

workhouse [ˈwɜːkhaʊs] (*pl* **workhouses** [-haʊzɪz]) *n* **1.** [in UK - HIST] hospice *m* **2.** [in US - prison] maison *f* de correction.

work-in *n occupation d'une entreprise par le personnel (avec poursuite du travail).*

working [ˈwɜːkɪŋ] ◇ *adj* **1.** [mother] qui travaille ▪ [population] actif ▪ **ordinary ~ people** les travailleurs ordinaires **2.** [day, hours] de travail ▪ **a ~ week of 40 hours** une semaine de 40 heures ▪ **he spent his entire ~ life with the firm** il a travaillé toute sa vie dans l'entreprise ▪ **a ~ breakfast/lunch** un petit déjeuner/déjeuner de travail **3.** [clothes, conditions] de travail **4.** [functioning - farm, factory, model] qui marche ▪ **in (good) ~ order** en (bon) état de marche **5.** [theory, definition] de travail ▪ [majority] suffisant ▪ [agreement] de circonstance ▪ [knowledge] adéquat, suffisant.
◇ *n* **1.** [work] travail *m* **2.** [operation - of machine] fonctionnement *m* **3.** [of mine] exploitation *f* ▪ [of clay, leather] travail *m*.

◆ **workings** *npl* **1.** [mechanism] mécanisme *m* ▪ *fig* [of government, system] rouages *mpl* ▪ **it's difficult to understand the ~s of his mind** il est difficile de savoir ce qu'il a dans la tête *OR* ce qui se passe dans sa tête **2.** MIN chantier *m* d'exploitation ▪ **old mine ~s** anciennes mines *fpl*.

working capital *n (U)* fonds *mpl* de roulement.

working class *n* : **the ~, the ~es** la classe ouvrière, le prolétariat.

◆ **working-class** *adj* [district, origins] ouvrier ▪ [accent] des classes populaires ▪ **she's ~** elle appartient à la classe ouvrière.

working group = **working party.**

working lunch *n* déjeuner *m* de travail.

working majority *n* majorité *f* suffisante.

working man *n UK* ouvrier *m*.

working men's club *n club d'ouvriers, comportant un bar et une scène où sont présentés des spectacles de music-hall.*

working party *n* **1.** [committee - for study] groupe *m* de travail ; [- for enquiry] commission *f* d'enquête **2.** [group - of prisoners, soldiers] groupe *m* de travail.

working title *n* titre *m* provisoire.

working woman *n* **1.** [worker] ouvrière *f*, employée *f* **2.** [woman with job] femme *f* qui travaille.

workload ['wɜ:kləʊd] *n* travail *m* à effectuer, charge *f* de travail ▪ **I still have a heavy ~** je suis encore surchargé de travail.

workman ['wɜ:kmən] (*pl* **workmen** [-mən]) *n* **1.** [manual worker] ouvrier *m* ➡ **workmen's compensation** *US* indemnité *f* pour accident de travail ▪ **a bad ~ blames his tools** *prov* les mauvais ouvriers ont toujours de mauvais outils *prov* **2.** [craftsman] artisan *m*.

workmanlike ['wɜ:kmənlaɪk] *adj* **1.** [efficient - approach, person] professionnel **2.** [well made - artefact] bien fait, soigné ▪ **he wrote a ~ report** il a fait un compte rendu très sérieux **3.** [serious - attempt, effort] sérieux.

workmanship ['wɜ:kmənʃɪp] *n (U)* **1.** [skill] métier *m*, maîtrise *f* **2.** [quality] exécution *f*, fabrication *f*.

workmate ['wɜ:kmeɪt] *n* camarade *mf* de travail.

workout ['wɜ:kaʊt] *n* séance *f* d'entraînement.

work party *n* [of soldiers] escouade *f* ▪ [of prisoners] groupe *m* de travail.

work permit [-,pɜ:mɪt] *n* permis *m* de travail.

workplace ['wɜ:kpleɪs] *n* lieu *m* de travail ▪ **in the ~** sur le lieu de travail.

workroom ['wɜ:krʊm] *n* salle *f* de travail.

works band *n* fanfare *m (d'une entreprise)*.

works committee, works council *n* comité *m* d'entreprise.

work-sharing *n* partage *m* du travail.

work sheet *n* COMPUT feuille *f* de travail.

workshop ['wɜ:kʃɒp] *n* **1.** INDUST [gen] atelier *m* **2.** [study group] atelier *m*, groupe *m* de travail.

workshy ['wɜ:kʃaɪ] *adj* fainéant, tire-au-flanc *(inv)*.

works manager *n* directeur *m*, - trice *f* d'usine.

workspace ['wɜ:kspeɪs] *n* COMPUT bureau *m*.

work space *n* [at home] coin-travail *m* ▪ [in office] espace *m* de travail.

workstation ['wɜ:k,steɪʃn] *n* COMPUT poste *m* OR station *f* de travail.

work-study *n* INDUST étude *f* des cadences.

work surface *n* surface *f* de travail.

worktop ['wɜ:ktɒp] *n* [in kitchen] plan *m* de travail.

work-to-rule *n UK* grève *f* du zèle.

work week *n US* semaine *f* de travail.

world [wɜ:ld] ◇ *n*

A.

1. [earth] monde *m* ▪ **to travel round the ~** faire le tour du monde, voyager autour du monde ▪ **to see the ~** voir du pays, courir le monde ▪ **throughout the ~** dans le monde entier ▪ **in this part of the ~** dans cette région ▪ **I'm the ~'s worst photographer** il n'y a pas pire photographe que moi ▪ **the ~ over, all over the ~** dans le monde entier, partout dans le monde
2. [planet] monde *m*
3. [universe] monde *m*, univers *m*

B.

1. [part of the world - HIST] & POL monde *m* ▪ **the developing ~** les pays *mpl* en voie de développement ▪ **the Spanish-speaking ~** le monde hispanophone
2. [society] monde *m* ▪ **to go up/down in the ~ : she's gone up in the ~** elle a fait du chemin ▪ **he's gone down in the ~** il a connu de meilleurs jours ▪ **to come into the ~** venir au monde ▪ **to bring a child into the ~** mettre un enfant au monde ▪ **to make one's way in the ~** faire son chemin ▪ **you have to take the ~ as you find it** il faut prendre les choses comme elles viennent
3. [general public] monde *m* ▪ **the news shook the ~** la nouvelle a ébranlé le monde entier ▌[people in general] **: we don't want the whole ~ to know** nous ne voulons pas que tout le monde le sache ▪ **(all) the ~ and his wife** *inf fig* le monde entier

C.

1. [existence, particular way of life] monde *m*, vie *f* ▪ **we live in different ~s** nous ne vivons pas sur la même planète ▪ **to be ~s apart** [in lifestyle] avoir des styles de vie complètement différents ; [in opinions] avoir des opinions complètement différentes ▌[realm] monde *m* ▪ **he lives in a ~ of his own** il vit dans un monde à lui ▪ **the child's ~** l'univers *m* des enfants
2. [field, domain] monde *m*, milieu *m*, milieux *mpl* ▪ **the publishing ~** le monde de l'édition
3. [group of living things] monde *m* ▪ **the animal/plant ~** le règne animal/végétal
4. RELIG monde *m* ▪ **he isn't long for this ~** il n'en a pas pour longtemps
5. *phr* **a holiday will do you a** *OR* **the ~ of good** des vacances vous feront le plus grand bien ▪ **it made a ~ of difference** ça a tout changé ▪ **there's a ~ of difference between them** il y a un monde entre eux ▪ **he thinks the ~ of his daughter** il a une admiration sans bornes pour sa fille ▪ **it means the ~ to me** c'est quelque chose qui me tient beaucoup à cœur.

◇ *comp* [champion, record] mondial, du monde ▪ [language, religion] universel ▪ **~ peace** la paix mondiale ▪ **~ opinion** l'opinion internationale ▪ **on a ~ scale** à l'échelle mondiale.

➡ **for all the world** *adv phr* exactement ▪ **she behaved for all the ~ as if she owned the place** elle faisait exactement comme si elle était chez elle.

➡ **for the world** *adv phr* **: I wouldn't hurt her for the ~** je ne lui ferais de mal pour rien au monde.

➡ **in the world** *adv phr* **1.** [for emphasis] **: nothing in the ~ would change my mind** rien au monde ne me ferait changer d'avis ▪ **I felt as if I hadn't a care in the ~** je me sentais libre de tout souci ▪ **we've got all the time in the ~** nous avons tout le *OR* tout notre temps ▪ **I wouldn't do it for all the money in the ~!** je ne le ferais pas pour tout l'or du monde! **2.** [expressing surprise, irritation, frustration] **: where in the ~ have you put it?** où l'avez-vous donc mis?

➡ **out of this world** *adj phr inf* extraordinaire, sensationnel.

World Bank *pr n* Banque *f* mondiale.

world-beater *n UK inf* [person] champion *m*, - onne *f* ▪ **this new car is going to be a ~** *fig* cette nouvelle voiture va faire un tabac.

world-class *adj* [player, runner] parmi les meilleurs du monde, de classe internationale.

World Cup *pr n* **: the ~** la Coupe du monde.

World Fair *pr n* exposition *f* universelle.

world-famous *adj* de renommée mondiale, célèbre dans le monde entier.

World Health Organization *pr n* Organisation *f* mondiale de la santé.

worldliness ['wɜ:ldlɪnɪs] *n* **1.** [materialism] matérialisme *m* **2.** [experience of the world] mondanité *f*.

worldly ['wɜ:ldlɪ] (*comp* **worldlier**, *superl* **worldliest**) *adj* **1.** [material - possessions, pleasures, matters] matériel, de ce monde, terrestre ▪ RELIG temporel, de ce monde ▪ **all my ~ goods** tout ce que je possède au monde **2.** [materialistic -

person, outlook] matérialiste **3.** [sophisticated - person] qui a l'expérience du monde ; [- attitude, manner] qui démontre une expérience du monde.

worldly-wise *adj* qui a l'expérience du monde.

world music *n* musiques *fpl* du monde.

world power *n* puissance *f* mondiale.

World Series *n* : **the ~** *le championnat américain de base-ball.*

World Service *pr n* RADIO *service étranger de la BBC.*

world-shattering *adj* [event, news] renversant, bouleversant.

World Trade Organization *n* COMM Organisation *f* mondiale du commerce.

world view *n vue métaphysique du monde.*

world war *n* guerre *f* mondiale ▪ **World War I, the First World War** la Première Guerre mondiale ▪ **World War II, the Second World War** la Seconde Guerre mondiale.

world-weary *adj* [person] las du monde.

worldwide ['wɜːldwaɪd] ◇ *adj* [depression, famine, reputation] mondial.
◇ *adv* partout dans le monde, dans le monde entier.

World Wide Web *n* : **the ~** le Web, la Toile.

worm [wɜːm] ◇ *n* **1.** [in earth, garden] ver *m* (de terre) ▪ [in fruit] ver *m* ▪ [for fishing] ver *m*, asticot *m* ▪ **the ~ has turned** *UK fig* il en a eu assez de se faire marcher dessus **2.** [parasite - in body] ver *m* **3.** *inf fig* [person] minable *mf* **4.** *lit* [troublesome thing] tourment *m*, tourments *mpl* ▪ **the ~ of jealousy** les affres *fpl* de la jalousie.
◇ *vt* **1.** [move] : **to ~ one's way under sthg** passer sous qqch à plat ventre *OR* en rampant ▪ **she ~ed her way through a gap in the fence** en se tortillant elle s'est faufilée par une ouverture dans la palissade **2.** *pej* [sneak] : **he ~ed his way into her affections** il a trouvé le chemin de son cœur *(par sournoiserie)* **3.** [dog, sheep] débarrasser de ses vers.
➡ **worm out** *vt sep* [information] soutirer ▪ **I tried to ~ the truth out of him** j'ai essayé de lui soutirer la vérité.

worm-eaten *adj* [apple] véreux ▪ [furniture] vermoulu, mangé aux vers ▪ *fig* [ancient] désuet, - ète *f*, antédiluvien.

worm's-eye view *n* PHOT & CIN contre-plongée *f* ▪ **he presents a ~ of events** *fig* il nous présente les événements vus par les humbles.

wormwood ['wɜːmwʊd] *n* **1.** [plant] armoise *f* **2.** *lit* [bitterness] fiel *m*, amertume *f*.

worn [wɔːn] ◇ *pp* ▷ **wear.**
◇ *adj* **1.** [shoes, rug, tyre] usé **2.** [weary - person] las, lasse *f*.

worn-out *adj* **1.** [shoes, tyre] complètement usé ▪ [rug, dress] usé jusqu'à la corde ▪ [battery] usé **2.** [person] épuisé, éreinté.

worried ['wʌrɪd] *adj* [person, look] inquiet, - ète *f* ▪ **I'm ~ that they may get lost** *OR* **in case they get lost** j'ai peur qu'ils ne se perdent ▪ **to be ~ about sthg/sb** être inquiet pour qqch/qqn ▪ **to be ~ sick** *OR* **to death (about sb)** être fou *OR* malade d'inquiétude (pour qqn) ▪ **you had me ~ for a minute** vous m'avez fait peur pendant une minute ▪ **I'm not ~ either way** ça m'est égal.

worriedly ['wʌrɪdlɪ] *adv* [say] avec un air inquiet.

worrier ['wʌrɪə^r] *n* anxieux *m*, - euse *f*, inquiet *m*, - ète *f* ▪ **he's a born ~** c'est un éternel inquiet.

worrisome ['wʌrɪsəm] *adj* *dated* inquiétant.

worry ['wʌrɪ] (*pret & pp* **worried**, *pl* **worries**) ◇ *vt* **1.** [make anxious] inquiéter, tracasser ▪ **you really worried me** je me suis vraiment inquiété à cause de toi ▪ **he was worried by her sudden disappearance** il était inquiet de sa disparition subite ▪ **I sometimes ~ that they'll never be found** parfois je crains qu'on ne les retrouve jamais ▪ **don't ~ your head** *inf* *OR* **yourself about the details** ne vous inquiétez pas pour les détails
2. [disturb, bother] inquiéter, ennuyer ▪ **it doesn't ~ me if you want to waste your life** cela m'est égal *OR* ne me gêne pas si vous voulez gâcher votre vie
3. [subj: dog - bone, ball] prendre entre les dents et secouer ; [- sheep] harceler.
◇ *vi* s'inquiéter, se faire du souci, se tracasser ▪ **to ~ about** *OR* **over sthg** s'inquiéter pour *OR* au sujet de qqch ▪ **she has enough to ~ about** elle a assez de soucis comme ça ▪ **there's nothing to ~ about** il n'y a pas lieu de s'inquiéter ▪ **don't ~** ne vous inquiétez *OR* tracassez pas ▪ **they'll be found, don't you ~** on va les trouver, ne vous en faites pas ▪ **not to ~!** ce n'est pas grave! ▪ **YOU should ~** *iron* ce n'est pas votre problème, il n'y a pas de raisons de vous en faire.
◇ *n* **1.** [anxiety] inquiétude *f*, souci *m* ▪ **money is a constant source of ~** l'argent est un perpétuel souci *OR* une perpétuelle source d'inquiétude ▪ **her sons are a constant ~ to her** ses fils lui causent constamment des soucis *OR* du souci ▪ **he was sick with ~ about her** il se rongeait les sangs pour elle *OR* à son sujet
2. [concern] sujet *m* d'inquiétude, souci *m* ▪ [problem] problème *m* ▪ **it's a real ~ for her** cela la tracasse vraiment ▪ **that's the least of my worries** c'est le moindre *OR* le cadet *OR* le dernier de mes soucis ▪ **no worries!** *inf* pas de problème!
➡ **worry at** *vt insep UK* = **worry** *(vt sense 3).*

worry beads *npl* chapelet *m*.

worryguts ['wʌrɪgʌts] *n UK inf* anxieux *m*, - euse *f*, éternel inquiet *m*, éternelle inquiète *f*.

worrying ['wʌrɪɪŋ] ◇ *adj* inquiétant ▪ **the ~ thing is that it could happen again** ce qu'il y a d'inquiétant *OR* ce qui est inquiétant, c'est que cela pourrait se reproduire.
◇ *n* inquiétude *f* ▪ **~ won't solve anything** cela ne résoudra rien de se faire du souci.

worryingly ['wʌrɪɪŋlɪ] *adv* : **the project is ~ late** le projet a pris un retard inquiétant.

worrywart ['wʌrɪwɔːt] *US inf* = **worryguts.**

worse [wɜːs] *(adj compar of bad, adv compar of badly)* ◇ *adj* **1.** [not as good, pleasant as] pire, plus mauvais ▪ **the news is even ~ than we expected** les nouvelles sont encore plus mauvaises que nous ne pensions ▪ **your writing is ~ than mine** votre écriture est pire que la mienne ▪ **my writing is bad, but yours is ~** j'écris mal, mais vous, c'est pire ▪ **the rain is ~ than ever** il pleut de plus en plus ▪ **things are ~ than you imagine** les choses vont plus mal que vous l'imaginez ▪ **it could have been ~!** ça aurait pu être pire! ▪ **I lost my money, and ~ still** *OR* **and what's ~, my passport** j'ai perdu mon argent, et ce qui est plus grave, mon passeport ▪ **~ than useless** complètement inutile ▪ **to get** *OR* **to grow ~** empirer, s'aggraver ▪ **to get ~ and ~** aller de mal en pis ▪ **his drug problem got ~** son problème de drogue ne s'est pas arrangé ▪ **things will get ~ before they get better** les choses ne sont pas près de s'améliorer ▪ **his memory is getting ~** sa mémoire est de moins en moins bonne ▪ **she's only making things** *OR* **matters ~ for herself** elle ne fait qu'aggraver son cas ▪ **and, to make matters ~, he swore at the policeman** et pour tout arranger, il a insulté le policier ▶ **~ things happen at sea!** on a vu pire!, ce n'est pas la fin du monde! ▪ **~ luck!** *inf* quelle poisse!^△
2. [in health] plus mal ▪ **I feel ~** je me sens encore plus mal *OR* encore moins bien ▪ **her headache got ~** son mal de tête s'est aggravé
3. *phr* **this carpet is looking rather the ~ for wear** cette moquette est plutôt défraîchie ▪ **he's looking/feeling rather the ~ for wear** [tired, old] il n'a pas l'air/il ne se sent pas très frais ; [drunk] il a l'air/il se sent plutôt éméché ; [ill] il n'a pas l'air/il ne se sent pas très bien ▪ **he was rather the ~ for drink** il était plutôt éméché.
◇ *adv* **1.** [less well] plus mal, moins bien ▪ **he behaved ~ than ever** il ne s'est jamais aussi mal conduit ▪ **you could** *OR* **might do ~ than (to) marry him** l'épouser, ce n'est pas ce que vous pourriez faire de pire ▪ **she doesn't think any the ~ of her for it** elle ne l'en estime pas moins pour ça
2. [more severely - snow, rain] plus fort.
◇ *n* pire *m* ▪ **there's ~ to come, ~ is to come** [in situation] le pire est à venir ; [in story] il y a pire encore ▪ **there's been a change for the ~** les choses se sont aggravées ▪ **to take a turn for the ~** [health, situation] se détériorer, se dégrader.

◆ **none the worse** *adj phr* pas plus mal ■ **he's apparently none the ~ for his drinking session last night** il n'a pas l'air de se ressentir de sa beuverie d'hier soir.

worsen ['wɜːsn] ◇ *vi* [depression, crisis, pain, illness] empirer, s'aggraver ■ [weather, situation] se gâter, se détériorer.
◇ *vt* [situation] empirer, rendre pire.

worsening ['wɜːsnɪŋ] ◇ *adj* [situation] qui empire ■ [health] qui se détériore ■ [weather] qui se gâte *OR* se détériore.
◇ *n* aggravation *f*, détérioration *f*.

worse-off ◇ *adj* **1.** [financially] moins riche, plus pauvre **2.** [in worse state] dans une situation moins favorable ■ **the country is no ~ for having a coalition government** le pays ne se porte pas plus mal d'avoir un gouvernement de coalition.
◇ *npl* : **the ~** les pauvres *mpl*, les moins nantis *mpl*.

worship ['wɜːʃɪp] (*UK pret & pp* **worshipped**, *cont* **worshipping**) (*US pret & pp* **worshiped**, *cont* **worshiping**) ◇ *n* **1.** RELIG [service] culte *m*, office *m* ■ [liturgy] liturgie *f* ■ [adoration] adoration *f* ■ **an act of ~** [veneration] un acte de dévotion ; [service] un culte, un office ■ **freedom of ~** la liberté de culte ■ **places of ~** les lieux du culte **2.** *fig* [veneration] adoration *f*, culte *m*.
◇ *vt* **1.** RELIG adorer, vénérer **2.** [person] adorer, vénérer ■ [money, possessions] vouer un culte à, avoir le culte de ■ **they worshipped the ground she walked on** ils vénéraient jusqu'au sol sur lequel elle marchait.
◇ *vi* faire ses dévotions ■ **the church where she worshipped for 10 years** l'église où elle a fait ses dévotions pendant 10 ans ■ **to ~ at the altar of success** *fig* vouer un culte au succès.
◆ **Worship** *n UK fml* [in titles] : **His Worship the Mayor** monsieur le Maire ■ **Your Worship** [to a judge] monsieur le Juge ; [to a mayor] monsieur le Maire.

worshiper *US* = **worshipper**.

worshipful ['wɜːʃɪpfʊl] *adj* **1.** [respectful] respectueux **2.** *UK fml* [in titles] : **the Worshipful Mayor of Portsmouth** monsieur le Maire de Portsmouth.

worshipper *UK*, **worshiper** *US* ['wɜːʃɪpər] *n* **1.** RELIG adorateur *m*, - trice *f*, fidèle *mf* **2.** *fig* [of possessions, person] adorateur *m*, - trice *f*.

worst [wɜːst] (*adj superl of bad, adv superl of badly*) ◇ *adj* **1.** [least good, pleasant etc] le pire, le plus mauvais ■ **it's the ~ book I've ever read** c'est le plus mauvais livre que j'aie jamais lu ■ **this is the ~ thing that could have happened** c'est la pire chose qui pouvait arriver ■ **and, ~ of all, I lost my keys** et le pire de tout, c'est que j'ai perdu mes clés ■ **we came off ~** [in deal] c'est nous qui étions perdants ; [in fight] c'est nous qui avons reçu le plus de coups ■ **I felt ~ of all just after the operation** c'est juste après l'opération que je me suis senti le plus mal **2.** [most severe, serious - disaster, error] le plus grave ; [- winter] le plus rude ■ **the fighting was ~ near the border** les combats les plus violents se sont déroulés près de la frontière.
◇ *adv* [most severely] : **the ~ affected** le plus affecté *OR* touché.
◇ *n* **1.** [worst thing] pire *m* ■ **the ~ that can happen** le pire qui puisse arriver ■ **the ~ of it is she knew all along** le pire, c'est qu'elle le savait depuis le début ■ **money brings out the ~ in people** l'argent réveille les pires instincts (chez les gens) ■ **I fear the ~** je crains le pire ■ **the ~ was yet to come** le pire restait à venir ▶ **if the ~ comes to the ~** au pire, dans le pire des cas ■ **he got the ~ of it** c'est lui qui s'en est le moins bien sorti ■ **do your ~!** *hum* allez-y, je suis prêt ■ **at its ~, at their ~** : **the fever was at its ~ last night** la fièvre était à son paroxysme hier soir ■ **things** *OR* **matters were at their ~** les affaires étaient au plus mal, les choses ne pouvaient pas aller plus mal **2.** [worst person] : **the ~** le/la pire de tous ■ **to be the ~ in the class** être le dernier de la classe.
◇ *vt lit* [opponent, rival] battre, avoir le dessus sur.
◆ **at (the) worst** *conj phr* au pire, dans le pire des cas.

worst- *in cpds* : **the ~dressed** le moins bien habillé ■ **to be the ~off** [financially] être le moins riche ; [in situation] s'en sortir le moins bien.

worst-case *adj* : **the ~ scenario** le scénario catastrophe.

worsted ['wʊstɪd] ◇ *n* worsted *m*, laine *f* peignée.
◇ *adj* [suit] en worsted, en laine peignée ■ **~ cloth** worsted *m*, laine *f* peignée.

worth [wɜːθ] ◇ *adj* **1.** [financially, in value] : **to be ~ £40,000** valoir 40 000 livres ■ **how much is the picture ~?** combien vaut le tableau? ■ **it isn't ~ much** cela ne vaut pas grand-chose ■ **his uncle is ~ several million pounds** la fortune de son oncle s'élève à plusieurs millions de livres ■ **it was ~ every penny** ça en valait vraiment la peine ■ **what's it ~ to you?** vous êtes prêt à y mettre combien? ■ **it isn't ~ the paper it's written on** *fig* ça ne vaut pas le papier sur lequel c'est écrit ▶ **to be ~ one's weight in gold** valoir son pesant d'or ■ **(to be) ~ one's salt** *UK* : **any proofreader ~ his salt would have spotted the mistake** n'importe quel correcteur digne de ce nom aurait relevé l'erreur
2. [emotionally] : **it's ~ a lot to me** j'y attache beaucoup de valeur *OR* de prix ■ **their friendship is ~ a lot to her** leur amitié a beaucoup de prix pour elle ■ **it's more than my job's ~ to cause a fuss** je ne veux pas risquer ma place en faisant des histoires
3. [valid, deserving] : **the church is (well) ~ a visit** l'église vaut la peine d'être visitée *OR* vaut le détour ■ **it's ~ a try** *OR* **trying** cela vaut la peine d'essayer ■ **it wasn't ~ the effort** cela ne valait pas la peine de faire un tel effort, ça n'en valait pas la peine ■ **is the film ~ seeing?** est-ce que le film vaut la peine d'être vu? ■ **don't bother to phone, it isn't ~ it** inutile de téléphoner, cela n'en vaut pas la peine ▶ **if a thing is ~ doing, it's ~ doing well** *prov* si une chose vaut la peine d'être faite, elle vaut la peine d'être bien faite ■ **the game isn't ~ the candle** *UK inf* le jeu n'en vaut pas la chandelle
4. *phr* **it would be ~ your while to check** *OR* **checking** vous auriez intérêt à vérifier ■ **it's not ~ (my) while waiting** cela ne vaut pas la peine d'attendre *OR* que j'attende ■ **I'll make it ~ your while** je vous récompenserai de votre peine ■ **I tried/shouted for all I was ~** j'ai essayé du mieux/crié aussi fort que j'ai pu ■ **for what it's ~** pour ce que cela vaut.
◇ *n* **1.** [in money, value] valeur *f* ■ **£2,000 ~ of damage** pour 2 000 livres de dégâts, des dégâts qui se montent à 2 000 livres ■ **he sold £50 ~ of ice cream** il a vendu pour 50 livres de glaces
2. [of person] valeur *f* ■ **she knows her own ~** elle sait ce qu'elle vaut, elle connaît sa propre valeur
3. [equivalent value] équivalent *m* ■ **a week's ~ of supplies** suffisamment de provisions pour une semaine.

worthily ['wɜːðɪlɪ] *adv* [live, behave] dignement.

worthless ['wɜːθlɪs] *adj* **1.** [goods, land etc] sans valeur, qui ne vaut rien **2.** [useless - attempt] inutile ; [- advice, suggestion] inutile, sans valeur **3.** [person] incapable, qui ne vaut rien.

worthlessness ['wɜːθlɪsnɪs] *n* **1.** [of goods, land etc] absence *f* totale de valeur **2.** [of attempt] inutilité *f* ■ [of advice, suggestion] inutilité *f* **3.** [of person] nullité *f*.

worthwhile [ˌwɜːθ'waɪl] *adj* **1.** [useful - action, visit] qui vaut la peine ; [- job] utile, qui a un sens ■ **they didn't think it was ~ buying** *OR* **to buy a new car** ils ne pensaient pas que ça valait la peine d'acheter une nouvelle voiture **2.** [deserving - cause, project, organization] louable, méritoire **3.** [interesting - book] qui vaut la peine d'être lu ; [- film] qui vaut la peine d'être vu.

worthy ['wɜːðɪ] ◇ *adj* (*comp* **worthier**, *superl* **worthiest**) **1.** [deserving - person] digne, méritant ; [- cause] louable, digne ■ **to be ~ of sthg** être digne de *OR* mériter qqch ■ **to be ~ to do sthg** être digne *OR* mériter de faire qqch ■ **she was a ~ winner** elle méritait bien de gagner ■ **it is ~ of note that...** il est intéressant de remarquer *OR* de noter que... **2.** *hum* excellent, brave.
◇ *n* (*pl* **worthies**) [important person] notable *mf* ■ *hum* brave citoyen *m*, - enne *f*.

wotcha, wotcher ['wɒtʃə] *interj UK inf dial* salut!

would [wʊd] ◇ *pt* ▷ **will**.
◇ *modal vb*

A.

1. [speculating, hypothesizing] : **I'm sure they ~ come if you asked them** je suis sûr qu'ils viendraient si vous le leur demandiez ■ **I wouldn't do that if I were you** je ne ferais pas ça si

j'étais vous *OR* à votre place ■ **you ~ think they had better things to do** on pourrait penser qu'ils ont mieux à faire ■ **they wouldn't have come if they'd known** ils ne seraient pas venus s'ils avaient su ■ **he wouldn't have finished without your help** il n'aurait pas terminé sans votre aide ■ **she ~ have been 16 by now** elle aurait 16 ans maintenant
2. [making polite offers, requests] : **~ you please be quiet!** voulez-vous vous taire, s'il vous plaît! ■ **~ you mind driving me home?** est-ce que cela vous dérangerait de me reconduire chez moi? ■ **~ you like to see her?** aimeriez-vous *OR* voudriez-vous la voir? ■ **~ you like another cup?** en voulez-vous encore une tasse? ■ **I'll do it for you – ~ you?** je vais m'en occuper – vraiment?
3. [expressing preferences, desires] : **I ~ prefer to go** *OR* **I ~ rather go alone** j'aimerais mieux *OR* je préférerais y aller seul ■ **I ~ have preferred to go** *OR* **I ~ rather have gone alone** j'aurais mieux aimé *OR* j'aurais préféré y aller seul ■ **I'd as soon not** j'aimerais mieux pas ■ **he'd rather** *OR* **sooner stay at home than go out dancing** il aimerait mieux rester *OR* il préférerait rester à la maison qu'aller danser

B.
1. [indicating willingness, responsiveness - subj: person, mechanism] : **they ~ give their lives for the cause** ils donneraient leur vie pour la cause ■ **she wouldn't touch alcohol** elle refusait de toucher à l'alcool ■ **I couldn't find anyone who ~ lend me a torch** je n'ai trouvé personne pour me prêter une lampe électrique ■ **the car wouldn't start** la voiture ne voulait pas démarrer
2. [indicating habitual or characteristic behaviour] : **he ~ smoke a cigar after dinner** il fumait un cigare après le dîner ■ **they ~ go and break something!** il fallait qu'ils aillent casser quelque chose! ■ **I didn't really enjoy the fish – you wouldn't, ~ you?** je n'ai pas tellement aimé le poisson – ça m'aurait étonné! ■ **he ~!** c'est bien de lui! ■ **he ~ say that, wouldn't he** il fallait qu'il dise ça
3. [expressing opinions] : **I ~ disagree there** je crains de n'être pas d'accord sur ce point ■ **I ~ imagine it's warmer than here** j'imagine qu'il fait plus chaud qu'ici ■ **I ~ think he'd be pleased** j'aurais cru que ça lui ferait plaisir
4. [giving advice] : **I ~ have a word with her about it(, if I were you)** moi, je lui en parlerais (à votre place)
5. [expressing surprise, incredulity] : **you wouldn't think she was only 15, ~ you?** on ne dirait pas qu'elle n'a que 15 ans, n'est-ce pas? ■ **who ~ have thought it?** qui l'aurait cru?
6. [indicating likelihood, probability] : **there was a woman there – that ~ be his wife** il y avait une femme – ça devait être sa femme

C.
1. [in reported speech] : **it was to be the last time I ~ see him before he left** c'était la dernière fois que je le voyais avant son départ
2. [used with 'have'] : **they ~ have been happy if it hadn't been for the war** ils auraient vécu heureux si la guerre n'était pas survenue ■ **if you ~ have told the truth, this ~ never have happened** *US* si tu m'avais dit la vérité, ça ne serait jamais arrivé
3. *(subjunctive use)* *fml* & *lit* [expressing wishes] : **~ that it were true!** si seulement c'était vrai!

would-be *adj* **1.** [hopeful] : **a ~ writer/MP** une personne qui veut être écrivain/député **2.** *pej* [so-called] prétendu, soi-disant *(inv)*.

wouldn't ['wʊdnt] = **would not**.

wouldst [wʊdst] *arch vb (2nd pers sg)* ▷ **would**.

would've ['wʊdəv] = **would have**.

wound¹ [wu:nd] ◇ *n* **1.** [physical injury] blessure *f*, plaie *f* ■ **a bullet ~** une blessure par balle ■ **she had three knife ~s** elle avait reçu trois coups de couteau ■ **they had serious head ~s** ils avaient été gravement blessés à la tête ■ **to dress a ~** panser une blessure *OR* une plaie **2.** *fig* [emotional or moral] blessure *f*.
◇ *vt* **1.** [physically] blesser ■ **she was ~ed in the foot** elle a été blessée au pied **2.** *fig* [emotionally] blesser ■ **to ~ sb's pride** heurter l'amour-propre de qqn, blesser qqn dans son amour-propre.

wound² [waʊnd] *pt & pp* ▷ **wind** *(twist)*.

wounded ['wu:ndɪd] ◇ *adj* **1.** [soldier, victim] blessé **2.** *fig* [feelings, pride] blessé.
◇ *npl* : **the ~** les blessés *mpl*.

wound-up [waʊnd-] *adj* **1.** [clock] remonté ■ [car window] remonté, fermé **2.** *inf* [tense - person] crispé, très tendu.

wove [wəʊv] *pt* ▷ **weave**.

woven ['wəʊvn] *pp* ▷ **weave**.

wow [waʊ] *inf* ◇ *interj* génial!, super!
◇ *n* **1.** : **it's a real ~!** c'est vraiment super! ■ **he's a ~ at hockey** c'est un super joueur de hockey **2.** ACOUST pleurage *m*.
◇ *vt* [impress] impressionner, emballer, subjuguer.

WP *n* (*abbrev of* **word processing, word processor**) TTX *m*.

WPC (*abbrev of* **woman police constable**) *n UK femme agent de police* ■ **~ Roberts** l'agent Roberts.

wpm (*written abbrev of* **words per minute**) mots/min.

WRAC (*abbrev of* **Women's Royal Army Corps**) *pr n section féminine de l'armée de terre britannique*.

wrack [ræk] *n* **1.** [seaweed] varech *m* **2.** = **rack** *(sense 5)*.

WRAF (*abbrev of* **Women's Royal Air Force**) *pr n section féminine de l'armée de l'air britannique*.

wraith [reɪθ] *n lit* apparition *f*, spectre *m*.

wraithlike ['reɪθlaɪk] *adj lit* spectral.

wrangle ['ræŋgl] ◇ *vi* se disputer, se chamailler ■ **to ~ about** *OR* **over sthg** se disputer à propos de qqch.
◇ *vt US* [cattle, horses] garder.
◇ *n* dispute *f*.

wrangler ['ræŋglər] *n US* [cowboy] cowboy *m*.

wrap [ræp] (*pret & pp* **wrapped**) ◇ *vt* **1.** [goods, parcel, gift, food] emballer, envelopper ■ **she wrapped the scarf in tissue paper** elle a emballé *OR* enveloppé l'écharpe dans du papier de soie **2.** [cocoon, envelop] envelopper, emmailloter ■ **the baby was wrapped in a blanket** le bébé était enveloppé dans une couverture **3.** [twist, wind] : **to ~ round** *OR* **around** enrouler ■ **she had a towel wrapped round her head** sa tête était enveloppée dans une serviette ■ **she had a towel wrapped round her body** elle s'était enveloppée dans une serviette ■ **he wrapped his arms round her** il l'a prise dans ses bras ■ **he wrapped the car round a tree** *inf fig* il s'est payé un arbre.
◇ *n* **1.** [housecoat] peignoir *m* ■ [shawl] châle *m* ■ [blanket, rug] couverture *f* **2.** CIN : **it's a ~!** c'est dans la boîte!
◆ **wraps** *npl fig* **to keep a plan/one's feelings under ~s** garder un plan secret/ses sentiments secrets.
◆ **wrap up** ◇ *vt sep* **1.** [goods, parcel, gift, food] envelopper, emballer, empaqueter ■ **he wrapped the sandwiches up in foil** il a enveloppé les sandwiches dans du papier d'aluminium **2.** [person - in clothes, blanket] envelopper ■ **~ him up in a blanket** enveloppez-le dans une couverture ■ **she was well wrapped up in a thick coat** elle était bien emmitouflée dans un épais manteau ■ **~ yourself up warmly** couvrez-vous bien **3.** *fig* **politicians are skilled at wrapping up bad news in an acceptable form** les politiciens s'y connaissent pour présenter les mauvaises nouvelles sous un jour acceptable **4.** *inf* [conclude - job] terminer, conclure ; [- deal, contract] conclure, régler ■ **let's get this matter wrapped up** finissons-en avec cette question **5.** *US* [summarize] résumer ■ **she wrapped up her talk with three points** elle a résumé son discours en trois points **6.** [engross] : **to be wrapped up in sthg** être absorbé par qqch ■ **they're wrapped up in their children** ils ne vivent que pour leurs enfants ■ **she's very wrapped up in herself** elle est très repliée sur elle-même.
◇ *vi insep* **1.** [dress] s'habiller, se couvrir ■ **~ up warmly** *OR* **well!** couvrez-vous bien! **2.**△ *UK* [shut up] : **~ up!** la ferme!△.

wraparound ['ræpə,raʊnd] ◇ *adj* [skirt] portefeuille *(inv)* ■ : **~ sunglasses** lunettes *fpl* de soleil panoramiques ■ **~ rear window** AUT lunette *f* arrière panoramique.
◇ *n* **1.** [skirt] jupe *f* portefeuille **2.** COMPUT mise à la ligne *f* automatique des mots.
◆ **wraparounds** *npl* [sunglasses] lunettes *fpl* de soleil panoramiques.

wrapover ['ræp,əʊvər] *adj* [dress, skirt] portefeuille *(inv)*.

wrapper ['ræpər] *n* **1.** [for sweet] papier *m* ▪ [for parcel] papier *m* d'emballage **2.** [cover - on book] jaquette *f* ; [- on magazine, newspaper] bande *f* **3.** [housecoat] peignoir *m*.

wrapping ['ræpɪŋ] *n* [on parcel] papier *m* d'emballage ▪ [on sweet] papier *m*.

wrapping paper *n* [for gift] papier *m* cadeau ▪ [for parcel] papier *m* d'emballage.

wrath [rɒθ] *n lit* colère *f*, courroux *m*.

wrathful ['rɒθfʊl] *adj lit* en colère, courroucé.

wreak [ri:k] *vt* **1.** (*pret & pp* **wreaked** *OR* **wrought** [rɔ:t]) [cause - damage, chaos] causer, provoquer ▪ **to ~ havoc** faire des ravages, mettre sens dessus dessous ▪ **the storm ~ed havoc with telephone communications** la tempête a sérieusement perturbé les communications téléphoniques ▪ **it ~ed havoc with my holiday plans** *fig* cela a bouleversé mes projets de vacances **2.** [inflict - revenge, anger] assouvir ▪ **to ~ vengeance on sb** assouvir sa vengeance sur qqn.

wreath [ri:θ] (*pl* **wreaths** [ri:ðz]) *n* **1.** [for funeral] couronne *f* ▪ **the President laid a ~ at the war memorial** le Président a déposé une gerbe au monument aux morts **2.** [garland] guirlande *f* ▪ **a laurel ~** une couronne de laurier **3.** *fig* [of mist] nappe *f* ▪ [of smoke] volute *f*.

wreathe [ri:ð] ◇ *vt* **1.** [shroud] envelopper ▪ **he sat ~d in smoke** il était assis dans un nuage de fumée ▪ **to be ~d in smiles** *fig* être rayonnant **2.** [with flowers - person] couronner ; [- grave, window] orner.
◇ *vi* [smoke] monter en volutes.

wreck [rek] ◇ *n* **1.** [wrecked remains - of ship] épave *f* ; [- of plane] avion *m* accidenté, épave *f* ; [- of train] train *m* accidenté ; [- of car, lorry, bus] véhicule *m* accidenté, épave *f* ▪ **the car was a ~** la voiture était une épave **2.** [wrecking - of ship] naufrage *m* ; [- of plane, car] accident *m* ; [- of train] déraillement *m* **3.** *inf* [dilapidated car] guimbarde *f* ▪ [old bike] clou *m* **4.** *inf* [person] épave *f*, loque *f* ▪ **he's a ~** [physically] c'est une épave ; [mentally] il est à bout ▪ **I must look a ~** je dois avoir une mine de déterré **5.** *fig* [of hopes, of plans] effondrement *m*, anéantissement *m*.
◇ *vt* **1.** [in accident, explosion - ship] provoquer le naufrage de ; [- car, plane] détruire complètement ; [- building] démolir ▪ **the tanker was ~ed off the African coast** le pétrolier a fait naufrage au large des côtes africaines **2.** [damage - furniture] casser, démolir ; [- mechanism] détruire, détraquer **3.** [upset - marriage, relationship] briser ; [- hopes, chances] anéantir ; [- health] briser, ruiner ; [- negotiations] faire échouer, saboter ▪ **she's ~ed my plans** elle a ruiné mes plans.

wreckage ['rekɪdʒ] *n* **1.** *(U)* [debris - from ship, car] débris *mpl* ; [- from building] décombres *mpl* ▪ **a body was found in the ~ of the plane** un corps a été trouvé dans les débris de l'avion **2.** [wrecked ship] épave *f*, navire *m* naufragé **3.** *fig* [of hopes, relationship] anéantissement *m*.

wrecked [rekt] *adj* **1.** [ship] naufragé ▪ [car, plane] complètement détruit ▪ [house] complètement démoli ▪ **~ remains** [of ship] épave *f* ; [of train, car] débris *mpl* ; [of building] décombres *mpl* ▪ **~ cars** épaves *fpl* d'automobiles, voitures *fpl* accidentées **2.** *fig* [relationship, hopes] anéanti **3.** *UK inf* [exhausted] épuisé, crevé **4.** △ *UK* [drunk] plein, bourré.

wrecker ['rekər] *n* **1.** [destroyer] destructeur *m*, - trice *f*, démolisseur *m*, - euse *f* ▪ **marriage-~** briseur *m*, - euse *f* de ménages **2.** *US* [demolition man - for buildings] démolisseur *m* ; [- for cars] ferrailleur *m*, casseur *m* **3.** *US* [breakdown van] dépanneuse *f* **4.** [of ships] naufrageur *m*.

wrecking bar *n* pied-de-biche *m*.

wren [ren] *n* roitelet *m*.

Wren [ren] *n UK auxiliaire féminine de la marine britannique.*

wrench [rentʃ] ◇ *vt* **1.** [pull] tirer violemment sur ▪ **she ~ed the door open** elle a ouvert la porte d'un geste violent ▪ **we'll have to ~ the lid off** nous allons être obligés de forcer le couvercle pour l'ouvrir ▪ **someone ~ed the bag out of my hands** *OR* **from my grasp** quelqu'un m'a arraché le sac des mains ▪ **to ~ o.s. free** se dégager d'un mouvement violent **2.** [eyes, mind] arracher, détacher **3.** [ankle, arm] se faire une entorse à ▪ **I've ~ed my shoulder** je me suis foulé l'épaule.
◇ *vi* : **he ~ed free of his bonds** *liter* il s'est dégagé de ses liens d'un mouvement violent ; *fig* il s'est libéré de ses liens.
◇ *n* **1.** [tug, twist] mouvement *m* violent *(de torsion)* ▪ **with a sudden ~ she pulled herself free** elle se dégagea d'un mouvement brusque ▪ **he gave the handle a ~** il a tiré brusquement *OR* violemment sur la poignée **2.** [to ankle, knee] entorse *f* ▪ **I gave my back a ~** je me suis donné *OR* fait un tour de reins **3.** *fig* [emotional] déchirement *m* **4.** TECH [spanner] clé *f*, clef *f* ▪ [adjustable] clé *f* anglaise ▪ [for wheels] clé *f* en croix ▶ **he threw a ~ into the works** *US* il nous a mis des bâtons dans les roues.

wrest [rest] *vt lit* **1.** [grab - object] arracher violemment ▪ **he ~ed the gun from me** *OR* **from my grasp** il m'a arraché violemment le fusil des mains **2.** [extract - truth, secret] arracher ▪ **he ~ed the truth from her** il lui a arraché la vérité **3.** [control, power] ravir, arracher ▪ **to ~ power from sb** ravir le pouvoir à qqn.

wrestle ['resl] ◇ *vi* **1.** SPORT [Greek, Sumo] lutter, pratiquer la lutte ▪ [freestyle] catcher, pratiquer le catch ▪ **to ~ with sb** lutter (corps à corps) avec qqn, se battre avec qqn **2.** *fig* [struggle] se débattre, lutter ▪ **he died after wrestling with a long illness** il mourut après avoir lutté contre une longue maladie ▪ **she ~d with her conscience** elle se débattait avec sa conscience **3.** [try to control] : **to ~ with sthg** se débattre avec qqch ▪ **the woman ~d to keep control of the car** la femme luttait pour garder le contrôle de la voiture.
◇ *vt* [fight - intruder, enemy] lutter contre ▪ SPORT [Greek, Sumo] rencontrer à la lutte ▪ [freestyle] rencontrer au catch ▪ **he ~d his attacker to the ground** en luttant avec son agresseur, il réussit à le clouer au sol.
◇ *n* lutte *f* ▪ **to have a ~ with sb** lutter avec *OR* contre qqn.

wrestler ['reslər] *n* SPORT [Greek, Sumo] lutteur *m*, - euse *f* ▪ [freestyle] catcheur *m*, - euse *f*.

wrestling ['reslɪŋ] ◇ *n* SPORT [Greek, Sumo] lutte *f* ▪ [freestyle] catch *m*.
◇ *comp* [hold, match - Greek, Sumo] de lutte ; [- freestyle] de catch.

wretch [retʃ] *n* **1.** [unfortunate person] pauvre diable *m*, malheureux *m*, - euse *f* **2.** *lit & hum* [scoundrel] scélérat *m*, - e *f*, misérable *mf* **3.** [child] vilain *m*, - e *f*, coquin *m*, - e *f*.

wretched ['retʃɪd] ◇ *adj* **1.** [awful, poor - dwelling, clothes] misérable ▪ **she receives a ~ wage** elle touche un salaire de misère **2.** [unhappy] malheureux ▪ [depressed] déprimé, démoralisé ▪ **he was** *OR* **felt ~ about what he had said** il se sentait coupable à cause de ce qu'il avait dit **3.** [ill] malade ▪ **the flu made me feel really ~** je me sentais vraiment très mal avec cette grippe **4.** *inf* [as expletive] fichu, maudit **5.** [abominable - behaviour, performance, weather] lamentable ▪ **I'm a ~ singer/writer** je suis un piètre chanteur/écrivain.
◇ *npl* : **the ~** les déshérités *mpl*.

wrick [rɪk] *UK* = **rick** *(vt sense 2, n sense 2)*.

wriggle ['rɪgl] ◇ *vt* **1.** [toes, fingers] tortiller **2.** [subj: person] : **he ~d his way under the fence** il est passé sous la clôture en se tortillant *OR* à plat ventre ▪ [subj: snake, worm] : **the worm was wriggling its way across the grass** le ver avançait dans l'herbe en se tortillant.
◇ *vi* [person] remuer, gigoter ▪ [snake, worm] se tortiller ▪ [fish] frétiller ▪ **to ~ along** [person] avancer en rampant *OR* à plat ventre ; [snake] avancer en se tortillant ▪ **the fish/the little boy ~d from her grasp** le poisson/le petit garçon réussit à s'échapper de ses mains en se tortillant ▪ **she ~d under the fence** elle est passée sous la clôture à plat ventre *OR* en se tortillant ▶ **to ~ free** *liter* se libérer en se tortillant ; *fig* s'en sortir.
◇ *n* : **to give a ~** [snake] se tortiller ; [fish] frétiller ; [person] se tortiller.

➡ **wriggle about** *UK*, **wriggle around** *vi insep* [eel, worm] se tortiller ▪ [fish] frétiller ▪ [person] gigoter, se trémousser.

◆ **wriggle out** *vi insep* **1.** [fish, snake] sortir ■ **the fish ~d out f the net** le poisson s'est échappé du filet en se tortillant . [person] se dégager (en se tortillant) ■ **I managed to ~ out f the situation** *fig* j'ai réussi à me sortir de cette situation.

◆ **wriggle out of** *vt insep* [evade] : **to ~ out of a task** se dé-obercà *OR* esquiver une tâche ■ **he ~d out of paying** il a trouvé n moyen d'éviter de payer.

riggly ['rɪglɪ] *adj* [eel, snake] qui se tortille ■ [fish] frétillant [person] remuant, qui gigote.

ring [rɪŋ] (*pret & pp* **wrung** [rʌŋ]) ◇ *vt* **1.** [wet cloth, clothes] ssorer, tordre ■ **he wrung the towel dry** il a essoré la ser-iette en la tordant ■ **she wrung the water from the sponge** elle exprimé l'eau de l'éponge **2.** [neck] tordre ■ **she wrung the nicken's neck** elle a tordu le cou au poulet ■ **I'll ~ his neck!** *fig* e vais lui tordre le cou! **3.** [hand - in handshake] serrer ■ **to ~ ne's hands (in despair)** se tordre les mains (de désespoir) **it's no use sitting there ~ing your hands** *fig* cela ne sert à rien e rester assis à vous désespérer **4.** [extract - confession] ar-acher ; [- money] extorquer ■ **I'll ~ the truth out of them** je vais eur arracher la vérité ■ **he's ~ing the maximum publicity from ne situation** il profite de la situation pour en tirer le maxi-num de publicité **5.** *fig* [heart] fendre.

◇ *vi* essorer ■ [on label] : **'do not ~'** 'ne pas essorer'.

◇ *n* : **give the cloth a ~** essorez la serpillière.

◆ **wring out** *vt sep* = **wring** *(vt senses 1 & 4)*.

ringer ['rɪŋə^r] *n* essoreuse *f* (à rouleaux) ■ **to put clothes hrough the ~** essorer des vêtements (à la machine) ■ **he has eally been through the ~** *fig* on lui en a fait voir de toutes les ouleurs.

ringing ['rɪŋɪŋ] *adj* : **~ (wet)** [clothes] complètement empé ; [person] complètement trempé, trempé jusqu'aux s ■ **the shirt was ~ with sweat** la chemise était trempée de ueur.

rinkle ['rɪŋkl] ◇ *vt* **1.** [nose] froncer ■ [brow] plisser **.** [skirt, carpet] faire des plis dans.

◇ *vi* **1.** [skin, hands] se rider ■ [brow] se contracter, se plisser [nose] se froncer, se plisser ■ [fruit] se ratatiner, se rider **.** [skirt, stocking] faire des plis.

◇ *n* **1.** [on skin, fruit] ride *f* **2.** [in dress, carpet] pli *m* ■ **there are till some ~s in the plan which need ironing out** *fig* il reste en-ore quelques difficultés à aplanir **3.** *UK inf dated* [trick] com-ine *f* ■ [hint] tuyau *m*.

◆ **wrinkle up** *vi insep & vt sep* = **wrinkle** *(vi & vt)*.

rinkled ['rɪŋkld] *adj* **1.** [skin, hands] ridé ■ [brow, nose] lissé, froncé ■ [fruit] ridé, ratatiné ■ **a ~ old man** un vieillard atatiné **2.** [rug, skirt] qui fait des plis ■ [stocking] qui fait des lis *OR* l'accordéon.

rinkly ['rɪŋklɪ] (*pl* **wrinklies**) ◇ *adj* **1.** [skin] ridé **2.** [stock-ıg] qui fait des plis.

◇ *n UK inf pej* vieux *m*, vieille *f*.

rist [rɪst] *n* poignet *m*.

ristband ['rɪstbænd] *n* [on shirt, blouse] poignet *m* ■ [sweat and] poignet *m* ■ [of watch] bracelet *m*.

ristlet ['rɪstlɪt] *n* bracelet *m*.

ristwatch ['rɪstwɒtʃ] *n* montre-bracelet *f*.

rit [rɪt] ◇ *pt & pp arch* ▷ **write**.

◇ *n* **1.** LAW ordonnance *f* ■ **to issue a ~ against sb** [for arrest] lan-er un mandat d'arrêt contre qqn ; [for libel] assigner qqn en ustice ■ **to serve a ~ on sb, to serve sb with a ~** assigner qn ● **~ of execution** titre *m* exécutoire ■ **~ of subpoena** as-ignation *f OR* citation *f* en justice **2.** POL [for elections] ordon-ance *f (émanant du président de la Chambre des commu-es et convoquant les députés pour un vote)*.

◇ *adj phr* **astonishment was ~ large on everybody's face** l'éton-ement se lisait sur tous les visages.

rite [raɪt] (*pret* **wrote** [rəʊt], *pp* **written** ['rɪtn], *arch pret & pp* **vrit** [rɪt]) ◇ *vt* **1.** [letter] écrire ■ [address, name] écrire, ins-rire ■ [initials] écrire, tracer ■ [prescription, cheque] écrire, aire ■ [will] faire ■ [application form] compléter, rédiger ■ **to ~ letter to sb** écrire *OR* envoyer une lettre à qqn ■ **I have some etters to ~** j'ai du courrier à faire ■ **they wrote me a letter of thanks** ils m'ont écrit pour me remercier ■ **he wrote her a postcard** il lui a envoyé une carte postale ■ **to ~ sb** *US* écrire à qqn ■ **it is written in the Bible "thou shalt love thy neighbour as thyself"** il est écrit dans la bible "tu aimeras ton prochain comme toi-même" ■ **perplexity was written all over his face** *fig* la perplexité se lisait sur son visage

2. [book] écrire ■ [article, report] écrire, faire ■ [essay] faire ■ [music] écrire, composer ■ **well written** bien écrit

3. [send letter about] écrire ■ **he wrote that he was getting married** il a écrit (pour annoncer) qu'il se mariait

4. [spell] écrire

5. COMPUT [program] écrire ■ [data - store] stocker, sauvegarder ; [- transfer] transférer.

◇ *vi* **1.** [gen] écrire ■ **to ~ in pencil/ink** écrire au crayon/à l'encre ■ **I don't ~ very well** je n'ai pas une belle écriture

2. [send letter] écrire ■ **to ~ to sb** écrire à qqn ■ **to ~ to thank/ invite sb** écrire pour remercier/inviter qqn ■ **have you written to let her know?** lui avez-vous écrit pour l'avertir? ■ **she wrote and told me about it** elle m'a écrit pour me le raconter ■ **please ~ (again) soon** écris-moi vite (à nouveau), s'il te plaît ■ **at the time of writing** au moment où j'écris ■ **I've written for a catalogue** j'ai écrit pour demander *OR* pour qu'on m'envoie un catalogue

3. [professionally - as author] écrire, être écrivain ; [- as journalist] écrire, être journaliste ■ **he ~s on home affairs for "The Economist"** il fait des articles de politique intérieure dans "The Economist" ■ **she ~s for "The Independent"** elle écrit dans "The Independent" ■ **he ~s on** *OR* **about archeology** il écrit sur l'archéologie, il traite de questions d'archéologie ■ **they wrote about their experiences in the Amazon** ils ont décrit leurs expériences en Amazonie

4. [pen, typewriter] écrire.

◆ **write away** *vi insep* **1.** [correspond] écrire

2. [order by post] écrire pour demander, commander par lettre ■ **I wrote away for a catalogue** j'ai écrit pour demander *OR* pour qu'on m'envoie un catalogue.

◆ **write back** *vi insep* [answer] répondre (à une lettre) ■ **please ~ back soon** réponds-moi vite, s'il te plaît ■ **he wrote back to say he couldn't come** il a répondu qu'il ne pouvait pas venir ■ **he wrote back rejecting their offer** il a renvoyé une lettre refusant leur offre.

◆ **write down** *vt sep* **1.** [note] écrire, noter ■ [put in writing] mettre par écrit

2. FIN & COMM [in price] réduire le prix de ■ [in value] réduire la valeur de ■ [undervalue] sous-évaluer.

◆ **write in** ◇ *vi insep* écrire ■ **hundreds wrote in to complain** des centaines de personnes ont écrit pour se plaindre.

◇ *vt sep* **1.** [on list, document - word, name] ajouter, insérer

2. *US* POL [add - name] ajouter, inscrire *(sur un bulletin de vote)* ■ [vote for - person] voter pour *(en ajoutant le nom sur le bulletin de vote)*.

◆ **write off** ◇ *vt sep* **1.** FIN [debt] passer aux profits et pertes

2. [consider lost, useless] faire une croix sur, considérer comme perdu ■ [cancel] renoncer à, annuler ■ **the plan had to be written off** le projet a dû être abandonné ■ **three months' hard work was simply written off** on a perdu trois mois de travail acharné ■ **he was written off as a failure** on a considéré qu'il n'y avait rien de bon à en tirer

3. [in accident - subj: insurance company] considérer comme irréparable, mettre à la casse ; [- subj: driver] rendre inutilisable ■ **she wrote off her new car** *UK* elle a complètement démoli sa voiture neuve

4. [letter, poem] écrire en vitesse.

◇ *vi insep* = **write away**.

◆ **write out** *vt sep* **1.** [report] écrire, rédiger ■ [list, cheque] faire, établir ■ **can you ~ the amount out in full?** pouvez-vous écrire la somme en toutes lettres?

2. [copy up - notes] recopier, mettre au propre

3. RADIO & TV [character] faire disparaître.

◆ **write up** *vt sep* **1.** [diary, impressions] écrire, rédiger ■ PRESS [event] faire un compte rendu de, rendre compte de ■ **he wrote up his ideas in a report** il a consigné ses idées dans un rapport

2. [copy up - notes, data] recopier, mettre au propre

3. FIN & COMM [in price] augmenter le prix de ■ [in value] augmenter la valeur de ■ [overvalue] surévaluer.

write head *n* TECH tête *f* d'enregistrement.

write-off *n* **1.** FIN [of bad debt] passage *m* par profits et pertes ■ [bad debt itself] perte *f* sèche **2.** [motor vehicle] : **to be a ~** être irréparable *OR* bon pour la casse.

write-protect *vt* COMPUT protéger contre l'écriture.

write-protected *adj* COMPUT [disk] protégé (en écriture).

writer ['raɪtəʳ] *n* [of novel, play] écrivain *mf*, auteur *mf* ■ [of letter] auteur *mf* ■ **a well-known ~ of novels/poetry** un romancier/poète connu ❯ **technical ~** rédacteur *m*, - trice *f* technique ■ **I'm a bad letter-~** je suis un mauvais correspondant.

writer's block *n* angoisse *f* de la page blanche.

writer's cramp *n* crampe *f* de l'écrivain.

write-up *n* **1.** [review] compte rendu *m*, critique *f* ■ **the play got a good ~** la pièce a eu une bonne critique *OR* a été bien accueillie par la critique ■ **the guide contains ~s of several ski resorts** le guide contient des notices descriptives sur plusieurs stations de ski **2.** *US* [of assets] surestimation *f*.

writhe [raɪð] *vi* **1.** [in pain] se tordre, se contorsionner ■ **to ~ in** *OR* **with agony** se tordre de douleur, être en proie à d'atroces souffrances **2.** *fig* **her remarks made him ~** [in disgust] ses remarques l'ont fait frémir ; [in embarrassment] ses remarques lui ont fait souffrir le martyre.
◆ **writhe about** *UK*, **writhe around** *vi insep* se tortiller ■ **to ~ about in pain** se tordre de douleur.

writing ['raɪtɪŋ] *n* **1.** [of books, letters] écriture *f* ■ **it's a good piece of ~** c'est bien écrit ■ **this is clear, concise ~** c'est un style clair et concis, c'est écrit avec clarté et concision ■ **the report was four years in the ~** il a fallu quatre ans pour rédiger le rapport ■ **at time of ~** PRESS à l'heure où nous mettons sous presse **2.** [handwriting] écriture *f* ■ **I can't read your ~** je ne peux pas déchiffrer votre écriture *OR* ce que vous avez écrit **3.** [written text] : **there was ~ all over the board** il n'y avait plus de place pour écrire quoi que ce soit sur le tableau noir ❯ **the ~'s on the wall** l'issue est inéluctable **4.** SCH [spelling] orthographe *f* ■ [written language] écriture *f* ■ **to learn reading and ~** apprendre à lire et à écrire, apprendre la lecture et l'écriture ■ **~ materials** matériel *m* nécessaire pour écrire.
◆ **writings** *npl* [written works] œuvre *f*, écrits *mpl*.
◆ **in writing** *adv phr* par écrit ■ **to put sthg in ~** mettre qqch par écrit ■ **you need her agreement in ~** il vous faut son accord écrit.

writing block *n* bloc *m* de papier à lettres.

writing case *n* nécessaire *m* à écrire.

writing desk *n* secrétaire *m (meuble)*.

writing pad *n* bloc-notes *m*.

writing paper *n* papier *m* à lettres.

written ['rɪtn] ◇ *pp* ▷ **write**.
◇ *adj* [form, text] écrit ■ **~ language** écrit *m* ■ **the ~ word** l'écrit.

WRNS (*abbrev of* **Women's Royal Naval Service**) *pr n section féminine de la marine de guerre britannique.*

wrong [rɒŋ] ◇ *adj* **1.** [incorrect - address, answer, information] mauvais, faux, fausse *f*, erroné ; [- decision] mauvais ■ MUS [note] faux, fausse *f* ■ TELEC [number] faux, fausse *f* ■ **to get things in the ~ order** mettre les choses dans le mauvais ordre ■ **to take the ~ road/train** se tromper de route/de train ■ **she went to the ~ address** elle s'est trompée d'adresse ■ **the biscuit went down the ~ way** j'ai avalé le gâteau de travers ■ **it was a ~ number** c'était une erreur ■ **to dial the ~ number** se tromper de numéro ■ **I'm sorry, you've got the ~ number** désolé, vous vous êtes trompé de numéro *OR* vous faites erreur ■ **the clock/my watch is ~** le réveil/ma montre n'est pas à l'heure
2. [mistaken - person] : **to be ~ (about sthg)** avoir tort *OR* se tromper (à propos de qqch) ■ **you were ~ to accuse him, it was ~ of you to accuse him** vous avez eu tort de l'accuser, vous n'auriez pas dû l'accuser ■ **to be ~ about sb** se tromper sur le compte de qqn ■ **how ~ can you be!** comme quoi on peut se tromper! ■ **I hope he won't get the ~ idea about me** j'espère qu'il ne se fera pas de fausses idées sur mon com ■ **I hope you won't take this the ~ way, but...** ne le prends mal, mais...
3. [unsuitable] mauvais, mal choisi ■ **you've got the ~ atti** vous n'avez pas l'attitude qu'il faut *OR* la bonne attitude **was the ~ thing to do/say** ce n'était pas la chose à faire/d ■ **I said all the ~ things** j'ai dit tout ce qu'il ne fallait pas d ■ **you're going about it in the ~ way** vous vous y prenez n ■ **it's the ~ way to deal with the situation** ce n'est pas com cela qu'il faut régler la situation ■ **I think you're in the ~** *liter* je pense que ce n'est pas le travail qu'il vous faut ; vous vous êtes trompé de métier! ■ **she was wearing th shoes for a long walk** elle n'avait pas les chaussures qui c viennent *OR* elle n'avait pas les bonnes chaussures p une randonnée
4. *phr* **he got hold of the ~ end of the stick** il a tout compris travers ■ **they got off on the ~ foot** ils se sont mal entenc au départ ■ **I'm (on) the ~ side of 50** *UK* j'ai 50 ans bien sonr ■ **to get out of bed on the ~ side** se lever du pied gauche ■ **get on the ~ side of sb** se faire mal voir de qqn
5. [immoral, bad] mal ■ [unjust] injuste ■ **cheating is ~** c'est n de tricher ■ **slavery is ~** l'esclavage est inacceptable ■ **it w ~ of him to take the money** ce n'était pas bien de sa part prendre l'argent ■ **what's ~ with reading comics?** qu'est qu'il y a de mal à lire des bandes dessinées? ■ **there's no ing ~ with it** il n'y a rien à redire à cela, il n'y a pas de ma cela ■ **it's ~ that anyone should have to live in poverty** il est juste que des gens soient obligés de vivre dans la misè
6. *(with 'something')* [amiss] : **something is ~** *OR* **there's so thing ~ with the lamp** la lampe ne marche pas bien *OR* a défaut ■ **something is ~** *OR* **there's something ~ with my elb** j'ai quelque chose au coude ■ **there's something ~ somewh** il y a quelque chose qui ne va pas quelque part ■ *(with 'no ing')* **there's nothing at all ~ with the clock** la pendule marc parfaitement bien ■ **there's nothing ~ with her decision/reas ing** sa décision/son raisonnement est parfaitement vala ■ **there's nothing ~ with you** vous êtes en parfaite sa ■ **there's nothing ~, thank you** tout va bien, merci ■ **the nothing ~ with your eyes/hearing!** vous avez de bons yeux/ bonnes oreilles! ■ *(with 'what's')* **what's ~?** qu'est-ce qui va pas? ■ **what's ~ with the car?** qu'est-ce qu'elle a, la voitu ■ **what's ~ with you?** qu'est-ce que vous avez? ■ **there's v little ~ with you** dans l'ensemble vous êtes en très bon santé ■ **there wasn't much ~ with the car** la voiture n'avait grand-chose ❯ **to be ~ in the head** *UK inf* avoir la tête fê *OR* le cerveau fêlé, être fêlé *OR* timbré
7. TEX : **the ~ side of the fabric** l'envers *m* du tissu ■ **~ side** à l'envers.
◇ *adv* mal ■ **I guessed ~** je suis tombé à côté, je me s trompé ■ **to get sthg ~ : I got the answer ~** je n'ai pas donn bonne réponse ■ **to get one's sums ~** MATHS faire des erre dans ses opérations ; *fig* se tromper dans ses calculs ■ **sh got her facts ~** elle se trompe, ce qu'elle avance est fa ■ **you've got it ~, I never said that** vous vous trompez *OR* v n'avez pas compris, je n'ai jamais dit cela ■ **to get sb ~ : d get me ~** comprenez-moi bien ■ **you've got her all ~** vous v trompez complètement sur son compte ■ **to go ~** [person] tromper ; [plan] mal marcher, mal tourner ; [deal] tombe l'eau ; [machine] tomber en panne ■ **something has gone ~ w the TV** la télé est tombée en panne ■ **something went ~ w her eyesight** elle a eu des ennuis avec sa vue ■ **you won't far ~ if you follow her advice** vous ne risquez guère de v tromper si vous suivez ses conseils ■ **you can't go ~ wit pair of jeans** vous êtes tranquille avec un jean ■ **you can't ~ with a good book** [for reading] vous ne risquez pas de v ennuyer avec un bon livre ; [as present] un bon livre, c plaît toujours ■ **when did things start going ~?** quand est que les choses ont commencé à se gâter? ■ **everything t could go ~ went ~** tout ce qui pouvait aller de travers est a de travers ■ **to turn out ~** [event] mal (se) terminer ; [calc tion] se révéler faux ; [person] mal tourner.
◇ *n* **1.** [immorality, immoral act] mal *m* ■ **to know the differe between right and ~** savoir distinguer le bien du mal ❯ **t ~s don't make a right** *prov* on ne répare pas une injustice une autre
2. [harm] tort *m*, injustice *f* ■ **to do sb ~** faire du tort à *OR* montrer injuste envers qqn ■ **he did them a great ~** il leu fait subir une grave injustice, il leur a fait (un) grand to

3. [error] tort *m*, erreur *f* ▪ **he can do no ~ in her eyes** tout ce qu'il fait trouve grâce à ses yeux
4. LAW tort *m*.
> *vt* faire du tort à, traiter injustement ▪ **she felt deeply ~ed** elle se sentait gravement lésée ▪ **she has been badly ~ed** [by words] on a dit à tort beaucoup de mal d'elle ; [by actions] on a agi de manière injuste envers elle.
◆ **in the wrong** *adj & adv phr* dans son tort ▪ **to be in the ~** être dans son tort, avoir tort.

wrongdoer [ˌrɒŋ'du:ər] *n* **1.** [delinquent] malfaiteur *m*, délinquant *m*, - e *f* **2.** [sinner] pécheur *m*, - eresse *f*.

wrongdoing [ˌrɒŋ'du:ɪŋ] *n* mal *m*, méfait *m*.

wrong-foot *vt* SPORT & *fig* prendre à contre-pied.

wrongful ['rɒŋfʊl] *adj* [unjust] injuste ▪ [unjustified] injustifié ▪ [illegal] illégal, illicite ▪ LAW : **~ arrest** arrestation *f* arbitraire ▪ **~ imprisonment** emprisonnement *m* injustifié ▪ **~ dismissal** INDUST renvoi *m* injustifié.

wrongfully ['rɒŋfʊlɪ] *adv* à tort.

wrongheaded [ˌrɒŋ'hedɪd] *adj* **1.** [person] buté **2.** [idea] erroné, fou *(before vowel or silent 'h'* **fol***)*, folle *f*.

wrongly ['rɒŋlɪ] *adv* **1.** [incorrectly] à tort, mal ▪ **this word is spelt ~** ce mot est mal écrit OR orthographié ▪ **I guessed ~** je suis tombé à côté, je me suis trompé **2.** [by mistake] par erreur, à tort.

wrote [rəʊt] *pt* ▻ **write**.

wrought [rɔ:t] <> *pt & pp arch* ▻ **work**.
> *adj lit* **wheels ~ by hand** des roues façonnées OR fabriquées à la main ▪ **carefully ~ prose** prose *f* finement ciselée ⊙ **~ copper** cuivre *m* martelé.

wrought iron *n* fer *m* forgé.
◆ **wrought-iron** *adj* en fer forgé.

wrought-up *adj* énervé.

wrung [rʌŋ] *pt & pp* ▻ **wring**.

WRVS (*abbrev of* **Women's Royal Voluntary Service**) *pr n association de femmes au service des déshérités.*

wry [raɪ] (*comp* **wrier** OR **wryer**, *superl* **wriest** OR **wryest**) *adj* **1.** [expression, glance - of distaste] désabusé **2.** [ironic - comment, smile] ironique, désabusé ▪ **~ humour** ironie *f*.

wryly ['raɪlɪ] *adv* de manière désabusée, ironiquement.

wt. (*written abbrev of* **weight**) pds.

WTO [ˌdʌblju:ti:'əʊ] (*abbrev of* **World Trade Organization**) *n* OMC *f*.

wurst [wɜ:st] *n grosse saucisse allemande.*

WV *written abbr of* **West Virginia**.

WW *written abbr of* **World War**.

WWF (*abbrev of* **Worldwide Fund for Nature**) *pr n* WWF *m*.

WWW *n* = **World Wide Web**.

WY *written abbr of* **Wyoming**.

wych elm [wɪtʃ-] *n* orme *m*.

Wyoming [waɪ'əʊmɪŋ] *pr n* Wyoming *m* ▪ **in ~** dans le Wyoming.

WYSIWYG ['wɪzɪwɪg] (*abbrev of* **what you see is what you get**) *n & adj* COMPUT *tel écran, tel écrit: ce que l'on voit sur l'écran est ce que l'on obtient à l'impression.*

x *n* MATHS x *m*.

x (*pl* **x's** *OR pl* **xs**), **X** (*pl* **X's** *OR pl* **Xs**) [eks] *n* [letter] x *m*, X *m*, *see also* **f**.

X (*pret & pp* **X-ed** *OR* **X'd**) ◇ *n* **1.** [unknown factor] X *m* ▪ **X marks the spot** l'endroit est marqué d'une croix ▪ **Mr X** monsieur X **2.** CIN film *m* interdit aux moins de 18 ans *(remplacé en 1982 par "18").*
◇ **1.** (*written abbrev of* **kiss**) *formule affectueuse placée après la signature à la fin d'une lettre* **2.** *written abbr of* **Christ**.
◇ *vt* marquer d'une croix.

x-axis *n* axe *m* des x, abscisse *f*.

X certificate *n* *UK* *signalait (jusqu'en 1982) un film interdit aux moins de 18 ans.*

X chromosome *n* chromosome *m* X.

x-coordinate *n* abscisse *f*.

xenophobia [,zenə'fəubjə] *n* xénophobie *f*.

xenophobic [,zenə'fəubɪk] *adj* xénophobe.

xerox ['zɪərɒks] *vt* photocopier.

Xerox® ['zɪərɒks] *n* **1.** [machine] copieur *m*, photocopieuse **2.** [process, copy] photocopie *f*.

XL (*written abbrev of* **extra-large**) *n* XL *m*.

Xmas *written abbr of* **Christmas**.

XML [,eksem'el] (*abbrev of* **Extensible Markup Language**) COMPUT XML *m*.

X-rated [-reɪtɪd] *adj* *dated* [film] interdit aux mineurs *OR* au moins de 18 ans.

x-ray, X-ray ◇ *vt* **1.** MED [examine - chest, ankle] radiographier, faire une radio de ; [- patient] faire une radio à **2.** [inspect - luggage] passer aux rayons X **3.** [treat] traiter au rayons X.
◇ *n* **1.** MED radio *f* ▪ **to have an ~** passer une radio ▪ **to take an ~ of sthg** radiographier qqch, faire une radiographie d qqch **2.** PHYS rayon *m* X.
◇ *comp* **1.** MED [examination] radioscopique ▪ [treatment] radiologique, par rayons X ▪ **~ photograph** radiographie *f*, radio *f* ▪ **~ therapy** radiothérapie *f* **2.** PHYS [astronomy, tube] rayons X.

xylophone ['zaɪləfəun] *n* xylophone *m*.

Y

y *n* MATHS y *m*.

y (*pl* **y's** *OR pl* **ys**)**, Y** (*pl* **Y's** *OR pl* **Ys**) [waɪ] *n* [letter] y *m*, Y *m*, *see also* **f**.

Y2K (*abbrev of* **the year 2000**) *n* : ~ [year] l'an 2000 ; [millennium bug] le bogue de l'an 2000.

yacht [jɒt] ◇ *n* [sailing boat] voilier *m* ■ [pleasure boat] yacht *m*.
◇ *comp* [race] de voiliers, de yachts ■ ~ **club** yacht-club *m*.
◇ *vi* faire du yachting ■ **to go ~ing** faire de la voile *OR* du yachting.

yachting ['jɒtɪŋ] ◇ *n* yachting *m*, navigation *f* de plaisance.
◇ *comp* [holiday] en yacht, sur l'eau ■ [magazine] de voile ■ [cap] de marin.

yachtsman ['jɒtsmən] (*pl* **yachtsmen** [-mən]) *n* yachtman *m*, yachtsman *m*.

yachtswoman ['jɒts,wʊmən] (*pl* **yachtswomen** [-,wɪmɪn]) *n* yachtwoman *f*.

yack [jæk] = **yak** *(n sense 2 & vi)*.

yackety-yak [,jækətɪ'jæk] *inf* ◇ *vi* jacasser.
◇ *n (U)* jacasserie *f*.

yahoo [jɑ:'hu:] (*pl* **yahoos**) *n* rustre *m*, butor *m*.

yak [jæk] (*pret & pp* **yakked**, *cont* **yakking**) ◇ *n* **1.** ZOOL yak *m*, yack *m* **2.** *inf (U) inf* jacasserie *f*.
◇ *vi inf* **to ~ on** *UK*, **to ~** jacasser.

Yale [jeɪl] *pr n* Yale *(prestigieuse université dans le Connecticut, faisant partie de la Ivy League)*.

Yale lock® [jeɪl-] *n* serrure *f* de sécurité *(à cylindre)*.

y'all [jɑ:l] *US inf* = **you-all**.

Yalta ['jæltə] *pr n* Yalta.

yam [jæm] *n* **1.** [plant, vegetable] igname *f* **2.** *US* CULIN patate *f* douce.

yang [jæŋ] *n* yang *m*.

Yangtze ['jæŋtsɪ] *pr n* : **the ~** le Yang-tseu-kiang, le Yangzi Jiang.

yank [jæŋk] ◇ *vt* [hair, sleeve] tirer brusquement (sur), tirer d'un coup sec ■ **he was ~ed to his feet** on l'a tiré brutalement pour l'obliger à se lever.
◇ *n* coup *m* sec ■ **I gave the wire/her hair a ~** j'ai tiré d'un coup sec sur le fil/sur ses cheveux.
◆ **yank off** *vt sep* [button, cover] arracher.
◆ **yank out** *vt sep* [nail, tooth] arracher.

Yank [jæŋk] *inf* ◇ *n* **1.** *UK pej* Amerloque *mf* **2.** *US* Yankee *mf*.
◇ *adj UK pej* amerloque.

Yankee ['jæŋkɪ] ◇ *n* **1.** *US* Yankee *mf* **2.** *UK inf pej* Amerloque *mf*.
◇ *adj* **1.** *US* yankee **2.** *UK inf pej* amerloque.

yap [jæp] (*pret & pp* **yapped**, *cont* **yapping**) ◇ *vi* **1.** [dog] japper **2.** [person] jacasser.
◇ *n* [yelp] jappement *m*.

yard [jɑ:d] *n* **1.** [of factory, farm, house, school] cour *f* **2.** [work site] chantier *m* ■ **builder's ~** chantier de construction **3.** [for storage] dépôt *m* **4.** RAIL voies *fpl* de garage **5.** [for animals - enclosure] enclos *m* ; [- pasture] pâturage *m* **6.** *UK* **the Yard** *inf* Scotland Yard **7.** *US* [backyard] cour *f* ■ [garden] jardin *m* **8.** [unit of measure] yard *m (0,914 m)* ■ **it was ten ~s wide** il avait dix mètres de large ■ **to buy cloth by the ~** acheter le tissu au mètre ■ **we still have ~s of green velvet** *fig* nous avons toujours des quantités de velours vert ➤ **his face was a ~ long** il en faisait une tête, il faisait une tête d'enterrement **9.** SPORT & *dated* **the 100 ~s, the 100 ~s' dash** le cent mètres **10.** NAUT vergue *f*.

yardarm ['jɑ:dɑ:m] *n* extrémité *f* d'une vergue carrée.

yard sale *n US* vide-greniers *m*.

yardstick ['jɑ:dstɪk] *n* **1.** [instrument] mètre *m (en bois ou en métal)* **2.** *fig* critère *m*.

yarmulke [jɑ:'mʊlkə] *n* kippa *f*.

yarn [jɑ:n] ◇ *n* **1.** TEX *(U)* fil *m (à tricoter ou à tisser)* **2.** [tall story] histoire *f* (incroyable *OR* invraisemblable) ■ [long story] longue histoire *f*.
◇ *vi* [tell tall stories] raconter des histoires ■ [tell long stories] raconter de longues histoires.

yashmak ['jæʃmæk] *n* litham *m*, litsam *m*.

yaw [jɔ:] ◇ *vi* **1.** [ship] être déporté, faire une embardée **2.** [plane, missile] faire un mouvement de lacet.
◇ *vt* faire dévier de sa trajectoire.
◇ *n* **1.** [of ship] écart *m*, embardée *f* **2.** [of plane, missile] mouvement *m* de lacet.

yawl [jɔ:l] *n* **1.** [sailing boat] yawl *m* **2.** [carried on ship] canot *m*.

yawn [jɔ:n] ◇ *vi* **1.** [person] bâiller **2.** [chasm, opening] être béant, s'ouvrir.
◇ *vt* [utter with yawn] dire en bâillant ■ **she was ~ing her head off** *inf* elle bâillait à se décrocher la mâchoire.
◇ *n* **1.** [of person] bâillement *m* ■ **to give a big ~** bâiller (bruyamment) la bouche grande ouverte **2.** *inf fig* **to be a ~** [meeting] être ennuyeux ; [film, book] être rasoir.

yawning ['jɔ:nɪŋ] ◇ *adj* **1.** [person] qui bâille **2.** [gap, chasm] béant.
◇ *n (U)* bâillement *m*, bâillements *mpl*.

y-axis *n* axe *m* des y *OR* des ordonnées.

Y chromosome *n* chromosome *m* Y.

y-coordinate *n* ordonnée *f*.

yd *written abbr of* **yard**.

ye [ji:] ◇ *pron arch* & BIBLE vous.
◇ *def art arch* ~ **olde inne** la vieille hostellerie.

YE OLDE

On utilise cette graphie ancienne de *the old* pour donner à des appellations souvent commerciales une apparence pseudo-historique : ainsi, dans une ville ancienne, on trouvera des salons de thé portant le nom de *ye olde tea shoppe*.

yea [jeɪ] ◇ *adv* **1.** [yes] oui ■ **you know you can say ~ or nay to the plan** vous savez bien que vous avez la faculté d'accepter ou de refuser ce projet **2.** *arch* & *lit* [indeed] voire, vraiment.
◇ *n* [in vote] oui *m*.

yeah [jeə] *adv* & *interj inf* [yes] ouais.

year [jɪəʳ] *n* **1.** [period of time] an *m*, année *f* ■ **this ~** cette année ■ **last ~** l'an dernier, l'année dernière ■ **next ~** l'année prochaine ■ **the ~ after next** dans deux ans ■ **~ by ~** d'année en année ■ **all (the) ~ round** (pendant) toute l'année ■ **~ in ~ out** année après année ■ **it was five ~s last Christmas** ça a fait cinq ans à Noël ■ **we'll have been here five ~s next Christmas** cela fera cinq ans à Noël que nous sommes là ■ **after ten ~s in politics** après dix ans passés dans la politique ▌ [with 'in'] : **in a few ~s, in a few ~s' time** dans quelques années ■ **in ten ~s, in ten ~s' time** dans dix ans ■ **in all my ~s as a social worker** au cours de toutes mes années d'assistante sociale ▌ [with 'for'] : **I haven't seen her for ~s** je ne l'ai pas vue depuis des années ■ **for a few ~s** pendant quelques années ■ **I haven't been home for two long ~s** cela fait deux longues années que je ne suis pas rentré chez moi ■ **for ~s and ~s** pendant des années ■ **she'll be busy writing her memoirs for ~s** elle en a pour des années de travail à écrire ses mémoires ▌ [with 'ago'] : **two ~s ago** il y a deux ans ■ **that was many ~s ago** cela remonte à bien des années ▌ [with 'last', 'take'] : **the batteries last (for) ~s** les piles durent des années ■ **it took me ~s to build up the collection** cela m' a demandé des années pour *OR* j'ai mis des années à rassembler cette collection ▌ [with 'earn', 'cost' etc] : **he earns over £40,000 a ~** il gagne plus de 40 000 livres par an ■ **it cost me a ~'s salary** cela m'a coûté un an de salaire
2. [in calendar] an *m*, année *f* ■ **in the ~ 1607** en (l'an) 1607 ■ **in the ~ of grace 1900** en l'an de grâce 1900 ➊ **since the ~ dot** *UK*, **since ~ one** *US* depuis une éternité, de tout temps
3. [in age] : **he is 15 ~s old** *OR* **of age** il a 15 ans ■ **the foundations are 4,000 ~s old** les fondations sont vieilles de 4 000 ans ■ **she died in her fiftieth ~** elle est morte dans sa cinquantième année ■ **she's young for her ~s** elle fait jeune pour son âge, elle ne fait pas son âge ■ **I'm getting on in ~s** je prends de l'âge ■ **the experience put ~s on/took ~s off her** l'expérience l'a beaucoup vieillie/rajeunie ■ **the carpet is beginning to show its ~s** la moquette commence à trahir son âge
4. SCH & UNIV année *f* ■ **he's in the first ~** [at school] ≃ il est en sixième ; [at college, university] il est en première année
5. [for wine, coin] année *f*.

yearbook ['jɪəbʊk] *n* annuaire *m*, recueil *m* annuel.

YEARBOOK

Aux États-Unis, les écoles, les universités et certaines colonies de vacances ont un *yearbook*, qui rassemble des photos et des adresses mais aussi des anecdotes sur l'année écoulée.

year-end ◇ *adj UK* de fin d'année ■ **a ~ report** un rapport annuel.
◇ *n* : **at the ~** à la fin de l'année, en fin d'année.

yearling ['jɪəlɪŋ] ◇ *n* ZOOL petit *m* d'un an ■ EQUIT yearling *m*.
◇ *adj* ZOOL (âgé) d'un an.

yearlong [ˌjɪə'lɒŋ] *adj* de toute une année ■ **a ~ drought** une sécheresse qui a duré toute une année.

yearly ['jɪəlɪ] (*pl* **yearlies**) ◇ *adj* annuel.
◇ *adv* annuellement.
◇ *n* PRESS publication *f* annuelle.

yearn [jɜ:n] *vi* **1.** [desire, crave] languir, aspirer ■ [pine] languir ■ **she ~ed for love** *OR* **to be loved** elle aspirait à l'amou elle avait très envie d'être aimée ■ **to ~ to do sthg** mour d'envie *OR* brûler de faire qqch ■ **she ~ed to see her hom again, she ~ed for home** elle avait la nostalgie du pays **2.** [be moved - person] s'attendrir, s'émouvoir ; [- heart] s'atter drir.

yearning ['jɜ:nɪŋ] *n* [longing] désir *m* ardent ■ [pining] nos talgie *f* ■ **he feels a constant ~ to see his old friends** *OR* **for his o friends** il n'aspire qu'à une chose, revoir ses vieux amis.

year-round *adj* [activity] qui dure toute l'année, sur tout l'année ■ [facility] qui fonctionne toute l'année.

yeast [ji:st] ◇ *n* levure *f*.
◇ *vi* mousser.

yeast infection *n* [vaginal thrush] mycose *f* vaginale.

yeasty ['ji:stɪ] (*comp* **yeastier**, *superl* **yeastiest**) *adj* **1.** [bread rolls - in taste] qui a un goût de levure ; [- in smell] à l'odeur d levure **2.** [frothy] écumeux, qui mousse **3.** *UK* [trivial, frivolous frivole, superficiel.

yell [jel] ◇ *vi* crier (à tue-tête) ■ **to ~ at sb** crier après qq ■ **to ~ about sthg** brailler au sujet de qqch ■ **to ~ at the top o one's voice** vociférer.
◇ *vt* [shout out] hurler, crier ■ [proclaim] clamer, crier ■ **he wa ~ing his head off** *inf* il beuglait comme un veau.
◇ *n* **1.** [shout] cri *m*, hurlement *m* ■ **to give a ~ of terror** pous ser un cri de terreur **2.** *US* [from students, supporters] cri *m* d ralliement ■ **the Buffstone ~** [students] le cri de ralliement de étudiants de Buffstone ; [supporters] le cri de ralliement de supporters de Buffstone.

yelling ['jelɪŋ] *n (U)* cris *mpl*, hurlements *mpl*.

yellow ['jeləʊ] ◇ *adj* **1.** [in colour] jaune ■ **the papers ha gone** *OR* **turned ~ with age** les papiers avaient jauni avec le temps ➊ **~ cab** *taxi new-yorkais* **2.** *inf* [cowardly] lâche.
◇ *n* **1.** [colour] jaune *m* **2.** [yolk] jaune *m* (d'œuf) **3.** [in snooker boule *f* jaune.
◇ *vi* jaunir ■ **to ~ with age** jaunir avec le temps.
◇ *vt* jaunir ■ **newspapers ~ed with age** des journaux jauni par le temps.

yellow-belly *n inf* trouillard *m*, - e *f*.

yellow card *n* FTBL carton *m* jaune.

yellow fever *n* fièvre *f* jaune.

yellowhammer ['jeləʊˌhæməʳ] *n* bruant *m* jaune ■ **the Yellowhammer State** l'Alabama.

yellow light *n US* feu *m* orange.

yellow line *n* bande *f* jaune ■ **to park on a ~** ≃ se mettre en stationnement irrégulier ■ **to be parked on a double ~** être en stationnement interdit.

YELLOW LINES

En Grande-Bretagne, une ligne jaune parallèle au trottoir signifie « arrêt autorisé réglementé » ; une double ligne jaune signifie « stationnement interdit ».

Yellow Pages® *npl* : **the ~** les Pages Jaunes.

yellow ribbon *n US ruban jaune arboré en signe de patriotisme et de solidarité avec ceux qui sont au combat, prisonniers politiques etc.*

Yellow River *pr n* : **the ~** le fleuve Jaune.

Yellow Sea *pr n* : **the ~** la mer Jaune.

yelp [jelp] ◇ *vi* [dog] japper, glapir ■ [person] crier, glapir.
◇ *n* [of dog] jappement *m*, glapissement *m* ■ [of person] cri *m*, glapissement *m*.

Yeltsin ['jeltsɪn] *pr n* : **Boris ~** Boris Eltsine.

Yemen ['jemən] *pr n* Yémen *m* ■ **in (the) ~** au Yémen ■ **the ~ Arab Republic** la République arabe du Yémen ■ **the People's Democratic Republic of ~** la République démocratique et populaire du Yémen ■ **the ~ Republic** la République du Yémen.

Yemeni ['jemənɪ] ◇ *n* Yéménite *mf*.
◇ *adj* yéménite.

yen [jen] *n* **1.** (*pl inv*) [currency] yen *m* **2.** *inf* [desire] envie *f* ■ **to have a ~ for sthg/to do sthg** avoir très envie de *OR* mourir d'envie de qqch/faire qqch.

yeoman ['jəumən] (*pl* **yeomen** [-mən]) *n* [in UK] yeoman *m*.

yeomanry ['jəumənrɪ] *n* yeomanry *f*, ensemble *m* des yeomen.

yep [jep] *interj inf* ouais.

yer [jɜː] *adj inf* votre, ton (*f* ta, *pl* tes).

yes [jes] ◇ *adv* **1.** [gen] oui ■ [in answer to negatives] si ■ [answering knock on door] oui (entrez) ■ [answering phone] allô, oui ■ [encouraging a speaker to continue] oui, et puis?, oui, et alors? ■ **to say/to vote ~** dire/voter oui ■ **is it raining? – ~ (it is)** est-ce qu'il pleut? – oui ■ **will you tell her? – ~ (I will)** le lui direz-vous? – oui (je vais le faire) ■ **oh ~?** [doubtful] c'est vrai? ■ **you don't like me, do you? – ~ I do!** vous ne m'aimez pas, n'est-ce pas? – mais si (voyons)! **2.** [introducing a contrary opinion] : **~ but...** oui *OR* d'accord mais... **3.** [in response to command or call] oui ■ **~, sir** oui *OR* bien, monsieur **4.** [indeed] en effet, vraiment ■ **she was rash, ~, terribly rash** elle a été imprudente, vraiment très imprudente.
◇ *n* [person, vote] : **to count the ~es** compter les oui *OR* les votes pour.
◇ *comp* : **~ vote** vote *m* pour.
◆ **yes and no** *adv phr* oui et non.

yes-man *n inf* béni-oui-oui *m inv*.

yesterday ['jestədɪ] ◇ *adv* **1.** hier ■ **~ morning/afternoon** hier matin/après-midi ■ **~ week** *UK*, **a week ~, a week ago ~** il y a huit jours ▶ **I wasn't born ~** je ne suis pas né de la dernière pluie **2.** [in the past] hier, naguère.
◇ *n* **1.** [day before] hier *m* ■ **~ was Monday** hier c'était lundi ■ **~'s programme** le programme d'hier ■ **the day before ~** avant-hier ■ **it seems like (only) ~** c'est comme si c'était hier **2.** [former times] temps *mpl* passés *OR* anciens ■ **~'s fashions** les coutumes d'hier *OR* d'autrefois ■ **all our ~s** tout notre passé.

yesteryear ['jestəjɪəʳ] *n fml & lit* temps *m* jadis.

yet [jet] ◇ *adv* **1.** [up to now] déjà ■ **is he here ~?** est-il déjà là? ■ **have you been to London ~?** êtes-vous déjà allés à Londres? ■ **did you go to the zoo ~?** *US* êtes-vous déjà allés au zoo?
2. [at the present time] : **not ~** pas encore ■ **not just ~** pas tout de suite ■ **she isn't here ~** elle n'est pas encore là
3. (*in affirmative statements*) [still] encore, toujours ■ **I have ~ to meet her** je ne l'ai pas encore rencontrée ■ **the best is ~ to come** le meilleur est encore à venir *OR* reste à venir ■ **there are another ten miles to go ~** il reste encore une quinzaine de kilomètres ■ **I won't be ready for another hour ~** j'en ai encore pour une heure ■ **they won't be here for another hour ~** ils ne seront pas là avant une heure ■ **they may ~ be found** on peut encore les retrouver, il se peut encore qu'on les retrouve ■ **they may ~ be alive** ils sont peut-être encore *OR* toujours en vie
4. (*with compar and superlatives*) [even] encore, même ■ **~ more expensive** encore plus cher ■ **~ more snow was expected** on prévoyait encore de la neige ■ **a life of parties and ~ more parties** une existence qui consiste à aller de fête en fête ■ [emphasizing amount, frequency etc] : **~ another bomb** encore une bombe ■ **~ again** encore une fois
5. [so far - in present] jusqu'ici, jusque-là ; [- in past] jusque-là ■ **it's her best play ~** c'est sa meilleure pièce
6. [despite everything] après tout, quand même ■ **she may ~ surprise you all** elle va peut-être vous surprendre tous après tout.
◇ *conj* [nevertheless] néanmoins, toutefois ■ [however] cependant, pourtant ■ [but] mais ■ **they had no income ~ they still had to pay taxes** ils n'avaient pas de revenus et pourtant ils devaient payer des impôts ■ **he was firm ~ kind** il était sévère mais juste.

yeti ['jetɪ] *n* yeti *m*.

yew [juː] *n* **1.** : **~ (tree)** if *m* **2.** [wood] (bois *m* d')if *m*.

Y-fronts® *npl* slip *m* kangourou.

YHA (*abbrev of* **Youth Hostels Association**) *pr n UK Fédération unie des Auberges de jeunesse.*

Yiddish ['jɪdɪʃ] ◇ *n* yiddish *m*.
◇ *adj* yiddish.

yield [jiːld] ◇ *vi* **1.** [give in - person] céder ■ [surrender] se rendre ■ **he refused to ~** il a refusé de céder *OR* fléchir ■ **to ~ to** [argument] céder *OR* s'incliner devant ; [criticism, force] céder devant ; [blackmail, demand] céder à ; [pressure, threat] céder sous ; [desire, temptation] succomber à, céder à ■ **the countryside has had to ~ to suburbia** la campagne a dû reculer au profit de la banlieue **2.** [break, bend - under weight, force] céder, fléchir **3.** *US* AUT céder le passage *OR* la priorité ■ **'yield'** 'cédez le passage' **4.** AGRIC [field] rapporter, rendre ■ [crop] rapporter.
◇ *vt* **1.** [produce, bring in - gen] produire, rapporter ; [- land, crops] produire, rapporter, donner ; [- results] donner ■ **the investment bond will ~ 11%** le bon d'épargne rapportera 11 % ■ **their research has ~ed some interesting results** leur recherche a fourni *OR* donné quelques résultats intéressants **2.** [relinquish, give up] céder, abandonner ■ **to ~ ground** MIL & *fig* céder du terrain **3.** *US* AUT : **to ~ right of way** céder la priorité.
◇ *n* **1.** AGRIC & INDUST [output] rendement *m*, rapport *m* ■ [of crops] récolte *f* ■ **high-~ crops** récoltes à rendement élevé ■ **~ per acre** ≃ rendement à l'hectare **2.** FIN [from investments] rapport *m*, rendement *m* ■ [profit] bénéfice *m*, bénéfices *mpl* ■ [from tax] recette *f*, rapport *m* ■ **an 8% ~ on investments** des investissements qui rapportent 8 %.
◇ *comp US* **~ sign** panneau *m* de priorité.
◆ **yield up** *vt sep UK* **1.** [surrender - town, prisoner] livrer ■ **he ~ed himself up to the police** il s'est livré à la police **2.** [reveal - secret] dévoiler.

yielding ['jiːldɪŋ] ◇ *adj* **1.** [soft - ground] mou (*before vowel or silent 'h'* **mol**), molle *f* **2.** [flexible - material, metal] flexible, extensible **3.** [person] complaisant, accommodant ■ [character] docile.
◇ *n* [of town] reddition *f* ■ [of rights, control] cession *f*.

yin [jɪn] *n* : **~ and yang** le yin et le yang.

yippee [*UK* jɪ'piː, *US* 'jɪpɪ] *interj inf* hourra.

YMCA (*abbrev of* **Young Men's Christian Association**) *pr n association chrétienne de jeunes gens (surtout connue pour ses centres d'hébergement).*

yo [jəu] *interj esp US inf* salut.

yob [jɒb] *n UK inf* loubard *m*.

yobbo ['jɒbəu] (*pl* **yobbos**) = **yob**.

yodel ['jəudl] (*UK pret & pp* **yodelled**, *cont* **yodelling**) (*US pret & pp* **yodeled**, *cont* **yodeling**) ◇ *vi* jodler, iodler.
◇ *n* tyrolienne *f*.

yoga ['jəugə] *n* yoga *m*.

yoghourt, yoghurt [*UK* 'jɒgət, *US* 'jəugərt] *n* yaourt *m*, yogourt *m*, yoghourt *m*.

yogi ['jəugɪ] *n* yogi *mf*.

yogurt [*UK* 'jɒgət, *US* 'jəugərt] = **yoghourt**.

yoke [jəuk] ◇ *n* **1.** [frame - for hitching oxen] joug *m* ; [- for carrying buckets] joug *m*, palanche *f* **2.** *fig* [burden, domination] joug *m* ■ **under the ~ of tyranny** sous le joug de la tyrannie **3.** [pair of animals] attelage *m*, paire *f* **4.** [of dress, skirt, blouse] empiècement *m* **5.** CONSTR [for beams] moise *f*, lien *m* **6.** *lit* **the ~ of marriage** les liens *mpl* du mariage.
◇ *vt* **1.** [oxen] atteler ■ **to ~ (up) oxen/bullocks to a plough** atteler des bouvillons/bœufs à une charrue **2.** [ideas, qualities] lier, joindre.

yokel ['jəukl] *n pej* péquenot *m*.

yolk [jəuk] *n* : **(egg) ~** jaune *m* (d'œuf).

Yom Kippur [ˌjɒm'kɪpəʳ] *n* Yom Kippour *m inv.*

yon [jɒn] *demonstrative adjective arch & dial* **~ tree** cet arbre-là, l'arbre là-bas.

yonder ['jɒndəʳ] ◇ *adj lit* **~ tree** l'arbre là-bas.
◇ *adv* là-bas ▪ **way over ~** loin là-bas.

yonks [jɒŋks] *n UK inf* **I haven't been there for ~** il y a une paie OR ça fait un bail que je n'y suis pas allé.

yoof [juːf] *adj UK inf* [television, programme] pour jeunes ▪ [culture] des jeunes.

yoo-hoo ['juːˌhuː] *interj* ohé.

YOP [jɒp] (*abbrev of* **Youth Opportunities Programme**) *n UK* **1.** [programme] ≃ TUC *mpl* **2.** *inf* [worker] ≃ tuciste *mf.*

yore [jɔːʳ] *n arch & lit* **in days of ~** au temps jadis.

Yorks. *written abbr of* **Yorkshire**.

Yorkshire pudding *n crêpe épaisse salée traditionnellement servie avec du rôti de bœuf.*

Yorkshire Ripper *pr n* : **the ~** *l'éventreur du Yorkshire, accusé en 1981 du meurtre de 13 femmes.*

Yorkshire terrier *n* yorkshire-terrier *m*, yorkshire *m.*

you [juː] *pron* **1.** [as plural subject] vous ▪ [as singular subject - polite use] vous ; [- familiar use] tu ▪ [as plural object] vous ▪ [as singular object - polite use] vous ; [- familiar use] te, t' *(before vowel or silent 'h')* ▪ **~ didn't ask** vous n'avez pas/tu n'as pas demandé ▪ **don't ~ dare!** je te le déconseille! ▪ **~ and I will go together** vous et moi/toi et moi irons ensemble ▪ **~ and yours** vous et les vôtres/toi et les tiens ▪ **~ there!** vous là-bas! ▪ **don't ~ say a word** je t'interdis de dire quoi que ce soit ▪ **she gave ~ the keys** elle vous a donné/elle t'a donné les clés
2. [after preposition] vous ▪ [familiar use] toi ▪ **all of ~** vous tous ▪ **with ~** avec vous/toi ▪ **for ~** pour vous/toi ▪ **that's men for ~** ah! les hommes! ▪ **she gave the keys to ~** elle vous a donné/elle t'a donné les clés ▪ **between ~ and me** entre nous
3. [before noun or adjective] : **~ bloody fool!**△ espèce de crétin!△ ▪ **~ sweetie!** oh, le mignon/la mignonne! ▪ **~ Americans are all the same** vous les Américains OR vous autres Américains, vous êtes tous pareils
4. [emphatic use] vous ▪ [familiar form] toi ▪ **~ mean they chose ~** tu veux dire qu'ils t'ont choisie toi ▪ **~ wouldn't do that, would ~?** vous ne feriez pas cela/tu ne ferais pas cela, n'est-ce pas?
5. [impersonal use] : **~ never know** on ne sait jamais ▪ **a hot bath does ~ a world of good** un bon bain chaud vous fait un bien immense ▪ **~ take the first on the left** prenez la première à gauche.

you-all *pron US inf dial* vous (tous).

you'd [juːd] **1.** = **you had 2.** = **you would**.

you-know-what *n inf euph* **does he know about the ~?** est-ce qu'il est au courant du... tu vois de quoi je veux parler OR ce que je veux dire?

you-know-who *n inf euph* qui tu sais, qui vous savez.

you'll [juːl] = **you will**.

young [jʌŋ] (*comp* **younger** ['jʌŋgəʳ], *superl* **youngest** ['jʌŋgɪst]) ◇ *adj* **1.** [in age, style, ideas - person, clothes] jeune ▪ **the ~ men and women of today** les jeunes gens et jeunes femmes d'aujourd'hui ▪ **a ~ woman** une jeune femme ▪ **~ people** les jeunes *mpl*, la jeunesse *f* ▪ **the ~er generation** la jeune génération ▪ **families with ~ children** les familles qui ont des enfants en bas âge ▪ **my ~er brother** mon frère cadet, mon petit frère ▪ **I'm ten years ~er than she is** j'ai dix ans de moins qu'elle ▪ **I'm not as ~ as I was!** je n'ai plus (mes) vingt ans! ▪ **you're only ~ once!** la jeunesse ne dure qu'un temps! ▪ **in my ~er days** dans ma jeunesse, quand j'étais jeune ▪ **how is ~ Christopher?** *UK* comment va le jeune Christopher? ▪ **the ~ Mr Ford, Mr Ford the ~er** le jeune M. Ford, M. Ford fils ▪ **now listen here ~ man!** écoutez-moi bien, jeune homme! ▪ **her ~ man** *dated* son petit ami, son amoureux ▪ **his ~ lady** *dated* sa petite amie ▪ **~ lady!** mademoiselle! ▪ **she's quite a ~ lady now** c'est une vraie jeune fille maintenant **2.** [youthful] jeune ▪ **he is ~ for 45** il fait jeune pour 45 ans ▪ **she is a ~ 45** elle a 45 ans, mais elle ne les fait pas ▪ **he's ~ for his age** il est jeune pour son âge, il ne fait pas son âge ▪ **to be ~ at heart** avoir la jeunesse du cœur **3.** [recent - grass, plant] nouveau *(before vowel or silent 'h' **nouvel**)*, nouvelle *f* ; [- wine] jeune, vert ▪ GEOL [- rock formation] jeune, récent.
◇ *npl* : **the ~** [people] les jeunes *mpl*, la jeunesse ; [animals] les petits *mpl* ▪ **a game suitable for ~ and old alike** un jeu pour les jeunes et les moins jeunes ▪ **to be with ~** [animal] être pleine OR grosse.

young blood *n* [new attitudes, ideas, people] sang *m* nouveau OR neuf.

youngish ['jʌŋɪʃ] *adj* plutôt jeune.

young-looking *adj* d'allure jeune.

young offender institution *n* [in UK] centre *m* de détention pour mineurs.

youngster ['jʌŋstəʳ] *n* **1.** [child] garçon *m*, fille *f*, gamin *m*, gamine *f* ▪ [youth] jeune homme *m*, jeune fille *f* **2.** EQUI jeune cheval *m.*

Young Turk *n* POL jeune-turc *m*, jeune-turque *f.*

your [jɔːʳ] *det* **1.** [addressing one or more people - polite use] votre *mf*, vos *mf pl* ▪ [addressing one person - familiar use] ton *m*, ta *f*, tes *mf pl* ▪ **~ book** votre/ton livre ▪ **~ car** votre/ta voiture ▪ **~ books** vos/tes livres
2. [with parts of body, clothes] : **don't put ~ hands in ~ pockets** ne mets pas tes mains dans les poches ▪ **hold on to ~ hat!** tenez bien votre chapeau! ▪ **I think you've broken ~ finger** je crois que vous vous êtes cassé le doigt ▪ **does ~ wrist hurt?** est-ce que tu as mal au poignet?
3. [emphatic form] : **is this ~ book or his?** est-ce que c'est votre livre ou le sien? ▪ **oh it's YOUR book, is it?** ah, c'est à toi ce livre! ▪ **that's YOUR problem** c'est TON problème
4. [impersonal use] : **if you don't stand up for ~ rights, no one else will** si vous ne défendez pas vos droits vous-même, personne ne le fera à votre place ▪ **swimming is good for ~ heart and lungs** la natation est un bon exercice pour le cœur et les poumons ▪ **where are ~ Churchills and ~ De Gaulles when you need them?** où sont vos Churchill et vos De Gaulle quand vous avez besoin d'eux? ▪ **it's not a film for ~ average cinemagoer** ce n'est pas un film pour n'importe quel public
5. [in titles] : **Your Highness** Votre Majesté *(à un roi, une reine un prince ou une princesse)* ▪ **Your Majesty** Votre Majesté *(à un roi ou une reine uniquement).*

you're [jɔːʳ] = **you are**.

yours [jɔːz] *pron* **1.** [addressing one or more people - polite use] le vôtre *m*, la vôtre *f*, les vôtres *mf pl* ▪ [addressing one person - familiar use] le tien *m*, la tienne *f*, les tiens *mpl*, les tiennes *f* ▪ **is this book ~?** est-ce que ce livre est à vous/toi? ▪ **is this car ~?** c'est votre/ta voiture? ▪ **are these books ~?** ces livres sont-ils à vous/toi? ▪ **is he a friend of ~?** est-ce un de vos/tes amis? ▪ **~ is an unenviable task** votre tâche est peu enviable ▪ **can't you control that wretched dog of ~?** vous ne pouvez pas retenir votre satané chien? **2.** [up to you] : **it is not ~ to decide** ce n'est pas à vous OR il ne vous appartient pas de décider **3.** *UK inf* [in offering drinks] : **what's ~?** qu'est-ce que vous buvez?, qu'est-ce que je vous sers? **4.** [in letter] : **~, Peter** ≃ bien à vous OR à bientôt, Peter ▪ **~ sincerely** cordialement vôtre ▪ **~ faithfully** ≃ veuillez agréer mes salutations distinguées.

yourself [jɔː'self] (*pl* **yourselves** [-'selvz]) *pron* **1.** [personally - gen] vous-même ; [- familiar use] toi-même ▪ **do it ~** faites-le vous-même/fais-le toi-même ▪ **do it yourselves** faites-le vous-mêmes ▪ **you've kept the best seats for yourselves** vous avez gardé les meilleures places pour vous ▪ **see for ~** tu n'as qu'à voir par toi-même ▪ **did you come by ~?** vous êtes venu tout seul? ▪ **did you mend the fuse (by) ~?** vous avez remplacé le fusible tout seul? ▪ **did you make it ~?** l'avez-vous fait vous-même? **2.** [reflexive use] : **did you hurt ~?** est-ce que vous vous êtes/tu t'es fait mal? ▪ **did you enjoy ~?** est-ce que c'était bien? ▪ **you were talking to ~** tu parlais tout seul ▪ **speak for ~!** parle pour toi! ▪ **just look at ~!** regarde-toi donc! ➔ **you don't seem ~ today** tu n'as pas l'air d'être dans ton assiette aujourd'hui **3.** [emphatic use] : **you told me ~, you ~ told me** vous me l'avez dit vous-même, c'est vous-même qui me l'avez dit ▪ **you must have known ~ that they wouldn't**

cept vous-même, vous auriez dû savoir qu'ils n'acceptent pas **4.** [impersonal use] : **you have to know how to look after ~ in the jungle** dans la jungle, il faut savoir se défendre tout seul *OR* se débrouiller soi-même ▪ **you're supposed to help ~** on est censé se servir soi-même.

urs truly *pron inf* bibi, mézigue.

uth [ju:θ] (*pl* **youths** [ju:ðz]) <> *n* **1.** [young age] jeunesse ▪ **in my ~** dans ma jeunesse, quand j'étais jeune **2.** [young man] adolescent *m*, jeune *m*.
npl [young people] : **the ~ of today** les jeunes *mpl OR* la jeunesse d'aujourd'hui.

uth club *n UK* ≃ maison *f* des jeunes.

uth custody *n UK* détention *f* de mineurs, éducation *f* surveillée.

uthful ['ju:θfʊl] *adj* **1.** [young - person] jeune ; [- appearance] allure jeune **2.** [typical of youth - idea] de jeunesse ; [- enthusiasm, expectations, attitude] juvénile.

uthfulness ['ju:θfʊlnɪs] *n* [of person] jeunesse *f* ▪ [of appearance] allure *f* jeune ▪ [of mind, ideas] jeunesse *f*, fraîcheur *f*.

uth hostel *n* auberge *f* de jeunesse.

uth hostelling *n (U)* **to go ~** passer ses vacances en auberges de jeunesse.

u've [ju:v] = **you have**.

wl [jaʊl] <> *vi* [cat] miauler (fort) ▪ [dog, person] hurler.
n [of cat] miaulement *m* (déchirant) ▪ [of dog, person] hurlement *m*.

-yo ['jəʊjəʊ] (*pl* **yo-yos**) *n* **1.** [toy] Yo-Yo® *m inv* **2.**△ *US* [fool] couillon *m*.

written abbr of **year**.

(*abbrev of* **your**) *adj* vtre, ton (*f* ta, *pl* tes).

(*abbrev of* **yours**) *pron* votre.

YTS (*abbrev of* **Youth Training Scheme**) *n (personne participant au) programme gouvernemental britannique d'insertion des jeunes dans la vie professionnelle.*

yucca ['jʌkə] *n* yucca *m*.

yuck [jʌk] *interj inf* berk, beurk.

yucky ['jʌkɪ] (*comp* **yuckier**, *superl* **yuckiest**) *adj inf* dégueulasse.

Yugoslav ['ju:gəʊˌslɑ:v] <> *n* Yougoslave *mf*.
<> *adj* yougoslave.

Yugoslavia [ˌju:gəʊ'slɑ:vɪə] *pr n* Yougoslavie *f* ▪ **in ~** en Yougoslavie.

Yugoslavian [ˌju:gəʊ'slɑ:vɪən] <> *n* Yougoslave *mf*.
<> *adj* yougoslave.

Yukon Territory ['ju:kɒn-] *pr n* territoire *m* du Yukon.

yule, Yule [ju:l] *n arch & lit* Noël *m*.

yule log, Yule log *n* bûche *f* de Noël.

yuletide, Yuletide ['ju:ltaɪd] *lit* <> *n* (époque *f* de) Noël *m* ▪ **at ~** à Noël.
<> *comp* [greetings, festivities] de Noël.

yummy ['jʌmɪ] (*comp* **yummier**, *superl* **yummiest**) *inf* <> *adj* [food] succulent, délicieux.
<> *interj* miam-miam.

yuppie, yuppy ['jʌpɪ] (*pl* **yuppies**) <> *n* yuppie *mf*, ≃ jeune cadre *m* dynamique.
<> *adj* [club] pour jeunes cadres dynamiques ▪ [lifestyle] des yuppies.

yuppie flu *n inf pej* syndrome *m* de fatigue chronique, syndrome *m* des yuppies.

yuppify ['jʌpɪfaɪ] *vt* : **to become yuppified** s'embourgeoiser.

YWCA (*abbrev of* **Young Women's Christian Association**) *pr n association chrétienne de jeunes filles (surtout connue pour ses centres d'hébergement).*

Z

z (*pl* **z's** *OR pl* **zs**)**, Z** (*pl* **Z's** *OR pl* **Zs**) [*UK* zed, *US* zi:] *n* z *m*, Z *m*, *see also* **f**.

Zagreb ['zɑ:greb] *pr n* Zagreb.

Zaïre [zɑ:'ɪəʳ] *pr n* Zaïre *m* ■ **in ~** au Zaïre.

Zaïrean [zɑ:'ɪərɪən] ◇ *n* Zaïrois *m*, - e *f*.
◇ *adj* zaïrois.

Zaïrese [zɑ:ɪə'ri:z] ◇ *n* Zaïrois *m*, - e *f*.
◇ *adj* zaïrois.

Zambia ['zæmbɪə] *pr n* Zambie *f* ■ **in ~** en Zambie.

Zambian ['zæmbɪən] ◇ *n* Zambien *m*, - enne *f*.
◇ *adj* zambien.

zany ['zeɪnɪ] (*comp* **zanier**, *superl* **zaniest**, *pl* **zanies**) *inf* ◇ *adj* farfelu, dingue, dingo.
◇ *n* THEAT bouffon *m*, zani *m*, zanni *m*.

Zanzibar [ˌzænzɪ'bɑ:ʳ] *pr n* Zanzibar *m* ■ **in ~** au Zanzibar.

zap [zæp] (*pret & pp* **zapped**, *cont* **zapping**) *inf* ◇ *vi* **1.** [go quickly] courir ■ **I'll ~ over to see her** je file la voir, je vais faire un saut chez elle **2.** TV zapper.
◇ *vt* **1.** [destroy by bombing - town] ravager, bombarder ; [- target] atteindre **2.** [kill - victim] tuer, descendre ; [- in video game] éliminer **3.** COMPUT [display, data] effacer, supprimer.
◇ *n* [energy] pêche *f*, punch *m*.
◇ *interj* vlan.

zappy ['zæpɪ] (*comp* **zappier**, *superl* **zappiest**) *adj UK inf* qui a la pêche, plein de punch.

z-axis *n* axe *m* des z.

zeal [zi:l] *n* zèle *m*, ferveur *f*, ardeur *f* ■ **she undertook the work with great ~** elle a entrepris le travail avec beaucoup de zèle.

zealot ['zelət] *n* fanatique *mf*, zélateur *m*, - trice *f*.

zealous ['zeləs] *adj* [worker, partisan] zélé, actif ■ [opponent] zélé, acharné.

zealously ['zeləslɪ] *adv* avec zèle *OR* ardeur.

zebra [*UK* 'zebrə, *US* 'zi:brə] (*pl inv OR pl* **zebras**) *n* zèbre *m*.

zebra crossing *n UK* passage *m* clouté *OR* pour piétons.

zed [zed] *UK*, **zee** [zi:] *US n* (lettre *f*) z *m*.

Zen [zen] ◇ *n* zen *m*.
◇ *adj* zen *(inv)* ■ **~ Buddhism** les préceptes *mpl* du zen, le bouddhisme zen.

zenith [*UK* 'zenɪθ, *US* 'zi:nəθ] *n* zénith *m* ■ **she had reached the ~ of her career** *fig* elle était au sommet *OR* au faîte *OR* à l'apogée de sa carrière.

zephyr ['zefəʳ] *n lit* & TEX zéphyr *m*.

zeppelin ['zepəlɪn] *n* zeppelin *m*.

zero [*UK* 'zɪərəʊ, *US* 'zi:rəʊ] (*pl* **zeros** *OR pl* **zeroes**) ◇ *n* **1.** M[ATH] zéro *m* **2.** [in temperature] zéro *m* ■ **40 below ~** 40 degrés [au-]dessous de zéro, moins 40 **3.** SPORT : **to win 3 ~** gagner [3 à] zéro **4.** [nothing, nought] : **our chances have been put at ~** on c[on]sidère que nos chances sont nulles.
◇ *comp* [altitude] zéro *(inv)* ■ [visibility] nul ■ **~ gravity** apes[an]teur *f* ■ **~ growth** croissance *f* zéro ■ **the project has ~ inte[rest] for me** le projet ne présente aucun intérêt pour moi.
◇ *vt* [instrument] régler sur zéro.
◆ **zero in on** *vt insep* **1.** MIL [aim for] se diriger *OR* piq[uer] droit sur ■ **the police ~ed in on the terrorists' hideout** *inf* la [po]lice a investi la cachette des terroristes **2.** *inf* [concentrate] se concentrer sur, faire porter tous ses efforts sur **3.** *inf* [pin-point] mettre le doigt sur.

zero hour *n* heure *f* H.

zero-rated [-ˌreɪtɪd] *adj* : **~ (for VAT)** exempt de TVA, [non] assujetti à la TVA.

zest [zest] *n* **1.** [piquancy] piquant *m*, saveur *f* **2.** [enthusia[sm]] enthousiasme *m*, entrain *m* ■ **~ for life** joie *f* de vivre **3.** C[ULIN] [of orange, lemon] zeste *m*.

zestful ['zestfʊl] *adj* [person] enthousiaste.

zeugma ['zju:gmə] *n* zeugma *m*, zeugme *m*.

Zeus [zju:s] *pr n* Zeus.

zigzag ['zɪgzæg] (*pret & pp* **zigzagged**, *cont* **zigzagg[ing]**)
◇ *vi* [walker, vehicle] avancer en zigzags, zigzaguer ■ [r[oad]] zigzaguer ■ [river] serpenter ■ **to ~ across/up the road** tra[ver]ser/monter la rue en zigzaguant.
◇ *n* [in design] zigzag *m* ■ [on road] lacet *m* ■ [in river] bouc[le]
◇ *adj* [path, line] en zigzag ■ [pattern] à zigzag *OR* zigzags.
◇ *adv* en zigzag.

zilch [zɪltʃ] *n US inf* que dalle.

zillion ['zɪljən] (*pl inv OR pl* **zillions**) *inf* ◇ *n* foultitude *f* ■ [we] **got ~s of replies** nous avons eu des tas et des tas *OR* des [tonnes] de réponses.
◇ *adj* : **for a ~ reasons** pour des tas *OR* une foultitude de [rai]sons.

Zimbabwe [zɪm'bɑ:bwɪ] *pr n* Zimbabwe *m* ■ **in ~** au Z[im]babwe.

Zimbabwean [zɪm'bɑ:bwɪən] ◇ *n* Zimbabwéen [*m*], - enne *f*.
◇ *adj* zimbabwéen.

Zimmer (frame)® ['zɪməʳ-] *n* déambulateur *m*.

zinc [zɪŋk] ◇ *n* zinc *m*.
◇ *comp* [chloride, sulphate, sulphide] de zinc ■ [ointmen[t]] l'oxyde de zinc ■ **~ white** oxyde *m* de zinc *(pigment)*.

ng [zɪŋ] *inf* ◇ *onom* zim.
▸ *n* **1.** [of bullet] sifflement *m* **2.** [of person] punch *m*.
▸ *vi* [projectile] siffler, passer dans un sifflement.

on ['zaɪən] *pr n* Sion.

onism ['zaɪənɪzm] *n* sionisme *m*.

onist ['zaɪənɪst] ◇ *n* sioniste *mf*.
▸ *adj* sioniste.

p [zɪp] (*pret & pp* **zipped**, *cont* **zipping**) ◇ *n* **1.** [fastener] fer-neture *f* Éclair® *OR* à glissière **2.** [sound of bullet] sifflement *n* **3.** *inf* [liveliness] vivacité *f*, entrain *m* **4.** *US* code *m* postal **5.** *US inf* [nothing] rien *m*.
▸ *vi* **1.** [with zip fastener] : **to ~ open/shut** s'ouvrir/se fermer à 'aide d'une fermeture Éclair® *OR* à glissière **2.** *inf* [verb of novement] : **to ~ past** passer comme une flèche ▪ **I zipped :hrough the book/my work** j'ai lu ce livre/fait mon travail en ıuatrième vitesse **3.** [arrow, bullet] siffler.
▸ *vt* **1.** [with zip fastener] : **to ~ sthg open/shut** fermer/ouvrir la 'ermeture Éclair® *OR* à glissière de qqch ▪ **I zipped myself nto my sleeping bag** je me suis mis dans mon sac de cou-:hage en tirant la fermeture **2.** *inf* [do quickly] : **I'll just ~ this :ake into the oven** je glisse en vitesse ce gâteau dans le four **3.** COMPUT zipper.
▸ **zip on** ◇ *vt sep* attacher (avec une fermeture à glis-sière).
▸ *vi insep* s'attacher avec une fermeture Éclair® *OR* à glis-sière.
▸ **zip up** ◇ *vt sep* **1.** [clothing, sleeping bag] fermer avec la 'ermeture Éclair® *OR* à glissière **2.** [subj: person] fermer la fermeture Éclair® *OR* à glissière de.
▸ *vi insep* [dress] se fermer avec une fermeture Éclair® *OR* à glissière.

p code, ZIP code *n US* code *m* postal.

ip disk® *n* COMPUT disque *m* zip.

ip drive® *n* COMPUT lecteur *m* de zips.

p fastener *n UK* fermeture *f* Éclair® *OR* à glissière.

p-on *adj* [flap, hood] qui s'attache avec une fermeture Éclair® *OR* à glissière.

pper ['zɪpəʳ] *US* = **zip fastener**.

ip-up *adj* [bag, coat] à fermeture Éclair®, zippé.

it [zɪt] *n inf* bouton *m (sur la peau)*.

ither ['zɪðəʳ] *n* cithare *f*.

izz [zɪz] *n UK inf* **to have a ~** faire un somme.

zodiac ['zəʊdɪæk] *n* zodiaque *m*.

zombie ['zɒmbɪ] *n* zombie *m*.

zonal ['zəʊnl] *adj* zonal.

zone [zəʊn] ◇ *n* **1.** [area] zone *f*, secteur *m* **2.** [sphere] zone *f*, domaine *m* **3.** GEOG & METEOR zone *f*.
◇ *vt* **1.** [partition] diviser en zones **2.** [classify] désigner.

zoning ['zəʊnɪŋ] *n* zonage *m*.

zonked [zɒŋkt] *adj inf* **1.** [exhausted] vanné, claqué **2.** [drunk] bourré ▪ [drugged] défoncé.

zoo [zu:] (*pl* **zoos**) *n* zoo *m*, jardin *m* zoologique.

zookeeper ['zu:ˌki:pəʳ] *n* gardien *m*, - enne *f* du zoo.

zoological [ˌzəʊə'lɒdʒɪkl] *adj* zoologique.

zoologist [zəʊ'ɒlədʒɪst] *n* zoologiste *mf*.

zoology [zəʊ'ɒlədʒɪ] *n* zoologie *f*.

zoom [zu:m] ◇ *vi inf* **1.** [verb of movement] : **the car ~ed up/down the hill** la voiture a monté/descendu la côte à toute allure ▪ **I'm just going to ~ into town to get some food** je vais faire un saut en ville pour acheter de quoi manger **2.** [prices, costs, sales] monter en flèche **3.** [engine] vrombir.
◇ *n* **1.** [of engine] vrombissement *m* **2.** PHOT [lens, effect] zoom *m*.
◇ *onom* : **~!** vroum!
▸ **zoom in** *vi insep* PHOT faire un zoom ▪ **the camera ~ed in on the laughing children** la caméra a fait un zoom sur les enfants en train de rire.
▸ **zoom off** *vi insep* filer.
▸ **zoom out** *vi insep* PHOT faire *OR* produire un effet d'éloignement avec le zoom.

zoom lens *n* zoom *m*.

zoot suit [zu:t-] *n* costume *m* zazou.

Zoroaster [ˌzɒrəʊ'æstəʳ] *pr n* Zoroastre.

Zoroastrian [ˌzɒrəʊ'æstrɪən] ◇ *adj* zoroastrien.
◇ *n* Zoroastrien *m*, - enne *f*.

zucchini [zu:'ki:nɪ] (*pl inv OR pl* **zucchinis**) *n US* courgette *f*.

Zulu ['zu:lu:] (*pl inv OR pl* **Zulus**) ◇ *n* **1.** [person] Zoulou *m*, - e *f* **2.** LING zoulou *m*.
◇ *adj* zoulou.

Zululand ['zu:lu:lænd] *pr n* Zoulouland *m*, Zululand *m*.

zygote ['zaɪgəʊt] *n* zygote *m*.

ENGLISH IRREGULAR VERBS
VERBES IRRÉGULIERS ANGLAIS

infinitif	prétérit	participe passé
arise	arose	arisen
awake	awoke	awoken
be	was, were	been
bear	bore	borne
beat	beat	beaten
become	became	become
befall	befell	befallen
begin	began	begun
behold	beheld	beheld
bend	bent	bent
beseech	besought	besought
beset	beset	beset
bet	bet, betted	bet, betted
bid	bid, bade	bid, bidden
bind	bound	bound
bite	bit	bitten
bleed	bled	bled
blow	blew	blown
break	broke	broken
breed	bred	bred
bring	brought	brought
build	built	built
burn	burnt, burned	burnt, burned
burst	burst	burst
buy	bought	bought
can	could	—
cast	cast	cast
catch	caught	caught
choose	chose	chosen
cling	clung	clung
come	came	come
cost	cost	cost
creep	crept	crept
cut	cut	cut
deal	dealt	dealt
dig	dug	dug
do	did	done
draw	drew	drawn
dream	dreamed, dreamt	dreamed, dreamt
drink	drank	drunk
drive	drove	driven
dwell	dwelt, dwelled	dwelt, dwelled
eat	ate	eaten
fall	fell	fallen
feed	fed	fed
feel	felt	felt
fight	fought	fought
find	found	found
flee	fled	fled
fling	flung	flung
fly	flew	flown
forbear	forbore	forborne
forbid	forbade	forbidden
forecast	forecast	forecast
forego	forewent	foregone
foresee	foresaw	foreseen
foretell	foretold	foretold
forget	forgot	forgotten
forgive	forgave	forgiven
forsake	forsook	forsaken
freeze	froze	frozen
get	got	got (*US* gotten)

infinitif	prétérit	participe passé
give	gave	given
go	went	gone
grind	ground	ground
grow	grew	grown
hang	hung, hanged	hung, hanged
have	had	had
hear	heard	heard
hide	hid	hidden
hit	hit	hit
hold	held	held
hurt	hurt	hurt
keep	kept	kept
kneel	knelt, kneeled	knelt, kneeled
know	knew	known
lay	laid	laid
lead	led	led
lean	leant, leaned	leant, leaned
leap	leapt, leaped	leapt, leaped
learn	learnt, learned	learnt, learned
leave	left	left
lend	lent	lent
let	let	let
lie	lay	lain
light	lit, lighted	lit, lighted
lose	lost	lost
make	made	made
may	might	—
mean	meant	meant
meet	met	met
mistake	mistook	mistaken
mow	mowed	mown, mowed
pay	paid	paid
put	put	put
quit	quit, quitted	quit, quitted
read	read	read
rend	rent	rent
rid	rid	rid
ride	rode	ridden
ring	rang	rung
rise	rose	risen
run	ran	run
saw	sawed	sawn
say	said	said
see	saw	seen
seek	sought	sought
sell	sold	sold
send	sent	sent
set	set	set
shake	shook	shaken
shall	should	—
shear	sheared	shorn, sheared
shed	shed	shed
shine	shone	shone
shoot	shot	shot
show	showed	shown
shrink	shrank	shrunk
shut	shut	shut
sing	sang	sung
sink	sank	sunk
sit	sat	sat
slay	slew	slain
sleep	slept	slept

infinitif	prétérit	participe passé
slide	slid	slid
sling	slung	slung
slink	slunk	slunk
slit	slit	slit
smell	smelt, smelled	smelt, smelled
sow	sowed	sown, sowed
speak	spoke	spoken
speed	sped, speeded	sped, speeded
spell	spelt, spelled	spelt, spelled
spend	spent	spent
spill	spilt, spilled	spilt, spilled
spin	spun	spun
spit	spat	spat
split	split	split
spoil	spoiled, spoilt	spoiled, spoilt
spread	spread	spread
spring	sprang	sprung
stand	stood	stood
steal	stole	stolen
stick	stuck	stuck
sting	stung	stung
stink	stank	stunk
stride	strode	stridden
strike	struck	struck, stricken
strive	strove	striven
swear	swore	sworn
sweep	swept	swept
swell	swelled	swollen, swelled
swim	swam	swum
swing	swung	swung
take	took	taken
teach	taught	taught
tear	tore	torn
tell	told	told
think	thought	thought
throw	threw	thrown
thrust	thrust	thrust
tread	trod	trodden
upset	upset	upset
wake	woke	woken
waylay	waylaid	waylaid
wear	wore	worn
weave	wove, weaved	woven, weaved
wed	wedded	wedded
weep	wept	wept
wet	wetted, wet	wetted, wet
will	would	—
win	won	won
wind	wound	wound
withdraw	withdrew	withdrawn
withhold	withheld	withheld
withstand	withstood	withstood
wring	wrung	wrung
write	wrote	written

Imprimé en Italie par Rotolito Lombarda S.p.A. - Mars 2007